Random House

RUSSIAN-ENGLISH DICTIONARY OF IDIOMS

Random House

RUSSIAN-ENGLISH DICTIONARY OF IDIOMS

Sophia Lubensky

RANDOM HOUSE

New York

Lubensky, Sophia.
    Random House Russian-English dictionary of idioms / Sophia
Lubensky.
        p.   cm.
    Includes bibliographical references and index.
    ISBN 0-679-40580-1
    1. Russian language—Idioms—Dictionaries. 2. Russian language—
Dictionaries—English.   I. Title.
PG2460.L83   1995
491.73′1—dc20   95-2424
                                                                         CIP

Composition by Harrison Prepress
Book design by Charlotte Staub

Manufactured in the United States of America
First Edition
New York   Toronto   London   Sydney   Auckland

CONTENTS

ACKNOWLEDGMENTS

During more than twelve years of work on the *Russian-English Dictionary of Idioms* I have received valuable help and contributions from many persons and sources. The dictionary has benefited enormously from their generosity, and it is with profound and sincere gratitude that I acknowledge my debt to them.

First and foremost, I wish to acknowledge a generous grant from the National Cryptologic School, Department of Defense, which made the publication of this dictionary possible.

Of all the individuals to whom tribute is due, I owe my greatest debt to Marjorie McShane, who worked with me on practically every aspect of the dictionary. Marjorie's talent, fine feeling for language and style, and critical flair helped to make the book much better than it would otherwise have been.

A very great debt is owed to my translation consultants, Charles Rougle and Rebecca Stanley, who have generously contributed to this volume and whose erudition and translation skills have significantly improved the dictionary.

I extend my special thanks to two outstanding linguists, Jurij Apresjan and Igor Mel'čuk, for their advice and assistance regarding linguistic matters. It was an inspiration to work with both of them, and their counsel has been invaluable.

Over the years I have benefited immeasurably from numerous discussions of linguistic and lexicographic problems with Catherine V. Chvany. I extend to her my boundless gratitude.

Many colleagues and friends on both sides of the Atlantic—linguists, translators, literary scholars—have generously assisted in my attempts to answer a multitude of questions related to the usage and stylistic register of idioms. These individuals filled out my endless questionnaires with knowledge and enduring patience, and I wish to express my appreciation to them all: Alina Israeli, Lidija Iordanskaja, Elena Krasnostchekova, Larisa Lebedeva, Olga Levchinskaya, the late Aleksei Mikhalyov, Eugene Ostrovsky, Slava Paperno, Alexander Penkovsky, Inna Sazonova, Veronika Telija, and Issa Zauber.

I offer unending thanks to my friends Nelly Zhuravlyova, Lena Jacobson, and Vladimir Savransky and all the members of the Savransky family, who provided me with fine and countless examples of idiomatic usage in speech. Many of the invented examples in this volume are theirs.

At the earlier stages of my work on this book I gained insights from discussions with the Slavicists Michael S. Flier, Robert A. Rothstein, Christopher A. Wertz, and Fruim Yurevich. Michael Scammell graciously helped me to find equivalents for several difficult idioms, and Lt. Col. James Holbrook, U.S. Army (Ret.), kindly assisted me with military expressions and usages. I would like to thank them all.

Many former graduate students at the State University of New York at Albany gave abundantly of their time and expertise to the dictionary. I wish to express my heartfelt appreciation to Nancy Downey, Erika Haber, and Eric Nehrbauer. Judith VanDyk and the late Michael Slattery earn special thanks for their work on the earliest version of this volume. I am also indebted to Monique Baran, Stephen C. Covell, Paul Dieterich, Eileen Fisher, Janet Hahn, Michael Harvey, Frank Kemp, Andrea Levin, Bruce McClelland, Catherine Meech, Madeleine Newell, Richard Reis, Carolyn Wieland, and Joanne Yasus. Many others made small but significant contributions, and I wish to thank them in the hope that they will forgive me for not recognizing each of them individually.

I am deeply obliged to my bibliographer, Kay L. Shaffer, and to all the knowledgeable and kindhearted people at the SUNY library who over the course of many years helped me in every possible way. My particular thanks go to Gregory C. Baron and the late Sara H. Stevenson.

I am ever grateful to Boris Yamrom for creating a special computer program to produce the Index for this volume. My sincere thanks also to Robert C. Atwood, who has been my indefatigable computer consultant.

Special appreciation goes to Henryk Baran, who as chair of the Department of Slavic Languages and Literatures at the University at Albany during the larger part of this undertaking offered constant support. I also wish to thank colleagues Alex M. Shane and Harlow Robinson for their encouragement, assistance, and generous willingness to share their personal libraries throughout the duration of this project.

After the final draft of the dictionary was completed, it was handed over to the care of Joyce O'Connor, who coordinated with the Random House staff as English-text editor and whose role in the project expanded greatly as the work went on. In addition to her excellent and much-appreciated editing, Joyce has been an unfailing source of support and encouragement, and to her I am especially indebted.

Over the course of preparing the manuscript for publication, I have worked hand in hand with Judy Kaplan, supervising copyeditor in the reference division at Random House. For her abiding patience and great assistance I wish to offer Judy my warmest thanks.

From the very beginning of my association with Random House I have worked closely with my project editor, Sol Steinmetz. To him I owe an enormous debt of gratitude for his advice, enthusiasm, and kindness. My sincerest thanks also to Enid Pearsons, senior editor at Random House Reference, for the benefit of her perceptiveness and critical thinking.

Finally, special recognition is due to Charles Levine, Vice President and Publisher of the Reference and Electronic Division of Random House, for his encouragement, support, and, if I may say so, vision.

While acknowledging with pleasure my indebtedness to those who helped me to produce this dictionary, I wish to emphasize that no one but myself is ultimately responsible for the content of the dictionary and the format in which the material is presented. My hope is that the finished product will justify the time and effort of all involved.

Sophia Lubensky,
January 1995

EXECUTIVE EDITOR
Sol Steinmetz

DEVELOPMENTAL EDITOR
Marjorie J. McShane

LINGUISTICS CONSULTANTS
Jurij Apresjan   Igor Mel'čuk

TRANSLATION CONSULTANTS
Charles Rougle   Rebecca Stanley

ENGLISH TEXT EDITOR
Joyce O'Connor

INDEX PROGRAM
Boris Yamrom

BIBLIOGRAPHY
Kay L. Shaffer

SUPERVISING COPYEDITOR
Judy Kaplan

PROOFREADERS
Nelly Zhuravlyova   Carole Cook

SAMPLE ENTRIES

HEAD MATTER

CASE GOVERNMENT

NUMBERS INDICATING
VARIOUS SENSES

DEFINITIONS

А-25 • А́ЛЬФА И ОМЕ́ГА *чего* *lit* [NP; sing only; fixed WO]
1. the beginning and the end of sth.: **the alpha and omega.**
2. the very essence, the most essential components of sth.: **the alpha and omega.**

Судилище явное и судилище тайное — вот альфа и омега нашей жизни (Мандельштам 2). Trials, "open" or secret, were the alpha and omega of our existence (2a).

ETYMOLOGICAL NOTE

< From the names of the first and last letters of the Greek alphabet. Used in the Bible (Rev. 1:8).

USAGE LABELS

RUSSIAN PATTERN

RUSSIAN NEGATIVE PATTERN

RELATED NOUN PHRASE

ENGLISH EQUIVALENTS

Б-68 • ИГРА́ТЬ В БИРЮ́ЛЬКИ *coll, disapprov* [VP; subj: human; often neg or infin with хватит, перестань(те) etc] to occupy o.s. with trifles (with the implication that one should be doing sth. serious, productive instead): X в бирюльки играет ≃ **X fritters ⟨fiddles⟩ away the time; X fiddles ⟨fools, putters⟩ around;** ‖ *Neg* X не в бирюльки играет ≃ [with an emphasis on the seriousness of the matter] **X is not playing games (with person Y).** ◦ **ИГРА́ В БИРЮ́ЛЬКИ** [NP] ≃ **fiddling ⟨fooling, puttering⟩ around; trifles; trifling matters.**

CITATION

AUTHOR AND BIBLIO-
GRAPHICAL REFERENCE

«А это ты нас не учи, что делать. — Он подступал к арестованному, красноречиво поигрывая деревянной кобурой у пояса. — Мы из тебя, ваше благородие, быстро гонор вышибем. Мы сюда не в бирюльки играть заявились» (Максимов 3). "Don't you tell us what to do."...He went up to the prisoner, eloquently fingering the wooden holster at his waist. "We'll soon cut you down to size. We haven't come here to fool around" (3a). ♦ «Кто подделывал икону?» — спросил Антон. «Не знаю!» — торопливо выпалил Вася... [Антон] передал фотоснимок [Васе] Сипенятину: «Узнаёте художника?» Тот, оценивающе прищурясь, натянуто усмехнулся: «Как волков флажками обложили». — «Вы что, думали, в бирюльки с вами играть будут?» (Чернёнок 2). "Who forged the icon?" Anton asked. "I don't know," Vasya burst out....[Anton] handed the picture to [Vasya] Sipeniatin. "Do you recognize the artist?" Vasya squinted as he appraised the picture and laughed nervously. "You've got him pegged." "Did you think we were going to play games with you?" (2a).

BIBLIOGRAPHICAL REFER-
ENCE FOR TRANSLATION

ETYMOLOGICAL NOTE

< From the name of an old game in which a large number of very small objects («бирюльки») were scattered on a table and the players tried to pull out one item at a time with a small hook without disturbing the other objects. Cf. **jackstraws, pick-up-sticks.**

Г-366 • ПРОСТИ́ ГО́СПОДИ[1] *obsoles, coll* [Invar; sent adv (parenth); fixed WO] used by the speaker to express his awareness that something he has just said or is about to say is phrased too sharply: **Lord ⟨God⟩ forgive me.**

«Чернышевского не читал, а так, если подумать… Прескучная, прости Господи, фигура!» (Набоков 1). "I've never read Chernyshevski, but when I come to think of it….A most boring, Lord forgive me, figure!" (1a).

Г-367 • ПРОСТИ́ ГО́СПОДИ[2] *euph, highly coll* [used as NP; Invar; fixed WO] a prostitute: **tart; hooker; strumpet; trollop; streetwalker; harlot.**

М-170 • КАК ОДНА́ МИНУ́ТА пролететь, пройти [как + NP; Invar; adv; usu. used with pfv verbs; fixed WO] (of a period of time usu. defined by some event, occasion etc) (to pass) very quickly, unnoticeably: **(be over) before one knows it; (fly) right by.**

Мы так ждали лета, а оно пролетело как одна минута. We couldn't wait for summer, and then it was over before we knew it.

П-489 • ПОЛОЖИ́ТЬ ⟨ПОСТА́ВИТЬ, ВЗЯТЬ⟩ (СЕБЕ́) ЗА ПРА́ВИЛО; ПОЛОЖИ́ТЬ ⟨ПОСТА́ВИТЬ, ВЗЯТЬ⟩ (СЕБЕ́) ПРА́ВИЛОМ [VP; subj: human; foll. by infin] to make it one's principle, custom (to do sth.): X поставил себе за правило (делать Y) ≃ **X made it a rule (to do Y); X made a point (of doing Y).**

Главный, по-видимому, поставил себе за правило соглашаться со всем и радоваться всему, что бы ни говорили ему окружающие, и выражать это словами «славно, славно…» (Булгаков 9). The chief had evidently made it a rule to agree with everything and to rejoice in everything his companions said to him, and to express this with the words, "Fine, fine…" (9a).

С-145 • С ЛЁГКИМ СЕ́РДЦЕМ; С ЛЁГКОЙ ДУШО́Й [PrepP; these forms only; usu. adv; fixed WO] feeling good, relieved, with a positive attitude etc: **with a light heart; lightheartedly.**

«Уж кого-кого, а тебя на свадьбу позову». Григорий шутливо хлопнул сестру по плечу и с лёгким сердцем пошёл с родного двора (Шолохов 5). "Don't worry, I'll invite you to the wedding if I invite anyone!" Grigory patted his sister's shoulder jokingly and left his father's house with a light heart (5a). ♦ «…Новому человеку позволительно стать человеко-богом… и, уж конечно, в новом чине, с лёгким сердцем перескочить всякую прежнюю нравственную преграду прежнего раба-человека, если оно понадобится» (Достоевский 2). "…The new man is allowed to become a man-god…and of course, in this new rank, to jump lightheartedly over any former moral obstacle of the former slave-man, if need be" (2a).

С-149 • ПРИНИМА́ТЬ/ПРИНЯ́ТЬ (БЛИ́ЗКО) К СЕ́РДЦУ *что* [VP; subj: human; if imper, only neg impfv] to react to sth. with great sensitivity, be deeply affected by sth. (usu. used in situations when one sympathizes deeply with another's misfortune or reacts to sth. more intensely than is warranted): X принимает Y (близко) к сердцу ≃ **X takes Y (right ⟨very much etc⟩) to heart.**

«Я бы очень желал не так живо чувствовать и не так близко принимать к сердцу всё, что ни случается» (Гоголь 3). "I wish I did not feel so keenly and did not take everything that happens so much to heart" (3a). ♦ Голубева этот разговор страшно заинтересовал. И он принял его близко к сердцу (Войнович 2). Golubev found this conversation terribly interesting. And he took it right to heart (2a).

GUIDE TO THE DICTIONARY

This dictionary presents some 13,000 Russian idioms in nearly 6,900 entries, and combines, in a rather unconventional manner, features of translational and learner's dictionaries. On the one hand, it attempts to provide sufficient English equivalents to cover any context a translator from Russian may encounter; on the other hand, it attempts to provide sufficient grammatical and explanatory information to allow the user to use the idioms actively. Since most of the equivalents presented in the dictionary are common to all varieties of the English language, it is hoped that all speakers of English will find it useful, even though in general the dictionary is based on American usage. Speakers of Russian may also benefit from the wide variety of English equivalents presented and from the illustrations of their usage in the examples and citations.

DISTINGUISHING FEATURES

The dictionary contains a number of features that distinguish it from existing dictionaries of Russian idioms.

Range of Entries

It includes not only traditional idioms but also several other types of fixed expressions not found in traditional monolingual or bilingual dictionaries of Russian idioms (see Types of Idioms under Idiomaticity, below).

Grammatical Descriptions

It includes a grammatical description for each entry, a feature generally not found in bilingual dictionaries and also not found in any existing comprehensive monolingual dictionary of Russian idioms. The grammatical description provides users with the information they need to learn to use the idioms productively.

Definitions

Definitions—another feature rarely found in bilingual dictionaries—are provided for each entry in order to:
1) describe minute semantic nuances that may not be conveyed by the English equivalents alone
2) help the user to determine which sense of a polysemous equivalent is intended in the given instance
3) provide the user with adequate information to create a context-specific translation if he or she should deem it necessary or preferable.

Usage Notes

When applicable, a usage note is provided in conjunction with (or, rarely, in place of) the definition. It describes the contexts in which the given idiom may be used and various other aspects of its usage—information that is for the most part absent in monolingual Russian dictionaries. Usage notes, like definitions, are given in English.

Equivalents

The equivalents—the English phrases that suitably render the Russian idiom—are intended to cover all possible contexts in which the given idiom can occur and to offer the translator a complete picture of the semantic range of the idiom. The equivalents presented were checked in contexts obtained from the following sources: approximately 250 works of Russian literature; all available monolingual general dictionaries; monolingual phraseological dictionaries; bilingual phraseological dictionaries; and linguistic works on Russian phraseology.

Variables and Patterns

The equivalents for verbal idioms are presented in patterns that employ the variables X, Y, and Z to indicate the subject, object(s), and, occasionally, location. This notation, which is widely accepted by linguists and is used in Mel'čuk and Zholkovsky's trailblazing "explanatory-combinatorial" dictionary of Russian[1] (and Mel'čuk's et al. dictionary of French[2]), has several advantages:

1) It allows for the presentation of a wide variety of equivalents that might otherwise not be presented for fear of confusion as to who is doing what, especially equivalents that reverse the Russian subject and object. For example, in Г-88 ПОПАДАТЬСЯ/ПОПАСТЬСЯ НА ГЛАЗА *кому...*, the use of variables allows for the inclusion of equivalents that have both X and Y as the subject:

> X попался на глаза Y-у ≃ **X caught Y's eye; Y caught sight of X; Y's eyes lighted ⟨lit⟩ on X** . . .

2) In Russian the full names of the variables employed can be declined in both the singular and the plural (X-a = икса, X-y = иксу, X-ов = иксов, Y-a = игрека, Y-y = игреку, Y-ов = игреков, Z-a = зета, Z-y = зету, Z-ов = зетов, etc.). Therefore, when used in patterns, the variables clearly show both the case and number of the corresponding Russian noun or pronoun. When used in the English equivalents, variables can show the possessive (X's, Y's, etc.).

3) It allows the explicit indication of those instances in which a noun (usually one used as a direct, indirect, or prepositional object) will be plural; for example, in Г-62 ГЛАЗА РАЗБЕГАЮТСЯ (*у кого*) the following pattern is presented.

> у X-a глаза разбегаются (от Y-ов) ≃ ...**X is dizzied by the multitude of Ys; it's more ⟨there are more Ys⟩ than the eyes can take in.**

4) It makes possible the illustration of special constructions in which a given idiom is often used, along with the English equivalents that best translate those special constructions. That is, in addition to the basic affirmative pattern (which is presented for practically all verbal idioms), these patterns are presented as applicable: negative, imperative, negative imperative, and verb used with a particular adverbial or adverbials. For example:

> P-222 • СХОДИТЬ/СОЙТИ С РУК...1.... X сошёл Y-у с рук ≃ **Y got away with X...;** ‖ *Neg* X не сойдёт Y-у с рук ≃ **Y will pay dearly for X...**

> Д-279 • ЗАБЫВАТЬ/ЗАБЫТЬ ДОРОГУ... X забыл дорогу к Y-у ≃ **X stopped going ⟨coming⟩ to Y's place...;** ‖ *Imper* забудь дорогу в наш дом ≃ **don't**

bother coming back here (ever) again; **don't come around here anymore**…

Д-355 • ПАДАТЬ/УПАСТЬ ДУХОМ… Х упал духом ≃ **X lost heart ⟨courage⟩**…; ‖ *Neg Imper* не падай духом ≃ **keep your spirits ⟨chin⟩ up; don't let it get you down**…

Н-158 • УНОСИТЬ/УНЕСТИ НОГИ… Х унёс ноги ≃ **X cleared out**…; ‖ Х еле ⟨едва, насилу⟩ ноги унёс ≃ **X escaped ⟨got away⟩ by the skin of his teeth**…

While the English equivalents provided for these special patterns tend to be best used in the specified construction, all or most of the equivalents for the basic affirmative pattern can usually be used in the negative, the imperative, the negative imperative, and with many adverbials.

The variables X, Y, and Z cover both genders for human nouns. In those few instances when an idiom can be used only with a female (or male) subject or object, gender specifications are included in the grammatical description; for example:

В-250 • ДАВАТЬ/ДАТЬ ВОЛЮ РУКАМ…2. [subj: usu. male]…Х даёт волю рукам ≃ **X lets his hands wander**…

С-144 • НОСИТЬ ПОД СЕРДЦЕМ *кого*…[VP; subj: human, female]…Х носила Y-а ⟨ребёнка⟩ под сердцем ≃ …**X was with child**…

When the subject or object in a Russian idiom can be either animate or inanimate, but the subject or object of one of its English equivalents can be only one or the other, the English animacy restrictions are indicated in the equivalent. "Person X," "person Y," and "person Z" designate animate subjects and objects, whereas "thing X," "thing Y," and "thing Z" designate inanimate subjects and objects (the word "thing" is used for all types of inanimate nouns). For example, the last equivalent in sense 2 of Г-85 can be used only with an abstract subject:

Г-85 • ОТКРЫВАТЬ/ОТКРЫТЬ… ГЛАЗА *кому (на кого-что)*…[subj: human or abstr]…**thing X was an eyeopener**…

The notation "thing X" shows that the subject for this equivalent must be inanimate, and the grammatical brackets indicate that any inanimate subject must be abstract.

The compiler's lexicographic conservatism militated against the introduction of variables and patterns. In the end, however, it became obvious that the above approach is significantly more user-friendly than the traditional one, and that it tremendously expands a lexicographer's possibilities for presenting a greater number of faithful translations in a clear and understandable fashion.

PRINCIPLES, DIMENSIONS, AND ATTRIBUTES OF THIS DICTIONARY

Idiomaticity

For the purposes of this dictionary, an idiom is interpreted as a nonfree combination of two or more words that acts as a semantic whole. In most cases, the meaning of an idiom cannot be predicted from the meanings of its components. An idiom is reproduced in speech as a readymade unit, and it functions as a part of speech or an independent sentence. This dictionary includes idioms per se as well as other phrases whose idiomaticity varies in degree and type.

Characteristics of Idioms

Idioms possess the following characteristic properties, which occur in various combinations:

1) Many idioms have a defective paradigm. The defectiveness of a paradigm may involve:

   a) *case* — For example, САМАЯ МАЛОСТЬ 'a tiny bit' is used only in the accusative case in one of its senses (самую малость)

   b) *number* — For example, ВЫСОКИЕ МАТЕРИИ 'lofty topics ⟨matters⟩' and СИЛЬНЫЕ МИРА СЕГО 'the mighty of this world' are used only in the plural; ДУРНОЙ ГЛАЗ 'the evil eye' and СТАНОВОЙ ХРЕБЕТ 'backbone' are used only in the singular

   c) *person* — For example, БОЮСЬ СКАЗАТЬ 'I'm not sure' is used only in the first person singular; НЕДОРОГО ВОЗЬМЁТ 'one won't think twice about doing sth.' is not used in the first person

   d) *tense/aspect* — For example, В МУТНОЙ ВОДЕ РЫБУ ЛОВИТЬ 'fish in troubled waters' is used only in the imperfective; КАМЕНЬ С ДУШИ СВАЛИЛСЯ 'a load was taken off s.o.'s mind', only in the perfective; В ЧЁМ ДУША ДЕРЖИТСЯ 's.o.'s body and soul are scarcely held together', only in the present;

ПОШЛА ПИСАТЬ ГУБЕРНИЯ 'there they go', only in the perfective past

   e) *finite versus nonfinite forms* — For example, НЕ ПРОПАДЁТ (as in За мной не пропадёт 'I will pay you ⟨him⟩ back') has no corresponding nonfinite forms (that is, no infinitive, participle, or verbal adverb)

2) Many idioms lack some syntactic functions of the type of phrase to which they belong. For example, some noun phrases are used only predicatively: НЕ ИГОЛКА 'not exactly invisible.' Others are used only or mainly as a subject or object (that is, not predicatively): ЦЕЛЫЙ КОРОБ новостей 'a whole lot (of news)'.

3) Some idioms are metaphorical extensions of nonidiomatic word combinations. For example, ПОДНИМАТЬ/ПОДНЯТЬ РУКУ has the literal meaning 'to raise one's hand/arm', as well as two idiomatic meanings:

   1. ~ *на кого* to (try to) harm s.o. physically
   2. ~ *на кого-что* to criticize openly and express strong disapproval of some person, idea, policy, school of thought etc.

   Another such example is ГОЛОВА БОЛИТ. While it literally means 's.o. has a headache', it has the idiomatic meaning 's.o. gives himself a headache over sth.'

4) Some idioms contain a unique lexical component not found elsewhere in the language. For example, ВО ВСЕОРУЖИИ 'fully armed', БИТЬ БАКЛУШИ 'twiddle one's thumbs', БЕЗ УМОЛКУ 'nonstop'.

5) Some components of idioms preserve archaic grammatical forms. For example, ТЕМНА ВОДА ВО ОБЛАЦЕХ 'it is all shrouded in darkness' has the old form of the locative plural of ОБЛАКО — ВО ОБЛАЦЕХ; СКРЕПЯ СЕРДЦЕ 'reluctantly' has the old form of the short active participle of the verb СКРЕПИТЬ — СКРЕПЯ (the cor-

responding modern form is the perfective verbal adverb СКРЕПИВ).

6) The role of the negative particle НЕ in idioms is often unpredictable.

  a) Some affirmative idioms cannot be used with negation at all: БАБУШКА НАДВОЕ СКАЗАЛА 'that remains to be seen'; КАМЕНЬ С ДУШИ СВАЛИЛСЯ 'a load was taken off s.o.'s mind'.

  b) In other idioms, used only with НЕ, the negative particle loses its meaning of negation: КОМАР НОСУ НЕ ПОДТОЧИТ '(it's) done to a T'.

  c) Idioms that can be used with and without negation comprise a rather heterogeneous group:

    i) The use of negation may produce the antonym of the affirmative idiom: ПО ВКУСУ/НЕ ПО ВКУСУ '(not) to s.o.'s taste ⟨liking⟩'

    ii) The idiom with negation may have a different number of senses than the corresponding affirmative idiom. For example, Л-14 В ЛАДУ has only one sense, '(be) friendly with s.o., have a good rapport with s.o.', whereas Л-15 НЕ В ЛАДУ has three senses:

      1. ~ *с кем*…one is in disagreement with s.o., has a strained relationship with s.o.

      2. ~ *с чем*…one cannot understand or master sth., cannot learn how to use, apply etc sth.

      3. *rare* ~ *с чем*…sth. is in discord with some other thing

    iii) The idiom may have the same meaning regardless of whether it is used with or without negation: (НЕ) ПРИШЕЙ КОБЫЛЕ ХВОСТ 'excess baggage'

7) Idioms differing only in verbal aspect may have different meanings as well as a different number of meanings. For example, Д-333 ВАЛЯТЬ ДУРАКА (the imperfective) has four meanings:

  1. to pretend not to understand, know about sth., feign stupidity (in order to fool s.o.)…

  2. to act in such a way as to amuse (and occasionally annoy) others with one's tricks, anecdotes etc; behave mischievously, in a silly manner…

  3. …to act irresponsibly, unintelligently, unseriously, make a stupid blunder…

  4. …to be idle, spend time lazily…

In contrast, СВАЛЯТЬ ДУРАКА (the perfective) has only one meaning, 'to make a blunder'. It is included at sense 3 of ВАЛЯТЬ ДУРАКА.

Types of Idioms

The overwhelming majority of entries included in the dictionary are idioms per se, or "traditional" idioms. This group includes idioms that function as a part of speech (ТЕЛЯЧЬИ НЕЖНОСТИ 'sloppy sentimentality'—noun phrase; ИЗ РЯДА ВОН ВЫХОДЯЩИЙ 'extraordinary'—adjective phrase; СЫГРАТЬ В ЯЩИК 'to kick the bucket'—verb phrase; ВКРИВЬ И ВКОСЬ 'every which way'—adverb phrase) and idioms that function as a sentence (БАБУШКА НАДВОЕ СКАЗАЛА 'that remains to be seen'; ЗАВАРИВАЕТСЯ/ЗАВАРИЛАСЬ КАША 'trouble is brewing'). The other types of fixed expressions included in the dictionary are:

1) Phrases serving as intensifiers, restrictive markers, etc., for the words with which they collocate. This group includes:

  a) pure intensifiers—for example, ДО ПОЛУСМЕРТИ 'intensely, to a very high degree'

  b) frozen similes—for example, красный КАК РАК '(as) red as a beet'; (глуп) КАК ПРОБКА '(as) dumb as they come'

  c) phrases that consist of a word and its intensifier—for example, ВОЛЧИЙ АППЕТИТ 'a ravenous ⟨voracious⟩ appetite'

2) Interjections used to express various emotions and reactions. For example, НУ И НУ! 'well, I'll be (damned)!'; ВОТ ТЕБЕ И РАЗ! 'well, I never!'

3) Formula phrases, that is, fixed phrases used in common communication situations (in greeting and in parting, when apologizing or responding to an apology, when thanking s.o., etc.). For example, ВСЕГО ХОРОШЕГО 'all the best!'; НЕ СТОИТ 'don't mention it'.

4) Grammatical, or function, idioms:

  a) prepositions—for example, ПО НАПРАВЛЕНИЮ *к кому-чему* 'toward'

  b) conjunctions—for example, ПЕРЕД ТЕМ КАК 'before'

  c) particles—for example, ТОГО И ГЛЯДИ '(one may do sth. ⟨sth. may happen⟩) any minute now'

5) Over 300 commonly used proverbs and sayings that occur in Russian literature and/or colloquial speech. For example, ЯБЛОКО ОТ ЯБЛОНИ НЕДАЛЕКО ПАДАЕТ 'the apple never falls far from the tree'.

6) Some *крылатые слова*, or "winged words," that is, commonly used quotations from works of Russian literature and poetry. For example, БЫЛИ КОГДА-ТО И МЫ РЫСАКАМИ 'we too had our hour of glory', from A.N. Apukhtin's poem "A Team of Bays" («Пара гнедых», 1895).

7) The dictionary follows the Russian lexicograpic tradition in including some other types of set phrases that are not strictly idiomatic, such as НЕСТИ/ПОНЕСТИ ВЗДОР ⟨АХИНЕЮ, БЕЛИБЕРДУ…⟩ 'spout drivel'.

The dictionary does not include composite terms such as ЦАРСКАЯ ВОДКА 'aqua regia', БЕЛАЯ ГОРЯЧКА 'delirium tremens', АНЮТИНЫ ГЛАЗКИ 'pansy', and the like, which can be found in comprehensive general bilingual dictionaries.

Etymological Groups

Etymologically, Russian idioms include the following groups:

1) Idioms rooted in Russian reality, past and present. For example, ПОПАДАТЬ/ПОПАСТЬ ВПРОСАК 'put one's foot in it', from the old practice of using a machine called «просак» for making rope; БЕЗ СУЧКА БЕЗ ЗАДОРИНКИ 'without a hitch', from the speech of carpenters and joiners; ИСКУССТВОВЕД В ШТАТСКОМ 'plain-clothes agent', referring to the KGB's widespread practice of recruiting informers. The source of such idioms is explained either in an etymological note at the end of the entry, or in the definition and/or usage note.

2) Idioms based on or derived from the Bible. For example, КАИНОВА ПЕЧАТЬ 'the mark of Cain'; МАННА НЕБЕСНАЯ 'manna from heaven'.

3) Idioms drawn from Greek and Roman mythology. For example, АХИЛЛЕСОВА ПЯТА 'Achilles heel'; АВГИЕВЫ КОНЮШНИ 'Augean stables'; ТАНТАЛОВЫ МУКИ 'the torments of Tantalus'.

4) Idioms that are full or partial loan translations of phrases

from other languages. For example, КАЖДОМУ СВОЁ 'to each his own' (from the Latin *suum cuique*); ВЕЩЬ В СЕБЕ 'thing-in-itself' (from the German *Ding an sich*); СТРОИТЬ КУРЫ 'pay court to s.o.' (partial loan translation of the French *faire la court*).

GRAMMAR

It is assumed that the user has a basic knowledge of Russian and English grammar and grammatical terminology. There are, however, several points that deserve special attention.

The term "copula," used widely in the grammatical descriptions, is understood to embrace a rather broad group of copula-like verbs. It includes both those verbs that are regularly used as copulas (that is, оказываться/оказаться, казаться/показаться, становиться/стать, делаться/сделаться, считаться, представляться, оставаться/остаться, бывать, and являться in its copular use) and some other verbs occasionally used as copulas (сидеть, стоять, and the like).

Some idioms are used as subject-complements only with the copular быть, which takes a zero form in the present tense. This is shown in the grammatical brackets of the entry or sense as быть$_\emptyset$.

Some idioms can be used both with copular быть$_\emptyset$, and with existential or possessive быть (which can be used in the present tense in the form есть). Such idioms are presented with two patterns, one with and one without есть. For example, НА ПРИМЕТЕ has the following two patterns:

у Y-a есть на примете один ⟨такой и т. п.⟩ X ≃ **Y has an ⟨a certain, one⟩ X in mind**...; ‖ (этот) X у Y-a давно на примете ≃ **Y has had an ⟨his⟩ eye on (this ⟨that⟩) X for (quite) some time**...

The user must be aware that when a verb is used as a participle or a verbal adverb (whether as part of an idiom or not), it changes its syntactic function. Such change of function is common to all Russian verbs and is therefore not specified for verbal idioms.

In the dictionary it is assumed that the grammatical subject may be in the nominative or the genitive case. This approach (suggested by a number of linguists including Mel'čuk 1974[3], Chvany 1975[4], and Apresjan 1980[5] and 1985[6]) differs from the traditional approach, which assigns the role of subject only to noun phrases in the nominative case. In addition, a noun phrase in the genitive case is considered to function as the subject in constructions where a quantifier functions as the predicate; for example, Денег у меня кот наплакал 'I have practically no money'.

In definitions and equivalents, the English pronouns "one," "one's," and "o.s." (for "oneself") correspond to the subject of the Russian clause, while the pronouns "s.o." and "s.o.'s" (for "someone" and "someone's") correspond to the object of the Russian clause (direct, indirect, and/or prepositional). For example, the idiom УТЕРЕТЬ НОС *кому*... has the definition 'to outdo s.o., prove one's superiority in sth.' Here, "s.o." corresponds to the Russian indirect object *кому*, and "one" refers to the Russian subject of the verb phrase. The abbreviated forms "s.o." and "sth." are used in all instances except when the phrases "someone else" and "something else" are irreplaceable elements in an equivalent. For example, С ЧУЖОГО ПЛЕЧА '...off someone else's back; someone else's castoff(s)'; НА ⟨ЗА⟩ ЧУЖОЙ СЧЕТ '...at someone else's expense;...on someone else's tab'. When the Russian verb has two

objects, "s.o." or "s.o.'s" is used in reference to only one of them; the other object is referred to as a "person" (or a "thing"), "another," etc.

In looking at the equivalents for Russian patterns, one must remember that the Russian and English tense-aspect forms do not fully correspond. For example, the Russian present tense (imperfective verbs only) can be rendered by the English simple present or present progressive; the Russian perfective past can be rendered by the English simple past, present perfect, or past perfect. The English tense-aspect forms most commonly used in patterns are the simple present and the simple past, but they should be viewed as models to be modified as contexts require.

ORDERING OF ENTRIES

Each entry begins with a letter-number indicator showing its placement in the dictionary, as:

П-537 • НА ПРИМЕТЕ...

Idiomatic homographs are listed as separate entries, each of which is marked by a superscript number:

П-490 • ПО ПРАВУ[1]...
П-491 • ПО ПРАВУ[2]...

Entries are ordered alphabetically by their key words in precisely the same form as the key words are used in the idioms. For example, ИЗ РЯДА ВОН ВЫХОДЯЩИЙ is entered under РЯДА (genitive singular) rather than РЯД (nominative singular).

Whenever possible, the key word is a content word. Content words are nouns (including substantivized adjectives and participles), adjectives, numerals, main verbs, adverbs, and pronouns. If a complex particle, conjunction, preposition, or interjection has a content word, the idiom is placed under that content word; for example, А МЕЖДУ ТЕМ '(and) yet' is placed under ТЕМ. Idioms not containing any content word (such as many interjections and complex particles) are entered under their first word; for example, АЙ ДА 'what (a)...!' is entered under АЙ.

According to this approach, an idiomatic noun phrase is entered under its noun. An idiomatic phrase containing two nouns is entered under the first noun, regardless of the cases the nouns are in. An adjective phrase is entered under its adjective (or the first adjective, if there is more than one), and a prepositional phrase is entered under the key word of the preposition's nominal complement. When the only noun in an idiom is a proper name (personal or geographical), the idiom is listed under that proper noun; for example, КАК МАМАЙ ПРОШЁЛ 'it's as if an army had marched through (some place)' is entered under МАМАЙ. One exception is СЫР-БОР ЗАГОРЕЛСЯ '(that's) what ⟨who⟩ sparked the whole thing'. Although СЫР is a short-form adjective, the idiom is placed under СЫР because of the hyphenated spelling.

Idiomatic verb phrases containing a noun are generally entered under the noun (or the first noun if an idiom contains more than one. For example, ПОЛУЧАТЬ/ПОЛУЧИТЬ ОГЛАСКУ 'become widely known' is listed under ОГЛАСКУ; ПОКУПАТЬ/КУПИТЬ КОТА В МЕШКЕ 'buy a pig in a poke' is listed under КОТА. This approach has been taken for pragmatic reasons, in order to spare the user the difficulty of dealing with Russian verbal aspect. The noun in a verbal idiom is the least changeable part of the idiom; only in

[xv]

rare cases can it change its number and/or gender. One exception is ГОДИ́ТЬСЯ В ОТЦЫ́ ⟨В МА́ТЕРИ, В СЫНОВЬЯ́ и т. п.⟩ 'be old ⟨young⟩ enough to be s.o.'s father ⟨mother, son etc⟩', which has changeable noun components and is entered under the verb. Verbal idioms not containing a noun are entered under the verb (or the first verb if there is more than one). For example, **РВАТЬ** И **МЕТА́ТЬ** 'to rant and rave'; И **ДУ́МАТЬ ЗАБЫ́ТЬ** 'to stop thinking about s.o. or sth.'

Within a group of idioms with the same key word, idioms are arranged alphabetically word by word (rather than letter by letter). For example, the entries for idioms with the key word МЕСТА́ are arranged in the following way:

ВЗЯТЬ С МЕ́СТА
ЖИВО́ГО МЕ́СТА НЕТ...
МЕСТА́ НЕ СТОЛЬ ОТДАЛЁННЫЕ
НЕ НАХОДИ́ТЬ... (СЕБЕ́) МЕ́СТА
НЕ СОЙТИ́ МНЕ... С (Э́ТОГО) МЕ́СТА
НЕ СХОДЯ́ С МЕ́СТА
НЕТ МЕ́СТА
НИ С МЕ́СТА
[etc.]

Prepositions are counted as separate words. Thus, С МЕ́СТА В КАРЬЕ́Р precedes СДВИ́НУТЬ С МЕ́СТА.

For the purposes of alphabetization, the Russian letters Е and Ё are treated as the same letter.

Each element in a hyphenated entry is treated as a separate word, as:

ЧТО ТАМ
ЧТО-ТО НЕ ТАК

ЧТО ТЫ!
ЧТО-ЧТО, А...

Optional elements in parentheses are counted in determining alphabetical order in the dictionary proper, as:

(В) ПЕ́РВОЕ ВРЕ́МЯ
(В) ПОСЛЕ́ДНЕЕ ВРЕ́МЯ
В СВОЁ ВРЕ́МЯ
В ТО ВРЕ́МЯ КАК
В ТО ЖЕ ВРЕ́МЯ

A slightly different approach has been taken in the Index, which is explained at the introduction to the Index.

Lexical, morphological, and orthographic variants in angle brackets are not counted in determining alphabetical order, as:

ПЕ́СЕНКА ⟨ПЕ́СНЯ⟩ СПЕ́ТА
ИЗ ПЕ́СНИ СЛО́ВА НЕ ВЫ́КИНЕШЬ

For verb phrases used in both the imperfective and the perfective, only the imperfective, which is given first, is counted in determining alphabetical order. For example, in МОЗО́ЛИТЬ/НАМОЗО́ЛИТЬ ГЛАЗА́ only the imperfective МОЗО́ЛИТЬ is counted in determining alphabetical order.

To ensure that the user can easily find any entry, the corpus of the dictionary is followed by an alphabetical Russian index. Each Russian entry is listed in the Index for each of its content words, and each content word is listed in the same form in which it occurs in the idiom. Sayings are listed under the first three content words plus all other particularly important words.

THE DICTIONARY ENTRY

Each dictionary entry has the following elements: a letter-number indicator, the head matter proper (rendered in boldface capital letters), grammatical information, a definition, and one or more English equivalents. The head matter proper includes variations and optional elements that constitute the idiom(s) being presented. Most entries have some or all of the following as well: collocates; an indication of case government; usage labels; a usage note; a Russian pattern or patterns (for verb phrases and selected other idioms); illustrations (literary citations and/or invented examples); and an etymological note.

HEAD MATTER

All entries are presented in their canonical variant(s), that is, in the form or forms common in Standard Russian. Regular word stress is marked for all polysyllabic words in the head matter, in synonyms presented in the various senses, and in related noun phrases. Stress may be marked on monosyllabic words to indicate phrasal stress in interjections (НУ И НУ́! 'how do you like that!') or to indicate unusual emphatic stress patterns (Я́ ТЕБЕ́! 'I'll teach you!').

Idioms that are synonymous with only one of the senses of a polysemous idiom do not appear in the head matter, but, rather, are listed at the applicable sense after the word "Also." For example, МЕ́ДНАЯ ГЛО́ТКА '(s.o. has) a lot of lung power' is synonymous with sense 2 of Г-146 ЛУЖЁНАЯ ГЛО́ТКА, and so is presented at the latter as: 2. Also: МЕ́ДНАЯ ГЛО́ТКА.

Noun and Adjective Phrases

Noun phrases used only in the singular or in both the singular and the plural are listed in the nominative singular: КАРТО́ЧНЫЙ ДО́МИК 'house of cards'. Noun phrases used only or commonly in the plural are listed in the plural: МЁРТВЫЕ ДУ́ШИ 'dead souls'; РАБО́ЧИЕ РУ́КИ 'manpower'; АХИ И О́ХИ 'ohs and ahs'. Adjective phrases used only in the singular or in both the singular and the plural are listed in the nominative singular, masculine: ВЕ́РНЫЙ САМОМУ́ СЕБЕ́ 'true to o.s.'

Verbal Idioms

Verbal idioms used in finite forms and in all or some of the nonfinite forms (the infinitive, participles, and verbal adverbs) are listed in the infinitive: ДУТЬ В ДУ́ДКУ 'play s.o.'s tune'; РВАТЬ И МЕТА́ТЬ 'rant and rave'. If an idiom is used in both the imperfective and the perfective aspects, the imperfective is entered first followed by a slash and the perfective: СТА́ВИТЬ/ПОСТА́ВИТЬ НА (СВОЁ) МЕ́СТО кого 'put s.o. in his place'. If only one aspectual form is listed, it means that the other aspect is not used in the given idiom or that the verb does not have an aspectual partner. For example, БИТЬ БАКЛУ́ШИ 'twiddle one's thumbs' is listed only in the imperfective, and НАВЯ́ЗНУТЬ В ЗУБА́Х 'bore s.o. to death' is listed only in the perfective because neither of these verbs has an aspectual partner. Verbal idioms that are used only in finite forms are generally listed in the third person singular present and perfective past forms (and have sentential definitions): БРОСАЕТ/БРОСИЛО В КРАСКУ…'s.o. flushes out of shame, embarrassment'. If no restrictions are stated, such idioms can be used in the future tense as well. Future-tense forms are presented in the head matter only for idioms that are used exclusively or predominantly in the future tense (usually the perfective future): НЕДОРОГО ВОЗЬМЁТ 'one won't think twice about doing sth.'; НЕ НАДЫШИТСЯ 'one dotes on s.o.' Idioms used only in one finite form are listed in that form: НЕ КАПЛЕТ 's.o. is not in any rush'; БОЮСЬ СКАЗАТЬ 'I'm not sure'. Idioms with one component functioning as the subject are presented in sentential form: ДУША УХОДИТ/УШЛА В ПЯТКИ 's.o.'s heart sinks into his boots'; УДАР ХВАТИЛ кого 's.o. had a seizure'.

An idiom containing the word НЕТ used as a predicate is described as a verb phrase (shown as VP). Numerous idioms with НЕТ are presented only in their present tense form: ИЗНОСУ НЕТ чему 'sth. doesn't wear out'. If no restrictions are stated for such idioms, they can be used in the past (не было) and future (не будет) tenses as well.

Idioms used only or most commonly in the negative are listed in the negative. Most idioms presented in the negative can never be used without negation: НЕ ВЫХОДИТ ⟨НЕ ИДЁТ, НЕЙДЁТ⟩ ИЗ ГОЛОВЫ 's.o. can't get sth. out of his mind'; НЕ ЗНАТЬ… ПОКОЯ 'know no peace'; НЕ ОСТАВАТЬСЯ/НЕ ОСТАТЬСЯ В ДОЛГУ 'pay s.o. back (in kind)'. Some idioms, however, while generally negative, can occasionally be used without negation; they are described as "used without negation to convey the opposite meaning." When the meaning of a negated phrase does not equal the meaning of the negation plus the meaning of the corresponding affirmative phrase, the negative and affirmative phrases are presented as separate entries:

Л-14 • В ЛАДУ…(to be) friendly with s.o., have a good rapport with s.o.…

Л-15 • НЕ В ЛАДУ…1. ~ с кем one is in disagreement with s.o., has a strained relationship with s.o.…
2. ~ с чем one cannot understand or master sth., cannot learn how to use, apply etc sth.…
3. rare ~ с чем sth. is in discord with some other thing…

Collocates and Case Government
For idioms with a limited range of *collocates*, the collocates (or the most typical of them) are listed, for example: С ВЕРХОМ налить, наполнить что '(fill etc sth.) to the brim'. When collocates differ for different senses of a polysemous idiom, they are listed separately in each sense, as at Н-229 НОСОМ К НОСУ:

1. ~ столкнуться, встретиться (to meet, run into one another) right up close, facing one another…
2. увидеть кого-что и т. п. ~ (to see s.o. or sth.) at close proximity…

Case government for both the main entry and its collocates is shown by the forms кого-чего, кому-чему, к кому, к чему, etc. Кого, кому, etc., must be replaced by human (or, occasionally, animal) nouns, whereas чего, чему, etc., can be replaced by inanimate or collective nouns, as: НЕ ПАРА кому 'one is not a (good) match for s.o.'; ПО СЕБЕ (sense 1) найти, выбрать кого-что '(to find, choose s.o. or sth.) coinciding with one's taste, of one's preference, commensurate with one's abilities, status etc'.

In instances when the main entry includes two or more synonymous idioms with the same government or collocates, the collocates and government are shown with the first idiom only, implying that they carry over to successive idioms. For example, Г-93 contains three synonymous idioms with the same government and collocates:

ПУЩЕ ГЛАЗА беречь кого-что, хранить что; ПАЧЕ ГЛАЗА ⟨ОКА⟩ obs…

If the verbal government differs for variants or synonyms, it is provided for each one, as: ПОКАЗЫВАТЬ ⟨УКАЗЫВАТЬ, ТЫКАТЬ⟩ ПАЛЬЦЕМ… (на кого-что); ТЫКАТЬ ПАЛЬЦЕМ… в кого.

The head matter for verbal idioms does not include related noun phrases; these are shown after the verbal equivalents following the symbol ○.

Proverbs and Sayings
Proverbs and sayings are given in their canonical forms. If part of a saying is used as an independent idiom, it is presented as a separate entry. For example, the saying ЛУЧШЕ СИНИЦА В РУКАХ, ЧЕМ ЖУРАВЛЬ В НЕБЕ 'a bird in the hand is worth two in the bush' has two offshoot idioms: СИНИЦА В РУКАХ 'the proverbial bird in the hand' and ЖУРАВЛЬ В НЕБЕ '(like) the proverbial two birds in the bush'. The full saying is given as one entry (at С-195), and each of its offshoots is entered separately (С-196, Ж-85) with an etymological note referring the user to the full saying.

Usage Labels
Usage labels are provided for Russian idioms only. When provided, usage labels follow the idiom to which they refer, whether it is located in the head matter of the entry or only at a given sense. The label or labels apply as well to any lexical variants, morphological variants, or synonymous idioms that appear in angle brackets. For example, in К-62 НА КАПЛЮ ⟨НА КАПЕЛЬКУ⟩ coll '(hardly) an ounce (of…)', the label *coll* refers to both КАПЛЮ and the КАПЕЛЬКУ variant. If synonymous idioms that are separated by a semicolon take the same usage label, it is preceded by the word *both* (for two variants) or *all* (for three or more variants). For example, the label *all coll* at С-452 refers to all four cited variants of the idiom:

ПО СОВЕСТИ; ПО СОВЕСТИ ГОВОРЯ ⟨СКАЗАТЬ, ПРИЗНАТЬСЯ⟩ all coll…speaking openly…

A label is placed within the angle brackets when it refers only to the variant inside those brackets. For example, the label *obs* at Л-68 refers only to the variant В РЕКУ ЗАБВЕНИЯ:

КАНУТЬ В ЛЕТУ ⟨В РЕКУ ЗАБВЕНИЯ obs⟩ lit… to disappear completely, be forgotten forever…

Usage labels fall into three main categories: temporal, stylistic, and emotive-expressive.

Stylistic and emotive-expressive labels should be seen as general, not absolute, guidelines for the interpretation and use of an idiom, since the nuances that an idiom can convey depend largely on contextual factors.

Temporal labels indicate an idiom's standing in relation to contemporary usage. These are the temporal labels used in the dictionary.

obs (obsolete) — The idiom is not used in contemporary literary or colloquial Russian.

[xvii]

obsoles (obsolescent) — The idiom is used rarely in contemporary literary or colloquial Russian and is perceived as becoming out of date.

old-fash (old-fashioned) — The idiom is used only or chiefly by older people.

rare — The idiom is used rarely and may be perceived as somewhat unusual.

recent — The idiom became common relatively recently.

Stylistic labels indicate the stylistic register of an idiom. Russian idioms presented without a stylistic label are stylistically neutral, meaning that they can be used under any circumstances and with any interlocutor. Two major factors have been considered in the assignment of stylistic labels: first, the circumstances in which an idiom can typically be used (a friendly conversation or letter, an official gathering, etc.); second, the ages and relative social status of the speaker, his interlocutor, and the person(s) referred to. While no stylistic labels are provided for English equivalents, an effort was made to find equivalents that are as close as possible to the stylistic register of the Russian. The following stylistic labels appear in the dictionary.

coll (colloquial) — The idiom is used in casual or informal speech and writing.

highly coll (highly colloquial) — The idiom is used in very casual speech and writing and is often colored by the speaker's emotive attitude; highly colloquial idioms are inappropriate in formal or semiformal situations.

substand (substandard) — The idiom is characterized by a deviation from grammatical or syntactical standards and/or by having a vernacular word as one of its components; it is used by less educated or uneducated people.

slang — The idiom has come into the spoken language from (or is still used predominantly in) the speech of a specific social group, profession, age group, etc. Such idioms are used in extremely casual speech; they are often metaphorical and sometimes sexually suggestive.

euph (euphemism) — The idiom is used as an inoffensive substitute for a vulgar, blasphemous, or shocking expression.

iron (ironic) — The idiom is used in a meaning opposite to its direct meaning.

lit (literary) — The idiom is characteristic of educated, well-read people and is used mainly, albeit not exclusively, in learned conversation and formal speech and writing (public speeches, scholarly essays, etc.).

rhet (rhetorical) — The idiom is used with the intention of producing a certain effect on the listener(s) or reader(s). It occurs mainly, but not only, in declamatory speech or in exhortative speech and writing.

elev (elevated) — The idiom is used in exalted (sometimes stilted) writing or very formal speech.

offic (official) — The idiom is used in formal, official contexts and/or belongs to bureaucratic jargon.

special — The idiom is used only or predominantly in specialized contexts.

folk poet (folkloric poetic) — The idiom comes from popular lore, especially folk tales, and preserves (to some degree or other) its folkloric, poetic overtones.

vulg (vulgar) — The idiom is socially or aesthetically in bad taste, or is generally considered indecent or obscene.

taboo — The idiom directly refers to sexual and/or scatological practices, and is unacceptable in standard contexts.

Occasionally, synonymous idioms of two different registers are grouped together in the same head entry, as: ГОЛОВА ВАРИТ *(у кого) coll*; КОТЕЛОК ВАРИТ *substand*; МОЗГИ ВАРЯТ *substand*…'s.o. is bright, intelligent'. The equivalents provided cover both colloquial and substandard variants.

Emotive-expressive labels describe the emotions commonly conveyed by the given idiom. The intensity of these emotions, expressed particularly clearly in colloquial speech, may be affected by such factors as the speaker's frame of mind, the relationship between the speaker and the interlocutor, and the status of the party to whom the idiom refers (the speaker himself, the interlocutor, or a third party). These are the emotive-expressive labels appearing in the dictionary.

humor (humorous)

iron or humor, *humor or iron* — Said with ironic or humorous intonation; the prevailing emotion comes first.

disapprov (disapproving)

derog (derogatory)

condes (condescending)

impol (impolite)

rude

GRAMMATICAL INFORMATION

The grammatical description is intended to supply the basic information needed to use an idiom actively in speech and writing. The majority of the terminology in the grammatical descriptions should be familiar to anyone who has studied a foreign language; exceptions are specified below.

The grammatical description appears within square brackets [ ] and refers to the Russian idiom and its variants and/or synonyms as presented in the head matter. If an idiom's variants and synonyms differ in structure and/or syntactic function from the main form, a description of each variant/synonym is provided. When different senses of a polysemous idiom require different grammatical information, grammatical brackets are included at each numbered sense.

An idiom is described according to its phrase type in those instances when it is used in all or most of the syntactic functions characteristic of the given type of phrase. The phrase types referred to in the grammatical brackets are noun phrase (NP), verb phrase (VP), adjective phrase (AdjP), adverb phrase (AdvP), and prepositional phrase (PrepP). To avoid complicating the grammatical description these labels are used as umbrella terms: NP encompasses both a noun and a noun phrase; VP both a verb and a verb phrase; and so on. (These grammatical labels and their syntactic parameters are described separately below.)

When an idiom is "frozen" and the description of the type of phrase (if altogether possible) would in no way help the user to use it correctly, it is described either as "Invar" (invariable) or as "these forms only." "Invar" indicates that the single form presented in the head matter is the only form used: Г-422 ГРУДЬ В ГРУДЬ [Invar; adv]. The label "these forms only" indicates that the multiple variants presented in the head matter are the only forms used: Д-300 ДОХНУТЬ ⟨ДЫХНУТЬ⟩ НЕКОГДА [these forms only; impers predic with быть∅]. The labels "Invar" and "these forms only" are also used to describe sentential idioms that are used only in the form or forms listed in the head matter: Б-5 БАБУШКА (ЕЩЁ) НАДВОЕ СКАЗАЛА ⟨ГАДАЛА⟩ [these forms only]. These two labels do not imply anything about the linear order of the components of an idiom, which is described separately.

When an idiom requires an object or complement to perform a specific syntactic function, its grammatical description includes an indication of the required object or complement: Л-74 ПО ЛИНИИ [...the resulting PrepP is adv or modif].

When an idiom functions only as a subject-complement, it is described in grammatical brackets as "subj-compl." In some instances, an idiomatic subject-complement can be used only with быть∅; such an idiom is described as "subj-compl with быть∅." In other instances, an idiomatic subject-complement can be used with other copular verbs, in which case it is described as "subj-compl with copula."

When an idiom that functions as an object-complement can be used only with a specific verb or verbs, the grammatical brackets present that verb or those verbs:

Ж-36 • В ЖИВЫХ [Invar; subj-compl with быть∅, остаться (subj:human) or obj-compl with застать (obj:human)]...

When an idiom that is not fixed in form (not "Invar" or "these forms only") is used as a subject- or object-complement, its gender and number are controlled by the subject or object, respectively.

Noun Phrases

As stated above, an idiom is described as "NP" when it is used in all or most of the typical syntactic functions of a noun phrase; that is, as a subject, an object, and a complement. For idioms in which one noun governs another or others, NP refers to the key word of the idiom: ВЛАСТИТЕЛЬ ДУМ 'molder of opinion'; КНИГА ЗА СЕМЬЮ ПЕЧАТЯМИ 'a closed book'; ПАРА ПУСТЯКОВ 'child's play'. Grammatical brackets indicate when an idiom is used only or predominantly in one or two of the above functions: К-307 ЦЕЛЫЙ КОРОБ [NP; sing only; subj or obj]. Grammatical brackets also indicate when an idiom is usually (or often) used as a vocative or appositive: Г-223 ШАЛЬНАЯ ГОЛОВА [NP; usu. appos, vocative, or subj-compl with copula (subj:human)].

Restrictions are provided for noun phrase idioms that are used only in one grammatical case; for example, sense 2 of М-17 САМАЯ МАЛОСТЬ... 'a tiny bit' has the restriction "accus only" (sense 1 has no restrictions with regard to case).

Restrictions are also given for noun phrase idioms used only in the singular or only in the plural: В-280 АДМИНИСТРАТИВНЫЙ ВОСТОРГ [NP; sing only] 'bureaucratic zeal'; Д-390 МЁРТВЫЕ ДУШИ [NP; pl only] 'dead souls'. Such restrictions are not presented for idioms whose key noun is used in the language only in the singular or only in the plural: Г-324 ГОРЕ ЛУКОВОЕ '(you) lummox' and Т-44 ТАРЫ-БАРЫ 'tittle-tattle'.

For idioms comprised of two nouns connected by a conjunction, the grammatical restriction "sing only" refers to each noun component of the idiom: ЦАРЬ И БОГ 'lord and master'; АЛЬФА И ОМЕГА 'the alpha and omega'. Similarly, АХИ И ОХИ 'ohs and ahs' is described as "pl only," which means that each of its components may be used only in the plural.

For idioms consisting of a noun in the nominative case plus another element, the restriction "sing only" or "pl only" refers only to the noun in the nominative case. It is understood that the remaining component(s) of the idiom can be used only in the form or forms shown in the head matter: for example, in the idioms ДОЛЯ ПРАВДЫ 'grain of truth', СУЕТА СУЕТ 'vanity of vanities', and БУРЯ В СТАКАНЕ ВОДЫ

'a tempest in a teapot', the indicator "sing only" refers just to the words ДОЛЯ, СУЕТА, and БУРЯ, respectively.

When a noun phrase that is used as a subject-complement can occur both in the nominative and in the instrumental case, the noun phrase is described as "subj-compl with copula, nom or instrum"; for example:

В-224 • ВОЛК В ОВЕЧЬЕЙ ШКУРЕ...[NP; usu. subj-compl with copula, nom or instrum (subj: human)...]...**wolf in sheep's clothing**...

Adjective Phrases

Adjective phrases (including participles) that contain long-form adjectives are presented in the nominative case only, in the masculine singular: ЦЕЛЫЙ И НЕВРЕДИМЫЙ 'safe and sound'. Adjective phrases that contain short-form adjectives are listed in the masculine singular: НИ ЖИВ НИ МЁРТВ 'more dead than alive'. If no restrictions are provided, the given adjective phrase can be used in other genders, in the plural, and (long-form only) in other cases as well.

An adjective phrase that can be placed only before or only after the word or phrase it modifies is described as "premodif" (premodifier) or "postmodif" (postmodifier), respectively.

An adjective phrase that is used as a subject-complement with a plural subject only is listed in the plural: ОДНИМ МИРОМ МАЗАНЫ 'tarred with the same brush'. An adjective phrase used as a subject- or object-complement is described similarly to a noun phrase used in these functions. For example, НЕ ЛИШНЕЕ ⟨НЕ ЛИШНЕ⟩ 'it wouldn't be (such) a bad idea (to do sth.)' is described as:

[AdjP; subj-compl with быть∅ (subj: infin or a clause) or obj-compl with находить, считать (1st var. only, obj: usu. deverbal noun or infin)]

Verb Phrases

A verb phrase is described as "VP" when it can be used in all or at least some finite and non-finite forms: ВЛЕЧЬ/ПОВЛЕЧЬ ЗА СОБОЙ *что* 'lead to (sth.)'.

Verbal idioms that function as predicates require that a subject (and often an object or objects) be added to them to create a complete utterance. To help the user to use such idioms actively, the grammatical brackets indicate the type(s) of subject and, if relevant, object(s) with which the given idiom is used: human noun, personal or geographical name, animal noun, collective noun, concrete noun (understood as denoting a thing), abstract noun, infinitive, and clause. For example, В-187 ЛИТЬ ВОДУ НА МЕЛЬНИЦУ (*чью, кого*) 'be grist to s.o.'s mill' has a human or abstract subject and is described as "VP; subj: human or abstr." When an idiom can be used only with a specific thematic group or a limited number of nouns as subjects and/or objects, this restriction is indicated:

К-112 • КАШИ ПРОСЯТ...[VP; subj: a noun denoting footwear or individual parts of shoes...] (s.o.'s boots, shoes etc) are in bad condition, in need of repair...

К-94 • СТАВИТЬ/ПОСТАВИТЬ НА КАРТУ *что* [VP; subj: human or collect; obj: abstr (usu. жизнь, честь etc)] to risk one's life, reputation, security etc in the hope of winning or gaining sth....

Д-7 • ДАВАТЬ/ДАТЬ СЕБЯ ЗНАТЬ...[VP; subj: abstr or concr...] to manifest itself, become noticeable...

Р-138 • НА РОДУ НАПИСАНО...[AdjP; subj-compl with быть∅ (subj: infin or a clause)...] sth. is predestined, preordained for s.o....

Restrictions are provided for verb phrases and sentences that are used only or usually in the specified tense-aspect and/or person form(s):

К-113 • МАЛО КАШИ ЕЛ/СЪЕЛ...[...2nd or 3rd pers; past only...] one is (too) inexperienced, young etc (for sth.)...

В-214 • НЕДОРОГО ⟨НЕ ДОРОГО⟩ ВОЗЬМЁТ... [...fut only...] one will do sth. (sth. bad, reprehensible, as denoted by the preceding verb) readily, without hesitation...

К-43 • КАМЕНЬ... С ДУШИ ⟨С СЕРДЦА⟩ СВАЛИЛСЯ у кого [...usu. past] s.o. experienced a sense of relief, felt liberated from his worries...

Some idioms are used only or predominantly in the generic «ты» form, perfective future. This feature is indicated in the grammatical brackets, along with the verb form itself:

К-32 • КАЛАЧОМ НЕ ЗАМАНИТЬ...[...usu. fut gener. 2nd pers sing не заманишь...] to be unable by any means to convince s.o. to go to some place or see s.o....

In those rare instances in which a verbal idiom consists of two verb forms, only one of which conjugates, the grammatical brackets specify "only *verb* conjugates":

Д-322 • И ДУМАТЬ ЗАБЫТЬ...[...only забыть conjugates...] to stop thinking about s.o. or sth....

Some infinitival idioms do not act as regular verb phrases in that they do not conjugate and are used only as the complement of given predicates. The entries for such idioms indicate the type of predicates with which the idiom can be used. For example, Г-33 ОТОРВАТЬ ГЛАЗ can be used with predicates like не мочь, не в силах, and нельзя; it is presented as follows:

Г-33 • не мочь, не в силах, нельзя и т. п. ОТОРВАТЬ ⟨ОТВЕСТИ⟩ ГЛАЗ от кого-чего...[Invar; infin compl of не мочь, не в силах etc (subj: human), infin compl of нельзя etc (impers)...] (to be unable) to stop looking at s.o. or sth....

Verb phrases that are often or most commonly used in the third person plural with an omitted subject are described as "3rd pers pl with indef. refer." For example, ПУСКАТЬ/ПУСТИТЬ КОЗЛА В ОГОРОД is such an idiom, and has the above grammatical description as well as the following illustrative pattern:

пустили козла в огород ≃ they put the cow to mind the corn; they put the wolf in charge of the sheep...

Idioms Functioning as Adverbials

Idioms that function as adverbials are divided into two groups based on their function. The first group, labeled "adv" (adverbial), comprises adverbials of manner, time, space, degree, cause, etc. The second group, labeled "sent adv" (sentence adverbial), comprises adverbial idioms that refer to the sentence or clause as a whole and are syntactically more detached from the elements of the sentence than adverbials belonging to the first group. Sentence adverbials may do the following:

* Indicate a manner of speaking (МЯГКО ВЫРАЖАЯСЬ 'putting it mildly'; ДРУГИМИ СЛОВАМИ 'in other words')
* Convey modality (ОТКРОВЕННО ГОВОРЯ 'frankly speaking'; ПО ПРАВДЕ ГОВОРЯ 'to tell (you) the truth')
* Express a value judgment (К НЕСЧАСТЬЮ 'unfortunately'; НА ДЕЛЕ 'in deed')

* Convey the possibility that something might happen (ЧЕГО ДОБРОГО 'for all one knows, s.o. ⟨sth.⟩ might...'; НЕ РОВЁН ЧАС 'who knows')
* Emphasize a statement or one of its parts (ЕСЛИ ХОТИТЕ 'if you will'; МОЖНО СКАЗАТЬ 'one might say'; НЕ ПРАВДА ЛИ? 'isn't that so?')
* Play an organizing role in a text or speech in various ways:
  1) by connecting two halves of a statement by means of a contrast (С ОДНОЙ СТОРОНЫ... С ДРУГОЙ СТОРОНЫ...'on the one hand...on the other (hand)')
  2) by marking a transition to a new topic (КСТАТИ СКАЗАТЬ 'incidentally')
  3) by introducing a summary (В ЗАКЛЮЧЕНИЕ 'in conclusion'), a specification (К ПРИМЕРУ 'for example'), a result (В РЕЗУЛЬТАТЕ 'as a result'; ТАКИМ ОБРАЗОМ 'consequently'), and so forth.

Most of the idioms used as adverbials or sentence adverbials cannot change in form and are therefore described as "Invar; adv," "Invar; sent adv," "these forms only; adv," or "these forms only; sent adv."

The grammatical brackets note when an idiom functioning as an adverbial occurs only or mainly with one verbal aspect:

В-11 • ВДОЛЬ И ПОПЕРЁК...1. [more often used with pfv verbs]...**far and wide**...

Г-47 • ВО ВСЕ ГЛАЗА...[...used with impfv verbs...]...**all eyes**...

There are some idiomatic Russian adverbials which, although positive in form and used with non-negated verbs, are negative in meaning; each such adverbial is described as "neg intensif" (negative intensifier). For example, разбираться... в чём КАК СВИНЬЯ В АПЕЛЬСИНАХ, literally 'to understand sth. like a pig understands oranges', means 'to understand absolutely nothing (with regard to sth.)'.

Adverbials used with a negated predicate are described as "used with negated verbs." This group of idioms consists mainly of НИ idioms such as НИ ЗА КАКИЕ БЛАГА (В МИРЕ) 'not for anything (in the world)'. The definitions for these idioms include an English negation (usually "not"), which corresponds to the combination of НЕ and НИ.

In adverbials of the type как + adjective (КАК ОШПАРЕННЫЙ 'as if one had been scalded') and как + noun (КАК БАРАН 'like a mule'), the adjective and noun, respectively, are always in the nominative case. Therefore such idioms are described as "nom only." These idioms are co-referential with the subject (or, less commonly, the object), and their adjectival or nominal components must agree with the subject or object in gender (adjectives only) and number (both adjectives and nouns).

Quantifiers

Quantifiers may function as predicates and/or adverbials. Quantifiers that function predicatively are described as "quantit subj-compl" (quantitative subject-complement). Some predicative quantifiers can be used only with быть∅ and are described as "quantit subj-compl with быть∅." Other predicative quantifiers can be used with a number of copular verbs and are described as "quantit subj-comp with copula." For example, КОТ НАПЛАКАЛ 'practically no...(at all)' and ХОТЬ ЗАВАЛИСЬ 'lots ⟨a lot⟩ of' are described as "quantit subj-compl with copula."

Quantifiers that function as adverbials—for example, КАК НА МАЛАНЬИНУ СВАДЬБУ '(cook) enough for an army'—are described as "adv (quantif)."

Interjections

The label "Interj" (interjection) describes idioms that express the speaker's emotional attitude toward, or emotive evaluation of, the person, thing, situation, etc., in question. Interjections are syntactically independent structures that can express different, and sometimes even opposite, emotions depending on the context and the speaker's intonation; for example, ЁЛКИ-ПАЛКИ can express annoyance, admiration, delight, surprise, and bewilderment, among others.

Formula Phrases

The label "formula phrase" describes situationally conditioned idioms used in communicative contexts. Such idioms are often referred to as "speech etiquette formulae" in Russian sources. They are used in greeting (СКОЛЬКО ЛЕТ, СКОЛЬКО ЗИМ! 'it's been ages!'), at parting (ВСЕГО ХОРОШЕГО ⟨ДОБРОГО⟩! 'all the best!'), when wishing someone something (СЧАСТЛИВОГО ПУТИ! 'have a good trip!'), in making a request (БУДЬ ДОБР ⟨БУДЬТЕ ДОБРЫ⟩ 'be so kind as to...'), in expressing gratitude (ПОКОРНО БЛАГОДАРЮ, sense 1, 'I humbly thank you'), in responding to an expression of thanks (НЕ СТОИТ 'don't mention it'), and the like.

Sentential Idioms

Sentential idioms fall into three basic groups:

1) *Idioms that need only a direct, indirect, or prepositional object to become a complete sentence.* For example, in order to become a complete sentence, НОГИ НЕ ДЕРЖАТ *кого* 's.o.'s legs won't support him' requires a direct object, and ВРЕМЯ РАБОТАЕТ *на кого* 'time is on s.o.'s side' requires a prepositional object. Such idioms are described as "VP$_{subj}$," which means that they contain both the subject and the predicate (or part of the predicate).

2) *Idioms that need быть$_\emptyset$ or another copular verb (and often an object) to become a complete sentence.* Such idioms are described as "VP$_{subj}$ with быть$_\emptyset$" or "VP$_{subj}$ with copula"; for example, ГАЙКА СЛАБА *у кого* 's.o. doesn't have it in him (to do sth.)' is described as "VP$_{subj}$ with copula."

3) *Idioms that are complete sentences as they are listed.* Such idioms are described as "sent." This group includes numerous sayings, adages, and крылатые слова ("winged words"), as: БАБУШКА НАДВОЕ СКАЗАЛА 'that remains to be seen'; РУКОПИСИ НЕ ГОРЯТ 'manuscripts don't burn'. Generally, such idioms can function in all or some of the following ways: as an independent sentence, as a clause in a compound sentence, or as the main or a subordinate clause in a complex sentence. Exceptions are specified.

Sayings

All proverbs and sayings are described as "saying" since, for the purposes of this dictionary, the difference between a proverb and a saying is irrelevant.

Word Order

When an idiom has a free order of elements, no reference to word order (WO) is made in the grammatical description. However, when an idiom has a fixed order of elements, it is described as "fixed WO", as: КАЛАНЧА ПОЖАРНАЯ [...fixed WO] 'beanpole'.

When the order of an idiom's components can be changed only in rare cases, the idiom is described as "usu. this WO."

When only one component of an idiom can change its position (and the rest cannot), this information is provided, as:

К-34 • **ДОВОДИТЬ/ДОВЕСТИ ДО БЕЛОГО КАЛЕНИЯ**...[...the verb may take the final position, otherwise fixed WO] to irritate s.o. past the limits of his endurance, make s.o. lose his self-control completely...

Д-11 • **ДОРОГО БЫ ДАЛ**...[...fixed WO with бы movable] one would be willing to give up, sacrifice sth. of great value in order to get sth. he really wants or make some desired event happen...

In the second example the grammatical description shows that **бы** can be placed before ДОРОГО or after ДАЛ.

When the word order of a noun phrase can change only when the noun phrase is used in a specified syntactic function, this information is provided: for example, ВОЛЧИЙ АППЕТИТ [fixed WO except when used as VP$_{subj}$ with copula] (as in Он ел с волчьим аппетитом 'He ate with a ravenous ⟨voracious⟩ appetite', but Аппетит у него волчий 'He has a ravenous ⟨voracious⟩ appetite').

Since "grammatical" idioms (conjunctions and prepositions) and hyphenated idioms always have fixed word order, the label "fixed WO" is not provided for them.

The labels "fixed WO" and "usu. this WO" apply to the idiom per se only and do not take into account placement of the copula, collocate(s), object(s), etc., whose typical placement is shown in patterns and citations.

It should be understood that even when a given idiom has fixed word order in standard literary and colloquial usage, this does not exclude its occasional use with a different word order in poetry, in utterances with shifted emphasis, or by an individual speaker or author for stylistic purposes. Thus, the idioms ОТ ПОЛНОТЫ ДУШИ ⟨СЕРДЦА⟩ 'from the fullness of one's heart' and НА ГОЛОДНЫЙ ЖЕЛУДОК 'on an empty stomach' are assigned the label "fixed WO" despite the existence of such well-known 19th-century citations as «Дай, обниму тебя от сердца полноты», "Let me embrace you now, from the fullness of my heart" (A.S. Griboedov) and «И кому же в ум пойдет на желудок петь голодный!», "And who would even think of singing on an empty stomach?" (I.A. Krylov).

DEFINITIONS AND USAGE NOTES

The definition and, where applicable, usage note are placed directly after the grammatical brackets. When possible, the definition is presented in the same form as the defined Russian idiom, that is,

* as a noun phrase for a Russian noun phrase: ВЛАСТИТЕЛЬ ДУМ [NP...] 'a person who has much influence on his contemporaries, an intellectual and spiritual leader'
* in the infinitive for a regular verb phrase presented in the infinitive: СЫГРАТЬ В ЯЩИК [VP...] 'to die')
* as an adjective phrase for a Russian adjective phrase: ЦЕЛЫЙ И НЕВРЕДИМЫЙ ⟨ЦЕЛ И НЕВРЕДИМ⟩ [AdjP...] 'unhurt, in fine condition')

* as an adverb for a Russian idiom functioning as an adverbial: НЕЖДАННО-НЕГАДАННО [AdvP...] '(to appear, arrive etc) suddenly, unexpectedly'

Idioms that function as sentences have sentential definitions; for example: БАБУШКА НАДВОЕ СКАЗАЛА...'it is yet unknown whether the event in question will happen or not (usu. the implication is that it will not happen)'.

In entries with two or more senses, each sense has its own definition, placed after the Arabic numeral introducing the sense.

Definitions and usage notes use generic "he" to refer to both sexes. In usage notes, "of" introduces the subject of the Russian phrase or the person or thing modified by the phrase; "in refer. to" indicates the object of the Russian phrase or the general situation surrounding the use of the idiom. For example:

М-142 • СИДЕТЬ МЕШКОМ на ком...(of a garment that is too large, wide etc) to fit poorly...

Л-55 • КТО В ЛЕС, КТО ПО ДРОВА...(often in refer. to singing and playing musical instruments) (people do sth.) without coordination among themselves, without agreement, cooperation...

Collocates in Definitions
The translations of collocates are generally given in parentheses as part of the definition. However, in those rare cases in which different collocates would require different wordings of the definition, the collocates are not included in the definition; for example: П-431 отдать на ПОТОК И РАЗГРАБЛЕНИЕ что, предать ПОТОКУ И РАЗГРАБЛЕНИЮ что...'complete destruction and widespread looting (of some place, country etc)'. Usage of the collocates is then shown in patterns:

Х-ы отдали Y на поток и разграбление ≃ **Xs surrendered Y to be ravaged and plundered ⟨pillaged and ruined⟩**; ‖ Х-ы предали Y потоку и разграблению ≃ **Xs ravaged and plundered ⟨pillaged and ruined⟩ Y.**

Prepositions, Conjunctions, Particles
No definition per se has been provided for most complex prepositions, complex conjunctions, and particles; instead, there is a usage note describing the relationship between the element(s) associated with the idiom and other elements of the context. In those cases where a definition per se has been provided, it follows the usage note. Some typical descriptions are:
* used to indicate the unexpected nature of the action that follows
* (used to introduce a clause, phrase etc whose information adds to, and is more important than, the information in the preceding statement)
* used to show that the situation or action presented in the main clause immediately follows the situation or action presented in the subordinate clause
* used to show that the truthfulness or realization of what is stated in the main clause is contingent upon the fulfillment of the condition stated in the subordinate clause

Interjections
Interjections are described in terms of the emotions they can convey; for example: НУ И НУ! used to express surprise, delight, displeasure, an ironic attitude etc.

ENGLISH EQUIVALENTS

The overwhelming majority of entries contain more than one English equivalent, since different contexts often require different translations of a given idiom. When a Russian idiom has several English equivalents, those that are most broadly applicable (or most similar to the Russian) are presented first, and those that are most restricted are presented last. Equivalents in a given entry may differ stylistically in order to cover 19th- as well as 20th-century contexts. Thus, a more formal equivalent might be more appropriate in a translation of 19th-century literature than in a translation of 20th-century colloquial speech.

Whenever possible, equivalents are presented in the same form as the Russian idiom, that is, an English noun phrase for a Russian noun phrase, an English verb phrase for a Russian verb phrase, and so forth. Equivalents for Russian idioms that function as complete sentences are presented in sentential form.

The notation "Cf." (which when given follows the last English equivalent in an entry) is used to introduce English idioms and sayings that, although not suggested for purposes of translation, provide insight into the meaning of the Russian idiom. Often such phrases (as "every Tom, Dick, and Harry" for КАЖДЫЙ ⟨ВСЯКИЙ⟩ ВСТРЕЧНЫЙ 'anyone and everyone') have a distinct national flavor, include typical American or British names, and the like. However, not all culturally bound elements are reserved for "Cf." Since substantial Russian communities can be found in English-speaking countries, the terms "ruble" and "kopeck," for example, are included with "penny," "dime," etc., in numerous English equivalents.

Collocates in Equivalents
In cases when it is impossible to present the English equivalent of a Russian idiom without collocates, the collocates are provided along with the equivalent (in parentheses, when possible). For example, many adverbial intensifiers cannot be translated without a verb. In such cases, the English equivalents are presented with their collocates, occasionally in a pattern, as in (И) В ГЛАЗА не видеть: Х (и) в глаза не видел Y-a ≃ **X has never set ⟨laid⟩ eyes on ⟨upon⟩ Y...**

Infinitives
Infinitives in the equivalents are presented without the infinitive marker "to," except in instances when "to" is a fixed component of the English equivalent, as in 'to tell (you) the truth' used as a sentence adverbial.

Articles
Noun phrases are generally presented without an article, but there are some exceptions. For example, the definite article "the" is provided when an idiom is not used without it (ЦАРСТВО НЕБЕСНОЕ, sense 1, 'the kingdom of heaven; the heavenly kingdom; the kingdom of God'); the indefinite article "a/an" may be added to indicate that the equivalent cannot be used without an article or specifier of some type (ФОМА НЕВЕРНЫЙ 'a doubting Thomas').

Illustrative Patterns
Some English equivalents are preceded by a Russian pattern that illustrates the use of the idiom in a sentence. Patterns are used for all verb phrases and for many idioms functioning as subject-complements.

Some Russian idioms that function as predicates do not contain a verb, and the temporal frame of the action must be interpolated from the context. In order to translate the Russian pattern, some temporal context must be assumed. The assumed temporal context is indicated in brackets preceding the English equivalents: for example, the pattern for **Н-161 НИ НОГОЙ** reads:

> X к Y-у ⟨в место Z⟩ ни ногой ≃ [in present contexts] **X doesn't set ⟨never sets⟩ foot in Y's house ⟨in place Z etc⟩**…

Occasionally, patterns are provided for context-specific uses of an idiom: for example, **Д-244 ПО ДОЛГУ** *чего* 'as sth. obliges ⟨requires⟩' has a separate pattern for по долгу службы 'as part of one's ⟨s.o.'s⟩ duties'. While the equivalents offered for по долгу службы can be used only for this collocation, some or all of the general equivalents for this idiom may also fit по долгу службы.

Restrictions

A restriction is presented in square brackets and applies to all equivalents that follow it, up to the next restriction, if there is one. English equivalents that can be used only in select contexts and should therefore be used cautiously are preceded by the restriction "in limited contexts." Other restrictions may point out syntactic or situational limitations, the collocates with which an equivalent may be used, or that element of a semantically rich Russian idiom that is stressed by the equivalents that follow; for example:

> **Б-198 • НАШ БРАТ**…[when used as obj or subj]…**people ⟨men, guys, fellows** etc⟩ **like us ⟨me⟩**;…[usu. when foll. by an appos] **we ⟨us⟩ writers ⟨workers** etc⟩; **our ⟨my⟩ fellow writers ⟨workers** etc⟩…

The entry **3-196 ЗАГОВАРИВАТЬ/ЗАГОВОРИТЬ ЗУБЫ** has the following restrictions: [esp. with the goal of avoiding an unpleasant topic]; [esp. with the goal of deceiving the interlocutor]; [esp. with the goal of obtaining sth. from s.o. or extricating o.s. from an uncomfortable situation].

When a Russian idiomatic preposition can be used with both animate and inanimate nouns, but its English equivalents have animate/inanimate restrictions, these restrictions are specified as part of the equivalent; for example:

> **С-610 • В СТОРОНУ**… 1. *кого-чего, чью*…**in the direction of s.o. ⟨sth.⟩; in s.o.'s direction; toward s.o. ⟨sth.⟩; s.o.'s way**…

CITATIONS AND EXAMPLES

Most of the entries in the dictionary are illustrated by citations from Russian and Soviet literature, each citation accompanied by a published translation. In the absence of clear, typical, or correctly translated citations, some entries are provided with invented examples. No excerpts from published translations have been retranslated for the purposes of this dictionary. Literary citations and invented examples are presented in the same order as their corresponding equivalents.

Not all equivalents are illustrated by examples, however, and only rarely is a single equivalent illustrated by more than one example. More than one example is provided for an equivalent only when the uses of the equivalent are significantly different in different citations (as when there can be substantially different types of subjects for a verbal idiom). For example, in **3-85 ЗАХОДИТЬ ДАЛЕКО** 'go too far', two citations are provided for the equivalent 'X has gone too far': one with a human subject—'The old man had gone too far'—and one with an abstract subject—'Matters have already gone too far'.

Style and Conventions

All citations from works of literature, memoirs, and so forth are followed by the author's name and the number that the given work has been assigned in the Bibliography. The English translation of the citation is followed by the same number plus a letter indicating which translation of the work has been cited (that is, if two translations of a work have been used, they are designated "a" and "b"). Illustrations that do not include an author's name at the end are invented examples provided by the compiler. When selecting literary citations for illustration, minor inaccuracies in translation have been disregarded if they do not harm the sense of the text or the effective illustration of the idiom. It must be kept in mind that a certain amount of freedom is acceptable, and even desirable, in literary translation, as the goal is to make the translation faithful to the original both in meaning and in style. However, some steps have been taken to draw the Russian and English versions of the citations closer together and to clarify points that may not be clear out of context.

For example, in some cases part of the Russian and/or English text has been elided in order to make the texts match better. When deletions are made in Russian, three ellipsis points replace the original punctuation; when deletions are made in English, three points represent omissions within a sentence and four represent omissions at the end of it or between sentences. There is no typographical difference between the author's/translator's ellipsis points and the compiler's.

In other cases a word in a citation is followed by square brackets providing information about that word (for example, that it is a nonce word, a phonetically spelled word, or an ungrammatical, dialectal, regional, or Ukrainian word). Square brackets in citations are also used to indicate pertinent names and pieces of information intended to clarify citation contexts.

Finally, some bracketed additions serve to make the Russian and English variants more similar. (It should be noted that such insertions do not imply that the translation is unfaithful; they merely reflect the reality that dictionary contexts are sometimes insufficient to present the situation clearly.) Wherever possible, wording found in the cited texts is used for such insertions. Such insertions are not made, however, in cases when a part of the citation may not be completely clear but the sense of the idiom is unaffected. For example, in **П-329 И ПОМИНА** нет (sense 1, 'sth. hasn't even been mentioned'), part of the English translation of the citation reads, "…Anisya's nose proclaimed…." This odd phrase, which cannot be fully understood without an explanation found earlier in the illustrative text, bears no direct relation to the idiom, so no explanation is provided.

When a speech impediment is shown through English spelling, as in some citations from Tolstoy, the affected words have been replaced by their correctly spelled counterparts in brackets. For example, in **ОТДУВАТЬСЯ СВОИМИ БОКАМИ** 'bear the brunt of sth.' the translation of the citation from Tolstoy's *War and Peace* reads, "This is certainly Scythian warfare. It's all [very] fine—except for those who bear the [brunt] of it." The translator has spelled the bracketed words as "vewy" and "bwunt."

Generally, the transliteration chosen by the translator is preserved for proper names in citations and for the names of characters in plays. However, since the designations of characters in Gogol's *The Government Inspector* are so different in different translations, the compiler has chosen to make uniform the names of the characters when indicating the speaker in citations. For example, although Городничий is translated as "Mayor," "Chief of Police," and "Prefect" in various translations, it is uniformly rendered "Mayor" in this dictionary.

Occasionally, two or more translations of the same citation are quoted. The user must be aware that translators' approaches differ, and so there may be significant differences in the cited translations. For example, two translations were used for Saltykov-Shchedrin's *История одного города* (*The History of a Town*). The names in this book are meaningful. One translator (Susan Brownsberger) chose to translate them into meaningful English names, while the other (I.P. Foote) transliterated them. Thus, "Melancholov" and "Dormousov" in the Brownsberger translation represent the same characters as "Grustilov" and "Bajbakov," respectively, in the Foote translation.

In some cases, the tense forms in the Russian and English versions of a citation do not coincide, but it would require a great amount of context to show why this is so. In such cases, the tense discrepancy has been overlooked. For example, in К-263 СВОДИТЬ КОНЦЫ С КОНЦАМИ 'make (both) ends meet' the beginning of the citation from Zalygin reads «...Мужикам, по их натуре, нужна любая техника...» (present tense) and the translation has "By their nature they [men] needed any sort of science..." (past tense).

Another lack of parallelism in citations concerns the use of quotation marks. Some Russian authors (as Aksyonov and Zinoviev) omit quotation marks in some of their works, while their translators have chosen not to do so. The authors' and translators' choices are retained in the presentation of citations.

Russian citations are presented exactly as they appear in the published text with the exception of a few archaic forms that have been replaced with contemporary ones. For example, in the entry Б-254 НИЧУТЬ НЕ БЫВАЛО the archaic того же дни in the Gogol citation has been replaced by the contemporary того же дня. In some cases, Western editions of Russian texts have been used as sources for citations. However, since these editions are not as carefully edited as most editions published in Russia and the former Soviet Union, Soviet/Russian editions have occasionally been used to check punctuation, spelling, etc.

The word «Бог» in the citations is capitalized when the source has it capitalized, and lowercase when the source has it lowercase.

The transliteration of proper names in invented examples and Russian names in etymological notes follows the transliteration system used in the *Handbook of Russian Literature*, edited by Victor Terras. The transliteration of authors' names in the Bibliography follows the spelling currently used by the Library of Congress (with diacritics omitted).

When a Russian author uses a nonstandard form of an idiom, the citation is preceded by the bracketed label "author's usage." When a Russian author uses an idiom either metaphorically or in an atypical context, the citation is preceded by the label "extended usage." For example, this label is found before the Goncharov citation in Г-232 ГЛАДИТЬ/ПОГЛАДИТЬ ПО ГОЛОВКЕ (sense 1, 'praise s.o., show one's approval to s.o.') because the subject is the abstract жизнь, rather than a human noun (which is typical for the idiom).

When the English translation of a citation translates the given idiom correctly but in a way that would not apply in most or any other contexts, the translation is preceded by the label "context transl" (contextual translation). Such translations of idioms are not included among the list of equivalents. Citations with contextual translations are presented in order to offer the user examples of creative and original approaches to translation.

When an idiom that originated in a work of Russian literature is illustrated by a citation from that same work, the citation is preceded by the label "source." For example, the idiom Р-388 КУВШИННОЕ РЫЛО 'jug snout' originated in Gogol's *Dead Souls*, so the *Dead Souls* citation containing the idiom has this label.

Every attempt has been made to cite literary illustrations from various authors in each entry. However, since individual authors tend to have a predilection for certain idioms, in some cases two citations from the same author may be presented in a given entry. This occurs only if the translations of those citations are considerably better that the translations of citations from other authors.

English translations of citations are rendered precisely as they occur in the published texts with two exceptions: spellings or orthographic forms that are not found in any mainstream American or British dictionary have been normalized, and the American system for quotation marks has been adopted throughout (that is, double quotes for direct speech, single quotes for a quote within a quote, and so on in order).

In some instances, a translator has come up with an original and creative translation of a Russian idiom or saying. When such translations are offered in this dictionary as regular English equivalents, the translator's version is acknowledged by citing the excerpt in question. For example, the saying ПАНЫ ДЕРУТСЯ, А У ХЛОПЦЕВ ⟨ХОЛОПОВ⟩ ЧУБЫ ТРЕЩАТ has two equivalents, both of which come from published translations, and both of which are illustrated by their respective citations: "the poor man always gets the blame" comes from a Nabokov citation (translated by Michael Scammell), and "when (the) masters fall out their men get the clout" comes from a Sholokhov citation (translated by Robert Daglish). All the translators' names are, of course, indicated in the Bibliography.

Every citation was cross-referenced to ensure that a citation used to illustrate idiom A, for example, does not have an incorrect equivalent for idiom B. Ideally, and in most cases, the translation of idiom B will be among the equivalents presented in entry B. However, in view of the fact that there are many criteria for a good overall translation apart from idiom translation, this rule has been relaxed in some instances. In no case has a citation been used for one idiom that has an incorrect translation of another idiom in it, but occasionally the translation of the secondary idiom may be bland, or correspond word for word to the definition of the idiom, or be correct only as a contextual translation, not as a general one.

ETYMOLOGICAL NOTES

Etymological information has been provided for those idioms where it might contribute to the user's understanding of a Russian idiom and help the translator to select an English equivalent. It has been provided for the following groups of idioms:

1) idioms from the Bible
2) idioms from works of Russian and Western literature
3) idioms from Russian folk tales
4) idioms that are loan translations of phrases from classical or modern languages
5) idioms that are rooted in Russian history and customs

For Biblical references, the King James Bible was used.

English titles of works of Russian literature are presented as they are known in English translation.

NOTES

1. Mel'čuk I.A., A.K. Zholkovsky. *Tolkovo-kombinatornyi slovar sovremennogo russkogo iazyka: Opyt semantiko-sintaksicheskogo opisaniia russkoi leksiki = Explanatory Combinatorial Dictionary of Modern Russian*. Wien: 1984. (Wiener Slawistischer Almanach. Sonderband; 14.)

2. *Dictionnaire explicatif et combinatoire du français contemporain*. Igor Mel'čuk avec Nadia Arbatchewsky-Jumarie, *et al.* Montréal: Les Presses de l'Université de Montréal, 1984. (*Recherches lexico-sémantiques;* 1)

3. Mel'čuk, Igor. *Opyt teorii lingvisticheskikh modelei "Smysl ↔ Tekst."* Moscow: Nauka, 1974.

4. Chvany, Catherine V. *On the Syntax of BE-Sentences in Russian.* Cambridge, Mass.: Slavica, 1975.

5. Apresjan, Jurij. *Tipy informatsii dlia poverkhnostno-semanticheskogo komponenta modeli smysl ↔ tekst.* Wien: 1980. (Wiener Slawistischer Almanach, Sonderband; 1.)

6. Apresjan, Jurij. "Sintaksicheskie priznaki leksem." *Russian Linguistics* 9 (2–3), 1985, 289–317.

ABBREVIATIONS
USED IN THE DICTIONARY

abstr   abstract (noun)
accus   accusative case
Adj   adjective
AdjP   adjective phrase
Adv   adverb
AdvP   adverb phrase
adv   adverbial
affirm   affirmative
anim   animate (noun)
appos   appositive
approv   approving
approx.   approximately
Cf.   compare
coll   colloquial
collect   collective (noun)
compar   comparative
compl   complement
concr   concrete (noun)
condes   condescending
condit   conditional
Conj   conjunction
contemp.   contemporary
context transl   contextual translation
dat   dative case
derog   derogatory
dial   dialectal
disapprov   disapproving
elev   elevated
esp.   especially
etc   et cetera
euph   euphemism
folk poet   folkloric poetic
foll. by   followed by
fut   future
gen   genitive case
gener.   generic

highly coll   highly colloquial
humor   humorous
imper/*Imper*   imperative
impers   impersonal
impfv   imperfective
impol   impolite
inanim   inanimate (noun)
indef. refer.   indefinite reference
indep. sent   independent sentence
indir obj   indirect object
infin   infinitive
instrum   instrumental case
intensif   intensifier
Interj   interjection
interrog   interrogative
Invar   invariable
iron   ironic
lit   literary
masc   masculine
mil   military
modif   modifier
neg/*Neg*   negative, negated
nom   nominative case
nonstand   nonstandard
NP   noun phrase
obj   object
obj-compl   object-complement
obs   obsolete
obsoles   obsolescent
occas.   occasionally
offic   official
old-fash   old-fashioned
orig.   originally
o.s.   oneself
parenth   parenthetical

Part   participle
pers   person, personal
pfv   perfective
pl   plural
postmodif   postmodifier
predic   predicate
premodif   premodifier
Prep   preposition
prep obj   prepositional object
PrepP   prepositional phrase
pres   present tense
quantif   quantifier
quantit   quantitative
refer.   reference
restr   restrictive
rhet   rhetorical
sent   sentence
sent adv   sentence adverbial
sing   singular
s.o.   someone
sth.   something
subj   subject
subj-compl   subject-complement
subord   subordinate
substand   substandard
ungrammat   ungrammatical
usu.   usually
var.   variant
Verbal Adv   verbal adverb
VP   verb phrase
VP_{subj} contains both the subject and the predicate
vulg   vulgar
WO   word order

SYMBOLS

бытьø   indicates copular быть
/   separates verbal aspects
⟨ ⟩   shows variants
( )   encloses optional elements
[ ]   used for grammatical information and compiler's comments
~   replaces an idiom in a pattern

≃   introduces English equivalents of Russian patterns
‖   introduces patterns
○   indicates related noun phrase for verbal idioms
♦   separates illustrations
<   introduces etymologies
(?)   indicates that the etymological information provided cannot be fully substantiated

РУССКИЙ АЛФАБИТ
RUSSIAN ALPHABET

А а	К к	Х х
Б б	Л л	Ц ц
В в	М м	Ч ч
Г г	Н н	Ш ш
Д д	О о	Щ щ
Е е	П п	ъ
Ё ё	Р р	ы
Ж ж	С с	ь
З з	Т т	Э э
И и	У у	Ю ю
Й й	Ф ф	Я я

RUSSIAN-ENGLISH
DICTIONARY
OF IDIOMS

A

A-1 • **ОТ А ДО Я** (прочитать, знать *что* и т. п.); **ОТ А ДО ЗЕТ**; **ОТ А́ЛЬФЫ ДО ОМЕ́ГИ** *lit;* **ОТ АЗА́ ДО И́ЖИЦЫ** *obs, lit* [PrepP; these forms only; adv; fixed WO] (to read sth.) from the very beginning to the very end; (to know sth.) thoroughly: [of books, journals etc] **(read sth.) from cover to cover;** [of documents] **(read sth.) from top to bottom; (know sth.) from A to Z; (know sth.) inside out.**

< Refers to the first and last letters of the Russian, Latin, Greek, and Slavonic alphabets, respectively.

A-2 • **БРАТЬ/ВЗЯТЬ НА АБОРДА́Ж** *кого-что* [VP; subj: human; obj: most often human] to take decisive action with s.o. or sth.: X взял Y-а на абордаж ≃ **X took ⟨tried⟩ a hard-nosed approach with person Y; X got tough with person Y; X tackled thing Y head-on.**

< From the French *abordage*. Originally meant "to attack an enemy vessel by coming alongside it and mooring with it for the purpose of hand-to-hand combat."

A-3 • **С ПЕ́РВОГО А́БЦУГА; ПО ПЕ́РВОМУ А́Б-ЦУГУ** *both obs* [PrepP; these forms only; adv; fixed WO] immediately, at or from the very beginning: **from the outset; from the very first; right from the start; right off; from the word go.**

A-4 • **ДЕ́ЛАТЬ АВА́НСЫ** *кому old-fash, coll, humor* [VP] **1.** [subj: human or collect] to approach s.o. (repeatedly) showing that one is well-disposed toward him (usu. in order to secure his support in sth. or to interest him in sth. — some deal, a job etc): X делает Y-у авансы ≃ **X makes advances toward ⟨to⟩ Y; X makes overtures to Y.**

Вы говорите, что эта фирма делает вам авансы? Учтите, у них очень плохая репутация. You say that firm is making overtures to you? Bear in mind that they have a very bad reputation.

2. [subj: human, female] to encourage a man (through coquettish behavior) to flirt with or court one: X делает Y-у авансы ≃ **X makes a play for Y; X makes a move on Y; X casts coquettish glances Y's way.**

A-5 • **АВО́СЬ ДА НЕБО́СЬ; АВО́СЬ, НЕБО́СЬ ДА КА́К-НИБУДЬ** *both obs, coll* [AdvP; these forms only; usu. indep. sent or clause; fixed WO] (used to describe s.o.'s lack of discipline, idleness, lack of initiative, or negligence) s.o. does nothing, thinking, assuming, or hoping that things will work out by themselves without his efforts: **somehow or other ⟨some way or other, one way or another⟩ (it will work out ⟨things will turn out all right** etc⟩).

A-6 • **НА АВО́СЬ** *coll* [PrepP; Invar; adv] (to venture sth.) counting on good fortune, success, even though chances may be against success: **on the off-chance; hoping for the best; trusting to luck; chance it;** [in limited contexts] **by guess and by God.**

...Они [Петька и Михаил] не с пустыми руками вернулись к избе. С рыбой... «Лиза, эво-то! Посмотри-ко!» — звонко закричал Петька, едва они завидели избу, и высоко над головой поднял рыбазанку с рыбой. «Да, — сказал Михаил... — А я думал: Ося-агент всё выбродил. Так, на авось кинулся» (Абрамов 1). ...They [Petka and Mikhail] did not go back empty-handed: there were fish... "Liza! Hey there! Look!" shouted Petka ringingly as soon as they caught sight of the house, and he lifted the string of fish high above his head. "Yes," said Mikhail....“I thought Osya the agent had fished the place out. I just threw out a line on the off-

chance" (1a). ♦ «Я не коммунхоз, на авось не работаю. И цена по совести. А тебе, как бывшему соседу, так и вовсе скидка» (Максимов 3). "I'm not the municipal repairs department when I work, I don't just hope for the best. And I'll give you an honest price. In fact, as a former neighbor, you get a discount anyway" (3a). ♦ [Городничий *(в сторону)*:] Не знаешь, с какой стороны и приняться. Ну да уж попробовать... Попробовать на авось. *(Вслух.)* Если вы точно имеете нужду в деньгах или в чём другом, то я готов служить сию минуту. Моя обязанность помогать проезжающим (Гоголь 4). [Mayor *(aside)*:] You don't know which side to tackle him [from]. But never mind that...let's have a go....Let's have a go and chance it. *(Aloud)* Should you in fact be short of money, or of anything else, I am prepared to be of immediate service to you. It is my duty to assist travellers (4b).

A-7 • **АД КРОМЕ́ШНЫЙ** [NP; sing only; usu. this WO] **1.** an extremely trying, unbearable situation or condition: **sheer hell ⟨torture, misery⟩; hell on earth; a nightmare;** ‖ ад кромешный на душе ⟨на сердце⟩ *у кого* ≃ **s.o. feels like hell; s.o. is going through hell.**

«Девочку придётся забрать, — подумал Виктор. — ...Если оставить Ирму здесь, в доме начнётся ад кромешный...» (Стругацкие 1). "I'll have to take the child," thought Victor. "...If Irma stays here, it'll be sheer hell" (1a).

2. utter confusion, unbearable noise, commotion: **sheer pandemonium; a hell of a racket.**

A-8 • **ОТ ⟨С⟩ АДА́МА** начинать (рассказ) и т. п. *obsoles* [PrepP; these forms only; adv or nonagreeing modif] (to begin a story etc) from something distant or unrelated: **from day one.**

A-9 • **В А́ДРЕС** *кого* ⟨**В** *чей* **А́ДРЕС⟩** высказываться, критика, похвала, аплодисменты и т. п. [PrepP; Invar; Prep; the resulting PrepP is adv or nonagreeing modif; can be used with collect noun] used to indicate the object of a statement, criticism, praise etc: **(address one's words** etc) **to s.o.; (direct ⟨aim⟩ one's words** etc) **at s.o.; (direct one's criticism** etc) **against s.o.; (criticism) of s.o.; (criticism) intended for s.o.; (praise ⟨applause⟩) for s.o.;** [in limited contexts] **(criticism ⟨praise⟩) comes s.o.'s way; (a remark) at s.o.'s expense.**

«Прежде чем скрещивать оружие с инженером Лопаткиным, — пробасил он, — я хочу сказать несколько слов критики в адрес почтенных представителей НИИ-Центролита» (Дудинцев 1). "Before I cross swords with Engineer Lopatkin," he growled, "I would like to address a few words of criticism to the respected representatives of C.S.I.F.R. [the Central Scientific Institute of Foundry Research]" (1a). ♦ Как только смолкли аплодисменты в адрес последнего из названных товарищей, вдруг вскочил редактор кенгурийской районной газеты... (Искандер 4). The moment the applause for the last-named comrade quieted down, the editor of the Kenguria district paper suddenly leaped to his feet... (4a). ♦ В тот вечер я услышал от дяди самую приятную похвалу, которую я когда-либо слышал в свой адрес (Искандер 4). That night, I heard from my uncle the pleasantest praise I have ever heard come my way (4a).

A-10 • **НЕ ПО А́ДРЕСУ** (обратиться, направить *что*, явиться и т. п.) [PrepP; Invar; adv or subj-compl with быть₀ (subj: abstr)] (to address a question, complaint etc, come etc) to the incorrect or an inappropriate person or place: **(to) the wrong person ⟨party, place** etc⟩; [usu. in refer. to criticism, rebukes etc] **bark up the wrong tree.**

«Лево сделал [плакат], в своей, свободной манере... Приношу... „Вы, говорит [шеф], Чупров, не по адресу обратились; такая, говорит, продукция для «Лайфа», может быть, и подходит, а для нас не годится"» (Аржак 1). "I painted a non-conformist one [poster], in my own, free manner....I took it to them....'You've brought it to the wrong place,' he [the Chief] says. 'This may be all right for *Life* but not for us'" (1a). ♦ «Медицина никакого отношения не имеет к вашим неприятностям, мы здесь затем, чтобы помогать людям, ваш протест в данном случае направлен не по адресу» (Марченко 2). [context transl] "The medical service has nothing to do with your problems. We are here to help people, so you should take your protest elsewhere" (2a).

A-11 • ПО А́ДРЕСУ [PrepP; Invar] **1.** писать, отправлять *что* и т. п. ~ [adv] (to write, send sth. etc) to the appropriate person or place: **to the right ⟨proper⟩ person ⟨place etc⟩;** [in limited contexts] **to where it belongs.**

Глядя снизу на этот подъём и последующий спуск, Кублицкий-Пиоттух всё больше наполнялся уверенностью, что приехал по адресу, что старик Лучников уникален и тоже предназначен Господом для особого дела... (Аксёнов 7). Observing ascent and descent from below, Kublitsky-Piottukh felt certain that he had come to the right place, that Luchnikov was his man, *the man predestined by God for the task he had in mind*... (7a).

2. высказываться, шутить, злословить, замечание и т. п. ~ *(кого, чьему)* [Prep; the resulting PrepP is usu. adv or nonagreeing modif; can be used with collect noun] (to say sth., make a joke, a remark is etc) about s.o., in reference to s.o.: **(a remark ⟨reproach etc⟩) addressed to s.o.; (gossip ⟨a remark etc⟩) directed at ⟨against⟩ s.o.; (some word etc is) applied to s.o.; (say sth. ⟨joke etc⟩) at s.o.'s expense.**

Речь, произнесённая им на банкете, была исполнена пьяного бахвальства и в конце содержала недвусмысленные упрёки и угрозы по адресу верхнедонцов (Шолохов 5). The speech he made at the banquet was full of drunken bragging and ended with some unambiguous reproaches and threats addressed to the Cossacks of the Upper Don (5a). ♦ Здесь опять послышались одобрительные смешки в публике, и всё по адресу прокурора (Достоевский 2). Here again approving chuckles came from the public, all directed at the prosecutor (2a). ♦ «Ну и тощи же вы, племяннички...» Это была шпилька по адресу дяди и тётки, которую он [дядя Федя] втайне недолюбливал за её столичную гордыню (Максимов 2). "How thin and peaky you are..." This was a dig at their mother, of whom he [Uncle Fedya] secretly disapproved because of her superior, big-city manner (2a). ♦ Сколько раз в жизни мне приходилось слышать слово "интеллигент" по своему адресу (Булгаков 12). How many times in my life have I heard the word "intellectual" applied to me! (12a). ♦ Что мне говорили о новой пьесе литераторы и парижские знатоки театра? Первые слова их трудно было понять, потому что в салонах закипела такая ругань по адресу Мольера, что вообще немыслимо было что-либо разобрать сразу (Булгаков 5). And what did the Paris literati and connoisseurs of the theater say about the new play? Their first response is difficult to make out, for the salons buzzed with so much abuse at Molière's expense that it was impossible to distinguish the words (5a).

A-12 • В (ПО́ЛНОМ) АЖУ́РЕ *coll* [PrepP; these forms only; subj-compl with copula (subj: usu. abstr, often всё)] in fine condition, in excellent shape: **in perfect order; A-OK; just so; tiptop; in tiptop shape; shipshape;** [in limited contexts] **(person X is) sitting pretty; (person X is) on velvet.** Cf. **in apple-pie order.**

...Люди бегут. И какие люди!.. Проверенные! И в местной партийной организации проверяли. И на райкоме характеристику утверждали. И выездная комиссия ЦК и КГБ всю подноготную бдительно изучала. И всё, как говорится, было в ажуре (Войнович 1). ...People *are* fleeing the country. And what people!...They'd all been checked out. The local Party organizations had run checks. Their files had been approved by the district committees. The Central Committee and the KGB commission on travel had vigilantly scrutinized all the ins and outs. Everything was, as they say,

tiptop... (1a). ♦ [Аким:] И вновь у тебя приличная жена и хорошая квартира. И по служебной линии всё в ажуре (Арбузов 3). [A.:] Once again, you have a decent wife and a good flat. At work you're on velvet (3a).

A-13 • НИ АЗА́ не знать, не смыслить, не понимать и т. п. *coll;* **(НИ) АЗА́ В ГЛАЗА́** *obsoles, coll* [NP$_{gen}$; these forms only; obj] (to know, understand) absolutely nothing (about sth.): **not (know ⟨understand⟩) a thing ⟨the first thing⟩ (about sth.); not (have) the foggiest ⟨the faintest⟩ idea ⟨notion⟩ (what sth. is about etc); not (know) the ABCs of sth.; not know from A to B about sth.;** [in limited contexts] **not (know) one's ABCs.**

«Я поставлю полные баллы во всех науках тому, кто ни аза не знает, да ведёт себя похвально...» (Гоголь 3). "I'll give top marks to a boy who doesn't even know his ABC's if his behavior is irreproachable..." (3e). ♦ «...Я очень рад, что вы занимаетесь естественными науками. Я слышал, что Либих сделал удивительные открытия насчёт удобрения полей...» — «Я к вашим услугам, Николай Петрович; но куда нам до Либиха! Сперва надо азбуке выучиться и потом уже взяться за книгу, а мы ещё аза в глаза не видали» (Тургенев 2). [context transl] "I must say I...am very glad that you are studying the natural sciences. I have heard that Liebig has made some astonishing discoveries to do with improving the soil..." "I'm at your service, Nikolai Petrovich; but Liebig is miles above our heads! One must learn the alphabet before beginning to read, and we don't know the first letter yet" (2c).

< From the name of the first letter of the Church Slavonic alphabet.

A-14 • ВХОДИ́ТЬ/ВОЙТИ́ ⟨ПРИХОДИ́ТЬ/ ПРИЙТИ́, ВПАДА́ТЬ/ВПАСТЬ⟩ В АЗА́РТ [VP; subj: human] to become extremely agitated, impassioned: X вошёл в азарт ≃ **X got all excited; X got all worked-up; X got carried away; X worked himself into a frenzy; X got into a lather.**

«Очень возможно, что куры у него вылупятся. Но ведь ни вы, ни я не можем сказать, какие это куры будут... Может быть, они подохнут через два дня. Может быть, их есть нельзя!.. Может быть, у них кости ломкие». Персиков вошёл в азарт и махал ладонью и загибал пальцы (Булгаков 10). "It is quite possible that the hens will hatch. But neither you nor I can say what sort of hens they will be....Maybe they'll die in a day or two. Maybe they'll be inedible!...Maybe their bones will be brittle." Persikov got all excited and waved his hands, crooking his index fingers (10b). ♦ Может, Харлампо и начинал мотыжить, чтобы показать тётушке Хрисуле, какой работящий муж будет у её племянницы, но постепенно он входил в азарт, в самозабвенье труда... (Искандер 5). Harlampo may have begun to hoe with the idea of showing Auntie Chrysoula what a hard-working husband her niece would have. But gradually he worked himself into a frenzy, into the self-oblivion of labor... (5a).

A-15 • С АЗО́В начинать *coll* [PrepP; Invar; adv] (to begin) from the very beginning, from the very first step: **(start) from scratch; (begin) from square one;** [in limited contexts] **(start) all over (again).**

< From the name of the first letter of the Church Slavonic alphabet.

A-16 • АЙ ДА...! *coll* [Interj; Invar; foll. by NP; fixed WO] used to express approval, admiration: [when foll. by an anim noun] **what (a)...!; good for you ⟨her, him etc⟩!; you are ⟨he is etc⟩ (really) quite a...!; atta boy ⟨girl⟩!; he ⟨she etc⟩ is really something!; ah, that...!; good job (...)!; well done (...)!;** [when foll. by an inanim noun] **what (a)...!; (now) that's ⟨here's, there's⟩ (a)...(for you)!; that's (really) quite a...!;** [when used ironically only] **some...!; some...he ⟨she, that etc⟩ is!**

«Поздравляю, господин исправник. Ай да бумага! По этим приметам немудрено будет вам отыскать Дубровского. Да

[2]

кто же не среднего роста, у кого не русые волосы, не прямой нос да не карие глаза!.. Нечего сказать, умные головушки приказные» (Пушкин 1). "I congratulate you, Mr Chief of Police. What a document! It'll be easy to trace Dubrovsky from such a description! Who is not of medium height? Who has not got fair hair — or a straight nose, or brown eyes?...I must say, these officials are clever fellows!" (1b). ♦ ...Совершенно неожиданно было получено письмо за подписями начальника и политрука музыкальной команды военной части номер такой-то, в котором родителям ефрейтора Аркадия Мансурова от лица командования выражалась благодарность за хорошее воспитание сына... Ай да Аркашка! (Залыгин 1). ...There came a completely unexpected letter signed by the C.O. and the political officer of the concert party of unit No. so-and-so, expressing official gratitude to the parents of Lance-corporal Arkady Mansurov for bringing him up so well....Good for you, Arkady! (1a). ♦ «Она [моя барыня] разрядится, точно пава, и ходит так важно; а кабы кто посмотрел, какие юбки да какие чулки носит, так срам посмотреть!..» Все, кроме Захара, засмеялись. «Ай да Татьяна Ивановна, мимо не попадёт!» — говорили одобрительно голоса (Гончаров 1). "She [my mistress] gets all dressed up in her finery and parades around like a peacock, but if you ever got a look at the petticoats and stockings she wears—it's a disgrace!..." Everyone except Zakhar laughed. "Ah, that Tatyana Ivanovna, she never misses!" they said approvingly (1b). ♦ Ай да герой! Собственной тени боится! Some hero! Afraid of his own shadow!

A-17 • **ЗАКЛЮЧИ́ТЕЛЬНЫЙ АККО́РД** *чего lit* [NP; sing only; often subj-compl with copula, nom or instrum (subj: usu. abstr); fixed WO] an event, action, phenomenon etc that concludes sth.: **final event; finale; culmination.**

A-18 • **В АККУРА́Т** *substand* [PrepP; Invar; nonagreeing modif] precisely (the amount, time, location etc stated): **exactly; right (before ⟨after etc⟩);** [when emphasizing the smallness of a quantity] **just; only.**

«Это так как есть!» — раздался чей-то свидетельский отзыв в толпе. «Кричал-то он [кучер], это правда, три раза ему [раздавленному лошадьми человеку] прокричал», — отозвался другой голос. «В аккурат три раза, все слышали!» — крикнул третий (Достоевский 3). "That's the way it was!" a witness called from the crowd. "He [the driver] yelled at him [the man who had been trampled under the horses' hoofs], all right, three times he yelled at him," sounded another voice. "Three times exactly, we all heard him!" shouted a third (3a). ♦ «Я тут у бугра сено косил, когда гляжу: летит [аэроплан]. И в аккурат, Нюрка, на твою крышу, на трубу прямо, да» (Войнович 2). "I'm over by the rise cutting hay when I see it [the plane] coming. Right for your roof, Nyurka, straight for your chimney" (2a).

A-19 • **В АККУРА́ТЕ** *substand* [PrepP; Invar; adv or subj-compl with copula (subj: всё, дела etc)] (to do sth.) properly, flawlessly, (be) in good order, in fine shape: **as it should be; to a T; (be) letter-perfect.**

A-20 • **ПИТА́ТЬСЯ АКРИ́ДАМИ (И МЁДОМ ⟨И ДИ́КИМ МЁДОМ⟩)** *lit, occas. humor* [VP; subj: human; usu. this WO] to eat poorly, limit one's food intake, usu. as a form of self-denial: **X питается акридами (и мёдом)** ≃ **X lives ⟨feeds⟩ on locusts and wild honey.**

«Будь уж последовательным. Надень рясу, прими схиму, уйди куда-нибудь в пещеры или в заброшенные каменоломни... сиди там и созерцай собственный пуп, как тибетский монах. Питайся акридами» (Трифонов 3). "Take your beliefs to their logical conclusion: put on the black habit, shave the top of your head, take your vows and go and live in a cave or in an abandoned stone-quarry...sit there and contemplate your navel, like a Tibetan lama. Live on locusts and wild honey" (3a). ♦ Пришедши туда, он [Феденька] предложит обывателям приносить покаяние, валяться на голой земле и питаться диким мёдом и акридами... (Салтыков-Щедрин 2). Having arrived there, Fedenka called the inhabitants to repentance and told them to roll about in the sand and feed on locusts and wild honey... (2a).

< From the Biblical account of John the Baptist, who lived in the wilderness and ate locusts and wild honey (Mark 1:6).

A-21 • **ДЕ́ЛАТЬ/СДЕ́ЛАТЬ АКЦЕ́НТ** *на чём* [VP; subj: human or collect] to accentuate (some idea), make (it) prominent (in a speech, statement, proposal etc): **X сделал акцент на Y-е** ≃ **X emphasized ⟨stressed, underscored, highlighted⟩ Y; X gave special emphasis to Y; X placed (the) emphasis on Y; X called attention to Y.**

A-22 • **РАССТАВЛЯ́ТЬ/РАССТА́ВИТЬ АКЦЕ́НТЫ** [VP; subj: human] (in making a speech, statement etc) to emphasize certain points, setting them apart from less important ones: **X расставил акценты** ≃ **X highlighted key points;** ‖ **X должен иначе ⟨правильно⟩ расставить акценты** ≃ **X should highlight different ⟨the right⟩ points.**

Я прочитал черновик вашего выступления и в общем с вами согласен, но думаю, что нужно иначе расставить акценты. I read the draft of your speech and basically concur, but I think different points should be highlighted. ♦ ...Подлости по отношению к Б.Л. [Пастернаку] от Слуцкого никто не ожидал. Напротив, сидя в задних рядах Дома кино вместе с Винокуровым, Евтушенко был уверен, что Слуцкий будет защищать Б.Л., и был обеспокоен последствиями. И потому в перерыве сказал: «Борис, будь осторожен». «Не беспокойся, все акценты будут расставлены правильно», — отвечал Слуцкий (Ивинская 1). [context transl] ...Nobody expected Slutski to play such a low trick on BL [Pasternak]. Indeed, Yevtushenko, as he sat with Vinokurov at the back of the meeting in Film House, was convinced that Slutski would speak in defense of BL and was worried at the possible consequences to Slutski himself. For this reason he said to him in the interval: "Be careful, Boris." "Don't worry," Slutski replied, "I shall know how to make my point in the right way" (1a).

A-23 • **А́КЦИИ** *чьи, кого-чего* **ПА́ДАЮТ/УПА́ЛИ** [VP_subj; fixed WO] s.o.'s (or sth.'s) chances for success are diminishing: **X-овы акции падают** ≃ **X's stock is falling; things are looking bleak for X; X's odds are getting worse.**

A-24 • **А́КЦИИ** *чьи, кого-чего* **ПОВЫША́ЮТСЯ/ПОВЫ́СИЛИСЬ ⟨ПОДНИМА́ЮТСЯ/ПОДНЯЛИ́СЬ⟩** [VP_subj; fixed WO] s.o.'s (or sth.'s) chances for success are improving: **X-овы акции повышаются** ≃ **X's stock is rising ⟨going up⟩; things are looking up ⟨better⟩ for X; X's prospects are getting brighter.**

A-25 • **А́ЛЬФА И ОМЕ́ГА** *чего lit* [NP; sing only; fixed WO]
1. the beginning and the end of sth.: **the alpha and omega.**

2. the very essence, the most essential components of sth.: **the alpha and omega.**

Судилище явное и судилище тайное — вот альфа и омега нашей жизни (Мандельштам 2). Trials, "open" or secret, were the alpha and omega of our existence (2a).

< From the names of the first and last letters of the Greek alphabet. Used in the Bible (Rev. 1:8).

A-26 • **УДАРЯ́ТЬСЯ/УДА́РИТЬСЯ ⟨ВПАДА́ТЬ/ВПАСТЬ, ВХОДИ́ТЬ/ВОЙТИ́** *obsoles*, **ВЛА́МЫВАТЬСЯ/ВЛОМИ́ТЬСЯ** *obsoles*⟩ **В АМБИ́ЦИЮ** *all coll* [VP; subj: human; usu. this WO] to express or display emphatically one's anger, hurt etc when one's pride has been wounded or when one interprets s.o.'s words or actions as offensive, show extreme edginess and stubbornness in defending one's (often unjustified) position: X ударился в амбицию ≃ **X got his back up**; [with the emphasis on one's being offended] **X took offense; X took umbrage (at sth.)**; [with the emphasis on the manner in which one expresses his annoyance] **X got into a huff ⟨a snit⟩**; [in limited contexts] **X picked a fight ⟨a quarrel⟩**; ‖ зачем ты ударяешься в амбицию? ≃ **don't be so touchy.**

Она молчала. Когда-то ударялась в амбицию, спорила со мной из-за каждого пустяка, теперь же новый метод – молчание (Трифонов 5). She was silent. At one time she would have taken offense and argued with me over every trifle, but now she had a new method: silence (5a). ♦ Тут тебя осенила новая блестящая мысль: воспользоваться скандалом и убежать от них вместе с Лидой под видом неудержимых эмоций... Как это делают пьяные, желающие впасть в амбицию, ты сказал, махая руками по всей комнате: «Лидия, я вас похищаю» (Терц 8). At this moment you had another brilliant idea: to take advantage of the scandal and run off with Lida on the pretext of uncontrollable emotion....Just as drunks do when they want to pick a quarrel, you waved your arms at the company and said, "Lida, I am taking you away" (8a). ♦ [Софья Егоровна:] Вы как-то странно смотрите [на меня]... преследуете... Точно шпионите!.. Вы не даёте мне покоя... [Платонов:] Всё! *(Встаёт.)* Merci за откровенность! *(Идёт к двери.)* [Софья Егоровна:] Вы сердитесь? *(Встаёт.)* Постойте, Михаил Васильич! Для чего же в амбицию вламываться? (Чехов 1). [S.E.:] You have this odd way of looking [at me]....and follow me about—as if you were spying on me....You won't leave me alone... [P.:] Finished? *(Gets up.)* Thanks for being frank. *(Moves towards the door.)* [S.E.:] Annoyed? *(Gets up.)* Don't go, don't be so touchy (1b).

A-27 • ОТКРЫВА́ТЬ/ОТКРЫ́ТЬ АМЕ́РИКУ ⟨-и⟩ *iron* [VP; subj: human; usu. pfv past; often used in the form «Открыл Америку!» as a response to s.o.'s statement] to discover for o.s. and announce aloud sth. that has long been known, that was discovered long ago: X открыл Америку ≃ **X reinvented the wheel**; [in limited contexts] **so what else is new?** ○ **ОТКРЫ́ТИЕ АМЕ́РИКИ** [NP] ≃ **reinventing the wheel.**

A-28 • ПРЕДАВА́ТЬ/ПРЕДА́ТЬ АНА́ФЕМЕ *кого-что* [VP; subj: human] **1.** *special* [subj: a noun denoting an ecclesiastical authority; often 3rd pers pl with indef. refer.] to pronounce s.o. excommunicated: X предал Y-а анафеме ≃ **X anathematized Y.**

2. *lit* to condemn, stigmatize s.o.: X предал Y-а анафеме ≃ **X anathematized ⟨execrated⟩ Y.**

С нашей стороны было невозможно заарканить Белинского; он слал нам грозные грамоты из Петербурга, отлучал нас, предавал анафеме и писал ещё злее в «Отечественных записках» (Герцен 2). On our side it was impossible to rope in Belinsky; he sent us threatening epistles from Petersburg, excommunicated and anathematised us, and wrote more angrily than ever in the *Notes of the Fatherland* (2a).

A-29 • АНДРО́НЫ Е́ДУТ *obs, coll* [VP$_{subj}$; Invar; fixed WO] **1.** [used as Interj] absurdity, foolish talk: **balderdash; tommyrot; hogwash; sheer nonsense.**

Какая же причина в мёртвых душах? Даже и причины нет. Это, выходит, просто: Андроны едут, чепуха, белиберда, сапоги всмятку! Это, просто, чёрт побери!.. (Гоголь 3). ...What reason could there be in dead souls? None whatsoever. It was all sheer nonsense, absurdity, moonshine! It was simply...oh, the Devil take it all!... (3c).

2. it is unknown whether sth. will come to pass: **it's a big question mark; that's an open question; we shall see what we shall see.**

A-30 • АНТИ́К С ГВОЗДИ́КОЙ ⟨С МАРМЕЛА́ДОМ⟩ *obs, coll, approv* [NP; sing only; subj-compl with copula, nom only (subj: any common noun); fixed WO] wonderful, delightful: **jim-dandy; a peach; a real gem; the bee's knees.**

A-31 • РАЗВОДИ́ТЬ АНТИМО́НИИ ⟨-ю⟩ *coll* [VP; subj: human] **1.** *~ с кем* to talk about insignificant matters, engage in idle chatter: X разводит антимонии ≃ **X is blabbing ⟨gabbing⟩; X is shooting the breeze (with person Y).**

2. *~ с кем* to treat s.o. with excessive gentleness, leniency: X с Y-ом антимонии разводит ≃ **X treats Y with kid gloves; X is too easy on Y; X is too soft with Y.**

3. [often infin with нечего, хватит, брось(те) etc] to observe superfluous social conventions: X разводит антимонии ≃ **X stands on ceremony**; ‖ брось(те) разводить антимонии ≃ **(oh, stop,) I don't want to hear another word about it**; [in limited contexts] **oh, don't be silly.**

A-32 • АППЕТИ́Т ПРИХО́ДИТ ВО ВРЕ́МЯ ЕДЫ́ [saying] your interest in or desire for sth. grows as you practice, experience, or learn it: **appetite comes ⟨grows⟩ with eating** ≃ **eating and scratching ⟨drinking⟩ want but a beginning.**

«Пока чай дойдёт, закусите», — Алферов обвёл рукой стол. «Спасибо, чай попью, а есть не хочу, завтракал». — «Ну, ну, смотрите, а захотите – ешьте, аппетит приходит во время еды» (Рыбаков 2). "Have a bite while the tea is brewing," he [Alferov] said, indicating the food. "Thank you, I'll have some tea, but I won't eat. I've already had breakfast," Sasha replied. "Well, just look and if you feel like it, eat something. The appetite grows with eating" (2a).

A-33 • ВО́ЛЧИЙ АППЕТИ́Т *coll* [NP; sing only; fixed WO except when used as VP$_{subj}$ with copula] (s.o. has) a very big appetite: **the appetite of a wolf; a ravenous ⟨voracious⟩ appetite.**

«У меня всегда появляется волчий аппетит от волнения» (Каверин 1). "Excitement always gives me the appetite of a wolf" (1a).

A-34 • ПРИЯ́ТНОГО АППЕТИ́ТА! *coll* [formula phrase; Invar; fixed WO] used as a wish that s.o. enjoy the meal he is eating or is about to eat: ***bon appétit!*; enjoy your meal ⟨your food etc⟩!; enjoy!; hearty appetite!**

Костерок оказался у небольшого причала, пылал уже затухающим пламенем, освещая нескольких то ли геологов, то ли рыбаков и край большой лодки. «Здравствуйте, товарищи! – Подойдя ближе, Золотарёв присел позади них на корточки. – Приятного аппетита» (Максимов 1). The dying flames of the bonfire, which turned out to be at a little mooring-stage, lit up the faces of a group of men—geologists perhaps, or fishermen—and the edge of a large boat. "Good evening, comrades! Enjoy your food." Zolotarev went up and crouched beside them (1a).

A-35 • КАК В АПТЕ́КЕ *coll, humor* [как + PrepP; Invar; adv] exactly (the right amount, measure etc): **precisely; to the drop ⟨ounce, gram etc⟩.**

«Ты всё делаешь точно по рецепту?» – «А как же! Полстакана сахару, десять грамм желатина, чайная ложка ликёра... Как в аптеке». "You go exactly by the recipe?" "Of course! Half a cup of sugar, ten grams of gelatin, and one teaspoon of liqueur...to the drop."

A-36 • БРАТЬ/ВЗЯТЬ НА АРА́ПА *кого highly coll* [VP; subj: human; often neg pfv fut, gener. 2nd pers sing не возьмёшь] to (try to) get sth. from s.o., make s.o. do as one wishes by telling him sth. deceitful (and getting him to act before he has had time to realize he is being tricked): X взял Y-а на арапа ≃ **X pulled a fast one on Y; Y was taken in by X; X hoodwinked Y; X threw dust in Y's eyes.**

Билеты на этот концерт давно распроданы, а попасть очень хочется. Решил я взять администратора на арапа: пришёл к нему, заговорил с акцентом, выдал себя за шведского журналиста — и вот они, билеты! The concert has been sold out for a long time, but I really wanted to go, so I decided to pull a fast one on the concert hall manager: I went up to him and, speaking with an accent, passed myself off as a Swedish journalist. And…here are the tickets!

A-37 • ЗАПРАВЛЯ́ТЬ АРА́ПА (кому) substand [VP; subj: human; often neg imper] to lie, make things up, tell far-fetched stories etc (in an attempt to dupe s.o. or make an impression): X Y-у арапа заправляет ≃ **X is trying to put one over on Y ⟨to take Y for a ride⟩; X is playing Y for a fool; [in limited contexts] X is spinning Y yarns; [of lighthearted kidding] X is putting Y on; X is pulling Y's leg.**

«Ты что, лавочку здесь собрал? Рука руку моет, да? В тюрьме соскучился? Ты мне арапа не заправляй, не таких обламывали!» (Максимов 3). "So you've got a gang of crooks here? Honor among thieves? Can't wait to go to prison, is that it? I'm warning you, don't try to take me for a ride, we've had tougher ones than you to handle" (3a). ♦ [author's usage] «Мы — коммунисты — всю жизнь… всю кровь свою… капля по капле… отдавали делу служения рабочему классу… угнетённому крестьянству. Мы привыкли бесстрашно глядеть смерти в глаза! Вы можете убить меня…» — «Слыхали!» — «Будет править арапа!» — «Дайте сказать!» — «А ну, замолчать!» (Шолохов 4). "We Communists have given our whole lives…all our blood…drop by drop…to the cause of serving the working class…the oppressed peasantry. We are used to looking death fearlessly in the face. You can kill me…" "We've heard that once!" "That's enough of your yarns!" "Let him speak!" "Shut up!" (4a).

A-38 • НА АРА́ПА highly coll [PrepP; Invar; adv] (to accomplish sth.) by acting insolently, in a brash manner, in a way that defies accepted rules or expected approaches: **bluff one's way through (sth.); wing it; finagle ⟨fast-talk⟩ one's way (into sth.** etc).

Я не успел подготовиться к экзамену, пошёл сдавать на арапа — и, представьте, сдал! I didn't have time to prepare for my exam, so I just winged it and, would you believe it, I passed! ♦ «На выставку пускают только по пригласительным билетам». — «Ничего, пройдём на арапа, не в первый раз». "You have to have a special invitation to get into this exhibit." "Don't worry, we'll fast-talk our way in—it won't be the first time."

A-39 • ТАЩИ́ТЬ/ЗАТАЩИ́ТЬ ⟨ПОТАЩИ́ТЬ, ТЯНУ́ТЬ/ЗАТЯНУ́ТЬ, ПОТЯНУ́ТЬ⟩ НА АРКА́НЕ кого куда coll [VP; subj: human; usu. neg pfv fut, gener. 2nd pers sing не затащишь, neg pfv infin (used as impers predic), or impfv infin with придётся, надо etc] to force s.o. to go (to some place): Х-а в место Y на аркане не затащишь ⟨не затащить⟩ ≃ **wild horses couldn't drag X to place Y; try as you might ⟨no matter what you do, however hard you try⟩, you won't get X to place Y;** ‖ Х-а в место Y на аркане тащить нужно ≃ **X has to be dragged ⟨you have to drag X⟩ to place Y.**

[Жарков:] [Егорьев] сказал — приду завтра, а скоро неделя этому завтра… Может, он просто не хочет. На аркане потяну, что ли (Розов 4). [Zh:] He [Yegorev] said he'd come tomorrow, and that was nearly a week ago….Perhaps he doesn't want to come. I can't drag him here, can I? (4a).

A-40 • ТЯЖЁЛАЯ АРТИЛЛЕ́РИЯ [NP; fixed WO] **1.** iron or humor a slow, sluggish person, or slow, sluggish people: a **slowpoke ⟨slowpokes⟩; dead weight; (one who is) hard to get moving.**

2. the most effective, powerful means of achieving sth. (to which one resorts when other means are exhausted): **heavy artillery; big guns; [in limited contexts] one's trump card.**

…Первым делом надо было Вику прописать… Как ни облучала Вера [обаянием] начальника паспортного стола — не помогало. Письмо народной артистки Куниной тоже оказалось пустым номером. Пришлось вывести на позиции тяжёлую артиллерию в лице «очень ответственного» из номера люкс… (Грекова 3). …First of all Vika had to be registered in her [Vera's] house….No matter how Vera sparkled at the director of the passport bureau it didn't help. A letter from People's Artist Kunina also didn't do the trick. She had to make use of heavy artillery in the form of a very important person staying in one of the luxury suites (3a).

A-41 • СДАВА́ТЬ/СДАТЬ В АРХИ́В [VP; subj: human; often 3rd pers pl with indef. refer., infin with надо, пора, рано etc, or short-form past passive Part] **1.** ~ кого to dismiss s.o., regarding him as unfit for some activity (usu. of a person unfit to fulfill his responsibilities at work because of his age, lack of abilities etc): Х-а сдали в архив ≃ **X was put ⟨turned, sent⟩ out to pasture; X was put on the shelf; X was written off as a has-been; X was sent to the glue factory; [in limited contexts] X is a back number.**

В то время, когда Козлику исполнилось тридцать лет, князь ещё не совсем был сдан в архив… (Салтыков-Щедрин 2). At the time Kozelkov reached the age of thirty, the prince had not been put on the shelf altogether… (2a). ♦ «Я хоть теперь сдан в архив, а… я психолог по-своему и физиогномист» (Тургенев 2). "Though I'm a back number now…I am something of a psychologist…in my own fashion, and a physiognomist" (2c).

2. ~ что to stop using sth. forever, consign sth. to oblivion as outdated, useless: X сдал Y в архив ≃ **X scrapped ⟨shelved⟩ Y; X put Y away for good; X relegated Y to the archives.**

«Увы! — с сожалением ответил Берлиоз, — ни одно из этих доказательств ничего не стоит, и человечество давно сдало их в архив» (Булгаков 9). "Alas!" Berlioz answered with regret. "None of these proofs is worth a thing, and humanity has long since scrapped them" (9a).

A-42 • (КАК ⟨БУ́ДТО, СЛО́ВНО, ТО́ЧНО⟩) АРШИ́Н ПРОГЛОТИ́Л coll, humor [(как etc +) VP; adv (variants with как etc) or predic with subj: human (all variants); past only; fixed WO] (a person who) has unnaturally straight posture (may refer to a permanent or a temporary characteristic): **straight as a ramrod; ramrod-straight; stiff as a poker; (one) looks like he has a broomstick ⟨a poker⟩ up his butt.**

«Я вот чего хотел-то: разводец бы нам организовать… Да что ты молчишь?» — как будто удивился [Дмитрий]… А она [Маруся] стоит и крикнуть не может… Ведь её — Дмитрий! Как же так?.. «Ну вот, будешь теперь стоять, как аршин проглотила…» (Суслов 1). "What I wanted was this: we should get a divorce….Why are you so quiet?" he [Dmitry] asked, as if he were surprised….And she [Marusia] stood there and couldn't cry out….It was her Dmitry! How could this be?…"So now you just stand there, stiff as a poker" (1a).

< «Аршин» is an old Russian measure of length (0.71 meter). The term also refers to a stick or ruler of that length (formerly used by merchants, tailors etc).

A-43 • МЕ́РИТЬ ⟨МЕ́РЯТЬ⟩ (кого-что) **НА** какой **АРШИ́Н ⟨**каким **АРШИ́НОМ, НА** какую **МЕ́Р(К)У,** какой **МЕ́Р(К)ОЙ⟩** [VP; subj: human] to evaluate s.o. or sth. by certain (as specified by the modifier) criteria: X мерит Y-а [AdjP] аршином ≃ **X measures ⟨judges⟩ Y by a [AdjP] yardstick; X judges ⟨measures⟩ Y by [AdjP] standards;** ‖ X мерит Y-а не на тот аршин ≃ **X measures Y by the wrong yardstick; X judges ⟨measures⟩ Y by the wrong standards.**

«…Народ другой стал с революции, как, скажи, заново народился! А они [генералы] всё старым аршином меряют» (Шолохов 5). "The people are different since the revolution, it's like they'd been born again! But these generals, they still measure everything by the old yardstick" (5a). ♦ «Прошу не мерять меня общими мерками. Я фигура особой породы – я таинственный в ночи!» (Аксёнов 6). "Please do not judge me by the common yardstick. I am a creature of a special breed, I am the mysterious being of the night" (6a). ♦ «…Подобных ему людей не приходится мерить обыкновенным аршином…» (Тургенев 2). "People like him can't be judged by ordinary standards" (2e).

< See A-42.

A-44 • МЕ́РИТЬ ⟨МЕ́РЯТЬ⟩ НА ОДИ́Н АРШИ́Н ⟨ОДНИ́М АРШИ́НОМ, НА ОДНУ́ МЕ́Р(К)У, ОД-НО́Й МЕ́Р(К)ОЙ⟩ *кого-что* [VP; subj: human; obj: pl, often всех, всё; often infin with нельзя, не надо etc; the verb may take the final position, otherwise fixed WO] to evaluate different people, things, phenomena by the same criteria, without taking into account their individual properties or qualities: X мерит Y-ов на один аршин ≃ **X measures Ys by the same yardstick; X judges ⟨measures⟩ Ys by the same standards.**

< See A-42.

A-45 • МЕ́РИТЬ ⟨МЕ́РЯТЬ⟩ НА СВОЙ АРШИ́Н ⟨СВОИ́М АРШИ́НОМ, НА СВОЮ́ МЕ́РКУ, СВОЕ́Й МЕ́РКОЙ, ПО СЕБЕ́⟩ *кого-что* [VP; subj: human; obj: often всех, всё; often infin with нельзя, не надо etc; the verb may take the final position, otherwise fixed WO] to evalute s.o. or sth. one-sidedly, subjectively, applying solely one's own criteria: X мерит Y-а на свой аршин ≃ **X measures Y by X's own yardstick ⟨measure⟩; X judges ⟨measures⟩ Y by X's own standards;** [in limited contexts] **X measures another man's foot by X's own last.**

«…Как всё переменилось! Пушкин, всю жизнь издевавшийся над рогами – и вдруг поборник женской чести и верности…» – …«Всё это так, но мы всё время забываем, что тогда было всё другое, другое всё тогда было. Вы меряете на свой аршин» (Битов 2). "…How everything changed! Pushkin, who all his life had mocked at horns – and suddenly he's the champion of his wife's honor and fidelity."…"That's all true, but we keep forgetting that things were different then, everything was different. You're measuring by your own yardstick" (2a). ♦ [Таня:] Вы по себе мерите. Не все же торопятся, как вы. Другие думают, размышляют… (Вампилов 3). [T.:] You're judging them by your own standards. Not everyone is in such a hurry as you. Some people think, meditate… (3a). ♦ [author's usage] «Знаешь, что он теперь про меня думает? Что сбегу с деньгами. Он всех людей по своей мерке мерит» (Евтушенко 2). "You know what he thinks now? That I'll run off with the money. He measures everyone in the world by his own standards" (2a).

< See A-42.

A-46 • ВИ́ДЕТЬ НА ТРИ АРШИ́НА ⟨НА ДВА АР-ШИ́НА, НА АРШИ́Н⟩ В ЗЕ́МЛЮ ⟨ПОД ЗЕМЛЁЙ, ПОД ЗЕ́МЛЮ⟩ *obs, coll* [VP; subj: human; the verb may take the final position, otherwise fixed WO] to be very observant, perceptive, astute: X на три аршина в землю видит ≃ **X never misses ⟨doesn't miss⟩ a trick ⟨a thing⟩; X is nobody's fool; you can't put one over on X; there are no flies on X.**

< See A-42.

A-47 • НАКАЛЯ́ТЬ/НАКАЛИ́ТЬ АТМОСФЕ́РУ *(где)* [VP; subj: human or abstr] to cause a situation to become tense, make people agitated: X накалил атмосферу ≃ **X generated tension;** ‖ атмосфера накалена ≃ **the atmosphere has become very heated.**

A-48 • РАЗРЯДИ́ТЬ АТМОСФЕ́РУ [VP; subj: human or abstr; often infin with надо, нужно etc or in a чтобы-clause] to alleviate the strain or anxiety in a situation, make people calmer, more relaxed: X разрядил атмосферу ≃ **X eased ⟨reduced⟩ the tension (in the air); X diffused the situation; X cooled things off ⟨down⟩;** [in limited contexts] **things simmered down.**

A-49 • КАК АУ́КНЕТСЯ, ТАК И ОТКЛИ́КНЕТСЯ [saying] you will be treated the same way as you treat others (often said when justifying the behavior of a person who repays unkindness or ill will with the same): ≃ **as you sow, so shall you reap; one ill ⟨good⟩ turn deserves another.**

A-50 • А́ХИ И ⟨ДА⟩ О́ХИ; О́ХИ И ⟨ДА⟩ А́ХИ *all coll* [NP; pl only; subj or obj] words used to express lamentation, regret, or delight, surprise etc: [lamentation, regret etc] **oh mes and oh mys; ohs and ahs; moans ⟨sighs⟩ and groans;** [delight, surprise etc] **oohs and ahs; gasps of delight and astonishment.**

«И матери моей хорошо: день её до того напичкан всякими занятиями, ахами да охами, что ей и опомниться некогда…» (Тургенев 2). "…Mother, too, is happy: her day is crammed with so many occupations, and so many oh's and ah's that she hasn't time to stop and think…" (2a). ♦ Надя привезла Ларе от всего дома поздравления и напутствия и в подарок от родителей драгоценность. Она вынула из саквояжа шкатулку… и, отщёлкнув крышку, передала Ларе редкой красоты ожерелье. Начались охи и ахи (Пастернак 1). Nadia had brought Lara the congratulations and good wishes of the whole family and a present from her parents. She took a jewel case out of her travelling bag, snapped it open, and held out a very beautiful necklace. There were gasps of delight and astonishment (1a).

A-51 • НЕ АХТИ́ КАК *coll* [AdvP; Invar; fixed WO] **1.** Also: **НЕ АХТИ́** *coll* [adv or impers predic] not very well; (it is) not very good, pleasant etc: **not particularly ⟨terribly, too⟩ well ⟨good⟩; not all that well ⟨good⟩.**

[Лёва:] В доме у вас не ахти. [Альберт:] Я это чувствую. [Лёва:] Молодец! [Альберт:] Но мне хочется, чтобы было хорошо (Розов 4). [L.:] Things are not too good at home just now, are they? [A.:] That's what I feel. [L.:] Good lad! [A.:] But I want them to be good (4a).

2. [adv; foll. by Adv or short-form Adj or Part denoting a positive quality, quantity, or distance] not very, not especially: **not particularly; not all that; not terribly ⟨too, exactly⟩.**

…Пока он [Гладышев] в горнице накачивал и разжигал примус, гость его остался в передней… Чонкин ещё не успел как следует рассмотреть то, что было в этой комнате, как яичница была готова, и Гладышев позвал его к столу. Здесь было тоже не ахти как убрано, но всё же почище, чем в передней… (Войнович 2). While Gladishev pumped and kindled the primus, his guest remained in the front room.…Chonkin had still not managed to have a proper look at everything in the room when the omelet was ready and Gladishev summoned him to the table. The back room too was not particularly tidy, but at least it was a bit cleaner than the front room (2a).

A-52 • НЕ АХТИ́ КАКО́Й *coll* [AdjP; fixed WO] **1.** Also: **НЕ АХТИ́** *coll* [modif (when foll. by NP) or subj-compl with copula, var. with какой – nom or instrum (subj: any common noun); var. не ахти is used as subj-compl only] not especially good, rather poor: **not so great ⟨hot⟩; not the best ⟨the greatest, the most brilliant etc⟩ (of…); not much of a…; nothing to rave ⟨to brag, to write home⟩ about.**

За окном стоял литой монотонный гул. Иссечённое песчаной пылью стекло мерно вибрировало… «Гляди, Коля, что на дворе делается!.. Страсть… Вот заехали, сам не рад будешь…» [Николай] пытался отшутиться… но по всему было видно, что настроение у него тоже не ахти (Максимов 3). From outside there came an unwavering, monotonous howl. The window vibrated rhythmically, lashed by fine sand…."Look what's going on outside, Kolya…it's terrifying….Look where we've landed ourselves—we shall regret it!" Nikolai tried to make a joke of it, although he was obviously not in the best of humor himself (3a). ♦ [Андрей:] …Вот вы фотограф; профессия, прямо скажем, не ахти какая, — это и был предел ваших мечтаний? (Розов 1). [A.:] …You are a photographer. It's not exactly the most brilliant profession. Well, is being a photographer the height of your ambition? (1a). ♦ «Акустика, конечно, не ахти, но ничего, работать можно» (Войнович 4). "Of course the acoustics are nothing to rave about, but it doesn't matter, we'll manage" (4a).

2. [modif; foll by Adj denoting a positive quality, quantity, or distance] not very, not especially: **not particularly; not all that; not terribly ⟨too, exactly⟩.**

Хотя роль Евдокии, жены Игната Тимофеевича, директорши сельской школы-семилетки, была не ахти какая завидная — очень уж лобовата, ревность, страдания, разговоры поучительные, — но Ляля надеялась всех поразить… (Трифонов 1). Although the role of Yevdokia, Ignat Timofeevich's wife and the principal of the seven-year village elementary school, was not a particularly enviable one—it was terribly overdone, with all sorts of jealousy, sufferings, and didactic conversations—still, Lyalya hoped to impress everyone… (1a).

A-53 • НЕ АХТИ́ СКО́ЛЬКО *кого-чего coll* [AdvP; Invar; quantit compl with copula (subj/gen: any common noun) or adv (quantif); fixed WO] a relatively small amount (of sth.), relatively few (people, things etc): **not very ⟨too⟩ much ⟨many⟩; anything but plentiful ⟨numerous⟩; not an overabundance;** [with count nouns only] **few and far between; only a handful.**

Денег у меня сейчас не ахти сколько, так что покупку телевизора придётся отложить. I don't have too much money at the moment, so I'll have to put off buying a TV.

Б

Б-1 • БАЗА́РНАЯ БА́БА *highly coll, rude* [NP; usu. obj, subj-compl with copula, nom or instrum (subj: human), or adv (after как)] a loud, abusive person: **fishwife; shrew;** ‖ кричать ⟨орать⟩ как базарная баба ≃ **scream ⟨shout etc⟩ like a fishwife.**

Б-2 • НЕ ЗНА́ЛА БА́БА ГО́РЯ, (ТАК) КУПИ́ЛА ⟨БА́БА⟩ ПОРОСЯ́; НЕ́ БЫ́ЛО У БА́БЫ ХЛОПО́Т ⟨ЗАБО́Т⟩, (ТАК) КУПИ́ЛА ⟨БА́БА⟩ ПОРОСЯ́ [saying] s.o. has caused himself much anxiety, trouble, or discomfort (said when new cares or worries arise for a person because of obligations or matters he has voluntarily undertaken): ≃ **trouble comes to him who seeks it; (it's) a trouble of his ⟨your etc⟩ own making.**

Б-3 • ПОДБИВА́ТЬ/ПОДБИ́ТЬ ⟨ПОДСЧИ́ТЫВАТЬ/ ПОДСЧИТА́ТЬ⟩ БА́БКИ *highly coll* [VP; subj: human] to examine and summarize the net results of sth.: **sum it up (and draw conclusions); sum up what one has done; [in limited contexts] sum it up and see what we've ⟨you've etc⟩ got; [in refer. to scoring in games] tally up the score(s).**

Три дня они заседали, обсуждали, а когда пришло время подбить бабки, оказалось, что ни до чего не договорились. For three days they discussed and debated, but when it came time to sum up what they had done, it turned out they had gotten nowhere. ♦ Ребята, все высказались? Тогда давайте подобьём бабки. OK, guys, has everyone said everything they wanted to? Then let's try to sum it up and see what we've got.

Б-4 • БА́БУШКА ВОРОЖИ́Т *кому obs, coll* [VP_subj; usu. pres; fixed WO] **1.** (s.o.) is very lucky, everything comes easy (for s.o.): Х-у бабушка ворожит ≃ **X is blessed with (good) luck; luck is (always) on X's side; X is never down on his luck.**

2. (s.o.) has the advantage of having influential friends, patronage: Х-у бабушка ворожит ≃ **X has friends in high places; X has a friend at court.**

Б-5 • БА́БУШКА (ЕЩЁ) НА́ДВОЕ СКАЗА́ЛА ⟨ГАДА́ЛА⟩ *coll* [VP_subj; these forms only; subj-compl with быть_ø (subj: usu. a clause) or indep. sent; ещё may take the initial position, otherwise fixed WO] it is yet unknown whether the event in question will happen or not (usu. the implication is that it will not happen): **that ⟨it⟩ remains to be seen; it's anybody's guess; that's ⟨it's⟩ an open question; it could go either way; we'll (just) have to wait and see.**

«Мы после обеда засядем в ералаш, и я его обыграю». — «Хе-хе-хе, посмотрим! Бабушка надвое сказала» (Тургенев 2). "We'll have a round of whist after dinner, and I'll clean him out." "He! he! he! We shall see! That remains to be seen" (2b). ♦ «Было время, товарищ Воробушкин... тобой детей пугали. Один бы ты и в жизнь не отплевался. Да и была бы жизнь, тоже бабушка надвое гадала...» (Максимов 3). "There was a time, Comrade Vorobushkin, when your name was used to scare children. On your own, you'd never have wriggled out of it as long as you lived. And whether you'd have lived at all is anybody's guess..." (3a). ♦ «...Тех — миллионы, которые не позволят вам попирать ногами свои священнейшие верования, которые раздавят вас!» — «Коли раздавят, туда и дорога, — промолвил Базаров. — Только бабушка ещё надвое сказала. Нас не так мало, как вы полагаете» (Тургенев 2). "...The others are millions, who won't let you trample their sacred traditions under foot, who will crush you!" "If we're crushed, serves us right," observed Bazarov. "But that's an open question. We are not so few as you suppose" (2b). ♦

«...Ваша власть и держится-то тридцать годов [*substand* = лет], и сколько ещё продержится — это ещё бабушка надвое сказала, а наша вера две тыщи [*phonetic spelling* = тысячи] лет стоит...» (Максимов 1). "Your power's been in existence thirty years, and how long it'll survive we'll have to wait and see, but our faith has lasted for two thousand years..." (1a).

Б-6 • ВО́Т ТЕБЕ, БА́БУШКА, И Ю́РЬЕВ ДЕНЬ! [saying] used to express the speaker's surprise, dismay, or disappointment over an unexpected occurrence which he has just discovered and which betrayed his expectations: ≃ **here's ⟨that's⟩ a fine ⟨nice⟩ how-d'ye do ⟨how-do-you-do⟩!; this is ⟨here's⟩ a fine kettle of fish!**

По левую сторону городничего: Земляника...; за ним судья... сделавший движенье губами, как бы хотел посвистать или произнесть: «Вот тебе, бабушка, и Юрьев день!» (Гоголь 4). On the left side of The Mayor stands Zemlyanika...; next to him is the Judge...making a movement with his lips as though he were going to whistle and say: "Here's a nice how-d'ye-do!" (4c).

< The origin of this saying is commonly linked to the ban in 1580–90 on the peasants' right to move from one landlord's estate to another's. Prior to this, peasants had had the right to move during the two weeks surrounding St. George's (or St. Yury's, Юрьев) Day, the day of the patron saint of field workers (Nov. 26, Old Style).

Б-7 • РАССКА́ЗЫВАЙ/РАССКАЖИ́ ЭТО СВОЕ́Й БА́БУШКЕ ⟨КОМУ́-НИБУДЬ ДРУГО́МУ, *less often* СВОЕ́Й ТЁТЕ⟩ *coll* [imper sent; usu. this WO (variants with бабушке and тёте)] (used to express one's strong disbelief of s.o.'s statement) I absolutely do not believe that: **you can't expect me to believe that; don't give me *that*; get outta ⟨out of⟩ here! Cf. tell it ⟨that⟩ to the marines!**

Б-8 • У БА́БЫ ВО́ЛОС ДО́ЛОГ, ДА ⟨А⟩ УМ КО́РОТОК [saying] (used to express the condescending opinion held by some men that women lack worldly wisdom) although a woman may be attractive, she lacks sound judgment: ≃ **long of hair and short of brains.**

Строже всего Семён хранил тайну от жены. Баба и есть баба — волос долог, да ум короток. Поведай, не утерпит — разнесёт по селу (Тендряков 1). Simon kept his secret carefully from his wife. A woman was a woman—long of hair and short of brains, as the saying is. In all likelihood she wouldn't be able to keep her mouth shut, and would go round telling everybody in the village (1a).

Б-9 • ПОДВОДИ́ТЬ/ПОДВЕСТИ́ *(какую)* **БА́ЗУ** *(под что) offic; in coll speech, often iron* [VP; subj: human or collect] to substantiate sth. (usu. with one's own interests in mind): X подводит [AdjP] базу (под Y) ≃ **X justifies Y on [AdjP] grounds; X produces a [AdjP] explanation (to back up ⟨to support⟩ Y); X makes a case for Y (based on...).**

Почему и зачем издан этот Указ — это мне всё равно. И нечего подводить под это научную базу и трепаться о революции (Аржак 1). I didn't care why the Decree had been put out. And there was no point in producing scientific explanations and in jabbering about the Revolution (1a).

Б-10 • ЗАБИВА́ТЬ/ЗАБИ́ТЬ ⟨ВКРУ́ЧИВАТЬ/ВКРУ-ТИ́ТЬ⟩ БА́КИ *кому slang* [VP; subj: human; usu. impfv] to deceive, intentionally mislead s.o.: X забивает Y-у баки ≃ **X is trying to con ⟨put one over on, fast-talk⟩ Y; X is pulling the wool over Y's eyes.**

«Когда-нибудь это должно произойти. Может быть, давно уже происходит. Внутри вида зарождается новый вид, а мы это называем генетической болезнью... Умные и все на подбор талантливые... Тогда что же это выходит? Тогда выходит, что они уже не люди. Зурзмансор мне просто баки забивал» (Стругацкие 1). "It's got to happen some time. Maybe it's been going on for a long time now. A new species arising out of an old one, and we call it a genetic illness....Intelligent and talented, every single one of them. And what does it lead to? That they're not human anymore. Zurzmansor was just pulling the wool over my eyes" (1a).

Б-11 • **БИТЬ БАКЛУ́ШИ** *coll, disapprov* [VP; subj: human] to be idle, do nothing: X бил баклуши ≃ **X twiddled his thumbs; X frittered away the ⟨his⟩ time; X sat around doing nothing; X goofed off;** [in limited contexts] **X killed time.**

[Аннушка:] Ты меня, братец, отпусти домой! На что я тебе! [Бессудный:] А дома что делать? Баклуши бить (Островский 8). [A.:] Brother, let me go home! What use am I to you? [B.:] What will you do at home? Twiddle your thumbs? (8a). ♦ Хлопнула дверь, дежурный по станции, проводя поезд, ушёл в свою каморку бить баклуши (Ерофеев 3). A door slammed: after seeing the train off, the stationmaster had gone into his little room to kill time (3a).

< «Баклуши», small chunks of wood chopped from large blocks, were once commonly used to make wooden objects. Chopping off chunks was considered an easy job.

Б-12 • **(И) КО́НЧЕН БАЛ** [sent; these forms only; fixed WO] that is the end of what has been going on, it is all over: **the party ⟨the game, the ball⟩ is over;** [in refer. to criminal activities, wrongdoings etc] **the jig ⟨the game⟩ is up.**

Каждое её слово камнем откладывалось в нём, всё утяжеляя и утяжеляя тёмный груз переполнявшей его горечи... Никогда раньше Золотарёву не приходилось испытывать подобной муки... И горячечно забываясь в ночи, он с отчаянием подытожил: «Кончен бал!» (Максимов 1). Every word she spoke fell like a stone upon him, making the dark burden of the anguish that filled him more and more unbearable....Zolotarev had never experienced such torment before....And as he drifted into feverish sleep he concluded in despair, "The ball is over!" (1a).

Б-13 • **БЕССТРУ́ННАЯ БАЛАЛА́ЙКА** *coll, disapprov* [NP; usu. sing; often subj-compl with copula, nom or instrum (subj: human), obj-compl with называть etc (obj: human), or vocative] a person who talks a lot but says nothing of substance: **windbag; gasbag; chatterbox.**

Б-14 • **ТРАВИ́ТЬ БАЛАНДУ́** *slang* [VP; subj: human] to babble, talk about trifles, make things up: X травит баланду ≃ **X is shooting the breeze ⟨the bull⟩; X is flapping his jaw; X is beating his gums.**

Б-15 • **ПОД БАЛДО́Й** *slang* [PrepP; Invar; usu. subj-compl with copula (subj: human)] (one is) somewhat intoxicated with alcohol, narcotics etc: **high; stoned; under the influence;** [in refer. to intoxication with alcohol only] **tipsy; tight; half-stewed.**

Б-16 • **БА́ЛОВЕНЬ СУДЬБЫ́ ⟨ФОРТУ́НЫ, СЧА́СТЬЯ⟩** *lit* [NP; usu. this WO] a lucky person: **fortune's child ⟨darling, favorite, minion⟩; child ⟨darling, favorite, minion⟩ of fortune.**

Я был поражён, что этот самый Бунин, счастливчик и баловень судьбы — как мне тогда казалось, — так глубоко не удовлетворён своим положением в литературе... (Катаев 3). I remember being astonished that this Bunin, this child of fortune—as he then seemed to me—should be so deeply dissatisfied with his position in literature... (3a).

Б-17 • **ПРОЛИВА́ТЬ/ПРОЛИ́ТЬ БАЛЬЗА́М** *на что,* often **НА РА́НЫ** *чьи, кого obsoles, often iron* [VP; subj: human or abstr] to console, soothe s.o.: X пролил бальзам на Y-овы раны ⟨на Y-ову душу⟩ ≃ **thing X was ⟨person X's words etc were⟩ as balm to Y's wounds ⟨soul⟩; thing X was ⟨person X's words were⟩ (like) a panacea for Y's wounds ⟨soul⟩.**

Б-18 • **ЗАДАВА́ТЬ/ЗАДА́ТЬ БА́НЮ** *кому highly coll* [VP; usu. pfv]. **1.** [subj: human] to scold s.o. sharply: X задал Y-у баню ≃ **X made it hot for Y; X gave Y what for; X let Y have it (with both barrels); X gave it to Y (good); X gave Y hell.**

Герой наш трухнул... порядком. Хотя... деревня Ноздрёва давно унеслась из вида... он всё ещё поглядывал назад со страхом, как бы ожидая, что вот-вот налетит погоня... «Эк, какую баню задал! Смотри ты какой!» (Гоголь 3). Our hero...had been considerably scared. Although...Nozdrev's village had long since vanished from sight...he was still casting apprehensive glances over his shoulder, as though expecting a pursuer to overtake him any moment...."He surely made it hot for me! What a character, that one!" (3c).

2. [subj: human (usu. pl) or collect] to overwhelm, defeat s.o. (usu. a hostile army, the enemy): X-ы задали баню Y-ам ≃ **Xs clobbered ⟨crushed, routed⟩ Ys; Xs ran Ys into the ground.**

3. [subj: human] to beat, thrash s.o.: X задал Y-у баню ≃ **X beat the tar ⟨the hell, the (living) daylights⟩ out of Y; X worked Y over; X gave Y a good working over ⟨going-over⟩.**

Б-19 • **КАК БАРА́Н** упереться *highly coll* [как + NP; nom only; adv (intensif)] (to resist sth.) very stubbornly: **(balk) like a mule; (be stubborn) as a mule; (be) bullheaded ⟨pigheaded⟩.**

Б-20 • **КАК БАРА́Н НА НО́ВЫЕ ВОРО́ТА** смотреть, уставиться и т. п. *highly coll, derog* [как + NP; Invar; adv; fixed WO] (to look, stare) in utter confusion, understanding nothing: **(stare) dumbly ⟨blankly⟩; (give s.o.) a blank stare.**

Б-21 • **НЕ БАРА́Н НАЧИХА́Л** *substand* [Invar; subj-compl with бытьø (subj: abstr or, rare, concr), pres only; fixed WO] sth. significant, sth. that should be taken into account: X — не баран начихал ≃ **X is nothing to sneeze at; X is no small thing; X is no trifle ⟨no trifling matter⟩.**

Б-22 • **ВЕРНЁМСЯ К НА́ШИМ БАРА́НАМ** [sent; Invar; fixed WO] let us return to the main topic of our conversation (used as a request to the interlocutor not to digress from the main topic; also used by the speaker to indicate a return to the main topic): **let's get back to the subject ⟨the matter⟩ at hand; let's return to the question at hand; let's get back to the point at issue; let's get back on track.**

< Loan translation of the French *revenons à ces moutons* or *retournons à nos moutons* ("let us return to our sheep"), from the medieval farce *Maistre Pierre Pathelin.*

Б-23 • **БАРА́ШЕК В БУМА́ЖКЕ** *obs* [NP; sing only; usu. obj; fixed WO] a bribe: **palm oil ⟨grease⟩; hush money.**

Б-24 • **СИДЕ́ТЬ БА́РИНОМ ⟨КАК БА́РИН⟩** *coll* [VP; subj: human] to be idle while everyone else is working cooperatively: X сидит барином ≃ **X sits around like royalty; X sits on his hands.**

Б-25 • **КИСЕ́ЙНАЯ БА́РЫШНЯ** *derog* [NP; usu. obj, subj-compl with copula, nom or instrum (subj: human), or adv (after как); fixed WO] a coddled person (usu. a young woman) who is unable to adjust to real life (orig., an affected and prudish young woman with petty interests): **pampered young lady; pampered darling**; [in limited contexts] **prim young lady.**

«Я кисейных барышень не люблю и вам такой быть не советую. Капризы извольте оставить» (Михайловская 1). "I don't like pampered young ladies and I don't advise you to become one. Please stop being capricious" (1a). ♦ Куражился он [Ужик] теперь только дома, над сёстрами: он, мол, рабочий класс, а они — кисейные барышни (Грекова 3). ...He [Uzhik] was able to play the big shot only at home with his sisters—a working-class man among prim young ladies (3a).

Б-26 • **БРАТЬ/ВЗЯТЬ БАРЬЕ́Р(Ы)** [VP; subj: human] to overcome obstacles to success: X возьмёт барьеры ≃ **X will cross ⟨surmount⟩ barriers; X will leap over hurdles.**

«Потребность в таком безделье — чаще всего неосознанная необходимость перескочить в том, что называется подсознанием, трудный барьер... Как часто я бессознательно и поражающе легко брал такие барьеры, стоило только мне перестать стараться и погрузиться в подобное безделие, в неожиданный сон» (Гладков 1). "The need for such idleness comes more often than not from an instinctive wish to leap over some difficult hurdle in the so-called subconscious....How often I have crossed such barriers unconsciously and with astonishing ease once I stopped trying and simply sank into idleness, into a sudden lethargy" (1a).

Б-27 • **НЕ ЛЕЗЬ ПОПЕРЁД БА́ТЬКИ В ПЕ́КЛО; ПРЕ́ЖДЕ ОТЦА́ ⟨БА́ТЬКИ⟩ В ПЕ́ТЛЮ НЕ СУ́ЙСЯ ⟨НЕ ЛЕЗЬ⟩** [saying] do not rush to undertake sth. risky or dangerous, let older and more experienced people make a move first: ≃ **don't rush ahead of people who know better; don't jump the gun.**

«Не спеши, — поморщился Коба. — Ты всегда спешишь поперёд батька [sic] в пекло» (Войнович 5). "Not so fast," said Comrade Koba, knitting his brows. "You're always jumping the gun" (5a).

Б-28 • **ПО БА́ТЮШКЕ (звать, величать** *кого*) *old-fash, coll* [PrepP; Invar; usu. adv] (to call, address s.o.) by the name derived from his or her father's name (by adding a suffix), which follows the first name and precedes the last name (in formal address, it is used in conjunction with the first name, whereas in uneducated or humorous speech it may be used alone): **patronymic.**

«Как, бишь, её зовут?» — спросил Базаров. «Фенечкой... Федосьей», — ответил Аркадий. «А по батюшке? Это тоже нужно знать». — «Николаевной» (Тургенев 2). "What did you say her name was?" asked Bazarov. "Fenichka...Fedosya," Arkady replied. "And her patronymic? One must know that too." "Nikolayevna" (2c).

Б-29 • **БА́ТЮШКИ МОЙ ⟨СВЕ́ТЫ⟩!** *obsoles, coll;* **БА́ТЮШКИ СВЯ́ТЫ!** *obsoles, substand;* **МА́ТУШКИ МОЙ ⟨СВЕ́ТЫ⟩!** *obs, coll* [Interj; these forms only; fixed WO] used to express amazement, admiration, fear etc: **(my) goodness (gracious)!; (my) gracious!; good heavens ⟨God, Lord⟩!; merciful heavens!; (good) God in heaven!; (holy) Mother of God!**

[Аркадина:] Как меня в Харькове принимали, батюшки мои, до сих пор голова кружится! (Чехов 6). [A.:] What a wonderful reception I had in Kharkov! My goodness, my head's still swimming! (6b). ♦ ...Нашему брату, хуторянину, высунуть нос из своего захолустья в большой свет — батюшки мои! — Это всё равно как, случается, иногда зайдёшь в покои великого пана: все обступят тебя и пойдут дурачить (Гоголь 5). For a villager like me to poke his nose out of his hole into the great world is—merciful heavens!—just like what happens if you go into the apartments of some fine gentleman: they all come around you and make you feel like a fool... (5a). ♦ «Ой, батюшки светы, дорогие товарищи, что с нами сделалось... Дрожим, ни живы ни мёртвы, язык

отнялся от ужаса!..» (Пастернак 1). "Oh, God in heaven, need I tell you the state we were in....We were shaking all over, half dead with fright and speechless with terror!" (1a).

Б-30 • **БАШ НА БАШ** *highly coll* [Invar; fixed WO] **1.** ~ **менять(ся), обменивать** и т. п. [adv] (in refer. to goods) (to exchange) one thing for another without additional payment, without adding anything: **(make) an even swap ⟨trade⟩.**

2. [subj-compl with бытьø (subj: usu. всё), adv, or indep. sent] an action (is undertaken), form of behavior (is demonstrated) etc in retaliation or reciprocation for a similar action, form of behavior etc: **tit for tat.**

Он [Мишка-сын] работал с Галибутаевым на одном производстве... То спросит какую-нибудь гадость, то толкнёт... Гонял его. Галибутаев... спуску тоже не давал. Баш на баш (Попов 1). He [Sonny Mishka] worked at the same factory as Galibutayev....One minute he'd be asking Galibutayev some filthy question, the next he'd be shoving him....Always after him....But [Galibutayev] would also let Sonny Mishka have it, when he got the chance. Tit for tat (1a).

Б-31 • **ПОД БАШМАКО́М ⟨ПОД БАШМАЧКО́М⟩** *чьим, (у) кого* **бытьø, находиться** и т. п. ог **держать** *кого;* **ПОД БАШМА́К** *чей, кого, к кому* **попадать** *all coll* [PrepP; these forms only; subj-compl with copula (subj: human) or obj-compl with держать (obj: human)] under the full control or influence of s.o., completely dependent on s.o. (usu. of a husband in relation to his wife): X под башмаком у женщины Y ≃ **X is under Y's thumb; X lets Y boss him around; [in limited contexts] X is henpecked ⟨a henpecked husband⟩;** ‖ Y держит X-а под башмаком ≃ **Y has ⟨keeps⟩ X under Y's thumb; Y has X wrapped around Y's little finger; [in limited contexts] Y wears the pants (in the family).**

Общее мнение было то, что Пьер был под башмаком своей жены, и действительно это было так. С самых первых дней их супружества Наташа заявила свои требования (Толстой 7). The general opinion was that Pierre was under his wife's thumb, which was really true. From the very first days of their married life Natasha had announced her demands (7b).

Б-32 • **БА́ШНЯ ИЗ СЛОНО́ВОЙ КО́СТИ** *lit* [NP; sing only; usu. obj; fixed WO] a place or state of isolation from the realities of life, esp. a preoccupation with remote intellectual pursuits rather than worldly affairs: **ivory tower.**

Думать, что в башне из слоновой кости он [Пастернак] охранял своё олимпийское спокойствие, — это абсурд (Ивинская 1). It is absurd to imagine that he [Pasternak] sat in an ivory tower, preserving an Olympian calm (1a).

< Loan translation of the French *tour d'ivoire.*

Б-33 • **НИ БЕ НИ МЕ (НИ КУКАРЕ́КУ)** *highly coll* [these forms only; fixed WO] **1.** ~ *(в чём)* [usu. predic with subj: human] one knows, understands etc nothing (about sth.): X (в Y-e) ни бе ни ме ≃ **X doesn't know ⟨understand⟩ a thing ⟨the first thing⟩ about Y; X doesn't know beans ⟨squat⟩ about Y; [in refer. to one's command of a foreign language, technical jargon etc] X doesn't know ⟨understand⟩ a word of Y; [in refer. to a foreign language only] X can't say two words in ⟨speak a word of⟩ Y.**

«И как это таких людей за границу посылают, когда они ни бе ни ме ни по-каковски?» (Трифонов 4). "And how is it they send such [people] abroad when they can't say two words in any other language?" (4a).

2. [predic (with subj: human) or obj] one says nothing, keeps silent: X (не говорит) ни бе ни ме ≃ **X doesn't say boo; X doesn't let out a peep; X doesn't utter a sound.**

Б-34 • **В БЕГА́Х** [PrepP; Invar; subj-compl with быть∅ (subj: human)] **1.** (one is) hiding from the police, the authorities, fleeing from the law: **on the run; on the lam; on the loose; in hiding.**

«Сегодня поздно вечером, гуляя в парке, я натолкнулся на какого-то человека, искавшего дорогу... Вид у него измученный, он, вероятно, несколько дней в бегах» (Федин 1). "Late this evening, while walking in the park, I came across a man trying to find his way....He looked exhausted, he has probably been on the run several days" (1a). ♦ «Директор в бегах... как раз мы его ищем. Есть подозрение, что сбежал с казённым золотом» (Искандер 3). "The director's in hiding...we're looking for him right now. He's suspected of absconding with government gold" (3a).

2. *coll* (one is) rushing around from place to place, incessantly running about taking care of business, doing chores etc: **on the move ⟨the run⟩; off ⟨out⟩ on errands; off ⟨out⟩ running errands; out and about; [in limited contexts] out running around.**

Б-35 • **НА БЕГУ́** [PrepP; Invar] **1.** [adv] while one is running: **as one runs.**

За машиной, рыдая и спотыкаясь, бежала Нюра... «Ваня! – кричала Нюра, давясь от рыданий. – Ванечка!» – и на бегу тянула руки к машине (Войнович 2). Sobbing and stumbling, Nyura ran after the truck...."Vanya!" cried Nyura, choking on her sobs. "Vanechka!" She reached her arms out to the truck as she ran (2a).

2. *coll* [usu. adv] (one does sth.) hastily, (one is, does sth.) in a hurry: **on the run; [in limited contexts] on the fly; (have) a quick (chat ⟨cry etc⟩).**

Около десяти, когда Ребров уже собрался уходить... появился Шахов, как обычно на бегу, второпях спросил, как дела у Реброва (Трифонов 1). At about ten o'clock, when Rebrov was just getting ready to leave...Shakhov appeared. He was on the run as usual and asked Rebrov hastily how his work was going (1a). ♦ «Ну конечно... я всегда бывала у Нюрка – зачем? Чтобы на бегу поплакаться в жилетку» (Залыгин 1). "Now, why was it I always used to go to Niurok? To have a quick cry on her shoulder, of course" (1a).

Б-36 • **СЕМЬ БЕД – ОДИ́Н ОТВЕ́Т** [saying] if the punishment for two transgressions of different magnitudes is the same, one might as well commit the more serious (and personally beneficial) one: ≃ **one might ⟨may⟩ as well be hanged for a sheep as (for) a lamb.**

...Он [Золотарёв] жёг мосты... он окончательно прощался с самим собою, ему не о чем было больше сожалеть и не в чем раскаиваться. Семь бед – один ответ! (Максимов 1). ...He [Zolotarev] burned his bridges....He bade himself a final goodbye, he had no more regrets now and no reason to repent. He might as well be hanged for a sheep as for a lamb! (1a).

Б-37 • **БЕДА́ (НИКОГДА́) НЕ ПРИХО́ДИТ ⟨НЕ ХО́ДИТ⟩ ОДНА́; БЕДА́ В ОДИНО́ЧКУ НЕ ХО́ДИТ** [saying] said when troubles or misfortunes follow one after another, when one misfortune seemingly evokes another: ≃ **troubles ⟨misfortunes⟩ never come singly; it never rains but it pours; when it rains, it pours.**

Беда в одиночку сроду не ходит: утром, по недогляду Гетька, племенной бугай Мирона Григорьевича распорол рогом лучшей кобылице-матке шею... Рану промыли. [Мирон Григорьевич] зашивал сам... Не успел Мирон Григорьевич отойти от колодца, из куреня прибежала Лукинична... Она отозвала мужа в сторону. «Наталья пришла, Гринич!.. Ушёл зятёк из дому!» (Шолохов 2). Troubles never come singly. That morning, because of Hetko's carelessness Miron Grigorievich's thoroughbred bull gored the neck of his best brood-mare....They washed the wound....[Miron] put in the stitches himself....But before he could step away from the well, Lukinichna

came running from the house....She called her husband aside. "Natalya has come back!...Our son-in-law's left home!" (2a).

Б-38 • **ЛИХА́ БЕДА́** *obsoles, coll* [NP; Invar; impers predic; foll. by infin; fixed WO] one must merely (do sth.): **one has only (to do sth.); one need only (do sth.).**

Б-39 • **ЛИХА́ БЕДА́ НАЧА́ЛО ⟨НАЧА́ТЬ⟩** [saying] beginning an endeavor is harder than continuing it once you have begun (may be used in refer. to both good deeds and reprehensible actions): ≃ **the first step is (always) the hardest; it's the first step that costs; the first blow is half the battle; a good start is half the race; well begun is half done; [in limited contexts] the first step is (always) the worst.**

[Большинцов:] Говорят, в этих делах лиха беда начать... (Тургенев 1). [B.:] They say, in these matters the first step is [the] hardest (1c). ♦ Лиха беда – начало. Одним словом, я аккуратнейшим образом, даже после ночной смены, посещала политзанятия у Евдокии Ивановны... (Гинзбург 2). As a good start is half the race, I made a point, even after my night shift, of attending punctiliously every one of Eudokia Ivanovna's political talks (2a). ♦ «Давайте выпьем!» – «Придётся. Лиха беда начало...» Лейтенант чокался с Григорием и поручиком, пил молча, почти не закусывал (Шолохов 5). "Let's drink!" "I suppose I'll have to. Oh well, the first step's the worst!" The English lieutenant clinked glasses with Grigory and his Russian companion and drank in silence, scarcely touching the food (5a).

Б-40 • **НЕ БЕДА́** *coll* [NP; Invar; subj-compl with быть∅ (subj: usu. это or a clause), pres only, or indep. sent] it is of no great consequence, it is not worth worrying about: **no matter; it doesn't matter; it's not so terrible; that's no misfortune.**

Когда я ухожу, он [Пастернак] снова церемонно извиняется, что не успел дочитать пьесу. «То есть, вернее, – я и не раскрыл её. Мне вчера помешали. Но это не беда. У нас будет повод снова вскоре встретиться, хорошо?» (Гладков 1). As I was leaving him [Pasternak], he again apologized very profusely for not having finished reading my play: "Or rather, I should say, I haven't even looked at it yet. I was interrupted yesterday. But no matter — we shall soon be meeting again, won't we?" (1a). ♦ «Простите великодушно за то, что заставил столько ждать...» – «Не беспокойтесь... ничего, несколько замешкались, не беда...» (Достоевский 1). "Be so generous as to forgive me for having kept you waiting so long..." "Don't worry...it's nothing, you're just a bit late, it doesn't matter..." (1a). ♦ В кабинете выпускающего происходила невероятная кутерьма и путаница. Он, совершенно бешеный, с красными глазами, метался, не зная, что делать... Метранпаж ходил за ним и, дыша винным духом, говорил: «Ну что же, Иван Вонифатьевич, не беда, пускай завтра утром выпускают экстренное приложение» (Булгаков 10). The night editor's office was in a state of pandemonium. The editor, furious, red-eyed, rushed about not knowing what to do....The makeup man followed him about, reeking of wine fumes and saying, "Oh, well, it's not so terrible, Ivan Vonifatievich, we can publish an extra supplement tomorrow" (10a). ♦ «Романтик сказал бы: я чувствую, что наши дороги начинают расходиться, а я просто говорю, что мы друг другу приелись». – «Евгений...» – «Душа моя, это не беда; то ли ещё на свете приедается!» (Тургенев 2). "A romantic would say, 'I feel our paths are beginning to diverge,' but I will simply say that we are tired of each other." "Oh Yevgeny...." "Dear lad, that's no misfortune; the world is full of things that pall on one" (2c).

Б-41 • **(НЕ) ВЕЛИКА́ БЕДА́** *coll* [NP; these forms only; usu. indep. sent or subj-compl with быть∅ (subj: a clause), pres only; fixed WO] it is not important, significant: **it's not the end of the world; it's ⟨that's⟩ no (great) tragedy; [in limited contexts] no problem.**

Я ушёл, недоумевая, почему всё это так его встревожило. Ну, даже если и испортил рыбу, подумаешь, велика беда (Кузнецов 1). I went away, wondering why all this had made him so apprehensive. What if he had spoiled the fish—that was no tragedy (1a). ♦ [Макарская:] Как же я могу тебя пустить, если я тебя не знаю! [Бусыгин:] Велика беда! Пожалуйста! Бусыгин Владимир Петрович. Студент (Вампилов 4). [M.:] How can I let you in if I don't know you? [B.:] No problem. Let me introduce myself: Vladimir Petrovich Busygin, a student (4a).

Б-42 • ПРИШЛА́ БЕДА́ – ОТВОРЯ́Й ⟨РАСТВОРЯ́Й, ОТКРЫВА́Й⟩ ВОРОТА́ [saying] if sth. unfortunate has happened, then you can expect more trouble to follow (said when misfortunes come one after another): ≃ **troubles ⟨misfortunes⟩ never come singly; it never rains but it pours; when it rains, it pours.**

Собрание вынесло рекомендацию освободить меня от обязанностей заведующего отделом... Тамара затеяла развод и раздел квартиры... Но пришла беда – открывай ворота. Не стало Ленки (Зиновьев 2). The Commission recommended that I should be relieved of the responsibilities of head of section....Tamara started divorce proceedings and demanded the division of our apartment....But troubles never come singly. Lenka died (2a).

Б-43 • ЧТО ЗА БЕДА́ coll [Invar; usu. a clause in a compound sent or the main clause in a complex sent; fixed WO] (used in refer. to some action, circumstance etc which is mentioned in the preceding context or is about to be mentioned) that is no cause for concern, that will not hurt anyone or anything: **what's ⟨where's⟩ the harm (in that)?; what harm is there in that?; what's wrong with that?; what does it matter?; it's no great matter.**

[Миловидов:] Ведь в окна огонь видно будет. [Евгения:] Так что ж за беда? У нас постоялый двор, всю ночь не гасим... (Островский 8). [M.:] The light will shine through the window! [E.:] Well, what's the harm in that? This is an inn. We don't put out the light all night (8a). ♦ «Г. прапорщик, вы сделали проступок, за который и я могу отвечать...» – «И полноте! что ж за беда? Ведь у нас давно всё пополам» (Лермонтов 1). "Ensign, you have committed an offense for which I, too, may be held responsible...." "Oh, come! Where's the harm? We've long shared everything, haven't we?" (1a). ♦ «Ну, да ежели бы меня и арестовали бы за то, что я здесь, что ж за беда?» (Толстой 5). "And even if they did arrest me for being here, what would it matter?" (5a). ♦ Проезжий... поглядывал в окно и посвистывал к великому неудовольствию смотрительши. «Вот бог послал свистуна, – говорила она вполголоса, – эк посвистывает, – чтоб он лопнул, окаянный басурман». – «...Что за беда, пускай себе свищет» (Пушкин 1). The traveler...looked through the window and whistled—an action that greatly annoyed the stationmaster's wife...."The Lord blessed us with a whistler," she muttered. "Ugh, he does whistle, may he be struck dumb, the damned infidel." "...It's no great matter: let him whistle" (1a).

Б-44 • БЕ́ДНОСТЬ НЕ ПОРО́К [saying] one should not be ashamed of one's poverty: ≃ **poverty is no crime ⟨vice, sin⟩.**

[Любим Карпыч:] Что он беден-то!.. Бедность не порок (Островский 2). [L.K.:] What if he is poor, eh?...Poverty is no crime (2a). ♦ «Сегодня вас не ждали, батюшка, говядинки не привезли», – промолвил Тимофеич... «И без говядинки обойдёмся... Бедность, говорят, не порок» (Тургенев 2). "They didn't expect you today, master, and the beef's not come," announced Timofeyich.... "We'll manage without the beef....Poverty, so they say, is no vice" (2e).

Б-45 • НА БЕДУ́ (чью) [PrepP; Invar; sent adv (usu. parenth)] (in refer. to an action or event) resulting in undesirable consequences (for s.o. or o.s.): **to one's ⟨s.o.'s⟩ misfortune; unluckily ⟨unfortunately⟩ (for one ⟨s.o.⟩); to one's ⟨s.o.'s⟩ cost; [in limited contexts] as luck would have it.**

«Множество лет тому назад, на мою беду, в дом ко мне пришёл бродячий художник и стал умирать от лихорадки» (Искандер 5). "Many years ago, to my misfortune, a wandering artist came to my house and began dying of a fever" (5a). ♦ Надобно было, на мою беду, чтоб вежливейший из генералов всех русских армий стал при мне говорить о войне (Герцен 1). Unluckily for me this most courteous of the generals of all the Russian armies had to begin speaking of the war in my presence (1a). ♦ «Они ещё пуще обиделись и начали меня неприлично за это ругать, а я... на беду себе, чтобы поправить обстоятельства, тут и рассказал очень образованный анекдот про Пирона... Они взяли да меня и высекли» (Достоевский 1). "...They got even more offended and began scolding me indecently, and I, unfortunately, tried to make things better by telling a very educated anecdote about Piron....Then they up and thrashed me" (1a). ♦ «Так, так научилась Параня, на свою беду, курить» (Абрамов 1). "Oh yes, that's how Paranya learned to smoke—to her cost" (1a). ♦ Б.Л. [Пастернак] сказал, что теперь он уже обязательно хочет посмотреть спектакль и не примет никаких отговорок. На беду заболела исполнительница главной роли Л.И. Добржанская и спектакли были отменены (Гладков 1). He [Pasternak] said I really must take him to see it [the production of my play] now, and he would not accept any excuses. But as luck would have it, the actress playing the leading part, L.I. Dobrzhanskaya, was ill at that moment and performances had been cancelled (1a).

Б-46 • НЕ БЕЗ чего [PrepP; Invar; Prep; the resulting PrepP is adv] with a certain degree (of sth.): **not without...; (with) some...; [in limited contexts] (with) a certain (amount of)...**

Не без страха глядел он и теперь на растворявшуюся дверь (Гоголь 3). It was not without fear, even now, that he watched the door opening (3b). ♦ ...Хотя чегемцы посмеивались над ним [Тимуром], однако относились к нему не без опаски (Искандер 5). Although the Chegemians snickered at him [Timur], they treated him with some caution (5a). ♦ Карасик изо всех сил старался выглядеть, как всегда, уверенным и властным, но получалось это у него не без натуги и смущения (Максимов 3). Karasik was trying his hardest to look as self-assured and authoritative as ever, but he could not avoid showing a certain strain and embarrassment (3a).

Б-47 • БЕ́ЗДНА ⟨КЛА́ДЕЗЬ⟩ ПРЕМУ́ДРОСТИ humor or iron [NP; sing only; fixed WO] a source, treasury of profound knowledge: **a wealth of knowledge; a storehouse of wisdom; [usu. of a person] a (veritable) font of wisdom.**

Б-48 • НА БЕЗРЫ́БЬЕ И РАК РЫ́БА [saying] in the absence of a better or needed person or thing, the one that is available will do: ≃ **better a ⟨one⟩ small fish than an empty dish; half a loaf is better than none ⟨no bread⟩; in the kingdom of the blind a ⟨the⟩ one-eyed man is king.**

Б-49 • ДО БЕЗУ́МИЯ [PrepP; Invar] **1.** ~ любить кого, влюбиться в кого, ненавидеть кого, кому хочется (с)делать что и т. п. [adv (intensif)] (to love, fall in love with, hate s.o.) intensely: **(love s.o.) to (the point of) distraction; (fall ⟨be⟩) passionately ⟨madly⟩ in love (with s.o.); (love ⟨hate⟩ s.o.) with a passion; (love s.o. ⟨want to do sth. etc⟩) desperately.**

Отец любил её до безумия, но обходился с нею со свойственным ему своенравием... (Пушкин 1). Her father loved her to distraction but treated her with his usual capriciousness... (1a). ♦ Бывали примеры, что женщины влюблялись в таких людей до безумия... (Лермонтов 1). There have been cases when women have fallen madly in love with men like him... (1b).

2. ~ какой, каков, как [modif] extremely, to the utmost degree: **terribly; awfully; exceedingly; incredibly.**

«Чем тебе не нравится твой начальник?» – «Он до безумия привередлив». "What don't you like about your supervisor?"

[12]

"He's terribly picky." ♦ Всё получилось до безумия нелепо: мы их ждали у левого входа, а они нас — у правого. The whole thing was incredibly ridiculous. We were waiting for them at the left entrance while they were waiting for us at the right.

Б-50 • БЕЛЕНЫ́ ОБЪЕ́ЛСЯ *highly coll, rude when addressed to the interlocutor* [VP; subj: human; past only; often after будто, как будто, словно, точно; often in questions; fixed WO] one behaves in an unreasonable fashion, as if he were crazy: X белены объелся ≃ **X is off his rocker ⟨trolley⟩; X is out of his gourd ⟨mind⟩; X is nuts ⟨loony⟩; X has cracked up; X has gone mad.**

"Что с вами, Руслан Павлович? Вы белены объелись?" (Трифонов 6). "...What's the matter with you, Ruslan Pavlovich? Are you off your rocker?" (6a). ♦ [Яичница:] ...Это не пройдёт тебе. Вот я тебя как сведу в полицию, так ты у меня будешь знать, как обманывать честных людей... *(Уходит.)* ...[Анучкин:] Признаюсь, любезнейшая, никак не думал я, чтобы вы стали так обманывать... *(Уходит.)* [Фёкла:] Белены объелись или выпили лишнее (Гоголь 1). [Kustard:] ...You won't get away with this. I'll set the police on you—that'll teach you to deceive honest folk...*(Goes out)*... [A.:] I must admit, my dear, I would never have believed that you could be so deceitful...*(Goes out)* [F.:] They've gone mad, or else they've had a drop too much (1a).

< «Белена» ("henbane") is a poisonous plant. Ingesting its seeds causes madness.

Б-51 • (ВЕРТЕ́ТЬСЯ ⟨КРУЖИ́ТЬСЯ, КРУТИ́ТЬСЯ⟩) КАК ⟨БУ́ДТО, СЛО́ВНО, ТО́ЧНО⟩ БЕ́ЛКА В КО-ЛЕСЕ́ *coll* [VP (with subj: human) or как etc + NP (these forms only; adv)] the verb may take the final position, otherwise fixed WO] to be incessantly bustling about, doing various things, occupied with various concerns: X вертится как белка в колесе ≃ **X is like a squirrel on a treadmill ⟨in a cage⟩; X is in a constant whirl; X is continually ⟨always⟩ on the go.**

...«[Виллон] жил в Париже, как белка в колесе, не зная ни минуты покоя» (Мандельштам 2). ..."[Villon] lived in Paris in a constant whirl—like a squirrel on a treadmill, never still for a moment" (2a).

Б-52 • РЕВЕ́ТЬ/ЗАРЕВЕ́ТЬ БЕЛУ́ГОЙ *coll* [VP; subj: human; usu. this WO] to (begin to) cry profusely, loudly, piercingly: X ревел белугой ≃ **X was crying hysterically; X was crying ⟨yelling, bawling⟩ his head off; [in limited contexts] X was howling like a jackal ⟨a hyena⟩.**

[Львов:] Скоро благословение? [Косых:] Должно, скоро. Зюзюшку в чувство приводят. Белугой ревёт, приданого жалко (Чехов 4). [L.:] Will the benediction be soon? [K.:] It should be soon. They're trying to bring Zyuzyushka around. She's howling like a jackal...upset about the dowry (4a).

Б-53 • РЫ́ТЬСЯ ⟨КОПА́ТЬСЯ⟩ В ГРЯ́ЗНОМ БЕЛЬЕ́ *кого, чьём* ⟨**В ЧУЖО́М ГРЯ́ЗНОМ БЕЛЬЕ́**⟩ *disapprov* [VP; subj: human; the verb may take the final position, otherwise fixed WO] to show an excessive interest in the intimate or unsavory details of other people's lives: X роется в Y-овом ⟨в чужом⟩ грязном белье ≃ **X pries ⟨snoops⟩ into Y's ⟨other people's⟩ personal affairs; X digs up dirt on Y ⟨on other people⟩; X sticks ⟨pokes⟩ his nose in(to) Y's ⟨other people's⟩ personal affairs.**

"Чем, кроме рыбалки, увлекается ваш Пётр Иванович?" — "Обожает рыться в грязном белье своих сотрудников". "What does your Pyotr Ivanovich like to do except go fishing?" "He loves to pry into his coworkers' personal affairs."

Б-54 • НИ БЕЛЬМЕ́СА ⟨НИ БУМ-БУ́М⟩ не знать, не понимать, не смыслить *(в чём) highly coll* [these forms only; obj (both variants) or predic with subj: human (2nd var.)] to know

or understand nothing (about sth.): X (в Y-е) не понимает ни бельмеса ⟨X в Y-е ни бум-бум⟩ ≃ **X doesn't know beans ⟨squat⟩ about Y; X doesn't know ⟨understand⟩ a thing ⟨the first thing⟩ about Y; X doesn't have the foggiest (notion) about Y; X doesn't have a clue about Y; [of one's command of a foreign language, technical jargon etc] X doesn't know ⟨understand⟩ a word of Y; [of a foreign language only] X can't say two words in ⟨speak a word of⟩ Y.**

«Играть не умеете! В миттельшпиле ни бум-бум...» (Аксёнов 3). "You don't know how to play! You don't know a thing about the midgame!" (3a). ♦ «Теперь [Херувимов] в направление тоже полез; сам ни бельмеса не чувствует, ну а я, разумеется, поощряю» (Достоевский 3). "Now he's [Cherubimov has] jumped onto the progressive bandwagon too; hasn't got the foggiest, of course, but naturally I encourage him" (3a). ♦ [Марина Дмитриевна:] Ты что же, ничего не соображал? [Лукашин:] Ни бум-бум... (Брагинский и Рязанов 1). [M.D.:] Didn't you know what was going on? [L.:] I hadn't a clue... (1a). ♦ [Анучкин:] Признаюсь, не зная французского языка, чрезвычайно трудно судить самому, знает ли женщина по-французски или нет. Как хозяйка дома, знает?.. [Кочкарёв:] Ни бельмеса (Гоголь 1). [A.:] I must admit that as I don't know French myself, it's awfully difficult for me to judge whether or not the young lady knows French. Do you think she does? [K.:] Not a word (1a). ♦ Однажды он стал читать Крымову стихи, потом прервал чтение, сказал: «Простите, вам, верно, не интересно». Крымов, усмехнувшись, ответил: «Скажу откровенно, не понял ни бельмеса» (Гроссман 2). Once he began reading some poems to Krymov, but then broke off and said: "I'm sorry. You're probably not in the least interested." Krymov grinned. "To be quite honest, I couldn't understand a word of it" (2a).

Б-55 • (КАК ⟨БУ́ДТО, СЛО́ВНО, ТО́ЧНО⟩) БЕЛЬМО́ В ⟨НА⟩ ГЛАЗУ́ *(у кого) coll, disapprov* [(как etc +) NP; subj-compl with бытьø (subj: human or concr) or adv (var. with как etc only); fixed WO] (a person or thing is) a source of constant irritation to s.o. by his or its presence: X (у Y-а) как бельмо на глазу ≃ **X is a thorn in Y's side ⟨flesh⟩; X is a thorn ⟨a burr⟩ in the side of Y; [in limited contexts] X sticks out like a sore thumb; thing X is an eyesore; thing X is a blot on the landscape.**

Опора своему брату и заступник всех обиженных... он [Браджеш] был, конечно, бельмом на глазу у раджи (Аллилуева 2). To his brother he [Brajesh] had been a real support, a protector to the wronged....As a result, he became a thorn in the side of the Raja (2a).

Б-56 • УСТРО́ИТЬ БЕНЕФИ́С *кому coll* [VP; subj: human] to scold, rebuke s.o. sharply (usu. in a noisy manner); to vent one's anger at s.o., punish him for his behavior: X устроил Y-у бенефис ≃ **X made it hot for Y; X gave it to Y; X had a few choice words for Y.**

Об администраторе гостиницы она сказала: «Я его предупредила: в следующий раз я ему устрою такой бенефис, что он после этого собственную маму примет за собственного папу» (Горенштейн 1). About the hotel manager she said: "I warned him that the next time I'd make it so hot for him he wouldn't be able to tell his own mother from his own father" (1a).

Б-57 • БЕРЕЖЁНОГО (И) БОГ БЕРЕЖЁТ [saying] a person who is cautious and alert avoids danger (said as advice to be careful, not to take risks, and also as a justification for taking what may seem to be unnecessary precautions): ≃ **God helps those who help themselves; better (to be) safe than sorry.**

Все эти предосторожности были, конечно, с запасом, но бережёного Бог бережёт (Солженицын 2). Some of these precautions, of course, proved not to have been strictly necessary, but God helps those who help themselves (2a).

Б-58 • НА́ША ⟨ВА́ША, ТВОЯ́⟩ БЕРЁТ/ВЗЯЛА́ *coll* [VP$_{subj}$; more often pfv; if impfv, pres only; fixed WO] we (you etc) are (or are about to be) victorious: **наша взяла ≃ we've won; our side (has) won; we're the winner(s) ⟨victor(s)⟩;** ‖ наша берёт ⟨возьмёт⟩ ≃ **we're winning ⟨going to win⟩; our side is winning ⟨going to win⟩; we're going to be the winner(s).**

...Я чувствовал, что за эту манеру стоять, повернувшись спиной возле самого носа, ломаться и показывать «мы-де победители — наша взяла» следовало бы их всех бросить в воду... (Герцен 2). ...I felt that in return for their manner of standing and turning their backs in our very faces, giving themselves airs and showing off, "We are the victors — our side won," they ought all to have been thrown into the water... (2a). ♦ «„Дураки, — говорю я им, — глупые несмышлёныши. Эту власть Гитлер не смог опрокинуть со своими танками, а вы что сможете со своей болтовнёй?.." — „Ничего, — говорит один из них, — это так кажется, что они сильные, наша возьмёт"» (Искандер 4). "'You fools,' I said to them, 'you're a couple of babes in the woods. Hitler couldn't topple this regime with all his tanks, and what can you do with your blather?...' 'Nuts,' says one of them. 'They only look strong, we're going to win'" (4a).

Б-59 • ДО БЕСКОНЕ́ЧНОСТИ [PrepP; Invar] **1.** [adv; used with impfv verbs] for a very long time: **to infinity; endlessly; till the end of time; forever; ad infinitum.**

Пить он мог до бесконечности, но мог и совсем не пить... (Достоевский 3). He could drink to infinity or not drink at all... (3a). ♦ «Посмотрите: вот нас двое умных людей, мы знаем заранее, что обо всём можно спорить до бесконечности...» (Лермонтов 1). "Now here we are, two intelligent people; we know in advance that everything can be argued about endlessly..." (1b). ♦ «Он мне всё рассказал: секретный институт... Вы знаете, Голем, они там у вас воображают, будто смогут вертеть генералом Пфердом до бесконечности» (Стругацкие 1). "He told me everything: a high-security think tank....You know, Golem, your friends over there imagine that they can manipulate General Pferd forever" (1a). ♦ «Надо подать проект, — подумал секретарь, — чтобы в каждом районе было два Учреждения. Тогда первое будет выполнять свои функции, а второе будет наблюдать, чтобы не пропало первое... А кто же будет наблюдать за другим Учреждением? Значит, нужно создать третье, а за третьим — четвёртое и так далее до бесконечности...» (Войнович 2). A resolution should be submitted, thought the Secretary, that there be two Institutions in each district. The first would carry out its usual functions and the second would keep an eye on the first so that it wouldn't disappear....But who's going to keep their eye on the second Institution? That means a third will have to be created, and a fourth for the third and so on, ad infinitum... (2a).

2. [modif or adv (intensif)] extremely: **to the nth degree; like you wouldn't believe;** [in limited contexts] **unbearably ⟨an unbearable...⟩; abysmally ⟨an abysmal...⟩; as** [AdjP] **as they come.**

Повторяю: всё это [рассказы иностранцев о России] в высшей степени преувеличено и до бесконечности невежественно... (Салтыков-Щедрин 2). All this [foreigners' portrayals of Russian life], I repeat, is not only shamelessly exaggerated, but also reveals a quite abysmal ignorance of the conditions in our country (2a).

Б-60 • РАССЫПА́ТЬСЯ МЕ́ЛКИМ БЕ́СОМ *перед кем coll* [VP; subj: human; the verb may take the final position, otherwise fixed WO] to try hard to impress s.o. in an attempt to gain his favor; to flatter s.o. in every way possible (often of a man trying to win a woman's affections): X рассыпался перед Y-ом мелким бесом ≃ **X fell all over himself to please ⟨to shine up to⟩ Y; X danced attendance (up)on Y;** [in limited contexts] **X waited on Y hand and foot.**

Егорша мелким бесом начал рассыпаться: Раечка, Раечка, дорогая соседка... (Абрамов 1). Egorsha started falling all over himself to shine up to her. "Raechka, Raechka, dear neighbor..." (1a). ♦ ...Парубки, в высоких козацких шапках, в тонких суконных свитках... с люльками в зубах, рассыпались перед ними [молодыми женщинами] мелким бесом... (Гоголь 5). ...The lads in high Cossack hats, in fine cloth jerkins...with a pipe in their teeth, danced attendance on them [the young women]... (5a).

Б-61 • ПРОДУВНА́Я БЕ́СТИЯ ⟨ШЕ́ЛЬМА⟩ *coll, disapprov* [NP; usu. sing; usu. subj-compl with copula, nom or instrum (subj: human); fixed WO] a sly, sneaky person, a swindler: **an out-and-out rogue; a sly fox; a slippery character.**

...Вошла чиновная особа — Самосвистов, эпикуреец, собой лихач... отличный товарищ, кутила и продувная бестия, как выражались о нём сами товарищи (Гоголь 3). ...In walked a certain official — one Samosvistov, an epicure, a daredevil, a capital companion, a rake, and an out-and-out rogue, as his own friends spoke of him (3c).

Б-62 • БЕ́ЛЫЙ БИЛЕ́Т [NP; fixed WO] a document certifying exemption from military service on medical grounds: **(be considered ⟨deemed etc⟩) unfit for military service; (have ⟨receive⟩) a medical deferment.** Cf. **NPQ (not physically qualified).**

Б-63 • ВО́ЛЧИЙ БИЛЕ́Т [NP; fixed WO] **1.** *obs* Also: ВО́ЛЧИЙ ПА́СПОРТ *obs* in tsarist Russia, a document affirming a person's political unreliability, corrupt, immoral behavior etc and thus denying him access to state jobs, universities etc: **blacklisting; (be) blacklisted; (be put on) a blacklist.**

Всё это была, конечно, политика. У Львовых мне казалось, что политика существует только для того, чтобы объяснить, почему Митю исключили с волчьим билетом. Как бы не так! (Каверин 1). All this, of course, was politics. When I was at the Lvovs, I imagined that the only point of politics was to explain why Mitya had been expelled and blacklisted. Nothing of the sort! (1a).

2. *coll* an extremely negative written evaluation (often a notation in s.o.'s work record) of s.o.'s work, political views, character etc: **a scathing evaluation ⟨character reference⟩.**

Б-64 • ЖЁЛТЫЙ БИЛЕ́Т *obs* [NP; fixed WO] in tsarist Russia, a passport printed on yellow paper stating that its holder was a prostitute: **a prostitute's ID ⟨ticket⟩.**

...Когда Амалия Ивановна вдруг закричала что-то про жёлтый билет, Катерина Ивановна отпихнула Соню и пустилась к Амалии Ивановне, чтобы немедленно привести свою угрозу, насчёт чепчика, в исполнение (Достоевский 3). ...When Mme Lippewechsel suddenly shouted something about a prostitute's ticket, Katerina Ivanovna repulsed Sonya and swooped on Mme Lippewechsel, intending to lose no more time in carrying out her threat concerning the bonnet (3a).

Б-65 • ПОЛОЖИ́ТЬ ⟨ВЫ́ЛОЖИТЬ⟩ БИЛЕ́Т ⟨ПАРТБИЛЕ́Т⟩ (НА СТОЛ) *coll* [VP; subj: human] to be expelled from or leave the Communist Party: X положил билет на стол ≃ **X turned ⟨handed⟩ in his (Party) card; X surrendered his Party card.**

Я спросила его [Абдуллина], что мне делать: оставаться в партии на таком положении, когда у тебя не хотят принимать взносов? Или положить билет на стол, дав этим новую пищу обвинениям? (Гинзбург 1). I asked Abdullin what I should do: stay in the party although my dues were being refused, or turn my card in and thereby invite fresh accusations (1a). ♦ «Парамошин, конечно, демагог, крикун... но и ты тоже хорош. К тебе всякий народ ходит, а у тебя в красном углу церковный парад. Так ведь и билет положить недолго!» (Максимов 3). "Paramoshin is a demagogue and a loudmouth, of course. But you're not one to talk — all sorts of people come to your house, and you've got a religious display in the place of honor. That way you'll be handing your party card in before you know where you are (3a).

Б-66 • ЖИТЬ БИРЮКÓМ [VP; subj: human] to be unsociable, live in seclusion: X живёт бирюком ≃ **X lives the life of ⟨lives like⟩ a recluse ⟨a hermit⟩.**

Б-67 • СМОТРÉТЬ ⟨ГЛЯДÉТЬ, СИДÉТЬ⟩ БИРЮ-КÓМ [VP; subj: human] to look gloomy, morose: X бирюком смотрит ≃ **X is being a (real) sourpuss; X is scowling.**

Б-68 • ИГРÁТЬ В БИРЮ́ЛЬКИ *coll, disapprov* [VP; subj: human; often neg or infin with хватит, перестань(те) etc] to occupy o.s. with trifles (with the implication that one should be doing sth. serious, productive instead): X в бирюльки играет ≃ **X fritters ⟨fiddles⟩ away the time; X fiddles ⟨fools, putters⟩ around;** ‖ *Neg* X не в бирюльки играет ≃ [with an emphasis on the seriousness of the matter] **X is not playing games (with person Y).** ○ **ИГРÁ В БИРЮ́ЛЬКИ** [NP] ≃ **fiddling ⟨fooling, puttering⟩ around; trifles; trifling matters.**

«А это ты нас не учи, что делать. — Он подступал к арестованному, красноречиво поигрывая деревянной кобурой у пояса. — Мы из тебя, ваше благородие, быстро гонор вышибем. Мы сюда не в бирюльки играть заявились» (Максимов 3). "Don't you tell us what to do."...He went up to the prisoner, eloquently fingering the wooden holster at his waist. "We'll soon cut you down to size. We haven't come here to fool around" (3a). ♦ «Кто подделывал икону?» — спросил Антон. «Не знаю!» — торопливо выпалил Вася... [Антон] передал фотоснимок [Васе] Сипенятину: «Узнаёте художника?» Тот, оценивающе прищурясь, натянуто усмехнулся: «Как волков флажками обложили»... «Вы что, думали, в бирюльки с вами играть будут?» (Чернёнок 2). "Who forged the icon?" Anton asked. "I don't know," Vasya burst out....[Anton] handed the picture to [Vasya] Sipeniatin. "Do you recognize the artist?" Vasya squinted as he appraised the picture and laughed nervously. "You've got him pegged." "Did you think we were going to play games with you?" (2a).

< From the name of an old game in which a large number of very small objects («бирюльки») were scattered on a table and the players tried to pull out one item at a time with a small hook without disturbing the other objects. Cf. **jackstraws, pick-up-sticks.**

Б-69 • МЕТÁТЬ ⟨РАССЫПÁТЬ⟩ БИ́СЕР ПЕРЕД СВИ́НЬЯМИ ⟨*перед кем*⟩ [VP; subj: human; often infin with зачем, хватит etc, or neg imper; usu. this WO] to try in vain to explain or prove sth. to a person or people who cannot or do not want to understand or appreciate it: X мечет бисер перед свиньями ≃ **X casts pearls before swine.**

< From the Bible (Matt. 7:6).

Б-70 • БИТЬ НАВЕРНЯКÁ *coll* [VP; subj: human; fixed WO] to act in a fashion that guarantees success, rules out any possibility of failure: X бил наверняка ≃ **X followed ⟨adopted⟩ a surefire ⟨foolproof⟩ plan of action; X made sure he wouldn't fail ⟨he'd get what he wanted etc⟩;** [in refer. to one's previously mentioned course of action] **it was a sure thing ⟨bet⟩;** [in limited contexts] **X went for the sure thing.**

Если вы хотите разоблачить Петрова, вам нужно бить наверняка: прежде всего соберите всё, что можно использовать как свидетельство, а потом уже действуйте. If you want to expose Petrov you'll have to follow a surefire plan of action: first of all, you've got to gather everything that can be used as evidence against him; then, you can make your move. ♦ Остап сразу же выяснил, что Провал для человека, лишённого предрассудков, может явиться доходной статьёй. «...Это, кажется, единственное место, куда пятигорцы пускают туристов без денег... Я

исправлю досадное упущение». И Остап поступил так, как подсказывали ему разум, здоровый инстинкт и создавшаяся ситуация. Он остановился у входа в Провал и, трепля в руках квитанционную книжку, время от времени вскрикивал: «Приобретайте билеты, граждане! Десять копеек!..» Остап бил наверняка. Пятигорцы в Провал не ходили, а с советского туриста содрать десять копеек за вход «куда-то» не представляло ни малейшего труда (Ильф и Петров 1). Ostap had seen at once that for a man without prejudice the Drop could be a source of income. "...It seems to be the only place where the people of Pyatigorsk allow the sight-seers in free. I will...rectify the sad omission." And Ostap acted as his reason, instinct, and the situation in hand prompted. He stationed himself at the entrance to the Drop and, rustling the receipt book, called out from time to time. "Buy your tickets here, citizens. Ten kopeks..." It was a sure bet. The citizens of Pyatigorsk never went to the Drop, and to fleece the Soviet tourists ten kopeks to see "Something" was no great difficulty (1a).

Б-71 • БИТЬ *кого* **НÉКОМУ** *coll* [impers predic with быть∅; pres or, rare, past; usu. this WO] s.o. deserves to be admonished or punished: бить X-а некому ≃ **what X needs is a good hiding ⟨talking-to⟩; X deserves a good swift kick ⟨dressing-down⟩.**

[author's usage] «Что ж у тебя с твоим генералом будет?» — «Я боюсь об этом думать». — «Ох, сечь тебя некому». — «Я не могла иначе поступить!» — сказала Евгения Николаевна (Гроссман 2). "So what's going to happen about this general of yours?" "I can't bear to think." "What you need is a good hiding." "But there just wasn't anything else I could do," pleaded Yevgenia (2a).

Б-72 • ВСЕХ БЛАГ [formula phrase; Invar; also used as obj of желать/пожелать; fixed WO] may everything go well for you (used when parting with s.o.): **all the best; best of luck; take care.**

Б-73 • НИ ЗА КАКИ́Е БЛÁГА ⟨СОКРÓВИЩА⟩ (В МИ́РЕ) *coll* [PrepP; these forms only; adv; used with negated verbs (usu. pfv fut or subjunctive); fixed WO] (one will not or would not do sth.) under any conditions or circumstances (used to express one's strong unwillingness to do sth. or accept s.o.'s suggestion): **not for anything (in the world ⟨on earth⟩); not for (all) the world; not for all the money in the world;** [in limited contexts] **nothing in the world (can persuade ⟨force etc⟩ one to do sth.); one has no desire in the world (to do sth.).** Cf. **not for all the tea in China.**

«Нравится досада!.. Отчего?» — «Не скажу». — «Скажите, пожалуйста, я прошу...» — «Ни за что, ни за какие блага!» (Гончаров 1). "You're glad I was vexed!...Why?" "I won't tell you!" "Please, do, I beg you." "Never! Not for anything in the world!" (1a). ♦ [Марья Андреевна:] Он [Беневоленский] мне не нравится, он мне противен!.. Я не пойду за него ни за какие сокровища! (Островский 1). [M.A.:] I don't like him [Benevolensky]. He is repulsive to me. I wouldn't marry him for all the money in the world (1a). ♦ Дядя Сандро был совершенно не подготовлен для встречи с девушкой, у которой при каждой улыбке на щеках возникают головокружительные ямочки, куда каждый раз душа дяди Сандро (предварительно раздвоившись) опускалась и ни за какие блага не желала оттуда выходить (Искандер 5). Uncle Sandro was completely unprepared to meet a girl whose every smile brought dizzying dimples to her cheeks. Every time she smiled, Uncle Sandro's soul split in half and fell into these two little traps, and had no desire in the world to climb out (5a).

Б-74 • СЧЕСТЬ ⟨ПОЧÉСТЬ, РАССУДИ́ТЬ *obs*⟩ **ЗА БЛÁГО** [VP; subj: human or collect; foll. by infin; fixed WO] to decide that one course of action is more beneficial than other options (and to undertake that course of action): X счёл за благо сделать Y ≃ **X saw fit to do Y; X thought ⟨deemed⟩ it best to do Y; X opted to do Y.**

Решение пленума ЦК было для него [Твардовского] обязательным не только административно, но и морально. Раз пленум ЦК почёл за благо снять Хрущёва – значит, действительно терпеть его эксперименты дальше было нельзя (Солженицын 2). For him [Tvardovsky] any decision taken by a plenum of the Central Committee had moral and not just executive force. If a plenum of the Central Committee had seen fit to remove Khrushchev, it meant that his experiments were indeed no longer to be tolerated (2a).

Б-75 • ПОКÓРНО ⟨ПОКÓРНЕЙШЕ⟩ БЛАГОДАРЮ́
[VP; 1st pers only; indep. sent] **1.** *obs* [fixed WO] used when addressing s.o. with a humble, polite expression of gratitude: **I humbly thank you; thank you kindly; (I am) much obliged.**

[Аркадина *(подаёт повару рубль)*:] Вот вам рубль на троих. [Повар:] Покорнейше благодарим, барыня (Чехов 6). [A. *(gives the Cook a ruble)*:] Here's a ruble for the three of you. [Cook:] Thank you kindly, madam (6b). ♦ [Ихарев:] Пара целковиков! *(Суёт ему в руку.)* [Алексей *(кланяясь)*:] Покорнейше благодарю (Гоголь 2). [I.:] Here's a couple of rubles for you! *(Thrusts them into his hand.)* [A. *(bowing)*:] Much obliged, Your Honor (2a).

2. *coll, iron* [in contemp. usage, WO is usu. благодарю покорно] used to express disagreement with sth., rejection of sth., or a negative reaction to some statement: [all said with ironic intonation] **much obliged, I'm sure; thanks a lot!; thank you very much!; I can't thank you enough;** [in limited contexts] **no, thank you!; thanks, but no thanks!**

[Работник:] Пожалуйте, Михаил Львович, за вами приехали. [Астров:] Откуда? [Работник:] С фабрики. [Астров *(с досадой)*:] Покорно благодарю (Чехов 3). [Labourer:] Will you come please, Dr. Astrov? You're wanted. [A.:] Who by? [L.:] The factory. [A. *(irritated)*:] Much obliged, I'm sure (3c). ♦ «Отчего вы не служите в армии?» – «После Аустерлица!» – мрачно сказал князь Андрей. – Нет, покорно благодарю, я дал себе слово, что служить в действующей русской армии я не буду» (Толстой 5). "Why aren't you serving in the army?" "After Austerlitz!" said Prince Andrew gloomily. "No, thank you very much! I have promised myself not to serve again in the active Russian army" (5b). ♦ «Вы видели, что в эти полгода делалось со мной? Чего вам хочется: полного торжества? Чтоб я зачах или рехнулся? Покорно благодарю!» (Гончаров 1). "You have seen what has happened to me in the last six months. What do you want: a complete triumph? Do you want me to waste away – go out of my mind? No, thank you!" (1b).

Б-76 • ПО БЛÁТУ достать, получить *что*, устроить *кого-что* и т. п. *coll* [PrepP; Invar; adv] (to get, receive, arrange sth., get s.o. a desired position etc) by using connections, with the help of influential friends, contacts etc, illicitly: **by pulling strings; through ⟨thanks to⟩ one's connections; by ⟨through⟩ knowing the right people; use influence (to get sth. etc); (one got ⟨obtained etc⟩ sth.) because one has pull ⟨connections⟩.**

Она курила длинные иностранные сигареты, которые доставала по блату... (Войнович 6). She smoked long foreign cigarettes that she got through her connections (6a). ♦ Мазила на выставку попасть не смог. Неврастеник, попавший на неё по блату, сказал, что выставка, конечно, любопытная. Но стоять часами в очередях из-за неё не стоит (Зиновьев 1). Dauber didn't manage to get in [to the exhibition] at all. Neurasthenic, who did manage to get in thanks to his connections, said that the exhibition was interesting enough, but not so interesting as to be worth queuing for hours to see (1a). ♦ Видно, друзья по блату устроили ему однодневный пропуск (Искандер 3). Evidently some friends had used influence to arrange a one-day pass for him (3a). ♦ ...Растление литературы дошло до того, что совершенно стёрлись всякие грани между профессиональным писателем и пришедшим по блату (Войнович 1). The corruption of literature has gone so far as to have obliterated all the boundary lines between the professional writer and those who are published because they have pull (1a).

Б-77 • ДЛЯ БЛЕЗИ́РУ ⟨-а⟩ *highly coll* [PrepP; these forms only; adv] in order to create a certain impression: **for show; for appearance' sake;** [in limited contexts] **as a smoke screen.**

[Андрей] Гуськов... пошагал к двери. Замок на ней, как и раньше, висел для блезиру: Гуськов дёрнул его – он тут же раскрылся (Распутин 2). Andrei...headed for the door....The lock on it, like before, was mostly for show; he pulled on it and it opened (2a). ♦ Другие договаривались до того, что в сущности Зейнаб по-настоящему живёт с удавом, а Марата держит при себе просто так, для блезира (Искандер 2). Others went so far as to say that in essence Zeinab lived *with* the boa in the real sense, and just kept Marat around as a smoke screen (2a).

Б-78 • ВО ВСЁМ БЛÉСКЕ *(чего)* [PrepP; Invar; subj-compl with быть∅ (subj: usu. human, animal, or concr), obj-compl with показать etc (obj: usu. human, animal, or concr), or adv; fixed WO] showing the full extent of one's or its perfection: **in all one's ⟨its⟩ glory ⟨splendor⟩; in one's ⟨its⟩ full splendor;** ∥ во всём блеске своей красоты ⟨своего остроумия и т. п.⟩ ≃ **as breathtakingly beautiful ⟨as brilliantly witty etc⟩ as ever.**

«И неужели, неужели вы из-за того только, чтоб обучить собаку, всё время не приходили!» – воскликнул с невольным укором Алёша. «Именно для того, – прокричал простодушнейшим образом Коля. – Я хотел показать его [пса] во всём блеске!» (Достоевский 1). "And can it be, can it be that you refused to come all this time only in order to train the dog!" Alyosha exclaimed with involuntary reproach. "That's precisely the reason," Kolya shouted in the most naive way. "I wanted to show him in all his glory!" (1a). ♦ Соколовский был налицо, несколько похудевший и бледный, но во всём блеске своего юмора (Герцен 1). Sokolovsky was present, pale and somewhat thinner, but as brilliantly amusing as ever (1a).

Б-79 • С БЛÉСКОМ [PrepP; Invar; adv] magnificently, excellently: **brilliantly; superbly;** [in limited contexts] **with flair;** [of the passing of exams, tests etc] **with flying colors.**

«На съездах и конференциях... Валентин Сергеевич с блеском доказывает, что наш план тесно связан с задачами третьего пятилетнего плана» (Каверин 1). "At congresses, at conferences...Valentin Sergeyevich brilliantly proves that our plan is closely connected with the tasks of the Third Five-Year Plan" (1a). ♦ ...На новом месте предприимчивый Поклен с ещё большим блеском развернул все приманки своей лавки (Булгаков 5). ...In the new place the enterprising Poquelin displayed his goods with even greater flair (5a).

Б-80 • ПÉРВЫЙ БЛИН (ВСЕГДÁ) КÓМОМ [saying] you cannot expect your first attempt to be successful (usu. said to justify a failed first effort): ≃ **the first try is bound to be a flop ⟨a washout⟩; the first time is always the hardest.**

Б-81 • ПЕЧЬ КАК БЛИНЫ́ *что coll* [VP; subj: human or collect; obj: pl; usu. pres] to produce things (often stories, articles etc) rapidly and in large quantities: X Y-и как блины печёт ≃ **X cranks out Ys ⟨Y after Y⟩; X turns ⟨knocks⟩ out Ys left and right.**

Б-82 • ЛОВИ́ТЬ ⟨ВЫИ́СКИВАТЬ и т. п.⟩ БЛОХ *highly coll* [VP; subj: usu. human or collect] to find fault with s.o. or sth. for small and unimportant deficiencies: X ловит блох ≃ **X nitpicks ⟨nit-picks⟩; X splits hairs; X picks (minor) holes in sth.**

Она заговорила о том, что всякая критика должна быть в первую очередь объективной, оценивать в целом, а потом уж выискивать блох (Трифонов 2). She said that criticism should above all be objective and should assess the work as a whole, and only then proceed to nit-picking (2a). ♦ После цепочки редакторов, трудившихся над книгой, цензору оставалось только вылавливать блох, чтобы оправдать свой кусок хлеба с маслом (Мандельштам 2). After a book had been thoroughly worked over by one editor after another, little remained for the censor to do except to pick a few minor holes here and there in order to justify the butter he got with his daily bread (2a).

Б-83 • КАК НА БЛЮ́ДЕЧКЕ ⟨БЛЮ́ДЕ⟩ ви́ден и т. п. *coll* [как + PrepP; these forms only; adv] (sth. can be seen) clearly, distinctly: **(be) in clear ⟨full⟩ view; (be) in plain sight;** [in limited contexts] **(be) as clear as anything.**

...День был чудесный, светлый и не жаркий; все горы видны были как на блюдечке (Лермонтов 1). It was...a really lovely day, bright but not too hot. The mountains all round were as clear as anything (1c).

Б-84 • НА БЛЮ́ДЕЧКЕ С ГОЛУБО́Й КАЁМОЧКОЙ преподноси́ть, подава́ть *что* и т. п.; **НА БЛЮ́ДЕЧКЕ (С ЗОЛОТО́Й КАЁМОЧКОЙ); НА БЛЮ́ДЕ** all *coll* [PrepP; these forms only; sent adv; fixed WO] (to give sth. to s.o., let s.o. have sth. etc) without the recipient's having to work hard to obtain it: **(hand s.o. sth. ⟨have sth. handed to one** etc⟩) **on a silver platter.**

[Андрей:] Слушай, я, наверно, оттого такой пустой, что мне всё на блюдечке подавалось — дома благополучие... сыт, одет... (Розов 1). [A.:] I'm probably so shallow because everything has been handed to me on a silver platter—the family is well-off...they feed and clothe me... (1a).

< The source of the first variant is *The Golden Calf* («Золотой телёнок») by Ilya Ilf and Evgeny Petrov, 1931, ch. 2. The original source of the last variant is possibly the Russian translation of the Bible. Cf. Matt. 14:8, Mark 6:25, in reference to Salome's demand that John the Baptist's head be given to her "in a charger."

Б-85 • НА БОБА́Х остаться, сидеть, оставить *кого coll* [PrepP; Invar; subj-compl with copula (subj: human) or obj-compl with оставить (obj: human)] (to end up, be, or leave s.o.) without sth. hoped for or counted on: **high and dry; empty-handed; out in the cold; with nothing.**

И вот она [революция] пришла... а он [Аверкий Степанович], прирождённый и постоянный рабочелюбец... очутился на бобах, не у дел, в опустевшем посёлке, из которого разбежались рабочие, частью шедшие тут за меньшевиками (Пастернак 1). Now it [the revolution] had come...but he [Averkii Stepanovich], the born and faithful champion of the proletariat...had been left high and dry; instead of being in the thick of things, he was in a remote village from which the workers—some of whom were Mensheviks—had fled! (1a). ♦ [Антонина Николаевна:] Я не спешила замуж, но сейчас это надо сделать. И быстрее, иначе я рискую остаться на бобах (Розов 3). [A.N.:] I haven't rushed to get married, but now it has to be done. And rather soon, or else I run the risk of being left empty-handed (3a). ♦ Каждый держатель облигации в глубине души не верит в возможность выигрыша. Зато он очень ревниво относится к облигациям своих соседей и знакомых. Он... боится того, что выиграют они, а он, всегдашний неудачник, снова останется на бобах (Ильф и Петров 1). In the depths of his heart no bond holder believes in the possibility of a win. At the same time he is jealous of his neighbors' and friends' bonds. He is...scared that they will win and that he, the eternal loser, will be left out in the cold (1a).

Б-86 • УБИ́ТЬ БОБРА́ *coll* [VP; subj: human; fixed WO]
1. *iron* to miscalculate, choosing the worst of the available options: X убил бобра ≃ **X put the saddle on the wrong horse; X put his eggs in the wrong basket;** [said with ironic intonation] **X**

picked a (real) winner; [in limited contexts] **X really did it this time; that was some catch.**
2. *obsoles* to acquire sth. of great value or achieve sth. remarkable: X убил бобра ≃ **X hit it big; X hit the jackpot.**

Б-87 • БОБЫ́ РАЗВОДИ́ТЬ *substand* [VP; subj: human; usu. this WO] **1.** to waste one's time on trifles, act very slowly, procrastinate: X бобы разводит ≃ **X fritters ⟨fiddles⟩ away the time;** [in limited contexts] **X drags his feet.**

[author's usage] «Чем в губернское правление-то шататься да пустяки на бобах разводить, лучше бы дело делать!» (Салтыков-Щедрин 2). "Instead of wasting his time in government departments and frittering away the precious minutes on some stupid trifles, he [the pompadour] should have been doing something!" (2a).
2. *obsoles* to talk about insignificant, frivolous matters (often in order to distract s.o. from sth.), engage in idle chatter: X бобы разводит ≃ **X is prattling (on); X is babbling;** [in limited contexts] **X is beating around ⟨about⟩ the bush;** ‖ X и Y бобы разводят ≃ **X and Y are gabbing; X and Y are shooting the breeze ⟨the bull⟩.**

Б-88 • БОГ ДАЁТ/ДАЛ *кого (кому) obs* [VP$_{subj}$; obj: сына, дочь, детей etc; usu. this WO] God has given s.o. (a child or children) for which s.o. feels thankful: бог дал Y-у X-а ≃ **God has blessed Y with X; Y is blessed with X.**

...Ребятишек Люсе бог не дал (Распутин 3). ...God had not blessed her [Liusia] with children (3a).

Б-89 • БОГ ДАЛ ⟨ПРИВЁЛ⟩ встретиться, свидеться и т. п. *obsoles* [VP$_{subj}$] it happened that s.o. had the occasion (to meet with another etc): **it is ⟨was⟩ God's will (that...); God (has) willed ⟨granted, ordained⟩ it ⟨that...⟩; (I didn't expect ⟨who would have thought etc⟩ that) the Lord would have us ⟨you, them⟩ (meet** etc⟩.

[Андрей:] Ты был когда-нибудь в Москве? [Ферапонт:] Не был. Не привёл бог (Чехов 5). [A.:] Were you ever in Moscow? [F.:] Never was. It was not God's will (5a). ♦ [Борис:] Ну, вот и поплакали вместе, привёл бог (Островский 6). [B.:] There now, we've had a cry together. God has granted us that (6d). ♦ «А, старый хрыч! — сказал ему Пугачёв. — Опять бог дал свидеться» (Пушкин 2). "You old grumbler!" Pugachev said to him. "So God has ordained that we should meet again" (2b). ♦ «...Думал найти вас в Грузии, а вот где бог дал свидеться...» (Лермонтов 1). "Thought I'd find you in Georgia, never dreaming the Lord would have us meet here..." (1b).

Б-90 • БОГ ⟨ГОСПО́ДЬ⟩ ДАЛ, БОГ ⟨ГОСПО́ДЬ⟩ И ВЗЯЛ *obs* [sent; these forms only; fixed WO] said with resignation upon s.o.'s death or upon the loss of sth.: ≃ **the Lord giveth and the Lord taketh away.**

< From the Bible (Job 1:21).

Б-91 • БОГ ДАСТ *coll* [VP$_{subj}$; Invar; sent adv (parenth)] I hope, one hopes (that things will turn out as desired): **God ⟨Lord⟩ willing; with God's help; I hope to God; God grant.**

«Ну, бог даст, ещё увидимся». Шофёр, поняв это как указание, надавил на газ, и машина рванулась (Евтушенко 2). "Well, God willing, we'll see each other again." The driver, interpreting this as a command, stepped on the gas, and the car sped away (2a). ♦ «Где же неприятель?» — «Неприятель недалече... Бог даст, всё будет ладно» (Пушкин 2). "And where is the enemy?" "The enemy isn't far off....With God's help we'll be all right" (2a). ♦ «...В первый раз я слышал такие вещи от 25-летнего человека и, бог даст, в последний...» (Лермонтов 1). "...It was the first time that I had heard such things from a man of twenty-five, and I hope to God it may also be the last..." (1a). ♦ «Не кричи, Натальюшка. Слезой тут не поможешь. Бог даст, живых-здоровых увидим» (Шолохов 5). "Don't cry, Natalya, dearie. Tears won't help. God grant we'll see them all again safe and sound" (5a).

Б-92 • БОГ ДАСТ ДЕНЬ, БОГ ДАСТ ПИЩУ; БОГ ДАСТ ДЕНЬ, ДАСТ И ПИЩУ; БУ́ДЕТ ДЕНЬ, БУ́ДЕТ ПИ́ЩА [saying] somehow or other everything will work out fine (usu. said to s.o. who is concerned about the future): ≃ **God will give the day, God will give us food ⟨will provide⟩.**

Я тратил все деньги… меня мало интересовало, что будет завтра. «Бог даст день, Бог даст пищу», – как говорила моя бабушка Вера (Лимонов 1). I spent all my money…I cared little about what the morrow would bring. "God will give the day, God will give us food," as my grandma Vera used to say (1a).

Б-93 • БОГ ⟨ГОСПО́ДЬ, АЛЛА́Х⟩ (ЕГО́ ⟨тебя и т. п.⟩) ЗНА́ЕТ ⟨ВЕ́ДАЕТ⟩; БОГ ВЕСТЬ *all coll* [VP_subj; these forms only; usu. the main clause in a complex sent or indep. sent; fixed WO] no one knows, it is impossible (for s.o.) to know: **God ⟨(the) Lord, heaven, goodness⟩ (only) knows; God alone knows.**

«Кто же я таков, по твоему разумению?» – «Бог тебя знает; но кто бы ты ни был, ты шутишь опасную шутку» (Пушкин 2). "And who am I then, in your opinion?" "God only knows; but whoever you may be, you're playing a dangerous game" (2a). ♦ …Он ездит и в свет, и читает: когда он успевает – бог весть (Гончаров 1). …There was his social life and his reading – heaven only knows how he found the time! (1b). ♦ Родители его были дворяне, но столбовые или личные – бог ведает (Гоголь 3). God alone knows whether his parents, who were of the nobility, were so by descent or personal merit (3d).

Б-94 • БОГ ЗНА́ЕТ ⟨ВЕСТЬ⟩ кто, что, как, какой, где, куда, откуда, почему, отчего, сколько *coll* [VP_subj; these forms only; fixed WO] **1.** [usu. the main clause in a complex sent; when foll. by an Adv, may be used as adv] no one knows (who, what, how etc): **God ⟨(the) Lord, heaven, goodness⟩ (only) knows (who ⟨what, how⟩).**

Выкопали всё, разузнали его [Чичикова] прежнюю историю. Бог весть, откуда всё это пронюхали… (Гоголь 3). Everything was dug up and all the past history of his [Chichikov's] life became known. God only knows how they got on the scent of it… (3a). ♦ Бог весть, почему нервничали встречавшие (Свирский 1). Heaven knows why the reception party should have been so nervous (1a). ♦ Дом Обломовых был когда-то богат и знаменит в своей стороне, но потом, бог знает отчего, всё беднел, мельчал… (Гончаров 1). The Oblomov family had once been rich and famous in its part of the country, but afterwards, goodness only knows why, it had grown poorer, lost all its influence… (1a).

2. [used as NP (when foll. by кто, что), AdjP (when foll. by какой), or AdvP (when foll. by где, куда etc)] used to express a strong emotional reaction – anger, indignation, bewilderment etc: **God ⟨(the) Lord, heaven, goodness⟩ (only) knows (who ⟨what, how⟩)!; what sort ⟨kind⟩ of (a) [NP] is he ⟨she, that⟩!;** [in limited contexts; said with ironic intonation] **some [NP] (I must say)!**

«Да ведь она тоже мне двоюродная тётка». – «Она вам тётка ещё бог знает какая: с мужниной стороны…» (Гоголь 3). "But, you know, she is a cousin of mine." "What sort of a cousin is she to you…only on your husband's side…" (3d).

Б-95 • БОГ ЗНА́ЕТ КА́К *obs* [AdvP; Invar; adv (intensif); fixed WO] to a great degree: **greatly; extremely; utterly.**

Наконец почувствовал он себя лучше и обрадовался бог знает как, когда увидел возможность выйти на свежий воздух (Гоголь 3). At last he felt better and was greatly overjoyed when he realized that he could…go out for a breath of fresh air (3a).

Б-96 • БОГ ЗНА́ЕТ СКО́ЛЬКО *чего coll* [AdvP; Invar; quantit compl with copula (subj/gen: any common noun) or adv (quantif); fixed WO; usu. said with emphatic intonation] a great number or amount (of people, things etc): **God knows how much ⟨many, long etc⟩; an enormous amount ⟨number, quantity etc⟩ of.**

«А ты что так беспокоишься, что я уезжаю. У нас с тобой ещё бог знает сколько времени до отъезда. Целая вечность времени, бессмертие!» (Достоевский 1). "And why do you worry so much about my leaving? You and I still have God knows how long before I go. A whole eternity of time, immortality!" (1a).

Б-97 • БОГ ЗНА́ЕТ ЧТО *coll* [NP; fixed WO; usu. said with emphatic intonation] **1.** ~ творится, начинается; городить, говорить и т. п. ~ [usu. subj or obj] sth. unimaginable, incredible, that elicits aggravation, indignation etc: **God ⟨Lord, goodness, heaven⟩ knows what (is going on); God ⟨Lord, goodness⟩ knows the sort of things (one is saying ⟨that are happening⟩ etc); all kinds of strange ⟨horrible etc⟩ things (are happening etc); (one said ⟨witnessed etc⟩) all sorts of bizarre ⟨wild etc⟩ things;** ‖ в месте X началось ~ ≃ **all hell broke loose in place X.**

«А не боялся, что я не спала ночь, бог знает что передумала?..» (Гончаров 1). "But you weren't afraid of my spending sleepless nights, thinking God knows what?…" (1b). ♦ «Он дурно выбирал свои знакомства… Сын князя Василия, он и один Долохов, они, говорят, бог знает что делали» (Толстой 4). "He made a bad choice of friends….Prince Vasily's son, he, and a certain Dolokhov, they say, have been up to heaven knows what!" (4a). ♦ Как я и ожидала, [в ЦК] нас с Борей повели в гардероб, а потом вверх по лестнице, а Иру не пропустили… Нас пригласили сесть… Боря начал первым и, конечно, с того, что потребовал пропуск для Иры. «Она меня будет отпаивать валерианкой». Поликарпов нахмурился: «…Зачем же девочку ещё путать? Она и так слышит Бог знает что!» (Ивинская 1). Just as I had thought, [at the Central Committee] Boria and I were taken through into the cloakroom, and then up the stairs, but Ira was not allowed to go with us….Boria and I were invited to sit down….Boria was the first to speak and he began, of course, by demanding a pass for Ira: "She will give me my valerian." Polikarpov frowned: "…Why involve the girl? Lord knows the sort of things she has to listen to as it is!" (1a). ♦ Когда объявили результаты голосования, в зале началось бог знает что: люди свистели, кричали, топали ногами. When the election results were announced, all hell broke loose in the auditorium: people started whistling, yelling, and stomping their feet.

2. [Invar; Interj; often preceded by это] used to express aggravation, indignation, extreme perplexity on account of sth.: **it's God ⟨Lord, goodness⟩ knows what!; God ⟨Lord, goodness⟩ (only) knows what's going on ⟨what it means etc⟩!**

3. ~ дать, отдать, заплатить, запросить и т. п. [accus only; obj] (to pay, charge, be willing to give etc) very much (for sth.): **God ⟨Lord⟩ knows what (one has to pay ⟨one will charge etc⟩); (pay ⟨charge etc⟩) an exorbitant ⟨enormous⟩ amount (of money);** [usu. fut, subjunctive, or infin with готов] **(give ⟨pay, bet etc⟩) anything; (give) anything in the world;** [subjunctive only] **what one wouldn't give ⟨pay etc⟩.**

«Клад! – закричал дед. – Я ставлю бог знает что, если не клад!» – и уже поплевал было в руки, чтобы копать, да спохватился, что нет при нём ни заступа, ни лопаты (Гоголь 5). "A treasure!" cried Grandad. "I'll bet anything it's a treasure!" And he was just about to spit on his hands to begin digging when he remembered that he had no spade or shovel with him (5a).

Б-98 • БОГ МИ́ЛОВАЛ *obs, coll* [VP_subj; past only; fixed WO] (s.o.) was saved from danger, things turned out well (for s.o.) because of God's help: **God was merciful ⟨kind⟩ (to s.o.); the**

[18]

Lord spared s.o.; by God's grace s.o. was spared; (s.o.) was lucky ⟨spared⟩.

«Доселе бог миловал. Всего-навсе [*obs* = всего-навсего] разграбили у меня один амбар...» (Пушкин 1). "So far the Lord has spared me. Until now, they've only plundered one of my barns..." (1b).

Б-99 • **БОГ НА ⟨В⟩ ПÓМОЩЬ; БОГ (НА ⟨В⟩) ПÓ-МОЧЬ; ПОМОГÁЙ БОГ** *all obs, coll* [formula phrase; these forms only; fixed WO] used as a wish for success to s.o. who is working on or undertaking sth.: **(may) God ⟨the Lord⟩ help ⟨bless etc⟩ you.**

«Вы не в армию?» – «Да». – «Помогай вам бог» (Шолохов 2). "Are you bound for the army?" "Yes." "May the Lord help you" (2a).

Б-100 • **БОГ ⟨ГОСПÓДЬ⟩ НЕ ВЫ́ДАСТ, СВИНЬЯ́ НЕ СЪЕСТ** [saying] God willing, things will turn out all right (usu. said when undertaking sth. risky, the outcome of which is uncertain): ≃ **(he) whom God ⟨the good Lord⟩ helps, nobody can harm.**

«Бог милостив: солдат у нас довольно, пороху много, пушку я вычистил. Авось дадим отпор Пугачёву. Господь не выдаст, свинья не съест!» (Пушкин 2). "God is merciful: we have soldiers enough, plenty of powder, and I have cleaned out the cannon. Perhaps we'll manage to repulse Pugachev. Whom God helps nobody can harm" (2b).

Б-101 • **БОГ НЕ ОБИ́ДЕЛ** *кого (чем)* [VP_subj; past only; used without negation to convey the opposite meaning; usu. this WO] s.o. is endowed with (a specified quality): бог X-а Y-ом не обидел ≃ **God didn't grudge X Y; the good Lord provided X with (plenty of) Y; nature blessed X ⟨X was blessed⟩ with Y; fortune favored X with Y.**

Ни лицом, ни фигурой Бог [Нюру] не обидел, красавицей, может, и не была, но и уродиной никто не считал (Войнович 2). God had grudged her [Nyura] neither face nor figure, and while she may not have been a beauty she was certainly no freak either (2a).

Б-102 • **(куда, откуда и т. п.) БОГ НЕСЁТ** *(кого)?;* **(зачем, откуда и т. п.) БОГ ПРИНЁС** *(кого)? both obs* [VP_subj; if impfv, pres only; fixed WO] (where) is s.o. going (or coming from)?; (why, from where etc) has s.o. come? (бог несёт is often used as a question addressed to a person going in the direction opposite to the speaker's): куда X-а бог несёт? ≃ **where (in the world) is X headed ⟨going, off to⟩?;** ‖ откуда X-а бог несёт? ≃ **where (in the world) is X coming from?;** ‖ зачем X-а бог принёс? ≃ **why (in the world) is X here ⟨did X come here⟩?; how come X is ⟨came⟩ here?; what brought X here?;** [when addressed to the interlocutor only] **what brings you here ⟨to these parts etc⟩?**

[Борис:] Кудряш, это ты? [Кудряш:] Я, Борис Григорьич!... Вас куда бог несёт? (Островский 6). [B.:] Kudryash, is that you? [K.:] It's me, Boris Grigorich!...Where're you headed? (6a). ♦ [Кума *(подходит к Матрёне)*:] Здорово, баушка [*ungrammat, phonetic spelling* = бабушка], отколь бог несёт? [Матрёна:] А из двора, милая. Сынка проведать пришла (Толстой 1). [Friend *(coming up to Matrena)*:] Good day, old woman, where in the world did you come from? [M.:] From home, of course, my dear. I came to see my son (1b). ♦ «А, ваше благородие! – сказал он мне с живостью. – Как поживаешь? Зачем тебя бог принёс?» (Пушкин 2). "Ah, Your Honor!" he said to me gaily, "how do you do? What brought you to these parts?" (2a).

Б-103 • **БОГ ⟨ГОСПÓДЬ⟩ ПРИБРÁЛ** *кого obsoles, coll* [VP_subj; fixed WO] s.o. died: X-а бог прибрал ≃ **God ⟨the Lord⟩ took X (home); X went to meet his Maker.**

Колдун посмотрел на воду и говорит: «Будет жить... Но лучше б его Господь прибрал» (Терц 3). The fortune-teller looked at the water and said: *"He will live....But it would be better if the Lord took him"* (3a).

Б-104 • **БОГ С ТОБÓЙ ⟨с вами, с ним, с ней, с ними⟩; ГОСПÓДЬ ⟨ХРИСТÓС *obs*⟩ С ТОБÓЙ ⟨с вами⟩** [indep. clause; these forms only; fixed WO] **1.** *rather elev* [variants с тобой ⟨с вами⟩ only] may everything be well with you: **God bless you; God ⟨Christ⟩ be with you.**

[Аня:] Я спать пойду. Спокойной ночи, мама... Прощай, дядя. [Гаев *(целует ей лицо, руки)*:] Господь с тобой (Чехов 2). [A.:] I'm going to bed. Good night, mama....Good night, Uncle. [G. *(kisses her face and hands)*:] God bless you (2a). ♦ «Коли найдёшь себе суженую, коли полюбишь другую – бог с тобою, Пётр Андреич...» (Пушкин 2). "If you find the one destined for you, if you grow to love another – God be with you, Pyotr Andreitch..." (2b). ♦ «...Пора мне, спасибо на угощении, Христос с вами» (Максимов 1). "...I must be off. Thanks for the hospitality and Christ be with you" (1a).

2. *coll* [more often variants с тобой ⟨с вами⟩] used to express agreement, concession, conciliation: **all right (then); so be it; have it your way; let s.o. have it his way; do as you like ⟨please⟩; let s.o. do as he pleases.**

«Ну, бог с вами, давайте по тридцати [рублей] и берите их [мёртвые души] себе!» (Гоголь 3). "Well then, all right, thirty rubles a soul and they're yours" (3e).

3. *coll* [usu. variants с тобой ⟨с вами⟩] how can you say or do that? (used to express reproach, disagreement, astonishment, fright etc): **good heavens ⟨Lord, God⟩!; my God ⟨Lord, goodness⟩!; for heaven's sake!; God ⟨heaven⟩ forbid!**

«Пойдём, мама, гулять», – говорит Илюша [Обломов]. «Что ты, бог с тобой! Теперь гулять, – отвечает она, – сыро, ножки простудишь...» (Гончаров 1). "Let's go for a walk, Mummy," said Oblomov. "Good heavens, child," she replied, "go for a walk at this hour! It's damp, you'll get your feet wet..." (1a). ♦ «Лучше всё это не было бы так роскошно. Я к роскоши не привыкла». – «Бог с тобой, какая роскошь? Обыкновенный уют» (Грекова 3). "It would be nicer if all this weren't so luxurious. I'm not used to luxury." "Good Lord, what luxury? Ordinary comfort" (3a). ♦ [Наталья:] Вы хотите, чтобы я тоже утопилась? Нетушки, князь, этого не случится. [Мятлев:] Господь с вами! (Окуджава 2). [Natalya:] You want me to drown myself, too? No, no, prince, that won't – [M.:] Heaven forbid! (2a).

4. [variants с ним ⟨с ней, с ними⟩ only; often foll. by a word or phrase denoting the person or thing in question] let us (or I should) not be concerned about s.o. or sth., let us not talk about s.o. or sth. anymore (because he or it is unimportant, is not deserving of our attention): **never mind s.o. ⟨sth.⟩; forget (about) s.o. ⟨sth.⟩; who cares (about s.o. ⟨sth.⟩).**

Бог с ней, с этой Картучихой, баба она и есть баба, но разве в Петербурге его [Александра Петровича] понимают? (Искандер 3). Never mind her, this Kartuchikha; she was only a woman. But would they understand him [Alexander Petrovich] in Petersburg? (3a). ♦ «Ты знаешь, – говорила Маргарита, – ...когда ты заснул вчера ночью, я читала про тьму, которая пришла со Средиземного моря... и эти идолы, ах, золотые идолы. Они почему-то мне всё время не дают покоя...» – «Всё это хорошо и мило, – отвечал мастер, куря и разбивая дым рукой, – и эти идолы, бог с ними, но что дальше получится, уж решительно непонятно!» (Булгаков 9). "You know," said Margarita, "when you fell asleep last night I read about the darkness which had come from the Mediterranean...and those idols, ah, those golden idols! For some reason they haunt me all the time..." "All this is fine and charming," said the Master, smoking and breaking up the smoke with his hand. "As for those idols – forget them....But I cannot imagine what will happen next!" (9a). ♦ ...Вот он бы так прожил до конца дней своих, в этой-то вот, внезапно возникшей – бог с ней, как она выглядит! – непрерывности своего существа (Битов 2). ...He would have liked to live just this way to the end of his days, live in this, the suddenly emergent – who cared how it looked! – uninterruptedness of his existence (2a).

Б-105 • БОГ ТРО́ИЦУ ЛЮ́БИТ [saying] the third person or thing, when added to two others, is likely to bring luck or a sense of completeness, the third attempt is likely to be successful: ≃ **three is the magic number; three ⟨third time⟩ is a charm; all good things come in threes; third time lucky.**

[Зилов:] Слушай! Бог троицу любит. Бросим третий раз. Решка – признаемся, орёл – нет (Вампилов 5). [Z.:] Listen! Three's a charm. Let's toss it a third time. Tails, we own up, heads, we don't (5b).

Б-106 • ВИ́ДИТ БОГ *coll* [VP_subj; Invar; usu. sent adv (parenth); usu. this WO] **1.** honestly, I swear I am telling the truth: **(as) God is my witness; honest to God ⟨to goodness⟩; by God;** [in limited contexts] **God ⟨Lord, goodness⟩ knows.**

«О, как я его [Ливерия] ненавижу! Видит Бог, я когда-нибудь убью его» (Пастернак 1). "God, how I hate him [Liberius]! As God is my witness, I'll murder him someday!" (1a). ♦ «Освободите [*regional* = освободите] дорогу, казаки! А то, видит бог, стрелять будем!» (Шолохов 3). "Clear out of the road, Cossacks! Or we'll start shooting, by God, we will!" (3a). ♦ [Муромский:] Двадцать четыре тысячи [серебром]... Где я их возьму? Их у меня нет, видит бог, нет... (Сухово-Кобылин 1). [M.:] Twenty-four thousand silver....Where will I get it? God knows, I don't have it... (1a).

2. as is obvious, of course, naturally: **God ⟨Lord, goodness⟩ knows.**

Скажу коротко, я уснул... Видит бог, дело прошлое, я изо всех сил крепился и, наконец, как это бывает на собраниях, если сидишь где-нибудь в задних рядах, решил на минуточку прикорнуть с тем, чтобы потом очнуться с посвежевшей головой (Искандер 3). To put it briefly, I fell asleep....Goodness knows, it doesn't matter anymore; I resisted with all my might and at last, as happens at meetings if you sit anywhere in the back rows, I decided to lean back a moment in order to awake with my mind refreshed (3a).

Б-107 • ВОТ (ТЕБЕ́ ⟨вам⟩) БОГ, А ВОТ ПОРО́Г [saying] (used when asking s.o. to leave some place, usu. after a disagreement, quarrel etc) go away: ≃ **there's the door, why don't you use it; good-bye and good riddance; here's your hat, what's your hurry?**

Б-108 • ДАВА́Й/ДАЙ БОГ НО́ГИ *coll* [these forms only; predic; subj: human or animal; usu. follows one or more predicates having the same subj; usu. impfv; usu. in past contexts; fixed WO] (s.o.) ran off quickly: X давай бог ноги ≃ **X took to his heels; X hightailed it; X beat it; X ran for his life; X took ⟨zipped⟩ off.**

«...Послушали бы вы, что рассказывает этот мошенник... Полез, говорит, в карман понюхать табаку и, вместо тавлинки, вытащил кусок чёртовой *свитки*, от которой вспыхнул красный огонь, а он давай бог ноги!» (Гоголь 5). "You should hear what this scoundrel says!...He says he put his hand in his pocket and instead of his snuff pulled out a bit of the devil's jacket and it burst into a red flame – and he took to his heels!" (5a). ♦ «Э! да ты, я вижу, Аркадий Николаевич, понимаешь любовь, как все новейшие молодые люди: цып, цып, цып, курочка, а как только курочка начинает приближаться, давай бог ноги!» (Тургенев 2). "Ugh! I can see, Arkady Nikolayevich, that your idea of love is the same as that of all the other young men of this new generation. 'Cluck, cluck, cluck,' you call to the hen, and the moment the hen comes anywhere near you, you run for your life!" (2c). ♦ «Сунул сумку к Алику в портфель и – дай бог ноги» (Чернёнок 2). "I stuck the bag in Alik's briefcase and zipped off" (2a).

Б-109 • ДАЙ БОГ [Invar; fixed WO] **1.** ~ *(кому)* [usu. indep. sent or sent adv (parenth)] used to express one's wish that sth. hoped-for be realized, come to pass: **God grant; I ⟨let's⟩ hope to God (that...);** [in limited contexts] **please God.**

[Городничий:] Да, признаюсь, господа, я, чёрт возьми, очень хочу быть генералом. [Лука Лукич:] И дай бог получить (Гоголь 4). [Mayor:] Yes, I must admit, ladies and gentlemen, God damn it, I very much want to be a general. [L.L.:] And God grant you get it (4a). ♦ «...Обстоятельства против нас. Наше время кончилось. По инерции ещё, может быть, протянется год-два. Может быть, ты успеешь в членкоры проскочить. Дай бог! Но путного ничего мы уже не сделаем» (Зиновьев 2). "...The circumstances are against us. Our time is over. We might have a year or two still, because of inertia. Perhaps you'll even have time enough to make it as corresponding member: I hope to God you do! But we won't get anything useful done" (2a). ♦ «Нужно проверить, – стоит на своём дедушка, – если он [Терещенко] не умер от белой горячки... и, дай бог, бросил пить, то лучшего защитника не надо» (Рыбаков 1). Grandfather stood his ground. "We have to check to see if he [Tereshchenko] hasn't already died of the DTs...and if, please God, he's stopped drinking, and if he has, then we won't need a better lawyer" (1a).

2. *coll* [adv (intensif) or predic (subj: usu. concr or abstr)] (used to emphasize the high degree of some quality or the intensity of some activity) incredibly (much, hard etc, as specified by the context): **like you wouldn't believe;** [in limited contexts] **like nobody's business; one hell of a [NP].**

На кухне твои друзья похозяйничали дай бог: перебили половину бокалов и даже не удосужились собрать осколки. Your friends messed up the kitchen like you wouldn't believe: they smashed half the wineglasses and didn't even bother to sweep up the pieces. ♦ Ты с этим парнем в драку не лезь: он боксёр, удар у него дай бог! Don't get into a fight with that guy. He's a boxer and has one hell of a punch!

Б-110 • ДАЙ БОГ ВСЯ́КОМУ ⟨ВСЕМ(...), КА́Ж-ДОМУ(...), ЛЮБО́МУ...⟩ *coll* [these forms only; usu. predic (with subj: any common noun); fixed WO] extremely, impressively strong, big, much etc (used to emphasize a very high degree of some positive quality or the intensity of some worthy activity): **as good ⟨much etc⟩ as anyone ⟨any man etc⟩ could want; (such a [NP]) that anyone ⟨any man etc⟩ would be thankful for; nobody could ask for (a) better [NP];** [in limited contexts] **may God give everybody as good.**

...На голых её [официантки] руках вздулись такие бицепсы, что дай бог любому мужику (Аксёнов 1). ...Her [the waitress's] bare arms swelled with biceps that any man would be thankful for (1a). ♦ С красителями мы ещё отстаём, но кожа – дай бог всем иметь такую кожу! (Рыбаков 1). Our dyes are a bit out of date, it's true, but nobody could ask for better leather (1a). ♦ [Марина:] Я на своё житьё, Микита, не жалюсь [*substand* = жалуюсь]. Моё житьё – дай бог всякому (Толстой 1). [M.:] I ain't complaining about my own life, Nikita. May God give everybody as good (1a).

Б-111 • ДАЙ БОГ ЗДОРО́ВЬЯ *кому* [Invar; indep. sent or sent adv (parenth); fixed WO] a wish for s.o.'s well-being: дай бог Х-у здоровья ≃ **(God) bless X; bless X's heart; (may) God grant X (good) health.**

«Ты... ты... всё приняла вчера?» – спросил я диким голосом. «Всё, батюшка милый, всё, – пела бабочка сдобным голосом, – дай вам бог здоровья за эти капли... полбаночки – как приехала, а полбаночки – как рукой сняло...» (Булгаков 6). "You...you...you mean to say you drank all this yesterday?" I asked, appalled. "All of it, sir, all of it," said the woman in her comfortable, sing song voice. "And God bless you for it...half the bottle when I got home and the other half when I went to bed. The pain just vanished..." (6a). ♦ Да, хорошие были люди, дай бог им здоровья, если они ещё живы (Искандер 4). Yes, they were good people, God grant them health, if they were still alive (4a).

Б-112 • ДАЙ БОГ ПА́МЯТИ ⟨ПА́МЯТЬ⟩ *coll* [these forms only; usu. indep. sent or sent adv (parenth); fixed WO] let me try to recall (used when trying hard to remember sth.): **(now) let me think ⟨see⟩; let me jog my memory; if only I could remember.**

[Анна Петровна:] Цветы повторяются каждую весну, а радости – нет. Кто мне сказал эту фразу? Дай бог памяти... Кажется, сам Николай сказал (Чехов 4). [A.P.:] Flowers come round every spring, but happiness doesn't. Who told me that? Now let me see. I think Nicholas himself said it (4b). ♦ «„Знаешь, – орёт, – что это – атаман ихний [*ungrammat* = их] Карла...“ – вот, запамятовал прозвищу [*ungrammat* = прозвище, used here instead of фамилию]... Э, да как его, дай бог памяти...» – «Карл Маркс?» – подсказал Штокман, ёжась в улыбке. – «Во-во!.. Он самый Карла Маркс...» – обрадовался Христоня (Шолохов 2). "'Do you know,' he says, 'that's their ataman Karl –' Oh darn it, I've forgotten his other name. What was it now, if only I could remember..." "Karl Marx?" Stokman suggested, barely suppressing a smile. "That's it! Karl Marx!" Khristonya burst out joyfully (2a).

Б-113 • КАК БОГ НА́ ДУШУ ПОЛО́ЖИТ *coll* [AdvP; Invar; adv; fixed WO] (to do sth.) whatever way one desires, or allowing things to happen as they might (may express the speaker's opinion that the action is carried out unsystematically, haphazardly, without concern for the result): **any which ⟨old⟩ way; however it strikes one's fancy; however it turns out; [in limited contexts] when(ever) the spirit moves one ⟨it⟩; letting matters take their course ⟨take care of themselves⟩.**

Тебе поручили серьёзное дело: делай всё как следует, а не как бог на душу положит. You've been given an important assignment – do it properly, not any old way. ♦ ...Радио нет, а ходики идут как им бог на душу положит, поэтому прежде, чем выйти на улицу, бабка шла узнавать время к соседям... (Кузнецов 1). We had no radio, and the wall clock ran when the spirit moved it. So before going into the street, Grandmother would call on the neighbors to find out the time... (1a). ♦ Подумать только! Я прожила столько лет и понятия не имела о таких сложных вещах. Жила просто так, как бог на душу положит (Михайловская 1). Just think! I have lived all these years and have had no notion of such complicated things. I have simply lived letting matters take their course (1a).

Б-114 • КАК БО́Г СВЯТ *obsoles, coll* [Invar; usu. this WO] **1.** [sent adv (parenth) or predic (with subj: это or a clause)] undoubtedly, definitely: **as sure as I'm standing here; surely; you can be darn sure.**

Между тем уважение к Надежде Петровне всё росло и росло. Купцы открыто говорили, что, «если бы не она, наша матушка, *он* [помпадур] бы, как свят бог, и нас всех, да и прах-то наш по ветру развеял!» (Салтыков-Щедрин 2). Meantime the respect in which Nadyezhda Petrovna was held grew and grew. The merchants were saying quite openly, "Were it not for her, that dear lady of ours, *he* [the pompadour] would surely have murdered us all by now and scattered our dust and ashes to the four winds!" (2a).

2. [sent adv (parenth) or indep. clause] (used to emphasize one's sincerity and trustworthiness) I swear, honestly: **I swear it; I swear to God!; (as) God is my witness; honest to God ⟨to goodness⟩; [in limited contexts] I swear before God; cross my heart (and hope to die).**

«Ты женишься, или я тебя прокляну, а имение, как бог свят! продам и промотаю, и тебе полушки не оставлю!» (Пушкин 3). "You will marry her or, I swear it, I'll curse you and sell up this whole estate and squander the money so that you won't get a single farthing" (3b). ♦ «Как вам не стыдно было, – сказал я ему сердито, – доносить на нас коменданту после того, как дали мне слово того не делать?» – «Как бог свят, я Ивану Кузьмичу того не говорил, – отвечал он, – Василиса Егоровна выведала всё от меня. Она всем и распорядилась без ведома коменданта» (Пушкин 2). "Didn't you feel any shame in denouncing us to the commandant," I asked him angrily, "when you'd given your word that you wouldn't?" "God is my witness, I said nothing to Ivan Kuzmich," he replied. "Vasilisa Egorovna wormed the secret out of me. It was she who saw to it all without the commandant's knowledge" (2a).

Б-115 • НЕ БОГ ВЕСТЬ ⟨ЗНА́ЕТ⟩ КАК *coll* [AdvP; these forms only; adv; fixed WO] **1.** not especially well, in a mediocre fashion: **not (all) that well; so-so; [in limited contexts] (be) not much of a [NP].**

Наконец, я вспомнил, как играют, и дело у нас пошло лучше. Джон тоже играл не Бог весть как, но постепенно, я говорю, дело пошло... (Лимонов 1). Finally I remembered how to play, and things started to go better. John wasn't much of a player either, but gradually, as I say, things got going... (1a).

2. [foll. by AdvP, short-form Adj, or Part denoting a positive quality, quantity, or distance] not very, not particularly: **not any too...; not all that...; not especially...**

Она его и раньше-то, своего собственного сына, не бог весть как хорошо знала, а теперь, через год разлуки? (Залыгин 1). Even before he went away she didn't know him any too well, her own son, so what might this year of absence have done? (1a).

Б-116 • НЕ БОГ ВЕСТЬ ⟨ЗНА́ЕТ⟩ КАКО́Й *coll* [AdjP; fixed WO] **1.** [modif (when foll. by NP) or subj-compl with copula (subj: any common noun)] not especially good, mediocre, not in any way special: **not all that good ⟨great etc⟩; not too ⟨terribly, particularly⟩ good ⟨great etc⟩; not much of a [NP]; nothing to brag ⟨write home⟩ about.**

Конечно, не Бог весть какая комната могла получиться из бывшего чулана, но да разве в хоромах дело? (Максимов 3). You couldn't make much of a home out of an old storeroom, true enough, but who wanted a mansion? (3a).

2. [modif; foll. by AdjP denoting a positive quality, quantity, or distance] not very, not particularly: **not all that...; not too ⟨terribly, especially⟩...; none too...**

...Она внезапно догадалась, что Никандров её не любит... Он её не преследовал, не ухаживал за ней... относился как ко всем вокруг неё. Ну, а когда она бросилась к нему, почему бы ему и не подобрать кусочек, если даже он и не бог весть какой лакомый? (Залыгин 1). [context transl] ...She suddenly realized that Nikandrov did not love her....He hadn't pursued her, hadn't paid court to her...he'd behaved towards her exactly as he behaved towards everybody else. But since she'd forced herself upon him why shouldn't he help himself, even if the morsel offered wasn't the choicest? (1a).

Б-117 • НЕ БОГ ВЕСТЬ ⟨ЗНА́ЕТ⟩ СКО́ЛЬКО (*кого-чего*) *coll* [AdvP; these forms only; usu. quantit compl with copula (subj/gen: human, concr, or abstr); fixed WO] relatively little, relatively few: **not very ⟨too⟩ much ⟨many⟩; anything but plentiful ⟨numerous⟩; not an overabundance; [with count nouns only] few and far between; only a handful.**

Б-118 • НЕ БОГ ВЕСТЬ ЧТО *coll* [NP; obj or subj-compl with copula (subj: concr or abstr); fixed WO] (sth. that is) nothing out of the ordinary, not very important or worthwhile: **nothing special; nothing to brag ⟨write home⟩ about; no great shakes; no big deal.**

«Муниципалитет составил петицию в департамент здравоохранения, господин Росшепер подпишется, вы, я надеюсь, тоже, но это не Бог весть что. Гласность нужна!» (Стругацкие 1). "The city council put together a petition to the

Department of Health. Mr. Rosheper will sign it, and you, I hope, will also sign it but that's no big deal. What I need is real publicity" (1a).

Б-119 • НЕ ДАЙ ⟨НЕ ПРИВЕДИ⟩ БОГ ⟨БОЖЕ, ГОСПОДИ⟩; НЕ ПРИВЕДИ ГОСПОДЬ *all coll* [these forms only; fixed WO] **1.** [indep. clause, sent adv (parenth), or predic (with subj: usu. infin)] (used to express concern that sth. disagreeable may happen, a warning to s.o. not to do sth., or the undesirability, inadmissibility of sth.) it would be bad, unfortunate if…: **God ⟨heaven⟩ forbid; (may) God preserve ⟨save⟩ s.o. (from sth.); God ⟨heaven⟩ help s.o. (if…); [in limited contexts] (avoid sth.) at all costs.**

«А если бы сбились с пути, да до утра, не приведи господи, закоченели бы как ледышки» (Айтматов 1). "What if you'd been lost right through until morning, God forbid? You'd have frozen solid, like icicles" (1b). ♦ …В первую же ночь тайному суровому испытанию подвергалась её любовь: не дай бог, не появился ли в ней какой-нибудь новый опыт (Трифонов 1). The very first night upon her return she would secretly be put to the test, and heaven forbid that her lovemaking reveal any new experience (1a). ♦ [Лука Лукич:] Не приведи бог служить по учёной части, всего боишься. Всякий мешается, всякому хочется показать, что он тоже умный человек (Гоголь 4). [L.L.:] God help anyone whose job has anything to do with education! Everybody interferes, everybody wants to show that he is an intelligent man too (4b). ♦ Они [Ирина Викторовна и Никандров] чувствовали необходимость сохранения некоторой дистанции между собой, чтобы, не дай бог, не случилось такой близости, когда одному известно о другом всё… (Залыгин 1). They [Irina Viktorovna and Nikandrov] felt it necessary to maintain a certain distance between each other, to avoid at all costs growing so close that each knew everything about the other… (1a).

2. [usu. predic (with subj: any common noun), indep. clause, or adv (intensif)] (a person or thing is) extremely bad, awful etc, (some undesirable quality is) very strongly manifested, (some undesirable action is carried out) with extreme intensity: **goodness ⟨God⟩, how [AdjP] one ⟨sth.⟩ is; one got ⟨sth. is etc⟩ incredibly [AdjP]; (s.o. ⟨sth.⟩) like I hope never to see ⟨hear etc⟩ again; God ⟨may the Lord⟩ save us ⟨you etc⟩ from such a [NP] ⟨from a [NP] like that⟩; God ⟨may the Lord⟩ spare you ⟨me etc⟩ a [NP] like that; [in limited contexts] I wouldn't wish him ⟨her, that etc⟩ on my worst enemy; [as a response to a question or a rejoinder to an exclamation] God, yes!; and how!; [in limited contexts] a God-awful [NP].**

«Когда я был ещё подпоручиком, раз, знаете, мы погуляли между собою, а ночью сделалась тревога; вот мы и вышли перед фрунт навеселе, да уж и досталось нам, как Алексей Петрович узнал: не дай господи, как он рассердился!» (Лермонтов 1). "When I was still a second lieutenant we all got a little high one time, and during the night there was an alarm; so we came out lit up in front of the soldiers, and did we get it from Aleksey Petrovich when he found out: goodness, how furious he was!" (1a). ♦ «Измаялась я с ней [Галькой], — стала жаловаться Степанида. — Ой девка, не приведи господь никому такую» (Распутин 1). "She's [Galia has] wore me out," began Stepanida plaintively. "The little beast! I wouldn't wish her on my worst enemy" (1a). ♦ «Поступайте в кондуктора! Вы не можете заниматься зоологией», — неслось из кабинета. «Строг?» — спрашивал котелок у Панкрата. «У, — не приведи бог», — отвечал Панкрат… (Булгаков 10). [context transl] "Go and get jobs as conductors! You aren't fit to study zoology," came from the office. "Strict, eh?" the derby asked Pankrat. "A holy terror," answered Pankrat (10a).

Б-120 • НЕ ПРИВЕДИ БОГ ⟨ГОСПОДИ⟩ СКОЛЬКО *coll* [AdvP; these forms only; quantit compl with copula (subj/gen: any common noun); fixed WO] a lot: **more…than you ⟨one⟩ can shake a stick at; scads ⟨oodles, loads⟩ of.**

Б-121 • ПОМИЛУЙ БОГ! *old-fash* [Interj; Invar; fixed WO] (used to express the speaker's strong disagreement with or objection to some suggestion, idea, or question—usu. one voiced by the interlocutor) absolutely not, I am appalled that such a thing has been suggested, asked: **(good) heavens, no!; goodness, no!; how could you even say ⟨think⟩ such a thing!; [in limited contexts] for God's ⟨goodness', heaven's⟩ sake (, of course not)!; not on your life!**

Б-122 • (САМ) БОГ ВЕЛИТ/ВЕЛЕЛ *(кому) coll;* И БОГ ВЕЛИТ/ВЕЛЕЛ *obs, coll* [VP_subj; past or pres; usu. used with infin; fixed WO] **1.** it is proper, normal (for s.o. to do sth.): Х-у сам бог велел сделать Y ≃ **it's only natural for X to do Y; it's in the order of things for X to do Y; it's only fitting that X do Y; [in limited contexts] who wouldn't do Y?**

«Странно, как хорошо я всё это помню. — Он обнаружил, что у него побелели щёки и кончик носа. — Вот таким я и был тогда, на такого орать сам Бог велел» (Стругацкие 1). "It's strange how well I remember it all." He discovered that his cheeks and the tip of his nose had turned pale. "That's the way I looked then—who wouldn't go after a guy who looked like that?" (1a).

2. (s.o.) must (do sth.): Х-у и бог велел сделать Y ≃ **it's X's (sacred) duty to do Y; it would be wrong for X not to do Y.**

«Подойди, подойди, любезный! Я и отцу-то твоему правду одна говорила, когда он в случае был, а тебе-то и бог велит» (Толстой 4). "Come on, come closer, my dear! I used to be the only one to tell that father of yours the truth in the days when he was a court favorite, and now it's my sacred duty to do the same for you" (4a).

Б-123 • СКОЛЬКО БОГ НА ДУШУ ПОЛОЖИТ *coll* [AdvP; Invar; usu. adv (quantif); fixed WO] however much or many one desires, an arbitrary amount (may express the speaker's opinion that the quantity in question is somehow inappropriate): **as much as one likes ⟨pleases, feels like, wants⟩; however much one likes ⟨would like etc⟩.**

Деньги мой бывший муж на ребёнка даёт, но нерегулярно и каждый раз — сколько бог на душу положит. My ex-husband pays me child support, but irregularly and each time however much he feels like.

Б-124 • СЧАСТЛИВ ТВОЙ ⟨его, её, ваш, их⟩ БОГ *old-fash* [sent; these forms only; fixed WO] s.o. is lucky (that he made the decision he did, that he acted as he did, that things turned out the way they did etc): счастлив твой ⟨его и т. п.⟩ бог ≃ **(you should) thank your ⟨he should thank his etc⟩ lucky stars; you ⟨he etc⟩ must have been born under a lucky star; lucky for you ⟨for her etc⟩.**

[Елена:] Счастлив ваш бог, что вы догадались мне об этом сказать (Булгаков 4). [E.:] Thank your lucky stars that you were smart enough to tell me about it (4a).

Б-125 • УБЕЙ ⟨ПОБЕЙ, РАЗРАЗИ, ДА РАЗРАЗИТ, ПОКАРАЙ⟩ МЕНЯ БОГ ⟨ГОСПОДЬ *obs*⟩ *coll* [these forms only; usu. this WO] **1.** [indep. sent, a clause in a compound sent, or sent adv (parenth)] (used to add emphasis to a statement or to convince the interlocutor that what is being stated is true) I swear: **may God strike me dead; I swear to God; honest to God; cross my heart (and hope to die).**

2. Also: УБЕЙ БОГ *coll* [main clause in a complex sent (often foll. by a если-clause), a clause in a compound sent (usu. foll. by a clause introduced by Conj «а» or «но»), or sent adv (parenth)] used to emphasize that one cannot or does not understand or believe sth., know sth. etc: [of understanding, knowing sth. etc] **God strike me (dead) if (I know ⟨understand etc⟩); I'll be damned ⟨darned, hanged⟩ if…; [in limited contexts] for the**

life of me (I can't understand ⟨remember etc⟩); **God help me if (I know ⟨understand⟩ etc);** [of believing s.o. or sth.] **there is no way in hell ⟨in the world⟩ (I will believe him ⟨her, that…⟩ etc);** **nothing in the world (could make me believe him ⟨her, that…⟩ etc).**

Откуда взялся этот писатель? Писатель Иванько. Всё-таки имею какое-то отношение к этому делу, слежу за новинками литературы, и — убей меня бог — если я хоть когда-нибудь слышал такую фамилию (Войнович 3). Where had this writer come from? The writer Ivanko. I still have some contact with that profession, follow the new literary figures, but God strike me if I've ever heard that name before (3a). ♦ …Самое тяжкое то, что нужно ждать почти сутки… Они [следователи] делают так специально, чтобы вызываемые больше волновались. Чтобы пришли уж тёпленькие, всё бы у них внутри тряслось и дрожало, ударишь пальцем — развалятся. Или, как говорят: *расколются*. Но, убей меня бог, если б я знал, в чём мне надо *колоться*! (Трифонов 5). Most distressing was the fact that I had almost twenty-four hours to wait.…They [the investigators] do that on purpose, so that you'll be more upset. So that when you come in, your resistance is already down, you're trembling and shaking inside, and then they just touch you with a finger and you crack. But God help me if I knew what I had to crack about (5a).

Б-126 • ЧЕМ БОГ ⟨ГОСПÓДЬ *obs*⟩ **ПОСЛÁЛ** угощать *кого*, **закусывать, завтракать** и т. п.; **ЧТО БОГ ПОСЛÁЛ** есть, отведать *both coll* [subord clause; past or, rare, fut; used as obj; fixed WO] (to treat s.o. to, snack on, breakfast on etc) whatever food happens to be available: **(give ⟨take⟩) potluck; whatever there is ⟨one has⟩; whatever is in the house; whatever is on ⟨at⟩ hand.**

Я чувствую, что как только мы покончим со сбором орехов, дядя возьмёт их [бойцов] к себе и угостит чем бог послал (Искандер 4). I have a feeling that as soon as we finish gathering nuts, Uncle will take the men home and give them potluck (4a). ♦ Зурин пригласил меня отобедать с ним вместе чем бог послал, по-солдатски (Пушкин 2). He [Zurin] invited me to take potluck with him as a fellow soldier (2a). ♦ [author's usage] …Семья наша простая и пища простая, ели что бог посылал… (Рыбаков 1). …Ours was a simple family and our food was simple; we ate whatever there was… (1a). ♦ «Я угостила его [генерала] чем бог послал, разговорились о том о сём, наконец и о Дубровском» (Пушкин 1). "I treated him [the general] to whatever was in the house, and we talked about this and that, mentioning at last Dubrovskii, too" (1a).

Б-127 • ЧТО БОГ ДАСТ *coll* [Invar; usu. indep. clause (often after «а там») or subord clause; fixed WO] (of an action or activity the outcome of which does not depend on the doer; expresses the speaker's hope for a favorable outcome) things will turn out the way they will turn out: **what(ever) will be will be; whatever God grants s.o.; we'll see what God ⟨the Lord⟩ has in store for us; we shall see (what comes next ⟨how things go etc⟩).**

«Здоров ли ты?»… Лукавый мальчишка здоровёхонек, но молчит. «Посиди-ка ты эту недельку дома, — скажет она, — а там — что бог даст» (Гончаров 1). "Do you feel well?" The sly little boy was quite well, but said nothing. "You had better stay at home this week," she would say, "then we shall see…" (1b).

Б-128 • ЧТО БОГ НÁ ДУШУ ПОЛÓЖИТ *coll* [subord clause; usu. used as obj; fixed WO] anything one desires (may express the speaker's opinion that the thing or phenomenon in question is somehow inappropriate, of poor quality etc): **whatever strikes one's fancy; whatever one feels like; (to say etc) whatever comes ⟨pops⟩ into one's head; whatever ⟨anything that⟩ comes to mind.**

Как-то я… решил посмотреть документацию уволенного математика. И глаза у меня буквально полезли на лоб. Он, оказывается, открыл тривиальную истину, что расчёты в этом звене вообще излишни и не влияют на последующие операции. И писал что бог на душу положит (Зиновьев 1). "Once…I decided to glance through the work of the mathematician who'd been fired. My eyes almost literally popped out. It turned out that he'd discovered the banal truth that calculations at this stage of the operation were totally unnecessary and had no influence on the subsequent stages. He just used to write whatever came into his head" (1a).

Б-129 • НА БÓГА НАДÉЙСЯ, А САМ НЕ ПЛОШÁЙ [saying] act decisively, intelligently, enterprisingly, not counting on favorable circumstances to help you: ≃ **God helps those who help themselves; (put your) trust in the Lord ⟨in God⟩, but keep your powder dry.** Cf. **praise the Lord and pass the ammunition.**

Б-130 • ПОБÓЙСЯ БÓГА; БÓГА БЫ ПОБОЯ́ЛСЯ *all coll* [indep. sent; usu. this WO] **1.** (used as an attempt to put s.o. to shame for unconscionable, inappropriate behavior, and/or as an attempt to convince him to change his behavior, reverse his decision etc) you (he etc) should be ashamed of yourself (himself etc): побойся бога ≃ **have you no fear of God?; have you no shame?;** [in limited contexts] **have a heart!; for God's ⟨goodness', pity's⟩ sake!**

[Саша:] Этот [отец] пьян, Николай пьян, Миша тоже… Хоть бы бога вы побоялись… если людей не стыдитесь! (Чехов 1). [S.:] Here's Father drunk, and so are Nicholas and Michael.…Have you no fear of God, even if you don't care what men think? (1b). ♦ «Кондрат Иванович! Ведь завод останется без специалистов… Побойтесь бога…» (Ильф и Петров 2). "Kondrat Ivanovich! The plant will be left without any specialists.…Have a heart!" (2a). ♦ «Пятьдесят [used in place of the correct form пятьдесят to show a Ukrainian accent] сегодня» — «Что ты, Явдоха?.. Побойся бога. Позавчера сорок, вчера сорок пять, сегодня пятьдесят. Ведь этак невозможно» (Булгаков 3). "Fifty kopecks today."…"What?…For pity's sake, Yavdokha — forty the day before yesterday, forty-five yesterday and now today it's fifty. You can't go on like this" (3a).

2. (used as an attempt to prevent s.o. from doing sth. imprudent, risky) be sensible: **be reasonable; come to your senses;** [in limited contexts] **don't tempt the gods ⟨the Lord⟩.**

«Ну, Савельич, — сказал я ему, — …я еду в Белогорскую крепость». — «Батюшка Пётр Андреич! — сказал добрый дядька дрожащим голосом. — Побойся бога; как тебе пускаться в дорогу в нынешнее время, когда никуда проезду нет от разбойников!» (Пушкин 2). "Well, Savelich," I said to him, "…I am going to Fort Belogorsk." "Petr Andreich, young master!" said my good-natured attendant in a trembling voice. "Don't tempt the Lord! How could you set out now, when all the roads are cut off by the brigands?" (2a).

Б-131 • РÁДИ БÓГА ⟨БÓГА РÁДИ *more emphatic*⟩ *coll*; **РÁДИ (САМОГÓ) ГÓСПОДА (БÓГА)** *obs, coll* [PrepP; these forms only; fixed WO] **1.** Also: **РÁДИ ВСЕГÓ СВЯТÓГО** *obsoles, coll* [sent adv (parenth); usu. used with imper] (used to express beseechment, entreaty) please, I implore you: **for God's ⟨goodness', heaven's, mercy's⟩ sake; I beg of you;** [in limited contexts] **for the sake of all that's holy.**

«Потише, сударь, ради бога потише. Проклятая клячонка моя не успевает за твоим долгоногим бесом» (Пушкин 2). "Easy, sir, for God's sake, easy! My damned nag can't keep up with your long-legged devil" (2a). ♦ «Ради бога успокойтесь, — сказала она, отняв у меня свою руку. — Вы ещё в опасности: рана может открыться. Поберегите себя хоть для меня» (Пушкин 2). "For heaven's sake, calm yourself," she said, withdrawing her hand. "You're still not out of danger: your wound may reopen. Take care of yourself, if only for my sake" (2a). ♦ «Вы, ради бога, простите меня, письмо-то я распечатал...» (Шолохов 2). "For mercy's sake, forgive me, but I unsealed the letter..." (2a). ♦ «Я его умолял: сожги ты бога свой пергамент! Но он вырвал его у меня из рук и убежал» (Булгаков 9). "I pleaded with him: 'Burn your parchment, I beg of you!' But he tore it from my hands and ran away" (9a). ♦ «Так у вас разве есть выкройка?»... – «Как же, сестра привезла». – «Душа моя, дайте её мне ради всего святого» (Гоголь 3). "So you've actually got the pattern!"..."Of course I have. My sister brought it along." "Darling, lend it to me for the sake of all that's holy" (3c).

2. [sent adv (parenth) or indep. sent] surely, naturally (used to express compliance with a request or agreement with a statement): **by all means!; of course!;** [in response to a request] **please do!;** [in response to a question or request with negated predic] **of course not!; certainly not!; heavens, no!**

«...Жалуйтесь, ради бога, хоть самому генералу Деникину! Сказал, не могу, – и не могу, вы русский язык понимаете?» (Шолохов 5). "...Complain by all means, to General Denikin himself, if you choose! I've said I can't and I can't, don't you understand the Russian language?" (5a). ♦ «Вы не возражаете, если я закурю?» – «Ради бога. Я сама курю». "Do you mind if I smoke?" "Of course not, I'm a smoker myself."

Б-132 • ЧЕМ БОГА́ТЫ, ТЕМ И РА́ДЫ [saying] you are welcome to share all that we (or I) have (usu. used when inviting a guest to enjoy all the—often modest—food, comforts etc that one has to offer; also used as an apology for not having anything more or better to offer): ≃ **what's mine ⟨ours⟩ is yours; you're welcome to what(ever) we ⟨I⟩ have; help yourself to whatever we ⟨I⟩ have;** [in limited contexts] **my home is your home; that's the best we have ⟨we've got⟩ (at the moment).**

«Вы кушайте, батюшка, кушайте... Чем богаты, как говорится...» (Максимов 3). "Eat, Pyotr Vasilievich, eat....What's ours is yours, as they say..." (3a).

Б-133 • НЕ БО́ГИ ГОРШКИ́ ОБЖИГА́ЮТ [saying] even an ordinary person can cope with sth. difficult (said to encourage or instill confidence in s.o. who is undertaking a task which is new to, or difficult for, him): ≃ **it can't be that hard; you can do anything you put your mind to; what ⟨whatever⟩ man has done man can do; any man can do what another man has done.**

Б-134 • БО́ГОМ ОБИ́ЖЕН(НЫЙ) obsoles [AdjP; subj-compl with бытьø (subj: human) or modif (long-form var. only); usu. this WO] (one is) unlucky, unfortunate: **forsaken by God; pitiable; unblessed; a hapless creature.**

Б-135 • ВСЁ (МЫ) ПОД БО́ГОМ ХО́ДИМ [saying] we never know what is going to happen to us, our fate is beyond our control (often in refer. to illness, death): ≃ **we are all in God's hands; we are all subject to God's will; we are all mortal.**

«Все мы, старуня, под богом ходим. Как он захочет, так и выйдет» (Распутин 3). "We are all in God's hands, old girl. It'll all turn out as He wills it" (3a). ♦ [Серебряков:] ...Все мы под богом ходим; я стар, болен и потому нахожу своевременным регулировать свои имущественные отношения постольку, поскольку они касаются моей семьи (Чехов 3). [S.:] ...We are all mortal. I am old, ill, and therefore find it timely to settle matters relating to my property, in so far as they concern my family (3a).

Б-136 • С БО́ГОМ old-fash [PrepP; Invar] **1.** [indep. sent or adv] (used to wish s.o. success—or occas. used as encouragement for a group that includes the speaker—before undertaking something new or setting out on a trip) may things go well: **(may) God be with you; God bless you; good luck to you;** [when the speaker participates in the undertaking in question] **with God's grace**

⟨**help, blessing**⟩; [as a wish for a pleasant journey only] **I wish you Godspeed ⟨good speed⟩; have a nice ⟨good etc⟩ trip.**

«Вы нынче ведь все влюблены. Ну, влюблена, так выходи за него замуж, — сердито смеясь, проговорила графиня, — с богом!» (Толстой 5). "You're all in love nowadays, it seems. Well, if you're in love, marry him," said the Countess, with a laugh of annoyance, "and God bless you!" (5a). ♦ Кетчер должен был ехать за заставу с Natalie, Астраков — воротиться, чтобы сказать мне, всё ли успешно и что делать. Я остался ждать с его милой, прекрасной женой... Наконец взошёл Астраков. Мы бросились к нему. «Всё идёт чудесно, они при мне ускакали!.. Ступай сейчас за Рогожскую заставу, там у мостика увидишь лошадей... С богом!» (Герцен 1). Ketscher was to drive out of the town with Natalie, and Astrakov was to come back and tell me whether everything had gone off successfully and what I was to do. I was left waiting with his beautiful, delightful wife....At last Astrakov came in, and we rushed to meet him. "Everything is going marvellously; I saw them gallop off....You go out at the Rogozhsky gate at once; there by the little bridge you will see the horses....Good luck to you!" (1a). ♦ «Итак, если нет препятствий, то с богом, можно бы приступить к совершению купчей крепости», — сказал Чичиков (Гоголь 3). "Well, then," Chichikov went on, "if there's nothing in our way, we can go ahead, with God's blessing, and draw up a purchase deed" (3e). ♦ «Ну вот и хорошо, вот всё и устроилось, поезжайте с Богом» (Стругацкие 1). "There, you see, everything's worked out, have a nice trip" (1a).

2. [adv] (used when dismissing s.o. peacefully, or in order to soften a command or suggestion that s.o. leave some place) you can, you should (leave, get out of here), it would be best if (you left, got out of here): **you'd better...; you'd be best off...;** [when dismissing s.o.] **you may (go ⟨leave now etc⟩).**

«Ты иди с богом, куда хотел, а я вот с Иваном Алексеевичем напишу все эти письма...» (Гончаров 1). "You'd better go about your business, and I'll write the letters with Alexeyev..." (1a).

Б-137 • НИ БО́ГУ СВЕ́ЧКА ⟨СВЕЧА́⟩ НИ ЧЁРТУ КОЧЕРГА́ highly coll, disapprov [NP; these forms only; subj-compl with copula (subj: usu. human); fixed WO] undistinguished, mediocre, devoid of striking characteristics: X ни богу свечка ни чёрту кочерга ≃ **X is lackluster ⟨run-of-the-mill, colorless⟩; neither this nor that; neither one thing nor the other.**

Б-138 • ОДНОМУ́ БО́ГУ ⟨ГО́СПОДУ, АЛЛА́ХУ⟩ ИЗВЕ́СТНО ⟨ВЕ́ДОМО obs⟩; **ОДИ́Н (ГОСПО́ДЬ-)БОГ ЗНА́ЕТ ⟨ВЕ́ДАЕТ** obs⟩ all coll [AdjP, usu. subj-compl with бытьø, subj: a clause (1st var.); VP_subj (2nd var.); pres or past; fixed WO] (it is) unknown to anyone: **God ⟨(the) Lord, heaven⟩ only knows; God alone knows ⟨can say⟩; only God knows.**

Эх, Мора, Мора... знать бы тебе, как [твоя жена], едва ты с глаз долой, бегает в избушку кладовщика-радиста Проскурина, а чем уж они там занимаются, одному Богу известно (Максимов 2). Ah, Mora, Mora...if only you knew that as soon as your back was turned your [wife] would run off to Proskurin, the radio operator and storeman. What they did together in Proskurin's hut, God only knows... (2a). ♦ О чём покойник спрашивал, зачем он умер или зачем жил, об этом один бог ведает (Гоголь 3). What the departed had wished to know, why he died, why he had lived, God alone can say (3e). ♦ [Астров:] Одному богу известно, в чём наше настоящее призвание (Чехов 3). [A.:] Only God knows what our real vocation is (3a).

Б-139 • ОТДАВА́ТЬ/ОТДА́ТЬ БО́ГУ ДУ́ШУ euph, coll [VP; subj: human; usu. pfv] to die: X отдал богу душу ≃ **X surrendered ⟨commended, gave up⟩ his soul to God; X departed this life ⟨this world, to God's care, to the hereafter⟩; X met ⟨went to meet⟩ his Maker; X gave up the ghost.**

Бедняга Тендел объелся на юбилее своего собственного столетия и отдал богу душу (Искандер 4). Poor Tendel had overeaten at his own centennial celebration and surrendered his soul to God (4a). ♦ «Умерла Клавдия Ивановна», — сообщил заказчик. «Ну, царствие небесное, — согласился Безенчук. — Преставилась, значит, старушка... Старушки, они всегда преставляются... Или богу душу отдают, — это смотря какая старушка. Ваша, например, маленькая и в теле, — значит, преставилась. А например, которая покрупнее да похудее — та, считается, богу душу отдаёт...» (Ильф и Петров 1). "Claudia Ivanovna's dead," his client informed him. "Well, God rest her soul," said Bezenchuk. "So the old lady's passed away. Old ladies pass away...or they depart this life. It depends who she is. Yours, for instance, was small and plump, so she passed away. But if it's one who's a bit bigger and thinner, then they say she has departed this life..." (1a). ♦ «Сообщаю вам, что наш Гришка чудок не отдал богу душу, а сейчас, слава богу, находится живой и здоровый...» (Шолохов 2). "I have to inform you that our Grisha nearly gave up the ghost, but that now, thank the Lord, he's alive and well..." (2a). ♦ [Щербук:] Чуть не убили... Думал, что богу душу отдам... (Чехов 1). [context transl] [Shch.:] They nearly killed me. I honestly thought my hour had come (1a).

Б-140 • РАЗВОДИ́ТЬ БОДЯ́ГУ *highly coll* [VP; subj: human] to engage in idle talk: X разводит бодягу ≃ **X is chewing the fat ⟨the rag⟩ (with s.o.); X is shooting the breeze ⟨the bull⟩ (with s.o.).**

Б-141 • СМЕ́РТНЫМ БО́ЕМ бить *кого coll* [NP_instrum; Invar; adv (intensif); used with impfv verbs; fixed WO] (to beat s.o.) unmercifully: **beat the (living) daylights ⟨the stuffing, the tar⟩ out of s.o.; beat s.o. to a pulp; beat s.o. black-and-blue;** [in refer. to a one-time beating] **give s.o. the hiding of his life.**

...Никого из своих сыновей дедушка так не бил, как Иосифа. Бил смертным боем (Рыбаков 1). ...Grandfather never beat his other sons as much as he did Yosif. He used to beat the living daylights out of him... (1a). ♦ В этот момент Петро не помнил, что собирался бить жену смертным боем... (Шолохов 3). At that moment Petro completely forgot that he had intended to give his wife the hiding of her life (3a).

Б-142 • БО́ЖЕ ⟨БОГ⟩ (ТЫ) МОЙ! *coll* [Interj; these forms only; fixed WO] used to express surprise, disbelief, delight, fear etc: **my God ⟨goodness, heavens⟩!; good God ⟨Lord, heavens, gracious, grief⟩!; goodness gracious!; God Almighty!; oh, Lord!**

[Анна Андреевна:] Ах, боже мой, какие ты, Антоша, слова произносишь (Гоголь 4). [A.A.:] Oh, my God, what language you use, Antosha! (4a). ♦ Вот опять нам пришло на ум утерейтское-ское дело. Кто из нас, следивших за перипетиями по передачам зарубежного радио, не приходил в изумление! Боже мой, из-за чего весь сыр-бор? Президент величайшей страны собирался кого-то подслушать. Всего-навсего (Войнович 3). Once again the Watergate affair comes to mind. Who among us, following its peripeteia on the foreign radio broadcasts, was not amazed? My heavens, what was all the commotion about? The President of the greatest country on earth wanted to eavesdrop on someone. That's all there was to it (3a). ♦ «Кока, — сказал администратор Арон Маркович, — и всё-таки вам придётся поехать в Томск». — «Боже мой, но ведь у меня почти начался отпуск!» (Семёнов 1). "Coca," said the impresario, Aron Markovich, "you still have to go to Tomsk, you know." "Good God, but my holiday has practically begun!" (1a). ♦ Вас обманывали, когда говорили вам, что это [«Божественная комедия» Данте] скучно. Скучно? Боже мой, здесь целый пожар фантазии! (Олеша 3). They deceived you who said it [Dante's *Divine Comedy*] was dull. Dull? Good Lord, there's a whole fire of imagination there! (3a). ♦ «Боже мой, когда я кому-нибудь неприятен, я стараюсь обходить его десятой дорогой» (Горенштейн 1). "God Almighty, when someone dislikes *me* I do my best to steer clear of him..." (1a).

Б-143 • БО́ЖЕ УПАСИ́ *coll* [VP_imper] **1.** ~ *(кого от чего).* Also: **УПАСИ́ ⟨СОХРАНИ́, ОБОРОНИ́ *obs*⟩ БОГ ⟨ГОСПО́ДЬ⟩; БО́ЖЕ СОХРАНИ́ ⟨ОБОРОНИ́ *obs*⟩; ИЗБА́ВИ БОГ ⟨БО́ЖЕ, ГО́СПОДИ⟩** [usu. indep. sent, sent adv (parenth), or predic (with subj: infin)] used to express caution, concern that sth. undesirable may happen, or a warning to s.o. not to do sth.: **God ⟨heaven⟩ forbid; (may) God preserve ⟨save⟩ s.o. (from sth.); God ⟨heaven⟩ help s.o. (if...);** [in limited contexts] **(don't do sth.) for God's ⟨heaven's⟩ sake.**

«Если вы заботитесь о своём пищеварении, мой добрый совет — не говорите за обедом о большевизме и о медицине. И, Боже вас сохрани, не читайте до обеда советских газет» (Булгаков 11). "If you care about your digestion, my advice is—don't talk about Bolshevism or medicine at the table. And, God forbid—never read Soviet newspapers before dinner" (11b). ♦ «Избави бог его [Абуталипа] от такого [от равнодушия детей]. Хватит ему и других горестей», — подумал Едигей (Айтматов 2). "God preserve him [Abutalip] from that [from his children's indifference]. He has enough other troubles," thought Yedigei (2a). ♦ Но боже упаси тебя сделать что-нибудь из ряда вон выходящее или, страшно подумать, выдающееся! (Зиновьев 1). But God help you if you produce something out of the ordinary, or, horror of horrors, outstanding! (1a). ♦ «...Здесь распространена трахома — упаси вас господь вытираться их полотенцами!» (Рыбаков 2). "...They've got trachoma, so never dry yourself with one of their towels, for God's sake!" (2a).

2. Also: **УПАСИ́ ⟨СОХРАНИ́, ОБОРОНИ́ *obs*⟩ БОГ ⟨ГОСПО́ДЬ⟩; БО́ЖЕ СОХРАНИ́ ⟨ОБОРОНИ́ *obs*⟩; ИЗБА́ВИ БОГ ⟨БО́ЖЕ, ГО́СПОДИ⟩** [indep. sent or sent adv (parenth)] used to express an emphatic denial of sth. that is, in fact, possible or may be assumed: **God ⟨heaven⟩ forbid!**

«Я не хочу пугать тебя, но временами у меня ощущение, будто не сегодня-завтра меня арестуют». — «Сохрани Бог, Юрочка» (Пастернак 1). "I don't want to worry you, but occasionally I have the feeling that they might arrest me any day." "God forbid, Yurochka" (1a). ♦ [Они] расскажут при случае, что они, Боже упаси, не антисемиты... (Свирский 1). [They] tell you whenever the opportunity occurs that they aren't anti-Semitic, heaven forbid (1a).

3. [usu. predic (with subj: any common noun), modif, or adv (intensif)] (a person or thing is) extremely bad, awful etc, (some undesirable quality is) very strongly manifested, (some undesirable action is carried out) with extreme intensity: **God ⟨may the Lord⟩ save us ⟨you etc⟩ from such a [NP] ⟨from a [NP] like that⟩; God ⟨may the Lord⟩ spare you ⟨me etc⟩ a [NP] like that; (sth.) like I hope never to see ⟨hear etc⟩ again; goodness ⟨God⟩, how [AdjP] one ⟨sth.⟩ is; God, how...!; a God-awful [NP]; God help us.**

И все [ведьмы], сколько ни было их там, как хмельные, отплясывали какого-то чертовского трепака. Пыль подняли боже упаси какую! (Гоголь 5). And the whole bunch of them [the witches] were dancing some sort of devil's jig as though they were drunk. What a dust they raised, God help us! (5a).

Б-144 • НИ БО́ЖЕ МО́Й *coll, often humor* [sent; Invar; fixed WO] certainly not, not under any circumstances (used as an emphatic negation of sth. or a negative reply to a question): **heavens ⟨good God⟩, no!; nothing of the kind ⟨sort⟩; nothing doing; not on your life!; by no means.**

Да ведь, может, [Гриша] не догадывается? Ни боже мой! Догадывается... (Трифонов 1). Was it possible that he [Grisha] hadn't guessed? Good God, no! He knew... (1a). ♦ [Лидия:] Вы знаете в Казани мадам Чурило-Пленкову?.. Она, говорят, разошлась с мужем. [Васильков:] Ни боже мой! (Островский 4). [L.:] Do you know Madam[e] Churilo-Plenkov in Kazan?...They say she's separated from her husband. [V.:] Not on your life! (4a). ♦ «Комары?» — осведомился Лавр Федотович. «...Нету их там. Муравьи разве что…» – «Хорошо, – констатировал Лавр Федотович. – Осы? Пчёлы?»… – «Ни боже мой», – сказал комендант (Стругацкие 3). "Are there mosquitoes?" inquired Lavr Fedotovich. "None. Some ants, maybe." "Well…" Lavr Fedotovich hesitated. "Wasps? Bees?"…"By no means" (3a).

Б-145 • ПОЧИ́ТЬ В БО́ЗЕ *obs* [VP; subj: human; fixed WO] to die: X почил в бозе ≃ **X joined ⟨met, went to meet⟩ his Maker; X went the way of all flesh.**

«Но не доехав до места назначения, папаша мой не выдержал обиды своего должностного понижения и почил, как говорится, в Бозе в номере парижской гостиницы…» (Максимов 2). "Before he reached his destination, however, my papa was unable to endure the affront of his political demotion, and he joined his Maker, as they say, in a Paris hotelroom…" (2a).

Б-146 • БОЙ-БА́БА; БОЙ-ДЕ́ВКА *both coll* [NP; usu. subj-compl with быть∅ (subj: human, female)] a clever, brave, determined woman or girl: X – бой-баба ⟨бой-девка⟩ ≃ **X is one helluva ⟨hell of a⟩ woman ⟨girl⟩; X is quite a woman ⟨girl⟩; X is a real firecracker.**

Б-147 • ДАВА́ТЬ/ДАТЬ БОЙ *(кому)* [VP; subj: human or collect; fixed WO] to speak out against, criticize s.o. openly, boldly: X дал бой (Y-у) ≃ **X rose up (in arms) against Y; X put up a fight; X crossed swords with Y; X gave battle to Y;** [in limited contexts] **X took a stand against Y.**

«Еще в тридцать четвёртом году группа пролетарских писателей давала бой Бухарину, сказавшему, что надо ориентироваться на Пастернака» (Ивинская 1). "Already in 1934 a group of proletarian writers rose up in arms against Bukharin for saying that everyone should take their cue from Pasternak…" (1a).

Б-148 • ОБЪЯВЛЯ́ТЬ/ОБЪЯВИ́ТЬ БОЙ *чему* [VP; subj: human or collect; fixed WO] to initiate a struggle, begin taking organized action (against sth. – usu. some negative phenomenon): X объявил бой Y-у ≃ **X declared war on Y; X waged war against ⟨on⟩ Y; X began a campaign against Y; X started a crusade against Y.**

Директор заявил, что пора объявить бой пьянству. The director announced that it was time to declare war on drunkenness.

Б-149 • РВА́ТЬСЯ В БОЙ [VP; subj: human or collect] to be keen on doing sth. and/or show one's eagerness to act decisively (in defense of some idea, stand etc, or in order to prove one is right, defeat one's opponent etc): X рвётся в бой ≃ **X is champing at the bit; X is raring to go ⟨to get into the thick of things** etc⟩; **X is itching to get into the action;** [in limited contexts] **X wants to plunge ahead.**

Б-150 • БОК О́ БОК; О́ БОК *both coll* [these forms only; the resulting phrase is adv] **1.** ~ *с кем-чем* **идти, ехать, стоять, находиться** и т. п. (to walk, ride, stand, be etc) next to each other, right beside (s.o. or sth.): **side by side (with); alongside (of); abreast;** [in limited contexts] **cheek by jowl (with).**

…Семён Тетерин и Дудырев, прислонив ружья к стволу берёзы, бок о бок отдыхают, отмахиваются от комаров (Тендряков 1). …Simon Teterin and Dudyrev, with their guns leaning against the trunk of a birch tree, were resting side by side, waving away the mosquitoes (1a). ♦ «Просьба у меня ко всем. Если такое случится, похороните здесь меня, вот тут, бок о бок с Казангапом» (Айтматов 2). "I have a request to you all. If anything happens, bury me here, side by side with Kazangap" (2a). ♦ Бок о бок со мной кипела работа… (Лившиц 1). Alongside of me work was going on in full swing… (1a). ♦ Лошади их шли шагом бок о бок, и Григорий искоса посматривал на Копылова, на его доб-

родушное лицо… (Шолохов 5). They were riding abreast. Grigory glanced sideways at Kopylov's good-natured face… (5a).

2. ~ *(с кем)* **жить, работать, воевать** и т. п. (of people only) (to live, work, fight etc) together: **side by side (with); shoulder to shoulder (with);** [in limited contexts] **cheek by jowl (with).**

Абхазцы… всегда отличались рыцарским отношением к женщине, тем более сейчас, при советской власти, когда равноправные мужчины и женщины бок о бок работают на стройках и колхозных полях (Искандер 3). Abkhazians…had always been noted for their chivalrous treatment of women, especially now, under Soviet rule, when men and women worked side by side with equal rights at construction sites and in kolkhoz fields (3a). ♦ «Поживу дома, а там услышу, как будут они идтить [*ungrammat* = идти] мимо, и пристану к полку», – отстранённо думал он о тех, с кем сражался вчера бок о бок (Шолохов 4). "I'll have a spell at home and then, when I hear them going past, I'll slip out and join them," he thought indifferently of those with whom only the day before he had been fighting shoulder to shoulder (4a).

Б-151 • (БРАТЬ/ВЗЯТЬ) ЗА БОКА́ *кого highly coll* [VP (with subj: human) or PrepP (used as predic, often as imper)] **1.** to censure, blame s.o., holding him responsible for sth. he has done wrong: X взял Y-а за бока ≃ **X called Y to account; X had Y on the carpet; X took Y to task.**

2. to compel, force s.o. to do sth.: X взял Y-а за бока ≃ **X put ⟨turned⟩ the heat on Y; X put the screws on Y; X strong-armed Y; X twisted Y's arm; X put pressure on Y.**

[Авдотья Назаровна:] Шутка ли, с пяти часов сижу, а она [Зинаида Савишна] хоть бы ржавою селёдкой попотчевала!.. [1-й гость:] …Со скуки да с голоду волком завоешь и людей грызть начнёшь… [Авдотья Назаровна:] Пойдём поищем, что ли… [1-й гость:] Тсс!.. Потихоньку! Шнапс, кажется, в столовой, в буфете стоит. Мы Егорушку за бока… Тсс!.. (Чехов 4). [A.N.:] It's no joke, I've been sitting here since five o'clock, and she [Zinaida Savishna] hasn't offered me so much as a piece of moldy herring!… [First Guest:] …I'm so bored and hungry, I could howl like a wolf and start gnawing on someone…. [A.N.:] Let's go and see if we can find— [First Guest:] Sh!…Quietly. I think there's some schnapps on the sideboard in the dining room. We'll put the screws on Yegorushka….Sh!… (4a). ♦ Не приехал бы некий Виктор в гости к брату, тот не выпил бы лишку и не умер, тётя Глаша не отдала бы иконы, Гартвиг их не привёз бы, Нюра не стала бы просить старую икону в больницу как раз в тот момент, когда приятели Кирилла взяли его за бока, и не случилось бы всего остального… (Трифонов 5). If a certain Viktor hadn't come to visit his brother, the brother wouldn't have drunk too much and died, Aunt Glasha wouldn't have given up her ikons, Gartvig wouldn't have brought them to us, Nyura wouldn't have started asking for the old ikon in the hospital just at the moment when Kirill's friends were putting pressure on him, and none of the rest would have happened… (5a).

Б-152 • НАМЯ́ТЬ ⟨НАЛОМА́ТЬ⟩ БОКА́ *кому substand* [VP; subj: human] **1.** Also: **ПОМЯ́ТЬ ⟨ОБЛОМА́ТЬ, НАГРЕ́ТЬ⟩ БОКА́** *кому substand* (often used as a threat) to beat, thrash s.o.: X намнёт Y-у бока ≃ **X will break Y's ribs; X will crack ⟨break⟩ a few of Y's ribs; X will knock Y around; X will beat Y up.**

«Бока ему [Егорше] наломать надо! С пьяных глаз зашёл к нам – Лизавету за него отдайте» (Абрамов 1). "I've got to crack a few ribs for him [Egorsha]! He comes to our house in his cups: 'Give me Lizaveta to marry,' he says" (1a).

2. [subj: human (usu. pl) or collect] to overwhelm, defeat s.o. (usu. a hostile army, the enemy): X-ы намяли Y-ам бока ≃ **Xs crushed ⟨routed, clobbered⟩ Ys.**

3. to scold s.o. severely, criticize s.o. harshly: X намял Y-у бока ≃ **X let Y have it (with both barrels); X gave Y what for; X came down hard on Y; X gave Y a tongue-lashing.**

Б-153 • ПОДНИМА́ТЬ/ПОДНЯ́ТЬ БОКА́Л(Ы) *за кого-что* [VP; subj: human] to offer a toast to or drink in honor of s.o. or sth.: X поднял бокал за Y-a ≃ **X drank to Y; X raised a ⟨his⟩ glass (to Y); X proposed a toast to Y; X held his glass high (in congratulation** etc).

До гроба, до поздних дней благодарный воспитанник, подняв бокал в день рождения своего чудного воспитателя, уже давно бывшего в могиле, оставался, закрыв глаза, и лил слёзы по нём (Гоголь 3). To the grave, to the very last days, the grateful pupil would raise a glass on the birthday of his wonderful teacher though he had long been in his grave, and closing his eyes, he would weep for him (3a).

Б-154 • ОТДУВА́ТЬСЯ СВОИ́МИ ⟨СО́БСТВЕН-НЫМИ⟩ БОКА́МИ *(за кого-что) coll* [VP; subj: human] to bear the negative consequences of sth. (usu. someone else's error, wrongdoing etc): X отдувается своими боками ≃ **X takes the rap (for sth.); X bears the brunt (of sth.); X pays with his own skin.**

«Вот и скифская война. Это всё хорошо, только не для тех, кто своими боками отдувается» (Толстой 6). "This is certainly Scythian warfare. It's all [very] fine—except for those who bear the [brunt] of it" (6a).

Б-155 • НА БОКОВУ́Ю *пора, отправиться* и т. п. *coll* [PrepP; Invar; adv (with the infin implied)] (it is time to, s.o. has to etc) go to sleep, (to leave some company etc to) go to bed: **(it's time etc to) hit the sack ⟨hit the hay, turn in, sack out, get some Zs⟩.**

«Теперь притащу Зосимова, он вам отрапортует, а затем и вы на боковую. Заморились, я вижу, донельзя» (Достоевский 3). "Now I'm going to get Zosimov. He'll report to you. Then you better hit the sack yourselves. I can see you're exhausted" (3b). ♦ [Сатин:] Теперь — выпей! [Клещ:] Спасибо! Да и на боковую пора... (Горький 3). [S.:] Now—bottoms up! [K.:] Thanks! And I guess it's time to turn in... (3a).

Б-156 • ВЫХОДИ́ТЬ/ВЫ́ЙТИ БО́КОМ *кому coll* [VP; subj: abstr or, less often, human, animal, or concr] to bring trouble to s.o.: X вышел Y-у боком ≃ **X gave ⟨caused⟩ Y (a lot of ⟨considerable etc⟩) trouble; thing X turned out bad(ly) for Y; X did Y (a lot of ⟨plenty of etc⟩) harm;** [in limited contexts] **Y ended up in trouble (because of X); Y got hurt when thing X misfired;** [in refer. to one's own mistake, misjudgment etc] **thing X boomeranged ⟨backfired, came home to roost⟩.**

...Подписку на заём в Пекашине из-за похорон Трофима Лобанова... пришлось отложить на два дня... «Этот старик нам ещё выйдет боком», — хмуро заметил Ганичев (Абрамов 1). ...Owing to the funeral of Trofim Lobanov...the Loan pledging had had to be postponed for two days.... "Dead or not, that old man'll give us trouble yet," said Ganichev grimly (1a). ♦ «Совсем он [Айрапет] отощал на этом деле». — «И про жену даже забыл, — добавил Лёня и посмотрел куда-то в угол. — Боком ему может выйти эта нефть» (Аксёнов 1). "He's [Airapet has] worn himself to a frazzle over this thing." "And forgotten about his wife, even," Lenya added, looking across the room. "This oil thing may turn out bad for him" (1a). ♦ ...Даже при встречах со знакомыми он избегал разговоров о политике. Хватит с него этой политики, она и так выходила ему боком (Шолохов 5). Even when meeting acquaintances he avoided any political discussion. He had had enough of politics; they had done him enough harm already (5a). ♦ «Ты ведёшь себя неправильно, — сказал Корытов. — ...Смотри, это боком может выйти» (Зиновьев 2). "Your conduct is unbecoming," said Korytov. "...Take care or you could end up in trouble" (2a). ♦ «Все наши российские горе-преобразователи, вроде Петра и его марксистских поклонников, умерли с чувством выполненного долга... а прожекты ихние [ungrammat = их] нам боком выходят» (Максимов 3). "All our crackpot Russian reformers, like Peter and his Marxist admirers, have died with a sense of duty well

done...and we're the ones who get hurt when their bright ideas misfire" (3a). ♦ ...Я написал в предисловии, что «считаю своим приятным долгом поблагодарить сотрудников КГБ и прокуратуры» за то, что они мою рукопись не изъяли, но мои насмешки вышли боком: некоторые на Западе приняли мою благодарность всерьёз (Амальрик 1). ...I said in my foreword that I felt pleasantly obliged to thank the KGB agents and the prosecutor's office for not having confiscated my manuscript. But my little joke at the expense of the KGB boomeranged: some people in the West took my expression of gratitude seriously (1a).

Б-157 • ПОД БО́КОМ ⟨ПО́Д БОКОМ⟩ *(у кого) coll* [PrepP; these forms only; adv or subj-compl with copula (subj: concr, a geographical name, a noun denoting an organization etc, or human] very near, in immediate proximity: **close ⟨near⟩ at hand; (right) close by; nearby ⟨near by⟩;** [in limited contexts] **right there ⟨here⟩; in s.o.'s immediate neighborhood; just ⟨right⟩ around the corner; (right) at s.o.'s side; (right) under s.o.'s nose; at ⟨on⟩ s.o.'s doorstep.**

...Стрелецкая слобода была у него под боком и он мог прибыть туда через полчаса (Салтыков-Щедрин 1). ...The Musketeers District was right close by and he could have been there in half an hour (1a). ♦ Тем была люба война на восстании, что под боком у каждого бойца был родимый курень. Надоедало ходить в заставы и секреты, надоедало в разъездах мотаться по буграм и перевалам, — казак отпрашивался у сотенного, ехал домой... (Шолохов 4). The one good thing about the insurgent war was that every Cossack had a home near by. When he grew tired of outpost duty or riding on patrol over hill and dale, he could ask permission of his squadron commander and go home... (4a). ♦ ...При нужде можно весь урожай одним мешком перетаскать — огород под боком... (Распутин 4). ...If you had to you could drag the entire harvest in one sack—for the garden was right there... (4a). ♦ ...Никак нельзя допустить, что господин Ратабон по рассеянности не заметил, что под боком у него играют актёры... (Булгаков 5). It surely cannot be assumed that Monsieur Ratabon had absent-mindedly failed to notice the actors playing in his immediate neighborhood... (5a). ♦ Приятно, в самом деле, иметь у себя под боком подземный мраморный дворец (Аксёнов 6). It really is very pleasant to have one's own subterranean marble palace just around the corner (6a). ♦ Всё ясно: Сталин хочет забрать его [Кирова] из Ленинграда, хочет иметь его под боком в Москве, хочет полного подчинения (Рыбаков 2). It was quite clear: Stalin wanted him [Kirov] out of Leningrad, he wanted him at his side in Moscow where he could keep him under full control (2a). ♦ Он опасался поначалу, не окажется ли его будущий зять с завихрениями, с интеллигентскими выкрутасами. Только такого ему не хватало под боком! (Ерофеев 3). [context transl] He had been worried at first that his future son-in-law would turn out to be one of those weird types with intellectual pretensions. That was all he needed—one of those right in his own family! (3a).

Б-158 • ЛЕЖА́ТЬ НА БОКУ́ ⟨НА ПЕЧИ́, НА ПЕ́ЧКЕ⟩ *coll* [VP; subj: human] to do nothing, be idle: X лежит на боку ≃ **X loafs (around); X lounges ⟨sits⟩ around.**

Б-159 • ПО́ БОКУ *кого-что highly coll* [PrepP; Invar; used as predic (with subj: human or impers), usu. in past or fut contexts, often as imper; if obj: inanim, it is usu. abstr] to free o.s. of s.o. or sth. (by getting rid of s.o., putting sth. to the side etc): X Y-a по боку ≃ [past context] **X dropped ⟨ditched⟩ Y; X got rid of person Y; X got person Y out of X's way ⟨hair⟩; X put ⟨set⟩ thing Y aside;** [in limited contexts] **there is no room for thing Y;** ‖ *Imper* Y-a по боку ≃ **to ⟨the⟩ hell with Y.**

«Меня от зарезанной курицы с души воротит, а здесь не курица – душа живая. Полномочия даны, а рука поднимется ли?» А полномочия ему даны были... недвусмысленные: жалость по боку (Максимов 3). "Seeing a hen's throat slit turns my stomach and this is a human being. I've been given full powers, but can

I bring myself to do it?" The full powers he'd been given were...unambiguous: there was no room for pity (3a).

Б-160 • ПОДХОДИ́ТЬ/ПОДОЙТИ́ С ДРУГО́ГО БО́КУ ⟨-а⟩ *(к кому-чему) coll* [VP; subj: human; the verb may take the final position, otherwise fixed WO] to try a different method of addressing s.o. or some matter: X подошёл к Y-у с другого боку ≃ **X tried a different approach with person Y ⟨to thing Y⟩; X looked at thing Y from a different ⟨another⟩ angle ⟨point of view, standpoint⟩.**

«А теперь, если с другого боку подойти: ведь наша дирекция совхоза только цифру понимает» (Гинзбург 2). "Look at it from another angle—the only thing our management understands is figures" (2a).

Б-161 • С БО́КУ НА́ БОК [PrepP; Invar; adv; fixed WO]
1. ~ ворочаться, переворачиваться и т. п. to be unable to sleep and keep changing the position one is lying in so as to get comfortable enough to fall asleep: X ворочался ~ ≃ **X turned ⟨tossed⟩ from side to side; X tossed and turned.**

Если Обломов поедет в театр или засидится у Ивана Герасимовича и долго не едет, ей не спится, она ворочается с боку на бок... (Гончаров 1). If Oblomov went to the theater or was late in coming home from Ivan Gerasimovich's, she was unable to sleep and tossed from side to side... (1b).

2. переваливаться ~ to walk in an awkward, swaying fashion: X переваливался ~ **X waddled (like a duck); X walked like a duck.**

Семёновна давно уже ждала невестку, чтобы сделать себе наконец послабление, и, дождавшись, расхворалась, у неё стали сильно отекать ноги, ходила она тяжело, переваливаясь с боку на бок, как утка (Распутин 2). Semyonovna had been waiting for a daughter-in-law for a long time so that she could relax a little, and when she finally got one she fell very sick, her legs swelled badly, and she walked with difficulty, waddling like a duck (2a).

Б-162 • С КАКО́ГО БО́КУ ⟨-а⟩ рассматривать *что,* интересовать *кого* и т. п. *coll* [PrepP; these forms only; adv; used in questions and subord clauses; fixed WO] from which aspect, in what relation: ~ X рассматривает Y? ≃ **from which angle ⟨side, direction, perspective⟩ does X look at Y?; [in limited contexts] how does X look at Y?; ‖ ~ X-а интересует Y? ≃ why should Y interest X?; in what way ⟨on what account⟩ does Y interest X?**

«Ты что, поссорился с Верой?» — «А тебя-то это с какого боку интересует?» "What happened, did you have a fight with Vera?" "Why should that interest you?"

Б-163 • (не знать, думать и т. п.,) С КАКО́ГО БО́КУ ⟨-а, С КАКО́Й СТОРОНЫ́⟩ ПОДОЙТИ́ ⟨ПОДСТУПИ́-ТЬСЯ⟩ *к кому coll* [subord clause; these forms only; fixed WO] (not to know, to wonder etc) how to address s.o. with sth. and/or whether s.o. is approachable: **(not know ⟨not be sure⟩) how to approach s.o.; (wonder) what would be the best approach to take with s.o.; (wonder ⟨not know⟩) which tack to try with s.o.; [in limited contexts] (be afraid) to come ⟨go⟩ near s.o.**

Он думал, с какой стороны лучше подойти к Лукину... (Войнович 6). He was wondering what the best approach to take with Lukin (6a). ♦ «...Не знаешь, с какого бока к тебе и подойти». — «Да ну!» (Абрамов 1). "We're afraid to come near you nowadays." "Come off it!" (1a).

Б-164 • БО́ЛЕЕ ИЛИ МЕ́НЕЕ [AdvP; Invar; fixed WO]
1. [modif] somewhat, relatively (but not completely): **more or less.**

Было непонятно, во-первых, как он [котёл] здесь очутился, а во-вторых, как он уцелел... Только успели найти более или

менее толковое объяснение этому чуду — было решено, что божество четвероногих подбросило этот котёл, чтобы крестьяне не расстраивались... (Искандер 3). They could not understand, in the first place, how it [the kettle] had gotten here, and in the second place, how it had survived....They could find only one more or less sensible explanation for this miracle: it was decided that the god of the four-legged had surreptitiously placed the kettle here so that the peasants would not fall into confusion... (3a). ♦ Он [старшина Песков] перебрал в уме все места, где мог бы быть Трофимович, но тот мог быть где угодно, и придумать сейчас что-нибудь более или менее вероятное старшине не так-то просто (Войнович 2). [context transl] He [Master Sergeant Peskov] mentally reviewed all the places Trofimovich could possibly be, but he could be anywhere and Peskov found it difficult to come up with one place which was any more likely than another (2a).

2. [adv] to a relatively large extent (but not completely): **more or less.**

«Ты ей доверяешь?» — «Более или менее». "Do you trust her?" "More or less."

Б-165 • БО́ЛЕЕ ⟨БО́ЛЬШЕ⟩ ТОГО́ [these forms only; usu. sent adv; fixed WO] in addition to and beyond what has just been stated (used to indicate the significance of the statement that follows): **(and) what is more; more than that; and not only that; moreover; on top of that; [in limited contexts] even worse.**

...Он [юный негодяй] при всём своём нахальстве никак не мог там [в доме дяди Сандро] показаться. Более того. Ему пришлось совсем уехать из наших мест (Искандер 3). ...Despite his considerable effrontery, he [the young reprobate] did not dare make an appearance there [at Uncle Sandro's]. More than that, he had to get out of our part of the world altogether (3a). ♦ ...С момента исключения [из Союза писателей] и до самого моего отъезда в декабре 1980 года ни в одной советской газете моё имя не было упомянуто ни разу. Больше того, чиновники из Союза писателей делали вид, что они о таком писателе даже не слышали... (Войнович 1). ...From the moment I was expelled [from the Writers' Union] until I left the country, in December 1980, my name was not mentioned in a single Soviet newspaper. Moreover, the officials in the Writers' Union pretended not to have ever heard of a writer named Voinovich... (1a). ♦ ...Остаётся признать, что сюринтендант Ратабон умышленно не предупредил труппу об уничтожении театра. Более того, он скрыл всякие приготовления к этому... (Булгаков 5). We must...conclude that Superintendent Ratabon had deliberately refrained from informing the company of the imminent demolition of its theater. Even worse, he concealed all the preparations for this action... (5a).

Б-166 • БО́ЛЕЕ ⟨БО́ЛЬШЕ⟩ ЧЕМ... [AdvP; these forms only; modif (intensif); fixed WO] extremely, to the highest degree: **more than [AdjP]; a more-than-[AdjP + NP]; [in limited contexts] (s.o. ⟨sth.⟩) couldn't be more [AdjP]; (s.o. ⟨sth.⟩ is) nothing if not [AdjP]; stranger than strange ⟨better than good, worse than bad etc⟩.**

...[Наши предки] остались верными начальстволюбию и только слегка позволили себе пособолезновать и попенять на своего более чем странного градоначальника (Салтыков-Щедрин 1). They [our forebears] remained faithful to archophilism, and only in passing allowed themselves to complain and reproach their more-than-strange town governor (1a). ♦ Ваше предложение более чем своевременно. Your suggestion is nothing if not timely.

Б-167 • ВСЁ БО́ЛЕЕ И БО́ЛЕЕ; ВСЁ БО́ЛЬШЕ И БО́ЛЬШЕ [AdvP; these forms only; adv (intensif); fixed WO] used to show increasing intensification of some action, feeling etc: **more and more.**

Он [Обломов] каждый день всё более и более дружился с хозяйкой: о любви и в ум ему не приходило... Он сближался с Агафьей Матвеевной — как будто подвигался к огню, от которого становится всё теплее и теплее, но которого любить нельзя (Гончаров 1). He [Oblomov] was becoming more and more friendly with [his landlady] every day; the thought of love never entered his head....He simply drew closer to Agafya Matveyevna as to a fire which makes one feel warmer and warmer, but is not loved (1b).

Б-168 • НЕ БОЛЕЕ ⟨НЕ БОЛЬШЕ⟩ (ТОГО) [these forms only; usu. sent adv (parenth); fixed WO] just what was stated, named, and not sth. more significant: **(and) nothing more; (and) that's all;** [in limited contexts] **(and) that's the extent of it.**

«А смерть... вы её, вероятно, видали близко в своей жизни... ведь она только смерть, не более» (Богданов 1). "As for death....I am sure you have seen it close up sometime in your life. Death, after all, is only that and nothing more" (1a). ♦ [Зилов:] Я женат... но мы с ней давно уже чужие люди, добрые друзья. Не больше (Вампилов 5). [Z.:] I'm married...but my wife and I have been strangers to each other for a long time. We're friends, good friends. That's all (5a).

Б-169 • БОЛЕЗНИ РОСТА [NP; fixed WO] **1.** [usu. pl] the emotional problems and rebelliousness one experiences during adolescence: **growing pains.**

2. [pl only] difficulties that arise in the developmental stages of an enterprise, a new phenomenon in social life etc: **growing pains.**

Б-170 • У КОГО ЧТО ⟨ЧТО У КОГО⟩ БОЛИТ, ТОТ О ТОМ И ГОВОРИТ [saying] a person unceasingly talks about what disturbs or concerns him: ≃ **you (always) talk about what ails you; the tongue ever turns to the ailing tooth.**

Извините, я долго задержался на этом, но у людей слабость говорить о своём деле. У кого что болит, тот о том и говорит, хотя, может быть, другого твои болячки не интересуют (Рыбаков 1). I'm sorry for going on about it, but then, everybody likes to talk about their profession, or as the saying goes, you talk about what ails you, though maybe your problems are not so interesting to anyone else (1a).

Б-171 • НУ ТЕБЯ ⟨его и т. п.⟩ В БОЛОТО! *highly coll, rather rude when addressed to the interlocutor* [Interj; these forms only; fixed WO] used to express irritation, anger, contempt directed at s.o. or sth., or a desire to be rid of s.o. or sth.: ну X-а в болото! ≃ **to hell ⟨to blazes⟩ with X!; to the devil with X!; (let X) go to hell ⟨to the devil⟩!; (let person X) go jump in the lake!; (why doesn't person X) beat it ⟨get lost⟩!**

«Пойти, что ль, пожрать. Ну их в болото», – решил пёс и вдруг получил сюрприз (Булгаков 11). Guess I'll go and eat something. To hell with them all, decided the dog, when he suddenly got a surprise (11a). ♦ «Почему, собственно, я так взволновался из-за того, что Берлиоз попал под трамвай? – рассуждал поэт. – В конечном счёте, ну его в болото!» (Булгаков 9). "Properly speaking, why did I get so upset when Berlioz fell under the streetcar?" the poet argued. "In the final analysis, to blazes with him!" (9a).

Б-172 • ВСЁ БОЛЬШЕ [AdvP; Invar; usu. adv; more often this WO] mainly, predominantly: **mostly; for the most part;** [in limited contexts] **most of...**

Тут же забрался и Фавори, но говорил мало, а всё больше слушал (Салтыков-Щедрин 2). Favori was also there, but he spoke little and mostly listened (2a). ♦ «Сколько ты времени провёл здесь всего?» – спросил Аркадий. «Года два сряду; потом мы наезжали. Мы вели бродячую жизнь; больше всё по городам шлялись» (Тургенев 2). "How long did you live here altogether?" asked Arkady. "Two years on end; then we travelled about. We led a roving life, wandering from town to town for the most part" (2b). ♦ «...Сюда всё больше шпана, рвачи, золотая рота за длинным рублём налетела...» (Максимов 1). "...Most of the people we get here these days are riff-raff, rabble, tramps on the lookout for easy money" (1a).

Б-173 • САМОЕ БОЛЬШЕЕ ⟨БОЛЬШОЕ⟩ [AdjP; these forms only; used as a restr marker; fixed WO] to an amount or extent not exceeding the one specified: **at (the) most; at the very most; no more than...**

[Ирина:] Он старый? [Тузенбах:] Нет, ничего. Самое большее лет сорок, сорок пять (Чехов 5). [I.:] Is he old? [T.:] No, not really. Forty – forty-five at most (5b). ♦ Господин полковник был немногим старше самого Турбина – было ему лет тридцать, самое большее тридцать два (Булгаков 3). The colonel was slightly older than Aleksei Turbin himself – about thirty, or thirty-two at the most (3a). ♦ «Я устроюсь скоро, очень скоро, Мари». – «Ну, как ты думаешь, с полгода, или...» – «...Месяца два, самое большее...» (Федин 1). "I'll get settled quickly, very quickly, Marie." "Well what do you think, in six months, or...?" "...Two months at the very most..." (1a).

Б-174 • В БОЛЬШИНСТВЕ (СВОЁМ) [PrepP; these forms only; nonagreeing modif or sent adv; fixed WO] the significantly larger part of (a specific group of people or things): **for the most part; mostly; the majority (of); most (of); the greater part of; predominantly.**

В приёмной было людно, посетители, в большинстве женщины, стояли в очереди у окошечкам... (Гроссман 2.) There were lots of people there [in the reception-room]; the visitors, mostly women, were standing in line in front of the windows (2a). ♦ ...Когда я познакомился ещё с несколькими его коллегами, я заметил, что кагебешники... в большинстве своём очень обидчивы (Войнович 1). ...When I got to know others of his colleagues in the KGB, I observed that the majority are quick to take offense (1a). ♦ ...Русские социал-демократы в большинстве своём пошли за большевиками... (Рыбаков 2). ...Most Russian Social Democrats had sided with the Bolsheviks... (2a). ♦ В большинстве офицеры были молодые, лишь у нескольких инеем белела седина (Шолохов 3). Most of the officers were young men; only a few were touched with a frosty grey (3a). ♦ «По ленинским местам» фильм должен был называться или как-то в этом духе, я... точно не помню. А места эти, ленинские, они, как известно, в большинстве своём за рубежами нашей отчизны находятся. Потому что товарищ Ленин в своё время был тоже как бы невозвращенец (Войнович 1). I don't remember exactly what it [the film] was to be called – "In the Footsteps of Lenin" – something like that. As we know, the greater part of those footsteps occurred outside the borders of our country. Because Comrade Lenin at one time had been something of a defector himself (1a).

Б-175 • ПО БОЛЬШОЙ играть, ходить *coll* [PrepP; Invar; adv] (to play cards) for large sums of money: X играет по большой ≃ **X plays for high stakes.**

Б-176 • САМ БОЛЬШОЙ *obs, substand* [AdjP; Invar; subj-compl with быть∅ (subj: human, male); fixed WO] (one is) entirely independent in his actions and judgments, acts as he chooses: X сам большой ≃ **X is his own boss ⟨master, man⟩.**

Б-177 • ПО БОЛЬШОМУ *euph, coll;* **ПО ТЯЖЁЛОМУ** *army slang* [PrepP; these forms only; adv (with the infin implied), usu. with хотеть, нужно etc) to move one's bowels: **do one's business; do ⟨go, make⟩ number two; take a crap.**

Б-178 • ВЛЕТАТЬ/ВЛЕТЕТЬ БОМБОЙ ⟨КАК БОМБА⟩ *coll* [VP; subj: human; usu. pfv] to run into some place swiftly, hurriedly: X влетел как бомба ≃ **X flew ⟨burst⟩ in like a bolt of lightning; X barreled in.**

Б-179 • С БОРОДОЙ *coll* [PrepP; Invar; nonagreeing modif or subj-compl with copula (subj: анекдот, шутка etc)] (of an anecdote, joke etc) old, stale, hackneyed: **so old it has whiskers ⟨moss⟩ on it; as old as the hills; a chestnut; (pretty) tired.**

Б-180 • В БО́РОДУ ⟨В УСЫ́⟩ смеяться, усмехаться и т. п. *coll* [PrepP; these forms only; adv] (to laugh) to o.s., (grin) unnoticeably etc: **laugh in ⟨grin into, chuckle into⟩ one's beard; laugh up ⟨in⟩ one's sleeve.**

А вор-новотор, сделавши такое пакостное дело, стоит, брюхо поглаживает да в бороду усмехается (Салтыков-Щедрин 1). And Thief-Among-Thieves, though he'd done such a dastardly deed, stands rubbing his belly and grinning into his beard (1a). ♦ ...К осени [Прокофий] увёл на новое хозяйство сгорбленную иноземку-жену. Шёл с ней за арбой с имуществом по хутору — высыпали на улицу все от мала до велика. Казаки посмеивались в бороды... (Шолохов 2). ...By autumn he [Prokofy] was able to take his bowed foreign wife to her new home. As he walked with her behind a wagon carrying all their belongings, the whole village, young and old, came out to watch. The men chuckled quietly into their beards... (2a).

Б-181 • ЗА ЧТО БОРО́ЛИСЬ, НА ТО И НАПОРО́ЛИСЬ [saying, contempt.] what we (you etc) have fought for and achieved has turned out to work against us (you etc): ≃ **what we ⟨you, they⟩ fought for has been our ⟨your, their⟩ undoing.**

Парадокс — я, который хочет нового больше всех, сам оказался жертвой этих новых отношений между мужчиной и женщиной. За что боролись — на то и напоролись (Лимонов 1). A paradox. I myself, who want the new more than anyone, proved to be the victim of these new relationships between man and woman. "What we fought for has been our undoing" (1a).

Б-182 • БОРО́ТЬСЯ С ⟨САМИ́М⟩ СОБО́Й [VP; subj: human] to try to overcome a certain feeling or desire in o.s., try to resolve an inner conflict: X боролся с собой ≃ **X struggled ⟨wrestled⟩ with himself; X did battle with himself; X fought an internal battle;** [in limited contexts] **X tried to stop himself (from doing sth.); X tried to force himself (to do sth.).**

Космонавт вообще любил драться. Вернее, не то чтобы любил — приходилось. Когда он видел какую-нибудь «морду», ему всегда хотелось врезать в неё. Он боролся с собой, воспитывал себя, но не получалось (Евтушенко 2). The cosmonaut liked fighting in general. Actually, it wasn't that he liked to fight—he had to. Whenever he saw a troublemaker, he wanted to smash his ugly face. He tried to stop himself, practiced self-control, but it didn't help (2a).

Б-183 • ВЫБРА́СЫВАТЬ/ВЫ́БРОСИТЬ ⟨БРОСА́ТЬ/БРО́СИТЬ, ВЫКИ́ДЫВАТЬ/ВЫ́КИНУТЬ, ВЫШВЫ́РИВАТЬ/ВЫ́ШВЫРНУТЬ⟩ ЗА́ БОРТ *кого-что* [VP; subj: human or collect; often past passive Part выброшен, выброшенный etc; usu. this WO] to dispose of sth. considered useless, dismiss s.o. considered unsuitable: X выбросил Y-a за борт ≃ **X threw Y overboard ⟨over the side⟩; X jettisoned Y;** [in contexts of firing] **X gave person Y the boot ⟨the sack, the ax⟩.**

Неперестроившихся делили на две группы: одним следовало помочь, других — выбросить за борт, как безнадёжных (Мандельштам 2). The "unreformed" were divided into two groups: those who could be "helped" to see the light and those it only remained to throw overboard as incorrigible (2a).

Б-184 • ЗА БОРТО́М оказаться, остаться, очутиться [PrepP; Invar; subj-compl with copula (subj: usu. human or concr)] (to end up being) rejected, not included in sth.: X оказался за бортом ≃ **X was left out (of sth.); X was thrown out; person X was counted out; person X was left on the sidelines ⟨out in the cold⟩.**

В третий «Камень» Мандельштам вернул несколько стихотворений, которые раньше оставались за бортом... (Мандельштам 2). In the third edition of *Stone* M[andelstam] included a few poems he had left out in the previous editions... (2a).

Б-185 • С БО́РУ ДА С СО́СЕНКИ набрать, собрать *кого-что,* **собраться и т. п.; С БО́РУ ПО СО́СЕНКЕ; И С БО́РУ И С СО́СЕНКИ** *all coll, disapprov* [PrepP; these forms only; adv or subj-compl with copula (subj: human or concr); fixed WO] (to assemble people or, less often, things, or to come together) unsystematically, arbitrarily: **take ⟨choose⟩ people etc) at random ⟨randomly, haphazardly⟩; a random collection ⟨assortment⟩;** [in limited contexts] **scratch crew ⟨team⟩; a mixed bag ⟨bunch⟩.**

На каждом объекте люди с бору да сосенки, во всём ни складу ни ладу... (Иоффе 1). People are chosen at random to do certain jobs, no rhyme or reason to it at all (1a). ♦ Начали раздражаться и свариться не только оттого, что перепились, но и оттого, что собрались в кучу не друзья, а с бору по сосенке (Трифонов 2). They began to get heated and quarrelsome not just because they had drunk too much but also because it wasn't a gathering of friends, rather just a random collection (2a).

Б-186 • СО́РОК БО́ЧЕК АРЕСТА́НТОВ наговорить *highly coll* [NP$_{accus}$; Invar; obj; fixed WO] (to produce) an outpouring of (usu. empty) words: **(a lot of) hot air; (a lot of) garbage ⟨blather⟩.**

Б-187 • БЕЗДО́ННАЯ БО́ЧКА *coll* [NP; sing only; fixed WO]
1. [usu. subj-compl with copula, nom or instrum (subj: human)] a person who can drink a lot of alcohol without getting drunk: X — бездонная бочка ≃ **X drinks like he's got a hollow leg; X can really hold his liquor.**
2. [subj-compl with copula, nom or instrum (subj: usu. a noun denoting an enterprise) or obj] sth. that requires perpetual monetary investments (which fail to bring about the desired result): **X is like a bottomless pit; X sucks up s.o.'s money; spending money on X is like pouring your money down the drain.**

Б-188 • БО́ЧКА ДАНАИ́Д *lit* [NP; sing only; fixed WO] futile, endless work: **Danaidean task.**

< From Greek mythology. The Danaidae were the 50 daughters of Danaus, 49 of whom were condemned eternally to pour water into a leaky vessel in Hades for having killed their husbands on their wedding night.

Б-189 • КАК БО́ЧКА *highly coll* [как + NP; Invar] **1. пить** ~ [adv (intensif)] (to drink liquor) in large quantities: **like a fish ⟨a sailor⟩; like there's no tomorrow.**
2. толстый ~ [modif (intensif)] extremely rotund: **(be) (as) fat as a (stuffed) pig; (look ⟨be⟩) like the side of a house; (be) as round as a barrel; (be) (as) big as a blimp ⟨a balloon⟩.**

Б-190 • ПОРОХОВА́Я БО́ЧКА; ПОРОХОВО́Й ПО́ГРЕБ [NP; fixed WO] a dangerous, potentially explosive situation or thing that may bring about drastic repercussions: **powder keg.**

«...Ты знаешь, на какой пороховой бочке мы живём, в какую клоаку превратился наш Остров... Тридцать девять одних только зарегистрированных политических партий. Масса экстремистских групп. Идиотская мода на марксизм распространяется, как инфлуэнца» (Аксёнов 7). "You are well aware that we are living on a powder keg...and you know what a sewer our Island has become. Thirty-nine officially registered political parties. Any number of extremist groups. And Marxism spreading like the flu" (7a).

Б-191 • КО ВСЯ́КОЙ ⟨К КА́ЖДОЙ⟩ БО́ЧКЕ ЗАТЫ́ЧКА *highly coll* [NP; usu. subj-compl with быть∅, nom or instrum (subj: human); fixed WO] **1.** *disapprov* a meddlesome person who wants to take part in everything that is going on: X —

ко всякой бочке затычка ≃ **X has a finger in every pie; X makes everything his business; X is a busybody ⟨a buttinsky⟩; X butts into everything.**

2. a person who is made to do all kinds of jobs, tasks etc, a person who serves in whatever capacity needed: X — ко всякой бочке затычка ≃ **X is a general factotum;** [in limited contexts] **X is chief cook and bottlewasher.**

Б-192 • КАТИ́ТЬ/ПОКАТИ́ТЬ БО́ЧКУ *на кого highly coll* [VP; subj: human] to blame s.o., charge s.o. (usu. a person who is not at fault) with some wrongdoing (for which he is subsequently punished): X катит бочку на Y-а ≃ **X is laying ⟨trying to lay⟩ the blame on Y; X is making ⟨trying to make⟩ Y a scapegoat ⟨a whipping boy, a fall guy⟩; X is pinning ⟨trying to pin, sticking, trying to stick⟩ it ⟨the blame⟩ on Y.**

Б-193 • БРАТЬ/ВЗЯТЬ С БО́Ю *что* [VP] **1.** *mil* [subj: collect or human (pl)] to capture the opponent's fortifications, territory etc by means of battle: X-ы взяли с бою Y ≃ **Xs took Y by force ⟨by storm⟩.**

Жители, издали завидев приближающееся войско, разбежались... и окопались в неприступной позиции. Пришлось брать с бою эту позицию... (Салтыков-Щедрин 1). The residents, having seen the troops approaching, had scattered...and entrenched themselves in an inaccessible position. The position would have to be taken by force... (1a). On seeing the approaching soldiers, the inhabitants had fled...entrenching themselves in an impregnable position. This position would have to be taken by storm (1b).

2. [subj: human] to obtain sth. by expending great effort, acting very resolutely: X берёт Y с бою ≃ **X fights (tooth and nail) for Y; X sweats for Y; X goes all out for Y; X goes to great pains ⟨lengths⟩ to get Y.**

[author's usage] ...Другой крупы в тот год нельзя было купить в Торфопродукте, да и ячневую-то с бою... (Солженицын 6). ...No other grain could be bought in Torfoprodukt that year, and even the barley you had to fight for... (6a).

Б-194 • БОЮ́СЬ СКАЗА́ТЬ ⟨НАЗВА́ТЬ и т. п.⟩ *coll* [VP; 1st pers sing only; fixed WO] (often used as a response to a question) I hesitate to say because I am not positive: **I'm not sure ⟨certain⟩; I can't say for sure; I don't know for sure; (it's) hard to say.**

«Фрадковы уже переехали?» — «Боюсь сказать, я их давно не видел». "Have the Fradkovs moved yet?" "I'm not sure—I haven't seen them in quite a while."

Б-195 • БРАЗДЫ́ ПРАВЛЕ́НИЯ *elev, occas. humor* [NP; subj or obj; fixed WO] governing power, rule, leadership: **the reins of government ⟨of power⟩.**

«Он [Людовик Святой] вздумал пойти в Иерусалим и *передал бразды правления* своей матери» (Толстой 2). "He [Louis the Pious] took it into his head to go to Jerusalem and *handed over the reins of government to his mother*" (2b). ♦ Первая [женщина], которая замыслила похитить бразды глуповского правления, была Ираида Лукинична Палеологова... (Салтыков-Щедрин 1). The first [woman] who contrived to seize the reins of power in Glupov was one Iraida Paleologova (1b).

Б-196 • БРАНЬ НА ВОРОТУ́ НЕ ВИ́СНЕТ [saying] verbal abuse, ridicule etc should be ignored inasmuch as it can cause no real harm: ≃ **hard words break no bones; sticks and stones may ⟨will⟩ break my bones, but names will never hurt me.**

Б-197 • ВАШ БРАТ *coll* [NP; sing only; often foll. by an appos denoting the class of people in question; when used as obj or (less often) subj, usu. refers to the class as a whole; when used as subj-compl with copula, nom only (subj: human), usu. refers to a specific individual within that class; fixed WO] (you and) a person or persons similar to you with regard to position, profession, social status, views etc (more often of males): [when used as obj or subj] **people ⟨men, guys, fellows etc⟩ like you; the likes of you;** [usu. when foll. by an appos] **you writers ⟨workers etc⟩;** [limited contexts] **your kind ⟨sort⟩; your lot; those ⟨people⟩ of your ilk;** [when used as subj-compl] **one of you (writers ⟨workers etc⟩); one of your kind ⟨sort⟩; one of your fellow writers ⟨workers etc⟩; your fellow writer ⟨worker etc⟩;** [in limited contexts] **one of your ilk.**

[Анна Петровна:] Денег у меня нет и не будет для вашего брата! (Чехов 1). [A.P.:] I have no money and I shall never have it for people like you (1a). ♦ «Разное [я] в жизни испытала; вашего брата — мужиков — должна бы уж хорошо знать» (Копелев 1). "I've seen a lot in life; I should know you men well by now" (1a). ♦ Комиссар поморщился и сказал: «Знаешь что, Чита? Иди-ка ты подальше со своим раскаянием. Я вашего брата тридцать пять лет ловлю, и все пластинку крутят, когда ко мне приводят» (Семёнов 1). The Commissioner frowned and said: "Do you know something, Cheetah? Go and take a running jump with your repentance. I've been catching your sort for thirty-five years now and they all sing the same tune when they're brought to me" (1a). ♦ «Это время прошло, когда с вами в вопросики-ответики играли. Сейчас некогда, вашего брата здесь целые банды» (Иоффе 1). ♦ "The time when we played games of questions and answers with you is now past. There's no time any more—there are hordes of your lot here now" (1a). ♦ [Мелузов:] Будешь совсем хорошей женщиной, такой, какой надо, как это нынче требуется от вашего брата (Островский 11). [context transl] [M.:] You'll be a thoroughly fine woman, such as you should be, such as is required of your sex nowadays (11a).

Б-198 • НАШ БРАТ *coll* [NP; sing only; often foll. by an appos denoting the class of people in question; when used as obj or (less often) subj, usu. refers to the class as a whole; when used as subj-compl with copula, nom only (subj: human), usu. refers to a specific individual within that class; fixed WO] (we or I and) a person or persons similar to us or me with regard to position, profession, social status, views etc (more often of males): [when used as obj or subj] **people ⟨men, guys, fellows etc⟩ like us ⟨me⟩; the likes of us ⟨me⟩;** [usu. when foll. by an appos] **we ⟨us⟩ writers ⟨workers etc⟩; our ⟨my⟩ fellow writers ⟨workers etc⟩;** [in limited contexts] **our (own) kind ⟨sort⟩; those ⟨people⟩ of our ilk;** [when used as subj-compl] **one of us (writers ⟨workers etc⟩); one of our kind ⟨sort⟩; one of our ⟨my⟩ fellow writers ⟨workers etc⟩; our ⟨my⟩ fellow writer ⟨worker etc⟩;** [in limited contexts] **one of our ilk.**

[Пепел:] Ты барин... было у тебя время, когда ты нашего брата за человека не считал... (Горький 3). [P.:] You're a gentleman, and once upon a time you didn't look on people like us as human beings (3d). ♦ «Она умна, — повторял он [чиновник], — мила, образованна, на нашего брата и не посмотрит» (Герцен 1). "She is intelligent," he [the clerk] repeated, "nice, cultured, but she won't look at fellows like us" (1a). ♦ «...Кто-то недавно мне говорил, что он возвратился в Россию, но в приказах по корпусу не было. Впрочем, до нашего брата вести поздно доходят» (Лермонтов 1). "Someone was telling me recently that he had returned to Russia, but there was nothing about it in divisional orders. But then news is late in reaching the likes of us" (1a). ♦ «Какова молодёжь-то, а, Феоктист? —сказал он. — Смеётся над нашим братом — стариками» (Толстой 5). "What are these young people coming to, eh, Feoktist?" he said. "Making fun of us old fellows!" (5a).

Б-199 • СВОЙ БРАТ *coll* [NP; sing only; often foll. by an appos denoting the class of people in question; when used as obj or (less often) subj, usu. refers to the class as a whole; when used as subj-compl with copula, nom only (subj: human), usu. refers to a specific individual within that class; fixed WO] a person or persons similar to the person or persons specified (by the appositive and/or context) with regard to position, profession, social status, views etc (more often of males): [when used as obj or subj] **people ⟨men, guys, fellows etc⟩ like us ⟨me, you etc⟩; the likes of us ⟨me, you, him, her, them⟩;** [usu. when foll. by an appos] **our ⟨my, your, his, her, their⟩ fellow writers ⟨workers etc⟩;** [in limited contexts] **our ⟨my, your, his, her, their⟩ kind ⟨sort⟩; those ⟨people⟩ of our ⟨your, their⟩ ilk;** [when used as subj-compl] **one of us ⟨you, them⟩; one of us ⟨you⟩ writers ⟨workers etc⟩; one of our ⟨your, their⟩ kind ⟨sort⟩; one of our ⟨my, your, his, her, their⟩ fellow writers ⟨workers etc⟩; our ⟨my, your, his, her, their⟩ fellow writer ⟨worker etc⟩;** [in limited contexts] **one of our ⟨your, their⟩ ilk.**

Обычно у Крымова складывались хорошие отношения со строевыми командирами, вполне сносные со штабными, а раздражённые и не всегда искренние со своим же братом политическими работниками (Гроссман 2). As a rule, he [Krymov] was able to establish good relations with officers in the field, tolerable relations with staff officers, and only awkward, rather insincere relations with his fellow political-workers (2a). ♦ Слуги также привязались к нему [Базарову], хотя он над ними подтрунивал: они чувствовали, что он всё-таки свой брат, не барин (Тургенев 2). The servants also grew attached to him [Bazarov], though he was always deriding them: they felt that none the less he was one of them, and not a master (2f).

Б-200 • СВОЙ СВОЕМУ́ ПОНЕВО́ЛЕ БРАТ ⟨ДРУГ⟩

[saying] people who share kinship, common interests, occupations etc usu. support and help one another (albeit sometimes reluctantly): ≃ **birds of a feather flock together;** [in limited contexts] **blood is thicker than water; the devil is kind to his own.**

Несколько зная язык, он писал статью начерно, оставляя пробелы, вкрапливая русские фразы и требуя от Фёдора Константиновича дословного перевода своих передовичных словец: ...чудеса в решете... пришла беда — растворяй ворота... свой своему поневоле брат (Набоков 1). Having a smattering of the language, he wrote his article out in rough, with gaps and Russian phrases interspersed, and demanded from Fyodor a literal translation of the usual phrases found in leaders: ...wonders never cease...troubles never come singly...birds of a feather flock together... (1a).

Б-201 • НА БРА́ТА ⟨НА́ НОС⟩ (приходится, давать *что* и т. п.) *coll* [PrepP; these forms only; prep obj] each (gets), (to give) to each: **for ⟨to⟩ every person ⟨man etc⟩; (to) a person ⟨a customer, a man etc⟩; per person ⟨customer, man etc⟩; a head; apiece.**

[Расплюев:] ...Ведь они [англичане] потому такими и стали, что у них теснота, духота, земли нет, по аршину на брата не приходится... (Сухово-Кобылин 2). [R.:] They [the English] got that way because they're so crowded, packed in like sardines (2a).

Б-202 • С БРА́ТА ⟨С НО́СА, С ГОЛОВЫ́⟩ (брать, получать *что* и т. п.) *coll* [PrepP; these forms only; prep obj] (to take, get sth.) from each: **from each ⟨every⟩ person ⟨man etc⟩; from each (and every) one (of us ⟨you, them⟩); a head; apiece; each.**

«Я здесь договорился с местной властью: вечером устраиваем сольный концерт. По полтиннику с носа» (Максимов 3). "I've arranged with the local authorities—we're putting on a one-man concert tonight. Half a ruble a head" (3a).

Б-203 • БРАТЬ/ВЗЯТЬ ⟨ПРИНИМА́ТЬ/ПРИНЯ́ТЬ⟩ НА СЕБЯ́ [VP; subj: human] **1.** ~ *что,* occas. *кого* [when

obj: human or collect, the implication is that one undertakes to do sth. for or involving the person or group in question] to undertake to carry out sth. or to accept responsibility for sth.: [obj: inanim] X **взял на себя Y ≃ X took Y upon himself; X took it upon himself to do Y; X assumed (responsibility for) Y; X took care of Y;** [in limited contexts] **X handled ⟨volunteered to handle⟩ Y;** ‖ X-у пришлось ⟨X был вынужден и т. п.⟩ взять на себя Y ≃ **Y fell onto X's shoulders;** ‖ [obj: human or collect] X взял Y-а на себя ≃ **X took ⟨took care of, handled⟩ Y.**

Не странно ли это: вот этот человек, недавно ещё совершенно незнакомый, сейчас уже знает обо мне так много, что взял на себя устройство моей судьбы (Аллилуева 2). Wasn't it strange, though: here was a man who recently had been a total stranger, and already he knew so much about me, had taken upon himself to settle my fate for me (2a). ♦ Навряд ли он [Маркс] мог побывать в Чегеме, даже если бы Энгельс, как всегда, бедняга, взял на себя расходы на это путешествие (Искандер 5). He [Marx] could hardly have been to Chegem, even if Engels—as always, poor fellow—assumed the expense of the trip (5a). ♦ «Но согласится ли она?! — воскликнул Аслан. — Она же меня любит. И как я ей в глаза посмотрю после этого?» — «Я всё беру на себя», — сказал дядя Сандро... (Искандер 5). "But will she consent?" Aslan exclaimed. "She loves me. How will I ever look her in the eye?" "I'll take care of everything," Uncle Sandro said... (5a). ♦ И Саша сказал только: «Если люди не могут жить вместе, они должны разойтись». Через месяц отец уехал на Ефремовский завод синтетического каучука. Так в шестнадцать лет Саше пришлось всё взять на себя (Рыбаков 2). All he [Sasha] had said was, "If people can't live together, they ought to separate." A month later his father went to work at the synthetic rubber factory in Efremov, and everything fell onto Sasha's shoulders, at the age of sixteen (2a). ♦ «Пойми, — сказала Лола, — я ведь не говорю, чтобы ты взял её [дочь] на себя. Я же знаю, что ты не возьмёшь, и слава Богу, что не возьмёшь, ты ни на что такое не годен» (Стругацкие 1). "Get it into your head," said Lola, "I'm not saying that you should take her [our daughter]. I'm well aware that you wouldn't, and thank God you wouldn't, you're no good at it" (1a). ♦ Уверяю вас, Петров против не выступит, я беру его на себя. I assure you Petrov won't speak out against you—I'll take care of him.

2. ~ *что* to assume leadership of sth.: X взял Y на себя ≃ **X took charge ⟨control, command⟩ of Y; X took over Y; X undertook to direct Y.**

Я знаю, что вы терпеть не можете административную работу, но всё же вам придётся взять на себя отдел патентов — больше некому. I know you can't stand administrative work, but nonetheless you *have* to take over the patent division—there's no one else who can do it.

3. ~ *что* to declare o.s. accountable (for another's guilt, wrongdoing, crime etc): X взял Y на себя ≃ **X took the blame ⟨the rap⟩ for Y; X took responsibility for Y; X claimed ⟨said etc⟩ that Y was (all) X's (own) doing.**

«Хочешь, возьму на себя дела ста восьмидесяти миллионов по обвинению в измене Родине?» (Алешковский 1). "Listen, if you want I'll take the rap for all the hundred and eighty million cases of treason against the motherland" (1a). ♦ На суде заведующий всё взял на себя, и остальных продавцов не тронули... (Искандер 4). The manager took full responsibility in court, and the other salesmen were not touched (4a). ♦ «Вот тут подельник твой в Верховный совет пишет, снисхождения к тебе просит, всё на себя берёт» (Максимов 2). "This partner of yours has written a petition to the Supreme Soviet asking for clemency for you, says it was all his doing" (2a). ♦ Надя прочно знала, много раз уже применяла: если брать на себя, не упрекать, что и он виноват, — Володя успокоится и отойдёт (Солженицын 5). [context transl] Nadya had a firm rule, often applied in the past. If she took Volodya's share of the blame on herself, he would cool off and come around (5a).

Б-204 • МНÓГО НА СЕБЯ́ БРАТЬ/ВЗЯТЬ *coll, rather impol when addressed to the interlocutor* [VP; subj: human] to overestimate one's capabilities, exceed the limits of one's authority, act in a way one has no right to etc: X много на себя берёт ≃ **X is biting off more than he can chew; X is taking on more than he can handle; X is getting in over his head; X is going too far;** [in refer. to one exceeding one's authority] **X is (way) out of line; X is overstepping his bounds.**

…[Я] взвалил его [баллон] на плечо… Пройдя первые десять ступенек, я понял, что слишком много взял на себя. Лет пять назад я мог пройти с таким баллоном втрое больше, теперь это было мне не под силу (Войнович 5). …I hefted the cylinder up on my shoulder.…After the first ten steps I realized that I'd bitten off more than I could chew. Five years ago I could have carried a cylinder like that three times as far, but now it was too much for me (5a). ♦ [Нина:] [Мой жених] волевой, целеустремлённый… Много он на себя не берёт, но он хозяин своему слову. Не то что некоторые (Вампилов 4). [N.:] He's [my fiancé is] headstrong and purposeful.…He won't take on more than he can handle, but he's as good as his word. Not like some… (4a).

Б-205 • БРЕД СИ́ВОЙ КОБЫ́ЛЫ *highly coll, rude* [NP; often subj-compl with copula, nom or instrum (subj: идея, статья, заявление, предложение, это, всё это etc); fixed WO] (some idea, article, statement, proposal etc is) nonsense, absurdity: **(a bunch of) baloney; raving nonsense; horsefeathers; hogwash;** [in limited contexts] **bullshit.**

Хотя сказали много умного и даже верного, Болтун заявил, что всё это бред сивой кобылы (Зиновьев 1). Although much of what was said was intelligent and even true, Chatterer said that it was nothing but raving nonsense (1a). ♦ «Вообрази, [Конский] пустил по нью-йоркскому фото снобистскую идею — русское фото нуждается в переводе на западные языки… Если же ты где-нибудь говоришь, что это бред сивой кобылы, тебя тут же зачисляют в восточные варвары…» (Аксёнов 12). "Just imagine, he's [Konsky has] started this snob idea in New York, that Russian photography requires translation into Western languages.…And if you dare say anywhere that it's all bullshit, you immediately become an Eastern Barbarian…" (12a).

Б-206 • РАЗРЕША́ТЬСЯ/РАЗРЕШИ́ТЬСЯ ОТ БРÉМЕНИ [VP; subj: human] **1.** ~ *(кем) lit* [subj: female] to bear a child: X разрешилась от бремени (Y-ом) ≃ **X gave birth (to Y); X brought Y into the world; X brought forth Y.**

Одна из невесток — Маша — была на последнем месяце и разрешилась от бремени сразу после переселения к нам (Рыбаков 1). One of her daughters-in-law, Masha, was in her last month of pregnancy and gave birth soon after moving to us (1a).

2. ~ *чем humor* to produce sth. (often a literary work) after lengthy preparation, effort: X разрешился от бремени Y-ом ≃ **X (finally ⟨recently etc⟩) brought forth Y; (in the end ⟨at long last etc⟩) X came out with Y.**

Б-207 • ПРОБИ́ТЬ БРЕШЬ *в чём* [VP; subj: abstr; usu. this WO] to do damage, harm to sth.: X пробил брешь в Y-е ≃ **X put a dent in Y; X dealt a (serious) blow to Y.**

Покупку швейной машины придётся отложить: это пробило бы большую брешь в нашем бюджете. We'll have to put off buying a sewing machine—that would really put a dent in our budget.

Б-208 • НЕ В БРОВЬ, А (ПРЯ́МО) В ГЛАЗ попадать, бить и т. п. *coll* [PrepP; these forms only; adv or subj-compl with copula (subj: слова, замечание etc); fixed WO] (to say sth.) aptly, addressing what is most essential, (some criticism, observation etc is) apt, exactly right: **hit the nail on the head; hit the bull's-eye; hit the mark; (be) right on target ⟨on the mark⟩.**

Б-209 • (И) БРÓВЬЮ ⟨ГЛА́ЗОМ, У́ХОМ, НÓСОМ, У́СОМ⟩ НЕ ВЕДЁТ/НЕ ПОВЁЛ; (И) БРÓВЬЮ НЕ ШЕВЕЛЬНУ́Л *all coll* [VP; subj: human; more often pfv past; usu. this WO] s.o. does not outwardly react to sth., does not display his emotions toward sth. said or done in his presence: X и бровью не повёл ≃ **X didn't bat ⟨blink⟩ an eye ⟨an eyelid⟩; X didn't turn a hair; X didn't raise an eyebrow;** [in limited contexts] **X didn't (even) seem to hear; X didn't show a flicker of interest.**

«Покажи тебе самую что ни есть раскрасавицу — ты даже глазом не поведёшь. Потому что биотоки отрицательные подключат» (Айтматов 2). "You could be shown the most ravishing creature you've ever set eyes on and you'll not even bat an eyelid. This will be because the bio-currents will cut out this feeling" (2a). ♦ «Борода-то у вас настоящая?» — спросила Таня. «Можете дёрнуть», — улыбнулся Востоков. Она с удовольствием дёрнула. Востоков даже и глазом не повёл (Аксёнов 7). "Is your beard real?" "You may pull it, if you like," Vostokov said, smiling. She gave it a good, stiff tug. Vostokov did not blink an eye (7a). ♦ «Привьет [used in place of the correct form привет to show a German accent], Марья Николаевна!» — огибая её, почтительно поклонился Штабель… Та и ухом не повела, продолжая одной ей ведомый разговор с самой собою (Максимов 3). Stabel bowed and spoke as he went around her. "How do you do, Maria Nikolaevna?…" She didn't turn a hair but continued her private conversation with herself (3a). ♦ Ардабьев вскочил с песка и вдруг закричал на весь берег, торжествующе размахивая руками: «Ар-да-би-о-ла!» …А рыбак с безнадёжной удочкой и ухом не повёл (Евтушенко 1). Ardabiev leapt up from the sand and suddenly shouted out to all the canalside, triumphantly waving his arms: "Ar-da-bio-la!"…But the fisherman with his despondent fishing-rod did not even seem to hear (1a).

Б-210 • (СТÓИТ) ТÓЛЬКО БРÓВЬЮ ⟨У́СОМ⟩ ПОВЕСТИ́ ⟨ШЕВЕЛЬНУ́ТЬ⟩ *(кому) coll* [VP; impers, pres or past (var. with стоит); infin only, impers predic (var. without стоит); a clause in a compound sent or the main clause in a complex sent (foll. by а как- or чтобы-clause)] a hint or indication from s.o. is sufficient (to get another to do sth.): X-у стоит только бровью повести ≃ **all X has to do is ⟨X need only⟩ drop a hint ⟨say the word, give the signal⟩;** [in limited contexts] **X just has to snap his fingers.**

Б-211 • НЕ ЗНА́Я ⟨НЕ СПРОСЯ́СЬ⟩ БРÓДУ, НЕ СУ́ЙСЯ В ВÓДУ [saying] do not attempt sth. unfamiliar to you unprepared (said when a person fails at some undertaking because of his lack of knowledge of it; also said as a warning against acting hastily, rashly): ≃ **look before you leap.**

…[Полицмейстер] мне заметил: «…Я бы ему, дураку, вздул бы спину, — не суйся, мол, в воду, не спросясь броду, — да и отпустил бы его восвояси, — все бы и были довольны…» (Герцен 1). …He [the *politsmeyster*] observed: "…I would have given the fool a good drubbing—to teach him to look before he leaps—and would have sent him home. Everyone would have been satisfied…" (1a).

Б-212 • ХОТЬ БРОСЬ *substand* [Invar; predic with subj: human, animal, concr, or abstr] (a person or thing is) useless: **good for nothing; no good (at all); of no value (at all); worthless.**

Пятьдесят пять лет ходил он на белом свете с уверенностью, что всё, что он ни делает, иначе и лучше сделано быть не может. И вдруг теперь в две недели Анисья доказала ему, что он — хоть брось… (Гончаров 1). He had lived in the world for fifty-five years in the conviction that nothing he did could be done better or differently, but it took Anisya only two weeks to show him that he was good for nothing… (1b).

Б-213 • ПИТЬ/ВЫ́ПИТЬ (НА) БРУДЕРША́ФТ ⟨НА ТЫ obs⟩ (с кем) [VP; subj: human; if there is no obj, subj: pl] to drink a special toast indicating that a new depth of feeling, a sort of brotherhood has developed between (two or more) individuals: X с Y-ом ⟨X и Y⟩ выпили на брудершафт ≃ **X and Y drank Brüderschaft ⟨brotherhood, fraternity⟩.**

Когда подали шампанское, все поздравили меня, и я выпил через руку «на ты» с Дубковым и Дмитрием и поцеловался с ними (Толстой 2). When the champagne was served everyone congratulated me and I drank *Brüderschaft* [sic], with linked arms, with Dubkov and Dmitri, and embraced them (2b).

Б-214 • ПО́ЛЗАТЬ НА БРЮ́ХЕ (перед кем) highly coll, derog [VP; subj: human] to be servile to, fawn before, s.o.: X ползает на брюхе перед Y-ом ≃ **X crawls on his belly (before ⟨to⟩ Y); X grovels (before Y); X kowtows ⟨bows and scrapes⟩ (to Y).**

Бретейль вспомнил [фон Шаумберга] и поморщился... Да, эти [немцы] чувствуют, что они победили. Они опьянели от победы... Зачем говорить с таким человеком о сотрудничестве? Его не сумели поставить на колени. Теперь он заставит нас ползать на брюхе (Эренбург 4). Breteuil remembered von Schaumberg and frowned....Yes; these Germans realized they were the conquerors. They were drunk with victory....What was the use of talking to such a man about collaboration? He had not been brought to his knees before and now he was forcing the French to crawl on their bellies (4a).

Б-215 • ВСЕ ТАМ БУ́ДЕМ [saying] everybody will die eventually: ≃ **we all have to go sometime; no one lives forever;** [in limited contexts] **all men are mortal.**

Посреди Старопанской площади... велись оживлённые разговоры, вызванные известием о тяжёлой болезни Клавдии Ивановны. Общее мнение собравшихся горожан сводилось к тому, что «все там будем»... (Ильф и Петров 1). In the middle of the square...an animated conversation was in progress following the news of Claudia Ivanovna's stroke. The general opinion of the assembled citizens could have been summed up as "We all have to go sometime"... (1a).

Б-216 • ВИ́ДНО БУ́ДЕТ [VP; impers; Invar; usu. a clause in a compound sent preceded by another clause; often after a там, а дальше etc] it will become clear in time, as matters progress, how one or s.o. should act or what some outcome will be: **(I will ⟨we can, you should etc⟩ do sth. and) see what happens; we shall ⟨we'll, I'll⟩ see;** [in limited contexts] **we'll ⟨let's, I'll etc⟩ see what's to be done; we ⟨you etc⟩ can sort things out later.**

«Практически мой вывод такой, что мы готовы заключить с вами договор, а там видно будет» (Солженицын 2). "The practical conclusion I draw is that we are prepared to sign a contract with you, and see what happens" (2a). ♦ Всю дорогу до самого хутора Григорий как-то несвязно и бестолково думал о недавнем, пытался хоть вехами наметить будущее, но мысль доходила до отдыха дома и дальше напарывалась на тупик. «Приеду, поотдохну трошки [regional = немного], залечу ранку, а там... – думал он... – Там видно будет» (Шолохов 3). All the way home Grigory thought disconnectedly and vaguely about the recent events, trying to make out at least a few landmarks for the future, but his thoughts got no farther than the idea of rest and recovery at home. I'll just have a bit of a rest at home and get my leg better, and then we'll see, he thought... (3a). ♦ [Телятев:] Во-первых, ты не вздумай стреляться в комнате... во-вторых, мы с тобой сначала пообедаем хорошенько, а там видно будет (Островский 4). [T.:] In the first place, don't think of having a duel in a room....In the second place, you and I'll have a good dinner first and then see what's to be done (4a). ♦ «Пусть [поступает на] гуманитарный! Хотя он ненавидит философию и бредит фи-

зикой. Лишь бы поступить, а там видно будет» (Зиновьев 2). "Let's settle for humanities! Even though he hates philosophy and dreams of physics. Just so long as he gets in, we can sort things out later" (2a).

Б-217 • ЖИ́РНО БУ́ДЕТ кому, для кого; БО́ЛЬНО ⟨СЛИ́ШКОМ⟩ ЖИ́РНО (БУ́ДЕТ) all highly coll [VP; impers or with subj: это or infin; these forms only; usu. this WO] (s.o.) is not worthy of sth., does not merit sth.: X-у жирно будет ≃ **that's too good ⟨nice⟩ for X; that's more than X deserves.**

[Олег:] Гена, ты плачешь, когда тебя отец бьёт? [Геннадий:] Как бы не так! Больно жирно ему будет (Розов 2). [O.:] Genna, do you cry when your father hits you? [G.:] Not likely! That'd be too nice for him (2a).

Б-218 • ТО ЛИ (ЕЩЁ) БУ́ДЕТ coll [VP_subj; these forms only; indep. clause (var. with ещё) or the main clause in a complex sent; fixed WO] some action, phenomenon etc (mentioned in the preceding context) will manifest itself on a larger scale, to a greater degree than it did before: **more is coming ⟨on the way⟩; more [NPs] are coming ⟨on the way⟩; there's more to come; there will be more [NPs]; you ain't seen nothin' yet; this is just the beginning (of sth.); I ⟨we etc⟩ haven't even begun to...yet;** [in limited contexts] **this is just the tip of the iceberg.**

«Как нас, однако, уже успели воспитать (то ли ещё будет!..): что что-нибудь непременно у тебя *должно* быть, что как-нибудь *именно так* должно быть, кроме, как *есть*, что как-нибудь *надо*, чтоб было» (Битов 2). ...How they've managed to condition us already (more to come!): that you absolutely *ought* to have something, that somehow you ought to have it *precisely* this way, other than as it *is*, that somehow you *must* have it (2a). ♦ «Это же смертоубийство учинил твой [верблюд] Каранар. А ты его спокойно отпускаешь в степь!» – «Не отпускал я его, Казаке. Сам он ушёл...». – «А ты и рад. Но подожди, то ли ещё будет» (Айтматов 2). "Your [camel] Karanar has started on a murderous course, yet you let him go out into the steppe without any qualms." "I didn't let him go out, Kazake. He just went of his own accord...." "So you're glad, are you? But, you see, there'll be more trouble" (2a).

Б-219 • ХУ́ДО ⟨ПЛО́ХО⟩ БУ́ДЕТ (кому) coll [VP; impers; these forms only; usu. a clause in a compound sent; preceded by one or more clauses expressing prohibition, warning etc; often after а то, не то, иначе etc] (if s.o. disobeys an order, fails to do what he should do etc) there will be trouble (for him and/or another or others): X-у худо будет ≃ **X will be sorry; X will be in hot water; X will have the devil to pay; X will come to a bad end;** [when the situation is already bad] **things will only get worse.**

«Раз подъехал к нему и говорю шутейно [substand = шутливо]: „Пора бы привалом стать, ваше благородие – товарищ Мелехов!" Ворохнул [substand, here = сверкнул] он на меня глазами, говорит: „Ты мне эти шутки брось, а то плохо будет"» (Шолохов 5). "One day I rides up to him and says joking like, 'Time to call a halt, Your Honour—Comrade Melekhov!' And you should have seen his eyes flash! 'Just you drop those jokes of yours, or you'll come to a bad end,' he says" (5a).

Б-220 • ЧТО БУ́ДЕТ, ТО БУ́ДЕТ [saying] (of an action undertaken without certainty as to its outcome, or of an event the outcome of which is uncertain) what is going to happen will happen the way it is destined to: ≃ **what(ever) will be will be; what(ever) happens happens; what(ever) will happen will happen;** [in limited contexts] **let the chips fall where they may.**

«Что будет – то будет, – сказала попадья, – а жаль, если не Владимир Андреевич будет нашим господином» (Пушкин 1). "What will be, will be," said the priest's wife. "But it'll be a pity if Vladimir Andreyevitch does not become our master" (1b). ♦ [Хлестаков:] Я заплачу, заплачу деньги, но у меня теперь нет!.. [Городничий (в сторону):] Не знаешь, с какой стороны и приняться... Ну да уж попробовать...! Что будет, то будет... (Вслух) Если вы точно имеете нужду в деньгах или в чём другом, то я готов служить сию минуту (Гоголь 4). [Kh.:] I'll pay, I'll pay the money, but right now I haven't any!... [Mayor (aside):] You don't know which way to take it. Well, let's try....What happens happens....(Aloud) If you need money specifically or anything else, why I am at your service this minute (4a).

Б-221 • **НАСИ́ЛЬНО МИЛ НЕ БУ́ДЕШЬ** [saying] a person cannot be forced to extend his affections to another, nor can he be forced to accept another's affections: ≃ **love cannot be compelled ⟨forced⟩; you can't force someone ⟨him, her etc⟩ to love ⟨like⟩ you; [in limited contexts] you can lead a horse to water, but you can't make him ⟨it⟩ drink.**

...Я подал заявление об увольнении ввиду возвращения в родной город, моя фабрика прислала запрос с просьбой вернуть меня обратно. Бойцов не хотел меня отпускать. «Чем мы вас обидели?» – «Ничем, – отвечаю, – но так сложились семейные обстоятельства, надо возвращаться домой». – «Ну что ж, – говорит, – насильно мил не будешь» (Рыбаков 1). ...I put in a request for a transfer to my home town; my own factory had written to ask whether I could be sent back. Boitsov didn't want me to go. "How did we offend you?" "You didn't," I replied. "Family circumstances, I have to go home." "Oh well, love can't be forced," he said (1a). ♦ [Пепел:] Ну... говори... [Василиса:] Что же говорить? Насильно мил не будешь... и не в моём это характере милости просить... (Горький 3). [P.:] Well, if you have anything to say – [V.:] What is there to say? You can't force one to like you – and it's not in my character to beg for alms (3b).

Б-222 • **БУ́ДТО БЫ 1.** [subord Conj; introduces a nominal clause] used to express doubt or uncertainty as to the reliability of what is stated in the clause that follows: **that (s.o. ⟨sth.⟩) seems to ⟨appears to⟩; that (s.o. ⟨sth.⟩) supposedly ⟨allegedly⟩; (a rumor ⟨a message etc⟩) alleging that...**

С первой санной оказией из города пришёл слух, будто бы Германия подписала перемирие... (Федин 1). With the first opportunity to use sleds a rumor came from town alleging that Germany had signed an armistice... (1a).

2. [subord Conj; introduces a compar clause] (used to convey the unreal, illusory nature of the comparison) just like it would be if: **as if ⟨though⟩; like; [in limited contexts] (so...that) one ⟨it etc⟩ seems to...**

Вы так смотрите, будто бы видите меня в первый раз! You're looking at me as if you were seeing me for the first time!

3. coll [Particle] used to express the speaker's doubt or uncertainty as to the reliability of the information contained in the statement as well as the source of that information: **allegedly; supposedly; ostensibly; apparently; purportedly; [in limited contexts] it seems that...**

...Переписывая по случаю летнего времени в беседке сада, он будто бы слышал, как Николай Гаврилович и Владислав Дмитриевич, ходя между собой под руку (чёрточка верная!), говорили о поклоне от их доброжелателей барским крестьянам... (Набоков 1). ...While doing his copying "on account of the summer weather in a garden pavilion," he allegedly heard Nikolay Gavrilovich and Vladislav Dmitrievich as they were strolling arm-in-arm (a not implausible detail), talking about greetings from well-wishers to the serfs... (1a). ♦ Наконец опросы перешли к защитнику, и тот первым делом начал узнавать о пакете, в котором «будто бы» спрятаны были Фёдором Павловичем три тысячи рублей для «известной особы» (Достоевский 2). Finally the questioning passed to the defense attorney, and he, first of all, began asking about the envelope in which Fyodor Pavlovich "supposedly" hid three thousand roubles for "a certain person" (2a). ♦ Жил будто бы на свете какой-то начальник, который вдруг встревожился мыслию, что никто из подчинённых не любит

его (Салтыков-Щедрин 1). It seemed that there had once lived in the world a chief who was suddenly disturbed by the thought that none of his subordinates loved him (1a).

Б-223 • **(Я) НЕ Я́ БУ́ДУ (, если не...)** highly coll [VP$_{subj}$; these forms only; the main clause in a complex sent; usu. this WO] (used to express certainty that some event or action did take, is taking, or will take place; also used to express one's firm resolve to do sth.) I am convinced, absolutely certain (of sth.), I am determined (to accomplish sth.): **if...I'll eat my hat; ...or I'll eat my hat; ...or my name isn't...; my name's not...if...; I'll be hanged ⟨damned⟩ if...; strike me blind ⟨dumb, dead etc⟩ if...; [in limited contexts, in refer. to one's resolve] I'll damn well see (to it) that...**

«Я как „Семерых козлят" по радио услыхала, так и сказала себе: „Не я буду, если эта женщина не будет у меня работать"»... (Гинзбург 2). "As soon as I heard the 'Seven Little Kids' on the radio, I said to myself, 'My name's not Kraevskaya if I don't get that woman onto my staff...'" (2a).

Б-224 • **ЗАГЛЯ́ДЫВАТЬ/ЗАГЛЯНУ́ТЬ В БУ́ДУЩЕЕ ⟨В ЗА́ВТРА, ВПЕРЁД⟩** [VP; subj: human] to (attempt to) envision future events, to contemplate the future: X заглядывает вперёд ≃ **X looks into the future; X looks ahead.**

[Аркадина:] И у меня правило: не заглядывать в будущее. Я никогда не думаю ни о старости, ни о смерти. Чему быть, того не миновать (Чехов 6). [A.:] And another thing: I make it a strict rule never to look into the future, never to worry about old age or death. What will be, will be (6b). ♦ [Фёдор:] Слава богу, я не пройдоха, не жулик... [Клавдия Васильевна:] Можешь им стать. [Фёдор:] Ты уже преувеличиваешь, мама. [Клавдия Васильевна:] Нет, я просто стараюсь всегда заглядывать вперёд (Розов 2). [F.:] Thank God, I'm not an impostor or a crook... [K.V.:] You may become one. [F.:] Now you're exaggerating, mother. [K.V.:] No, I'm simply trying to look ahead (2a).

Б-225 • **В БУ́ДУЩЕМ** [PrepP; Invar; adv] at some time(s) or during some period yet to come: **in the future; tomorrow; someday.**

«Думаю, что те знания, которые достал тут, в окопах, пригодятся в будущем...» (Шолохов 3). "I think the knowledge I've gained here in the trenches will come in useful in the future..." (3a).

Б-226 • **БУДЬ БЛАГОНАДЁЖЕН ⟨БУ́ДЬТЕ БЛАГО-НАДЁЖНЫ⟩** obs [formula phrase; these forms only; fixed WO] have complete confidence, have no doubts: **have no fear!; fear not!; rest assured; doubt not.**

Б-227 • **БУДЬ ДОБР ⟨БУ́ДЬТЕ ДОБРЫ́ or ДО́БРЫ, БУДЬ ЛЮБЕ́ЗЕН, БУ́ДЬТЕ ЛЮБЕ́ЗНЫ⟩** [formula phrase; these forms only; fixed WO] **1.** (used to express a polite request) be obliging and do what I am asking you to do: **(please ⟨would you⟩) be so kind as to...; would you be kind enough to...; would you please ⟨kindly, mind⟩...; might I trouble you to ⟨for a⟩...; do me a favor and...**

[Серебряков:] Друзья мои, пришлите мне чай в кабинет, будьте добры! (Чехов 3). [S.:] My friends, be so kind as to have my tea brought to the study (3a). ♦ В прихожей заверещал звонок... Скрипач поднял голову и попросил: «Откройте дверь, будьте любезны» (Семёнов 1). ...The doorbell tinkled in the hall. The violinist lifted his head and said: "Do me a favour and open the door, will you?" (1a).

2. (used to express a demand that may go against the will of the person addressed) do what I am telling you (even if you do not want to): **make sure that (you do ⟨don't do⟩ sth.); be sure (to do ⟨not to do⟩ sth.); be sure and (do sth.); make it a point (not) to...;**

see that you (do ⟨don't do⟩ sth.); **if you please**; [with ironic intonation] **please ⟨would you⟩ be so kind as to (not)…**; **would you be kind enough (not) to…**; **would you please ⟨kindly, mind⟩ (not)…**

«Потрудись отправиться в Орлеан, – сказал Поклен-отец… – и держи экзамен на юридическом факультете. Получи учёную степень. Будь так добр, не провались, ибо денег на тебя ухлопано порядочно» (Булгаков 5). "You will now be kind enough to take a trip to Orléans," said Poquelin the elder…"and take an examination in jurisprudence. You must get a degree. And see that you don't fail, for I spent plenty of money on you" (5a). ♦ [Кай:] А слёзы нам ни к чему. Без них, будьте любезны (Арбузов 2). [K.:] Tears won't help. No tears, if you please (2a).

Б-228 • БУДЬ ЗДОРÓВ¹ ⟨БУ́ДЬТЕ ЗДОРÓВЫ⟩ [VP_imper; fixed WO] **1.** [formula phrase; these forms only] used to wish s.o. well upon parting: **take care (of yourself ⟨-selves⟩); stay well!**; [in limited contexts] **take it easy; all the best; good luck (to you).**

«…Передай ему привет, а сама будь здорова!» (Рыбаков 1). "Give him my regards, and take care of yourself!" (1a). ♦ «Мы ещё увидимся, – сказал он. – Я тебе буду писать». – «Ну, будь здоров» (Грекова 3). "We'll see each other again," he said. "I'll write to you." "Well, all the best" (3a). ♦ «Прощайте-с и будьте здоровы». – «Я убеждена, что мы не в последний раз видимся», – произнесла Анна Сергеевна с невольным движением (Тургенев 2). "Good-bye, and good luck to you." "I am certain we are not seeing each other for the last time," Anna Sergeyevna declared with an involuntary gesture (2b).

2. [formula phrase; these forms only] (used to wish good health to s.o. who has just sneezed) may you be healthy: **(God) bless you!; gesundheit!**

Кто-то чихнул, и ты не сказал «будь здоров» – штраф (Зиновьев 1). If someone sneezes and you don't say "Bless you"—a fine (1a). ♦ …[Павор] извлёк… большой мокрый платок и принялся сморкаться и чихать. Жалкое зрелище… «Меня этот город доконает… Р-р-рум-чж-ж-жах! Ох…» – «Будьте здоровы», – сказал Виктор (Стругацкие 1). He [Pavor] retrieved a huge, wet handkerchief… and started sneezing and blowing his nose. It was a piteous sight.…"This town is driving me crazy. He-he-hep chuuu! Oh, hell." "Gesundheit," said Victor (1a).

3. Also: **БУ́ДЕМ ЗДОРÓВЫ** [formula phrase; these forms only] (used when toasting as a wish for good health) may you (or we all) have good health: **(here's) to your (good) health!; to good health!; cheers!**

Григорий присел к столу… Оставшееся в бутылке Степан разлил поровну в стаканы, поднял на Григория задёрнутые какой-то дымкой глаза. «За всё хорошее!» – «Будем здоровы!» Чокнулись. Выпили (Шолохов 5). Grigory seated himself at the table.…Stepan filled their glasses evenly with what was left in the bottle and raised his strangely misted eyes. "To all that's good!" "Your good health!" They clinked glasses and drank (5a).

4. *coll, iron* [indep. clause; if used as a clause in a complex sent, takes the final position] (let s.o.) get out, go away (used to express one's displeasure with s.o., one's desire to get rid of s.o. etc): **(let s.o.) clear out ⟨hit the road⟩!; good riddance!**

Люди у нас в цеху хорошие, не поладишь с ними – будь здоров! We've got good people in our shop. If you don't get along with them—clear out!

Б-229 • БУДЬ ЗДОРÓВ² *slang* [Invar] **1.** [predic (subj: any common noun)] excellent, superior, of the highest quality: **top-notch; topflight; first-class; first-rate; one ⟨a, some⟩ helluva…**

Попроси Васю помочь с компьютером. Он будь здоров какой специалист. Ask Vasya for help with the computer. He's a topnotch specialist.

2. [usu. adv (intensif)] (used to emphasize the high degree of some quality or the intensity of some activity) very much or many,

very strong, big etc: **like you wouldn't believe; like nobody's business; really ⟨incredibly⟩** [AdjP or AdvP]; [in limited contexts] **plenty(!).**

Больше всех зарабатывают шахтеры — он [Коля] и подался на шахту. Работал он там… будь здоров! Он и умеет работать… (Марченко 1). The biggest wages are earned by miners, so Kolya decided to go down the mines. He worked away there like nobody's business. He liked work and knew how to go about it… (1a). ♦ «Да и необходимости у него нет заниматься рискованными подделками, Алик на элементарной халтуре будь здоров зарабатывает» (Чернёнок 1). "And he doesn't need to take on the risk of forgery. Alik makes plenty by elementary hackwork" (1a).

Б-230 • БУДЬ ТЫ ⟨он и т. п.⟩ НЕЛА́ДЕН *highly coll* [VP_imper; 2nd and 3rd pers only; indep. clause or sent adv (parenth); fixed WO] (used to express dissatisfaction, disapproval, displeasure etc) s.o. or sth. (mentioned in the preceding context) is extremely irritating, deserves to be rejected, scorned: **blast ⟨curse, damn⟩ you ⟨him etc⟩; the devil take you ⟨him etc⟩; to ⟨the⟩ hell with you ⟨him etc⟩; (this) damn** [NP].

После массажей Картучихи, будь она неладна, и осмотра ремонтных мастерских кормление пеликанов было третьим по силе воздействия успокаивающим средством Александра Петровича (Искандер 3). Next to being massaged by Kartuchikha, blast her, and inspecting the repair shops, feeding the pelicans was third in its power to soothe Alexander Petrovich (3a). ♦ Собираясь прибить лису, [Едигей] вспомнил вдруг, как кто-то рассказывал, то ли кто из тех приезжих типов, то ли фотограф, с которым о боге беседовал, то ли ещё кто-то, да нет же, Сабитжан рассказывал, будь он неладен, о посмертном переселении душ (Айтматов 2). As he had prepared to throw the stone at the fox, he had remembered something that someone had once told him—either a visitor, or a photographer with whom he had talked about God, or someone else—no, it had been Sabitzhan; the devil take him.…It had been about the transmigration of souls after death (2a).

Б-231 • БУДЬ ТЫ ⟨он и т. п.⟩ (ТРИ́ЖДЫ) ПРÓКЛЯТ *highly coll* [VP_imper; 2nd and 3rd pers only; indep. clause or sent adv (parenth); fixed WO] (used to express strong dissatisfaction, disapproval, displeasure etc) s.o. or sth. (mentioned in the preceding context) is abhorrent, deserves to be harshly rejected, cursed: будь X (трижды) проклят ≃ **(God) damn X (to hell); to ⟨the⟩ hell with X; X can go to (bloody) hell; may X be (thrice) damned!**

…[Скопенко] сморщился, словно от зубной боли, сорвавшись почти на крик. «Да будь они [женщины] все прокляты, всем им одна цена, любая ни за грош продаст!» (Максимов 2). …He [Skopenko] grimaced, as though from toothache, and his next words were almost shouted: "Damn them [women], they're all the same—they'll all cheat on you as soon as look at you!" (2a). ♦ Иосиф Джугашвили… въезжает в раскрытые ворота своего двора… Мать… выглядывает из кухни и улыбается сыну. Добрая, старая мать с морщинистым лицом… Добрая. Будь ты проклята!!! (Искандер 3). Iosif Dzhugashvili…drives through the open gates of his yard.…His mother…glances out of the kitchen and smiles at her son. His kind old mother with her wrinkled face.…His kind old…Damn her to hell! (3a). ♦ [Саяпин:] Он *(показывает на дверь кабинета Кушака)* требует статью. Что будем делать? Так он этого не оставит… [Зилов:] Опять статья. Будь она проклята (Вампилов 5). [S. *(indicating the door to Kushak's office):*] He's yelling for the article. What are we going to do? He won't let it drop… [Z.:] The hell with the article (5b). ♦ «…По мне, его кобыла и с матерью – да будь они прокляты! – а я жеребца не дам обскакать!» (Шолохов 2). "…His mare and its mother can go to bloody hell for all I care, but I won't let him beat the stallion!" (2a). ♦ …В трагических ролях он [Мольер] имел в лучшем случае средний успех… Но лишь только после трагедии давали фарс и Мольер, переодевшись, превращался из Цезаря в Сганареля, дело менялось в ту же минуту: публика начинала хохотать, публика аплодировала, происходили овации... Разгримировываясь после спектакля или снимая маску, Мольер, заикаясь, говорил в уборной: «Что это за народец, будь он трижды проклят!.. Я не понимаю...» (Булгаков 5). In tragic roles he [Molière] had at best a fair to middling success....But as soon as farce followed tragedy, and Molière transformed himself from Caesar into Sganarelle, there was an immediate change: the audience roared with laughter, applauded, and gave him ovations....Removing his makeup after the show, or taking off his mask, Molière would stutter in his dressing room: "Idiots, may they be thrice damned! I can't understand it..." (5a).

Б-232 • БУДЬ ЧТО БУ́ДЕТ [imper sent; Invar; fixed WO] (used to emphasize one's determination to pursue a certain course of action—usu. one that may have unwelcome or dangerous repercussions) despite what may happen: **come what may; [in limited contexts] come hell or high water; no matter what; let the chips fall where they may; regardless; I'll take my chances.**

[Михаил] походил-походил вокруг да около и поехал в район: будь что будет, пускай под суд его отдадут, а он должен увидеть Варвару. Своими глазами (Абрамов 1). Не [Mikhail] had walked around and around, and then had gone to the district center: let them take him to court, but come what may he had to see Varvara—with his own eyes (1a). ♦ Я подумал: «Будь что будет, подписывать акт я не стану» (Войнович 5). I thought to myself: No matter what, I won't sign [the document] (5a). ♦ Я решил смирить свою гордость, бежать от этого урода и вернуться к своему старику, а там будь что будет (Искандер 3). I decided to swallow my pride, run away from this monster, and return to my old man; I'd take my chances there (3a).

Б-233 • БУДЬ Я (ТРИ́ЖДЫ) ПРО́КЛЯТ (, если...) *highly coll* [VP$_{imper}$; 1st pers only; fixed WO] an oath used by the speaker to emphasize the truth of a statement: **I'll be damned ⟨darned, hanged⟩ if...**

Б-234 • НЕ ТЕМ БУДЬ ПОМЯ́НУТ *obsoles, coll* [VP$_{imper}$; sent adv (parenth); cannot be addressed to the interlocutor; fixed WO] (used after making a negative statement about the characteristics or actions of some person or group with whom the speaker had contact in the past) it is unfortunate that I have nothing better to say about this person (or these people): **(I'm) sorry to say; sad to say.**

Б-235 • БУ́ДЬТЕ ПОКО́ЙНЫ [VP$_{imper}$; fixed WO] **1.** *obs* Also: **БУДЬ ПОКО́ЕН** [2nd pers only; indep. clause] there is no reason to be concerned about that, do not be disturbed by that: **set your mind at rest ⟨at ease⟩.**

[Алексей:] ...Изволите говорить насчёт блох? Уж будьте покойны. Если блоха или клоп укусит, уж это наша ответственность... (Гоголь 2). [A.:] Your honor means fleas? Set your mind at rest. If a flea or bug bites you, we take the responsibility... (2b).

2. *coll* [Invar; sent adv (parenth)] undoubtedly: **rest assured; you can be sure of that; no doubt about it; you can bank ⟨count, bet⟩ on it; for sure; don't (you) worry.**

«Дождались станишники [phonetic spelling = станичники] своего часа. И уж они, будьте покойны, они своё возьмут» (Максимов 3). "This is just what the Cossacks have been waiting for. They'll take their revenge, don't you worry" (3a).

Б-236 • БУ́КВА В БУ́КВУ повторять, запоминать, передавать *что и т. п.* [Invar; adv; fixed WO] (to repeat, memorize, recount etc sth.) exactly as sth. was said, written etc: **word for word; verbatim; literally.**

Вот мой разговор с I... Я воспроизвожу этот разговор буква в букву — потому что он, как мне кажется, будет иметь

огромное, решающее значение для судьбы Единого Государства... (Замятин 1). Here is my conversation with I-330....I shall reproduce the conversation word for word, for it seems to me that it may have an enormous and decisive importance for the fate of the United State... (1b).

Б-237 • БУ́КВА ЗАКО́НА [NP; sing only; fixed WO] a formal interpretation of the law (based on its literal meaning as opposed to its spirit): **the letter of the law.**

Голос следователя был почтительно-бережный... «Поверьте, мы не формалисты, хватающиеся за букву закона. Мы понимаем очевидную невиновность как Митягина, так и вашу. Но поставьте себя на наше место. Представьте, что мы прикроем это дело, не доведём до суда» (Тендряков 1). [The Assistant Prosecutor's] voice was respectful and soothing.... "Believe me, we are not just pedants sticking to the letter of the law. We know that neither you nor Mityagin is really guilty. But put yourself in our place. Imagine if we just covered up this business, and didn't bring it to trial" (1a).

Б-238 • МЁРТВОЙ БУ́КВОЙ [NP$_{instrum}$; Invar; subj-compl with быть$_∅$ (past or fut), оставаться (subj: закон, декрет etc); fixed WO] (some law, decree etc remains) in existence only on paper, (sth. is) without practical application: **(become ⟨be⟩) a dead letter.**

Б-239 • С БОЛЬШО́Й БУ́КВЫ [PrepP; Invar; nonagreeing postmodif; fixed WO] (a person, thing, or phenomenon that is) an embodiment of the highest degree of the quality or type described: **(spelled) with a capital** [letter as specified]; **with a capital letter.**

Что вам сказать? Это был Момент, Момент с большой буквы. Это была любовь-молния (Рыбаков 1). What can one say? This was the Moment, with a capital M. It was love at first sight (1a).

Б-240 • СМОТРЕ́ТЬ ⟨ГЛЯДЕ́ТЬ⟩ БУ́КОЙ *coll* [VP; subj: human] to look gloomy, unfriendly, unsociable: X смотрит букой ≃ **X looks sullen; X is lowering ⟨glowering⟩; X has ⟨is going around with⟩ a long face; X is wearing a frown ⟨a glum expression⟩.**

Б-241 • БРАТЬ/ВЗЯТЬ НА БУКСИ́Р *кого-что* [VP; subj and obj: human or collect] to aid s.o., help s.o. improve his performance by sharing one's own experience, expertise with him: X взял Y-а на буксир ≃ **X took Y in tow; X helped Y along.**

Б-242 • НА БУЛА́ВКИ ⟨НА ИГО́ЛКИ⟩ давать, получа́ть (деньги) *obs* [PrepP; these forms only; usu. nonagreeing modif] (to give to or receive from s.o.) small amounts of money for minor or incidental expenses: **pin money; pocket money.**

[Лидия:] ...Ни муж мой, ни мои обожатели не хотят ссудить меня... ничтожной суммой на булавки (Островский 4). [L.:] ...Neither my husband nor my worshippers want to lend me a paltry sum for pin-money (4a).

Б-243 • БУМА́ГА НЕ КРАСНЕ́ЕТ; БУМА́ГА ВСЁ СТЕ́РПИТ [VP$_{subj}$; these forms only; fixed WO] (used to express an ironic or scornful attitude toward sth. written or published because it contains lies, tendentiousness etc) paper can bear absolutely anything: **paper won't ⟨doesn't⟩ blush; pen and ink never blush.**

«Алексей Фёдорович, — писала она, — ...я не могу больше жить, если не скажу вам того, что родилось в моём сердце, а этого никто, кроме нас двоих, не должен до времени знать. Но как я вам скажу то, что я так хочу вам сказать? Бумага, говорят, не краснеет, уверяю вас, что это неправда и что краснеет она так же точно, как и я теперь вся» (Достоевский 1). "Alexei Fyodorovich," she wrote, "...I cannot live any longer without telling you what has been born in my heart, and this no one but the two of us should know for the time being. But how shall I tell you that which I want so much to tell you? Paper, they say, does not blush, but I assure you that it is not true, and that it is blushing now just as I am blushing all over" (1a).

< The first variant of this phrase goes back to Cicero's *Epistulae ad Familiares*, "Epistula non erubescit," V, 12, I.

Б-244 • **НА БУМА́ГЕ** [PrepP; Invar; usu. sent adv] as presented or described in a document, written statement etc (in contrast to what exists in actuality): **on paper.**

[Треплев:] Как легко, доктор, быть философом на бумаге и как это трудно на деле! (Чехов 6). [T.:] How easy it is, Doctor, to be a philosopher on paper and how hard it is in life! (6d).

Б-245 • **ЛОЖИ́ТЬСЯ/ЛЕЧЬ НА БУМА́ГУ ⟨ПОД ПЕРО́⟩** [VP; subj: abstr (often слова)] to be expressed in written form: слова легли на бумагу ≃ **the words were written down; the words found their way to paper;** ‖ слова легко ложились на бумагу ≃ **the words were flowing ⟨coming easily, falling into place⟩;** ‖ *Neg* слова не ложатся на бумагу ≃ **the words (just) won't come; person X cannot find the right words ⟨cannot get his ideas down on paper⟩.**

Б-246 • **МАРА́ТЬ БУМА́ГУ** usu. *derog* [VP; subj: human] (usu. of a bad, untalented writer, occas. of anyone involved in writing sth.) to write sth. of no significance, of poor quality etc: X марает бумагу ≃ **X is writing something unimportant ⟨worthless, of no value etc⟩; X is scribbling something or other;** [when characterizing an untalented writer or poet] **X is a scribbler ⟨a hack, a literary drudge⟩;** [in limited contexts] **X is a poetaster.**

Б-247 • **БУ́РЯ В СТАКА́НЕ ВОДЫ́** [NP; sing only; usu. subj-compl with copula, nom or instrum (subj: abstr); fixed WO] a lot of commotion, a big disturbance, heated arguing etc, all about sth. unimportant: **a tempest ⟨a storm⟩ in a teapot ⟨a teacup⟩.**

И вот Хаим Ягудин объявляет, что вся возня вокруг этой истории... — буря в стакане воды (Рыбаков 1). He [Khaim Yagudin] declared that all the fuss over this business was...a storm in a teacup (1a).

Б-248 • **ПРИКЛА́ДЫВАТЬСЯ К БУТЫ́ЛКЕ ⟨К РЮ́МКЕ, К РЮ́МОЧКЕ⟩; ЗАГЛЯ́ДЫВАТЬ В БУ-ТЫ́ЛКУ ⟨В РЮ́МКУ, В РЮ́МОЧКУ⟩** all *highly coll* [VP; subj: human; often infin with стать, начать] to drink alcohol regularly: X начал прикладываться к бутылке ≃ **X took to ⟨started hitting⟩ the bottle ⟨the sauce⟩; X began tippling.**

«Надломился он [Зарванцев] как-то... Мельчить стал, в рюмочку заглядывать» (Чернёнок 1). "He [Zarvantsev] cracked somehow....He started degenerating, hitting the bottle" (1a).

Б-249 • **ЛЕЗТЬ/ПОЛЕ́ЗТЬ В БУТЫ́ЛКУ** *coll* ⟨**В ПУЗЫ́РЬ** *substand*⟩ [VP; subj: human] to become irritated, lose one's temper (usu. over sth. unimportant): X полез в бутылку ≃ **X got (all) worked ⟨riled⟩ up; X flew off the handle; X got into a snit;** [of expressing one's irritation by acting arrogantly] **X got (all) uppity.**

«Ну чего ты, понимаешь, в бутылку лезешь?» — попытался урезонить Егоршу Михаил (Абрамов 1). "What is there to get worked up about?" Mikhail tried to appeal to Yegorsha (1b). ♦ «...Я ему [Тимофею]: "Сколько колонн у Большого театра?" А он мне, как обыкновенно: "Шесть!" А я ему: "Плохо, видно, ты считал. Пальцев, мол, не хватило для счёту". Тут Тимо-

фей обидится, полезет в бутылку» (Войнович 5). "...I'll say: How many columns on the Bolshoi Theater? And like always he'll [Timofei will] say: Six! Then I'll say: Looks like you're no good at counting. Maybe you don't have enough fingers. Then Timofei'll get offended and fly off the handle..." (5a). ♦ [author's usage] [Калошин:] С вами по-хорошему — вы не понимаете, начинаешь с вами по закону — вы в бутылку (Вампилов 1). [K.:] Try being polite, and you don't understand. Start laying down the law, and you get all uppity (1a).

Б-250 • **РАЗДАВИ́ТЬ БУТЫ́ЛКУ** *highly coll* [VP; subj: human, usu. pl] to drink a bottle of liquor (with s.o.): X и Y раздавили бутылку ≃ **X and Y killed ⟨split⟩ a bottle;** [in limited contexts] **X and Y made short work of a bottle.**

Кто-то предложил «раздавить бутылку» — возражений особых не было. Взяли в магазине три поллитровки, пошли в столовую ткацкой фабрики... (Войнович 5). Someone proposed killing a bottle of vodka and nobody had any special objection. We bought three half liters in a store, then went to the cafeteria in a textile factory... (5a).

Б-251 • **С БУ́ХТЫ-БАРА́ХТЫ ⟨С БУ́ХТА-БАРА́ХТА** *obs*⟩ сделать, сказать *что* и т. п. *coll* [PrepP; these forms only; adv] (to do, say sth.) rashly, suddenly, without taking time to think, without preparation or deliberation: **(do ⟨say⟩ sth.) without thinking ⟨out of the blue, all of a sudden⟩; (do sth.) on the spur of the moment; (say sth.) off the top of one's head;** [in limited contexts] **(do sth.) just like that.**

[Бабакина:] И эти дела не делаются так, с бухты-барахты (Чехов 4). [B.:] And these things are not done like that, just out of the blue... (4a). ♦ Был он нетороплив, рассудителен, и уж если говорил что-то — это было окончательно, весомо, не с бухты-барахты (Буковский 1). He was slow-moving and meditative, and if he ever said anything, it was his final word, carefully weighed, never off the top of his head (1a). ♦ «Почитайте, пожалуйста, если вам не трудно читать на улице, здесь. Я стихи люблю». Он посмотрел на меня с сомнением — как это так читать неизвестно кому с бухты-барахты? (Чуковская 2). "Please do read a little if it is not too difficult for you to read here, in the open. I love poetry." He looked at me dubiously, wondering how on earth he could read to someone he didn't know just like that, but he took out the papers (2a).

Б-252 • **КАК НЕ БЫВА́ЛО** *кого-чего coll* [VP; subj/gen: more often inanim; Invar; fixed WO] (a person or thing) disappeared, went away completely: X-a как не бывало ≃ **X vanished (without a trace); there is no trace (left) of X; it is as if X had never existed ⟨been⟩; thing X is completely gone.**

Молодецким движением Борис вскинул на плечо посылку, взял в руки чемодан. Усталости его как не бывало (Рыбаков 2). Boris swung the parcel up onto his shoulder with a spirited gesture and picked up his own suitcase. His fatigue had vanished (2a). ♦ Раздался треск и грохот... Через несколько минут крайней избы как не бывало... (Салтыков-Щедрин 1). There came a resounding crack and a crash....In a few moments the hut on the end was completely gone... (1a).

Б-253 • **КАК НИ В ЧЁМ НЕ БЫВА́ЛО** делать *что*, вести себя и т. п. *coll* [AdvP; Invar; adv or sent adv; fixed WO] (to do sth., behave) in a manner suggesting that one has not been affected by the preceding or concurrent events (which would be expected to elicit some reaction): **as if ⟨though⟩ nothing (had) happened ⟨were happening⟩; as if ⟨though⟩ nothing were wrong;** [in limited contexts] **as if one had never seen ⟨heard etc⟩; as if ⟨though⟩ it were the most natural thing in the world; just as one used to do.**

Заветная была у него [Джульбарса] мечта — покусать собственного хозяина, и он таки её осуществил — придавшись, что тот ему наступил на лапу... Когда хозяин наутро пришёл к нему, весь перебинтованный, Джульбарс его поприветствовал как ни в чём не бывало... (Владимов 1). His [Djulbars's] cherished dream was to bite his own master, and he succeeded in carrying it out, with the excuse that his master had trodden on his paw....When his master came to him next morning all bandaged up, Djulbars greeted him as though nothing had happened... (1a). ♦ ...Взрослые, к великому огорчению, не поступали так, как считал справедливым мальчик. Они делали всё наоборот. Приедет Орозкул домой уже подвыпивший. Его встречают как ни в чём не бывало (Айтматов 1). ...Unfortunately, the grown-ups did not do the things the boy thought would be just. They did everything the other way around. Orozkul would come home tipsy, and they would welcome him as if nothing were wrong (1a). ♦ ...[Митенька] не давал слушателю никакой возможности сделать возражение, а если последний ухитрялся как-нибудь ввернуть свое словечко, то Митенька не смущался и этим: выслушав возражение, соглашался с ним и вновь начинал гудеть как ни в чём не бывало (Салтыков-Щедрин 2). ...He [Mitenka] would give his listener no chance of getting a word in edgeways, and if the latter did succeed by some miracle in putting in a word, Mitenka was not in the least put out: he listened to what the other man had to say and, having expressed complete agreement with him, resumed his buzzing, as if he had never been interrupted (2a). ♦ И вот уже (25.4) с напечатанным письмом я шагаю в редакцию «Литературной газеты»... Два заместителя [редактора Чаковского]... ошарашенные моим приходом, встречают меня настороженно-предупредительно. Как ни в чём не бывало, как будто я их завсегдатай, кладу им на стол своё письмишко (Солженицын 2). On 25 April I strolled to the offices of *Literaturnaya Gazeta* with a typewritten letter....His [the editor Chakovsky's] two deputies...were flabbergasted by my appearance and met me with guarded politeness. As though it were the most natural thing in the world, as though I were one of their regular clients, I laid my little letter on a desk before them (2a).

Б-254 • **НИЧУ́ТЬ ⟨НИЧЕГО́** *obs*⟩ **НЕ БЫВА́ЛО** *coll* [sent; these forms only; fixed WO] (used to emphasize that sth. turned out differently than expected, presumed, described etc) absolutely not, not at all (what has been suggested, claimed etc): **nothing of the sort ⟨kind⟩ (happens); far from it; that isn't ⟨wasn't⟩ the case (at all).**

«Теща насыпала ещё [галушек]; думает, гость наелся и будет убирать меньше. Ничего не бывало. Ещё лучше стал уплетать!» (Гоголь 5). "My mother-in-law put out some more [dumplings]; she thought the visitor had had enough and would take less. Nothing of the sort: he began gulping them down faster than ever..." (5a). ♦ «Всё думаешь: с завтрашнего дня начнёшь новую жизнь, с завтрашнего дня сядешь на диету — ничуть не бывало: к вечеру того же дня так объешься, что... язык не ворочается...» (Гоголь 3). "You keep thinking that from tomorrow you'll start a new life, that from tomorrow you will go on a diet, but nothing of the sort happens: on the evening of that very day you gorge yourself so much that...you can hardly utter a word" (3a). ♦ Я часто себя спрашиваю, зачем я так упорно добиваюсь любви молоденькой девочки, которую обольстить я не хочу и на которой никогда не женюсь?.. Если б она казалась мне непобедимой красавицей, то может быть, я бы завлёкся трудностию предприятия. Но ничуть не бывало! (Лермонтов 3). I often ask myself why it is that I so persistently seek to win the love of a young girl whom I do not wish to seduce and whom I shall never marry....Were she an unconquerable beauty, the difficulty of the undertaking might serve as an inducement....But far from it! (1b). I often wonder why I'm trying so hard to win the love of a girl I have no desire to seduce and whom I'd never marry....If she were some unattainable beauty I might have been attracted by the difficulty of the undertaking. But that isn't the case... (1c).

Б-255 • **КАК БЫК** *coll* [как + NP; nom only] **1. здоров ~** [sing only; modif] (of a person, usu. a man, in very good health)

completely (healthy): **healthy as a horse ⟨an ox⟩; (as) fit as a fiddle.**

«Шунечка, ты болен?» — «Ерунда. Здоров как бык, просто устал» (Грекова 3). "Shunechka, are you sick?" "Nonsense. Healthy as a horse, just tired" (3a). ♦ «Ты когда-нибудь болел так, чтобы заново вкус жизни ощутить?» — «Что-то не помню, — со всей непосредственностью ответил Едигей. — Разве что после контузии...» — «Да ты здоров как бык! — рассмеялся Елизаров. — Я вообще-то и не об этом» (Айтматов 2). "Have you ever been ill and then recovered, with a new taste for life?" "I don't remember," Yedigei answered ingenuously, "perhaps after my shellshock, though..." "Oh, you're as healthy as an ox, now!" Yelizarov laughed. "But I'm not talking about health..." (2a).

2. сильный, здоровый ~ [sing only; modif] (of a strong, solidly built man) extremely (strong): **(as) strong as a bull ⟨an ox, a horse⟩; sturdy as an ox.**

«Да что с тобой говорить! Здоровый как бык, а ума...» — дед Момун безнадёжно махал рукой (Айтматов 1). "Ah, what's the use of talking to you. Strong as an ox, and the brain of an...." And Grandpa Momun would shake his head hopelessly (1a).

3. ~ упереться [adv (intensif)] (to resist sth.) very stubbornly: **(balk) like a mule; (be) stubborn ⟨as balky⟩ as a mule; (be) bullheaded ⟨pigheaded⟩.**

[Кашкина (*подражая Ларисе*):] «Он [Шаманов] упёрся как бык... не знаю уж, кем он себя вообразил, но он тронулся, это точно» (Вампилов 2). [K. *imitating Larisa*:] "He [Shamanov] was stubborn as a mule....I don't know who he thought he was, but he went nutty, that's for sure" (2b).

Б-256 • **БРАТЬ/ВЗЯТЬ ⟨ХВАТА́ТЬ/СХВАТИ́ТЬ⟩ БЫКА́ ЗА РОГА́** *coll* [VP; subj: human; fixed WO] to take bold, resolute action, immediately and bravely addressing the most essential, difficult aspects of the matter: X взял быка за рога ≃ **X took the bull by the horns.**

«Сколько лет, сколько зим!» — «Вот гостя тебе из Москвы привёз». — Шилов брал быка за рога. — Чем привечать будешь?» (Максимов 1). "Haven't seen you out here for ages!" "I've brought you a visitor from Moscow." Shilov took the bull by the horns: "What can you offer us?" (1a).

Б-257 • **БЫЛ ДА СПЛЫЛ** *coll* [VP; subj: any common noun (often omitted); past only; fixed WO] (a person or thing) was present somewhere, or (a thing) was in s.o.'s possession, but is no longer: (X) был да сплыл ≃ **X was here ⟨s.o. *did* have X etc⟩, but not anymore ⟨any longer⟩; X was here ⟨s.o. *did* have X etc⟩ but it's all gone now; here today, gone tomorrow; here one day ⟨minute⟩, gone the next; [in limited contexts] X came and went ⟨has come and gone⟩.**

[author's usage] Я встал и сказал: «Да ладно уж... Сказано — сделано. Сбрею [бороду]. Считайте, что её уже нет. Была и сплыла» (Аксёнов 1). I stood up and said, "Well, okay then....No sooner said than done. I'll shave it [my beard] off. Think of it as already gone. Come and went" (1a). ♦ «Так и молодость пройдёт, жизнь — она короткая». — «Была у меня молодость да сплыла», — потерянно вздохнула она (Максимов 1). [context transl] "And so your youth will slip by. Life is short!" "I was young once, but that's all past," she sighed distractedly... (1a).

Б-258 • **И БЫЛ ТАКО́В** *coll* [VP; subj: human or animal (more often male); past only; preceded by one or more verbs (usu. pfv past); occas. used in fut contexts] one ran away, disappeared (from sight): X... и был таков ≃ **and off ⟨away⟩ X went; and that's ⟨that was⟩ the last anyone ⟨I, we etc⟩ saw of X; and X was gone (before you ⟨I, we etc⟩ knew it); and X was off in a flash; and X skipped; [in limited contexts] and X up and ran away.**

«Так вот, сударь, как настоящие-то начальники принимали! — вздыхали глуповцы, — а это что! Фыркнул какую-то нелепицу, да и был таков!» (Салтыков-Щедрин 1). "Now that, sir, is the way *real* governors received you!" sighed the Foolovites. "But this one! Splutters some kind of fol-de-rol and off he goes!" (1a). ♦ [Варвара:] Да, что сделаешь? [Катерина:] Что мне только захочется, то и сделаю. [Варвара:] Сделай, попробуй, так тебя здесь заедят. [Катерина:] А что мне! Я уйду, да и была такова (Островский 6). [V.:] Yes, what will you do? [K.:] Whatever I take a fancy to. [V.:] Well, do it, just try it; and they will fairly eat you alive. [K.:] What do I care! I'll go away; that's the last they'll see of me (6e). ♦ Проснувшись... [Аркадий] переоделся в гражданское, навёл на себя всяческий блеск и марафет – и был таков (Залыгин 1). On waking...he [Arkady] changed into civilian clothes, spruced himself up and was gone (1a). ♦ [Дуня:] Только сумеешь ли ты с этакой женой жить? Ты смотри, не загуби чужого веку даром. Грех тебе будет. Остепенись, да живи хорошенько. Это ведь не со мной: жили, жили, да и был таков. *(Утирает глаза.)* (Островский 1). [D.:] Only will you know how to live with a woman like her? Look out that you don't destroy another's life for nothing. It'd be a sin for you. Come to your senses, and live properly. It wasn't so with me: we lived, we lived for a while, and then you skipped. *(She wipes her eyes.)* (1b).

Б-259 • КАК ⟨В ЧЁМ⟩ БЫЛ coll [subord clause; past only; fixed WO] without having or being given a chance to change clothes: **(just) as one was; in what one had on ⟨was wearing⟩.**

Войдя к себе, он бросился на диван, так, как был (Достоевский 3). Entering his room, he threw himself on his couch as he was (3a). ♦ Разбудили нас Чудаков и Евдощук. Они, как были, в шапках и тулупах, грохотали сапогами по настилу, вытаскивали свои чемоданы и орали: «Подъём!» (Аксёнов 1). Chudakov and Yevdoshchuk woke us up. Just as they were, in their hats and sheepskins, their boots clumping on the floorboards, they pulled out their suitcases and roared: "Rise and shine!" (1a).

Б-260 • КТО БЫ (ТО) НИ БЫЛ [NP; nom only; used as appos or subord clause; fixed WO] regardless of who a person is; any person: **no matter who he is; whoever it ⟨he⟩ may ⟨might⟩ be.**

[Ирина:] Человек должен трудиться, работать в поте лица, кто бы он ни был... (Чехов 5). [I.:] Man must work, he must toil by the sweat of his brow, no matter who he is... (5a).

Б-261 • БЫЛА́ НЕ БЫЛА́ coll [Invar; indep. clause or sent adv (parenth)] (used to express one's resolve to do sth. risky – usu. after some hesitation – in the hope of achieving success) I will go ahead and risk it: **here goes (nothing); whatever happens happens; (I ⟨we etc⟩ will do sth.) come what may; you only live once.**

«Эх, была не была! – крикнул Скороход, снимая с ног жернова. – Прыгаю через радугу!» (Искандер 5). "Well, here goes," Highspeed shouted, removing the millstones from his feet. "I'm going to jump over the rainbow!" (5a). ♦ «Я вижу, вас что-то смущает?» – «Так точно, смущает, товарищ Сталин». – «Что же именно вас смущает?» А, была не была, Дрынов решился (Войнович 4). "I see something's bothering you." "Yes, sir, there is, Comrade Stalin." "So just what is it?" Here goes nothing, thought Drinov (4a). ♦ «Как, батя, советуешь – слезать или не слезать?» – в последний раз понадеялся он на проводника. «Слезай!» – махнул рукой проводник и отступил в сторону, освобождая проход. «Была не была», – решился Алтынник (Войнович 5). "What's your advice, old man, get off here or not?" he asked, pinning his last hopes on the conductor. "Get off!" The conductor waved his hand and stepped aside, clearing the way. "Whatever happens happens," decided Altinnik (5a). ♦ Иногда при ударе карт по столу вырывались выражения: «А! была не была, не с чего, так с бубен!» или же просто восклицания: «черви! червоточина!..» (Гоголь 3). Now and then as the cards landed on the table with a bang, certain exclamations would escape the players: "Come what may, I'll play diamonds if there is nothing else!" or just ejaculations: "Hey, hearts – heartaches!"... (3c).

Б-262 • ГДЕ БЫ ТО НИ БЫЛО; КУДА́ БЫ ТО НИ БЫЛО [AdvP; these forms only; adv; fixed WO] any (or to any) place, regardless of where: **anywhere (at all ⟨whatsoever, whatever⟩); [in limited contexts] it doesn't matter where; no matter where; wherever.**

Б-263 • КАК БЫ ТО ⟨ТАМ⟩ НИ БЫЛО [AdvP; these forms only; usu. sent adv (parenth); usu. in the initial position; fixed WO] whatever the circumstances or situation may be, regardless of whether the preceding statement is true (or, in the case of several preceding statements, which of them is true), even though that might be true, it is irrelevant: **whatever the case ⟨the cause, the reason⟩ (may be); however that ⟨this⟩ may be; whatever the truth of the matter is; [in limited contexts] be that as it may; at any rate.**

Сейчас мне не совсем понятно, почему, собственно, потребовалось вмешательство бабушки: ведь я был достаточно взрослым мальчиком... По всей вероятности, бабушка была послана, так сказать, для отчёта. Как бы то ни было, этот день... соединён именно с бабушкой... (Олеша 3). It isn't entirely clear to me now just why my grandmother's intervention was required; I was, after all, quite sufficiently grown-up to have gone by myself....Most likely, my grandmother was sent to keep account, so to speak. Whatever the reason, that day...is united with the memory of my grandmother (3a). ♦ [Глуповцы] стали доискиваться, откуда явилась Пфейферша. Одни говорили, что она не более как интриганка... Другие утверждали, что Пфейферша... вышла замуж за Пфейфера единственно затем, чтобы соединиться с Грустиловым... Как бы то ни было, нельзя отвергать, что это была женщина далеко не дюжинная (Салтыков-Щедрин 1). They [the Foolovites] began trying to find out where Mme Pfeifer had come from. Some said that she was no more than an intriguer....Others alleged that...[she] had married Pfeifer only in order to be united with Melancholov....However that may be, it cannot be denied that she was far from an ordinary woman (1a). ♦ Публика эта разделилась на два лагеря. Часть её... решительно во всём обвиняла Надежду Петровну... Другая часть, напротив, оправдывала её... Как бы то ни было, но Надежда Петровна стала удостоверяться, что уважение к ней с каждым днём умаляется (Салтыков-Щедрин 2). The public was divided into two camps. One section...was firmly of the opinion that Nadezhda Petrovna was to blame....The other section of public opinion, however, stoutly defended her....Whatever the truth of the matter was, Nadezhda Petrovna began to notice that the respect in which she had been held was beginning to fritter away daily (2a). ♦ Не оттого ли, может быть, шагала она [Ольга] так уверенно по этому пути, что по временам слышала рядом другие, ещё более уверенные шаги «друга», которому верила, и с ними соразмеряла свой шаг. Как бы то ни было, но в редкой девице встретишь такую простоту и естественную свободу взгляда, слова, поступка (Гончаров 1). Quite likely she [Olga] walked so confidently through life because she heard at times beside her the still more confident footsteps of her "friend" whom she trusted and with whom she tried to keep in step. Be that as it may, there were few girls who possessed such a simplicity and spontaneity of opinions, words, and actions (1a).

Б-264 • КАКО́Й БЫ ТО НИ́ БЫЛО [AdjP; modif; fixed WO] any: **any... (at all ⟨whatsoever, whatever⟩); [in limited contexts] any sort ⟨kind⟩ of; no matter what sort ⟨kind⟩ (of).**

При настоящих, усложнённых формах государственной и общественной жизни в Европе возможно ли придумать какое бы то ни было событие, которое бы не было предписано, указано, приказано государями, министрами, парламентами, газетами? (Толстой 7). With the present complex forms of political and social life in Europe, can one think of any event that would not have been prescribed, decreed, or ordered by monarchs, ministers, parliaments, or newspapers? (7a). ♦ Только при полном отсутствии каких бы то ни было сведений об общественной жизни тайна будет сохранена (Зиновьев 1). The secret can only be preserved in the complete absence of any data at all about social life (1a). ♦ ...Как бы ни хотел учёный быть объективным, одним последовательным перечислением известных фактов — он уже рисует, даже помимо воли, определённую жизненную картину и расстановку сил в нашем сознании. Но... в этой картине неизбежно отсутствует какая бы то ни было полнота... (Битов 2). ...However objective a scholar may wish to be, let him merely enumerate a sequence of known facts and he is already, even against his will, drawing a well-defined picture of life and an arrangement of forces in our consciousness. But...that picture inevitably lacks any sort of completeness... (2a). ♦ Он так устал от целого месяца этой сосредоточенной тоски своей и мрачного возбуждения, что хотя одну минуту хотелось ему вздохнуть в другом мире, хоть бы в каком бы то ни было... (Достоевский 3). After a whole month of concentrated melancholy and gloomy excitement, he was so weary he wanted to take breath in some other world, no matter what kind (3b).

Б-265 • **КОГДА́ БЫ ТО НИ́ БЫЛО** [AdvP; Invar; adv; fixed WO] at any time, regardless of when: **anytime (at all ⟨whatsoever, whatever⟩);** [in limited contexts] **no matter when; whenever.**

Б-266 • **КТО БЫ ТО НИ́ БЫЛО** [NP; obj or, usu. as a response to a question, subj; often used with a negated predic; fixed WO] any person, regardless of who: **anyone ⟨anybody⟩ at all; anyone whatever;** [in limited contexts] **no matter who;** [after a compar form] **than anyone ⟨anybody⟩ else.**

Явясь по двадцатому году к отцу, положительно в вертеп грязного разврата, он, целомудренный и чистый, лишь молча удалялся, когда глядеть было нестерпимо, но без малейшего вида презрения или осуждения кому бы то ни было (Достоевский 1). Coming to his father in his twentieth year, precisely into that den of dirty iniquity, he, chaste and pure, would simply retire quietly when it was unbearable to watch, yet without the least expression of contempt or condemnation of anyone at all (1a). ♦ ...Лёва не мог подозревать кого бы то ни было в чём бы то ни было... — тем более, незнакомого человека... (Битов 2). ...Lyova was incapable of suspecting anyone whatever of anything whatever...especially a man he didn't know... (2a). ♦ Лёвин дом оттаивал, и будто это именно бездомный дядя Митя создал им дом. Дяде Мите позволялось многое, больше, чем кому бы то ни было, и больше, чем себе (Битов 2). Lyova's house thawed out, and it was as though homeless Uncle Mitya had created a home for them. To Uncle Mitya they permitted much; more than to anyone else, and more than to themselves (2a).

Б-267 • **НЕ ТУ́Т-ТО БЫ́ЛО** coll [sent; Invar; often a clause in a compound sent (often after но, да); fixed WO] (of unrealized hopes, expectations, usu. when attempting to accomplish sth.) the desired or expected event (as specified by the preceding context) did not happen, the desired or expected result was not achieved etc: **nothing doing; no such luck; nothing of the kind ⟨the sort⟩ (happened); it ⟨things etc⟩ didn't work out (that way);** [in limited contexts] **far from it; it was not to be.**

...К нему [старому кучеру] подбежала фрейлейн Мари и объявила ему о своём желании зарезать гусака собственноручно. Конечно, он отговаривал её, упрашивал, пригрозил даже нажаловаться. Не тут-то было! (Федин 1). ...Fräulein Marie ran up to him [the old coachman] and announced her desire to cut the goose's neck personally. Of course he tried to talk her out of it, begged, threatened even to complain about her. Nothing doing! (1a). ♦ «Иди домой!...» – крикнул ей Чунка по-русски. Но не тут-то было! (Искандер 5). "Go home!..." Chunka yelled to her in Russian. No such luck (5a). ♦ Он [Тентетников] уничтожил вовсе всякие приносы холста, ягод, грибов и орехов, наполовину сбавил с них других работ, думая, что бабы обратят это время на домашнее хозяйство... Не тут-то было (Гоголь 3). He [Tentet-

nikov] had exempted them from any deliveries of homespun linen, berries, mushrooms and nuts, he had halved their other obligatory labours, with the idea that the women would give more time to their household affairs....But nothing of the sort! (3d). ♦ Видимо, замешкались в совхозе с разными делами; и когда время поджало, решили одним разом, всеми машинами вывезти заготовленное сено. Но не тут-то было!.. (Айтматов 1). Evidently they'd dawdled with various jobs on the state farm and now that time was pressing, decided to bring in the waiting hay with all the lorries in one go. But it didn't work out... (1b). ♦ Я думал, что после этих мешков не скоро отдышится этот осёл. Но не тут-то было! (Искандер 3). I thought it would take a while for the donkey to catch his breath after those sacks. But far from it! (3a). ♦ Прошёл слух, что я выступал у курчатовцев, и стали приходить мне многие приглашения... И в этих учреждениях всё как будто было устроено, разрешено директорами, повешены объявления... — но не тут-то было! не дремали и там [в КГБ] (Солженицын 2). The news that I had appeared at the Kurchatov Institute got around, and invitations began to arrive in large numbers....These institutions seemed to have everything arranged — directors had given their permission, notices had been put up... — but it was not to be! *They* [the KGB] were not to be caught napping (2a).

Б-268 • **ПОЧЕМУ́ БЫ ТО НИ́ БЫЛО** [AdvP; Invar; adv; fixed WO] because of any circumstances: **for any reason (at all ⟨whatsoever, whatever⟩); for whatever reason;** [in limited contexts] **no matter what the reason (may be); whatever the reason (may be).**

Характер у Никиты для бизнеса неподходящий. Если он почему бы то ни было решит заняться коммерцией, у него наверняка ничего не выйдет. Nikita's personality isn't suited for business. If he for whatever reason decides to try it, he'll certainly fail.

Б-269 • **СКО́ЛЬКО БЫ ТО НИ́ БЫЛО** [AdvP; Invar; adv; fixed WO] any number or quantity, regardless of how much or how many: **however much ⟨many⟩;** [in limited contexts] **it doesn't matter how much ⟨many⟩; no matter how much ⟨many⟩.**

Б-270 • **ЧЕЙ БЫ ТО НИ́ БЫЛО** [AdjP; modif; fixed WO] any person's, regardless of whose: **anyone's ⟨anybody's⟩; it doesn't matter whose.**

«Чьи лыжи можно взять?» – «Да чьи бы то ни было». "Whose skis can I take?" "Anybody's."

Б-271 • **ЧТО БЫ ТО НИ́ БЫЛО** [NP; usu. obj; fixed WO] any thing, regardless of what: **anything (at all ⟨whatsoever, whatever⟩);** [in limited contexts] **no matter what; any of it.**

Ему [Марку Крысобою] прокуратор приказал сдать преступника начальнику тайной службы и при этом передать ему распоряжение прокуратора о том, чтобы... команде тайной службы под страхом тяжкой кары запрещено о чём бы то ни было разговаривать с Иешуа или отвечать на какие-либо его вопросы (Булгаков 9). He [Mark Rat-Killer] was ordered by the Procurator to turn the criminal over to the chief of the secret service, and to relay the Procurator's command that...the soldiers of the secret service detachment be forbidden, under threat of severe punishment, to speak with Yeshua about anything, or to answer any of his questions (9a). ♦ ...Лёва не мог подозревать кого бы то ни было в чём бы то ни было... — тем более, незнакомого человека... (Битов 2). ...Lyova was incapable of suspecting anyone whatever of anything whatever...especially a man he didn't know... (2a).

Б-272 • **ЧТОБЫ НЕПОВА́ДНО БЫ́ЛО ⟨ЧТОБЫ НЕ́ БЫЛО ПОВА́ДНО⟩** (кому) coll [these forms only; subord clause; the main clause indicates how s.o. was or will be punished, or expresses a threat to punish s.o.; fixed WO] (s.o. was or will be punished, rebuked etc for some wrongdoing) so that he or another will not commit a similar wrongdoing (again): чтобы (X-у) неповадно было ≃ **(in order) to teach X a lesson; as a lesson to X; so that X will know better ⟨think twice⟩ next time.**

Как известно, наши хозяева умели предсказывать будущее, пользуясь... научными методами, а также действительно действенным методом устрашения и расправы не над виновными или сопротивляющимися, а над кем попало, чтобы другим не было повадно (Мандельштам 2). As we all know, our rulers were able to foretell the future...with the aid of "scientific principles," and also influenced its course by that most efficient means of intimidation which consists in persecuting not the guilty or the recalcitrant, but anybody who happens to come to hand—just as a lesson to the rest (2a).

Б-273 • ЧТОБ ПУ́СТО БЫ́ЛО *кому-чему*, usu. тебе, ему и т. п. *substand* [Interj; Invar; usu. this WO] **1.** used to express annoyance, strong irritation, anger caused by s.o. or sth.: чтоб X-у пусто было! ≃ **damn X; to hell with X!; X can go to hell; may person X rot ⟨roast⟩ in hell (, damn him!); may place X crumble to the ground.**

[Авдотья Назаровна:] Чтоб тебе пусто было, с ног сшиб! (Чехов 4). [A.N.:] You nearly knocked me over, damn you (4b). ♦ [Зилов:] Знать вас больше не желаю! Подонки!.. Чтоб вам пусто было! (Вампилов 5). [Z.:] I've had it with you! Scum!...Roast in hell, damn you! (5b). ♦ «И на мое еврейское счастье я таки в конце концов попал в эту самую консерваторию, чтоб ей было пусто, и даже почти кончил её, спасибо, война помешала» (Максимов 1). "And, with my Jewish luck, I ended up entering the famous Conservatoire itself, may it crumble to the ground, and I almost finished my course, but luckily the war intervened" (1a).

2. used to express admiration, surprise caused by sth.: **well, I'll be damned ⟨darned⟩!; (hot) damn!**

Б-274 • БЫЛЬЁМ ⟨БЫ́ЛЬЮ, ТРАВО́Й⟩ ПОРОСЛО́ [VP; subj: abstr, usu. всё, (всё) это; usu. past; fixed WO] (sth.) has been completely forgotten (usu. sth. that happened long ago): всё быльем поросло ≃ **it's (all) long forgotten; it's all gone and forgotten; it's all (long since) dead and buried ⟨gone⟩; it's all ancient history;** [in limited contexts] **it's long dead.**

В те благословенные времена советская молодёжь не воротила нос от советских же символов... Я помню, в моде были «будённовки», сталинские френчи и даже сталинские усы. Давно это было, да быльём поросло (Войнович 1). In those hallowed days, Soviet youth did not turn up its nose at Soviet symbols....I can remember when army caps, Stalin jackets, and even Stalin mustaches were in style. But those times were long ago and are long forgotten (1a). ♦ Много позже, когда всё, так сказать, быльём поросло, Лёва взглянул однажды на её кольцо... — и вдруг всё ожило и завертелось перед его глазами, воскресло и ощущение того вечера с Митишатьевым, и всех последовавших дней... (Битов 2). Much later, when the issue was long dead, so to speak, Lyova glanced at her ring one day...—and suddenly it all came back to life and started spinning before his eyes. The feeling of that night with Mitishatyev revived, too, and of all the days that had followed... (2a).

< Part of the saying «Что было, то прошло (и быльём поросло)». See Б-275.

Б-275 • ЧТО БЫ́ЛО, ТО ПРОШЛО́ (И БЫЛЬЁМ ПОРОСЛО́) [saying] what has passed has passed, and there is no point in dwelling on it: ≃ **it's all water under the bridge ⟨over the dam⟩; things past cannot be recalled;** [when emphasizing that a past difference between people should be forgotten] **let bygones be bygones.**

Б-276 • С БЫСТРОТО́Ю ⟨-ой⟩ МО́ЛНИИ [PrepP; these forms only; adv; usu. used with pfv verbs; fixed WO] very swiftly: **with lightning speed;** [in limited contexts] **like wildfire.**

Раскольников сел, не сводя с него [Порфирия Петровича] глаз... Оба следили друг за другом, но только что взгляды их встречались, оба, с быстротою молнии, отводили их один от другого (Достоевский 3). Raskolnikov sat down without taking his eyes off him [Porfiry Petrovich]....Each watched the other, but the moment their eyes met, they both, with lightning speed, averted them again (3a).

Б-277 • БЫТЬ ПО СЕМУ́ *obs, now humor* [sent; Invar; fixed WO] (used to express the speaker's agreement with, support of some suggestion, idea etc) let it be that way: **so be it.**

Предоставить актёрам его высочества герцога Орлеанского... зал в Малом Бурбоне, утвердить им пенсию, незначенную герцогом Орлеанским. Играть им в очередь с итальянской труппой... И быть по сему! (Булгаков 5). It was decreed that the Players of His Highness Duc d'Orléans...be given a hall at the Petit Bourbon and confirmed in the pension declared by the Duc d'Orléans. They were to take turns with the Italian troupe....And so be it! (5a).

< Originally, the written formula phrase used by tsars and tsarinas at the end of official documents to express their support, approval etc of the material contained therein.

Б-278 • ДОЛЖНО́ БЫТЬ [Invar; sent adv (parenth); fixed WO] presumably: **probably; (as) likely as not; most likely; in all likelihood ⟨probability⟩;** [in pres and past contexts] **must** [+ infin]; [in limited contexts] **I suppose; chances are.**

Должно быть, слова в старину читались медленнее... (Терц 3). In the old days people probably read much more slowly... (3a). ♦ [Вошедший] буркнул что-то и, должно быть, сел (Солженицын 12). The man muttered something and then must have sat down (12a). ♦ [Анна Петровна:] Где Софья? [Войницев:] Должно быть, у себя... (Чехов 1). [A.P.:] Where's Sophia? [V.:] In her room, I suppose (1a).

Б-279 • НА́ДО БЫТЬ *substand* [Invar; sent adv (parenth); fixed WO] presumably: **probably; (as) like as not;** [in pres and past contexts] **must** [+ infin].

Б-280 • ТАК И БЫТЬ *coll* [Invar; indep. clause or sent adv (parenth); fixed WO] (used to express the speaker's concession, agreement to repeated requests etc) let it be as you wish or as the circumstances require: **all right (then); very well; so be it;** [in limited contexts] **that's ⟨it's⟩ all right; oh well.**

Шунечка... целовал ей руки, не хотел никуда её отпускать — даже в аптеку. «Ну, так и быть, иди, только приходи скорей» (Грекова 3). He [Shunechka] kissed her hands and didn't want to let her go anywhere, even to the pharmacy. "Well, all right, go, but come back right away" (3a). ♦ «Пусть он [мой клиент] обманул отца знаками, пусть он проник к нему — я сказал уже, что ни на одну минуту не верю этой легенде, но пусть, так и быть, предположим её на одну минуту!» (Достоевский 2). "Suppose he [my client] did deceive his father with the signals, suppose he did get in—I have already said that I do not for a moment believe this legend, but very well, let us suppose it for the moment!" (2a). ♦ «Добро, — сказала комендантша, — так и быть, отправим Машу. А меня и во сне не проси: не поеду» (Пушкин 2). "All right," said the commandant's wife, "so be it: we'll send Masha away. But don't dream of asking me: I won't go" (2b). ♦ «...Это целая история. Но я тебе, так и быть, расскажу, потому что ты преданный нашему народу человек, хоть и сидишь верхом на муле» (Искандер 3). "...That's another story. That's all right, I'll tell it to you, because you're a man devoted to our people, even if you do ride a mule" (3a). ♦ «Два часа только до обеда, что успеешь сделать в два часа? — Ничего. А дела куча. Так и быть, письмо отложу до следующей почты, а план набросаю завтра» (Гончаров 1). "Only two hours left before dinner, and what can one do in two hours? Nothing. And there's lots to be done. Oh well, I shall have to put off my letter till the next post and jot down the plan to-morrow" (1a).

Б-281 • ТАК ТОМУ́ И БЫТЬ [Invar; indep. clause; fixed WO]
1. let it be that way: **so be it.**

Наверно, Лизка в своей простоте подумала: раз уж люди решили — свадьбе быть, то так тому и быть. Поздно теперь отступать (Абрамов 1). Most likely Lizka, in her innocence, thought, if they've all decided there's going to be a wedding, then so be it. It's too late to back down now (1a).

2. (used to express concession to the inevitability of sth.) that is just how it has to be: **that's the way it is ⟨it goes, it was meant to be⟩; that's (just) the way of things; it (simply) has to be that ⟨this⟩ way; it has to happen; there's no getting around it.**

[Анна Петровна:] Жалко расставаться с гнёздышком, но что же поделаешь, голубчик мой? Не воротишь... Так тому и быть, значит... (Чехов 1). [A.P.:] It hurts to say good-bye to your nice little home, but what can you do, dear? You can't put the clock back now. So that's the way of things (1b). ♦ ...Варя выбрала этот путь ещё в школе: мальчишки, губная помада, тряпки. Нина и тогда ничего не могла с ней поделать, ничего не может сделать и сейчас. Значит, так тому и быть! (Рыбаков 2). ...Varya had chosen her life while still at school. She had gone out with lots of boys, used lipstick, spent all her money on clothes. Even then Nina had been unable to control her, and she certainly couldn't now. It had to happen (2a).

Б-282 • ЧЕМУ́ БЫТЬ, ТОГО́ ⟨ТОМУ́⟩ НЕ МИНОВА́ТЬ [saying] you cannot avoid what must happen (said with certainty that what is fated to happen will happen regardless of how a person acts): ≃ **what must be must be; what ⟨whatever⟩ will ⟨is to⟩ be will be; what's got to be has got to be; there's no avoiding the inevitable.**

Жалоба Мими, единица и ключик! Хуже ничего не могло со мной случиться... «Что со мной будет? А-а-ах! что я наделал?! — говорил я вслух, прохаживаясь по мягкому ковру кабинета. — Э! — сказал я сам себе, доставая конфеты и сигары, — чему быть, тому не миновать...» (Толстой 2). Mimi's complaint, the bad mark, the key! Nothing worse could happen to me... "What will become of me? O-oh dear, what have I done!" I said aloud, walking over the soft carpet in the study. "Ha!" I said to myself as I got the candy and cigars, *"what must be, must be..."* (2b). ♦ [Аркадина:] И у меня правило: не заглядывать в будущее. Я никогда не думаю ни о старости, ни о смерти. Чему быть, того не миновать (Чехов 6). [A.:] And another thing: I make it a strict rule never to look into the future, never to worry about old age or death. What will be, will be (6b). ♦ «Чего надумал, Андрейка, умней не мог, мне же ещё и саботаж пришьют. — В увещевающем тоне Хохлушкина сквозило тоскливое безразличие. — Чему быть, того не миновать» (Максимов 1). "What are you thinking of, Andreika? Use your brains, they'll start pinning sabotage on me as well." In Khokhlushkin's admonishing tone there was an element of melancholy indifference. "What is to be will be" (1a).

Б-283 • БЫТЬ БЫЧКУ́ НА ВЕРЁВОЧКЕ [saying] **1.** a person will not escape the consequences of what he has done, will not escape punishment: ≃ **you ⟨he etc⟩ will get your ⟨his etc⟩ just deserts; you will get your comeuppance; you won't get away with it ⟨get off the hook⟩ (this time).**

2. (of men) s.o. cannot escape proposing and getting married: ≃ **he will be snared ⟨roped in⟩ all right; he took the bait — now he's hooked for good; there's no way he can get off the hook now.**

Б-284 • ВЫХОДИ́ТЬ/ВЫ́ЙТИ ИЗ БЮДЖЕ́ТА [VP; subj: human or collect] to spend too much money, more than one planned to or should have: X вышел из бюджета ≃ **X exceeded ⟨went through, went over⟩ his budget; X put a hole in his budget.**

«Мне нужны деньги». — «Но у вас же их никогда нет. Вы ведь вечно рыщете за полтинником». — «Я купил мебель и вышел из бюджета» (Ильф и Петров 1). "I need the money." "But you never have any. You're always trying to cadge half-roubles." "I bought some furniture and went through my budget" (1a).

В

В-1 • **ВАГО́Н И МА́ЛЕНЬКАЯ ТЕЛЕ́ЖКА** *чего coll, usu. humor* [NP; often quantit compl with copula (subj/gen: usu. concr or abstr); fixed WO] a great number, a great deal: **oodles; scads; barrels; scores;** [in limited contexts] **a whole truckload; enough to feed ⟨clothe etc⟩ an army.**

«Что нового в управлении?» – «Новостей вагон и маленькая тележка», – сказал Сидоркин (Войнович 5). "What's new over our way?" "I've got scads of news," said Sidorkin (5a). ♦ «Жена, – говорит, – перед отправкой вещей нанесла вагон и маленькую тележку» (Марченко 1). "My wife," he said, "brought along enough things to clothe an army just before I was due to leave" (1a).

В-2 • **ДЛЯ (ПУ́ЩЕЙ ⟨БО́ЛЬШЕЙ⟩) ВА́ЖНОСТИ** [PrepP; these forms only; adv; fixed WO] in order to create an effect: **to make an impression; just to impress (s.o.); to make o.s. look more important; just for show.**

Насчёт газет и журналов приезжие, конечно, пыль пустили в глаза боранлинцам для пущей важности... (Айтматов 2). In claiming to represent newspapers and magazines, the visitors were, of course, deceiving the people of Boranly—it was just to impress them (2a).

В-3 • **ВЕЛИКА́ ⟨Э́КА, ЧТО́ ЗА⟩ ВА́ЖНОСТЬ!** *coll* [sent; these forms only; fixed WO] (usu. used as a response to the preceding statement, rhetorical question, suggestion etc) that (fact, circumstance etc) is of no importance: **what (does it ⟨that⟩) matter?; as if that ⟨it⟩ mattered!;** [in limited contexts] **so what!; and what of it?; big deal!**

«Тебе бы следовало уважать в нём моего приятеля...» – «Уважать немца? – с величайшим презрением сказал Тарантьев. – За что это?» – «Я уж тебе сказал, хоть бы за то, что он вместе со мной рос и учился». – «Велика важность!» (Гончаров 1). "You ought to respect him as my friend..." "To respect a German?" Tarantyev said with the utmost contempt. "Why should I?" "But I've just told you—if for nothing else then because we grew up and went to the same school together." "What does that matter?" (1a). ♦ [Лебедев:] Что ж тебе ещё нужно? Денег нет? Велика важность! Не в деньгах счастье... (Чехов 4). [L.:] What more do you want? You may be hard up, but what matter? Money doesn't bring happiness (4b). ♦ «Я начинаю соглашаться с дядей, – заметил Аркадий, – ты решительно дурного мнения о русских». – «Эка важность!» (Тургенев 2). "I am beginning to agree with my uncle," remarked Arkady; "you most certainly have a poor opinion of Russians." "As if that mattered!" (2e).

В-4 • **НЕ ВЕЛИКА́ ВА́ЖНОСТЬ** *coll* [NP; Invar; indep. clause or subj-compl with быть∅ (subj: usu. infin); fixed WO] it is unimportant, nothing to be concerned about: **no problem; no big deal ⟨thing⟩; it's ⟨that's⟩ nothing.**

«Тебе придётся долго ждать поезда». – «Всего два часа, не велика важность». "You'll have a long wait for the train." "Just two hours—no big deal."

В-5 • **ДЕВЯ́ТЫЙ ВАЛ** [NP; sing only; fixed WO] **1.** the strongest and most dangerous wave during a storm at sea: **ninth wave.**

А – выход на Западе двух моих романов сразу – дубль?! Как на гавайском прибое у Джека Лондона, стоя в рост на гладкой доске, никак не держась, ничем не припутан, на гребне девятого вала, в раздире лёгких ветра – угадываю: предчувствую: а это – пройдёт! (Солженицын 2). But—two novels of mine appearing simultaneously in the West? A *double?* I felt like the Hawaiian surf riders described by Jack London, standing upright on a smooth board, with nothing to hold on to, nothing to hamper me, on the crest of the ninth wave, my lungs bursting from the rush of air. I divined, I sensed, that it would work! (2a).

2. the strongest manifestation of a serious menace, the apex of sth.: **mighty ⟨surging⟩ wave; climactic moment.**

В-6 • **ВАЛО́М ВАЛИ́ТЬ/ПОВАЛИ́ТЬ** *coll* [VP; usu. this WO] **1.** ~ *(куда)* [subj: human pl or collect] to go or come (somewhere) in great numbers: Х-ы валом валят (в место Y) ≃ **Xs are flocking ⟨thronging, streaming⟩ (to place Y); Xs are coming ⟨going⟩ in droves; Xs are going to ⟨heading for etc⟩ place Y en masse.**

Несмотря на травлю, поднятую охранителями передвижнических и мирискуснических традиций, москвичи валом валили на выставку... (Лившиц 1). Despite the persecution begun by the guardians of the traditions of the Wanderers and the World of Art, Muscovites flocked to the exhibition... (1a). ♦ [author's usage] Публике пьеса чрезвычайно понравилась, и на второе и следующие представления народ пошёл валом... (Булгаков 5). The play elicited instant enthusiasm, and the public thronged to the following performances... (5a). ♦ ...Солдатики в трубу трубили, песни пели, носками сапогов играли, пыль столбом по улицам поднимали, и всё проходили, всё проходили. «Валом валит солдат!» – говорили глуповцы... (Салтыков-Щедрин 1). [context transl] ...The soldiers trumped their trumpets and sang their songs, the shining toes of their boots rose and fell, raising a column of dust in the streets, and still they passed on without end. "There's millions of them!" said the Glupovites... (1b). ♦ [extended usage] В хрущёвские либеральные времена чиновники стали просачиваться в литературу, а при Брежневе повалили в неё валом (Войнович 1). In the liberal Khrushchev period, officials began infiltrating literature, and under Brezhnev, they burst into literature en masse (1a).

2. [subj: usu. concr (pl or mass) or count abstr] (of letters, complaints, news, troubles etc; also of snow, steam etc) to come (or come out of) somewhere continually and in large amounts: Х валом валил ≃ **X kept (on) coming (in ⟨down etc⟩); there was a constant stream of X; there was no end to X; X came ⟨kept⟩ pouring ⟨streaming⟩ in ⟨out⟩;** [of mail etc] **(I am ⟨he is etc⟩) flooded with X;** [of snow] **X came down ⟨fell⟩ thick and fast.**

Что-то я не припомню в своей жизни, чтобы 1-го мая шёл снег. А вот идёт, и не то что идёт, а валом валил с утра и за полчаса едва не покрыл всю землю (Терц 3). I don't somehow seem to remember snow falling on May 1st ever before. But it happened this morning, and it came down so thick and fast that almost the whole earth was covered over in half an hour (3a).

В-7 • **ЛЮБОПЫ́ТНОЙ ВАРВА́РЕ НОС ОТОРВА́ЛИ** [saying] a person who is excessively curious and asks questions about other people's affairs brings trouble to himself (usu. used as a warning not to ask questions, not to interfere): ≃ **curiosity killed the cat.**

«Ты кто?.. С какого эшелона?» – «Мы с Ожерелья... А тебе что?» – «Ничего... Спрашиваю просто». – «Любопытной Варваре нос оторвали» (Максимов 2). "Who are you?...What train are you from?" "We've come from Ozherelye....So what?" "Oh, nothing...I was just asking." "Curiosity killed the cat" (2a).

В-8 • **КАК ⟨БУ́ДТО, СЛО́ВНО, ТО́ЧНО⟩ ВА́РОМ ОБДА́ЛО** *кого obs, substand* [VP; impers; usu. past; fixed WO] s.o. experienced anxiety, fright: Х-а как варом обдало ≃ **it threw X ⟨X broke⟩ into a cold sweat; it threw X ⟨X was thrown⟩ into a panic; it startled the hell out of X.**

[Нелькин:] ...Подымаюсь, знаете, на лестницу, да и посматриваю: куда, мол, тут? Как звякнет он [колокольчик] мне над самым ухом, так меня как варом обдало! Уж не чувствую, как меня в гостиную ноги-то вкатили (Сухово-Кобылин 2). [N.:] Well, as I was saying, I had just started up the stairs and was just getting my bearings when the bell clanged right over my head! It threw me into a cold sweat! I can hardly remember how my legs propelled me into the drawing room (2a).

В-9 • И ВА́ШИХ НЕ́Т *slang* [indep. clause; Invar; usu. used after a clause expressing a threat; fixed WO] (of s.o. who experienced or will experience complete failure, ruin, who perished or will perish) and your life (career, undertaking etc) will be finished, over: **and that's the end of you; and you're done for; and you've had it; and it's all over (for you); and you're a goner.**

«Молчать! У меня с социально-опасными разговор короткий. Пулю в лоб, и ваших нет...» (Максимов 3). "Silence! I don't waste words on socially dangerous prisoners. A bullet in the head and that's the end of you"(3a).

В-10 • СОЛО́МЕННЫЙ ВДОВЕ́Ц ⟨СОЛО́МЕННАЯ ВДОВА́⟩ [NP] a person who is temporarily separated from or not living with his or her spouse: **grass widower ⟨widow⟩.**

< Loan translation of the German *Strohwitwer, Strohwitwe.*

В-11 • ВДОЛЬ И ПОПЕРЁК [AdvP; Invar; adv; fixed WO]
1. usu. **пройти, исходить, изъездить** и т. п. *что* ~ [more often used with pfv verbs] (to travel etc) throughout the whole of a given space, in all directions: **far and wide; the length and breadth of sth.; all over; back and forth; from one end to the other.**

«Сторона мне знакомая... исхожена и изъезжена вдоль и поперёк» (Пушкин 2). "As for knowing this land...I've traveled the length and breadth of it, on horseback and on foot..." (2a). ♦ В рейсах за желудёвыми шляпками и майскими жуками он облазил едва ли не каждую пядь, вдоль и поперёк исплавал все здешние пруды, держал в памяти самые потаённые стёжки (Максимов 2). On expeditions hunting for acorns or maybugs he crawled over practically every inch of the park, swam back and forth across all of its ponds, knew all the remotest trails and paths (2a). ♦ «Но, положим, вояж — это роскошь, и не все в состоянии и обязаны пользоваться этим средством; а Россия? Я видел Россию вдоль и поперёк» (Гончаров 2). "But, after all, travel [abroad] is a luxury, and not everyone can afford it, nor is everyone obliged to undertake it. And Russia? I have traveled from one end of Russia to the other" (1b).

2. знать, изучить и т. п. *кого-что* ~ *coll* [obj: more often inanim] (to learn, know s.o. or sth.) very well, down to the minutest details: **inside out; backward and forward; through and through.**

По физике у нас хороший преподаватель, свой предмет он знает вдоль и поперёк. We have a good physics teacher, he knows his subject inside out.

В-12 • БЕЗ ВЕ́ДОМА *чьего, кого* [PrepP; Invar; the resulting PrepP is adv] (to do sth.) without s.o.'s being aware of it or without asking the permission of s.o. (who is supposed to be notified or asked): **without s.o.'s knowledge ⟨the knowledge of s.o.⟩; unbeknown(st) to s.o.; without informing s.o.; without asking s.o.'s permission.**

«Я рассказал обо всём моему дяде Рязанову, но не просил его вмешиваться. Он сам, без моего ведома попросил Будягина позвонить директору института Глинской» (Рыбаков 2). "I told my uncle Ryazanov about my case, but I didn't ask him to get involved. He went to Budyagin without my knowledge and asked him to telephone Glinskaya, the director of the institute" (2a). ♦ Люди жили, работали, рождались и умирали и всё это без ведома соответствующих органов... (Войнович 2). People were living, working, having children, and dying, and all without the knowledge of the proper agencies (2a). ♦ ...Всем лучшим гостям

подали уху стерляжью, а штаб-офицеру, — разумеется, без ведома хозяина, — досталась уха из окуней (Салтыков-Щедрин 1). ...All the most important guests were given sterlet soup, while the staff-officer was served — of course, unbeknown to his host — with perch soup (1b).

В-13 • С ВЕ́ДОМА *чьего, кого* [PrepP; Invar; the resulting PrepP is adv] (to do sth.) with s.o.'s being aware of it or after having received the permission of s.o. (who is supposed to be notified or asked): **with s.o.'s knowledge ⟨the knowledge of s.o.⟩; with s.o.'s permission;** [in limited contexts] **with s.o.'s connivance.**

Пале-рояльская труппа в том же декабре с ужасом узнала, что Бургонский отель начал репетировать «Александра Великого» и что это делается с ведома Расина (Булгаков 5). That same December the Palais Royal troupe learned to its dismay that the Bourgogne had begun rehearsals of *Alexander*, and that this was being done with Racine's knowledge (5a). ♦ Стали доискиваться, откуда явилась Пфейферша. Одни говорили, что она не более как интриганка, которая, с ведома мужа, задумала овладеть Грустиловым... (Салтыков-Щедрин 1). They began trying to find out where Mme Pfeifer had come from. Some said that she was no more than an intriguer, who with her husband's connivance planned to gain control of Melancholov... (1a).

В-14 • лить, хлынуть КАК ИЗ ВЕДРА́ *coll* [как + PrepP; Invar; adv] (usu. of rain) (to rain, pour) heavily: **(come down) in buckets ⟨in bucketfuls, in torrents, in sheets⟩; (rain) buckets; (rain ⟨pour⟩) cats and dogs.**

[Зилов *(поднимает трубку, набирает номер)*:] ...Льёт как из ведра... Привет, Дима... Поздравляю, старик, ты оказался прав... Да вот насчёт дождя, чёрт бы его подрал! (Вампилов 5). [Z. *(takes receiver, dials number)*:] ...It's coming down in buckets...Hullo, Dima...Congratulations, you were right...About the blasted rain of course (5a). ♦ Косой дождь, гонимый сильным ветром, лил как из ведра (Толстой 2). The slanting rain, driven by a strong wind, pours down in bucketfuls (2b). ♦ Да, это был дождь, тот, что «как из ведра», тот, что падает перед настоящей календарной весной, расталкивая ветки можжевельника и корешки молочая (Эренбург 2). It was the kind of rain of which one says, "It came down in sheets"; the kind of rain that heralds the real spring, stirring the branches of the juniper and the roots of the wort (2a).

В-15 • ВЕК ВЕКОВА́ТЬ *obsoles, coll* [VP; subj: human; usu. this WO] to spend one's life or the rest of one's life (in a humble position or circumstances, in one's native—usu. humble—setting): X будет век вековать ≃ **X will live out his life ⟨days⟩.**

...Уж лучше век одной вековать, чем с таким связывать свою жизнь... (Войнович 5). ...Better to live out your life alone than to join it with someone like that... (5a). ♦ ...В тёмном молчании этом [Пётр Васильевич] проглядел и прослушал дыхание собственной дочери за перегородкой. Проглядел, что, схоронив мать, восемнадцатилетней девчонкой осталась она вековать свой век рядом с ним и с тех пор, вот уже без малого двадцать лет, ходит за ним... (Максимов 3). ...In his black silence he [Pyotr Vasilievich] had no eyes for his daughter, no ears for the living being on the other side of the wall, the eighteen-year-old girl who after her mother's funeral stayed behind to live out her days at his side, and for nearly twenty years now had looked after him... (3a).

В-16 • ВЕК ЖИВИ́, ВЕК УЧИ́СЬ [saying] there are always things you do not know, you can keep learning throughout your life (said as advice to keep studying or, jokingly, when a person learns sth. he did not know before): ≃ **(you) live and learn; it's never too late to learn.**

В-17 • ДОЖИВА́ТЬ СВОЙ ВЕК [VP] **1.** [subj: human] to live the end of one's life (often used with an adv of manner, place etc): X доживал свой век ≃ **X lived out his life** ⟨**days, last years**⟩; **X lived out the rest of his life** ⟨**days**⟩; **X lived** ⟨**spent**⟩ **the last years of his life.**

Больной, озлобленный, всеми забытый, доживал Козырь свой век… (Салтыков-Щедрин 1). Hotspur lived out his life sick, embittered, forgotten by all (1a). ♦ …Как только он… увидал стариков московских, ничего не желающих и никуда не спеша доживающих свой век, увидал старушек… московские балы и московский Английский клуб, – он почувствовал себя дома, в тихом пристанище (Толстой 5). …When he again saw old Muscovites quietly living out their days, desiring nothing, hurrying nowhere, old Moscow ladies… Moscow balls and the English Club, he felt himself at home in a quiet haven (5a). ♦ …У младшего [сына], у Михаила, который один из всех не уехал из деревни, старуха [Анна] и доживала свой век (Распутин 3). Anna was living out her last years with her younger son Mikhail, the only one who had not left the village… (3a).

2. [subj: concr, abstr, or collect] to fall gradually out of use: X доживал свой век ≃ **X lived** ⟨**finished**⟩ **out its days.**

Трамвай доживал свой век вместе с этими домами… (Евтушенко 1). The tram had lived out its days together with these houses… (1a).

В-18 • ЗАЕДА́ТЬ/ЗАЕ́СТЬ ВЕК чей ⟨**ЖИЗНЬ** чью**, ЧУ-ЖО́Й ВЕК, ЧУЖУ́Ю ЖИЗНЬ**⟩ all coll [VP; subj: human; usu. impfv] by oppressing s.o., doing harm to s.o., to make his life unbearable: X заедает Y-ов ⟨чужой⟩ век ≃ **X ruins** ⟨**spoils, embitters**⟩ **Y's** ⟨**another's**⟩ **life; X makes Y's** ⟨**another's**⟩ **life miserable; X torments Y** ⟨**another person**⟩; **X makes life a torture for Y** ⟨**someone else**⟩.

[Любим Карпыч:] …Я бедных не грабил, чужого веку не заедал… (Островский 2). [L.K.:] …I didn't rob the poor, I didn't ruin another's life… (2a). ♦ [Ислаев:] …Хоть я и простой человек – а настолько понимаю, что чужую жизнь заедать не годится… (Тургенев 1). [I.:] …Though I am a simple man, I have this much sense: I know that it isn't a good thing to embitter another man's life… (1b). ♦ Иван застонал протяжно, боднул воздух и двинулся к Никишкину: «Ржа ты, ржа, – захлёбываясь, говорил он… – Дай я плюну на тебя, чтоб издох ты, пёс!.. Что же ты нам век заедаешь?..» (Максимов 3). Ivan groaned aloud, swung his head angrily and advanced on Nikishkin. "You're like a blight.…I want to spit on you. I hope you die like the dog you are. Why should you live to torment us all our lives?" (3a).

В-19 • МАФУСА́ИЛОВ ВЕК жить, прожить, отжить; **МАФУСА́ИЛОВЫ ГОДА́** ⟨**ЛЕТА́**⟩ all obs, lit [NP; these forms only; obj] (to live) a very long life: **(live) as long as Methuselah; (live to be) as old as Methuselah.**

< From the Church Slavonic variant of the name of the Biblical patriarch *Methuselah,* who lived to be 962 (Gen. 5:25–27).

В-20 • МЫ́КАТЬ ВЕК ⟨**ЖИЗНЬ** obsoles⟩ substand [VP; subj: human] to have a hard life, suffer hardships: X мыкает век ≃ **X is struggling to get by** ⟨**to keep body and soul together**⟩; **X is having a tough time of it; X has fallen on hard times; X is going through the mill; X is just scraping by.**

В-21 • ОТЖИВА́ТЬ/ОТЖИ́ТЬ СВОЙ ВЕК ⟨**СВОЁ ВРЕ́МЯ**⟩ [VP; usu. pfv] **1.** Also: **ОТЖИВА́ТЬ/ОТ-ЖИ́ТЬ СВОЁ** [subj: human] to have lived one's allotted years: X отжил свой век ≃ **X has lived his life** ⟨**share**⟩; [in limited contexts] **X has already had a long life.**

…Мысли [Спиридона] были о дочери. Жена, как и он, отжили уже своё (Солженицын 3). …His [Spiridon's] thoughts dwelled on his daughter. His wife and he had already lived their share (3a). ♦ [Подхалюзин:] Что об вас-то толковать! Вы, Самсон

Силыч, отжили свой век… (Островский 10). [P.:] Why talk about you! You, Samson Silych, have already lived a long life… (10b).

2. [subj: abstr or concr] to become out-of-date, go out of use, be no longer popular, in fashion: X отжил свой век ≃ **X has outlived its usefulness; X has outlived** ⟨**had**⟩ **its day; X has become passé** ⟨**a thing of the past**⟩; [in limited contexts] **X has seen better days.**

Марксизм и прочие «измы» не привлекают молодые умы: «измы» отжили свой век (Аллилуева 2). Marxism and all other "isms" do not attract these young minds; "isms" have outlived their day (2a).

В-22 • ИСПОКО́Н ⟨**СПОКО́Н** substand⟩ **ВЕ́КА** ⟨**-ов, -у** obs⟩; **ОТ ВЕ́КА (ВЕКО́В)** [AdvP; these forms only; adv; usu. used with impfv verbs; fixed WO] starting long ago and continuing up until the present (or the moment indicated): **from** ⟨**since**⟩ **time immemorial; from** ⟨**since**⟩ **the (very) beginning of time; from the dawn of time; for centuries.**

…Какой-то человек вошёл на пустырь с косой в руках и начал сечь травяные рощи, росшие здесь испокон века (Платонов 1). …Some man came into the field with a scythe and began to hack away at the grass thickets that had grown there from time immemorial (1a). ♦ «Бог дал простолюдину язык вовсе не для разглагольствований, а для лизания сапог своего господина, каковой господин положен простолюдину от века…» (Стругацкие 4). "God didn't give them [simple folk] a tongue for talking, but for licking the boots of their master, the noble lord, who has been placed above them from the very beginning of time…" (4a). ♦ «По умершим молятся люди испокон веков» (Айтматов 2). "People have been praying over the dead for centuries" (2a).

В-23 • ЖИТЬ В ВЕКА́Х elev [VP; subj: human or abstr] to be remembered by posterity for a long time, always: X будет жить в веках ≃ **X will live forever; X will live (on) through the ages; X will never be forgotten.**

В-24 • АДА́МОВЫ ВЕ́КИ ⟨**ВРЕМЕНА́**⟩ obs [NP; pl only] ancient times: **the days of creation; antiquity; (from) time immemorial.**

В-25 • А́РЕДОВЫ ⟨**А́РИДОВЫ**⟩ **ВЕ́КИ** жить, прожить obs, lit [NP; pl only] (to live) a very long life: **(live) as long as Jared; (live to be) as old as Jared.**

< From the Church Slavonic variant of the name of the Biblical patriarch *Jared,* who lived to be 962 (Gen. 5:20).

В-26 • В КО́И-ТО ⟨**В КО́И**⟩ **ВЕ́КИ** coll [PrepP; these forms only; adv; most often used with pfv past verbs; when used with impfv or pfv fut verbs, usu. denotes a repeated action; fixed WO] finally, for the first time in a long period or after a long wait: **at (long) last; after all this time; after an eternity (of waiting** ⟨**of silence** etc⟩**);** [of repeated actions] **once in a blue moon; once in a great while.**

«…Зачем ты это сделал [загнал полицмейстера в клозет]? Ты его не любишь?» – «Давайте об этом не будем», – предложил Виктор. «Так, а о чём же мы будем?.. В кои веки случилось что-то интересное, и сразу – не будем» (Стругацкие 1). "…Why did you do it [lock the police chief in the lavatory]? Don't you like him?" "Let's not talk about it," proposed Viktor. "Then what will we talk about?…At long last something interesting happens, and right away we can't talk about it" (1a). ♦ …Близилось открытое и общемосковское – в кои-то веки! – собрание советских писателей… (Свирский 1). The open, all-Moscow conference of Soviet writers was approaching after an eternity of silence (1a). ♦ Ефим и Наташа приехали в субботу, как раз к тому дню, когда было решено *накрыть стол*… В кои веки собрались все вместе… (Рыбаков 1). Yefim and Natasha arrived on a Saturday, the very day we had decided to 'have a spread'... —once in a blue moon the whole family got together... (1a).

В-27 • ВО ВЕ́КИ ВЕКО́В *elev* [PrepP; Invar; adv; usu. used with fut verbs or with verbs denoting a wish, promise etc; fixed WO] **1.** Also: **ОТНЫ́НЕ И ВО ВЕ́КИ ВЕКО́В** eternally, for all time: **forever ⟨for ever⟩ (and ever); for ages on end; unto ages of ages; (for)evermore ⟨for ever more⟩; till the end of time.**

...Иов, хваля господа, служит не только ему, но послужит и всему созданию его в роды и роды и во веки веков, ибо к тому и предназначен был (Достоевский 1). ...Job, praising God, does not only serve him, but will also serve his whole creation, from generation to generation and unto ages of ages, for to this he was destined (1a). ♦ Да будет проклято царствование Николая во веки веков, аминь! (Герцен 1). May the reign of Nicholas be damned for ever and ever! Amen! (1a).

2. [used with negated verbs] not at any future time: **never; not ever; nevermore; not in a million years.**

В-28 • НА ВЕ́КИ ВЕ́ЧНЫЕ ⟨ВЕКО́В⟩ *elev* [PrepP; these forms only; adv; fixed WO] eternally, for all time: **forever ⟨for ever⟩ (and ever); (for)evermore ⟨for ever more⟩; till the end of time; for ages on end; unto ages of ages; forever and a day.**

Осталось, как ему теперь казалось, недостаточно ясным, что с Ларою он порывает навсегда, на веки вечные (Пастернак 1). He felt now that he had not made it clear enough to Lara that he was breaking with her for good, forever (1a). ♦ [Бакченин:] На веки вечные это будет самое святое воспоминание! (Панова 1). [B.:] It will be my most sacred memory forever and ever (1a). ♦ Так что отныне и на веки веков Сталин войдёт в историю как автор многих работ... (Зиновьев 2). So, now and for ever more Stalin goes down in history as the author of many books... (2a). ♦ Какая-то как бы идея воцарялась в уме его — и уже на всю жизнь и на веки веков (Достоевский 1). Some sort of idea, as it were, was coming to reign in his mind—now for the whole of his life and unto ages of ages (1a).

В-29 • (КАК ⟨СЛО́ВНО⟩) ПО ЩУ́ЧЬЕМУ ВЕЛЕ́НЬЮ ⟨-ию⟩ *coll* [(как etc +) PrepP; these forms only; adv; fixed WO] in a most miraculous way, without anyone's intercession: **as if by magic; as if by some magic formula; (as though) at the wave of a (magic) wand.**

Огромные мольберты с натянутыми на подрамки и загрунтованными холстами, словно по щучьему велению, выросли за одну ночь в разных углах мастерской (Лившиц 1). In the space of a single night huge easels, their canvases primed and on stretchers, grew up in various corners of the studio, as if by magic (1a). ♦ На пороге, словно по щучьему веленью, вырос второй помощник (Максимов 2). As though at the wave of a wand, the Second Officer materialized in the doorway (2a).

< Part of the saying «По щучьему велению, по моему хотению». From the fairy tale about Emelya who set free the pike («щука») he had caught. The grateful pike promised that whatever Emelya wished would be granted as soon as he said «По щучьему велению, по моему хотению...».

В-30 • ДУ́ТАЯ ВЕЛИЧИНА́ [NP; often subj-compl with copula, nom or instrum (subj: human)] a person whose scholarly or professional reputation is greatly exaggerated, has no factual basis: X — дутая величина ≃ **X is not what he's cracked up to be; X's reputation is overblown; X is a fraud.**

В-31 • ИДТИ́/ПОЙТИ́ ПОД ВЕНЕ́Ц ⟨К ВЕНЦУ́⟩ *obs* [VP; subj: human] to marry, take a husband or wife: X пошёл под венец ≃ **X went to the altar; X went ⟨walked⟩ down the aisle; X wedded person Y.**

[Квашня:] Не-ет, говорю, милый, с этим ты от меня — поди прочь. Я, говорю, это испытала... и теперь уж — ни за сто печёных раков — под венец не пойду! (Горький 3). [K:] Oh, no, my friend, says I, keep away from me with that. I went through all that before, says I, and now you won't make me go to the altar even if you give me a hundred boiled crawfish (3b).

В-32 • ТЕРНО́ВЫЙ ВЕНЕ́Ц *lit* [NP; sing only] (symbol of) suffering, torment: **crown of thorns.**

«Сын за царя и отечество терновый венец принял...» (Шолохов 2). "Your son wore a crown of thorns for the tsar and the fatherland..." (2a).

< From the Biblical account of the crown of thorns that the soldiers put on Jesus' head before he was crucified (Matt. 27:29 et al.).

В-33 • ВЫДЕ́ЛЫВАТЬ ⟨ВЫПИ́СЫВАТЬ, ПИСА́ТЬ⟩ (НОГА́МИ) ВЕНЗЕЛЯ́ *coll* ⟨**КРЕНДЕЛЯ́** *coll*, **КРЕ́НДЕЛИ** *coll*, **МЫСЛЕ́ТЕ** *obs*⟩; **ВЫВОДИ́ТЬ ⟨ПИСА́ТЬ** и т. п.⟩ **ВАВИЛО́НЫ** *obs* [VP; subj: human] (usu. of a drunken person) to walk with an unsteady, weaving gait: X выписывал (ногами) вензеля ≃ **X was staggering along; X was weaving (unsteadily) along.**

В-34 • ОТ ВЕРБЛЮ́ДА *coll, humor* [PrepP; Invar; used as indep. sent] used as a way to avoid directly answering the question: «Откуда?» — "Where (did you get that, did that come etc) from?": **aren't *we* curious; wouldn't *you* like to know.**

В-35 • ЛЕ́ГЧЕ ВЕРБЛЮ́ДУ ПРОЙТИ́ СКВОЗЬ ⟨В⟩ ИГО́ЛЬНОЕ УШКО́ (, чем ⟨нежели⟩...) [main clause in a compar complex sent] it would be easier to accomplish the impossible (than to accomplish the action in question which, presumably, should be possible): **it is easier for a camel to pass ⟨go⟩ through the eye of a needle (than...).**

...Легче верблюду пройти в угольное ушко, чем тюрзаку-террористу получить пропуск на члена семьи [для въезда на Колыму] (Гинзбург 2). It was easier for a camel to go through the eye of a needle than for someone who had been imprisoned as a terrorist to obtain a permit for a relative [to come to Kolyma] (2a).

< From the Bible: "It is easier for a camel to go through the eye of a needle than for a rich man to enter into the kingdom of God" (Matt. 19:24 et al.).

В-36 • ВЕРЁВКА ПЛА́ЧЕТ *по ком coll* [VP_subj; usu. pres; fixed WO] **1.** s.o. deserves strict punishment, deserves to be whipped: по X-у верёвка плачет ≃ **X is cruising for a bruising; what X needs is a good ⟨sound⟩ hiding ⟨thrashing⟩; X is asking for it.**

2. Also: **ПЕТЛЯ́ ПЛА́ЧЕТ** s.o. should be hanged: по X-у верёвка плачет ≃ **X deserves the gallows ⟨to be strung up⟩; X is asking for the noose ⟨the hangman's knot⟩.**

В-37 • ВИТЬ ВЕРЁВКИ *из кого coll* [VP; subj: human] to subject s.o. (usu. a meek or weak-willed person) to one's will, be able to make s.o. do exactly as one wants: X из Y-а верёвки вьёт ≃ **X wraps ⟨twists⟩ Y (a)round X's little finger; X walks all over Y; X has Y jumping through hoops; X bosses ⟨pushes⟩ Y around.**

«Знаешь, нам иногда до крайности необходимо вить друг из друга верёвки». — «Необходимо... а почему?» — «Наверное, потому, что мы не можем обойтись без того, чтобы не вить верёвок из самих себя. Ну если так, наступает момент, когда приобретённые навыки обязательно нужно на ком-то испробовать» (Залыгин 1). "You know, sometimes it's absolutely essential to wrap people round your little finger." "Essential? Why's that?" "I suppose because we can't get by if we don't wrap ourselves round our own little fingers. And that being so there comes a time when we absolutely have to test our acquired skills on somebody else" (1a). ♦ «Вот эдак кажинный [substand = каждый] раз, майор за ей [substand = ней], она — от него, не баба, а стервь, верёвки из нашего брата вьёт...» (Максимов 1). "That's the way it happens every time. The major chases after her—she runs away from him. She's not a woman—she's a witch. She twists our lads round her little finger..." (1a).

B-38 • СКО́ЛЬКО ⟨КАК⟩ ВЕРЁВОЧКЕ НИ ВИ́ТЬСЯ, А КОНЕ́Ц БУ́ДЕТ; СКО́ЛЬКО ВЕРЁВОЧКУ ⟨ВЕ-РЁВКУ⟩ НИ ВИТЬ, А КОНЦУ́ БЫТЬ [saying] underhanded dealings, depraved behavior etc, no matter how long they continue, will eventually be stopped: ≃ **the pitcher goes often to the well, but is broken at last; the pitcher goes once too often to the well;** [in limited contexts] **it will catch up with you in the end.**

«Воровал мой оголец, как ни попадя [ungrammat = всё, что попадётся]. Я тряпьё на базар таскала. Сколько верёвочке ни виться... Сгорели мы, как шведы. Он подельников выгораживал, всё на себя взял, ему на всю катушку, а мне, по моей глупости, — пять без поражения» (Максимов 3). "He stole everything he could lay his hands on, this man of mine. I used to take it all down to the market to sell. It caught up with us in the end. We went up in smoke. He wouldn't squeal on his mates, he took all the blame, so they gave him the full treatment and I got five years without deprivation of rights for being stupid" (3a).

B-39 • ОДНО́Й ВЕРЁВОЧКОЙ ⟨ВЕРЁВКОЙ, ЦЕПО́ЧКОЙ⟩ СВЯ́ЗАН с кем all coll [AdjP; subj-compl with быть∅ (subj: human); usu. pres] (two or more people are) equally involved in sth.: X с Y-ом ⟨X и Y⟩ связаны одной верёвочкой ≃ **X and Y are in it together; X is (just) as mixed up in it as Y (is); X is as much a part of it as Y (is).**

«Стабильность восстановится, и с облегчением вздохнут прежде всего в Москве... В конце концов, там же тоже есть люди, понимающие, что мы все связаны одной цепочкой...» (Аксёнов 7). "Stability will be restored, and everyone will breathe more easily, especially in Moscow....Even in Moscow there are people who understand we're all in it together" (7a).

B-40 • ВЕ́РНЫЙ ⟨ВЕ́РЕН⟩ (САМОМУ́) СЕБЕ́ [AdjP; modif (long-form var. only) or subj-compl with copula (subj: human); fixed WO] (one is) consistent in carrying out one's views or displaying one's character, habits: **(one is ⟨remains⟩) true to o.s.; (one is ⟨remains⟩) true to form; (one acts) in character.**

Опомниться! Быть верным себе, не изменять своим привычкам. А то всё полетит прахом (Пастернак 1). He must come to his senses. He must be true to himself and to his habits. Otherwise everything would go up in smoke (1a).

B-41 • ВЕ́РОЙ И ПРА́ВДОЙ служить кому; **ВЕ́РОЙ-ПРА́ВДОЙ** [NP_instrum; these forms only; adv; fixed WO] **1.** (of a person) (to serve s.o.) devotedly, honestly, with complete loyalty, (to render s.o.) good service (usu. over a long period of time): **(do s.o.) yeoman ⟨yeoman's⟩ service; (serve s.o.) loyally and well; (serve s.o.) faithfully (and truly); (be) a true and faithful servant;** [when the period of service is indicated] **(give ten years ⟨a lifetime etc⟩ of) true and faithful service.**

«Я, соколик, верой-правдой своему белому царю служил» (Шолохов 4). "Young man, I served my tsar loyally and well" (4a). ♦ «Послужи мне верой и правдою, и я тебя пожалую и в фельдмаршалы и в князья» (Пушкин 2). "Serve me faithfully and truly, and I will make you field-marshal and prince" (2b). ♦ «Пусть видят все, весь Петербург, как милостыни просят дети благородного отца, который всю жизнь служил верою и правдой и, можно сказать, умер на службе» (Достоевский 3). "Let everybody see, let the whole of St. Petersburg see these children begging for alms, although they had a respectable father who gave a lifetime of true and faithful service and even died, you might say, in harness" (3a).

2. (of an everyday item, piece of clothing, tool etc) (to serve s.o.) reliably for a long period of time: **(serve s.o.) long and well; (do s.o.) yeoman ⟨yeoman's⟩ service; [in limited contexts] never let s.o. down.**

Мы расстелили прямо на пол старую фланелевую шаль нашей няни Фимы, — уже десятый год она служила мне верой и правдой на всех этапах!.. (Гинзбург 2). We spread out on the floor the old flannel shawl belonging to my nurse, Fima, which had already done me yeoman service in all my journeyings under escort... (2a).

B-42 • ПО ВСЕ́Й ВЕРОЯ́ТНОСТИ [PrepP; Invar; sent adv (parenth); fixed WO] apparently, judging by what can be seen or what is known: **in all probability ⟨likelihood⟩; most likely; to ⟨by, from⟩ all appearances; probably.**

«Нет добродетели, если нет бессмертия». — «Блаженны вы, коли так веруете, или уже очень несчастны!» — «Почему несчастен?» — ...«Потому что, по всей вероятности, не веруете сами по себе в бессмертие вашей души, ни даже в то, что написали о церкви и о церковном вопросе» (Достоевский 1). "There is no virtue if there is no immortality." "You are blessed if you believe so, or else most unhappy!" "Why unhappy?"..."Because in all likelihood you yourself do not believe either in the immortality of your soul or even in what you have written about the Church and the Church question" (1a). ♦ Сейчас мне не совсем понятно, почему, собственно, потребовалось вмешательство бабушки: ведь я был достаточно взрослым мальчиком... По всей вероятности, бабушка была послана, так сказать, для отчёта (Олеша 3). It isn't entirely clear to me now just why my grandmother's intervention was required; I was after all, quite sufficiently grown-up to have gone by myself....Most likely, my grandmother was sent to keep account, so to speak (3a). ♦ «Вас, по всей вероятности, удивит принятое мною решение...» (Шолохов 2). "You will probably be surprised by my decision..." (2a).

B-43 • ЗА СЕМЬ ВЁРСТ КИСЕЛЯ́ ХЛЕБА́ТЬ ⟨ЕСТЬ⟩ ехать, идти и т. п. coll [VP; infin only; usu. this WO] to go to some place a long distance away in vain (or without any special need; the place in question is implied or specified by the context): X поехал за семь вёрст киселя хлебать ≃ **X went all that way for nothing; X went (all that way) on a wild-goose chase.**

[author's usage] «Захар, ты недавно просился у меня в гости на ту сторону, в Гороховую, что ли, так вот, ступай теперь!» — с лихорадочным волнением говорил Обломов. «Не пойду», — решительно отвечал Захар. «Нет, ты ступай!.. Теперь же, сейчас!..» — «Да куда я пойду семь вёрст киселя есть?» (Гончаров 1). "Zakhar," Oblomov said with feverish agitation, "the other day you asked my permission to go and see your friends in Gorokhovaya Street, didn't you? Well, you may go now!" "I won't go, sir," Zakhar replied emphatically. "Oh yes, you will!...You're going now—at once!..." "But why should I go all that way for nothing?" (1a). ♦ [author's usage] «Ты поедешь?» — спросил Павел Петрович. — «Нет; а ты?» — «И я не поеду. Очень нужно тащиться за пятьдесят вёрст киселя есть» (Тургенев 2). "Are you going?" asked Pavel Petrovich. "No; are you?" "No, I won't go either. Much object there would be in dragging oneself over thirty miles on a wild-goose chase" (2b).

B-44 • СЕМЬ ВЁРСТ ДО НЕБЕ́С (И ВСЁ ЛЕ́СОМ) наговорить, наобещать и т. п. coll, humor or iron [NP; these forms only; adv (quantif); fixed WO] (to say) a lot of things which are either not true or are presented in an unintelligible, long-winded fashion, (to make) a lot of promises (that one has no intention of keeping): наговорить ~ ≃ **say all kinds of things; talk a lot of hot air; go on at a great rate and leave s.o. baffled;** ‖

наобещать ~ ≃ **make s.o. a cartload of (empty) promises; promise s.o. the moon (and the stars).**

В-45 • КОЛÓМЕНСКАЯ ВЕРСТÁ; С ⟨В⟩ КОЛÓМЕН-СКУЮ ВЕРСТУ́ *all coll, humor* [NP, sing only (1st var.); PrepP, adv or nonagreeing modif (2nd var.)] (of a person) very tall: **tall as a beanpole; beanpole; (long,) tall drink of water.**

[Любим Карпыч:] Остался я после отца, видишь ты, малмалёхонек, с коломенскую версту, лет двадцати несмышлёночек (Островский 2). [L.K.:] I was left when my father died, just a kid tall as a bean pole, a little fool of twenty (2a).

< From a comparison of a very tall person with a "verst pole," i.e., a very high roadside pole marking a *verst* (an old Russian unit of length, about 1.06 km, used prior to the introduction of the metric system). Such poles were placed by order of Tsar Aleksei Mikhailovich on the road from Moscow to the village of Kolomenskoye, where the tsars resided in the summer.

В-46 • ЗА ВЕРСТУ́ [PrepP; Invar; adv] **1.** (being) at a relatively great distance (from some person, thing etc): **a mile away; far off; (so) far away.**

[Восмибратов:] Что же будет вам угодно-с? [Несчастливцев:] Не могу же я с тобой за версту разговаривать (Островский 7). [V.:] Now what is it I can do for you, sir? [N.:] I can't talk to you standing a mile away (7c).

2. ~ **видно, слышно, тянет, пахнет** и т. п. (sth. can be seen, heard, smelled etc) for a relatively great distance: **(from) a mile away ⟨off⟩; (from) far off; for miles.**

Дернула же меня нелёгкая ещё обшить телогрейку у ворота этой драной кошкой! За версту видать вчерашнюю каторжанку (Гинзбург 2). It must have been the devil's prompting that caused me to sew that strip of moulting cat fur onto the collar of my jacket! Anybody could see from a mile away that I was an ex-convict (2a). ♦ «Вот эдакая какая-нибудь глупость, какая-нибудь пошлейшая мелочь, весь замысел может испортить! Да, слишком приметная шляпа... Смешная, потому и приметная... К моим лохмотьям непременно нужна фуражка, хотя бы старый блин какой-нибудь, а не этот урод. Никто таких не носит, за версту заметят, запомнят...» (Достоевский 3). "Some such idiocy as this, some incredibly trivial detail can ruin the whole plan! Yes, a hat that's too conspicuous...Ridiculous and therefore conspicuous...My rags definitely call for a cap, no matter how old and flat, but not this monstrosity. Nobody wears them, it would be seen a mile off and remembered..." (3a). ♦ ...Вспоминалась ему [Гипатову] первая практика – в горах, на строительстве рудника, куда Назаренко не поехал, достав справку о временной нетрудоспособности в связи с гипотонией. Это Гипатов помнил точно; они ещё все смеялись...: живой гипотоник ходил по институту и жаловался на головные боли, а от него за версту несло водкой и духами (Семёнов 1). ...He [Gipatov] recalled their first practice trip–to the mountains where a mine was being built–on which Nazaryenko did not go, having obtained a certificate to say he was temporarily excused from work on the grounds of low blood pressure. Gipatov remembered this precisely; they had all laughed about it...: here was a living specimen of low blood pressure walking about the Institute and complaining of headaches, while the smell of vodka and lotion about him carried for miles (1a).

< «Верста» is an old Russian unit of length, about 1.06 km, that was used prior to the introduction of the metric system.

В-47 • МÉРИТЬ ⟨-ять⟩ ВЁРСТЫ *obs, coll* [VP; subj: human] to walk a great distance: **X мерил вёрсты ≃ X covered many miles on foot.**

< See В-46.

В-48 • ОБХОДИ́ТЬ/ОБОЙТИ́ ЗА ТРИ ВЕРСТЫ́ ⟨ЗА ВЕРСТУ́⟩ *кого coll* [VP; subj: human; the verb may take the final position, otherwise fixed WO] to (try to) avoid, keep away from s.o.: X обходит Y-а за три версты ≃ **X steers ⟨keeps⟩ clear of Y; X gives Y a wide ⟨the widest possible⟩ berth; X goes miles ⟨a mile⟩ out of his way to avoid Y; X keeps his distance (from Y).**

...Зэк, который вот таким образом «нарушает», старается не попадаться на глаза, офицера обойдёт за три версты (Марченко 1). ...A con who commits a "violation" in this way takes good care not to be seen and gives all officers the widest possible berth (1a). ♦ «И чего только вы с ней связались, скажите на милость! Её – эту Дёмину – у нас на заводе даже начальство за версту обходит, лишь бы не разговаривать» (Максимов 2). "What in God's name possessed you to tangle with Dyomina? Here at the shipyard even the bosses will go a mile out of their way to avoid having to talk to her" (2a).

< See В-46.

В-49 • ДАВÁТЬ/ДАТЬ ВÉРУ *кому-чему* [VP; subj: human] to believe, have confidence in s.o. or sth.: X даёт веру Y-у ≃ **X puts ⟨places⟩ his trust ⟨faith⟩ in Y; X has ⟨puts⟩ trust ⟨faith⟩ in Y; X gives credence to thing Y; ‖ *Neg* X Y-у веры не даёт ≃ X doesn't buy ⟨fall for⟩ thing Y; X doesn't take stock in thing Y.**

«А вот ты наш, казак, и мы тебе веры больше даём [, чем агитаторам]...» (Шолохов 3). "But you here, you're one of us, a Cossack, we've got more trust in you [than in the agitators]..." (3a). ♦ «Баба – кошка: кто погладил – к тому и ластится. А ты не верь, веры не давай» (Шолохов 2). "A woman's like a cat; she cuddles up to anyone who pets her. Don't trust 'em, don't put no faith in 'em!" (2a).

В-50 • НА ВÉРУ *obs* [PrepP; Invar; adv] trustingly, relying on the honesty, good will of s.o.: **on trust; on faith.**

Читать бумаги по всем отделениям было решительно невозможно, надобно было подписывать на веру (Герцен 2). To read the papers concerning all the departments was absolutely impossible, so one had to sign them on trust (2a).

В-51 • ОБРАЩÁТЬ/ОБРАТИ́ТЬ В СВОЮ́ ВÉРУ *кого* [VP; subj: human; often infin with пытаться, надеяться etc; usu. this WO] to persuade or induce s.o. to adopt one's beliefs, approaches etc: X пытается обратить Y-а в свою веру ≃ **X is trying to convert Y (to X's views); X is trying to bring Y around to X's way of thinking; X is trying to win Y over to X's side ⟨to X's way of thinking⟩.**

Пока ехали, Антон без умолку болтал о своей новой идеологии, может быть, он решил за дорогу до аэропорта обратить и дедушку в свою веру (Аксёнов 7). All the way to the airport Anton babbled on about his new ideology, as if trying to convert his grandfather in the time alloted (7a). ♦ [Майор] вызвал меня по поводу голодовки и дактилоскопии, а занесло куда: и про законность, и про эмиграцию, и в психологию ударился... Ведь не надеялся же он... сразу обратить меня в свою веру... (Марченко 2). He [the major] called me in on account of a hunger strike and fingerprinting, and off he went in all directions–legality, emigration, psychology. Surely he did not think that he could convert me to his views... (2a).

В-52 • ПРИНИМÁТЬ/ПРИНЯ́ТЬ НА ВÉРУ *что* [VP; subj: human] to believe sth. trustingly, without evidence or investigation: X принял Y на веру ≃ **X accepted ⟨took⟩ Y on trust ⟨on faith, as an article of faith⟩; X took person Y's word for it.**

Её совершенно не занимало, прилежно ли автор держится исторической правды, – она принимала это на веру, – ибо если бы это было не так, то просто не стоило бы писать книгу (Набоков 1). She was completely unconcerned whether or not the author clung assiduously to historical truth–she took that on trust, for if it were not thus it would simply not have been worth writing the book

(1a). ♦ «Нигилист — это человек... который не принимает ни одного принципа на веру, каким бы уважением ни был окружён этот принцип» (Тургенев 2). "A nihilist is a man who...accepts no principle whatsoever as an article of faith, however great the respect in which that principle may be generally held" (2e). ♦ «Хорошо, я готов принять на веру. Хороши ваши стихи, скажите сами?» (Булгаков 9). "Very well, I am prepared to take your word for it. Are your poems good? Tell me yourself!" (9a).

B-53 • БРАТЬ/ВЗЯТЬ ВЕРХ [VP] **1.** ~ *(над кем, где)*. Also: **ЗАБИРА́ТЬ/ЗАБРА́ТЬ ВЕРХ** [subj: human or collect] to get control over s.o. (or in some place), subject s.o. to one's will: X взял верх (над Y-ом ⟨в месте Z⟩) ≃ **X got ⟨gained, had⟩ the upper hand (over Y); X dominated Y; X held sway over Y; X had everything ⟨it all⟩ his own way (in place Z); X took over (in place Z);** [in limited contexts] **X took ⟨had⟩ Y well in hand.**

А особенно дома Дементьев умел брать верх над Главным: Твардовский и кричал на него, и кулаком стучал, а чаще соглашался (Солженицын 2). It was particularly easy for Dementyev to get the upper hand when he and the chief were at home. Tvardovsky might shout and hammer the table, but more often than not he would agree in the end (2a). ♦ «Так вы полагаете, что он [Базаров] имел большое влияние на Анну Сергеевну?» – «Да. Но над ней никто долго взять верх не может...» – «Почему вы это думаете?» – «Она очень горда... она очень дорожит своею независимостью» (Тургенев 2). "So you think that he [Bazarov] had a great influence on Anna Sergeevna?" "Yes. But no one can dominate her for long..." "Why do you think that?" "She is very proud...she greatly treasures her independence" (2f). ♦ Каждый дом, квартира... деревня, не говоря уж о городах и областях, получили своего верховода (сначала их было по нескольку, потом один брал верх), который распоряжался, инструктировал, отдавал приказания... (Мандельштам 2). Every house, apartment, and village, not to mention every town and province, had its little tyrant (at first there would be several, until a single one took over), who gave orders and instructions... (2a).

2. ~ *(над кем-чем)*. Also: **ОДЕ́РЖИВАТЬ/ ОДЕРЖА́ТЬ ВЕРХ** [subj: human or abstr; if subj: human, obj is also human; if subj: abstr, obj is also abstr] to overpower, overcome (s.o. or sth.), turn out to be stronger: X взял верх (над Y-ом) ≃ **X got ⟨gained, had⟩ the upper hand (over Y); X got the better of Y; X got the best of Y ⟨of it⟩; X won out (over Y); X prevailed (over Y); person X came out on top.**

...Гоголь невольно примиряет смехом, его огромный комический талант берёт верх над негодованием (Герцен 1). ...Gogol cannot help conciliating one with his laughter; his enormous comic talent gets the upper hand of his indignation (1a). ♦ Эти детки часто спорили друг с другом о разных вызывающих житейских предметах, причем Настя, как старшая, всегда одерживала верх... (Достоевский 1). The children often argued with each other about various provocative matters of life, and Nastya, being older, always had the upper hand... (1a). ♦ ...Мало-помалу любопытство взяло верх, и однажды, когда полициймейстер явился утром, по обыкновению, то новый помпадур не выдержал. «А что... эта старая... какова?» (Салтыков-Щедрин 2). ...By and by his curiosity got the better of him and one day as the police commissioner, as usual, appeared at his office in the morning, the new pompadour could restrain himself no longer. "And...er...what about that one...the one before, you know...what sort of person is she?" (2a). ♦ Как ни отбивались стрельчата... но сила, по обыкновению, взяла верх (Салтыков-Щедрин 1). However hard the musketeer sons fought back...force won out, as usual (1a). ♦ Он готовил ответы на те вопросы, которые ему, может быть, зададут... надеясь, что в данном конкретном случае почему-то возьмут верх его доводы и соображения здравого смысла (Войнович 4). He was preparing answers to the questions which would be asked him; that is, he was hoping that, in the specific case at hand, his arguments and the considerations of common

sense would prevail (4a). ♦ ...Рассказчик всегда преследовал одну цель — доказать себе и своему слушателю, что он с честью вышел из невыносимого положения и взял верх над тем, кто на него наседал (Мандельштам 2). [context transl] ...The speaker's object is always the same: to prove to himself and the listener that he emerged with honor from an impossible situation and managed to outwit the person putting pressure on him... (2a).

B-54 • ДЕРЖА́ТЬ ВЕРХ *над кем, где* [VP; subj: human] to dominate, control s.o., be the master (in some place): X держит верх над Y-ом ⟨в месте Z⟩ ≃ **X is in charge of Y ⟨in place Z⟩; X has the final say (in place Z); X is calling the shots (in place Z); X rules the roost;** [in limited contexts] **X wears the pants (in the family).**

B-55 • НАХВАТА́ТЬСЯ ВЕРХО́В ⟨ВЕРХУ́ШЕК, ВЕРШКО́В⟩; ХВАТА́ТЬ ВЕРХИ́ ⟨ВЕРХУ́ШКИ, ВЕРШКИ́⟩ *all coll, derog;* **СКОЛЬЗИ́ТЬ ПО ВЕРХА́М** [VP; subj: human] to study sth. superficially, in a brief and cursory manner: X нахватался верхов ≃ **X scratched ⟨skimmed⟩ the surface; X got a smattering of...; X just got ⟨picked up⟩ the basics.**

«Так нельзя, господа, готовиться в высшее учебное заведение; вы все хотите только мундир носить с синим воротником; верхов нахватаетесь и думаете, что вы можете быть студентами; нет, господа, надо основательно изучать предмет...» (Толстой 2). "That's no way, gentlemen, to prepare for entry to an establishment of higher learning; all you want is a uniform to wear with a blue collar; you skim the surface a bit and you think you can be students; no, gentlemen, you have to have a thorough knowledge of your subject" (2b).

B-56 • С ВЕ́РХОМ *налить, наполнить, насыпать что coll* [PrepP; Invar; adv] (to fill, pour sth.) to the very top of the container, vessel: **to the brim; to the rim; to overflowing.**

Ведро с верхом было наполнено сочащимися янтарными и тёмно-коричневыми сотами (Искандер 5). The pail was full to the brim with oozing combs, amber and dark brown (5a).

B-57 • НА ВЕРХУ́ БЛАЖЕ́НСТВА быть₀, чувствовать себя etc. *coll* [PrepP; Invar; subj-compl with copula (subj: human); fixed WO] (to be, feel) elated: **on top of the world; in a state of perfect bliss; on cloud nine; walking ⟨treading⟩ on air; euphoric.**

B-58 • ВЕРШИ́ТЕЛЬ СУ́ДЕБ *lit* [NP; fixed WO] a person who possesses great power, controls the fates of other people: **maker ⟨master⟩ of destinies.**

...К тому времени, когда прогремела «Школа мужей», министра Фуке уже называли вершителем судеб. Вершитель судеб решил устроить у себя в поместье Во празднества для короля (Булгаков 5). By the time that *The School for Husbands* was winning its resounding success, Fouquet was already known as the maker of destinies. And the maker of destinies decided to arrange an entertainment for the King at his Vaux estate (5a).

B-59 • ИМЕ́ТЬ ВЕС [VP; subj: human] to be influential, have authority in society, in a certain group etc: X имеет вес ≃ **X carries weight; X has influence ⟨clout, pull⟩.**

Жирмунского поддерживала целая толпа докторов наук... и академик Шишмарёв, но Ахманова с Любарской имели несравненно больше весу и побеждали на всех этапах (Мандельштам 2). Zhirmunski was supported by a whole cohort of Doctors of Science... and by academician Shishmarev, but Akhmanova and Liubarskaya had infinitely more influence and got their way at all stages (2a).

B-60 • НА ВЕС ЗО́ЛОТА быть₀, ценить *кого*, **цениться** *coll, approv* [PrepP; Invar; adv or subj-compl with быть₀ (subj:

human, animal, concr, or abstr); fixed WO] (to be, consider s.o. or sth. to be, be considered to be etc) very valuable, precious: **worth one's ⟨its⟩ weight in gold.**

[Лорд:] В наше время, Савва Лукич, такие авторы на вес золота (Булгаков 1). [L.:] In our times, Savva Lukich, authors like him are worth their weight in gold (1a).

В-61 • УДЕ́ЛЬНЫЙ ВЕС *кого-чего (в чём)* [NP; sing only; usu. subj or obj; fixed WO] the comparative role, significance of s.o. or sth.: **relative worth ⟨importance⟩ of s.o. ⟨sth.⟩; role of s.o. ⟨sth.⟩; weight of sth.**

Слова «Тартюф» и «Обманщик» не сходили с языков в Париже, и 11-го числа грянула новость. Весь Париж стал читать послание архиепископа. Оно было составлено очень внушительно... Удельный вес этого послания был слишком значителен, это было понятно даже наивным людям, и парижане поняли, что дело «Обманщика» проиграно (Булгаков 5). *Tartuffe* and *The Impostor* were on all tongues in Paris, and on the eleventh a new misfortune struck. All Paris was reading a message from the Archbishop. It was worded most solemnly....The weight of this message was too great, as even the most naïve people could see, and the Parisians understood that *The Impostor* was a lost cause (5a).

В-62 • ВЕСТИ́/ПОВЕСТИ́ СЕБЯ́ *как* [VP; subj: human] to comport o.s. in a particular way (as specified by the adv): X ведёт себя... ≃ **X behaves ⟨acts⟩...; X conducts himself...;** [in limited contexts] **X carries himself...**

...Люди формально ведут себя так, как должны вести себя искренние члены Братии (Зиновьев 1). ...People behave formally as sincere members of the Brotherhood should behave (1a). ♦ Нюра, увидев Чонкина, смешалась и опустила глаза, но потом, поняв, что так вести себя глупо, подняла их... (Войнович 2). Nyura was embarrassed to see Chonkin and dropped her eyes. Then, realizing she was acting foolishly, she brought her eyes back up again... (2a). ♦ Что до того, как вести себя, соблюсти тон... то в этом они [дамы города N.] опередили даже дам петербургских и московских (Гоголь 3). As to the ways in which they [the ladies of the town of N—] conducted themselves, maintained the elevated tone...—in these things they surpassed even the ladies of Petersburg and Moscow (3c). ♦ «Вообще её [Лолу] губит то, что она очень много говорит. В девицах она была тихая, молчаливая, таинственная. Есть такие девицы, которые от рождения знают, как себя вести. Она знала» (Стругацкие 1). "...The thing that spoils her [Lola] is that she talks a lot. When she was younger she was quiet, reticent, mysterious. There are women who know from birth how to carry themselves. She knew" (1a).

В-63 • ПРОПА́СТЬ БЕ́З ВЕСТИ [VP; subj: human] to disappear, leaving no sign of where one has gone or what has happened to one: X пропал без вести ≃ **X disappeared ⟨vanished⟩ without a trace;** [in military contexts] **X is missing in action.**

В-64 • ХУДЫ́Е ВЕ́СТИ НЕ ЛЕЖА́Т НА МЕ́СТЕ ⟨НЕ СИДЯ́Т НА НАСЕ́СТЕ⟩ [saying] disturbing information is quickly spread: ≃ **bad ⟨ill⟩ news travels fast;** [said ironically] **good news travels fast.**

29, 30, 31-го я слушал по всем радиостанциям, как идёт моё интервью, ликовал и дописывал... «Письмо вождям». А тем временем выкопан был «Архипелаг», и – худые вести не сидят на насесте – 1-го сентября пришли мне сказать об этом, ещё не совсем точно. 3-го – уже наверняка (Солженицын 2). On 29, 30, 31 August I heard my press statement broadcast by all the radio stations, and jubilantly finished writing...my *Letter to the Leaders*. Meanwhile, *Gulag* had been dug up. Bad news travels fast, and on 1 September someone came to warn me, although he was rather vague about it. On the third we knew for certain (2a).

В-65 • НА ВЕСУ́ *держать что* (less often *кого*), *держаться* и т. п. [PrepP; Invar; adv] (to hold, keep etc sth. or, occas., s.o) in a hanging position, without support from below or supported only by a person's hand(s): **(hold s.o. or sth. ⟨keep s.o. or sth., remain etc⟩) suspended ⟨dangling⟩ in midair ⟨mid-air⟩; (hold s.o. ⟨sth.⟩) in midair; hanging in midair; (hold ⟨keep etc⟩ sth.) balanced (in one's hand ⟨hands⟩);** [in limited contexts] **(weigh sth.) in one's hand(s); hold up sth.**

Гай ухватывает Лёнчика за горло обеими руками, перетягивает за стену и держит на весу (Солженицын 8). Gai grabs Lennie by the throat with both hands, pushes him over the wall and holds him there in mid-air (8a). ♦ Вместо того чтоб держать посылку бережно на весу, неопытный посланец кинул её на дно телеги... (Салтыков-Щедрин 1). Instead of keeping the parcel carefully balanced, the inexperienced messenger tossed it into the bottom of the wagon... (1a). ♦ ...Евсей щепал лучину. Ловко, красиво сбегал с полена тонкий розовато-белый ремень... А когда этот ремень совсем отделился от полена, Евсей не дал ему упасть на пол, а быстро подхватил его и покачал на весу: а ну-ка, скажи, друг-приятель, на что ты пригоден... и бросил отдельно, в сторону от растопки, – надо полагать, для дела (Абрамов 1). ...Evsei was chopping kindling. A thin pinkish-white strip came beautifully away from the log....And when the strip had detached itself completely from the log, Evsei did not let it fall to the ground, but quickly caught it up and weighed it in his hand: Well now, my dear friend, tell me what you're fit for....Then he tossed it over to a place separate from the kindling, presumably to use for some job (1a). ♦ ...Два ружья разом грохнули, хрипло завизжала Калинка, бросившаяся под ноги качнувшемуся вперёд медведю... Дудырев и Митягин стояли не шевелясь, держа на весу всё ещё сочившиеся дымком (Тендряков 1). ...Two rifles cracked simultaneously. Kalinka gave a hoarse yelp and threw herself at the feet of the bear as he swayed forward....Dudyrev and Mityagin stood stock-still, holding up their rifles which were still smoking (1a).

В-66 • ВЕСЬ НАРУ́ЖУ; ВСЁ НАРУ́ЖУ *у кого* both coll [AdjP; subj-compl with быть∅, subj: human (1st var.); VP_subj with быть∅ (2nd var.); usu. pres; fixed WO] (a person is) extremely open, spontaneous in the expression of his thoughts and emotions: X весь ⟨у X-а всё⟩ наружу ≃ **X is an open book; X is very ⟨completely⟩ open about everything.**

Лена ничего не умеет скрыть, у неё всё наружу. Lena can't hide anything—she's an open book.

В-67 • БРОСА́ТЬ/БРО́СИТЬ ⟨ВЫБРА́СЫВАТЬ/ВЫ́БРОСИТЬ⟩ НА ВЕ́ТЕР[1] ⟨НА́ ВЕТЕР⟩ деньги, имущество и т. п.; **ПУСКА́ТЬ/ПУСТИ́ТЬ ⟨ШВЫРЯ́ТЬ/ШВЫРНУ́ТЬ, КИДА́ТЬ/КИ́НУТЬ⟩ НА ВЕ́ТЕР ⟨НА́ ВЕТЕР⟩** all coll, disapprov [VP; subj: human] to spend (money), fritter away (one's fortune) to no purpose, senselessly: X бросает деньги на ветер ≃ **X throws money to the (four) winds; X throws money away; X throws money out the window ⟨down the drain⟩; X squanders (away) money.**

«...Бросать денег на ветер я не стану. Уж пусть меня в этом извинят!» (Гоголь 3). "...I am not going to throw my money to the four winds. Here they must excuse me!" (3c). ♦ «...Кто за каждую копейку дрожит, у того их [денег] не будет». – «Как же не будет, если он их не бросает зря на ветер, не пропивает, как ты?» (Распутин 1). "A person who counts every kopeck'll never have money." "Why won't he if he doesn't throw it away and doesn't drink it up like you do?" (1a). ♦ Давать деньги Терещенко – это значит выбрасывать их на ветер... (Рыбаков 1). Giving money to Tereshchenko was like throwing it down the drain... (1a).

В-68 • БРОСА́ТЬ/БРО́СИТЬ НА ВЕ́ТЕР[2] ⟨НА́ ВЕ́ТЕР⟩ слова; **ГОВОРИ́ТЬ ⟨БОЛТА́ТЬ⟩ НА ВЕ́ТЕР ⟨НА́ ВЕТЕР⟩** all coll [VP; subj: human; often neg, esp. 1st var.] to speak without thinking, make rash promises that will not be fulfilled: X слов на ветер не бросает ≃ **X doesn't throw words around; X doesn't speak lightly; X is as good as his word; X lives up to his word; X means what he says.**

Все знали, что Болтун — не дурак, слов на ветер зря не бросает (Зиновьев 1). Everyone knew that Chatterer was no fool, that he never spoke lightly (1a). ♦ Его вызвали в Москву… и дали важное задание по выпуску танков, знали, что Ефим задание выполнит, он слов на ветер не бросал (Рыбаков 1). He [Yefim] had been called to Moscow…and given an important assignment on tank output, which they knew he would deliver, as he was always as good as his word (1a). ♦ Он довольно долго молчал, а затем сказал — неторопливо, сосредоточенно — слова, которые я не могу забыть до сих пор, прибавив: «Я своих слов на ветер не бросаю» (Катаев 3). He was silent for a time, then he said — with unhurried concentration — something that I have not forgotten to this day, and added: "I mean what I say" (3a).

B-69 • ВЕ́ТЕР В ГОЛОВЕ́ ⟨гуля́ет, бро́дит, свисти́т⟩ *у кого́ coll, disapprov* [NP; Invar; VP$_{subj}$ with бытьø or subj; usu. pres] s.o. is light-minded, frivolous (often said by older people when characterizing the young): у X-а ветер в голове ≃ **X is flighty ⟨harebrained, lightheaded⟩; X never has a serious thought in his head.**

B-70 • ВЕ́ТЕР ⟨СВИСТИ́Т⟩ В КАРМА́НАХ *чьих* ⟨В КАРМА́НЕ *чьём*⟩, *у кого́ coll, humor* [VP$_{subj}$] s.o. has no money: у X-а ветер свистел в карманах ≃ **X didn't have a penny ⟨a dime, a kopeck etc⟩ to his name; X didn't have a (red) cent; X was (flat) broke; X's pockets were empty.**

B-71 • КУДА́ ВЕ́ТЕР ДУ́ЕТ *coll, disapprov* [VP$_{subj}$; Invar; usu. this WO] **1. знать, понима́ть** и т. п. ~ . Also: ОТКУ́ДА ВЕ́ТЕР ДУ́ЕТ [subord clause] (to understand) whose views, opinions etc one should adhere to, which line of behavior is in one's best interests (usu. of a person who adjusts his opinions and behavior to those of his superiors): X знает, куда ⟨откуда⟩ ветер дует ≃ **X knows ⟨sees etc⟩ which way ⟨how, in which direction, from which direction⟩ the wind blows ⟨is blowing⟩; X trims his sails to ⟨before⟩ the wind.**

Его поддержало несколько Завторангов [*nonce word*]… которые сразу смекнули, куда дует ветер (Зиновьев 1). He was supported by a number of Secradeps…who immediately divined which way the wind was blowing (1a). ♦ Тридцать седьмой [год] покатил антисемитское колесо быстрее. Сталин в документе ТАСС собственноручно «исправил» фамилию Зиновьева и Каменева, сообщив населению о дореволюционных фамилиях жертв террористического процесса — Радомысльский и Розенфельд. Как оживились… карьеристы, которые уловили, наконец, откуда ветер дует… (Свирский 1). The year 1937 set the anti-Semitic wheel turning faster. In a TASS document Stalin personally "corrected" the names of Zinoviev and Kamenev, telling the population the pre-Revolutionary names of these victims of the process of the terror — Radomyslsky and Rosenfeld. That encouraged…the careerists, who could finally be sure which direction the wind was blowing (1a).

2. идти, смотреть и т. п. ~ [subord clause or, rare, predic with subj: human (sing or pl)] lacking strong principles or out of selfish motives, to change one's views according to circumstances, prevalent opinions etc: X идёт куда ветер дует ≃ **X changes ⟨goes, swims, flows⟩ with the tide; X is a weathercock ⟨weather vane⟩.**

B-72 • С ВЕТЕРКО́М прокати́ть *кого́*, прокати́ться и т. п. *coll* [PrepP; Invar; adv] (to ride, race, go) with great speed: **like the wind; quick as the wind.**

«Ну, как поедем? С ветерком? — спросил Егорша. — У меня *сам* другой езды не признаёт» (Абрамов 1). "Well, how

shall we ride? Like the wind?" asked Egorsha. "The Boss won't ride any other way" (1a). ♦ «Ну что же, валяй, — сказал он. — Только сначала съезди к Кате Очкиной, покойника на кладбище отвези». — «Мы его мигом! С ветерком!» — обрадовался Лёха и побежал к дверям (Войнович 5). "All right then, go," he said. "But first drop in on Katya Ochkin and take Ochkin's body over to the cemetery." "In two shakes! Quick as the wind!" In high spirits, Lekha started running for the door (5a).

B-73 • С ВЕТЕРКО́М В ГОЛОВЕ́ *coll* [PrepP; Invar; usu. subj-compl with copula (subj: human); often used after another compl with which it is contrasted; fixed WO] light-minded, frivolous: **kind of ⟨a little etc⟩ flighty; somewhat lightheaded ⟨giddy⟩.**

Он парень неглупый, но с ветерком в голове. He's a pretty smart guy, but kind of flighty.

B-74 • ИЩИ́ ⟨ДОГОНЯ́Й⟩ ВЕ́ТРА В ПО́ЛЕ; ИЩИ́-СВИЩИ́ ⟨ВЕ́ТРА В ПО́ЛЕ⟩; ИЩИ́ ДА СВИЩИ́ *all coll* [imper sent; these forms only; often after тепе́рь, тогда́ etc; fixed WO] (usu. in refer. to people) it is no use searching, you will not be able to find s.o. or sth. (said when s.o. or sth. has disappeared completely and is impossible to locate): **you can (go) whistle for him ⟨her etc⟩; you'll never find ⟨see⟩ him ⟨it etc⟩ again; he ⟨it etc⟩ is gone with the wind.**

[Хороших:] А теперь где те геологи? [Дергачёв:] Ищи-свищи (Вампилов 2). [Kh.:] And where are them geologists now? [D.:] You can go whistle for them (2b).

B-75 • МОЧИ́ТЬСЯ ПРОТИВ ВЕ́ТРА *slang* [VP; subj: human] to do sth. that goes against a general tendency, prevailing policies etc: X мочится против ветра ≃ **X is pissing ⟨spitting⟩ in(to) the wind.**

«Там перед самой зоной старик один обитает… пасеку обихаживает, рыбкой промышляет для офицерского стола. Нам тоже не отказывает, сообразительный старикан, против ветра не мочится» (Максимов 1). "There's an old man just outside the zone…— he looks after the bees and earns a living by supplying fish for the officers' table. He won't refuse us either. A quick-witted old fellow, he is. He won't piss in the wind" (1a).

B-76 • ПОПУ́ТНОГО ВЕ́ТРА [formula phrase; Invar; fixed WO] good wishes to s.o. who is embarking on a sea voyage (usu. to sailors setting out to sea): **smooth sailing!; bon voyage!**

B-77 • ВЕ́ТРОМ ШАТА́ЕТ *кого́ coll* [VP; impers; fixed WO] (a person is) unable to walk steadily, hardly able to stand up (from weakness, old age, drunkenness etc): X-а ветром шатает ≃ **a (good) breeze could knock ⟨blow⟩ X over; [in limited contexts] X trembles in the wind; (X is so drunk) he can't stand up straight.**

«…Колыма, Воркута, Тайшет. Так ведь там от истощения подыхали пачками, доходяг буквально ветром шатало…» (Марченко 1). "…Kolyma, Vorkuta, Taishet. There they used to die like flies from exhaustion, 'goners' would literally tremble in the wind…" (1a).

B-78 • КАК ⟨БУ́ДТО, СЛО́ВНО, ТО́ЧНО⟩ ВЕ́ТРОМ СДУ́ЛО ⟨СДУВА́ЛО/СДУ́НУЛО⟩ *кого́-что coll, occas. humor* [VP; impers; usu. pfv past; fixed WO] s.o. or sth. disappeared very quickly, speedily: X-а как ветром сдуло ≃ **person X was off like the wind; X vanished ⟨disappeared, was gone⟩ in a flash ⟨in an instant, in a wink⟩; it is as if X evaporated into thin air; thing X evaporated into thin air.**

…Он закричал: «По трамвайной линии немцы идут! Пошли!» И меня как ветром сдуло (Кузнецов 1). …He called out: "The Germans are coming down the tramline! Let's go!" I was off like the wind (1b). ♦ «Цыть!» – сказал Губошлёп. И улыбку его как ветром сдуло (Шукшин 1). "Shut up!" hissed Fat Lip. And his smile was gone in an instant (1a).

B-79 • КАКИ́М ВЕ́ТРОМ ⟨КАКИ́МИ ВЕТРА́МИ, КАКИ́МИ ВЕ́ТРАМИ⟩ ЗАНЕСЛО́ *кого (куда)*?; **КАКО́Й ВЕ́ТЕР ЗАНЁС ⟨КАКИ́Е ВЕ́ТРЫ ЗАНЕСЛИ́⟩?; КАКИ́М ВЕ́ТРОМ ⟨КАКИ́МИ ВЕТРА́МИ⟩?** *all coll* [VP, impers, past only (var. with занесло); VP$_{subj}$, past only (variants with занёс, занесли); indep sent, these forms only, always addressed to the hearer (variants without the verb); fixed WO] what caused s.o. to come to a certain place? (often used to express surprise when meeting s.o. unexpectedly): каким ветром X-а занесло в место Y? ≃ **what brings ⟨brought⟩ X to place Y?; what on earth ⟨in the world⟩ brings ⟨brought⟩ X to place Y?; what (good) wind brings ⟨blew⟩ X to place Y?**

«Лучше скажите, каким вас ветром занесло? Больше года тут, и всё не могли собраться, удосужиться?» (Пастернак 1). "Better tell me what brought you here. You've been around more than a year and you never found a moment to come till now" (1a). ♦ Он увидел хуторян – и вислые воронёно-чёрные усы его дрогнули в улыбке. «...Каким вас ветром занесло?» (Шолохов 3). At the sight of the men from his own village, his drooping burnished moustache twitched into a smile. "…What wind brings you here?" (3a).

B-80 • ПОДБИ́ТЫЙ ⟨ПОДБИ́Т⟩ ВЕ́ТРОМ ⟨ВЕТЕРКО́М⟩ *coll* [AdjP; modif (long-form var. only) or subj-compl with copula (subj: a noun denoting an item of outerwear)] thin, offering little protection from the cold: **skimpy; flimsy; (like) cheesecloth.**

B-81 • ДО ВЕ́ТРУ пойти, выйти, хотеть и т. п. *substand* [PrepP; Invar; adv] (to go, go outside etc) in order to urinate or defecate: **(go outside) to relieve o.s. ⟨to answer the call of nature⟩; (go to ⟨use etc⟩) the outhouse; (go out) to do one's business.**

«Что вам нужно, зачем стучите?» – «Выйти до ветру», – заявил дед глубоким басом проповедника. «Господи, да у вас же в номере туалет!» (Грекова 3). "What do you want? Why are you carrying on like this?" "Need the outhouse," the old man intoned in the deep bass voice of a preacher. "Good Lord, you've got a toilet in your room!" (3a). ♦ ...Самая любимая их байка была о начальнике экспедиции, который вышел утром «до ветру» и, сидя за сугробом, почувствовал, что кто-то лизнул его сзади (Войнович 6). ...Their favorite story was about an expedition chief who went out "to do his business" one morning and, as he was crouching behind a snowdrift, felt someone lick his behind (6a).

B-82 • ПУСКА́ТЬ/ПУСТИ́ТЬ ПО́ ВЕТРУ ⟨ПО ВЕ́ТРУ⟩ деньги, состояние, имущество и т. п. [VP; subj: human] to spend (money) wastefully, fritter away (one's fortune) to no purpose, senselessly: X пустил деньги по ветру ≃ **X threw money to the (four) winds; X threw money out the window ⟨down the drain⟩; X squandered (away) money.**

...Через двадцать лет упорных трудов мой старик уже имел всё – и детей, и хозяйство, и огромный загон скота... А теперь что? А теперь всем колхозом они не имеют столько скота, сколько он один тогда имел. Пустомели, всё по ветру пустили! (Искандер 3). ...After twenty years of unrelenting labor my old man had it all – children, a farm, and a huge pen of stock....And now what? Now they don't have as much stock in the whole kolkhoz as he alone had then. Big talk, but they've thrown it all to the winds! (3a). ♦ «Ваши брильянты!» – закричал он, пугаясь силы своего голоса. – В стул! Кто вас надоумил? Почему вы не дали их мне?» – «Как же было дать вам брильянты, когда вы пустили по ветру имение моей дочери?» – спокойно и зло молвила старуха (Ильф и Петров 1). "Your jewels!" he cried, startled at the loudness of his own voice. "In a chair? Who induced you

to do that? Why didn't you give them to me?" "Why should I have given them to you when you squandered away my daughter's estate?" said the old woman quietly and viciously (1a).

B-83 • ДО́БРЫЙ ВЕ́ЧЕР [formula phrase; Invar; fixed WO] a greeting used upon meeting s.o. in the evening: **good evening; hello.**

«Простите за беспокойство, фрау Майер. Разве Курта нет дома?» – «Ах, герр Старцов! Добрый вечер» (Федин 1). "Excuse the disturbance, Frau Maier. Isn't Kurt at home?" "Ah, Herr Startsov! Good evening" (1a).

B-84 • ЕЩЁ НЕ ВЕ́ЧЕР *recent, coll* [sent; Invar; fixed WO] there remains time before the conclusion of sth. (to accomplish sth. not yet accomplished, prove o.s., turn around a course of events etc): **it's not too late (to do sth.); there's still time; it's not over yet; it's not over till it's over; we're ⟨they're etc⟩ not through yet; nothing is set in stone yet;** [in limited contexts] **the final act has yet to be played out ⟨the final scene has yet to be acted out⟩.** Cf. **the opera isn't over till the fat lady sings.**

«Вашу команду бьют!» – «Ничего, ещё не вечер, они ещё себя покажут». "Your team is getting killed!" "That's OK, there's still time. They'll show what they can do yet."

B-85 • КА́НУТЬ В ВЕ́ЧНОСТЬ *lit* [VP; subj: usu. abstr] to disappear forever, cease to be remembered: X канет в вечность ≃ **X will pass ⟨sink⟩ into oblivion; X will be totally ⟨long⟩ forgotten.**

Антологию запретили, потому что О. М[андельштам] не включил в неё поэтов, которым уже тогда покровительствовало государство, то есть пролетарских. Их имена канули в вечность, и мне не припомнить, о ком шла речь (Мандельштам 1). The anthology was eventually forbidden by the censor because O. M[andelstam] had not included any of the "proletarian" poets who were already being sponsored by the State. Their names are now totally forgotten, and I do not remember which ones it was proposed to include (1a).

B-86 • ОТОЙТИ́ В ВЕ́ЧНОСТЬ *elev* [VP] **1.** [subj: human] to die: X отошёл в вечность ≃ **X went to his eternal rest; X departed this life; X left this world; X awoke to life immortal; X joined the choir invisible.**

2. [subj: usu. abstr] to disappear forever, cease to be remembered: X отошёл в вечность ≃ **X has passed ⟨sunk⟩ into oblivion; X is long ⟨totally⟩ forgotten.**

B-87 • КАК НА ВЕ́ШАЛКЕ сидеть, висеть, болтаться *на ком coll* [как + PrepP; Invar; adv] (some piece of clothing fits) poorly because it is too large: костюм ⟨пальто и т. п.⟩ висит на X-е ~ ≃ **that suit ⟨coat etc⟩ (just) hangs on X; X is swimming in that suit ⟨coat etc⟩; you could fit two of him ⟨you etc⟩ in that suit ⟨coat etc⟩.**

B-88 • НАЗЫВА́ТЬ/НАЗВА́ТЬ ВЕ́ЩИ СВОИ́МИ ⟨СО́БСТВЕННЫМИ, НАСТОЯ́ЩИМИ⟩ ИМЕНА́МИ [VP; subj: human; often impfv infin with любить, привыкнуть, не хотеть etc; fixed WO] to speak of s.o. or sth. very plainly and straightforwardly, not resorting to euphemisms or toning down one's wording: X будет называть вещи своими именами ≃ **X will call a spade a spade; X will call things by their own ⟨real, right⟩ names.**

Вообще резкость суждений у нас осуждалась всеми кругами без исключения... Называть вещи своими именами считалось неприличным... (Мандельштам 2). By now, in fact, everybody without exception, whatever circle he belonged to, disapproved of any blunt expression of opinion....It was thought improper to call a spade a spade... (2a). ♦ Одиннадцать лет правления

Хрущёва будут помнить потому, что он попытался назвать вещи своими именами (Аллилуева 2). The eleven years of Khrushchev's rule will be remembered for his effort to call things by their real names (2a).

B-89 • СМОТРÉТЬ ⟨ГЛЯДÉТЬ⟩ НА ВÉЩИ *как* [VP; subj: human] to consider, regard things in a particular way (as specified by the adv): X смотрит на вещи… ≃ **X sees ⟨views, looks at, looks upon⟩ things ⟨the matter, the situation⟩** [AdvP]; **X takes a** [AdjP] **view (of things).**

Трудно сказать, когда Крикун начал систематически изучать материалы периода Хозяина, касающиеся репрессий… Он давно чувствовал, что именно здесь зарыта собака… Тогда иначе смотрели на вещи и не могли предполагать, что слова, казавшиеся им вполне справедливыми, много лет спустя станут свидетельством страшных преступлений (Зиновьев 1). It is hard to say precisely when Bawler began his systematic study of materials regarding repression in the period of the Boss.…He had long felt that this was the crux of the matter.…In those days people saw things differently, and could not suppose that words which then seemed just would later be seen as evidence of atrocious crimes (1a). ♦ «Конечно, нужно смотреть на вещи трезво…» (Эренбург 4). "Of course…we must look at the matter in a sober light" (4a). ♦ «Он [мой поверенный] смотрит на эти вещи гораздо мрачнее» (Пастернак 1). "My lawyer takes a much gloomier view [of these matters]" (1a).

B-90 • ВЕЩЬ В СЕБÉ *lit* [NP; usu. subj-compl with copula (subj: abstr, concr, or—by extension—human); fixed WO] (of phenomena which are) unfathomable to the human mind; *by extension* (of a person whose personality, mindset etc is) enigmatic, difficult to understand: **thing-in-itself ⟨things-in-themselves⟩; closed book.**

< Loan translation of the German *Ding an sich* (from Immanuel Kant's *Critique of Pure Reason*, 1781).

B-91 • ВЗАД И ВПЕРЁД ⟨ВЗАД-ВПЕРЁД⟩ ходить, расхаживать, бегать, метаться и т. п. [AdvP; these forms only; adv; fixed WO] (to walk, pace, run etc) first in one direction and then in another, from one place to another and back again repeatedly: **back and forth; to and fro; up and down; hither and thither;** [in limited contexts] **backward(s) and forward(s).**

«…[Печорин] выскочил в другую комнату. Я зашёл к нему; он сложа руки прохаживался угрюмый взад и вперёд» (Лермонтов 1). "Pechorin…rushed into the next room. I went there; he was gloomily pacing to and fro, with his arms folded on his chest" (1a). ♦ …Отказавшись от ужина и оставшись один в маленькой комнатке, он долго ходил и не взад и вперёд… (Толстой 5). …Refusing supper, he remained alone in the little room, pacing up and down for a long time… (5a). ♦ Дуняша бегала взад и вперёд как угорелая и то и дело хлопала дверьми (Тургенев 2). Dunyasha ran hither and thither like one possessed and kept banging the doors (2e). ♦ Она ходила взад и вперёд по своей небольшой комнате, сжав руки на груди, с запёкшимися губами и неровно, прерывисто дышала (Достоевский 3). She was walking backward and forward about her small room, her hands pressed to her bosom, her lips parched, and she was breathing unevenly and jerkily (3a). ♦ Солдаты шныряли беспрестанно взад и вперёд мимо пожара… (Толстой 6). Soldiers were continually rushing backwards and forwards near it [the fire]… (6b). ♦ Несмотря на мерзкую погоду и слякоть, щегольские коляски пролетали взад и вперёд (Гоголь 3). In spite of the foul weather and the muddy roads, elegant carriages kept driving rapidly back and forth (3a). [context transl] Despite the filthy weather and the mud, there was a rapid coming and going of smart carriages (3d).

B-92 • НИ ВЗАД НИ ВПЕРЁД *coll* [AdvP; Invar; fixed WO] **1. Also: НИ ВЗАД И НИ ВПЕРЁД** [adv or predic (subj: human, animal, or a noun denoting a vehicle)] (some person, animal, or vehicle is) unable to move in any direction, (does) not move from one's or its place: X ни взад ни вперёд ≃ **X won't ⟨can't⟩ move ⟨go⟩ backward or forward; X won't move ⟨go⟩ one way or the other ⟨either one way or the other⟩; X won't move an inch; X won't budge (an inch).**

Машина застряла в грязи — и ни взад ни вперёд. The car got stuck in the mud and couldn't go backward or forward.

2. [predic with subj: abstr, concr, or human] (of a person's work, matters etc, or of a person who is trying to do a project, task etc) not to show any progress, be in the same state: X ни взад ни вперёд ≃ **X is making no progress ⟨headway⟩; X is at a (complete) standstill; there is absolutely no progress with thing X; X isn't getting anywhere.**

B-93 • НА ВЗВÓДЕ *highly coll* [PrepP; Invar; usu. subj-compl with copula (subj: human)] **1. Also: НА ПÉРВОМ ⟨ВТОРÓМ⟩ ВЗВÓДЕ** [fixed WO] (one is) in a state of inebriation: X на взводе ≃ **X is feeling no pain; X is in his cups; X is tipsy ⟨loaded⟩; X is under the influence; X is the worse for drink.**

После того как они, наконец, с помощью Осипа устроились и Антонина, вычистив и вымыв отведённую им комнату, сбегала в ларёк и накрыла на стол, комендант, уже на изрядном взводе, явился к ним в гости… (Максимов 3). When they had finally settled in with Osip's help, and Antonina had dusted and mopped the room, run down to the shop, and laid the table, the house manager, who was already well loaded, invited himself in (3a).

2. (one is) annoyed or agitated: X был на взводе ≃ **X was worked up; X was on edge; X was keyed ⟨wrought⟩ up.**

B-94 • НА ТРÉТЬЕМ ⟨НА СЕДЬМÓМ⟩ ВЗВÓДЕ *coll* [PrepP; these forms only; usu. subj-compl with copula (subj: human); fixed WO] (one is) in a state of strong inebriation: X был на третьем взводе ≃ **X was dead drunk; X was three sheets in ⟨to⟩ the wind; X was tanked.**

B-95 • БРОСÁТЬ/БРÓСИТЬ ⟨КИДÁТЬ/КИ́НУТЬ⟩ ВЗГЛЯД [VP; subj: human; fixed WO] **1.** ~ *на кого-что* to look quickly, briefly at s.o. or sth.: X бросил взгляд на Y-а ≃ **X cast a glance at Y; X gave Y a look; X glanced at Y.**

Временами он [Харлампо] бросал взгляд на свою невесту и тётушку Хрисулу, стараясь внушить им своим взглядом, что вот он здесь сидит с дедушкой Хабугом, что он в сущности в этом доме не какой-нибудь там нанятый пастух, а почти член семьи (Искандер 5). From time to time he [Harlampo] would cast a glance at his bride and Auntie Chrysoula, trying to impress on them that here he was, sitting with Grandpa Khabug, he wasn't actually just a hired shepherd in this house, he was practically a member of the family (5a). ♦ Грушницкий бросил на меня недовольный взгляд (Лермонтов 1). Grushnitsky gave me a look of displeasure (1c). ♦ Они деловито проезжают мимо вас, безусловно разговаривая между собой и именно о вас, да-да, они кидают на вас взгляды, когда проезжают мимо (Олеша 3). They ride by you in a businesslike way, undoubtedly talking among themselves and certainly about you; indeed they glance at you as they go by (3a).

2. ~ *на что* to think briefly about sth., return to sth. in one's thoughts: X бросил взгляд на Y ≃ **X went back in his mind to Y; X looked ⟨glanced⟩ back on Y; X cast a (swift ⟨quick etc⟩) glance at Y; X took a look at Y.**

Не стану час за часом следить за своими воспоминаниями, но брошу быстрый взгляд на главнейшие из них… (Толстой 2). I shall not trace my recollections hour by hour, but shall cast a swift glance at the most important ones… (2b).

B-96 • НА ВЗГЛЯД *coll* [PrepP; Invar] **1.** [adv] outwardly: **in appearance; from the looks of; to look at.**

На взгляд он был человек видный; черты лица его были не лишены приятности, но в эту приятность, казалось, чересчур было передано сахару... (Гоголь 3). In appearance he was an impressive-looking man; his features were rather pleasant, but this pleasantness, one could not help feeling, had much too much sugar in it... (3a).

2. ~ чей, кого. Also: **НА ГЛАЗ** ⟨**-а**⟩ *obs* [the resulting PrepP is sent adv (usu. parenth)] according to s.o.'s opinion, belief: на X-ов взгляд ≃ **to X's mind; in X's opinion** ⟨**view, book**⟩; **as** ⟨**the way**⟩ **X sees it; the way X looks at it;** [in limited contexts] **what** ⟨**which**⟩ **one considers** ⟨**would consider**⟩...

И тут Абесаломон Нартович нам выдал, на мой взгляд, хорошую новеллу (Искандер 4). At this point Abesalomon Nartovich produced what to my mind was a good short story (4a). ♦ Она сильно изменилась в лице, похудела и пожелтела, хотя вот уже почти две недели как могла выходить со двора. Но, на взгляд Алёши, лицо её стало как бы ещё привлекательнее, и он любил, входя к ней, встречать её взгляд (Достоевский 2). Her face was greatly changed, she had become thin and sallow, though for almost two weeks she had already been able to go out. But in Alyosha's opinion her face had become even more attractive, as it were, and he loved meeting her eyes when he entered her room (2a). ♦ В тридцать шестом году он рассорился с отцом — строгим, деспотичным, не желавшим мириться с кинематографическими, на его взгляд несерьёзными, увлечениями сына... (Некрасов 1). In 1936 he had quarreled with his father, who was strict, despotic, and did not wish to countenance his son's frivolous (as he saw it) enthusiasm for the movies... (1a). ♦ [В старину,] по сравнению с позднейшей убористой печатью, на странице помещалось мало знаков. Маленькая, на наш взгляд, повестушка растягивалась на волюм... (Терц 3). Compared to the very close print of a later age, [in the old days] there were fewer letters to a page. A story which we would now consider short filled a whole volume... (3a).

В-97 • НА ПЕ́РВЫЙ ВЗГЛЯД [PrepP; Invar; sent adv (occas. parenth); fixed WO] on first impression: **at first sight** ⟨**glance, blush**⟩; **on the face of it.**

...Отношение Бориса Леонидовича [Пастернака] к этой проблеме было сложным, иногда временами даже на первый взгляд по-детски наивным и смешным (Ивинская 1). BL's [Pasternak's] attitude to the whole problem was, it must be said, complicated—and at times contradictory, or even at first sight naïve and comic (1a). ♦ В общем-то, лицо Мансурова было довольно красивым, особенно на первый взгляд: лоб, глаза, но крупное и как будто бы значительное (Залыгин 1). Taken as a whole Mansurov's face was quite handsome, especially at first glance: the brow, the eyes—everything was strong and seemed to be filled with meaning (1a). ♦ Слова, на первый взгляд, были самыми незначительными — о погоде, о житейском, о мелочах разных, — но откровение общности коснулось их [Лашкова и Ивана]... (Максимов 3). On the face of it nothing they [Lashkov and Ivan] said was of the slightest importance—they talked about the weather, about daily routines, about all sorts of trivialities—but they both sensed a deep affinity... (3a).

В-98 • С ПЕ́РВОГО ВЗГЛЯ́ДА ⟨**-у** *obs*⟩ [PrepP; these forms only; adv; fixed WO] **1.** Also: **ПО ПЕ́РВОМУ ВЗГЛЯ́ДУ** *obs* [more often used with pfv verbs] immediately: **at a glance; at first sight** ⟨**glance**⟩; **the moment** ⟨**the minute**⟩ **one sets** ⟨**lays**⟩ **eyes on (s.o.** ⟨**sth.**⟩**); the moment** ⟨**the minute**⟩ **one sees (s.o.** ⟨**sth.**⟩**); right away; at once.**

Юре хорошо было с дядей. Он был похож на маму... Как у неё, у него было дворянское чувство равенства со всеми живущими. Он так же, как она, понимал всё с первого взгляда... (Пастернак 1). Yura enjoyed being with his uncle. He reminded him of his mother....He had the same aristocratic sense of equality with all living creatures and the same gift of taking in everything at a glance... (1a). ♦ «Вы мне что-то с первого взгляда понравились!» (Шукшин 1). "There was something about you I liked the minute I laid eyes on you!" (1a). ♦ Меня он, кажется,

совсем не узнал, а Митю узнал, разумеется, с первого взгляда (Каверин 1). I don't think he recognised me, but Mitya, of course, he knew the moment he saw him (1a). ♦ Есть ведь на свете чуткие, сердобольные люди, примечающие с первого взгляда, что неладное происходит с человеком (Айтматов 2). There are in this world compassionate, sensitive people who can notice at once when something is wrong with a person (2a).

2. Also: **ПРИ ПЕ́РВОМ ВЗГЛЯ́ДЕ** *obs* on first impression: **at first sight** ⟨**glance, blush**⟩; **on the face of it.**

...Теперь, глядя на отца, я начинала смутно догадываться, что он не так уж счастлив, как могло показаться с первого взгляда (Каверин 1). ...Now, when I looked at my father, I began vaguely to suspect that he was not so happy as might appear at first sight (1a). ♦ Комната, где лежал Илья Ильич, с первого взгляда казалась прекрасно убранною (Гончаров 1). The room in which Oblomov was lying seemed at first glance to be splendidly furnished (1a).

В-99 • НЕСТИ́/ПОНЕСТИ́ ВЗДОР ⟨**АХИНЕ́Ю, БЕЛИБЕРДУ́, ГАЛИМАТЬЮ́, ДИЧЬ, Е́РЕСЬ, ЕРУНДУ́, ОКОЛЁСИЦУ, ОКОЛЕ́СИЦУ, ЧЕПУХУ́, ЧУШЬ, ГИЛЬ** *obs*, **ОКОЛЁСИНУ** *obs*, **ОКОЛЁСНУЮ** *obs*⟩; **МОЛО́ТЬ ВЗДОР** ⟨**ГАЛИМАТЬЮ́, ЕРУНДУ́, ЧЕПУХУ́**⟩; **ПОРО́ТЬ ВЗДОР** ⟨**АХИНЕ́Ю, ГАЛИМАТЬЮ́, ДИЧЬ, ЕРУНДУ́, ЧЕПУХУ́, ЧУШЬ**⟩; **ГОРОДИ́ТЬ/НАГОРОДИ́ТЬ ВЗДОР** ⟨**ЕРУНДУ́, ОКОЛЁСИЦУ, ЧЕПУХУ́, ЧУШЬ**⟩; **ПЛЕСТИ́ АХИНЕ́Ю** ⟨**Е́РЕСЬ, ОКОЛЁСИЦУ**⟩; **БОЛТА́ТЬ ЕРУНДУ́** ⟨**ЧЕПУХУ́**⟩ *all coll* [VP; subj: human] to say ridiculous things: X несёт вздор ≃ **X spouts** ⟨**talks, spews**⟩ **drivel** ⟨**nonsense, gibberish, rubbish**⟩; **X babbles nonsense; X spouts bosh; X comes out with all sorts** ⟨**kinds**⟩ **of nonsense** ⟨**rubbish, drivel**⟩; **X talks blather** ⟨**a lot of rot**⟩; **X blathers away;** ‖ *Neg Imper* не пори ерунду ≃ [in limited contexts] **don't give me all that stuff and nonsense!**

Андрей тронул; колокольчик зазвенел. «Прощай, Пётр Ильич! Тебе последняя слеза!..» — «Не пьян ведь, а какую ахинею порет!» — подумал вслед ему Пётр Ильич (Достоевский 1). Andrei got going; the bells jingled. "Farewell, Pyotr Ilyich! For you, for you is my last tear!..." "He's not drunk, but what drivel he's spouting!" Pyotr Ilyich thought, watching him go (1a). ♦ Поначалу мне почудилось, будто Дудин намеренно нёс околесицу, облегчая возможность его опровергать и вообще стремясь всему заседанию придать пародийный характер (Эткинд 1). At first I imagined that Dudin was deliberately talking nonsense so as to be more easily refuted and generally so as to make the whole meeting look like a parody (1a). ♦ «Столько лет молчал... и вдруг нагородил столько ахинеи» (Достоевский 1). "For so many years I was silent...and suddenly I spewed out so much gibberish!" (1a). ♦ «Простите, — после паузы заговорил Берлиоз, поглядывая на мелющего чепуху иностранца, — при чём здесь подсолнечное масло... и какая Аннушка?» (Булгаков 9). "Forgive me," Berlioz spoke after a pause, glancing at the foreigner who was babbling such nonsense, "but what has sunflower oil to do with it? And who is Annushka?" (9a). ♦ Когда мои знакомые просят меня рассказать, что изображено на рисунках ЭН, я теряюсь и несу какую-то чепуху (Зиновьев 1). When my acquaintances ask me to explain E.N.'s drawings, I become confused and come out with all kinds of rubbish (1a). ♦ «Наконец старик опьянел и уже стал молоть такую околесицу, что его и племянницы перестали понимать» (Искандер 5). "Finally the old man got drunk, and by now he was talking such blather that even his nieces had ceased to understand" (5a).

В-100 • ВЗДОХНУ́ТЬ НЕ́КОГДА *кому coll* [Invar; impers predic with быть∅] s.o. is extremely busy: X-у вздохнуть было некогда ≃ **X didn't even have time to breathe** ⟨**to catch his breath**⟩.

B-101 • СВОБО́ДНО ⟨-ее⟩ ВЗДОХНУ́ТЬ [VP; subj: human; usu. past] to feel relief (after being freed from some cares, worries, obligations): X вздохнул свободно ≃ **X drew free breath; X breathed freely ⟨easy⟩ again; X breathed a sigh of relief.**

В первый раз свободно вздохнули глуповцы и поняли, что жить «без утеснения» не в пример лучше, чем жить «с утеснением» (Салтыков-Щедрин 1). For the first time the Foolovites drew free breath and realized that to live "without oppression" was far better than to live "with oppression" (1a).

B-102 • НЕ ВЗДУ́МАЙ(ТЕ) *coll* [VP_imper; these forms only; usu. foll. by infin] (used when forbidding s.o. to do sth.) you are not to do that: **don't even think about it ⟨doing sth.⟩; don't take it into your head (to do sth.); don't you dare (to do sth.); [in limited contexts] don't (even) try (to do sth.).**

...Видавшие виды дамы просто обязаны предупреждать молодёжь женского пола [по поводу таких мужчин, как Никандров]: «И не вздумайте! Кроме головной боли, ничего не маячит!» (Залыгин 1). Seasoned women had a duty to warn the younger of their sex about men like him [Nikandrov]: "Don't even think about it! You'll get yourself nothing but a headache!" (1a). ♦ «...Ты не вздумай ему сказать про... того парня, которого я сдуру взял в кассу» (Семёнов 1). "...Don't take it into your head to say anything about...that kid I took to the bank" (1a). ♦ Митягин давно уже по-соседски упрашивал Семёна Тетерина взять его на медвежью охоту... Семён дал ему свою старенькую одностволку, наказал: «Не вздумай лезть наперёд, не на зайца идём» (Тендряков 1). For a long time Mityagin had been begging Simon Teterin to do him a favour, as a neighbour, by taking him on a bear hunt....Simon gave him his old rifle, and said: "Don't try to get in front, we're not after hares" (1a).

B-103 • НЕ ВЗЫЩИ́(ТЕ) *coll* [imper sent; these forms only] do not be offended; be tolerant: **no offense (intended); don't ⟨you mustn't⟩ hold it against me ⟨us etc⟩; (I) hope you don't mind; don't be (too) hard on me ⟨us etc⟩; forgive me ⟨us etc⟩; sorry (, but...).**

«Не взыщи, друг, я тут стеганул вашу лошадь невзначай...» (Искандер 5). "No offence, friend, I didn't mean to lash your horse..." (5a). ♦ «Ну, ладно, слушай [*Ukrainian* = слушай] мою правду колкую, не взыщи, я тебе всё в глаза скажу» (Пастернак 1). "Now, I'll tell you the whole truth if you want it, I'll say it to your face, but you mustn't hold it against me" (1a). ♦ «И вам... Иван Алексеич, забыла капусты к котлетам приготовить, — прибавила она, обращаясь к Алексееву. — Не взыщите» (Гончаров 1). "And I'm afraid I forgot to cook some cabbage for your cutlets, Ivan Alexeyevich," she added, turning to Alexeyev. "I hope you don't mind" (1a). ♦ «Не узнал, не взыщи!» — крикнул мне Тендел... (Искандер 3). "Sorry, but I don't recognize you!" Tendel shouted at me... (3a).

B-104 • ВСЕМ ВЗЯЛ *coll, approv* [VP; subj: human; past only; fixed WO] one has every positive attribute, is superior: X всем взял ≃ **X has (got) everything; X has (got) it all; X is a fine figure of a man ⟨a woman etc⟩; [in limited contexts] X is good at everything.**

«У вас — девка невеста, у нас — жених... Не снюхаемся ли каким случаем?»... — «Наша не засидится. Девка... всем взяла: что на полях, что дома...» (Шолохов 2). "You've got a girl of marriageable age; we've got a lad....Could we come to an agreement by any chance?"..."Our girl won't be left on the shelf....She's good at everything, whether it be on the farm or in the house" (2a).

B-105 • ОТКУ́ДА ⟨С ЧЕГО́⟩ ТЫ ⟨он и т. п.⟩ ВЗЯЛ? [sent; past only; usu. addressed to the hearer; fixed WO] how did you arrive at that thought?: **what makes you think that ⟨that...⟩?; where did you ⟨he etc⟩ get that idea ⟨the idea that...⟩?; what ⟨whatever⟩ gave you ⟨him etc⟩ that idea ⟨the idea that...⟩?**

«С чего ты, например, взял, что, что бы я ни говорил вслух — втайне... я страдаю?» (Битов 2). "What makes you think, for example, that no matter what I say aloud I'm secretly suffering?..." (2a). ♦ [Галина:] Нет, ты его [ребёнка] не хочешь, я знаю. [Зилов:] Да нет, с чего ты это взяла? Я не против... (Вампилов 5) [G.:] No, I can see you don't want one [a baby]. [Z.:] Now where'd you get that idea? I've nothing against it... (5a). ♦ «Откуда ты, собственно, взяла, что у тебя [нет]... никакой доброты?» (Стругацкие 1). "Where did you get the idea that you completely lack kindness?" (1a). ♦ «Ты стареешь, Золотарёв». — «С чего ты взяла?» — «Становишься сентиментальным» (Максимов 1). "You're getting old, Zolotarev." "What gives you that idea?" "You're becoming sentimental" (1a).

B-106 • ОТКУ́ДА ЧТО ВЗЯЛО́СЬ! *coll* [sent; Invar; fixed WO] it manifested itself suddenly, unexpectedly: **whatever brought that on?; where did that come from?; goodness knows how (it happened)!; [in limited contexts] will wonders never cease!**

...[Соня] носилась разгорячённая, суматошная, предовольная и готова была, кажется, приковать себя к этой квартире. А ведь тоже деревенская баба, с князьями да дворянами не возжалась [*nonstand* = не водилась], красивой жизни не нюхала, но... распушилась, откуда что и взялось? (Распутин 4). ...[Sonya] raced around excited, animated, bustling, ever so happy and apparently ready to live forever in that apartment. And yet she was a country woman too, she didn't hang around with princes and nobles, she hadn't tasted the good life, but...she took to it right away. Where did that come from? (4a). ♦ [Наталья Петровна:] Давно ли, кажется, всё было так тихо, так покойно в этом доме... и вдруг... откуда что взялось! Право, мы все с ума сошли (Тургенев 1). [N.P.:] It seems only a little while ago everything was so quiet and peaceful in this house...and all at once...goodness knows how! Really, we've all gone out of our minds (1a).

B-107 • ВЗЯ́ТКИ ГЛА́ДКИ *с кого coll, often disapprov* [sent; Invar; fixed WO] it is futile to attempt to hold s.o. responsible for sth. or get sth. out of him (because of his character traits, attitude, circumstances, financial situation etc): с X-а взятки гладки ≃ **you ⟨he etc⟩ won't get much ⟨anything⟩ out of X; you won't get anywhere with X; you're wasting your time on X; there is nothing you ⟨he etc⟩ can do to X; X cannot be called to account; [when s.o. cannot be blamed or punished for sth. because his accusers lack proof] you've ⟨they've etc⟩ got nothing on X.**

«Новенький полковник... донесёт, и придётся отвечать...» — «...С меня взятки гладки!» (Шолохов 5). "The new colonel...will report this, and you'll have to answer for it...." "...They won't get much out of me!" (5a). ♦ [Кречинский:] ...Проглядел невесту; теперь на меня глаза пялить нечего: с меня, приятель, взятки гладки... (Сухово-Кобылин 2). [K.:] You've already lost your sweetheart—there's no sense in staring...at me like that now. You won't get anywhere with me, my friend... (2b). ♦ С патронами Дарья и не дала бы [Богодулу берданку]: у него ума достанет и пальнуть... Теперь только этого и не хватало. С него взятки гладки (Распутин 4). Darya wouldn't have considered giving it [the rifle] to him [Bogodul] loaded: he just might shoot it if he got angry....That's all they needed now. There was nothing they could do to him... (4a). ♦ «Что ж, смотрите, я — не боюсь! Вы же видите — я занят делом, я люблю свою Лиду и с меня взятки гладки...» (Терц 8). "Okay, look! I'm not afraid! You can see that I'm busy making love to my Lida, and you've got nothing on me..." (8a). ♦ Лучников легонько отодвинул Фредди и прошёл к дверям. Выходя, успел заметить, как Бутурлин разводит руками, — дескать, ну вот, с меня, мол, и взятки гладки (Аксёнов 7). [context transl] Luchnikov moved Freddy gently aside and made his way to the door unimpeded. Leaving the room, he caught a glimpse of Buturlin throwing up his hands as if to say, Well, what did you expect? I've done what I could (7a).

В-108 • ВЗЯТЬ ДА ⟨ДА И, И⟩... *coll* [VP; subj: any noun; imper возьми да etc is used with any pers (sing or pl), usu. in refer. to the past; foll. by another verb in the same form; fixed WO] (to do sth., to happen) unexpectedly, suddenly: X возьми да и сделай Y ≃ **person X up and did Y; all of a sudden X did Y;** ‖ X взял бы да сделал Y ≃ [in limited contexts] **X could do Y.**

«У мамы отпуск, у папы отпуск, у меня каникулы, вот мы сюда и приехали на пять дней покататься на лыжах». — «Прямо так вот взяли и приехали?» — «Ну да» (Войнович 1). "Mama's on vacation, Papa's on vacation, and it's school break, so we came to ski for five days." "You just up and came?" "That's right" (1a). ♦ [Нина:] Слушай, Васька... Гад ты, и больше никто. Взяла бы тебя и убила (Вампилов 4). [N.:] Listen, Vaska....You're a creep, that's all. I could kill you (4b).

В-109 • ВЫСТАВЛЯ́ТЬ/ВЫ́СТАВИТЬ НА ВИД *что, rare кого;* **ВЫСТАВЛЯ́ТЬ/ВЫ́СТАВИТЬ НАПОКА́З ⟨НАРУ́ЖУ⟩** [VP; subj: human or abstr] to reveal sth., make sth. visible: X выставляет на вид Y ≃ **X exhibits ⟨discloses, exposes⟩ Y; X makes Y known; person X puts Y on display; person X lets everyone see Y;** [in limited contexts] **person X shows off Y.**

Перечитывая эти записки, я убедился в искренности того, кто так беспощадно выставлял наружу собственные слабости и пороки (Лермонтов 1). While reading over these notes, I became convinced of the sincerity of this man who so mercilessly exhibited his own failings and vices (1a). Reading over these notes again, I felt convinced of the sincerity of the man who so ruthlessly exposed his own failings and vices (1c). ♦ Веру вызывали в школу: «Ваш сын ведёт себя демонстративно, выставляет на вид своё высокое развитие» (Грекова 3). Vera was called in to school, where the teacher told her, "Your son is impertinent, and keeps showing off his high level of development" (3a).

В-110 • ДЕ́ЛАТЬ/СДЕ́ЛАТЬ ВИД [VP; subj: human; usu. foll. by a что-clause; usu. this WO] to feign (sth.), take the semblance (of sth.): X сделал вид ≃ **X pretended (that ⟨to⟩...); X acted ⟨looked⟩ as if...; X made out (that...); X made believe (that...); X gave the impression (that...).**

Вы можете на него накричать, он не обидится (хотя в интересах дела может сделать вид, что обиделся)... (Войнович 3). You can scream at him and he won't be offended (though in the interests of the case he may pretend he is offended)... (3a). ♦ Дежурные сделали вид, что не слышат, и вышли (Солженицын 3). The duty officers acted as if they had not heard him and went out (3a). ♦ «Изобразите на словах, обманно, готовность уступить, сделайте вид, будто вас можно уговорить» (Пастернак 1). "You'll have to pretend, let her think that you might be willing to change your mind, look as if you might allow yourself to be persuaded" (1a). ♦ «Имейте в виду, в ссылке ни один человек не скажет вам правды: кто сидит за дело — делает вид, что сидит ни за что...» (Рыбаков 2). "Remember this: nobody in exile ever tells the truth—if someone's here because there was a real case against him, he makes out he's here for nothing..." (2a). ♦ Строев же... прыгая через ступеньки, спешил к зрительному залу. На сцену он проник не через зал, а сбоку, через ворота на сцену, пробрался к посту, а оттуда к рампе... и стал, искусно делая вид, что присутствует он здесь уже давным-давно (Булгаков 12). Stroyev...came leaping downstairs and onto the stage, which he reached through the scenery dock without crossing the auditorium, and...took up a position in the wings near the footlights, skillfully giving the impression that he had been there all the time (12a).

В-111 • НА ВИД; С ⟨ПО⟩ ВИ́ДУ [PrepP; these forms only; adv or modif] the way (a person or thing) seems when perceived visually: **look (like); look to be;** [AdjP]**-looking;** [NP or AdjP] **to look at; to look at s.o. ⟨sth.⟩; from the looks of s.o. ⟨sth.⟩; in appearance; give the appearance of...; seemingly; seem...to the eye; look to the eye like...; appear to the eye to be...; on the outside.**

Только два человека, с виду похожие на мелких базарных торговцев, мирно пивши в углу кофе, не принимали никакого участия в этих сетованиях (Эренбург 2). Only two people, who looked like bazaar merchants, sitting quietly in their corner drinking coffee, took no part in any of these lamentations (2a). ♦ Они [посетители] вступили в комнату почти одновременно со старцем... В келье ещё раньше их дожидались выхода старца два скитские иеромонаха... Кроме того, ожидал, стоя в уголку (и всё время потом оставался стоя), молодой паренёк, лет двадцати двух на вид, в статском сюртуке... (Достоевский 1). They [the visitors] came into the room almost at the same moment as the elder....Two hieromonks of the hermitage were already in the cell awaiting the elder....Besides them, there stood in the corner (and remained standing there all the while) a young fellow who looked to be about twenty-two and was dressed in an ordinary frock coat... (1a). ♦ ...Слушая его щёлкающую речь и глядя на его аккуратные черты, трудно было представить себе внежизненный опыт этого здорового с виду, кругленького... человека... (Набоков 1). ...When one listened to his sprightly speech and looked at his regular features, it was difficult to imagine the unearthly experiences of this healthy-looking, plump little man... (1a). ♦ Вероятно, я был в те времена очень жалким на вид — болезненный, бледный, маленький (Олеша 3). Probably I was at that time rather pitiful to look at: sickly, pale, small (3a). ♦ На вид Пастернаку можно было дать не более 47–48 лет (Ивинская 1). To look at him one would not have given Pasternak more than forty-seven or forty-eight (1a). ♦ ...Ведь вы молоды, вам на вид не дашь и шестнадцати (Соколов 1). ...You're young, after all, from the looks of you you're not more than sixteen (1a). ♦ Пьер почти не изменился в своих внешних приёмах. На вид он был точно таким же, каким он был прежде (Толстой 7). Outwardly Pierre had hardly changed at all. In appearance he was just the same as before (7a). ♦ И хотя с виду Лёва был спокоен и рассудителен, я видел, что он напряжён, как струна... (Рыбаков 1). Although Lyova gave the appearance of calm and common sense, I could tell he was under terrible strain... (1a). ♦ Вообще судя, странно было, что молодой человек, столь учёный, столь гордый и осторожный на вид, вдруг явился в такой безобразный дом... (Достоевский 1). Generally considered, it was strange that so learned, so proud, and seemingly so prudent a young man should suddenly appear in such a scandalous house... (1a). ♦ Пузыри газа лопались и подымались — гигантские, как целые планеты! И невесомые на вид (Обухова 1). Bubbles of gas burst and flew up—enormous as planets, yet seeming weightless to the eye (1a).

В-112 • НАПУСКА́ТЬ/НАПУСТИ́ТЬ НА СЕБЯ́ ВИД *какой* [VP; subj: human] (to try) to look a certain way (as denoted by the modifier): X напустил на себя [AdjP] вид ≃ **X took ⟨put⟩ on a [AdjP] expression; X assumed a look ⟨an air⟩ of** [NP denoting the same quality as the Russian AdjP]; **X pretended to be** [AdjP].

...Он, с жадностью ловя каждое слово [тёщи], напускал на себя уныло-спокойный и даже рассеянный вид, отчего тёща скрытно негодовала... (Трифонов 1). ...As he greedily took in her [his mother-in-law's] every word, he would take on a calmly subdued and even absentminded expression which his mother-in-law secretly resented (1a). ♦ Тут Ляля насторожилась, хотя напустила на себя равнодушный вид (Трифонов 1). Though she assumed a look of indifference, Lyalya listened with interest... (1a).

В-113 • ПРИВОДИ́ТЬ/ПРИВЕСТИ́ В БО́ЖЕСКИЙ ⟨ХРИСТИА́НСКИЙ⟩ ВИД *кого-что;* **ПРИДАВА́ТЬ/ПРИДА́ТЬ БО́ЖЕСКИЙ ⟨ХРИСТИА́НСКИЙ⟩ ВИД** *кому-чему coll, often humor* [VP; subj: human; the verb may take the final position, otherwise fixed WO] to make s.o. or sth. look neat, orderly in appearance, put sth. in order: X привёл Y-a ⟨себя⟩ в христианский вид ≃ **X made Y ⟨himself⟩ presentable; X tidied ⟨spruced, fixed⟩ Y ⟨himself⟩ up.**

В-114 • СТА́ВИТЬ/ПОСТА́ВИТЬ НА ВИД *кому offic*
[VP; subj: human; often 3rd pers pl with indef. refer.] to reproach one's subordinate officially (about his errors, oversights at work etc): X поставил Y-y на вид ≃ **X reprimanded ⟨chided⟩ Y; X formally censured Y;** [in limited contexts] **X pointed out to Y (that…).**

«За неправильное использование семенного фонда председателю т. Першину поставить на вид» (Абрамов 1). "Comrade Chairman Pershin to be reprimanded for misuse of seed stocks" (1a). ♦ [Гетман:] Я давно уже хотел поставить на вид вам и другим адъютантам, что следует говорить по-украински (Булгаков 4). [Hetman:] I've long been meaning to point out to you and the other aides that you ought to speak Ukrainian (4b).

В-115 • ДЛЯ ВИ́ДА ⟨-y⟩; ДЛЯ ВИ́ДИМОСТИ *all coll*
[PrepP; these forms only; adv] in order to create a certain impression: **for appearance' ⟨form's⟩ sake; for the sake of appearance;** [in limited contexts] **(one) puts up ⟨on⟩ a (little) show of…; (one) makes a pretense of…; (in order) to make it look good.**

Предполагалось продолжать действия пяти последних градоначальников, усугубив лишь элемент гривуазности, внесённой виконтом дю Шарио, и сдобрив его, для вида, известным колоритом сантиментальности (Салтыков-Щедрин 1). The intention was to continue the activities of the last five town governors, but with the element of ribaldry introduced by the Vicomte du Chariot intensified and enriched with a certain coloring of sentimentality for appearance' sake (1a). ♦ Привыкли [к Радеку] как к своему, только для виду считается — польская партия (Солженицын 5). They'd got used to thinking of him [Radek] as one of themselves—he was a "Polish comrade" only for form's sake (5a). ♦ Под «первым посвящением» «Поэмы без героя» стоит дата — 27 декабря. Это годовщина смерти Мандельштама… Ахматова сначала поставила 28 декабря, потому что кто-то дал ей это число, и она поверила. Мне же она не верила, считая, что я могу всё перепутать, а она — никогда. Мне пришлось принести ей бумажку из загса, она поспорила, для виду… (Мандельштам 2). The date under the "First Dedication" of *Poem Without a Hero* is December 27. This is the date of M[andelstam]'s death.…At first Akhmatova put a different one: December 28. This is what someone had told her, and she accepted it without question. She did not believe what I told her because she was convinced that—unlike herself—I always got things wrong. I had to bring her the slip of paper from the Register Office, and even then she put up a little show of resistance (2a). ♦ «Куда в такую спозаранку?» — «Рыбалить». Дед, любивший рыбу, для видимости запротивился… (Шолохов 2). "Where are you off to so early?" "Fishing." The old man had a weakness for fish but he made a pretense of opposing Mitka's designs (2b).

В-116 • НЕ ПОДАВА́ТЬ/НЕ ПОДА́ТЬ ⟨НЕ ПОКА́ЗЫВАТЬ/НЕ ПОКАЗА́ТЬ⟩ ВИ́ДА ⟨-y⟩ [VP; subj: human; often a clause in a compound sent after Conj «но», a main clause in a complex sent with a что-clause, or a main or subord clause in a complex sent containing a clause of concession] not to reveal (some thought, feeling, desire, intention etc): X не подал вида ≃ **X didn't let on (that…); X didn't show it ⟨that…⟩; X didn't let it ⟨anything etc⟩ show; X gave no sign (that… ⟨of it etc⟩).**

Встреча с Чонкиным её [Нюру] тоже взволновала, но она не подала виду… (Войнович 2). Encountering Chonkin had excited Nyura as well, but she didn't let on… (2a). ♦ …Ничего он не чувствовал, кроме благодарности за то, что [Наденька]

пришла. Он, конечно, и вида не подал (Ерофеев 3). All that remained was gratitude that she [Nadya] had come. Of course he didn't let a bit of this show (3a). ♦ …Она мне нравилась, и, как мне казалось, я тоже ей не был безразличен, хотя она и не подавала виду (Рыбаков 1). I liked her and I thought that she wasn't entirely neutral towards me, though she gave no sign either way (1a).

В-117 • НЕ ВИДА́Л *кого-чего coll* [VP; subj: human; subj follows the verb; past only] one does not want or have need of (s.o. or sth.): не видал X Y-a ≃ **what the heck would X need Y for?; X doesn't need Y; who needs Y (anyway)?; as if X needed Y!**

«Куда ты дела, разбойница, бумагу?» — «Ей-богу, барин, не видывала, опричь [obs = кроме] небольшого лоскутка, которым изволили прикрыть рюмку»… — «Врёшь, ты снесла пономарёнку, он маракует, так ты ему и снесла». — «Да пономарёнок, если захочет, так достанет себе бумаги. Не видал он вашего лоскутка!» (Гоголь 3). "What have you done with the sheet of paper, you thief?" "I swear I haven't seen any paper, master, except the little scrap you used to cover the glass."…"You took it over to the sacristan—he can write, so you gave it to him." "But, master, if the sacristan wanted paper, he could get some himself. He doesn't need your bit" (3e).

В-118 • ЧЕГО́ Я ⟨ты и т. п.⟩ ТАМ ⟨ТУТ, ЗДЕСЬ⟩ НЕ ВИДА́Л ⟨НЕ ВИ́ДЕЛ⟩? *highly coll* [VP_subj; past only; usu. indep. sent; fixed WO] there is no reason why I (you etc) need to or would want to go there (or stay here): чего X там ⟨тут⟩ не видал? ≃ **why on earth (would X want to) go there ⟨stay here⟩?; what's the point of going there ⟨staying here etc⟩?; X won't see anything there ⟨here⟩ he hasn't seen before; what does X want there ⟨around here⟩?; who needs it?**

Так было с Францией — вдруг [Сергей] сказал, что исчезло всякое желание ехать… Сказал ей: «Чего я там не видел? То, что мне нужно, я могу найти только здесь…» (Трифонов 3). …He [Sergei] had decided against the trip to France. He suddenly announced that he had lost all desire to go.…He said to her, "What's the point of going to France? Everything that I need can be found [only] here" (3a). ♦ «Говорил я тебе, чудаку, не связывайся… Майор узнает, на фронт пойдёшь, а чего ты там не видел на фронте-то, или не навоевался?» (Максимов 1). "I told you, you crank, don't get involved.…If the major finds out you'll be off to the front, and you won't see anything there you haven't seen before. Haven't you had enough of fighting?" (1a). ♦ Первые же слова Егорши: «Здорово, невеста!» — …полымем одели её щёки. Но она не растерялась: «Проваливай! Чего здесь не видал?.. Нечего тебе тут делать» (Абрамов 1). Egorsha's first words—"Hi there, fiancée!"—…brought a blush to her cheeks. But she did not lose her head. "Get lost! What do you want around here?…There's nothing here for you" (1a).

В-119 • ГДЕ (Э́ТО) ВИ́ДАНО?; ГДЕ Ж(Е) Э́ТО ВИ́ДАНО? *all coll* [indep. clause; often foll. by a чтобы-clause; fixed WO] used to express a negative attitude toward sth., indignation etc: **where did you ever see (such a thing ⟨anything like it etc⟩)?; who ever saw ⟨who's ever seen⟩ (such a thing ⟨the likes of it etc⟩)?; who ⟨who's⟩ ever heard of (such a thing ⟨anything like it etc⟩)?; it's (just ⟨simply⟩) unheard of.**

«Наляпали золота кусками, аж отваливается. Где это видано, чтобы столько тратить!» (Сологуб 1). "They've scattered pieces of gold in the sky, and it's already falling off. Where did you ever see such waste!" (1a). ♦ «Они говорят — где ж это видано, чтоб человек проживал непрописанный в Москве» (Булгаков 11). "They say—who ever saw such a thing, for a man to live in Moscow unregistered?" (11a). ♦ «Степановна… кур твоих испортили. Где ж это видано! Ведь таких и курьих болезней нет! Это твоих кур кто-то заколдовал» (Булгаков 10). "Stepanovna…I'll say your chickens got the evil eye. Who's ever seen the likes of it? Why, there ain't no chicken sickness of this kind! Somebody sure bewitched your chickens" (10a). ♦ «Да где ж это видано, чтобы народ сам по себе собирался без всякого контроля со стороны руководства?» (Войнович 2). "Who ever heard of people assembling all by themselves, without any control on the part of the leadership?" (2a). ♦ «Личные интересы поставил товарищ выше общественных! Где это видано?» (Аксёнов 1). "This comrade has put his personal interests before his social obligations! It's unheard of!" (1a).

В-120 • В ВИ́ДАХ *чего obs* [PrepP; Invar; Prep; usu. foll. by a deverbal noun; the resulting PrepP is adv] for the purpose of: **(in order) to (do sth.); with the goal of (doing sth.).**

...Слух о богатствах, скрывающихся якобы в недрах земли, есть не более как выдумка, пущенная экспертом от наук в видах легчайшего получения из казны денег... (Салтыков-Щедрин 2). [context transl] ...The rumours about the riches hidden in the bowels of the earth was a pure invention of the scientific expert who wanted the State to pay his travelling expenses... (2a).

В-121 • В ВИ́ДЕ [PrepP; Invar; Prep; the resulting PrepP is usu. adv] **1.** ~ *чего* resembling, having the shape of: **in the form ⟨shape⟩ of; shaped like; like.**

Если даже допустить какие-то возможности объединения усилий интеллектуалов, например – в виде особого журнала, вы всё равно в принципе не измените ситуацию (Зиновьев 1). Even if we accept the possibility of some combination of effort by the intellectuals, for instance in the form of some particular journal, you still won't change the system in principle (1a). ♦ ...Градоначальниково тело, облечённое в вицмундир, сидело за письменным столом, а перед ним, на кипе недоимочных реестров, лежала, в виде щегольского пресс-папье, совершенно пустая градоначальникова голова... (Салтыков-Щедрин 1). The gubernatorial body, arrayed in civil uniform, was sitting at the desk, and there before him on a stack of tax arrears registers, like a rakish paperweight, lay the completely empty gubernatorial head... (1a).

2. ~ *чего* in the capacity of: **as; by way of.**

«„...Нельзя [напечатать вашу историю], направлению повредить может. Разве в виде шутки?" Ну в шутку-то, подумал, будет неостроумно. Так и не напечатали» (Достоевский 2). "'...We can't do it [publish your story], it might harm our tendency. Or perhaps only as a joke?' Well, I thought, as a joke it wouldn't be very witty. So they simply didn't publish it" (2a). ♦ ...Она спросила, будут ли есть сосиски эти люди и буду ли есть сосиски я. Я сказал, что да, буду... «Он столько ест!» – сказала она им в виде шутки (Лимонов 1). ...She asked would these people eat sausages, and would I have sausages. I said yes....“He eats so much!” she told them, by way of a joke (1a).

3. ~ *кого* having adopted the appearance of someone else: **in the form of; looking like; dressed (up) as.**

Олег не мог забыть спасённую им девушку. Она являлась ему во сне в виде прекрасной русалки. Oleg couldn't get the girl he had rescued out of his mind. She kept appearing to him in a dream in the form of a beautiful mermaid.

В-122 • В ЛУ́ЧШЕМ ВИ́ДЕ *highly coll* [PrepP; Invar; adv or subj-compl with быть₀ (subj: human or abstr, often всё); fixed WO] in the best way, very well: **(just) fine; in fine fashion; in the best possible way; (one is ⟨one looks, sth. is going etc⟩) as well as could be; (one ⟨sth.⟩) couldn't be better; (one) couldn't look better;** [in limited contexts] **as well as one can; in the proper manner;** ‖ проявить ⟨показать, выставить⟩ себя ~ ≃ **show o.s. at one's best; show o.s. in the best (possible) light;** ‖ всё будет в лучшем виде ≃ **everything will be shipshape.**

[Фёдор Иванович:] Придёт письмо. И вообще всё будет в лучшем виде, вот увидишь (Розов 3). [F.I.:] A letter will come....And everything will be fine, you'll see (3a). ♦ «Вот он [Аркадий], Прокофьич, – начал Николай Петрович, – приехал к нам наконец... Что? как ты его находишь?» – «В лучшем виде-с», – проговорил старик... (Тургенев 2). "So here

is the young master, Prokofyich," began Nikolai Petrovich. "Come back to us at last....Well? How do you think he looks?" "Couldn't look better, sir," said the old man... (2c). ♦ «Комбат грит [*ungram-mat*=говорит] мне: надо, мол, Федя, надо. А я ему: надо, мол, значит надо, заделаем в лучшем виде...» (Максимов 1). "The battalion commander says to me: we've got to, Fedya, we've got to. So I say to him, well if we've got to, we've got to, we'll do it as well as we can..." (1a). ♦ «Брат, постой... ведь тут всё-таки одно дело ты мне до сих пор не разъяснил: ведь ты жених [Катерины Ивановны], ведь ты всё-таки жених?..» – «Я жених... произошло всё в Москве, по моём приезде, с парадом, с образами, и в лучшем виде» (Достоевский 1). "Wait, brother...you still haven't explained one thing to me: are you her [Katerina Ivanovna's] fiancé, are you really her fiancé?..." "I am her fiancé...; it all happened in Moscow after my arrival, with pomp, with icons, in the proper manner" (1a). ♦ ...Да, я хорошо помню, что Перилло хотел уволить меня... Но, подумав, он дал мне испытательный срок – две недели, и чтобы не вылететь с работы, я решил проявить себя в лучшем виде (Соколов 1). ...Yes, I remember quite well that Perillo wanted to fire me....But after thinking it over he gave me a probationary period – two weeks, and so as not to get kicked out of work I decided to show myself at my best (1a). ♦ Нет, ты объясни тогда: что ты называешь ханжеством? Ну, всё то, что делается не от сердца, а с задней мыслью, с желанием выставить себя в лучшем виде (Трифонов 4). No, you explain then: what do you call phony? Well, everything that's done not from the heart, but with an ulterior motive, with the desire to show oneself in the best light (4a).

В-123 • В ЧИ́СТОМ ВИ́ДЕ [PrepP; Invar; adv or nonagreeing modif; fixed WO] in the form in which s.o. or sth. naturally exists, functions etc, without any additions, admixtures, embellishments etc: **in its ⟨their⟩ pure(st) form; in pure form; in its ⟨their⟩ pure state; (just) as it ⟨he etc⟩ is;** [in limited contexts] **pure and simple.**

Колония была заключена в сравнительно изолированное помещение с целью наблюдать законы крысиной жизни в чистом виде (Зиновьев 1). The colony was housed in a fairly isolated environment with the aim of observing the laws of rodent life in their pure form (1a). ♦ Коммунистический мир – это сюрреализм в чистом виде... (Аксёнов 12). The communist world is surrealism in pure form... (12a). ♦ Возможно, крупицы искусства, как соль, всыпаны в жизнь. Художнику предоставляется их обнаружить, выпарить и собрать в чистом виде (Терц 3). It could be that particles of art are strewn like grains of salt throughout our existence, and that the artist's job is to discover them, refine them and gather them together in their pure state (3a).

В-124 • ПРИ ВИ́ДЕ *кого-чего* [PrepP; Invar; Prep; the resulting PrepP is adv] when seeing s.o. or sth.: **at the sight of; (up)on seeing; when one sees.**

При виде своих коммерческих врагов Безенчук отчаянно махнул рукой... (Ильф и Петров 1). At the sight of his business rivals, Bezenchuk waved his hand in despair... (1a). ♦ «...Только так, только этим восклицанием я мог выразить свой восторг при виде её [Вали]» (Олеша 2). "That exclamation was the only way I could express my ecstasy when I saw her [Valia]" (2a).

В-125 • ТО́ЛЬКО меня ⟨его и т. п.⟩ И ВИ́ДЕЛИ; ТО́ЛЬКО меня ⟨его и т. п.⟩ И ВИ́ДЕЛ *all coll* [VP; subj: human; 3rd pers pl with indef. refer. (1st var.); past or, rare, subjunctive; the idiom can be used in fut contexts; fixed WO] s.o. disappeared swiftly, vanished (the context may imply that the person will not return): только Y-а и видели ⟨только X Y-а и видел⟩ ≃ **Y was gone in a flash; Y was out of here ⟨there⟩ in no time;** [with the emphasis on the permanence of s.o.'s leaving] **that's the last you ⟨X⟩ (ever) saw of Y; X has seen the last of Y.**

[Шабельский:] Эх, милейшая Сарра, выиграй я сто или двести тысяч, показал бы я вам, где раки зимуют!.. Только бы вы меня и видели (Чехов 4). [Sh.:] Ah, my dear Sarah, if I won a few hundred thousand roubles, I'd show you a thing or two. I'd be out of here in no time... (4b). ♦ «Говорю тебе, такой одной весточки жду. Придёт весточка, вскочу – полечу, только вы меня здесь и видели» (Достоевский 1). "I told you, I'm expecting a certain message. When it comes, I'll jump up and fly away, and that will be the last you ever see of me" (1a). ♦ [Глафира:] ...Она хорошо знает, что если я вырвусь от неё замуж, так она только меня и видела (Островский 5). [G.:] ...She knows very well, that if I once escape from her through marriage, she will have seen the last of me (5a).

В-126 • **ВИ́ДЕТЬ НАСКВО́ЗЬ** *кого* [VP; subj: human] to understand s.o.'s true nature (often, beneath a deceptive appearance), discern s.o.'s thoughts, intentions: X видит Y-а насквозь ≃ **X sees ⟨can see⟩ (right) through Y; X reads Y like a book; X knows Y inside out.**

«Я вижу вас насквозь, прокурор! Вы ведь так и думали, что я сейчас вскочу, уцеплюсь за то, что вы мне подсказываете, и закричу во всё горло: „Ай, это Смердяков, вот убийца!“ Признайтесь, что вы это думали...» (Достоевский 1). "I see right through you, prosecutor! You thought I'd jump up at once, snatch your prompting, and shout at the top of my lungs: 'Aie, it's Smerdyakov, he's the murderer!' Admit that's what you thought..." (1a). ♦ «Я знаю этого художника». – «Вы не можете знать ни этой картины, ни художника! – закричал обер-лейтенант и ударил ладонью по столу. – Я вижу вас насквозь! Вы не увернётесь от меня!» (Федин 1). "I know that artist." "You can't know either that picture or that artist," shouted the Ober-lieutenant and banged his palm on the desk. "I can see right through you! You won't get away from me!" (1a).

В-127 • **ВИ́ДЕТЬ НЕ МО́ЖЕТ** *кого-что coll* [VP; subj: human; fixed WO] one cannot tolerate s.o. or sth., one strongly dislikes s.o. or sth.: X видеть Y-а не может ≃ **X can't bear ⟨stand, stomach⟩ Y; X can't bear ⟨stand, stomach⟩ the sight ⟨the thought⟩ of Y; (just) the sight ⟨the thought⟩ of Y makes X sick ⟨ill⟩.**

[Васенька:] Вы мне все осточертели! *(Бусыгину.)* И ты тоже! Пусти, тебе говорят! Я и видеть-то вас не могу! (Вампилов 4). [V.:] I'm sick to death of all of you! *(To Busygin)* Of you too! Let go! Do you hear? I can't bear the sight of any of you! (4a).

В-128 • **ВИ́ДИМО-НЕВИ́ДИМО** *кого-чего coll;* **И ВИ́ДИМО И НЕВИ́ДИМО** *obs, coll* [AdvP; these forms only; usu. quantit compl with copula (subj/gen: any common noun) or adv (quantif)] a great many, an infinite number: **countless numbers of; in countless numbers; multitudes ⟨a multitude⟩ of; no end of ⟨to⟩; endless** [NPs]; **a whole slew of; hordes ⟨myriads, thousands, hundreds⟩ of; huge numbers of.**

[Астров:] На этом озере жили лебеди, гуси, утки, и, как говорят старики, птицы всякой была сила, видимо-невидимо... (Чехов 3). [A.:] On this lake there were swans, geese, ducks, and, as the old people say, a powerful lot of birds of all sorts, no end of them... (3a). ♦ Везде что-то гремит, свистит, скрежещет, народу видимо-невидимо, с авоськами, с портфелями, все куда-то торопятся... (Войнович 1). No matter where you went, something was booming, whistling, gnashing, and endless crowds with net shopping bags and briefcases swept by in a hurry... (1a). ♦ [Серёжа Быстрицын] сидит, бывало, на своём месте и всё над чем-то копается. Или кораблик из бумаги делает, или домик вырезывает, или стругает что-нибудь... Наделал он этих корабликов видимо-невидимо... (Салтыков-Щедрин 2). He'd [Sergey Bystritsyn would] sit at his desk quietly, always working away at something. He'd either be making a boat out of a piece of paper, or cutting out a house, or fashioning a piece of wood into the shape of something or other....He built hundreds of boats... (2a).

В-129 • **ПО (ВСЕЙ) ВИ́ДИМОСТИ** [PrepP; these forms only; sent adv (parenth); fixed WO] judging from the way it seems:

apparently; from ⟨to, by⟩ all appearances; (s.o.) appears to...; it appears (that...).

С того письма, нет, уже с «Августа» начинается процесс раскола моих читателей, потери сторонников, и со мной остаётся меньше, чем уходит. На «ура» принимали меня, пока я был, по видимости, только против сталинских злоупотреблений, тут и всё общество было со мной (Солженицын 2). It is not from this letter, but earlier, from the appearance of *August 1914*, that we must date the schizm among my readers, the steady loss of supporters, with more leaving me than remained behind. I was received with 'hurrahs' as long as I appeared to be against Stalinist abuses only; thus far the entire Soviet public was with me (2a).

В-130 • **ВИ́ДИШЬ ⟨-те⟩ ЛИ** *coll* [these forms only; sent adv (parenth)] **1.** used to introduce an explanation or to attract the interlocutor's attention to the statement to which it belongs: **you see.**

[Таня:] Вы это серьёзно? [Колесов:] Что? [Таня:] Да вот приглашаете на свадьбу... [Колесов:] С полной ответственностью. Видите ли, женится мой друг, и на свадьбе я обещал прийти с самой симпатичной девушкой в городе (Вампилов 3). [T.:] Are you serious about it? [K.:] About what? [T.:] About inviting me to a wedding... [K.:] I take full responsibility. You see, a friend of mine is getting married and I promised to bring the prettiest girl in town to the wedding (3b).

2. used to express a sarcastic reaction to sth., or one's annoyance, indignation etc at sth.: **if you please; wouldn't you know it; can ⟨could⟩ you believe it.**

[Львов:] У несчастной жены всё счастье в том, чтобы он был возле неё, она дышит им, умоляет его провести с нею хоть один вечер, а он... он не может... Ему, видите ли, дома душно и тесно (Чехов 4). [L.:] ...His unfortunate wife's entire happiness is in having him near her; he's the breath of life to her, she begs him to spend just one evening with her, and he...he cannot....He, if you please, feels cramped and stifled at home (4a). ♦ «Они [профсоюзы] возомнили себя, видите ли, школой коммунизма! Тогда как последней являемся мы, органы [КГБ]!» (Алешковский 1). "Can you believe it, they [the trade unions] think they're the school for communism, when everyone knows it's us, the agency [the KGB]" (1a).

В-131 • **ВОТ ВИ́ДИШЬ ⟨-те⟩!** *coll* [indep. sent; these forms only] used to emphasize the correctness of a statement, prediction etc made earlier by the speaker: **there you are; there you have it; there, you see; (you) see!;** [in limited contexts] **I told you so!; what did I tell you!;** [when the statement, prediction etc is repeated after the idiom] **I told you...**

«Ну что ж, – сказал Киров, – если есть необходимость, поеду [в Казахстан]». – «Необходимость есть, ты это сам хорошо понимаешь, да и потом, – Сталин показал на листки конспекта по истории, – эта работа, я вижу, тебя не слишком увлекает, так ведь?» – «Да, это так, – подтвердил Киров, – какой я историк...» – «Вот видишь!» (Рыбаков 2). "Well, if it's necessary," Kirov said, "I'll go [to Kazakhstan]." "It is necessary, as you well know. And anyway," – Stalin nodded at the notes on the history project – "you don't seem terribly taken with this work. Am I right?" "Yes, you're right," Kirov confirmed. "I'm no historian...." "Well, there you are!" (2a). ♦ «...Друзья у тебя все были евреи». – «Как так все? Кто, например?» – «Тот же Тимофеев хотя бы. Или Москвин». – «Да не евреи же они!» – «Евреи», – неколебимо сказал Митишатьев. «Сдурел я, что ли! – вдруг спохватился Лёва. – А хоть бы и евреи, мне-то что?» – «Вот видишь...» – удовлетворённо сказал Митишатьев (Битов 2). "...All your friends were Jews." "What do you mean, all? Who, for example?" "Timofeev, for one. Or Moskvin." "But they're not Jews!" "They're Jews," Mitishatyev said unshakably. "How stupid can I be!" Lyova said, suddenly remembering. "Even if they are Jews, what do I care?" "There, you see," Mitishatyev said with satisfaction (2a).

В-132 • **КАК ВИ́ДИШЬ** ⟨-те⟩ *coll* [these forms only; sent adv (parenth)] as is now apparent to you: **as you (can) see.**

[Виктория:] Что вы делаете? [Калошин:] Я?.. Лежу, как видите (Вампилов 1). [V.:] What are you doing? [K.:] Me?...Just lying down, as you see (1a).

В-133 • **КАК ВИ́ДНО** [Invar; sent adv (parenth); fixed WO] according to what can be seen, deduced: **evidently; apparently;** [in limited contexts] **probably.**

Он [Пугачёв] остановился; его окружили, и, как видно, по его повелению четыре человека отделились и во весь опор подскакали под самую крепость (Пушкин 2). He [Pugachev] stopped; his men gathered around him; and evidently by his command, four of them peeled off from the group and galloped right up to the fort at full speed (2a). ♦ Чемодан внесли кучер Селифан... и лакей Петрушка, малый лет тридцати, в просторном подержанном сюртуке, как видно, с барского плеча... (Гоголь 3). The trunk was brought in by Selifan, the coachman...and Petrushka, the valet, a fellow of about thirty, wearing a shabby loose frock coat (apparently at one time his master's)... (3c). ♦ ...В гневе [Пантелей Прокофьевич] доходил до беспамятства и, как видно, этим раньше времени состарил свою когда-то красивую, а теперь сплошь опутанную паутиной морщин, дородную жену (Шолохов 2). In anger he [Pantelei Prokofievich] would go berserk, and it was probably this that had prematurely aged his buxom wife, whose once beautiful face was now a web of wrinkles (2a).

В-134 • **НИ ПОД КАКИ́М ВИ́ДОМ** *coll* [PrepP; Invar; adv; used with negated verbs; fixed WO] never, not for any reason, no matter what the circumstances: **not on any account; on no account; not under any circumstances ⟨condition(s), pretext⟩; under no circumstances ⟨condition(s), pretext⟩ (whatsoever);** [in limited contexts] **not for anyone ⟨anything⟩.**

«Наташа! Ты можешь про меня всё, что хочешь. Считай меня, если хочешь, безумцем, но помни одно: когда вернёшься домой — не вздумай ходить в Гнездниковский. Такой переулок, возле площади Пушкина, улицы Горького. Не заглядывай туда ни под каким видом» (Терц 2). "Natasha! Think what you like about me, call me a madman if you like, but remember one thing: when you get back, keep away from Gnezdnikovsky. You know the street — near Pushkin Square and Gorki Street. Don't go there on any account..." (2a). ♦ ...Барин накрепко запирался сам с вечера каждую ночь вот уже всю неделю и даже Григорию ни под каким видом не позволял стучать к себе (Достоевский 1). ...For the whole past week the master had been locking himself up securely in the evening, every night, and would not allow even Grigory to knock for him under any circumstances (1a). ♦ ...Швейцару дан был строжайший приказ не принимать ни в какое время и ни под каким видом Чичикова (Гоголь 3). The doorman was given the strictest orders not to admit Chichikov at any time nor under any pretext whatsoever (3c). ♦ [Коринкина:] ...Не заводите никакого разговора о детях. [Незнамов:] О детях? Что такое? Почему? [Дудукин:] Ах, да, да, да! Ни под каким видом, господа, ни под каким видом! (Островский 3). [K.:] ...Don't mention children.... [N.:] Why not? Why shouldn't we? [D.:] Ah, yes, quite right. Under no circumstances, gentlemen; under no circumstances! (3a). ♦ Отказаться от частной практики старик не пожелал ни под каким видом... (Рыбаков 2). The old man wouldn't give up his private income for anyone (2a). ♦ Меня звала приятельница, хозяйка шумного однокомнатного дома, куда захаживал сам Агранов и его будущие жертвы. Днём Мандельштам иногда соглашался зайти на минутку в этот дом, но вечером ни под каким видом (Мандельштам 2). [context transl] I was invited out by a woman I knew, the mistress of a noisy one-room apartment frequented by none other than Agranov — and his future victims. M[andelstam] would sometimes agree to go there for a minute or two during the daytime, but nothing would have induced him to set foot in the place in the evening (2a).

В-135 • **ПОД ВИ́ДОМ** [PrepP; Invar; Prep; the resulting PrepP is usu. adv] **1.** ~ *чего* using sth. as an excuse: **under ⟨on⟩ (the) pretext of; under ⟨on⟩ (the) pretense of.**

Известно, что сочинители иногда, под видом требования советов, ищут благосклонного слушателя (Пушкин 2). It is well-known that authors, under pretext of seeking advice, sometimes attempt to find a benevolent listener (2b). ♦ Тут тебя осенила новая блестящая мысль: воспользоваться скандалом и убежать от них вместе с Лидой под видом неудержимых эмоций (Терц 8). At this moment you had another brilliant idea: to take advantage of the scandal and run off with Lida on the pretext of uncontrollable emotion (8a). ♦ ...Шумилов далее сказал, чтобы он, Михаил, срочно написал и передал по телефону донесение: такой-то и такой-то под видом болезни дезертировал с лесного фронта, бывший военнопленный... (Абрамов 1). ...Shumilov said further that Mikhail should immediately write out a report and transmit it by telephone: so and so, under pretense of illness, deserted from the forest front, a former prisoner of war... (1b). ♦ «...Я знаю, что есть масоны и масоны, и надеюсь, что вы не принадлежите к тем, которые под видом спасения рода человеческого хотят погубить Россию» (Толстой 6). "...I know that there are Masons and Masons. I hope that you are not one of those who, on the pretense of saving the human race, are doing their best to destroy Russia" (6a).

2. ~ *кого-чего* representing o.s., s.o., or sth. falsely (as s.o. or sth. else): **under ⟨in⟩ the guise of; passing o.s. ⟨s.o., sth.⟩ off as;** [of a person only] **posing as.**

Римская история была в нём [романе], собственно, ни при чём. Изображены были под видом римлян видные парижане (Булгаков 5). Properly speaking, Rome had nothing to do with the story at all. Under the guise of Romans, the novel depicted eminent Parisians (5a). ♦ ...В 71 году была уже попытка Лопатина [освободить Чернышевского], в которой всё несуразно: и то, как в Лондоне он вдруг бросил переводить «Капитал»... и путешествие в Иркутск под видом члена географического общества... (Набоков 1). ...In 1871, there was Lopatin's attempt [to free Chernyshevski] in which everything was absurd: the way he suddenly abandoned the Russian translation of *Das Kapital*...; his journey to Irkutsk in the guise of a member of the Geographical Society... (1a).

В-136 • **С УБИ́ТЫМ ВИ́ДОМ** *coll* [PrepP; Invar; adv; fixed WO] exhibiting a despairing expression: **with a crushed ⟨crestfallen⟩ look; looking crushed ⟨dejected, depressed, crestfallen, like misery itself⟩.**

Лукашин с убитым видом выслушал эту директиву (Абрамов 1). Lukashin listened to that directive with a crushed look (1a). ♦ ...Он прямо обвинил Раскольникова в преднамеренном оскорблении Петра Петровича [Лужина]... «Он ещё до болезни это придумал», — прибавил он. «Я тоже так думаю», — сказала Пульхерия Александровна с убитым видом (Достоевский 3). ...He accused Raskolnikov directly of having planned in advance to insult Mr. Luzhin....“He planned it before his illness,” he added. “I think so too,” said Mrs. Raskolnikov, looking crushed (3a). ♦ Даже Петра, вышедшего из горницы с убитым видом, на минуту развеселил смех (Шолохов 4). Even Petro, who had come out of the front room looking like misery itself, was cheered for a minute by the laughter (4a).

В-137 • **В ВИДУ́** *чего obs* [PrepP; Invar; Prep; the resulting PrepP is subj-compl with copula (subj: human, collect, or concr) or adv] within visible distance: **within view of; within ⟨in⟩ sight of;** [in limited contexts] **in full view of.**

Войска авангарда расположились впереди Вишау, в виду цепи неприятельской, уступавшей нам место при малейшей перестрелке в продолжение всего дня (Толстой 4). The troops of the vanguard were stationed before Wischau within sight of the enemy line, which all day long had yielded ground to us at the least skirmish (4a). ♦ «Это ужасно», — начал в виду их собственной деревни Юрий Андреевич (Пастернак 1). "It's terrible," said Yurii

Andreievich when they were in sight of their own village (1a). ♦ Не успели обыватели оглянуться, как из экипажа выскочил Байбаков, а следом за ним в виду всей толпы очутился точь-в-точь такой же градоначальник, как и тот, который, за минуту перед тем, был привезён в телеге исправником! (Салтыков-Щедрин 1). Before the townsfolk could look around, out of the carriage jumped Dormousov, and behind him, in full view of the crowd, appeared a town governor who was the spit and image of the one the commissioner had brought by cart the moment before! (1a).

В-138 • ИМЕ́ТЬ В ВИДУ́ [VP; fixed WO] **1.** ~ *кого-что* [subj: usu. human, occas. collect or журнал, статья etc] to intend to indicate s.o. or sth., convey sth.: X имеет в виду Y-a ≃ **person X has Y in mind; person X means Y; X is referring to Y;** [in limited contexts] **person X is thinking of Y.**

Такой разговор не состоялся, и я не знаю, что имел в виду Твардовский (Солженицын 2). No such conversation ever took place, and I still don't know what Tvardovsky had in mind (2a). ♦ Когда говорят о цензуре, то имеют в виду прежде всего специальное учреждение, Главлит... (Войнович 1). When people speak of censorship, they're primarily referring to a special institution, Glavlit... (1a).

2. ~ (*кого-что*). Also: **ПОИМЕ́ТЬ В ВИДУ́** *highly coll* [subj: human; usu. infin with надо, нужно etc or imper; often foll. by a что-clause] to include s.o. or sth. in one's considerations, take s.o. or sth. into consideration: имей это в виду ≃ **bear ⟨keep⟩ it ⟨that, this⟩ in mind; remember that ⟨this⟩;** ‖ имей в виду, что... ≃ **bear ⟨keep⟩ in mind that...; mind that...; remember that...; consider that...**

«...Сейчас мы тебя отправим в камеру. Но имей в виду следующее: я скажу Сударю, что ты молчишь и, таким образом, берёшь на себя роль главаря банды» (Семёнов 1). "We'll send you down to the cells now. But bear this in mind: I shall tell Squire that you're refusing to talk and are thus taking on the role of gang leader" (1a). ♦ [Я] рассматривал книжечку... и размышлял: говорить подлецу или промолчать? Решил — молчать. Иметь в виду на крайний случай (Трифонов 5). I gazed...at the diary...and debated whether to confront him with it or to say nothing. I decided to say nothing and to keep this in mind for some future occasion (5a). ♦ «Имейте в виду, в ссылке ни один человек не скажет вам правды...» (Рыбаков 2). "Remember this: nobody in exile ever tells the truth..." (2a).

3. *coll* ~ *что, что (с)делать* [subj: human] to have the intention or goal to do sth.: X имеет в виду (сделать Y) ≃ **X intends ⟨means, plans⟩ (to do Y); X has it in mind (to do Y).**

«Вы сказали больше, чем имели в виду, и я вам за это благодарен...» (Гладков 1). "You said more than you intended, and I am grateful to you for it..." (1a). ♦ Заговорили о деле моего друга и потом не очень тактично, но и не имея в виду обидеть его, перешли на рассказы о смертоубийствах вообще (Искандер 4). They began to talk about my friend's case and then—not very tactfully, but without meaning to offend him—moved on to accounts of murders in general (4a).

В-139 • НА ВИДУ́ [PrepP; Invar] **1.** ~ (*у кого*) [subj-compl with copula (subj: human or concr) or adv] (fully) visible (to s.o.): **in plain ⟨full⟩ view (of s.o.); within s.o.'s view; (can be) seen; before s.o.'s eyes; in front of s.o.;** [in limited contexts] **exposed; out in the open;** ‖ *Neg* не на виду ≃ **out of (s.o.'s) sight ⟨view⟩; out of view ⟨sight⟩ (of s.o.);** ‖ у всех на виду ≃ **for all to see; in front of everybody; in public;** ‖ жить у всех на виду ≃ **live a completely open life.**

А разве не сам я, когда прилетела «рама» и все полезли по щелям, стоял на виду? (Окуджава 1). Wasn't it me who remained in full view when the Heinkel swooped down and everyone jumped into the trenches? (1a). ♦ В обоих отделениях столовой кухня была отделена от общего зала стеклянной перегородкой, чтобы неряхи-повара всё время были на виду у рабочих (Искандер

3). In each department of the dining room, the kitchen was divided from the public hall by a glass partition so that the slovenly cooks were within the workers' view at all times (3a). ♦ Да, лучше вечером, — почему я решила завтра утром? Днём всё на виду, сейчас уже темнеет, мало фонарей. Да, надо сегодня, сейчас же, зачем я откладываю? (Аллилуева 2). Yes, it would be better to do it all in the evening. Why did I ever think of the morning? In the daytime everything could be seen; now it was getting dark, lights were few. Yes, it must happen today, at once; why was I putting it off? (2a). ♦ ...Времена тяжёлые, у властей приступ служебного рвения, намекнули кому-то, что плохо де работаете, а он [Виктор] — вот он... голенький, глаза руками зажал, а весь на виду (Стругацкие 1). ...The times were hard, the authorities were having an attack of official zeal, the hint's been given, you aren't doing your work, gentlemen, and there he [Victor] was...naked, covering his eyes with his fists and utterly exposed (1a). ♦ Ксана на приставания Иосифа не отвечала, но городок маленький, южный, всё на виду, все видят, как Иосиф вяжется к Ксане, и этот факт её компрометирует... (Рыбаков 1). Ksana didn't respond to his [Yosif's] passes, but it was a small town in the south, where everything is out in the open, everyone could see that Yosif was trying to get involved with her, he was compromising her... (1a). ♦ Илья Терентьевич Хоробров задней стороной лаборатории, не на виду у начальства, тяжёлой поступью прошёл за стеллаж к Потапову (Солженицын 3). Ilya Terentevich Khorobrov, in the rear of the laboratory and out of sight of the chiefs, walked with heavy tread behind the wall of shelves to Potapov (3a). ♦ В общем, они ходили в лес и, как вы догадываетесь, располагались не на виду у дачного общества, а в стороне (Рыбаков 1). So they would go into the forest and, as you might guess, they would settle themselves down somewhat out of the way, out of view of summer visitors (1a). ♦ Праздновать труса у всех на виду? Никогда! (Аксёнов 12). "Be cowards in public? Never!" (12a). ♦ «Живу я на виду у всех. Чем дышу, всякий в городе знает» (Максимов 3). "I live a completely open life. Everybody in town knows what I live for" (3a).

2. [usu. subj-compl with быть∅ (subj: human)] to occupy a highly visible position (occas., esp. formerly, used in refer. to a position that attracts the attention of influential people, promises a successful career): X был на виду ≃ **X was in the public eye; X was (in a position) where he could be noticed; X was in the limelight; X had everybody's attention; X was exposed ⟨conspicuous⟩.**

Этот человек, проживший так открыто, так напоказ, так на виду — оказался самым скрытным, самым невидимым и унёс свою тайну в могилу (Битов 2). This man who lived so openly, so on display, so in the public eye, turns out to have been the most secretive, the most invisible. He has carried his secret to the grave (2a). ♦ «...Перейдя в гвардию, я на виду, — продолжал Берг, — и вакансии в гвардейской пехоте гораздо чаще» (Толстой 4). "...By transferring to the Guards, I shall be where I can be noticed," Berg continued, "and vacancies occur more frequently in the Foot Guards" (4a). ♦ ...Эти люди ждали. Больше двадцати лет ждали. Копили ненависть. Кое-чему научились. Защитились. Напечатались. Продвинулись. Не на виду, на периферии. Но продвинулись (Зиновьев 1). ...These people were waiting. They'd been waiting for more than twenty years. They had built up enormous reserves of bitter hatred. They had learnt something. They had defended their theses. They had been published. They had risen. Never in the limelight, always on the fringes. But they had risen (1a). ♦ [Репников:] Сейчас он на виду, герой, жертва несправедливости! (Вампилов 3). [R.:] Right now, he's got everybody's attention, he's a hero, a victim of injustice! (3b). ♦ «Я боюсь, что тут мы будем больше на виду, чем в Москве, откуда бежали в поисках незаметности» (Пастернак 1). "I am afraid that after leaving Moscow to escape notice, we are going to be even more conspicuous here" (1a).

В-140 • ТЕРЯ́ТЬ/ПОТЕРЯ́ТЬ ИЗ ВИ́ДУ [VP; subj: human] **1.** ~ *кого-что*. Also: **ТЕРЯ́ТЬ/ПОТЕРЯ́ТЬ ИЗ**

ВИ́ДА ⟨ИЗ ГЛАЗ *obs*⟩ not to see s.o. or sth. anymore: X потерял Y-а из виду ≃ **X lost sight of Y; X let Y out of X's sight.**

Взяв на плечи каждый по узлу, они пустились вдоль по берегу, и скоро я потерял их из виду (Лермонтов 1). Each shouldering a bundle, they set out along the shore and I soon lost sight of them (1b).

2. ~ *кого* to stop meeting with s.o., cease keeping in contact with s.o. or keeping o.s. informed about s.o.: X потерял Y-а из виду ≃ **X lost touch with Y; X lost track of Y.**

Мы надолго потеряли её [Сусанну] из виду и вдруг встретили в период наших блужданий по Москве тридцать седьмого года (Мандельштам 2). For a long time we lost touch with her [Susanna]—until we suddenly ran into her again during our wanderings around Moscow in 1937 (2a). ♦ [Филипп:] ...На фронте я потерял Алекса из виду, и с тех пор он не возвращался в наш город (Солженицын 11). [Ph.:] ...I lost track of Alex at the front and since then he's never come back to our town (11a).

B-141 • УПУСКА́ТЬ/УПУСТИ́ТЬ ⟨ВЫПУСКА́ТЬ/ ВЫ́ПУСТИТЬ⟩ ИЗ ВИ́ДУ ⟨-а⟩ [VP; subj: human] **1.** ~ *кого-что*. Also: **УПУСКА́ТЬ/УПУСТИ́ТЬ ⟨ВЫПУС- КА́ТЬ/ВЫ́ПУСТИТЬ⟩ ИЗ ⟨С⟩ ГЛАЗ** *obs* [often neg; if affirm, fixed WO] to keep s.o. within the field of one's vision: X не упускал Y-а из виду ≃ **X did not let Y out of X's sight; X did not lose sight of Y.**

Пока я рассказывал ему [этому человеку] что и как, косясь на собаку и стараясь не упускать её из виду, он качал головой, прицокивал языком... (Искандер 6). Glancing sideways at the dog and trying not to let it out of my sight, I began filling him [the man] in on the details, while he for his part kept shaking his head and clicking his tongue (6a). ♦ ...[Чонкин] торопился, боясь упустить из виду Плечевого, спина которого то исчезала, то вновь появлялась перед глазами (Войнович 2). ...He [Chonkin] kept hurrying for fear of losing sight of Burly, whose back kept disappearing, then reappearing up ahead (2a).

2. ~ *кого-что* [often neg; if affirm, fixed WO] to stop keeping o.s. informed about s.o. (or sth.), stop keeping up one's acquaintance with s.o., following s.o.'s career or the changes in his life: X не упускал Y-а из виду ≃ **X did not lose ⟨never lost⟩ sight of Y; X didn't lose touch with person Y;** [in limited contexts] **X kept tabs on Y.**

[Треплев:] Дебютировала она под Москвой в дачном театре, потом уехала в провинцию. Тогда я не упускал её из виду и некоторое время куда она, туда и я (Чехов 6). [T.:] She made her debut in a summer theater near Moscow, then went to the provinces. At that time I never lost sight of her; wherever she went, I followed (6a).

3. ~ *что* [often foll. by a что-clause; fixed WO] not to consider sth., not to include sth. in one's calculations as a result of one's oversight: X упустил из виду Y ⟨что...⟩ ≃ **X lost sight of Y ⟨of the fact that...⟩; X overlooked ⟨forgot (about), neglected, missed⟩ Y ⟨the fact that...⟩; X failed to see Y ⟨that...⟩; X failed to take Y into account; X failed to take account of Y ⟨of the fact that...⟩.**

Деятельность его [Наполеона] в Москве так же изумительна и гениальна, как и везде... Он не упускает из виду... ни блага народов России, ни управления делами Парижа, ни дипломатических соображений о предстоящих условиях мира (Толстой 7). His [Napoleon's] activity in Moscow was just as amazing and as charged with genius as it had been elsewhere....He did not lose sight either of the welfare of the people of Russia, or of the direction of affairs in Paris, or of diplomatic considerations concerning the terms of the anticipated peace (7a). ♦ ...Дорогая Наташа, я упустил из виду главное: план (Олеша 1). ...Dear Natasha, I have overlooked the most important thing: the Plan (1a). ♦ Тут он перевёл

на меня свою приветливость, напоминая, что присутствие моей личности он ни на минуту не упускал из виду и теперь готов целиком заняться мной (Искандер 4). Now he transferred his cordiality to me, reminding me that he had not forgotten my presence for a moment and was now ready to devote his full attention to me (4a). ♦ «...Ты упустил из виду важное дело: ты не спросил, каков мужик у Чичикова» (Гоголь 1). "...You have missed an important point: you haven't asked what Chichikov's peasants are like" (3d). ♦ ...Он упустил из виду... что народы, даже самые зрелые, не могут благоденствовать слишком продолжительное время, не рискуя впасть в грубый материализм... (Салтыков-Щедрин 1). ...He failed to see...that even the most mature nations cannot live long in a state of prosperity without the risk of lapsing into crude materialism (1b).

B-142 • ВИДА́ТЬ ⟨ВИ́ДЫВАТЬ⟩ ВИ́ДЫ *coll* [VP; usu. this WO] **1.** Also: **ВИДА́ТЬ ⟨ВИ́ДЫВАТЬ⟩ ВСЯ́КИЕ ВИ́ДЫ** [subj: human; often active past Part] to have experienced much in life, endured various troubles: X видал виды ≃ **X has been through plenty (in his time ⟨life, lifetime⟩); X has seen much ⟨a great deal, a lot⟩ in his time ⟨day, life, lifetime⟩; X has seen all sorts ⟨kinds⟩ of things (in his time etc); X has been through the mill; X has been around ⟨around the block⟩; X is schooled in the ways of the world;** ‖ видавший виды ≃ **seasoned; battle-scarred.**

Фомин с силой сжал ногами бока коня, послал его в толпу. Народ шарахнулся в разные стороны. В широком кругу осталась одна вдова. Она видала всякие виды и потому спокойно глядела на оскаленную морду фоминского коня, на бледное от бешенства лицо всадника (Шолохов 5). Fomin dug his heels into his horse's flanks and rode into the crowd. It drew back, leaving only the widow in the middle of a wide circle. She had seen much in her time, so she looked up imperturbably at the horse's bared teeth and the furious face of its rider (5a). ♦ Они слушали неумолчную трескотню словоохотливой и видавшей виды девушки (Пастернак 1). ...They listened to the incessant chatter of the garrulous girl, who had seen a great deal in her life (1a). ♦ У Моси был неистовый темперамент южанина и не вполне безукоризненная биография мальчишки, видавшего за свои двадцать три года всякие виды (Катаев 1). Mosya had the violent temperament of a southerner, and the not entirely faultless biography of a gamin who had seen all sorts of things in the course of his twenty-three years (1a). ♦ ...Кирпиченко вдруг увидел, что ей [Ларисе] под тридцать, что она видала виды (Аксёнов 5). ...Kirpichenko suddenly saw that she [Larisa] was getting on for thirty and that she had been around (5a). ♦ И кому-то нужно с таким человеком [, как Никандров,] связываться?.. Видавшие виды дамы были обязаны предупреждать молодёжь женского пола: «И не вздумайте! Кроме головной боли, ничего не маячит!» (Залыгин 1). Who needed to get involved with a man like him [Nikandrov]? Seasoned women had a duty to warn the younger of their sex about men like him: "Don't even think about it! You'll get yourself nothing but a headache!" (1a).

2. [subj: concr] (of various devices, machines etc, often of furniture, clothes, footwear etc) to have been used a great deal, show signs of much wear: X видал виды ≃ **X looks ⟨is⟩ the worse for wear; X has seen better days; X is timeworn ⟨worn-out, well-worn, shabby⟩.**

B-143 • ИМЕ́ТЬ ВИ́ДЫ *на кого-что* [VP; subj: human; fixed WO] to have definite goals, plans, intentions regarding s.o. or sth., count on s.o. or sth. in some way (occas. to have hope of marrying s.o.): X имеет виды на Y-а ≃ **X has his eye on Y; X has certain ideas concerning ⟨about⟩ Y;** [usu. in refer. to marriage, sexual pursuit] **X has designs on Y.**

...Сидоров разрешил Грише посетить гетто только в январе или феврале сорок второго года, а может быть, сам послал в гетто, у Сидорова были свои виды на наш город, вернее, на нашу железнодорожную станцию (Рыбаков 1). ...Sidorov could permit Grisha to visit the ghetto only in January or February of 1942. He may have even sent him there, as he had his eye on our town, on the railway station, to be precise (1a). ♦ ...Княжна Марья не переставая думала о том, как ей должно держать себя в отношении Ростова. То она решала, что она не выйдет в гостиную, когда он приедет к тётке... то ей приходило в голову, что её тётка и губернаторша имеют какие-то виды на неё и Ростова... (Толстой 7). ...Princess Marya never ceased thinking about how she ought to behave to him [Rostov]. First she decided not to go into the drawing room when he came to see her aunt...then it occurred to her that her aunt and the Governor's wife had certain ideas concerning herself and Rostov... (7a). ♦ [Купавина:] ...Если замечу, что он [Беркутов] имеет виды на меня, я полюбезничаю с ним, потом посмеюсь и отпущу его в Петербург ни с чем (Островский 5). [K.:] ...If I find that he [Berkutov] has designs on me, I'll flirt with him, then laugh at him, and send him back to Petersburg (5a).

В-144 • **(ЕЩЁ) ВИ́ЛАМИ НА ⟨ПО⟩ ВОДЕ́ ПИ́САНО** *coll* [AdjP; subj-compl with бытьø (subj: usu. это, всё, всё это, or a clause); usu. pres; usu. this WO] it is as yet unclear how things will turn out or whether sth. (usu. sth. desired) will come to pass, be realized etc: это вилами на воде писано ≃ **it remains to be seen; it's ⟨things are⟩ still up in the air; it could go either way;** [in limited contexts] **it's uncertain, to say the least.**

...Небольшого ума требует, взглянув на всё, понять, что выигрыш тут мал и временен и всё совершенно вилами по воде писано: выигрыш ли ещё это, — а скорее всего, что и нет... (Битов 2). ...It doesn't take much intelligence to realize, all things considered, that the gain here is small and temporary and it's still up in the air whether it *is* a gain, more likely it's not... (2a). ♦ [author's usage] После войны [Настя] домой не вернулась... Её судьба после возвращения была бы вилами по воде писана. Сталин не любил людей, которые в чужестранстве побывали... (Войнович 1). She [Nastya] didn't return to the Soviet Union after the war....Had she returned, her own fate would have been uncertain, to say the least. Stalin had no liking for people who had spent time in foreign countries... (1a).

В-145 • **ПО ВИНЕ́** *чьей, кого-чего* [PrepP; Invar; the resulting PrepP is adv] caused by (s.o. or sth.): **because of s.o. ⟨sth.⟩; (sth. is) (all) s.o.'s ⟨sth.'s⟩ fault.**

В-146 • **ЗЕ́ЛЕН ВИНОГРА́Д** [sent (with copula); usu. pres] said when s.o. criticizes, badmouths sth. unjustly, simply because he himself does not possess it or cannot get it: **that's just sour grapes; the grapes are sour.**

Я был стыдлив от природы, но стыдливость моя ещё увеличивалась убеждением в моей уродливости... Я был слишком самолюбив, чтобы привыкнуть к своему положению, утешался, как лисица, уверяя себя, что виноград ещё зелен, то есть старался презирать все удовольствия, доставляемые приятной наружностью, которыми на моих глазах пользовался Володя и которым я от души завидовал... (Толстой 2). I was bashful by nature, but my bashfulness was increased by the conviction that I was ugly....I was too vain to reconcile myself to my situation and comforted myself, like the fox, by reassuring myself that the grapes were still sour; that is, I tried to despise all the pleasures that were obtainable through a pleasant appearance, that Volodya enjoyed before my eyes and that I envied with all my heart (2b).

< From Ivan Krylov's fable "The Fox and the Grapes" («Лисица и Виноград»), 1808. English source: Aesop's fable.

В-147 • **ВИ́НТИКОВ ⟨ВИ́НТИКА, ША́РИКОВ, ЗА-КЛЁПОК, ЗАКЛЁПКИ, КЛЁПОК, КЛЁПКИ⟩ (В ГОЛОВЕ́) НЕ ХВАТА́ЕТ ⟨НЕДОСТАЁТ⟩** *у кого all highly coll* [VP; impers] s.o. is dense, slow-witted, acts strangely,

as if he is slightly insane: у X-а винтиков не хватает ≃ **X has a screw ⟨a few screws⟩ loose; X has bats in his belfry; X (acts as if he) has lost his marbles; X is a bit cracked ⟨touched in the head⟩;** [in limited contexts] **X is off his rocker; X has gone batty.**

У неё, как казалось Михаилу, и раньше кое-каких винтиков недоставало, а после смерти мужа она и совсем ослабла головой (Абрамов 1). Mikhail vaguely remembered that she had always had a few screws loose, but that after her husband's death she had gone quite weak in the head (1a). ♦ Почему ты моешь посуду шампунем? У тебя что, винтиков в голове не хватает? Why are you washing the dishes with shampoo? Have you lost your marbles?

В-148 • **СТА́ВИТЬ/ПОСТА́ВИТЬ ⟨ВМЕНЯ́ТЬ/ВМЕ-НИ́ТЬ** *lit*⟩ **В ВИНУ́** *кому что* [VP; subj: human or collect] to accuse s.o. of sth., consider s.o. guilty of sth., or reprimand s.o. for sth.: X ставит Y-у в вину Z ≃ **X blames Y for Z; X holds Y to blame for Z; X holds Y accountable ⟨responsible⟩ for Z; X points the finger at Y (for Z); X takes Y to task for Z.**

Наконец Аракчеев объявил моему отцу, что император велел его освободить, не ставя ему в вину, что он взял пропуск от неприятельского начальства... (Герцен 1). At last Arakcheyev informed my father that the Tsar had ordered his release, and did not hold him to blame for accepting a permit from the enemy... (1a). ♦ Есть высказывания Толстого о Наполеоне, где он снижает величие последнего, ставя ему в вину его... "суетливость", как он определяет (Олеша 3). ♦ There are Tolstoy's observations on Napoleon, where he reduces the grandeur of the latter, taking him to task...for his "fussiness," as he calls it (3a).

В-149 • **ВНОСИ́ТЬ/ВНЕСТИ́ СВОЙ ⟨** or *какой*⟩ **ВКЛАД** *во что* [VP; subj: human; the verb may take the final position, otherwise fixed WO] to participate in sth. and benefit it by one's labor or involvement: X внёс свой ⟨[AdjP]⟩ вклад в Y ≃ **X made his ⟨a + [AdjP]⟩ contribution to Y; X did his share ⟨part⟩ for Y.**

Таким путём ибанцы [*nonce word*] внесли ценный вклад в мировую культуру (Зиновьев 1). So the Ibanskians made an important contribution to world culture (1a).

В-150 • **КАК ⟨СЛО́ВНО, ТО́ЧНО** *rare*⟩ **ВКО́ПАННЫЙ** остановился, стоит, замер и т. п. [как + AdjP; nom only; adv] (of people, animals, or, less often, vehicles) (to stop) abruptly, remaining motionless, (to stand) completely still: X остановился ⟨стоял⟩ как вкопанный ≃ **X stopped dead; X stopped ⟨sth. stopped X⟩ in his ⟨its⟩ tracks; X stood stock-still; X came to a dead halt ⟨stop⟩;** [of a person or animal only] **X stood (as if) rooted to the spot ⟨the ground⟩; X froze on the spot ⟨in his tracks⟩; X was frozen ⟨riveted, glued⟩ to the spot.**

...Приблизившись к реке, [Угрюм-Бурчеев] встал как вкопанный (Салтыков-Щедрин 1). ...When [Gloom-Grumblev] came near the river, he stopped dead (1a). ♦ «Алексей!» — крикнул ему издали отец, завидев его, — сегодня же переезжай ко мне совсем, и подушку и тюфяк тащи...» Алёша остановился как вкопанный, молча и внимательно наблюдая сцену (Достоевский 1). "Aleksei!" his father cried from far off when he saw him, "move back in with me today, for good, bring your pillow and mattress...." Alyosha stopped in his tracks, silently and attentively observing the scene (1a). ♦ И вдруг недалеко от полицейского участка машина остановилась как вкопанная: посреди дороги валялся разбитый арбуз (Искандер 3). Suddenly, near the police station, the car came to a dead halt: in the middle of the road lay a crushed watermelon (3a). ♦ ...Сколько ни хлыстал их кучер, они [кони] не двигались и стояли как вкопанные (Гоголь 3). ...They [the horses] would not move however much the driver whipped them, and stood as if rooted to the ground (3a).

В-151 • **ВКРИВЬ И ВКОСЬ; ВКОСЬ И ВКРИВЬ** *obs* [AdvP; these forms only; adv] **1.** Also: **И ВКРИВЬ И ВКОСЬ** [fixed WO] (of numerous disorderly lines made when writing, drawing, stitching etc, of tracks left by vehicles or people, of a person's gait etc) unsystematically, in an irregular or disorderly fashion, in different ways or directions: **in all (different) directions; every which way; all over (the place ⟨the paper etc⟩); this way and that (way);** [in limited contexts] **crisscrossing (in all directions);** [in limited contexts] **all askew;** ‖ написано ⟨напечатано⟩ вкривь и вкось ≃ **written ⟨printed⟩ at all angles (across the page).**

Столы были сдвинуты со своих, геометрией подсказанных, правильных мест и стояли то там, то сям, вкривь и вкось... (Битов 2). The tables had been moved from their geometrically suggested correct places to stand here and there, every which way (2a). ♦ Для довершения сходства [с медведем] фрак на нём был совершенно медвежьего цвета, рукава длинны, панталоны длинны, ступнями ступал он и вкривь и вкось и наступал беспрестанно на чужие ноги (Гоголь 3). To complete the resemblance [to a bear], his frock coat was precisely the color of a bear's pelt, with sleeves and trousers that were too long; he set his feet down clumsily, this way and that way, and was continually treading on other people's feet (3c). ♦ С ними [оловянными солдатиками] происходило что-то совсем необыкновенное... Усы, нарисованные вкривь и вкось, стали на свои места и начали шевелиться... (Салтыков-Щедрин 1). Something quite unusual was happening to [the tin soldiers]....Their mustaches, painted all askew, rose up in their places and began to twitch... (1a).

2. (sth. is going, progressing) poorly; (sth. is done) not as it should be (done): **all wrong; sloppily; any old way; twisted and awry.**

И мне плохо. Плохо оттого, что всё идёт у нас с Юркой вкривь и вкось, и он этого не замечает (Михайловская 1). And I feel rotten. Because everything between Yuri and me is twisted and awry and he fails to notice it (1a).

3. толковать *(что),* судить и т. п. ~. Also: **ВКРИВЬ ⟨ВКОСЬ⟩ И ВПРЯМЬ** *obs, coll* [fixed WO] (to interpret sth.) the way one wants to (with the implication that one's interpretation is incorrect or unfounded, that one distorts the phenomenon's true nature or meaning): **in any way one likes; every which way;** [in limited contexts] **(interpret etc sth.) to suit one's own interests.**

«Давно пора понять, что это всё — пустые фразы, которые можно толковать вкривь и вкось» (Зиновьев 2). "It's high time to realise that all that is just empty phrases which you can interpret in any way you like" (2a). ♦ ...[Троекуров] мало заботился о выигрыше им затеянного дела, Шабашкин за него хлопотал, действуя от его имени, страща и подкупая судей и толкуя вкривь и впрямь всевозможные указы (Пушкин 1). [Troekurov] cared...little about winning the case he had initiated. It was Shabashkin who kept busy on his behalf, acting in his name, intimidating and bribing judges, and interpreting every possible edict every which way (1a).

В-152 • **ВХОДИТЬ/ВОЙТИ ВО ВКУС** *(чего)* [VP; subj: human] to begin to derive pleasure from some newly undertaken activity as one familiarizes o.s. with it and continues to pursue it: X вошёл во вкус (Y-а) ≃ **X developed ⟨acquired, got⟩ a taste for it ⟨for Y⟩; X developed a liking for it ⟨for Y⟩; X got into the swing of it ⟨of Y⟩; X got into ⟨hit⟩ his stride; X grew to like it ⟨Y⟩; X warmed (up) to it ⟨to Y⟩; X took to it ⟨to Y⟩; X began to enjoy himself ⟨it, Y⟩;** [in limited contexts] **Y began to grow on X.**

Они [люди, которых использовали для массовых убийств,] слепо доверялись начальникам, а потом входили во вкус убийства и издевательства (Мандельштам 2). Trusting blindly in their superiors, they [those people who were employed in the

carrying out of mass murder] soon developed a taste for killing and torture (2a). ♦ ...Он женился на этой красивой девушке, сыграл свадьбу, а примерно через две недели после женитьбы собрался в горы, потому что начиналось лето. Односельчане в шутку говорили ему, как это он не боится бросать без присмотра молоденькую жену, когда она только-только вошла во вкус (Искандер 4). ...He married this beautiful girl, celebrated the wedding, but about two weeks after the marriage made ready to go to the mountains, because it was the beginning of summer. The villagers jokingly asked him how come he wasn't afraid to leave a little young wife without supervision when she was just getting a taste for it (4a). ♦ «...Вообразите, что вы, например, начнёте управлять, распоряжаться и другими и собою, вообще, так сказать, входить во вкус, и вдруг у вас... кхе... кхе... саркома лёгкого... И вот ваше управление закончилось!» (Булгаков 9). "...Imagine yourself, for example, trying to govern, to manage both others and yourself, just getting into the swing of it, when suddenly you develop...hm, hm...cancer of the lung....And all your management is done with!" (9a). ♦ ...С каждым словом становился он [Лужин] всё привязчивее и раздражительнее, точно во вкус входил (Достоевский 3). ...He [Mr. Luzhin] became more and more pugnacious and more and more irritable with every word, as though getting into his stride (3a). ♦ ...Иван Васильевич, всё более входя во вкус, стал подробно рассказывать, как работать над этим материалом (Булгаков 12). ...Ivan Vasilievich, warming increasingly to his job, began telling me exactly how I should rework my material (12a). ♦ Он сам не заметил, как постепенно вошёл во вкус работы и стал во всём помогать Алексею (Максимов 3). Unconsciously he began to enjoy himself and to help Alexei with the rest of his job (3a).

В-153 • **НА ВКУС** *чей, кого* [PrepP; Invar; the resulting PrepP is sent adv] from the standpoint of s.o.'s notions about what is beautiful, right etc: **to s.o.'s taste; to s.o.'s mind ⟨way of thinking⟩.**

«Я решился драться с вами... Вы, на мой вкус, здесь лишний... я вас презираю...» (Тургенев 2). "I have decided to fight a duel with you....To my taste, you are superfluous here...I despise you..." (2f).

В-154 • **НА ВКУС (И) НА ЦВЕТ ТОВАРИЩЕЙ ⟨-ща⟩ НЕТ** [saying] everyone has his own likes, dislikes, preferences etc; often what one person likes, another does not: ≃ **there is no accounting for taste; every man to his taste; different strokes for different folks; tastes differ.**

«Вы так любите этого Пастернака?» — ...«Дело не в том, что я его так люблю, — терпеливо сказала я. — Мне не за него обидно, а за вас. Как легко вы отрекаетесь по чьему-то наущению от наших великих радостей...» — «Но ведь, как говорится, на вкус и на цвет товарищей нет» (Чуковская 2). "Do you really like that Pasternak so much?" "It isn't a question of me being very fond of him," I said patiently. "It's not him I'm sorry for, but you. How lightly you forego our great pleasures at someone else's instigation...." "But, as they say, there's no accounting for taste" (2a).

В-155 • **О ВКУСАХ НЕ СПОРЯТ** [saying] every person has his own tastes, one has to be tolerant of another's likes and dislikes: ≃ **there is no accounting for taste; every man to his taste;** [in limited contexts] **one man's meat is another man's poison.**

В-156 • **ВО ВКУСЕ** [PrepP; Invar; the resulting PrepP is subj-compl with copula or nonagreeing modif] **1.** ~ *чьём, кого* [subj: any noun] (a person or thing is) appealing to s.o., suited to s.o.'s preferences: X в Y-овом вкусе ≃ **X is to Y's taste ⟨liking⟩; X suits Y's taste; X suits ⟨pleases⟩ Y's fancy; X suits Y fine.**

«Обе женщины одна другой лучше, обе мировой стандарт и обе в моем вкусе» (Искандер 2) "The women are one prettier than the other, both world-class, and both to my taste" (2a).

2. ~ *кого-чего, каком* [subj: usu. concr or abstr; also used as adv] (sth. is, is done etc) in a certain (as specified by the context) mode, in a manner characteristic of a well-known writer, architect etc, or some movement, trend etc: **in the style ⟨manner⟩ of; in the [AdjP] style ⟨manner, fashion⟩; like that ⟨those⟩ of ⟨in⟩;** [in limited contexts] **along the lines of; on the order of;** [as modif only] **à la;** [of a suit, dress etc] **of [AdjP] cut.**

Подъезжая к Арбатову, он не мог не любоваться чистыми и весёлыми избами крестьян и каменным господским домом, выстроенным во вкусе английских замков (Пушкин 1). Approaching Arbatovo, he could not help admiring the peasants' clean and cheerful cottages and the landlord's stone house, built in the style of an English castle (1a). Approaching Arbatovo, he could not but admire the clean and cheerful-looking peasants' cottages and the big stone house, built along the lines of an English castle (1b). ♦ Усадьба, в которой жила Анна Сергеевна, стояла на пологом открытом холме, в недальнем расстоянии от жёлтой каменной церкви с зелёною крышей, белыми колоннами и живописью al fresco над главным входом, представлявшею «Воскресение Христово» в «итальянском» вкусе (Тургенев 2). Anna Sergeyevna's country house stood on the slope of a bare hill not far from a yellow stone church with a green roof, white columns, and a fresco over the main entrance representing the Resurrection of Christ in the "Italian" style (2c). ♦ «Да разве это не поэма?.. Слабоумный идиот Смердяков, преображённый в какого-то байроновского героя, мстящего обществу за свою незаконнорождённость, — разве это не поэма в байроновском вкусе?» (Достоевский 2). "Is this not a poem?...The feebleminded idiot Smerdyakov, transformed into some sort of Byronic hero revenging himself upon society for his illegitimate birth—is this not a poem in the Byronic fashion?" (2a). ♦ [Астров:] Здесь есть лесничество, полуразрушенные усадьбы во вкусе Тургенева... (Чехов 3). [A.:] We've the forest reservation and the tumble-down country houses and gardens like those in Turgenev (3c). ♦ Павел Петрович присел к столу. На нём был изящный утренний, в английском вкусе, костюм... (Тургенев 2). Pavel Petrovich sat down at the table. He was wearing an elegant morning suit of English cut... (2f).

В-157 • **СО ВКУ́СОМ** [PrepP; Invar] **1.** [adv] (to do sth.) with pleasure, happily: **with relish; with (great) gusto; enjoy(ing) sth.**

На крыльце стояла женщина лет сорока, могучего телосложения, в... рваном сарафане. И со вкусом, звучно шлёпала комаров на загорелых плечах и на ляжках (Войнович 1). A powerfully built woman of around forty, wearing a torn sundress, was standing on the porch. Loudly and with great gusto, she was slapping mosquitoes on her sunburned shoulders and thighs (1a). ♦ Ещё лёжа он знал, что ровно в семь встанет... Потом он не спеша, со вкусом поплескается перед рукомойником... (Максимов 3). Lying there in bed he knew that at seven sharp he would get up....Then he would enjoy a leisurely splash at the washstand... (3a).

2. [adv or nonagreeing modif] displaying or possessing an artistic flair, a feeling for the refined: **in (very) good ⟨in excellent⟩ taste; with taste; (a man ⟨a woman⟩) of ⟨with⟩ taste; tastefully (dressed ⟨decorated etc⟩).**

«...Хорош фрак?» — «Отличный! С большим вкусом сшит...» (Гончаров 1). "...How do you like my coat?"..."Splendid! In very good taste" (1b). ♦ Зала рестации превратилась в залу благородного собрания. В 9 часов все съехались. Княгиня с дочерью явились из последних; многие дамы посмотрели на неё с завистью и недоброжелательством, потому что княжна Мери одевается со вкусом (Лермонтов 1). The restaurant's ballroom was transformed into that of the Club of the Nobility. By nine o'clock everybody had arrived. The old princess and her daughter were among the last to appear: many ladies looked at her with envy and ill will because princess Mary dresses with taste (1a). ♦ Мы недавно посмотрели фильм «Евангелие от Матфея»... И вот мнения разделились: одни были потрясены, а другим — «понравилось, но...». Такое разделение нормально, но любопытно то, что и в том и в другом лагере было приблизительно поровну людей: умных и глупых, со вкусом и безвкусных... (Битов 2). We recently saw the film *The Gospel According to Matthew*....Opinion was divided: some people were deeply impressed, and others "liked it, but..." Such a division is normal, but the puzzling thing was that both camps, in approximately equal numbers, included people who were: wise and foolish, with taste and without... (2a). ♦ Госпожа Хохлакова-мать, дама богатая и всегда со вкусом одетая, была ещё довольно молодая и очень миловидная собою особа... (Достоевский 1). Madame Khokhlakov, the mother, a wealthy woman, always tastefully dressed, was still fairly young and quite attractive... (1a).

В-158 • **ПО ВКУ́СУ** *кому* [PrepP; Invar; subj-compl with быть∅, прийтись (subj: usu. human or abstr); often neg] (a person, quality etc is) appealing to s.o.: X Y-у не по вкусу ≃ **X is not to Y's taste ⟨liking⟩; X doesn't suit Y's taste; X doesn't suit ⟨please⟩ Y's fancy; Y doesn't care for X.**

Простак Фейербах был Чернышевскому больше по вкусу [, чем Гегель] (Набоков 1). The simpleton Feuerbach was much more to Chernyshevski's taste [than Hegel] (1a). ♦ «Вы оба страшно не по вкусу здешним жрецам Фемиды» (Пастернак 1). "Neither of you are at all to the liking of the local priests of Themis" (1a). ♦ Глуповская распущенность пришлась ему [Грустилову] по вкусу (Салтыков-Щедрин 1). The dissoluteness of Foolov suited his [Grustilov's] taste (1a).

В-159 • **ВЛАДЕ́ТЬ СОБО́Й** [VP; subj: human; usu. this WO] to be able to suppress one's feelings, hold back the expression of one's emotions: X владеет собой ≃ **X has self-control; X has control of himself; X controls himself; X is in command ⟨in possession⟩ of himself;** ‖ учись владеть собой ≃ **you must learn to exercise self-control;** ‖ *Neg* X не владеет собой ≃ **X has lost self-control; X cannot ⟨is not able to⟩ control himself.**

Луи Блан — и это большая сила и очень редкое свойство — мастерски владеет собой, в нём много выдержки, и он... никогда не выходит из себя в споре, не перестаёт весело улыбаться... (Герцен 3). Louis Blanc—and it is a great strength and a very rare quality—has complete self-control; he has a great deal of firmness and...never loses his temper in argument, never stops smiling good-humouredly... (3a). ♦ [Соня:] У меня уже нет гордости, нет сил владеть собой... (Чехов 3). [S.:] I have no pride left, no strength to control myself... (3a). ♦ Видно было, что он [Орсини]... никогда вполне не отдаётся и удивительно владеет собой... (Герцен 2). It was evident that he [Orsini]...never fully let himself go and was wonderfully in command of himself... (2a). ♦ ...Вместо плакавшей сейчас в каком-то надрыве своего чувства бедной оскорблённой девушки явилась вдруг женщина, совершенно владеющая собой... (Достоевский 1). ...Instead of the poor, insulted girl who had just been crying in a sort of strain of emotion, there suddenly appeared a woman in complete possession of herself... (1a). ♦ ...Злоба вскипела в нём [Орозкуле] ко всему и ко всему... Пусть провалится этот мир, где всё устроено не так, как требуется, не так, как положено Орозкулу по его достоинствам и по должности! Уже не владея собой, Орозкул повёл коня по кустарнику прямо на крутой спуск (Айтматов 1). ...Anger boiled within him [Orozkul] against everything and everybody....To hell with the whole world, where everything was wrong, where Orozkul was not appreciated according to his merits and position. No longer able to control himself, Orozkul led the horse across the underbrush directly to a steep descent (1a).

В-160 • **В МОЕ́Й ⟨твоей и т. п.⟩ ВЛА́СТИ ⟨ВО́ЛЕ⟩** [PrepP; these forms only; subj-compl with copula; fixed WO] **1.** [subj: infin or это; often neg] (doing sth. is) within s.o.'s ability, authority etc: сделать X не в Y-овой власти ≃ **it's not (with)in Y's power to do X; Y is not in a position to do X; Y doesn't have the wherewithal to do X.**

...Если б статья была в своё время опубликована, то не в вашей власти было бы ограждать читателя от знакомства с ней... (Битов 2). ...If the article had been published in its own day, you wouldn't be in a position to shield the reader from an acquaintance with it... (2a).

2. Also: **ВО ВЛА́СТИ** *кого* [subj: usu. human or collect] (a person or thing is) under s.o.'s control completely, (a person is) dependent upon or defenseless against s.o.: X был во власти Y-а ≃ **X was in Y's power; X was at the mercy of Y; X was in Y's hands.**

Насмешка Пугачёва возвратила мне бодрость. Я спокойно отвечал, что я нахожусь в его власти и что он волен поступать со мною, как ему будет угодно (Пушкин 2). Pugachev's taunting manner restored my courage. I answered calmly that I was in his power and he was free to deal with me in whatever way he thought fit (2a). ♦ «Голова моя в твоей власти: отпустишь меня — спасибо; казнишь — бог тебе судья...» (Пушкин 2). "My life is in your hands: if you let me go, I'll be grateful; if you execute me, God shall be your judge..." (2a).

B-161 • **ВО ВЛА́СТИ ⟨ПОД ВЛА́СТЬЮ⟩** *чего* [PrepP; these forms only; the resulting PrepP is subj-compl with copula (subj: human)] (a person is) overcome by sth., fully absorbed in sth. (that elicits a strong emotional response): X во власти Y-а ≃ **X is in the power ⟨the grip⟩ of Y; X is overpowered ⟨gripped, overwhelmed⟩ by Y; X is under the spell of Y.**

...Я молчу, я весь во власти необыкновенного ритма и серебряного звука трубы (Казаков 2). ...I'm quiet, I'm entirely in the power of that extraordinary rhythm and the silvery sound of the trumpet (2a). ♦ ...Она опять во власти какой-то навязчивой идеи, смотрит в одну точку с тем же сосредоточенным, напряжённым, упрямым выражением (Рыбаков 2). ...She was obviously in the grip of some new obsession, gazing at a single spot with her fixed, tense, stubborn stare (2a). ♦ «Он сидит ночью один, весь во власти охватившей его душу любви — единственной, неповторимой любви...» (Катаев 3). "He sits there alone in the night, completely overpowered by the love that has taken possession of his soul, unique, inimitable..." (3a).

B-162 • **У ВЛА́СТИ быть₀, стоять, продержаться** и т. п. [PrepP; Invar; subj-compl with copula (subj: human or collect) or adv] (to be, remain etc) in a position of leadership, (to be) a ruler: X (стоит) у власти ≃ **X is in power ⟨in control, at the helm⟩; X is holding the reins; the government ⟨power etc⟩ is in X's hands;** ‖ X стал у власти ≃ **X took power ⟨control, the helm, the reins of government⟩; X took over.**

...Строительству этих ресторанов Абесаломон Нартович уделял особенно большое внимание, когда был у власти (Искандер 4). ...Abesalomon Nartovich had devoted particular attention to the construction of these restaurants when he was in power (4a). ♦ «Крымов принимает меня, а так как он знает, кого из офицеров к нему посылают, то прямо заявляет следующее: „У власти люди, сознательно ведущие страну к гибельному концу"...» (Шолохов 3). "Krymov receives me and, since he knows what kind of officers are being sent to him, he comes straight out with the following statement: 'The government is in the hands of men who are deliberately leading the country to destruction'" (3a). ♦ «Несомненно, будет правительственный переворот, у власти станет Корнилов» (Шолохов 3). "There will certainly be a *coup d'état* and Kornilov will take over" (3a).

B-163 • **ВЛАСТИ́ТЕЛЬ ДУМ** *(чьих, кого)* lit [NP; fixed WO] a person who has much influence on his contemporaries, an intellectual and spiritual leader: **molder of opinion; dominant ⟨major⟩ influence.**

...За пятьдесят лет прогрессивной критики, от Белинского до Михайловского, не было ни одного властителя дум, который не произвёлся бы над поэзией Фета (Набоков 1).

...During fifty years of utilitarian criticism, from Belinski to Mikhailovski, there was not a single molder of opinion who did not take the opportunity to jeer at the poems of Fet (1a). ♦ Не знает он, что о ненавистном во все школьные годы физике станет когда-нибудь вспоминать с теплотою, а о кумире и властителе дум завуче — с содроганием (Битов 2). He doesn't know that someday he will come to remember with warmth the physics teacher he has hated throughout his school years, and will shudder to remember the principal, his idol and dominant influence (2a).

< From Aleksandr Pushkin's poem "To the Sea" («К морю»), 1824. Used by Pushkin in reference to Napoleon and Byron.

B-164 • **ВА́ША ВЛАСТЬ** obs [NP; Invar; indep. sent or clause] you may do whatever you would like to: **as you like ⟨wish, please⟩; please ⟨suit⟩ yourself.**

B-165 • **ОТДАВА́ТЬСЯ/ОТДА́ТЬСЯ ВО ВЛАСТЬ** *кого-чего;* **ОТДАВА́ТЬСЯ/ОТДА́ТЬСЯ ⟨ПРЕДАВА́ТЬСЯ/ПРЕДА́ТЬСЯ⟩ ВЛА́СТИ** *кого-чего* all lit [VP; subj: human] to submit o.s. to s.o. or sth. (voluntarily or instinctively), come under the influence of s.o. or sth.: X отдался во власть Y-а ≃ **X gave himself over to Y; X came under the power of Y.**

B-166 • **ТЕРЯ́ТЬ/ПОТЕРЯ́ТЬ ВЛАСТЬ НАД СОБО́Й** [VP; subj: human] to lose one's composure: X потерял власть над собой ≃ **X lost his self-control ⟨self-restraint, presence of mind⟩; X lost control of himself.**

...Дарья на четвереньках ползла за ними на крыльцо; целуя, хватала негнущиеся, мёрзлые руки мужа. Григорий отталкивал её ногой, чувствовал, что ещё миг — и он потеряет над собой власть (Шолохов 4). ...Darya crawled after them on to the porch, snatching at and kissing her husband's stiff, frozen hands. Grigory pushed her away with his foot, feeling that in another second he would lose control of himself (4a).

B-167 • **СКО́ЛЬКО ВЛЕ́ЗЕТ** coll [AdvP; Invar; adv; usu. used with impfv imper or with можешь, можете foll. by infin of another verb; fixed WO] (to do sth.) without limit or restriction, to one's complete satisfaction: **to one's heart's content; as much ⟨as long as⟩ as one likes ⟨pleases, wants⟩.**

Перед тем и после того — смейся сколько влезет, а во время этого — не моги (Терц 1). Before the event and after it you could laugh to your heart's content, but during it—no (1a).

B-168 • **НЕ ВЛЕ́ЗЕШЬ** *в кого* coll [VP; neg pfv fut, gener. 2nd pers sing only] it is impossible to know s.o.'s true thoughts, intentions, qualities etc: **you can't read s.o.'s mind; you can't see inside s.o.'s head; you can't tell what s.o. is (really) like.**

[Анна Петровна:] Нравится ли он [твой жених] тебе? Признаться сказать, скоренько дело-то сделали: кто его знает, в него не влезешь (Островский 1). [A.P.:] Do you like him [your fiancé]? I must admit the thing was done pretty quickly. Who knows? You can't tell what he's like (1b).

B-169 • **ВЛЕЧЬ/ПОВЛЕ́ЧЬ ЗА СОБО́Й** *что* [VP; subj: abstr; fixed WO] to cause sth. to happen, have sth. as a consequence: X влечёт за собой Y ≃ **X brings about ⟨on, with it⟩ Y; X leads to Y; X results in Y; X brings Y in X's wake; Y ensues ⟨results⟩ from X.**

«„Сын мой, — виляет патер, — по неисповедимым судьбам провидения всё восполняется и видимая беда влечёт иногда за собою чрезвычайную, хотя и невидимую выгоду"» (Достоевский 2). "'My son,' the priest hedged, 'through the inscrutable decrees of Providence everything has its recompense, and a visible calamity sometimes brings with it a great, if invisible, profit'" (2a). ♦ Очевидно было, что странное это фокусирование влечёт за собой искажение нашей реальной социалистической действительности... (Аксёнов 12). It was obvious that this strange focusing led to distortions of the "real" socialist reality... (12a). ♦ ...Царь Николай стеганул камчой брата Ленина, совершенно не подозревая, какие грандиозные исторические события повлечёт за собой эта мгновенная вспышка царского гнева (Искандер 5). ...Czar Nicholas lashed Lenin's brother with his quirt, never suspecting what vast historical events would ensue from this instantaneous flare of czarist wrath (5a).

В-170 • ВМÉСТЕ ТÉСНО, А ВРОЗЬ СКУ́ЧНО [saying] some (usu. two) people find it hard to be together because they argue or irritate each other, yet find it hard to be apart because they care for and miss each other (said of or by such people): ≃ **you can't live with 'em and you can't live without 'em; they ⟨we etc⟩ can't be ⟨live, stand to be⟩ together, but they ⟨we etc⟩ can't be ⟨live, stand to be⟩ apart.**

В-171 • ВНÉШНОСТЬ ⟨НАРУ́ЖНОСТЬ⟩ ОБМÁН-ЧИВА [saying] one cannot judge sth.'s value by its exterior or s.o.'s inner qualities by his appearance: ≃ **appearances are deceptive ⟨deceiving⟩; appearances cannot be trusted; don't ⟨you can't⟩ judge a book by its cover; beauty is but ⟨only⟩ skin-deep.**

В-172 • ПРИНИМÁТЬ/ПРИНЯ́ТЬ ВО ВНИМÁНИЕ *что* [VP; subj: human or collect; often infin with надо, нужно, должен; often foll. by a что-clause] to include sth. in one's deliberations or calculations: X должен принять во внимание Y ≃ **X must take Y into account; X must take account of Y; X must take ⟨bring⟩ Y into consideration; X must consider Y; X must bear ⟨keep⟩ Y in mind;** [in limited contexts] **X must allow for Y;** ‖ принимая во внимание, что... ≃ **in view of the fact that...**

...Субъективно он честный человек, не вор, не жулик, не чужак, и суд должен принять это во внимание (Рыбаков 1). Subjectively...he was an honest man, he was not a thief, or a swindler, or an intruder, and the court should take this into account (1a). ♦ Уклонист заметил, что творчество во внимание принимать вообще не нужно, ибо дело идёт к тому, что в деятельности писателей, художников и прочих представителей творческих профессий... творческий элемент катастрофически сокращается... (Зиновьев 1). Deviationist said there was no need to bring creative work into consideration since, the way things were going, the creative element in the work of writers, artists and other representatives of the creative professions...was diminishing catastrophically... (1a). ♦ Я тебе поясню на примере нашего учреждения, сказал Болтун. Оно типично для целой категории учреждений, активно участвующих в определении характера власти. А только их и надо в данном случае принимать во внимание (Зиновьев 1). "Well, I'll explain it to you," said Chatterer; "take the example of the institute where I work. It's typical of the whole range of institutes which take an active part in determining the nature of power. And those are the only ones which should be considered here" (1a). ♦ «...Нужно принять во внимание, что вот тут-то и есть мораль, тут-то и заключена мораль...» (Гоголь 3). "...We must allow for the fact that it is precisely here that the moral of the story lies..." (3e). ♦ «[Вы] поступили неправильно... поставили сержанта Токареву в ложное положение, но, принимая во внимание, что вы боевой офицер, я это дело прекращаю...» (Рыбаков 1). "...You acted improperly....You placed Sergeant Tokareva in a false position, but in view of the fact that you're a combat officer, I'm closing the case" (1a).

В-173 • ОСТАВЛЯ́ТЬ/ОСТÁВИТЬ БЕЗ ВНИМÁНИЯ *что* [VP; subj: human or collect] not to pay attention to sth., to consider sth. not worthy of regard: X оставил без внимания Y ≃ **X took no notice of Y; X paid no heed to Y; X ignored ⟨disregarded⟩ Y; X brushed Y aside.**

Крупной ошибкой, которую сделал в этот период жизни своей Мольер, была следующая: он прислушивался к тому плохому, что о нём говорят, и оскорбления, которые ему следовало оставлять без всякого внимания, задевали его (Булгаков 5). During this period of his life, Molière made the serious mistake of listening to the evil spoken of him. The insults which he should have ignored cut him to the quick (5a).

В-174 • ЖИВÁЯ ВОДÁ *folk* [NP; usu. this WO] in fairy tales, a wonder-working water that brings the dead back to life: **elixir of life.**

«А в магазине – что хочешь, только живой воды нет. Лишь бы – твои деньги» (Терц 3). "And the store sold anything you like except the Elixir of Life. Provided you had the money" (3a).

В-175 • СЕДЬМÁЯ ⟨ДЕСЯ́ТАЯ⟩ ВОДÁ НА КИСЕЛÉ *coll, humor or iron* [NP; usu. subj-compl with copula (subj: human); fixed WO] a very distant relative: **second ⟨third etc⟩ cousin twice removed; a cousin seven ⟨ten etc⟩ times removed.**

Лена спросила шёпотом: «Откуда здесь Бубрик?» Дмитриев, подавив в себе чувство неприятного удивления, сказал: «Ну, как же? Он какой-то наш родственник, седьмая вода на киселе» (Трифонов 4). Lena asked in a whisper: "Why's Bubrik here?" Dmitriev, stifling a feeling of unpleasant surprise, said: "Well, so? He's related somehow. Second cousin twice removed" (4a). ♦ Родственник был так себе, десятая вода на киселе, но он был в числе тех, кому принц помогал (Искандер 3). He wasn't much of a relative, a cousin ten times removed, but he was among those whom the prince helped (3a).

В-176 • ТЕМНÁ ВОДÁ ВО ÓБЛАЦЕХ *lit, humor or iron* [sent; Invar; fixed WO] sth. is obscure, unclear: **it is all shrouded in darkness; it's as clear as mud.**

«Знаете, – сказал Штрум, – у меня удивительное чувство. Мне кажется, что упорство наше в Сталинграде – это упорство Ньютона, упорство Эйнштейна; что победа на Волге знаменует торжество идей Эйнштейна, словом, понимаете, вот такое чувство». Шишаков недоумённо усмехнулся, слегка покачал головой. «Неужели не понимаете меня, Алексей Алексеевич?» – сказал Штрум. «Да, темна вода во облацех», – сказал, улыбаясь, оказавшийся рядом молодой человек из отдела науки (Гроссман 2). "Do you know," said Victor, "I've got an extraordinary feeling. As though our determination at Stalingrad is the determination of Newton, the determination of Einstein. As though our victory on the Volga symbolizes the triumph of Einstein's ideas. Well, you know what I mean..." Shishakov gave a perplexed smile and gently shook his head. "Don't you understand me, Aleksey Alekseyevich?" said Victor. "It's as clear as mud," said the young man from the scientific section, who was now standing beside Victor (2a).

< From the Church Slavonic text of the Bible (Russian text, Psalter 17:12; cf. Ps. 18:11, King James Version). «Во облацех» is the old form of the locative plural of the word «облако».

В-177 • В МУ́ТНОЙ ВОДÉ РЫ́БУ ЛОВИ́ТЬ *disapprov* [VP; subj: human; often infin with пытаться, любить, хватит etc] to take advantage of a troubled situation or s.o.'s difficulties: X в мутной воде рыбу ловит ≃ **X fishes in troubled waters.**

[Золотилов:] Взгляни ты на себя... Ты изнурён, ты кашляешь, и кашляешь нехорошо... К нам отовсюду доходят слухи, что ты пьёшь... Я убеждён, что эта госпожа поддерживает в тебе эту несчастную наклонность, чтобы ловчей в мутной воде рыбу ловить (Писемский 1). [Z.:] Just look at yourself....You are worn out: you are coughing, and coughing like a sick man....Rumors come to us from all quarters that you are drinking....I am also convinced that this woman encourages you in this unfortunate weakness, because it is easier to fish in troubled waters (1a).

< Loan translation of the French *pêcher en eau trouble.*

В-178 • КАК ВО́ДИТСЯ [Invar; sent adv (parenth); fixed WO] as is generally or always the case: **as usual; as is customary; as is one's ⟨the⟩ custom;** [in limited contexts] **as people do.**

Плечевой хотел сообщить лётчику ещё ряд сведений из жизни окрестных селений, но тут набежал народ. Первыми подоспели, как водится, пацаны (Войнович 2). Burly was about to provide the pilot with further information on the life of the neighboring settlements when people started running up. As usual, the kids were the first ones on the scene (2a). ♦ …Как водится, приехали родственники молодых мужей и развезли их по своим сёлам (Искандер 5). …As is customary, the husbands' relatives arrived and took them home to their villages (5a). ♦ Как-то ещё в Москве я оказался в одной интеллигентной компании. Сидя на кухне, пили чай и, как водится, обсуждали все или почти все местные и мировые проблемы и события (Войнович 1). One day in Moscow I found myself with a group of intellectuals. They sat in the kitchen, drank tea, and, as is their custom, discussed all, or nearly all, local and world problems and events (1a). ♦ Ну, посидели они, как водится, выпили джин или виски… почесали языками да и пора расходиться (Войнович 1). They sat together for a while, as people do, drinking whiskey or gin…shooting the breeze until it was time for Rabinovich to go (1a).

В-179 • ВОДО́Й НЕ РАЗОЛЬЁШЬ *кого (с кем);* **ВОДО́Й НЕ РАЗЛИ́ТЬ** *both coll* [VP; neg pfv fut, gener. 2nd pers sing не разольёшь (1st var.); impers predic with бытьø (2nd var.); fixed WO] (the named people) are always together, have a very close relationship: Х-а и Y-а ⟨Х-а с Y-ом⟩ водой не разольёшь ≃ **X and Y are inseparable; nothing can part X and Y; X and Y are (as) thick as thieves.**

«Ладно, иди, — понятливо отвернулся Тихон и выпустил его руку, — вас ведь всё одно водой не разольёшь, старый да малый…» (Максимов 2). "All right, off you go." Tikhon turned away understandingly and let go of Vlad's hand. "I guess you two are pretty well inseparable, even though one's old and the other's young…" (2a). ♦ …Какими друзьями они были, водой не разлить! (Эренбург 1). …What friends they were, nothing could part them! (1a). ♦ «Ты раньше… не любил Мишечкиных. А теперь тебя с ними водой не разольёшь…» (Евтушенко 1). "You never liked the Mishechkins…before. But now you're thick as thieves with them" (1a).

В-180 • КАК ⟨БУ́ДТО, СЛО́ВНО, ТО́ЧНО⟩ ВОДО́Й СМЫ́ЛО *кого-что coll* [VP; impers; past only; fixed WO] s.o. or sth. disappeared quickly and completely: Х-а как водой смыло ≃ **X disappeared ⟨was gone⟩ in a flash; X disappeared without a trace; X vanished (into thin air); (it's as if) thing X evaporated.**

В-181 • ОКАТИ́ТЬ ⟨ОБЛИ́ТЬ⟩ ХОЛО́ДНОЙ ВОДО́Й ⟨УША́ТОМ ХОЛО́ДНОЙ ВОДЫ́⟩ *кого;* **КАК ⟨БУ́ДТО, СЛО́ВНО, ТО́ЧНО⟩ ХОЛО́ДНОЙ ВОДО́Й ОКАТИ́ТЬ ⟨ОБЛИ́ТЬ⟩; ВЫ́ЛИТЬ УША́Т ХОЛО́ДНОЙ ВОДЫ́** *на кого all coll* [VP; subj: human or abstr; var. with как can be impers: окатило; often 3rd pers pl with indef. refer.] to discourage s.o., dampen s.o.'s zeal or enthusiasm: X окатил Y-а холодной водой ≃ **X threw ⟨poured⟩ cold water over ⟨on⟩ Y ⟨Y's plans etc⟩; X threw a bucket ⟨a pail⟩ of cold water over Y; thing X made Y feel as though someone had thrown ⟨poured⟩ cold water over ⟨on⟩ him; thing X made Y feel as though someone had thrown a bucket ⟨a pail⟩ of cold water over ⟨on⟩ him;** [in limited contexts] **person X rained on Y's parade.**

…Спокойствие Зинаиды меня точно холодной водой окатило. Я понял, что я дитя в её глазах, — и мне стало очень тяжело! (Тургенев 3). …Zinaida's composure made me feel as though someone had poured cold water over me: I realised that I was a child in her eyes—and I felt very unhappy! (3a). ♦ Сосед Павел Сочава на всю улицу иронически сказал: «А вот и Толя награбил! Иди скажи своей матери, чтобы она тебя выпорола». Меня словно окатили холодной водой (Кузнецов 1). …Our neighbor Pavel Sochava remarked loudly and ironically, for the whole street to hear, "So Tolya has been plundering, too. Go on home and tell your mother to give you a good spanking." I felt as though someone had thrown a pail of cold water over me (1a).

В-182 • ВОЗИ́ТЬ ВО́ДУ *на ком coll* [VP; subj: human] to burden s.o. with hard, demeaning work: X возит воду на Y-е ≃ **X makes Y do the donkey work; X has made Y X's drudge;** [in limited contexts] **X walks all over Y.**

«На таких, как вы, только воду и возить, лучше скотины не отыщешь» (Максимов 3). "People like you are born to do the donkey work, there's no finer beast of burden" (3a). ♦ [author's usage] [Бусыгин:] Ты сам сказал, что ты мой друг. [Сильва:] Ну правильно, друг. Но нельзя же сено на мне возить (Вампилов 4). [B.:] You said yourself that you're my friend. [S.:] That's true, I am. But that doesn't mean you can walk all over me (4a).

В-183 • ВЫВОДИ́ТЬ/ВЫ́ВЕСТИ НА ЧИ́СТУЮ ⟨СВЕ́ЖУЮ *obs⟩* **ВО́ДУ** *кого-что coll* [VP; subj: human; often pfv fut (usu. denoting a threat) or infin with надо, нужно, пора, хотеть, решить etc; the verb may take the final position, otherwise fixed WO] to expose s.o.'s shady dealings, secretive intrigues etc, disclose s.o.'s true (usu. harmful) intentions: X выведет Y-а на чистую воду ≃ **X will show up person Y; X will show Y for what Y (really) is; X will bring thing Y (out) into the open; X will blow the lid off thing Y;** [in limited contexts] **X will smoke person Y out; X will blow the whistle on Y; X will bring Y to justice; X will pull the plug on person Y; X will bring person Y to book.**

«Я, конечно, не знаю, какой будет у него подход. Но если ему, скажем просто, хочется вывести на чистую воду прогрессивных критиков, то ему не стоит стараться: Волынский и Айхенвальд уже давно это сделали» (Набоков 1). "Of course I don't know what his approach will be. But if he, let's speak plainly, wants to show up the progressive critics then it's not worth the effort: Volynski and Eichenwald did this long ago" (1a). ♦ …Цель такой критики — вывести на чистую воду порочность той или иной теории, научной школы, художественного или нравственного принципа, заставить свою жертву принять требования собрания, то есть «исправиться» (Эткинд 1). The aim of such criticism is to bring out into the open the failings of such and such a theory, a scientific school, or an artistic or moral principle, and to oblige its victim to comply with the demands of the meeting, in other words, to "correct himself" (1a). ♦ «Ежели бы я был разбойник, я бы просил милости, а то я сужусь за то, что вывожу на чистую воду разбойников» (Толстой 5). "If I were a [robber] I might ask for mercy, but I'm being court-martialed for [bringing robbers] to book" (5a).

В-184 • КАК ⟨БУ́ДТО, СЛО́ВНО, ТО́ЧНО⟩ В ВО́ДУ ГЛЯДЕ́Л ⟨СМОТРЕ́Л⟩ *coll* [VP; subj: human; past only; fixed WO] (as if) one knew beforehand that sth. was going to happen, foresaw sth., had a presentiment about sth.: X как в воду глядел ≃ **X must have been looking in ⟨X must have had⟩ a crystal ball; X must have second sight; it's as if X knew it all beforehand ⟨in advance⟩;** [in limited contexts] **X's words turned out to be all too true; X's words ⟨remarks etc⟩ were prophetic.**

Нуца знала, что муж её уже завёлся и теперь ещё долго будет пить, скорее всего всю ночь… Она как в воду смотрела (Искандер 5). Noutsa knew that her husband was off; he'd drink a long time now, most likely all the night….She must have been looking in a crystal ball (5a). ♦ «Ну что ж, — сказал парторг, — я вижу, мы не договорились… С такими взглядами можно далеко докатиться». И действительно, парторг как в воду глядел. Наш учёный вскоре докатился в столыпинском вагоне до Колымы (Войнович 4). "All right, then," said the Party organizer. "Clearly we don't see eye to eye.…With views like those you'll go far." The Party organizer must have had a crystal ball. Our scientist in no time had gone as far as Kolyma, in a prison train (4a). ♦ «…Пока я член Политбюро, у меня есть всё. А вот когда меня выгонят, тогда неизвестно, что будет.…» И как в воду глядел, выгнали-таки его (Войнович 1). "…As long as I'm a member of the Politburo, I have everything I want. But nobody knows what'll happen when they kick me out…" A prophetic remark, because later on he was kicked out of the Politburo (1a).

В-185 • КАК ⟨БУ́ДТО, СЛО́ВНО, ТО́ЧНО⟩ В ВО́ДУ КА́НУЛ coll [VP; subj: usu. human, animal, or concr; past only; usu. this WO] (a person, thing etc) vanished completely: X как в воду канул ≃ **X (has) vanished into thin air; X (has) disappeared ⟨vanished⟩ without a trace;** [in limited contexts] **the earth seems to have swallowed X up.**

В это время из дамских благовонных уст к нему устремилось множество намёков и вопросов, проникнутых насквозь тонкостию и любезностию… Но он отвечал на всё решительным невниманием, и приятные фразы канули как в воду (Гоголь 3). At that moment a great many hints and questions full of the most polite and refined subtleties were fired at him from the fragrant lips of the ladies.…But Chichikov paid no attention whatever and the agreeable phrases vanished into thin air (3a). ♦ Изварин посидел немного и ушёл, а наутро исчез, — как в воду канул (Шолохов 3). They sat talking for a while, then Izvarin left, and by morning he had disappeared without a trace (3a). ♦ Известный всей решительно Москве знаменитый театральный администратор канул как в воду (Булгаков 9). This man, known to the entire theatrical world of Moscow, seemed to have vanished without a trace (9b). ♦ «С той поры Пряжкину не видели?» — …спросил Антон. «Нет. Люся как в воду канула» (Чернёнок 2). "You haven't seen Priazhkina since?" Anton asked. "No. The earth swallowed her up, it seems" (2a).

В-186 • КАК ⟨БУ́ДТО, СЛО́ВНО, ТО́ЧНО⟩ В ВО́ДУ ОПУ́ЩЕННЫЙ (ходит, сидит и т. п.) coll [как + AdjP; nom only; subj-compl with copula (subj: human), detached modif, or adv; fixed WO] (one is, looks etc) extremely sad about sth., dispirited: **depressed; dejected; crestfallen; downcast; down in the dumps ⟨in the mouth⟩; forlorn(ly).**

…[Доктор] вышел из комнаты, как в воду опущенный, с чувством недоброго предзнаменования (Пастернак 1). …He [the doctor] went out of the room depressed and with a feeling of foreboding (1a). ♦ Он задумался и вдруг тихо спросил: «Жозет, эта женщина наша?» — «Нет». — «А я думал, что наша. Не понимал, почему она как в воду опущенная…» (Эренбург 1). He became lost in thought and then suddenly inquired in a low voice: "Josette, is that woman one of us?" "No." "I thought she was. I couldn't understand why she looked so dejected" (1a). ♦ Руслан сидит как в воду опущенный, на себя непохож (Трифонов 6). Ruslan sits there crestfallen, not himself (6a). ♦ Аксинья не вмешивалась в разговор, сидела на кровати, как в воду опущенная (Шолохов 2). Aksinya took no part in the conversation and sat forlornly on the bed… (2a).

В-187 • ЛИТЬ ВО́ДУ НА МЕ́ЛЬНИЦУ чью, кого lit, often media [VP; subj: human or abstr] to further s.o.'s cause (often that of one's opponent, the opposite party, or s.o. undeserving) indirectly or unintentionally by one's actions or behavior: X льёт воду на мельницу Y-a ≃ **thing X is grist to ⟨for⟩ Y's mill; X brings ⟨adds⟩ grist to Y's mill; X provides grist for Y's mill; person X is playing into Y's hands.**

На очередном заседании политбюро (тогда — «президиума») стал Никита [Хрущёв] требовать от членов согласия на опубликование [«Ивана Денисовича»]… Многие отмалчивались («Чего молчите?» — требовал Никита), кто-то осмелился спросить: «А на чью мельницу это будет воду лить?» (Солженицын 2). At a regular meeting of the Politburo (or Presidium, as it then was) Nikita [Khrushchev] sought agreement to the publication of the story [Ivan Denisovich].…Several made no comment ("Why don't you say something?" Nikita demanded), and someone ventured to ask "whose mill would it be grist to?" (2a). ♦ …Коллеги на очередном партийном собрании… просили Шевчука осознать свою ошибку и признать, что, хотя его высказывание, может быть, и не носило намеренно провокационного характера, объективно оно льёт воду на мельницу наших врагов (Войнович 4). …His [Shevchuk's] colleagues, at the next Party meeting, asked Shevchuk to realize his error and to acknowledge that, although his statement was perhaps not of a deliberately provocative nature, it did, objectively, provide grist for the mills of our enemies (4a).

В-188 • МУТИ́ТЬ ВО́ДУ coll, usu. disapprov [VP; subj: human] **1.** to confuse a certain matter intentionally, muddle some facts (usu. trying to deceive s.o., misrepresent the real situation): X мутит воду ≃ **X is muddying the water(s); X is confusing the issue.**

«Фантастика всё это… Никакого удава в горах нет и никогда не было»… — «Всё-таки до меня ещё не полностью доходит, что всё это значит». — «А надо, чтоб дошло, надо… Давайте зададим себе вопрос: кто мутит воду, кто распускает слухи? Бригадир Потапов» (Домбровский 1). "The whole story is pure science-fiction. There is no boa-constrictor up in those hills and never was."…"I still don't see what it's all supposed to mean." "Well, it's time you realised what it means.…Now let us ask ourselves this question—who is muddying the water, who is spreading rumours? Brigade-leader Potapov" (1a).

2. to sow discord between people: X мутит воду ≃ **X is stirring up trouble; X is stirring things up; X is causing ⟨making⟩ trouble.**

Второй раз предупреждает её Подрезов насчёт молельни… А может, Марфа тут ни при чём? Когда она отличалась набожностью? Может, это Евсей Мошкин воду мутит? (Абрамов 1). This was the second time Podrezov had warned her about the prayer house.…But maybe it had nothing to do with Marfa. She had never been especially devout. Perhaps it was Evsei Moshkin stirring up trouble (1a). ♦ [Сильва:] Хату поджёг он (указывает на Бусыгина), а не кто-нибудь. И воду тут у вас мутит тоже он (Вампилов 4). [S.:] He set fire to the cottage, (Indicating Busygin) and not someone else. And he stirred up things here too (4b).

В-189 • НОСИ́ТЬ ⟨ТАСКА́ТЬ, ЧЕ́РПАТЬ⟩ ВО́ДУ РЕШЕТО́М; НОСИ́ТЬ ⟨ТАСКА́ТЬ⟩ ВО́ДУ В РЕШЕТЕ́ all coll, iron or humor [VP; subj: human; usu. infin after всё равно что or то же самое, что] to do sth. knowing that one's efforts, actions are in vain: делать X — всё равно что воду решетом носить ≃ **doing X is like trying to carry ⟨draw⟩ water in a sieve; doing X is like plowing the sands.**

Дмитрий человек упрямый, спорить с ним — всё равно что воду решетом носить. Dmitry is a stubborn person: arguing with him is like trying to carry water in a sieve.

В-190 • ТОЛО́ЧЬ ВО́ДУ (В СТУ́ПЕ) coll, disapprov [VP; subj: human] to do something absolutely fruitless, useless for a long period of time (often used in situations when one engages in empty talk instead of taking action in some matter): X толчёт воду в ступе ≃ **X is beating the air; X is pouring water through a sieve; X is milling the wind; X is plowing the sand;** [of idle talk only] **X is jabbering ⟨talking in circles⟩.**

«За границу мы вас не выпустим! — сказал он [Суслов]… — Будут провокации». — «Какие провокации? При чём тут провокации?»… — «Вас там сразу же окружат корреспонденты. Вы не знаете, что это такое, — словом, политические провокации будут на каждом шагу. Мы вас же хотим уберечь от всего этого». Это было всё равно что толочь воду в ступе. Мы говорили о разном и с разных точек зрения (Аллилуева 2). "We shall not let you go abroad!" he [Suslov] said.… "There'll be provocations." "What provocations? What have provocations got to do with this?"…"You'll be instantly surrounded by newsmen. You don't know what it's like. In short, there will be political provocations at every step. We want to save you from it." It was like beating the air. We spoke of different things from different points of view (2a). ♦ Мысли жгут так сильно, что он… не ощущал, как набрякшие ноги распирали голенища сапог… Все мы были беспощадны к врагам революции. Почему же революция беспощадна к нам? А может быть, потому и беспощадна. А может быть, не революция, какая же этот капитан [из органов безопасности] революция, это – чёрная сотня, шпана. Он толок воду в ступе, а время шло (Гроссман 2). His thoughts burned so fiercely that…he no longer even felt how his swollen legs were bursting open the tops of his boots.…We were merciless towards the enemies of the Revolution. Why has the Revolution been so merciless towards us? Perhaps for that very reason. Or maybe it hasn't got anything to do with the Revolution. What's this captain [from the security organs] got to do with the Revolution? He's just a thug, a member of the Black Hundreds. There he had been, just milling the wind, while time had been passing (2a). ♦ [Кречинский:] Ну довольно! считай! А то ведь ты рад воду толочь (Сухово-Кобылин 2). [K.:] Enough of that! Count! You and that everlasting jabbering of yours!… (2b).

B-191 • ХОТЬ В ВО́ДУ; ХОТЬ В О́МУТ ⟨В ПРО́-РУБЬ⟩ (ГОЛОВО́Й); ХОТЬ (С МОСТА́) В РЕ́КУ all coll [хоть + PrepP; these forms only; usu. subord clause (often introduced by что)] (a situation is so hopeless that) a person wants to drown himself, commit suicide, thinking that that is the only solution: **one could jump ⟨throw o.s.⟩ off a bridge; one might (go and) drown o.s.; one wants to end it all; one is simply ⟨absolutely⟩ desperate.**

Видно было, что человек дошёл до черты, погиб и ищет последнего выхода, а не удастся, то хоть сейчас и в воду (Достоевский 1). Here obviously was a man at the end of his rope, facing ruin and looking for a last way out, and if he did not find it, he might just go and drown himself (1a). ♦ «Вот видите, я уж после узнал всю эту штуку: Григорий Александрович до того его [Азамата] задразнил, что хоть в воду; раз он ему и скажи: „Вижу, Азамат, что тебе больно понравилась эта лошадь; а не видать тебе её как своего затылка!"» (Лермонтов 1). "You see, I got the whole story later. Grigori Alexandrovich egged him [Azamat] on to a point when the lad was simply desperate. Finally he put it point-blank: 'I can see, Azamat, that you want that horse very badly. Yet you have as little chance of getting it as of seeing the back of your own head'" (1b).

B-192 • ВО́ДЫ В РОТ НАБРА́ТЬ coll [VP; subj: human; usu. past, often after как, будто, словно, точно] (often used when contrasting a person's silence with his initial intention to speak, his usual talkativeness, the expectation that he speak etc) to maintain complete silence, as if one had lost the ability to speak: X (как) воды в рот набрал ≃ **X won't say a word; X (has) clammed up;** [of concealing a secret, not objecting to sth. etc] **X is keeping his mouth shut;** ‖ ты что, воды в рот набрал? ≃ **has the cat got your tongue?; have you lost your tongue?**

«Давно ли ещё о празднике причитали, а тут воды в рот набрали…» (Абрамов 1). "Not long ago they were wailing over the holiday, and now they won't say a word!" (1b). ♦ …Когда в конце он поставил вопрос о распределении имущества бежавших с белыми, – ответили молчанием. «Чего ж вы воды в рот набрали?» – досадуя, спросил Иван Алексеевич (Шолохов 4). …When he concluded with the proposal to share out the property of those who had fled with the Whites, the response was silence. "What's the matter? Have you lost your tongues?" Ivan exclaimed angrily (4a). ♦ «А ты думал, что стариков можно толкать, пихать… а они

будут сидеть, как воды в рот набравши» (Ерофеев 3). [context transl] "And I suppose you thought that you could give an old man like him a shove and a kick…and he would just sit and take it without a murmur" (3a).

B-193 • ВО́ДЫ ⟨ВОДО́Й obs⟩ НЕ ЗАМУТИ́Т coll, approv or iron [VP; subj: human; these forms only; fixed WO] one is quiet, modest, very gentle: X воды не замутит ≃ **X wouldn't hurt ⟨harm⟩ a fly; X is (as) meek ⟨gentle⟩ as a lamb; X isn't the kind ⟨the sort⟩ to give ⟨cause⟩ (anyone) trouble.**

Это был тщедушный мужик с задублённым, изрезанным глубокими морщинами кротким лицом, один из тех, про кого обычно говорят – воды не замутит (Тендряков 1). He was a small man with a meek expression on his weather-beaten, deeply-furrowed peasant's face – not the sort who would ever give trouble (1a).

B-194 • много, немало, сколько, столько ВОДЫ́ УТЕКЛО́ (с тех пор, с того времени и т. п.) coll [VP_subj; usu. past; the verb is usu. in the final position] much time has passed, many changes have taken place (since the moment or event indicated): **much ⟨so much, a lot of etc⟩ water has flowed ⟨passed, gone⟩ under the bridge (since…); so much ⟨a lot of etc⟩ water has flowed by; a lot ⟨so much⟩ has happened.**

…Прошло уже четыре года с тех пор, как старик привёз в этот дом из губернского города восемнадцатилетнюю девочку, робкую, застенчивую, тоненькую, худенькую, задумчивую и грустную, и с тех пор много утекло воды (Достоевский 1). …It had already been four years since the old man had brought the timid, shy, eighteen-year-old girl, delicate, thin, pensive, and sad, to this house from the provincial capital, and since then much water had flowed under the bridge (1a). ♦ «Да, княжна, – сказал, наконец, Николай, грустно улыбаясь, – недавно кажется, а сколько воды утекло с тех пор, как мы с вами в первый раз виделись в Богучарове» (Толстой 7). "Yes, Princess," said Nikolai at last, smiling sadly, "it seems not so long ago since we first met at Bogucharovo, but how much water has flowed under the bridge since then!" (7a). ♦ Много воды утекло с той весенней поры, как, выпроводив именитых Андреевых сватов, она изо всех многочисленных своих воздыхателей выбрала Серёгу Агуреева, самого что ни на есть отпетого свиридовского гуляку. (Максимов 3). A lot of water had passed under the bridge since that spring when she had shown Andrei's matchmakers the door and, from a host of admirers, chosen Sergei Agureev, the most hopeless layabout in Sviridovo (3a). ♦ Сколько же воды утекло с того вечера! Нет больше в живых Насти Гаврилиной… (Абрамов 1). How much water had flowed by since that evening! Nastya Gavrilina was no longer alive (1a). ♦ За год утечёт много воды, многое изменится, Вадим Павлович скоро уедет, и эта блажь у Дины пройдёт (Рыбаков 1). …A lot could happen in a year, a lot could change, Vadim Pavlovich would soon be going away and Dina's infatuation would pass (1a).

B-195 • ВЫХОДИ́ТЬ/ВЫ́ЙТИ СУХИ́М ИЗ ВОДЫ́ coll, usu. disapprov [VP; subj: human] (of a crafty, cunning, or lucky person) to escape well-deserved punishment, remain unpunished, uncompromised: X вышел сухим из воды ≃ **X got off ⟨away⟩ scot-free; X emerged ⟨came out⟩ unscathed; X came away without a scratch; X waltzed away from it;** [in limited contexts] **X landed on his feet; X beat the rap; X got off.**

Рассказывал обо всём этом Иван не стыдясь, а как будто хвастаясь: вот, мол, какой я ловкий, вот какой я хитрый, украл – и вышел сухим из воды (Марченко 1). Ivan told us all this without the least trace of shame and even as though proud of himself, as if to say: look how clever I am, look how crafty I am – I managed to steal the stuff and I got away scot free (1a). ♦ Дрынов отличался тем, что свободно и быстро ориентировался в любой, самой сложной ситуации, правда, из всех возможных решений всегда выбирая самое глупое. Это не помешало ему выйти сухим из воды… (Войнович 2). Drinov was distinguished by his ability to easily and quickly get his bearings in any, even the most complex, situation, though, on the other hand, of all possible decisions, he invariably made the most stupid one. This did not, however, prevent him from always landing on his feet... (2a). ♦ Жизнь Жолио была бурной. Много раз его привлекали к ответственности то за вымогательство, то за клевету; он всегда выходил сухим из воды: говорили, будто он слишком много знает о прошлом различных государственных деятелей (Эренбург 4). Joliot's career had been a stormy one. He had been before the courts a number of times, sometimes for extortion, sometimes for libel, but never failed to get off; he was said to know too much about the pasts of various politicians (4a).

B-196 • **ТИ́ШЕ ВОДЫ́, НИ́ЖЕ ТРАВЫ́** быть₀, вести себя, держаться и т. п. coll [AdjP; Invar; subj-compl with copula (subj: human) or adv; fixed WO] one is timid, humble, self-effacing; one behaves timidly, humbly: X (держится) тише воды, ниже травы ≃ **X is ⟨keeps⟩ (as) quiet as a mouse; X is (as) gentle ⟨meek⟩ as a lamb; you'd never hear a peep from ⟨out of⟩ X.**

«И чего на него нашло такое? Никому никогда не перечил, тише воды, ниже травы был — и на тебе вдруг!» (Айтматов 1). "What's come over him? He never crossed anyone, always quiet as a mouse, and now—look at him" (1a). "What on earth's come over him? He never crossed anybody, he was meek as a lamb—then this all of a sudden" (1b).

B-197 • **ЧИ́СТОЙ ⟨ЧИСТЕ́ЙШЕЙ⟩ ВОДЫ́** [NP_{gen}; these forms only; nonagreeing modif; fixed WO] **1.** *special* (of a precious stone) of high quality, absolutely clear: **of the first water; flawless.**

2. *coll* [most often used with nouns referring to a negative quality] (sth. is) the most genuine, authentic (example of some object, phenomenon etc), (s.o.) embodies some trait to the highest degree possible: **of the first order ⟨water⟩; sheer; thoroughgoing; true; par excellence; pure and simple.**

...Если он решил поднять такой вопрос на партсобрании, то «это чистой воды демагогия» (Эренбург 3). ...For him to raise the issue at a Party meeting was "demagogy of the first order" (3a). ♦ [Шаманов:] Ты славная девочка, ты прелесть, но то, что ты сейчас сказала, — это ты выбрось из головы. Это чистейшей воды безумие (Вампилов 2). [Sh.:] You're charming, you're adorable, but what you've just said—you must put it out of your mind. It's sheer madness (2a). ♦ А Александр Васильевич, между прочим, чистой воды догматик (Стругацкие 4). Incidentally, Alexander Vassilevitch is a dogmatist par excellence (4a). ♦ «Авантюрист чистой воды!» — говорил о нём мой отец, но не с осуждением, а даже с некоторой завистью (Паустовский 1). "An adventurer, pure and simple," my father used to say of him, but with a certain envy rather than with disapproval (1a). ♦ Жил рядом со мной в Пскове маляр, бывший партизан... ещё и сейчас сталинец чистой воды (Мандельштам 1). [context transl] I remember one of my neighbors in Pskov, a house painter and former partisan who is still a die-hard Stalinist (1a).

B-198 • **ВОЖЖА́ ⟨ШЛЕЯ́⟩ ПОД ХВОСТ ПОПА́ЛА** кому substand [VP_{subj}] s.o. behaves strangely, wildly, as if possessed by sth.: X-у вожжа под хвост попала ≃ **something got ⟨must have got(ten)⟩ into X; something came over X.**

B-199 • **ОПУСКА́ТЬ/ОПУСТИ́ТЬ ⟨ВЫПУСКА́ТЬ/ВЫ́ПУСТИТЬ** и т. п.⟩ **ВО́ЖЖИ** coll [VP; subj: human] to lessen control (over one's subordinates or anyone under one's control), relax discipline: X опустил вожжи ≃ **X loosened ⟨slackened, eased up on⟩ the reins.**

Стоит нам хоть чуть-чуть опустить вожжи — и сын начинает приносить двойки. Whenever we ease up on the reins even the slightest bit, our son starts bringing home Ds.

B-200 • **ПРИБИРА́ТЬ/ПРИБРА́ТЬ ВО́ЖЖИ К РУ-КА́М; ДЕРЖА́ТЬ ВО́ЖЖИ В РУКА́Х** both coll [VP; subj: human] to concentrate power or leadership in one's hands, taking full control of sth. or some group of people: X прибрал вожжи к рукам ≃ **X seized ⟨took⟩ the reins of power; X took the reins of power into his hand(s).**

B-201 • **ДА ТО́ЛЬКО ВО́З И НЫ́НЕ ТА́М** [sent; fixed WO] (usu. in refer. to long and useless discussions that lead nowhere) sth. is not moving, progressing: **but so far there has been no headway ⟨progress⟩; but things are still right where they started; but it (still) hasn't gotten past the talking stage.**

< From Ivan Krylov's fable "Swan, Pike and Crab" («Лебедь, Щука и Рак»), 1816.

B-202 • **БЕЗ ВОЗВРА́ТА** [PrepP; Invar; adv] **1.** irreversibly, forever: **irrevocably; for good; never to return; and will never return.**

Я понял, что молодость прошла без возврата. I realized that my youth was gone, never to return.

2. давать, брать что ~ coll (to give sth. to s.o.) without asking him to return it, (to take, borrow sth.) without planning to return it: [in refer. to giving sth.] **for good; for keeps;** [in refer. to taking, borrowing sth.] **never returning it ⟨them⟩; never intending to return it ⟨them⟩; with no intention of returning it ⟨them⟩.**

Ваня завёл себе привычку брать книги у друзей без возврата. Vanya made a habit of borrowing his friends' books and never returning them.

B-203 • **ВЗЛЕТА́ТЬ/ВЗЛЕТЕ́ТЬ НА ВО́ЗДУХ** [VP; usu. pfv; fixed WO] **1.** Also: **ВЗЛЕТА́ТЬ/ВЗЛЕТЕ́ТЬ В ВО́З-ДУХ** [subj: concr or, less often, animal or human] to explode or be destroyed in an explosion: X взлетел на воздух ≃ **X was blown to bits ⟨to pieces, to smithereens⟩; X was blown up ⟨blown sky-high⟩; thing X blew up.**

Предвидя конечную гибель, она решилась умереть геройскою смертью и, собрав награбленные в казне деньги, в виду всех взлетела на воздух вместе с казначеем и бухгалтером (Салтыков-Щедрин 1). [context transl] Foreseeing ultimate ruin, she resolved to die an heroic death. Gathering up the money she had garnered from the treasury, in full view of everyone she blew herself up together with the treasurer and bookkeeper (1a).

2. [subj: abstr] (of plans, hopes, dreams) to fall through, end in nothing: X взлетел на воздух ≃ **X went up in smoke; X was blown to smithereens.**

B-204 • **КАК ВО́ЗДУХ** нужен, необходим и т. п. кому [как + NP; Invar; adv (intensif)] (s.o. needs some person or thing) very much: X нужен Y-у ~ ≃ **Y needs X as much as the air Y breathes; X is as necessary to Y as the air Y breathes; Y needs X as much as air to breathe.**

После падения Франции я не раз встречал людей... разлагаемых потребностью политической деятельности... Им надобно как воздух сцена и зрители... (Герцен 1). After the fall of France I more than once met people...who were disintegrated by the craving for public activity....A stage and spectators are as necessary to them as the air they breathe... (1a). ♦ Главное было передохнуть... Передышка нам была нужна как воздух (Мандельштам 2). ...The main thing for us was to have a break....We needed this as much as air to breathe (2a).

B-205 • **ПО́РТИТЬ/ИСПО́РТИТЬ ВО́ЗДУХ** euph, highly coll [VP; subj: human] to expel foul-smelling gas through one's anus: X испортил воздух ≃ **X let one fly; X broke wind; X cut one ⟨the cheese⟩.**

В-206 • **НА (СВЕ́ЖЕМ ⟨ОТКРЫ́ТОМ, ЧИ́СТОМ, ВО́ЛЬНОМ⟩) ВО́ЗДУХЕ быть₀, бывать и т. п.; НА (СВЕ́ЖИЙ ⟨ОТКРЫ́ТЫЙ, ЧИ́СТЫЙ, ВО́ЛЬНЫЙ⟩) ВО́ЗДУХ выйти, вырваться и т. п.** [PrepP; these forms only; adv (all variants) or subj-compl with copula, subj: usu. human (variants with воздухе)] outside of a house or building: (be ⟨go, spend time etc⟩) **outdoors ⟨outside, out of doors⟩; (be ⟨be held etc⟩) in the open air; (get some ⟨be out in the, go out(side) for a breath of etc⟩) (fresh) air.**

...Не переставать бормотать: «Правь, Эндурия, правь!» — [я] скатился с третьего этажа и вырвался на воздух (Искандер 5). Without ceasing to mutter "Rule, Enduria, rule!" I raced down from the third floor and lunged outdoors (5a). ♦ ...Там на чистом воздухе, окружённый высшим духовенством, стоял коленопреклонённый митрополит и молился — да мимо идёт чаша сия (Герцен 1). There in the open air, surrounded by the higher clergy, the Metropolitan genuflected and prayed that his cup might pass (1a). ♦ [Васенька:] Ты мало бываешь на воздухе (Вампилов 4). [V.:] You don't get enough fresh air (4a). ♦ Наконец почувствовал он себя лучше и обрадовался бог знает как, когда увидел возможность выйти на свежий воздух (Гоголь 3). At last he felt better and was greatly overjoyed when he realized that he could at last go out for a breath of fresh air (3a).

В-207 • **НОСИ́ТЬСЯ В ВО́ЗДУХЕ** *lit* [VP; subj: abstr] (of some idea, event etc) to be anticipated, foreseen, intuited etc by many people: X носится в воздухе ≃ **X is in the air;** [in limited contexts] **(people etc) sense X.**

Идея реорганизации института вообще-то не новая — это давно уже носится в воздухе. The idea to reorganize the institute is not new—it's been in the air for quite a while now.

В-208 • **ПОВИСА́ТЬ/ПОВИ́СНУТЬ В ВО́ЗДУХЕ** [VP; fixed WO] **1.** [subj: usu. рука, нога] having interrupted a movement before it is completed, to remain motionless in that position: рука ⟨нога⟩ повисла в воздухе ≃ **s.o.'s arm ⟨leg⟩ remained ⟨was left⟩ suspended in midair.**

2. *coll.* Also: **ВИСЕ́ТЬ В ВО́ЗДУХЕ** *coll* [subj: human or abstr (дело, поездка, планы etc)] to be in a state of uncertainty, in an indefinite position: X повис в воздухе ≃ **X was left hanging; X was up in the air; X was in (a state of) limbo.**

Из-за маминой болезни моя командировка в Прагу повисла в воздухе. Because of my mother's illness, my business trip to Prague is up in the air.

3. [subj: слова, возражения etc] (of s.o.'s remarks, objections etc) to receive no reaction, response, or support (from others): X повис в воздухе ≃ **X fell on deaf ears; X was of ⟨to⟩ no avail.**

[Бывший партийный работник] стал агитатором в каком-то техникуме, в Ленинграде... Пришёл поторопить своих подопечных в день выборов — никто идти не хочет. Он говорит: «Вам надо с нас пример брать — мы революцию делали»... А ему отвечают: «А кто вас просил революцию делать? Раньше лучше жилось...» Вся его революционная фразеология повисла в воздухе... (Мандельштам 1). ...Не [a former Party official] had taken on the job of giving political instruction in a Leningrad technical college....On one election day he had come to the college early to get all the students out to vote, but none of them wanted to. He said they should take an example from people like himself who had "made the Revolution."...To this they replied that nobody had asked him to make a revolution and that people had been better off before. This had left him speechless, and the whole of his "revolutionary" claptrap had been to no avail (1a).

В-209 • **МЫШИ́НАЯ ВОЗНЯ́ ⟨БЕГОТНЯ́, СУЕТА́, СУ́ТОЛОКА⟩** *disapprov* [NP; usu. subj or obj; usu. this WO] pursuit of trivial and/or vain interests accompanied by excessive bustle (and sometimes involving intriguing): **(one is wrapped up in etc) petty cares ⟨concerns⟩;** [in limited contexts] **petty scheming ⟨machinations⟩.**

Весь отдел занимается мышиной вознёй: один добывает путёвку в санаторий, другой — прибавку к зарплате, третий интригует против начальника... Работа, естественно, стоит. The whole department is wrapped up in petty concerns: this one is trying to get a pass to a health resort, that one—a salary increase, a third is plotting against the boss....Naturally, work is at a standstill. ♦ В прошлом году от него [романа Пастернака] отказался «Новый мир». Котов собирался его печатать в Гослитиздате, но умер, а остальным не до этого — все заняты мышиной карьеристской вознёй (Гладков 1). The previous year it [Pasternak's novel] had been turned down by *Novy Mir*. Kotov had been going to publish it in the State Publishing House for Literature, *Goslitizdat*, but had died, and all the rest of the people there had no time at all for it—they were too busy with their petty careerist scheming (1a).

В-210 • **ВХОДИ́ТЬ/ВОЙТИ́ ⟨ВСТУПА́ТЬ/ВСТУПИ́ТЬ⟩ В ВО́ЗРАСТ ⟨В ГОДА́, В ЛЕТА́⟩** *obs* [VP; subj: human] to become mature, develop into an adult: X вошёл в возраст ≃ **X came of age; X reached maturity ⟨adulthood, manhood, womanhood⟩; X grew to manhood ⟨womanhood⟩.**

В-211 • **ВЫХОДИ́ТЬ/ВЫ́ЙТИ ИЗ ВО́ЗРАСТА ⟨ИЗ ЛЕТ⟩** [VP; subj: human] to exceed the age limit (when one is eligible to enroll in sth., able to perform a certain job, required to serve in a certain capacity etc): X вышел из возраста ≃ **X is overage; X is past ⟨over⟩ the age limit; X is too old (for sth.);** [in limited contexts] **X is past the age of eligibility.**

В-212 • **НА ВО́ЗРАСТЕ** *obs* [PrepP; Invar; subj-compl with copula (subj: human, usu. female)] one is an adult, has reached maturity: X на возрасте ≃ **X is a grown woman ⟨man⟩; X has come of age.**

В-213 • **ЧТО С ВО́ЗУ ⟨-а⟩ УПА́ЛО, ТО (И) ПРОПА́ЛО** [saying] what happened in the past cannot be changed, what is lost or gone will not be returned: ≃ **it's no use ⟨there's no use (in), there's no point (in), what's the use of, what's the use in⟩ crying over spilt ⟨spilled⟩ milk; what's done is done.**

«...Не думаешь с женой жить?» — «Давнишний сказ... отгутарили [*regional*, here = уже обсудили]...» — «Не думаешь, стал[о] быть?» — «Стал[о] быть, так... что с возу упало, то пропало» (Шолохов 2). "...You're not thinking of living with your wife?" "That's an old story....It's all over and done with." "So you won't?" "So I won't....What's the use of crying over spilt milk" (2a). ♦ [Ананий:] ...Какой бы там внутри червяк ни сидел, всё прощаю и забываю; ну, по пословице, что с возу упало, то пропало, — не воротишь! (Писемский 1). [A.:] ...No matter what's eating me up inside, I try to forgive and forget; as they say: "What's done is done; you can't bring back the past!" (1a).

В-214 • **НЕДО́РОГО ⟨НЕ ДО́РОГО⟩ ВОЗЬМЁТ** *coll* [VP; subj: human; not used in the 1st pers; fut only; usu. used after another verb (in pfv fut or infin); fixed WO] one will do sth. (sth. bad, reprehensible, as denoted by the preceding verb) readily, without hesitation: X сделает Y — недорого возьмёт ≃ **X won't ⟨wouldn't⟩ think twice about doing Y; it won't ⟨wouldn't⟩ take much to make X do Y ⟨to get X to do Y⟩.**

[Телятев:] Хотите, с миллионщиком познакомлю? [Надежда Антоновна:] Да ты... и солгать не дорого возьмёшь (Островский 4). [T.:] May I introduce you to a millionaire? [N.A.:] Oh...it doesn't take much to make *you* lie (4a).

В-215 • **ЧЬЯ ВОЗЬМЁТ** *coll* [VP_subj; usu. fut, occas. past; fixed WO] who will achieve victory: **who'll ⟨who's going to⟩ win**

(out); who'll come out ahead; who'll win the day; who'll get the upper hand; who'll hold the winning card; [in limited contexts] who is the better man.

«Это ещё неизвестно, чья возьмёт», — бормочет фотограф... (Искандер 4). "No one knows yet who's going to win out," the photographer murmurs... (4a). ♦ «Чья возьмёт на этот раз, мы ещё посмотрим», — сказал Дмитрий Алексеевич, угрожающе глядя в сторону (Дудинцев 1). "It remains to be seen who will get the upper hand this time," Dmitri said with a menacing look (1a). ♦ Чем виновата Раечка? Прибежала к нему [Михаилу] по первому слову — радостная, сияющая, на всё готова. А он начал... показывать Егорше свою власть над девкой. Вот, мол, какой я, грязный, небритый, нечёсаный, прямо с поля... а давай потягаемся — чья возьмёт? (Абрамов 1). What had Raechka done? She had come running to him [Mikhail] at his first word, happy, radiant, ready for anything. But he had started... showing Egorsha his power over the girl. Look at me: a dirty, unshaven, unkempt fellow straight off the field...but let's see which of us is the better man! (1a).

В-216 • ЧТО ВОЗЬМЁШЬ ⟨ВЗЯТЬ⟩ *с кого-чего coll, often condes* [VP; pfv fut, gener. 2nd pers sing возьмёшь (1st var.) or impers predic (2nd var.); these forms only; fixed WO] (the behavior, action, statement in question) is typical (of s.o.), one cannot expect anything better (from s.o.): что с Х-а возьмёшь? ≃ **what (else) could ⟨can⟩ you expect from X?; what do you expect from X?**

Когда ибанцы [nonce word] узнали (с разрешения начальства, разумеется), что китайцы на стены домов и заборы вешают листки со всякого рода хвалебными критическими заметками, называемые дадзыбао, они надрывались от хохота... Впрочем, что с них взять! (Зиновьев 1). When the people of Ibansk discovered (with, of course, the permission of the authorities) that the Chinese covered their walls and fences with placards carrying all kinds of criticism or eulogies, called Da-Tsi-Bao, they went into hoots of laughter....What else could you expect from the Chinese! (1a). ♦ ...Не было в этих коротких словах ни злости, ни обиды на сына, оставившего её без крова и хлеба, — один... всепрощающий смысл: мол, такой он у меня уродился, что с него взять?! (Распутин 4). ...There was no anger or bitterness in those brief words against her son, who had left her without shelter or bread—only...[an] all-forgiving meaning: that's the way he was born to me, what can you expect from him? (4a).

В-217 • ОТКУ́ДА НИ ВОЗЬМИ́СЬ *появился, выбежал, выскочил и т. п. coll* [AdvP; Invar; adv; most often used with verbs in pfv past; fixed WO] (a person or thing appears etc) totally unexpectedly, from an unknown place or source: **(from) out of the blue; (from) out of nowhere; out of a ⟨the⟩ clear blue sky; all of a sudden, (from) out of nowhere.**

Иногда на своём пути встречаешь доброго человека, и он возникает неожиданно, откуда ни возьмись, словно вестник, чтобы сказать: держись, ещё не всё потеряно, голову выше — уныние запрещено... (Мандельштам 2). Now and then you run into a kind person, someone who suddenly appears when you least expect it, like a messenger out of the blue telling you all is not lost, to hold your head high and never despair (2a). ♦ ...Откуда ни возьмись, у чугунной решётки вспыхнул огонёчек и стал приближаться к веранде (Булгаков 9). ...A little light flared up from out of nowhere near the wrought-iron fence and floated toward the veranda (9a). ♦ Настроение у них [шофёров] было отличное — погода неплохая, а тут ещё, откуда ни возьмись, какой-то ушастый и головастый сорванец выбегает навстречу каждой машине, ошалев от дикой радости (Айтматов 1). The drivers were in a pleasant mood—the weather was fine, and here, all of a sudden, out of nowhere, came this lop-eared, roundheaded kid, meeting every truck as though crazed with joy (1a).

В-218 • ДА́РОМ НЕ ВОЗЬМУ́ *кого-чего or что;* **ДА́РОМ НЕ НА́ДО ⟨НЕ НУ́ЖНО⟩** *кому кого-чего all coll, derog* [VP, subj: human, fut only (1st var.); impers predic with быть∅, usu. pres (variants with не надо, не нужно); usu. this WO] one does not want or need s.o. or sth. at all: X-у Y-a даром не надо ≃ **X wouldn't have ⟨take⟩ Y as a gift; X wouldn't take Y (even) if you paid X.**

«Нет, я больше молодых люблю... Помню, я завучем был на Кубани, в Тбилисской, станица такая есть, литературу вёл в седьмом, так от меня полкласса беременными ходили... А учительницы эти у меня во где, даром не надо, лучше онанизмом заниматься буду» (Максимов 2). "No, I like 'em young....When I was principal of a village school at a place called Tbilisskaya in the Kuban, I taught literature to the seventh grade and half the class was pregnant by me....But as for the women teachers, I couldn't stand them, wouldn't have 'em as a gift—I'd rather masturbate" (2a).

В-219 • КАК ВОЛ *работать, трудиться coll* [как + NP; nom only; adv] (to work) excessively, indefatigably: **(work) like an ox ⟨a horse, a mule, a dog⟩.**

«...Я так требую с мужиков, как нигде. У меня работай — первое... Я и сам работаю как вол, и мужики у меня...» (Гоголь 3). "...I demand of my peasants more than anyone else does. Work comes first with me....I myself work like an ox and my peasants do the same..." (3a). ♦ [Войницкий:] Я обожал этого профессора, этого жалкого подагрика, я работал на него как вол! (Чехов 3). [V.:] I adored that Professor, that miserable, gouty nonentity; I worked for him like a horse (3b).

В-220 • ВОЛА́ ВЕРТЕ́ТЬ ⟨КРУТИ́ТЬ⟩ *substand, disapprov* [VP; subj: human; usu. neg imper or infin with брось(те), хватит etc; usu. this WO] to speak nonsensically, assert sth. ridiculous intentionally: X вола вертит ≃ **X talks (a lot of) nonsense ⟨rubbish⟩; X spins (person Y) a yarn; X talks through his hat.**

«Что касается Криворучко, — сказал Саша, — то на бюро я рассказал про случай с лопатами». — «Какие лопаты?» — перебил его Столпер. — «Лопаты на стройке, кладовщика не было...» — «Не крутите вола! — рассвирепел Столпер. — Отвечайте: почему вы защищали Криворучко?» (Рыбаков 2). "As far as Krivoruchko is concerned, I told the committee meeting about the problem with the shovels." "What shovels?" Stolper broke in. "Shovels, to work on the building, the storekeeper wasn't there—" "Stop talking rubbish," Stolper interrupted him savagely. "Answer the question—why did you defend Krivoruchko?" (2a).

В-221 • ПО СВОЕ́Й ⟨ПО ДО́БРОЙ⟩ ВО́ЛЕ [PrepP; these forms only; adv; fixed WO] voluntarily: **of one's own free will; of one's own accord ⟨volition⟩;** ‖ *Neg* не по своей воле ≃ **against one's will ⟨wishes⟩; under duress.**

Люди разделились на два лагеря: на уходящих и на остающихся. Первые, независимо от того, уходили ли они по доброй воле или по принуждению, считали себя героями (Лившиц 1). People were divided into two camps: those who were leaving and those who were staying behind. The former, independent of whether they were leaving of their own free will or by coercion, considered themselves to be heroes (1a).

В-222 • ВОЛЕ́Й-НЕВО́ЛЕЙ [AdvP; Invar; adv] regardless of whether desired or not: **willy-nilly; like it or not; have no choice but to...**

Марлен Михайлович... знал, что звуки, исторгнутые «Видным лицом», волей-неволей нарушат общее молчание... (Аксёнов 7). He [Marlen Mikhailovich] knew that the Important Personage, by producing the slightest sound, would willy-nilly break the others' silence... (7a). ♦ Волей-неволей ему [Кузьме] приходилось... постоянно думать об одном и том же: где достать деньги? (Распутин 1). Like it or not, he [Kuzma] was forced to think of only one thing: where could he get money? (1a). ♦ ...Она [Анисья] не управится одна, и Агафья Матвеевна, волей-неволей, сама работает на кухне... (Гончаров 1). She [Anisya] could not manage alone, and Agafya Matveyevna had no choice but to work in the kitchen herself... (1b).

< Loan translation of the Latin *volens nolens*, which is also used in Russian both in its Latin form and in transliteration.

В-223 • ВО́ЛЕЮ СУДЬБЫ́ ⟨СУДЕ́Б⟩; ПО ВО́ЛЕ СУДЬБЫ́ ⟨СУДЕ́Б⟩ *all lit* [NP_instrum or PrepP; these forms only; sent adv; fixed WO] as a result of circumstances (over which one has no control): **by the will ⟨the hand⟩ of fate; as fate (has) willed; as the fates (have) decreed; (one ⟨s.o.⟩ has been) fated (to do sth.); it is one's ⟨s.o.'s⟩ fate (to do sth.).**

Оказавшись волею судеб первыми свидетелями внеземной общественной жизни, мы испытываем сложные чувства... (Айтматов 2). Since we have been fated to be the first to see an extraterrestrial civilization... we are experiencing complicated reactions... (2a). ♦ [Андрей:] ...Это и был предел ваших мечтаний? [Маша:] Конечно, нет... Но волею судеб я стала фотографом, и мне нравится эта работа (Розов 1). [A.:] Well, is being a photographer the height of your ambition? [M.:] Of course not....It was my fate to become one. But I like it now... (1a).

В-224 • ВОЛК В ОВЕ́ЧЬЕЙ ШКУ́РЕ *coll, disapprov* [NP; usu. subj-compl with copula, nom or instrum (subj: human); fixed WO] a person who has evil intentions but covers them up, appears harmless or friendly: **wolf in sheep's clothing.**

Мы «злые», лишь по недоразумению восхитившие наименование «добрых». Мы волки в овечьей шкуре (Салтыков-Щедрин 2). It was we who were "the wicked" who merely appropriated the name of "the good" owing to a misunderstanding. We were the wolves in sheep's clothing (2a).

< Russian source: the Bible (Matt. 7:15); English source: Aesop's fables and the Bible.

В-225 • КАК ВОЛК голоден *coll* [как + NP; nom only; modif (intensif)] very (hungry): **(hungry) as a wolf ⟨a bear⟩.**

«Разве что на дороге случилось?» — «Ничего не случилось... так, замешкались немного. Зато мы теперь голодны как волки» (Тургенев 2). "Did anything happen on the road?" "Nothing happened...we were rather slow. But we're as hungry as wolves now" (2b).

В-226 • МОРСКО́Й ВОЛК *coll* [NP; usu. subj-compl with copula, nom or instrum (subj: human, male) or obj; fixed WO] an experienced sailor: **sea dog ⟨sea-dog⟩; old salt.**

«...Меня окрестили здесь морским волком, а меня тошнит, когда я проезжаю мостом через Эльбу...» (Федин 1). "...They've called me a sea-dog here, but it makes me sick to cross the bridge over the Elbe..." (1a).

В-227 • ТРА́ВЛЕНЫЙ ⟨СТА́РЫЙ, СТРЕ́ЛЯНЫЙ⟩ ВОЛК; ТРА́ВЛЕНЫЙ ЗВЕРЬ *all coll* [NP; often subj-compl with copula, nom or instrum (subj: human, usu. male); fixed WO] a man who has been through much adversity, survived many dangers, and acquired much experience in life: **old hand; (one) has seen it all; [in limited contexts] (one is) battle-scarred; (one) has been there and back.**

В-228 • КАК ⟨СКО́ЛЬКО⟩ ВО́ЛКА НИ КОРМИ́, (А) ОН (ВСЁ) В ЛЕС СМО́ТРИТ ⟨ГЛЯДИ́Т⟩ [saying] no matter how you try to change s.o., win s.o. over, his true nature, feelings, habits etc will surface: ≃ **a leopard cannot change its spots; once a wolf always a wolf; nature is stronger than nurture; what is bred in the bone will come out in the flesh.**

В-229 • С ВОЛКА́МИ ЖИТЬ – ПО-ВО́ЛЧЬИ ВЫТЬ [saying] a person should adapt himself to the habits and customs of those in whose society he finds himself: ≃ **he that lives with the wolves learns to howl; when in Rome, do as the Romans do.**

Как въехали они в нашу квартиру — Николай Николаевич с Ниночкой, я им сразу сказал: «Коля! — говорю, — Ниночка! держите ухо востро. Не поддавайтесь на провокацию. Живите как в отдалении. А я возле вас погреюсь на старости лет». – «Нет! — отвечает Ниночка. — С волками жить — по-волчьи выть» (Терц 5). When they moved into our apartment—Nikolay Nikolayevich and Ninochka, that is—I told them at once: "Nicky," I said, "Ninochka! Keep your ears open. Don't give in to provocation. Keep your distance. And I'll warm myself at your hearth in my old age." "No!" Ninochka answered. "When in Rome, do as the Romans do" (5a).

В-230 • И ВО́ЛКИ СЫ́ТЫ, И О́ВЦЫ ЦЕ́ЛЫ [saying; often used as a subord clause introduced by чтобы] sth. satisfies both parties involved, both opposing sides (usu. said in situations when a person is trying to please two people or parties with different interests or views): ≃ **the wolves are sated and the sheep intact; we ⟨you etc⟩ have pleased everyone; we ⟨you etc⟩ have managed to keep everyone happy; Peter has been paid without robbing Paul.**

[Мамаев:] В какие отношения ты поставил себя к тётке? [Глумов:] Я человек благовоспитанный, учтивости меня учить не надо. [Мамаев:] Ну, вот и глупо... Женщины не прощают тому, кто не замечает их красоты... [Ты] имеешь больше свободы, чем просто знакомый; можешь иногда... лишний раз ручку поцеловать. Она женщина темперамента сангвинического... очень легко может увлечься каким-нибудь франтом... А тут, понимаешь ты... свой, испытанный человек. И волки сыты, и овцы целы (Островский 9). [M.:] What are your relations with your aunt? [G.:] I have had a proper upbringing, it is not necessary to teach me how to respect my elders. [M.:] Poppycock!...Women never forgive a person for not noticing their beauty....You can take more liberties than just an acquaintance. Might kiss her hand an extra time or so....Your aunt, she's very temperamental...she could easily fall for some dandy....But you, you're one of the family, one to be trusted. In this way the wolves are sated and the sheep intact (9b). ♦ «Мы всё хотим, чтоб и волки были сытые, и овцы целые, а Каледин, он не так думает. Нами перехвачен приказ об аресте всех участников вот этого съезда» (Шолохов 3). "We want to please everyone, but that's not what Kaledin wants. We've just intercepted his order that everyone taking part in this congress is to be arrested" (3a). ♦ Несколько зная язык, он писал статью начерно, оставляя пробелы, вкрапливая русские фразы и требуя от Фёдора Константиновича дословного перевода своих передовичных словец: ...пришла беда – растворяй ворота, и волки сыты, и овцы целы... (Набоков 1). Having a smattering of the language, he wrote his article out in rough, with gaps and Russian phrases interspersed, and demanded from Fyodor a literal translation of the usual phrases found in leaders: ...troubles never come singly, Peter's been paid without robbing Paul... (1a).

В-231 • ВОЛКО́В БОЯ́ТЬСЯ – В ЛЕС НЕ ХОДИ́ТЬ [saying] once you are determined to do sth., you must not let impending difficulties or risks deter you (said to encourage o.s. or another person when undertaking a dangerous or unknown affair involving risk): ≃ **if you're going to play with matches ⟨fire⟩, you can't be afraid of getting burned; nothing ventured, nothing gained; risk nothing, win nothing.**

В-232 • ВО́ЛКОМ ВЫТЬ/ВЗВЫТЬ *coll* [VP; subj: human; fixed WO] to complain bitterly (about one's suffering, hardships): X волком взвоет ≃ **X will start howling; X will ⟨thing Y will make X⟩ moan and groan.**

[75]

B-233 • СМОТРЕ́ТЬ ⟨ГЛЯДЕ́ТЬ⟩ ВО́ЛКОМ (на кого) *coll* [VP; subj: human] to look (at s.o.) angrily, in a hostile way: X (на Y-а) волком смотрит ≃ **X scowls ⟨glowers, glares⟩ (at Y); X looks daggers at Y; X gives ⟨keeps giving⟩ Y dirty ⟨nasty⟩ looks.**

…Администратор смотрел на меня волком, пока я, как бы извиняясь за свой «запорожец», не подарил ему пачку венгерских фломастеров (Войнович 1). The head clerk scowled at me until, in apology for my Zaporozhets, I gave him a package of Hungarian felt-tip pens as a present (1a). ♦ «Так вот ты… запер его [полицмейстера], беднягу, в сортирной кабинке, припёр дверцу метлой и не выпускал…» – «Серьёзно? – сказал Виктор. – Ну и ну. То-то он сегодня на меня весь день волком смотрит» (Стругацкие 1). "What happened…is that you backed him [the police chief] into the toilet. Then you barricaded the door with a broom and refused to let him out…" "No kidding," said Viktor. "How do you like that? No wonder he's been giving me dirty looks all day" (1a). ♦ Если бы [священник] сопротивлялся, если бы пробовал блажить, если бы, наконец, хоть смотрел волком, Андрею было бы куда легче (Максимов 3). If the priest had resisted, or put on an act, or even given him a nasty look, Andrei would have felt much better (3a).

B-234 • ХОТЬ ВО́ЛКОМ ВОЙ *coll* [хоть + VP$_{imper}$; Invar; predic or subord clause; fixed WO] (used to express despair, hopelessness, impotence) (it is) an intolerable, untenable situation: **it's enough to make you ⟨a grown man⟩ cry; you could just scream; it's more than one can bear ⟨take⟩.**

B-235 • ДО СЕДЫ́Х ВОЛО́С (дожить и т. п.) [PrepP; Invar; adv; fixed WO] (of a person) (to have lived etc) until old age: **till one goes ⟨grows⟩ gray; till one's hair turns ⟨begins to turn⟩ gray; into (one's) old age.**

«Что ж, тебе не хотелось бы так пожить?»… – «И весь век так?» – спросил Штольц. – До седых волос, до гробовой доски. Это жизнь!» (Гончаров 1). "Now, wouldn't you like to live like that?"…"To live like that all the time?" "Till you grow gray—till you are laid in the grave! That is life!" (1b). ♦ …Сам [Тарантьев] как двадцать пять лет назад определился в какую-то канцелярию писцом, так в этой должности и дожил до седых волос (Гончаров 1). …Having entered a government office as a clerk some twenty-five years earlier, he [Tarantyev] had remained in the same job till his hair began to turn gray (1b).

B-236 • НА ВО́ЛОС; НА ВОЛОСО́К *both obs* [PrepP; these forms only] **1.** [adv or modif; often preceded by хоть] (even) a little: **(even) the slightest ⟨tiniest⟩ bit; (even) in the slightest way;** [in limited contexts] **(even) by a hairbreadth ⟨a hairsbreadth** etc⟩.

«…Захочу ли я хоть на волос стеснять твою жизнь, твои привычки?» (Тургенев 2). "…Would I want to interfere, even in the slightest way, with your life, with your habits?" (2d). ♦ …Штольц не мог уловить у ней на лице и в словах… даже искры чувства, которое хоть бы на волос выходило за границы тёплой, сердечной, но обыкновенной дружбы (Гончаров 1). …Stolz was unable to detect in her face or her words…a spark of feeling which by a hairbreadth exceeded the limits of warm, affectionate, but ordinary friendship (1b).

2. [adv (intensif); used with negated verbs] not at all: **not the slightest ⟨tiniest⟩ bit; not in the least ⟨the slightest⟩; not a bit ⟨an inch⟩;** [in limited contexts] **not by (so much as) a hairbreadth.**

B-237 • НИ НА́ ВОЛОС; НИ НА ВОЛОСО́К *both coll* [PrepP; these forms only; adv (intensif); used with negated verbs] not at all: **not the slightest ⟨tiniest⟩ bit; not in the least ⟨the slightest⟩; not a bit ⟨an inch⟩;** [in limited contexts] **not by (so much as) a hairbreadth ⟨a hairsbreadth** etc⟩.

Стряпала [Маргарита Антоновна] строго по рецептам, как иногда делают это мужчины, не отступая ни на волос от предписанных норм… (Грекова 3). She [Margarita Antonovna] cooked strictly by the recipes, the way men sometimes do, not deviating an inch… (3a). ♦ …Надя воспитывала в себе последовательность: не отклонять с пути Володю ни на волосок — так ни на волосок (Солженицын 5). …Nadya had schooled herself to follow rigid rules. Volodya must not be deflected from his path by so much as a hairbreadth (5a). ♦ «Я — по закону-с! Не отступая-с… ни на шаг-с… ни на волос-с!» (Салтыков-Щедрин 2). "I'm acting according to law! Without deviating by a single step…not by a hair's breadth, sir!" (2a).

B-238 • НЕ ТРО́НУТЬ ВОЛОСКА́ чьего, у кого *obs, coll* [VP; subj: human] not to cause s.o. any harm, not injure or hit s.o.: X не тронет Y-ова волоска ≃ **X won't touch ⟨harm, hurt⟩ a hair of Y's head.**

«Нет, дитя моё, никто не тронет волоска твоего. Ты вырастешь на славу отчизны…» (Гоголь 5). "No, my child, no one shall touch a hair of your head. You shall grow up to the glory of your fatherland…"(5a).

B-239 • ВИСЕ́ТЬ ⟨ДЕРЖА́ТЬСЯ⟩/ПОВИ́СНУТЬ НА ВОЛОСКЕ́ ⟨НА НИ́ТОЧКЕ, НА НИ́ТКЕ⟩ [VP; subj: human or abstr, often жизнь; if subj: human, usu. one's life or career is involved] to be in a perilous position or condition, be threatened by imminent danger, ruin, or death: X висит на волоске ≃ **X is hanging by a thread; person X is within a hairbreadth ⟨a hairsbreadth** etc⟩ **of death; person X is on the brink of death;** [in limited contexts] **X is within a hairbreadth of disaster ⟨ruin⟩; X is on the brink of disaster ⟨ruin⟩; thing X is touch and go.**

Долгое время жизнь князя висела на волоске (Окуджава 2). His [the prince's] life hung by a thread for a long time (2a). ♦ «Жить в городе стало невозможно, скажите спасибо вашему Голему — кстати, вы знаете, что Голем — скрытый коммунист?.. Да-да, уверяю вас, есть материалы… он на ниточке висит, ваш Голем…» (Стругацкие 1). "It's impossible to live in this town, for which you can say thank you to your buddy Golem—incidentally, are you aware of his Communist leanings? Yes, I assure you, we have evidence; he's hanging by a thread, your Golem" (1a). ♦ [Елена Федотовна:] Ты обострил с ним отношения?.. Ах, молчишь… Ты повис на волоске! (Салынский 1). [E.F.:] You've spoilt your relations with him? Why don't you answer?…You are on the brink of disaster! (1a). ♦ …Мне претила ложь и скука старой семьи, и я участвовала в её разрушении. Выход я нашла в свободном союзе. Случайно мой путь удался, но всё всегда висело на волоске (Мандельштам 2). …Repelled by the hypocrisy and tedium of conventional family life, I helped to undermine it…by seeking my own solution in a free union based on love, not marriage. It so happens that in my particular case it succeeded—though it was very much always touch and go (2a).

< From the story of Damocles, courtier of the Syracusan tyrant Dionysius in classical mythology. At a banquet, Dionysius had Damocles seated under a sword suspended by a single hair to show him how precarious power and the ruler's happiness were.

B-240 • НА ВОЛОСО́К ⟨НА ВОЛОСКЕ́, НА ВО́ЛОС *obs*⟩ от чего [PrepP; these forms only; subj-compl with copula (subj: usu. human or collect; prep obj: usu. от смерти, от гибели etc); usu. used with past verbs] one is very close (to death, ruin etc) (if used with a past-form verb, refers to danger or trouble that one has managed to avoid): X был на волосок от Y-а ≃ **X was within a hairbreadth ⟨a hairsbreadth** etc, **an inch, a whisker⟩ of Y; X was a hairbreadth away (from Y); X escaped Y by a hairbreadth ⟨by the skin of X's teeth⟩; X was on the verge (of Y).**

Ужасной была поездка в Москву по вызову Ярославского. Вот когда я была на волосок от самоубийства! (Гинзбург 1). The journey back to Moscow at Yaroslavsky's summons was terrible. I was within a hair's breadth of suicide (1a). ♦ ...Из парадного вынесли Ольгу, покрытую, как покойница, клеймёной больничной простынёй, и... Лёва, враз забыв обо всём, судорожно потянулся к сестре: «Олюшка, как же это ты?» ...Но [врач] взял актёра за пуговицу плаща: «Вам, милый, не следует здесь находиться. Вы сами на волосок от этого. Максимум покоя, минимум – эмоций» (Максимов 3). ...They carried Olga out of the main door, covered with a stenciled hospital sheet, as though she were dead....Lyova became oblivious of everything else and drifted after his sister, shaking convulsively. "Olga, little sister, what is happening to you?"...[The doctor] took hold of the actor by a button on his raincoat. "You shouldn't be here, my dear man. You're on the verge yourself. Maximum of quiet, minimum of excitement..." (3a).

B-241 • ВО́ЛОСЫ СТАНО́ВЯТСЯ/СТА́ЛИ ⟨ВСТАЮ́Т/ ВСТА́ЛИ, ПОДНИМА́ЮТСЯ/ПОДНЯЛИ́СЬ⟩ ДЫ́-БОМ (у кого от чего or при виде чего) coll [VP$_{subj}$] s.o. experiences intense fear, horror (caused by sth.): у Х-а волосы стали дыбом (от Y-а) ≃ **Y made X's hair stand on end; X's hair stood on end;** [in limited contexts] **it was enough to make X's hair stand on end; Y filled X with horror.**

[Городничий:] О, я знаю вас: вы если начнёте говорить о сотворении мира, просто волосы дыбом поднимаются (Гоголь 4). [Mayor:] Oh, I know you. When you start talking about the creation of the world, it makes my hair stand on end (4c). ♦ ...Шесть месяцев её связи с Комаровским превысили меру Лариного терпения. Он... тонко и незаметно напоминал ей о её поругании. Эти напоминания приводили Лару в то именно смятение, которое требуется сластолюбцу от женщины. Смятение это отдавало Лару во всё больший плен чувственного кошмара, от которого у неё вставали волосы дыбом при отрезвлении (Пастернак 1). ...Six months of Lara's liaison with Komarovsky had driven her beyond the limits of her endurance. He...subtly reminded her of her shame. These reminders brought her to just that state of confusion that a lecher requires in a woman. As a result, Lara felt herself sinking ever deeper into a nightmare of sensuality which filled her with horror whenever she awoke from it (1a).

B-242 • ПРИТЯ́ГИВАТЬ/ПРИТЯНУ́ТЬ ЗА ВО́ЛОСЫ ⟨ЗА́ ВОЛОСЫ, ЗА́ УШИ⟩ что [VP; subj: human; usu. short-form past passive Part; usu. this WO] to introduce or try to use sth. (usu. an argument or example) that is completely unrelated to the matter in question: Y притянут за волосы ≃ **Y is forced ⟨contrived, extraneous, far-fetched⟩; Y has no bearing (upon this issue ⟨this case etc⟩);** ‖ X притягивает Y-и за волосы ≃ **X is bringing in extraneous Ys; X is forcing ⟨pushing⟩ it.**

B-243 • РВАТЬ ⟨ДРАТЬ substand⟩ НА СЕБЕ́ ВО́ЛОСЫ coll [VP; subj: human; often fut or infin with готов, должен] to experience utter despair or become very angry with o.s. (often after having realized that undesirable consequences of sth. could have been avoided): X рвёт на себе волосы ≃ **X is tearing his hair (out); X is tearing out his hair;** [in limited contexts] **X could kick himself.**

[author's usage] Блудов велел, чтоб каждое губернское правление издавало свои «Ведомости» и чтоб каждая «Ведомость» имела свою неофициальную часть для статей исторических, литературных и проч. Сказано – сделано, и вот пятьдесят губернских правлений рвут себе волосы над неофициальной частью (Герцен 1). ...Bludov commanded every provincial government to publish its own newspaper, which was to have an unofficial part for articles on historical, literary, and other subjects. No sooner said than done, and the officials in fifty provinces were tearing their hair over this unofficial part (1a). ♦ Когда два-три часа назад

ей сказали, что Митрий лежит у зарода на Марьиных лугах — отощал, идти не может, — Марфа готова была волосы рвать на себе. Господи! За что ей ещё такое наказание? (Абрамов 1). A few hours earlier, when they had told her that Mitry was lying by the hayrick in Mariny Luga, emaciated and unable to walk, Marfa had been ready to tear out her hair. God! Not another cross to bear! (1a).

B-244 • ВЕРТЕ́ТЬСЯ ВОЛЧКО́М [VP] 1. [subj: concr] to rotate without stopping: X вертелся волчком ≃ **X was spinning like a top.**

Он два раза испытал это страшное мучительное чувство страха смерти... Первый раз он испытал это чувство тогда, когда граната волчком вертелась перед ним и он смотрел на жнивьё, на кусты, на небо и знал, что перед ним была смерть (Толстой 7). Twice he had experienced that agonizing feeling, the dread of death....The first time he had felt it was when the shell had spun like a top in front of him, and he had looked at the stubble field, at the bushes, and the sky, and knew that he was face to face with death (7a).

2. [subj: human] to be in constant motion (while standing or sitting in one place): X вертится волчком ≃ **X can't hold ⟨stand, sit⟩ still;** [in limited contexts] **X is fidgety; X has ants in his pants.**

3. [subj: human] to bustle, busy o.s. without taking any time to sit down and rest: X вертится волчком ≃ **X is (always) buzzing about ⟨around⟩; X is (always) on the go ⟨the run⟩; X is (always) running around (like crazy); X is (always) busy as a bee.**

[Лебедев:] В наше время, бывало, день-деньской с лекциями бьёшься, а как только настал вечер, идёшь прямо куда-нибудь на огонь и до самой зари волчком вертишься... (Чехов 4). [L.:] Now, in our time you'd sweat away at your lectures all day long, then you'd make for the bright lights in the evening and buzz around till the crack of dawn (4b).

B-245 • КАК ⟨БУ́ДТО, СЛО́ВНО, ТО́ЧНО⟩ ПО ВОЛ-ШЕБСТВУ́ [как etc + PrepP; these forms only; adv] in a miraculous way: **as if by magic ⟨a miracle⟩;** [in limited contexts] **(appear) as if out of nowhere.**

Я до сих пор не могу привыкнуть к компьютеру: нажимаешь клавишу — и, как по волшебству, сразу же получаешь нужные тебе данные. I still can't get used to computers: you hit a key and, as if by magic, get the data you need instantly.

B-246 • ТЯНУ́ТЬ ⟨РАЗВОДИ́ТЬ⟩ ВОЛЫ́НКУ highly coll, disapprov [VP; subj: human] to act very slowly, procrastinate in dealing with s.o. or sth.: X тянет волынку ≃ **X is dragging things ⟨it⟩ out; X is dragging his feet;** [in limited contexts] **X is stalling; X is taking his own sweet time (about thing Y ⟨it⟩).**

«...Аркашка с ней [Ириной] долго канителиться не будет, поиграет и прогонит... Он ведь не в отца, не такой, чтобы тянуть волынку годами!» (Залыгин 1). "Arkady won't waste much time on her [Irina]. He'll have his bit of fun then kick her out....He doesn't take after his father, he won't drag it out for years" (1a).

B-247 • БРАТЬ/ВЗЯТЬ ВО́ЛЮ obs [VP; subj: human; can be used with infin of another verb] to behave willfully, inconsiderately toward others: X взял волю ≃ **X took liberties with person Y; X made free with person Y; X became impudent; X was being insolent;** [in limited contexts] **X bossed person Y around ⟨about⟩.**

«...Сестра она вам не родная, а сведённая, а вот какую волю взяла» (Достоевский 3). "She's not your real sister, only a stepsister, and look how she bosses you about" (3a).

B-248 • ДАВА́ТЬ/ДАТЬ ВО́ЛЮ [VP; subj: human] 1. ~ кому to allow s.o. to act, behave as he chooses: X дал волю Y-у

≃ **X gave free ⟨full⟩ rein to Y;** ‖ дай Y-у волю [used as condit] ≃ **if Y could; if Y had the opportunity; (if) given the chance, Y would…; if you ⟨we etc⟩ let Y have Y's way;** ‖ Х дал себе волю ≃ **X let himself go; X gave in to himself.**

[Неля (задумчиво):] Дай мне волю, я бы убила вас (Арбузов 2). [N. (thoughtfully):] I'd kill you, if I could (2a). ♦ [Джульбарс,] свирепейший [из псов], дай только волю, наверняка бы загрыз какого-нибудь лагерника насмерть… (Владимов 1). [The dog] Djulbars, the fiercest of the fierce, if given the chance, would no doubt have cheerfully bitten a prisoner to death (1a). ♦ «Много мы с вами, грабителями, понастроим, дай вам волю — всё бы разворовали» (Максимов 2). "A lot we'd get built if we let you robbers have your way—you'd pinch everything" (2a). ♦ [Войницкий:] Дайте себе волю хоть раз в жизни, влюбитесь поскорее в какого-нибудь водяного по самые уши… (Чехов 3). [V.:] Let yourself go for once in your life, fall head over heels in love with some water sprite… (3a). ♦ «Что ж это я в самом деле? — сказал он вслух с досадой, — надо совесть знать: пора за дело! Дай только себе волю, так и…» (Гончаров 1). "Now, what am I doing?" he said aloud, in annoyance. "Enough of this! Time to set to work! If one gives in to oneself…" (1b).

2. ~ *чему* [indir obj: usu. слезам, чувствам, переживаниям, мечтам etc] to allow for free expression of (one's emotions, occas. after having suppressed them), not to hold back (one's emotions, tears etc): Х дал волю Y-ам ≃ **X gave vent ⟨way⟩ to Ys; X gave free ⟨full⟩ rein to Ys;** [in limited contexts] **X let Ys get the better of him; X made no attempt to subdue ⟨suppress etc⟩ his Ys;** [in refer. to tears only] **X let his tears flow freely.**

Меня это взорвало… но в такой ситуации нельзя давать волю чувствам, надо сдерживать себя… (Рыбаков 1). I thought I would explode…but in a situation like that, you can't give vent to your feelings, you must control yourself… (1a). ♦ …Пушкари остановились на городской площади и решились дожидаться тут до свету. Многие присели на землю и дали волю слезам (Салтыков-Щедрин 1). …The cannoneers remained behind on the town square and decided to wait there till daylight. Many sat down on the ground and gave way to tears (1a). ♦ В самый день приезда в Яреськи всё было как будто хорошо. Чуть-чуть, возможно, напряжённо, но Вадим объяснял это тем, что мать боится дать волю своим чувствам (Некрасов 1). The first day in Yareski everything seemed to be all right. The atmosphere was possibly a little bit tense, but Vadim felt the explanation lay in what he imagined was his mother's reluctance to give free rein to her feelings (1a). ♦ «Нельзя давать такой воли тревожным мыслям» (Пастернак 1). "You mustn't let your worries get the better of you" (1a). ♦ Она побежала в свою комнату, заперлась и дала волю своим слезам… (Пушкин 1). She ran to her room, locked herself in, and let her tears flow freely… (1a).

B-249 • ДАВА́ТЬ/ДАТЬ ВО́ЛЮ КУЛАКА́М *coll* [VP; subj: human] to beat s.o. (unmercifully): Х даёт волю кулакам ≃ **X is free ⟨hasty⟩ with his fists; X lets fly ⟨loose⟩ with his fists;** ‖ *Neg Imper* кулакам воли не давай ≃ **keep your fists to yourself.**

[Городничий:] Да сказать Держиморде, чтобы не слишком давал воли кулакам своим (Гоголь 4). [Mayor:] And tell Derzhimorda not to be too free with his fists (4c). [Mayor:] And tell Constable Derzhimorda to keep his fists to himself (4e).

B-250 • ДАВА́ТЬ/ДАТЬ ВО́ЛЮ РУКА́М *coll* [VP; subj: human] **1.** to beat s.o. (unmercifully): Х даёт волю рукам ≃ **X is free ⟨hasty⟩ with his fists; X lets fly ⟨loose⟩ with his fists;** ‖ *Neg Imper* рукам воли не давай ≃ **keep your fists to yourself.**

Одно, что иногда мучило Николая по отношению к его хозяйничанию, это была его вспыльчивость в соединении с его старою гусарскою привычкой давать волю рукам. В первое время он не видел в этом ничего предосудительного, но на второй год своей женитьбы его взгляд на такого рода рас-

правы вдруг изменился (Толстой 7). One thing that plagued Nikolai in connection with his management of the estate was his quick temper together with the old hussar habit of being free with his fists. At first he saw nothing reprehensible in this, but in the second year of his marriage his opinion of this sort of chastisement suddenly changed (7a). ♦ [Скотинин (бросаясь на Митрофана):] Ох ты чушка проклятая!.. [Правдин (не допуская Скотинина):] Господин Скотинин! Рукам воли не давай! (Фонвизин 1). [S. (attacking Mitrofan):] Oh! You cursed pig! [P. (halting Skotinin):] Mr. Skotinin! Don't be too hasty with your fists! (1d).

2. [subj: usu. male] (usu. in refer. to a man's behavior toward a woman) to grab, touch, try to embrace s.o.: Х даёт волю рукам ≃ **X lets his hands wander; X puts his hands where they don't belong;** [in limited contexts] **X has his hands all over person Y.**

B-251 • ДАВА́ТЬ/ДАТЬ ВО́ЛЮ ЯЗЫКУ́ *coll* [VP; subj: human] to say more than one should, not restrain o.s.: Х дал волю языку ≃ **X gave free ⟨full⟩ rein to his tongue.**

Хлынувшие вслед за ним [Петром Житовым] из клуба бабы едва не сбили его с ног. А когда выбрались на твёрдую, накатанную дорогу, дали волю своим языкам (Абрамов 1). Pouring out of the club building after him [Pyotr Zhitov], the women nearly knocked him off his feet. Once they reached the hard-surfaced road they gave free rein to their tongues (1a).

B-252 • БУДЬ ⟨БЫЛА́ БЫ⟩ МОЯ́ ⟨твоя и т. п.⟩ ВО́ЛЯ; МОЯ́ ⟨твоя и т. п.⟩ БЫ ВО́ЛЯ [subord clause, condit; these forms only; fixed WO] if I (you etc) were to decide how the problem, matter in question would be handled: **if it were up to me ⟨you etc⟩; if I ⟨you etc⟩ had (it) my ⟨your etc⟩ way; if I ⟨you etc⟩ were in charge.**

…Была бы воля Ершова, он генералу Гудзю полком не доверил бы командовать, не то что корпусом (Гроссман 2). If it had been up to him, Yershov wouldn't have trusted Gudz with a regiment, let alone a whole corps (2a). ♦ «Хочу спросить, когда ты пирушку устраиваешь?»… — «Послезавтра», — сказал Тендел… «Теймыра думаешь звать?» — «Как же его не позвать, разрази его молния, сосед!» — «Правильно, зови его вместе с женой!» — «…Моя бы воля, я бы их в адское пекло пригласил!» (Искандер 5). "I wanted to ask, when are you having your party?"…"Day after tomorrow," Tendel said.…"Are you thinking of inviting Temyr?" "How can we help it, may he be struck by lightning! He's a neighbor!" "Right; invite him, and his wife too!"…"If I had my way, I'd invite them to hellfire!" (5a).

B-253 • ВО́ЛЬНОМУ ВО́ЛЯ *coll* [sent; Invar; fixed WO] (said—occas. with resignation—to or of a person when he acts or is about to act the way he wants to; often his behavior is considered imprudent or foolish by the speaker) one can do as he wishes: **one can ⟨may⟩ do as one likes ⟨pleases⟩; let one have it his ⟨her etc⟩ way; it's your ⟨his etc⟩ decision; to each his own;** [in limited contexts] **nobody is forcing you ⟨him etc⟩;** [when addressed to the hearer only] **do as you like; have it your way; suit yourself.**

Надев фартуки, мы перетирали фарш с водой… Я напоролся в фарше на что-то, порезался: кусочек полуды… «Люди будут есть?» — «Помалкивай. Вольному воля. Пусть не жрут» (Кузнецов 1). After putting on aprons, we kneaded the ground meat in water.…I struck on something in the ground meat and cut myself: a piece of tin.…"Are people going to eat that?" "Quiet. They can do as they like. They don't have to" (1a). ♦ «Я провожу тебя, если ты боишься, — сказал он ей, — ты мне позволишь идти подле себя?» — «А кто те [substand = тебе] мешает? — отвечала Лиза, — вольному воля, а дорога мирская» (Пушкин 3). "I'll accompany you if you're afraid," he said. "Allow me to walk beside you?" "Who's to stop you?" Lisa replied. "You may do as you please; anyone is free to use the road" (3b). ♦ «Пусть государь и его ближайшие слуги выдумывают уставы и определяют необходимый цвет исподнего, чтобы тем самым противостоять европейским заразам. Вольному воля» (Окуджава 2). "Let the tsar and his intimate servants dream up laws that determine the required color for underwear, thereby countering European infections. To each his own" (2a). ♦ ...Сойдясь в упор с недвижным взглядом хозяина, [Золотарёв] понял, что тот заранее отказывался долее слушать гостя. «Как знаешь, – выходя, замкнулся Золотарёв, – вольному воля!» (Максимов 1). ♦ ...Catching Matvei's motionless gaze [Zolotarev] realized that he had already decided not to listen to him any longer. "As you wish," he thought sullenly as he went out, "nobody's forcing you" (1a).

< Reduced version of the saying «Вольному воля, спасённому рай».

В-254 • **ВОЛЯ ВА́ША ⟨ТВОЯ́⟩** *coll* [these forms only] **1.** [indep. sent] (said in response to s.o.'s statement expressing or implying his intention to act in a certain way) you can do whatever you want to: **(do) as you wish ⟨please⟩; do as you like; it's up to you; suit yourself ⟨-selves⟩; have it your way.**

«Много ль за часы-то, Алёна Ивановна?»... – «Полтора рубля-с и процент вперёд, коли хотите-с». – «Полтора рубля!» – вскрикнул молодой человек. «Ваша воля». – И старуха протянула ему обратно часы (Достоевский 3). "Do I get much for the watch then, Alyona Ivanovna?"..."One and a half rubles with interest in advance, if you like." "One and a half rubles!" cried the young man. "It's up to you," and the old woman handed the watch back to him (3a).

2. [sent adv (usu. parenth); fixed WO] used to express the speaker's refusal to do what has been suggested or demanded; also used to express the speaker's disagreement with or objection to some statement, action etc that he considers unreasonable, ludicrous etc: **say what you will ⟨like, want⟩ (, but...); (you may ⟨can⟩) think what you will ⟨wish⟩ (, but...);** [in limited contexts] **that's all very well, but...**

Вот этого самого незнакомца в берете, воля ваша, Стёпа в своём кабинете вчера никак не видал (Булгаков 9). Say what you will, but Styopa had not seen this stranger in the beret at his office at all (9a). ♦ «Угодно вам заряжать?» – спросил Павел Петрович, вынимая из ящика пистолеты. «Нет; заряжайте вы, а я шаги отмеривать стану... Раз, два, три...» – «Евгений Васильич, – с трудом пролепетал Пётр (он дрожал, как в лихорадке), – воля ваша, я отойду». – «Четыре... пять... Отойди, братец, отойди...» (Тургенев 2). "Would you care to load?" inquired Pavel Petrovich, taking the pistols out of the box. "No, you load while I measure out the paces....One, two, three..." "Please sir," Piotr faltered with an effort (he was trembling as if he had fever) "say what you like, but I am going farther off." "Four...five...all right, move away, my good fellow, move away..." (3c). ♦ «Но только, воля ваша, здесь не мёртвые души, здесь скрывается что-то другое» (Гоголь 3). "You may think what you will, but this is not a matter of dead souls; there is something else behind all this" (3c). ♦ «...Намерен я тебя женить». – «На ком это, батюшка?» – спросил изумлённый Алексей. – «На Лизавете Григорьевне Муромской...» – «Воля ваша, Лиза Муромская мне вовсе не нравится». – «После понравится. Стерпится, слюбится» (Пушкин 3). "...I intend to get you a wife." "Who would that be, father?" asked the astonished Aleksei. "Lizaveta Grigorevna Muromskaia...." "That's all very well, but I don't like Liza Muromskaia in the least." "You'll grow to like her. Love comes with time" (3a).

В-255 • **ПОСЛЕ́ДНЯЯ ВО́ЛЯ** *чья, кого obsoles, lit* [NP; fixed WO] the expression of a person's final wishes before his death: **last will and testament; last ⟨dying⟩ wish.**

В-256 • **(МНО́ГО) ВООБРАЖА́ТЬ О СЕБЕ́** *coll;* **МНО́ГО ⟨ВЫСОКО́⟩ ДУ́МАТЬ ⟨МНИТЬ** *lit⟩* **О СЕБЕ́** [VP; subj: human] to behave haughtily, consider o.s. better, more important, or cleverer than one really is: X много воображает о себе ≃ **X thinks too ⟨quite⟩ highly of him-**

self; **X thinks a lot ⟨too much⟩ of himself; X has a very high ⟨too high an⟩ opinion of himself; X has a swelled head ⟨an inflated ego⟩.**

[Мурзавецкая:] А Евлампия теперь с деньгами-то, пожалуй, очень высоко думает о себе: тот ей не пара, другой не жених (Островский 5). [M.:] Eulampe, rolling in money as she is now, no doubt thinks a lot of herself: No man is good enough for her (5b). ♦ Кажется, вся беда его характера заключалась в том, что думал он о себе несколько выше, чем позволяли его истинные достоинства (Достоевский 1). It appeared the whole trouble with his character was that he had a somewhat higher opinion of himself than his real virtues warranted (1a).

В-257 • **БРАТЬ/ВЗЯТЬ ⟨ПРИНИМА́ТЬ/ПРИНЯ́ТЬ⟩ НА ВООРУЖЕ́НИЕ** *что* [VP; subj: human or collect] to (begin to) make active use of (some device, idea, method, theory etc): X взял на вооружение Y ≃ **X added Y to ⟨made Y part of⟩ his arsenal; X adopted ⟨seized upon⟩ Y; X put Y to use; X started using Y.**

«Вопросник. Беру словечко на вооружение. Кратко и точно. У вас, наверное, есть ещё в таком роде, вы ж газетный работник» (Иоффе 1). "'Questionnaire!' I'm going to adopt this word. Brief and exact. You probably have a few more like that—after all, you are a journalist" (1a).

В-258 • **БОЛЬНО́Й ВОПРО́С** [NP; fixed WO] a pressing problem that has no easy solution: **touchy ⟨thorny⟩ issue ⟨question⟩; sore subject.**

В-259 • **ВОПРО́С ЖИ́ЗНИ И ⟨ИЛИ⟩ СМЕ́РТИ** [NP; usu. sing; fixed WO] an extremely important matter: **matter of life and death; (matter) of utmost importance.**

«Знаете, Саша, – с сердцем возразил Борис, – ссыльных устроил сюда [в столовую «Заготпушнины»] я. Теперь мне, конечно, наплевать, я уезжаю. Но для тех, кто остаётся, это вопрос жизни и смерти» (Рыбаков 2). "Look, Sasha," Boris objected vehemently, "I arranged it so the exiles could come in here [to the Fur Procurement Trust Canteen]. Now that I'm going, it doesn't affect me, of course, but for those who are staying here, it's a matter of life and death" (2a).

< Loan translation of the French *question de vie et de mort.*

В-260 • **СТА́ВИТЬ/ПОСТА́ВИТЬ ВОПРО́С РЕБРО́М** [VP; subj: human; usu. this WO] to say sth. or ask sth. straightforwardly, in an abrupt manner: X поставил вопрос ребром ≃ **X posed the issue ⟨put the question⟩ point-blank; X put the question bluntly ⟨squarely⟩.**

Эта дама... поставила вопрос ребром: или я убираю квартиру, или должен идти домой (Лимонов 1). The lady...posed the issue point-blank: Either I cleaned the apartment or I had to go home (1a). ♦ «Не можете ли вы сообщить... откуда вы взяли вдруг столько денег, тогда как из дела оказывается по расчёту времени даже, что вы не заходили домой?» Прокурор немножко поморщился от вопроса, поставленного так ребром, но не прервал Николая Парфёновича (Достоевский 1). "Would you mind informing us...as to where you suddenly got so much money, when it appears from the evidence, even from the simple reckoning of time, that you did not stop at your own lodgings?" The prosecutor winced slightly at the bluntness with which the question had been put, but he did not interrupt Nikolai Parfenovich (1a). ♦ [Ипполит:] Сегодня, Надя, в последний час старого года, я намерен поставить вопрос ребром. Хватит водить меня за нос! [Надя:] Чем ты недоволен? [Ипполит:] Своим холостым положением. И я предлагаю... [Надя (перебивает):] Сядь! (Брагинский и Рязанов 1). [I.:] Today, Nadya, in the last hour of the old year, I intend to put the question squarely. No more leading me on like this! [N.:] What's wrong? [I.:] My bachelor status. And I propose... [N. (interrupting):] Please, sit down (1a).

B-261 • СТА́ВИТЬ/ПОСТА́ВИТЬ ПОД ВОПРО́С что [VP; subj: human] to dispute, query sth.: X поставил под вопрос Y ≃ **X called Y in(to) question; X raised doubts about Y; X questioned Y.**

«Что же тут, сравнивается наша мощь с силёнками белых? Ставится под вопрос успех военного решения проблемы?» (Аксёнов 7). "Are you putting those puny Whites on a par with us? Are you questioning the success of a military solution to the problem?" (7a).

B-262 • ЧТО ЗА ВОПРО́С! *coll* [sent; Invar; fixed WO] used to express one's astonishment at or emphatic reply to an unnecessary or ridiculous question: **what a question!; what kind of question is that!; what do you mean!; what ⟨where etc⟩ do you think!;** [in limited contexts] **who ⟨what, where etc⟩ else!**

«Ты где сегодня ужинаешь, Амвросий?» — «Что за вопрос, конечно, здесь, дорогой Фока!» (Булгаков 9). "Where are you dining tonight, Amvrosy?" "What a question—here, of course, my dear Foka!" (9a).

B-263 • ПОД (БОЛЬШИ́М) ВОПРО́СОМ быть₀, оставаться, находиться и т. п. [PrepP; these forms only; subj-compl with copula (subj: abstr); fixed WO] (of plans, future prospects etc) (to be, remain etc) uncertain, undecided, dubious: **open to question; up in the air; a (big) question mark; (pretty) iffy.**

«Они что, собираются разводиться?» — «Это пока под вопросом». "What, are they planning to get a divorce?" "At this point it's up in the air."

B-264 • ВОР У ВО́РА ДУБИ́НКУ УКРА́Л [saying] a swindler cheated another swindler: ≃ **one thief robs another.**

B-265 • НЕ ПО́ЙМАН – НЕ ВОР [saying] a person should not be considered guilty of a wrongdoing if he is not caught at the scene of the crime (said when there is no irrefutable evidence of s.o.'s guilt; sometimes said with regret when s.o.'s obvious guilt cannot be proven): ≃ **innocent until proven guilty; a thief isn't a thief unless you catch him in the act; a thief isn't a thief till he's caught (in the act).**

«А откуда вам известно про его штуки?» — «Говорили в институте...» — «Чего ж вы ему тогда холку не намылили?» — «Не пойман – не вор» (Семёнов 1). "How do you come to know so much about his tricks?" "They were talked about at the Institute...." "Why didn't you settle his hash at that time?" "You're not a thief till you're caught" (1a).

B-266 • НА ВО́РЕ ША́ПКА ГОРИ́Т [saying] a person who is guilty of sth. cannot hide his guilt (said when a person unwittingly shows himself to be guilty through his behavior or words in a case when he otherwise would not have been suspect): ≃ **that's his ⟨her⟩ guilty conscience speaking.**

B-267 • СТРЕ́ЛЯНЫЙ ⟨СТА́РЫЙ⟩ ВОРОБЕ́Й; СТРЕ́ЛЯНАЯ ПТИ́ЦА *all coll* [NP; usu. sing; often subj-compl with copula (subj: human); fixed WO] an experienced, worldly-wise person who is not easily fooled: **wise old bird; old hand; no novice;** [in limited contexts] **(one) wasn't born yesterday.**

Конечно, Исидор Маркович прав — он опытнейший врач, старый воробей, его приглашают на консультации в другие города... (Трифонов 4). Isidor Markovich was right, of course—he's an experienced surgeon, an old hand, they invite him for consultations in other cities... (4a).

< From the saying «Старого воробья на мякине не проведёшь». See B-268.

B-268 • СТА́РОГО ВОРОБЬЯ́ НА МЯКИ́НЕ НЕ ПРОВЕДЁШЬ [saying] you cannot outwit or deceive an experi-

enced, worldly-wise person (said in praise of o.s. or another person who, thanks to his experience, is able to see through s.o.'s sly intentions or deception): ≃ **he ⟨she etc⟩ is too old a bird to be caught with chaff; you can't catch old birds with chaff; an old fox isn't easily snared.**

< «Мякина» is the husks and stalks separated in the winnowing and threshing of grain and certain other crops.

B-269 • ВО́РОН ВО́РОНУ ГЛАЗ НЕ ВЫ́КЛЮЕТ [saying] people who share common—usu. mercenary—interests act together and do not betray one another: ≃ **a crow doesn't peck out the eye of another crow.**

B-270 • ВОРО́Н ⟨ГА́ЛОК, МУХ⟩ СЧИТА́ТЬ; ВОРО́Н ⟨МУХ⟩ ЛОВИ́ТЬ *all coll, disapprov* [VP; subj: human] **1.** [often pres (in questions), neg imper, or infin with хватит, нечего etc] to look around aimlessly, absent-mindedly, getting distracted from what one is doing: X ворон считает ≃ **X stands ⟨sits etc⟩ gaping; X stands ⟨sits etc⟩ there just looking (around);** || *Neg Imper* ворон не считай ≃ [in limited contexts; with verbs of motion] **look ⟨watch⟩ where you're going.**

«Чего ворон-то считаете? — закричала Анна и замахала рукой. — Не видите, кто приехал?» (Абрамов 1). "Are you going to stand there just looking?" Anna waved her arms. "Don't you see who's come?" (1b). ♦ «Как пройти в управление, к Дудыреву?» — «Топай прямо да ворон не считай. Толкнут ненароком...» Семён направился по обочине дороги, оглядываясь во все стороны (Тендряков 1). "Can you tell me how to get to the Director's office, to Dudyrev?" "Straight ahead, only look where you're going, or there'll be an accident." Simon made his way along the path by the road, looking around him on all sides (1a).

2. to spend time aimlessly, lazily, be idle: X ворон считает ≃ **X loafs (around); X twiddles ⟨sits around twiddling⟩ his thumbs; X does absolutely nothing; X sits on his hands; X goofs off.**

Прекрати ворон считать! Сейчас же садись за уроки! Quit goofing off! Sit down and do your homework right now!

3. to be inactive (in a situation when some action is required or expected): X ворон считает ≃ **X (stands back ⟨by⟩ and) does nothing; X sits on his hands; X takes no action.**

Вопрос о том, какому отделу отдать освободившееся помещение, ещё не решён, но если вы будете ворон считать, то ваш отдел его точно не получит. It has yet to be decided which department will get the offices that have been vacated, but if you don't take action yours certainly won't.

B-271 • КУДА́ ВО́РОН КОСТЕ́Й НЕ ЗАНОСИ́Л (выслать, загнать *кого*, попасть и т. п.) *coll* [subord clause (usu. after туда); fixed WO] (to exile, send s.o.) very far away, to a most remote place: **to the back of beyond; to the middle of nowhere; to the land of no return.**

B-272 • ЧЁРНЫЙ ВО́РОН ⟨ВОРОНО́К⟩; ЧЁРНАЯ МАРУ́СЯ *all coll* [NP; fixed WO] a police wagon for transporting prisoners: **Black Maria.**

Я думал, что на улице меня ждёт «чёрный ворон», куда меня втащат, заламывая руки. Но никакого «ворона» не было, и мой провожатый предложил мне пройти пешком (Войнович 1). I expected there to be a Black Maria outside, that my arm would be twisted as I was thrown inside. But there was no police van waiting, and my escort suggested that we go on foot (1a).

B-273 • БЕ́ЛАЯ ВОРО́НА *coll* [NP; sing only; usu. subj-compl with copula, nom or instrum (subj: human) or obj-compl with считать, называть etc (obj: human); fixed WO] a person who is vastly different from those around him, unlike all the rest: X был

⟨казался⟩ белой вороной ≃ **X was the odd man ⟨one⟩ out; X was ⟨seemed to be⟩ out of place (among ⟨in⟩...); X stood ⟨stuck⟩ out like a sore thumb.**

Среди советских писателей он [Эренбург] был и оставался белой вороной. С ним единственным я поддерживала все годы (Мандельштам 2). He [Ehrenburg] was always the odd man out among the Soviet writers, and the only one I maintained relations with all through the years (2a). ♦ Среди Цыганковых Сима выглядела белой вороной (Максимов 3). Sima was the odd one out among the Tsygankovs (3a). ♦ ...Все обрадовались, прочтя фамилию Лозинского в списке первых писателей, награждённых орденами. В этом списке он был белой вороной... (Мандельштам 1). ...Everybody was pleased to see Lozinski's name in the list of the first writers ever to receive Soviet decorations. He was quite out of place in this company... (1a). ♦ Среди унылых, бездельничающих, сидящих здесь в шубах прочих литераторов, он [Пастернак], чьи мысли прежде всего в своей работе, как белая ворона (Гладков 1). With his thoughts first and foremost on his work, he [Pasternak] seems utterly out of place among the others, who sit there glumly in their fur coats, doing nothing (1a). ♦ В школе трактористов, куда Влада определили по просьбе мастера, он выглядел белой вороной (Максимов 2). In the school for tractor drivers, whither Vlad had been transferred at the foreman's request, he stuck out like a sore thumb (2a).

В-274 • ВОРО́НА В ПАВЛИ́НЬИХ ПЕ́РЬЯХ *derog* [NP; usu. sing; often subj-compl with copula, nom or instrum (subj: human); fixed WO] a person who tries in vain to appear better or more important than he is in reality: **jay ⟨jackdaw⟩ in peacock's feathers ⟨plumes⟩.**

< (?) Loan translation of the French *"Le Geai paré des plumes du paon"* (title of La Fontaine's fable). It came into widespread usage through Ivan Krylov's fable "The Crow" («Ворона»), 1825.

В-275 • ПУ́ГАНАЯ ВОРО́НА (И) КУСТА́ БОЙТСЯ [saying] a person who has been frightened by sth. or has suffered because of sth. becomes extremely wary and begins to fear even those things which are not dangerous: ≃ **once bitten ⟨burned etc⟩ twice shy.**

Подозрительная дружба Фомина с Капариным не осталась незамеченной. Несколько коммунистов из батальона устроили за ними слежку, сообщили о своих подозрениях начальнику политбюро Дончека Артемьеву... «Пуганая ворона куста боится, — смеясь, сказал Артемьев. — Капарин этот — трус, да разве он на что-либо решится? За Фоминым будем смотреть... только едва ли и Фомин отважится на выступление» (Шолохов 5). The suspicious friendship between Fomin and Kaparin did not pass unnoticed. Some of the Communists in the battalion started keeping a watch on them and reported their suspicions to Artemyev, head of the political Bureau of the Don Emergency Commission....“Once frightened twice shy,” Artemyev said, laughing. “That Kaparin is a coward. D'you think he'd ever dare to start anything? We'll watch Fomin...but I shouldn't think even Fomin would risk any action” (5a).

В-276 • ПРОКАТИ́ТЬ НА ВОРОНЫ́Х *кого obsoles, iron* [VP; subj: human, pl; often 3rd pers pl with indef. refer.] to vote against s.o., not elect s.o.: Х-ы прокатили Y-а на вороных ≃ **Xs blackballed Y; Xs voted Y down; [in limited contexts] Xs voted Y out of office; Y was well and truly beaten.**

...Он изъявил готовность баллотироваться... Против обыкновения, его прокатили на вороных (Салтыков-Щедрин 2). He...expressed his readiness to run for election....But against all expectation, he was well and truly beaten (1a).

< This is a play on words. The word «вороной» usually means a black horse, but here it denotes the color of black balls used to represent negative ballots (19th cent.).

В-277 • ОТ ВОРО́Т ПОВОРО́Т (дать, показать *кому,* **получить** и т. п.) *coll, occas. humor* [NP; Invar; usu. obj or indep. sent; fixed WO] (to give s.o., receive etc) a categorical refusal or negative response to a request, suggestion etc (often in the context of matchmaking): Х дал Y-у от ворот поворот ≃ **X gave Y the gate ⟨the brush-off⟩; X brushed Y off; X sent Y packing ⟨about Y's business⟩; X turned thumbs down on Y; X turned Y down ⟨away⟩; ‖ Y получил от ворот поворот ≃ Y got the gate ⟨the brush-off⟩; Y was sent packing ⟨about his business⟩; Y got a flat rejection ⟨refusal⟩; Y was turned down ⟨away⟩; [in limited contexts] good-bye to...**

Его [Михаила] удивил яркий свет в своей избе, который он увидел ещё от задних воротец... Так, так, подумал Михаил. Сваты... Дадим от ворот поворот, но так, чтобы сватам обиды не было (Абрамов 1). He [Mikhail] was surprised by the bright light in his house, which he noticed from the back gate....So that's it, thought Mikhail. Matchmakers....We'll send 'em about their business, but don't let's offend the matchmakers (1a). ♦ «Ну, после этого опять началось. Куда ни ткнёмся, всюду нам от ворот поворот...» (Айтматов 2). “Well, after that, naturally everything started up again. Wherever we go, we're turned away” (2a). ♦ [author's usage] [Афанасий:] Одну четвёрку [на вступительных экзаменах] он имеет? Имеет. Получит вторую — всё. Поворот от ворот... (Розов 1). [A.:] He has one B [on the entrance exams] and will likely get another. That means good-bye to the Agronomy Academy... (1a).

В-278 • У ВОРО́Т; У ДВЕРЕ́Й [PrepP; these forms only; subj-compl with copula] **1.** [subj: abstr, often the name of a month, a noun denoting a season etc] sth. is very close, sth. will come very soon, in the immediate future: Х у ворот ≃ **X is just ⟨right⟩ around the corner; X is close ⟨near⟩ at hand; X is almost upon us; it's almost X.**

2. [subj: human (usu. pl) or collect] some people are in immediate proximity (to s.o.), nearby: Х-ы у ворот ≃ **Xs are ⟨right⟩ at the doorstep; Xs are ⟨knocking⟩ at person Y's ⟨the⟩ door; Xs are at the gate(s); Xs are almost upon person Y.**

Обезумевшими глазами [люди] хватали с обрывков нового приказа на стенах бесстрашные слова: «ЗА ДЕЛО! ВСЕ В РЯДЫ! БЕЙТЕ ТРЕВОГУ, ВРАГ У ВОРОТ!» (Федин 1). Their [the people's] panic-stricken eyes grasped the fearless words from scraps of a new order on the walls: “TO WORK! EVERYONE TO THE RANKS! SOUND THE ALARM, ENEMY AT THE GATES!” (1a).

В-279 • НИ В КАКИ́Е ВОРО́ТА НЕ ЛЕ́ЗЕТ; НИ В КАКИ́Е ВОРО́ТА *both coll, disapprov* [VP (1st var.) or PrepP, Invar, subj-compl with бытьø (2nd var.); subj: abstr, often это; pres or, rare, past; the verb may take the initial position, otherwise fixed WO] sth. is absolutely unacceptable, outrageous (used to express one's indignation at s.o.'s actions, some events etc): это ни в какие ворота не лезет ≃ **this is really too much; this is the limit; it's an outrage; this ⟨it⟩ simply won't do; this is really going too far.**

«Чёрт знает что! Запретить коммунисту пропаганду марксизма-ленинизма! Ни в какие ворота не лезет!» (Гинзбург 1). “Damn it all, this is really too much! How can you forbid a Communist to carry on Marxist propaganda?” (1b). ♦ Милый Костя, это уж наглость... ни в какие ворота! (Трифонов 1). ...My dear Kostya, this is sheer effrontery...—it simply won't do! (1a).

В-280 • АДМИНИСТРАТИ́ВНЫЙ ВОСТО́РГ *iron* [NP; sing only; fixed WO] excessive devotion to and enjoyment of administrative activities: **bureaucratic zeal ⟨enthusiasm, ecstasy, rapture⟩.**

B-281 • ТЕЛЯ́ЧИЙ ВОСТО́РГ *usu. iron* [NP; sing only; fixed WO] overexpressive or unfounded joy: **wild enthusiasm; foolish euphoria; childlike glee(fulness).**

...Телячий восторг от предвкушения возврата в жизнь лишил меня разума, умения читать газеты, сопоставлять факты... (Гинзбург 2). ...Foolish euphoria, as I enjoyed in advance my return to life, robbed me of the ability to think, to read the papers, to compare the facts... (2a). ♦ Описывая прогулку по Москве в ту памятную для меня июльскую ночь, я сейчас спрашиваю себя: не был ли я слишком опьянён собственным успехом и похвалами Б.Л. [Пастернака] и не переношу ли я на него своё настроение, в котором было что-то от телячьего восторга, — и отвечаю себе — нет (Гладков 1). Describing at this distance in time that memorable July night I cannot help wondering whether I was not so intoxicated by my own success and Pasternak's praise that I am imputing to him my own state of mind—which was one of almost childlike gleefulness. But I think not. (1a).

B-282 • ВОТ-ВО́Т *coll* [AdvP; Invar; adv] (sth. will happen) very soon: **any minute ⟨moment, day, time⟩ (now); at any minute ⟨moment⟩; in no time at all; be about to...**

Близился полдень, и пахарь уже настораживал слух в сторону дома, что вот-вот жена его должна позвать обедать, да и быкам пора передохнуть (Искандер 4). It was getting near noon, and the plowman had an ear cocked toward the house: any minute now his wife would be calling him to dinner, and besides it was time to rest the oxen (4a). ♦ «Пощёчина общественному вкусу», к этому времени уже отпечатанная в Москве, вот-вот должна была поступить в продажу (Лившиц 1). *A Slap in the Face of Public Taste* had already been printed in Moscow and was due to go on sale any day (1a). ♦ «[Татьяна] ещё не приехала». — «Вот-вот будет». — «Теперь уж скоро» (Распутин 3). "She's [Tatyana is] not here yet." "Any time now." "She won't be long" (3a). ♦ Дождик шёл с утра, и казалось, что вот-вот он пройдёт и на небе расчистит, как вслед за непродолжительною остановкой припускал дождик ещё сильнее (Толстой 7). Rain had been falling since morning, and it seemed as if at any moment it might cease and the sky clear, but after a brief respite it began raining again harder than before (7a).

B-283 • ВОТ, ВОТ *coll* [indep. sent] precisely (used to express agreement with the interlocutor's words, occas. with an implication that the speaker has already thought or said the same thing): **exactly; that's right; that's just it; [in limited contexts] hear that?; what did I tell you?; there you are.**

[Иванов:] Чувствую, что сегодняшнее моё напряжение разрешится чем-нибудь... Или я сломаю что-нибудь, или... [Саша:] Вот, вот, это именно и нужно. Сломай что-нибудь, разбей или закричи (Чехов 4). [I.:] ...I'm so tense, I feel something's bound to snap. I'll either smash something or... [S.:] That's right—it's just what you need. Break something, smash things or start shouting (4b). ♦ [Семён:] Приказали прийти? [Леонид Фёдорович:] Да, да... Так вот, дружок, ты так же делай, как давеча, садись и отдавайся чувству. А сам ничего не думай. [Семён:] Чего ж думать? Что думать, то хуже. [Леонид Фёдорович:] Вот, вот, вот (Толстой 3). [S.:] Did you call me? [L.F.:] That's right....Now, my friend, you'll do just what you did before—sit down and abandon yourself to your feelings. But don't think. [S.:] Why think? It's only worse if you do. [L.F.:] That's just it (3a). ♦ «Конечно, ты прав, — сказала она. — Менять что-либо поздно. Особенно мне — женщине...» — «Вот, вот!» — откликнулся Курильский... (Залыгин 1). "You're right, of course," she said. "It's too late to change anything. Specially for me, a woman..." "What did I tell you?" exclaimed Kurilsky... (1a).

B-284 • ЯДРЁНА ВОШЬ! *vulg* [Interj; Invar; fixed WO] used to express a very strong emotion—admiration, joy, surprise, indignation etc: **well I'll be damned!; hot damn!; (holy) shit ⟨crap⟩!; son of a gun!; for crying out loud!**

«Они проскочили! — завопил Кеша. — Проскочили, ядрёна вошь!» И замахал расщеплённым веслом первой лодке (Евтушенко 2). "They made it!" Kesha yelled. "They made it, son of a gun!" And he waved the splintered oar at the first boat (2a).

B-285 • ВПЛОТЬ ДО [Invar; Prep] **1.** ~ *чего* all the way up to (the point in time or space indicated by the noun that follows): **right up to ⟨until⟩.**

Вплоть до войны вокзалы были ещё забиты снявшимися с места крестьянами (Мандельштам 1). Right up to the last war, the railroad stations were still crowded with uprooted peasants (1a).

2. ~ *кого-чего* not barring even (some person, thing, or action): **right up to; (up to and) including; (right) down to; on down to.**

[Мне] угрожали убийством... устраивали всякие другие провокации (вплоть до того, что моим престарелым родителям объявили однажды, что я погиб) (Войнович 1). I was threatened with death...all sorts of other provocations were made (right up to telling my aged parents that I had been killed) (1a). ♦ «А что, если я не сдам всё-таки дом?» — «Не сдашь? — Силаев посмотрел мне в глаза. — Тогда все меры. Вплоть до увольнения» (Войнович 5). "And what if I won't turn the building over?" "If you won't?" Silaev looked me right in the eye. "Then we'll take any measures we have to, including firing you" (5a). ♦ ...[Чернышевский] перевёл целую библиотеку, использовал все жанры вплоть до стихов... (Набоков 1). ...[Chernyshevski] translated a whole library, cultivated all genres right down to poetry... (1a).

B-286 • ВПРЕДЬ ДО *чего offic* [Invar; Prep] for the span of time between the present or the moment indicated, and some subsequent event: **until (such time as); up to the time (when ⟨that etc⟩); pending.**

Ламуаньон был совершенно вежлив, но в конце разговора на представления «Обманщика» выдать разрешение отказался категорически, впредь до решения этого дела королём (Булгаков 5). Lamoignon was irreproachably cordial, but in the end he categorically refused to grant his permission to perform *The Impostor* until the King decided the matter (5a).

B-287 • ВО ВРЕД *кому-чему* [PrepP; Invar; usu. subj-compl with copula (subj: usu. abstr)] (sth. is) damaging (for s.o. or sth.): **(be) harmful ⟨detrimental, hazardous⟩ to s.o. ⟨sth.⟩; (be) bad ⟨no good⟩ for s.o. ⟨sth.⟩; do s.o. ⟨sth.⟩ harm; do damage to sth.; not do s.o. ⟨sth.⟩ any good; [in limited contexts] (be) unhealthy for s.o.**

Опыт Нюрка пошёл, должно быть, ей во вред (Залыгин 1). All Niurok's experience couldn't have done her any good (1a).

B-288 • С НЕЗАПА́МЯТНЫХ ВРЕМЁН [PrepP; Invar; adv; usu. used with impfv verbs; fixed WO] starting long ago and continuing up until the present (or the moment indicated): **from time immemorial; from day one; [in limited contexts] since time immemorial.**

В тот год [знаменитый певец] Рой Ройсон отдыхал в Крыму. Ну, отдыхает человек — ничего особенного. Так наши товарищи и туда в Крым проникли к Рой Ройсону и передали, что... у нас с незапамятных времён живут негры (Искандер 4). That year [the celebrated singer] Roy Royson vacationed in the Crimea. Well, a man takes a vacation—nothing special. So our comrades even got to Roy Royson there in the Crimea and informed him that we've had Negroes living here from time immemorial (4a).

B-289 • ВО ВСЕ ВРЕМЕНА́ *lit* [PrepP; Invar; adv; fixed WO] in all periods of time, at all stages of man's existence: **in all times; in every time ⟨age⟩; always.**

Во все времена существовали и будут существовать богатые и бедные, счастливые и несчастные. There always have been and always will be the rich and the poor, the happy and the unhappy.

B-290 • ПО ВРЕМЕНА́М [PrepP; Invar: adv; used with impfv verbs] sometimes, at varying intervals: **from time to time; at times; (every) now and then; now and again; occasionally.**

Новый градоначальник заперся в своем кабинете, не ел, не пил и всё что-то скрёб пером. По временам он выбегал в зал, кидал письмоводителю кипу исписанных листков… и вновь скрывался в кабинете (Салтыков-Щедрин 1). The new governor shut himself up in his office, did not eat, did not drink, and was always scratching away with his pen. From time to time he ran out to the hall, tossed the scrivener a stack of sheets covered with writing…and again disappeared into his office (1a). ♦ …По временам, видя, что в ней мелькают не совсем обыкновенные черты ума, взгляды… он недоумевал, откуда далось ей это… (Гончаров 1). …At times, seeing that she had quite original ideas and qualities of mind…he wondered where she got it all… (1a). ♦ Ветер по временам приносил мне их разговор (Лермонтов 1). Now and then snatches of their conversation reached me down wind (1e). ♦ Эти пароксизмы гордости и тщеславия посещают иногда самых бедных и забитых людей и, по временам, обращаются у них в раздражительную, неудержимую потребность (Достоевский 3). These paroxysms of pride and vanity sometimes occur even with the poorest and most crushed of people and are occasionally transformed into an irritating, irresistible craving (3a).

B-291 • ПО ТЕМ ВРЕМЕНА́М [PrepP; Invar; adv; fixed WO] pertaining to standards, points of view, customs etc characteristic of a certain period (in the life of a people, state etc): **for those times ⟨days⟩; by the standards of the time(s).**

Тридцать рублей в месяц как комендант Цика и столько же как участник ансамбля — неплохие деньги по тем временам, прямо-таки хорошие деньги… (Искандер 3). Thirty rubles a month as superintendent at the CEC, and as much again as a member of the ensemble—not bad money for those times, downright decent money… (3a). ♦ …Центр Магадана выглядел вполне благопристойно, даже по тем временам шикарно… (Аксёнов 6). The center of Magadan…looked thoroughly respectable, and indeed, by the standards of the time, quite splendid… (6a).

B-292 • СО ВРЕ́МЕНЕМ [PrepP; Invar; adv] with the passing of time, subsequently: **in time; with time; as time goes by ⟨on⟩; by and by;** [in limited contexts, in refer. to future action] **given time; in due time; one day.**

…Хотя со временем бабушка освоилась с хозяйством и с семьёй, но она так и осталась на вторых ролях (Рыбаков 1). …Although in time she [grandmother] learned to cope with the house and the family, she always played a supporting role (1a). ♦ Со временем буквы, написанные чернильным карандашом, слились, и многих слов вовсе нельзя было разобрать… (Шолохов 5). As time went by, the words scrawled in indelible pencil grew blurred, and many of them became illegible… (5a). ♦ «Он [Иегова] станет со временем переделывать землю всё лучше и лучше, до бесконечного, уму непостижимого совершенства и жить на ней нескончаемо вместе с бессмертными людьми» (Терц 3). "As time goes on he [Jehovah] will…transform the earth, making it better and better, till it reaches a perfection beyond our understanding, and will live on it for ever and ever, together with immortal men" (3a). ♦ Его [Гладышева] разговоры насчёт замечательного гибрида невесты ещё терпели… надеясь, впрочем, что дурь эта у Гладышева со временем пройдёт сама по себе (Войнович 2). The girls would put up with his [Gladishev's] discourses on his remarkable hybrid…meanwhile hoping that given time this foolishness would pass from Gladishev by itself (2a). ♦ …Объяснять ему всё это, конечно, незачем, он сам, со временем, всё поймёт и разберётся… (Битов 2). …There was no reason, of course, to explain it all to him, in due time he himself would understand and get it all figured out… (2a).

B-293 • ТЕМ ВРЕ́МЕНЕМ [NP_instrum; Invar; sent adv; fixed WO] concurrently with (the action, activity etc mentioned in the preceding context): **meanwhile; in the meantime.**

У метро Краснопресненская людской поток подхватил Ефима, втянул в подземелье и, сильно помятого, вынес наружу на станции Аэропорт. Тем временем Трёшкин двигался к тому же конечному пункту совершенно иным путём (Войнович 6). At the Krasnaya Presnya metro the stream of humanity caught Yefim, pulled him underground, and ejected him, badly rumpled, at Airport Station. Meanwhile, Vaska [Tryoshkin] was proceeding to the same terminal by a completely different route (6a).

B-294 • В СКО́РОМ ВРЕ́МЕНИ [PrepP; Invar; adv; fixed WO] in the near future: **in a short time; soon; shortly; before long;** [in limited contexts] **shortly thereafter.**

«…Предупреждаю тебя, милый Родя, как увидишься с ним в Петербурге, что произойдёт в очень скором времени, то не суди слишком быстро и пылко, как это и свойственно тебе…» (Достоевский 3). "…Let me warn you, dear Rodya, when you see him in St. Petersburg, which you will do in a very short time, don't be too quick and vehement in your judgment, as you usually are…" (3a). ♦ Весело шутя с предводительшей, он рассказывал ей, что в скором времени ожидается такая выкройка дамских платьев, что можно будет по прямой линии видеть паркет, на котором стоит женщина (Салтыков-Щедрин 1). Merrily joking with the marshal's wife, he was telling her that ladies' dresses would soon be so décolleté that you could see clear down to the parquet on which a woman stood (1a). ♦ …[Николай Петрович] блаженствовал со своею Машей сперва на даче около Лесного института, потом в городе… наконец — в деревне, где он поселился окончательно и где у него в скором времени родился сын Аркадий (Тургенев 2). At first they [Nikolai Petrovich and Masha] lived in a country villa near the Institute of Forestry, then in town…and finally in the country where he settled down for good and where before long his son, Arkady, was born (2c). ♦ Рассказав затем о пропавшей трёшкинской кошке, Фишкин… прошлёпал к себе вниз, а в скором времени на лестнице появился Ефим в дублёнке… (Войнович 6). After telling Yefim about Vaska Tryoshkin's lost cat, Fishkin…shuffled downstairs to his apartment. Shortly thereafter, Yefim appeared in a sheepskin coat… (6a).

B-295 • ДО ВРЕ́МЕНИ [PrepP; Invar; adv] **1.** *obs* for the meantime, until a moment when the situation changes and some opportunity arises: **for the time being; for the present;** [in limited contexts] **for now; until the time is right.**

…С тем убеждением прожил я годы подпольного писательства, что я не один такой сдержанный и хитрый. Что десятков несколько нас таких — замкнутых, упорных одиночек… Несколько десятков нас таких, и всем дышать нелегко, но до времени никак нельзя нам открыться даже друг другу (Солженицын 2). …I lived through those years as an underground writer in the conviction that I was not the only aloof and cunning one. That there were dozens of stubborn, self-contained individuals like me.…Yes, dozens and dozens of us, all suffering from lack of air—but for the present it was impossible for us to come out into the open and reveal ourselves even to each other (2a).

2. before the time that is customary, appropriate, or expected under normal circumstances: **before one's ⟨its⟩ time; too soon; prematurely; sooner ⟨earlier⟩ than one ⟨it⟩ should; too early;** [in limited contexts] **ahead of time.**

Теперь уже могло показаться странным, но Митишатьев был ещё школьным товарищем Лёвы. Просто Митишатьев до времени полысел и обрюзг (Битов 2). Mitishatyev had been a schoolmate of Lyova's, although by now it was hard to believe. He had gone bald and flabby before his time… (2a). ♦ Костанжогло ещё более поразил Чичикова смуглостью лица, жёсткостью чёрных волос, местами до времени поседевших, живым выраженьем глаз… (Гоголь 3). Chichikov was struck even more by the swarthiness of his [Kostanjoglo's] face, the coarseness of his black hair, gone prematurely grey in places, the lively expression of his eyes… (3a). ♦ Лучше прийти к месту позже (собаки всё равно наведут по следу), чем нагрянуть до времени, спугнуть зверя (Тендряков 1). It was better to get to the place later (the dogs would be able to pick up the scent) than to appear too early and frighten the bear away… (1a).

B-296 • **КО ВРÉМЕНИ** [PrepP; Invar] **1.** [adv] timely, opportunely: **on time; in (good) time; at the right ⟨proper⟩ time.**

«…Я за час управлюсь, как раз приду ко времени» (Семёнов 1). "I'll be through in an hour and can get there just on time" (1a). ♦ Семён Тетерин поднялся с земли… «Пора и нам. Солнце-то низко. Как раз ко времени поспеем» (Тендряков 1). Simon Teterin got up from the ground. "Time for us to be going too. The sun is getting low. We'll be there just at the right time" (1a).

2. *Neg* **НЕ КО ВРÉМЕНИ** [adv or subj-compl with copula (subj: human, abstr, or, rare, concr)] at an inappropriate time; (sth. is) inopportune: **(show up at ⟨happen at, choose etc⟩) the wrong ⟨a bad⟩ time; the time is not right for sth.; sth. is untimely; this is not ⟨is hardly⟩ the time (for sth. ⟨to do sth.⟩).**

Видя, что Евгений Николаевич собирает книги, Кузьма приподнялся. «Может, я не ко времени?» (Распутин 1). Seeing Evgeny Nikolaevich gather up his books, Kuzma got up as if to go. "I'm afraid I chose the wrong time…" (1a). ♦ Кирилл сам открыл ему [Кошевому] дверь в горницу… «Проходи, Кошевой, садись, гостем будешь…» Приход его был явно не ко времени (Шолохов 5). Kirill himself opened the door into the front room…. "Come in, Koshevoi, sit down and make yourself at home…." His arrival was clearly untimely (5a). ♦ [Глафира:] Не к месту… не ко времени разговоры эти (Горький 2). [G.:] This isn't the place…nor the time, for that kind of talk (2b). ♦ «Тебя-то уж отпоминали, как Гришку моего…» Сказал [Пантелей Прокофьевич] и досадливо осёкся: не ко времени вспомнил (Шолохов 4). "We'd said our prayers of remembrance for you, like for my Grigory…" Pantelei broke off vexedly; it was hardly the time to recall such things (4a).

B-297 • **ОТСТАВÁТЬ/ОТСТÁТЬ ОТ ВРÉМЕНИ ⟨ОТ ВÉКА⟩** [VP; subj: human or abstr] to become or be backward, old-fashioned: X отстаёт от времени ≃ **X lags ⟨has fallen⟩ behind the times; X can't keep up with the times.**

Отец… не хотел, чтоб сын его отставал от времени, и пожелал поучить чему-нибудь, кроме мудрёной науки хождения по делам (Гончаров 1). The father…did not want his son to lag behind the times and wished him to learn something besides the tricky business of legal practice (1a). The father…wanted his son to keep up with the times and to learn something besides the abstruse art of legal matters… (1b). ♦ «Время его [Сергея Леонидовича] вышло, поняла? Запутался он, не годится, отстал безнадёжно». Ляля засмеялась. «От кого отстал? От тебя, что ли?» — «От *времени*, моя милая!» (Трифонов 1). "His [Sergei Leonidovich's] day is past, do you understand? He's made a mess of things, he's not up to the job—he's fallen hopelessly behind." Lyalya burst out laughing. "Behind whom? Behind you, I suppose." "Behind the *times*, my dear!" (1a).

B-298 • **РÁНЬШЕ ⟨ПРÉЖДЕ⟩ ВРÉМЕНИ; РÁНЬШЕ СРÓКА** [AdvP or PrepP; these forms only; adv] before the time that is customary, appropriate, or to be expected under normal circumstances: **before one's ⟨its⟩ time; too soon; prematurely; sooner ⟨earlier⟩ than one ⟨it⟩ should; too early; [in limited contexts] ahead of time.**

…В гневе [Пантелей Прокофьевич] доходил до беспамятства и, как видно, этим раньше времени состарил свою когда-то красивую, а теперь сплошь опутанную паутиной морщин, дородную жену (Шолохов 2). In anger he [Pantelei Prokofievich] would go berserk, and it was probably this that had prematurely aged his buxom wife, whose once beautiful face was now

a web of wrinkles (2a). ♦ «Стоит ли прежде времени раскрывать перед Юрием Павловичем наши карты?» (Чернёнок 1). "Should we reveal our cards to Yuri Pavlovich ahead of time?" (1a).

B-299 • **(В) ПÉРВОЕ ВРÉМЯ** [PrepP or NP; these forms only; adv; fixed WO] in the beginning, during the initial period (of some activity, process, s.o.'s stay somewhere etc): **at first; initially; [in limited contexts] early on; in those ⟨these⟩ first days ⟨weeks etc⟩; in the first days ⟨hours etc⟩ (of sth.).**

Одно, что иногда мучило Николая по отношению к его хозяйничанию, это была его вспыльчивость в соединении с его старою гусарскою привычкой давать волю рукам. В первое время он не видел в этом ничего предосудительного, но на второй год своей женитьбы его взгляд на такого рода расправы вдруг изменился (Толстой 7). One thing that plagued Nikolai in connection with his management of the estate was his quick temper together with the old hussar habit of being free with his fists. At first he saw nothing reprehensible in this, but in the second year of his marriage his opinion of this sort of chastisement suddenly changed (7a). ♦ Более всех других в это первое время как делами Пьера, так и им самим овладел князь Василий (Толстой 4). In those first days, more than anyone else Prince Vasily took charge of Pierre's affairs, and of Pierre himself (4a).

B-300 • **(В) ПОСЛÉДНЕЕ ВРÉМЯ** [PrepP or NP; these forms only; adv; fixed WO] in the period immediately preceding (and often including) the present: **recently; lately; of late; latterly; [in limited contexts] over ⟨during⟩ the last ⟨past⟩ few weeks ⟨months⟩.**

…В последнее время доктор проявлял признаки неблагонадёжности — …под подушкой у него нашли книгу Авторханова «Технология власти»… (Войнович 6). The doctor had recently been showing signs of ideological unreliability. Avtorkhanov's book *The Technology of Power* had been found under his pillow (6a). ♦ В последнее время у него был довольно мрачный вид, но здесь, в горах, он сумел сбросить свои заботы и заметно повеселел (Искандер 4). Lately he had been looking rather grim, but here in the mountains he had managed to throw off his worries and had brightened noticeably (4a). ♦ …В последнее время хоть мальчик и не любил переходить в своих шалостях известной черты, но начались шалости, испугавшие мать не на шутку… (Достоевский 1). Of late…though the boy did not like to overstep a certain line in his pranks, there began to be some pranks that genuinely frightened his mother… (1a). ♦ …Князь Василью нужно было решить дела с Пьером, который… последнее время проводил целые дни дома, то есть у князя Василья, у которого он жил… (Толстой 4). …Prince Vasili had to settle matters with Pierre, who…had latterly spent whole days at home, that is in Prince Vasili's house where he was staying… (4b). ♦ Ко многому я привык в последнее время… Но к тому, что мне смутно чудилось теперь в Зинаиде, — я привыкнуть не мог… (Тургенев 3). I had got used to many things during the last few weeks.…But what I seemed to be dimly discerning now in Zinaida I could never become used to… (3a).

B-301 • **В СВОЁ ВРÉМЯ** [PrepP; Invar; adv; fixed WO] **1.** at some time in the past, formerly: **in one's ⟨its⟩ time ⟨day⟩; at one time; there was a time when…; at one point; [in limited contexts] in its own time ⟨day⟩.**

«А чудковат у тебя дядя», — говорил Аркадию Базаров… «Да ведь ты не знаешь, — ответил Аркадий, — ведь он львом был в своё время» (Тургенев 2). "A bit of an eccentric, your uncle," said Bazarov to Arkady.…"Ah, but you don't know," replied Arkady. "You see he was a society lion in his time" (2e). ♦ «…Старик у нас охотник, медведя валил в своё время» (Айтматов 1). "…Our old man here is a hunter, he's gotten even bears in his day" (1a). ♦ «По ленинским местам» фильм должен был называться или как-то в этом духе, я, признаться, точно не помню. А места эти, ленинские, они, как известно, в большинстве своём за рубежами нашей отчизны находятся. Потому что товарищ Ленин в своё время был тоже как бы невозвращенец (Войнович 1). I don't remember exactly what it [the film] was to be called—"In the Footsteps of Lenin"—something like that. As we know, the greater part of those footsteps occurred outside the borders of our country. Because Comrade Lenin at one time had been something of a defector himself (1a). ♦ В своё время можно было издать книгу на английском языке здесь и продать за границей (Зиновьев 1). There was a time when it was possible to publish a book in English here and sell it abroad (1a). ♦ В своё время популярность Зощенко, Ахматовой, Пастернака и Солженицына резко возросла после того, как советская пропаганда подвергла их уничтожающей критике... (Войнович 1). At one point, Mikhail Zoshchenko, Anna Akhmatova, Boris Pasternak, and Alexander Solzhenitsyn became considerably more popular after Soviet propaganda subjected them to withering criticism... (1a). ♦ Ведь если б статья была в своё время опубликована, то не в вашей власти было бы ограждать читателя от знакомства с ней... (Битов 2). After all, if the article had been published in its own day, you wouldn't be in a position to shield the reader from an acquaintance with it... (2a).

2. [usu. used with verbs in pfv fut] at the appropriate time, when it becomes necessary: **in due time ⟨course⟩; (all) in good time; when the ⟨one's, its⟩ time comes.**

«Он [император] шёл с Родзянко и, проходя мимо меня... сказал по-английски: „Вот моя славная гвардия. Ею в своё время я побью карту Вильгельма"» (Шолохов 2). "He [the Emperor] came in with Rodzyanko and as he passed he...said in English, 'These are my gallant guardsmen. In due course I'll use them to trump Wilhelm's card'" (2a). ♦ В доме все спали — и Маргарита Антоновна, и Вика. Ещё узнают [об аварии] в своё время (Грекова 3). Both Margarita Antonovna and Vika were asleep. They'd find out [about the accident] in good time (3a). ♦ Вощев поглядел на людей и решил кое-как жить, раз они терпят и живут: он вместе с ними произошёл и умрёт в своё время неразлучно с людьми (Платонов 1). Voshchev glanced at the men and decided to live somehow, since they also endured and lived: he came into the world with them, and he would die when his time came inseparably from them (1a).

В-302 • В ТО ВРЕ́МЯ КАК *lit* [subord Conj] **1.** [contrastive-concessive] while at the same time: **whereas; while;** [in limited contexts] **although; even though.**

Какое ему [Орозкулу] было дело до этого дурацкого портфеля, до этого брошенного родителями мальчишки, племянника жены, если сам он был так обижен судьбой, если бог не дал ему сына собственного, своей крови, в то время как другим дарит детей щедро, без счёта?.. (Айтматов 1). What did he [Orozkul] care about that stupid schoolbag, about that brat abandoned by his parents, when he himself was so wronged by life, when God didn't see fit to grant him a son of his own, his own flesh and blood, while others were blessed with all the children they could want (1a). ♦ «Помешала хозяйка квартиры, которая вызвала её в коридор и, я слышал, попросила у неё взаймы денег. Она отказала, в то время как деньги у неё были» (Шолохов 2). "We were interrupted by her landlady, who called her out into the corridor and, as I heard, asked her for a loan. She refused, although she had the money" (2a). ♦ «Я мог бы назвать вам десятки писателей, переведённых на иностранные языки, в то время как они не заслуживают даже того, чтоб их печатали на их родном языке» (Булгаков 5). [context transl] "I can name you dozens of writers translated into foreign languages who do not even deserve to be published in their own" (5a).

2. [temporal] during the time that: **while; when.**

В то время как глуповцы с тоскою перешёптывались... к сборищу незаметно подъехали столь известные обывателям градоначальнические дрожки (Салтыков-Щедрин 1). While the Foolovites were whispering among themselves in anguish...the gubernatorial carriage which the townsfolk knew so well drove up to the gathering unnoticed (1a).

В-303 • В ТО́ ЖЕ ВРЕ́МЯ [PrepP; Invar; sent adv; when used after Conj «но», «но и», and, in some contexts, «и», emphasizes contrast; fixed WO] (some action, event etc occurs) simultaneously with another previously mentioned one, (some quality, feeling etc is present in s.o. or sth.) along with another previously mentioned one (a contrast may be implied): **at the same time; simultaneously; at once;** [when the English equivalent is placed before the first of the two connected phrases or clauses] **while;** [only when a contrast is implied] **(and) yet.**

«Спросите любого из ваших же мужиков, в ком из нас — в вас или во мне — он скорее признает соотечественника. Вы и говорить-то с ним не умеете». — «А вы говорите с ним и презираете его в то же время» (Тургенев 2). "Ask any of your peasants which of us—you or me—he would more readily acknowledge as a fellow-countryman. You don't even know how to talk to them." "While you talk to them and despise them at the same time" (2c). ♦ Дядя Сандро был рад... что ему не изменило его тогда ещё только брезжущее чутьё на возможности гостеприимства, заложенные в малознакомых людях. Впоследствии... он это чутьё развил до степени абсолютного слуха, что отчасти позволило ему стать знаменитым в наших краях тамадой, так сказать, самой весёлой и в то же время самой печальной звездой на небосклоне свадебных и поминальных пиршеств (Искандер 3). Uncle Sandro was happy...that his already sensitive nose for the possibilities of finding hospitality among people he barely knew had not betrayed him. In later years...he developed this sense to the point of absolute pitch. It was largely responsible for his becoming a celebrated tamada, or toastmaster, in our part of the world—at once the merriest and the saddest star, as it were, in the firmament of marriage and funeral feasts (3a). ♦ Изощрённость этого сионистского издевательства Давида Аракишвили состояла в том, что, оставляя дом на имя несуществующего племянника, он в то же время всех своих существующих племянников забрал с собой (Искандер 3). One refinement of this Zionist mockery of David Arakishvili's was that while he left his house in the name of a nonexistent nephew, he took all his existing nephews with him (3a). ♦ «Я и не скрываюсь: я люблю то, что вы называете комфортом, и в то же время я мало желаю жить» (Тургенев 2). "I don't deny that I love what you call comfort and yet I have little desire to live" (2a).

В-304 • ВО ВРЕ́МЯ *чего* [PrepP; Invar; Prep; the resulting PrepP is adv] over the course of (sth.), at some point in the course of: **during; at the time of; when there is ⟨are⟩...;** [in limited contexts] **on; as; in.**

Во время его выступления несколько раз его перебивали с места наши местные патриоты... (Искандер 4). During his speech he was interrupted several times from the floor by our local patriots... (4a). ♦ «Во время ареста обвиняемый... оказал вооружённое сопротивление» (Войнович 4). "At the time of the arrest, the accused...showed armed resistance..." (4a). ♦ Вчера я приехал в Пятигорск, нанял квартиру на краю города, на самом высоком месте, у подошвы Машука: во время грозы облака будут спускаться до моей кровли (Лермонтов 1). Yesterday I arrived in Pyatigorsk and rented rooms on the outskirts of the town, at its highest part, at the foot of Mount Mashuk. When there is a storm, the clouds will come right down to my roof (1d). ♦ Во время охотничьих походов за турами никто не мог угнаться за ним [Железным Коленом]... (Искандер 4). On ibex-hunting expeditions, no one could keep up with him [Iron Knee]... (4a). ♦ Молодой человек, литератор Жан-Донно де Визе, первый выступил в печати по поводу «Школы жён». Статья де Визе показывает, что во время её сочинения душа автора была раздираема пополам (Булгаков 5). A young writer, Jean Donneau de Visé, was the first to comment in print on *The School for Wives*. De Visé's article clearly shows that its author's soul was torn in two as he composed it (5a). ♦ Чего не скажешь в запале, особенно во время войны! (Рыбаков 1). ...You say all sorts of things in the heat of the moment, especially in wartime (1a).

В-305 • **ВО ВРЕ́МЯ О́НО** ⟨**ВО ВРЕМЕНА́ О́НЫ** *obs*⟩ *lit, often humor or iron*; **В О́НЫ ДНИ** *obs, now humor* [PrepP; these forms only; adv; fixed WO (variants with время, времена)] at some time in the (distant) past, very long ago: **in (the) days of yore; in days of old; in the olden days; in olden times; in bygone days; in days gone by;** [in limited contexts] **once upon a time.**

…Слог его лился свободно и местами выразительно и красноречиво, как в «оны дни», когда он мечтал со Штольцем о трудовой жизни, о путешествии (Гончаров 1). …He wrote freely, at times even eloquently and expressively, as in "the days of yore" when he had shared Stolz's dream of a life of work and travel (1b). ♦ «Сколько… надо было погубить душ и опозорить честных репутаций, чтобы получить одного только праведного Иова, на котором меня так зло поддели во время оно!» (Достоевский 2). "…How many souls had to be destroyed, and honest reputations put to shame, in order to get just one righteous Job, with whom they baited me so wickedly in olden times!" (2a). ♦ [Платонов:] Мне хотелось бы знать, узнает она меня или нет? Я когда-то был с ней знаком немножко и… [Войницев:] Знакомы? С Соней? [Платонов:] Был во время оно… Когда ещё был студентом, кажется (Чехов 1). [P.:] I'd like to see if she recognizes me. I once knew her slightly, and— [V.:] You knew Sonya? [P.:] Once upon a time—in my student days… (1b).

В-306 • **ВРЕ́МЯ — ДЕ́НЬГИ** [saying] time is valuable, it should not be spent frivolously: **time is money.**

В-307 • **ВРЕ́МЯ** ⟨**ДЕ́ЛО**⟩ **НЕ ТЕ́РПИТ** ⟨**НЕ ЖДЁТ**⟩ [VP_subj; pres only (variants with терпит); fixed WO] (used in refer. to some urgent matter that should be handled without delay) s.o. should not procrastinate, s.o. must act immediately: **(there is) no time to lose** ⟨**to waste**⟩; **time is running out; time is (running) short; it can't** ⟨**won't**⟩ **wait; the matter is of the utmost urgency;** [in limited contexts] **time waits** ⟨**time and tide wait**⟩ **for no man.**

[Дононов:] Когда официально будем оформляться? [Павел Михайлович:] Время не терпит, хоть сегодня (Погодин 1). [D.:] When will we officially fill out the papers? [P.M.:] No time to lose; today if possible (1a). ♦ «Дело не ждёт и… необходимо приступить к нему немедленно» (Салтыков-Щедрин 2). "…The matter is of the utmost urgency and…we must set to work immediately" (2a). ♦ Описывать свои злоключения в ремстрой-конторе не буду, они знакомы каждому… «Ждите», — говорят. Ждать-то нам не впервой, но время, как говорится, не ждёт (Войнович 3). I shall not describe my misadventures at the maintenance and construction department, everyone knows what that's like.…"Wait," they said. Well, it wouldn't be the first time we waited, but time, as they say, waits for no man (3a).

В-308 • **ВРЕ́МЯ ОТ ВРЕ́МЕНИ; ОТ ВРЕ́МЕНИ ДО ВРЕ́МЕНИ** *obs* [these forms only; adv; used with impfv verbs; fixed WO] sometimes, at variable intervals: **from time to time; (every) now and then; now and again; every so often; (every) once in a while; on occasion; occasionally.**

Мать поехала мне покупать… что — я не знал — одну из тех чудаковатых вещей, на которые время от времени я зарился с жадностью брюхатой женщины… (Набоков 1). Mother had gone to buy me—I did not know what exactly—one of those freakish things that from time to time I coveted with the greed of a pregnant woman… (1a). ♦ Время от времени ворота открываются, и во двор, рыча и переваливаясь, вползают грузовики с грузом, выползают без груза (Грекова 2). Every now and then the gates swing open to allow a loaded lorry to enter, snorting and lurching, or an empty lorry to emerge (2a). ♦ Время от времени… заглядывал дед Тихон (Максимов 2). …Great-Uncle Tikhon would now and again make a visit (2a). ♦ …Я не любил строй и в столовую или по утрам в уборную пробираться предпочитал в одиночку.

Чаще всего эта операция мне удавалась, но… и я время от времени попадался (Войнович 5). …I had no love for formation and preferred to make my own way to the mess hall or the latrine in the morning. Usually I was successful, but…I did get caught every once in a while (5a). ♦ Он [Бухарин] бегал по огромному кабинету и время от времени останавливался передо мной с очередным вопросом… «Было свидание [с Мандельштамом]?» (Мандельштам 1). He [Bukharin] paced rapidly up and down his huge office, occasionally stopping in front of me to ask another question. "Have you been to see him [Mandelstam]?" (1a).

В-309 • **ВРЕ́МЯ РАБО́ТАЕТ** *на кого* [VP_subj; fixed WO] the passing of time will benefit s.o.'s situation, cause etc; after a time s.o. will win out, prove himself correct etc: время работает на X-а ≃ **time is on X's side; X has time on his side.**

В ближайшие месяцы всё выяснится, время работает на нас… (Искандер 6). In a very few months we shall see for ourselves; time is on our side… (6a).

< Apparently, a partial loan translation of the English phrase "time is on our side."

В-310 • **ВРЕ́МЯ** ⟨**ДЕ́ЛО**⟩ **ТЕ́РПИТ** [VP_subj; pres only: fixed WO] there is still time remaining (to undertake, decide, set about doing sth. etc), haste is not necessary: **there is still (plenty of) time; there is no (particular) hurry; there is no rush; it can wait.**

О дороге, о мостах писал он, что время терпит, что мужики охотнее предпочитают переваливаться через гору и через овраг до торгового села, чем работать над устройством новой дороги и мостов (Гончаров 1). With regard to the road and bridges, he wrote that there was no particular hurry, since the peasants preferred going over the hill and through the ravine to the village where the market was held to working on the construction of a new road and bridges (1b). ♦ «…Время терпит, время терпит-с, и всё это одни пустяки-с! Я, напротив, так рад, что вы наконец-то к нам прибыли…» (Достоевский 3). "There's no rush, no rush, these are all trifles! And I'm so glad you finally have come to see us…" (3b). ♦ [author's usage] Ипполит Матвеевич и сам понимал, что у пришедшего дело маленькое, что оно терпит, а потому… углубился в бумаги (Ильф и Петров 1). Ippolit Matveyevich also felt the young man's business was a trifling one and could wait, and so he…immersed himself in the papers (1a).

В-311 • **ВСЁ ВРЕ́МЯ** [NP; Invar; adv; used with impfv verbs; fixed WO] incessantly, repeatedly: **all the time; always; constantly; continually; at all times;** [in limited contexts] **keep** ⟨**never stop**⟩ **(doing sth.); in constant (fear** ⟨**expectation, denial** etc⟩**);** [when another concurrent action is specified or implied] **the whole time; all the while.**

«Ты знаешь, — говорила Маргарита, — …когда ты заснул вчера ночью, я читала про тьму, которая пришла со Средиземного моря… и эти идолы, ах, золотые идолы. Они почему-то мне всё время не дают покоя…» (Булгаков 9). "You know," said Margarita, "when you fell asleep last night I read about the darkness which had come from the Mediterranean…and those idols, ah, those golden idols! For some reason they haunt me all the time…" (9a). ♦ Они [мои сторонники] меня всё время учат: «Тише, тише, вы всё не так делаете…» (Войнович 3). They're [my supporters are] always telling me, "Calm down, calm down, you do everything wrong…" (3a). ♦ Что он [Павел Литвинов] внук Максима Литвинова, бесконечно повторяло и западное радио; тогда всё время подчёркивалось, что такой-то — сын или внук такого-то, дескать, диссиденты, люди не «с улицы»… (Амальрик 1). The fact that he [Pavel Litvinov] was Maxim Litvinov's grandson was endlessly repeated in radio broadcasts from the West. In those days, it was constantly being emphasized that such-and-such a person was the son or grandson of somebody-or-other, as if to say that the dissidents were not just "anybody" (1a). ♦ В обоих отделениях столовой кухня была отделена от общего зала стеклянной перегородкой, чтобы неряхи-повара всё время были на виду у рабочих (Искандер 3). In each department of the dining room, the kitchen was divided from the public hall by a glass partition so that the slovenly cooks were within the workers' view at all times (3a). ♦ «Мы всё время забываем, что тогда было всё другое, другое всё тогда было» (Битов 2). "…We keep forgetting that things were different then, everything was different" (2a). ♦ «Ты в последние дни стал какой-то нервный… ничего не ешь и всё время куришь» (Войнович 2). "The last few days you've gotten, I don't know, nervous…you're not eating, and you never stop smoking" (2a). ♦ Он [председатель] всё время ждал, что вот приедет какая-нибудь инспекция и ревизия, и тогда он получит за всё и сполна (Войнович 2). He [the chairman] lived in constant expectation of the arrival of some committee of inspection—then he'd pay for everything and in full (2a). ♦ Сейчас Чита говорил чётко, подобострастно глядя на оперативников, всё время кивая головой (Семёнов 1). Now Cheetah was speaking clearly, gazing at the detectives obsequiously and nodding his head the whole time (1a). ♦ «Стыдно и позорно!» — своим отроческим голосом, дрожащим от волнения, и весь покраснев, крикнул вдруг Калганов, всё время молчавший (Достоевский 1). "A shame and a disgrace!" Kalganov, who had been silent all the while, suddenly cried in his adolescent voice, trembling with excitement and blushing all over (1a).

В-312 • ВСЕМУ́ ⟨ВСЁ В⟩ СВОЁ ВРЕ́МЯ [saying] one should not rush things or show undue impatience, things should be done when the time is appropriate: ≃ **everything in its season ⟨in its own good time⟩.**

Помяните моё слово, пройдёт немного времени, и всё, о чём вы, молодые, мечтаете, разрешат. Всему своё время (Зиновьев 1). Just mark my words: it won't be much longer before everything that all you young chaps dream about will be permitted. Everything in its own good time (1a).

В-313 • ВЫИ́ГРЫВАТЬ/ВЫ́ИГРАТЬ ВРЕ́МЯ [VP; subj: human or collect] to gain time by using dilatory tactics (hoping that a more opportune time to do sth. will arise, in order to allow o.s. more time to accomplish sth. etc): X выигрывает время ≃ **X is playing ⟨stalling⟩ for time; X is buying time;** ‖ Х-у надо выиграть время ≃ **X needs to gain time.**

…Выигрывая время, Каледин закончил совещание ходом на оттяжку: «Донское правительство обсудит предложение ревкома и в письменной форме даст ответ к десяти часам утра назавтра» (Шолохов 3). …Playing for time, Kaledin closed the proceedings with a further delaying move. "The Don Government will discuss the Revolutionary Committee's proposal and an answer will be given in writing by 10 o'clock tomorrow morning" (3a).

В-314 • ДЕ́ТСКОЕ ВРЕ́МЯ [NP; sing only; usu. subj-compl with бытьø, nom only (subj: a phrase denoting a point in time) or VP_subj with бытьø] (said at some point in the evening or night to encourage s.o. to stay longer at one's place, to engage in some activity, not to go to bed yet etc) it is early, even children are still awake: **it's still early; it's too early; the night is (still) young.**

«Сейчас… 12 часов, для нас с тобой это детское время, а позвонить сейчас простому человеку, такому, как эта девица, — значит обидеть её» (Лимонов 1). "…It's twelve o'clock. The night is young for you and me, but it would be an insult to go calling up an ordinary person like that girl" (1a).

В-315 • НА ВРЕ́МЯ [PrepP; Invar; adv] for a limited time: **for a while; for a time; temporarily; [in limited contexts] for the time being; for the nonce;** ‖ давать ⟨брать⟩ что ~ ≃ **give ⟨take⟩ sth. on loan.**

Со свойственной ему практичностью он живо прикинул возможные последствия — на тот случай, если бы Лизка подняла шум. Во-первых, забудь на время дорогу в Пе-

кашино… (Абрамов 1). With his customary pragmatism he quickly assessed the possible consequences in the event that Lizka should raise a stink. First of all, he could forget about visits to Pekashino for a while (1a). ♦ Сердце было убито: там на время затихла жизнь (Гончаров 1). His heart was dead: life had ceased there for a time (1a). ♦ …Сам градоначальник, по-видимому, прекратил на время критический анализ недоимочных реестров и погрузился в сон (Салтыков-Щедрин 1). …The governor himself appeared to have temporarily abandoned his review of the tax arrears registers and fallen asleep (1b). ♦ …Ему на вездеходе компании «Ойл Аляска» лично Стен Гетс прислал свой сакс, в подарок или на время, точно неизвестно… (Аксёнов 6). …Stan Getz sent him his own sax on an Oil Alaska snowcat—whether as a gift or on loan isn't clear… (6a).

В-316 • НА ПЕ́РВОЕ ВРЕ́МЯ [PrepP; Invar; adv; fixed WO] for the initial period (of some undertaking, project etc), for the beginning period (of a longer span of time): **for starters; to start with; for the first little while; [in refer. to the present and immediate future only] for the time being; for now.**

«Не перейти ли мне во флигель, Николай Петрович?» — «Это зачем?» — «Я думаю, не лучше ли будет на первое время» (Тургенев 2). "Hadn't I better move back to the wing, Nikolai Petrovich?" "What for?" "I was thinking it would be best for the time being" (2a).

В-317 • ОДНО́ ВРЕ́МЯ [NP; Invar; adv; usu. used with impfv verbs; fixed WO] there was a time when: **at one time ⟨point⟩; for a ⟨some⟩ time; for a while; once.**

«Акселерация? Это что-то связанное с преждевременным созреванием? Слыхал. Об этом одно время шумели…» (Стругацкие 1). "Acceleration? That's something connected with premature maturation? I've heard about it. At one time there was a lot of talk on the topic" (1a). ♦ …Моя двухкомнатная квартира стоила семь тысяч рублей. Я её купил, потому что одно время получал довольно приличные гонорары (Войнович 1). …My two-room apartment cost seven thousand rubles. I was able to buy it because I received rather large royalties at one point (1a). ♦ …Обезображивать такого красавца, как [верблюд] Каранар, — прокалывать ему ноздри… [у Едигея] рука не поднималась… Подумывал одно время кастрировать и тоже не посмел… (Айтматов 2). …To spoil such a handsome beast as [the camel] Karanar—to pierce his nostrils… Yedigei could not bring himself to do that.…Once he considered castrating him, but he did not do that either… (2a).

В-318 • СА́МОЕ ВРЕ́МЯ [NP; Invar; usu. impers predic with бытьø; foll. by infin; fixed WO] (it is) the appropriate moment (to do sth.): самое время (X-у) делать Y ≃ **now is ⟨this might be etc⟩ the right ⟨the perfect, the very, an ideal etc⟩ time (for X) to do Y; this is ⟨that might be etc⟩ the ideal ⟨a perfect etc⟩ moment (for X) to do Y; now etc is (just) the time (for X) to do Y; the time is right (for X) to do Y; if ever there was a time (for X) to do Y, this is it.**

…Я уезжаю с Юркой на юг! Он сказал вчера, что мы с ним поедем. Если меня отпустят… И если — самое главное! — тётя Муза разрешит мне. Я вчера робела поговорить с тётей Музой. А сейчас мы обе торопимся на работу и самое время поговорить (Михайловская 1). …Yuri and I are going to the south! He told me yesterday that we would go. If they will let me off.…And if—most important of all—Aunt Musa gives me her permission. Yesterday I hesitated to talk to Aunt Musa. Now we are both in a hurry to go to work and this might be the right time to talk (1a). ♦ Все студенческие пять лет мечтал он прочесть заветную эту книгу [«Капитал»] и не раз брал её в институтской библиотеке…но никогда не оставалось времени… И даже когда проходили политэкономию, самое время было читать «Капитал» — преподаватель отговаривал: «Утонете!» (Солженицын 12). All the five years that he had been a student, he had dreamt of reading this cherished book [*Das Kapital*]. He had borrowed it time and again from the university library...but he had never managed to find the time....Even when they were doing political economy, the very time to read *Das Kapital*, the lecturer had advised them against it—"It's too much for you" (12a). ♦ Тут бы, конечно, самое время сиониста зацапать и передать в руки закона... (Войнович 6). This, of course, was the ideal moment to seize the Zionist and deliver him into the hands of the law (6a). ♦ Когда общественной жизни нет... тогда самое время удариться в мистику (Войнович 1). When there is no public life...that's the time to get hooked on mysticism (1a). ♦ Я заказывал. Я не скупился. Коньяк — так «Отборный», прекрасно. Не время мне было скупиться и зажимать монету. Самое время было разойтись вовсю (Аксёнов 2). I did the ordering. I spared no expense. Cognac — "Select," the best. This was no time for me to scrimp and save. If ever there was a time to go all out, this was it (2a).

В-319 • ТЯНУ́ТЬ ВРЕ́МЯ [VP; subj: human or collect] to use delaying tactics (in bringing sth. about): X тянет время ≃ **X is stalling (for time); X is dragging it out; X is dragging his feet; X is temporizing;** [in limited contexts] **X is playing for time;** ‖ *Neg* чтобы не тянуть время ≃ **(in order) to save time; so as not to waste time.**

«Вы спрашиваете, что у меня с квартирой?» — Сергей Сергеевич тянет время, пытаясь понять, что именно известно Борису Ивановичу (Войнович 3). "You're asking what's with my apartment?" Sergei Sergeevich stalls for time, trying to figure out exactly what Boris Ivanovich knows (3a). ♦ «Чтобы не тянуть время, скажу: женщина, которой принадлежала эта сумка, скончалась» (Чернёнок 2). "To save time I'll tell you that the woman who owned this purse is dead" (2a).

В-320 • УБИВА́ТЬ/УБИ́ТЬ ВРЕ́МЯ *coll* [VP; subj: human or collect]   **1.** to spend time doing nothing important, occupying o.s. with trifles: X убивает время ≃ **X fritters away the time; X wastes his time on trifles.**

2. to (try to) make some period of time pass quickly, fill up some period of time (often one's leisure time) with some activity (so as not to be bored etc): X убивал время ≃ **X killed time; X passed the time.**

«Время-то надо убить, правда? В дороге шахматы — милое дело», — добродушно приговаривал Г.О., расставляя фигуры (Аксёнов 9). "We've got to kill time, right?...you can't beat a game of chess on a trip," G.O. chatted as he arranged the chessmen (9a). ♦ Фомин и его соратники каждый по-своему убивали время: ...Фомин и Чумаков без устали играли в самодельные, вырезанные из бумаги карты; Григорий бродил по острову, подолгу просиживал возле воды (Шолохов 5). Fomin and his men each found their own ways of passing the time....Fomin and Chumakov played indefatigably with makeshift cards; Grigory roamed about the island and sat for long hours by the water (5a).

В-321 • ВРИ, ДА НЕ ЗАВИРА́ЙСЯ *coll* [imper sent; fixed WO] when lying, at least know when to stop: **if you're going to lie, at least make it good; come on, at least make your lies believable; aren't you going overboard ⟨a bit too far⟩?**

«Вчера Женя показал мне, как пользоваться компьютером, а сегодня я уже сам написал программу!» — «Слушай, ты ври, да не завирайся». "Yesterday Zhenya showed me how to use the computer and today I already wrote my own program!" "Listen, if you're going to lie, at least make it good."

В-322 • ВРО́ДЕ БЫ ⟨КАК *coll*⟩   **1.** [subord Conj; introduces a compar clause] used to convey the hypothetical, provisional nature of a comparison; the var. вроде как may also be used to convey the approximate nature of a comparison: **as if ⟨though⟩; (just) like.**

Кузьма Кузьмич упёрся — не пробьёшь. Головой кивает, вроде бы сочувствует, а губы поджал — значит, при своём

мнении! (Абрамов 1). Kuzma Kuzmich dug in his heels, and nothing would budge him. He nodded his head as if he sympathized, but his lips were pursed, meaning, I'm sticking to my guns! (1a).

2. [Particle] used to express doubt or uncertainty as to the reliability of a statement or to tone down, moderate a statement: **seemingly; it seems; it would seem;** [in limited contexts] **(s.o. ⟨sth.⟩) seems (to); sort of; rather; you ⟨one⟩ would think;** [when the reliability of the source of information is in doubt] **supposedly; allegedly.**

Этот вроде бы не очень грамотный старик знает историю Армении, как биографию соседей по улице (Искандер 5). This seemingly illiterate old man knew the history of Armenia like the biography of a neighbor down the street (5a). ♦ Когда общественной жизни нет... тогда самое время удариться в мистику. Дело вроде бы не совсем советское, но в отличие от, допустим, распространения или хотя бы чтения самиздата, безопасное (Войнович 1). When there is no public life...that's the time to get hooked on mysticism. Not a particularly Soviet thing to do, it would seem, but—unlike, say, distributing or even just reading samizdat—it's safe (1a). ♦ [Кушак:] ...Она [жена] там одна, а я в гости... веселиться... Ведь это... мм... неэтично вроде бы (Вампилов 5). [K.:] ...She's [my wife is] all alone there, and I go out enjoying myself...It's...sort of...unethical (5a). [K.:] ...She's [my wife is] there alone, whereas I'm with friends, having a good time... That's... umm... rather unethical (5b). ♦ Они не виделись больше пяти лет, и вроде бы полагалось обняться... (Аксёнов 12). They hadn't seen each other in over five years and, you would think, they should have embraced... (12a). ♦ Мне было бы морально гораздо проще, если бы я думал, что все подонки и негодяи, но здесь вроде бы говорит человек, разделяющий мои взгляды (Войнович 3). It would have been much easier for me morally if I had thought that they were all scum and scoundrels, but here was a man who had supposedly shared my views (3a).

В-323 • ВРЯД ⟨НАВРЯ́Д *coll*, **ЕДВА́⟩ ЛИ** [Particle] it is dubious: **it is doubtful ⟨unlikely, hardly likely⟩ (that...); probably (...) not; I doubt it; I doubt if ⟨whether⟩...;** [in limited contexts] **hardly; scarcely.**

...Едва ли и мать воочию видела то бескрайнее небо... (Обухова 1). ...It is doubtful that even her mother had seen that endless sky... (1a). ♦ Мои пращуры любили сначала по праву брачной ночи, потом — за деньги. Едва ли кто-нибудь из них любил своих жён (Федин 1). My forefathers loved at first according to the *droit de seigneur*, then for money. It is unlikely that any of them loved their wives (1a). ♦ Не знаю, жив ли он сейчас. Вряд ли (Гинзбург 2). I don't know whether he's alive now. It's hardly likely (2a). ♦ «...В хозяйстве [твой отец] вряд ли смыслит, но он добряк» (Тургенев 2). "...It's hardly likely that he [your father] understands farming, but he is a good-natured man" (2d). ♦ «Ну как, сдадим к празднику объект?» — «Вряд ли» (Войнович 5). "So, how about it, we'll hand over the building by the holiday?" "I doubt it" (5a). ♦ [Грекова:] Вы так привыкли к разного рода резкостям, что мои слова едва ли будут вам в диковинку... (Чехов 1). [G.:] You're so used to all kinds of rudeness, I doubt if what I say will surprise you at all (1b). ♦ «Количество дохода определить нельзя. При нынешнем беспорядке едва ли вы получите больше трёх тысяч...» (Гончаров 1). "It is impossible to tell you what your income amounts to. In the present rather confused state of affairs you will hardly receive more than three thousand..." (1a). ♦ ...«Видному лицу» такое высокомерие к новому любимчику вряд ли понравится (Аксёнов 7). The Important Personage would scarcely countenance an overbearing attitude towards his new favorite (7a). ♦ «Выздоровеет? Можно надеяться?» — «Едва ли. Умрёт девочка...» (Шолохов 2). [context transl] "Will she get better? Is there hope?" "Very little. She'll probably die..." (2a).

В-324 • ВОТ И ВСЁ; И ВСЁ *both coll* [sent; these forms only; usu. the concluding clause in a compound sent; fixed WO] and this concludes the matter, there is nothing else to add (to what has been said, done, or enumerated): **(and) that's it** ⟨**that, final**⟩; **(and) that's all there is to it; (and) that's the end of it** ⟨**that**⟩.

[Алексей:] Я не остановлюсь. [Андрей:] Остановишься, и всё (Розов 1). [Aleksei:] I'm not staying. [Andrei:] You are staying with us, and that's final (1a). ♦ [Платонов:] Я погубил тебя, вот и всё! Да и не тебя одну... (Чехов 1). [P.:] I've ruined you, and that's all there is to it. And not only you (1a).

B-325 • **ВСЁ ЖЕ** [Particle; often after contrastive Conj «но» or «а» or Conj «и»] notwithstanding or in contrast to some expressed or implied circumstance, fact, event etc: **all the same; still; (and) yet; nevertheless; nonetheless; even so;** [in limited contexts] **X did do sth.** ⟨*has done sth. etc*⟩; **at any rate.**

[Маша:] Я вам по совести: если бы он [Константин] ранил себя серьёзно, то я не стала бы жить ни одной минуты. А всё же я храбрая. Вот взяла и решила: вырву эту любовь из своего сердца, с корнем вырву (Чехов 6). [M.:] I'll tell you honestly: if he'd [Konstantin had] hurt himself seriously, I wouldn't have gone on living, not for one minute. But all the same I've got courage. So I up and decided: I'll rip this love right out of my heart, rip it out by the roots (6c). ♦ Если в рассказе Петра Александровича могло быть преувеличение, то всё же должно было быть и нечто похожее на правду (Достоевский 1). Though Pyotr Alexandrovich may have exaggerated, still there must have been some semblance of truth in his story (1a). ♦ ...По рассказу дяди Сандро, это самое должностное лицо, к которому он обращался со своим предложением, не встало с места при его появлении в кабинете, а также не встало с места, когда он уходил. Возможно, говорил дядя Сандро, он этим хотел показать, что очень прочно сидит на своём месте. Всё же через некоторое время это самое должностное лицо вынуждено было покинуть своё место, якобы в связи с переходом на другую работу... (Искандер 3). ...According to Uncle Sandro, the official to whom he took this suggestion did not stand up when he came into the office and did not stand up when he left, either. Possibly, Uncle Sandro said, he meant to imply that he sat as solidly in his job as in his chair. Nevertheless, after a while this same official was forced to leave his job, supposedly in connection with a transfer to another one... (3a). ♦ «Она [Цветаева] так говорила [, что не любит театр и не тянется к театру,] и всё же написала несколько пьес. Вы сами свидетельствуете, что это превосходная пьеса» (Гладков 1). "She [Tsvetayeva] may have said this [that she does not herself like the theatre and is not drawn to it], yet even so she wrote several plays—and you yourself say this is an excellent one" (1a). ♦ ...Он [дядя Сандро] стал просить помочь ему выхлопотать пенсию... «Дядя Сандро, — сказал я, — но ведь у вас нет трудового стажа»... Между прочим, пенсию он всё же получил той же зимой (Искандер 3). ...He [Uncle Sandro] began asking for help in wangling a pension....«Uncle Sandro,» I said, «you don't have any work record.»...By the way, he did receive a pension, that very winter (3a). ♦ ...Этот Дмитрий Фёдорович был один только из трёх сыновей Фёдора Павловича, который рос в убеждении, что он всё же имеет некоторое состояние и когда достигнет совершенных лет, то будет независим (Достоевский 1). ...This Dmitri Fyodorovich was the only one of Fyodor Pavlovich's three sons who grew up in the conviction that he, at any rate, had some property and would be independent when he came of age (1a).

B-326 • **ВСЕ** ⟨**ВСЁ**⟩ **И ВСЯ** *lit* [NP; subj or obj; вся is Invar; usu. this WO] all people and things without exception: **everyone and everything; all and sundry.**

...Такое отношение к окружающим, как у Гартвига — тайная насмешливость надо всем и вся, — приводит меня в ярость (Трифонов 5). ...The sort of attitude that Gartvig has—his secret mockery of everyone and everything—makes me furious (5a).

B-327 • **ВСЁ РАВНО́** [Invar; fixed WO] **1.** ~ (*кому*). Also: **ВСЁ ОДНО́** ⟨**ЕДИНО́**⟩ *substand* [subj-compl with copula (subj: это or a clause) or impers predic with copula] (may refer to the subjective reaction, desire etc of the person involved, or to

objective reality) (the difference, if any, between two or more expressed or implied options is) unimportant (to s.o.), of little or no significance (to s.o.): **X-у все равно** ≃ **it's all the same (to X); it comes to the same thing; it doesn't make any difference (to X); it doesn't matter (to X); X doesn't care;** [in limited contexts] **X is past caring.**

Будет говорить русский? Не всё ли равно? Пусть (Федин 1). A Russian will speak? Isn't it all the same? Let him (1a). ♦ «...Все мы, что человеки, что скоты — всё едино; все помрём и все к чёртовой матери пойдём!» (Салтыков-Щедрин 1). "Whether we're men or beasts, it comes to the same thing: we shall all die and go to the Devil!" (1b). ♦ «Может быть, вы мне, господин профессор, хотя описание вашей камеры дадите? — заискивающе и скорбно говорил механический человек, — ведь вам теперь всё равно...» (Булгаков 10). "Perhaps, Mr. Professor, you would give me at least a description of your chamber?" the mechanical man said ingratiatingly and mournfully. "After all, it makes no difference to you now..." (10b). ♦ Ах, какая тебе разница, кто он... не всё ли равно! (Битов 2). Oh, what do you care who it was—what does it matter! (2a). ♦ «Дети так не говорят. Это даже не грубость, это — жестокость, и даже не жестокость, а просто ей всё равно» (Стругацкие 1). "Children don't talk like that. It's not even rudeness, it's cruelty, no, not even cruelty—she simply doesn't care" (1a). ♦ «История показала, что специалисты могут ошибаться. Партия — никогда». По бесстрастному лицу помощника Марлен Михайлович понял, что в этот момент он слегка пережал, прозвучал слегка — не-совсем-в-ту-степь, но ему как-то уже было всё равно (Аксёнов 7). "History has shown that experts make mistakes. The Party never makes mistakes." The blank face of the Important Personage's assistant told him [Marlen Mikhailovich] that this time he had gone a bit too far, but by now he was past caring (7a).

2. Also: **ВСЁ ОДНО́** ⟨**ЕДИНО́**⟩ *substand* [adv] under any circumstances, regardless of what happens: **in any case** ⟨**event**⟩; **whatever happens;** [in limited contexts] **one way or another; anyway; all the same;** [with a negated verb] **there is no way (that s.o. will do sth.** ⟨**that sth. will happen** etc⟩.

Когда Маяна выходила замуж, городской родственник тайно, через людей передал подарок для Маяны... Подарок... был богатый, и тётя Маша... переправила его дочери. Дочка не приняла ничего, велев передать матери, что туфли ей... малы, а подарок она всё равно брать не будет (Искандер 4). ...When Mayana got married, the city relative secretly sent a present for her, through other people....It was a rich gift, and Aunt Masha...forwarded it to her daughter. The daughter accepted nothing, returning a message to her mother that the shoes were too small for her, and she would not take the present in any case (4a). ♦ «Всё равно [Марченко] даст отпечатки [пальцев], не добром, так силой. Заковать его в наручники — и катай!» (Марченко 2). "One way or another, willing or not, we'll get his [Marchenko's] fingerprints. Put the cuffs on him and let's go!" (2a). ♦ Полесов стоял в очередях главным образом из принципа. Денег у него не было, и купить он всё равно ничего не мог (Ильф и Петров 1). Polesov stood in line chiefly for reasons of principle. He had no money, so he could not buy anything, anyway (1a).

3. [Particle] despite some (indicated or implied) circumstances: **all the same; nevertheless; nonetheless; still.**

Кладбище напоминало карликовый город... Возле нескольких могил стояли табуретки с вином и закуской... Я знал, что это такой обычай, приносить на могилу еду и питьё, но всё равно сделалось ещё страшнее (Искандер 6). The cemetery resembled a city of dwarfs....I noticed several small stools on which food and wine had been placed....I had heard of the custom of offering up food and drink to the dead, but nonetheless the sight of these stools frightened me all the more (6a). ♦ «Теперь уж и без офицера всё кончено, хотя бы он и не явился он вовсе, то всё равно всё было бы кончено...» (Достоевский 1). "It's all finished now, even without the officer, even if he hadn't come at all, it would still be finished..." (1a).

B-328 • ВСЁ РАВНО́ ⟨ОДНО́⟩ ЧТО ⟨КАК⟩... [these forms only; used as compar Conj] similar or equivalent to: **(just) like; (just) the same as;** [in limited contexts] **as good ⟨bad, pleasant etc⟩ as; no better than.**

...Штольц думал, что если внести в сонную жизнь Обломова присутствие молодой, симпатичной, умной, живой и отчасти насмешливой женщины — это всё равно что внести в мрачную комнату лампу... (Гончаров 1). ...He [Stolz] thought that to bring an attractive, intelligent, lively, and somewhat ironical young woman into Oblomov's somnolent life would be like taking a lamp into a gloomy room... (1b). ♦ «Отправить жену в ночь с ружьём — всё равно что отправить её в ночь с чужим мужчиной» (Искандер 5). "Sending a woman out into the night with a gun is the same as sending her out into the night with a strange man" (5a). ♦ «...Мы вот с тобой попали в женское общество, и нам было приятно; но бросить подобное общество — всё равно что в жаркий день холодною водой окатиться» (Тургенев 2). "...You and I fell into the society of women, and we found it pleasant; but leaving such society is as grand as throwing icy water over yourself on a sultry day" (2d). ♦ ...Не хватило у него [Валентинова] стойкости против Мартова, а значит, стал всё равно как и меньшевик (Солженицын 5). ...He [Valentinov] had lacked the stamina to stand up to Martov and had become no better than a Menshevik himself (5a).

B-329 • ЗА ВСЁ ПРО ВСЁ *obs, coll* [PrepP; Invar; fixed WO]
1. ругать, бранить, наказывать и т. п. *кого* ~ [adv] (to scold, punish etc s.o.) for everything possible, for all sorts of things: **for everything under the sun; for anything and everything; for everything imaginable.**
2. ~ заплатить, (от)дать и т. п. *кому что;* наказание ~ [prep obj] (to pay the named amount of money, receive the named extent of punishment etc) for everything in total (that one has bought, done etc): **for everything altogether; for all of it (together).**

B-330 • И ВСЁ ТАКО́Е (ПРО́ЧЕЕ) *coll* [NP; fixed WO] and other similar things (used at the end of an enumeration to indicate that it could be extended to include similar objects or phenomena): **and so on (and so forth ⟨on⟩); and so forth; and all that; and things of that sort; and the ⟨such⟩ like; et cetera; etc.; and whatnot; and what have you; and all that sort of thing; and (all) the rest; and more of the same; and so on in the same vein; and more to that effect.**

«Анатолий Николаевич каждый год мне помогает найти мастеров по ремонту квартиры. Понимаете, побелка-покраска и всё такое» (Чернёнок 2). "Anatoly Nikolaevich helps me find workmen for my apartment every year. You know, whitewashing, painting, and so on" (2a). ♦ [Булычов:] Ты говоришь — высшая власть... от бога... И всё такое, ну а Дума-то — как? Откуда? (Горький 2). [B.:] You talk about the higher powers...the will of God and all that. But what about the Duma? Where does that come in? (2a). ♦ [Сорин:] Мне, брат, в деревне как-то не того, и, понятная вещь, никогда я тут не привыкну. Вчера лёг в десять и сегодня утром проснулся в девять с таким чувством, как будто от долгого спанья у меня мозг прилип к черепу и всё такое (Чехов 6). [S.:] For some reason, my boy, I'm not quite myself in the country, and, it stands to reason, I'll never get accustomed to it. I went to bed at ten o'clock last night and woke up at nine this morning feeling as though my brain were stuck to my skull from sleeping so long, and all that sort of thing (6a). ♦ Хочешь ты в членкоры [Академии Наук] попасть!.. Да и как не хотеть! Положение. Почёт. Квартира. Денежки. Распределитель закрытый. И всё такое прочее (Зиновьев 2). You just want to be a corresponding member [of the Academy of Sciences]!... And why not? Position. Honours. An apartment. Cash. The special privilege shop. And all the rest (2a).

B-331 • И ВСЁ ТУТ *coll* [sent; Invar; usu. the concluding clause in a compound sent; fixed WO] there is nothing more to be said or done, there is nothing to talk about (used after a statement, order etc to emphasize its finality): **and that's that; and that's all there is to it;** [in limited contexts] **nothing else ⟨nothing but a [NP]⟩ (will do ⟨will satisfy s.o. etc⟩);** [when a threat is implied] **...or else.**

«Главный врач мне приказал с ним сидеть, потому что он, то есть Росшепер, без меня не мог. Не мог — и всё тут. Ничего не мог. Даже помочиться» (Стругацкие 1). "The head doctor ordered me to sit with him because he, that is, Rosheper, couldn't manage without me. He couldn't, and that's that. He couldn't do anything. Even urinate" (1a). ♦ ...Орозкул поленился карабкаться в горы и решил отделаться от сородича первой попавшейся лесиной. Тот ни в какую: подавай ему настоящее сосновое бревно — и всё тут! (Айтматов 1). Orozkul was too lazy to clamber for the log, and he decided to get rid of his clansman with any old piece of timber. But the fellow wouldn't have it. Nothing but a genuine pine log would do (1a). ♦ «Взяли и тятю моего за грудки: пишись [в колхоз] и всё тут!» (Максимов 2). "They grabbed hold of my dad and told him to sign on [to join the collective farm] or else" (2a).

B-332 • НА ВСЁ ПРО ВСЁ оставить, осталось, иметь, нужно и т. п. *obsoles, highly coll* [PrepP; Invar; adv; fixed WO] (to leave s.o., be left with, have, need etc the named amount of money, objects etc to cover all one's or s.o.'s needs, expenses etc: **(all) in all; altogether; all told.**

B-333 • НЕ ВСЁ ЖЕ *кому что делать* [Particle] s.o. should not or cannot continue doing what he is doing indefinitely (may focus on his need to make a change in the future, on the fact that he spends too much time engaging in the given activity etc), some phenomenon cannot continue indefinitely or happen all the time: не всё же Х-у делать Y ≃ **X can't go on doing Y forever; thing X can't go on ⟨continue⟩ forever;** [with the focus on spending too much time on one activity] **person X can't ⟨shouldn't⟩ spend all his time doing Y;** ‖ не всё же дождю ⟨снегу и т. п. ⟩ идти ≃ **it can't go on raining ⟨snowing etc⟩ forever.**

[Колесов:] Итак, дома ты не ночевала... В первый раз? [Таня:] Да, в первый раз. [Колесов:] Ну что ж. В конце концов не всё же тебе ночевать дома (Вампилов 3). [K.:] So, you didn't spend the night at home....For the first time? [T.:] Yes, for the first time. [K.:] Well....You can't go on spending the night at home forever, after all (3b). ♦ Не расстраивайся из-за погоды: не всё же дождю идти — ещё успеем и позагорать и поплавать. Don't let the weather get you down: it can't go on raining forever. We'll still have time to get a tan and go swimming.

B-334 • ВСЕГО́-НА́ВСЕГО ⟨ВСЕГО́-НА́ВСЕ *obs*⟩ [AdvP; these forms only; used as a restr marker] merely, and nothing more: **only; just; no more than; nothing but; at (the) most;** [when used as an indep. sent] **that's all (there is to it).**

...У бедного Петруся всего-навсего была одна серая свитка... (Гоголь 5). ...Poor Petro had only one gray jacket... (5a). ♦ После некоторых колебаний я... отдал [управдому] паспорта и военный билет, из которого управдом узнал, видимо, с некоторым разочарованием, что я всего-навсего рядовой (Войнович 3). After some hesitation, I gave him [the building manager] the passports and my military service card, from which the building manager learned, apparently with some disappointment, that I was just rank-and-file (3a). ♦ Я опоздала на концерт всего-навсего на пять минут, но в зал меня уже не пустили. I was only at most five minutes late for the concert, but they still wouldn't let me in. ♦ Вот опять нам пришло на ум уотергейтское дело. Кто из нас, следивших за его перипетиями по передачам зарубежного радио, не приходил в изумление! Боже мой, из-за чего весь сыр-бор? Президент величайшей страны собирается кого-то подслушать. Всего-навсего (Войнович 3). Once again the Watergate affair comes to mind. Who among us, following its peripeteia on the foreign radio broadcasts, was not amazed? My heavens, what was all the commotion about? The President of the greatest country on earth wanted to eavesdrop on someone. That's all there was to it (3a).

B-335 • ВСЕГО́ НИЧЕГО́ *(кого-чего) coll* [NP; Invar; quantit subj-compl with copula (subj/nom or gen: human, abstr, or concr) or adv (quantif); fixed WO] very little, very few: **practically ⟨almost⟩ nothing ⟨none, no...⟩ (at all); practically ⟨almost, next to⟩ nothing ⟨none, no...⟩; nothing ⟨none, no...⟩ to speak of; hardly anything ⟨any...⟩.**

Она сказала Андрею в тот разговор, когда он пристал с расспросами, что человек живёт на свете всего ничего (Распутин 4). She had told Andrei when he was pestering her with questions that man lives almost no time at all (4a). ♦ [Алёна:] У шампанского есть одна особенность. Когда наливают, кажется, что через край, а осядет пена — оказывается, всего ничего, на донышке... (Панова 1). [A.:] There's a special thing about champagne. When it's poured, you think it will spill over, but when the foam has settled, it turns out that there's practically nothing, only a little on the bottom... (1a). ♦ [Охранники] между собой диву давались, когда сроку-то оставалось всего ничего... (Гинзбург 2). ...Among themselves [the guards] couldn't figure out why anyone should want to try to escape when he had hardly any time left to serve... (2a).

B-336 • ПРЕ́ЖДЕ ВСЕГО́ [PrepP; Invar] **1.** [subj-compl with copula (subj: abstr) or obj-compl with ставить (obj: abstr)] (sth. is) most important, more important than anything else: X — прежде всего ≃ **X is ⟨person Y sets X⟩ above all else; X before everything; X comes first; X matters most.**

Полковник был утомлён дорожными лишениями, однообразным степным пейзажем, скучными разговорами и всем сложным комплексом обязанностей представителя великой державы, но интересы королевской службы—прежде всего! (Шолохов 5). The colonel had been wearied by the hardships of travel, the monotonous steppe scenery, the tedious conversation and all the other complex duties of a representative of a great power, but he set the interests of His Majesty's service above all else (5a).

2. [adv] first in order or priority, before all else: **first of all; above all; first and foremost; first;** [in limited contexts] **the first thing to do is...**

...Глуповцам это дело не прошло даром. Как и водится, бригадирские грехи прежде всего отразились на них (Салтыков-Щедрин 1). The affair was not without consequence for the Foolovites....As usual, the brigadier's sins were visited first of all upon them (1a). ♦ ...Давая оценку той или иной женщине или девушке, абхазцы вообще, а чегемцы в особенности, прежде всего ценят это качество [степень лёгкости, с которой женщина обслуживает свой дом и особенно гостей] (Искандер 5). ...When appraising some woman or girl, Abkhazians in general and Chegemians in particular prize this quality [the degree of lightness with which a woman served her household and especially her guests] above all (5a). ♦ Нужны радикальные реформы! Прежде всего надо давать более свободными поездки за границу (Зиновьев 2). Radical reforms are needed! The first thing would be to make foreign travel easier (2a).

3. [adv] predominantly, basically: **primarily; chiefly; mainly; most of all; more than anything else.**

Когда говорят о цензуре, то имеют в виду прежде всего специальное учреждение, Главлит... (Войнович 1). When people speak of censorship, they're primarily referring to a special institution, Glavlit... (1a). ♦ Нюрок и тут взбеленилась: «...Неужели ты не видишь, что он давно умеет делать, чтобы за него всё делали?.. Он всегда кого-нибудь эксплуатирует — мать, отца, каких-то там приятелей, а прежде всего приятельниц!» (Залыгин 1). Niurok lost her temper completely: "...Can't you see he knows how to arrange things so that other people do everything for

him?... He's forever exploiting somebody—his mother, his father, his friends, but most of all his girlfriends" (1a).

B-337 • СВЕРХ ВСЕГО́ [PrepP; Invar; adv] in addition to all the rest: **on top of everything (else); on top of it all; to top it all off; in addition to everything else.**

«...Лучше шампанского подавай, долг на тебе, сама знаешь!» — «Вправду долг. Ведь я, Алёша, ему за тебя шампанского всего обещала, коль тебя приведёт» (Достоевский 1). "You'd better bring us champagne, you owe it to me, you know!" "It's true, I owe it to him. I promised him champagne, Alyosha, on top of everything else, if he brought you to me" (1a).

B-338 • ПРИ ВСЁМ (ПРИ) ТОМ *coll;* **СО ⟨ЗА⟩ ВСЕМ ТЕМ** *obs, coll* [PrepP; these forms only; sent adv; fixed WO] notwithstanding sth.: **(but) for all that; nonetheless; in spite of that ⟨there being etc⟩; regardless of that ⟨there being etc⟩; (and) yet.**

Услышав, что даже издержки по купчей он [Чичиков] принимает на себя, Плюшкин заключил, что гость должен быть совершенно глуп... При всём том он однако ж не мог скрыть своей радости... (Гоголь 3). Hearing that Chichikov was even taking the expenses of the deed of purchase on himself, Plyushkin concluded that his visitor must be an utter fool....For all that, he could not conceal his joy... (3a). ♦ Развращение нравов развивалось не по дням, а по часам. Появились кокотки...; мужчины завели жилетки с неслыханными вырезками, которые совершенно обнажали грудь... И за всем тем [глуповцы] продолжали считать себя самым мудрым народом в мире (Салтыков-Щедрин 1). Moral corruption grew by leaps and bounds. Cocottes...appeared; men acquired waistcoats with unprecedented decolletage which completely bared the chest....Nonetheless, they [the Foolovites] continued to consider themselves the wisest people on earth (1a). ♦ ...К сорока годам... решил он [Гладышев]... жениться, хотя это оказалось делом нелёгким, при всём том, что невест в деревне было в избытке (Войнович 2). ...As his forties drew near, Gladishev decided to marry....However, this turned out to be no simple matter in spite of there being a surplus of marriageable girls in the village (2a). ♦ Лотта безобразна, редковолоса, лишена бровей и ресниц и за всем тем с ожесточением упрекает его [Агатона] в том, что он загубил её молодость (Салтыков-Щедрин 2). Lotta is a very plain woman, her hair is thin, she has neither eyebrows nor eyelashes, and yet she keeps abusing him [Agathon] for having ruined her youth (2a).

B-339 • ПО ВСЕМУ́ видно, выходит, ясно и т. п. [PrepP; Invar; the resulting phrase is indep. clause or sent adv (parenth)] judging by all available signs, outward manifestations etc: **to ⟨by⟩ all appearances; by all indications; judging by all appearances; (judging) by what one can tell; it looks like;** [in limited contexts] **obviously.**

Чонкин, по всему выходило, вроде даже в каком-то лучшем положении, чем другие. Вроде как бронёй защищён он от фронта тюремными стенами (Войнович 4). To all appearances Chonkin was in a better position than other men. As if he were protected from the front by the armor of prison walls (4a). ♦ За окном стоял литой монотонный гул. Иссечённое песчаной пылью стекло мерно вибрировало... «Гляди, Коля, что на дворе делается!.. Страсть... Вот заехали, сам не рад будешь...» [Николай] пытался отшутиться... но по всему было видно, что настроение у него тоже не ахти (Максимов 3). From outside there came an unwavering, monotonous howl. The window vibrated rhythmically, lashed by fine sand...."Look what's going on outside, Kolya...it's terrifying....Look where we've landed ourselves—we shall regret it!" Nikolai tried to make a joke of it, although he was obviously not in the best of humor himself (3a).

B-340 • ВО ВСЕОРУ́ЖИИ *lit* [PrepP; Invar; usu. subj-compl with copula (subj: human or collect) or adv] **1.** (one is) completely ready (for sth.): **fully armed; fully ⟨totally⟩ prepared; all ⟨quite⟩ ready.**

...Крестьянская реформа не только не застигла его врасплох, как других, но, напротив того, он встретил её во всеоружии и сразу сумел поставить своё хозяйство на новую ногу (Салтыков-Щедрин 2). ...The peasant reform did not catch him unawares as it did the others. On the contrary, he was quite ready for it, meeting it fully armed, as it were, and he was able to reorganize his farm immediately in accordance with the new requirements of the time (2a).

2. ~ *чего* possessing sth. (knowledge, talent etc) to a very high degree: **with a full arsenal of; fully ⟨well-⟩ equipped with;** ‖ ~ знаний ≃ **in full command ⟨with a full mastery⟩ of the facts ⟨the subject⟩.**

В-341 • ВСЕРЬЁЗ И НАДÓЛГО *coll, often humor* [AdvP; Invar; usu. adv; fixed WO] for a long period of time and in a serious, fundamental etc way: **for a good long while ⟨time⟩;** [in limited contexts] **(sth. is) not easily or quickly remedied ⟨fixed⟩.**

Похоже, что экономический спад затянулся всерьёз и надолго. It looks like the recession will last for a good long time. ♦ В Ртищеве они застряли всерьёз и надолго (Максимов 3). [context transl] In Rtishchev they got well and truly stuck (3a).

В-342 • ВО ВСЕУСЛЫ́ШАНИЕ заявить, объявить *что* и т. п. *lit* [PrepP; Invar; adv] (to declare, announce sth.) so that everyone can hear it, in order to make it common knowledge: **for all (the world) to hear; for everyone to hear; to anyone who cares to listen; publicly.**

Он во всеуслышанье заявил... что прекрасно помнит Тендела ещё в те времена, когда тот имел вполне приличный (для своего рода), ничем не повреждённый нос (Искандер 3). He said for all to hear...that he well remembered Tendel in the days when he had a perfectly decent nose (for his clan), in no way damaged (3a). ♦ В классе, в который недавно перевели сына, учится огромный неповоротливый мальчик... [Ребята] катаются на нём верхом и даже... окрестили «лошадью»... Сын сказал во всеуслышанье, что он никому не позволит бить «лошадь»... (Свирский 1). In my son's new class there was a huge, clumsy boy....The children used to ride him around the room, which earned him the nickname of Horse....My son said to anyone who cared to listen that he wouldn't allow anyone to beat up the Horse (1a). ♦ [Львов:] Николай Алексеевич Иванов, объявляю во всеуслышание, что вы подлец! (Чехов 4). [L.:] Nikolai Alekseyevich Ivanov, I wish to state publicly that you are a scoundrel! (4a).

В-343 • ВСЕХ И КÁЖДОГО; ВСЕМ И КÁЖДОМУ [NP; these forms only; obj; fixed WO] absolutely everyone without exception: **anyone and everyone; anybody and everybody; one and all; all and sundry; each and every one; everybody ⟨everyone⟩ under the sun; everybody ⟨everyone⟩ and his uncle ⟨brother⟩.** Cf. **every Tom, Dick, and Harry.**

...[Помощник градоначальника] всем и каждому наказал хранить по этому предмету глубочайшую тайну... (Салтыков-Щедрин 1). ...[The assistant town governor] bade one and all to maintain the deepest secrecy on the subject... (1a). ♦ Матвей Ильич был настоящим «героем праздника», губернский предводитель объявлял всем и каждому, что он приехал собственно из уважения к нему... (Тургенев 2). Matvey Il'ich was the true hero of the hour. The Marshal of the Nobility informed all and sundry that he had consented to come out of respect for him (2e).

В-344 • ВСЛЕД ЗА *кем-чем* [Invar; Prep] (immediately) coming after s.o. or sth. (in time or space): **(right) after; on the heels of;** [in limited contexts] **in s.o.'s ⟨sth.'s⟩ wake;** [in refer. to

space] **(right) behind;** [with verbs of motion] **follow (s.o. ⟨sth.⟩) (in ⟨out etc⟩); followed by.**

...Щащико вдруг остановился, к чему-то прислушался и с криком «Ложись!» сам бросился на землю. Дядя Сандро шлёпнулся вслед за ним... (Искандер 3). ...Shashiko suddenly stopped, listened to something, and with the cry "Get down!" threw himself to the ground. Uncle Sandro flopped down after him... (3a). ♦ Тальберг... глянул на часы и неожиданно добавил: «Елена, пойдём-ка на пару слов...» Елена торопливо ушла вслед за ним на половину Тальбергов в спальню... (Булгаков 3). Talberg...glanced at his watch an added unexpectedly: "Elena, I must have a word with you in our room..." Elena hastily followed him out into the bedroom in the Talbergs' half of the apartment... (3a). ♦ Красивая борзая собака с голубым ошейником вбежала в гостиную, стуча ногтями по полу, а вслед за нею вошла девушка лет восемнадцати... (Тургенев 2). A beautiful white borzoi with a pale blue collar ran into the drawing-room, the nails on its paws tapping on the floor; it was followed by a girl of eighteen... (2c).

В-345 • ВСЛЕД ЗА ТЕМ [AdvP; Invar; sent adv; fixed WO] following that which precedes in time: **after that; next.**

...В 1812 году французами одержана победа под Москвой, Москва взята, и вслед за тем, без новых сражений, не Россия перестала существовать, а перестала существовать шестисоттысячная армия, потом наполеоновская Франция (Толстой 7). ...In 1812, the French win a victory near Moscow. Moscow is taken, and after that, with no further battles, it is not Russia that ceases to exist, but the French army of six hundred thousand, and then Napoleonic France itself (7a).

В-346 • КТО РÁНО ВСТАЁТ, ТОМУ́ БОГ (ПО)ДАЁТ [saying] he who rises early and acts without delay enjoys success: ≃ **the early bird catches the worm.**

Я уж и не помню, как Дегтярёв отвёл меня спать на топчане... Чуть свет он уже тормошил: «На базар, на базар! Кто рано встаёт, тому бог подаёт!» (Кузнецов 1). I can't even remember how Degtyarev got me to my makeshift cot....He shook me awake when it was barely light outside. "To the bazaar, to the bazaar! The early bird catches the worm!" (1a).

В-347 • КÁЖДЫЙ ⟨ВСЯ́КИЙ⟩ ВСТРЕ́ЧНЫЙ; (КÁЖДЫЙ ⟨ВСЯ́КИЙ⟩) ВСТРЕ́ЧНЫЙ И ПОПЕ-РЕ́ЧНЫЙ ⟨ВСТРЕ́ЧНЫЙ-ПОПЕРЕ́ЧНЫЙ⟩ *all coll* [NP; sing only (variants with каждый or всякий); usu. obj; fixed WO] any person, everyone without discrimination (usu. of people who are complete strangers or are not the right people for the action in question): **anyone and everyone; anybody and everybody; one and all; everyone who crosses one's path; every stranger one meets;** [in limited contexts] **(people) right and left ⟨left and right⟩; (people) right, left, and center.** Cf. **every Tom, Dick, and Harry.**

И ещё очень важное он [Твардовский] требовал: чтобы я *никому не говорил,* что отобран у меня роман! — иначе *нежелательная огласка* сильно затруднит положение... Чьё положение??.. *верхов* или моё? Нежелательная?.. Да огласка — одно моё спасение! Я буду рассказывать каждому встречному! (Солженицын 2). Не [Tvardovsky] had another very important request to make: I *must tell no one* that the novel had been taken from me! Otherwise, *undesirable publicity* would make the situation much more difficult....Make whose situation more difficult? That of the *top people* — or my own? *Undesirable* publicity?...But that was the one thing that could save me! I would tell anybody and everybody! (2a). ♦ «У азиатов, знаете, обычай всех встречных и поперечных приглашать на свадьбу» (Лермонтов 1). "With those Asiatics, you know, it is the custom to invite one and all to their weddings" (1a). ♦ Иван возмущённо жаловался каждому встречному-поперечному: «Это разве по Богу над стариком среди бела дня измываться?» (Максимов 3). ...[Ivan] complained indignantly to everyone who crossed his path. "Is it God's will, knocking an old man about in broad daylight?" (3a). ♦ Он был убеждён, что... он сотворён богом так, что должен жить в тридцать тысяч дохода и занимать всегда высшее положение в обществе. Он так твёрдо верил в это, что, глядя на него, и другие были убеждены в этом и не отказывали ему ни в высшем положении в свете, ни в деньгах, которые он, очевидно без отдачи, занимал у встречного и поперечного (Толстой 5). He believed that...God had created him to spend thirty thousand a year and always to occupy a prominent position in society. He was so firmly convinced of this that looking at him others were persuaded of it too, and refused him neither a leading place in society nor the money he borrowed right and left, obviously with no notion of repaying it (5a). ♦ «Из этого, впрочем, вовсе не следует, чтобы Ньютон имел право убивать кого вздумается, направо и налево попадающихся, или воровать каждый день на базаре» (Достоевский 3). "It doesn't at all follow from this, however, that Newton had the right to kill whoever he pleased, right, left, and center, or to go thieving in the market place" (3a).

B-348 • ПЕ́РВЫЙ ВСТРЕ́ЧНЫЙ *occas. disapprov* [NP; sing only; subj or obj; fixed WO] **1.** the first person one encounters: **the first person to come ⟨to happen⟩ along; the first person one meets ⟨sees, comes across⟩; the first passerby.**

Самба как будто не замечал гражданских бурь, которые потрясали в те годы Париж. Иногда он удивлённо спрашивал первого встречного: «Кто это стреляет?» (Эренбург 1). Sembat did not seem to notice the civil storms shaking Paris in those years. Sometimes he would inquire in surprise of the first passerby: "Who's that shooting?" (1a).

2. any person without discrimination: **anyone who comes one's way; anyone ⟨anybody⟩ at all; anyone one meets ⟨sees, comes across⟩; a complete ⟨total⟩ stranger.**

...Самим есть нечего, а он [Илья] единственный кусок отдавал первому встречному (Распутин 3). ...When his [Ilia's] own family had nothing to eat he would give the last crust to a complete stranger (3a).

B-349 • И ВСЯ НЕДОЛГА́; ВО́Т (ТЕБЕ́) И ВСЯ НЕДОЛГА́ *both highly coll* [sent; these forms only; usu. the concluding clause in a compound sent; the preceding clause usu. has a verb in fut, imper, or subjunctive; fixed WO] (used in refer. to the preceding action, problem etc to emphasize that it can or will be done, solved etc quickly and easily) and with that the matter is finished, there is nothing more to be said about it: **and that's that ⟨it⟩; and that's the end of it; and that's all (there is to it); and that settles ⟨does⟩ it.**

Сам по себе процесс выглядел делом нехитрым: помпа, вашгерд — ящик с ситами, наподобие улья, — вот и вся, казалось, недолга... (Максимов 2). The process itself seems fairly uncomplicated: a pump, a buddle (a box looking like a large beehive that contained a series of sieves), and that was all... (2a).

B-350 • БЕЗ(О) ВСЯ́КИХ *highly coll* [PrepP; these forms only; usu. adv] (one does sth.) without argument or doubts, unreservedly: **without a moment's hesitation; without a second thought; no questions asked; right away;** [when used with a command] **(and) no nonsense ⟨backtalk, arguments⟩; and no (ifs, ands, or) buts about it.**

Если бы мне предложили работу в этой лаборатории, я бы пошла туда безо всяких. If I were offered a job in that laboratory, I'd take it without a moment's hesitation. ♦ А что я могу сделать, если сам министр приказал: «Принять Кочкина на работу — и без всяких!»? What can I do when the minister himself ordered: "Give Kochkin a job, and no ifs, ands, or buts about it!"?

B-351 • ВСЯ́КАЯ ВСЯ́ЧИНА *coll* [NP; sing only; fixed WO] **1.** [obj or subj] the most diverse things, objects, phenomena: **all sorts ⟨kinds⟩ of things ⟨stuff⟩;** [of material objects] **sundries;** **(all kinds of) odds and ends; odd items;** [when introduced by Conj «и» at the end of an enumeration] **and what have you.**

Мужик и работники заткнули дыру всякой всячиной (Герцен 1). The peasant and the others plugged the hole with all sorts of things (1a). ♦ «Что везёшь к нам?» — спросил мой старик. «Ткани для женских платьев и мужских рубашек, — сказал Самуил, — галоши с загнутыми носками, какие обожают абхазцы, стёкла для ламп, иголки для швейных машин, нитки, пуговицы, чуму, холеру и другую всякую всячину» (Искандер 3). "What are you bringing us?" my old man asked. "Yard goods for women's dresses and men's shirts," Samuel said, "galoshes with turned-up toes of the kind Abkhazians adore, lamp chimneys, sewing-machine needles, thread, buttons, plague, cholera, and other sundries" (3a). ♦ Хотел он ей [птице] тут же размозжить голову, но вспомнил, что рядом, в Гаграх, живёт принц Ольденбургский и от скуки покупает всякую всячину (Искандер 3). He wanted to smash its [the bird's] head then and there, but remembered that nearby in Gagra lived a Prince Oldenburgsky who bought odd items out of boredom (3a).

2. [usu. prep obj; used with verbs of speaking] different things, topics, subjects (of conversation, discussion, reading, or contemplation): **anything and everything; everything under the sun; all sorts ⟨kinds⟩ of things; this and that.**

Так, разговаривая о всякой всячине, они шли по дороге (Искандер 5). Thus they walked along the road, talking of anything and everything (5a). ♦ Там мы жарили картошку на электрической плитке, прозванной «камином», распивали крепчайший чай и толковали о всякой всячине... (Копелев 1). There we fried potatoes on a hotplate, dubbed "the fireplace," drank the strongest tea, and talked about everything under the sun (1a). ♦ Ему хотелось на постоялый двор, к... Козлевичу, с которым так приятно попить чаю и покалякать о всякой всячине (Ильф и Петров 2). He was longing to get back to the tavern, to...Kozlevich, with whom it was so nice to drink tea and chat about this and that (2a).

B-352 • жить КАК НА ВУЛКА́НЕ *coll* [как + PrepP; Invar; adv] (to live) in a potentially dangerous situation, expecting sth. unpleasant, disastrous to happen: **(be living) on top of a volcano; (be sitting) on a time bomb ⟨a volcano⟩.**

«Живём мы, знаете, как на вулкане... Всё может произойти...» (Ильф и Петров 1). "We're living on top of a volcano, you know. Anything can happen" (1a). ♦ «Интересно, постигаете ли вы, на каком мы тут и без вас вулкане?» — «...Жена совершенно права. И без вас не сладко» (Пастернак 1). "I wonder if you realize what a volcano we are sitting on even without you here?" "...My wife is quite right. Things are bad enough without you" (1a).

B-353 • ИДУ́ НА ВЫ *obs, now coll, often humor* [sent; Invar; fixed WO] I am going to attack you (in contempt. usage, I intend to oppose you, argue against your point of view etc): **I come against ye!**

Бородавкин вспомнил, что великий князь Святослав Игоревич, прежде нежели побеждать врагов, всегда посылал сказать: иду на вы! — и, руководствуясь этим примером, командировал своего ординарца к стрельцам с таким же приветствием (Салтыков-Щедрин 1). Wartkin remembered that Grand Prince Svyatoslav Igorevich, before conquering his enemies, always sent ahead to say, "I come against ye!" Guided by this example, he dispatched his orderly to the musketeers with the same greeting (1a).

< According to Russian chroniclers, this phrase was used by Prince Svyatoslav (10th cent.) as a declaration of war. In old Russian, the pronoun «вы» had two forms of the accusative case: the full form «васъ» and the short, or enclitic, form «вы».

B-354 • НА ВЫ *с кем быть₀*, переходить; называть *кого*, обращаться *к кому;* **ГОВОРИ́ТЬ ВЫ** *кому* [PrepP, Invar, subj-compl with copula or adv (1st var.); VP (2nd var.); subj:

human] (to begin) to use the «вы» (formal "you") form of address when speaking to or with s.o.: X с Y-ом на вы ≃ **X is on formal terms with Y; X and Y are on formal terms with each other; X addresses Y ⟨X and Y address each other⟩ formally ⟨in the formal way⟩;** ‖ X должен говорить Y-у вы ≃ [in limited contexts] **X must treat Y with respect.** ○ ОБРАЩЕ́НИЕ НА ВЫ [NP; sing only] **the formal way one addresses s.o. ⟨one is addressed⟩.**

...В кухне он называл меня на «вы» и мне это понравилось, а теперь вдруг на «ты» (Каверин 1). ...In the kitchen, he had spoken to me in the formal way in which grown-ups are addressed and I had liked it, but now he had suddenly changed for the familiar form (1a). ♦ «А ты мне „ты" не говори, — сказал Прохор улыбчиво, — ты мне „вы" должен говорить» (Семёнов 1). "And don't you be so familiar," said Prokhor smilingly, "you must treat me with respect" (1a). ♦ Тёща сказала, что Наташка... слишком высоко себя ставит, а нас презирает. Я спросил, откуда это видно. Тёща сказала, что это видно из её обращения ко всем на «вы» из подчёркнутой вежливости (Зиновьев 2). My mother-in-law said that Natashka...obviously thinks herself very superior and despises us. I asked her what made her think that. My mother-in-law said it was clear from the formal and excessively polite way she addressed everyone (2a).

В-355 • НА ВЫ́БОР *(чей)* **давать, предлагать** и т. п. [PrepP; Invar; adv or nonagreeing modif] allowing s.o. to select from two or more things: **(give ⟨offer⟩ s.o.) a choice; (have ⟨give s.o., offer s.o.⟩ several things) to choose from ⟨between⟩; (have) one's choice; (take) whatever one would like;** ‖ бери любой [NP] ~ ≃ **take any ⟨whichever⟩ [NP] you please ⟨you'd like etc⟩;** ‖ любой [NP] ~ ≃ **any ⟨whichever⟩ [NP] one chooses ⟨wants etc⟩.**

[Альда:] Если б вы дали мне на выбор две одинаковых конфеты — я б не выбрала (Солженицын 11). [A.:] If you'd given me two identical pieces of candy to choose between—I wouldn't have been able to choose (11a). ♦ «Ты человек проверенный... Член партии со стажем... И вообще мы тебя знаем... Будешь сопровождать... архив... Бери любой классный вагон на выбор» (Максимов 3). "You've proved yourself reliable...and you're an old party member...And, well, we know you, so you will go with the records...Take any passenger carriage you please" (3a). ♦ Сижу вот, пишу, на эти берёзы поглядываю. А надоест, куплю билет и поеду, куда захочу. Хоть в Америку, хоть в Италию... Любая страна на выбор (Войнович 1). I sit here and write, gazing out at those birches. If I get bored, I can buy a ticket and travel wherever I please. To the United States, to Italy...to any country I choose (1a).

В-356 • ВЫВОДИ́ТЬ/ВЫ́ВЕСТИ ИЗ СЕБЯ́ *кого* [VP; subj: human or abstr] to make s.o. lose his self-control, irritate s.o. badly: **X вывел Y-а из себя ≃ X made Y lose Y's temper ⟨cool⟩; X drove Y crazy ⟨berserk, out of Y's wits⟩; X got Y's dander up; X drove Y up the wall; thing X got Y's back up; X exasperated Y.**

«А сюрпризик-то не хотите разве посмотреть?» — захихикал Порфирий, опять схватывая его [Раскольникова] немного повыше локтя и останавливая у дверей. Он, видимо, становился всё веселее и игривее, что окончательно выводило из себя Раскольникова (Достоевский 3). "But don't you want to take a look at my little surprise?" giggled Porfiry, again taking him [Raskolnikov] just above the elbow and stopping him in the doorway. He was clearly growing ever more cheerful and playful, which drove Raskolnikov completely berserk (3a). ♦ [Говорящий – мул] В одном месте из калитки выскочила мерзкая собачонка и с визгливым лаем долго бежала за мной... Конечно, я бы мог её одним ударом копыта отбросить в сторону, но это означало бы признаться, что она выводит меня из себя (Искандер 3). [The speaker is a mule] In one place a loathsome little dog jumped out of a gate and ran after me for a long time, barking shrilly....Of course I

could have flung her aside with one blow of my hoof, but that would have meant admitting that she was driving me out of my wits (3a). ♦ К концу обыска я настолько вывел Шилова из себя, что он отказался оставить мне протокол... (Амальрик 1). By the end of the search I had driven Shilov up the wall—so much so that he refused to leave a copy of the search report with me (1a). ♦ Господин Ней нервничал. Его выводил из себя этот ужасный, неподобный вой (Эренбург 2). ...M. Ney was nervous. The awful howling of the wind exasperated him (2a).

В-357 • ВЫВОДИ́ТЬ/ВЫ́ВЕСТИ НАРУ́ЖУ *что obsoles* [VP; subj: usu. human] to make sth. (usu. some reprehensible designs, actions etc) evident to everyone, expose sth.: **X вывел наружу Y ≃ X brought Y to light; X brought Y (out) into the open; X took the wraps off Y; X unmasked Y; X blew the lid off Y.**

В-358 • ВЫВОРА́ЧИВАЕТ/ВЫ́ВЕРНУЛО ⟨ВЫ́ВОРОТИЛО⟩ НАИЗНА́НКУ *кого highly coll* [VP; impers] s.o. is very nauseated, vomiting: **X-а выворачивало наизнанку ≃ X was sick to his stomach; X was green around the gills; X was barfing ⟨puking⟩ his brains out.**

В-359 • ВЫВОРА́ЧИВАТЬ/ВЫ́ВЕРНУТЬ ⟨ВЫ́ВОРОТИТЬ⟩ НАИЗНА́НКУ *coll* [VP; subj: human] **1.** ~ *что* to interpret and/or present sth. incorrectly, falsely (may refer to an intentional distortion or an honest mistake): **X вывернул Y наизнанку ≃ X turned Y inside out;** [of an intentional distortion] **X twisted Y around ⟨about⟩;** [of an honest mistake] **X got Y all wrong ⟨backward⟩; X misconstrued ⟨misinterpreted⟩ Y.**

Что Виктору ни скажешь, он всё выворачивает наизнанку. No matter what you tell Viktor, he turns it inside out.

2. ~ *кого-что* to comprehend and reveal the true essence of s.o. or sth.: **X вывернул наизнанку Y-а ≃ X showed Y up for what Y really is ⟨was⟩; X got to the bottom of thing Y;** [in limited contexts] **X got to the heart of the matter.**

Эта экономическая теория только кажется новаторской: выверни её наизнанку и увидишь, что в основе её лежат старые марксистские догмы. This economic theory only seems innovative: when you get to the bottom of it you see that it's based on old Marxist dogmas.

В-360 • ВЫВОРА́ЧИВАТЬСЯ/ВЫ́ВЕРНУТЬСЯ НАИЗНА́НКУ *coll* [VP; subj: human] to try very hard (to do sth.), resort to whatever means are necessary (to attain or accomplish sth.): **X вывернется наизнанку ≃ X will bend over backward; X will go to any lengths; X will knock himself out; X will do his damnedest ⟨darnedest⟩.**

Мы готовы вывернуться наизнанку, чтобы наш сын получил высшее образование. We're willing to go to any lengths to give our son the opportunity for a higher education. ♦ Обуви в магазинах не было, и Николаю пришлось вывернуться наизнанку, чтобы достать жене зимние сапоги. With no shoes to be found in the stores, Nikolai had to knock himself out to get his wife a pair of winter boots.

В-361 • ВЫДАВА́ТЬ/ВЫ́ДАТЬ ⟨ОТДАВА́ТЬ/ОТДА́ТЬ⟩ ЗА́МУЖ *кого* (за *кого*) [VP; subj: human; obj: human, female] to give one's daughter, sister etc in marriage: **X выдал женщину Y замуж ≃ X married off Y ⟨married Y off⟩;** [in limited contexts] **X found Y a husband ⟨found a husband for Y⟩.**

[Атуева:] Что ж тут думать? Вы думаньем дочь замуж не отдадите (Сухово-Кобылин 2). [A.:] What is there to think about? You won't marry off your daughter by just thinking (2b). ♦ От времени до времени Кирила Петрович выдавал некоторых из них [горничных] замуж... (Пушкин 1). From time to time Kirila Petrovitch found husbands for some of them [maidservants]... (1b).

В-362 • ВЫДАВА́ТЬ/ВЫ́ДАТЬ СЕБЯ́ [VP] **1.** ~ *(чем кому)* [subj: human or animal] to reveal one's presence: X выдал себя ≃ **X gave himself away; X made his presence known.**

2. ~ *(чем)* [subj: human] to reveal involuntarily one's true feelings, state of mind, attitude etc: X выдал себя ≃ **X gave himself away; X gave away his true feelings.**

…Однажды вечером отец позвал Евгения к себе… «Ты простишь мне вмешательство в твои личные дела. Но я хочу знать, как ты думаешь поступить с Аксиньей?» Торопливостью, с какой стал закуривать, Евгений выдал себя… «Не знаю… Просто не знаю…» — чистосердечно признался он (Шолохов 4). …One evening his [Yevgeny's] father called him in….″Forgive my intruding in your personal affairs. But I want to know what you intend to do about Aksinya.″ Yevgeny gave himself away by the haste with which he lighted a cigarette….″I don't know.…I simply don't know,″ he confessed frankly (4a).

В-363 • НЕ ВЫ́ДАЙ(ТЕ) *coll* [VP$_{imper}$; these forms only] **1.** *obs* do not abandon me (or us), help me (or us) (used as an appeal for help): **don't turn your back on me ⟨us⟩; don't run out on me ⟨us⟩; don't leave me ⟨us⟩ in the lurch.**

2. do not disappoint me (or us) (used to urge s.o. to apply all his efforts to the work he is doing or is about to do): **don't let me ⟨us⟩ down; don't fail me ⟨us⟩ now.**

В-364 • НА ВЫ́ДАНЬЕ *substand* [PrepP; Invar; subj-compl with copula (subj: human, female) or nonagreeing modif] at an age when a young woman is expected to get married: **of marriageable age; marriageable.**

«Одна беда: Маша; девка на выданье, а какое у ней приданое? Частый гребень, да веник, да алтын денег…» (Пушкин 2). ″There's just one problem: Masha. She's of marriageable age, but what does she have for a dowry? A fine-tooth comb, a besom, and a three-kopeck piece…″ (2a).

В-365 • ХОТЬ ВЫ́ЖМИ *coll* [хоть + VP$_{imper}$; Invar; subj-compl with быть$_\emptyset$ (subj: concr)] (of clothing) thoroughly wet (from rain, perspiration etc): **wringing ⟨soaking, sopping⟩ wet; soaked (through); drenched; wet right through.**

Платье на тебе — хоть выжми. Скорее переоденься, а то простудишься. Your dress is sopping wet. Hurry up and get changed or you'll catch cold.

В-366 • С ВЫ́ЗОВОМ *сказать, ответить, посмотреть* и т. п. [PrepP; Invar; adv] (to say, answer, look etc) in a provoking manner: **with a challenge; challengingly; defiantly;** [in limited contexts] **as a challenge.**

«Могу предложить очную ставку. Пригласить Звонкову?» — спокойно спросил Антон. Глаза Сипенятина растерянно заметались, но ответил он с вызовом: «Приглашай!» (Чернёнок 2). ″I can suggest a meeting. Shall I call in Zvonkova?″ Anton asked calmly. Sipeniatin's eyes darted about nervously, but he answered with a challenge. ″Go ahead!″ (2a). ♦ «Ты мне что-то хотел сказать?» — спросил он [дядя Сандро] у меня с вызовом (Искандер 4). ″Was there something you wanted to tell me?″ he [Uncle Sandro] asked me challengingly (4a). ♦ Когда Нина спросила, кто даёт ей заграничные патефонные пластинки, [Варя] нагло прищурилась. «Ведь я работаю на японскую разведку. Разве ты не знаешь?» С вызовом сказала, нарывалась на скандал (Рыбаков 2). When Nina asked her [Varya] who gave her foreign phonograph records, she pulled an insolent face and said, ″I work for Japanese intelligence. Didn't you know?″ She said it as a challenge, trying to provoke a quarrel (2a).

В-367 • В ВЫ́ИГРЫШЕ [PrepP; Invar; subj-compl with copula] **1.** [subj: human] one is winning at cards: X был ⟨оказался⟩ в выигрыше ≃ **X was winning ⟨the winner⟩; X came out the winner; X was ⟨came out⟩ ahead of the game.**

[Степан] вошёл в кухню, плотно притворил дверь, зажёг спичку. Был он в выигрыше (играли на спички), оттого мирен и сонлив (Шолохов 2). He [Stepan] went into the kitchen, closed the door firmly and lighted a match. After winning at cards (they had been playing for matches), he was in a peaceful, sleepy mood (2a).

2. [subj: human or collect] a person or group has or gets the advantage (in sth.): X будет ⟨останется⟩ в выигрыше ≃ **X will get the better end of it ⟨of the deal etc⟩; X will come out ahead (of the game);** [in limited contexts] **X will be better off.**

Не вмешивайся ни в какие конфликты на работе — и ты будешь в выигрыше. Avoid getting mixed up in any disputes at work and you'll come out ahead of the game. ♦ «Я не уверен, надо ли мне выступить и сказать, как я отношусь к этому предложению». — «Не уверен — промолчи: будешь в выигрыше». ″I'm not sure if I should speak out about where I stand on this proposal.″ ″If you're not sure, you'd be better off keeping quiet.″

В-368 • ВЫ́КРАСИТЬ ДА ⟨И⟩ ВЫ́БРОСИТЬ *что coll* [VP; usu. infin used as impers predic] (of things that are worn out, falling to pieces, in terrible condition) sth. should be thrown away, discarded: X [accus] только выкрасить да выбросить ≃ **X belongs in the garbage ⟨the trash⟩ ⟨can⟩; X is ready ⟨fit⟩ for the junk heap; X deserves to be deep-sixed ⟨chucked, trashed⟩; one should (just) deep-six ⟨chuck, trash⟩ X.**

Зачем переделывать это старое платье? Его только выкрасить да выбросить. Why bother to fix up that old dress? You should just chuck it.

В-369 • НА́-КА ⟨НА́-КАСЬ, НА́-КАСЯ, НА́⟩, ВЫ́-КУСИ! *substand, rude* [Interj; these forms only; fixed WO] emphatically no (used to express one's categorical refusal to do sth., refutation of some statement etc): [when refusing to do sth.] **no (frigging) way!; you can whistle for it!; not on your life!; nothing doing!; like hell I ⟨we⟩ will!; I'll see you in hell first!;** [when refuting a statement] **what (a load of) crap!; that's bullshit!;** [when emphasizing a previous statement of refusal etc] **put that in your pipe (and smoke it)!**

«В лес ехать надо». — «Мне? В лес?» — «Да». — «…На этот раз на, выкуси! Не поеду!» — «Поедешь. Своей волей не поедешь — по суду отправим» (Абрамов 1). ″…You've got to go out to the forest.″ ″Me? To the forest?″ ″Yes.″ ″…This time you can whistle for it! I'm not going!″ ″Yes you are. If not of your own free will, then the court will make you go!″ (1a). ♦ «Правильно! Ты думаешь человек человеку кто? Друг? Товарищ? Братишка? На-ка, выкуси! Человек человеку люпус ест! [transliteration of the Latin *lupus est* = волк]» (Войнович 4). ″Right! What do you think man is to man? A friend? A comrade? A brother? Ha-ha, what crap! Man is like a wolf to his fellow man″ (4a). ♦ «Ступай, откель [*ungrammat* = откуда] пришёл! А Гришку твоего, захочу — с костями съем и ответа держать не буду!.. Вот на!.. Выкуси!» (Шолохов 2). ″Go back to where you came from! And if I want your Grishka, I'll have him, bones and all, and won't answer to anyone for it!…So there! Put that in your pipe!″ (2a).

< The idiom may be accompanied by one of two gestures: a "fig" gesture, in which one's hand is extended, clenched in a fist with the palm usually facing up and the thumb placed between the index and middle fingers; or an obscene gesture, by which the left fist is placed in the crook of the right arm and the right elbow is bent, bringing the forearm all the way up.

В-370 • ВЫНЬ ДА ПОЛО́ЖЬ *(кому, кого-что) highly coll* [VP$_{imper}$; Invar; predic; fixed WO] do sth. or give sth. to s.o. immediately: **give sth. to s.o. ⟨produce sth., do it etc⟩ on the spot ⟨right away, at once⟩;** [in pres contexts only] **give sth. to s.o. here and now;** [in past contexts only] **give sth. to s.o. there and then;** [in limited contexts] **come on, let's have it ⟨him etc⟩;**

[when threatening s.o.] **hand s.o. over** ⟨**cough sth. up** etc⟩ **or else.**

«Уж как мне этого Бонапарта захотелось! – говаривала она [Марфа Терентьевна] Беневоленскому, – кажется, ничего бы не пожалела, только бы глазком на него взглянуть!» Сначала Беневоленский сердился... но так как Марфа Терентьевна не унималась, а всё больше приставала к градоначальнику: вынь да положь Бонапарта, то под конец он изнемог (Салтыков-Щедрин 1). "How I'm taken with that Bonaparte!" she [Marfa Terentevna] used to say to Benevolensky. "I think there is nothing I wouldn't give just to peep at him once!" At first, Benevolensky would grow angry....But Marfa Terentevna would not desist and grew even more importunate, insisting that Benevolensky should produce her Bonaparte at once, and in the end he gave way (1b). ♦ Мне передали, что Твардовский срочно хочет меня видеть. Это было 8 июня... Я ответил А.Т. [Твардовскому], что – совершенно невозможно, приеду 12-го. Он очень расстроился... Потом, говорят, ходил по редакции обиженный и разбитый. Это – всегда в нём так, если возгорелось – то вынь да положь, погодить ему нельзя (Солженицын 2). ...A message reached me that Tvardovsky urgently wanted to see me. This was on 8 June....My answer to A.T. [Tvardovsky] was that it was absolutely impossible, and I would come to see him on the twelfth. He was very upset....I have heard that after our conversation he wandered from room to room, looking hurt and disconsolate. It was always the same with him: if he set his heart on something, it was "Come on, let's have it!" He couldn't bear to wait (2a). ♦ ...Рита сказала: «Молодцы твои родственники. Так и впились клешнями, вынь да положь им Гартвига» (Трифонов 5). ...Rita said, "Your relatives are really something. The way they dug in with their claws—it was hand over Gartvig or else!" (5a).

В-371 • МЯ́ГКО ВЫРАЖА́ЯСЬ ⟨ГОВОРЯ́⟩ [these forms only; sent adv (parenth); fixed WO] used to indicate that the speaker is intentionally avoiding phrasing sth. harshly, abruptly: **putting ⟨to put⟩ it mildly.**

«Обвинять меня в несчастье, случившемся с Саней, мягко говоря, – откровенная нелепость» (Чернёнок 2). "Accusing me of the misfortune that befell Sanya is, to put it mildly, a blatant absurdity" (2a).

В-372 • ИЗВИНИ́(ТЕ) ⟨ПРОСТИ́(ТЕ)⟩ ЗА ВЫРА-ЖЕ́НИЕ *coll;* **ИЗВИНЯ́ЮСЬ ЗА ВЫРАЖЕ́НИЕ** *substand* [these forms only; sent adv (parenth); fixed WO] used to ask the listener's indulgence when the speaker uses improper, vulgar language: **(if you'll) pardon the expression ⟨my language⟩; excuse the expression.** Cf. **excuse ⟨pardon⟩ my French.**

[Маргарита:] Ах вы, шкура вы эдакая, извиняюсь за выражение (Эрдман 1). [M.:] Oh you...you tramp, you! If you'll pardon the expression (1a). ♦ Мне на принципы так же насрать [*taboo*], извини за выражение, как и тебе (Алешковский 1). I feel the same way about principles you do—fuck 'em, excuse the expression (1a).

В-373 • С ВЫРАЖЕ́НИЕМ читать, декламировать, петь и т. п. [PrepP; Invar; adv] (to read, recite, sing etc sth.) with emotional appeal, expressively: **with feeling; with expression (in one's voice); with (genuine) emotion; in an expressive voice.**

...Какой-то несостоявшийся артист, встав в позу, читал с выражением поэму Маяковского «Хорошо» (Войнович 4). ...Some failed actor, striking a pose, was reciting Mayakovsky's poem "It's Good" with genuine emotion (4a). ♦ Балашов развернул общую тетрадь в картонном переплёте и начал читать громко, с выражением, не вставляя ни единого своего слова (Войнович 2). Balashov opened up a standard cardboard-covered notebook and began to read in a loud expressive voice without using a single word of his own (2a).

В-374 • БЕЗ ВЫРАЖЕ́НИЯ читать, говорить и т. п. [PrepP; Invar; adv] (to read sth., speak etc) in a monotone, unexpressively: **without feeling; without expression (in one's voice); without emotion; flatly.**

В-375 • ВЫБИРА́ТЬ ВЫРАЖЕ́НИЯ ⟨СЛОВА́⟩ [VP; subj: human; often imper or neg] to phrase carefully what one is saying (in order not to offend s.o. or make a mistake): **выбирай(те) выражения ≃ choose your words carefully; watch what you're saying;** [in limited contexts] **watch your tongue;** ‖ *Neg* X не выбирал выражений ≃ **X did not mince words.**

«Расскажите-ка, Максим Петрович, что за подпольное издание вы затеяли?» – «Ого! – сказал Ого. – Начинается свистопляска!» – «Выбирайте выражения!» – рявкнул вождь (Аксёнов 12). "Tell me, Maxim Petrovich, what is this underground publication you've come up with?" "Oho!" said Ogo. "The witch-hunt begins." "Choose your words carefully!" the leader barked (12a).

В-376 • НА ВЫ́РОСТ ⟨НА РОСТ⟩ шить, покупать и т. п. *coll* [PrepP; these forms only; adv or nonagreeing modif] (usu. of children's clothing) (to sew, buy a piece of clothing etc) too big in order to allow for the wearer's growth: **with room for s.o. to grow; with room (for s.o.) to grow into; to give s.o. room to grow (into); so (that) s.o. won't outgrow it too quickly.**

Московское платье оказалось превосходно: коричневые полуфрачки с бронзовыми пуговками были сшиты в обтяжку – не так, как в деревне нам шивали, на рост... (Толстой 2). Our Moscow clothes turned out to be superb: the brown dress coats had bronze buttons and were made close-fitting—not like they had been made in the country, with room for you to grow... (2b). ♦ Я – маленький гимназист в платье на вырост (Олеша 5). I am a small schoolboy wearing clothes that are too big so that I won't outgrow them too quickly (5a).

В-377 • ВЫ́СЛУГА ЛЕТ [NP; sing only; fixed WO] the period of continuous employment which entitles the employee to receive special benefits, privileges etc: **long service.**

В Германии до сих пор судят нацистов, а наши вонючие псы получают пенсии, а то и ордена за выслугу лет (Аксёнов 6). In Germany they are still indicting Nazis and bringing them to justice, but our stinking hell hounds are getting pensions and even long-service medals (6a).

В-378 • НА ВЫСОТЕ́ быть₀, оказаться, чувствовать себя и т. п.; **НА ДО́ЛЖНОЙ ВЫСОТЕ́** [PrepP; these forms only; subj-compl with copula] **1.** Also: **НА ВЫСОТЕ́ ПОЛОЖЕ́НИЯ** [subj: human or collect] (to be, feel that one is etc) performing in the best, most fitting manner in a given situation, demonstrating the daring, courage etc required under particular circumstances: X был ⟨оказался⟩ на высоте (положения) ≃ **X rose ⟨measured up⟩ to the occasion; X was equal to the occasion ⟨to the task⟩; X rose to ⟨met⟩ the challenge;** [in limited contexts] **X lived up to person Y's expectations; X was at his best;** ‖ *Neg* X был ⟨оказался⟩ не на высоте ≃ **X fell short of expectations ⟨of the mark⟩.**

...По слухам, которые распространяли чегемцы... Маяна в первую же брачную ночь сломала своему почтенному мужу два ребра... Но опять же, если верить чегемским слухам, старик оказался на высоте, потому что, будучи человеком со сломанными рёбрами, он, по крайней мере, успел зачать ещё двух детей, если первого ребёнка, как предполагали чегемцы, он успел зачать до того, как треснули его рёбра (Искандер 4). ...According to rumors that the Chegemians spread...on their wedding night Mayana broke two of her venerable husband's ribs....What is more, if we are to believe Chegem rumors, the old man rose to the occasion, because, even as a man with broken ribs, at least he succeeded in begetting two more children, if, as the Chegemians hypothesized, he had succeeded in begetting the first child before his ribs got cracked (4a). ♦ ...Он [Кирилл] оказался на высоте – сдержал своё обещание... (Лимонов 1). ...He [Kirill] lived up to my expectations and kept his promise... (1a).

2. [subj: human, collect, abstr, or concr] (to be, feel that one is etc) able to satisfy the highest demands, excellent in quality: **X на высоте ≃ X is first-rate ⟨topnotch⟩;** [in limited contexts] **person X is at his best;** ‖ [usu. with negated predic or in questions] **X был не на высоте ≃ X did not measure up; X was not up to the mark ⟨to snuff, to scratch, to par, to it⟩.**

«Ваши разговоры были записаны, когда вы звонили в [американское] посольство. Наша техника на высоте и позволила разоблачить ваши преступные замыслы...» (Копелев 1). "Your conversations were recorded when you called the [American] embassy. Our technology is first-rate and has allowed us to expose your criminal plans..." (1a). ♦ [Нина:] Отец у тебя отличный, Алька. Судьба ему определилась невесёлая... Не спорь с ним сегодня. Ни слова... [Альберт (помотал головой):] Я и не собирался ехать, а он подумал... [Нина:] Ладно, ладно, Жук, мы должны быть на высоте (Розов 4). [N.:] You have a splendid father, Al. It's just that life hasn't treated him too well....Don't argue with him today. Not one word... [A. (shaking his head):] I never even thought of going, and he thought... [N.:] Yes, I know what you mean, old man, but we've got to be at our best now (4a). ♦ «Как работают заводы, какие у вас впечатления от личности Фосса, на высоте ли, по-вашему, химики?» – быстро спрашивал он [Эйхман] (Гроссман 2). "How are the factories getting on? What are your impressions of Voss? Do you think the chemists are up to it?" he [Eichmann] asked rapidly (2a).

В-379 • С ВЫСОТЫ́ ПТИ́ЧЬЕГО ПОЛЁТА; С ПТИ́ЧЬЕГО ПОЛЁТА [PrepP; these forms only; adv; fixed WO] **1.** seen from high up, from a place allowing one to see everything: **(get, have) a bird's-eye view (of sth.); (look at sth.) from a bird's-eye view.**

С утра до вечера сидел он, сгорбившись, перед лестничным окном второго этажа во флигеле и оттуда – как бы с высоты птичьего полёта – печально и трезво оглядывал двор (Максимов 3). From morning to night he sat hunched up by the staircase window on the second floor of the outbuilding, where he had a sad and sober bird's-eye view of the yard (3a). ♦ Оказалось, что все они [пятеро мужчин, которых привезли в районный вытрезвитель,] видели в ту ночь один и тот же сон – кучу разноцветных котят на зелёной мокрой траве. Вначале вроде бы как из окна, потом как бы с птичьего полёта, потом всё выше, выше... (Аксёнов 6). It seemed that they [the five men brought to the precinct sobering-up station] had all had the same dream: a litter of different colored kittens on wet green grass. At first it was as if they were looking at them out of a window, then apparently from a bird's-eye view, then higher and higher... (6a).

2. судить (о ком-чем), рассматривать что и т. п. ~ (to judge s.o. or sth., examine sth. etc) cursorily, without an in-depth analysis: **(give ⟨get⟩) a bird's-eye view (of a subject etc); (judge sth.) superficially;** [in limited contexts] **judge a book by its cover.**

В-380 • С ВЫСОТЫ́ СВОЕГО́ ВЕЛИ́ЧИЯ смотреть, взирать на кого-что, сказать что и т. п. iron [PrepP; Invar; adv; fixed WO] (to look at s.o. or sth., say sth. etc) haughtily, condescendingly, with an excessive sense of self-importance: **look down one's nose (at s.o. ⟨sth.⟩); (look at ⟨say sth. to⟩ s.o.) condescendingly; (say sth.) pompously; one thinks he is ⟨behaves as if he were⟩ God's gift to mankind ⟨to the world⟩.**

«Я такими мелкими делами не занимаюсь, – процедил хозяин роскошного кабинета с высоты своего величия. – Обратитесь с этим вопросом к моему секретарю». "I don't deal with such trifling matters," said the occupant of the luxurious office condescendingly. "Take your question to my secretary."

В-381 • ХОТЬ НА ВЫ́СТАВКУ кого-что coll, occas. iron [хоть + PrepP; Invar; usu. subj-compl with бытьø (subj: any common noun) or adv] (looking) wonderful, beautiful: **s.o. ⟨sth.⟩ could be placed on exhibition; s.o. ⟨sth.⟩ could be sent to ⟨shown at⟩ an exhibition; s.o. ⟨sth.⟩ is fit for an exhibition; s.o. is ⟨looks⟩ (as) pretty as a picture; s.o. ⟨sth.⟩ is) picture perfect.**

«А чудаковат у тебя дядя... Щегольство какое в деревне, подумаешь! Ногти-то, ногти, хоть на выставку посылай!» (Тургенев 2). "Queer fellow, that uncle of yours....Fancy all that foppery out in the country! And talk about nails, why, they could be placed on exhibition!" (2a).

В-382 • НА ВЫ́СТРЕЛ подходить, подъезжать и т. п. к кому-чему [PrepP; Invar; adv] at a distance near enough to be reached by a bullet or shell when fired from a weapon; *by extension* very nearby: **within firing ⟨close⟩ range; within shooting distance; (come ⟨get etc⟩) anywhere near (s.o. ⟨sth.⟩).**

Петро не велел им [жителям хутора] подходить даже на выстрел к казачьей цепи. Но одно появление их произвело на красных заметное воздействие (Шолохов 4). Petro would not allow the village folk to come anywhere near the Cossack positions. But their mere appearance on the scene produced a noticeable impression on the Reds... (4a).

В-383 • НА ПУ́ШЕЧНЫЙ ВЫ́СТРЕЛ не подпускать, не допускать кого к кому-чему, не подходить к кому-чему [PrepP; Invar; adv; fixed WO] (not to allow s.o. to see some person or appear in some place) at all, (to avoid some person or place) entirely: **X-а нельзя на пушечный выстрел подпускать к Y-у ≃ X should ⟨must⟩ not be allowed within firing ⟨shooting⟩ range of Y (no matter what); X should not ⟨cannot⟩ under any circumstances be allowed in place Y ⟨near person Y, to see person Y etc⟩; X should ⟨must⟩ not be allowed in place Y ⟨near person Y etc⟩ no matter what;** ‖ **X к Y-у на пушечный выстрел не подойдёт ≃ X won't go anywhere near Y (no matter what); X won't go near Y for anything;** [in limited contexts] **X won't ⟨wouldn't⟩ touch Y with a ten-foot pole.**

...Давным-давно известно, кому из писателей можно дать слово... а кого нельзя и к трибуне подпускать и на пушечный выстрел (Свирский 1). ...They'd known for a long time which writers could be allowed to speak....And they knew who couldn't under any circumstances be allowed on the platform (1a).

В-384 • ХОЛОСТО́Й ВЫ́СТРЕЛ iron [NP; fixed WO] sth. worthless, useless that has not fulfilled or will not fulfill its intended purpose: **like firing a blank (cartridge); (like) a shot from a stage pistol.**

Хорошо, что письмо осталось при мне. Иначе получился бы холостой выстрел (Олеша 2). It's lucky that I kept the letter. Otherwise it would have been like firing a blank (2a). ♦ Тупо задуманный, занудно подготовленный якировский процесс пролетел холостым выстрелом, никого не поразив, никого не напугав, только позором для ГБ (Солженицын 2). The Yakir trial, a crass idea fumblingly executed, was a shot from a stage pistol, which hit no one, frightened no one, and merely brought disgrace on the KGB (2a).

В-385 • ДАВА́ТЬ/ДАТЬ ВЫ́ХОД ⟨ИСХО́Д⟩ чему [VP; subj: human or, rare, abstr; usu. pfv] to allow o.s. to express (some emotion) without constraint: **X дал выход Y-у ≃ person X gave vent ⟨free rein⟩ to Y; person X freely expressed Y; X let loose Y; X unleashed Y.**

До последней минуты Рита не могла поверить своему счастью и только получив выигрыш, дала выход своему лико ванию. Until the last moment Rita couldn't believe her luck, and it was only after she had received her winnings that she let loose her joy.

B-386 • **ВЫХОДЕЦ С ТОГО СВЕТА** [NP; fixed WO] in popular belief, the spirit of a deceased person: **ghost; apparition; phantom; specter; s.o. who has returned ⟨come back⟩ from the grave ⟨the dead⟩.**

B-387 • **ВЫХОДИ́ТЬ/ВЫ́ЙТИ ЗА́МУЖ** *(за кого)* [VP; subj: human, female] to take (s.o.) in marriage, take a husband: X вышла замуж (за Y-а) ≃ **X married Y; X got married.**

[Ольга:] Всё хорошо, всё от бога, но мне кажется, если бы я вышла замуж и целый день сидела дома, то это было бы лучше (Чехов 5). It's all good, all from God, but it seems to me that if I had married and stayed at home all day, it would have been better (5a).

B-388 • **ВЫХОДИ́ТЬ/ВЫ́ЙТИ ИЗ СЕБЯ́** [VP; subj: human] to become enraged, explode with anger: X вышел из себя ≃ **X lost his temper ⟨self-control⟩; X lost control of himself; X flew off the handle; X blew up; X was beside himself;** [in limited contexts] **X flew into a rage.**

[Глафира:] Без меня начинается в доме ералаш: то не так, – другое не по вас... Вы начинаете выходить из себя... (Островский 5). [G.:] When I am gone, confusion begins. This thing is wrong; the other doesn't suit you....You begin to lose your temper (5a). ♦ Пока Марей не выйдет из себя, он отличается невыносимым терпением... (Мандельштам 2). As long as Marei does not lose control of himself he is distinguished by an excruciating capacity for endurance... (2a). ♦ «Это разорение! Это ни на что не похоже!» – говорил Обломов, выходя из себя (Гончаров 1). "That's devastating! Absolutely unheard of!" exclaimed Oblomov, beside himself (1b).

B-389 • **ЗА ВЫ́ЧЕТОМ** *чего* [PrepP; Invar; the resulting PrepP is adv] **1.** upon deduction of: **after deducting;** [of taxes and other deductions from one's pay] **after;** [the English equivalent and its obj precede the NP denoting the final sum] **less; minus.**

«Сколько ты получаешь?» – «За вычетом налогов и алиментов – четыре тысячи рублей». "How much do you make?" "Less taxes and alimony, four thousand rubles."

2. excluding: **except for; with the exception of; apart from; save; not counting; outside of.**

...Мой актив, за вычетом вещей, разбросанных по будетлянским [from «будетляне», a Slavonic name for the Futurists coined by Velimir Khlebnikov] сборникам, сводился в ту пору к одной лишь «Флейте Марсия»... (Лившиц 1). ...Apart from pieces scattered throughout the budetliane miscellanies, my assets at that time amounted merely to the *Flute of Marsyas* (1a).

B-390 • **ВЕСЬ ВЫ́ШЕЛ** *coll* [VP; past only; often used as part of the statement Был (...), да весь вышел; fixed WO] **1.** [subj: human or animal (usu. omitted)] one no longer possesses some (usu. positive) quality that he once possessed (said of a person whose energy has been spent, talent has gone unrealized or been used up, beauty has faded etc): **(one's talent ⟨creativity, energy etc⟩) is all gone; one has lost (his spark ⟨spunk, sense of humor etc⟩);** [in response to the interlocutor's remark stating that a person possesses or used to possess a certain quality] **not anymore; there's none of that left now.**

«Твой дядя очень изменился. Раньше он был бодрым, энергичным». – «Был, да весь вышел». "Your uncle has really changed. He used to be upbeat and energetic." "Used to be, but not anymore."

2. [subj: concr, usu. a noun denoting an appliance, machine, gadget etc] sth. no longer functions (usu. from long use): X весь вышел ≃ **X died; X is no more.**

B-391 • **НЕ ВЫ́ШЕЛ** *чем coll* [VP; subj: human; past only] s.o. lacks a particular quality (usu. beauty, intelligence etc): X Y-ом не вышел ≃ **X is short on Y; X is not as [AdjP] as he could be;** [in limited contexts] **X is not big in the Y department;** ‖ X лицом ⟨умом⟩ не вышел ≃ **X is not much to look at ⟨not much of a brain etc⟩; X ростом не вышел ≃ X ⟨X's body⟩ is puny.**

И что из того, что он [Митрий] не вышел телом? Разве его вина? А она-то [Марфа] сама вышла? (Абрамов 1). So what if his [Mitry's] body was puny? Was that his fault? Was her [Marfa's] body that marvelous? (1a).

B-392 • **КАК БЫ ЧЕГО НЕ ВЫ́ШЛО** [sent; Invar; fixed WO] (usu. reflects s.o.'s cowardliness, extreme indecisiveness, alarmism etc) sth. bad, unpleasant, dangerous etc might happen: **all sorts of things could happen; you never know what might happen; that may lead to trouble;** [in limited contexts] **you ⟨one⟩ can never be too careful.**

А вдруг как раз в день рождения матери приехал Аркашка? Приехал и ждет её?.. А она ходит в чистом поле сама по себе и ничего-то не знает... И вообще – как бы чего не вышло, уж очень умиротворённым и спокойным оказался нынче день, а за спокойствием всегда что-нибудь да кроется (Залыгин 1). But what if Arkady had turned up at home, on his mother's birthday? What if he was waiting for her now?... And she'd been wandering gaily in the open fields, never thinking he might be there....All sorts of things could have happened! The day had been too serenely calm, and there was always something lurking under a calm surface (1a). ♦ ...Они [местные власти] требовали эти стихи на предварительный просмотр. А просмотрев, бывало, запрещали представление. Причем мотивировки запрещений были разнообразные. Наичаще такая: «Наш народ бедный, и нечего ему тратить деньги на ваши представления». Бывали и ответы загадочные: «Боимся, как бы чего не вышло благодаря вашим представлениям» (Булгаков 5). ...They [the local authorities] demanded to see the script and, having seen it, often forbade its performance, giving a variety of reasons. The most frequent of these reasons was: "Our people are poor, and there is no need for them to waste money on your shows." There were also enigmatic answers, such as "We are afraid that your shows may lead to trouble..." (5a).

< From Anton Chekhov's "Man in a Case" («Человек в футляре»), 1898.

B-393 • **ВЕРТЕ́ТЬСЯ ⟨ВИ́ТЬСЯ⟩ ВЬЮНО́М** [VP; subj: human] **1.** to move quickly from one place to another, be in motion all the time: X вертелся вьюном ≃ **X was scurrying ⟨bustling⟩ about.**

2. ~ *около кого* to flatter s.o., be excessively (and usu. insincerely) attentive to s.o. (usu. in order to gain s.o.'s favor): X вьётся вьюном около Y-а ≃ **X is playing up to Y; X is dancing attendance on Y.**

[author's usage] «Илья Золотарёв... в большие начальники вышел, другие кругом него вьюном крутятся...» (Максимов 1). "He [Ilya Zolotarev] has become an important boss; the others dance attendance on him" (1a).

B-394 • **НЕ ВЯ́ЖЕТСЯ** [VP; subj: дело, разговор etc; pres or past] sth. (usu. some project, s.o.'s work, a conversation etc) is not going as it should, as was expected or hoped: X не вяжется ≃ **X isn't coming out right; X isn't jelling; X isn't coming together;** [of a conversation] **X is flagging.**

...[Митенька] делал всевозможные усилия, чтоб соблюсти приличие и заговорить с своею соседкой по левую сторону, но разговор решительно не вязался... (Салтыков-Щедрин 2). ...[Mitenka] did his best to observe the rules of decorum by engaging the lady on his left in conversation, which, however, flagged badly... (2a).

Г

Г-1 • ТИ́ХАЯ ГА́ВАНЬ [NP; sing only; fixed WO] a place (job etc) that provides protection from hardship, danger etc, a sanctuary: **quiet ⟨peaceful, safe⟩ haven; peaceful abode; safe refuge ⟨shelter⟩.**

«Какой-то процент ведь уцелел же? Так вот я попал в этот процент. Я ушёл в чистую биологию – нашёл себе тихую гавань!..» (Солженицын 10). "A certain percentage managed to survive, didn't they? Well, I was part of that percentage. I withdrew into the study of pure biology, I found myself a quiet haven (10a). ♦ Она [Д. Камминс] встретила меня не как «нанимателя дома», а как друга, уставшего после многих передряг, нашедшего, наконец, тихую гавань (Аллилуева 2). She [Mrs. Commins] treated me not as a future tenant, but as a friend who, exhausted after many hardships, had at last found a peaceful abode (2a).

Г-2 • ДАТЬ ГАЗ; ПРИБАВЛЯ́ТЬ/ПРИБА́ВИТЬ ⟨ПОДДАВА́ТЬ/ПОДДА́ТЬ coll⟩ ГА́ЗУ [VP; subj: human (all variants) or a noun denoting a vehicle (var. with прибавлять)] (of a person) to cause a vehicle to go faster, accelerate, (of a vehicle) to go faster, accelerate: X прибавил газу ≃ **X sped up;** [subj: human only] **X stepped on it ⟨on the gas⟩; X gave it ⟨her⟩ the gun; X put the pedal to the metal.**

Происходит нечто позорное, подумал Огородников. Я бегу от русских под защитой американской машины... Однако, что делать дальше? Сейчас они прибавят газу, и я останусь наедине с нашими мазуриками (Аксёнов 12). Something shameful is happening, thought Ogorodnikov. I am running from Russians under cover of an American car....However, what do I do next? They're going to speed up and I'll be left alone with our boys (12a).

Г-3 • СБАВЛЯ́ТЬ/СБА́ВИТЬ ГАЗ [VP; subj: human or a noun denoting a vehicle] (of a person) to cause a vehicle to go more slowly, decelerate, (of a vehicle) to decrease speed: X сбавил газ ≃ **X slowed down;** [subj: human only] **X eased off ⟨up on⟩ the gas; X backed off the pedal.**

Г-4 • ПОД ГА́ЗОМ slang [PrepP; Invar; subj-compl with copula (subj: human) or obj-compl with видеть кого etc (obj: human)] one is in a state of intoxication (more often, mild): **tight; tipsy; under the influence.**

[Авдонин:] Побежал я, короче говоря, в контору. Комнату просить. Очень плохо соображал... [Третий коммунист:] Под газом? [Авдонин:] Какой – под газом! Рано утром (Салынский 1). [А.:] ...To put it briefly, I ran to the office to ask for a room. I hardly knew what I was doing.... [Third communist:] Were you tight? [А.:] I wasn't tight at all. It was early in the morning (1a).

Г-5 • НА ПО́ЛНОМ ГАЗУ́ ехать, мчаться и т. п. coll [PrepP; Invar; adv (intensif); fixed WO] (of a car, truck etc) (to go, race etc) very fast, with great speed: **(go ⟨race along etc⟩) at full ⟨top, breakneck⟩ speed; burn up the road.**

Г-6 • ГА́ЙКА ЗАСЛА́БИЛА у кого substand, rude [VP$_{subj}$] s.o. became very frightened, lost his nerve, behaved in a cowardly way: у Х-а гайка заслабила ≃ **X got cold feet; X turned yellow; X chickened out.**

Г-7 • ГА́ЙКА СЛАБА́ у кого highly coll [Invar; VP$_{subj}$ with copula; usu. pres; usu. used with infin] s.o. lacks the ability, energy, willpower etc (to undertake or accomplish sth.): гайка у Х-а слаба (сделать Y) ≃ **X doesn't have it in him (to do Y); X doesn't have what it takes (to do Y); X isn't made of the right stuff;** [in limited contexts] **X doesn't have the guts (to do Y); X isn't man ⟨woman⟩ enough (to do Y).**

Г-8 • ЗАКРУ́ЧИВАТЬ/ЗАКРУТИ́ТЬ ⟨ЗАВИ́НЧИ-ВАТЬ/ЗАВИНТИ́ТЬ⟩ ГА́ЙКИ; ПОДКРУ́ЧИВАТЬ/ПОДКРУТИ́ТЬ ГА́ЙКИ (кому) all highly coll [VP; subj: human] (usu. of a superior toward subordinates, a government toward its people, the head of a family toward other family members etc) to become more strict, oppressive with s.o.: X закрутил гайки ≃ **X tightened ⟨turned⟩ the screws (on person Y); X put the screws on person Y; X cracked down (on person Y).** ○ **ЗАКРУ́ЧИВАНИЕ ⟨ЗАВИ́НЧИВАНИЕ⟩ ГА́ЕК** [NP] ≃ **screw-tightening (process); crackdown.**

И ведь извне нам опять грозят – атомные бомбы, западно-немецкие реваншисты, все, кого пугают наши победы... И значит, опять надо закручивать гайки? (Копелев 1). And we were threatened from without also—the atom bomb, West German revanchists, everyone who was frightened by our victories. And did that mean that we had to tighten the screws again? (1a). ♦ Гангут познакомился с Лучниковым, как ни странно, на Острове. Он был одним из первых «советикусов» на Ялтинском кинофестивале. В тот год случилась какая-то странная пауза в генеральном деле «закручивания гаек», и ему вдруг разрешили повезти свою вторую картину на внеконкурсный показ (Аксёнов 7). Strange to say, Gangut met Luchnikov on the Island. Gangut was one of the first specimens of *homo soveticus* at the Yalta Film Festival. There had been an unprecedented lull in the screw-tightening process, and he was suddenly permitted to show his second film *hors concours* (7a).

Г-9 • С ГА́КОМ highly coll [PrepP; Invar; usu. used after a Num as a postmodif] (used when making an approximate estimate of the quantity, measure etc of sth.) with an excess, above some measure: **...and then some; ...odd; more than...; ...or more; ...or better.**

«В общем, до конца года ещё далеко, – сказал Михаил. – Тысячу-то [трудодней] наколотим. И даже с гаком» (Абрамов 1). "And the end of the year's still a long way away," Mikhail had said. "We'll run up a thousand [workdays] or better" (1a).

Г-10 • ЗАКЛА́ДЫВАТЬ/ЗАЛОЖИ́ТЬ ⟨ЗАЛИВА́ТЬ/ЗАЛИ́ТЬ⟩ ЗА ГА́ЛСТУК euph, old-fash [VP; subj: human] to drink alcohol, usu. in considerable amounts: X закладывает за галстук ≃ **X hits the bottle; X boozes (it up); X bends an elbow.**

Г-11 • (И) НИКАКИ́Х ГВОЗДЕ́Й coll [these forms only; sent; usu. the concluding clause in a compound sent or indep. sent; often used after a verb denoting a command, decision etc that should be carried out; fixed WO] (used to emphasize the categorical nature of an order, the finality of a decision etc) no objection or discussion will be tolerated: **and that's that; and that's final; and I ⟨he etc⟩ won't take no for an answer; and I ⟨he etc⟩ won't hear of anything else;** [when used with a command] **and no (ifs, ands, or) buts (about it); and no argument(s) ⟨back talk, nonsense⟩.**

...Как здорово она [Яковлева] отбрила этого Бударина: «Всё, с этим вопросом покончено». И никаких гвоздей! Участвовать в нарушении закона она не может (Войнович 3). How soundly she [Yakovleva] rebuked that Budarin: "That's all, the matter is finished." And that was that! She would not be an accessory to a violation of the law (3a). ♦ «Ты ж знаешь мою Дусю, расплакалась: „Поехали выручать сынулю!“ – и никаких гвоздей» (Чернёнок 1). "You know my Dusya, she starts wailing, 'Let's go save our son!'—and won't hear of anything else" (1a).

Г-12 • **ГВОЗДЁМ ЗАСЕ́СТЬ ⟨СИДЕ́ТЬ⟩ В ГОЛОВЕ́** *чей, у кого* ⟨**В МОЗГУ́** *чьём, у кого*⟩ *coll;* **ЗАСЕ́СТЬ ⟨СИДЕ́ТЬ⟩ В ГОЛОВЕ́** *чей, у кого* ⟨**В МОЗГУ́** *чьём, у кого*⟩ [VP; subj: abstr (all variants) or a clause (var. without гвоздём)] (of a persistent thought, idea etc) not to leave s.o.'s mind, to dominate s.o.'s thoughts persistently: X гвоздём сидит у Y-а в голове ≃ **X preys on Y's mind; X has lodged (itself) in Y's head; X haunts Y.**

[Маша:] …Не выходит у меня из головы… Просто возмутительно. Сидит гвоздём в голове, не могу молчать. Я про Андрея… Заложил он этот дом в банке, и все деньги забрала его жена, а ведь дом принадлежит не ему одному, а нам четверым! (Чехов 5). [M.:] I can't get it out of my head. It's simply disgraceful. It preys on my mind. I can't keep silent. I mean about Andrey. He's mortgaged the house to a bank, and his wife's grabbed all the money, but the house doesn't belong to him alone, does it? It belongs to all four of us (5b). ♦ Он [доктор Герценштубе] был добр и человеколюбив, лечил бедных больных и крестьян даром, сам ходил в их конуры и избы и оставлял деньги на лекарство, но притом был и упрям, как мул. Сбить его с его идеи, если она заседа у него в голове, было невозможно (Достоевский 2). He [Dr. Herzenstube] was kind and philanthropic, treated poor patients and peasants for nothing, visited their hovels and cottages himself, and left them money for medications, yet for all that he was stubborn as a mule. Once an idea had lodged itself in his head, it was impossible to shake it out of him (2a).

Г-13 • **ГДЕ(…) НИ…; ГДЕ Б(Ы)(…) НИ…; КУДА́(…) НИ…; КУДА́ Б(Ы)(…) НИ…** [AdvP; these forms only; adv; fixed WO] in or to any location: **wherever; no matter where;** [in limited contexts] **anywhere; anyplace; in whatever direction.**

Где бы ни появлялась Тали, повсюду она вносила тот избыток жизненных сил, которыми её наградила природа (Искандер 3). Wherever Tali went, she introduced the excess of vitality that nature had conferred on her (3a). ♦ «Поедешь на конгресс какой-нибудь, дай знать. Я приеду повидать тебя, где бы я ни был» (Зиновьев 2). "If you come to a congress anywhere, let me know. I'll come and see you no matter where I am" (2a). ♦ Куда бы ни направился движущийся корабль, впереди его всегда будет видна струя рассекаемых им волн (Толстой 7). In whatever direction a ship moves, the billowing waves created by the prow cleaving the water will always be discernible (7a). ♦ «Куда ни придёшь на вечерок, обязательно окажешься рядом с древним отпрыском. Это у нас-то, через столько-то лет — и вдруг такая тяга у интеллигентов к голубой крови!..» (Битов 2). [context transl] "Any party you go to, you're bound to find yourself next to some ancient scion. Here we are, after so many years—and suddenly the intellectuals have such a fascination with blue blood!" (2a).

Г-14 • **ВЗЛЕТЕ́ТЬ НА ГЕЛИКО́Н** *obs, lit* [VP; subj: human] to become a poet: X взлетел на Геликон ≃ **X ascended the heights of (Mount) Helicon.**

< Mount *Helicon* was regarded by ancient Greeks as the abode of the Muses.

Г-15 • **СВА́ДЕБНЫЙ ГЕНЕРА́Л** *obs, now iron or humor* [NP] an important, high-ranking guest at a celebration or ceremony invited to add importance to the event: **a very important personage ⟨a VIP⟩; high-muck-a-muck.**

Г-16 • **ДО́БРЫЙ ГЕ́НИЙ** *чей lit* [NP; sing only] a person who exerts a beneficial influence on s.o., who helps, protects, and does beneficial things for s.o.: **guardian angel; good fairy.**

[Аллочка Токарева], почувствовавшая ко мне симпатию, была в течение всего месяца, проведённого мной на владивостокском транзите, моим добрым гением. Она очень тактично и доброжелательно вводила меня в новый для меня мир (Гинзбург 1). [Allochka Tokareva] took a fancy to me and acted

as my good fairy during the whole month that I spent in the transit camp, instructing me kindly and tactfully in the conditions of my new life (1b).

Г-17 • **ЗЛОЙ ГЕ́НИЙ** *чей lit* [NP; sing only] a person who has a strong negative influence on s.o., who causes s.o. harm: **evil genius.** Cf. **Svengali.**

Г-18 • **ГЕРО́Й НЕ МОЕГО́ ⟨твоего, вашего, её⟩ РОМА́НА** [NP; subj-compl with copula (subj: human, male); fixed WO] some man is not the kind of man that impresses me (you, her) or that I (you, she) might fall in love with: X — герой не моего романа ≃ **X is not my type (of hero); X is not my idea of a romantic hero.**

< From Aleksandr Griboedov's *Woe from Wit* («Горе от ума»), 1824.

Г-19 • **ГИГА́НТ МЫ́СЛИ** *iron* [NP; fixed WO] (in refer. to a person whose pretensions to intellect are unjustified) a great thinker: **mental giant; mastermind; genius.**

[source] «Вы знаете, кто это сидит?» — спросил Остап, показывая на Ипполита Матвеевича. «Как же, — ответил Кислярский, — это господин Воробьянинов». — «Это, — сказал Остап, — гигант мысли, отец русской демократии, особа, приближенная к императору» (Ильф и Петров 1). "Do you know who that is sitting there?" asked Ostap, pointing to Ippolit Matveyevich. "Of course," said Kislarsky. "It's Mr. Vorobyaninov." "That," said Ostap, "is the mastermind, the father of Russian democracy and a person close to the emperor" (1a).

< From *The Twelve Chairs* («Двенадцать стульев»), 1928, by Ilya Ilf and Evgeny Petrov.

Г-20 • **ВО ГЛАВЕ́** [PrepP; Invar] **1.** идти, маршировать и т. п. ~ *кого-чего* [the resulting PrepP is subj-compl with copula (subj: human or collect) or adv] (to walk, march etc) in front, ahead of others: **at the head (of sth.); leading (s.o. ⟨sth.⟩); in the lead;** [in limited contexts] **in the first row.**

Полгода назад он [Коля] шёл с лопатой через плечо во главе комсомольского воскресника и пел во всю глотку — а сейчас даже о боли своей не мог рассказать громче шёпота (Солженицын 10). Six months ago he [Kolya] had been striding along, a spade over his shoulder, at the head of a Young Communists' Sunday working party, singing at the top of his voice. Now he could not raise his voice above a whisper, even when talking about his pain (10a).

2. быть∅, стоять, (в)стать и т. п. ~ [the resulting PrepP is subj-compl with copula (subj: human or collect) or obj-compl with поставить *кого* etc (obj: human or collect)] (to be) in a position of authority, (to take over) as leader (of s.o. or sth.): **(be ⟨put s.o.⟩) at the head (of sth.); (be ⟨become⟩) s.o.'s leader; (be ⟨become⟩) leader of sth.; (be ⟨leave s.o. etc⟩) in charge (of sth.); take command of sth.;** [in limited contexts] **take the lead (in sth.); spearhead (sth.).**

По-видимому, он про себя рассуждал так: сегодня женщину поставили во главе государства, а завтра поставят во главе стола (Искандер 4). He apparently reasoned thus: Today they've put a woman at the head of the government, tomorrow they'll put her at the head of the table (4a). ♦ [Лорд:] Во главе вас станет ваш царь Кири-Куки 1-ый, а я окажу помощь (Булгаков 1). [Lord:] Your Tsar Kiri-Kuki the First will be our leader, and I will assist (1a). ♦ «Я бы, товарищи, ещё трижды подумал, оставлять ли его во главе столь ответственного участка, как Лаборатория № 4» (Аксёнов 6). "I would think twice, comrades, before leaving him in charge of such a sensitive department as Laboratory Number 4" (6a). ♦ [Яков Фомин] стал во главе мятежного полка, но… за спиной Фомина правила делами и руководила Фоминым группа большевистски настроенных казаков (Шолохов 4). [Yakov Fomin] took command of the insurgent regiment, but…behind him stood a group of Bolshevik-minded Cossacks who held the reins of power (4a).

3. ~ *с кем* [the resulting PrepP is nonagreeing modif] having s.o. as leader: **with s.o. at the head; under the leadership of; led ⟨headed⟩ by.**

В дежурное помещение, поддерживая друг друга, явилась невероятная компания во главе с известным в городе гражданином, директором санатория имени XIX партсъезда, генералом в отставке Чувиковым (Аксёнов 6). The duty room was invaded by an incredible rabble of people, supporting one another, who were led by a well-known citizen of Yalta, director of the Nineteenth Party Congress Sanatorium, retired Major-General Chuvikov (6a). ♦ …Она [труппа] однажды явилась во главе с Шарлем Лагранжем и сообщила Мольеру, что ввиду того, что он соединяет с необыкновенными способностями честность и приятное обращение, труппа просит его не беспокоиться: актёры не уйдут искать счастья на стороне, какие бы выгодные предложения им ни делали (Булгаков 5). …One day his [Molière's] players came to him, headed by Charles La Grange, and assured him that, in view of his fairness and kindness, as well as his extraordinary talents, he had nothing to worry about—they would not leave to seek their fortunes elsewhere no matter how tempting the offers they received (5a).

Г-21 • СТА́ВИТЬ/ПОСТА́ВИТЬ ⟨КЛАСТЬ/ПОЛО-ЖИ́ТЬ⟩ ВО ГЛАВУ́ УГЛА́ *что lit* [VP; subj: human; the verb may take the final position, otherwise fixed WO] to consider sth. to be vital, of extremely great importance, more important than anything else: X ставит Y во главу угла ≃ **X puts Y ahead of everything else; X puts Y at the top ⟨the head⟩ of the list; X assigns primary importance to Y; X considers Y (to be) of paramount importance; X gives Y top ⟨first⟩ priority; X makes Y X's top priority.**

Г-22 • ГЛАЗ ДА ГЛАЗ нужен *за кем-чем coll* [NP; Invar; subj] s.o. or sth. should be kept under strict, constant supervision: за Х-ом нужен глаз да глаз ≃ **X has to be watched all the time ⟨constantly⟩; X must be closely watched; person Y must keep a close eye on ⟨a constant watch over⟩ X.**

Второй период [нашей совместной жизни] ознаменовался тем, что я перестала быть добычей, украденной Европой, девчонкой, за которой нужен глаз да глаз. Нас стало двое (Мандельштам 2). The noteworthy thing about this second period [of our life together] was that he [Mandelstam] ceased to treat me as a prize he had carried off, a Europa abducted by Zeus, a little girl who had to be watched all the time. We now became a real couple (2a). ♦ Надо же! За арестантом, который тянет голодовку почти два месяца, нужен глаз да глаз: «склонен к побегу» (Марченко 2). What will they think of next! A prisoner who maintains a hunger strike for nearly two months must be closely watched, as he displays "tendencies to try to escape" (2a).

Г-23 • ГЛАЗ НАМЁТАН ⟨НАБИ́Т⟩ *чей, у кого, в чём, на чём;* НАМЁТАННЫЙ ГЛАЗ (*у кого*) *all coll* [these forms only (variants with short-form Part); NP, sing only (var. with long-form Part); VP$_{subj}$ with copula (all variants) or subj or indir obj (last var.)] s.o. has experience and skill in some area and can easily evaluate things within that area (with regard to their classification, worth etc) just by looking at them: у X-a (в Y-e) глаз намётан ≃ **X has a trained ⟨practiced, experienced⟩ eye; X has an eye ⟨a good eye⟩ for Y.**

«У моряка намётанный глаз, и притом наган на шнуре. Он сразу видит — имущий класс… Матрос хвать наган и хлоп его [доктора] как муху» (Пастернак 1). "A sailor has a trained eye and a gun. He takes a look at him [the doctor] and what does he see? A member of the propertied classes….He pulls out his gun—and goodbye" (1a). ♦ Намётанным глазом сразу вижу: умрёт к вечеру (Гинзбург 2). With my practiced eye I could see immediately that he

would be dead by evening (2a). ♦ Тут только дядя Сандро обратил внимание на то, что сидящие за столом уже порядочно выпили. Теперь он присмотрелся к ним своим намётанным глазом и определил, что выпито уже по двенадцать-тринадцать фужеров (Искандер 3). Only now did Uncle Sandro turn his attention to the fact that those sitting at the table had had a great deal to drink. Now he trained his experienced eye on them and determined that they had already consumed twelve to thirteen glasses apiece (3a).

Г-24 • ДУРНО́Й ГЛАЗ *coll;* ХУДО́Й ⟨ЛИХО́Й, ЧЁРНЫЙ⟩ ГЛАЗ *obsoles, coll* [NP; sing only; usu. this WO] (a look believed to have) the power to bring harm or bad luck to the recipient: **the evil eye.**

«…Мать Фреда говорила, помнится, что у них [мокрецов] дурной глаз… и что накликают они нам войну, мор и голод…» (Стругацкие 1). "I remember Fred's mother saying that they [the slimies] had the evil eye…and that they'd bring us war, pestilence, and famine" (1a).

Г-25 • ЛАСКА́ТЬ ГЛАЗ ⟨ВЗОР⟩ [VP; subj: concr; usu. pres or past] to be pleasant to look at: X ласкает глаз ≃ **X pleases ⟨is pleasing to⟩ the eye.**

Где-то вдалеке море сливалось с небом, всё вокруг ласкало глаз. Somewhere in the distance the sea drifted into the sky, and everything around pleased the eye.

Г-26 • НА ГЛАЗ ⟨НА ГЛАЗО́К⟩ определять, прикидывать [PrepP; these forms only; adv] (to measure sth., judge the size of sth. etc) just by looking and approximating, without using any measuring devices: **(measure ⟨judge etc⟩ sth.) by eye; (tell) by looking.**

Покупать скот нужен опыт, надо на глаз определить, как откормлена скотина, сколько в ней ценного мяса, сколько жира… (Рыбаков 1). It takes experience to buy animals, you have to be able to judge by eye what the animal has been fed on, how much valuable meat there is on it, and how much fat… (1a). ♦ «Я и так на глаз вижу, сколько там пудов в мешках!» (Искандер 5). "Anyway, I can tell by looking how many pounds there are in the sacks!" (5a).

Г-27 • НАСКО́ЛЬКО ⟨КУДА́, СКО́ЛЬКО⟩ ХВАТА́ЕТ ⟨ХВАТА́Л⟩ ГЛАЗ; НАСКО́ЛЬКО ⟨КУДА́, СКО́ЛЬКО⟩ ХВАТА́ЛО ГЛАЗ ⟨ГЛА́ЗА, ГЛА́ЗУ⟩ [VP$_{subj}$ or VP, impers; used as subord clause; more often this WO] for the whole distance that can be seen: **as far as the eye can ⟨could⟩ see.**

Насколько хватало глазу, поле было засыпано людьми и узлами (Федин 1). As far as the eye could see the field was scattered with people and bundles (1a).

Г-28 • НЕ КАЗА́ТЬ ⟨НЕ ПОКА́ЗЫВАТЬ/НЕ ПОКАЗА́ТЬ⟩ ГЛАЗ (*куда, к кому*) *coll* [VP; subj: human] not to visit s.o., not to go or come to some place: X (к Y-у ⟨в место Z⟩) глаз не кажет ≃ **X hasn't shown his face (at Y's place ⟨in place Z⟩); X doesn't show himself at Y's place ⟨in place Z⟩; X hasn't been to see Y ⟨to place Z, in place Z⟩; X is keeping away from Y;** ‖ ты что ⟨почему и т. п.⟩ глаз не кажешь? ≃ **where have you been hiding ⟨keeping⟩ yourself?**

«Забыли совсем, Лев Львович, старика. Вторую неделю глаз не кажете» (Максимов 3). "Thought you'd quite forgotten an old man, Lev Lvovich. Haven't shown your face for over a week now" (3a). ♦ «Ты чего ж это глаз не кажешь?» (Шолохов 2). "Why haven't you been to see us?" (2b). ♦ В Рубежин приехали к обеду. Фомин действительно оказался дома. Он встретил Петра по-хорошему… «Ты что-то, односум, и глаз не кажешь», — говорил Фомин протяжно, приятным баском… (Шолохов 4). They reached Rubezhin at dinner-time. Fomin was indeed at home. He greeted Petro affably.…"Where've you been hiding yourself, chum?" Fomin drawled in his pleasant bass… (4a).

Г-29 • НЕ ОСУША́ТЬ ГЛАЗ *lit* [VP; subj:human] to weep unconsolably for a long period of time, cry much: X не осушает глаз ≃ **X is crying his eyes 〈heart〉 out; X keeps crying all the time; X is in tears all the time; X has been crying 〈weeping etc〉 for days 〈hours etc〉 (without drying his eyes 〈without stopping, nonstop〉).**

Когда Василий *содержался в части*, Маша по целым дням, не осушая глаз, жаловалась на свою горькую судьбу Гаше… и, презирая брань и побои своего дяди, потихоньку бегала в полицию навещать и утешать своего друга… (Толстой 2). When Vasily was being *kept in detention*, Masha wept for whole days without drying her eyes, complained of her bitter fate to Gasha…and, scorning her uncle's abuse and blows, ran to the police station in secret in order to visit and console her friend (2b).

Г-30 • НЕ ОТРЫВА́ТЬ 〈НЕ ОТВОДИ́ТЬ〉 ГЛАЗ *от кого-чего* [VP; subj: human] to look at s.o. or sth. intently, steadily: X не отрывал глаз от Y-a ≃ **X didn't 〈couldn't〉 take his eyes 〈gaze〉 off Y; X kept his eyes on Y (the whole time); X's eyes were fixed on 〈glued to〉 Y; X didn't remove his eyes from Y.**

(Входит Треплев и садится на скамеечке у ног Сорина. Маша всё время не отрывает от него глаз.) [Дорн:] Мы мешаем Константину Гавриловичу работать. [Треплев:] Нет, ничего (Чехов 6). *(Treplev enters and sits on a stool at Sorin's feet. Masha never takes her eyes off him.)* [D.:] We're keeping Konstantin Gavrilovich from his work. [T.:] No, it doesn't matter (6a).

Г-31 • НЕ СВОДИ́ТЬ 〈НЕ СПУСКА́ТЬ〉 ГЛАЗ 〈ВЗГЛЯ́ДА, ВЗО́РА〉 *с кого-чего* [VP; subj: human] **1.** to look at s.o. or sth. intently, steadily: X не сводил глаз с Y-a ≃ **X didn't 〈couldn't〉 take his eyes 〈gaze〉 off Y; X kept his eyes on Y (the whole time); X's eyes were fixed on 〈glued to〉 Y; X didn't remove his eyes from Y.**

Прокурор хоть и не смеялся, но зорко, не спуская глаз, разглядывал Митю, как бы не желая упустить ни малейшего словечка, ни малейшего движения его… (Достоевский 1). The prosecutor, though he did not laugh, was studying Mitya intently, without taking his eyes off him, as if not wishing to miss the least word, the least movement… (1a). ♦ Мне было вовсе свободно идти в шагах трёх, не спуская взгляда с той девушки… (Набоков 1). I was quite free to walk at about three paces distance without taking my gaze off that girl… (1a). ♦ …Я шёл, не шевелясь и не убыстряя шагов, чувствуя, что главное – не сводить глаз с крышки гроба (Искандер 6). …I continued to walk, not moving one extra muscle and not accelerating my steps, knowing that I must keep my eyes on the coffin lid, no matter what (6a). ♦ Азазелло… одетый, как и Воланд, в чёрное, неподвижно стоял невдалеке от своего повелителя, так же как и он не спуская глаз с города (Булгаков 9). Azazello…dressed in black like Woland, stood motionless not far from his master, his eyes also fixed on the city (9a). ♦ Приезжий отступил на шаг, не сводя глаз с Кознака, потом накрылся шляпой (Булгаков 5). The visitor stepped back without removing his eyes from Cosnac, and replaced his hat (5a).

2. to observe, watch s.o. or sth. carefully, closely: X не спускал глаз с Y-a ≃ **X kept an eye 〈a close eye〉 on Y; X kept (a) constant watch on 〈over〉 Y; X didn't let Y out of X's sight; X kept (close) tabs on Y; X watched person Y's every move.**

…Один из юнкеров стоял на часах у двери, не спуская глаз с мотоциклетки у подъезда… (Булгаков 3). A cadet stood on guard at the door keeping constant watch on the motor-cycle and sidecar parked outside… (3a). ♦ «Если ты вылетишь из Новосибирска утром, то как раз успеешь встретить Реваза Давидовича. Встретишь и – глаз с него не спускай» (Чернёнок 1). "If you

leave Novosibirsk in the morning, you'll get there in time to meet Revaz Davidovich. Meet him and don't let him out of your sight" (1a).

Г-32 • НЕ СМЫКА́ТЬ/НЕ СОМКНУ́ТЬ ГЛАЗ [VP; subj: human] not to sleep at all or not be able to fall asleep: X не сомкнул глаз ≃ **X didn't 〈couldn't〉 sleep a wink; X didn't have 〈get〉 a wink of sleep; X didn't get any sleep (at all); X kept 〈stayed〉 awake;** [in limited contexts] **X couldn't get back to sleep.**

Всю ночь мы не смыкали глаз. Мы счастливы возвращением к людям (Гинзбург 1). That night, neither of us slept a wink. We were happy to be among people again… (1a). ♦ …Если б понадобилось, например, просидеть всю ночь подле постели барина, не смыкая глаз, и от этого бы зависело здоровье или даже жизнь барина, Захар непременно бы заснул (Гончаров 1). [If] he had had to keep awake by his master's bedside all night because his master's health and even life depended on it, Zakhar would most certainly have fallen asleep (1a). ♦ «Бывает, муха пролетит, ты проснёшься, а до утра глаз не сомкнёшь, а тут шум, споры, переполох, а тебя не добудиться» (Пастернак 1). "Sometimes, a fly will wake you up and you can't get back to sleep till morning, and here you slept through all this row and I simply couldn't get you to wake up" (1a).

Г-33 • не мочь, не в силах, нельзя и т. п. ОТОРВА́ТЬ 〈ОТВЕСТИ́〉 ГЛАЗ *от кого-чего;* **НЕ ОТОРВА́ТЬ 〈НЕ ОТВЕСТИ́〉 ГЛАЗ** [VP; these forms only; infin compl of не мочь, не в силах etc (subj: human), infin compl of нельзя etc (impers), or neg infin used as impers predic] (to be unable) to stop looking at s.o. or sth. (usu. because of his or its beauty, power to captivate, transfix etc): X не мог оторвать глаз от Y-a ≃ **X couldn't take his eyes 〈gaze〉 off Y; X couldn't tear himself away from Y.**

Приближение весны сказывалось только в совершенно ослепительном великолепии чистого снега и в разноцветном сверкании на нём солнечных лучей. От этого зрелища нельзя было оторвать глаз (Гинзбург 1). The only sign of the approach of spring was the blinding splendour of the clean snow and the iridescent play of the sun's rays on it. One couldn't take one's eyes off it… (1a). ♦ Глаз не могу оторвать от картины поединка героя ирландских саг Кухулина с Фердиадом (Терц 3). I cannot tear myself away from [the account of] the combat between two heroes of the Irish sagas, Cuchulainn and Fer Diad (3a).

Г-34 • ПОЛОЖИ́ТЬ ГЛАЗ *на кого highly coll* [VP; subj: human (more often male)] to become actively interested in s.o., pay special attention to s.o. (often in refer. to one's being physically attracted to s.o. and desiring an intimate relationship with him or her): X (давно) положил глаз на Y-a ≃ **X took notice 〈note〉 of Y (quite a while ago); X has been keeping an eye on Y (for quite a while);** [in refer. to one's being physically attracted to s.o.] **X has had his eye on Y (for quite a while); X took a fancy to Y (quite a while ago); X has had a yen for Y (for quite a while).**

А Иосиф вернулся из армии в семнадцатом, и вот рядом красивая молодая солдатка без мужа, Иосиф, естественно, положил на неё глаз… (Рыбаков 1). Now, Yosif came back from the army in 1917, and there, living right next door, was a soldier's pretty young wife, minus a husband. Naturally, Yosif had his eye on her (1a). ♦ «Всё бы ничего, да один обехэсник [from ОБХСС — Отдел борьбы с хищениями и спекуляцией] на меня глаз положил» (Максимов 3). "Everything would have been all right if this cop from the embezzlement and illegal trading department hadn't taken a fancy to me" (3a).

Г-35 • РА́ДИ 〈ДЛЯ〉 ПРЕКРА́СНЫХ ГЛАЗ *чьих, кого;* **ЗА ПРЕКРА́СНЫЕ 〈КРАСИ́ВЫЕ〉 ГЛАЗА́** *all coll* [PrepP; these forms only; adv; fixed WO] (to do sth.) simply out of a desire to help s.o., without being motivated by self-interest: **out of sheer**

goodness of heart; out of the goodness of one's heart; out of sheer kindness; just to please (s.o.).

Едва ли Анфим благодетельствует Ларисе Фёдоровне ради её прекрасных глаз (Пастернак 1). It was hardly likely that Samdeviatov helped Lara out of sheer goodness of heart (1a).

Г-36 • РА́ДОВАТЬ ГЛАЗ ⟨ВЗОР⟩ [VP; subj: concr; usu. pres or past] to be pleasant to look at: X радует глаз ≃ **X is delightful ⟨a pleasure⟩ to behold; X is a feast ⟨a treat⟩ for the eye(s); X pleases the eye; X delights one's eyes.**

[author's usage] «...Наш город издревле прославлен своими базарами, банями, портом, крепостью, храмом Великому Весовщику и многими другими радующими глаза делами рук человеческих» (Искандер 5). "Our city has been famed from earliest times for its bazaars, baths, harbor, fort, temple to the Great Weighmaster, and many other works of man delightful to behold" (5a). ♦ Сидим мы, бывало, вчетвером... в любимой его [нашего доброго старого начальника] угловой комнате; в камине приятно тлеют дрова; в стороне, на столе, шипит самовар, желтеет только что сбитое сливочное масло, и радуют взоры румяные булки... (Салтыков-Щедрин 2). The four of us...used to sit in his [our good old governor's] beloved corner room, the wood smouldering pleasantly in the fireplace, the *samovar* hissing on a side-table, the butter just out of the churn—a lovely, yellow pile on a plate—and the appetizing, well-browned rolls delighting our eyes... (2a).

Г-37 • С БЕЗУ́МНЫХ ГЛАЗ *obs, substand* [PrepP; Invar; sent adv; fixed WO] in a state of extreme agitation or complete loss of self-control: **in one's madness ⟨crazed state⟩; having gone mad; having lost one's head.**

[Расплюев:] Однако не качнул бы он [Кречинский] меня с безумных-то глаз... (Сухово-Кобылин 2) [R.:] I better be on the lookout or he'll [Krechinsky will] do me in...in his madness... (2a).

Г-38 • С ГЛАЗ ДОЛО́Й ⟨С ГЛАЗ (чьих)⟩ уходить, прогонять *кого*, убирать *что* и т. п. *coll* [PrepP; these forms only; adv (both variants) or indep. sent (1st var.); fixed WO] (to go, send s.o., take sth. etc) away from some person, so that one (s.o. or sth.) will not be in view of that person; or (to go, send s.o., take sth. etc) away from some place, so that one (s.o. or sth.) will not be present at that place: [of a person] уйти ⟨убраться и т. п.⟩ ~ ≃ **get out of sight; make o.s. scarce;** ‖ уходи ⟨убирайся⟩ ~! ≃ **(get) out of my sight!; get ⟨clear⟩ out (of here)!;** ‖ прогнать *кого* ~ ≃ **get s.o. out of one's ⟨another's⟩ sight; see to it that s.o. is kicked out of some place;** ‖ [of a thing] убрать *что* ~ ≃ **get ⟨put⟩ sth. out of one's ⟨s.o.'s⟩ sight; remove sth. from sight ⟨view⟩.**

...Выходит, что общество... совсем не охранено, ибо хоть и отсекается вредный член механически и ссылается далеко, с глаз долой, но на его место тотчас же появляется другой преступник, а может, и два другие (Достоевский 1). ...It turns out that society...is not protected at all, for although the harmful member is mechanically cut off and sent far away out of sight, another criminal appears at once to take his place, perhaps even two (1a). ♦ «Ступай, ступай себе только с глаз моих! Бог с тобой!» – говорил бедный Тентетников... (Гоголь 3). "Go, go now, only get out of my sight," poor Tentetnikov would say... (3c). ♦ Обломов поклонился иронически Захару и сделал в высшей степени оскорблённое лицо... «С глаз долой!» – повелительно сказал Обломов, указывая рукой на дверь (Гончаров 1). He [Oblomov] made a mocking bow to Zakhar and looked deeply offended...."Out of my sight!" Oblomov commanded, pointing to the door (1b). ♦ «Да убери ты их [часы] с глаз моих, убери, Христа ради» (Распутин 2). "Just get it [the watch] out of my sight, away, for Christ's sake" (2a). ♦ Эх, Мора, Мора... знать бы тебе, как [твоя жена], едва ты с глаз долой, бегает в избушку кладовщика-радиста Проскурина, а чем уж они там занимаются, одному Богу известно. Только, надо полагать,

не морзянку слушают (Максимов 2). [context transl] Ah, Mora, Mora...if only you knew that as soon as your back was turned your [wife] would run off to Proskurin, the radio operator and storeman. What they did together in Proskurin's hut, God only knows, but they probably did not listen to Morse code... (2a).

Г-39 • С ГЛАЗ ДОЛО́Й – ИЗ СЕ́РДЦА ВОН [saying] when you do not see s.o. for a long time, you forget about him, stop thinking about him (occas. used as a reproach to a person who fails to keep in contact with one): ≃ **out of sight, out of mind; seldom seen, soon forgotten.**

«...Ты меня послушай, хоть я и старая и неучёная... Капкан, Евгенья, капкан [во]круг тебя вьётся... Беги, покуда цела... С глаз долой – из сердца вон!» (Гинзбург 1). "You listen to me even though I'm old and ignorant. They're setting a trap for you, Genia, and you'd better run while you still can....'Out of sight, out of mind'..." (1b).

Г-40 • С ПЬЯ́НЫХ ГЛАЗ *coll* [PrepP; Invar; adv; fixed WO] in a state of intoxication: **(being ⟨when, because one is⟩) drunk ⟨smashed, loaded, tight, in his cups etc⟩.**

«Ну что ж, идти как идти, – сказал Мольер, – но вот в чём дело, друзья. Нехорошо топиться ночью после ужина, потому что люди скажут, что мы сделали это с пьяных глаз» (Булгаков 5). "Well, if that's what we are going to do, let's do it," said Molière. "But there's one thing that troubles me, my friends. It isn't right for us to drown ourselves at night, after supper. People will say we did it because we were drunk" (5a). ♦ «Бока ему наломать надо! С пьяных глаз зашёл к нам – Лизавету за него отдайте» (Абрамов 1). "I've got to crack a few ribs for him! He comes to our house in his cups: 'Give me Lizaveta to marry,' he says" (1a).

Г-41 • СВОЙ ГЛАЗ – АЛМА́З (, А ЧУЖО́Й – СТЕКЛО́); СВОЙ ГЛАЗ ⟨ГЛАЗО́К⟩ – СМОТРО́К [saying] it is preferable to see sth. oneself and make one's own conclusions, as opposed to relying on another's interpretation of it: ≃ **your own eye is the best spy; it is better to trust the eye than the ear; one eye has more faith than two ears.**

...[Коровьев] выложил председателю пять новеньких банковских пачек. Произошло подсчитывание, пересыпаемое шуточками и прибаутками Коровьева, вроде «денежка счёт любит», «свой глазок – смоторок» и прочего такого же (Булгаков 9). ...He [Koroviev] stacked five bundles of new bank notes before the chairman. There was a careful count, interspersed with Koroviev's little quips and pleasantries, such as "money loves to be counted," "your own eye is the best spy," and so on in the same vein (9a).

Г-42 • СКРЫВА́ТЬСЯ/СКРЫ́ТЬСЯ ⟨ИСЧЕЗА́ТЬ/ИСЧЕ́ЗНУТЬ⟩ ИЗ ГЛАЗ ⟨ИЗ ВИ́ДА, И́З ВИДУ⟩; СКРЫВА́ТЬСЯ/СКРЫ́ТЬСЯ С ГЛАЗ [VP; subj: human, animal, or concr] to cease to be visible: X скрылся из глаз ≃ **X disappeared from sight ⟨from view⟩; X passed out of sight ⟨out of view⟩; X vanished from sight; X faded ⟨receded⟩ from view.**

Я следил за ней [девушкой], пока она со своими спутницами не скрылась из глаз (Искандер 6). I followed her [the girl] with my eyes until she and her companions had disappeared from sight (6a). ♦ Белый пароход удалялся. Уже не различить было в бинокль его труб. Скоро он скроется из виду (Айтматов 1). The white steamship steamed away. By this time, you couldn't make out its funnels in the binoculars. Soon it would pass out of sight (1b).

Г-43 • ХОТЬ ГЛАЗ ⟨ГЛАЗА́⟩ ВЫ́КОЛИ ⟨КОЛИ́ *obsoles*⟩ *coll* [хоть + VP$_{imper}$; usu. subord clause after темно, темнота, тьма и т. п.; fixed WO] (there is) total darkness, absolutely nothing is visible: **(it's) pitch-black; (it's) pitch-dark; (it's) so dark (that) you can't see your hand before ⟨in front of⟩ your face.**

На дворе было темно, хоть глаз выколи. Тяжёлые, холодные тучи лежали на вершинах окрестных гор... (Лермонтов 1). It was pitch black outside. The mountains were capped by cold, heavy clouds... (1c). ♦ Я вышел из кибитки. Буран ещё продолжался, хотя с меньшею силою. Было так темно, что хоть глаз выколи (Пушкин 2). I stepped out of the wagon. The blizzard was still blowing, though with lesser force by now. It was pitch-dark: you couldn't see your hand before your face (2a).

Г-44 • БИТЬ В ГЛАЗА́ *(кому)* [VP; subj: concr or abstr] to stand out to such an extent that one cannot fail to notice it: X бьёт (Y-у) в глаза ≃ **Y cannot help noticing ⟨but notice⟩ X;** [in limited contexts] **X is striking;** [in limited contexts; of things that evoke a negative reaction from the speaker] **X is hard on the eyes; X hurts the eye(s).**

...Город никак не уступал другим губернским городам: сильно била в глаза жёлтая краска на каменных домах и скромно темнела серая на деревянных (Гоголь 3). [The town] in no way yielded to the other provincial towns—the paint on the stone houses was the usual yellow and just as hard on the eyes, while the paint on the wooden houses showed as a modestly dark gray, quite unexceptional (3a).

Г-45 • БРОСА́ТЬСЯ/БРО́СИТЬСЯ ⟨КИДА́ТЬСЯ/КИ́НУТЬСЯ⟩ В ГЛАЗА́ *(кому)* [VP] **1.** ~ *(чем)* [subj: usu. concr or human] to attract s.o.'s gaze, be noticed because of one's or its prominence: X бросался в глаза ≃ **X caught the eye; X was striking ⟨conspicuous⟩; one couldn't help but notice ⟨one couldn't help noticing⟩ X;** ‖ Y-у бросился в глаза X ≃ **X caught Y's eye; X struck Y's eye; Y couldn't help but notice ⟨Y couldn't help noticing, Y couldn't help but see⟩ X;** ‖ первым Y-у в глаза бросился X ≃ **X was the first (person ⟨thing⟩) to meet ⟨catch⟩ Y's eye;** ‖ *Neg* X не бросается в глаза ≃ **X is inconspicuous;** [in limited contexts] **person X keeps a low profile.**

Остальные [красноармейцы] были бледны, безличны. Один он бросался в глаза дюжим складом плеч и татарским энергичным лицом (Шолохов 4). The others [the Red Army men] were a pale, faceless lot. Only he caught the eye with his massive shoulders and energetic Tatar face (4a). ♦ Во втором ряду с правого фланга, с которого коляска обгоняла роты, невольно бросался в глаза голубоглазый солдат, Долохов... (Толстой 4). Conspicuous in the second file from the right flank, the side on which the carriage was passing, was the blue-eyed soldier, Dolokhov... (4a). ♦ Иногда он выглядел много старше: бросались в глаза отёки, болезненная серость кожи, сутулость... (Эренбург 4). Sometimes he looked much older. One could not help noticing the dropsical puffiness, the morbid greyness of his skin, and the stoop of his shoulders (4a). ♦ Многовёдерный блестящий самовар за прилавком первым бросался в глаза... (Булгаков 12). The first thing to meet the eye behind the counter was a gleaming samovar of several gallons' capacity... (12a). ♦ Багратион оглянул свою свиту своими большими, ничего не выражающими, невыспавшимися глазами, и невольно замиравшее от волнения и надежды детское лицо Ростова первое бросилось ему в глаза (Толстой 4). Bagration cast his large, sleepy, expressionless eyes over his suite and the boyish face of Rostov, whose heart was throbbing with excitement, was the first to catch his eye (4a). ♦ ...Monsieur Перси не был шумным человеком, даже наоборот — был бессловесен, тих и не бросался в глаза (Федин 1). ...Monsieur Percy was not a noisy man, he was even, on the contrary, wordless, quiet and inconspicuous (1a).

2. [subj: usu. abstr] (of a personality trait, an aspect of some phenomenon etc) to attract attention to itself by being prominent: X бросался (Y-у) в глаза ≃ **X was striking ⟨evident, apparent⟩; X struck Y; Y was struck by X; Y couldn't help noticing ⟨but notice⟩ X.**

Также в европейском искусстве бросается в глаза графичность, геометрическая терпкость, колючесть изображения (Терц 3). Also striking in European art is its graphic quality, its geometric starkness, its trenchant way of depicting things (3a). ♦ Сглаживающие, приукрашающие, искажающие свойства памяти коллективной, то есть исторической, и личной особенно бросаются в глаза в эпохи, когда рушатся устои, на которых держалось общество (Мандельштам 2). The capacity of memory, both collective and individual, to gloss over, improve on, or distort the facts is particularly evident at periods when the foundations of a society are collapsing (2a). ♦ Я плохо знаю театр, но кое-какие различия между актёром и поэтом сразу бросаются в глаза... (Мандельштам 2). I do not know much about the theater, but certain differences between the actor and the poet are immediately apparent... (2a). ♦ «Господину Замётову прежде всего ваш гнев и ваша открытая смелость в глаза бросилась: ну как это в трактире вдруг брякнуть: „Я убил!"» (Достоевский 3). "What struck Mr. Zamyotov most of all was your wrath and your open daring, suddenly to blurt out in the tavern: 'I killed her!'" (3c). ♦ Даже при беглом чтении [«Доктора Живаго»] в глаза бросается много самоповторений, или, вернее, автоцитат (Гладков 1). Even on a cursory reading [of *Doctor Zhivago*] one is struck by the number of times he repeats things he has said somewhere else before... (1a).

Г-46 • В ГЛАЗА́ *кому* говорить *что*, смеяться, лгать, называть *кого чем*, хвалить, бранить *кого* и т. п. [PrepP; Invar; adv] (to say sth., laugh at s.o., lie to s.o., call s.o. sth., praise s.o., scold s.o. etc) openly, directly addressing the person in question: **(right ⟨straight⟩) to s.o.'s face; (laugh) in s.o.'s face; (tell s.o. sth.) face to face.**

Если бы Т. кто-нибудь назвал в глаза лицемером, он искренне огорчился бы (Гладков 1). If anyone had ever called T. a hypocrite to his face, he would have been genuinely shocked (1a). ♦ [Христиан:] А первого министра я назову в глаза дураком... (Шварц 1). [Ch.:] As for the Prime Minister, I'll call him a fool straight to his face (1a). ♦ «Они за глаза всякую ерунду говорят, а в глаза смеются» (Сологуб 1). "They spread all sorts of scandal behind your back and then laugh in your face" (1a).

Г-47 • ВО ВСЕ ГЛАЗА́ ⟨В О́БА ГЛА́ЗА *rare*⟩ смотреть, глядеть *на кого-что coll* [PrepP; these forms only; adv; used with impfv verbs; fixed WO] (to look, stare at s.o. or sth.) with one's full attention, completely absorbed in what is happening, intensely, trying not to miss anything: **be ⟨look at s.o., stare at sth.⟩ all eyes; (stare etc at s.o. ⟨sth.⟩) wide-eyed ⟨with wide-open eyes⟩; (look) hard (at s.o. ⟨sth.⟩); fix one's eyes (on s.o. ⟨sth.⟩); (look etc at s.o. ⟨sth.⟩) with rapt attention.**

«Экий чёрт!» — думал Чичиков, глядя на него [Костанжогло] в оба глаза... (Гоголь 3). "What a devil!" thought Chichikov, looking at him [Kostanzhoglo], all eyes (3c). ♦ Видимо, он [человек с лопатой] так был поражён, что товарищ Сталин вдруг оказался в такой близости от него, что, забыв про все инструкции, во все глаза смотрел на него (Искандер 3). Evidently he [the man with the shovel] was so thrilled that Comrade Stalin had suddenly appeared so close to him that he forgot all his instructions and stared at him openly, all eyes (3a). ♦ «Да разве после одного счастья бывает другое, потом третье, такое же?» — спрашивала она, глядя на него во все глаза (Гончаров 1). "Do you really think that one happiness is followed by another, and then a third, exactly like it?" she asked, looking at him wide-eyed (1b). ♦ Сольц во все глаза смотрел на Сашу, видимо, не понимая, что вообще происходит... (Рыбаков 2). Solts looked hard at Sasha, apparently unable to understand...what was going on in general... (2a). ♦ Она стояла под порогом, словно приросшая к полу, и во все глаза смотрела на подходившего к ней мужа (Абрамов 1). She stood at the foot of the porch steps as if rooted to the spot, and fixed her eyes on her approaching husband (1a).

Г-48 • (ВСЕ) ГЛАЗА́ ПРОГЛЯДЕ́ТЬ ⟨ПРОСМОТ-РЕ́ТЬ⟩ *coll* [VP; subj: human] **1.** Also: (ВСЕ) ГЛАЗА́ ВЫ́СМОТРЕТЬ *coll* to exhaust o.s. by staring into the distance for a long time in anticipation of the arrival of s.o. or sth.: X все глаза проглядел ≃ **X has ⟨had⟩ worn himself out watching for person Y; X's eyes were tired from watching the door ⟨the horizon etc⟩;** [in limited contexts] **X had his eyes on ⟨fixed on, glued to⟩ the door the whole time; X kept watching the door the whole time.**

[Варвара Капитоновна:] Вот вы, Вероника!.. Здравствуйте, здравствуйте! Боренька все глаза на двери просмотрел (Розов 3). [V.K.:] Veronika, here you are!...Hello, hello! Borenka kept watching the door the whole time (3a).

2. ~ *(на кого-что) obsoles* to look at s.o. steadily, constantly (out of interest, because of emotional attachment etc): X все глаза проглядел (на Y-а) ≃ **X couldn't ⟨didn't⟩ take his eyes off ⟨of⟩ Y; X never took his eyes off ⟨of⟩ Y.**

[Курчаев:] Тётка в вас влюблена... [Глумов:] Каким же это образом? [Курчаев:] В театре видела, все глаза проглядел... (Островский 9). [K.:] ...My aunt is...in love with you. [G.:] How did that happen? [K.:] She saw you at the theatre, couldn't take her eyes off of you... (9b).

Г-49 • ВЫ́ПЛАКАТЬ ⟨ПРОПЛА́КАТЬ⟩ (ВСЕ) ГЛАЗА́ *coll* [VP; subj: human, usu. female] to cry a lot, to the point where one can cry no more: X выплакала все глаза ≃ **X cried her eyes ⟨heart⟩ out; X cried herself out; X had no more tears (left) to cry ⟨weep⟩.**

Через четыре месяца бедная Маяна, бросив школу, внезапно возвратилась домой, неся в руке свой красный фанерный чемодан, а в животе плод от этого ужасного хитреца. Тёте Маше кое-как удалось замять эту историю, и бедняга Маяна, выплакав все глаза, поняла, что на богатыря теперь нечего рассчитывать (Искандер 4). Four months later poor Mayana quit school and suddenly returned home, carrying the red plywood suitcase in her hand and the child of this terrible deceiver in her belly. Aunt Masha somehow managed to hush up the story, and poor Mayana, after crying her eyes out, came to understand that she must give up hope for her hero (4a).

Г-50 • ГЛАЗА́ БЕ́ГАЮТ [VP$_{subj}$; fixed WO] **1.** ~ *чьи, (у) кого disapprov* s.o. glances rapidly in different directions in order to avoid looking directly into another's eyes (usu. because he fears that eye contact will betray his guilt, fraudulence etc): глаза у Х-а бегают ≃ **X has shifty ⟨darting⟩ eyes; X's eyes dart ⟨keep darting about⟩.**

...Взгляд [Лёвы] оттого был подозрительным, что глазки автора бегали... (Битов 2). ...Lyova's glance was suspicious because the author had shifty eyes (2a). ♦ Положительному герою [в идеальном произведении социалистического реализма] противостоит отрицательный. Он... родину спасать не хочет, знамя спасать не хочет, от выполнения планов уклоняется. Руки у него потные, глаза бегают, изо рта пахнет гнилыми зубами (Войнович 1). The positive hero [in the ideal work of socialist realism] is opposed by a negative figure....He is unwilling to save the Motherland and the flag, and seeks to avoid fulfilling the plan. He has sweaty palms, darting eyes, and the smell of rotting teeth on his breath (1a). ♦ В чёрной бороде его показывалась проседь; живые большие глаза так и бегали (Пушкин 2). His black beard was beginning to go grey; his large lively eyes were for ever darting about (2b).

2. ГЛАЗА́ *чьи, кого* БЕ́ГАЮТ *по чему.* Also: БЕ́ГАТЬ ГЛАЗА́МИ *по чему* [VP; subj: human] s.o. moves his eyes quickly over (some place, text etc) in the process of surveying it, trying to get a general picture of what is there etc: Х-овы глаза бегали по месту Y ⟨по Y-ам⟩ ≃ **X's eyes darted ⟨shot⟩ around place Y ⟨from one Y to another⟩; X's eyes strayed about place Y;** [in refer. to a text] **X's eyes ran quickly over the lines ⟨along the lines, down the page etc⟩.**

Он медленно проводил своими длинными пальцами по бакенбардам, а глаза его бегали по углам (Тургенев 2). He slowly passed his fingers over his side whiskers, while his eyes strayed about the room (2b). ♦ Иван Матвеевич взял письмо и привычными глазами бегал по строкам, а письмо слегка дрожало в его пальцах (Гончаров 1). Ivan Matveyevich took the letter..., his eyes running quickly along the lines, while his hands trembled slightly (1a).

Г-51 • ГЛАЗА́ БЫ (МОИ́) НЕ ГЛЯДЕ́ЛИ ⟨НЕ СМОТРЕ́ЛИ⟩ *(на кого-что);* ГЛАЗА́ БЫ (МОИ́) НЕ ВИДА́ЛИ ⟨НЕ ВИ́ДЕЛИ⟩ *(кого-чего) all coll* [VP$_{subj}$; these forms only; usu. this WO] it is unpleasant, painful, or disgusting to look (at s.o. or sth.): глаза бы (мои) не глядели на X-а ≃ **I don't even want to see ⟨to look at⟩ X; I can't stand the sight of X; X is not a pretty sight; it's no sight for my eyes.**

Утром [Марья] встанет, заткнёт космы за плат и пошла растрёпа растрёпой. Ворот рубахи не застёгнут, груди болтаются, крест на грязном гайтане болтается – глаза бы не глядели (Абрамов 1). She [Marya] would get up in the morning, tuck her mane under a scarf and go around looking like a blowzy slut. The neck of her shirt undone, her breasts flopping around, her cross bobbing on its filthy strap: not a pretty sight (1a). ♦ [Марина:] Давеча подняли шум, пальбу – срам один! [Телегин:] Да, сюжет, достойный кисти Айвазовского. [Марина:] Глаза бы мои не глядели (Чехов 3). [M.:] The row they made this afternoon and all that shooting, a thorough disgrace I call it. [T.:] Yes, it was a subject worthy of the brush of Ayvazovsky. [M.:] It was no sight for my old eyes (3c).

Г-52 • ГЛАЗА́ В ГЛАЗА́ *видеть кого-что,* **столкну́ться** *с кем* и т. п.; ЛИЦО́ В ЛИЦО́ [Invar; adv or nonagreeing modif] (to see s.o. or sth.) right by, close up, (to run) directly, right (into one another etc): **face to face.**

...И ему самому доводилось не раз бывать понятым при арестах, просто он никогда не предполагал, что вот такая, глаза в глаза, встреча с ними посреди безлюдной степи может так жгуче и горестно в нём отозваться... (Максимов 3). He had been called on more than once to witness an arrest himself. But he had never imagined that an encounter like this, face to face on the empty steppe, would affect him so painfully (3a).

Г-53 • ГЛАЗА́ НА ЗАТЫ́ЛКЕ *у кого coll, humor* [VP$_{subj}$ with быть$_\emptyset$, pres only] **1.** (in refer. to an inattentive, absent-minded person) s.o. is not watching, paying attention to what he is doing or what is going on around him: у X-а глаза на затылке ≃ **X is out of it; X's mind is somewhere else;** ‖ [in questions only] у тебя что, глаза на затылке? ≃ **what, are you daydreaming ⟨woolgathering⟩?**

2. s.o. notices everything happening around him, does not miss anything: у X-а глаза на затылке ≃ **X has eyes in the back of his head; X doesn't miss a trick.**

Г-54 • ГЛАЗА́ НА ЛОБ ЛЕ́ЗУТ/ПОЛЕ́ЗЛИ *у кого (от чего) coll* [VP$_{subj}$] s.o.'s eyes suddenly open wide from amazement, surprise, pain, fright etc: у X-а глаза на лоб полезли ≃ **X's eyes (nearly) popped ⟨bugged⟩ out (of his head) (from fright ⟨in surprise etc⟩); X's eyes started from ⟨out of⟩ his head (in surprise etc); X's eyes started from ⟨out of⟩ their sockets.**

«Я в тулупе, а под тулупом стёганая одежда... и то, пока сдам перегон, глаза на лоб лезут» (Айтматов 2). "I'm wearing my sheepskin coat, and under that the quilted things...but each time I step outside to give the signal to leave, my eyes nearly pop out from the cold" (2a). ♦ ...Абесаломон Нартович не был бы Абесаломоном Нартовичем, если бы он, написав книгу о певчих птицах Абхазии, не внёс бы в неё нечто такое, от чего у специалиста глаза полезут на лоб… (Искандер 4). …Abesalomon Nartovich would not have been Abesalomon Nartovich if, in writing a book about the songbirds of Abkhazia, he had failed to insert something that would make a specialist's eyes start from his head… (4a). ♦ Он назвал мне свою фамилию, и у меня глаза на лоб полезли. «Неужели тот самый?» – спросил я (Зиновьев 2). He told me his name and my eyes started out of my head. "Is that really who you are?" I asked (2a).

Г-55 • **ГЛАЗА́ НА МО́КРОМ МЕ́СТЕ** (у кого) coll [VP_subj with быть₀; Invar; fixed WO (except in questions)] s.o. cries often, is inclined to cry, or is ready to start crying: у X-а глаза (всегда) на мокром месте ≃ X is (always) on the verge of tears; X is (always) ready to burst into tears; X is (always) ready to turn on the waterworks; X is one for turning on the waterworks; [in reference to s.o.'s state at a given moment] X is about to cry ⟨to burst into tears⟩; X's eyes are brimming ⟨filled⟩ with tears.

[Трилецкий:] Будем теперь плакать… Кстати, глаза на мокром месте… (Чехов 1). [T.:] Now we're going to cry—we've always been one for turning on the waterworks, haven't we? (1b). ♦ [Я] видел, что у неё глаза на мокром месте, но она не хотела этого показывать и ушла (Трифонов 5). I could see that she was about to cry, but she didn't want to show her emotion and left the room (5a).

Г-56 • **ГЛАЗА́ НАВЫ́КАТ(Е)** [NP; pl only] eyes that jut out: **protruding** ⟨**bulging**⟩ **eyes.**

«Вы не поверите, как вы нас самих ободряете, Дмитрий Фёдорович, вашею этою готовностью…» – заговорил Николай Парфёнович с оживлённым видом и с видимым удовольствием, засиявшим в больших светло-серых навыкате, очень близоруких впрочем, глазах его… (Достоевский 1). "You would not believe how encouraged we are, Dmitri Fyodorovich, by this readiness of yours…," Nikolai Parfenovich started saying, with an animated look and with visible pleasure shining in his big, protruding, pale gray, and, by the way, extremely myopic eyes… (1a). ♦ Наш замполит, капитан Сазонов – типичный замполит, тупой, обрюзгший, с красной бычьей шеей и глазами навыкате, – был особенно ревнив (Буковский 1). Captain Sazonov, a typical commissar—stupid, flabby, with a red bull neck and bulging eyes—was the most jealous of all (1a).

Г-57 • **ГЛАЗА́ НЕ ОСУША́ЮТСЯ** чьи, у кого lit [VP_subj; usu. this WO] s.o. is unable to or does not stop crying: глаза X-овы не осушаются ≃ X cannot stop the tears; the tears keep coming; the tears keep ⟨won't stop⟩ flowing from X's eyes; X keeps on ⟨cannot stop⟩ crying.

Г-58 • **ГЛАЗА́** (чьи) **НЕ ОТРЫВА́ЮТСЯ** от кого-чего; **ВЗГЛЯД** (чей) **НЕ ОТРЫВА́ЕТСЯ** [VP_subj; fixed WO] s.o. looks at some person or thing steadily, intently: X-овы глаза не отрываются от Y-а ≃ X does not ⟨cannot⟩ take his eyes ⟨gaze⟩ off Y; X's eyes are ⟨X's gaze is⟩ fixed on Y; X's eyes are glued to Y.

Г-59 • **ГЛАЗА́ НЕ ПРОСЫХА́ЮТ** у кого coll [VP_subj; usu. this WO] s.o. is constantly crying: у X-а глаза не просыхают ≃ X never stops crying; X cries nonstop; X (just) keeps on crying.

Г-60 • **ГЛАЗА́ ОТКРЫВА́ЮТСЯ/ОТКРЫ́ЛИСЬ** у кого (на что) [VP_subj; more often pfv] having rid himself of delusions or misconceptions, s.o. begins to understand the situation as it really is: у X-а открылись глаза (на Y) ≃ X's eyes have been opened (to Y); the scales fell ⟨have fallen⟩ from X's eyes.

[Войницкий:] …Теперь у меня открылись глаза! Я всё вижу! Пишешь ты об искусстве, но ничего не понимаешь в искусстве! (Чехов 3). [V.:] …Now my eyes have been opened. Everything's perfectly clear. You write about art, but you haven't the faintest idea what art is all about (3c). ♦ Выросла она в Галиции, жадно читала советских писателей и верила каждому слову… Из первого вуза, где она работала, её выгнали по пятому пункту. Она сочла это местной ошибкой, но, когда выяснилось, что пятый пункт стал центром внимания и на идиллию соцреализма полагаться нельзя, у неё вдруг открылись глаза (Мандельштам 2). She had grown up in Galicia, where she eagerly read Soviet writers and believed every word they said.…In the first college where she worked she had been dismissed because of Point Five [the entry in Soviet passports indicating a person's ethnic origin. If used without specification, usu. refers to Jews]. She had put this down as a "local mistake," but when Point Five proved to be a major issue and the idylls of socialist realism had worn thin, the scales suddenly fell from her eyes (2a).

Г-61 • как, стыдно, страшно и т. п. **ГЛАЗА́ ПОКАЗА́ТЬ** кому куда coll [VP; subj: human; usu. infin, used as subj (with стыдно, страшно etc), in infin clause (after как), or as infin compl of не мочь etc] s.o. is ashamed to appear somewhere: X-у стыдно глаза показать (в место Y) ≃ X can't ⟨is ashamed to, is afraid to, doesn't dare to⟩ show his face (in place Y); X can't face person Z.

[Анна Петровна:] Мне теперь глаза показать никуда нельзя (Островский 1). [A.P.:] I can't show my face anywhere now (1b).

Г-62 • **ГЛАЗА́ РАЗБЕГА́ЮТСЯ/РАЗБЕЖА́ЛИСЬ** (у кого от чего) coll [VP_subj] s.o. cannot concentrate visually or fix his gaze on any one thing, owing to a great number and diversity of objects, impressions etc: у X-а глаза разбегаются (от Y-ов) ≃ X doesn't know ⟨X scarcely knows⟩ where to look (first ⟨next⟩); X doesn't know ⟨scarcely knows⟩ which way to look; X doesn't know ⟨X scarcely knows⟩ what ⟨whom⟩ to look at first ⟨next⟩; X is dizzied by the multitude of Ys; it's more ⟨there are more Ys⟩ than the eyes can take in.

В ослепительных белых и чёрных лимузинах ехали, весело разговаривая, офицеры в высоких картузах с серебром. У нас с Шуркой разбежались глаза и захватило дыхание (Кузнецов 1). The officers in their tall peaked caps with silver braid travelled in dazzling black and white limousines, chatting cheerfully among themselves. We, Shurka and I, caught our breath and scarcely knew where to look next (1b). ♦ Для Пьера, воспитанного за границей, этот вечер Анны Павловны был первый, который он видел в России. Он знал, что тут собрана вся интеллигенция Петербурга, и у него, как у ребёнка в игрушечной лавке, разбегались глаза (Толстой 4). Pierre had been educated abroad, and this reception at Anna Pavlovna's was the first he had attended in Russia. He knew that all the intellectual lights of Petersburg were gathered there and, like a child in a toy shop, did not know which way to look… (4b). ♦ …У случайного посетителя [Дома] Грибоедова начинали разбегаться глаза от надписей, пестревших на ореховых тёткиных дверях… (Булгаков 9). …The chance visitor at Griboyedov's [Griboyedov House] was all but dizzied by the multitude of signs peppering the aunt's heavy walnut doors… (9a).

Г-63 • **ГЛАЗА́** ⟨(**ГЛАЗА́ И**) **ЗУ́БЫ**⟩ **РАЗГОРЕ́ЛИСЬ** у кого (на что) coll, occas. disapprov or humor [VP_subj; usu. this WO] s.o. has developed a strong desire to obtain, appropriate sth.: у X-а глаза разгорелись на Y ≃ X has his heart set on Y; X has his sights (set) on Y; X has his eye on Y; X is dying ⟨itching⟩ to get Y.

Г-64 • **ГЛАЗА́ СЛИПА́ЮТСЯ** ⟨**ЗАКРЫВА́ЮТСЯ**⟩ чьи, у кого coll [VP_subj] s.o. wants to sleep very badly: у X-а глаза слипаются ≃ X can't ⟨can hardly, can barely, can scarcely⟩

keep his eyes open; X's eyes won't stay open; X's eyelids are drooping ⟨heavy⟩.

...Почему прежде, бывало, с восьми часов вечера у ней слипаются глаза, а в девять... она ложится – и уже никакая пушка не разбудит её до шести часов? (Гончаров 1). ...Why was it that before, she could hardly keep her eyes open at eight o'clock in the evening...she used to go to bed at nine, and a cannon could not have wakened her till six o'clock in the morning? (1a). ♦ [author's usage] [Платонов:] Спать хочу ужасно, глаза слиплись, но нет сил уснуть... (Чехов 1). [P.:] I feel terribly sleepy. I can hardly keep my eyes open and yet I can't sleep (1a). [P.:] I'm terribly sleepy and my eyes won't stay open, but I can't sleep (1b).

Г-65 • ГЛАЗА́ СЛОМА́ЕШЬ; ГЛАЗА́ СЛОМА́ТЬ МО́ЖНО both coll [VP; pfv fut, gener. 2nd pers sing сломаешь (1st var.); impers predic with бытьø (2nd var.)] sth. is extremely difficult to read, illegible: **you could go blind ⟨crazy⟩ (trying to figure ⟨make⟩ it out).**

Г-66 • ДЕ́ЛАТЬ/СДЕ́ЛАТЬ БОЛЬШИ́Е ⟨КРУ́ГЛЫЕ⟩ ГЛАЗА́; СМОТРЕ́ТЬ БОЛЬШИ́МИ ⟨КРУ́ГЛЫМИ⟩ ГЛАЗА́МИ на кого-что [VP; subj: human; the verb may take the final position, otherwise fixed WO] to open one's eyes wide, expressing one's extreme surprise, look at s.o. or sth. with eyes wide open in surprise: X сделал большие глаза ≃ **X was wide-eyed; X's eyes grew big(ger);** ‖ X смотрел на Y-а большими глазами ≃ **X looked at Y wide-eyed ⟨with wide eyes⟩.**

Делая большие глаза... Елена Павловна рассказывала, что солдаты совсем не пленных ищут, а грабят... (Кузнецов 1). Wide-eyed...Yelena Pavlovna related that the soldiers were not looking for prisoners at all, but simply plundering (1a). ♦ В том, что гости привезли вино, не могло быть сомнений хотя бы потому, что Агаша ежеминутно делала большие глаза... (Каверин 1). That the visitors had brought wine there could be no doubt, if only because Agasha's eyes grew bigger every minute... (1a).

Г-67 • ДЕ́ЛАТЬ/СДЕ́ЛАТЬ СТРА́ШНЫЕ ГЛАЗА́ ⟨СТРА́ШНОЕ ЛИЦО́⟩ coll [VP; subj: human; usu. this WO] to express one's fear, relay a warning to s.o., alert s.o. to some threat etc through the look in one's eyes or on one's face: X сделал страшные глаза ≃ **X gave (person Y) a look ⟨a glance⟩ of warning; X gave (person Y) a warning look ⟨glance⟩; X gave (person Y) a menacing ⟨dreadful⟩ look; X darted a dreadful look (at person or thing Y); X made a terrifying face.**

Хозяин переводил и, делая страшные глаза, косился на щёлкающую камчу, но дядя Сандро предпочёл не заметить намёка (Искандер 3). The host translated, darting dreadful looks at the flicking quirt, but Uncle Sandro preferred not to take the hint (3a). ♦ [Надя (вбегает):] Тётя Таня, он глуп, этот поручик!.. И он, должно быть, бьёт солдат... Кричит, делает страшное лицо... (Горький 1). [N.:] Aunt Tanya, he's a fool, that Lieutenant. And he probably beats the soldiers. He shouts, makes terrifying faces... (1a).

Г-68 • ЗА ГЛАЗА́[1] [PrepP; Invar; adv] **1.** ~ называть кого кем-чем, говорить что о ком, смеяться над кем и т. п. (to call s.o. sth., say sth. about s.o., laugh at s.o.) in s.o.'s absence: **behind s.o.'s back; not to s.o.'s face; when s.o. isn't around ⟨present⟩.**

Лицо у неё, как всегда, было спокойным и немного сонным. За глаза её называли «Мадам Флегма» (Аржак 1). Her face was as always calm and a little sleepy. Behind her back they called her "Lady Phlegmatic" (1a).

2. ~ купить, снять что, нанять кого и т. п. (to buy, rent, hire etc) without seeing sth. or meeting s.o. first: **sight unseen; without even having set ⟨laid⟩ eyes on (s.o. ⟨sth.⟩).**

«Куда изволите вы ехать?» – спросил он [Дубровский] его [француза]. «В ближний город, – отвечал француз, – оттуда

отправляюсь к одному помещику, который нанял меня за глаза в учители» (Пушкин 1). "Where you are going?" he [Dubrovsky] asked him [the Frenchman]. "To the next town," the Frenchman replied, "and from there to the estate of a landowner who has engaged me as a tutor without ever having set eyes on me" (1b).

Г-69 • ** кому **ЗА ГЛАЗА́[2] хватит, достаточно, довольно и т. п. чего, less often кого coll [PrepP; Invar; modif] (the quantity or amount of sth. or the number of people is) entirely sufficient, (sth. is even) more than sufficient: X-у Y-а ~ хватит ≃ **Y is quite ⟨more than⟩ enough for X; Y is more than X needs ⟨will ever need⟩.**

Я никогда не спал много, в тюрьме без всякого движения мне за глаза было достаточно четырёх часов сна... (Герцен 1). I have never been a great sleeper, and in prison, where I had no exercise, four hours' sleep was quite enough for me... (1a). ♦ «Ну, зачем вам, зачем вам столько денег?» – «Как зачем? Как зачем?» – кипятился Ипполит Матвеевич. Остап чистосердечно смеялся и приникал щекой к мокрому рукаву своего друга по концессии. «Ну что вы купите, Киса? Ну что? Ведь у вас нет никакой фантазии. Ей-богу, пятнадцать тысяч вам за глаза хватит...» (Ильф и Петров 1). "What would you want with all that money?" "What do you mean, what would I want?" Ippolit Matveyevich seethed with rage. Ostap laughed heartily and rubbed his cheek against his partner's wet sleeve. "Well, what would you buy, Kisa? You haven't any imagination. Honestly, fifteen thousand is more than enough for you" (1a). ♦ Она легко соскочила с нар и выгребла из кучи в углу два холщовых мешочка – с порохом и дробью. «Половину отсыпь, а половину я отцу увезу, это он заказывал». – «Мне и половины за глаза достанет» – обрадованно засуетился над мешочками Андрей (Распутин 2). She leaped down lightly from the plank bed and pulled out two burlap bags from the pile in the corner – one with powder and the other with shot. "Pour off half to you and the other half I'll bring to your father, he ordered it." "Half is more than I'll ever need," Andrei said, happily puttering over the bags (2a).

Г-70 • ЗАВОДИ́ТЬ/ЗАВЕСТИ́ ГЛАЗА́ [VP; subj: human] **1.** Also: **ЗАКА́ТЫВАТЬ/ЗАКАТИ́ТЬ ГЛАЗА́** (of a person who is sick, about to faint etc; also of a person who wants to express some strong emotion or attract another's attention when flirting) to raise one's eyes so that the pupils are under the upper eyelids: X завёл глаза ≃ [of a sick person] **X rolled up ⟨back⟩ his eyes; X's eyes rolled back;** [when expressing a strong emotion etc] **X turned up his eyes; X rolled his eyes.**

...Истерика Катерины Ивановны кончилась обмороком, затем наступила «ужасная, страшная слабость, она легла, завела глаза и стала бредить» (Достоевский 1). ...Katerina Ivanovna's hysterics had ended in a fainting spell, then she felt "terrible, horrible weakness, she lay down, rolled up her eyes, and became delirious" (1a). ♦ «Вы Безухову скажите, чтоб он приезжал. Я его запишу. Что, он с женою?» – спросил он. Анна Михайловна завела глаза, и на лице её выразилась глубокая скорбь... «Ах, мой друг, он очень несчастлив», – сказала она (Толстой 5). "Tell Bezukhov to come. I'll put his name down. Is his wife with him?" he asked. Anna Mikhailovna turned up her eyes and an expression of profound sorrow came over her face. "Ah, my friend, he is most unfortunate," she said (5a).

2. obs to close one's eyes and fall asleep: X завёл глаза ≃ **X shut his eyes and nodded ⟨dropped, dozed⟩ off.**

Г-71 • ЗАКРЫВА́ТЬ/ЗАКРЫ́ТЬ ГЛАЗА́[1] **1.** ~ кому to be with a dying person in his last moments and shut his eyes after death: X закрыл Y-у глаза ≃ **X closed Y's eyes.**

...Отец его, дед, дети, внучата и гости сидели или лежали в ленивом покое, зная, что есть в доме... непокладные руки, которые обошьют их, накормят, напоят... спать положат, а при смерти закроют им глаза... (Гончаров 1). ...The father, grandfather, children, grandchildren, and guests, all sat or lay about, indolent and idle, knowing that they were continually attended by…untiring hands, which were there to sew for them, to give them food and drink…put them to bed, and close their eyes when they were dead (1b).

2. [pfv only] to expire: **X закрыл глаза** ≃ **X died; X passed on ⟨away⟩.**

[Бабушка:] Сейчас я могла бы спокойно закрыть глаза, он окружён любящей, дружной семьёй (Панова 1). [Grandmother:] Now I'm ready to die peacefully, content that he's surrounded by a devoted, closely knit family (1a).

Г-72 • ЗАКРЫВА́ТЬ/ЗАКРЫ́ТЬ ГЛАЗА́² *на что* [VP; subj: human; often infin with нельзя, (не) надо etc] to ignore sth. (usu. sth. important, some problem etc) intentionally, stop o.s. deliberately from paying attention to or becoming concerned with sth.: **X закрывает глаза на Y** ≃ **X closes ⟨shuts⟩ his eyes to Y; X turns a blind eye to Y;** [in limited contexts] **X is blind to Y.**

Некоторые из наиболее радикальных «заграничных русских» закрывают глаза на интеллектуальную жизнь Советской страны… (Эткинд 1). Some of the most radical émigré Russians close their eyes to the intellectual life of the Soviet Union… (1a). ♦ В той жизни, которую мы прожили, люди со здоровой психикой невольно закрывали глаза на действительность, чтобы не принять её за бред (Мандельштам 1). In our sort of life people of sound mind had to shut their eyes to their surroundings—otherwise they would have thought they were having hallucinations (1a). ♦ Начальство, до того закрывавшее глаза на истязание юноши, испугалось огласки и поспешило откомандировать его в полковую швальню (Лившиц 1). Before that the authorities had turned a blind eye to the torturing of the young man, but they became afraid of the publicity and hastened to post him to the regimental tailor's shop (1a).

Г-73 • ЗАЛИВА́ТЬ/ЗАЛИ́ТЬ ⟨НАЛИВА́ТЬ/НАЛИ́ТЬ⟩ ГЛАЗА́ ⟨ЗЕ́НКИ *vulg*, **ШАРЫ́** *vulg⟩ substand* [VP; subj: human] to get drunk: **X залил глаза** ≃ **X got ⟨was⟩ soused ⟨pie-eyed⟩; X drank himself cockeyed ⟨under the table⟩.**

«Не успел человек заявиться, он рюмку выпрашивать… Он ведь шары нальёт — море по колено!» (Абрамов 1). "The man's scarcely back home and already he's scrounging for a drink.…He'll go and get himself so pie-eyed he'll be all Dutch courage" (1a). ♦ «Не понимаешь ты человеческого отношения. Тебе что — абы зенки налить» (Аксёнов 1). "You don't understand it when a body treats you decent. All's you want is to drink yourself cockeyed" (1a).

Г-74 • ЗАМА́ЗЫВАТЬ/ЗАМА́ЗАТЬ ГЛАЗА́ *кому substand* [VP; subj: human] to mislead s.o. intentionally, give s.o. a false impression of sth., deceive s.o.: **X замазывает Y-у глаза** ≃ **X throws dust in Y's eyes; X pulls the wool over Y's eyes.**

Г-75 • ЗАПУСКА́ТЬ/ЗАПУСТИ́ТЬ ГЛАЗА́ ⟨ГЛАЗЕНА́ПА *obs⟩ highly coll* [VP; subj: human] **1.** ~ *куда* to glance furtively, hurriedly at sth. (one should not): **X запускает глаза в ⟨на etc⟩ Y** ≃ **X sneaks peeks ⟨a peek, looks, a look⟩ at ⟨in, into⟩ Y; X steals glances ⟨a glance⟩ at Y.**

Как только Шурочка вышла из комнаты, молодой человек запустил глаза в её раскрытый дневник, лежавший на столе. The moment Shurochka left the room, the young man sneaked a peek at her open diary lying on the table.

2. ~ *на что* to show a mercenary interest in sth. in the hope of obtaining it: **X запускает глаза на Y** ≃ **X is eyeing Y; X has (got) his eye on Y.**

[Кочкарёв:] …[Дом невесты] не только заложен, да за два года ещё проценты не выплачены. Да в сенате есть ещё брат, который тоже запускает глаза на дом; сутяги такого свет не производил… (Гоголь 1). [K.:] Not only is it [the young lady's house] mortgaged, the interest hasn't been paid for two years. And there's a brother in the Senate who's got his eye on the property—a shyster; you've never seen anything like him (1b).

3. ~ *на кого* to look at a person (of the opposite sex) with desire: **X запускает глаза на Y-а** ≃ **X has his eye on Y.**

«Заметили, как Фуфков переживает? На новопреставленную смотрел, слёзы градом… А рядом муж». — «Он всю жизнь на неё запускал глазенапа» (Пастернак 1). "Did you see how upset Fufkov was? Looking at her [the deceased], tears pouring down his face.…Standing next to her husband at that." "He always had his eye on her" (1a).

Г-76 • (И) В ГЛАЗА́ не видать, не видеть *кого-что* or *чего coll* [PrepP; these forms only; adv; used with past tense] (not to have seen s.o. or sth.) ever: **X (и) в глаза не видел Y-а** ≃ **X has never set ⟨laid⟩ eyes on ⟨upon⟩ Y; X has never so much as seen Y; X has never even seen Y.**

Из 12 ораторов, выступавших на заседании, я знаком только с четырьмя. Остальных никогда в глаза не видел, а если и видел, то едва ли узнал бы (Эткинд 1). Of the twelve speakers at the meeting, I only know four. The rest I have never set eyes on, or if I have met them, I would be hard put to recognize them (1a). ♦ Жители ликовали; ещё не видав в глаза вновь назначенного правителя, они уже рассказывали об нём анекдоты и называли его «красавчиком» и «умницей» (Салтыков-Щедрин 1.) The inhabitants rejoiced; though they had not yet laid eyes on their newly appointed ruler, they were already telling anecdotes about him and calling him a "bright boy" and a "handsome laddy" (1a). ♦ «Ваня говорил, что у этого француза славная дочка. Может, ты с ней?..» — «Я её и в глаза не видал» (Эренбург 2). "Vanya says this Frenchman has a nice daughter; perhaps you're in love with her?" "I've never so much as seen her" (2a).

Г-77 • КОЛО́ТЬ ГЛАЗА́ ⟨ГЛАЗ *obs⟩ coll* [VP] **1.** ~ *кому (чем)* [subj: human] to remind s.o. consistently of, reproach s.o. for etc (some shortcoming, mistake, foolish behavior etc): **X колол Y-у глаза Z-ом** ≃ **X kept ⟨was⟩ throwing Z in Y's face ⟨teeth⟩; X kept ⟨was⟩ throwing Z up to Y; X was ⟨kept⟩ rubbing Y's nose in it.**

…Он [мой отец] был не только честный и порядочный человек, у него была голова на плечах… И хотя некоторые подбирали ключи под моего отца, кололи [директору фабрики] Сидорову глаза, что отец из Швейцарии, но Сидоров не обращал на это внимания — (Рыбаков 1). Father wasn't just honest and decent, he also had a good head on his shoulders.…Though some people tried to trip father up by throwing his Swiss nationality in [the manager] Sidorov's face, Sidorov took no notice… (1a). ♦ [Чеглов:] Что ж ты мне всё этой любовью колешь глаза? (Писемский 1). [Ch.:] Why do you throw this love in my teeth all the time? (1a).

2. ~ *(кому)* [subj: concr or abstr] to irritate s.o., be disagreeable to s.o.: **X колет глаза Y-у** ≃ **X sets Y's teeth on edge; X gets under Y's skin; X gets on Y's nerves; X gets Y's goat;** [of sth. that makes an unpleasant visual impression] **X offends the eye; X hurts the eye(s); X is an eyesore.**

[Мамаева:] Если вы видите, что умный человек бедно одет, живёт в дурной квартире, едет на плохом извозчике, — это вас не поражает, не колет вам глаз… (Островский 9). [M.:] If you happen to see a clever man poorly dressed, living in an ugly apartment, riding in second-rate cabs—…this doesn't startle you, or set your teeth on edge (9c).

Г-78 • КУДА́ ГЛАЗА́ ГЛЯДЯ́Т *coll* [Invar; adv; fixed WO] **1. идти, брести, бежать** и т. п. ~ (to walk, roam, run etc) without choosing a specific direction, without a prepared plan, indifferent to where one ends up (often used in cases when one is escaping from a dangerous, intolerable, volatile etc situation; also used when s.o. is deep in thought, emotionally distraught etc): **уйти ⟨убежать** и т. п.⟩ ~ ≃ **leave ⟨run away** etc⟩ **not caring**

where one is going; go anywhere (just to get out of here ⟨there etc⟩); ‖ брести ~ ≃ **wander aimlessly ⟨randomly, at random⟩; go wherever one's legs carry ⟨take⟩ one; go wherever one's feet take one; walk without thinking ⟨paying attention to⟩ where one is going; go ⟨walk etc⟩ heedlessly ⟨blindly etc⟩;** ‖ беги ~! ≃ **run away, go anywhere at all!; get out of here ⟨there⟩, it doesn't matter where you go!; go anywhere, just get out of here ⟨there⟩!**

[extended usage] …Если дождь пойдёт или гроза начнётся, не знают ковыли, куда им приткнуться. Мечутся, падают, прижимаются к земле. Были бы ноги, убежали бы, наверное, куда глаза глядят... (Айтматов 1). …If it rained or stormed, the feather grass went frantic, it did not know what to do, where to hide. It tossed and flattened, pressed itself against the earth. If it had feet, it surely would run away, just anywhere at all (1a). ♦ …Он хотел было поворотить назад, к дому, но домой идти ему стало вдруг ужасно противно... и он пошёл куда глаза глядят (Достоевский 3). …He was about to turn back and go home, but the thought of going home suddenly repelled him....He walked on at random (3a).

2. идти, ехать, отправляться и т. п. ~ **(to walk, go, set off) wherever one chooses, desires (without restrictions or limitations): wherever one's fancy takes one; wherever one feels like (going); wherever the spirit moves one; wherever one's legs (will) carry ⟨take⟩ one; wherever one's feet (will) take one.**

И вдруг мелькнула в голове [у Орозкула] отчаянная мысль: «А плюну на всё и уйду куда глаза глядят!» (Айтматов 1). Suddenly a desperate thought flashed across his [Orozkul's] mind: "I'll spit on all this and get out. Just leave for wherever my fancy takes me" (1b).

Г-79 • ЛЕЗТЬ В ⟨НА⟩ ГЛАЗА́ *(кому)* coll [VP] **1.** [subj: human] to try to attract s.o.'s attention to o.s. by remaining constantly in his presence, within his view: X лезет на глаза (Y-у) ≃ **X is trying to get ⟨make⟩ himself noticed; X is trying to make Y notice X.**

Мой помощник всегда лезет на глаза, особенно когда появляются репортёры. My assistant is always trying to get himself noticed, especially when there are reporters around.

2. [subj: human, concr, or abstr] to attract attention to o.s. or itself, be noticeable: X лезет в глаза ≃ **X catches the ⟨one's⟩ eye; X grabs person Y's attention; X calls attention to himself ⟨itself⟩.**

Первое, что лезет в глаза, когда разворачиваешь газету, — это огромная реклама бюро путешествий «Вокруг света». The first thing to catch your eye when you open the newspaper is a huge ad for the travel agency Around the World.

Г-80 • ЛО́ПНИ (МОЙ) ГЛАЗА́ substand [VP_imper; these forms only; usu. a main clause in a complex sent or indep. sent; often foll. by a clause introduced by Conj если, коли etc] (used as an oath to emphasize the truth or accuracy of one's statement) I swear that what I say is true: **strike me blind ⟨dead⟩ if...; I'll be darned ⟨damned⟩ if...**

«Что я вижу! — закричала жена Кязыма и, бросив свою лопаточку, тоже подбежала ко мне. — Лопни мои глаза, если это не Арапка!» (Искандер 3). "What do I see!" cried Kyazym's wife. She dropped her spatula and ran over too. "Strike me blind if it isn't Blackamoor!" (3a).

Г-81 • МОЗО́ЛИТЬ/НАМОЗО́ЛИТЬ ГЛАЗА́ *кому* highly coll [VP] **1.** [subj: human or concr] to be annoying, irritate s.o. with one's or its constant presence: X мозолит Y-у глаза ≃ **X is a pain in the neck (to Y); X drives Y crazy; thing X is an eyesore (to Y); X is a nuisance (to Y); person X makes a nuisance of himself.**

«Мастера — они всегда мозолят людям глаза и от них отделываются при первой же возможности» (Максимов 2). "Such men [master-craftsmen] are always a pain in the neck to others, and they get rid of them at the first available opportunity" (2a). ♦ «Да за каким он дьяволом мне сдался? — рассердился Михаил. — И так каждый день глаза мозолит» (Абрамов 1). "What the hell do I want to see *him* for?" said Mikhail angrily. "He drives me crazy every day as it is" (1a). ♦ Или вот ходики с отломанной стрелкой. И ходики, и отломанная стрелка мозолили ему [Петру Васильевичу] глаза лет уже не менее сорока, но только теперь Петру Васильевичу подумалось: «А стрелка-то отломана, да...» (Максимов 3). Then there was the wall-clock with the broken hand. The clock and the broken hand had been an eyesore to him [Pyotr Vasilievich] for a good forty years, yet only now did the thought enter his head: "Hm, the hand's broken off..." (3a). ♦ «Я предупреждал [ссыльных]: приходите [в столовую] часам к двум, когда сотрудники уже пообедали, не шумите, не мозольте глаза, тихо, мирно, аккуратно» (Рыбаков 2). "I warned them [the exiles] all not to get here [to the canteen] before two o'clock, after the employees have eaten, and not to make any noise, not to be a nuisance, but to be quiet, peaceable, and tidy" (2a). ♦ [Лапшин:] Я к нашим в гостиницу проеду, а ты поди отсюда. Покушал — и поди, не мозоль глаза (Розов 2). [L.:] I'm going to see our lot in the hotel. You make yourself scarce. You've had your bit. So off you go, don't make a nuisance of yourself (2a).

2. ~ *чем* [subj: human] to pester s.o. with constant complaints about sth., reproaches etc: X мозолит Y-у глаза Z-ом ≃ **X is (always) bugging Y about Z; X is (getting) after Y about Z; X is on Y's case about Z.**

Г-82 • НАВОСТРИ́ТЬ ГЛАЗА́ *на кого-что* highly coll [VP; subj: human] to look attentively, watchfully (at s.o. or sth.): X навострил глаза на Y-а ≃ **X gazed intently at Y; X fixed his eyes on Y; X was all eyes.**

…Девочка навострила на него глаза, ожидая, что он сделает с сухарями (Гончаров 1). …The little girl still gazed intently at him, waiting to see what he would do with the cakes (1b). ♦ Ребёнок, навострив уши и глаза, страстно впивался в рассказ (Гончаров 1). The child, all eyes and ears, listened to the story with passionate absorption (1b).

Г-83 • НЕ ЗНАТЬ, КУДА́ ГЛАЗА́ ДЕВА́ТЬ/ДЕТЬ coll [VP (subj: human) + subord clause (these forms only)] to experience a feeling of embarrassment, awkwardness, shame: X не знал, куда глаза девать ≃ **X didn't know where ⟨which way⟩ to look; X didn't know where to hide (from embarrassment etc).**

«Стали снимать [меня с должности председателя] — ни у людей, ни у райкома слова доброго для меня не нашлось». Михаил не знал, куда и глаза девать: это ведь его стараниями так отблагодарили [iron] Анфису Петровну (Абрамов 1). "When they decided to throw me out, nobody from the village or the District Committee could find a good word to say about me." Mikhail did not know which way to look. After all, it was his doing that they had shown their gratitude to Anfisa Petrovna in that way (1a).

Г-84 • ОТВОДИ́ТЬ/ОТВЕСТИ́ ГЛАЗА́ *кому* coll [VP; subj: human] to mislead s.o. intentionally, give s.o. a false impression of sth., deceive s.o.: X отводит Y-у глаза ≃ **X throws dust in Y's eyes; X pulls the wool over Y's eyes; X deludes Y.**

Представляя слуг и рабов распутными зверями, планта́торы отводят глаза другим и заглушают крики совести в себе (Герцен 1). By picturing servants and slaves as degraded animals, the slave-owners throw dust in people's eyes and stifle the voice of conscience in themselves (1a). ♦ «...Буду опять его [журнал] издавать и непременно в либеральном и атеистическом направлении, с социалистическим оттенком, с маленьким даже лоском социализма, но держа ухо востро, то есть, в сущности, держа нашим и вашим и отводя глаза дуракам»

(Достоевский 1). "...I will go on publishing it [the journal], most certainly with a liberal and atheistic slant, with a socialistic tinge, with even a little gloss of socialism, but with my ears open, that is, essentially, running with the hare and hunting with the hounds, and pulling the wool over the fools' eyes" (1a). ◆ [Трофимов:] ...Очевидно, все хорошие разговоры у нас для того только, чтобы отвести глаза себе и другим (Чехов 2). [T.:] It's obvious that all our fine talk is merely to delude ourselves and others (2a).

Г-85 • ОТКРЫВА́ТЬ/ОТКРЫ́ТЬ ⟨РАСКРЫВА́ТЬ/ РАСКРЫ́ТЬ⟩ ГЛАЗА́ [VP; usu. pfv past; fixed WO] **1. ~ (на что)** [subj: human] to begin to see a situation as it really is or people as they really are: X открыл глаза (на Y) ≃ **X opened his eyes (to Y); X saw the light.**

[Люди] просыпались от вынужденной спячки периода Хозяина, открывали глаза на действительность и рвались развернуть свои творческие потенции, зажимавшиеся столько десятилетий (Зиновьев 1). ...People were beginning to wake up after the forced hibernation of the Boss period, to open their eyes to reality, impatient to give full rein to their creative potential which had been repressed for so many decades (1a). ◆ [Платонов:] Ты первая перестанешь заблуждаться! Ты первая откроешь глаза и оставишь меня! (Чехов 1). [P.:] You'll be the first to realize the error of your ways and see the light. You'll leave me first (1b).

2. ~ кому (на кого-что) [subj: human or abstr] to show s.o. that his perceptions of sth. are erroneous, help s.o. to comprehend the true nature of some person or phenomenon: X открыл Y-у глаза на Z-а ≃ **X opened Y's eyes ⟨the eyes of Y⟩ to Z; X made ⟨helped⟩ Y see what...Z is; X showed Y the truth about Z; thing X was an eyeopener ⟨eye-opener⟩.**

«Его речь мне просто глаза открыла на многое» (Чуковская 2). "His speech opened my eyes to a lot of things" (2a). ◆ «Иванько воспользовался тем, что, к сожалению, Борис Иванович [Стукалин, председатель Государственного комитета по делам издательств], слишком мягок и доверчив... В таком случае не открыть ли нам глаза доверчивому Борису Ивановичу на одного из его ближайших соратников? (Войнович 3). "Ivanko took advantage of the fact that, unfortunately, Boris Ivanovich [Stukalin, Chairman of the State Committee on Publishing] is too soft and credulous."...But, in that case, shouldn't we open the eyes of the credulous Boris Ivanovich to one of his closest comrades-in-arms? (3a). ◆ Глебов принял лекарство и прилёг одетый на тахту, думая о том, что сегодня надо бы наконец, если всё будет благополучно и дочка вернётся живая, поговорить с нею о Толмачёве. Раскрыть глаза на это ничтожество (Трифонов 2). Glebov took his medication and lay down fully dressed on the couch, thinking how today—provided all was well and she actually returned alive—he must talk to his daughter about Tolmachev and make her see what a nonentity this young man was (2a). ◆ В Олю он окончательно влюбился после велосипедной прогулки с ней и с Яшей по Шварцвальду, которая, как потом он показывал на следствии, «нам всем троим открыла глаза»... (Набоков 1). He fell in love with Olya conclusively after a bicycle ride with her and Yasha in the Black Forest, a tour which, as he later testified at the inquest, "was an eye-opener for all three of us"... (1a).

Г-86 • ПЛЕВА́ТЬ/НАПЛЕВА́ТЬ ⟨ПЛЮ́НУТЬ⟩ В ГЛАЗА́ highly coll ⟨**В ЛИЦО́, В РО́ЖУ** substand, rude⟩ **кому** [VP; subj: human or collect] to express extreme contempt or disrespect for s.o. in a harsh manner: X наплевал в глаза Y-у ≃ **X spat in Y's eye ⟨face⟩.**

«...Того и гляди, пойдёшь на старости лет по миру!» — «Мне, однако же, сказывали... что у вас более тысячи душ». — «А кто это сказывал? А вы бы... наплевали в глаза тому, который это сказывал!» (Гоголь 3). "...If I don't watch out, I'll be forced to go begging in my old age." "But I was told you possessed over a thousand souls...." "Who told you that? You ought to have spat in the eye of the man who goes around saying such things" (3e). ◆ На лице [Иванько] ничего, кроме страдания. Ещё бы!.. Ему же не

просто не дали, чего он хотел. Ему в лицо плюнули, его не признали достаточно большим человеком (Войнович 3). On his [Ivanko's] face was nothing but suffering. Of course!...They didn't just fail to give him what he wanted; they spit in his face, they did not recognize him as a big enough man (3a).

Г-87 • ПОКА́ЗЫВАТЬСЯ ⟨КАЗА́ТЬСЯ obs, substand⟩/ ПОКАЗА́ТЬСЯ НА ГЛАЗА́ кому coll [VP; subj: human; if impfv, usu. neg (often neg imper) or with a negated verb denoting a command, prohibition; often pfv infin with нельзя, не мочь, бояться, как etc] to appear before s.o. or at s.o.'s place: X боится показаться на глаза Y-у ≃ **X is afraid to show ⟨of showing⟩ his face to Y; X is afraid to show himself at Y's place ⟨before Y⟩;** [in limited contexts] **X is afraid of facing ⟨can't face⟩ Y;** ‖ Neg Imper не показывайся на глаза Y-у ≃ **don't let Y set eyes on you; keep out of Y's sight.**

«Теперь ступай и больше на глаза мне не показывайся» (Бунин 1). "Be off with you now and never show your face to me again" (1a). ◆ Она [сестра Присциллы] водила меня в местные магазины, потом купила мне платья и мелочи сама, — мне было лучше не показываться на глаза публике (Аллилуева 2). She [Priscilla's sister] used to take me shopping. Later she bought me some dresses and a few other things on her own—it was best for me not to show myself in public (2a). ◆ «Как покажусь я на глаза господам? Что скажут они, как узнают, что дитя пьёт и играет» (Пушкин 2). "How can I ever face the master and mistress? What'll they say when they hear that their child drinks and gambles?" (2a). ◆ «Уходи, Виктор, и не показывайся мне больше на глаза, не доводи до краю...» (Максимов 1). "Go away, Viktor, and don't let me ever set eyes on you again. Don't push me too far" (1a).

Г-88 • ПОПАДА́ТЬСЯ/ПОПА́СТЬСЯ ⟨ПОПАДА́ТЬ/ ПОПА́СТЬ⟩ НА ГЛАЗА́ кому [VP; subj: human, animal, or concr; often neg infin after стараться or in infin clause introduced by чтобы] to happen to be seen or met by s.o., or to attract s.o.'s attention: X попался на глаза Y-у ≃ **X caught Y's eye; Y caught sight of X; Y's eyes lighted ⟨lit⟩ on X;** [in limited contexts] **thing X came to Y's notice ⟨to the notice of Y⟩; Y came across thing X; thing X turned up;** ‖ Neg [or with negated predic; of people only] X не хотел ⟨X старался не etc⟩ попадаться Y-у на глаза ≃ **X tried to keep out of Y's sight;** [in limited contexts] **X didn't want ⟨tried not⟩ to invite attention;** ‖ Neg Imper [usu. used as a warning or threat] не попадайся Y-у на глаза ≃ **stay ⟨keep⟩ out of Y's sight.**

Конечно же, и шкаф, и граммофон попадались ему на глаза множество раз, но лишь сейчас он отметил их... (Максимов 3). Of course, the cupboard and the gramophone had caught his eye countless times in the past but he had never before taken notice of them... (3a). ◆ Сначала она его дичилась и однажды, перед вечером, встретив его на узкой тропинке, проложенной пешеходами через ржаное поле, зашла в высокую, густую рожь... чтобы только не попасться ему на глаза (Тургенев 2). At first she avoided him, and one day, late in the afternoon, meeting him on a narrow path that walkers had made across a ryefield, she turned into the dense, tall rye...so that he would not catch sight of her (2f). ◆ Бирюков подошёл к книжному стеллажу, задумчиво стал разглядывать шеренги книг. На глаза попался полный ряд старинных изданий (Чернёнок 1). Birukov went over to the bookshelf and looked thoughtfully over the ranks of books. His eyes lit on a row of old editions (1a). ◆ Практика показала, что... эти надписи обязательно попадут на глаза кому нужно (Буковский 1). Practice showed that these inscriptions would invariably come to the notice of whomever they were meant for (1a). ◆ Среди совершенно непонятных для меня стихов, напечатанных вкривь и вкось, даже, кажется, кое-где вверх ногами... мне попался на глаза футуристический сборник «Садок судей»... (Катаев 3). Among these poems of which I could not understand a word, printed at all angles across the page, and sometimes even upside down…I came across a futurist collection called *A Stew of Judges*… (3a). ♦ Она невольно отворачивалась от меня… невольно; вот что было горько, вот что меня сокрушало! Но делать было нечего — и я старался не попадаться ей на глаза… (Тургенев 3). Involuntarily she turned away from me…involuntarily; it was that which was so bitter, so crushing—but there was nothing I could do. I did my best to keep out of her sight… (3b). ♦ И без того обездоленная слухами о своём классовом происхождении, совесть его [председателя] окончательно замолкла и в распрях его страстей уже не принимала никакого участия, как бедная родственница, лишний рот, незаметно устраивалась где-нибудь в уголке, чтобы не слишком попадаться на глаза… (Искандер 3). His [the Chairman's] conscience, which had already been harassed and impoverished anyway by rumors about his class origin, was silenced for good and took no sides in the feuding among his passions—like a poor female relative, an extra mouth to feed, who fixes herself up in some out-of-the-way corner lest she invite too much attention… (3a).

Г-89 • ПРОДИРА́ТЬ/ПРОДРА́ТЬ ГЛАЗА́ *highly coll;* **ПРОТИРА́ТЬ/ПРОТЕРЕ́ТЬ ГЛАЗА́** *coll;* **ПРОДИРА́ТЬ/ПРОДРА́ТЬ ЗЕ́НКИ ⟨ГЛАЗЕНА́ПА** *obs⟩ substand, rude* [VP; subj: human] to awaken from sleep: X продрал глаза ≃ **X opened his eyes; X woke up;** [in limited contexts] **X rubbed the sleep out of his eyes.**

[Кухарка:] Только, господи благослови, глаза продерут, сейчас самовар… Только самовара два отопьют, уж третий ставь (Толстой 3). [Woman Cook:] God bless us, as soon as they open their eyes, they have to have their samovar….No sooner have they finished two samovars than they need a third (3a). ♦ «Я и сегодня пришёл в камеру только в третьем часу ночи. И заснул не сразу… Утром еле глаза продрал…» (Копелев 1). "I only got in last night from working after two in the morning. And I couldn't fall asleep right away….I could barely open my eyes in the morning… (1a). ♦ Едва продирал я глаза по утрам — тянуло меня не к роману, а Предупреждение ещё раз переписать, это было сильней меня, так во мне и ходило (Солженицын 2). As soon as I rubbed the sleep out of my eyes in the morning I longed to get to my novel, but the urge to rewrite my Warning just once more would be too strong for me, I was so worked up about it (2a).

Г-90 • ПРОТЕРЕ́ТЬ ГЛАЗА́ [VP; subj: human] **1.** *highly coll* [usu. imper] (to begin) to see things as they are, think clearly: протри глаза! ≃ **open your eyes!; wake up (to reality)!; come to your senses!**

2. ~ *чему,* usu. деньгам, денежкам *obs, substand.* Also: **ПРОТЕРЕ́ТЬ ГЛА́ЗКИ** to waste money, spend money senselessly: X протёр глаза деньгам ≃ **X squandered the money; X blew the money ⟨a fortune⟩.**

3. ~ *кому obs, substand.* Also: **ПРОТЕРЕ́ТЬ ГЛА́ЗКИ** to prove one's superiority over s.o. in sth., outdo s.o.: X протёр глаза Y-у ≃ **X showed Y up; X got the better ⟨the best⟩ of Y.**

Г-91 • ПРЯ́ТАТЬ ГЛАЗА́ ⟨ВЗГЛЯД, ВЗОР⟩ [VP; subj: human] to avoid or be afraid of looking directly at another or others: X прятал глаза ≃ **X hid his eyes (from Y); X avoided Y's eyes; X averted his eyes; X wouldn't look at Y; X wouldn't ⟨took care not to⟩ look Y in the eye; X avoided eye contact (with Y).**

«Я получил в тот день полное удовлетворение, — вспоминал Иван Петрович. — Отец был напуган. Долго затем искал его взгляда, но он прятал глаза» (Олеша 2). "That day was completely satisfying," Ivan Babichev reminisced. "Father was scared. For a long time afterward, when I tried to look into his eyes, he hid them from me" (2b). ♦ «Оно надо же, беда свалилась… Кто ж гадал…» — виновато забормотал он, пряча глаза (Тендряков 1). "What a thing to happen to me…you never can tell…." he muttered guiltily, avoiding Simon's eyes (1a). ♦ В 11 часов — звонок, при-

бежала секретарша из СП [Союза писателей], очень поспешная, глаза как-то прячет и суетливо суёт мне отпечатанную бумажку, что сегодня в 3 часа дня совещание об *идейном воспитании* писателей (Солженицын 2). At 11 A.M. there was a ring at the door, and a flustered secretary from the Writer's Union rushed in. Taking care not to look me in the eye, she fumblingly thrust a scrap of typewritten paper into my hand, announcing a conference on the *ideological education* of writers at 3 P.M. that same day (2a).

Г-92 • ПУСКА́ТЬ/ПУСТИ́ТЬ НА ГЛАЗА́ *кого к кому coll* [VP; subj: human; usu. neg or neg imper] to allow s.o. to come to one's or another person's home or office: X не пустил Y-а к себе ⟨к Z-у⟩ на глаза ≃ **X didn't let Y set foot in X's ⟨Z's⟩ place ⟨office etc⟩; X didn't let Y show Y's face in X's ⟨Z's⟩ house ⟨office etc⟩;** ‖ *Neg Imper* не пускай Y-а ко мне ⟨к Z-у⟩ на глаза ≃ **keep Y out of my ⟨Z's⟩ sight.**

[Кречинский:] Нелькина вы больше на глаза к себе не пустите (Сухово-Кобылин 2). [K:] And you'll never let Nelkin set foot in your house again (2a).

Г-93 • ПУ́ЩЕ ГЛА́ЗА беречь *кого-что,* хранить *что;* **ПА́ЧЕ ГЛА́ЗА ⟨О́КА⟩** *obs* [AdvP; these forms only; adv; fixed WO] (to treat s.o. or sth. that one cherishes, that is very valuable etc) as very dear, (to guard, watch over sth. valuable) vigilantly, attentively: **(cherish ⟨treasure⟩ s.o. ⟨sth.⟩) more than life itself ⟨more than one's life⟩; (guard sth.) with one's life.**

[Мигаев:] Да, чудак, давно б я его [портсигар] заложил, да нельзя — дарёный, в знак памяти, пуще глазу его берегу (Островский 11). [M.:] I'd have pawned it [the cigar case] long ago, but I mustn't; it was given to me as a token of remembrance. I treasure it more than my life (11a).

Г-94 • РАЗУ́Й ГЛАЗА́ ⟨БЕ́ЛЬМА⟩ *substand, rude* [VP$_{imper}$; these forms only] look carefully, take a close look: **open ⟨use⟩ your eyes; open your peepers.**

Г-95 • РЕ́ЗАТЬ ГЛАЗА́ ⟨ГЛАЗ⟩ *(кому чем)* [VP] **1.** [subj: usu. concr] to have an unpleasant effect upon the (or s.o.'s) eyes (usu. by being too bright or colorful): X режет глаза ≃ **X hurts the ⟨s.o.'s⟩ eye(s); X offends the eye; X is an eyesore.**

Одета она была безвкусно, яркое платье в огромных цветах резало глаз. She was dressed tastelessly: her bright dress with huge flowers offended the eye.

2. [subj: abstr] to make a negative impression on s.o. by deviating conspicuously from the proper or expected form, manner etc: X режет глаза (Y-ом) ≃ **X is glaring; X is glaringly [AdjP].**

Эта статья режет глаза своей научной несостоятельностью. Scientifically, this article is glaringly unsound.

Г-96 • СМОТРЕ́ТЬ ⟨ГЛЯДЕ́ТЬ⟩ В ГЛАЗА́¹ *кому coll* [VP; subj: human] to try to please s.o., fawn upon s.o.: X смотрит Y-у в глаза ≃ **X dances attendance on Y; X tries to anticipate Y's every wish; X plays up to Y; X falls all over Y.**

«Я и Иван Матвеич ухаживали за тобой… словно крепостные, служили тебе, на цыпочках ходили, в глаза смотрели…» (Гончаров 1). "Ivan Matveyevich and I took care of you, we waited on you as if we were your serfs, walked on tiptoe, tried to anticipate your every wish…" (1b).

Г-97 • СМОТРЕ́ТЬ ⟨ГЛЯДЕ́ТЬ⟩ В ГЛАЗА́² ⟨В ЛИЦО́⟩ *чему* [VP; subj: human; indir obj: опасности, трудностям, фактам etc; often infin with надо, должен etc] not to fear sth., to confront sth. boldly: X должен смотреть в глаза Y-у ≃ **X has to look Y straight ⟨right⟩ in the eye; X has to face (up to) Y; X has to meet Y head-on.**

«...Нет, нет, поймите правильно! Кто-кто, а уж я-то не поклонник газетных штампов. Но факты есть факты, и надо смотреть им в глаза...» (Аржак 1). "...No, no, don't misunderstand me. You know me, I'm the last man in the world to be impressed by newspaper clichés. But facts are facts, and you've got to face them..." (1a).

Г-98 • СМОТРЕ́ТЬ ⟨ГЛЯДЕ́ТЬ⟩ ПРЯ́МО ⟨СМЕ́ЛО⟩ В ГЛАЗА́ *кому* [VP; subj: human; often infin compl of мочь] to feel that one is acting honestly, honorably, that one does not have to be ashamed of his actions before s.o.: X может прямо смотреть Y-у в глаза ≃ **X can look Y straight in the eye.**

[author's usage] До сих пор он покойно жил, никого не боялся, любому и каждому мог без опаски смотреть в глаза (Тендряков 1) Up till now he had lived quietly, fearing no one, and able to look any man straight in the eye (1a).

Г-99 • СОВА́ТЬСЯ/СУ́НУТЬСЯ НА ⟨В⟩ ГЛАЗА́ *кому* *coll* [VP; subj: human] to attempt to gain s.o.'s attention by constantly appearing before him or staying close to him: X совался на глаза Y-у ≃ **X thrust ⟨threw⟩ himself on Y ⟨at Y, in Y's path⟩.**

Вовремя посторониться — вот всё, что было нужно... Но они [глуповцы] сообразили это поздно, и в первое время, по примеру всех начальстволюбивых народов... совались ему [градоначальнику] на глаза (Салтыков-Щедрин 1). All you had to do was to get out of the way in time....But they [the Glupovites] understood it only later, and at first followed the example of all peoples who love their superiors, thrusting themselves in his [the town governor's] path... (1b).

Г-100 • ТАРА́ЩИТЬ ⟨ВЫ́ТАРАЩИТЬ, ПУ́ЧИТЬ, ВЫ́ПУЧИТЬ, ВЫКА́ТЫВАТЬ/ВЫ́КАТИТЬ⟩ ГЛАЗА́ *(на кого-что)* *highly coll;* **ПЯ́ЛИТЬ ⟨ВЫ́ПЯЛИТЬ, ЛУПИ́ТЬ, ВЫ́ЛУПИТЬ⟩ ГЛАЗА́** *substand;* **ПЯ́ЛИТЬ ⟨ВЫ́ПЯЛИТЬ, ПУ́ЧИТЬ, ВЫ́ПУЧИТЬ, ЛУПИ́ТЬ, ВЫ́ЛУПИТЬ⟩ ЗЕ́НКИ ⟨БЕ́ЛЬМА⟩** *substand, rude* [VP; subj: human] to look (at s.o. or sth.) intently, raptly, opening one's eyes wide: X таращил глаза на Y-а ≃ **X was staring at Y (, wide-eyed); X was gawking at Y; X's eyes were popping ⟨bugging⟩ out (of X's head); X's eyes were bulging ⟨goggling, bugging⟩ (with fright ⟨in disbelief etc⟩);** [usu. of looking at s.o. or sth. one wants; often used when making advances to a person of the opposite sex] **X was eyeing ⟨ogling⟩ Y;** ‖ [in questions and *Neg Imper*] ты что пялишь глаза? ≃ **why are you staring like that?**

«Вот этот жёлтый господин в очках, — продолжал Обломов, — пристал ко мне: читал ли я речь какого-то депутата, и глаза вытаращил на меня, когда я сказал, что не читаю газет» (Гончаров 1). "That sallow-faced gentleman in spectacles who attached himself to me," Oblomov continued, "kept asking whether I had read the speech of some French deputy or other, and stared at me, wide-eyed, when I told him I didn't read the papers" (1b). ♦ «Ну что... — он [инвалид] обратился к Ермолкину, — что глаза вылупил?» (Войнович 4). "What are you gawking at?" he [the invalid] said to Ermolkin (4a). ♦ «Смотрите на неё [хозяйку]: вытаращила глаза, чувствует, что мы о ней говорим, а не может понять...» (Достоевский 3). "Look at her [the landlady]: her eyes are popping out, she realizes we're talking about her, but she can't make it out..." (3a). ♦ Зина, испуганно таращя глаза, ушла с календарём, а человек покачал укоризненно головою (Булгаков 11). Zina, her eyes bulging with fright, hurried out with the calendar, and the man shook his head deploringly (11a). ♦ «А ведь он [жилец] пялит глаза на мою сестру...» — шёпотом прибавил он. «Что ты?» — с изумлением сказал Тарантьев (Гончаров 1). "You know," he added in a whisper, "he's [the tenant has] been eyeing my sister." "Really?" Tarantyev said, in astonishment (1b). ♦ «На пирожки-то глаз не пяль, не дам, тебе вредно...»

(Достоевский 2). "Don't ogle the pirozhki, you won't get any, they're not good for you..." (2a). ♦ «Когда тронемся, неизвестно, может, через час, а может, через месяц...» — «Тронемся в восемнадцать ноль-ноль... Не пяль глаза, у меня сведения из первых рук» (Максимов 3). "There's no knowing when we'll get away from here....It may be an hour and it may be a month...." "We'll be off at eighteen hundred hours....No need to stare like that. I've got firsthand information" (3a).

Г-101 • ТЫ́КАТЬ В ГЛАЗА́ ⟨В НОС⟩ *кому что* *or* *кемчем* *highly coll, rude* [VP; subj: human] to mention sth. or remind s.o. of sth. (usu. his inadequacies, failures, or one's own or another's positive qualities, achievements) repeatedly and obtrusively, with the goal of reproaching him, making him feel guilty for sth., embarrassing him etc: X тычет Y-у в глаза Z-ом ≃ **X throws ⟨keeps throwing⟩ Z in Y's face; X casts ⟨keeps casting⟩ Z in Y's teeth; X throws ⟨keeps throwing⟩ Z up to Y; X will never let Y forget Z.**

[extended usage; говорящий — мул] Я же, например, не оспариваю, что собаки преданы своих хозяевам. Да это и в самом деле так. Но то, что эту преданность они всё время тычут в глаза, забывая о собственном достоинстве, тоже не признак ума (Искандер 3). [The speaker is a mule] I don't deny, for example, that dogs are devoted to their masters. This really is true. But the way they always cast this devotion in your teeth, forgetting their own dignity, is no sign of intelligence either (3a). ♦ [Бурмистр:] К какому слову ты тут межёвку-то приплёл? Что ты мне тем тычешь в глаза? (Писемский 1). [Bailiff:] What do you bring up the measuring of the land for? Why do you throw that up to me? (1a).

Г-102 • НЕ ВЕ́РИТЬ/НЕ ПОВЕ́РИТЬ (СВОИ́М) ГЛАЗА́М *coll* [VP; subj: human] to be extremely surprised at sth. one has seen: X глазам (своим) не верил ≃ **X couldn't believe his eyes; X could scarcely ⟨hardly⟩ believe his eyes; X wondered if he was seeing straight ⟨seeing things⟩; X did a double take.**

«Маралы! Маралы!» — вне себя от испуга и радости вскричал дед Момун. И замолк, будто не веря своим глазам (Айтматов 1). "Deer! Deer!" Grandfather Momun cried out, beside himself with fright and joy. And instantly fell silent, as though he did not believe his eyes (1a). ♦ ...Клеманс глазам не верила, когда Жано принёс первую получку (Эренбург 4). ...Clémence could scarcely believe her eyes when Jeannot brought home his first pay-envelope (4a). ♦ И вдруг рядом я прочёл такое, что не поверил своим глазам... (Кузнецов 1). Then my eye fell on something next to the poster which made me wonder if I was seeing straight (1b).

Г-103 • ПО ГЛАЗА́М ВИ́ДЕТЬ ⟨ВИ́ДНО⟩ [VP, subj: human (var. with видеть); Invar, usu. subj-compl with быть∅, subj: usu. a clause or это (var. with видно)] to draw a conclusion (about what s.o. is thinking or feeling, what kind of person s.o. is etc) by looking at the expression in s.o.'s eyes: X по глазам видит (, что ⟨как и т. п.⟩...) ≃ **X sees ⟨can see⟩ it in Y's eyes; X sees ⟨can see⟩ in Y's eyes that...; X sees ⟨can see, can tell⟩ by ⟨from, by the look in⟩ Y's eyes (that...); Y's eyes show ⟨tell⟩ (X) (that ⟨how much etc⟩...).**

[Елена Андреевна:] Вы не любите её, по глазам вижу... (Чехов 3). [Е.А.:] You don't love her, I see it in your eyes... (3a). ♦ «Ну, рассказывайте, как было дело». Рассказываю и вижу по её глазам: ей это неинтересно (Войнович 3). "Well, tell me how it happened." I tell her and see by her eyes that she's bored (3a). ♦ [Мольер:] Лжёшь, по глазам вижу, что лжёшь! (Булгаков 8). [M.:] You're lying, I can see by your eyes that you're lying! (8a). ♦ [Аметистов:] По глазам всегда видно, есть ли у человека деньги или нет (Булгаков 7). [A.:] You can always tell from his eyes whether a person has money or not (7a). ♦ «Вам это интересно? Не говорите, что понятно, не поверю. А вот что интересно, вижу по глазам» (Копелев 1). "Does that interest you? Don't tell me that you understand; I won't believe it. But I can see by the look in your eyes that you're interested (1a). ♦ ...По глазам её замутнённым можно было видеть, что болезнь измотала её (Солженицын 6). Her bleary eyes showed how much her illness had exhausted her (6b).

Г-104 • ВЕРТЕ́ТЬСЯ ПЕРЕД ГЛАЗА́МИ 〈НА ГЛАЗА́Х〉 (у кого) coll [VP; subj: human; often used with постоянно, всегда etc] to stay near s.o., vexing, annoying him with one's presence: X вертится у Y-а перед глазами ≃ **X hangs 〈keeps hanging〉 around (Y); X hovers about; X hovers around Y.**

[Иванов:] Всегда ты, дядя, перед глазами вертишься, не даёшь поговорить наедине! (Чехов 4). [I.:] You're always hanging around, Uncle, you never give me a chance to talk to anyone alone! (4a).

Г-105 • ВПИВА́ТЬСЯ/ВПИ́ТЬСЯ ГЛАЗА́МИ 〈ВЗГЛЯ́ДОМ〉 в кого-что [VP; subj: human] to gaze steadily at s.o. or sth. without taking one's eyes off him or it: X впился глазами в Y-а ≃ **X stared (hard) at Y; X fixed his eyes 〈gaze〉 on Y; X riveted his eyes on Y; X's eyes were 〈X had his eyes〉 glued to 〈on〉 Y;** [in limited contexts] **X devoured Y with X's eyes.**

Я жадно впивалась взглядом в каждую дверь, точно можно было через её толщу увидать томящихся в камерах людей (Гинзбург 1). I stared hard at each door, as though I could see right through to the people inside (1b). ♦ Тётушка Хрисула впивалась в них глазами, и они под её взглядом как-то замирали... (Искандер 5). Auntie Chrysoula fixed her eyes on them, and under her gaze they stood rooted to the spot... (5a). ♦ Раскольников так и впился в него [Лебезятникова] глазами, как бы подхватывая и взвешивая каждое слово (Достоевский 3). Raskolnikov riveted his eyes on him [Lebezyatnikov], as if snatching at every word and weighing it (3a). ♦ По тому, как полковой командир салютовал главнокомандующему, впиваясь в него глазами... видно было, что он исполнял свои обязанности подчинённого ещё с большим наслаждением, чем обязанности начальника (Толстой 4). From the manner in which the regimental commander saluted Kutuzov...with his eyes glued on him...it was clear that his duties as a subordinate were executed with even greater delight than his duties as a commanding officer (4a). ♦ [Телятев:] ...Он [Васильков] стоит поодаль, так и впился глазами [в Лидию] (Островский 4). [T.:] ...There he [Vassilkov] was, some distance away, simply devouring Lydia with his eyes (4b).

Г-106 • ВСТАВА́ТЬ/ВСТАТЬ ПЕРЕД ГЛАЗА́МИ чьими, (у) кого [VP; subj: usu. human or concr] (usu. of some past event, or some person or thing with which s.o. had contact in the past) to appear in s.o.'s mind very clearly, in full detail: X встаёт у Y-а перед глазами ≃ **Y can see X now; Y can see X in Y's mind's eye; X arises 〈appears〉 before Y; X comes back to Y (as if it were yesterday); Y can visualize X.**

Как ни старался Григорий, уехав в поле, забыть о своём горе, в мыслях он неизбежно возвращался к этому... Перед глазами его вставала живая, улыбающаяся Наталья. Он вспоминал её фигуру, походку, манеру поправлять волосы... (Шолохов 5). Try as he would, even out in the fields Grigory could not forget his grief; it was for ever in his thoughts....The living, smiling Natalya would arise before him. He would recall her figure, her walk, her way of patting her hair into place... (5a). ♦ У Нины Петровны встали перед глазами трудные военные годы, нужда и лишения. Those difficult war years, all the hardship and poverty, came back to Nina Petrovna as if it were yesterday.

Г-107 • ЕСТЬ 〈ПОЕДА́ТЬ, ПОЖИРА́ТЬ〉 ГЛАЗА́МИ кого-что coll [VP; subj: human; more often this WO] to look at s.o. or sth. intently, without diverting one's gaze, usu. with desire or obsequiousness: X ел Y-а глазами ≃ **X devoured Y with X's**

eyes; X eyed Y greedily; X ogled Y; X watched Y with a hungry look (in X's eyes); X drank Y in with X's eyes.

«Сидоркин, вы там опять в шахматы режетесь?» — «Никак нет!» — рявкает Сидоркин и нагло ест начальство глазами (Войнович 5). "Sidorkin, are you playing chess over there?" "Of course not!" barked Sidorkin, devouring the chief with his impudent eyes (5a). ♦ Грушницкий целый вечер преследовал княжну, танцевал или с нею, или vis-à-vis; он пожирал её глазами, вздыхал и надоедал ей мольбами и упрёками (Лермонтов 1). Grushnitski followed the princess about the whole evening, dancing either with her or vis-à-vis. He eyed her greedily, sighed, and bored her with entreaties and reproaches (1d).

Г-108 • ИГРА́ТЬ ГЛАЗА́МИ [VP; subj: human; often Verbal Adv] to glance at s.o. in a flirtatious manner, trying to gain his or her interest: X играл глазами ≃ **X was flirting with his eyes; X was making eyes at person Y; X was casting coquettish glances person Y's way.**

Г-109 • МЕ́РИТЬ/СМЕ́РИТЬ ГЛАЗА́МИ 〈ВЗГЛЯ́ДОМ〉 кого [VP; subj: human] to look at s.o. intently as if evaluating him: X смерил Y-а глазами ≃ **X looked Y up and down; X looked Y over; X measured Y with X's gaze 〈eyes〉; X sized Y up; X gave Y the once-over;** ‖ X смерил Y-а [AdjP] взглядом ≃ **X measured Y with a [AdjP] look.**

Самозванцы встретились и смерили друг друга глазами (Салтыков-Щедрин 1). The pretenders met and looked each other up and down (1b). ♦ Орозкул даже приостановился, смерил старика взглядом (Айтматов 1). Orozkul stopped short and measured the old man with his gaze (1b). ♦ Противники стояли, вцепившись в ножки [стула], как коты или боксёры, мерили друг друга взглядами, похаживая из стороны в сторону (Ильф и Петров 1). The two opponents stood clutching the chair and, moving from side to side, sized one another up like cats or boxers (1a). ♦ [author's usage] Стоявшие кучкою поодаль любопытные мешали знахарке. Она недобрым взглядом смеривала их с головы до ног (Пастернак 1). The knot of curious onlookers who stood at a distance annoyed the witch, and she measured them from top to toe with a hostile look (1a).

Г-110 • ПЕРЕД ГЛАЗА́МИ у кого [PrepP; Invar; subj-compl with copula (subj: usu. abstr or concr) or adv] (some person or thing is, sth. happens etc) close to s.o., so that he should be aware of him or it: **right in front of s.o. 〈of s.o.'s eyes, of s.o.'s face〉; (right) before s.o.'s eyes; (right) under s.o.'s nose;** [usu. of death, ruin etc] **(sth. is) staring s.o. in the face.**

Пьер почти не изменился в своих внешних приёмах. На вид он был точно таким же, каким он был прежде. Так же, как и прежде, он был рассеян и казался занятым не тем, что было перед глазами, а чем-то своим, особенным (Толстой 7). Outwardly Pierre had hardly changed at all. In appearance he was just the same as before. Also as before, he was absentminded and seemed to be concerned not with what was before his eyes, but with something exclusively his own (7a).

Г-111 • ПРОБЕГА́ТЬ/ПРОБЕЖА́ТЬ ГЛАЗА́МИ что [VP; subj: human] to glance over (a text etc) quickly: X пробежал глазами Y ≃ **X ran his eyes over Y; X skimmed (through) Y; X scanned Y.**

...Как-то через несколько дней ему под руку попалось всё тот же шахматный журнальчик [«8 x 8»], он перелистал его, ища недостроенных мест, и, когда оказалось, что всё уже сделано, пробежал глазами отрывок в два столбца из юношеского дневника Чернышевского... (Набоков 1). ...A few days later he happened to come across that same copy of [the chess magazine] 8 x 8; he leafed through it, looking for unfinished bits, and when all the problems turned out to be solved, he ran his eyes over the two-column extract from Chernyshevski's youthful diary... (1a). ♦ Вот вы читаете эти истории. Может быть, где-то спокойно пробегаете глазами, может быть, где-то (моя вина) скучаете… (Кузнецов 1). Here you are, reading these accounts. Perhaps there are pages you skim through casually; perhaps there are others (my fault) where you yawn… (1a).

Г-112 • ПРОВОЖА́ТЬ/ПРОВОДИ́ТЬ ГЛАЗА́МИ ⟨ВЗГЛЯ́ДОМ, ВЗО́РОМ⟩ *кого-что* [VP; subj: human; fixed WO] to watch steadily as s.o. or sth. moves away from one, keeping one's eyes fixed on him or it: X проводил Y-а глазами ≃ **X followed Y with X's eyes; X's eyes followed Y.**

…Защитник возвестил, что он свои вопросы господину Ракитину кончил. Господин Ракитин сошёл со сцены несколько подсаленный… Фетюкович, провожая его глазами, как бы говорил, указывая публике: «вот, дескать, каковы ваши благородные обвинители!» (Достоевский 2). …The defense attorney announced that he had finished questioning Mr. Rakitin. Mr. Rakitin left the stage somewhat besmirched.…Fetyukovich, following him with his eyes, seemed to be saying, intending it for the public: "So there goes one of your noble accusers!" (2a). ♦ Степан выехал за ворот торопким шагом, сидел в седле, как вкопанный, а Аксинья шла рядом… Григорий провожал их долгим, неморгающим взглядом (Шолохов 2). Stepan rode out of the gate at a brisk walk, sitting like a rock in the saddle. Aksinya kept pace with him.…Grigory's eyes followed them to the turn in a long unblinking stare (2a).

Г-113 • ПРОНЗА́ТЬ/ПРОНЗИ́ТЬ ГЛАЗА́МИ ⟨ВЗГЛЯ́ДОМ⟩ *кого* [VP; subj: human; usu. this WO] to look at s.o. sharply, scrutinizingly: X пронзил Y-а глазами ≃ **X pierced Y with X's eyes ⟨gaze⟩.**

Штольц и Обломов остались вдвоём, молча и неподвижно глядя друг на друга. Штольц так и пронзал его глазами (Гончаров 1). Stolz and Oblomov were left alone, looking silently and motionlessly at each other. Stolz seemed to pierce him with his gaze (1a).

Г-114 • С ЗАКРЫ́ТЫМИ ГЛАЗА́МИ [PrepP; Invar; adv; fixed WO] **1.** (to undertake sth. serious, risky) imprudently, unthinkingly: **with one's eyes closed; blindly.**

То, что ты собираешься сделать, может плохо кончиться для тебя. Хорошо ли ты всё обдумал? Такой шаг нельзя делать с закрытыми глазами. What you're planning to do could turn out badly for you. Have you thought it all through? You can't take a step like this with your eyes closed.

2. without wavering: **without thinking twice; without (giving it) a second thought.**

Г-115 • С КАКИ́МИ ГЛАЗА́МИ появиться, показаться *к кому, у кого, где*; **КАКИ́МИ ГЛАЗА́МИ** смотреть, глядеть в глаза *кому* both coll [PrepP (1st var.) or NP_{instrum} (2nd var.); these forms only; adv; often after не знать (1st var.); fixed WO] (not to know) how to act, behave in s.o.'s presence out of shame, embarrassment etc: **(not know) how to face s.o.; (not know) how one can ever face s.o. (again); (be) ashamed to show one's face (in front of s.o.); (feel that one cannot) look s.o. (straight) in the eye.**

Обломов не знал, с какими глазами покажется он к Ольге, что будет говорить она, что будет говорить он… (Гончаров 1). Oblomov did not know how to face Olga, what to say to her, or what she would say to him… (1b). ♦ «И что я теперь? Куда я гожусь? Какими глазами я стану смотреть теперь в глаза всякому почтенному отцу семейства?» (Гоголь 3). "And what am I now? What am I good for? How can I look a respectable father of a family straight in the eye?" (3e).

Г-116 • С ОТКРЫ́ТЫМИ ГЛАЗА́МИ [PrepP; Invar; adv; fixed WO] (to do sth.) knowingly, fully aware of the consequences: **with open eyes; with one's eyes (wide) open.**

Мы начинаем кампанию протеста с открытыми глазами, прекрасно представляя себе все возможные последствия. We are starting the protest movement with our eyes wide open, well aware of all the possible consequences.

Г-117 • СВЕРКА́ТЬ/СВЕРКНУ́ТЬ ГЛАЗА́МИ *(на кого)* [VP; subj: human] to give (s.o.) a brief, angry look: X сверкнул глазами ≃ **X flashed his eyes; X's eyes flashed; X's eyes glinted (with anger ⟨with fury etc⟩).**

«…Потрудитесь снять и носки». — «Вы не шутите? Это действительно так необходимо?» — сверкнул глазами Митя. «Нам не до шуток», — строго отпарировал Николай Парфёнович (Достоевский 1). "…May I also trouble you to take off your socks?" "You must be joking! Is it really so necessary?" Mitya flashed his eyes. "This is no time for joking," Nikolai Parfenovich parried sternly (1a). ♦ «Я вот имею офицерский чин с германской войны. Кровью его заслужил! А как попаду в офицерское общество — так вроде как из хаты на мороз выйду в одних подштанниках. Таким от них холодом на меня попрёт, что аж всей спиной его чую!» — Григорий бешено сверкнул глазами и незаметно для себя повысил голос (Шолохов 5). "Take me, I've had officer's rank since the German war. I earned it with my own blood! But as soon as I find myself in officers' company, it's like going out into the frost in my underpants. The cold shoulder they give me sends shivers down my back!" Grigory's eyes glinted with fury and, without noticing it, he raised his voice (5a).

Г-118 • СВОИ́МИ ⟨(СВОИ́МИ) СО́БСТВЕННЫМИ⟩ ГЛАЗА́МИ видеть *кого-что*, убедиться *в чём* и т. п. [NP_{instrum}; these forms only; adv; fixed WO] (to see s.o. or sth.) personally, (to become convinced of sth.) through one's own observation: **(see s.o. ⟨sth.⟩) with one's own (two) eyes; (see sth.) for o.s.**

«Я своими глазами видел, как какая-то неопрятная девушка подливала из ведра в ваш громадный самовар сырую воду…» (Булгаков 9). "I saw with my own eyes how some slattern poured unboiled water from a pail into your huge samovar…" (9a). ♦ На досуге и без помех я раскачивался… и даже в Историческом музее, в двух шагах от Кремля, работал — дали официальное разрешение, и только приходили чекисты своими глазами меня обсмотреть, как я тут (Солженицын 2). With so much spare time, and so few hindrances, I was able to get into my stride…and even to work in the Historical Museum, a stone's throw from the Kremlin. (I obtained official permission, and all that happened was that the Chekists came along to see for themselves what I was doing there) (2a).

Г-119 • СМОТРЕ́ТЬ ⟨ГЛЯДЕ́ТЬ⟩ ГЛАЗА́МИ *чьими* or *кого на кого-что* [VP; subj: human] to view things as another person does because one is under that person's influence: X смотрит на Y-а глазами Z-а ≃ **X looks at Y ⟨sees Y⟩ through the eyes of Z ⟨through Z's eyes⟩; X sees Y Z's way.**

Я смотрела на всё глазами Мандельштама и потому видела то, чего не видели другие (Мандельштам 2). I looked at it all through the eyes of M[andelstam] and hence saw things that others did not see (2a). ♦ Варя одна не бросила его мать, была рядом с ней в самые тяжёлые дни… Нежность к этой мужественной девочке пронзила Сашу. А он читал ей нотации, смотрел на неё глазами Нины. До чего же узок был его взгляд тогда! (Рыбаков 2). Only Varya had stood by his [Sasha's] mother in her most difficult days.…He was filled with tender feelings for this brave girl. And he had lectured her, seeing her through Nina's eyes! How narrow his point of view had been in those days! (2a).

Г-120 • СМОТРЕ́ТЬ/ПОСМОТРЕ́ТЬ ⟨ГЛЯДЕ́ТЬ/ПОГЛЯДЕ́ТЬ, ВЗГЛЯНУ́ТЬ⟩ ДРУГИ́МИ ⟨ИНЫ́МИ⟩ ГЛАЗА́МИ *на кого-что* [VP; subj: human] to evaluate or regard s.o. or sth. differently (than previously or than someone else does): X смотрит на Y-а другими глазами ≃ **X sees Y in**

a different light ⟨from a different perspective⟩; X looks at Y from a (whole) different angle; X differs (from person Z) in his view of Y; X takes a different view of Y (than person Z).

Новый ходок, Пахомыч, взглянул на дело несколько иными глазами, нежели несчастный его предшественник (Салтыков-Щедрин 1). The new envoy, Pakhomych, differed somewhat from his unfortunate predecessor in his view of the affair (1a).

Г-121 • СТОЯ́ТЬ ⟨МАЯ́ЧИТЬ coll⟩ ПЕРЕД ГЛАЗА́МИ *чьими, у кого;* **СТОЯ́ТЬ В ГЛАЗА́Х** *у кого* [VP; subj: usu. human or concr] (usu. of some past event, or some person or thing with which s.o. had contact in the past) to be continually present in s.o.'s thoughts: X стоит у Y-а перед глазами ≃ **X is always on ⟨in the forefront of⟩ Y's mind; X is forever before Y's eyes; X keeps rising up before Y's eyes; Y cannot help thinking of X; Y cannot get X out of Y's mind;** [in limited contexts] **thing X haunts Y.**

О чём бы кто ни заговорил, он [Вадим] сейчас же вспоминает какую-то историю из «тех лет» [когда он был в лагере и в ссылке]... Это можно понять — всё ещё слишком свежо, не успело зарасти, стоит перед глазами (Некрасов 1). No matter what anybody started to talk about, it would at once remind him [Vadim] of some story from "those years" [when he was in the camp and in exile]....That one could understand—those days were so fresh and recent, they were always in the forefront of his mind, the memories hadn't had time to heal (1a). ♦ ...У нас с О.М[андельштамом] в глазах стоял Ломинадзе, отозванный для казни из Тифлиса, когда О.М. вёл с ним переговоры о том, чтобы остаться на архивной работе в Тифлисе (Мандельштам 1). ...M[andelstam] and I couldn't help thinking of Lominadze, who was recalled to Moscow for his execution while we were in Tiflis talking with him about the possibility of M[andelstam] staying there to work in the archives (1a).

Г-122 • СТРЕЛЯ́ТЬ/СТРЕЛЬНУ́ТЬ ГЛАЗА́МИ *coll* [VP; subj: human] **1.** to glance rapidly at s.o. or sth., around some place etc: X стрелял глазами ≃ **X was ⟨kept⟩ casting quick glances at Y ⟨all around, all over place Z etc⟩;** ‖ X стрельнул глазами (в сторону Y-а) ≃ **X cast ⟨shot⟩ a (quick) glance at Y.**

2. Also: **СТРЕЛЯ́ТЬ/СТРЕЛЬНУ́ТЬ ГЛА́ЗКАМИ; ПОСТРЕ́ЛИВАТЬ ГЛАЗА́МИ ⟨ГЛА́ЗКАМИ⟩** *all coll* [usu. impfv] to glance flirtatiously (at s.o.): X стреляет глазами ≃ **X is making eyes at ⟨is ogling⟩ person Y; X keeps giving person Y the eye.**

Г-123 • ХЛО́ПАТЬ ГЛАЗА́МИ *coll;* **ЛУ́ПАТЬ ГЛАЗА́МИ** *substand, both often disapprov or iron* [VP; subj: human] **1.** to open one's eyes wide and blink them (in surprise, confusion, embarrassment etc): X хлопал глазами ≃ **X (just) stood ⟨sat⟩ there blinking (dumbly ⟨confusedly etc⟩); X stood ⟨sat etc⟩ there blinking in bewilderment ⟨confusion, surprise, embarrassment etc⟩;** ‖ ты что глазами хлопаешь? ≃ **why are you blinking (at me) like that?**

[Пепел:] Вчера, при свидетелях, я тебе продал часы за десять рублей... три — получил, семь — подай! Чего глазами хлопаешь? (Горький 3). [P.:] Yesterday, before witnesses, I sold you a watch for ten rubles. I received three rubles, now hand over the other seven. Why are you blinking at me like that? (3b).

2. to be idle, not take action when immediate action is called for: X хлопает глазами ≃ **X sits on his hands; X doesn't lift a finger; X (sits back and) does nothing.**

«Из-под носа дочь уводят... а ты, старый хрыч, глазами хлопаешь!» (Максимов 3). "Your daughter's being carried off under your very nose... and you don't lift a finger, you silly old devil" (3a).

Г-124 • ША́РИТЬ ГЛАЗА́МИ ⟨ВЗГЛЯ́ДОМ⟩ *по чему,* less often *по кому coll* [VP; subj: human] to look at the whole of (some place, thing, or, less often, person) intently, moving one's eyes over all parts in an attempt not to miss anything: X шарил глазами по Y-у ≃ **X looked Y over intently; X scanned Y;** [usu. of looking at s.o. or sth. with desire] **X eyed Y.**

Г-125 • ШНЫРЯ́ТЬ ГЛАЗА́МИ *по чему,* often **по сторонам** *highly coll* [VP; subj: human] to shift one's eyes anxiously from one thing (or person) to another, look stealthily around some place: X шнырял глазами (по комнате ⟨по сторонам etc⟩) ≃ **X was casting furtive glances (about the room ⟨from side to side etc⟩); X's eyes were darting about (the room etc); X was casting his eyes about (the room etc).**

Г-126 • В ГЛАЗА́Х *чьих, кого* [PrepP; Invar; the resulting PrepP is sent adv] according to s.o.'s perception or opinion: **in the eyes of s.o.; in s.o.'s eyes ⟨estimation, opinion⟩; as s.o. sees it;** [in limited contexts] **s.o. looks on s.o. ⟨sth.⟩ as (on)...; to s.o.**

Выше всего он ставил настойчивость в достижении целей: это было признаком характера в его глазах... (Гончаров 1). Persistence in the pursuit of a certain aim was a quality he valued most; it was a mark of character in his eyes... (1a). ♦ ...Собственно против отца у меня не было никакого дурного чувства. Напротив: он как будто ещё вырос в моих глазах... (Тургенев 3). ...I bore no ill will against my father. On the contrary, he seemed to have risen in my estimation... (1a). ♦ «Я не скрываюсь: я люблю то, что вы называете комфортом, и в то же время я мало желаю жить. Примирите это противоречие как знаете. Впрочем, это всё в ваших глазах романтизм» (Тургенев 2). "I don't deny that I love what you call comfort and yet I have little desire to live. Try and reconcile those inconsistencies if you can. In any case it's all romanticism to you" (2a). ♦ Она вздохнула, но, кажется, больше от радости, что опасения её кончились и она не падает в глазах мужа, а напротив... (Гончаров 1). [context transl] She sighed, but it seemed to be a sigh of happiness that her apprehensions were over and that she had not fallen in her husband's esteem, but quite the contrary (1b).

Г-127 • В ГЛАЗА́Х ТЕМНЕ́ЕТ/ПОТЕМНЕ́ЛО ⟨МУ́ТИТСЯ/ПОМУТИ́ЛОСЬ, ЗАМУТИ́ЛОСЬ, ЗЕЛЕНЕ́ЕТ/ПОЗЕЛЕНЕ́ЛО⟩ *у кого coll* [VP; impers; more often pfv] s.o. ceases to see clearly, s.o.'s vision is distorted (because of fatigue, illness, a blow etc), or s.o. ceases to see at all (directly after a blow or as one loses consciousness): у X-а потемнело в глазах ≃ **everything went black; everything became blurred (before X's eyes); everything started to spin (before X's eyes); X saw ⟨began to see⟩ spots before his eyes; X felt dizzy.**

Раз утром, когда я встал с постели, у меня всё сразу потемнело в глазах (Богданов 1). One morning as I was getting up everything suddenly went black... (1a). ♦ И опять у Юрия Андреевича стало мутиться в глазах и голове (Пастернак 1). Once again everything in his [Yurii Andreievich's] head and before his eyes became confused, blurred (1a). ♦ У меня потемнело в глазах, рот наполнился хиной, заболели зубы, а проклятый нобль всё говорил и говорил... (Стругацкие 3). I was beginning to see spots before my eyes, bile was rising, and my teeth ached, and the damned *noble vieux* went on talking (3a). ♦ Как с ней [Томой] получится, Кирпиченко не знал и старался не глядеть не неё, а как только взглядывал, у него темнело в глазах (Аксёнов 5). Kirpichenko didn't know how things would turn out with her [Toma] and tried not to look at her, but every time he did look he felt dizzy (5a).

Г-128 • В ГЛАЗА́Х ЧЁРТИКИ ⟨ЧЕРТЕНЯ́ТА⟩ (ПРЫ́ГАЮТ) *у кого coll* [VP$_{subj}$ (with быть$_\emptyset$ if the verb is omitted)] s.o.'s eyes sparkle merrily: у X-а в глазах чёртики (прыгают) ≃ **X's eyes twinkle; X has a twinkle ⟨a gleam⟩ in his eye(s);** [in limited contexts] **X has mischief in his eye(s).**

Г-129 • ДВОЙТСЯ ⟨ТРОЙТСЯ⟩ В ГЛАЗА́Х *у кого* [VP; impers or, rare, with subj: human or concrete] s.o. sees two or three images of a single object: у X-а двоится в глазах ≃ **X is seeing double; X is seeing two ⟨three⟩ of...**

«...У природы двоилось в глазах, когда она создавала нас...» (Набоков 1). "...Nature was seeing double when she created us..." (1a).

Г-130 • НА ГЛАЗА́Х [PrepP; Invar] **1.** ~ *чьих, у кого* [the resulting PrepP is sent adv] in such a way as to be visible, noticeable, known etc: **(right) before s.o.'s (very) eyes; in front of s.o.; in s.o.'s presence;** ∥ на глазах у всех ≃ **for all to see; in plain ⟨full⟩ view (of everyone); openly; right out in the open.**

[Михаил:] Извольте видеть, какая ситуация! Служащий ваш, которого вы оборвали за дерзость, фамильярничает на ваших глазах с женой брата вашего компаньона... (Горький 1). [M.:] There's a situation for you, if you please. Your employee, whom you've cut short for impertinence, permits himself, before your very eyes, to be familiar with the wife of your partner's brother (1a). ♦ В углу стояла огромная параша, которой *все* – и мужчины и женщины – пользовались открыто, на глазах у всех (Гинзбург 1). In the corner stood an enormous bucket which everyone, men and women alike, used in full view of one another (1b). ♦ Фашисты на глазах у всех формировали боевые отряды... (Эренбург 4). The fascists were openly forming military detachments... (4a).

2. ~ *чьих, у кого* [the resulting PrepP is sent adv] (sth. happens) during s.o.'s life, giving him the opportunity to have personal knowledge of it: **before s.o.'s (very) eyes; in ⟨during⟩ s.o.'s lifetime; to witness...**

Мало было людей на свете, которых бы он [мой отец] в самом деле любил: Голохвастов был в том числе. Он вырос на его глазах, им гордилась вся семья... (Герцен 2). There were few people in the world that he [my father] really liked and Golokhvastov was one of them. He had grown up before his eyes and the whole family was proud of him (2a). ♦ Литературная карьера товарища Сизова началась почти на моих глазах (Войнович 1). Comrade Sizov's literary career had begun before my very eyes (1a).

3. [adv] (sth. happens) surprisingly quickly (bringing about a radical change in the situation, s.o.'s or sth.'s state of being etc): **right before your ⟨s.o.'s⟩ eyes; (right) before your ⟨s.o.'s⟩ very eyes; [in limited contexts] dramatically.**

...Два-три крохотных события, две-три случайные встречи, и мир, взлелеянный с такой любовью, с таким тщанием, начинал терять устойчивость, трещать по швам, разваливаться на глазах (Максимов 3). Two or three trivial events, two or three chance meetings, and the world he had cherished with such loving care began to crumble, fall apart, disintegrate before his very eyes (3a). ♦ Слух о зловещем высказывании члена Политбюро быстро рассыпался по Москве, и отношение к Ефиму людей на глазах менялось. Некоторые его знакомые перестали с ним здороваться... (Войнович 6). The report of the Politburo member's statement regarding foreign elements spread rapidly throughout Moscow, and people's behavior toward Yefim changed dramatically. Some of his acquaintances stopped greeting him... (6a).

Г-131 • РЯБИ́Т/ЗАРЯБИ́ЛО В ГЛАЗА́Х *у кого (от чего)* [VP; impers] s.o. experiences the sensation of having various spots, colors, or images race and change quickly before his eyes: у X-а рябит в глазах (от Y-ов) ≃ **X sees spots (before his eyes); Ys ⟨spots, things⟩ are flashing ⟨dancing⟩ before X's eyes; Ys dazzle the eye; X is dazzled (by Ys); Ys make X's head spin ⟨swim⟩.**

До шести часов, когда уже зарябило в глазах, Ребров просидел в библиотеке, исписав страниц двадцать – боже мой, для чего же? – разных фактов и соображений, почерпнутых из жизни Ивана Гавриловича и из его сочинений. Потом пошёл в кафе «Националь» ужинать (Трифонов 1). By six that evening he had managed to fill up some twenty pages of a notebook – my God, what on earth for?! – with various facts and ideas drawn from Ivan Gavrilovich's life and writings. Then, as spots were already dancing before his eyes, he left the library and set off to have supper in the cafe of the Hotel National (1a). ♦ В лавках и перед лавками бурлила такая жизнь, что звенело в ушах, в глазах рябило (Булгаков 5). In the shops and in the street before them life ran riot, dazzling the eye and setting up a ringing in the ears (5a). ♦ Она вспомнила, что маленький порывистый грек ей нравился всегда... Только от его мельтешения у неё, бывало, рябило в глазах... (Искандер 3). She recalled that she had always liked the impetuous little Greek....The only trouble was that his endless flitting about used to make her head spin (3a).

Г-132 • СТРО́ИТЬ ⟨ДЕ́ЛАТЬ⟩ ГЛА́ЗКИ *кому coll* [VP; subj: human, usu. female] to look at s.o. flirtatiously in an attempt to attract his or her attention: X строит глазки Y-у ≃ **X is making (sheep's ⟨goo-goo⟩) eyes at Y.**

Г-133 • (хоть, хотя бы) ОДНИ́М ГЛАЗКО́М ⟨ГЛА́ЗОМ⟩ взглянуть, посмотреть *на кого-что* и т. п. *coll* [NP$_{instrum}$; these forms only; adv; used with pfv verbs; fixed WO] (to look, glance at s.o. or sth.) quickly, (if only) for a moment: **take ⟨get⟩ a quick look ⟨glance⟩ (at s.o. ⟨sth.⟩); (catch) a glimpse (of s.o. ⟨sth.⟩); (if only one could have) just one (quick) look (at s.o. ⟨sth.⟩); (if one could just have) a (quick) peek (at s.o. ⟨sth.⟩); have a look (at s.o. ⟨sth.⟩), however fleeting.**

[Повариха:] Кукла сделана из особой массы. Её сделал великий мастер. Мне удалось увидеть её одним глазом (Олеша 7). [Cook:] The doll was made from a special paste. It was made by a great craftsman. I had the chance to get a quick look at her (7a). ♦ Ей очень хотелось под каким-нибудь предлогом пойти к Мелеховым, побывать там хоть минутку, хоть одним глазком взглянуть на Григория. Просто немыслимо было думать, что он тут, рядом, и не видеть его (Шолохов 5). She was longing to go to the Melekhovs on some pretext and spend a few minutes there, just to catch a glimpse of Grigory. It was unbearable to think that he was so close and yet not be able to see him (5a). ♦ ...Ещё ей хотелось хоть одним глазком, хоть краешком глаза взглянуть на Егоршу: как он сегодня-то, на трезвую голову? (Абрамов 1). ...She also wanted to have a peek at Yegorsha, if only out of the corner of one eye: how is he today, sober? (1b). ♦ Маньяк – из долгосрочных больных: каждый вечер должен, хоть одним глазком, посмотреть на покойников в морге (Терц 3). A psychopath from among the chronically ill patients: every evening he must have a look, however fleeting, at the corpses in the morgue... (3a).

Г-134 • ГЛА́ЗОМ НЕ МОРГНУ́ТЬ *coll* [VP; subj: human; often Verbal Adv, used with pfv verbs] **1.** [used in conjunction with another pfv verb denoting the action in question; when the idiom is in fut (or, occas., subjunctive), it is usu. used with убьёт, зарежет, обманет (убил бы etc)] not to hesitate, waver, or pause before doing sth.: X глазом не моргнул ≃ **X didn't think twice; X (did sth.) without (giving it) a second thought;** ∥ глазом не моргнув ≃ **without thinking twice; without (giving it) a second thought.**

2. [usu. past, often after хоть бы] not to show any signs of emotion (agitation, fear, anxiety etc) on one's face: X глазом не моргнул ≃ **X didn't bat an eye ⟨an eyelid, an eyelash⟩; X didn't turn a hair;** ∥ глазом не моргнув ≃ **without batting an eye ⟨an eyelid, an eyelash⟩; without turning a hair.**

«Дайте мне взаймы рублей пятьдесят, я вам отдам не позже чем послезавтра...» ...Она была смущена ещё больше, чем я, но и глазом не моргнула. «Ах, пожалуйста, пожалуйста» (Катаев 2). "Lend me fifty roubles [or so] and I'll give it back to you not later than the day after tomorrow."...She was even more embarrassed than I, but she didn't bat an eyelid. "Oh, of course, of course" (2a).

Г-135 • не успел (И) ГЛА́ЗОМ МОРГНУ́ТЬ ⟨МИГ-НУ́ТЬ⟩ *coll* [these forms only; infin compl of не успел, often used in neg pfv fut, gener. 2nd pers sing не успеешь; usu. the 1st clause in a complex sent, foll. by a clause introduced by Conj «как» or «а»] (some person did not have time) to realize sth. or react to sth. (because it happened so quickly): X не успел глазом моргнуть ≃ **before X could bat an eye ⟨an eyelid, an eyelash⟩; before X had time to blink; before X knew it.** Cf. **before X can ⟨could⟩ say Jack Robinson.**

«Не мой [ребёнок]», — сказал Алтынник и облизнул губы. «Ах, не твой? – вскрикнула Людмила. – Вот тебе!» И Алтынник не успел глазом моргнуть, как свёрток очутился в пыли у его ног (Войнович 5). "It's not mine [my child]," said Altinnik, licking his lips. "Ach, it's not yours?" screeched Ludmilla. "Here, you take him!" Before Altinnik could bat an eye, the bundle was in the dust at his feet (5a).

Г-136 • КАКИ́М ГЛА́ЗОМ ⟨КАКИ́МИ ГЛАЗА́МИ⟩ посмотреть, взглянуть *на что coll* [NP_instrum; these forms only; adv; fixed WO] the way (one perceives sth.), the perspective (from which one views sth.): **what (point of) view (one takes of sth.); how (one feels about ⟨looks at⟩ sth.); what angle ⟨stance⟩ (one takes).**

Г-137 • КУДА́ НИ КИНЬ ⟨НИ КИ́НЕШЬ⟩ ГЛА́ЗОМ ⟨ВЗГЛЯ́ДОМ, ВЗГЛЯД⟩ [subord clause; these forms only; the verb may take the final position, otherwise fixed WO] everywhere, regardless of where you look (used to characterize the vast expanse one can see or whatever lies within this expanse): **wherever ⟨no matter where, whichever way⟩ you look; wherever you cast your gaze ⟨eye(s)⟩.**

Набережная Тесьмы вспоминалась мне, плоты, плоты, куда ни кинь взгляд, и утренний парок над ними, и шум у пристани... (Каверин 1). I remembered the Tesma embankment, rafts, rafts, wherever you looked, and the morning mist rising over us, and the noise and the wharves... (1a).

Г-138 • НЕВООРУЖЁННЫМ ГЛА́ЗОМ видеть, разглядеть, видно и т. п. [NP_instrum; Invar; adv; fixed WO] **1.** Also: ПРОСТЫ́М ГЛА́ЗОМ (to be able to see s.o. or sth., sth. is visible etc) with the eye alone, without the aid of any optical instrument: **with the naked ⟨unaided⟩ eye; with one's naked eye.**

А коршуны в поисках прохлады забирались невесть в какую высь – их невозможно было разглядеть простым глазом (Айтматов 2). Meanwhile, the kites were trying to get cool by soaring to such heights that you could no longer see them with the naked eye (2a). ♦ Не только все французские войска, но сам Наполеон со штабом находился... так близко от наших войск, что Наполеон простым глазом мог в нашем войске отличать конного от пешего (Толстой 4). The whole French army, and even Napoleon himself with his staff were...so close to our forces that Napoleon could distinguish a cavalryman from an infantryman with his naked eye (4a).

2. *often humor* (to discern sth., sth. is obvious etc) without careful examination or one's needing any special knowledge: **(be obvious) to the untrained eye; (even) an untrained eye (can see it).**

«Вы, конечно, знаете, что Клава беременна?» – «В общем... Конечно... я догадывался...» – «В общем, конечно, – передразнила она [гинеколог]. – Что там догадываться? Это – извините меня – видно невооружённым глазом» (Войнович 5). "You know of course that Klava is pregnant." "Of course. I'd just about guessed." "Just about guessed," she [the gynecologist] mimicked me. "But what's there to guess? You'll excuse me, but it's obvious even to the untrained eye" (5a).

Г-139 • ОДНИ́М ГЛА́ЗОМ наблюдать, присматривать, следить *за кем-чем* и т. п. *coll* [NP_instrum; Invar; adv] (to observe, look after s.o. or sth.) not giving him or it one's full attention, while doing something else: **(keep ⟨have⟩) one eye on s.o. ⟨sth.⟩.**

Бабушка что-то шила и одним глазом присматривала за детьми. Grandmother kept one eye on the kids while doing some sewing.

Г-140 • В ЧУЖО́М ГЛАЗУ́ СУЧО́К ВИ́ДИМ, А В СВОЁМ (И) БРЕВНА́ НЕ ЗАМЕЧА́ЕМ [saying] we notice minor shortcomings in other people while being unaware of our own far more serious faults: ≃ **one sees the speck ⟨the splinter, the mote⟩ in another's ⟨one's brother's⟩ eye and ignores the log ⟨the plank⟩ in his own.**

< From the Bible (Matt. 7:3, Luke 6:41).

Г-141 • НИ В ОДНО́М ГЛАЗУ́ ⟨ГЛА́ЗЕ *obs*⟩; ХОТЬ БЫ В ОДНО́М ГЛАЗУ́ ⟨ГЛА́ЗЕ *obs*⟩ all *coll* [PrepP or хоть бы + PrepP; these forms only] **1.** [subj-compl with быть∅ (subj: human); usu. preceded by one or more predicates] one is not at all drunk, scared, tired etc (as specified by the preceding context): X... ни в одном глазу ≃ **X isn't drunk ⟨scared, tired etc⟩ in the least; X isn't the least ⟨the slightest⟩ bit drunk ⟨scared, tired etc⟩; X is far from drunk ⟨scared, tired etc⟩; X is dead ⟨stone-cold⟩ sober; X is wide awake;** [in limited contexts] **X can't sleep a wink;** [when used in response to a question] **not in the least ⟨the slightest⟩; not a bit.**

На следующий день в вагоне с утра появился Мозговой, вновь ни в одном глазу, как всегда, резкий в слове и в движении (Максимов 1). The next morning Mozgovoy entered the carriage stone-cold sober, as laconic of word and gesture as ever (1a).

2. сна, страха, хмеля, усталости и т. п. *(у кого)* ~ [subj-compl with не быть∅; subj/gen: abstr (сна, страха etc); pres or past (var. with ни), pres only (var. with хоть)] s.o. does not (sleep) at all, is not (scared, drunk, tired etc) at all: сна ⟨страха, хмеля, усталости и т. п.⟩ (у Y-а) ни в одном глазу ≃ **Y is far from asleep ⟨scared, drunk, tired etc⟩; Y is wide awake; Y isn't scared ⟨drunk, tired etc⟩ in the least; Y isn't the least ⟨the slightest⟩ bit scared ⟨drunk, tired etc⟩; Y is dead ⟨stone-cold⟩ sober;** [in limited contexts] **Y can't sleep a wink.**

Утром Альбина заспешила на работу, робко пытаясь разбудить его [Лёву]: у него сна ни в одном глазу не было, но он мычал, как бы не в силах проснуться, и глаз не разлеплял (Битов 2). In the morning Albina hurriedly left for work, timidly trying to wake him [Lyova]. He was far from asleep, but he mumbled as if unable to rouse himself and would not unstick his eyes (2a).

Г-142 • С ГЛА́ЗУ НА ГЛАЗ говорить, беседовать, оставаться и т. п., разговор, беседа и т. п. *coll;* ГЛАЗ НА ГЛАЗ *obs;* МЕЖДУ ЧЕТЫРЁХ ГЛАЗ *obs* [PrepP; these forms only; adv or nonagreeing modif; fixed WO] (to talk) privately, (to remain) solely with one other person, excluding anyone else: **in private; alone (with s.o.); tête-à-tête;** [in limited contexts] **without witnesses; confidentially.**

«Нам нужно поговорить с глазу на глаз» (Эренбург 4). "We've got something to talk about in private" (4a). ♦ «Останься ради меня... Я ни с какой стороны не боюсь очутиться с глазу на глаз с ним [Комаровским]. Но это тягостно» (Пастернак 1). "Please don't go, for my sake....It isn't that I'm frightened of being alone with him [Komarovsky], but it's painful" (1a). ♦ В этом состоянии мама позирует Гайку, находится с ним один на один, с глазу на глаз, два часа в день (Рыбаков 1). It was in this state that mother posed for Gaik, completely alone with him, *tête-à-tête* for two hours every day (1a). ♦ ...Неужели Нобелевская премия – воровская добыча, что её надо передавать с глазу на глаз в закрытой комнате?.. (Солженицын 2). ...Surely the Nobel prize ought not to be handed over without witnesses, behind closed doors, as though we were thieves dividing our booty (2a). ♦ Перед отправкой арестованных в гостиницу «Метрополь», где они должны были содержаться под стражей, Алексеев с глазу на глаз о чём-то в течение двадцати минут беседовал с Корниловым... (Шолохов 3). Before sending them to the Hotel Metropole, where they were to be kept under guard, Alexeyev spoke confidentially with Kornilov for about twenty minutes... (3a).

Г-143 • **ГЛАС ВОПИЮ́ЩЕГО В ПУСТЫ́НЕ; ГЛАС ⟨ГО́ЛОС⟩, ВОПИЮ́ЩИЙ В ПУСТЫ́НЕ** *all lit* [NP; sing only] an appeal disregarded by everyone, unheeded: **a voice (crying) in the wilderness.**

Призыв Солженицына [«жить не по лжи»] остаётся гласом вопиющего в пустыне (Эткинд 1). Solzhenitsyn's appeal ["not to live by lies"] has remained a voice crying in the wilderness (1a).

< From the Bible (Isa. 40:3, Matt. 3:3 etc).

Г-144 • **НИ ГЛА́СА НИ ВОЗДЫХА́НИЯ** *obs* [NP_gen; Invar; used as subj/gen with быть_ø; fixed WO] (there is) complete silence (in some place): **dead ⟨utter, total⟩ silence.**

Г-145 • **ПРЕДАВА́ТЬ/ПРЕДА́ТЬ ГЛА́СНОСТИ** *что* [VP; subj: human or пресса, газета etc; often infin with должен, нужно etc; fixed WO] to make sth. (often sth. hitherto concealed) widely known, open to public judgment: X предал гласности Y ≃ **X made Y public (knowledge);** [in limited contexts] **X gave Y publicity.**

Выйдя в 1966 году из лагеря, я считал, что написать и предать гласности то, чему я был свидетелем, — это мой гражданский долг (Марченко 2). When I was discharged from prison camp in 1966, I considered it my civic duty to write down and make public what I had seen (2a). ♦ [author's usage] Ротшильд заключал тем, что, в случае дальнейших проволочек, он должен будет дать гласность этому делу через журналы для предупреждения других капиталистов (Герцен 2). Rothschild wound up by saying that in case of further delays he would have to give the matter publicity through the press, in order to warn other capitalists (2a).

Г-146 • **ЛУЖЁНАЯ ГЛО́ТКА** *(у кого) substand* [NP; often VP_subj with быть_ø] **1.** (s.o. has) the capacity to drink much alcohol without getting drunk: у X-а лужёная глотка ≃ **X has a hollow leg; X can drink you ⟨anyone etc⟩ under the table; X can (really) hold his liquor.**

2. Also: **МЕ́ДНАЯ ГЛО́ТКА** *(у кого) substand* [fixed WO] (s.o. has) the ability to shout, swear, sing etc loudly and for a long time: у X-а лужёная глотка ≃ **X has a lot of lung power; X has a terrific ⟨powerful⟩ set of lungs;** [in refer. to swearing etc] **X has a mouth on him like you wouldn't believe.**

Г-147 • **ЗАТЫКА́ТЬ/ЗАТКНУ́ТЬ ГЛО́ТКУ ⟨ГО́РЛО⟩** *кому highly coll, rude* [VP; subj: human] to force s.o. to be silent, prevent s.o. in a harsh manner from speaking, voicing his opinion: X заткнул Y-у глотку ≃ **X shut Y's mouth; X shut Y up; X made Y keep Y's (big) mouth shut; X gagged Y; X put a muzzle on Y.**

...[Партийный лектор] объяснил, что сборник [стихов Осипа Мандельштама] издан, чтобы продемонстрировать Западу свободу печати. «...Мы издали Мандельштама, чтобы заткнуть им глотку». — «Заткните и нам тоже!» — раздался голос из зала (Войнович 1). ...A Party lecturer explained that the volume [of poems by Osip Mandelstam] had been published to demonstrate our freedom of the press to the West. "...We have published Mandelstam in order to shut their mouths." "Shut ours too!"

came a voice from the audience (1a). ♦ «У меня достаточно способов заткнуть глотку говорунам» (Максимов 3). "I've got ways of shutting up loud mouths" (3a). ♦ Каждому ясно: когда экономика в паршивом состоянии, лучше затеять войну, чтобы сразу всем заткнуть глотки (Стругацкие 2). Everyone knew that when a country's economy was in rotten shape, the easiest dodge was to start a war as a pretext for gagging everyone immediately (2a).

Г-148 • **В ГЛУБИНЕ́ ВЕКО́В** [PrepP; Invar; sent adv; fixed WO] in the distant past: **in times past; in ancient times; in the remote past; long, long ago.**

Г-149 • **В ГЛУБИНЕ́ ДУШИ́ ⟨СЕ́РДЦА⟩** [PrepP; these forms only; sent adv; usu. used with impfv verbs; fixed WO] (in refer. to one's innermost feelings, thoughts) internally, secretly: **in one's heart of hearts; in the depths of one's soul ⟨heart⟩; deep in one's heart ⟨soul⟩; deep down (in one's soul ⟨heart⟩); deep down inside.**

Я остался в совершенном одиночестве на земле, но, признаюсь, в глубине души обрадовался (Булгаков 12). I was now totally alone in the world but I confess that in my heart of hearts I was glad (12a). ♦ Он знал, что в глубине души Лена довольна, самое трудное сделано: она сказала (Трифонов 4). He knew that in the depths of her soul Lena was satisfied, the most difficult thing had been done: she'd spoken (4a). ♦ Они [раковые больные] могли признаваться, что верят, или отрицать, но все они до одного в глубине души верили, что такой врач, или такой травник, или такая старуха-бабка где-то живёт, и только надо узнать — где, получить это лекарство — и они спасены (Солженицын 10). These people [the cancer patients] might have admitted or denied that they believed in such a thing, but all of them, to a man, felt, deep in their hearts, that there really was such a doctor, such a dispenser of herbs or such an old village woman living somewhere, and that they only had to learn where, take that medicine, and they would be saved (10b). ♦ Радуясь за неё [дочь], он в глубине души ревновал её к Николаю, постепенно заместившему отца в сердце дочери... (Максимов 3). He was glad for her [his daughter], but deep down he felt jealous of Nikolai, who had gradually replaced her father in his daughter's heart (3a).

Г-150 • **ДО ГЛУБИНЫ́ ДУШИ́ ⟨СЕ́РДЦА** *obsoles, lit*⟩ волновать, трогать, потрясать, поражать и т. п. [PrepP; these forms only; adv; fixed WO] (to worry, move, affect s.o. etc) profoundly, intensely: **to the (very) depths of one's soul ⟨being⟩; deeply; terribly.**

Некий Плаписсон, усердный посетитель парижских салонов, возмущённый до глубины души содержанием пьесы, сидя на сцене, при каждой остроте или трюке обращал багровое от злобы лицо к партеру и кричал: «Смейся же, партер! Смейся!» (Булгаков 5). A certain Monsieur Plapisson, a faithful habitué of Paris salons, who had a stage seat, was outraged by the play to the depths of his soul. At every witticism or stunt, he turned his apoplectic face to the parterre, shouting furiously, "Laugh, parterre! Go on, laugh!" (5a). ♦ Справедливости ради должен сказать, что и меня дразнили, хотя, правда, и очень редко, но зато оскорбляли до глубины души (Кузнецов 1). In fairness I have to say that I used also to be teased; not very often, it's true, but it deeply offended me (1b).

Г-151 • **ИЗ ГЛУБИНЫ́ ВЕКО́В ⟨ПРО́ШЛОГО⟩** [PrepP; these forms only; adv; fixed WO] from the distant past: **from ancient times; from the remote past; from long, long ago.**

Г-152 • **ОТ ГЛУБИНЫ́ ДУШИ́** желать, сказать *что* и т. п. [PrepP; Invar; adv; fixed WO] (to wish sth.) very deeply, (to say sth.) with great feeling: **from the depths of one's soul; with one's whole being; with all one's heart.**

Г-153 • **ТОГО́ И ГЛЯДИ́** ⟨**ЖДИ, СМОТРИ́**⟩; **ТОГО́ ГЛЯДИ́** *all coll* [Particle; fixed WO] (sth. unpleasant, and often unexpected, might happen) momentarily (its reason is often specified in the preceding context): (one may or will do sth. ⟨sth. may happen, it looks as if sth. will happen⟩) any minute now ⟨(at) any minute, (at) any moment, before you ⟨we etc⟩ know it⟩; (the) next thing you know (sth. will happen); you can never ⟨never can⟩ tell when you ⟨s.o., sth.⟩ might...; [in limited contexts] if one doesn't watch out; unless one watches out; if one isn't careful; one has to be careful (not to...).

«Ишь ты, месяц-то, как вертухай на стене, — усмехнулся Саня. — Того и гляди пальнёт!» (Аксёнов 6). "Say, look at that moon, like a guard on a prison wall," said Sanya, laughing. "Any minute now it'll open fire on us" (6a). ♦ «...Я тебе за эти же деньги не только продам рощу, но буду и сторожить её до твоего приезда. А то сейчас самый сезон. Того и гляди налетят греки и армяне, и от твоих каштанов ничего не останется» (Искандер 3). "For that price, not only will I sell you the grove, I'll guard it till you come back. Besides, this is the height of the season. Any minute the Greeks and Armenians will descend on it, and there'll be nothing left of your chestnuts" (3a). ♦ И так он чувствовал, что мигает чаще и чаще, и вот того и гляди брызнут слёзы (Гончаров 1). He felt that he was blinking more and more and that any moment tears would start in his eyes (1a). ♦ [Лебедев:] Столько, брат, про тебя по уезду сплетен ходит, что того и гляди к тебе товарищ прокурора приедет... (Чехов 4). [L.:] There's so much gossip going around about you that before you know it, my boy, the assistant prosecutor will be dropping in on you... (4a). ♦ «...Избиратели недовольны, некоторые город покидают, идёт брожение, того и гляди начнутся самосуды, окружная администрация бездействует...» (Стругацкие 1). "The voters are dissatisfied, some of them have left, there are rumblings, the next thing you know there'll be lynchings, and the district administration does nothing" (1a). ♦ «...Чего ты боишься?» — «Как чего боюсь, батюшка Кирила Петрович, а Дубровского-то; того и гляди попадёшься ему в лапы» (Пушкин 1). "What are you afraid of?" "What indeed, dear sir Kirila Petrovich! Dubrovskii, that's what! You can never tell when you might fall into his clutches" (1a). ♦ «Землишка маленькая, мужик ленив, работать не любит, думает, как бы в кабак... того и гляди, пойдёшь на старости лет по миру!» (Гоголь 3). "I have only a very small piece of land here, the peasants are lazy—they don't like to work and all they think about is drinking....So if I don't watch out, I'll be forced to go begging in my old age" (3e).

Г-154 • **НАВОДИ́ТЬ/НАВЕСТИ́ ГЛЯ́НЕЦ** *на что coll* [VP; subj: human or collect] to make the final improvements on sth., bring sth. to a good, acceptable, finished state (occas. used when sth. bad is made to appear deceptively good): X наводит глянец на Y ≃ X is putting a gloss ⟨a finish⟩ on Y; X is putting the final ⟨finishing⟩ touches on Y; X is polishing Y (up); [in refer. to sth. bad made to appear good] X is putting a positive gloss ⟨face⟩ on Y.

Г-155 • **МЕНЯ́ТЬ** ⟨**СМЕНЯ́ТЬ**⟩/**СМЕНИ́ТЬ** ⟨**ПЕРЕМЕНИ́ТЬ, ПРЕЛОЖИ́ТЬ** *obs,* **ПОЛОЖИ́ТЬ** *obs*⟩ **ГНЕВ НА МИ́ЛОСТЬ** [VP; subj: human; usu. pfv (past or Verbal Adv); usu. this WO] to cease being angry at s.o. and start treating him kindly: X сменил гнев на милость ≃ X relented; X's anger changed ⟨gave way⟩ to pity ⟨mercy etc⟩; X's heart softened.

Сам флигель-адъютант первый, сменив гнев на милость, говорил, что он «никакого зла сделать старосте не хочет...» (Герцен 1). The adjutant himself, relenting, was the first to declare that he "wished the man no harm..." (1a). ♦ Он [Чик] боялся, что, когда они напьются и уйдут отсюда, ему придётся по всему городу нести одежду Керопчика, если Мотя не сменит гнев на милость (Искандер 1). He [Chik] was afraid that when they got drunk and left he would have to carry Keropchik's clothes all through town, if Motya's anger didn't change to pity (1a).

Г-156 • **ВИТЬ/СВИТЬ (СЕБЕ́) ГНЕЗДО́** *lit* [VP] **1.** [subj: human] to set up one's family life, make a comfortable home for o.s.: X свил себе гнездо ≃ X built his nest; X built himself a nest; X built a nest for himself.

...[Анна Сергеевна] подала ему [Базарову] сложенный листок почтовой бумаги. Это было письмо от Аркадия: он в нём просил руки её сестры... «Так ты задумал гнездо себе свить? — говорил он в тот же день Аркадию... — Что ж? Дело хорошее» (Тургенев 2). ...[Anna Sergeevna] handed him [Bazarov] a folded sheet of notepaper. It was a letter from Arkady, in which he asked for her sister's hand...."So you've decided to build a nest for yourself?" he was saying the same day to Arkady...."Well, not a bad idea" (2a).

2. ~ *где* [subj: human] to establish residence or remain in some place permanently or for a long time: X свил себе гнездо в месте Y ≃ X put down roots in place Y; X settled (down) in place Y; X made place Y his home.

3. ~ *где* [subj: abstr] to become fixed, firmly established (in some place, in s.o.'s mind etc): X свил себе гнездо в Y-е ≃ X took root in Y.

Публика... заключила, что измена свила себе гнездо в самом Глупове... (Салтыков-Щедрин 1). The assemblage...concluded that treachery had taken root right in Foolov (1a).

Г-157 • **ОСИ́НОЕ ГНЕЗДО́** [NP; usu. sing; fixed WO] a group or crowd of hostile, malicious, or socially dangerous people, or their dwelling or whereabouts: **hornet's nest.**

В те времена он считал, что все меньшевики эндурского происхождения. Конечно, он знал, что у них есть всякие местные прихвостни, но сама родина меньшевизма, самое осиное гнездо, самая идейная пчеломатка, по его мнению, обитала в Эндурске (Искандер 3). In those days he believed all Mensheviks came from Endursk. Of course he knew they had a bunch of local stooges around here, but in his opinion Endursk was the true motherland of Menshevism, its hornet's nest, its ideological queen bee (3a).

Г-158 • **НЕ ГОВОРИ́ ГОП, ПОКА́ НЕ ПЕРЕПРЫ́ГНЕШЬ** ⟨**НЕ ПЕРЕСКО́ЧИШЬ**⟩ [saying] do not consider sth. finished until it is brought to a conclusion (said to or of a person who is too self-confident, who celebrates his success before it is ensured): ≃ **don't count your chickens before they are hatched; don't whistle ⟨halloo⟩ till you are out of the wood(s); don't speak too soon; there's many a slip 'twixt ⟨betwixt, between⟩ the cup and the lip.**

Г-159 • **(А ⟨НУ⟩) ЧТО Я ⟨вам⟩ ГОВОРИ́Л!** *coll* [sent; fixed WO] used to express the speaker's reaction upon learning that sth. he maintained earlier has been confirmed: **what did I tell you!; (that's) just ⟨exactly⟩ what I said!; just like I said!; didn't I tell you!; I told you so!**

«Знаешь, Вере действительно за сорок!» — «А что я говорила!» "You know, Vera really is over forty!" "What did I tell you!"

Г-160 • **ГОВОРИ́Т КАК ПИ́ШЕТ** *coll* [VP; subj: human; pres only; fixed WO] one speaks smoothly and articulately: X говорит как пишет ≃ **X has a silver tongue; X is silver-tongued; X has a way with words; [when reacting to a speech etc] quite a piece ⟨a bit⟩ of oratory!; what an eloquent presentation!**

Ваш завкафедрой говорит как пишет, но когда пытаешься потом вспомнить, о чём шла речь, понимаешь, что это были пустые слова. Your department chair has a silver tongue, but when you try to remember afterward what he was talking about, you realize it was all just empty words.

Г-161 • **САМ ЗА СЕБЯ ГОВОРИ́Т** [VP; subj: usu. abstr] some fact, quality etc is so obvious or attests to sth. so clearly that it does not require any explanation, proof etc: X сам за себя говорит ≃ **X speaks for itself; X is self-evident.**

Придворные объяснили князю Андрею невнимание к нему государя тем, что его величество был недоволен тем, что Болконский не служил с 1805 года. «Я сам знаю, как мы не властны в своих симпатиях и антипатиях, – думал князь Андрей, – ...но дело будет говорить само за себя» (Толстой 5). Courtiers explained to Prince Andrei that the Tsar's disregard of him was due to His Majesty's displeasure at Bolkonsky's not having served since 1805. "I know myself that one cannot help one's likes and dislikes," thought Prince Andrei, "...but the project will speak for itself" (5a).

Г-162 • **(И) НЕ ГОВОРИ́(ТЕ)** coll [usu. indep. sent; these forms only] (used to express total agreement with the interlocutor in his evaluation of sth., more often of sth. bad, unpleasant etc) yes, of course, definitely: **you can say that again!; I'll say!; that's for sure!; you bet!; no argument there ⟨here⟩!;** [in limited contexts] **don't even suggest such a thing; perish the thought!**

«Ну и геройским сынком сподобил тебя господь!..» И польщённый в отцовских чувствах Пантелей Прокофьевич охотно согласился: «И не говори!» (Шолохов 5). "That's a real hero of a son God granted you!..." And with his paternal feelings thus flattered Pantelei readily agreed, "You can say that again!" (5a). ♦ [Валя:] Он меня вызвал, а я говорю: «Я устала, Борис Палыч». И села. Представляешь? У него прямо челюсть отвисла. И ребята смотрят, ничего не понимают. А я села, и всё. [Валентин:] Красиво! [Валя:] Не говори! (Рощин 1). [V.:] He called me out, and I said: "I'm tired, Boris Pavlovich." And I sat down again. Can you imagine? His jaw dropped. And the boys and girls stared; they couldn't understand it. And I sat down, and that was all. [Valentin:] Lovely! [V.:] I'll say! (1b). ♦ «Чуть было не прошёл мимо великого начинания». – «А что если бы прошли?» – говорил я. «Не говори», – отвечал Платон Самсонович и снова вздрагивал (Искандер 6). "To think that I almost let this great undertaking slip through my fingers!" "Well, and what if you had?" I would ask. "Don't even suggest such a thing," he [Platon Samsonovich] would answer, wincing once again (6a).

Г-163 • **ЧТО ⟨КАК⟩ НИ ГОВОРИ́(ТЕ)** coll [these forms only; sent adv (parenth) or indep. clause; often foll. by a clause introduced by Conj «а»; fixed WO] regardless of any contrary opinions or judgments that may be voiced or held (the opinion or judgment that follows is the correct one): **say what you like; no matter what you say ⟨anyone says⟩; whatever you say.**

Подарок, что ни говори, был богатый (Искандер 4). Say what you like, it was a rich gift... (4a). ♦ Баба Дуня тащила свою добычу. Ноша была нелёгкая. Одной соли пуд, да мыла тридцать шесть кусков по четыреста граммов каждый... Что ни говори, тяжесть получилась порядочная (Войнович 2). Granny Dunya was lugging her booty home. It was no light burden. The pood of salt alone was thirty-six pounds, then there were the thirty-six bars of soap, four hundred grams each....No matter what you say, a respectable load (2a). ♦ «Во-первых, власть новая... Во-вторых, что там ни говори, они за простой народ, в этом их сила» (Пастернак 1). "To begin with, it's a new government....And then, whatever you say, they are on the side of the common people, that's their strength" (1a).

Г-164 • **КАК ГОВОРИ́ТСЯ** [Invar; sent adv (parenth); fixed WO] as it has become accepted to say: **as ⟨like⟩ they say; as the saying ⟨the expression⟩ goes; to borrow a phrase.**

«Так что до сегодняшнего дня мне было, как говорится, до фени, живёт ли где-то подобный Шевчук или нет» (Войнович 4). "So, up until today, I couldn't have, as they say, given a good goddamn whether there was any such Shevchuk alive anywhere" (4a). ♦ Нам, как говорится, не то обидно, что этот безумный мир принимает многих гениальных людей принимает за сумасшедших (Искандер 5). It doesn't bother us, as the saying goes, that this mad world takes many geniuses for madmen (5a).

Г-165 • **(ЕЩЁ) НИ О ЧЁМ НЕ ГОВОРИ́ТЬ** coll [VP; subj: abstr; 3rd pers or Part; pres or past; the verb is usu. in the final position] (of some action, quality etc) not to provide sufficient grounds for drawing conclusions: X (ещё) ни о чём не говорит ≃ **X doesn't mean anything ⟨a thing⟩; X doesn't prove anything; X tells one ⟨you⟩ nothing; X says nothing; X is of no significance.**

...С какой стати он, то есть скот, должен предчувствовать человеческое кровопролитие и тревожиться по этому поводу, непонятно. Ссылка на то, что скот перестал кричать, как только началась перестрелка, тоже ни о чём не говорит (Искандер 3). ...No one knows why they – the livestock, that is – should have had a premonition of human bloodshed and been anxious on that account. The fact that the livestock ceased to cry out as soon as the shooting started doesn't mean anything either (3a). ♦ То, что у Коли Смирнова над верхней губой модные усики, ни о чём ещё не говорит. Он самый настоящий корифей. Нет переводчика, который хоть раз в жизни не обратился бы к нему с вопросом (Михайловская 1). The fact that Kolya Smirnov has a modish mustache on his upper lip is of no significance. He is a real star. There is no interpreter who has not asked him a question at least once in his lifetime (1a).

Г-166 • **НЕ́ЧЕГО И ГОВОРИ́ТЬ, что...** or о ком-чём, про кого-что coll [these forms only; impers predic with быть∅, usu. pres; и always precedes говорить] **1.** it is so obvious that it does not even have to be stated: нечего и говорить, что... ≃ **needless to say; it goes without saying (that...); of course;** ‖ об X-е нечего и говорить ≃ **one need hardly mention ⟨say anything about⟩ X;** [when the person or thing in question is juxtaposed with a person or thing in the preceding context] **to say nothing of X; not to mention X.**

«Нечего и говорить о том, что мы приняли решение вашего превосходительства к непременному исполнению...» (Салтыков-Щедрин 2). "Needless to say, we accepted your excellency's decision and put it into effect immediately" (2a). ♦ Ближе – яснее – господин. Вы думаете, я сужу по пальто? Вздор. Пальто теперь очень многие и из пролетариев носят. Правда, воротники не такие, об этом и говорить нечего, но всё же издали можно спутать (Булгаков 11). As he came closer it was obvious that he was a gentleman. I suppose you thought I recognized him by his overcoat? Nonsense. Even lots of proletarians wear overcoats nowadays. I admit they don't usually have collars like this one, of course, but, even so, you can sometimes be mistaken at a distance (11b). ♦ Нечего и говорить о том, как утешительно было находить в письмах незнакомых людей отклик на то сокровенное, что годами вынашивалось молчком (Гинзбург 2). I need hardly say how reassuring it was to discover in letters from unknown people their reaction to inner secrets that for long years had been cherished in silence (2a). ♦ Не до всего доходили руки старика, посев уменьшился, а про остальное уж и говорить нечего (Шолохов 3). The old man could not cope with everything; he had even reduced his sowings, not to mention other things (3a).

2. sth. or s.o. is excluded altogether (as a possibility): об X-е нечего и говорить ≃ **X is out of the question;** [in limited contexts] **there is no question of (person Y's) doing thing X.**

О поездке в Прагу нечего и говорить. Going to Prague is out of the question. ♦ [author's usage] ...Маргарите решительно нечего было надеть, так как все её вещи остались в особняке, и хоть этот особняк был очень недалеко, конечно, нечего было и толковать о том, чтобы пойти туда и взять там свои вещи (Булгаков 9). ...Margarita had nothing to put on, since all her things remained in her house, and though it was not far, there was, of course, no question of her going there to take her clothes (9a).

Г-167 • **ЧТО И ГОВОРИ́ТЬ; (ДА) ЧТО (ТАМ ⟨ТУТ, И⟩) ГОВОРИ́ТЬ** *all coll* [these forms only; indep. clause or sent adv (parent); fixed WO] definitely, undoubtedly, truly (used to emphasize that there is no reason to argue or disagree with the statement that precedes or follows): **no question ⟨doubt⟩ about it; true; that's for sure; to be sure; sure enough; it can't be denied;** [in limited contexts] **really and truly.**

«Ну, при нём-то [председателе сельсовета] не будут подкладывать», — сказал он, опуская бинокль. «Что и говорить, при нём не посмеют», — согласились женщины... (Искандер 3). "Well, with him [the chairman of the village soviet] there they won't cheat," he said, lowering the binoculars. "No question about it, with him there they won't dare," the women agreed... (3a). ♦ [Комсорг:] Вон у химиков, вы посмотрите, у них дела гораздо хуже. Да что говорить! (Вампилов 3). [Komsomol Organizer:] In the chemistry department it's much worse, that's for sure! (3a). ♦ Да что тут говорить, вопиющую несправедливость её [Фаины] упорства мог снести только Лёва... (Битов 2). Really and truly, only Lyova could have borne the flagrant injustice of her [Faina's] stubbornness... (2a).

Г-168 • **ЧТО ТЫ ГОВОРИ́ШЬ ⟨ВЫ ГОВОРИ́ТЕ⟩!** *coll* [indep. sent; these forms only; fixed WO] (used to express surprise, amazement, or disbelief at sth. said) can it really be true? is it true?: **well, what do you know!; you don't say!; what are you saying!; you don't mean that!;** [in limited contexts] **you're kidding!**

«Дядя Сандро!.. А я вас ищу по всему городу...» — «Что ты говоришь!» — оживился дядя Сандро... (Искандер 3). "Uncle Sandro!...I've been looking for you all over town...." "Well, what do you know!" Uncle Sandro said, reviving (3a). ♦ «А знаете фамилию этого молодого вьюноши [obs = юноши]? — вдруг, точно угадывая его мысль, спросил Соколов. — Чей он родич?» — «Понятия не имею...». Соколов, приблизив губы к уху Штрума, зашептал. «Что вы говорите!» — воскликнул Штрум (Гроссман 2). "Do you know the surname of the young grandee?" Sokolov asked suddenly, as though reading Viktor's thoughts. "Do you realize whose relative he is?" "I've no idea." Sokolov leant over and whispered in Viktor's ear. "You don't say!" exclaimed Viktor (2a). ♦ «[Муразов] десять миллионов, говорят, нажил». — «Какое десять! Перевалило за сорок! Скоро половина России будет в его руках». — «Что вы говорите!» — вскрикнул Чичиков... (Гоголь 3). "...He's [Murazov has] accumulated ten million, they say." "Ten million! He must be worth more than forty by now. Pretty soon half of Russia will be in his hands." "What are you saying!" said Chichikov... (3b).

Г-169 • **ВООБЩЕ́ ГОВОРЯ́** [Invar; sent adv (parent); fixed WO] when considered in general terms: **generally speaking.**

Вообще говоря, он [Григорий Васильевич Кутузов] был честен и неподкупен (Достоевский 1). Generally speaking, he [Grigory Vasilievich Kutuzov] was honest and incorruptible (1a).

Г-170 • **ИНА́ЧЕ ГОВОРЯ́** [Invar; sent adv (parent); fixed WO] expressed differently (used to introduce a statement that conveys the meaning of the preceding statement but phrases it differently): **in other words; to put it another way; that is (to say).**

...Кроме комиссий на станции есть *некомиссии*, иначе говоря, люди, не являющиеся членами комиссий, они стоят вне этого, заняты на других работах или вообще не служат (Соколов 1). ...Besides the commissions there is a *noncommission* at the station too, or to put it another way, people who are not members of commissions, they stand outside them, employed at other jobs, they don't work here at all (1a). ♦ С появлением Рыцаря всё в доме окончательно встало на свои места. Иначе говоря, Ирина Викторовна не болела, Мансуров-Курильский снова вошёл в роль по части ценных указаний, хотя и высказывал их в более

лояльной форме... (Залыгин 1). With the appearance of the Knight everything in the house found its level. That is, Irina Viktorovna was no longer ill, Mansurov-Kurilsky resumed his role of order-giver, although he was fairer about it now... (1a).

Г-171 • **КОРО́ЧЕ ⟨КО́РОТКО⟩ ГОВОРЯ́** [these forms only; sent adv (parent); fixed WO] if the essence of the matter is to be summarized, stated briefly, then it is as follows (usu. used by the speaker before summarizing an account, explanation etc, or when he realizes he is failing to express himself clearly and tries to present the matter more succinctly): **in short; to make a long story short; in a word; in brief; to put it briefly; to be brief.**

...Пока находился он [Кириленко] на своём высоком посту... чего у него только не было. И квартиры, и дачи с отгороженными от людей лесами, полями, реками и километрами морских побережий... Короче говоря, важный был человек Кириленко, не нам с вами чета (Войнович 1). ...As long as he held his high position...Kirilinko wanted for nothing. He had apartments and dachas fenced off from the world by forests, fields, rivers, and miles of ocean front....In short, Kirilinko was an important man, not like you and me (1a). ♦ ...В тот день они [дядя Сандро и абрек Щащико] славно попили грушевой водки и Щащико ещё раз приходил в Большой Дом... Коротко говоря, знаменитый абрек больше дядю Сандро в вероломных замыслах не подозревал (Искандер 3). ...They [Uncle Sandro and the abrek Shashiko] drank gloriously of pear brandy that day. Shashiko came again to the Big House more than once....To make a long story short, the famous abrek never again suspected Uncle Sandro of perfidious plots (3a). ♦ Однажды я прочёл записку Брежнева. В одиннадцати строках этой записки было одиннадцать грамматических ошибок. Короче говоря, Брежнев, как и большинство сталинских выдвиженцев, представлял собой вполне мелкую личность, был малокультурен и необразован (Войнович 1). I once read a note written in Brezhnev's hand. It was eleven lines long and contained eleven grammatical errors. In a word, Brezhnev, like the majority of people who rose under Stalin, was a complete nonentity as a personality and had little culture and little education (1a). ♦ [Авдонин:] Побежал я, короче говоря, в контору. Комнату просить. Очень плохо соображал... (Салынский 1). [A.:] ...To put it briefly, I ran to the office to ask for a room. I hardly knew what I was doing... (1a).

Г-172 • **МЕЖДУ НА́МИ ГОВОРЯ́; МЕЖДУ НА́МИ** *both coll* [Verbal Adv (1st var.), PrepP (2nd var.); these forms only; sent adv, parent (both variants) or subj-compl with быть⊘, остаться (subj: usu. это or этот разговор, наша беседа etc — 2nd var.)] as a secret that should not be known to anyone other than ourselves: **(just ⟨strictly etc⟩) between us ⟨you and me, ourselves⟩; between you, me, and the lamppost ⟨bedpost, back porch etc⟩.**

...В газетах появилось мрачное имя Чомбе. (Между нами говоря, правильнее было бы сказать Чомба.) (Искандер 4). ...The name of Tshombe appeared in the papers. (Just between us, it would be more correct to say Tshomba.) (4a). ♦ [Гусь:] Я ведь к вам отчасти по делу. Только это между нами (Булгаков 7). [G.:] I have come to see you partly on business. Only this is just between you and me (7a). ♦ Говоря строго между нами... я соврал тебе давеча про наше хорошее положение. Положение у нас хуже некуда (Терц 6). Strictly between ourselves...I told you a lie when I said that things were not as bad as they might be. The fact is, they couldn't be worse (6a).

Г-173 • **НЕ ГОВОРЯ́ (УЖЕ́ ⟨УЖ⟩)** *о ком-чём;* **Я УЖЕ́ ⟨УЖ⟩ НЕ ГОВОРЮ́** *о ком-чём* [Verbal Adv (1st var.); VP_subj, я is always in the initial position (2nd var.); these forms only] and also, in addition to, as well as: **not to mention; to say nothing of; let alone; not to speak of (sth. ⟨s.o., the fact that...⟩); quite apart from the fact that...; never mind (sth. ⟨s.o., the fact that...⟩).**

А как быть [жителям села] с освящённой древними традициями необходимостью побывать на свадьбе и других родовых торжествах? А дежурство у постели больного родственника? А годовщина смерти, а сорокадневье? Я уж не говорю о свежих похоронах (Искандер 3). What were they [the villagers] to do about the necessity, sanctified by ancient tradition, of attending a wedding or any other clan celebration? And the vigil at the bedside of a sick relative? And the anniversary of a death, or the fortieth-day memorial feast? Not to mention the funeral itself! (3a). ♦ [Львов:] В вашем голосе, в вашей интонации, не говоря уже о словах, столько бездушного эгоизма... (Чехов 4). [L.:] In your voice, your intonation, to say nothing of your words, there is so much callous egotism... (4a). [L.:] Your voice and tone, let alone your actual words, are so insensitive, selfish... (4b). ♦ Коллекцию имперских полотен пришлось пополнять союзными национальными цветами. Это отнимало время, не говоря о том, что почти всякий день надо было выбрать комбинацию одиннадцати флагов из семнадцати, чтобы расцветить ими фасад дома (Федин 1). The collection of imperial linen had to be reinforced by the allied national colors. This took time, not to speak of the fact that nearly every day one had to choose a combination of eleven flags from seventeen in order to decorate the house façade with them (1a). ♦ «Вот видишь ли, Евгений, — промолвил Аркадий, оканчивая свой рассказ, — как несправедливо ты судишь о дяде! Я уже не говорю о том, что он не раз выручал отца из беды, отдавал ему все свои деньги... но он всякому рад помочь...» (Тургенев 2). "So you see, Yevgeny," said Arkady, finishing his story, "how unfairly you jump to conclusions about Uncle! Quite apart from the fact that he has often helped my father out of trouble and given him all his money...he is always glad to help anybody..." (2e). ♦ Перестраиваются города. Октябрьская площадь, рядом с которой мы жили когда-то, совершенно изменила облик. Не говоря уже о том, что возникли новые африканские государства. Двадцать лет! (Трифонов 5). Whole cities are rebuilt. October Square, which we once lived right next to, had changed its appearance completely. Never mind the fact that new states have arisen in Africa. Twenty years! (5a).

Г-174 • ОТКРОВЕ́ННО ⟨ЧЕ́СТНО⟩ ГОВОРЯ́; ОТКРОВЕ́ННО СКАЗА́ТЬ [these forms only; sent adv (parenth); fixed WO] speaking honestly: **frankly speaking; to be (perfectly ⟨quite⟩) frank ⟨honest⟩; I must admit.**

«Откровенно говоря, мне самой было бы не очень интересно восстанавливать всё, что я чувствовала по этому поводу, когда была курсисткой» (Набоков 1). "Frankly speaking, I myself wouldn't be very interested in resuscitating everything that I felt in this connection when I was a college student..." (1a). ♦ ...Пётр Васильевич, взявший уже себе за правило готовиться здесь к любым фокусам, откровенно говоря, ожидал, что [новый знакомый] в любую минуту может выкинуть какое-нибудь «коленце». (Максимов 3). ...Pyotr Vasilievich had already made it a rule to be ready for all sorts of antics in this place, and, to be frank, he was expecting funny business at any moment... (3a). ♦ «Вы понимаете, о чём я говорю?» — «Да откровенно говоря, нет...» (Домбровский 1). "Do you see what I'm driving at?" "Well, to be quite honest, no I don't" (1a).

Г-175 • ПО́ПРОСТУ ГОВОРЯ́ ⟨СКАЗА́ТЬ⟩ coll [these forms only; sent adv (parenth)] speaking directly: **to put it plainly; quite simply; simply put ⟨stated⟩; [in limited contexts] to put it bluntly; to be blunt.**

Чёрт сбил с толку обоих чиновников: чиновники, говоря попросту, перебесились и перессорились ни за что (Гоголь 3). The Devil led the two officials astray: the officials, to put it plainly, went crazy and fell out with each other for no reason whatsoever (3c).

Г-176 • СО́БСТВЕННО ГОВОРЯ́ [Invar; fixed WO] **1.** [sent adv (parenth)] (used in conjunction with a statement that specifies the situation, provides a more precise phrasing of sth.

stated earlier etc) in reality, in truth: **actually; after all; strictly speaking; in fact; as a matter of fact.**

Собственно говоря, именно Октябрь и привил ему начальную тягу ко всякого рода машинам... (Аксёнов 12). It was actually October who infected him with a passion for all sorts of machinery... (12a). ♦ ...Почему он [Сталин] созвал совещание секретарей райкомов только Западной Грузии, дядя Сандро так и не понял. По-видимому, секретари райкомов Восточной Грузии в чём-то провинились... Так думал дядя Сандро, напрягая свой любознательный ум, хотя это, собственно говоря, не входило в его обязанности коменданта Цика... (Искандер 3). ...Why he [Stalin] had called a conference of the secretaries of the district committees of only western Georgia, Uncle Sandro simply could not understand. Apparently the district committee secretaries of eastern Georgia had committed some offense....Or so thought Uncle Sandro, exerting his inquisitive mind—although strictly speaking this was not within his purview as superintendent at the CEC... (3a). ♦ Мне было горько, что меня не приняли в комсомол. Но я не только убеждена была, что так и надо, но даже и вопросов не задавала, а почему, собственно говоря, так надо? (Орлова 1). I was miserable because I had not been accepted into the Komsomol. But not only was I convinced that that was the way it should have been, I did not even ask any questions, such as why in fact should it have been like that? (1a).

2. [used as Particle with interrog and relative pronouns, adverbs etc] used to emphasize, draw attention to some word or phrase: **exactly; precisely; just.**

«Почему же, собственно говоря, вы себя выдаёте за папу товарища Сталина?» — «Потому что я и есть папа товарища Сталина. Мой сын, товарищ Зиновий Сталин, самый известный в Гомеле зубной техник». — «Вот оно что!» (Войнович 2). "...Just why are you trying to pass yourself off as Comrade Stalin's papa?" "Because I am the father of Comrade Stalin. My son, Comrade Zinovy Stalin, is the most-well-known dental technician in Gomel." "So that's it!" (2a).

Г-177 • ГОВОРЯ́Т ⟨ГОВОРЮ́⟩ ВАМ ⟨ТЕБЕ́⟩ coll [VP; subj: implied; these forms only; often used as sent adv (parenth); usu. this WO] used to emphasize a statement or make a command more emphatic: **I'm telling you; I tell you; I've ⟨we've⟩ (already) told you.**

[Анна Андреевна:] Кто ж бы это такой был? [Марья Антоновна:] Это Добчинский, маменька... [Анна Андреевна:] Ну вот: нарочно, чтобы только поспорить. Говорят тебе — не Добчинский (Гоголь 4). [A.A.:] Whoever could it be? [M.A.:] It's Mr Dobbin, Mummy.... [A.A.:] There now, you said that deliberately, simply for the sake of argument. I tell you it is not Mr Dobbin (4b). ♦ «Словоблудие — у тебя! — с новой запальчивостью отсёк дланью Сологдин. — Если вы всё выводите из этих трёх законов...» — «Да говорят тебе: не выводим!» — «Из законов — не выводите?» — изумился Сологдин. «Нет!» — «Так что они тогда — пришей кобыле хвост?» (Солженицын 3). "The high-flown, empty verbiage is all yours!" said Sologdin in a new outburst of vehemence, cutting him off with a wave of his hand. "If you deduce everything from those three laws—" "But I've told you—we don't." "You don't?" Sologdin asked in surprise. "No!" "Well then, what are the laws good for?" (3a).

Г-178 • ХОДИ́ТЬ ⟨ВЫСТУПА́ТЬ⟩ ГО́ГОЛЕМ coll [VP; subj: human] to walk with a self-important, arrogant air: X ходит гоголем ≃ **X struts about; X struts like a peacock ⟨a bantam (rooster)⟩; X swaggers.**

[Офицерским жёнам] тоже скучно в тесном офицерском посёлке, расположенном обычно рядом с лагерем, вдали от больших населённых пунктов. Развлечений никаких, даже кино нет... Одна надежда — завести роман в лагере, с зэком помоложе. Разумеется, избраннику завидует весь лагерь, и он ходит гоголем — первый парень на деревне (Буковский 1). [The officers' wives] too found life boring, for in the cramped officers' quarters, which were usually situated next to the camp and far away from any population centers, there were no amusements, not even a movie....Their only distraction was to start a romance with one of the young cons in the camp. Of course, the entire camp would be green with envy at the lucky fellow, and he would strut like a bantam—the cock of the village (1a).

Г-179 • **ГОД ОТ ГО́ДА ⟨ОТ ГО́ДУ, О́Т ГОДУ⟩; С ГО́ДУ ⟨-а⟩ НА́ ГОД** [these forms only; adv; used with impfv verbs; fixed WO] as the years go by: **with every ⟨each⟩ passing year; from year to year; year by year; from one year to the next; every year.**

Национальность... Вот пятый пункт... Он [Штрум] не знал, что год от года будут сгущаться вокруг этого пятого пункта мрачные страсти (Гроссман 2). Nationality...Point five....He [Shtrum] wasn't to know what dark passions would gather year by year around this point (2a). ♦ Год от году холодела кровь. Жалился [regional = жаловался] дед Гришака Наталье — любимой внучке: «Шерстяные чулки, а не греют мои ноженьки» (Шолохов 2). Every year his [Grandad Grishaka's] blood grew colder. He would complain to his favourite grand-daughter Natalya. "Even these woollen socks don't keep my feet warm any longer" (2a).

Г-180 • **ГОДА́ ⟨ГО́ДЫ⟩ ВЫ́ШЛИ** *кому, чьи substand* [VP$_{subj}$] **1.** s.o. has become an adult, reached a suitable age for sth. (often marriage): года Х-у вышли ≃ X is ⟨has come⟩ of age; [in limited contexts] X is old enough; [of a young woman considered ready for marriage] X is of marriageable age.

[2-ой мужик:] Что же замуж не выдают? Года-то уж небось вышли? (Толстой 3). [Second Peasant:] Why don't they marry them off? They're old enough, aren't they? (3a).

2. s.o. is beyond the maximum age allowed for sth.: года Х-овы вышли ≃ X is past ⟨has passed⟩ the age limit ⟨the cutoff age⟩; X is overage ⟨too old⟩ (for sth.).

Г-181 • **ИЗ ГО́ДА В ГОД ⟨И́З ГОДУ В ГОД⟩** [PrepP; these forms only; adv; used with impfv verbs; fixed WO] (used to convey the constant, uninterrupted nature of an action) every year, over the course of several or many years: **year after year; from year to year; year in (,) year out; year in and year out.**

[Алекс:] ...Честно говоря, надоело как-то [преподавать детишкам]. Из года в год параграфы — потом спрашивать, опять параграфы — и опять каждого спрашивать (Солженицын 11). [A.:] ...To be frank, I just got fed up [with teaching kids]. Year after year going through sections of a textbook, questioning the kids on them, then some more out of the textbook, and then again questioning the kids one after the other (11a). ♦ Так путешествовали мы из года в год, так путешествуем мы из года в год, так будем путешествовать мы из года в год... (Аксёнов 6). So we traveled from year to year, so we travel from year to year, so we will travel from year to year (6a). ♦ «Возьмите очереди. Раз постоять — пустяк. Сто раз — пустяк. А если изо дня в день, из года в год?» (Зиновьев 2). "Take queues. To stand in line once is nothing. To stand in line a hundred times is nothing. But if it's day in day out, year in year out? (2a).

Г-182 • **ОБЕ́ЩАННОГО ТРИ ГО́ДА ЖДУТ** [saying] said jokingly when the fulfillment of a promise is delayed for a long time or when a person does not believe in the fulfillment of s.o.'s promise: ≃ **between promising and performing a man may marry his daughter;** [in limited contexts] **promises are made ⟨meant⟩ to be broken; promises demand patience.**

Г-183 • **НЕ ПО ГОДА́М ⟨ЛЕТА́М, ВО́ЗРАСТУ⟩** [PrepP; these forms only] **1.** ~ *какой, каков etc* [usu. modif or adv] not in accordance with one's age: **for one's age; beyond one's years; for someone his ⟨her etc⟩ age; for a man ⟨woman etc⟩ of**

his ⟨her etc⟩ **age;** [in refer. to an unusually mature young person] **(have) an old head on young shoulders;** ‖ X одевается не по возрасту ≃ **X doesn't dress in keeping with his years ⟨age⟩.**

Тендел вскочил со скамейки, костистый, не по годам проворный старик, и глянул издали на Кязыма... (Искандер 5). Tendel jumped up from the bench. A bony old man, agile for his age, he looked at Kyazym from afar... (5a). ♦ У меня есть приятель, ещё совсем молодой, но умный и мрачный не по возрасту (Мандельштам 1). I have a certain acquaintance who, though still quite young, is both wise and gloomy beyond his years (1a).

2. ~ *(кому)* [subj-compl with быть$_\emptyset$ (subj: abstr or infin)] not befitting s.o.'s age, not within s.o.'s capacity because of his age: X (Y-у) не по годам ≃ **X is unbecoming at Y's age; X is inappropriate for someone Y's age; Y is too old for X; Y is past X ⟨that sort of thing⟩.**

Я вздохнул и отвернулся. Да, да, конечно, моя страсть не по возрасту (Искандер 3). I sighed and looked away. No, of course such passion was unbecoming at my age (3a). ♦ [Суходолов:] ...Трудно мне переживать какую-то детскую, глупенькую встречу... Не по возрасту, не по положению!.. (Погодин 1). [S.:] ...I find it hard to go through a silly, childlike encounter....I'm too old for it; it doesn't go with my position!... (1a).

Г-184 • **С ГОДА́МИ; С ЛЕТА́МИ** [PrepP; these forms only; sent adv] with the progression of time: **with the (passing) years; over the years; as the years pass ⟨go by⟩; in time.**

С годами у неё стал слишком развязываться язык, сказывался, видно, возраст... (Максимов 1). With the passing years her tongue had begun to wag too freely—evidently the effect of age... (1a). ♦ Я думаю, что настоящие люди — это те, кто с годами не утрачивает детской веры в разумность мира... (Искандер 6). The best people, I think, are those who over the years have managed to retain this childhood faith in the world's rationality (6a). ♦ Вероятно, с летами она успела бы помириться с своим положением... (Гончаров 1). It is possible that, as the years passed, she would have become reconciled to her position... (1a). ♦ С годами мы со многим примиряемся, ничего не поделаешь — жизнь... Но в пятнадцать лет! (Рыбаков 1). As the years go by, we learn to accept all kinds of things, we resign ourselves—that's life—but at the age of fifteen! (1a). ♦ Ну, вероятно, с годами Олег сумеет устроиться лучше (Солженицын 10). [context transl] ...Oh well, he [Oleg] would probably find himself something better in a few years' time (10a).

Г-185 • **В ГОДА́Х; В ЛЕТА́Х** [PrepP; these forms only; subj-compl with быть$_\emptyset$ (subj: human) or nonagreeing modif] older, elderly: X в годах ≃ **X is getting on in years; X is advanced in years; X is no youngster.**

Дельце, о котором просил хозяин, касалось его сбежавшей жены. Начал он издалека, говоря, что он уже не мальчик, чтобы есть что попало и как попало, а человек в летах, и ему нужен человек, который мог бы приготовить и подать ему пищу (Искандер 4). The favor that Omar had requested concerned his runaway wife. He began in a roundabout way, saying that he was no longer a boy, to eat any old thing fixed any old way; he was a man getting on in years, he needed a person who could prepare and serve his food for him (4a). ♦ Хотя и в годах, ему было лет, наверно, под пятьдесят, но мужчина, надо сказать, красавец (Рыбаков 1). He was no youngster, around fifty or so, but he was a good-looking man, I must say (1a).

Г-186 • **КУДА́ Э́ТО ГОДИ́ТСЯ!** *coll* [sent; Invar; fixed WO] this is utterly inappropriate, unacceptable (used to express a harsh judgment of or negative attitude toward sth.): **this is just ⟨really⟩ too much!; how could you ⟨he etc⟩ do such a thing!; how can this be!**

Почему мне об этом раньше не сказали? Куда это годится! Why wasn't I told about this before? This is really too much!

Г-187 • **НИКУДА́ НЕ ГОДИ́ТСЯ** *coll* [VP; subj: human, abstr, or concr; fixed WO] some person (thing, phenomenon) is totally unsuitable, does not meet the required or desired standards, some action or situation is totally unacceptable: X никуда не годится ≃ **X just won't do; X will never do; X is no good (at all); X is good for nothing; X is not good for anything; person X is utterly incompetent; thing X is utterly worthless; X is of no use (whatsoever);** [in limited contexts] **X is an utter waste of time.**

«Язык! – вскрикивал литератор (тот, который оказался сволочью), – язык, главное! Язык никуда не годится» (Булгаков 12). "The language!" cried one of the writers (the one who turned out to be such a swine). "The language is the trouble. It's no good" (12a). ♦ ...Стихи всё равно никуда не годились, как подавляющее большинство описательных стихов... (Катаев 3). ...The verses were no good at all, like most descriptive verses... (3a). ♦ [Яков:] Так вот я – из третьей группы. К ней принадлежат все лентяи, бродяги, монахи, нищие и другие приживалы мира сего. [Надя:] Скучно ты говоришь, дядя! И совсем ты не такой, а просто – ты добрый, мягкий. [Яков:] То есть никуда не гожусь (Горький 1). [Ya.:] That's me—the third category. To this category belong all the lazy loafers, the tramps, monks, beggars and other parasites of this world. [N.:] Why do you say such tiresome things, uncle? And you're not like that at all. You're just kind and soft-hearted. [Ya.:] In other words, good-for-nothing (1c). ♦ «Да, – угрюмо сказал Передонов, – вы взяли себе в голову, что я никуда не гожусь, а я постоянно о гимназии забочусь» (Сологуб 1). "That's right," said the sullen Peredonov, "you've taken it into your head that I'm not good for anything, even though I am constantly concerned about the gymnasium" (1a). ♦ Кутузову пожалован Георгий 1-й степени; государь оказывал ему почайшие почести; но неудовольствие государя против фельдмаршала было известно каждому. Соблюдалось приличие, и государь показывал первый пример этого; но все знали, что старик виноват и никуда не годится (Толстой 7). Kutuzov had received the Order of St. George, First Class; the Tsar had conferred on him the highest honors, but everyone was aware of his dissatisfaction with the Field Marshal. The proprieties were observed and the Tsar was the first to set the example, but everyone knew that the old man was at fault and utterly incompetent (7a). ♦ «...[Я] гаснул и тратил по мелочи жизнь и ум... Даже самолюбие – на что оно тратилось? Чтоб заказывать платье у известного портного? Чтоб попасть в известный дом?.. Или я не понял этой жизни, или она никуда не годится...» (Гончаров 1). "...[I was] fading out, wasting my mind, my life, on trifles....Even my self-respect—what was that wasted on? On ordering clothes from a famous tailor? On being invited to a celebrated house?...Either I failed to understand that life, or it was utterly worthless..." (1b). ♦ «Третьего дня, я смотрю, он [твой отец] Пушкина читает, – продолжал... Базаров. – Растолкуй ему, пожалуйста, что это никуда не годится» (Тургенев 2). "The other day I found him [your father] reading Pushkin," Bazarov resumed. "Tell him what an utter waste of time it is" (2a).

Г-188 • **ГОДИ́ТЬСЯ В ОТЦЫ́ ⟨В МА́ТЕРИ, В СЫНО-ВЬЯ́** и т. п.⟩ *кому* [VP; subj: human] to be the appropriate age to be s.o.'s father (mother, son etc): X годится Y-у в отцы ⟨в сыновья⟩ ≃ **X is old ⟨young⟩ enough to be Y's father ⟨son⟩; X could ⟨might well⟩ be Y's father ⟨son⟩.**

[Шаманов *(по телефону)*:] Девушка?.. Да, интересная... Успокойся, старина. Ты ей в отцы годишься... (Вампилов 2). [Sh. *(into the telephone)*:] The girl?...Yes, not bad....Relax, my friend. You're old enough to be her father (2b). ♦ «Вы говорите, что он [Аркадий] неравнодушен ко мне, и мне самой всегда казалось, что я ему нравлюсь. Я знаю, что я гожусь ему в тётки, но я не хочу скрывать от вас, что я стала чаще думать о нём» (Тургенев 2). "You say that he's [Arkady is] not indifferent to me, and it did always seem to me as though he was attracted to me. I know that I

might well be his aunt, but I will not conceal from you that I have begun to think about him more often" (2e).

Г-189 • **НИКУДА́ НЕ ГО́ДНЫЙ** [AdjP; modif; fixed WO] very bad, poor in quality, not fit for anything: **(absolutely) worthless; (perfectly) useless; lousy; no-good; not ⟨no longer⟩ good for anything.**

...Великий Лев Толстой совершенно спокойно, не считаясь ни с чем, подверг уничтожающей критике самого Шекспира, взявши под сомнение не только ценность его мыслей, но и просто-напросто высмеяв его как весьма посредственного – точнее, никуда не годного – сочинителя (Катаев 3). ...The great Leo Tolstoy...quite calmly and without regard for anything or anyone, had subjected Shakespeare himself to annihilating criticism, not only casting doubt on the value of his ideas but simply ridiculing him as an extremely mediocre, or rather, perfectly useless scribbler (3a). ♦ «Женись стариком, никуда не годным... А то пропадёт всё, и то в тебе есть хорошего и высокого» (Толстой 4). "Marry when you are old and no longer good for anything, otherwise all that is fine and noble in you will be lost..." (4a).

Г-190 • **БЕЗ ГО́ДУ НЕДЕ́ЛЯ ⟨-ю⟩** *coll* [PrepP; these forms only; fixed WO] **1.** [adv; usu. used with impfv verbs] for a very brief period of time: **(only) a very short time; just a brief while; next to no time; (for) only a few days; (be) (completely) new (in some place);** [in limited contexts] **only just (arrived ⟨began to work etc⟩ somewhere).**

«Вы... в полку без году неделя; нынче здесь, завтра перешли куда в адъютантики; вам наплевать, что говорить будут: „Между павлоградскими офицерами воры!"» (Толстой 4). "You...have been in the regiment a very short time; you're here today, tomorrow you'll go off somewhere as an adjutant, and it's all the same to you if they say: 'There are thieves among the Pavlograd officers!'" (4a). ♦ «С тобой я знакома без году неделю, а он [кабан Борька] у меня живёт, почитай, уже два года» (Войнович 2). "I've known you only a few days, but you've got to remember he's [the hog Borka has] been living here two years already" (2a). ♦ [У Ляли] колотилось сердце, и набегали всякие слова, злые, справедливые, которые не были сказаны. А почему Милютина, которая в театре без году неделя?.. – и так далее и тому подобное (Трифонов 1). Her [Lyalya's] heart was pounding, and all of the just and nasty things that she had left unsaid came rushing to mind. And why should Milyutina, who was completely new in the theater?...—and so forth and so on (1a). ♦ ...Комиссар дивизии раздражал его [Крымова]: без году неделя на фронте, а представляется ветераном... (Гроссман 2). ...He [Krymov] was irritated by this commissar. He'd only just been sent to the front and he put on the airs of a veteran (2a).

2. *often condes* or *disapprov* [nonagreeing modif of NP denoting a person's profession, position etc and used as subj-compl] recent, inexperienced: **new; green; a greenhorn.**

Ты инженер без году неделя, а уже лезешь других учить. As an engineer you're still green, and already you're trying to teach others how to do things.

Г-191 • **ГО́ДЫ ⟨ГОДА́⟩ ПОДХО́ДЯТ/ПОДОШЛИ́** *кому substand* [VP$_{subj}$] s.o. has reached the age when he should do sth.: годы X-у подошли ≃ **X is at that age (when...); it's (high) time for X (to do sth.).**

Г-192 • **СКО́ЛЬКО ГОЛО́В, СТО́ЛЬКО (И) УМО́В** [saying] there are as many different opinions as there are people: ≃ **so many men, so many minds.**

Г-193 • **АДА́МОВА ГОЛОВА́** [NP; fixed WO] a representation of a human skull, often with two crossed bones underneath (as a symbol of death, poison etc): **death's-head; the sign of a ⟨the⟩ skull; skull and crossbones;** [in refer. to a pirate's flag with a skull and crossbones] **Jolly Roger.**

...Взглянув ещё раз на руку нового знакомца, [Пьер] ближе рассмотрел перстень. Он увидал на нём адамову голову, знак масонства (Толстой 5). ...Glancing once more at the stranger's hands he [Pierre] looked more closely at his ring with its death's-head — a Masonic symbol (5a). ♦ Говорили, говорили мистики, что было время, когда красавец не носил фрака, а был опоясан широким кожаным поясом, из-за которого торчали рукояти пистолетов, а его волосы воронова крыла были повязаны алым шёлком, и плыл в Караибском море под его командой бриг под чёрным гробовым флагом с адамовой головой (Булгаков 9). It was said, it was said by mystics that there had been a time when the handsome man did not wear a frock coat, but a wide leather belt with revolvers tucked into it, and his raven hair was tied with scarlet silk, and he commanded a brig that sailed the Caribbean under a dead black flag bearing the sign of the skull (9a).

Г-194 • БАРА́НЬЯ ГОЛОВА́ *highly coll, rude* [NP] a dense, stupid person: **lamebrain; dumbbell; dunce; fathead; blockhead; idiot; moron.**

Опять эта баранья голова лезет со своими непрошеными советами! Again this idiot is butting in with unwanted advice!

Г-195 • БУ́ЙНАЯ ⟨БЕДО́ВАЯ⟩ ГОЛОВА́ *coll* ⟨ГОЛО́ВУШКА *folk*⟩ [NP; fixed WO] a daring, reckless person: **(bold) daredevil; plucky devil; hotspur; madcap.**

Вдруг что-то похожее на песню поразило мой слух. «...Стану морю кланяться/ Я низёхонько:/ „Уж не тронь ты, злое море,/ Мою лодочку:/ Везёт моя лодочка/ Вещи драгоценные,/ Правит ею в тёмну ночь/ Буйная головушка"» (Лермонтов 1). Suddenly something like a song caught my ear. "The angry ocean then I pray,/Bending low before him:/'Spare my barque, O fearsome one!'—/Thus do I implore him.—/'Precious goods are stowed on board!'—/Fierce the sea is foaming!/—Keep her safe—a madcap steers/Through the gloaming!'" (1b).

Г-196 • ВЕ́ТРЕНАЯ ГОЛОВА́ *coll* ⟨ГОЛО́ВУШКА *folk*⟩ [NP; fixed WO] a frivolous, unreliable person: **airhead; bubblehead; dingbat; scatterbrain; featherbrain; (be) featherbrained ⟨scatterbrained, flighty⟩.**

«Свинкин ветреная голова. Иногда чёрт знает какие тебе итоги выведет, перепутает все справки» (Гончаров 1). "Svinkin is scatterbrained: sometimes you wonder what the devil he'll come up with next. He's always mixing up the reports" (1b).

Г-197 • ГОЛОВА́ БОЛИ́Т (*у кого, чья*) *за кого, о ком-чём coll* [VP$_{subj}$; fixed WO] s.o. is anxious, worries about another or about sth.: (у Х-а) голова болит за Y-a ≃ **X gives himself a headache over Y; X loses sleep over Y.**

«Слушай, я тебе ещё раз повторяю: это не твоё дело! За что преследовать врага, как с ним обходиться, к какому наказанию привлечь его — это мы знаем! Пусть твоя голова не болит» (Айтматов 2). "Listen, I'll repeat—it's none of your business! We know how to deal with this sort of thing—how to sniff out an enemy, how to treat him, how to punish him. Don't give yourself a headache over this!" (2a).

Г-198 • ГОЛОВА́ В ГО́ЛОВУ *идти coll* [Invar; adv; fixed WO] (of horses etc racing; *by extension* of two people or groups competing in sth.) (to be) even, (be going) at the same pace, neither one ahead of or behind the other: **neck and neck; dead even.**

Г-199 • ГОЛОВА́ ВА́РИТ (*у кого*) *coll;* КОТЕЛО́К ВА́РИТ *substand;* МОЗГИ́ ВА́РЯТ *substand* [VP$_{subj}$; usu. this WO] **1.** s.o. is bright, intelligent: у Х-а голова ⟨котелок⟩ варит ≃ **X has a good head on his shoulders; X's head is screwed on straight; X has a lot ⟨X is really⟩ on the ball; X is one smart cookie; X has (the) smarts; X has brains.**

2. [neg only] s.o. cannot think clearly (because of fatigue, illness etc): у Х-а голова не варит ≃ **X can't think straight; X's brain refuses to function; X's brain is on the blink; X's brain is mush ⟨fried⟩.**

Г-200 • ГОЛОВА́ ВСКРУЖИ́ЛАСЬ *чья, у кого (от чего)* [VP$_{subj}$] (having been affected by praise, flattery, or success) s.o. has become conceited, has lost the ability to look upon his behavior or actions realistically, critically: у Х-а (от Y-a) вскружилась голова ≃ **X has (gotten) a swelled ⟨big⟩ head; Y gave X a swelled ⟨big⟩ head; Y turned ⟨went (right) to⟩ X's head.**

Г-201 • ГОЛОВА́ ЕЛО́ВАЯ *highly coll, rude* [NP; usu. sing; usu. vocative] a stupid, senseless person: **numskull; dumbbell; nitwit.**

Г-202 • ГОЛОВА́ ЗАБИ́ТА *у кого чем* [VP$_{subj}$ with быть$_\emptyset$] **1.** [indir obj: usu. pl] s.o. has many concerns or thoughts about s.o. or sth.: у Х-а голова забита заботами ⟨хлопотами, всякими делами и т. п.⟩ ≃ **X has a lot on his mind;** [in limited contexts] **X is weighed down with concerns;** ‖ голова у Х-а забита мыслями об Y-e ⟨[AdjP] мыслями⟩ ≃ **X's head is filled with thoughts of Y ⟨with [AdjP] thoughts⟩; X's mind is on Y.**

2. s.o.'s mind is overburdened with some (usu. unnecessary) information or knowledge: у Х-а голова забита Y-ом ≃ **X's head is chock-full of Y; X's head is filled ⟨crammed, stuffed, cluttered⟩ with Y.**

Г-203 • ГОЛОВА́ (И) ДВА У́ХА *highly coll, disapprov, occas. humor* [NP; these forms only; usu. vocative; fixed WO] a slow-witted, inattentive person: **(you) lummox ⟨lamebrain, knucklehead⟩.**

Г-204 • ГОЛОВА́ ИДЁТ/ПОШЛА́ КРУ́ГОМ *чья, у кого coll* [VP$_{subj}$] **1.** s.o. experiences dizziness (caused by fatigue, alcohol, noise, shock etc): у Х-а голова идёт кругом ≃ **X's head is spinning ⟨whirling, reeling, going (a)round⟩; X feels dizzy; thing Y makes X's head spin ⟨whirl, reel⟩.**

«Но я же это сделал не нарочно!» — «Именно это вас и спасает, — объяснил Лужин, — если бы вы сделали *это* нарочно, мы бы вас расстреляли». У Ермолкина голова пошла кругом. Он обмяк (Войнович 4). "But I didn't do it on purpose." "That's just what's going to save you," explained Luzhin. "Had you done it on purpose, we'd have you shot." Ermolkin's head was spinning. His body slackened (4a). ♦ ...Я наелся... до того наелся, что голова пошла кругом, меня качало, как пьяного... (Кузнецов 1). I ate and ate, to the point when my head was going round and I was swaying like a drunk... (1b).

2. s.o. loses the ability to think clearly (because he has too many concerns, too many things to do, is under the influence of too many impressions etc): у Х-а голова идёт кругом ≃ **X's head is in a whirl ⟨a daze etc⟩; X's head is whirling ⟨spinning etc⟩; thing Y makes X's head spin ⟨whirl etc⟩.**

«Уж не знаю, право, как и быть, — жаловалась Варвара. — Поверите ли, голова кругом идёт» (Сологуб 1). "I really don't know what to do," complained Varvara....."Believe me, my head's in a whirl" (1a). ♦ «Как Керенского звали?» — «Александр Фёдорович». — «Во. А царь был Николай Александрович. Стало быть, евонный [*ungrammat* = его] сын». У Талдыкина голова кругом пошла (Войнович 2). "What was Kerensky's name?" "Alexander Fyodorovich." "Ya see! And the tsar was Nikolai Alexandrovich. So, he had to be Kerensky's son." Taldikin's head was whirling (2a). ♦ [Кири:] Три дня всего прошло, как я управляю нашим проклятым островом, а... от этого жемчуга у меня голова кругом идёт (Булгаков 1). [K.:] Only three days have passed since I've been running this damned island, and...my head is spinning because of those pearls! (1a).

Г-205 • ГОЛОВА́ НА ПЛЕЧА́Х *у кого;* ИМЕ́ТЬ ГО́ЛОВУ НА ПЛЕЧА́Х *both coll* [VP$_{subj}$ with быть∅ or быть (1st var.); VP, subj: human (2nd var.); usu. pres; fixed WO] s.o. is intelligent, sharp, sensible: у X-а (есть) голова на плечах ≃ **X has a good head (on his shoulders); X has a brain ⟨has brains⟩ (in his head); X has (plenty of) common sense.**

«Голова у тебя на плечах есть, я твой формуляр библиотечный смотрел да и так за тобой приглядывал» (Максимов 2). "You have a good head on your shoulders. I've been looking at your library card, and I've been keeping an eye on you in general" (2a). ♦ «Приказ приказом, — возразил Максим, — а у нас тоже есть головы на плечах» (Стругацкие 2). "An order is an order," retorted Maxim. "OK. But we, too, have brains in our heads" (2a).

Г-206 • ГОЛОВА́ ПУ́ХНЕТ/РАСПУ́ХЛА *у кого (от чего) coll* [VP$_{subj}$; usu. impfv; usu. this WO] s.o. loses the ability to think clearly because of excessive work, concerns, noise etc, s.o. is in a state of extreme mental exertion: у X-а голова пухнет (от Y-а) ≃ **Y makes X's head spin ⟨reel⟩; X's head is spinning ⟨reeling⟩; Y gives X a headache; X feels like ⟨that, as if⟩ his head is about to explode (from Y).**

«...Пишут, пишут... конгресс, немцы какие-то... Голова пухнет» (Булгаков 11). "They...write and write all that crap... all about some congress and some Germans....Makes my head reel" (11b).

Г-207 • ГОЛОВА́ САДО́ВАЯ *highly coll, disapprov, occas. humor* [NP; usu. sing; usu. vocative; fixed WO] a slow-witted, inattentive, doltish person: **cabbagehead ⟨cabbage-head⟩; blockhead; dimwit; numskull ⟨numbskull⟩; dummy; lummox.**

«Иди, собирайся, голова садовая!» (Максимов 2). "Go on, pack your things, cabbage-head" (2a). ♦ «У всех ребятишки. А заём-то зачем, голова садова[я]? Чтобы этим самым ребятишкам хорошую жизнь устроить. Так?» (Абрамов 1). "Everyone has kids. What's the point of the Loan, numbskull? To give these very kids a good life. Right?" (1a).

Г-208 • ГОЛОВА́ СОЛО́МОЙ ⟨МЯКИ́НОЙ, ТРУХО́Й⟩ НАБИ́ТА *у кого all highly coll, rude* [VP$_{subj}$ with быть∅; pres only] s.o. is stupid, muddleheaded, slow-witted: у X-а голова соломой набита ≃ **X has mush for brains.**

Г-209 • ГОЛОВА́ ⟨БАШКА́ *substand*⟩ ТРЕЩИ́Т ⟨РАСКА́ЛЫВАЕТСЯ, РАЗЛА́МЫВАЕТСЯ⟩ *у кого coll* [VP$_{subj}$] s.o. has a very bad headache (usu. caused by drinking, fatigue, or overwork): у X-а голова трещит ≃ **X's head is splitting ⟨throbbing, pounding⟩; X has a splitting ⟨throbbing, pounding⟩ headache.**

[Фёдор:] Я не вникаю в денежные вопросы, мама. У меня от одной работы голова трещит (Розов 2). [F.:] I don't go into these money questions, mother. My head's splitting with the amount of work I have to get through (2a).

Г-210 • ГОРЯ́ЧАЯ ГОЛОВА́ *coll* [NP; usu. appos or subj-compl with быть∅ (subj: human); fixed WO] a quick-tempered, easily excited, impetuous person: **hothead; (be) hotheaded ⟨hot-tempered, hot-blooded⟩.**

«Я просил вас, герр Майер, не говорить со мною на эту тему». — «Я не думал, что вы такая горячая голова», — ответил Майер... (Федин 1). "I requested you, Herr Maier, not to talk to me about this subject!" "I didn't think you were such a hothead," replied Maier... (1a).

Г-211 • ДУБО́ВАЯ ГОЛОВА́ *highly coll, rude;* ДУБО́ВАЯ БАШКА́ *substand, rude* [NP] a dull, obtuse person: **blockhead; dolt; numskull; dumbbell; meathead.**

[Ox:] Что же ты, дубовая башка, так дерёшься? (Сухово-Кобылин 3). [O.:] What are you brawling about, blockhead? (3a).

Г-212 • ДУ́РЬЯ ⟨МЯКИ́ННАЯ⟩ ГОЛОВА́ *highly coll, rude;* ДУ́РЬЯ ⟨МЯКИ́ННАЯ⟩ БАШКА́ *substand, rude* [NP; usu. vocative] a stupid person, fool: **cabbagehead; bonehead; fathead; featherbrain; dumbbell; goof; nincompoop.**

«Что это? Постой, что это?» — «Не что, а кто, дурья голова» (Грекова 2). "What's that? Stop, what's that?" "Not what, but who, fathead" (2a). ♦ «Не будем об этом говорить». — «Ну и о баране нечего говорить». — «Да пойми ты, дурья голова», — опять начал объяснять Илья (Абрамов 1). "Let's not discuss it." "Then there's no point discussing the sheep either." "Can't you understand, you featherbrain?" Ilya started to explain again (1a). ♦ «Чего мелешь... дурья голова? — возмущённо перебил один [казак]. — Ты неграмотный, так думаешь, и всем темно, как тебе?» (Шолохов 3). "What are you babbling about, you goof?" another Cossack interrupted indignantly. "You can't read, so you think we're all as ignorant as you are?" (3a).

Г-213 • ДЫРЯ́ВАЯ ГОЛОВА́ *coll* [NP] **1.** [usu. appos, vocative, or subj-compl with быть∅ (subj: human)] a person who has a very bad memory, is absent-minded, forgetful: **scatterbrain; featherbrain.**

2. ~ *у кого* [VP$_{subj}$ with быть∅; pres only] s.o. has a very bad memory, is forgetful, absent-minded: у X-а дырявая голова ≃ **X is scatterbrained; X has a brain ⟨a head⟩ like a sieve.**

Г-214 • ЗАБУБЁННАЯ ГОЛОВА́ *coll* ⟨ГОЛО́ВУШКА *folk*⟩ [NP; often appos; usu. this WO] a reckless, hotheaded person: **daredevil; hotspur; plucky devil; madcap.**

Г-215 • КРУ́ЖИТСЯ/ЗАКРУЖИ́ЛАСЬ ГОЛОВА́ *чья, у кого (от чего);* ЗАКРУЖИ́ЛОСЬ В ГОЛОВЕ́ *у кого (от чего)* [VP$_{subj}$ (1st var.); VP, impers (2nd var.)] **1.** s.o. experiences dizziness (from exhaustion, overwork etc): у X-а кружится голова (от Y-а) ≃ **X's head is swimming ⟨spinning, reeling etc⟩; X's head is going (a)round; Y is making X's head swim ⟨spin, reel etc⟩; X feels ⟨is getting⟩ dizzy ⟨lightheaded⟩.**

Дина глянула вниз, и у неё закружилась голова — так ей показалось высоко (Кузнецов 1). Dina looked down and her head swam, she seemed to be so high up (1b). ♦ «Давай поцелуемся мы с тобой по-братскому [*ungrammat* = по-братски], без злобы. И — ещё одну [бутылку твина] трахнем». — «Больше не буду. Голова у меня и так чего-то кружится» (Семёнов 1). "Let's embrace one another like brothers, without malice. And — let's have another one." "No more for me. My head's going round a bit as it is" (1a). ♦ Воспоминание о Средней Азии отложилось в его памяти одним цветовым пятном: нежно-зелёное на голубом с ослепительными вкраплениями белого. И все города рифмуются... а в них — устремлённые ввысь минареты и башни над убогой бескрылостью плоских кровель... И всё это залито прозрачным и вязким, словно желе, зноем, от которого до обморочности сладко кружится голова (Максимов 2). Central Asia is recorded in his memory as one splash of color: pale green on sky-blue with dazzling flecks of white. And cities with names that all rhyme with each other...; in them minarets and towers soaring above humble, earthbound, flat roofs....And all of it bathed in a sticky, translucent, sultry heat that makes your head reel deliciously until you nearly faint (2a).

2. s.o. is so overwhelmed (by success, troubles, responsibilities etc) that he loses the ability to think clearly, evaluate things soberly: у X-а кружится голова (от Y-а) ≃ **X's head is spinning ⟨swimming, in a whirl etc⟩; Y makes X's head spin ⟨swim, reel etc⟩; X feels lightheaded ⟨dizzy, giddy⟩.**

[Аркадина:] Как меня в Харькове принимали, батюшки мои, до сих пор голова кружится! (Чехов 6). [A.:] How I was received in Kharkov! My gracious, my head's still in a whirl! (6c). ♦

...Он [Маршак] завёл штат младших редакторов, постепенно продвигая их в старшие, которые точили, шлифовали и подпиливали каждую фразу, каждое слово, каждый оборот... У них кружилась голова от мысли, что они собственными руками делают литературу (Мандельштам 2). ...He [Marshak] created a special staff of junior editors, gradually promoting them to senior status, who polished, filed, and honed every sentence, every word and turn of phrase....The thought that they were creating literature with their own hands fairly made their heads spin... (2a).

Г-216 • **ОТЧА́ЯННАЯ ГОЛОВА́** *coll* ⟨**ГОЛО́ВУШКА** *folk*, **БАШКА́** *substand*⟩ [NP; usu. this WO] a recklessly bold person: **a (real) daredevil; a plucky devil; a hotspur; a madcap.**

«...Вот пример: в нашей-то части, старуху-то убили. Ведь уж, кажется, отчаянная башка, среди бела дня на все риски рискнул, одним чудом спасся...» (Достоевский 3). "Take, for example, this old woman who was murdered in our precinct. It looks like the work of a real daredevil; he risked it all in broad daylight, got away only by a miracle..." (3c). ♦ «Жалкие люди!» — сказал я штабс-капитану, указывая на наших грязных хозяев... «Преглупый народ, — отвечал он. — ...Наши кабардинцы или чеченцы, хотя разбойники, голыши, зато отчаянные башки, а у этих и к оружию никакой охоты нет...» (Лермонтов 1). "They're a pathetic lot," I said, pointing to our filthy hosts...."As stupid as they come!" he replied. "...Our friends the Kabardians or the Chechens—robbers and vagabonds they may be, but they're plucky devils for all that. Why, this lot don't even bother about weapons" (1c).

Г-217 • **ПУСТА́Я ГОЛОВА́** *coll* ⟨**БАШКА́** *substand*⟩ [NP]
1. [usu. appos, vocative, or subj-compl with быть$_\varnothing$ (subj: human); fixed WO] a stupid, empty-headed person: **blockhead; knucklehead; cabbagehead; dunce; dummy.**

[Кречинский:] Ты мне не финти, пустая голова! [Расплюев:] Чем же я пустая голова? За что вы меня каждодневно ругаете? (Сухово-Кобылин 2). [K.:] None of your tricks, you blockhead. [R.:] Why am I a blockhead? Why do you keep raking me over the coals day after day? (2a).

2. ~ *у кого* [usu. VP$_{subj}$ with быть$_\varnothing$; pres only] s.o. is stupid, empty-headed: у Х-а пустая голова ≃ **X is a blockhead ⟨a knucklehead, a cabbagehead, a dunce, a dummy, a dimwit⟩; X is dimwitted.**

Г-218 • **СВЕ́ТЛАЯ ГОЛОВА́** [NP] **1.** *occas. iron* [fixed WO] an intelligent, lucid, logical person: **a brilliant ⟨sharp, fine⟩ mind; [in limited contexts] have a brilliant ⟨sharp, fine, very good⟩ mind.**

...Оба они [Маша и Митя]... были направлены... на один и тот же завод, но в разные бригады... Развёрнутое красное знамя часто делилось между этими бригадами, пока чья-то светлая голова не додумалась до такой умной идеи [устроить комсомольскую свадьбу двух передовых бригадиров] (Попов 1). They both [Masha and Mitya]...were sent to the same factory but to different work brigades....The unfurled red banner passed back and forth, again and again, between these two work brigades until some brilliant mind came up with an extremely clever idea [to arrange a Young Communist wedding of the two exemplary team leaders] (1a). ♦ Безусловно, дедушка Рахленко — мудрейший человек, светлая голова... (Рыбаков 1). Without doubt, grandfather Rakhlenko was a very wise man, he had a very good mind... (1a).

2. ~ *у кого, обладать светлой головой и т. п.* [usu. VP$_{subj}$ with быть$_\varnothing$ or obj] s.o. has plenty of intelligence, the ability to think logically: у Х-а светлая голова ≃ **X has a brilliant ⟨sharp, fine, very good⟩ mind.**

«Какой светлой головой надо обладать, — продолжал Тенгиз, — ...чтобы в наше нелёгкое время прожить, нигде не работая на себя, а целиком отдавая свою жизнь за наши с вами интересы» (Искандер 3). "What a fine mind he [Uncle Sandro] must have," Tengiz continued, "in order to get by in our difficult times without working for a living, devoting his life wholly to your interests and mine" (3a).

Г-219 • **СВОЯ́ ГОЛОВА́ НА ПЛЕЧА́Х** *у кого coll* [VP$_{subj}$ with быть$_\varnothing$ or быть; usu. pres; fixed WO] s.o. is capable of figuring sth. out, making a decision, planning a course of action etc independently (when used in refer. to o.s., expresses one's reluctance to follow another's advice, one's refusal to tolerate another's interference etc): у Х-а (есть) своя голова на плечах ≃ **X can think for himself; X can decide sth. ⟨figure sth. out, work sth. out etc⟩ on his own ⟨by himself, alone⟩.**

Г-220 • **ТЯЖЁЛАЯ ГОЛОВА́** *у кого (от чего)* [VP$_{subj}$ with быть$_\varnothing$] s.o. has a feeling of sluggishness, heaviness in the head as a result of fatigue, indisposition, intoxication etc: голова у Х-а тяжёлая ≃ **X's head is ⟨feels⟩ heavy; X's head is ⟨feels⟩ like lead; X's head feels as if ⟨like⟩ it weighs a ton.**

Она не понимает, что всю ночь мне снился сон и что сейчас голова у меня тяжёлая и мысли тяжёлые, неповоротливые (Михайловская 1). She doesn't know about the dream I had all night long and that now my head is heavy and my thoughts heavy and sluggish (1a).

Г-221 • **У́МНАЯ ГОЛОВА́** ⟨**ГОЛО́ВУШКА**⟩ *coll, occas. iron* [NP; often appos or vocative; fixed WO] a sensible, intelligent person: **a clever one ⟨fellow, girl etc⟩; (a real ⟨a total, you⟩) brain; (one is) so clever.**

«Поздравляю, господин исправник. Ай да бумага! По этим приметам немудрено будет вам отыскать Дубровского. Да кто же не среднего роста, у кого не русые волосы, не прямой нос да не карие глаза!.. Нечего сказать, умные головушки приказные» (Пушкин 1). "I congratulate you, Mr Chief of police. What a document! It'll be easy to trace Dubrovsky from such a description! Who is not of medium height? Who has not got fair hair — or a straight nose, or brown eyes?...I must say, these officials are clever fellows!" (1b). ♦ [Шабельский:] Для всех ты, гениальная башка, изобретаешь и учишь всех, как жить, а меня хоть бы раз поучил... Поучи-ка, умная голова, укажи выход... (Чехов 4). [Sh.:] You're such a mastermind, always concocting plans for everyone, teaching everyone how to live, but you've never yet taught me anything....Come on, give me an idea, if you're so clever, show me a way out (4a).

Г-222 • **ЧУГУ́ННАЯ ГОЛОВА́** *coll* [NP] **1.** *rude.* Also: **ЧУГУ́ННЫЕ МОЗГИ́** *coll, rude* [usu. appos, vocative, or subj-compl with copula (subj: human)] a very stupid, slow-witted person: **lamebrain; numskull; bonehead; blockhead; dolt.**

2. ~ *(у кого)* [VP$_{subj}$ with быть$_\varnothing$ or obj] s.o. has a feeling of sluggishness, heaviness in the head: голова (у Х-а) была чугунная ≃ **X's head was ⟨felt⟩ heavy; X's head was ⟨felt⟩ like lead; X's head felt as if ⟨like⟩ it weighed a ton;** ‖ ходить ⟨лежать и т. п.⟩ с чугунной головой ≃ **(walk ⟨lie etc⟩ around) with a leaden head.**

Г-223 • **ШАЛЬНА́Я ГОЛОВА́** *coll* [NP; usu. appos, vocative, or subj-compl with copula (subj: human)] an impulsive, reckless person: **daredevil; hotspur; madcap.**

Г-224 • **В ГОЛОВА́Х** *сидеть, висеть, быть$_\varnothing$ и т. п.*; **В ГО́ЛОВЫ** ⟨**-у**⟩ *класть, ставить что и т. п.* [PrepP; Invar; adv] at or near the spot where the head is laid when one lies down: **at the head of the bed; by ⟨at, near⟩ s.o.'s head.**

В шалаше... за перегородкою, раненый Дубровский лежал на походной кровати. Перед ним на столике лежали его пистолеты, а сабля висела в головах (Пушкин 1). In the hut...on a camp bed behind a partition, lay the wounded Dubrovskii. His pistols sat on a small table next to him and his saber hung on the wall at the head of the bed (1a).

Г-225 • О ДВУ́Х ГОЛОВА́Х *obs, folk* [PrepP; Invar; usu. subj-compl with быть∅ (subj: human); usu. in rhetorical questions or neg; fixed WO] (usu. of a recklessly brave person, one who is ready to risk his life) it is as if one were protected from death (*by extension* from punishment etc): X о двух головах, что ли? ≃ **X acts as if he had nine lives ⟨were immune to death, were indestructible⟩; what, does X think he has nine lives?;** ‖ X не о двух головах ≃ **X doesn't have nine lives; X isn't immune to death; X isn't indestructible.**

Г-226 • ВЕРТЕ́ТЬСЯ В ГОЛОВЕ́ *у кого* [VP; subj: abstr; usu. pres or past] **1.** (of sth. well-known, familiar, that escapes s.o.'s memory at a given moment) not to come to s.o.'s mind despite the feeling that he is about to recall it: X вертится у Y-а в голове ≃ **X is on ⟨at⟩ the tip of Y's tongue.**

2. to come to mind continually, recur in s.o.'s thoughts: X вертится у Y-а в голове ≃ **X is ⟨keeps⟩ running ⟨going⟩ through Y's head ⟨mind⟩; X keeps popping into Y's head.**

Я, например, даже думаю иногда одними ругательствами. Они всё время вертятся в голове (Кожевников 1). For example, sometimes I think in nothing but curse words. They're always running through my head (1a).

Г-227 • МУТИ́ТСЯ/ПОМУТИ́ЛОСЬ В ГОЛОВЕ́ *у кого* *coll* [VP; impers] s.o. experiences dizziness, is in a state of semiconsciousness (from fatigue, weakness, anxiety): у X-а помутилось в голове ≃ **X's head was swimming ⟨spinning etc⟩; X was ⟨felt⟩ dizzy ⟨lightheaded⟩.**

[Лопахин:] Погодите, господа, сделайте милость, у меня в голове помутилось, говорить не могу... (Чехов 2). [L.:] Kindly wait a moment, ladies and gentlemen, my head is swimming, I can't talk... (2a).

Г-228 • НЕ УКЛА́ДЫВАЕТСЯ ⟨НЕ УМЕЩА́ЕТСЯ *rare*⟩ **В ГОЛОВЕ́** (*чьей, у кого*) **⟨В СОЗНА́НИИ** (*чьём, у кого*)⟩ [VP] **1.** [subj: a clause, это, or abstr. (usu. мысль о том, что...); if subj is a clause, it usu. follows the idiom; usu. impfv pres or past; affirm with the opposite meaning is rare] (sth. is) unacceptable, incomprehensible (used to express s.o.'s inability to understand the logic of sth., unwillingness to accept some fact as true etc): X не укладывается у Y-а в голове ≃ **X is beyond Y ⟨Y's comprehension⟩; Y cannot fathom ⟨understand, comprehend⟩ X; Y finds it difficult to accept X;** [in limited contexts] **Y just ⟨simply⟩ cannot believe X.**

...Одно только никак не укладывалось у Лёши в голове — зачем отцу нужно было выводить из строя эту самую печь? Неужели он думал, что вместе с этой печью рухнет всё советское государство? (Войнович 2). ...There was just one thing Lyosha found difficult to accept—why had his father wanted to put that particular furnace out of commission? Could he really have thought the loss of this one furnace would cause the entire Soviet state to collapse? (2a). ♦ [author's usage] В Калинине я прожила до самой эвакуации, почти два года, и никто меня не тронул, хотя в моем деле лежал неиспользованный ордер на мой арест... В её [Татьяны Васильевны] голове не могло уложиться, что «они» [чекисты] хотели кого-то взять и не взяли, потому что не нашли... (Мандельштам 1). I lived in Kalinin nearly two years—right till the evacuation after the war broke out—and I was left alone, even though the warrant for my arrest must still have been lying, unused, in my file....She [Tatiana Vasilievna] just could not believe that "they" [the Chekists] would ever fail to arrest anyone they were after, and that I had escaped because I had not been there when they came (1a).

2. *coll* [subj: это, often omitted; neg impfv only; used as Interj] used to express indignation, incredulity, incomprehension etc: **it's ⟨that's⟩ beyond me ⟨my comprehension⟩!; it's ⟨that's⟩ beyond belief!; it's ⟨that's⟩ incredible ⟨unbelievable, unthinkable, outrageous⟩!**

«Это не укладывается в голове! — воскликнула Лена, изумлённо вертя в руках газету. — Это чёрным по белому и всерьёз... После всех... философий, великих наук и литератур открыто наконец, что чрезмерное образование — зло» (Кузнецов 1). "It's incredible!" Lena exclaimed, bewildered, twisting the newspaper in her hands. "Here it is in black and white, in all seriousness. After...all the philosophers, the great scientists and writers, it is finally discovered that too much education is an evil" (1a).

Г-229 • УЛОЖИ́ТЬ В ГОЛОВЕ́ ⟨В СОЗНА́НИИ⟩ *что obs* [VP; subj: human; often infin compl of не мочь etc] to comprehend sth.: X не может уложить в голове Y ≃ **X cannot understand Y; Y is beyond X ⟨X's comprehension⟩.**

Г-230 • ХОДИ́ТЬ НА ГОЛОВЕ́ ⟨НА ГОЛОВА́Х⟩ *coll, usu. disapprov* [VP; subj: human or collect] (usu. of children) to behave mischievously, disobediently, make noise: X на голове ходит ≃ **X is making a racket ⟨a commotion⟩; X is raising ⟨making⟩ a ruckus; X is horsing around; X is going ⟨running⟩ wild;** [in limited contexts] **it's a three-ring circus.**

Г-231 • ШУМИ́Т/ЗАШУМЕ́ЛО В ГОЛОВЕ́ (*у кого*) [VP; impers] s.o. feels an aching, heavy sensation in his head (from intoxication, fatigue etc): у X-а шумит в голове (от Y-а) ≃ **X's head is pounding ⟨throbbing⟩ (from Y); there's a roaring ⟨X has a roar⟩ in X's head;** [indicating a light degree of intoxication] **X is fuzzy ⟨tipsy⟩.**

Я сказал, что мы пили за здоровье тёти Зины водку, а теперь надо выпить портвейна. В голове шумело, хотелось какого-то движения (Кожевников 1). I said that since we'd drunk to Aunt Zina with the vodka, now we should do it with the port. There was a roar in my head and I wanted some kind of action (1a). ♦ «...Вот что можно: предварительно закусить с ним [Обломовым] и выпить; он смородиновку-то любит. Как в голове зашумит, ты и мигни мне: я и войду с письмецом-то. Он и не посмотрит сумму, подпишет...» (Гончаров 1). "What you could do...would be to have a friendly snack with him [Oblomov] first; he's very fond of currant vodka. As soon as he gets a bit fuzzy, you can give me the sign, and I'll come in with the IOU. He won't even look at the amount, he'll just sign it..." (1b).

Г-232 • ГЛА́ДИТЬ/ПОГЛА́ДИТЬ ПО ГОЛО́ВКЕ ⟨ПО ГОЛОВЕ́ *rare*⟩ (*кого*) *coll* [VP; subj: human or collect] **1.** ~ (*за что*) [often in questions or neg] to praise s.o., show one's approval to s.o.: X погладил Y-а по головке ≃ **X gave Y a pat on the back; X patted Y on the back;** [in limited contexts] **X patted Y on the head ⟨gave Y a pat on the head⟩.**

«Если я, например, захочу быть императором... Или... взорву памятник Пушкину на Тверского бульвара... По головке погладите?» (Терц 7). "Suppose I took it into my head to become an emperor....or...to blow up the Pushkin Monument on the Tverskoy Boulevard....Would you pat me on the back for that?" (7a). ♦ [extended usage] «Что случилось?» — «Да что: жизнь трогает!» — «И слава богу!» — сказал Штольц. «Как слава богу! Если б она всё по голове гладила, а то пристаёт, как, бывало, в школе с смирным ученику забияки...» (Гончаров 1). "What's happened?" "Why, life doesn't leave me alone." "Thank goodness it doesn't!" said Stolz. "Thank goodness indeed! If it just went on patting me on the head, but it keeps pestering me just as naughty boys pester a quiet boy at school..." (1a).

2. ~ *за что* [neg only; usu. 3rd pers pl with indef. refer.; the verb is usu. in the final position] to punish s.o., hold s.o. responsible for sth.: X-а (за Y) по головке не погладят ≃ **they won't pat X on the back for (doing) Y; they won't be too happy with X for (doing) Y; X won't get a medal ⟨any medals, any praise,**

any thanks〉 for (doing) Y; [in limited contexts] **X can get (himself) into hot water for Y 〈for doing Y, because of Y〉.**

«Вы уже написали заявление?» – «Нет». – «И не пишите! – зашептала Кипарисова... – Не пишите, ради вашего сына. За такое заявление по головке не погладят» (Чуковская 1). "You've already written the appeal?" "No." "Then don't write any!" whispered Kiparisova....Don't write, for the sake of your son. They're not going to pat you on the back for an appeal like that..." (1a). ♦ «Я так рад, что не убил тебя... Не хватало только редактора „Курьера" убить. По головке бы за это не погладили» (Аксёнов 7). "I'm glad I didn't kill you....I don't think they would have been too happy with me for killing the editor of the *Courier*" (7a). ♦ «Я думаю, тебе как члену партии известно, что за такие вещи по голове не гладят»... (Дудинцев 1). "You, as a member of the Party, ought to know that you won't get any medals for a business like this"... (1a). ♦ «Что он [клоун] делает!? Нет, вы только посмотрите, что он делает!? Ведь за это по головке не погладят» (Максимов 3). "What's he [the clown] think he's doing? Just look at him – what on earth is he doing? He won't get any thanks for this" (3a). ♦ Мы уезжали в Армению, и мне не захотелось везти с собой единственный экземпляр «Четвёртой [прозы]». Время хоть и было нежнейшим, но за эту прозу О. М[андельштама] бы по головке не погладили (Мандельштам 1). When we left for Armenia, I did not want to take the only copy of "Fourth Prose." Although the climate was very good at the moment, M[andelstam] could still have got into hot water because of it (1a).

Г-233 • С 〈В〉 БУЛА́ВОЧНУЮ ГОЛО́ВКУ [PrepP; these forms only; nonagreeing modif; fixed WO] very small, tiny: **the size of a pinhead.**

На ноге у Маши было крошечное, с булавочную головку пятнышко – след укуса змеи. Masha had a tiny spot the size of a pinhead on her leg – the final trace of a snakebite.

Г-234 • ВИСЕ́ТЬ НАД ГОЛОВО́Й [VP; subj: usu. abstr]
1. (of a disaster, death, sth. dangerous etc) to be imminent, threaten, impend: X висит над головой ≃ **X is looming (in the distance 〈on the horizon, in front of person Y〉); X is in the offing; X is hanging over person Y 〈over person Y's head〉.**

На фронте, где смерть постоянно висела над головой, он вёл себя геройски, а тюрьма его сломала. At the front, where death was constantly looming, he acted heroically, but prison broke him.

2. Also: **ВИСЕ́ТЬ НА НОСУ́** *coll* (of sth. that causes the person involved concern, sth. he does not have the time, means, or desire to handle) to need to be handled, done etc immediately, without delay, be imperative: X висит над головой ≃ **X is hanging over person Y 〈over person Y's head〉; X is staring person Y in the face.**

Обе соседки в бригаде строителей, самой лёгкой и аристократической на ОЛПе – не висит норма над головой, остаются в зоне (всегда можно словчить в барак погреться), а главное – постоянная работа... (Иоффе 1). Both my neighbors were on the construction team, the least onerous and the most "aristocratic" in the camp. No quotas hung over their heads, they stayed in the main zone (always possible to sneak into the barracks for a warm-up) and most important of all, the work was permanent... (1a).

Г-235 • ВЫДАВА́ТЬ/ВЫ́ДАТЬ ГОЛОВО́Й *кого (кому) obs* [VP; subj: human] to give a person over to s.o. who will harm or mistreat him: X выдал Y-а головой (Z-у) ≃ **X turned 〈handed〉 Y over to Z; X delivered Y into Z's hands.**

Г-236 • ЗАПЛАТИ́ТЬ ГОЛОВО́Й *за что;* **ПОПЛА́ТИ́ТЬСЯ ГОЛОВО́Й 〈ЖИ́ЗНЬЮ〉** *(за что)* [VP; subj: human] to perish, be put to death (as retribution for sth.): X заплатил головой за Y ≃ **X paid for Y with X's life.**

Никто не сомневался, что за эти стихи он [Мандельштам] поплатится жизнью (Мандельштам 1). ...None of us doubted that for verse like this he [Mandelstam] would pay with his life (1a).

Г-237 • ОТВЕЧА́ТЬ/ОТВЕ́ТИТЬ ГОЛОВО́Й *за кого-что* [VP; subj: human or collect; usu. pres or fut] to bear full responsibility for s.o. or sth. and be the one to receive harsh punishment (sometimes even death) should s.o. or sth. fail (may be used as a threat): X отвечает за Y-а головой ≃ **the responsibility for Y is on X's head;** ‖ [used as a threat] ты отвечаешь головой за Y-а! ≃ **(if anything goes wrong** etc**) you'll pay 〈answer〉 with your life!; Y is on your head!**

«За каждую подлость по отношению ко мне или к моим друзьям вы ответите головой» (Стругацкие 4). "For any foul play, involving myself or any of my friends, you'll have to pay with your own life!" (4a). ♦ «Запри их [пьяных начальников], пускай... проспятся, чтобы на людях в таком виде не показывались, головой отвечаешь, Самохин, понял?» (Максимов 1). "Lock them [the drunk bosses] in. Let them sleep it off...and don't let them appear in public looking like that. It's on your head, Samokhin, do you understand me?" (1a).

Г-238 • РУЧА́ТЬСЯ/ПОРУЧИ́ТЬСЯ ГОЛОВО́Й *(за кого-что)* [VP; subj: human; often foll. by a что-clause] to assure (s.o. of sth.), guarantee (sth.) emphatically, be prepared to be held accountable (for s.o. or sth.): X ручается головой (за Y-а) ≃ **X vouches for Y with X's life; X would 〈is prepared to etc〉 stake 〈bet〉 his life on thing Y; X is willing to bet his life that...; X swears that...; [in limited contexts] X says he'd stake his life on thing Y 〈bet his life that...〉; X is betting his reputation on Y.**

Много ещё говорил полковник о том, как привести людей к благополучию... Он ручался головой, что если только одеть половину русских мужиков в немецкие штаны, – науки возвысятся, торговля подымется, и золотой век настанет в России (Гоголь 3). The colonel had a great deal more to say about how people were to achieve happiness and prosperity....He said he'd bet his life that if half of the Russian peasants were dressed in German trousers, the level of culture would rise, trade would improve, and the golden age would dawn in Russia (3a). ♦ Я ручаюсь головой, что, если бы я привёл откуда-нибудь свежего человека на репетицию [«Чёрного снега»], он пришёл бы в величайшее изумление (Булгаков 12). I swear that if I were to bring a layman into a rehearsal [of *Black Snow*] he would be amazed (12a).

Г-239 • С ГОЛОВО́Й[1] *coll* [PrepP; Invar] **1. парень, малый, человек** и т. п. ~ *approv* [subj-compl with copula (subj: human) or nonagreeing modif] very smart, sensible, capable: **have 〈with〉 a good head on one's shoulders; have 〈with〉 brains 〈a brain, smarts〉.**

«Ты, парень, вижу – с головой, понимаешь, что – к чему» (Максимов 3). "I can see you've got a head on your shoulders, boy. You understand things" (3a). ♦ Подобрал он [Шутиков], конечно, толковых людей. Люди были с головой (Дудинцев 1). Certainly he [Shutikov] had picked highly competent men for this, men with brains (1a).

2. [adv] (to do sth.) sensibly, intelligently: **use 〈using〉 one's head 〈brain(s)〉.**

«Работаю безотказно. В своём деле спец не из последних... Работаю с головой...» (Копелев 1). "I work nonstop. In my field I'm not the least of specialists....I use my head" (1a).

Г-240 • С ГОЛОВО́Й[2] [PrepP; Invar; adv (intensif)] **1.** ~ **уйти, окунуться, погрузиться** *во что,* **увязнуть** *в чём,* **отдаться** *чему* и т. п. (to give o.s. over to sth.) wholly, fully: X с головой ушёл в Y ≃ **X became completely absorbed in Y; X became thoroughly 〈totally〉 engrossed in Y; X plunged 〈threw himself〉 into Y.**

Он [Королёв] с головой окунулся в проектирование сразу двух объектов — ракеты и планера с жидкотопливным ракетным двигателем (Владимиров 1). He [Korolyov] became completely absorbed in the design of two machines at the same time — a rocket and a glider equipped with a liquid-fuel jet motor (1a). ♦ ...К коммунизму он [Лежан] пришёл путём долгих размышлений, а сделав выводы, с головой окунулся в повседневную политическую работу (Эренбург 1). He [Lejean] had accepted Communism after long reflection, but had then plunged into everyday political activity (1a).

2. выдавать ~ *кого,* often **себя** [subj: abstr or concr (var. without себя), or human (var. with себя] (to reveal s.o.'s or one's own involvement in sth.) conclusively, leaving no room for doubt: X выдал Y-а с головой ≃ **X gave Y away completely; X was a dead giveaway; X betrayed Y;** ‖ Y выдал себя с головой ≃ **Y gave himself away completely; Y betrayed himself.**

Миша утверждал, что письмо написано не им, но стиль выдавал его с головой. Misha asserted that he wasn't the one who wrote the letter, but the style was a dead giveaway. ♦ ...Через несколько дней после этого разговора был ещё случай, когда он [Едигей] выдал себя с головой и долго каялся, мучился после этого... (Айтматов 2). A few days after this conversation, there was an occasion when he [Yedigei] gave himself away completely, and he regretted it and suffered from it for a long time afterwards... (2a). ♦ Лёва угощал и, симулируя беспечность: о том, о сём, — всё подбирался к цели. И когда, наконец, не узнавая свой голос, сразу выдав себя с головой (хотя все силы его были направлены, чтобы вопрос был безразличен и между прочим), всё-таки задал его, то неповторимая улыбочка вдруг подёрнула губы Митишатьева... (Битов 2). He [Lyova] bought the drinks and all the while—feigning unconcern, talking of this and that—kept sneaking up on his goal. When at last, not recognizing his own voice, betraying himself at once (though he bent every effort to make his question indifferent and casual)—when he did ask it, Mitishatyev's lips suddenly twitched in an inimitable little smile... (2a).

Г-241 • С НЕПОКРЫ́ТОЙ ГОЛОВО́Й [PrepP; Invar; often subj-compl with copula (subj: human); fixed WO] without a head covering: **with one's head bare ⟨uncovered⟩; bareheaded; without a hat; with nothing ⟨not wearing anything⟩ on one's head.**

...В скором времени на лестнице появился Ефим в дублёнке и красном шарфе, с непокрытою головой (Войнович 6). Shortly thereafter, Yefim appeared in a sheepskin coat, a red muffler, and with his head bare (6a).

Г-242 • ХОТЬ ГОЛОВО́Й ОБ СТЕ́НУ ⟨СТЕ́НКУ⟩ БЕ́ЙСЯ *coll* [хоть + VP$_{imper}$; these forms only; usu. indep. or subord clause] (used to express despair, helplessness, or the inability to find a way out of a difficult, hopeless situation) I feel (he feels etc) desperate and unable to cope: **it's enough to make you ⟨me etc⟩ cry ⟨scream, climb the wall(s)⟩; it's more than one ⟨I etc⟩ can bear ⟨take, stand⟩.**

Г-243 • ЗАДАВА́ТЬ/ЗАДА́ТЬ ⟨ДАВА́ТЬ/ДАТЬ, УСТРА́ИВАТЬ/УСТРО́ИТЬ⟩ ГОЛОВОМО́ЙКУ *кому coll* [VP; subj: human] to scold s.o. severely, rebuke s.o. harshly: X задал Y-у головомойку ≃ **X gave Y a dressing-down ⟨a tongue-lashing, the business⟩; X bawled ⟨chewed⟩ Y out; X told Y off; X gave it to Y in spades ⟨but good⟩.**

Г-244 • ПОЛУЧА́ТЬ/ПОЛУЧИ́ТЬ ГОЛОВОМО́ЙКУ *coll* [VP; subj: human] to receive a scolding, harsh rebuke: X получил головомойку ≃ **X got a dressing-down ⟨a tongue-lashing⟩; X got bawled ⟨chewed⟩ out; X got it in spades ⟨but good⟩.**

Г-245 • ВБИВА́ТЬ/ВБИТЬ ⟨ВКОЛА́ЧИВАТЬ/ВКОЛОТИ́ТЬ, ВДА́ЛБЛИВАТЬ/ВДОЛБИ́ТЬ, ВТЕМЯ́-

ШИВАТЬ/ВТЕМЯ́ШИТЬ *substand*⟩ **В ГО́ЛОВУ** *coll* ⟨**В БАШКУ́** *substand*⟩ *кому что* [VP; subj: human] **1.** to make s.o. memorize or master sth. by using persistent repetition: X вбивает Y-у в голову Z ≃ **X keeps drumming ⟨pounding⟩ Z into Y's head ⟨into Y⟩; X keeps hammering ⟨beating⟩ Z into Y's head ⟨into Y⟩.**

Наши тюремщики: закрутить режим!.. Какие сейчас могут быть церемонии с врагами народа! Ведь война! Ведь фашисты! Тут действует, видимо, инерция клишированных формул, вбиваемых в головы с детства (Гинзбург 2). *Our jailers* were obsessed with tightening everything up. "What's the point of pussyfooting around with enemies of the people? There's a war on, after all, against the fascists!" This attitude was evidently the product of inertia; the inertia of set phrases, hammered into people's heads since childhood (2a).

2. [often foll. by a что-clause] to impress sth. on s.o. insistently, (to try to) convince s.o. of sth.: X вбил Y-у в голову Z ≃ **X got ⟨put, drove, knocked, hammered, beat, drummed, dinned⟩ Z into Y's head; X got Z through Y's head; [in limited contexts] X drove Z home to Y;** ‖ *Neg* X не может вбить Z Y-у в голову ≃ [usu. when said in anger about a futile attempt] **X can't knock ⟨hammer etc⟩ Z into Y's (thick) skull.**

«...Мне, признаюсь, одно больно: я надеялся именно теперь тесно и дружески сойтись с Аркадием, а выходит, что я остался позади, он ушёл вперёд, и понять мы друг друга не можем». — «Да почему он ушёл вперёд? И чем он от нас так уж очень отличается? — с нетерпением воскликнул Павел Петрович. — Это всё ему в голову синьор этот вбил, нигилист этот» (Тургенев 2). "...I confess it's very painful to me: just as I hoped to establish a real, close friendship with Arkady it turns out that I have been left behind; he's gone on ahead and we can't understand one another." "But why do you say he's gone on ahead? And wherein is he so different from us?" exclaimed Pavel Petrovich impatiently. "It's that *signor* who has put all these ideas into his head, that nihilist" (2e). ♦ «Большевики вдалбливают им в головы, что надо войну кончать, вернее, превращать её в гражданскую» (Шолохов 3). "The Bolsheviks keep drumming it into their heads that the war must be brought to an end, or rather, turned into a civil war" (3a). ♦ ...Поди, вдолби им [семидольцам] в головы, что Семён Иваныч Голосов... в известном отношении ничем не отличён от любого семидольца, достигшего двадцати двух лет (Федин 1). Just try to din it into their [the Semidolians'] heads that Semyon Ivanich Golosov...was in certain respects not a bit different from any Semidolian who had reached the age of twenty-two (1a). ♦ [Кречинский:] Разве я вам в платеже отказываю? Я прошу вас... подождать два, три дня... Или вы нарочно пришли дурака разыгрывать, что я вам не могу вдолбить в голову, что теперь, сию минуту, у меня денег нет и отдать их не могу!.. (Сухово-Кобылин 2). [K.:] Am I refusing to pay you? I'm merely asking you...to wait two or three days....Or have you come here deliberately to play the fool? Can't I knock it into that thick skull of yours that now, this minute, I don't have any money and I can't pay you back! (2b).

Г-246 • ВБИВА́ТЬ/ВБИТЬ ⟨ЗАБИРА́ТЬ/ЗАБРА́ТЬ, БРАТЬ/ВЗЯТЬ, ЗАБИВА́ТЬ/ЗАБИ́ТЬ, ВТЕМЯ́ШИВАТЬ/ВТЕМЯ́ШИТЬ *substand*⟩ **СЕБЕ́ В ГО́ЛОВУ** *coll* ⟨**В БАШКУ́** *substand*⟩ *что* [VP; subj: human; often foll. by a что-clause] to convince o.s. of sth. (usu. some idea that becomes fixed in one's head), adhere stubbornly to sth. (often a wrong or foolish notion or idea): X вбил себе в голову, что... ≃ **X got ⟨took⟩ it into his head that...; X got an idea ⟨a notion⟩ into his head that...; [in rude contexts only] X got ⟨took⟩ it into his (thick) skull ⟨head⟩ that...**

«Я тебя спрашиваю, как ты мог забрать такую нелепость себе в голову?» — повторил Обломов (Гончаров 1). "I ask you: how did you ever get such a preposterous idea into your head?" Oblomov repeated (1b). ♦ «Да, — угрюмо сказал Передонов, —

вы взяли себе в голову, что я никуда не гожусь, а я постоянно о гимназии забочусь» (Сологуб 1). "That's right," said the sullen Peredonov, "you've taken it into your head that I'm not good for anything, even though I am constantly concerned about the gymnasium" (1a). ♦ «Втемяшил себе в башку жениться, — он [Михаил] бросил короткий, разъярённый взгляд на Егоршу, — твоё дело» (Абрамов 1). "If you've got it into your skull to get married,"—he [Mikhail] cast a quick, furious look at Egorsha—"that's your business" (1a).

Г-247 • ВЕ́ШАТЬ/ПОВЕ́СИТЬ ⟨ОПУСКА́ТЬ/ОПУ-СТИ́ТЬ⟩ ГО́ЛОВУ coll [VP; subj: human] to become depressed, crestfallen, lose hope: X повесил голову ≃ **X lost heart; X was ⟨looked⟩ dejected ⟨downcast, discouraged, despondent, dispirited, down in the mouth⟩;** ‖ Neg Imper не вешай голову ≃ **keep your chin up!; cheer up!**

«Вчера папа будильник сломал и был в отчаянии. Последние часы в доме. Стал чинить, ковырял, ковырял, ничего не выходило. Часовщик на углу три фунта хлеба запросил, неслыханная цена... Папа совсем голову повесил» (Пастернак 1). "Yesterday Father broke the alarm clock...he was terribly upset, it was our only clock. He tried to repair it, he tinkered and tinkered with it, but he got nowhere. The clockmaker around the corner wanted a ridiculous price—three pounds of bread....Father was completely dejected" (1a). ♦ Вздумал он [Тентетников] было попробовать какую-то школу [для мужиков]... завести, но от этого вышла такая чепуха, что он и голову повесил; лучше было и не задумывать (Гоголь 3). He [Tentetnikov] attempted to set up some sort of school for his peasants but the outcome of it was so nonsensical that he was utterly discouraged—it would have been better had he not even thought of it! (3c).

Г-248 • ВЗБРЕДА́ТЬ/ВЗБРЕСТИ́ В ГО́ЛОВУ ⟨НА УМ, НА МЫСЛЬ⟩ кому coll [VP; impers or with subj: abstr (usu. что, ничего etc)] (of a thought, idea etc, occas. a strange or absurd one) to come to s.o. suddenly: X-у взбрело в голову ≃ **it came ⟨popped⟩ into X's head; it (suddenly) occurred to X; X got ⟨had⟩ an idea; X got the idea (to do sth.); [in limited contexts] X took ⟨got⟩ it into his head (to do sth.); X came up with the idea (to do sth.);** ‖ X говорит ⟨пишет и т. п.⟩ что взбредёт в голову ≃ **X says ⟨writes etc⟩ whatever comes to mind ⟨into his head⟩; X says ⟨writes etc⟩ whatever he feels like;** ‖ ...когда ⟨где и т. п.⟩ X-у взбредёт в голову ≃ **whenever ⟨wherever etc⟩ X feels like it.**

Конечно, можно было бы привести иную, лучшую причину, но ничего иного не взбрело тогда [Чичикову] на ум (Гоголь 3). Of course he [Chichikov] might have given another and a better reason, but nothing else occurred to him at the moment (3c). ♦ «Поверьте мне, я хорошо знаю эту систему. У них никому ничего не взбредает в голову без указания свыше» (Войнович 2). "Believe me, I know the system. Nobody gets any ideas without orders from above" (2a). ♦ ...С самого начала была полная уверенность в том, что никому в голову не взбредёт этими свободами воспользоваться (Зиновьев 1). ...From the very beginning there was complete certainty that no one would ever take it into his head to make use of these freedoms (1a). ♦ ...Там [в Советском Союзе] не хватает... одной важной вещи — свободы... Я говорю вообще о свободе. В том числе свободе не ходить на эти митинги и собрания, говорить что хочешь, писать что на ум взбредёт, а если всё опостылело, плюнуть и уехать в Принстон, Кембридж, Мюнхен... (Войнович 1). ...There is something lacking there [in the Soviet Union] that does matter—freedom....What I mean here is freedom in general. Including the freedom not to attend rallies and assemblies, the freedom to say what you want, to write whatever comes to mind, and if it all comes to nothing, to kiss it goodbye and go off to Princeton, Cambridge, Munich... (1a). ♦ ...Самым невероятным мне всегда казалось именно это: как тогдашняя — пусть даже зачаточная — государственная власть могла допустить, что люди жили без всякого подобия нашей

Скрижали... вставали и ложились спать когда им взбредёт в голову... (Замятин 1). ...Most incredible of all, it seems to me, is that the state authority of that time—no matter how rudimentary—could allow men to live without anything like our Table...getting up and going to bed whenever they felt like it (1a).

Г-249 • ГО́ЛОВУ ПРОЗАКЛА́ДЫВАЮ ⟨готов ПРОЗАКЛА́ДЫВАТЬ⟩ coll [VP; subj: я (often omitted); these forms only; usu. foll. by a что-clause; fixed WO] I assure, guarantee (that sth. will happen, s.o. will do sth. etc): **I'd ⟨I'll⟩ stake ⟨bet⟩ my life.**

«Вы рассмотрите: вот, например, каретник Михеев! ведь больше никаких экипажей и не делал, как только рессорные... А Пробка Степан, плотник! Я голову прозакладаю [ungrammat = прозакладываю], если вы где сыщете такого мужика» (Гоголь 3). "Now, just have a look. Take Mikheyev, the wheelwright, for instance. He never made a carriage that wasn't on springs....And Stepan Probka, the carpenter. I'll stake my life you'd never find another peasant like him" (3a).

Г-250 • ДАВА́ТЬ/ДАТЬ ГО́ЛОВУ ⟨РУ́КУ⟩ НА ОТСЕЧЕ́НИЕ (кому) coll [VP; subj: human; usu. 1st pers sing pres or fut, or infin with готов, мочь etc; usu. foll. by a что-clause] to assert, vouch for sth. with absolute confidence, conviction: даю голову на отсечение, что... ≃ **I'd bet ⟨stake⟩ my life that... ⟨on it⟩; I'd bet my right arm that...**

Не дам голову на отсечение, но не исключено, что КГБ узнал о моей книге (Амальрик 1). I wouldn't bet my life on it, but I think it quite possible that the KGB found out about my book (1a). ♦ «Ну что же мне сказать, — ответил Юра, беспокойно заёрзал по стулу, встал, прошёлся и снова сел. — Во-первых, завтра вам станет лучше, — есть признаки, даю вам голову на отсечение» (Пастернак 1). "Well, what is there for me to say?" replied Yura. He fidgeted on his chair, got up, paced the room, and sat down again. "In the first place, you'll feel better tomorrow. There are clear indications—I'd stake my life on it—that you've passed the crisis" (1a). ♦ «Голову отдам на отсечение, они в этом своём заведении наверняка принимали и высшее московское начальство» (Зиновьев 2). "I'd bet my right arm that some of the biggest bosses from Moscow have been invited to enjoy the delights of their establishment" (2a).

Г-251 • ЗАБИВА́ТЬ/ЗАБИ́ТЬ ГО́ЛОВУ coll; **ЗАБИВА́ТЬ/ЗАБИ́ТЬ МОЗГИ́** substand [VP; subj: human] **1.** ~ кому чем to overload s.o.'s (or one's own) memory with much information or knowledge, often unnecessary: X забивает Y-у голову Z-ом ≃ **X fills ⟨stuffs⟩ Y's head ⟨mind⟩ with Z; X stuffs ⟨fills⟩ Y's head full of Z; X clutters (up) Y's mind with Z.**

«Ну и дед у тебя! — искренне подивился солдат. — Интересный дед. Только забивает он тебе голову всякой чепухой» (Айтматов 1). "You've quite a grandpa, haven't you!" the soldier said admiringly. "An interesting grandpa. But he fills your head with all sorts of nonsense" (1a). "That's some grandfather you have," said the soldier with genuine wonder. "A very interesting grandfather. Only he stuffs your head with all kinds of rubbish" (1b).

2. to overload, burden o.s. with obligations or concerns regarding s.o. or sth.: X забивает (себе) голову Y-ом ≃ **X weighs himself down with Y.**

Г-252 • ПОЛОЖИ́ТЬ ⟨СЛОЖИ́ТЬ⟩ (СВОЮ́) ГО́ЛОВУ ⟨(СВОЙ) ГО́ЛОВЫ⟩ (за кого-что) lit [VP; subj: human; usu. pfv] to perish, lose or sacrifice one's life (for s.o. or sth.): X сложил голову (за Y-а) ≃ **X laid down his life (for Y); X gave (up) his life (for Y).**

Один [из её сыновей] умер блестяще, окружённый признанием врагов... хотя и не за своё дело сложил голову (Герцен 1). One [of her sons] died gloriously, amid the esteem of his enemies...though it was not for his own cause he laid down his life (1a).

♦ Другие в его [Юрочки] возрасте и в Берлине побывали, и чёрт знает ещё где («Кое-кто и голову там положил», — перебил его в этом месте Вадим Петрович, но он тут же ответил: «Положили, знаю, но было за что положить») (Некрасов 1). Other men of his [Yurochka's] age had been to Berlin and God knows where else ("Some of them gave their lives in Berlin," Vadim Petrovich interrupted him at this point, but Yurochka replied without hesitation: "They gave their lives, I know, but they had something to give them for") (1a).

Г-253 • КРУЖИ́ТЬ/ВСКРУЖИ́ТЬ ⟨ЗАКРУЖИ́ТЬ⟩ ГО́ЛОВУ *кому* [VP] **1.** [subj: abstr or human] to influence s.o. in such a way that he loses the ability to assess a situation sensibly; often, to make s.o. conceited: X вскружил Y-у голову ≃ **thing X ⟨person X's praise, person X's flattery etc⟩ turned Y's head ⟨went to Y's head, made Y's head spin, set Y's head in a whirl⟩; Y was giddy with thing X.**

Петербург и две-три аристократические гостиные вскружили ей [жене Огарёва] голову. Ей хотелось внешнего блеска, её тешило богатство (Герцен 2). Petersburg and two or three aristocratic drawing-rooms had turned her [Ogarev's wife's] head. She wished for outward glitter, she found pleasure in the thought of wealth (2a). ♦ Подхватившая Влада восхитительная лёгкость кружила ему голову, никогда ещё он не чувствовал себя таким уверенным и свободным (Максимов 2). The buoyant thrill which had seized Vlad made his head spin; never before had he felt so self-assured and so free (2a). ♦ Вместе с любовью иные чувства кружили голову Пьера (Эренбург 4). ...It was not only love that had set Pierre's head in a whirl (4a).

2. [subj: human] to infatuate s.o., cause s.o. to fall in love with one: X вскружил Y-у голову ≃ **X turned Y's head; X swept Y off Y's feet.**

«Тебе вскружил голову этот... как его? Твой француз. Платэ» (Свирский 1). "That Frenchman of yours, what's his name, Plate, has turned your head" (1a).

Г-254 • КРУТИ́ТЬ/ЗАКРУТИ́ТЬ ГО́ЛОВУ *кому coll* [VP; subj: human] to charm s.o. so that he or she falls in love with one: X закрутил Y-у голову ≃ **X turned Y's head; X made Y fall for X.**

Г-255 • ЛЕЗТЬ/ПОЛЕ́ЗТЬ В ГО́ЛОВУ *(кому)* [VP; subj: abstr (usu. мысли, чушь, вздор, глупости etc); more often impfv] (of certain thoughts, strange ideas, absurdities etc, as specified) to arise in s.o.'s consciousness again and again (usu. against the person's will): X лезет Y-у в голову ≃ **X keeps creeping ⟨popping⟩ into Y's head ⟨mind⟩; X keeps coming to mind; Y cannot get X out of Y's head ⟨mind⟩.**

«Еда и на ум не идёт, сон от меня бежит, всякие дурные мыслишки в голову лезут...» (Шолохов 1). "I couldn't even think of eating and couldn't sleep, and all sorts of black thoughts kept creeping into my head" (1b). ♦ ...Сегодня [Куницеру] всё лезла в голову утренняя дичь: и металлолом, и арбуз с ложкой, и глиняный бульдог вместо Нины Николаевны... (Аксёнов 6). Today...he [Kunitser] could not get this morning's strange happenings out of his head: the scrap metal, the watermelon and the spoon, the clay bulldog sitting in Nina Nikolayevna's place... (6a).

Г-256 • ЛОМА́ТЬ ⟨ПОЛОМА́ТЬ⟩ (СЕБЕ́) ГО́ЛОВУ *(над чем)* [VP; subj: human; usu. impfv; often impfv infin with зачем, незачем, не стоит, не надо etc] to think hard, trying to comprehend something complex or find a solution to a difficult problem: X ломает (себе) голову (над Y-ом) ≃ **X racks his brains (over Y); X cudgels his brains; X puzzles over Y;** ‖ *Neg Imper* не ломай себе голову (над Y-ом) ≃ **don't trouble your head (about Y).**

«Мы, знаешь, — заключил он [Сивак], — долго голову на правлении ломали, кто же это такой может быть?» (Макси-

мов 2). "Well," Sivak went on, "we at the farm office racked our brains for a long time wondering who that could be" (2a). ♦ Как ни ломают головы, определения поэзии нет и не будет (Мандельштам 2). People may cudgel their brains as much as they like, but they will never find a definition for poetry (2a). ♦ «О прошлом вспоминать незачем, — возразил Базаров, — а что касается до будущего, то о нём тоже не стоит голову ломать, потому что я намерен немедленно улизнуть» (Тургенев 2). "There is no point in dwelling on the past," Bazarov replied, "and as for the future, it's not worth your troubling your head about that either, seeing that I intend to make my departure from here at once" (2c).

Г-257 • МОРО́ЧИТЬ/ЗАМОРО́ЧИТЬ ГО́ЛОВУ *кому coll;* **ДУРИ́ТЬ/ЗАДУРИ́ТЬ ГО́ЛОВУ** *highly coll* [VP; subj: human; often in questions, neg imper, or infin with перестань, нечего etc] **1.** to deceive, intentionally mislead s.o.: X морочит Y-у голову ≃ **X is pulling the wool over Y's eyes; X is leading Y up ⟨down⟩ the garden path; X is trying to put something over on Y; X is playing games with Y;** [in limited contexts] **X is making ⟨trying to make⟩ a fool of Y;** ‖ *Neg Imper* не морочь мне голову ≃ **don't take me for a fool.**

«Ты поверь мне... я знаю, ты мне не веришь, но сейчас поверь, я ведь давно вам говорю: нельзя здесь оставаться... Голем тебе голову заморочил, пьяница носатая...» (Стругацкие 1). "Believe me. I know you don't believe me, but believe me now, I've been telling you for a long time, we can't stay here. Golem pulled the wool over your eyes, the long-nosed drunk" (1a). ♦ Когда же я... провозгласил заключительную фразу рассказа, то Бунин некоторое время молчал... а затем ледяным голосом спросил: «И это всё?» — «Всё», — сказал я. «Так какого же вы чёрта, — вдруг заорал Бунин, стукнув кулаком по столу с такой силой, что подпрыгнула пепельница, — так какого же вы чёрта битых сорок пять минут морочили нам голову» (Катаев 3). When I uttered the concluding sentence of the story, Bunin said nothing for a time.... "Is that all?" he asked icily. "Yes," I said. "...Then why the devil," he shouted suddenly, banging on the table with his fist with such force that the ashtray bounced, "then why the devil have you been leading us up the garden path for the last forty-five minutes or more?" (3a). ♦ «Едике, дорогой, только ты... голову мне не морочь» (Айтматов 2). "Yedigei, my dear fellow, don't take me for a fool..." (2a).

2. ~ *(кем-чем)* to annoy or distract s.o. with trifling matters, unnecessary chatter, absurd requests etc: X морочит Y-у голову (Z-ом) ≃ **X is driving Y crazy (with Z); X makes Y's head spin; X makes Y dizzy; X is pestering Y (with Z).**

«Послушайте, — взмолился лётчик, — что вы мне голову морочите? Зачем мне говорить с народом? Мне с начальством поговорить надо» (Войнович 2). "Listen," implored the pilot. "Why are you trying to drive me crazy? Why should I talk with the people? I need to talk with my superiors" (2a). ♦ «Дали бы ей [тётушке Хрисуле] чего-нибудь пожевать, авось замолкнет», — говорил кто-нибудь по-абхазски, когда она своим лопотанием слегка заморачивала всем голову (Искандер 5). "Give her [Auntie Chrysoula] something to nibble on and she might shut up," someone would say in Abkhazian when she had everyone dizzy with her jabbering (5a).

3. to captivate s.o., cause s.o. to fall in love with one: X задурил Y-у голову ≃ **X turned Y's head; X made Y fall for X.**

Когда-то я дурил голову одной девочке, ей было тринадцать, а мне четырнадцать (Трифонов 5). Once I managed to turn a certain girl's head. She was thirteen and I was fourteen (5a).

Г-258 • МЫ́ЛИТЬ/НАМЫ́ЛИТЬ ⟨ПУ́ДРИТЬ/НАПУ́ДРИТЬ *obs,* **МЫТЬ/ВЫ́МЫТЬ** *obs⟩* **ГО́ЛОВУ** *кому (за что) highly coll* [VP; subj: human] to scold, reprimand s.o. severely: X намылил Y-у голову ≃ **X gave Y a (good) dressing-down ⟨tongue-lashing⟩; X pinned Y's ears back; X**

chewed ⟨bawled⟩ Y out; X let Y have it; X laid Y out in lavender.

«Товарищ Яконов! Только что у меня были товарищи из Политуправления и очень-таки намылили голову» (Солженицын 3). "Comrade Yakonov! Some comrades from the Political Section just came to see me, and they gave me a good dressing-down" (3a).

Г-259 • НА чью ГО́ЛОВУ ⟨НА́ ГО́ЛОВУ кому⟩ свалиться, обрушиться, посыпаться и т. п. [PrepP; these forms only; the resulting PrepP is prep obj] (to befall, happen to) s.o.: **(fall ⟨come down etc⟩) (up)on s.o.'s head.**

...Хорошо, если удастся ему [станционному смотрителю] скоро избавиться от непрошенного гостя; но если не случится лошадей?.. Боже! Какие ругательства, какие угрозы посыплются на его голову! (Пушкин 3). ...The postmaster is fortunate if he succeeds in getting rid of his uninvited guest quickly. But if there should happen to be no horses?... Heavens, what curses, what threats are poured down upon his head! (3b). ♦ Лашков ещё натягивал пиджак, чтобы бежать за уполномоченным, а кто-то уже кричал сверху: «Ироды! Куда по подзору сапожищами-то! И зачем только принесло вас на нашу голову!» (Максимов 3). [context transl] While Lashkov was still pulling on his coat to go and fetch the block sergeant he heard somebody shouting from above. "Monsters! Get those ugly great boots off my tablecloth. Why were you sent to plague us?" (3a).

Г-260 • НА́ ГО́ЛОВУ ⟨НА ДВЕ ГОЛОВЫ́ и т. п.⟩ ВЫ́ШЕ кого coll; **ГОЛОВО́Й ВЫ́ШЕ** obs [AdjP; these forms only; subj-compl with быть∅ (subj: human or collect)] one is much more intelligent, experienced, informed (than someone else): X на голову выше Y-a ≃ **X is ⟨stands⟩ head and shoulders above Y; X is a cut above Y; X can run circles ⟨rings⟩ around Y.**

...Никанор сразу понял, что Курода-сан художник настоящий, на голову выше его, Никанора (Евтушенко 2). ...Nikanor realized immediately that Kuroda-san was a real artist, standing head and shoulders above him (2a).

Г-261 • НА МОЮ́ ⟨твою́ и т. п.⟩ ГО́ЛОВУ coll [PrepP; these forms only; sent adv (occas. parenth); more often used with pfv past verbs; fixed WO] (of some action, occurrence etc) causing me (you etc) inconvenience, difficulties, trouble: **unfortunately for me ⟨you etc⟩; to my ⟨your etc⟩ misfortune ⟨detriment, dismay⟩; [in limited contexts] it's a disaster for me ⟨you etc⟩; I am ⟨you are etc⟩ in for trouble.**

На мою голову Тамурка вспомнила, что у меня приближается день рождения (Зиновьев 2). To my dismay Tamurka remembered that my birthday was drawing near (2a). ♦ [Анчугин:] Отправили меня с тобой на мою голову. Я три месяца не пил, а ты, змей, за три дня всего меня испортил (Вампилов 1). [A.:] It was a disaster for me to be sent here with you. I hadn't had a drink for three months, and you've made a complete write-off of me in three days, you snake (1a).

Г-262 • НА СВЕ́ЖУЮ ГО́ЛОВУ [PrepP; Invar; sent adv; fixed WO] when one is not tired or after one has rested (usu. after a night's sleep): **when ⟨while⟩ one ⟨one's mind⟩ is fresh; with a clear head; when ⟨while⟩ one's head is clear.**

«Не получается у меня задача». — «Это потому что ты устал. Подумай над ней завтра, на свежую голову». "I can't figure out this problem." "That's because you're tired. Work on it tomorrow, when your mind is fresh."

Г-263 • НА СВОЮ́ ГО́ЛОВУ; СЕБЕ́ НА ГО́ЛОВУ ⟨НА́ ГО́ЛОВУ⟩ all coll [PrepP; these forms only; sent adv (occas. parenth); more often used with verbs in pfv past; fixed WO] causing trouble for o.s. (by doing sth.): X сделал Y на

свою голову ≃ **X did Y to X's own misfortune ⟨detriment, harm⟩; X brought ⟨called⟩ it ⟨trouble etc⟩ upon himself when he did Y; X brought ⟨called⟩ it ⟨trouble etc⟩ down upon his own head when he did Y; [in limited contexts] Y bounced back at X; X was paid back for Y; X stored up trouble for himself (by doing Y).**

Прежний заведующий... боялся Ужика и трусливо переводил его из класса в класс. Довёл бы и до окончания школы, но Ужик, на свою голову, добился-таки его увольнения... (Грекова 3). The former principal...was afraid of Uzhik and promoted him from grade to grade. He would have graduated him, but Uzhik, to his own misfortune, managed to get him fired (3a). ♦ Когда однажды, в 55 году, расписавшись о Пушкине, он [Чернышевский] захотел дать пример «бессмысленного сочетания слов», то привёл мимоходом тут же выдуманное «синий звук», — на свою голову напророчив пробивший через полвека блоковский «звонко-синий час» (Набоков 1). Once in 1855, when expatiating on Pushkin and wishing to give an example of "a senseless combination of words," he [Chernyshevski] hastily cited a "blue sound" of his own invention—prophetically calling down upon his own head Blok's "blue-ringing hour" that was to chime half a century later (1a). ♦ Да, конечно, за наши встречи я наговорил ей много лишнего, на свою голову... (Ерофеев 3). ...Well, yes, I have spoken a bit too loosely with her during our meetings, things that might bounce back at me... (3a). ♦ «...Про меня написали, что я была „милым другом" вашего брата...» — «Этого быть не может! Где же и как написали?» — «...Вот здесь в газете „Слухи", в петербургской... Я ужасно люблю слухи, и подписалась, и вот себе на голову: вот они какие оказались слухи» (Достоевский 2). "...They also wrote about me, that I was your brother's 'dear friend'..." "It can't be! Where and how did they write it?" "...Here, in the newspaper *Rumors*, from Petersburg....I'm terribly fond of rumors, so I subscribed, and now I've been paid back for it, this is the sort of rumors they turned out to be" (2a). ♦ ...Почти уверен я был, что не решатся [исключить меня из Союза писателей], и обнаглел в своей безнаказанности. Да нет, ясно вижу: им же это невыгодно, на свою они голову, зачем? Отняла им злоба ум (Солженицын 2). I had been almost certain that they would not [expel me from the Writers' Union], and this false sense of security had made me impudent. Still, I could see clearly that all this would do them no good, that they were storing up trouble for themselves. Malice had robbed them of their wits (2a).

Г-264 • НАВЯ́ЗЫВАТЬСЯ/НАВЯЗА́ТЬСЯ НА ГО́ЛОВУ ⟨НА ШЕ́Ю⟩ чью, кому coll [VP; subj: human] to impose one's presence upon s.o. intrusively, thereby annoying or becoming a burden to him: X навязался на Y-ову голову ≃ **X thrust ⟨forced, foisted⟩ himself (up)on Y.**

Мы не хотели брать с собой Романа, но он навязался нам на голову, а обижать его отказом не хотелось. We didn't want to take Roman along, but he forced himself on us, and we would have hated to offend him by turning him away.

Г-265 • НЕ ИДЁТ ⟨НЕЙДЁТ⟩/НЕ ПОЙДЁТ В ГО́ЛОВУ ⟨НА УМ⟩ (кому) coll [VP; if pfv, fut only] **1.** [subj: abstr, concr, or, rare, human] the thought of sth. (or of doing sth.) does not occupy s.o.'s mind; s.o. does not feel like doing sth. (often because of his preoccupation with something else): X не шёл в голову Y-у ≃ **Y couldn't (even) think of X; [in limited contexts] X never ⟨hadn't⟩ entered Y's head ⟨mind⟩;** ‖ Y-у ничего не идёт в голову ≃ **Y can't keep his mind on anything; [in limited contexts] Y can't think of anything;** ‖ (Y-у) ничего больше не идёт в голову ≃ **Y can think of nothing else; that's all Y can think about.**

«Ответа из дома нет, и я, признаться, затосковал. Еда и на ум не идёт, сон от меня бежит, всякие дурные мыслишки в голову лезут...» (Шолохов 1). "There had been no answer from home and I must say I began to feel very uneasy. I couldn't even think of

[133]

eating and couldn't sleep, and all sorts of black thoughts kept creeping into my head" (1b). ♦ «Я пьян? Батюшка Владимир Андреевич, бог свидетель, ни единой капли во рту не было... да и пойдёт ли вино на ум...» (Пушкин 1). "Me drunk? Vladimir Andreyevitch, master, as God is my witness, I haven't touched a drop all evening, nor has it entered my head to do so" (1b). ♦ Я изнывал в отсутствие Зинаиды: ничего мне на ум не шло, всё из рук валилось, я по целым дням напряжённо думал о ней... (Тургенев 3). Away from Zinaida, I languished: I could not think of anything, I had not the heart to do anything, and for days on end all my thoughts revolved round her (3a).

2. [subj: a noun denoting some material, a subject matter etc that can be learned or memorized (often ничего)] (sth.) is not remembered or comprehended by s.o.; s.o. cannot retain sth. in his memory: X не идёт (Y-у) в голову ≃ **X doesn't stick (in Y's mind); Y can't make X stick (in Y's mind); X doesn't sink in.**

Г-266 • ОЧЕРТЯ́ ГО́ЛОВУ *coll* [Verbal Adv; Invar; adv; fixed WO] **1.** ~ броситься, кинуться и т. п. (to rush into sth., do sth.) recklessly, thoughtlessly: **(rush ⟨plunge, throw o.s. etc⟩) headlong (into sth.); (throw o.s. etc) rashly (into sth.); throwing caution to the winds.**

«Вот что значит говорить очертя голову обо всём, чего ты не понимаешь и не можешь понять...» (Герцен 1). "This is what comes of rushing headlong into conversation about all sorts of things you don't understand and can't understand..." (1a). ♦ «...Неужели ты думаешь, что я как дурак пошёл, очертя голову? Я пошёл как умник, и это-то меня и сгубило!» (Достоевский 3). "Do you think I plunged headlong like a fool? No, I was clever about it—that's how I came to grief" (3b). ♦ ...Она [Фрида Вигдорова] очертя голову бросалась во все дела, где была попрана справедливость и где можно было надеяться её восстановить (Эткинд 1). ...She [Frida Vigdorova] threw herself headlong into any cases where justice had been interfered with and there seemed some hope of restoring it (1a).

2. бежать, мчаться и т. п. ~ (to run, race) very quickly, impetuously: **at breakneck speed; for all one is worth; like a bat out of hell.**

Завернув за угол, бухгалтер незаметно перекрестился и побежал очертя голову (Ильф и Петров 2). He [the bookkeeper] turned the corner, surreptitiously crossed himself and ran for all he was worth (2b).

< Apparently, a blend of сломя голову (which influenced the meaning) and очертить кругом (which refers to the old custom of drawing a line around oneself or another person in order to obtain protection from evil forces). Очертя is the old form of the short active participle of очертить; the corresponding modern form is the perfective verbal adverb очертив.

Г-267 • ПОВИ́ННУЮ ГО́ЛОВУ (И) МЕЧ НЕ СЕЧЁТ [saying] a person who confesses to a misdeed is not punished (said when forgiving a guilty person who has confessed and repented or by the guilty person himself admitting to his guilt and hoping for forgiveness): ≃ **a fault confessed is half redressed; a sin confessed is half forgiven.**

[Г-жа Простакова *(стоя на коленях)*:] Ах, мои батюшки, повинную голову меч не сечёт... Не губите меня (Фонвизин 1). [Mrs. P. *(standing on her knees)*:] Oh, my masters, a sin confessed is half forgiven....Don't ruin me! (1a).

Г-268 • ПОДНИМА́ТЬ/ПОДНЯ́ТЬ ГО́ЛОВУ ⟨-ы⟩ *occas. disapprov* [VP; subj: human (usu. pl), collect, or abstr (denoting a political trend, school of thought etc); usu. pres or pfv past; fixed WO] to become confident of one's strength and begin to take action: X поднимает голову ≃ **X is getting ⟨growing⟩ active; X is rising up;** [of a phenomenon regarded as negative] **thing X is rearing its (ugly) head.**

«По округу наблюдаются волнения. Оставшаяся белогвардейщина поднимает голову и начинает смущать трудовое казачество» (Шолохов 4). "There have been signs of unrest in the district. The White Guard elements who have stayed behind are getting active and sowing confusion among the working Cossacks" (4a). ♦ «А то, что Европа, не выдержав произвола, подняла голову, это что, по-вашему?.. Я имею в виду революцию, князь...» (Окуджава 2). "What do you call the fact that Europe, no longer tolerating arbitrary rule, has risen up? I'm referring to revolution, Prince" (2a).

Г-269 • ПОСЫПА́ТЬ/ПОСЫ́ПАТЬ (СЕБЕ́) ГО́ЛОВУ ⟨ГЛАВУ́⟩ ПЕ́ПЛОМ *obs, lit* [VP; subj: human] to express profound grief or repentance (in contemp. usage, usu. used in refer. to an excessive display of grief over sth. insignificant): X посыпает (себе) голову пеплом ≃ **X puts on ⟨is in⟩ sackcloth and ashes.**

< Cf. the Bible (Esther 4:1 et al.).

Г-270 • ПРИКЛОНИ́ТЬ ГО́ЛОВУ *где, куда lit* [VP; subj: human; usu. infin with мочь, не знать etc] to find a place to live, shelter: X-у негде ⟨некуда⟩ голову приклонить ≃ **X has nowhere to lay his head ⟨to hang his hat⟩;** ‖ X не знает, куда голову приклонить ≃ **X doesn't know where to lay his head.**

Хотя уж ему не казалось теперь подвигом переехать с квартиры... и не прилечь целый день, но он не знал, где и на ночь приклонить голову (Гончаров 1). Although it no longer seemed a heroic feat to him to move from his apartment...or refrain from lying down for a whole day, he still had not found a place to lay his head at night (1b).

Г-271 • ПРИХОДИ́ТЬ/ПРИЙТИ́ В ГО́ЛОВУ ⟨НА УМ, В УМ *obs*, **НА МЫСЛЬ** *obs*⟩ *кому coll;* **ВХОДИ́ТЬ/ВОЙТИ́ В ГО́ЛОВУ ⟨В УМ, В МЫСЛЬ⟩** *obs, coll;* **ВСПАДА́ТЬ/ВСПАСТЬ НА УМ ⟨НА МЫСЛЬ⟩** *obs* [VP; subj: abstr (usu. мысль, идея etc), (rare) concr or human, a clause, or infin; when foll. by infin, may convey s.o.'s intention or desire to do sth.] to arise in s.o.'s consciousness: Y-у пришёл в голову X ≃ **X came into ⟨entered⟩ Y's head ⟨mind⟩; X crossed Y's mind; X occurred to Y; X came to mind;** [in limited contexts] **Y thought of X; it struck Y;** ‖ Y-у невольно пришло в голову, что... ≃ **Y couldn't help thinking that...**

«Мне тотчас же пришёл в голову опять ещё вопрос: что Софья Семёновна, прежде чем заметит, пожалуй, чего доброго, потеряет деньги...» (Достоевский 3). "...Another question immediately came into my head also: that Miss Marmeladov might well, for all I knew, lose the money before she noticed it..." (3a). ♦ Когда приходил к нему [Манилову] мужик и, почесавши рукою затылок, говорил: «Барин, позволь отлучиться на работу, подать заработать», — «Ступай», — говорил он, куря трубку, и ему даже в голову не приходило, что мужик шёл пьянствовать (Гоголь 3). Whenever a peasant came to him [Manilov] and, scratching the back of his head, said, "Master, give me leave to get an outside job, to pay off my taxes," Manilov invariably answered "Go," and puffed at his pipe; and it never entered his head that the peasant was merely off on a drunken spree (3d). ♦ ...Иногда мне приходит на ум, что я что-то напутал в жизни, не сделал чего-то самого главного, а чего именно — никак не могу вспомнить (Войнович 5). ...Sometimes the thought crosses my mind that I've somehow messed up, that I've left the most important thing undone, but for the life of me, I can't remember just what that thing is (5a). ♦ В Лефортове удивительная библиотека: все книги, что конфисковывались у «врагов народа» за полвека, видно, стеклись сюда. По всей стране «чистили» библиотеки, жгли «вредные» книги — здесь же всё сохранилось, как в оазисе. Никому не приходило в голову чистить библиотеку тюрьмы КГБ... (Буковский 1). Lefortovo had a wonderful library—it looked as if all the books confiscated from the enemies of the people over half a century had ended up here. Up and down the country they had "purged" libraries and burned "pernicious" books, while in here, everything was preserved as in an oasis. It had never occurred to anyone to purge the libraries of the KGB prisons... (1a). ♦ Когда хочешь определить, где корни творчества Хемингуэя, на ум не приходит ни английская, ни французская, ни американская литература (Олеша 3). When you wish to determine where the roots of Hemingway's creative work lie, you don't think of English, French, or American literature (3a). ♦ В его голосе звучало такое искреннее убеждение, такая несомненная решимость, что мне невольно пришло на мысль: да, если этот человек не попадёт под суд, то он покажет, где раки зимуют! (Салтыков-Щедрин 2). There was such sincere conviction in his voice, such indomitable resolution in every word he uttered that I couldn't help thinking, "Ah, if this man's lucky enough to escape being put on trial, he'll certainly show them what's what!" (2a). ♦ Хотя мы и представительствовали в искусстве определённые социально-политические тенденции, однако никому из нас, разумеется, и во сне не приходило в голову, что где-то... у него лежит такой мандат: мы ещё в тринадцатом году перегрызли бы горло всякому, кто попытался бы уверить нас в этом... (Лившиц 1). [context transl] Although we represented definite socio-political tendencies in art, not one of us would have dreamed that he possessed such a mandate. In 1913 we would have throttled anyone who attempted to convince us of this... (1a).

Г-272 • **ПРЯ́ТАТЬ/СПРЯ́ТАТЬ ГО́ЛОВУ ПОД КРЫЛО́** *obsoles, lit* [VP; subj: human] to hide, run away from reality, life: X прячет голову под крыло ≃ **X buries his head in the sand.**

Г-273 • **САДИ́ТЬСЯ/СЕСТЬ НА́ ГОЛОВУ** *кому coll* [VP; subj: human] to subject s.o. to one's will, force him to satisfy one's whims by exploiting his meekness: X сядет Y-у на голову ≃ **X will walk ⟨be⟩ all over Y; X will take advantage of Y; X will push ⟨boss⟩ Y around.**

«Если мы это так оставим, эндурцы совсем на голову сядут!» (Искандер 5). "If we let it go on like this, the Endurskies will be all over us!" (5a). ♦ Климентьева передёргивало, когда Нержин сошвыривал с ног ботинки. Ведь это было намеренное оскорбление его надзирателя. Если не заступаться за надзирателей – арестанты сядут на голову и администрации (Солженицын 3). Klimentiev had winced when Nerzhin kicked off his shoes. After all, that was a deliberate insult to his guard. If one did not stand behind the guards, the prisoners would take advantage of the administration [as well] (3a).

Г-274 • **СКЛОНЯ́ТЬ/СКЛОНИ́ТЬ ГО́ЛОВУ** *перед кем-чем elev* [VP; subj: human or collect] **1.** to acknowledge defeat, surrender: X склонил голову перед Y-ом ≃ **X bowed his head before Y; X bowed to Y.**

[Москва] склонила голову перед Петром, потому что в звериной лапе его была будущность России (Герцен 1). [Moscow] bowed her head before Peter because the future of Russia lay in his brutal grip (1a).

2. to admire, revere s.o. or sth., hold s.o. or sth. in high esteem: X склоняет голову перед Y-ом ≃ **X bows his head respectfully to ⟨before⟩ Y; X bows down before Y; [in limited contexts] X takes his hat off to Y.**

«Я склоняю голову перед тем, что вам пришлось пережить, отец Гур. Но я от души осуждаю вас за то, что вы сдались» (Стругацкие 4). "I bow my head respectfully before all you have had to go through, Father Gur. But I condemn you with all my soul for giving up!" (4a). ♦ «Протяните руку падшему человеку... Любите его, помните в нём самого себя и обращайтесь с ним, как с собой, – тогда я... склоню перед вами голову...» (Гончаров 1). "Stretch out your hand to the fallen man....Love him;

see yourself in him, and treat him as you would yourself—then I will...bow down before you" (1b).

Г-275 • **СЛОМЯ́ ГО́ЛОВУ** *бежать, мчаться, нестись* и т. п. *coll* [Verbal Adv; Invar; adv (intensif); fixed WO] (to run, race, rush etc) very fast, impetuously: **(run ⟨gallop etc⟩) at breakneck speed; (run ⟨race etc⟩) like mad; (race etc) as fast as one's legs ⟨feet⟩ will carry one; (rush) headlong ⟨madly⟩; nearly break one's neck (running etc).**

Никогда он не садился верхом на Алабаша и никогда не скакал так по двору сломя голову (Айтматов 1). He had never mounted Alabash and never galloped across the yard at such breakneck speed (1a). ♦ ...Марфа Игнатьевна бросилась от окна, выбежала из сада, отворила воротный запор и побежала сломя голову на зады к соседке Марье Кондратьевне (Достоевский 1). ...Marfa Ignatievna rushed away from the window, ran out of the garden, unlocked the gates, and ran like mad through the back lane to her neighbor, Maria Kondratievna (1a). ♦ ...Заслышав родную речь, сперва летим, как безумные, на её звук: «Вы русские?» И тут же, опомнившись и даже не дослушав ответа, сломя голову кидаемся наутёк (Войнович 1). ...Hearing our own language we first run like madmen toward the sound, saying: "Are you Russian?" But then at once we come to our senses and, without waiting for an answer, dash away as fast as our feet will carry us (1a). ♦ Эти самые люди, которые идут рядом с ним в похоронной процессии, встречали его появление аплодисментами, льстивыми улыбками, сломя голову кидались выполнять любое его желание (Войнович 1). The same people who were now walking with him in the funeral procession had greeted his every appearance with applause and smiles of flattery, and had rushed headlong to carry out any wish of his (1a). ♦ ...К воротам дома подъехала принадлежавшая госпоже Хохлаковой карета. Штабс-капитан, ждавший всё утро доктора, сломя голову бросился к воротам встречать его. Маменька подобралась и напустила на себя важности (Достоевский 1). ...A carriage belonging to Madame Khokhlakov drove up to the gates of the house. The captain, who had been expecting the doctor all morning, rushed out to meet him. Mama pulled herself together and assumed an important air (1a). ♦ «Забыли, как из той же Западной Украины бежали сломя голову, когда там не прогуливаться, а воевать пришлось» (Максимов 3). "They've forgotten how they nearly broke their necks running away from that very same western Ukraine when it came to fighting there, instead of picnicking" (3a).

< «Сломя» is the old form of the short active participle of the verb «сломить»; the corresponding modern form is the perfective verbal adverb «сломив».

Г-276 • **СНЯ́ВШИ ГО́ЛОВУ, ПО ВОЛОСА́М НЕ ПЛА́ЧУТ** [saying] after an irreparable act has been committed or a permanent loss suffered, it is futile to grieve over it (or insignificant details related to it): ≃ **if you sell the cow, you sell her milk; there is no use ⟨point, sense⟩ (in) crying over spilt ⟨spilled⟩ milk.**

«Я боюсь, что тут мы будем больше на виду, чем в Москве, откуда бежали в поисках незаметности. Конечно, делать теперь нечего. Снявши голову, по волосам не плачут. Но лучше не высказываться, скрываться, держаться скромнее» (Пастернак 1). "I am afraid that after leaving Moscow to escape notice, we are going to be even more conspicuous here. Not that there is anything to be done about it, and there certainly isn't any sense in crying over spilt milk. But we'd better stay in the background and keep quiet" (1a).

Г-277 • **СНЯТЬ ГО́ЛОВУ** *с кого, кому coll* [VP; subj: human] **1.** Also: **СОРВА́ТЬ ГО́ЛОВУ** *с кого highly coll* to kill s.o. (usu. in combat or in battle): X голову снимет с Y-а ≃ **X will blow Y's head off; X will finish Y off; X will put an end to Y.**

2. ~ *(за что)*. Also: **СОРВА́ТЬ ГО́ЛОВУ** *с кого (за что) highly coll* [often used as a threat] to punish s.o. severely: X с Y-а голову снимет (за Z) ≃ **X will have Y's head; Z will cost Y Y's head; Y's head will roll; X will wring ⟨break⟩ Y's neck.**

«Слушай мою команду... Крючок, заводи. Зеф, в башню! Гай, проверь нижние люки... Да тщательно проверь, голову сниму!» (Стругацкие 2). "Obey my orders....Hook, you drive. Zef, to the turret! Guy, check the lower hatches. And thoroughly, or I'll have your head!" (2a). ♦ Конечно, вчера он [пьяный] наболтал по телефону лишнего... Раньше бы и за это голову сняли, а теперь ничего, теперь времена либеральные... (Войнович 1). Of course, he [the drunk] blabbed more than he should have on the phone yesterday....In the old days, that would have cost him his head; but it's nothing now; these are liberal times... (1a). ♦ «...У меня здесь секретная документация, если что, голову с меня сымут [*substand* = снимут]...» (Максимов 2). "...I'm carrying secret documents, and if anything happens to them my head will roll..." (2a).

Г-278 • **СОВА́ТЬ/СУ́НУТЬ ГО́ЛОВУ В ПЕ́ТЛЮ; СО-ВА́ТЬСЯ В ПЕ́ТЛЮ** *both coll* [VP; subj: human] **1.** to take one's own life by hanging: X сунул голову в петлю ≃ **X hanged himself; X put the noose around his neck.**

2. to undertake sth. risky that may jeopardize one's life, career etc: X суёт голову в петлю ≃ **X is sticking his head in the noose; X is risking his neck; X is putting his life ⟨career etc⟩ on the line.**

Г-279 • **ТЕРЯ́ТЬ/ПОТЕРЯ́ТЬ ГО́ЛОВУ** *coll* [VP; subj: human] **1.** ~ *(от чего)* to lose one's poise, common sense, not know how to act (in a difficult situation): X потерял голову ≃ **X lost his head ⟨senses⟩; X panicked; [in limited contexts] X went to pieces; ‖ *Neg* X не потерял голову ⟨-ы⟩ ≃ X kept his head ⟨his cool, his wits about him⟩; X kept a level head.**

[Надежда Антоновна:] Я совершенно потеряла голову. Что нам делать!.. У нас опять накопилась пропасть долгов (Островский 4). [N.A.:] I have lost my head completely. What are we to do?...We're up to our necks in debt again (4b). ♦ Как полусонный бродил он без цели по городу, не будучи в состоянии решить, он ли сошёл с ума, чиновники ли потеряли голову, во сне ли всё это делается или наяву заварилась дурь почище сна (Гоголь 3). Like a sleepwalker, he stalked the streets of the town, unable to make up his mind whether it was he who had gone mad or the officials who had lost their senses, whether he was dreaming or and all this idiotic nonsense was happening while he was wide awake (3e). ♦ ...Потеряв голову, опозорясь с нобелевской церемонией, власти прекратили публичную травлю... (Солженицын 2). ...Having panicked, and disgraced themselves over the Nobel ceremony, the authorities stopped hounding me publicly... (2a).

2. ~ *(от чего)* to become conceited, get a false sense of one's own importance, abilities etc, usu. from praise, success etc: X потерял голову (от Y-а) ≃ **Y went to X's head; X had ⟨got⟩ a swelled head; X was ⟨became⟩ giddy (with success).**

3. ~ *(от кого)* [pfv only] to fall passionately in love with s.o., become completely infatuated with s.o.: X потерял голову (от Y-а) ≃ **X (completely) lost his head (over Y); X fell head over heels in love (with Y); X fell hard for Y.**

...На четвёртый год замужества, встретив Люсьена, Муш потеряла голову (Эренбург 4). ...In her fourth year of married life Mouche met Lucien and lost her head completely (4a).

Г-280 • **УДАРЯ́ТЬ/УДА́РИТЬ ⟨БРОСА́ТЬСЯ/БРО-СИ́ТЬСЯ, КИДА́ТЬСЯ/КИ́НУТЬСЯ⟩ В ГО́ЛОВУ** *(кому)* [VP; subj: a noun denoting an alcoholic drink or an emotion, intense experience etc] to have an intoxicating effect: X ударил Y-у в голову ≃ **X went ⟨rushed⟩ to Y's head.**

[Наталья Петровна:] Этот человек меня заразил своею молодостью... С непривычки мне всё это в голову бросилось,

как вино... (Тургенев 1). [N.P.:] This man has infected me with his youth....I'm not used to this, it's gone to my head like wine (1c).

Г-281 • **ХВАТА́ТЬСЯ/СХВАТИ́ТЬСЯ ЗА́ ГО́ЛОВУ** *coll* [VP; subj: human] to experience horror, utter confusion, extreme astonishment and display it by grabbing one's head with one's hands (usu. when one realizes that he or another has done sth. absurd, inexcusable, or potentially harmful): X схватился за голову ≃ **X clutched his head (in despair ⟨in horror etc⟩); X tore (at) his hair (in anguish ⟨in despair etc⟩).**

Гапка только за голову хваталась: надо пахать, нужна лошадь (а где взять?), нужен плуг, борона, зерно, да засеять столько, что и двум мужикам не под силу (Кузнецов 1). Gapka could only clutch her head in despair. She had to plow, and to do so she needed a horse (where was she to get one?), a plow, a harrow and grain; and even then she would have to sow more than two men could (1a). ♦ Пале-рояльская труппа... с ужасом узнала, что Бургонский Отель начал репетировать «Александра Великого»... Директор Пале-Рояля просто схватился за голову, потому что ясно было совершенно, что сборы на «Александра» упадут при параллельной постановке у бургонцев (Булгаков 5). ...The Palais Royal troupe learned to its dismay that the Bourgogne had begun rehearsals of *Alexander*....The director of the Palais Royal simply clutched his head in consternation, for it was entirely clear that the income from *Alexander* would drop if there was a parallel production at the Bourgogne (5a).

Г-282 • **ЧЕРЕЗ ГО́ЛОВУ** *чью, кого coll* [PrepP; Invar; the resulting PrepP is adv] (one takes some action) bypassing a person or people whom one is supposed or expected to address or inform first (and usu. contacting a third party directly, often s.o. of a higher rank): **over s.o.'s head ⟨over the head of s.o.⟩.**

[Старший администратор] Зайцева была из тех администраторов, которые свою малую, временную власть над людьми воспринимают как великую, вечную... То, что Борис Григорьевич советовался с Верой через её, старшего администратора, голову, раздражало её безмерно (Грекова 3). [The senior administrator] Zaitseva was one of those administrators who perceive their limited temporary power over people as great and permanent....The fact that Boris Grigorievich sought advice from Vera over the senior administrator's head irritated her enormously (3a).

Г-283 • **БЕЗ ГОЛОВЫ́** *coll* [PrepP; Invar] **1.** [subj-compl with copula (subj: human)] unintelligent, foolish: **brainless; dumb; a (total) fool; a dimwit.**

Нужно совсем без головы быть, чтобы так промокнуть и не переодеться! You'd have to be a total fool not to change your clothes after getting so wet!

2. [adv] (to do sth., act) imprudently, rashly: **without using one's head; thoughtlessly; recklessly.**

Реформу цен провели без головы — как, впрочем, и все остальные реформы. Price reforms were instituted recklessly—but then again so were all the other reforms.

Г-284 • **ВАЛИ́ТЬ ⟨СВА́ЛИВАТЬ/СВАЛИ́ТЬ, ПЕРЕ-КЛА́ДЫВАТЬ⟩ С БОЛЬНО́Й ГОЛОВЫ́ НА ЗДО-РО́ВУЮ** *coll* [VP; subj: human] (to try) to take the blame from s.o. who is guilty and put it on s.o. who is not guilty: X валит с больной головы на здоровую ≃ **X shifts ⟨is trying to shift⟩ the blame to someone else ⟨to someone else's shoulders⟩; X lays the blame at someone else's door(step); X pins it ⟨the blame, the rap⟩ on someone else; X hangs the blame on someone else.**

[Матрёна:] Что ж ты на меня-то сворачиваешь? Ты, деушка, мотри [*ungrammat* = девушка, смотри], с больной головы на здоровую не сворачивай (Толстой 1). [M.:] Why do you throw the blame on me? Look out, girlie, don't shift the blame to someone else's shoulders (1b). ♦ Она [Анфиса] начала оправдываться: не колхоза это, дескать, вина. Сплавщики виноваты. Они бон ставили. «Ты, Анфиса Петровна, с больной головы на здоровую не вали» (Абрамов 1). She [Anfisa] began to cover herself: the *kolkhoz* was not to blame. It was the timber floaters' fault. It was they who had erected the dam. "Anfisa Petrovna, don't go laying the blame at someone else's door" (1a).

Г-285 • **ВЫБИВА́ТЬ/ВЫ́БИТЬ ИЗ ГОЛОВЫ́** *что coll* [VP; subj: human; usu. infin with не мочь, надо, стараться etc; fixed WO] to free o.s. from a persistent thought, idea etc: X-у надо выбить из головы Y ≃ **X should get Y out of X's head; X should get rid of Y; X should drive Y from ⟨out of⟩ X's head; X should shake Y ⟨the thought of Y⟩.**

«Казбич не являлся снова. Только не знаю почему, я не мог выбить из головы мысль, что он недаром приезжал и затевает что-нибудь худое» (Лермонтов 1). "Kazbich didn't show up again. Still, for some reason I couldn't get rid of the idea that he'd come for a purpose and was up to some devilry" (1c).

Г-286 • **ВЫ́БРОСИТЬ ⟨ВЫ́КИНУТЬ⟩ ИЗ ГОЛОВЫ́ ⟨ИЗ ПА́МЯТИ** *rare⟩ кого-что coll* [VP; subj: human; usu. imper or infin with не мочь, надо, пытаться etc] to forget s.o. or sth. intentionally, stop thinking about s.o. or sth.: X не может выбросить Y-а из головы ≃ **X cannot get Y out of X's mind ⟨head⟩; X cannot put Y out of X's mind ⟨head⟩; X cannot dismiss thing Y from X's memory ⟨mind⟩;** ‖ *Imper* выброси Y-а из головы ≃ **put Y out of mind.**

Конечно, ни она [мать], ни отец, ни кто из нас не могли выкинуть Лёву из памяти... (Рыбаков 1). Naturally, neither mother nor father, nor any of us, could get Lyova out of our minds... (1a). ♦ «Запомни, Сарра, – сказала мама, – никаких партизан тут нет, не было и быть не может. Выбрось из головы и не повторяй этих глупостей» (Рыбаков 1). "Just remember, Sarah," mother told her, "there are no partisans here, there never have been and it couldn't happen. Get the whole idea out of your head and don't repeat such nonsense" (1a). ♦ «Выбрось из головы! Не мучься по пустякам!» (Искандер 5). "Put it out of mind! Don't trouble yourself over nothing!" (5a). ♦ Она [Люся] забыла, что когда-то боронила, пахала... Да, боронила, пахала – подумать только! Странно, что и это, не разобрав, она выкинула из памяти... (Распутин 3). She [Liusia] had forgotten that she had harrowed and ploughed....Yes, imagine it! She had actually harrowed and ploughed. How strange it was that she had indiscriminately dismissed even this from her memory... (3a).

Г-287 • **ВЫЛЕТА́ТЬ/ВЫ́ЛЕТЕТЬ ⟨ВЫСКА́КИВАТЬ/ВЫ́СКОЧИТЬ, УЛЕТУ́ЧИВАТЬСЯ/УЛЕТУ́ЧИТЬСЯ** и т. п.⟩ **ИЗ ГОЛОВЫ́** *чьей, у кого coll;* **ВЫЛЕТА́ТЬ/ВЫ́ЛЕТЕТЬ ⟨ВЫСКА́КИВАТЬ/ВЫ́СКОЧИТЬ, ВЫПАДА́ТЬ/ВЫ́ПАСТЬ** и т. п.⟩ **ИЗ ПА́МЯТИ; ИЗ ГОЛОВЫ́ ⟨ИЗ ПА́МЯТИ, ИЗ УМА́⟩ ВОН** *coll* [VP (subj: usu. abstr or a clause) or impers predic (variants with вон)] to be forgotten (by s.o.) suddenly and completely: X вылетел у Y-а из головы ≃ **X slipped Y's mind ⟨memory⟩; X has gone (clean ⟨clear, right etc⟩) out of Y's head ⟨mind⟩; X escaped Y ⟨Y's memory⟩; Y forgot all about X.**

Мы прикатили на трёх машинах в это уединённое абхазское село по причине, которая сейчас совершенно выветрилась у меня из головы (Искандер 4). We came rolling into this isolated Abkhazian village in three cars, for a reason that has now completely slipped my mind (4a). ♦ «Как я назвал его [Шевцова], не помнишь?» – «Не притворяйся, старик!» – «Клянусь, я забыл, всё вылетело из головы» (Аксёнов 6). "What did I call him [Shevtsov], do you remember?" "Don't try and kid me, old man!" "I swear I've forgotten it – it's gone clean out of my head" (6a). ♦ ...Уже Шухов совсем намерился в санчасть, как его озарило, что ведь сегодня утром до развода назначил ему длинный латыш из седьмого барака прийти купить два стакана самосада, а Шухов захлопотался, из головы вон (Солженицын 7). ...Shu-

khov had made up his mind to go to sick bay, when it suddenly dawned on him that he had arranged with the lanky Latvian in Hut 7 to buy two tumblers full of homegrown tobacco that morning. With so much to do, it had gone clean out of his mind (7c). ♦ «Знаком вам этот предмет?» – показал он [следователь] его [медный пестик] Мите. «Ах, да! – мрачно усмехнулся он, – как не знаком!..» – «Вы о нём упомянуть забыли», – заметил следователь. «...Из памяти только вылетело» (Достоевский 1). "Are you familiar with this object?" he [the district attorney] showed it [a brass pestle] to Mitya. "Ah, yes!" Mitya grinned gloomily, "indeed I am!..." "You forgot to mention it," the district attorney observed. "...It just escaped my memory" (1a). ♦ [Колесов:] Через месяц эта сказка вылетит у тебя из головы (Вампилов 3). [K.:] In a month you'll forget all about this fairy tale (3b).

Г-288 • **ВЫ́ШЕ ГОЛОВЫ́** *чего (у кого) coll* [PrepP; Invar; quantit subj-compl with copula (subj/gen: usu. дел, работы, забот etc)] s.o. has too much (work to do), too many (concerns etc): **(be) up to one's neck ⟨ears⟩ in sth.; (be) loaded (down) ⟨swamped⟩ with sth.**

...Александр Иванович Ларичев... – командир строгий, толковый, разумно требовательный. Дел у него выше головы... (Грекова 3). ...Alexander Larichev was...a tough, intelligent, reasonably demanding commander – and he was loaded with work (3a).

Г-289 • **ВЫ́ШЕ ГОЛОВЫ́ НЕ ПРЫ́ГНЕШЬ** [saying] you cannot do more than what is within your power or abilities (said with regret when a person has put forth great effort and still has not attained what was wanted): ≃ **a man ⟨you, one etc⟩ can do no more than he ⟨you, one etc⟩ can (do); you ⟨one, a person etc⟩ can only do so much.**

Г-290 • **ГО́ЛОВЫ ЛЕТЯ́Т/ПОЛЕТЕ́ЛИ** *coll* [VP_subj] several (or many) people suffer terribly (often used when certain people are fired from their jobs, are being scapegoated for sth., are the victims of a change in the political climate etc): головы полетят ≃ **heads will roll.**

Г-291 • **НЕ ВЫХО́ДИТ ⟨НЕ ИДЁТ, НЕЙДЁТ** *rare⟩* **ИЗ ГОЛОВЫ́** *у кого, чьей, кого;* **НЕ ВЫХО́ДИТ ⟨НЕ ИДЁТ, НЕЙДЁТ** *rare⟩* **ИЗ ПА́МЯТИ ⟨ИЗ УМА́⟩** [VP; subj: human, concr, or abstr; usu. 3rd pers, pres or past] a person (or thing) comes to mind persistently, is not forgotten by s.o.'s thoughts, is not forgotten by s.o.: X не выходил у Y-а из головы ≃ **Y couldn't get X out of Y's mind ⟨head⟩; thing X wouldn't go out of ⟨leave⟩ Y's mind; X was constantly on Y's mind; Y's mind kept going back to X; [in limited contexts] thing X stuck (fast) in Y's mind; thing X haunted Y; thing X kept running through Y's head.**

[Негина:] У меня бенефис из головы нейдёт... (Островский 11). [N.:] I can't get the benefit out of my head... (11a). ♦ ...Не по себе ей было, всё не шёл у ней из головы этот проклятущий след от папоротниковой ветки на нежной ноге её девочки, повыше колена (Искандер 3). ...She did not feel right, her mind kept going back to the accursed mark from the fern frond on her little girl's tender leg, above the knee (3a). ♦ «Дети! – промолвила она громко, – что, любовь чувство напускное?» Но ни Катя, ни Аркадий её даже не поняли. Они её дичились; невольно подслушанный разговор не выходил у них из головы (Тургенев 2). "Children!" she said aloud, "is love an affectation?" But neither Katya nor Arkady even understood her. They were shy of her; the conversation they had involuntarily overheard stuck fast in their minds (2a). ♦ С этой минуты настойчивый взгляд Ольги не выходил из головы Обломова. Напрасно он во весь рост лёг на спину, напрасно брал самые ленивые и покойные позы – не спится, да и только (Гончаров 1). From that moment Olga's persistent gaze haunted Oblomov. In vain did he stretch out full length on his back, in vain did he assume the laziest and most comfortable positions—he simply could not go to sleep (1a). ♦ Одна мысль не выходила у меня из головы: как могла она... решиться на такой поступок... (Тургенев 3). One thought kept running through my head: How could she...have made up her mind to do such a thing... (3a).

Г-292 • НЕ СНОСИ́ТЬ ГОЛОВЫ́ *кому coll* [VP; infin only; impers predic; fixed WO] s.o. will not escape punishment, reprisal, s.o. will perish (often used as a warning or threat): не сносить X-у головы ≃ X's head will roll; X will be as good as dead; X will ⟨is sure to⟩ come to a bad end.

«[Азамат] такой хитрец: ведь смекнул, что не сносить ему головы, если б он попался» (Лермонтов 1). "[Azamat] was no fool, you see, and reckoned he'd be as good as dead if ever he was caught" (1c). ♦ «Шапку-то сыми [*substand* = сними], нехристь! Кто же под образа садится в шапке? Ох, Яков, не сносить тебе головы...» (Шолохов 5). "Take your hat off, infidel! Who sits under the ikon in his hat? Mark my words, Yakov, you'll come to a bad end" (5a).

Г-293 • С ⟨ОТ⟩ ГОЛОВЫ́ ДО НОГ ⟨ДО ПЯТ, ДО ПЯ́ТОК *coll*⟩; С НОГ ДО ГОЛОВЫ́ [PrepP; these forms only; fixed WO] **1.** [adv or modif] including the entirety of one's body, being: мокрый ⟨облить, обдать *кого чем*, осмотреть *кого*, одетый *во что* и т. п.⟩ ~ ≃ be wet ⟨drench s.o., cover s.o. with sth., look s.o. over, be dressed in sth. etc⟩ from head to foot ⟨from head to toe, from top to toe⟩; ‖ осмотреть ⟨смерить взглядом⟩ *кого* ~ ≃ look s.o. up and down; give s.o. the once-over; ‖ [of a thought, emotion etc] X завладел Y-ом ~ ≃ Y was completely overcome ⟨overwhelmed⟩ by X; Y was seized by X; ‖ одеть *кого* ~ ⟨*во что*⟩ ≃ give ⟨buy⟩ s.o. a full ⟨complete⟩ set of clothing.

Влад хочет встать, подняться, чтобы пойти туда, к зелёной воде под берегом, но здесь хлёсткая боль пронизывает его с головы до ног... (Максимов 2). Vlad wanted to get up and walk down the beach to the green water's edge, but at that moment a searing pain shot through him from head to foot (2a). ♦ Варвара скептическим взглядом окинула его [Егоршу] с ног до головы (Абрамов 1). Varvara sized him [Egorsha] up skeptically from head to toe (1a). ♦ Стоявшие кучкою поодаль любопытные мешали знахарке. Она недобрым взглядом смеривала их с головы до ног (Пастернак 1). The knot of curious onlookers who stood at a distance annoyed the witch, and she measured them from top to toe with a hostile look (1a). ♦ Жена директора смерила её взглядом с ног до головы (Чуковская 1). The director's wife looked her up and down (1a). ♦ Эта Ира чем-то так очаровала всемогущую Гридасову, что та снабдила её чистым паспортом, одела с ног до головы в одежду со своего плеча и на свой счёт отправила на материк (Гинзбург 2). Ira had somehow cast such a spell on the omnipotent Gridasova that the latter had provided her with a perfectly clean passport, given her a complete set of clothing from her own wardrobe, and paid for her passage back to the mainland (2a). ♦ В голосе своего коллеги Пчёлкин уловил нечто такое, что с ног до головы прохватило его ознобом... (Катаев 3). [context transl] Pcholkin detected in his colleague's voice something that sent a shiver all the way up his spine (3a).

2. вооружить *кого*, вооружённый ~ [adv or modif] (to be) fully (armed): (armed) to the teeth ⟨to the hilt⟩.

3. [nonagreeing modif] (one is a person of a certain type) in every respect, in every way: every inch a ⟨the⟩ [NP]; a [NP] through and through; a [NP] from head to toe ⟨to foot⟩; a [NP] all the way; [in limited contexts] a [NP] born and bred.

...Чехов, как большинство его современников, был чужд изобразительному искусству и понимал культуру главным образом как просвещение. Он был «литератором» с ног до головы... (Терц 3). ...Like most of his contemporaries, Chekhov was indifferent to the visual arts and understood culture mainly as education. He was a "literary man" from head to foot... (3a).

Г-294 • С ГОЛОВЫ́ НА́ НОГИ поставить, перевернуть *что* [PrepP; Invar; adv; fixed WO] (in refer. to an issue, problem etc that has been previously distorted, misconstrued) (to approach, examine sth.) correctly, appropriately: (put sth.) in the right ⟨proper⟩ perspective; (approach sth.) from the right angle.

Г-295 • ГО́ЛОД НЕ ТЁТКА [saying] hunger is a serious matter, hunger leaves you little choice (used to explain or justify why a person is eating sth. he does not like, doing sth. he would not ordinarily do, being especially resourceful etc): ≃ hunger is no joke.

[Любим Карпыч:] Нет, брат, воровать скверно! Это штука стара, её бросить пора... Да ведь голод-то не тётка, что-нибудь надобно делать! (Островский 2). [L.K.:] No, brother, stealing's a bad business, and an old one to boot; time to have done with it. But hunger's no joke, a man's got to eat (2b).

< Abbreviated variant of the saying «Голод не тётка, пирожка не поднесёт ⟨не подсунет⟩».

Г-296 • МОРИ́ТЬ ГО́ЛОДОМ *кого* [VP; subj: human] to keep s.o. very hungry: X морит Y-а голодом ≃ X is starving Y (to death); ‖ X морит себя голодом ≃ X is starving himself; X is depriving himself of food; [in limited contexts] X is on a hunger strike.

«Неужто и компот дают [в лагере]?»... — «Это где какой начальник. Один голодом морит, а другой, если хочет, чтобы план выполняли, и накормит тебя, и оденет потеплее, только работай на совесть» (Войнович 2). "They actually serve compote in there [the camp]?"..."Depends on your boss. One'll starve you to death, another one, if he wants to fulfill the plan, will feed you and dress you warm, as long as you give it everything you've got, that's all" (2a). Его [Мандельштама] преследует страх отравы — ...и он морит себя голодом, совершенно не дотрагиваясь до казённой баланды (Мандельштам 1). Terrified of being poisoned, he [Mandelstam] was starving himself, refusing to touch the soup on which the prisoners were fed (1a). ♦ Нашего же героя юность была кондитерскими околдована, так что потом, моря себя голодом в крепости, он — в «Что делать?» — наполнял иную реплику невольным воплем желудочной лирики... (Набоков 1). Our hero's youth had been bewitched by pastry shops, so that later, while on [a] hunger strike in the fortress, he—in *What to Do?*—filled this or that speech with an involuntary howl of gastric lyricism... (1a).

Г-297 • В ГО́ЛОС [PrepP; Invar; adv] **1.** ~ кричать, плакать и т. п. *substand* (to scream, cry etc) at a great volume, so that everyone can hear: (yell ⟨shout etc⟩) at the top of one's voice ⟨lungs⟩; (weep ⟨wail, lament etc⟩) loudly; (cry) aloud.

«Ах ты, мошенник эдакий! Ведь я тебе кричал в голос: сворачивай... направо! Пьян ты, что ли?» (Гоголь 3). "Hey you, damned fool, I was hollering to you at the top of my voice. Keep to the right!... Are you drunk, or what?" (3c). ♦ [Гладышев] толкнул Нюру ногой в живот. Нюра упала в борозду и завыла в голос (Войнович 2). [Gladyshev] gave Nyura a shove in the stomach with his foot. Nyura fell back into a furrow and began howling at the top of her lungs (2a). ♦ Плача в голос, обращаясь к умершему отцу, растрёпанная и опухшая, горько сетовала она по-бабьи на свою нескладную судьбину, что некому её ни понять, ни приветить... (Айтматов 2). Weeping loudly, all dishevelled and with tear-swollen eyes, she deplored her fate, as women will, complaining to her dead father that no one understood or appreciated her... (2a).

2. ~ ответить, воскликнуть и т. п. *obs* (to answer, exclaim sth. etc) all together, simultaneously: in ⟨with⟩ one voice; in unison; in chorus.

«Ну что, дураки... зачем вы вздумали бунтовать?» — «Виноваты, государь ты наш», — отвечали они [мужики] в голос (Пушкин 2). "Well, fools...what made you rebel?" "We're guilty, master," they [the peasants] answered in unison (2a).

3. ~ **утверждать, повторять** *что* и т. п. *obs* (to assert, repeat etc sth.) showing complete accord: **with one voice; unanimously; in unison; as one.**

Г-298 • **В ОДИ́Н ГО́ЛОС** [PrepP; Invar; adv; fixed WO] **1.** ~ **сказать, воскликнуть** и т. п. [more often used with pfv verbs] (to say, exclaim etc sth.) all together, simultaneously: **in ⟨with⟩ one voice; with a single voice; in unison; in chorus.**

«Моя первая любовь принадлежит действительно к числу не совсем обыкновенных»... – «А!» – промолвили хозяин и Сергей Николаевич в один голос (Тургенев 3). "It so happens that my first love was not exactly ordinary"...."Ah!" the host and Sergei Nikolaich exclaimed in one voice (3c). ♦ «Последние находки в Сахаре и Месопотамии позволяют думать, что в далёкие времена на Земле побывали пришельцы из космоса». – «Может быть, те самые марсиане?» в один голос ахнули дамы (Аксёнов 2). "Recent discoveries in the Sahara and Mesopotamia give us reason to think that in far-off times the Earth was visited by strangers from outer space." "Perhaps these same Martians?" The ladies oohed and aahed with one voice (2a). ♦ «Здорово живёшь, Домаха!» – гаркнули в один голос граждане. «Здравствуйте!» (Салтыков-Щедрин 1). "How are you doing, Domashka?" roared the citizens with a single voice. "Hallo there!" (1b). ♦ Вскоре вернулись все женщины и... принялись за работу. Примерно через час в сарай вошёл мальчик и сказал, что у Цицы девятнадцать шнуров [нанизанного табака]. «Не может быть!» – в один голос воскликнули все женщины... (Искандер 3). Soon all the women returned...and got back to work. About an hour later the little boy came into the shed and said that Tsitsa had nineteen strings [of tobacco strung]. "Impossible!" all the women exclaimed in unison... (3a).

2. ~ **утверждать, повторять, заявлять** и т. п. (to assert, repeat, declare etc sth.) showing complete accord: **with one voice; unanimously; (be) unanimous (in declaring sth. etc); in unison; as one.**

Все [киевские гимназистки] в один голос говорили, что на её [Маруси] месте они бы ни за что не могли выйти замуж за азиата, хотя бы и сына короля (Паустовский 1). With one voice they [the Kiev schoolgirls] declared that not for anything would they, in her [Marusya's] place, have married an Asiatic, even if he was the son of a king (1b). ♦ Скоро все разошлись по домам, различно толкуя о причудах Вулича и, вероятно, в один голос называя меня эгоистом... (Лермонтов 1). Soon everyone left, each giving his own interpretation of Vulic's eccentric behaviour on the way home, and, probably, unanimously branding me an egoist... (1b). ♦ ...Когда маршал Брежнев начал издавать свою трёхтомную мифологию, все советские классики, секретари Союза писателей, Герои Социалистического Труда и лауреаты в один голос устно и печатно объявили книги маршала неподражаемыми шедеврами... (Войнович 1). When Marshal Brezhnev began to publish his three-volume book of mythology, all the leading lights of Soviet literature, the secretaries of the Writers' Union, the heroes of socialist labor, and all the other prize winners were unanimous in declaring, both verbally and in print, that these books were inimitable masterpieces... (1a). ♦ Тут все, кроме Чунки, стали в один голос утверждать, что лошади здесь подняться не смогли бы... (Искандер 3). Now everyone but Chunka began to affirm in unison that the horses could never have climbed this bank... (3a).

Г-299 • **ВО ВЕСЬ ⟨В ПО́ЛНЫЙ⟩ ГО́ЛОС** [PrepP; these forms only; adv; fixed WO] **1.** ~ **кричать, орать, вопить, петь** и т. п. [intensif] (to shout, yell, sing etc) very loudly: **at the top of one's voice ⟨lungs⟩; with all one's lung power; (scream) one's head off.**

Он [обросший бородой человек] стоял... на коленях и вопил во весь голос, взывая к людям, чтобы они спасли, помогли, потому что его везут на расстрел (Мандельштам 2). He [the bearded man] was on his knees, shouting at the top of his voice,

imploring people to help and save him from being shot (2a). ♦ ...Приняв стойку «смирно», [капитан] произнёс во весь голос, словно командовал: «Здравствуйте, товарищ Сталин!» (Войнович 2). ...Standing at attention, [the captain] pronounced at the top of his lungs, as if barking out an order: "Hello, Comrade Stalin!" (2a). ♦ ...Мы, дети, во весь голос орали за ним [Законоучителем] тексты (Замятин 1). ...We children would yell the prescribed texts after him [the priest] with all our lung power (1b).

2. ~ **говорить, заявлять** и т. п. Also: **ПО́ЛНЫМ ГО́ЛОСОМ** [NP_instrum; Invar; fixed WO] (to speak, assert, declare etc sth.) openly, without hesitation or fear: **speak out ⟨up⟩; let one's voice be heard; [in limited contexts] speak one's mind.**

Все эти вопросы остаются открытыми – не только для иностранцев, но и для нас; в этом не разобраться, пока мы во весь голос не заговорим о нашем прошлом, настоящем и будущем (Мандельштам 1). All these questions will remain open, both for foreigners and for ourselves, until we are able to speak up about our past, present and future (1a).

Г-300 • **ГО́ЛОС СРЫВА́ЕТСЯ/СОРВА́ЛСЯ** *у кого* [VP_subj] **1.** s.o.'s voice changes sharply, often becoming temporarily silent or jumping into a higher register (often caused by stress, strong emotion, or tiredness of the vocal cords): голос у X-а сорвался ≃ **X's voice cracked ⟨broke, gave out⟩; X's voice failed him.**

...[Ольга] хотела было также сказать: «прощай», но голос у ней на половине слова сорвался... (Гончаров 1). ...She [Olga] tried to say "good-bye," but her voice broke in the middle of the word (1b).

2. s.o.'s voice produces a false note in singing (usu. from straining the vocal cords on a high note): голос у X-а сорвался ≃ **X's voice broke ⟨cracked⟩; [in limited contexts] X hit a clinker ⟨a clam⟩.**

Г-301 • **ПОВЫША́ТЬ/ПОВЫ́СИТЬ ГО́ЛОС** [VP; subj: human] **1.** to (begin to) speak at a higher volume than before (in order to be heard at a distance etc): X повысил голос ≃ **X raised his voice; X spoke ⟨began to speak⟩ louder ⟨more loudly⟩;** ‖ *Neg* X не повышал голоса ≃ **X kept ⟨held⟩ his voice down; X didn't raise ⟨never raised⟩ his voice.**

Хотя он стоял довольно далеко от нас и говорил не повышая голоса, мы отчётливо слышали каждое слово. Although he was standing relatively far from us and spoke without raising his voice, we heard every word he said distinctly.

2. ~ *(на кого).* Also: **ПОВЫША́ТЬ/ПОВЫ́СИТЬ ТОН** to (begin to) speak at a higher volume as a result of irritation, exasperation etc, or in order to sound more authoritative: X повысил голос (на Y-а) ≃ **X raised his voice (to Y).**

В первый раз за всю жизнь он повысил голос во гневе (Айтматов 1). For the first time in his life he raised his voice in anger (1a). ♦ Битый час он доказывал рыжей врачихе, что плоскостопие недостаточный повод, чтоб ошиваться в тылу. Он повышал на неё голос, льстил и даже пытался соблазнить... (Войнович 2). For a good hour he tried to prove to the red-haired woman doctor that being flat-footed was insufficient grounds for being forced to idle in the rear. He raised his voice to her, tried flattery, and even attempted to seduce her... (2a).

Г-302 • **ПОДАВА́ТЬ/ПОДА́ТЬ ГО́ЛОС** [VP] **1.** [subj: human or animal] (of people) to make one's presence known by saying sth.; (of animals) to make its presence known by producing its characteristic sounds: [of people] X подал голос ≃ **X opened his mouth; [in limited contexts] X found his tongue; X chimed in;** ‖ *Neg* X не подавал голоса ≃ **X held his tongue; X kept his mouth shut;** ‖ [of animals] X подаёт голос ≃ **X is making itself ⟨himself, herself⟩ heard; X is reminding us ⟨you etc⟩ of its**

⟨his, her⟩ presence; X let out a bark ⟨a neigh, a moo, a chirp etc⟩.

[Тарелкин:] Ох, ох, – разбойники – что вы? [Расплюев:] Ага – голос подал! (Сухово-Кобылин 3). [T.:] Oh, oh—criminals—what are you doing? [R.:] Aha! He's found his tongue again! (3a).

2. [subj: human] to voice one's opinions: X подал голос ≃ **X made himself ⟨his voice⟩ heard; X let his voice be heard; X spoke up;** [in limited contexts] **X found his voice.**

Жёлчный агроном после этого письма [Платона Самсоновича], видимо, больше не пытался спорить, зато вежливый зоотехник продолжал подавать голос (Искандер 6). Platon Samsonovich's reply apparently silenced the acrimonious agronomist for good. The polite livestock expert, however, continued to make himself heard (6a). ♦ Самое удивительное, что ещё копошатся люди, которые пробуют подать голос сквозь толщу воды, со дна океана. Среди них и я, хотя мне точно известно, какие нужны сверхчеловеческие усилия, чтобы сохранить кучку рукописей (Мандельштам 2). The most astonishing thing is that there are still a few people with just enough life in them to try making their voices heard, but only through an immense volume of water, from the bottom of the ocean, as it were. Among them I count myself—and I know, if anybody does, what superhuman efforts are needed just to preserve a handful of manuscripts (2a). ♦ Раз, когда Илья Нетёсов подал голос насчёт того, чтобы поблагодарить Анфису Петровну, [Михаилу] показалось, что Анфиса Петровна кого-то ищет глазами в зале. Может, его искала? (Абрамов 1). When Ilya Netyosov had spoken up about thanking Anfisa Petrovna, [Mikhail] had thought he had seen her searching for someone in the room. For him maybe? (1a).

3. [subj: human] to send s.o. a letter, inform s.o. about o.s.: X подал голос ≃ **X dropped (person Y) a line;** ‖ X не подаёт голоса ≃ **X hasn't been heard from.**

4. ~ *за кого-что* [subj: human] to vote for s.o. or sth.: X подал голос за Y-а ≃ **X cast his vote for Y; X gave Y his vote; X said yes to Y.**

Г-303 • ПОДНИМА́ТЬ ⟨ПОДЫМА́ТЬ⟩/ПОДНЯ́ТЬ ГО́ЛОС *lit* [VP; subj: human or collect] **1.** ~ *против кого-чего; в защиту кого-чего, за кого-что* to speak up resolutely, publicly (in opposition to or support of s.o. or sth.): X поднял голос против ⟨в защиту⟩ Y-а ≃ **X raised his voice against ⟨in defense of⟩ Y.**

2. to assert o.s., one's rights, some claims etc: X поднял голос ≃ **X spoke out; X made his voice heard.**

«...Если они [такие люди, как Иван Лукич,] сейчас выступят против Сталина, то от этого, кроме ещё нескольких тысяч покойников, ничего не будет, а вред большой. Ведь настанет время, когда они смогут поднять свой голос» (Гинзбург 1). "...If they [people like Ivan Lukich] stand up against Stalin now no good will come of it, it'll only be death for a few more thousand people. A time will come for them to speak out..." (1b). ♦ Из всех этих партий, в то самое время, как князь Андрей приехал к армии, собралась ещё одна, девятая партия, начинавшая поднимать свой голос. Это была партия людей старых, разумных, государственно-опытных... (Толстой 6). Just at the time Prince Andrei reached the army, another, a ninth party was being formed and beginning to make its voice heard. This was the party of the elders—judicious, capable men, experienced in government affairs... (6a).

Г-304 • ПОНИЖА́ТЬ/ПОНИ́ЗИТЬ ГО́ЛОС [VP; subj: human] to (begin to) speak at a lower volume: X понизил голос ≃ **X lowered his voice; X spoke ⟨started speaking⟩ more softly.**

Капарин глянул в сторону... Фомина и Чумакова и, хотя расстояние до них было порядочное и они никак не могли слышать происходившего разговора, понизил голос. «Я знаю ваши отношения с Фоминым и другими» (Шолохов 5). Kaparin

glanced in the direction of Fomin and Chumakov and, although they were a good distance away and could not possibly hear him, he lowered his voice. "I know what your relationship is with Fomin and the others" (5a).

Г-305 • СРЫВА́ТЬ/СОРВА́ТЬ ГО́ЛОС [VP; subj: human] to lose temporarily the ability to speak (from too much shouting, screaming etc): X сорвал голос ≃ **X lost his voice;** [in limited contexts] **X strained his voice.**

Г-306 • ПЕТЬ ⟨ГОВОРИ́ТЬ⟩ С ЧУЖО́ГО ⟨ТВОЕГО́ и т. п.⟩ ГО́ЛОСА *coll, disapprov* [VP; subj: human] being influenced by another person (or other people) and not having one's own opinion, to repeat the thoughts, opinions of that person (or those people): X поёт с чужого голоса ≃ **X is parroting someone else's words ⟨ideas, views⟩; X takes his opinions from others;** [in limited contexts] **X has no mind of his own.**

Люди, дававшие направление разговорам... не показывались в клубе, а собирались по домам, в своих интимных кружках, и москвичи, говорившие с чужих голосов (к которым принадлежал и Илья Андреич Ростов), оставались на короткое время без определённого суждения о деле войны и без руководителей (Толстой 5). The men who set the course in conversation...did not show themselves at the Club, but met in intimate circles in their own homes, and those Muscovites who took their opinions from others (Count Ilya Andreyevich Rostov among them) remained for a while without any definite views in regard to the war, and without guidance (5a). ♦ С зэком-историком они стараются не спорить. А когда такой, как я, ссылается на статью из журнала, на документ, словом, на печатное слово — они убеждены, что ты говоришь с чужого голоса, что кто-то из зэков ведёт в лагере враждебную пропаганду... (Марченко 1). [context transl] They tried not to argue with a con who was a historian. But when somebody like me referred to an article in a magazine or a document, in short any printed source, they were convinced he was repeating it from hearsay, that one of the cons in the camp was spreading hostile propaganda... (1a).

Г-307 • С ГО́ЛОСА ⟨-у⟩ учить, запоминать [PrepP; these forms only; adv] (to learn, memorize sth.) solely by listening to it: **by ear.**

Г-308 • В ГО́ЛОСЕ [PrepP; Invar; subj-compl with copula (subj: human)] one is in good vocal form: **in good voice.**

[Лорд:] Браво, браво! Моя дорогая, вы сегодня в голосе, как никогда! (Булгаков 1). [L.:] Bravo, bravo! You have never been in better voice than tonight, my dear! (1a).

Г-309 • ДУРНЫ́М ГО́ЛОСОМ кричать, орать, визжать и т. п. *coll* [NP$_{instrum}$; usu. sing; adv; fixed WO] (to scream, yell etc) hysterically: **(scream) in a wild ⟨an unnatural⟩ voice; howl (with grief ⟨with pain etc⟩); scream bloody murder.**

«„Уведомляю Вас..."» – начала Дуняшка и, сползая с лавки, дрожа, крикнула дурным голосом: – Батя! Батянюшка!.. Ой, ма-а-ама! Гриша наш... Ох! Ох, Гришу... убили!» (Шолохов 2). "'I have to inform you...'" Dunyashka began, then slid off the bench, howling with grief. "Oh, Father! Father!...Oh, Mother! Our Grisha...Oh! oh! oh!...he's been killed!" (2a).

Г-310 • НЕ СВОИ́М ГО́ЛОСОМ кричать, орать, вопить, голосить и т. п. *coll* [NP$_{instrum}$; Invar; adv (intensif); fixed WO] (to yell, scream etc) very loudly, hysterically (usu. because of shock, fear, nervousness etc): **in a voice not one's own; in a voice that could no longer be recognized as one's own; in an unnatural ⟨a wild⟩ voice.**

...Ночью, вопя от жути не своим голосом, с керосиновым факелом за спиною, носился он [пожарный вестовой] по городу (Федин 1). ...At night, wailing with terror in a voice not his own, he [the fire warden] had rushed about the town with a kerosene torch on his back (1a). ♦ ...Он вскочил... и не своим голосом закричал: «Разорю!» (Салтыков-Щедрин 2). ...He jumped up and...screamed in a voice that could no longer be recognized as his own—"I'll ruin you!" (2a). ♦ И с самим человеком творилось столько непонятного: живёт-живёт человек долго и хорошо—ничего, да вдруг заговорит такое непутное, или учнёт [*substand* = начнёт] кричать на своим голосом... (Гончаров 1). And so many mysterious things happened to people, too; a man might live for years happily without mishap, and all of a sudden he would begin to talk strangely or scream in a wild voice... (1a).

Г-311 • ГОЛЬ НА ВЫ́ДУМКИ ХИТРА́ [saying] the shortage or absence of sth. forces a person to be resourceful: ≃ **necessity is the mother of invention.**

Это было, конечно, очень сложным, дорогим и неудобным решением. Но это *было* решением!.. Поистине печальная русская поговорка «голь на выдумки хитра» оправдалась здесь с полной точностью! (Владимиров 1). It was, of course, a very complicated, costly and clumsy solution of the problem. But it was a solution none the less....There is in Russian as in English a saying that "necessity is the mother of invention," and it seemed on this occasion to have been demonstrated in practice (1a).

Г-312 • ГОЛЬ ПЕРЕКА́ТНАЯ ⟨КАБА́ЦКАЯ *obs*⟩ *coll* [NP; sing only; usu. this WO] a penniless vagrant (or vagrants), person(s) living in utter poverty: **bum(s); tramp(s); (one is) down-and-out; the riffraff;** [in limited contexts] **(one) owns nothing but his skin.**

Они люди... а я что... я голь перекатная. К моим 30 у меня ничего нет и не будет (Лимонов 1). They're people...and what am I...down-and-out. At 30 I don't have a thing, and never will (1a). ♦ «Много их в Петербурге, молоденьких дур, сегодня в атласе да бархате, а завтра, поглядишь, метут улицу вместе с голью кабацкою» (Пушкин 3). "There are many young fools like her in Petersburg—today attired in satin and velvet, tomorrow sweeping the streets with the riffraff of the town" (3b). ♦ [Отрадина:] Богат [твой жених]? [Шелавина:] Какое богатство! Голь перекатная! (Островский 3). [O.:] Is he [your fiancé] rich? [Sh.:] Rich? He owns nothing but his skin (3a).

Г-313 • ГОРА́ РОДИЛА́ МЫШЬ [sent; fixed WO] great efforts yielded insignificant results, or a person promised much but delivered little: **the mountain brought forth a mouse.**

< The source of the Russian idiom is most likely Horace (65–8 B.C., *Ars poetica*: 139, "*Parturient montes, nascetur ridiculus mus*," "Mountains will heave in childbirth, and a silly little mouse will be born") or Aesop through Phaedrus.

Г-314 • ГОРА́ С ГОРО́Й НЕ СХО́ДИТСЯ, А ЧЕЛОВЕ́К С ЧЕЛОВЕ́КОМ ⟨ВСЕГДА́⟩ СОЙДЁТСЯ [saying] usu. said at an unexpected meeting or when parting for an unspecified amount of time: ≃ **mountains never greet, but friends ⟨men⟩ may (always) meet.**

Г-315 • Е́СЛИ ГОРА́ НЕ ИДЁТ К МАГОМЕ́ТУ, ТО МАГОМЕ́Т ИДЁТ К ГОРЕ́ [saying] if the person or thing s.o. wants does not come to him, he must make the effort to attain what he wants himself: **if the mountain will not come to Muhammad ⟨Mohammed etc⟩, Muhammad must go to the mountain.**

Он [дед]... сватался на базаре к приезжим колхозницам... но у одиноких старух были на селе свои хаты, переселяться в голодный город они не хотели... Дед это скоро понял и сообразил, что если гора не идёт к Магомету, то Магомет идёт к горе. Он срочно полюбил одну старую одинокую колхозницу из Литвиновки по имени баба Наталка... и отправился... в село (Кузнецов 1). He [Grandfather] wooed the collective-farm women at the bazaar....But the old single women had cottages of their own in the countryside and did not want to move to the starving city....Grandfather soon realized this, and understood that if the mountain would not come to Mohammed, Mohammed would have to go to the mountain. He hurriedly fell in love, therefore, with a single collective-farm woman named Granny Natalka from the village of Litvinovka...and went off to the village... (1a).

Г-316 • ⟨КАК ⟨БУ́ДТО, СЛО́ВНО, ТО́ЧНО⟩⟩ ГОРА́ С ПЛЕЧ ⟨СВАЛИ́ЛАСЬ⟩ (*у кого*) *coll* [(как etc +) VP$_{subj}$; these forms only; usu. this WO] s.o.'s state of anxiety, preoccupation with concerns has ended and s.o. feels enormously relieved: (у X-а) как гора с плеч (свалилась) ≃ **(it's ⟨X feels⟩) as if a (terrible) load ⟨a (terrible) burden, a (great) weight⟩ has been lifted from X's shoulders; (it's) a load ⟨a burden, a weight⟩ off X's shoulders ⟨mind⟩; a burden ⟨a weight⟩ fell from X's shoulders; (it's) like a mountain (has been) lifted from X's shoulders.**

[Катерина:] Вот мне теперь гораздо легче сделалось; точно гора с плеч свалилась (Островский 6). [K.:] I feel better now, as if a great weight had been lifted from my shoulders (6f). ♦ «Какое следствие! Никакого следствия не будет!..» — «Что ты, кум! Как гора с плеч! Выпьем!» — сказал Тарантьев (Гончаров 1). "Who's going to prosecute you? There won't be any prosecution...." "You don't say so, old man! Ugh, what a weight off my mind! Let's have a drink!" said Tarantyev (1a).

Г-317 • КТО ВО ЧТО ГОРА́ЗД [Invar; usu. indep. clause; fixed WO] each person is doing whatever he is capable of or chooses to in whatever way he wants: **everyone is doing his own thing; everyone is doing whatever he can ⟨wants, feels like etc⟩;** [in limited contexts] **everyone is saying ⟨trying etc⟩ whatever he can think of.**

«Что обо мне гутарят по хутору?»... — «Господь их знает... Разное брешут, кто во что горазд» (Шолохов 5). "What are they saying about me in the village?"..."God knows....They're saying all kinds o' things, whatever they can think of" (5a).

Г-318 • НЕ ЗА ГОРА́МИ *coll* [PrepP; Invar; subj-compl with copula] **1.** [subj: concr, collect, or human] some place (organization, person) is a short distance (from somewhere), nearby: **not (very ⟨too, that, so⟩) far away.**

2. [subj: abstr] (of an event or the time of an event) sth. will occur soon, in the near future: **(sth.) is not (too ⟨very⟩) far away ⟨off⟩; (sth.) will happen any day now; (sth.) is close at hand;** [in limited contexts] **(sth.) is getting closer every day.**

...Он [Мандельштам] уже знал, что над ним нависла смертельная опасность и гибель не за горами (Мандельштам 2). ...He [Mandelstam] knew by now that he was in mortal danger and that his end was not far away (2a). ♦ Снова, как и в прошлом году в это время, стало казаться, что победа не за горами (Гладков 1). Again—as at the same time the previous year—it was beginning to seem that victory was not far off (1a). ♦ Пролетарская революция в тылу у противника не за горами (Максимов 2.) "Any day now a proletarian revolution will break out on the enemy's home front" (2a). ♦ «Вы, товарищ Чонкин, по политподготовке отстаёте от большинства других бойцов... А ведь не за горами инспекторская поверка. С чем вы к ней придёте?» (Войнович 2). "In political training, you, Comrade Chonkin, are lagging far behind most of the rest of the men....The check on political training is getting closer every day and what are you going to have to show when it comes?" (2a).

Г-319 • ГОРБА́ТОГО МОГИ́ЛА ИСПРА́ВИТ [saying] a person's deep-rooted shortcomings, habits etc are impossible to correct, a person's nature cannot change: ≃ **a leopard cannot change his ⟨its⟩ spots; can the leopard change his ⟨its⟩ spots?; what's bred in the bone...**

«Всерьёз обиделись мужики, не вернутся». — «Не плясать же мне перед ними? — сорвал на нём [старом ветеринаре] досаду Андрей. — Когда-никогда, всё одно подвели бы. Горбатого могила исправит» (Максимов 3). "They've [the peasants have] really taken offense. They won't be back." Andrei vented his annoyance on him [the old veterinarian]. "What am I supposed to do, dance for them? They'd have let us down sooner or later anyway. The leopard can't change his spots" (3a).

Г-320 • СВОИ́М ⟨СО́БСТВЕННЫМ⟩ ГОРБО́М зарабатывать, добывать *что* и т. п. [NP_{instrum}; these forms only; adv; fixed WO] (to earn, attain sth.) through one's own hard work: **with one's own sweat; by the sweat of one's brow; by one's own toil; by dint of hard work ⟨labor⟩.**

…Над тобой стоят дармоеды-надзиратели… тебя попрекают куском хлеба, который ты заработал своим горбом (Марченко 1). …You have these parasitical warders standing over you, grudging you the crust of bread that you've earned with your own sweat (1a). ♦ Все подтверждают и другое — [Мигулин] образованный, книгочей, грамотней его не сыскать, сначала учился в церковноприходской, потом в гимназии, в Новочеркасском юнкерском, и всё своим горбом, натужливыми стараниями… (Трифонов 6). Everyone claims that he [Migulin] has other qualities besides: that he is educated, that a better read, more literate man you won't find. First he went to the parish school, then to the high school and Novocherkassk Cadet College, and all by the sweat of his…brow, by his own strenuous efforts (6a).

Г-321 • ЧУЖИ́М ГОРБО́М наживать, добывать *что* coll [NP_{instrum}; Invar; adv; fixed WO] (to acquire, gain sth.) through someone else's hard work: **(by) cashing in on other people's labors; (by) letting others do (all) the work for one.**

Г-322 • НА СВОЁМ ⟨НА СО́БСТВЕННОМ⟩ ГОРБУ́ испытать, испробовать *что*; НА СВОЕ́Й ⟨НА СО́БСТВЕННОЙ⟩ СПИНЕ́ all coll [PrepP; these forms only; sent adv] (of a person) (to know, learn sth.) from one's own hard experience: X испытал Y на своём горбу ≃ **X learned Y the hard way; X learned Y by bitter experience; X learned Y in the school of hard knocks.**

Г-323 • НА ЧУЖО́М ГОРБУ́ ⟨НА ЧУЖО́Й СПИНЕ́⟩ В РАЙ ВЪЕ́ХАТЬ highly coll, disapprov [VP; subj: human; often infin with хочет, думает etc; fixed WO] to use s.o.'s hard work to one's own advantage: X хочет на чужом горбу в рай въехать ≃ **X wants to reap where he hasn't sown; X wants to profit from the fruits of others' labors.**

Г-324 • ГО́РЕ ЛУ́КОВОЕ coll, humor [NP; usu. used as vocative; fixed WO] a sluggish person who bungles everything: **(you) lummox; (you) oaf; (you) blunderer.**

Подошла и накинулась на Чонкина Нюра: «Ах ты, горе луковое, да кого ж ты уговариваешь и кого жалеешь? Он тебя жалел, когда из ружья целил? Он тебя убить хотел!» (Войнович 2). Nyura came up to Chonkin and started in on him. "Ach, Vanya, you blunderer. Whose mind are you trying to change, who are you feeling sorry for? Was he feeling sorry for you when he aimed the gun at your head? He wanted to kill you!" (2a).

Г-325 • ГО́РЕ МЫ́КАТЬ; НАМЫ́КАТЬСЯ ГО́РЯ both obsoles, coll [VP; subj: human; more often this WO (1st var.)] to experience hardship, adversity, suffering, extreme poverty: X горе мыкал ≃ **X led a wretched ⟨hard⟩ life; X lived in hardship.**

«Кабы не барыня, дай бог ей здоровье! — прибавил Захар, крестясь, — давно бы сгиб я на морозе. Она одежонку на зиму даёт и хлеба сколько хочешь… Да из-за меня и её стали попрекать, и я ушёл… Вот теперь второй год мыкаю горе…» (Гончаров 1). "If it wasn't for the mistress — God bless her! — I'd have

perished long ago in the frost. She gives me some clothes for the winter and as much bread as I want…but they began nagging at her on my account, so I just walked out of the house, sir. Aye, sir, it'll be two years soon since I began leading this wretched life…" (1a).

Г-326 • ЗАВИВА́ТЬ/ЗАВИ́ТЬ ГО́РЕ ВЕРЁВОЧКОЙ folk [VP; subj: human; often pfv imper or fut (1st pers)] to stop fretting, worrying, grieving: завей горе верёвочкой ≃ **put your worries ⟨cares, troubles, sorrows etc⟩ behind you; pack up your cares ⟨troubles etc⟩; forget your troubles ⟨sorrows etc⟩.**

«Геологом мечтала [стать]. А теперь, — круглые… глаза её [Валентины] на мгновение помертвели, — завей горе верёвочкой!..» (Максимов 3). "I dreamt of being a geologist. But now…" Her [Valentina's] round eyes…went blank for a moment. "…Let's forget our troubles" (3a).

Г-327 • ЗАЛИВА́ТЬ/ЗАЛИ́ТЬ ГО́РЕ ⟨ТОСКУ́⟩ (чем) [VP; subj: human] to suppress a feeling of grief by drinking: X заливает горе ≃ **X is drowning his sorrows ⟨troubles, woes etc⟩; X is drinking away ⟨drinking to forget⟩ his sorrows ⟨troubles, woes etc⟩.**

Шарманщика не было дома — он всё ещё заливал своё горе с приятелями… (Паустовский 1). [The organ grinder] was still out with his friends, drowning his sorrows in the pubs (1a).

Г-328 • НА ГО́РЕ чьё, кому [PrepP; Invar; the resulting PrepP is sent adv] (of an action or event) resulting in grave consequences (for s.o. or o.s.): **to s.o.'s ⟨one's (own)⟩ misfortune; to s.o.'s ⟨one's (own)⟩ grief ⟨sorrow⟩.**

Да, показал дед Крессе, на горе Поклену-отцу, его сыну ход в Бургонский Отель! (Булгаков 5). Yes, to the misfortune of Poquelin the elder, grandfather Cressé had shown the boy the way to the Hôtel de Bourgogne! (5a).

Г-329 • исчезнуть, пропасть С ГОРИЗО́НТА (чьего) [PrepP; Invar; the resulting PrepP is adv] (to stop associating) with a certain group of people: X исчез с (Y-ова) горизонта ≃ **X disappeared from the scene ⟨from Y's circle⟩; X left the scene ⟨the picture⟩; X disappeared from sight ⟨from view⟩; X dropped out of sight ⟨the picture⟩.**

А в скором времени исчез с горизонта и сам Жёлудев Н.А. Его сняли «за нетактичное поведение» (Грекова 3). …Soon Zheludev, N.A. disappeared from the scene. He was removed for "tactless behavior" (3a). ♦ Прошло полтора года… Удар, нанесённый Лопаткину, оказался как раз тем предельным усилием его противников, которого он опасался и ждал. Изобретатель исчез с горизонта (Дудинцев 1). A year and a half had gone by. The blow that had been struck at Lopatkin proved to be that final effort of his opponents which he had feared and expected. The inventor disappeared from sight (1a).

Г-330 • появиться, возникнуть НА ГОРИЗО́НТЕ чьём [PrepP; Invar; the resulting PrepP is adv] (to begin to associate) with a given group of people: X появился на Y-овом горизонте ≃ **X appeared ⟨came⟩ on the scene; X came into the picture; X entered Y's circle.**

Г-331 • НЕ ГОРИ́Т (у кого) coll [VP; this form only; impers or with subj: это] there is no need to hurry: (у X-а) не горит ≃ **there's no (big) rush ⟨hurry⟩; it can wait; X is in no rush ⟨no hurry⟩.**

Вы можете отложить эту работу на завтра — не горит. You can put off that work till tomorrow — there's no rush.

Г-332 • СТАНОВИ́ТЬСЯ/СТАТЬ ⟨ВСТАТЬ⟩ ПОПЕРЁК ГО́РЛА кому, у кого coll [VP; subj: human or abstr; usu. pfv] to become unbearable for s.o., vex s.o.: X стал Y-у поперёк горла ≃ **X stuck in Y's throat ⟨craw, gullet⟩; X got Y's goat.**

«Поперёк горла вам Лашковы встали, потому как Лашковы по совести, по справедливости жизнь устроить хочут [*ungrammat* = хотят]» (Максимов 3). "The Lashkovs stick in your craw because the Lashkovs want to bring some honor and justice into life" (3a). ♦ ...Вот что ему, Михаилу, поперёк горла – Егоршина спесь (Абрамов 1). ...What got Mikhail's goat was Egorsha's arrogance (1a).

Г-333 • СТОЯ́ТЬ ПОПЕРЁК ГО́РЛА *у кого coll* [VP; subj: human or abstr] to annoy, vex, irritate s.o. greatly: **X стоит у Y-а поперёк горла ≃ X sticks in Y's throat ⟨craw, gullet⟩; X is a thorn in Y's side ⟨flesh⟩.**

В Москве двадцатых годов шутить было не с кем. Шутки Петеньки и одесситов стояли поперёк горла (Мандельштам 2). In the Moscow of the twenties there was nobody to exchange jokes with. The jokes of Petia and the Odessans stuck in one's gullet (2a). ♦ ...Вообще посадили [меня] не за то – был, не был дома, а за то, что я, какой есть, не гожусь в этой стране, вечно я им поперёк горла, а они мне (Марченко 2). ...I was being sent up not because of whether or not I was home, but because I was who I was. This country was not the place for me: I was a thorn in their flesh and they in mine (2a).

Г-334 • ЗАСТРЕВА́ТЬ/ЗАСТРЯ́ТЬ В ГО́РЛЕ *у кого coll* [VP; subj: слова, упрёк(и) etc] (of a statement, reproach etc) to be left unsaid, unfinished (because the speaker cannot bring himself to say it, is overwhelmed by emotion, is embarrassed or ashamed, realizes that what he is about to say is offensive etc): **слова застряли у X-а в горле ≃ the words stuck in X's throat; the words didn't ⟨wouldn't⟩ come out.**

Басмановой предложили обмен... Пришёл мужчина в зелёной велюровой шляпе, подал Басмановой эту мысль и ушёл. Мы думали, она возмутится, пойдёт красными пятнами, бросит свой отказ вслед велюровой шляпе – ничуть! Басманова зашла к нам в комнату... и плавным голосом пересказала нам эту мысль, и даже слова не застревали у неё в горле, а лились не иссякая... (Михайловская 1). Basmanova was offered an exchange of rooms....A man in a green velvet hat came to see Basmanova, made the suggestion and left. We thought she would be indignant, that her face would flush, that she would hurl her refusal at the velvet hat – not at all! Basmanova came to our room...and in a smooth voice, told us of the idea. The words did not stick in her throat, they poured out in an endless stream (1a).

Г-335 • БРАТЬ/ВЗЯТЬ ⟨ХВАТА́ТЬ/СХВАТИ́ТЬ⟩ ЗА ГО́РЛО ⟨ЗА ГЛО́ТКУ⟩ *кого;* **НАСТУПА́ТЬ/НА-СТУПИ́ТЬ НА ГО́РЛО ⟨НА ГЛО́ТКУ⟩** *кому all coll* [VP; subj: human] to coerce, force s.o. to (begin to) act in a certain fashion: **X взял Y-а за горло ≃ X took ⟨got, grabbed⟩ Y by the throat.**

Как только приедет Мансур, нужно взять его за горло: пускай одолжит рублей триста, потом с издательством рассчитается (Трифонов 5). As soon as Mansur arrives I'll have to take him by the throat. Let him lend me 300 rubles or so, and later on he can settle with the publishing house (5a). ♦ «Ты, оказывается, против иностранного вмешательства? Но, по-моему, когда за горло берут – рад будешь любой помощи» (Шолохов 5). "So you're against foreign intervention? But in my view, when someone's got you by the throat you should be glad of any help you can get" (5a).

Г-336 • БРАТЬ/ВЗЯТЬ НА ГО́РЛО ⟨НА ГЛО́ТКУ⟩ *кого highly coll* [VP; subj: human] (to try) to gain the advantage over s.o., make s.o. submit, by shouting at him: **X берёт Y-а на горло ≃ X tries to gain the upper hand by shouting at Y; X tries to get ⟨force⟩ Y to back down by shouting at him; [in limited contexts] X starts a shouting match with Y.**

...Я начал скандалить, требовать свои книги... Конечно, дежурный офицер сначала поругался со мной с полчаса для приличия, попытался взять на горло. Но уж знали они меня достаточно, сидел я у них третий раз, – понимали, что не уймусь, и книги отдали (Буковский 1). ...I kicked up a fuss, demanded my books....For the sake of appearances, the duty officer swore at me for half an hour or so and tried to force me to back down, but they knew me well by now. (This was my third time in Lefortovo.) They realized I wouldn't budge, and they gave me the books (1a). ♦ ...Осташенко побагровел: «Ты меня на горло не бери, Костюковский! – заорал он на меня. – Ты тут демагогией не занимайся, тунеядец!» (Аксёнов 1). ...Ostashenko turned purple. "Don't you start a shouting match with me, Kostyukovsky!" he bawled at me. "Don't you pull any of your demagoguery on me, you parasite!" (1a).

Г-337 • ВО ВСЁ ГО́РЛО ⟨ВО ВСЮ ГЛО́ТКУ⟩ *кричать, орать, хохотать, петь* и т. п. *coll* [PrepP; these forms only; adv (intensif)] (to shout, yell, laugh, sing etc) very loudly: **at the top of one's lungs ⟨voice⟩; [in refer. to laughter] roar ⟨howl, shriek, screech, bellow⟩ with laughter; double over with laughter; [in refer. to singing] belt out (a song ⟨a tune, a number etc⟩).**

Схватившись за руки, [стрельцы] бродили вереницей по улице и, дабы навсегда изгнать из среды своей дух робости, во всё горло орали (Салтыков-Щедрин 1). [The musketeers] zigzagged down the streets with arms linked, yelling at the top of their lungs so as to drive the spirit of timidity forever from their midst (1a). ♦ Полгода назад он [Коля] шёл с лопатой через плечо во главе комсомольского воскресника и пел во всю глотку, а сейчас даже о боли своей не мог рассказать громче шёпота (Солженицын 10). Six months ago he [Kolya] had been striding along, a spade over his shoulder, at the head of a Young Communists' Sunday working party, singing at the top of his voice. Now he could not raise his voice above a whisper, even when talking about his pain (10a). ♦ Чумаков, откинувшись назад, захохотал во всё горло. Он смеялся так, что на глазах его выступили слёзы (Шолохов 5). Chumakov leaned back and roared with laughter. He laughed so hard that tears came to his eyes (5a). ♦ В зал ввалилась компания молодых людей, и сразу стало шумно. Молодые люди... обсели столик в дальнем углу и принялись громко разговаривать и хохотать во всё горло (Стругацкие 1). A group of teenagers burst into the hall, and it immediately got noisy....[They] took over a table in a far corner and started talking and doubling over with laughter (1a).

Г-338 • ДЕРЖА́ТЬ ЗА ГО́РЛО *кого coll* [VP; subj: human or abstr] to coerce, force s.o. to act in a certain fashion: **X держит Y-а за горло ≃ X has Y by the throat; X has backed Y into a corner.**

Чувство бессильного протеста, когда тебя держат за горло, может толкнуть на любые крайности (Марченко 2). When they have you by the throat your feeling of helpless protest may drive you to any extremes (2a).

Г-339 • ДРАТЬ ⟨*less often* **РВАТЬ⟩ ГО́РЛО ⟨ГЛО́ТКУ⟩** *highly coll;* **НАДРЫВА́ТЬ ⟨НАДСА́ЖИВАТЬ⟩ ГО́РЛО ⟨ГЛО́ТКУ⟩** *coll* [VP; subj: human] to speak, shout etc very loudly: **X драл горло ≃ X made ⟨shouted⟩ himself hoarse; X screamed his lungs out; || *Neg Imper* не дери горло ≃ shut your trap; quit hollering.**

...Якулов не мог спокойно слышать о симюльтанэ и надсаживал себе глотку, крича, что Делонэ ограбил его... (Лившиц 1). ...Yakulov couldn't hear of Simultanism without getting worked up and he made himself hoarse shouting that Delauney had robbed him... (1a). ♦ Людям после долгого шагания с пением хотелось посидеть немного молча, и чтобы теперь кто-нибудь другой отдувался за них и драл свою глотку (Пастернак 1). After all the walking and singing people were glad to sit quietly for a while and let others do their work for them, shouting themselves hoarse

(1a). ♦ Хозяин… слыша крик и чуя, что гости перессорились, тотчас явился в комнату. «Ты чего кричишь, глотку рвёшь?» – обратился он к Врублевскому с какою-то непонятною даже невежливостью (Достоевский 1). The innkeeper…hearing shouts and seeing that his guests were quarreling, came into the room at once. "What are you yelling about? Shut your trap!" he addressed Vrublevsky with a sort of discourtesy that was even impossible to explain (1a). ♦ «Что вы тут горло дерёте! Базар, что ли, здесь!» – крикнул я, подходя к одной кучке (Салтыков-Щедрин 2). [context transl] "What are you kicking up such an infernal din for?" I shouted, approaching one group. "Do you think you are in a market place or what?" (2a).

Г-340 • ПЕРЕГРЫ́ЗТЬ ГО́РЛО *кому coll* [VP; subj: human; usu. fut (often used as a threat), subjunctive, or infin with готов etc] to deal or settle accounts with s.o. very harshly: X перегрызёт Y-у горло ≃ **X will slit ⟨cut⟩ Y's throat; X will go for Y's throat ⟨for the jugular⟩; X will wring Y's neck; X will throttle Y.**

Хотя мы и представительствовали в искусстве определённые социально-политические тенденции, однако никому из нас, разумеется, и во сне не приходило в голову, что где-то… у него лежит такой мандат: мы ещё в тринадцатом году перегрызли бы горло всякому, кто попытался бы уверить нас в этом… (Лившиц 1). Although we represented definite sociopolitical tendencies in art, not one of us would have dreamed that he possessed such a mandate. In 1913 we would have throttled anyone who attempted to convince us of this… (1a).

Г-341 • ПЕРЕХВА́ТЫВАТЬ/ПЕРЕХВАТИ́ТЬ ГО́РЛО *у кого, кому* [VP; impers or with subj: спазм(а), что-то etc] to be unable to speak because of strong emotion: у X-а перехватило горло ≃ **X was choked (with hate ⟨rage etc⟩); X was ⟨felt⟩ (all) choked up; X had ⟨got, felt⟩ a lump in his throat;** ‖ спазма перехватила X-у горло ≃ **a spasm seized X's throat.**

Он [Зотов] даже сказать ей ничего не мог, ему горло перехватило ненавистью (Солженицын 12). He [Zotov] was so choked with hate that he could not even speak (12a). ♦ …Теперь у меня так горло перехватило, что я бы, наверное, не смог сделать и глотка (Искандер 3). …Now I had such a lump in my throat that I probably couldn't even have taken a swallow (3a). ♦ …Вдруг впереди, над… степью, как птица, взлетел мужественный грубоватый голос запевалы… Словно что-то оборвалось внутри Григория… Внезапно нахлынувшие рыдания потрясли его тело, спазма перехватила горло. Глотая слёзы, он жадно ждал, когда запевала начнёт… (Шолохов 5). …Suddenly the brave, rather harsh voice of a songleader soared up like a bird over the steppe….Something seemed to snap inside Grigory….A sudden fit of sobbing shook his body and a spasm seized his throat. Swallowing his tears, he waited eagerly for the leader to begin again… (5a).

Г-342 • ПО ГО́РЛО *coll* [PrepP; Invar] **1.** ~ **занят, загружен, завален работой** и т. п. [modif or adv (intensif)] (one is) extremely (busy, overloaded with work etc): **(be) up to one's neck ⟨ears, eyes, elbows⟩ in sth.; have one's hands full; (be) overburdened ⟨weighed down, swamped⟩ (with work etc); (be) buried under a pile of work.**

Кириллов отвечал поспешно и бойко: «Мне, Ардальон Борисыч, нет времени особенно углубляться в городские отношения и слухи, я по горло завален делом» (Сологуб 1). "I have no time, Ardal'on Borisych," replied Kirillov hurriedly, "to get mixed up in town relations and gossip—I'm up to my neck in work" (1a).

2. дел, работы, забот и т. п. *у кого* ~ [quantit subj-compl with copula (subj/gen: abstr)] s.o. has a great quantity (of work, troubles etc), so much that it deeply concerns him: у X-а дел ~ ≃ **X is up to his neck ⟨ears, eyes, elbows⟩ in work; X has his**

hands full; X has enough work and more; X has more than enough to do; X is knee-deep in work; X is overburdened ⟨weighed down, swamped⟩ (with work etc).

[Зоя:] Я знаю, что у вас дела по горло (Булгаков 7). [Z.:] I know you are up to your ears in work (7a). ♦ …Как случилось, что однажды конвой недоглядел, оставил щель в седьмом вагоне во время стоянки? По-человечески понять можно, у конвоя тоже было дел по горло (Гинзбург 1). Once an extraordinary thing happened: the guards omitted to bar our door at one of the stops. Humanly speaking, this was understandable: they had their hands full all day… (1b). ♦ «Желание сажать есть. Лагерей хватает. Работы, которую могут выполнить заключённые, по горло» (Зиновьев 2). "There is still a desire to put people in prison and there are plenty of camps. There is enough work and more which prisoners could do" (2a). ♦ Даже вохровцам недосуг заняться охотой или рыбной ловлей. У них дел по горло (Гинзбург 2). Even the armed guards had no time to spare for hunting or fishing. They had more than enough to get through as it was (2a).

3. быть₀, сидеть, увязнуть в долгах ~ ; **влезать, залезать в долги** ~ [adv (intensif)] (to be in debt, get into debt) beyond any measure: X в долгах ~ ≃ **X is up to his neck ⟨ears⟩ in debt; X is mired ⟨buried⟩ in debt(s); X is swamped with debts; X is deep in the hole ⟨in debt⟩.**

Г-343 • ПРОМОЧИ́ТЬ ГО́РЛО ⟨ГЛО́ТКУ⟩ *coll* [VP; subj: human] to drink some alcohol: X промочит горло ≃ **X will wet his whistle; X will take ⟨have⟩ a (little) nip; X will have a drop (of wine etc); X will have a shot ⟨a slug, a snort⟩ (of whiskey etc).**

Он [Охотников] почему-то полагал, что всем приходящим надо дать что-нибудь пожевать или промочить глотку (Аксёнов 12). For some reason Alexei [Okhotnikov] felt that all guests had to be given something to chew on or to wet their whistles with (12a).

Г-344 • РАСПУСКА́ТЬ/РАСПУСТИ́ТЬ ГО́РЛО ⟨ГЛО́ТКУ⟩ *highly coll, rude* [VP; subj: human] (to begin) to yell, curse very loudly: X распустил горло ≃ **X started yelling ⟨screaming, cursing⟩ his (bloody) head off.**

Г-345 • СЫТ ПО ГО́РЛО *coll* [AdjP; subj-compl with быть₀ (subj: human)] **1.** one is completely sated: X сыт по горло ≃ **X is stuffed (to the gills); X couldn't eat another bite; X has had more than his fill.**

«Положить тебе ещё жаркого?» – «Спасибо, больше не могу. Сыт по горло». "Would you like some more stew?" "No, thanks, I couldn't eat another bite. I'm stuffed to the gills."

2. ~ *(чем)* one has had more than a sufficient amount of sth. (often, of sth. unpleasant): X сыт по горло (Y-ом) ≃ **X has had it (up to here) with Y; X is fed up (to the teeth) with Y; X has had more than his fill ⟨more than enough⟩ (of Y); X has had all he can take (of Y); X is sick to death of Y.**

Поздно вечером Максим понял, что сыт по горло этим городом… (Стругацкие 2). By late evening Maxim had had it with the city (2a). ♦ «Слушай, дед… иди-ка ты отсюдова [*ungrammat* = отсюда] к чёртовой матери. Я этими байками сыт по горло» (Максимов 2). "Listen, Grandpa, why don't you go to bloody hell. I'm fed up to the teeth with your bedtime stories" (3a). ♦ Первый «Пролог» – невозвратимая утрата, второй – дань самоуспокоенной старости в эпоху доброго цезаря, когда Ахматова искала внепространственных бед и страстей, хотя нам вполне хватало посюсторонних несчастий. Я ими сыта по горло (Мандельштам 2). The first *Prologue* is an irreparable loss, but the second is a self-indulgence of her [Akhmatova's] complacent old age, when she tried to invent torments and passions outside space—as though the ones on this side of the fence were not enough for us! I have had much more than my fill (2a). ♦ Маша, всегда жадная до операций… теперь, кажется, была сыта по горло (Грекова 3). Masha, always eager to operate…now had more than enough (3a).

Г-346 • **БРАТЬ/ВЗЯТЬ ГÓРЛОМ** *highly coll* [VP; subj: human; usu. impfv] to get what one wants by shouting, swearing etc., make s.o. submit by being aggressively loud: X горлом берёт ≃ X **gets his way by shouting ⟨cursing etc⟩**; [in limited contexts] X **rants and raves until he gets his way.**

Г-347 • **ПОДСТУПÁТЬ/ПОДСТУПИ́ТЬ ⟨ПОДКÁТЫ- ВАТЬ(СЯ)/ПОДКАТИ́ТЬ(СЯ)⟩ К ГÓРЛУ** *(чьему, у кого)* [VP; subj: usu. слёзы, рыдания etc or impers] (of tears, sobbing, emotion etc) to overwhelm, stifle s.o. so that he is unable to speak: X подступил ⟨X-ы подступили⟩ к Y-ову горлу ≃ X ⟨Xs⟩ **choked Y; Y got choked up; Y felt choked by tears ⟨emotion⟩**; [of tears only] **Xs welled in Y's eyes**; [of feelings] X **welled up (in Y)**; [of a cry, scream etc] X **rose in Y's throat**; ‖ у Y-а подступило к горлу ≃ **a lump rose in Y's throat; Y got a lump in his throat.**

В середине фразы князь Андрей замолчал и почувствовал неожиданно, что к его горлу подступают слёзы, возможность которых он не знал за собой (Толстой 5). Suddenly in the middle of a sentence, he [Prince Andrei] fell silent, feeling choked by tears, a thing he would not have believed possible for him (5a). ♦ Он должен был что-то крикнуть, потому что крик подступал к горлу... но вместо крика ткнул в спину извозчика и выдавил из горла через силу: «Гони!» (Федин 1). He should have cried out, because a cry had risen in his throat...but instead of crying out he prodded the cabby in the back and with a tremendous effort forced from his throat: "Drive on!" (1a). ♦ Ему вспомнились жёлтые круги вокруг глаз [мокреца]. Подкатило к горлу (Стругацкие 1). He remembered the yellow circles around the [slimy's] eyes. A lump rose in his throat (1a).

Г-348 • **ЗÁ ГОРОДОМ** *жить, находиться и т. п.;* **ЗÁ ГОРОД** *поехать, отправиться и т. п.* [PrepP; these forms only; adv or subj-compl with copula (subj: human or concr)] (to live, be located, go etc) outside of an urban area: **(live etc) in the country; (go etc) to the country; (live, go etc) out of town; (live etc) outside of the city.**

Завтра обещают хорошую погоду, давай поедем за город собирать грибы. They say it's going to be nice tomorrow—let's go out to the country and pick mushrooms.

Г-349 • **ДУЙ ⟨РАЗДУ́Й⟩ ТЕБЯ́ ⟨его и т. п.⟩ ГОРÓЙ!** *substand, humor* [Interj; these forms only; fixed WO] a jokingly abusive expression of vexation, surprise, reluctant admiration: **the hell with you ⟨him etc⟩; to hell ⟨blazes⟩ with you ⟨him etc⟩; the devil take you ⟨him etc⟩; a pox ⟨a plague⟩ on you ⟨him etc⟩.**

[Митрич:] Ишь, дуй его горой, налакался как. Доверху (Толстой 1). [M.:] But look at *him,* the hell with him, the way he swilled it up (1a).

Г-350 • **СТОЯ́ТЬ ⟨СТАТЬ, ВСТАТЬ⟩ ГОРÓЙ** *за кого- что* [VP; subj: human or collect] to defend, support s.o. or sth. in every way: X горой стоит за Y-a ≃ X **is behind Y all the way; X backs Y (up) to the hilt ⟨the maximum, the fullest⟩; X is for Y one hundred percent; Y receives X's full backing ⟨support⟩; X stands ⟨sticks⟩ up (loyally) for Y; X is a champion of thing Y.**

[elliptical usage] «Несомненно, будет правительственный переворот, у власти станет Корнилов. Армия ведь за него горой» (Шолохов 3). "There will certainly be a *coup d'état* and Kornilov will take over. The army is backing him up to the hilt" (3a). ♦ ...Когда на конкурс пришло стихотворение лыхнинского бухгалтера под тем же названием, Платон Самсонович стал за него горой... (Искандер 6). ...When the Lykhninsky accountant submitted his poem of the same title, it received Platon Samsonovich's full backing... (6a). ♦ Правда, всегда были читатели, которые горой стояли за него и клялись его именем, но

О.М[андельштам] как-то невольно отталкивался от них (Мандельштам 1). True, there were always readers who stood up for him and swore by him, but M[andelstam] was somehow, despite himself, repelled by them (1a). ♦ Они [банда Курочкина] целиком составили отдельный взвод, крепко сколоченный и державшийся несколько обособленно ото всех остальных. И в боях и на отдыхе они действовали сплочённо, стояли друг за друга горой... (Шолохов 5). They [Kurochkin's band] formed a whole troop and held themselves aloof from the others. Whether fighting or resting they acted together and stood up loyally for each other... (5a). ♦ «Давно пора», — сказал Филимонов, который пришёл к нам всего два месяца назад, прямо из института, и горой стоит за передовые методы (Войнович 5). "It's about time," said Filimonov, who'd been with us all of two months. He was fresh from the institute and a champion of the progressive approach (5a).

Г-351 • **ИДТИ́/ПОЙТИ́ В ГÓРУ** [VP; fixed WO] **1.** Also: **ЛЕЗТЬ/ПОЛÉЗТЬ В ГÓРУ** *coll,* **ПЕРÉТЬ В ГÓРУ** *substand* [subj: human] to improve one's status or job, gain influence, importance, succeed in one's career: X идёт в гору ≃ X **is coming ⟨moving⟩ up in the world; X is rising in the world ⟨rising higher and higher⟩; X is making his way in the world;** [in limited contexts] X **is climbing the ladder of success; X is rising ⟨moving⟩ up the ladder of promotion; X's stock is going up; X is making headway; X is doing very well for himself.**

Василий был на фронте со своей дивизией, потом — корпусом. Он шёл и шёл в гору — генерал, ордена, медали, — и всё больше пил (Аллилуева 1). Vasily was at the front with his division, and later his corps. He rose higher and higher. He became a general. He was awarded orders and medals. And he was drinking more and more (1a). ♦ У Сенатора был повар необычайного таланта, трудолюбивый, трезвый, он шёл в гору; сам Сенатор хлопотал, чтоб его приняли в кухню государя, где тогда был знаменитый повар-француз (Герцен 1). The Senator had a cook, Alexey, a sober, industrious man of exceptional talent who made his way in the world. The Senator himself got him taken into the Tsar's kitchen, where there was at that time a celebrated French cook (1a). ♦ ...Петро быстро и гладко шёл в гору, получил под осень шестнадцатого года вахмистра, заработал, подлизываясь к командиру сотни, два креста и уже поговаривал в письмах о том, что бьётся над тем, чтобы послали его подучиться в офицерскую школу (Шолохов 3). ...Petro was rising quickly and smoothly up the ladder of promotion; in the autumn of 1916 he had received the rank of sergeant-major and earned himself two crosses by sucking up to the squadron commander, and now he spoke in his letters of trying to get himself sent to an officers' training school (3a). ♦ Складка брюк и та могла удостоверить, что Халыбьеву теперь не приходится весь день валяться на сальном диване, что он, наконец, пошёл в гору (Эренбург 2). The crease in his trousers alone proved that Halibieff no longer need spend his time sprawling on a greasy sofa, that he was at last making headway (2a). ♦ Щёкин спросил: «Говорят, твоя жена пошла в гору?» (Трифонов 1). "I hear that your wife's doing very well for herself," said Shchyokin (1a).

2. [subj: abstr (often дела) or a noun denoting an enterprise, business etc] to develop successfully, make progress: X пошёл в гору ≃ X **was on the rise; things were looking up; X began to prosper ⟨was prospering⟩;** [in limited contexts] X **was on the increase; X was going well.**

Вечером, в ожидании радиопереклички, они с Ганичевым подсчитали: подписка пошла в гору (Абрамов 1). In the evening, while waiting for the radio linkup, he [Lukashin] and Ganichev tallied the pledges and saw that things were looking up (1a). ♦ Лишь только вдовьины дела пошли в гору, вдову обложили таким налогом, что куроводство чуть-чуть не прекратилось... (Булгаков 10). As soon as the widow's affairs began to prosper, the government clapped such a tax upon her that her chicken-breeding activities were on the verge of coming to an end (10a).

3. [subj: a noun denoting stocks, securities etc] to increase in value, cost: Х-ы идут в гору ≃ **Xs are going up; Xs are soaring ⟨rising, climbing⟩.**

«Не имея курсов Нью-Йорка, трудно сказать что-нибудь определённое. Но я не продавал бы... Как только всё уляжется, эти бумаги пойдут в гору» (Эренбург 4). "It's impossible to say anything definite without having the New York quotations. But I wouldn't risk it. When everything calms down, those stocks will go up" (4a). ♦ [Бабакина:] Выигрышные билеты, душечка Зинаида Савишна, опять пошли шибко в гору (Чехов 4). [В.:] Lottery tickets are simply soaring again, darling (4b).

Г-352 • **ИДТИ/ПОЙТИ ⟨КАТИ́ТЬСЯ/ПОКАТИ́ТЬСЯ** *coll*⟩ **ПО́Д ГОРУ ⟨ПОД ГО́РУ, ПОД ГО́РКУ** *coll*, **ПОД УКЛО́Н⟩** [VP] **1.** Also: **ИДТИ́/ПОЙТИ́ ⟨КАТИ́ТЬСЯ/ПОКАТИ́ТЬСЯ⟩ ВНИЗ** *coll* [subj: abstr. (often дела) or a noun denoting an enterprise, business etc] to deteriorate sharply: X пошёл под гору ≃ **X went ⟨plunged⟩ downhill; X took a turn for the worse.**

Тут дела немецкой революции пошли быстро под гору... (Герцен 2). Then the fortunes of the German Revolution went rapidly downhill... (2a).

2. *coll*. Also: **КАТИ́ТЬСЯ/ПОКАТИ́ТЬСЯ ВНИЗ** *coll* [subj: human] to deteriorate morally: X покатился под горку ≃ **X really went downhill; X went wrong ⟨astray⟩.**

3. [subj: abstr] (of a season, month, day etc, or of s.o.'s life) to approach its end: X идёт под гору ≃ **X is nearing the ⟨its⟩ end; X is coming ⟨is drawing⟩ to an end ⟨a close⟩; X is waning ⟨ebbing, almost over⟩; [of a period of time] X is making its exit; X is on its way out; X is winding down.**

Сколько Настёна помнила, никогда в эту пору так не заметало. Вот тебе и весна – март покатился под горку (Распутин 2). As long as Nastyona could remember, it never snowed like this at this time of the year. Some spring – and March was almost over (2a). ♦ Петухи покричали и утихли, но после них в ночи что-то потрескивало, подрагивало – ночь, торопясь, шла под уклон (Распутин 3). The cocks had fallen silent, but after them the night was filled with creaking and trembling noises as it hurried to make its exit (3a).

Г-353 • **КАК НА КА́МЕННУЮ ГО́РУ ⟨СТЕ́НУ** *obs*⟩ **надеяться, полагаться** *на кого-что coll* [как + PrepP; these forms only; adv] (to rely on s.o. or sth.) absolutely, completely: X надеется на Y-а ~ ≃ **X has complete faith in Y; X relies fully on Y; X puts all his trust in Y; X counts on Y one hundred percent.**

Г-354 • **НА КУДЫ́КИНУ ГО́РУ** *highly coll* [PrepP; Invar; used as indep. sent; fixed WO] (said, usu. with irritation, as a way to avoid directly answering the question «Куда идёшь?» – "Where are you going?") does it make a difference to you?: **what do you care?; what's it to you?; aren't *we* curious; wouldn't *you* like to know.**

Г-355 • **ОТ ГОРШКА́ ДВА ⟨ТРИ⟩ ВЕРШКА́** *coll* [NP; these forms only; usu. predic with subj: human, often omitted; fixed WO] (of a child or, less often, an adult) very small in height: **knee-high to a grasshopper; a little bit of a thing; peewee; half pint; pint-size** ([NP]); [accompanied by the gesture of placing the hand at a level indicating a short height] **no bigger ⟨taller, higher⟩ than this.**

«Вон слыхал про Мамлакат, от горшка два вершка, а с самим вождём за ручку здоровается [*ungrammat* = здоровается]» (Максимов 2). "You've heard about Mamlakat – only knee-high to a grasshopper she was, but she got to meet Stalin" (2a).

< «Вершок» is an old unit of linear measurement equal to 4.4 cm.

Г-356 • **ХОТЬ ГОРШКО́М НАЗОВИ́, ТО́ЛЬКО В ПЕ́ЧКУ НЕ СТАВЬ** [saying] offensive words can be tolerated as long as they are not accompanied by actions: ≃ **hard words break no bones; sticks and stones may break my bones, but names will never hurt me.**

Г-357 • **ПОД ГОРШО́К стричь** *кого*, **постричься, стрижка** *obsoles, coll* [PrepP; Invar; adv or nonagreeing modif] (to cut s.o.'s hair, have one's hair cut etc) in a straight line around the head: **(give s.o. ⟨get⟩) a bowl (hair)cut; (cut s.o.'s hair ⟨have one's hair cut⟩) in peasant style.**

< From the old way of cutting hair by putting a bowl upside down on a person's head and cutting off or trimming only the hair that stuck out below the bowl.

Г-358 • **ВОРОТИ́ТЬ/СВОРОТИ́ТЬ ⟨СВЕРНУ́ТЬ** и т. п.⟩ **ГО́РЫ ⟨ГО́РУ⟩; ВОРО́ЧАТЬ ⟨ДВИ́ГАТЬ** и т. п.⟩ **ГОРА́МИ ⟨ГО́РЫ⟩** [VP; subj: human; more often pfv; often infin with готов, способен, мочь etc] to accomplish a great task requiring tremendous energy, determination, resourcefulness etc: X горы своротит ≃ **X will move mountains.**

По молодости он спешил двумя руками сворачивать горы в одиночку, обгонял проторённый общий порядок офицерского учения, а едва кончив академию, предлагал реформу генерального штаба и военного министерства (Солженицын 1). In his youth he had been in a hurry to move mountains single-handed. The routine of a regular officer's training was too slow for him, and he was hardly out of the academy when he put forward a plan for the reform of the General Staff and the War Ministry (1a).

Г-359 • **ЗОЛОТЫ́Е ⟨ЗЛАТЫ́Е⟩ ГО́РЫ сулить, обещать** и т. п. [NP; pl only; obj or (with verbs in passive) subj; fixed WO] (to promise s.o.) exaggerated amounts of sth., great riches, everything imaginable: **(promise s.o.) the moon (and the stars); (promise s.o.) mountains of gold ⟨a gold mine, the world⟩.**

Бургонцы и Театр на Болоте, пользуясь тем, что Мольер временно остался без театра, стали сманивать актёров. Они сулили золотые горы мольеровским комедиантам... (Булгаков 5). Taking advantage of the fact that Molière was temporarily without a theater, the Hôtel de Bourgogne and the Marais did everything they could to tempt his actors away from him. They promised his players mountains of gold (5a). ♦ Маляр безнадёжно махнул рукой... и пошёл между койками к двери, истошно выкрикивая на ходу: «Вербовщик, гадёныш, золотые горы сулил, а вышло по семь бумаг на рыло и – крышка!.. Вот-те и заработки!..» (Максимов 3). The painter waved his hand helplessly...and passed between the rows of beds on his way to the door, yelling at the top of his voice as he went. "That rat of an agent promised us a gold mine, and it works out at seventy rubles per head, and that's it....That's what you get when you try to earn a bit!" (3a).

Г-360 • **ПИТЬ/ЗАПИ́ТЬ ГО́РЬКУЮ ⟨МЁРТВУЮ** *obsoles*⟩ *coll* [VP; subj: human] to drink, get drunk unrestrainedly: X пьёт горькую ≃ **X drinks himself blind ⟨silly, unconscious, into a stupor, into oblivion⟩; X drinks like a fish.**

Все чаще и чаще он стал запивать мёртвую, пока, наконец, это не стало его бедой и болезнью (Максимов 3). He drank himself into a stupor with increasing frequency until it became a disease and ruined him (3a). ♦ ...Мастер Безенчук пил горькую и даже однажды пытался заложить в ломбарде свой выставочный гроб (Ильф и Петров 1). ...Bezenchuk drank like a fish and had once tried to pawn his best sample coffin (1a).

Г-361 • **И ГО́РЯ ⟨ГО́РЮШКА⟩ МА́ЛО** *кому coll* [these forms only; impers predic; used as a clause in a compound sent or as an indep. sent contrasted with the preceding context; usu. introduced by Conj «а»; fixed WO] **1.** *often disapprov* s.o.

shows no concern for, pays no attention to, s.o. or sth. (in a situation where he should or is expected to behave otherwise): X-у и горя мало ≃ **X couldn't ⟨could⟩ care less; X doesn't care (a fig ⟨one way or another⟩); X doesn't give a damn ⟨a hoot, a fig⟩; what does it matter to X?; it doesn't worry X (at all ⟨much⟩); X takes no notice of it.**

...Удивил Лизку возчик, который сиднем сидел в стороне. Надрывайтесь, рвите, мужики, жилы, а мне и горюшка мало (Абрамов 1). Lizka was amazed to see the driver sitting on his backside, apart from the others. Bust your guts, boys, knock yourselves out! I could care less (1a). ♦ [Кочкарёв:] Ведь вот что досадно: [Подколёсин] вышел себе — ему и горя мало (Гоголь 1). [K.:] What's so annoying is that he [Podkoliosin] has walked off, he doesn't care... (1c). [K.:] Now what really kills me is that he's [Podkolyosin has] gone off—he just doesn't give a damn (1b). ♦ Бывало, что ни случится — придёт ли Вонифатий доложить, что сахару нет, выйдет ли наружу какая-нибудь дрянная сплетня, поссорятся ли гости, — она только кудрями встряхнёт... — и горя ей мало (Тургенев 3). Whatever happened, whether Vonifaty came in to announce that there was no sugar left, or whether some unsavoury piece of scandal came to light, or her guests began to quarrel, she would only shake her curls...and take no notice of it (3a).

2. *usu. approv* problems or difficulties do not affect s.o.: X-у и горя мало ≃ **it's nothing to X; it doesn't bother ⟨ruffle⟩ X a bit ⟨at all⟩; [in limited contexts] X hasn't ⟨doesn't have, hasn't got⟩ a care in the world.**

(За стеной скрипка активизируется). [Анчугин:] А этому *(жест головой в сторону стены)* горя мало. Пилит и пилит (Вампилов 1). *(The violin in the next room warms up.)* [A.:] *(Nodding towards the wall.)* Hasn't a care in the world, that guy. Keeps on sawing away (1a).

Г-362 • **С ГО́РЯ** пить, запить и т. п. [PrepP; Invar; adv] (to drink) because of unhappiness, in order to dull one's suffering, emotional pain: X с горя запил ≃ **X drank from grief; X drowned his sorrows; X sought solace in a ⟨the⟩ bottle.**

Статский советник, по русскому обычаю, с горя запил... (Гоголь 3). [The official] followed Russian custom and sought solace in the bottle (3e).

Г-363 • **ХЛЕБНУ́ТЬ ⟨ХВАТИ́ТЬ⟩ ГО́РЯ ⟨ГО́РЮШКА, ЛИ́ХА⟩** *coll* [VP; subj: human] to experience much hardship, misfortune in life: X хлебнул горя ≃ **X has had ⟨seen⟩ his share of suffering ⟨grief⟩; X has had more than his share of trouble ⟨hard luck⟩; X has taken ⟨been through⟩ a lot; X's lot has been hard; X has had it rough ⟨tough⟩.**

Впоследствии она сама попала за колючую проволоку, хлебнула горя, но то, как и почему она не простилась с отцом, которого больше не увидела, не могло не остаться пятном на её душе (Мандельштам 2). Later she wound up behind barbed wire herself and had her own share of suffering, but she never ceased to be troubled in her mind at not having said goodbye to her father, whom she never saw again (2a). ♦ «В войну [мадам Бранд] попала в Германию, горя, я думаю, не пригубила, а хлебнула взахлёб» (Михайловская 1). "During the war she [Madame Brand] found herself in Germany, where, I think, she had her share of grief" (1a). ♦ «Нас в этих ротах недаром смертниками звали. До одного выкашивало. Как я выжил? Как я выжил? Однако, вообрази, весь этот кровавый ад был счастьем по сравнению с ужасами концлагеря...» — «Да, брат, хлебнул ты горя» (Пастернак 1). "They called our company the death squad. It was practically wiped out. How and why I survived, I don't know. And yet—would you believe it—all that utter hell was nothing, it was bliss compared to the horrors of the concentration camp...." "Yes, poor fellow. You've taken a lot" (1a).

Г-364 • **ВСЫ́ПАТЬ ⟨ВЛЕПИ́ТЬ⟩ ГОРЯ́ЧИХ** кому *obsoles, substand* [VP; subj: human] to beat, whip, flog s.o.: X

всыпал Y-у горячих ≃ **X gave Y a good thrashing ⟨hiding, beating⟩; X tanned Y's hide; X whipped Y but good.**

[author's usage] [Платонов:] Закати-ка мне chinini sulphurici... [Трилецкий:] Закатить бы тебе сотню-другую горячих! (Чехов 1). [P.:] Let me have some quinine. Lots of it. [T.:] What you want is a good thrashing! (1a). ♦ Всыпали и Мишке по приговору двадцать горячих. Но ещё горячее боли был стыд. Вся станица — и стар и мал — смотрела (Шолохов 3). [context transl] Mishka was also given his twenty strokes. But the disgrace stung more than any pain, for the whole stanitsa—yound and old—was looking on (3a).

Г-365 • **ПОРО́ТЬ ГОРЯ́ЧКУ** *coll, disapprov* [VP; subj: human; often neg imper or infin with не надо, не стоит etc] to act with unnecessary haste, temper, irritation: не пори горячку ≃ **don't do anything rash; don't rush into it ⟨into anything⟩; don't do anything in the heat of the moment; don't plunge headlong (into it ⟨into anything⟩); [in limited contexts] look before you leap.**

[author's usage] Нет, не напороть бы горячки. Люди неповинные пострадают (Солженицын 2). No, mustn't do anything rash. Innocent people would suffer (2a). ♦ Рита советовалась с Ларисой. Та сказала: обождать, не пороть горячки (Трифонов 5). Rita discussed the matter with Larisa, and Larisa advised her to wait awhile and not rush into anything (5a). ♦ Так и вертелось на языке, влепить бы прямым текстом, но сдержался. Нет, нет, пороть горячку не будем. Этот козырь выложим напоследок (Трифонов 6). It was on the tip of his tongue to say it, to slap her in the face with it, but he restrained himself. No, no; not in the heat of the moment. We'll keep that trump card for last (6a).

Г-366 • **ПРОСТИ́ ГО́СПОДИ**[1] *obsoles, coll* [Invar; sent adv (parenth); fixed WO] used by the speaker to express his awareness that something he has just said or is about to say is phrased too sharply: **Lord ⟨God⟩ forgive me.**

«Чернышевского не читал, а так, если подумать... Прескучная, прости Господи, фигура!» (Набоков 1). "I've never read Chernyshevski, but when I come to think of it....A most boring, Lord forgive me, figure!" (1a).

Г-367 • **ПРОСТИ́ ГО́СПОДИ**[2] *euph, highly coll* [used as NP; Invar; fixed WO] a prostitute: **tart; hooker; strumpet; trollop; streetwalker; harlot.**

Г-368 • **В ГОСТЯ́Х ХОРОШО́, А ДО́МА ЛУ́ЧШЕ** [saying] although it is nice to visit other people and places, there is no place one likes to be more than in his own home: ≃ **(be it ever so humble,) there's no place like home; East or West, home is best.**

[Пашка:] Вот, говорят, в гостях хорошо, а дома лучше. Может, правда? Может, хватит мне шататься? Здесь дом, хозяйство, леспромхоз — работы навалом (Вампилов 2). [P.:] They say there's no place like home. Maybe it's true, huh? Maybe I've had enough bumming around? There's a house here to run, the lumber camp—lots of work (2b).

Г-369 • **НА ВСЁМ ГОТО́ВОМ** жить [PrepP; Invar; adv; fixed WO] (to live) having food, housing (and sometimes clothes) provided by s.o. (often without having any household duties): **all one's needs are provided for; everything one needs is provided; (have) bed ⟨room⟩ and board provided; be provided with board ⟨food⟩ and lodgings; [in limited contexts] everything is done for ⟨handed to⟩ one.**

«...На всём готовом будешь жить. Что тут размышлять? Переезжай да и конец...» (Гончаров 1) "You will be provided with board and lodgings. Why hesitate? Move—and that's the end of it" (1a). ♦ «Послушай, Верочка. Ты... жила в семье на всём готовом. Я тебя не осуждаю, я хочу тебе добра и только добра... Мы с тобой муж и жена. У каждого из нас есть права и есть обязанности. Моя обязанность — служить, приносить домой деньги. Твоя обязанность – вести дом» (Грекова 3). "Listen, Verochka....You've lived in a family where everything was done for you. I don't blame you. I wish you the best and only the best....You and I are husband and wife. Each of us has his rights and duties. My duty is to work, to bring home money. Your duty is to take care of the house" (3a).

Г-370 • **ПОД ГРА́ДУСОМ** *coll;* **В ГРА́ДУСЕ** *obs, coll;* **ПОД КУРАЖО́М** *obs, coll;* **В ⟨НА⟩ КУРАЖЕ́** *obs, coll* [PrepP; these forms only; usu. subj-compl with copula (subj: human)] in a state of intoxication, usu. mild: X был под гра́дусом ≃ **X was under the influence; X was feeling good ⟨no pain⟩; X was tipsy ⟨high, tight⟩; X had had one too many.**

Г-371 • **ДЕ́ВЯТЬ ГРАММ** *euph, coll* [NP; subj or obj; fixed WO] the bullet that kills s.o. (usu. at an execution): **nine grams of lead; a dose of lead.**

«Меня брали уже дважды, сейчас я еду домой, но скоро они возьмут меня в третий раз и теперь уже навсегда. Третий раз я не выдержу... Лучше бы уж сразу девять грамм в затылок...» (Максимов 2). "They arrested me twice; I'm on my way home now, but before long they'll get me a third time, and then it'll be for good. I won't hold out a third time....It would be better if they gave you nine grams of lead in the back of the neck..." (2a). ♦ «Миновали тебя вовремя твои девять грамм, ваше преподобие...» (Максимов 3). "Pity you missed your dose of lead when it was your time to go, Your Reverence" (3a).

Г-372 • **КИТА́ЙСКАЯ ⟨ТАРАБА́РСКАЯ⟩ ГРА́МОТА** *(для кого) coll* [NP; sing only; usu. subj-compl with copula (subj: concr or abstr); fixed WO] sth. completely incomprehensible, beyond s.o.'s ability to understand: X для Y-а китайская грамота ≃ **it's Greek ⟨double-dutch⟩ to Y; X is beyond Y ⟨Y's comprehension⟩; X is over Y's head.**

Нехитрая механика занимательной болтовни была для него [Хлебникова] китайской грамотой (Лившиц 1). The facile mechanics of entertaining small talk was double-dutch to him [Khlebnikov] (1a).

Г-373 • **ФИ́ЛЬКИНА ГРА́МОТА** *coll, derog* [NP; sing only; fixed WO] a legally invalid, crudely written, obscure document: **a mere ⟨meaningless, useless, worthless⟩ piece ⟨scrap⟩ of paper; just a piece of paper.**

Друг мой прочитал договор и, к великому моему удивлению, рассердился на меня. «Это что за филькина грамота?» (Булгаков 12). My friend read the contract and to my great astonishment lost his temper with me. "This is nothing but a useless scrap of paper!" (12a).

Г-374 • **НИ ГРА́НА** *чего* [NP_gen; Invar; the resulting phrase is usu. subj/gen with нет, не осталось] not the smallest amount of: **not a ⟨one⟩ grain ⟨ounce, bit, iota⟩ of.**

«Я...никогда и в глаза не видела ни одного из обвинённых, не только что всех, — сказала я. – Но в словах, которые о них пишутся, нет ни грана правды. За это я ручаться могу...» (Чуковская 2). "I have never seen one of the accused with my own eyes, let alone all of them," I said. "But there's not one grain of truth in what they write about them. That I can vouch for..." (2a).

Г-375 • **НА ГРА́НИ** *чего* [PrepP; Invar; the resulting PrepP is subj-compl with copula (subj: human, collect, or abstr) or, rare, nonagreeing postmodif] at the moment or stage just before the onset of a different emotion, phenomenon, event etc: **on the verge ⟨brink⟩ of;** [as postmodif] **to the point of.**

Так почему же я ощущаю себя на грани физической катастрофы? (Довлатов 1). So why, then, do I feel on the verge of a physical catastrophe? (1a). ♦ ...Вся наша страна стоит на грани

нового, может быть, ещё более таинственного, чем революция, исторического периода... (Аксёнов 7). Our country stands on the brink of a new and perhaps more mysterious historical adventure than the Revolution (7a). ♦ В быту тётя Дуся проявляла бережливость на грани скупости (Гинзбург 2). In her everyday dealings Aunt Dusya was thrifty almost to the point of miserliness (2a).

Г-376 • **СТИРА́ТЬ/СТЕРЕ́ТЬ ГРА́НИ ⟨ГРАНЬ⟩** *между кем, между чем* [VP; subj: usu. abstr; fixed WO] to make it so that the differences distinguishing, separating two or more groups or phenomena disappear: X стёр грани между Y-ом и Z-ом ≃ **X obliterated ⟨erased, eliminated⟩ the distinctions ⟨the differences, the boundaries, boundary lines⟩ between Y and Z; X broke down the boundaries between Y and Z.**

Г-377 • **СТИРА́ЮТСЯ/СТЁРЛИСЬ ГРА́НИ** *между кем, между чем* [VP_subj; usu. this WO] the differences distinguishing, separating two or more groups or phenomena are disappearing: стёрлись грани между X-ом и Y-ом ≃ **the boundaries ⟨boundary lines, distinctions, differences⟩ between X and Y were obliterated ⟨erased, eliminated⟩;** ‖ стираются грани между X-ом и Y-ом ≃ **the distinctions ⟨the boundaries⟩ between X and Y are becoming blurred; the line between X and Y is becoming blurred; the boundaries ⟨the differences⟩ between X and Y are melting away.**

...Растление литературы дошло до того, что совершенно стёрлись всякие грани между профессиональным писателем и пришедшим по блату (Войнович 1). The corruption of literature has gone so far as to have obliterated all the boundary lines between the professional writer and those who are published because they have pull (1a). ♦ ...Её увлекла праздничность этого вечера... атмосфера мужского, военного, солдатского единения, когда стираются грани субординации... (Рыбаков 2). ...She was taken with the festive atmosphere of this occasion:...the atmosphere of masculine, martial unity, when the boundaries of seniority became blurred... (2a).

Г-378 • **ЗА ГРАНИ́ЦЕЙ** *быть₀, находиться* и т. п.; **ЗА ГРАНИ́ЦУ** *поехать* и т. п.; **ИЗ-ЗА ГРАНИ́ЦЫ** *вернуться* и т. п. [PrepP; Invar; subj-compl with copula (subj: human, a noun denoting an enterprise, a geographical name etc) or adv] in, to, or from a foreign country or foreign countries: **(be ⟨go, return from** etc⟩**) abroad;** [in limited contexts] **(be** etc**) overseas.**

Для Пьера, воспитанного за границей, этот вечер Анны Павловны был первый, который он видел в России (Толстой 4). Pierre had been educated abroad, and this soirée of Anna Pavlovna's was the first he had ever attended in Russia (4a). ♦ [Известный советский критик] долго допытывался, когда и каким образом мне удалось вернуться из-за границы (Войнович 1). ...He [a well-known Soviet critic] went on and on, questioning me about when and by what means I had managed to return from abroad (1a).

Г-379 • **ПРОВОДИ́ТЬ/ПРОВЕСТИ́ ГРАНЬ** *между кем, между чем* [VP; subj: human or collect] to set up distinctions (usu. exact, definite ones) between two or more phenomena, persons etc: X проводит грань между Y-ом и Z-ом ≃ **X draws a line ⟨a boundary, boundary lines⟩ between Y and Z; X differentiates ⟨makes a distinction⟩ between Y and Z.**

«...Конечно, иногда бывает довольно затруднительно провести достаточно чёткую грань между простой оговоркой и продуманным преступлением» (Войнович 5). "...Of course at times it is quite difficult to draw a sufficiently clear boundary between a simple slip of the tongue and a premeditated offense" (5a).

Г-380 • **ПОД ГРЕБЁНКУ** *стричь кого-что, стрижка* [PrepP; Invar; adv or nonagreeing modif] (to cut s.o.'s hair etc) very short: **(s.o.'s hair is) close cropped; a close-cropped hair-cut; (wear one's hair) cropped close; crop s.o.'s hair; (wear ⟨give s.o.⟩) a crew cut.**

...Он стриг волосы под гребёнку, и неровности его черепа, обнажённые таким образом, поразили бы френолога странным сплетением противоположных наклонностей (Лермонтов 1). His hair is close cropped, and shows up the bumps of his skull, which would astonish a phrenologist by their strange mixture of opposing tendencies (1c). ...He wore his hair cropped close, and the irregularities of his skull thus exposed would have astounded a phrenologist by their queer combination of contradictory inclinations (1b).

Г-381 • СТРИЧЬ/ОСТРИ́ЧЬ ⟨ПОДСТРИГА́ТЬ/ПОД-СТРИ́ЧЬ⟩ ПОД ОДНУ́ ГРЕБЁНКУ *кого coll* [VP; subj: human; usu. impfv; obj: pl, often всех] to regard different people, different groups, or all people as if they were identical in some respect, without considering their differences: X стрижёт всех под одну гребёнку ≃ **X treats everyone ⟨everybody, all [NPs]⟩ as if they were (all) alike ⟨the same⟩; X puts everyone ⟨everybody, all [NPs]⟩ on the same level; X lumps everyone ⟨everybody, all [NPs]⟩ together;** [in limited contexts] **X reduces everyone ⟨everybody, all [NPs]⟩ to the same level.**

К работе с детьми Веру подпускать нельзя: тут нужен индивидуальный подход, а она всех стрижёт под одну гребёнку. Vera mustn't be allowed to work with children: that requires an individual approach, whereas she treats all children as if they were alike. ♦ Я приветствовал нацистов, потому что они провозгласили принцип духовной иерархии. А теперь они стригут всех под одну гребёнку (Эренбург 1). I welcomed the Nazis because they had proclaimed the principle of an intellectual hierarchy. Now they're putting everybody on the same level (1a). ♦ [author's usage] Самому-то Кильдигсу двадцать пять [лет] дали. Это полоса была раньше такая счастливая: всем под гребёнку десять давали. А с сорок девятого такая полоса пошла — всем по двадцать пять... (Солженицын 7). [context transl] Kildigs himself was serving twenty-five years. In happier days everybody got a flat ten. But in '49 a new phase set in: everybody got twenty-five... (7c).

Г-382 • БРАТЬ/ВЗЯТЬ ⟨ПРИНИМА́ТЬ/ПРИНЯ́ТЬ⟩ ГРЕХ НА́ ДУШУ [VP; subj: human; often neg, neg imper, or infin with negated form of хотеть, заставлять etc] **1.** to take moral responsibility for a reprehensible deed: X не хочет брать грех на душу ≃ **X doesn't want (to have) this sin on his conscience.**

2. Also: **ХВАТИ́ТЬ ГРЕХА́ НА́ ДУШУ** *obs, coll* to commit a reprehensible deed: X взял грех на душу ≃ **X committed a sin; X took a sin upon his soul.**

«Это правда?» — Жанна ожила. «Честное слово», — сказал Дмитрий Алексеевич, твёрдо беря на душу новый грех (Дудинцев 1). "Is that really true?" Jeanne asked, brightening. "Word of honor!" Lopatkin said stolidly, taking yet one more sin upon his soul (1a).

Г-383 • ВВОДИ́ТЬ/ВВЕСТИ́ В ГРЕХ *кого coll* [subj: human or abstr] **1.** to tempt, seduce s.o.: X ввёл Y-а в грех ≃ **X led Y into sin; X led Y astray; X corrupted Y.**

[Костылёв:] Прости господи... опять ты меня, Василиса, во грех ввела... (Горький 3). [K.:] God forgive me—you've led me into sin again, Vassilissa (3b). ♦ [Барыня:] Много, много народу в грех введёшь! (Островский 6). [Gentlewoman:] Ah, yes, my pretty one, you're going to lead many, many men astray (6c).

2. to irritate, provoke s.o.: X Y-а в грех вводит ≃ **X gets Y (all) worked ⟨steamed⟩ up; X pushes Y too far; X makes Y hot under the collar; X makes Y lose Y's cool.**

Г-384 • ГРЕХ ⟨СМЕХ⟩ ОДИ́Н (, а не...) *coll, disapprov* [NP; these forms only; fixed WO] one is completely incompetent,

unqualified, ill-suited (for the position, role etc specified in the preceding context), sth. is of very poor quality, useless, does not properly fulfill its role or function: **one ⟨sth.⟩ is a poor excuse for a [NP]; there's no way you can call one ⟨sth.⟩ a [NP];** [in limited contexts] **one ⟨sth.⟩ is a joke (, not a [NP]).**

Какой из него начальник! Грех один, а не начальник. Him—a boss? He's a joke, not a boss.

Г-385 • ЕСТЬ (ТАКО́Й ⟨ТОТ⟩) ГРЕХ *(за кем) coll* [VP_subj; pres or past; fixed WO] that is true, (the behavior or action in question) does or did take place (said to confirm a statement about one's own or another's undesirable action, habit etc, be it real or simply viewed as such): **I'm sorry to say I did ⟨he does etc⟩;** [of a habit etc] **I have ⟨he has etc⟩ that failing ⟨weakness⟩;** [when the speaker responds to a statement referring to his short-coming, wrongdoing etc] **I (have to) admit it; I (must) confess; I own up;** [in limited contexts] **guilty as charged.**

«Говорят, ты выпиваешь». — «Есть такой грех». "They say you've been hitting the bottle." "I'm sorry to say I have." ♦ [Устинья Наумовна:] Всё, чай, друг на друга любуетесь да миндальничаете. [Подхалюзин:] Есть тот грех, Устинья Наумовна, есть тот грех! (Островский 10). [U.N.:] I suppose you're all the time billing and cooing. [P.:] We have that failing, Ustinya Naumovna; we have it (10b). ♦ Сознавайтесь, Жеребятников, брали деньги у иностранца по имени Лерой? Жеребятников от напряжения часто мигал, будто глаза засорил. Был грех, сознавался он (Аксёнов 12). "Confess, Zherebyatnikov, did you take money from a foreigner named Leroy?" Zherebyatnikov blinks from the pressure, as if there is something in his eye. "I admit it," he confesses (12a). ♦ «Вы раньше спортом занимались?» — «Был грех. До тридцати пяти годков футбол гонял, пока не выдохся» (Чернёнок 1). "You used to be an athlete?" "I confess. I chased a soccer ball around until I was thirty-five and worn out" (1a). ♦ «Вы опираетесь на Хунту, сеньор Сиракузерс», — дрожащим от возмущения голосом говорю я... «Есть грех, иногда опираюсь» (Аксёнов 3). "You lean on Junta for support, señor Syracuzers," I said in a voice quivering with indignation....."I own up, sometimes I do a bit of leaning" (3a).

Г-386 • КАК НА ГРЕХ; НА ГРЕХ *both coll* [как + PrepP (1st var.) or PrepP (2nd var.); these forms only; sent adv (parenth); 1st var. more common] unfortunately, as if to thwart s.o.'s plans or harm s.o.: **as luck ⟨ill luck, bad luck, fate⟩ would have it; (it is) just s.o.'s luck (that...);** as if to spite s.o.; [in limited contexts] **to add to s.o.'s troubles ⟨woes⟩; to make things ⟨matters⟩ worse.**

Приходил домой какой-нибудь оборванный, обовшивевший и худой, но долгожданный хозяин, и в хате начиналась радостная, бестолковая суета... растерявшаяся от счастья хозяйка то кидалась накрывать на стол, то бежала к сундуку, чтобы достать чистую пару мужниного белья. А бельишко, как на грех, оказывалось незаштопанным, а дрожащие пальцы хозяйки никак не могли продеть нитку в игольное ушко... (Шолохов 5). When a tattered, lice-ridden, half-starved but long-awaited husband did appear, the house would be filled with joyful fuss and bustle....The wife, beside herself with joy, would dart to and fro, now to lay the table, now to take some clean under-clothes for her husband from the chest. But the underclothes, as luck would have it, would turn out to be unmended, and with her trembling hands she would be quite unable to thread a needle... (5a). ♦ Комсорг, который всегда занимался этими делами, как на грех заболел (Войнович 5). ...As bad luck would have it, the Komsomol organizer, who usually took care of such things, was out sick (5a). ♦ Время шло, а Анне Савишне лучше не становилось... Ещё, как на грех, тошнота привязалась (Грекова 3). Time passed and Anna Savishna did not get better....To make things worse, nausea set in (3a).

Г-387 • дурён, страшен **КАК СМЕ́РТНЫЙ ГРЕХ** *coll* [как + NP; Invar; modif (intensif); fixed WO] extremely, excessively (ugly): **(as) ugly as sin; his ⟨her⟩ face would stop a clock.**

Г-388 • **НЕ ГРЕХ** *кому coll* [NP; Invar; impers predic with быть∅; used with pfv infin; usu. pres or subjunctive] it would not be inappropriate, it would be good for s.o. (to do sth.): Х-у не грех сделать Y ≃ **it wouldn't be half bad if X did Y; it wouldn't be a bad thing ⟨idea⟩ for X to do Y; it wouldn't hurt X to do Y; [in limited contexts] there's no harm in doing Y.**

Товарищ Ростова, разговорившись о женщинах, стал смеяться Ростову, говоря, что он всех хитрее и что ему бы не грех познакомить товарищей с спасённою им хорошенькой полькой (Толстой 5). One of his [Rostov's] comrades, talking of women, began to twit Rostov, saying that he was the sliest of them all, that it would not be half bad if he introduced them to the pretty little Polish woman he had rescued (5a). ♦ «Им бы самим у него поучиться не грех, да за науку в ножки поклониться…» (Максимов 1). "It wouldn't be a bad idea for them to come and learn from him and bow down in gratitude to him…" (1a). ♦ [Хороших:] Илья! Не пил бы ты больше, а шёл бы лучше в собес или куда там… *(Дергачёву.)* А тебе то самое: не грех бы и остановиться, об работе подумать (Вампилов 2). [Kh.:] Ilya! You'd be better off going down to the Social Security Office, or somewheres, instead of drinking anymore. *(To Dergachev.)* And you too. It wouldn't hurt you to stop right there and start thinking about some work (2b).

Г-389 • **СМЕ́РТНЫЙ ГРЕХ** [NP; usu. this WO] a grievous sin, an unpardonable act: **deadly ⟨mortal, cardinal⟩ sin.**

«В чём же вы провинились?» – «Да не мы… Соседи. Нам заодно досталось…» – «А те что?» – «Да без малого все семь смертных грехов» (Пастернак 1). "What have you done?" "We didn't do anything, it was our neighbors; we got it too for good measure…." "And what crime had they committed?" "Just about all the seven deadly sins…" (1a). ♦ …Мы с Ритой ещё вертелись и прятались за слова, обвиняя друг друга во всех смертных грехах и не замечая за собой главного (Трифонов 5). …Rita and I continued to rationalize and hide behind words, accusing each other of all the mortal sins and missing the real point (5a).

Г-390 • **ДО́ЛГО ЛИ ДО ГРЕХА́ ⟨ДО БЕДЫ́⟩; НЕДО́ЛГО (И) ДО ГРЕХА́ ⟨ДО БЕДЫ́⟩** *all coll* [sent; these forms only; fixed WO] (used, usu. as a question or exclamation, to connect the description of events in the preceding context with that of their potential or real consequences in the context that follows) sth. unpleasant or irreparable could easily happen (at any moment, under such circumstances, or if s.o. does sth.): **that can easily lead to trouble; something bad may happen; anything can happen; trouble is never far off.**

«Только с огнём… осторожнее обращайтесь, потому что тут недолго и до греха. Имущества свои попалите, сами погорите – что хорошего!» (Салтыков-Щедрин 1). "Only…be careful how you handle fire, because that can easily lead to trouble. You burn your property, you burn yourselves—and what's the good of that?" (1b). ♦ «Не пишет жена… А, может быть, заболели! Долго ли в эвакуации до беды» (Гроссман 2). "My wife still hasn't written….Maybe they've fallen ill. Anything can happen when you're evacuated" (2a).

Г-391 • **ОТ ГРЕХА́ ПОДА́ЛЬШЕ** *coll* [AdvP; Invar; adv; usu. this WO] in order to avoid some conflict, misfortune, a fight etc: **(in order) to be ⟨to get s.o. etc⟩ out of harm's way; (in order) to get ⟨to keep⟩ away from trouble ⟨from temptation⟩; (in order) to keep (s.o.) ⟨to stay⟩ out of trouble; (in order) to flee from temptation ⟨from trouble⟩; (in order) to steer clear of trouble ⟨of temptation⟩; before something happens to one.**

«Пока нас не трогают и силком не берут в часть, надо… уезжать от греха подальше…» (Шолохов 5). "We've got to get out of harm's way…before someone recruits us by force…" (5a). ♦ «…Я пойду узнаю, как там дела». И пошёл [Едигей] с потемневшим, неприязненным лицом, подальше от греха. Брови его сошлись на переносице (Айтматов 2). "…I will go and see how things are out there." Off he [Yedigei] went, his face dark and hostile, to get away from temptation, his brows furrowed with anger (2a). ♦ …Оба [брата] исчезли в ночь перед арестом Ивана Хохлушкина. Матвей всегда отличался скрытностью и, видно почуяв неладное, ушёл и увёл за собой брата… от греха подальше (Максимов 1). …They [the two brothers] both disappeared the night before Ivan Khokhlushkin was arrested. Matvei was always secretive and he'd evidently got wind of something being up, for he had gone off, taking his brother with him, so as to keep him out of trouble (1a). ♦ Пока полк выстраивался на дороге, генерал вместе с Ревкиным сел в бронетранспортёр и уехал. Уехал от греха подальше и Голубев (Войнович 2). While the regiment was forming on the road, the general and Revkin climbed into the armored carrier and drove away. Golubev drove away as well, before something happened to him too (2a).

Г-392 • **ЧТО ⟨ЧЕГО́, НЕ́ЧЕГО⟩ (И) ГРЕХА́ ТАИ́ТЬ** *coll* [these forms only; sent adv (parenth); usu. this WO] it is pointless to (try to) conceal sth., one must acknowledge sth.: **there is no (use) denying ⟨hiding⟩ it ⟨the fact that…⟩; why deny it ⟨that…⟩; it's ⟨there's⟩ no use pretending (that…); why hide it ⟨the truth⟩?; you can't get away from it ⟨the fact that…⟩; [in limited contexts] I must ⟨might as well⟩ admit ⟨confess⟩ that…; I ⟨we⟩ don't deny it.**

Всех, что греха таить, беспокоили огромные остатки закусок и напитков, все потянулись к столу (Аксёнов 6). There was no hiding the fact that everyone was worried by the huge amount of leftover food and drink, and they all surged toward the table (6a). ♦ «Что, брат, прозяб?» – «Как не прозябнуть в одном худеньком армяке? Был тулуп, да что греха таить? Заложил вечор у целовальника: мороз показался не велик» (Пушкин 2). "How are you doing, my good fellow? Are you all frozen?" "I should think I am, in nothing but a thin jerkin. I had a sheepskin jacket, but, why deny it, I pawned it at a tavern last night: the frost didn't seem that fierce then" (2a). ♦ …Что греха таить, ревновал Пётр Васильевич дочь к зятю… (Максимов 3). It's no use pretending that Pyotr Vasilievich wasn't jealous of his son-in-law… (3a). ♦ Что греха таить, было такое – поверил он своему странному сну (Войнович 2). Why hide it? He really had believed his strange dream (2a). ♦ «Среди обитателей Нахаловки было немало передовых, революционно настроенных рабочих, но, чего греха таить, достаточно было и преступного элемента…» (Чернёнок 1). "Among the residents of Nakhalovka were a few front-line revolutionary workers, but, why hide the truth, there were plenty of criminals…" (1a). ♦ Шли молча; против моховского дома Иван Алексеевич, не выдержавший тошного молчания… сказал: «Нечего греха таить: с фронта пришли большевиками, а зараз [*regional* = сейчас] в кусты лезем!» (Шолохов 3). They walked on without speaking. As they were passing Mokhov's house, Ivan could bear the hateful silence no longer and…said, "You can't get away from it. We were Bolsheviks when we came home from the front, and now we're running for cover!" (3a). ♦ «Всегда с старшими детьми мудрят, хотят сделать что-нибудь необыкновенное», – сказала гостья. – «Что греха таить, ma chère! Графинюшка мудрила с Верой», – сказал граф (Толстой 4). "People always try too hard with their first children, they want to make something exceptional of them," said the visitor. "We don't deny it, ma chère! Our little Countess tried too hard with Vera," said the Count (4a).

Г-393 • **С ГРЕХО́М ПОПОЛА́М** *coll* [AdvP; Invar; adv; fixed WO] **1.** Also: **С ГО́РЕМ ПОПОЛА́М** *coll* with difficulty and almost not succeeding: **(just) barely; (just) barely manage (to do sth.); just scrape through (sth.); [in limited**

contexts] **by the skin of one's teeth**; [of one's ability to do sth.] **after a fashion.**

Антифашистский роман, в центре – интересный образ эсэсовца. Написанный в той субъективной манере, которая уже протискивалась, хотя и с грехом пополам, в узкие щели наших издательств и журналов (Орлова 1). It was an antifascist novel with a very powerful portrait of an SS officer, written in that subjective fashion that just barely allowed it to squeeze through the narrow cracks of our publishing houses and journals (1a). ♦ [Сарафанов:] У меня было звание капитана, меня оставляли в армии. С грехом пополам я демобилизовался (Вампилов 4). [S.:] I was a captain in the army and they wanted me to stay. I just barely managed to get a discharge (4b). ♦ «Ты говоришь по-испански?» – «С грехом пополам». "Do you speak Spanish?" "After a fashion."

2. *obs* through deception, trickery: **in an underhand(ed) way; by dishonest means.**

Г-394 • СЪЕСТЬ ГРИБ *obs* [VP; subj: human] not to receive or obtain what one desires, to have one's expectations unfulfilled: X съел гриб ≃ **X lost out (on sth.); X had his hopes dashed; X's hopes were dashed.**

Г-395 • КАК ГРИБЫ́ (ПОСЛЕ ДОЖДЯ́) расти, вырастать и т. п. *coll* [как + NP; these forms only; adv] (to appear, grow etc) swiftly and in abundance: **(pop up ⟨spring up, spring forth etc⟩) like mushrooms (after a rain); (spring ⟨pop⟩ up) all over.**

Г-396 • ВГОНЯ́ТЬ/ВОГНА́ТЬ ⟨ЗАГНА́ТЬ, УЛОЖИ́ТЬ, СВОДИ́ТЬ/СВЕСТИ́⟩ В ГРОБ кого *coll* [VP; subj: human or, less often, abstr; usu. pfv] to cause s.o.'s death (by treating him cruelly, worrying him excessively etc): X Y-а в гроб вгонит ≃ **X will drive Y to the ⟨to an early⟩ grave; X will send Y to the ⟨to Y's, to an early⟩ grave; X will be the death of Y.**

«Мой муж – тиран, он – ужасный, ужасный человек... Он меня в гроб вгонит...» (Сологуб 1). "My husband is a tyrant. He is a terrible, terrible man....He is driving me to the grave..." (1a). ♦ «Господи, за что же мне это такое наказание, – трясясь от негодования, причитала мать. – ...Ты скоро вгонишь меня в гроб раньше времени, негодяй!.. Сил моих больше нет!» (Максимов 2). "Lord, what have I done to deserve this punishment?" his mother wailed, shaking with indignation. "You'll drive me to an early grave, you little horror!...I've reached the end of my tether!" (2a). ♦ «Стрельба идёт тёмная, всё живое похоронилось, а он [Григорий] в одну душу: „Найди её [Аксинью], иначе в гроб вгоню!"» (Шолохов 4). "Here they are blazing away at us, every living thing's taken cover, but he [Grigory] keeps at me, 'Find her [Aksinya] or I'll send you to your grave!'" (4a).

Г-397 • ГРОБ ПОВА́ПЛЕННЫЙ *obs* [NP] a phenomenon, thing, or person whose presentable appearance belies its or his repulsive nature: **a whited sepulcher.**
< From the Bible (Matt. 23:27).

Г-398 • КРА́ШЕ В ГРОБ КЛАДУ́Т *coll* [Invar; indep. clause or subj-compl with бытьø (subj: usu. вид у кого); fixed WO] s.o. looks sickly, pale, thin, exhausted: (вид у X-а –) краше в гроб кладут ≃ **X looks like death warmed over ⟨like living death, like a goner⟩.**

Г-399 • ПО ГРОБ ЖИ́ЗНИ ⟨ДНЕЙ obs⟩ *coll* [PrepP; these forms only; sent adv; fixed WO] until death, to the end of one's life: **to one's dying day; till ⟨until⟩ (the day) one dies; as long as one lives.**

Да, по гроб жизни должен быть благодарен покойному Берлиозу обитатель квартиры № 84... за то, что председа-тель МАССОЛИТа попал под трамвай, и за то, что траурное заседание назначили как раз на этот вечер (Булгаков 9). Yes, the tenant of apartment 84 ought to be grateful to his dying day to the late Berlioz [chairman of the board of MASSOLIT] for falling under the streetcar and for the memorial meeting which had been set for just that evening (9a). ♦ «В колхозе работа – это ладно, это своё. А только хлебушек уберём – уж снег, лесозаготовки. По гроб жизни буду помнить я эти лесозаготовки» (Распутин 2). "The work in the kolkhoz – all right, that's our own work. But as soon as we harvested the grain – there was the snow and the logging to do. I'll remember that logging until the day I die" (2a).

Г-400 • ХОТЬ В ГРОБ ЛОЖИ́СЬ *coll* [хоть + VP_imper; Invar; usu. used as subord clause; fixed WO] (used to express despair, hopelessness) there is no escape from a desperate situation: **there is nothing (left) to do but lie down and die; you ⟨person X⟩ might just as well lie down and die; you might as well kill yourself.**

Г-401 • ДО ГРО́БА [PrepP; Invar; adv or nonagreeing modif] to the end of one's life, to one's death: **to the ⟨one's very⟩ grave; till the grave; till ⟨until⟩ (the day) one dies; to ⟨till⟩ one's dying day; until death;** [in contexts of love and marriage] **till death do us part; as long as we both shall live;** [as modif] **lifelong; everlasting; undying;** ‖ враги ~ ≃ **mortal enemies.**

[Петрин:] Учёное звание за мной до гроба останется... (Чехов 1). [P.:] I shall carry my degree to the grave with me (1a). ♦ «Николая моего опять посадили. Теперь ждать буду. Сколько нужно. До гроба» (Максимов 3). "My Nikolai has been put in prison again. But now I shall be waiting for him. For as long as it takes. Till I die" (3a). ♦ Когда-то мы с женой дали слово любить друг друга до гроба и даже за гробом (Катаев 2). Once upon a time my wife and I had promised to love each other until death, and even beyond it (2a). ♦ ...Любовь её высказалась только в безграничной преданности [Обломову] до гроба (Гончаров 1). Her love found its only expression in a boundless and lifelong devotion to him [Oblomov] (1b). ♦ «Знаете, я весь последний месяц говорил себе: „Или мы разом с ним сойдёмся друзьями навеки, или с первого же раза разойдёмся врагами до гроба!"» (Достоевский 1). "You know, all this past month I've been saying to myself: 'He and I will either become close friends at once and forever, or from the first we'll part as mortal enemies!'" (1a).

Г-402 • В ГРОБУ́ ВИДА́Л ⟨ВИ́ДЕЛ⟩ кого-что *substand, rude* [VP; subj: human (usu. a pronoun); past only; usu. this WO] used to express a sharply scornful attitude toward s.o. or sth.: в гробу X видал Y-а ≃ **X couldn't care less about Y; X doesn't give a damn ⟨a shit⟩ about Y; Y can go to hell; to ⟨the⟩ hell with Y.**

Экономист в гробу видел литературные произведения бывшего мужа Елены... (Лимонов 1). The economist could not have cared less about Elena's ex-husband's literary works... (1a). ♦ ...В гробу я видал твою тягу просечь [author's usage = понять] тайны материи (Алешковский 1). I didn't give a shit about [your] longing to penetrate the secrets of matter (1a). ♦ [Сильва:] В гробу бы я её видел, такую любовь (Вампилов 4). [S.:] To hell with that kind of love (4c).

Г-403 • ПЕРЕВОРА́ЧИВАТЬСЯ ⟨ПЕРЕВЁРТЫВАТЬСЯ⟩/ПЕРЕВЕРНУ́ТЬСЯ В ГРОБУ́ [VP; subj: human; usu. subjunctive or, less often, pfv fut] (of a deceased person) one would become extremely indignant, horrified (if he found out about this): X перевернулся бы в гробу ≃ **X would turn (over) in his grave; X would roll over ⟨be spinning⟩ in his grave; X would die a second death.**

Г-404 • ГРОМ НЕ ГРЯ́НЕТ, МУЖИ́К НЕ ПЕРЕКРЕ́СТИТСЯ [saying] a careless person procrastinates doing what is necessary until forced by circumstances (said, usu. ironically or humorously, when a person gets into trouble by procrastinating too long): ≃ he ⟨she etc⟩ **won't lock the barn door till after the horse is stolen**; [in limited contexts] **don't wait for the flood to start building your ark.**

Г-405 • **КАК** ⟨**БУ́ДТО, СЛО́ВНО, ТО́ЧНО**⟩ **ГРОМ СРЕДИ́ Я́СНОГО НЕ́БА** *coll* [как etc + NP; these forms only; usu. adv or subj-compl with бытьø (subj: abstr); fixed WO] sth. happened unexpectedly, suddenly (usu. an unfortunate event, a misfortune that has befallen s.o.): **(like) a bolt from ⟨out of⟩ the blue; out of a ⟨the⟩ clear (blue) sky.**

«После того, как меня отпустили из милиции, куда я был отправлен завучем из-за бульдога, я пошёл в школу, но там завуч сказал мне, что я из школы исключён и к экзаменам на аттестат зрелости допущен не буду. Это было как гром среди ясного неба» (Семёнов 1). "After I had been released from the police station where the director of studies sent me because of the bulldog, I returned to school, but the director of studies told me that I had been expelled and that I would not be admitted to the matriculation examinations. This was like a bolt from the blue" (1a). ♦ Как гром среди ясного неба прозвучал для нас приказ Севлага о ликвидации в Тасканском лагере женского отделения… (Гинзбург 2). The order from Sevlag for the liquidation of the women's section of the Taskan camp…came like a bolt out of the blue (2a).

Г-406 • **РАЗРАЗИ́** ⟨**ПОРАЗИ́, УБЕ́Й**⟩ **МЕНЯ́ ГРОМ (НА Э́ТОМ МЕ́СТЕ); ДА** ⟨**ПУСТЬ, ПУСКА́Й**⟩ **РАЗРАЗИ́Т** ⟨**ПОРАЗИ́Т**⟩ **МЕНЯ́ ГРОМ; РАЗРАЗИ́** ⟨**ПОРАЗИ́**⟩ **МЕНЯ́ СИ́ЛЫ НЕБЕ́СНЫЕ; ДА** ⟨**ПУСТЬ, ПУСКА́Й**⟩ **РАЗРАЗЯ́Т** ⟨**ПОРАЗЯ́Т**⟩ **МЕНЯ́ СИ́ЛЫ НЕБЕ́СНЫЕ** *all highly coll* [these forms only; indep. sent, main clause in a complex sent (usu. foll. by a если-clause), a clause in a compound sent (usu. foll. by a clause introduced by Conj «но»), or sent adv (parenth)] an oath used by the speaker to emphasize the truth of a statement: **(may) God strike me dead (if I'm lying); may lightning strike me (if…).**

[Настя:] Ей-богу… было это! Всё было!.. Студент он… француз был… Гастошей звали… с чёрной бородкой… в лаковых сапогах ходил… разрази меня гром на этом месте! И так он меня любил… так любил! (Горький 3). [N.:] I swear it happened! Everything happened just as I told you. He was a student—a Frenchman—Gaston his name was—he had a little black beard and patent leather shoes.…God strike me dead if I'm lying! And he loved me so passionately—so passionately! (3e).

Г-407 • **РАЗРАЗИ́** ⟨**ПОРАЗИ́**⟩ **ТЕБЯ́** ⟨**вас, его, её, их**⟩ **ГРОМ** ⟨**-ом**⟩; **ДА** ⟨**ПУСТЬ**⟩ **РАЗРАЗИ́Т ТЕБЯ́** ⟨**его и т. д.**⟩ **БОГ** ⟨**ГОСПО́ДЬ**⟩ *all substand* [these forms only; usu. a clause in a compound sent or sent adv (parenth)] used to express indignation, surprise etc: **damn ⟨darn⟩ it ⟨you etc⟩!**

Г-408 • **КАК ГРО́МОМ ПОРАЗИ́ТЬ** ⟨**ОГЛУШИ́ТЬ**⟩ *кого* [VP; subj: usu. abstr; often past passive Part как громом поражённый; usu. this WO] to come as a total shock, dumbfound s.o.: X Y-а как громом поразил ≃ **X struck ⟨hit⟩ Y like a bolt of lightning; X came as a bombshell; X hit Y like a ton of bricks;** ‖ как громом поражённый ≃ **thunderstruck; as if struck by lightning; stunned as by a thunderclap.**

Оба они [оба парня]… стали исчезать в пучине. Мы все стояли как громом поражённые (Попов 1). The two of them [young men]…began to disappear beneath the waves.…We all stood there, thunderstruck (1a). ♦ «Дорогие друзья, — лучезарно сказал космонавт, — я хочу, чтобы мы за этим прекрасным столом выпили за комсомол, воспитавший нас…» Молодой хозяин, услышав этот тост, застыл, как поражённый громом (Искандер 4). "Dear friends," the cosmonaut said radiantly, "I pro-

pose that we at this excellent table drink a toast to the Komsomol that has nurtured us.…" When he heard that, the young host stopped dead as if struck by lightning (4a). ♦ Наутро город встал как громом поражённый, потому что история приняла размеры странные и чудовищные. На Персональной улице к полудню осталось в живых только три курицы… (Булгаков 10). When the town awakened in the morning, it was stunned as by a thunderclap, for the affair assumed strange and monstrous proportions. By noontime, only three hens were still alive on Personal Street… (10a).

Г-409 • **МЕТА́ТЬ ГРО́МЫ И МО́ЛНИИ** ⟨**ГРО́МЫ-МО́ЛНИИ, ГРОМ И МО́ЛНИЮ, ГРО́МЫ**⟩ *(на кого)* *coll* [VP; subj: human; fixed WO] (usu. of a person in authority) to upbraid s.o. angrily, indignantly, usu. threatening to punish him severely: X мечет громы и молнии ≃ **X is ranting and raving; X is raging and fuming.**

Подрезов не стал метать громы и молнии — видно, отметал ещё у себя на бюро (Абрамов 1). Podrezov did not rant and rave; obviously he had finished with that at the Bureau meeting (1a). ♦ [author's usage] …Поскольку весь командный состав батальона… именно тем, в основном, и занимался, что вылавливал курсантов, ходящих вне строя, не удивительно, что и я время от времени попадался. И тогда на мою голову метались громы и молнии (Войнович 5). [context transl] …Since the main concern of the battalion's entire staff of commanding officers…was the nabbing of cadets out of formation, it's not surprising that I did get caught once in a while. And when I did, thunder and lightning would come crashing down on my head (5a).

Г-410 • **ГРОШ ЦЕНА́ (В БАЗА́РНЫЙ ДЕНЬ)** *кому-чему;* **ЛО́МАНЫЙ** ⟨**МЕ́ДНЫЙ**⟩ **ГРОШ ЦЕНА́** *all coll, derog* [these forms only; VP_subj with бытьø, pres only; fixed WO] s.o. or sth. is of no value: грош цена X-у ≃ **X is worthless ⟨useless⟩; X isn't worth a (damn) thing; thing X isn't worth a (tinker's) damn; thing X isn't worth a kopeck ⟨two cents, a (plug) nickel, a (red) cent, a brass farthing etc⟩.**

Это ведь только в спорте судьи и противники дают тебе обрести лучшую форму — грош цена этим рекордам (Буковский 1). It's only in sport that referees and competitors wait for you to reach your best form—records achieved that way are not worth a damn (1a).

< See Г-417.

Г-411 • **НА ГРОШ** ⟨**НА КОПЕ́ЙКУ**⟩ *coll* [PrepP; these forms only] **1.** ~ *чего (у кого, где)* [quantit subj-compl with copula (subj/gen: usu. abstr) or quantif of subj/gen] s.o. has a very small amount (of some quality—intelligence, ability etc): **(hardly) an ounce ⟨a scrap, a shred⟩ (of [NP]); next to no [NP].**

Таланта у него на грош, а считает себя великим писателем. He has next to no talent, yet considers himself a great writer.

2. ~ *делать* [adv] (to do) very little: **(do) practically ⟨next to, almost⟩ nothing.**

< See Г-417.

Г-412 • **(НИ ⟨И⟩) В ГРОШ НЕ СТА́ВИТЬ** *кого-что;* **(И) В МЕ́ДНЫЙ ГРОШ НЕ СТА́ВИТЬ; НИ ВО ЧТО НЕ СТА́ВИТЬ** ⟨**НЕ СЧИТА́ТЬ**⟩; **НИ ЗА ЧТО СЧИТА́ТЬ** *all coll* [VP; subj: human] to have a very low opinion of s.o. or sth., consider s.o. or sth. to be of no value, regard s.o. or sth. with contempt: X Y-а (ни) в грош не ставит ≃ **X doesn't set (much ⟨great, any⟩) store by Y; X thinks very little of Y; X snaps his fingers at Y; X scorns Y.**

Марье грамота вовсе не далась. Да она ни во что и не ставила учение (Абрамов 1). Marya had no talent at all for reading and writing. Nor did she set any store by learning (1a). ♦ Я ни во что не ставлю русскую эмиграцию… (Лимонов 1). I think very little of the Russian emigration… (1a). ♦ Всю жизнь не ставит в грош докторов, а кончится тем, что обратится наконец к бабе, которая лечит зашёптываньями и заплёвками... (Гоголь 3). ...All his life he'll scorn doctors and will end up going to some old peasant woman who will treat him with incantations and spittle... (3e).

< See Г-417.

Г-413 • НИ ЗА ГРОШ ⟨КОПÉЙКУ⟩ пропасть, погибнуть и т. п. *coll* [PrepP; these forms only; adv] (of people) (to perish, be destroyed etc) to no purpose, absolutely futilely: **(all) for nothing ⟨naught⟩; (all) in vain.**

Здесь ни за что погиб мой отец... Ни за грош пропала моя собственная жизнь (Зиновьев 1). "My father died here for nothing....My own life has been ruined for nothing" (1a).

< See Г-417.

Г-414 • НИ НА ГРОШ; (И) НА ГРОШ; (НИ) НА КОПÉЙКУ *all coll;* **НИ НА ⟨ЛÓМАНУЮ⟩ ПОЛÚШКУ** *obs, coll* [PrepP; these forms only] **1.** ~ *чего* **(нет)** *(у кого, где)* [quantit compl with negated copula (subj/gen: abstr); when variants without ни are used, negated copula or нет cannot be omitted] some quality is completely absent (in s.o. or sth.): (у X-a) Y-a ни на грош ≃ **X doesn't have ⟨there isn't⟩ a scrap ⟨a drop, a lick, an ounce, a grain⟩ of Y; X doesn't have ⟨there isn't⟩ the least ⟨slightest, tiniest⟩ bit ⟨drop, scrap⟩ of Y.**

...Он [Грушницкий] из тех людей, которые на все случаи жизни имеют готовые пышные фразы... В их душе часто много добрых свойств, но ни на грош поэзии (Лермонтов 1). ...He [Grushnitski] is one of those people who, for every occasion in life, have ready-made pompous phrases....Their souls often possess many good qualities, but not an ounce of poetry (1a).

2. ~ **не верить** *кому, во что* [adv (intensif)] (not to believe s.o., sth., or in sth.) even to the slightest degree: Х не верит Y-у ~ ≃ **X doesn't believe a word ⟨a thing⟩ Y says; X doesn't believe Y for a minute; X doesn't believe ⟨trust⟩ Y at all; X doesn't trust Y one bit.**

«Это иезуит, русский то есть. Как у благородного существа, в нём это затаённое негодование кипит на то, что надо представляться... святыню на себя натягивать». — «Да ведь он же верует в бога». — «Ни на грош. А ты не знал?» (Достоевский 1). "He's a Jesuit, a Russian one, that is. As a noble person, he has this hidden indignation seething in him because he has to pretend...to put on all this holiness." "But he does believe in God." "Not for a minute. Didn't you know?" (1a). ♦ Тому, что писали немецкие газеты, нельзя было верить и на грош (Кузнецов 1). The German newspapers could not be believed at all... (1a).

< See Г-417 and Г-418.

Г-415 • БЕЗ ГРОШÁ ⟨КОПÉЙКИ⟩ (В КАРМÁНЕ) быть₀, сидеть, остаться и т. п.; **БЕЗ ГРОШÁ ⟨КОПÉЙКИ⟩ денег** *all coll;* **БЕЗ КОПЬЯ́** *substand* [PrepP; these forms only; usu. subj-compl with copula (subj: human); fixed WO] (to be, be left etc) without any money at all: **(be etc) without a kopeck ⟨a penny, a (red) cent, a dime etc⟩; (be etc) without a kopeck ⟨a penny etc⟩ to one's name; not (have) a kopeck ⟨a penny, a (red) cent, a dime etc⟩; (be) penniless ⟨(flat) broke⟩.**

Во всём городе... говорили, что он тогда, укатив с Грушенькой в Мокрое, «просадил в одну ночь и следующий за тем день три тысячи разом и воротился с кутежа без гроша, в чём мать родила» (Достоевский 1). ...The whole town was saying that he had driven off to Mokroye with Grushenka then, "squandered three thousand at once in a night and a day, and came back from the spree without a kopeck, naked as the day he was born" (1a). ♦ ...В тот день Владу было не до шуток. Голодный, без копейки денег... он сразу сделался игрушкой в руках судеб, от которых, как известно, спасенья нет (Максимов 2). At the time...Vlad was in no mood for jokes. Hungry, without a kopeck to his

name...he became a plaything in the hands of fate—from which, as we know, there is no salvation (2a). ♦ Как только приедет Мансур, нужно взять его за горло: пусть одолжит рублей триста, потом с издательством рассчитается. Всё-таки нету совести. Знает, что сижу без гроша... (Трифонов 5). As soon as Mansur arrives I'll have to take him by the throat. Let him lend me 300 rubles or so, and later on he can settle with the publishing house. That man really has no conscience. He knows that I'm stuck here without a penny. (5a). ♦ Объективно говоря, такие фигуры в революционной эмиграции неизбежны — эти неопрятные юноши с блуждающими глазами, недоразвитые... Они вечно голодные, без гроша... (Солженицын 5). Objectively speaking, there was no avoiding such figures in émigré revolutionary circles—slovenly, vacant-looking young men with unformed minds....They were everlastingly hungry and penniless (5a).

< See Г-417.

Г-416 • ГРОША́ МÉДНОГО ⟨ЛÓМАНОГО⟩ НЕ СТÓИТ; НИ ⟨И⟩ ГРОША́ НЕ СТÓИТ *all coll* [VP; subj: abstr, less often concr or human; pres or, rare, past] some thing (person etc) is of no value, is worthless: X гроша медного не стоит ≃ **X isn't worth a damn (thing); thing X isn't worth a kopeck ⟨a (red) cent, two cents, a (plug) nickel, a brass farthing etc⟩.**

Вот ты говоришь, что воспоминания не стоят ни гроша, но ты не прав (Аксёнов 6). You were saying that memories aren't worth a damn, but you're wrong (6a). ♦ Секреты, находившиеся за дверью, не стоили и гроша (Войнович 5). The secrets kept behind that door weren't worth a kopeck (5a). ♦ «Мне сказывали, что в Риме наши художники в Ватикан ни ногой. Рафаэля считают чуть не за дурака, потому что это, мол, авторитет; а сами бессильны и бесплодны до гадости...» — «По-моему, — возразил Базаров, — Рафаэль гроша медного не стоит, да и они не лучше его» (Тургенев 2). "I am told that in Rome our artists never set foot in the Vatican. Raphael they practically regard as a fool because, if you please, he is an authority. Yet they themselves are so impotent and sterile...." "To my mind," retorted Bazarov, "Raphael's not worth a brass farthing; and they are no better" (2c). ♦ Есть только один момент для осмысления происходящего по горячим следам, когда ещё сочится кровь и аргументация «продажных перьев» не стоит ни гроша (Мандельштам 2). [context transl] ...The only possible moment at which to make proper sense of events is immediately afterwards, while they are still fresh, before the blood has congealed and the special pleading of the "hired hacks" can still be seen for what it is worth (2a).

< See Г-417.

Г-417 • НÉ БЫЛО НИ ГРОША́ ⟨НИ ГРÓША⟩, ДА (И) ВДРУГ АЛТÝН [saying] suddenly there is a lot of something that had been completely lacking (said in response to unexpected money, luck etc): ≃ **it's rags to riches; yesterday a pauper, today a king.**

< «Грош» is an old coin worth half a kopeck; «алтын» is an old coin worth three kopecks. Neither is any longer in use.

Г-418 • НИ ГРОША́ нет *у кого,* **не дать, не получить** и т. п.; **НИ КОПÉЙКИ ⟨-éечки⟩ (денег)** *all coll;* **НИ КОПЬЯ́** *substand;* **НИ ПОЛÚШКИ ⟨НИ АЛТЫ́НА⟩** *obs, coll* [NP_gen; these forms only; subj/gen or obj] (to have, give, receive etc) no money, nothing at all: **not (so much as) a kopeck ⟨a penny, a (red) cent, a dime etc⟩ (to one's name); (be) without a kopeck ⟨a penny, a dime etc⟩; (be) penniless;** [in limited contexts] **(completely) cleaned ⟨tapped⟩ out.**

[Сатин:] Клещ, дай пятак! [Клещ:] Пошёл к чёрту! Много вас тут... [Сатин:] Чего ты ругаешься? Ведь у тебя нет ни гроша, я знаю... (Горький 3). [S.:] ...Klestch, give me five kopecks! [K.:] Go to hell! There are too many of your kind around here. [S.:] What are you cursing for? I know you haven't a kopeck (3b). ♦

Дело в том, что у меня как раз не было ни копейки денег и я очень рассчитывал на эти две тысячи (Булгаков 12). The fact was that I hadn't a kopeck to my name and I was counting heavily on that two thousand (12a). ♦ [Следователь и прокурор] нашли нужным факт этот [продажу часов] в подробности записать, ввиду вторичного подтверждения того обстоятельства, что у него [Мити] и накануне не было уже ни гроша почти денег (Достоевский 1). ...They [the district attorney and the prosecutor] found it necessary to record this fact [Mitya's having sold the watch] in detail, seeing in it a second confirmation of the circumstance that even a day before he [Mitya] had been almost without a kopeck (1a). ♦ «Жених, жених!» — написано у всех на лбу, а он [Обломов] ещё не просил согласия тётки, у него ни гроша денег нет, и он не знает, когда будут... (Гончаров 1). "The bridegroom, the bridegroom!" was written all over their faces; yet he [Oblomov] had not asked her aunt's consent, and was not only penniless but did not know when he would receive any money... (1b).

< For «грош», «алтын» see Г-417. «Полушка» is an old copper coin worth one fourth of a kopeck.

Г-419 • ЗА ГРОШИ́ ⟨ЗА ГРОШ, ЗА КОПЕ́ЙКУ⟩ купить, продать *что* и т. п. *coll* [PrepP; these forms only; adv] (to buy, sell sth. etc) very cheaply, almost for free, (to work, do sth.) for scanty payment: **for a song; for a pittance; for next to nothing.**

[Незнамов:] Его [Шмагу], конечно, нельзя считать образцом нравственности; он не задумается за грош продать лучшего своего друга... (Островский 3). [N.:] To be sure he [Shmaga] is not exactly a model of moral integrity; he would sell his best friend for a song... (3a). ♦ Не имея степени, я работала за гроши, то и дело теряя работу во имя бдительности... (Мандельштам 2). Without my degree, I was forced to work for a pittance and was always being kicked out of jobs in the name of "vigilance" (2a).

< See Г-417.

Г-420 • БРАТЬ/ВЗЯТЬ ЗА ГРУ́ДКИ *кого substand* [VP; subj: human] **1.** Also: **ХВАТА́ТЬ/СХВАТИ́ТЬ ЗА ГРУ́ДКИ** *substand* to take hold of s.o. by the clothing covering his chest, usu. while threatening him or demanding sth.: X схватил Y-а за грудки ≃ **X grabbed ⟨got⟩ Y by the shirtfront ⟨by the front of the shirt, by the lapels⟩.**

...Дедушка берёт приказчика за грудки, вытаскивает из-за прилавка и выкидывает из магазина... на мостовую (Рыбаков 1). ...Grandfather grabbed the assistant by the shirtfront, dragged him out of the entrance and threw him into the street (1a). ♦ «Ты, старый козёл! — она [Кукуша] перегнулась через стол и схватила его [Лукина] за грудки. — Если ты сам лично не принесёшь моему мужу шапку, я тебе...» (Войнович 6). "...You son of a bitch!" She [Kukusha] reached across the desk and seized him [Lukin] by the lapels. "If you don't personally bring my husband a hat, so help me I'll—" (6a).

2. to use force, put pressure on s.o. in order to make him do sth.: X взял Y-а за грудки ≃ **X grabbed hold of Y; X bullied Y (into doing sth.); X strong-armed Y.**

«Взяли и тятю моего за грудки: пишись [в колхоз] и всё тут!» (Максимов 2). "They grabbed hold of my dad and told him to sign on [to join the collective farm] or else" (2a).

Г-421 • БИТЬ СЕБЯ́ В ГРУДЬ [VP; subj: human] to repent in front of others, try to convince s.o. of one's sincere regret over sth. one did: X бил себя в грудь ≃ **X beat his breast.**

«...Из всех я самый подлый гад! Пусть! Каждый день моей жизни я, бия [obs] себя в грудь, обещал исправиться и каждый день творил всё те же пакости» (Достоевский 1). "...Of all I am the lowest vermin! So be it! Every day of my life I've been beating my breast and promising to reform, and every day I've done the same vile things" (1a).

Г-422 • ГРУДЬ В ГРУДЬ столкнуться, сойтись и т. п. [Invar; adv; fixed WO] (two parties meet, stand etc) very closely, so that hardly any distance separates them: **face-to-face; eyeball-to-eyeball; right up close.**

Г-423 • ГРУДЬ НА ГРУДЬ идти, двигаться и т. п. *obsoles* [Invar; adv; fixed WO] (to move, advance) one man (unit etc) upon another in a fight or battle: **one against the other; one-on-one.**

Г-424 • ГРУДЬ С ГРУ́ДЬЮ сойтись, схватиться, столкнуться, биться и т. п. [Invar; adv; fixed WO] (to fight s.o.) coming into direct contact with one's adversary, enemy: **in hand-to-hand combat; at close quarters.**

Г-425 • И́ЛИ ⟨ЛИ́БО⟩ ГРУДЬ В КРЕСТА́Х, И́ЛИ ⟨ЛИ́БО⟩ ГОЛОВА́ В КУСТА́Х [saying] one will either achieve all he sets out to achieve, or will fail miserably (used by the speaker in reference to his own or another's determination, readiness to risk everything in order to accomplish or obtain what he wants): ≃ **it's do or die; it's all or nothing; it will make me ⟨you etc⟩ or break me ⟨you etc⟩; win big or lose big.**

Г-426 • НАДСА́ЖИВАТЬ ⟨НАДРЫВА́ТЬ⟩ ГРУДЬ *coll* [VP; subj: human] to speak, argue, shout etc very loudly: X надсаживал грудь ≃ **X screamed his lungs out ⟨his head off⟩; X screamed ⟨made, shouted⟩ himself hoarse.**

Г-427 • СТОЯ́ТЬ ⟨СТАТЬ, ВСТАТЬ⟩ ГРУ́ДЬЮ (*за кого-что*) *elev* [VP; subj: human or collect] to defend, fight for s.o. or sth. courageously: X стоял грудью за Y-а ≃ **X defended ⟨protected⟩ Y with everything X had; X bravely defended Y; [in limited contexts] X took a firm stand for Y; X stood firm;** ‖ [in military contexts] X-ы стояли грудью (за Y) ≃ **Xs defended Y with their lives; Xs fought courageously (for Y); [in limited contexts] Xs put their lives on the line.**

Пусть только кто-нибудь попробует задеть её детей — она станет за них грудью. Just let anyone try to harm her children — she'll protect them with everything she has.

Г-428 • НАЗВА́ЛСЯ ГРУ́ЗДЕМ, ПОЛЕЗА́Й В КУ́ЗОВ [saying] once you have committed yourself to sth., do not complain that it is too difficult or try to back out of it, just finish it (addressed to a person who tries to extricate himself from a commitment upon realizing the difficulties or unpleasant consequences it involves; or said when a person who has voluntarily taken on a commitment encounters difficulties but will not allow himself to relinquish his responsibilities): ≃ **if you pledge, don't hedge; if a job is once begun, never leave it till it's done; in for a penny, in for a pound.**

Г-429 • ЛЕЖА́ТЬ МЁРТВЫМ ГРУ́ЗОМ [VP; subj: abstr or concr; the verb may take the final position, otherwise fixed WO] to go unused, be without application: X лежит мёртвым грузом ≃ **X lies dormant ⟨fallow⟩; X (just) lies ⟨sits⟩ there (doing nothing); X sits idle.**

Г-430 • ВЫТА́СКИВАТЬ/ВЫ́ТАЩИТЬ ИЗ ГРЯ́ЗИ *кого coll* [VP; subj: human] to help s.o. get out of degrading, socially humiliating circumstances, help s.o. out of poverty: X вытащил Y-а из грязи ≃ **X pulled ⟨helped⟩ Y (up) out of the gutter.**

Г-431 • ИЗ ГРЯ́ЗИ (ДА) В КНЯ́ЗИ выйти, вылезти *coll* [PrepP; these forms only; adv or indep. sent; fixed WO] (to move) from poverty or a low social position to a recognized place in society: **(go) from rags to riches; (go) from bottom to top.**

По бесформенному полю скачут, как блохи, выскочки, из рабов в императоры, из грязи в князи... (Терц 3). In the vast formless plains men jumped about like fleas—upstart slaves moved from rags to riches and became Emperors... (3a). ♦ ...Они [советские вожди] в результате кровавых чисток толпами выходили из грязи в князи... оказывались генералами и губернаторами и вершили судьбами тысяч людей (Войнович 1). ...As a result of the bloody purges, they [the Soviet leaders] went from bottom to top—suddenly becoming generals and governors, who could decide the fate of thousands (1a).

Г-432 • ВТА́ПТЫВАТЬ/ВТОПТА́ТЬ ⟨ЗАТА́ПТЫВАТЬ/ЗАТОПТА́ТЬ⟩ В ГРЯЗЬ *кого-что disapprov* [VP; subj: human; more often pfv] to defame s.o. publicly in an insulting way, sparing him no abuse, bring accusations (usu. unjust) against s.o.: X втоптал Y-а в грязь ≃ X trampled Y in the mud; X dragged person Y ⟨Y's name⟩ through the mud ⟨the mire, the muck⟩; X threw ⟨slung, flung⟩ mud ⟨dirt⟩ at Y; X blackened person Y's name ⟨reputation⟩.

[У Ленина была] способность не колеблясь втоптать [противника] в грязь... — непонятным образом соединённая с милой улыбкой, с застенчивой деликатностью (Гроссман 1). [Lenin had] the capacity to trample an opponent in the mud with no hesitation...paradoxically combined with a kind smile and shy sensitivity (1a). ♦ [Глаголев 1:] Удачно однажды выразился Платонов... Мы, сказал он, поумнели по части женщин, а поумнеть по части женщин значит втоптать самого себя и женщину в грязь... (Чехов 1). [G. Sr.:] Platonov once put it very well. We've grown more intelligent about women, he said, and to become more intelligent about women means to drag women as well as ourselves through the mire (1a).

Г-433 • МЕСИ́ТЬ ГРЯЗЬ *coll* [VP; subj: human] to walk in the mud, walk along a muddy road: X месил грязь ≃ X waded ⟨trudged, sloshed, slogged⟩ through the mud.

Изо дня в день месил я вязкую грязь на плацу... (Лившиц 1). Day after day I waded through the sticky mud on the parade-ground... (1a).

Г-434 • БРОСА́ТЬ/БРО́СИТЬ ⟨КИДА́ТЬ/КИ́НУТЬ⟩ ГРЯ́ЗЬЮ *в кого;* ЗАБРА́СЫВАТЬ/ЗАБРОСА́ТЬ ⟨ЗАКИ́ДЫВАТЬ/ЗАКИДА́ТЬ⟩ ГРЯ́ЗЬЮ ⟨КАМНЯ́МИ⟩ *кого disapprov* [VP; subj: human] to defame, vilify s.o.: X бросает в Y-а грязью ≃ X throws ⟨slings, flings⟩ mud ⟨dirt⟩ at Y; X blackens Y's name ⟨reputation⟩; X besmirches Y's good name ⟨Y's reputation⟩; X heaps abuse on Y.

Г-435 • ЗАРАСТА́ТЬ/ЗАРАСТИ́ ГРЯ́ЗЬЮ *coll* [VP; subj: human] to reach an extreme level of untidiness, negligence: X зарос грязью ≃ X is ⟨has become⟩ a walking pigpen ⟨pigsty⟩; X's place is ⟨has turned into⟩ a pigsty ⟨a pigpen⟩; X is (en)crusted with dirt.

[author's usage] Если б доктор Гааз не прислал Соколовскому связку своего белья, он зарос бы в грязи (Герцен 1). If Dr. Haas had not sent Sokolovsky a bundle of his own linen he would have been crusted with dirt (1a).

Г-436 • ОБЛИВА́ТЬ/ОБЛИ́ТЬ ⟨ПОЛИВА́ТЬ/ПОЛИ́ТЬ⟩ ГРЯ́ЗЬЮ ⟨ПОМО́ЯМИ *coll*⟩ *кого;* ЛИТЬ ГРЯЗЬ ⟨ПОМО́И *coll*⟩ *на кого disapprov* [VP; subj: human] to disgrace, defame s.o. unjustly, bring accusations (usu. unjust) against s.o.: X обливает Y-а грязью ≃ X throws ⟨slings, flings⟩ mud ⟨dirt⟩ at Y; X covers Y's name in mud ⟨dirt⟩; X heaps abuse on Y; X besmirches Y's reputation ⟨good name⟩.

...Даже ТАССу пришлось отзываться — но как же отозваться на мой призыв молодёжи — не лгать, а выстаивать мужественно? Вот как: «Солженицын обливает грязью советскую молодёжь, что у неё нет мужества» (Солженицын 2). ...Even Tass had to take notice—but how could it respond to my exhortation to the young not to lie, but to stand up for the truth courageously? This was how: "Solzhenitsyn slings mud at the young Soviet generation, accuses them of lacking courage" (2a). ♦ Откройте любой лист газеты того времени, и вы увидите, как часто завтрашние жертвы, чтобы спастись, обливали грязью жертвы сегодняшнего дня (Гладков 1). Look at any newspaper from those days and you will see how tomorrow's victims, trying to save their own skins, heaped abuse on today's (1a).

Г-437 • СМЕ́ШИВАТЬ/СМЕША́ТЬ С ГРЯ́ЗЬЮ ⟨С ДЕРЬМО́М *vulg*⟩ *кого usu. disapprov* [VP; subj: human; more often pfv] to slander s.o. publicly, harshly, denigrate s.o., not sparing him any abuse: X смешал Y-а с грязью ≃ X dragged Y ⟨Y's name⟩ through the mud ⟨the mire, the muck⟩; X threw ⟨slung, flung⟩ mud ⟨dirt⟩ at Y; X blackened Y's name ⟨reputation⟩.

«Послушай, Луи, я тебя не понимаю. К чему эти комплименты? Разве ты не поддерживал Дюгара? А он меня каждый день смешивал с грязью» (Эренбург 4). "Look here, Louis," said Tessa, "I don't understand what you're driving at. Why all these compliments? Haven't you been supporting Dugard? Well, he's been slinging mud at me day after day" (4a). ♦ Твёрдо знали одно: прежде он [Соколовский] работал на Урале, изругал директора, тот смешал его с грязью... (Эренбург 3). Only one thing was known for certain—his [Sokolovsky's] last job had been in the Urals; there he had quarrelled with his chief who had then blackened his name... (3a).

Г-438 • ГУБА́ ⟨ГУ́БА⟩ НЕ ДУ́РА *у кого highly coll* [VP$_{subj}$ with быть$_\emptyset$ (present only); fixed WO] s.o. knows how to choose the very best, has a keen understanding of quality: у X-а губа не дура ≃ X has good taste; X's taste isn't bad; X doesn't have bad taste; X is no fool when it comes to...; X knows a good thing when he sees it ⟨one⟩.

«Кто это? — спросил его Базаров... — Какая хорошенькая!» ...Аркадий, не без замешательства, объяснил ему в коротких словах, кто была Фенечка. «Ага! — промолвил Базаров, — у твоего отца, видно, губа не дура» (Тургенев 2). "Who's that?" Bazarov inquired...."What a pretty girl!"...Arkady, not without embarrassment, explained to him briefly who Fenichka was. "Aha!" remarked Bazarov. "That shows your father's got good taste" (2c). ♦ [Митя:] ...Я весь тут-с: я вашу дочку полюбил душою-с. [Гордей Карпыч:] Как, чай, не любить! У тебя губа-то не дура! (Островский 2). [M.:] Here I am; I've fallen in love with your daughter with all my heart and soul. [G.K.:] Well, how could you help loving her? Your taste isn't bad! (2a). ♦ Собакевич... опрокинул половину бараньего бока к себе на тарелку, съел всё, обгрыз, обсосал до последней косточки. «Да, — подумал Чичиков, — у этого губа не дура» (Гоголь 3). Sobakevich... overturned half the side of mutton onto his plate, and ate it all up, gnawing clean and sucking dry every bit of a bone. "Yes," reflected Chichikov, "this fellow is no fool when it comes to his belly" (3b). ♦ [Телятев:] ...Что ж бы ты думал, на кого он [Васильков] так уставился?.. На [Лидию] Чебоксарову. [Глумов:] У него губа-то не дура (Островский 4). [T.:] ...What do you think he [Vassilkov] was staring at?...He was staring at sweet Lydia! [G.:] He certainly knows a good thing when he sees one (4b).

Г-439 • ПОШЛА́ ПИСА́ТЬ ГУБЕ́РНИЯ; (И) ПОШЛО́ ⟨ПОШЛА́⟩ ПИСА́ТЬ *coll, humor* [VP$_{subj}$ (1st var.) or VP$_{impers}$ (2nd var.); these forms only; fixed WO] things started up, some action was undertaken etc in a very intense manner, everything was set in motion (and developed rapidly): **there they go; off they go ⟨went⟩; things really began to take off;** [of arguments etc] **the fireworks started.**

Галопад летел во всю пропалую: почтмейстерша, капитан-исправник, дама с голубым пером... всё поднялось и понеслось... «Вона! Пошла писать губерния!» — проговорил Чичиков... (Гоголь 3). The dancing was going full tilt: the postmaster's wife, the police captain, a lady with a pale blue feather...—all of them had taken off and were now rushing and swirling about. "There they go!" Chichikov muttered... (3e). ♦ Общий хохот покрыл его [Луки Савича] голос... Все хохочут долго, дружно... Только начнут умолкать, кто-нибудь подхватит опять — и пошло писать (Гончаров 1). His [Luka Savich's] voice was drowned in the general laughter....They all laughed and laughed in unison....When the laughter began to die down, someone would start it anew and—off they went again (1a). ♦ Егорша потолкался с недельку в райцентре, всё разнюхал, повыведал, тому зубы заговорил, этому заговорил — сел на райкомовскую легковуху. И пошла писать губерния. Куда ни заехал, куда ни заявился — первый человек (Абрамов 1). Egorsha lingered for a week or so in the district center, had a good sniff around, wormed out some information, sweet-talked this one, sweet-talked that one, and...became the District Committee chauffeur. Then things really began to take off. Whomever he paid a call on, wherever he appeared, he was like a VIP (1a).

< The source of the first variant is Nikolai Gogol's *Dead Souls* («Мёртвые души»), 1842.

Г-440 • НАДУВА́ТЬ/НАДУ́ТЬ ГУ́БЫ ⟨ГУ́БКИ⟩ *coll* [VP; subj: human] to push out one's lips in an expression of anger, offense, or sulkiness, look sullen: X надул губы ≃ **X pouted; X made a moue ⟨a sour face⟩.**

[Бессудный *(Аннушке):*] А ты что губы-то надула! (Островский 8). [B. *(To Annushka):*] What are *you* pouting about? (8a).

Г-441 • РАЗЖИМА́ТЬ/РАЗЖА́ТЬ ГУ́БЫ ⟨ЗУ́БЫ *obs*⟩ *coll* [VP; subj: human; often neg or neg Verbal Adv] to say sth., speak: X губ не разожмёт ≃ **X won't (so much as) open his mouth; X won't utter a sound ⟨a word⟩.**

Г-442 • НИ ГУГУ́ *coll* [Invar] **1.** [usu. predic with subj: human or collect; usu. used in present or past contexts; because of the absence of a verb in Russian, the tense of the verb in the English equivalent must be determined by the context] one keeps silent, does not say anything: X ни гугу ≃ [past context] **X didn't say ⟨breathe⟩ a word; X didn't make ⟨utter, let out⟩ a ⟨one⟩ peep; X kept mum; there wasn't ⟨s.o. didn't hear⟩ a peep ⟨a sound, a word⟩ from ⟨out of⟩ X.**

...Они здесь только покурить: дыма табачного в рот наберут, ни гугу (Ерофеев 3). ...They just went out there for a smoke, took a drag or two of tobacco smoke into their lungs, and never made a peep (3a). ♦ ...[Местная газета «Большевистские темпы»] печатала чёрт-те чего, а о пропавшем Учреждении — ни гугу (Войнович 2). ...[The local newspaper *Bolshevik Tempos*] was printing all sorts of rubbish, but that the Institution had vanished, not one peep (2a).

2. *от кого, откуда* ~ [subj (with не быть₀)] there has been no news, letter, response from some person or organization: от X-а ни гугу ≃ **there hasn't been a ⟨any⟩ word from X; there is no word from X; person Y hasn't heard a thing from X.**

3. ~ *(кому о ком-чём)* [used as imper] do not tell anyone (or a certain person) about sth.: X-у ⟨никому⟩ (об Y-е) ни гугу ≃ **don't ⟨you mustn't⟩ say ⟨breathe⟩ a word to X ⟨to anyone⟩ (about Y); not a word to X ⟨to anyone⟩ (about Y); don't ⟨you mustn't⟩ make ⟨utter⟩ a peep ⟨a sound⟩ to X (about Y); keep mum (about Y).**

Говоря строго между нами, только уж ты, профессор, об этом никому ни гугу, — я соврал тебе давеча про наше хорошее положение. Положение у нас хуже некуда (Терц 6). Strictly between ourselves—but you really mustn't breathe a word, Professor—I told you a lie when I said that things were not as bad as they might be. The fact is, they couldn't be worse (6a). ♦ У меня гениальная идея, сказал Претендент, и они перешли на шёпот.

Только никому ни гугу, сказал Претендент (Зиновьев 1). "I've had a marvellous idea," said Claimant, and the rest of the conversation was held in whispers. "Not a word to anyone," said Claimant (1a).

Г-443 • ВЗЯ́ЛСЯ ЗА ГУЖ, НЕ ГОВОРИ́, ЧТО НЕ ДЮЖ [saying] once you have begun sth., do not complain that it is too difficult or try to back out of it, just finish it (said by, to, or about a person who has voluntarily taken on a commitment and then encounters difficulties but will not allow himself to relinquish his responsibilities; also used to reproach a person who, because of difficulties encountered in an undertaking, wants to back out of it): ≃ **if you pledge, don't hedge; if a job is once begun, never leave it till it's done; it's no good turning back halfway; in for a penny, in for a pound.**

Он [Аркадий] застал Базарова в трактире, где они остановились, и долго его уговаривал пойти к губернатору. «Нечего делать! — сказал, наконец, Базаров. — Взялся за гуж — не говори, что не дюж! Приехали смотреть помещиков — давай их смотреть!» (Тургенев 2). He [Arkady] found Bazarov in the inn where they were staying and set himself to persuade him to visit the governor. "Since there's no way out of it!" said Bazarov at last. "It's no good turning back halfway! We came to have a look at the landlords, so let's go and have a look at them!" (2e).

Г-444 • ДРАЗНИ́ТЬ/РАЗДРАЗНИ́ТЬ ГУСЕ́Й *coll* [VP; subj: human; usu. impfv; often infin with зачем, не надо etc, or neg infin after чтобы] to irritate, anger s.o., usu. pointlessly (often, one's superior(s) or s.o. who is in a position to make trouble for one): не надо ⟨зачем⟩ гусей дразнить ≃ **don't ⟨why⟩ make waves ⟨trouble⟩; don't ⟨why⟩ stir things up; don't ruffle any ⟨s.o.'s⟩ feathers; don't rub s.o. the wrong way.**

«Кто форинов [*author's usage* = иностранцев] пригласил? Ты, Маккар? — строго спросил Самсик. — Зачем, ребята? Зачем гусей-то дразнить?» «Зачем гусей дразнить?» — это, можно сказать, было лозунгом их поколения (Аксёнов 6). "Who invited the foreigners? Was it you, Makkar?" asked Samsik sternly. "Why, kids? Why make waves?" "Why make waves?" This, one might say, was the slogan of Samsik's generation (6a). ♦ «Есть некоторый коммунистический стиль. Мало кто подходит под эту мерку. Но никто так явно не нарушает этой манеры жить и думать, как вы, Юрий Андреевич. Не понимаю, зачем гусей дразнить» (Пастернак 1). [context transl] "There exists a certain Communist style, Yurii Andreievich. Few people measure up to it. But no one flouts that way of life and thought as openly as you do. Why you have to flirt with danger, I can't imagine" (1a).

< From Ivan Krylov's fable "Geese" («Гуси»), 1811.

Г-445 • НЕ ГУ́СТО *(кого-чего* or *с чем, у кого, где) coll* [Invar; usu. quantit subj-compl with copula (subj/gen: any common noun) or quantit impers predic with быть₀] (s.o. has, in some place there is) a small quantity (of some type of person or thing): у X-а Y-а ⟨Y-ов, с Y-ом, с Y-ами⟩ не густо ≃ **X doesn't have much Y ⟨many Ys, a great variety of Ys⟩; X hardly ⟨scarcely⟩ has any Ys; X has practically nothing ⟨no Y(s)⟩; X has just a few Ys; [in refer. to money] X is low ⟨short⟩ on cash ⟨on funds⟩.**

[Галя *(Андрею):*] Эх ты, хозяин! Твой брат, наверно, устал с дороги, умыться хочет... [Андрей:] Да, да. *(Алексею)* Пойдём. [Вадим *(взяв чемодан Алексея):*] Остальные вещи в прихожей? [Алексей:] Тут всё! *(встряхнул чемодан):* Не густо! (Розов 1). [Galya *(to Andrei):*] Hey, you—host! Your cousin is probably tired from the trip, would like to wash up... [Andrei:] Yes, yes...In a minute. [Vadim *(Picking up Aleksei's "suitcase"):*] Are the rest of your things in the entry? [Aleksei:] That is all I have. [Vadim *(shaking the "suitcase"):*] Not much here! (1a). ♦ ...По части музыкальных инструментов, надо прямо сказать, в Чегеме не густо — абхазская чамгури, греческая кеменджа у нескольких греческих семей, живущих здесь, да международная гитара (Искандер 3). ...As regards musical instruments, it must be plainly stated that Chegem did not have a great variety—the Abkhazian *chamguri*, the Greek *kementzes* played by some of the local Greek families, and the international guitar (3a).

Г-446 • ГУСЬ ЛА́ПЧАТЫЙ *highly coll, disapprov* [NP; usu. sing; usu. subj-compl with быть∅, pres only (subj: human, male), or vocative; fixed WO] a sly, crafty person: **sly (old) fox ⟨devil⟩; shifty rascal; scoundrel.**

Г-447 • ГУСЬ СВИНЬЕ́ НЕ ТОВА́РИЩ [saying] people who have different social standings, characters, habits etc do not belong together: ≃ **oil and water don't mix.**

Укрощённое самолюбие недавнего «пахана» ревновало к упрямой гордыне залётного шкета. [Мастер] преследовал Влада с упорным злорадством человека, глубоко уязвлённого в своём понимании человечества... «Где нам в лаптях до вас в калошах, значит? Гусь свинье не товарищ, говоришь?» (Максимов 2). This one-time gang boss, his self-esteem crippled, was jealous of the obstinate pride shown by the cheeky young newcomer. He persecuted Vlad with the resolute malice of someone bitterly disillusioned with the human race....“Too big and mighty for us, eh? Oil and water don't mix, is that it?” (2a).

Г-448 • ХОРО́Ш ⟨КАКО́В, НУ И, ЧТО ЗА и т. п.⟩ ГУСЬ *highly coll* [Interj; these forms only; fixed WO] used to express one's scornful or ironic attitude toward s.o. (rarely toward o.s.), usu. in regard to negative qualities—dishonesty, trickery, unreliability etc: **what a rascal ⟨a louse, a weasel etc⟩; [in limited contexts] I know your ⟨his⟩ type; I am ⟨you are, he is⟩ a fine one to talk; I've got your ⟨his⟩ number.**

Ягодный уполномоченный... тоскливо вздыхал: «Убьёт он [отец Ксюты] меня... Ведь он же меня отцом считает [*dial* = считает]. Впутала меня девка...» Ко всему прочему история встречи с чернобородым незнакомцем [, от которого она забеременела], сбивчиво рассказанная Ксютой, навела ягодного уполномоченного на размышления о жизни вообще и о собственной в частности. «Я ведь тоже хорош гусь, — думал Тихон Тихонович. — Чо [*dial* = что], со мной такого не бывало, чо ли?.. Может, и мои детишки, мне неизвестные, на свете копошатся?» (Евтушенко 2). The berry commissioner...sighed heavily. *He'll [Ksiuta's father will] kill me....He thinks I'm the father. The girl got me mixed up in this....Aside from every-* thing else, Ksiuta's somewhat confused account of her meeting with the black-bearded stranger [who made her pregnant] set the berry commissioner to musing about life in general and his own in particular. *I'm a fine one to talk,* thought Tikhon Tikhonovich. *Haven't things like that ever happened to me?...Maybe I have children that I don't know about, walking this earth?* (2a). ♦ Ему [Михаилу] очень понравилось, как Иван Дмитриевич срезал Петра Житова. Твёрдо и в то же время не обидно. Дескать, учти, любезный. Я сразу понял, что ты за гусь. Каждое дело вспрыскивать — вот ты из каких (Абрамов 1). He [Mikhail] was very pleased with the way Ivan Dmitrievich had cut Pyotr Zhitov off. Firmly and at the same time without causing offense. As if saying, “Look out, my dear fellow. I've got your number, all right. You're the kind who likes to lubricate every occasion...” (1a).

Г-449 • КАК С ГУ́СЯ ВОДА́ *с кого, кому coll, usu. disapprov* [как + NP; Invar; usu. compl of быть∅ (impers) or subj-compl with быть∅ (subj: всё); fixed WO] s.o. is utterly indifferent to sth., does not react to sth.; sth. does not affect s.o. at all: **(it is) like water off a duck's back.**

[Кочкарёв:] Ведь вот что досадно: [Подколёсин] вышел себе — ему и горя мало. С него всё это так, как с гуся вода — вот что нестерпимо! (Гоголь 1). [K.:] That's what's so annoying. He's [Podkolyosin has] gone off—it doesn't worry him much, it's just like water off a duck's back—that's what's unbearable! (1a).

Г-450 • ГАДА́ТЬ НА КОФЕ́ЙНОЙ ГУ́ЩЕ ⟨НА БОБА́Х⟩ *coll, usu. disapprov* [VP; subj: human; usu. this WO] to make guesses or suppositions that are totally without foundation or are based on insufficient knowledge, information etc: X гадал на кофейной гуще ≃ **X was taking shots in the dark; X was taking ⟨making⟩ wild guesses; [in limited contexts] X was reading tea leaves.** ○ ГАДА́НИЕ НА КОФЕ́ЙНОЙ ГУ́ЩЕ ⟨НА БОБА́Х⟩ [NP] ≃ **shots in the dark; wild guesses; guesswork; [in limited contexts] reading tea leaves.**

Зачем гадать на кофейной гуще, когда можно взять справочник и посмотреть? Why take wild guesses when you can just look up the facts in a reference book? ♦ [author's usage] Как известно, наши хозяева умели предсказывать будущее, пользуясь не кофейной гущей, а научными методами... (Мандельштам 2). As we all know, our rulers were able to foretell the future not by reading tea leaves, but with the aid of “scientific principles”... (2a).

Д-1 • ДА И... [coord Conj] **1.** [connective] used to connect two successive words, phrases, or clauses: **and**; [when connecting negated units] **and did not ⟨was not etc⟩...either; nor...**

[Атуева:] А вот вам Нелькин дался! Вы бы его в свете посмотрели, так, думаю, другое бы сказали. Ведь это просто срамота! Вот вчера выхлопотала ему приглашение у княгини — стащила на бал. Приехал. Что ж вы думаете? Залез в угол, да и торчит там... (Сухово-Кобылин 2). [A.:] You and your Nelkin! You'd change your mind about him if you saw him in society. He is positively a disgrace! Why, only yesterday I got him an invitation from the countess. I dragged him to the ball—and what do you think? He slunk into a corner and crouched there... (2a). ♦ ...[Юра] даже не смотрел в сторону мясного, да и выпивкой не очень интересовался, а только рубал свои апельсинчики так, что за ушами трещало (Аксёнов 1). Yura...hadn't even looked at the meat dish and wasn't even interested in the drinks, either, but was only digging into his oranges, wolfing them down (1a).

2. [connective] used to indicate the unexpected nature of the action that follows: **and (then); and end up (doing sth.);** [in limited contexts] **and in the end.**

«Купит вот тот каналья повар... кота, обдерёт его да и подаёт на стол вместо зайца» (Гоголь 3). "That scoundrel of a cook they have...he'd buy a cat, skin it and then serve it up in place of a hare" (3d). ♦ Олег готовился, готовился к экзаменам, да и провалился. Oleg studied intensely for his exams and ended up failing them. ♦ ...[Когда] понадобилось написать бумагу в полицию, он взял лист бумаги, перо, думал, думал, да и послал за писарем (Гончаров 1). ...[When] he had to write to the police, he took a sheet of paper and pen, spent a long time thinking over it, and in the end sent for a clerk (1a).

3. [connective] (used to introduce a clause, phrase etc whose information adds to, and is usu. more important than, the information in the preceding statement) and furthermore: **(and) besides; (and) anyway; (and) after all; moreover; and indeed; and what's more.**

Близился полдень, и пахарь уже настораживал слух в сторону дома, что вот-вот жена его должна позвать обедать, да и быкам пора передохнуть (Искандер 4). It was getting near noon, and the plowman had an ear cocked toward the house: any minute now his wife would be calling him to dinner, and besides it was time to rest the oxen (4a). ♦ Обыватели не только ценили такую ровность характера, но даже усматривали в ней признаки доблести; да и нельзя было не ценить... (Салтыков-Щедрин 2). The citizens of our town not only appreciated such a steadfastness of disposition, but even seemed to discern in it unmistakable signs of heroism. Besides, it was quite impossible not to appreciate it... (2a). ♦ Что сталось с старухой и с бедным слепым — не знаю. Да и какое дело мне до радостей и бедствий человеческих... (Лермонтов 1). I've no idea what became of the old woman and the poor blind boy. And anyway, the joys and tribulations of mankind are of no concern to me... (1c). ♦ ...Он решил, что детям будет полезно послушать рассказы о его подвигах, да и не каждый день к ним заворачивает такой гость, как Сандро из Чегема (Искандер 3). ...He decided that the children would profit by hearing tales of his feats; after all, it wasn't every day that they had a guest like Sandro of Chegem (3a).

4. [contrastive] used to connect contrasting clauses or parts of a sentence: **and ⟨but, yet⟩ even.**

«Один там только есть порядочный человек: прокурор; да и тот, если сказать правду, свинья» (Гоголь 3). "There's only one decent man among them, the public prosecutor, and even he, to tell the truth, is a dirty swine" (3a).

Д-2 • ДА НУ?⟨!⟩ *coll* [Interj; Invar; fixed WO] (used as an expression of surprise, incredulity etc in response to s.o.'s state-

ment) is that in fact true?: **you don't say!; is that so?; come ⟨go⟩ on!; really?; you've got to be kidding!;** [when expressing utter disbelief] **come off it!**

«Ты слышал? — говорит он мне. — Иванько отказался от своих притязаний». — «Да ну!» — «Абсолютно точно» (Войнович 3). "Did you hear?" he said to me. "Ivanko gave up his claim." "Come on!" "Absolutely" (3a). ♦ «Говори же!» — «Ничего особенного! Просто меня собираются пригласить в Михайловский театр» (Каверин 1). "Well, tell me!" "Oh, it's nothing special. Just that I'm being offered a job at the Mikhailovsky Theatre." "Go on!" (1a). ♦ «...Не знаешь, с какого бока к тебе и подойти». — «Да ну!» (Абрамов 1). "We're afraid to come near you nowadays." "Come off it!" (1a).

Д-3 • ДАВА́ТЬ/ДАТЬ ЗНАТЬ [VP; usu. this WO] **1.** ~ *кому (о чём)* [subj: human or collect; if there is no prep obj, often foll. by a clause introduced by что, когда etc] to inform s.o. (of sth.): X дал Y-y знать (о Z-e ⟨, что...⟩) ≃ **X let Y know (about Z ⟨that...⟩); X sent word to Y (that...).**

Попрощались [Гриша и Николай Демьянович] мирно, условились, что Николай Демьянович поглядит, подумает и через денька три-четыре даст знать (Трифонов 1). ...The two men [Grisha and Nikolai Demianovich] parted on peaceful terms, with the understanding that Nikolai Demianovich would look over the manuscripts, think about them, and let him know in three or four days (1a).

2. ~ *(кому)* [subj: human or collect; foll. by a что-clause] to make sth. understood (through a gesture, facial expression, mode of behavior etc): X дал (Y-y) знать, что... ≃ **X made it clear ⟨plain⟩ that...; X let Y know that...; X let it be known that...; X gave Y to understand that...; (by doing sth.) X showed that...**

Некоторые сотрудники нашей редакции перестали со мной здороваться... Другие мужественно продолжали со мной здороваться, но при этом явно давали знать, что употребляют на это столько душевных сил, что я не должен удивляться, если в скором времени они надорвутся от этой перегрузки (Искандер 4). ...Several people on the newspaper staff stopped saying hello to me....Others bravely continued to say hello to me, but made it plain that this took so much spiritual strength that I must not be surprised if they collapsed under the strain before long (4a). ♦ Управляющий лёгким поклоном-кивком дал знать, что распоряжение, и при том не без личного удовольствия, принято к сведению (Искандер 3). The bailiff, with a slight bow and a nod, let it be known that the disposition had been noted, and not without personal satisfaction (3a). ♦ Подчеркнув абсурдность замечания вождя относительно цыплят, Тенгиз, как бы во избежание кривотолков, дал знать слушателям, что реплика эта представляла из себя только шутку... (Искандер 3). By stressing the absurdity of the Leader's remark about the chickens, Tengiz, as if to prevent false rumors, gave his listeners to understand that this retort was merely a joke... (3a). ♦ Анатоль не отпускал англичанина, и, несмотря на то, что тот, кивая, давал знать, что всё он понял, Анатоль переводил ему слова Долохова по-английски (Толстой 4). Anatole did not release him, and though [the Englishman] kept nodding to show that he understood, Anatole went on translating Dolokhov's words into English (4b).

3. [subj: abstr, usu. a noun denoting some sound, movement etc; foll. by a что-clause] to indicate, evince (sth.): X давал знать, что... ≃ **X showed that...; X gave evidence to the fact that...; X was a sign that...;** [in refer. to s.o.'s unsuccessful attempt(s) to conceal some emotion] **X gave away that...**

Д-4 • ДАВА́ТЬ/ДАТЬ О СЕБЕ́ ЗНАТЬ [VP] **1.** ~ *(кому)* [subj: human] to communicate (with s.o.), send (s.o.)

information about o.s.: X дал о себе знать ⟨Y-у⟩ ≃ **X let Y know how X was doing ⟨how things were going with X etc⟩; X sent word about himself (to Y); [in limited contexts] Y has heard from X; X was ⟨got⟩ in touch (with Y); X dropped Y a line;** ‖ *Neg* X не даёт о себе знать ≃ **X hasn't been heard from.**

2. [subj: human or animal] not to let one's presence go unnoticed or be forgotten: X даёт о себе знать ≃ **X makes his ⟨its⟩ presence known; X makes himself ⟨itself⟩ heard.**

Кязым открыл ворота и пересёк двор, удивляясь и настораживаясь от того, что собака не даёт о себе знать (Искандер 5). Kyazym opened the gate and crossed the yard, surprised and on his guard because the dog had not made her presence known (5a). ♦ Если б его [скот], как обычно, выпустили на выгон, может быть, он и не кричал бы. Но... голодный скот, находясь взаперти, всегда даёт о себе знать... (Искандер 3). If they [the livestock] had been turned out to graze on the common as usual, perhaps they would not have cried out. But...hungry animals who find themselves penned up always make themselves heard... (3a).

3. [subj: abstr or concr] (often of illness, a wound etc) to surface, manifest itself: X даёт о себе знать ≃ **X makes itself felt; X has its effect on person Y;** [of chronic illness, an ailing part of the body etc] **X acts up;** [of age, hardship, illness etc] **X is beginning to take its toll.**

Ветра не было. Шторм шёл где-то далеко в открытом море, а здесь он лишь давал о себе знать мощными, но чуть ленивыми ударами по пляжам (Аксёнов 8). There was no wind. The storm was somewhere way out in the open sea, and it only made itself felt here by pounding at the beaches with powerful, if slightly indolent blows (8a). ♦ «Настроение у меня хорошее... падает, только когда гипертония разгуливается. Она у меня давно, и вполне терпимая, но иногда всё-таки даёт о себе знать» (Грекова 3). "My mood is good...and goes bad only when high blood pressure takes over. I've had it for a long time, and it's quite bearable, but now and then it acts up" (3a). ♦ Помяните моё слово, эта ошибка ещё даст о себе знать роковым образом (Зиновьев 1). [context transl] Mark my words, this mistake will have fateful consequences in the future (1a).

Д-5 • ДАВА́ТЬ/ДАТЬ ПОНЯ́ТЬ ⟨ПОЧУ́ВСТВО-ВАТЬ⟩ (кому) что; ДАВА́ТЬ ЧУ́ВСТВОВАТЬ [VP; subj: human; usu. foll. by a что-clause; fixed WO] to make (sth.) felt or understood: X дал Y-у понять, что... ≃ **X gave Y to understand that...; X let Y know that...; X made it clear ⟨plain⟩ that...; X got the message across (that...); X conveyed to Y that...;** [in limited contexts] **X's manner ⟨attitude etc⟩ suggested that...;** ‖ давая понять, что... ≃ [in limited contexts] **as if to say that...**

В конце концов, Колчерукий сумел успокоить его [родственника], дав понять, что убить никогда не поздно, если окажется, что Сандро виноват (Искандер 3). In the end, Bad Hand managed to soothe him [the relative] by giving him to understand that it was never too late to kill Sandro if it turned out he was guilty (3a). ♦ Я дал ей [княжне Мери] почувствовать очень запутанной фразой, что она мне давно нравится (Лермонтов 1). In a muddled sentence I let her [Princess Mary] know that I had long been attracted to her (1c). ♦ Тарантьев вообще постоянно был груб в обращении со всеми, не исключая и приятелей, как будто давал чувствовать, что, заговаривая с человеком, даже обедая или ужиная у него, он делает ему большую честь (Гончаров 1). ...[Tarantyev] was generally rude to everyone, including his friends, as though making it clear that he bestowed a great honour on a person by talking to him or having dinner or supper at his place (1a). ♦ ...Всем своим видом [Ефим] давал понять, что пишет о хороших людях потому, что сам хороший и в жизни замечает только хорошее... (Войнович 6). ...His [Yefim's] whole manner suggested that he wrote about decent people because he himself was decent and saw only the good in life... (6a). ♦ Профессор снисходительно улыбнулся, давая понять, что студент ещё молод и

зелен, и ему следует кое-что объяснить (Войнович 1). The professor smiled condescendingly, as if to say that the student was still young and green, and required enlightening (1a).

Д-6 • ДАВА́ТЬ/ДАТЬ ПРИКУРИ́ТЬ ⟨ПИ́ТЬ⟩ кому highly coll [VP; usu. pfv; fixed WO] **1.** [subj: human] to scold s.o. severely, punish s.o.: X дал Y-у прикурить ≃ **X let Y have it (with both barrels); X gave Y the business ⟨what for⟩; X gave it to Y (but good); X showed Y what's what; X gave Y hell; Y caught hell (from X).**

...Своему начальнику леспонкта он тоже сумеет ответить. Кубики тебе даём? Даём... И завтра он ещё даст кое-кому прикурить (Абрамов 1). ...He had an answer ready for his logging boss too: I produce the goods, don't I?...And tomorrow he would show certain people what's what (1a).

2. [subj: human (usu. pl) or collect] to overwhelm, defeat s.o. (usu. a hostile army, the enemy): X-ы дали Y-ам прикурить ≃ **Xs crushed ⟨clobbered, creamed⟩ Ys; Xs gave Ys a licking; Xs beat the pants off Ys.**

Д-7 • ДАВА́ТЬ/ДАТЬ СЕБЯ́ ЗНАТЬ ⟨ЧУ́ВСТВО-ВАТЬ⟩; ДАТЬ СЕБЯ́ ПОЧУ́ВСТВОВАТЬ [VP; subj: abstr or concr; usu. this WO] to manifest itself, become noticeable: X даёт о себе знать ≃ **X makes itself felt; X has its effect on person Y;** [of chronic illess, an ailing part of the body etc] **X acts up;** [of age, hardship, illness etc] **X is beginning to take its toll;** [of age, illness etc] **X is beginning to tell on person Y.**

После той, батумской истории Влад навсегда зарёкся ввязываться в авантюры, подпадающие под какую-либо статью уголовного кодекса, но голод уже давал себя знать, да и роль, отведённая ему напарником в предстоящей операции, ограничивалась минимальным риском (Максимов 2). After the business in Batum, Vlad had sworn never to get mixed up in any adventures likely to be covered by some article of the Criminal Code, but hunger was already making itself felt, and his role of accomplice in the proposed operation involved only a minimum of risk (2a).

Д-8 • ПОД ДАВЛЕ́НИЕМ кого-чего [PrepP; Invar; the resulting PrepP is adv] as a result of a constraining influence (of s.o. or sth. upon a person): **at the insistence of s.o.; under pressure from s.o.; under the pressure of sth.; bowing to sth.;** [in limited contexts] **under duress.**

Очень часто раненое животное, заслышав шорох, бросается на выстрел охотника, бежит вперёд, назад и само ускоряет свой конец. То же самое делал Наполеон под давлением всего своего войска (Толстой 7). Very often a wounded animal, hearing a rustle, rushes straight at the hunter's gun, runs forward and back again, and hastens its own end. Napoleon, under pressure from his whole army, did the same thing (7b).

Д-9 • ДАВНО́ БЫ ТАК! coll [sent; Invar; usu. this WO] (used to express the speaker's approval of s.o.'s long awaited and desired action or decision) finally!: **(it's) about time (, too)!; high time!; none ⟨not a moment⟩ too soon!; at long last;** [in limited contexts] **this is how it should have been all along.**

[Кочкарёв:] Да вы, сударыня, видите: он просит руки вашей... Спрашивает только, согласны ли вы его осчастливить... [Агафья Тихоновна:] Я никак не смею думать, чтобы я могла составить счастие... А, впрочем, я согласна. [Кочкарёв:] Натурально, натурально, так бы давно! (Гоголь 1). [К.:] Now you see, ma'am: he's asking for your hand....He's only asking, will you agree to make him happy?... [A.T.:] I can't dare to think that I could bestow happiness...but...I agree. [K.:] Naturally! Naturally! About time, too! (2a). ♦ Увидя меня, он смутился; но вскоре оправился, протянул мне руку, говоря: «И ты наш? Давно бы так!» (Пушкин 2). When he saw me he became confused, but he soon recovered himself and offered his hand, saying, "So you, too, are on our side? High time!" (2a). ♦ [Анна Петровна:] Я вам дам поесть! [Трилецкий:] Давно бы так (Чехов 1). [А.Р.:] I'll give you something to eat. [T.:] And not a moment too soon (1b).

Д-10 • ЗА ДА́ВНОСТЬЮ ЛЕТ ⟨ВРЕ́МЕНИ⟩ [PrepP; these forms only; adv; fixed WO] (it is impossible to recall, determine etc sth. that existed or took place in the past) because so much time has passed since then: **after so many ⟨after all these⟩ years; after all this time; sth. was ⟨happened etc⟩ so long ago that…;** [in limited contexts] **at this late date.**

Что за дамочка была у Шикалова и какая между ними приключилась история, автор за давностью лет, признаться, не помнит… (Войнович 2). To tell you the truth, after all these years the author can no longer recall what sort of lady Shikalov had or what adventures they shared… (2a). ♦ Фёдор Павлович не мог указать ему [Алёше], где похоронил свою вторую супругу, потому что никогда не бывал на её могиле, после того как засыпали гроб, а за давностью лет и совсем запамятовал, где её тогда хоронили… (Достоевский 1). Fyodor Pavlovich could not show him [Alyosha] where he had buried his second wife, because he had never visited her grave after her coffin was covered with earth, and it was all so long ago that he just could not recall where they had buried her… (1a). ♦ Сколько ещё она прождала своей очереди, сейчас, за давностью лет, установить уже никак невозможно… (Войнович 4). How much longer she waited for her turn cannot, at this late date, be determined… (4a).

Д-11 • ДО́РОГО БЫ ДАЛ, чтобы… or за что; МНО́ГО БЫ ⟨ЧЕГО́ БЫ НЕ⟩ ДАЛ [VP; subj: human (usu. a pronoun); subjunctive only; fixed WO with бы movable] one would be willing to give up, sacrifice sth. of great value in order to get sth. he really wants or make some desired event happen: дорого бы X дал ≃ **X would give ⟨have given⟩ anything ⟨a lot, a great deal, much⟩; what X wouldn't give ⟨have given⟩; X would pay ⟨have paid⟩ dearly; X would give ⟨have given⟩ his right arm.**

«…Пишите для театра. Это редкий вид дарования, и я много дал бы, чтобы им обладать…» (Гладков 1). "…Write for the theatre. This is a very rare kind of gift and I would give a great deal to possess it myself…" (1a). ♦ …Он закрывал глаза; он много дал бы, чтобы не слышать гармоник и саксофонов! (Эренбург 4). He closed his eyes; he would have given anything to silence those accordions and saxophones! (4a). ♦ Что делает теперь Вера? — думал я… Я бы дорого дал, чтоб в эту минуту пожать её руку (Лермонтов 1). I wondered what Vera was doing at that moment. I'd have given a lot to press her hand just then (1c). ♦ …[Ракитин] позволил себе выразиться об Аграфене Александровне несколько презрительно, как о «содержанке купца Самсонова». Дорого дал бы он потом, чтобы воротить своё словечко… (Достоевский 2). …[Rakitin] allowed himself to refer to Agrafena Alexandrovna somewhat contemptuously as "the merchant Samsonov's kept woman." He would have given much afterwards to take that little phrase back… (2a). ♦ «Моя жена, — продолжал князь Андрей, — прекрасная женщина. Это одна из тех редких женщин, с которою можно быть покойным за свою честь; но, боже мой, чего бы я не дал теперь, чтобы не быть женатым!» (Толстой 4). "My wife," Prince Andrei continued, "is an excellent woman, one of those rare women with whom a man's honor is secure, but, my God, what wouldn't I give not to be married now!" (4a). ♦ Дорого дала бы я тогда, чтобы понять смысл всего происходящего (Гинзбург 1). What wouldn't I have given in those days to understand the meaning of what was going on (1b).

Д-12 • НЕ ДА́ЛЕЕ ⟨НЕ ДА́ЛЬШЕ⟩ чего (пойти) [these forms only; the resulting AdvP is usu. adv] not (to move) any higher in rank than (the rank specified in the context): **not (get) further than…; not (rise) above the rank of; rank no higher than…**

…Люди степенные и занимающие важные должности как-то немного тяжеловаты в разговорах с дамами; на это мас-

тера господа поручики и никак не далее капитанских чинов (Гоголь 3). …Sedate men and those occupying important posts are a trifle clumsy in their converse with ladies; the real masters of this art are lieutenants and certainly not anyone above the rank of captain (3b).

Д-13 • НЕ ДА́ЛЕЕ ⟨НЕ ДА́ЛЬШЕ⟩ КАК ⟨ЧЕМ⟩… [AdvP; these forms only; used as a restr marker; the resulting AdvP is adv; fixed WO] (of time) precisely at or not before (the indicated time in the past), precisely at or not later than (the indicated time in the future); (of place) precisely at (the place indicated): [in refer. to the past] ~ вчера ⟨неделю назад, пять минут назад и т. п.⟩ ≃ **only yesterday ⟨a week ago, five minutes ago etc⟩; just yesterday ⟨a week ago, five minutes ago etc⟩; not ⟨no⟩ more than a week ⟨five minutes etc⟩ ago;** [in limited contexts; when used to point out that the event in question took place at the same time as some previously mentioned related event] **that very ⟨night ⟨day etc⟩);** ‖ [in refer. to the future] ~ завтра ⟨в будущем году и т. п.⟩ ≃ **not ⟨no⟩ later than tomorrow ⟨next year etc⟩; tomorrow ⟨next year etc⟩, and no later;** ‖ [in refer. to a place] **right in ⟨at⟩ this ⟨that⟩…; in ⟨at⟩ this ⟨that⟩ very…**

«А ты знаешь, что этот депутат не далее как вчера политическое убежище попросил?» — «Не может, — режиссёр говорит, — быть!» (Войнович 1). "Are you aware that this deputy only yesterday requested political asylum in the West?" "That can't be!" says the director (1a). ♦ Павел Петрович сказал нам: дорогой коллега, как славно, что имя, произнесённое вами не далее как минуту назад, растворилось, рассеялось в воздухе… (Соколов 1). Pavel Petrovich told us: dear colleague, how glorious it is that the name you uttered not more than a minute ago dissolved, dissipated in the air… (1a). ♦ «Не далее как дней пять тому назад, в одном здешнем, по преимуществу дамском, обществе он торжественно заявил… что на всей земле нет решительно ничего такого, что бы заставляло людей любить себе подобных…» (Достоевский 1). "No more than five days ago, at a local gathering, predominantly of ladies, he solemnly announced…that there is decidedly nothing in the whole world that would make men love their fellow men…" (1a).

Д-14 • ДАЛЕКО́ кому-чему ДО кого-чего [Invar; impers predic with быть₀] some person (or thing) does not compare with, is very inferior to some other person (or thing): X-у далеко до Y-а ≃ **X is no match for Y; X can't hold a candle to Y; X comes nowhere near Y; X is no comparison to Y; X is not in the same class ⟨league⟩ as Y; X is a far cry from Y.**

[Мелания:] Зобунова — лекариха знаменитая. Докторам — далеко до неё! (Горький 2). [M.:] Zobunova's a famous healer. The doctors come nowhere near her! (2a).

Д-15 • ДАЛЕКО́ ЗА [Invar] **1.** далеко ⟨далёко⟩ за полночь [the resulting AdvP is adv or impers predic with быть₀] much later than: **(till) well ⟨way, long⟩ past midnight; (till) well ⟨long⟩ after midnight; far ⟨late⟩ into the night.**

Пошли толки, расспросы; говорил больше Аркадий, особенно за ужином, который продолжался далеко за полночь (Тургенев 2). They all began to talk and ask questions. Arkady chattered most, especially at supper, which lasted till well past midnight (2c). ♦ Время утекло далеко за полночь… Из окна виден был тёмный шпиль адмиралтейской башни и жёлтый половодный разлив огней (Шолохов 3). The time was long past midnight.…The dark spire of the Admiralty tower and a yellow flood of lights could be seen from the window (3a). ♦ …Густой мрак окутывал улицы и дома, и только в одной из комнат градоначальнической квартиры мерцал, далеко за полночь, зловещий свет (Салтыков-Щедрин 1). …Thick gloom enveloped the streets and houses, and only in one of the rooms of the governor's apartment did a sinister light glimmer, far into the night (1a).

2. (кому) ~ [foll. by a Num; the resulting AdvP is usu. impers predic with бытьø] (of a person's age) much more than: **well ⟨way, considerably⟩ over [Num]; way past [Num]; much older than [Num].**

Перед войной мы с ним [дедушкой] ездили в Ленинград, ему было уже далеко за семьдесят... (Рыбаков 1). Before the war, we went to Leningrad together when he [my grandfather] was already well over seventy... (1a).

Д-16 • ДАЛЕКО́ НЕ [Particle; Invar; used as intensified negation] not at all: **far from (it); not (...) by any means; a long way from (doing sth. ⟨being...⟩);** [in limited contexts] **anything but (...); not anywhere ⟨nowhere⟩ near...; not (...) by a long shot; no [NP];** ‖ далеко не все ⟨не каждый и т. п.⟩ ≃ [in limited contexts] **very few.**

Впрочем, большая ошибка считать, что все французы брюнеты. Далеко не все (Рыбаков 1). As a matter of fact, it's a mistake to imagine all Frenchmen as dark-haired. Far from it... (1a). ♦ Знаю, что я далеко не исчерпал всех случаев помпадурской деятельности... (Салтыков-Щедрин 2). I am aware, of course, that I have not by any means exhausted the subject of pompadour activity... (2a). ♦ ...Только глупые люди думают, что животные лишь мыкают да блеют. Нет, животные далеко не только мыкают да блеют! (Искандер 5). ...It's only foolish people who think that animals merely moo and bleat. No, animals are a long way from mere mooing and bleating! (5a). ♦ В милицию [об исчезновении Юрия Андреевича] не заявляли, чтобы не напоминать властям о человеке, хотя и прописанном и не судившемся, но в современном понимании далеко не образцовом (Пастернак 1). They did not report him [Yurii Andreievich] as missing to the police. Although he was registered and had no police record, it was better not to draw the attention of the authorities to a man who, by the standards of the day, lived anything but an exemplary life (1a). ♦ ...В том виде, в каком Глупов предстал глазам его, город этот далеко не отвечал его идеалам (Салтыков-Щедрин 1). ...Foolov, as it appeared to his eyes, did not come anywhere near his ideal (1a). ♦ [Зилов:] Слышите? Ваши приличия мне опротивели. [Кушак (негодует):] Ну знаешь ли! Я далеко не ханжа, но это уже слишком! (Вампилов 5). [Z.:] Do you hear? I'm sick to death of your decency. [K. (indignant):] Now look here! I'm no prude, but this is a bit much! (5a). ♦ В Учреждение, возглавляемое капитаном Милягой, граждане почти всегда писали письма без обратного адреса... В таких письмах содержались обычно мелкие доносы... К чести Учреждения надо сказать, что оно принимало меры далеко не по каждому такому сигналу, иначе на воле не осталось бы ни одного человека (Войнович 2). Citizens almost always wrote letters to the Institution headed by Milyaga without a return address....As a rule, such letters contained petty denunciations....It must be said, to the Institution's credit, that very few such letters ever caused it to take measures; otherwise there would not have been a single person left free in the country (2a).

Д-17 • В ДАЛЬНЕ́ЙШЕМ [PrepP; Invar; usu. adv or sent adv] **1.** from some point in time onward: [in present and future contexts] **in the future; from now ⟨this point, this moment⟩ on; henceforth;** [in limited contexts] **future...;** [in past contexts] **afterward(s); from then ⟨that point, that moment⟩ on;** [in limited contexts] **as time went by.**

Некоторые довольно интеллигентные люди, замечая отдельные недостатки, которые всё ещё имеют место в нашей стране, думают: а что, если слегка потеснить большевиков, чтобы в дальнейшем, устранив эти недостатки, перестать их теснить? (Искандер 4). There are certain rather well-informed people who notice the isolated shortcomings that still exist in our country and think: What if we crowd the Bolsheviks a little, with the idea that we'll stop crowding them in the future, when we've eliminated these deficiencies? (4a). ♦ «Казачество окажет вам, Лавр Георгиевич, всемерную поддержку. Нам остаётся согласовать

вопрос о совместных действиях в дальнейшем» (Шолохов 3). "The Cossacks will give you full support, Lavr Georgievich. All we have to do now is settle the question of our future co-operation" (3a). ♦ Я не был убеждён, что это Маяковский, также не был убеждён в этом и Катаев, но мы в дальнейшем всё больше укреплялись в той уверенности, что, конечно же, это был Маяковский (Олеша 3). I wasn't really convinced that it was Mayakovsky, nor was Kataev, but afterwards we became more and more certain that of course it had been he (3a).

2. (presented, referred to etc) subsequently (in the book, manuscript, or document in question): **below; hereafter; henceforth.**

Главы, посвящённые цветам, не имеют особой связи с описанным в дальнейшем (Федин 1). The chapters devoted to flowers have no particular connection with what is described below (1a).

Д-18 • ДА́ЛЬШЕ – БО́ЛЬШЕ; ДА́ЛЕЕ – БО́ЛЕЕ [sent; these forms only; usu. used in past contexts; fixed WO] (usu. in refer. to sth. disagreeable) the longer a process, activity etc continues, the more intense it becomes: **as time went on, it got ⟨grew⟩ worse (and worse); (then) it went from bad to worse; it went downhill from there.**

[Анисья:] Ничегохонько не угадывала, а у них [Акулины и Никиты] согласье уж было. [Кума:] О-о, дело-то какое! [Анисья:] Дальше – больше, вижу, от меня хорониться стали (Толстой 1). [A.:] It never occurred to me that there might already have been an understanding between them [Akulina and Nikita]. [K.:] Oh, dear, what a disgraceful business! [A.:] And as time went on, it got worse and worse, and they began to hide from me (1c). ♦ Ворюга [Федька], повадки волчьи. А началось всё с пустяков – с кочешка капусты, с репки, с горстки зерна, которые он начал припрятывать от семьи. Потом дальше – больше: в чужой рот полез (Абрамов 1). [context transl] He [Fedka] was a crook – greedy as a wolf. It began with piddling little stuff: a head of cabbage, a turnip, or a handful of grain that he hid from the rest of the family. And it took off from there, until he was stealing the food out of everyone else's mouth (1a).

Д-19 • Я ТЕБЕ́ ⟨те substand, вам и т. п.⟩ ДА́М ⟨ЗАДА́М, ПОКАЖУ́⟩!; Я ТЕБЕ́! all coll [sent; usu. 1st or 3rd pers; fut only; fixed WO] used to express a threat to punish or a threatening reproach (sometimes the interlocutor's last word or remark is repeated): **I'll teach ⟨show⟩ you ⟨him etc⟩!; I'll give it to you ⟨him etc⟩!;** [when part of the interlocutor's statement is repeated only] **don't even think about...!; don't you dare...!**

«А ты, Захарка, пострелёнок, куда опять бежишь? – кричал потом [барин]. – Вот я тебе дам бегать!.. Пошёл назад, в прихожую!» (Гончаров 1). "And you, Zakharka, where are you running off to, you little scamp?" he [the master] shouted. "I'll teach you to run!...Back to the hall with you!" (1b). ♦ «Мне, Гришка, обидно...» – «Ну?» – «Да как же, – Митька длинно ругнулся, – он не он, сотник, так и задаётся... Я ему покажу!» (Шолохов 2). "It riles me, Grishka." "What does?" "Well, look!" Mitka swore at great length. "The way he shows off just because he's a lieutenant....I'll show him!" (2a). ♦ Ростов злобно оглянулся на Ильина и, не отвечая ему, быстрыми шагами направился к деревне. «Я им покажу, я им задам, разбойникам!» – говорил он про себя (Толстой 6). Rostov gave Ilyin a wrathful look, and without replying, strode in the direction of the village. "I'll show them! I'll give it to them, those ruffians!" he said to himself (6a).

Д-20 • ДА́МА СЕ́РДЦА usu. humor [NP; usu. sing; fixed WO] a beloved woman, sweetheart: **lady ⟨queen⟩ of one's ⟨s.o.'s⟩ heart; ladylove.**

...А утром Абрамов, истёртый молодой человек тридцати двух лет, осторожненько выходил на зорьке, дабы не скомпрометировать даму сердца перед соседями (Попов 1). The next morning, Abramov, a worn-looking man of thirty-two, was leaving the house at dawn, ever so cautiously, so as not to compromise the lady of his heart in the eyes of her neighbors (1a).

Д-21 • **В ДА́МКАХ** *coll* [PrepP; Invar; subj-compl with copula (subj: human), usu. pres] one is in an advantageous position, one is a winner: X — в дамках ≃ **X has it ⟨the game⟩ all wrapped ⟨sewed⟩ up; X is sitting pretty; it's in the bag (for X).**

Пленных не брать! Вот так! Раз, два и в дамках! Современная война – стремительная штука! (Аксёнов 6). Take no prisoners! Just like that. One, two, three and it's in the bag! Speed is the essence of modern warfare! (6a).

Д-22 • **ОТДАВА́ТЬ/ОТДА́ТЬ ⟨ПЛАТИ́ТЬ/ЗАПЛАТИ́ТЬ и т. п.⟩ ДАНЬ** *lit* [VP; subj: human; fixed WO] **1.** ~ *(чего) кому-чему* to appreciate s.o. or sth. in full measure for his or its merit, show one's appreciation for s.o. or sth.: X отдал Y-у дань (Z-а) ≃ **X paid homage to Y ⟨X paid Y the homage of Z⟩; X paid tribute to Y;** [in limited contexts] **X gave person Y credit for Z.**

«...Посмотрите на себя: может ли мужчина, встретя вас, не заплатить вам дань удивления... хотя взглядом?» (Гончаров 1). "...Look at yourself: what man could fail to pay you the homage of admiration — if only with his eyes?" (1b). ♦ Такой путь менее тернист, чем обычный, который предполагал ученичество у шумевших тогда официальных метров символизма – у Бальмонта, Брюсова или Вячеслава Иванова (им Мандельштам, конечно, отдал дань, но не столь большую, как другие) (Мандельштам 2). There was a less thorny path than the one that in those years usually required an apprenticeship with the acknowledged masters of Symbolism: Balmont, Briusov, or Viacheslav Ivanov, then at the height of their fame. (M[andelstam] naturally paid them due tribute, but to a lesser degree than others did) (2a). ♦ И отдавая дань уму моей матери, надо сказать, что вела она себя с Ивановскими идеально, в том смысле, что запрятала подальше свою дерзость и строптивость (Рыбаков 1). It should also be said, giving my mother credit for intelligence, that she behaved perfectly with the Ivanovskys, and kept her rudeness and obstinacy well out of sight (1a).

2. ~ *чему* to comply with sth., yield to sth.: X отдаёт дань Y-у ≃ **X pays tribute to Y; X makes concessions to Y; X respects Y;** [in limited contexts] **X succumbs ⟨gives in⟩ to Y.**

Он [Вертинский] отдавал дань моде, отражал те настроения, которые влияли в ту эпоху даже на таких серьёзных деятелей искусства, как Александр Блок, Алексей Толстой, Владимир Маяковский (Олеша 3). He [Vertinsky] paid tribute to fashion, reflecting those attitudes which in that epoch influenced even such serious artistic figures as Alexander Blok, Alexey Tolstoy, and Vladimir Mayakovsky (3a). ♦ Ему известно, что люди, отдыхая, болтают. Он решает отдать какую-то дань общечеловеческим обыкновениям (Олеша 2). He knows that when people are relaxing they usually chat. He decides to respect certain human habits (2a). ♦ Ходасевич – человек старой школы. Он верил в необходимость провокации для уничтожения человека. Кроме того, он отдал дань современному стилю и в каждом встречном подозревал провокатора (Мандельштам 2). Khodasevich was a man of the old school who believed that provocation was essential to the business of destroying a chosen victim, and furthermore, he had succumbed to the new fashion of seeing a spy in everyone who came along (2a).

3. ~ *кому-чему* to pay attention to s.o. or sth. (often, in one's writings, speech etc): X отдал дань Y-у ≃ **X gave Y Y's due; X gave Y credit; X paid homage to Y.**

Д-23 • **ДАР РЕ́ЧИ ⟨СЛО́ВА⟩** [NP; sing only; usu. subj or obj; fixed WO] **1.** обрести, потерять, утратить дар речи, лишиться дара речи и т. п. (to regain, lose etc) the ability to speak: **the power ⟨the gift⟩ of speech; (the use of) one's voice;** [in refer. to losing the ability to speak only] **(be ⟨become⟩**

speechless; (be) dumbstruck ⟨struck dumb, at a loss for words⟩; lose one's tongue.**

«Ты что, а? – глухо сказал он [старик], прижимая к себе внука. – Ты что, а? Ты что?» – И кроме этих слов, он не мог произнести ничего, словно утратил дар речи (Айтматов 1). "What is it, eh?" he [the old man] said hoarsely, pressing the boy to himself. "What is it, eh? What is it?" He seemed unable to say any other word, as though he had lost the power of speech (1a). ♦ «Фроська я, слышите, люди, я – Фроська!» – выкрикивала она с таким остервенелым наслаждением, как будто после долгой немоты вновь обрела вдруг дар речи (Войнович 2). "I'm Froska, people, listen to me, I'm Froska!" she kept shouting with frenzied delight, as if she had just suddenly regained the gift of speech after years of being mute (2a). ♦ «Владимир Ипатьич... этот негодяй вывел змей вместо кур...» – «Что такое? – ответил Персиков, и лицо его сделалось бурым... – Вы шутите, Пётр Степанович... Откуда?» Иванов онемел на мгновение, потом получил дар слова и, тыча пальцем в открытый ящик... сказал: «Вот оттуда» (Булгаков 10). "Vladimir Ipatyich...that scoundrel has hatched snakes instead of chickens..." "What?" Persikov screamed, and his face became purple. "You're joking, Pyotr Stepanovich.... Where from?" Ivanov was speechless for a moment, then he regained his voice, and poking his finger at the open crate...he said, "That's where" (10a). ♦ «Есть мужчины, которые теряют дар речи от... вида округлившегося женского брюха» (Окуджава 2). "There are men who become speechless when faced with a rounded female belly" (2a). ♦ Это был «Мир фантазии» – детский книжный базар, разбитый на нашем бульваре... Кит обомлел. Он не мог сдвинуться с места, не зная, к кому бежать – к Коту ли, к Царевичу, к Лебедю... В первые минуты он словно лишился дара речи, лишь вращал своими большими глазами и что-то беззвучно шептал (Аксёнов 4). It was Fantasy World, a children's book fair set up on our boulevard....Whale was overwhelmed. He did not know where to run first — the Cat, the Prince, the Swan. For a moment or so he stood as if struck dumb: he just rolled his big eyes and whispered soundlessly (4a).

2. the ability to speak beautifully, expressively: **(have) the gift of eloquence ⟨gab⟩; (have) a way with words; (have) the power of expression;** [in limited contexts] **(have mastered) the art of conversation; (be) silver-tongued;** [with нет] **(s.o. is) not much of a speaker.**

...Собакевич вошёл, как говорится, в самую силу речи, откуда взялись рысь и дар слова... (Гоголь 3). ...Sobakevich had got into the vein, as they say. Whence came this gift of gab and the pace of his speech? (3b). ...Sobakevich had hit the peak of his eloquence, as they say, and his pace and power of expression were truly surprising (3c). ♦ [Львов:] Не могу я вам высказать, нет у меня дара слова, но... но вы мне глубоко несимпатичны! (Чехов 4). [L.:] I can't put it properly, I'm not much of a speaker, but — but I do most thoroughly dislike you (4b).

Д-24 • **НА ДАРМОВЩИ́НУ ⟨ДАРМОВЩИ́НКУ, ДАРОВЩИ́НУ, ДАРОВЩИ́НКУ⟩** *highly coll, often disapprov;* **НА ЧУЖАЧКА́** *substand* [PrepP; these forms only; adv] (to get or do sth. for which payment is normally required) without spending any money, without cost to o.s.: **free; for free; free of charge; for nothing;** [in limited contexts] **at s.o.'s ⟨someone else's⟩ expense;** [with the NP implied by the context; usu. of food and/or drinks] **(for) a free** [NP]; [when the translation of the idiom incorporates the Russian verb; usu. in refer. to the repeated or prolonged exploitation of s.o.'s hospitality] **freeload.**

Рысс стакан за стаканом дул цинандали. Платили какие-то физики из Новосибирска, и барабанщик старался побыстрее на дармовщину «поймать кайф» (Аксёнов 6). Ryss was drinking glass after glass of Tsinandali, a Georgian white wine. Some physicists from Novosibirsk were paying, and the drummer was trying to get high as quickly as possible at their expense (6a). ♦ Все, все были тут, критики тайные, насмешники, презиратели, все на

[162]

дармовщинку сбежались... (Трифонов 1). All of them, all of these secret critics and scoffers were here. They had all come running for free drinks and a free meal (1a).

Д-25 • **ДА́РОМ ЧТО** *coll* [subord Conj, concessive] notwithstanding (the fact that): **(even) though; although; despite ⟨in spite of⟩ (the fact that ⟨s.o.'s doing sth. etc⟩)**; [in limited contexts] **it doesn't matter that...; I ⟨you etc⟩ may...but**; ‖ даром что профессор ⟨умный и т. п.⟩ ≃ **professor ⟨intelligent etc⟩ or not...**

«Да вот не развалилось же [крыльцо], даром что шестнадцать лет без поправки стоит» (Гончаров 1). "They [the front steps] haven't fallen down, though they have stood there for sixteen years without any repairs" (1a). ♦ «Маше здесь оставаться не гоже. Отправим её в Оренбург... Да и тебе советовал бы с нею туда же отправиться; даром что ты старуха, а посмотри что с тобою будет, коли возьмут фортецию приступом» (Пушкин 2). "It won't do for Masha to stay here. Let us send her to Orenburg....And I would advise you to go there with her; although you're an old woman, consider what would happen to you if the fortress were taken" (2b). ♦ Мужичок ехал рысцой на белой лошадке по тёмной узкой дорожке вдоль самой рощи; он весь был ясно виден, весь, до заплаты на плече, даром что ехал в тени... (Тургенев 2). A peasant on a white nag went at a trot along the dark, narrow path close beside the copse; his whole figure was clearly visible even to the patch on his shoulder, in spite of his being in the shade... (2b). ♦ [Анисья:] ...На дуру-то, на Акулину, погляди... Даром что дура, забрала себе в голову: я, говорит, хозяйка (Толстой 1). [A.:] ...Take a look at the half-wit, at Akulina....Don't matter she's an idiot, she's gotten it into her head: I'm the lady of the house, she says (1a). ♦ «Да куда мне за ней! Я даром что моложе, а не выстоять мне столько!» (Гончаров 1). "...I'm afraid I can't keep up with her! I may be the younger one, but I can't stand as long as she can!" (1a). ♦ «...Чей он прозвищем?.. Листницкий... Очки носит. Ну, да нехай [*regional* = пусть] я, в очках, а жеребца не дамся обогнать!» (Шолохов 2). "...What's his name?...Listnitsky....Wears glasses. Well, let him! Glasses or not, I'm not going to let him get past the stallion!" (2a).

Д-26 • **ДАРЫ́ ДАНА́ЙЦЕВ** *lit* [NP; pl only; fixed WO] a treacherous gift intended to bring disaster, destroy its recipient(s): **beware of Greeks bearing gifts; gifts borne by Greeks.**

< From the legend of the large wooden horse built by the Greeks and taken by the Trojans into their city as a gift. Later, the Greeks who had hidden inside the hollow horse climbed out, opened the gates of Troy to their army, and seized the city. Described in Homer's *Odyssey* (VIII, 492–520) and Virgil's *Aeneid* (II, 45–49).

Д-27 • **КРУ́ГЛАЯ ДА́ТА** [NP; usu. subj or obj; fixed WO] an anniversary counted in round numbers that are usu. multiples of ten or twenty-five: **(good ⟨nice⟩) round figure.**

Кстати, сказал директор Ларька, скоро юбилей основания Ларька. Пятьдесят лет. Да, круглая дата (Зиновьев 1). By the way, said the director of the Shop, it'll soon be the fiftieth anniversary of our foundation. It's a good round figure (1a).

Д-28 • **НИ ДАТЬ НИ ВЗЯТЬ** *coll* [Invar; fixed WO]
1. [modif] a person (or thing) looks absolutely the same as another person (or thing): **(look) exactly ⟨just⟩ like (s.o. ⟨sth.⟩); for all the world like (s.o. ⟨sth.⟩); (s.o. ⟨sth.⟩) could (easily) have been a [NP]; like a regular [NP]; a real [NP]; a [NP] nothing less ⟨nothing less than a [NP]⟩.**

Ещё и ещё падали на стол снимки, и вот мелькнул покатый, тупой (ни дать ни взять мучной ларь) архиерейский дом... (Домбровский 1). More and more photographs fell onto the table. I caught a glimpse of a squat, square archbishop's palace (looking exactly like a flour-bin)... (1a). ♦ Пантелей Прокофьевич с Ильи-

ничной – в заду брички рядком, ни дать ни взять – молодые (Шолохов 2). Pantelei and Ilyinichna, seated side by side at the back of the wagon, suddenly looked for all the world like a young couple (2a). ♦ Его [солдата] лицо было очень обыкновенное, будничное, чем-то знакомое – ни дать ни взять слесарь со «Спорта»... (Кузнецов 1). His [the soldier's] was a very ordinary, everyday type of face which had something familiar about it – he could easily have been a mechanic from the Sport Factory... (1b). ♦ Машина остановилась точно там, где нужно было: между Огородниковым и фон Дерецки. Последний, когда первый начал говорить, приосанился и нацепил на нос очки в железной оправе, ни дать ни взять теоретик из Пном-Пеня (Аксёнов 12). The machine stopped just where it should have: in the center of the table, between Ogorodnikov and Von Deretzki. When the former began speaking, the latter straightened up and put on wire-rim glasses, like a regular theoretician from Phnom Penh (12a). ♦ [Гвардеец:] Это даже невероятно... чтобы солдату да вдруг приснился такой волшебный сон... кукла разгуливает по дворцу... Удивительное дело. Ишь ты... Ну, ни дать ни взять – живая девочка (Олеша 7). [G.:] It's incredible that a soldier should have such a magical dream...a doll goes strolling round the palace.... Amazing. How d'you like that! A live girl...nothing less (7a).

2. [adv or sent adv; often foll. by a как-clause or phrase] (to do sth.) in precisely the same way that someone else does it: **just ⟨exactly⟩ like; for all the world like ⟨as if⟩; exactly ⟨just⟩ how ⟨the way⟩ (someone else does it).**

...Люди на пароходе, в море, разговаривают и смеются беззаботно, ни дать ни взять как на твёрдой земле... (Тургенев 2). ...People on a steamer at sea talk and laugh light-heartedly, for all the world as if they were on dry land... (2c). ♦ Дворня хохотала, дружно сочувствуя... лакею, прибившему казачка... «Вот, вот этак же, ни дать ни взять, бывало, мой прежний барин – начал опять тот же лакей, что всё перебивал Захара, – ты, бывало, думаешь, как бы повеселиться, а он вдруг, словно угадает, что ты думал, идёт мимо, да и ухватит вот этак, вот как Матвей Мосеич Андрюшку» (Гончаров 1). [the translation of the idiom combines it with the preceding adverbial] The servants laughed, sympathizing with the footman who had beaten the boy.... "That's exactly the way my former master used to carry on!" said the footman who kept interrupting Zakhar. "Just when you'd think of having a little fun, suddenly he seemed to guess what was in your mind, and he'd grab you, just as Matvei Moseich grabbed Andryushka" (1b).

Д-29 • **ДАЮ́Т – БЕРИ́, БЬЮТ – БЕГИ́** [saying] accept what you are given, run away from what is harmful: ≃ **don't refuse a gift, don't accept a blow; when offered something good accept it gratefully, when in danger beat a fast retreat; [when only the first half of the saying is used] take what you're given (and be thankful); don't look a gift horse in the mouth.**

«Берите [деньги], раз даю! Не на вовсе ведь. Взаймы». – «Конечно! В течение года я всё выплачу, Дуся. А может, расписку написать, чтобы тебе спокойнее было?» – предложила я. По лицу тёти Дуси пробежало лёгкое раздражение. «Пословицу знаете: бьют – беги, дают – бери!.. Неужто не поверю на слово? Не первый день знаемся...» (Гинзбург 2). "Take it [the money], since I've given it to you! It's not as if I'm throwing the money away – it's on loan." "Of course! I'll pay it back within the year, Dusya. But perhaps you'd feel happier if I gave you a receipt," I ventured. A look of mild irritation flitted across Aunt Dusya's face. "You know the saying: 'Don't accept a blow, don't refuse a gift.'...You think I wouldn't take your word for it? We've known each other some time now..." (2a).

Д-30 • **НИ ДВА НИ ПОЛТОРА́** *coll* [Invar; subj-compl with copula (subj: usu. abstr), modif, or adv; fixed WO] neither one thing nor another, sth. that is difficult to identify: **neither this nor that; neither fish nor fowl.**

...Эти волосы дурацкие, ни два ни полтора: полудлинные, неухоженные... (Грекова 1). ...This stupid hair of mine, neither this nor that, too long, unkempt... (1a).

Д-31 • КАК ДВА́ЖДЫ ДВА (ЧЕТЫ́РЕ) *coll* [как + NP; these forms only; fixed WO] **1. ясно, понятно ~** [modif] absolutely, completely (clear, understandable): **as clear ⟨simple⟩ as twice ⟨two times⟩ two makes ⟨is⟩ four; as clear ⟨plain⟩ as can be; (as) plain as day.**

Отдельно от общих... способностей ума, чувствительности, художнического чувства, существует частная, более или менее развитая в различных кружках общества и особенно в семействах, которую я назову *пониманием*... Ни с кем, как с Володей, с которым мы развивались в одинаковых условиях, не довели мы этой способности до такой тонкости. Уже и папа давно отстал от нас, и многое, что для нас было так же ясно, как дважды два, было ему непонятно (Толстой 2). Apart from the general faculties...of intelligence, sensibility, and artistic feeling, there is a particular faculty, developed to a greater or lesser degree in various circles of society and especially in families, that I choose to call *understanding*....With no one was this faculty developed to such a pitch of subtlety as with Volodya and myself, who had grown up together in identical circumstances. Even Papa was far behind us in this respect and much that was as clear as twice two makes four to us was incomprehensible to him (2b).

2. доказать, растолковать и т. п. ~ [adv; usu. used with pfv verbs] (to prove) convincingly, (to explain) clearly, completely: **(prove) beyond a shadow of a doubt; (make it) perfectly (clear); (make it clear) in no uncertain terms.**

...[Капитан] как дважды два объяснил Капе, что хотя она и является вольнонаёмной, но служба в военном учреждении в военное время обязывает её выполнять приказания беспрекословно, точно и в срок... (Войнович 2). ...[The captain] made it perfectly clear to Kapa that although she was a civilian her position in a military institution during wartime obliged her to carry out orders unquestioningly, to the letter and to the minute... (2a).

3. [adv; used with pfv verbs, usu. fut] (sth. will happen) definitely, certainly: **as sure as twice ⟨two times⟩ two makes ⟨is⟩ four; as sure as I'm standing here; as sure as God made little (green) apples.**

«Дело известное, что мужик: на новой земле, да заняться ещё хлебопашеством, да ничего у него нет, ни избы, ни двора, убежит, как дважды два, навострит так лыжи, что и следа не отыщешь» (Гоголь 3). "You know perfectly well what a Russian peasant is like: settle him on new land and set him to till it, with nothing prepared for him, neither cottage nor farmstead, and, well, he'll run away, as sure as twice two makes four. He'll take to his heels and you won't find a trace of him" (3a).

Д-32 • ЗАКРЫВА́ТЬ/ЗАКРЫ́ТЬ ДВЕ́РИ ДО́МА *перед кем;* often *чьи* **ДВЕ́РИ ЗАКРЫ́ТЫ ⟨ДВЕРЬ** *чьего* **ДО́МА ЗАКРЫ́ТА⟩** *для кого all obsoles, lit* [VP, subj: human (1st var.); VP_subj with бытьø (2nd var.); fixed WO (1st var.), usu. this WO (2nd var.)] to refuse to receive s.o. into one's home: X закрыл двери (своего) дома перед Y-ом ≃ **X shut ⟨closed⟩ his door(s) to Y; X barred Y from X's home; Y is not ⟨no longer⟩ welcome (in X's home).**

«...Я бы очень желал доказать вам, что вы насчёт меня ошибались...» – «Вам это будет довольно трудно...» – «Отчего же?» – «Оттого, что вы у нас не бываете, а эти балы, вероятно, не часто будут повторяться». Это значит, подумал я, что их двери для меня навеки закрыты (Лермонтов 1). "...I would wish very much to prove to you that you are mistaken about me." "You will find this rather difficult." "Why so?" "Because you do not come to our house, and these balls will probably not take place very often." "This means," I thought, "that their door is closed to me forever" (1a).

Д-33 • ОТКРЫВА́ТЬ/ОТКРЫ́ТЬ ДВЕ́РИ ⟨ДВЕРЬ⟩ *кому-чему куда lit* [VP; subj: usu. abstr or concr, occas. human; indir obj: usu. human; usu. this WO] to give s.o. (or sth.) easy access (to some institution, desirable place of work or research etc): X открыл Y-у двери в место Z ≃ **X opened the doors of place Z for Y; X is Y's ticket to place Z.**

Д-34 • ВЫСТАВЛЯ́ТЬ/ВЫ́СТАВИТЬ ЗА ДВЕРЬ *кого coll* [VP; subj: human] to eject s.o. (from one's home, office etc): X выставил Y-a за дверь ≃ **X turned ⟨threw, kicked⟩ Y out (of the house etc); X threw ⟨kicked, shoved⟩ Y out the door; X sent Y packing; X gave Y the (old) heave-ho.**

«Ну, как у вас подвигается роман с очаровательной Наташей Н?.. Смотрите, как бы её маман в один прекрасный день, несмотря на весь свой аристократизм, не выставила вас за дверь» (Катаев 3). "And how is your affair with the charming Natasha N. proceeding?...Mind her mother doesn't turn you out of the house one fine day, for all her gentility" (3a). ♦ «Надеюсь, вы не будете так негостеприимны и не выставите меня за дверь в такой час» (Пастернак 1). "I hope you aren't going to be so inhospitable as to throw me out at this hour of the night!" (1a).

Д-35 • ДВЕРЬ В ДВЕРЬ *(с кем-чем)* **жить, находиться, бытьø** и т. п. [Invar; adv] (to live, be located) next to or opposite one another: **right ⟨just, only⟩ next-door (to each other); side by side; [in limited contexts] (right) across from; across the way from.**

...Стёпа басит, что... как только всё утрясётся... он сейчас же прикатит наше пианино обратно, благо живём-то дверь в дверь (Гинзбург 2). ...Stepan muttered that...as soon as things quieted down...he could roll the piano straight back again, since we were only next door (2a).

Д-36 • ЛОМИ́ТЬСЯ В ОТКРЫ́ТУЮ ДВЕРЬ ⟨В ОТКРЫ́ТЫЕ ДВЕ́РИ⟩ [VP; subj: human; often infin with зачем, незачем, не стоит etc; the verb may take the final position, otherwise fixed WO] to argue or try to prove sth. that is already obvious, well-known, and that no one disputes: X ломится в открытую дверь ≃ **X is forcing an open door; X is belaboring ⟨restating, trying to prove⟩ the obvious; [in limited contexts] X is preaching to the converted.**

«Николаев утверждает, что наши рабочие не готовы активно участвовать в управлении заводом». – «Зачем он ломится в открытую дверь?» "Nikolaev maintains that our workers aren't ready to participate actively in the management of the plant." "Why is he bothering to restate the obvious?"

< Loan translation of the French *enfoncer une porte ouverte.*

Д-37 • СТУЧА́ТЬСЯ В ДВЕРЬ *чью* **⟨В ДВЕ́РИ** *чьи*⟩ or *кого-чего* [VP] **1.** *coll* [subj: human] to approach s.o. or go to some place(s) repeatedly, persistently requesting sth., trying to obtain sth.: X стучится в Y-ову дверь ≃ **X goes knocking on ⟨at⟩ Y's door;** ‖ X стучится в двери мест Y-ов ≃ **X goes knocking on the doors of places Y; X makes the rounds of places Y;** ‖ X стучится во все двери ≃ **X knocks ⟨raps, beats⟩ on every door; X beats down every door.**

Прошло года четыре. Я только что вышел из университета и не знал ещё хорошенько, что мне начать с собою, в какую дверь стучаться... (Тургенев 3). Four years passed. I had just left the university and had not quite made up my mind what to do with myself, at what door to knock... (3a).

2. *lit* [subj: abstr] (often of sth. unwelcome – poverty, misfortune etc) to approach steadily, be close at hand: X стучится в (Y-ову) дверь ≃ **X is knocking at the ⟨Y's⟩ door; X is at ⟨on⟩ the ⟨Y's⟩ doorstep; X is breathing down Y's neck; X is looming nearer and nearer.**

Д-38 • УКА́ЗЫВАТЬ/УКАЗА́ТЬ ⟨ПОКА́ЗЫВАТЬ/ ПОКАЗА́ТЬ⟩ (НА) ДВЕРЬ *кому* [VP; subj: human] to demand that s.o. leave, drive s.o. out: X указал Y-у на дверь ≃ **X showed Y the door.**

Вообще всякая неожиданная бытовая неурядица, а особенно несвоевременный незваный гость, бесцельная потеря времени – больше всего изводили [Ленина] и выбивали из рабочего состояния... Но есть этика эмиграции, и ты беззащитен против таких посетителей, ты не можешь просто указать им на дверь или не пустить... (Солженицын 5). In general, any unexpected upset to his [Lenin's] daily routine, especially an uninvited and untimely guest, any pointless waste of time, so exasperated and unsettled him that he was incapable of work....But the émigré world has its own code of behavior and you are defenseless against such visitors, you cannot simply show them the door or refuse to let them in (5a).

Д-39 • ХЛО́ПНУТЬ ДВЕ́РЬЮ [VP; subj: human; fixed WO] to leave some place in an ostentatious manner, showing indignation, anger etc: X хлопнул дверью ≃ **X stormed ⟨stomped⟩ out; X left in a huff;** [in limited contexts] **X slammed the door.**

Девушке было предложено покинуть дом, ибо её поведение было расценено как посягательство на наследство. Гордая Александрина хлопнула дверью, имея при себе небольшой сундучок с нехитрым скарбом и горькие воспоминания (Окуджава 2). ...She [Alexandrina] was asked to leave the house, since her behavior was seen as an attempt to gain the inheritance. Proud Alexandrina slammed the door, taking with her a small trunk with her few possessions and her bitter memories (2a).

Д-40 • ПРИ ЗАКРЫ́ТЫХ ДВЕРЯ́Х [PrepP; Invar; adv; fixed WO] in the presence of involved (often official) parties only, without an outside audience: **behind closed doors.**

«Я не приду на ваше заседание, потому что оно будет происходить при закрытых дверях, втайне от общественности...» (Войнович 1). "I'm not coming to your meeting because it will be held behind closed doors, in secret, out of public view..." (1a).

Д-41 • НА СВОИ́Х (НА) ДВОИ́Х идти, прийти, добираться, прибывать и т. п. *coll, humor* [PrepP; these forms only; adv; fixed WO] (to go, get to some place etc) on foot: **on one's own two feet ⟨legs⟩; under one's own power ⟨steam⟩; hoof ⟨foot⟩ it;** [in limited contexts] **on ⟨by⟩ shanks' ⟨shank's⟩ mare.**

Обычно к приезду сезонниц все ребятишки в радиусе двухсот километров начинают наводить блеск на свою амуницию, стригутся под канадскую полечку и торопятся в порт Петрово на всех видах транспорта, а то и на своих на двоих (Аксёнов 1). Usually, toward the time the summer girls arrive, all the guys make with the spit and polish, get themselves a ducktail haircut, and hasten to the port of Petrovo on all forms of transport, or else on their own two feet (1a). ♦ [extended usage] Хочешь не хочешь, а приходится согласиться с Андреем, что на своих двоих... за сегодняшней жизнью не поспеть (Распутин 4). Andrei was right—and you had to agree with him whether you wanted to or not— you can't keep up with today's life on shank's mare... (4a).

Д-42 • НА ДВОР ходить, пойти, надо, хотеть и т. п. *substand* [PrepP; Invar; adv] (to go outside) in order to defecate or urinate: **go outside to relieve o.s. ⟨to answer the call of nature⟩; use ⟨go to⟩ the outhouse; (one) has to go.**

Чонкин из-за укрытия бдительно следил за своими противниками. Они лежали в грязи... «Пущай лежат, покуда меня не сменят». – «А если тебе на двор надо будет?» – «Если на двор... Тогда ты посторожишь» (Войнович 2). From his cover, Chonkin kept a vigilant eye on his enemies. They were all lying in the mud now....''They can lie there until someone relieves me." "But what if you have to go to the outhouse?" "If I have to....Then you can stand

guard a few minutes" (2a). ♦ Капитан через стол тормошил Чонкина двумя связанными руками и настойчиво требовал: «Слышь ты, скотина, проснись! На двор хочу!» (Войнович 2). The captain was pulling on Chonkin from across the table with his two bound hands, demanding insistently: "Hey, you dummy, wake up! I have to go!" (2a).

Д-43 • ПРОХОДНО́Й ДВОР *disapprov* [NP; sing only; often subj-compl with copula (subj: concr)] an apartment, office etc where people who do not belong there come and go at all times (thus encroaching on the people who live, work etc there): **(like) a public thoroughfare; (like) a hotel ⟨an open house⟩.**

[Ольга:] Наш сад как проходной двор, через него и ходят и ездят (Чехов 5). [O.:] Our garden's like a public thoroughfare. Everyone walks and drives through it (5b).

Д-44 • НА ДВОРЕ́ [PrepP; Invar] **1.** [adv] outside of a building, in the open: **outside; outdoors; out-of-doors.**

Пьер поспешно оделся и выбежал на крыльцо. На дворе было ясно, свежо, росисто и весело (Толстой 6). Pierre hastily dressed and ran out to the porch. Outside it was fresh and dewy, a bright, clear day (6a).

2. *coll* [subj-compl with быть∅ (subj: usu. a noun denoting a season, month, part of a day etc)] sth. is soon to come, very near: X на дворе ≃ **X is close ⟨near⟩ at hand; it's almost X; X is coming up; X is just ⟨right⟩ around the corner.**

Д-45 • КО ДВОРУ́ *(где, кому)* быть∅, прийтись, оказаться *coll* [PrepP; Invar; subj-compl with copula (subj: human or, rare, concr or abstr); usu. used with pfv past; usu. neg] s.o. or sth. is welcome (at some place), suited or corresponding to s.o.'s (or some kind of) requirements: X пришёлся ко двору (в месте Y) ≃ **X fitted well ⟨aptly⟩ (into place Y); X fitted right in (at place Y); thing X filled the bill;** ‖ *Neg* X пришёлся не ко двору (в месте Y) ≃ **X didn't fit in (at place Y); X was out of place (at place Y).**

Наталья пришлась Мелеховым ко двору (Шолохов 2). Natalya fitted well into the Melekhov household (2a). ♦ Перед тем, как написать стихи о свадьбе и черепахе, Мандельштам перелистал у меня в комнате томик переводов Вячеслава Иванова из Алкея и Сафо... Из переводов и пришёл «пёстрый сапожок»... Пришёлся он ко двору, потому что за отсутствием пристойной обуви я носила нелепые казанские сапожки с киевской ярмарки... (Мандельштам 2). Before writing his poem about the wedding and the tortoise, M[andelstam] had sat in my room glancing through a slender tome of Viacheslav Ivanov's translations of Alcaeus and Sappho....It was here that he got the words "brightly colored boot"....It happened to fit very aptly, since for want of proper shoes, I was wearing a grotesque pair of Kazan boots which I had bought at the Kiev fair... (2a). ♦ Вадима смущало отношение матери и сестры к Кире. Правда, пожаловаться на то, что они относятся к ней дурно, он не мог. Внешне всё было очень хорошо. И всё же Вадим чувствовал, что Кира здесь как-то не пришлась ко двору (Некрасов 1). Vadim was disconcerted by his mother's and sister's attitude to Kira. He could not, it was true, say that they treated her badly. On the surface everything was fine. Nevertheless Vadim felt that Kira somehow did not fit in here (1a).

Д-46 • СТА́РАЯ ДЕ́ВА [NP; fixed WO] a woman past her youth who has never married, has no sexual experience: **old maid; spinster.**

Она знала: либо за Игоря, либо в старые девы. Она не могла без него (Ерофеев 3). She knew that it was either marry Igor or become an old maid. She couldn't live without him (3a).

Д-47 • ДЕВА́ТЬ/ДЕТЬ НЕ́КУДА *кого-чего (у кого or где) coll* [these forms only; usu. quantit subj-compl with copula (subj/ gen: any common noun); usu. impfv] an extremely large amount, an excess: Х-ов у Y-а ⟨в месте Z⟩ — девать некуда ≃ **Y has more Xs than he knows what to do with; Y has enough Xs and then some; there are more Xs in place Z than you can shake a stick at; Xs are a dime a dozen in place Z; Y has Xs coming out of Y's ears.**

Пристанет [Басаврюк], бывало, к красным девушкам: надарит лент, серёг, монист — девать некуда! (Гоголь 5). Sometimes he'd [Basavriuk would] set upon the girls, heap ribbons, earrings, necklaces on them, till they did not know what to do with them (5a).

Д-48 • ДЕВА́ТЬСЯ/ДЕ́ТЬСЯ НЕ́КУДА *(кому)* [these forms only; impers predic with бытьø] **1.** s.o. has no place to go for entertainment, nothing with which to fill time: Х-у некуда было деваться ≃ **X had nowhere to go (and nothing to do); X had no way to kill time.**

2. [usu. impfv; usu. this WO] s.o. has no other choice of action, is forced by circumstances to act in a certain way (as specified by the context): Х-у деваться некуда ≃ **X has ⟨there is⟩ no (other) alternative ⟨way out⟩; X has no other recourse (but...); there is nothing X can do (about sth.); there is nothing else to do (but...); there is nothing for it (but...); [in limited contexts] there is no going ⟨turning⟩ back.**

И Фрейдкин, как всякий кулак, за этот кредит брал проценты. Беднякам деваться некуда... (Рыбаков 1). ...Like any kulak, Freidkin charged interest. There was nothing the poor people could do... (1a). ♦ ...Все они [адвокаты] тут друг за друга, у них профессиональная солидарность, и если я без всяких оснований перейду к другому адвокату, то он встретит меня не лучшим образом. Деваться, вижу, некуда, и я ему [Терещенко] всё выкладываю (Рыбаков 1). ...They [the lawyers] were all for each other in that place, they had their professional solidarity, so if I had gone to another lawyer, without any cause whatever, he wouldn't have treated me any better. I saw there was nothing else to do but tell him [Tereshchenko] everything (1a).

Д-49 • КРА́СНАЯ ДЕ́ВИЦА ⟨ДЕ́ВУШКА *obsoles, coll,* **ДЕ́ВКА** *substand*⟩ [NP; fixed WO] a very shy and timid young man: **shrinking violet; (be) like a shy girl ⟨maiden⟩; (be) like a blushing virgin.**

«А тут, знаешь, народ какой? Робеют...» – «...„Робеют!“ – злобно бледнея, прокричал Кудинов и ёрзнул в кресле, будто жару сыпану.ли ему на сиденье. – Все вы как красные девки!» (Шолохов 4). "The folk up there, you know what they're like? They're scared..." "...'Scared!'" Kudinov shouted, turning pale with anger, and squirmed in his chair as if someone had thrown hot coals on the seat. "You're like a lot of blushing virgins" (4a).

Д-50 • В ДЕ́ВКАХ остаться, засидеться, сидеть и т. п. *highly coll, rather rude when addressed to the interlocutor* [PrepP; Invar; usu. subj-compl with copula (subj: human, female)] (to remain, be) unmarried: Х осталась в девках ≃ **X remained ⟨was⟩ an old maid ⟨a spinster⟩; X was left on the shelf;** ‖ X засиделась ⟨сидит⟩ в девках ≃ **X hasn't found anybody ⟨the right man⟩ yet; X is still single ⟨alone⟩.**

«Дура ты, Люська, – засмеялась Сима, – эдак ты даже при твоей красоте в девках останешься» (Аксёнов 1). "You're a dope, Lusya," laughed Sima. "At that rate you'll be an old maid for all your good looks" (1a). ♦ «И к чему ей [Марье] выходить замуж? – думал он. – Наверно, быть несчастною... И кто её возьмёт из любви? Дурна, неловка. Возьмут за связи, за богатство. И разве не живут в девках? Ещё счастливее!» (Толстой 4). "And why should she [Marya] marry?" he thought. "Probably to be unhappy....And who would marry Marya for love? Plain, awkward. They'd take her for her connections, for her wealth. And aren't there plenty of women living as spinsters? And better off!" (4a). ♦ Не одна Нюра, конечно, в девках сидела, но у других хоть были либо родители, либо братья и сёстры, либо ещё кто, а у неё –

никого (Войнович 2). Of course Nyura wasn't the only one who hadn't found anybody, but the others at least had their parents or their brothers and sisters. Nyura had no one (2a).

Д-51 • МЕНЯ́ТЬ/ПЕРЕМЕНИ́ТЬ ⟨СМЕНИ́ТЬ⟩ ДЕКОРА́ЦИИ [VP; subj: human; often infin with пора, надо etc; fixed WO] to make changes in one's physical surroundings, one's behavior, the outward manifestations of one's views etc (usu. in an attempt to conform to changed circumstances) (in contemp. usage often used in political contexts with the implication that one is trying to create the impression that he has changed his views, convictions etc although he has not): X переменил декорации ≃ [usu. in refer. to changing one's physical surroundings] **X changed his décor; X changed things around; X made some changes; X changed the face ⟨the look⟩ of things; X put a new face ⟨a fresh face, a new look⟩ on things; X gave his office ⟨his kitchen etc⟩ a face-lift;** ‖ Х-ы переменили декорации ≃ [in refer. to changing one's views etc] **Xs changed their tune; Xs did an about-face; Xs shifted their position;** ‖ Х-у пора переменить декорации ≃ **X needs a change of scenery; it's time for X to make a change.** ○ **ПЕРЕМЕ́НА ДЕКОРА́ЦИЙ** [NP; sing only] ≃ [usu. in refer. to one's changing his physical surroundings] **change of décor; new face on things; new look; face-lift;** [in refer. to one's changing his views etc] **change of tune; change of heart; about-face.**

Вчерашние коммунисты быстро переменили декорации и стали выдавать себя за демократов. Yesterday's communists quickly changed their tune and started passing themselves off as democrats.

Д-52 • ЗАПЛЕ́ЧНЫХ ДЕЛ МА́СТЕР; ЗАПЛЕ́ЧНЫЙ МА́СТЕР *euph, lit* [NP; fixed WO] one who performs executions: **headsman; (master) executioner; hangman; butcher.**

«Тебя не поймут... эти заплечные мастера нового застенка. Но не падай духом. История всё разберёт» (Пастернак 1). "...These master executioners of the new torture chambers will never understand you! But don't lose heart. History will tell the truth" (1a).

Д-53 • НАДЕ́ЛАТЬ ДЕЛ *coll;* **НАДЕ́ЛАТЬ ДЕЛО́В** *substand* [VP; subj: human] to do sth. reprehensible: X наделал дел ≃ **X made trouble.**

Как только кто-нибудь начинал кричать, чтобы его отпустили, на нём мгновенно повисали три-четыре человека, так, чтобы всем ясно было — не отпускают парня, а то наделал бы он делов (Искандер 3). As soon as someone began shouting to be turned loose, three or four men instantly hung on him so as to make it clear to everyone that they would not turn the fellow loose, or he'd make trouble (3a).

Д-54 • НЕ У ДЕЛ бытьø, остаться и т. п. [PrepP; Invar; subj-compl with copula (subj: human) or, rare, nonagreeing postmodif] (to be, remain etc) without work (often as a result of a firing, retirement, or dismissal): X не у дел ≃ **X is out of work ⟨out of a job⟩; X is not working.**

Когда мы жили вместе, она была не у дел по болезни и подрабатывала у меня, помогая по хозяйству (Мандельштам 2). At the time when we lived in the same apartment, she was out of work because of ill-health and I gave her a little money for helping with my housework (2a). ♦ Муж [Сони] — бывший лётчик, в отставке по болезни. Больно ударила его эта отставка. Не мог примириться, что не у дел (Грекова 3). Her [Sonya's] husband was a former pilot, retired because of illness. That retirement had hit him hard. He couldn't live with the fact that he wasn't working (3a). ♦ И вот она [революция] пришла... а он [Аверкий Степанович], прирождённый и постоянный рабочелюбец... очутился на бобах, не у дел, в опустевшем посёлке, из которого разбежались рабочие, частью шедшие тут за меньшевиками

(Пастернак 1). [context transl] Now it [the revolution] had come…but he [Averkii Stepanovich], the born and faithful champion of the proletariat…had been left high and dry; instead of being in the thick of things, he was in a remote village from which the workers—some of whom were Mensheviks—had fled! (1a).

Д-55 • **ДЕЛА́ ИДУ́Т, КОНТО́РА ПИ́ШЕТ** [saying] things continue to go on as they normally do (said, usu. humorously or ironically, about a person's or institution's activities that carry on despite outside circumstances; usu. said in response to the question «Как дела?»—"How are things going?"): ≃ **(things are) plugging along, same as always; everything's fine—business as usual.**

Д-56 • **ДЕЛА́ КАК СА́ЖА БЕЛА́** [saying] things could be better (said, usu. humorously or ironically, in response to the question «Как дела?»—"How are things going?"—when matters are going badly or when a person prefers to give a vague reply, implying that things are not going well): ≃ **don't ask; could be better.**

Д-57 • **НЕТ ДЕ́ЛА** *кому до кого-чего* or *до того, как и т. п.* [VP; impers; pres or past] s.o. is indifferent to, not interested in or concerned about s.o. or sth.: X-у нет дела до Y-а ≃ **X doesn't care about Y; Y is of no concern to X; X is not in the least concerned about Y; X doesn't want (to have) anything to do with Y;** [in limited contexts] **X minds his own business;** ‖ X-у нет никакого дела до Y-а ≃ **X couldn't ⟨could⟩ care less about Y; X doesn't care a ⟨one⟩ bit about Y;** [in limited contexts] **X doesn't give a damn ⟨a hoot⟩ about Y.**

[Трилецкий:] Что случилось? А ты и не знаешь? Тебе и дела нет до этого? Тебе некогда? (Чехов 1). [T.:] What's happened? Don't you know? Don't you care? Are you too busy? (1a). ♦ …Однажды в тусклом номере гостиницы в Казани он, пробуждённый тяжким и сумеречным похмельем, вдруг увидел себя со стороны маленьким, затерянным и жалким существом, до которого никому, ну вовсе никому на свете нет дела (Максимов 3). …One evening in a dingy hotel room in Kazan he woke up with a heavy hangover and suddenly saw himself from outside: a small, lost, pathetic creature, of no concern to anybody in the whole world (3a). ♦ …Ему нет дела, что в истории о нём не останется следа… (Стругацкие 4). …He is not in the least concerned that history won't even wonder who he was… (4a). ♦ «Алёша, голубчик, завтра-то, завтра-то что будет? Вот ведь что меня мучит! Одну только меня и мучит! Смотрю на всех, никто-то об том не думает, никому-то до этого и дела нет никакого» (Достоевский 2). "Alyosha, darling, tomorrow, what will happen tomorrow? That's what torments me! And I'm the only one it torments! I look at everyone, and no one is thinking about it, no one wants to have anything to do with it" (2a). ♦ Ему до этого дома нет никакого дела, важно поскорее отделаться и сообщить начальству, что всё в порядке (Войнович 5). He didn't care a bit about the building. All he wanted was to be done with it quickly and report to the authorities that everything was in good order (5a). ♦ «Кто там в школу ходит, кто там плачет — дела мне нет никакого» (Айтматов 1). "I don't give a damn who goes to school or who's crying over there" (1b).

Д-58 • **НУ И ДЕЛА́!** *coll* [Interj; Invar; fixed WO] used to express surprise (occas. flavored by irony), indignation, disapproval or ironic approval etc : **(well,) I'll be darned ⟨damned⟩!; how about that!; (well,) what do you know!; well, I'll be!; well, I never!; who'd have thought it!; you don't say!**

…Среди сопровождавших принца лиц один был на сильном подозрении, что понимает по-русски, хотя и скрывает это. Оказывается, на предыдущем банкете, когда ему подали литровый рог, с тем чтобы он, сказав пару тёплых слов, выпил его, он растерялся и как будто по-русски прошептал: «Ну и дела…» (Искандер 4). …One of the people in the prince's escort was strongly suspected of understanding Russian, although he tried to hide the fact. At a previous banquet, when they served him a liter horn, expecting him to say a few heartfelt words and drink it off, he lost his head and allegedly whispered in Russian, "Well, I'll be darned!" (4a).

Д-59 • **ЧТО́** *кому-чему* **ДЕ́ЛАЕТСЯ!** *coll* [VP_subj; pres only; fixed WO] s.o. or sth. is the same as always, has not changed (and there is no reason why he or it should be otherwise, or anyone should think otherwise): что X-у делается? ≃ **what could (possibly) happen to X?; what could be wrong with X?;** [in limited contexts; in refer. to a person, usu. in response to the question «X здоров?»] **why wouldn't X be?**

«Я считаю долгом предостеречь вас. Нашему брату, старому холостяку, можно сюда ходить: что нам делается? Мы народ прокалённый, нас ничем не проберёшь; а у вас кожица ещё нежная…» (Тургенев 3). "I consider it my duty to warn you. It is all very well for people like me—for old bachelors—to go on coming here. What could possibly happen to us? We are a hard-boiled lot; you cannot do much to us. But you have a tender skin" (3b). ♦ На другой день, только что Обломов проснулся… Захар, подавая ему чай, сказал, что когда он ходил в булочную, так встретил барышню… «Ну?» — нетерпеливо спросил Обломов. «Ну, кланяться приказали, спрашивали, здоровы ли вы, что делаете». — «Что ж ты сказал?» — «Сказал, что здоровы; что, мол, ему делается?..» (Гончаров 1). Next morning, as soon as Oblomov woke up…Zakhar, who had brought him his breakfast, told him that he had met the young lady on his way to the baker's.…"Well?" Oblomov asked impatiently. "Well, sir, she sent you her greetings, and asked how you were and what you were doing." "What did you say?" "Me, sir? I said that you were all right—what could be wrong with you?" (1a). The next morning, as soon as Oblomov woke up…Zakhar brought him his breakfast and told him that he had met the young lady on his way to the baker's.…"Well?" inquired Oblomov impatiently. "Well, she sends you her greetings, asks how you are and what you are doing." "What did you say?" "I said you were well. 'Why wouldn't he be?' I said" (1b).

Д-60 • **ДЕ́ЛАТЬ НЕ́ЧЕГО** [Invar; impers predic with быть_ø, pres or past; used as sent or sent adv (parenth)] s.o. has no alternative, s.o. must, against his will, give in and do precisely (what is specified by the following context): **there is nothing one can do (about it ⟨except…⟩); there is nothing (else) to do (but…); there is nothing to be done (about it); there is nothing for it (but…); there is no way out of it; there's no help for it; it can't be helped; one has no choice (but…); there is no escaping it; it cannot be avoided.**

Их [Лёву и Фаину] рассадили порознь — это был принцип компании. Лёве он показался глупым, и Лёва досадовал — но делать было нечего… (Битов 2). They [Lyova and Faina] were seated separately—this was a principle of the group. It struck Lyova as silly, and he felt annoyed, but there was nothing he could do… (2a). ♦ «Нечего делать, надо будить», — сказал Щербинин, вставая и подходя к человеку в ночном колпаке, укрытому шинелью… (Толстой 7). "There's nothing to be done, we'll have to wake him," said Shcherbinin, rising and going up to the man in the nightcap who lay covered by a greatcoat (7b). ♦ Я должен был нанять быков, чтоб втащить мою тележку на эту проклятую гору… Нечего делать, я нанял шесть быков и несколько осетин (Лермонтов 1). I saw I would need oxen to haul my carriage to the top of the confounded mountain.…There was nothing for it but to hire six oxen and several Ossetians (1b). ♦ «Любезный Пётр Андреевич, пожалуйста, пришли мне с моим мальчиком сто рублей, которые ты мне вчера проиграл…» Делать было нечего. Я… приказал [Савельичу] отдать мальчику сто рублей (Пушкин 2). "My dear Petr Andreevich, be so good as to send me by my serving boy the hundred rubles I won from you yesterday.…" There was no way out of it.…[I] ordered him [Savelich] to hand the boy a hundred rubles (2a). ♦ «…За что вы ему [Ракитину] отказали [от дома]—я и от него не слыхал...» – «Ну, так я вам это всё открою и, нечего делать, покаюсь, потому что тут есть одна черта, в которой я, может быть, сама виновата» (Достоевский 2). "...Why you closed your door to him [Rakitin] – that he didn't tell me..." "Well, then I'll reveal it all to you and – since there's no help for it – I'll confess, because there's a point here that may be my own fault" (2a). ♦ Он застал Базарова в трактире, где они остановились, и долго его уговаривал пойти к губернатору. «Нечего делать! – сказал, наконец, Базаров. – ...Приехали смотреть помещиков – давай их смотреть!» (Тургенев 2). He found Bazarov at the inn where they were staying and was a long while persuading him to go with him to the Governor's. "Well, it can't be helped," said Bazarov at last. "...We came to look at the gentry; let's look at them!" (2b). ♦ «...Конечно, я понимал: если нас девушки предали – нам хана, потому что в этом случае моя [девушка] первым делом должна была отдать им [немцам] пистолет. Но делать нечего, тихо открываю дверь и быстро поднимаюсь по лестнице» (Искандер 5). "...Of course I realized it was curtains for us if the girls had betrayed us, because if they had, mine must have given them [the Germans] the pistol first thing. But I had no choice, I quietly opened the door and quickly climbed the stairs" (5a).

Д-61 • ДЕ́ЛАТЬ/СДЕ́ЛАТЬ 〈ХОДИ́ТЬ/СХОДИ́ТЬ〉 ПОД СЕБЯ́ coll [VP; subj: human] (usu. of a seriously ill, bedridden person) to urinate or defecate in one's bed or, occas., in one's clothing: X сделал под себя ≃ **X wet his bed 〈pants〉; X wet the bed; X messed 〈went in〉 his bed 〈pants〉; X had an 〈a little〉 accident.**

[extended usage] Он [Лёва] занимался своей незапятнанной стариной и не изменял ей, и эта определённость его снискала к себе доверие в определённой интеллигентной среде, иногда называемой либеральной. Эта-то его чистоплотность... была и не чистоплотностью вовсе, а, быть может, лишь инстинктивным или фамильным нежеланием ходить под себя, попросту кое-какая культурная привычка к санитарным нормам... (Битов 2). He [Lyova] studied his own unsullied antiquity and did not betray it, and his definiteness won him the trust of a definite intellectual milieu sometimes called liberal. This cleanliness of his...wasn't cleanliness at all, it may have been merely an instinctive or familial reluctance to go in the bed, just a certain cultured habit of sanitation... (2a).

Д-62 • ОТ НЕ́ЧЕГО ДЕ́ЛАТЬ coll [Invar; sent adv; fixed WO] (to do sth.) out of a lack of anything to occupy one's time, without any particular aim in mind: **for want 〈lack〉 of anything 〈something〉 better to do; having nothing better to do; just to pass 〈while away〉 the time; with 〈having〉 time on one's hands.**

По ночам дед [Гордей] сторожил в мастерских, а днём от нечего делать бродил по деревне (Распутин 1). At night he [old Gordei] served as watchman in the kolkhoz workshops and in the daytime, for want of anything better to do, went wandering about the village (1a). ♦ «Ты кокетничаешь, – подумал он, – ты скучаешь и дразнишь меня от нечего делать...» (Тургенев 2). "You're playing the coquette," he thought to himself. "You are bored, and teasing me for want of something better to do..." (2c). ♦ Его друзья от нечего делать... отправились гулять... (Набоков 1). His friends, having nothing better to do...went out for a stroll... (1a). ♦ «И что это за нелепая фигура! – скажете вы возмущённо. – Где тут пример для подрастающего поколения? И где автор увидел такого в кавычках героя?» И я, автор, прижатый к стенке и пойманный, что называется, с поличным, должен буду признаться, что нигде я его не видел, выдумал из своей головы и вовсе не для примера, а просто от нечего делать (Войнович 2). "What a sorry sight he makes!" you will say indignantly. "What kind of example is this for the younger generation? And just where has the author seen a quote unquote hero like this?" And I, the author, my back to the wall and caught, as they say, red-handed, will have to admit that I never saw him anywhere, that I thought him up with

my own head, and not to use him as an example but simply to while away the time (2a). ♦ Была середина дня, палило солнце, время стояло на месте, начальство не появлялось. От нечего делать люди, слово по слову, разговорились (Войнович 2). It was midday, the sun was scorching, time stood still, the authorities had not yet appeared. With time on their hands, people began to exchange a few words and ended up talking (2a).

Д-63 • В СА́МОМ ДЕ́ЛЕ [PrepP; Invar; fixed WO] **1.** [usu. adv] (in refer. to the nature of s.o. or sth.) in actuality (as opposed to as perceived, portrayed etc by s.o.): **in reality; in (actual) fact; really; actually.**

Он [Давид] почувствовал впервые, что и он смертен, не по-сказочному, а в самом деле, с невероятной очевидностью (Гроссман 2). For the first time David felt very clearly that he himself was mortal, not just in a fairy-tale way, but in actual fact (2a). ♦ Одни почитают меня хуже, другие лучше, чем я в самом деле... (Лермонтов 1). Some think me worse, others better, than I really am (1d). Some deem me worse, others better than I actually am (1a).

2. [Particle or sent adv (often parenth)] used to confirm or ask for confirmation of sth. stated previously; also used to express one's agreement with, seconding of etc sth. said by another: **in fact; actually; really; indeed.**

Конечно, сказать, что я это [мещанскую ненависть жены Марата ко всякого рода чудачествам] заметил и принял к сведению, было бы неточно. Я в самом деле это заметил, но тогда подумал, что... это мне показалось (Искандер 2). Of course, it would be imprecise to say that I noticed this [Marat's wife's bourgeois hatred for any kind of eccentricity] and took it into account. I did in fact notice it, but at the time I thought I was imagining things (2a). ♦ Многие очевидцы этого утра теперь утверждают, что скот села Анхара предчувствовал начало боя, хотя с достоверностью этого утверждения трудно согласиться... Так как голодный скот, находясь взаперти, всегда даёт о себе знать, теперь трудно установить, в самом деле он предчувствовал кровопролитие или нет (Искандер 3). Many eyewitnesses now claim that the livestock of the village of Ankhara had a premonition the battle would begin that morning, although this claim is hard to authenticate....Since hungry animals who find themselves penned up always make themselves heard, it is difficult to establish now whether they actually had a premonition of bloodshed or not (3a). ♦ «Свинкин дело потерял!» – «В самом деле? Что ж директор?» – спросил Обломов дрожащим голосом (Гончаров 1). "Svinkin lost a file of documents." "Really? What did the director do?" Oblomov asked in an unsteady voice (1b). ♦ «Кто тебе сказал, что Монина собираются уволить?» – «Декан». – «В самом деле?» – «В самом деле». "Who told you they were planning on firing Monin?" "The dean." "Really?" "Really." ♦ «...Я этого так не оставлю, я позвоню, я пойду к Каретникову, ему ничего не стоит, ему стоит только снять трубку...» ...Откликаясь на просьбы Ефима, Каретников и в самом деле кому-то звонил или писал письма на своём депутатском бланке и... отказа на его звонки или письма, как правило, не бывало (Войнович 6). "...I won't leave it at this. I'll call Karetnikov. I'll go see Karetnikov. All Karetnikov has to do is pick up the phone..." Karetnikov had indeed made phone calls on Yefim's behalf, or written letters, using his official stationery, and his calls and his letters always did their work (6a).

3. [sent adv; often preceded by Conj «и»] used to introduce a statement justifying, supporting etc sth. previously stated: **indeed; after all.**

«Как ты едешь? Ну же, потрогивай!» И в самом деле, Селифан давно уже ехал зажмуря глаза, изредка только потряхивая впросонках вожжами по бокам дремавших тоже лошадей... (Гоголь 3). "You call this driving? Come on, put your whip to them, get going!" And indeed Selifan had been driving for a long time with his eyes closed, only now and then flipping the reins against the flanks of the horses, who were dozing too (3c). ♦ ...В комнату вошла... симпатичная женщина в белом чистом халате и сказала Ивану: «Доброе утро!» Иван не ответил, так как счёл это приветствие в данных условиях неуместным. В самом деле, засадили здорового человека в лечебницу... (Булгаков 9). Into the room came a kind-looking woman in a clean white coverall and said to Ivan, "Good morning!" Ivan did not reply, as he felt the greeting out of place in the circumstances. They had, after all, dumped a perfectly healthy man in the hospital... (9b).

4. [Particle] used to intensify an expression of indignation, annoyance, surprise etc, or to intensify a request or demand that s.o. do (or stop doing) sth.: **really!; honestly!;** [with прекрати, перестань etc] **(stop...,) will you?;** [when used with a negated word or phrase] **certainly (not)!**

«Экий я дурак в самом деле!» (Гоголь 3). "What a fool I am, really!" (3b). "Oh, what a fool I am, honestly!" (3a). ♦ [Ислаев:] Michel, однако ты ненадолго уезжаешь?.. [Ракитин:] Не знаю, право... Я думаю... надолго... [Ислаев:] Ведь тебя здесь заменить некому. Не Большинцов же в самом деле! (Тургенев 1). [I.:] Michel, you aren't going to leave us for long, are you?... [R.:] I really don't know....I think...for a long time... [I.:] But we have no one to replace you here! Certainly not Bolshintsov! (1b).

Д-64 • **НА ДЕ́ЛЕ** [PrepP; Invar; usu. adv] in actuality, in action (as distinguished from words): **in deed; in one's deeds; in practice; in life; in actual fact; in actuality; in reality;** [in limited contexts] **learn by experience.**

Он скептик и матерьялист, как все почти медики, а вместе с этим поэт, и не на шутку, — поэт на деле всегда и часто на словах... (Лермонтов 1). He is a sceptic and a materialist like most medical men, but he is also a poet, and that quite in earnest—a poet in all his deeds and frequently in words... (1b). ♦ [Треплев:] Как легко, доктор, быть философом на бумаге и как это трудно на деле! (Чехов 6). [T.:] How easy it is, Doctor, to be a philosopher on paper, and how hard it is in life! (6d). ♦ На словах провозглашался исторический материализм, на деле чистейший идеализм (Орлова 1). Historical materialism was being professed in words, but it was pure idealism in actual fact (1a). ♦ ...В ту пору у нас слишком уж даже выделанно напрашивался на свою роль шута, любил выскакивать и веселить господ, с видимым равенством конечно, но на деле совершенным пред ними хамом (Достоевский 1). ...At that time he was even overzealously establishing himself as a buffoon, and loved to pop up and amuse the gentlemen, ostensibly as an equal, of course, though in reality he was an absolute master beside them (1a). ♦ «Ну, насчёт общины... поговорите лучше с вашим братцем. Он теперь, кажется, изведал на деле, что такое община, круговая порука, трезвость и тому подобные штучки» (Тургенев 2). "Well, so far as the commune is concerned...you'd better talk with your brother about it. I think he has now learned by experience what the commune is: mutual responsibility, sobriety, and all that kind of thing" (2f).

Д-65 • **НА СА́МОМ ДЕ́ЛЕ** [PrepP; Invar; fixed WO] **1.** [usu. adv; often preceded by Conj «а»] (in refer. to the nature of s.o. or sth.) in actuality (as opposed to as perceived, portrayed etc by s.o.): **in reality; in (actual) fact; really; actually; the reality is ⟨was...⟩.**

Все провозглашённые советской конституцией права и свободы являются фикцией. Право на труд на самом деле является обязанностью (Войнович 1). All the rights and freedoms proclaimed in the Soviet constitution are fictions. The right to work is in fact a duty (1a). ♦ Вера Лазаревна жила недалеко, через два дома, и приходила к Лене почти ежедневно под предлогом «помочь Наташеньке» и «облегчить Ленусе», а на самом деле с единственной целью — беспардонно вмешиваться в чужую жизнь (Трифонов 4). Vera Lazarevna lived not far away, two buildings from them, and came to Lena's almost daily on the pretext of "helping Natashenka" and "making things easier for Lenusha," but in actual fact with one sole aim—to unforgivably interfere in someone else's life (4a). ♦ «...Боюсь, что никто не может подтвердить, что... то, что вы нам рассказывали, происходило на самом деле» (Булгаков 9). "...I am afraid no one can confirm to us that the

things you spoke of really happened" (9a). ♦ Торговал он с рук разной, необходимой в казачьем обиходе рухлядью... и два раза в год ездил в Воронеж, будто за товаром, а на самом деле доносил, что в станице пока-де спокойно и казаки нового злодейства не умышляют (Шолохов 2). He traded in various odds and ends that were of use to Cossacks...and twice a year he travelled to Voronezh ostensibly to replenish his stocks, but actually to report that the stanitsa was calm and the Cossacks were not plotting any fresh mischief (2a). ♦ Михаил тоже вышел из избы, и под тем же самым предлогом — вроде и ему дышать нечем... а на самом-то деле он вышел, чтобы не остаться с глазу на глаз с новоявленным зятьком... (Абрамов 1). Mikhail went out too, and under the same pretext: that he could not breathe....The reality was that he had left so as not to be alone with his newly proclaimed brother-in-law (1a).

2. [Particle] used to intensify an expression of indignation, annoyance, surprise etc or to intensify a request or demand that s.o. do (or stop doing) sth.: **really!; honestly!;** [with прекрати, перестань etc] **(stop...,) will you!;** [when used with a negated word or phrase] **certainly (not)!**

Д-66 • **ПРИ ДЕ́ЛЕ** coll [PrepP; Invar; subj-compl with copula (subj: human)] one is occupied, engaged in some kind of activity: X при деле ≃ **X has something to keep him busy ⟨to keep himself occupied⟩; X has something to do; X is ⟨keeps (himself)⟩ busy;** [in limited contexts] **X is in business; X has a job.**

Достоинство человека здесь [в этом городке] определяется одной фразой: «Строит дом». Строит дом — значит, порядочный человек, приличный человек, достойный человек. Строит дом — значит, человек при деле... значит человек пустил корень... (Искандер 6). In this town a man's whole worth was defined by the phrase: "He's building a house." A man who's building a house is an honest man, a decent and deserving man. A man who's building a house is a man who keeps himself busy...a man who has put down roots (6a). ♦ ...Коля Зархиди снова оказался при деле. В ближайший год он наладил закупку табака у населения, переработку и дальнейшую продажу за границей (Искандер 3). Kolya Zarhidis found himself back in business. The next year he organized the purchase of tobacco from the population, its processing and subsequent sale abroad (3a). ♦ Мне двадцать три, хорошо зарабатываю, голод, слава богу, кончился, карточки отменили, отец при деле на фабрике... дома только Генрих, Дина, Саша и маленький Игорёк (Рыбаков 1). I was twenty-three, earning good money, the famine was over, thank God, ration cards were a thing of the past, father had his job at the factory...and at home there were only Genrikh, Dina, Sasha and little Igorek (1a).

Д-67 • **ДЕЛИ́ТЬ НЕ́ЧЕГО** кому (с кем) coll [Invar; impers predic with быть₀; if used without prep obj, indir obj refers to two or more parties] there is no basis for conflict (between two or more individuals or groups of people): X-у с Y-ом ⟨X-у и Y-у⟩ делить нечего ≃ **X has (got) no bone to pick with Y; X has (got) no quarrel with Y; X and Y have (got) nothing to argue about; there's nothing for X and Y to quarrel over; there is no bone of contention between X and Y.**

«Я, — объяснил Гусев Петру Васильевичу жизненную позицию при случайной встрече в день отъезда того в эвакуацию, — человек маленький. По мне, какая ни есть власть, всё едино... Мне с немцами делить нечего... Не пропаду» (Максимов 3). On the day of Pyotr Vasilievich's evacuation, Gusev happened to meet him, and explained his philosophy of life. "I'm a man of no importance. I don't care what kind of government we have, it's all the same to me....I've got no quarrel with the Germans....I shan't come to any harm" (3a). ♦ «...Делить нам с тобой нечего, езжай с богом!» (Шолохов 5). "There's nothing for us to quarrel over, so go and God be with you!" (5a).

Д-68 • **БОЛЬШО́Е ⟨ВЕЛИ́КОЕ⟩ ДЕ́ЛО; БОЛЬШИ́Е ДЕЛА́** all coll [NP; these forms only; used as Interj or sent adv;

fixed WO] used to express a sarcastic attitude, disdain etc toward sth.: **big deal!**; [in limited contexts] **as if it mattered; as if it could make (all) that much (of a) difference.**

Следующий сюрприз ждал Куницера в гардеробе собственного института. Новый гардеробщик прищуренным чекистским взглядом смотрел на него... Да ладно, большое дело — новый гардеробщик! Отдал пальто, получил номерок, отдал номерок, взял пальто, вот и все отношения (Аксёнов 6). The next surprise awaited Kunitser in the cloakroom of his own institute. A new attendant was looking at him with the frowning stare of a KGB officer....OK, big deal! A new cloakroom attendant! He handed in his coat, got a tag, gave in his tag and got his coat back—that was the sum of his dealings with the man (6a).

Д-69 • БРА́ТЬСЯ/ВЗЯ́ТЬСЯ НЕ ЗА СВОЁ ДЕ́ЛО [VP; subj: human; the verb may take the final position, otherwise fixed WO] (to begin) to do sth. that one is not trained for or competent in: X взялся не за своё дело ≃ **X took on a job he couldn't handle; X bit off more than he could chew; X got in over his head; X is the wrong man for the job;** ‖ за своё ли дело X взялся? ≃ **is X the right man for the job?**

Какие только наседки мне за все эти годы ни попадались: и наглые, и робкие, и умные, и глупые. Бывали уж такие хитрецы, что никак бы не догадаться. А в 67-м сидел со мной некто Присовский — до того глупый парень, что даже легенду свою складно рассказать не мог, запутался... Другого, в 71-ом году, мне даже жалко стало. Совсем не годился человек для этой роли, не за своё дело взялся (Буковский 1). The snoopers I have had through the years—some insolent, some timid, some intelligent, some stupid, some so cunning that you'd never have guessed. On the other hand, I shared a cell in 1967 with a certain Prisovsky, who was so stupid that he couldn't even tell his story properly and got all mixed up....There was another one in 1971—I even felt sorry for him, he was completely the wrong man for the job (1a).

Д-70 • В ТОМ-ТО И ДЕ́ЛО ⟨ШТУ́КА coll⟩ (, что...) [sent; these forms only; main clause in a complex sent; fixed WO] that is the main point, the most important factor: **that's just ⟨precisely⟩ the point; that's (just) it ⟨the thing, the problem, the trouble⟩; that's the whole point; the whole point is that...**

Дед смеётся: в том-то и дело, говорит он, что пророк сам не знает, что он пророк... (Айтматов 1). Grandpa laughs: that's just the point, he says—the prophet doesn't know himself that he's a prophet... (1a). ♦ ...Ерёменко, будь он простой ученик, до десятого класса никак бы не добрался, но в том-то и дело, что он был не простой ученик, а номенклатурный... (Войнович 1). Had Eremenko been an ordinary student, he would never have made it to the tenth grade; but that was precisely the point, he was no ordinary student. He was a member of the power elite, the *nomenklatura* (1a). ♦ [Синбар:] Значит, вы едете домой. [Тилия:] В том-то и дело, что нет (Солженицын 11). [S.:] You're going right home then. [T.:] That's just it, I'm not! (11a). ♦ «А что ты думаешь, застрелюсь, как не достану трех тысяч отдать? В том-то и дело, что не застрелюсь» (Достоевский 1). "What do you think, that I'll shoot myself if I can't find three thousand roubles to give back to her? That's just the thing: I won't shoot myself" (1a). ♦ «А у вас есть и беглые?» — быстро спросил Чичиков, очнувшись. «В том-то и дело, что есть» (Гоголь 3). "So you have some runaways as well?" Chichikov asked, quickly pricking up his ears. "Yes, that's just the trouble" (3e). ♦ «А людей надо о-очень любить. Иначе к-какой смысл нам работать? В том-то и дело: нет смысла...» (Семёнов 1). "But one should l-love people. Otherwise, what's the s-sense of our work? That's the whole point: there's no sense..." (1a). ♦ Это не было ни в воскресенье, ни в какой-нибудь праздник. В том-то и дело, что это был будний, обыкновенный день... (Олеша 3). It was neither on a Sunday, nor indeed on any holiday at all. The whole point is that it was an ordinary working day... (3a).

Д-71 • В ЧЁМ ДЕ́ЛО? [sent; Invar; often a subord clause in a complex sent; fixed WO] what is taking place or took place?: **what's going on?; what's happening?; what's up?; what's the matter ⟨the problem, the trouble⟩?; what's it ⟨this⟩ all about?;** [in limited contexts] **what's wrong?**

[Филипп:] Слушай, я почти не знаю этой семьи, мы месяца не знакомы. В чём тут дело? Она на тридцать лет моложе. Как это получилось? (Солженицын 11). [P.:] Listen, I scarcely know this family, I first met them less than a month ago. What's going on here exactly? She is thirty years younger than he. How did it happen? (11a). ♦ [Николка:] Алёша, может быть, ты пошлёшь меня узнать, в чём дело в штабе? (Булгаков 4). [N.:] Alyosha, maybe you'd send me to find out what's happening at headquarters? (4b). ♦ Опять звонок. На этот раз звонит наш общий со старушкой знакомый. Она ему звонила, рыдала, жаловалась, и он хочет выяснить, в чём дело, почему я её обидел (Войнович 3). The phone again. This time it was a mutual acquaintance of the old woman and mine. She had called him, sobbing and complaining, and he wanted to know what the problem was, why I had offended her (3a). ♦ Городской голова, Яков Аникиевич Скучаев, встретил Передонова на пороге своей гостиной... Скучаев был весьма польщён тем, что к нему пришли. Он не совсем понимал, для чего это и в чём тут дело, но из политики не показывал и вида, что не понимает (Сологуб 1). The mayor, Yakov Anikievich Skuchaev, met Peredonov at the entrance to his living room....Skuchaev was extremely flattered that Peredonov had come to him. He did not completely understand what it was all about, but he had sense enough not to show that (1a).

Д-72 • ВИ́ДАННОЕ ЛИ (Э́ТО) ДЕ́ЛО coll [sent; these forms only; often the main clause in a complex sent foll. by a чтобы-clause; fixed WO] used to express a negative attitude toward sth., indignation etc: **who ever saw ⟨who's ever seen⟩ such a thing ⟨anything like it, the likes of it⟩?; who ⟨who's⟩ ever heard of such a thing ⟨of anything like it⟩?; it's (just ⟨simply⟩) unheard of; whoever heard the like?**

«А это на что похоже, что вчера только восемь фунтов пшена отпустила, опять спрашивают... А я пшена не отпущу... Нет, я потачки за барское добро не дам. Ну виданное ли это дело — восемь фунтов?» (Толстой 2). "And what sort of game is this? Only yesterday I let them have eight pounds of rice and now they're asking for more!...I'm not giving you any more rice....No, I'm not letting anybody take liberties with the master's things. Well, who ever heard of such a thing—eight pounds?" (2b).

Д-73 • ВИ́ДИМОЕ ДЕ́ЛО substand [NP; Invar; used as sent adv (parenth) or indep. sent; fixed WO] that is quite apparent, there is no doubt about it: **that's for sure; sure thing; that's (crystal) clear; that's obvious ⟨evident⟩.**

[Анисья:] Сейчас [Пётр] за Марфой, за сестрой родной, посылает. Должно, об деньгах. [Матрёна:] Видимое дело (Толстой 1). [A.:] He's [Petr is] just sending for Marfa, his own sister. Must be about the money. [M.:] Sure thing (1b). [A.:] He's [Pyotr is] sending for Marfa now, for his own sister. Must be about the money. [M.:] That's clear (1a). ♦ [Мурзавецкая:] Что ж это такое, Вукол, а? [Чугунов:] Насмешка. [Мурзавецкая:] Над кем? [Чугунов:] Над вами, видимое дело (Островский 5). [M.:] What do you think of this, eh, Vukol? [Ch.:] An affront. [M.:] To whom? [Ch.:] To you, that's evident (5a).

Д-74 • ВСТУПА́ТЬ/ВСТУПИ́ТЬ В ДЕ́ЛО [VP; subj: human, collect, or concr] to begin to act: X вступил в дело ≃ **X went into action; thing X came into play;** [in limited contexts] **X was called ⟨brought⟩ into play;** ‖ в дело вступили пушки ⟨пулемёты, пулемётчики и т. п.⟩ ≃ **the artillery ⟨the machine guns, the machine-gunners etc⟩ opened fire.**

Публика стала окружать негодяев, и тогда в дело вступил Коровьев (Булгаков 9). As customers began edging up to the rogues and surrounding them, Koroviev went into action (9b). ♦ Немецким пулемётам ещё рано было вступать в дело (Свирский 1). It was still too early for the German machine gunners to open fire (1a).

Д-75 • **ГИ́БЛОЕ ⟨ПРОПА́ЩЕЕ⟩ ДЕ́ЛО** [NP; sing only; subj-compl with copula, nom or instrum (subj: usu. infin or это, often omitted)] doing sth. is futile and may, in addition, result in unfavorable consequences: **lost cause; losing proposition; hopeless undertaking; (sth. is) hopeless.**

…Спорить с Юркой об архитектуре – дело гиблое (Михайловская 1). …It is a lost cause, arguing with Yuri about architecture (1a). ♦ В общем, лично мне это надоело… Артель «Напрасный труд». Мы пробурили этот живописный распадок в двух местах и сейчас бурили в третьем. Гиблое дело – нет здесь её [нефти] (Аксёнов 1). Actually, I for one was fed up with it… The "Labor-in-Vain Co-op." We drilled this picturesque ravine in two spots and now we were drilling in a third. A losing proposition – there isn't any [oil] here (1a). ♦ Весь январь сорок седьмого года я провёл на Ярославском вокзале… С семи утра встречал пригородные поезда, вечером с пяти и до двенадцати ночи их провожал… Гиблое дело… Нет Гали (Рыбаков 1). I spent the whole of January 1947 at Yaroslav Station.…From seven in the morning I met the suburban trains and from five o'clock to midnight I watched them leave.…It was hopeless. No Galya (1a).

Д-76 • **ГОВОРИ́ТЬ ДЕ́ЛО** (кому) coll [VP; subj: human] to say sth. worth listening to: X дело говорит ≃ **X is talking sense; X has a point; what X says is very much to the point; [in limited contexts] X is making sense.**

«Фельдмаршал мой, кажется, говорит дело. Как ты думаешь?» (Пушкин 2). "My field-marshal seems to be talking sense. What do you think?" (2b). ♦ «Полковник Воротынцев говорит дело. Я для себя беру здесь много поучительного» (Солженицын 1). "What Colonel Vorotyntsev says is very much to the point. I am learning a lot from him" (1a).

Д-77 • **ДЕ́ЛАТЬ/СДЕ́ЛАТЬ СВОЁ ДЕ́ЛО** [VP] **1.** [subj: human] to perform one's specific function or role: X делал своё дело ≃ **X did his work ⟨job, thing⟩; X went about his business; [in limited contexts] X did his part; X did what he was supposed to ⟨had to⟩ do.**

В саду уже порядочно и иностранных корреспондентов, фоторепортёров и кинооператоров. Они – спокойные, деловитые… и умело, без лишней суеты делают своё дело (Гладков 1). By now there were also a good many foreign correspondents, photographers and newsreel men in the garden. They were calm and business-like…they did their job impassively, without fuss (1a). ♦ «Мужики… делают своё дело, ни за чем не тянутся; а теперь развратятся!» (Гончаров 1). "The peasants…went about their business and asked for nothing, but now they'll be corrupted!" (1a). ♦ Нет, полностью отрицать заслуги того, который сидел в метро, я не буду. Он [Сталин] тоже своё дело делал: и трубку курил, и жирным пальцем глобус мусолил, указывая, куда какую кинуть дивизию… (Войнович 4). No. I will not completely deny the merits of the man who lived in the metro. He [Stalin] did his part too—he smoked his pipe, he soiled his globe with a greasy finger, indicating where a division was to be hurled… (4a). ♦ В двадцатых годах все понемногу учили Мандельштама, в тридцатых на него показывали пальцами, а он жил, поплёвывая, в окружении дикарей и делал своё дело (Мандельштам 2). In the twenties everybody tried to reason with M[andelstam], but in the thirties they were already pointing their fingers at him; not concealing his distaste, he went on living among the barbarians and did what he had to do (2a).

2. [subj: abstr or concr] to produce its usual result, influence s.o., make itself felt: X делал ⟨сделал⟩ своё дело ≃ **X did its work ⟨job⟩; X began to have ⟨X had⟩ its effect ⟨way⟩; [of age, illness etc] X began to take ⟨X had taken⟩ its toll; [impfv only] X began to tell on person Y.**

Иногда, уязвлённые пренебрежением покупателей, чегемцы увозили назад свои продукты, говоря: ничего, сами съедим. Впрочем, таких гордецов оставалось всё меньше и меньше, деспотия рынка делала своё дело (Искандер 3). Sometimes, stung by the contempt of the customers, the Chegemians would cart their produce back: All right, then, we'll eat it ourselves. As time went on, however, there were fewer and fewer people so arrogant; the despotism of the marketplace did its work (3a). ♦ …В общем, это хорошо, что меня показали по телевизору. Слух об этом сегодня же облетит всю Москву и сделает своё дело (Зиновьев 2). …On the whole it's a good thing that I've been seen on television. The news'll be round all Moscow by this evening, and it'll have its effect (2a). ♦ Быть может, возраст всё же делает своё дело с проплешинами и серебряными искорками, вместе с разными «звоночками», появляется и у их хамоватого поколения вкус к истинной дружбе? (Аксёнов 6). Perhaps age was, after all, beginning to tell on them, and along with patches of mold, spots before the eyes, and ringing in the ears, even their boorish generation was developing a taste for true friendship? (6a).

Д-78 • **ДЕ́ЛО В ТОМ…** [Invar; main clause (with быть$_\emptyset$) in a complex sent; pres or past; often foll. by a что-clause] the essence of the matter, the most important factor is as follows: **the point ⟨the thing⟩ is; the fact (of the matter) is; [in limited contexts] the trouble is; what matters is;** ‖ Neg дело не в том… ≃ **it's not a question of…**

Дело в том, что ожидаемая критика центральной газеты не повторилась (Искандер 4). The point is that the central newspaper did not, as expected, repeat its critique (4a). ♦ Ученик такой-то, позвольте мне, автору, снова прервать ваше повествование. Дело в том, что книгу пора заканчивать: у меня вышла бумага (Соколов 1). Student so-and-so, allow me, the author, to interrupt your narrative again. The thing is that it's time to end the book: I'm out of paper (1a). ♦ «Вы где учились?» Тут приходится открыть маленькую тайну. Дело в том, что я окончил в университете два факультета и скрывал это (Булгаков 12). "Where did you study?" Here I must reveal a little secret. The fact is that I graduated from two faculties at the university, but I would not admit to it (12a). ♦ Почему же все эти противоречивые чувства, свойственные нормальным людям, когда они собираются жениться, выражает не лицо Аслана… а именно лицо дяди Сандро, столь решительного во всех случаях жизни? Дело в том, что дядя Сандро влюблён в невесту своего друга, и она, судя по всему, тоже в него влюблена (Искандер 5). …Why are all these contradictory feelings, which are characteristic of normal men when they are about to get married, expressed not on Aslan's face…but on that of Uncle Sandro, who is so resolute under all of life's circumstances? The trouble is that Uncle Sandro is in love with his friend's bride, and by all indications she is in love with him too (5a). ♦ Дело… не в том, плохое или хорошее право. Дело в том, есть или нет какое-то право вообще (Зиновьев 1). "What matters…is not whether a law is bad or good. What matters is whether or not the law exists" (1a).

Д-79 • **ДЕ́ЛО В ШЛЯ́ПЕ** coll [Invar; VP$_{subj}$ with быть$_\emptyset$, usu. pres, also fut or subjunctive; often a clause in a compound (after Conj «и») or complex sent; usu. preceded by one or more clauses; fixed WO] the success of some undertaking, effort etc is assured, the desired outcome is or will be achieved: **it's in the bag; it's a sure thing; it's a cinch; it's as good as done; it's all sewn up; that does it ⟨the trick⟩; [in limited contexts] one's got it made.**

«Прежде молодым людям приходилось учиться; не хотелось им прослыть за невежд, так они поневоле трудились. А теперь им стоит сказать: всё на свете вздор! – и дело в шляпе» (Тургенев 2). "Before, young men had to study; they didn't want to be known for ignoramuses so they had to work, whether they liked it or not. And now all they have to do is to say 'Everything in the world is rubbish!'—and it's all in the bag for them" (2e). "Formerly young people were faced with having to study; they were averse to becoming known as ignoramuses; so, like it or not, they worked hard. But now all they have to do is to say 'Everything in the world is bosh!' – and that does it" (2d). ♦ «Поздравляю, старик! Только сейчас твою рожу по телевизору показали. Правда, в толпе и на сотую долю секунды, но для начала и то хлеб. Теперь твоё дело в шляпе» (Зиновьев 2). "Congratulations, old man! I have just seen your mug on television. It's true you were only one of a crowd, and you were only there for about a hundredth of a second, but it's something for a start. Now you've got it made" (2a).

Д-80 • **ДЕ́ЛО ДЕ́ЛАТЬ** [VP; subj: human; usu. this WO] **1.** to be engaged in work, occupy o.s. with some activity: X дело делает ≃ **X keeps (himself) busy; X attends to his work;** ‖ Х-у надо дело делать ≃ **X should be doing something;** ‖ давайте дело делать ≃ **let's get to work.**

«Чем в губернское правление-то шататься... лучше бы дело делать!» (Салтыков-Щедрин 2). "Instead of wasting his time in government departments...he should have been doing something!" (2a). ♦ Вышинский? Законченный негодяй. Всю жизнь был меньшевиком, понятно, в меньшевиках можно дела не делать, только краснобайствовать (Рыбаков 2). What about Vyshinsky? He was a thoroughbred scoundrel. All his life he'd been a Menshevik. That was understandable: among the Mensheviks you didn't have to do anything, other than engage in rhetoric (2a).

2. to do sth. needed, important: X дело делает ≃ **X is doing real work; X is doing something worthwhile ⟨useful etc⟩.**

«Эхе, хе! двенадцать часов! – сказал наконец Чичиков, взглянув на часы. – Что ж я так закопался? Да ещё пусть бы дело делал...» (Гоголь 3). "Oh, my, it's twelve o'clock already," said Chichikov, glancing at his watch. "Why have I been lingering over the stuff so long? Had I been doing something worthwhile, it wouldn't have been so bad..." (3c).

Д-81 • **(это) ДЕ́ЛО ДЕСЯ́ТОЕ ⟨ДЕВЯ́ТОЕ** obs, **ДВАД-ЦА́ТОЕ⟩** coll [NP; these forms only; subj-compl with быть∅ (subj: abstr, это, infin, or concr); pres only; fixed WO] **1.** sth. is not very important or essential: X — дело десятое ≃ **X is of little ⟨minor⟩ significance; X is no (very) great matter.**

...В течение нескольких дней [Василий Иванович], ни к селу ни к городу, всё твердил: «Ну, это дело девятое!» – потому только, что сын его, узнав, что он ходил к заутрене, употребил это выражение (Тургенев 2). For several days on end he kept on repeating at utterly inappropriate moments "Well, that's no very great matter!" simply because his son had used the expression on hearing that he attended matins (2e).

2. doing sth. is uncomplicated, simple: сделать X – дело десятое ≃ **doing X is a snap ⟨a cinch, no sweat, a piece of cake, as easy as pie⟩.**

Д-82 • **ДЕ́ЛО ДОХО́ДИТ/ДОШЛО́ ДО** [VP_subj] **1.** ~ чего things arrive at (a specific end): дело дошло до X-a ≃ **it came (down) to X; it ⟨this, things⟩ ended (up) in X;** ‖ если дело дойдёт до этого ≃ **if things come ⟨if it comes⟩ to that;** ‖ дело дошло до того, что... ≃ **it ⟨things⟩ reached ⟨got to⟩ the point where...**

Штаб-ротмистр на широкой и степенной кобыле шагом ехал навстречу Денисову. Штаб-ротмистр, с своими длинными усами, был серьёзен, как и всегда, только глаза его блестели больше обыкновенного. «Да что? – сказал он Денисову. – Не дойдёт дело до драки. Вот увидишь, назад уйдём» (Толстой 4). The staff captain on his steady, broad-backed mare rode at a walk to meet him [Denisov]. His face with its long moustache was serious as always, but his eyes were brighter than usual. "Well," he said to Denisov, "it won't come to a fight. You'll see, we'll move back again" (4a). ♦ Дядя Сандро... понимал, как легко будет Щащико, если дело дойдёт до этого, вскинуть винтовку и убить его (Искандер 3). Uncle Sandro...realized how easy it would be for Shashiko, if things came to that, to raise his rifle and kill

him (3a). ♦ Дело дошло до того, что сам Крыс... перестал спокойно спать по ночам... (Зиновьев 1). Things reached the point where Rat himself...stopped sleeping peacefully at nights... (1a).

2. ~ кого-чего s.o.'s or sth.'s turn arrives: дело дошло до X-a ≃ **X's turn came; it was X's turn.**

Князь Андрей простым глазом увидал внизу направо поднимавшуюся навстречу апшеронцам густую колонну французов, не дальше пятисот шагов от того места, где стоял Кутузов. «Вот она, наступила решительная минута! Дошло до меня дело», — подумал князь Андрей и, ударив лошадь, подъехал к Кутузову (Толстой 4). With the naked eye Prince Andrew saw below them to the right, not more than five hundred paces from where Kutuzov was standing, a dense French column coming up to meet the Apsherons. "Here it is! The decisive moment has arrived. My turn has come," thought Prince Andrew, and striking his horse he rode up to Kutuzov (4b).

Д-83 • **ДЕ́ЛО ЖИТЕ́ЙСКОЕ** coll [NP; Invar; subj-compl with быть∅ (subj: это, often omitted); pres only; fixed WO] this is a common occurrence, nothing unusual: **it happens; these ⟨those⟩ things happen; things like this ⟨that⟩ happen; it's nothing out of the ordinary; there's nothing out of the ordinary about it.**

Что, совсем нет денег? Возьмите у меня 20 рублей до получки. Дело житейское, со всяким может случиться. What, are you out of cash? Here's 20 roubles till payday. These things happen, it could happen to anyone. ♦ [Фёкла:] ...Уж каких женихов тебе припасла!.. Сегодня же иные и прибудут... [Агафья Тихоновна:] Как же сегодня? Душа моя, Фёкла Ивановна, я боюсь. [Фёкла:] И, не пугайся, мать моя! дело житейское. Придут, посмотрят, больше ничего (Гоголь 1). [F.:] You should see what suitors I've collected for you....Some of them will be here this very day.... [A.T.:] What! Today! Oh my dear Fyokla Ivanovna, I'm terrified. [F.:] Don't be frightened, my dear, there's nothing out of the ordinary about it. They'll come, they'll take a look at you and that's all (1a).

Д-84 • **ДЕ́ЛО ИДЁТ/ПОШЛО́** к чему [VP_subj; fixed WO] sth. is approaching, sth. is about to happen: дело идёт к X-у ≃ **things are heading toward ⟨to⟩ X; things are moving toward X; things are heading straight for X; it looks as if ⟨like⟩ there is going to be X; X is coming; the way things are going, there is bound to be X; [in limited contexts] X is in the air; X is brewing; [in refer. to seasons, holidays etc] X is on the way.**

Он прекрасно понимал, куда идёт дело — к роковому моменту, к скандалу, к катастрофе, к разоблачению! (Аксёнов 6). He knew perfectly well where things were heading—to the moment of truth, to a scandal, to catastrophe, to exposure! (6a). ♦ «Ну что ж, — помрачнел старший великан, — видно, дело идёт к свадьбе» (Искандер 5). "Well then," the eldest giant said darkly, "evidently things are moving toward a wedding" (5a).

Д-85 • **ДЕ́ЛО МА́СТЕРА БОИ́ТСЯ** [saying] a skillful person can handle any job quickly and well (said in praise of a person who shows ability and skill in his work): ≃ **know-how gets the job done best.**

Д-86 • **ДЕ́ЛО НАЖИВНО́Е** coll [NP; Invar; subj-compl with быть∅ (subj: concr, abstr, or, rare, human); pres only; fixed WO] (of money, material possessions etc or knowledge, some skill etc) sth. can or will be acquired eventually; (of a spouse, friends etc) some person can or will be gotten, won over eventually: X — дело наживное ≃ **it ⟨thing X⟩ will come with time; it's (just) a matter ⟨a question⟩ of time; [of knowledge or skills] one will pick it ⟨thing X⟩ up as one goes along; [of friends or money] X can (always) be made; there are always Xs ⟨there is always X⟩ to be made; [of a spouse or material possessions] X can (always) be gotten; [of material possessions only] there are always Xs to be had; X can be bought again.**

«Отпускные мои все до копейки кончились, а без денег далеко не разбежишься...» – «Деньги – дело наживное», – сказал Антон (Чернёнок 2). "I've spent the last cent of my vacation money, and you can't go far without money." "Money can be made," Anton said (2a). ♦ «...Ко мне приходил офицер, просят, чтобы дать несколько подвод под раненых. Ведь это всё дело наживное; а каково им оставаться, подумай!..» (Толстой 6). "...An officer came to me...they are begging me to let them have a few carts for the wounded....After all, it's only a question of a few things that can easily be bought again, and think what it means for them to be left behind!..." (6a).

Д-87 • ДЕЛО НЕ СТАНЕТ ⟨НЕ ПОСТОИТ obs⟩ за кем-чем coll [VP_subj; fut only; fixed WO] there will be no delay (in some matter) caused by s.o. or sth.: за X-ом дело не станет ≃ **X won't hold things up; doing thing X will be no problem at all ⟨shouldn't pose a problem, shouldn't be difficult, ought to be easy enough etc⟩; person X won't stand in the way; person X will see to it that the matter is not dragged out;** [in refer. to s.o.'s reliability, readiness to provide help etc] **person Y can count on X.**

...[Владимир] поехал искать свидетелей между соседними помещиками. Первый, к кому явился он, отставной сорокалетний корнет Дравин, согласился с охотою... Он уговорил Владимира остаться у него отобедать и уверил его, что за другими двумя свидетелями дело не станет (Пушкин 3). ...He [Vladimir] went in search of potential witnesses among the landowners of the neighborhood. The first one he called on, a forty-year-old retired cavalry officer by the name of Dravin, consented with pleasure....He persuaded Vladimir to stay for dinner, assuring him that finding two more witnesses would be no problem at all (3a). ♦ «Идите к Ивану Григорьевичу, – сказал Иван Антонович голосом несколько поласковее, – пусть он даст приказ... а за нами дело не постоит» (Гоголь 3). "Go and see Ivan Grigorievich," Ivan Antonovich said in a more friendly tone. "If he issues the order, we'll see to it that the matter is not dragged out" (3e). ♦ «Эта княжна Лиговская пренесносная девчонка! Вообразите, толкнула меня и не извинилась... Уж её надо бы проучить...» – «За этим дело не станет!» – отвечал услужливый капитан... (Лермонтов 1). [context transl] "This young Princess Ligovskaya is a minx. Think of it, she bumped into me and did not bother to apologise....It would do her good to be taught a lesson...." "Leave it to me!" replied the obliging captain... (1b).

Д-88 • ДЕЛО НЕЧИСТО coll [NP; Invar; VP_subj with copula; pres or, rare, past; fixed WO] sth. is suspicious, may be not entirely legal: **it looks ⟨seems⟩ crooked ⟨fishy, shady, underhanded, slippery⟩; this is a crooked ⟨fishy, shady⟩ business; there's something going on here ⟨there⟩;** [in limited contexts] **there's more here than meets the eye.**

Д-89 • ДЕЛО НЕШУТОЧНОЕ; ШУТОЧНОЕ (ЛИ) ДЕЛО both coll [NP; these forms only; subj-compl with copula (subj: usu. infin or это); fixed WO] sth. is very serious, must be treated seriously: (делать) X – дело нешуточное ≃ **(doing) X is no ⟨not a⟩ laughing matter; (doing) X is no joke ⟨no joking matter, nothing to laugh at⟩.**

Потолкуйте с любым мыслящим человеком, и он вам скажет... что вступать в единоборство со Сперанским – дело нешуточное (Ерофеев 3). Talk with any thinking person and he will tell you...that taking on Speransky personally is not a laughing matter (3a). ♦ ...В наш просвещённый век утерять из виду целый город с самостоятельною цивилизацией и с громадными богатствами в недрах земли – дело нешуточное (Салтыков-Щедрин 2). ...To lose a whole city with an independent civilization and untold riches buried in the bowels of the earth is no joke in our present enlightened age (2a).

Д-90 • ДЕЛО ПАХНЕТ КЕРОСИНОМ highly coll [sent; pres or past; fixed WO] this is a bad situation, nothing good will come of it (used when s.o. is about to fail, when it is clear that a conflict is about to arise, when s.o. realizes that sth. desired will not materialize etc): **things are in a bad way; this means trouble; person X is in big ⟨a heap of⟩ trouble.**

Д-91 • ДЕЛО (чьё) ПЛОХО coll; **ДЕЛО ДРЯНЬ ⟨ШВАХ⟩** highly coll [NP; these forms only; VP_subj with быть_ø, pres only] **1.** s.o. is in very bad physical condition, is very ill, seriously injured etc: (X-ово) дело дрянь ≃ **X is in bad shape ⟨in a bad way⟩; things look bad.**

...Ему [Рослякову] было очень страшно опустить глаза, чтобы рану посмотреть... «Что? – спросил [Росляков] сестру, стоявшую всё время возле него с нашатырём и шприцем. – Дрянь дело?» – «Да что вы, – ответила сестра. – Пустяки...» (Семёнов 1). ...He [Roslyakov] was terrified of lowering his head to look at the wound... "How is it?" said Roslyakov to the nurse who stood beside him the whole time, holding the sal ammoniac and a hypodermic. "Do things look bad?" "What do you mean?" replied the nurse, "nonsense..." (1a).

2. the situation is extremely unfavorable (for s.o.), nothing good will come of it: (X-ово) дело дрянь ≃ **it ⟨this⟩ is (a) bad business; this means trouble; things are in a bad way; things look bad (for X); X is in trouble ⟨in hot water, in a real mess⟩; the situation is bad.**

Прокурор давеча сказал – дело плохо, кто-то должен сесть в тюрьму (Тендряков 1). The Prosecutor had said yesterday that it was a bad business, and that someone could go to prison for it (1a). ♦ ...[Дядя Сандро] уныло поднялся в дом, где не только не нашли Тали, а, наоборот, обнаружили, что исчез патефон... Тут всем стало ясно, что дело плохо, и стали искать её обратные следы... (Искандер). He [Uncle Sandro] climbed dolefully up to the house, where they not only had not found Tali, but, on the contrary, had discovered that the phonograph was gone....By now it was clear to everyone that this was bad business. They began hunting for her return tracks... (3a). ♦ ...Жена прокурора... стала уверять [Хабуга], что прокурора нет дома, что он завтра будет у себя в кабинете и что он вообще теперь про дела разговаривает только у себя в кабинете. Тут старый Хабуг понял, что дело плохо, но решил подождать до следующего дня (Искандер 3). ...The magistrate's wife...assured him [Khabug] that the magistrate was not home, that he would be in his office tomorrow, and that nowadays he generally discussed business only in his office. Old Khabug realized that this meant trouble, but he decided to wait until the next day (3a). ♦ Он [адвокат] меня слушает, изредка задаёт вопросы, прикрывая рот ладонью, – признак, что алкаш... Я вижу перед собой алкаша, понимаю, что дело плохо... с таким алкашом мы дело проиграем... (Рыбаков 1). He [the lawyer] listened to me, putting a question occasionally, and covering his mouth with his hand, the sure sign of a drunk....I was looking at an alcoholic and I knew the situation was bad...with an alcoholic like this one we would lose the case... (1a).

Д-92 • ДЕЛО ПРОШЛОЕ coll [NP; Invar; sent adv (parenth) or subj-compl with быть_ø (subj: usu. abstr or это), pres only; fixed WO] it is already over and is not important now: **that's a thing of the past; that's all over now; that's all in the past; it doesn't matter anymore ⟨any more⟩; what's done is done.**

«Дело прошлое, а кто старое вспомянет – тому глаз вон» (Шолохов 5). "It's all over now, so let bygones be bygones" (5a). ♦ [Золотуев:] Ну, говорит ему [ревизору] продавец, дело прошлое, а скажи-ка ты теперь мне, дорогой товарищ, откровенно: сколько тебе тогда дать надо было? (Вампилов 3). [Z.:] Well, the salesclerk says to him [the inspector general], all that's in the past. But tell me honestly, dear comrade, how much should I have offered you then? (3b). ♦ Скажу коротко, я уснул... Видит бог, дело прошлое, я изо всех сил крепился и наконец, как это бывает на собраниях, если сидишь где-нибудь в задних рядах, решил на минуточку прикорнуть, с тем чтобы потом очнуться с посвежевшей головой (Искандер 3). To put it briefly, I fell asleep.... Goodness knows, it doesn't matter any more; I resisted with all my might and at last, as happens at meetings if you sit anywhere in the back rows, I decided to lean back a moment in order to awake with my mind refreshed (3a).

Д-93 • **ДЕ́ЛО РУК** *чьих, кого usu. disapprov* [NP; sing only; usu. subj-compl with copula, nom or instrum (subj: это, abstr, or concr denoting the result of some action) or obj] sth. has been executed, carried out, or masterminded, by none other than the person specified (usu. used in refer. to reprehensible actions): это дело рук X-а ≃ **this is X's handiwork ⟨doing⟩; this is the work of X; X ⟨it is X who⟩ has done it; this has been arranged by X; X is behind this ⟨it⟩;** [in limited contexts] **X is to blame (for this).**

«Пропавший из машины бензин — это дело рук Реваза» (Чернёнок 2). "That missing gas—that's Revaz's handiwork" (2a). ♦ Обоих парней убили в ту же ночь, как привели в тюрьму... Камера была большая, дружная, так и не дознались, чьих рук дело (Рыбаков 2). The two boys had been murdered the night they arrived at the prison....They had been put in a big cell, where the inmates were all friends, so it had been impossible to find out who had done it (2a). ♦ Путешествие в Армению, квартира, пайки, договоры на последующие издания. — всё это дело рук Бухарина (Мандельштам 1). The journey to Armenia, our apartment and ration cards, contracts for future volumes.—all this was arranged by Bukharin (1a). ♦ «Да ведь как же *мы* всё время лжём... как *мы* извращаем историю... да ведь Катынский-то лес — это же *наших* рук дело...» (Аксёнов 7). "We never stop lying, you know what I mean? We're constantly distorting history: the Katyn Forest incident—we're completely to blame" (7a).

Д-94 • **ДЕ́ЛО СЛУ́ЧАЯ** [NP; sing only; subj-compl with быть₀, nom or instrum (subj: это, abstr, concr, infin, or a clause); fixed WO] what happens depends on chance, is beyond s.o.'s control: X дело случая ≃ **X is a matter of luck ⟨chance, fortuity⟩; X is a question of luck;** ‖ это ⟨сделать X⟩ дело случая ≃ **it ⟨doing X⟩ is (all) a matter of luck ⟨chance, fortuity⟩; it ⟨doing X⟩ is (all) a question of luck; it's (all) up to chance ⟨fate⟩.**

Всё в этой области определялось инстинктом-вдохновением, всякая удача была делом случая, неожиданностью для самого поэта (Лившиц 1). In this area everything depended on instinct and inspiration. Every success was a matter of fortuity, and surprised the poet himself (1a). ♦ «Добывайте командировку, — говорил ему носильщик в белом фартуке. — Надо каждый день наведываться. Поезда теперь редкость, дело случая» (Пастернак 1). "You must get a priority," a porter in a white apron told him. "Then you must come every day to ask if there is a train. Trains are rare nowadays, it's a question of luck" (1a).

Д-95 • **ДЕ́ЛО** *(чьё)* ⟨**ДЕЛА́** *(чьи)*⟩ **ТАБА́К** ⟨**ТРУБА́**⟩ *highly coll* [NP; these forms only; used as VP_subj with быть₀, pres only] s.o. is in a desperate situation that is sure to end badly (for him): дело (X-ово) табак ≃ **X is in trouble ⟨in hot water, in a real mess⟩; X is done for; all is lost (for X); things are bad ⟨hopeless, in a bad way⟩ (for X); X is up the creek (without a paddle); it's all over for X;** [in limited contexts] **it's curtains for X.**

[Кривой Зоб:] Без руки ты — никуда не годишься!.. Нет руки — и человека нет! Табак твоё дело!.. (Горький 3). [K.Z.:] Without a hand you're good for nothing!...Having no hand is as being no man! You're done for!... (3a). ♦ «А что, хлопцы, дело табак? — сказал дед. — Киев сдают» (Кузнецов 1). "Well, boys, all is lost, eh?" said Grandfather. "They're surrendering Kiev" (1a). ♦ Дед заговорил о том, о чём Кузьма со страхом думал и сам:

денег в деревне немного... Но не мог же Кузьма согласиться с дедом, что да, дело табак, он не имел права даже так думать. И он сказал: «Найдём, дед, найдём» (Распутин 1). The old man had put into words Kuzma's own fears. There was very little money in the village....But Kuzma could not accept the old man's conclusions that things were hopeless. He had no right to think so, and he said: "We'll find a way out, Grandad" (1a). ♦ «Ох, парень, я сам вижу, что дело наше — табак, а всё как-то не верится...» — вздохнул Прохор (Шолохов 5). "Ay, lad, I can see for myself we're up the creek, but I still can't believe it somehow..." Prokhor sighed (5a).

Д-96 • **ДЕ́ЛО ХОЗЯ́ЙСКОЕ** *coll* [NP; Invar; used as an indep. remark or subj-compl with быть₀ (subj: это, abstr, infin, or a clause), pres only; fixed WO] sth. (usu. a decision to act in a specific way) rests with s.o., s.o. can do what he wants: это дело хозяйское ≃ **it's up to you ⟨him etc⟩; it's your ⟨his etc⟩ choice ⟨decision, business⟩; do ⟨let him etc do⟩ what you think ⟨he thinks etc⟩ best;** [in limited contexts] **suit yourself ⟨-selves⟩.**

«Так пойдёшь ужинать?» — «Не хочется». — «Дело хозяйское. Как хочешь» (Залыгин 1). "Are you going to get supper?" "I don't feel like it." "Suit yourself. Do as you like" (1a).

Д-97 • **ДО́ХЛОЕ ДЕ́ЛО; ДО́ХЛЫЙ НО́МЕР** *both highly coll* [NP; sing only; subj-compl with copula, nom or instrum (subj: это, abstr, or infin), pres only] some undertaking is doomed to fail: это дохлое дело ≃ **it's a lost cause; it's a bad business;** [in limited contexts] **the game ⟨the jig⟩ is up.**

«Капарин... с тобой вчера об чём-то долго разговаривал... Дохлое это дело, когда из пятерых двое начинают наиздальке держаться, секреты разводить...» (Шолохов 5). "Yesterday he [Kaparin] had a very long talk with you....It's a bad business when two out of five keep apart from the others, having secrets..." (5a). ♦ «Какая жалость, что вы нам дали нам как-нибудь знать. Нужно было бы Ванду Михайловну послать к нам через чёрный ход», — говорил Николка, капая со свечи стеарином. «Ну, брат, не очень-то, — отозвался Мышлаевский, — когда уже они [бандиты] были в квартире, это, друг, дело довольно дохлое. Ты думаешь, они не стали бы защищаться? Ещё как» (Булгаков 3). "What a pity you didn't warn us somehow. You should have sent Wanda Mikhailovna up to us by the back door," said Nikolka, wax dripping from his candle. "That wouldn't have done much good," Myshlaevsky objected. "By the time they [the burglars] were in the apartment the game was up. You don't believe they wouldn't have put up a fight, do you? Of course they would—and how" (3a).

Д-98 • **ДРУГО́Е** ⟨**ИНО́Е**⟩ **ДЕ́ЛО** [NP; these forms only] **1.** [subj-compl with быть₀ (subj: usu. это or a clause); often preceded by тогда, теперь] that changes (or would change) the situation: **that's another ⟨a different⟩ story (altogether); that's (quite) another ⟨a different⟩ matter; (now) it's (very ⟨totally⟩) different; things are ⟨will be⟩ different; that's different ⟨something else altogether⟩;** [in fut and condit clauses] **things ⟨everything⟩ will ⟨would⟩ be different.**

...Как можно управлять таким способом неодушевлённым предметом? Если внутри предмета человек находится, тогда другое дело: он исполняет указания — делай так, делай этак (Айтматов 2). How on earth could you control a soulless object in that way? If there was a man inside that object, then that was another story—he would carry out the orders, do this, do that, as he was told (2a). ♦ «Ну, прикажут тебя тронуть — другое дело, я присягу давал или не давал?» (Владимов 1). "Of course, if I'm ordered to lay hands on you, that's another matter. I took the oath of allegiance when I joined the army, didn't I?" (1a). ♦ ...Она едет в Крым ради него, он просил её, она согласилась поехать, но ни на что другое согласия не давала... Другое дело, если бы она влюбилась... (Рыбаков 2). She was going to the Crimea for his sake—he had asked her and she had agreed, but that was all she had agreed to....It would be different if she were in love with him... (2a). ♦ «Да вы *освободите меня от марксизма-ленинизма*, тогда другое дело. А пока — мы на нём стоим» (Солженицын 2). "Well, *emancipate me from Marxism-Leninism*, and things will be different. Till then, it's on Marxism-Leninism that we take our stand" (2a). ♦ [Анна Петровна:] Как бы папенька-то твой не мотал без памяти, так бы другое дело было, а то оставил нас почти ни с чем (Островский 1). [A.P.:] If only your papa hadn't spent his money like water, then everything'd be different. As it is, he left us almost nothing at all (1a). ♦ «Почему ж бы я мог быть известен про Дмитрия Фёдоровича: другое дело, кабы я при них сторожем состоял?» — тихо, раздельно и пренебрежительно ответил Смердяков (Достоевский 1). [context transl] "Why should I be informed as to Dmitri Fyodorovich? It's not as if I were his keeper," Smerdyakov answered quietly, distinctly, and superciliously (1a).

2. [subj-compl with быть∅ (subj: any noun or infin)] a person (thing etc) is very different from another person (thing etc) mentioned previously: X — другое дело ≃ **X is ⟨that's⟩ (quite) another ⟨a different⟩ matter; X is ⟨it's⟩ another ⟨a different⟩ story; X is something else (entirely);** ‖ одно дело... и (совсем) другое дело... ≃ **it's one thing...but ⟨and⟩ (quite) another...**

«А я что такое? Обломов — больше ничего. Вот Штольц — другое дело: Штольц — ум... уменье управлять собой, другими...» (Гончаров 1). "But what am I? Oblomov—nothing more. Stolz, now, is another matter: Stolz has intelligence...he knows how to control himself and others..." (1b). ♦ «Ты знаешь: нарисовал этот Евдокимов похабную карикатуру на декана...» — «Который её заслуживал! Ну, скажи, нет! Ты ведь сам его терпеть не можешь». Игорь невольно оглянулся на дверь. «Я — другое дело, — сказал он кисло. — Не вали, пожалуйста, всех в одну кучу» (Ерофеев 3). "You know that Evdokimov drew a smutty caricature of the Dean..." "And he deserved it. Go on, deny it! You know you can't stand him yourself." Igor couldn't keep himself from glancing at the door. "What I think is something else entirely," he said in a sour voice. "Please don't put everyone in the same bag..." (3a). ♦ «...Одно дело попасть молотком в стекло критику Латунскому и совсем другое дело — ему же в сердце» (Булгаков 9). "It's one thing to hit Latunsky's window with a hammer, but quite another to hit the critic's heart" (9a).

3. [main clause in a complex sent, foll. by a что-clause] it should be mentioned, however, that... (used to detract from the merit of sth. previously mentioned): **(the fact) that...is another matter; ...but that's another matter ⟨story⟩.**

Ляля очень хорошенькая. Другое дело, что она круглая дура. Lyalya is very pretty. The fact that she doesn't have a brain in her head is another matter.

Д-99 • ЕСТЬ ТАКОЕ ДЕЛО coll [sent; Invar; fixed WO] used to express ready agreement to do sth.: **it's a deal!; agreed!; sure thing!;** [in limited contexts] **right away!**

Д-100 • ЗА ДЕЛО(!)[1] [sent; Invar] (usu. used as a command or prompting) start working or let us start working): **let's) get down ⟨back⟩ to work; let's) get to it ⟨to work⟩!; to work!**

«Теперь за дело!» — прошептал один сообщник. «Ну нет, — заявила Мари, — я теперь займусь изучением [документов]». Слово это прозвучало торжественно, и все согласились, что без изучения приступить к делу нельзя (Федин 1). "Now to work!" whispered one accomplice. "Oh, no," announced Marie, "now I shall do some studying." This word rang out solemnly and all agreed that to get down to work without studying [the documents] was impossible (1a).

Д-101 • ЗА ДЕЛО(!)[2] наказать, наградить, посадить (в тюрьму) и т. п. [PrepP; Invar; adv] (to punish, reward, imprison etc s.o.) deservedly, in correspondence with s.o.'s deeds: **(and) rightly so; s.o. deserves ⟨has earned⟩ sth. ⟨it⟩; for good reason; for a (good) reason; with good reason ⟨cause⟩; for what s.o. did; for cause;** [in limited contexts] **there is a real case against s.o.**

[Фира:] Слушай, мы узнали — завтра день рождения Анны Сергеевны. [Олег:] Физички? [Фира:] Да, ей исполняется семьдесят лет... Надо срочно в стенгазету вклеить стихи — напиши. [Олег:] Ей? Ни за что! Она мне тройку... закатила. [Фира:] Так за дело!.. Ты же ничего не знал (Розов 2). [F.:] We've just heard that tomorrow is Anna Sergeyevna's birthday. [O.:] The physics teacher? [F.:] Yes, she'll be seventy....We must have some verses for the wall newspaper. We'll stick them in somehow. Write something. [O.:] To her? Never! She's...given me a "fair." [F.:] But you deserved it!...You didn't know a thing (2a). ♦ Он гордился тем, что, в отличие от массы политических заключённых, сидел за дело: написал статью под заголовком «Государство Ленина-Сталина» и давал её читать студентам (Гроссман 2). He was proud of the fact that, unlike the majority of the political prisoners, he was there [in the camp] for a reason: he had written an article entitled "The State of Lenin and Stalin" and distributed it to his students (2a). ♦ «Я именно *заслуженно* пострадал... Словечко-то какое! Заслуженно! Меня посадили за *дело*» (Битов 2). "I suffered *deservedly*! What a word! Deserv-edly! They put me away for what I *did*" (2a). ♦ «Случалось, [принц Ольденбургский] поваров палкой бивал, но всегда за дело» (Искандер 3). "Sometimes he [Prince Oldenburgsky] used to beat the cooks with his cane, but always for cause" (3a). ♦ «Имейте в виду, в ссылке ни один человек не скажет вам правды: кто сидит за дело — делает вид, что сидит ни за что...» (Рыбаков 2). "Remember this: nobody in exile ever tells the truth—if someone's here because there was a real case against him, he makes out he's here for nothing..." (2a).

Д-102 • ЗА МАЛЫМ ⟨ЗА НЕБОЛЬШИМ, ЗА НЕМНОГИМ⟩ ДЕЛО СТАЛО coll, iron [sent; these forms only] the completion of some matter, realization of some plan etc is contingent upon some factor that is presented as small but, in fact, is absolutely crucial: **there's only one little thing left (to be done etc); there's only one last little hurdle; there's only one little detail that has to be taken care of; there's (only) one small ⟨last⟩ hitch; there remains just one minor ⟨small⟩ problem.**

Д-103 • ЗА ЧЕМ ⟨ЗА КЕМ, ЗА ТЕМ и т. п.⟩ ДЕЛО СТАЛО? coll [sent; these forms only; fixed WO] what or who is impeding progress in some matter?: **what's the hitch ⟨the holdup⟩?; what's ⟨who's⟩ standing in the ⟨your etc⟩ way?; what's ⟨who's⟩ stopping ⟨preventing⟩ you (from doing sth.)?**

Она устраивала выставку, и я сказал Коломийченко, что неплохо было бы пригласить Гюзель. «За чем дело стало», — сказал лучший покровитель искусств... (Амальрик 1). She was organizing an exhibit, and I told Kolomiychenko that it wouldn't be a bad idea to invite Gusel to show some of her work there. "Well," said the best local patron of the arts, "what's the hitch?" (1a). ♦ [Аннушка:] [У вас] приданого нет. [Отрадина:] Так ты думаешь, что только за тем и дело стало? (Островский 3). [A.:] You've got no money. [O.:] You think that is what is standing in the way? (3a). ♦ [Кочкарёв:] Разве тебе не нравится женатая жизнь, что ли? [Подколёсин:] Нет... нравится. [Кочкарёв:] Ну, так что ж? За чем дело стало? (Гоголь 1). [K.:] Don't you like the idea of married life? [P.:] No...I like it. [K.:] What is it then? What's stopping you? (1b).

Д-104 • И ДЕЛО С КОНЦОМ; И ДЕЛУ КОНЕЦ both coll [sent; these forms only; usu. the concluding clause in a compound or complex sent; usu. refers to the completion of sth. in the future; fixed WO] and then everything will be finished: **and that will be the end of it ⟨the matter, the business⟩; and that will be that ⟨it⟩; and it will all be over;** [in limited contexts, usu. after imper] **and (let's) leave it at that.**

Толпе этот ответ не понравился, да и вообще она ожидала не того. Ей казалось, что Грустилов, как только приведут к нему Линкина, разорвёт его пополам — и дело с концом (Салтыков-Щедрин 1). This reply was not much to the liking of the crowd, who had anyway expected something quite different. They had supposed that as soon as they brought Linkin to Grustilov, the governor would tear him in two, and that would be the end of it (1b). ♦ «На железной дороге, в нескольких перегонах отсюда стоит казачий полк. Красный, преданный. Их вызовут, бунтовщиков окружат и дело с концом» (Пастернак 1). "There is a Cossack regiment stationed a short distance down the railway.…It's Red, it's loyal. It will be called out, the rebels will be surrounded, and that will be the end of the business" (1a). ♦ …В те времена женились — и дело с концом, автомашин с разноцветными лентами и куклами на радиаторах не было (Рыбаков 1). In those days you just got married and that was that, no cars tied with coloured ribbons and dolls on the radiators? (1a). ♦ «А зачем тебе делать эту идеологию? Плюнь! Изучай себе наше общество, и дело с концом» (Зиновьев 2). "But why do you want to produce this ideology? Forget it! Just go ahead with your study of our society, and leave it at that!" (2a).

Д-105 • **И ТО́ ДЕ́ЛО** *highly coll* [sent; Invar; fixed WO] (used to express agreement with the words of one's interlocutor) right, correct: **it's ⟨that's, 'tis⟩ true; quite ⟨you're⟩ right; you've got a point (there); I see your point; there's something in that; you may be right about that;** [in limited contexts] **that's reasonable enough.**

«Нечего мне под старость лет расставаться с тобою да искать одинокой могилы на чужой сторонке. Вместе жить, вместе и умирать». — «И то дело», — сказал комендант (Пушкин 2). "There is no earthly reason why I should part with you in my old age and seek a lonely grave in a strange place. Together we have lived, together we will die." "You may be right about that," said the commandant (2a).

Д-106 • **ИЗВЕ́СТНОЕ ДЕ́ЛО** *highly coll* [NP; Invar; sent adv (parenth) or an indep. remark; more often this WO] (used to emphasize that what is stated contains nothing surprising) as could be expected: **(quite) naturally; sure enough; sure thing;** [in limited contexts] **you know how it is; that's for sure.**

«Ослица эта, например, известная. „Валаам, Валаам, говорит… не ходи туда, сам пожалеешь". Ну, известное дело, он не послушал, пошёл» (Пастернак 1). "Take the famous she-ass, for instance. 'Balaam, Balaam,' she says, 'listen to me, don't go that way…you'll be sorry.' Well, naturally, he wouldn't listen, he went on" (1a). ♦ «Заграница, — говорил Александр Семёнович, выкладывая яйца на деревянный стол, — разве это наши мужицкие яйца… Все, вероятно, брамапутры, чёрт их возьми! немецкие…» — «Известное дело», — подтверждал охранитель, любуясь яйцами (Булгаков 10). "That's Europe for you," said Alexander Semyonovich, laying out the eggs on the wooden table. "What did you expect—our measly little peasant eggs? They must be Brahmaputras, all of them, the devil take 'em! German." "Sure thing," echoed the guard, admiring the eggs (10a). ♦ «…Ехал [я] по грязи, в одном хуторе машину мою занесло, а тут корова подвернулась, я и сбил её с ног. Ну, известное дело, бабы крик подняли…» (Шолохов 1). "I was driving along a muddy road through a village and I went into a skid. There happened to be a cow in the way and I knocked it over. Well, you know how it is—the women raised a hullabaloo…" (1c).

Д-107 • **ИМЕ́ТЬ ДЕ́ЛО** [VP; subj: human or collect]   **1.** ~ *с кем-чем* to encounter, come across s.o. or sth. (a rare phenomenon, strange fact, unusual personality etc): **X имеет дело с Y-ом ≃ X is dealing with Y; X is faced ⟨confronted⟩ with thing Y; X meets with thing Y;** [in refer. to people or phenomena that challenge or threaten one] **X is up against;** ‖ **X знает ⟨понимает и т. п.⟩, с кем ⟨чем⟩ он имеет дело ≃** [in limited contexts] **X knows ⟨understands etc⟩ who ⟨what⟩ Y is.**

Мы имеем дело с явлением, которое наука пока объяснить не может. We are dealing with a phenomenon that science has not yet been able to explain. ♦ Его [императора] крайне забавляло, что она [девушка] не догадывалась вовсе, с кем имеет дело, и

держала себя с ним на равных (Окуджава 2). He [the emperor] was vastly amused that she [the girl] had no idea who he was and behaved as though they were equals (2a).

2. ~ *с кем* [obj: human or collect; often infin with можно, нельзя, трудно, приятно, не хочу, не советую etc] to have or enter into some kind of relations with s.o. (occas. in refer. to an argument, fight, or punishment): **X имеет дело с Y-ом ≃ X deals ⟨has dealings⟩ with Y;** ‖ **X не хочет иметь дело с Y-ом ≃ X doesn't want to deal ⟨have (any) dealings, have any truck, be involved⟩ with Y; X doesn't want (to have) anything to do with Y;** ‖ **X будет иметь дело с Y-ом ≃** [used as a threat] **X will have Y to reckon with.**

«Ведь нельзя же иметь дело с человеком, который никого не слушает!» (Булгаков 12). "How can one deal with a man who never listens to anybody?" (12a). ♦ Ипполит Матвеевич никогда ещё не имел дела с таким темпераментным молодым человеком, как Бендер… (Ильф и Петров 1). Ippolit Matveyevich had never had dealings with so spirited a young man as Ostap Bender… (1a). ♦ Социальное действие… есть действие [индивида] по отношению к другому индивиду или к другим индивидам… К числу таких действий относятся часто встречающиеся действия, которые можно обозначить как действия «Я готов на всё, что вам угодно», «На меня можно рассчитывать», «Я с вами не хочу иметь дела» и т. п. (Зиновьев 1). A social action…is an action [of an individual] directed towards another individual or to other individuals.…Such actions include frequent examples of the type "I am willing to do anything you want," "You can count on me," "I don't want anything to do with you," and so on (1a).

3. ~ *с чем* [prep obj: usu. a noun denoting an instrument, gadget, object, or material one works with] to make use of sth.: **X имел дело с Y-ом ≃ X used ⟨dealt with, handled⟩ Y.**

Я никогда не имел дела с электронным микроскопом, но уверен, что научусь быстро. I've never used an electron microscope before, but I'm sure I'll learn quickly.

Д-108 • **КАКО́Е ⟨ЧТО ЗА⟩ ДЕ́ЛО** *кому (до кого-чего)* *coll* [VP_subj with быть∅; these forms only; var. with что за is usu. pres; fixed WO] sth. has absolutely no bearing on s.o.'s life or affairs, and s.o. is entirely unconcerned about and indifferent to it: **какое X-у дело до Y-а? ≃ what has thing Y ⟨it⟩ got to do with X?; what business is it of X's?; what does X care (about Y)?; Y is ⟨that's⟩ no concern of X's; thing Y is of no concern to X; why should it concern X?; what's it to X?;** ‖ **кому какое дело до Y-а? ≃ who cares about Y?**

[Михаил:] Рабочие каждый праздник бьют друг друга по зубам, — какое нам до этого дело? (Горький 1). [M.:] Every holiday the workers go around bashing each other on the jaw—what's it got to do with us? (1b). ♦ «Хорошо, смейтесь, да ведь государство погибнет без правительства». — «А мне что за дело!» (Герцен 3). "All right: laugh; but the State will perish, you know, without a government." "And what business is that of mine?" (3a). ♦ Какое ему было дело до этого дурацкого портфеля, до брошенного родителями мальчишки, племянника жены… (Айтматов 1). What did he care about a stupid briefcase, about his wife's nephew, a kid abandoned by his parents… (1b). ♦ Что сталось с старухой и с бедным слепым — не знаю. Да и какое дело мне до радостей и бедствий человеческих… (Лермонтов 1). I've no idea what became of the old woman and the poor blind boy. And anyway, the joys and tribulations of mankind are of no concern to me… (1c). ♦ …Во всём виновата Зоя… если бы не она, я бы и думать не стал об этом проклятом Дне убийств. Какое мне дело до него? (Аржак 1). …It was all Zoya's fault. If it hadn't been for her I wouldn't have given that damned Murder Day a second thought. Why should it concern me? (1a). ♦ «И какое им [этой гордой знати] дело, есть ли ум под нумерованной фуражкой и сердце под толстой шинелью?» (Лермонтов 1). "What is it to them [these haughty aristocrats] if there is an intellect under a numbered cap and a heart beneath a thick greatcoat?" (1b). ♦ Кому какое дело, приветливая или огрызающаяся улыбка играет у него на устах? (Салтыков-Щедрин 2). Who cares whether the smile that plays on his lips is kindly or caustic? (2a).

Д-109 • **КОМУ́ КАКО́Е ДЕ́ЛО, ЧТО КУМА́ С КУ́МОМ СИДЕ́ЛА** [saying] it should not (or does not) concern anyone other than the persons involved (said in response to an allusion to s.o.'s intimate relations): ≃ **that's nobody's business but their own; that's their ⟨his etc⟩ affair (, not yours ⟨ours etc⟩).**

Д-110 • **КО́НЧИЛ ДЕ́ЛО – ГУЛЯ́Й СМЕ́ЛО** [saying] after you have finished your work, you can put it out of your mind and rest: ≃ **work is done, time for fun; work well done makes rest sweet.**

Д-111 • **ЛЕЗТЬ ⟨СОВА́ТЬСЯ⟩ НЕ В СВОЁ ДЕ́ЛО** *coll, rather rude;* **ВМЕ́ШИВАТЬСЯ НЕ В СВОЁ ДЕ́ЛО** [VP; subj: human; often neg imper] to interfere in sth. that has no relation to one: X лезет не в своё дело ≃ **X sticks ⟨pokes⟩ his nose into person Y's ⟨someone else's⟩ business; X messes in ⟨butts into⟩ someone else's affairs; X interferes in other people's business;** ‖ *Neg Imper* не лезь ⟨не суйся⟩ не в своё дело ≃ **mind your own business; keep out of this; keep out of what does not concern you; stay in your own backyard.**

«Если ты заблудилась, — всё звончей кричала Люда, чуя победу, — вместо монастыря попала в аспирантуру, — так сиди в углу и не будь свекровью. Надоело! Старая дева!» — «Людка! Не смей!» — закричала Оленька. «А чего она не в своё дело...?» (Солженицын 3). "If you got lost on the way," Lyuda shouted even louder, sensing victory, "and instead of landing in a nunnery you turned up here doing graduate work, all right then, sit there in your corner, but don't act like such a stepmother. It makes me sick. Old maid!" "Lyuda, don't you dare!" Olenka screamed. "Then what's she doing sticking her nose into everyone else's business?" (3a). ♦ [author's usage] Казангап, патриарх бороанлинцев, притом очень тактичный, никогда не вмешивавшийся не в свои дела, пребывал ещё в полной силе и крепком здравии (Айтматов 2). At that time, Kazangap, as the patriarch of the people of Boranly, was always very tactful, never interfering in other people's business, and was still proud and in excellent health (2a). ♦ «Они [женщины] ничего не посмеют сказать председателю, он им ответит: не лезьте не в своё дело» (Рыбаков 2). "They [the women] wouldn't dare say anything to the manager—he'd only tell them to mind their own business" (2a). ♦ Фигура приближается к машине. Это солдат. Он весь в снегу. Пола шинели оторвана. «Чем побито?» — спрашивает Карпов... «Пулями побило!» — говорю я. «Не суйтесь не в своё дело», — говорит Карпов (Окуджава 1). The figure comes up to the car. It's a soldier. He's covered in snow. One side of his greatcoat has been ripped off. "What were they hit by?" asks Karpov.... "Hit by bullets," I say. "You keep out of this," says Karpov (1a).

Д-112 • **МИ́ЛОЕ ДЕ́ЛО** *coll* [NP; Invar; fixed WO] **1.** [subj-compl with быть∅ (subj: concr, abstr, or infin), pres only, or indep. sent] sth. is most satisfying, agreeable, enjoyable: X — (самое) милое дело ≃ **X is the best ⟨the greatest⟩ (thing); X is a great thing; you can't beat X.**

«Одно жалею, — говорил он, — не я ему [Сталину], живоглоту любимому, гроб делал... На крышку изнутри самшит бы я пустил... Нет, лучше сандал, он пахнет... Спи только, родной, не просыпайся! Самое тебе милое дело — спать» (Владимов 1). "There's only one thing I regret," he said, "and that is that I didn't make Stalin's coffin, the dear old monster....I'd have lined the cover with boxwood....No, sandalwood's better; it has a strong scent....Just so as you stay asleep, old pal, and don't wake up! The best thing you ever did was sleep" (1a). ♦ «Время-то надо убить, правда? В дороге шахматы — милое дело», — доб-

родушно приговаривал Г.О., расставляя фигуры (Аксёнов 9). "We've got to kill time, right?...you can't beat a game of chess on a trip," G.O. chattered as he arranged the chessmen (9a).

2. *iron* [Interj] how wonderful (used ironically to express dissatisfaction, surprise, indignation etc): **that's just great ⟨terrific⟩!; (oh) great, just great!;** [in limited contexts] **just what I need!; just what I wanted ⟨needed⟩ to hear!**

Д-113 • **МИНУ́ТНОЕ ДЕ́ЛО** *coll* [NP; sing only; subj-compl with copula, nom or instrum (subj: usu. infin or это), or obj] an uncomplicated job, task etc that takes very little time to do: **(it) only takes a minute; it can be done in a flash ⟨in no time⟩;** [in limited contexts] **(it's) nothing; (it's) a snap ⟨a breeze, a cinch etc⟩.**

Д-114 • **МОЁ ⟨твоё, ваше и т. п.⟩ ДЕ́ЛО** [NP; these forms only; subj-compl with быть∅ (subj: usu. это or infin) or indep. sent] **1.** it concerns me (you etc), the decision is mine (yours etc): **that's my ⟨your etc⟩ business ⟨concern, affair⟩; it's my ⟨your etc⟩ choice; that's up to me ⟨you etc⟩;** [2nd and 3rd persons only] **have it your (own) way ⟨let him have it his (own) way etc⟩;** [when addressed to the hearer] **as you wish; suit yourself ⟨-selves⟩.**

То, что я пишу о себе, — дело моё. Но пишу и о других, а это не только моё дело (Орлова 1). What I write about myself is my own affair. But what I write about others is not just my affair alone (1a). ♦ «Зачем мне говорить с народом? Мне с начальством поговорить надо»... — «Дело ваше... Только я думаю, с народом поговорить никогда не мешает» (Войнович 2). "Why should I talk with the people? I need to talk with my superiors."..."It's up to you....It's just that I think it never hurts to have a talk with the people" (2a). ♦ [Платонов:] Не дадите руки, юноша? [Венгерович 2:] Я не подаю милостыни. [Платонов:] Не подаёте? Ваше дело... (Чехов 1). [P.:] So you won't shake hands, boy? [V.:] I don't feel all that charitable. [P.:] So you won't shake hands? Have it your own way (1b). ♦ «Я в проигрыше, и я кончаю», — сказал он... — «Ваше дело», — ответил Коля (Искандер 3). "I'm the loser, and I quit," he said...."As you wish," Kolya replied (3a).

2. *Neg* **НЕ МОЁ ⟨не твоё и т. п.⟩ ДЕ́ЛО** [usu. this WO] (with 2nd and 3rd persons, often used to express a flat refusal to tell s.o. sth. or allow s.o. to interfere in some matter) it does not concern me (you etc): **it's ⟨that's⟩ none of my ⟨your etc⟩ business; it's ⟨that's⟩ no concern of mine ⟨yours etc⟩; it's ⟨that's⟩ not my ⟨your etc⟩ concern; that's ⟨it's⟩ got nothing to do with me ⟨you etc⟩; what's that ⟨it⟩ to me ⟨to you etc⟩?**

[Клещ:] А ты слезай с печи-то да убирай квартиру... чего нежишься? [Актёр:] Это дело не твоё... [Клещ:] А вот Василиса придёт — она тебе покажет, чьё дело... (Горький: 3). [K.:] You'd better come down off the stove and clean the place up—You've been loafing up there long enough. [A.:] That's none of your business. [K.:] Wait till Vassilissa comes in—she'll show you whose business it is (3b). ♦ За три года тюрьмы Таджихон всё ещё не привыкла к тому, что забота о народном хозяйстве страны теперь не её дело (Гинзбург 1). After three years in prison she [Tadjikhon] had not yet got used to the idea that the nation's economy was no longer her concern (1a). ♦ ...Он [Очкин] взял в руки бутылку с остатками вина и повертел её в руках. «Тут на двоих уж, считай, ничего не осталось», — сказал он и с надеждой посмотрел на Николая. «Не твоё дело», — грубо сказал Николай... (Войнович 5). Ochkin picked up the bottle with what was left of the wine, turning it back and forth in his hands. "Look, there's not enough left there for two," he said, looking hopefully over at Nikolai. "What's it to you," said Nikolai crudely... (5a).

Д-115 • **МОЁ ⟨твоё и т. п.⟩ ДЕ́ЛО МА́ЛЕНЬКОЕ** [sent; these forms only; most often 1st pers; fixed WO] (used by the speaker to justify himself for not being, or wanting to be, involved in sth.; also used to express the speaker's opinion that another should not get involved in sth.) it does not concern me (you etc) (because I, you etc have a small, insignificant role in the matter in question, hold little or no power); I (you etc) cannot be held responsible (for sth.): X-ово дело маленькое ≃ **that's not up to X; it's not X's affair; it has little ⟨nothing⟩ to do with X; it's none of X's business ⟨concern⟩; it's not X's place to get involved; X has no place getting involved;** [in limited contexts] **X is just a little guy; X's job is to obey.**

Уродилось, не уродилось на полях — твоё дело маленькое. Пайка тебе обеспечена (Абрамов 1). Whether the crops ripened or whether they didn't—nothing to do with you. You got your rations regardless (1a). ♦ «Бродяга он, не бродяга, хуй [*taboo*] его знает, — сказал Алёшка, — тёмный человек. Ну, да наше дело маленькое, нам с ним не детей крестить» (Лимонов 1). "He may be a bum or he may not, how the fuck should I know," Alyoshka said. "A shady character. Well, it's none of our business, we don't have to be buddies with him..." (1a). ♦ «Надо полагать — Королёвка?» — сотник указал на деревушку глазами. Вахмистр подъехал к нему молча. Выражение его лица без слов говорило: «Вам лучше знать. Наше дело маленькое» (Шолохов 2). "That must be Korolevka?" the lieutenant indicated the village with his eyes. The sergeant-major rode up to him without replying. His expression said without words, "You know best. Our job is to obey" (2a).

Д-116 • МОЁ ⟨твоё и т. п.⟩ ДЕ́ЛО (–) СТОРОНА́ *coll* [sent; these forms only; fixed WO] (used by the speaker to justify himself for not being, or wanting to be, involved in sth.; also used to express the speaker's opinion that another should not get involved in sth.) I am (you are etc) not or should not be involved in sth.: X-ово дело сторона ≃ **it has nothing to do with X; X has nothing to do with it; it's not X's affair; it's no business ⟨concern⟩ of X's; it's none of X's business ⟨concern⟩; X is not involved ⟨mixed up⟩ in it; it's not X's place to get involved; X has no place getting involved.**

[Матрёна:] Коли чего коснётся, моё дело сторона, я знать не знаю, ведать не ведаю, — крест поцелую, никаких порошков не давала и не видала и не слыхала, какие такие порошки бывают (Толстой 1). [M.:] If it ever comes to something, I had nothing to do with it, I don't know nothing about nothing—I'll swear on the cross I never gave no powders, never saw no powders, and never heard nothing about there being such powders (1a). ♦ Судорожно впиваясь в рукав мужа, Антонина испуганно выдохнула: «Коля...» — «Тише, Тоня, тише. — Её дрожь передалась ему, он тревожно напрягся и побелел. — Наше дело сторона. Пойдём...» (Максимов 3). Digging her nails into her husband's sleeve, Antonina spoke his name in a terrified whisper. "Be quiet, Tonya, be quiet." He felt her trembling, and went tense and pale with anxiety. "It's none of our business. Let's go" (3a). ♦ «Ты, Илья Никанорыч, не подумай чего, наше дело — сторона, мы люди маленькие... Ванька сам по себе, а я сам по себе, у меня к евонным [*ungrammat* = его] затеям никакого касательства» (Максимов 1). "Ilya Nikanorych, please don't get the wrong idea. We're not mixed up in this, we're just simple people!...Vanka went his way and I went mine. I had nothing to do with what he was up to" (1a).

Д-117 • МО́КРОЕ ДЕ́ЛО *slang* [NP; fixed WO] homicide: **murder; killing; slaying; bump(ing) s.o. off; off(ing) s.o.**

«Вот так, гражданин инспектор, было...» — «Продолжайте», — сухо сказал Антон. Сипенятин вздохнул... «Чего продолжать... Трухнул не меньше Алика. Кому охота по мокрому делу садиться?..» (Чернёнок 2). "That's how it happened, citizen inspector..." "Go on," Anton said dryly. Sipeniatin sighed....'Why go on...I was as scared as Alik. Who wants to serve time for murder?" (2a).

Д-118 • МЫ́СЛИМОЕ ⟨МЫ́СЛИМО *substand*⟩ **ЛИ ДЕ́ЛО** *coll* [sent; these forms only; usu. the main clause in a complex sent (often foll. by a чтобы-clause), a clause in a com-

pound sent, or indep. sent (often used as an exclamation or rhetorical question); fixed WO] (used to express one's displeasure, resentment, indignation etc over some action or occurrence) this is unacceptable, unimaginable: **is it conceivable ⟨possible⟩ that...?;** [in limited contexts] **it's beyond me; it's ⟨that's⟩ (simply) unheard of.**

«Подумай сама, — начинает старший, — мыслимое ли дело, чтобы немцы подпустили этого прохвоста [Петлюру] близко к городу?» (Булгаков 3). "Now just think," Alexei began. "Is is conceivable that the Germans should let that scoundrel Petlyura come anywhere near the city?" (3a). ♦ «Ну, мыслимое ли это дело: русские, православные люди сцепились между собой, и удержу нету» (Шолохов 5). "Ay, it's beyond me! Russians, true Christians, going for each other like this and there's no pulling you apart" (5a).

Д-119 • НЕ ДЕ́ЛО [NP; Invar; subj-compl with быть⌀ (subj: infin or abstr), pres only, or obj (usu. of затеваешь, затеял etc)] doing sth. is improper, inappropriate (used to express disapproval of s.o.'s actions, plans etc): **(that's ⟨doing sth. is⟩) not a good idea; (that's) not the (right) thing (to do); (s.o.) shouldn't (do sth.); it's wrong ⟨not right⟩ (to do sth.); (s.o. has) no business (doing sth.);** [in limited contexts] **get the idea out of your head.**

«...Пришёл я к вам, братцы, — не дело вы затеяли рыть эти места» (Пильняк 1). "...I have come to you, lads—you have no business digging these places" (1a). ♦ «...Слыхано ли дело, — подьячие задумали нами владеть, подьячие гонят наших господ с барского двора... Эк они храпят, окаянные; всех бы разом, так и концы в воду». Дубровский нахмурился. «Послушай, Архип, — сказал он, немного помолчав, — не дело ты затеял» (Пушкин 1). "Whoever heard of clerks imagining that they can take us over, that they can drive our masters out of their house? How they snore, the wretches! If we bumped them off now, no one would be any the wiser." Dubrovsky frowned. "Listen, Arkhip," he said after a slight pause. "Get the idea out of your head" (1b).

Д-120 • НЕ ТВОЁ ⟨его и т. п.⟩ СОБА́ЧЬЕ ДЕ́ЛО *substand, rude* [sent; these forms only; fixed WO] it absolutely does not concern you (him etc), does not have any relation to you (him etc): **it's none of your ⟨his etc⟩ goddamn(ed) ⟨damn, fucking⟩ business; don't stick your nose where it doesn't belong; keep your nose out of my ⟨our, other people's etc⟩ business.**

Всё это должно делаться не так, и не их это собачье дело, не они за это отвечают, и никто их не просит заниматься таким просветительством... (Стругацкие 1). This is not the way it should be done. And it's none of their goddamned business, it's not their responsibility, no one asked them to engage in educational activities (1a).

Д-121 • НО́ВОЕ ДЕ́ЛО! *highly coll* [Interj; Invar; fixed WO] used to express displeasure or surprise in response to sth. unpleasant or unexpected: **(that's) just great!; how do you like that!; that ⟨this⟩ beats everything ⟨all⟩!; I can't believe this!**

Д-122 • ПЕ́РВОЕ ДЕ́ЛО [NP; Invar; fixed WO] **1.** *coll* [subj-compl with быть⌀ (subj: infin or any common noun)] the most important matter: **the main ⟨first⟩ thing; the (most) important thing; (that's) what counts most;** [in limited contexts] **you don't get far without...**

[Анна Петровна:] Как ты мрачен... Что ж делать?.. Будь умницей, Сержель! Первое дело — хладнокровие (Чехов 1). [A.P.:] Don't look so gloomy. You can't do anything about it....Be wise, Sergey. The important thing now is not to give way to despair (1a). ♦ [Виктория:] По одёжке, значит, встречаете? [Калошин:] А ты думала? На этой работе глаз — первое дело... [Виктория:] А что — одежда? Есть большие люди, а одеваются скромно...

(Вампилов 1). [V.:] You mean you treat all guests according to their clothes? [K.:] What do you think? In this job you don't get far without sharp eyes.... [V.:] What do clothes tell you? Plenty of important people dress modestly... (1a).

2. *substand* [sent adv (parenth)] before (doing) anything else: **(the) first thing; first of all; in the first place; first (off); to begin ⟨start⟩ with.**

[Рисположенский:] Вот, первое дело, Самсон Силыч, надобно дом да лавки заложить либо продать (Островский 10). [R.:] Well, the first thing, Samson Silych, the house and shops must be mortgaged, or sold (10a).

Д-123 • **ПЛЁВОЕ ДЕ́ЛО** *highly coll* [NP; sing only; usu. subj-compl with copula, nom or instrum (subj: infin or abstr, often это)] **1.** doing sth. is very easy, does not require any effort: **(it's) a snap ⟨a cinch, a breeze⟩; (that's) nothing; (as) easy as pie; (as) easy as falling off a log.**

Собрать автомат за 25 секунд с завязанными глазами было для Мосина плёвым делом. Reassembling a submachine gun in 25 seconds with his eyes blindfolded was a snap for Mosin. ♦ [author's usage] «По мне, мужики, чего ни делается, всё к лучшему, сунут нашим корешам от силы по пятерику [пять лет тюрьмы] за соучастие, детский срок, плёвое дело...» (Максимов 1). [context transl] "In my opinion, lads, whatever happens is for the best. They'll give our mates five years at the most for complicity—kids' stuff, hardly worth bothering about" (1a).

2. doing sth. reprehensible (unethical etc) is easy for s.o., elicits in s.o. no feelings of regret, remorse etc: сделать Y для X-а — плёвое дело ≃ **X doesn't feel the least bit bad about ⟨guilty for⟩ doing Y; X doesn't feel bad at all about doing Y; X doesn't think it's ⟨doesn't consider it⟩ any big deal to do Y;** [in limited contexts] **X would do Y to s.o. as soon as look at him.**

Д-124 • **ПОНЯ́ТНОЕ ДЕ́ЛО; ПОНЯ́ТНАЯ ВЕЩЬ** *both coll* [NP; these forms only; usu. sent adv (parenth) or indep. sent; fixed WO] (used to emphasize that what is stated is entirely logical, understandable) as is apparent: **sure enough; naturally; it stands to reason; quite understandable ⟨-ably⟩.**

«Мать отправляет свою дочь-отца искать – ага. „Иди, – говорит, – в забегаловку, опять он, такой-сякой, наверно, там". Он, понятное дело, там...» (Распутин 3). "Mum sends her daughter out to find Dad. 'Look in the boozer,' she says. 'That's where he'll be, the old so-and-so.' Sure enough, he's there..." (3a). ♦ [Сорин:] Мне, брат, в деревне как-то не того, и, понятная вещь, никогда я тут не привыкну. Вчера лёг в десять и сегодня утром проснулся в девять с таким чувством, как будто от долгого спанья у меня мозг прилип к черепу и всё такое (Чехов 6). [S.:] For some reason, my boy, I'm not quite myself in the country, and, it stands to reason, I'll never get accustomed to it. I went to bed at ten o'clock last night and woke up at nine this morning feeling as though my brain were stuck to my skull from sleeping so long, and all that sort of thing (6a). ♦ «[Раскольников] всё хандрит, – продолжал Разумихин, – бельё мы сейчас переменили, так чуть не заплакал». – «Понятное дело; бельё можно бы и после, коль сам не желает...» (Достоевский 3). "He's [Raskolnikov is] down in the mouth," continued Razumikhin. "We just changed his underwear and he almost started crying." "Quite understandable. The underwear could have waited if he didn't want it..." (3a).

Д-125 • **ПОСЛЕ́ДНЕЕ ДЕ́ЛО** *coll* [NP; Invar; subj-compl with бытьₒ (subj: abstr, infin, or a clause), usu. pres] **1.** [fixed WO] some situation (doing sth. etc) is very bad, not good at all: [of a situation etc] **things are as bad as can be; things are really bad; things are in a bad way; things have hit ⟨reached⟩ rock bottom;** [in limited contexts] **it's (the beginning of) the end;** [of doing sth.] **(doing sth. is) as low as you can get; despicable; you can't get lower than (doing sth.).**

...Хозяин добавил: «Твой муж никому зла сделать не мог – последнее дело, если таких берут...» (Мандельштам 1). And the old man added: "Your husband could never have done harm to anyone. If they are arresting people like him, things must be really bad" (1a). ♦ «Ох, уж эти мне базары! Нет, что вы на это скажете? Уж если они немцев перестанут бояться... последнее дело» (Булгаков 3). "Hell—these market women! How'd you like that? Once they stop being afraid of the Germans...it's the beginning of the end" (3a).

2. sth. is of negligible importance within the framework of the matter in question: **completely unimportant; means nothing;** [in limited contexts] **the last thing (you think of etc); the last thing on one's list; the least of one's concerns ⟨worries⟩.**

[Беневоленский:] Теперь я вас спрошу, что такое красота в мужчине? – Последнее дело (Островский 1). [B.:] Now I ask you, what are good looks in a man, exactly? It's the last thing you think of (1a).

Д-126 • **ПРИШИВА́ТЬ/ПРИШИ́ТЬ ⟨ШИТЬ, МОТА́ТЬ/НАМОТА́ТЬ и т. п.⟩ ДЕ́ЛО** *(кому) slang* [VP; subj: human] to make an accusation against s.o. (usu. a false one), fabricate a charge against s.o., incriminate s.o. falsely: X шьёт Y-у дело ≃ **X is trying to frame Y; X is cooking up charges ⟨something⟩ against Y; X is building ⟨making⟩ a case against Y.**

«Боюсь я, Петя, Парамошина этого. Смерть как боюсь. Нету у меня силы против его речей. Как заговорит, чую — тону я. Ты ему: „работать надо". А он тебе: „мировой империализм"... Чуть что не по его – дело шьёт... в попустительстве обвиняет» (Максимов 3). "I'm frightened of that Paramoshin, Petya. Frightened to death. I'm powerless against his endless speechmaking. As soon as he starts talking, I feel as if I'm drowning. You say to him, 'There's work to be done,' and he answers 'world imperialism.'...If the least little thing doesn't suit him, he cooks something up...accuses you of covering up for people" (3a). ♦ «Стукачи старались... На меня дунули, будто сказал, что у немцев хорошие самолёты... И ещё стали мотать дело, что в мастерских большой износ инструментов. Вредительство!» (Копелев 1). "The stoolies worked hard. They said that I supposedly said that the Germans had good planes. And they began building a case on the fact that the instruments were wearing out too fast in the shops. Sabotage!" (1a).

Д-127 • **ПУСТО́Е ДЕ́ЛО** *coll* [NP; sing only; subj-compl with copula, nom or instrum (subj: abstr or infin)] a vain endeavor: X ⟨делать X⟩ – пустое дело ≃ **X ⟨doing X⟩ is a waste of time (and energy); it's pointless (to do X); it's ⟨there's⟩ no use (doing X); X ⟨doing X⟩ is useless ⟨worthless⟩.**

Пойти в кино – пустое дело. Раз в год мелькнёт мало-мальски терпимый фильм. А всё остальное – дрянь (Зиновьев 2). Going to the cinema is a waste of time. You might see a half-way tolerable film once a year—everything else is rubbish (2a). ♦ «...Туда [на космодром] нас не пустят». – «Так если не идти, то не пустят. А если потребовать, то и пустят...» Сабитжан метнул на Едигея раздражённый взгляд. «Оставь, старик, это пустое дело. А на меня не рассчитывай» (Айтматов 2). "...They won't let us inside [the cosmodrome]." "If we don't try, then of course they won't let us in. But if we demand, then they will...." Sabitzhan gave Yedigei a look full of irritation. "Leave it alone, old man, it's pointless to try. Don't count on my help" (2a).

Д-128 • **РАЗ ТАКО́Е ДЕ́ЛО** *coll* [subord clause; Invar; usu. precedes the main clause; fixed WO] if matters are like that (as described in the preceding context): **if that's the case; that being the case; if that's the way things are; if that's how it is.**

[Говорящий – мул] Я одного не пойму, почему все эти люди, прежде чем их схватят, никуда не бегут. Да что они, стреножены, что ли?! Раз такое дело – бегите в горы, в леса, кто вас там отыщет?! (Искандер 3). [The speaker is a mule] One thing I'll never understand is why all those people don't run away somewhere before they get caught. What are they, hobbled? If that's the way things are—run to the hills, to the woods, who'll find you there? (3a). ♦ Одного кинорежиссёра как-то давным-давно... записали в очередь на квартиру... Очередь двигалась ужасно медленно... Наконец, кто-то, кто поумнее, ему говорит: «Ты... будешь в этой очереди стоять до второго пришествия или до тех пор, пока какому-нибудь нужному человеку на лапу не дашь»... — «Ладно, — думает, — раз такое дело, один раз дам всё-таки взятку, а больше уж никогда не буду» (Войнович 1). Long ago...a certain film director signed up on a waiting list for an apartment....The waiting list was very slow in moving....Finally, someone cleverer than he told him: "You'll be on that waiting list until the Second Coming or until you grease the right person's palm." All right, he thought, if that's how it is, I'll give a bribe this time, but never again (1a).

Д-129 • СЛЫ́ХАННОЕ ⟨СЛЫ́ХАНО *substand*⟩ **ЛИ ДЕ́ЛО** *coll* [sent; these forms only; usu. the main clause in a complex sent (often foll. by a чтобы-clause), a clause in a compound sent, or indep. sent (often used as an exclamation or rhetorical question); fixed WO] (used to express one's indignation over or strongly negative attitude toward some action or occurrence) this is unacceptable, outrageous, utterly unreasonable, should not be: **whoever ⟨who's ever⟩ heard of such a thing ⟨of anything like it⟩?; whoever heard of...?; it's ⟨just ⟨simply⟩⟩ unheard of ⟨unbelievable⟩; this ⟨that, it⟩ beats all.**

«...Слыхано ли дело, — подьячие задумали нами владеть, подьячие гонят наших господ с барского двора...» (Пушкин 1). "Whoever heard of clerks imagining that they can take us over, that they can drive our masters out of their house?" (1b). ♦ «Слыхано ль дело, меня две власти приставили следить за лесом, а этот безродный грек заставляет меня следить за скотом» (Искандер 5). "It beats all—two regimes have appointed me to watch over the forest, but that kinless Greek is forcing me to watch the animals" (5a).

Д-130 • СТА́ТОЧНОЕ ЛИ ДЕ́ЛО *obs* [sent; Invar; usu. the main clause in a complex sent (often foll. by a чтобы-clause), a clause in a compound sent, or indep. sent (often used as an exclamation or rhetorical question); fixed WO] (used to express one's displeasure, resentment etc over some action, occurrence, suggestion etc) this is unacceptable, impermissible, utterly unreasonable: **how can such a thing be (possible)?; can such a thing really be?; how is that ⟨it⟩ possible?; is it conceivable that...?; it is hardly possible that...**

«Статочное ли дело, чтоб... барин давно не нашёл себе невесты, кабы захотел жениться...» (Гончаров 1). "...It was hardly possible that our master would not have found a wife long ago had he meant to marry..." (1b).

Д-131 • СТРА́ННОЕ ⟨ЧУ́ДНОЕ *substand*⟩ **ДЕ́ЛО; СТРА́ННАЯ ВЕЩЬ** [NP; these forms only; usu. sent adv (parenth); fixed WO] (used to emphasize the unexpected, unusual, or illogical nature of the statement that follows, which is often contrasted with a preceding statement) surprisingly, unbelievably: **strangely (enough); strange to say; strange thing; strange as it may ⟨might⟩ seem; [in limited contexts] it's strange.**

Наконец-то и Леонид Иванович дождался этой чести — подписал статью, которую для него сочинил тот же Невраев. Но — странное дело! — став автором газетного подвала, Леонид Иванович не освободился от того чувства, которое вызывало на его лице чуть заметную, презрительную усмешку (Дудинцев 1). So finally Drozdov, too, lived to experience the honor of signing an article that had been written for him by that same Nevraev. But strangely enough, although he was now the author of a newspaper feature, Drozdov could still not rid himself of the emotion that had always brought a faint, contemptuous smile to his face

(1a). ♦ ...Иван Фёдорович, расставшись с Алёшей, пошёл домой, и в дом Фёдора Павловича. Но странное дело, на него напала вдруг тоска нестерпимая... (Достоевский 1). ...Ivan Fyodorovich, on parting from Alyosha, went home to Fyodor Pavlovich's house. But strangely, an unbearable anguish suddenly came over him... (1a). ♦ Он молился, и — странное дело! — почти всегда приходила к нему откуда-нибудь неожиданная помощь... (Гоголь 3). He prayed and, strange to say, almost invariably some unexpected help would come to him from somewhere... (3a). He would pray, and—strange thing—almost invariably he received help from some unexpected quarter... (3d). ♦ Странное дело: давеча он направлялся к Катерине Ивановне в чрезвычайном смущении, теперь же не чувствовал никакого... (Достоевский 1). It was strange: earlier he had set out to see Katerina Ivanovna in great embarrassment, but now he felt none... (1a).

Д-132 • ТО И ДЕ́ЛО [Invar; adv; used with impfv verbs; fixed WO] (one does sth., sth. happens) often, frequently: **over and over (again); again and again; time and (time) again; [in limited contexts] constantly; continually; keep (doing sth.).**

«Генерал Кондратенко», — то и дело повторяла бабушка (Олеша 3). "General Kondratenko," my grandmother repeated over and over (3a). ♦ «Байрон», — то и дело слышалось из его уст... (Олеша 3). "Byron," we heard from his lips again and again... (3a). ♦ Это был человек, которого нельзя не заметить. На пустой, заснеженной улице он привлекал внимание тем, что то и дело оглядывался (Терц 8). This was a man whom one could not fail to notice. In the empty, snow-swept street he attracted attention by constantly looking over his shoulder (8a). ♦ Было без четверти час; но Карл Иваныч, казалось, и не думал о том, чтобы отпустить нас: он то и дело задавал новые уроки. Скука и аппетит увеличивались в одинаковой мере (Толстой 2). It was a quarter to one. But Karl Ivanych apparently had no intention of letting us go: he kept setting us new tasks. Lassitude and hunger increased in equal proportion (2c).

Д-133 • ТО ЛИ ДЕ́ЛО *coll, approv* [Invar; subj-compl with бытьø (subj: any noun), pres only, or Particle; initial position only; fixed WO] s.o. or sth. is entirely different from, and better than, someone or something else (used to express approval, a positive evaluation of the person, thing etc that is about to be named as opposed to the one named previously): **то ли дело X ≃ X is quite another matter; X is a different story; thing X ⟨with person X it⟩ is a different matter (altogether); thing X is quite a different thing; X is not like that at all; X is not at all like [NP].**

«Всё может случиться: ну, как лопнет [компания], вот я и без гроша. То ли дело в банк» (Гончаров 1). "...Anything might happen—such as your company going bankrupt and leaving me without a penny. A bank is quite another matter" (1b). ♦ «А старик, оказывается, в первую мировую войну был у нас в плену и немного говорит по-русски. Но лучше бы он совсем не говорил. Путается, хочет всё объяснить... То ли дело эти молодые немочки, всё с полуслова понимают...» (Искандер 5). "It turned out the old man had been a prisoner of ours in the First World War and spoke a little Russian. But he would have done better not to talk at all. He kept getting tangled up, wanting to explain everything....The girls were a different story, they picked up on everything right away" (5a). ♦ На что борода — и та [у Момуна] не удалась. Посмешище одно. На голом подбородке две-три волосинки рыжеватые — вот и вся борода. То ли дело видишь: вдруг едет по дороге осанистый старик... (Айтматов 1). Even his [Momun's] beard was nothing but a joke. Two or three reddish hairs on his chin—that was all there was to it. He wasn't at all like some stately old man you might see riding down the road... (1a). ♦ «Вот жизнь-то человеческая! — поучительно произнёс Илья Иванович. — Один умирает, другой родится, третий женится, а мы вот всё стареемся: не то что год на год, день на день не приходится! Зачем это так? То ли бы дело, если б каждый день как вчера, вчера как завтра!..» (Гончаров 1). [context transl] "Such is man's

[180]

life!" Ilya Ivanovich pronounced sententiously. "One man dies, another is born, a third is married, and we keep growing older....There are no two days alike, let alone two years. Why should it be so? Wouldn't it have been nice if every day were like the day before, yesterday just like tomorrow?" (1b).

Д-134 • УДИВИ́ТЕЛЬНОЕ ДЕ́ЛО [NP; Invar; indep. sent or clause; fixed WO] used to express surprise, astonishment: **(it's) amazing ⟨astonishing⟩; (it's) an amazing ⟨astonishing⟩ thing; (it's) a most extraordinary thing; it's truly extraordinary.**

[Гвардеец:] Это даже невероятно... чтобы солдату да вдруг приснился такой волшебный сон... кукла разгуливает по дворцу... Удивительное дело. Ишь ты... Ну, ни дать ни взять — живая девочка (Олеша 7). [G.:] It's incredible that a soldier should have such a magical dream...a doll goes strolling round the palace....Amazing. How d'you like that! A live girl...nothing less (7a). ♦ [Почтмейстер:] Удивительное дело, господа! Чиновник, которого мы приняли за ревизора, был не ревизор (Гоголь 4). [Postmaster:] An astonishing thing, ladies and gentlemen! The official whom we took to be the government inspector, was not the inspector at all (4d). [Postmaster:] A most extraordinary thing, ladies and gentlemen! The civil servant we took to be the Government Inspector, is not the Government Inspector at all (4c).

Д-135 • ХОРО́ШЕНЬКОЕ ⟨ХОРО́ШЕЕ⟩ ДЕ́ЛО! *coll* [NP; these forms only; used as indep. sent or sent adv (parenth); fixed WO] used to express disapproval of or indignation at sth. (usu. in refer. to the preceding statement, which may be repeated after the idiom): **I like that!; a fine thing ⟨state of affairs⟩ (indeed)!; isn't that just dandy!**

«С вас, Шариков, 130 рублей. Потрудитесь внести». — «Хорошенькое дело, — ответил Шариков, испугавшись, — это за что такое?» (Булгаков 11). "Your share is one hundred thirty rubles, Sharikov. Kindly pay up." "A fine thing," Sharikov became alarmed. "What's this for?" (11a). ♦ ...Здесь, в палате, даже радио нет, и в коридоре нет, хорошенькое дело! (Солженицын 10). ...Here in the ward there wasn't even a radio, and there wasn't one in the corridor either—a fine state of affairs! (10a).

Д-136 • ЧЁРНОЕ ДЕ́ЛО *lit* [NP; fixed WO] a reprehensible, despicable action or crime: **dirty deed; heinous act ⟨crime⟩.**

«История всё разберёт. Потомство пригвоздит к позорному столбу бурбонов комиссародержавия и их чёрное дело» (Пастернак 1). "History will tell the truth. Posterity will pillory the Bourbons of the commissarocracy together with their dirty deeds" (1a).

Д-137 • Я́СНОЕ ДЕ́ЛО *coll* [NP; Invar; sent adv (parenth) or the main clause in a complex sent; fixed WO] (used to emphasize that what is stated is completely evident, logical) as is apparent: **naturally; obviously; evidently; no doubt ⟨no question⟩ (about it); no two ways about it; sure enough; it's clear enough ⟨quite clear⟩.**

Ясное дело, мне хотелось бы познакомиться с ним... (Соколов 1). Naturally I would like to make his acquaintance... (1a). ♦ «Мне и вправду скоро нелегко придётся, а если ещё и ты не будешь верить, что мне тогда останется?» — «Без меня, ясное дело, было бы лучше» (Распутин 2). "I really will have a hard time soon, and if you don't believe in me, then what will I have left?" "Obviously, it would be easier without me" (2a). ♦ ...Когда-то здесь были богатые травянистые места, климат был иной, дождь выпадало в три раза больше. Ну, ясное дело, и жизнь оттого была иная (Айтматов 2). ...Once upon a time there were rich grassy places here and a different climate, with three times the present rainfall. Evidently life here was quite different then (2a). ♦ «Ясное дело, девушка втрескалась в него по уши» (Искандер 5). "No question, the girl was head over heels in love with him" (5a). ♦ ...Крушения не прекращались. Тогда-то и была создана комиссия... Уполномоченный особого отдела... вызывал их

[членов комиссии] по одному и чуть не плакал, упрашивая их поторопиться. «Бросьте вы канитель разводить! Ясное дело — враг орудует» (Максимов 3). ...The crashes went on. At this point a commission of inquiry was set up....The representative of the security branch...called them [the members of the commission] in one by one and almost wept as he begged them to come to a verdict. "Stop dragging it out! It's clear enough—the enemy is at work" (3a).

Д-138 • ГРЕ́ШНЫМ ДЕ́ЛОМ *coll, occas. humor* [NP$_{instrum}$; Invar; sent adv (often parenth); fixed WO] used by the speaker to admit his own or another's mistake, weakness, oversight etc, or to inquire if another (often the interlocutor) has made a mistake, given in to a weakness, overlooked sth. etc: **I'm afraid; much as I hate to admit ⟨say⟩ it; I'm ashamed to say; sad to say; [in refer. to the interlocutor or a third party only] you ⟨he etc⟩ didn't go and (do sth.), did you ⟨he etc⟩?**

«Они [два студента] как-то очень просто и хорошо обратились к старику. Он даже прослезился. Грешным делом, и я тоже» (Некрасов 1). "What they [two students] said to the old man was very simple, direct, sincere. He even shed a few tears. I'm afraid I did, too" (1a). ♦ Когда я поступал в ресторан, у меня грешным делом мелькала мысль, что я... смогу завести какие-то знакомства (Лимонов 1). When I started at the restaurant, I am ashamed to say, I had the fleeting thought that I...could make some contacts (1a).

Д-139 • МА́ЛЫМ ДЕ́ЛОМ *obs, substand* [NP$_{instrum}$; Invar; adv; usu. used with pfv verbs; fixed WO] not much: **a (wee ⟨tiny⟩) bit; a little.**

[Телятев:] ...[Васильков] спросил бутылку шампанского, потом другую, ну, мы и выпили малым делом (Островский 4). [T.:] ...[Vasilkov] ordered a bottle of champagne, then another. Well, we had a bit of a drink (4a).

Д-140 • МЕ́ЖДУ ДЕ́ЛОМ ⟨ДЕЛ *obs*⟩ [PrepP; these forms only; adv] in one's free moments, during intervals between other engagements: **in between other things ⟨one's other activities⟩; betweentimes ⟨betweenwhiles⟩; [in limited contexts] when one has ⟨can spare⟩ a minute ⟨a moment⟩; when one can snatch a free moment; when one has a spare moment ⟨a moment to spare⟩; on the side.**

...Каждое посещение театра [Юра] считал праздником. Поэтому никогда не понимал Сашу Панкратова, Нину, забегавших в театр между делом... (Рыбаков 2). For him [Yuri], going to the theater was like taking a holiday. He could never understand Sasha Pankratov or Nina, who would go to the theater in between their other activities... (2a).

Д-141 • ПЕ́РВЫМ ДЕ́ЛОМ ⟨ДО́ЛГОМ⟩ *coll* [NP$_{instrum}$; these forms only; adv; fixed WO] before (doing) anything else: **first of all; in the first place; first (off); first thing; the first thing (one does is...); to begin ⟨start⟩ with.**

Наконец опросы перешли к защитнику, и тот первым делом начал узнавать о пакете, в котором «будто бы» спрятаны были Фёдором Павловичем три тысячи рублей для «известной особы» (Достоевский 2). Finally the questioning passed to the defense attorney, and he, first of all, began asking about the envelope in which Fyodor Pavlovich "supposedly" hid three thousand roubles for "a certain person" (2a). ♦ Маленькие картинки Леонардо в том алтаре, в который вделаны они в Эрмитаже, трудно оценить мне, который первым делом не хочет поверить, что писал Леонардо... (Олеша 3). The little pictures by Leonardo in the altar into which they are set in the Hermitage are difficult for me to appreciate, since in the first place I don't want to believe that they are Leonardo's... (3a). ♦ Мой старик, конечно, стал расспрашивать абхазского арапа насчёт колхозных дел. Первым долгом он у него спросил, не заставляют ли их сажать эвкалипты (Искандер 3). My old man, of course, began by asking the Abkhazian blackamoor about kolkhoz affairs. First off he asked whether they were making them plant eucalyptuses (3a). ♦ На Иркутской пересылке я снова первым долгом влип в историю, хоть к этому и не стремился (Марченко 2). At the Irkutsk transit point I got involved first thing in another incident, although I was not looking for trouble (2a). ♦ Нюра, пригнувшись, кинулась к избе… Вбежав в избу, она первым делом обратила внимание на крышку подпола, но в этом смысле всё было в порядке… (Войнович 2). Doubled over, Nyura dashed to the hut….The first thing Nyura did in the hut was to check the cellar door, but everything was fine in that respect… (2a). ♦ Первым делом она [комсомолка] обвинила меня в сочинении закона Гримма и Раска, который я навязывала студентам (Мандельштам 2). To begin with, she [the young woman member of the Komsomol] accused me of inventing Grimm's and Rask's law and forcing it down the students' throats (2a).

Д-142 • БЛИ́ЖЕ К ДЕ́ЛУ [Invar; fixed WO] **1.** Also: **К ДЕ́ЛУ(!)** [usu. indep. sent] (used as a prompt, appeal, or command) do not digress, speak relevantly: **get ⟨come, stick⟩ to the point; get (down) to business; get (down) to the business at hand; to business!; get down to brass tacks.**

«Но к делу, к делу, Маргарита Николаевна. Вы женщина весьма умная и, конечно, уже догадались о том, кто наш хозяин» (Булгаков 9). "But come to the point, Margarita Nikolayevna. You are a very intelligent woman and have naturally guessed who our host is" (9b). ♦ [Авдонин:] Побежал я, короче говоря, в контору. Комнату просить. Очень плохо соображал… [Третий коммунист:] Под газом? [Авдонин:] Какой — под газом! Рано утром. [Яблоков:] Ближе к делу, Авдонин (Салынский 1). [A.:] …To put it briefly, I ran to the office to ask for a room. I hardly knew what I was doing…. [Third communist:] Were you tight? [A.:] I wasn't tight at all. It was early in the morning. [Ya:] Stick to the point, Avdonin (1a). ♦ «Теперь к делу: что вам сказала княгиня Лиговская обо мне?» (Лермонтов 1). "Now, to business! What did the old Princess Ligovskoy say to you about me?" (1a).

2. [AdjP; subj-compl with бытьø (subj: это), usu. pres] this is more relevant than what was said before: **this is more to the point; [in limited contexts] now you're talking.**

[Галя:] Хорошо, если ты хочешь откровенности — пожалуйста: во-первых… [Андрей:] Слушай, нельзя ли прямо в-десятых! [Галя:] Хорошо! В-двадцать-пятых! [Андрей:] Вот это ближе к делу (Розов 1). [G.:] All right—if you want me to be frank—first… [A.:] Listen, could you make it short and start with "tenthly"! [G.:] All right! Twenty-fifthly!… [A.:] Now you're talking (1a).

Д-143 • ГОВОРИ́ТЬ ПО ДЕ́ЛУ coll [VP; subj: human] to talk about the essence of what is being discussed: X говорит по делу ≃ **X speaks ⟨gets⟩ to the heart of the matter; X speaks ⟨gets⟩ to the point;** ‖ X говорит не по делу ≃ **X has gone off on ⟨at⟩ a tangent.**

[Вася:] Теперь во всех домах такие [люстры]… [Любин муж:] Это научились, что говорить. Теперь ведь точно под квартиры всё делают, мебель там и люстры. По площади всё рассчитано. Кровать сюда, стол сюда. А иначе и не встанет… [Адамыч:] Ага. Я вот ещё когда лифтёром был — теперь-то на автоматику перевели — я телеграммки ношу… (*Спохватывается, что не по делу говорит.*) Квартиры, точно, похожие (Рощин 2). [V.:] All the buildings have fixtures like that now…. [Lyuba's husband:] No question about it, they have it all down to a science now. Everything's made exactly to fit the apartment, you know, furniture, or chandeliers. The bed goes here, the table, there. Otherwise, they don't fit…. [A.:] That's so. And when I was still an elevator operator—now they're all automatic—I deliver telegrams….(*Remembering suddenly that he has gone off on a tangent.*) Apartments, it's the truth, they're all alike (2a).

Д-144 • ДЕ́ЛУ ВРЕ́МЯ, (А) ПОТЕ́ХЕ ЧАС [saying] one should spend most of his time and energy on work and relax only when his work is done: ≃ **business before pleasure.**

Д-145 • ИДТИ́ К ДЕ́ЛУ obsoles [VP; subj: abstr; often neg] to be pertinent, relevant to the matter in question: X идёт к делу ≃ **X is related to the matter at hand; X is to the point;** ‖ Neg X к делу не идёт ≃ **X has ⟨bears⟩ no relation to the matter at hand; X is beside the point.**

Для чего он дрался с мародёром? Пьер отвечал, что он защищал женщину, что защита оскорбляемой женщины есть обязанность каждого человека, что… Его остановили: это не шло к делу (Толстой 7). Why had he fought the marauder? Pierre answered that he was 'protecting a woman,' and that 'to protect a woman who was being insulted, was the duty of every man; that'…They interrupted him, for this was not to the point (7b).

Д-146 • ПО ДЕ́ЛУ наказывать, ругать, критиковать кого coll [PrepP; Invar; adv] (to punish, berate, criticize s.o.) deservedly: **for a (good) reason; for good reason; with good reason ⟨cause⟩; (the punishment ⟨the criticism etc⟩ is) well-deserved.**

Вконец раздобревший хозяин кинулся было в магазин за добавкой, но гость решительно перевернул свой стакан вверх дном: «Я… пас». — «Что так?» — «Папашка не любит, когда посреди работы». — «Строг?» — «Да как сказать. Строг не строг, а порядок любит. Если и осадит, так по делу» (Максимов 3). Completely mellowed by now, he wanted to run to the shop for fresh supplies, but his guest resolutely turned his glass upside down. "I pass…." "How's that?" "The old man doesn't like it in the middle of a job." "So he's strict?" "I don't know if I'd say that. He isn't exactly strict, but he likes things to be proper. If he takes you down a peg, it's always for a good reason" (3a).

Д-147 • НЕ СЧИТА́ТЬ ДЕ́НЕГ [VP; subj: human] (of s.o. who is wealthy) to spend one's wealth lavishly, extravagantly: X денег не считает ≃ **X spends money right and left ⟨left and right⟩; X spends money like water ⟨like there was no tomorrow⟩.**

Д-148 • ПЛА́КАЛИ чьи **ДЕ́НЕЖКИ** highly coll [VP$_{subj}$; past only; fixed WO] (of money that has been spent unwisely or of money loaned out that has not been and never will be paid back) s.o.'s money is gone forever: плакали X-овы денежки ≃ **X's money is lost for good; X's money is down the drain;** [usu. of money loaned out, an investment that seems sure to fail etc] **X can kiss his money good-bye; X can say good-bye to his money; X can forget about ever seeing his ⟨that⟩ money again.**

«Нам платят за убитых и пленных дополнительное вознаграждение…» — «Нет, господа, раненых мы вам не отдадим, — возразил профессор Аббас. — Они нуждаются в лечении». — «Не отдадут, не отдадут, — горько заплакал блондин-атлет. — Плакали наши денежки, ребята…» (Аксёнов 6). "We get paid extra money for dead bodies and prisoners…." "No, gentlemen, we will not hand over the wounded," objected Professor Abbas. "They need treatment." "They won't give them up," said the blond athlete, bursting into bitter tears. "We can say good-bye to our money, boys" (6a).

Д-149 • НИКУДА́ НЕ ДЕ́НЕШЬСЯ ⟨НЕ ДЕ́ТЬСЯ⟩ (от чего) coll [VP; subj: human; usu. neg pfv fut, gener. 2nd pers sing не денешься; fixed WO] **1.** because of the circumstances, sth. cannot be avoided: **there is no way around it; there is no getting out of it; there is no way out (of it); you have no choice (but to…); [in limited contexts] you can't escape.**

Убийц прогнали. А на Лёльке клеймо: «была в оккупации». И она, и её мама, и её «двоюродная» теперь не полноценные граждане... От анкеты никуда не денешься: анкета – шлагбаум, опущенный перед их жизнями (Чуковская 2). The murderers had been driven out. But Lyolka was branded: "[She] was in the occupation." And she and her mother and cousin were no longer full-fledged citizens....You couldn't escape filling out forms: these forms were like a barrier placed in front of their lives (2a).

2. one cannot change or overlook some unpleasant or disturbing fact, state of affairs etc: **there is no getting around ⟨away from⟩ it ⟨that⟩; there is no avoiding it.**

«...Ломаться, я думаю, [Наташка] не должна, потому что хоть какой там каблук ни подставляй, а хроменькая есть хроменькая, никуда не денешься» (Войнович 5). "...I don't think she'll [Natashka will] be finicky, because no matter what kind of heel you put on, a cripple's still a cripple, no getting around that" (5a). ♦ Правда ли, что – давний сотрудник Охранного отделения? Тут – никуда не деться, этого не скрыть (Солженицын 1). Was it true that he was an Okhrana agent of long standing? There was no getting away from that. Concealment was impossible (1a).

Д-150 • В ОДИ́Н ПРЕКРА́СНЫЙ ДЕНЬ; В ОДНО́ ПРЕКРА́СНОЕ ВРЕ́МЯ *rather lit* [PrepP; these forms only; sent adv; fixed WO] on one particular, significant, or memorable day, on a given day, occasion, at a certain point (often used as a stylistic device to give the flavor of a fairy tale, epic, or the like): **one fine day;** [in refer. to the future] **one of these days.**

...В один прекрасный день в нашей газете прошёл слушок, что картина Таркилова кому-то наверху не понравилась... (Искандер 4). ...One fine day the rumor went around at our newspaper that somebody high up did not like Tarkilov's painting... (4a).

Д-151 • ВЧЕРА́ШНИЙ ДЕНЬ *(чего)* [NP; sing only; often subj-compl with copula (subj: abstr) or (when used in gen) non-agreeing postmodif; fixed WO] (that which belongs to) the past: **(be) a thing of the past; (be) yesterday's** [NP]; [in limited contexts] **(be) behind the times; (be living) in the past; (be) passé ⟨outmoded⟩.**

«...Не считайте меня глухим консерватором, человеком вчерашнего дня» (Аксёнов 6). "You would be wrong...to regard me as a dull conservative, one of yesterday's men" (6a). ♦ Теория, на которую опирается ваш эксперимент, уже не представляет никакого интереса, это вчерашний день науки. The theory on which your experiment is based is no longer of any interest, it's a thing of the past.

Д-152 • ДЕНЬ А́НГЕЛА *obs* [NP; sing only; fixed WO] the day when the Russian Orthodox church honors the saint after whom one is named: **s.o.'s name day; s.o.'s saint's day.**

«Поздравь меня, – воскликнул вдруг Базаров, – сегодня 22-е июня, день моего ангела» (Тургенев 2). "Wish me many happy returns," Bazarov suddenly exclaimed. "Today's the twenty-second of June, my name day" (2c). ♦ [Кулыгин:] Дорогая сестра, позволь мне поздравить тебя с днём твоего ангела и... поднести тебе в подарок вот эту книжку... (Чехов 5). [K.:] My dear sister, allow me to congratulate you on your saint's day and...to present this book to you as a gift... (5c).

Д-153 • ДЕНЬ В ДЕНЬ [Invar; adv; fixed WO] precisely (on the day named): **to the day; right to the very day.**

...Последняя часть романа подписана 4-ым апреля 63 года, а ровно день в день три года спустя и произошло покушение [на царя] (Набоков 1). ...The last part of the novel was signed on April 4, 1863, and exactly three years later to the day the attempt [to assassinate the Tsar] took place (1a). ♦ «...Я тебе рассказывала, кажется, как Кирюша день в день, час в час предсказал покойнику папеньке его кончину» (Толстой 2). "I believe I told you how Kiryusha prophesied the end of poor Papa, right to the very day and hour" (2b).

Д-154 • ДЕНЬ-ДЕНЬСКО́Й *coll* [AdvP; Invar; adv] throughout, for the entire day: **all day long; the whole day long ⟨through⟩.**

[Лебедев:] В наше время, бывало, день-деньской с лекциями бьёшься... (Чехов 4). [L.:] Now, in our time you'd sweat away at your lectures all day long... (4b).

Д-155 • ДЕНЬ И НОЧЬ; ДНЁМ И НО́ЧЬЮ; ДЕ́ННО И НО́ЩНО [NP or AdvP; these forms only; adv; used with impfv verbs; fixed WO (1st and last variants)] constantly, all the time: **day and night; night and day;** [in limited contexts] **twenty-four hours a day; (a)round the clock.**

Пфейферша денно и нощно приставала к Грустилову, в особенности преследуя его перепискою... (Салтыков-Щедрин 1). Mme Pfeifer badgered Melancholov day and night, especially tormenting him with letters (1a).

Д-156 • ДЕНЬ ОТКРЫ́ТЫХ ДВЕРЕ́Й [NP; sing only; fixed WO] a day when an institution of higher learning is open for all potential applicants to visit: **open house.**

Д-157 • ДЕНЬ ОТО ДНЯ [Invar; adv; used with impfv verbs; fixed WO] gradually, little by little: **with every ⟨each⟩ passing day; from one day to the next; from day to day; day by day; with each new day;** [in limited contexts; usu. with compar form of Adj used as subj-compl] **every day.**

Настороженность [Лилит] таяла день ото дня (Обухова 1). Her [Lilith's] wariness melted away from one day to the next (1a). ♦ «...Жизнь моя становится пустее день ото дня...» (Лермонтов 1). "...My life becomes more empty day by day..." (1a). "...My life gets emptier every day" (1c).

Д-158 • ДО́БРЫЙ ДЕНЬ [formula phrase; Invar; fixed WO] a greeting used upon meeting s.o. during the day: **good afternoon; good day; hello;** [in limited contexts] **good morning.**

Когда он вернулся, в номере сидел Павор. «Добрый день», – сказал Павор, ослепительно улыбаясь (Стругацкие 1). When he returned, Pavor was sitting in his room. "Good afternoon," said Pavor with a blinding smile (1a). ♦ Она прищурилась на прохожего... «Добрый день», – сказала она. «Добрый день», – ответил Андрей... (Федин 1). She wrinkled her eyes at the passer-by...."Good day," she said. "Good day," replied Andrei... (1a). ♦ «Добрый день», – сказал командир. Верочка, не смутившись, ответила: «Добрый день» (Грекова 3). "Good morning," said the commander. "Good morning," answered Verochka, unabashed (3a).

Д-159 • ЗА́ВТРАШНИЙ ДЕНЬ *(чего)* [NP; sing only; usu. obj or subj-compl with copula (subj: abstr or concr)] (that which will exist in or belong to) the time yet to come: **tomorrow; the future; the morrow;** [in limited contexts] **tomorrow's** [NP].

[Астров:] ...Озябший, голодный, больной человек, чтобы спасти остатки жизни, чтобы сберечь своих детей, инстинктивно, бессознательно хватается за всё, чем только можно утолить голод, согреться, разрушает всё, не думая о завтрашнем дне... (Чехов 3). [A.:] ...A man who is freezing, hungry, sick to save what is left of life for his children, instinctively, unconsciously grabs at anything that might satisfy his hunger or warm him, and in doing so destroys everything without a thought for tomorrow... (3a). ♦ Россо зарабатывал много, но никогда не был уверен в завтрашнем дне... (Лившиц 1). Rosso earnt [sic] a lot of money, but he was never certain of the morrow... (1a). ♦ «Поверь мне, – сказал он, – что ежели бы что зависело от распоряжений штабов, то я бы был там и делал бы распоряжения, а вместо того я имею честь служить здесь, в полку, вот с этими господами, и считаю, что от нас действительно будет зависеть завтрашний день, а не от них...» (Толстой 6). "You may be sure," he continued, "that if things depended on arrangements made by the staff, I should be there, making those arrangements, instead of which I have the honor of serving here in the regiment with these gentlemen, and I consider that tomorrow's battle, in fact, will depend on us rather than on them…" (6a).

Д-160 • ИСКА́ТЬ ВЧЕРА́ШНИЙ ДЕНЬ ⟨ВЧЕРА́Ш-НЕГО ДНЯ⟩ *coll* [VP; subj: human] to waste time trying to find or bring back sth. that is irretrievably gone: X ищет вчерашний день ≃ **X is trying to bring back yesterday.**

Д-161 • КА́ЖДЫЙ БО́ЖИЙ ДЕНЬ *coll* [NP; Invar; adv; used with impfv verbs; fixed WO] daily: **every blessed day.**

Д-162 • ясно КАК (БО́ЖИЙ) ДЕНЬ *coll* [как + NP; these forms only; modif; fixed WO] (sth. is) completely (clear, obvious): **(as) plain ⟨clear⟩ as day ⟨daylight⟩; crystal clear.**

…Ведь это же ясно как божий день: не приди Джамхух со своими друзьями, Гунда была бы навеки обречена жить без мужа! (Искандер 5). After all, it was plain as day: had Jamkhoukh not arrived with his friends, Gunda would have been forever doomed to live without a husband! (5a). ♦ «Одно, что тяжело для меня… — это образ мыслей отца в религиозном отношении. Я не понимаю, как человек с таким огромным умом не может видеть того, что ясно, как день, и может так заблуждаться?» (Толстой 4). "The only thing that is hard for me…is Father's attitude to religion. I cannot understand how a man of such tremendous intelligence can fail to see what is as clear as day, and can fall into such error" (4a).

Д-163 • ПО СЕЙ ⟨СЕГО́ДНЯШНИЙ⟩ ДЕНЬ; ДО НАСТОЯ́ЩЕГО ДНЯ; ДО Э́ТОГО ⟨НАСТОЯ́-ЩЕГО, СЕГО́⟩ ВРЕ́МЕНИ [PrepP; these forms only; adv; fixed WO] up to the present time, even now: **to this (very) day; to the present day; even today.**

…На рынке [в Таллинне]… моим приятельницам приходилось слышать: «Вот придут белые корабли, всех вас отсюда выгонят». Белых кораблей ждали, ждут и по сей день (Орлова 1). At the market [in Tallinn] my friends occasionally heard: "When the White ships come, then all of you will be driven out of here." They were waiting for the White ships and they're waiting for them to this day (1a). ♦ Кое-что из этих рукописей сохранилось по сегодняшний день, но большая часть погибла во время двух арестов [Мандельштама]… (Мандельштам 1). Some of these manuscripts have survived to the present day, but the bulk of them disappeared at the time of his [Mandelstam's] two arrests (1a). ♦ «Недаром и по сей день наши русские бабы — все матери — молятся, каются в грехах — богоматери: она простит, поймёт грехи, ради материнства…» (Пильняк 1). "Not without reason, even today, do our Russian peasant women—mothers all—pray, confess their sins—to the Virgin: she forgives, accepts sins, for the sake of motherhood…" (1a).

Д-164 • ЧЁРНЫЙ ДЕНЬ *(чей)*; отложить, спрятать *что* и т. п. НА ⟨ПРО *obs*⟩ ЧЁРНЫЙ ДЕНЬ *coll* [NP (1st var.); PrepP, these forms only, adv (2nd var.); fixed WO] a time of misfortune, need in s.o.'s life (esp. a time of possible want in the future for which one saves in the present): **rainy day; hard times; bleak ⟨dark⟩ day(s);** ‖ отложить ⟨припасти, спрятать и т. п.⟩ *что* на чёрный день ≃ **put away ⟨put by, put aside, save etc⟩ (money) for a rainy day.**

Удержалось у него тысячонок десяток, запрятанных про чёрный день… (Гоголь 3). All he managed to keep was some ten thousand roubles put away for a rainy day… (3c).

Д-165 • СОРИ́ТЬ ⟨БРОСА́ТЬ(СЯ), ШВЫРЯ́ТЬ(СЯ), СЫ́ПАТЬ⟩ ДЕНЬГА́МИ *coll* [VP; subj: human] to spend money carelessly, extravagantly, often wastefully: X сорит деньгами ≃ **X throws (his) money around ⟨away⟩; X blows**

⟨**squanders**⟩ **(his) money; X spends money like water;** [in limited contexts] **money burns a hole in X's pocket.**

«…Он [подсудимый] в ту же ночь кутил, сорил деньгами, у него обнаружено полторы тысячи рублей — откуда же он взял их?» (Достоевский 2). "…That night he [the defendant] was carousing, throwing money away, he was found with fifteen hundred roubles—where did he get it?" (2a). ♦ «Доцент твой приехал деньгами сорить?» — спросил Пашков (Чернёнок 1). "Your professor is here to blow money?" Pashkov asked (1a). ♦ [Гаев:] Сестра не отвыкла ещё сорить деньгами (Чехов 2). [G.:] My sister hasn't yet lost her habit of squandering money (2a).

Д-166 • НЕ В ДЕНЬГА́Х СЧА́СТЬЕ [saying] money alone does not make one happy: ≃ **money isn't everything; money can't buy ⟨doesn't bring⟩ happiness.**

[Лебедев:] Ты Сашу любишь, она тебя любит… Оба вы здоровые, умные, нравственные, и сыты, слава богу, и одеты… Что ж тебе ещё нужно? Денег нет? Велика важность! Не в деньгах счастье… (Чехов 4). [L.:] You love Sasha, she loves you….You're both healthy, intelligent, decent people. You have enough to eat, thank God, and you've clothes on your back. What more do you want? You may be hard up, but what matter? Money doesn't bring happiness (4b).

Д-167 • ПРИ ДЕНЬГА́Х *coll* [PrepP; Invar; subj-compl with быть∅, оказаться (subj: human); often neg] one is in possession of money: X при деньгах ≃ **X has (some) money;** [in limited contexts] **X is well-to-do; X is in the money;** ‖ *Neg* X не при деньгах ≃ **X is out ⟨short⟩ of cash ⟨funds⟩; X is low on funds; X is strapped for money ⟨cash⟩.**

Приехал как-то в гостиницу дед из глубинки… Просил самолучший номер… Дед уплатил вперёд за три дня и не поморщился (видно, был при деньгах) (Грекова 3). Once a very old man came to the hotel from the sticks….He asked for the very best room….Without a murmur the old man paid in advance for three days. Apparently he had money (3a). ♦ После истории с накидкой он вёл себя так, будто ничего не случилось: такова жизнь игрока… сегодня при деньгах, завтра зубы на полку… (Рыбаков 2). After the business of the fur wrap, he acted as if nothing had happened: such was the life of a gambler—today you're in the money, tomorrow you have to tighten your belt (2a). ♦ «Четыреста двадцать пять. А?»… — «А может быть, тысячу триста? Мне, право, неловко, но я сейчас не при деньгах, а мне портному платить…» — …«У нас… как-то и прецедентов-то не было, чтобы мы авторам деньги при договоре выдавали, но уж для вас… четыреста двадцать пять!» (Булгаков 12). "How about four hundred and twenty-five rubles?"…"Thirteen hundred perhaps? I feel rather embarrassed because I'm out of funds for the moment and I have to pay my tailor…"…"We don't…exactly have any precedents for paying our authors in cash on signature of the contract, but in your case…four hundred and twenty-five!" (12a).

Д-168 • БЕ́ШЕНЫЕ ДЕ́НЬГИ *coll* [NP; usu. this WO] **1.** a very large sum of money (paid for sth., to s.o., charged for sth. etc): **(cost) a fortune; prodigious sum(s) (of money); fantastic sum (of money); ton of money; (cost) an arm and a leg;** [in limited contexts] **that kind of money.**

Теперь у него просто мастерская, но подпольная, так как патент стоит бешеных денег… (Кузнецов 1). Now he had only a workshop—an underground one, since a license cost an arm and a leg (1a). ♦ «Им же всем нужно деньги платить! Много тысяч денег! Где же их взять». — «…Деньги дадут сборы». — «Кто же у нас будет платить такие бешеные деньги?» (Ильф и Петров 1). "They would all have to be paid. Many thousands of roubles! Where would we get it?" "…The money will come from collections." "And who do you think is going to pay that kind of money?" (1a).

2. money obtained easily and unexpectedly and therefore spent recklessly, extravagantly: **easy money.**

[Телятев:] Вот и мне доставались всё бешеные [деньги], никак их в кармане не удержишь. Знаете ли, я недавно догадался, отчего у нас с вами бешеные деньги? Оттого, что не мы сами их наживали (Островский 4). [T.:] I, too, got easy money, money that came easily and went easily. Only recently I understood why your money and my money was easy money. It was because we did not earn it ourselves (4b).

Д-169 • **ДЕ́НЬГИ НА БО́ЧКУ (класть, выкладывать и т. п.)** *coll* [NP; Invar; usu. obj or indep. sent; fixed WO] to pay right away, produce payment at the time of sale: **cash on the barrel(head); pay cash up front; pay on the spot.**

Д-170 • **ДЕ́НЬГИ НЕ ПА́ХНУТ** *often disapprov* [sent; pres only; fixed WO] it does not matter that the money in question has been obtained by unseemly means or from unsavory sources: **money has no smell.**

< Loan translation of the Latin *pecunia non olet*. According to the Roman biographer Suetonius (*Vespasian*, XXIII, 3), the emperor Vespasian (1st cent. A.D.) introduced a tax on public lavatories. When his son Titus objected to this tax, he held a coin to Titus' nose and asked whether it smelled. Hearing that it did not, the emperor replied, "Yet it's made from urine."

Д-171 • **ДЕ́НЬГИ ⟨ДЕ́НЕЖКИ⟩ СЧЁТ ЛЮ́БЯТ; ДЕ́НЕЖКА СЧЁТ ЛЮ́БИТ** [saying] monetary matters require careful, precise handling (often said when counting money before handing it to s.o. or upon receiving it): ≃ **money likes ⟨loves⟩ to be counted.**

…[Коровьев] выложил председателю пять новеньких банковских пачек. Произошло подсчитывание, пересыпаемое шуточками и прибаутками Коровьева, вроде «денежка счёт любит», «свой глазок — смотрок» и прочего такого же (Булгаков 9). …He [Koroviev] stacked five bundles of new bank notes before the chairman. There was a careful count, interspersed with Koroviev's little quips and pleasantries, such as "money loves to be counted," "your own eye is the best spy," and so on in the same vein (9a).

Д-172 • **НА МЕ́ДНЫЕ ДЕ́НЬГИ ⟨ГРОШИ́⟩ учиться, учить кого, воспитываться и т. п.** *obs* [PrepP; these forms only; adv; fixed WO] (to study, provide for s.o.'s study, be raised etc) with meager, poor, insufficient funds: **(have to) scrape together money ⟨funds⟩ (to study etc); (have to) scrape up pennies (for one's ⟨s.o.'s⟩ education etc); be too poor to get ⟨give s.o.⟩ decent schooling ⟨a decent education⟩; study ⟨go to school etc⟩ on a shoestring.**

Стоило ли воспитывать их [мальчиков], на медные гроши учить живописи, если они занимаются такой мазнёй, да ещё выдают её за последнее откровение! (Лившиц 1). Was it worth bringing them [the boys] up, scraping together the money to let them study painting, if they do such daubing and, moreover, present it as the latest revelation! (1a). ♦ «Пётр Петрович и не скрывает, что учился на медные деньги, и даже хвалится тем, что сам себе дорогу проложил», — заметила Авдотья Романовна… (Достоевский 3). "Pyotr Petrovich makes it no secret that he had to scrape up pennies for his education, and even boasts of having made his own way in life," Avdotya Romanovna remarked… (3c). ♦ «Чему же однако?.. чему [вас] научить?» — сказал Костанжогло. — Я и сам учился на медные деньги» (Гоголь 3). "But what can I teach you, sir? What?" said Kostanjoglo, looking a little embarrassed. "I was too poor to get a decent education myself" (3a).

Д-173 • **НИ ЗА КАКИ́Е ДЕ́НЬГИ** *coll* [PrepP; Invar; adv; used with negated verbs] **1.** not even for a very large sum of money (can sth. be bought, will s.o. sell sth. etc): **not for any price ⟨money⟩; not at any price.**

Самое лучшее бы сейчас — не вздыхать, а достать лошадь. Но лошади сейчас — она это знала — ни за какие деньги не купить в Пекашине (Абрамов 1). The best thing now would be to stop sighing and get hold of a horse. But nowadays in Pekashino horses weren't to be had for any money, and she knew it (1a). ♦ «„А-68" — превосходные бомбардировщики. Что же вам мешает достать ещё?» — «Нам не продают. Ни за какие деньги» (Эренбург 4). "The A 68's are excellent bombers. What prevents your getting any more?" "They won't sell us any. Not at any price" (4a).

2. not under any circumstances: **not (do sth.) at any price; not (do sth.) for all the money in the world ⟨for any money, for anything⟩; there is no way (in the world) (one would ⟨could⟩ do sth.).** Cf. **not for all the tea in China.**

Раз в неделю баба Нила… ехала трамваями на Даниловский рынок за зеленью, сухими грибами, щавелем, шиповником. А уж сколько чая из шиповника было пито! Сейчас этого пойла ни за какие деньги в рот не взять (Трифонов 2). Once a week Nila would…ride the streetcars to the Danilovsky market for greens, dried mushrooms, sorrel and rose-hips. God, the gallons of rose-hip tea they drank! Nowadays he couldn't stand the stuff at any price (2a).

Д-174 • **ШАЛЬНЫ́Е ДЕ́НЬГИ** [NP; fixed WO except when used as VP$_{subj}$ with быть$_\emptyset$] money (usu. a large sum) obtained easily, without any effort on s.o.'s part: **easy money.**

[1-й мужик:] А тысячу-то [доктору] отдали? [Яков:] А то как же?.. [2-й мужик:] То-то шальные деньги-то (Толстой 3). [First Peasant:] And did they give him [the doctor] the thousand? [Ya.:] I should say they did. [Second Peasant:] That's real easy money (3a).

Д-175 • **ЗАШИБА́ТЬ/ЗАШИБИ́ТЬ ДЕНЬГУ́ ⟨МОНЕ́ТУ⟩** *substand* [VP; subj: human] to earn, make money: X зашибает деньгу ≃ **X is making some ⟨a few⟩ bucks;** [in limited contexts] **X is raking in the dough; X is trying to make a fast buck.**

Д-176 • **ПЛЕВА́ТЬ ⟨НАПЛЕВА́ТЬ⟩ С ВЫСО́КОГО ДЕ́РЕВА (кому) на кого-что** *highly coll* [VP; subj: human; usu. infin compl of быть$_\emptyset$ (impers, var. with кому), impfv past (used in pres or past contexts), or imper] s.o. considers some person or thing unimportant, inconsequential, s.o. is contemptuous of some person or thing: X-у плевать на Y-а с высокого дерева ≃ **X doesn't give a damn ⟨a tinker's damn, a hoot⟩ about Y; X doesn't care ⟨give⟩ a fig about Y; X couldn't ⟨could⟩ care less about Y.**

Доктор говорит… для меня все люди равны, и ссылается на клятву Гиппократа, которую он, между прочим, не давал… Администратору… на Гиппократа этого с высокого дерева наплевать… (Войнович 1). The doctor said: "…All people are the same for me." He was referring to the Hippocratic Oath, which, by the way, he had not taken….The hotel manager could not have cared less about the Hippocratic Oath… (1a).

Д-177 • **ПОТЁМКИНСКИЕ ДЕРЕ́ВНИ** *lit, iron* [NP; usu. pl; fixed WO] fakery, a deceptive front that conceals the miserable state of affairs behind the external splendor: **Potemkin villages; window dressing;** [in limited contexts] **(do ⟨have⟩ sth.) just for show; (put up) a façade.**

…Родители Рахили спокойно дожидались приезда Ивановских. Готовились не они… готовился город… И хотя ни сама Рахиль, ни её родители не собирались устраивать потёмкинские деревни, не хотели показухи… но город был взбудоражен… (Рыбаков 1). Calmly Rachel's parents awaited the arrival of the Ivanovskys. It wasn't they who were getting ready for their arrival, but the town….Although neither Rachel nor her parents intended to do anything just for show, or to put up any façades, the whole town was in a state of agitation… (1a).

< From the name of Prince Grigory Potyomkin (often transliterated as *Potemkin*), who constructed artificial villages along the route of Catherine the Great's journey to the south in order to show the empress the prosperity of the new territory acquired by Russia in 1787 after the annexation of the Crimea.

Д-178 • **ЗА ДЕРЕ́ВЬЯМИ ⟨ИЗ-ЗА ДЕРЕ́ВЬЕВ⟩ ЛЕ́СА НЕ ВИ́ДЕТЬ** *disapprov* [VP; subj: human; usu. pres] not to have a complete understanding of the whole because one pays too much attention to minor details: X за деревьями леса не видит ≃ **X doesn't ⟨can't⟩ see the forest ⟨the wood(s)⟩ for the trees; X misses the forest for the trees.**

Многие из них [моих современников] всю жизнь ждали революцию, но увидев её будни, испугались и отвернулись. А были и другие — они боялись собственного испуга: ещё проморгаешь, из-за деревьев не увидишь леса... (Мандельштам 1). Many of them [my contemporaries] had awaited the Revolution all their lives, but at the sight of what it meant in terms of everyday life, they were horrified and looked away. Then there were others who were frightened of their own fears and were terrified of not seeing the wood for the trees (1a).

Д-179 • **ДЕРЖА́ТЬ ⟨ОСТАВЛЯ́ТЬ/ОСТА́ВИТЬ⟩ ПРИ СЕБЕ́** [VP; subj: human] **1.** ~ *кого* to make s.o. stay near one (so that one can easily make use of his services, oversee his work, supervise his behavior etc): X держит Y-а при себе ≃ **X keeps Y close by (X); X keeps Y around; X keeps Y with X;** [when Y is X's subordinate] **X keeps Y on.**

В общем, отец мой Якоб был младший, был любимчик, и его мама, моя будущая бабушка, старалась держать его при себе... (Рыбаков 1). As my father, Jakob, was the youngest and the favourite, his mother, my grandmother-to-be, tended to keep him close by her (1a). ♦ Юный негодяй был влюблён в княгиню... Княгиня была без ума от дяди Сандро. Всё-таки он надеялся на что-то... Возможно, она его не прогоняла, потому что он подхлёстывал дядю Сандро на всё новые и новые любовные подвиги. А может, она его держала при себе на случай, если дядя Сандро внезапно выйдет из строя (Искандер 3). The young reprobate was in love with the princess....The princess was mad about Uncle Sandro. Nevertheless, he had hopes....Possibly she refrained from banishing him because he spurred Uncle Sandro to ever more inventive feats of love. Or perhaps she kept him around just in case Uncle Sandro suddenly became disabled (3a). ♦ «Я тебя вызвал, чтоб оставить при себе». – «Благодарю вашу светлость, — отвечал князь Андрей, — но я боюсь, что не гожусь больше для штабов...» (Толстой 6). "I sent for you because I want to keep you with me." "I thank you, Your Highness, but I fear I am no longer fit for staff work," replied Prince Andrei... (6a). ♦ Он [князь] бы давно его [адъютанта] выгнал, но, подозревая, что адъютант отчасти следит за ним и время от времени доносит на него в Петербург, нарочно из гордости продолжал оставлять его при себе (Искандер 3). He [the prince] would have fired him [his aide-de-camp] long ago, but since he suspected the aide-de-camp of watching him and occasionally denouncing him to Petersburg, he kept him on purposely, out of pride (3a).

2. ~ *что* [obj: usu. свои мысли, взгляды, советы etc] not to let others know (one's thoughts, views etc), not tell others: X держит Y при себе ≃ **X keeps Y to himself;** [in limited contexts] **X keeps ⟨holds⟩ Y in(side).**

«Володя, чтобы не было недоразумений. Я разделяю линию партии. Будем держать свои взгляды при себе. Ни к чему бесполезные споры» (Рыбаков 2). "Volodya, just so there won't be any misunderstandings, I want you to know that I accept the Party line. Let's keep our views to ourselves. No need to have pointless arguments" (2a). ♦ Одна, совсем одна [Настёна] среди людей: ни с кем ни поговорить, ни поплакаться, всё надо держать при себе (Распутин 2). She [Nastyona] was alone, completely alone amid

all these people: there was no one to talk to, to cry to, she had to keep it all in (2a).

Д-180 • **ДЕРЖА́ТЬ СЕБЯ́** [VP; subj: human] **1.** to assume a particular posture while walking, sitting, talking etc: X держит себя [AdvP] ≃ **X carries ⟨holds, bears⟩ himself** [AdvP]; ‖ искусство ⟨умение⟩ держать себя ≃ **perfection of manner.**

[Милашин:] Однако это ужасно! В целый вечер она не сказала со мной ни одного слова... А как она нынче хороша-то! Как держит себя! (Островский 1). [M.:] Really, this is awful! The whole evening she hasn't said a single word to me....But how pretty she is to-day! How she bears herself! (1b). ♦ «Не правда ли, она [Элен] восхитительна?.. Для такой молодой девушки и такой такт, такое мастерское уменье держать себя!» (Толстой 4). "Isn't she [Ellen] ravishing?...And such tact for so young a girl, such absolute perfection of manner!" (4a).

2. to act in a certain manner (as specified by the context), maintain a particular kind of behavior: X держит себя [AdvP] ≃ **X behaves ⟨conducts himself, comports himself⟩** [AdvP].

Направляясь в мурьёвскую глушь, я, помнится, ещё в Москве давал себе слово держать себя солидно (Булгаков 6). Back in Moscow, when I found out that I was to go to remote Muryovo, I had promised myself that I would behave in a dignified manner (6a). ♦ [Тальберг:] Ты женщина умная и прекрасно воспитана. Ты прекрасно понимаешь, как нужно держать себя, чтобы не бросить тень на фамилию Тальберг (Булгаков 4). [T.:] You are an intelligent woman of excellent upbringing. You understand quite well how you must conduct yourself so as not to cast a shadow on the Talberg name (4a). ♦ Он [Володя] во всём стоял выше меня: в забавах, в учении, в ссорах, в умении держать себя... (Толстой 2). He [Volodya] was superior to me in everything: in games, in studies, in quarrels, and in his ability to comport himself well... (2b).

Д-181 • **ТА́К ДЕРЖА́ТЬ!** [Interj; Invar; fixed WO] **1.** *nautical* a command to the helmsman to keep to the charted course: **mind your rudder!; steady as she goes!**

2. (you are doing everything well, correctly,) continue acting the same way: **keep it up!; stay on ⟨the⟩ course!; keep up the good work!; that's the way to do it!; way to go!;** [in limited contexts] **atta boy ⟨girl⟩!**

Д-182 • **ТО́ЛЬКО ДЕРЖИ́СЬ!** *coll* [Invar; used as an indep. clause or subord clause (usu. introduced by Conj что and often correlated with так, такой etc in the preceding clause); usu. this WO] used to emphasize the extreme intensity of the previously mentioned action, quality etc (more often used in refer. to sth. disagreeable): **like you wouldn't believe!; you'd never believe!;** [in limited contexts] **and how!**

«Он такие штуки может выделывать, что только держись! Он заранее знал, что Берлиоз попадёт под трамвай» (Булгаков 9). "He can do things you'd never believe! He knew in advance that Berlioz was going to fall under a streetcar!" (9b). ♦ «Ты думаешь, они меня надуют?» – «Да они же мошенники! Так надуют, что только держись!» "Do you think they'll cheat me?" "They're swindlers! Of course they'll cheat you—and how!"

Д-183 • **ЗАДАВА́ТЬ/ЗАДА́ТЬ ⟨ДАВА́ТЬ/ДАТЬ⟩ ДЁРУ**[1] *substand* [VP; subj: human] **1.** to run away in a great hurry: X дал дёру ≃ **X took to his heels; X hightailed it; X ran ⟨made a run⟩ for it; X made tracks.**

Как только медведь отошёл на несколько шагов, Тендел дал дёру и бежал до самого Чегема, по дороге прихватив сломанное ружьё (Искандер 3). As soon as the bear went off a few steps Tendel took to his heels and ran all the way to Chegem, grabbing his broken gun on the way (3a). ♦ «Вижу, уже могу просунуться — гимнастёрка трещит, по спине дерёт, пролез и дал дёру!» (Кузнецов 1). "I saw that I could just squeeze through; I heard my tunic being ripped, the barbed wire scraping down my back, but I got through and ran for it!" (1b).

2. to leave s.o. (usu. a spouse or romantic partner) or sth. (usu. a job) abruptly and forever: X дал дёру ≃ **X ditched ⟨dumped, dropped⟩ Y; X walked out on Y; X bagged thing Y.**

Ахматова говорит, что ехать надо, иначе Пунин (Николаша) «даст дёру» (Мандельштам 2). Akhmatova said she must go, or else Punin ("Nikolasha") would "walk out" on her (2a).

Д-184 • ЗАДАВА́ТЬ/ЗАДА́ТЬ ⟨ДАВА́ТЬ/ДАТЬ⟩ ДЁРУ² *кому substand* [VP; subj: human] **1.** to punish s.o. by hitting him with a rod or strap: X задал Y-у дёру ≃ **X gave Y a (good) whipping ⟨beating, thrashing⟩; X tanned Y's hide; X took a stick to Y.**

2. to scold s.o. severely, rebuke s.o. harshly: X задал Y-у дёру ≃ **X gave Y a (good) tongue-lashing; X gave Y a piece of X's mind; X told Y off; X told Y a thing or two.**

Д-185 • ДЕРЬМО́ НА ПА́ЛОЧКЕ *vulg* [NP; often subj-compl with copula, nom or instrum (subj: any common noun or pers name); fixed WO] an absolutely worthless, repulsive, despicable person or thing: **pile ⟨lump, piece⟩ of shit.**

«...На тех [политических заключённых] надо было тебе поглядеть, братишка, надо было поглядеть тебе, чтобы понять, какое дерьмо на палочке может быть человек!.. Каким же холуём, братишка, надо заделаться, чтобы в холуйстве своём всех холуёв геройством переплюнуть?» (Максимов 2). "...You should have seen those politicals, brother—you should have seen them if you want to know how human beings can turn themselves into lumps of shit....What sort of an arse-licker have you got to be to make a virtue out of breaking records for arse-licking?" (2a).

Д-186 • НЕ (ИЗ) РО́БКОГО ⟨ТРУСЛИ́ВОГО⟩ ДЕ-СЯ́ТКА *coll, approv* [NP_gen or PrepP; these forms only; subj-compl with copula (subj: human) or nonagreeing modif; fixed WO] brave: **no coward; not easily scared; not the timid type; not (one) of the timid sort; [in limited contexts] a bold ⟨courageous⟩ spirit.**

«Василиса Егоровна прехрабрая дама, — заметил важно Швабрин. — Иван Кузьмич может это засвидетельствовать». — «Да, слышь ты, — сказал Иван Кузьмич, — баба-то не робкого десятка» (Пушкин 2). "Vassilissa Yegorovna is a very brave woman," Shvabrin observed solemnly. "Ivan Kuzmitch can bear witness to that." "Yes, indeed," said Ivan Kuzmitch, "my wife isn't one of the timid sort" (2b). ♦ Конечно, нашлись, как и везде бывает, кое-кто не робкого десятка, которые не теряли присутствия духа, но их было весьма немного: почтмейстер один только (Гоголь 3). Of course, as is generally the case, there were to be found some courageous spirits who had not lost their presence of mind, but they were far from many—as a matter of fact, there was only one: the Postmaster (3b).

Д-187 • НЕ (ИЗ) ХРА́БРОГО ДЕСЯ́ТКА *coll* [NP_gen or PrepP; these forms only; subj-compl with copula (subj: human) or postmodif; fixed WO] not at all brave: **no hero; not the bravest of men ⟨women⟩.**

«Ехать ближним путём через Кистенёвский лес я не осмелился, а пустился в объезд...» — «Эге! — прервал Кирила Петрович, — да ты, знать, не из храброго десятка; чего ты боишься?» (Пушкин 1). "I didn't dare take the short cut through the Kistenevka wood, so I took the roundabout way..." "What!" Kirila Petrovich broke in. "Well, you're certainly no hero. What are you afraid of?" (1b). ♦ Ему... всё это было не только неприятно, но и противно, однако он, человек далеко не храброго десятка, исправно выполнял задание партийной организации (Эткинд 1). He...found the whole business not merely disagreeable but repul-

sive, but not being the bravest of men he was obediently carrying out the instructions of the Party organization (1a).

Д-188 • НЕ ДЕТЕ́Й КРЕСТИ́ТЬ *кому с кем coll* [VP; infin only; impers predic; fixed WO] nothing is tying s.o. to someone else, there are and will be no close relations between the two (or more) persons in question: X-у с Y-ом не детей крестить ≃ **X doesn't have to be (best) friends ⟨buddies⟩ with Y; X doesn't have to be Y's best friend ⟨bosom buddy⟩; [in limited contexts] X doesn't owe Y anything.**

«Бродяга он [Джонни], не бродяга, хуй [*taboo*] его знает, — сказал Алёшка, — тёмный человек. Ну, да наше дело маленькое, нам с ним не детей крестить...» (Лимонов 1). "He [Johnny] may be a bum or he may not, how the fuck should I know," Alyoshka said. "A shady character. Well, it's none of our business, we don't have to be buddies with him..." (1a).

Д-189 • ДЕТИ́ШКАМ ⟨РЕБЯТИ́ШКАМ⟩ НА МОЛО-ЧИ́ШКО заработать, получить, остаться и т. п. *coll, humor* [PrepP; these forms only; obj; fixed WO] (to earn, get, be left with etc) a small amount of money: **a few ⟨a couple of⟩ bucks; a little something; [in limited contexts] (earn enough ⟨try etc⟩) to make ends meet ⟨to get by⟩.**

...От большевиков [офицеры] бежали, к белым не пристали, понемножку жили, спорили о судьбах России, зарабатывали детишкам на молочишко и страстно желали конца войны (Шолохов 4). Having fled from the Bolsheviks without joining the Whites, they [the officers] led a hole-and-corner existence, arguing about Russia's destiny, trying to make ends meet, and wishing only for the war to end (4a).

Д-190 • ВПАДА́ТЬ/ВПАСТЬ В ДЕ́ТСТВО ⟨В МЛА-ДЕ́НЧЕСТВО⟩ [VP; subj: human] **1.** to lose one's mental faculties because of old age: X впадает в детство ≃ **X is entering ⟨falling into⟩ his second childhood; X is getting ⟨becoming⟩ senile; X is in his dotage.**

«Не все в старости впадают в детство», — сказала Тёща... (Зиновьев 2). "Not all old people fall into a second childhood," observed my mother-in-law (2a).

2. Also: **ВПАДА́ТЬ/ВПАСТЬ В РЕБЯ́ЧЕСТВО** to act, think etc as a child would: X впадает в детство ≃ **X behaves like a (little) child ⟨kid⟩; [in limited contexts] X is experiencing ⟨enjoying etc⟩ his second childhood; X is being childish.**

Д-191 • (И) ДЁШЕВО И СЕРДИ́ТО *coll* [AdvP; these forms only; adv, subj-compl with быть∅ (subj: это), or indep. sent; fixed WO] for a reasonable price and of good quality: **(both) cheap and good ⟨cheaply and well⟩; a real bargain; [in limited contexts] (both) cheap and effective.**

[Доктор:] ...Волноваться-то очень незачем. [Барыня:] Да ведь как же? Полную дезинфекцию надо. [Доктор:] Нет, что ж полную, это дорого слишком, рублей триста, а то и больше станет. А я вам дёшево и сердито устрою (Толстой 3). [Doctor:] ...There's no reason to get very excited. [A.P.:] What do you mean? There'll have to be a complete disinfection. [Doctor:] No, why a complete disinfection? That's too expensive. That could run to some three hundred rubles, or even more. I'll fix you one that's cheap and effective (3a).

Д-192 • НА ДИ́ВО; НА УДИВЛЕ́НИЕ [PrepP; these forms only] **1.** [subj-compl with copula (subj: usu. concr or abstr)] sth. is very good, excellent: **a real wonder ⟨marvel⟩; wonderful; marvelous.**

Земля славная, и урожай всегда бывал на диво; но на заколдованном месте никогда не было ничего доброго (Гоголь 5). It's marvelous ground and there is always a wonderful crop on it; but there has never been anything good on that bewitched place (5a).

2. ~ *какой, каков* и т. п. [modif (intensif)] very, extremely: **amazingly; remarkably; uncommonly; exceptionally; wondrously.**

Конец августа был погожий и сухой на диво (Шолохов 5). The end of August was wondrously fine and dry (5a).

3. [adv or modif] very well, excellently: **wonderfully (well); amazingly (well); splendidly.**

Его казаки были экипированы на диво. У всех было в достатке патронов, на всех была справная одежда и добротная обувь − всё добытое с пленных красноармейцев (Шолохов 4). His Cossacks were splendidly equipped. They had plenty of ammunition and their clothing and footwear, all taken from captured Red Army men, were in excellent condition (4a).

4. ~ *(кому-чему)* [the resulting PrepP is sent adv; indir obj: human or collect] so as to evoke wonder, admiration etc: **to the amazement ⟨astonishment, delight⟩ of; [in limited contexts] in a way marvelous to see; to the surprise of.**

[Телятев:] А вот пьёт [Васильков] шампанское, так на диво: отчётливо, методически, точно воду зельтерскую (Островский 4). [T.:] ...He [Vasilkov] drinks champagne in a way marvelous to see: carefully, methodically, just as if it were seltzer water (4a). ♦ «Нет, так не пойдёт! Желаете счастья зятю и дочери, а сами не пьёте», − упрекнул Кокетай засмущавшегося деда Момуна. «Ну разве что за счастье, я что ж», − заторопился старик. На удивление всем, он ахнул до дна почти полный стакан водки... (Айтматов 1). "No, no, that will not do! You toast to the happiness of your daughter and your son-in-law and then don't drink yourself," Koketay reproached the embarrassed Momun. "Well, if it's to happiness, sure..." he mumbled hurriedly. And, to everyone's surprise, he gulped down almost a full glass in a single breath (1a).

Д-193 • ДИ́ВУ ДАВА́ТЬСЯ/ДА́ТЬСЯ *coll* [VP; subj: human; more often impfv past; fixed WO] to be very surprised (at sth.): X диву давался ≃ **X was amazed ⟨astonished⟩; X wondered ⟨marveled⟩; [in limited contexts] it was just ⟨simply⟩ amazing; it was hard to believe.**

Пройдёт время, и люди будут диву даваться, как можно было за такое судить (Зиновьев 1). "As time goes by people will start being amazed that anyone could have been tried on charges like that" (1a). ♦ Обернулась Рябая Хромая Старуха, глянула − диву далась, стоит перед ней олениха, матка маралья (Айтматов 1). The pockmarked Lame Old Woman turned, looked, and wondered: before her stood a deer, a mother deer (1a). ♦ Она? Она! − сразу узнал, никогда не видавши в жизни! Он − диву давался, что так легко её нашёл... (Солженицын 1). She? Yes, it was she! He recognized her at once, though he had never seen her in his life. He marveled that he had found her so easily (1a). ♦ [Рябцов:] Зачем руки связали?.. Не хочу я этого! Развязывай! [Другой рабочий *(Квачу)*:] Господин жандарм! Можно? Парень смирный... Мы диву даёмся... как это он? (Горький 1). [R.:] What did you tie my hands for?...I won't have it! Untie them! [Another Worker *(to Kvatch)*:] May we, sir? The fellow is quiet enough. It's hard to believe he could have been the one... (1c). ♦ Вохровцы... между собой диву давались: чего это бежать, когда сроку-то оставалось всего ничего... (Гинзбург 2). [context transl] ...Among themselves they [the guards] couldn't figure out why anyone should want to try to escape when he had hardly any time left to serve... (2a).

Д-194 • В ДИКО́ВИНКУ ⟨В ДИКО́ВИНУ⟩ *coll* [PrepP; these forms only; subj-compl with copula] **1.** ~ *(кому)* [subj: abstr, concr, human, or infin] a person (thing etc) is unusual, surprising to s.o.: X Y-у в диковинку ≃ **Y has never seen anything like X before; thing X surprises Y; Y is surprised at thing X; ‖** *Neg* X Y-у не в диковинку ≃ **thing X is nothing new ⟨unusual⟩ to Y; there is nothing surprising ⟨unusual⟩ about X; thing X is not unusual with Y; thing X comes as no surprise (to Y); thing X is by no means uncommon; [in limited contexts]**

X is ⟨such things etc are⟩ not unknown; thing X won't take Y by surprise.

...Этот парень ей [Рахили] в диковинку. Не только потому, что он из Швейцарии, она об этой Швейцарии понятия не имела, просто она никогда не видела, чтобы еврейский парень был голубоглазый блондин... (Рыбаков 1). She [Rachel] had never seen anything like this boy before. It wasn't only that he came from Switzerland, which didn't mean anything to her, anyway, but she had never seen a Jewish boy with fair hair and blue eyes... (1a). ♦ [Грекова:] Вы так привыкли к разного рода резкостям, что мои слова едва ли будут вам в диковинку... (Чехов 1). [G.:] You're so used to all kinds of rudeness, I doubt if what I say will surprise you at all (1b). ♦ Матросы всюду матросы... Хороший шторм им не в диковину (Эренбург 2). A sailor is always a sailor....A good storm is nothing new to him (2a). ♦ Что Ноздрёв лгун отъявленный, это было известно всем, и вовсе не было в диковинку слышать от него решительную бессмыслицу... (Гоголь 3). That Nozdrev was an archliar was a fact known to all, and there was nothing surprising in hearing him tell the wildest fabrications... (3c). That Nozdryov was an inveterate liar was a fact they all knew and it was nothing unusual to hear him talk the most absurd nonsense... (3a). ♦ ...В первую минуту гнева [Троекуров] хотел было со всеми своими дворовыми учинить нападение на Кистенёвку... Таковые подвиги были ему не в диковину (Пушкин 1). ...In the first moment of anger [Troekurov] wanted to gather all his men and fall upon Kistenevka....Such exploits were not unusual with him (1a). ♦ ...На базаре откуда-то появился в продаже спирт, и уже не в диковинку было видеть в те дни пьяных... офицеров (Шолохов 3). ...Illicitly distilled spirits appeared on sale at the markets and it was by no means an uncommon sight to see drunken officers...in the streets (3a). ♦ Случались кое-где ограбления, изнасилования, но во время войны в любых войсках такое не в диковинку... (Копелев 1). There were a few robberies and rapes, but in wartime in any army such incidents are not unknown (1a).

2. [subj: any common noun, often animal] a person (thing etc) is an uncommon phenomenon: **rare thing; rarity; oddity.**

Д-195 • ПОД ДИКТО́ВКУ *чью, кого* [PrepP; Invar; the resulting PrepP is adv] (one does sth.) as directed, suggested, ordered etc by another: **at s.o.'s urging ⟨prompting, suggestion, behest, bidding⟩; at the urging ⟨the prompting, the suggestion, the behest, the bidding⟩ of; under orders from.**

У Романа нет своего мнения, он всё делает под диктовку своей жены. Roman never thinks for himself − everything he does is at his wife's prompting.

Д-196 • КРУТИ́ТЬ/ПРОКРУТИ́ТЬ ⟨ПРОВЕРНУ́ТЬ⟩ ДИНА́МО *кому recent, slang* [VP; subj: human] to be deceitful in one's relationship with s.o., ultimately rejecting s.o. (usu. in refer. to relations between the sexes): X крутит Y-у динамо ≃ **X is giving Y the runaround; ‖ X прокрутил Y-у динамо ≃ X gave Y the brush-off ⟨the heave-ho⟩; X dumped Y.**

[Сильва:] Ты любишь девушку − она крутит тебе динамо. Нормальное явление. (Вампилов 4). [S.:] You're in love with a girl and she's giving you the runaround. It happens all the time (4b). ♦ [Кушак:] Она [женщина] сбежала... Что это значит?.. Как это называется? [Зилов:] Динамо. [Кушак:] Что? [Зилов *(с раздражением)*:] Динамо. Это называется прокрутить динамо... Она вам провернула динамо (Вампилов 5). [K.:] She's [the woman has] run away....What's the meaning of this?...I don't know what to call it... [Z.:] The heave-ho. [K.:] What? [Z. *(irritated)*:] It's called the heave-ho....She's given you the heave-ho (5a).

Д-197 • ЧЕМ БЫ ДИТЯ́ НИ ТЕ́ШИЛОСЬ, ЛИШЬ БЫ НЕ ПЛА́КАЛО [saying; often only the first half of the saying is used] let a person do what he wants as long as he is satisfied (said when condescendingly referring to s.o.'s pursuits, actions etc, which are not serious, not worthy of attention): ≃ **as long as you**

are ⟨he is etc⟩ happy; if it makes you ⟨him etc⟩ happy; anything that keeps you ⟨him etc⟩ happy; [in limited contexts] whatever makes your ⟨his etc⟩ boat float; anything to make it easier for you ⟨him etc⟩.

Вскоре после той их первой встречи в чайной Фёдор стал замечать, что старики его наладились подолгу отлучаться на выпасы к Загладину, приохотив к этому и соседей. Сначала он лишь посмеивался над старческой блажью: чем бы дитя ни тешилось. (Максимов 1). Soon after their first meeting in the tearoom, Fyodor had begun to notice that his old folk had taken to making extended visits to Zagladin's pastures, taking their neighbors along with them. At first he had merely laughed at the old couple's whim: anything that keeps them happy! (1a). ♦ «Меня вы забудете, — начал он опять, — мёртвый живому не товарищ. Отец вам будет говорить, что вот, мол, какого человека Россия теряет... Это чепуха; но не разуверяйте старика. Чем бы дитя ни тешилось... вы знаете» (Тургенев 2). "You'll forget me," he began again; "the dead are no companions for the living. My father will tell you what a man Russia is losing—that's nonsense; but don't disillusion the old man. Anything to make it easier for him—you know" (2e).

Д-198 • ПЕТЬ/ПРОПЕ́ТЬ ДИФИРА́МБЫ *кому-чему lit;* **ПЕТЬ/СПЕТЬ ПАНЕГИ́РИК** *obs, lit* [VP; subj: human] to praise s.o., s.o.'s merits excessively: X поёт Y-у дифирамбы ≃ **X heaps ⟨lavishes⟩ praise(s) on Y; X sings the praises of Y; X showers Y with praise(s) ⟨compliments⟩.**

Д-199 • ДО ДНА [PrepP; Invar; adv] **1.** выпить, осушить *что* etc ~ (to empty one's glass) completely: **drink it ⟨a glass etc⟩ (right) down; down it ⟨a glass, one's vodka etc⟩; gulp down (a glass ⟨one's drink etc⟩); drain a ⟨one's⟩ glass; toss it ⟨one's drink⟩ down; drink it to the last drop;** [used as a toast to cheer others to finish their drinks] **bottoms up!**

Довольный эффектом, он [граф] допил до дна бокал... (Аксёнов 7). ...Satisfied with the effect he [the count] had produced, he downed the rest of his champagne (7a). ♦ «Нет, так не пойдёт! Желаете счастья зятю и дочери, а сами не пьёте», — упрекнул Кокетай засмущавшегося деда Момуна. «Ну разве что за счастье, я что ж», — заторопился старик. На удивление всем, он ахнул до дна почти полный стакан водки... (Айтматов 1). "No, no, that will not do! You toast to the happiness of your daughter and your son-in-law and then don't drink yourself," Koketay reproached the embarrassed Momun. "Well, if it's for happiness, sure..." he mumbled hurriedly. And, to everyone's surprise, he gulped down almost a full glass in a single breath (1a). ♦ Мужчины смотрели восторженно: «Людмила Петровна, за вас! До дна! Все пьют за Людмилу Петровну!» (Трифонов 1). The men gazed at her in delight and exclaimed, "To you, Liudmila Petrovna! Bottoms up! Everybody drink to Liudmila Petrovna!" (1a).

2. испытать, понять, исследовать *что* etc ~ (to experience sth.) profoundly, (to understand, study sth.) completely: **fully; to the fullest (measure); in full measure; to the ⟨its, their⟩ very core.**

Смысл каждой беседы: себя без надобности не открыв — собеседника понять, понять до дна (Солженицын 5). The purpose of any conversation is to understand your partner fully without unnecessarily exposing yourself (5a). ♦ Он и веру, и древность, красоту, музыку, людей кругом себя трогал с одинаковым ледяным рвением — изучал. Не просто узнавал, а *изучал*... до последней капли, до дна (Трифонов 5). He approached religious faith, antiquity, beauty, music, and the people around him all with the same icy zeal and subjected them to the same scrutiny. He did not merely learn about them, but he analyzed them inside and out, to their very core (5a).

Д-200 • СО ДНА МО́РЯ ⟨МОРСКО́ГО⟩ достать, добыть *кого-что;* **НА ДНЕ МО́РЯ ⟨МОРСКО́М⟩ найти, сыскать** *кого-что all coll* [PrepP; these forms only; adv; used

with pfv verbs; fixed WO] (to reach, find s.o. or sth.) without fail, no matter how difficult it is, no matter where he or it might be: **(even if one has to dredge s.o. ⟨sth.⟩ up) from the bottom of the sea; (even if s.o. ⟨sth.⟩ is) at the bottom of the sea.**

«Пафнуткина, Рябых, Нехвалёных живыми или мёртвыми. Хоть со дна морского [достать]» (Пастернак 1). "I want Pafnutkin, Riabikh, and Nekhvalenykh, dead or alive. I don't care if you have to dredge them up from the bottom of the sea" (1a).

Д-201 • (ЧТОБ) НИ ДНА НИ ПОКРЫ́ШКИ *кому-чему highly coll* [indep. sent or clause; these forms only; fixed WO] used to express ill will toward s.o. or sth., wish the worst for s.o. or sth.: чтоб X-у ни дна ни покрышки ≃ **(god)damn X; blast X; may X rot in hell.**

«Помню, учили мы про них [эсеров] на политзанятиях, так я думала — они давно вымерли... И вдруг рядом... Вот компания, понимаешь! Чтоб ему ни дна ни покрышки, этому следователю!» (Гинзбург 1). "When we learned about them [Social Revolutionaries] at our political study groups, I thought they'd died out a long time ago and now they turn up here. Some company! All I can say is, damn the investigators who lumped us together!" (1b).

Д-202 • НА ДНЕ быть₀, оказаться и т. п.; **НА ДНО** опускаться, попасть; **ДО ДНА** докатиться [PrepP; these forms only; usu. subj-compl with copula (subj: human)] (to descend to) the lower levels of society, (to be) in déclassé surroundings: X оказался на дне ⟨докатился до дна etc⟩ ≃ **X was down and out; X ended up in the gutter ⟨on the garbage heap, on skid row⟩; X ended up among the dregs of society; X descended to the lower depths;** [in limited contexts] **X hit rock bottom.**

[Глебов] что-то когда-то слышал о том, что Шулепа пропал, докатился до дна... (Трифонов 2). He [Glebov] remembered hearing some time ago that Shulepa had dropped out of sight and had probably ended up somewhere on the garbage heap (2a). ♦ Проходимцу с высшим образованием не надо опускаться на «дно». Он может прекрасно спиваться и на высоких должностях, которых у нас великое множество (Зиновьев 2). There's no need for a careerist with higher education to descend to the "lower depths"; he can perfectly well become an alcoholic in one of the high positions which we have in abundance (2a).

Д-203 • ДНЕВА́ТЬ И НОЧЕВА́ТЬ *у кого, где coll* [VP; subj: human; fixed WO] to be at a specified place constantly, spend almost all one's time there: X днюет и ночует в месте Y ≃ **X is at place Y day and night; X spends day and night at place Y; X spends all day and all night at place Y; X practically lives at place Y.**

«...В этом дурацком, как вы его называете, сигнале (я бы попросту назвала его доносом!) сказано, что Сергей Павлович днюет и ночует у Ларичевой?» (Грекова 3). "...In this idiotic 'complaint,' as you call it—I would simply call it a denunciation—it states that Sergei Pavlovich spends day and night at Laricheva's?" (3a). ♦ «...[Брат] днюет и ночует в камышах, на люди совсем не показывается...» (Максимов 1). "...[My brother] spends all day and night in the reeds. He never sees anyone..." (1a).

Д-204 • ЖИТЬ СЕГО́ДНЯШНИМ ДНЁМ [VP; subj: human; usu. this WO] **1.** to be concerned with the present, live in the present, not thinking about the future: X живёт сегодняшним днём ≃ **X lives for the moment ⟨the present, the day, today⟩; X takes one day at a time; X takes life ⟨it⟩ as it comes, one day at a time; X lives from one day to the next ⟨from day to day⟩.**

Мы жили сегодняшним днём, не ожидая от будущего ничего, кроме мелких пакостей (Окуджава 2). We lived for the day, expecting nothing from the future except petty irritations (2a).

2. to show interest in current events, preserve ties with reality: X живёт сегодняшним днём ≃ **X keeps up on ⟨with⟩ things**

⟨what's happening, the news, the latest happenings⟩; **X keeps himself informed**; **X keeps abreast of the news ⟨the times⟩.**

Д-205 • ДНИ СОЧТЕНЫ́ *чьи, кого* [VP$_{subj}$ with быть$_\emptyset$; fixed WO] **1.** s.o. has a very short time left to live: X-овы дни сочтены ≃ **X's days are numbered**; **X has only a few days left to live**; **X hasn't long to live**; **X is not long for this world**; **time is running out for X.**

[Львов:] Близкий вам человек погибает… дни его со-чтены… (Чехов 4). [L.:] Someone close to you is dying…her days are numbered… (4a).

2. s.o. has very little time left in power, leadership etc: дни X-а сочтены ≃ **X's days are numbered.**

Д-206 • СЧИ́ТАННЫЕ ДНИ (остаются *до чего*) [NP; pl only; used as subj; fixed WO] little time (remains until sth.): до X-а остаются считанные дни ≃ **there are precious few ⟨only a few⟩ days left before X**; **X is only a few days off**; **X will be here any day now**; **X will be here before you know it**; [in limited contexts] **time is running out ⟨getting short, ticking away⟩.**

До экзаменов остаются считанные дни, а я ещё и не начинала готовиться. There are only a few days left before my exams and I haven't even started studying yet.

Д-207 • ЗОЛОТО́Е ДНО [NP; fixed WO] an inexhaustible source of profit: **gold mine**; **mother lode**; **treasure-trove.**

«Вы на юг? Никогда не посоветовал бы». — «Но почему, почему? Я говорю вам — золотое дно, золотое дно» (Федин 1). "You going south? I wouldn't advise it." "But why, why? I'm telling you, it's a gold mine, a gold mine" (1a).

Д-208 • ВВЕРХ ⟨КВЕ́РХУ *obs*⟩ **ДНОМ** [AdvP; these forms only; fixed WO] **1. пойти, идти ~** [adv; often used in sentences with subj: всё] (in refer. to s.o.'s everyday life, general goings-on, the activities of a certain group or within a certain sphere etc) (to be going or begin to go) in a way contrary to normal, in a disorderly fashion, not the proper way: **(be going) topsy-turvy.**

С приездом свекрови всё у нас в доме пошло вверх дном. When my mother-in-law arrived everything at home started going topsy-turvy.

2. перевернуть, перерыть и т. п. *что*, **быть$_\emptyset$ ~** [obj-compl with перевернуть etc (obj: concr or abstr, often всё) or, less often, subj-compl with быть$_\emptyset$ (subj: concr or abstr, often всё)] (used in refer. to the furnishings, objects etc in some place, to the typical routine of some organization, to s.o.'s way of life etc) (to bring sth., be brought) into a state of disorder, confusion: **(turn sth. ⟨everything⟩) upside down**; **(be ⟨end up⟩) topsy-turvy.**

Что вам сказать? Что можно сказать, когда вдруг приходят, устраивают обыск и уводят твоего отца, тихого человека, переворачивают всё вверх дном, ищут ворованное, деньги и ценности, как будто не понимают, что будь отец вор, то он бы всё из дома унёс (Рыбаков 1). What can you say? What can you say when they suddenly come and search your house and take your father away, a harmless man, and when they turn everything in the house upside down in the search for stolen goods and money and valuables, as if they don't realize that, had father really been a thief, he would have got everything out of the house during the six months of the investigation! (1a). ♦ Тридцать первого августа, в субботу, в доме Ростовых всё казалось перевёрнутым вверх дном. Все двери были растворены, вся мебель вынесена или переставлена, зеркала, картины сняты (Толстой 6). On Saturday, the thirty-first of August, everything in the Rostov house seemed topsy-turvy. All the doors were open, the furniture had been carried out or displaced, and the mirrors and pictures taken down (6a).

Д-209 • ИДТИ́/ПОЙТИ́ КО ДНУ ⟨НА ДНО⟩ *coll* [VP] **1.** [subj: human or collect] to be failing miserably, be losing, be

almost ruined: X идёт ко дну ≃ **X is going under**; **X is going to end ⟨wind⟩ up on the rocks**; **X is headed for disaster ⟨ruin⟩.**

2. *disapprov* [subj: human] to degenerate, decline morally: X идёт ко дну ≃ **X is going downhill ⟨to wrack and ruin, to the dogs⟩**; [in limited contexts] **X is (slowly) turning into a bum.**

Д-210 • ИЗО ДНЯ́ ⟨И́ЗО ДНЯ⟩ В ДЕ́НЬ [PrepP; these forms only; adv; used with impfv verbs; fixed WO] every day, one day after another: **day after day**; **from day to day**; **day by day**; **from one day to the next**; **day in, day out ⟨day in and day out⟩**; **every single day.**

Мы только слышали пулемётные очереди через разные промежутки: та-та-та, та-та… Два года изо дня в день я слышал, и это стоит в моих ушах сегодня (Кузнецов 1). We could only hear bursts of machine-gun fire at various intervals: ta-ta-ta, ta-ta….For two long years I could hear them, day after day, and even now they still ring in my ears (1b). ♦ Машина проверяла качество работы и давала ей оценку. Итоги шли в Машину-Сумматор… И так — изо дня в день (Зиновьев 1). The Computer checked the quality of the work and gave it a mark. The results were then passed to the Totalising Computer….Thus it went on from day to day (1a). ♦ «Возьмите очереди. Раз постоять — пустяк. Сто раз — пустяк. А если изо дня в день, из года в год?» (Зиновьев 2). "Take queues. To stand in line once is nothing. To stand in line a hundred times is nothing. But if it's day in day out, year in year out?" (2a).

Д-211 • ПЕРЕБИВА́ТЬСЯ СО ДНЯ НА́ ДЕНЬ *coll* [VP; subj: human; usu. this WO] to live badly, poorly, be in a state of need: X перебивается со дня на день ≃ **X lives from hand to mouth**; **X scrapes ⟨struggles⟩ along**; **X struggles on from day to day**; **X barely makes it from one day to the next.**

Мы никогда не отличались богатством, но до войны в нашей среде никто не мог похвастаться даже относительным благополучием. Все перебивались со дня на день (Мандельштам 1). People like us had never at any time been rich, but before the war nobody in our circle could even say that he was comparatively well-off. Everybody lived from hand to mouth (1a). ♦ Остались дети одни с матерью, кой-как перебиваясь с дня на день (Герцен 1). The children were left with their mother, struggling on somehow from day to day (1a).

Д-212 • СО ДНЯ НА́ ДЕНЬ [PrepP; Invar; adv; fixed WO] **1.** [usu. used with impfv pres or past, or pfv fut] (sth. is expected to happen) very soon: **any day (now)**; **at any moment**; **any time (now).**

Об успехе мартовских запусков было широко объявлено в советских газетах. Это привело в возбуждение аккредитованных в Москве иностранных журналистов — они понимали, что Советский Союз постарается запустить человека на орбиту раньше американцев, и ждали, что это произойдёт со дня на день (Владимиров 1). The Soviet press gave a great deal of publicity to the successful launchings in March. This aroused the interest of the foreign correspondents in Moscow who then realised that the Soviet Union was trying to put a man into orbit before the Americans did and were expecting it to happen any day (1a). ♦ «Вот расписание вашей медицинской части на случай выступления из лагеря. Телеги с партизанскими семьями уже близко. Лагерные разногласия сегодня будут улажены. Со дня на день можно ждать, что мы снимемся» (Пастернак 1). "Here are your marching orders for the medical unit. The convoy with the partisans' families is quite near and the dissensions inside the camp will be settled by this evening, so we can expect to move any day now" (1a). ♦ Со дня на день я ждала ареста, потому что жёны обычно разделяли участь мужей (Мандельштам 2). I expected to be arrested myself at any moment: wives generally shared their husbands' fate at that time (2a).

2. ~ **откладывать, переносить** *что* (to postpone sth. etc) repeatedly, day after day: **(put sth. off) from one day to the next ⟨from day to day⟩; keep putting sth. off.**

…Этой суммы было недостаточно, и Фёдор Константинович решил написать в Америку дяде Олегу, постоянно помогавшему его матери. Составление этого письма он со дня на день откладывал… (Набоков 1). …The sum was insufficient, and Fyodor decided to write to Uncle Oleg in America, who regularly helped his mother.…The composition of this letter was put off from day to day… (1a).

Д-213 • СРЕДИ ⟨СРЕДЬ⟩ БЕ́ЛА ⟨БЕ́ЛОГО⟩ ДНЯ *coll* [PrepP; these forms only; adv; fixed WO] (sth. unlawful, shameful, unconventional, unexpected etc is done) during the daylight hours, so that everyone can see it: **in broad daylight.**

…Самым неприятным, самым скандальным и неразрешимым из всех этих случаев был случай похищения головы покойного литератора Берлиоза прямо из гроба в грибоедовском зале, произведённого среди бела дня (Булгаков 9). …The most unpleasant, the most scandalous and insoluble of all these incidents was the theft of the head of the late editor Berlioz directly from his coffin in the Griboyedov hall, perpetrated in broad daylight (9a).

Д-214 • ТРЕ́ТЬЕГО ДНЯ *coll* [NP$_{gen}$; Invar; adv; fixed WO] two days prior to the day in question: **two days ago;** [when the point of refer. is the moment of speech] **the day before yesterday; the other day;** [when the point of refer. is a certain moment in the past] **two days before.**

«Всё думаю: „Ведь уж как такой меня, скверную, презирать теперь должен". И третьего дня это думала, как от барышни сюда бежала» (Достоевский 1). "I keep thinking: 'How a man like him must despise a bad woman like me.' I thought the same thing two days ago, as I was running home from the young lady's" (1a). ♦ «Погодите, мы вас переделаем». – «Кто меня переделает? Вы?» – «Кто? – Сестра; Порфирий Платонович, с которым вы уже не ссоритесь; тётушка, которую вы третьего дня проводили в церковь» (Тургенев 2). "You just wait…we shall transform you." "Who will transform me? You?" "Who? My sister, and Porfiry Platonych, whom you've stopped arguing with, and auntie, whom you escorted to church the day before yesterday" (2c). ♦ «Третьего дня, за обедом, я не знал, куда смотреть, хоть под стол залезть, когда началось терзание репутаций отсутствующих…» (Гончаров 1). "The other day at dinner I didn't know where to look, I wanted to crawl under the table when they began tearing to pieces the reputations of people who didn't happen to be present" (1b). ♦ Прокурор же показался мне, да и не мне, а всем, очень уж как-то бледным, почти с зелёным лицом, почему-то как бы внезапно похудевшим в одну, может быть, ночь, потому что я всего только третьего дня видел его совсем ещё в своём виде (Достоевский 2). To me, and not only to me but to everyone, the prosecutor looked somehow too pale, with an almost green face, which for some reason seemed suddenly to have grown very thin, perhaps overnight, since I had seen him just two days before looking quite himself (2a).

Д-215 • НЕ ПО ДНЯМ, А ПО ЧАСА́М расти, развиваться, изменяться и т. п. *coll* [PrepP; Invar; adv; fixed WO] (to grow, change etc) very rapidly: **by the hour; by hours rather than by days; not by the day, but by the hour; by leaps and bounds.**

…Над ней [старухой] поохали, поахали, радуясь и удивляясь тому, что она поправляется не по дням, а по часам… (Распутин 3). …They'd all oohed and aahed, surprised and pleased to hear that she [the old lady] was getting better by the hour… (3a). ♦ Она как будто слушала курс жизни не по дням, а по часам (Гончаров 1). She seemed to be going through the course of life by hours rather than by days (1a). ♦ Развращение нравов развивалось не по дням, а по часам (Салтыков-Щедрин 1). Moral corruption grew by leaps and bounds (1a).

Д-216 • НА ДНЯХ [PrepP; Invar; adv] **1.** very recently, not long ago: **a few days ago ⟨back⟩; the other day; a day or two ⟨so⟩ ago.**

На днях в очередном мучительном разговоре о Чехословакии кто-то сказал: не надо при детях (Орлова 1). A few days ago, during a really painful conversation about Czechoslovakia, someone said: "Don't say anything in front of the children" (1a). ♦ Он [Пастернак] рассказывает, что на днях кончил перевод «Ромео и Джульетты»… (Гладков 1). He [Pasternak] told me that he finished [his version of] *Romeo and Juliette* the other day… (1a). ♦ …Расскажу о том, как мы на днях лишились своего начальника (Салтыков-Щедрин 2). I'd better tell you how we lost our chief a day or two ago (2a).

2. very soon, on one of the following days: **within a few ⟨a matter of⟩ days; in a few days; some day soon; any day now; in a day or two ⟨so⟩; shortly;** [in limited contexts] **be about (to do sth. ⟨to happen⟩).**

Мама сказала, что на днях возьмёт меня домой… (Каверин 1). Mother told me that within a few days she would take me home… (1a). ♦ …Дома на днях должны уже были сносить (Попов 1). …The houses were going to be torn down within a matter of days (1a). ♦ «Мы по душам говорили сегодня, и она сказала, что я её физически не удовлетворяю. Разрыв ещё не оформлен, на днях, наверное» (Шолохов 2). "We had a heart-to-heart talk today and she told me I don't satisfy her physically. The break is not yet official, in a few days probably" (2a). ♦ Он сшил себе новую пару платья и хвастался, что на днях откроет в Глупове такой магазин, что самому Винтергальтеру в нос бросится (Салтыков-Щедрин 1). He had a new suit made and boasted that any day now he would open such a store in Foolov that Winterhalter himself would have to sit up and take notice (1a). ♦ «На днях вы ко мне придёте по вызову, как свидетель. Мы ещё вспомним эту беседу. До свидания» (Тендряков 1). "In a day or two I shall summon you officially as a witness. We shall then come back to what we're talking about now. Goodbye" (1a). ♦ «…[Я] тебе на днях вышлю денег, сколько могу больше» (Достоевский 3). "…I'll send you some money in a day or so, as much as I can manage" (3a). ♦ Тут много было [у Ленина] и других расстройств. С Радеком — вперемежку дружба и ссоры… То ссора с Усиевичем… То — слух, что Швейцария на днях втянется в войну, жутковато… (Солженицын 5). There were many other things to disturb him [Lenin]. He and Radek…were friends one day and quarreling the next.…Then there was his quarrel with Usievich.…Then there was the spine-chilling rumor that Switzerland would shortly be drawn into the war… (5a). ♦ Володя на днях поступает в университет… (Толстой 2). Volodya is about to enter the university… (2b).

Д-217 • кому НЕ ДО кого-чего [Invar; the resulting PrepP is impers predic with быть$_\theta$] s.o. does not have the time or desire, is not in the proper frame of mind etc to handle, think about, or deal with some person or matter: **X-у не до Y-a ≃ X isn't ⟨doesn't feel⟩ up to thing Y; X can't be bothered with Y; X has no time for Y; this is no time for thing Y; X is not in the mood ⟨in no mood⟩ for Y; X has other things on his mind (than thing Y); X has better ⟨more important⟩ things to think about (than Y);** [in limited contexts] **X doesn't feel much like doing thing Y; X isn't into it ⟨thing Y⟩.**

В другое время Чонкин подивился бы незаурядному дарованию Плечевого, но теперь было не до того (Войнович 2). Another time Chonkin would have stopped to marvel at Burly's unusual talent, but he wasn't up to it at that particular moment (2a). ♦ Редко когда тётка Бекей бывает в добром настроении. Чаще – мрачная и раздражённая – она не замечает своего племянника. Ей не до него (Айтматов 1). Aunt Bekey was seldom in a good mood. Most of the time, gloomy and irritable, she paid no attention to her nephew. She couldn't be bothered with him (1a). ♦ На чём всё-таки подорвались Мотя и Броня? Может быть, играли с найденной миной или гранатой? Им, знаете, было не до игр (Рыбаков 1). How had Motya and Bronya blown themselves up? Maybe they were playing with a mine they'd found, or a grenade? They had no time for games… (1a). ♦ «Молчите, — шепнула она, — нынче не до шуток» (Окуджава 2). "Shh," she whispered, "this is no time for jokes" (2a). ♦ Он начал было побаиваться, чтобы [чиновники] не узнали его экипажа, но им было не до того (Гоголь 3). He felt apprehensive lest they [the officials] should recognize his carriage but they were not in the mood for noticing such things (3c). ♦ На днях, посмотрев на лес, который всегда был далёким и недоступным, я вдруг подумал, что это мой лес, и удивился такой свободе мыслей. Что значит весна. В последний год, полагаю, мне будет уже не до этих тонкостей (Терц 3). The other day, looking out at the forest which has always been so remote and inaccessible, I suddenly conceived of it as *my* forest and felt surprised at such freedom of thought. That's what spring does for you. During my last year here I imagine that I shall have other things on my mind than fine points such as this (3a). ♦ Работники скупки и домовой лавки, которые были ограблены… пришли в управление для того, чтобы опознать одного из грабителей. В кабинете у Садчикова посадили трёх парней, приглашённых студентов-практикантов из университета. Студенты всё время улыбались и весело переглядывались — это была их первая практика. Садчиков сказал: «Вы это, х-хлопцы, бросьте. Мы сейчас приведём т-того парня, так ему не до улыбок. Ясно?» (Семёнов 1). The staff of the pawnshop that had been robbed…had come to headquarters in order to identify one of the thieves. Three students doing their practical work at the university had been invited to Sadchikov's office. They smiled and looked at one another cheerfully the whole time—this was their first case. Sadchikov said: "Right, pack it up, l-lads. We're going to bring the other b-boy in now and he doesn't feel much like laughing. Got it?" (1a).

Д-218 • **ДО ДОБРА́ НЕ ДОВО́ДИТ/НЕ ДОВЕДЁТ** *(кого)* coll [VP; subj: usu. abstr; usu. pres or fut; more often this WO] sth. will result in negative consequences (for s.o.): X (Y-a) до добра не доведёт ≃ **X will lead to no good.**

Д-219 • **ОТ ДОБРА́ ДОБРА́ НЕ И́ЩУТ** [saying] since the present situation is (relatively) favorable, it is better to leave things as they are than to make a change and risk making things worse: ≃ **(better to) leave ⟨let⟩ well enough alone;** [in limited contexts] **don't rock the boat; why seek anything better than what you already have?**

И зачем ей было от добра искать добра — ведь этот человек уже неплохо отнёсся к ней к такой, какой она была… (Залыгин 1). And why should she seek anything better than what she already had? He liked her well enough as she was (1a).

Д-220 • **ДОБРО́ БЫ** coll [subord Conj, condit; often foll. by a clause introduced by Conj «а то» or «но»] (usu. used to introduce a clause expressing an unreal or hardly realizable condition) (sth.) would be acceptable, understandable, justifiable etc if: **if only; if at least; it would be all right ⟨a different matter, something else, very well, one thing⟩ if;** [in limited contexts] **one could understand it if.**

«Есть некоторый коммунистический стиль. Мало кто подходит под эту мерку. Но никто так явно не нарушает этой манеры жить и думать, как вы, Юрий Андреевич… Вы — насмешка над этим миром, его оскорбление. Добро бы это было вашею тайной. Но тут есть… люди из Москвы. Нутро ваше им известно досконально» (Пастернак 1). "There exists a certain Communist style, Yurii Andreievich. Few people measure up to it. But no one flouts that way of life and thought as openly as you do….You are a living mockery of that whole world, a walking insult to it. If at least your past were your own secret—but there are people from Moscow who know you inside out" (1a). ♦ [Осип:] …Вишь ты, нужно в каждом городе показать себя. (*Дразнит его*

[Хлестакова].) «Эй, Осип, ступай посмотри комнату, лучшую, да обед спроси самый лучший…» Добро бы было в самом деле что-нибудь путное, а то ведь елистратишка [*obs, derog* = мелкий чиновник] простой (Гоголь 4). [О.:] He has, you see, to show off in every town! (*Mimicking him [Khlestakov].*) "I say, Osip, go and book me a room, the best room you can find, and order me the best dinner they have…." It would have been all right if he had really been someone, but he is just a copying clerk! (4c). ♦ Хоть околей, хоть издохни в лесу, а в барак без нормы не возвращайся… И добро бы хоть они, бедные, пайку свою съедали, а то ведь нет. Детям сперва надо голодный рот заткнуть (Абрамов 1). It didn't matter if you caved in and dropped down dead [in the forest], but woe betide you if you came back to the barracks without filling your quota….It would have been one thing if the poor creatures could have eaten their own rations, but no—first they had to stop up the hungry mouths of their children (1a). ♦ «„Пусть, говорит [чёрт], ты шёл из гордости, но ведь всё же была и надежда, что уличат Смердякова и сошлют в каторгу… Но вот умер Смердяков, повесился — ну и кто ж тебе там на суде теперь-то одному поверит?.. И добро бы ты, говорит, в добродетель верил: пусть не поверят мне, для принципа иду. Но ведь ты поросёнок, как Фёдор Павлович, и что тебе добродетель?"» (Достоевский 2). "'Suppose you were to go out of pride,' he [the devil] said, 'but still there would also be the hope that Smerdyakov would be convicted and sent to hard labor….But now Smerdyakov is dead, he's hanged himself—so who's going to believe just you alone there in court?…And one could understand it,' he said, 'if you believed in virtue: let them not believe me, I'm going for the sake of principle. But you are a little pig, like Fyodor Pavlovich, and what is virtue to you?'" (2a).

Д-221 • **ЧЕГО́ ДО́БРОГО** coll [Invar; sent adv (parenth); usu. used in declarative sentences (with pfv fut, subjunctive, or могу, может etc + the infin of another verb); also used in questions containing не… ли; the potential nature of the action, event etc expressed by the Russian idiom (or the Russian idiom in conjunction with мочь) is usu. conveyed in English through "might" or "may"; fixed WO] (sth. is) entirely possible (usu. used in refer. to the possibility that sth. disagreeable or undesirable may occur): **for all one knows, s.o. ⟨sth.⟩ might ⟨may⟩…; who can tell ⟨you never know⟩, s.o. ⟨sth.⟩ might…; s.o. ⟨sth.⟩ might easily ⟨very well⟩…; s.o. ⟨sth.⟩ might even…; perhaps…(you never can tell);** [in limited contexts] **s.o. might take it into his head (to do sth.); you're ⟨he's etc⟩ not by any chance (going to do sth., are you ⟨is he etc⟩)?;** [when the speaker emphasizes his strong negative reaction to the possibility in question] **I'm afraid s.o. ⟨sth.⟩ might…**

…И от мысли, что где-нибудь… он, чего доброго, может встретиться с тревожными, скорбными глазами этого господина, всё вокруг принималось жить по-ночному, как природа во время затмения (Набоков 1). …The thought that somewhere…for all he knew, he might meet the anxious, mournful eyes of this gentleman, caused everything around him to assume nocturnal habits of life, like nature during an eclipse (1a). ♦ «Я тебя, говорит [генерал], не оставлю. Чего доброго, я ещё в дядья тебе запишусь…» (Пастернак 1). "I won't leave you this way, he [the General] said….Who can tell, I might put myself down as your uncle…" (1a). ♦ «…Отказать [отказаться от вызова на дуэль] было невозможно; ведь он меня, чего доброго, ударил бы, и тогда… Тогда пришлось бы задушить его, как котёнка» (Тургенев 2). "…It was impossible to refuse [the duel]; why, he might easily have hit me, and then….Then I'd have had to strangle him like a kitten" (2e). ♦ Какой-то сволочной, под сибирского деланный, кот-бродяга вынырнул из-за водосточной трубы и, несмотря на вьюгу, учуял краковскую [колбасу]. Пёс Шарик свету невзвидел при мысли, что богатый чудак, подбирающий раненых псов в подворотне, чего доброго, и этого вора прихватит с собой… (Булгаков 11). A mangy stray tom, pretending to be Siberian, dived out from behind a drainpipe; he had caught a whiff of the sausage despite the storm. [The dog] Sharik went blind with rage at the thought that the rich eccentric who picked up wounded mutts in gateways might take it into his head to bring along that thief as well (11a). ♦ [Кулыгин:] Если тринадцать за столом, то, значит, есть тут влюблённые. Уж не вы ли, Иван Романович, чего доброго... (Чехов 5). [К.:] If there are thirteen at the table it means that someone here is in love. It's not you by any chance, Ivan Romanovich? (5a). ♦ [Артемий Филиппович:] ...Уж [городничий] и в генералы лезет. Чего доброго, может и будет генералом (Гоголь 4). [A.F.:] ...He's [the Mayor is] bucking for general. I'm afraid that maybe he'll be a general at that (4a). ♦ Больше всего она [Ахматова] боялась, чтобы какие-нибудь авангардисты не оторвали их [её и Мандельштама] друг от друга, зачислив его посмертно в футуристы, в братья Хлебникову или, чего доброго, в Леф (Мандельштам 2). [context transl] What she [Akhmatova] feared most of all was that some avant-gardists might try to dissociate them [her and Mandelstam] by making him posthumously into a Futurist, a fellow spirit of Khlebnikov, or even, perish the thought, a member of LEF (2a).

Д-222 • ПОМИНА́ТЬ/ПОМЯНУ́ТЬ ⟨ВСПОМИНА́ТЬ/ВСПО́МНИТЬ⟩ ДОБРО́М ⟨ДО́БРЫМ СЛО́ВОМ⟩
кого-что [VP; subj: human; obj: usu. human] when remembering s.o. or sth., to say or recall good things about him or it: X поминал Y-а добрым словом ≃ **X had a kind word for person Y; X had a kind word to say about person Y; X had nice ⟨only good⟩ things to say about Y; X remembered person Y kindly ⟨with a kind word⟩; X remembered Y fondly; X spoke kindly ⟨fondly⟩ of person Y; X had fond memories of Y.**

«Стойте! Неужто вы желаете помянуть добрым словом Обломова?» (Набоков 1). "Stop right there! Don't tell me you have a kind word for Oblomov..." (1a). ♦ Нигде так пышно не справляются поминки, как в Грузии: угощают всю улицу, чтобы добром поминали покойника, а потом каждый год опять пьют вино возле могилы (Аллилуева 2). Nowhere are wakes so sumptuous as in Georgia: they treat the entire street, so that the deceased may be kindly remembered; and every year thereafter they drink wine around the grave (2a). ♦ [Астров:] Сел я, закрыл глаза — вот этак, и думаю: те, которые будут жить через сто-двести лет после нас и для которых мы теперь пробиваем дорогу, помянут ли нас добрым словом? (Чехов 3). [A.:] I sat down, shut my eyes—just like this—and started to think: people who live a hundred or a couple of hundred years after us, and for whom we are now clearing the way, will they remember us with a kind word? (3e).

Д-223 • К ДОБРУ́ [PrepP; Invar; usu. subj-compl with бытьø
(subj: usu. abstr or a clause, often это), pres only] sth. is a good sign: **it's ⟨that's⟩ (a sign of) good luck; it's ⟨that's⟩ a good omen; it bodes well; that's lucky.**

[Варя:] Что ещё тут? [Дуняша:] Блюдечко разбила... [Варя:] Это к добру (Чехов 2). [V.:] What's going on here? [D.:] I broke a saucer. [V.:] That's good luck (2a).

Д-224 • НЕ К ДОБРУ́ [PrepP; Invar; subj-compl with бытьø
(subj: usu. abstr or a clause, often это), pres only, or adv] sth. forebodes ill fortune, harmful consequences: X не к добру ≃ **no good will come of X; X will lead to no good; X bodes ill ⟨no good⟩; X is not a good sign; X is a bad omen ⟨sign⟩; X is bad luck; X means trouble.**

[Колесов:] Опять ты замуж собираешься? Это не к добру... (Вампилов 3). [K.:] You're planning to get married again? No good will come of it... (3b). ♦ Он шёл и думал: Неужели его будут судить? Неужели возможна такая жестокость: по прошествии стольких лет его судить? Ах, эта смена Суда! Ах, не к добру! (Солженицын 10). Moving along, he was lost in reflections: Would they really put him on trial? Was such cruelty possible? Were they going to try him so many years after the events? Ah, that replacement of the Court. It could lead to no good! (10b). ♦ «Вы посудите, Иван

Григорьевич: пятый десяток живу, ни разу не был болен; хоть бы горло заболело, веред [obs, substand = нарыв] или чирей выскочил... Нет, не к добру! Когда-нибудь придётся поплатиться за это» (Гоголь 3). "Just judge for yourself, Ivan Grigoriyevich: here I'm going on my fifth decade and I haven't been sick even once—haven't had as much as a sore throat, never even as much as a boil or carbuncle....No, that doesn't bode any good! Some time or other I'll have to pay for it" (3b). "See for yourself, Ivan Grigoriyevich, I'm going on fifty now and I've never been sick. Not even a sore throat or a boil or anything....It's not a good sign—someday I'll have to pay for it..." (3e). ♦ В тут ночь мне приснились иконы. Сон не к добру (Мандельштам 1). That night I dreamed of ikons—this is always regarded as a bad omen (1a). ♦ Шалико почувствовал, что её [Хикур] внезапный отъезд не к добру (Искандер 4). Shaliko had sensed that Khikur's sudden departure meant trouble (4a).

Д-225 • ВТИРА́ТЬСЯ/ВТЕРЕ́ТЬСЯ ⟨ВКРА́ДЫВАТЬСЯ/ВКРА́СТЬСЯ, ВЛЕЗА́ТЬ/ВЛЕЗТЬ⟩ В ДОВЕ́РИЕ к кому coll, disapprov [VP; subj: human] (to try) to obtain s.o.'s trust by using whatever (often underhand) means are necessary (usu. with the goal of personal gain): X втёрся в доверие к Y-у ≃ **X wormed ⟨weaseled⟩ his way into Y's confidence; X wormed himself into Y's confidence; X stole into Y's confidence; X insinuated himself into Y's trust ⟨confidence⟩.**

[Иосиф] умел улыбаться, и когда улыбался, то это был ангел, втирался в доверие к людям и потом их обманывал (Рыбаков 1). He [Yosif] knew how to smile, and when he did he could look like an angel and worm his way into your confidence, and then stab you in the back (1a). ♦ Самый хитрый человек не мог бы искуснее вкрасться в доверие княжны, вызывая её воспоминания лучшего времени молодости и выказывая к ним сочувствие (Толстой 7). The most cunning man could not have stolen into the Princess's confidence more cleverly, evoking memories of the best times of her youth and showing sympathy with them (7a). ♦ Вероятно, [Александр] думал, что я притворяюсь «честнягой», рассчитывая на особую благосклонность начальства и, значит, дурак, либо хочу втереться в доверие к товарищам и, значит, опасен (Копелев 1). He [Aleksandr] must have thought that I was playing at being very "honest," hoping for special favor from the bosses, and therefore a fool, or hoping to insinuate myself into the trust of my comrades, and therefore dangerous (1a).

Д-226 • ВХОДИ́ТЬ/ВОЙТИ́ В ДОВЕ́РИЕ к кому [VP;
subj: human] to get s.o. to trust one: X вошёл в доверие к Y-у ≃ **X gained Y's trust ⟨confidence⟩; X earned ⟨won⟩ Y's trust.**

Д-227 • ВЫХОДИ́ТЬ/ВЫ́ЙТИ ИЗ ДОВЕ́РИЯ у кого
[VP; subj: human] to fail to keep s.o.'s trust: X вышел из доверия у Y-а ≃ **X lost Y's confidence ⟨trust⟩; Y lost confidence ⟨his trust⟩ in X; Y no longer trusted X.**

«Нет, Павел Миронович, на вас я больше надеяться не могу. Хватит. Вы из доверия вышли» (Распутин 4). "No, Pavel Mironovich, I can't count on you anymore. Enough. I no longer trust you" (4a).

Д-228 • В ДОВЕРШЕ́НИЕ ⟨К ДОВЕРШЕ́НИЮ, ДЛЯ ДОВЕРШЕ́НИЯ⟩ чего [PrepP; these forms only; the resulting PrepP is sent adv] as a final addition to (the circumstances, events, features etc mentioned in the preceding context and usu. summarized by the complement of the idiom): **to crown ⟨cap, complete, add to⟩ sth.;** ‖ в довершение ⟨к довершению⟩ всего ≃ **to top it (all) off; on top of everything else; on top of all this ⟨that⟩;** ‖ в довершение несчастья ⟨беды и т. п.⟩ ≃ **to make things ⟨matters⟩ worse.**

Только они [друзья] дошли до ручья, как увидели, что навстречу им идёт человек могучего сложения и несёт на плечах дом... На вершине крыши сидел золотистый петух... К довершению всех этих странностей на веранде дома стояла женщина... (Искандер 5). Just as they [the friends] reached the brook they saw a powerfully built man coming toward them, carrying a house on his shoulders....On the roof-peak sat a golden rooster.…To crown all these oddities, a woman stood on the veranda... (5a). ♦ Сидевшие вокруг его [Тентетникова] господа показались ему так похожими на учеников. К довершению сходства, иные из них читали глупый переводной роман... (Гоголь 3). ...The young gentlemen who were sitting around him [Tentetnikov] reminded him of a lot of schoolboys. To complete the similarity, some of them were reading a stupid foreign novel... (3a). ♦ К довершению бедствия, глуповцы взялись за ум (Салтыков-Щедрин 1). To add to the disaster, the Foolovites came to their senses (1a). ♦ Начал [бригадир] требовать, чтоб обыватели по сторонам не зевали, а смотрели в оба, и к довершению всего устроил такую кутерьму, которая могла бы очень дурно для него кончиться... (Салтыков-Щедрин 1). He [the brigadier] began to demand that the townsfolk not stand around gaping but keep their eyes peeled. To top it all off, he staged a ruckus that might have ended very badly for him... (1a). ♦ В произнесённых им невзначай каких-то сухих и обыкновенных словах [дамы] нашли колкие намёки. В довершение бед какой-то из молодых людей сочинил... сатирические стихи на танцевавшее общество... (Гоголь 3). They [the ladies] discovered sarcastic allusions in the few indifferent and ordinary words he had uttered at random. To make things worse, one of the young men composed some satirical verses on the dancers... (3a).

Д-229 • ТЕРЯ́ТЬСЯ В ДОГА́ДКАХ ⟨В ПРЕДПОЛО-ЖЕ́НИЯХ⟩ [VP; subj: human; fixed WO] to be making various suppositions without knowing which of them provides an explanation or answer: X терялся в догадках ≃ **X was lost in conjecture; X was racking his brains trying to figure it out; X drowned in surmise;** [when the focus is on one's final inability to come to a conclusion] **X was at a loss (to know...); X couldn't figure it out.**

К двенадцати часам следующего дня по «Геркулесу» пополз слух о том, что начальник [Полыхаев] заперся с каким-то посетителем в своём пальмовом зале и вот уже три часа не отзывается ни на стук Серны Михайловны, ни на вызовы по внутреннему телефону. Геркулесовцы терялись в догадках (Ильф и Петров 2). Toward midday the next day the rumor went around that Polykhayev had locked himself in his hall of palms with a visitor and hadn't responded to Serna Mikhailovna's knocking or the internal telephone calls for three hours. The Herculeans were lost in conjecture (2a). ♦ Марат терялся в догадках, стараясь узнать степень полномочий этих двух деревенских верзил (Искандер 2). Marat drowned in surmise when he tried to figure out exactly how much authority these two village giants had (2a). ♦ Но кто же брал на себя труд уведомить отца моего о моём поведении?.. Я терялся в догадках (Пушкин 2). But who then took it on himself to inform my father of my conduct?...I was at a loss (2a). ♦ Он терялся в догадках. Был убеждён, что его арестовали из-за истории в институте... Если институт — не повод для ареста, значит, повод другой, прокурор счёл его убедительным (Рыбаков 2). He couldn't figure it out. He'd been sure they'd arrested him because of what happened at the institute....If the institute wasn't the reason for his arrest, that meant there was another one, and that the prosecutor had found it convincing (2a).

Д-230 • ПОСЛЕ ДО́ЖДИЧКА ⟨ДО́ЖДИКА⟩ В ЧЕТ-ВЕ́РГ coll, humor or iron [PrepP; these forms only; adv; often used as indep. sent in response to the question «Когда..?»; fixed WO] it is not known when, perhaps never: **God knows when;** [in response to a question] **God only knows!;** [in limited contexts] **your guess is as good as mine;** [with the implication that sth. will never happen] **when hell freezes over.**

«Когда родители дадут тебе деньги на машину?» — «После дождичка в четверг! Лучше возьми ссуду в банке». "When are your parents going to give you the money for a car?" "God only knows! I'd be better off taking out a loan from the bank."

Д-231 • ЗОЛОТО́Й ДОЖДЬ (чего) [NP; sing only; fixed WO] riches, large sums of money (by extension large amounts of benefits, awards, prizes etc): **golden rain (of sth.); shower of golden rain; shower of gold ⟨wealth⟩.**

...Когда-то [бывший литературный маршал] заседал в президиумах, громил своих неудачливых собратьев, требовал их крови, издавался огромными тиражами, сыпался на него золотой дождь наград, денег и привилегий, и сам он... поверил, что заслужил это своим выдающимся вкладом в литературу (Войнович 1). At one time, he [a former field marshal of literature] had presided over presidiums, thundered against his hapless fellow writers, demanded their blood. His books were printed in enormous editions, a golden rain of prizes, money, and privileges fell upon him, and...he believed he'd earned it all (1a).

< Loan translation of the German *Goldregen*. From the Greek myth of Zeus, who was so captivated by Danaë's beauty that, in order to reach her, he turned himself into golden rain and impregnated her.

Д-232 • ТО, ЧТО ДО́КТОР ПРОПИСА́Л coll [Invar; usu. indep. sent or subj-compl with быть∅ (subj: concr or abstr); fixed WO] exactly what is required, needed, suitable, pleasing in a given situation: **just what the doctor ordered.**

«Отлично, — пробормотал Тюлькин, опрокинув рюмку и подцепив вилкой маринованный гриб, — то, что доктор прописал». "First-rate," muttered Tyulkin right after knocking back a shot of vodka and scooping up a marinated mushroom with his fork, "just what the doctor ordered."

Д-233 • В ДОЛГ [PrepP; Invar; adv] **1. давать, брать, просить** что ~ to give, receive, or request sth. (often money) for some period of time, on the condition that it (or its equivalent) will be returned later: **(give ⟨get, ask for etc⟩) a loan (of...); (give ⟨get etc⟩) money on loan; lend (sth.); borrow (sth.).**

Что ни двор — то вексель у Сергея Платоновича: зелёненькая с оранжевым позументом бумажка — за косилку, за набранную дочери справу (подошло время девку замуж отдавать, а на Парамоновской ссыпке прижимают с ценой на пшеницу, — «Дай в долг, Платонович!»), мало ли за что ещё... (Шолохов 2). There was scarcely a farm that had not given Sergei Platonovich a green slip with an orange border promising to pay for a reaper, for a daughter's dowry (time for the girl to be married but wheat prices were low at the Paramonov elevator, so "Give us a loan, Platonovich!"), and for all kinds of other things (2a). ♦ Руслан Павлович. Хам, алкоголик... Ходит по дачам, просит по трояку, по пятёрке в долг — опохмелиться... И как совести хватает? Ведь инженер, с высшим образованием... (Трифонов 6). Ruslan Pavlovich. A lout and an alcoholic. Goes around the dachas asking for a loan of three, five rubles to go for a dose of the hair of the dog. Has the man no shame? After all, he's an engineer; he has higher education (6a).

2. (to provide or receive some good or service) without requiring or providing immediate payment, on the condition that payment will follow: **on credit;** [in limited contexts] **(give ⟨extend⟩) credit.**

Костенко подходил к подъезду, в котором жил профессор. Он даже не подходил, а, правильнее сказать, подбегал, потому что такси он найти не смог, а если бы и нашёл, то вряд ли уговорил бы шофёра везти его в долг, без денег (Семёнов 1). Kostyenko walked up to the block of flats in which the professor lived. In fact he did not walk but ran up, because he had been unable to find a taxi, and even if he had it was unlikely that he would have been able to persuade him to take him on credit, with no money (1a). ♦ В магазине всегда пусто. Там на двери сильная пружина. Там работает пожилая женщина. Она добрая, потому что даёт в долг (Соколов 1). The store is always empty. The spring on the door is a strong one. An aging woman works there. She is kind, because she gives credit (1a).

3. жить ~ (to live) on money that one has borrowed: **(live) on credit ⟨on borrowed money⟩.**

[Трофимов:] ...Ваша мать, вы, дядя уже не замечаете, что вы живёте в долг... (Чехов 2). [T.:] ...Your mother, you yourself, your uncle—you don't realize that you're actually living on credit (2c).

Д-234 • ДОЛГ ПЛАТЕЖÓМ КРÁСЕН [saying] a kind (or, occas., hostile) act is reciprocated (said when s.o. responds to another's action or attitude in a similar way): ≃ **one good ⟨bad⟩ turn deserves another;** [in limited contexts] **you scratch my back and I'll scratch yours.**

«Ах! Я было и забыл благодарить тебя за лошадь и за тулуп. Без тебя я не добрался бы до города и замёрз бы на дороге»... Пугачёв развеселился. «Долг платежом красен», — сказал он (Пушкин 2). "Oh, I almost forgot to thank you for the horse and the coat. Without your help I would've never reached the city and would've frozen on the highway."...Pugachev cheered up. "One good turn deserves another," he said... (2a).

Д-235 • ОТДАВÁТЬ/ОТДÁТЬ ПОСЛÉДНИЙ ДОЛГ *кому lit* [VP; subj: human; usu. this WO] to bid farewell to a dead person, usu. by attending his burial: X отдал последний долг Y-y ≃ **X paid his last respects to Y; X said a final ⟨last⟩ farewell to Y.**

Причастившись и особоровавшись, он тихо умер, и на другой день толпа знакомых, приехавших отдать последний долг покойнику, наполняла наёмную квартиру Ростовых (Толстой 7). Having received communion and the final anointing, he died peacefully, and the following day the throng of acquaintances who came to pay their last respects to the deceased filled the house rented by the Rostovs (7a).

Д-236 • В ДОЛГÁХ быть₀, сидеть, увязнуть *coll* [PrepP; Invar; subj-compl with copula (subj: human)] to have debts (usu. large ones): X сидит в долгах ≃ **X is in debt ⟨in hock, in the hole⟩;** [in limited contexts] **X is in the red;** ‖ X весь ⟨кругом⟩ в долгах ≃ **X is deep ⟨up to his neck, up to his ears⟩ in debt; X is deep in the hole; X is saddled with debts;** [in limited contexts] **X owes everyone money.**

Всё, кажется, прожил, кругом в долгах, ниоткуда никаких средств, а задаёт обед... (Гоголь 3). To all appearances such a one has spent all he had, he is up to his ears in debt, he has nowhere to turn for money, and yet he will give a banquet... (3a).

Д-237 • ВЛЕЗÁТЬ/ВЛЕЗТЬ ⟨ЗАЛЕЗÁТЬ/ЗАЛÉЗТЬ, ВХОДИ́ТЬ/ВОЙТИ́⟩ В ДОЛГИ́ ⟨В ДОЛГ⟩ *coll* [VP; subj: human] to incur debts (usu. large ones): X влез в долги ≃ **X got (himself) into debt; X ran ⟨went⟩ into debt; X ran up (big ⟨huge etc⟩) debts; X got deep in debt ⟨in the hole⟩; X got up to his ears ⟨his neck⟩ in debt.**

Будучи расточителен и честолюбив, он позволял себе роскошные прихоти; играл в карты и входил в долги, не заботясь о будущем... (Пушкин 1). Prodigal and ambitious, he indulged himself in extravagant habits, played at cards, got into debt, and gave no thought to the future... (1a). ♦ Он не был жаден, но любил широко жить, не отказывал ни в чём семье и любовницам, легко влезал в долги (Эренбург 4). He was not greedy, but he liked to live on a grand scale. He never refused anything to his family or mistresses and easily ran into debt (4a).

Д-238 • ДÓЛГО ЛИ *coll* [AdvP; Invar; impers predic; used with infin] (sth., often sth. disagreeable, unpleasant, could happen) easily: **(sth. could happen ⟨you could get into trouble etc⟩) before you know ⟨knew⟩ it; it wouldn't ⟨doesn't⟩ take much (for sth. to happen); it's ⟨it would be⟩ easy (to do sth.).**

Не выходи сегодня на улицу: очень скользко, долго ли ногу сломать. Don't go outside today, it's really slippery, before you know it, you could fall and break a leg. ♦ [Катерина:] Долго ли в беду попасть! А там и плачься всю жизнь... (Островский 6). [K.:] It's easy to get into trouble. And if I do, I can spend the rest of my life in tears... (6f).

Д-239 • ДÓЛГО ЛИ, КÓРОТКО ЛИ *folk* [AdvP; Invar; adv; fixed WO] for some (unknown and inconsequential) amount of time: **for a time, a long time or a short time; for a while, it doesn't matter how long; how long (s.o. was doing sth. ⟨sth. was going on etc⟩) is no matter.**

Долго ли, коротко ли они так жили, только в начале 1776 года, в тот самый кабак, где они в свободное время благодушествовали, зашёл бригадир (Салтыков-Щедрин 1). They lived thus for a time, a long time or a short time, but in 1776, near the first of the year, the brigadier dropped into the very same tavern where they whiled away their leisure hours (1a).

Д-240 • КАК ДÓЛГО [AdvP; Invar; adv; fixed WO] (for) how much time: **how long;** [in limited contexts] **how much longer.**

С торжественным победным маршем сливалась песня... Петя не знал, как долго это продолжалось: он наслаждался, всё время удивлялся своему наслаждению и жалел, что некому сообщить его (Толстой 7). The voices blended with the triumphal victory march....How long this lasted Petya could not tell; he delighted in it, wondering all the while at his delight and regretting that there was no one to share it (7a).

Д-241 • В ДОЛГУ́ [PrepP; Invar; the resulting PrepP is subj-compl with copula (subj: human)] **1.** ~ *у кого* one is financially beholden to s.o.: X в долгу у Y-a ≃ **X owes Y money; X is in debt to Y.**

2. ~ *у кого, перед кем* one feels obligated, very grateful to s.o. (for a favor, his kindness etc): X в долгу перед Y-ом ≃ **X is ⟨feels⟩ indebted to Y; X is in Y's debt; X owes Y (one); X owes Y a debt of gratitude.**

...Она [Светланочка] существовала доподлинно и со страстью не вчерашней, не завтрашней, а сегодняшней и даже сиюминутной жизни. Вот этим, этой страстью жить, она и была нынче так близка Ирине Викторовне, за эту же страсть Ирина Викторовна оставалась в долгу перед Светланочкой (Залыгин 1). She [Svetlana] lived fully and with a love of life—not life yesterday or life tomorrow, but life today, this very minute. It was in this love of life that she was so close to Irina Viktorovna. For this Irina Viktorovna was indebted to Svetlana (1a). ♦ «Я ему сказал, решайте сами, я не хочу быть ему обязанным, не хочу быть в долгу» (Рыбаков 2). "I told him to decide for himself. I don't want to be under any obligation to him; I don't want to be in his debt" (2a).

Д-242 • В ДОЛГУ́ КАК В ШЕЛКУ́ *coll* [PrepP; Invar; subj-compl with быть₀ (subj: human); fixed WO] one owes large amounts of money: X в долгу как в шелку ≃ **X is buried ⟨drowning⟩ in debt; X is up to his ears ⟨his neck⟩ in debt; X is deep in the hole.**

Д-243 • НЕ ОСТАВÁТЬСЯ/НЕ ОСТÁТЬСЯ В ДОЛГУ́ *(у кого, перед кем)* [VP; subj: human; usu. pfv] to respond to s.o.'s attitude, action etc with the same kind of attitude, a similar action etc; occas., to remunerate s.o. for a favor: X не остался у Y-a в долгу ≃ **X repaid Y; X paid Y back (in kind); X returned the favor ⟨the compliment⟩;** [in limited contexts] **X replied in the same vein ⟨manner⟩;** [in refer. to a favor, kindness etc only] **X made it up to Y;** [in refer. to a conflict, fight, revenge etc only] **X paid Y back with interest; X got even with Y; X gave Y as good as X got; X got back at Y.**

«Ты меня пожалела, а я в долгу не останусь!.. Ты, что понадобится, говори» (Шолохов 2). "You've been good to me, lass, and I'm going to pay you back!...So you just say if there's anything you need" (2a). ♦ «...Не только никаких Тихоновых и большинства Союза [писателей] нет для меня и я их отрицаю, но я не упускал случая открыто и прямо заявлять. И они, разумеется, правы, что в долгу у меня не остаются» (Гладков 1). "...Not only do Tikhonov and his like as well as most other members of the Union of Writers no longer exist for me, not only do I deny them, but I also lose no opportunity of saying so openly and plainly. And they, of course, are quite right to pay me back in kind" (1a). ♦ Квиты! Ты мне насолила, жизнь разломала, и я не осталась в долгу. Сполна рассчитался (Абрамов 1). We're even! You did me dirt and smashed my life, and I've returned the compliment. So the score is settled (1a). ♦ Два дня спустя Дмитрий Алексеевич [Лопаткин] получил протокол заседания технического совета... Протокол заканчивался фразой: «Постановили признать нецелесообразным...» — дальше шли такие же знакомые слова... [Он] привычной рукой написал жалобу на имя начальника технического управления министерства (Дудинцев 1). Two days later Lopatkin received the minutes of the technical council's session....The minutes ended with the words: "it was decided to consider it unsuitable..." after which came other no-less-familiar phrases....He replied in the same vein...writing with a practiced hand a complaint addressed to the chief of the technical department of the Ministry (1a). ♦ «...Наташенька, не сердись на меня, — сказал я. — Это было очень важно. Я в долгу не останусь...» (Зиновьев 2). "...Natasha, don't be angry with me," I said. "It was very important. But I'll make it up to you..." (2a). ♦ Говорят, его [Ситникова] кто-то недавно побил, но он в долгу не остался: в одной тёмной статейке, тиснутой в одном тёмном журнальце, он намекнул, что побивший его — трус (Тургенев 2). There is talk of someone having beaten him [Sitnikov] not so long ago, but Sitnikov paid this fellow back with interest: in an obscure little article, published in an obscure little journalette, he hinted that the man who had beaten him up is a coward (2d). Rumour has it that he [Sitnikov] recently received a thrashing, but he got even with his assailant: in an insidious little paragraph squeezed into an insidious little journal he insinuated that his assailant was a coward (2a). ♦ Вышел оттуда [из чулана] Егорша покачиваясь, насквозь мокрый, будто вынырнул из воды, но довольный. «Досталось маленько, — сказал он, отряхиваясь и звонко шлёпая себя по мокрой груди. — Ну да я тоже не остался в долгу. Целое ведро на Раечку вылил» (Абрамов 1). Egorsha emerged [from the storeroom] — slightly unsteady and soaked through as if he had just taken a swim — but pleased. "I caught it a little," he said, shaking himself dry and slapping his chest. "But I gave as good as I got. I poured a whole bucketful over Raechka" (1a).

Д-244 • ПО ДО́ЛГУ *чего* [PrepP; Invar; the resulting PrepP is adv] in order to meet the demands dictated by or intrinsic to sth.: **as (sth.) obliges ⟨requires⟩; from a sense of obligation (to act in a certain way); out of...;** ‖ по долгу службы ≃ **as part of one's ⟨s.o.'s⟩ duties ⟨responsibilities etc⟩;** ‖ по долгу чести ≃ **true to one's honor.**

Главный редактор издательства М.М. Смирнов, добросовестный и образованный человек, прочитал, как это полагалось ему по долгу службы, всю книгу от первой до последней страницы (Эткинд 1). The chief editor of the publishing house, Mikhail Smirnov...a conscientious and educated person, had read the book from cover to cover, as his post obliged him to (1a). ♦ Я кое-как стал изъяснять ему должность секунданта, но Иван Игнатьич никак не мог меня понять. «Воля ваша, — сказал он. — Коли уж мне и вмешаться в это дело, так разве пойти к Ивану Кузьмичу да донести ему по долгу службы, что в фортеции умышляется злодейство...» (Пушкин 2). I tried to explain the role of a second to him as best I could, but Ivan Ignatich was incapable of comprehending it. "Say what you will," he declared, "if I'm to get mixed up in this business at all, it will be to go and report to Ivan Kuzmich, as my duty requires, that an evil scheme...is being hatched in the fort..." (2a). ♦ Время от времени по долгу родства заглядывал дед Тихон (Максимов 2). From a sense of family

obligation, Great-Uncle Tikhon would now and again make a visit (2a). ♦ Мы приходили в посольство... а затем уносили посольские судки с обедом и пачку газет, из которых Мандельштаму полагалось по долгу службы делать вырезки (Мандельштам 2). We used to go to the embassy...and then take away our meals in covered dishes, together with the newspapers from which M[andelstam] was supposed to make cuttings as part of his official work (2a). ♦ «[Когда] Временное правительство... потребовало от меня оставления должности верховного главнокомандующего, я, как казак, по долгу совести и чести вынужден был отказаться от исполнения этого требования...» (Шолохов 3). "...When the Provisional Government...demanded my resignation from the post of Supreme Commander-in-Chief, I, true to my Cossack honour and conscience, felt compelled to reject that demand..." (3a).

Д-245 • В ДО́ЛЕ *с кем, у кого быть∅*; **В ДО́ЛЮ** *с кем войти*; **В ДО́ЛЮ принять, взять** *кого* [PrepP; these forms only; the resulting PrepP is subj-compl with copula (subj: human) or adv] (to be, become, take s.o. as) an associate in some business or undertaking of mutual interest: **go shares ⟨halves⟩ with s.o.; join s.o. ⟨take s.o. on⟩ as (a) partner; be partners ⟨in partnership⟩ (with s.o.); go ⟨be⟩ in on it ⟨on sth.⟩ (with s.o.); come into one's share.**

Сначала им [табачнику Коле и его жене Даше] пришлось довольно туго, но потом, во времена нэпа, персидский коммерсант снова открыл свою кофейню-кондитерскую, на этот раз осторожно назвав её «Кейфующий пролетарий». Он взял в долю бывшего табачника... (Искандер 3). At first they [the tobacco merchant Kolya and his wife Dasha] were rather hard up. Then, during the era of the New Economic Policy, the Persian merchant opened his coffeehouse and bake shop again — this time cautiously naming it the Idle Proletariat — and took on the former tobacco merchant as partner... (3a). ♦ Младший продавец, когда начали продавать мёд из запасной бочки, видно, кое о чём догадался... Шалико никак не мог решить — заткнуть ему рот парой тридцаток или не стоит унижаться? Не стоит, наконец решил он, пусть с моё поишачит, а потом будет в долю входить (Искандер 4). The junior salesman must have caught on when they began selling honey from the reserved barrel....Shaliko could not decide: should he stop the man's mouth with a pair of thirty-ruble bills, or was it worth demeaning himself? It's not worth it, he decided finally; let him do as much scutwork as I did, and then he'll come into his share (4a).

Д-246 • ОТДАВА́ТЬ/ОТДА́ТЬ ДО́ЛЖНОЕ *кому-чему*; **ОТДАВА́ТЬ/ОТДА́ТЬ (ДО́ЛЖНУЮ ⟨ПО́ЛНУЮ⟩) СПРАВЕДЛИ́ВОСТЬ** [VP; subj: human; often infin with надо, нужно; fixed WO] to appreciate s.o. or sth., acknowledge s.o.'s merit, abilities, skills etc: X отдаёт Y-у должное ≃ **X gives Y Y's due; X has to hand it to Y;** ‖ надо отдать Y-у должное ≃ **X has to give person Y credit; (Y is...,) you've got to ⟨X must⟩ grant him that; in all justice ⟨fairness (to Y)⟩...;** [usu. when contrasted with the preceding statement] **...(but) to do Y justice;** [in limited contexts] **let us give credit where credit is due;** ‖ нельзя ⟨X не может⟩ не отдать Y-у должное ≃ **X cannot but recognize thing Y ⟨person Y's abilities, achievements etc⟩.**

Гартвиг — человек особый. В чём-то я ему завидовал, за что-то глубоко его презирал... Но, разумеется, и отдавал ему должное: свой предмет он знает великолепно, и, главное, знает то, *что нужно знать*, и Кирилла натаскал здорово (Трифонов 5). Gartwig was no ordinary individual. There were some things about him I envied, and other things I was deeply contemptuous of....But I did of course give him his due: he knew his subject inside and out, and more to the point, he knew what it was *necessary* to know and did a fine job of coaching Kirill (5a). ♦ Марлен Михайлович... внимательно следил за лицами всей компании... Чаще всего взгляд Марлена Михайловича задерживался на «Видном лице» и всякий раз он отдавал ему должное — никак не проникнешь за эту маску (Аксёнов 7). Marlen Mikhailovich...kept close tabs on the faces of the entire crew....The Important Personage received more than his share of attention, of course, and Marlen Mikhailovich had to hand it to him; that mask of his was impenetrable (7a). ♦ Взяв всё это во внимание, Тюфяев, и тут нельзя ему не отдать справедливости, представлял министерству о том, чтоб им дать льготы и отсрочки (Герцен 1). Taking all this into consideration, Tyufayev—and one must give him credit for it—asked the Ministry to grant postponements and exemptions (1a). ♦ [Дорн:] Да, её папенька порядочная таки скотина, надо отдать ему полную справедливость (Чехов 6). [D.:] Yes, her papa is rather a beast, I must grant him that (6d). ♦ Кончилось всё это тем, что Иванов соорудил камеру и в неё действительно уловил красный луч. И надо отдать справедливости, уловил мастерски: луч вышел жирный, сантиметра 4 в поперечнике, острый и сильный (Булгаков 10). This all ended with Ivanov finishing the construction of a chamber and actually capturing the red ray in it. And in all justice, it was an expert job: the ray came out thick,—almost four centimeters in diameter—sharp and powerful (10b). ♦ Мне приятно было думать, что Зинаида не может, однако, не отдать справедливости моей решимости, моему героизму... (Тургенев 3). I was glad to think that Zinaida could not but recognise my resolution, my heroism (3a).

Д-247 • ДОЛОЖУ́ (Я) ВАМ ⟨ТЕБЕ́⟩ *coll* [sent; these forms only; used as sent adv (parenth); fixed WO] used when telling one's hearer(s) about sth. unusual, astonishing, outrageous: **I ⟨I'll⟩ tell you; I've got to tell you; let me tell you.**

«Ну и в историйку я недавно влип, доложу тебе», — начал он... (Искандер 2). "Well, I'll tell you, I really fell into something once not so long ago," he began... (2a). ♦ Был я, доложу я вам, слаб, капризен и прозрачен — прозрачен, как хрустальное яйцо (Набоков 1). I was, let me tell you, weak, capricious and transparent—as transparent as a cut-glass egg (1a).

Д-248 • НА ДО́ЛЮ *чью, кого* ог *кому* **выпасть, прийтись, достаться** [PrepP; Invar; the resulting PrepP is subj-compl with выпасть etc (subj: usu. abstr or infin, occas. concr)] (to become) s.o.'s destiny, responsibility, share of sth. etc: **X выпал на долю Y-а ≃ Y was fated ⟨it was Y's fate⟩ to experience ⟨to have etc⟩ X; Y was destined to experience ⟨to have etc⟩ X; fate bestowed X upon Y; X befell Y; X fell to Y's lot; X was Y's lot (in life); Y was fated to live through X; Y got X; Y ended up with ⟨getting, having to do etc⟩ X; as for Y, he got X.**

[Нина:] ...Другим же, как, например, вам, — вы один из миллиона, — выпала на долю жизнь интересная, светлая, полная значения... (Чехов 6). [N.:] But others, you, for instance, you—one in a million—are fated to have such interesting, bright, happy lives, lives worthwhile, full of significance (6b). ♦ ...[Мать] шептала [Андрею] о блестящем призвании то воина, то писателя, мечтала с ним о высокой роли, какая выпадает иным на долю... (Гончаров 1). ...[Andrey's mother] whispered to him about the brilliant calling of a soldier or a writer, and dreamed with him of the exalted part some men are destined to play (1a). ♦ ...Мы говорили, что Пастернак прожил очень счастливую жизнь, остался верен себе и равен себе, не часто такой жребий выпадает на долю русского поэта (Орлова 1). We said that Pasternak had lived a very fortunate life: in spite of all the difficulties he had remained true to himself and equal to himself. It isn't often that such a destiny befalls a Russian poet (1a). ♦ «Увы, жив», — воскликнули мы, — ибо как не предпочесть казнь смертную, содрогания висельника в своём ужасном коконе, тем похоронам, которые спустя двадцать пять бессмысленных лет выпали на долю Чернышевского (Набоков 1). "Alas, alive," we exclaimed, for how could one not prefer the death penalty, the convulsions of the hanged man in his hideous cocoon, to that funeral which twenty-five insipid years later fell to Chernyshevski's lot (1a). ♦ На экзамене по физике

на мою долю достался, как всегда, самый трудный вопрос. At my physics exam I ended up, as usual, with the hardest question. ♦ Королевские обойщики (их было несколько человек) службу при короле несли в очередь, причём на долю Поклена-отца приходились весенние месяцы: апрель, май и июнь (Булгаков 5). [context transl] The Royal Upholsterers (there were several of them) served the King in turn. Poquelin the elder's period of service was during the spring months of April, May, and June (5a).

Д-249 • есть ДО́ЛЯ ПРА́ВДЫ ⟨И́СТИНЫ⟩ *в чём* [NP; sing only; used as subj; fixed WO] there is sth. true (in s.o.'s remark, some statement etc): **grain ⟨bit, element, kernel⟩ of truth; some truth.**

...Тесса был обеспокоен; невольно вспоминал слова Дессера: «Бедный старый клоп». Конечно, Дессер рехнулся, но есть в его обидных словах доля правды... (Эренбург 4). ...He [Tessa] felt anxious. He could not help remembering Desser's remark: "Poor old bug." Of course, Desser was out of his mind, but there was a grain of truth in the offensive remark (4a). ♦ Дядя Сандро... говорил, что этого человека сняли именно потому, что он в своё время принял у себя в кабинете его, дядю Сандро, с недопустимой, по абхазским обычаям, степенью хамства. Я было посмеялся этому предположению, но потом решил, что в его словах всё-таки есть доля истины (Искандер 3). ...Uncle Sandro said the reason they fired the man was that in his time he had received him, Uncle Sandro, with a degree of rudeness impermissible by Abkhazian custom. I started to snicker at this hypothesis, but then I decided the remark did contain a kernel of truth (3a). ♦ Лансье томился: что, если есть доля правды в словах этого русского? (Эренбург 1). Lancier was tormented with anxiety: suppose there was some truth in what that Russian had said? (1a).

Д-250 • ЛЬВИ́НАЯ ДО́ЛЯ *(чего)* [NP; sing only; usu. used as subj or obj; fixed WO] the larger or largest (and usu. better) part (of sth.): **the lion's share; the greater part (of sth.); [in limited contexts] the bulk (of sth.).**

По моим расчётам, «монстр» [ракета] Королёва должен был весить на старте около 400 тонн, и львиная доля этого гигантского веса приходилась на двадцать слабых, но тяжёлых двигателей, которые должны были поднимать самих себя (Владимиров 1). According to my calculations, Korolyov's monster [of a rocket] must have weighed around 400 tons on the ground, and the greater part of this tremendous weight was accounted for by the 20 small-thrust but heavy engines which had to lift themselves into space (1a). ♦ Наконец, на допросах мы начали разбирать бумаги, стихи и записки, собранные следователем [Семёновым]. Львиная доля шла на уничтожение, в печь, а некоторые возвращались родным (Ивинская 1). Eventually [during my interrogation], we began to go through all the papers with poems and notes which [the investigator] Semionov had collected together. The bulk of them were afterward destroyed, though some were returned to my relatives (1a).

< Loan translation of the French *la part du lion*, from one of Aesop's fables.

Д-251 • ВВОДИ́ТЬ/ВВЕСТИ́ В *(чей)* **ДОМ** *кого* [VP; subj: human] to bring s.o. to one's own home or the home of one's relatives, friends etc in order to introduce him to one's family, relatives etc (and help him to become accepted by them): **X ввёл Y-а в (свой) дом ⟨в Z-ов дом⟩ ≃ X brought Y home to meet X's family; X brought Y to Z's place so X could meet Z (and Z's family ⟨friends⟩); X had Y over to X's place so Y could get to know X's family ⟨friends⟩; X introduced Y to X's family ⟨to Z, to Z's family etc⟩.**

Д-252 • ПУБЛИ́ЧНЫЙ ДОМ; ДОМ ТЕРПИ́МОСТИ *obs* [NP; fixed WO] a house of prostitution: **brothel; bawdyhouse; cathouse; house of ill repute ⟨ill fame⟩.**

Семья Лансье приютилась в маленькой гостинице возле порта; прежде здесь останавливались мелкие колониальные чиновники, матросы, солдаты, пропивавшие свои сбережения в окрестных кабачках и домах терпимости (Эренбург 1). The Lanciers took refuge in a small hotel near the docks, formerly frequented by minor colonial officials, sailors and soldiers who squandered their savings in the neighboring taverns and brothels (1a).

Д-253 • СУМАСШЕ́ДШИЙ ДОМ coll [NP; fixed WO]

1. Also: **ЖЁЛТЫЙ ДОМ** obs, coll a hospital for the mentally ill: **lunatic ⟨insane⟩ asylum; madhouse; nut house.**

Судьба обошлась с ней неласково: сыновья её, один — спортивный журналист, другой — актёр, оказались неудачниками, невестка почти безвылазно обитала в жёлтом доме, внуки росли пугливыми и болезненными... (Максимов 2). Fate had been unkind to her: of her two sons—one a sports journalist, the other an actor—both had turned out to be failures, her daughter-in-law spent almost all her time in the lunatic asylum, her grandsons were growing up timorous and sickly... (2a). ♦ Базаров...считал рыцарские чувства чем-то вроде уродства или болезни и не однажды выражал своё удивление: почему не посадили в жёлтый дом Тоггенбурга со всеми миннезингерами и трубадурами? (Тургенев 2). Bazarov...regarded chivalrous feelings as something in the nature of a deformation or disease, and more than once expressed his surprise that Toggenburg with all his minnesingers and troubadours had not been put away in a madhouse (2f).

2. [sing only] complete disorder, a noisy uproar, commotion: **a madhouse; pandemonium;** [in limited contexts] **a three-ring circus.**

«И без вас не сладко. Собачья жизнь, сумасшедший дом...» (Пастернак 1). "Things are bad enough without you. It's a dog's life, a madhouse..." (1a).

Д-254 • КАК (У СЕБЯ́) ДО́МА чувствовать себя, быть₀ [как + AdvP; these forms only; subj-compl with copula (subj: human); often used with imper; fixed WO] to feel comfortable, relaxed, not shy or embarrassed: **feel ⟨quite ⟨very much⟩⟩ at home; be quite ⟨very much⟩ at home; feel ⟨be⟩ (quite ⟨very much⟩) at ease;** [in limited contexts] **make o.s. at home; be so much at home; feel like one of the family.**

«Вы, кажется, стараетесь по обязанности хозяйки занять меня? — спросил Обломов. — Напрасно!» — «Отчего напрасно? Я хочу, чтоб вам не было скучно, чтоб вы были здесь как дома, чтоб вам было ловко, свободно, легко...» (Гончаров 1). "Do you feel it your duty as a hostess to entertain me?" Oblomov asked. "You needn't, you know." "Why not? I don't want you to be bored. I want you to feel at home here, to be comfortable and at your ease..." (1b). ♦ Холостяк Дюма у доктора чувствовал себя как дома (Эренбург 1). Dumas, the bachelor, felt quite at home at the doctor's house... (1a). ♦ ...С Катей Аркадий был как дома; он обращался с ней снисходительно, не мешал ей высказывать впечатления, возбуждённые в ней музыкой, чтением повестей, стихов и прочими пустяками... (Тургенев 2). With Katya...Arkady was quite at ease; he was indulgent, and gave her free rein to voice her impressions inspired by music, by the reading of a book or poetry and similar trifles...(2a). ♦ В кабинете дядюшка попросил гостей сесть и расположиться как дома, а сам вышел (Толстой 5). 'Uncle' asked his visitors to sit down and make themselves at home, and then went out of the room (5b). ♦ По мнению Демьяна, Маяковский погиб, потому что вторгся в область, где он, Демьян, чувствует себя как дома, но для Маяковского чуждую (Мандельштам 1). In Demian's view, Mayakovski had died because he had trespassed on territory to which he was a stranger—the same political territory in which he (Demian) was so much at home (1a).

Д-255 • НЕ ВСЕ ДО́МА у кого highly coll, derog [Invar; VP_subj with быть₀, usu. pres; fixed WO] s.o. is eccentric, has quirks, acts strangely, as if he is not quite normal: у X-а не все дома ≃ X isn't playing with a full deck; X doesn't have both oars in the water; X isn't all there; X isn't quite right in the head; X's elevator doesn't go to the top floor; X has a screw loose; X has bats in his belfry; [in limited contexts] **(there's) nobody home upstairs.**

Циолковский пошёл вниз по оврагу, опять полудумая-полубормоча: «...Один разум без воли — это ничто, и одна воля без разума тоже ничто...» Главарь оправил косоворотку, оглядел дружков... Один из оборванцев приложил палец к виску, покрутил — мол, не все дома у Птицы [Циолковского] (Евтушенко 2). ...Tsiolkovsky went down the ravine, again lost in thought and muttering.... "Intelligence without will is nothing, and so is will without intelligence." The leader adjusted his shirt and looked over at his pals....One of them put his finger to his temple and twirled it—that Bird wasn't playing with a full deck (2a). ♦ «Послушайте, вы, — сказал Ревкин, — вам надо срочно обратиться к врачу, вы больны, у вас не все дома» (Войнович 4). "Listen, you," said Revkin, "you should see a doctor immediately, you're a sick man, you're not all there" (4a). ♦ Старый шлиссельбуржец — говорят, что над его кроватью висели кандалы, — он отличался крутым нравом. Проще говоря, у него не все были дома: в Ленинграде, заведуя там госиздатом, он безумствовал, как хотел (Мандельштам 2). A former veteran of Schlusselberg—it is said that he still kept his manacles hanging over his bed—he was noted for his vile temper. He was, in fact, not quite right in the head. As head of the State Publishing House in Leningrad, he had behaved outrageously... (2a).

Д-256 • ОТБИВА́ТЬСЯ/ОТБИ́ТЬСЯ ОТ ДО́МА coll [VP; subj: human; usu. pfv past] (to begin) to spend very little time at home, lose interest in family affairs: X отбился от дома ≃ X forgot (about) his family; X never ⟨hardly ever⟩ spent any time at home ⟨with his family⟩; [in limited contexts] **it was as if X forgot that he had a family.**

Мать не видела Василия неделями: он всё время проводил у Жанны и совершенно отбился от дома. Vasily's mother didn't see him for weeks: he was spending all his time at Zhanna's and totally forgot about his family.

Д-257 • ОТКА́ЗЫВАТЬ/ОТКАЗА́ТЬ ОТ ДО́МА кому obs [VP; subj: human] to stop receiving s.o. in one's home (because one harbors bad feelings toward s.o., no longer wants to associate with s.o. etc): X отказал Y-у от дома ≃ X closed his door to Y; X forbade ⟨did not allow, did not permit⟩ Y to visit ⟨to come to⟩ X's house; X forbade Y to visit X; X told Y (that) Y was no longer welcome in X's home.

«О, ему надо дать урок, чтоб этого вперёд не было! Попрошу ma tante отказать ему от дома: он не должен забываться...» (Гончаров 1). "He must be taught a lesson, so it doesn't happen again! I'll tell ma tante not to permit him to come to the house: he must not again forget himself" (1b). ♦ [Машенька:] Курчаеву не отказывайте от дому, пусть ездит (Островский 9). [M.:] Please, don't forbid Kurchaev to visit us. Let him come as before (9a).

Д-258 • В ЛУ́ЧШИХ ДОМА́Х ФИЛАДЕ́ЛЬФИИ iron or humor [PrepP; Invar; sent adv] among refined and fashionable people: **in the best ⟨finest⟩ homes; in polite society.**

Я заметил: «Герасим Иванович, по-моему, так не принято в лучших домах Филадельфии: учить жену, как она должна вести себя с мужем!» (Трифонов 5). ...I remarked, "I don't believe, Gerasim Ivanovich, that it's customary in polite society to teach a wife how she should behave with her husband!" (5a).

< From *The Twelve Chairs* («Двенадцать стульев»), 1928, by Ilya Ilf and Evgeny Petrov.

Д-259 • В ДО́МЕ ПОВЕ́ШЕННОГО НЕ ГОВОРЯ́Т О ВЕРЁВКЕ [saying] one should not speak in another person's presence about things that remind that person of his weaknesses, shortcomings etc: ≃ **don't mention rope in the house of a hanged man.**

[Шабельский:] Да, я был молод и глуп, в своё время… обличал мерзавцев и мошенников, но никогда в жизни я воров не называл в лицо ворами и в доме повешенного не говорил о верёвке. Я был воспитан (Чехов 4). [Sh.:] Yes, I was young and foolish, and in my time I, too…expos[ed] frauds and scoundrels, but I never in my life called a thief a thief to his face, nor mentioned rope in the house of a hanged man. I was properly brought up (4a).

Д-260 • КА́РТОЧНЫЙ ДО́МИК [NP; sing only; fixed WO] a plan, idea, hope etc that is unfounded, does not have a solid basis, will most likely fail: **house of cards;** ‖ рухнуть ⟨рассыпаться etc⟩ как карточный домик ≃ **topple ⟨crumble, fall apart⟩ like a house of cards.**

«…Преступная „фирма" стала рушиться, словно карточный домик» (Чернёнок 2). "…Their shady business began crumbling like a house of cards" (2a).

Д-261 • ЖИТЬ ОДНИ́М ДО́МОМ (с кем) [VP; subj: human; if there is no prep obj, subj: pl] (usu. of people who do not belong to the same nuclear family or who are not related by blood) to share living quarters and home expenses (with s.o.): X и Y живут одним домом ⟨X живёт одним домом с Y-ом⟩ ≃ **X and Y share a home ⟨the same household⟩; X and Y live as one family ⟨household⟩.**

Д-262 • НЕСТИ́ (И) С ДО́НА И С МО́РЯ obs, rare, substand [VP; subj: human; fixed WO] to say nonsensical, stupid things: X несёт и с Дона и с моря ≃ **X talks ⟨spouts⟩ drivel; X spouts bosh ⟨bunk⟩; X talks blather; X spouts ⟨spews⟩ gibberish ⟨rubbish⟩.**

Д-263 • БОЛЬША́Я ДОРО́ГА [NP; fixed WO] **1.** obs a well-built road connecting large population centers: **highroad; main road ⟨thoroughfare⟩; highway.**

«Как вы могли велеть, чтоб мне не давали лошадей? Что это за вздор — на большой дороге останавливать проезжающих?» (Герцен 1). "How could you give orders that I shouldn't have horses? What nonsense is this, stopping travellers on the highroad?" (1a). ♦ Около деревни Праца Ростову велено было искать Кутузова и государя… По большой дороге, на которую он выехал, толпились коляски, экипажи всех сортов, русские и австрийские солдаты всех родов войск, раненые и нераненые (Толстой 4). Rostov had been ordered to look for Kutuzov and the Tsar near the village of Pratzen….The highway on which he had come out was teeming with calashes and vehicles of all sorts, with Russian and Austrian soldiers of all arms, some wounded and some not (4a).

2. [sing only] the correct, main course of development of sth., the one that will lead to further progress, advancement etc: **the right direction; the right track;** [in limited contexts] **(be ⟨get sth. etc⟩ back on track.**

«Помнишь, Анфиса, как он сказал на собрании? Меня, говорит, либо на кладбище отвезёте, либо я выведу на большую дорогу [колхоз] „Новую жизнь"» (Абрамов 1). "You remember, Anfisa, what he said at the meeting? He said, 'If I don't get New Life Kolkhoz back on track, you can just cart me away to the cemetery'" (1a).

Д-264 • ПРЯМА́Я ДОРО́ГА ⟨ПРЯМО́Й ПУТЬ⟩ к чему, куда [NP; sing only; fixed WO] **1.** the most direct, shortest route to sth. (glory, crime, ruin etc): **straight road to;** [in limited contexts] **shortcut to.**

Отец [моей кузины] был отчаянный игрок… Сын его, уланский юнкер, единственный брат кузины, очень добрый юноша, шёл прямым путём к гибели: девятнадцати лет он

уже был более страстный игрок, нежели отец (Герцен 1). Her [my cousin's] father was a desperate gambler….His son, an ensign in the Uhlans, my cousin's only brother and a very good-natured youth, was going the straight road to ruin: at nineteen he was already a more passionate gambler than his father (1a).

2. a decent, honest means of achieving sth. or a life lived in an honest way: **(do sth. ⟨live⟩) on the straight and narrow; (do sth.) by the straight and narrow; (do sth.) (by) sticking to the straight and narrow; (follow ⟨take, stick to⟩) the straight road.**

«Покривил, не спорю, покривил. Что ж делать? Но ведь покривил только тогда, когда увидел, что прямой дорогой не возьмёшь…» (Гоголь 3). "I have acted against my conscience; I don't deny it, I have….What can be done about it? But I acted crookedly only when I saw that the straight road would not get me anywhere…" (3c).

Д-265 • СТОЛБОВА́Я ДОРО́ГА [NP] **1.** obs a large post road with poles indicating distance in versts (verst = an old Russian measure of linear distance, approx. two thirds of a mile): **highroad; main road ⟨thoroughfare⟩; highway.**

А Чичиков в довольном расположении духа сидел в своей бричке, катившейся давно по столбовой дороге (Гоголь 3). As for Chichikov, he was in a contented frame of mind, sitting in his britska, which had for some time been rolling along the highroad (3c).

2. ~ (чего) [sing only; fixed WO] the principal direction of movement or development of sth.: **mainstream; main current;** [in limited contexts] **highroad.**

Вторая категория — это писатели побочные, идущие не по столбовой дороге советской литературы, а где-то в стороне от неё (Войнович 1). The second category is made up of writers who do not travel the highroad of Soviet literature, but are off somewhere to the side (1a).

Д-266 • ТО́РНАЯ ДОРО́ГА lit [NP; fixed WO] **1.** obs broad possibilities, opportunities in life: **an open path in life.**

2. an unoriginal path in life (taken by everyone or by most people): **the beaten path ⟨track⟩; the well-traveled road.**

Я впоследствии не раз встречал эти натуры… Они умно рассуждают, не отступая от данных; они ещё умнее поступают, не сходя с торной дороги; они настоящие современники своего времени, своего общества (Герцен 2). I have since more than once met these characters….They are intelligent in their judgments, never deviating from their data; they are still more intelligent in their conduct, never stepping aside from the beaten track; they are the true contemporaries of their age, of their society (2a).

Д-267 • ТУДА́ И ДОРО́ГА coll [sent; Invar; fixed WO] **1.** ~ кому usu. disapprov s.o. deserves precisely that (which is specified by the preceding context), there is no reason to pity him: туда X-у и дорога ≃ **(it) serves X right; X got what ⟨no more than⟩ he deserved; X asked ⟨was asking⟩ for it;** [in limited contexts] **X had it coming (to him).**

Дело идёт к развязке, сказал Неврастеник. Редколлегию разогнали. Претендент продал Мыслителя, Социолога и Супругу. Из редколлегии их выгнали… Туда им и дорога, сказал Болтун (Зиновьев 1). "Here comes the dénouement," said Neurasthenic: "The editorial committee has been dissolved. Claimant has sold out Thinker, Sociologist and Wife. They've been expelled from the editorial board…" "Serves them right," said Chatterer (1a).

2. ~ чему it is not worth regretting, being distressed over the loss of sth.: туда X-у и дорога ≃ **X won't be missed; X isn't worth losing sleep over; X is no great loss;** [in limited contexts] **and a very good thing at that; and a very good thing, if you ask me;** [in refer. to discarding sth.] **that's where X belongs!**

[Любим Карпыч:] Вот я этот капитал взял да пропил, промотал. Туда ему и дорога! (Островский 2). [L.K.:] So I took it [the money] and squandered it. Drank it up. And a very good thing, if you ask me (2b). ♦ «...Свой-то пистолет схватил, оборотился назад, да швырком, вверх, в лес и пустил: „Туда, кричу, тебе и дорога!"» (Достоевский 1). "...I seized my pistol, turned around, and sent it hurtling up into the trees: 'That's where you belong!'" (1a).

Д-268 • **НА ДОРО́ГЕ ⟨НА У́ЛИЦЕ, НА ПОЛУ́, НА ЗЕМЛЕ́⟩ НЕ ВАЛЯ́ЕТСЯ** *coll* [VP; pres only; fixed WO]
1. [subj: usu. concr] sth. cannot be obtained easily, without effort: X на дороге не валяется ≃ **you don't ⟨won't⟩ find X lying around (in ⟨on⟩ the street); you don't ⟨won't⟩ find X (just) waiting to be picked up ⟨be found⟩; X won't just fall into your lap; X can't be had just for the asking;** [usu. of money] **X doesn't grow on trees.**

«...На заём стали подписываться. Я без памяти-то на триста рублей подписалась... И Лизка, глупая, пятьдесят рублей выкинула...» — «Пущай [*ungrammat* = пускай]», — миролюбиво сказал Михаил... «Да ведь деньги-то не щепа — на улице не валяются» (Абрамов 1). "...Everyone began signing up for the Loan. Without thinking, I put myself down for three hundred rubles....And Lizka, silly girl, threw in fifty rubles....Let her," said Mikhail peaceably....But money isn't wood chips—you don't find it lying around on the street" (1a).

2. [subj: human (often pl), abstr, or concr] some type of person (thing etc) is rare, not often found: [of people or things] X-ы ⟨такие [NPs], как X,⟩ на дороге не валяются ≃ **Xs ⟨[NPs] like X⟩ are hard ⟨not easy⟩ to come by; Xs ⟨[NPs] like X⟩ don't come along every day; Xs ⟨[NPs] like X⟩ are few and far between; there aren't (that) many Xs about ⟨around⟩ (these days);** ‖ [of qualities etc] X на дороге не валяется ≃ **X is hard ⟨not easy⟩ to come by.**

«Рекомендую: Золотарёв, Илья Никанорыч... кадровый товарищ, такие нынче на дороге не валяются...» (Максимов 1). "Let me introduce you: Ilya Nikanorych Zolotarev. He's...an experienced comrade. There aren't that many of them about these days..." (1a).

Д-269 • **ПО ДОРО́ГЕ; ПО ПУТИ́** [PrepP; these forms only]
1. [adv] while one or s.o. is going some place, during a trip: **along the way; on the way; en route; as one is walking ⟨riding, driving⟩;** [in limited contexts] **on the voyage (somewhere).**

По дороге он мне рассказывал о роскоши правительственных охот, куда он допускался в качестве опытного егеря... (Искандер 4). Along the way he told me about the splendor of government hunts, to which he was admitted as an expert huntsman (4a). ♦ ...Вдруг звонок в дверь. Иду открывать, мысленно по дороге чертыхаясь: кого ещё там нелёгкая на ночь глядя принесла? (Войнович 1). ...All of a sudden the doorbell rang. I went to the door, cursing on the way: Who the hell could it be at this time of night? (1a). ♦ По пути [домой Николай] отправлял ей [своей невесте] письма с лоцманами (Солженицын 1). On the voyage home he [Nikolai] sent her [his fiancée] letters by pilot boats (1a).

2. ~ зайти, заехать, заглянуть *куда, к кому* [adv] (to stop by somewhere, stop in to see s.o. etc) while going somewhere else: **on the ⟨one's⟩ way (to...); while on one's way; while ⟨when⟩ passing by.**

...Прежде, чем к князю, по дороге надо было заехать к Ивиным (Толстой 2). ...On the way to the Prince's I had to call in at the Ivins (2b).

3. [subj-compl with copula (subj: concr) or sent adv] (located) at some point along s.o.'s (planned, intended) route or in the general direction s.o. is going: **(right) on s.o.'s way ⟨route⟩; (right) on the way;** ‖ *Neg* не по пути ≃ **out of s.o.'s ⟨the⟩ way.**

Ты не занесёшь мой костюм в химчистку, если тебе по дороге? Could you take my suit to the cleaners if it's on your way? ♦ «У меня очень покойная коляска... я могу вас подвезти, а Евгений Васильич может взять ваш тарантас...» — «Да

помилуйте, вам совсем не по дороге, и до меня далеко». — «Это ничего, ничего...» (Тургенев 2). "I have a very comfortable carriage....I can take you, and Yevgeny Vasilich can have your tarantass...." "But of course not, it is quite out of your way, and it is a long distance to my home." "It's nothing, nothing..." (2f).

4. ~ *кому (с кем)* [compl of copula, impers] (s.o. is going) in the same direction as someone else: X-у и Y-у ⟨X-у с Y-ом⟩ было по дороге ≃ **X was going the same way as Y; X and Y were going the same way; X was going Y's way; X was going ⟨X's route took him⟩ in the same direction as Y;** ‖ *Neg* X-у с Y-ом было не по пути ≃ **X and Y were going in different directions; our ⟨your, their⟩ paths parted ⟨diverged⟩.**

«...Меня поманил шофёр захудалой машины, сказал так добродушно — ну вот, нам по пути, садись, подвезу...» (Иоффе 1). "...The driver of a car, a rather shabby car, beckoned to me and said, there now, we are going the same way—get in and I'll give you a lift" (1a). ♦ Обратно, из школы, Толе было по пути с заключёнными... (Аксёнов 6). On the way back from school, Tolya's route took him in the same direction as the prisoners... (6a).

5. ~ *кому с кем* [compl of copula, impers; in the affirm, the var. по пути is more common; more often neg] having common interests, outlooks, sharing the same convictions etc: X-у с Y-ом по пути ≃ **X goes along with Y; X and Y think alike; X's aims ⟨views etc⟩ are the same as Y's;** ‖ *Neg* X-у с Y-ом (больше) не по пути ≃ **X and Y have come to a parting of the ways.**

Большой делец, он [Эфрос] откровенно соблазнял Мандельштама устройством материальных дел, если он согласится на создание литературной группы, — «вы нам нужны»... Мандельштам отказался наотрез. Каждому в отдельности он сказал, почему ему с ним не по пути... (Мандельштам 2). A great operator, he [Efros] frankly tried to tempt M[andelstam] with the prospect of being able to do well for himself if he would agree to the creation of a literary group ("We need you")....M[andelstam] refused outright. He told those present—each in turn—why he could not go along with them... (2a). ♦ «Вы, я вижу, бескорыстно любите деньги. Скажите, какая сумма вам нравится?» — «Пять тысяч», — быстро ответил Балаганов. «В месяц?» — «В год». — «Тогда мне с вами не по пути. Мне нужно пятьсот тысяч». (Ильф и Петров 2). "You, I see, love money. Tell me, how much would you like?" "Five thousand," Balaganov promptly replied. "A month?" "A year." "Then we don't think alike. I need five hundred thousand" (2a). ♦ «Смертельно жаль Потебню и его товарищей, — говорил я Бакунину, — и тем больше, что вряд по дороге ли им с поляками...» (Герцен 3). "I am mortally sorry for Potebnya and his comrades," I said to Bakunin, "and the more so that I doubt whether their aims are the same as those of the Poles" (3a). ♦ Нам не по пути с Юркой. Странно, правда? А ведь так бывает (Михайловская 1). Yuri and I came to a parting of the ways. Strange, isn't it? But it happens (1a).

Д-270 • **ПОЙТИ́ ПО ПЛОХО́Й ⟨ХУДО́Й, ДУРНО́Й⟩ ДОРО́ГЕ ⟨ДОРО́ЖКЕ⟩; ПОЙТИ́ ПО ПЛОХО́МУ ПУТИ́** *coll* [VP; subj: human] to degenerate morally, become depraved, dishonest etc: X пошёл по плохой дороге ≃ **X went wrong ⟨astray⟩; X fell into bad ⟨sinful, evil⟩ ways.**

Д-271 • **С ДОРО́ГИ** [PrepP; Invar] **1. устать, отдохнуть, перекусить** и т. п. ~ [adv or subj-compl with быть∅ (subj: human)] (to be tired, get some rest, have a bite to eat etc) immediately following a trip or journey: **(be tired ⟨rest up⟩ etc)) from a ⟨the, one's⟩ trip; (be tired ⟨rest up⟩ etc)) after one's ⟨the⟩ journey; (one has been) on the road;** [in limited contexts] **(come in) off the road.**

[Галя:] Твой брат, наверно, устал с дороги, умыться хочет... (Розов 1). [G.:] Your cousin is probably tired from the trip, would like to wash up... (1a). ♦ «Лихоманка вас забери! — ругалась Ильинична, уже в полночь выпроваживая гостей. — ...Служивый наш ишо [*ungrammat* = ещё] не отдыхал с дороги» (Шолохов 3). "Drat you!" Ilyinichna scolded as she turned the guests out at midnight. "...Our soldier hasn't even had time for a rest after his journey" (3a). ♦ На другое утро приезжие спали с дороги до десятого часа (Толстой 5). Next morning, after the journey, the travelers slept till ten o'clock (5a). ♦ «Ну, допросили? А теперь покормить надо — человек с дороги» (Шукшин 1). "Well, have you asked all your questions? It's time to eat now—our guest has been on the road a long time" (1a). ♦ Она вдруг посмотрела на меня искоса и снизу так, как будто влюбилась в меня с этого, как бы с первого взгляда, как будто я какой-нибудь ковбой и только что с дороги вошёл сюда в пыльных сапогах... (Аксёнов 1). She suddenly looked up at me with a sidelong glance, as if she had just now fallen in love with me, love at first sight, as if I were some cowboy and had just come in off the road in my dusty boots... (1a).

2. написать, послать телеграмму *кому* и т. п. ~ [adv] (to write, send s.o. a telegram etc) during a trip: **(from some place) on the way (to...); while on the road; while (one is) traveling.**

«Ты напиши с дороги». — «Непременно, непременно» (Федин 1). "Write on the way." "Definitely, definitely" (1a).

Д-272 • ИДТИ́ ПРЯМО́Й ДОРО́ГОЙ ⟨ПРЯМЫ́М ПУТЁМ⟩ [VP; subj: human; usu. this WO] to live honestly and properly, possess moral integrity: X идёт прямой дорогой ≃ **X keeps to the straight and narrow; X follows the straight and narrow path.**

Д-273 • ИДТИ́/ПОЙТИ́ СВОЕ́Й ДОРО́ГОЙ ⟨СВОИ́М ПУТЁМ⟩ [VP; subj: human; fixed WO] **1.** to act independently, following a course one has chosen oneself, not falling under the influence of others: X идёт своей дорогой ≃ **X goes his own way; X follows his own path.**

Останови он [Штольц] тогда внимание на ней [Ольге], он бы сообразил, что она идёт почти одна своей дорогой, оберегаемая поверхностным надзором тётки от крайностей, но что не тяготеют над ней, многочисленной опекой, авторитеты... бабушек, тёток... (Гончаров 1). Had he [Stolz] turned his attention to her [Olga] at that time, he would have realized that she was going her own way almost alone, guarded from extremes by her aunt's superficial surveillance, but not opressed by the authority of a profusion of...grandmothers and aunts... (1b). ♦ Будах тихо проговорил: «Тогда, господи, сотри нас с лица земли и создай заново более совершенными... или, ещё лучше, оставь нас и дай нам идти своей дорогой» (Стругацкие 4). Suddenly Budach spoke softly: "Then, oh, Lord, remove us from the face of the earth and create us anew, make us better men this time, more perfect beings. Or, better still—leave us the way we are, but ordain that we can follow our own path!" (4a).

2. [imper only] do not get involved in this—your opinion is not welcome, go away: иди своей дорогой ≃ **keep ⟨stay⟩ out of this ⟨it⟩; leave us ⟨them⟩ alone; don't interfere; butt out; keep your nose out of it.**

Д-274 • ОБХОДИ́ТЬ/ОБОЙТИ́ ДЕСЯ́ТОЙ ДОРО́ГОЙ *кого-что* coll [VP; subj: human; obj: human or a noun denoting some place or organization] to (try to) avoid s.o. or sth., maintain a distance from s.o. or some place: X обходит Y-а десятой дорогой ≃ **X steers ⟨keeps⟩ clear of Y; X goes miles ⟨a mile⟩ out of his way to avoid Y; X gives a wide ⟨the widest possible⟩ berth to person Y.**

«Боже мой, когда я кому-нибудь неприятен, я стараюсь обходить его десятой дорогой» (Горенштейн 1). "God Almighty, when someone dislikes *me* I do my best to steer clear of him..." (1a).

Д-275 • В ДОРО́ГУ [PrepP; Invar; adv] in order to be used on a trip, while traveling: **for the trip ⟨the road, the ride⟩; on the trip ⟨the road⟩.**

Возьми в дорогу что-нибудь почитать. Take something to read on the trip.

Д-276 • ВЫВОДИ́ТЬ/ВЫ́ВЕСТИ НА ДОРО́ГУ ⟨НА ПУТЬ⟩ *кого* [VP] **1.** [subj: human] to help s.o. become independent, obtain a secure place in life: X вывел Y-а на дорогу ≃ **X helped Y find Y's way in life ⟨in the world⟩; [in limited contexts] X helped Y get a ⟨Y's⟩ start in life; X got Y started ⟨off to a good start⟩ in life.**

2. [subj: human or abstr] to help s.o. develop good values, understand things properly, correctly: X вывел Y-а на дорогу ≃ **X set ⟨put⟩ Y on the right path; X put Y on the right track; X pointed Y in the right direction.**

Именно стихи пробили дорогу прозе в таинственных каналах самозародившихся читателей. Читатель появился совершенно неожиданно... Он научился отбирать то, что ему нужно, а стихи, двинувшиеся к нему, преобразовали его и вывели на дорогу (Мандельштам 2). It was poetry that blazed the trail for prose along the mysterious byways leading to the new readers who suddenly sprang up from nowhere. These readers emerged quite unexpectedly....They learned to pick out what they needed, and the poetry that came into their hands transfigured them and set them on the right path (2a).

Д-277 • ВЫХОДИ́ТЬ/ВЫ́ЙТИ ⟨ВЫБИВА́ТЬСЯ/ВЫ́-БИТЬСЯ⟩ НА (ШИРО́КУЮ) ДОРО́ГУ [VP; subj: human] to grow independent, achieve success in life, in one's career etc by one's own efforts: X вышел на широкую дорогу ≃ **X found ⟨made⟩ his way in life ⟨in the world⟩.**

Д-278 • ДАВА́ТЬ/ДАТЬ ⟨УСТУПА́ТЬ/УСТУПИ́ТЬ⟩ ДОРО́ГУ *кому* [VP; subj: human] **1.** to allow s.o. to go by one or enter some place by moving aside: X дал Y-у дорогу ≃ **X made way (for Y); X stepped ⟨got⟩ out of Y's ⟨the⟩ way; X let Y pass (by X); [in limited contexts] X yielded the right of way.**

По мере того как кортеж приближался, толпы глуповцев расступались и давали дорогу (Салтыков-Щедрин 1). As the cortege drew near, the crowds [of Foolovites] parted and the Foolovites made way (1a). ♦ Рослый германец стал пробираться через толпу. На него глядели враждебно. Даже не давали дороги (Сологуб 1). The sturdy German began to make his way through the crowd. Everyone glanced hostilely at him. They did not even make way for him (1a). ♦ Этот невысокий человек... пристально-холодным взглядом стал вглядываться в князя Андрея, идя прямо на него и, видимо, ожидая, чтобы князь Андрей поклонился ему или дал дорогу (Толстой 4). This small man...fixing his cold, intent gaze on Prince Andrei, walked straight toward him, apparently expecting him to bow or step out of his way (4a). ♦ ...Она и по улице шла так, будто все обязаны уступать ей дорогу... (Рыбаков 1). ...She even walked along the street as though everyone else should get out of her way... (1a). ♦ Он что-то хотел сказать ещё, но в это время поднялся князь Василий с дочерью, и мужчины встали, чтобы дать им дорогу (Толстой 4). He was about to say something more, but at that moment Prince Vasily and his daughter got up to go and the gentlemen stood up to let them pass (4a).

2. to give s.o. an opportunity to progress ahead of o.s. in some field, the workplace etc: X дал дорогу Y-у ≃ **X made room ⟨way⟩ for Y; X gave way to Y; X opened the way to Y.**

В театре засилье великовозрастных актрис, их давно пора убрать, дать дорогу молодым (Рыбаков 1). The theatre was dominated by ancient actresses who should have been got rid of ages ago to make room for younger ones (1a). ♦ А чего они [Социолог и Мыслитель] хотят? Напечатать труд, продуманный десятилетиями? У них его нет! Дать дорогу подлинному таланту? (Зиновьев 1). "And what do they [Sociologist and Thinker] want? To publish their life's work? But it doesn't exist! To open the way to genuine talents?" (1a).

Д-279 • ЗАБЫВА́ТЬ/ЗАБЫ́ТЬ ДОРО́ГУ к кому, куда *coll* [VP; subj: human; usu. pfv past] to stop visiting s.o., frequenting some place (often as a consequence of a quarrel, an offense or insult, the breakup of a relationship etc): X забыл дорогу к Y-у ≃ **X stopped going ⟨coming⟩ to Y's place; X no longer goes ⟨comes⟩ to Y's place; X stopped visiting Y;** ‖ [following a quarrel etc] X может забыть дорогу в место Z ≃ **X can forget about visiting ⟨visits to⟩ place Z;** ‖ *Imper* забудь дорогу в наш дом ≃ **don't bother coming back here; don't come here (ever) again; don't come around here anymore.**

Со свойственной ему практичностью он живо прикинул возможные последствия — на тот случай, если бы Лизка подняла шум. Во-первых, забудь на время дорогу в Пекашино... (Абрамов 1). With his customary pragmatism he quickly assessed the possible consequences in the event that Lizka should raise a stink. First of all, he could forget about visits to Pekashino for a while (1a).

Д-280 • ЗАСТУПА́ТЬ/ЗАСТУПИ́ТЬ ДОРО́ГУ кому *substand* [VP; subj: human] **1.** to move in front of s.o. in order to interrupt or stop his movement: X заступил Y-у дорогу ≃ **X barred ⟨stood in⟩ Y's ⟨the⟩ way; X blocked ⟨stood in⟩ Y's path.**

Едва Пётр Васильевич тронулся с места, знакомая старушка, вынырнув неведомо откуда, заступила ему дорогу (Максимов 3). As soon as Pyotr Vasilievich stirred from his place, the same old woman bobbed up out of nowhere to bar his way (3a).

2. to prevent s.o. from advancing (often, from progressing ahead of o.s.) in some field, the workplace, a (potential) romantic involvement etc: X заступил Y-у дорогу ≃ **X barred ⟨got in, stood in⟩ Y's ⟨the⟩ way; X blocked Y's path.**

Я когда-то ухаживал за Валей, но ничего из этого не вышло: мой лучший друг заступил дорогу. At one time I was trying to win Valya over, but nothing came of it: my best friend stood in my way.

Д-281 • НА ДОРО́ГУ [PrepP; Invar; adv] **1.** поесть, выпить, закурить ~ (to eat, drink sth., have a smoke) before setting out on a trip: **(have a bite ⟨a cigarette etc⟩) before going ⟨hitting the road⟩; (have a bite ⟨have one, let's have one etc⟩) for the road.**

Тётя Зина сказала, что дядю Сашу надо отвести домой... Мы выпили на дорогу (Кожевников 1). Aunt Zina said that Uncle Sasha had better be taken home....We had a drink for the road (1a).

2. to be used on a trip, while traveling: **for the ⟨one's⟩ trip ⟨journey⟩.**

...Он вынул бумажник и спросил, не нужно ли мне денег на дорогу (Герцен 1). ...He took out his notecase and asked if I did not need some money for the journey (1a).

Д-282 • НАХОДИ́ТЬ/НАЙТИ́ ДОРО́ГУ ⟨ПУТЬ, ДО́СТУП⟩ К СЕ́РДЦУ чьему, кого [VP; subj: human] to attain, evoke s.o.'s favor, love etc: X нашёл дорогу к сердцу Y-а ≃ **X found a ⟨his⟩ way (in)to Y's heart; X won Y's heart ⟨love, affection etc⟩; X found a place in Y's heart.**

Д-283 • ПЕРЕБЕГА́ТЬ/ПЕРЕБЕЖА́ТЬ ⟨ПЕРЕХОДИ́ТЬ/ПЕРЕЙТИ́, ПЕРЕБИВА́ТЬ/ПЕРЕБИ́ТЬ *obs*⟩ ДОРО́ГУ ⟨ДОРО́ЖКУ⟩ кому *coll* [VP; subj: human; more often pfv past] to block s.o.'s attempt to attain sth., usu. by attaining it first: X перебежал Y-у дорожку ≃ **X got ⟨stood⟩ in Y's way; X beat Y to it ⟨to the punch, to the draw⟩; X stole a march on Y; X stole Y's thunder; X snatched sth. from under Y's nose.**

«Ты это про Лашковых брось... Тебе Лашковы дорогу не переходили». — «Зато я им, — Александра даже не старалась

скрыть своего мстительного торжества, — перешла» (Максимов 3). "Keep the Lashkovs out of it. The Lashkovs have never got in your way." "No, I got in theirs." Alexandra was openly savoring her revenge (3a).

Д-284 • ПРОБИВА́ТЬ/ПРОБИ́ТЬ СЕБЕ́ ДОРО́ГУ ⟨ПУТЬ⟩ [VP; subj: human] (to strive) to achieve a good position in some field, success in life: X пробил себе дорогу ≃ **X made his way (in the world); X managed to get somewhere in life; X moved up in the world;** [in limited contexts] **X made it.**

Д-285 • ПРОКЛА́ДЫВАТЬ ⟨ПРОЛАГА́ТЬ⟩/ПРОЛОЖИ́ТЬ ⟨ПРОБИВА́ТЬ/ПРОБИ́ТЬ⟩ ДОРО́ГУ (кому-чему) [VP; subj: usu. human or abstr] to create conditions favorable for the development, growth of sth. or for s.o.'s activities: X проложил дорогу (Y-у) ≃ **X blazed a ⟨the⟩ trail (for Y); X forged ⟨laid down⟩ a path (for Y); X paved ⟨cleared⟩ the way (for Y).**

...Стихи вещь летучая — их нельзя ни спрятать, ни запереть. Именно стихи пробили дорогу прозе в таинственных каналах самозародившихся читателей (Мандельштам 2). ...Poetry is an elusive thing that can neither be hidden nor locked away. It was poetry that blazed the trail for prose along the mysterious byways leading to the new readers who suddenly sprung up from nowhere (2a). ♦ Это люди, выдвигающие новые идеи и прокладывающие новые пути в области духовной культуры человечества (Зиновьев 1). "They're people who put forward new ideas and who lay down new paths in the field of mankind's spiritual culture" (1a). ♦ [Астров:] Сел я, закрыл глаза — вот этак, и думаю: те, которые будут жить через сто-двести лет после нас и для которых мы теперь пробиваем дорогу, помянут ли нас добрым словом? (Чехов 3). [A.:] I sat down, shut my eyes — just like this — and started to think: people who live a hundred or a couple of hundred years after us, and for whom we are now clearing the way, will they remember us with a kind word? (3e).

Д-286 • ПРОКЛА́ДЫВАТЬ/ПРОЛОЖИ́ТЬ СЕБЕ́ ДОРО́ГУ [VP] **1.** [subj: human or collect] (in refer. to physical movement) to push ahead aggressively, removing obstacles or overcoming opposition as one goes: X проложил себе дорогу ≃ **X forced ⟨made, fought⟩ his way through.**

Растопчин рассказывал про то, как русские были смяты бежавшими австрийцами и должны были штыком прокладывать себе дорогу сквозь беглецов (Толстой 5). Rostopchin was describing how the Russians had been overwhelmed by fleeing Austrians, and had to force their way through them with bayonets (5a).

2. [subj: human] (to strive) to achieve a good position in some field, success in life: X прокладывает себе дорогу ≃ **X is making ⟨trying to make⟩ his (own) way (in the world ⟨in life⟩); X is trying to get somewhere in life.**

В станкевичевском кругу только он и Боткин были достаточные и совершенно обеспеченные люди. Другие представляли самый разнообразный пролетариат... Вероятно, каждому из них отец с матерью, благословляя на жизнь, говорили — и кто осмелится упрекнуть их за это? — «Ну, смотри же, учись хорошенько; а выучишься, прокладывай себе дорогу, тебе неоткуда ждать наследства...» (Герцен 2). In Stankevich's circle only he and Botkin were well-to-do and completely free from financial anxieties. The others made up a very mixed proletariat....Probably the father and mother of each one of them when giving him their blessing had said — and who will presume to reproach them for it — "Come, mind you work hard at your books; and when you've done with your studying you must make your own way, there's nobody you can expect to leave you anything..." (2a). ♦ «Пётр Петрович и не скрывает, что учился на медные деньги, и даже хвалится тем, что сам себе дорогу проложил», — заметила Авдотья Романовна... (Достоевский 3). "Pyotr Petrovich makes it no secret that he had to scrape up pennies for his education, and even boasts of having made his own way in life," Avdotya Romanovna remarked… (3c).

Д-287 • **СЕБЕ́ ДОРО́ЖЕ; СЕБЕ́ ДОРО́ЖЕ СТО́ИТ** *coll* [AdjP, Invar, subj-compl with быть∅, стать etc (1st var.); VP, usu. pres (2nd var.); subj: abstr or infin (occas. omitted); fixed WO] sth. (or doing sth.) does not justify the effort, will have unpleasant consequences, will affect s.o. adversely: **it's likely to cost person X dearly; it's more trouble ⟨bother, hassle⟩ than it's worth; person X stands to lose more than he gains.**

Д-288 • **ПРОТОРЁННАЯ ДОРО́ЖКА; ИЗБИ́ТАЯ ДОРО́ГА ⟨ДОРО́ЖКА⟩** *all coll, occas. iron* [NP; fixed WO] the usual, familiar, conventional way: **the beaten track ⟨path⟩; the well-worn path; tried-and-true methods;** ‖ не идти по проторённой дорожке ≃ **stay off the beaten track ⟨path⟩.** Cf. **take the road less traveled** (from Robert Frost's poem "The Road Not Taken," 1915).

Д-289 • **ВСТРЕЧА́ТЬСЯ/ВСТРЕ́ТИТЬСЯ ⟨СТА́ЛКИ-ВАТЬСЯ/СТОЛКНУ́ТЬСЯ⟩ НА У́ЗКОЙ ДО-РО́ЖКЕ ⟨ДОРО́ГЕ⟩** *(с кем)* [VP; subj: human; if there is no obj, subj: pl; usu. this WO] to come into conflict with s.o., be mutually hostile: **X и Y ⟨X с Y-ом⟩ встретились на узкой дорожке** ≃ **X ran ⟨fell⟩ afoul ⟨foul⟩ of Y; X clashed ⟨locked horns⟩ with Y.**

Я его [Грушницкого] понял, и он за это меня не любит… Я его также не люблю: я чувствую, что мы когда-нибудь с ним столкнёмся на узкой дороге, и одному из нас несдобровать (Лермонтов 1). I see through him [Grushnitsky] and he dislikes me for it.…I do not like him either, and I feel we are bound to fall foul of each other one day with rueful consequences for one of us (1b).

Д-290 • **КАК ДОСКА́ худой, тощий** *coll* [как + NP; Invar; adv (intensif)] (of a person) very (thin): **(thin) as a rail ⟨a reed⟩; (thin ⟨skinny⟩) as a toothpick; pencil thin.**

Д-291 • **СТОЯ́ТЬ НА ОДНО́Й ДОСКЕ́** *(с кем-чем)* [VP; subj: human or abstr; if subj: human, obj is also human; if subj: abstr, obj is also abstr; fixed WO] to be equal to someone or something else in some respect(s), be of equal standing: **X стоит на одной доске с Y-ом ⟨X и Y стоят на одной доске⟩** ≃ **X is on the same level as ⟨with⟩ Y; X is on the level of Y; X is in the same class ⟨league, category⟩ as Y; X is on a par with Y; person X is on person Y's level.**

«Ежели ты ждёшь от себя чего-нибудь впереди, то на каждом шагу ты будешь чувствовать, что для тебя всё кончено, всё закрыто, кроме гостиной, где ты будешь стоять на одной доске с придворным лакеем и идиотом…» (Толстой 4). "If you expect anything of yourself in the future, you will feel at every step that all is over, all is closed to you except the drawing room, where you will be on the level of a court lackey and an idiot…" (4a).

Д-292 • **ДО ГРОБОВО́Й ДОСКИ́** [PrepP; Invar; adv or, rare, postmodif; fixed WO] to the end of one's life, for as long as one lives: **to ⟨till⟩ one's dying day; till the day one dies; till ⟨to⟩ the end of one's days; to the grave; till one is laid in the grave;** [in refer. to marriage] **till death do us part.**

Этого броска в Москву Владу не забыть до гробовой доски (Максимов 2). To his dying day Vlad will never forget that dash to Moscow (2a). ♦ «Что ж, тебе не хотелось бы так пожить?..» — «И весь век так?»… «До седых волос, до гробовой доски. Это жизнь!» (Гончаров 1). "Now, wouldn't you like to live like that?…" "To live like that all the time?" "Till you grow gray—till you are laid in the grave! That is life!" (1b). ♦ [Катерина:] Ведь я замужем, ведь мне с мужем жить до гробовой доски… (Островский 6). [K.:] I am a married woman. I must live with my husband till death do us part (6b).

Д-293 • **В ДО́СКУ пьян(ый), напиться** *highly coll, disapprov* [PrepP; Invar; modif or adv (intensif)] (to be or become) very drunk: **(be ⟨get⟩) drunk as a skunk; (be ⟨get⟩) smashed ⟨bombed⟩; (be ⟨get⟩) completely plastered.**

«Давно мы с тобой не пили, Лёха, — удовлетворённо похахатывал гость, — вернусь, напьёмся — нальёмся в драбадан». — «В доску!». — «В лоск!» (Максимов 1). "You and I haven't had a drink for ages, Lyonya," the visitor chuckled contentedly. "When I get back we'll get stuck in—we'll get drunk as lords!" "Completely plastered!" "Out of our skulls!" (1a).

Д-294 • **СВОЙ В ДО́СКУ; СВОЙ ПА́РЕНЬ В ДО́СКУ** *both highly coll* [NP; often subj-compl with copula (subj: human); usu. this WO (1st var.)] genuinely close (in convictions, values etc) and trusted, accepted by the group in question: **one of our ⟨your, their⟩ own; one of the gang ⟨the guys etc⟩; one of us ⟨you, them, ours, yours, theirs⟩ (all right).**

Тут мы собутыльники… А за дверями Павильона мы социальные индивиды, устраивающие свои делишки. Тут ты свой в доску парень. А там ты активист. Карьерист, точнее говоря (Зиновьев 1). "We're all drinking companions here.…But as soon as we get outside the doors of the Pavilion we're social individuals going about our own little affairs. In here you're just one of the lads. Out there you're an activist, or rather a careerist" (1a). ♦ Дважды уже мимо Пантелея прошли дружинники… «Боятся, что иностранец», — подумал Пантелей… «Который час, не скажете?» — спросил дружинник. Решили, наконец, выяснить — иностранец или наш. Сейчас он им покажет, что в доску свой, несмотря на длинные волосы и замшевые кеды. «У вас рубля случайно не будет, папаша? — хриплым голосом ответил он вопросом на вопрос. — Душа горит…» Дружина испустила вздох облегчения — свой парень! (Аксёнов 6). [context transl] Twice already a group of vigilantes had walked past Pantelei.…They're afraid I'm a foreigner, thought Pantelei.…"What's the time, please?" asked one of the vigilantes. They had finally decided to find out whether he was a foreigner or one of ours. He would now show them that he was one hundred percent Soviet, in spite of his long hair and suede sneakers. "You wouldn't happen to have a ruble to spare, would you, dad?" He answered their question with another question in a hoarse, desperate voice. "My soul's on fire…" The vigilantes gave a sigh of relief—he's one of ours all right! (6a).

Д-295 • **СТА́ВИТЬ/ПОСТА́ВИТЬ НА ОДНУ́ ДО́СКУ** *кого с кем, что с чем* [VP; subj: human or collect] to consider two people or groups (or, rare, things) equal, the same in some respect(s), disregarding their individuality (with the implication that one of the two is better, more worthy than the other): **X ставит Y-а на одну доску с Z-ом** ≃ **X puts ⟨places⟩ Y in the same class ⟨league, category⟩ as ⟨with⟩ Z; X puts ⟨places⟩ Y on the same level with ⟨as⟩ Z; X puts ⟨places⟩ Y on a par ⟨a level⟩ with Z.**

…Нельзя ставить Убожко на одну доску с тем, кто сознательно писал и действовал враждебно (Амальрик 1). …[Ubozhko] should not be put in the same class with those who deliberately wrote and acted in a subversive manner (1a). ♦ Вот я и считаю, что его [Тихонова] нельзя ставить на одну доску с Луговским. Этот был совсем иного склада… (Мандельштам 1). I do not think he [Tikhonov] can be put in the same category as Lugovskoi, who was a completely different type… (1a). ♦ [Золотилов:] …Господа, поймите вы: главное то, что вы тут пьяницу мужика ставите на одну доску с дворянином… (Писемский 1). [Z.:] …Gentlemen, pray understand: the point is that you are putting a drunken peasant on the same level with a nobleman… (1a). ♦ Над товарищами он [Сазонов] старался брать верх и никого не ставил на одну доску с собой. Оттого они его больше уважали, чем любили (Герцен 2). He [Sazonov] tried to dominate his comrades, and put no one on a level with himself. That was why they respected him more than they liked him (2a).

Д-296 • СТАНОВИ́ТЬСЯ/СТАТЬ ⟨ВСТАТЬ⟩ НА ОДНУ́ ДО́СКУ *с кем* [VP; subj: human] to become comparable to s.o. in some respect(s) (usu. to s.o. who is or whom the speaker considers to be inferior, not equal in status etc to one): X становится на одну доску с Y-ом ≃ X puts himself on the same level as ⟨with⟩ Y; X lowers himself to Y's level; X stoops to Y's level.

Д-297 • НИ́ЖЕ *чьего* **ДОСТО́ИНСТВА; НИ́ЖЕ СВОЕ́ГО ДОСТО́ИНСТВА** [AdjP; these forms only; subj-compl with быть₀ (subj: usu. abstr or infin) or obj-compl with считать (obj: usu abstr or infin); fixed WO] sth. is demeaning for s.o.; (one considers sth.) demeaning for o.s.: X ⟨делать X⟩ ниже Y-ова достоинства ≃ (Y feels that) X ⟨doing X⟩ is beneath Y ⟨Y's dignity⟩; ‖ Y считает X ⟨делать X⟩ ниже своего достоинства ≃ Y considers X ⟨doing X⟩ beneath him ⟨his dignity⟩; Y won't lower himself to X ⟨to do X⟩; Y won't stoop to X; Y considers himself above that ⟨doing X⟩.

Стоявшие кучкою поодаль любопытные мешали знахарке. Она недобрым взглядом смеривала их с головы до ног. Но было ниже её достоинства признаваться, что они её стесняют (Пастернак 1). The knot of curious onlookers who stood at a distance annoyed the witch, and she measured them from top to toe with a hostile look. But…she felt that it was beneath her dignity to admit that they embarrassed her (1a).

Д-298 • ОЦЕ́НИВАТЬ/ОЦЕНИ́ТЬ ПО ДОСТО́ИНСТВУ *кого-что* [VP; subj: human or collect; usu. pfv; fixed WO] to evaluate s.o. or sth. correctly (either positively or negatively): X оценил Y-а по достоинству ≃ [in refer. to a positive evaluation] X recognized person Y's worth ⟨the worth of thing Y⟩; X saw person Y's true worth ⟨the true worth of thing Y⟩; X recognized the merit of thing Y; X appreciated ⟨recognized⟩ the value of thing Y; X assessed ⟨evaluated⟩ thing Y at its true worth; [in limited contexts] X gave Y Y's due; [in refer. to a negative evaluation] X saw Y for what Y really is; ‖ *Neg* X не оценил Y-а по достоинству ≃ X did not properly ⟨sufficiently⟩ appreciate Y.

Имеет значение то, что там, куда Кожевников отнёс рукопись, её прочли и, в отличие от некоторых издателей, редакторов, критиков и литературоведов, сразу оценили её по достоинству (Войнович 1). The important thing was that the people to whom Kozhevnikov gave the novel read it through and, unlike certain publishers, editors, critics, and literary scholars, saw its true worth right away (1a). ♦ «А я, — продолжал Обломов голосом оскорблённого и не оценённого по достоинству человека, — ещё забочусь день и ночь…» (Гончаров 1). "And here I am, worrying day and night," Oblomov went on, in the injured tone of a man who feels he is not properly appreciated… (1b).

Д-299 • ДОХНУ́ТЬ ⟨ДЫХНУ́ТЬ *substand*⟩ **НЕ́ГДЕ ⟨НЕЛЬЗЯ́, НЕ́ЧЕМ⟩** *coll* [these forms only; impers predic with быть₀; pres or past] some place is extremely crowded, there are too many people or things there: there's no room to breathe ⟨no breathing room, no elbow room, no room to turn around⟩.

[Таня:] Скоро на голову будут ставить [мебель]. Дохнуть нечем (Розов 2). [T.:] They'll soon be piling furniture on our heads. There's no room to breathe as it is (2a).

Д-300 • ДОХНУ́ТЬ ⟨ДЫХНУ́ТЬ *substand*⟩ **НЕ́КОГДА** *(кому)* [these forms only; impers predic with быть₀; pres or past] s.o. is very busy, excessively burdened with work: (X-у) дохнуть некогда ≃ X has no time to catch his breath ⟨to take a breather⟩; X has to work without a break.

Д-301 • МА́МЕНЬКИНА ДО́ЧКА *coll, disapprov* [NP; subj-compl with copula (subj: human, female) or obj; fixed WO] a girl or young woman whose character has been adversely affected by the excessive indulgence shown her by her family: **pampered girl ⟨young woman, young lady, little thing, darling⟩; spoiled (little) girl; (little) princess.**

Зачем вы берёте в поход эту маменькину дочку? Она через два часа начнёт хныкать и проситься домой. Why are you taking that pampered little thing hiking with you? After two hours she'll be whining to go home.

Д-302 • СУ́ЧЬЯ ⟨СОБА́ЧЬЯ⟩ ДОЧЬ *substand, rude* [NP; fixed WO] an expletive (often used as vocative) in refer. to a woman: **bitch.**

[Фёкла:] А Иван-то Павлович… Такой видный из себя, толстый; как закричит на меня: «Ты мне не толкуй пустяков, что невеста такая и этакая, ты скажи напрямик, сколько за ней движимого и недвижимого?» — «Столько-то и сколько-то, отец мой!» — «Ты врёшь, собачья дочь!» Да ещё, мать моя, вклеил такое словцо, что и неприлично тебе сказать (Гоголь 1). [F.:] And there's Ivan Pavlovich….Very handsome—stout. The way he yells at me: "Don't give me any nonsense, that she's such and such a lady. Give it to me straight—what's she got in property and how much in ready cash?" "So much and so much, my good sir." "You're lying! Bitch!" Yes, my dear, and he stuck in another word, only it wouldn't be polite to repeat it (1b).

Д-303 • ПОСЛЕ ДРА́КИ КУЛАКА́МИ НЕ МА́ШУТ [saying] it is senseless to show one's indignation about, or try to take measures concerning, a matter that has already been completed (said when one tries to rectify a matter or situation when it is too late): ≃ **why throw punches when the fight is over; you don't shake your fist when the fight is over; there's no use locking the barn door after the horse is gone ⟨stolen⟩; it is easy to be wise ⟨bold⟩ after the event.**

…Если уж быть до конца честным, надо признаться, что, будь моя статья об этой декаде более яркой, хотя бы в лучших её местах, думаю, не пожалели бы на меня медали. Но, как говорится, после драки кулаками не машут (Искандер 4). …To be perfectly honest, I think the truth is that they would have coughed up a medal for me, if my write-up on the festival—even just the key passages—had been more brilliant. But, as the saying goes, you don't shake your fist when the fight is over (4a).

Д-304 • ДАВА́ТЬ/ДАТЬ ⟨ЗАДАВА́ТЬ/ЗАДА́ТЬ⟩ ДРА́ПА ⟨ДРА́ПУ, ДРАПАКА́, ДРА́ЛА, ТЯ́ГУ, ТЁКУ, ЛАТАТЫ́⟩ *substand* [VP; subj: human or animal; more often pfv] to run away quickly (usu. in order to escape danger, pursuit etc): X дал драпа ≃ **X made off; X made tracks; X turned tail; X hightailed ⟨beat⟩ it; X cut and ran; X bolted (from some place); person X took to his heels (out of some place); person X split; [in limited contexts] person X flew the coop.**

[Гаттерас:] Катера нет! Всё ясно! Сэр! Черти дали тягу в вашем катере! (Булгаков 1). [G.:] The launch is gone! Everything's clear! Sir! The devils have made off in your launch! (1a). ♦ [Шервинский:] Слушайте, Алексей Васильевич, внимательно: гетман драпу дал… Драпанул!.. Серьёзно говорю… (Булгаков 4). [Sh.:] Listen, Aleksei Vasilyevich, carefully: the Hetman's turned tail…Beat it!…I'm telling you seriously… (4b). [Sh.:] Listen carefully, Alexei Vasilievich: the Hetman has flown the coop.…*Flown the coop!*…Yes I'm serious… (4a). ♦ «Ну нет, думаю, надо рвать когти, пока армяне меня не застукали в этом доме. Беру кружку, потихоньку прихватываю ружьё и как будто на кухню, а сам даю драпака» (Искандер 2). "Well, no, I think, I'd better get the hell out before the Armenians find me in this house. I take the cup, quietly pick up my rifle, and as if I am going to the kitchen, I take to my heels out of there" (2a).

Д-305 • **НЕ ДРЕМА́ТЬ** [VP; subj: human, collect, or animal; usu. past or pres] to be vigilant, watchful, ready to act: X не дремлет ≃ **X is wide-awake; X keeps his eyes open; X is not asleep; X is on the alert ⟨the lookout, his guard⟩; X is not to be caught napping.**

В то время, когда Ираида беспечно торжествовала победу, неустрашимый штаб-офицер не дремал и, руководясь пословицей: «Выбивай клин клином», научил некоторую авантюристку, Клементинку де Бурбон, предъявить права свои (Салтыков-Щедрин 1). While Iraidka was unconcernedly celebrating her victory, the intrepid staff-officer was not asleep. Guided by the proverb "One nail drives out another," he found an adventuress, a certain Clementinka de Bourbon, and put her up to presenting a claim (1a). ♦ Прошёл слух, что я выступал у курчатовцев, и стали приходить мне многие приглашения... И в этих учреждениях всё как будто было устроено, разрешено директорами, повешены объявления, напечатаны и розданы пригласительные билеты, — но не тут-то было! Не дремали и там [в КГБ] (Солженицын 2). The news that I had appeared at the Kurchatov Institute got around, and invitations began to arrive in large numbers....These institutions seemed to have everything arranged—directors had given their permission, notices had been put up, invitation cards were printed and distributed—but it was not to be! *They* [the KGB] were not to be caught napping (2a).

Д-306 • **НАЛОМА́ТЬ ДРОВ** coll, disapprov [VP; subj: human] to make a lot of blunders, do very foolish things (usu. as a result of reckless, rash behavior, careless decision making): X наломал дров ≃ **X screwed ⟨botched, messed⟩ things up; X screwed ⟨botched, messed⟩ it (all) up; X made a (real) mess of things;** [in limited contexts] **X got himself in(to) a mess ⟨a fix⟩;** ‖ *Neg Imper* не наломай дров ≃ **don't do anything stupid.**

«Наверно, одурел Алик от страха... Когда после регистрации билета он на своём „Запорожце" укатил из аэропорта, мне чутьё подсказывало, наломает дров» (Чернёнок 2). "Alik must have freaked out....When he drove off [from the airport] in his Zaporozhets after registering the ticket, my instincts told me that he would screw things up" (2a). ♦ «Эх, молодость, молодость, наломают дров, а потом: „Дядя, выручай!"» (Максимов 2). "Ah, you young people—get yourselves in a mess and then come yelling for help!" (2a). ♦ Что ты думаешь делать? — Горбун с тревогой следил за его [Влада] лихорадочным одеванием. — Куда пойдёшь?» — «Ещё не знаю». — «Не наломай дров» (Максимов 2). "What are you going to do?" The hunchback anxiously watched Vlad as he feverishly got dressed. "Where will you go?" "I don't know yet." "Don't do anything stupid" (2a).

Д-307 • **КАК НА ДРОЖЖА́Х** расти, подниматься и т. п. coll [как + PrepP; Invar; adv (intensif)] (of a person—usu. an adolescent, a city, a house under construction etc) (to grow) very quickly: **(grow) by leaps and bounds; (grow) like mad ⟨crazy⟩;** [of a building, city etc] **(grow) like a mushroom;** [in limited contexts, usu. of a teenager] **(grow) like a weed ⟨a beanstalk⟩; shoot up.**

Дом водопроводчика поднимался, как на дрожжах: ряд за рядом, ряд за рядом... из первосортного огнеупора, в два с половиной кирпича... (Максимов 3). The plumber's house was growing by leaps and bounds: row by row, it rose, each row two-and-a-half thicknesses of the best firebrick (3a). ♦ [Жарков:] Москва как на дрожжах поднимается (Розов 4). [Zh.:] Moscow is growing like a mushroom (4a).

Д-308 • **ДРУГ ДО́МА** [NP; usu. subj-compl with copula (subj: human) or obj-compl with считать (obj: human)] **1.** a person who is on friendly terms with the entire family: **friend of the family; family friend;** [in limited contexts] **(consider s.o.) one ⟨part⟩ of the family.**

Тут и объявляется старик-пьяница, о котором мы помянули вскользь... Был он когда-то, когда Лёвы не было, другом дома, любил бабушку и маму... (Битов 2). Now a drunk appears on the scene, an old man we have mentioned in passing....At some time, before Lyova existed, he had been a family friend, he had loved Grandma and Mama... (2a).

2. euph, humor (of a male) the wife's lover: **special friend.**

Д-309 • **ДРУГ ДРУ́ГА ⟨ДРУ́ЖКУ** coll⟩; **ДРУГ ДРУ́ГУ ⟨ДРУ́ЖКЕ** coll⟩; **ДРУГ НА ДРУ́ГА ⟨НА ДРУ́ЖКУ** coll⟩; **ДРУГ О ДРУ́ГЕ ⟨О ДРУ́ЖКЕ** coll⟩ и т. п. [NP (has no nom case); sing only; fixed WO] each of two or more (people, things etc) does sth. to the other(s) (used to indicate a reciprocal action or relationship): **(to ⟨about, against, near etc⟩) each other ⟨one another⟩; one after ⟨against, over, without etc⟩ the other;** [in limited contexts] **each other's; one another's.**

Они впервые стояли рядом — зять и свояк. За столом они не сказали друг дружке ни слова (Абрамов 1). It was the first time they had stood side by side—as brothers-in-law. They had not said a word to each other at the table (1a). ♦ «Доктор! Решительно нам нельзя разговаривать: мы читаем в душе друг у друга» (Лермонтов 1). "Upon my word, Doctor, it's impossible for us to talk together. We read each other's minds" (1c).

< «Друг» is the short form of the adjective «другой».

Д-310 • **СКАЖИ́ МНЕ, КТО ТВОЙ ДРУГ, И Я СКАЖУ́ (ТЕБЕ́), КТО ТЫ** [saying] you can judge a person's character, views etc by the sort of people with whom he associates: ≃ **a man is known by the company he keeps;** [in limited contexts] **birds of a feather (flock together)!**

Д-311 • **СТА́РЫЙ ДРУГ ЛУ́ЧШЕ НО́ВЫХ ДВУХ** [saying] there is a special loyalty and devotion that exists only between old friends (and therefore one should treasure his old friends): ≃ **old friends (and old wine) are best; there's no friend like an old friend; never exchange an old friend for a new one; make new friends but keep the old (, one is silver and the other gold).**

Д-312 • **ДЛЯ ДРУ́ГА ⟨ДЛЯ МИ́ЛОГО ДРУЖКА́⟩ (И) СЕМЬ ВЁРСТ НЕ ОКО́ЛИЦА** [saying] even a long distance seems short when you are traveling to see a friend or a loved one: ≃ **distance won't keep loved ones ⟨(two) friends⟩ apart; the road ⟨the way⟩ to a friend's house is never long; love ⟨friendship⟩ laughs at distance.**

...Вдруг отворилась дверь его комнаты и предстал Ноздрёв... «Вот говорит пословица: для друга семь вёрст не околица!» — говорил он, снимая картуз (Гоголь 3). ...The door of his room suddenly opened and Nozdrev appeared. "You know, there's truth in the saying that distance won't keep two friends apart," Nozdrev said, taking off his cap (3e). ♦ Он [старый князь] подошёл к князю Василью. «Ну, здравствуй, здравствуй; рад видеть». — «Для мила дружка семь вёрст не околица», — заговорил князь Василий, как всегда, быстро, самоуверенно и фамильярно (Толстой 4). He [the old Prince] went up to Prince Vasily. "Well, how do you do, how do you do, glad to see you." "Friendship laughs at distance," said Prince Vasily in his usual rapid, self-assured, familiar tone (4a).

Д-313 • **БУДЬ ДРУ́ГОМ ⟨ДРУГ⟩** coll [imper sent; these forms only; fixed WO] (when addressing s.o., used to ask a favor or express an emphatic request) please, be kind and do this: **be a pal ⟨a sport⟩; do me ⟨a guy, a gal⟩ a favor.**

«Пошли, Вася, будь другом, за компанию» (Максимов 3). "Come on, Vasilii, be a pal, keep us company" (3a).

Д-314 • **ДРУ́ЖБА ДРУ́ЖБОЙ, А СЛУ́ЖБА СЛУ́ЖБОЙ** [saying] friendly relations should not influence or interfere with official or business relations: ≃ **business and friendship ⟨pleasure⟩ don't mix; never mix business and ⟨with⟩ pleasure.**

[Кушак:] Они [ваш муж и Зилов] допустили серьёзную ошибку в работе. Я бы сказал – непростительную ошибку. [Валерия:] Вот как?.. Так взгрейте их как следует!.. Мужа я прошу наказать со всей строгостью... Каждому – по заслугам... Дружба дружбой, а служба... (Вампилов 5). [K.:] They've [your husband and Zilov have] committed a serious error in their work. An unforgivable error, in my opinion. [V.:] Have they now?...Then give them everything they deserve! Kindly punish my husband with all the severity of the law....They should both get their just desserts....Business and friendship don't mix... (5a).

Д-315 • ДРУЗЬЯ́ ПОЗНАЮ́ТСЯ ⟨УЗНАЮ́ТСЯ⟩ В БЕДЕ́ [saying] a person who helps when one is in trouble is a true friend (said of a person who either was helpful in a time of need or, conversely, was callous to the person in trouble): ≃ **a friend in need is a friend indeed; adversity shows (you) your true friends ⟨who your friends are⟩; you know who your (real) friends are when times are bad ⟨in times of trouble, when trouble comes** etc⟩.

Сергей Сергеевич охотно сообщает [члену правления], что он против снятия Турганова не имеет никаких возражений. Раз председатель [Турганов] злоупотребил своей властью и доверием коллектива, то он, Сергей Сергеевич Иванько, как коммунист, решительно его осуждает. Несколько дней спустя дошла до нас новая весть: на заседании какой-то высокой инстанции Иванько в пух и прах разгромил готовившийся к печати сборник Турганова... Друзья познаются в беде (Войнович 3). Sergei Sergeevich readily informed him [a board member] that he had no objections to Turganov's removal. Since the Chairman [Turganov] abused his power and the confidence of the collective, he, Sergei Sergeevich Ivanko, as a Communist, must resolutely censure him. Several days later, a new piece of news reached us: at a meeting of some high board, Ivanko completely wrecked the chances of the Turganov collection that was being prepared for publication....You know who your friends are when times are bad (3a).

Д-316 • ДАВА́ТЬ/ДАТЬ ⟨ВРЕ́ЗАТЬ⟩ ДУ́БА ⟨ДУ́-БАРЯ, ДУБАРЯ́⟩ *substand* [VP; subj: human; usu. pfv] to die: X дал дуба ≃ **X kicked the bucket; X cashed in (his chips); X croaked.**

«...В Летнем саду выступал какой-то силач, который ложился под машину. Я посмотрел, а потом пошёл к директору и спрашиваю: „Сколько вы мне дадите, если я тоже лягу?" Он говорит: „А если ты дуба дашь, кто тогда отвечать будет?"» (Каверин 1). "There was a strong man performing at the Summer Garden; he used to lie down and let a car drive over him. I watched his act and then went to the manager and asked him how much he would pay me if I were to do the same. He replied: 'And who'll be responsible if you kick the bucket?'" (1a). ♦ Если я врежу... дубаря раньше тебя, Коля, ты положи, пожалуйста, в мой гроб электробритву «Эра» и маленькие ножнички... (Алешковский 1). Hey, Kolya, if I croak before you do...you put an Era electric shaver and a pair of nail clippers in my coffin, okay? (1a).

Д-317 • ДУБИ́НА СТОЕРО́СОВАЯ; ДУРА́К ⟨БОЛ-ВА́Н⟩ СТОЕРО́СОВЫЙ *all highly coll, rude* [NP; usu. this WO] a very stupid person: **blockhead; numskull; dumbbell; bonehead; dunce; boob; dope.**

Д-318 • ДУТЬ В ДУ́ДКУ *чью, кого coll, often disapprov* [VP; subj: human; obj: human or collect] to serve s.o.'s goals by one's actions, further s.o.'s cause, act with s.o.'s goals or needs in mind: X дует в дудку Y-a ≃ **X plays ⟨sings⟩ Y's tune; X acts in the interests of Y;** ‖ X дует в свою дудку ≃ **X looks out for his (own) best interests.**

Д-319 • ПЛЯСА́ТЬ/ПОПЛЯСА́ТЬ ПОД ДУ́ДКУ ⟨ДУ́-ДОЧКУ⟩ *чью, кого* ⟨**ПО ДУ́ДКЕ** or **ДУ́ДОЧКЕ** *чьей, кого*⟩ *coll, disapprov* [VP; subj: human; usu. impfv] to submit to s.o. completely, allow one's behavior and actions to be swayed by the will, desires of another: X пляшет под Y-ову ⟨под чужую⟩ дудку ≃ **X dances to Y's ⟨to someone else's, to another's, to another man's⟩ tune;** [in limited contexts] **X sings in whatever key Y plays ⟨adopts⟩.**

«...Живи по-своему и не пляши ни по чьей дудке, это лучше всего» (Толстой 2). "Live your own life and don't dance to anybody's tune, that's best of all" (2b). ♦ Белокурый был один из тех людей, в характере которых на первый взгляд есть какое-то упорство... Кажется, никогда [они] не согласятся на то, что явно противоположно их образу мыслей... и в особенности не согласятся плясать по чужой дудке (Гоголь 3). The fair-haired man was one whose character at first sight seemed to have a streak of obstinacy....[Such men] never seem to agree with anything that contradicts their way of thinking...and above all, they never agree to dancing to another man's tune... (3d).

Д-320 • В ОДНУ́ ⟨В ТУ ЖЕ⟩ ДУДУ́ ⟨ДУ́ДКУ⟩ ДУ-ДЕ́ТЬ *(с кем) coll* [VP; subj: human; the verb may take the initial position, otherwise fixed WO] **1.** to pursue the same course of action as another or others; (of two or more people) to act similarly: X и Y в одну дуду дудят ≃ **X and Y do ⟨are up to⟩ the same thing.**

2. to repeat, usu. incessantly, another's opinion, judgment etc (usu. having adopted it as one's own); (of two or more people) to voice, usu. incessantly, the same opinion, judgment etc; to repeat incessantly one's own opinion, judgment etc: X дудит в одну дуду с Y-ом ≃ **X plays ⟨pipes⟩ the same tune as Y; X sings the same song as Y; X takes the same line as Y;** [in limited contexts] **X parrots what Y says;** ‖ X и Y ⟨X с Y-ом⟩ дудят в одну дуду ≃ **X and Y play ⟨sing, pipe⟩ the same tune; X and Y sing the same song; X and Y take the same line;** ‖ X дудит в одну дуду ≃ **X keeps harping on the same string ⟨thing, subject⟩; X keeps repeating the same thing over and over.**

«Вы читали сегодня газеты? – посапывая, спросил толстяк. – Наш Сергей Дмитриевич целую речь произнёс...» – «Да, ужасная гадость, – сказала я... – Вот обедаешь каждый день с человеком, человек как человек, и вдруг он начинает дудеть в одну дуду с негодяями...» (Чуковская 2). "Have you read the papers today?" the stout gentleman asked wheezing. "Our Sergei Dimitriyevich made a whole speech...." "Yes, it was disgusting," I said...."Every day you eat with a person who is a man like any other man, and suddenly he starts playing the same tune as those scoundrels..." (2a). ♦ ...Тюремное начальство обо мне не забывало... Настаивали, чтобы я снял голодовку... В одну эту дудку... дудели и начальник тюрьмы, и прокурор, и врач, и мой сокамерник (Марченко 2). ...The prison officials had not forgotten about me....[They] insisted that I end my hunger strike....They all piped the same tune – the prison commander, the prosecutor, the doctor and my cellmate (2a).

Д-321 • ДУ́МАТЬ И ⟨ДА⟩ ГАДА́ТЬ; ДУ́МАТЬ-ГАДА́ТЬ *both coll* [VP; subj: human; usu. foll. by a subord clause; fixed WO] to ponder sth., make suppositions: X думал и гадал ≃ **X was turning it over in his mind ⟨head⟩; X was mulling it over; X was puzzling over it; X was wondering ⟨guessing⟩.**

Пока чегемцы думали и гадали, что бы значили чудеса в дупле молельного дерева и чем окончится спор Сико с охотничьим кланом, из села Анхара, где жил Колчерукий, стали доходить слухи о таинственном исчезновении колхозного бухгалтера (Искандер 3). While the Chegemians were still wondering what the miracles in the hollow of the Prayer Tree might mean and how Siko's quarrel with the hunter's clan would end, they began hearing rumors from the village of Ankhara, where Bad Hand lived, about the mysterious disappearance of the kolkhoz bookkeeper (3a).

Д-322 • **И ДУ́МАТЬ ЗАБЫ́ТЬ** *о ком-чём coll* [VP; subj: human; only забыть conjugates; past form is used in both past and present contexts; «и» always precedes думать] to stop thinking about s.o. or sth.: X об Y-е и думать забыл ≃ **X forgot (about) Y and never thought about him ⟨it etc⟩ again; X put Y out of X's mind completely; X didn't (even) think about Y anymore; Y was the last thing on X's mind;** ‖ *Imper* об Y-е и думать забудь ≃ **don't even think about Y ⟨about doing Y⟩;** [in limited contexts] **just forget the whole idea.**

«…О Мишке Кошевом с нонешнего [*regional* = нынешнего] дня и думать позабудь»… – «Вы, братушка, знаете? – Сердцу не прикажешь!» (Шолохов 5). "…Forget Mishka Koshevoi and never think of him again."…"Surely you should know, brother? We can't tell our hearts what to feel!" (5a). ♦ Пошла вторая рюмка [коньяка]. Про чай и думать забыли (Аксёнов 7). They were on their second round of cognac. Tea was the last thing on anyone's mind (7a).

Д-323 • **НА́ДО ДУ́МАТЬ ⟨ПОЛАГА́ТЬ⟩** [these forms only; fixed WO] **1.** [sent adv (parenth) or main clause in a complex sent foll. by a что-clause] probably: **I ⟨one may⟩ suppose; presumably; it seems; most likely; chances are (that…); in all likelihood ⟨probability⟩;** [in response to a question] **I suppose so.**

…Он выплыл наконец в залу. Надо думать, что ощущал он некоторое довольно сильное любопытство (Достоевский 1). …He came finally sailing into the drawing room. One may suppose he felt a certain rather strong curiosity (1a). ♦ …Какой процент отказывается [сотрудничать с чекистами]? Этого учесть нельзя. Надо думать, что их количество увеличивалось в периоды ослабления террора (Мандельштам 1). …What percentage refused [to cooperate with the Chekists]? There's no way of knowing. Presumably their number increased in periods when the terror slackened off (1a). ♦ Надо думать, что неплохо жилось ему [Митьке] в отступлении, за Донцом: лёгкий защитный френч так и распирали широченные Митькины плечи… (Шолохов 5). Life, it seemed, had been not unkind to Mitka in the retreat across the Donets; his light field-service tunic was stretched taut across his massively broad shoulders… (5a). ♦ Следствие расположилось в кабинете Варенухи, куда и стало по очереди вызывать тех служащих Варьете, которые были свидетелями вчерашних происшествий во время сеанса… Афиши-то были? Были… Откуда взялся этот маг-то самый? А кто ж его знает. Стало быть, с ним заключали договор? «Надо полагать», – отвечал… Василий Степанович (Булгаков 9). The detectives settled into Varenukha's office, where one after the other they called in all the members of the Variety staff who had witnessed the events of the previous evening.…Had there been any posters advertising the performance? Yes, there had.…Where did this magician come from? Nobody knew. Had a contract been signed? "I suppose so," replied Vassily Stepanovich… (9b).

2. [indep. sent] (used as an affirmative answer to a question or as a remark corroborating the interlocutor's statement) yes, of course: **I should say ⟨think⟩ so; he ⟨it etc⟩ sure ⟨certainly⟩ is ⟨does, has, will etc⟩; indeed he ⟨it etc⟩ is ⟨does, has, will etc⟩; I'll say;** [in response to a statement with negated predic] **he ⟨it etc⟩ certainly isn't ⟨doesn't etc⟩.**

«Он тебя не подведёт». – «Надо думать». "He won't let you down." "He certainly won't."

Д-324 • **НЕ ДУ́МАТЬ ⟨НЕ ЖДА́ТЬ⟩, НЕ ГАДА́ТЬ; НЕ ДУ́МАТЬ И НЕ ГАДА́ТЬ** *all coll* [VP; subj: human; past only; often foll. by a что-clause; fixed WO] not to suppose, think, expect (sth. or that sth. will happen; said in retrospect after the event in question has already occurred): X не думал, не

гадал ≃ **X never thought or dreamed; X never thought ⟨dreamed, imagined⟩; it never (even) entered X's head;** [in limited contexts] **X could never have foretold.**

[Полина Андреевна:] Никто не думал и не гадал, что из вас, Костя, выйдет настоящий писатель (Чехов 6). [P.A.:] Nobody ever thought or dreamed that you'd turn out to be a real author, Kostya (6a). [P.A.:] Nobody ever dreamed that you'd make a real writer, Kostya (6c). ♦ Ардабьев-младший сжимал в руках портфель с крохотным африканским крокодилом, никогда не думавшим не гадавшим попасть со своего озера почти к самому Байкалу (Евтушенко 1). The youngest son gripped the briefcase made with the tiny African crocodile, which could never have foretold that it would find its way from its own waters almost to Lake Baikal itself (1a).

Д-325 • **НЕ́ЧЕГО И ДУ́МАТЬ ⟨МЕЧТА́ТЬ⟩** *о чём, что (с)делать* [Invar; infin compl of быть₀, impers; «и» always precedes the full verb] it is impossible (to do sth.), s.o. should not even think of (doing) sth.: об X-е нечего и думать ≃ **it is not worth (even) thinking about (doing) X; it is useless (even) to think of (doing) X; X is out of the question; there's no way (in the world) that person Y can do X;** [in limited contexts] **it is no use even to hope for X.**

Нечего было и думать на трамвае добраться до вокзала за пятнадцать минут (Каверин 1). It was useless to think of getting to the station by tram in fifteen minutes (1a). ♦ Коня он отвёл на конюшню – нечего и думать было ехать обратно, не покормив его… (Абрамов 1). He had taken the horse to the stable – it was out of the question to ride back without feeding it… (1a). ♦ …[Анна Сергеевна] вошла в кабинет. Доктор успел шепнуть ей, что нечего и думать о выздоровлении больного (Тургенев 2). …[Anna Sergeyevna] entered the study. Her doctor managed to whisper to her that it was no use even to hope for the patient's recovery (2c).

Д-326 • **Я ДУ́МАЮ!** *coll* [sent; Invar; fixed WO] (used to express one's emphatic agreement with the interlocutor's statement or affirmative response to a question) definitely, certainly: **(but) of course!; naturally!; what do you think!; you said it!; I'll say!**

«Это ведь настоящий мех?» – «Я думаю! Посмотри на цену!» "This is real fur, isn't it?" "But of course! Look at the price!"

Д-327 • **НЕ ДО́ЛГО ДУ́МАЯ ⟨ДУ́МАЮЧИ⟩** *coll* [Verbal Adv; these forms only; sent adv; fixed WO] (one does sth.) instantly, without vacillating: **without thinking twice; without giving it a second thought; without a moment's hesitation.**

…Мы, не долго думая, приняли это предложение (Искандер 4). …We accepted the suggestion without thinking twice (4a). ♦ [Анна Петровна:] Будь вы свободны, я, недолго думая, сделалась бы вашей женой… (Чехов 1). [A.P.:] If you were free, I'd marry you without giving it a second thought… (1a).

Д-328 • **ВСЯ́КИЙ ⟨КА́ЖДЫЙ⟩ ДУРА́К МО́ЖЕТ/СМО́ЖЕТ** *coll* [VP_subj; these forms only; usu. preceded by infin or это; fixed WO] (doing sth. is so easy that) anyone can do it: **any fool ⟨idiot, half-wit⟩ can (do sth.).**

Когда я рассказал ему об убийстве президента Кеннеди и о том, что убийцу нашли, он спокойно меня выслушал и, обращаясь ко мне, как бы давая мне дружеский совет, сказал: «Если ты собираешься убить человека, ты должен это сделать так, чтобы тебя не нашли… А так убить каждый дурак может» (Искандер 3). When I told him about the murder of President Kennedy and how they had found the murderer, he heard me out calmly and turned to me as if giving me a piece of friendly advice. "If you're planning to murder a man, you ought to do it in such a way that they don't find you. Any fool can murder the way he did" (3a).

Д-329 • **ДУРА́К ДУРАКО́М ⟨ДУ́РА ДУ́РОЙ⟩** *coll* [NP; these forms only; subj-compl with copula (subj: human); fixed WO] **1.** a very stupid person: **complete ⟨utter, prize⟩ fool; complete ⟨first-class⟩ idiot.**

«Да, — проговорил он, ни на кого не глядя, — беда пожить этак годков пять в деревне, в отдалении от великих умов!.. Дурак дураком станешь» (Тургенев 2). "Yes," he said, without looking at anyone, "what a calamity it is to have spent five years in the country like this, far from the mighty intellects! One becomes a complete fool" (2c).

2. a person who ends up appearing stupid or foolish: **(one) makes a (real) fool of o.s.; (one) looks like a (real) fool; (one) makes an ass of o.s.**

«...Меня опять обвели вокруг пальца, и я опять дурак дураком, второй раз за этот день...» (Стругацкие 1). "...I came out looking like an ass again, a real fool for the second time today" (1a).

Д-330 • НАБИ́ТЫЙ ⟨КРУ́ГЛЫЙ, ПЕ́ТЫЙ *obs*⟩ **ДУ-РА́К** *highly coll* [NP] a very stupid person: **total ⟨utter, complete, absolute, prize⟩ fool; fool through and through; out-and-out fool; complete ⟨absolute, total⟩ idiot; (real) dope;** [in limited contexts] **(one) doesn't have a brain in his head.**

«Дура!» — сказал он тихо. Она отшатнулась, как от удара. «Как?» — «Дура! Дура набитая» (Войнович 4). "Fool!" he said softly. She recoiled as if from a blow. "What?" "Fool! Total fool" (4a). ♦ «Лобачевского знала вся Казань, — писал он из Сибири сыновьям, — вся Казань единодушно говорила, что он круглый дурак...» (Набоков 1). "All Kazan knew Lobachevski," he wrote to his sons from Siberia..."all Kazan was of the unanimous opinion that the man was a complete fool..." (1a). ♦ И вот тут-то меня озарило: да ты просто бестолочь, Веничка, ты круглый дурак... (Ерофеев 1). And then, suddenly, it dawned on me: "Venichka, what a blockhead you are, you're an out-and-out fool" (1a). ♦ ...С дамами... в особенности, если они круглые дуры, следует при всех обстоятельствах оставаться вежливым (Чуковская 2). ...Under all circumstances one must remain polite in the company of ladies...especially if they are complete idiots (2a). ♦ Вот ещё дура-набитая! В жизни такой не видал (Абрамов 1). What a dope she was! He'd never seen anything like it (1a).

Д-331 • НЕ БУДЬ ДУРА́К ⟨ДУ́РА⟩ *highly coll;* **НЕ БУДЬ ДУРЁН ⟨ДУРНА́⟩** *substand* [не будь + NP or AdjP; NP or AdjP agrees with the subj, не будь is used with sing or pl subj; detached modif; fixed WO] (of a person or animal) being intelligent enough to make a shrewd, timely decision regarding how to act in a given situation: **(being) no fool; (being) nobody's fool; (being) no dummy ⟨dumbbell⟩.**

«...Пришёл [купец] и говорит: „Я такой-то и такой, хочу, когда смерть подберёт, на вашем острову, на высоком яру быть похоронетым [*ungrammat* = похороненным]. А за то я поставлю вам церкву христовую". Мужики, не будь дураки, согласились» (Распутин 4). "...He came to them and said: 'I'm so-and-so, and when death takes me, I want to be buried on a high hill on your island. And I'll build you a Christian church for that.' The men, being no fools, agreed" (4a). ♦ ...Он написал записку на склад, чтобы старухе выдали сколько надо пшена и масла. Старуха, не будь дура, отнесла записку не на склад, а в музей Революции, где получила такую сумму, что купила под Москвой домик, коровку... (Войнович 5). He wrote a note to the storehouse ordering that the old woman be issued as much millet and butter as she needed. The old woman, no fool, did not take the note to the storehouse but to the Museum of the Revolution, where she sold it for enough money to buy herself a little house near Moscow and a cow... (5a).

Д-332 • НЕ ДУРА́К ⟨НЕ ДУ́РА⟩ выпить, поесть, по-спать, поухаживать *за кем,* **по части** *чего* **и т. п.** *coll* [NP; subj-compl with быть∅, nom only (subj: human)] a person who enjoys and is good at (drinking, eating, sleeping, courting etc): X не дурак сделать Y ≃ **X is no slouch when it comes to doing Y; X does know how to do Y; when it comes to doing Y, X is a real pro;** [in limited contexts] **X can do Y with the best of them;** [in refer. to one's taste in clothing] **X is quite the dresser.**

[Аркадина:] На мне был удивительный туалет... Что-что, а уж одеться я не дура (Чехов 6). [A.:] I wore a lovely dress. Say what you like, but I do know how to dress (6b).

Д-333 • ВАЛЯ́ТЬ ⟨ЛОМА́ТЬ, КО́РЧИТЬ⟩ ДУРАКА́ *coll, disapprov;* **ВАЛЯ́ТЬ ⟨ЛОМА́ТЬ, КО́РЧИТЬ⟩ ВА́НЬКУ ⟨ДУ́РОЧКУ⟩** *highly coll, disapprov* [VP; subj: human] **1.** Also: **СТРО́ИТЬ ДУ́РОЧКУ** *highly coll, disapprov* to pretend not to understand, know about (sth.), feign stupidity (in order to fool s.o.): X валяет дурака ≃ **X plays the fool; X plays dumb.**

«А за что меня судить?» — «Я могу п-повторить ещё раз...» — «Не надо ваньку валять, — сказал Костенко... — Это у тебя только со Шрезелем такие номера проходили...» — «Я не понимаю, о чём вы говорите». — «З-значит, ты отказываешься давать показания?» (Семёнов 1). "But why will I be taken to court?" "I c-can repeat it for you..." "It's no good you playing the fool," said Kostyenko.... "It was only with Shresel that you could get by with that sort of game...." "I don't know what you're talking about." "D-does that mean you refuse to give evidence?" (1a). ♦ «Слушайте, Чонкин, — возбудился Запятаев, — я же вам не следователь. Зачем вы со мной дурака валяете?» (Войнович 4). "Listen, Chonkin," — Zapyataev grew excited — "I'm not interrogating you, why play dumb with me?" (4a).

2. to act in such a way as to amuse (and occas. annoy) others with one's tricks, anecdotes etc, behave mischievously, in a silly manner: X валял дурака ≃ **X was playing ⟨acting⟩ the fool; X was monkeying ⟨clowning, fooling⟩ around;** [in limited contexts] **X was up to his (usual) tricks;** ‖ хватит валять дурака! ≃ **quit fooling around!; cut (out) the monkey business.**

...Судя по грохоту кастрюль, доносившемуся из кухни, можно было допустить, что Бегемот находится именно там, валяя дурака, по своему обыкновению (Булгаков 9). ...To judge from the clatter of saucepans coming from the kitchen Behemoth was presumably there, playing the fool as usual (9b).

3. Also: **СВАЛЯ́ТЬ ДУРАКА́ ⟨ВА́НЬКУ, ДУ́РОЧКУ⟩** [if impfv, often neg imper or infin with хватит, брось etc] to act irresponsibly, unintelligently, unseriously, make a stupid blunder: X валяет дурака ≃ **X is fooling around; X is being a fool; X is being stupid;** ‖ X свалял дурака ≃ **X did a stupid thing; X put his foot in it ⟨in(to) his mouth⟩; X pulled a boner; X goofed (up); X blew it; X made a fool (out) of himself;** ‖ *Neg Imper* не валяй дурака ≃ **quit fooling (around)!; don't be a fool!**

[Лопахин:] Я-то хорош, какого дурака свалял! Нарочно приехал сюда, чтобы [Любовь Андреевну и Аню] на станции встретить, и вдруг проспал... (Чехов 2). [L.:] I'm a fine one! What a fool I've made of myself! Came here on purpose to meet them [Lyubov Andreyevna and Anya] at the station, and then overslept... (2a). ♦ ...Затрещал телефон. «Да!» — крикнул [Иван Савельевич] Варенуха. «Иван Савельевич?» — осведомилась трубка препротивным гнусавым голосом. «Его нету в театре!» — крикнул было Варенуха, но трубка тотчас его перебила: «Не валяйте дурака, Иван Савельевич, а слушайте. Телеграммы эти никуда не носите и никому не показывайте» (Булгаков 9). ...The telephone rang. "Yes!" cried [Ivan Savelievich] Varenukha. "Ivan Savelievich?" the receiver inquired in a most repulsive nasal voice. "He is not in the theater!" Varenukha began, but the receiver immediately interrupted him: "Quit fooling, Ivan Savelievich, and listen. Do not take those telegrams anywhere, and do not show them to anyone" (9a).

4. [variants with валять only] to be idle, spend time lazily: X валял дурака ≃ **X fooled ⟨fiddled⟩ away the ⟨his⟩ time; X goofed off.**

Как тебе не стыдно! Все работают, а ты дурака валяешь. You should be ashamed of yourself! Everyone else is working while you're goofing off.

Д-334 • НАШЁЛ ДУРАКА́ ⟨ДУ́Р(ОЧК)У, ДУРА-КО́В⟩!; ИЩИ́ ДУРАКА́ ⟨ДУ́Р(ОЧК)У, ДУРА-КО́В⟩!; НЕТ ДУРАКО́В! *all highly coll, iron* [Interj; these forms only; more often this WO] used to express disagreement, one's refusal to do or believe sth.: **I am not as stupid as you ⟨they etc⟩ think; what kind of fool do you ⟨they etc⟩ take me for ⟨think I am⟩?; I'm not such a fool (as to do ⟨believe etc⟩ that!); find yourself ⟨let them etc find themselves⟩ another patsy ⟨sucker, fall guy, dupe⟩;** Cf. **tell it to the marines!**

[Себейкин:] Я за своё отвечаю, а за всех отвечать дураков нету! (Рощин 2). [S.:] I answer for my own work, but to answer for everybody? I'm not such a fool! (2a).

Д-335 • НЕ НА ДУРАКА́ ⟨ДУ́РУ, ПРОСТАКА́⟩ НА-ПА́Л *highly coll* [sent; past only; fixed WO] you are (he is etc) underestimating the intelligence of the person with whom you are (he is etc) dealing (usu. used in contexts when the interlocutor underestimates the speaker's intelligence): **I'm not the fool you take me for ⟨he's not the fool you take him for etc⟩; what do you take me for ⟨what do they take her for etc⟩, a fool?; you ⟨he etc⟩ shouldn't take me ⟨her etc⟩ for a fool.**

«...Я камердинер молодого барина»... Но Лиза поглядела на него и засмеялась. «А лжёшь, – сказала она, – не на дуру напал. Вижу, что ты сам барин» (Пушкин 3). "I am the young master's valet."...But Lisa looked at him and laughed. "You're lying," she said. "I'm not the fool you take me for. I can see that you are the young master himself" (3b).

Д-336 • РАЗЫ́ГРЫВАТЬ/РАЗЫГРА́ТЬ ДУРАКА́ ⟨ДУ́РУ⟩ [VP; subj: human] **1.** to pretend not to understand, know about sth., feign stupidity (in order to fool s.o.): X дурака разыгрывает ≃ **X plays the fool; X plays dumb.**

[Кречинский:] ...Вы нарочно пришли дурака разыгрывать, что я вам не могу вдолбить в голову, что теперь, сию минуту, у меня денег нет и отдать их я не могу!.. (Сухово-Кобылин 2). [K.:] ...Have you come here deliberately to play the fool? Can't I knock it into that thick skull of yours that now, this minute, I don't have any money and I can't pay you back! (2b).

2. *obs* [pfv only] to make a blunder, do sth. stupid: X разыграл дурака ≃ **X made a fool ⟨an ass⟩ (out) of himself; X put his foot in it;** [in limited contexts] **X put his foot in(to) his mouth.**

[Войницкий:] Разыграть такого дурака: стрелять два раза и ни разу не попасть! (Чехов 3). [V.:] To have made such a fool of myself: fired twice and missed him! (3b).

Д-337 • ДУРАКА́М ⟨ДУРАКУ́⟩ ЗАКО́Н НЕ ПИ́САН [saying] stupid, foolhardy people do not observe the rules (said of a person who, in the speaker's opinion, acts or behaves strangely, not according to common sense and the accepted standards of behavior): ≃ **there's no knowing ⟨telling⟩ with a fool; there's no knowing ⟨telling⟩ what a fool will do;** [in limited contexts] **fools rush in where angels fear to tread.**

[Катенька:] А как же Иван Андреевич... без вас? [Безенчук:] А уж это как желает. Дуракам закон не писан (Арбузов 1). [K.:] But what will Ivan do without you? [B.:] That's his business. There's no knowing with a fool! (1a).

Д-338 • В ДУРАКА́Х ⟨В ДУ́РАХ *obs*⟩ быть₀, остаться, оставить *кого* и т. п. *coll* [PrepP; these forms only; subj-compl with copula (subj: human or collect) or obj-compl with оставить (obj: human or collect)] (to be, end up, put s.o.) in a stupid, ludicrous situation: X остался в дураках ≃ **X made a fool ⟨an ass, a jackass, a monkey⟩ (out) of himself; X was made a fool ⟨an ass⟩ of; X ended up looking like a fool; X ended up with egg on his face;** ‖ Y оставил X-а в дураках ≃ **Y made a fool ⟨an ass, a jackass, a monkey⟩ (out) of X; Y left X with egg on X's face.**

Депутаты считали, что Дессер остался в дураках: поддерживал Народный фронт, хотел предотвратить войну резолюциями Лиги наций (Эренбург 4). The deputies thought he [Desser] had made a fool of himself; he had supported the Popular front and wanted to prevent war with airy resolutions by the League of Nations (4a). ♦ «...Неужели вы думаете, что кампания кончена?» – «Я вот что думаю. Австрия осталась в дурах, а она к этому не привыкла. И она отплатит» (Толстой 4). "...Do you really think the campaign is over?" "This is what I think. Austria has been made a fool of, and she is not used to it. She will retaliate" (4a). ♦ Говорят, что... была у них [двух таможенных чиновников] ссора за какую-то бабёнку... но что оба чиновника были в дураках и бабёнкой воспользовался какой-то штабс-капитан Шамшарёв (Гоголь 3). It is said...that they [the two customs officials] had quarrelled violently over some young woman...but that she had made fools of both customs officials and some Major Shamsharyov had got the pretty creature in the end (3a).

Д-339 • БЕЗ ДУРАКО́В *highly coll* [PrepP; Invar; sent adv or indep. sent] earnestly, seriously, without exaggerating or lying: **no kidding ⟨joking⟩; all kidding ⟨joking⟩ aside.**

«Тост, конечно, за хозяйку, за её гостеприимный дом, за её сердце, сказал я, вобравшее в себя ум всех этих книг и нежность всех этих ковров. Без дураков, здорово сказал...» (Искандер 2). "Of course the toast is to our hostess, for the hospitality of her house, for her heart, I say, which has absorbed the wisdom of all these books and the soft tenderness of all these carpets. No kidding, it was a great toast..." (2a).

Д-340 • ВЫБИВА́ТЬ/ВЫ́БИТЬ ⟨ВЫШИБА́ТЬ/ВЫ-ШИБИТЬ, ВЫКОЛА́ЧИВАТЬ/ВЫ́КОЛОТИТЬ⟩ ДУРЬ из кого ⟨ИЗ ГОЛОВЫ́ чьей, у кого⟩ *coll, occas. rude* [VP; subj: human; usu. pfv; often infin (with надо, пора), fut (1st pers sing, used as a threat), or subjunctive] by using strong measures, to force s.o. to give up a bad habit, relinquish a wrong idea, cease to engage in some reprehensible behavior etc: X выбьет дурь из Y-а ⟨у Y-а из головы⟩ ≃ **X will knock the nonsense out of Y's head ⟨out of Y⟩; X will knock ⟨pound, talk⟩ some sense into Y's head ⟨into Y⟩.**

[author's usage] «Слушай ты, мыслитель, я из тебя эту дурь окопную быстро вышибу...» (Максимов 1). [context transl] "Listen, philosopher, it's not going to take me very long to knock your shell-shock out of you" (1a).

Д-341 • ВЫБРА́СЫВАТЬ/ВЫ́БРОСИТЬ ⟨ВЫКИ́ДЫВАТЬ/ВЫ́КИНУТЬ⟩ ДУРЬ ИЗ ГОЛОВЫ́ *coll* [VP; subj: human; usu. pfv; often infin with надо, пора] to give up a bad habit, relinquish a wrong idea, stop engaging in some reprehensible behavior etc: X-у надо выбросить дурь из головы ≃ **X should get ⟨put⟩ this ⟨that⟩ nonsense ⟨foolishness⟩ out of his head; X should put this ⟨that⟩ nonsense behind him; X should forget ⟨stop⟩ this ⟨that⟩ nonsense (completely).**

«Мне говорили, сказывали, что Варуха с парнем связалась, ну, я не верила». – «А теперь веришь». – «Выбрось эту дурь из головы. Посмешила людей и хватит» (Абрамов 1). "...They were saying Varukha is involved with the boy. Well, I didn't believe it...." "And now you do believe it?" "Just put that nonsense out of your head. You've made people laugh—and that's enough" (1b).

Д-342 • ВО ВЕСЬ ДУХ ⟨МАХ, ОПО́Р⟩ бежать, мчаться, нестись, пустить лошадь и т. п. *coll* [PrepP; these forms only; adv; fixed WO] (of a person, a horse, or, rare, a horse-driven carriage) (to run, race along etc) very fast, with great speed, headlong: **at top ⟨full⟩ speed; (at) full tilt; as fast as one can (go); as fast as one's legs can carry one; for all one is worth;** [of a horse] **(race along ⟨go⟩) at a full gallop; (put one's horse) to a full gallop; (go ⟨make one's horse go⟩) flat-out.**

Он [Пугачёв] остановился; его окружили, и, как видно, по его повелению четыре человека отделились и во весь опор подскакали под самую крепость (Пушкин 2). He [Pugachev] stopped; his men gathered around him; and evidently by his command, four of them peeled off from the group and galloped right up to the fort at full speed (2a). ♦ Лошади летели во весь опор, карету мягко встряхивало... (Окуджава 2). The horses raced along at full speed, the carriage rolling slightly... (2a). ♦ ...Сейчас он, конечно, уже на конюшне, дрожащими от волнения и спешки, путающимися, не слушающимися руками запрягает Савраску и немедленно во весь дух пустится нахлёстывать следом, так что нагонит их ещё в поле, до въезда в лес (Пастернак 1). ...At the moment, of course, he's in the stable, hurrying, excited, fumbling with the harness, and he'll rush after us full tilt and catch up with us before we get into the forest (1a). ♦ ...[Чичиков] сел в бричку и велел Селифану погонять лошадей во весь дух (Гоголь 3). Chichikov...got into his carriage and told Selifan to drive as fast as he could (3a). ♦ ...Ты бежал во весь дух, сам не зная куда, обезумевший от счастья (Олеша 3). ...You ran for all you were worth, yourself not knowing where, out of your wits with happiness (3a). ♦ Кавалергарды скакали, но ещё удерживая лошадей. Ростов уже видел их лица и услышал команду: «Марш, марш!», произнесённую офицером, выпустившим во весь мах свою кровную лошадь (Толстой 4). The Horse Guards were galloping but still holding in their horses. Rostov could now see their faces and hear the command: "Charge!" shouted by an officer putting his thoroughbred to a full gallop (4a).

Д-343 • ВЫШИБА́ТЬ/ВЫ́ШИБИТЬ ДУХ ⟨ДУ́ШУ⟩ из кого substand [VP; subj: human] to kill s.o. on the spot (usu. with a blow or blows): X вышиб дух из Y-а ≃ **X bumped ⟨knocked, finished⟩ Y off.**

Внизу в теплушке разговаривали двое. Один спрашивал другого: «Ну как, угомонили своих? Доломали хвосты им?» – «Это лавочников, что ли?» – «Ну да, лабазников». – «...Из которых для примеру вышибли дух, ну остальные и присмирели» (Пастернак 1). Two men were talking underneath his bunk. "Well, have they had their tails twisted yet? Are they keeping quiet now?" "The shopkeepers, you mean?" "That's right. The grain merchants." "...As soon as a few were bumped off by way of example, all the others piped down" (1a).

Д-344 • ДУХ ⟨ДУША́⟩ ВОН (из кого) substand [sent; these forms only; fixed WO] s.o. suddenly died: (из X-а) дух вон ≃ **X kicked off; X dropped dead; X croaked; X gave up the ghost.**

Д-345 • ДУХ ⟨ДЫХА́НИЕ⟩ ЗАХВА́ТЫВАЕТ/ЗАХВАТИ́ЛО ⟨ЗАНИМА́ЕТ/ЗА́НЯЛО coll, **СПЁРЛО** obs, substand⟩ у кого (от чего); **ДУХ ⟨ДЫХА́НИЕ⟩ ЗАНИМА́ЕТСЯ/ЗАНЯЛСЯ́ ⟨-лось⟩** coll; **ПЕРЕХВА́ТЫВАЕТ/ПЕРЕХВАТИ́ЛО ДЫХА́НИЕ ⟨ДУХ** coll⟩ у кого [VP; impers (1st and last groups) or VP_subj (2nd group); more often past] **1.** Also: **ПЕРЕХВА́ТЫВАЕТ/ПЕРЕХВАТИ́ЛО** чьё **ДЫХА́НИЕ** [VP; subj: abstr] s.o.'s breathing stops for a moment (because of exposure to bitter cold etc), or s.o. breathes with great effort (as a result of fast running, intense physical exertion etc): у X-а захватило (от Y-а) ≃ **Y took X's breath away; X couldn't catch his breath; X gasped for air ⟨breath⟩;** [as a result of physical exertion] **X was short ⟨out⟩ of breath.**

Вода в горных реках всегда холодная, дух занимает, но потом привыкаешь (Айтматов 1). The water in mountain streams is always cold—it takes your breath away, then you get used to it (1a). ♦ От силы удара у Махаза перехватило дыхание... (Искандер 4). [context transl] The force of the blow knocked the wind out of Makhaz... (4a).

2. s.o. takes an unusually long, deep etc breath (as an expression of wonder, surprise, fear etc): у X-а дух захватило (от Y-а)

≃ **Y took X's breath away; X caught his breath; X was breathless (with Y); X gasped (in surprise** etc).

[author's usage] ...Тройка летела, «пожирая пространство», и по мере приближения к цели опять-таки мысль о ней [Грушеньке], о ней одной, всё сильнее и сильнее захватывала ему дух и отгоняла все остальные страшные призраки от его сердца (Достоевский 1). ...The troika went flying on, "devouring space," and the closer he came to his goal, the more powerfully the thought of her [Grushenka] again, of her alone, took his breath away and drove all the other terrible phantoms from his heart (1a). ♦ В ослепительных белых и чёрных лимузинах ехали, весело разговаривая, офицеры в высоких картузах с серебром. У нас с Шуркой разбежались глаза и захватило дыхание (Кузнецов 1). The officers in their tall peaked caps with silver braid travelled in dazzling black and white limousines, chatting cheerfully among themselves. We, Shurka and I, caught our breath and scarcely knew where to look next (1b). ♦ Равнодушно не мог выстоять на балконе никакой гость и посетитель. От изумленья у него захватывало в груди дух, и он только вскрикивал: «Господи, как здесь просторно!» (Гоголь 3). No guest or visitor could stand unmoved on the balcony. He would be breathless with surprise and he could only exclaim: "Lord, what a magnificent view!" (3a).

Д-346 • ИСПУСТИ́ТЬ ДУХ obs; **ИСПУСКА́ТЬ/ИСПУСТИ́ТЬ ПОСЛЕ́ДНИЙ ВЗДОХ** obs, lit [VP; subj: human; usu. pfv past; usu. this WO] to die: X испустил дух ≃ **X breathed his last; X gave up the ghost; X drew his last breath; X departed this life ⟨world⟩.**

...[Эти дикие существа] с такою зверскою жадностью набросились на пищу, что тут же объелись и испустили дух (Салтыков-Щедрин 1). ...[The wild creatures] fell upon the food with such bestial greed that they overate, and then and there breathed their last (1a). ♦ «...Старому жулику из княжеского рода не пришлось торжествовать победу: он испустил дух в одно мгновение с Мастером, только куда менее героически...» (Максимов 2). "...The old rogue of princely blood was not fated to celebrate his triumph: he gave up the ghost at the very same moment as did the Master-Craftsman, only far less heroically..." (2a). ♦ ...Он [дед Одоевцев] испустил дух под вопли старухи, на руках у слесаря Пушкина (Битов 2). He [Grandfather Odoevtsev] departed this world, to the wails of the old woman, in the arms of Pushkin the locksmith (2a).

Д-347 • НА́ ДУХ ⟨НА ДУ́Х⟩ не переносить, не принимать кого-что и т. п. highly coll [PrepP; these forms only; adv (intensif); used with impfv verbs] (to be) absolutely (unable to bear s.o. or sth.): X Y-а на дух не переносит ≃ **X cannot stand ⟨stomach⟩ Y; X hates person Y's guts; Y makes X sick (to X's stomach).**

«Ведь он единственный человек, с кем Сергей Кириллович может разговаривать! Хотя и с ним спорит... Но остальных на дух не принимает» (Трифонов 6). "You see, he's the only person Sergei Kirillovich can talk to! Even though he argues with him. But he can't stomach the others..." (6a).

Д-348 • ПЕРЕВОДИ́ТЬ/ПЕРЕВЕСТИ́ ДУХ ⟨ДЫХА́НИЕ⟩ [VP; subj: human] **1.** to breathe in deeply, pause to breathe (esp. after strenuous physical effort, because one is frightened etc): X перевёл дух ≃ **X caught ⟨recovered, drew⟩ his breath; X took ⟨drew⟩ a deep breath; X got his breath back;** ‖ X едва ⟨еле, с трудом, тяжело⟩ переводил дух ≃ **X was short ⟨out⟩ of breath; X was struggling ⟨gasping⟩ for breath; X was struggling to catch ⟨to get⟩ his breath.**

Трудно сказать, чем кончился бы монолог Ярцева, если бы его не прервал дневальный Алимов. Видно, Алимов бежал от самого городка, потому что долго не мог перевести дух, и, приложив руку к пилотке, тяжело дышал, молча глядя на Ярцева (Войнович 2). There's no telling how Yartsev's monologue would have ended if it hadn't been interrupted by Alimov, the orderly. Alimov had clearly run the whole distance from camp, for it took him a long time to catch his breath. Panting, frozen in a salute, he looked at Yartsev without saying a single word (2a). ♦ Арестованный пошатнулся… перевёл дыхание и ответил хрипло: «Я понял тебя. Не бей меня» (Булгаков 9). The prisoner swayed.…He drew his breath and answered hoarsely: "I understand you. Don't hit me" (9a). ♦ Академик Флоринский, прежде чем заговорить, несколько раз кивнул, опёрся посильнее на трость. «Я рад слышать здесь положительный отзыв профессора Авдиева…» Он перевёл дух… и стал диктовать сидящей сзади него стенографистке… (Дудинцев 1). Before he began to speak Academician Florinsky nodded repeatedly and tightened his hold on the stick on which he was leaning. "I am glad to hear Professor Avdiyev's positive opinion here.…" He took a deep breath and began dictating to the stenographer sitting behind him… (1a). ♦ …Поняв, что тот [Тимур] рано или поздно поймает его кисть своими челюстями, [Кязым] с такой силой вывернул ему руки, что тот, застонав, повалился. Кязым, с трудом переводя дыхание, положил ключ в карман (Искандер 5). Realizing that sooner or later Timur would catch his hand in his jaws, he [Kyazym] wrenched Timur's arm so hard that he let out a groan and fell. Struggling for breath, Kyazym put the key in his pocket (5a). ♦ Через несколько мгновений он [Скороход] обогнал старуху… Вскоре, тяжело дыша, прибежала и старуха. «Молодец, Страусиная Нога, — зло прошипел старший великан, — на таких состязаниях и второе место почётно». — «Я сделала всё, что могла», — сказала старуха, с трудом переводя дыхание (Искандер 5). He [Highspeed] overtook the old woman in a few instants.…Before long the old woman too arrived, panting hard. "Well done, Ostrich Leg," the eldest giant hissed spitefully. "In a contest like this even second place is honorable." "I did all I could," the old woman said, struggling to get her breath (5a).

2. to take a short break, respite: X перевёл дух ≃ **X caught his breath; X took a breather; X got his breath (back); X came up for air.**

Точно демонстрируя на собственном примере возможности новой динамики, Маринетти двоился, выбрасывая в стороны руки, ноги, ударяя кулаком по пюпитру, мотая головой, сверкая белками, скаля зубы, глотая воду стакан за стаканом, не останавливаясь ни на секунду, чтобы перевести дыхание (Лившиц 1). As if demonstrating the potential of the new dynamics by his own example, Marinetti split into two, throwing out his legs and arms in all directions, banging his fist on the desk, reeling about, showing the whites of his eyes, baring his teeth, swallowing glass after glass of water and not stopping for a moment to get his breath back (1a).

Д-349 • В ДУ́ХЕ[1] *coll* [PrepP; Invar; subj-compl with copula (subj: human)] one is in a cheerful, happy mood: X был в духе ≃ **X was in high ⟨good, great⟩ spirits; X was in a good ⟨great⟩ mood ⟨frame of mind⟩.**

Я был в духе, импровизировал разные необыкновенные истории; княжна сидела против меня и слушала мой вздор с таким глубоким, напряжённым, даже нежным вниманием, что мне стало совестно (Лермонтов 1). I was in high spirits, I improvised all kinds of extraordinary stories: the young princess sat opposite me and listened to my tosh with such deep, tense, even tender attention that I felt ashamed of myself (1a).

Д-350 • В ДУ́ХЕ[2] [PrepP; Invar; Prep] **1.** ~ *кого-чего, чьём, каком* [the resulting PrepP is subj-compl with copula (subj: concr, abstr, or human), adv, or postmodif] (in a way) typical or characteristic of s.o. or sth. (as specified by the context): в духе X-а ⟨в X-овом духе⟩ ≃ **in the spirit of X; in the manner of person X; along the lines of thing X; in keeping with thing X; on the order of thing X; [in limited contexts] thing Y has a little of X in it; (that's) person X's style ⟨way⟩; (the sort of thing)**

person X likes; ‖ в [AdjP] духе ≃ **in a [AdjP] spirit ⟨vein, manner⟩.**

Письмо начиналось очень решительно, именно так: «Нет, я должна к тебе писать!» Потом говорено было о том, что есть тайное сочувствие между душами… Окончанье письма отзывалось даже решительным отчаяньем… Письмо было написано в духе тогдашнего времени (Гоголь 3). The letter began in a very determined tone, in these words: "No, I really must write to you!" Then it went on to say that there *was* a mysterious affinity of souls.…The end of the letter echoed downright despair.…The letter was written in the spirit of the day (3c). ♦ Усугубилась его [Чернышевского] манера логических рассуждений — «в духе тёзки его тестя», как вычурно выражается Страннолюбский (Набоков 1). His [Chernyshevski's] trick of logical reasoning was intensified — "in the manner of his father-in-law's namesake," as Strannolyubski so whimsically puts it (1a). ♦ На северном хвостике косы был ещё в духе Дикого Запада посёлочек, под названием Малый Бем и Копейка (Аксёнов 7). At the northernmost tip of the spit was a small town called Bem-Minor-and-a-Kopeck that had a little of the Wild West in it… (7a). ♦ Она мне очень нравилась, эта книга [«Чудо-богатырь Суворов»]… Она была составлена в патриотическом духе… (Олеша 3). That book [*The Wonderful Warrior Suvorov*] pleased me very much.…It was written in a patriotic spirit… (3a). ♦ Когда он говорил о себе, то всегда в мрачно-юмористическом духе (Набоков 1). When he spoke of himself it was always in a gloomily humorous vein (1a).

2. ~ *чьём, кого* [the resulting PrepP is subj-compl with copula (subj: human, abstr, or concr) or postmodif] a person or thing is of a type, category etc that appeals to s.o., that s.o. approves of: X в Y-овом духе ≃ **X is Y's sort ⟨kind⟩ of person ⟨thing⟩; X is the sort of person ⟨thing⟩ Y likes.**

Я уверен, что мои новые друзья тебе понравятся, они вполне в твоём духе. I'm sure you'll like my new friends, they're your sort of people. ♦ [Суходолов:] Вот, видишь, вдали в дымке мачты… Это «Старые причалы». В твоём духе, поэтическое место… (Погодин 1). [S.:] There, you see those masts in the distant, smoky haze? That's "Old Harbor." The sort of thing you like, a poetic place (1a).

3. В ТОМ ЖЕ ⟨В ТАКО́М (ЖЕ), В Э́ТОМ (ЖЕ)⟩ ДУ́ХЕ [adv, postmodif, or subj-compl with copula (subj: human, abstr, or concr); fixed WO] in a way similar to what was stated or implied previously: **along these ⟨those⟩ ⟨same⟩ lines; in the same vein ⟨spirit, manner, way⟩;** ‖ что-то в этом духе ≃ **something like that.**

[Сарафанов:] Я подумал, что её, может быть, смущает разница в возрасте, может, боится, что её осудят, или… думает, что я настроен против… В этом духе я с ней и разговаривал, разубеждал её… (Вампилов 4). [S.:] I thought maybe she was bothered by the difference in age. Maybe she was afraid she'd be criticized…or thinks I'm against it.…I talked to her along those lines, tried to convince her I wasn't against it… (4b). ♦ Ребров ему [Сергею Леонидовичу] что-то про справку, а тот — про то, что зол на весь мир, находится в опаснейшем, мизантропическом настроении… мы погибнем от лицемерия и что-то ещё в таком духе (Трифонов 1). No sooner had Rebrov said something to him about the certificate than Sergei Leonidovich declared that he was mad at the whole world, that he was in an extremely negative, misanthropic mood…that hypocrisy would be our downfall — and more in the same vein (1a). ♦ «По ленинским местам» фильм должен был называться или как-то в этом духе, я, признаться, точно не помню. А места эти, ленинские, они, как известно, в большинстве своём за рубежами нашей отчизны находятся. Потому что товарищ Ленин в своё время был тоже как бы невозвращенец (Войнович 1). I don't remember exactly what it [the film] was to be called — "In the Footsteps of Lenin" — something like that. As we know, the greater part of those footsteps occurred outside the borders of our country. Because Comrade Lenin at one time had been something of a defector himself (1a).

4. В ТОМ ⟨В ТАКО́М⟩ ДУ́ХЕ, что... [adv; fixed WO] approximately as follows: **to the effect that; in the vein that.**

[Отставной активист] высказывался в том духе, что... квартира в жилтовариществе советских фотографов превратилась в пристанище для сборищ с определённой подкладкой, с сомнительным душком (Аксёнов 12). ...The retired activist expressed himself to the effect that...an apartment in a housing community for Soviet photographers had been "turned into a haven for gatherings of a certain element, with a dubious air" (12a). ♦ Он уже хотел было выразиться в таком духе, что, наслышась о добродетелях [Плюшкина]... почёл долгом принести лично дань уважения, но спохватился и почувствовал, что это слишком (Гоголь 3). He was about to venture an explanation in the vein that having heard of Pliushkin's virtues...he had deemed it his duty to pay him his due tribute of respect in person, but he reined up in time, realizing that it would be spreading it too thickly (3c).

Д-351 • НЕ В ДУ́ХЕ [PrepP; Invar; subj-compl with copula (subj: human)] **1.** *coll.* Also: **НЕ В ДУХА́Х** *substand, humor* one is not cheerful, one is discontent, displeased, irritable: X не в духе ≃ **X is in a bad ⟨dismal, foul, rotten, lousy, nasty⟩ mood; X is out of sorts ⟨humor⟩; X is in low spirits; X is in (a) bad ⟨(an) ill⟩ humor; X is down in the dumps.**

Карл Иваныч был очень не в духе. Это было заметно по его сдвинутым бровям и по тому, как он швырнул свой сюртук в комод... (Толстой 2). Karl Ivanich was in an extremely bad mood. This was evident from his lowering brows and from the way he flung his coat into the wardrobe... (2b). ♦ Николай Васильевич был в тот день не в духе, мрачноват и вовсе ничего не замечал (Трифонов 2). Nikolai Vasilievich was out of sorts that day, gloomy and unaware of anything around him (2a). ♦ «Верно, Андрей рассказал [Ольге], что на мне были вчера надеты чулки разные или рубашка наизнанку!» – заключил он и поехал домой не в духе... (Гончаров 1). "Andrei probably told her [Olga] I had on unmatched socks yesterday, or that I put my shirt on inside out!" he concluded, and went home in low spirits... (1b) ♦ ...Сейчас Дмитрий Алексеевич может оказаться не в духе. Возможно, что ему ни с кем не хочется разговаривать... (Дудинцев 1). ...Dmitri Alexeyevich might be in a bad humor. He might not want to talk to anyone... (1a).

2. *obs* [foll. by infin] one is not disposed (to do sth.): X не в духе делать Y ≃ **X is not in the mood to do Y; X is in no mood to do Y; X is not up to doing Y; X doesn't feel (much) like doing Y.**

«Если б вы знали, какая мучит меня забота!» – «Я всё знаю», – отвечал я... «Тем лучше: я не в духе рассказывать» (Лермонтов 1). "If only you knew how worried I am." "I know about everything," I replied...."That's just as well, I'm not in the mood to tell you" (1d).

Д-352 • ВОСПРЯ́НУТЬ ДУ́ХОМ [VP; subj: human; fixed WO] having overcome a feeling of despondency, to feel braver, more positive: X воспрянул духом ≃ **X recovered ⟨regained⟩ his spirits; X took heart ⟨courage⟩; X felt in better spirits; X's spirits rose.**

Доживая жизнь при добром цезаре, Ахматова воспрянула духом (Мандельштам 2). Living out her last few years under a good Caesar, Akhmatova recovered her spirits (2a). ♦ ...Я посоветовал [Лёше Иванченко] составить «график роста числа активных читателей» как свидетельство успешной работы библиотеки. «Но оно не растёт...» – «Тем лучше, давай бумагу!» – сказал я и через несколько минут изобразил график... Увидев, что рост достигается так легко, Иванченко воспрял духом и решил, что удержится на месте культорга (Амальрик 1). I advised him [Lesha Ivanchenko] to draw up a graph showing the "rise in the number of active readers" as evidence of how much work was being done in the library. "But there hasn't been any such rise...." "So much the better," I said. "Just give me a piece of paper." In a few minutes I had drawn a graph....When he saw how easy it was to achieve a growth in readership...Lesha took heart and decided he would be able to hang onto his job as culture organizer (1a). ♦ Вырвавшись из толпы, в сравнительном безлюдье и спокойствии территории уголовников, оба они [Л. и Мандельштам] воспряли духом (Мандельштам 1). Away from the crowd, in the comparative peace of this waste lot reserved for the criminals, both of them [L. and Mandelstam] felt in better spirits (1a).

Д-353 • НИ́ЩИЕ ДУ́ХОМ *lit* [NP] people who do not have spiritual interests or intelligence: **the poor in spirit.**

Если в небесное царство входят нищие духом, представляю себе, как там весело (Набоков 1). If the poor in spirit enter the heavenly kingdom I can imagine how gay it is there (1a).

< From the Bible (Matt. 5:3), where it is used in reference to humble and meek people.

Д-354 • ОДНИ́М ⟨ЕДИ́НЫМ⟩ ДУ́ХОМ *coll* [NP$_{instrum}$; these forms only; adv; usu. used with pfv verbs; fixed WO] **1.** ~ **выпить, проглотить** *что;* **проговорить, прочитать** *что* и т. п. (to drink, say etc sth.) all at once, without stopping: **without pausing for breath; without taking a breath; without coming up for air;** [in refer. to drinking sth.] **in one go;** [in limited contexts] **in one ⟨a single⟩ gulp; in one swallow ⟨motion⟩;** [in refer. to saying, stating sth.] **in one ⟨a single⟩ breath.**

При сих словах он взял стакан, перекрестился и выпил одним духом (Пушкин 2). With these words he took the glass, crossed himself, and drank the vodka down in one gulp (2a). ♦ Прыгающей рукой поднёс Стёпа стопку к устам, а незнакомец одним духом проглотил содержимое своей стопки (Булгаков 9). Styopa brought his tumbler to his lips with a shaking hand, and the stranger emptied his in a single gulp (9a). ♦ «Я вот её [водку] сейчас в рот взять не могу, а он [столяр] выльет пол-литра в кружку от бачка, крутанёт – и всё одним духом до дна» (Домбровский 1). "I couldn't touch a drop [of vodka] in this weather, but he [the carpenter] pours himself out a half-liter, swills it round – and downs the lot in one go" (1a). ♦ Он выложил свою претензию единым духом (Максимов 3). He stated his complaint in a single breath... (3a).

2. (to do sth.) very quickly, in a single moment: **in no time (at all); in a jiffy ⟨a flash, a trice⟩; in nothing ⟨no time⟩ flat; in ⟨at⟩ one fell swoop; in one go.**

Д-355 • ПА́ДАТЬ/УПА́СТЬ ⟨ПАСТЬ *obs*⟩ **ДУ́ХОМ** [VP; subj: human; more often pfv past or neg imper] to become despondent, despair: X упал духом ≃ **X lost heart ⟨courage⟩; X fell ⟨sank⟩ into despair; X became ⟨was⟩ disheartened ⟨downhearted, depressed, dispirited, demoralized⟩; X lost ⟨gave up⟩ (all) hope;** [in limited contexts] **X's spirits fell;** ‖ *Neg Imper* не падай духом ≃ **keep your spirits ⟨chin⟩ up; don't let it get you down.**

«Володя, не нужно падать духом. Я тоже часто бываю в таком состоянии» (Эренбург 3). "Don't lose heart, Volodya. I often do myself..." (3a). ♦ Шалико почувствовал, что её [Хикур] внезапный отъезд не к добру... Неужели она забеременела и, как сестра её, ничего не сказав ему, уехала в деревню?!.. Ничего, главное не падать духом, сказал он себе... (Искандер 4). Shaliko had sensed that Khikur's sudden departure meant trouble....Could she really have gotten pregnant and gone off to the country without saying anything to him, just like her sister?...Never mind; whatever you do, don't lose courage, he told himself... (4a). ♦ Не находил Едигей ответа, сокрушался, переживал, падал духом и снова обнадёживал себя безнадёжными грёзами... (Айтматов 2). Finding no answer to his dilemma, he [Yedigei] was overwhelmed, suffered and became downhearted and tried once more to raise his hopes with hopeless dreams... (2a). ♦ Вообще, сила западной гневной реакции [на травлю Сахарова и Солженицына] была неожиданна для всех – и для самого Запада... и тем более для наших властей... И, спасаясь из этого состояния, 13-го сентября правительство сняло глушение западных передач... И как же взбодрилось наше *общество*, так недавно столь упавшее духом, что даже отказалось от Самиздата! (Солженицын 2). All in all, the force of the West's angry reaction [to the vicious press campaign against Sakharov and Solzhenitsyn] was a surprise to everyone: to the West itself...and even more of a surprise to our rulers....On 13 September the government tried to escape from this situation by putting a stop to jamming....How it cheered our *public*, who just a little while ago had been so demoralized that they had even given up samizdat (2a). ♦ ...Он [академик] советовал Гладышеву не падать духом и, ссылаясь на пример древних алхимиков, утверждал, что в науке никакой труд не бывает напрасным, можно искать одно, а найти другое (Войнович 2). ...He [the academician] advised Gladishev to keep his spirits up and, citing the example of the ancient alchemists, pointed out that in science no work is ever done in vain, one thing is sought and another found (2a).

Д-356 • ПИТА́ТЬСЯ СВЯТЫ́М ДУ́ХОМ *coll* [VP; subj: human] to eat absolutely nothing: X питается святым духом ≃ **X lives on thin air.**

Д-357 • СВЯТЫ́М ДУ́ХОМ *coll, iron* [NP_instrum; Invar; adv; usu. this WO] **1.** [often with negated predic] (sth. happens) as if by its own effort: **(all) by itself; on its own; (sth. will) take care of itself.**

«Это ты перевёз на дачу холодильник?» – «А кто же ещё? Не святым же духом он туда попал!» "Was it you who moved the refrigerator to the dacha?" "Who else? It didn't get there by itself!"

2. ~ узнать *что humor* (to figure out or learn sth.) from an unexpected or unusual source that one does not want to reveal: **a little bird told one.**

Д-358 • СОБИРА́ТЬСЯ/СОБРА́ТЬСЯ С ДУ́ХОМ; НАБИРА́ТЬСЯ/НАБРА́ТЬСЯ ДУ́ХУ ⟨-а⟩ *coll* [VP; subj: human; usu. pfv; often pfv Verbal Adv or infin with не мочь, трудно, надо etc; usu. this WO] to force o.s. to overcome one's timidity, self-doubt, nervousness etc (so that one can carry out some action requiring courage or self-confidence): X собрался с духом ≃ **X plucked ⟨got⟩ up his courage; X gathered ⟨mustered, summoned⟩ (up) his courage; X summoned up the strength; X geared himself up; X got ⟨plucked⟩ up his nerve; X braced up; X brought himself to (do sth.).**

...[Шагинян] громко спросила: «А вы здесь зачем? Что, вы Мандельштама надеетесь напечатать?» ...Я собралась с духом и сказала, что сейчас пришла по своим делам, но Мандельштама, пусть она не сомневается, обязательно напечатают... (Мандельштам 2). ...[Shaginian] asked in a loud voice: "And what are you doing here? Hoping to publish Mandelstam or something?"...I plucked up my courage and said that I was there on my own business at the moment, but that Mandelstam would certainly be published–of which she need have no doubt (2a). ♦ «Министр или вельможа подходит к одному, к другому... Наконец, сударь мой, к Копейкину. Копейкин, собравшись с духом: „Так и так, ваше превосходительство: проливал кровь, лишился... руки и ноги, работать не могу, осмеливаюсь просить монаршей милости"» (Гоголь 3). "The high dignitary or the minister, one after another....At last, my dear sir, he comes up to Kopeikin. Kopeikin musters up all his courage and says, 'This is how it is, Your Excellency; I've shed my blood, lost...my arm and leg, I cannot work....May I make so bold as to beg for some dispensation of grace from our Monarch?'" (3c).

Д-359 • КАК НА ДУХУ́ (рас)сказать *что*, **признаться в** *чём* и т. п. *coll* [как + PrepP; Invar; adv or, rare, subj-compl with быть∅ (subj: human)] (to say, confess to it) frankly, openly, concealing nothing: **as if confessing it to a ⟨the⟩ priest; [in limited contexts] as God is my witness; I swear to God.**

«Я с тобой буду как на духу – не таскали мы оттуда [из магазина] ни одной крупинки» (Распутин 1). "I'll be as honest with you as if I was confessing to the priest: not a grain of anything have we taken from that store" (1a). ♦ «Я тебе вот что скажу, Саша. Верь моему слову, как на духу: ни разу в жизни ни тютелькой для себя не попользовался. Только для других» (Грекова 3). "I'll tell you. Believe me, Sasha, I swear to God, never in my life did I do *anything* for myself. Only for others..." (3a).

Д-360 • ХВАТА́ЕТ/ХВАТИ́ЛО ⟨ДОСТАЁТ/ДОСТА́ЛО⟩ ДУ́ХУ *у кого, что (с)делать* or *на что coll* [VP; impers; often neg; neg for the 2nd var. is недостаёт, недостало etc] **1.** s.o. has the resolve, courage etc (to do sth.): у Х-а не хватает ⟨недостаёт⟩ духу сделать Y ≃ **X doesn't have the nerve to do Y; X can't get up enough ⟨the⟩ nerve to do Y; X lacks the courage to do Y; X doesn't dare to do Y; X doesn't have the guts to do Y; X can't bring himself to do Y; X doesn't have the heart to do Y.**

...Чувствуя, что у меня никогда недостанет духу поднести свой подарок, я спрятался за спину Карла Иваныча... (Толстой 2). ...Sensing that I would never have the nerve to step forward with my present, I hid myself behind Karl Ivanich... (2b). ♦ [Саша:] Виноват же Иванов только, что у него слабый характер и не хватает духа прогнать от себя этого Боркина... (Чехов 4). [S.:] Ivanov is guilty of nothing except a weak character, he lacks the courage to turn that Borkin out (4a). ♦ «Беда большая. Умер наш Абуталип!.. Как же нам быть? У кого из нас хватит духу сказать им [его семье] такое?..» (Айтматов 2). "There's been a real tragedy. Our Abutalip is dead!...What can we do? Which of us has the heart to tell them [his family] this?" (2a).

2. s.o. has the impudence, insolence (to do sth.): у Х-а хватило духу сделать Y ≃ **X had ⟨got⟩ the cheek ⟨the gall, the nerve⟩ to do Y;** || *Neg* у Х-а не хватит духу сделать Y ≃ **X wouldn't dare (to) do Y.**

[Саша:] ...Как у вас хватает духа говорить всё это про человека, который не сделал вам никакого зла? (Чехов 4). [S.:] How dare you talk like this about someone who never did you any harm? (4b).

Д-361 • ЧТО ЕСТЬ ⟨БЫ́ЛО⟩ ДУ́ХУ *coll* [these forms only; adv (intensif); fixed WO] **1.** бежать, мчаться и т. п. ~ (of a person or animal) (to run, race etc) very fast, with maximum effort: **for all one is worth; as fast as one's legs can carry one; as fast as one can (go); with all one's might.**

2. кричать, орать, вопить и т. п. ~ (to yell, scream, shriek etc) very loudly, as loud as one can: **for all one is worth; at the top of one's lungs ⟨voice⟩; with all one's might; (yell ⟨scream⟩) one's lungs out.**

Д-362 • ЧТОБЫ ДУ́ХУ *чьего* **НЕ́ БЫЛО** *(где) highly coll;* **ЧТОБЫ ДУ́ХОМ** *чьим* **НЕ ПА́ХЛО** *substand* [sent; these forms only; fixed WO] (used as an emphatic demand) s.o. should not appear at some place or (esp. in direct address) should leave some place immediately and not reappear ever again: чтобы духу Х-ового в месте Y не было ≃ **X is not ⟨never⟩ to show his face at place Y (again); X had better not (ever) show his face at place Y (again); X is not to set foot at place Y (again); person Z never wants to set eyes on X ⟨to see X's face (at place Y)⟩ (again); person Z doesn't want to see hide nor hair of X;** || чтобы духу твоего здесь не было! ≃ **get ⟨clear⟩ out of here!; get out of my sight (and stay out)!; never let me set eyes on you again!; don't let me see ⟨find, catch⟩ you here again!**

...Супруга Стёпы якобы обнаружилась на Божедомке, где, как болтали, директор Варьете, используя свои бесчисленные знакомства, ухитрился добыть ей комнату, но с одним условием, чтобы духу её не было на Садовой улице... (Булгаков 9). As for Styopa's wife, she was allegedly discovered on

Bozhedomka Street where, gossip had it, the director of the Variety Theater had managed, with the aid of his innumerable acquaintances, to find her a room, but on one condition: she was never to show her face on Sadovaya... (9a). ♦ [Василиса:] Я тебе... сказала, чтобы духа твоего не было здесь... а ты опять пришёл? (Горький 3). [V.:] I told you not to set foot in here again...and here you are... (3c). ♦ «...Потом [Александр Третий] говорит: „Дайте карандаш!" — и тут же начертал резолюцию на телеграмме: „Чтоб духу его [Эшаппара] в Петербурге не было. Александр". И лёг спать» (Булгаков 12). "Then he [Alexander III] said: 'Give me a pencil!' And he immediately scribbled a memorandum on the telegram form: 'I never want to see his [Echappard's] face in Petersburg again. Alexander.' And went back to sleep" (12a). ♦ [Варя:] Ты смеешь мне говорить это! (Вспылив.) Ты смеешь? Значит, я ничего не понимаю? Убирайся же вон отсюда! Сию минуту!.. Чтобы духу твоего здесь не было! (Чехов 2). [V.:] How dare you talk to me like that! (Flaring up.) How dare you! So I don't know what I'm talking about, don't I? Then get out of here! This instant!...You clear out of here! (2c). ♦ «Ну чего, подлый человек, от неё [Маши] добиваешься?.. Вон пошёл. Чтобы духу твоего не было» (Толстой 2). "Well, villain, what are you trying to get from her [Masha] now?...Clear out. Out of my sight" (2b). ♦ «А, присудил!.. присудил! — сказал старик тихим голосом и, как показалось князю Андрею, с смущением, но потом вдруг он вскочил и закричал: — Вон, вон! Чтобы духу твоего тут не было!..» (Толстой 6). "Ah, he has passed judgment...he has passed judgment," said the old man in a low voice and, as it seemed to Prince Andrei, with a certain embarrassment, but the next moment he sprang to his feet and shouted: "Out—get out! Never let me set eyes on you again!" (6a).

Д-363 • В ЧЁМ (ТО́ЛЬКО) ДУША́ ДЕ́РЖИТСЯ; ЕЛЕ-ЕЛЕ́ ДУША́ В ТЕ́ЛЕ *coll* [sent; these forms only; только can be placed after душа, otherwise fixed WO] s.o. is frail, sickly, ill: **X's body and soul are scarcely held together; X is as weak as could be;** [in limited contexts] **weak as X is.**

«Тебе бы всё душить да резать. Что ты за богатырь? Поглядеть, так в чём душа держится. Сам в могилу смотришь, а других губишь» (Пушкин 2). "All you ever want is to strangle and slaughter. A great hero, aren't you? Look at you, your body and soul are scarcely held together. One foot's already in the grave, but you still cut other people's throats" (2a). ♦ Саша родился недоношенный, два килограмма двести граммов... Мама пролежала в больнице дней, наверно, десять, а может быть, и двадцать, потом мы её вместе с Сашей забрали домой... Всё сосредоточилось на Саше. Сами понимаете, два килограмма двести граммов! Слабый, в чём душа держится, не кричит, пищит едва-едва... (Рыбаков 1). Sasha was born premature and weighed only four and a half pounds....Mother stayed in the hospital for ten days or maybe three weeks, and then we took her home together with Sasha....Everyone's attention turned to Sasha. Can you imagine, only four and a half pounds! He was as weak as could be, he didn't cry and could barely give a squeak... (1a). ♦ «Ну, куда ты пустишься такой, кожа да кости, еле душа в теле? Неужто опять пешком? Да ведь не дойдёшь ты!» (Пастернак 1). "How could you travel, weak as you are, nothing but skin and bones? Do you really imagine you could go on foot? You would never get there" (1a).

Д-364 • ДУША́ (СЕ́РДЦЕ) БОЛИ́Т [VP$_{subj}$; most often pres] **1.** ~ *чья* (чьё), *у кого*. Also: СЕ́РДЦЕ НО́ЕТ (ЩЕМИ́Т) s.o. experiences anguish, emotional suffering: у X-а душа болит ≃ **X's heart aches; X is sick at heart.**

У меня так болит душа, когда я думаю о его [Мандельштама] последних днях... (Мандельштам 2). My heart aches so much when I think of his [Mandelstam's] last days... (2a).

2. ~ *у кого за кого-что*. Also: ДУША́ (СЕ́РДЦЕ) ПЕРЕБОЛЕ́ЛА (-о) [obj: human or collect] s.o. experiences deep concern, anxiety, emotional pain in response to another's (or others') distressing situation: у X-а душа болит за Y-а ≃ **X's heart aches (bleeds, breaks) for Y.**

[Полина Андреевна:] Сердце моё за тебя переболело. Я ведь всё вижу, всё понимаю (Чехов 6). [P.A.:] My heart aches for you. I see it all, you know, I understand (6a).

Д-365 • ДУША́ В ДУ́ШУ *жить (с кем) coll* [Invar; adv; if there is no prep obj, subj: pl; fixed WO] (two or more persons live) peacefully, happily, in complete agreement, fully understanding each other: X и Y ⟨X с Y-ом⟩ живут душа в душу ≃ **X and Y live in complete ⟨perfect⟩ harmony; X and Y get on ⟨along⟩ beautifully; X and Y live on the best of terms;** [of a couple] **X and Y live like two lovebirds.**

Помню, лет десять тому назад я поселился в Орехово-Зуеве. К тому времени, как я поселился, в моей комнате уже жило четверо, я стал у них пятым. Мы жили душа в душу, и ссор не было никаких (Ерофеев 1). I remember ten years ago I moved to Orekhovo-Zuevo. At that same time, there were four other people living in the same room. I was the fifth. We lived in complete harmony, and there weren't any quarrels among us (1a). ♦ [Репникова:] ...У нас всё прекрасно. Живём душа в душу. Все нам завидуют (Вампилов 3). [R.:] ...Everything is just fine with us. We live in perfect harmony. Everyone envies us (3b). ♦ С Вовкой... Вера жила душа в душу — кормила его, бранила, воспитывала... (Грекова 3). Vera got on beautifully with Vovka: fed him, scolded him, raised him (3a). ♦ Худой, со втянутыми щеками Чекмарь, устроившись с своими делами, поглядывал на барина, с которым он жил тридцать лет душа в душу, и, понимая его приятное расположение духа, ждал приятного разговора (Толстой 5). After seeing to his duties, the thin, hollow-cheeked Chekmar glanced at his master, with whom he had lived on the best of terms for thirty years, and, perceiving that he was in a genial humor, looked forward to a pleasant chat (5a). ♦ «...[Мы] жили душа в душу, песнями хлебали, припевками закусывали, впроголодь, да весело» (Максимов 2). "We lived like two lovebirds, we had a song for soup and the chorus for dessert—we were starving but we were happy" (2a).

Д-366 • ДУША́ МОЯ́ *old-fash, coll* [NP; Invar; used as vocative; usu. this WO] a friendly, familiar way of addressing s.o.: **(my) dear(est) ⟨darling⟩;** [in limited contexts] **(my) love;** [man to woman] **my sweet;** [man to man] **my good man; my dear chap;** [man to a younger man or a boy] **dear lad.**

«Щи, моя душа, сегодня очень хороши!» — сказал Собакевич... (Гоголь 3). "The cabbage soup is very good today, my dear," said Sobakevich... (3a). "The cabbage soup is very good today, my love!" said Sobakevich... (3c). ♦ «Так у вас разве есть выкройка?»... — «Как же, сестра привезла». — «Душа моя, дайте её мне ради всего святого» (Гоголь 3). "So you've actually got the pattern!"..."Of course I have. My sister brought it along." "Darling, lend it to me for the sake of all that's holy" (3c). ♦ «Романтик сказал бы: я чувствую, что наши дороги начинают расходиться, а я просто говорю, что мы друг другу приелись. — «Евгений...» — «Душа моя, это не беда; то ли ещё на свете приедается!» (Тургенев 2). "A romantic would say, 'I feel our paths are beginning to diverge,' but I will simply say that we are tired of each other." "Oh Yevgeny...." "Dear lad, that's no misfortune; the world is full of things that pall on one" (2c).

Д-367 • ДУША́ *чья* ⟨СЕ́РДЦЕ *чьё*⟩, *(у) кого* НАДРЫВА́ЕТСЯ [VP$_{subj}$; usu. this WO] s.o. experiences emotional anguish, sorrow, compassion (for another): душа у X-а надрывается ≃ **X's heart is torn to pieces ⟨ripped out⟩; X's heart bleeds for ⟨goes out to⟩ person Y; X is terribly ⟨frightfully etc⟩ upset.**

Даже мальчишкой Семён не плакал... А тут надрывается душа, кипят слёзы, вот-вот вырвутся... (Тендряков 1). Even as a little boy Simon never cried....But now he was so upset, tears were welling up inside him... (1a).

Д-368 • ДУША́ НАРАСПА́ШКУ (*у кого*) *coll* [NP; sing only; usu. subj-compl with быть∅ (subj: human), VP_subj with быть∅ (var. with *у кого*), or appos; pres or (less often) past; fixed WO] s.o. is frank, straightforward, open, unpretentious in his relations with people: X ⟨у Х-а⟩ − душа нараспашку ≃ **X is open-hearted;** [in limited contexts] **X wears his heart on his sleeve; X opens his heart to people.**

Фамилия этого хитрого наседки была Грицай... Я, конечно, виду не показывал, что разгадал его, − напротив, был с ним душа нараспашку, лучший друг, и таким образом многое через него всё-таки сделал (Буковский 1). This cunning informer's name was Gritsai....I didn't let on, of course, that I had guessed what Gritsai was. On the contrary, I pretended to open my heart to him, made him my best friend, and in that way managed to accomplish quite a bit through him (1a).

Д-369 • ДУША́ *чья* ⟨СЕ́РДЦЕ *чьё*⟩, *у кого* НЕ ЛЕЖИ́Т [VP_subj; pres or past] **1.** ~ *к кому* s.o. does not like another, does not enjoy another's company: у Х-а душа не лежит к Y-у ≃ **X doesn't (really) care for Y; Y doesn't appeal to X.**

[Пепел:] Красивая ты, Васка, − а никогда не лежало у меня сердце к тебе... (Горький 3). [P.:] You're beautiful, Vassilisa. But I never really cared for you... (3e).

2. ~ *к чему* or *что делать* the idea of doing sth. is not attractive to s.o.: у Х-а душа не лежит к Y-у ⟨делать Z⟩ ≃ **X doesn't (really) care for Y; Y doesn't appeal to X;** [in limited contexts] **X doesn't feel like doing Z;** [in refer. to a job etc] **X's heart isn't in it; X has no heart for the job.**

Несколько дней он провёл в угнетающем безделье. Попробовал было кое-что смастерить в Аксиньином хозяйстве и тотчас почувствовал, что ничего не может делать. Ни к чему не лежала душа (Шолохов 5). For a few days he lived in a state of oppressive idleness. He tried to do a few jobs in Aksinya's yard but at once felt that there was nothing he could put his hands to. Nothing appealed to him (5a). ♦ ...Никанор открыл было прежнюю москательную лавку, но душа у него к этому делу не лежала (Евтушенко 2). Nikanor tried reopening his father's shop, but his heart wasn't in it (2a).

Д-370 • ДУША́ ⟨СЕ́РДЦЕ⟩ НЕ НА МЕ́СТЕ (*у кого*) *coll* [VP_subj with быть∅; these forms only; fixed WO] s.o. feels restless, very alarmed (usu. in expectation of possible trouble or a potential misfortune for s.o. dear, or out of concern for sth. dear): у Х-а душа не на месте ≃ **X is awfully worried; X is worried sick; X's heart is in his mouth;** [in limited contexts] **X is on tenterhooks ⟨on pins and needles⟩.**

[Городничий:] Да говорите, ради бога, что такое? У меня сердце не на месте (Гоголь 4). [Mayor:] So tell us, for God's sake, what is it? My heart's in my mouth (4a).

Д-371 • ДУША́ НЕ ПРИНИМА́ЕТ *highly coll* [VP_subj; fixed WO] s.o. has absolutely no desire, or finds it repulsive, to eat or drink sth.: **it (just) won't go down; person X couldn't eat a ⟨another⟩ bite; person X couldn't drink a ⟨another⟩ drop; (just) the thought of food ⟨drinking⟩ makes person X sick.**

Анна Савишна, бледно улыбаясь, брала кусочек, переминала его дёснами, но потом сплёвывала украдкой, чтобы не обидеть Маргариту Антоновну, − больно уж та гордилась своей стряпнёй... Да что поделать, если душа не принимает, кто бы ни стряпал, хоть повар-расповар (Грекова 3). Anna Savishna, smiling weakly, took a piece, mashed it with her gums, and then spit it out stealthily so as not to offend Margarita Antonovna, who was really proud of her concoctions. But what can you do if it just won't go down, no matter who made it, even a five-star chef (3a).

Д-372 • ДУША́ О́БЩЕСТВА [NP; sing only; usu. subj-compl with copula (subj: human); fixed WO] the most lively, charismatic,

and witty member of a social gathering: **the life (and soul) of the party.**

...Профессор математики, Владимир Андреевич Т., ленинградец, образованный, ироничный говорун, привык везде быть «душою общества» и задавать тон (Копелев 1). ...A professor of mathematics, Vladimir Andreevich T., a Leningrader, and an educated, ironic talker...was used to always being the "life of the party" and setting the tone (1a). ♦ Ух, дядя Митя веселился на свадьбе! Читал куплеты, разыгрывал с тёщей сценки, пел, плясал − в общем, был душой общества (Аксёнов 10). Oh, how Old Mitya enjoyed himself at the wedding! He recited couplets, acted scenes with his mother-in-law, sang and danced−in short, he was the life and soul of the party (10a).

Д-373 • ДУША́ ⟨СЕ́РДЦЕ⟩ ПЕРЕВОРА́ЧИВАЕТСЯ/ПЕРЕВЕРНУ́ЛАСЬ ⟨-лось⟩ *у кого, в ком (от чего) coll* [VP_subj; usu. this WO] s.o. experiences strong feelings of pity, compassion for another (caused by another's suffering): у Х-а душа переворачивается (от Y-ова плача ⟨Y-овых страданий и т. п.⟩) ≃ **Y's sobbing ⟨suffering etc⟩ cuts X to the heart; X's heart goes out to Y; it ⟨Y's suffering etc⟩ wrings X's heart.**

«Поедем отсюда, ради бога! Я на неё [убитую женщину] глядеть не могу. У меня сердце переворачивается!» (Шолохов 5). "Let's get out of here for God's sake! I can't look at her [the dead woman]. It fair wrings my heart!" (5a).

Д-374 • ДУША́ УХО́ДИТ/УШЛА́ В ПЯ́ТКИ (*у кого, от чего*); ДУША́ В ПЯ́ТКАХ *coll* [VP_subj (1st var.); Invar, VP_subj with быть∅ (2nd var.); the verb may take the final position (1st var.); fixed WO (2nd var.)] s.o. experiences very strong fear: у Х-а душа ушла в пятки ≃ **X's heart sank into ⟨to⟩ his boots ⟨shoes⟩;** [in limited contexts] **X got the shakes.**

Однажды, убирая мастерскую, [я] решился и стянул кольцо колбасы, запрятал в снег под окном... Уходя домой, полез в снег − нет колбасы. Тут у меня душа ушла в пятки: выгонит Дегтярёв (Кузнецов 1). One day, while cleaning up the shop, I mustered up the courage to steal a ring of sausage which I hid in the snow under the window....When I was leaving for home I dug under the snow and−no sausage. My heart sank into my boots. Degtyarev would surely throw me out (1a). ♦ Липман вынул из чемодана пакет, развернул, там лежал пластинчатый [зубной] протез... Сталин в изумлении поднял брови. Ведь он ему ясно сказал, что предпочитает золотой, даже ударил кулаком по креслу, и у врача душа ушла в пятки (Рыбаков 2). He [Lipman] took a package out of his case and unwrapped it to reveal a plastic [dental] plate....Stalin raised his eyebrows in amazement. He had said plainly enough that he preferred gold, he'd even hit the arm of his chair with his fist, and the dentist's heart had sunk to his boots (2a). ♦ «Странный крик», − сказал Максим. «Странный − не знаю, − возразил Зеф, − но страшноватый. Ночью как начнут орать по всему лесу, душа в пятки уходит» (Стругацкие 2). "It's a strange cry." "Strange−I don't know, but it's damned frightening. When those screams start tearing through the forest at night, you get the shakes" (2a).

Д-375 • ЗА́ЯЧЬЯ ДУША́ *coll, disapprov* [NP; fixed WO] **1.** [subj-compl with copula (subj: human), appos, or vocative] a cowardly, timid person: **yellowbelly; scaredy-cat; jellyfish; chicken.**

Испуганно озираясь, за мной вышмыгнул доцент И-лев... Я утешил эту заячью душу, как мог (Битов 2). Senior Lecturer N., glancing fearfully over his shoulder, darted out after me....I comforted the yellowbelly as best I could (2a).

2. ~ *у кого* [VP_subj with copula] s.o. is cowardly, timid: у Х-а заячья душа ≃ **X is as yellow as they come; X is chicken-hearted ⟨chicken-livered, lily-livered, yellow-bellied⟩; X has no backbone.**

Д-376 • НИ ОДНА́ (ЖИВА́Я) ДУША́ coll [NP; sing only; subj or obj; fixed WO] no one: **not a ⟨one⟩ (living) soul; not a single (living ⟨blessed⟩) soul.**

«...Ни одна душа не будет знать об этом посещении» (Булгаков 9). "...Not a soul will know about this visit" (9a).

Д-377 • ПОКА́ ДУША́ ДЕ́РЖИТСЯ В ТЕ́ЛЕ coll [subord clause; Invar; the verb may take the final position, otherwise fixed WO] for as long as s.o. is alive, has strength: **for as long as s.o. has a spark ⟨a breath⟩ of life left in him; for as long as s.o. has some life left in him.**

Д-378 • ЧЕРНИ́ЛЬНАЯ ДУША́ derog [NP; usu. sing; fixed WO] **1.** obs a petty official (who quibbles over trivial matters): **pettifogger; petty scrivener.**

2. coll. Also: **БУМА́ЖНАЯ ДУША́** coll, derog a callous, petty bureaucrat; by extension any person with bureaucratic tendencies, esp. in minor matters: **paper shuffler; paper-pusher; pettifogger.**

...Кто-то уже пожаловался. Кляузники! Их ещё не успеешь прижать как следует, а они уже бегут с жалобами. Что за люди, что за чернильные души! (Войнович 3). Someone must have complained. Tattletales! You barely have time to really put the pressure on them before they run off to complain. What people, what pettifoggers! (3a).

Д-379 • ЧУЖА́Я ДУША́ – ПОТЁМКИ [saying] you cannot find out or know what is in another person's soul, what he thinks, what kind of person he is (said when it is difficult to understand a person's true nature, his mood, behavior, intentions): ≃ **another person's soul ⟨the human heart⟩ is a mystery; one person's soul is (always) a mystery to another; you can never see into another heart.**

[Кабанов:] Да какие ж, маменька, у неё грехи такие могут быть особенные! Все такие же, как и у всех у нас.... [Кабанова:] А ты почём знаешь? Чужая душа потёмки (Островский 6). [Kabanov:] But, Mama, what kind of special sins can she have? Just the same as all the rest of us.... [Kabanova:] And how do you know? The human heart is a mystery (6a). ♦ Нехорошо всё вышло, очень нехорошо! А я думал, что Лена меня любит. Когда новый год встречали, сказал Брайнину: «Выпьем за Лену, замечательная жена...» Чужая душа – потёмки, это бесспорно (Эренбург 3). "It's bad, it's very bad the way it has worked out. And I thought Lena loved me. Last New Year, I said to Brainin: 'Let's drink to Lena, she's a wonderful wife.' You can never see into another heart, no doubt about it" (3a).

Д-380 • ПО ДУША́М ⟨ПО ДУШЕ́ obs⟩ поговорить, побеседовать с кем; разговор, беседа и т. п. [PrepP; these forms only; adv or nonagreeing modif] (to talk with s.o.) frankly, candidly, freely, without hiding anything: поговорить ~ ≃ **have a heart-to-heart ⟨an intimate⟩ talk (with s.o.); have a heart-to-heart (with s.o.); talk ⟨speak⟩ to s.o. heart to heart;** ‖ разговор ~ ≃ **a heart-to-heart (talk); a candid conversation ⟨talk⟩.**

Времени до отхода поезда было предостаточно, и они славно посидели, и выпили, и потолковали по душам на прощание (Айтматов 2). There had been plenty of time before the train left, and they had sat there enjoying a drink and having a heart-to-heart talk before they parted (2a). ♦ Был... ещё один человек, с которым она могла поговорить по душам, – Степан Андреянович (Абрамов 1). ...There was one other person she could speak with heart to heart: Stepan Andreyanovich (1a).

Д-381 • В ДУШЕ́ [PrepP; Invar] **1.** ~ надеяться, удивляться, радоваться, признавать что, осуждать кого-что, бояться, смеяться над кем-чем и т. п. [adv] (to hope, be surprised, be happy, admit sth., condemn s.o. or sth., be afraid, laugh at s.o. or sth. etc) deep within o.s.: **in one's heart of hearts; (deep) in one's heart ⟨soul⟩; deep down (inside); deep inside; at heart; inwardly; secretly.**

Он в душе очень обрадовался предложению своего приятеля, но почёл обязанностию скрыть своё чувство (Тургенев 2). In his heart of hearts he was highly delighted with his friend's suggestion but thought it a duty to conceal his feelings (2c). ♦ Дессер окончил политехникум; года два он проработал как инженер и в душе считал, что деньги их погубили: ради них он изменил своему призванию (Эренбург 4). Desser had taken his degree at the Polytechnic School. He had worked for two years as an engineer, and in his heart he considered that money had ruined him. He had betrayed his profession for the sake of lucre (4a). ♦ Я не мог не признаться в душе, что поведение моё в симбирском трактире было глупо... (Пушкин 2). Deep down I could not help recognizing that my behavior at the Simbirsk inn had been foolish... (2a). ♦ Люди, потерявшие «я», делятся на две категории. Одни, подобно мне, погружаются в оцепенение... В душе они часто таят безумную надежду прорваться в будущее, где снова обретут себя, потому что там будут восстановлены все ценности в их извечной форме (Мандельштам 2). People suffering from loss of identity are divided into two types: some, as I did, sink into a torpor....Deep inside them they often cherish the mad hope of surviving to a future in which they will recover their lost selves—something that will be possible only when true values have come into their own again (2a). ♦ ...В душе Михаил был немало удивлён: с чего это вдруг вспомнил о нём Егорша? (Абрамов 1). ...Inwardly Mikhail was quite surprised: why had Egorsha suddenly remembered him? (1a). ♦ Люба... так странно смотрела [на него], точно над собой же подсмеивалась в душе, точно говорила себе, изумлённая своим поступком: «Ну, не дура ли я? Что затеяла-то?» (Шукшин 1). She [Lyuba] looked at him so strangely, that it seemed as though she was secretly laughing at herself, as if to say, astonished at her behavior: "You're a fool, aren't you? What have you gotten yourself into?" (1a).

2. [nonagreeing postmodif or adv] in one's real nature, in spite of appearances: **at heart.**

...У вдовушки, безутешно оплакивающей мужа, погибшего под Сталинградом, была мания: она упрашивала дядю каждый вечер на ужин надевать унтер-офицерский мундир её незабвенного Пауля. Дядя, артист в душе, оказывал снисхождение к женской сентиментальности и, посмеиваясь, влезал в мундир (Евтушенко 2). The widow's husband had been killed near Stalingrad, and her inconsolable grief for him took the form of a particular mania: Every evening she begged Uncle to wear her precious Paul's noncom uniform at supper. Uncle, an actor at heart, consented to this sentimental charade and laughingly got into the uniform (2a).

Д-382 • КАК ДУШЕ́ (чьей, кого) **УГО́ДНО** coll [subord clause with быть₀; usu. used as adv; usu. pres; fixed WO] (to do sth.) the way one wants: как (X-овой) душе угодно ≃ **as X pleases ⟨likes⟩; (in) any way X pleases ⟨likes⟩.**

«Будь нашим гостем. А с утра — как душе твоей угодно» (Айтматов 2). "Be our dear guest, and tomorrow morning you can do as you please" (2a).

Д-383 • НА ДУШЕ́ ⟨НА СЕ́РДЦЕ⟩ у кого радостно, легко, спокойно, грустно, тяжело, горько, тревожно и т. п. [PrepP; these forms only; usu. adv] (s.o. experiences the emotional state specified by the context) inwardly: **(there is an emptiness ⟨a heaviness, bitterness etc⟩) in s.o.'s soul ⟨heart⟩; s.o.'s heart is full of (joy ⟨happiness, sadness etc⟩); s.o.'s heart (is light ⟨heavy, grieved, sad, happy, peaceful etc⟩); (s.o. feels bitter ⟨joyful, happy, empty etc⟩) at heart; (s.o. is ⟨feels⟩) lighthearted ⟨heavy-hearted etc⟩; [in limited contexts] s.o.'s spirit (is uneasy);** ‖ у X-а спокойно на душе ≃ **X has peace in his soul; X's soul is at peace; X has peace of mind; X's mind is at rest.**

На сердце у Григория сладостная пустота (Шолохов 2). There was a sweet void in Grigory's heart (2a). ♦ Хотя был ещё день и совсем светло, у доктора было такое чувство, точно он поздним вечером стоит в тёмном дремучем лесу своей жизни. Такой мрак был у него на душе, так ему было печально (Пастернак 1). Although it was early in the afternoon and full daylight, the doctor felt as if he were standing late at night in the dark forest of his life. Such was the darkness in his soul, such was his dejection (1a). ♦ ...[Ростов] чувствовал себя весёлым, смелым, решительным... Утро было ясное, лошадь под ним была добрая. На душе его было радостно и счастливо (Толстой 4). ...[Rostov] felt cheerful, resolute and fearless....It was a bright morning, he had a good horse under him, and his heart was full of joy and happiness (4a). ♦ Опять весна, и у меня очень легко на душе. Я люблю весну (Казаков 2). It was spring again...and my heart was light. I love spring (2a). ♦ «...Мы все живём на пустом свете, — разве у тебя спокойно на душе?» (Платонов 1). "We are all living in an empty world—do you really have peace in your soul?" (1b). "We all live in an empty world—do *you* have peace of mind?" (1a).

Д-384 • ПО ДУШЕ́ ⟨ПО́ СЕ́РДЦУ⟩ *кому* бытьθ, прийти́сь [PrepP; these forms only; subj-compl with copula (subj: usu. human or abstr) or postmodif] to be pleasing to, liked by s.o.: X пришёлся Y-у по душе ≃ **X appealed to Y ⟨to Y's heart⟩; X was to Y's liking ⟨taste⟩; Y took a fancy ⟨a shine⟩ to X; Y was fond of person X; Y felt drawn to X; Y went for thing X;** ‖ *Neg* X Y-у не по душе ≃ **Y doesn't care for X;** [in refer. to a decision, response, plan etc] **thing X doesn't sit too well with Y;** [in refer. to some food, medicine, environmental conditions etc] **thing X doesn't agree with Y.**

Сталин был против постановки «Гамлета», вероятно, потому же, почему он был против «Макбета» и «Бориса Годунова» — изображение образа властителя, запятнавшего себя на пути к власти преступлением, было ему не по душе (Гладков 1). Stalin was probably against it [putting on *Hamlet*] for the same reason that he was against putting on *Macbeth* or *Boris Godunov*: such portraits of rulers whose road to power had been strewn with corpses did not appeal to him in the least (1a). ♦ Незнакомец понравился Жаннет, хотя был он немолод и некрасив... Этот человек... пришёлся ей по сердцу (Эренбург 4). Jeannette liked the stranger, although he was neither young nor handsome....This man...had something that appealed to her heart (4a). ♦ ...Закон, каков бы он ни был... всё-таки имеет ограничивающую силу, которая никогда честолюбцам не по душе (Салтыков-Щедрин 1). A law, whatever it may be...still has a limiting force, which is never to the liking of the ambitious (1a). ♦ Я думаю, она презирает коммунальные квартиры и служба в таком нарядном доме ей очень по душе (Чуковская 2). How she must despise communal flats! It must be very much to her taste to work in such a smart place (2a). ♦ И очень [Солженицын] по душе мне пришёлся. Сильный, пытливый разум, проницательный и всегда предельно целеустремлённый (Копелев 1). And I had taken quite a fancy to him [Solzhenitsyn]. His strong, questioning mind was penetrating and always maximally goal-oriented (1a). ♦ Был ему по сердцу один человек: тот тоже не давал ему покоя; он любил и новости, и свет, и науку, и всю жизнь... (Гончаров 1). There was only one man he was fond of, and he, too, gave him no peace: a man interested in the latest news, in people, learning, and in life as a whole... (1b). ♦ «...Она [княжна Болконская] мне очень нравится, она по сердцу мне...» (Толстой 7). "I like her [Princess Bolkonskaya] very much, I feel drawn to her..." (7a). ♦ Можно болеть, можно всю жизнь делать работу не по душе, но нужно ощущать себя человеком (Трифонов 5). ...A person can get sick, a person can spend his whole life working at something he doesn't really care for, but what is important is to feel himself a human being (5a).

Д-385 • СКО́ЛЬКО ДУШЕ́ УГО́ДНО *coll* [subord clause with бытьθ; used as adv; usu. pres; fixed WO] (to do sth.) without any limitations, restrictions, to the extent one wants: **to one's heart's content; (for) as long as one likes ⟨pleases⟩; as much as one likes ⟨pleases⟩; (for) as long as one's heart desires; as much as one's heart desires.**

«Она под вымышленной фамилией, под которой все меня узнавали, высмеивала меня сколько душе угодно в стенгазете» (Пастернак 1). "...She made fun of me to her heart's content in the wall newspaper, referring to me by some invented name that everyone could see through" (1a). ♦ [Бугров:] ...Жить можете тут сколько вашей душе угодно, хоть до Рождества... (Чехов 1). [B.:] You can live here as long as you like—till Christmas, even (1b).

Д-386 • ЧИТА́ТЬ В ДУШЕ́ ⟨В СЕ́РДЦЕ⟩ *у кого obs* [VP; subj: human] to understand clearly what s.o.'s thoughts, desires, intentions etc are: X читает у Y-а в душе ≃ **X can see into Y's heart; X reads Y's mind; X can read Y like a book.**

«Доктор! Решительно нам нельзя разговаривать: мы читаем в душе друг у друга» (Лермонтов 1). "Upon my word, Doctor, it's impossible for us to talk together. We read each other's minds" (1c).

Д-387 • ЧТО ДУШЕ́ УГО́ДНО *coll* [subord clause with бытьθ; usu. used as subj or obj; usu. pres; fixed WO] whatever one wants or likes: **whatever ⟨anything⟩ your heart desires;** [in limited contexts] **anything you could ever want.**

Приезжайте к нам на дачу. У нас там есть и лес, и озеро, и горы — словом, всё, что душе угодно. Come visit us at our dacha: we've got woods, a lake, mountains—in a word, anything you could ever want.

Д-388 • ДЛЯ ДУШИ́ *coll* [PrepP; Invar; usu. adv or, rare, nonagreeing modif] (one does sth.) in order to satisfy one's inner (usu. intellectual, spiritual) needs, desires: **for the good of one's (own) soul; to nourish the spirit; to lift ⟨stimulate⟩ the soul; (just) for (one's own) pleasure.**

...[Маршак] излагал на среднем языке шекспировские сонеты и писал мерзкие политические стишонки. Для души он завёл целую коробку гладкой мудрости, вызывавшей умиление даже у начальства (Мандельштам 2). ...He [Marshak] produced Shakespeare's sonnets in a commonplace Russian translation and wrote nasty political doggerel for the newspapers. For the good of his own soul he had devised a glib philosophy which he could spout endlessly, plucking at the heartstrings even of his masters (2a). ♦ ...Вспоминаю я о литкружке с удовольствием, он как-то возвышал нас. Когда перед тобой весь день подмётки, каблуки и союзки, то хочется чего-то для души, одной танцплощадки мало (Рыбаков 1). ...I recall the literary circle with pleasure, as it somehow gave one a lift. After all, when you've spent the whole day looking at soles, heels, and uppers, you need something to nourish the spirit, and the dance hall isn't enough (1a). ♦ В свободное время она много читала, перечла всю классику (совсем по-новому, не по-школьному, а для души) (Грекова 3). In her free time she read a lot, even reread all the classics (not the way she'd read them in school, but just for pleasure) (3a).

Д-389 • ДУШИ́ НЕ ЧА́ЯТЬ *в ком coll* [VP; subj: human] to love s.o. deeply, be extremely fond of s.o.: X в Y-е души не чает ≃ **X adores Y; X thinks the world of Y;** [usu. in refer. to an older person's affection for a younger person, often among relatives] **X dotes on Y; Y is the apple of X's eye;** [often in refer. to a romantic relationship or to a younger person's admiration for an older person] **X worships Y; X worships the ground Y walks ⟨treads⟩ on.**

[Катерина:] Маменька во мне души не чаяла, наряжала меня, как куклу, работать не принуждала... (Островский 6). [K.:] My Mama adored me, dressed me up like a doll, didn't force me to work... (6d). ♦ ...Антон лечил и самого Тимошкина и его... жену Валю от подлинных и воображаемых болезней, и они оба души не чаяли в обходительном докторе (Гинзбург 2).

Anton was personally treating Timoshkin and his...wife, Valya, for illnesses real and imaginary, and they thought the world of the attentive doctor (2a). ♦ Верный, надёжный, родной, быть может, единственный на свете человек, который души в мальчике не чаял, был таким вот простецким, чудаковатым стариком, которого умники прозвали Расторопным Момуном... (Айтматов 1). Sure, secure, and terribly dear—perhaps the only person on earth who doted on the boy turned out to be this simple, slightly outlandish old man whom clever types called Efficacious Momun... (1b). ♦ Перед ним [моим сыном] трудная, но благодарная жизнь врача, у него и милая работящая жена, и в нём души не чает его отец (Аллилуева 2). At present the hard but gratifying life of a doctor lies ahead of him [my son]; he has a sweet, hard-working wife, and he is the apple of his father's eye (2a). ♦ [Шпигельский:] Ведь он в вас души не чает, Вера Александровна... (Тургенев 1). [Sh.:] Why, he worships the ground you tread on, Vera Alexandrovna... (1a).

Д-390 • **МЁРТВЫЕ ДУ́ШИ** [NP; pl only; fixed WO] people counted fictitiously somewhere (orig. used in refer. to serfs who had died in the period between two censuses but were still counted in the rolls): **dead souls.**

Они с Ганичевым подсчитали: подписка [на заём] пошла в гору. Нажим помог. Но до плановой цифры всё ещё было далеко. Тогда Лукашин опять стал доказывать, что добрая треть этой суммы падает на мёртвых душ, на тех, кто только на бумаге числится в колхозе (Абрамов 1). ...He and Ganichev tallied the pledges [to contribute to the government loan] and saw that things were looking up. The pressure had helped, but they were still far from the Plan target. Lukashin again tried to show that a good third of the target sum fell on dead souls; that is, on people who were in the *kolkhoz* on paper only (1a).

< The title of a novel by Nikolai Gogol, 1842.

Д-391 • **НИ (ОДНО́Й) ДУШИ́ ⟨НИ (ОДНО́Й) ЖИ-ВО́Й ДУШИ́, НИ ЕДИ́НОЙ (ЖИВО́Й) ДУШИ́⟩** нет, не видно, не встретилось, не встретить и т. п. *coll* [NP_gen; these forms only; used as subj/gen or obj; fixed WO] (there is, to see etc) no one, not one person: **(there is) not a (living) soul (in sight ⟨to be seen⟩); (there is) not a single living soul (in sight ⟨to be seen⟩); (not to see ⟨meet etc⟩) a single (living ⟨blessed⟩) soul.**

Мы выходим в поле. На этот раз мы совсем одни в пустом поле. Ни души не видно ни впереди, ни сзади (Казаков 2). We'd already reached the field. This time the field was empty and we were all alone. Not a soul to be seen ahead or behind (2a). ♦ Неживое всё кругом какое-то и до того унылое, что так и тянет повеситься на этой осине у мостика. Ни дуновения ветерка, ни шевеления облака и ни живой души (Булгаков 9). The surroundings looked so lifeless and miserable that one might easily have been tempted to hang oneself on that aspen by the little bridge. Not a breath of wind, not a cloud, not a living soul (9b). ♦ Юра прошёл по дорожке, обсаженной цветами, и очутился перед двухэтажной дачей... Ни души, ни звука (Рыбаков 2). [context transl] Yuri walked along the path edged with flowers and found himself before a two-story dacha....There was no sign of life (2a).

Д-392 • **ОТ (ВСЕ́Й) ДУШИ́** желать *кому чего*, надеяться, что..., благодарить *кого за что*, поздравлять *кого с чем*, говорить *(кому что)*, жаль *кому кого*, дарить *кому что*, смеяться и т. п. [PrepP; these forms only; adv or, rare, nonagreeing postmodif] in a sincere, completely frank manner, with great feeling: **(hope ⟨wish sth., thank s.o. etc⟩) with all one's heart; (thank s.o. ⟨wish sth. etc⟩) from the bottom of one's heart; sincerely (hope ⟨congratulate s.o. etc⟩); (laugh ⟨thank s.o. etc⟩) heartily; (give ⟨offer etc⟩ sth. to s.o.) from the heart; (say sth. ⟨speak⟩) straight ⟨right⟩ from the heart; (laugh) wholeheartedly; [in limited contexts] (speak out) as one

pleases; (condemn s.o.) with all one's soul; ‖ Х-у ~ жаль Y-а ≃ X is ⟨feels⟩ very sorry for Y; X's heart goes out to Y; ‖ X-у ~ жаль, что... ≃ X sincerely regrets that...; ‖ Neg делать *что* не от души ≃ do sth. halfheartedly; ‖ говорить не от души ≃ say sth. insincerely.**

«Позвольте вас поблагодарить от всей души!» (Булгаков 9). "Allow me to thank you with all my heart!" (9b). ♦ Машенька слушала, широко открыв глаза; видно было, что она не только глубоко сочувствует мне, но от всей души желает, чтобы со мной ничего подобного больше никогда не случалось (Каверин 1). Mashenka listened, opening her eyes wide. It was clear that she not only sympathised deeply with me, but from the bottom of her heart wished that nothing like this should ever happen to me again (1a). ♦ «Вот сейчас в «Советской» все руку жали, говорили: „Мы вас поздравляем, мой милый". Или так: „Поздравляем от души, любезный"» (Трифонов 1). "Why, just now in the Sovietskaya [hotel] everyone was shaking my hand and saying, 'We congratulate you, dear man.' Or else they'd say, 'We sincerely congratulate you, dear man'" (1a). ♦ Я старался понравиться княгине, шутил, заставлял её несколько раз смеяться от души... (Лермонтов 1). I did my best to charm the old princess, told jokes and made her laugh heartily several times (1b). ♦ [Бургомистр:] Пожалуйста, сынок, я отвечу тебе попросту, от души (Шварц 2). [Mayor:] Of course, Sonny, I'll answer you straight—straight from the heart (2a). ♦ [Надя:] Он очень хорошо сказал, так... от души! (Горький 1). [N.:] He said that so nicely, you know, right from the heart (1b). ♦ В лагерь он ехал с простодушной радостью, что хоть выскажется там от души (Солженицын 3). He went off to camp with a simple-hearted feeling of gladness—at least there he could speak out as he pleased (3a). ♦ [Васильков *(Телятеву)*:] Прощай, друг, мне тебя от души жаль. Ты завтра будешь без крова и без пищи (Островский 4). [V. *(To Telyatev)*:] Good-bye, old man. I am very sorry for you. Tomorrow you won't have anything to eat and no roof over your head (4b). ♦ В трудные для себя времена они [перечисленные мною писатели] даже пытались сочинить что-нибудь панегирическое о Ленине и Сталине. Но справедливости ради надо сказать, делали они это неохотно, неумело, не от души (Войнович 1). In the more trying times, they [the writers mentioned above] even attempted to compose panegyrics to Lenin and Stalin. But, for the sake of fairness, it must be said that they did this unwillingly, clumsily, and halfheartedly (1a).

Д-393 • **С ДУШИ́ ВОРО́ТИТ ⟨РВЁТ, ТЯ́НЕТ⟩** *highly coll* [VP; impers; fixed WO] **1.** s.o. is nauseated (by some food, the sight of sth., some smell etc): **it turns X's stomach; it makes X sick (to his stomach); it makes X vomit ⟨retch, throw up, gag⟩.**

«Меня от зарезанной курицы с души воротит, а здесь не курица – душа живая» (Максимов 3). "Seeing a hen's throat slit turns my stomach. And this is a human being" (3a).

2. s.o. is repulsed, disgusted (by some person, action, matter etc), cannot tolerate (s.o. or sth.): **it makes X sick to look at sth. ⟨listen to s.o. etc⟩; it ⟨being with s.o., watching sth. etc⟩ turns X's stomach; it ⟨seeing sth. etc⟩ makes X want to throw up ⟨vomit⟩.**

«Ну, не выдумывай. Пошли». – «Не хочу, – сказал Гай. – Ну их всех! С души воротит, невозможно». – «Глупости. Прекрасные люди, очень тебя уважают» (Стругацкие 2). "No excuses. Let's go!" "I don't want to," replied Guy. "The hell with all of them! It makes me sick to look at them. I can't." "Nonsense. They're fine people and have a great deal of respect for you" (2a).

Д-394 • **С ДУШКО́М** *coll* [PrepP; Invar; subj-compl with copula or nonagreeing modif] **1.** [subj: a noun denoting food] not fresh, decaying: X с душком ≃ **X is going bad; X is spoiling; X smells bad ⟨like it's going bad⟩.**

Выброси эту рыбу, она с душком. Throw out this fish—it's going bad.

2. с (каким) душко́м disapprov [subj: human, collect, or abstr; while in Russian the modifier may be only implied, the English equivalent in most cases will specify it] (used to show that the speaker thinks the views of some person or group, the direction taken by a newspaper, some theory etc has a tendency to be ethically, politically etc wrong; in the Soviet context was also used to show that some phenomenon contradicted official ideology) sth. is undesirable, harmful, marked by some unacceptable (as implied or specified by the context) tendency: X с (нехорошим) душком ≃ **X has a nasty smell to it;** ‖ X с либеральным ⟨консервативным, антисемитским и т. п.⟩ душком ≃ **X is tainted by liberalism ⟨conservatism, anti-Semitism etc⟩;** ‖ X с сомнительным душком ≃ **X has a dubious ⟨doubtful⟩ air (about it ⟨him⟩ etc).**

…Преуменьшать значения молитвы… нельзя. Далеко зашёл старик. С душком, с нехорошим душком молитва (Абрамов 1). …The importance of the prayer could not be underestimated. The old man had gone too far. It had a nasty smell to it, that prayer (1a). ♦ …Он [отставной активист] высказался в том духе, что… квартира в жилтовариществе советских фотографов превратилась в пристанище для сборищ с определённого подкладкой, с сомнительным душком (Аксёнов 12). …The retired activist expressed himself to the effect that…an apartment in a housing community for Soviet photographers has been "turned into a haven for gatherings of a certain element, with a dubious air" (12a).

Д-395 • БОЛЕ́ТЬ ДУШО́Й ⟨СЕ́РДЦЕМ⟩ [VP; subj: human] **1.** to experience anguish, emotional pain: X болел душой ≃ **X's heart ached; X was sick at heart.**

Не болел он душой, не терялся никогда в сложных, трудных или новых обстоятельствах… (Гончаров 1). His heart did not ache, he never lost his presence of mind in new, difficult, or complicated situations… (1a).

2. ~ за кого-что, о ком-чём to experience deep concern in response to another's (or others') distressing state of affairs, over some cause etc: X болеет душой за Y-а ≃ **X's heart aches ⟨bleeds⟩ for Y.**

Д-396 • ВСЕЙ ДУШО́Й ⟨ВСЕМ СЕ́РДЦЕМ⟩ [NP$_{instrum}$; these forms only; fixed WO] **1. ~ любить** *кого,* **верить, сочувствовать** *кому,* **чувствовать** *что* и т. п. [adv (intensif)] (to love, feel for s.o. etc) very deeply, (to trust s.o.) entirely, (to sense sth.) acutely: **with all one's heart ⟨soul⟩; with (all one's) heart and soul; [in limited contexts] heart and soul; wholeheartedly; with one's entire being; with everything ⟨all⟩ one has; with everything that is in one.**

Большие добрые и умные глаза Тушина с сочувствием и состраданием устремлялись на него [Ростова]. Он видел, что Тушин всею душой хотел и ничем не мог помочь ему (Толстой 4). Tushin's large, kind, intelligent eyes were fixed on him [Rostov] with compassion and concern. Rostov saw that he wanted with all his heart to help him but could do nothing (4a). ♦ «Он, может быть, жаждал увидеть отца после долголетней разлуки… и всею душой жаждал оправдать и обнять отца своего!» (Достоевский 2). "Perhaps he longed to see his father after so many years of separation…and longed with all his soul to vindicate his father and embrace him!" (2a). ♦ …Он всей душой ощущал, что ничего так не согревает человека во вселенском холоде, как добрый костёр человеческой дружбы (Искандер 5). He sensed with heart and soul that nothing so warms a man in the universal cold as the kind campfire of human friendship (5a). ♦ Он хотя и знал, но не верил всею душою до последней минуты в оставление Москвы… (Толстой 6). Though he knew it was coming, he did not till the last moment wholeheartedly believe that Moscow would be abandoned… (6b).

---

2. к кому ~ [predic with subj: human; used in pres or, less often, past contexts] one relates to s.o. in a sincere manner: X к Y-у ~ ≃ **X comes to Y with an open heart; X comes to Y in (all) good faith.**

[Мечеткин:] Значит, вы меня разыграли? Я к вам всей душой, а вы ко мне?.. (Вампилов 2). [M.:] So you were just making fun of me. I came to you with an open heart, and you?… (2a). ♦ «…Мы к нему [князю] всей душой, а он послал нас искать князя глупого!» (Салтыков-Щедрин 1). "We went to him [the prince] in all good faith, and he sent us to seek a foolish prince!" (1a).

Д-397 • ДУШО́Й И ТЕ́ЛОМ [NP$_{instrum}$; Invar; adv] with one's entire being, totally: **body and soul; [in limited contexts] heart and soul.**

Из предыдущей главы уже видно, в чём состоял главный предмет его вкуса и склонностей, а потому не диво, что он скоро погрузился весь в него и телом и душою (Гоголь 3). The preceding chapter revealed the main subject of his interests and inclinations, and therefore it is not surprising that he soon became immersed in it body and soul (3c).

Д-398 • ЗА ДУШО́Й *(у кого)* **нет, не иметь** *чего,* **есть** *что* [PrepP; Invar; adv; usu. used with negated predic] (s.o. does not have anything, s.o. has sth.) of s.o.'s own: [in refer. to money, material possessions] у X-а нет ни копейки ⟨ни гроша etc⟩ за душой ≃ **X doesn't have ⟨is without⟩ a kopeck ⟨a penny, a cent etc⟩ to his name; X is (flat) broke;** ‖ [in refer. to convictions, spiritual values, morals etc] что у X-а ~? ≃ **what is (going on) inside (of) X?; what is in X's heart ⟨soul⟩?; what does X believe in?; what are the principles ⟨beliefs etc⟩ that guide X?; what principles does X live by?;** ‖ у X-а нет ничего ~ ≃ **X's soul is a wasteland ⟨a void⟩; X is without beliefs or convictions; X has no spiritual fiber; X's heart is empty.**

…В тринадцатом году она [«Бродячая Собака», ночной клуб] была единственным островком в ночном Петербурге, где литературная и артистическая молодёжь, в виде общего правила, не имевшая ни гроша за душой, чувствовала себя как дома (Лившиц 1). …In 1913 it [the *Stray Dog* night-club] was the only haven in night-time Petersburg where the literary and artistic youth (usually without a penny to its name) could feel at home (1a). ♦ О Дессере думают: всесилен. В газетах его называют «некоронованным королём». А он — нищий. У него ничего за душой (Эренбург 4). They thought he [Desser] was all-powerful. They [the newspapers] called him the "uncrowned king." And in reality he was destitute. His heart was empty (4a). ♦ Интеллигенция… на досуге занялась переоценкой ценностей – это был период массовой капитуляции [перед новым режимом]… Психологически всех толкал на капитуляцию страх остаться в одиночестве и в стороне от общего движения… Но самое главное это то, что у самих капитулянтов ничего за душой не было (Мандельштам 1). [context transl] The intellectuals…set about a leisurely "revaluation of all values." This was the period of mass surrender [to the new regime]….Psychological factors that worked in favor of capitulation were the fear of being left out in the cold, of not moving with the times….But the main thing was that those who surrendered had nothing of their own to offer (1a).

Д-399 • КРИВИ́ТЬ/ПОКРИВИ́ТЬ ДУШО́Й *(перед кем, в чём; против чего)* coll [VP; subj: human; fixed WO] to say sth. one knows to be false or do sth. one knows to be wrong, ignoring one's conscience (usu. pretending to be sincere while attempting to deceive s.o. or o.s.): X кривит душой (перед Y-ом) ≃ **X is lying (to Y); X is bending the truth; X is playing false (with Y); X isn't being straight (with Y); [in limited contexts] X is going ⟨acting etc⟩ against his conscience (in doing sth.);** ‖ X кривит душой перед самим собой ≃ **X is deceiving ⟨trying to deceive⟩ himself;** ‖ не кривя душой ≃

without dissembling; [in limited contexts] **without holding any-thing back.**

«Нюся?» – «Она. – Он подмигнул мне. – Ничего девка?» – «Красивая». Возможно, я покривил душой, но что я мог ещё сказать (Войнович 5). "Nyusa?" "That's her, all right." He winked at me. "Good stuff?" "Beautiful," I said. "Perhaps I was bending the truth, but what else could I do? (5a). ♦ «Он [председатель], дьявол, на нас взъелся... А из-за чего?..» Тут Лизка немного покривила душой. На самом-то деле она знала, из-за чего взъелся на них председатель (Абрамов 1). "That monster [the Chairman] is out to get us....And for what?..." Lizka was playing somewhat false here. She did in fact know why the Chairman was out to get them... (1a). ♦ ...Александров садится в сознании выполненного долга и избегнутой опасности. В самом деле, он не покривил душой, дурного не сказал, товарища не пре-дал... (Эткинд 1). ...Aleksandrov can sit down with the feeling of duty done and danger avoided. And indeed he has not spoken against his conscience or said anything shameful; he has not betrayed his comrade... (1a). ♦ Кровь кинулась Григорию в голову, когда напал глазами на свой курень... «Не щипет [ungrammat = щиплет] глаза?» – улыбнулся Пантелей Прокофьевич, оглядываясь, и Григорий, не лукавя и не кривя душой, со-знался: «щипет... да ишо [ungrammat = ещё] как!..» (Шолохов 3). The blood rushed to Grigory's head as his eyes rested on his own home...."Aren't your eyes stinging?" Pantelei smiled as he looked round at his son, and Grigory without dissem-bling, "Yes they are – that they are!" (3a). ♦ «...С кем и за кого мы? Давайте же поговорим по-товарищески, не кривя душой» (Шолохов 3). "Who are we with? Who do we support?...Let's talk it over in a spirit of comradeship without holding anything back" (3a).

Д-400 • НИ ДУШО́Й НИ ТЕ́ЛОМ не виноват *в чём*, не **причастен** *к чему* и т. п. *obs, coll* [NP$_{instrum}$; these forms only; adv (intensif); usu. this WO] absolutely not (guilty etc): **(not guilty,) neither in thought nor deed; (not at fault) in thought or deed; not at all (to blame).**

[Городничий:] Ах, боже мой! Я ей-ей не виноват ни душою ни телом (Гоголь 4). [Mayor:] No, no! So help me God, I'm not guilty! Neither in thought nor deed! (4b).

Д-401 • ОТДЫХА́ТЬ/ОТДОХНУ́ТЬ ДУШО́Й ⟨СЕ́РД-ЦЕМ⟩ [VP; subj: human] to free o.s. from anxiety and stress, often through a pleasant distraction: X отдыхал душой ≃ **X found peace of mind ⟨inner peace⟩; X's mind ⟨soul⟩ was at rest.**

Нажив миллионы, Жюль Дессер остался верен привычкам детства: он отдыхал душой, играя в шашки со стариком садовником... (Эренбург 4). Having made his millions, Desser remained faithful to the habits of his childhood. He found peace of mind over a game of chess with his old gardener (4a). ♦ [Ланцелот:] Ты их [твоих хозяев] не любишь? [Кот:] Люблю каждым волоском моего меха, и лапами, и усами, но им грозит огром-ное горе. Я отдыхаю душой, только когда они уходят со двора (Шварц 2). [L.:] Don't you like them [your masters]? [Cat:] I love them with every hair of my fur and with my paws and whiskers, too, but a terrible sorrow is in store for them. My mind is only at rest when they're out of the house (2a).

Д-402 • С ДОРОГО́Й ДУШО́Й *coll* [PrepP; Invar; adv; usu. used with pfv verbs (fut or subjunctive); fixed WO] (to do sth.) very willingly: **(be) (only too) happy ⟨glad⟩ (to do sth.); gladly; (be) delighted (to do sth.); with pleasure.**

Согласен ли Илья Максимович встать за наковальню? «А почему не согласен, – ответил Илья. – Я кузнечное дело люблю. Вот только с лесом развяжусь – и с дорогой душой» (Абрамов 1). Would Ilya Maximovich agree to man the anvil? "Why not?" he replied. "I like smithing. Once I'm through with the timber I'd be happy to" (1a). ♦ «Всё бесполезно. Я бы с дорогой душою послужил Григорию Пантелеевичу, но говорю честно: помочь

не могу» (Шолохов 5). "It's hopeless. I'd be only too glad to help Grigory Panteleyevich, but, honestly, there's nothing I can do" (5a). ♦ «Поймите, что здесь, в Городе, он [гетман] набрал бы пятидесятитысячную армию, и какую армию! Отборную, лучшую, потому что все юнкера, все студенты, гимназисты, офицеры, а их тысячи в Городе, все пошли бы с дорогою душой» (Булгаков 3). "Here in the City alone he [the Hetman] could have had a volunteer army of fifty thousand men – and what an army! An élite, none but the very best, because all the officer-cadets, all the students and high school boys and all the officers – and there are thousands of them in the City – would have gladly joined up" (3a).

Д-403 • С ДУШО́Й *coll, approv* [PrepP; Invar; adv] (to do sth.) with enthusiasm, devotion: **with spirit ⟨feeling, zeal, zest⟩; put(ting) one's heart into it ⟨sth.⟩; [in limited contexts] with heart.**

...А как работали, разве так, как теперь? С огоньком работали, с душой (Суслов 1). And how they worked, not at all like now! They worked with zest, with spirit (1a). ♦ Встал Гриша, повёл ещё шире, раздольнее... И геологический парень тоже запел, хотя и не шибко красиво, но с душой (Евтушенко 2). Grisha rose and sang even more broadly, with bravura....And the geologist also joined in, though not very beautifully, but with feeling (2a). ♦ «Когда-то, раньше, молодой, ты любил петь „Назови мне такую обитель", помнишь?.. „Где бы русский мужик не стонал", помнишь? Хорошо пел, с душой, добрый был, жалел мужика» (Рыбаков 2). "Don't you remember, when you were young and used to sing 'Find me the village where the Russian peasant doesn't groan'? You sang it well, with heart, you were good, you pitied the peasant" (2a).

Д-404 • С ОТКРЫ́ТОЙ ДУШО́Й; С ОТКРЫ́ТЫМ СЕ́РДЦЕМ [PrepP; these forms only; usu. adv; fixed WO] in a totally frank, straightforward manner: **with an open ⟨a sincere⟩ heart; with one's heart laid open; [in limited contexts] (be) open and honest (with s.o.).**

[Генрих:] Мне давно хочется поговорить с тобою наедине, по-дружески, с открытой душой (Шварц 2). [H.:] For a long time I've wanted to have a talk with you alone, to talk to you as a friend, with an open heart (2a). ♦ «Ты-то отдал своё [оружие]? А?»... – «Сдал, конечно [phonetic spelling = конечно], Яков Ефимыч, ты не подумай... Я с открытой душой» (Шолохов 4). "Have you given up yours [your weapons]? Eh?"..."Of course, I have, Yakov Yefimovich. You mustn't think....I'm being open and honest with you" (4a).

Д-405 • СТОЯ́ТЬ ⟨ТОРЧА́ТЬ highly coll, СИДЕ́ТЬ rare⟩ НАД ДУШО́Й (*чьей, у кого*) *coll, disapprov* [VP; subj: human] to weary s.o. with one's presence, exasperate s.o. with one's importunity: X стоит над душой у Y-а ≃ **X is ⟨Y has X⟩ breathing down Y's neck; X is pestering Y; X is looking over Y's shoulder;** ‖ *Neg Imper* не стой над душой ≃ **get off my back.**

«Восемь посылок с английской литературой. Помогите просмотреть и разобраться!» – «Одни не можете?» – «Одни не можем!» – «Вот как?!» – «А так: у нас над душой стоит Василий Никандрович и требует. А мы – одни не можем» (Залыгин 1). "Eight parcels of English books. Come and help us go through them and sort them out!" "Can't you cope by yourselves?" "No." "Really?" "Really. We've got Vasily Nikandrovich breathing down our necks and insisting, and we can't do it on our own" (1a). ♦ Если она [девушка] ошибалась, а иногда она ошибалась и оттого, что председатель на неё смотрел и Кязым стоял над душой, он говорил: «А ну перещёлкай [= пересчитай на счётах] наново!» (Искандер 5). If she [the girl] made a mistake – and sometimes she made mistakes precisely because the chairman was watching and Kyazym was pestering her – he said, "Well, do it over [on the abacus]!" (5a).

Д-406 • БЕРЕДИ́ТЬ/РАЗБЕРЕДИ́ТЬ ДУ́ШУ ⟨СЕ́РД-ЦЕ⟩ (кому) [VP; subj: human or abstr] to evoke painful memories (in s.o.): X бередит душу Y-у ≃ **X stirs (up) old feelings (in Y); thing X torments Y's soul.**

…Его не манит сюда приехать, посмотреть, как живут свои и не свои, походить по старым, с детства знакомым местам и разбередить этим душу… (Распутин 1). Nothing would induce him to come back and see how his kinsmen and friends were getting on and to stir old feelings by roaming through scenes connected with his childhood (1a).

Д-407 • БРАТЬ/ВЗЯТЬ ⟨ЗАБИРА́ТЬ/ЗАБРА́ТЬ, ХВА-ТА́ТЬ⟩ ЗА́ ДУШУ ⟨ЗА́ СЕРДЦЕ⟩ coll [VP; subj: usu. abstr] (usu. of a song, melancholy music, poetry etc) to move, affect, trouble s.o. deeply, cause s.o. to feel deep emotion: X берёт за душу ≃ **X touches ⟨grips, clutches at⟩ the ⟨person Y's⟩ heart; X goes straight ⟨right⟩ to the ⟨person Y's⟩ heart;** [in limited contexts] **X tugs ⟨pulls⟩ at person Y's heartstrings.**

«Играй». – «А что бы ты хотел?» – «Это тебе лучше знать, Эрлеке. Мастер сам знает, что ему сподручней. Конечно, старинные вещи – они как бы роднее. Не знаю отчего, за душу берут, думы навевают» (Айтматов 2). "Do play some more." "And what would you like?" "You know best, Erleke. The artist himself knows what he has to play. Of course, I prefer the old things, they're dearer to me. I don't know why, but they touch the heart and feed one's thoughts" (2a). ♦ Что в ней, в этой песне? Что зовёт, и рыдает, и хватает за сердце? (Гоголь 3). What is there in it, in that song? What is there in it that calls, and sobs, and grips my heart? (3c). What is there in that song? What is it that calls, and sobs, and clutches at my heart? (3a). ♦ …В объявлении… говорилось: «Жившая здесь обезьянка ослепла от бессмысленной жестокости одного из посетителей. Злой человек сыпнул табака в глаза макаке-резус»… Больше всего простотою ребёнка хватало написанное за сердце (Солженицын 10). It [the notice] said: "The little monkey that used to live here was blinded because of the senseless cruelty of one of the visitors. An evil man threw tobacco into the Macaque Rhesus's eyes."…What went straight to his heart was the childish simplicity with which it was written (10a).

Д-408 • В ОДНУ́ ДУ́ШУ твердить, повторять что и т. п. coll [PrepP; Invar; adv; used with impfv verbs; fixed WO] (to repeat) the same thing many times, (to say sth.) repeatedly, persistently: **(repeat sth. etc) over and over (again); (keep saying etc) one and the same thing;** [in refer. to nagging, making persistent demands of s.o. etc] **keep at s.o. (to do sth.).**

«Стрельба идёт тёмная, всё живое похоронилось, а он [Григорий] в одну душу: „Найди её [Аксинью], иначе в гроб вгоню!"» (Шолохов 4). "Here they are blazing away at us, every living thing's taken cover, but he [Grigory] keeps at me, 'Find her [Aksinya] or I'll send you to your grave!'" (4a).

Д-409 • ВКЛА́ДЫВАТЬ ⟨ВЛАГА́ТЬ⟩/ВЛОЖИ́ТЬ ДУ́ШУ ⟨СЕ́РДЦЕ⟩ во что [VP; subj: human] to apply all one's energy, efforts, abilities to sth., do sth. with great dedication: X вкладывает душу в Y = **X puts (his) heart and soul into Y; X puts his (whole) heart ⟨soul⟩ into Y; X gives himself wholly ⟨entirely⟩ to Y.**

…Мне в этот же приезд предстояло уговориться обо всём с М. В. Матюшиным и Е. Г. Гуро, вкладывавшими, по словам Давида, душу в издание сборника (Лившиц 1). On this particular visit I was to arrange everything with M. V. Matiushin and E. G. Guro who, in David's words, had put their heart and soul into the publication of the miscellany (1a). ♦ Платон Самсонович вложил в него [очерк] всю свою душу (Искандер 6). Platon Samsonovich had put heart and soul into this article… (6a). ♦ «Мы, маменька, сегодня пойдём гулять?» – вдруг спрашивал он среди молитвы. «Пойдём, душенька», – торопливо говорила она, не отводя от иконы глаз и спеша договорить святые слова. Мальчик вяло повторял их, но мать влагала в них всю свою душу (Гончаров 1). "Are we going for a walk to-day, Mummy?" he suddenly asked in the middle of the prayer. "Yes, darling," she replied hurriedly, without taking her eyes off the ikon and hastening to finish the holy words. The boy repeated them listlessly, but his mother put her whole soul into them (1a).

Д-410 • ВЛЕЗА́ТЬ/ВЛЕЗТЬ ⟨ЛЕЗТЬ, ЗАЛЕЗА́ТЬ/ЗА-ЛЕ́ЗТЬ⟩ В ДУ́ШУ чью, кого, (к) кому [VP; subj: human] **1.** coll to understand the inner world of another person, anticipate his thoughts, moods, feelings: X влез Y-у в душу ≃ **X got inside Y's head ⟨soul⟩.**

2. coll, usu. disapprov to inquire in very close detail about s.o.'s personal life, interfere in s.o.'s private affairs: X лезет к Y-у в душу ≃ **X pries into Y's feelings; X pries into Y's (very) soul.**

«Зачем он всё это мне рассказывает? – закипала в Андрее лютая и необъяснимая для него самого злость. – Что ему надо от меня? Какие такие у него права есть влезать ко мне в душу?» (Максимов 3). A fierce anger, which he couldn't have explained to himself, took hold of Andrei. "Why is he telling me all this? What does he want from me? What right has he got to come prying into my feelings?" (3a). ♦ [Сангвиник:] Послушайте, батенька, а как вы сюда попали? [Холерик:] Не ваше дело! Я к вам в душу не лезу! (Аксёнов 11). [S.:] Listen, old buddy, how did you get here? [Ch.:] None of your business! I don't go prying into your soul (11a). ♦ Сначала старухи переберут весь околоток, кто как живёт, кто что делает; они проникнут не только в семейный быт, в закулисную жизнь, но в сокровенные помыслы и намерения каждого, влезут в душу… (Гончаров 1). The ladies would begin by talking over the whole neighborhood, discussing how this one lived, what that one did, not only going into everyone's domestic life and what went on behind the scenes, but prying into their innermost thoughts and motives, into their very souls… (1b).

3. coll to (try to) win s.o.'s confidence by any means, (try to) obtain s.o.'s favor (usu. out of selfish or mercenary motives): X влез к Y-у в душу ≃ **X wormed ⟨weaseled, wheedled⟩ his way into Y's confidence; X wormed himself into Y's confidence; X gained Y's confidence.**

[Мурзавецкая:] Я тебя свезу сегодня к Купавиной: подружись с ней, да в душу-то к ней влезь: она женщина не хитрая; а тебя учить нечего (Островский 5). [M.:] I'm going to take you with me to-day to Madam Kupavin's. Make friends with her; gain her confidence. She is not a clever woman, – but I needn't instruct you (5a).

4. substand to become the object of s.o.'s affection, love, respect etc, become very dear to s.o.: X влез Y-у в душу ≃ **X won Y's heart; X won Y over;** [in limited contexts] **Y fell for X.**

Д-411 • ВХОДИ́ТЬ/ВОЙТИ́ В ДУ́ШУ чью ⟨В СЕ́РДЦЕ чьё⟩, кого [VP] **1.** [subj: human] to become the object of s.o.'s affection, love, respect etc, become very dear to s.o.: X влез Y-у в душу ≃ **X won ⟨stole⟩ Y's heart; X won Y over.**

Работящая Наталья вошла свёкрам в душу (Шолохов 2). The diligent Natalya soon won the hearts of her father- and mother-in-law (2a).

2. [subj: abstr] to worry s.o., affect s.o. deeply: X вошёл в душу Y-а ≃ **Y took X to heart; Y responded to X with Y's whole heart; X struck a chord in Y's heart.**

Д-412 • ВЫВОРА́ЧИВАТЬ/ВЫ́ВЕРНУТЬ ДУ́ШУ чью, кого, кому; ДУ́ШУ ВЫВОРА́ЧИВАЕТ coll [VP; subj: human or abstr (1st var.); impers (2nd var.)] to have a strong emotional effect on s.o., cause s.o. to feel great pain, anguish: X Y-у душу выворачивает ≃ **X tears Y up inside; X breaks ⟨wrenches⟩ Y's heart; X shakes Y up (inside); thing X is heartrending.**

[Варя:] …Этот, Марк Александрович, как он на пианино играет. Просто душу выворачивает… (Розов 3). [V.:] …That

Mark Alexandrovich, how he plays the piano. He just breaks your heart… (3a).

Д-413 • ВЫВОРА́ЧИВАТЬ/ВЫ́ВЕРНУТЬ ДУ́ШУ (НАИЗНА́НКУ) *перед кем coll* [VP; subj: human] to tell s.o. all one's innermost thoughts, private feelings, concerns etc: X вывернул душу перед Y-ом ≃ **X bared his soul ⟨heart⟩ to ⟨before⟩ Y; X laid bare his soul ⟨heart⟩ before ⟨to⟩ Y.**

Д-414 • ВЫКЛА́ДЫВАТЬ/ВЫ́ЛОЖИТЬ ДУ́ШУ *кому coll* [VP; subj: human] to share one's thoughts, feelings openly with s.o.: X выложил Y-у душу ≃ **X opened his heart ⟨his soul⟩ to Y; X poured out his soul ⟨his heart⟩ to Y; X opened up to Y.**

Д-415 • ВЫМА́ТЫВАТЬ/ВЫ́МОТАТЬ (ВСЮ) ДУ́ШУ *(кому, из кого);* ВЫТЯ́ГИВАТЬ/ВЫ́ТЯНУТЬ (ВСЮ) ДУ́ШУ *(из кого) coll* [VP; subj: usu. human, occas. abstr] to vex, torment, or pester s.o. to the point where he is exhausted (physically or mentally): X из Y-а (всю) душу вымотал ≃ **X wore Y out.**

(На платформе звонок.) [Домна Пантелевна:] Ай! Поехали. [Великатов:] Успокойтесь, Домна Пантелевна, без вас не уедут… [Домна Пантелевна:] Напугали до смерти. Они этими звонками проклятыми всю душу вымотают (Островский 11). *(Bell heard from platform.)* [D.P.:] Aie! Aie! They've gone!… [V.:] Don't worry, Domna Panteleyevna, they won't go without you…. [D.P.:] I was frightened to death! They've worn me out with their accursed bells! (11a).

Д-416 • ВЫНИМА́ТЬ/ВЫ́НУТЬ ДУ́ШУ *(из кого)* [VP; subj: human] **1.** *highly coll* to torment s.o. to the point of exhaustion with threats, reprimands etc: X из Y-а душу вынет ≃ **X will put Y through the wringer;** [in limited contexts] **X will rake Y over the coals.**

Лейтенант нервничал. Он только утром вернулся из области, где подполковник Лужин всю ночь вынимал из него душу… выспрашивая все подробности и детали того случая… (Войнович 4). The lieutenant was nervous. That very morning he had returned from the district, where Lieutenant Colonel Luzhin had raked him over the coals all night…questioning him about all the details and particulars of the incident… (4a).

2. *substand* to kill s.o. by beating or torturing him: X вынет душу из Y-а ≃ **X will beat ⟨torture⟩ Y to death.**

Д-417 • ВЫ́ТРЯСТИ ДУ́ШУ *из кого substand* [VP] **1.** [usu. impers] s.o. is exhausted from a ride on a bad, bumpy road or in an uncomfortable vehicle: из X-а душу вытрясло ≃ **X had his insides shaken (up); it shook (up) X's innards.**

2. [subj: human] to harrass s.o., torment s.o. with threats, demands etc: X из Y-а душу вытрясет ≃ **X will hound Y (with threats** etc); [used as a threat] **X will shake the life ⟨the stuffing, the hell⟩ out of Y.**

Попался бы он [Писатель] мне сейчас на глаза, я из него душу бы вытряс (Войнович 5). If he [the Writer] had appeared in front of me at that moment, I'd have shaken the life out of him (5a).

Д-418 • ЗА МИ́ЛУЮ ДУ́ШУ *coll* [PrepP; Invar; adv] **1.** (to do sth.) very willingly, with great enthusiasm, delight: **(be) more than happy (to do sth.); (be) only too glad ⟨happy⟩ (to do sth.); with great pleasure; happily; gladly;** [in limited contexts] **to one's heart's content;** ‖ съесть ⟨сожрать *substand*⟩ *что* ~ ≃ **relish ⟨savor⟩ every bite (of sth.);** ‖ повеселиться ~ ≃ **have the time of one's life.**

«А ведь она [Нинка]… и правда понесла бы их [бутылки с водкой] сдавать… А там за милу[ю] душу приняли бы за те же двенадцать копеек» (Распутин 3). "She [Ninka] really would have done it too. She'd have taken them [the bottles full of vodka] back….And they'd have been only too glad to give her twelve kopecks for them, same as for the empties" (3a). ♦ Тогда вой усилился, словно воющий решил во время перерыва повыть за милую душу (Аксёнов 6). Then the wailing grew louder, as though the wailer had decided that during the lunch break he would wail to his heart's content (6a). ♦ Он заговорщически подмигнул мне: не пропадём, мол, погуляемся за милую душу! (Аксёнов 6). He gave me a conspiratorial wink, meaning: We're not going to waste our stay here; we're going to have the time of our lives, aren't we?! (6a).

2. [usu. used with pfv verbs] (to do sth.) without deliberating, immediately, with no qualms: **without thinking twice; without a moment's hesitation; just like that; (right) then and there;** [in limited contexts] **in a snap.**

Не ввязывайся в драку с Петром — может прихлопнуть за милую душу. Don't get in a fight with Pyotr, he could kill you just like that. ♦ Эти суки могут тебя обратать и в международной зоне аэропорта, и на борту самолета запереть в сортирный чуланчик, как недавно поступили с нежной балериной В., и в братской республике захрапоут за милую душу (Аксёнов 12). Those animals could get him back even from the international zone or lock him into the toilet on board a plane, he knew, as they recently did with the delicate ballerina V., and they could grab him in a snap in a "fraternal republic" (12a).

3. [used with pfv verbs] certainly, unquestionably, without any doubt: **for (darn) sure; sure as anything; (there's ⟨there are⟩) no two ways about it.**

Д-419 • ЗАГЛЯ́ДЫВАТЬ/ЗАГЛЯНУ́ТЬ В ДУ́ШУ *чью* ⟨В СЕ́РДЦЕ *чьё*⟩, *кого, кому* [VP; subj: human; often pfv infin with пытаться] (to attempt) to understand s.o.'s innermost thoughts, feelings: X пытался заглянуть Y-у в душу ≃ **X tried to peer ⟨look⟩ into (the depths of) Y's soul; X tried to peer ⟨look⟩ into the hidden places of Y's heart; X tried to peer ⟨look⟩ into the depths of Y's being;** ‖ загляни себе в душу ≃ **look into your own soul; search your heart.**

«Нет, я положу конец этому, — сказал он, — я загляну ей в душу, как прежде, и завтра — или буду счастлив, или уеду!» (Гончаров 1). "No, I shall put an end to this," he said. "I will look into her soul as I used to, and tomorrow—I shall either be happy or go away!" (1b). ♦ «А раскаяние хоть испытываешь какое-то?» — спрашиваю я. Мнётся некоторое время, как бы заглядывая себе в душу: «Да нет, ничего вроде не испытываю» (Амальрик 1). "But don't you feel at least a little bit sorry that you did it?" I would ask. Then, after some hesitation, as if my interlocutor were looking into his own soul, would come the reply: "No, I can't say as I really feel sorry" (1a).

Д-420 • ЗАКРА́ДЫВАТЬСЯ/ЗАКРА́СТЬСЯ В ДУ́ШУ *чью* ⟨В СЕ́РДЦЕ *чьё*⟩, *кого, (к) кому* [VP; subj: abstr] (of feelings, thoughts etc) to arise involuntarily, either spontaneously or in a gradual, almost imperceptible manner: X закрался в Y-ову душу ≃ [of doubt, suspicion] **X crept ⟨stole⟩ into Y's soul ⟨mind⟩; X (a)rose in Y ⟨in Y's mind⟩;** [of sadness, grief etc] **X came over Y;** [of love] **X stirred in Y's heart.**

Вдруг что-то шумно упало в воду: я хвать за пояс — пистолета нет. О, тут ужасное подозрение закралось мне в душу… (Лермонтов 1). Suddenly, something fell into the water, with a noisy splash; my hand flew to my belt—my pistol was gone. Ah, what a terrible suspicion stole into my soul! (1a). ♦ Лукашин осматривается, не зная, что делать дальше, как вдруг сомнение закрадывается в его душу (Брагинский и Рязанов 1). Lukashin looks round not knowing what to do and suddenly a doubt rises in his mind (1a).

Д-421 • ЗАПАДА́ТЬ/ЗАПА́СТЬ В ДУ́ШУ ⟨В ГО́ЛОВУ, В ПА́МЯТЬ⟩ *(чью, кому),* ⟨В УМ *(чей)*⟩ [VP;

subj: abstr (usu. слова, мысль, образ etc)] having produced a strong impression on s.o., to be remembered by him for a very long time: X запал Y-у в душу ≃ **X was engraved (up)on Y's heart; X was etched in Y's memory; X remained (fresh) in Y's memory; X became unforgettable.**

«Он не мог не видеть, какое глубочайшее впечатление произвели на людей проникновенные, западающие в душу слова нашего любимого вождя» (Войнович 4). "He could not help but see what a profound impression the heartfelt, unforgettable words of our beloved leader made on these people" (4a).

Д-422 • ИЗЛИВА́ТЬ/ИЗЛИ́ТЬ ДУ́ШУ (кому, перед кем)
[VP; subj: human; often pfv infin with хочется, нужно etc] to reveal candidly to s.o. one's anxieties, worries, innermost feelings: X изливал душу (Y-у) ≃ **X poured out his soul ⟨heart⟩ (to Y); X bared his soul ⟨heart⟩ to ⟨before⟩ Y; X unburdened his heart (to Y).**

...Никто не молчал, все сразу говорили, гудели, галдели, и общий рокот как волнами бил по комнате. Ну, ещё бы! — российская любовь излить душу (Солженицын 5). ...Not one of them [was] silent, all [were] talking at once, babbling and bawling, so that the general din swept across the room in waves. Nothing surprising in that! The Russian loves to pour out his heart (5a). ♦ Захмелевший Мальчик... рвался кому-нибудь излить душу (Зиновьев 1). The Boy, who was rather tipsy by this time...tried to find someone to pour out his soul to (1a). ♦ Так оно бывает зачастую — смерть отца явилась для неё поводом выплакаться, излить принародно душу, всё то, что давно не находило открытого выхода в слове (Айтматов 2). As so often happens, the death of her father opened the floodgates, giving her a reason to bare her soul before everyone — to say all the things which had long been bottled up inside her, unexpressed in words (2a).

Д-423 • КЛАСТЬ/ПОЛОЖИ́ТЬ ДУ́ШУ [VP; subj: human]
1. *за кого-что* to sacrifice one's life (in order to save, protect s.o. or sth.): X душу положит за Y-a ≃ **X will give up ⟨lay down⟩ his life for Y.**

2. ~ *на что* to put much effort, all one's energy into sth., devote o.s. completely to sth.: X положил душу на Y ≃ **X put his heart and soul into Y; X put his whole being into Y; X gave himself completely ⟨entirely⟩ to Y; X gave Y ⟨it⟩ his all ⟨all he had⟩.**

Д-424 • НАДРЫВА́ТЬ/НАДОРВА́ТЬ ДУ́ШУ (чью) ⟨СЕ́РДЦЕ (чьё)⟩, (кого, кому) [VP; subj: human or abstr; usu. impfv] to arouse anguish, pain in s.o., make s.o. extremely depressed: X надрывает Y-у душу ≃ **X makes Y's heart ache; X torments Y; X breaks ⟨thing X wrings⟩ Y's heart.**

Д-425 • ОБЛЕГЧА́ТЬ/ОБЛЕГЧИ́ТЬ ДУ́ШУ ⟨СЕ́РД-ЦЕ⟩ [VP; subj: human; usu. pfv infin with хочется, не терпится *кому* etc or pfv Verbal Adv облегчив душу] to rid o.s. of one's worries, concerns, of things that weigh heavily on one's soul, esp. by talking about them: X облегчил душу ≃ **X eased ⟨relieved⟩ his mind; X unburdened ⟨relieved⟩ his soul; X put ⟨set⟩ his mind at rest ⟨at ease⟩; X got it off his chest; X took a load off his mind.**

«Вы напрасно взяли такое сравнение...» » — «Не напрасно, господа, не напрасно!» — вскипел опять Митя, хотя и, видимо облегчив душу выходкой внезапного гнева, начал уже опять добреть с каждым словом (Достоевский 1). "You shouldn't make such comparisons...." "Why shouldn't I, gentlemen, why shouldn't I!" Mitya boiled up again, though he had apparently unburdened his soul with this outburst of sudden anger and was growing kinder again with every word (1a). ♦ ...Княжна Марья вслух произнесла то ласкательное слово, которое он сказал ей в день смерти. «Ду - ше - нь - ка!» — повторила княжна Марья

это слово и зарыдала облегчающими душу слезами (Толстой 6). ...Princess Marya said aloud the term of endearment he had uttered on the day of his death. "'Dear-est!'" she repeated and sobbed, her tears relieving her soul (6a). ♦ Ей [Наташе] не терпелось облегчить душу и рассказать... всё то, что мне без её признаний было отлично известно... (Терц 2). She [Natasha] just couldn't wait to put her mind at rest and tell me what I knew perfectly well without her owning up to it... (2a).

Д-426 • ОТВОДИ́ТЬ/ОТВЕСТИ́ ДУ́ШУ ⟨СЕ́РДЦЕ *obs*⟩ (с кем, на ком) *coll* [VP; subj: human] **1.** (с кем, в чём) to relieve o.s. of emotional stress, find a sense of calm, soothe o.s. by having a frank conversation with s.o. or doing sth. relaxing: X отвёл душу (с Y-ом ⟨в Z-e⟩) ≃ **X unburdened himself ⟨his heart, his soul⟩ (to Y); X eased his mind (by talking to Y ⟨doing Z⟩); X relieved tension (by doing Z); X calmed himself (by talking to Y ⟨doing Z⟩); [in limited contexts] X got it off his chest; X blew off steam.**

...Впервые за их недолгую, но богатую событиями совместную жизнь Пётр Васильевич постеснялся перебить жену за этим её занятием [молитвой]: «Каждому своё, пускай отведёт душу» (Максимов 3). For the first time in their brief but eventful life together, Pyotr Vasilievich hadn't the heart to interrupt his wife at this occupation of hers [praying]. "To each his own, let her unburden herself" (3a). ♦ Мне захотелось отвести с ним душу, и я, взяв его под руку, отделил от компании (Искандер 4). I had an urge to unburden my heart to him. Taking him by the arm, I drew him apart from the company (4a).

2. (на ком-чём) to relieve o.s. of intense anger, frustration etc by directing it at some innocent person or thing: ‖ X отвёл душу (на Y-e) ≃ **X vented ⟨let out⟩ his feelings ⟨frustration etc⟩ on Y; X took it out on Y.**

...Полицейские отводили душу на жёнах забастовщиков, которые пытались пробраться к воротам... (Эренбург 4). The gendarmes vented their feelings on the wives of the strikers who tried to get through to the gates... (4a). ♦ Снова в директоре взыграла жёлчь. Старший сын Роман год тому назад ушёл из семьи. Отец отводил душу на младших (Олеша 2). The father's bile rose. Roman, his eldest son, had left home a year earlier. The father was taking it out on his younger sons (2a).

Д-427 • ОТКРЫВА́ТЬ/ОТКРЫ́ТЬ ДУ́ШУ кому; РАС-КРЫВА́ТЬ/РАСКРЫ́ТЬ ДУ́ШУ кому, перед кем; РАСПА́ХИВАТЬ/РАСПАХНУ́ТЬ ДУ́ШУ перед кем [VP; subj: human] to tell s.o. openly one's intimate feelings, worries etc: X открыл Y-у душу ≃ **X opened his heart ⟨his soul⟩ to Y; X opened up to Y; [in limited contexts] X unburdened his soul ⟨his heart, himself⟩ to Y.**

«Хотите ли, доктор, — отвечал я ему, — чтоб я раскрыл вам мою душу?» (Лермонтов 1). "Do you want me to open my heart to you, Doctor?" I said (1c). ♦ [Андрей:] Говорю вам как другу, единственному человеку, которому могу открыть свою душу (Чехов 5). [A.:] I say this to you as to a friend, the only man I can open my soul to (5c). ♦ ...В «Правде» появился подвал Шагинян, где она рассказывала, как подсудимые охотно открывают душу своим следователям и «сотрудничают с ними» на допросах... (Мандельштам 1). ...Shaginian wrote a half-page article in *Pravda* saying how gladly persons under investigation unburdened themselves to their interrogators and "co-operated" with them at their interrogations (1a).

Д-428 • ОТПУСТИ́ТЬ ДУ́ШУ НА ПОКАЯ́НИЕ [VP; subj: human; usu. imper; fixed WO] **1.** *obs* to have mercy on s.o., not kill or harm s.o.: отпустите душу на покаяние ≃ **spare me; spare my life; let me go ⟨be⟩.**

[Голос Земляники:] Отпустите, господа, хоть душу на покаяние, совсем прижали (Гоголь 4). [Z.'s Voice:] Don't crush me, gentlemen, for goodness' sake! Let me go (4c). ♦ Несколько разбойников вытащили на крыльцо Василису Егоровну, растрёпанную и раздетую донага... «Батюшки мои! – кричала бедная старушка. – Отпустите душу на покаяние» (Пушкин 2). Several brigands had just dragged Vasilisa Egorovna, disheveled and stripped naked, out on the porch..."Please, my dear fellows," shouted the poor old woman, "let me be" (2a).

2. *coll, usu. humor* to stop annoying s.o., leave s.o. alone: отпусти душу на покаяние ≃ **leave me in peace; let me be.**

Отпусти душу на покаяние! Я на все твои вопросы уже десять раз ответил. Let me be! I've already answered all your questions ten times over.

Д-429 • ПЕРЕВОРА́ЧИВАТЬ 〈ПЕРЕВЁРТЫВАТЬ obs〉/ПЕРЕВЕРНУ́ТЬ 〈ПЕРЕВОРОТИ́ТЬ〉 (ВСЮ) ДУ́ШУ чью, кого, кому [VP; subj: human or abstr] to disturb s.o. deeply, affect s.o. very strongly: X перевернул Y-ову душу ≃ **X shook Y (up);** [in limited contexts] **X almost broke Y's heart.**

Д-430 • ПЛЕВА́ТЬ/НАПЛЕВА́ТЬ 〈ПЛЮ́НУТЬ〉 В ДУ́ШУ кому coll [VP; subj: human] to insult what is most dear, sacred to s.o.: X наплевал Y-у в душу ≃ **X trampled on Y's feelings; X stomped all over Y's feelings.**

[Дор.:] А если кого и полюбишь, то его-то и бойся всех более. [Анна:] Да? [Дор.:] За твою ласку он тебя не пожалеет. Наплюёт в душу и посмеётся (Арбузов 1). [D.:] And if you should fall in love, fear him more than anyone else. [A.:] Really? [D.:] He won't spare you because you're fond of him. He'll trample on your feelings and laugh (1a).

Д-431 • ПО чью ДУ́ШУ (прийти, явиться и т. п.) *coll* [PrepP; Invar; the resulting PrepP is adv or predic (subj: human)] (to come in order to summon, see etc) a certain person (as specified by the modifier): X пришёл по Y-ову душу ≃ **X has come for 〈after〉 Y; X has come to get Y; Y is the one X wants 〈needs, has come for〉;** [in limited contexts] **X has tracked Y down; X is after Y's skin 〈hide, head〉; X is out to get Y; X is out for Y's blood.**

«А мы по вашу душу, хлопцы!» (Аксёнов 6). "We've tracked you down, boys!" (6a). ♦ Если они [конница] свищут в пяти верстах, то спрашивается, на что надеется гетман? Ведь по его душу свищут!.. Может быть, немцы за него заступятся? (Булгаков 3). If the cavalry is only three miles out of town, people asked, what hope can there be for the Hetman? And it's his blood they're out for....Perhaps the Germans will back him up? (3a).

Д-432 • ТРАВИ́ТЬ ДУ́ШУ 〈СЕ́РДЦЕ〉 кому coll [VP; subj: human or abstr; often infin (with зачем, незачем, ни к чему, не хочется etc) or neg imper] to cause s.o. emotional pain, often by saying sth. that upsets, distresses etc him: не трави Y-у душу ≃ **don't torment Y; don't make Y 〈Y's life〉 more miserable;** [in limited contexts] **don't rub salt into the wound 〈into Y's wounds〉.**

Эти детские воспоминания... травили [Саше] душу: для чего воспитывал в себе волю, для чего ковал характер? (Рыбаков 2). These memories of his childhood tormented him [Sasha] now: Why had he cultivated such willpower, why had he toughened his character? (2a). ♦ «Пойдём, Надька, на Максима посмотрим. Посмотрим, какие теперь мужики, и обратно». – «А чё [ungrammat = что] на него глядеть? Только душу травить. На чужое счастье не наглядишься» (Распутин 2). "Come on, Nadya, let's go take a look at Maxim. Let's see what the men look like now, and then we'll come back." "What is there to see? It'll just make me more miserable. You won't get any satisfaction looking at another's happiness" (2a).

Д-433 • ТЯНУ́ТЬ ЗА́ ДУШУ (кого) coll [VP] **1.** Also: **ТЯНУ́ТЬ ДУ́ШУ** (из кого, кому) coll [subj: human] to vex,

exasperate s.o. to an extreme degree (by one's annoying actions, pestering, deliberate slowness in recounting or relating sth. etc): X тянет из Y-а душу ≃ **X torments 〈tortures, harrows〉 Y; X makes Y 〈Y's life〉 miserable; X puts Y through torture;** [in refer. to persistent annoying actions] **X pesters 〈bugs〉 Y;** [in refer. to causing s.o. anxiety by being slow or reluctant to tell him sth.] **X keeps Y hanging; X has Y on pins and needles; X is keeping Y on tenterhooks.**

Ну что ты своими расспросами из меня душу тянешь? Why do you have to keep bugging me with your questions? ♦ «Понимаешь, какая штука, Лашков... Как бы это тебе...» – «Не тяни душу, Александр Петрович!» – «В общем, заходил тут ко мне один, интересовался: кто, мол, да что, мол, ты такое...» (Максимов 3). "Well, it's like this, Lashkov, see...how can I put it?" "Don't keep me on tenterhooks, Alexander Petrovich." "Well, then, a man called on me, wanted to know about you, who you were, what you were like..." (3a).

2. [subj: a noun denoting emotionally disturbing sounds, or a person or instrument producing such sounds] to cause s.o. emotional anguish, make him feel alarmed: X тянет Y-а за душу ≃ **X 〈person X's singing, person X's violin playing etc〉 is heartrending 〈tugs at Y's heartstrings, pulls at Y's heartstrings〉.**

Д-434 • НА ДЫБЫ́ [PrepP; Invar] **1.** стать, встать, подняться, поднять коня и т. п. [adv] (used in refer. to an animal, often a horse) (to rise up, go up, make a horse go up etc) on one's or its back legs, with the forelegs lifted up and the body in a vertical position: X встал на дыбы ≃ **X stood (up) on its hind legs;** [of a horse only] **X reared (up);** ‖ Y поднял коня ~ ≃ **person Y reared his horse.**

Помню только: рейс наш сопровождался тем, что вдоль дороги все собаки вставали на дыбы (Олеша 4). Still I do remember one thing, but only that: all the dogs stood up on their hind legs as we roared past them (4a).

2. стать, встать, подняться и т. п. ~ [adv] (of an object that is supposed to be positioned along a horizontal plane, as a wagon, car, or raft) (to end up etc) in a vertical position with one end at the bottom and the other at the top: X встал на дыбы ≃ **X got upended; X ended up tipped straight up in the air; X got tipped up on its end.**

3. Also: **СТАНОВИ́ТЬСЯ/СТАТЬ 〈ВСТАВА́ТЬ/ВСТАТЬ** и т. п.〉 **НА ДЫБЫ́** [subj-compl with copula or VP; subj: human, collect, or, rare, abstr] to protest sharply: X встал на дыбы ≃ [of a person] **X put up a fight; X bristled; X kicked up a fuss;** [of s.o.'s pride etc] **X reared up.**

Значит, сбросили немцы листовки, где упоминали Гамсуна, одна такая листовка попалась Гале, и она показала её Нине: смотри, мол, каков твой Гамсун... Нина, конечно, на дыбы: не может этого быть... (Рыбаков 1). So, the Germans had dropped these leaflets, which mentioned Hamsun, Galya got hold of one of them and showed it to Nina, as if to say, look at this Hamsun of yours! Nina, of course, bristled, it couldn't be true (1a). ♦ Базаров побледнел при одной этой мысли; вся его гордость так и поднялась на дыбы (Тургенев 2). Bazarov paled at the very thought; all his pride reared up within him (2c).

Д-435 • В ДЫМ substand [PrepP; Invar; adv (intensif)] **1.** ~ пьян(ый), напиться и т. п. Also: **В ДЫМИ́НУ; В ДРЕЗИ́НУ; В ДРАБАДА́Н** all substand (to be, get) extremely drunk: **stinking 〈blind, dead〉 drunk; drunk 〈stoned〉 out of one's mind; drunk as a skunk; pie-eyed; pickled; drunk as a lord.**

И опять ему снилась какая-то чертовщина. Бабка Наталья... протягивала ему горсть мятых вишен... А потом покойный начальник службы движения Егоркин... честил его на чём свет стоит... Следом за Егоркиным, выплыла из небытия собственная его — Лашкова — свадьба, на которой приходившийся ему тестем забойщик Илья Парфёныч Махоткин, пьяный в дымину, лез к нему целоваться... (Максимов 3). Once again all hell was let loose in his dreams. Granny Natalya...offered him a handful of dried [sic] cherries....Next comes Yegorkin, the traffic manager, long since dead...cursing him up hill and down dale....After Yegorkin, his own wedding floated up from oblivion, with his father-in-law Ilya Parfenich Makhotkin, a coal miner, stinking drunk, sidling up to kiss him... (3a). ♦ «Давно мы с тобой не пили, Лёха, — удовлетворённо похохатывал гость, — вернусь, напьёмся — нальёмся в драбадан». — «В доску!» — «В лоск!» (Максимов 1). "You and I haven't had a drink for ages, Lyonya," the visitor chuckled contentedly. "When I get back we'll get stuck in—we'll get drunk as lords!" "Completely plastered!" "Out of our skulls!" (1a).

2. [used with pfv verbs] ~ **поругаться, разругаться** *(с кем)* и т. п. (to have quarreled with s.o.) viciously: X и Y поругались в дым ≃ **X and Y had a terrible quarrel ⟨run-in⟩;** [in limited contexts] **X and Y made the fur ⟨the feathers⟩ fly.**

Д-436 • ДЫМ (СТОЍТ ⟨ИДЁТ/ПОШЁЛ⟩) КОРО-МЍСЛОМ ⟨СТОЛБО́М⟩ *(где)* coll [VP_subj (variants with verbs) or VP_subj with быть_ø; коромыслом is always in the final position] there is great activity, noise, disorder etc (in some place): дым стоял коромыслом ≃ **all hell broke ⟨was let⟩ loose; there was a fearful commotion; there was bedlam ⟨utter chaos⟩; things were ⟨went⟩ wild.**

Росшепер занимал три палаты. В первой недавно жрали... В смежной палате дым стоял коромыслом. На гигантской Росшеперовой кровати брыкались полураздетые нездешние девчонки (Стругацкие 1). Rosheper had a three-room suite. The first one contained the remains of a recent feast....In the adjoining room all hell had broken loose. Half-naked girls, imported from the capital, were kicking their legs on Rosheper's enormous bed (1a). ♦ В храмовском чулане стоял дым коромыслом (Максимов 3). All hell was let loose in Khramov's attic (3a). ♦ Представляете картину? Кухня. Дым коромыслом (Терц 5). Can you imagine the scene? A fearful commotion in the kitchen (5a). ♦ Деревянные коробки поселковых клубов распирало гремучей матерщиной и хмельным перегаром, в грязных и холодных гостиницах круглые сутки стоял дым коромыслом (Максимов 3). The workers' clubs were little wooden boxes bursting with earsplitting obscenities and alcoholic fumes. Each day in the filthy, unheated hotels was twenty-four hours of bedlam (3a).

Д-437 • НЕТ ДЫ́МА ⟨-у⟩ БЕЗ ОГНЯ́; ДЫ́МА БЕЗ ОГНЯ́ НЕ БЫВА́ЕТ [saying] there is always a reason why people begin to talk about s.o. or sth. (usu. said when it is believed that rumors, gossip etc have some basis): ≃ **there is no smoke without fire; where there's smoke, there's fire.**

Со злости он [Передонов] лгал на княгиню несообразные вещи. Рассказывал Рутилову да Володину, что был прежде её любовником... [Рутилов] думал, что без огня дыма не бывает: что-то, думал он, было между Передоновым и княгинею (Сологуб 1). In his anger Peredonov made up absurd stories about the Princess. He told Rutilov and Volodin too that he had formerly been her lover....[Rutilov] thought that there is no smoke without fire and that there had been something between Peredonov and the Princess (1a).

Д-438 • ДО ДЫР зачитанный, зачитывать *что* и т. п. *coll* [PrepP; Invar; modif or adv] (some book, journal etc has been read) so much that it is falling apart, the ink is smeared etc: **(sth. is read) to tatters and smudges; (sth. is read) till it's frayed and dog-eared.**

Все ничтожнейшие брошюры, выходившие в Берлине... где только упоминалось о Гегеле, выписывались,

зачитывались до дыр... (Герцен 2). Every insignificant pamphlet published in Berlin...was ordered and read to tatters and smudges...if only there was a mention of Hegel in it (2a).

Д-439 • ДЫ́РКА ОТ БУ́БЛИКА *coll, iron* [NP; sing only; fixed WO] (to get, be left with etc) absolutely nothing: **a whole lot of nothing; big (fat) zero ⟨nothing⟩;** [when contrasting s.o. who gets nothing with a person who gets a lot] **one person gets the doughnut, another gets the hole.**

Д-440 • ЛЕЗТЬ ВО ВСЕ ДЫ́РКИ *highly coll, usu. disapprov* [VP; subj: human; the verb may take the final position, otherwise fixed WO] to interfere or try to participate in too many things, showing excessive curiosity, being obtrusive, getting involved where one is not invited (and thus annoying others): X лезет во все дырки ≃ **X butts into everything; X sticks ⟨pokes⟩ his nose into everything; X meddles ⟨has a hand⟩ in everything;** [in limited contexts] **X is everywhere.**

Приехали тесть с тёщей. Лезут во все дырки, учат меня жить, настраивают жену против меня — настоящий ад! My in-laws have come to visit. They butt into everything, tell me how to live, and try to turn my wife against me. It's sheer hell!

Д-441 • ЗАТЫКА́ТЬ/ЗАТКНУ́ТЬ ДЫ́РЫ ⟨ДЫРУ́, ПРОРЕ́ХИ, ПРОРЕ́ХУ⟩ *coll* [VP; subj: human] to use s.o. or sth. to compensate immediately and temporarily for a deficiency in some area: X заткнул дыры ≃ **X used Y to fill in the gaps;** [in limited contexts] **X used person Y as a fill-in ⟨a stand-in⟩; X used thing Y to tide X over (for a little while); X used thing Y as a stopgap (measure).**

Начальство постоянно затыкает Корнейчуком дыры, давая ему задания, за которые никто не хочет браться. The administration is always using Korneichuk to fill in the gaps, giving him assignments no one else wants to handle.

Д-442 • ЗАТАИ́В ДЫХА́НИЕ [Verbal Adv; Invar; adv; fixed WO] **1. ждать, следить** *за кем-чем* и т. п. ~ (to wait, watch etc s.o. or sth.) anxiously, worriedly, intently (often when one is in danger, is afraid of frightening s.o. or sth. away, is awaiting s.o.'s reaction to an important question etc): **holding one's breath; with bated breath; scarcely ⟨hardly⟩ daring to breathe.**

...Рогатая мать-олениха всё смотрела и смотрела на мальчика. Затаив дыхание, мальчик вышел из-за камня... (Айтматов 1). ...She [the Horned Mother Deer] still looked and looked at the boy. Holding his breath, the boy came out from behind the rock... (1a). ♦ Шла обычная жизнь с обычными ночными обысками и арестами, ловлей «повторников» и прочими радостями. Люди трудились, затаив дыхание... (Мандельштам 2). This was just business as usual for us: night searches and arrests, the tracking down of people who had been in prison before, and other such joys. Everybody got on with his work, scarcely daring to breathe... (2a).

2. слушать *кого-что,* **следить** *за кем-чем* и т. п. (to listen to, watch s.o. or sth.) very attentively, with great interest: **with bated breath; with rapt attention.**

Сцену смерту Клеопатры и финальные сцены все слушают, затаив дыхание... (Гладков 1). We all listened with bated breath to the part about Cleopatra's death and the closing scenes (1a).

Д-443 • ДО ПОСЛЕ́ДНЕГО ДЫХА́НИЯ ⟨ИЗДЫХА́-НИЯ *obs,* **ВЗДО́ХА⟩** *lit* [PrepP; these forms only; adv; fixed WO] **1.** to the end of one's life, all one's life: **till ⟨to⟩ one's dying day; till ⟨to⟩ the end of one's days.**

«Я до последнего дыхания её [Россию] любить буду» (Гроссман 2). "I'll love Russia till my dying day" (2a).

2. биться, сражаться, защищать *кого-что* и т. п. ~ (to fight, defend s.o. or sth.) to the point of sacrificing one's life:

(right up) to one's dying ⟨last⟩ breath; to the ⟨one's⟩ death; to the bitter end.

«Долг наш защищать крепость до последнего нашего издыхания; об этом и говорить нечего. Но надобно подумать о безопасности женщин» (Пушкин 2). "...It is our duty to defend the fort to our last breath; that goes without saying. But we must think of the safety of the women" (2a).

Д-444 • **НЕ ПЕРЕВОДЯ́ ДЫХА́НИЯ** ⟨ДУ́ХА *obs*, ДУ́ХУ *obs*⟩ [Verbal Adv; these forms only; adv; fixed WO] **1.** ~ **вы́пить, осуши́ть** *что* и т. п. (to drink sth. etc) all at once, without stopping: **without pausing for breath; without taking a breath; in one go;** [in limited contexts] **in one ⟨a single⟩ gulp; in one swallow ⟨motion⟩.**

Изверг этот взял стакан, налил его до невозможной полноты и вылил его себе внутрь, не переводя дыхания... (Герцен 1). The monster took a tumbler, filled it incredibly full and drank it down without taking [a] breath... (1a).

2. работать, трудиться и т. п. ~ (to work etc) without stopping or pausing to rest: **nonstop; without a break.**

Д-445 • **Е́ЛЕ ⟨ЕДВА́, ЧУТЬ⟩ ДЫША́ТЬ** *coll* [VP; fixed WO] **1.** [subj: human] to be very weak, decrepit, or incurably ill: X еле дышит ≃ **X is on his last legs; X is on his way out; X is declining ⟨failing, sinking fast⟩.**

2. [subj: concr] to become dilapidated, useless, unable to carry out its function: X еле дышит ≃ **X is on its last legs; X is on its way out; X is about to fall apart; X has just about had it; X is dying;** [of a campfire etc] **X is dying down ⟨going out⟩.**

Мне нужна новая пишущая машинка, моя еле дышит. I need a new typewriter—mine is on its last legs.

Д-446 • **ЧЕМ ДЫ́ШИТ** *coll* [VP; subj: human; pres only; fixed WO] what interests, plans etc motivate one's actions and behavior: ...чем X дышит ≃ **...what X lives by; ...what makes X tick;** [in limited contexts] **...what X lives for.**

...Он для того, казалось, и начал этот разговор, чтобы слышать, что имеет ответить сын, что нажил он за последние, не связанные с домом годы самостоятельной жизни, чем дышит и какими правилами руководится (Распутин 4). He had brought up the subject to hear what his son would say, what he had become in the last years of independent life away from home, what he lived by and what principles guided him (4a). ♦ «Да вот товарищ Борщёв, — сказал он [Молоков] с легким сарказмом, — предлагает мне вместе с ним отстраниться от активной деятельности, уйти во внутреннюю эмиграцию». Но Борщёв был тоже парень не промах. «Дурак ты! — сказал он, поднимаясь и расправляя грудь. — Я тебя только пощупать хотел, чем ты дышишь» (Войнович 5). "Comrade Borshchev here," he [Molokov] said with a touch of sarcasm, "was just suggesting that he and I abandon our political activities and join the inner emigration." But you couldn't put anything over on Borshchev either. "You fool!" he said, rising and smoothing his chest. "I only wanted to feel you out and see what makes you tick" (5a). ♦ «Как же так выходит, секретарь? Живу я на виду у всех. Чем дышу, всякий в городе знает. С чем в революцию пришёл — тоже известно. Первым начинал и не последний кончил» (Максимов 3). "How do you make that out, secretary? I live a completely open life. Everybody in town knows what I live for. What I did for the revolution is also well known. I was one of the first to begin and the last to stop" (3a).

Д-447 • **ЧЁРТОВА ДЮ́ЖИНА** *coll, usu. humor* [NP; sing only; fixed WO] thirteen: **baker's dozen.**

< According to popular belief the number thirteen is unlucky (therefore «чёртова», "the devil's").

Е

Е-1 • **ГАЛО́ПОМ ПО ЕВРО́ПАМ** скакать, делать *что* *coll, disapprov* [Invar; adv; fixed WO] (usu. in refer. to traveling, reading, making a survey of sth. etc) (to do sth.) quickly and superficially: **(give sth.) a superficial ⟨quick⟩ look**; [in refer. to traveling, visiting museums etc] **(take) a whirlwind tour; just (hit) the high points ⟨highlights⟩**; [with the emphasis on treating sth. superficially] **barely ⟨hardly⟩ scratch the surface.** Cf. **Cook's tour; if it's Tuesday, this must be Belgium.**

Е-2 • **ЕДВА́ ТО́ЛЬКО ⟨ЛИШЬ⟩...; ЕДВА́ (ТО́ЛЬКО)... КАК** [subord Conj, temporal] used to show that the situation or action presented in the main clause immediately follows the situation or action presented in the subordinate clause: **hardly ⟨scarcely, barely, just⟩...when; no sooner...than; just as; as soon as; the moment ⟨the minute⟩...**

Едва он сделал шаг, как снова засвистело, и начальник связи поспешно отступил и прихлопнул дверь, — мина разорвалась метрах в десяти (Гроссман 2). He'd barely taken a step...when there was another whistle; he ducked back and closed the door as another mortar-bomb burst only ten metres away (2a). ♦ ...Едва Владимир выехал за околицу в поле, как поднялся ветер и сделалась такая метель, что он ничего не взвидел (Пушкин 3). ...No sooner had he [Vladimir] left the village behind and entered the fields than the wind rose, and such a blizzard developed that he could not see anything (3a). ♦ Едва только мы вышли из дому, начался проливной дождь. The moment we stepped out of the house it started to pour.

Е-3 • **ТИ́ШЕ Е́ДЕШЬ – ДА́ЛЬШЕ БУ́ДЕШЬ** [saying] you will accomplish what you set out to do faster if you do not rush (said jokingly to justify one's slow pace, or as advice not to try to work too fast): ≃ **haste makes waste; slow and steady wins the race; the more haste the less ⟨worse⟩ speed; more hurry, less speed; make haste slowly.**

Е-4 • **ЕДУ́Н НАПА́Л** *(на кого) substand, humor* [VP$_{subj}$; past only; fixed WO] s.o. is overcome by an intense desire to eat: на Х-а едун напал ≃ **all X wants to do (today etc) is eat ⟨stuff his face etc⟩; X is dying to have something to eat; X has an irresistible ⟨unbelievable etc⟩ desire to eat; X can't (seem to) stop eating.**

Е-5 • **С ЧЕМ ЕГО́ ⟨её, их⟩ ЕДЯ́Т** *coll, humor* [VP; 3rd pers pl with indef. refer. only; used as a subord clause (usu. after интересно, надо посмотреть, понять etc) or a question; fixed WO] (one wonders, wants to know, understands etc) what the essential characteristics of the person or thing just mentioned are, or what the meaning of the word or phrase in question is: с чем его ⟨её⟩ едят? ≃ **what is it?; what is he ⟨she, it⟩ (really) like?; what sort of person ⟨administrator etc⟩ is he ⟨she⟩?**; [in refer. to a device, machine etc] **how (exactly) does it work?; what (exactly) does it do ⟨is it used for⟩?; what's it for?**; [in refer. to a word or phrase] **what does that mean?**; ‖ я понял, с чем его ⟨её⟩ едят ≃ **I figured him ⟨her, it⟩ out; I got the hang of it; I got a handle on it.**

«У тебя есть модем?» — «А что это такое и с чем его едят?» "Do you have a modem?" "What's that, and what does it do?"

Е-6 • **(И) ЕЖУ́ ПОНЯ́ТНО** *highly coll* [these forms only; subj-compl with быть$_\emptyset$ (subj: это or a clause), pres only; fixed WO] the essence of some statement (action, fact etc) is so obvious, so clear that it is impossible not to understand it: это ~ ≃ **anyone ⟨any fool, any half-wit etc⟩ could tell ⟨see⟩ (that); it's (as) plain as day.**

Нина говорит, что не красит волосы, но и ежу понятно, что это неправда. Nina says she doesn't dye her hair, but any fool can see it's not true.

Е-7 • **Е́ЗДИТЬ ВЕРХО́М** *на ком coll, disapprov* [VP; subj: human or collect] to exploit s.o. whom one has subjected to one's will, use a person for one's own ends, make s.o. do what one wants: X ездит верхом на Y-е ≃ **X pushes ⟨bosses, orders⟩ Y around; X walks all over Y**; [in limited contexts] **X has Y wrapped around X's little finger.**

Е-8 • **ЕЙ-БО́ГУ** *coll* [Interj; Invar] used to express an emphatic confirmation or reinforcement of some statement (occas. colored by irritation, surprise etc): **really (and truly); honestly; honest to God; by God**; [in limited contexts] **I swear (to God).**

[Марья Андреевна:] Иван Иваныч, вы меня любите? [Милашин:] Люблю, Марья Андреевна, ей-богу, люблю!.. Я для вас готов жизнию пожертвовать (Островский 1). [М.А.:] Ivan Ivanych, do you love me? [M.:] I love you, Marya Andrevna, really and truly I love you....I'm ready to sacrifice my life for your sake (1a). ♦ «...Кадровые офицеры – все негодяи, ей-богу! Вы ведь из казаков? Да? Вот вашими руками они и хотят каштанчики из огня таскать» (Шолохов 4). "...The regular officers, they're all scoundrels, honestly they are! You're a Cossack, aren't you? Well, they want to use you to do their dirty work for them" (4a). ♦ «Вот ты всегда утверждал, что я глуп; ей-богу, брат, есть глупее меня!» (Достоевский 3). "Now, you've always maintained that I'm stupid: by God, brother, there are some that are stupider!" (3c). ♦ «Куда ты дела, разбойница, бумагу?» – «Ей-богу, барин, не видывала, опричь [*obs* = кроме] небольшого лоскутка, которым изволили прикрыть рюмку» (Гоголь 3). "What have you done with the sheet of paper, you thief?" "I swear I haven't seen any paper, master, except the little scrap you used to cover the glass" (3e). ♦ «Вам всё кажется, что у меня какие-то цели, а потому и глядите на меня подозрительно... Но как я ни желаю сойтись с вами, я всё-таки не возьму на себя труда разуверять вас в противном. Ей-богу, игра не стоит свеч...» (Достоевский 3). "You seem to think the whole time that I have certain ulterior motives and therefore you look upon me with suspicion....But no matter how much I'd like to be friends with you, I'm still not going to take upon myself the labor of convincing you to the contrary. The game's not worth the candle, I swear to God..." (3a).

Е-9 • **ЁЛКИ-ПА́ЛКИ ⟨ЁЛКИ-МОТА́ЛКИ, ЁЛКИ ЗЕЛЁНЫЕ⟩!** *highly coll* [Interj; these forms only; fixed WO] used to express annoyance, admiration, delight, surprise, bewilderment etc: **for crying out loud!; hell's bells!**; [in refer. to annoyance only] **drat!; hang it (all)!; shoot!**; [usu. in refer. to delight] **hot dog ⟨damn⟩!**; [usu. in refer. to surprise or bewilderment] **holy mackerel ⟨cow⟩!; what do you know!; well, I'll be!; balls of fire!**; [usu. in refer. to anxiety] **goodness gracious!; oh my!; dear me!**

Часовой, увидев такого странного человека, сразу подумал: ёлки-палки, шпион (Войнович 1). Catching sight of this odd individual, the sentry immediately thought: For crying out loud, a spy (1a). ♦ И показывает Вовик из-за пазухи чудо-юдо – апельсин. «Можешь потрогать». Трогаю – апельсин. Ёлки-моталки, апельсин! (Аксёнов 1). And Vovik opens his coat and shows me something wonderful—an orange. "You can touch it." I touch it—an orange. Hell's bells, an orange! (1a). ♦ «Смотрю: ёлки-палки, что время делает с нами! Разве я когда-нибудь узнал бы в этом облысевшем, как и я, человеке того молодого, как звон, красавца-лётчика в далёком сорок четвёртом году...» (Искандер 5). "I looked—balls of fire, what time does to us! How would I ever have recognized this man, now grown bald like me, as that handsome airman, young as a chime in faraway '44..." (5a).

E-10 • МЕЛИ́, ЕМЕ́ЛЯ, ТВОЯ́ НЕДЕ́ЛЯ [saying; often used in the abbreviated form «Мели, Емеля»] (said mockingly or sarcastically) you can talk as much as you want, but nobody takes what you say seriously: ≃ **keep ⟨go right on⟩ talking, (but) nobody's listening; talk all you like, but don't expect us to take you seriously; anything you say; sure, keep ⟨go right on⟩ talking; yeah, right.**

< «Мели» is the imperative of «молоть», "to grind." «Емеля» is a diminutive of the male name «Емельян». Formerly, in peasant families in Russia there was a weekly alternation of certain household chores among family members. One such chore was grinding flour.

E-11 • ЕРУНДА́ ⟨ЧЕПУХА́⟩ НА ПО́СТНОМ МА́СЛЕ *highly coll* [NP; fixed WO] (in refer. to stupid, meaningless, or insignificant talk, thoughts, actions etc) foolishness, not deserving of attention: **a bunch ⟨a lot⟩ of nonsense ⟨baloney, rubbish, bull etc⟩; hogwash; crapola; stuff and nonsense; horsefeathers; (unbelievable) drivel.**

Иногда она смеялась, иногда злилась, но более всего изумлялась тому, что чепуха на постном масле — все эти медиумы, планшетки, низшие духи, высшие духи, загробные голоса — дотащилась до наших дней (Трифонов 3). Sometimes they made her laugh, sometimes angry, but above all she was amazed that so much unbelievable drivel—all these mediums, planchettes, lower spirits, higher spirits, voices from beyond the grave—had actually persisted into the present day (3a).

E-12 • Е́СЛИ БЫ ДА КАБЫ́ *coll, often humor* [Invar; usu. indep. remark; fixed WO] just wishing for sth. will not make it come true: **if wishes were horses...**

< Part of the saying «Если бы да кабы, да во рту росли грибы, то был бы не рот, а целый огород».

E-13 • ЕСТЬ НЕМНО́ГО *coll;* **ЕСТЬ МАЛЕ́НЬКО** *substand* [sent; these forms only; usu. this WO] (used as a gentle confirmation of an observation, a thought, s.o.'s statement, or in response to a question) that is true to a certain extent: **there's some truth to that ⟨it⟩; there's a measure ⟨a grain⟩ of truth in that;** [in limited contexts] **one ⟨you⟩ could say that; one ⟨you⟩ might say so; your ⟨his etc⟩ words have a ring of truth to them; there's truth in what you say ⟨he says etc⟩.**

E-14 • ЕСТЬ ПРО́СИТ *highly coll* [VP; subj: usu. a noun denoting footwear, parts of footwear, or clothes; pres or past] s.o.'s shoes (clothes etc) are in bad condition, in need of repair: X есть просит ≃ **X needs mending; X needs to be patched (up); X is worn out; X is in sad shape; X has holes in it;** [of footwear only] **X needs to be taken to the shoemaker.**

E-15 • ...И ЕСТЬ *substand* [Particle] used as part of either an answer or a rejoinder to provide an affirmative response or confirm that the person, thing, action etc in question is, in reality, precisely as he or it has been described (whereas in Russian a relevant word from the preceding context is always repeated before the idiom, some English equivalents do not require such repetition): *that he ⟨it etc⟩ is;* **...he ⟨it etc⟩ is; ...is what he ⟨it etc⟩ is all right; he ⟨it etc⟩ sure is; (yup ⟨ay(e) etc⟩,) that's him ⟨her, it etc⟩;** [with verbs] *that* **I ⟨you etc⟩ did; I ⟨he etc⟩ sure did.**

«По современным нормам, она просто святая». — «Святая и есть» (Битов 2). "By modern standards she's a saint." "A saint she is" (2a). ♦ «Ну, поворачивайся, толстобородый!» — обратился Базаров к ямщику. «Слышь, Митюха, — подхватил другой... ямщик... — барин-то тебя как прозвал? Толстобородый и есть» (Тургенев 2). "Well, stir your stumps, greatbeard!" said Bazarov to the driver of the stage horses. "Hear that, Mitya!" cried his mate...."Hear what the gentleman called ye? Greatbeard—it's what you are all right" (2a). ♦ «Помощниками Деникина нас величают... А кто же мы? Выходит, что помощники и есть, нечего обижаться. Правда-матка глаза заколола...» (Шолохов 4). "They call us accomplices of Denikin....And what are we? That's just what we are. So why get huffy about it? It stings because it's true" (4a). ♦ «Гляди, Григорий, никак Майданниковых пристань?» — «Она и есть» (Шолохов 2). "Look, Grigory, isn't that the Maidannikovs' pier?" "Ay, that's it" (2a).

E-16 • КАК ЕСТЬ *substand* [intensif Particle] **1.** completely and positively: **absolutely;** ‖ ~ **ничего** ≃ **nothing at all; nothing whatsoever; not a damn ⟨blessed⟩ thing;** ‖ **всё как есть** ≃ **the whole deal ⟨scoop⟩; the whole kit and caboodle;** ‖ **один** ~ ≃ **completely ⟨utterly⟩ alone; all alone;** [in limited contexts] **(all) alone in the world.**

2. (used to emphasize that a person or thing has all the qualities characteristic of whatever he or it is being called) genuine: **a real ⟨an honest-to-goodness, a true⟩** [NP]; **a** [NP] **if ever there was one.**

3. *obs* (used to emphasize the truth of a statement) definitely: **you bet (one did ⟨will etc⟩); one sure (did ⟨will etc⟩).**

E-17 • КАКО́Й НИ (НА) ЕСТЬ *coll* [AdjP; modif; fixed WO] it is inconsequential what kind; any representative(s) of the group in question (often with the implication that even an inferior one or ones is or are better than nothing): **any (kind ⟨sort⟩) at all; any that's available ⟨you have handy etc⟩; some sort of; a..., it doesn't matter what kind;** [in limited contexts] **what ⟨whatever⟩** [NP] **one has ⟨there is etc⟩.**

«Где у вас штопор? Дайте нож — колбасу нарезать. И какие ни на есть тарелки. Рюмки? Вот они» (Аржак 2). "Where's the corkscrew? Give me a knife to cut the sausage. And any plates you have handy. Glasses? There they are" (2a). ♦ [Кусаев] из кожи лез вон, чтоб... в лагере в какие ни на есть начальники попасть (Иоффе 1). ...In camp, [Kusayev] was eager to do his utmost to become some sort of chief (1a). ♦ «...Аграфена Александровна для того и выйдут за них, чтобы всё на себя отписать и какие ни на есть капиталы на себя перевести-с» (Достоевский 1). "...Agrafena Alexandrovna will marry him in order to get it all down in her name and transfer whatever capital there is to herself, sir" (1a).

E-18 • КТО НИ (НА) ЕСТЬ *coll* [NP; subj or obj; fixed WO] it is inconsequential who, any person or people who might be involved, regardless of who he or they might be: **anyone ⟨anybody⟩ at all; absolutely anyone ⟨anybody⟩; anyone, it doesn't matter who; anyone who is available ⟨who can etc⟩;** [only when все or каждый is stated or implied] **anyone and everyone; everyone and his brother ⟨uncle etc⟩.**

Заприте шкаф с документацией: нельзя, чтобы кто ни на есть приходил и брал то, что ему нужно. Lock the file cabinet: we can't have anyone and everyone coming and taking whatever they need.

E-19 • ПОЕДО́М ЕСТЬ/СЪЕСТЬ *(кого) coll* [VP; usu. impfv; if pfv, usu. fut; more often this WO] **1.** [subj: a noun denoting insects (комары, мошкара etc)] to bite s.o. continuously: комары ⟨мошкара и т. п.⟩ (Y-а) поедом едят ≃ **mosquitoes ⟨gnats etc⟩ are eating Y alive.**

2. [subj: human] to make life horrible for s.o., usu. through incessant faultfinding, reproaches etc: X Y-а поедом ест ≃ **X is eating Y alive; X makes Y's life miserable; X never lets up (on Y); X is forever ⟨always⟩ on Y's case ⟨back⟩;** [in limited contexts] **X keeps ⟨is always etc⟩ nagging at Y; all X does is ⟨knows is to⟩ nag, nag, nag; X bullies Y.**

«Тёмен, ленив, поди, русский мужичок... Ты видел, как он сало солит? Набросает в бочку кусками и рад. А попробуй кто в деревне покоптить или повялить, поедом съедят...» (Максимов 3). "He's just ignorant and idle, the Russian peasant....Have you ever seen how he salts fat bacon? Throws lumps of it into a barrel and thinks he's smart. Just let anybody in the village try smoking or dry-curing it: They'll eat him alive..." (3a). ♦ [Кабанов:] ...[Мать] всё приставала: «Женись да женись, я хоть бы поглядела на тебя, на женатого»! А теперь поедом ест, проходу не даёт – всё за тебя (Островский 6). [K.:] ...She [Mother] never stopped saying, "Get married, that's what you should do, get married. If only I'd see you married." And now she never lets up, never gives me a minute's peace. And all because of you (6f). ♦ «Вот, Семерик, какая у тебя была жена, а ты её всю жизнь поедом ел!» (Кузнецов 1). "Look, Semerik, what a wonderful wife you had, yet you kept nagging at her all her life!" (1b). ♦ [Анисья:] Ни работы от тебя, ни радости. Только поедом ешь (Толстой 1). [A.:] One gets neither work nor pleasure out of you. All you know is to nag, nag, nag (1c). ♦ [Кулигин:] И не от воров они запираются, а чтоб люди не видали, как они своих домашних едят поедом да семью тиранят (Островский 6). [K.:] It wasn't to keep thieves out that they bolted themselves in, but to prevent people from seeing the way they bully their servants and oppress their families (6d).

E-20 • СКÓЛЬКО НИ (НА) ЕСТЬ *coll* [AdvP; these forms only; adv; fixed WO] it is inconsequential how much or many, all belonging to the group or type in question (when in refer. to s.o.'s needing, desiring etc sth., often implies that even an insufficient amount is better than nothing): **however much (there is ⟨you have etc⟩); however many (there are ⟨you have etc⟩); whatever (you've got ⟨is available etc⟩); as much ⟨many⟩ as (you've got etc);** [only when всё or все is stated or implied] **every single one ⟨last bit, last one etc⟩.**

«...Стоят ли, батюшка Дмитрий Фёдорович, здешние мужики такой ласки, али вот девки?.. Ему ли, нашему мужику, цигарки курить, а ты им давал. Ведь от него смердит, от разбойника. А девки все, сколько их ни есть, вшивые» (Достоевский 1). "...Are they worth such pampering, our peasants, or the girls, Dmitri Fyodorovich?...It's not for our peasant to smoke cigars—and you did give them out. They all stink, the bandits. And the girls have lice, every last one of them" (1a).

E-21 • ТАК (ОНÓ) И ЕСТЬ *coll* [sent; these forms only; fixed WO] some assumption (conclusion, suspicion, statement etc) is entirely correct: **just as I thought ⟨he said etc⟩; and so it is ⟨it was, one does etc⟩; right you are ⟨I was etc⟩; you're ⟨I was etc⟩ right;** [when the idiom is used to confirm the expected existence, presence etc of s.o. or sth.] **there he ⟨it etc⟩ is.**

«Ах, вот и Феня с письмом! Ну, так и есть, опять от поляков, опять денег просят!» (Достоевский 2). "Ah, here's Fenya with a letter! Well, just as I thought, it's from the Poles again, asking for money again" (2a). ♦ Вдруг слышу быстрые и неровные шаги... Верно, Грушницкий... Так и есть! (Лермонтов 1). Suddenly I heard quick, uneven steps....Probably Grushnitsky... and so it was (1b). ♦ [Шаманов:] У меня такое впечатление, что ты хочешь от меня чего-то невозможного. [Кашкина:] Боюсь, что так оно и есть (Вампилов 2). [Sh.:] I have the impression you expect the impossible of me. [K.:] I'm afraid you're right (2a).

E-22 • ЧТО НИ (НА) ЕСТЬ¹ *coll* [NP; subj or obj; fixed WO] it is inconsequential what; anything, regardless of what it might be: **anything at all; absolutely anything; anything, it doesn't matter what; anything that's available ⟨handy etc⟩;** [only when всё is stated or implied] **anything and everything; anything in the world.**

«Что тебе дать поесть?» – «Что ни на есть, лишь бы побыстрее». "What shall I get you to eat?" "Anything at all, as long as it's quick." ♦ Ноздрёв во многих отношениях был многосторонний человек... В ту же минуту он предлагал вам ехать куда угодно, хоть на край света, войти в какое хотите предприятие, менять всё, что ни есть, на всё, что хотите (Гоголь 3). Nozdryov was a man of great versatility in many ways....In the same breath he would offer to go with you anywhere you liked, even to the ends of the earth, to become your partner in any enterprise you might choose, to exchange anything in the world for anything you like (3a).

E-23 • (самый) ЧТО НИ (НА) ЕСТЬ² *coll* [intensif Particle; usu. preceded by самый; foll. by NP or AdjP; fixed WO] used to express that s.o. or sth. exhibits the highest or most extreme degree possible (of the characteristic named) or represents the ultimate example (of the type, group etc named): **the most ⟨the worst etc⟩...you can imagine ⟨imaginable, in the world, you've ever seen, you've ever set eyes on, that ever existed etc⟩; a...if ever there was one;** [in limited contexts] **s.o. ⟨sth.⟩ couldn't be (a) more...**

...Через год, в мае, было подано от имени его сыновей (он, конечно, об этом не знал) прошение, в самом что ни на есть пышном, душещипательном стиле... (Набоков 1). A year later, in May, a petition was submitted in his sons' names (he, of course, knew nothing of this), in the most florid and tear-jerking style imaginable (1a). ♦ Самая что ни на есть пытка и с питьём и с оправкой (Марченко 1). It's the worst kind of torture you can imagine, both with the drinking and the toilet (1a). ♦ «Покажи тебе самую что ни есть раскрасавицу – ты даже глазом не поведёшь. Потому что биотоки отрицательные подключат» (Айтматов 2). "You could be shown the most ravishing creature you've ever set eyes on and you'll not even bat an eyelid. This will be because the bio-currents will cut out this feeling" (2a). ♦ «Ну, а теперь, друзья-товарищи и граждане-враги, – говорит Дзюба, – нехай выступает перед нами самая что ни на есть реакционная шкура мракобеса...» (Алешковский 1). "Now, comrade-friends and citizen-enemies," said Dziuba, "we're going to hear a speech by the most reactionary obscurantist asshole who ever existed..." (1a). ♦ Упомянули Антона. Я сказал, что он самый что ни на есть русский, глубинный русский... (Зиновьев 2). [context transl] Anton's name was mentioned. I said that he was the most Russian of Russians, profoundly Russian... (2a).

E-24 • ВСЁ ЕЩЁ [AdvP; Invar; adv; fixed WO] used to emphasize that the action in question continues up to the present moment or continued up to the specified moment in the past: **still;** [in limited contexts] **keep ⟨go on⟩ (doing sth.);** [with negated verbs] **not (...) yet.**

Смердяков, как и давеча, совсем не пугаясь, всё пытливо следил за ним [Иваном]. Всё ещё он никак не мог победить своей недоверчивости... (Достоевский 2). Smerdyakov kept watching him [Ivan] inquisitively, as before, with no trace of fear. He still could not manage to get over his mistrust... (2a).

E-25 • ЕЩЁ БЫ! *coll* [AdvP; Invar; used as affirm particle; may be foll. by не + a relevant word or phrase from the preceding context: ещё бы я не знал, ещё бы (мне) не знать, ещё бы не серьёзно etc] **1.** used as an emphatic affirmative response to a question or rejoinder to a statement: **(but) of course (I do ⟨he was etc⟩)!; and how!; I'll say!; I should say so!; you said it!; you bet!**

«Но по сравнению с общими работами ведь здесь и вправду лучше вам?» – «Ещё бы!» (Гинзбург 2). "But compared to manual labor outside, you really are better off here, aren't you?" "And how!" (2a). ♦ [Букин:] Итак, на свадьбе будет ректор. Ты рада? [Маша:] Ещё бы (Вампилов 3). [B.:] And so the Provost is coming to the wedding. Are you glad? [M.:] I'll say (3b). ♦ [Городничий:] Как ты думаешь, Анна Андреевна: можно влезть в генералы? [Анна Андреевна:] Ещё бы! конечно, можно (Гоголь 4). [Mayor:] What do you think, Anna Andreyevna?

Could I become a general? [A.A.:] I should say so! Indeed you can (4f). ♦ [Катя:] Мне не нравится в Москве... У нас лучше, верно? [Алексей:] Ещё бы! (Розов 1). [K.:] I don't like it here, in Moscow. Where we live, it's better—true? [A.:] You said it! (1a). ♦ «Марджи, ну а вы, конечно, знаете, кто такой Макс Огородников?» — «Ещё бы!» (Аксёнов 12). "Margie, of course, you know who Mr. Ogorodnikov is?" "You bet!" (12a). ♦ «Ты это серьёзно?» — тихо спросил Малькольмов. «Ещё бы не серьёзно» (Аксёнов 6). [context transl] "Do you mean that seriously?" Malkolmov asked quietly. "Never been more serious" (6a).

2. there is nothing unusual (in what has been stated), nothing different could be expected (usu. foll. by an explanation as to why): **(there's) nothing surprising about ⟨in⟩ that; no wonder; of course (not);** [in limited contexts] **how could s.o. not (do sth.) ⟨sth. not (happen) etc⟩.**

...Никто не молчал, все сразу говорили, гудели, галдели, и общий рокот как волнами бил по комнате. Ну, ещё бы! — российская любовь излить душу (Солженицын 5). ...Not one of them [was] silent, all [were] talking at once, babbling and bawling, so that the general din swept across the room in waves. Nothing surprising in that! The Russian loves to pour out his heart (5a). ♦ Уходя, он скользнул взглядом по моей офицерской шашке «за храбрость» с анненским красным темляком, одиноко висевшей на пустой летней вешалке, и, как мне показалось, болезненно усмехнулся. Ещё бы: город занят неприятелем, а в квартире на виду у всех вызывающе висит русское офицерское оружие! (Катаев 3). When about to leave, he let his eye rest for a moment on my officer's sword, with its red St Anne sword-knot "for bravery," which hung forlornly on the empty summer hat-stand, and, so it seemed to me, a pained smile crossed his lips. No wonder. The city was occupied by enemy troops, and here, hung up challengingly for all to see, were the arms of a Russian officer! (3a). ♦ «Впрочем, мы друг друга понять не можем; я по крайней мере не имею чести вас понимать». — «Ещё бы! — воскликнул Базаров. — Человек всё в состоянии понять — и как трепещет эфир и что на солнце происходит; а как другой человек может иначе сморкаться, чем он сам сморкается, этого он понять не в состоянии» (Тургенев 2). "We cannot understand one another; or, at least, I have not the honour of understanding you." "Of course not!" exclaimed Bazarov. "Man is capable of understanding everything—the vibration of ether and what's going on in the sun; but why another person should blow his nose differently from him—that, he's incapable of understanding" (2c).

E-26 • ЕЩЁ И ЕЩЁ [AdvP; Invar; adv; fixed WO] (to do sth., sth. happens) repeatedly, each instance being followed by another (often with the action becoming more intense with each repetition): **again and (yet) again; over and over (again); time and (time) again;** [in limited contexts] **more and more.**

Он [Раскольников] спешил к Свидригайлову... Дорогой один вопрос особенно мучил его: был ли Свидригайлов у Порфирия? Сколько он мог судить и в чём бы он присягнул — нет, не был! Он подумал ещё и ещё, припомнил всё посещение Порфирия, сообразил: нет, не был, конечно, не был! (Достоевский 3). He [Raskolnikov] was hurrying to Svidrigailov....One question especially tormented him on the way: had Svidrigailov gone to Porfiry? No, as far as he was able to judge, he had not—he would have sworn to it! He thought it over again and again, recalled Porfiry's

entire visit, and realized: no, he had not; of course he had not! (3c). ♦ Ещё и ещё падали на стол снимки, и вот мелькнул покатый, тупой (ни дать ни взять мучной ларь) архиерейский дом... (Домбровский 1). More and more photographs fell onto the table. I caught a glimpse of a squat, square archbishop's palace (looking exactly like a flour-bin)... (1a).

E-27 • (И ⟨ДА⟩) ЕЩЁ КА́К coll [these forms only; adv (intensif) or indep. sent; may be foll. by the verb used in the preceding context; more often this WO] used to emphasize the intensity of an action, desire, quality, characteristic etc, and/or the certainty that an action did or will occur: **and how!; you bet (s.o. ⟨sth.⟩ will ⟨does etc⟩)!; doesn't ⟨wouldn't etc⟩ s.o. just!; (s.o. ⟨sth.⟩ is ⟨does, will etc⟩,) all right; that one did ⟨it will etc⟩;** [as a response] **you can say that again!**

«Скучал?» — спрашивает она. «Ещё как», — отвечаю я (Аксёнов 8). "Did you miss me?" she would ask. "And how!" I would reply (8a). ♦ [Ким:] Я тоже буду таким... таким... [Алла:] Не будешь. [Ким:] Почему это? Ещё как буду! Вот увидишь (Розов 4). [K.:] I'm going to be like them. [A.:] You never will be. [K.:] Why not? You bet I will! Wait and see (4a). ♦ А ведь если [Антонина] не лучше других была, то и не хуже, право! Мужика ей не хотелось? Ещё как! (Максимов 3). If she [Antonina] was no better-looking than most, she was no worse either. Didn't she want a husband? Didn't she just! (3a). ♦ [Колесов:] Пойти к геологам, авось рассмешат... [Маша:] Ещё как рассмешат (Вампилов 3). [K.:] I'm going to join the geologists, perhaps they can make me laugh. [M.:] They'll make you laugh all right (3a). ♦ Кровь кинулась Григорию в голову, когда напал глазами на свой курень... «Не щипет [ingrammat = щиплет] глаза?» — улыбнулся Пантелей Прокофьевич, оглядываясь, и Григорий, не лукавя и не кривя душой, сознался: «щипет... да ишо [ingrammat = ещё] как!..» (Шолохов 3). The blood rushed to Grigory's head as his eyes rested on his own home....."Aren't your eyes stinging?" Pantelei smiled as he looked round at his son, and Grigory confessed frankly and without dissembling, "Yes they are—that they are!" (3a).

E-28 • (НУ) ВО́Т ЕЩЁ! coll, impol [Interj; these forms only; fixed WO] (used as a response in a dialogue when one resents a question put to him, pointedly refuses to do what is asked of him, or strongly disagrees with the interlocutor's statement) what you are saying, suggesting, asking is preposterous: **what do you mean!; the ⟨like⟩ hell I was ⟨did, am etc⟩; what (on earth) are you talking about!; you've got to be kidding!; you must be out of your mind!; don't be ridiculous!;** [in limited contexts] **what ⟨whatever⟩ next!; of course not!; that's a good one!; what kind of (a) question is that!**

[Подколёсин:] Послушай, Илья Фомич, знаешь ли что? Поезжай-ка ты сам. [Кочкарёв:] Ну, вот ещё: с ума сошёл разве? (Гоголь 1). [P.:] Listen, Ilya Fomich; I tell you what! You go by yourself. [K.:] Whatever next! Have you taken leave of your senses? (1a). ♦ «Переоденешься в сухое и ляжешь в постель», — сказал Виктор. «Вот ещё!» — сказала Ирма (Стругацкие 1). "You'll change into something dry and get into bed," said Victor. "That's a good one!" said Irma (1a). ♦ «А не знаешь, уехал он с Анфисой Петровной?» — «Вот ещё!» (Абрамов 1). "D'you know if he left again with Anfisa Petrovna?" "What kind of question is that?" (1a).

Ж-1 • **БРАТЬ/ВЗЯТЬ ЗА ЖА́БРЫ** *кого highly coll* [VP; subj: human] to pressure s.o. into acting or force s.o. to act as one demands: X взял Y-а за жабры ≃ **X put the screws ⟨the squeeze⟩ on Y; X put ⟨turned⟩ the heat on Y; X took ⟨grabbed, got⟩ Y by the throat; X strong-armed Y.**

Полный комплект [номеров] по идее должен был быть у секретаря Лодера, агента Органов… Но когда его взяли за жабры, выяснилось, что он загнал его на чёрном рынке за валюту атташе одного посольства (Зиновьев 1). In theory Idleader's secretary, a secret police agent…should have had a full set [of copies]….But when the screws were put on him, it turned out that he had sold them on the black market to an attaché from a foreign embassy in exchange for foreign currency (1a).

Ж-2 • **БРОСА́ТЬ/БРО́СИТЬ ⟨КИДА́ТЬ/КИ́НУТЬ⟩ В ЖАР (И В ХО́ЛОД ⟨И ХО́ЛОД⟩)** *кого (от чего)*; **БРОСА́ТЬ ⟨КИДА́ТЬ⟩ ТО В ЖАР, ТО В ХО́ЛОД** [VP; impers; last var.: impfv only, fixed WO with the verb movable] s.o. becomes extremely agitated, experiences anxiety, alarm: X-а бросает в жар (и холод) ≃ **X breaks into ⟨out in⟩ a cold sweat; X feels hot (and cold) all over; X gets hot and cold by ⟨in⟩ turns.**

Ольга не показывалась… и время тянулось медленно. Обломова опять стало кидать в жар и холод (Гончаров 1). …Olga did not show herself, and time dragged on slowly. Oblomov was again getting hot and cold in turns (1a).

Ж-3 • **ПА́ХНЕТ/ЗАПА́ХЛО ЖА́РЕНЫМ** *highly coll* [VP; impers] **1.** sth. promises profit: it ⟨sth.⟩ **smells of money; there's money to be made.**

У этого спекулянта большие связи, он всегда знает, где пахнет жареным. This speculator has good connections and always knows where there's money to be made.

2. Also: **ПА́ХНЕТ/ЗАПА́ХЛО ПАЛЁНЫМ** *highly coll* danger from or punishment for some wrongdoing, illegal actions etc is imminent: **one smells trouble (coming); there's danger in the air; it looks like they've got me ⟨you etc⟩; it looks like the jig is up.**

«Так, — сказал Губошлёп, не утрачивая своей загадочной весёлости. — Что-то палёным пахнет» (Шукшин 1). "Damn," said Fat Lip, without losing his enigmatic gaiety. "It looks like they've got us" (1a).

Ж-4 • **НИ ЖА́РКО ⟨НИ ТЕПЛО́⟩ НИ ХО́ЛОДНО** *кому от чего*; **НИ ХО́ЛОДНО НИ ЖА́РКО** *all coll* [these forms only; impers predic with быть∅; usu. pres] sth. makes no difference to s.o.: X-у от Y-а ни жарко ни холодно ≃ **X doesn't care (one way or the other); Y doesn't matter (to X) one way or the other; it's all the same to X; X is neither hot nor cold about Y; [in limited contexts] for all X cares.**

…В глазах большинства это были единичные жертвы, от исчезновения которых городу было ни тепло ни холодно… (Салтыков-Щедрин 2). …In the eyes of the majority, these were but isolated victims whose disappearance did not matter one way or the other (2a). ♦ Шагинян и сейчас продолжает плодотворную деятельность. При разборе дел всяких «подписантов» она суёт слуховую трубку им в лицо, чтобы не упустить ни слова. Пусть живёт хоть до ста лет вместе с Фединым и присными. Мне от этого ни холодно ни жарко (Мандельштам 2). Even now Shaginian has not ceased her fruitful labors. Attending meetings at which "protest signers" are called to account, she thrusts her ear trumpet right in their faces, not to miss a single word. For all I care, she can live to be a hundred years, together with Fedin and his tribe (2a).

Ж-5 • **С ЖА́РОМ** [PrepP; Invar; adv] (to do sth.) with excitement, emotional intensity: (say sth. ⟨answer etc⟩) **fervently ⟨with ardor, ardently, zealously, hotly⟩; (speak ⟨say sth. etc⟩ with great feeling; (object ⟨argue, debate sth. etc⟩) heatedly ⟨with a passion, vehemently⟩; (undertake sth. ⟨set about sth. etc⟩) eagerly ⟨with enthusiasm⟩; (kiss s.o.) passionately.**

«Ручаюсь вам за успех», — отвечал я с жаром (Пушкин 2). "I'll vouch for our success," I answered fervently (2a). "I guarantee success," I replied with ardour (2b). ♦ «Я не от твоих речей покраснел и не за твои дела, а за то, что я то же самое, что и ты». — «Ты-то? Ну, хватил немного далеко». — «Нет, не далеко», — с жаром проговорил Алёша (Достоевский 1). "I blushed not at your words and not at your deeds, but because I'm the same as you." "You? Well, that's going a bit too far." "No, not too far," Alyosha said hotly (1a). ♦ Аркадий с жаром заговорил о покойнице; а Базаров между тем принялся рассматривать альбомы (Тургенев 2). Arkady began to speak with great feeling about his dead mother, while Bazarov sat and looked through some albums (2c). ♦ Пикейные жилеты в числе сорока человек уже оправились от потрясения… и с жаром толковали о пан-Европе… (Ильф и Петров 2). The forty piqué vests had now recovered from their shock…and were heatedly discussing Pan-Europe… (2a).

Ж-6 • **ДАВА́ТЬ/ДАТЬ ⟨ЗАДАВА́ТЬ/ЗАДА́ТЬ⟩ ЖА́РУ** *кому highly coll* [VP; subj: human; usu. pfv] **1.** to scold s.o. severely: X дал Y-у жару ≃ **X gave Y hell; X gave it to Y good; X chewed ⟨bawled⟩ Y out; X raked Y over the coals; X let Y have it (with both barrels); Y caught hell (from X).**

2. [subj: usu. pl] to fight s.o. (usu. a hostile army, the enemy) vehemently; to overwhelm, defeat s.o.: X-ы задали Y-ам жару ≃ **Xs gave it to Ys hot; Xs crushed ⟨clobbered, routed⟩ Ys; Xs ran Ys into the ground.**

Перестрелка стала стихать, и из боковой улицы высыпали оживлённые говором солдаты. «Цел, Петров?» — спрашивал один. «Задали, брат, [французам] жару. Теперь не сунутся», — говорил другой (Толстой 4). When the shooting on both sides began to die down, soldiers in animated conversation streamed out of a side street. "Not hurt, Petrov?" asked one. "We gave it to them [the French] hot, brother. They won't mess around with us again," said another (4a).

3. to do sth. very intensely, with maximum effort: X даёт жару ≃ **X is going all out; X is really going at it ⟨at his work etc⟩; X is going at it ⟨at his work etc⟩ hammer and tongs; [usu. in refer. to a physical activity, task etc] X is (doing sth.) with might and main.**

Ж-7 • **ПОДДАВА́ТЬ/ПОДДА́ТЬ ЖА́РУ ⟨ПА́РУ⟩** *highly coll* [VP] **1.** Also: **ПОДБАВЛЯ́ТЬ/ПОДБА́ВИТЬ ЖА́РУ** [subj: human] to make an already intense or difficult situation even more intense, volatile etc by one's actions or words (usu. by provoking greater anger or hostility): X поддал жару ≃ **X added fuel to the fire ⟨the flames⟩; X stoked the fire; X fanned the flames; X added to the commotion ⟨the excitement, the uproar etc⟩.**

Всё началось с маленькой бумажки… «С получением сего, — значилось в бумажке, — *предлагается* вам в недельный срок освободить помещение бывш. гостиницы „Каир"…» — «Как! — нервно вскричал начальник „Геркулеса". — Они пишут мне „предлагается!" Мне, подчинённому непосредственно центру! Да что они, с ума там посходили? А?» — «Они бы ещё написали „предписывается"», — поддала жару Серна Михайловна (Ильф и Петров 2). It all began with a small piece of paper…."With effect from receipt of this," the note read, "you are *instructed* to vacate the premises of the former Cairo Hotel within one week...." "What!" screeched the head of the Hercules. "They say I'm instructed! Me! Someone who's directly responsible to Moscow! Have they gone mad or something!" "They might just [as well have] said 'directed,'" said Serna Mikhailovna, adding fuel to the fire (2a). ♦ «...Вчера я, спьяну, проболтался ему, дорогой идучи, о разных глупостях... о разных... между прочим, что ты боишься, будто он... наклонен к помешательству...»... — «Ну, а мы вчера ещё жару поддали, ты то есть, этими рассказами-то... о маляре-то; хорош разговор, когда он, может, сам на этом с ума сошёл!» (Достоевский 3). "Yesterday, when drunk, I blabbed all sorts of trash to him on the way home...all sorts...among other things that you were afraid he might be...inclined to madness...."..."Well, and then we stoked the fire yesterday, or rather you did, with those stories...about the painter; a fine thing to talk about when that's maybe what's driving him crazy!" (3a). ♦ ...В первый же вечер он [Сергей] поразил Ольгу Васильевну потрясающим искусством [читать слова наоборот]... Произвело огромное впечатление. Влад подбавлял жару: «Да что там — гений! Самый обыкновенный гений...» (Трифонов 3). ...On that first evening he [Sergei] had amazed Olga with this bizarre skill [of being able to say words backward]....It produced an enormous impression. Vlad added to the excitement by announcing, "But he's a genius. A plain, ordinary genius" (3a).

2. [subj: human] to begin to act more energetically: поддайте жару! ≃ **get it in gear!; step up the pace!; get (it) moving!;** [in refer. to physical labor only] **put some muscle into it!**

3. ~ *(кому)* [subj: usu. human, occas. abstr] to incite, induce s.o. to act more energetically, increase s.o.'s interest in sth.: X поддал Y-у жару ≃ **X spurred Y on; X fired Y up; X kindled a fire ⟨a flame⟩ in Y.**

Ж-8 • ЖЕВА́ТЬ ⟨ПЕРЕЖЁВЫВАТЬ⟩ ЖВА́ЧКУ [VP; subj: human] to repeat sth. again and again in a tedious and irksome manner: X будет пережёвывать жвачку ≃ **X will go on and on about the same thing; X will harp on the same string; X will rehash the same old thing; X will repeat the same old stuff (over and over again).**

На семинарах было очень скучно: докладчики один за другим жевали одну и ту же жвачку. The seminars were really boring: one speaker after another rehashed the same old thing.

Ж-9 • ЖДАТЬ НЕ ДОЖДА́ТЬСЯ *кого-чего coll* [VP; subj: human; fixed WO] to await s.o. or sth. with impatience: X ждёт не дождётся Y-а ≃ **X can't ⟨can hardly⟩ wait for thing Y ⟨for person Y to do sth.⟩; X is anxiously awaiting thing Y; X is waiting anxiously for thing Y ⟨for person Y to do sth.⟩.**

[Гомыра:] Вася, заглянув правде в глаза. Мы с тобой уезжаем? Уезжаем. А они остаются. Что, неправда?.. Они ждут не дождутся, когда мы уедем (Вампилов 3). [G.:] Vasia, let's face the truth. Are you and I going away? We are. And they're staying. Isn't that true?...They can't wait for us to go (3a). ♦ ...А у кого есть шуба — ждут не дождутся хоть нескольких морозных дней (Солженицын 10). Those who had heavy winter coats could hardly wait for a few frosty days (10b).

Ж-10 • СЕ́МЕРО ОДНОГО́ НЕ ЖДУТ [saying] several or many people do not have to wait for one person (said to a person who forces others to wait for him; also said when a group does not or cannot wait for one person): ≃ **one should not keep many waiting.**

Ж-11 • НА ВСЮ ЖЕЛЕ́ЗКУ *highly coll* [PrepP; Invar; adv (intensif); fixed WO] **1.** [used with subj: human] **жать, нажимать, нажать** и т. п. ~ (to press one's foot down on a gas pedal) as hard as possible (thus making a vehicle go at its maximum speed): X жал на всю железку ≃ **X stepped on it; X threw it into high gear; X floored it; X put the pedal to the metal.**

«Командир нашей автороты спрашивает: „Проскочишь, Соколов?"... — „Какой разговор! — отвечаю ему. — Я должен проскочить, и баста!" — „Ну, — говорит, — дуй! Жми на всю железку!"» (Шолохов 1). "'Can you get through, Sokolov?' asks the commander of our company....'What are you talking about!' I told him. 'I've got to get through, and that's that.' 'Get cracking then,' he says, 'and step on it!'" (1c). ♦ «Куда?..» Бирюков показал на удаляющуюся «Волгу». «За ней, чтобы не упустить». «На всю железку можно?» — «Жми!» (Чернёнок 1). "Where to?" Birukov pointed to the Volga ahead. "Follow that car and don't lose it." "Can I floor it?" "Go ahead!" (1a).

2. работать, делать *что* ~. Also: **НА ПО́ЛНУЮ ЖЕ-ЛЕ́ЗКУ** (to work, do sth.) to one's full capacity, at one's full potential: **(go) all out; giving it all ⟨everything⟩ one's got; giving it one's best shot;** [usu. in refer. to a physical task] **with might and main; going (the) whole hog;** [in limited contexts] **going great guns.**

3. жить ~ (to live one's life) taking advantage of all the opportunities life has to offer: **(live life) to the fullest.**

Ж-12 • КУЙ ЖЕЛЕ́ЗО, ПОКА́ ГОРЯЧО́ [saying] take advantage of opportunity the moment it comes: **strike while the iron is hot; make hay while the sun shines.**

«Непостоянны сильные мира сего, — говорил Мольер Мадлене, — и дал бы я совет всем комедиантам. Если ты попал в милость, сразу хватай всё, что тебе полагается. Не теряй времени, куй железо, пока горячо» (Булгаков 5). "How inconstant are the mighty of this world," Molière said to Madeleine. "And I would give this advice to all players: if you happen to win favor, seize everything you can at once. Lose no time, strike while the iron is hot" (5a).

Ж-13 • ВЫЖИГА́ТЬ/ВЫ́ЖЕЧЬ КАЛЁНЫМ ЖЕЛЕ́-ЗОМ *что* [VP; subj: human; often infin with надо, нужно, следует; the verb may take the final position, otherwise fixed WO] to destroy, eradicate sth. (usu. some negative phenomenon) ruthlessly: X будет калёным железом выжигать Y ≃ **X will eliminate ⟨annihilate, obliterate, wipe out⟩ Y.**

Ж-14 • НА ПУСТО́Й ⟨ТО́ЩИЙ, ГОЛО́ДНЫЙ⟩ ЖЕ-ЛУ́ДОК *coll;* **НА ГОЛО́ДНОЕ БРЮ́ХО** *highly coll, rude* [PrepP; these forms only; adv; fixed WO] when a person is hungry: **on an empty stomach ⟨belly⟩.**

...Замечал Ленин, что сегодняшний библиотекарь не всегда ходит обедать. Подошёл к нему, спросил. Не пойдёт. А нельзя в перерыв остаться? Можно. Вот это удача... На пустой желудок лучше работается. И лишний час (Солженицын 5). ...Lenin had noticed that the librarian on duty today did not always go to lunch. He went over and inquired. No, he wasn't going. Was it at all possible to stay through the lunch break? It was. Here was a bit of luck....It was easier to work on an empty stomach. And he would gain time (5a). ♦ «...Тухлая краска, тридцать градусов Реомюра, спёртый воздух, куча людей, рассказ об убийстве лица, у которого был накануне, и всё это — на голодное брюхо! Да как тут не случиться обмороку!» (Достоевский 3). "...Stinking paint, eighty degrees, stifling air, a crowd of people, talk about the murder of somebody he had visited the day before—and all this on an empty belly. How could anybody not faint!" (3a).

Ж-15 • НА СЫ́ТЫЙ ЖЕЛУ́ДОК *coll;* **НА СЫ́ТОЕ БРЮ́ХО** *highly coll, rude* [PrepP; these forms only; adv; fixed WO] when a person's appetite is satisfied, when he has already eaten: **on a full stomach ⟨belly⟩.**

Ребята... начали играть в перекличку с эхом. Приятное занятие, особенно на сытое брюхо (Абрамов 1). ...The boys started playing echoes. A pleasant occupation, especially on a full stomach (1a). The boys...began to call to the echo, a pleasant occupation especially on a full belly (1b).

Ж-16 • **БЕЗ МЕНЯ́ МЕНЯ́ ЖЕНИ́ЛИ** *usu. humor* [saying] sth. concerning me was decided (or done in my name) without my knowing about it or consenting to it: ≃ **before I knew what was happening you ⟨they⟩ up and volunteered me; you ⟨they⟩ made me a [NP] without my knowledge; you ⟨they⟩ got me into it without my knowledge.**

Алик Неяркий вскочил, едва покосившись на нас смущённым глазом — что, мол, поделаешь, профессором заделали, без меня меня женили (Аксёнов 6). Alik Neyarky jumped up, with an embarrassed sideways glance in our direction, implying that it wasn't his fault they had made him a professor without his knowledge (6a).

Ж-17 • **СМОТРЕ́ТЬ ЖЕНИХО́М** *highly coll* [VP; subj: human] to look very happy, content: X смотрит женихом ≃ **X is ⟨looks⟩ (as) happy as a lark; X is walking ⟨floating⟩ on air; X looks radiant.**

Ж-18 • **НЕ ЗНАТЬ ЖЕ́НЩИН ⟨НИ ОДНО́Й ЖЕ́Н-ЩИНЫ⟩** [VP; subj: human, male; fixed WO] to be a virgin: X не знал женщин ≃ **X has never known ⟨been with, lain with⟩ a woman.**

Ж-19 • **МЫШИ́НЫЙ ЖЕРЕ́БЧИК** *obs* [NP; fixed WO] an old man who likes to court young women: **old wooer.**

< From Nikolai Gogol's *Dead Souls* («Мёртвые души»), Vol. I, ch. 8, 1842.

Ж-20 • **ПАСТЬ ЖЕ́РТВОЙ** *чего* [VP; subj: human; fixed WO] to suffer greatly or perish because of sth.: X пал жертвой Y-а ≃ **X fell victim ⟨prey⟩ to Y.**

Два года с половиной я прожил с великим художником и видел, как под бременем гонений и несчастий разлагался этот сильный человек, павший жертвою приказно-казарменного самовластия... (Герцен 1). For two years and a half I lived with the great artist and saw the strong man, who had fallen victim to the autocracy of red-tape officialdom and barrack-discipline...breaking down under the weight of persecution and misery (1a). ♦ ...Желая высказать в прозе свои заветные мысли и наблюдения, но избрав для этого традиционную форму романа... он [Пастернак] пал жертвой ложного стремления к занимательности, доступной драматичности, фабульности (Гладков 1). ...When Pasternak chose the traditional form of the novel as a vehicle for the expression of his most cherished ideas and observations, he fell prey to a misplaced desire to hold the reader's attention by "telling a story" with readily-understood elements of drama in it (1a).

Ж-21 • **ПРИНОСИ́ТЬ/ПРИНЕСТИ́ В ЖЕ́РТВУ** *кого-что (кому-чему)* [VP; subj: human; usu. this WO] to give up a person, group, cause etc, allowing him or it to be hurt or destroyed, for the benefit of another person, group, cause etc: X принёс Y-а в жертву Z-у ≃ **X sacrificed Y to Z; X offered Y in ⟨up as a⟩ sacrifice;** ‖ X принёс себя в жертву ≃ **X sacrificed himself; X offered himself in ⟨up as a⟩ sacrifice.**

«...Приносить семью в жертву какому-то сумасшествию [тебе] не стыдно?» (Пастернак 1). "...Aren't you ashamed to sacrifice your family to some crazy notion?" (1a). ♦ «...Он [Христос] родился в момент того душевного порыва, когда его народ, сам того не сознавая, приносил себя в жертву, обрёк себя на распятие во имя рождения христианской цивилизации...» (Горенштейн 1). "...He [Christ] was born at a moment of psychic upsurge, when his people, without realizing it, offered themselves in sacrifice, doomed themselves to crucifixion for the sake of giving birth to Christian civilization" (1a). ♦ [Элен] сквозь слёзы говорила... что она никогда не была женою своего мужа, что она была принесена в жертву (Толстой 6). ...[Ellen] tearfully asserted...that she had never been her husband's wife; that she had been offered up as a sacrifice (6a).

Ж-22 • **ПРИНОСИ́ТЬ/ПРИНЕСТИ́ ЖЕ́РТВУ ⟨ЖЕ́РТ-ВЫ⟩** *(кому-чему)* [VP; subj: human] to give up sth. important, vital to one's interests, well-being etc for the sake of another person or some cause: X принёс жертву Y-у ≃ **X made a sacrifice for Y.**

Кутузов никогда не говорил... о жертвах, которые он приносит отечеству, о том, что он намерен совершить или совершил: он вообще ничего не говорил о себе, не играл никакой роли, казался всегда самым простым и обыкновенным человеком... (Толстой 7). Kutuzov never talked of...the sacrifices he was making for the fatherland, or of what he meant to do or had done: in general he said nothing about himself, adopted no pose, always appeared to be the simplest and most ordinary of men... (7a).

Ж-23 • **КРАСИ́ВЫЙ ⟨БЛАГОРО́ДНЫЙ, ШИРО́-КИЙ⟩ ЖЕСТ** [NP; fixed WO] a deliberate action done merely for effect, in order to create a good (but not necessarily true) impression: **grand ⟨noble, pretty, showy⟩ gesture;** *beau geste.*

Его нежелание идти к родственникам показалось ей [Ольге] чрезвычайно обидным. Те делали благородный жест — у кого бы он занял такую сумму? у дружков-приятелей? чёрта с два! (Трифонов 3). His unwillingness to see his relatives struck Olga as extremely hurtful. They had made a noble gesture: who else would lend them such a large sum of money? Their friends? Like hell they would! (3a). ♦ [Шаманов:] *(По телефону.)* К начальнику?.. А что такое?.. Вызывают в город?.. Знаю, получил повестку... Ну да, тот самый процесс... Да, послезавтра. А мне всё равно — хоть сегодня, — я не еду... Зачем? Там уже всё решено, а с меня хватит... Всё. Я не любитель красивых жестов... (Вампилов 2). [Sh.:] *(Into the phone.)* The chief's asking for me?...What for?...Expects me to come to town?...I know, I got the notice. That's it, the same trial....Uh-huh, day after tomorrow. A lot of difference it makes, I wouldn't go even if it was today....What's the sense? Everything's been decided. I've had enough, thanks. I'm not a lover of pretty gestures... (2a).

Ж-24 • **ЖИВ-ЗДОРО́В ⟨ЖИВ И ЗДОРО́В, ЖИВО́Й-ЗДОРО́ВЫЙ, ЖИВО́Й И ЗДОРО́ВЫЙ⟩** *coll* [AdjP; usu. subj-compl with copula (subj: human); fixed WO] one is safe and unharmed, in good health: **safe and sound; alive and well ⟨kicking⟩.**

«Говорю тебе, [Григорий] живой и здоровый, морду наел во какую!»... Аксинья слушала, как в чаду... Она опомнилась только у мелеховской калитки (Шолохов 5). "I tell you he's [Grigory is] safe and sound, and real fat in the face!"...Aksinya listened as if in a trance. She came to herself only at the Melekhovs' gate (5a). ♦ [Аркадина:] До свидания, мои дорогие... Если будем живы и здоровы, летом опять увидимся... (Чехов 6). [A.:] Good-bye, my dears....If we are alive and well, we'll meet again next summer... (6a).

Ж-25 • **НИ ЖИВ НИ МЁРТВ; НИ ЖИВО́Й НИ МЁРТВЫЙ** *both coll* [AdjP; subj-compl with copula (subj: human) or detached modif; fixed WO] extremely frightened or aggrieved: **more dead than alive; scared stiff ⟨to death⟩; half dead with fright.**

Она [моя мать] не знала, что думать, ей приходило в голову, что его [Павла Ивановича] убили или что его хотят убить, и потом её. Она взяла меня на руки и, ни живая ни мёртвая, дрожа всем телом, пошла за старостой (Герцен 1). She [my mother] did not know what to think; the idea occurred to her that they had killed him [Pavel Ivanovich], or that they meant to kill him and afterwards her. She took me in her arms, and trembling all over, more dead than alive, followed the elder (1a). ♦ «Ой, батюшки светы... что с нами сделалось... Дрожим, ни живы ни мёртвы, язык отнялся от ужаса...» (Пастернак 1). "Oh, God in heaven, need I tell you the state we were in....We were shaking all over, half dead with fright and speechless with terror!" (1a).

Ж-26 • **ЗА ЗДОРО́ВО ЖИВЁШЬ;** *less common* **ЗДОРО́ВО ЖИВЁШЬ** *both highly coll* [Invar; adv; fixed WO] **1.** рабо́тать, дава́ть *что кому,* де́лать *что для кого* и т. п. ~ (to work, give s.o. sth., do sth. for s.o. etc) for free, without receiving compensation: **for nothing; just ⟨free⟩ for the asking.**

«Ко мне часто прихо́дят: то пятёрку, то деся́тку дай. Друго́й раз после́дний отдаю́. Пра́вда, люблю́, чтобы возвраща́ли, за здоро́во живёшь тоже рабо́тать неохо́та» (Распу́тин 1). "They often come to me for a fiver, or a tenner, and often it's the last one I've got. True, I expect to get paid back. Nobody wants to work for nothing" (1a). ♦ [Анчу́гин:] Сто рубле́й [дать незнако́мым лю́дям] про́сто так, за здоро́во живёшь – ну кто тебе́ пове́рит, сам посуди́... (Вампи́лов 1). [A.:] Handing over a hundred rubles [to strangers] just like that, just for the asking – who'd believe you? Judge for yourself... (1a).

2. (to so sth.) without any reason or basis: **without rhyme or reason; for no reason (at all); just for the heck ⟨hell⟩ of it.**

[Андре́й:] Пора́ уже́ оста́вить э́ти глу́пости и не ду́ться так, здоро́во живёшь (Че́хов 5). [A.:] It's about time you stopped this silliness...pouting like this without rhyme or reason... (5d). ♦ Влад встал, подавля́я волне́ние и дога́дываясь, что секрета́рь райко́ма не посеща́л слу́шателей тра́кторных ку́рсов за здоро́во живёшь... (Макси́мов 2). [context transl] Vlad stood up, trying to control his nerves and guessing that the district Party secretary had not paid a visit to the tractor school just to pass the time of day... (2a).

Ж-27 • **ЗДОРО́ВО ЖИВЁШЬ ⟨ЖИВЁТЕ⟩!** *substand* [formula phrase; these forms only; fixed WO] (among uneducated people) a salutation upon meeting: **hey (there); hi ya; how do; how you doin'.**

«Здоро́во живёшь, Дома́ха!» – га́ркнули в один го́лос гра́ждане. «Здра́вствуйте!» (Салтыко́в-Щедри́н 1). "Hey there, Domashka!" the citizens barked with one voice. "Hello!" (1a).

Ж-28 • **КАК ЖИВЁШЬ-МО́ЖЕШЬ ⟨ЖИВЁТЕ-МО́ЖЕТЕ⟩?** *old-fash, coll* [formula phrase; these forms only; fixed WO] (a question asked upon meeting a friend or acquaintance) how are you?: **how are you doing ⟨getting on, getting along⟩?; how's it going?; how're things going?; how goes it?; how's life ⟨the world⟩ treating you?**

[Агра́фена Кондра́тьевна:] Сади́ться ми́лости про́сим; как живёте-мо́жете? (Остро́вский 10). [A.K.:] Please sit down, won't you? How are you getting along? (10b). [A.K.:] Sit down, you're more than welcome. How're things going? (10a). ♦ [author's usage] [Исла́ев *(...обора́чивается ко входя́щему Беля́еву):*] А... э́то вы! Ну... ну, как мо́жете? [Беля́ев:] Сла́ва бо́гу, Арка́дий Серге́ич (Турге́нев 1). [I. *(...turns to Beliayev, who has just entered):*] Oh, it's you...well, how goes it? [B.:] Very well, thank you, Arkady Sergeyich (1d).

Ж-29 • **ЖИВИ́ И ЖИТЬ ДАВА́Й ДРУГИ́М** [saying; used in all finite forms] be concerned with your own affairs and do not interfere with other people, let them live as they wish (in contempt. usage, sometimes used ironically with reference to people involved in shady dealings): ≃ **live and let live.**

Так вот глу́по и бессла́вно зако́нчил свой жи́зненный путь прокуро́р Евпракси́н, кото́рый роди́лся, может быть, для чего́-то хоро́шего, кото́рый хоте́л, может быть, лю́дям добра́, а приноси́л зло. И сам, как говори́тся, не жил, и други́м жить не дава́л (Войно́вич 4). Thus, stupidly and ingloriously, did Prosecutor Evpraksein end his life, he, who, perhaps, had been born to do some good and who perhaps wished people well but did them harm....As the saying goes, he neither lived nor let live (4a).

Ж-30 • **ЗАДЕВА́ТЬ/ЗАДЕ́ТЬ ⟨ЗАБИРА́ТЬ/ЗАБРА́ТЬ, ЗАТРА́ГИВАТЬ/ЗАТРО́НУТЬ** и т. п.⟩ **ЗА ЖИВО́Е** *кого coll* [VP; subj: human or abstr; more often pfv] **1.** [often impers] to hurt s.o. by saying or doing sth. that is particularly painful for him, wound s.o.'s pride: X заде́л Y-a за живо́е ≃ **X cut ⟨stung⟩ Y to the quick; X got Y where it hurts; X touched ⟨hit⟩ a (raw) nerve.**

[Ли́почка:] Кого́ не заде́нет за живо́е: все подру́ги с мужья́ми давно́, а я сло́вно сирота́ кака́я! (Остро́вский 10). [L.:] Who wouldn't be cut to the quick? All my girl friends have been married forever, while I stand around like an orphan (10a). ♦ [author's usage] Он встал из-за стола́ и ухмыля́лся уже́ по-ино́му, злора́дно: ага́, пойма́л за живо́е! (Ко́пелев 1). He rose from his desk and smirked a different way now, maliciously: aha, got you where it hurts! (1a).

2. Also: **БРАТЬ/ВЗЯТЬ ЗА ЖИВО́Е** to touch s.o.'s innermost feelings: X заде́л Y-a за живо́е ≃ **X moved ⟨touched⟩ Y very deeply; thing X cut Y to the heart.**

Серьёзное чте́ние утомля́ло его́. Мысли́телям не удало́сь расшевели́ть в нём жа́жду к умозри́тельным и́стинам. Зато́ поэ́ты заде́ли его́ за живо́е: он стал ю́ношей, как все (Гончаро́в 1). Serious reading exhausted him. The philosophers were unable to arouse in him a thirst for speculative thought....However, the poets touched him deeply, and he became a youth like any other (1b).

Ж-31 • **ПО ЖИВО́МУ РЕ́ЗАТЬ** [VP; subj: human; usu. infin with тру́дно, бо́льно etc] to force o.s. to break off relations, ties with s.o. or sth. dear: тру́дно ре́зать по живо́му ≃ **it's hard to cut ⟨sever⟩ the ties that bind; it's hard to cut the cords.**

Ж-32 • **ЖИВО́Т ⟨ЖИВОТЫ́, ЖИВО́ТИКИ⟩ ПОДВО́ДИТ/ПОДВЕЛО́ ⟨ПОДТЯНУ́ЛО⟩** *(у кого) highly coll* [VP; impers] **1.** (in refer. to a temporary condition that is not life-threatening) s.o. is very hungry: у Х-а живо́т подво́дит ≃ **X has a gnawing in (the pit of) his stomach; X has hunger pains; X is ravenous ⟨famished, dying of hunger etc⟩.**

Дай что-нибу́дь перекуси́ть, совсе́м живо́т подвело́. Give me something to snack on, I'm famished.

2. (in refer. to a life-threatening situation) s.o. lives in want, is perishing for lack of food: у Х-а живо́т подвело́ ≃ **X is starving; X is half-starved.**

Ж-33 • **НАДРЫВА́ТЬ/НАДОРВА́ТЬ ЖИВО́ТИКИ ⟨ЖИВО́Т, ЖИВОТЫ́, КИШКИ́⟩** (со сме́ху, от хо́хота и т. п.) *substand* [VP; subj: human; often pfv fut, gener. 2nd pers sing надорвёшь] to laugh very hard, to the point of exhaustion: Х-ы живо́тики надорва́ли ≃ **Xs were in stitches; Xs (nearly ⟨almost⟩) split ⟨burst⟩ their sides laughing; Xs (nearly) busted a gut laughing; Xs (nearly) died laughing.**

«...Быва́ло, по це́лым часа́м [от Печо́рина] сло́ва не добьёшься, зато́ уж иногда́ как начнёт расска́зывать, так живо́тики надорвёшь со сме́ха» (Ле́рмонтов 1). "...Sometimes you couldn't get a word out of him [Pechorin] for hours on end, but when he occasionally did start telling stories you'd split your sides laughing" (1b). ♦ «Крепкоголо́вые» хихи́кали и надрыва́ли живо́тики, ви́дя, как крикли́вый господи́н... вдруг прику́сывал язычо́к... (Салтыко́в-Щедри́н 2). The "die-hards" first sniggered and then nearly burst their sides laughing as they watched the clamourous gentleman...suddenly biting his tongue... (2a).

Ж-34 • **ПОДТЯ́ГИВАТЬ/ПОДТЯНУ́ТЬ ЖИВО́Т ⟨ЖИВОТЫ́⟩** *coll* [VP; subj: human; often infin with пришло́сь, на́до etc; fixed WO] to eat less than one would like (as a result of one's financial circumstances, the unavailability of food etc): Х-у пришло́сь подтяну́ть живо́т ≃ **X had to tighten his belt.**

Ж-35 • **ХВАТА́ТЬСЯ ⟨ДЕРЖА́ТЬСЯ⟩ ЗА ЖИВОТЫ́ ⟨ЗА ЖИВО́ТИКИ, ЗА ЖИВО́Т, ЗА БОКА́⟩** *coll* [VP; subj: human, usu. pl] to shake with laughter, laugh profusely: Х-ы хвата́лись за животы́ ≃ **Xs (nearly ⟨almost⟩) split ⟨burst⟩**

their sides laughing; Xs were in stitches; Xs roared with laughter; Xs held their sides.

Зал взрывается от смеха. Люди хватаются за животы, визжат и стонут... (Распутин 1). The audience burst out laughing. People rocked and roared and held their sides... (1a).

Ж-36 • **В ЖИВЫ́Х** [PrepP; Invar; subj-compl with быть∅, остаться (subj: human) or obj-compl with застать (obj: human)] (one is, one remained, or to find s.o.) living, not deceased: X остался в живых ≃ **X survived; X remained alive** ⟨**among the living**⟩; [in limited contexts] **X lived;** ‖ *Neg* X-а нет в живых ≃ **X is no more; X is no longer alive** ⟨**with us**⟩; **X is gone** ⟨**dead**⟩.

Лукашин, вернувшись с лесозаготовок, застал Трофима ещё в живых, но уже без памяти (Абрамов 1). When he had gotten back from the forest, Lukashin had found Trofim still alive but already unconscious (1a). ♦ Они [врачи] дали ему понять, что припадок этот был даже необыкновенный, продолжался и повторялся несколько дней, так что жизнь пациента была в решительной опасности, и что только теперь, после принятых мер, можно уже сказать утвердительно, что больной останется в живых... (Достоевский 2). They [the doctors] gave him to understand that the fit was even an exceptional one, that it had persisted and recurred over several days, so that the patient's life was decidedly in danger, and that only now, after the measures taken, was it possible to say affirmatively that the patient would live... (2a). ♦ Сердце его исполнено было печальных предчувствий, он боялся уже не застать отца в живых... (Пушкин 1). His heart was full of sad forebodings: he feared his father might be dead by the time he reached home... (1a).

Ж-37 • **БО́ЛЬШЕ ЖИ́ЗНИ!** *highly coll* [sent; Invar; used as imper; fixed WO] a call to work, act, do sth. more energetically: **show some life!; put some life into it!; get with it!; look alive!; get it into** ⟨**high**⟩ **gear!;** [in limited contexts] **shake a leg!; put some elbow grease into it!**

Ж-38 • **В ЖИ́ЗНИ** ⟨**В ЖИЗНЬ**⟩ *coll* [PrepP; Invar; used with negated (usu. pfv) verbs to intensify negation] not ever: **never in one's life; not in a lifetime; never** ⟨**ever**⟩; [in limited contexts] **such** [NP] **as one has never seen** ⟨**met etc**⟩ **in one's entire life; the best** ⟨**greatest** etc⟩ [NP] **one has ever seen** ⟨**met** etc⟩ **in one's life.**

Летом, когда мама была у сестры на даче, она [Катя] приходила к нему, глаза сердитые, стеснялась сидевших у подъезда женщин. «Пялят зенки. Больше в жизни не приду» (Рыбаков 2). She [Katya] came to see him in the summer, when his mother was away at her sister's dacha. Her eyes were angry and she was embarrassed by the women sitting at the entrance. "All eyes! I'll never come here again in my life!" (2a). ♦ ...Вам в жизни не разрешить эту задачу (Терц 1). ...You won't solve this problem in a lifetime (1a). ♦ Абарчук постепенно различил в полумраке лицо Магара. Он не узнал бы его... умирающий старик!.. Ощущая на себе взгляд Магара, он подумал: «Тоже, наверно, считает: в жизни б не узнал» (Гроссман 2). Gradually, in the half-light, he [Abarchuk] made out Magar's face. He would never have recognized him...he was an old man who was about to die....Sensing that Magar was looking at him, he thought: "He's probably thinking the same thing—" "Well, I'd never have recognized him" (2a). ♦ ...Встретил меня старый и седой слуга с тёмным, медного цвета, лицом... и такими глубокими морщинами на лбу и на висках, каких я в жизни не видывал... (Тургенев 3). ...I was met by a grey-haired old servant with a face the colour of dark copper...and the deepest wrinkles on his forehead and temples I had ever seen in my life (3b).

Ж-39 • **ВОЗВРАЩА́ТЬ/ВОЗВРАТИ́ТЬ** ⟨**ВЕРНУ́ТЬ**⟩ **К ЖИ́ЗНИ** *кого* [VP] **1.** [subj: human, concr, or abstr] to restore s.o. quickly or suddenly to consciousness: X возвратил Y-а к жизни ≃ **X revived Y; X brought Y around; X brought Y to; X brought Y back to life.**

[extended usage] ...Господин Мольер получил официальное извещение от парижских властей о том, что пьеса его «Смешные драгоценные» к дальнейшим представлениям воспрещается... [Он] тут же набросал в голове черновик защитительной речи: «Ваше величество! Здесь очевидное недоразумение!» ...Пьеса была отправлена на просмотр королю... Мольер куда-то поехал наводить справки и кланяться, а вернувшись, решил прибегнуть ещё к одному способу, для того чтобы вернуть пьесу к жизни (Булгаков 5). Monsieur de Molière received official notice from the Paris authorities, banning all further performances of *The Precious Ladies Ridiculed*....He immediately drew up a letter in his mind, defending the play: "Your Majesty! This is an obvious misunderstanding!"...The play was sent to the King....Molière went somewhere to make inquiries and to bow; and, on returning, he decided to resort to yet another method of bringing his play back to life (5a).

2. [subj: human] to cure, heal a very sick or severely wounded person: X возвратил Y-а к жизни ≃ **X brought Y back** ⟨**restored Y**⟩ **to health; X saved Y's life.**

Ж-40 • **ВЫЗЫВА́ТЬ/ВЫ́ЗВАТЬ К ЖИ́ЗНИ** *что* [VP; subj: concr or abstr; fixed WO] to generate sth., serve as a catalyst for sth., or illuminate sth. previously hidden: X вызвал к жизни Y ≃ **X gave rise** ⟨**birth**⟩ **to Y; X sparked** ⟨**triggered**⟩ **Y; X brought Y to life.**

Нам здорово повезло, и мы видим Рембрандта в один из солнечных апрельских дней, когда освещение вызывает к жизни всё богатство и глубину красок (Михайловская 1). We were very lucky since we viewed Rembrandt on one of those sunny April days, when the lighting brings to life all the richness and depth of the colors (1a).

Ж-41 • **ВЫЧЁРКИВАТЬ/ВЫ́ЧЕРКНУТЬ ИЗ СВОЕ́Й ЖИ́ЗНИ** *кого* [VP; subj: human; the verb may take the final position, otherwise fixed WO] to stop considering s.o. (usu. a friend, lover etc) a part of one's life (usu. following a breakup, falling-out etc): X вычеркнул Y-а из своей жизни ≃ **X cut** ⟨**crossed**⟩ **Y out of X's life; X severed Y from X's life; Y ceased to exist for X.**

[author's usage] Если она не ответит мне и на это письмо, то всё — вычеркну тогда её из своей личной жизни (Аксёнов 1). If she didn't answer this letter either, then that was it—I'd cross her out of my personal life (1a).

Ж-42 • **ДАВА́ТЬ/ДАТЬ ЖИ́ЗНИ** *highly coll* [VP; subj: human; most often pfv] **1.** *кому* ~ to scold s.o. severely: X дал жизни Y-у ≃ **X gave it to Y good; X gave Y hell** ⟨**what for**⟩; **X chewed** ⟨**bawled**⟩ **Y out; X lowered the boom on Y; X let Y have it (with both barrels); Y caught hell (from X).**

«...Ваше счастье, что не встретили нашего коменданта, не раздевшись, а в пальто, он бы вам дал жизни...» (Гроссман 2). "You're lucky you didn't meet the commandant still in your outdoor coat. He really would have given you what for..." (2a).

2. ~ *кому* [subj: human (usu. pl) or collect] to fight s.o. (usu. a hostile army, the enemy) vehemently, overwhelming or defeating him: X-ы дадут Y-ам жизни ≃ **Xs will crush** ⟨**rout, clobber**⟩ **Ys; Xs will run** ⟨**drive**⟩ **Ys into the ground.**

3. ~ *кому* to beat, thrash s.o.: X дал жизни Y-у ≃ **X beat Y up; X beat the (living) daylights out of Y; X beat Y within an inch of Y's life.**

...Пантелей подумал, что, расправившись с Вадимом, вернётся и даст жизни грязному шакалу-антисемиту... (Аксёнов 6). ...Pantelei decided that, once he had dealt with Vadim, he would come back and beat up this filthy anti-Semite jackal...(6a).

4. to work, do sth. using all one's strength and energy: X даст жизни ≃ **X will go all out; X will go at it ⟨at his work etc⟩ hammer and tongs;** [usu. in refer. to a physical task] **X will (do sth.) with might and main;** [in limited contexts] **X will show them what he can do.**

Ж-43 • **ЖИЗНИ (СВОЕЙ) НЕ ЖАЛЕ́ТЬ** *coll;* **ЖИВОТА́ (СВОЕГО́) НЕ ЖАЛЕ́ТЬ** *obs* [VP; subj: human; fixed WO] to do sth. selflessly, with complete dedication: X жизни (своей) не жалеет ≃ **X doesn't spare himself; X gives his all.**

«...Пыли-то, грязи-то, боже мой! Вон, вон, погляди-ка в углах-то — ничего не делаешь!» — «Уж коли я ничего не делаю... — заговорил Захар обиженным голосом, — стараюсь, жизни не жалею!» (Гончаров 1). "The dust! The dirt! Oh, Lord! There, go on, have a look into the corners. You don't do anything!" "Well then, seeing I don't do anything..." Zakhar began in an injured tone. "I do my best. I don't spare myself" (1b).

Ж-44 • **ЛИША́ТЬ/ЛИШИ́ТЬ ⟨РЕША́ТЬ/РЕШИ́ТЬ** *substand⟩* **ЖИ́ЗНИ** *кого* [VP; subj: human; usu. pfv] to kill s.o.: X лишил Y-а жизни ≃ **X took Y's life; X did Y in; X did away with Y;** ‖ X лишил себя жизни ≃ **X took his own life; X did himself in.**

Чем больше других людей успевал он [Сталин] лишить жизни, тем настойчивей угнетал его постоянный ужас за свою (Солженицын 3). ...The more people's lives he [Stalin] took, the more he was oppressed by constant terror for his own (3a). ♦ «У него всё теперь, всё на земле совокупилось в Илюше, и умри Илюша, он или с ума сойдёт с горя, или лишит себя жизни» (Достоевский 1). "For him, now, everything on earth has come together in Ilyusha, and if Ilyusha dies, he will either go out of his mind from grief or take his own life" (1a).

Ж-45 • **ЛИША́ТЬСЯ/ЛИШИ́ТЬСЯ ⟨РЕША́ТЬСЯ/РЕШИ́ТЬСЯ** *substand⟩* **ЖИ́ЗНИ** [VP; subj: human; usu. pfv] to die, perish: X лишился жизни ≃ **X lost his life; X paid with his life; X got killed; it cost X his life.**

«Вы уедете, а мы должны оставаться?.. Ваше добро будем оберегать!.. Через него, может, и жизни лишишься!.. Не останусь я!» (Шолохов 4). "So you'll go away while we stay here?...And we look after your property for you!...Then get killed for its sake!...I'm not staying here!" (4a). ♦ *(Сатин пятится задом, отталкивая Василису, которая... пытается ударить сестру...)* [Василиса:] Прочь, каторжник! Жизни решусь, а — растерзаю... (Горький 3). *(Satin walks backward, pushing off Vasilisa, who is trying to get at her sister...)* [V.:] Get away, jail-bird! It may cost me my life, but I'll tear her to pieces! (3d). ♦ [Анисья:] Ты слушай, Микита: коли ты за себя Марину возьмёшь, я не знаю, что над собой сделаю... Жизни решусь! (Толстой 1). [context transl] [A.:] Listen, Nikita: if you're going to marry Marina, I don't know what I'll do to myself....I'll kill myself! (1b).

Ж-46 • **ОТСТАВА́ТЬ/ОТСТА́ТЬ ОТ ЖИ́ЗНИ** [VP; subj: human; fixed WO] to be or become backward, old-fashioned: X отстаёт от жизни ≃ **X lags ⟨falls, is⟩ behind the times.**

Ж-47 • **УХОДИ́ТЬ/УЙТИ́ ИЗ ЖИ́ЗНИ** *lit* [VP; subj: human; more often pfv; usu. this WO] to die: X ушёл из жизни ≃ **X left this world; X passed on ⟨away⟩.**

Ж-48 • **ВДОХНУ́ТЬ ЖИЗНЬ** *в кого, во что* [VP; subj: human] to enliven s.o. or sth., spur s.o. to activity: X вдохнул жизнь в Y-а ≃ **X breathed life into thing Y; X livened Y up.**

Этой труппе нужен режиссёр, который сумел бы вдохнуть жизнь в их спектакли. This theatrical company needs a director who can breathe some life into their productions.

Ж-49 • **ВОПЛОЩА́ТЬ/ВОПЛОТИ́ТЬ ⟨ПРЕТВОРЯ́ТЬ/ПРЕТВОРИ́ТЬ⟩ В ЖИЗНЬ** *что* [VP; subj: human] (in refer. to an idea, a dream, a plan etc) to make sth. happen, actualize sth.: X воплотил Y в жизнь ≃ **X turned Y into (a) reality; X made Y a reality; X realized Y; X put Y into effect;** [in refer. to dreams only] **X made Y come true.**

«До чего испохабили прекрасную идею», — сказал я. «Почему же испохабили, — возразил Антон. — Как раз наоборот, воплотили в жизнь» (Зиновьев 2). "See how far a noble idea has been degraded," I said. "Why degraded?" objected Anton. "It's the very opposite, the idea has actually been realised" (2a). ♦ Как-то внезапно созрело у Натальи решение сходить в Ягодное к Аксинье — вымолить, упросить её вернуть Григория... Толкаемая подсознательным чувством, она стремилась скорей претворить внезапное своё решение в жизнь (Шолохов 2). The decision to go to Aksinya at Yagodnoye and beg her to give Grigory back suddenly ripened in Natalya's mind....Driven by an unconscious urge, she set about putting her sudden decision into effect at once (2a).

Ж-50 • **ВХОДИ́ТЬ/ВОЙТИ́ В ЖИЗНЬ** [VP] **1.** Also: **ВХОДИ́ТЬ/ВОЙТИ́ В БЫТ** [subj: abstr] to become an accepted, common phenomenon in life: X вошёл в жизнь ≃ **X became a part of (everyday) life; X became rooted in daily life.**

Этот обычай давно вошёл в жизнь. This custom became a part of life long ago.

2. ~ *чью, какую, чего* [subj: human] to adapt to and become an active participant in new surroundings, a new environment: X вошёл в Y-ову жизнь ≃ **X adapted to Y's way of life ⟨Y's life style⟩;** ‖ X быстро вошёл в городскую жизнь ⟨в жизнь института и т. п.⟩ ≃ **X quickly got into the swing of city ⟨institute etc⟩ life; X quickly adapted ⟨adjusted⟩ to city ⟨institute etc⟩ life.**

3. Also: **ВСТУПА́ТЬ/ВСТУПИ́ТЬ В ЖИЗНЬ** [subj: human] to begin to function as an independent member of society: X вступает в жизнь ≃ **X is starting ⟨setting⟩ out in life.**

Ж-51 • **ДАРОВА́ТЬ ⟨ПОДАРИ́ТЬ⟩ ЖИЗНЬ** *кому obsoles* [VP; subj: human] to show clemency to a person condemned to death: X даровал Y-у жизнь ≃ **X pardoned Y.**

Ж-52 • **ДАТЬ ЖИЗНЬ** *кому lit* [VP; subj: human, usu. denoting parents or a parent] to beget or give birth to a child: X-ы дали ⟨X дал(а)⟩ жизнь Y-у ≃ **Xs ⟨X⟩ gave life to Y;** [of the father only] **X sired ⟨fathered⟩ Y.**

Когда [жена этого господина] стала беременна первым ребёнком и поведала ему это, он вдруг смутился: «Даю жизнь, а сам отнял жизнь» (Достоевский 1). When she [this gentleman's wife] became pregnant with their first child and told him of it, he suddenly became troubled: "I am giving life, but I have taken a life" (1a). ♦ Папа Нессельроде махровый монархист, а ведь она [Лидочка] благоговеет перед своим папой, потому что он дал ей жизнь! (Аксёнов 7). Papa Nesselrode is a dyed-in-the-wool monarchist, and Lidochka worships him: he sired her, after all (7a).

Ж-53 • **ДО́РОГО ПРОДАВА́ТЬ/ПРОДА́ТЬ ⟨ОТДАВА́ТЬ/ОТДА́ТЬ⟩ СВОЮ́ ЖИЗНЬ** [VP; subj: human] to fight fiercely before being killed in a battle, confrontation etc, causing the enemy great difficulty and substantial losses in destroying one: X дорого продаст свою жизнь ≃ **X will go down fighting; X won't go down without a fight; X will fight to the death; X will put up a ferocious struggle ⟨a hell of a fight⟩ right to the end ⟨before being wiped out⟩ etc.**

Ж-54 • **ЖИЗНЬ ПРОЖИ́ТЬ — НЕ ПО́ЛЕ ПЕРЕЙТИ́** [saying] life is complicated, and to live it is not easy: ≃ **life is no ⟨not a⟩ bed of roses; life is not all smooth sailing.**

Ж-55 • **КЛАСТЬ/ПОЛОЖИ́ТЬ ЖИЗНЬ ⟨ЖИВО́Т (СВОЙ)** *obs⟩* [VP; subj: human; usu. pfv] **1.** ~ *(за кого-*

что) lit to perish, lose or sacrifice one's life (for s.o. or sth.): X положил жизнь (за Y-а) ≃ **X laid down his life (for Y); X gave (up) his life (for Y).**

«Свет ты мой, Иван Кузьмич, удалая солдатская головушка! Не тронули тебя ни штыки прусские, ни пули турецкие; не в честном бою положил ты свой живот, а сгинул от беглого каторжника!» (Пушкин 2). "Ivan Kuzmich, light of my life, brave soldier heart! You escaped both the Prussians' bayonets and the Turks' bullets unscathed; it was not your lot to lay down your life in honest battle; you had to perish at the hands of an escaped convict!" (2a).

2. ~ *(на что)* to expend maximum effort, energy etc (on sth.): X положил жизнь на Y ≃ **X gave his whole self to Y; X dedicated ⟨devoted⟩ himself ⟨his life⟩ (to Y).**

Ж-56 • КОНЧА́ТЬ/КО́НЧИТЬ ЖИЗНЬ ⟨(СВОЙ) ВЕК⟩ *obs* [VP; subj: human; most often pfv] to die: X кончил жизнь ≃ **X passed away ⟨on⟩; X left ⟨departed⟩ this world.**

Ж-57 • НЕ ЖИЗНЬ ⟨НЕ ЖИТЬЁ⟩, А МА́СЛЕНИЦА ⟨МАЛИ́НА⟩ *(у кого) highly coll* [NP; subj-compl with бытьø (subj: это) or VP_subj with бытьø; fixed WO] s.o. has a wonderful life: у X-а не жизнь, а масленица ≃ **X is in clover; X lives high on ⟨off⟩ the hog; X has it made.**

Ж-58 • НЕ НА ЖИЗНЬ ⟨ЖИВО́Т *obs*⟩, **А НА́ СМЕРТЬ ⟨НА СМЕ́РТЬ⟩** *lit* [PrepP; Invar; fixed WO] **1. биться, сражаться** и т. п. ~ ; **борьба, война** и т. п. ~ [adv (intensif, more often used with impfv verbs) or postmodif] (to struggle, fight) to an ultimate conclusion, ruthlessly, not sparing one's life: **fight to the death ⟨to the bitter end⟩; wage a life-and-death struggle; [in limited contexts] fight (against) s.o. tooth and nail.**

В СССР сейчас во всём борются не на жизнь, а на смерть партия Памяти с партией Надежды, партия прошлого с партией будущего (Аллилуева 2). At present in the USSR there is a constant life-and-death struggle between the Party of Memory and the Party of Hope, the Party of the Past and the Party of the Future (2a).

2. рассердиться, испугаться, перепугать *кого* и т. п. ~ [adv (intensif)] (to get angry, get scared, frighten s.o. etc) to an extreme degree, very intensely: рассердиться ~ ≃ **fly into a wild ⟨deadly⟩ rage; get furious;** ‖ испугаться ~ ≃ **get scared stiff ⟨out of one's wits⟩; get the life scared out of one;** ‖ перепугать *кого* ~ ≃ **scare s.o. stiff ⟨out of s.o.'s wits⟩; scare the life out of s.o.;** ‖ враждовать ~ ≃ **be sworn ⟨mortal⟩ enemies;** ‖ избить *кого* ~ ≃ beat ⟨**thrash**⟩ **s.o. within an inch of s.o.'s life;** ‖ ругать *кого* ~ ≃ **curse ⟨chew⟩ s.o. out; curse s.o. for all one is worth.**

Автор чрезвычайно затрудняется, как назвать ему обеих дам таким образом, чтобы опять не рассердились на него... Назвать выдуманною фамилией опасно. Какое ни придумай имя, уж непременно найдётся в каком-нибудь углу нашего государства... кто-нибудь носящий его и непременно рассердится не на живот, а на смерть, станет говорить, что автор нарочно приезжал секретно с тем, чтобы выведать всё, что он такое сам, и в каком тулупчике ходит... (Гоголь 3). The author is in a quandary how to name these two ladies without rousing anger....To invent names for them would be dangerous. However fictitious the name, there will always be someone in some out-of-the-way corner of our empire...who will lay some claim to it, fly into a deadly rage, and start proclaiming that the author had paid a secret visit with the express purpose of finding out who he was and what sort of sheepskin coat he wore... (3d). ♦ Сиделец говорил, что она, во-первых, ему не платит долг, во-вторых, разобидела его в собственной его лавке и, мало того, обещала исколотить его не на живот, а на смерть руками своих приверженцев (Герцен 1). The shopkeeper declared that, in the first place, she had not paid what she owed him, and, in the second, had insulted him in his own shop and, what was

---

more, threatened that he should be thrashed within an inch of his life by her followers (1a).

Ж-59 • НИ В ЖИЗНЬ ⟨ЖИСТЬ⟩ *substand* [PrepP; these forms only; adv; used with negated pfv verbs (fut, subjunctive, or infin) to intensify negation; fixed WO] under no circumstances, not ever: **not ⟨never⟩ in a lifetime; not ⟨never⟩ in a million years; never (ever); [in limited contexts] not on your life.**

[Шелавина:] ...А сколько тут денег, ни в жизнь мне не счесть (Островский 3). [Sh.:] And all the bank notes! I couldn't count them in a lifetime (3a). ♦ [Брылов:] Вишь ты, зав. производством, на литейщиков какая худая слава! Чтоб я, Брылов, позволил ребятам налево лить? Да ни в жисть! (Солженицын 8) [B.:] You see what a reputation we've got in the foundry? Imagine, me, Brylov, letting my boys make things to sell on the side. Never in a million years (8a). ♦ «[Она] пьяная была?» — «Почему непременно пьяная?» — «Трезвый человек ни в жизнь с балкона не вывалится» (Чернёнок 1). "Was she drunk?" "Why drunk?" "A sober person would never fall off a balcony" (1a).

Ж-60 • ОТДАВА́ТЬ/ОТДА́ТЬ ЖИЗНЬ [VP; subj: human] **1.** ~ *кому-чему* to devote all one's time and effort to s.o. or sth.: X отдал жизнь Y-у ≃ **X devoted ⟨dedicated, gave⟩ his life to Y.**

[Ирина:] Завтра я поеду одна, буду учить в школе и всю свою жизнь отдам тем, кому она, может быть, нужна (Чехов 5). [I.:] Tomorrow I shall go away alone; I shall teach in a school, and I shall give my life to those who may need it (5b).

2. ~ *за кого-что* to sacrifice one's life for s.o. or sth.: X отдал жизнь за Y-а ≃ **X laid down his life for Y; X died for Y; X gave (up) his life for Y.**

Неблагодарный, я же тебя спас от смерти, я же готов за тебя жизнь отдать, а ты ничего этого не понимаешь (Искандер 3). Ingrate—I saved you from death, I'd lay down my life for you, and you understand nothing of this (3a).

Ж-61 • ОТРАВЛЯ́ТЬ ЖИЗНЬ *чью, кого, кому* ⟨**СУЩЕСТВОВА́НИЕ** *чьё, кого, кому*⟩ [VP; subj: human or abstr] to make s.o.'s life difficult, intolerable: X отравляет Y-у жизнь ≃ **X poisons Y's existence ⟨life⟩; X makes Y's life miserable ⟨difficult, unbearable, a torment⟩; X is the bane of Y's existence.**

Компаньонка стала осторожнее, но, питая теперь личную ненависть и желая на ней [Natalie] выместить обиду и унижение, она отравляла ей жизнь мелкими, косвенными средствами... (Герцен 1). ...The "lady companion" was more on her guard, but, now cherishing a personal hatred for Natalie, and desirous of avenging her own injury and humiliation, she poisoned her existence by petty, indirect means (1a). ♦ Варенуха прятался сейчас в кабинете у финдиректора от контрамарочников, которые отравляли ему жизнь, в особенности в дни перемены программы. А сегодня как раз и был такой день (Булгаков 9). Varenukha had taken refuge in the financial manager's office to escape from the seekers of free passes who were the bane of his existence, especially during the periods of program changes. And today was just such a day (9a).

Ж-62 • ПРОВОДИ́ТЬ/ПРОВЕСТИ́ В ЖИЗНЬ *что lit, often media* [VP; subj: human, often pl] to put sth. (a plan, a decision etc) into effect: X-ы провели Y в жизнь ≃ **Xs carried out Y; Xs made Y a reality; Xs put Y into practice; Xs implemented Y on a practical level ⟨scale⟩.**

Он [председатель] приложит все силы, чтобы принятое решение было проведено в жизнь без проволочек (Войнович 3). He [the Chairman] would use all his powers to see that their decision was carried out without delay (3a).

Ж-63 • ПРОЖИГА́ТЬ ЖИЗНЬ [VP; subj: human] to spend one's time engaging in pleasant diversions, pursue pleasure: X прожигает жизнь ≃ **X lives it up; X leads a fast life; X lives a life of pleasure; X lives (life) in the fast lane.** ○ **ПРОЖИГА́-ТЕЛЬ ⟨ПРОЖИГА́ТЕЛЬНИЦА⟩ ЖИ́ЗНИ** [NP] ≃ **pleasure-seeker; fast liver; [in limited contexts] playboy ⟨playgirl⟩.**

По-видимому, арбатовцы не представляли себе, как это можно пользоваться автомобилем в трезвом виде, и считали автотелегу Козлевича гнездом разврата, где обязательно нужно вести себя разухабисто, издавать непотребные крики и вообще прожигать жизнь (Ильф и Петров 2). The citizens of Arbatov were evidently unable to imagine how the car could be utilized in a state of sobriety, and thought of Kozlevich's motor as a den of iniquity, in which you just had to let your hair down, make undignified noises, and generally live it up (2a). Evidently the Arbatovites could not imagine how one could use an automobile while sober, and considered the horseless carriage of Kozlevich a nest of lechery in which one must perforce behave boisterously amid unnecessary cries and generally lead a fast life (2b). ♦ Каждый человек, которому дано, хотя бы на мгновенье, высунуться из житейской суеты, сознаёт нешуточность данного ему судьбой дара жизни. Он не может не понимать, что дар этот ограничен во времени и надо использовать его наилучшим образом. Между прочим, прожигатели жизни — это не люди, которые махнули рукой на дар жизни, а люди, которые так понимают ценность жизни и последовательно осуществляют накопление этой ценности (Искандер 3). Every man to whom it is granted to lift himself above the vain bustle of the world, if only for a moment, realizes the solemnity of the gift of life that fate has given him. He cannot fail to understand that this gift is limited in time and he must use it as best he can. Incidentally, fast livers are not men who have given up on the gift of life but men who understand the value of life in this way and are therefore seeing to it that they accumulate this value (3a).

Ж-64 • СОБА́ЧЬЯ ЖИЗНЬ *highly coll* [NP; sing only; may be used as VP$_{subj}$ with быть$_\emptyset$] a miserable existence, a life full of troubles or unhappiness: **dog's life; lousy life.**

«И без вас не сладко. Собачья жизнь, сумасшедший дом. Всё время между двух огней...» (Пастернак 1). "Things are bad enough without you. It's a dog's life, a madhouse. I am caught between two fires" (1a).

Ж-65 • УСТРА́ИВАТЬ/УСТРО́ИТЬ ВЕСЁЛУЮ ЖИЗНЬ *кому highly coll, iron* [VP; subj: human; usu. pfv; the verb may take the final position, otherwise fixed WO] to cause s.o. trouble, discomfort etc (by sharply reprimanding him, punishing him, being unreasonably demanding etc): X устроил Y-у весёлую жизнь ≃ **X made Y's life miserable; X made Y's life hell (on earth);** [of reprimanding s.o. only] **X gave Y hell ⟨what for⟩; X gave Y a good tongue-lashing ⟨dressing-down⟩.**

Дома я решил сказать, что часы у меня украли в гостинице. Дядя... воспринял эту новость болезненно... «С попутным рейсом заеду и устрою им [администрации гостиницы] весёлую жизнь!» — пообещал он на ходу, выскакивая на улицу (Искандер 6). I decided to tell everyone at home that my watch had been stolen from my hotel room. My uncle took the news very badly.... "The next time I pass through that town I'm going to stop off at that hotel and give 'em [the hotel management] hell!" was my uncle's parting shot as he went dashing out onto the street (6a).

Ж-66 • ИГРА́ТЬ ЖИ́ЗНЬЮ И СМЕ́РТЬЮ; ИГРА́ТЬ СО СМЕ́РТЬЮ; ИГРА́ТЬ (СВОЕ́Й) ЖИ́ЗНЬЮ [VP; subj: human] to put o.s. in a life-threatening situation, disregarding danger: X играл жизнью и смертью ≃ **X risked ⟨gambled with⟩ his life; X played with death; X flirted with danger ⟨with death⟩; X put his life on the line; X took his life in his hands.**

[Шеметова:] Нелепость, безумие — так играть своей жизнью, когда конец [войны] завиднелся! (Панова 1). [Sh.:] It's stupidity, madness to risk your life like that when the end [of the war] is in sight (1a). ♦ «Вы мужчина, вы — вольный казак... Сумасбродствовать, играть своей жизнью ваше священное право. Но Лариса Фёдоровна человек несвободный. Она мать» (Пастернак 1). "...You are a man, Yurii Andreievich, you are your own master, and you have a perfect right to gamble with your life if you feel like it. But Larisa Feodorovna is not a free agent. She is a mother..." (1a). ♦ О боевых делах он рассказывал неохотно, но мне-то было известно со стороны, как он там [на Кавказе] играл со смертью (Окуджава 2). He didn't like talking about military affairs, but I knew from others how he had played with death down there [in the Caucasus] (2a).

Ж-67 • МЕ́ЖДУ ЖИ́ЗНЬЮ И СМЕ́РТЬЮ [PrepP; Invar; usu. subj-compl with copula (subj: human); fixed WO] in a very serious, life-threatening condition: **between life and death; with one's life hanging in the balance ⟨by a thread⟩.**

«Как, вы воротились из Австралии?» — спросил я его... «Нет-с, не из Австралии, а из больницы, где пролежал месяца три между жизнью и смертью...» (Герцен 3). "What, have you come back from Australia?" I asked him.... "No, not from Australia, but from the hospital where I have been lying for three months between life and death..." (3a).

Ж-68 • ЖИЛ-БЫ́Л *folk* [VP; subj: human; past only; always precedes subj] the stock phrase used at the beginning of folk tales: **once upon a time (there was ⟨were, lived⟩).**

«Жил-был, здравствовал, изучал математику и прочие точные науки и никогда не думал, что стану таким „шовинистом"» (Шолохов 2). "Once upon a time I was a student of mathematics and other exact sciences. Little did I think I should live to become such a 'jingoist'" (2a).

Ж-69 • ЧТОБ Я ТАК ЖИЛ! *highly coll* [Interj; Invar; fixed WO] **1.** used by the speaker to emphasize the truth of a statement or that a promise will be realized: **(as) sure as I'm standing here; (as) God is my witness; or my name isn't...**

Видел я это, видел собственными глазами, чтоб я так жил! I saw the whole thing, saw it with my own two eyes, sure as I'm standing here!

2. used to express strong surprise, delight: **well, I'll be!; holy mackerel ⟨cow⟩!; what do you know!**

«Ты знаешь, что Борис выиграл в лотерею машину?» — «Чтоб я так жил!» "Did you hear that Boris won a car in the lottery?" "Holy mackerel!"

Ж-70 • ОТ ЖИЛЕ́ТКИ РУКАВА́ получить, достаться *кому и т. п. coll* [NP; Invar; obj or subj; usu. this WO] (to receive, get) absolutely nothing: **a (whole) lot of nothing; not a blessed thing.**

Они нам много чего наобещали, а как до дела дошло — получили мы от жилетки рукава. They promised us the world, but when it came right down to it, all we got was a whole lot of nothing.

Ж-71 • ПЛА́КАТЬСЯ/ПОПЛА́КАТЬСЯ ⟨ПЛА́КАТЬ/ ПОПЛА́КАТЬ⟩ В ЖИЛЕ́ТКУ *(кому) coll* [VP; subj: human; usu. this WO] to complain about one's lot in an attempt to evoke sympathy: X плачется Y-у в жилетку ≃ **X cries ⟨has a cry⟩ on Y's shoulder.**

«Ну конечно... я всегда бывала у Нюрка — зачем? Чтобы на бегу поплакаться в жилетку» (Залыгин 1). "Now, why was it I always used to go to Niurok? To have a quick cry on her shoulder, of course" (1a).

Ж-72 • НЕ ЖИЛЕ́Ц (НА СВЕ́ТЕ ⟨НА БЕ́ЛОМ СВЕ́ТЕ, НА Э́ТОМ СВЕ́ТЕ⟩) [NP; these forms only; subj-compl with быть$_\emptyset$ (subj: human); the masc form жилец is used with both male and female subjects; usu. pres] one is expected to die soon (usu. because of serious illness, old age etc): X не жилец на белом свете ≃ **X is not long for this world; X doesn't have long ⟨much longer⟩ to live.**

«Насчёт него [Ильи], твоя правда, брат, клеймо на нём, печать каинова, не жилец он...» (Максимов 1). "As for him [Ilya], you are right, brother, he has the brand on him, the mark of Cain; he is not long for this world" (1a). ♦ Старуха слышала, как загудела корова, но не стала кричать Надю: пускай привыкнет подниматься сама, а она всё равно не жилец на этом свете (Распутин 3). She [the old lady] heard the cow starting its morning lowing, but did not call out to Nadia: Nadia would have to get used to getting up by herself, since she, Anna, hadn't much longer to live (3a).

Ж-73 • ПОПАДА́ТЬ/ПОПА́СТЬ В (СА́МУЮ) ЖИ́ЛКУ ⟨ЖИ́ЛУ⟩ *obs* [VP; subj: human] to do or say the proper thing at the proper time: X попал в жилку ≃ **X said ⟨suggested, did⟩ just the right thing; X did ⟨said⟩ just what the occasion called for.**

Ж-74 • ТЯНУ́ТЬ ЖИ́ЛЫ; ВЫТЯ́ГИВАТЬ/ВЫ́ТЯ-НУТЬ ⟨ВЫМА́ТЫВАТЬ/ВЫ́МОТАТЬ⟩ (ВСЕ) ЖИ́ЛЫ *из кого all highly coll* [VP; subj: human] to torment, exhaust s.o. by making excessive demands on him, constantly pestering him, or exploiting him with hard work: X вытянул из Y-а все жилы ≃ **X plagued ⟨tortured, tormented⟩ the life out of Y; X wore Y out;** [in limited contexts] **X worked Y to death.**

Конечно, попадись мне вместо полковника какой-нибудь либеральный доцентик (бывают такие доцентики, дотошные, из евреев), уж он бы жилы из меня повытягивал: где тут свобода воли и какую особую роль играет личность в истории? (Терц 2). Of course, I was lucky to be with the colonel rather than one of those liberal-minded university types (you know the sort I mean: very sharp and Jews, mostly) who would have plagued the life out of me about free will and the role of the personality in history (2a). ♦ «Вот попал [в тюрьму], чёрт шелудивый, а я с тремя [детьми] живи, — и все колготят: хлеба! И иде [*ungrammat* = где] я его возьму, хлеба-то? Жилы они из меня все вытянули» (Максимов 3). "Got caught [and sent to prison], the miserable devil, and left me with three [children] on my hands, and all they can yell about is food. Where'm I supposed to get it from? They've tortured the life out of me..." (3a).

Ж-75 • СПУСКА́ТЬ/СПУСТИ́ТЬ ⟨РАСТРЯСА́ТЬ/РАСТРЯСТИ́⟩ ЖИР ⟨ЖИРО́К⟩; СГОНЯ́ТЬ/СО-ГНА́ТЬ ⟨СБРА́СЫВАТЬ/СБРО́СИТЬ⟩ ЖИР *all coll* [VP; subj: human; usu. pfv fut, imper, or infin with надо, полезно etc] (of an overweight person) to lose weight: X-у надо жир растрясти ≃ **X should shed ⟨take off, get rid of⟩ some flab ⟨fat, blubber, poundage⟩.**

Плавайте и ходите побольше, вам полезно жирок растрясти. You should try walking and swimming more, it would do you good to get rid of some flab.

Ж-76 • ЗАПЛЫВА́ТЬ/ЗАПЛЫ́ТЬ ЖИ́РОМ ⟨ЖИР-КО́М⟩ *coll* [VP; subj: human; more often pfv] to grow obese, become very fat: X заплыл жиром ≃ **X has turned into a (real) butterball ⟨a tub of lard⟩; X is covered in rolls ⟨layers⟩ of fat.**

«Вы знаете, Оленька, — мягким кошачьим голоском говорила эта огромная заплывшая жиром туша, — разрешите мне показать этот роман вышестоящему лицу» (Ивинская 1). "I tell you what, Olenka," she said in a soft, purring voice—she was a woman of enormous bulk, covered in rolls of fat—"let me show the novel to someone high up" (1a).

Ж-77 • НЕ ДО ЖИ́РУ, БЫТЬ БЫ ЖИ́ВУ [saying; often only the first half of the saying is used] you have to be satisfied with what little you have or is available, since anything more is unattain-

able: ≃ **you have to be happy with what you've got ⟨what you can get⟩; beggars can't be choosers;** [in limited contexts] **count your blessings.**

...[Строители] станут планировать жильё с расчётом на эти бараки. Раз стоят [бараки], — значит, жить можно, мало ли что некрасиво и неудобно — не до жиру, быть бы живу (Тендряков 1). ...[The builders] would take these barracks into account in planning future housing needs. Since they [the barracks] were already there, they would argue, people might as well stay in them, in spite of the fact that they were ugly and inconvenient: beggars couldn't be choosers (1a).

Ж-78 • С ЖИ́РУ БЕСИ́ТЬСЯ *coll disapprov* [VP; subj: human or collect; usu. this WO] (of one who is deemed to have been spoiled by a satiated, idle life devoid of troubles) to behave in a fussy, capricious manner: X с жиру бесится ≃ **it's X's plushy ⟨cushy⟩ life that makes him act so fussy ⟨behave capriciously, act like this etc⟩; X doesn't know when he's well off; X is too well off for his own good; X does what he does for want of anything better to do.**

[author's usage] [Старый повар:] Вишь, черти проклятые! С жиру-то! Черти!.. (Толстой 3). [Old Cook:] See what the damned devils have done! It's their plushy life that makes them do this. The devils! (3a). ♦ Андрей натянуто рассмеялся: «Сейчас она скажет: вы ублюдки, с жиру беситесь». — «Вы ублюдки, — сказала Таня, — и с жиру вы точно беситесь» (Аксёнов 7). Andrei gave a forced laugh and said, "Just you watch. Now she'll tell us we're a pack of animals and don't know when we're well off." "Well, you are a pack of animals," Tanya said, "and even if I don't understand all the ins and outs of your politics, I can tell you don't know when you're well off" (7a).

Ж-79 • С ⟨ОТ⟩ ЖИ́РУ ЛО́ПАТЬСЯ/ЛО́ПНУТЬ *highly coll, derog* [VP; subj: human; pfv past is not used in the affirm; more often this WO] to get very fat (usu. from inactivity, an idle life style): X с жиру лопнет ≃ **X will become ⟨be⟩ a tub of lard; X will be ⟨get⟩ as fat as a pig; X will be ⟨become⟩ as big as a house ⟨a horse, a barn⟩.**

Ж-80 • ЖИТЬ ПРИПЕВА́ЮЧИ *coll* [VP; subj: human; fixed WO] to live very well, in prosperity, be content with life: X живёт припеваючи ≃ **X lives in clover; X lives high on ⟨off⟩ the hog; X lives like a king ⟨a queen⟩; X has it made.**

[Скотинин:] Ты будешь жить со мною припеваючи. Десять тысяч твоего доходу! (Фонвизин 1). [S.:] You and me'll live in clover. Ten thousand of your income! (1a). ♦ ...[Брат Агафьи Матвеевны] рассчитал, какой стол должны они держать, как уменьшить издержки... сколько она может получить за цыплят, за капусту, и решил, что со всем этим можно жить припеваючи (Гончаров 1). He [Agafya Matveyevna's brother] reckoned how much they needed for food, how they could reduce expenses...and after estimating what she received from her chickens and cabbages, he decided that with what they had they could live like kings (1b).

Ж-81 • ЖИТЬЯ́ НЕТ ⟨НЕ СТА́ЛО⟩ *(кому) от кого-чего highly coll* [VP; impers] s.o.'s life is or has become difficult because of the insults, carping, or annoying behavior of another: X-у житья нет от Y-а ≃ **Y gives X no peace; Y makes X's life miserable ⟨impossible, unbearable, intolerable⟩; Y is the bane of X's existence ⟨life⟩; things are impossible ⟨unbearable, intolerable⟩ for X (because of Y).**

[Гаттерас:] Я вас уверяю, лорд, этой проклятой птице необходимо свернуть голову. От неё житья нет (Булгаков 1). [G.:] My lord, I tell you that damned bird must have its head yanked off. He makes life impossible (1a). ♦ «За письмо прости. Но другого выхода не было. Житья не стало» (Айтматов 2). "Forgive me for my letter, but there was no other way. Things had become impossible" (2a). ♦ «Ах, этот Захар: житья нет от него!» (Гончаров 1). "Oh, that Zakhar! He's the bane of my life!" (1b).

Ж-82 • **НЕ ДАВА́ТЬ/НЕ ДАТЬ ЖИТЬЯ́** *кому highly coll* [VP; subj: human; if pfv, usu. fut] to make s.o.'s life unbearable, intolerable (usu. by nagging or making excessive requests, demands): X житья Y-у не даёт ≃ **X gives Y no peace; X makes Y's life miserable ⟨impossible⟩; X doesn't let up ⟨never lets up⟩ (on Y).**

[Калошин:] [Жена] житья мне не давала, так пусть хоть даст помереть по-человечески (Вампилов 1). [K.:] She [my wife] gave me no peace in life. The least she can do is let me die in peace (1a). ♦ Думал мальчик и о том, что если Орозкул выгонит деда с работы, то бабка житья не даст старику (Айтматов 1). ...The lad thought too that if Orozkul kicked grandfather out of his job, old grandma would make the old man's life impossible (1b).

Ж-83 • **БРОСА́ТЬ/БРО́СИТЬ ⟨КИДА́ТЬ/КИ́НУТЬ, МЕТА́ТЬ/МЕТНУ́ТЬ⟩ ЖРЕ́БИЙ** [VP; subj: human, usu. pl] to decide, determine sth. by chance (usu. by choosing blindly among objects, each of which has an assigned outcome): X-ы бросили жребий ≃ **Xs cast ⟨drew⟩ lots.**

[Агафья Тихоновна:] Право, такое затруднение — выбор!.. Я думаю, лучше всего кинуть жребий. Положиться во всём на волю божию: кто выкинется, тот и муж (Гоголь 1). [A.T.:] Ah, how difficult it is to choose!...I believe it would be best to cast lots. Rely on God's will in everything. Whichever is drawn shall be my husband (1c). ♦ «Что же, мы друг друга будем обыскивать?» — «Вас первого, Листницкий!» — крикнул молодой безусый сотник Раздорцев. «Давайте жребий метнём». — «По алфавиту» (Шолохов 3). "Are we expected to search each other?" "Your turn first, Listnitsky!" young, beardless Lieutenant Razdortsev called out. "Let's draw lots." "Take us in alphabetical order" (3a).

Ж-84 • **ЖРЕ́БИЙ БРО́ШЕН** *lit* [sent; Invar; fixed WO] a decision has been made and cannot be revoked: **the die is cast.**

[Тузенбах:] Жребий брошен. Вы знаете, Мария Сергеевна, я подал в отставку (Чехов 5). [T.:] The die is cast. You know, Maria Sergeyevna, I have sent in my resignation (5a).

< A translation of the Latin *alea iacta est*, ascribed to Julius Caesar.

Ж-85 • **ЖУРА́ВЛЬ В НЕ́БЕ** *coll* [NP; sing only; fixed WO] sth. desirable yet extremely difficult to obtain, achieve etc: **(like) the proverbial two birds in the bush.**

...Он давно бы хотел в таможню, но удерживали текущие разные выгоды по строительной комиссии, и он рассуждал справедливо, что таможня, как бы то ни было, всё ещё не более как журавль в небе, а комиссия уже была синица в руках (Гоголь 3). ...He had been longing to get into the Customs, but had been held back by sundry current benefits accruing from the Building Commission, and he had reasoned, justly enough, that the Customs was, after all, no more than the proverbial two birds in the bush whereas the Building Commission was an actual bird in the hand (3b).

< From the proverb «Лучше синица в руках, чем журавль в небе» ("A bird in the hand is worth two in the bush"). See C-195.

Ж-86 • **ДО ЖУ́ТИ** *coll* [PrepP; Invar; modif or adv (intensif)] very, to an extreme degree: **awfully; horribly; terribly; incredibly; dreadfully.**

...Николай Гаврилович прижимал салфетку к сердцу, грозил проткнуть себе вилкой грудь. В свою очередь, она притворялась сердитой. Он просил прощения (всё это до жути не смешно)... (Набоков 1). ...Nikolay Gavrilovich, miming jealousy, would press a napkin to his heart and threaten to pierce his breast with a fork. In her turn she would pretend to be cross with him. He would then beg forgiveness (all this is horribly unfunny)... (1a).

З

З-1 • **(взвешивать) (все) ЗА И ПРО́ТИВ; ПРО И КО́Н-ТРА** *lit* [NP; these forms only; subj or obj; fixed WO] (to consider) the arguments in favor of and against sth.: **(weigh) (all) the pros and cons; (weigh ⟨consider, look at⟩) the pluses and minuses.**

З-2 • **ПРЕДАВА́ТЬ/ПРЕДА́ТЬ ЗАБВЕ́НИЮ** *что obsoles, lit* [VP; subj: human; fixed WO] to put sth. out of one's memory forever: X предал Y забвению ≃ **X consigned Y to oblivion.**

По поводу [разбитого] сервиза, ввиду того, что у Елены, конечно, даже язык не повернётся и вообще это хамство и мещанство — сервиз предать забвению (Булгаков 3). As for the smashed dinner service, since Elena could naturally not bring herself to complain about it, and to complain would in any case be insufferably vulgar and rude, they agreed to consign it to…oblivion (3a).

З-3 • **ЗАБЕГА́ТЬ/ЗАБЕЖА́ТЬ ВПЕРЁД** [VP; subj: human; fixed WO] **1.** to do sth. prematurely or in advance, interrupting the logical order, progression of events, actions etc: X забегает вперёд ≃ **X is getting (way) ahead of himself; X is rushing things; X is anticipating (matters ⟨events, things⟩); X is rushing ⟨jumping⟩ ahead.**

Забегая вперёд, скажу лишь одно: он [Иван Фёдорович] был теперь, в этот вечер, именно как раз накануне белой горячки, которая наконец уже вполне овладела его издавна расстроенным, но упорно сопротивлявшимся болезни организмом (Достоевский 2). Getting ahead of myself, I will say only one thing: he [Ivan Fyodorovich] was, that evening, precisely just on the verge of brain fever, which finally took complete possession of his organism, long in disorder but stubbornly refusing to succumb (2a). ♦ [Бусыгин:] Ну, не будем забегать вперёд, но вы мне уже нравитесь (Вампилов 4). [B.:] I don't want to rush things but you know what? I already like you (4c). ♦ …Борис Леонидович [Пастернак] учился у жизни и истории. И взгляды его на некоторые фундаментальные события века существенно эволюционировали. Иногда это проявлялось самым неожиданным образом. Забегая вперёд, вспомню об одном эпизоде из того времени, когда роман «Доктор Живаго» уже перешёл границу… (Ивинская 1). BL [Pasternak] was able to learn from life and history, and his views on certain basic events of our age underwent a substantial change. This was sometimes demonstrated in unexpected ways—as, for example, in an incident which—anticipating a little—I will mention here, though it happened many years later, at the time when *Doctor Zhivago* had already appeared abroad… (1a).

2. *obs* [usu. pfv] to forestall, outstrip s.o. by attaining or obtaining sth. first: X забежал вперёд ≃ **X got ahead of person Y; X eclipsed person Y's efforts; X beat person Y to it; X got there first.**

З-4 • **ВВОДИ́ТЬ/ВВЕСТИ́ В ЗАБЛУЖДЕ́НИЕ** *кого* [VP; subj: human or abstr] to misinform, disorient, deceive s.o.: X вводит Y-а в заблуждение ≃ **X is misleading ⟨deluding⟩ Y; [in limited contexts] person X is stringing Y along; person X is trying to fool Y (into thinking ⟨believing⟩ that…); X is leading Y astray.**

…Николая Ивановича [Бухарина] я ввела в заблуждение вполне сознательно, с холодным расчётом — нельзя отпугивать единственного защитника (Мандельштам 1). …I misled Bukharin quite deliberately, out of a calculated desire not to frighten off my only ally (1a). ♦ Никакие неологизмы… не могли ввести ни меня, ни Маяковского в заблуждение (Лившиц 1). No neologisms…could lead Maiakovsky or myself astray (1a). ♦ «Вы понимаете, чем это пахнет?.. Ложное показание с целью ввести в заблуждение правосудие» (Тендряков 1). [context transl] "You understand what this looks like?…False evidence with the aim of perverting the course of justice" (1a).

З-5 • **ВЫВОДИ́ТЬ/ВЫ́ВЕСТИ ИЗ ЗАБЛУЖДЕ́НИЯ** *кого* [VP; subj: human or abstr] to reveal the true state of affairs to s.o. who perceives it incorrectly: X вывел Y-а из заблуждения ≃ **X freed ⟨divested, stripped⟩ Y of Y's delusions ⟨illusions⟩ (about Z); X set Y straight (about Z); person X set ⟨put⟩ Y right (about Z).**

…Я стал бояться, чтобы она не приняла меня за дурака, и решился во что бы то ни стало вывести её из такого заблуждения на мой счёт (Толстой 2). …I began to fear that she would take me for a fool and resolved, come what may, to divest her of any such delusions on that score (2b). …I began to be afraid she would take me for a fool and decided to set her straight about me at any price (2d).

З-6 • **НЕ МОЯ́ ⟨твоя, его и т. п.⟩ ЗАБО́ТА ⟨ПЕЧА́ЛЬ⟩** *coll* [NP; Invar; subj-compl with быть∅ (subj: usu. abstr, often это)] sth. does not involve me (you etc), does not cause me (should not cause you etc) any anxiety, is of no interest to me (should be of no interest to you etc): это не Х-ова забота ≃ **that's not X's concern ⟨worry⟩; that's no business of X's; that's none of X's business; it's not X's headache ⟨problem⟩.**

[Валерия:] Вадим Андреевич, мы опаздываем. А Зилову, знаете, задержите ему отпуск. На недельку. Если он вовремя не попадёт на охоту… [Зилов:] Это не твоя забота (Вампилов 5). [V.:] Vadim Andreich, we're late. As for Zilov, hold up his vacation. For a week. If he can't go hunting on time… [Z.:] That's not your concern (5b). ♦ [Анютка:] Помрёт, должно, ребёночек-то?.. Куды [*substand* = куда] ж они его [ребёнка] денут? [Митрич:] Туда и денут, куда надо. Не твоя печаль (Толстой 1). [A.:] It'll die, I bet, the little baby?…Where'll they put it? [M.:] They'll put it where they got to. Not your worry (1a). ♦ «Зачем ему твой заячий тулуп? Он его пропьёт, собака, в первом кабаке». — «Это, старинушка, уж не твоя печаль, — сказал мой бродяга, — пропью ли я его или нет» (Пушкин 2). "Why give him your hareskin coat? The dog will only sell it for a drink at the first pub he gets to." "It's none of your business, old man," my vagabond said, "whether I sell it or not" (2b). ♦ …Не обращайте внимания на все эти мелочи, это в самом деле не ваша забота, дорогой (Аксёнов 12). "Don't pay attention to all these trifles, it's not really your headache, dear boy" (12a).

З-7 • **НЕ́ БЫЛО ЗАБО́ТЫ!** *highly coll* [Interj; Invar; fixed WO] used to express one's displeasure at, disappointment because of etc some unexpected trouble or worry: **that's the last thing I need ⟨want⟩!; just what I need(ed)!; as if I didn't have enough problems ⟨enough to do, enough to worry about⟩ already ⟨as it is⟩!**

«Тебе придётся съездить к Тихоновым и отвезти им этот пакет». — «Ну вот, не было заботы! Они живут на другом конце города!». "You'll have to stop by the Tikhonovs' place and deliver this package." "Great, that's the last thing I need! They live clear across town!"

З-8 • **С ОТКРЫ́ТЫМ ⟨С ПО́ДНЯТЫМ⟩ ЗАБРА́ЛОМ** *lit* [PrepP; these forms only; adv; fixed WO] (to do sth.) with complete openness, directness: **straightforwardly; boldly; openly; [in refer. to expressing one's formerly undisclosed views, opinions etc] (come) out in the open.**

Рыцарь без страха и упрёка, географ шёл один против всех с открытым забралом… (Соколов 1). …Daring and irreproachable, the geographer moved openly against everyone… (1a). ♦ «Объясните: почему *именно* Панкратов защищал Криворучко?» — «Панкратов за это тоже исключён», — отрезал Баулин. «Нет, не за это! — закричал Столпер. — Его исключили, когда он уже выступил с открытым забралом» (Рыбаков 2). "Explain to me, why precisely was it *Pankratov* who defended Krivoruchko?" "Pankratov has been expelled for it," Baulin retorted. "No, it wasn't for that!" Stolper yelled. "He was expelled only after he'd come out in the open" (2a).

3-9 • ЗАБЫВА́ТЬ/ЗАБЫ́ТЬ СЕБЯ́ *(для кого)* [VP; subj: human] to behave in a selfless, generous manner for the benefit of another, others, or some cause: X забывает себя (для других) ≃ **X sacrifices himself (for others); X puts others ahead of himself.**

3-10 • СЕБЯ́ НЕ ЗАБЫВА́ТЬ/НЕ ЗАБЫ́ТЬ [VP; subj: human] not to overlook one's own interests: X себя не забывает ≃ **X doesn't forget about himself; X takes ⟨doesn't forget to take⟩ care of himself;** [in limited contexts] **X looks ⟨watches⟩ out for himself; X doesn't lose sight of his own interests; X watches out for ⟨takes care of⟩ number one.**

[Золотуев:] Работа у него была интересная, он за прилавком стоял. Людей он не обижал и себя, конечно, не забывал (Вампилов 3). [Z.:] His work was interesting, he was a counter man. He was fair to people but he didn't forget about himself either (3b). ♦ …[Граф] усердно подливал вина своим соседям, не забывая и себя (Толстой 4). [context transl] …He [the Count] diligently filled his neighbors' glasses, not forgetting his own (4a).

3-11 • ЧТО Я ⟨ты он и т. п.⟩ ТАМ ⟨ТУТ⟩ ЗАБЫ́Л ⟨ПОТЕРЯ́Л⟩? *highly coll* [sent; these forms only; fixed WO] there is no reason why I (you etc) need to or would want to go there (or stay here): **why ⟨on earth ⟨in the world⟩⟩ would I ⟨you etc⟩ want to go there ⟨to stay here⟩?; what(ever) for?**

«Куда это ты идёшь?» — «На собрание». — «Что ты там забыл?» "Where are you going?" "To the meeting." "Why on earth would you want to go there?"

3-12 • НЕ ЗАБЫ́ТЬ *coll* [VP; subj: human; usu. fut] **1.** *кого* ~ to do sth. nice, kind, helpful for s.o. (in reciprocation for a favor, as recompense for a service, occas. as an act of patronage etc): X Y-a не забудет ≃ **X will do Y a good turn; X will make it worth Y's while; X will return the favor; X will do what he can for Y.**

2. ~ *кому чего* to harbor bad feelings toward s.o. (for some offense etc): X не забудет Y-у Z-a ≃ **X will never forgive Y (for) Z; X will never forget Z.**

Этого оскорбления я тебе не забуду. I'll never forgive you that insult.

3-13 • ХОТЬ ЗАВАЛИ́СЬ *чего highly coll* [хоть + VP$_{imper}$; Invar; quantit subj-compl with copula (subj/gen: usu. inanim); fixed WO] an abundance, a great deal of (things): **lots ⟨a lot⟩ of; heaps ⟨a heap⟩ of; tons ⟨a ton⟩ of; loads ⟨a load⟩ of; scads of; oodles of.**

Карандашей у меня хоть завались, бери сколько тебе нужно. I've got tons of pencils, take as many as you'd like.

3-14 • ВО ВСЕ НОСОВЫ́Е ЗАВЁРТКИ ⟨ВО ВСЮ НО-СОВУ́Ю ЗАВЁРТКУ⟩ храпеть *obs, substand, humor* [PrepP; these forms only; adv; fixed WO] (to snore) very loudly: **saw wood; (snore) like a chain ⟨buzz⟩ saw.**

[author's usage] День, кажется, был заключён порцией холодной телятины, бутылкою кислых щей и крепким сном во всю насосную завёртку, как выражаются в иных местах обширного русского государства (Гоголь 3). [context transl] The day was apparently concluded by a portion of cold veal, a pint of sour cabbage soup, and a sound sleep in which he snored away like a suction pump in full blast, as is the saying in some parts of our spacious Russian empire (3a).

3-15 • ДЫМОВА́Я ЗАВЕ́СА [NP; sing only; fixed WO] words, promises etc used to disguise s.o.'s actual designs, plans, intentions: **smoke screen.**

Слова про отчима Ольга Васильевна расценила как дымовую завесу и вовсе на них не отозвалась (Трифонов 3). Olga interpreted the reference to her stepfather as a smoke screen and did not pursue the subject (3a).

3-16 • ЗАВЕ́СА ПА́ДАЕТ/УПА́ЛА ⟨СПАДА́ЕТ/ СПА́ЛА⟩ (С ГЛАЗ *чьих*) *lit* [VP$_{subj}$; usu. pfv] what had previously been unclear to s.o. becomes evident, s.o. suddenly becomes aware of the truth and realizes that he had been mistaken: завеса упала с X-овых глаз ≃ **the scales fell from X's eyes.**

3-17 • ПРИПОДНИМА́ТЬ/ПРИПОДНЯ́ТЬ ЗАВЕ́СУ *(чего) (над чем)*; **ПРИОТКРЫВА́ТЬ/ПРИОТКРЫ́ТЬ ЗАВЕ́СУ** *над чем all lit* [VP; subj: human or abstr] to reveal sth. previously hidden, make it known: X приподнял завесу (тайны) над Y-ом ≃ **X lifted the veil of secrecy ⟨mystery⟩ from Y ⟨that hung over Y etc⟩; X took the wraps off Y.**

«Elle est bien malheureuse», — прибавила Анна Павловна. Полагая, что этими словами Анна Павловна слегка приподнимала завесу тайны над болезнью графини, один неосторожный молодой человек позволил себе выразить удивление тому, что не призваны известные врачи, а лечит графиню шарлатан, который может дать опасные средства (Толстой 7). "She is so unfortunate!" added Anna Pavlovna. Supposing that by these words Anna Pavlovna was slightly lifting the veil of mystery that hung over the Countess's illness, one imprudent young man ventured to express surprise that well-known doctors had not been called in and that the Countess was being treated by a charlatan who might apply dangerous remedies (7a).

3-18 • СРЫВА́ТЬ/СОРВА́ТЬ ⟨СНИМА́ТЬ/СНЯТЬ⟩ ЗАВЕ́СУ ⟨ПОКРО́В(Ы)⟩ *с чего lit* [VP; subj: usu. human] to reveal, make known the formerly hidden nature (of some reprehensible phenomenon, action etc): X сорвал завесу с Y-a ≃ **X exposed ⟨unmasked⟩ Y.**

3-19 • ЗАВИ́ДКИ БЕРУ́Т *(кого) substand* [VP$_{subj}$; usu. pres; fixed WO] s.o. feels envious (of another's success, desirable qualities etc): X-a завидки берут ≃ **X is ⟨it makes X⟩ (really) jealous ⟨envious⟩; X is ⟨it makes X⟩ green with envy; X wishes he were as** [AdjP] **as s.o. ⟨could do sth. as** [AdvP] **as s.o. etc⟩.**

«Ешь да спи, вот и вся теперь твоя работа. Ах, завидки берут!» (Максимов 3). "Eat and sleep, that's only work you have to do here. I'm really jealous" (3a). ♦ «Как это ты быстро всё понимаешь? Просто завидки берут — до чего толковая девка» (Распутин 3). "You do catch on fast! I wish I was as quick. What a clever girl!" (3a).

3-20 • В ЗАВИ́СИМОСТИ *от чего* [PrepP; Invar; Prep] being contingent (on sth.): **depending on ⟨upon⟩; according to.**

В зависимости от возраста, социального положения, партийности и образовательного уровня каждый человек получает пропаганду в том виде, какой, по мнению властей, доступен его пониманию (Войнович 1). Depending on age, social position, Party membership, and educational level, every person is given propaganda in a form that the authorities deem appropriate for him (1a). ♦ «Одна и та же строка может быть признана хорошей или плохой, в зависимости от того, в какой поэтической системе она находится…» (Гладков 1). "The same line may be considered good or bad according to which kind of poetic system it occurs in…" (1a).

3-21 • **НА ЗА́ВИСТЬ** *coll* [PrepP; Invar; modif or subj-compl with copula (subj: inanim)] so or such as to evoke feelings of envy in others: **(so pretty ⟨smart, well etc⟩) it makes you ⟨it's enough to make you⟩ jealous ⟨envious, green with envy⟩; an enviable [NP]; enviably.**

Подавальщица, румяная на зависть, приветливо указала мне моё место... (Чуковская 2). A waitress, with an enviable glow on her cheeks, showed me to my place... (2a).

3-22 • **(И) В ЗАВО́ДЕ НЕТ** *чего*, less often *кого (у кого, где)* *substand* [VP; pres or past] **1.** [subj/gen: usu. concr, abstr, animal, or, less often, human] (some person does not have or some place is devoid of s.o. or sth.) entirely: у Y-а X-а и в заводе нет ⟨не было⟩! ≃ **Y doesn't have ⟨never had⟩ any X!**

2. [subj/gen: usu. этого, такого (in conjunction with a чтобы-clause)] sth. is absolutely not done (by s.o. or in some place): у Y-а ⟨в месте Z⟩ этого ⟨такого⟩ и в заводе нет ≃ **none of that kind of stuff goes on with Y ⟨in place Z⟩; there's (never) nothing like that with Y ⟨in place Z⟩; Y doesn't allow any ⟨none⟩ of that in place Z ⟨here, there⟩.**

«В чём отказывали [своим детям]? Чего для них жалели?» — ...«Я видела, как вы своего-то [сына] ремнём гоняли, а у нас дома в заводе такого не было» (Стругацкие 1). "What did we deny them [our children]? What didn't we do for them?"... "You liked to strap yours [your son], I saw it, but in our house there was never nothing like that" (1a).

3-23 • **ТИ́ХАЯ ЗА́ВОДЬ** [NP; sing only; fixed WO] a quiet, undisturbed place where one feels protected from the outside world: **quiet ⟨peaceful⟩ haven; safe ⟨sheltered⟩ refuge; [in limited contexts] quiet little backwater.**

...Много лет спустя бывал я часто у своих знакомых... Однажды я неожиданно застал их в ожесточённом споре. Вся семья, включая старую бабку, спорила о Ленине... На следующий день я зашёл к ним опять — и опять застал их в споре о Ленине... И так недели две... Пропала моя тихая заводь, где можно было отдохнуть душой (Буковский 1). Some years later, I had some friends I often used to visit....One day I was surprised to find the entire family, including the ancient grandmother, engaged in a violent argument about Lenin....The following day I saw them again, and again they were arguing about Lenin....And so it continued for a couple of weeks. The peaceful haven where I had been able to refresh my soul was destroyed (1a). ♦ Прощай, деткомбинат, моя тихая заводь! (Гинзбург 2). Good-by, children's home, my quiet little backwater (2a).

3-24 • **ДО ЗА́ВТРА** *coll* [formula phrase; Invar] parting words said to a person or persons whom one expects to see the next day: **see you tomorrow; till tomorrow.**

3-25 • **КОРМИ́ТЬ ЗА́ВТРАКАМИ ⟨ОБЕЩА́НИЯМИ⟩** *кого coll* [VP; subj: human] to promise s.o. repeatedly that one will do sth. in the immediate future and not fulfill one's promises: X кормит Y-а завтраками ≃ **X feeds Y promises; X hands Y a line ⟨a story⟩; X is all talk and no action.**

Опять то же самое: «Приходите завтра, директор вас примет». Они меня завтраками кормят уже неделю. It's the same old story: "Come back tomorrow and the director will see you." They've been feeding me promises for a week now.

3-26 • **ПОД ⟨ПО⟩ (СА́МУЮ) ЗАВЯ́ЗКУ** *highly coll* [PrepP; these forms only; fixed WO] **1.** наполнить, нагрузить, набить *что (чем* or, less often, *кем)* ~ [usu. adv] (to fill, load etc sth.) to its uppermost physical capacity, to a point beyond which it is impossible, unadvisable, unrealistic etc to go: **to the limit; right to the top; chock-full ⟨chockful⟩; full up; to the breaking ⟨bursting etc⟩ point; (so that) there isn't room for (more ⟨another [NP] etc⟩).**

«...Нагрузили мою машину снарядами по самую завязку»... (Шолохов 1). "...My lorry was loaded with shells right to the top..." (1a). "We loaded up my lorry chockful of shells" (1c). ♦ «...Мы этого вашего Чонкина в настоящий момент до себя [*substand* = к себе] взять не можем, мест [*substand* = мест] нету. Гарнизонная гауптвахта — под завязку» (Войнович 4). "We are not taking that Chonkin of yours at the present moment because we have no room here. The garrison guardhouse is full up" (4a). ♦ «Вот это квас! Аж дух зашибает. Погоди, бабка, не уноси. Сейчас я сбегаю по малому делу, ещё выпью, а то уж некуда, под завязку» (Войнович 5). "That's kvass. Takes your breath away. Hold on, don't take it away. I'll go run and take a leak and then I'll have some more. There isn't room for another drop in me right now" (5a).

2. ~ *чего (у кого, в ком)* [quantit subj-compl with copula (subj/gen: abstr or concr) or adv] (of work, some emotion, some quality etc) sth. is present in the most extreme (usu. maximum) amount possible, tolerable etc: у Y-а X-а ~ ≃ **Y has all the X he can handle; Y is up to his neck ⟨his ears etc⟩ in X; [of work only] Y is swamped ⟨plowed under, snowed under⟩ with X.**

3-27 • **ИГРА́ТЬ В ЗАГА́ДКИ; ГОВОРИ́ТЬ ЗАГА́ДКАМИ** [VP; subj: human] to speak evasively, enigmatically, in a roundabout way: X играет в загадки ≃ **X talks ⟨speaks⟩ in riddles; [in limited contexts] X beats around ⟨about⟩ the bush.**

Не надо играть в загадки, говори прямо. Stop talking in riddles and tell it straight.

3-28 • **НА ЗАГЛЯДЕ́НЬЕ** *(кому) coll* [PrepP; Invar; modif, subj-compl with copula (subj: usu. concr or human), or adv; indir obj: всем, другим etc] (of things or, less often, people that one stares at in admiration) remarkable, remarkably: **marvelous ⟨amazing, incredible⟩; marvelously ⟨amazingly, incredibly⟩; a sight to see ⟨to behold⟩;** ‖ всем ~ ≃ **so [AdjP or AdvP] that people stop and stare; so [AdjP or AdvP] that people look upon one ⟨it⟩ with wonder.**

Почерк у тебя на загляденье, я никогда не видела более красивого почерка. Your handwriting is incredible, I've never seen prettier.

3-29 • **ДО МОРКО́ВКИНА ЗА́ГОВЕНЬЯ** *highly coll, humor* [PrepP; Invar; adv; fixed WO] for an indefinitely long time: **till doomsday; till hell freezes over; till the end of time; till the cows come home.**

Снова ходили они вокруг дерева, трогали его топорами, пытались рубить и оставляли эти попытки: топоры, соскребая тонкую гарь, отскакивали от ствола, как от резины... «Пилу надо». — «Пилой ты его до морковкиного заговенья будешь ширкать [*substand* = пилить]» (Распутин 4). They circled the tree again, touching it with their axes, trying to chop it and dropping their attempts: the axes, scraping off a thin layer of burned wood, pushed off from the trunk as if it were rubber...."We need a saw." "You'll be sawing till doomsday" (4a).

3-30 • **ЗА́ГОВОР МОЛЧА́НИЯ** *(против кого)* [NP; sing only; fixed WO] a (usu. unspoken) understanding between many people (often members of the media) not to discuss, mention etc sth.: **conspiracy of silence; [in limited contexts] (sth. is) suppressed altogether.**

Вокруг одних имён был заговор молчания, другие имена поносились в печати и в постановлениях... (Мандельштам 2). The names of some poets were simply suppressed altogether, while others were denounced in the press and in Party decrees... (2a).

< Loan translation of the French phrase *une conspiration du silence*.

3-31 • **В ЗАГО́НЕ** [PrepP; Invar] **1.** жить, расти, быть~ *obsoles* [adv or subj-compl with быть~ (subj: human)] (to live, grow up etc) without receiving sufficient supervision, nurturing etc from one's parent(s) or guardian(s): **without receiving proper care; without being properly cared for; (be) neglected.**

2. ~ *(у кого, где)* [subj-compl with copula (subj: human or collect)] (often used in refer. to the status of a person, group, department etc at some workplace, in the eyes of the management etc) a person (group etc) is disregarded, considered unimportant, treated poorly etc: X в загоне (у Y-a ⟨в месте Z⟩) ≃ **X is treated as if he ⟨it etc⟩ didn't matter (by Y ⟨at place Z⟩); X is treated like he ⟨it⟩ doesn't matter (by Y ⟨at place Z⟩); X is treated like a nonentity (by Y ⟨at place Z⟩); X gets second-rate treatment; X is low on Y's list of priorities; X is suffering from neglect; X is neglected (by Y).**

Похоже, что наш отдел скоро закроют, — он давно уже у начальства в загоне. It looks as if our department might be shut down soon—the administration's been treating it like a nonentity for quite a while now.

3-32 • НА ЗАДВО́РКАХ *(чего)* **быть₀, держать** *кого-что coll* [PrepP; Invar; usu. subj-compl with copula (subj: human, collect, or abstr) or obj-compl with держать (obj: human, collect, or abstr)] (of or in refer. to a person) (to be, keep s.o.) in a secondary, disadvantageous role or position; (of or in refer. to an issue, proposal etc) (to be, keep sth.) out of the focus of attention, ignore (sth.): **be ⟨be kept, keep s.o. or sth.⟩ in the background;** [of or in refer. to a person] **take ⟨be forced to take etc⟩ a back seat;** [of or in refer. to an issue, proposal etc] **(be ⟨be put, put sth.⟩) on the back burner.**

Казачьи офицеры были на задворках... движение по службе было слабым... (Шолохов 3). The Cossack officers had been kept in the background...; promotion had been slow... (3b). ♦ Конечно, и Васькин за это время преуспел. Но — с большим отставанием и в меньших масштабах [, чем я], на задворках, так сказать (Зиновьев 2). Of course, during the same period Vaskin, too, came to succeed. But he was very much behind me, on a lower scale—forced, one might say, to take a back seat (2a).

3-33 • ЗА́ДОМ НАПЕРЁД [AdvP; Invar; adv; fixed WO] with the back side forward: **backward; back to front; the wrong way (a)round.**

Ты надела шляпу задом наперёд. You put your hat on backward.

3-34 • НЕ ТУДА́ ЗАЕ́ХАТЬ *highly coll* [VP; subj: human; usu. past; usu. this WO] to make an inappropriate digression from the topic under discussion, say sth. unfitting: X не туда заехал ≃ [with the focus on straying from the topic at hand] **X got off course ⟨off the track⟩;** [with the focus on the inappropriateness of a comment] **X went too far; X said something he shouldn't have; X shouldn't have said that; X ⟨X's remark etc⟩ was out of line.**

«Напрасно ты упомянул о наркотиках. Этой темы в разговорах с Беллой лучше не касаться». — «Да, я и сам сразу понял, что не туда заехал». "You shouldn't have brought up narcotics. It's better to steer clear of that topic when talking to Bella." "Yes, I knew right away that I said something I shouldn't have."

3-35 • БЕЗ ЗАЗРЕ́НИЯ СО́ВЕСТИ *coll* [PrepP; Invar; adv; fixed WO] without feeling ashamed (of one's actions or words), without feeling guilty: **without any pangs of conscience; without a ⟨the slightest⟩ twinge of conscience; without a qualm ⟨any qualms⟩ (of conscience); without any scruples; without compunction.**

[Трилецкий:] Вот как нужно жить на этом свете! Посадил беззащитную женщину за шахматы да и обчистил её без зазрения совести на десять целкачей [*substand* = целковых рублей] (Чехов 1). [T.:] That's the way to get on in this world. Put a

defenceless woman at a chessboard and clean her out of ten rubles without the slightest twinge of conscience (1a). ♦ ...[Крючков] рассказывал о «подвиге»... врал без зазрения совести... (Шолохов 2). ...He [Kryuchkov] described his "exploit"...lying without a qualm of conscience... (2a). ♦ ...Мои крупицы [слова и выражения из моих рукописей], даже в искажённом виде, помогли ему быстро сделать блистательную карьеру, и теперь без зазрения совести он потреблял плоды славы, которые по праву принадлежали мне одному (Терц 4). ...The crumbs from my table [words and expressions from my manuscripts], even in distorted form, had helped him rapidly to achieve a brilliant career, and now, without any qualms of conscience, he was consuming the fruits of glory which by rights belonged to me alone (4a).

3-36 • ГОНЯ́ТЬСЯ ⟨ГНА́ТЬСЯ⟩/ПОГНА́ТЬСЯ ЗА ДВУМЯ́ ЗА́ЙЦАМИ *coll* [VP; subj: human; the verb may take the final position, otherwise fixed WO] to attempt to reach two different goals, accomplish two different things at the same time: X погнался за двумя зайцами ≃ **X chased two hares at the same time.**

< From the proverb «За двумя зайцами погонишься, ни одного не поймаешь». See 3-37.

3-37 • ЗА ДВУМЯ́ ЗА́ЙЦАМИ ПОГО́НИШЬСЯ, НИ ОДНОГО́ НЕ ПОЙМА́ЕШЬ [saying] if you try to do several things at the same time, you will not do any of them well or finish anything: **if you chase ⟨run⟩ after two hares, you will catch neither; he who chases two hares catches neither; if you choose two hares, both will escape you.**

3-38 • УБИВА́ТЬ/УБИ́ТЬ ДВУХ ЗА́ЙЦЕВ [VP; subj: human; usu. pfv] to accomplish two important things at once, realize two goals through a single action (the notion of a single action may either be expressed by adverbials like сразу, одним ударом, одновременно etc, or be implied): X убил двух зайцев ≃ **X killed two birds with one stone.**

Я помню растерянный вид Мандельштама, когда мы вернулись домой, поглядев, как происходит изъятие [церковного имущества]... Предложение [патриарха] Тихона [организовать помощь голодающим] отклонили, а теперь вопят, что церковники не жалеют голодающих и прячут свои сокровища. Одним ударом убивали двух зайцев: загребали золото и порочили церковников (Мандельштам 2). I remember the appalled look on M[andelstam]'s face as we returned home after watching the "confiscation" [of church property] for a while....[Patriarch] Tikhon's proposal [to organize aid for the starving] had been turned down, and now they were shrieking that the church people had no pity for the starving and were hoarding their treasures. In this way they were killing two birds with one stone: while vilifying the church, they were also grabbing its gold (2a).

3-39 • НЕ ЗАКА́ЖЕШЬ *кому obsoles, substand* [VP; this form (gener. 2nd pers sing) only; usu. used with the infin of another verb] you cannot forbid s.o. to do sth.: **you can't stop ⟨prevent⟩ s.o. (from doing sth.); there is no law against (doing) sth.**

[Гурмыжская:] Хоть я и выше подозрений, но, если б нашлись злые языки, вы можете объяснить, в чём дело. [Милонов:] ...Кто же смеет... [Бодаев:] Ну, отчего же не сметь? Никому не закажешь (Островский 7). [G.:] I am above suspicion, as you know. But if you chance to hear evil gossip, you will be able to explain what's going on. [M.:] ...Who on earth would dare... [B.:] Well, why on earth shouldn't a person dare? You can't stop a person, can you? (7b). [G.:] Everyone knows I am above suspicion, but sometimes evil tongues will wag, so now you can explain the truth. [M.:] ...Who could possibly dare—? [B.:] Of course they'll dare, there's no law against it (7c).

3-40 • **НА ЗАКА́З** [PrepP; Invar; adv or nonagreeing modif] (of clothes, footwear etc) made according to the buyer's wishes: **made-to-order; custom-made; tailor-made; made to measure.**

Туфли мы покупаем готовыми, а костюм стараемся сшить на заказ (Рыбаков 1). Shoes we buy ready-made, whereas we like to have our suits made to measure (1a).

3-41 • **КАК ПО ЗАКА́ЗУ; КАК НА ЗАКА́З** [как + PrepP; these forms only] **1.** [subj-compl with быть∅, стоять etc (subj: usu. погода, утро, день etc)] beautiful, remarkable: X как по заказу ≃ it's as if X were made to order; X could have been made to order; X couldn't be better ⟨more perfect⟩; you couldn't ask for better ⟨for (a) better X⟩.

Вечер был как по заказу. Днём, после полудня, хлестнул дружный ливень – с луга домой прибежали насквозь мокрые, – а потом опять солнце, опять тепло... (Абрамов 1). The evening could have been made to order. In the afternoon, there was a sudden, welcome downpour—people came running home from the fields soaked through—and then it was sunny and warm again... (1a). ♦ Кузьма сидел и вспоминал сентябрь сорок седьмого года. Поспели хлеба... Погода стояла как на заказ – ни одной тучки (Распутин 1). As Kuzma sat there he recalled what had happened in September 1947. The corn was ripe....The weather could not have been more perfect for harvesting. Not a cloud in the sky (1a).

2. [adv] excellently, flawlessly, precisely as desired: **perfectly; swimmingly; (sth.) couldn't have gone ⟨been, come out etc⟩ better; without a hitch.**

Нина очень волновалась перед интервью, но всё прошло как по заказу. Nina was really nervous before her interview, but everything went swimmingly.

3-42 • **ПО ЗАКА́ЗУ** [PrepP; Invar; adv] in response to a request, in fulfillment of an order, assignment: **on demand; by request; [in limited contexts] to order.**

«Расскажите нам о своих путешествиях». – «В другой раз, не люблю рассказывать по заказу». "Tell us about your travels." "Some other time. I don't like to tell about them on demand." ♦ В это время он [Мольер] заканчивал работу над пьесой «Учёные женщины», написанной им не по заказу, а для себя (Булгаков 5). He [Molière] was at that time completing his work on *The Learned Ladies*, which he had written, not to order, but for himself (5a).

3-43 • **СТА́РОГО ЗАКА́ЛА; СТА́РОЙ ЗАКВА́СКИ** *both coll* [NP_gen; these forms only; nonagreeing modif; fixed WO] (a person) who has old-fashioned ways, adheres to old-fashioned ideas etc: **of the old school ⟨stamp⟩.**

...Нивелляторы старого закала, подобные Угрюм-Бурчееву, действовали в простоте души, единственно по инстинктивному отвращению от кривой линии и всяких зигзагов и извилин (Салтыков-Щедрин 1). ...The levellers of the old school, such as Ugryum-Burcheev, acted in the simplicity of their hearts, solely in response to their instinctive abhorrence for crooked lines and any kind of zigzag or curve (1b). ♦ ...Это был человек старого закала, не разделявший новейших воззрений (Тургенев 2). ...He was a man of the old stamp and did not accept the modern views (2a).

3-44 • **НА ЗАКА́ТЕ ДНЕЙ ⟨ЖИ́ЗНИ⟩** *lit* [PrepP; these forms only; adv; more often used with pfv verbs; fixed WO] in a person's old age: **in the twilight ⟨autumn⟩ of one's life; in the sunset of one's days; in one's declining years.**

...На самом закате жизни он сочиняет произведение, в котором мечту воплощает... (Набоков 1). ...In the very twilight of his life he composes a work in which he embodies his dream... (1a). ♦ Больной, озлобленный, всеми забытый, доживал Козырь свой век и на закате дней вдруг почувствовал прилив «дурных страстей»... (Салтыков-Щедрин 1). Hotspur lived out his life sick, embittered, forgotten by all. In the sunset of his days he suddenly felt an upsurge of "evil passions"... (1a). ♦ «На закате дней своих он убеждается ясно, что лишь советы великого страшного духа могли бы хоть сколько-нибудь устроить в сносном порядке малосильных бунтовщиков...» (Достоевский 1). "In his declining years he comes to the clear conviction that only the counsels of the great and dread spirit could at least somehow organize the feeble rebels..." (1a).

3-45 • **БИ́ТЬСЯ/ПОБИ́ТЬСЯ ОБ ЗАКЛА́Д** [VP; subj: human] **1.** ~ *(с кем)*. Also: **УДА́РИТЬСЯ ОБ ЗАКЛА́Д** *obs* to stake sth. on the outcome of an uncertain issue, event etc, usu. in return for a similar pledge by another: X побился об заклад (с Y-ом) ≃ X bet ⟨wagered⟩ Y (five rubles etc); X bet on it; X laid ⟨made, placed⟩ a bet ⟨a wager⟩ on it.

Прежде всего пошли они обсматривать конюшню, где видели... гнедого жеребца, на вид и неказистого, но за которого Ноздрёв божился, что заплатил десять тысяч. «Десяти тысяч ты за него не дал, – заметил зять. – Он и одной не стоит»... – «Ну, хочешь, побьёмся об заклад!» – сказал Ноздрёв. Об заклад зять не хотел биться (Гоголь 3). First they went to the stables; there they found...a bay stallion, not much to look at, but for which, so he swore, Nozdrev had paid ten thousand rubles. "You didn't pay ten thousand for him," his brother-in-law said. "He's even worth one thousand"...."Would you like to bet on it?" But his brother-in-law didn't wish to bet (3e).

2. *coll* [pres 1st pers sing бьюсь... only] I assure you, I am ready to swear (that what I am stating is true, that my prediction, guess is correct etc): **I ⟨I'll⟩ bet (you); I ⟨I'll⟩ bet you anything; I'm ready to bet.**

«...Я бьюсь об заклад, что нынче он узнал Бэлу» (Лермонтов 1). "...I'll bet you anything that he recognized Bela today" (1a). ♦ «Дворца не обещаю, – уверенно добавил Лёвушкин, – но что [дом] сто лет простоит – об заклад бьюсь» (Максимов 3). "I can't promise a palace," added Lyovushkin, "but I'm ready to bet it'll [the house will] stand a hundred years" (3a).

3-46 • **В ЗАКЛЮЧЕ́НИЕ** [PrepP; Invar; sent adv] (used to introduce the final point in a speech or writing, topic of discussion, event in a series of events etc) finally, lastly: **in conclusion; in closing; conclude ⟨end⟩ by (saying sth.); conclude ⟨end⟩ with (sth.); (in order) to conclude (a discussion ⟨a speech etc⟩).**

«В заключение команда выздоравливающих исполнит патриотические песни...» (Федин 1). "In conclusion a team of convalescents will perform patriotic songs..." (1a). ♦ Скажу в заключение, что он [Печорин] был вообще очень недурён... (Лермонтов 1). Let me conclude by saying that he [Pechorin] was on the whole rather good-looking... (1c). ♦ В заключение Марк Александрович в резкой форме критиковал неисправных поставщиков (Рыбаков 2). He [Mark Alexandrovich] concluded with sharp criticism of faulty suppliers (2a).

3-47 • **ВСТУПИ́ТЬ В ЗАКО́Н; ПРИНЯ́ТЬ ЗАКО́Н** *both obs, substand* [VP; subj: human, male] to get married (to s.o.): X вступил в закон ≃ **X got hitched.**

3-48 • **ЗАКО́Н НЕ ПИ́САН** *кому, для кого coll, often disapprov* [VP_subj; this form only; fixed WO] s.o. disregards generally accepted norms, rules of conduct: для X-а закон не писан ≃ **the law is not written ⟨made⟩ for X; X is a law unto himself; the law doesn't ⟨the rules don't⟩ apply to X; X doesn't play ⟨live⟩ by the rules; X doesn't go by the book.**

«...[В вашей статье] проводится некоторый намёк на то, что существуют на свете будто бы некоторые такие лица, которые могут... то есть не то что могут, а полное право имеют совершать всякие бесчинства и преступления, и что для них будто бы и закон не писан» (Достоевский 3). "...[In your article] a certain hint is presented that there supposedly exist in the world certain persons who can...that is, who not only can but are fully entitled to commit all sorts of crimes and excesses and to whom the law supposedly does not apply" (3c). ♦ «Мсьё Вольдемар [играет в фанты] с нами в первый раз, и сегодня для него закон не писан» (Тургенев 3). "M'sieu Woldemar is here [playing a game of forfeits with us] for the first time, and today the rules do not apply to him" (3a).

3-49 • ЗАКО́Н ЧТО ДЫ́ШЛО: КУДА́ ПОВЕРНУ́Л ⟨ПОВЕРНЁШЬ⟩, ТУДА́ И ВЫ́ШЛО [saying] a law may be interpreted in many different ways (refers to the reality that those who have the power and/or means can find ways of escaping punishment when breaking the law): ≃ **every law has a loophole; one law for the rich and another for the poor.**

3-50 • ВНЕ ЗАКО́НА быть∅, находиться, объявить *кого* и т. п. [PrepP; Invar; usu. subj-compl with copula (subj: human) or obj-compl with объявить (obj: human)] outside the protection of the law: X был ⟨X-а объявили⟩ вне закона ≃ **X was outlawed; X was declared ⟨branded⟩ an outlaw ⟨an outcast⟩.**

…[Союзники] заставили Наполеона отречься от престола и послали его на остров Эльбу, не лишая его сана императора и оказывая ему всякое уважение, несмотря на то, что пять лет тому назад и год после этого все его считали разбойником вне закона (Толстой 7). …[The allies] forced Napoleon to abdicate, and sent him to the island of Elba, without divesting him of the title of Emperor and showing him every respect, despite the fact that five years before and one year later everyone regarded him as a brigand and outlaw (7a). ♦ Исключённый из Союза писателей, я был объявлен как бы вне закона (Войнович 1). Expelled from the Writers' Union, I had been declared something of an outcast (1a).

3-51 • В ЗАКО́НЕ *с кем* жить, быть∅ и т. п. *obs, substand* [PrepP; Invar; subj-compl with copula (subj: human) or adv] (to be) legally married (to s.o.): **(be) lawfully married; (live) in lawful marriage ⟨holy wedlock⟩; (be) bound in holy wedlock.**

[Кабанова:] Ведь ты… с ней [с женой] в законе живёшь. Али [*substand* = или], по-вашему, закон ничего не значит? (Островский 6). [K.:] After all…you're living with her [your wife] in lawful marriage. Or, to your way of thinking, doesn't lawful marriage mean anything? (6a).

3-52 • НА ЗАКУ́СКУ *coll* [PrepP; Invar; adv] (to announce, present, perform etc sth.) as the last item in a series, (save sth.) for the final segment, the conclusion of (some event, activity etc): **for ⟨as⟩ one's final (announcement ⟨number etc⟩); (here's ⟨one finished up with etc⟩) one last ⟨final⟩ (joke ⟨announcement etc⟩); [when the final number, announcement etc is intended to be esp. pleasing] as a final ⟨special⟩ treat; saving the best for last (, here's…); to top off (the concert ⟨the show etc⟩); as one's finale.**

3-53 • НА ЗАМЕ́ТКЕ ⟨НА ЗАМЕЧА́НИИ *obs*⟩ *у кого* [PrepP; these forms only; subj-compl with быть∅ (subj: human); prep obj: often a noun denoting the police, security organs etc] one is the object of close observation: X на заметке у Y-а ≃ **X is under surveillance; Y keeps tabs on X; Y has ⟨keeps⟩ an eye on X.**

«Слушайте, Виктор, – сказал Голем. – Я позволил вам болтать на эту тему только для того, чтобы вы испугались и не лезли в чужую кашу. Вам это совершенно ни к чему. Вы и так уже на заметке…» (Стругацкие 1). "Listen, Victor," said Golem. "I've allowed you to shoot your mouth off on this topic only to get you scared, to stop you from sticking your nose into other people's business. This isn't doing you any good. They've got an eye on you as it is" (1a).

3-54 • БРАТЬ/ВЗЯТЬ НА ЗАМЕ́ТКУ [VP] **1.** ~ *что* [subj: human] to write sth. down in order not to forget it: X взял Y на заметку ≃ **X made a note of Y; X took Y down.**

«А ну-ка, возьми себе на заметку: двадцать пятого октября на бюро райкома» (Абрамов 1). "Now then, just make a note of this: October twenty-fifth you're to come down to the District Committee office" (1a).

2. ~ *кого-что* [subj: human or collect] (usu. in refer. to a person who shows promise in some area, a promising undertaking etc) to pay special attention to s.o. or sth.: X возьмёт Y-а на заметку ≃ **X will take notice ⟨note⟩ of Y; X will keep an eye on Y; X will make a mental note of thing Y.**

«Я ведь тебя ещё в карантине на заметку взял» (Максимов 2). "I've been keeping an eye on you since you first arrived in quarantine" (2a).

3. ~ *кого.* Also: **БРАТЬ/ВЗЯТЬ НА ЗАМЕЧА́НИЕ** *obs* [subj: human or collect, often a noun denoting the police, security organs etc] to consider s.o. among those who must be kept under observation (as a political threat, a bad influence on society, a troublemaker etc): X взял Y-а на заметку ≃ **X took note ⟨notice⟩ of Y; X started keeping tabs on Y; [in limited contexts] Y became a marked man.**

…Если бы я был такой умный, продемонстрировал кагебешникам знание законов и высокий уровень правосознания, они бы уже тогда взяли меня на заметку, и как бы сложилась моя судьба, никому не известно (Войнович 1). …If I had been clever and had demonstrated my knowledge of the law and my highly developed sense of justice, they [the KGB] would have taken note of me at the time, and my life would have become more complicated (1a). ♦ [Чекисты] приглашали людей обычно не на Лубянку, а на специально содержавшиеся с этой целью квартиры. Отказывающихся держали там часами, бесконечно долго, предлагая «подумать». Из вызовов тайны не делали: они служили важным звеном в системе устрашения, а также способствовали проверке гражданских чувств – упрямцев брали на заметку и при случае с ними расправлялись (Мандельштам 1). They [the Chekists] generally invited people for these interviews not to the Lubianka, but to apartments specially allotted for the purpose. The uncooperative were kept for hours on end and urged to "think again." No secret was made of all this—it was an important element in the general system of intimidation, as well as being a good way of testing a person's "loyalty." The stubborn became marked men and were "dealt with" as opportunity arose (1a).

3-55 • ПОПАДА́ТЬ/ПОПА́СТЬ НА ЗАМЕ́ТКУ ⟨НА ЗАМЕЧА́НИЕ *obs*⟩ *(кому, кого)* [VP; subj: human; indir obj: often a noun denoting the police, security organs etc] to become noticed as involved in sth., usu. sth. reprehensible: X попал на заметку (Y-у) ≃ **X drew the attention of Y; X was placed under surveillance ⟨observation⟩ (by Y); X became an object of scrutiny (by Y).**

3-56 • С ЗАМИРА́НИЕМ СЕ́РДЦА; С ЗАМИРА́Ю-ЩИМ СЕ́РДЦЕМ [PrepP; these forms only; adv] in a state of nervous expectation or high anxiety: **with (one's) heart pounding; with a pounding heart; one's heart stands still (as…); with one's heart in one's mouth.**

3-57 • ЗА ⟨ПОД⟩ СЕМЬЮ́ ЗАМКА́МИ [PrepP; these forms only; usu. adv or subj-compl with copula] **1.** [subj: usu. human or concr] well guarded: **under lock and key; locked up tight(ly); guarded day and night; under seven locks.**

[Расплюев:] Под семью печатями и за семью замками лежит стекло… (Сухово-Кобылин 2). [R.:] A piece of glass is lying there under seven seals and seven locks… (2b).

2. [subj: abstr] well-hidden, inaccessible (often of a person's feelings): **buried deep (down) inside; hidden away;** [in limited contexts] **(be) a deep dark secret.**

Зная, что Людмила Николаевна замужем, Рыжков хранил свои чувства к ней за семью замками. Knowing that Lyudmila Nikolayevna was married, Ryzhkov kept his feelings for her buried deep down inside.

3-58 • **НА ЗАМКЕ́ ⟨ПОД ЗАМКО́М⟩ быть∅, держать кого-что и т. п.; НА ЗАМО́К посадить кого; ПОД ЗАМО́К спрятать что** [PrepP; these forms only; subj-compl with copula (subj: concr or human) or obj-compl with держать etc (obj: concr or human)] (to be, keep s.o. or sth. etc) confined, securely shut up: **under lock and key; locked up ⟨away⟩;** [in refer. to money, valuables etc] **in safekeeping.**

«Такое отродье надо держать на замке!» (Федин 1). "Offspring like that should be kept under lock and key!" (1a). ♦ Василиса Егоровна возвратилась домой... и узнала, что во время её отсутствия было у Ивана Кузьмича совещание и что Палашка была под замком (Пушкин 2). ...When she [Vasilisa Egorovna] returned home, she learned that Ivan Kuzmich had called a meeting and locked Palashka up in her absence (2a). ♦ ...Главное, об этом ни слова никому не говорить, потому что бог знает ещё что из этого выйдет, а деньги поскорее под замок... (Достоевский 3). ...The main thing was not to say a word to anyone about this, since God only knew what else might come of it and the money should immediately be placed in safekeeping... (3a).

3-59 • **ВОЗДУ́ШНЫЕ ЗА́МКИ (строить)** [NP; pl only; usu. obj] daydreams, hopes that are unlikely to become reality: **(build) castles in the air.** Cf. **castles in Spain.**

...Пока вы намечаете программы великих преобразований, строите воздушные замки... или пытаетесь рассмотреть в микроскоп Х-хромосому, наш скромный труженик своими востренькими глазками бдительно следит, нельзя ли под видом борьбы с чуждой идеологией что-нибудь у вас оттяпать... (Войнович 3). ...While you plan great reform programs, build castles in the air...or try to see an X chromosome through a microscope, our humble drudge, with his sharp little eyes, watches carefully to see if, under the guise of struggling against alien ideology, he can get something from you... (3a).

3-60 • **ПОЦЕЛОВА́ТЬ ЗАМО́К** coll; **ПОЦЕЛОВА́ТЬ ПРОБО́Й** substand [VP; subj: human] (to go to s.o.'s residence or some office and) not to find anyone there: X поцеловал замок ≃ **no one was in ⟨(at) home, there⟩; not a soul was there.**

«Ты заходил к Саше?» — «Да, но поцеловал замок и ушёл». "Did you drop by Sasha's?" "Yes, but no one was home, so I left."

3-61 • **ЗАМЫКА́ТЬСЯ/ЗАМКНУ́ТЬСЯ В (САМО́М) СЕБЕ́** [VP; subj: human] to become unsociable, avoid people: X замкнулся в себе ≃ **X withdrew into himself; X retreated into his shell.**

После смерти сына Катя замкнулась в себе, перестала видеться даже с друзьями. After the death of her son Katya withdrew into herself and stopped seeing even her friends.

3-62 • **ПОД ЗА́НАВЕС** [PrepP; Invar; adv] right before the conclusion of sth., at the very end of sth. (often used in refer. to one's saving the most effective statement, remark, item etc for the end of a written piece, speech, recital etc): **as ⟨just before⟩ the curtain falls ⟨comes down⟩; at ⟨before⟩ curtainfall ⟨curtain-fall⟩.**

И наконец [в конце статьи], так сказать, под занавес, я наносил заключительный удар. Но как раз в это место статьи и вкралась опечатка, из-за которой впоследствии и поднялось столько шума (Домбровский 1). Finally, [at the end of the article,] just before curtain-fall as it were, I delivered the conclusive blow. But it so happened that a printer's error crept into the article at that very point and it was this which was the cause of all the subsequent trouble (1a).

< From an old custom among playwrights of giving actors especially effective lines at the very end of a play, act, or scene.

3-63 • **НЕ ЗАНИМА́ТЬ** кому чего or где кого-чего coll; **НЕ ЗАНИМА́ТЬ СТАТЬ** substand [VP; infin only; quantit subj-compl with быть∅; subj/gen: usu. abstr (var. with кому чего), concr or, less often, human (var. with где кого-чего); usu. pres] s.o. possesses a generous amount of some quality (more often a positive one), in some place there is more than a sufficient quantity of some thing or of people of a certain group (profession etc): X-a Y-у не занимать ≃ **Y has plenty of X; Y is not lacking in ⟨not short on⟩ X; you can't deny Y his X; there's no disputing Y's X;** ‖ в месте Y X-ов не занимать ≃ **there are plenty ⟨there is no lack⟩ of Xs in place Y; there are all kinds of Xs in place Y.**

Лукерья опять усмехнулась и сказала: «Да уж чего-чего, а красоты твоей невестушке не занимать» (Абрамов 1). Lukerya grinned again and said, "Yes, there's one thing you can't deny your daughter-in-law, and that's beauty" (1a).

3-64 • **ПОД ЗАПА́Л; В ЗАПА́ЛЕ** both coll [PrepP; these forms only; adv] impulsively, driven by an outburst of feeling: **in the heat of the moment; in a fit ⟨a burst⟩ of temper;** [in limited contexts] **when one is ⟨gets⟩ hot under the collar.**

Чего не скажешь в запале, особенно во время войны! (Рыбаков 1). ...You say all sorts of things in the heat of the moment, especially in wartime (1a).

3-65 • **ПРО ЗАПА́С держать, оставить что** и т. п. coll [PrepP; Invar; usu. adv] (to keep, save etc sth.) for use when needed: **in reserve; as a reserve; in store; on hand;** [in limited contexts] **in case of need.**

Странно, что все мы, безумные и нормальные, никогда не расстаёмся с этой надеждой: самоубийство — это тот ресурс, который мы держим про запас, и почему-то верим, что никогда не поздно к нему прибегнуть (Мандельштам 1). It is strange that all of us, whether mad or not, never give up this one hope: suicide is the last resort, which we keep in reserve, believing that it is never too late to use it (1a). ♦ Принц Ольденбургский требовал для кормления пеликанов самой свежей рыбы, поэтому боцман всегда держал про запас сачок, наполненный рыбой и опущенный в море (Искандер 3). Prince Oldenburgsky demanded the very freshest fish to feed the pelicans, which is why the harbormaster always kept on hand a net full of fish, submerged in the sea (3a).

3-66 • **В ЗАПА́СЕ** [PrepP; Invar; usu. subj-compl with copula (subj: any common noun)] kept for later use, ready to be used: **in reserve; (have ⟨keep etc⟩ sth.) ready;** [in limited contexts] **(have ⟨keep etc⟩ sth.) up one's sleeve.**

...Он [защитник] всех прокурорских свидетелей сумел вовремя «подвести» и, по возможности, сбить, а главное, подмарать их нравственную репутацию... Все были убеждены, что какой-нибудь большой и окончательной пользы он всеми этими «подмарываниями» не мог достичь и, вероятно, это сам лучше всех понимает, имея какую-то свою идею в запасе, какое-то ещё пока припрятанное оружие защиты, которое вдруг и обнаружит, когда придёт срок (Достоевский 2). ...He [the defense attorney] had been able to "take down" all the witnesses for the prosecution, to throw them off as much as possible, and, above all, to cast a slight taint on their moral reputations....Everyone was convinced that he could achieve no great and ultimate advantage by all these "slight taints," and that he probably knew it better than anyone, holding ready some idea of his own, some still hidden weapon of defense that he would suddenly reveal when the time came (2a).

З-67 • **БЕЗ ЗАПИ́НКИ** сказать, ответить и т. п. [PrepP; Invar; adv] **1.** (to say sth., answer etc) fluently, smoothly: **without stumbling once; without stumbling over a single word; without a flub** ⟨a fumble etc⟩.

Капитан сделал паузу, ещё раз без запинки повторил просьбу, и, поблагодарив за внимание, исчез с экрана (Чернёнок 2). The captain paused, repeated the request without a flub, thanked them for their attention, and disappeared from the screen (2a).

2. (to say sth., answer etc) without vacillation: **without (a moment's) hesitation; without thinking twice; unhesitatingly.**

«Зачем ты здесь?» — говорит капитан-исправник. «Отпущен на оброк», — отвечаешь ты без запинки (Гоголь 3). "What are you doing here?" says the police captain. "I've been allowed to go on payment of tax," you reply without a moment's hesitation (3a). ♦ «Что такое общество?» — задал он себе вопрос и тотчас же без запинки отвечал, что общество составляют les dames et les messieurs (Салтыков-Щедрин 2). "What is society?" he asked himself, and he immediately and unhesitatingly replied that society consisted of les dames and les messieurs (2a).

З-68 • **ДО́РОГО ЗАПЛАТИ́ТЬ** за что [VP; subj: human; fixed WO] **1.** [usu. subjunctive, often foll. by за то, чтобы…] to (be willing to) sacrifice sth. of great value in order to get sth. one really wants or make some desired event happen: X до́рого бы заплатил ≃ **X would give** ⟨**pay, do**⟩ **anything; what X wouldn't give** ⟨**pay, do**⟩.

Дорого бы я заплатил за то, чтобы хоть на несколько минут увидеть родителей. What I wouldn't give to see my parents, even if only for a few minutes.

2. to suffer grave consequences as a result of sth. (some reprehensible action, wrongdoing, mistake etc): X дорого заплатил за Y ≃ **X paid dearly for Y; X paid a high price for Y; X had hell** ⟨**the devil**⟩ **to pay for Y; Y cost X dearly.**

Иван Петрович дорого заплатил за своё легкомыслие: жена, узнав, что он провёл ночь со своей секретаршей, ушла от него и забрала с собой ребёнка. Ivan Petrovich paid dearly for his foolishness: his wife, having found out that he spent the night with his secretary, left him and took their child with her.

З-69 • **ПОД ЗАПРЕ́ТОМ** [PrepP; Invar; subj-compl with copula (subj: concr or abstr)] sth. is prohibited: X находится под запретом ≃ **X is banned** ⟨**forbidden, proscribed, tabooed, outlawed**⟩.

В течение многих лет книги религиозных философов были в России под запретом. For many years, books written by religious philosophers were banned in Russia.

З-70 • **ДО ПОСЛЕ́ДНЕЙ ЗАПЯТО́Й** знать, изучать что и т. п. coll [PrepP; Invar; adv; fixed WO] (to know, learn etc sth.) thoroughly, including the minutest details: **(right) down to the last** ⟨**smallest, finest**⟩ **detail.**

Лида знает этот учебник до последней запятой: она преподаёт по нему уже десять лет. Lida knows that textbook down to the last detail: she's been teaching from it for the past ten years.

З-71 • **ХОТЬ ЗАРЕ́ЖЬ(ТЕ)** coll [хоть + VP$_{imper}$; these forms only; subord clause] **1.** ~ не понимаю, не помню, не знаю, не верю, не сделаю и т. п. [used with negated verbs in the 1st pers; when the idiom is used with verbs in the 2nd pers, they usu. occur in the pfv fut (не поймёшь etc) and have a generic meaning] one absolutely cannot (understand, remember, believe etc sth.), one absolutely does not (have any knowledge of sth.), or one absolutely will not (do sth.): **(even) if my** ⟨**his** etc⟩ **life depended on it; for the life of me** ⟨**him** etc⟩; [1st pers only] **(I'll be) damned if I (know** ⟨**can** etc⟩**); I'm** ⟨**I'll be**⟩ **hanged if…**

«Бывало, он приводил к нам в крепость баранов и продавал дёшево, только никогда не торговался: что запросит, давай,

— хоть зарежь, не уступит» (Лермонтов 1). "Occasionally he brought rams to us at the fort and sold them cheap, but he never bargained: you had to pay him what he asked; he would never cut a price even if his life depended on it" (1b). ♦ [Лебедев:] Или я отупел от старости, или все вы очень уж умны стали, а только я, хоть зарежьте, ничего не понимаю (Чехов 4). [L.:] Either I'm old and dotty, or else you've all grown far too clever. Anyway, I'm hanged if I can make it out (4b).

2. нужен, необходим и т. п. ~ a person or thing is very much (needed): **desperately; (very) badly; in the worst way.**

«…Ты должен мне дать три тысячи взаймы. Нужны, брат, хоть зарежь!» (Гоголь 3). "…You must lend me three thousand rubles. I need the money desperately" (3c).

З-72 • **ДО ЗАРЕ́ЗУ** нужен, нужно, хочется кому и т. п. coll [PrepP; Invar; adv (intensif)] (sth. is needed, s.o. needs or wants sth., s.o. needs or wants to do sth.) very much: **desperately; very badly; in the worst way;** [with хочется only] **(have an) irresistible (desire).**

Взволнованно заикаясь, он принялся рассказывать, что пишет по творчеству Шукшина кандидатскую, что ему до зарезу нужен этот двухтомник… (Чернёнок 2). Stammering excitedly, he started telling him that he was writing a dissertation on Shukshin, that he desperately needed the two-volume collection… (2a). ♦ …Он сказал: «Мне нужны пять тысяч. До зарезу» (Эренбург 4). "I need five thousand," he said. "I need it very badly" (4a). ♦ «…Лиза ввела меня в непредвиденный расход. Ей до зарезу захотелось пообедать в хорошем ресторане и купить себе шёлковые чулки» (Шолохов 2). "…Liza put me to an unexpected expense. She suddenly had an irresistible desire to dine at a good restaurant and buy herself a pair of silk stockings" (2a).

З-73 • **ОТ ЗАРИ́ ДО ЗАРИ́** [PrepP; Invar; adv; fixed WO] **1.** all day, from early morning till late evening: **from dawn to** ⟨**till**⟩ **dusk; from sunrise to** ⟨**till**⟩ **sunset; from sunup** ⟨**to**⟩ **till sundown.**

От зари до зари кишели люди в воде, вбивая в дно реки сваи… (Салтыков-Щедрин 1). From dawn to dusk people swarmed about in the water, knocking the piles to the bottom of the river… (1a). ♦ Работаю [в лагере] по девять часов, а здесь ему [Голубеву] приходится крутиться от зари до зари… (Войнович 2). In here [the camp] you worked nine hours, where here Golubev had to run around from dawn till dusk (2a).

2. all night: **from sunset to** ⟨**till**⟩ **sunrise; from sundown to** ⟨**till**⟩ **sunup; all night long; all through the night.**

З-74 • **В ЗАРО́ДЫШЕ** [PrepP; Invar] **1.** быть$_\varnothing$, существовать, находиться ~ [subj-compl with copula (subj: abstr or collect)] (to be, exist) in an incipient state: **in an embryonic state** ⟨**stage**⟩.

Эти политические тенденции существовали в зародыше ещё двадцать лет назад. These political tendencies already existed in an embryonic state twenty years ago.

2. уничтожать, душить что ~ [obj-compl with уничтожать etc (obj: abstr or collect)] (to destroy sth.) in the earliest stage of its existence, before it has time to develop: **nip sth. in the bud; squelch sth. at its very outset;** [in limited contexts] **smother sth. in its crib; strangle sth. at birth.**

…Настоящие учёные и научные результаты, хотя их и было ничтожно мало, не переходили ни во что и с намёками не считались. Их следовало уничтожить в зародыше (Зиновьев 1). …The true scientists and their results, although there were distressingly few of them, were not transformed into anything and paid no attention to any hints. So they had to be nipped in the bud (1a). ♦ Будь Виктор один, они бы его искалечили, но с тыла на них набежал Тэдди, который свято исповедовал золотое правило всех вышибал — гасить любую драку в самом зародыше… (Стругацкие 1). Had Victor been alone, they would have mutilated him. But along came Teddy, bounding in from the rear, devout observer of the bouncer's golden rule to squelch all fights at their very outset (1a). ♦ Аппарат надо сохранить, аппарат надо укреплять, но надо в зародыше убить в нём самостоятельность... (Рыбаков 2). The organization had to be preserved and strengthened, but its independence had to be strangled at birth... (2a).

3-75 • ПО ЗАСЛУ́ГАМ (воздать *кому,* **выдать** *кому coll,* **получить) [PrepP; Invar; usu. adv]** (to reward or punish s.o.) according to what he deserves, (to be rewarded or punished) according to what one deserves: [in refer. to rewarding s.o.] X-у воздадут ~ ≃ **X will be given (due) credit; X will be given his due ⟨his just reward⟩;** ‖ [in refer. to punishment] X получил ⟨X-у выдали⟩ ~ ≃ **X got ⟨received⟩ his just deserts; X got what he deserved ⟨what was coming to him⟩; X got what he asked for.**

[Кушак:] Смотрите, Валерия. Если вы думаете, что теперь им всё сойдёт с рук, — вы ошибаетесь. [Валерия:] Ещё бы. Каждому — по заслугам (Вампилов 5). [K.:] Look here, Valeriya. If you think they're going to get off scot free now, you're mistaken. [V.:] Of course. To each his just deserts (5b). ♦ У папы прекрасное настроение, вчера у него было тяжёлое заседание, он говорит, что дьявольски устал, но зато все получили по заслугам (Соколов 1). Papa is in a splendid mood, yesterday he had a difficult meeting, he said that he was devilishly tired, but then everybody got what they deserved (1a). ♦ "...В ваших руках — моя судьба, и вы снисходительны к ней, может быть не по заслугам" (Федин 1). [context transl] "My fate is in your hands and perhaps I don't deserve your indulgence" (1a).

3-76 • НЕ ЗАСТА́ВИТЬ СЕБЯ́ ДО́ЛГО ПРОСИ́ТЬ ⟨УПРА́ШИВАТЬ и т. п.⟩ *coll* **[VP; subj: human]** to agree readily to fulfill a request or accept a suggestion: X не заставил себя долго просить ≃ **X didn't wait to be asked twice; X agreed right away; X agreed at once.**

Даниель де Кознак был осведомлён о пребывании Мольера в Лангедоке... Он немедленно послал гонца с приказанием разыскать директора труппы и вручить ему приглашение его высочества прибыть вместе со всею труппой в замок де ла Гранж. Нужно ли говорить, что старый клермонец, а ныне комедиант не заставил себя долго упрашивать? (Булгаков 5). Daniel de Cosnac knew of Molière's presence in Languedoc....He sent a messenger at once with orders to seek out the director of the troupe and convey to him an invitation from His Highness to come with the entire company to La Grange. Needless to say, the former Clermont student and present comedian did not wait to be asked twice (5a).

3-77 • ЗАСТАВЛЯ́ТЬ/ЗАСТА́ВИТЬ СЕБЯ́ ЖДАТЬ [VP; subj: human or abstr] not to arrive when desired or expected, to be delayed: X заставил себя ждать ≃ **X kept person Y waiting; X made person Y wait for him ⟨it⟩;** [in limited contexts] **thing X eluded person Y.**

Я затворил за собою дверь моей комнаты, засветил свечу и бросился на постель; только сон на этот раз заставил себя ждать более обыкновенного (Лермонтов 1). I closed the door of my room behind me, lit a candle, and threw myself onto the bed, but this time sleep kept me waiting longer than usual (1d). I locked the door of my room, lighted a candle and flung myself on the bed; tonight, however, sleep eluded me longer than usual (1b).

3-78 • НЕ ЗАСТАВЛЯ́ТЬ/НЕ ЗАСТА́ВИТЬ СЕБЯ́ (ДО́ЛГО) ЖДАТЬ [VP; subj: human or abstr] to come, arrive promptly: X не заставил себя ждать ≃ **X wasted little ⟨no⟩ time; thing X was not long in coming; X did not keep person Y waiting; X did not make person Y wait long.**

«Я сейчас зайду к тебе». — «Заходи». Казангап не заставил себя ждать. (Айтматов 2). "I'll drop in in a few minutes." "Come along as soon as you're ready." Kazangap wasted little time (2a). ♦

Новые преследования не заставили себя ждать. На этот раз несчастье непосредственно выросло из моих трудов праведных (Гинзбург 2). A new wave of persecutions was not long in coming. This time the misfortune arose from my own righteous labors (2a). ♦ Смею надеяться, что успех не заставит себя долго ждать... (Соколов 1). I trust that success will not make me wait long... (1a).

3-79 • ЗАСТА́ТЬ ⟨ЗАСТИ́ГНУТЬ⟩ ВРАСПЛО́Х *кого* **[VP; subj: human or abstr]** to appear suddenly, surprise s.o. when he is unprepared: X застал Y-а врасплох ≃ **X caught ⟨took⟩ Y unaware(s); X caught Y off guard; X caught Y napping; X took Y by surprise.**

Он [Хлебников] поражал необычностью своих внутренних масштабов, инородностью своей мысли... Неожиданность ходов этой мысли застигала хлебниковского собеседника врасплох (Лившиц 1). He [Khlebnikov] amazed one by his extraordinary inner dimensions, by his heterogeneity of thought....The unexpected currents of this thought would catch Khlebnikov's collocutor unawares (1a). ♦ Красивая роль руководителя народного чувства так понравилась Растопчину, он так сжился с нею, что необходимость выйти из этой роли, необходимость оставления Москвы без всякого героического эффекта застала его врасплох... (Толстой 6). The illustrious role of leader of popular feeling so delighted Rostopchin, and he had grown so accustomed to it, that the necessity of relinquishing it and surrendering Moscow with no heroic display of any kind took him unawares... (6a). ♦ Как ни готовился он к своей участи, но сейчас появление этих серых людей застало его врасплох (Войнович 2). No matter how much he had prepared himself for his fate, the sudden appearance of the men in gray had caught him off guard (2a). ♦ В эту ночь около хутора Малого Громчонка полк красноармейцев переправился через Дон на сбитых из досок и брёвен плотах. Громковская сотня была застигнута врасплох, так как большинство казаков в эту ночь гуляло (Шолохов 5). That night near the village of Maly Gromchonok a Red Army regiment crossed the Don on makeshift rafts. The Gromchonok squadron was taken by surprise because most of its men that night were celebrating (5a).

3-80 • вопрос НА ЗАСЫ́ПКУ *coll* **[PrepP; Invar; nonagreeing modif]** (a question that is) very difficult and intended to baffle s.o.: **a stumper.**

...Задал Гладышев мерину вопрос, что называется, «на засыпку»: «А вот ты мне скажи, Ося, ежели тебя, к примеру, на фронт возьмут, ты за кого воевать будешь — за наших или за немцев?» (Войнович 2). ...[Gladishev] posed the gelding a question of the sort known as "stumpers." "Now answer me this, Osya: If, for example, they send you to the front, who are you going to fight for, us or the Germans?" (2a).

3-81 • БЕЗ ЗАТЕ́Й [PrepP; Invar; adv; often preceded by попросту, просто etc] simply, without pretense: **without any to-do ⟨fuss⟩; without whimsy ⟨fanfare⟩; without trying to be too clever.**

«Взял я как-то клочок бумаги... натянул на левую руку перчатку и написал: „Во время пребывания в Англии Галчинский был завербован британской разведкой". И подписал простенько, без затей: „Зоркий глаз"» (Войнович 4). "I took a scrap of paper...put a glove on my left hand, and wrote: 'During his stay in England Galchinsky was recruited by British Intelligence.' Then I signed it simply, without any to-do, Eagle Eye" (4a). ♦ И к окнам, под образа, поставили на табуретках гроб, сколоченный без затей (Солженицын 6). [context transl] Under the icons, near the windows, they stood a rough unadorned coffin on a row of stools (6a).

3-82 • ЗАТЕ́М ЧТО *obs* **[subord Conj;** introduces a clause of reason] for the reason that: **because; since; as.**

3-83 • В ЗАТЫ́ЛОК идти, шагать, стоять, строиться и т. п. [PrepP; Invar; adv] (to walk, march, stand, line up etc) in a row, with each person positioned immediately behind another: **(in) single file; Indian file; in a file; one behind the other.**

Тропинка была узкая, и нам пришлось идти в затылок. The path was narrow, and we had to walk single file.

3-84 • ЧЕСА́ТЬ ЗАТЫ́ЛОК ⟨ЗАТЫ́ЛКИ, В ЗАТЫ́ЛКЕ, В ЗАТЫ́ЛКАХ⟩ *highly coll* [VP; subj: human] **1.** to be puzzled, perplexed by sth.: X чешет затылок ≃ **X scratches his head (in bewilderment ⟨in wonder etc⟩); X scratches his head and wonders; X is at a loss.**

Инженеры часто затылки чесали: дорога, к примеру, далеко недостаточно загрунтована, а по нарядам шлака отсыпано вдвое больше, чем по проекту... (Иоффе 1). The engineers often scratched their heads in wonder—a road, for instance, was by no means sufficiently primed and yet, according to the register, twice as much clinker had been used as should have been according to plan... (1a).

2. *disapprov* to do nothing, usu. when one should be working: X чесал в затылке ≃ **X stood around gaping; X sat around and did nothing.**

3-85 • ЗАХОДИ́ТЬ/ЗАЙТИ́ (СЛИ́ШКОМ) ДАЛЕКО́; (СЛИ́ШКОМ) ДАЛЕКО́ ХВАТИ́ТЬ [VP; subj: human (all variants) or abstr (variants with заходить/зайти only); when слишком is not directly stated, it is implied] (of a person) to go beyond the accepted norms in one's behavior or speech, (of a joke) to go beyond the permissible, beyond what is considered in good taste, (of an argument, matter etc) to go beyond a critical point, the point at which its course might have been reversed: X зашёл слишком далеко ≃ **X has gone too far; that's going too far; person X has overstepped the limits ⟨the bounds⟩; [in limited contexts] person X is pushing it; [of a matter etc] things have gotten out of hand; the situation has become ⟨has gotten⟩ serious.**

...Преуменьшать значения молитвы... нельзя. Далеко зашёл старик. С душком, с нехорошим душком молитва (Абрамов 1). ...The importance of the prayer could not be underestimated. The old man had gone too far. It had a nasty smell to it, that prayer (1a). ♦ «Monsieur le vicomte совершенно справедливо полагает, что дела зашли уже слишком далеко. Я думаю, что трудно будет возвратиться к старому» (Толстой 4). "Monsieur le Vicomte quite rightly supposes that matters have already gone too far. I think it will be difficult to return to the old régime" (4b). ♦ «Послушай, Ольга, — заговорил он, наконец, торжественно, — под опасением возбудить в тебе досаду, навлечь на себя упрёки, я должен, однако ж, решительно сказать, что мы зашли далеко» (Гончаров 1). "Listen, Olga," he said at last, very gravely, "at the risk of annoying you and incurring your reproaches, I must tell you, very definitely, that we have gone too far" (1b). ♦ «Я не от твоих речей покраснел и не за твои дела, а за то, что я то же самое, что и ты». — «Ты-то? Ну, хватил немного далеко». — «Нет, не далеко», — с жаром проговорил Алёша (Достоевский 1). "I blushed not at your words, and not at your deeds, but because I'm the same as you." "You? Well, that's going a bit too far." "No, not too far," Alyosha said hotly (1a). ♦ Куртка на зелёно-коричневой пижаме расстёгивалась крупными пуговицами и не была тесна, и, кажется, бы не трудно было её снять, но при вытягивании рук отдалось в шее, и Павел Николаевич простонал. О, как далеко зашло дело! (Солженицын 10). His green and brown pajama jacket had large buttons and was the right size. No one would have thought it could be difficult to take off. But when he stretched his arms it pulled at his neck and Pavel Nikolayevich groaned. The situation was serious! (10a). ♦ Ведь был же в её жизни период, когда она знала о любви всё! Только посмотрит на какую-нибудь парочку... и всё ясно — далеко ли зашло дело, на какой оно стадии... (Залыгин 1). [context transl] Hadn't there been a time in her life when she knew all there was to know about love? She only

had to glance at any couple... to see everything—how far advanced the romance was, what stage it had reached... (1a).

3-86 • ОДНО́ (ТО́ЛЬКО) ЗВА́НИЕ осталось (*от чего*); **ОДНО́ (ТО́ЛЬКО) ЗВА́НИЕ (, что...)** *all highly coll* [NP; sing only; often the main clause in a complex sent] s.o. or sth. is referred to by some name that he or it does not seem to merit, no longer merits etc (not displaying the characteristic qualities associated with that name): от X-а одно звание осталось ≃ **X is a [NP] in name only; only the name (of X) remains ⟨is left⟩.**

3-87 • И ЗВА́НИЯ НЕТ *кого-чего* or *кому-чему obs, substand* [VP; impers; usu. pres] there is no sign of s.o. or sth., s.o. or sth. is completely absent, has disappeared or ceased to exist: X-а и звания нет ≃ **there isn't (even) a trace of X; there isn't a hint of thing X.**

3-88 • МНО́ГО ЗВА́НЫХ, НО МА́ЛО И́ЗБРАННЫХ [sent; Invar; fixed WO] very few of the many who desire to enter an elite group have the ability or good fortune to succeed, few of the many working in the fields of science, art etc have real talent or a genuine calling: **many are called, but few are chosen.**

«Много званых, но мало избранных, — так начал он речь свою, — очень рад, господа, что имею дело с почтенными представителями одного из почтеннейших сословий нашего любимого отечества...» (Салтыков-Щедрин 2). "Many have been called, but few chosen," he began his speech. "I'm very happy, gentlemen, that I shall be dealing today with the worthy representatives of one of the worthiest estates of our beloved country..." (2a).

< From the Bible (Matt. 22:14).

3-89 • ЗВЁЗД С НЕ́БА НЕ ХВАТА́ТЬ *coll* [VP; subj: human; usu. 3rd pers; pres or past] to be average, not especially intelligent, have mediocre abilities: X звёзд с неба не хватает ≃ **X won't set the world on fire; X is nothing out of the ordinary; X is no genius.**

[Нина:] Он простой, скромный парень. Допустим, он звёзд с неба не хватает, ну и что? (Вампилов 4). [N.:] He's a simple, modest fellow. Admittedly, he's no genius, but so what? (4b).

3-90 • ВОСХОДЯ́ЩАЯ ЗВЕЗДА́ (*чего*); **ВОСХОДЯ́ЩЕЕ СВЕТИ́ЛО** [NP; usu. sing; fixed WO] a person beginning to acquire widespread renown in some field: **a rising star; an up-and-coming [NP].**

Когда настроение духа становилось совершенно невыносимым, на помощь приходило вино, и небольшая компания, состоящая из старых одноклассников Мольера... а кроме них — Лафонтена, Буало и восходящей звезды — Жана Расина, собиралась время от времени то в кабачке Белого Барана, то в Еловой Шишке (Булгаков 5). When things became unbearable, Molière took refuge in wine and a small company of former classmates, with the addition of La Fontaine, Boileau, and the rising star, Jean Racine, which gathered from time to time either at the Mouton Blanc tavern or at the Croix de Lorraine (5a).

3-91 • ЗВЕЗДА́ ПЕ́РВОЙ ВЕЛИЧИНЫ́ [NP; fixed WO] a well-known person who has become famous for his achievements in some field: **star of the first magnitude; one of the brightest stars (in some field); [in limited contexts] superstar.**

...Широкому кругу читателей он [Бунин] был мало заметен среди шумной толпы — как он с горечью выразился — «литературного базара». Его затмевали звёзды первой величины, чьи имена были на устах у всех: Короленко, Куприн, Горький, Леонид Андреев, Мережковский, Фёдор Сологуб... (Катаев 3). ...For the wider public he [Bunin] did not stand out from among the noisy crowd of what he bitterly called the "literary bazaar." He was overshadowed by stars of the first magnitude, whose names were on every lip: Korolenko, Kuprin, Gorky, Leonid Andreyev, Merezhkovsky, Fyodor Sologub… (3a).

3-92 • ПУТЕВО́ДНАЯ ЗВЕЗДА́ [NP; sing only; usu. this WO] a person, idea etc directing s.o.'s life, activities, providing guidance: **guiding light 〈star〉; lodestar.**

Она мигом взвесила свою власть над ним [Обломовым], и ей нравилась эта роль путеводной звезды, луча света, который она разольёт над стоячим озером и отразится в нём (Гончаров 1). Swiftly she gauged her power over him [Oblomov]: she liked the role of guiding star, of a beam of light shed on a stagnant pool and reflected by it (1b).

3-93 • РОДИ́ТЬСЯ ПОД СЧАСТЛИ́ВОЙ ЗВЕЗДО́Й [VP; subj: human] to be very lucky, be fortunate in everything: X родился под счастливой звездой ≃ **X was born under a lucky star.**

Под счастливой звездой родился критик Латунский. Она спасла его от встречи с Маргаритой, ставшей ведьмой в эту пятницу! (Булгаков 9). The critic Latunsky had been born under a lucky star—it saved him from meeting with Margarita, who had become a witch that Friday (9a).

3-94 • ВЕ́РИТЬ В (СЧАСТЛИ́ВУЮ) ЗВЕЗДУ́ *чью* [VP; subj: human] to believe that one (or someone else) will have good fortune in life: X верит в свою 〈Y-ову〉 счастливую звезду ≃ **X believes in his 〈Y's〉 lucky star; X believes that he 〈Y〉 was born under a lucky star; X believes that luck is on his 〈Y's〉 side.**

И хотя дядя Сандро верил в свою звезду, как никто в мире, он всё-таки сильно волновался (Искандер 5). If ever anyone believed in his lucky star it was Uncle Sandro, yet he was still very worried (5a).

3-95 • ДО ЗВЕЗДЫ́ *obs* [PrepP; Invar; adv] until it has become dark: **till the first stars appear; till nightfall; till night falls; until dark 〈darkness〉.**

3-96 • СЧИТА́ТЬ ЗВЁЗДЫ *lit* [VP; subj: human] **1.** to be a dreamer, fantasize: X считает звёзды ≃ **X has his head in the clouds; X is a stargazer 〈a daydreamer〉; X is stargazing 〈daydreaming〉.**

2. to gape, be idle: X считал звёзды ≃ **X stared into space; X loafed around; X frittered away his 〈the〉 time.**

3-97 • ХВАТА́ТЬ ЗВЁЗДЫ С НЕ́БА *coll, approv* [VP; subj: human; usu. 3rd pers; pres or past] to be distinguished by unusual abilities, be capable of great achievements: X хватает звёзды с неба ≃ **X will set the world on fire; X is one of the brightest lights (in some field).**

Вадим Афанасьевич никаких звёзд с неба хватать не собирался, но он гордился – и заслуженно – своей специальностью, своими знаниями в одной узкой области (Аксёнов 3). Vadim Afanasyevich had no intentions of setting the world on fire, but he was proud, justifiably, of his specialty, his knowledge in one narrow field (3a).

3-98 • БУДИ́ТЬ/ПРОБУДИ́ТЬ 〈РАЗБУДИ́ТЬ〉 ЗВЕ́РЯ *в ком coll, often humor* [VP; subj: human or abstr; usu. past or neg imper] to awaken s.o.'s crude instincts: X пробудил зверя в Y-е ≃ **X brought out the beast in Y; X aroused 〈brought out〉 Y's baser 〈animal〉 instincts.**

3-99 • СЛЫ́ШАЛ ЗВОН, ДА НЕ ЗНА́ЕШЬ 〈НЕ ЗНА́ЕТ〉, ГДЕ ОН [saying] you have (he has etc) muddled, confused, and are incorrectly or incompletely relaying some information: ≃ **you've 〈he's etc〉 got it all wrong; you don't 〈he**

doesn't etc〉 **know what you're 〈he's etc〉 talking about; you've 〈he's etc〉 got everything all mixed up 〈all backward〉.**

3-100 • ОТ ЗВОНКА́ ДО ЗВОНКА́ отсидеть, отработать и т. п. *coll* [PrepP; Invar; adv; more often used with pfv verbs] (to serve in prison, stay at work etc) the entire required length of time, (to participate in sth.) from the very beginning to the very end: **(participate in sth. etc) from start to finish 〈(the) beginning to (the) end, the first day to the last etc〉; (stick out) the whole day 〈year etc〉; [in refer. to work only] (put in) a full day; (stay) till the whistle blows; [in refer. to prison, a labor camp etc] (serve out) one's 〈the〉 full term 〈sentence〉; (do one's) full time 〈five years etc〉.**

При старом начальнике можно было уйти раньше, если не было работы, а теперь приходится отсиживать от звонка до звонка. Under the old boss we could go home early if there wasn't any work to be done, but now we have to stick out the whole day. ♦ «За икону я три года от звонка до звонка в зоне оттрубил» (Чернёнок 2). "I did my full three years for the icon" (2a).

3-101 • ЗАДАВА́ТЬ/ЗАДА́ТЬ ЗВО́НУ *кому substand* [VP; subj: human; usu. pfv] to scold s.o. severely: X задал звону Y-у ≃ **X gave it to Y (good); X gave Y hell; X let Y have it (with both barrels 〈in spades〉); X raked Y over the coals; Y caught hell (from X).**

3-102 • ПУСТО́Й ЗВУК [NP; usu. sing; often subj-compl with copula (subj: abstr)] words, statements etc perceived by s.o. as lacking sense, meaning, or not deserving of attention: **(just 〈nothing more than〉) empty 〈meaningless〉 words 〈phrases〉; merely words; (sth.) rings hollow (for s.o.).**

3-103 • НИ ЗВУ́КА [NP_gen; Invar] **1.** [used as subj/gen (with implied predic не слышно)] (in some place) it is totally quiet: **(there is) not a sound to be heard.**

Юра прошёл по дорожке, обсаженной цветами, и очутился перед двухэтажной дачей… Ни души, ни звука (Рыбаков 2). [context transl] Yuri walked along the path edged with flowers and found himself before a two-story dacha.…There was no sign of life (2a).

2. ~ *(кому о ком-чём)*, ~ **нет** *о ком-чём (где)* [usu. predic (subj: human) or subj_gen] (may be used as a request or command to be silent, not to tell s.o. about sth.) one does not utter a word (about some person or thing) to s.o., not a word is written somewhere (about some person or thing): X ни звука (о Z-е) ≃ [past context] **X didn't say anything 〈a word〉 (about Z); X didn't breathe a word (about Z);** ‖ *Imper* Y-у (о Z-е) ни звука ≃ **don't say anything 〈a word〉 (about Z) to Y; not 〈don't breathe〉 a word (about Z) to Y; not a peep to Y (about Z);** ‖ в книге 〈статье и т. п.〉 нет ни звука о Z-е ≃ **the book 〈article etc〉 doesn't mention 〈say anything about〉 Z; there is nothing about Z in the book 〈the article etc〉.**

[Я] получил французскую премию «за лучшую книгу года» (дубль – и за «Раковый [корпус]», и за «Круг» [«В круге первом»]) – наши ни звука (Солженицын 2). I was awarded a French prize for "best book of the year" (for *Cancer Ward* and *The First Circle* jointly), and *on our side* not a word was said (2a). ♦ «Сергей Львович, – сказал он, войдя к хозяину, – у меня должен переночевать один товарищ. Это необходимо… Слышите? И – молчок. Никому ни звука» (Федин 1). "Sergei Lvovich," he said, going to the landlord's room, "a comrade has to spend the night with me. It's essential.…Do you hear? And—mum's the word. Not a peep to anyone" (1a).

3-104 • НИ ЗГИ (НЕ ВИ́ДНО 〈НЕ ВИДА́ТЬ〉); ЗГИ НЕ ВИ́ДНО 〈НЕ ВИДА́ТЬ〉; (НИ) ЗГИ НЕ ВИ́ДЕТЬ

all coll [impers sent with быть∅ or VP, subj: human (var. with не видеть)] it is so dark that nothing can be seen, discerned: **it is pitch-black ⟨pitch-dark⟩; there is pitch-darkness (all around)**; ‖ X не видел ни зги ≃ **X couldn't see a thing (in the dark); X couldn't see an inch before his face; X couldn't see his hand in front of his face**.

Глубокая, полная тишина стояла в доме. Но минут через десять я снова услышала, как внизу, в вестибюле, прогудела дверь. Я вскочила и подбежала к окну. Раздвинула занавески. Ни зги, но ясно слышно, как заводят машину (Чуковская 2). A deep, absolute silence pervaded the house. But ten minutes later I heard the hiss of the door again in the hall downstairs. I jumped up and ran to the window. I drew the curtains aside. It was pitch-black but I could clearly hear the starting of a car (2a). ♦ Селифан, не видя ни зги, направил лошадей так прямо на деревню... (Гоголь 3). Selifan, though he could not see a thing, directed the horses straight to the village... (3a). ♦ «Неужели вы едете, не дождавшись дня? — спросил шотландец. — Зги не видать...» (Герцен 2). "Surely you are not going on without waiting for daylight?" asked the Scotsman. "One can't see an inch before one's face..." (2a).

3-105 • (ЗА) ВА́ШЕ ⟨ТВОЁ⟩ ЗДОРО́ВЬЕ! [formula phrase; these forms only; fixed WO] a wish that the person to whom the toast is raised enjoy health, good fortune: **(here's) to your health!; (to) good health!; here's to you!**

[Студзинский:] Елена Васильевна очень красивая. Ваше здоровье! (Булгаков 4). [S.:] Elena Vasilievna is very beautiful. To your health! (4a).

3-106 • НА ЗДОРО́ВЬЕ coll [PrepP; Invar; often used with imper] **1.** [adv or formula phrase] (usu. used to encourage s.o. to eat or drink when offered, or as a response to s.o.'s thanks) may it prove beneficial: [when offering food or drink] **(please) help yourself; eat ⟨drink⟩ in good health; take as much as you like**; ‖ пусть X ест ⟨пьёт⟩ ~ ≃ **let X ⟨X is welcome to⟩ help himself; may X eat ⟨drink⟩ in good health; let X ⟨X is welcome to⟩ take as much as he likes**; ‖ [in response to s.o.'s thanks] **you're (very) welcome; you're welcome, I'm sure; my pleasure**.

[Рисположенский:] Я, Аграфена Кондратьевна, рюмочку выпью. [Аграфена Кондратьевна:] Кушай, батюшко, на здоровье! (Островский 10). [R.:] I'll just try a drop or two, Agrafena Kondratevna. [A.K.:] Please help yourself, my dear fellow (10a).

2. [adv] (if a person, animal etc wants to do sth., let him go ahead and do it) as long as or as much as he wants: **to one's heart's content; as much ⟨long⟩ as one likes; and welcome to it**.

[Саша:] Папа, ведь это ложь! [Лебедев:] Ну, так что же? Пусть себе мелют на здоровье... (Чехов 4). [S.:] Papa, that's a lie! [L.:] Well, what does it matter? Let them babble on to their heart's content... (4a). ♦ «Умоляю, уйми ты эту... как её... твою мамочку! Я же творческим трудом занят!!» — «Ну и твори себе на здоровье...» (Зиновьев 2). "Please, I beg you, can't you do something to calm down this...this...your dear mama? Here I am trying to do some creative work!" "Well create as much as you like..." (2a). ♦ Разосланные по всем городам и селам Абхазии гонцы рассказывали народу, что Джамхух – Сын Оленя, просыпаясь, по утрам жуёт жвачку. Но народ спокойно отнёсся к этому известию... «Пусть себе жуёт жвачку на здоровье, лишь бы помогал нам советами и предсказаниями» (Искандер 5). The heralds who had been sent through all the cities and villages of Abkhazia told the people that Jamkhoukh, Son of the Deer, chewed his cud when he woke up in the morning. But the people took this news in stride.... "Let him chew his cud, and welcome to it, so long as he helps us with advice and predictions" (5a).

3-107 • НАЧА́ТЬ ЗА ЗДРА́ВИЕ, А КО́НЧИТЬ ⟨СВЕСТИ́⟩ ЗА УПОКО́Й coll [VP; subj: human; usu. past; fixed WO] (of the disparity between a good beginning and a bad ending in words and actions) to begin pleasantly but end sadly, unpleas-

antly: X-ы ⟨X и Y⟩ начали за здравие, а кончили за упокой ≃ **Xs ⟨X and Y⟩ started out smiling and ⟨but⟩ ended up crying; Xs ⟨X and Y⟩ began with laughter and ⟨but⟩ ended with tears; X and Y met as friends and ⟨but⟩ parted as enemies; X and Y started out playing and ⟨but⟩ ended up fighting**.

Каждые первые две строки свидетельствовали для Лёвы о бесспорном природном гении Лермонтова; если бы всё оно [стихотворение] было составлено из этих первых строк минус вторые, то всё было бы так же хорошо, почти как у Пушкина. Но зато вторые две... боже! зачем же так! всё насмарку; начал за здравие, кончил за упокой... (Битов 2). [context transl] For Lyova, the first two lines of each stanza bespoke Lermontov's indisputable natural genius; if the whole poem had been made up of these first lines, minus the second ones, it would have been just as good, almost, as Pushkin's. But then the second two...good God, why does he do it! The whole thing falls flat, he goes from the sublime to the ridiculous (2a).

3-108 • ЗДРА́ВИЯ ЖЕЛА́Ю ⟨-ем⟩! [formula phrase; these forms only; fixed WO] a form of greeting used in the army by one of lower rank in answer to the greeting of s.o. of higher rank: **good day, sir!**

Я знаю, старые кавказцы любят поговорить, порассказать; им так редко это удаётся: другой лет пять стоит где-нибудь в захолустье с ротой, и целые пять лет ему никто не скажет здравствуйте (потому что фельдфебель говорит здравия желаю) (Лермонтов 1). I know that Caucasian veterans love to talk; they so rarely have the opportunity. He would be another five years with a company in some remote place, and for five whole years no one would say "hello" to him (because a sergeant-major always says "good day, sir!") (1d).

3-109 • ВО́Т ТЕБЕ́ И ЗДРА́ВСТВУЙ(ТЕ)! highly coll; **ВО́Т ТЕ (И) ЗДРА́ВСТВУЙ(ТЕ)!** substand [Interj; these forms only; fixed WO] used to express bewilderment, vexation, surprise etc: **how do you like that!; well, I like that!; (well,) this is a fine how-do-you-do!; (well,) if that don't beat all!; isn't that just dandy!**

3-110 • ЗА ТРИ́ДЕВЯТЬ ЗЕМЕ́ЛЬ (от кого-чего) coll or folk poet [PrepP; Invar; adv or subj-compl with copula (subj: usu. human or concr); fixed WO] very far away: **at ⟨to⟩ the other end of the world; far, far away; a long, long way (away)**; [in limited contexts] **in ⟨to⟩ a faraway land**; [in refer. to location only] **miles ⟨oceans⟩ apart**; [in refer. to direction only] **to the ends of the earth**.

Через минуту они уже были за тридевять земель, врывались на скорости 90 в тоннельный мрак под площадью Маяковского (Аксёнов 6). A minute later they were already at the other end of the world, tearing along at ninety kilometers into the gloom of the tunnel under Mayakovsky Square (6a). ♦ [Эльза:] Эти чудовища сторожат нас. А мы ушли от них за тридевять земель (Шварц 2). [E.:] Those monsters are watching us. But we managed to get a long, long way from them (2a). ♦ «И хотя бы ты был за тридевять земель, но жив, всё равно, невыносима эта мысль, что ты жив и всё знаешь, и меня судишь» (Достоевский 1). "And even if you had been in a faraway land, but still alive, the thought that you were alive and knew everything, and were judging me, would in any case have been unbearable" (1a). ♦ Конечно, это были смешные письма — хотя бы потому, что почти в каждом письме он сообщал, что ему «живётся всё хуже и хуже», как будто мы были за тридевять земель друг от друга (Каверин 1). Of course these were ridiculous letters, if only because in nearly every one he informed me that "his life grew worse and worse," as though we were miles apart (1a).

3-111 • ПРЕДАВА́ТЬ/ПРЕДА́ТЬ ЗЕМЛЕ́ кого lit [VP; subj: human] to inter s.o.: X предал Y-a ⟨тело Y-a⟩ земле ≃ **X**

committed Y ⟨Y's body⟩ to the earth; X consigned Y ⟨Y's body⟩ to the grave; X laid Y to rest; X buried Y.

И предали Настёну земле среди своих, только чуть с краешку, у покосившейся изгороди (Распутин 2). They committed Nastyona to the earth among her own, but over to the side by the sagging fence (2a). ♦ …Под Вязьмой Саню в клочья разорвало снарядом, так что нечего было и земле предать (Абрамов 1). …Sanya had been blown to pieces by a shell at the battle of Vyazma: there was nothing even left to bury (1a).

3-112 • СРОВНЯ́ТЬ С ЗЕМЛЁЙ *что* [VP; subj: human (often pl) or collect] to demolish sth. (often a town, village etc) utterly, esp. during wartime: X-ы сровняли Y с землёй ≃ **Xs (totally) destroyed Y; Xs razed ⟨leveled⟩ Y to the ground; Xs laid Y waste; Xs tore ⟨pulled⟩ Y down; Xs plowed Y under.**

Женщинам нечего было терять, и они крыли директора густым южнорусским матом… Но он не успокоился, пока не сровнял с землёй и не засыпал их жалкое логово (Мандельштам 2). The women had nothing to lose, and they started cursing the director in a south Russian accent, using the foulest words they knew.…But the director went on undeterred until he had destroyed their pitiful burrow and filled in the hole where it had stood (2a).

3-113 • ЗЕМЛИ́ ПОД СОБО́Й НЕ СЛЫ́ШАТЬ ⟨НЕ ЧУ́ЯТЬ⟩ *obs* [VP; subj: human; pres or past] to be very happy, in ecstasy (over sth.): X земли под собой не слышал ≃ **X was walking on air; X was beside himself (with joy** etc**); X was on top of the world.**

3-114 • ИЗ-ПОД ЗЕМЛИ́ достать, добыть *кого-что*; **ПОД ЗЕМЛЁЙ** найти *кого-что* both coll [PrepP; these forms only; adv] (to reach, find s.o. or sth.) without fail, no matter how difficult it is, no matter where he or it might be: **(get sth. ⟨find s.o.** etc⟩**) at any cost ⟨at all costs, no matter what the cost, by whatever means necessary, no matter what it takes⟩.**

«Это сыпняк, и притом в довольно тяжёлой форме. Она порядком мучится, бедняжка. Я бы посоветовал поместить её в больницу… Тolько из-под земли достаньте извозчика…» (Пастернак 1). "…She's got typhus—a severe case, poor thing; she must be feeling pretty wretched. My advice to you is to put her in a hospital.…Now, get a cab at any cost…" (1a).

3-115 • КАК ⟨БУ́ДТО, СЛО́ВНО, ТО́ЧНО⟩ ИЗ-ПОД ЗЕМЛИ́ ⟨ИЗ ЗЕМЛИ́⟩ вырасти, появиться *coll* [как etc + PrepP; these forms only; adv; fixed WO] (to appear) suddenly, unexpectedly: **(as if ⟨as though⟩) out of nowhere; (spring up) from nowhere; as if out of the ground; as if out of thin air; as if by magic.**

Тотчас рядом с нею [Лилит] , словно из-под земли, вырос Смарагд… (Обухова 1). At once, as though out of nowhere, Emerald appeared beside her [Lilith]… (1a). ♦ Сначала одинокие хлопки, а потом радостный шквал рукоплесканий приветствовал двадцать кипарисовых рыцарей, как бы выросших из-под земли во главе с Платоном Панцулая (Искандер 3). At first isolated claps, then a joyous squall of applause greeted the twenty cypresslike knights who had sprung up from nowhere, led by Platon Pantsulaya (3a). ♦ Бутылка, сало, хлеб, холодная картошка с луком появлялись, одно за другим, будто из-под земли (Максимов 2). A bottle, some bacon, bread, cold potatoes and onions all appeared as if by magic (2a).

3-116 • ОТ ЗЕМЛИ́ НЕ ВИДА́ТЬ ⟨НЕ ВИ́ДНО⟩ *кого* highly coll [these forms only; impers predic with быть₀; usu. pres] (in refer. to the height of a child or an adult who is the size of a child) very small: X-а от земли не видать ≃ **X is very short ⟨little⟩; X is pint-size; X is knee-high to a grasshopper; X is a half pint ⟨a little bit of a thing⟩.**

3-117 • ГОТО́В ⟨РАД⟩ СКВОЗЬ ЗЕ́МЛЮ ПРОВА-ЛИ́ТЬСЯ; ХОТЬ ⟨ЛУ́ЧШЕ⟩ СКВОЗЬ ЗЕ́МЛЮ ПРОВАЛИ́ТЬСЯ *кому all coll* [subj-compl with быть₀, subj: human (variants with готов, рад); impers predic with быть₀ (variants with хоть, лучше)] to feel like hiding, disappearing out of embarrassment, shame: X готов сквозь землю провалиться ≃ **X wishes the earth would ⟨could⟩ swallow him up; X wants to sink into ⟨to fall through⟩ the ground; X wants to ⟨wishes he could⟩ sink through the floor.**

…Лизке так стыдно стало за себя перед братом, что она готова была сквозь землю провалиться (Абрамов 1). Lizka felt so ashamed of herself in front of her brother that she wished the earth could swallow her up (1a). ♦ «Не поверишь, лучше сквозь землю провалиться, чем в такое дурацкое положение попадать…» (Чернёнок 2). "You won't believe it but it's better to fall through the ground than to find yourself in a situation like that" (2a). ♦ Но не всё смешил её Штольц: через полчаса она слушала его с любопытством и с удвоенным любопытством переносила глаза на Обломова, а Обломову от этих взглядов − хоть сквозь землю провалиться (Гончаров 1). But he [Stoltz] did not make her laugh all the time; half an hour later she was listening to him with interest and from time to time glancing at Oblomov with even greater interest. Because of those glances Oblomov wanted to sink through the floor (1b).

3-118 • ЗЕ́МЛЮ ЕСТЬ БУ́ДУ *substand* [sent; this form only; usu. this WO] I swear that I am telling the truth (or that I will fulfill my promise): **may lightning strike me (dead); may God strike me dead; may I eat dirt.**

«Степановна, землю буду есть, что кур твоих испортили. Где ж это видано! Ведь таких и курьих болезней нет! Это твоих кур кто-то заколдовал» (Булгаков 10). "Stepanovna, may I eat dirt, but I'll say your chickens got the evil eye. Who's ever seen the likes of it? Why, there ain't no chicken sickness of this kind! Somebody sure bewitched your chickens" (10a).

3-119 • ЗЕ́МЛЮ РО́ЕТ *highly coll* [VP; subj: human; usu. this WO] one engages in ceaseless activity, makes every effort to achieve or obtain sth. (usu. motivated by selfish considerations): X землю рыть будет ≃ **X will do his damnedest; X will go to any length ⟨to great lengths⟩; X will move heaven and earth.**

…В НЭП [период новой экономической политики] выделили группу ИТР, инженерно-технических работников, а писатели рыли землю, чтобы стать «инженерами человеческих душ» и получить свою долю (Мандельштам 2). During NEP [the New Economic Policy], engineers and technicians were picked out to become a favored group, and writers began to move heaven and earth to be recognized as "engineers of human souls," thus making certain of a share in the cake (2a).

3-120 • КАК ⟨БУ́ДТО, СЛО́ВНО, ТО́ЧНО⟩ СКВОЗЬ ЗЕ́МЛЮ ПРОВАЛИ́ЛСЯ; ПРОВА́ЛИВАТЬСЯ/ ПРОВАЛИ́ТЬСЯ СКВОЗЬ ЗЕ́МЛЮ *all coll* [как etc + VP, usu. pfv past (1st var.); VP with subj: human, animal, or concr (2nd var.); the verb is usu. in the final position (1st var.)] to disappear unexpectedly, leaving no trace: X как сквозь землю провалился ≃ **it is as if the earth had swallowed X (up); it is as if X had been swallowed up by the earth; X has ⟨seems to have⟩ vanished into thin air ⟨from the face of the earth⟩.**

«Он прогостил около двух недель, часто отлучаясь в Юрятин, и вдруг исчез, как сквозь землю провалился» (Пастернак 1). "He stayed about two weeks, went often to Yuriatin, and then vanished suddenly as if the earth had swallowed him" (1a). ♦ Что же, позвольте вас спросить: он [Воланд] провалился, что ли, сквозь землю… или же, как утверждают некоторые, вовсе не приезжал в Москву? (Булгаков 9). What could it mean? Had Woland been swallowed up by the earth or had he, as some claimed, never come to Moscow at all? (9b). ♦ Иван сделал попытку ухватить негодяя за рукав, но промахнулся и ровно ничего не поймал. Регент как сквозь землю провалился (Булгаков 9). Ivan tried to catch the rogue by the sleeve, but missed and caught exactly nothing: the choirmaster seemed to have vanished into thin air (9a).

З-121 • ЧТОБ МНЕ СКВОЗЬ ЗЕ́МЛЮ ПРОВА-ЛИ́ТЬСЯ!; ПРОВАЛИ́ТЬСЯ МНЕ СКВОЗЬ ЗЕ́МЛЮ ⟨В ТАРТАРАРЫ́⟩!; ЧТОБ МНЕ ПРОВА-ЛИ́ТЬСЯ (В ТАРТАРАРЫ́)! *all highly coll* [Interj; these forms only; fixed WO] I swear that I am telling the truth (or that I will fulfill my promise): **may the earth swallow me up; may the earth open up and swallow me; may I drop dead; may I burn in hell; may lightning strike me (dead); may I be struck (dead) by lightning.**

Провалиться мне сквозь землю, если не докажу, что я прав. May the earth swallow me up if I don't prove I'm right.

З-122 • ЧТОБ ТЕБЕ́ ⟨ему, ей, вам, им⟩ СКВОЗЬ ЗЕ́МЛЮ ПРОВАЛИ́ТЬСЯ!; ЧТОБ ТЕБЕ́ ⟨ему и т. п.⟩ ПРОВА-ЛИ́ТЬСЯ (В ТАРТАРАРЫ́)! *all highly coll, rude* [Interj; these forms only; fixed WO] used to express one's intense annoyance, vexation, anger directed at s.o.: **why don't you ⟨doesn't he etc⟩ go to hell!; to hell with you ⟨him etc⟩!; may you ⟨he etc⟩ burn in hell!; God damn you ⟨him etc⟩!**

Никанор Иванович... подхватил на вилку три куска селёдки... и в это время позвонили... Проглотив слюну, Никанор Иванович заворчал, как пёс: «А чтоб вам провалиться! Поесть не дадут» (Булгаков 9). Nikanor Ivanovich...picked up three slices of herring with his fork...at this moment the doorbell rang...Swallowing his saliva, Nikanor Ivanovich growled like a dog: "Why don't they go to hell! A man can't eat in peace…" (9a).

З-123 • ЗЕМЛЯ́ ГОРИ́Т ПОД НОГА́МИ *чьими, у кого* [VP_subj; pres or past; fixed WO] **1.** usu. **словно ⟨как будто⟩ земля горит под ногами** s.o. is compelled to run away from some place or to some place very quickly: Х убегал, как будто земля горела у него под ногами ≃ **X ran off like the wind ⟨like greased lightning⟩.**

2. s.o. is in a difficult, dangerous situation: земля горела у Х-а под ногами ≃ **X was sitting ⟨living⟩ on a volcano; X was in hot water; things were getting hot for X.**

З-124 • ЗЕМЛЯ́ ДЕ́РЖИТСЯ на таких..., на таких ⟨людях⟩, как... и т. п. *coll* [VP_subj; pres only; fixed WO] the highest moral standards, behavior of exceptional virtue is exhibited (by the person or people in question and their like): **(such people are) the salt of the earth; (it's X and his kind who) keep the world ⟨the globe⟩ turning.**

[author's usage] «Меня в деревне Иван Акимычем кликали. Калачёв фамилиё [*ungrammat* = фамилия]...» Пожалуй, Влад и до этого знал: такими калачёвыми земля держится... (Максимов 2). "Back home they call me Ivan Akimych. Kalachev's my last name...." Vlad already knew that it was Kalachev and his kind who keep the globe turning... (2a).

З-125 • ЗЕМЛЯ́ ПЛЫВЁТ/ПОПЛЫЛА́ ПОД НО-ГА́МИ *у кого* [VP_subj; usu. pres or past; fixed WO] s.o. experiences extreme agitation, a strong attack of emotion: земля поплыла у Х-а под ногами ≃ **the ground ⟨the earth⟩ trembled ⟨shook⟩ beneath X's feet; (it seemed to X that) the whole world turned upside down.**

Я взял конверт и взглянул на адрес. Земля поплыла у меня под ногами, и стены стали валиться на меня... Почерк Нэтти! (Богданов 1). I took the envelope and glanced at the address. The

ground trembled beneath my feet and the walls came crashing down around me....Netti's handwriting! (1a).

З-126 • (И) КАК (ТО́ЛЬКО ⟨ЕЩЁ⟩) ЗЕМЛЯ́ НО́СИТ ⟨ТЕ́РПИТ, ДЕ́РЖИТ⟩ *кого highly coll* [VP_subj; pres only; fixed WO] how can the mere existence of s.o. be possible, permissible (usu. in refer. to a scoundrel, rascal): как только Х-а земля носит ≃ **how the earth can tolerate X's presence is beyond me; how the earth can bear to have X's feet on it beats me; why doesn't the earth swallow X (up)?; it's a wonder the earth doesn't open and swallow X (up); it's a wonder people like X are allowed to live.**

«Сука ты сука, Бочкарёв, и другого названия тебе нету. И как только земля тебя по себе носит, Бочкарёв?» (Максимов 3). "You're a bastard, Bochkarev, a lousy bastard, there's no other word for you. How the earth can bear to have your feet on it beats me, Bochkarev" (3a). ♦ «Какими ты глазами на меня [, на свою сестру,] глядишь? И-и-и, бессовестный!.. Как тебя земля держит!» (Шолохов 2). "How can you look like this at your sister? Have you no shame? It's a wonder the earth don't open and swallow you up!" (2a).

З-127 • ОБЕТОВА́ННАЯ ЗЕМЛЯ́ ⟨СТРАНА́⟩; ОБЕ-ТОВА́ННЫЙ КРАЙ *all lit* [NP; usu. sing] a place in which life promises to be prosperous, where people hope to become happy and successful: **the promised land; the land of promise; the land of milk and honey.**

Обетованная земля при наступлении французов была Москва, при отступлении была родина (Толстой 7). The promised land for the French when they invaded Russia was Moscow; when they retreated it was their native land (7a).

< From the Bible (Heb. 11:9).

З-128 • ПУСТЬ ⟨ДА⟩ БУ́ДЕТ ЗЕМЛЯ́ ПУ́ХОМ *кому* [VP_subj; these forms only] parting words said when wishing the deceased peace: пусть будет Х-у земля пухом ≃ **may X ⟨X's soul⟩ rest in peace; God rest X ⟨X's soul⟩.**

...[Она] мне родная тёща, родная мать моей родной жены, пусть земля им обеим будет пухом... (Рыбаков 1). ...She was my mother-in-law, my own wife's mother, may both their dear souls rest in peace (1a).

З-129 • В ЗЕНИ́ТЕ *чего lit* [PrepP; Invar; the resulting PrepP is usu. subj-compl with copula (subj: human) or obj-compl with застать *кого* etc (obj: human)] at the moment or during a period when one enjoys maximum (fame, recognition), has maximum success (in one's career, life) etc: **at the peak (of one's ⟨s.o.'s⟩ fame etc); at the high ⟨crowning⟩ point (of one's ⟨s.o.'s⟩ career etc); in the prime ⟨at the zenith⟩ (of one's ⟨s.o.'s⟩ life etc).**

Агафья Матвеевна была в зените своей жизни; она жила и чувствовала, что жила полно, как прежде никогда не жила... (Гончаров 1). Agafya Matveyevna was in the prime of her life. She lived feeling that her life was full as it had never been before (1a). Agafya Matveyevna was at the zenith of her existence: she lived feeling that her life had never been so full before... (1b).

З-130 • КАК ЗЕНИ́ЦУ О́КА ⟨ПА́ЧЕ ЗЕНИ́ЦЫ О́КА *obs*, **ПУ́ЩЕ ЗЕНИ́ЦЫ О́КА** *obs*⟩ **беречь, хранить, лелеять** *кого-что* [как + NP (1st var.) or AdvP; these forms only; adv; fixed WO] (in refer. to a person or thing that one cherishes, that is very valuable etc) (to treat s.o. or sth.) as very dear, (to guard, watch over sth.) vigilantly, attentively: **(guard ⟨cherish⟩ s.o. ⟨sth.⟩) like the apple of one's eye ⟨one's dearest possession⟩; (cherish ⟨treasure⟩ s.o. ⟨sth.⟩) more than one's life ⟨more than life itself⟩; (guard s.o. ⟨sth.⟩) with one's life.**

«Куда ты собрался, чудак?.. Куда ты хочешь тащить грудного младенца, которого тебе поручили беречь как зеницу ока?» (Каверин 2). "Where do you think you're going, you idiot?…Where are you off to with that infant you are supposed to cherish like the apple of your eye?" (2a). ♦ «Вот вам книга… Это моя собственная книга. Берегите как зеницу ока» (Копелев 1). "Here's a book for you….This is my own copy. Guard it with your life" (1a).

3-131 • ЗЛА НЕ ПО́МНИТЬ *(на ком obs)*; **ЗЛА НЕ ДЕР-ЖА́ТЬ** *(на кого) coll* [VP; subj: human; usu. this WO] not to feel resentment toward s.o., to forgive s.o. (after a falling-out, after he has offended one etc): X зла (на Y-е) не помнит ≃ **X bears Y no grudge ⟨malice⟩; X doesn't hold anything against Y; X is letting bygones be bygones.**

За тем, что было написано, стоял, конечно, намёк на то, что Нюра зла не помнит и готова примириться, если Иван не будет упрямиться (Войнович 2). Everything about the note hinted that Nyura bore him no grudge and was ready to make up if Ivan wouldn't stay stubborn (2a). ♦ [Марина:] Погубил ты меня ни за что, обманул… Убил ты меня, да я на тебя зла не держу (Толстой 1). [M.:] You've ruined me for nothing. You've deceived me….You've killed me. But I bear you no malice (1c). ♦ «Он всё одно как и учёный человек теперя [*ungrammat* = теперь]», — восхищался Пантелей Прокофьевич, явно польщённый тем, что Степан его хлебом-солью не побрезговал и, зла не помня, пришёл (Шолохов 4). "He's like a real learned man now," Pantelei proclaimed admiringly, evidently flattered that Stepan had not scorned his hospitality and let bygones be bygones (4a).

3-132 • ЗЛО БЕРЁТ/ВЗЯЛО́ ⟨РАЗБИРА́ЕТ/РАЗО-БРА́ЛО⟩ *кого (на кого)*; **ЗЛОСТЬ БЕРЁТ/ВЗЯЛА́ ⟨РАЗБИРА́ЕТ/РАЗОБРАЛА́⟩** *all coll* [VP$_{subj}$; usu. pres or past] s.o. gets very angry (at another or on account of sth.): X-a зло взяло (на Y-a) ≃ **X got ⟨was⟩ mad (at Y); X got ⟨was⟩ furious (with Y); Y ⟨that⟩ made X furious.**

[Спор] с Бухариным [Ленин] не довёл до публичности, объяснился в письмах. А перед его отъездом такая злость на него взяла — не ответил ему (Солженицын 5). He [Lenin] had confined his argument with Bukharin to letters, and had not let it come out into the open. But he had been too furious to answer the letter Bukharin had written before his departure (5a). ♦ [Васюта:] Я вот, к примеру, по копейке собираю, никак внучку одеть не могу, а вы на водку — сотнями, сотнями фугуете [*sl* = тратите]. Зло меня берёт (Вампилов 1). [V.:] Take me, for instance. I have to save every kopeck to dress my grand-daughter, and here you go splurging hundreds and hundreds on booze. Makes me furious (1a).

3-133 • СРЫВА́ТЬ/СОРВА́ТЬ ЗЛО ⟨СЕ́РДЦЕ obs⟩ *на ком*, less often *на чём coll* [VP; subj: human] to let out one's anger by shouting at or hurting an innocent person (animal), or by striking, breaking etc some object: X сорвал зло на Y-е ≃ **X took it out on Y; X vented ⟨took out, poured out⟩ his fury ⟨frustration, wrath etc⟩ on Y; X vented his spleen on Y.**

«На старичишке решила зло сорвать… Ты бы в городе кой-кому рёбра пересчитала бы…» (Искандер 4). "Had to take it out on a wretched old man….If you were going to break anyone's ribs, it should have been someone in the city" (4a). ♦ …Если бы мы срывали зло на истинных виновниках дерьма нашей судьбы, то перед кем же тогда, спрашивается, Коля, мы извинялись бы, замаливали грехи?.. (Алешковский 1). If we took out our anger on the guys who're really to blame for all the shit in our lives, who could we apologize to afterward, who could we ask to forgive us? (1a). ♦ [author's usage] Встречала [Аксинья] где-нибудь Гришку и, бледнея, несла мимо красивое, стосковавшееся по нём тело… Чувствовал Гришка после встречи с ней сосущую тоску. Без причины злобствовал, рвал зло на Дуняшке, на матери… (Шолохов 2). If she [Aksinya] happened to meet Grigory somewhere, she would turn pale and carry her beautiful yearning body past him….After the encounter Grigory would feel the undertow of that

yearning. He would lose his temper for no reason, vent his fury on Dunyashka and his mother… (2a).

3-134 • УПОТРЕБИ́ТЬ ВО ЗЛО *что lit* [VP; subj: human; obj: usu. abstr (доверие, расположение, гостеприимство, знания etc)] to use, exploit sth. (s.o.'s trust, s.o.'s friendliness, s.o.'s hospitality, one's own knowledge etc) in a despicable, base manner that harms another or others: X употребил во зло Y ≃ **X used Y for evil purposes; X put Y to evil ends; X made (a) bad use of Y; X used Y against person Z; [in limited contexts] X abused Y.**

Их потомки, вооружённые высокими знаниями, употребили их во зло (Обухова 1). Their descendants, armed with great knowledge, put it to evil ends (1a). ♦ …Я предложил Чичерину прочесть ненапечатанную тетрадь о Кетчере и прочёл её всю. Я много раз раскаивался в этом, не потому, чтоб он во зло употребил читанное мною, а потому, что мне было больно и досадно, что я в сорок пять лет мог разоблачать наше прошедшее перед чёрствым человеком… (Герцен 2). …I offered to read Chicherin my unpublished chapter about Ketscher, and I read him the whole of it. I have many times repented of this, not because he made a bad use of what I read, but because I was vexed and pained that at forty-five I was capable of exposing our past before an unfeeling man… (2a).

3-135 • ЗЛО́БА ДНЯ [NP; usu. sing] a topical question, sth. that attracts general attention: **the topic of the day; a burning question ⟨issue, topic⟩; the latest news.**

3-136 • НА ЗЛО́БУ ДНЯ [PrepP; Invar; nonagreeing postmodif or prep obj] (related to a matter, topic) of widespread interest or concern that attracts general attention: **topical; dealing with the topic of the day.**

«Только знаете… Газета… Политический орган райкома. Нам бы что-нибудь на злобу дня…» (Максимов 2). "The trouble is…er, this newspaper…is the political organ of the District Committee. We really need something topical…" (2a).

3-137 • ЛО́ПАТЬСЯ ОТ ЗЛО́СТИ *highly coll* [VP; subj: human] to be extremely angry, irritated: X лопался от злости ≃ **X seethed with anger ⟨rage⟩; X was beside himself with anger ⟨rage⟩; X was hopping ⟨boiling⟩ mad.**

3-138 • ЛО́ПНУТЬ СО ⟨ОТ⟩ ЗЛО́СТИ *highly coll* [VP; subj: human; often fut, past with чуть не, or infin with можно] to lose control of o.s. from anger, express one's extreme anger in an intense manner: X лопнет со злости ≃ **X will fly into a rage; X will explode in anger; X will hit the roof ⟨the ceiling⟩; X will throw a fit; X will blow his stack ⟨his top⟩.**

3-139 • ОТОГРЕВА́ТЬ/ОТОГРЕ́ТЬ ⟨ПРИГРЕВА́ТЬ/ПРИГРЕ́ТЬ, СОГРЕВА́ТЬ/СОГРЕ́ТЬ⟩ ЗМЕЮ́ НА ГРУДИ́ ⟨ЗА ПА́ЗУХОЙ⟩ [VP; subj: human; usu. pfv past] to lavish attention, care on a person who later turns out to be ungrateful, treacherous: X отогрел змею на груди ≃ **X warmed ⟨nourished, harbored⟩ a snake ⟨a serpent⟩ in his bosom.**

«А ты, — продолжал, не слушая его, Обломов, — ты бы постыдился выговорить-то! Вот какую змею [я] отогрел на груди!» (Гончаров 1). "And you," Oblomov went on, without listening to him — "you ought to be ashamed to say such things. That's the sort of snake I've warmed in my bosom!" (1a). ♦ Рюхин тяжело дышал, был красен и думал только об одном, что он отогрел у себя на груди змею, что он принял участие в том, кто оказался… злобным врагом (Булгаков 9). Ryukhin, breathing heavily, turned red, there was only one thought in his mind — that he had nourished a serpent in his bosom, that he had tried to help someone who…had treacherously turned on him (9b).

3-140 • ЗМЕЯ́ ПОДКОЛО́ДНАЯ *rather folk, usu. rude, derog* [NP; sing only; usu. this WO] (often used when addressing a person, usu. a woman) an insidious, dangerous person: **a snake in the grass; a viper;** [when addressing s.o.] **you snake in the grass; you viper.**

«Лариосика постиг ужасный удар... Милочка Рубцова, на которой, как вы знаете, он женился год тому назад, оказалась подколодной змеёй» (Булгаков 3). "Lariosik has had a most terrible blow....You know he married Milochka Rubtsova a year ago. Well, she has turned out to be a snake in the grass!" (3a). ♦ [Ананий:] Молчи уж, по крайности, змея подколодная! (Писемский 1). [A.:] At least hold your tongue, you viper! (1a).

3-141 • ДО ЗЕЛЁНОГО ЗМИ́Я допиться, упиться и т. п. *coll* [PrepP; Invar; adv; fixed WO] (to get drunk) to the point of hallucinations: **(get) blind ⟨dead⟩ drunk; drink o.s. under the table ⟨into a stupor⟩.**

3-142 • ЗНА́ЕМ МЫ ВАС! *coll, iron* [Interj; Invar; fixed WO] (we do not trust you because) we know more about you and the type of people you represent than what you reveal about yourself or what you appear to be: **we ⟨I⟩ know you (all too well)!; we ⟨I⟩ know what you're ⟨your lot is⟩ like; we ⟨I⟩ know the likes of you; we ⟨I⟩ know (all about) your type ⟨you fellows etc⟩;** [in limited contexts] **we ⟨I⟩ know what kind of [NP] you are; we ⟨I⟩ know what you're up to.**

Была [шкатулочка у меня] полна, а нынче совсем опустела!» — «Полно врать, Антон Панфутьич. Знаем мы вас; куда тебе деньги тратить, дома живёшь свинья свиньёй, никого не принимаешь, своих мужиков обдираешь...» (Пушкин 1). "It [my little coffer] used to be full, but by now it's entirely empty." "Enough of fibbing, Anton Pafnutich. We know you all too well: what would you be spending money on? You live at home like a pig in a sty, never inviting anybody and fleecing your peasants..." (1a). ♦ «...Я сам плохо играю!» — «Знаем мы, как вы плохо играете!» — сказал Ноздрёв, выступая шашкой (Гоголь 3). "...I play poorly myself." "We know all about you fellows who claim to play poorly!" said Nozdrev, advancing one of his checkers (3b). ♦ "...I'm not such a good player myself." "I know what kind of a not-too-good player you are," Nozdrev said, moving a checker (3e).

3-143 • КТО́ (ЕГО́ ⟨её и т. п.⟩) ЗНА́ЕТ *coll* [sent; these forms only; fixed WO] no one knows, it is impossible (for s.o.) to know (often used to express the speaker's indifference to s.o. or sth.): **who knows; who can tell ⟨say⟩; you can never tell;** [in limited contexts] **there's no telling; how should I know?**

Кто знает, быть может, пустыня и представляет в его [идиота] глазах именно ту обстановку, которая изображает собой идеал человеческого общежития? (Салтыков-Щедрин 1). Who knows, perhaps in his [the idiot's] eyes the desert is the environment that best represents the ideal communal life for mankind? (1a). ♦ «Утверждают будто бы бич Божий наш и кара небесная, комиссар Стрельников, это оживший Антипов. Легенда, конечно. И непохоже. А впрочем, кто его знает. Всё может быть» (Пастернак 1). "Some people say this scourge of ours, Commissar Strelnikov, is Antipov risen from the dead. But that's only a silly rumor, of course. It's most unlikely. Though, who can tell, anything is possible" (1a). ♦ «А кто его знает, где платок?» — ворчал он, обходя вокруг комнату и ощупывая каждый стул... (Гончаров 1). "How should I know where your handkerchief is?" he grumbled, walking around the room and feeling every chair with his hand... (1a).

3-144 • ТО́ЛЬКО И ЗНА́ЕТ ⟨ДЕ́ЛАЕТ⟩, что... *coll* [VP; subj: human; pres or past; foll. by another verb; fixed WO] one does only or mainly (the specified activity): **X только и знает, что... ≃ X does nothing but...; all X (ever) does is...; ...that's all X does; X spends all his time...**

...Его [Обломова] всё тянет в ту сторону, где только и знают, что гуляют, где нет забот и печалей... (Гончаров 1). ...He [Oblomov] was always drawn to the land where people do nothing but have a good time and where there are no worries or sorrows... (1a). ♦ Коля числился на работе, хотя целыми днями только и делал, что пил кофе и водку за счёт бывших друзей... (Искандер 3). Although Kolya showed up at work, all he did day in and day out was drink coffee and brandy [*sic*] at the expense of his former friends... (3a). ♦ «Из окна острога он [разбойник] только и делал, что смотрел на играющих в тюремном дворе детей» (Достоевский 1). "He [the robber] spent all his time at the window, watching the children playing in the prison yard" (1a).

3-145 • ЗНА́ЕШЬ ⟨-ете⟩ ЛИ *coll* [these forms only; sent adv (parenth)] used to attract the hearer's attention to what has been said or to emphasize the speaker's attitude toward sth.: **you know.**

«Ну, с талантами, знаете ли, расправляться проще простого» (Войнович 4). "But, you know, nothing could be simpler than making short work of talented people" (4a).

3-146 • КАК ЗНА́ЕШЬ *coll* [usu. indep. sent; 2nd or 3rd pers only; fixed WO] do as you want, he (she etc) can do as he (she etc) wants: [in direct address] **(do) as you wish ⟨please, like, choose⟩; (you can) do as ⟨what⟩ you like; suit yourself; you know (what's) best; do as ⟨what⟩ you think best;** [in limited contexts] **if you're sure;** [in refer. to a 3rd party] **X can do ⟨let X do⟩ as ⟨what⟩ he wishes ⟨pleases, likes, chooses, thinks best⟩; X can suit himself; X knows best; X knows what's best for him;** [in limited contexts] **if X is sure.**

...Сойдясь в упор с недвижным взглядом хозяина, [Золотарёв] понял, что тот заранее отказывался долее слушать гостя. «Как знаешь, — выходя, замкнулся Золотарёв, — вольному воля!» (Максимов 1). ...Catching Matvei's motionless gaze he [Zolotarev] realized that he had already decided not to listen to him any longer. "As you wish," he thought sullenly as he went out, "nobody's forcing you" (1a). ♦ [Бусыгин:] Ты как знаешь, а я пока останусь. Ненадолго (Вампилов 4). [B.:] You can do as you like, but I'm staying for a while. Not for long (4a). ♦ «Ладно, пойду», — сказала Нюра, поднимаясь. «Ну, как знаете. Люди для вас стараются, хотят сделать, как лучше, а вы...» (Войнович 4). "All right, I'm leaving," said Nyura, rising. "Well, suit yourself. People are trying to help you. They want to make the best of it, but you..." (4a). ♦ [Большов:] Да ты бы посидел немножко. [Рисположенский:] Нет, ей-богу, Самсон Силыч, не время. Я уж к вам завтра пораньше зайду. [Большов:] Ну, как знаешь! (Островский 10). [B.:] Why don't you stay a bit longer? [R.:] No, really and truly, Samson Silych, I haven't time. I'll drop by tomorrow as soon as possible. [B.:] Well, you know best (10a). ♦ «...Поешь с нами хотя бы мамалыгу с кислым молоком...» — «Нет-нет, — отвечает Лилиша — я совсем не хочу есть». — «Ну ладно, как знаешь», — говорит тётушка... (Искандер 4). "At least have some mush and yogurt with us..." "No, no," Lilisha answers. "I'm not hungry at all." "Well, all right, if you're sure," Auntie says... (4a). ♦ Пётр Ильич встал и объявил, что пойдёт теперь прямо к исправнику и всё ему расскажет, а там как тот сам знает (Достоевский 1). Pyotr Ilyich stood up and announced that he would now go directly to the police commissioner and tell him everything, and let him do as he thinks best (1a).

3-147 • НЕ ЗНА́ЕШЬ, ГДЕ НАЙДЁШЬ, ГДЕ ПОТЕ-РЯ́ЕШЬ [saying] you can meet with unexpected success and unexpected failure at any time: ≃ **anything can happen; you never know what fate may hold ⟨what fate has in store for you⟩; you never know what's around the corner.**

3-148 • НУ́ ЗНА́ЕШЬ ⟨-ете⟩ ЛИ! *highly coll* [Interj; these forms only] used to express one's indignation at, strong disagreement with etc s.o.: **(well,) really!; now look here!; well, I never!**

[256]

[Зилов:] Слышите? Ваши приличия мне опротивели. [Кушак *(негодует)*:] Ну знаешь ли! Я далеко не ханжа, но это уже слишком! (Вампилов 5). [Z.:] Do you hear? I'm sick to death of your decency. [K. *(indignant)*:] Now look here! I'm no prude, but this is a bit much! (5a).

3-149 • ЗНАЙ НА́ШИХ! *highly coll* [Interj; Invar; fixed WO] (used to express self-satisfaction, self-praise, bravado) look at how talented, brave, invincible etc (as specified by the context) I am (we are): **look at what I ⟨we⟩ can do!; I ⟨we⟩ showed 'em what I ⟨we⟩ could do!; impressed you, didn't I ⟨we⟩?; get a load of me ⟨us⟩!**

3-150 • ЗНАЙ СЕБЕ́ *highly coll* [Particle; Invar; foll. by a finite form of an impfv verb; fixed WO] one continues to do sth. (despite another's command to stop, not paying attention to what is happening around him etc): **keep (doing sth.); keep ⟨go⟩ (right) on (doing sth.); keep etc (doing sth.) regardless.**

[Фёкла:] Всё сидит в халате да трубку знай себе покуривает (Гоголь 1). [F.:] He goes on sitting here in his dressing-gown and smoking away at his pipe! (1a).

3-151 • ТАК И ЗНАЙ(ТЕ) *coll* [indep. clause; these forms only; fixed WO] (used to intensify a prediction, threat, or comment about a state of affairs) sth. is or will be precisely as I say, I assure you: **you can be sure of that ⟨of one thing…⟩; you can be sure (that…); that's for sure; I mean it; you can count on that; mark my words; [in limited contexts] do you hear me?**

[Валентина:] Было, не было — тебе-то что? Было бы, если бы он [Шаманов] захотел! Так и знай (Вампилов 2). [V.:] Whether it happened or not—what's it to you? You can be sure of one thing—it *would* have happened if he'd [Shamanov had] wanted it to (2a). ♦ Радиопереклички созывались в году часто. Заело с посевной — радиоперекличка… Не выполняется план по сдаче хлеба — так и знай, будет перекличка (Абрамов 1). Radio linkups were called frequently during the year. If there was a hitch in the sowing campaign—radio linkup….If the Grain Requisition Plan was not being fulfilled, you could be sure there would be a radio linkup (1a). ♦ «Там тебе не верили и тут веры большой давать не будут, так и знай!» (Шолохов 5). "They didn't trust you over there, and back here they won't trust you [much] either, you can count on that!" (5a). ♦ …Хотя язык у неё и чесался, рассказывать побоялась, памятуя Прохорово наставление: «Так и знай: скажешь об этом кому хоть слово — положу тебя головой на дровосеку, язык твой поганый на аршин вытяну и отрублю» (Шолохов 5). …Although she was itching to speak, she was afraid, remembering Prokhor's warning, "Mark my words. If you so much as breathe a word to anyone about it, I'll put your head on the chopping block, pull your tongue out till it's a yard long, and cut it off" (5a). ♦ «Дома весь вечер будешь сидеть — так и знай» (Распутин 2). "You're going to spend the whole evening home, do you hear me?" (2a).

3-152 • ТО И ЗНАЙ *obsoles, coll* [Invar; adv; used with impfv verbs; fixed WO] repeatedly, almost all the time: **constantly; over and over (again); time and (time) again.**

3-153 • В ЗНАК *чего* [PrepP; Invar; Prep] as an expression, indication (of sth.): **as a sign of ⟨that…⟩; as a token ⟨a symbol⟩ of; in token of; by way of indicating that…; (in order) to show (sth.);** ‖ в знак согласия ⟨сочувствия, признательности и т. п.⟩ ≃ **in agreement ⟨sympathy, appreciation etc⟩.**

Чёрт его знает, какой реакции он ожидал на свою благодушную отповедь. То ли они начнут смущённо переглядываться, или лица их озарятся пониманием, или некий вздох облегчения пронесётся по залу в знак того, что недоразумение благополучно разъяснилось, и теперь можно всё начинать сначала, на новой, более реалистической основе… (Стругацкие 1). God only knows what kind of reaction he expected from his well-intended lecture. Either that they'd start exchanging embarrassed glances, or that their faces would light up with understanding, or that a sigh of relief would flood through the hall as a sign that the misunderstanding had passed and they could begin again on a new, more realistic basis (1a). ♦ [Войницкий:] В знак мира и согласия я принесу сейчас букет роз… (Чехов 3). [V.:] As a token of peace and harmony I am going to bring you a bouquet of roses… (3a). ♦ «…В знак чистосердечия, я прошу вас открыть мне главное ваше пристрастие» (Толстой 5). "…In token of sincerity, I ask you to disclose to me your chief passion" (5a). ♦ «Надо посоветоваться с товарищами», — сказал редактор [Автандил Автандилович] и включил вентилятор в знак того, что летучка окончена (Искандер 6). "I'll have to consult some colleagues on this," said Avtandil Avtandilovich. Then by way of indicating that the meeting was adjourned, he switched on his office fan (6a). ♦ Он понимает намёк на возможный арест Юли и кивает мне в знак того, что понял (Гинзбург 2). He understood this reference to the possibility of Julia's being arrested and gave me a nod to show that he had understood (2a). ♦ «…Ты видишь, как я тебя люблю; я всё готов отдать, чтоб тебя развеселить: я хочу, чтоб ты была счастлива… Скажи, ты будешь веселей?» Она призадумалась… потом улыбнулась ласково и кивнула головой в знак согласия (Лермонтов 1). "You can see how I love you. I am ready to do anything to cheer you: I want you to be happy.…Tell me, you will be more cheerful?" She thought for a moment…then smiled tenderly and nodded in agreement (1b).

3-154 • В ЗНАК ПА́МЯТИ [PrepP; Invar; usu. adv] (in refer. to sth. given or received as a gift) so that the recipient will be reminded in the future of s.o. or sth. special, dear etc to him in the past: **as a (token of) remembrance; as a keepsake; to remember s.o. ⟨sth.⟩ by.**

[Мигаев:] Да, чудак, давно б я его [портсигар] заложил, да нельзя — дарёный, в знак памяти… (Островский 11). [M.:] I'd have pawned it [the cigar case] long ago, but I mustn't; it was given to me as a token of remembrance (11a).

3-155 • ДАВА́ТЬ/ДАТЬ ⟨ПОДАВА́ТЬ/ПОДА́ТЬ *obs*⟩ **ЗНАК** *(кому)* [VP; subj: human] to make s.o. aware of sth., use a signal to warn s.o.: Х подал знак Y-у ≃ **X gave Y the ⟨a⟩ signal ⟨sign⟩ (to do sth.); X signaled (to) Y (to do sth.); [in refer. to signaling with one's eyes] X gave Y the eye.**

Когда же [Митя] рассказал, как он решился наконец дать отцу *знак*, что пришла Грушенька и чтобы тот отворил окно, то прокурор и следователь совсем не обратили внимание на слово «знак», как бы не поняв вовсе, какое значение имеет тут это слово… (Достоевский 1). When he [Mitya] told how he finally made up his mind to give his father the *signal* that Grushenka had come, so that he would open the window, the prosecutor and the district attorney paid no attention to the word "signal," as if they had no idea at all of the word's significance here… (1a). ♦ …[Император] подал рукою знак. Раздался одинокий выстрел сигнальной пушки, и войска, с разных сторон обложившие Москву, двинулись в Москву… (Толстой 6). …[The Emperor] gave a sign with his hand. A single report of a signalling-gun followed, and the troops, who were already spread out on different sides of Moscow, moved into the city… (6b). ♦ Пугачёв задремал, сидя на своём месте; товарищи его встали и дали мне знак оставить его (Пушкин 2). Pugachev went to sleep, sitting in his place; his comrades stood up and gave me the sign to leave him (2b). Pugachev fell asleep in his chair; his comrades rose and signaled to me to leave him (2a).

3-156 • СТА́ВИТЬ/ПОСТА́ВИТЬ ЗНАК РА́ВЕНСТВА *между кем (и кем), между чем (и чем)* [VP; subj: human; often infin with (не) мочь, можно, нельзя etc] to regard two or more people or things as being identical, equivalent, or similar: X ставит знак равенства между Y-ом и Z-ом ≃ **X equates Y with Z; X considers Y and Z (to be) equal; X puts Y and Z on**

the same level ⟨in the same category⟩; X considers Y (to be) on a par with Z.

«Но не принимает ли товарищ Киров преданность себе за преданность партии? Не ставит ли товарищ Киров знак равенства между собой и партией?» (Рыбаков 2). "But perhaps Comrade Kirov is mistaking devotion to him for devotion to the Party? Is Comrade Kirov equating himself with the Party?" (2a).

3-157 • ПОД ЗНА́КОМ *чего lit* [PrepP; Invar; the resulting PrepP is adv] impacted, characterized, guided by sth.: **marked ⟨colored, influenced⟩ by.**

3-158 • С ПЕ́РВОГО ЗНАКО́МСТВА [PrepP; Invar; adv; fixed WO] immediately, from the first encounter: **from the first meeting; from the very beginning ⟨start, first⟩.**

3-159 • ША́ПОЧНОЕ ⟨ШЛЯ́ПОЧНОЕ *obs*⟩ **ЗНАКО́М-СТВО** *coll* [NP; usu. sing] a superficial, casual acquaintanceship: **(have) (only) a nodding ⟨passing, fleeting⟩ acquaintance (with s.o.); (be) (only) on nodding terms (with s.o.);** [in limited contexts] **(be) mere acquaintances.**

[Анастасия Ефремовна:] Петя, у тебя нет знакомств в Бауманском училище? [Пётр Иванович:] Нет. У Николая Афанасьевича я встречал Коробова, но это так — шапочное знакомство (Розов 1). [А.Е.:] Petya, do you know anyone at the Bauman Institute? [P.I.:] No, I once met Korobov at Nikolai Afanasievich's, but just that once. We have only a nodding acquaintance (1a). ♦ «Да, так о Жилинском... Умный человек, эрудит, но с ним будьте начеку». — «Я с ним почти не общаюсь, так, шапочное знакомство» (Рыбаков 2). "Yes, about Zhilinsky. He's a clever man, very well read, but be on your guard with him." "I have very little to do with him. We're only on nodding terms" (2a). ♦ «Плохое настроение у неё [Сани Холодовой] было?» — спросил Антон. «Не сказал бы... Наверное, осторожничала — знакомство-то наше было, как говорится, шапочное» (Чернёнок 1). "Was she [Sanya Kholodova] in a bad mood?" Anton asked. "I wouldn't say that....She was careful, I think; we were mere acquaintances" (1a).

3-160 • ПО ЗНАКО́МСТВУ достать *что,* **устроить** *кого-что и т. п. coll* [PrepP; Invar; adv] (to get, arrange sth., get s.o. a desired position etc) by using connections, with the help of influential friends, contacts etc: **through ⟨thanks to⟩ one's connections; by pulling strings; through pull; by ⟨through⟩ knowing the right people; through some useful contact(s).**

[Алексей:] Как это ты серебряную медаль получила? [Галя:] По знакомству (Розов 1). [А.:] How did you manage to get a silver medal? [G.:] Through pull (1a). ♦ [Колесов:] Сержант, нам бы здесь местечко — тихо, по знакомству. А, сержант? (Вампилов 3). [К.:] Sergeant, we wouldn't mind getting a plot here ourselves, on the side, through some useful contact. Eh, sergeant? (3a).

3-161 • ША́ПОЧНЫЙ ЗНАКО́МЫЙ *coll* [NP; usu. obj or subj-compl with copula (subj: human)] a casual acquaintance, with whom one only exchanges greetings upon meeting: **a nodding ⟨passing, fleeting⟩ acquaintance.**

3-162 • ПРИВОДИ́ТЬ/ПРИВЕСТИ́ К ОДНОМУ́ ⟨К ЕДИ́НОМУ, К О́БЩЕМУ⟩ ЗНАМЕНА́ТЕЛЮ *кого-что lit* [VP; subj: human; often infin with нельзя, невозможно etc] to equalize two or more objects, phenomena, or, less often, people in some respect: X пытался привести Y и Z к общему знаменателю ≃ **X tried to reduce Y and Z to a common denominator.**

3-163 • ПОД ЗНА́МЕНЕМ *чего rhet* [PrepP; Invar; the resulting PrepP is adv] guided, driven by sth.: **under ⟨beneath⟩ the banner of; in the name of.**

Она [Анна Николаевна] шла в революцию под знаменем долга и жертвы, я — под знаменем моего свободного желания (Богданов 1). She [Anna Nikolaevna] had entered the revolution under the banner of duty and sacrifice, while I had joined it under the banner of my own free will (1a).

3-164 • ЗНАМЕ́НИЕ ВРЕ́МЕНИ *lit* [NP; usu. sing; usu. obj or subj-compl with copula (subj: abstr); fixed WO] a phenomenon typical of a certain period: **a sign ⟨a symbol⟩ of the times.**

«Анкет перестали бояться, — ядовито заключил Митишатьев, — вот знамение времени, так сказать... Вот и хвастают?» — «Почему же хвастают? — с трудом разлепил губы, сказал Готтих. — Вот я, например, барон, а не хвастаюсь же?» (Битов 2). "People have stopped being afraid of the origin question on official forms," Mitishatyev concluded venomously. "A sign of the times, as it were. So they boast." "But why boast?" Gottich said, prying open his lips with difficulty. "Take me, for example, I'm a baron and I don't boast, do I?" (2a).

3-165 • ВЫСОКО́ ДЕРЖА́ТЬ ЗНА́МЯ *(чего, чьё) elev* [VP; subj: human; fixed WO] to maintain certain ideals, hold them sacred: X высоко держал знамя Y-а ≃ **X held high the banner ⟨the flag⟩ of Y; X kept the flag of Y flying.**

3-166 • ПОДНИМА́ТЬ/ПОДНЯ́ТЬ ЗНА́МЯ *чего elev* [VP; subj: human; fixed WO] to begin fighting for sth., in the name of sth.: X поднял знамя Y-а ≃ **X raised the banner of Y.**

3-167 • СТАНОВИ́ТЬСЯ/СТАТЬ ⟨ВСТАТЬ⟩ ПОД ЗНА́МЯ ⟨ПОД ЗНАМЁНА⟩ *кого-чего lit* [VP; subj: human; fixed WO] to join s.o., some group or movement in order to struggle for their side, defend their interests: X-ы встали под знамя Y-ов ≃ **Xs rallied to the banner of Ys; Xs united under ⟨beneath⟩ the banner of Ys; Xs joined the ranks of Ys.**

Наконец, после долгой отлучки возвратился ещё один член правления, человек активный и от Иванько независимый... Вернувшийся из отлучки сразу заявил, что разрушения дома он ни за что не потерпит. Положение стало меняться. Почувствовав сильную руку, мои сторонники сразу встали под знамёна приехавшего... (Войнович 3). Finally, another member of the board returned after a long absence, an energetic man and one independent of Ivanko....He immediately declared that under no circumstances would he endure the destruction of the building. The situation began to change. Sensing a strong hand, my supporters united beneath the banner of the returnee (3a).

3-168 • ЗНАТЬ НЕ ЗНА́Ю ⟨не знает и т. п.⟩ (, ВЕ́ДАТЬ НЕ ВЕ́ДАЮ ⟨не ведает и т. п.⟩) *coll* [VP; subj: human; usu. pres; when 2nd pers form is used, it is usu. in subord clauses (e.g., after «Говори, что...», «Ты притворяешься, что...» etc); fixed WO] (in refer. to one's complete lack of knowledge, information about sth., or one's reluctance to admit sth.) I have (he has etc) no information about it: знать не знаю, ведать не ведаю ≃ **I know nothing (whatsoever) about it; I don't know a thing (, not a thing); I don't know what s.o. is talking about; I haven't the slightest ⟨the faintest⟩ idea (what s.o. is talking about).**

«Сверх того за огород и продовольствие из оного капустой, репой и прочими овощами... — читал Иван Матвеевич, — примерно двести пятьдесят рублей...» — «Какой огород? Какая капуста? Я и знать не знаю, что вы!» — почти грозно возражал Обломов (Гончаров 1). "In addition," Ivan Matveyevich read, "for kitchen garden produce, such as cabbages, turnips, and other vegetables...approximately two hundred and fifty roubles...." "What kitchen garden? What cabbages? What are you talking about? I know nothing about it!" Oblomov rejoined almost menacingly (1a). ♦ Некоторое время Байбаков запирался и ничего, кроме «знать не знаю, ведать не ведаю», не отвечал... (Салтыков-

Щедрин 1). At first Baibakov refused to say anything and answered only: "I don't know a thing, not a thing!" (1b).

З-169 • **ЗНАТЬ НЕ ХОЧУ́** ⟨не хо́чет и т. п.⟩ *кого-что coll* [VP; subj: human; usu. 1st or 3rd pers; usu. this WO] I do not (he does not etc) want to have dealings with s.o., be involved in sth., sacrifice time to s.o. or sth. etc: X Y-а знать не хо́чет ≃ **X doesn't want (to have) anything to do with Y; X doesn't want to hear about Y; X doesn't want to know person Y; X doesn't want to know about thing Y;** [in limited contexts] **X will not hear of Y.**

Пфуль был один из тех теоретиков, которые так любят свою теорию, что забывают цель теории — приложение её к практике; он из любви к теории ненавидел всякую практику и знать её не хотел (Толстой 6). He [Pfühl] was one of those theoreticians who so love their theory that they lose sight of the theory's object — its practical application. His passion for theory made him despise all practical considerations and he would not hear of them (6a).

З-170 • **ЗНАТЬ ПРО СЕБЯ́** *obsoles, substand* [VP; subj: human; often imper (sing)] to hold sth. secret, not talk about it: знай про себя ≃ **keep it ⟨things⟩ to yourself; keep it under your hat; keep quiet ⟨mum⟩ about it; don't spill the beans.**

[Анисья:] …Ты на чьи деньги гуляешь?.. На мои. [Акулина:] Как же, твои! Украсть хотела, да не пришлось. Уйди, ты! *(Хочет пройти, толкает.)* [Анисья:] Ты что толкаешься-то? Я те толкану. [Акулина:] Толкану? Ну-ка, сунься. *(Напирает на неё.)* …Молчала бы, про себя бы знала (Толстой 1). [An.:] Whose money do you have your sprees with?… With mine! [Ak.:] What do you mean, yours! You wanted to steal it, but didn't get the chance to. Get out, you! *(Tries to get by, pushes)* [An.:] What're you pushing for? I'll push you! [Ak.:] Push me? All right, come on. *(Advances toward her)* …You better shut up, keep things to yourself (1a).

З-171 • **ИНТЕРЕ́СНО ЗНАТЬ** *coll* [Invar; main clause in a complex sent; fixed WO] I would like to learn, find out (sth.): **I wonder; I'd be interested to know; I'd like to know; it will be interesting to see ⟨to find out etc⟩;** [in limited contexts] **I can't wait to hear ⟨to see etc⟩.**

Детям дали трудное задание по биологии. Интересно знать, как они с ним справятся. The kids were given a hard biology assignment. I wonder how well they'll be able to handle it. ♦ Уроки кончились в час, а сейчас пять часов! Интересно знать, где ты был всё это время! School was over at one o'clock, and it's already five! I'd like to know where you've been all this time!

З-172 • **КАК ⟨ПОЧЁМ⟩ ЗНАТЬ** *coll* [indep. sent or sent adv (parenth); these forms only; fixed WO] although it is not known, it is entirely possible (when used as a rejoinder, may imply that the opposite may be true): **who knows?; you never know ⟨one never knows⟩; you ⟨one⟩ never can tell; who can tell?; how can you ⟨one⟩ tell?; how can you ⟨one⟩ be sure?; there's no telling ⟨knowing⟩; I ⟨he, it etc⟩ might…**

«…Поздно мне каяться. Для меня не будет помилования. Буду продолжать как начал. Как знать? Авось и удастся!» (Пушкин 2). "It's too late for me to repent. There'll be no mercy for me. I will continue as I have begun. Who knows? Perhaps I'll succeed" (2b). ♦ «Вы — не Достоевский», — сказала гражданка, сбиваемая с толку Коровьевым. «Ну, почём знать, почём знать», — ответил тот (Булгаков 9). "You are not Dostoevsky," said the woman, somewhat rattled by Koroviev's logic. "You never can tell, you never can tell," he answered (9a). ♦ «Всех же не выгонишь и не посадишь». — «Как знать, — сказал Антон. — Если нужно, могут посадить и всех» (Зиновьев 2). "And they can't expel everyone or send them all to jail." "How can you tell?" said Anton. "If they had to, they wouldn't be past jailing everybody" (2a).

З-173 • **МНО́ГО БУ́ДЕШЬ ЗНАТЬ – СКО́РО СОСТА́-РИШЬСЯ** [saying] said in answer to s.o.'s excessive curiosity as a refusal to explain, tell sth.: ≃ **curiosity killed the cat; ask me no questions, I'll tell you no lies; that's for me to know and (for) you to find out.**

«Я завтра к батьке уезжаю», — проговорил Базаров. Аркадий приподнялся и опёрся на локоть. Он и удивился и почему-то обрадовался. «А! — промолвил он. — И ты от этого грустен?» Базаров зевнул. «Много будешь знать, состареешься [*obs* = состаришься]» (Тургенев 2). "I'm going to my father's tomorrow," announced Bazarov. Arkady propped himself up on his elbow. He was surprised and yet somehow glad. "Ah!" he said. "Is that why you're sad?" Bazarov yawned. "Curiosity killed the cat" (2a). ♦ «А куда полетишь?» — «Много знать будешь, скоро состаришься» (Достоевский 1). "Where will you fly to?" "Ask me no questions, I'll tell you no lies" (1a).

З-174 • **НЕ ЗНАТЬ, КУДА́ ДЕВА́ТЬСЯ/ДЕ́ТЬСЯ ⟨ДЕТЬ СЕБЯ́⟩** ⟨от стыда́, смуще́ния и т. п.⟩ *coll* [VP; subj: human; only знать conjugates; usu. impfv деваться; fixed WO] to experience a feeling of intense embarrassment, awkwardness, shame: X не знал, куда деваться ≃ **X didn't know where ⟨which way⟩ to look ⟨turn⟩ (from embarrassment ⟨for shame etc⟩); X didn't know where to hide (from embarrassment ⟨for shame etc⟩); X was so embarrassed ⟨ashamed etc⟩ he didn't know what to do (with himself); X was about to ⟨thought he'd etc⟩ die (from embarrassment etc).**

«Деньги… должны храниться в госбанке, в специальных сухих и хорошо охраняемых помещениях, а отнюдь не в тёткином погребе, где их могут… попортить крысы! Право, стыдно, Канавкин! Ведь вы же взрослый человек». Канавкин уж не знал, куда и деваться, и только колупал пальцем борт своего пиджачка (Булгаков 9). "Money…should be kept in the State Bank, in dry and specially guarded strong rooms, but never in your aunt's cellar, where…the rats may get at it. Really, Kanavkin, you should be ashamed — you, a grown man!" Kanavkin did not know which way to look and could only twist the hem of his jacket with his finger (9b). ♦ «Ну, чья взяла, троцкисты?» — обратился он к ним [чегемцам], яростно улыбаясь. Чегемцы не только не стали оспаривать свою принадлежность к этому опасному политическому течению, о существовании которого, впрочем, они и не подозревали, а просто не знали, куда деть себя от стыда (Искандер 3). "Well, who won, you Trotskyites?" he said [to the Chegemians], grinning savagely. Not only did the Chegemians make no effort to dispute their membership in this dangerous political movement — whose existence, however, they had not even suspected — they simply did not know where to hide for shame (3a). ♦ «Ты огорчил барина!» — с расстановкой произнёс Илья Ильич и пристально смотрел на Захара, наслаждаясь его смущением. Захар не знал, куда деваться от тоски… (Гончаров 1). "You have grieved your master!" Oblomov spoke in a measured tone, fixing his gaze on Zakhar and enjoying his discomfort. Zakhar was so miserable he did not know what to do (1b).

З-175 • **НЕ ЗНАТЬ, КУДА́ СЕБЯ́ ДЕВА́ТЬ/ДЕТЬ** *coll* [VP; subj: human; only знать conjugates; fixed WO] not to know what to occupy o.s. with, what to do: X не знает, куда себя деть ≃ **X doesn't know what to do with himself; X is at loose ends.**

З-176 • **ПОЧЁМ МНЕ ⟨тебе́ и т. п.⟩ ЗНАТЬ; ПОЧЁМ Я ЗНА́Ю ⟨ты зна́ешь и т. п.⟩** *all coll* [sent; these forms only; fixed WO] I (you etc) do not know at all, have no idea (often used in answer to a question): **how could I ⟨you etc⟩ (possibly) know?; I ⟨you etc⟩ haven't the foggiest ⟨the faintest⟩ (idea);** [1st pers only] **how (on earth) should I know?; search ⟨beats⟩ me; I'm sure I don't know.**

[Трагик:] Где мой Вася? Где мой Вася? [Нароков:] А я почём знаю (Островский 11). [T.:] Where's my Vasya? Where's my Vasya? [N.:] How should I know? (11a). ♦ «А им кто сказывал?» —

«Я почём знаю!» (Гончаров 1). "And who told them?" "I'm sure I don't know, sir" (1a).

3-177 • ЧТО ЗНА́ЧИТ [Invar; used as Particle; usu. foll. by NP or infin; fixed WO] that is the effect or inherent nature of: **that's…for you; that's ⟨this is⟩ what comes of…; that's what…means; that's what…does (for you);** [in limited contexts] **that's what I call…**

«Вот, дорогой, что значит гений! Можно и веру переменить» (Шолохов 2). "That's genius for you, my dear fellow! It can make you change your faith" (2a). ♦ Аркадий бросился на шею к своему бывшему наставнику и другу, и слёзы так и брызнули у него из глаз. «Что значит молодость!» – произнёс спокойно Базаров (Тургенев 2). Arkady flung himself on the neck of his former mentor and friend, and the tears fairly gushed from his eyes. "That's what comes of being young!" Bazarov commented calmly (2b). ♦ Что значит быть красивой — всё само получается, плывёт в руки (Рыбаков 2). That's what being beautiful meant. Everything just dropped into your lap (2a). ♦ На днях, посмотрев на лес, который всегда был далёким и недоступным, я вдруг подумал, что это мой лес, и удивился такой свободе мыслей. Что значит весна. В последний год, полагаю, мне будет уже не до этих тонкостей (Терц 3). The other day, looking out at the forest which has always been so remote and inaccessible, I suddenly conceived of it as *my* forest and felt surprised at such freedom of thought. That's what spring does for you. During my last year here I imagine that I shall have other things on my mind than fine points such as this (3a). ♦ «Молодец! – повторил он, отдуваясь. – Вот что значит еврейская голова!» (Войнович 6). "Good job!" he repeated, panting. "That's what I call Jewish smarts" (6a).

3-178 • НИЧЕГО́ НЕ ЗНА́ЧИТЬ [VP; subj: abstr, human, or collect; fixed WO] to have no significance, be unimportant: X ничего не значит ≃ **thing X doesn't mean anything ⟨a thing⟩; thing X doesn't matter; thing X is inconsequential; person X doesn't have any clout ⟨say (in anything), pull etc⟩; person X is a nonentity (in his family ⟨at work etc⟩).**

[Кабанова:] Ведь ты… с ней [с женой] в законе живёшь. Али [*substand* = или], по-вашему, закон ничего не значит? (Островский 6). [K.:] After all…you're living with her [your wife] in lawful marriage. Or, to your way of thinking, doesn't lawful marriage mean anything? (6a). ♦ [Хороших:] Думаешь, заступился он за тебя, значит, что ж?.. Да ничего не значит!.. Не замечал он тебя и не замечает (Вампилов 2). [Kh.:] You think because he defended you it means something, is that it?…But it doesn't mean a thing!…He never noticed you before and he doesn't now (2b).

3-179 • КАК НЕ ЗНА́Ю КТО *coll* [Invar; adv (intensif); fixed WO] to an extreme extent, very intensely: **like you wouldn't believe;** ‖ врать ~ ≃ **lie like a rug;** ‖ объесться ~ ≃ **stuff o.s. to the gills; overeat like I don't know what;** ‖ устать ~ ≃ **be dead tired ⟨dog-tired⟩; be beat ⟨whipped⟩.**

[Репникова:] Опять ворчишь? Не понимаю, чем ты недовольна. [Таня:] Вечно объедимся, как не знаю кто, а потом весь вечер перевариваем… (Вампилов 3). [R.:] Are you grumbling again? I don't understand what's bothering you. [T.:] We always overeat like I don't know what, and then spend the whole evening digesting… (3a).

3-180 • ИЗ ДВУХ ЗОЛ МÉНЬШЕЕ выбрать [NP; obj; usu. this WO] (to choose) sth. that is, although undesirable, somewhat better than the available alternative: **(choose) the lesser of two evils.**

Но всё-таки я пожал эту руку. Значит, если бы я не пожал её, я бы чувствовал себя ещё хуже? Из двух зол я выбираю меньшее? Почему оно меньшее? (Искандер 4). Yet, despite it all, I did shake the hand. Does that mean that if I hadn't I would have felt even worse? Am I choosing the lesser of two evils? Why is it the lesser? (4a).

< Modified loan translation of the Latin *ex malis eligere minima* (Cicero, *De officiis*, III, 1, 3).

3-181 • КУПА́ТЬСЯ В ЗО́ЛОТЕ *coll* [VP; subj: human] to be very rich: X купается в золоте ≃ **X is rolling in money ⟨dough⟩; X is made of money; X has money to burn.**

3-182 • МАЛ ЗОЛОТНИ́К, ДА ДО́РОГ [saying] small in size but very valuable (said of a small person who has many good qualities; also of sth. small in size but very important or valuable): ≃ **good things come in small packages.**

3-183 • НЕ ВСЁ ТО ЗО́ЛОТО, ЧТО БЛЕСТИ́Т [saying] a person or thing may not be as good, valuable etc as he or it appears to be on the surface: **all that glitters is not gold; all is not gold that glitters.**

3-184 • ЗУБ НА́ ЗУБ НЕ ПОПАДА́ЕТ *у кого (от чего) coll* [VP$_{subj}$; pres or past; usu. this WO] s.o. is trembling violently (from the cold, fear etc): у X-а зуб на зуб не попадает ≃ **X's teeth are chattering; X cannot keep his teeth from chattering.**

«На третье утро повели меня грязного, застылого, зуб на зуб не попадает, в дом, в чистую комнату» (Копелев 1). "On the third morning they took me, filthy, chilled, my teeth chattering, into the house, into a clean room" (1a). ♦ «…Все мы на холодном ветру продрогли, как собаки, зуб на зуб не попадает» (Шолохов 1). "…We were shivering like dogs in the bitter wind, we couldn't keep our teeth from chattering" (1a).

3-185 • ИМÉТЬ ЗУБ *на кого, против кого coll* [VP; subj: human] to have bitter feelings toward s.o. (and, often, to want to cause s.o. harm): X имеет зуб на Y-а ≃ **X has it in for Y; X has ⟨nurses, harbors⟩ a grudge against Y; X bears Y a grudge; X is down on Y; X feels resentment toward Y.**

[Саяпин:] Он (*показывает на дверь кабинета [Кушака]*) требует статью… Так он этого не оставит… Ты имей в виду, он имеет на тебя зуб за новоселье (Вампилов 5). [S. (*Indicating the door to Kushak's office*):] He's yelling for the article.…He won't let it drop.…Remember, he's got it in for you because of the house-warming (5b). ♦ Бартелеми имел на Курне какой-то зуб за письма, посланные ему через Курне из Франции, которые до него не дошли (Герцен 3). Barthélemy had a grudge against Cournet about some letters which had been sent to him from France through Cournet and had never reached him (3a).

< Loan translation of the French *avoir une dent contre (quelqu'un).*

3-186 • НА ОДИ́Н ЗУБ *чего highly coll* [PrepP; Invar; adv or subj-compl with быть$_\emptyset$ (subj/gen: a noun denoting food); fixed WO] (the amount of food in question) is very small, not nearly enough to satisfy (s.o.): **only enough to whet one's appetite; hardly ⟨not⟩ enough to fill a cavity; not enough to feed a bird; just ⟨barely⟩ a mouthful.**

Коле этого бутерброда — на один зуб, дай ему ещё что-нибудь. Give Kolya something else—that sandwich is only enough to whet his appetite.

3-187 • НИ В ЗУБ НОГО́Й *(в чём, по чему);* **НИ В ЗУБ (ТОЛКНУ́ТЬ)** *all highly coll* [PrepP; these forms only; predic; subj: human; fixed WO] one knows, understands etc absolutely nothing (about sth.): в Y-е X ни в зуб ногой ≃ **X doesn't know beans ⟨the first thing, a damn thing⟩ about Y; Y is a closed book to X.**

«Книжный язык он, может, и знал, но настоящий, народный — ни в зуб» (Трифонов 2). "He may know the literary language, but he doesn't know a damn thing about the language that real people speak" (2a). ♦ [Кречинский:] Помилуйте, Пётр Константиныч! Да что вы его спрашиваете? Ведь он только по полям с собаками ездит; ведь он по хозяйству ни в зуб толкнуть... (Сухово-Кобылин 2). [K.:] For heaven's sake, Piotr Konstantinych, why ask him about such things. He never goes near a field except with his hunting dogs. Farming is a closed book to him (2a).

З-188 • **НЕ ПО ЗУБА́М** *кому highly coll* [PrepP; Invar; subj-compl with copula] **1.** [subj: a noun denoting food] sth. is very tough, difficult for s.o. to chew: X Y-у не по зубам ≃ **X is too hard (for Y to chew); Y can't chew X; X can't manage Y.**

«...Вот здесь хороший кусочек оленьего мяса. Правда, мне он не по зубам. Он немножко жилистый...» (Гинзбург 2). "Here's a nice bit of venison for you. The fact is I can't manage it. It's too stringy for me" (2a).

2. [subj: abstr] sth. is too difficult, complicated for s.o. to cope with: X Y-у не по зубам ≃ **X is over Y's head; X is too much for Y (to handle); X is more than Y can handle ⟨manage⟩; Y doesn't have what it takes (to do X).**

Не давай детям эту задачу. Она слишком трудная, им не по зубам. Don't give the kids this problem. It's too hard, it will be over their heads.

З-189 • **ЗУБА́МИ ДЕРЖА́ТЬСЯ** *за что highly coll* [VP; subj: human; fixed WO] to value sth. very highly and do everything possible not to lose it: X зубами держится за Y ≃ **X hangs on to Y for dear life ⟨for all X is worth⟩; X holds fast to Y.**

Бондарев этой должности долго добивался, и теперь он за неё зубами держится. Bondarev worked long and hard to get this position and now he hangs on to it for dear life.

З-190 • **ЩЁЛКАТЬ ЗУБА́МИ (от голода)** *substand* [VP; subj: human] to be or go hungry: X щёлкал зубами (от голода) ≃ **X was starving ⟨half-starved, famished, dying of hunger⟩; [in limited contexts] X's stomach was growling.**

З-191 • **НАВЯ́ЗНУТЬ В ЗУБА́Х** *(у кого) highly coll* [VP; subj: usu. abstr; usu. past] to become unbearably boring, annoying to s.o. (because of its monotony, endless repetitions etc): X навяз у Y-а в зубах ≃ **X bored Y to death ⟨to tears⟩; Y was sick to death ⟨sick and tired⟩ of X; Y had had enough of X; Y was fed up (to the teeth) with X; Y had had it up to here (with X); [of a topic of conversation, discussion etc] X had been talked to death ⟨into the ground⟩.**

[author's usage] Мне было скучно объяснять навязшие на зубах российские несчастья, но пришлось (Лимонов 1). It was boring for me to explain Russia's misfortunes, I was sick to death of them, but I had to (1a). ♦ «Сегодня уже все знают, что есть человек. Что с человеком делать — вот вопрос. Да и то, признаться, уже навяз в зубах» (Стругацкие 1). "Today everybody knows what man is. The problem is what to do with him. And even that one's been talked to death" (1a).

З-192 • **ДО ЗУБО́В вооружён(ный)** *coll* [PrepP; Invar; adv or modif] fully equipped with the necessary weapons, tools etc: **armed to the teeth ⟨to the hilt⟩.**

«Да ты не бойся, я вооружён до зубов». Он хлопнул себя по карману «сафари», где... лежала «беретта» (Аксёнов 7). "Don't worry. I'm armed to the teeth." He patted the pocket of his safari jacket where he kept the Beretta (7a).

З-193 • **НА ЗУБО́К** *coll* [PrepP; Invar; prep obj or nonagreeing postmodif] as a present to a newborn: **(as) a gift for s.o.'s ⟨the⟩ new baby.**

З-194 • **ПОПАДА́ТЬ(СЯ)/ПОПА́СТЬ(СЯ) НА ЗУБО́К ⟨НА́ ЗУБ *less common*⟩ (к) кому** *coll* [VP; subj: human] to

become the object of s.o.'s mockery, biting criticism, gossip: X попал к Y-у на зубок ≃ **X became the butt of Y's ridicule ⟨criticism, sarcasm etc⟩; X became ⟨was⟩ the target of Y's tongue; Y got his teeth into X.**

[Хлестаков:] А уж Тряпичкину точно, если кто попадёт на зубок — берегись, отца родного не пощадит для словца... (Гоголь 4). [Kh.:] Now if Tryapichkin gets his teeth into anybody — watch out! He wouldn't spare his own father for a wisecrack (4f).

З-195 • **В ЗУ́БЫ дать, сунуть и т. п. кому что** *highly coll* [PrepP; Invar; adv] (to give sth., often a bribe) directly to s.o.: **slip ⟨shove⟩ s.o. sth. ⟨sth. to s.o.⟩.**

«Возьму такси, скажу — на курорт. Пятёрку в зубы — что он, в чемоданы лезть будет?» (Семёнов 1). "I'll take a taxi and head for the coast. If I shove him a fiver he's not likely to poke his nose into my affairs, is he?" (1a).

З-196 • **ЗАГОВА́РИВАТЬ/ЗАГОВОРИ́ТЬ ЗУ́БЫ кому** *coll, usu. disapprov* [VP; subj: human; usu. impfv, often neg imper] to (try to) distract the interlocutor by talking about extraneous matters (with the goal of avoiding an unpleasant topic, deceiving the interlocutor, persuading him to act as one wishes etc): X Y-у зубы заговаривает ≃ **X is fooling Y with smooth talk ⟨with fine words⟩; X is spinning (Y) a fine yarn;** [esp. with the goal of avoiding an unpleasant topic] **X is putting Y off with fine words;** [esp. with the goal of deceiving the interlocutor] **X is pulling the wool over Y's eyes;** [esp. with the goal of obtaining sth. from s.o. or extricating o.s. from an uncomfortable situation] **X is sweet-talking ⟨fast-talking⟩ Y.**

Больной завозился... Кое-кто из солдат засмеялся. «Жалеете вы его, ребятки, напрасно. Жалостью не поможешь, не такое теперь время. Вас тоже пожалеть надо...» Семидолец перебил его: «Ты зубы-то не заговаривай, мил-человек, мы сами с усами. Ты... скажи, что тебе про Расею [*ungrammat* = Россию] известно?» (Федин 1). The sick man began to toss about....One or two of the soldiers laughed. "Your pity for him is a waste of time, boys. Pity won't help him, it's not the time for it now. You are also to be pitied...." The man from Semidol cut him short: "Don't you spin us no fine yarns, kind sir, we know what's what. You tell us...what you know about Russia" (1a). ♦ [Войницкий:] ...Если бы можно было прожить остаток жизни как-нибудь по-новому... Начать новую жизнь... Подскажи мне, как начать... [Астров (*кричит сердито*):] Перестань!.. Ты мне зубов не заговаривай, однако. Ты отдай то, что взял у меня (Чехов 3). [V.:] ...If only it were possible to live through the rest of life in some new way!...To begin a new life....Tell me how to begin... [A. (*shouts angrily*):] Stop it!...Don't try to put me off with fine words. Give me back what you took from me (3a). ♦ «Ах, мошенник, мошенник, — качая головой, говорил Воланд, — каждый раз, как партия его в безнадёжном положении, он начинает заговаривать зубы, подобно самому последнему шарлатану...» (Булгаков 9). "Oh, you swindler, you swindler," Woland said, shaking his head. "Every time he is about to lose a game, he'll try to pull the wool over your eyes, like the worst charlatan" (9a).

З-197 • **ЗУ́БЫ СЪЕСТЬ ⟨ПРОЕ́СТЬ⟩ на чём, в чём** *highly coll, approv* [VP; subj: human; past only with resultative meaning; usu. this WO] to gain much experience, acquire substantial knowledge in some field through extensive practice: X зубы съел на Y-е ≃ **X knows Y inside out; X knows the tricks of the trade; X is an expert at ⟨in⟩ Y; X is a past master at Y; X knows a lot about Y; X knows his stuff ⟨business, onions⟩;** [in limited contexts] **X is an old hand ⟨pro⟩ at Y.**

Вепрь, зубы съевший в вопросе влияния экономики на политику, предсказывал эту войну ещё несколько лет назад (Стругацкие 2). Vepr, who knew a lot about the influence of economics on politics, had predicted this war several years ago (2a).

З-198 • (КЛАСТЬ/ПОЛОЖИ́ТЬ) ЗУ́БЫ НА ПО́ЛКУ *coll* [VP or NP (used as predic); subj: human; often infin with пришлось, придётся] to experience need, be hungry: X-у придётся положить зубы на полку ≃ **X will have to go hungry; X will have to go ⟨do⟩ without (food ⟨the necessities⟩); X will have to tighten his belt.**

После истории с накидкой он вёл себя так, будто ничего не случилось: такова жизнь игрока... сегодня при деньгах, завтра зубы на полку... (Рыбаков 2). After the business of the fur wrap, he acted as if nothing had happened: such was the life of a gambler—today you're in the money, tomorrow you have to tighten your belt (2a).

З-199 • ЛОМА́ТЬ/СЛОМА́ТЬ ⟨ОБЛОМА́ТЬ⟩ (себе) ЗУ́БЫ *на ком-чём, об кого, обо что coll* [VP; subj: human; usu. pfv] to suffer a crushing defeat, fail miserably in sth.: X сломал зубы (на Y-е) ≃ **X came to grief (over Y); X got the worst of it (in dealing with person Y); X came a cropper (in venture Y);** [in limited contexts] **X got crushed ⟨wiped out⟩.**

З-200 • ПОКА́ЗЫВАТЬ/ПОКАЗА́ТЬ ЗУ́БЫ *(кому) coll* [VP; subj: human; fixed WO] **1.** to respond to some question or remark angrily, rudely, in a curt manner: X показал (Y-у) зубы ≃ **X retorted sharply; X snapped (back) at Y; X bit Y's head off.**

2. to display the malicious side of one's nature, display hostility, a readiness to repulse s.o.: X показал зубы ≃ **X showed ⟨bared⟩ his teeth ⟨fangs⟩.**

...Он убивается, пулю таскает то Дудыреву, то следователю... Их мутит от этой пули, зубы показывают, как [собака] Калинка при виде палки (Тендряков 1). ...He was eating his heart out, taking that bullet around, first to Dudyrev, then to the Assistant Prosecutor. They hated this bullet, almost baring their teeth at it, like Kalinka [the dog] at the sight of a stick (1a).

З-201 • СКА́ЛИТЬ ЗУ́БЫ *substand* [VP; subj: human] to react to sth. (s.o.'s behavior, words etc) by smiling, laughing etc (sometimes as a form of mockery): что зубы скалишь? ≃ **what are you grinning ⟨laughing, smiling, snickering, smirking etc⟩ at?; what's so funny?**

Казачок отошёл шага на два, остановился и глядел с улыбкой на Захара. «Что скалишь зубы-то?» – с яростью захрипел Захар (Гончаров 1). The boy walked away a few yards and stopped, looking at Zakhar with a smile. "What are you grinning at?" Zakhar growled furiously (1a). ♦ «Что он там, в немецкой школе, что ли, сидит да уроки учит? Врёт он!.. Я бы его в острог... Обломов расхохотался. «Что зубы-то скалишь? Не правду, что ли, я говорю?» – сказал Тарантьев (Гончаров 1). "What's he doing there—sitting in some German school doing his lessons? Nonsense!...I'd put him in jail...." Oblomov burst out laughing. "What's so funny?" asked Tarantyev. "What I say is true, isn't it?" (1b).

З-202 • СКВОЗЬ ЗУ́БЫ *coll* [PrepP; Invar; adv] **1.** говори́ть, бормота́ть и т. п. ~ (to say, whisper etc sth.) very softly and indistinctly: **under one's breath; through one's teeth.**

«А хорошо бы было...» – чуть слышно сквозь зубы сказал Римский (Булгаков 9). "Would be a good thing..." Rimsky muttered almost inaudibly through his teeth (9a).

2. процеди́ть, провора́чить и т. п. ~ (to utter sth., grumble) with displeasure, angrily, or antagonistically, condescendingly: **through ⟨with⟩ clenched teeth; through ⟨between⟩ one's teeth;** [in limited contexts] **under one's breath.**

И говорит он не сквозь зубы, не вынужденно. Он возбуждён, он проводит литературные параллели, он художественно говорит (Войнович 3). And he wasn't speaking through his teeth, he wasn't being forced. He was excited, he was drawing literary parallels, he was speaking *artistically* (3a). ♦ Её [мою сестру] нельзя было узнать... Слова цедит сквозь зубы (Зиновьев 2). [context transl] She [my sister] was totally unrecognizable. She spat her words out (2a).

З-203 • СТИ́СНУТЬ ЗУ́БЫ [VP; subj: human; usu. Verbal Adv or imper] to suppress one's pain, grief etc (and preserve self-control under trying circumstances): стиснув зубы ≃ **gritting one's teeth.**

Сапоги примёрзли. Абуталип морщился, стиснув зубы, стонал, когда все дружно пытались стащить их с ног (Айтматов 2). The boots were frozen on his feet. Abutalip frowned, gritting his teeth and groaning when everyone tried to take them off (2a).

З-204 • ТОЧИ́ТЬ ⟨ВОСТРИ́ТЬ, ОСТРИ́ТЬ⟩ ЗУ́БЫ ⟨ЗУБ⟩ *coll* [VP; subj: human] **1.** ~ *на кого-что, против кого* to feel spite toward (a person, organization etc), be determined to cause (him or it) harm: X точит зубы на Y-а ≃ **X has it in for Y; X has ⟨bears, nurses⟩ a grudge against Y; X is out to get Y;** [in limited contexts] **Y comes under fire (from X).**

...Он [Сталин] спокойно, даже равнодушно сказал [Кирову]: «...Если вместо тебя придёт другой человек и так же хорошо будет справляться с Ленинградом, то они [ленинградские коммунисты] поймут, что дело не только в товарище Кирове, а дело в партии... И на твоего преемника уже не будут точить зубы» (Рыбаков 2). ...He [Stalin] spoke blandly, almost with indifference: "...If someone else were to take your place and to cope with Leningrad as well as you do, they'd [the Leningrad Communists would] realize that success isn't just a question of Comrade Kirov, but of the Party....And they wouldn't have a grudge against your successor" (2a). ♦ На наш Отдел точат зубы потому, что он приличнее всех выглядит (Зиновьев 2). Our Section comes under fire because it produces a better impression than all the others (2a).

2. ~ *на что*, less common *на кого* to seek to seize, take possession of, or have sth. or s.o.: X точит зубы на Y ≃ **X is anxious ⟨itching, eager⟩ to get hold of Y; X is dying to get his hands on Y; X has (set) his sights on Y; X wants Y in the worst way; X hankers for Y; X is after Y.**

«Настоящий мордаш, – продолжал Ноздрёв. – Я, признаюсь, давно острил зубы на мордаша» (Гоголь 3). "A real bulldog," Nozdryov went on. "I must confess I have been anxious to get hold of a bulldog for a long time" (3a). "A real pug," Nozdrev went on. "I must confess I've been hankering for a pug for a long time" (3b). "A purebred pug," Nozdrev said. "I confess I've been after a pug for a long time" (3e).

З-205 • ЧЕСА́ТЬ/ПОЧЕСА́ТЬ ЗУ́БЫ ⟨ЗУ́БКИ⟩ *substand, often disapprov* [VP; subj: human] to talk about trifles, babble: X чешет зубы ≃ **X shoots the breeze ⟨the bull⟩; X wags his tongue; X chews the fat; X chitchats.**

З-206 • КАК ЗЮ́ЗЯ напи́ться, пьян и т. п. *slang* [как + NP; Invar; adv (intensif) or modif] (to get or be drunk) to excess: X напи́лся ~ ≃ **X got ⟨was⟩ drunk as a skunk; X got ⟨was⟩ plastered ⟨smashed, bombed etc⟩; X drank himself into a stupor ⟨under the table⟩.**

«А ты тоже ничего не помнишь?» – спросил его Виктор. «Это насчёт вчерашнего?» – «Да, насчёт вчерашнего... Напился, как зюзя», – сказал Виктор, обращаясь к Голему... (Стругацкие 1). "So you don't remember either?" Victor asked him. "You mean last night?" "Yes, last night. I drank myself into a stupor," said Victor, turning to Golem... (1a).

И

И-1 • ВО ВСЮ ИВА́НОВСКУЮ *highly coll* [PrepP; Invar; adv (intensif); used with impfv verbs] (one does sth., sth. goes on) at a very high level of intensity: **with all one's ⟨its⟩ might; for all one ⟨it⟩ is worth;** [in limited contexts] **to beat the band;** ‖ кричать ~ ≃ **shout at the top of one's lungs ⟨voice⟩;** ‖ храпеть ~ ≃ **snore like a chain ⟨buzz⟩ saw;** ‖ шуметь ~ ≃ **make enough noise to wake the dead;** ‖ гони ⟨валяй, жми⟩ ~ ≃ **go full tilt ⟨steam⟩; step on it;** ‖ цвести ~ ≃ **be in full bloom;** ‖ солнце светит ~ ≃ **the sun is beating down.**

< There are two common explanations of the origin of this idiom, one connecting it with Ivanovskaya Square, the place in the Kremlin where the tsar's decrees were announced for all to hear, and the other connecting it with the Bell Tower of Ivan the Great, also located within the Kremlin. The latter explanation traces the idiom to an expression used by bell ringers, «Звонить во всю колокольную фамилию» ("to ring all the bells in the bell tower"). The full complement of bells in the Bell Tower of Ivan the Great was called «ивановская».

И-2 • КАК ⟨БУ́ДТО, СЛО́ВНО, ТО́ЧНО⟩ ИГО́ЛКА В СТОГУ́ ⟨В СТО́ГЕ⟩ СЕ́НА исчезнуть, затеряться; **ИГО́ЛКА В СЕ́НЕ ⟨В СТОГУ́ СЕ́НА⟩** [(как etc +) NP; adv (variants with как); fixed WO] (a person, thing etc that has vanished and is) very difficult or almost impossible to find: **like a needle in a haystack; a needle that has vanished in a haystack.**

Он [Влад] ещё долго петлял под составами, перескакивал через десятки тормозных площадок, кружился по стрелкам, но когда ему показалось, что главное позади и вот-вот он канет в ночи, как иголка в стогу сена, перед ним вдруг возникла из ничего неосвещённая стена станции, и дальше пути не было (Максимов 2). For a long while he [Vlad] dodged under the cars, leaped over a dozen brake-platforms and raced over switches; but just when it seemed the worst was over and at any moment he could vanish into the night like a needle in a haystack, an unlit wall suddenly reared up in front of him and there was nowhere left to go (2a). ♦ Главная удача нищего — найти потерянное, но найти своё «я» труднее, чем иголку в сене (Мандельштам 2). A beggar's greatest windfall is to pick up something that has been lost, but to regain one's own "self" is harder than finding a needle in a haystack (2a). ♦ Прошло несколько дней с тех пор, как исчезло ведомство капитана Миляги, но в районе никто этого не заметил. И ведь пропала не иголка в сене, а солидное Учреждение, занимавшее в ряду других учреждений весьма заметное место (Войнович 2). Several days had passed since Captain Milyaga's department had vanished, but nobody in the district seemed to notice. And after all it wasn't a needle that had vanished in a haystack but a reputable Institution which occupied a prominent place among other institutions (2a).

И-3 • КУДА́ ИГО́ЛКА, ТУДА́ И НИ́ТКА [saying] (usu. in refer. to the influence a man has over his wife, but occas. in refer. to the influence parents have over their children etc; usu. refers to s.o.'s following another in a physical or geographical sense, but may also refer to s.o.'s adopting another's point of view, values etc) where one person goes (what one person does etc), the other will go (will do etc): **where the needle goes, the thread follows ⟨will follow⟩.**

И-4 • НЕ ИГО́ЛКА [NP; usu. subj-compl with быть∅ (subj: human, concr, or abstr); pres only] a person or thing is not so small that he or it cannot be seen, found etc: X не иголка ≃ **X is not exactly invisible; X is not someone ⟨something⟩ you can easily**

miss; [in limited contexts] **X is not a needle that can get lost in a haystack.**

«Лиза, Лиза! — замахала руками Раечка. — Где ты была? Мы вчера просто с ума сходили...» Лизка подождала, пока Раечка не подбежала к ней, сказала: «А чего сходить-то? Я ведь не иголка – в сене не потеряюсь» (Абрамов 1). "Liza, Liza!" shouted Raechka, waving her arms. "Where've you been? We were going out of our minds yesterday." Lizka waited for Raechka to run up to her before saying, "What on earth for? I'm not a needle–I won't get lost in the haystack!" (1a).

И-5 • КАК ⟨БУ́ДТО, СЛО́ВНО, ТО́ЧНО⟩ НА ИГО́Л- КАХ *coll* [как etc + PrepP; these forms only; subj-compl with быть∅, сидеть (subj: human)] one is in a state of agitation, anxiety, expectation etc: X сидит как на иголках ≃ **X is on pins and needles; X is on tenterhooks;** [when eagerly anticipating the ending of s.o.'s gripping story, a captivating movie etc] **X is on the edge of his seat.**

И-6 • ДО ИГО́ЛКИ описать, перечислить и т. п. *obs* [PrepP; Invar; adv] (to describe, enumerate sth.) omitting nothing, in minute detail: **(down) to the last ⟨smallest, finest⟩ detail.**

И-7 • ИГО́ЛКИ НЕ ПОДПУ́СТИШЬ ⟨НЕ ПОД- ТО́ЧИШЬ⟩ *(под кого-что);* **НЕЛЬЗЯ́ ИГО́ЛКИ ПОД- ПУСТИ́ТЬ ⟨ПОДТОЧИ́ТЬ⟩** *all obs, coll* [VP; neg pfv fut, gener. 2nd pers sing не подпустишь etc or impers predic with быть∅ (var. with нельзя); fixed WO (with нельзя movable)] you will find nothing to criticize (in s.o. or sth.): (под X-а) иголки не подпустишь ≃ **you cannot find fault with X; you will find no fault in X; X is absolutely unassailable; X is beyond reproach.**

«Стригуны» молчали; они понимали, что слова Собачкина очень последовательны и что со стороны логики под них нельзя иголки подточить... (Салтыков-Щедрин 2). The "colts" were silent; for they realized that Sobachkin's words were very logical and that, from the point of view of pure logic, they were absolutely unassailable (2a).

И-8 • ИГО́ЛКУ ⟨ИГО́ЛКИ⟩ НЕ́ГДЕ ⟨НЕ́КУДА⟩ ВОТКНУ́ТЬ *где coll* [impers predic with быть∅; these forms only; fixed WO] (some place is) very crowded with people: **there is no room to swing a cat; (some place) is packed ⟨jammed⟩ to the rafters.**

И-9 • С ИГО́ЛОЧКИ *coll* [PrepP; Invar] **1.** Also: **С ИГО́ЛКИ** [nonagreeing modif or subj-compl with copula (subj: a noun denoting clothes); often preceded by новый, новенький etc, which does not require a separate translation] completely new and, usu., well-made and fashionable: **brand-new; (brand) spanking new; fresh new** [NP]; **fresh from the tailor ⟨the tailor's⟩.**

Ты стоишь передо мною, одетый в новый с иголочки костюм... в новой шляпе, сдвинутой на затылок чуть больше, чем следовало бы (Михайловская 1). You are standing before me, dressed in a brand-new suit...wearing a new hat pushed back on your head a little more than it should be (1a). ♦ [Дарья:] [У Аксиньи] шубку новенькую украли, с иголочки (Островский 1). [D.:] Somebody stole her [Aksinya's] new coat, brand spanking new it was (1a). ♦ ...Он явился ужасным франтом, в новом с иголочки сюртуке (Достоевский 2). ...He appeared a terrible dandy, in a fresh new frock coat (2a).

2. одеваться, быть∅ одетым ~ [adv] (to dress, be dressed) in completely new, well-made, and fashionable clothes: **(dress) impeccably ⟨immaculately⟩; (wear) a brand-new outfit.**

О разведке у нас знают из кинофильмов. Служит под боком у Гитлера наш смельчак, одет с иголочки, побрит, надушен, водит за нос и Гиммлера, и Бормана, и Кальтенбруннера... (Рыбаков 1). People...know about intelligence from what they've seen in the movies. Our daring agent is operating right under Hitler's nose, dressed immaculately, clean-shaven and perfumed, leading Himmler, Bormann and Kaltenbrunner up the garden path... (1a).

3. [usu. nonagreeing modif] (of objects, equipment, gadgets etc) completely new: **brand-new; fresh from the factory ⟨off the assembly line⟩; just built ⟨made, manufactured etc⟩.**

И-10 • ИГРА́ ВООБРАЖЕ́НИЯ [NP; sing only; fixed WO] sth. imaginary: **figment of s.o.'s imagination.**

И-11 • ИГРА́ НЕ СТО́ИТ СВЕЧ [saying; used without negation in the opposite meaning] the results, profits etc gained from doing sth. are not worth the effort, trouble, or expense involved: **the game isn't worth the candle; it's not worth the effort.**

«Вам всё кажется, что у меня какие-то цели, а потому и глядите на меня подозрительно... Но как я ни желаю сойтись с вами, я всё-таки не возьму на себя труда разуверять вас в противном. Ей-богу, игра не стоит свеч...» (Достоевский 3). "You seem to think the whole time that I have certain ulterior motives and therefore you look upon me with suspicion....But no matter how much I'd like to be friends with you, I'm still not going to take upon myself the labor of convincing you to the contrary. The game's not worth the candle, I swear to God..." (3a). ♦ ...Конечно, научиться писать плохо не так-то легко, потому что приходится выдерживать адскую конкуренцию, но игра стоит свеч, и если вы действительно научитесь писать паршиво, хуже всех, то мировая популярность вам обеспечена (Катаев 2). Of course it's not so easy to learn to write badly because there is such a devil of a lot of competition, but it's well worth the effort and if you can really learn to write lousily, worse than anybody else, then world fame is guaranteed (2a).

И-12 • ИГРА́ ПРИРО́ДЫ [NP; sing only; fixed WO] an exceptional, rare phenomenon, a deviation from the norm: **freak ⟨caprice⟩ of nature;** [in limited contexts] **trick ⟨joke⟩ played by nature.**

[Колесов:] Вы меня заинтриговали. Хулиган — и разводите орхидеи. Игра природы (Вампилов 3). [К.:] You intrigue me. A hooligan and you cultivate orchids. A freak of nature (3b). ♦ [Муров:] Третьего дня я был в театре; говорить о том впечатлении, которое ваша игра производит на зрителей, я не стану. Это вам и без меня известно, но я был поражён ещё необыкновенным сходством, которое вы имеете с одной женщиной, мне когда-то знакомой... Такой игры природы не может быть... Вы Любовь Ивановна Отрадина? [Кручинина:] Да, я Любовь Ивановна Отрадина (Островский 3). [M.:] The day before yesterday I was at the theatre. I will not attempt to tell you what an impression your acting made on everyone, you know that without my telling. But I was struck by the likeness you bear to a woman I once knew....Nature can hardly have played such a trick....Are you not Lubov Ivanovna Otradina? [A.:] Yes, I am Lubov Ivanovna Otradina (3a).

И-13 • ИГРА́ СЛОВ [NP; sing only; fixed WO] using words in a witty manner based on the substitution of one word (or meaning) for another: **wordplay; play on words.**

По-твоему выходит, что от воли самих людей не зависит ничто, говорит Мазила. Почему? Потому что от них зависит всё, говорит Болтун. Это игра слов, говорит Мазила (Зиновьев 1). "From what you say," said Dauber, "nothing depends on the will of men. Why not?" "Because everything depends on it," said Chatterer. "That's just a play on words," said Dauber (1a).

< Loan translation of the French *jeu de mots.*

И-14 • ИГРА́ СЛУ́ЧАЯ ⟨СУДЬБЫ́ *lit*⟩ [NP; sing only; fixed WO] a chance occurrence, unexpected turn of events, or unforeseen set of circumstances: **twist ⟨whim, quirk, trick⟩ of fate; the play of chance.**

Я не знал, какой этаж выбрать для чистоты эксперимента. Почему-то я остановился на третьем. Он мне показался наиболее свободным от игры случая (Искандер 5). I didn't know what floor to choose for an unbiased experiment. For some reason I settled on the third. It struck me as being the freest from the play of chance (5a).

И-15 • ИГРА́ТЬ В ОПА́СНУЮ ИГРУ́ [VP; subj: human; the verb may take the final position, otherwise fixed WO] to be involved in an undertaking that could have dangerous consequences: X играет в опасную игру ≃ **X is playing with fire ⟨dynamite⟩.**

И-16 • РАСКРЫВА́ТЬ/РАСКРЫ́ТЬ ИГРУ́ чью [VP; subj: human; usu. pfv] to uncover and usu. reveal s.o.'s secret plans, intentions: X раскрыл Y-ову игру ≃ **X exposed ⟨saw through⟩ Y's game.**

И-17 • КАК ⟨СЛО́ВНО⟩ ИГРУ́ШКА [как etc + NP; usu. subj-compl with быть∅, получиться etc (subj: human or concr)] a person or thing is nice-looking, refined: **pretty as a picture; lovely.**

И-18 • ДЕ́ТСКИЕ ИГРУ́ШКИ; ДЕ́ТСКАЯ ИГРУ́ШКА ⟨ЗАБА́ВА⟩ [NP; usu. subj-compl with copula, nom or instrum (subj: concr or abstr); fixed WO] a trifle, sth. that is not serious (as compared to something else; the comparison is usu. directly expressed in the context): **child's play.**

Тогда мне казалось, что страдания мои безмерны. Но через несколько месяцев я узнала, что мой конвейер был детской игрушкой сравнительно с тем, что практиковалось позднее, начиная с июня 1937 года (Гинзбург 1). It seemed to me then that my suffering was beyond measure. But in a few months' time I was to realize that my spell on the conveyor belt had been child's play compared with what was meted out to others, from June 1937 on (1b).

И-19 • ВЫХОДИ́ТЬ/ВЫ́ЙТИ ИЗ ИГРЫ́ [VP; subj: human or collect; usu. this WO] to cease to participate in some matter, quit: X вышел из игры ≃ **X bowed ⟨dropped⟩ out (of the game); X was out of the game; X quit ⟨withdrew from⟩ the game; X called it quits.**

Эти принципы просты и доступны всем. Но предварительно их кто-то должен сформулировать профессионально строго. Это мог бы сделать Болтун. Но после той истории он, кажется, вышел из игры (Зиновьев 1). These principles are simple and accessible to all. But in preparation someone must formulate them in a rigorously professional manner. Chatterer could do it, but evidently he has dropped out after all this business (1a). ♦ «Если никогда нет ни одной минуты ни удовлетворения, ни радости, то что же тогда? И я хорошо вижу, что мне надо выйти из игры!» (Булгаков 5). "If there is never a single moment of satisfaction, of joy, then what's the good of it? I see very clearly that it's time for me to bow out of the game!" (5a). ♦ «Теперь скоро всё кончится — немцы пойдут на Лондон. Дело двух-трёх месяцев... Мы вышли из игры, и это наш плюс» (Эренбург 4). "It will soon be all over. The Germans will go for London. It's only a matter of two or three months. We're out of the game and that's to our advantage" (4a).

И-20 • ПО ИДЕ́Е [PrepP; Invar; sent adv] as conceived, according to the idea, plan underlying sth.: **in theory; in principle;** [in limited contexts] **the idea is (that...).**

КК и ММ — наши друзья. По идее они должны помогать мне всеми доступными средствами (Зиновьев 1). "K.K. and

M. M. are our friends. In theory they ought to go to any lengths to help me" (1a). ♦ Кто поверит, что один из ведущих советских теоретиков марксизма (а значит, по идее — невежда, начётчик, мракобес, бездарь) может размышлять подобным образом (Зиновьев 2). Who would ever have believed that one of our leading Soviet Marxist theorists (which is to say in principle a boor, a dogmatist, an obscurantist and an oaf) could think in this way! (2a). ♦ По идее подземное движение устроено так, что машины набирают всё большую скорость и выносятся на горбы магистралей, держа стрелки уже на второй половине спидометров (Аксёнов 7). The idea was to enable the underground traffic to pick up enough speed so that by the time a car reached the entrance ramp of its choice, its needle had moved over to the second half of the speedometer (7a).

И-21 • **ИДЕ́Я ФИКС** [NP; fixed WO] a persistent thought, idea: **fixed idea; idée fixe; obsession.**

И-22 • **ИДИ́ ТЫ!** *highly coll* [Interj; Invar; fixed WO] used to express amazement bordering on incredulity, delight etc: **no kidding ⟨fooling⟩!; you don't say!; is that so?**

[Мерещун:] Так вот, если вы хотите производительность труда — я вам человека нашёл... Ради производительности труда родного отца на лесоповал пошлёт. [Овчухов:] Иди ты! Такого мне и надо! (Солженицын 8). [M.:] Listen, if you want to increase productivity, I've found just the man....He'd send his own father out into the forest if it would help his production figures. [O.:] Is that so? He sounds ideal (8a).

И-23 • **ИДИ́ (ТЫ) ⟨ИДИ́ТЕ (ВЫ)⟩ (КУДА́) ПОДА́ЛЬШЕ! (А НЕ) ПОШЁЛ БЫ ТЫ ⟨он и т. п.⟩ (КУДА́) ПОДА́ЛЬШЕ!** *all substand, rude* [sent; fixed WO] used to express the speaker's intense annoyance with s.o., his desire to be rid of s.o. etc: **to hell with you ⟨him etc⟩!; (why don't you ⟨doesn't he etc⟩) get lost ⟨beat it, drop dead, go to hell, take a running jump, take a flying leap, go jump in the lake, go fly a kite⟩!**

Как видим, Толя вполне мог и не откликнуться на ужасное имя, снабжённое к тому же давно отправленной восвояси приставкой [«фон»], всё было по закону, он Боков Анатолий Аполлинариевич, идите вы все подальше! (Аксёнов 6). As we can see, Tolya had every right not to respond to that awful name with its telltale "von," which, in any case, had long since been sent back to the place it came from; his legal name was Anatoly Apollinarievich Bokov, and to hell with the whole bunch of you! (6a). ♦ Комиссар поморщился и сказал: «Знаешь что, Чита? Иди-ка ты подальше со своим раскаянием. Я вашего брата тридцать пять лет ловлю, я на одну пластинку крутят, когда ко мне приводят» (Семёнов 1). The Commissioner frowned and said: "Do you know something, Cheetah? Go and take a running jump with your repentance. I've been catching your sort for thirty-five years now and they all sing the same tune when they're brought to me (1a).

И-24 • **АРКА́ДСКАЯ ИДИ́ЛЛИЯ** *lit, occas. iron* [NP; sing only; fixed WO] a serene life, a quiet peaceful existence: **Arcadian existence ⟨life, idyll⟩.**

< From *Arcadia*, the name of a region of ancient Greece known for the pastoral contentment of its people.

И-25 • **ИДТИ́/ПОЙТИ́ ⟨ИГРА́ТЬ/СЫГРА́ТЬ⟩ ВА-БА́НК** [VP; subj: human; more often pfv; fixed WO] to act desperately, putting everything at risk (usu. striving to achieve sth. significant): X пошёл ва-банк ≃ **X put everything on the line; X (went ahead and) risked everything ⟨all⟩; X went for broke; X shot the works; [in limited contexts] X went for the jackpot; X risked everything ⟨it all⟩ on one throw (of the dice).**

Королёва предупредили, что прежний темп работы после выписки из больницы равносилен для него смертному при-

говору... Но длительный отдых в то время означал для Королёва нечто вполне определённое: провал попытки обогнать американцев с выводом человека на орбиту... Королёв пошёл ва-банк... До того он состязался со временем и с косной технологией; теперь вступил в поединок с самой смертью (Владимиров 1). Korolyov was warned that for him to continue to work after his release from hospital at the same pace as before would be equivalent to a death sentence....But to take a long convalescence at that time would have meant only one thing for Korolyov: the failure of the attempt to overtake the Americans in the race to put a man into orbit....Korolyov decided to go ahead and risk everything....Previously he had been competing with time and with inadequate technology; now he entered into a duel with death itself (1a). ♦ [author's usage] Прохор приглядывался, выжидал, думал. Встретился с Сударем. Убил с ним Копытова, завладел оружием. Проверил Сударя на мелочах. А завтра решил сыграть ва-банк (Семёнов 1). Prokhor examined his surroundings, bided his time and thought. Then he met Squire. Together they murdered Kopytov and gained possession of his revolver. He tested Squire in various minor enterprises. And now tomorrow he had resolved to go for the jackpot (1a).

И-26 • **ИДТИ́/ПОЙТИ́ ВПРОК** *кому* [VP; subj: usu. abstr] to be beneficial to s.o., improve s.o.'s well-being, health etc: X пойдёт Y-у впрок ≃ **X will do Y good; Y will profit by ⟨from⟩ X; X will have a beneficial effect on Y.**

Не знаю... Леонид Владимирович, пошёл бы ему этот разговор впрок, если бы не твои пайковые обеды в актёрской столовой в саду «Эрмитаж» в голодном сорок втором году, которые ты по-братски делил с ним пополам... (Максимов 2). I doubt, Leonid Vladimirovich, whether this conversation with you would have done him any good, had it not been for the meals, obtained on your special ration card at the actors' canteen in the Hermitage Gardens during that hungry year of 1942, which you shared equally with him like a brother (2a). ♦ «Я вижу, друзья, — сказал Джамхух, — наше путешествие идёт вам впрок» (Искандер 5). "Friends, I can see you're profiting by our journey," Jamkhoukh said (5a). ♦ Небритый спешил и жадничал, когда ел арбузы... Только всё ему не шло впрок, был он худой, изнурённый, и с утра никогда не понять: не то недоспал, не то переспал, но арбузы любил (Ерофеев 2). The unshaven one was always in a greedy hurry when he ate watermelons....But all this eating seemed to have no effect on him. He was skinny and emaciated, and in the morning it was hard to tell whether he hadn't gotten enough sleep or had overslept. But he did love watermelons (2a).

И-27 • **ИДТИ́/ПОЙТИ́ ВРАЗРЕ́З** *с чем* [VP; subj: abstr] to contradict sth., disagree with sth. completely: X идёт вразрез с Y-ом ≃ **X goes against Y; X runs counter to Y; X is in direct contradiction to Y; X is out of tune with Y; X flies in the face of Y.**

Было бы тягостным недоразумением и шло бы вразрез с прямыми намерениями автора, если бы полемика с прошлым о прошлом, проходящая через эту книгу, была истолкована как желание оживить литературное движение, скончавшееся ровным счётом восемнадцать лет назад (Лившиц 1). It would be an onerous misunderstanding and would go against the author's immediate intentions, if the polemics with the past about the past which run through this book, were to be interpreted as a wish to resurrect a literary movement which died exactly eighteen years ago (1a). ♦ О.М[андельштам] всегда знал, что его понятия идут вразрез с временем... но после «Четвёртой прозы» это его уже не страшило (Мандельштам 1). M[andelstam] always knew that his ideas were out of tune with the times...but after writing the "Fourth Prose" he was no longer worried about it (1a).

И-28 • **ИДТИ́/ПОЙТИ́ НАВСТРЕ́ЧУ** *кому-чему* [VP; subj: human or collect; usu. this WO; when indir obj: human or collect, the person's or group's needs, requests, desires etc are implied] to satisfy s.o.'s needs, requests, desires, make concessions in order to reach an agreement etc: X пошёл навстречу Y-у ⟨нуждам, просьбам и т. п. Y-а⟩ ≃ **X accommodated ⟨obliged⟩ person Y; X catered to person Y's needs; X fulfilled ⟨complied with⟩ person Y's request(s);** [with the emphasis on making concessions] **X met person Y halfway.**

…[Никандров] заявил, что никто и никогда не узнает конца этой истории, если библиотека сию же минуту не пойдёт ему навстречу (Залыгин 1). …[Nikandrov] declared that nobody would ever hear the rest of the story if the library didn't *this minute* meet him halfway (1a).

И-29 • ИДТИ́ ⟨ПЕРЕ́ТЬ *substand*⟩ **НАПРОЛО́М** [VP; subj: human; often infin with надо, нужно, должен, решил etc] to act decisively, overcoming any obstacles, sometimes by cruel, harsh means (in order to achieve one's goal): X шёл напролом ≃ **X forged ⟨barged, barreled⟩ ahead; X pressed on regardless; X (forged ahead and) let nothing ⟨no obstacles⟩ stop him; X let nothing stand ⟨get⟩ in his way;** [in limited contexts] **X stopped at nothing.**

Может, я правда чего-то не понял, может, у Иванько какие-то особые обстоятельства, а я пру напролом, ослеплённый жаждой расширения площади? (Войнович 3). Maybe I really didn't understand something, maybe there were some special circumstances in Ivanko's case, and I was barging ahead, blinded by my craving for expanded living space (3a). ♦ Идиоты вообще очень опасны, и даже не потому, что они непременно злы... а потому, что они чужды всяким соображениям и всегда идут напролом... (Салтыков-Щедрин 1). Idiots in general are very dangerous people, not because they are necessarily evil...but because they are alien to any kind of reasoning and invariably press on regardless... (1b). ♦ «Если уже избрана цель, уж нужно идти напролом» (Гоголь 3). "Once the goal has been chosen, you must forge ahead, letting no obstacles stop you" (3b). "...If you've once decided to get something, then you must stop at nothing" (3a).

И-30 • ИДТИ́/ПОЙТИ́ НАСМА́РКУ *coll* [subj: abstr (usu. планы, усилия, работа, разговор etc)] to yield no positive result, end in nothing: X пошёл насмарку ≃ **X came to nothing ⟨naught⟩; X went ⟨was⟩ (all) for naught; X went down the drain ⟨the tube(s)⟩; X went by the board.**

…Как только он её [Зину] видел вновь, вся эта подсознательная работа по уничтожению её образа, которого он всё больше боялся, шла насмарку... (Набоков 1). …As soon as he saw her [Zina] again, all this subconscious work directed at the destruction of her image, whose power he feared more and more, went by the board... (1a).

И-31 • НЕ ИДТИ́ ДА́ЛЬШЕ *чего* [VP; subj: human or abstr] to stop at sth., some point: X не идёт дальше Y-а ≃ **X doesn't go any further than Y; Y is as far as X goes.**

Его понятие о «долге» не шло далее всеобщего равенства перед шпицрутеном... (Салтыков-Щедрин 1). His concept of "duty" went no further than universal equality before the rod... (1a).

И-32 • И И́ЖЕ С НИМ ⟨С НИ́МИ⟩ *lit, iron* [и + NP; these forms only; used after a personal noun, often a person's name; fixed WO] (in refer. to people who are close to the person named in terms of views, position etc) and those who are like him: **and others of that ilk ⟨sort⟩; and company;** *et al.*

Почему не сказал никто: «Докусов — и иже с ним — совершил преступления против человечества»? (Эткинд 1). Why did no one say: "Dokusov (and others of that ilk) committed a crime against humanity"? (1a). ♦ [Колосовитов:] Герцен Маркса и иже с ним знаете как называл? *Серная банда!* (Солженицын 9). [K.:] Do you know what he [Herzen] called Marx, *et al.*? *A sulphuric band!* (9a).

И-33 • ПРОПИСА́ТЬ И́ЖИЦУ *кому lit, occas. humor* [VP; subj: human] to scold, punish, deal with s.o. (sometimes with one's enemies) severely (often used as a threat): X пропишет Y-у ижицу ≃ **X will teach Y a (good) lesson; X will teach Y a lesson Y won't forget.**

И-34 • НЕ КРАСНА́ ИЗБА́ УГЛА́МИ, А КРАСНА́ ПИРОГА́МИ [saying] it is not outward appearance or splendor that makes a home nice, but hospitable hosts: ≃ **a hearty welcome is the best dish on the table.**

И-35 • ВО ИЗБЕЖА́НИЕ *чего* [PrepP; Invar; Prep; the resulting PrepP is adv] in order to keep sth. from happening: **(in order) to avoid ⟨prevent, avert⟩ sth.**

Полковник Емышев... украл двести казённых рублей, но, пойманный с поличным, вынужден был их вернуть и уйти с работы во избежание более серьёзных последствий (Войнович 3). …Colonel Emyshev stole two hundred rubles of state funds, but, caught red-handed, he was forced to return them and leave work in order to avoid more serious consequences (3a). ♦ «Значит, они его всё-таки схватили?» — «И увезли. Скажите спасибо, что вас не прихватили — во избежание утечки информации» (Стругацкие 1). "In other words, they got him anyway?" "And carried him away. You can say thank you that they didn't seize you as well to avoid leaving any witnesses" (1a). ♦ Подчеркнув абсурдность замечания вождя относительно цыплят, Тенгиз, как бы во избежание кривотолков, дал знать слушателям, что реплика эта представляла из себя только шутку... (Искандер 3). By stressing the absurdity of the Leader's remark about the chickens, Tengiz, as if to prevent false rumors, gave his listeners to understand that this retort was merely a joke... (3a).

И-36 • ИЗБИЕ́НИЕ МЛАДЕ́НЦЕВ *lit, humor or iron* [NP; sing only; fixed WO] excessively strict measures, severe demands directed toward the young and inexperienced, severe criticism of their work: **slaughter ⟨massacre⟩ of the innocents.**

< From the Biblical account of King Herod's massacre of the infants in Bethlehem (Matt. 2:16).

И-37 • ИЗБУ́ШКА НА КУ́РЬИХ НО́ЖКАХ [NP; usu. sing] **1.** *folk* the hut perched on chicken legs belonging to Baba Yaga, a witch in Russian folk tales: **a hut on chicken legs; Baba Yaga's hut.**

2. *coll* a small rickety house: **a hut on wobbly stilts; a ramshackle old cottage.**

«А пока что мне вполне достаточно одного острова из группы Курильских островов, вас, милые жители этого острова, избушки на курьих ножках да милой жены!» (Залыгин 1). "But for the moment I'm perfectly content with what I've got now: one island in the Kurile chain; you, my dear islanders; a hut on wobbly stilts, and a pretty wife" (1a).

И-38 • В ИЗБЫ́ТКЕ; С ИЗБЫ́ТКОМ [PrepP; Invar; quantit subj-compl with copula (subj/gen: any common noun) or adv] in excess: **quite ⟨more than⟩ enough; in abundance; (have ⟨there is⟩) a surplus (of).**

Поскольку здесь всего в избытке, то все потребности удовлетворяются, и... Вот в этом-то и состоит суть дела (Зиновьев 1). Since we have more than enough of everything, all needs are satisfed and...That is the essence of the matter (1a). ♦ …К сорока годам... решил он [Гладышев]... жениться, хотя это оказалось делом нелёгким, при всём том, что невест в деревне было в избытке (Войнович 2). …As his forties drew near, Gladishev decided to marry....However, this turned out to be no simple matter in spite of there being a surplus of marriageable girls in the village (2a).

И-39 • КАК ИЗВЕ́СТНО [Invar; sent adv (parenth); fixed WO] as is clear to all: **as everyone knows; as we (all) know.**

«По ленинским местам» фильм должен был называться или как-то в этом духе, я, признаться, точно не помню. А места эти, ленинские, они, как известно, в большинстве своём за рубежами нашей отчизны находятся. Потому что товарищ Ленин в своё время был тоже как бы невозвращенец (Войнович 1). I don't remember exactly what it [the film] was to be called—"In the Footsteps of Lenin"—something like that. As we know, the greater part of those footsteps occurred outside the borders of our country. Because Comrade Lenin at one time had been something of a defector himself (1a).

И-40 • СТА́ВИТЬ/ПОСТА́ВИТЬ В ИЗВЕ́СТНОСТЬ

кого (о чём) offic [VP; subj: human] to inform s.o. (of sth.): X поставил в известность Y-a о Z-e ≃ **X made Y aware of Z; X notified ⟨apprised⟩ Y of Z; X made Z known to Y; X brought (it) to Y's attention (that…); X acquainted Y with Z.**

«Я вас спрашиваю, вопрос улучшения ваших жилищных условий рассматривался уже на общем собрании?» — «Да», — выдавливает из себя Сергей Сергеевич. «Почему же вы не поставили меня об этом в известность?» (Войнович 3). "I'm asking you if the question of improvement of your housing conditions had already been considered at a general assembly?" "Yes," Sergei Sergeevich forces out. "Why didn't you make me aware of this?" (3a). ♦ Тут номенклатурная логика: подчинённому (мне) не надо знать всего, что знает начальник (он [Твардовский]). И подчинённый (я) не мог же написать такого, о чём не поставлен в известность начальник (он) (Солженицын 2). That is the logic of the officeholding hierarchy: a subordinate (I) must not know all his superior (Tvardovsky) knows. And the subordinate (I) could not have written anything of which his superior (Tvardovsky) had not been notified (2a). ♦ «…О плане этом вы будете в своё время поставлены мною в известность…» (Салтыков-Щедрин 2). "I shall acquaint you with the plan in good time…" (2a).

И-41 • ИЗВИНИ́ ПОДВИ́НЬСЯ ⟨ИЗВИНИ́ТЕ ПО-ДВИ́НЬТЕСЬ⟩

substand [VP; imper only] used to express one's categorical refusal to do sth., tolerate sth., allow s.o. to do sth. etc, or to express one's strong conviction that another is mistaken: **you've ⟨he's etc⟩ got to be kidding; no way!; nothing doing!; thanks but no thanks; forget it!;** [when one leaves a person or situation one can no longer tolerate] **(it's) pardon me and that's that.**

«И вопрос, Нюрка, в настоящий период стоит либо так, либо эдак, либо я, либо кабан, даю тебе на размышление пять с лишним минут, а затем собираю свои манатки и извини подвинься» (Войнович 2). "And so the question right now is—one or the other, me or the hog. I'll give you five minutes to think it over, a little more than five. Then I'll get my stuff and it's pardon me and that's that" (2a).

И-42 • НЕТ, УЖ ⟨Э́ТО⟩ ИЗВИНИ́(ТЕ); НЕТ, ИЗВИ-НИ́(ТЕ)

coll [Interj; these forms only] used to express a protest, one's disagreement with sth.: **well, excuse me!; sorry, no way!; I beg your pardon!; no, that's asking too much!**

Я многое ему прощал: и обиды, и невнимание, и невыплаченные долги, но простить предательство — нет, уж это извините! I forgave him a lot: his insults, his lack of consideration, and his unpaid debts; but forgive betrayal? No, that's asking too much!

И-43 • КАК ИЗВО́ЗЧИК ругаться, браниться и т. п.

highly coll [как + NP; nom only; adv] (to swear) fiercely: **(swear) like a trooper ⟨a truckdriver⟩.**

И-44 • ЧЕГО́ ИЗВО́ЛИТЕ

[Invar; fixed WO] **1.** *obs* [indep. sent] (used as a deferential question) what would you like me to do for you?: **in what way may I serve you?; what would you like?; what can ⟨might⟩ I do for you?;** [in limited contexts] **yes, sir ⟨ma'am⟩?**

«Захар!» — сказал он. «Чего изволите?» — вяло отозвался Захар (Гончаров 1). "Zakhar!" he said. "Yes, sir?" Zakhar responded listlessly (1a).

2. *derog* [usu. nonagreeing postmodif] used to characterize the behavior of a person who, lacking in convictions, principles etc, behaves obsequiously, is prepared to do or say whatever is most personally advantageous under the given circumstances: **(have ⟨take⟩) an at-your-service (attitude etc); a whatever-you-say-sir (attitude ⟨role etc⟩);** [in limited contexts] **(be) a yes-man ⟨-woman⟩.**

Поглядев на удостоверение с печатью Большого дома, Прокофьев стал в позицию «чего изволите?» и уступил — без попыток сопротивления (Эткинд 1). Having seen this document with the stamp of the Big House, Prokofiev took up an "at your service" attitude and gave in without the slightest resistance (1a).

И-45 • ИЗВО́ЛИШЬ ⟨-те⟩ ВИ́ДЕТЬ

obs [sent adv; these forms only; fixed WO] used to introduce an explanation or to attract the interlocutor's attention to the statement to which it belongs: **you see.**

«Вот (он набил трубку, затянулся и начал рассказывать), — вот, изволите видеть, я тогда стоял в крепости за Тереком с ротой — этому скоро пять лет» (Лермонтов 1). "Well," he filled and lit his pipe, took a long draw on it, and began the story, "you see, I was stationed at the time at a fort beyond the Terek with a company—that was nearly five years back" (1b).

И-46 • ИЗВО́ЛЬТЕ РА́ДОВАТЬСЯ

iron [Invar; usu. sent adv (parenth); fixed WO] used to express one's disappointment at, dissatisfaction with etc sth. unpleasant (usu. sth. that is the opposite of what was expected, hoped for etc): **wouldn't you know it!**

Представь себе: у меня уже чемодан был упакован, и вдруг за два часа до поезда звонит начальник, изволите радоваться, сообщает, что поездка в Париж отменяется. Picture it: my suitcase is all packed, and suddenly, two hours before the train is to leave, the boss calls and, wouldn't you know it, tells me my trip to Paris is off.

И-47 • ПРИ ПОСЛЕ́ДНЕМ ИЗДЫХА́НИИ

obs when used of a person [PrepP; Invar; subj-compl with быть∅ (subj: human or animal); fixed WO] one is close to the moment of his death: X был при последнем издыхании ≃ **person X was at his last gasp; person X was breathing his last; person X was on the verge of death; animal X was about to die.**

«Удивительно, как он [Мармеладов] ещё очнулся, — шепнул потихоньку доктор Раскольникову… — Сейчас умрёт». — «Неужели никакой надежды?» — «Ни малейшей! При последнем издыхании…» (Достоевский 3). "It's amazing that he [Marmeladov] even recovered consciousness," the doctor whispered softly to Raskolnikov.…"He'll die very soon." "Is there no hope at all?" "Not the slightest! He's at his last gasp…" (3a). ♦ Два казака, встретившие меня и следившие за убийцей, подоспели, подняли раненого, но он был уже при последнем издыхании… (Лермонтов 1). The two Cossacks who had met me and who were on the lookout for the murderer, came along; they picked up the wounded officer, but he was already breathing his last… (1a).

И-48 • ИЗЖИВА́ТЬ/ИЗЖИ́ТЬ СЕБЯ́

[VP; subj: usu. abstr] (of an idea, tradition, approach etc) to become antiquated, no longer be useful, accepted, utilized etc: X изжил себя ≃ **X became outdated ⟨outmoded, obsolete, passé, a thing of the past⟩; X lost its usefulness.**

Вы должны разработать новую, современную методику, а не цепляться за старые, давно изжившие себя методы. You need to develop new, modern methods and not stick to old ones that are long outmoded.

И-49 • С ИЗЛИ́ШКОМ окупить *что*, окупиться, компенси́ровать *кому что* и т. п. [PrepP; Invar; adv] (to cover the cost of sth., pay for itself, compensate s.o. for sth. etc) to an even greater extent than (expected, necessary etc): **more than (adequately); (all…) and then some; (all…) and more.**

В кооперативе дела идут очень хорошо: все наши старания, время и деньги уже окупились с излишком. Things at the co-op are going really well: we've already been more than compensated for all the time, effort, and money we invested in it.

И-50 • ИЗМЕНЯ́ТЬ/ИЗМЕНИ́ТЬ (САМОМУ́) СЕБЕ́ [VP; subj: human; usu. this WO] to act against one's nature, habits, or beliefs: X изменил (самому) себе ≃ **X was untrue ⟨false⟩ to himself; X went against his convictions ⟨principles⟩.**

Для русских историков… Наполеон есть предмет восхищения и восторга…. Кутузов же, тот человек, который от начала и до конца своей деятельности в 1812 году… ни разу ни одним действием, ни словом не изменяя себе, являет необычайный в истории пример самоотвержения и сознания в настоящем будущего значения события, – Кутузов представляется им чем-то неопределённым и жалким… (Толстой 7). For Russian historians…Napoleon is the object of adulation and enthusiasm….But Kutuzov, the man who from the beginning to the end of his activity in 1812…was never once by word or deed false to himself, who presents an example rare in history of self-sacrifice and of present insight into the future significance of events – Kutuzov seems to them something indeterminate and pitiful… (7a).

И-51 • БРАТЬ/ВЗЯТЬ ИЗМО́РОМ ⟨НА ИЗМО́Р⟩ [VP]
1. ~ *кого-что* [subj: human or collect] to seize, gain possession of (a fortress etc) by surrounding it and waiting for its inhabitants to exhaust their resources: Х-ы взяли Y-ов измором ≃ **Xs starved Ys into surrender ⟨submission⟩; Xs starved Ys out.**

Взять крепость штурмом они не смогли и решили взять её измором. They couldn't take the fortress by storm, so they decided to starve the inhabitants out.

2. ~ *кого* [subj: human] to (try to) force s.o. to do sth. against his will by besieging him with persistent and irksome requests, actions etc: Х берёт Y-а на измор ≃ **X is wearing ⟨trying to wear⟩ Y down ⟨out⟩; X is nagging ⟨hounding⟩ Y (into doing sth.); X is wearing ⟨trying to wear⟩ down Y's resistance.**

И-52 • НА ИЗНО́С работать *coll* [PrepP; Invar; adv] (to work) to the point of complete exhaustion, giving o.s. fully to the task at hand: **(work o.s.) to death ⟨to a frazzle⟩; (work) at full stretch.**

…Королёв, сам работавший «на полный износ» и рисковавший жизнью, считал риск возможным и необходимым в космонавтике – особенно в той авантюрной космонавтике, в которую был теперь вовлечён силою событий (Владимиров 1). …Korolyov, who had himself been working at full stretch and risking his own life, recognised the possibility and even the inevitability of risk in space flight, especially in the more adventurous form of space flight into which he had been drawn by force of circumstances (1a).

И-53 • ИЗНО́СУ ⟨ИЗНО́СА, СНО́СУ, СНО́СА⟩ НЕТ [VP; impers] **1.** ~ *чему*. Also: **ИЗНО́СУ ⟨СНО́СУ⟩ НЕ ЗНАТЬ** [VP; subj: a noun denoting clothes, footwear etc] sth. is very durable: X-у износу нет ≃ **X doesn't ⟨won't, will never⟩ wear out; X never wears out; X will stand any amount of hard wear; X will last (forever ⟨indefinitely⟩).**

«Между прочим, хороший материал, говорят… Ему сносу нет…» (Искандер 5). "By the way, they say it's good material. Doesn't wear out" (5a). ♦ …Носки и рукавицы в палец толщиной вязала мать, и не было тем носкам и рукавицам износу (Распутин 4). …His mother had made mittens and socks a finger thick and those socks and mittens never wore out (4a).

2. ~ *кому rare* s.o. is in good shape, despite being old or middle-aged: X-у сносу нет ≃ **X is ⟨looks⟩ none the worse for wear; X wears ⟨has aged⟩ well; the years haven't changed ⟨aged, told on⟩ X a bit.**

[Лебедев:] А тебе, старая скворешня, и сносу нет. Лет тридцать я тебя старухой знаю… (Чехов 4). [L.:] You look none the worse for wear, you old windbag. I remember you as an old woman thirty years ago (4b). [L.:] You know, old magpie, you wear well. You've been an old woman ever since I've known you – for the last thirty years (4a).

И-54 • МЕТА́ТЬ ИКРУ́ *substand, rude* [VP; subj: human] to make a loud and unpleasant fuss (usu. over sth. trivial), express one's anger in an outward, sometimes offensive, manner: X мечет икру ≃ **X is kicking up a fuss; X is raising ⟨making⟩ a stink.**

И-55 • ЧТО ИМЕ́ЕМ, НЕ ХРАНИ́М, ПОТЕРЯ́ВШИ, ПЛА́ЧЕМ [saying] we begin to value things only after we lose them: ≃ **we only know the worth of water when the well is dry; you never miss the water till the well runs dry; you don't know what you've got ⟨you have⟩ till you lose it.**

И-56 • С И́МЕНЕМ [PrepP; nonagreeing postmodif] (of a person) famous: **a [NP] with a name; a (big-)name [NP]; well-known;** ‖ с мировым именем ≃ **a [NP] with a world reputation; world-renowned.**

Удивительное какое-то стало замечаться в обществе пренебрежение к художнику с именем (Аксёнов 12). He had begun noticing society's astonishing disdain for any artist with a name (12a). ♦ …В большом, хорошо знакомом русским берлинцам зале… состоялся открытый литературный вечер… Сперва читал писатель с именем, в своё время печатавшийся во всех русских журналах… (Набоков 1). …In a large hall which was well known to Berlin Russians…an open literary evening was held….First to read was a name writer who in his time had appeared in all the Russian reviews… (1a). ♦ «…Баранова никто не знает, – он подумал и улыбнулся самодовольно, – а я писатель с мировым именем» (Войнович 6). "…Kostya [Baranov] is unknown," he added with a smug grin, "and I'm a writer with a world reputation!" (6a).

И-57 • ОТ И́МЕНИ *кого* ⟨**ОТ** *чьего* **И́МЕНИ**⟩; **ОТ ЛИЦА́** *кого-чего all lit* [PrepP; these forms only; the resulting PrepP is adv; от лица is usu. used with a pl or collect noun] expressing the opinion of s.o., on s.o.'s instructions, referring to s.o.: **on ⟨in⟩ behalf of; in s.o.'s name; in the name of; (speaking ⟨as spokesman etc⟩) for; [in limited contexts] from.**

«Мы вас все здесь, если только осмелюсь выразиться от лица всех, все мы готовы признать вас за благородного в основе своей молодого человека, но увы! увлечённого некоторыми страстями в степени несколько излишней…» (Достоевский 1). "All of us here, if I may be so bold as to express myself on behalf of all, all of us are prepared to recognize you as a young man who is noble in principle, though one, alas, carried away by certain passions to a somewhat inordinate degree…" (1a). ♦ Приказав от имени главнокомандующего исполнить упущенное, князь Андрей поскакал назад (Толстой 4). Having given orders in the commander-in-chief's name to rectify this omission, Prince Andrew galloped back (4b). ♦ [Тесть:] У всех налито?.. Ну хорошо. Так что разрешите от лица стола… поднять этот тост… (Рощин 2). [Father-in-law:] Does everybody have a glass?…All right. So then allow me, speaking for the table…to raise this toast… (2a). ♦ «Пошли им от нашего имени бутылку вина и плиточку шоколада для женщины», – сказал Валико… (Искандер 6). "Bring them a bottle of wine from us, and a bar of chocolate for the lady," ordered Valiko (6a). ♦ Через час урядник принёс мне пропуск, подписанный каракульками Пугачёва, и позвал меня к нему от его имени (Пушкин 2). [context transl] An hour later, the sergeant brought me my safe-conduct, signed with Pugachev's scrawl, and told me that Pugachev wished to see me (2b).

И-58 • СИДЕ́ТЬ КАК ИМЕНИ́ННИК ⟨ИМЕНИ́ННИ-ЦА⟩ *coll* [VP; subj: human] to do nothing, sit idly while others work: X сидит как именинник ≃ **X is sitting around like royalty.**

И-59 • СМОТРЕ́ТЬ ИМЕНИ́ННИКОМ ⟨ИМЕНИ́Н-НИЦЕЙ⟩ *obsoles, coll, humor* [VP; subj: human] to look very happy, content: X смотрит именинником ≃ **X is ⟨looks⟩ happy as a lark; X is walking ⟨floating⟩ on air; X looks radiant ⟨all aglow⟩.**

И-60 • ЧЕ́РСТВЫЕ ИМЕНИ́НЫ *coll* [NP; fixed WO] the day following the celebration of a person's name day, when people may come over to offer belated congratulations, eat food left over from the party etc: **the day after s.o.'s name day;** ‖ приходить на чёрствые именины ≃ **come ⟨go⟩ over s.o.'s place for leftover birthday cake; come over** etc **to wish s.o. a belated happy name day.**

< The idiom refers to the fact that on the day after a party the cakes are already stale («чёрствые»).

И-61 • НИЧЕГО́ НЕ ИМЕ́ТЬ ПРО́ТИВ *кого-чего* [VP; subj: human] not to harbor any bad feelings toward s.o. or have any objections to sth.: X ничего не имеет против Y-а ≃ **X doesn't have anything ⟨X has nothing⟩ against Y.**

Безумный и нераскаянный Жан-Батист ответил, что он охотно отказывается от звания [королевского камердинера] и ничего не будет иметь против того, чтобы отец передал звание тому из сыновей, которому он пожелает (Булгаков 5). The mad and unrepentant Jean-Baptiste replied that he would willingly give up the title [of Royal Valet] and had nothing against its being turned over to any of the sons his father chose (5a).

И-62 • ВО И́МЯ *кого-чего rather elev* [PrepP; Invar; Prep] for s.o. or sth., in honor of s.o. or sth.: **in the name of; in s.o.'s ⟨sth.'s⟩ name; for the sake of.**

Все самые гнусные преступления в истории совершались во имя добра (Зиновьев 1). "The vilest crimes of history have been committed in the name of good" (1a). ♦ Русская проза, какие преступления совершаются во имя твоё! (Набоков 1). Russian prose, what crimes are committed in thy name! (1a). ♦ Если совершить величайшее безрассудство во имя любви можно в молодые годы, то понять его и, быть может, пожалеть, что в твоей жизни такого не было, можно лишь в зрелые (Рыбаков 1). If you have to be young to commit an act of extreme folly for the sake of love, then perhaps you have to be getting on in years to be able to understand such an act, and maybe to regret that nothing like it had happened in your own life (1a).

И-63 • И́МЯ (ЖЕ) ИМ ЛЕГИО́Н *lit* [sent; these forms only; fixed WO] there are very many of them: **they are ⟨their name is⟩ legion.**

Нет, нет, отшвыривание, низвержение этих стариков, а имя им легион, было бы трагической ошибкой для государства... (Аксёнов 7). No, getting rid of these old fogies, eliminating them—and they are legion—would be a tragic mistake for the state... (7a).

< From the Bible (Luke 8:30, Mark 5:9).

И-64 • НА И́МЯ *кого* ⟨**НА чьё И́МЯ**⟩ [PrepP; these forms only; the resulting PrepP is adv or postmodif] **1.** писать, посылать *что, письмо* и т. п. ~ for the person whose name is written on (some letter, package etc): **addressed to; (address ⟨write, send⟩ sth.) to.**

Сказать ли всю истину: по секрету, он даже заготовил на имя известного нашего географа, К.И. Арсеньева, довольно странную резолюцию... (Салтыков-Щедрин 1). If the whole

truth be told, he even prepared in secret a rather strange resolution addressed to our well-known geographer, K.I. Arseniev (1a). ♦ Теперь я писала заявление, считая, что появились шансы на благоприятный ответ. Я писала на имя Ворошилова (Гинзбург 2). I was now writing a petition in the belief that there was a chance of getting a favorable answer to it. I addressed it to Voroshilov... (2a).

2. записать, купить *что* и т. п. ~ (while executing a transaction, closing a deal etc, to use) s.o.'s or one's own name for the legal record: **in ⟨under⟩ s.o.'s name; in the name of;** ‖ на своё имя ≃ **in ⟨under⟩ one's own name.**

Изощрённость этого сионистского издевательства Давида Аракишвили состояла в том, что, оставляя дом на имя несуществующего племянника, он в то же время всех своих существующих племянников забрал с собой (Искандер 3). One refinement of this Zionist mockery of David Arakishvili's was that while he left his house in the name of a nonexistent nephew, he took all his existent nephews with him (3a). ♦ ...На всякий случай, если немцев не дождёмся, надо готовить путь и через Англию. Пусть, например, Карпинский готовит: берёт проездные бумаги на своё имя, а фотографию приложим мою (Солженицын 5). ...Just in case the Germans are too slow, we must also make preparations to travel through England. Tell Karpinsky, for instance, to get a transit visa in his own name, and we can put my photograph on it (5a).

И-65 • СДЕ́ЛАТЬ ⟨СОСТА́ВИТЬ *obs*⟩ **СЕБЕ́ И́МЯ** *(в чём) lit* [VP; subj: human; fixed WO] to achieve recognition, distinguish o.s. (in some field): X сделал себе имя ≃ **X made a name for himself; X earned ⟨built up⟩ a reputation for himself; X won his spurs.**

Этим исследованием она сделала себе имя в науке. Thanks to that research, she made a name for herself in science.

И-66 • НЕ ИНА́ЧЕ (КАК) [restr Particle; these forms only; var. without как is often parenth; var. with как always precedes the word, phrase, or clause to which it refers; fixed WO] used to express the speaker's belief that his (or, occas., another's) supposition is correct, even though he does not know it for a fact: **must [+ infin]; I am ⟨he is etc⟩ sure ⟨certain⟩; without a doubt; no doubt; (that's) for sure ⟨for certain⟩; (there's) no doubt about it ⟨that⟩;** [in limited contexts] **I bet.**

Илья вошёл в избу запыхавшись — не иначе как бежал... (Абрамов 1). Ilya came into the house out of breath—he must have run (1b). ♦ [Булычов:] Пропьют государство. [Башкин:] Не иначе (Горький 2). [B.:] They'll sell the state for a drink. [B.:] For certain (2b).

И-67 • ИНВАЛИ́Д ПЯ́ТОЙ ГРУ́ППЫ ⟨ПЯ́ТОГО ПУ́НКТА⟩ *euph, coll* [NP; fixed WO] a Jew (used predominantly by Jews themselves to imply some form of discrimination against them): **victim of Point Five.**

«Евреев бьют»... «Инвалиды пятого пункта», острили порой студенты отделения русской литературы. Не зло острили, даже сочувственно (Свирский 1). "They're beating the Jews."..."Victims of Point Five." The students of the Russian literature department sometimes wisecracked. They weren't malicious jokes—more often sympathetic (1a).

< Refers to the fifth line in Soviet internal passports, which designates nationality, and (in the first variant) to disability categories, of which there are, in fact, only three.

И-68 • ИЗ СПОРТИ́ВНОГО ИНТЕРЕ́СА *coll, occas. humor* [PrepP; Invar; adv; fixed WO] (to do sth.) out of a desire to test one's abilities and/or for the enjoyment of the process itself, not striving to reap material advantage, career advancement etc: **for the sport of it; for (the) love of the game; for the fun of it; for kicks; for the challenge.**

И-69 • **В ИНТЕРЕ́САХ** *чего* [PrepP; Invar; Prep; the resulting PrepP is adv] in order to help, support sth.: **in the interests of; for the sake of.**

Вы можете на него [генерала Ильина] накричать, он не обидится (хотя в интересах дела может сделать вид, что обиделся)... (Войнович 3). You can scream at him [General Ilin] and he won't be offended (though in the interests of the case he may pretend he is offended)... (3a). ♦ [Таня:] ...Диплом ты выменял у моего отца на меня?.. Откуда я знаю, может, ты снова меня променяешь. В интересах дела (Вампилов 3). [T.:] ...You bartered me for the diploma with my father?...How do I know you won't barter me again. For the sake of your work (3b).

И-70 • **ПРИ ПИ́КОВОМ ИНТЕРЕ́СЕ** *остаться, оказаться* и т. п., *оставить кого coll* [PrepP; Invar; subj-compl with copula (subj: human) or obj-compl with оставить (obj: human); fixed WO] (to end up, leave s.o.) without sth. counted on or hoped for: **holding the bag; out in the cold; high and dry; (get ⟨end up with etc⟩) nothing for one's pains ⟨trouble⟩.**

Все его сотрудники получили прибавку к зарплате, а он опять остался при пиковом интересе. All of his coworkers got a raise, but he was left out in the cold again.

И-71 • **ИО́В МНОГОСТРАДА́ЛЬНЫЙ** [NP; sing only; fixed WO] a person suffering from continual misfortunes: **long-suffering Job.**

«Я, ты знаешь: одна нога в гробу, бездна забот, болезни, ну, Иов многострадальный» (Герцен 2). "I have one foot in the grave, as you know, and no end of worries and infirmities; I am a long-suffering Job, in fact" (2a).

< From the name of the upright man in the Bible who suffered many calamities (Book of Job).

И-72 • **ИРО́НИЯ СУДЬБЫ́** [NP; fixed WO]; often **ПО ИРО́НИИ СУДЬБЫ́** [PrepP; Invar; adv] a strange, absurd occurrence: **quirk ⟨twist⟩ of fate; irony of fate.**

По иронии судьбы или даже самого председателя профкома Платон Самсонович был отправлен в горный санаторий имени бывшего Козлотура (Искандер 6). Whether due to a quirk of fate or to some quirk of the committee chairman, Platon Samsonovich was sent off to a mountain health resort which until very recently had been named in honor of the goatibex (6a). ♦ По иронии судьбы он очутился в камере с белобородым дедушкой, известным работником охранки... (Мандельштам 2). By an irony of fate he had found himself sharing a cell with a white-bearded old man who had once been a well-known Okhrana official... (2a).

И-73 • **ИСКА́ТЕЛЬ ПРИКЛЮЧЕ́НИЙ** [NP; fixed WO] **1.** *obs* a person who travels in unexplored places: **adventure seeker; adventurer.**

2. *euph, disapprov.* Also: (of a woman) **ИСКА́ТЕЛЬ-НИЦА ПРИКЛЮЧЕ́НИЙ** a person who seeks social position, material gain etc by questionable or unscrupulous means: **adventurer ⟨adventuress⟩; schemer;** [in limited contexts] **fortune hunter;** [of a woman only] **gold digger.**

И-74 • **ЗА ИСКЛЮЧЕ́НИЕМ** *кого-чего* [PrepP; Invar; Prep] excepting, besides: **with the exception of; except (for); apart from; save.**

...Он помог сохранить имущество Коли Зархиди, которое, за исключением настенного зеркала, проломанного буфета и других мелочей, полностью перешло в руки советской власти (Искандер 3). ...He helped preserve Kolya Zarhidis' property, which, with the exception of the wall mirror, the broken sideboard, and other trifles, passed intact into the hands of the Soviet authorities (3a). ♦ «Было нас пять человек. Все — интеллигенты, за исключением меня...» (Терц 3). "There was five of us. All intellectuals except me..." (3a).

И-75 • **И́СКРА БО́ЖЬЯ** (*у кого, в ком*) *obs* [NP; sing only; fixed WO] **1.** (s.o. has) talent, prominent natural ability: **God-given talent; God-given gift.**

2. noble impulses, high aspirations: **high ideals; divine spark.**

[Андрей:] ...Жёны обманывают мужей, а мужья лгут, делают вид, что ничего не видят, ничего не слышат, и неотразимо пошлое влияние гнетёт детей, и искра божья гаснет в них, и они становятся такими же жалкими, похожими друг на друга мертвецами, как их отцы и матери... (Чехов 5). [A.:] ...The wives deceive their husbands, the husbands tell lies, pretend not to see anything, not to hear anything; and their profoundly vulgar influence has so crushing an effect on their children that the divine spark in them is extinguished and they become just as pitiable corpses, and as like to one another, as their fathers and mothers (5b).

И-76 • **ЗАРОНИ́ТЬ И́СКРУ ⟨СЕ́МЯ, ЗЕРНО́⟩** *чего (в кого, в чью душу) lit* [VP; subj: human or abstr; indir obj: usu. abstr; usu. this WO] to arouse a certain feeling (in s.o.), cause a certain reaction to sth.: X заронил искру надежды ⟨сомнения, подозрения, скептицизма и т. п.⟩ в Y-a ≃ X sparked ⟨awakened⟩ hope ⟨doubt, suspicion, skepticism etc⟩ in Y; X sparked ⟨awakened⟩ in Y a feeling of hope ⟨doubt, suspicion, skepticism etc⟩; thing X gave rise to Y's hopes ⟨doubts, suspicions, skepticism etc⟩.

Разговор этот заронил в него искру подозрения относительно истинных намерений директора. This conversation gave rise to his suspicions as to the director's true intentions.

И-77 • **И́СКРЫ ИЗ ГЛАЗ ПОСЫ́ПАЛИСЬ** *у кого coll* [VP_subj] s.o. experiences such sharp pain from a blow to the head or face that it seems to him that lights are flashing before his eyes: у X-a искры из глаз посыпались ≃ **X saw stars.**

[author's usage] «...Если он сейчас начнёт про дятла, который умрёт от сотрясения мозга, я так его трахну вот этой головешкой по голове, что он сам умрёт от сотрясения мозга! А перед смертью у него столько искр посыплется из глаз, что они затмят звёздное небо...» (Искандер 5). "If he starts in about the woodpecker who'll die of concussion, I'll conk him on the head with this brand so hard that he'll die of concussion himself! And before he dies he'll see so many stars...that they'll eclipse the starry sky" (5a).

И-78 • **ИСКУССТВОВЕ́Д В ШТА́ТСКОМ** *euph, coll* [NP; fixed WO] a KGB agent in plain clothes or an informer secretly collaborating with the KGB: **man on the agency payroll; plainclothes agent.**

И-79 • **ВНОВЬ ИСПЕЧЁННЫЙ** *coll, humor* [AdjP; modif; fixed WO] (s.o. who) has just received a certain position, title, degree etc: **brand-new; new; newly ⟨freshly⟩ minted; newly fledged.**

Разрешите представить вам нашего вновь испечённого инженера. Let me introduce to you our newly fledged engineer.

И-80 • **БРАТЬ/ВЗЯТЬ НА ИСПУ́Г** *кого highly coll* [VP; subj: human; often infin with пытаться, хотеть etc or neg imper] to intimidate s.o., thereby forcing him to act in a certain way: X взял Y-a на испуг ≃ **X used scare tactics (on Y); X scared Y into doing sth.; X gave Y a scare;** [in limited contexts] **X frightened ⟨scared⟩ Y off.**

«А я думаю, сперва язык твой обсудить надо! Понял? А то он у тебя разболтался — гаек не хватает». — «Давай, давай, Всё на испуг взять хочешь, товарищ Ганичев» (Абрамов 1). "First of all, I think we should discuss your tongue! Hear that? It's gotten so loose, it's obviously missing some screws." "All right! Scare tactics, eh, Comrade Ganichev?" (1a). ♦ «Видите ли, я ведь именно за эту квартиру дрался не только потому, что она мне очень нужна. Я ведь утверждал, что принципиально борюсь именно за неё. А теперь получится так, что Иванько меня на испуг не взял, так за деньги купил» (Войнович 3). "You see, I wasn't fighting for this apartment just because I needed it badly. I told everyone I was struggling for it on principle. And now people will think that Ivanko couldn't frighten me off, so he bought me for money" (3a).

И-81 • ОТДЕ́ЛЫВАТЬСЯ/ОТДЕ́ЛАТЬСЯ ЛЁГКИМ ИСПУ́ГОМ *coll* [VP; subj: human] to get out of a situation that might have had serious negative consequences for one without serious loss or injury: X отделался лёгким испугом ≃ **X got off lightly ⟨(pretty) easy⟩; X got off with only a scare.**

Рыбаков мог получить несколько лет тюрьмы за то, что избил подчинённого, но вступился его высокопоставленный тесть, и он отделался лёгким испугом: был временно понижен в должности. Rybakov could have gotten a few years in prison for beating up one of his subordinates, but his high-ranking father-in-law intervened and he got off easy, with a temporary demotion.

И-82 • А́ЗБУЧНАЯ И́СТИНА [NP; fixed WO except when used as VP_subj with быть_ø] a very simple statement or thought known to all: **elementary ⟨simple, basic⟩ truth; truism.**

И Крикун понял азбучные истины бытия. Если начальство думает, что делает тебе добро, оно в самом деле делает тебе добро (Зиновьев 1). And Bawler came to understand one of the elementary truths of existence. If the leadership thinks that they are doing you good, then they are indeed doing you good (1a). ♦ «Да кто его [Пушкина] понимал! кто его вообще понимал!.. Вяземский? Баратынский? Но они… не понимали его тоже. Вам ли мне пересказывать эти азбучные истины…» (Битов 2). "But who understood him [Pushkin]! Who ever understood him!... Vyazemsky? Baratynsky?...But they, too, didn't understand him. Do I have to repeat these truisms for you?" (2a). ♦ [Алекс:] *Зачем — наука?* [Филипп:] Ты просто разыгрываешь меня? В чём ты видишь тут вопрос? Азбучные истины! (Солженицын 11). [context transl] [A.:] *What* is science *for?* [Ph.:] You must be pulling my leg? Where is the problem? It's all so elementary! (11a).

И-83 • ПРОПИСНА́Я И́СТИНА [NP; fixed WO except when used as VP_subj with быть_ø] an overused, trite phrase, statement etc that is devoid of originality and known to all: **boring ⟨oft-repeated⟩ truism; (old) hackneyed truth; (well-worn) cliché; copybook maxim.**

[Бакченин:] Ты меня только прописями не долбай. Прописные истины — не для моего положения (Панова 1). [B.:] Don't you start lecturing me in clichés. Old hackneyed truths aren't for me in my position (1a). ♦ «Оступиться, Наталья Михайловна, легко — вылечить подвёрнутую ногу трудно. Истина, конечно, прописная, может быть, поэтому её часто забывают» (Чернёнок 2). "It's easy to trip and hard to mend a sprained limb, Natalya Mikhailovna. It's a cliché, of course; maybe that's why it's so often forgotten" (2a).

И-84 • ВОЙТИ́ В ИСТО́РИЮ *rather lit* [VP; subj: human or abstr; more often pfv] to become well-known, make an impact on history, be remembered into the future: X войдёт в историю ≃ **X will go down in history ⟨in the history books, in the record books⟩; X will earn a place in history; thing X ⟨person X's name⟩ will be added to the history books; X will make history.**

Так что отныне и на веки веков Сталин войдёт в историю как автор многих работ… (Зиновьев 2). So, now and for ever more Stalin goes down in history as the author of many books… (2a).

И-85 • ПОПАДА́ТЬ/ПОПА́СТЬ В ИСТО́РИЮ *coll;* **ВЛИПА́ТЬ/ВЛИ́ПНУТЬ В ИСТО́РИЮ** *highly coll* [VP; subj: human; more often pfv; usu. this WO] to become involved in an unpleasant incident or sth. blameworthy: X попал в историю ≃ **X got (himself) into a mess ⟨a fix⟩; X got involved in an unpleasant incident ⟨scene etc⟩; X got (himself) into an un-**

pleasant ⟨embarrassing etc⟩ situation; **X walked right into trouble.**

…Он [Чонкин] твёрдо решил, что теперь никогда в жизни не будет задавать никаких вопросов, а то ещё влипнешь в такую историю, что и не выпутаешься (Войнович 2). Chonkin firmly resolved that from there on in he would never ask another question, and that way keep himself from getting into a mess so bad there'd be no getting out (2a). ♦ На Иркутской пересылке я снова первым долгом влип в историю, хоть к этому и не стремился (Марченко 2). At the Irkutsk transit point I got involved first thing in another incident, although I was not looking for trouble (2a). ♦ [Гомыра:] По кустам он [Вася Букин] никогда не прятался, друзей в беде не бросал. Я это к тому говорю, что раз уж он попал в такую историю, то пусть он знает… *(Обращаясь к Букину.)* Короче, если что, то знай, Вася, у тебя есть друзья, которые не бросят тебя на произвол судьбы (Вампилов 3). [G.:] He's [Vasia Bukin has] never chickened out of anything, never left a friend in the lurch. I'm saying this so that, since he's got himself into a situation like this, he'll know… *(Turns to Bukin.)* In other words, if anything happens, Vasia, you know you've got friends who won't just leave you to your fate (3a).

И-86 • ВЕ́ЧНАЯ ⟨ОБЫ́ЧНАЯ⟩ ИСТО́РИЯ *coll* [NP; sing only; used as sent; fixed WO] (of actions, events etc, usu. disagreeable or annoying ones) this is what always happens, this is the same as always: **(it's) the same old story ⟨thing⟩ (all over again); (it's) the usual story; there ⟨here⟩ we go again.**

«Вечная история: власти узнают о событиях после всех» (Федин 1). "The same old story: the authorities are the last to learn of events" (1a).

И-87 • ИСТО́РИЯ С ГЕОГРА́ФИЕЙ *old-fash, coll, humor* [NP; sing only; usu. used in exclamations after вот так; fixed WO] an unexpected turn of affairs, a difficulty that is not easy to resolve: **that's ⟨this is⟩ a fine ⟨nice, pretty⟩ kettle of fish!**

«А где же ключ?» — «Ой, боюсь, что я забыла его дома». — «Вот так история с географией!» "Where's the key?" "Oops, I'm afraid I left it home." "This is a fine kettle of fish!"

И-88 • ИСТО́РИЯ УМА́ЛЧИВАЕТ *о ком-чём occas.* *humor or iron* [VP_subj; this form only; fixed WO] sth. remains unknown, unrevealed, is not spoken of, discussed etc: об X-е история умалчивает ≃ **history is silent about ⟨on⟩ X; history passes ⟨glosses⟩ over X in silence;** [humor or iron only] **X is a deep dark secret.**

На какой-то олимпиаде в прошлые годы — какой точно и в какие годы, история умалчивает — Хэлоуэй завоевал то ли золотую, то ли серебряную, то ли бронзовую медаль по метанию диска… (Аксёнов 7). At one or another of the Olympics — history glosses over the date in silence — Halloway won either a gold or a silver or a bronze medal for the discus throw… (7a).

И-89 • СОВСЕ́М ДРУГА́Я ИСТО́РИЯ [NP; sing only; subj or subj-compl with copula (subj: usu. abstr or это); fixed WO] sth. (is) completely, absolutely different (from the way it is supposed to be, what is expected, what is hoped for etc): **a different ⟨another⟩ story altogether; a horse of a different ⟨of another⟩ color; something else altogether.**

И-90 • КАК ИСТУКА́Н *стоять, сидеть coll* [как + NP; nom only; adv] **1.** (to stand or sit) motionless: **like a statue ⟨a stone⟩.**

2. (to stand or sit somewhere) clearly not understanding anything, mindlessly, not reacting: **like a zombie ⟨a dummy⟩.**

Осуждённый сидел как истукан, не слыша обращённых к нему вопросов. The convict sat there like a zombie, not hearing the questions addressed to him.

И-91 • НА ⟨В obsoles⟩ ИСХО́ДЕ [PrepP; these forms only] **1. ~** *чего.* Also: **К ИСХО́ДУ** [the resulting PrepP is adv] during the last part of sth.: **at the end ⟨close⟩ of; toward the end of; as sth. is drawing to a close; as sth. is nearing its end.**

К началу нашего повествования, на исходе довольно сумбурной редакционной ночи... мы видим издателя-редактора этой газеты Андрея Арсениевича Лучникова в его личных апартаментах, на «верхотуре» (Аксёнов 7). As our story begins—at the end of a hard night at the teletype machines...we find the publisher-editor of the *Courier*...Andrei Arsenievich Luchnikov, in his suite atop a skyscraper (7a).

2. [subj-compl with быть∅ (subj: concr or abstr)] sth. is approaching or coming to an end: X на исходе ≃ **X is almost gone; X is running short ⟨low, out⟩; (s.o.) is running out of X; X is petering out; X is almost at an end ⟨finished⟩;** [in time-related contexts only] **X is drawing to a close ⟨to an end⟩; X is winding down;** [of s.o.'s strength only] **X is giving out;** [of patience only] **X is wearing thin;** [of food, supplies etc only] **X is nearing rock bottom;** ‖ апрель ⟨третий час и т. п.⟩ ~ ≃ **it's nearly ⟨almost⟩ May ⟨three o'clock etc⟩.**

«Ну ладно, — сдалась Раиса. — Пуд [соли] дам, а больше и не проси». — «Ну давай хоть пуд», — уступила и старуха, предвидя, что время её на исходе (Войнович 2). "Well, all right," yielded Raisa. "I'll give you a pood [of salt], but don't ask me for more." "A pood'll be fine." Sensing that time was running short, Granny Dunya in her turn yielded (2a). ♦ [Трилецкий:] Трагедия на исходе, трагик! На исходе-с! (Чехов 1). [T.:] The tragedy is almost at an end, tragedian! Yes, sir, almost at an end (1a). ♦ Март был уже на исходе, когда, однажды вечером, она ему сказала: «У меня, кажется, для вас что-то имеется» (Набоков 1). March was drawing to an end when, one evening, she said to him: "I think I have something for you" (1a). ♦ Говорят, что [штрафной лагерь] Известковую обычный человек выдержать никак не может, тем более если сидит уже восьмой год и силёнки на исходе (Гинзбург 2). People said that an ordinary person had no chance of surviving at Izvestkovaya [punishment camp], especially one in her eighth year inside, whose strength was giving out (2a). ♦ Час пятый в исходе; проспал! (Достоевский 3). It was nearly five o'clock; he had overslept! (3a). ♦ «Э! да чёрт с ним совсем, с письмом-то!.. Я отвык деловые письма писать. А вот уж третий час в исходе» (Гончаров 1). "Oh, to hell with the letter!...I've lost the knack of writing business letters. Good Lord, it's almost three o'clock!" (1a).

И-92 • ПОДВОДИ́ТЬ/ПОДВЕСТИ́ ИТО́Г ⟨ИТО́ГИ⟩ *(чего, чему)* [VP; subj: usu. human or collect, occas. книга, статья etc] (in refer. to one's life, accomplishments etc, or some movement, historical period etc) to examine and summarize the net results of sth.: X подвёл итог (Y-a or Y-y) ≃ **X summed Y ⟨it⟩ up (and drew some conclusions); X made ⟨did⟩ a summing up of Y; X summed up what he had done ⟨accomplished etc⟩; X took stock (of Y); X drew up a balance sheet; X came to ⟨made⟩ some conclusions.**

Эти не по сезону перемены действуют на психику с такой силой, что, проснувшись в такое внезапно оказывающееся холодным и пасмурным утро, вдруг с раздирающей грустью начинаешь думать о жизни, подводить итоги, ничего не ждёшь (Олеша 3). These out-of-season changes act on the psyche with such force that, waking up on a morning turned suddenly cold and gray, you immediately begin to think about life with a heart-rending sadness, you begin to sum it up, expecting nothing (3a). ♦ Теперь сам он [Стрельников] был одержим сходным припадком саморазоблачения, всего себя переоценивал, всему подводил итог, всё видел в жаровом, изуродованном, бредовом извращении (Пастернак 1). Now he [Strelnikov] was himself swayed by the impulse to unmask himself, to reappraise his whole life, to draw up a balance sheet, while monstrously distorting everything in his feverish excitement (1a). ♦ Ну что ж, пора подвести некоторые итоги, пора выстроить по ранжиру должностных лиц, вступивших по такому ерундовому делу на путь прямого нарушения... советских законов (Войнович 3). Well, now it's time to come to some conclusions, time to arrange in order of importance the public servants who, over such a trivial matter, headed toward direct violation of Soviet law... (3a).

И-93 • В ⟨КОНЕ́ЧНОМ⟩ ИТО́ГЕ [PrepP; these forms only; sent adv] as a final result, after everything has been considered: **in the end; in the long run; in the final analysis; when all is said and done.**

«...Дмитрий Фёдорович в итоге ещё мне же должен, да не сколько-нибудь, а несколько тысяч-с, на что имею все документы!» (Достоевский 1). "...Dmitri Fyodorovich in the end owes me money, and not just a trifle but several thousand, sir, I've got it all on paper" (1a). ♦ «В испанском вопросе мы должны быть сугубо осторожны... Англичане стоят за реставрацию. Альфонс или Франко — это деталь. Во всяком случае Сити предпочитает генерала барселонским анархистам. В итоге Франция окажется одна...» (Эренбург 4). "We must be doubly cautious over the Spanish question....The British are in favour of restoration. Alfonso or Franco — that's a detail. In any case the City prefers the general to the anarchists of Barcelona. In the long run France will find herself alone" (4a). ♦ Человеку дано стать палачом, так же как и дано не становиться им. В конечном итоге выбор за нами (Искандер 3). Man is given the choice of becoming a hangman, just as he is given the choice of not becoming one. In the final analysis, the choice is ours (3a).

Й

Й-1 • НИ НА 〈ОДНУ́ 〈ЕДИ́НУЮ〉〉 ЙО́ТУ; И НА ЙО́ТУ *all lit* [PrepP; these forms only; adv (intensif); used with negated verbs; fixed WO] not at all, not in the least: **not one 〈an〉 iota; not one 〈a〉 jot 〈whit〉**.

«...Ну что же, — обратился он к поэту, — успеха я вам желать не буду, потому что в успех этот ни на йоту не верю» (Булгаков 9). "Well," he turned to the poet, "I shall not wish you success, for I do not have an iota of confidence in your success" (9a). ♦ «Из этой фразы, братцы, я делаю совершенно определённый вывод, что Лучников ни на йоту не изменил свою позицию...» (Аксёнов 7). "From these words I conclude beyond a shadow of a doubt that Luchnikov has not modified his position one jot..." (7a).

< From the name of the ninth letter of the Greek alphabet. Cf. the Bible (Matt. 5:18).

Й-2 • НИ 〈ОДНО́Й 〈ЕДИ́НОЙ〉〉 ЙО́ТЫ *lit* [NP$_{gen}$; these forms only; fixed WO] **1. не знать, не понимать ~ ; не уступить, не выполнить** и т. п. **~** *(из чего)* [obj] (to know, understand etc) nothing at all (about sth.), (to carry out, yield etc) none (of sth.) at all: не знать 〈не понимать и т. п.〉 ~ ≃ **not know 〈understand** etc〉 **one iota (of sth.); know 〈understand〉 not a whit 〈one iota〉 (of sth.); not know 〈understand** etc〉 **a single thing 〈the first thing〉 (about sth.); ‖** не уступить ~ ≃ **not give an inch; not yield in the slightest; not yield one iota; ‖** не выполнить ~ ≃ **not carry out even one iota (of sth.).**

С одной стороны, он понимал, что не выполнил ни одной йоты из программы, начертанной правителем канцелярии; с другой стороны, ему казалось, что программа эта должна выполниться сама собой, без всякого его содействия (Салтыков-Щедрин 2). He realized, on the one hand, that he had not carried out one iota...of the program his chief secretary had outlined for him, but, on the other, it seemed to him that that program had a good chance of coming off by itself without any interference from him (2a).

2. ~ *чего* **нет, не осталось** и т. п. [quantif of subj/gen] (there is, there remains etc) absolutely none (of sth.): **not one 〈a single〉 iota (of sth.); not a jot (of sth.).**

Я смотрела «Ярь» — в ней нет ни одной йоты подлинной поэзии, ни одного настоящего слова (Мандельштам 2). I have looked at *Yar.* There is not one iota of real poetry in it, not a single genuine word (2a).

< See Й-1.

К

К-1 • ПОД КАБЛУКÓМ ⟨ПОД КАБЛУЧКÓМ *humor*⟩ *чьим, (у) кого* **быть₀, находиться** и т. п. *or* **держать** *кого coll* [PrepP; these forms only; subj-compl with copula (subj: human) or obj-compl with держать (obj: human)] completely under the control or influence of s.o., entirely dependent on s.o. (often of a husband in relation to his wife): X под каблуком у Y-а ≃ **X is under Y's thumb; X lets Y boss him around;** ‖ Y держит X-а под каблуком ≃ **Y keeps X under Y's thumb; Y has X wrapped around Y's little finger;** [only of a husband in relation to his wife] X под каблуком у женщины Y ≃ **X is henpecked ⟨a henpecked husband⟩;** [in limited contexts] **Y wears the pants in the family.**

«Ну, ты-то, Гриш, никогда под каблуком не будешь», — польстила кладовщица... (Евтушенко 2). "Come on, Grisha, you'll never let anyone boss you around"... (2a). ♦ ...Наташка молодец. Правда, она держит Антона под каблуком. Но это ему на пользу (Зиновьев 2). ...Natasha is wonderful. It's true she keeps Anton under her thumb, but it's for his own good (2a). ♦ [Марина Дмитриевна:] Боюсь, что... ты будешь у жены под каблуком... [Лукашин:] Мама! Я разделю общую мужскую участь (Брагинский и Рязанов 1). [M.D.:] I'm afraid you're going to be a henpecked husband. [L.:] Mother! I'll only be sharing the common fate of all males (1a).

К-2 • В КАВЫ́ЧКАХ *iron* [PrepP; Invar; nonagreeing modif] in appearance or by name but not in fact, not deserving of his or its name (because he or it does not possess the required qualities, properties etc): **quote unquote; so-called.**

...Боец последнего года службы Иван Чонкин был маленького роста, кривоногий, да ещё и с красными ушами. «И что это за нелепая фигура! — скажете вы возмущённо. — Где тут пример для подрастающего поколения? И где автор увидел такого в кавычках героя?» (Войнович 2). ...Ivan Chonkin, the soldier with one year left to serve, was short of stature, bowlegged, and even had red ears. "What a sorry sight he makes!" you will say indignantly. "What kind of example is this for the younger generation? And just where has the author seen a quote unquote hero like this?" (2a).

К-3 • РАЗДУВÁТЬ/РАЗДÝТЬ КАДИ́ЛО *highly coll* [VP; subj: human] **1.** to expand a business, enterprise, or launch some activity successfully: X раздует кадило ≃ **X will get it going great guns; X will make a go of it;** [in limited contexts] **X will drum up business.**

2. to turn an unimportant matter into an object of excessive discussion, investigation etc by attaching unwarranted significance to it: X раздует кадило ≃ **X will blow things ⟨it⟩ (all) out of proportion; X will make a big to-do about it; X will make ⟨kick up⟩ a fuss; X will raise a hue and cry.**

К-4 • КÁЖДОМУ СВОЁ [sent; Invar; fixed WO] each person has his own fate, purpose in life, as well as his own concerns, gifts, tastes etc: **to each his own;** [in limited contexts] **everybody is different; it's a matter of taste; each to his own taste.**

...Ирина Викторовна вообще не боялась никаких на свете машин, не испытывала страха от того, что роботы могут вытеснить человека из жизни или стихийно взбунтоваться, как об этом написано у многих довольно умных, но теперь уже не оригинальных авторов... Пустяки! Каждому своё, машине — машинное, человеку — человеческое (Залыгин 1). There was no machine in the world that held any terrors for her [Irina Viktorovna], and she never feared that robots might displace humans or spontaneously revolt, as so many clever but no longer original writers had suggested. What nonsense that was! To each his own — the

mechanical to the machine, the human to the human (1a). ♦ В них [стихах, написанных сознательным способом,] исчезает чудо стихотворчества, но они нравятся неискушённому читателю, потому что в них наличествует элемент пересказа, готовой мысли. Мне такие стихи не нужны. Каждому — своё (Мандельштам 2). Such verse [written in premeditated fashion], though lacking the miraculous quality of spontaneous creation, always appeals to the unschooled reader because it "tells a story" or conveys a ready-made idea. I can do without this kind of verse. It's a matter of taste (2a).

< Loan translation of the Latin *suum cuique*.

К-5 • ВÓЛЬНЫЙ КАЗÁК *coll* [NP; usu. sing; subj-compl with быть₀ (subj: human), nom only, usu. pres; fixed WO] a completely independent person, free to act as he chooses: X вольный казак ≃ **X is his ⟨her⟩ own master ⟨man, mistress, woman, agent⟩; X is the master of his fate; X is a free man ⟨woman, agent⟩; X is as free as a bird.**

«Вы мужчина, вы — вольный казак... Сумасбродствовать, играть своей жизнью ваше священное право. Но Лариса Фёдоровна человек несвободный. Она мать» (Пастернак 1). "...You are a man, Yurii Andreievich, you are your own master, and you have a perfect right to gamble with your life if you feel like it. But Larisa Feodorovna is not a free agent. She is a mother..." (1a). ♦ [Борис:] Не говори, пожалуйста, таких слов, не печаль меня... [Катерина:] Да, тебе хорошо, ты вольный казак, а я!.. [Борис:] Никто и не узнает про нашу любовь (Островский 6). [B.:] Don't say such things, please, don't make me sad... [K.:] It's easy for you, you're a free man, but me! [B.:] No one will ever know about our love (6a). ♦ «Теперь ты вольный казак: можешь выступать, можешь не выступать, как хочешь. Хозяин — барин» (Трифонов 2). "Now you're a free agent: you may speak or not speak — suit yourself. The decision is yours" (2a).

К-6 • КАЗÁЛОСЬ БЫ [Invar; sent adv (parenth)] seemingly, ostensibly: **it would ⟨might⟩ seem; you ⟨one⟩ would think ⟨suppose⟩;** [in limited contexts] **apparently.**

...[Иванько] обменял квартиру маленькую двухкомнатную на большую трёхкомнатную, обставил её привозной мебелью... Казалось бы, что ещё человеку нужно? (Войнович 3). ...[Ivanko] traded a small two-room apartment for a large three-roomer, furnished it with imported furniture....It would seem a man could want no more (3a). ♦ Казалось бы, чего тут хитрого, ещё при царе Горохе телефоны умели проверять на слух, но ваши работники, Абрам Менделевич, оказывается, не умеют...» (Копелев 1). "You would think there was nothing so complicated about it, even in the olden days they knew how to test telephones by ear, but your workers, Abram Mendelevich, it turns out, don't know how" (1a). ♦ Этот, казалось бы, простенький вопрос почему-то расстроил сидящего, так что он даже изменился в лице (Булгаков 9). This apparently simple question upset the man behind the desk so much that a complete change came over his expression (9b).

К-7 • КАК КАЗÁЛОСЬ [Invar; sent adv (parenth); fixed WO] as could be readily seen, visibly: **apparently; evidently; appear ⟨seem⟩ to.**

О себе приезжий, как казалось, избегал много говорить... (Гоголь 3). The newcomer apparently avoided saying a great deal about himself... (3a). The newcomer seemed to avoid saying much about himself... (3c).

К-8 • ЕГИ́ПЕТСКАЯ КАЗНЬ *lit* [NP] a horrendous calamity, horrible punishment: **one of the ten plagues of Egypt; one of ten Egyptian plagues.**

[Платонов:] Ты ли это, Осип? Что с тобой? На лице у тебя написаны все десять египетских казней! (Чехов 1). [P.:] Is this you, Osip? What's wrong? You look as if you'd suffered all ten plagues of Egypt (1b).

< From the Biblical account of ten calamities visited upon Egypt by God when Pharaoh refused to free the Jews from bondage (Ex. 7-12; Deut. 4:34, 6:22; I Sam. 4:8).

К-9 • **А (ТО) КАК ЖЕ!** *coll* [Interj; these forms only; fixed WO] naturally, certainly (used as a response to a да-нет question, or as a rejoinder): **(but) of course!; of course I will ⟨I am** etc⟩**; of course, what do you expect?; sure (enough)!; sure I will ⟨I am** etc⟩**!; you bet!; and how!; what else?; I should say so!; I should say I will ⟨he did** etc⟩**!**

«Собираешься на службу?» — «А то как же?» (Шолохов 2). "Getting ready for the army?" "Of course" (2a). ♦ «И как это вы не боитесь, барин, право!» – обратился к Пьеру красноро́жий широкий солдат... «А ты разве боишься?» – спросил Пьер. «А то как же?» – ответил солдат (Толстой 6). "How is it you're not afraid, sir? Really, now!" a red-faced, broad-shouldered soldier asked Pierre....“Are you afraid, then?" asked Pierre. "Of course, what do you expect?" replied the soldier (6a). ♦ [Бусыгин:] Я тебя как-то видел. На главной улице. [Сильва:] А как же! Я принимаю там с восьми до одиннадцати. Каждый вечер (Вампилов 4). [B.:] I've seen you before. On the main street. [S.:] Sure! I hold court there from eight to eleven. Every evening (4a). ♦ «А ты могёшь [*ungrammat* = можешь] дать освобождение?» – «Конечно, могу». – «Бумажку напишешь?» – «А то как же!» (Шолохов 5). "Can ye give me my release?" "Of course, I can." "Will you put it on paper?" "Sure I will" (5a). ♦ «Грибы, должно, пойдут после этого дождя», – сказала Анфиса. «Пойдут», – вяло отозвался Лукашин. «Люди уже носят». – «Грибы? А то как же! Харч». (Абрамов 1). "There should be some mushrooms after this rain," Anfisa said. "Yes," Lukashin answered limply. "People are already bringing them in." "Mushrooms? You bet – good grub" (1a). ♦ [1-й мужик:] А тысячу-то отдали? [Яков:] А то как же?.. [2-й мужик:] То-то шальные деньги-то (Толстой 3). [First Peasant:] And did they give him the thousand? [Ya.:] I should say they did. [Second Peasant:] That's real easy money (3a).

К-10 • **ВОТ КАК** *coll* [Invar; fixed WO] **1.** [Interj (an exclamation or question)] used to express surprise, astonishment etc, occas. mixed with incredulity, indignation: **is that so ⟨right, it⟩?; really!; I see!; so that's how it is ⟨what's going on** etc⟩**!; well now!; dear me!; upon my word!; how about that!**

[Вера:] У нас в пансионе одна барышня писала стихи. [Беляев:] Вот как! и хорошие? (Тургенев 1). [V.:] At my boarding-school a girl used to write poetry. [B.:] Is that so? Was it good poetry? (1e). ♦ [Репников:] Да понимаешь ли ты, что этот прохвост пришёл сюда в расчёте, что ты ему поможешь? [Таня:] Ах, вот как? (Вампилов 3). [R.:] Do you realize that scoundrel came here counting on you to help him? [T.:] Oh, is that it? (3b). ♦ «Нет, Тимофей Лобанов не дезертир, – сказал Кузьма Кузьмич. – Не из таких». – «Не их таких? Вот как!» (Абрамов 1). "No – Timofei Lobanov isn't a deserter," said Kuzma Kuzmich. "He's not that kind." "Not that kind! Really!" (1b). ♦ «Свидетели показывают, что у „Мотодрома" Люся высадилась из светло-серой „Волги", которую мы преследовали»... – «Кому принадлежит „Волга"?» – «Ревазу Давидовичу Степнадзе». – «Вот как!..» – удивился начальник отдела (Чернёнок 1). "Witnesses testified that Lusya got out at the Motodrom stop from a light gray Volga – the one we were pursuing.”...“Who owns the Volga?" "Revaz Davidovich Stepnadze." "So that's how it is!" The chief was surprised (1a). ♦ «...Когда-то отец из меня кузнеца хотел сделать. Кузница у нас была». – «Вот как! – с волнением сказал Илья. – Дак, значит, мы с тобой тёзки, товарищ Лукашин?» – «В каком смысле?» – «А в том, что у моего отца тоже кузница была» (Абрамов 1).

"...There was a time when my father wanted to make a blacksmith out of me. We used to have a forge." "Well now!" said Ilya with emotion. "That makes us cousins, doesn't it, Comrade Lukashin?" "How so?" "I mean, my father had a forge too" (1a). ♦ «Сегодня я сижу да читаю Пушкина... Вдруг Аркадий подходит ко мне и молча, с этаким ласковым сожалением на лице, тихонько, как у ребёнка, отнял у меня книгу и положил передо мной другую, немецкую... улыбнулся и ушёл, и Пушкина унёс». – «Вот как!» (Тургенев 2). "Today I was sitting reading Pushkin....All of a sudden Arkady comes up to me and, without saying a word, with a look, you know, of kindly commiseration, gently takes the book away from me as if I were a child, puts another one in front of me, a German one...smiles, and goes away, carrying Pushkin off with him." "Dear me!" (2a). "Today I was sitting reading Pushkin....Suddenly Arkady comes up to me and without a word, as gently as if I were a child, with an affectionate look of pity on his face, took away my book and put another before me, a German book....Then he gave me a smile and went out, carrying Pushkin off with him." "Upon my word!" (2c).

2. ~ **нужен, надоел** и т. п. Also: **ВО КАК** *substand* [adv (intensif) or modif] (a person or thing is needed by s.o., boring to s.o. etc) to an extreme, the utmost degree (often accompanied by a gesture in which the speaker raises the edge of his index finger to his throat): **like you wouldn't believe; awfully; terribly; really; [in refer. to annoyance etc] s.o. has had it (up to here) (with sth.); sth. is more than one can take ⟨handle⟩.**

«А время тяжёлое, и нам урожай этот во как нужен. Так?» (Войнович 4). "Times are rough and we really need this harvest, right?" (4a). ♦ [Кудимов:] Парни! Что за формальность? Мне эта субординация *(показывает)* во как осточертела! (Вампилов 4). [K.:] Come on, fellers! Let's have a bit less of this formality. I've had seniority and juniority up to here. *(Points)* (4a). ♦ «Своей у тебя жизни, что ли, нет, чтобы так-то вокруг смотреть! Мне своей жизни – во как хватает – я всего этого не замечаю, на что твоя сила ушла...» (Битов 2). "Perhaps you don't have a life of your own, to be looking around you like this! My own life is more than I can handle, I don't notice all these things that you've poured your strength into—" (2a).

К-11 • **КАК БУДТО (БЫ)** **1.** Also: **КАК ЕСЛИ БЫ** [subord Conj; introduces a compar clause] (used to convey the unreal, illusory nature of the comparison) just like it would be if: **as if ⟨though⟩; like; [in limited contexts] (so...that) one ⟨it** etc⟩ **seems to...**

[Елена Андреевна:] Ты говоришь о своей старости таким тоном, как будто все мы виноваты, что ты стар (Чехов 3). [E.A.:] You speak of your old age as if we were to blame for it (3a). ♦ [Сорин:] Мне, брат, в деревне как-то не того, и, понятная вещь, никогда я тут не привыкну. Вчера лёг в десять и сегодня утром проснулся в девять с таким чувством, как будто от долгого спанья у меня мозг прилип к черепу и всё такое (Чехов 6). [S.:] For some reason, my boy, I'm not quite myself in the country, and, it stands to reason, I'll never get accustomed to it. I went to bed at ten o'clock last night and woke up at nine this morning feeling as though my brain were stuck to my skull from sleeping so long, and all that sort of thing (6a). ♦ «Вы смотрите! – говорил он [бригадир] обывателям, – как только меня завидите, так сейчас в тазы бейте, а потом зачинайте поздравлять, как будто я и невесть откуда приехал!» (Салтыков-Щедрин 1). "Mind you!" he [the brigadier] said to the townsfolk. "Soon as you see me, you bang on dishpans, and then start congratulating me like I'd ridden in from goodness knows where!" (1a). ♦ Потом разрешили одеться и выдали под расписку постель: матрац, такой твёрдый и тяжёлый, как будто его набили кирпичами... (Марченко 1). Then I was allowed to get dressed and sign out some bedding: a mattress that was so hard and heavy it seemed to be filled with bricks... (1a).

2. [Particle] used to express the speaker's doubt or uncertainty as to the reliability of the information in the statement (usu. when the speaker is uncertain of his own interpretation, understanding etc of the situation; less often when the speaker is uncertain of the reliability of an outside source of information): **(s.o. 〈sth.〉) seems (to); it seems that…; it is as if; (s.o. 〈sth.〉) looks (as if); apparently;** [when the reliability of the source of information is in doubt] **allegedly; ostensibly; supposedly; purportedly.**

Голос у него был прекрасный, громкий и симпатичный, и даже в самом голосе этом как будто заслышалось уже нечто искреннее и простодушное (Достоевский 2). His voice was beautiful, loud, and attractive, and even in this voice itself one seemed to hear something genuine and guileless (2a). ♦ «Флигелёк-то плох – вот беда». – «Помилуй, папаша, – подхватил Аркадий, – ты как будто извиняешься…» (Тургенев 2). "The little lodge is so horrid – that's the worst of it." "Goodness, dad," interposed Arkady, "it's as if you were apologising…" (2b). ♦ «От кого я бы это?» – задумчиво говорил Обломов, рассматривая адрес. – Рука как будто знакомая…» (Гончаров 1). "Who could it be from?" mused Oblomov, examining the address. "The handwriting looks familiar…" (1b). ♦ Возле дома, на цветной клумбе, лежала ничком молодая женщина в тёмно-вишнёвом купальнике. Она как будто легла загорать и, разбросив руки, уснула (Чернёнок 1). Near the house, in the flower bed, a young woman in a dark-cherry bathing suit lay facedown. She looked as if she had been sunbathing and had fallen asleep with her arms spread out (1a). ♦ Берия как будто пытался узнать у него тайну прохладительных напитков, а Логидзе не открывал этой тайны (Искандер 4). Beria apparently tried to find out the secret of the soft drinks from him, but Logidze would not reveal it (4a). ♦ «По субботам тебя как будто подменяют. Это от предчувствия свиданья» (Федин 1). [context transl] "On Saturdays you're like a new man. That's from your anticipation of a date" (1a).

К-12 • КАК БЫ…   1. [Particle] used to show that the object, action etc named is almost, but not exactly, what is named: **(a) kind of; something of; seem to…; (it is) as if 〈though〉; as it were;** [in limited contexts] **seemingly.**

…Между ними [ёлками] образовалась как бы аллейка… (Набоков 1). …They [the fir trees] formed between them a kind of small avenue… (1a). ♦ Исключённый из Союза писателей, я был объявлен как бы вне закона (Войнович 1). Expelled from the Writers' Union, I had been declared something of an outcast (1a). ♦ Иван хотел было кинуться к окну; но что-то как бы вдруг связало ему ноги и руки (Достоевский 2). Ivan wanted to rush to the window, but something seemed suddenly to bind his legs and arms (2a). ♦ Когда я, нарушив правила литературного тона, сам оказался в повествовании в качестве героя, то впервые как бы поколебалась социальная структура Лёвы… (Битов 2). When I violated literary etiquette by turning up in the narrative myself in the capacity of hero, it was as if Lyova's social structure had been shaken for the first time (2a). ♦ Публика долго лица его не знала. Его нигде не видать. Уже знаменитый, он как бы остаётся за кулисами своей деятельной, говорливой мысли (Набоков 1). For a long time the public did not know his face. Nowhere was he seen. Already famous, he remained as it were in the wings of his busy, talkative thought (1a).

2. [subord Conj, compar] (used to introduce an interpretation of what is stated in the main clause; the interpretation takes the form of an unreal comparison) (sth. is done, happens, looks etc) the way it would if…: **as if 〈though〉.**

Он продолжал стоять возле своего столика, как бы сочувствуя мне по поводу этой неприятной новости (Искандер 4). He continued to stand by his desk, as though sympathizing with me over this disagreeable news (4a).

3. obs, substand [subord Conj, condit] used to introduce a conditional clause: **if (only);** [with neg predic only] **were it not for; had it not been for.**

[Анна Петровна:] Как бы папенька-то твой не мотал без памяти, так бы другое дело было, а то оставил нас почти ни с чем (Островский 1). [A.P.:] If only your papa hadn't spent his money like water, then everything'd be different. As it is, he left us almost nothing at all (1a).

К-13 • КАК БЫ (…) НЕ…   1. [subord Conj; introduces a nominal clause; usu. used after the words бояться, страх etc in the main clause] used to introduce a clause expressing a supposition that sth. undesirable may occur or may have occurred: **(be afraid 〈fear etc〉) that (s.o. 〈sth.〉) might 〈may〉.**

Больше всего Аслан боится, как бы кто не подумал, что он боится своего происхождения (Искандер 5). What Aslan fears above all is that someone might think he feared his lineage (5a).

2. [Particle] used to introduce a supposition that something undesirable may occur or may have occurred: **what if.**

«Как бы он нас не опозорил, дядя Сандро…» (Искандер 3). "What if he puts us to shame, Uncle Sandro?" (3a).

К-14 • КАК БЫ НЕ ТА́К! coll; **КАК НЕ ТА́К!** substand [Interj; these forms only; fixed WO] used to express strong disagreement, objection, refusal, refutation: **not at all!; not a chance!; fat chance; not on your life!; not by a long shot!; nothing of the sort 〈kind〉!; no way!;** [in limited contexts] **not if I can help it.**

«Я это дело, которым руководил, разваливал как только мог. И вы думаете, меня за это схватили? Как бы не так, меня за это орденом наградили» (Войнович 4). "I did the best I could to ruin the work I supervised. And do you think I was picked up for that? Not at all, I was awarded a medal" (4a). ♦ [Всеволод:] А вы думаете, господа, вожди наши эмигрантские – были очень подвижны умом? Русский народ спрашивать? Как бы не так! (Солженицын 9). [V.:] And did you imagine, gentlemen, that our émigré leaders were any brighter? Do you think they would bother to consult the Russian people? Not a chance! (9a). ♦ За тем, что было написано, стоял, конечно, намёк на то, что Нюра зла не помнит и готова примириться, если Иван не будет упрямиться. «Как бы не так», – вслух сказал он… (Войнович 2). Everything about the note hinted that Nyura bore him no grudge and was ready to make up if Ivan wouldn't stay stubborn. "Fat chance," said Chonkin aloud… (2a). ♦ Всё это была, конечно, политика. У Львовых мне казалось, что политика существует только для того, чтобы объяснить, почему Митю исключили с волчьим билетом. Как бы не так! (Каверин 1). All this, of course, was politics. When I was at the Lvovs, I imagined that the only point of politics was to explain why Mitya had been expelled and blacklisted. Nothing of the sort! (1a). ♦ «Может быть, опять случится услужить чем-нибудь друг другу». – «Да, как бы не так!» – думал про себя Чичиков, садясь в бричку (Гоголь 3). "Perhaps we may be able to be of service to each other again one day." "Not if I can help it," thought Chichikov to himself as he got into his carriage (3a).

К-15 • КА́К ЖЕ coll [Particle]   **1.** Also: **КА́К ЖЕ, КА́К ЖЕ** coll [used as an affirmative response to a question or in support of a statement] certainly, it is clear or agreed (without needing to be stated or proven): **(yes 〈but, why〉,) of course; of course I do 〈will etc〉; yes, indeed (I do etc); sure(ly); naturally;** [in limited contexts] **well then (, well then);** [in response to "Do you mind…?", "Do you object to…?" etc] **of course not (, of course not).**

«Может быть, помните? Я вам рассказывал об Абуталипе Куттыбаеве». – «А, ну как же, как же! Прекрасно помню» (Айтматов 2). "Perhaps you'll remember – I told you once about Abutalip Kuttybaev." "Oh, yes, of course, indeed I do! I remember well now" (2a). ♦ «Ах да, конечно же, „Капитаны", „Африка", „Нигер"… Как же, как же, в наше время все гимназисты от этих стихов [Гумилёва] с ума сходили» (Копелев 1). "Ah yes, of course, 'Captains,' 'Africa,' 'The Niger.' But of course, in our day all the Gymnasium students were crazy about some of his [Gumilev's] poems" (1a). ♦ «Разве вы ездите верхом?» – «Как же! К нынешнему дню и фрак нарочно заказывал» (Гончаров 1). "But do you ride?" "Of course I do! I had the coat specially made for to-day" (1a). ♦ «У меня для вас письмо от сына, от Алексея Сергеевича». – «А-а-а! Как же, как же!» (Федин 1). "I have a letter for you from your son, from Aleksei Sergeyevich." "A-a-ah! Well then, well then" (1a). ♦ «Мне нужно кое о чём переговорить, так не хотите ли заехать ко мне?» — «Как же, как же», — сказал поспешно Хлобуев и вышел с ним (Гоголь 3). "There's something I'd like to discuss with you. Would you mind coming to my house?" "Of course not, of course not," Khlobuyev said hastily and went out with him (3a).

2. used to express disagreement, doubt that sth. said by the interlocutor is as stated (the speaker often repeats the part of the interlocutor's statement with which he disagrees): **that's what you think!; (oh) sure!; yeah, right!;** [in limited contexts] **sure one does ⟨will etc⟩.**

[Катерина:] И на воле-то он словно связанный. [Варвара:] Да, как же, связанный! Он как выедет, так запьёт (Островский 6). [K.:] So, even on his own, it's just as if he were still tied to her. [V.:] That's what you think! As soon as he leaves here, he'll start in drinking (6f). ♦ «Ленту, что ли, привезли? – спросил я. – Опять „Девушку с гитарой"?» – «Как же, ленту, дожидайся!» – ответил Чудаков (Аксёнов 1). "What, did you bring a movie?" I asked. "*The Girl with the Guitar* again?" "Oh sure, a movie, that's a good one!" answered Chudakov (1a). ♦ «Ты думаешь, ты любишь?! Как же! Да ты за человека никого не считаешь» (Битов 2). "You think you love? Sure! But you don't consider anyone a person" (2a). ♦ [Бусыгин:] Он говорил, что он сам сочиняет музыку. [Нина (насмешливо):] Ну как же (Вампилов 4). [B.:] He said he composed music himself. [N. (ironically):] Sure he does (4a).

К-16 • КАК (...) НИ... [subord Conj] **1.** Also: **КАК БЫ (...) НИ...** [concessive] regardless of to what extent or degree: **however (great ⟨much etc⟩)...; no matter how (great ⟨much etc⟩)...; (as) much as...;** [in limited contexts] **for all one's ⟨its⟩...; ...as one is; despite one's ⟨s.o.'s⟩ best efforts (to do sth.);** ‖ **как (это) ни странно ≃ curiously ⟨oddly⟩ enough; strange as it may seem;** [in limited contexts] **strange to say;** ‖ **как он ни старался... ≃ try as he might ⟨would⟩.**

Есть такие люди, в которых, как ни бейся, не возбудишь никак духа вражды, мщения и т. п. Что ни делай с ними, они всё ласкаются (Гончаров 1). There are people in whom, however hard you try, you cannot arouse any feeling of hostility, revenge, etc. Whatever you do to them, they go on being nice to you (1a). ♦ Что бы он ни говорил себе, как бы он ни взвинчивал себя, как бы он себя ни настраивал, ему было противно (Стругацкие 1). No matter what he told himself, no matter how much he steeled himself or tried to overcome it, he was still disgusted (1a). ♦ [Лукашин:] Как здесь ни приятно, мне пора... (Брагинский и Рязанов 1). [L.:] Well, much as I enjoy your company, it's time for me to be going (1a). ♦ Как ни владела собою Одинцова, как ни стояла выше всяких предрассудков, но и ей было неловко, когда она явилась в столовую к обеду (Тургенев 2). For all her self-possession and freedom from the conventions Madame Odintsov felt distinctly ill at ease when she entered the dining room for dinner (2c). ♦ ...Как ни потрясло их описанное выше зрелище, они не увлеклись ни модными в то время революционными идеями, ни соблазнами, представляемыми анархией... (Салтыков-Щедрин 1). Shocked as they were by the scene which has been described, they were not carried away by any of the revolutionary ideas then in fashion, nor by the temptations offered by the prospect of anarchy (1b). ♦ Как ни отвлекали тётушку Хрисулу, через некоторое время она забеспокоилась... (Искандер 5). Despite everyone's best efforts to distract Auntie Chrysoula, she became uneasy after a while... (5a). ♦ Как это ни странно, подумал я, но и в моей судьбе есть некоторая доля Рогозинского варианта (Зиновьев 2). Curiously enough, I thought to myself, my own case has something in common with that of Rogozin (2a). ♦ Гангут познакомился с Лучниковым, как ни странно, на Острове (Аксёнов 7). Strange to say, Gangut met Luchnikov on the Island (7a). ♦ Как ни старался Григорий, уехав в поле, забыть о своём горе, в мыслях он неизбежно возвращался к этому (Шоло-

хов 5). Try as he would, even out in the fields Grigory could not forget his grief; it was for ever in his thoughts (5a).

2. [temporal] every time that: **whenever; no matter when; it doesn't matter when.**

Тебе как ни позвонишь, телефон всегда занят. Whenever I call you, the line is always busy.

К-17 • КАК-НИКА́К *coll* [AdvP; Invar; usu. sent adv (occas. parenth)] **1.** used to introduce an explanation of or justification for what is stated in the immediate context; occas. adds the additional implication that the person, thing etc in question is not of very good quality: **after all.**

[Зилов:] Напрасно ты не доверяешь технике. Ей как-никак принадлежит будущее (Вампилов 5). [Z.:] You're wrong to mistrust machinery. After all, the future belongs to it (5a).

2. regardless of the circumstances, regardless of how things turn out: **no matter what (happens).**

Мы поняли, что как-никак, а неприятного разговора с отцом не избежать. We understood that, no matter what, there was no avoiding an unpleasant conversation with Father.

К-18 • КАК ⟨ЛИШЬ, ЧУТЬ⟩ ТО́ЛЬКО...; ТО́ЛЬКО ЛИШЬ... [subord Conj, temporal] used to show that the situation or action presented in the main clause immediately follows the situation or action presented in the subordinate clause: **as soon as; just as; hardly ⟨scarcely, just⟩...when; no sooner...than; the moment ⟨the minute⟩...**

«Я боюсь больше всего, что ты разорвёшь письмо, как только узнаешь мой почерк» (Федин 1). "I'm most of all afraid that you will tear up the letter as soon as you recognize my handwriting" (1a). ♦ Как только они скрылись за воротами, тётя Катя... побежала в сарай... (Искандер 3). As soon as they disappeared beyond the gate, Aunt Katya...ran to the barn... (3a). ♦ Как только рукопись попала в редакции двух популярнейших толстых журналов, началось пятилетнее плаванье по бурным волнам Самиздата (Гинзбург 2). No sooner did the manuscript reach the editorial board of Moscow's two most popular literary journals, than it began a five-year voyage over the stormy waves of *samizdat* (2a). ♦ Как только Щащико, распахнув дверь, выстрелил, почти одновременно раздался выстрел офицера... (Искандер 3). The moment Shashiko opened the door and fired, almost simultaneously, the officer's shot rang out (3a).

К-19 • КРО́МЕ КАК... [subord Conj; introduces a clause of exception] other than: **except; but; save; saving.**

Садчиков ничего не мог с собой поделать. Он не мог сейчас думать ни о чём другом, кроме как об убитом парне (Семёнов 1). Sadchikov could not do a thing with himself. He could not think of anything else at the moment except the dead man (1a). ♦ «Тот, кто правил землёй, шляпы ни перед кем никогда, кроме как перед дамами, не снимал...» (Булгаков 5). "The one who ruled the earth had never removed his hat before anyone but ladies..." (5a).

К-20 • ЛИШЬ БЫ КАК *coll* [AdvP; Invar; adv; fixed WO] (to do sth.) carelessly, negligently, without regard for quality: **slapdash; in a slapdash ⟨slipshod⟩ manner; any which ⟨old⟩ way.**

К-21 • КАКО́Е ТАМ ⟨ТУТ⟩! *coll* [these forms only; fixed WO] **1.** [Particle] used to express disagreement with some statement or to correct one's own words (the part of the statement that is objected to or corrected is repeated): **(but) what am I ⟨are you⟩ saying ⟨talking about⟩...!; what do you mean,...!;** [in limited contexts] **don't call it...**

Нас там было человек пятнадцать, — да нет, какое там пятнадцать, не меньше тридцати. There were about fifteen of us there – but wait, what am I saying, fifteen – there were no fewer than thirty.

2. [Interj] used to express a negative reaction to a suggestion, request etc, express one's opinion that some suggestion is unrealistic, some undertaking is futile etc: **no way!; nothing doing!; not on your (sweet) life!; not a chance!;** [in limited contexts] **far from it.**

...Лукашин начал действовать. Не прямо, конечно, чтобы встретились, как мужчина с мужчиной, и давай по-деловому, раз уж так всё получилось. Какое там! До встречи ли ему, когда его от одного имени Григория трясёт... (Абрамов 1). ...Lukashin had started to act. Not directly, of course. Not a meeting in man-to-man, "let's get on with it since this is the way things have worked out" fashion. Not on your sweet life! How could he be in a mood to meet with Grigory when the mere mention of his name made him quiver?... (1a).

К-22 • ВО́Т КАКО́Й... *coll;* **ВО́ КАКО́Й** *substand* [AdjP; modif; fixed WO] very good (big, strong etc): **one hell ⟨heck⟩ of a [NP]; quite a [NP]; some [NP]!; incredibly [AdjP].**

Он во какой механик! He's one hell of a mechanic! ♦ «Говорю тебе, [Григорий] живой и здоровый, морду наел во какую!»... Аксинья слушала, как в чаду... Она опомнилась только у мелеховской калитки (Шолохов 5). [context transl] "I tell you he's [Grigory is] safe and sound, and real fat in the face!"...Aksinya listened as if in a trance. She came to herself only at the Melekhovs' gate (5a).

К-23 • КАКО́Й (...) НИ...; КАКО́Й БЫ (...) НИ... [AdjP; used as subord Conj, concessive] **1.** notwithstanding how great (strong etc): **however ⟨no matter how, regardless of how⟩ great ⟨strong etc⟩.**

«Нигилист — это человек... который не принимает ни одного принципа на веру, каким бы уважением ни был окружён этот принцип» (Тургенев 2). "A nihilist is a man who...accepts no principle whatsoever as an article of faith, however great the respect in which that principle may be generally held" (2e). ♦ ...Она [труппа] однажды явилась во главе с Шарлем Лагранжем и сообщила Мольеру, что ввиду того, что он соединяет с необыкновенными способностями честность и приятное обращение, труппа просит его не беспокоиться: актёры не уйдут искать счастья на стороне, какие бы выгодные предложения им ни делали (Булгаков 5). ...One day his [Molière's] players came to him, headed by Charles La Grange, and assured him that, in view of his fairness and kindness, as well as his extraordinary talents, he had nothing to worry about—they would not leave to seek their fortunes elsewhere no matter how tempting the offers they received (5a).

2. any at all: **no matter what (kind ⟨sort⟩ of); it doesn't matter what (kind ⟨sort⟩ of).**

...«Какая бы чума на нашу голову ни свалилась, а эндурцам, глядишь, всё на пользу» (Искандер 5). "No matter what plague lands on us, it works out to the Endurskies' advantage" (5a).

К-24 • КАКО́Й-НИКАКО́Й *substand* [AdjP; modif] perhaps (a person, thing, phenomenon is) not adequate, not very good, but at least he or it is there, available etc: **какой-никакой X ≃ a bad ⟨poor etc⟩ X perhaps, but an X all the same; bad ⟨poor etc⟩ as X is, still he ⟨it etc⟩ is an X; bad ⟨poor etc⟩ as he ⟨it etc⟩ is, he ⟨it etc⟩ is an X all the same; not much of an X, but an X (all the same); (at least) some sort of an X.**

Первый весенний день. Как-то не верится: и солнышко припекает, и слегка закапало. Какая-никакая худенькая весна показалась (Терц 3). The first spring day. It's hard to credit: the sun is quite hot and a few drops of melted snow fall pitapat from the roof. Still a poor and feeble thing perhaps, but spring all the same (3a). ♦ «А хоронить будете по-православному иль по-гражданскому?» — «По-граждански». — «Тогда дороже». — «Это почему же?» — «Как сказать... От православного какой-никакой доход: глядишь, за крестиком накажут посмотреть, чтобы не слямзили...» (Федин 1). "D'you want a Christian burial or a civil

one?" "A civil one." "Then it's dearer." "Why is that?" "How shall I put it... From a Christian one you get some sort of profit: maybe they'll tell you to watch the cross, so's no one swipes it..." (1a).

К-25 • КАКО́Й ТАКО́Й... *highly coll* [AdjP; modif; fixed WO] used to express the speaker's attitude (surprise, incredulity, rejection etc) toward the person, thing, or phenomenon denoted by the noun that follows: **какой такой X? ≃ what X?; who is this X?; (just) what sort ⟨kind⟩ of X (is this ⟨does one have etc⟩)?; X!; what do you mean, X?; what's this about X?**

«Зачем он всё это мне рассказывает? — закипала в Андрее лютая и необъяснимая для него самого злость. — Что ему надо от меня? Какие такие у него права есть влезать ко мне в душу?» (Максимов 3). A fierce anger, which he couldn't have explained to himself, took hold of Andrei. "Why is he telling me all this? What does he want from me? What right has he got to come prying into my feelings?" (3a). ♦ «Я хочу рассказать тебе о Саше». — «Какой такой Саша? Вчера был Коля, а сегодня уже Саша?» "I want to tell you about Sasha." "Who is this Sasha? Yesterday it was Kolya, and today it's Sasha?" ♦ «...Я [деньги] в хозяйкин чепчик зашил». — „В какой такой чепчик?" — „Я у ней взял, у неё валялся, старая коленкоровая дрянь"» (Достоевский 2). "...I sewed it [the money] up in my landlady's bonnet." 'What sort of bonnet?' 'I took it from her, it was lying about, an old calico rag'" (2a). ♦ «Откуда валюту взял?»... — «Бог истинный, бог всемогущий, — заговорил Никанор Иванович, — всё видит... В руках никогда не держал и не подозревал, какая такая валюта!» (Булгаков 9). "Where did you get foreign exchange?"..."God, the true and the almighty," Nikanor Ivanovich pattered, "sees everything....I never had it in my hands, and never knew the looks of it. Foreign exchange!" (9a).

К-26 • КАКО́Й ТАМ ⟨ТУТ⟩...! *coll* [AdjP; modif; fixed WO] used to express disagreement with some statement or to correct one's own words (the part of the statement that is objected to or corrected is repeated): **what do you mean,...?; (but) what am I ⟨are you⟩ saying ⟨talking about⟩...?;** [in limited contexts] **how can you call it ⟨him etc⟩...?; don't call it ⟨him etc⟩...; some [NP]!**

«Кто же у нас будет платить такие бешеные деньги? Васюкинцы...» — «Какие там васюкинцы! Васюкинцы денег платить не будут. Они будут их по-лу-чать!» (Ильф и Петров 1). "And who do you think is going to pay that kind of money? The people of Vasyuki?" "What do you mean, the people of Vasyuki? The people of Vasyuki are not going to pay any money, they're going to receive it" (1a). ♦ [Колесов:] Как свадьба? Где муж? [Маша:] Где, в том-то и дело!.. Сбежала я от него, Коля, прямо со свадьбы. [Колесов:] Как — со свадьбы? Почему? [Маша:] Да не свадьба была! Какая там свадьба. Неохота рассказывать (Вампилов 3). [K.:] How was the wedding? Where's your husband? [M.:] Where, that's just the point!...I ran away from him, Kolya, right at the wedding. [K.:] What do you mean, at the wedding? Why? [M.:] It wasn't a wedding! Don't call it a wedding. I don't feel like talking about it (3b). ♦ В вуз он и не пытался пойти, какой там вуз с его знаниями, кроме того — возраст (Залыгин 1). [context transl] He didn't even try for university—how could he with his knowledge? Besides, there was his age (1a).

К-27 • ХОТЬ КАКО́Й; КАКО́Й ХО́ЧЕШЬ ⟨хотите⟩ *both coll* [AdjP; these forms only; modif; fixed WO] regardless of which or what kind: **(absolutely) any ⟨any kind of, any sort of⟩; any [NP] you like ⟨can think of⟩; whichever ⟨whichever kind, whatever etc⟩ (you like).**

Дайте им какое хотите щекотливое сватство, какую хотите торжественную свадьбу или именины — справят по всем правилам, без малейшего упущения (Гончаров 1). Given any sort of ticklish matchmaking, a festal wedding, or a name day, and it was invariably celebrated according to the rules, down to the last detail (1b). ♦ [Катерина:] Да неужели же ты разлюбил меня?

[Кабанов:] Да не разлюбил; а с этакой-то неволи от какой хочешь красавицы жены убежишь! (Островский 6). [context transl] [K.:] Have you stopped loving me? [K-ov:] No, that I haven't, but the fairest wife in the world couldn't keep her husband from trying to escape from a prison like this (6b).

К-28 • **НИ В КАКУ́Ю** *highly coll* [PrepP; Invar; predic (with subj: human, collect, or animal) or adv; fixed WO] one absolutely and categorically refuses, is unwilling etc (to agree to sth., accept sth. etc): X – ни в какую ≃ **X won't ⟨wouldn't⟩ have it; X will ⟨would⟩ have none of it; X won't ⟨wouldn't⟩ budge; X won't ⟨wouldn't⟩ hear of it;** ‖ [when used as adv] **not (do sth.) on any account; not (do sth.) for anything;** [when used as indep. remark] **no way.**

Главным действующим лицом в Базеле была моя бабушка Эльфрида, и бабушка Эльфрида – ни в какую!.. Чтобы её Якоб, такой Якоб, вдруг женился, да ещё на дочери сапожника, об этом не может быть и речи (Рыбаков 1). The chief character in Basel was my grandmother, Elfrieda, and grandmother Elfrieda would simply have none of it!... That her Jakob should all of a sudden get married, and to the daughter of a bootmaker, was simply out of the question (1a). ♦ Лукашин, когда стали утверждать сенокосные группы, – ни в какую (Абрамов 1). Lukashin wouldn't hear of it when they began setting up the harvest groups (1a). ♦ «...Старик у нас охотник, медведя валил в своё время. Я ему и говорю: „Вот тебе ружьё, старик, стреляй!" А он ни в какую» (Айтматов 1). "...The old man's a hunter—he's dealt with bear in his time. So I say to him, here's the rifle, old man—you shoot. But he won't do it for anything" (1b). ♦ ...Павел хорошо понимал, что матери здесь [в посёлке] не привыкнуть. Ни в какую (Распутин 4). ...Pavel knew that his mother would never get used to it [the settlement]. No way (4a).

К-29 • **КАЛАНЧА́ ПОЖА́РНАЯ** *coll, humor* [NP; sing only; often used as appos or vocative; fixed WO] a very tall (and usu. thin) person: **beanpole; (long,) tall drink of water;** [in refer. to a man only] **highpockets.**

К-30 • **ТЁРТЫЙ КАЛА́Ч** *coll, occas. disapprov* [NP; more often sing; often subj-compl with copula, usu. nom (subj: human); fixed WO] a person who has experienced a lot, is worldly-wise and very difficult to deceive: X – тёртый калач ≃ **X wasn't born yesterday; X has been around; X has been around the block; X knows his way around ⟨about⟩;** [in limited contexts] **X is nobody's fool; X is an old hand ⟨pro, stager⟩.**

«Что за чудесная женщина Анна Сергеевна», — воскликнул Аркадий... «Да... но чудо – не она, а её сестра». – «Как? эта смугленькая?» – «Да, эта смугленькая. Это вот свежо, и нетронуто, и пугливо, и молчаливо, и всё, что хочешь... Из этой ещё что вздумаешь, то и сделаешь; а та – тёртый калач» (Тургенев 2). "What a wonderful woman Anna Sergeyevna is," exclaimed Arkady...."Yes....But the miracle's not her but her sister." "What? That little brown creature?" "Yes, that little brown creature. There you have something fresh and untouched and wild and silent and—anything you like....You could still make anything you like out of her; but the elder—she already knows her way about" (2e).

К-31 • **КАЛАЧО́М НЕ ВЫ́МАНИТЬ** *кого откуда coll* [VP; subj: human; usu. fut gener. 2nd pers sing не выманишь; fixed WO] to be unable by any means to force s.o. to leave some place: X-а из места Y калачом не выманишь ≃ **you won't ⟨can't, couldn't⟩ get X out of place Y for love (n)or money ⟨for anything (in the world)⟩; wild horses won't ⟨can't, couldn't⟩ drag X away from ⟨out of⟩ place Y.**

«Пса в столовой прикармливаете, – раздался женский голос, – а потом его отсюда калачом не выманишь» (Булгаков 11). "If you feed a dog at the table," said a woman's voice, "you won't get him out of here afterward for love or money" (11b).

К-32 • **КАЛАЧО́М НЕ ЗАМАНИ́ТЬ** *кого куда coll* [VP; subj: human; usu. fut gener. 2nd pers sing не заманишь; fixed WO] to be unable by any means to convince s.o. to go to some place or see s.o.: X-а в место Y калачом не заманишь ≃ **you won't ⟨can't, couldn't⟩ get X (to come ⟨go⟩) to place Y for love (n)or money ⟨at any price⟩; nothing will ⟨can, could⟩ (ever) tempt X to come ⟨to go⟩ to place Y; nothing will ⟨can, could⟩ lure X to place Y.**

[Вася:] Калачом в театр не заманишь. Так ты и ожидай! (Островский 11). [V.] You won't get them to the theatre for love or money—that's what *you're* soon going to find out! (11a). ♦ [Астров:] Уехали. Профессор рад небось! Его теперь сюда и калачом не заманишь (Чехов 3). [A.:] They've gone. The professor is happy, that's certain. Nothing could ever tempt him to come back here now (3a).

К-33 • **ДО ГРЕ́ЧЕСКИХ КАЛЕ́НД** отложить, отсрочить *что и т. п. lit, iron* [PrepP; Invar; adv; fixed WO] (to postpone sth.) indefinitely: **till ⟨until⟩ the Greek calends; till the millennium; till the end of time.**

< Loan translation of the Latin *ad Calendas Graecas.* Ascribed to the Roman emperor Augustus (63 B.C.–A.D. 14).

К-34 • **ДОВОДИ́ТЬ/ДОВЕСТИ́ ДО БЕ́ЛОГО КАЛЕ́НИЯ** *кого coll* [VP; subj: human or abstr; the verb may take the final position, otherwise fixed WO] to irritate s.o. past the limits of his endurance, make s.o. lose his self-control completely: X довёл Y-а до белого каления ≃ **X provoked Y to a (white) rage; X made Y livid (with rage); X roused Y to fury; X made Y see red; X made Y's blood boil; X burned Y up.**

А Лизка считала себя виноватой: она вечор своими глупыми слезами довела брата до белого каления (Абрамов 1). Lizka felt she was to blame, having provoked her brother to a white rage the day before with her silly tears (1a). ♦ ...Меня раздражало (да и сейчас иногда доводит до белого каления) – с какой тупостью целыми днями, годами дуются в домино... (Терц 3). ...I have always been irritated (and even now I am sometimes roused to fury) to see how vacuously people play dominoes for days on end... (3a). ♦ «Нет, я не могу успокоиться! Это он меня довёл до белого каления!» (Булгаков 2). "No, I can't calm down! He burns me up!" (2a).

К-35 • **ДОХОДИ́ТЬ/ДОЙТИ́ ДО БЕ́ЛОГО КАЛЕ́НИЯ** *coll* [VP; subj: human; the verb may take the final position, otherwise fixed WO] to become irritated beyond the limits of one's endurance, lose one's self-control completely: X дошёл до белого каления ≃ **X flew into a (white) rage; X became furious; X saw red; X's blood boiled; X was livid.**

К-36 • **КАЛИ́Ф ⟨ХАЛИ́Ф⟩ НА ЧАС** *lit* [NP; often subj-compl with copula, nom or instrum (subj: human); fixed WO] (usu. of a man) a person who has received or wields power for a short time: **king ⟨queen⟩ for a day.**

«Несомненно, будет правительственный переворот, у власти станет Корнилов... Керенский между двумя жерновами, – не тот, так другой его сотрёт... Он – калиф на час» (Шолохов 3). "There will certainly be a *coup d'état* and Kornilov will take over....Kerensky is between two fires—if one doesn't get him, the other will....He's only king for a day" (3a).

< Loan translation: part of the title of a story from the *Arabian Nights.*

К-37 • **БРОСА́ТЬ/БРО́СИТЬ ⟨КИДА́ТЬ/КИ́НУТЬ, ПУСКА́ТЬ/ПУСТИ́ТЬ⟩ КА́МЕНЬ ⟨КА́МНЕМ⟩** *в кого;* **БРОСА́ТЬ КАМЕ́НЬЯ(МИ)** *all disapprov* [VP; subj: human] to speak condemningly of s.o., make accusations (often unjustly) against s.o.: X бросит в Y-а камень ≃ **X will cast ⟨throw⟩ stones at Y.**

Когда же Помпадурша была... сослана в монастырь и пострижена под именем инокини Нимфодоры, то он [Грустилов] первый бросил в неё камнем и написал «Повесть о некоторой многолюбивой жене», в которой делал очень ясные намёки на прежнюю свою благодетельницу (Салтыков-Щедрин 1). But when [Madame de] Pompadour...was exiled to a monastery and took the veil under the name of Nimfodora, he [Melancholov] was the first to cast stones at her; he wrote the "Story of a Certain Woman of Many Loves," in which he made very clear allusions to his former benefactress (1a).

< From the Biblical account of the adulterous woman (John 8:7).

К-38 • ВÉШАТЬ/ПОВÉСИТЬ (СЕБÉ) КÁМЕНЬ НА ШÉЮ [VP; subj: human] to take upon o.s. (voluntarily, but usu. reluctantly) sth. burdensome (such as concern for s.o., support of s.o. etc): X повесил себе камень на шею ≃ **X hung a millstone (a)round his neck.**

К-39 • ДЕРЖÁТЬ ⟨НОСИ́ТЬ⟩ КÁМЕНЬ ЗА ПÁЗУ-ХОЙ *(на кого, против кого)* coll [VP; subj: human; the verb may take the final position, otherwise fixed WO] to bear secret malice, feel deep resentment toward s.o. and want to make trouble for him: X держит камень за пазухой (на Y-а) ≃ **X harbors ⟨nurses⟩ a hidden grudge against Y; X harbors ill will ⟨evil intentions⟩ toward Y; X has it in for Y (secretly).**

К-40 • КÁМЕНЬ НА ДУШÉ ⟨НÁ СЕРДЦЕ, НА СÉРДЦЕ⟩ *у кого* [NP; sing only; often VP$_{subj}$ with copula] s.o. feels sad, depressed, aggrieved: у Х-а на душе камень ≃ **X's heart is heavy; X has a heavy heart; X's heart is like lead; there is a weight on X's heart.**

Отвязав лошадь, я шагом пустился домой. У меня на сердце был камень. Солнце казалось мне тускло, лучи его меня не грели (Лермонтов 1). I untethered my horse and set off slowly home. My heart was like lead, the sun seemed to have lost its brightness, and I felt no warmth from its rays (1c). ♦ «Хорошо, я замолчу, — сказал он, — только, ради бога, не уходите так, а то у меня на душе останется такой камень...» (Гончаров 1). "Very well, I shall say no more," he said. "Only, please, don't go away like this, or there will be such a weight on my heart!" (1b).

К-41 • КÁМЕНЬ НА ШÉЕ *(для кого)* [NP; sing only; often subj-compl with copula, nom or instrum (subj: human, collect, or abstr); fixed WO] a heavy burden (on s.o.): **millstone ⟨albatross⟩ (a)round s.o.'s neck.**

И вот однажды ему [деду] взбрело в голову, что мы с мамой для него — камень на шее... «Живите за стенкой сами по себе, а я буду вещи менять, богатую бабу искать» (Кузнецов 1). Suddenly the idea came into his [Grandpa's] head that my mother and I were a millstone round his neck....«You live on your own, on your side of the partition, and I'll go bartering things and try to find a rich widow" (1b).

К-42 • КÁМЕНЬ ПРЕТКНОВÉНИЯ *lit* [NP; sing only; subj-compl with copula, nom or instrum (subj: abstr, concr, or human); fixed WO] an impediment, obstacle, difficulty: **stumbling block.**

По вечерам ходил я и в сад... Главный предмет занятий и разговоров было волокитство и подсматривание друг за другом... Я был страшным камнем преткновения для всей тайной полиции нашего сада, дамы и мужчины удивлялись моей скрытности... (Герцен 1). In the evenings I used to walk into the garden....The chief subject of talk and interest was flirtation and spying on one another....I was a terrible stumbling block for all the

secret police in our garden; the ladies and the men wondered at my reserve... (1a).

< From the Bible (Isa. 8:14, Rom. 9:32–33 et al.).

К-43 • КÁМЕНЬ ⟨КÁМЕНЬ *чего rare, lit*⟩ **С ДУШИ́ ⟨С СÉРДЦА⟩ СВАЛИ́ЛСЯ** *у кого* [VP$_{subj}$; usu. past] s.o. experienced a sense of relief, felt liberated from his worries: у Х-а камень с души свалился ≃ **a load ⟨a great weight⟩ was taken off X's mind; that was a load ⟨a great weight⟩ off X's mind; X's soul was relieved (of a tremendous load).**

«Подите сюда, — проговорил Ростов, хватая Телянина за руку... — Это деньги Денисова, вы их взяли...» — прошептал он ему над ухом. «Что?.. Что?.. Как вы смеете? Что?..» — проговорил Телянин. Но эти слова звучали жалобным, отчаянным криком и мольбой о прощении. Как только Ростов услыхал этот звук голоса, с души его свалился огромный камень сомнения (Толстой 4). "Come here," said Rostov, seizing Telyanin by the arm....«That is Denisov's money—you took it," he whispered in his ear. "What? What? How dare you! What?" babbled Telyanin. But the words came out like a piteous, despairing cry and a plea for a pardon. As soon as Rostov heard the sound of his voice, his soul was relieved of a tremendous load of doubt (4a).

К-44 • КРАЕУГÓЛЬНЫЙ КÁМЕНЬ *чего lit* [NP; usu. sing; usu. subj-compl with copula, nom or instrum (subj: usu. abstr), obj-compl with считать etc (obj: usu. abstr), or obj of положить, заложить; fixed WO] the fundamental basis of sth., the most important part: **cornerstone.**

Он обнял совокупность явлений, лежавших в районе его духовного ока, и вынужден был согласиться, что весь мир стоит на этом краеугольном камне (Салтыков-Щедрин 2). With his mind's eye he encompassed the interdependence of every event within the circumference of his own experience and he was driven to admit that the whole world was balanced on that cornerstone (2a).

К-45 • ПОД ЛЕЖÁЧИЙ ⟨ЛЕЖÁЧ⟩ КÁМЕНЬ (И) ВОДÁ НЕ ТЕЧЁТ [saying] if a person makes no effort, he will make no progress, get nowhere (said when s.o. is inactive and does nothing toward attaining some goal, furthering some matter etc): ≃ **nothing ventured, nothing gained; no work, no money; no bees, no honey; no song, no supper; the sleeping fox catches no chickens.**

К-46 • ПРÓБНЫЙ КÁМЕНЬ *(кого-чего, для кого-чего) lit* [NP; sing only; usu. subj-compl with copula, nom or instrum (subj: abstr) or obj-compl with считать etc (obj: abstr); fixed WO] an action, event, circumstance etc that reveals the essence, characteristic qualities of s.o. or sth.: **touchstone.**

Социализм и реализм остаются до сих пор пробными камнями, брошенными на путях революции и науки (Герцен 1). Socialism and realism remain to this day the touchstones flung on the paths of revolution and science (1a).

К-47 • БРОСÁТЬ ⟨КИДÁТЬ⟩ КÁМЕШЕК ⟨КÁ-МЕШКИ, КÁМЕНЬ, КÁМНИ⟩ В *чей* **ОГОРÓД** coll [VP; subj: human] in conversation, to hint, usu. disapprovingly or ironically, at sth. concerning another person (who may or may not be present) without directly referring to that person: X бросает камешки в Y-ов огород ≃ [translations vary depending on the speaker's attitude—sarcastic, ironic, joking etc—toward the person in question] **X needles Y; X takes pokes at Y; X makes digs at Y; X takes shots at Y; X makes snide remarks about Y.** ○ **КÁМЕШЕК ⟨КÁМЕШКИ** и т. п.⟩ **В** *чей* **ОГОРÓД** [NP] ≃ **dig (at s.o.); snide remark (about s.o.);** ‖ это не в мой огород камешек? ≃ **that wasn't aimed ⟨directed⟩ at *me*, was it?; could that have been aimed ⟨directed⟩ at me?; you aren't referring to *me*, are you?;** ‖ это в чей огород камешек? ≃ **at**

whom is that ⟨could that be⟩ aimed ⟨directed⟩?; to whom are you referring?

[author's usage] [Лиза:] Я говорю: представьте, маменька, он не имеет никакой политики в разговоре и даже такие слова говорит, что совсем неучтиво. [Разлюляев:] Это не в наш ли огород? [Лиза:] Не об вас речь (Островский 2). [L.:] So I said: Fancy that, mama! No tact when he talks to you—why, he even uses impolite words. [R.:] That aimed at me? [L.:] Pooh! I'm not even *thinking* about you (2b).

К-48 • **КА́МНИ ВОПИЮ́Т/ВОЗОПИ́ЛИ** *lit* [VP$_{subj}$; fixed WO] (sth. is so horrendous, monstrous that) even stones, if they could speak, would express their indignation: камни возопиют ≃ **the stones would cry out.**

< From the Bible (Luke 19:40).

К-49 • **ПОДВО́ДНЫЕ КА́МНИ ⟨КА́МЕШКИ⟩** [NP; sing rare; fixed WO] unseen, concealed difficulties, obstacles, dangers: **pitfalls; hidden dangers ⟨catches⟩.**

К-50 • **КА́МНЯ НА КА́МНЕ НЕ ОСТАВЛЯ́ТЬ/НЕ ОСТА́ВИТЬ ⟨НЕ ОСТАЁТСЯ/НЕ ОСТА́ЛОСЬ⟩** *от чего lit, rhet* [VP (1st var.), VP$_{subj/gen}$ (2nd var.); more often pfv past; the verb may take the initial position] **1.** [subj: human or collect (1st var.)] to destroy sth. (or sth. is destroyed) totally, mercilessly: X камня на камне не оставил от Y-a ≃ **X did not leave ⟨X left not⟩ one stone standing (upon another); X razed Y to the ground;** ‖ от Y-a камня на камне не осталось ≃ **not one stone was left standing (upon another); no stone was left standing; there was not one stone left upon another; Y was razed to the ground.**

Целый день преследовали маленькие негодяи злосчастную вдову… покуда она не пришла в исступление и не начала прорицать. Смысл этих прорицаний объяснился лишь впоследствии, когда в Глупов прибыл Угрюм-Бурчеев и не оставил в городе камня на камне (Салтыков-Щедрин 1). The little rascals pursued the ill-fated widow for a whole day…until at last she went into a frenzy and began to prophesy. The meaning of her prophecies became clear only later, when Gloom-Grumblev arrived in Foolov and razed it to the ground (1a). ♦ Приходит еврей к раввину и спрашивает: «Ребе, ты мудрый человек, скажи: будет война или не будет?» — «Войны не будет, — отвечает ребе, — но будет такая борьба за мир, что камня на камне не останется» (Буковский 1). …A Jew goes to his rabbi and asks: "Rabbi, you are a very wise man. Tell me, is there going to be a war or not?" "There will be no war," replies the rabbi, "but there will be such a struggle for peace that no stone will be left standing" (1a). ♦ После недолгих колебаний он решил так: сначала разрушить город, а потом уже приступить и к реке… Через полтора или два месяца он не оставлял уже камня на камне (Салтыков-Щедрин 1). After brief vacillation he decided: destroy the town first, and then start on the river.…After a month or two there was not one stone left upon another (1a).

2. [subj: human or abstr (1st var.)] to disprove, rebut sth. (or sth. is disproved, rebutted) thoroughly, unequivocally: X камня на камне не оставил от Y-a ≃ **X left nothing of Y; X tore ⟨cut⟩ Y to pieces;** ‖ от Y-a камня на камне не осталось ≃ **nothing was left of Y; Y was torn ⟨cut⟩ to pieces.**

Всё попало под удар переменных измерений, под губительные лучи той теории относительности, что вдохновила нашего пастора на дерзкую вивисекцию и не оставила камня на камне от подопытного кролика… (Терц 3). Everything was exposed to these variable dimensions, to the fatal rays of a relativity theory which inspired the good Dean to a vivisection so daring that nothing was left of his guinea-pig…(3a).

< From the Bible (Matt. 24:2, Mark 13:2).

К-51 • **ХРОНОЛОГИ́ЧЕСКАЯ КАНВА́** *lit* [NP; sing only; usu. this WO] a consecutive listing of facts pertaining to a specific historical period, the life and activities of a well-known figure etc: **chronological outline; chronology.**

К-52 • **ТЯНУ́ТЬ ⟨РАЗВОДИ́ТЬ/РАЗВЕСТИ́⟩ КАНИ́ТЕЛЬ** *coll, disapprov* [VP; subj: human] **1.** to be very slow in doing sth., delay sth. intentionally: X тянет канитель ≃ **X is dragging it ⟨things⟩ out; X is dragging his feet; X is stalling.**

«Вечером со сватами приду, — объявил Егорша… — Чего тут канитель разводить? Ты войди в моё положение. Мне так и эдак жениться надо» (Абрамов 1). "This evening I'm coming over with the matchmakers," announced Egorsha.…"Why drag it out? Put yourself in my position. One way or another I'm going to have to get married" (1a).

2. to talk for a long time in a monotonous, boring manner: X тянул канитель ≃ **X went ⟨droned⟩ on and on.**

К-53 • **ИДТИ́/ПОЙТИ́ В КАНО́ССУ** *lit* [VP; subj: human; often neg] to forsake one's pride and humble o.s. before s.o., acknowledging one's defeat: X в Каноссу не пойдёт ≃ **X will not go to Canossa.**

< From the name of a castle in Italy where the Holy Roman emperor Henry IV of Germany did penance before Pope Gregory VII in 1077.

К-54 • **НЕБЕ́СНАЯ КАНЦЕЛЯ́РИЯ** *recent, coll, humor or iron* [NP; sing only; subj or obj] forces seemingly in control of nature: **the Man Upstairs; the Powers That Be.**

«…Ведь нас не так уж много, старик, — мы все на учёте в небесной канцелярии» (Аксёнов 6). [context transl] "…After all, there aren't so many of us left, old man. We're all numbered in the Big Ledger in the sky" (6a).

К-55 • **КАПИТА́Л ПРИОБРЕСТИ́ И НЕВИ́ННОСТЬ СОБЛЮСТИ́** [VP; subj: human; usu. infin with хочет(ся), можно etc; usu. this WO] to obtain advantage for o.s. (often material success or financial gain) without acting unethically or damaging one's reputation: X-у хочется и капитал приобрести и невинность соблюсти ≃ **X wants to have his cake and eat it too; X wants (to get ⟨to enjoy⟩) the best of both worlds.**

< From Mikhail Saltykov-Shchedrin's *Trifles of Life* («Мелочи жизни»), 1877, et al.

К-56 • **НЕ КА́ПЛЕТ** *над кем coll* [VP; impers; this form only] s.o. is not under time constraints, there is no reason why s.o. need hurry: над X-ом не каплет ≃ **X is not in any rush ⟨hurry⟩; [in limited contexts] what's the rush ⟨the hurry⟩?; where's the fire?; the sky isn't falling.**

[Анна Ивановна:] Что ж ты, бандурист, когда на мне женишься? [Гуслин:] А вот когда от Гордея Карпыча разрешение выйдет [*ungrammat* = выйдет]. Куда нам торопиться-то, над нами не каплет (Островский 2). [A.I.:] When are you going to marry me, my brave guitarist? [G.:] As soon as Gordei Karpych gives his permission. What's the hurry? The sky's not falling (2b).

К-57 • **ДО (ПОСЛЕ́ДНЕЙ) КА́ПЛИ ⟨КА́ПЕЛЬКИ⟩** *coll* [PrepP; these forms only; adv; usu. used with pfv verbs] **1. выпить, осушить** *что* ~ (to drink, drain) everything in one's glass, leaving nothing: **(down) to the last drop.**

…Арину Власьевну [Василий Иванович] заставил выпить рюмку до последней капельки (Тургенев 2). He [Vasily Ivanovich] made Arina Vlasievna drink her glassful down to the last drop (2f).

2. ~ **исчерпать, израсходовать (силы, энергию** и т. п.**), изучить, рассказать** *что* и т. п. completely, totally: исчерпать ⟨израсходовать⟩ силы ⟨энергию и т. п.⟩ ~ ≃ **spend one's strength ⟨energy etc⟩ to the last drop; utterly exhaust o.s.;** ‖ изучить *что* ~ ≃ **learn sth. down to the smallest detail; learn sth. inside out;** ‖ рассказать всё ~ ≃ **recount everything down to the last detail.**

Это было поразительное ощущение – дядя Митя стоял перед ним в дверях, старый, несчастный, уничтоженный человек, тративший в день до капли свои силы, чтобы больше никогда не быть униженным (Битов 2). It was an astonishing sensation – Uncle Mitya stood before him in the doorway, an old, unhappy, destroyed man, who spent his day's strength, to the last drop, on never again being humiliated... (2a).

К-58 • ДО ПОСЛЕ́ДНЕЙ КА́ПЛИ КРО́ВИ биться, сражаться, бороться и т. п. [PrepP; Invar; adv; used with impfv verbs; fixed WO] (to fight, struggle etc) sacrificing everything (and, in contexts involving physical conflict, not sparing one's own life): **to the last drop of one's blood; to the death.**

«Вы заступаетесь за этих бабёнок?» – «Не за бабёнок, а за права женщин, которые я поклялась защищать до последней капли крови» (Тургенев 2). "Are you going to stand up for those silly females?" "Not for silly females, no, but for the rights of women which I have sworn to defend to the last drop of my blood" (2a).

К-59 • КАК ДВЕ КА́ПЛИ ВОДЫ́ похож(ий), походить *на кого-что* и т. п.; **ДВЕ КА́ПЛИ ВОДЫ́** *both coll* [(как +) NP; these forms only; usu. modif or adv (1st var.) or subj-compl with быть∅, subj: human (2nd var.); fixed WO] (resembling s.o. or sth.) very closely, (looking) completely alike: **like ⟨as (a)like as⟩ two peas (in a pod); the spitting ⟨the spit and⟩ image of; carbon copy of; perfect facsimile of.**

«Когда ты в кабинете говорил, я смотрела на тебя, – заговорила Наташа, видимо стараясь отогнать набежавшее облако. – Ну, две капли воды ты на него похож, на мальчика». (Она так называла сына.) (Толстой 7). "...While you were talking in the study I was looking at you," Natasha began, obviously trying to dispel the cloud that had come over them. "You are as like as two peas – two peas – just like the boy." (She meant their little son.) (7a). ♦ Хозяйка дома выбежала сама на крыльцо... [Она] походила, как две капли воды, на Платонова... (Гоголь 3). The mistress of the house herself ran out on the front steps. She...and Platonov were as like as two peas in a pod... (3b). ♦ «Да посмотрите на меня! – кричала Берта, похожая на своего отца, как две капли воды, – посмотрите на меня! Какая я узбечка? Какая я русская? Я – негритянка и хочу быть негритянкой!» (Аллилуева 2). "But look at me!" cried Bertha, who was the spit and image of her father. "Look at me: What kind of Uzbek or Russian am I? I am a Negro and I want to remain a Negro!" (2a). ♦ [author's usage] Для зачтения доклада в помощь Заибану рационализаторы изготовили Робота, как две капли похожего на Заибана (Зиновьев 1). To help in the delivery of this speech by Leadiban the inventive and creative scientists made a Robot, a perfect facsimile of Leadiban himself (1a).

К-60 • КА́ПЛИ ⟨НИ КА́ПЛИ, МА́КОВОЙ РО-СИ́НКИ⟩ В РОТ НЕ БРАТЬ/НЕ ВЗЯТЬ *coll* [VP; subj: human; more often impfv; in var. with капли, капли always precedes the verb] not to drink alcohol at all: X капли в рот не берёт ≃ **X doesn't touch ⟨take⟩ a drop; X never touches ⟨takes⟩ a drop;** [in limited contexts] **X is a teetotaler.**

Начинаю понимать его тактику. И до меня постепенно доходит, что министерский ум в данном случае не у моего брата Лёвы, а у пропойцы Терещенко, который, кстати сказать, во время процесса не взял в рот ни капли... (Рыбаков 1). I began to understand his tactics, and to see that it wasn't Lyova who had the mind of a politician, in this case, but the old boozer Tereshchenko, who, incidentally, didn't touch a drop during the entire trial... (1a). ♦ «Вот что значит трезвость, – отвечал мне

старик, – он капли вина в рот не берёт» (Герцен 1). "That's what sobriety does," the old man answered; "he never takes a drop of liquor" (1a).

К-61 • НИ КА́ПЛИ ⟨НИ КА́ПЕЛЬКИ⟩ *coll* [NP$_{gen}$; these forms only] **1.** ~ *чего* нет, не осталось и т. п. [quantif of subj/gen] (there is, there remains, s.o. has etc) absolutely none (of sth.): **not a ⟨one⟩ drop of; not an ounce ⟨a hint, a trace⟩ of; no [NP] at all.**

Я не чувствовал рук, они онемели на ледяном пруте, и у меня не оставалось ни капли силы, чтобы подтянуться (Кузнецов 1). I could not feel my hands – they were numb from the icy bar – and I had not a drop of strength left to pull myself up (1a). ♦ До сих пор я не знаю, как назвать это состояние... В нём не было ни капли восторженности. Наоборот, оно приносило покой и отдых (Паустовский 1). Even now I don't know what to call this mood....There was not a trace of exaltation in it. On the contrary, it brought peace and quiet (1b). ♦ «Видите: мы сперва это дело кончим, пистолеты-то, вы мне их отдайте, а вот ваши деньги... потому что мне очень, очень нужно... и времени, времени ни капли...» (Достоевский 1). "Look: first let's finish this business, the pistols, I mean, give them back to me, and here's your money...because I really, really must...and I have no time, no time at all..." (1a).

2. Also: **НИ НА КА́ПЛЮ ⟨КА́ПЕЛЬКУ⟩** *coll* [adv (intensif)] not at all, not to any extent: **not a bit; not the least bit; not in the least ⟨the slightest⟩.**

Господи! За тридцать лет она [тётка] не изменилась ни капли (Битов 1). My God, in thirty years she [Auntie] hasn't changed a bit (1a). ♦ «Дурачок, ты много выпил». – «Я ни капельки не пьяный» (Максимов 3). "You've had too much to drink, silly." "I'm not the least bit drunk" (3a). ♦ [Генрих:] Тебя это не тревожит? [Бургомистр:] Ни капельки (Шварц 2). [H.:] Tell me, doesn't this worry you? [Mayor:] Not in the least (2a).

К-62 • НА КА́ПЛЮ ⟨НА КА́ПЕЛЬКУ⟩ *чего (у кого, в ком) coll* [PrepP; these forms only; quantit subj-compl with copula (subj/gen: abstr) or quantif of subj/gen] s.o. has a very small amount (of some quality, skill etc): **(hardly) an ounce (of [NP]); next to no [NP].**

К-63 • КА́ПЛЯ В КА́ПЛЮ похож(ий), походить *на кого-что coll* [Invar; modif or adv; fixed WO] (resembling s.o. or sth.) very closely; completely alike: **like ⟨as (a)like as⟩ two peas (in a pod); carbon copy of; the spitting ⟨the spit and⟩ image of; perfect facsimile of; identical; exactly alike.**

К-64 • КА́ПЛЯ В МО́РЕ *coll* [NP; sing only; usu. subj-compl with copula, nom or instrum (subj: usu. inanim, occas. human); fixed WO] an insignificant amount (when compared with the amount that is needed, was previously available etc): **drop in the bucket ⟨in the ocean⟩.**

«По моим подсчётам, на книгах, присланных Саней, Реваз получил прибыли не меньше двадцати тысяч. Но это капля в море» (Чернёнок 2). "According to my calculations, Revaz made at least twenty thousand on the books Sanya sent him. But that's a drop in the bucket" (2a). ♦ Среди них, конечно, найдётся несколько человек, которые всё поймут. Но это – капля в море (Зиновьев 1). Of course there are among them a few people who will understand everything. But they are a drop in the ocean (1a).

К-65 • КА́ПЛЯ ЗА КА́ПЛЕЙ; (КА́ПЛЯ) ПО КА́ПЛЕ; ПО КА́ПЛЯМ [these forms only; adv; usu. used with impfv verbs; fixed WO] gradually, slowly, by degrees: **drop by drop; bit by bit; little by little.**

[Ольга:] И в самом деле, за эти четыре года, пока служу в гимназии, я чувствую, как из меня выходят каждый день по каплям и силы и молодость (Чехов 5). [О.:] And really, all these four years while I've been working at school, I've felt as though my strength and my youth were draining out of me drop by drop (5b).

К-66 • **КА́ПЛЯ** ⟨**ЧАСТИ́ЦА**⟩ **МОЕГО́** ⟨**твоего и т. п.**⟩ **МЁДУ есть** *в чём coll, often humor* [NP; sing only; VP$_{subj}$ with быть; fixed WO] I (you etc) also participated in sth., contributed to sth.: **I** ⟨**you etc**⟩ **had a hand in it, too; I** ⟨**you etc**⟩ **had a finger in the pie; I** ⟨**you etc**⟩ **made a** ⟨**my, your etc**⟩ **contribution (to sth.)**; [in limited contexts] **I** ⟨**you etc**⟩ **put in my** ⟨**your etc**⟩ **two cents' worth.**

< From Ivan Krylov's fable "Eagle and Bee" («Орёл и Пчела»), 1813.

К-67 • **ПОСЛЕ́ДНЯЯ КА́ПЛЯ; КА́ПЛЯ, ПЕРЕПОЛ-НИ́ВШАЯ ЧА́ШУ** *lit* [NP; sing only; usu. subj-compl with copula, nom or instrum (subj: abstr); fixed WO] the final (often minor) aggravation that, when added to existing troubles, makes the situation unbearable, forces s.o. to lose his patience etc: **the last straw; the straw that broke the camel's back.**

И вот однажды появился по всем поселённым единицам приказ, возвещавший о назначении шпионов. Это была капля, переполнившая чашу... (Салтыков-Щедрин 1). One day an order proclaiming the appointment of spies appeared in all settlement units. This was the last straw... (1a).

К-68 • **РУБИ́ТЬ/ИЗРУБИ́ТЬ В КАПУ́СТУ** *кого;* **ИЗ-РУБИ́ТЬ** ⟨**ИСКРОШИ́ТЬ**⟩ **В ЛАПШУ́** *all coll* [VP; subj: human or collect] to kill, destroy s.o. (usu. in refer. to killing one's enemy with a saber etc; often used as a threat): X изрубит Y-a в капусту ≃ **X will make mincemeat (out) of Y; X will cut** ⟨**tear, rip**⟩ **Y to shreds** ⟨**to ribbons, to pieces**⟩.

[Варравин:] Если бы он теперь мне в лапу попался, да я бы его, мошенника, в лапшу искрошил... (Сухово-Кобылин 3). [V.:] If he fell into my clutches now, I'd make mincemeat out of the bastard... (3a).

К-69 • **БРАТЬ/ВЗЯТЬ НА КАРАНДА́Ш** *что* [VP; subj: human; usu. this WO] to write sth. down (in order to remember it later): X берёт Y на карандаш ≃ **X makes a note of Y; X notes Y (down); X jots down Y; X takes notes (on Y)**; [in limited contexts] **X reaches for a pencil.**

Он [писатель] был неплохой парень, и мы все к нему быстро привыкли, только неприятно было, что он всё берёт на карандаш (Аксёнов 1). He [the writer] wasn't a bad guy, and we all quickly got used to him, only it was annoying the way he was always reaching for a pencil (1a).

К-70 • **В КАРАНДАШЕ́** (**выполнить, сделать рисунок, чертёж** и т. п.) [PrepP; Invar; adv or nonagreeing postmodif] (to do a drawing, produce a draft etc) using a pencil: **(do a drawing** ⟨**a sketch is done etc**⟩**) in pencil; (do) a pencil (sketch** etc**); pencil (a drawing** etc**).**

К-71 • **БРАТЬ/ВЗЯТЬ** ⟨**ДЕ́ЛАТЬ/СДЕ́ЛАТЬ**⟩ **НА КА-РАУ́Л** *mil* [VP; subj: human or collect; fixed WO] to salute s.o. with a particular rifle maneuver: X взял на караул ≃ **X presented arms.**

Часовой у комендатуры, из новичков, в необмятом пыльнике и в берете, натянутом на уши, сделал ей «на караул» (Стругацкие 2). The sentry in front of the CO's headquarters, a recent recruit wearing an unwrinkled trench coat and a beret pulled down over his ears, presented arms (2a).

К-72 • **КРИЧА́ТЬ КАРАУ́Л** *coll* [VP; subj: human] **1.** Also: **КРИ́КНУТЬ** ⟨**ЗАКРИЧА́ТЬ**⟩ **КАРАУ́Л** to call out for help when in danger: X кричал караул ≃ **X cried (out) for help; X screamed** ⟨**shouted**⟩ **for help.**

...Он потребовал от Петрухи: «Кричи». — «Чё [*ungrammat* = что] кричи?» — не понял тот. — «Что хошь [*ungrammat* = хочешь!] кричи. Хоть караул. Есть же тут где-то живые люди или что?» (Распутин 4). ...He told Petrukha: "Shout." "Shout what?" He didn't understand. "Whatever you want. Scream for help if you want. There are living people around here somewhere" (4a).

2. to call others' attention to some trouble, transgression etc in an attempt to enlist their intervention: X кричит караул ≃ **X sounds** ⟨**raises**⟩ **the alarm; X sounds the alert**; [in limited contexts] **X cries foul.**

К-73 • **ПОЧЁТНЫЙ КАРАУ́Л** [NP; sing only; fixed WO] a special body of persons designated to show great respect, veneration for s.o. on ceremonial occasions: **guard of honor; honor guard.**

Народу было ещё не слишком много. По углам гроба бесшумно сменялся почётный караул (Катаев 3). There were still not too many people present. The guard of honor changed silently at each corner of the coffin (3a).

К-74 • **ХОТЬ КАРАУ́Л КРИЧИ́** *coll* [хоть + VP$_{imper}$; Invar; predic or subord clause; usu. this WO] (used to express despair, helplessness) the situation is so trying, hopeless that some person feels desperate: **you** ⟨**he etc**⟩ **could just cry** ⟨**scream, climb the walls**⟩**; it's enough to make you** ⟨**him** etc⟩ **cry** ⟨**scream, climb the walls**⟩.

К-75 • **КАРАЧУ́Н ПРИШЁЛ** *кому obs, substand* [VP$_{subj}$; fixed WO] s.o. suddenly died: X-у карачун пришёл ≃ **X up and died; X cashed in (his chips).**

К-76 • **СТА́РАЯ КАРГА́** *highly coll, rude* [NP; sing only; fixed WO] an insulting name for an old woman: **old bag** ⟨**hag, bat, crone**⟩.

«Чего смотрите, как сычи? Ну, кто святой, плюнь на меня... А ты что, старая карга, губами жуёшь?» (Максимов 3). "What are you staring at like owls? Spit on me, then—if you're such saints....And what are you mouthing and mumbling about, you old bag?" (3a).

К-77 • **ВЫ́ТРЯСТИ КАРМА́Н** *substand;* **ВЫВОРА́ЧИ-ВАТЬ/ВЫ́ВЕРНУТЬ КАРМА́НЫ** *coll* [VP; subj: human] **1. вытрясти карман** *чей, у кого;* **выворачивать карманы** *чьи, кому* to make s.o. spend all his money: X вытряс Y-ов карман ≃ **X emptied Y's pockets; X cleaned Y out.**

2. Also: **ВЫВОРА́ЧИВАТЬ/ВЫ́ВЕРНУТЬ СВОЙ КАРМА́НЫ** to spend or give away all one's money: X вывернул карманы ≃ **X emptied his pockets; woman X emptied her purse; X gave (person Y) everything** ⟨**all**⟩ **X had.**

[Золотуев:] Нашёл он того ревизора и даёт ему с перепугу всё, что у него было. Все карманы вывернул (Вампилов 3). [Z.:] He finds that inspector and out of fright gives him everything he's got. Empties all his pockets (3b). ♦ Анна Андреевна пошла к Булгаковым и вернулась, тронутая поведением Елены Сергеевны, которая заплакала, услышав о высылке, и буквально вывернула карманы (Мандельштам 1). Akhmatova went to the Bulgakovs and returned very touched by the reaction of Elena Sergeyevna, Bulgakov's wife, who burst into tears when she heard about our exile and gave us everything she had (1a).

К-78 • **ДЕРЖИ́ КАРМА́Н** ⟨**ШИ́РЕ**⟩ *highly coll* [imper sent; these forms only; fixed WO] (used in refer. to false expectations, calculations etc) do not hope for or count on sth., it is not or will not be so: **not a chance; don't bet on it; don't hold your breath; (there's) no way (in hell); like** ⟨**the**⟩ **hell I** ⟨**he etc**⟩ **will** ⟨**am etc**⟩**; fat chance!; I wouldn't be too** ⟨**so**⟩ **sure.**

«Только и подходит ко мне самый этот молодец: „Слепа, бабушка?.. А отчего, мол, ты слепа?" — „От бога, говорю, ваше высокое благородие". – „Какой тут бог, от воспы [*nongrammat* = оспы], чай?" – это он-то всё говорит. „А воспа-то, говорю, от кого же?" – „Ну да, от бога, держи карман! Вы, говорит, в сырости да в нечистоте всю жизнь копаетесь, а бог виноват!"» (Салтыков-Щедрин 1). "Just then this same fellow comes up to me. 'Blind, grandma?...And what made you blind?' says he. 'God, Your Worship,' says I. 'What's God got to do with it! It was the smallpox, probably?' That's what he keeps saying. 'And who,' I say, 'sent the smallpox?' 'God?' he says, 'not a chance! You people root around in dampness and dirt all your lives, and God's to blame!'" (1a). ♦ [Лорд:] Ну, вот что. Коротко. Нам сейчас нужно отплывать в Европу. Пойми, король, что у тебя был жулик. [Сизи:] Ах, ах! Дух Вайдуа его накажет. [Гаттерас:] Конечно, держи карман шире (Булгаков 1). [L.:] Well, here's what we'll do. In brief. We have to sail back to Europe right now. Please understand, King, that you had a swindler here. [S.:] Oh! Oh! The spirit of Vaydua will punish him! [H.:] Don't hold your breath (1a). ♦ [Пищик:] Отдам, милая... Сумма пустяшная... [Любовь Андреевна:] Ну, хорошо, Леонид даст... Ты дай, Леонид. [Гаев:] Дам я ему, держи карман (Чехов 2). [P.:] I'll pay you back, dear lady. Such a trifling sum. [L.A.:] Oh, all right. Leonid will let you have it. Let him have it, Leonid. [G.:] Let him have it? The hell I will (2b).

K-79 • ЗАЛЕЗА́ТЬ/ЗАЛЕ́ЗТЬ В КАРМА́Н *чей, (к) кому coll, disapprov* [VP; subj: human] to make illegal, fraudulent use of s.o.'s goods, rob s.o.: X залезает к Y-у в карман ≃ **X slips ⟨has, puts⟩ his hand in Y's pocket ⟨purse⟩; X puts ⟨has⟩ his hand in the till.**

Жулик никому не доверяет, никому не позволяет себя надуть, а сам надувает всех... а у честного лопуха – недостача, он горит, и бухгалтер горит, и директор горит, хотя все они честнейшие люди и не залезали в государственный карман (Рыбаков 1). A crook trusts nobody, he doesn't let anyone con him, he does the conning....But if an honest scatterbrain shows one shortage, he's had it, the accountant's had it, the manager's had it, all of them absolutely honest and none of them with his hand in the state's purse (1a).

K-80 • КЛАСТЬ/ПОЛОЖИ́ТЬ (себе) В КАРМА́Н *что coll* [VP; subj: human; obj: a noun denoting money] to take money (or, less often, goods) as one's own (often in situations when one is not entitled to it, has not earned it, or is acting unscrupulously in appropriating it): X положил (себе) в карман Y ≃ **X put Y in(to) his (own) pocket; X pocketed Y; X filled his (own) pockets with Y; X helped himself to Y.**

Администратор... экономил командировочные деньги, доставал фиктивные гостиничные счета, а разницу в деньгах клал к себе в карман (Искандер 2). ...The manager economized on travel expenses, got fictitious hotel bills, and put the difference – in cash – into his own pocket (2a). ♦ «...Разбой, говорю, не тот делает, кто берёт провиант, чтобы кормить своих солдат, а тот, кто берёт его, чтобы класть в карман!» (Толстой 5). "'A [robber],' I tell him, 'is not a man who takes [provisions] to feed his soldiers, but a man who steals to fill his own pockets'" (5a).

K-81 • НАБИВА́ТЬ/НАБИ́ТЬ КАРМА́Н ⟨МОШНУ́, КОШЕЛЁК⟩ *substand* [VP; subj: human] to become rich, make a fortune (usu. by dishonest means): X набил карман ≃ **X lined ⟨filled⟩ his pockets; X stuffed his pockets full of money; [in limited contexts] X feathered his nest.**

Пока он крал, делал всякие сделки и махинации да набивал себе карман, никто его не трогал, всё ему с рук сходило (Буковский 1). While he was stealing, fixing deals and other illicit operations, and filling his pockets, nobody touched him and he got away scot-free (1a). ♦ [Городничий:] Ещё мальчишка, «Отче наша» не знаешь, а уж обмериваешь; а как разопрёт тебе брюхо да набьёшь себе карман, так и заважничал! (Гоголь 4). [Mayor:] When you are small boys, before you can repeat the Lord's Prayer, you know how to give short measure. And as soon as you grow

a big belly and stuff your pockets full of money, you start giving yourself airs (4c).

K-82 • ТО́ЛСТЫЙ ⟨ТУГО́Й⟩ КАРМА́Н ⟨КОШЕЛЁК⟩ *(у кого)*; ТО́ЛСТАЯ ⟨ТУГА́Я⟩ МОШНА́ *all coll* [NP; usu. sing; fixed WO except when used as VP$_{subj}$ with быть$_\varnothing$] s.o. has a lot of money: у X-а толстый карман ≃ **X has a fat wallet; X has a big thick wallet; X is rolling in money; X has money to burn; X has deep pockets.**

K-83 • ТО́ЩИЙ ⟨ПУСТО́Й⟩ КАРМА́Н ⟨КОШЕЛЁК⟩ *(у кого) coll* [NP; usu. sing; fixed WO except when used as VP$_{subj}$ with быть$_\varnothing$] s.o. has very little or no money: у X-а тощий карман ≃ **X's pockets are empty; X is hard up (for money ⟨cash⟩).**

K-84 • В КАРМА́НЕ *у кого coll* [PrepP; Invar; subj-compl with быть$_\varnothing$ (subj: usu. concr or, less often, human)] sth. is sure to be gotten by s.o., sth. is guaranteed to s.o.: X у Y-а в кармане ≃ **X is as good as in Y's pocket; thing X is in the bag; Y can count X Y's (own); X is a sure thing.**

«...Сударыня, эти три тысячи, которыми вы так великодушно меня обещали ссудить...» – «Вас не минуют, Дмитрий Фёдорович, – тотчас же перерезала госпожа Хохлакова, – эти три тысячи всё равно что у вас в кармане, и не три тысячи, а три миллиона...» (Достоевский 1). "Madame, this three thousand, which you have so generously promised to lend me..." "You will get it, Dmitri Fyodorovich," Madame Khokhlakov at once cut him short, "you may consider it as good as in your pocket, and not three thousand, but three million..." (1a).

K-85 • БИТЬ ⟨УДАРЯ́ТЬ/УДА́РИТЬ⟩ ПО КАРМА́НУ *кого coll* [VP; subj: human or abstr] to cause s.o. financial damage, loss: X ударил Y-а по карману ≃ **X hit Y in the ⟨Y's⟩ wallet ⟨pocketbook⟩; thing X made (quite) a dent in Y's wallet ⟨budget⟩.**

...С Образцовым [я] решил рассчитаться – не убить, как предлагал Гаврилыч, но ударить по карману... самому больному его месту (Амальрик 1). I had decided to settle accounts with him: not to kill him, as the old zek Gavrilych had suggested, but...to hit him where it would hurt him the most – in his wallet (1a).

K-86 • НЕ ПО КАРМА́НУ *кому coll* [PrepP; Invar; subj-compl with copula (subj: concr or abstr); used without negation to convey the opposite meaning] sth. is too expensive for s.o.: X Y-у не по карману ≃ **X is beyond Y's means; X is more than Y can afford; Y can't afford X; X is out of Y's reach ⟨(price) range⟩;** ‖ X Y-у по карману ≃ **X is within Y's means.**

«Я прожил жизнь», – сказал Эдик, отодвинув брезгливо тарелку с абсолютно непережёвываемым мясом и пюре из гнилой картошки... «Смотрите, что мы едим! А ведь это – одно из лучших кафе в Москве. Не всякому по карману такое!» (Зиновьев 2). "I have lived out my life," said Edik, pushing aside with distaste his plate of resolutely unchewable meat and mouldy mashed potatoes.... "Just look at what we're eating! And yet this is one of the best restaurants in Moscow, beyond most people's means!" (2a). ♦ Ни моим детям, ни большинству моих друзей я не разрешаю поездку за границу даже с туристской целью. Впрочем, такой туризм им и не по карману (Аллилуева 2). Neither my children nor the majority of my friends will be granted permission to go abroad even as tourists. None of them could afford a tourist trip anyway (2a). ♦ Открываю дверь – сзади ещё пассажирский салон, человек на 20 – и *совершенно пуст*! Ну, эта роскошь социализму по карману (Солженицын 2). I open the door and there behind is another passenger compartment with room for twenty – completely empty! Never mind; socialism can afford such luxuries (2a).

K-87 • КА́РТА БИ́ТА ⟨УБИ́ТА⟩ *чья, кого* [VP$_{subj}$ with быть$_\varnothing$; usu. pres; fixed WO] s.o. has experienced complete failure, ruin: X-ова карта бита ≃ **the game is over for X; the jig is up for X; X's ace has been trumped.**

...Что бы он [Демагог] ни думал и ни говорил, он невольно выталкивался на роль главаря одной из враждующих тенденций в жизни страны. И это не выдумка. Если бы даже всё это специально выдумали Хозяин и его приспешники, это стало реальностью. ...Иначе карта Демагога не была бы бита (Зиновьев 1). ...Whatever he [Demagogue] may have thought or said, he was involuntarily thrust into the position of leader of one of the warring tendencies in the life of the country. And that is not a fabrication. Even if all this had been specifically dreamt up by the Boss and his entourage, it would have become a reality. Otherwise Demagogue's ace would not have been trumped (1a).

К-88 • ПОСЛЕ́ДНЯЯ КА́РТА [NP; sing only; fixed WO] the last remaining possibility of changing the situation in s.o.'s favor: **last hope 〈chance, resort〉.**

К-89 • СТОЯ́ТЬ НА КА́РТЕ [VP; subj: usu. abstr] to be in jeopardy, at risk: X стоит на карте ≃ **X is on the line; X is at stake;** [of s.o.'s life] **X is 〈hangs, is hanging〉 in the balance.**

К-90 • КАК КАРТИ́НКА; КАК НА КАРТИ́НКЕ [как + NP or PrepP; these forms only; usu. subj-compl with copula (subj: human or concr) or modif] very beautiful: **(as) pretty as a picture 〈a postcard〉; (as) pretty as can be.**

К-91 • одет(ый) ПО КАРТИ́НКЕ *obs* [PrepP; Invar; modifier or adv] (dressed) in keeping with the latest fashion: **(dressed) in the latest finery; (be) a fashion plate.**

К-92 • НЕ КАРТО́ШКА *coll, humor* [NP; sing only; subj-compl with быть∅ (subj: abstr)] some serious, significant thing, no trifle: X не картошка ≃ **X is nothing to sneeze at; X is no laughing matter 〈no joke〉; X is not something to be fooled with.**

К-93 • СТА́ВИТЬ/ПОСТА́ВИТЬ ВСЁ НА ОДНУ́ КА́РТУ [VP; subj: human] to place all one's hopes in, base all one's plans on one person, thing, or event: X поставил всё на одну карту ≃ **X put all his eggs in(to) one basket.**

К-94 • СТА́ВИТЬ/ПОСТА́ВИТЬ НА КА́РТУ *что* [VP; subj: human or collect; obj: abstr (usu. жизнь, честь etc)] to risk one's life, reputation, security etc in the hope of winning or gaining sth.: X поставил на карту Y ≃ **X staked Y; X laid 〈put〉 Y on the line;** [in limited contexts] **X endangered Y;** ‖ Y поставлен на карту ≃ **Y is at stake;** ‖ X поставит всё на карту ≃ **X will risk it all; X will go for broke; X will lay it all on the line.**

...Двадцать раз жизнь свою, даже честь поставлю на карту... но свободы моей не продам (Лермонтов 1). ...Twenty times I can stake my life, even my honor, but my freedom I shall never sell (1b). ♦ ...Излагая столь ясно свои либеральные убеждения, он [Феденька] ведь и рисковал. Он ставил на карту всё своё административное будущее... (Салтыков-Щедрин 2). ...By declaring his liberal convictions in so uncompromising a way, Fedenka ran a certain risk. As a matter of fact, he endangered his whole administrative future... (2a). ♦ ...Конечно, у всех на языке одно слово «адвокат», и не просто адвокат, а адвокат из адвокатов — на карту поставлена жизнь отца (Рыбаков 1). Of course, everyone thought of the same thing, which was to get a lawyer, not just any lawyer, but the best in the business, as father's life was at stake (1a).

К-95 • УБИ́ТЬ 〈ПОБИ́ТЬ〉 КА́РТУ *(чью, кого)* [VP; subj: human or collect] by taking an appropriate course of action, to thwart s.o.'s plans, defeat s.o., ruin s.o.'s chances for success etc:

X убил Y-ову карту ≃ **X trumped Y's card;** ‖ Y-ова карта убита 〈бита〉 ≃ **Y's card is beaten.**

«Он [император] шёл с Родзянко и, проходя мимо меня... сказал по-английски: "Вот моя славная гвардия. Ею в своё время я побью карту Вильгельма"» (Шолохов 2). "He [the Emperor] came in with Rodzyanko and as he passed he...said in English, 'These are my gallant guardsmen. In due course I'll use them to trump Wilhelm's card'" (2a). ♦ «А я всё-таки скажу, что человек, который всю свою жизнь поставил на карту женской любви и, когда ему эту карту убили, раскис и опустился до того, что ни на что не стал способен, этакой человек — не мужчина...» (Тургенев 2). "I must say, though, that a man who has staked his whole life on the card of a woman's love and who, when that card is beaten, falls to pieces and lets himself go to the dogs—a fellow like that is not a man..." (2a).

К-96 • ДЕРЖА́ТЬ КА́РТЫ К ОРДЕНА́М *coll* [VP; subj: human; fixed WO with the verb movable] to be secretive, keep one's plans, intentions to o.s.: X держит карты к орденам ≃ **X holds 〈keeps, plays〉 his cards close to his 〈the〉 chest 〈vest〉; X plays (it) close to the vest.**

К-97 • (И) КА́РТЫ 〈КНИ́ГИ〉 В РУ́КИ *кому coll* [sent; these forms only; fixed WO] s.o.'s knowledge, experience etc make him best suited for some job, task: X-у и карты в руки ≃ **this is right up X's alley; this is X's department 〈specialty〉; this is (right) in X's line; X is just the person (to do sth.).**

Молись! Молись — тебе говорят, пьяная рожа! Как это — забыл? Откуда я знаю? Это ты должен знать! Ты — человек, а не я. Тебе и карты в руки. А мне нельзя, не полагается (Терц 5). Pray! Say your prayers, I tell you, you drunken bastard! What do you mean, you've forgotten them? How am I supposed to know? It's you who have to know. It's you who's human, not me. This is right up your alley. I'm not allowed to; it's not done (5a).

К-98 • ПУ́ТАТЬ/СПУ́ТАТЬ 〈ПОПУ́ТАТЬ, МЕША́ТЬ/СМЕША́ТЬ〉 (ВСЕ) КА́РТЫ *чьи, кого, кому* [VP; subj: human or abstr] to thwart, frustrate s.o.'s plans, designs: X спутал Y-у (все) карты ≃ **X spoiled Y's game; X upset Y's applecart; X spiked Y's guns.**

Уверен, тебя не пустят и на общую выставку, ибо ты спутаешь им карты (Зиновьев 1). "...I'm sure they won't let you anywhere near a general exhibition, because you'd spoil their game" (1a).

К-99 • РАСКРЫВА́ТЬ/РАСКРЫ́ТЬ 〈ОТКРЫВА́ТЬ/ОТКРЫ́ТЬ〉 (СВОЙ) КА́РТЫ *(кому, перед кем)* [VP; subj: human] to cease hiding one's plans, intentions: X раскрыл свои карты (Y-у) ≃ **X put 〈laid〉 his cards on the table; X showed his cards 〈his hand〉 (to Y); X tipped his hand; X revealed his cards (to Y);** ‖ *Neg* X не раскрывал карт ≃ **X played 〈kept, held〉 his cards close to the 〈his〉 chest 〈vest〉; X played (it) close to the vest.**

«Я поразился, что он раскрыл нынче свои карты... Знает, что взглядов этих из нас никто не может разделять, а для чего-то разоткровенничался» (Шолохов 3). "I was surprised that he put his cards on the table....He knows that none of us can possibly share these views, but for some reason he opened up" (3a). ♦ А приводят ли мои рассуждения о юморе к некоторой опасной потере чувства юмора? В таком случае беру свои слова назад. Или даже лучше — раскрываю карты. Эти страницы на самом деле написаны с одобрения самых высших инстанций для выявления людей, которые своими улыбками или тем более смехом... обнаруживают свою диалектическую неблагонадёжность (Искандер 4). Won't my discussion of humor lead to a certain dangerous loss of sense of humor? In that case I immediately take back my words. Or even better, I lay my cards on the table. These pages were actually written with the approval of the highest courts, in order to detect people who by smiling, or especially by laughing, reveal their dialectical unreliability (4a). ♦ «Пулемёт-чики – все поголовно большевики. Он [Бунчук] их сумел настроить. Я поразился, что он раскрыл нынче свои карты» (Шолохов 3). "The machine-gunners are Bolsheviks to the last man. He's [Bunchuk has] certainly succeeded in winning them over. I was astonished when he showed his hand today" (3b). ♦ «Стоит ли прежде времени раскрывать перед Юрием Павловичем [Демен-ским] наши карты? Деменский или потрясён случив-шимся, или хранит тайну…» (Чернёнок 1). "Should we reveal our cards to Yuri Pavlovich [Demensky] ahead of time? Demensky is either shocked by the incident or hiding a secret…" (1a).

К-100 • ДЕ́ЛАТЬ/СДЕ́ЛАТЬ КАРЬЕ́РУ [VP; subj: human] to progress steadily or strive to progress in one's job, ascending to a point where one has a good position and is considered a success in his chosen field: X сделал карьеру ≃ **X made himself a career; X made ⟨carved out⟩ a career for himself.**

Князь Иван Иваныч в конце прошлого столетия… сделал ещё в очень молодых летах блестящую карьеру (Толстой 2). While he was still very young at the end of the last century, Prince Ivan Ivanych had made himself a brilliant career… (2c). ♦ Этот генерал за короткий срок сделал головокружительную карьеру, потому что четыре года назад он носил ещё одну шпалу и командовал ротой. Но однажды ему крупно повезло… С тех пор дела его шли как по маслу (Войнович 2). The general had made a fabulous career for himself in a very short span of time. Four years before, he still wore only a single stripe and commanded a company. But then he had one great piece of luck.…From then on, things could not have gone better for him (2a).

К-101 • ЧТО КАСА́ЕТСЯ (до) кого-чего (, ТО…) var. with до obs [used as subord Conj, correlative] with respect to, concerning s.o. or sth.: что касается X-а ≃ **as for X; as far as X goes ⟨is concerned⟩; as regards X; as concerns X;** [in limited contexts] **for person X's part;** ‖ что касается меня ≃ **speaking for myself.**

Те [очевидцы], что остались, рассказывают по-разному, а некоторые и вовсе не помнят… Что касается меня, то я собрал в кучу всё, что слышал по данному поводу, и прибавил кое-что от себя, прибавил, может быть, даже больше, чем слышал (Войнович 2). Those [eyewitnesses] that are [left] tell all kinds of different stories and some can't remember anything at all.…As for me, I've heaped up everything I heard on the subject and added a little something of my own as well, could be I even added more than I heard (2a). ♦ «Что до меня касается, то я убеждён только в одном», – сказал доктор. «В чём это?» – спросил я. «В том, – отвечал он, – что рано или поздно в одно прекрасное утро я умру» (Лермонтов 1). "As far as I am concerned, I am sure only of one thing," said the doctor. "What's that?" I asked.…"That sooner or later," he replied, "one fine day I shall die…" (1d). ♦ Что касается двух пехотных рот, опять враньё (Искандер 3). As regards the two infantry companies—more lies (3a). ♦ Что касается до вну-треннего содержания «Летописца», то оно по преимуществу фантастическое… (Салтыков-Щедрин 1). As concerns the Chronicle's subject matter, it is for the most part fantastical… (1a).

К-102 • НЕ ОТХОДЯ́ ОТ КА́ССЫ coll [Verbal Adv; Invar; adv; fixed WO] at this (or that) moment and in this (or that) place: **right here; here and now; right there; there and then; on the spot; right away.**

«Почему сорван график…? Отвечайте, или я вас всех, не отходя от кассы, перестреляю, сукины сыны!» (Алешков-ский 1). "Who interrupted the schedule…? You tell me, or I'll blow your brains out right here, you s.o.b.'s!" (1a). ♦ Некоторые из тех женщин, у кого были небольшие сроки и кто успел выйти из лагеря ещё до начала войны, но без права выезда на ма-терик… перешагнув порог лагеря, стремительно вступали в колымские браки, абсолютно не стесняясь мезальянсов… Вот, например, новелла о том, как Соня Больц «вышла

замуж, не отходя от кассы» (Гинзбург 2). [context transl] Some of the women who had short sentences or who had managed to get out of the camps before the outbreak of war but without the right to return to the mainland…rushed headlong into Kolyma marriages as soon as they were through the camp gates, totally disregarding the possibility of mésalliances.…For example, there was the story of Sonya Bolts's "instantaneous" marriage (2a).

К-103 • НА ВСЮ ⟨ПО́ЛНУЮ⟩ КАТУ́ШКУ highly coll [PrepP; these forms only; adv (intensif); fixed WO] **1.** (one does sth. or, less often, sth. is operating) to one's or its full capacity, to the fullest extent possible: **to the fullest; to the max; giving it all ⟨everything⟩ one's got; giving it one's best shot; going (the) whole hog; with might and main;** [in refer. to volume or capacity] **(at) full blast;** ‖ жить ~ ≃ **make the most of one's life; live life to the fullest;** ‖ веселиться ⟨праздновать⟩ ~ ≃ **live ⟨whoop⟩ it up; have the time of one's life;** [in limited contexts] **have a big bash;** [of a party] **be in full swing;** ‖ влюбиться ~ ≃ **be ⟨fall⟩ head over heels in love; fall for s.o. hook, line, and sinker;** ‖ высказаться ~ ≃ **hold nothing back; leave nothing unsaid.**

Он мог опять привести её к себе, в свою комнату. …Но сдерживала примитивная мужская осторожность. Возобно-вить отношения – да. Но не на полную катушку (Рыбаков 2). [context transl] He'd be able to take her to his room again.…But he was restrained by a primitive male cautiousness. They would rekindle their affair, fine, but this time he wasn't going to get in too deep (2a).

2. наказать кого, взыскать с кого, влетело, досталось кому – и т. п. (to punish s.o., s.o. is punished etc) extremely severely: X-а наказали ⟨X-у влетело⟩ ~ ≃ **X got ⟨they gave X⟩ the full treatment ⟨the works⟩; X got it ⟨they gave it to X⟩ (but) good; they went hard on X; X was shown ⟨they showed X⟩ no mercy; they threw the book at X.**

«Воровал мой оголец, как ни попадя [ungrammat = всё, что попадётся]. Я тряпьё на базар таскала. Сколько верёвочке ни виться… Он подельников выгораживал, всё на себя взял, ему на всю катушку…» (Максимов 3). "He stole everything he could lay his hands on, this man of mine. I used to take it all down to the market to sell. It caught up with us in the end.…He wouldn't squeal on his mates, he took all the blame, so they gave him the full treat-ment…" (3a).

К-104 • ТРИ́ШКИН КАФТА́Н [NP; sing only; fixed WO] a situation in which rectifying one inadequacy, defect etc results in another inadequacy, defect etc: **rob(bing) Peter to pay Paul.**

< From Ivan Krylov's fable "Trishka's Coat" («Тришкин каф-тан»), 1815, in which Trishka attempts to patch his old coat by first cutting off a quarter of the sleeves to cover the elbows and then having to cut off the flaps and tails to lengthen the sleeves.

К-105 • В КА́ЧЕСТВЕ кого-чего [PrepP; Invar; Prep] in the function of: **as; in the ⟨one's⟩ capacity of; in one's capacity as; by way of; in one's role of.**

[Колесов:] Уверяю вас, я здесь не в качестве жениха (Вампилов 3). [K.:] I assure you, I am not here as a suitor (3a). ♦ Когда я, нарушив правила литературного тона, сам оказался в повествовании в качестве героя, то впервые как бы поколебалась социальная структура Лёвы… (Битов 2). When I violated literary etiquette by turning up in the narrative myself in the capacity of hero, it was as if Lyova's social structure had been shaken for the first time (2a). ♦ Пётр, который в качестве усовершенствованного слуги не подошёл к ручке барича, а только издали поклонился ему, снова скрылся под воротами (Тургенев 2). Pyotr, who in his role of superior modern servant had not come up to kiss the young master's hand but had merely bowed to him from a distance, disappeared once again through the gateway (2e).

К-106 • **БЕРЁЗОВАЯ КАША** *obs* [NP; sing only] punishment with a rod: **(get ⟨give s.o.⟩) the rod; (get ⟨give s.o.⟩) a taste of the rod; (get ⟨give s.o.⟩) a few strokes of the birch; (get ⟨give s.o.⟩) a (good) flogging.**

К-107 • **ГРЕ́ЧНЕВАЯ КА́ША САМА́ СЕБЯ́ ХВА́ЛИТ** [saying] an immodest person boasts about his own positive qualities, talents, and accomplishments: ≃ **you ⟨they etc⟩ are tooting ⟨blowing⟩ your ⟨their etc⟩ own horn; you ⟨they etc⟩ are patting yourself ⟨themselves etc⟩ on the back;** [in limited contexts, when the speaker considers s.o.'s self-praise unjustified] **every ass likes to hear himself bray.**

К-108 • **ЗАВА́РИВАЕТСЯ/ЗАВАРИ́ЛАСЬ КА́ША** *coll* [VP_subj; more often pfv] a difficult, troublesome, unpleasant matter is developing: **trouble is brewing; it is becoming an awful ⟨a terrible, a fine⟩ mess; things are getting out of hand.**

Только хорошо знавшие папу люди понимали и знали, что виноватое выражение у него от смущения... от того, что именно из-за него заварилась такая каша... (Рыбаков 1). [context transl] Only those who knew him [my father] well understood that his guilty expression came from the embarrassment...he felt at being the main cause...of this terrible mess... (1a).

К-109 • **КА́ША В ГОЛОВЕ́** *чьей, у кого coll* [NP; Invar; VP_subj with быть∅] s.o.'s thoughts are totally confused: у X-а в голове каша ≃ **X's head is in a muddle; X's thoughts are jumbled; X's brain is mush; X's head is full of mush.**

Множество мыслей вертелось у меня в голове... Меня должно было радовать то обстоятельство, что редактор появился у меня... Но, с другой стороны, роман ему мог не понравиться... Кроме того, я чувствовал, что самоубийство, прерванное на самом интересном месте, теперь уж не состоится... Вообще в голове была каша... (Булгаков 12). A host of thoughts whirled in my head....I should have been delighted at his [the editor's] coming to see me....On the other hand he might not like my novel....Apart from that I felt that my suicide, interrupted at the crucial point, was off....My head was in a thorough muddle... (12a).

К-110 • **КА́ША ВО РТУ** *у кого coll* [NP; Invar; VP_subj with быть∅, usu. pres] s.o. speaks unclearly, indistinctly: у X-а каша во рту ≃ **X sounds like ⟨as if⟩ he's got marbles in his mouth; X mumbles ⟨mutters⟩.**

К-111 • **КА́ШИ ⟨ПИ́ВА obs⟩ НЕ СВА́РИШЬ ⟨НЕ СВА́РИТЬ⟩** *с кем coll, disapprov* [VP; neg pfv fut, gener. 2nd pers sing не сваришь or infin (used as impers predic) only; fixed WO] you will not be able to reach an agreement, accomplish anything etc with s.o.: с X-ом каши не сваришь ≃ **you won't ⟨can't⟩ get anywhere with X; you'll get nowhere with X.**

К-112 • **КА́ШИ ПРО́СЯТ** *coll* [VP; subj: a noun denoting heavy, sturdy footwear or individual parts of shoes or boots; pres or past] s.o.'s boots (shoes etc) are in bad condition, in need of repair: X-ы каши просят ≃ **Xs need mending ⟨to be repaired⟩; Xs need to be taken to the shoemaker('s); Xs have holes in them; Xs are worn out.**

«Главное, у него тогда было платьишко скверное, штанишки наверх лезут, а сапоги каши просят» (Достоевский 1). "The main thing was that he had such shabby clothes then, and his pants were riding up, and his boots had holes in them" (1a).

К-113 • **МА́ЛО КА́ШИ ЕЛ/СЪЕЛ** *coll* [VP; subj: human; 2nd or 3rd pers; past only; fixed WO] one is (too) inexperienced, young etc (for sth.): X мало каши ел ≃ **X is (too) green; X is a greenhorn ⟨a tenderfoot⟩; X is (still) wet behind the ears.**

К-114 • **ТАСКА́ТЬ КАШТА́НЫ ИЗ ОГНЯ́** *для кого, кому lit* [VP; subj: human] to do sth. difficult, unpleasant, or dangerous while another enjoys the results of one's efforts: X таскает каштаны из огня для Y-а ≃ **X pulls Y's chestnuts out of the fire; X does Y's dirty work for Y.**

[author's usage] «...Кадровые офицеры – все негодяи, ей-богу! Вы ведь из казаков? Да? Вот вашими руками они и хотят каштанчики из огня таскать» (Шолохов 4). "...The regular officers, they're all scoundrels, honestly they are! You're a Cossack, aren't you? Well, they want to use you to do their dirty work for them" (4a).

< Loan translation of the French *tirer les marrons du feu* (from the fable "Le Singe et le chat" by Jean de La Fontaine, 1621–95).

К-115 • **ЗАВА́РИВАТЬ/ЗАВАРИ́ТЬ КА́ШУ** *coll* [VP; subj: human or collect; usu. pfv] to cause a situation that brings about troublesome or unpleasant consequences: X заварил кашу ≃ **X made ⟨stirred up, cooked up⟩ a (fine) mess; X made ⟨stirred up⟩ trouble.**

...Делая исключение для отца и матери, Миша постепенно преисполнился презрением к взрослым, заварившим кашу, которой они не в силах расхлебать (Пастернак 1). ...Making an exception only for his parents, he [Misha] gradually became contemptuous of all grownups who had made this mess and were unable to clear it up (1a). ♦ – Нет, надо уходить Андрею... Или выходить и сдаваться: когда по своей воле, надежды на пощаду больше... Какую заварил кашу... какую кашу... к чему! (Распутин 2). No, Andrei had to leave....Or come out and turn himself in: when it's voluntary, there's more hope of clemency....What a mess he stirred up...what a mess...and what for! (2a). ♦ [author's usage] «Казаки-то мутятся... Нашкодили, а зараз [Ukrainian = сейчас] побаиваются. Заварили мы кашу...» (Шолохов 3). "The Cossacks are worried....They've done the damage, and now they're afraid. We've cooked up a fine mess for ourselves" (3b).

< From the saying «Сам кашу заварил, сам и расхлёбывай». See К-118.

К-116 • **КА́ШУ ⟨-и⟩ МА́СЛОМ НЕ ИСПО́РТИШЬ** [saying] sth. good or useful cannot be harmful, even in large amounts: ≃ **butter never spoils the porridge; you can't spoil porridge with butter; you can't have too much of a good thing.**

...Товарищ Коба провозгласил первый тост: «Дорогие друзья, – сказал он, – я пригласил вас сюда для того, чтобы... отметить самую короткую ночь...» – «Ура!» – крикнул Вершилов. «Не спеши, – поморщился Коба. – ...Я также хочу провозгласить тост за самого мудрого нашего деятеля...» Вершилов на всякий случай хотел ещё раз крикнуть «ура», зная, что каши маслом не испортишь, но товарищ Коба на этот раз успел плюнуть прямо в открытый для выкрика рот (Войнович 5). Comrade Koba proposed the first toast. "Dear friends," he said, "I invited you here to celebrate...the shortest night of the year...." "Hurrah!" cried Vershilov. "Not so fast," said Comrade Koba, knitting his brows. "...I also want to propose a toast to our wisest statesman...." Vershilov was about to shout "Hurrah!" just to be on the safe side, realizing that butter never spoils the porridge, but this time Comrade Koba managed to spit directly into Vershilov's open mouth (5a).

К-117 • **РАСХЛЁБЫВАТЬ КА́ШУ** *coll* [VP; subj: human or collect; often with пусть, надо, нужно, приходится etc] to rectify a difficult, troublesome, or unpleasant matter: X-у пришлось расхлёбывать кашу ≃ **X had to clear it ⟨things⟩ up; X had to straighten it ⟨things⟩ out; X had to deal with the mess; X had to get himself ⟨person Y⟩ out of trouble ⟨a mess, a jam⟩.**

...Делая исключение для отца и матери, Миша постепенно преисполнился презрением к взрослым, заварившим кашу, которой они не в силах расхлебать (Пастернак 1). ...Making an exception only for his parents, he [Misha] gradually became contemptuous of all grownups who had made this mess and were unable to clear it up (1a). ♦ «Давно приехать изволили?» – прибавил он снисходительно, как бы поощряя сконфузившегося посетителя. «Да вот только сегодня… Кашу вашу здешнюю расхлёбывать» (Достоевский 2). "Did you come long ago, sir?" he added condescendingly, as though encouraging a shy visitor. "Just today… To deal with this mess here" (2a). ♦ «Мало того что ты чуть не утопил мальчика из прекрасной семьи, – сердито говорил женский голос, – теперь ещё эта история, о которой говорит весь город!.. Расхлёбывай сам эту кашу» (Каверин 1). "It wasn't enough that you nearly drowned a boy of good family," said a woman's angry voice. "Now there has to be this affair, with the whole town talking about it….You'll have to get out of this trouble by yourself" (1a).

< From the saying «Сам кашу заварил, сам и расхлёбывай». See K-118.

К-118 • САМ КА́ШУ ЗАВАРИ́Л, САМ И РАСХЛЁ-БЫВАЙ [saying] you have caused an unpleasant, troublesome situation and now you must face the consequences and remedy it yourself (said when the speaker or another person withdraws from participation in something troublesome started by someone else, or refuses to help s.o. rectify a situation): ≃ **you have made this mess, now you must clear it up; you have made your bed and now you must ⟨can⟩ lie in it; as a man makes his bed, so must he lie; as you brew, so must you drink.**

[Калошин:] Где он? Куда ушёл? Куда? [Виктория:] Я не знаю. Может, в милицию. [Калошин:] Что же делать? [Виктория:] Вот уж не знаю. Вы кашу заварили, вы и расхлёбывайте (Вампилов 1). [K.:] Where is he? Where did he go? Which way? [V.:] I don't know. To the police, maybe. [K.:] What shall I do? [V.:] How should I know? You've made your bed, now you can lie in it (1a).

К-119 • ВОЗВОДИ́ТЬ/ВОЗВЕСТИ́ В КВАДРА́Т *что rare* [VP; subj: human] to exaggerate sth. significantly, presenting it as more important than it really is: X возведёт Y в квадрат ≃ **X will make ⟨far⟩ too much of Y; X will blow Y (all) out of proportion.**

К-120 • В КВАДРА́ТЕ [PrepP; Invar; nonagreeing postmodif] (usu. used with nouns referring to a negative quality) (one possesses a given quality or a given quality is manifested) to a high degree: **a complete [NP]; a total [NP]; an utter [NP];** [in limited contexts] **twice the [NP].**

Его начальник – дурак в квадрате. His boss is a complete fool.

К-121 • КВАДРАТУ́РА КРУ́ГА *lit* [NP; sing only; fixed WO] an insoluble matter, problem: **(be like) squaring ⟨trying to square⟩ the circle.**

К-122 • КИРПИЧА́ ПРО́СИТ *substand, rude* [VP; subj: рожа, морда, харя etc; pres only] s.o.'s face is ugly, repulsive: у X-а рожа кирпича просит ≃ **X's mug ⟨face⟩ would stop a clock; X is (as) ugly as sin.**

К-123 • ВЫХОДИ́ТЬ/ВЫ́ЙТИ ИЗ-ПОД КИ́СТИ *чьей, кого lit* [VP; subj: a noun denoting an artist's work; usu. pfv] to be painted by s.o.: X вышел из-под кисти Y-а ≃ **X came from the brush of Y ⟨from Y's brush⟩; X was the work of Y ⟨Y's work⟩.**

К-124 • НА́ШЕ ВАМ С КИ́СТОЧКОЙ *substand, humor* [Interj; Invar; fixed WO] **1.** Also: **НА́ШЕ ВАМ ⟨С КИ́СТОЧКОЙ⟩; СО́РОК ОДНО́ С КИ́СТОЧКОЙ** *all substand, humor* a salutation used in greeting: **howdy (do); how-(de)-do.**

2. a parting wish that things go well for s.o.: **(good-bye and) good luck; so long and best wishes.**

«Так, Лашков, так, Вася, – отчеканила она. – Так. Выходит, о шкуре своей печёшься? А я как?.. Как я? Поматросил и бросил. Наше вам, мол, с кисточкой? Спасибо, Вася, только временить и ждать тебя я не собираюсь…» (Максимов 3). "All right, Lashkov, all right, Vasilii," she said slowly and distinctly. "Right. So you're worried about your own skin, are you? And what about me?…What about me? You've had your fun, and now it's good-bye and good luck? Thanks, Vasilii, but I won't be hanging around to wait for you…" (3a).

К-125 • ВЛАДЕ́ТЬ КИ́СТЬЮ [VP; subj: human] to paint very well, expertly: X владеет кистью ≃ **X has a mastery of the brush; X is a master of the brush; X knows how to ply ⟨wield⟩ the brush.**

«По-моему, вы хорошо владеете кистью» (Чернёнок 1). "It seems to me you have a good mastery of the brush" (1a).

К-126 • держаться, покоиться и т. п. НА ТРЁХ КИТА́Х *lit* [NP; fixed WO] (to be based, founded etc) on three basic principles: **on three foundations;** [in limited contexts] **three things (that) count.**

«Соображать надо. Колыма-то, она на трёх китах держится: мат, блат и туфта. Вот и выбирай, который кит тебе подходящий», – загадочно сказал Костик (Гинзбург 1). "You've got to use your brains. Listen—only three things count in Kolyma: swearing, thieving, and window dressing. You just make your choice," he said cryptically (1b).

< Apparently from the ancient belief that the earth is balanced on the backs of three whales («на трёх китах»).

К-127 • КИШМЯ́ КИШЕ́ТЬ *coll* [VP; fixed WO] **1.** [subj: animal (pl or collect)] to be present (usu. in a lake, river, forest etc) in large numbers: в месте Y кишмя кишат X-ы ≃ **there are tons ⟨throngs, zillions etc⟩ of Xs in place Y; there is a swarm of Xs in place Y;** [usu. in refer. to insects and small creatures] **there is ⟨there swarms⟩ an army of Xs in place Y.**

Около оголившихся корней того дуба, под которым я сидел, по серой, сухой земле… кишмя кишели муравьи (Толстой 2). Around the uncovered roots of the oak tree under which I sat and over the dry gray earth…there swarmed an army of ants (2b).

2. ~ *кем-чем* [subj: a noun denoting a place] to contain a large number of living organisms: место X кишмя кишит Y-ами ≃ **place X is alive ⟨crawling, teeming, swarming⟩ with Ys; place X abounds with Ys; place X is jumping with Ys;** [in limited contexts] **place X is infested with Ys.**

К-128 • КИШКА́ ТОНКА́ ⟨ТО́НКАЯ⟩ *у кого substand* [VP_subj with быть_ø; usu. pres; usu. used with infin] **1.** s.o. does not have the strength, courage, ability, or know-how to do sth.: у X-а кишка тонка ≃ **X doesn't have what it takes; X doesn't have it in him; X hasn't got the guts; X isn't man ⟨woman⟩ enough;** [in limited contexts] **X's muscle can't match person Y's.**

«За два убийства и вооружённое ограбление полагается расстрел. Это ты знаешь. Чита, конечно, вместе с тобой не убивал – у него кишка тонка. Значит, убивал ты один» (Семёнов 1). "For two murders and armed robbery the sentence is shooting. You know that. Cheetah, of course, didn't participate in the murders—he hasn't got the guts for that. That means that you alone did the murdering" (1a). ♦ «Вот что, папанечка, – серые, калмыцкого сечения глаза её светились нескрываемой яростью, – спасибочки тебе за хлеб, за соль, только хвост тебе поднимать против моего Витьки кишка тонка» (Максимов 3). Her slanted, gray Kalmyk eyes flashed with undisguised fury. "Listen, dear Father, we thank you kindly for your hospitality, but don't start ordering Victor around, you aren't man enough for that" (3a).

2. s.o. does not have the means to pay for sth.: у Х-а кишка тонка ≃ **X hasn't got the dough ⟨the cash⟩.**

К-129 • **ВЫМА́ТЫВАТЬ/ВЫ́МОТАТЬ ⟨ВЫТЯ́ГИ-ВАТЬ/ВЫ́ТЯНУТЬ⟩ (ВСЕ) КИШКИ́** *из кого substand* [VP; subj: human] to exasperate, torment s.o.: Х из Y-а все кишки вымотал ≃ **X bugged the hell out of Y; X drove Y crazy ⟨nuts, up the wall⟩.**

К-130 • **ВЫ́ПУСТИТЬ КИШКИ́** *из кого, кому substand* [VP; subj: human] to kill, slaughter s.o.: Х выпустил кишки из Y-а ≃ **X ripped Y's guts out.**

«Женщин не тронут». — «Жидов тронут, это верно...» — «И офицеров. Всем им кишки повыпустят» (Булгаков 3). "They won't touch women." "They'll touch the Jews all right, that's for sure...." "And the officers. They'll rip their guts out" (3a).

К-131 • **ПОКА́ЗЫВАТЬ/ПОКАЗА́ТЬ КЛАСС ⟨МА́РКУ⟩** *highly coll* [VP; subj: human or collect] to do sth. perfectly, show one's mastery of sth.: Х показал класс ≃ **X did a first-class job; X showed fine ⟨top⟩ form; X showed his stuff.**

Через несколько минут мы были на шоссе. Сергей показывал класс... «Чудо! – кричал я на ухо Сергею. – Скорость! Двадцатый век, Серёжа!» (Аксёнов 1). Within a few minutes we were on the highway. Sergei was showing his stuff...."A marvel!" I shouted in Sergei's ear. "Speed! The twentieth century, Sergei!" (1a).

К-132 • **КЛЕЩА́МИ НЕ ВЫ́ТЯНЕШЬ ⟨НЕ ВЫ́ТА-ЩИШЬ⟩** *слова, ответа, признания и т. п. из кого coll* [VP; neg pfv fut, gener. 2nd pers sing only; fixed WO] there is no way you will be able to make s.o. say sth., answer a question, admit to sth. etc: из Х-а Y-а клещами не вытянешь ≃ **wild horses couldn't drag it out of X; you can't ⟨couldn't⟩ pry it out of X (with a crowbar); you won't ⟨can't⟩ get a word ⟨an answer etc⟩ out of X.**

К-133 • **КЛЕЩА́МИ ТАЩИ́ТЬ ⟨ВЫТЯ́ГИВАТЬ⟩** *слово, ответ и т. п. из кого coll* [VP; subj: human; usu. infin with надо, нужно, приходится etc; usu. this WO] to have difficulty getting s.o. to talk, answer: Х-у приходится из Y-а ответ ⟨каждое слово⟩ клещами тащить ≃ **X has to drag ⟨coax⟩ an answer ⟨every word⟩ out of Y; X has to force Y to open Y's mouth.**

К-134 • **ВБИВА́ТЬ/ВБИТЬ КЛИН** [VP] **1.** ~ *между чем и чем, во что* [subj: human or collect] to force apart, disunite (armies, military units, or two component parts of an army or military unit) by driving one's forces between them (or it): Х вбил клин между Y-ом и Z-ом ≃ **X drove a wedge between Y and Z.**

2. ~ *между кем и кем, между чем и чем* [subj: human or abstr] to cause alienation, dissociation, hostility (between two or more people, groups etc): Х вбил клин между Y-ом и Z-ом ≃ **X drove a wedge between Y and Z; X caused a rift between Y and Z.**

...Видимо, оно [институтское руководство] полагало, что профессор Эткинд ещё пригодится. Хоть и «вбил клин» между партией и литературой, но лекции читает, семинары проводит, с аспирантами занимается... (Эткинд 1). ...They [those in charge of the Institute] obviously thought that Professor Etkind could still be of some service. Although he had "driven a wedge" between the Party and literature, he was still giving lectures, running seminars, supervising graduate work... (1a).

К-135 • **КЛИН КЛИ́НОМ ВЫШИБА́ЮТ ⟨ВЫБИ-ВА́ЮТ, ВЫШИБА́ЕТСЯ, ВЫБИВА́ЕТСЯ⟩** [saying;

other finite forms and infin are also used] the undesirable consequences of some action are neutralized, some condition is remedied etc by the same means that brought about the consequences or gave rise to the condition: ≃ **fight fire with fire; one nail drives out another;** [in refer. to a hangover] **a hair of the dog (that bit you ⟨him⟩ etc).**

В то время, когда Ираида беспечно торжествовала победу, неустрашимый штаб-офицер не дремал и, руководясь пословицей: «Выбивай клин клином», научил некоторую авантюристку, Клемантинку де Бурбон, предъявить права свои (Салтыков-Щедрин 1). While Iraidka was unconcernedly celebrating her victory, the intrepid staff-officer was not asleep. Guided by the proverb "One nail drives out another," he found an adventuress, a certain Clementinka de Bourbon, and put her up to presenting a claim (1a).

К-136 • **КУДА́ НИ КИНЬ, ВЕЗДЕ́ ⟨ВСЁ, ВСЮ́ДУ⟩ КЛИН** [saying] anything one tries or does is futile because the given problem cannot be solved, the given situation cannot be resolved etc: ≃ **every avenue is ⟨comes up⟩ a dead end; there's no way out.**

Куда ни кинь – везде клин. Что же делать? К кому завтра пойти [за деньгами]? А к кому пойдёшь? Не к кому (Распутин 1). Every avenue was a dead end. What was he to do? Whom to ask for money tomorrow? As if there was anybody to ask! Nobody (1a).

К-137 • **КЛИ́НОМ ⟨ДУБИ́НОЙ, ГВОЗДЁМ⟩ НЕ ВЫ́-ШИБЕШЬ ⟨НЕ ВЫ́КОЛОТИШЬ⟩** *что* or *чего, из кого coll* [VP; neg pfv fut, gener. 2nd pers sing only; fixed WO] it is impossible by any means to make s.o. give up some idea, plan etc: Y ⟨Y-а⟩ из Х-а клином не вышибешь ≃ **you won't ⟨couldn't⟩ knock Y out of X with a sledgehammer.**

К-138 • **ПОДБИВА́ТЬ/ПОДБИ́ТЬ КЛИ́НЬЯ** *к кому, под кого highly coll, humor* [VP; subj: human, male; usu. impfv] to flirt with a woman, seek her affections: Х подбивает клинья к женщине Y ≃ **X is chasing (after) Y; X is after Y; X is making a play for Y.**

К-139 • **КЛИ́КАТЬ/КЛИ́КНУТЬ КЛИЧ** [VP; subj: human] **1.** ~ *(к кому obs) elev* to address people with a call, summons to do sth. (usu. when appealing to all the members of a given group, community etc to unite for a common cause): Х кликнул клич ≃ **X made an appeal (to the people); X sent out a ⟨the⟩ call; X sounded ⟨issued⟩ a call;** [in limited contexts] **X went to the people; X sent out a call to arms.**

Обыкновенно Бородавкин, напившись утром чаю, кликал клич; сбегались оловянные солдатики... (Салтыков-Щедрин 1). Usually, after Wartkin had drunk his morning tea, he would send out a call; the tin soldiers would come running... (1a). ♦ Он говорил, что нынче народ разбирал оружие в Кремле, что в афише Растопчина хотя и сказано, что он клич кликнет дня за два, но что уж сделано распоряжение наверное о том, чтобы завтра весь народ шёл на Три Горы с оружием, и что там будет большое сражение (Толстой 6). He said the people had been getting arms in the Kremlin and that though Rostopchin's broadsheet had said that he would sound a call two or three days in advance, the order had certainly already been given for everyone to go armed to the Three Hills to-morrow, and that there would be a big battle there (6b). ♦ ...Он [начальник] решился испытать своих подчинённых и кликнуть клич. «Кто хочет доказать, что любит меня... тот пусть отрубит указательный палец правой руки своей!» Никто, однако ж, на клич не спешил... (Салтыков-Щедрин 1). ...He [the chief] decided to test his subordinates and issued a call. "Whoso wishes to prove he loves me...shall cut off the index finger of his right hand!" No one, however, hastened to the call (1a).

2. *coll* [pfv only] to appeal to friends, colleagues etc for help: X кликнул клич ≃ **X called for ⟨in the⟩ reinforcements; X called in ⟨up⟩ the troops.**

К-140 • В ⟨НА⟩ КЛО́ЧЬЯ разорвать, разнести и т. п. *кого coll* [PrepP; these forms only; adv; the verb is usu. pfv fut (used as a threat) or subjunctive] (to inflict upon s.o.) great physical harm: X разорвёт Y-а в клочья ≃ **X will rip ⟨tear⟩ Y to pieces ⟨shreds⟩; X will tear Y limb from limb.**

Правители спасли Правдеца от народа. Не сделай они этого, народ разорвал бы его в клочья (Зиновьев 1). The rulers have saved Truth-teller from the people. Had they not done this, the people would have torn him to shreds (1a).

К-141 • (ПОПО́ЛЬЗОВАТЬСЯ) НАСЧЁТ КЛУБ-НИ́ЧКИ *obs, euph, humor* [VP or PrepP (used as predic); subj: human, male] to succeed in seducing a woman (or a number of women): X попользовался насчёт клубнички ≃ **X enjoyed a piece of cheesecake.**

[source] «А Кувшинников, то есть это такая бестия, подсел к ней и на французском языке подпускает ей такие комплименты... Поверишь ли, простых баб не пропустил. Это он называет: попользоваться насчёт клубнички» (Гоголь 3). "But Kuvshinnikov, that's the sort of beastly fellow he is, sat down beside her and started showering such compliments in French....I know you won't believe me, but he wouldn't let ordinary peasant women alone. That's what he calls 'enjoying a piece of cheesecake'" (3a).

< From Nikolai Gogol's *Dead Souls* («Мёртвые души»), 1842.

К-142 • КЛУБО́К ⟨КОМ, КОМО́К⟩ В ГО́РЛЕ (СТОИ́Т ⟨ЗАСТРЯ́Л и т. п.⟩); КЛУБО́К ⟨КОМ, КОМО́К⟩ К ГО́РЛУ ПОДСТУПИ́Л ⟨ПОДКАТИ́Л(СЯ)⟩ [NP or VP$_{subj}$] s.o. experiences a spasmodic, painful constriction in his throat (as a result of intense emotion): комок стоит в горле ≃ **person X has ⟨gets⟩ a lump ⟨a knot⟩ in his throat;** ∥ ком(ок) подкатил к горлу ≃ **a lump rose in person X's throat.**

...Саша сообразил, что Сольц вызывает всех причастных к его, Сашиному, делу. Первый раз за эти месяцы сердце его дрогнуло и к горлу подкатил ком (Рыбаков 2). ...Sasha realized that Solts wanted to summon everyone connected with his case. For the first time, his heart thumped and a lump rose in his throat (2a).

К-143 • ВОТ ТАК КЛЮ́КВА! *coll* [Interj; Invar; fixed WO] used to express one's disappointment at an unexpected, unpleasant occurrence as well as one's surprise that things turned out that way: **(well,) this is a fine kettle of fish!; well, this is a fine pickle!; what a pickle!**

«Вот так клюква! – подумал он, не обнаружив ключа на обычном месте. – Что же теперь делать?» "Well, this is a fine kettle of fish," he thought, not having found the key in its usual place. "What do I do now?"

К-144 • РАЗВЕ́СИСТАЯ КЛЮ́КВА *humor or iron* [NP; sing only; fixed WO] a totally improbable, nonsensical story betraying the storyteller's complete ignorance of the subject matter; a pure fabrication: **tall tale ⟨story⟩; cock-and-bull story; fable.**

< Originally used in reference to ignorant descriptions of Russia by foreigners, this phrase is thought to come from an account by a Frenchman (possibly Alexandre Dumas père, 1802–70) of his sitting *sous l'ombre d'un kliukva majestueux* ("in the shade of a majestic cranberry").

К-145 • БИТЬ/ЗАБИ́ТЬ ⟨КИПЕ́ТЬ/ЗАКИПЕ́ТЬ⟩ КЛЮЧО́М [VP] **1.** [subj: a noun denoting some fluid] to come rushing, bubbling out (of some place, container etc) with great force: X забил ключом ≃ **X gushed forth; X spurted (out); X spouted.**

2. ~ *(где, у кого, в ком)* [subj: abstr, often жизнь, радость, счастье, энергия etc] (of life) to flourish, (of joy, energy etc) to exhibit itself with great intensity: X бил ключом ≃ [of life] **X was booming; X was surging on ⟨forth⟩; X was in full swing;** ∥ X бил (в Y-е) ключом ≃ [of joy, happiness, energy etc] **X was bursting forth; X was bubbling over inside Y; Y was bubbling over with X; X was coursing through Y's veins.**

Жизнь как будто налаживалась, многим казалось, что она бьёт ключом, но каждый день мы узнавали что-нибудь новое, наводившее ужас и уничтожавшее всякую надежду на исцеление (Мандельштам 2). ...Life seemed to be on the mend, and to many it even seemed to be booming, but every day brought something new to fill us with horror and destroy any hope of recovery (2a). ♦ [Сильва:] А, мсьё Сарафанов! *(Подходит.)* Жизнь бьёт ключом! (Вампилов 4). [S.:] Ah, Monsieur Sarafanov! *(Coming closer.)* Life surges on (4a). ♦ Одним словом, в ней как будто... ещё совершался тот процесс вчерашней жизни, когда счастье полным ключом било в её жилах... (Салтыков-Щедрин 2). In short, the processes of her former life seemed still to go on within her...a life where happiness coursed gaily through her veins... (2a). ♦ Вообще жизнь в городе, где собирались Штаты, всегда начинала бить ключом (Булгаков 5). [context transl] Generally, wherever the Estates met, life always quickened (5a).

К-146 • АННИБА́ЛОВА ⟨АННИБА́ЛОВСКАЯ⟩ КЛЯ́ТВА *lit* [NP; sing only; fixed WO] a firm resolution to fight against s.o. or sth. to the very end: **Hannibalian oath.**

< From the name of the Carthaginian general *Hannibal* (247?–83 B.C.), who, according to ancient historians, at the age of ten took an oath to be an irreconcilable enemy of Rome.

К-147 • КНИ́ГА ЗА СЕМЬЮ ПЕЧА́ТЯМИ *(для кого) lit* [NP; sing only; subj-compl with copula, nom or instrum (subj: abstr, often это); fixed WO] sth. utterly incomprehensible, beyond s.o.'s ability to understand: X (для Y-а) – книга за семью печатями ≃ **X is a closed book ⟨a mystery⟩ to Y; X is beyond Y's comprehension ⟨understanding, reach, grasp⟩.**

< (?) From the Bible (Rev. 5:1).

К-148 • СМОТРЕ́ТЬ ⟨ГЛЯДЕ́ТЬ⟩ В КНИ́ГУ И ВИ́ДЕТЬ ФИ́ГУ *highly coll, humor* [VP; subj: human; fixed WO] to read sth. without understanding the sense of it: X смотрит в книгу и видит фигу ≃ **X stares at the pages and doesn't get a word (of it) ⟨understand a thing etc⟩.**

К-149 • НАЖИМА́ТЬ/НАЖА́ТЬ (НА ВСЕ) КНО́ПКИ *coll* [VP; subj: human] to make use of all one's opportunities, contacts etc (in order to achieve one's goal): X нажал на все кнопки ≃ **X pulled (a few ⟨all the right⟩) strings; X used his pull ⟨influence, connections⟩.**

К-150 • ЧЁРНОГО КОБЕЛЯ́ НЕ ОТМО́ЕШЬ ДО-БЕЛА́ [saying] a person's deep-rooted shortcomings, deficiencies etc are impossible to correct: ≃ **a ⟨the⟩ leopard cannot change his spots; can a ⟨the⟩ leopard change his spots?; what's bred in the bone...**

К-151 • (НЕ) ПРИШЕ́Й КОБЫ́ЛЕ ХВОСТ; НЕ ПРИ-ШЕ́Й НЕ ПРИСТЕГНИ́ *all substand* [VP$_{imper}$; these forms only; usu. predic with subj: human or inanim; fixed WO] a person (thing etc) is superfluous, unneeded, unrelated to some matter: X – пришей кобыле хвост ≃ **X is excess baggage; person X is a useless appendage ⟨a fifth wheel⟩; X is entirely out of place; person X is a square peg in a round hole;** [in limited contexts] **X is good for nothing; what is X good for?**

«Словоблудие — у тебя! — с новой запальчивостью отсёк дланью Сологдин. — Если вы всё выводите из этих трёх законов...» — «Да говорят тебе: *не выводим!*» — «Из законов — не выводите?» — изумился Сологдин. «Нет!» — «Так что они тогда — пришей кобыле хвост?» (Солженицын 3). "The high-flown, empty verbiage is all yours!" said Sologdin in a new outburst of vehemence, cutting him off with a wave of his hand. "If you deduce everything from those three laws—" "But I've told you—we *don't*." "You don't?" Sologdin asked in surprise. "No!" "Well then, what are the laws good for?" (3a).

К-152 • ВЫЗЫВА́ТЬ/ВЫ́ЗВАТЬ НА КОВЁР *кого recent, coll* [VP; subj: human (a noun denoting some authority)] to call s.o. to be reprimanded, respond to some charges against him etc: X вызвал Y-а на ковёр ≃ **X called ⟨had⟩ Y on the carpet.**

< Apparently a loan translation of the English "to call on the carpet."

К-153 • НИ ЗА КАКИ́Е КОВРИ́ЖКИ ⟨ПРЯ́НИКИ *rare*⟩ *coll* [PrepP; these forms only; adv; used with negated verbs; fixed WO] under no circumstances: **not (do sth.) for anything (in the world); not (do sth.) for any money ⟨for love (n)or money⟩; there is no way (one would ⟨could⟩ do sth.); (doing sth. is) the last thing one wants ⟨would ever want⟩ to do.** Cf. **not for all the tea in China.**

«...Теперь в Кремль проси меня работать идти, не пойду ни за какие коврижки!» (Коротюков 1). "If you asked me to work in the Kremlin, I wouldn't do it for anything in the world" (1a). ♦ «...Ни за какие коврижки я не оставлю старика» (Максимов 3). "...I wouldn't leave the old man, not for any money" (3a). ♦ ...Ружьё есть ружьё, это не корыто, с ним ни за какие пряники бы не смог расстаться он ни за какие пряники бы не смог (Распутин 4). ...A gun's a gun and not a trough, and there was no way he could part with it (4a). ♦ ...Его в конце концов отпустили, хотя в магазине работать не позволили. Но он бы туда и сам ни за какие пряники больше не пошёл... (Распутин 1). ...In the end they let him go, merely forbidding him to run the shop any more. But that...was the last thing he wanted to do (1a).

К-154 • КОГДА́ Б⟨Ы⟩ *obsoles, lit* [subord Conj, condit] on the condition that: **if (only); [with neg predic only] were it not for; had it not been for.**

К-155 • КОГДА́ (...) НИ...; КОГДА́ БЫ (...) НИ... [subord Conj, temporal] at whatever time: **whenever; no matter when.**

К-156 • КОГДА́ КА́К *coll* [sent; Invar] differently at different times: **all ⟨it (all)⟩ depends; it varies.**

«Я спрашиваю, какой у тебя заработок — ага, сколько ты денег в месяц получаешь?» — «Заработок... Когда как, Илья» (Распутин 3). "I meant, how much do you earn? What do they pay you a month?" "Pay?...All depends, Ilia" (3a).

К-157 • ОБЛОМА́ТЬ КО́ГТИ *кому coll* [VP; subj: human] to deprive s.o. of the opportunity to do harm (to another or others): X обломает Y-у когти ≃ **X will pull out Y's claws; X will render Y harmless.**

К-158 • ПОКА́ЗЫВАТЬ/ПОКАЗА́ТЬ (СВОИ́) КО́ГТИ ⟨КОГОТКИ́ *coll*⟩ (*кому*); ВЫПУСКА́ТЬ/ВЫ́ПУ-СТИТЬ КО́ГТИ *coll* [VP; subj: human or collect] to show hostility toward s.o., act in a confrontational manner, (display a readiness to) fight back when provoked: X показал Y-у когти ≃ **X showed ⟨Y⟩ X's claws ⟨teeth⟩; X bared his teeth (at Y).**

Тюфяев знал своих гостей насквозь, презирал их, показывал им иногда когти и вообще обращался с ними в том роде, как хозяин обращается с своими собаками... (Герцен 1).

Tyufyayev knew his guests through and through, despised them, showed them his claws at times, and altogether treated them as a master treats his dogs... (1a).

К-159 • РВАТЬ/РВАНУ́ТЬ КО́ГТИ (*откуда*) *substand* [VP; subj: human; usu. impfv; often imper or infin with пора, пришлось, надо, нужно etc] to run away from some place, usu. in order to escape danger, avoid pursuit etc: рви когти ≃ **beat it; split; get the hell out (of here ⟨there⟩); [in limited contexts] blow the joint.**

[Сильва:] Говорю тебе по-дружески, предупреждаю: рвём когти, пока не поздно (Вампилов 4). [S.:] I'm telling you as a friend. I'm warning you: let's beat it before it's too late (4b). ♦ «Оторвалось у меня что-то внутри, и словно мне кто сказал: беги, говорит, рви когти... Ну, я и рванул» (Стругацкие 1). "And it was like something snapped inside me, like some voice was telling me, 'Beat it, buddy, split...' So I split" (1a). ♦ «Ну нет, думаю, надо рвать когти, пока армяне меня не застукали в этом доме» (Искандер 2). "Well, no, I think, I'd better get the hell out before the Armenians find me in this house" (2a). ♦ Влад сразу узнал размашистые каракули напарника: «Рви когти. Этот чмур [*prison slang, here* = человек] тебе поможет. Сергей» (Максимов 2). Vlad immediately recognized his partner's bold scrawl: "Blow the joint. This guy will help you. Sergei" (2a).

К-160 • ГУСИ́НАЯ КО́ЖА [NP; sing only] tiny, temporary bumps on the skin caused by cold or fear: **goose flesh ⟨bumps, pimples⟩.**

К-161 • (ОДНА́) КО́ЖА ДА КО́СТИ *coll* [NP; these forms only; subj-compl with быть₀ (subj: human or animal), detached modif, subj with остались, осталась, or indep. remark; usu. this WO] one is extremely thin, emaciated: **(nothing but) skin and bone(s); bag of bones.**

«Ну, куда ты пустишься такой, кожа да кости, еле душа в теле? Неужто опять пешком? Да ведь не дойдёшь ты!» (Пастернак 1). "How could you travel, weak as you are, nothing but skin and bones? Do you really imagine you could go on foot? You would never get there" (1a).

К-162 • ИЗ КО́ЖИ ⟨ИЗ ШКУ́РЫ *substand*⟩ (ВОН) ЛЕЗТЬ ⟨ВЫЛЕЗА́ТЬ⟩ *coll* [VP; subj: human or collect; often foll. by a чтобы-clause] to make special efforts (to do sth.), try very hard: X из кожи вон лезет ≃ **X goes out of his way; X bends ⟨falls⟩ over backward; X falls (all) over himself; X does his utmost; X goes all out; X (practically) kills himself (trying to accomplish sth.).**

На воле, там у себя, он был одним из «руководящих товарищей», теперь из кожи лез вон, чтоб и в лагере в какие ни на есть начальники попасть (Иоффе 1). Formerly, while at liberty, he had been a "leading comrade" and now in camp, was eager to do his utmost to become some sort of chief (1a). ♦ Городишко у нас гонористый, из кожи вон лезет, чтобы всё было как у больших (Аксёнов 1). Our little town puts on airs, goes all out to have everything like the big cities (1a). ♦ «А я про что говорю? — суетился Рабинович. — Каждая порядочная цель сама себя поедает. Из кожи вылезаешь, чтоб до неё добраться, а чуть добрался — глядь — всё наоборот» (Терц 7). "What was I telling you?" fidgeted Rabinovich. "Every decent End consumes itself. You kill yourself trying to reach it, and by the time you get there it's been turned inside out" (7a). ♦ «Видишь, Родион: слушай и скажи своё мнение. Я хочу. Я из кожи лез вчера с ними и тебя поджидал; я и им про тебя говорил, что приедешь...» (Достоевский 3). "Look here, Rodion; listen and then give us your opinion. I want you to. I practically killed myself trying to convince them yesterday, and was waiting for you; I even told them you were coming..." (3a).

К-163 • НИ КО́ЖИ НИ РО́ЖИ (*у кого*) *highly coll, derog*; НИ КО́ЖИ, НИ РО́ЖИ, НИ ВЕ́ДЕНИЯ *у кого obs*

[NP_gen; these forms only; subj/gen with быть∅ or detached modif; fixed WO] s.o. is very homely and usu. thin: (у X-а) ~ ≃ [equivalents vary depending on the speaker's attitude to the person addressed or described] **X is not much to look at; X is no feast for the eyes; X is (as) ugly as sin.**

Он долго думал, долго ловил какую-нибудь угловатую черту, за которую можно было бы уцепиться, в наружности, в манерах или в характере этого лица, наконец, махнув рукой, выражался так: «А у этого ни кожи, ни рожи, ни ведения» (Гончаров 1). He would ponder, try to seize on some outstanding feature of the face, the figure, or the manner of the man, then say with a shrug: "He's not much to look at and he doesn't know anything" (1a).

К-164 • НА КО́ЗЕ НЕ ПОДЪЕ́ДЕШЬ *к кому highly coll* [VP; neg pfv fut, gener. 2nd pers sing не подъедешь only; fixed WO] it is impossible to address s.o. (about sth.), catch s.o.'s attention, turn s.o.'s attention to o.s. (because of his sternness, intractability, self-importance etc): к X-у на козе не подъедешь ≃ **X is hard to approach; there's no approaching X.**

[author's usage] [Матюшев:] А Добротин ещё больше силу теперь почувствовал. Нужно поговорить с ним о городских делах, так и не знаю, на какой козе к нему подъехать (Салынский 1). [context transl] [M.:] Dobrotin feels even stronger these days. I'll have to have a word with him about urban development, but I don't know what approach to take (1a).

К-165 • КОЗЁЛ ОТПУЩЕ́НИЯ [NP; fixed WO] a person (or group) blamed for the faults or misdeeds of others: **scapegoat; whipping boy.**

Они узаконивали беззаконие, наши песенные двадцатые годы. Поиски козлов отпущения становились привычны (Свирский 1). They legalized illegality, our much-vaunted twenties. It became customary to look for scapegoats (1a). ♦ Говорили, что бериевцы то ли между собой, то ли с кем-то из обслуги судачили: «Ну, что Лаврентий Павлович? Будто он один, а другие, нынешние, ни при чём? Все решения были общие. Просто нужен был козёл отпущения!» (Марченко 1). They also said that the Beria men had been heard to say, either among themselves or to someone doing orderly duty: "Well, what about Lavrenty Beria? Do you think he was the only one and that those men up there now had nothing to do with it? All decisions were taken unanimously. He's just the one they used as a whipping boy!" (1a).

< From an ancient Jewish rite described in the Bible. On Yom Kippur the high priest laid his hands on the head of a goat, symbolically transferring the sins of the people to it, and then let the goat loose in the wilderness (Lev. 16:5–22).

К-166 • ДРАТЬ КОЗЛА́ *substand* [VP; subj: human or collect] to sing poorly, with an unpleasant voice, or to play a musical instrument off-key: X драл козла ≃ **X was rasping ⟨wheezing, screeching, croaking etc⟩ out a tune ⟨a song etc⟩; X was torturing his instrument ⟨person Y's ears⟩.**

К-167 • ЗАБИВА́ТЬ/ЗАБИ́ТЬ «КОЗЛА́» *highly coll* [VP; subj: human, usu. pl] to play a game of dominoes: X-ы забивают «козла» ≃ **Xs are playing dominoes.**

Во дворе никого не было, только четверо под деревянным грибком забивали «козла» (Евтушенко 1). There wasn't anyone in the yard, apart from four men playing dominoes under a wooden mushroom meant for children (1a).

К-168 • КАК ⟨ЧТО⟩ ОТ КОЗЛА́ МОЛОКА́ *coll, disapprov* [как etc + PrepP; these forms only; subj-compl with быть∅ (subj/gen: пользы, толку etc); fixed WO] s.o. or sth. is of absolutely no use, help etc: пользы от X-а как от козла молока ≃ **X is (about) as useful as tits on a boar; X is good for nothing; one gets as much good out of X as milk from a he-goat; trying to get some use out of X is like trying to get milk out of a billy goat.**

«Старика мирного убивать — это тоже война?» — «...Такие, как дед Гришака, и настраивали казаков сопротив нас... От него пользы было, как от козла молока, а вреда много» (Шолохов 5). "Killing a peaceable old man — is that war too?" "...It was old men like Grandad Grishaka who set the Cossacks against us....We got as much good out of him as milk from a he-goat. But he did a lot of harm" (5a).

К-169 • ПУСКА́ТЬ/ПУСТИ́ТЬ КОЗЛА́ В ОГОРО́Д *coll* [VP; subj: human; more often pfv past; often 3rd pers pl with indef. refer.; the verb may take the final position, otherwise fixed WO] to allow s.o. access to some place where he may be esp. harmful or to some thing that he wants to use or exploit for personal gain: пустили козла в огород ≃ **they put the cow to mind the corn; they put the wolf in charge of the sheep; they put the fox to guard the henhouse ⟨the chickens⟩.**

Весна девятнадцатого: наступает Деникин, полыхает восстание... Мигулина отзывают в Москву, в Смоленск... *Убрали — значит, есть повод.* Оставлять Мигулина на Дону во время казачьего бунта? Пустить козла в огород? (Трифонов 6). ...Spring 1919. Denikin was advancing, the uprising was blazing away. Migulin was recalled to Moscow, then to Smolensk.... *If they kicked him out, then there was a reason for it.* Leave Migulin on the Don during the Cossack mutiny? Put a wolf in charge of the sheep? (6a).

К-170 • СТРО́ИТЬ КО́ЗНИ *(против кого)* [VP; subj: human] to devise secret, malicious plans against s.o.: X строит козни против Y-а ≃ **X hatches ⟨cooks up⟩ plots ⟨schemes⟩ against Y; X plots intrigues against Y; X connives against Y.**

К-171 • КАК СИ́ДОРОВУ КО́ЗУ *драть, лупить, пороть кого coll* [как + NP; Invar; adv (intensif); fixed WO] (to flog, thrash s.o.) cruelly, unmercifully: X выдрал Y-а ~ ≃ **X beat the crap ⟨the stuffing, the tar, the (living) daylights⟩ out of Y; X worked Y over (but) good; X beat Y black-and-blue.**

К-172 • ОТСТАВНО́Й КОЗЫ́ БАРАБА́НЩИК *obs, iron or humor* [NP; fixed WO] an unimportant, insignificant person disregarded by everyone (because of low standing in society, at the workplace etc): **small fry ⟨potatoes, change⟩.**

< From a popular fair attraction of the past involving a goat and a drummer. According to some sources (V. I. Dal, M. I. Mikhelson et al.) a drummer kept time while a tame bear and a boy dressed as a goat paraded around. According to other sources (N. M. Shansky et al.) the drummer (usually a retired, «отставной», army drummer) beat out the sound backstage while a live goat stomped on an onstage drum (stomping its foot on any available object is a goat's natural way of indicating hunger).

К-173 • БРАТЬ/ВЗЯТЬ ⟨ДЕ́ЛАТЬ/СДЕ́ЛАТЬ⟩ ПОД КОЗЫРЁК [VP; subj: human; fixed WO] to greet (s.o.) in military fashion, raising one's hand to the visor of one's cap: X взял под козырёк ≃ **X saluted.**

...[Блондин-провожатый в штатском] взял под козырёк, желая нам счастливого пути... (Мандельштам 1). ...[The fair-haired escort in civilian clothes] saluted as he wished us a happy journey... (1a).

К-174 • ХОДИ́ТЬ КО́ЗЫРЕМ *coll* [VP; subj: human] to look overconfident, arrogant, carry o.s. in a self-important fashion: X ходит козырем ≃ **X struts about; X swaggers; X looks smug ⟨cocky⟩.**

К-175 • КО́ЗЫРЬ ⟨-и⟩ В РУКА́Х *у кого (против кого); давать КО́ЗЫРЬ ⟨-и⟩ В РУ́КИ кому all coll* [NP; usu. obj (both variants) or VP_subj with copula (1st var.)] sth. that gives s.o.

the advantage over another, puts s.o. in a favorable, winning position: **(have ⟨hold, hand s.o. etc⟩) a trump card; (hold ⟨give s.o. etc⟩) the high card(s); (have ⟨give s.o. etc⟩) a powerful card to play; (keep ⟨have⟩) an ace up one's sleeve; (have) an ace in the hole; (have) a hole card; [in limited contexts] (be) one up on s.o.**

Женщина… уходит, и Ася шепчет в необыкновенном волнении: «Она не должна знать! Я потом объясню. Она догадывается, но мы не дадим ей козыри в руки» (Трифонов 6). …The woman goes out, and Asya whispers to me with surprising agitation, "She must not know! I'll explain later. She guesses, but we won't hand her the trump cards so easily" (6a).

К-176 • **ПРИ СВОЍХ КОЗЫРЯ́Х** оставаться *coll* [PrepP; Invar; adv] (to end up) in the same situation, condition in which one started, (to be left) with what one had before: **(end up etc) back where one started (from); (end up etc) (no better and) no worse off than when one began; (be left etc) with what one began with.**

К-177 • **ВБИТЬ ⟨ЗАБИ́ТЬ⟩ ОСИ́НОВЫЙ КОЛ** *во что* ⟨**В МОГИ́ЛУ** *кого-чего*⟩ *lit or media* [VP; subj: human, collect, or abstr] to destroy, put an end to s.o. or sth., render s.o. or sth. harmless: **Х вбил осиновый кол в могилу Y-a ≃ X hammered the last nail in Y's coffin; X buried Y for good ⟨once and for all⟩; X did away with Y (for good).**

< From the old superstitious custom of driving a stake («кол») into the ground in the place where it was thought that a sorcerer or witch was buried in order to prevent his or her rising from the grave.

К-178 • **ХОТЬ КОЛ НА ГОЛОВЕ́ ТЕШИ́** *кому substand* [хоть + VP_imper; Invar; indep. or subord clause; usu. this WO] (s.o. is so stubborn, stupid, lazy etc that) it is utterly impossible to convince him of sth., make him understand sth., or make him do sth.: **Х-у хоть кол на голове теши ≃ there's no way to beat it into X's thick head; there's no way to beat it into that thick head ⟨skull⟩ of X's; no matter what you say, X won't listen ⟨no matter what you do, X won't give in etc⟩; it's ⟨talking to X is⟩ like talking to a (brick) wall ⟨to the wall⟩.**

К-179 • **НИ КОЛА́ НИ ДВОРА́** (*у кого*) *coll* [NP_gen; Invar; subj/gen with не бытьø or obj of не иметь; fixed WO] s.o. has absolutely nothing (usu. refers to s.o.'s extreme poverty, need, occas. to s.o.'s having no place to live): **у Х-а ~ ≃ X doesn't have a thing (to his name); X has neither house nor home.**

[Золотуев:] Посадил он того продавца на десять лет… И вот выходит наш продавец на свободу. Садился – жена у него оставалась, интересная баба. На пятнадцать лет моложе его была. А вернулся – ни кола ни двора. Ни одной близкой души (Вампилов 3). [Z.:] He put that salesman in prison for ten years.…And then our salesman comes out. When he went in he still had a wife, a nice-looker. Fifteen years younger than him. But when he came back – What's he got? Nothing. Not a thing. Not one person he could turn to (3a). ♦ Почему вдова переехала из Ивановки сюда, где у неё ни кола, ни двора?.. (Рыбаков 1). Why did the widow move from Ivanovka to this place, where she had neither house nor home?… (1a).

К-180 • **КАТИ́СЬ КОЛБАСО́Й ⟨КОЛБА́СКОЙ⟩!** *substand, rude* [VP_imper; usu. indep. sent; fixed WO] go away, leave: **beat it!; scram!; get (the hell) out (of here)!; clear out!**

[Мышлаевский:] А чем же, старик, печи топить? [Максим:] Дровами, батюшка, дровами. [Мышлаевский:] А где у тебя дрова? [Максим:] У нас дров нету. [Мышлаевский:] Ну, катись отсюда… колбасой к чёртовой матери! (Булгаков 4).

[Myshl.:] And what are we supposed to put in the stoves, old man? [Ma.:] Firewood, sir, firewood. [Myshl.:] And where is your firewood? [Ma.:] We don't have any firewood. [Myshl.:] Well then get the bloody hell out of here… (4a).

К-181 • **ВЫБИВА́ТЬ/ВЫ́БИТЬ ⟨ВЫШИБА́ТЬ/ВЫ́-ШИБИТЬ⟩ ИЗ КОЛЕИ́** *кого* [VP; subj: abstr; more often pfv past; usu. this WO] to disturb the daily rhythm of s.o.'s life, s.o.'s daily habits: **Х выбил Y-а из колеи ≃ X disrupted the ⟨Y's⟩ (entire) routine; X threw ⟨knocked⟩ Y out of Y's groove ⟨out of gear⟩; X threw Y off balance; X unsettled Y.**

Профессор Персиков совершенно измучился и заработался в последние три недели. Куриные события выбили его из колеи и навалили на него двойную тяжесть (Булгаков 10). Professor Persikov had worked himself to the point of exhaustion. For three weeks the chicken events disrupted his entire routine and doubled his duties and burdens (10a). ♦ Свидание с внуком снова выбило Петра Васильевича из колеи (Максимов 3). His meeting with his grandson threw Pyotr Vasilievich off balance again (3a).

К-182 • **ВЫБИВА́ТЬСЯ/ВЫ́БИТЬСЯ ⟨ВЫХОДИ́ТЬ/ВЫ́ЙТИ⟩ ИЗ КОЛЕИ́** [VP; subj: human or abstr; more often pfv past; usu. this WO] (of a person) to have one's customary life style, schedule etc disrupted; (of s.o.'s life) to be disrupted: **Х выбился из колеи ≃ X was (thrown) out of joint ⟨whack⟩; X got out of his ⟨its⟩ groove; person X's routine was upset; person X's life became unsettled.**

[Войницкий:] С тех пор, как здесь живёт профессор со своею супругой, жизнь выбилась из колеи… Сплю не вовремя, за завтраком и обедом ем разные кабули, пью вина… нездорово всё это! (Чехов 3). [V.:] Ever since the professor and his wife came here to live, life has been out of joint.…I sleep at odd hours, eat all sorts of spicy sauces for lunch and dinner, drink wine – all bad for the health! (3a).

К-183 • **ДО СЕДЬМО́ГО КОЛЕ́НА** [PrepP; Invar; usu. modif or adv; fixed WO] extending back through many generations: **(way back) to the seventh generation.**

К-184 • **ПРЕКЛОНЯ́ТЬ/ПРЕКЛОНИ́ТЬ КОЛЕ́НИ ⟨-а⟩** *перед кем-чем elev* [VP; subj: human] **1.** to treat s.o. with the deepest respect, reverence: **X преклоняет колени перед Y-ом ≃ X pays homage to Y; X affords Y the greatest respect.**

2. [often neg] to submit to s.o.'s authority: **X не преклонит колен перед Y-ом ≃ X will not get ⟨go⟩ down on his knees before ⟨to⟩ Y; X will not bow down to ⟨before⟩ Y.**

К-185 • **СТА́ВИТЬ/ПОСТА́ВИТЬ НА КОЛЕ́НИ** *кого* [VP; subj: human or collect] to force s.o. into submission, subordinate s.o.: **X поставил Y-а на колени ≃ X brought ⟨forced⟩ Y to Y's knees; X had Y on Y's knees.**

«Мы ещё могли победить, если бы пустили в ход ФАУ-3. Ведь уже ФАУ-1 и ФАУ-2 деморализовали англичан. ФАУ-3 поставило бы их и янки на колени» (Копелев 1). "We still might have won if we had used the V-3. Even the V-1 and V-2 had demoralized the British. The V-3 would have brought them and the Yankees to their knees" (1a).

К-186 • **СТАНОВИ́ТЬСЯ/СТАТЬ НА КОЛЕ́НИ** *перед кем* [VP; subj: human or collect; often neg] to submit, subordinate o.s. to s.o.: **X не станет на колени перед Y-ом ≃ X will not be brought ⟨forced⟩ to his knees; Y will not get ⟨have⟩ X on X's knees; X will not kneel (down) before ⟨to⟩ Y; X will not go down on his knees before ⟨to⟩ Y.**

К-187 • **СЛАБ В КОЛЕ́НКАХ** *highly coll* [AdjP; subj-compl with copula (subj: human)] one is lacking the courage or skill to do sth.: X слаб в коленках ≃ **X doesn't have what it takes; X doesn't have the guts ⟨the pluck, the nerve, the stomach⟩.**

K-188 • КОЛЕ́НКИ ⟨КОЛЕ́НИ⟩ ПОДГИБА́ЮТСЯ *у кого;* КОЛЕ́НКИ ДРОЖА́Т *all coll* [VP$_{subj}$] s.o. experiences an intense feeling of nervousness, fear: у Х-а коленки подгибаются ≃ **X's knees are shaking; X's knees are knocking (together); X is shaking ⟨quaking⟩ in his boots; X is shaking in his shoes.**

Мы приехали в Сен-Антони поздно вечером и, не скрою, у меня подгибались коленки. У меня какой-то суеверный трепет перед храмами, монастырями, священниками... (Аллилуева 2). We arrived in San-Antoni late in the evening. I confess my knees shook. Temples, monasteries, priests make me tremble superstitiously (2a).

K-189 • (ДАВА́ТЬ/ДАТЬ) КОЛЕ́НКОЙ ⟨КОЛЕ́НОМ⟩ ПОД ЗАД *кому highly coll, rude* [VP or PrepP (used as predic); subj: human] to reject s.o., throw s.o. out rudely: X дал Y-у коленкой под зад ≃ **X kicked ⟨booted⟩ Y ⟨Y's butt, Y's ass⟩ out (of place Z); X threw Y out on Y's ear ⟨ass⟩;** [in limited contexts] **X gave Y the bum's rush.**

K-190 • ДРУГО́Й ⟨ИНО́Й, НЕ ТОТ⟩ КОЛЕНКО́Р ⟨ТАБА́К⟩ *highly coll* [NP; sing only; subj-compl with copula (subj: usu. это, occas. any noun or a clause); fixed WO] that changes (or would change) the situation: **(that's) a horse of another ⟨a different⟩ color; (that's) a card of a different suit; (that's) a bird of another feather; (that's) another ⟨a different⟩ kettle of fish.**

«...Я к вам совсем по другому делу, связанному сугубо с производством, а не то, чтоб всё жрать да разбазаривать». — «Ну, это тогда совсем другой коленкор» (Попов 1). "...I'm here on totally different business, strictly related to production, and not to eating up and selling off everything." "Well, that's a horse of a different color" (1a).

K-191 • ОТКА́ЛЫВАТЬ/ОТКОЛО́ТЬ КОЛЕ́НЦЕ ⟨КОЛЕ́НЦА⟩ *coll* [VP; subj: human; var. with pl коленца is usu. impfv, var. with sing коленце is usu. pfv] **1.** Also: ВЫДЕ́ЛЫВАТЬ КОЛЕ́НЦЕ ⟨КОЛЕ́НЦА⟩ *coll* to dance joyfully, executing intricate patterns: X откалывал коленца ≃ **X was cutting capers; X was capering (about).**

[author's usage] Беспутную оную Клемантинку посадили в клетку и вывезли на площадь; атаманы-молодцы подходили и дразнили её. Некоторые, более добродушные, потчевали водкой, но требовали, чтобы она за это откинула какое-нибудь коленце (Салтыков-Щедрин 1). The wanton Klemantinka was put in a cage and carried out on to the square; the brave lads went up to her and taunted her. Some of the better-natured ones gave her vodka, but told her to cut them a caper in return (1b).

2. Also: ВЫКИ́ДЫВАТЬ/ВЫ́КИНУТЬ КОЛЕ́НЦЕ ⟨КОЛЕ́НЦА⟩ *coll* to do sth. unusual, unexpected, often absurd: X выкинул коленце ≃ **X pulled a stunt ⟨a caper⟩; X pulled some funny business.**

И хотя трезвость суждений и выказывала в новом знакомце человека в своём уме и памяти, Пётр Васильевич, взявший уже себе за правило готовиться здесь к любым фокусам, откровенно говоря, ожидал, что тот в любую минуту может выкинуть какое-нибудь «коленце»... (Максимов 3). Although his new acquaintance's sensible remarks seemed to show that he was in full possession of his faculties, Pyotr Vasilievich had already made it a rule to be ready for all sorts of antics in this place, and, to be frank, he was expecting funny business at any moment (3a). ♦ [extended usage] ...С такой обидной смертью Семён встретился впервые. Шёл парень к зазнобе... рассчитывал, верно, жениться, обзавестись семьёй — и на вот, подвернулся. Не бо-

лел, не воевал, на медведей не ходил. В старину говорили: на роду написано. Пустое! Просто жизнь коленца выкидывает (Тендряков 1). [context transl] ...This was the first time Simon had seen such senseless death. The young man had been to see his girl friend and was probably thinking of getting married and starting a family — and then this had to happen. He hadn't been ill, or getting into fights, or hunting bears. In the old days they would have said it was his fate from birth. What rubbish! It was just a matter of the queer tricks life plays on you (1a).

K-192 • СТОЯ́ТЬ НА КОЛЕ́НЯХ *(перед кем) lit* [VP; subj: human or collect] to be in a state of submission, be subordinated to s.o.: X стоит на коленях (перед Y-ом) ≃ **X is on his knees (before ⟨to⟩ Y); Y has X on X's knees.**

...Меня не печатали и лишали куска хлеба ещё два года (до конца 1972), после чего власти, полагая, что я уже прочно стою на коленях, решили меня простить и даже издали одновременно две мои книги (Войнович 1). ...They stopped publishing me and kept me from earning a living for another two years, until the end of 1972. Then, assuming that they had me on my knees, the authorities decided to forgive me, and even published two of my books at the same time (1a).

K-193 • ПОДМА́ЗЫВАТЬ/ПОДМА́ЗАТЬ КОЛЁСА *(кому) obs* [VP; subj: human] to give a bribe (to s.o.): X подмазал колёса (Y-у) ≃ **X greased Y's palm.**

K-194 • НА КОЛЁСАХ [PrepP; Invar] **1.** *recent* [subj-compl with быть$_\emptyset$ (subj: human or collect)] one has a car or motorcycle: **(one has) wheels.**

2. *coll* [subj-compl with copula (subj: human) or adv] traveling extensively: **always on the road ⟨on the move⟩; living out of a suitcase.**

Работа у меня — сплошные командировки, живу на колёсах. My work is nothing but business trips — I'm always on the road.

3. [subj-compl with copula (subj: collect, usu. a noun denoting an organization, factory etc)] moving (or about to start moving) from one location to another: **in transit.**

K-195 • КАК НЕМА́ЗАНОЕ ⟨НЕСМА́ЗАННОЕ, НЕПОДМА́ЗАННОЕ⟩ КОЛЕСО́ скрипеть [как + NP; these forms only; adv] **1.** to make squeaking, irritating sounds: **(squeak ⟨creak⟩) like an unoiled hinge ⟨a rusty hinge, an old cart wheel⟩; (squeak) like an ungreased wheel.**

2. (of an enterprise, business etc) not (to work out) well, (to develop) poorly, with difficulty: **(wobble along) on squeaky wheels; (creak) like an ungreased wheel.**

Недавно заведённое на новый лад хозяйство скрипело, как немазаное колесо... (Тургенев 2). The estate had only recently been put on to the new system, whose mechanism still creaked like an ungreased wheel... (2c).

K-196 • ПОВЕРНУ́ТЬ КОЛЕСО́ ИСТО́РИИ ВСПЯТЬ ⟨НАЗА́Д⟩ *lit* [VP; subj: human; usu. infin with пытаться, хотеть etc] to (attempt to) halt the natural course of historical development, return to the past: Х-ы пытались повернуть колесо истории вспять ≃ **Xs tried to turn back the clock (of history); Xs tried to turn back the hands of time.**

[author's usage] Да, говорили одни, процессы истории необратимы. Историю не повернёшь вспять, говорили другие (Зиновьев 1). "Yes," some of them said, "the tide of history cannot be turned back." "You can't turn back the clock of history," said others (1a).

K-197 • ПЯ́ТОЕ КОЛЕСО́ В ТЕЛЕ́ГЕ ⟨В КОЛЕСНИ́ЦЕ⟩ *coll* [NP; sing only; subj-compl with copula, nom or instrum (subj: human); fixed WO] an extra, unnecessary, superfluous person: **fifth wheel; odd man out.**

К-198 • **ВХОДИ́ТЬ/ВОЙТИ́** ⟨**ПОПАДА́ТЬ/ПО-ПА́СТЬ**⟩ **В (СВОЮ́ ⟨ОБЫ́ЧНУЮ, ПРИВЫ́ЧНУЮ** и т. п.⟩) **КОЛЕЮ́** [VP; fixed WO] **1.** [subj: human] to return to one's usual life style: X вошёл в (свою) колею ≃ **X settled ⟨got back⟩ into the (old) groove ⟨into his (old) routine⟩; X returned to his former routine.**

Он вернулся в Россию, попытался зажить старою жизнью, но уже не мог попасть в прежнюю колею (Тургенев 2). He returned to Russia and tried to take up his former life but could not get back into the old groove (2c). He returned to Russia, tried to take up his old life, but found it impossible to return to his former routine (2e).

2. Also: **ВХОДИ́ТЬ/ВОЙТИ́** ⟨**ВОЗВРАЩА́ТЬСЯ/ВЕРНУ́ТЬСЯ**⟩ **В (СВОЁ ⟨ОБЫ́ЧНОЕ, ПРИВЫ́Ч-НОЕ** и т. п.⟩) **РУ́СЛО** [subj: abstr, often жизнь, всё] to return to being the way it usu. is: X вошёл в свою колею ≃ **X settled ⟨got back⟩ into the (old) groove ⟨into its (old) routine⟩; X returned to normal ⟨to its normal course⟩; X got ⟨was⟩ back to normal; X got ⟨was⟩ back on course.**

Жизнь снова вошла в свою колею. Дирижёр и Гайк уехали, а мы остались на своих, так сказать, местах, при своих занятиях (Рыбаков 1). Life returned to normal. The conductor and Gaik left, and we were, so to speak, back in our proper places, going on as usual (1a). ♦ Жизнь вернулась в прежнюю колею: день неизбежно сменялся тьмой ночи (Обухова 1). Life had returned to its normal course: the day was inevitably followed by the darkness of the night (1a). ♦ «Всё ерунда, не обращайте внимания. Всё объяснится, всё войдёт в свою колею» (Аржак 2). "The whole thing is nonsense so take no notice of it. Everything will be cleared up and everything will be back to normal" (2a).

К-199 • **НЕ ПЛЮ́Й В КОЛО́ДЕЦ, ПРИГОДИ́ТСЯ ВОДЫ́ НАПИ́ТЬСЯ** [saying] do not do harm to or show disregard for another person because, in the future, you may come to need his help or support: ≃ **cast no dirt in the well that gives you water; don't spit into the well, you may have to ⟨need to⟩ drink from it one day ⟨someday⟩; don't spit into a cup from which you may someday drink; chickens will always come home to roost.**

[author's usage] После обряда он [поп Виссарион] поздравил молодых, назидательно сказал: «Вот, молодой советский товарищ, как бывает в жизни: в прошлом году вы собственноручно сожгли мой дом... а сегодня мне пришлось вас венчать... Не плюй, говорят, в колодец, ибо он может пригодиться» (Шолохов 5). After the [wedding] ceremony he [Father Vissarion] congratulated the young couple, and said didactically, "So there you are, young Soviet comrade, that's how it is in life. Last year you burnt down my house with your own hands...and today I have to marry you. Don't spit into the well, they say, because you may need to drink from it one day" (5a).

К-200 • **(все) НА ОДНУ́ КОЛО́ДКУ (сшиты, скроены, сделаны)** coll [PrepP; Invar; subj-compl with copula (subj: human, pl) or adv; fixed WO] (two or more people are) very similar to one another, identical in some respect (esp. in regard to shortcomings): (все) X-ы ⟨X-ы и Y-и и т. п.⟩ на одну колодку (сшиты) ≃ **Xs ⟨Xs and Ys⟩ are (all) cut from the same cloth; Xs ⟨Xs and Ys⟩ are cast in the same mold; Xs ⟨Xs and Ys⟩ are birds of a feather ⟨are (all) of the same ilk⟩; [in limited contexts] like father, like son; like mother, like daughter.**

К-201 • **БИТЬ ВО ВСЕ КОЛОКОЛА́; УДАРЯ́ТЬ/УДА́РИТЬ В ⟨ВО ВСЕ⟩ КОЛОКОЛА́** all coll [VP; subj: human or collect] to arouse concern over sth., call attention to sth. (a disturbance, transgression etc): X бьёт во все колокола ≃ **X sounds ⟨raises⟩ the alarm.**

[Клавдия Васильевна:] Но ты пришёл ещё раз, ещё, ещё, и всё в нетрезвом виде. Я ударила во все колокола: я подняла школу, комсомол, и мы вытащили тебя из этой компании (Розов 2). [K.V.:] But you came home drunk time after time. So I sounded the alarm. I roused the school, the Komsomol, and we dragged you away from that bunch you were going with (2a).

К-202 • **ЗВОНИ́ТЬ/ЗАЗВОНИ́ТЬ** ⟨**РАЗЗВОНИ́ТЬ, ТРЕЗВО́НИТЬ/РАСТРЕЗВО́НИТЬ**⟩ **В ⟨ВО ВСЕ⟩ КОЛОКОЛА́** highly coll [VP; subj: human] to tell everyone about sth., spread news, rumors: X звонит во все колокола ≃ **X shouts it ⟨the news etc⟩ from the housetops ⟨from the rooftops, on every street corner⟩; X spreads it all over ⟨far and wide⟩; X lets the whole world know; X tells it to the whole world.**

К-203 • **КОЛОКОЛА́ ЛИТЬ** obs, coll [VP; subj: human] to disseminate gossip or stories that are impossible to believe: X льёт колокола ≃ **X spreads gossip; X tells tall tales.**

< From an old superstitious belief that spreading gossip and unbelievable stories at the time when a new bell («колокол») is being cast will make them sound better.

К-204 • **СМОТРЕ́ТЬ ⟨ГЛЯДЕ́ТЬ⟩ СО СВОЕ́Й КО-ЛОКО́ЛЬНИ** (на кого-что) coll [VP; subj: human] to make one-sided judgments about s.o. or sth. based entirely on one's own limited perspective: X смотрит на Y-а со своей колокольни ≃ **X sees ⟨judges, looks at⟩ Y ⟨things⟩ solely from X's own point of view; X takes a narrow view of Y.**

Она смотрит со своей колокольни и не видит многого, не помнит, не хочет знать (Трифонов 6). She took a narrow view of things—there was much she did not see, did not remember and did not want to hear (6a).

К-205 • **СТОЯ́ТЬ КОЛО́М** coll [VP; subj: a noun denoting a piece of clothing, fabric etc] to be inflexible, hard: X стоял колом ≃ **X was ⟨became, turned⟩ (as) stiff as a board; X was like cardboard.**

Промокшая юбка подмёрзла на ветру и стояла колом. The wet skirt froze in the wind and turned stiff as a board.

К-206 • **СТОЯ́ТЬ/(В)СТАТЬ КОЛО́М В ГО́РЛЕ** у кого, кому highly coll [VP] **1.** [subj: a noun denoting some food] to be unpalatable, inedible, disgusting: X стоит у Y-а колом в горле ≃ **X sticks in Y's throat; X won't go down.**

2. Also: **СТОЯ́ТЬ/(В)СТАТЬ КО́СТЬЮ В ГО́РЛЕ ⟨В ГЛО́ТКЕ⟩** (кому) coll [subj: abstr or concr] to annoy, aggravate s.o. extremely: X стоит у Y-а колом в горле ≃ **X sticks in Y's throat (like a bone); X is a thorn in Y's side.**

Этот проклятый New Lanark вообще костью стоит в горле людей, постоянно обвиняющих социализм в утопиях... (Герцен 3). That cursed New Lanark stuck in the throats of people who perpetually accused socialism of Utopianism... (3a).

К-207 • **ПЯ́ТАЯ КОЛО́ННА** [NP; sing only; fixed WO] people secretly collaborating with an enemy invading the country they live in: **fifth column.**

< Loan translation of the Spanish *la quinta columna*, originally used by General Emilio Mola during the Spanish Civil War (1936–39) in reference to the Franco supporters within Madrid at the time when Mola was leading four columns of Franco's troops against the city.

К-208 • **КОЛО́СС НА ГЛИ́НЯНЫХ НОГА́Х** lit [NP; fixed WO] (often of a country) sth. that appears mighty, invincible, but is in fact weak and can be easily destroyed: **colossus with feet of clay.**

В парламентских кулуарах говорили о лапландской руде, о «колоссе на глиняных ногах», о сочувствии Рима. Депутаты приехали, чтобы убедиться в солидности линии Мажино… (Эренбург 4). In the parliamentary lobbies there was a good deal of talk about the core in Lapland, the "colossus with feet of clay," and the sympathy of Rome. The deputies were visiting the front to reassure themselves as to the solidity of the Maginot Line (4a).

< From the Biblical account of the image seen in a dream by Nebuchadnezzar, king of Babylon, and interpreted as a symbol of Babylon and its future destruction (Dan. 2:31–45).

К-209 • ПОД СТЕКЛЯ́ННЫМ КОЛПАКО́М жить, находиться, держать *кого*; **ПОД СТЕКЛЯ́ННЫЙ КОЛПА́К** посадить, поместить *кого* [PrepP; these forms only; usu. subj-compl with copula (subj: human) or obj-compl with держать etc (obj: human); fixed WO] (to be, keep s.o. etc) isolated from the difficulties and hardships of life, hard work etc: **(be ⟨turn s.o. into, live like⟩) a hothouse flower; (live as if ⟨keep s.o., wrap s.o.⟩) in cotton wool.**

К-210 • СТОЯ́ТЬ У КОЛЫБЕ́ЛИ *чего lit* [VP; subj: human] to contribute to the emergence of sth. new: X стоял у колыбели Y-а ≃ **X helped conceive ⟨create, give birth to⟩ Y.**

К-211 • КАК ⟨БУ́ДТО и т. п.⟩ ПО КОМА́НДЕ *coll* [как + PrepP; Invar; adv] (of two or more people, animals, or things) (to do sth.) simultaneously, so that it looks as if s.o. had ordered them to do it: **as if on command; as if at a command.**

Гусары не оглядывались, но при каждом звуке пролетающего ядра, будто по команде, весь эскадрон с своими однообразно-разнообразными лицами, сдерживая дыханье, пока летело ядро, приподнимался на стременах и снова опускался (Толстой 4). The hussars did not look back, but at the sound of every cannonball that flew past them, as if at a command, the whole squadron, their faces all so alike yet so different, held its breath, rising in the stirrups and sinking back again (4a).

К-212 • КОМА́Р НО́СА ⟨-у⟩ НЕ ПОДТО́ЧИТ ⟨НЕ ПОДТОЧИ́Л БЫ⟩ *coll* [VP$_{subj}$; these forms only; used as indep. sent or subord clause (introduced by что or, if subjunctive, by чтобы, often after a main clause containing так); fixed WO] sth. is done so flawlessly that no defects can be found: **(it is) a precise ⟨beautiful, very neat⟩ job; (it's) done to a T ⟨to perfection⟩.**

Выходит, всё делается по правилам — комар носу не подточит (Эткинд 1). So everything was being done according to the rules — a beautiful job (1a). ♦ «Выкопал я ей яму, как тайничку полагается, книзу шире, кувшином, узким горлом вверх. Яму тоже дымом сушили, обогревали. В самую, самую метель. Спрятали картошку… землёй забросали. Комар носу не подточит» (Пастернак 1). "So I made the pit in the proper way for a hiding place, wide at the bottom and narrow at the top, like a jug, and we started a fire again and warmed and dried the pit with the smoke — all in a howling blizzard. Then we put the potatoes into the pit and the earth back on top. A very neat job it was" (1a).

К-213 • ВЕЛИ́КИЙ КОМБИНА́ТОР *coll, usu. humor or iron* [NP; usu. sing; fixed WO] a clever (and usu. likable) swindler: **great schemer; smooth ⟨shrewd⟩ operator.**

[source] Великий комбинатор не любил ксендзов (Ильф и Петров 2). The great schemer did not like Catholic priests (2b).

< The appellation of Ostap Bender, hero of the novels *The Twelve Chairs* («Двенадцать стульев»), 1928, and *The Golden Calf* («Золотой телёнок»), 1931, by Ilya Ilf and Evgeny Petrov.

К-214 • КОМБИНА́ЦИЯ ИЗ ТРЁХ ПА́ЛЬЦЕВ *euph, coll* [NP; sing only] a gesture of derision, contempt, rejection, which consists of extending one's fist, usu. palm upward, with the thumb placed between the index and middle fingers: **fig.**

К-215 • ЛОМА́ТЬ ⟨ИГРА́ТЬ, РАЗЫ́ГРЫВАТЬ⟩ КОМЕ́ДИЮ *(перед кем) coll, usu. disapprov* [VP; subj: human] to pretend, behave insincerely, hypocritically (with s.o.), speak untruthfully etc: X ломает комедию (перед Y-ом) ≃ **X is playacting ⟨play-acting⟩; X is putting on an act ⟨a show⟩ (for Y); X is playing a farce; X is playing false with Y; [in limited contexts] X is giving Y a song and dance.**

Всё начинало злить меня. Какого чёрта я здесь сижу? Если она мне нужна как женщина, то почему я трачу время, ломаю комедию (Лимонов 1). It all began to irritate me. What the hell was I sitting here for? If I needed her as a woman, then why was I wasting time play-acting? (1a). ♦ «Да у тебя белая горячка, что ль! — заревел взбесившийся наконец Разумихин. — Чего ты комедии-то разыгрываешь! Даже меня сбил с толку…» (Достоевский 3). "Have you got brain fever or what?" Razumikhin bellowed, finally enraged. "What is this farce you're playing? You've even got me all screwed up…" (3c).

К-216 • КУ́КОЛЬНАЯ КОМЕ́ДИЯ [NP; sing only; fixed WO] a false show (of sth.), a hypocritical action: **farce; humbug.**

Карл Иваныч рассердился, поставил меня на колени, твердил, что это упрямство, кукольная комедия… (Толстой 2). Karl Ivanych got angry, ordered me on my knees and kept saying that it was obstinacy and all humbug… (2c).

К-217 • КОММЕНТА́РИИ ИЗЛИ́ШНИ [sent; Invar; fixed WO] the situation is perfectly clear, understandable without any (further) explanation: **no more need be said; no explanation required ⟨necessary⟩.**

К-218 • ВОДИ́ТЬ КОМПА́НИЮ *с кем coll* [VP; subj: human] to associate, be friends, spend time with s.o.: X водит компанию с Y-ом ≃ **X keeps company with Y; X hangs ⟨pals⟩ around with Y; X hangs out with Y; X hobnobs with Y; [in limited contexts] X rubs shoulders with Y.**

[Пелагея Егоровна:] Мне, говорит, здесь не с кем компанию водить, все, говорит, сволочь… (Островский 2). [context transl] [P.E.:] No worthy company for me here, says he; they're all scum here, says he (2b).

К-219 • ЗА КОМПА́НИЮ *(с кем);* **ДЛЯ КОМПА́НИИ** *both coll* [PrepP; these forms only; adv] (in refer. to one's or s.o.'s participation in an activity in which one or s.o. would not have engaged had others not been engaging in it) (to do sth.) with another or others when he is or they are doing it, (to get s.o. to do sth. or take s.o.) with one when one is doing sth.: **(come ⟨go etc⟩) along with s.o.; (take s.o. etc) along with one; join in; join s.o.; (do sth.) because s.o. is doing it; [when a person participates in sth. in order to make it more enjoyable for another or others] (do sth.) to keep s.o. company; (take s.o. with one etc) to keep one company; for company.**

Алёша цирк не любит, но у нас был лишний билет, и он решил пойти за компанию. Alyosha doesn't like the circus, but since we had an extra ticket he decided to come along with us. ♦ [Галина:] …Бывал ли ты когда-нибудь в церкви? [Зилов:] Да. Раз мы заходили с ребятами. По пьянке. А ты? [Галина:] А я с бабушкой. За компанию (Вампилов 5). [G.:] Have you ever been to church? [Z.:] Yes. Looked in once with some of my mates, when we were drunk. Have you? [G.:] I went with my grandmother. To keep her company (5a). ♦ «Пошли, Вася, будь другом, за компанию» (Максимов 3). "Come on, Vasilii, be a pal, keep us company" (3a). ♦ По-моему, они даже не держали кухарку, а столовались у соседей, куда иногда за компанию затаскивали и меня пить чай или ужинать в большой компании московских беженцев, где я познакомился с некоторыми известными людьми (Катаев 3). I believe they did not even have a cook. Instead they ate with their neighbours. Sometimes they took me in there with them for company to have tea or supper with a large gathering of Moscow refugees, where I met many famous people (3a).

К-220 • **ПОДДЕРЖÁТЬ КОМПÁНИЮ** *coll* [VP; subj: human] to enter into some activity planned and participated in by some group of people: X поддержит компанию ≃ **X will join in; X will join us ⟨you, them⟩.**

К-221 • **СОСТÁВИТЬ КОМПÁНИЮ** *кому* [VP; subj: human] to do with another or others what he or they are doing: X составит Y-у компанию ≃ **X will join Y; X will come ⟨go⟩ (along) with Y;** [in limited contexts] **X will keep Y company.**

Гость ждал и именно сидел как приживальщик, только что сошедший сверху из отведённой ему комнаты вниз к чаю составить хозяину компанию, но смирно молчавший ввиду того, что хозяин занят и об чём-то нахмуренно думает… (Достоевский 2). The visitor sat and waited precisely like a sponger who had just come down from upstairs, from the room assigned to him, to keep his host company at tea, but was humbly silent, since the host was preoccupied and scowling at the thought of something… (2a).

К-222 • **…И КОМПÁНИЯ** *derog* [NP; sing only; used after a personal noun (often a person's name)] (the person named) and his friends, companions: X и компания ≃ **X and company; X and his gang ⟨buddies, chums, pals, crowd, crew⟩.**

К-223 • **НЕ КОМПÁНИЯ** *кому;* **КАКÁЯ КОМПÁНИЯ** [NP; these forms only; subj-compl with быть∅ (subj: human), pres only] a person does not suit another person (or persons) as a friend, companion etc: X Y-у не компания ≃ **X is no ⟨not good, not the proper⟩ company for Y.**

К-224 • **ТЁПЛАЯ КОМПÁНИЯ ⟨КОМПÁШКА** *slang*⟩ *coll* [NP; sing only; fixed WO] **1.** a nice, friendly group of people (who usu. have fun together): **nice crowd ⟨bunch⟩; friendly ⟨merry⟩ gang; fun group ⟨bunch⟩.**

2. *rather derog* a group of people united by and involved in some reprehensible, base activity: [said with ironic intonation] **lovely bunch ⟨group etc⟩; charming crew ⟨crowd etc⟩;** [when used as Interj] **what a bunch!;** [in limited contexts] **seedy ⟨unsavory⟩ bunch ⟨crew etc⟩.**

К-225 • **СТÁВИТЬ/ПОСТÁВИТЬ НÁ КОН** *что coll* [VP; subj: human] to risk (one's life, reputation etc), expose o.s. to danger in the hope of winning, gaining sth.: X поставил на кон Y ≃ **X put ⟨laid⟩ Y on the line.**

Зимой он целый день выстоял на морозе напротив милиции, где, как он узнал, Варвара работала уборщицей. Можно сказать, жизнь свою на кон ставил… И всё ради неё (Абрамов 1). Once that winter he had stood a whole day in the freezing cold, opposite the police station where he had learned Varvara was working as a cleaning woman. You might say he had put his whole life on the line.…And all for her sake (1a).

К-226 • **С КОНДАЧКÁ** [PrepP; Invar] **1.** *highly coll* [adv] (to do sth.) without thinking, without giving the matter serious consideration: **(do sth.) at the drop of a hat; (say sth.) off the top of one's head; offhand; just like that.**

«…Пойдём на прогулку, я тебе объясню. Это надо серьёзно говорить, не с кондачка» (Копелев 1). "When we go for a walk, I'll explain. That requires serious talk, not off the top of your head" (1a).

2. обращаться *с кем,* **вести себя** *~ obs* [adv or subj-compl with быть∅ (subj: human)] (to treat s.o., behave) too informally, without the due formalities: **unceremonious(ly); irreverent(ly); discourteous(ly).**

К-227 • **ДО КОНДИ́ЦИИ дойти, довести** *кого-что coll,* *usu. humor or iron* [PrepP; Invar; adv] (to reach, bring s.o. or sth.

to) the state expected, desired etc in the given circumstances: **(whip ⟨get⟩ s.o. ⟨sth.⟩) into shape;** [in refer. to inanim objects only] **(be) done.**

К-228 • **КОНДРÁШКА ХВАТИ́Л ⟨СТУ́КНУЛ, ПРИ-ШИ́Б⟩** *кого substand;* **КОНДРÁТИЙ ХВАТИ́Л** *obs, substand* [VP∅ₛᵤᵦⱼ] s.o. suddenly became paralyzed or died as the result of an apoplectic stroke: X-а кондрашка хватит ≃ **X will drop dead from a stroke ⟨from apoplexy⟩; X will have ⟨will suffer⟩ a stroke; s.o. ⟨sth.⟩ will give X a stroke.**

«…А вас, если так будете надуваться и наливаться кровью, скоро кондрашка хватит!» (Амальрик 1). "As for you, if you go swelling up with anger until you're red in the face, you'll soon drop dead from apoplexy" (1a). ♦ «От таких новостей кондрашка может хватить» (Грекова 3). "News like that can give you a stroke" (3a).

< According to historian Sergey Solovyov, this phrase might be related to the name of *Кондратий (Кондрашка)* Булавин, who led the peasant uprising of 1707. Cited in M.I. Mikhelson, «Русская мысль и речь. Своё и чужое. Опыт русской фразеологии» (St. Petersburg: 1912) and other sources.

К-229 • **НА КОНÉ** *coll* [PrepP; Invar; subj-compl with copula (subj: human)] one is in an advantageous, winning position: X на коне ≃ **X is riding high (in the saddle); X is sitting pretty; X is in the catbird seat;** [in limited contexts] **X is in the saddle.**

К-230 • **В КОНÉЦ разорить, испортить** *кого-что,* **измучить** *кого,* **измучиться** и т. п. *coll* [PrepP; Invar; adv; usu. used with pfv verbs] (to ruin s.o. or sth., exhaust s.o., be exhausted etc) entirely, absolutely: **completely; totally; utterly;** [in limited contexts] **for good; beyond salvation.**

К-231 • **В ОДИ́Н КОНÉЦ поездка, билет, ехать** и т. п. *coll* [PrepP; Invar; nonagreeing modif or adv; fixed WO] (a trip, a ticket, to travel etc) in one direction only: **one way;** ‖ билет ~ ≃ **one-way ticket;** ‖ стоимость билета ~ ≃ **one-way fare.**

К-232 • **И КОНÉЦ** *coll* [sent; Invar; usu. the concluding clause in a compound or complex sent] **1.** and there is nothing more to add (to what has been said or done), no further argument or discussion will be of any avail: **and that's the end of it ⟨of that⟩; and that's it ⟨that's that, that's final⟩.**

«Любовь? Что это такое, ты хочешь спросить? А это только обозначение обязанностей. Да. Пошлое и… легкомысленное обозначение, которое позволяет человеку в любой момент отказаться от своих самых главных обязанностей: разлюбил, и конец, а там хоть трава не расти…» (Залыгин 1). "Love? You mean, what is it? It's only another name for duty. A tasteless and flippant name…which permits people to abandon their most important obligations whenever they feel like it, so that they can say: 'I don't love her any more, and that's the end of it, and I don't care what happens now…'" (1a).

2. and then (after the action in question has been undertaken) the matter will be concluded, the problem in question will be resolved etc: **and that will be the end of it ⟨the matter, the business⟩; and that will be that ⟨it⟩; and it will all be over; and that will settle it; (do sth.) and be done with it.**

«Что тут размышлять? Переезжай да и конец!» (Гончаров 1). "Why hesitate? Move, and be done with it!" (1b).

К-233 • **КОНÉЦ – (ВСЕМУ́) ДÉЛУ ВЕНÉЦ; КОНÉЦ ВЕНЧÁЕТ ДÉЛО** [saying] the successful conclusion of some undertaking makes the undertaking on the whole a success: ≃ **the end crowns the work.**

К-234 • НА КАКО́Й КОНЕ́Ц? *obs, coll* [PrepP; Invar; adv; fixed WO] why, with what goal: **to what end?; what would be the point ⟨the purpose⟩?**

Логики нет никакой в мёртвых душах, как же покупать мёртвые души? Где ж дурак такой возьмётся?.. И на какой конец, к какому делу можно приткнуть эти мёртвые души? (Гоголь 3). There was no logic to them [dead souls]. How could one buy dead souls and where would you find a big enough fool to buy them?...And to what end, for what purpose could he use dead souls? (3c).

К-235 • НА ХУДО́Й КОНЕ́Ц *coll* [PrepP; Invar; sent adv (occas. parenth); fixed WO] in the worst case, under the most disagreeable circumstances: **if (the) worst comes to (the) worst; if worse comes to worse; at worst; at the (very) worst;** [in limited contexts] **at (the very) least.**

«Ты представляешь себе, какой поднимется шум, когда кто-нибудь из них для начала преподнесёт читающей публике „Ревизора" или, на самый худой конец, „Евгения Онегина"!» (Булгаков 9). "Can you imagine the furore when one of them will, as a starter, present the reading public with an *Inspector General* or, if worst comes to worst, a *Yevgeny Onegin*?" (9a). ♦ Если бы была нужда, на худой конец можно было бы придумать легенду и о вилле фон Фрейлебен. Но нужды нет (Федин 1). If there were a need to and worse came to worse, it would be possible to invent a legend about the Villa von Freileben as well. But there is no need (1a). ♦ «Итак, друзья мои, мы, по всей вероятности, будем сматываться отсюда», – сказал Дима... «На родину предков?» – спросил Антон. «Ты с ума сошёл, – возмутился Дима. – В Канаду или США. На худой конец – в Париж» (Зиновьев 2). "Well, then, my friends, we'll probably be pushing off quite soon," said Dima....."To return to the land of your forefathers?" Anton asked. "You must be off your head," said Dima, indignantly. "To Canada, or to the States. Paris at worst" (2a). ♦ «Что тебе стоило согласиться или на худой конец промолчать?» (Распутин 2). "What would it have cost you to agree or at least to say nothing?" (2a). ♦ Когда разгорелось пламя, Пётр Житов в ознаменование нынешнего исторического события... предложил выбить памятную медаль или на худой конец сковать подкову на счастье (Абрамов 1). When the flames were blazing, Pyotr Zhitov proposed that to mark this historic event...a memorial medal be struck, or that at the very least a lucky horseshoe be forged (1a).

К-236 • ОДИ́Н КОНЕ́Ц *coll* [NP; Invar; usu. indep. clause] (in refer. to sth. unavoidable, often death) there is no choice, a sad outcome is inevitable: **it (all) comes (down) to the same thing in the end; it all ends up the same way.**

К-237 • ПОД КОНЕ́Ц [PrepP; Invar; adv] **1.** ~ *(чего)* when sth. is approaching its conclusion: **toward ⟨near⟩ the end (of sth.).**

В начале следствия, как заметил О. М[андельштам], следователь держался гораздо агрессивнее, чем под конец (Мандельштам 1). At the beginning of the interrogation, M[andelstam] noticed, the interrogator had behaved much more agressively than toward the end (1a).

2. used to introduce the final event in a series: **in the end; finally.**

Их обгоняли конные, и Прохор, не выдержав, останавливал проезжавших, здоровался, спрашивал, куда едут... под конец говорил: «Зря едете» (Шолохов 5). If anyone on horseback overtook them, he [Prokhor] could not resist stopping him with a greeting and asking where they were heading for...and in the end he would say, "You're making a mistake to go on" (5a). ♦ Года три-четыре по смерти второй жены он [Фёдор Павлович] отправился на юг России и под конец очутился в Одессе, где и прожил сряду несколько лет (Достоевский 1). Three or four years after his second wife's death, he [Fyodor Pavlovich] set off for the south of Russia and finally wound up in Odessa, where he lived for several years in a row... (1a).

К-238 • ПОЛОЖИ́ТЬ КОНЕ́Ц *чему* [VP; subj: human or abstr; fixed WO] to stop, terminate sth.: X положил конец Y-у ≃ **X put an end ⟨a stop⟩ to Y; X called a halt (to Y).**

Если исторический опыт нашей эпохи не поможет людям положить конец воинствующему своеволию, останется только совершить последний и логический шаг – самоуничтожение (Мандельштам 2). If the historical experience of our times does not help people to put an end to unbridled license, then there remains only the last logical step: self-destruction (2a).

К-239 • ВНЕ КОНКУРЕ́НЦИИ *coll;* **ВНЕ КО́НКУРСА** [PrepP; these forms only; subj-compl with copula (subj: human, abstr, or concr)] unequaled, better than the rest, better than all possible rivals: X был вне конкуренции ≃ **X was beyond comparison ⟨beyond compare⟩; X was unsurpassed; person X was head and shoulders above the rest.**

К-240 • ШАРА́ШКИНА КОНТО́РА *coll, usu. derog* [NP; sing only; fixed WO] a questionable, suspicious, untrustworthy business, shop, enterprise etc: **shady ⟨dubious⟩ business ⟨outfit etc⟩;** [in limited contexts] **fly-by-night outfit ⟨enterprise etc⟩.**

К-241 • СДЕ́ЛАТЬ КОНФЕ́ТКУ *из чего coll* [VP; subj: human] to improve sth. dramatically, make sth. worthless into sth. superior: X сделал из Y-а конфетку ≃ **X turned Y into a (real) masterpiece ⟨work of art⟩; X made a real (little) jewel out of Y.**

О боже, сказал Мыслитель, прочитав статью Киса. Какая мразь!.. Конечно, кое-какие мыслишки в статье есть... Поработать над ней пару вечеров, хороший материал можно сделать. И Мыслитель углубился в работу. И работа его увлекла. Как говорила потом Супруга, Мыслитель сделал из статьи Киса конфетку (Зиновьев 1). Oh, God, said Thinker, as he read through an article by Puss. What rubbish!...Of course, there are a few tiny signs of thought in the article....If I worked on it for a couple of evenings it might turn out quite well. So Thinker buckled [down] and found the work inspiring. As Wife later said, Thinker made a real little jewel out of Puss's article (1a).

К-242 • БЕЗ КОНЦА́ [PrepP; Invar; adv] (used to characterize an action that continues uninterruptedly or is carried out repeatedly) over or for a very long period of time, seemingly without end: **endlessly; forever;** [in limited contexts] **never stop (doing sth.).**

Час проходит за часом, а мы всё ходим, говорим и ходим. По Москве можно ходить без конца (Казаков 2). The hours pass, and we're still walking, talking, and walking. You can walk around Moscow endlessly (2a). ♦ «Какова скотина! Почему я должен без конца делать ему одолжение?» (Трифонов 5). "What a cad! Why should I forever be doing him favors?" (5a). ♦ [Иванов:] Нет, замучил я себя, люди мучают меня без конца... Просто сил моих нет! (Чехов 4). [I.:] Really, I've worn myself out and people never stop bothering me. I'm at the end of my tether (4b).

К-243 • БЕЗ КОНЦА́ И (БЕЗ) КРА́Я ⟨-ю⟩; БЕЗ КОНЦА́-КРА́Ю [PrepP; these forms only; fixed WO] **1.** [adv, nonagreeing modif, or quantit subj-compl with copula (subj: a noun denoting some expanse)] (to be or seem to be) without an end: X тянулся ~ ≃ **X stretched endlessly into the distance; X stretched boundlessly into the horizon; X went on without end into the distance.**

2. *чего* ~ [quantit subj-compl with copula (subj/gen: usu. abstr or concr)] (in some place there is) a great number or quantity of sth.: X-ов было ~ ≃ **there was no end of Xs; there were hordes ⟨scads, droves etc⟩ of Xs.**

К-244 • В ОБА КОНЦА́ поездка, билет, ехать и т. п. *coll* [PrepP; Invar; nonagreeing modif or adv; fixed WO] (a trip, a ticket, to travel etc) to a place and back again: **(make) a round trip; (travel) there and back;** ‖ билет ~ ≃ **round-trip ticket;** ‖ стоимость билета ~ ≃ **round-trip fare.**

У меня всего 500 рублей – на билет в оба конца не хватит. I've only got five hundred rubles – that's not enough for a round-trip ticket.

К-245 • ДО КОНЦА́ [PrepP; Invar; adv or modif] entirely, wholly: **completely; fully; totally;** [in limited contexts] **in its entirety; complete ⟨entire⟩** [NP]; ‖ если (уж) быть до конца честным ⟨откровенным⟩ ≃ **to be perfectly honest ⟨frank⟩.**

...Только Лиля, одна Лиля понимает меня, только с ней я могу быть до конца откровенным (Казаков 2). Only Lilya, Lilya alone understood me, only with her could I be completely open (2a). ♦ Вот уже столько лет мы дружим с этим длинным [американцем], а всё никак не можем до конца понять друг друга (Аксёнов 6). This tall American and I have been friends for years now, yet we can never fully understand each other (6a). ♦ ...Митишатьев – в этом было даже какое-то безволие, погружение в порок – не удержался и добавил, что, если уж быть до конца честным... так он вернулся всё-таки [к Фаине] тогда, когда Лёва поехал домой... (Битов 2). Mitishatyev could not resist adding (there was even something spineless about this, an immersion in vice) that to be totally honest...he *had* gone back [to Faina's] that night, after Lyova went home... (2a). ♦ «Ксения Макаровна, почему не говорите правду до конца?» (Чернёнок 1). "Ksenya Makarovna, why aren't you telling the complete truth?" (1a). ♦ ...Если уж быть до конца честным, надо признаться, что, будь моя статья об этой декаде более яркой, хотя бы в лучших её местах, думаю, не пожалели бы на меня медали (Искандер 4). ...To be perfectly honest, I think the truth is that they would have coughed up a medal for me, if my write-up on the festival – even just the key passages – had been more brilliant (4a).

К-246 • ДО КОНЦА́ ⟨ДО КО́НЧИКОВ⟩ НОГТЕ́Й [PrepP; these forms only; nonagreeing modif; fixed WO] (one is a certain type of person) entirely, in every way: **(a [NP]) to the ⟨one's⟩ fingertips; every inch (a ⟨the⟩ [NP]); (a [NP]) to the core; (a [NP]) through and through.**

...С такими людьми я ещё никогда не встречался, сразу видно: утончённый, изысканно-простой, до кончиков ногтей интеллигентный... (Катаев 3). ...Such people were quite beyond my ken. I saw at once that he was refined and yet exquisitely natural, an intellectual to the very fingertips (3a).

К-247 • ДО КОНЦА́ (СВОИ́Х) ДНЕЙ [PrepP; these forms only; adv; fixed WO] to the end of one's life, until one dies: **to ⟨till⟩ the end of one's days; to one's dying day; as long as one lives.**

Старик настолько оправился, что через некоторое время пошёл работать мясником в одну из своих бывших лавок, где проработал до конца своих дней (Искандер 3). The old man was so much improved that he eventually took a job as a butcher in one of his former shops, where he worked to the end of his days (3a).

К-248 • ДО ПОБЕ́ДНОГО КОНЦА́ [PrepP; Invar; adv; fixed WO] **1.** довести *что* ~ (to bring sth.) to the point of complete and final success: **to a triumphant conclusion; to a successful finish ⟨close, end⟩.**

2. сидеть *где,* ждать *кого* и т. п. ~ *coll* (to stay somewhere, wait for s.o. etc) resolutely, until sth. in progress is finished or s.o. expected appears: **sit ⟨wait⟩ it out; (stay) till ⟨until⟩ the last gun is fired.**

«Давно ждёшь, Евгений Николаевич?» – «Так, давненько уже. Но решил сидеть до победного конца» (Распутин 1). "Have you been waiting long, Evgeny Nikolaevich?" "Pretty long, but I decided to sit it out" (1a).

К-249 • ДОВОДИ́ТЬ/ДОВЕСТИ́ ДО КОНЦА́ *что* [VP: subj: human] to bring sth. to its conclusion, reach a final result: X довёл Y до конца ≃ **X saw ⟨carried⟩ Y through (to the end); X carried Y to the end; X pursued Y to the end; X wound Y up;** [in limited contexts] **X rounded off Y; X got to the bottom of it ⟨Y⟩.**

Ленин... писал: Сталин капризен. Но вместе с тем он терпелив, настойчив и задуманное *всегда* доводит до конца (Рыбаков 2). Lenin had written that Stalin was capricious. But he was also patient and persistent, and he always carried his intentions through to the end (2a). ♦ Что я мог сказать Марату? Что рок никогда не останавливается на полпути, а всегда до конца доводит свой безжалостный замысел? (Искандер 2). What could I say to Marat? That Fate never stops halfway, but always carries its pitiless design to the end! (2a). ♦ ...Мы теперь... избираем последние жертвы и доводим дело до конца (Зиновьев 1). "...We are now choosing our last victims and rounding off the affair" (1a). ♦ ...Юра провёл это расследование в тихости, никому ни слова. Он решил довести до конца – кто ж из двух расхититель... (Солженицын 10). Yuri had conducted his investigation quietly, without breathing a word to anyone. He had made up his mind to get to the bottom of it, to find out which of the two girls was the embezzler (10a).

К-250 • ИЗ КОНЦА́ В КОНЕ́Ц пройти, проехать, изъездить *что* и т. п. [PrepP; Invar; adv; usu. used with pfv verbs; fixed WO] over the whole area or length of sth.: **from one end to the other; from end to end; all over; (throughout) the entire length of (the land ⟨the country etc⟩).**

Сколько раз уже (тысячу раз)... [я] проходил по Москве с севера на юг, с запада на восток, из конца в конец... – и ни разу не видел Кремля (Ерофеев 1). How many times (thousands) I've walked...across Moscow from north to south, east to west, from one end to the other...and never did I see the Kremlin (1a).

К-251 • КОНЦА́-КРА́Ю ⟨-я⟩ ⟨КОНЦА́ И КРА́Ю, НИ КОНЦА́ НИ КРА́Ю, КОНЦА́⟩ НЕТ ⟨НЕСТЬ *obs,* НЕ ВИ́ДНО, НЕ ВИДА́ТЬ⟩ [VP_subj/gen (variants with нет) or VP_subj/gen with быть∅, usu. pres (variants with не видно, не видать)] **1.** ~ *чему* sth. extends extremely far into the distance, seemingly without end: X-у конца-краю не видно ≃ **X has no bounds; X has no end (or limit); X goes on forever; you can't see where X starts or (where it) ends.**

И как нет, казалось, конца и края бегущей воде, нет и веку деревне... (Распутин 4). And just as the flowing water seemed to have no end or limit, the village seemed ageless... (4a).

2. ~ *чему* sth. lasts an extremely long time, seemingly forever: X-у конца-краю нет ≃ **there's no end to X; X goes on and on; X goes on endlessly; X lasts an eternity.**

Для обитателей нашей улицы эта семья была идеалом, витриной достигнутого счастья... Они не только дают полюбоваться своим счастьем, от щедрот его и соседям немало перепадает... Вот так они жили на нашей улице, и, казалось, конца и края не будет этой благодати. И вдруг однажды всё разлетелось на куски! Вахтанг был убит на охоте случайным выстрелом товарища (Искандер 5). To the residents of our street this family was an ideal, a showcase of achieved happiness....Not only were the neighbors allowed to admire their happiness, they also came in for a goodly share in its abundance....Thus they lived on our street, and it seemed there would be no end to this abundance. And suddenly one day everything fell apart! Vakhtang was accidentally shot to death by a comrade while hunting (5a).

3. ~ *кому-чему* there is an extremely large number of people or things, or an extremely large quantity of sth. (in some place, in s.o.'s possession etc), there seems to be an infinite number or quantity: X-ам конца-краю нет ≃ **there's no end (or limit) to (the) Xs; Xs are endless; Xs are ⟨seem⟩ inexhaustible.**

В те времена я ему нравился как хороший слушатель его любовных приключений. Этим приключениям не было ни конца ни края... (Искандер 2). He liked me then because I was a good audience for his stories of romantic adventure. There was no end or limit to these adventures... (2a). ♦ Богатств было пропасть, и конца им не видно было... (Толстой 6). There was an abundance of wealth: it seemed inexhaustible... (6a).

К-252 • НЕ С ТОГО́ КОНЦА́ начинать *что,* **браться** *за что* и т. п. *coll* [PrepP; Invar; adv; fixed WO] (to begin, undertake sth.) incorrectly, using the wrong approach, means etc: **(begin ⟨start⟩ sth.) from ⟨at⟩ the wrong end; (begin ⟨approach⟩ sth.) the wrong way; (approach s.o. ⟨sth.⟩) from the wrong angle;** [in limited contexts] **put the cart before the horse.**

«Снимут судимость! – зло воскликнул Нержин, и глаза его сузились. – Да откуда вы взяли, что я хочу этой подачки: хорошо работал, так, мол, освобождайся?! Мы тебя *прощаем!* Нет, Пётр Трофимович!.. Не с того конца! Пусть признают сперва, что за образ мыслей нельзя сажать – а там *мы* посмотрим – прощаем ли!» (Солженицын 3). "They'll remove the conviction from my record!" Nerzhin cried angrily, his eyes narrowing. "Where did you get the idea that I want that little gift? 'You've worked well, so we'll free you, forgive you.' No, Pyotr Trofimovich!...You're beginning at the wrong end. Let them admit first that it's not right to put people in prison for their way of thinking, and then *we* will decide whether we will forgive *them*" (3a). ♦ Лицо у Егорши вытянулось. Жалко, чёрт побери! Не с того, видно, конца заход сделал (Абрамов 1). Egorsha's face fell. What a shame, goddammit! Obviously, he'd approached her from the wrong angle (1a).

К-253 • С КОНЦА́МИ *highly coll* [PrepP; Invar; usu. adv] (one left, disappeared etc) without leaving any trace and/or forever: **(and) that was the end of him ⟨her etc⟩; (and) he ⟨she etc⟩ was never seen or heard from again; (and) he ⟨she etc⟩ was gone for good.**

К-254 • В КОНЦЕ́ КОНЦО́В [PrepP; Invar; usu. sent adv (often parenth); fixed WO] **1.** as the final result when some (action, series of actions, process etc) is over, when everything related to the situation at hand has been considered: **in the end; in the final analysis; when all is said and done; after all.**

Я был избавлен от необходимости собирать справки о личности Иванько, сведения о нём сыпались на меня на каждом шагу... В конце концов я узнал, что Иванько Сергей Сергеевич... родственник бывшего председателя КГБ Семичастного... (Войнович 3). I was spared the necessity of gathering information on Ivanko—reports on him rained down on me....In the end I learned that Ivanko, Sergei Sergeevich...was a relative of the former director of the KGB, Semichastny... (3a). ♦ В ранней молодости я стыдился своих ушей. Теперь я к ним привык. В конце концов они не очень мешали мне в жизни (Войнович 5). Though I was ashamed of my ears in my early youth, now I've grown used to them. In the final analysis they haven't been that much of a hindrance to me in this life (5a).

2. used to add emotional emphasis to some statement, express dissatisfaction, impatience etc: **really; after all.**

«У меня изменилось мнение. Могло же оно измениться? Мы не догматики, в конце концов!» (Ерофеев 3). "I've changed my mind. Can't one change one's mind? We're not dogmatists, after all!" (3a).

К-255 • КОНЦО́В НЕ НАЙТИ́ ⟨НЕ СЫСКА́ТЬ⟩ *coll* [VP; subj: human; usu. infin (used as impers predic) or neg pfv fut, gener. 2nd pers sing не найдёшь, не сыщешь; fixed WO] it is impossible to find out the reason for sth., understand sth., uncover who is to blame for sth. etc: концов не найти ⟨не найдёшь⟩ ≃ **it's impossible ⟨no one will ever be able etc⟩ to**

put the pieces together ⟨figure it out, puzzle it out, get to the bottom of it⟩; you can't ⟨they'll never be able to etc⟩ figure ⟨puzzle⟩ out who did ⟨organized, was behind etc⟩ it; we ⟨you etc⟩ can't make head(s) or tail(s) (out) of it; [in limited contexts] **there's no way it can be traced (back to s.o.).**

Мы знаем, что с фабрики воруют товары и сбывают их на сторону. Должно быть, работает целая группа, но всё организовано так, что концов не найти. We know that goods are being stolen from the factory and sold on the side. A whole group of people must be involved, but everything's organized in such a way that we can't get to the bottom of it. ♦ Ты не хочешь, чтобы они знали, что бандероль от тебя? Пришли её мне, я отправлю её отсюда без обратного адреса, чтобы и концов не нашли. You don't want them to know the package is from you? Then send it to me and I'll send it to them without any return address so there will be no way to trace it back to you. ♦ ...Ничего вроде бы и не изменилось, вот только завезённые на склад дублёнки для рядового начальства, включая и инструкторов, опять куда-то делись, концов не сыскать (Бахтин 1). [context transl] ...It seemed that nothing really had changed, except that the *dublyonkas* brought to the warehouse for ordinary officials, including instructors, once again disappeared without a trace (1a).

К-256 • СО ВСЕХ КОНЦО́В земли, страны и т. п. [PrepP; Invar; adv; fixed WO] from everywhere: **from all parts (of the world ⟨the country etc⟩); from all sides ⟨quarters⟩; from all over (the place); from every corner of the world ⟨the globe⟩; from the four corners of the globe ⟨the earth⟩.**

К-257 • ВО ВСЕ КОНЦЫ́ посылать, рассылать *кого-что,* скакать и т. п. [PrepP; Invar; adv; fixed WO] to various, many different destinations, everywhere: **in all directions; all over (the place); to the four corners of the globe ⟨the earth⟩;** [in limited contexts] **to the four winds.**

Как-то осенью Мари исчезла. Целый день нельзя было её сыскать, и вечером вилла Урбах забила тревогу. Люди были посланы во все концы (Федин 1). One autumn Marie disappeared. For a whole day she could not be found and in the evening the Villa Urbach sounded the alarm. Men were sent in all directions (1a). ♦ [Зилов:] Разошлёт такие письма во все концы и лежит... ждёт (Вампилов 5). [Z.:] He sends out letters like this all over the place, and settles down to wait... (5a).

К-258 • (И) КОНЦЫ́ В ВО́ДУ *coll* [NP; these forms only; usu. used as a clause in a compound or complex sent preceded by one or more clauses; fixed WO] (and) no bits of evidence (from a reprehensible action, crime etc) will be left for anyone to discover, no one will ever find out about it: **and no traces will be left behind; (and) none ⟨no one⟩ will be (any) the wiser; and no one will ⟨would⟩ know the difference.**

«Ешьте, не стесняйтесь. Я знаю: вы постоянно испытываете дьявольский аппетит, особенно в гостях». – «Что скажет Вера Николаевна!» – воскликнул я. «...Мы с вами сейчас расправимся со всем этим... затем отнесём посуду на кухню – и концы в воду» (Катаев 3). "Eat, man, don't be shy. I know you always have a devilish appetite, particularly when you're dining out." "What will Vera Nikolayevna say!" I exclaimed. "...We'll soon finish this off...take the dishes back to the kitchen—and no one will be any the wiser" (3a).

К-259 • КОНЦЫ́ С КОНЦА́МИ НЕ СХО́ДЯТСЯ [VP_subj; the verb may take the initial position, otherwise fixed WO] **1.** ~ (*у кого*) *coll.* Also: **КОНЦЫ́ С КОНЦА́МИ едва ⟨еле-еле и т. п.⟩ СХО́ДЯТСЯ** *coll* one can barely support himself (and his family) on the money he has, earns etc: у X-а концы с концами не сходятся ≃ **X can barely make ⟨has trouble making etc⟩ ends meet; X can barely keep his head above water; X can barely keep body and soul together.**

Семья у нас большая, работает только муж, концы с концами не сходятся. We have a big family and only my husband works, so we have trouble making ends meet.

2. ~ (*в чём*) there is a contradiction, a lack of necessary agreement between various aspects of some matter, lines of argumentation etc: **it doesn't add up; there are a lot of loose ends; it doesn't (all) fit together; it's full of holes;** [in refer. to a story] **it doesn't hang together.**

Сначала он [Виктор] всё ожидал удара по затылку, прямо по желваку... а потом решил: вряд ли. Концы с концами не сходились (Стругацкие 1). At first he [Victor] kept on waiting for a blow on the back of his head, right on his lump, then he decided it was unlikely. It didn't fit together (1a). ♦ Он утверждает, что не виноват, но в его рассказах концы с концами не сходятся (Марченко 2). According to him, he was innocent, but his story did not hang together (2a).

3. the final results of a calculation (usu. of receipts and expenditures, debits and credits etc) are not what they should be, are not as expected: **the accounts do not balance (out); it doesn't add up.**

К-260 • ОТДАВА́ТЬ/ОТДА́ТЬ КОНЦЫ́[1] *nautical* [VP; subj: human; usu. pfv imper or infin used as a command; fixed WO] to release the ropes or cables that hold a ship at its moorings: отдать концы! ≃ **cast off!; let go!**

К-261 • ОТДАВА́ТЬ/ОТДА́ТЬ КОНЦЫ́[2] *substand* [VP; subj: human; usu. this WO] **1.** to die: X отдал концы ≃ **X kicked off; X kicked the bucket; X cashed in (his chips); X turned up his toes.**

Без дачи и поликлиники на Грановского [Александр Иванович] давно бы отдал концы (Ерофеев 3). Without a summer cottage and the special clinics on Granovsky Street he [Alexander Ivanovich] would have kicked the bucket long ago (3a).

2. to run away, run off: X отдал концы ≃ **X took off; X took to his heels; X split (the scene); X lit ⟨cut⟩ out (of place Y); X cut and ran;** [in limited contexts] **X flew the coop.**

К-262 • ПРЯ́ТАТЬ/СПРЯ́ТАТЬ ⟨ХОРОНИ́ТЬ/СХОРОНИ́ТЬ⟩ КОНЦЫ́ (В ВО́ДУ) *coll* [VP; subj: human; often infin with уметь, пытаться, можно, надо etc; the verb may take the final position, otherwise fixed WO] to hide the traces, destroy the evidence of some reprehensible or criminal action: X прячет концы в воду ≃ **X covers his tracks; X destroys the traces; X hides what he is doing.**

...За двадцать пять лет свидетель Икс присмирел, научился лукавить и прятать концы в воду (Эткинд 1). ...Over twenty-five years witness X had quieted down and learned cunning and the art of covering his tracks (1a). ♦ Боялся он погони, боялся, что через полчаса, через четверть часа уже выйдет, пожалуй, инструкция следить за ним; стало быть, во что бы ни стало, надо было... схоронить концы (Достоевский 3). He feared pursuit, he feared that in half an hour, or in a quarter of an hour, most likely, the order would go out for him to be followed; come what may, therefore, he had to destroy the traces... (3a). ♦ Карда – деревня большая, и концы в воду там спрятать можно (Распутин 2). Karda was a big village, and it was easy to hide what you were doing (2a).

К-263 • СВОДИ́ТЬ/СВЕСТИ́ КОНЦЫ́ С КОНЦА́МИ [VP; the verb may take the final position, otherwise fixed WO] **1.** *coll* [subj: human; often used with едва, еле, кое-как, с трудом etc] to manage to survive (albeit with difficulty) on one's pay, the resources available to one etc: X едва сводит концы с концами ≃ **X barely makes (both) ends meet; X hardly keeps his head above water; X barely scrapes ⟨gets⟩ by.**

Итак, я предполагал, что разбогатею на моих метафорах... Но это был дешёвый товар, и я даже не сводил

концов с концами (Олеша 3). And so I thought I would grow rich on my metaphors....But those were cheap goods, and I couldn't even make ends meet (3a).

2. Also: **СВЯ́ЗЫВАТЬ/СВЯЗА́ТЬ КОНЦЫ́ С КОНЦА́МИ** [subj: human or abstr] to make various parts of sth. (a theory, the plot of a story etc) jibe, fit together, form a congruous whole: X свёл концы с концами ≃ **X tied up the loose ends; X tied everything together; X made things add up.**

...Мужикам, по их натуре нужна любая техника, лишь бы она была новой, любая теория, лишь бы она сводила какие-нибудь концы с какими-нибудь другими концами, а женщинам? Им-то какое дело до всего этого, если в этом начисто отсутствовали проблемы семьи, брака, деторождения, воспитания, домоустройства, любви, вообще человеческой психологии и морали? (Залыгин 1). By their nature they [men] needed any sort of science as long as it was new, any theory as long as it tied up one or two loose ends, but what did women need? What did they care about any of this, if it was utterly barren of family problems, marital problems, problems of childbirth, child-rearing, home management, love, and all of human psychology and morality? (1a).

К-264 • ВСЁ ХОРОШО́, ЧТО ХОРОШО́ КОНЧА́ЕТСЯ [saying] when sth. troublesome ends happily or positively, one must not dwell on the difficulties encountered along the way (said with relief, joy after trouble or danger has been successfully avoided or endured without substantial loss): ≃ **all's ⟨all is⟩ well that ends well.**

К-265 • КОНЧА́ТЬСЯ/КО́НЧИТЬСЯ ⟨ЗАКА́НЧИВАТЬСЯ/ЗАКО́НЧИТЬСЯ⟩ НИЧЕ́М [VP; subj: abstr; fixed WO] to turn out unsuccessfully, not produce the desired results: X кончился ничем ≃ **X came to nothing ⟨to naught⟩; X went nowhere;** [in limited contexts] **X got person Y nowhere.**

Одно обстоятельство чуть было не разбудило его [Тентетникова], чуть было не произвело переворота в его характере. Случилось что-то похожее на любовь. Но и тут дело кончилось ничем (Гоголь 3). There was one thing that nearly awakened him [Tentetnikov] from his slumber and nearly brought about a complete transformation of his character. It was something very much like love. But this too came to nothing (3a). There was one circumstance, however, that all but awakened Tentetnikov, all but brought about a transformation in his character. He experienced something like love, but here too things came to naught (3c). ♦ Григорий выучил его [Смердякова] грамоте и, когда минуло ему лет двенадцать, стал учить священной истории. Но дело кончилось тотчас же ничем (Достоевский 1). Grigory taught him [Smerdyakov] to read and write and, when he was twelve, began teaching him the Scriptures. But that immediately went nowhere (1a). ♦ Разговор, казалось, закончился ничем (Тендряков 1). The conversation had not really got him anywhere (1a).

К-266 • ПЛО́ХО ⟨ДУ́РНО *obs*, **СКВЕ́РНО** *obs*⟩ **КО́НЧИТЬ** [VP; subj: human] to end up in an unfortunate, irreversibly depraved state or position, have one's life go to ruin: X плохо кончит ≃ **X will come to a bad ⟨to no good⟩ end; X will meet with a bad ⟨an unhappy⟩ fate ⟨end⟩.**

«Чем он располагает к себе? Это обречённый. Я думаю, он плохо кончит» (Пастернак 1). "What is it that makes one like him? He is a doomed man. I believe that he'll come to a bad end" (1a).

К-267 • КОНЬ (ЕЩЁ) НЕ ВАЛЯ́ЛСЯ *у кого, где coll* [VP_subj; these forms only; fixed WO with ещё movable] s.o. has not yet begun sth. or made significant progress toward the realization of sth.: у X-а конь ещё не валялся ≃ **X hasn't (yet) gotten it in gear; things haven't gotten ⟨started⟩ moving (yet); things haven't gotten off the ground (yet).**

К-268 • КО́НЬ (И) О ЧЕТЫРЁХ НОГА́Х, ДА (И ТО ⟨И ТОТ⟩) СПОТЫКА́ЕТСЯ [saying] anyone can err (said in justification of one's or s.o.'s mistake, negligence, oversight etc): ≃ **the horse has four legs and yet he ⟨it⟩ stumbles; horses have four legs and still they stumble; we all make mistakes; we're only human; nobody's perfect.**

«Злодеи не злодеи, а твои ребята таки пошарили да порастаскали. Не гневись: конь и о четырёх ногах, да спотыкается» (Пушкин 2). "Brigands or no brigands, but it was your lads as went ransacking and plundering. Don't be angry with 'em: the horse has four legs and yet he stumbles" (2a). ♦ «Ошибки были, — быстро сказал Хлебовводов. — Люди не ангелы. И на старуху бывает проруха. Конь о четырёх ногах и то спотыкается» (Стругацкие 3). "There have been mistakes," Khlebovvodov said quickly. "People are not angels. Anyone can make a mistake. Horses have four legs and still they stumble" (3a).

К-269 • ТРОЯ́НСКИЙ КОНЬ *lit* [NP; sing only; fixed WO] a subversive, harmful device, action, group of people etc that is disguised as something good: **Trojan horse.**

< From the legend of the large hollow wooden horse that the Greeks presented to the Trojans as a gift. When the Trojans took the horse into Troy, the Greek soldiers hiding inside the horse emerged and opened the gates of the city to the Greek army. Described in Homer's *Odyssey* (VIII, 492–520 etc) and Virgil's *Aeneid* (II, 15ff).

К-270 • САДИ́ТЬСЯ/СЕСТЬ НА СВОЕГО́ (ЛЮБИ́-МОГО) КОНЬКА́; ОСЕДЛА́ТЬ СВОЕГО́ (ЛЮБИ́-МОГО) КОНЬКА́ [VP; subj: human; fixed WO] to begin to speak on one's favorite topic: X сел на своего (любимого) конька ≃ **X mounted ⟨climbed onto, rode⟩ his (favorite) hobbyhorse; X launched into ⟨got off on⟩ his pet subject ⟨topic⟩; X got on his soapbox.**

«Ох, не говори так! Сглазишь...» При такой моей реплике Антон тут же садился на своего конька. Да, он не видел в тюрьмах и лагерях более суеверных людей, чем бывшие коммунисты (Гинзбург 2). "Please don't say that. You'll bring me bad luck." At this Anton mounted his hobbyhorse. He proclaimed that he had met no more superstitious people in the prisons and camps than the former Communists (2a).

К-271 • ОТБРО́СИТЬ КОНЬКИ́ *slang* [VP; subj: human] to die: X отбросил коньки ≃ **X kicked off; X kicked the bucket; X croaked; X turned up his toes; X cashed in ⟨his chips⟩.**

«Если же она даст показания да после этого коньки отбросит, большой срок... схлопотать можем» (Чернёнок 2). "But if she makes a statement and then kicks off, we'll get a stiff sentence..." (2a).

К-272 • ДАРЁНОМУ ⟨ДАРОВО́МУ⟩ КОНЮ́ В ЗУ́БЫ НЕ СМО́ТРЯТ [saying] one should not complain about, or look for faults in, sth. that is freely offered or received as a gift (said when a person receives sth. that he does not like and would not have chosen himself): ≃ **don't ⟨never⟩ look a gift horse in the mouth.**

К-273 • А́ВГИЕВЫ КОНЮ́ШНИ *lit* [NP; pl only; fixed WO]
1. a very dirty or cluttered place: **Augean stables.**
2. extreme disorder, a neglected state of affairs: **Augean stables; gigantic ⟨hopeless, dire⟩ mess.**

Крупные промышленники, за исключением Дессера, поддержали кандидатуру Гранделя... Прошёл месяц. Грандель показал себя неутомимым работником... Грандель говорил: «Коммунисты... Дессер... Это — авгиевы конюшни. Прежде чем начать, нужно чистить, чистить и чистить!» (Эренбург 4). All the big industrialists, with the exception of Desser, backed Grandel....A month went by. Grandel proved to be an indefatigable worker...."It's the Communists and Desser," he said. "It's worse than the Augean stables! We've got to clean them out before anything can be done" (4a). ♦ Люди медленно и упорно фальсифицируют деталь за деталью, частность за частностью, а собранные вместе они составляют ткань истории. Пройдёт ещё полстолетия, и разобраться в этих авгиевых конюшнях не сможет никто (Мандельштам 2). ...[People] go on slowly, stubbornly, embroidering the facts, inventing one detail after another, weaving them together to re-create the fabric of "history." Fifty years hence nobody will ever be able to clean up this gigantic mess (2a).

< From the name of *Augeas*, legendary king of Elis, whose stables (which sheltered 3000 oxen) had not been cleaned for thirty years. Cleaning the Augean stables was one of the twelve labors of Hercules.

К-274 • НЕ В КОНЯ́ КОРМ *coll* [Invar; indep. sent or subj-compl with быть₀; fixed WO] **1.** [subj: concr (a noun denoting food, drinks etc)] sth. does not have the expected beneficial effect on s.o.: X не в коня корм ≃ **X doesn't ⟨didn't etc⟩ do person Y any good.**

2. [subj: concr or abstr] sth. is not or cannot be properly appreciated by s.o.: (X) не в коня корм ≃ **X is ⟨it's⟩ wasted ⟨lost⟩ on person Y; person Y can't appreciate X ⟨it⟩; you would be wasting X ⟨it⟩ on person Y; X ⟨it⟩ is a waste of time ⟨energy etc⟩.**

«Не могу больше, не полечу! Пусть судят: больше вышки не дадут, а дальше фронта не пошлют. Я не лягавый, я — лётчик-истребитель! Хватит!..» Но речь его теперь была — не в коня корм: каждого уже одолевала своя собственная болячка (Максимов 1). "I can't take it any more, I'm going to stop flying. Let them put me before a court-martial. They can't do more than shoot me. They can't send me further than the front. I'm not a cop—I'm a fighter-pilot. I've had enough!..." But by this time his speech was a waste of time. Each of them was overwhelmed by his own ills (1a).

К-275 • КРУ́ГЛАЯ ⟨КРУ́ГЛЕНЬКАЯ⟩ КОПЕ́ЕЧКА *obs* [NP; sing only; fixed WO] a large sum of money: **pretty penny; hefty ⟨tidy⟩ sum.**

К-276 • ВЛЕТА́ТЬ/ВЛЕТЕ́ТЬ ⟨ВСКОЧИ́ТЬ, ОБОЙ-ТИ́СЬ, СТАТЬ и т. п.⟩ В КОПЕ́ЕЧКУ ⟨В КОПЕ́ЙКУ⟩ (кому) *coll* [VP; subj: concr or abstr; usu. pfv] to cost a very large amount, require large expenditures: X влетел (Y-у) в копеечку ≃ **X cost (Y) a pretty penny ⟨a small fortune, an arm and a leg⟩.**

[Серафима:] В это время ей, может быть, траур шьют. И какая портниха! Мадам Софи. Это встанет в копейку, Семён Семёнович (Эрдман 1). [S.:] At this very minute they could be sewing her mourning outfit. And what a dressmaker—Madame Sophie. It'll cost a pretty penny, Semyon Semyonovich (1a). ♦ «Понимаешь, отец, мне эта справка в большую копеечку обошлась» (Максимов 2). "You see, dad, just getting that permit cost me a small fortune" (2a).

К-277 • КАК ОДНА́ КОПЕ́ЙКА ⟨КОПЕ́ЕЧКА⟩ *obs, coll* [как + NP; these forms only; nonagreeing modif; used with a phrase denoting a sum of money that is either objectively, or perceived by the speaker to be, large; fixed WO] exactly (the named amount of money): **precisely; to the kopeck ⟨the penny, the cent etc⟩; [in limited contexts] ...no less.**

К-278 • КОПЕ́ЙКА В КОПЕ́ЙКУ; КОПЕ́ЕЧКА В КО-ПЕ́ЕЧКУ *both obs, coll* [NP; these forms only; nonagreeing modif; often used with a phrase denoting an amount of money; fixed WO] (used to emphasize the precision with which a monetary matter is handled; often used when counting money exactly, precisely: **(down) to the (last) kopeck ⟨penny, cent etc⟩; kopeck for kopeck ⟨penny for penny, cent for cent⟩.**

Возвращаю тебе долг — одиннадцать тысяч рублей копейка в копейку. Here's the money I owe you—eleven thousand rubles, down to the last kopeck.

К-279 • КОПÉЙКА РУБЛЬ БЕРЕЖЁТ [saying] frugality in small matters leads to an accumulation of great material gains: ≃ **a penny saved is a penny gained ⟨earned⟩; little gains make heavy purses; penny and penny laid up will be many; take care of the pennies and the dollars will take care of themselves.**

К-280 • ДО (ПОСЛÉДНЕЙ) КОПÉЙКИ ⟨КО-ПÉЕЧКИ⟩ истратить, заплатить, получить, прокутить и т. п. что coll [PrepP; these forms only; adv] (to spend, pay, squander etc a certain amount of money) completely, with nothing left over, (to receive a certain amount of money) in full: **(spend ⟨get, pay etc⟩ a certain amount of money) (down) to the last kopeck ⟨penny, cent etc⟩; (spend ⟨pay, receive etc⟩) every last kopeck ⟨penny, cent etc⟩ (of...); (spend ⟨squander, blow etc⟩) one's last kopeck ⟨penny, cent etc⟩; (spend ⟨blow, squander etc⟩) the last kopeck ⟨penny, cent etc⟩ of...**

[Аркадина:] Говорят, её покойная мать завещала мужу всё своё громадное состояние, всё до копейки... (Чехов 6). [A.:] They say her mother, who's dead, willed her husband all her enormous fortune, down to the last kopeck (6c). ♦ «Отпускные мои все до копейки кончились...» (Чернёнок 2). "I've spent the last cent of my vacation money..." (2a).

К-281 • ДРОЖÁТЬ ⟨ТРЯСТИ́СЬ⟩ НАД (КÁЖДОЙ) КОПÉЙКОЙ ⟨ЗА КÁЖДУЮ КОПÉЙКУ regional⟩ all coll, disapprov [VP; subj: human] to be miserly, excessively thrifty: X дрожит над каждой копейкой ≃ **X pinches pennies; X trembles at the thought of parting with a kopeck ⟨a penny⟩; X counts every kopeck ⟨penny⟩; X hangs onto every kopeck ⟨penny⟩.**

«А кто за каждую копейку дрожит, у того их [денег] не будет». — «Как же не будет, если он их не бросает зря на ветер, не пропивает, как ты?» — «А так. Они [деньги] поймут, что он жмот, и — с приветом!» (Распутин 1). "A person who counts every kopeck'll never have money." "Why won't he if he doesn't throw it away and doesn't drink it up like you do?" "Well, he won't, I tell you. Money'll see he's stingy and run in the opposite direction" (1a).

К-282 • ЗА КОПÉЙКУ ⟨ЗА ГРОШ⟩ УДÁВИТСЯ highly coll, derog [VP; subj: human; fixed WO] one is extremely frugal, miserly: X за копейку удавится ≃ **X pinches pennies; X hangs onto every kopeck ⟨penny⟩ for dear life; X is a cheapskate ⟨a skinflint, a tightwad⟩.**

К-283 • КАК ОДНУ́ КОПÉЙКУ ⟨КОПÉЕЧКУ⟩ coll [как + NP; these forms only; nonagreeing modif; used with a phrase denoting a sum of money that is either objectively, or perceived by the speaker to be, large; fixed WO] **1. прокутить, истратить** и т. п. **что** ~ (to squander, spend etc the named amount of money) completely, with nothing left over: **(down) to the last kopeck ⟨penny, cent etc⟩; squander ⟨spend etc⟩ every last kopeck ⟨penny, cent etc⟩ (of...); [in limited contexts— usu. in refer. to a large sum of money] (spend) as if it were nothing.**

«Есть свидетели, что он [подсудимый] прокутил в селе Мокром все эти три тысячи, взятые у госпожи Верховцевой, за месяц перед катастрофой, разом, как одну копейку...» (Достоевский 2). "There are witnesses that the whole three thousand he [the defendant] took from Miss Verkhovtsev was squandered in the

village of Mokroye a month before the catastrophe, at one go, to the last kopeck..." (2a).

2. заплатить, выложить и т. п. **что** ~ (to pay etc) exactly (the named amount of money): **precisely; to the ⟨a⟩ kopeck ⟨penny etc⟩; [in limited contexts] ...no less.**

«Сам видел, в руках у них видел три тысячи как одну копеечку...» (Достоевский 2). "I myself saw it, I saw three thousand to a kopeck in his hands..." (2a).

К-284 • ПОСЛÉДНЮЮ КОПÉЙКУ ⟨ПОСЛÉДНИЙ ГРОШ⟩ РЕБРÓМ СТÁВИТЬ/ПОСТÁВИТЬ obs, coll [VP; subj: human] to spend all one's remaining money on sth. (often out of vanity): X последнюю копейку ребром поставит ≃ **X will spend his last kopeck ⟨penny, cent etc⟩ (to show off).**

К-285 • СЧИТÁТЬ (КÁЖДУЮ) КОПÉЙКУ; СЧИ-ТÁТЬ КОПÉЙКИ all highly coll [VP; subj: human] to spend one's money very sparingly, be very careful in how one spends one's money (usu. because one is poor, has very little money): X считает каждую копейку ≃ **X counts every kopeck ⟨penny etc⟩.**

Живётся им тяжело, приходится считать каждую копейку. Things are tough for them, they have to count every penny.

К-286 • С КОПЫ́Т (ДОЛÓЙ) slang [PrepP; these forms only; predic with subj: human; the idiom can be used in past, pres, and fut contexts] **1.** one falls, crashes to the ground: X — с копыт долой ≃ [in past contexts] **X keeled over; X fell in a heap; X went down like a ton of bricks; X was ⟨got⟩ knocked (clean) off his feet.**

2. one dies: X — с копыт долой ≃ [in past contexts] **X kicked off; X kicked the bucket; X croaked; X turned up his toes; X cashed in (his chips).**

К-287 • ОТКИ́НУТЬ ⟨ОТБРÓСИТЬ⟩ КОПЫ́ТА slang [VP; subj: human or animal] to die: X отбросит копыта ≃ **X will kick off; X will kick the bucket; X will croak; X will turn up his toes; X will cash in (his chips); [in limited contexts] X will be pushing up daisies ⟨kicking up the daisies⟩.**

«Немцы наши дрейфят, — когда он [Сталин] копыта откинет, начнётся заваруха...» (Копелев 1). "Our Germans are scared—when he [Stalin] kicks off, a real mess will start..." (1a). ♦ «Направляют меня в сотню, в третий взвод. А я же страшный охотник воевать! Два раза сходил в атаку, а потом думаю: „Тут мне и копыта откинуть придётся! Надо искать какую-нибудь дыру, а то пропадёшь ты, Проша!.."» (Шолохов 5). "[I] got sent to the squadron, in the third troop. And me so keen on fighting! Well, I rode in a couple of charges, and then I thought, 'You'll be kicking up the daisies before long at this rate! You'll have to find a loophole, Prokhor, or you'll be done for!'" (5a).

К-288 • ЛОМÁТЬ/ПОЛОМÁТЬ КÓПЬЯ (с кем, из-за кого-чего, за что) [VP; subj: human; usu. impfv] to argue heatedly, fight vehemently with s.o. over sth., defending one's position or a third party's interests: X будет ломать копья с Y-ом (из-за Z-a) ≃ **X will cross swords ⟨lock horns⟩ with Y (over Z); X will go to war over Z; [in limited contexts] X will break a lance with Y (over Z).**

Вообще одновременность такого восприятия следовало признать довольно относительной. Нам, поэтам, ломать копья тут было не из-за чего (Лившиц 1). Generally speaking, this kind of simultaneous perception had to be recognized as somewhat relative. We poets had no reason to go to war over it (1a). ♦ Он и Маццини, бывши социалистами прежде социализма, сделались его врагами, когда он стал переходить из общих стремлений в новую революционную силу. Много поломал я копий с обоими... (Герцен 2). Fazy and Mazzini, who had been socialists in the days before socialism, became its enemies when it began to pass from general aspirations into a new revolutionary force. Many a lance I have broken with both of them... (2a).

К-289 • СЖИГА́ТЬ ⟨ЖЕЧЬ⟩/СЖЕЧЬ (СВОИ́) КО-РАБЛИ́; СЖИГА́ТЬ ⟨ЖЕЧЬ⟩/СЖЕЧЬ (ВСЕ ⟨СВОИ́, ЗА СОБО́Й⟩) МОСТЫ́ *all lit* [VP; subj: human; usu. this WO] breaking resolutely with the past, to take an irrevocable step that makes turning back impossible: X сжигает свои корабли ≃ **X is burning his bridges ⟨boats⟩ (behind him).**

Боб Рейл сел возле меня. «А вы понимаете, что сжигаете все мосты за собой? – спросил он серьёзно... – Готовы ли вы к этому?» (Аллилуева 2). Bob Rayle sat down beside me, saying in great earnestness: "Do you realize that you are burning your bridges behind you?...Are you prepared for such a step?" (2a). ♦ Назади была верная погибель; впереди была надежда. Корабли были сожжены; [для французов] не было другого спасения, кроме совокупного бегства, и на это совокупное бегство были устремлены все силы французов (Толстой 7). Behind the French lay certain destruction; before them lay hope. They had burned their boats; there was no salvation save in running away, and the whole strength of the French was bent on this collective flight (7a).

К-290 • БОЛЬШО́МУ КОРАБЛЮ́ – БОЛЬШО́Е ПЛА́-ВАНИЕ [saying] an outstanding person needs ample opportunity and unbounded freedom to allow his abilities to manifest themselves fully (often said when wishing well to a person who has deservedly been given the opportunity to demonstrate his abilities): ≃ **a big ship needs a big sea; a great ship asks for deeper water; great ships need deep waters.**

«...За буйные поступки и за вызов на поединок ссылают его [подсудимого] в один из отдалённых пограничных городков нашей благодатной России. Там он служит, там и кутит, и конечно – большому кораблю большое и плавание. Нам надо средств-с, средств прежде всего...» (Достоевский 2). "...For riotous conduct, for a challenge to a duel, he [the accused] is exiled to one of the remote frontier towns of our bounteous Russia. There he serves, there he carouses, and of course a big ship needs a big sea. We need money, money above all..." (1a). ♦ [Городничий:] Да, признаюсь, господа, я, чёрт возьми, очень хочу быть генералом. [Лука Лукич:] И дай бог получить... [Аммос Фёдорович:] Большому кораблю большое плаванье (Гоголь 4). [Mayor:] Yes, I must admit, ladies and gentlemen, God damn it, I very much want to be a general. [L.L.:] And God grant you get it.... [A.F.:] Great ships need deep waters (4a).

К-291 • С КОРАБЛЯ́ НА БАЛ (попасть) [PrepP; Invar; adv or predic with subj: human; fixed WO] one unexpectedly finds himself, usu. immediately upon returning from a trip, at a gathering of people (a party, large celebration, an official meeting etc): **straight from one's travels into the social scene; one minute a traveler, the next a socialite; (it's) off the plane ⟨boat etc⟩ and into the party.**

< From Aleksandr Pushkin's *Eugene Onegin* («Евгений Онегин»), 1833, ch. 8, 13.

К-292 • В КО́РЕНЬ разорить *кого-что,* разрушить *что* и т. п. *coll* [PrepP; Invar; adv (intensif)] (to ruin, destroy s.o. or sth.) entirely, wholly: **totally; completely; utterly.**

К-293 • ПОД КО́РЕНЬ [PrepP; Invar; adv] **1.** рубить, срезать, косить и т. п. *что* ~ (to chop down, cut etc a tree, bush, plant, or, occas., a pole, mast etc) at the very root or bottom: **(chop sth. off) at the roots; (chop sth. down) at the base; [in limited contexts] (raze sth.) to the ground.**

Председатель его [колхоза]... свёл под корень изрядно гектаров леса... (Солженицын 6). ...[The chairman] had razed a considerable area of forest to the ground... (6b).

2. ~ подорвать, разрушить и т. п. *что* [obj: abstr (здоровье, авторитет, жизнь, промышленность etc)] (to damage or harm s.o.'s health, s.o.'s life, the economy, undermine s.o.'s authority etc) thoroughly and irreversibly: **wreak havoc (on ⟨upon⟩ sth.); play havoc (with sth.); do irreversible damage (to sth.).**

3. ~ истреблять, уничтожать и т. п. *кого-что* [obj: human pl or collect] (to kill) everyone (in some place, belonging to some group etc), not leaving anyone out: **to the last man; to a man; sparing no one; [in limited contexts] mow down s.o. ⟨sth.⟩; wipe out s.o. ⟨sth.⟩.**

«То все профессора, все инженеры стали вредителями, а он – верит?.. То все его друзья и знакомые – враги народа, а он – верит?.. То целые народы... срезают под корень – а он верит?» (Солженицын 10). "Suddenly all the professors and all the engineers turn out to be wreckers, and he believes it!...His own friends and acquaintances are unmasked as enemies of the people, and he believes it!...Whole nations...are mown down, and he believes it!" (10a).

К-294 • ПОДРУБА́ТЬ/ПОДРУБИ́ТЬ ⟨ПОДРЕЗА́ТЬ/ПОДРЕ́ЗАТЬ, ПОДКОСИ́ТЬ, ПОДСЕ́ЧЬ⟩ ПОД КО́-РЕНЬ *кого-что coll* [VP; subj: human or abstr] to damage the very basis of sth., do s.o. or sth. irreparable harm: X подрубил Y-а под корень ≃ **X did great damage to Y; thing X undermined the roots of thing Y; thing X undermined thing Y at the root ⟨the core⟩; X struck Y a mortal ⟨fatal⟩ blow.**

К-295 • СМОТРЕ́ТЬ ⟨ГЛЯДЕ́ТЬ и т. п.⟩ В КО́РЕНЬ [VP; subj: human; often imper or infin with надо, нужно, если etc] to delve into the very essence of some matter: X смотрит в корень ≃ **X gets to the root ⟨the heart, the crux, the bottom⟩ of the matter ⟨the problem etc⟩; X gets (right) down to the nub of the matter ⟨the problem etc⟩;** ‖ *Imper* смотри в корень ≃ **look beneath the surface.**

Все поняли, как глубоко и мудро судит наш сосед, и все устыдились того, что до него никто не сумел взглянуть вот так... в самый корень (Михайловская 1). We all understood how profoundly and wisely our neighbor evaluated the situation and we all were embarrassed that we had failed to get to the root of the matter (1a).

К-296 • НА ВСЕ ⟨О́БЕ *rare*⟩ КО́РКИ ругать, бранить, честить и т. п. *кого coll* [PrepP; these forms only; adv (intensif); fixed WO] (to swear at s.o., scold s.o.) vehemently: X ругал Y-а ~ ≃ **X gave Y a good tongue-lashing; X called Y every name in the book; X gave Y a (good) dressing-down ⟨going-over⟩; X chewed ⟨bawled⟩ Y out.**

К-297 • ОТ КО́РКИ ДО КО́РКИ читать, прочитывать, учить, знать и т. п. *что coll* [PrepP; Invar; adv; fixed WO] (to read, learn, memorize etc sth.) completely, not leaving anything out, (to know sth.) thoroughly, in all its details: **(read sth. ⟨read sth. through⟩) from cover to cover; (read ⟨memorize, learn⟩ sth.) from beginning to end; (read etc sth.) from top to bottom; (read sth. through etc) from end to end ⟨from start to finish⟩; (know ⟨learn⟩ sth.) backward and forward.**

Старик читает справочник по элементарной математике. Сынок прислал соседу. Ничего не понимает. Какие-то синусы-косинусы. Всё равно читает. От корки до корки... (Терц 3). An old man is reading a text-book on elementary mathematics sent to the man in the next bunk by his son. He doesn't understand a word of it – all this business about sines and cosines. But all the same he reads right through, from cover to cover... (3a). ♦ [Калошин:] Сколько раз вам указывалось, чтобы анкеты заполнялись от корки до корки (Вампилов 1). [K.:] How many times have you been told to get those forms filled in from top to bottom... (1a). ♦ ...Он с утра отправлялся в село за газетами. Затем… прочитывал их от корки до корки, старательно подчёркивая наиболее, по его мнению, значительные места… (Максимов 3). …First thing in the morning he went down to the village for the papers. Next, he read them through from end to end, carefully underlining what he considered to be the most significant passages… (3a). ♦ Ганичев взял у него районку [районную газету] и все четыре полоски просмотрел от корки до корки (Абрамов 1). Ganichev took the paper from him and looked through all four pages from start to finish (1a).

К-298 • ПОДНО́ЖНЫЙ КОРМ [NP; sing only; usu. subj or obj; fixed WO] **1.** *coll, usu. humor* food at no cost: **free food ⟨grub, eats⟩.**

В геологической экспедиции мне понравилось: весь день на воздухе, подножный корм, работы немного. I liked the geological expedition: out in the fresh air all day long, free food, and not too much work.

2. *obs* whatever means of subsistence one can acquire from chance sources (when one has no steady source of income etc): **whatever crumbs ⟨morsels, crusts⟩ one can get; chance morsel; (get hold of ⟨pick up etc⟩) what food one can.**

…Он [камердинер] продал какие-то брёвна, чтоб не умереть с голоду. Сенатор, возвратившись в Россию, принялся приводить в порядок своё имение и наконец добрался до брёвен. В наказание он отобрал его должность и отправил его в опалу. Старик, обременённый семьёй, поплёлся на подножный корм (Герцен 1). …He [the valet] sold some beams to escape starvation. The Senator, on his return to Russia, proceeded to set his estate in order, and at last came to the beams. He punished his former valet by sending him away in disgrace, depriving him of his duties. The old man, burdened with a family, trudged off to pick up what food he could (1a).

К-299 • У КОРМИ́ЛА (власти, правления и т. п.) *lit* [PrepP; Invar; subj-compl with copula (subj: human)] (to be, serve) in a position of leadership or control: **at the helm; [in limited contexts] at the helm of state.**

«Вы поставлены, так сказать, у кормила общественного спокойствия, а с общественным спокойствием — по крайней мере, таково моё мнение — в сильной степени связано общественное благосостояние» (Салтыков-Щедрин 2). "You have been placed, as it were, at the helm of public security, and with public security, — this, at any rate, is my opinion, public well-being is inextricably bound up" (2a).

К-300 • В КО́РНЕ [PrepP; Invar; adv] **1.** ~ **изменить** *что*, **измениться, не соглашаться и т. п.** to change sth., change, disagree etc) totally, entirely: **radically; completely; absolutely; fundamentally.**

…Ему в корне чужды были побуждения к бунту… (Айтматов 2). …He was absolutely impervious to any incitement to revolt… (2a).

2. пресечь, истребить и т. п. *что* ~ (to destroy sth.) at the very source, completely, (to stop sth.) just as it is getting started: **(nip sth.) in the bud; root out sth; (cut off sth.) at the root.**

Сидоров был настоящий хозяин, знал производство… всякие махинации пресекал в корне. При нём фабрика процветала… (Рыбаков 1). Sidorov was a fine boss who knew all about production.…[He] would nip any attempt at deception in the bud. The factory flourished under him (1a). ♦ Советским детям не полагается никакой самостоятельности, они должны делать то и только то, что им сказано. Резвость, озорство, подвижность — естественные свойства нормально развитого ребёнка — советская школа стремится истребить в корне… (Буковский 1). Soviet children are not supposed to exhibit any independence; they have to do only what they are told. Playfulness, mischievousness, restlessness—the natural attributes of a normal child—are rooted out at all costs (1a). ♦ «Ну что ж, Филипп, в управлении ты хозяин, бюро обкома знает только тебя.

Любые сепаратные действия Запорожца пресекай в корне, мы тебя поддержим» (Рыбаков 2). "Well, Philip, you're the boss of your organization. The bureau only acknowledges you. You must cut off any of Zaporozhets' separate operations at the root. And we'll support you" (2a).

К-301 • ДО КОРНЕ́Й ВОЛО́С [PrepP; Invar; fixed WO] **1. покраснеть** ~ [adv (intensif)] (to blush) very deeply, to an extreme degree: **(blush) to the roots of one's hair; (turn ⟨go⟩) bright red.**

Покраснев до корней волос, я стоял в полуоткрытых дверях и слушал молодой, твёрдый стук его каблуков, сбегавших с четвёртого этажа вниз… (Катаев 3). Blushing to the roots of my hair, I stood at the half-open door and listened to the sound of his young firm footsteps as he ran downstairs from the third floor… (3a).

2. [nonagreeing modif] (one is a certain type of person) entirely, in every way: **(a [NP]) to the (very) marrow of one's bones; every inch (a ⟨the⟩ [NP]); (a [NP]) to the core.**

Он всю жизнь прожил в России, но остался немцем до корней волос. He lived his whole life in Russia but remained a German to the very marrow of his bones.

К-302 • ВЫРЫВА́ТЬ/ВЫ́РВАТЬ С КО́РНЕМ *что* [VP; subj: human] to eliminate (some phenomenon, strong feeling, habit etc) completely: X с корнем вырвал Y ≃ **X tore ⟨ripped, pulled⟩ Y out by the roots; X rooted out Y; X uprooted Y.**

Все единодушно соглашались, что крамолу следует вырвать с корнем… (Салтыков-Щедрин 1). All were unanimously agreed that sedition must be torn out by the roots… (1a). They were all agreed that treason should be uprooted… (1b). ♦ [Маша:] …[Я] взяла и решила: вырву эту любовь из своего сердца, с корнем вырву (Чехов 6). [M.:] …I up and decided: I'll rip this love right out of my heart, rip it out by the roots (6c).

К-303 • ПУСКА́ТЬ/ПУСТИ́ТЬ КО́РНИ [VP] **1.** ~ *(где)* [subj: human] to settle down or be settled down in some place (which one makes his permanent home, where one raises his family, becomes part of the community etc): X пустил корни в месте Y ≃ **X put ⟨set⟩ down roots (in place Y).**

Когда мы покидали Москву, писатели ещё не были привилегированным сословием, а сейчас они пускали корни и обдумывали, как бы им сохранить свои привилегии (Мандельштам 1). At the time we left Moscow for exile, the writers had not yet become a privileged caste, but now they were putting down roots and figuring out ways of keeping their privileges (1a). ♦ …Ещё до японской войны пришёл в Атамановку… переселенец Андрей Сивый с двумя сыновьями… Один из его сыновей не пришёл с германской, а второго в тридцатом году раскулачили и вместе с семьёй куда-то выслали. Так и не пустил переселенец Андрей Сивый корни на новой земле (Распутин 2). …Back before the Russo-Japanese War a man called Andrei Sivy and his two sons had moved to Atamanovka.…One of his sons never came back from World War I, and the second was declared a kulak and he and his wife were exiled somewhere. So old Andrei Sivy never did set down roots in his new land (2a).

2. ~ *(в ком-чём, в кого-что)* [subj: abstr] (of some feeling, habit, phenomenon etc) to become firmly established, become ingrained (in some person, group of people, in life etc): X пустил корни (в Y-е) ≃ **X took root (in Y); X put down (its) roots; X became ⟨was⟩ deeply rooted (in Y).**

Не успело ещё пагубное двоевластие пустить зловредные свои корни, как из губернии прибыл рассыльный… (Салтыков-Щедрин 1). Before the ruinous diarchy could put down its pernicious roots, a courier arrived from the provincial capital… (1a). ♦ Нет. Уж если демагогические навыки, привитые мне всем воспитанием, пустили в моём сознании такие глубокие корни, что я не могу сейчас дать самостоятельного анализа положения в стране и партии, то буду руководствоваться просто голосом совести (Гинзбург 1). No; if the demagogic habits of mind I had been trained in were so deeply rooted in me that I could not now make an independent analysis of the situation in the country and the Party, then I would be guided simply by the voice of my conscience (1b).

К-304 • **НА КОРНЮ́** [PrepP; Invar; adv] **1.** while (some grain, crop etc is) still in the field and uncut, unmown: **before it's ⟨they are⟩ harvested ⟨cut down⟩; on the stalk; (while) standing in the fields.**

[Боркин:] Возьму вот и продам завтра тройку! Да-с!.. Овёс на корню продал, а завтра возьму и рожь продам (Чехов 4). [B.:] See if I don't [up and] sell the troika tomorrow! Yes, sir! I sold the oats before they were harvested, and you just see if I don't [up and] sell the rye too (4a).

2. засо́хнуть, увя́нуть, зача́хнуть и т. п. ~ (usu. of positive undertakings, aspirations etc) (to wither, fade away) while just beginning to develop: **(wither) on the vine.**

...Не погнушался Твардовский пойти сам и в типографию «Известий» и там дал понять какому-то начальнику, что с «Корпусом» — не самоуправство, а *есть такое мнение*, и надо поторопиться... Совершился акт «набора»... Но очень скоро в ЦК очнулись, подправились... — и засохло всё на корню (Солженицын 2). ...Tvardovsky did not think it beneath him to visit *Izvestia*'s printing shops in person, and convey to some manager or other that he was not exceeding his authority in the matter of *Cancer Ward*, but that Somebody was of the same opinion, and that haste was therefore necessary....The deed was done, the type was set....But the Central Committee soon woke up to its mistake and set about rectifying it....The whole enterprise withered on the vine (2a).

К-305 • **ВРАСТА́ТЬ/ВРАСТИ́ КОРНЯ́МИ** *во что;* **ПРИРАСТА́ТЬ/ПРИРАСТИ́ КОРНЯ́МИ** *к чему* [VP; subj: human] having settled down in a place for a long time, to become very accustomed, attached to it: X врос корнями в место Y ≃ **X put down roots in place Y; X became rooted in place Y.**

Самая неприятная личность и опаснейший соперник — некий Летунов Руслан Павлович. Всё летуновское гнездо. Они там вросли корнями (Трифонов 6). The most disagreeable individual and the most dangerous rival was a certain Ruslan Pavlovich Letunov. That whole Letunov nest. They had put their roots down there (6a).

К-306 • **УХОДИ́ТЬ КОРНЯ́МИ** *во что* [VP; subj: usu. abstr] to have its origins in the past, in some phenomenon in the past: X уходит корнями в Y ≃ **X traces its roots back to Y; X is rooted ⟨has its roots⟩ in Y.**

Вопрос, уходящий корнями в державинский век простоты, крепостного права, мужицкой галантности, был опрометчивым (Ерофеев 4). His question, though it could trace its roots back to the age of Derzhavin, back to an age of simplicity, serfdom, and crude gallantry, was a trifle ill-considered (4a).

К-307 • **ЦЕ́ЛЫЙ КО́РОБ** новостей, вестей *coll* [NP; sing only; subj or obj] a great deal (of news): **a whole lot; all sorts ⟨kinds⟩; loads; heaps; (be) plum full of; (be) chock-full of.**

К-308 • **С ТРИ КО́РОБА** наговорить, наобещать, наврать и т. п. *coll, often disapprov* [PrepP; Invar; adv (quantif); fixed WO] (to talk, promise, lie etc) far too much (usu. saying things that, in the speaker's judgment, are not true or relevant, making promises that will not be kept etc): наговорить (кому) ~ ≃ **talk s.o.'s ear off; talk nonstop; run off at the mouth;** [in limited contexts] **fill s.o.'s head with stories;** ‖ наговорить (кому) ~ чепухи ≃ **say all kinds of odd ⟨strange etc⟩ things; spout ⟨talk⟩ a lot of nonsense;** ‖ наобещать (кому) ~ ≃ **make s.o. a cartload ⟨a barrelful⟩ of promises;** ‖ наврать (кому) ~ ≃ **tell s.o. a pack ⟨all kinds⟩ of lies.**

...У Сони... две сестры в Иркутске... Приезжая из города, когда удавалось туда вырваться, недобро смотрела на ухваты да чугунки, а однажды попробовала сманить в Иркутск и Павла. Ей там нагородили с три короба, как хорошо да ладно, культурно да уважительно... (Распутин 4). ...Sonya had two sisters in Irkutsk....When she came back from a visit in the city, whenever she managed to get away, she would look with loathing at the oven prongs and cast iron pots, and once she even tried to lure Pavel to the city. They had filled her head with stories about how good and fine it was, how cultured and respectable... (4a). ♦ Фронта он боялся как огня, литературной войны не вёл и в пьяном виде мог наговорить с три короба чепухи (Мандельштам 1). ...He had been scared stiff at the front, never involved himself in the "literary war," and when he was drunk he could say all kinds of odd things (1a). ♦ «Так ты, значит, хочешь писать книгу о дипломатах?»... — «"Хочешь", "не хочешь" — не решается, Инк, так просто, как в новогодних интервью. Но запастись заранее материалами... Не всякого дипломата расспросишь. Спасибо, что ты — родственник». — «И твой выбор доказывает твою проницательность. Посторонний дипломат, во-первых, наврёт тебе с три короба. Ведь у нас есть, что скрывать» (Солженицын 3). "Well, I take it you want to write a book about diplomats?"..."What you want, Innokenty, and what you don't want, isn't decided as simply as it sounds in New Year's interviews. You store up material ahead of time; you can't ask just any diplomat. I'm lucky you're a relative." "You're wise. A diplomat who was a stranger to you would tell you all kinds of lies. After all, we have things to cover up" (3a).

К-309 • **ДО́ЙНАЯ КОРО́ВА** *coll, usu. disapprov* [NP; usu. sing] a person, organization etc continuously used by s.o. as a source of material goods, exploited shamelessly: **milk ⟨milch⟩ cow; cash cow; meal ticket;** [in limited contexts] **(one is) milking s.o. ⟨sth.⟩ for all he ⟨it⟩ is worth.**

...На нас... смотрели как на дойных коров, и отношение к нам то улучшалось, то ухудшалось в зависимости от количества и качества удоя, который давал начальству каждый из нас. По прибытии нашем в роту нас медленно ощупывали, заранее стараясь определить, какое количество жизненных благ можно от нас получить... (Лившиц 1). ...We were regarded as milch cows, and attitudes to us got better or worse depending on the quantity and quality of the milk yield which each of us presented to the authorities. When one of us arrived in the company, they mentally felt us over, trying to predetermine the number of earthly blessings which they could extract from us... (1a).

К-310 • **КАК ⟨БУ́ДТО, СЛО́ВНО, ТО́ЧНО⟩ КОРО́ВА ЯЗЫКО́М СЛИЗА́ЛА ⟨СЛИЗНУ́ЛА⟩** *кого-что;* **КАК ЯЗЫКО́М СЛИЗНУ́ЛО** *all coll* [VP$_{subj}$ or VP, impers; these forms only; fixed WO] (s.o. or sth.) disappeared quickly and completely: X-а как корова языком слизала ≃ **X vanished ⟨disappeared⟩ into thin air; X vanished ⟨disappeared⟩ without a trace; person X did a disappearing act.**

...Даже здесь [Нинке] было слышно, как Надя ищет хлеб, который будто корова языком слизнула (Распутин 3). ...Even at this distance she [Ninka] could hear her mother looking for the roll, which seemed to have vanished into thin air (3a).

К-311 • **ЧЬЯ БЫ КОРО́ВА МЫЧА́ЛА, А ТВОЯ́ ⟨его, её⟩ ⟨БЫ⟩ МОЛЧА́ЛА** [saying] you have (he has, she has) the exact same faults for which you are (he is, she is) criticizing another: ≃ **the pot calls ⟨it's the pot calling⟩ the kettle black; look who's talking!; it takes one to know one.**

К-312 • идёт, пристало **КАК (К) КОРО́ВЕ СЕДЛО́** *кому coll* [как + NP (or PrepP); these forms only; adv (neg intensif);

fixed WO] (sth. does not suit, befit s.o.) at all: **(be) like putting a saddle on a cow;** [of clothes] **(look) ridiculous on s.o.**

[Аммос Фёдорович:] Вот уж кому пристало генеральство, как корове седло! (Гоголь 4). [A.F.:] If they make him a general, it'll be like putting a saddle on a cow (4e).

К-313 • сидит **КАК НА КОРÓВЕ СЕДЛÓ** *coll* [как + PrepP; Invar; adv; fixed WO] (of ill-fitting clothes) (sth. does) not fit s.o. at all, (is) the wrong size, cut etc for s.o.: **(sth.) looks ridiculous ⟨like hell⟩ on s.o.;** [in limited contexts] **(sth.) looks like a clown suit on s.o.**

К-314 • **БÓЖЬЯ КОРÓВКА** [NP; fixed WO] **1.** one of any number of small, round beetles, often bright red with black spots: **ladybug; ladybeetle; ladybird.**

2. *coll* [usu. sing; often subj-compl with copula, nom or instrum (subj: human)] a quiet, inoffensive person who does not know how to stand up for himself: **gentle ⟨meek⟩ as a lamb; (little) mouse; (such) a docile ⟨submissive⟩ person ⟨man etc⟩;** [in limited contexts] **wouldn't hurt a fly.**

К-315 • **КОРÓЛЬ-ТО ГÓЛЫЙ; ГÓЛЫЙ КОРÓЛЬ** [VP$_{subj}$ with copula, used as indep. sent (1st var.); NP, sing only (2nd var.); fixed WO] a person whose scholarly reputation, authority in some field etc turns out to be completely ungrounded, a theory that turns out to be false etc: **but the emperor has nothing on at all!; the emperor has no clothes; an emperor without (any) clothes.**

«Ты мелкий эгоист и себялюбец. На этом моя сторона заканчивает дискуссию». – «А ты голый король, – ответил Юра, – генерал без армии. На этом моя сторона тоже заканчивает дискуссию» (Рыбаков 2). "You're small-minded, vain, conceited, and that's the end of it as far as I'm concerned." "And you're an emperor without any clothes, a general without an army. And that's the end of it as far as *I'm* concerned" (2a).

< From the Russian translation of Hans Christian Andersen's "Emperor's New Clothes," 1837.

К-316 • **НА КÓРТОЧКАХ** сидеть; **НА КÓРТОЧКИ** сесть, присесть [PrepP; these forms only; adv] (to be sitting, assume a position) with one's knees deeply bent, supporting one's weight on the feet or balancing o.s. on the balls of the feet: **squat (down); sit ⟨squat (down)⟩ on one's haunches ⟨heels⟩; crouch.**

Тэдди пристально на него [Виктора] посмотрел, потом вздохнул; крякнув, присел на корточки, покопался под стойкой и выставил перед Виктором пузырёк с нашатырным спиртом и початую пачку чая (Стругацкие 1). Teddy stared at him [Victor] for a moment and sighed. Grunting, he squatted down, rummaged around under the bar, and came up with a bottle of liquid ammonia and an opened packet of tea (1a). ♦ В то утро он продал Николаю Гавриловичу (оба присели на корточки подле груды книг) неразрезанный ещё Фейербаха (Набоков 1). That morning he sold Nikolay Gavrilovich (both of them squatting on their haunches beside a pile of books) a still uncut volume of Feuerbach (1a). ♦ Костерок оказался у небольшого причала, пылал уже затухающим пламенем, освещая нескольких то ли геологов, то ли рыбаков и край большой лодки. «Здравствуйте, товарищи! – Подойдя ближе, Золотарёв присел позади них на корточки. – Приятного аппетита» (Максимов 1). The dying flames of the bonfire, which turned out to be at a little mooring-stage, lit up the faces of a group of men—geologists perhaps, or fishermen—and the edge of a large boat. "Good evening, comrades! Enjoy your food." Zolotarev went up and crouched beside them (1a).

К-317 • **У РАЗБИ́ТОГО КОРЫ́ТА** остаться, оказаться, сидеть и т. п.; **К РАЗБИ́ТОМУ КОРЫ́ТУ** вернуться *both coll* [PrepP; these forms only; subj-compl with copula (subj:

human) or adv; fixed WO] (to be left) with nothing, having lost all one had gained, having had one's hopes in sth. thwarted etc: **(be) left) empty-handed; (be) left) with zilch;** [in limited contexts] **(be) no better off than when one started; (be) back to square one; (be) (right) back where one started; (be) back where one started again.**

Денежная реформа разорила его: деньги, которые он копил десять лет, превратились в бумагу, и он остался у разбитого корыта. The monetary reform impoverished him: the money he'd been saving for ten years turned into worthless paper and he was left with nothing. ♦ Думаю, получив срок, Убожко по крайней мере был утешен, что «невеста» осталась у разбитого корыта... (Амальрик 1). I would guess that when Ubozhko was sentenced, he at least felt consoled by the fact that his "ex-wife" was no better off than when she started... (1a). ♦ Вот мы и сидим опять у разбитого корыта, сказал Клеветник (Зиновьев 1). "We're back where we started again," said Slanderer (1a).

< From Aleksandr Pushkin's tale "The Fisherman and the Goldfish" («Сказка о рыбаке и рыбке»), 1835, in which the magic goldfish punishes the fisherman's greedy wife by taking back everything it has given her, leaving her with the same broken washtub she had before the goldfish appeared on the scene.

К-318 • **НАШЛÁ КОСÁ НА КÁМЕНЬ** [saying] a person has met another who is his equal with regard to a specific quality (stubbornness, shrewdness etc; usu. used when two parties are involved in an argument, irreconcilable conflict etc and neither is willing to yield): ≃ **diamond cut diamond; when Greek meets Greek; one has met his match; it's a clash of wills.**

...Циммерман не выполняет приказа Севлага... Она пустилась в конфликт со своим начальством из Севлага. «Коса на камень нашла... надеемся, всё будет хорошо. Вряд ли Селезнёв допустит, чтобы Циммерманша над ним верх взяла» (Гинзбург 2). ...Zimmerman was not carrying out Sevlag's instructions....She was challenging her own superiors in Sevlag. "When Greek meets Greek... Let's hope all will be well. It's hardly likely that Sevlag will allow Zimmerman to get the upper hand" (2a). ♦ Он [царь Николай] побледнел, щёки задрожали у него, и глаза сделались ещё свирепее; тем же взглядом отвечала ему дочь... Николай встал, – он почувствовал, что нашла коса на камень (Герцен 1). The Tsar turned pale, his cheeks twitched, and his eyes grew still more ferocious; his daughter met him with the same look in hers....Nicholas got up: he felt that he had met his match (1a).

К-319 • **ДО КОСТÉЙ** промокнуть, промёрзнуть и т. п. *coll* [PrepP; Invar; adv (intensif)] (to get) extremely (wet, cold etc): промокнуть ~ ≃ **be ⟨get⟩ soaked to the skin; be ⟨get⟩ totally drenched; be ⟨get⟩ soaked through;** ‖ промёрзнуть ⟨продрогнуть⟩ ~ ≃ **be ⟨get⟩ chilled to the bone ⟨the marrow⟩; be ⟨get⟩ chilled through and through;** ‖ холод ⟨мороз, ветер⟩ пронизывает ⟨пробирает⟩ *кого* ~ ≃ **the cold ⟨the wind⟩ pierces ⟨cuts⟩ s.o. to the bone; the cold ⟨the wind⟩ pierces right through to s.o.'s bones.**

...Тут появляются Галя с Ниной, бедные девочки, продрогли до костей, прямо из пурги... (Рыбаков 1). ...Then Galya and Nina turned up, chilled to the bone, poor girls, straight out of a blizzard... (1a). ♦ Он [Михаил] выстоял у неё на крыльце чуть ли не всю ночь и вернулся домой на рассвете злой, продрогший до костей (Абрамов 1). He [Mikhail] had spent nearly the whole night standing on her porch steps and had returned home at dawn—furious, and chilled to the marrow (1a). ♦ ...Мокрый, злой ветер России пронизывал его до костей... (Аксёнов 7). ...Russia's evil wet wind had pierced right through to his bones... (7a).

К-320 • **КОСТÉЙ НЕ СОБЕРЁШЬ ⟨НЕ СОБРÁТЬ⟩** *coll* [VP; subj: human; usu. neg pfv fut, gener. 2nd pers sing не соберёшь; fixed WO] you will be destroyed, you will perish (in some battle, while doing sth. dangerous etc): **you'll never come**

⟨get⟩ back alive; you'll never come ⟨get⟩ out of it alive; that will be the end of you; [in limited contexts] you've had it.

«Знаешь, Кемал, — говорит, — надо кончать с этим». — «Почему кончать?» — спрашиваю. «Затаскают. Потом костей не соберёшь» (Искандер 5). "'You know, Kemal,' he says, 'we have to end this.' 'Why end it?' I ask. 'They'll haul us in. We'll never get back alive'" (5a). ♦ «Не нравится мне что-то в последнее время эта печка [вулкан]... копоти больно много, не загудеть ли собралась? Если по-настоящему разойдётся, костей не соберём, такая у неё слава (Максимов 1). "Somehow I haven't liked the look of that stove [the volcano] recently....There's a hell of a lot of soot. Can it really be going to erupt? If it goes up properly we've had it—at least that's its reputation" (1a).

K-321 • ПЕРЕЛОМА́ТЬ (ВСЕ) КО́СТИ *кому highly coll* [VP; subj: human; usu. fut (used as a threat) or subjunctive] to beat s.o. up, mutilate s.o.: X Y-у все кости переломает ≃ **X will break every bone in Y's body; X will break all Y's bones.**

«Признавайся — помилуем, не признаешься — шкуру с тебя сдерём, кости переломаем и повесим как шпиона...» (Копелев 1). "Confess and we'll pardon you; don't confess, we'll skin you alive, break all your bones, and hang you as a spy" (1a).

K-322 • РАЗМИНА́ТЬ/РАЗМЯ́ТЬ КО́СТИ ⟨КО́-СТОЧКИ⟩ *coll* [VP; subj: human] to move around a bit, usu. after sitting in one place for a long time: X размял кости ≃ **X stretched his legs.**

K-323 • СЛОЖИ́ТЬ (СВОИ́) КО́СТИ *(где) elev* [VP; subj: human] to perish, die (often, in battle or while doing sth. dangerous): X сложит свои кости ≃ **X will meet his death ⟨his end⟩;** [in refer. to death from natural causes, usu. old age] **X will lay his bones to rest.**

«Ну уж мне, старухе, давно бы пора сложить старые кости на покой...» (Толстой 2). "It's high time an old woman like me laid her bones to rest..." (2b).

K-324 • ВОЕ́ННАЯ ⟨СОЛДА́ТСКАЯ⟩ КО́СТОЧКА *coll* [NP; sing only; usu. subj-compl with быть₀ (subj: human, male); fixed WO] a man from a military family or with a military background who possesses the qualities characteristic of a military person: **an officer ⟨a soldier⟩ through and through; an officer ⟨a soldier⟩ to the core ⟨the marrow⟩; every inch a soldier ⟨an officer⟩; soldier's soldier; army man.**

Он [Николай Тихонов] умел покорять людей... Его приход в литературу встретили радостно: Коля молодой, Коля живой, Коля непосредственный... Он новый человек, он военная косточка, он удивительный рассказчик (Мандельштам 1). He [Nikolai Tikhonov]...was good at winning people over. His literary debut was greeted with joy by all those who spoke of him in such glowing terms as a man of the new generation, a wonderful story-teller—and every inch a soldier to boot (1a). ♦ «Подполковник Г., видать, не из вертухаев. Строевик, военная косточка» (Копелев 1). "...Lieutenant Colonel G., he's not one of the screws. He's a line officer, an army man" (1a).

K-325 • РАБО́ЧАЯ КО́СТОЧКА *coll* [NP; sing only; usu. subj-compl with быть₀ (subj: human); fixed WO] a person from a working-class family or with a working-class background: **a worker, body and soul; natural-born worker; a worker born and bred.**

«...Она с молоком матери впитала любовь к труду, рабочая косточка...» (Орлова 1). "...She has been nurtured on her mother's milk with a love for work, she's a worker, body and soul" (1a).

K-326 • РАЗБИРА́ТЬ/РАЗОБРА́ТЬ ПО КО́СТОЧКАМ *кого-что coll* [VP; subj: human] **1.** to analyze the qualities of s.o. or sth. thoroughly, covering all the fine points: X разобрал Y-а по косточкам ≃ **X scrutinized Y from every angle; X put Y under a microscope ⟨a magnifying glass⟩; X examined thing Y in (great) detail; X took thing Y apart.**

2. to criticize s.o. or sth. severely, gossip about s.o. unkindly: X разобрал Y-а по косточкам ≃ **X picked ⟨tore⟩ Y to pieces.**

[author's usage] [Курчаев:] У вас, говорят, дневник какой-то есть, где вы всех по косточке разобрали (Островский 9). [K.:] They say you keep a diary in which you pick everybody to pieces (9b).

K-327 • ПЕРЕМЫВА́ТЬ ⟨МЫ́ТЬ⟩/ПЕРЕМЫ́ТЬ КО́-СТОЧКИ ⟨КО́СТИ⟩ *(кому, чьи) coll* [VP; subj: human, pl; more often impfv] to talk unkindly about s.o. behind his back, discuss and criticize s.o.'s behavior in detail: X-ы перемывают косточки Y-у ≃ **Xs are picking ⟨tearing⟩ Y to pieces; Xs are gossiping about Y; Xs are dishing the dirt about Y.**

«Слыхал, наверно, что тут про меня плели?.. Ну про фронтовика моего? Слыхал. Был тут у нас в войну один человек... Ну дак от него письмо. Сюда собирается... То-то опять начнут перемывать косточки...» (Абрамов 1). "I'm sure you've heard the gossip about me, haven't you?...You know—about my soldier. You heard. About the man who was here during the war....Well, the letter's from him. He's planning on coming here, so they'll start tearing me to pieces again soon" (1a). ♦ Женщины оживают, встряхиваются, их освежённый мозг вспоминает совершенно неожиданного человека, чьи косточки они, оказывается, забыли перемыть (Искандер 3). The women would revive and rouse themselves, their refreshed minds would suddenly recall that there was someone they had completely forgotten to gossip about (3a).

< The phrase originates in the ancient custom of giving a deceased person a second burial. While performing the customary ritual of washing the exhumed remains, i.e., the bones («косточки»), in preparation for reburial, people recalled and spoke of the deceased.

K-328 • БЕ́ЛАЯ КОСТЬ *obs* [NP; sing only, but may refer to one or more persons; fixed WO] (a person or persons) of distinguished lineage, (a member or members) of a high social or privileged group: **blue blood(s);** [as modif] **blue-blooded;** [in refer. to a group only] **the cream of society;** [contemp. usage, said sarcastically] **first-class citizen(s);** [in limited contexts] **bigwig(s).**

«Мы казаки, белая кость, а ты гужеед, скотина, тебе навоз копать» (Трифонов 6). "We're Cossacks, blue bloods, and you're damned coachmen, you swine; your place is digging manure" (6a). ♦ «Мы с тобой в этой халупе вдвоём [*ungrammat* = вдвоём] обитаем, белая кость там, — он кивнул в окно, — в особняка живёт» (Максимов 1). "You and I will live in this hovel together while the bigwigs are over there in the big house," he nodded out of the window (1a).

K-329 • ЧЁРНАЯ КОСТЬ *obs* [NP; sing only, but may refer to one or more persons; fixed WO] (a person or people) of undistinguished lineage, not (a member or members) of the upper class or any privileged group: **common ⟨ordinary⟩ person ⟨people, worker(s) etc⟩; run-of-the-mill peasant(s) ⟨worker(s) etc⟩; of humble birth;** [in refer. to a group only] **common ⟨ordinary, plain⟩ folk;** [contemp. usage, said sarcastically] **second-class citizen(s).**

[author's usage] Вот обратите внимание на Андрея Арсеньича, вот западная школа, вот тренаж, ни жириночки. Аристократы, хе-хе, а мы мужицкая кость (Аксёнов 7). Have a look at Andrei Arsenievich over there. That's the Western look for you. Not an ounce of fat. They keep in shape. They're blue bloods, after all, and we're just your run-of-the-mill peasants (7a). ♦ Оказывается, свободных номеров в гостинице сколько угодно. «Для китайцев... Нам не дают, мы чёрная кость» (Гинзбург 2). Apparently there were any number of vacant rooms in the hotel. "They're all for the Chinese. They're not for us; we're second-class citizens" (2a).

K-330 • ЛЕЧЬ КОСТЬМИ́ [VP; subj: human] **1.** ~ *(за кого-что) elev.* Also: **ПОЛЕ́ЧЬ КОСТЬМИ́** *obs* to perish, fall in battle (usu. in a fight for a just cause): X ляжет костьми (за Y-a) ≃ **X will lay down his life (for Y); X will give (up) his life (for Y).**

…Он [рыцарь] всегда готов был лечь костьми за то, что считал правым… (Герцен 2). …He [the knight] was always ready to lay down his life for what he thought right… (2a).

2. [usu. fut foll. by Conj «a» or «но» and another pfv verb] to exert every effort in order to accomplish sth. (when used in the 1st pers, expresses the speaker's firm resolve to accomplish sth.): X костьми ляжет ≃ **X will do his damnedest ⟨darnedest⟩; X will go all out; X will do it even if it kills him; X will knock himself out.**

< «Костьми» is the old instrumental plural form of «кость» (the contemporary form is «костями»).

K-331 • В КОСТЮ́МЕ АДА́МА; В КОСТЮ́МЕ Е́ВЫ [PrepP; these forms only; modif or subj-compl with copula (subj: human); of a man (1st var.); of a woman (2nd var.); fixed WO] naked, without any clothes on: **in one's birthday suit; in the altogether; without a stitch (on); in the raw ⟨the buff⟩; au naturel.**

K-332 • НА КОСТЯ́Х *(кого, чьих)* **строить, воздвигать** *что* и т. п. [PrepP; Invar; the resulting PrepP is adv] (to build, erect sth.) through the labors and great suffering (of many people): X построен на костях ≃ **X is built on the bones of many men; X is built on dead men's bones; X was built at the cost of many (human) lives;** ‖ X построен на костях Y-ов ≃ **X is built on the bones of Ys.**

[extended usage] «Разрушить старый мир и на его костях построить новый — это очень старая идея. И ни разу пока она ещё не привела к желаемым результатам» (Стругацкие 1). "To destroy the old world and build up a new one on its bones is a very old idea. And never once has it brought the desired results" (1a).

K-333 • КАК КОТ НА СМЕТА́НУ смотреть *на кого-что coll, humor* [как + NP; Invar; adv; fixed WO] (to look at s.o. or sth.) with desire, lust: **like ⟨the way⟩ a cat looks at a canary; licking one's chops.**

K-334 • КОТ НАПЛА́КАЛ *кого-чего coll* [Invar; quantit subj-compl with copula (subj/gen: any common noun); fixed WO] very little, very few: **practically ⟨almost⟩ no…(at all); practically none ⟨nothing⟩; no…to speak of; next to no…; hardly any…; precious little.**

…В ГУМе [Государственном универсальном магазине] людей до чёрта, а товаров кот наплакал, а здесь всё совершенно наоборот… (Войнович 1). …GUM is packed with people and there are no goods to speak of; in our store it's the exact opposite (1a). ♦ «Когда ты этого дурноеда сбудешь с рук?.. У самих хлеба осталось — кот наплакал, а ты его, чёрта горбатого, содержишь, кормишь каждый день» (Шолохов 5). "When will you get rid of this sponger?…We've got precious little grain left for ourselves, and you keep that hunchbacked devil here, feeding him every day" (5a).

K-335 • ПОКУПА́ТЬ/КУПИ́ТЬ КОТА́ В МЕШКЕ́ *coll* [VP; subj: human; the verb may take the final position, otherwise fixed WO] to buy, get etc sth. without having seen it, without having carefully examined its quality: X купил кота в мешке ≃ **X bought a pig in a poke; X bought thing Y sight unseen.** ○ **КОТ В МЕШКЕ́** [NP; sing only] ≃ **a pig in a poke.**

«Гляну пойду для порядка на животину твою. Потом и порешим. А то вроде как кота в мешке обговариваю» (Максимов 3). "I'll go and take a look at your animals [*sic*], just to do things properly. Then we'll decide. I won't want to buy a pig in a poke" (3a).

< Loan translation of the French *acheter chat en poche.*

K-336 • ТЯНУ́ТЬ КОТА́ ЗА ХВОСТ *coll, disapprov* [VP; subj: human; often neg imper; fixed WO] to talk tediously, too slowly, not to the point, or be slow to answer a question: X тянет кота за хвост ≃ **X hems and haws; X beats around ⟨about⟩ the bush; X drags it out;** ‖ *Neg Imper* не тяни кота за хвост ≃ **spit it out; get to the point.**

K-337 • КАК ⟨С⟩ ПИВНО́Й КОТЁЛ голова [как + NP or PrepP; these forms only; nonagreeing modif or subj-compl with copula (subj: голова); fixed WO] (s.o.'s head is) very large: **(a head) the size of a pumpkin; giant ⟨enormous⟩ head.**

K-338 • О́БЩИЙ КОТЁЛ *coll* [NP; sing only; fixed WO] common resources (money, goods etc) contributed and used by members of a given group: **pool; kitty; common pot;** ‖ класть ⟨отдавать и т. п.⟩ всё в общий котёл ≃ **pool everything.**

…Разграбив где-либо лавку… всё валили в общий взводный котёл и делили добычу поровну, строго соблюдая принцип равенства (Шолохов 5). …When they had looted some village shop…they would pool everything and then share it out fairly, strictly observing the principle of equality (5a).

K-339 • ВАРИ́ТЬСЯ В *каком* **КОТЛЕ́** [VP; subj: human] to be a member, usu. for a considerable amount of time, of a certain group or body of people (as specified by the modifier), absorbing their views, approaches etc: X варился в нашем ⟨в этом⟩ котле ≃ **X was one of us ⟨that crowd, their group, that circle etc⟩; X was a part of that crowd ⟨their group etc⟩.**

K-340 • (КАК ⟨СЛО́ВНО, ТО́ЧНО⟩) В КОТЛЕ́ КИПЕ́ТЬ ⟨ВАРИ́ТЬСЯ⟩ *coll* [(как etc +) VP; subj: human; fixed WO] to be extremely nervous, worried about sth., be in a greatly agitated state (usu. for an extended period of time): X как в котле кипит ≃ **X is in a sweat; X is in a state; X is all keyed-up.**

K-341 • НЕ ВСЁ КОТУ́ МА́СЛЕНИЦА (, БЫВА́ЕТ И ВЕЛИ́КИЙ ПОСТ) [saying] life is not made up of pleasures alone—troubles and difficulties also occur (said when a time full of worries and cares comes to replace a period that is pleasant and carefree): ≃ **every day is not Sunday ⟨a holiday⟩; into each life a little rain must fall;** [in limited contexts] **all good things (must) come to an end.**

K-342 • ДРА́НАЯ ⟨ОБО́ДРАННАЯ⟩ КО́ШКА *highly coll, derog* [NP; usu. sing] a skinny, emaciated, pathetic-looking woman: **(look like) a stray ⟨starved⟩ cat.**

K-343 • ЗНА́ЕТ ⟨ЧУ́ЕТ⟩ КО́ШКА, ЧЬЁ МЯ́СО СЪЕ́ЛА [saying] a person knows that he is guilty (said of a person whose behavior suggests that he is aware of his wrongdoing): ≃ **that's your ⟨his etc⟩ guilty conscience speaking; he ⟨she etc⟩ knows who he ⟨she etc⟩ wronged; he ⟨she etc⟩ knows what he ⟨she etc⟩ did (wrong);** [in questions] **a guilty conscience, eh?**

«А ты, — Семён направил тяжёлый взгляд на Митягина, — крой [= иди] в Пожнёвку. Сообщи бригадиру Михайле о сыне [о том, что его сына убили]…» …Митягин сжался. «Ты сам, Семён, сходи… Не могу… — попросил он угасшим голосом. — Не неволь, как же к человеку с эдаким…» Семён взял Митягина за плечо, сурово вгляделся в него. «Иль чует кошка, чьё мясо съела?» — «Да ведь я не один стрелял...» — «Двое стреляли. Один медведя свалил [= убил], другой человека. И сдаётся [substand = кажется] мне: ты с ружьём-то похуже справляешься» (Тендряков 1). "And you," Simon looked somberly at Mityagin, "go to Pozhnevka. Tell Mikhailo Lyskov what's happened to his son [that he has been killed]."...Mityagin seemed to cringe. "You go, Simon, I can't," he said in a faint voice. "I can't do it, how can I go to a man and tell him..." Simon put a hand on Mityagin's shoulder and looked sternly into his face. "A guilty conscience, eh?" "But I wasn't the only one to shoot." "There were two shots. One hit the bear and the other this boy. And the way I reckon: you are not so handy with a gun..." (1a).

К-344 • КАК КÓШКА С СОБÁКОЙ жить (с кем), **быть_0** coll [как + NP; Invar; adv or, less often, subj-compl with быть_0 (subj: human); if there is no prep obj, subj: pl; fixed WO] (two parties are) constantly quarreling, in constant conflict with each other: **(fight ⟨quarrel⟩) like cat(s) and dog(s).**

Степанида жила в большом, на две семьи, доме вдвоём с племянницей Галькой... Мир их почему-то не брал, и они жили как кошка с собакой... (Распутин 1). Stepanida lived in a big two-storey house with her niece Galia....They could not get on together, indeed they quarrelled like cat and dog... (1a).

К-345 • КАК УГОРÉЛАЯ КÓШКА метаться, бегать, бежать и т. п. coll [как + NP; nom only; adv; fixed WO] (to rush about, run somewhere) in a frenzy, not noticing anything around one: **like a singed ⟨scalded⟩ cat; like a chicken with its head (cut) off.**

[Анна Андреевна:] Что за ветреность такая! Вдруг вбежала, как угорелая кошка (Гоголь 4). [A.A.:] What sort of thoughtlessness is that! You just suddenly run in like a singed cat (4a).

К-346 • (ЧЁРНАЯ ⟨СÉРАЯ⟩) КÓШКА ПРОБЕЖÁЛА ⟨ПРОСКОЧÍЛА⟩ между кем coll [VP_subj] a quarrel, disagreement has taken place (between two or more people) and they — temporarily or, occas., permanently — stay angry at each other: между Х-ом и Y-ом пробежала (чёрная) кошка ≃ **something came between X and Y; X and Y had a falling-out ⟨a tiff⟩;** [in limited contexts] **there is bad blood between X and Y.**

«Без тебя и когда вот так у нас какая-то кошка пробежит, я как будто пропал и ничего не могу» (Толстой 7). "Without you, or when something comes between us like this, I feel lost and can do nothing" (7a). ♦ ...Раз, не сказав никому, [Печорин] отправился стрелять, — целое утро пропадал; раз и другой, всё чаще и чаще... Нехорошо, подумал я: верно, между ними [Печориным и Бэлой] чёрная кошка проскочила! (Лермонтов 1). ...One day, without telling anybody, he [Pechorin] was off to shoot, was gone the whole morning—this happened once, and it happened again, and became more and more frequent. "That's bad," I thought, "no doubt, they [Pechorin and Bela] must have had a tiff" (1a).

К-347 • ИГРÁТЬ В КÓШКИ-МЫШКИ с кем coll [VP; subj: human] to try to outwit, deceive s.o. (usu. in a conversation, often by exploiting one's advantageous position): X играет с Y-ом в кошки-мышки ≃ **X is playing cat and mouse with Y; X is playing a cat-and-mouse game with Y.** ○ **ИГРÁ В КÓШКИ-МЫШКИ** [NP] ≃ **a cat-and-mouse game.**

«Стыдно, Панкратов! Не играйте с нами в кошки-мышки. Мы осведомлённее, чем вы думаете» (Рыбаков 2). "You should be ashamed of yourself, Pankratov, playing cat and mouse with us. We know more than you think" (2a). ♦ Христофорович, играя в кошки-мышки с О. М[андельштамом] и только намекая ему на аресты по его делу родных и близких, вёл себя по высокому следовательскому рангу... (Мандельштам 1). In playing this cat-and-mouse game with M[andelstam] and only hinting that his family and friends had been arrested, Christophorovich was behaving like a top-level interrogator... (1a).

К-348 • КÓШКИ СКРЕБÚТ НА ДУШÉ ⟨НА СÉРДЦЕ⟩ у кого; СКРЕБЁТ НА ДУШÉ ⟨НÁ СЕРДЦЕ⟩ all coll [VP_subj (variants with кошки) or VP, impers (variants with скребёт)] s.o. experiences (and often tries to conceal from others) strong feelings of unrest, anxiety, worry etc (caused by pangs of conscience, a premonition of coming troubles etc): у Х-а на душе скребут кошки ≃ **there's a gnawing in X's heart; something is gnawing at X's heart; X feels torn up ⟨apart⟩ inside; X feels miserable ⟨distressed, upset etc⟩.**

Когда летом [актёры] приехали из Саратова и [Гриша] Ребров встречал её [Лялю] на вокзале, Корнилович нарочно громким, шутовским голосом говорил Ляле: «Ну что, Лялечка, признаемся Грише во всём? А? Давай признаемся!» Актеры хохотали, Гриша силился улыбаться, а на душе кошки скребли: чёрт их знает, а вдруг? (Трифонов 1). When the company had come back from Saratov that previous summer and [Grisha] Rebrov had gone to the railroad station to meet her [Lyalya], Kornilovich had spoken up in an intentionally loud, jesting voice, "Well, Lyalechka, shall we confess everything to Grisha? Shall we? Let's tell him!" The actors had roared with laughter and Grisha had done his best to smile, but inside he felt torn apart: who could be sure, perhaps something had actually gone on between them? (1a). ♦ За годы супружеской жизни Вера Платоновна выучилась улыбаться, какие бы кошки ни скребли на душе, быть всегда свежей, подтянутой, энергичной (Грекова 3). During their years together, Vera had learned to smile regardless of how miserable she felt, to look fresh and lively always (3a).

К-349 • НÓЧЬЮ ⟨В ТЕМНОТÉ⟩ ВСЕ КÓШКИ СÉРЫ [saying] differences between people, things etc of a certain kind are indistinguishable in the dark, or under circumstances that obscure those differences: **all cats are gray in the dark.**

К-350 • КРÁЕМ ⟨КРÁЕШКОМ⟩ ГЛÁЗА coll [these forms only; adv; fixed WO] **1.** ~ **видеть кого-что взглянуть на кого-что** и т. п. (to see sth.) for a brief moment, in passing: **(see s.o. ⟨sth.⟩) out of the corner of one's ⟨one, an⟩ eye; catch ⟨have, get⟩ a glimpse of s.o. ⟨sth.⟩; catch sight of s.o. ⟨sth.⟩.**

Кто-то схватил её руку и, больно сжав пальцы, потянул к рампе. Она поклонилась, краем глаза увидела, кто тянул: Макеев (Трифонов 1). Someone grabbed her by the hand, and squeezing her fingers painfully, dragged her to the footlights. She bowed and saw out of the corner of her eye that it was Makeev (1a). ♦ ...Ещё ей хотелось хоть одним глазком, хоть краешком глаза взглянуть на Егоршу: как он сегодня-то, на трезвую голову? (Абрамов 1). ...She also wanted to have a peek at Yegorsha, if only out of the corner of one eye: how is he today, sober? (1b). ♦ [Нина:] ...Он точно знает, что ему в жизни надо... [Бусыгин:] Покажи мне его. Дай хоть краем глаза на него взглянуть. [Нина:] Вечером увидишь (Вампилов 4). [N.:] ...He knows exactly what he wants in life.... [B.:] I want to see him. Show him to me. Let me at least have a glimpse of him. [N.:] You'll see him this evening (4b).

2. ~ **наблюдать** и т. п. **за кем** (to watch s.o.) without focusing all one's attention on him, while doing something else: **(watch s.o.) out of the corner of one's eye.**

«Ты из России приехал или из Кенгурска?» — спросил старший родственник... «Из Кенгура», — сказал милиционер, краем глаза последил за правой рукой младшего родственника (Искандер 3). "Are you from Russia or from Kengursk?" the elder relative asked....."From Kengur," the policeman said, watching the younger relative's right hand out of the corner of his eye (3a).

К-351 • КРÁЕМ ⟨КРÁЕШКОМ⟩ ÚХА; ОДНÍМ ÚХОМ all coll [these forms only; adv; fixed WO] **1.** ~ **слышать что, о чём** (to hear sth.) accidentally: **happen to hear; half hear; (hear) by chance ⟨by accident⟩.**

...Я в тот день одним ухом слышал — и изумился: ещё одна полная неожиданность — Твардовский нисколько не возмущён моим письмом съезду, даже доволен им! (Солженицын 2). ...That very day I half heard something that amazed me. Here was another complete surprise. Tvardovsky was not the least bit indignant about my letter to the congress; indeed, he was pleased with it! (2a).

2. ~ слушать *(кого-что)* (to listen to s.o. or sth.) inattentively: **(listen) with half an ear; half listen.**

Я краем уха прислушиваюсь к тому, о чём разговаривают Антон и Сашка (Зиновьев 2). I listened with half an ear to what Anton and Sashka were discussing (2a).

К-352 • БИТЬ 〈ЛИ́ТЬСЯ, ПЕРЕЛИВА́ТЬСЯ〉 ЧЕРЕЗ КРАЙ [VP; subj: abstr] (usu. of energy, a certain quality, or a feeling) to manifest itself, come forth with great force, in abundance: X бьёт через край ≃ **X is bursting forth; X is overflowing 〈brimming over〉; s.o. 〈sth.〉 is bursting with X; s.o. is overflowing 〈bubbling over〉 with X.**

«Счастье льётся через край, так хочется жить... а тут вдруг примешивается какая-то горечь...» (Гончаров 1). "My happiness is brimming over, I so want to live—and now suddenly it is mixed with a kind of bitterness!" (1b).

К-353 • НА КРАЙ СВЕ́ТА 〈ЗЕМЛИ́〉 идти, бежать, пойти *(за кем)*, **увезти** *кого* **и т. п.** *coll* [PrepP; these forms only; adv; usu. used with verbs in pfv fut or subjunctive; fixed WO] (to go, run, take s.o. etc) someplace very far away, (to follow s.o.) anywhere, even to a place very far away: **to the end of the earth 〈the world〉; to the (very) ends of the earth; to the back of beyond;** [in limited contexts] **somewhere far, far away.**

Он [господин] наклонился к Шарику, пытливо глянул ему в глаза и неожиданно провёл рукой в перчатке интимно и ласково по Шарикову животу... «Ступай за мной. — Он пощёлкал пальцами. — Фить-фить!» За вами идти? Да на край света (Булгаков 11). He [the gentleman] bent down to Sharik, peered into his eyes, and suddenly passed his gloved hand intimately and caressingly over Sharik's belly....“Come on, follow me.” He snapped his fingers, “Whuit, whuit!” Follow you? Why, to the end of the world (11a). ♦ Раскольников почувствовал и понял в эту минуту, раз навсегда, что Соня теперь с ним навеки и пойдёт за ним хоть на край света, куда бы ему ни вышла судьба (Достоевский 3). At this moment Raskolnikov felt and understood, once and for all, that Sonya would be with him always now and would follow him even to the very ends of the earth, wherever he was fated to be sent (3a). ♦ «Ах, если бы он встретился мне раньше. Я бы побежала за ним на край света» (Дудинцев 1). "If only I had met him sooner! I would have followed him to the ends of the earth!" (1a). ♦ «Всё мне опротивело... ушла бы я на край света, не могу я это вынести, не могу сладить...» (Тургенев 3). "I'm sick and tired of it all....I wish I could go away somewhere, far, far away. I can't bear it; I can't do anything about it..." (3a).

К-354 • НЕПОЧА́ТЫЙ КРАЙ *чего coll;* **НЕПОЧА́ТЫЙ У́ГОЛ** *obs* [NP; sing only; often quantit subj-compl with copula (subj/gen: abstr or concr); usu. this WO] an enormous number or quantity: **a host; (have) no end of; (there is) no end to; an abundance; a wealth; plenty;** [in limited contexts] **(be) snowed under (with sth.).**

Путь Хлебникова был для меня запретен. Да и кому, кроме него, оказался бы он под силу? Меня и не тянуло в ту сторону: передо мной расстилался непочатый край иных задач... (Лившиц 1). For me the path chosen by Khlebnikov was a forbidden one. And who, apart from him, would have found the strength to pursue it? I was not tempted in that direction: before me unfolded a host of different problems... (1a). ♦ Работы у тамошних партий — край непочатый (Алешковский 1). The parties there were just snowed under with work (1a).

К-355 • ХВАТА́ТЬ *obs*/**ХВАТИ́ТЬ 〈ПЕРЕХВАТИ́ТЬ, ПЕРЕЛИВА́ТЬ** *obs*〉 **ЧЕРЕЗ КРАЙ** *coll, often disapprov* [VP; subj: human; usu. pfv] to do or say (usu. on impulse) sth. inappropriate, excessive, exaggerate sth.: X хватил через край ≃ **X took 〈carried〉 it 〈things〉 a bit too far; X went (a little) overboard 〈too far〉; X carried it 〈things〉 to extremes; X overstated his case.**

Шовинизм Василия Смирнова, пояснила она, проявлялся лишь в словах, а не в делах. В высказываниях, а не в поступках. И надо, мол, судить, Смирнова так, как он сам о том просит — не по словам, а по делам. Тут уж и некоторые члены комиссии задвигались... И даже переглянулись. Не хватила через край? (Свирский 1). Vasily Smirnov's chauvinism, she explained, was revealed only in his words, not in his actions. In what he said rather than in what he did. And we must judge Smirnov as he himself asked—not by his words but by deeds. At this point several members of the commission began to stir....They even exchanged glances. Hadn't she gone too far this time? (1a).

К-356 • ХЛЕБНУ́ТЬ ЧЕРЕЗ КРАЙ *coll* [VP; subj: human]
1. ~ **горя, нужды** to experience much (sorrow and/or need): X хлебнул горя через край ≃ **X has had (more than) his share of sorrow 〈misfortune, hard times〉; X has had (a lot) more than enough; X has drunk his cup to the bitter dregs; X has known a lot of sorrow 〈grief etc〉.**

«...Уж хватит! Хлебнули через край! — вспыхнул неожиданно Грязнов. — Мы тут бедствуем, во вшах погибаем, а семьи наши там нужду принимают...» (Шолохов 3). “...We've had enough! A lot more than enough!” Gryaznov burst out unexpectedly. “Here we are going through hell, getting eaten up by lice while our families go hungry” (3a). ♦ ...Зачем душу людям травить, и без того хлебнули... горя через край (Айтматов 2). Why make their life more miserable, when they had...drunk their cup to the bitter dregs? (2a).

2. to drink too much: X хлебнул через край ≃ **X had one too many; X had a drop too much; X exceeded his limit.**

К-357 • ЧЕРЕЗ КРАЙ *чего coll* [PrepP; Invar; usu. quantit subj-compl with copula (subj/gen: abstr or concr)] (s.o. has or in some place there is) a very large quantity or excessive amount of sth.: **limitless; without limit; enough and to spare;** [in refer. to undesirable things, often personality traits considered undesirable when present to an excessive degree] **far too much.**

Мама ведёт активный образ жизни, энергии у неё через край. Mom leads a very active life, she has energy enough and to spare.

К-358 • ВПАДА́ТЬ 〈ВДАВА́ТЬСЯ〉 В КРА́ЙНОСТИ [VP; subj: human] to go considerably beyond what is reasonable, logical, true, or correct (in one's argumentation, actions etc), often going from one extreme to the other: X впадает в крайности ≃ **X goes 〈is driven〉 to extremes; X carries 〈takes〉 it 〈things〉 to extremes; X goes 〈carries things〉 too far.**

«Итак... вы повстанец?» — «Я не говорю этого, баронесса, — опять-таки, зачем впадать в крайности?» (Салтыков-Щедрин 2). “So you're a...revolutionary?” “I didn't say that, baroness! Again, why go to extremes?” (2a).

К-359 • ДО КРА́ЙНОСТИ [PrepP; Invar; modif or adv (intensif)] to a great degree, far beyond a normal level: **in the extreme; to an extreme; terribly; to the utmost; no end;** [in limited contexts] **to the limit;** [with negated predic] **(not...) at all;** [as modif only] **extremely; absolutely.**

...Литературная жизнь ему уже успела опротиветь до крайности... (Битов 2). ...The literary life had begun to disgust him in the extreme... (2a). ♦ [Астров:] Когда бываю в таком состоянии, то становлюсь нахальным и наглым до крайности

(Чехов 3). [А.:] When I'm in this state I get terribly bumptious and impudent (3c). ♦ Всё в Шухове было напряжено до крайности — вот сейчас нарядчик в дверях заорёт (Солженицын 7). Every fiber in his [Shukhov's] body was tensed to the utmost: the work assigner would be bellowing at the door any moment now (7c). ♦ Нынче его напряжение действовало на Ирину Викторовну особенно, наверное, потому, что она и сама-то тоже до крайности была напряжена (Залыгин 1). Now Irina Viktorovna felt the strain in him more than ever, doubtless because she was strained to the limit herself (1a). ♦ «А мне до крайности не нравится эта затея», — злобно поглядывая на афишу сквозь роговые очки, ворчал Римский... (Булгаков 9). "Well, I don't care for this business at all," Rimsky grumbled, glancing at the playbill angrily through his horn-rimmed glasses (9a). ♦ Этот добродушный и несколько ленивый правитель вдруг сделался деятелен и настойчив до крайности... (Салтыков-Щедрин 1). This genial and somewhat lazy ruler suddenly became extremely energetic and persistent... (1a). ♦ «Знаешь, нам иногда до крайности необходимо вить друг из друга верёвки». — «Необходимо... а почему?» — «Наверное, потому, что мы не можем обойтись без того, чтобы не вить верёвок из самих себя. Ну а если так, наступает момент, когда приобретённые навыки обязательно нужно на ком-то испробовать» (Залыгин 1). "You know, sometimes it's absolutely essential to wrap people round your little finger." "Essential? Why's that?" "I suppose because we can't get by if we don't wrap ourselves round our own little fingers. And that being so there comes a time when we absolutely have to test our acquired skills on somebody else" (1a).

К-360 • ДОВОДИ́ТЬ/ДОВЕСТИ́ ДО КРА́ЙНОСТИ [VP; subj: human or abstr] **1.** ~ *кого* to cause s.o. to lose his composure: X довёл Y-а до крайности ≃ **X pushed Y too far; X drove Y over the edge ⟨the brink⟩; X pushed Y past Y's limit;** [in limited contexts] **Y (had) reached his limit.**

...Может быть, эта легенда возникла как галлюцинация в мозгу у людей, доведённых до крайности (Рыбаков 1). ...Maybe this legend arose like a hallucination in the minds of people who had reached their limit (1a).

2. ~ *что* to take (some matter, line of reasoning etc) beyond the usual limits: X довёл Y до крайности ≃ **X took Y to extremes ⟨to its extreme⟩.**

Такой метод оценки, доведённый до крайности, был бы ещё глупее, чем подход к писателям и критикам как к выразителям общих мыслей (Набоков 1). Such a method of evaluation, taken to its extreme, would be even sillier than approaching writers and critics as exponents of general ideas (1a). ♦ Три месяца до ареста жена уговаривала меня не объявлять голодовку, хоть не бессрочную: «Двух недель достаточно. Ну, пусть три недели...» — торговалась она со мной, а я смеялся и говорил, что вытяну несколько месяцев и непременно сниму [голодовку], не доводя дело до крайности. Я и сам не стремился к смерти (Марченко 2). [context transl] Three months before I was arrested, my wife urged me not to go on a hunger strike, or at least not for an unlimited period. She bargained with me: "Two weeks is enough. Well, maybe three weeks...." I laughed and said I would be able to hold out for several months and would definitely quit before reaching a critical point. I had no desire to die (2a).

К-361 • ВПАДА́ТЬ/ВПАСТЬ ⟨ВДАВА́ТЬСЯ/ВДА́ТЬСЯ⟩ В КРА́ЙНОСТЬ *(какую)* [VP; subj: human] to overdo sth., show a lack of moderation in one's judgment, reaction to sth. etc: X впадает в крайность ≃ **X goes to extremes;** ‖ X впадает в другую ⟨обратную⟩ крайность ≃ **X goes to the other ⟨the opposite⟩ extreme; X goes to the opposite end of the scale.**

С того самого дня Чик потерял интерес к людям с холодными стальными глазами. Он даже впал в обратную крайность, то есть, увидев человека с такими глазами, он начинал подозревать его в преступных склонностях... (Искандер 1). After that day Chik lost interest in people with cold and steely eyes. He

even went to the opposite extreme, that is, when he saw a person with eyes like that he started to suspect him of criminal tendencies... (1a).

К-362 • ИДТИ́/ПОЙТИ́ НА КРА́ЙНОСТЬ; ПРИБЕ-ГА́ТЬ/ПРИБЕ́ГНУТЬ К КРА́ЙНОСТИ [VP; subj: human] to resort to extreme means: X пошёл на крайность ≃ **X took drastic ⟨extreme, severe⟩ measures;** [in limited contexts] **X went to the brink.**

К-363 • ВО ВСЕЙ (СВОЕ́Й) КРАСЕ́ [PrepP; these forms only; usu. adv; fixed WO with своей movable] **1.** showing, displaying all one's or its grandeur, magnificence: **in all one's ⟨its⟩ beauty ⟨glory, splendor⟩.**

Весна, долго задерживаемая холодами, вдруг началась во всей красе своей, и жизнь заиграла повсюду (Гоголь 3). The spring which had been held back for a long time by frosts, suddenly arrived in all its beauty and everything came to life everywhere (3a). ♦ Перед Владимиром [Сканщиным]... стоял во всей красе совсем уже было утраченный объект — Максим Петрович Огородников! (Аксёнов 12). There before Skanshchin stood the long-lost object in all his glory—Maxim Petrovich Ogorodnikov! (12a). ♦ Наконец павлин предстал перед ним во всей своей красе (Алешковский 1). Finally the peacock displayed itself in all its glory... (1a).

2. (показать себя, проявить себя) ~ *iron* (of a person) (to display, show o.s.) in an unappealing manner or light: **in all one's splendor ⟨glory⟩.**

[Валентина:] Мы только на секундочку! [Татьяна (шёпотом):] Только взглянуть на твоего... [Надя:] ...Ну что ж, проходите... Знакомьтесь... вот он, во всей красе (Брагинский и Рязанов 1). [V.:] We've only dropped in for a second! [T. (in a whisper):] Just to have a peep at your... [N.:] ...Well, come in... Let me introduce you... Here he is, in all his splendour (1a).

К-364 • В МРА́ЧНЫХ ⟨ЧЁРНЫХ, РО́ЗОВЫХ и т. п.⟩ КРА́СКАХ описывать, рисовать, видеть и т. п. *кого-что*; МРА́ЧНЫМИ ⟨ЧЁРНЫМИ, РО́ЗОВЫМИ и т. п.⟩ КРА́СКАМИ описывать, рисовать и т. п. *кого-что* [PrepP or NP$_{instrum}$; these forms only; adv; fixed WO] (to describe, paint, see etc s.o. or sth.) in a certain way (as specified by the modifier): **(portray etc s.o. ⟨sth.⟩) in dark ⟨somber, rosy etc⟩ colors ⟨hues, tones⟩; (see etc s.o. ⟨sth.⟩) in the worst ⟨the best, a rosy etc⟩ light;** [in positive contexts only] **(see etc s.o. ⟨sth.⟩) through rose-colored glasses.**

Очертил Бездомный главное действующее лицо своей поэмы... очень чёрными красками... (Булгаков 9). Homeless had portrayed the principal character of his poem...in very dark hues (9a).

К-365 • СГУЩА́ТЬ/СГУСТИ́ТЬ КРА́СКИ [VP; subj: human; if pfv, usu. past; if impfv, usu. pres, past, or infin with не стоит, не надо, не будем etc; usu. this WO] to overstate sth., making it seem considerably worse, gloomier etc or more important, better etc than it is in reality: X сгустил краски ≃ **X laid ⟨put, spread⟩ it on thick ⟨with a trowel⟩; X piled it on (thick); X (grossly) exaggerated (it ⟨things⟩);** [in refer. to an exaggeratedly negative portrayal of sth.] **X painted too black ⟨gloomy, dismal⟩ a picture (of things).**

«Мой добрый Александр в благородном негодовании собрался было ехать в Петербург и помочь Вам... но по размышлении решил, что Вы, как всегда, несколько сгустили краски» (Окуджава 2). "My dear Alexander in a fury of righteousness wanted to go to Petersburg to help you...but on second thought decided that you, as usual, may have exaggerated a bit" (2a). ♦ Я слушал тебя, сказал Мазила, и у меня всё время было такое ощущение, будто я через какой-то мощный прибор наблюдаю, как медленно и неуклонно образуется раковая опухоль у близкого мне существа, но не могу предпринять ничего, чтобы помешать этому. Не будем сгущать краски, сказал Карьерист (Зиновьев 1). "While I've been listening to you," said Dauber, "I've been having a growing feeling that I was observing through a microscope a cancerous tumour developing in the body of a man I am fond of, and that I couldn't do a thing to stop it." "We mustn't paint too black a picture," said Careerist (1a). ♦ «Это не мемуары, это политическая акция. Акция, направленная на извращение истории нашей партии...» — «Я думаю, вы несколько сгущаете краски», — нахмурился Киров... (Рыбаков 2). [context transl] "These are not memoirs, this is a political act. It is an act aimed at distorting the history of our Party...." "I think you're over-reacting," Kirov said with a frown (2a).

К-366 • **БРОСА́ЕТ/БРО́СИЛО В КРА́СКУ** *кого coll* [VP; impers] s.o. flushes out of shame, embarrassment: Х-а бросило в краску ≃ **X blushed; it ⟨s.o.'s words etc⟩ made X blush; X ⟨X's face⟩ turned (beet) red; X ⟨X's face⟩ turned crimson.**

[Варя:] Зачем это вы, Антонина Николаевна, Мишу обидели? Как нехорошо сказали — наелся. Меня прямо в краску бросило (Розов 3). [V.:] Antonina Nikolayevna, what did you insult Misha for? How wrong of you to say that he stuffed himself full. It actually made me blush (3a).

К-367 • **ВГОНЯ́ТЬ/ВОГНА́ТЬ ⟨ВВОДИ́ТЬ/ВВЕСТИ́⟩ В КРА́СКУ** *кого* [VP; subj: human or abstr] to cause s.o. to flush with embarrassment: Х вогнал Y-а в краску ≃ **X made Y blush; X made Y turn (beet) red; X made Y turn crimson.**

...За три года житья в лесу Егорша образовался. Стыда никакого — сам первый похабник стал. Глаз синий в щёлку, голову набок, и лучше с ним не связывайся — кого угодно в краску вгонит (Абрамов 1). ...In his three years in the forest, Yegorsha grew up. No embarrassment remained. He became the bawdiest of them all. One blue eye closed to a slit, his head tilted to one side—better not tangle with him—he could make anyone blush (1b).

К-368 • **НЕ ЖАЛЕ́ТЬ/НЕ ПОЖАЛЕ́ТЬ ⟨НЕ ЩАДИ́ТЬ/НЕ ПОЩАДИ́ТЬ⟩ КРА́СОК; НЕ СКУПИ́ТЬСЯ/НЕ ПОСКУПИ́ТЬСЯ НА КРА́СКИ** [VP; subj: human] to describe sth. with special vividness, very expressively, often exaggerating: Х не жалел красок ≃ **X spared no words;** [in limited contexts] **X laid it on thick ⟨with a trowel⟩.**

Дядя Сандро... не скупясь на краски, рассказал историю поимки чёрного лебедя (Искандер 3). Sparing no words, he [Uncle Sandro] told the story of the capture of the black swan (3a).

К-369 • **ВО́ СТО КРА́Т; ВО МНО́ГО КРА́Т** [PrepP; these forms only; adv; used with compar form of Adj or Adv; fixed WO] many times, much (better, worse, more etc): **a hundred times; a hundredfold; far...**

...В сердцах простых чувство красоты и величия природы сильнее, живее во сто крат, чем в нас... (Лермонтов 1). ...Simple hearts feel the beauty and majesty of nature a hundred times more keenly than do we... (1b).

К-370 • **НА КРАЮ́ ГИ́БЕЛИ ⟨ПРО́ПАСТИ⟩** [PrepP; these forms only; usu. subj-compl with copula (subj: human or collect); fixed WO] one is very close to serious, mortal danger: **on the brink ⟨the verge⟩ of disaster ⟨catastrophe, ruin⟩; on the edge ⟨the brink⟩ of the ⟨an⟩ abyss; on the edge of the precipice.**

Во время войн в Италии он несколько раз находится на краю гибели и всякий раз спасается неожиданным образом (Толстой 7). During the wars in Italy he is several times on the brink of disaster and each time is saved in some unexpected way (7a). ♦ [Лунц] всё рос да рос и уж совсем, видимо, стал считать себя неуязвимым, как вдруг в один миг оказался на краю пропасти (Буков-

ский 1). Lunts...continued to grow and grow, and it seems that he had already come to regard himself as invulnerable, when suddenly, overnight, he found himself on the edge of an abyss (1a).

К-371 • **НА КРАЮ́ МОГИ́ЛЫ ⟨ГРО́БА⟩; У КРА́Я МОГИ́ЛЫ ⟨ГРО́БА⟩** [PrepP; these forms only; subj-compl with copula (subj: human); fixed WO] one is close to death, about to die: **(be) at death's door; (have) one foot in the grave; (be ⟨lie⟩) between life and death.**

«Видно, тебе не довольно, что я, благодаря тебе, ранен и целый месяц был на краю гроба: ты и мать мою хочешь уморить» (Пушкин 2). "It seems that you are not content that, thanks to you, I should be wounded and at death's door for a whole month; you wish to kill my mother as well" (2b). ♦ Открылась сильная горячка, и бедная больная две недели находилась у края гроба (Пушкин 3). A violent fever developed, and for two weeks the poor girl lay between life and death (3b).

К-372 • **НА КРАЮ́ СВЕ́ТА ⟨ЗЕМЛИ́⟩** *coll* [PrepP; these forms only; adv or subj-compl with copula (subj: human, collect, or concr); fixed WO] very far away: **at the end of the earth ⟨the world⟩; at the (very) ends of the earth; at the back of beyond;** [in limited contexts] **somewhere far, far away.**

«Я не сделаю ни шага, пока вы не дадите мне возможность повидать сына. Он в школе. Остаётся на краю земли, один, без куска хлеба. Я должна поговорить с ним перед расставаньем...» (Гинзбург 2). "I won't take a step until you let me see my son. He's at school. He will be left behind out here at the end of the earth, all alone, with no means of support. I must talk to him before we are parted..." (2a). ♦ [Ветхая церковь], может, потому и держится, что — на краю света и мало к себе гостей привлекает... (Терц 6). ...Perhaps the reason it [the ancient church] was still standing was that it was indeed at the end of the world, where few visitors came... (6a).

К-373 • **ИЗ КРА́Я В КРА́Й** [PrepP; Invar; adv; fixed WO] over the whole area or length of some expanse of land, in all directions: **from one end to the other; from end to end; all across the land ⟨the country etc⟩; (throughout) the length and breadth of (the land ⟨the country etc⟩); all over.**

К-374 • **(КАК) ИЗ ГОЛО́ДНОГО КРА́Я** *coll* [(как +) PrepP; these forms only; adv or subj-compl with бытьø (subj: human); fixed WO] (to look emaciated, eat hungrily etc) as if one were starving, without food for a long time: **(look ⟨eat⟩) as if one hadn't eaten for days; (look ⟨eat⟩) as if one were on the brink of starvation; (eat) as if one had never seen food before;** ‖ *Neg* не из голодного края ≃ **it's not the first time one has seen food.**

Пили красное и по неполной рюмке, губы вытирали чистыми платками, закусывая, оставляли на тарелке малость: не из голодного края, мол (Максимов 3). They drank red wine, not quite filling the glasses; they dabbed at their lips with clean handkerchiefs; and when they ate they left a little on the plate: It's not the first time we've seen food, you know! (3a).

К-375 • **ОТ КРА́Я (И) ДО КРА́Я** [PrepP; these forms only; adv; fixed WO] the entire space from end to end: **from one end to the other;** [in limited contexts] **the whole land ⟨country etc⟩; the length and breadth of (the land ⟨the country etc⟩).**

К-376 • **В НА́ШИХ ⟨ВА́ШИХ⟩ КРАЯ́Х; В НА́ШИ ⟨ВА́ШИ⟩ КРАЯ́** [PrepP; these forms only; adv; fixed WO] in or to the area or region where I (we, you) live: **in our ⟨your⟩ part ⟨corner⟩ of the world; in our ⟨your⟩ neck of the woods;** [in limited contexts] **in our ⟨these, those⟩ parts; (a)round here ⟨there⟩.**

Дядя Сандро был рад, что остановил выбор на этом доме, что ему не изменило его тогда ещё только брезжащее чутьё на возможности гостеприимства, заложенные в малознакомых людях. Впоследствии беспрерывными упражнениями он это чутьё развил до степени абсолютного слуха, что отчасти позволило ему стать знаменитым в наших краях тамадой... (Искандер 3). Uncle Sandro was happy that his choice had fixed on this house, that his already sensitive nose for the possibilities of finding hospitality among people he barely knew had not betrayed him. In later years, with continuing practice, he developed this sense to the point of absolute pitch. It was largely responsible for his becoming a celebrated tamada, or toastmaster, in our part of the world... (3a).

К-377 • В КРЕДИ́Т покупать, отпускать и т. п. *что* [PrepP; Invar; adv] (to purchase, sell sth. etc) with the agreement that payment will follow, be made later: **on credit; (give ⟨receive⟩) credit.**

...Все деповские покупали мясо у Кусиела. В кредит (Рыбаков 1). All the people from the depot bought their meat from Kusiel, on credit (1a). ♦ Жёны теперь приходили к воротам не с провизией, но с жалобами: деньги вышли, а лавочники не отпускают в кредит (Эренбург 4). Wives were now coming to the gates with complaints instead of provisions; their money was all spent and the shopkeepers refused to give credit (4a).

К-378 • ПО́ЛЬЗОВАТЬСЯ КРЕДИ́ТОМ *(у кого) coll* [VP; subj: human; fixed WO] to enjoy s.o.'s favor, be trusted by s.o.: X пользуется кредитом у Y-a ≃ **X is in good standing with Y; X stands in well with Y; X is in Y's good graces ⟨good books⟩.**

Для него директор не сделает ничего, скорее наоборот, а если Людмила попросит — может сделать. Она... пользуется кредитом (Трифонов 1). [The executive director] wouldn't do anything for him—in fact, just the opposite—but if Liudmila asked, perhaps he'd do it. She was in his good graces... (1a).

К-379 • ВЫКИ́ДЫВАТЬ ⟨ВЫПИ́СЫВАТЬ, ВЫДЕ́-ЛЫВАТЬ⟩ КРЕНДЕЛЯ́; ВЫПИ́СЫВАТЬ ⟨ВЫДЕ́-ЛЫВАТЬ⟩ КУРБЕ́ТЫ *obs;* ВЫВОДИ́ТЬ ВЕНЗЕЛЯ́ *all coll* [VP; subj: human] to dance joyfully, executing intricate patterns: X выкидывал кренделя ≃ **X was cutting capers; X was capering (about).**

[author's usage] Просто дрянь бал, не в русском духе, не в русской натуре... Иной даже, стоя в паре, переговаривается с другим об важном деле, а ногами в то же самое время, как козлёнок, вензеля направо и налево... (Гоголь 3). And that ball of theirs is nothing but so much rubbish; it's not in the Russian spirit, it does not suit the Russian character....Some fellows, standing with their dance partners, might be exchanging remarks about some important matter and at the same time cutting capers with their legs, now to the right, now to the left, like young goats... (3c).

К-380 • ВО́Т ТЕБЕ́ ⟨ТЕ, ВАМ⟩ КРЕСТ! *obs, substand* [Interj; fixed WO] used by the speaker to emphasize the truth of a statement: **cross my heart (and hope to die); I swear to God; as God is my witness ⟨judge⟩.**

[Трубач:] И — вот вам крест! — некоторым труба помогает (Горький 2). [Trumpeter:] And—cross my heart—my trumpet does help some folks (2b).

К-381 • НЕСТИ́ (свой) КРЕСТ [VP; subj: human] to endure trials, suffering, the difficulties allotted to one: X несёт (свой) крест ≃ **X bears ⟨carries⟩ his ⟨a⟩ cross; X has his cross to bear.**

[Алла:] Ты обречён на честность. Она твой крест... Ты будешь нести его до конца (Розов 4). [A.:] You're doomed to honesty. It's your cross and you'll carry it all your life (4a).

< From the Biblical account of how Jesus bore his cross to the place of his crucifixion (John 19:17 et al.).

К-382 • СТА́ВИТЬ/ПОСТА́ВИТЬ КРЕСТ [VP; subj: human or collect; usu. this WO] **1.** ~ *на ком, на кого* having

become disillusioned with s.o., to cease hoping for anything good from him: X поставил крест на Y-е ≃ **X gave up on Y (as hopeless); X gave Y up as hopeless; X wrote Y off.**

Всякий раз его сознание, описав фантастический логический круг, взмыв спиралью, обернувшись, находило объяснение любому человеческому поступку с гуманистической точки зрения, когда ещё не всё потеряно, рано ставить крест и т. д. (Битов 2). His consciousness would travel a fantastic logical circle, spiraling up and back, to find an explanation for any man's deed from the humanistic viewpoint—when all was not lost, it was still too early to give the man up as hopeless, and so forth (2a).

2. ~ *на чём, на что* having become convinced that sth. is worthless, some undertaking is sure to fail etc, to stop thinking about it, stop investing time, energy etc into it: X поставил крест на Y-е ≃ **X gave Y up as hopeless ⟨lost, a waste of time etc⟩; X kissed Y good-bye ⟨goodbye⟩; X wrote Y off; X called it quits with Y.**

...Михаил решил: немедля, сегодня же ехать за сеном на Среднюю Синельгу. Сена на Средней Синельге оставалось возов пятнадцать, и, если не вывезти его сейчас, в эти два-три дня, пока ещё не поплыла дорога, ставь крест на сене (Абрамов 1). ...Mikhail resolved to go to Middle Sinelga immediately and fetch the hay. There were about fifteen cartloads of hay left there, and unless it was picked up in the next two or three days, before the road was awash, you could kiss the whole lot goodbye (1a). ♦ Кириллов — самый опасный из всех бесов Достоевского. Он не случайно поселился в одном доме с Шатовым. Они заключат союз, и тогда можно будет на всём поставить крест (Мандельштам 2). [context transl] Kirillov is the most dangerous of all Dostoevski's "possessed," and not for nothing does he go to live in the same house as Shatov. One day the two could form an alliance—and then it will be the end of everything (2a).

К-383 • КРЕСТА́ НЕТ *на ком obs, substand* [VP; impers; pres only; fixed WO] what s.o. is doing is indecent and shows how dishonorable s.o. is: креста на X-е нет ≃ **X has no conscience ⟨no mercy, no heart⟩; there is no fear of God in X; X knows no shame; it's not Christian!**

Лашков ещё натягивал пиджак, чтобы бежать за уполномоченным, а кто-то уже кричал сверху: «Ироды! Куда по подзору сапожищами-то! И зачем только принесло вас на нашу голову! Креста на вас нету!» (Максимов 3). [context transl] While Lashkov was still pulling on his coat to go and fetch the block sergeant he heard somebody shouting from above. "Monsters! Get those ugly great boots off my tablecloth. Why were you sent to plague us? Bastards!" (3a). ♦ «...Мужики по три рубля с подводы просят — креста на них нет!» (Толстой 6). "...The peasants are asking as much as three rubles for a cart and horse—it's not Christian!" (6a).

К-384 • БОЕВО́Е КРЕЩЕ́НИЕ [NP; sing only; fixed WO] **1.** one's or s.o.'s first participation in battle: **baptism of fire.**

«Самохин? Фёдор Тихонович? Девятнадцатого года рождения? — Майор, не глядя на него, резко перелистывал папку... — Комсомолец? Из крестьян?.. Прошёл боевое крещение?» (Максимов 1). "Samokhin? Fyodor Tikhonovich? Born in '19?" Without looking at him, the major jerkily leafed through the file....."Member of the Komsomol? Of peasant origin?...Gone through the baptism of fire?" (1a).

2. one's or s.o.'s first serious experience (in some type of endeavor, work etc): **baptism of fire.**

...Незадолго до приезда в Москву его [Лёву] впервые посадили и через несколько дней выпустили. Это было, так сказать, боевым крещением (Мандельштам 2). Not long before he [Lev] came to us in Moscow he had been arrested for the first time and then released a few days later. This was, so to speak, his baptism of fire (2a).

К-385 • **КРИВА́Я ВЫВО́ЗИТ/ВЫ́ВЕЗЕТ** ⟨**ВЫНО́-СИТ/ВЫ́НЕСЕТ**⟩ *кого coll* [VP_subj; usu. pfv fut; if impfv, usu. refers to repeated occurrences; fixed WO] (s.o. hopes that, there is a possibility that etc) pure chance will help s.o. in some situation: (X-a) кривая вывезет ≃ **luck will be on X's side; things will go X's way; things will work out (for X); the chips will fall X's way; something will turn up.**

«...Подсудимому должно же было прийти в голову опасение, что он слишком много накричал по городу предварительно и что это может весьма послужить к его уличению и его обвинению, когда он исполнит задуманное. Но уж что же делать, факт огласки был совершён, его не воротишь, и, наконец, вывозила же прежде кривая, вывезет и теперь» (Достоевский 2). "...The fear must have occurred to the defendant that he had shouted around town too much beforehand and that it would go a long way towards exposing and accusing him once he had carried out his plan. But there was no help for it, the fact of publication had been accomplished, it could not be taken back, and, after all, things had always worked out before, so they would work out now as well" (2a).

К-386 • **КУДА́ КРИВА́Я ВЫ́ВЕЗЕТ** ⟨**ВЫ́НЕСЕТ, ВЫ́ВЕДЕТ,** less often **НИ ВЫ́ВЕЗЕТ, НИ ВЫ́НЕСЕТ**⟩ *substand* [VP_subj; these forms only; used as adv or a clause in a complex or compound sent; fixed WO] (to wait and see) how a situation will develop, what its outcome will be (without interfering in it): **(wait and see) how it turns ⟨things turn⟩ out; (wait and see) what happens; (wait and see) what will come of it.**

К-387 • **НА КРИВО́Й** ⟨**НА КОЗЕ́, НА ВОРОНЫ́Х, НА САВРА́СОЙ**⟩ **НЕ ОБЪЕ́ДЕШЬ** *кого highly coll* [VP; neg pfv fut, gener. 2nd pers sing не объедешь only; usu. this WO] you cannot outwit, deceive s.o.: X-a на кривой не объедешь ≃ **you can't trick ⟨bamboozle, outsmart, put anything over on⟩ X; you can't pull the wool over X's eyes; you can't take X for a ride; you have to get up pretty early in the morning to fool X.**

[author's usage] Видят головотяпы, что вор-новотор кругом на кривой их объехал, а на попятный уж не смеют (Салтыков-Щедрин 1). The Knockheads saw that Thief-Among-Thieves had bamboozled them, but they didn't dare back out (1a).

К-388 • **(ПОСЛЕ́ДНИЙ) КРИК МО́ДЫ** [NP; sing only; fixed WO] the most recent style (of dressing, behaving etc), which is striking in its novelty: **the latest fashion; the latest thing (in fashion); [in limited contexts] all the rage.**

[Публика] хлопала сногсшибательного покроя фраку, цилиндру невиданного фасона, альпийской белизне гетр. Рукоплескала последнему крику моды... (Лившиц 1). They [the audience] applauded the stunning cut of his morning-coat, the unique style of this top-hat and the Alpine whiteness of his gaiters. They applauded the latest fashion... (1a).

< Adapted loan translation of the French *dernier cri*.

К-389 • **КРИ́КОМ** ⟨**КРИЧМЯ́**⟩ **КРИЧА́ТЬ** *coll* [VP; subj: human; fixed WO (var. with криком)] to shout very loudly, as loudly as one can: X криком кричал ≃ **X shouted ⟨yelled, screamed⟩ at the top of his voice ⟨lungs⟩; X cried ⟨shouted, screamed⟩ his head off; X screamed his lungs out; X shouted for all he was worth.**

К довершению содома, кричал кричмя дворовый ребятишка, получивший от матери затрещину... (Гоголь 3). To make the uproar more complete, one of the house-serfs, a little boy who had been slapped by his mother, was screaming at the top of his voice... (3a). ♦ По вечерам, возвращаясь с поля, Михаил частенько слышит ликующие голоса своих братьев в сосняке за деревней, и хоть криком кричи — не зазовёшь домой (Абрамов 1). Returning from the field in the evenings, Mikhail would often hear the exultant voices of his brothers in the pine forest back of the village. And

though he would shout for all he was worth, his shouts would not bring them home (1a).

К-390 • **НИ́ЖЕ ВСЯ́КОЙ КРИ́ТИКИ; НЕ ВЫДЕ́Р-ЖИВАТЬ (НИКАКО́Й) КРИ́ТИКИ** [AdjP, subj-compl with copula (1st var.); VP (2nd var.); subj: usu. abstr or concr, occas. human; fixed WO (1st var.)] to be of very poor quality, not meet even the most modest requirements or standards: X ниже всякой критики ≃ **X is beyond ⟨beneath (all)⟩ criticism; [in limited contexts] X is beyond ⟨beneath⟩ consideration; [of an argument, idea, theory etc] X does not hold water.**

К-391 • **В КРОВИ́** *у кого* [PrepP; Invar; subj-compl with быть₀ (subj: abstr)] sth. is inherent in s.o., present from birth: X у Y-а в крови ≃ **X is ⟨runs⟩ in Y's blood; Y has X in Y's blood.**

Лёва охотно становился тем, кем его хотели видеть Бланк — человеком «породы», той культуры и порядочности, которая в крови... (Битов 2). Lyova eagerly became the man Blank wished to see in him—a man of "breeding," of culture, of the decency that is in the blood... (2a).

К-392 • **ЖА́ЖДАТЬ КРО́ВИ** *coll* [VP; subj: human or collect] to strive to cause trouble for s.o., seek to punish or take revenge on s.o.: X жаждет крови ≃ **X is out for blood; X is after person Y's scalp; X is out to get person Y; X is bloodthirsty.**

К-393 • **КУПА́ТЬСЯ** ⟨**УТОПА́ТЬ**⟩ **В КРОВИ́** [VP; subj: human; fixed WO] to commit many murders, massive slaughter, be responsible for much bloodshed: X купался в крови ≃ **X had the blood of many people on his hands ⟨head⟩; X's hands were stained with the blood of many (people); X's hands were steeped in blood.**

К-394 • **НАПИ́ТЬСЯ** ⟨**НАСОСА́ТЬСЯ**⟩ **КРО́ВИ** *чьей coll* [VP; subj: human; usu. this WO] to torment s.o. terribly (by exploitation, malicious insults, beatings etc): X напился Y-овой крови ≃ **X sucked (out) Y's blood.**

К-395 • **ТОПИ́ТЬ/ПОТОПИ́ТЬ В КРОВИ́** *что lit* [VP; subj: human or collect; obj: usu. collect—a noun denoting a political movement, an inhabited area etc (implying the participants or inhabitants therein)] to slaughter indiscriminately (one's political opponents, participants in a specified movement, those living in a specified place etc): X-ы потопили революцию ⟨город и т. п.⟩ в крови ≃ **Xs massacred ⟨slaughtered, wiped out⟩ the revolutionaries ⟨the city's inhabitants etc⟩;** ‖ восстание потопили в крови ≃ **the uprising turned into a bloodbath.**

К-396 • **(НИ) КРОВИ́НКИ** ⟨**КРОВИ́НОЧКИ**⟩ **В** ⟨**НА**⟩ **ЛИЦЕ́ НЕТ** ⟨**НЕ ОСТА́ЛОСЬ**⟩ *у кого;* **БЕЗ КРО-ВИ́НКИ** ⟨**КРОВИ́НОЧКИ**⟩ **В ЛИЦЕ́** *all coll* [VP_subj/gen (1st var.); PrepP, detached modif or subj-compl with copula; subj: human (variants with без); fixed WO (variants with без)] s.o. is or became very pale: у X-а ни кровинки в лице не было ⟨не осталось⟩ ≃ **all the blood drained from X's face; X was ⟨turned⟩ deathly ⟨ghastly⟩ pale; X was ⟨turned⟩ (as) white as a sheet; X didn't have a drop of blood in his face.**

Выдвинув вперёд себя кулаки на столе и откинувшись на высокую спинку плетёного стула, дед [Пётр] сидел... без кровинки в лице... (Максимов 3). He [Grandpa Pyotr] sat there, leaning back against the wicker chair, his fists thrust out before him on the table...with not a drop of blood in his face... (3a).

К-397 • **В КРОВЬ** ⟨**ДО КРО́ВИ, ДО КРОВИ́**⟩ **разбить** *что,* **избить** *кого и т. п.* [PrepP; these forms only; adv] (to injure a body part, beat s.o.) to the point where blood flows: **till it ⟨one, s.o.⟩ bleeds; (s.o. ⟨s.o.'s nose etc⟩ is) bloodied ⟨bleeding⟩; bloody (s.o.'s nose etc)**; [in refer. to hands and feet only] **work one's hands ⟨feet⟩ into blisters.**

Лошади, в кровь иссечённые мухами, крутили хвостами и недружно натягивали постромки (Шолохов 2). The horses, their backs bloodied by flies, swung their tails and pulled jerkily at the traces (2a). ♦ «Помилуй, Иван Богданыч... не проходит дня, чтоб он без синего пятна воротился, а намедни нос до крови разбил» (Гончаров 1). "For heaven's sake, Ivan Bogdanych!...Not a day passes that he doesn't come home with a bruise, and the other day he came back with his nose bleeding!" (1b). ♦ ...Пчёлкин выскочил из брички и некоторое время с яростной независимостью шёл по дороге... Он сразу же разбил себе ноги в кровь и принуждён был сесть обратно... (Катаев 3). ...Pcholkin jumped out of the *britzka* and for a time stomped along in furious independence....He soon worked his feet into blisters, however, and was compelled to resume his seat... (3a).

К-398 • **ГОЛУБА́Я КРОВЬ**; usu. *кто* **ГОЛУБО́Й КРО́ВИ**, *у кого* **ГОЛУБА́Я КРОВЬ**, or **В ЖИ́ЛАХ** *у кого* **ТЕЧЁТ ГОЛУБА́Я КРОВЬ** all obs [NP; fixed WO except when used as VP_subj with быть_∅] (one or s.o. has, s.o. is a person of etc) noble, aristocratic lineage: **blue blood;** [as modif] **blue-blooded;** ‖ у Х-а в жилах течёт голубая кровь ≃ **noble ⟨aristocratic⟩ blood flows in X's veins; X has noble ⟨aristocratic⟩ blood in his veins.**

Следует отметить, что юноши голубой крови были отделены от сыновей богатых буржуа, к числу которых принадлежал Жан-Батист. Принцы и маркизы были пансионерами лицея, имели свою собственную прислугу, своих преподавателей, отдельные часы для занятий, так же как и отдельные залы (Булгаков 5). It must be noted...that the youths of blue blood were segregated from the sons of the wealthy bourgeois, of whom Jean-Baptiste was one. Princes and marquises were boarders at the lycée, with their own servants, their own instructors, their own separate hours of study, as well as their own separate classrooms (5a). ♦ «Какие все вы сейчас довольные, радостные, счастливые – все: и купцы, и биржевые маклеры, и чиновники разных рангов, и помещики, и люди голубой крови!» (Шолохов 3). "How smug, contented, and happy you all are, merchants and stockbrokers, officials of one rank or another, landowners, blue-blooded aristocrats!" (3a).

К-399 • **КРОВЬ БРО́СИЛАСЬ ⟨КИ́НУЛАСЬ, УДА́РИЛА⟩ В ГО́ЛОВУ** *кому* [VP_subj; fixed WO] s.o. reached a state of extreme excitement, frenzy (from indignation, anger etc): кровь бросилась Х-у в голову ≃ **the blood rushed to X's head.**

Он хотел только подразнить меня; но каждое его слово протекло ядом по всем моим жилам. Кровь бросилась мне в голову (Тургенев 3). He just wanted to tease me, but every word he uttered ran like poison through my veins. The blood rushed to my head (3a).

К-400 • **КРОВЬ ⟨КРА́СКА⟩ БРО́СИЛАСЬ ⟨КИ́НУ-ЛАСЬ⟩ В ЛИЦО́** *(чьё, кому, кого)*; **КРОВЬ ПРИ-ЛИЛА́ К ЛИЦУ́** *(чьему, кого)* [VP_subj; fixed WO] s.o. became red in the face (from embarrassment, shame, annoyance etc): кровь бросилась Х-у в лицо ≃ **the blood rushed to X's face ⟨cheeks⟩; X flushed; X blushed; X turned (bright ⟨beet⟩) red.**

«Теперь и я не боюсь! – бодро сказал он [Обломов]. – С вами не страшна судьба!» – «Эти слова я недавно где-то читала... У Сю, кажется... только их там говорит женщина мужчине...» У Обломова краска бросилась в лицо (Гончаров 1). "I'm not afraid any more," he [Oblomov] said cheerfully. "With you I do not fear the future." "I read that phrase somewhere recently – in Sue, I think. Only there it was the woman who said it to the man."...Oblomov flushed (1b).

К-401 • **КРОВЬ ГОВОРИ́Т/ЗАГОВОРИ́ЛА** *в ком* [VP_subj; fixed WO] **1.** s.o. becomes impassioned, has an emotional outburst: в X-е кровь говорит ≃ **X's blood is up.**

2. feelings of family loyalty, solidarity arise in s.o., s.o. feels an interconnectedness with his family: в X-е кровь говорит ≃ **feelings of kinship well up inside X; X is seized by feelings of kinship;** [in limited contexts] **blood is thicker than water.**

К-402 • **КРОВЬ ЗА КРОВЬ** [NP; Invar; usu. indep. sent; fixed WO] avenging a killing by a killing: **a life for a life; an eye for an eye (and a tooth for a tooth).**

К-403 • **КРОВЬ КИПИ́Т/ЗАКИПЕ́ЛА ⟨ИГРА́ЕТ/ЗАИГРА́ЛА, РАЗЫГРА́ЛАСЬ, ГОРИ́Т/РАЗГОРЕ́-ЛАСЬ, БРО́ДИТ⟩** *в ком;* **КРОВЬ ИГРА́ЕТ/ЗАИГРА́ЛА В ЖИ́ЛАХ** *у кого* [VP_subj; usu. this WO] **1.** [usu. impfv] s.o. has a surplus of energy, vitality (may refer to sensuality): в X-е кровь кипит ≃ **X's blood is racing; X's blood runs hot; X is bursting with energy ⟨with life⟩; X is full of life ⟨energy, pep, vim and vigor⟩; X's juices are flowing.**

2. s.o. experiences strong emotion, is seized by passion, has a rush of feeling, burns with anger etc: кровь в X-е кипит ≃ **X's blood is on fire; X's blood courses in ⟨through⟩ his veins;** [usu. in refer. to intense anger] **X's blood boils; it makes X's blood boil; X's blood is up.**

«На тротуаре, видит, идёт какая-то стройная англичанка, как лебедь, можете себе представить, эдакой. Мой Копейкин, кровь-то, знаете, разыгралась в нём, побежал было за ней на своей деревяшке, трюх-трюх следом...» (Гоголь 3). "As he was walking along the pavement, he saw a tall and slender Englishwoman coming towards him, like a swan, yes, sir, like a real swan, in a manner of speaking. Poor old Kopeikin – his blood, you see, was on fire – started running after her, his wooden leg clip-clopping on the pavement" (3a). ♦ ...Эти [петербуржцы] ничем не увлекутся, в них не кипит кровь, вино не вскружит им голову (Герцен 2). ...These Petersburg men are never carried away by anything: their blood never boils, and wine does not turn their heads (2a).

К-404 • **КРОВЬ С МОЛОКО́М** coll [NP; sing only; usu. subj-compl with быть_∅ or modif; fixed WO] **1.** [subj: human] (one is) very healthy-looking, with good facial color: **the (very) picture of health; bursting with health; (have) the freshest of complexions; (have) a country-fresh look;** [of a woman] **(as) fresh as a daisy ⟨as the morning dew⟩;** [of a man] **hale and hearty.**

...Это был мужчина весёлый, краснощёкий, кровь с молоком (Салтыков-Щедрин 2). ...He was a cheerful man, ruddy-faced and the picture of health (2a). ♦ ...[Мне] 55 лет, не тот я уже, 27-летний, кровь с молоком, фронтовик, в первой камере спрошенный: с какого курорта? (Солженицын 2). I was fifty-five, and not the twenty-seven-year-old straight from the front and bursting with health, who had been asked in the first cell he saw, "What holiday resort have you just come from?" (2a). ♦ [author's usage] Хозяйка дома выбежала сама на крыльцо. Свежа она была, как кровь с молоком... (Гоголь 3). The lady of the house came running out on to the front steps herself. She was as fresh as a daisy... (3a).

2. [subj: лицо, щёки] (s.o.'s face is, cheeks are) healthy-looking, rubicund: **(s.o. has) the freshest of complexions;** [in refer. to a woman] **(like) peaches and cream;** [of a man] **ruddy.**

К-405 • **КРОВЬ СТЫ́НЕТ ⟨ЛЕДЕНЕ́ЕТ, ХОЛО-ДЕ́ЕТ⟩/ЗАСТЫ́ЛА (В ЖИ́ЛАХ)** *(чья, у кого)* lit; **КРОВЬ ЗАСТЫВА́ЕТ В ЖИ́ЛАХ** obs [VP_subj; usu. this WO] s.o. experiences extreme fear, horror: у X-а кровь стынет в жилах ≃ **X's blood freezes ⟨runs cold⟩; X's blood turns to ice water (in X's veins); thing Y makes X's blood curdle.**

К-406 • ЛЕДЕНИ́ТЬ КРОВЬ ⟨ДУ́ШУ⟩ *чью, кому;* **ЛЕДЕНИ́ТЬ СЕ́РДЦЕ** *чьё, кому* [VP; subj: abstr or impers] to frighten s.o. horribly: X леденит Y-у кровь ≃ **X chills Y's blood; X makes Y's blood freeze ⟨curdle, run cold⟩; X makes Y's blood turn to ice water (in Y's veins); Y's blood freezes ⟨curdles, runs cold⟩.**

Что только слышал Фриц Платтен от этого человека, своего рока и судьбы своей! – леденило кровь иногда… (Солженицын 5). The things Fritz Platten heard from this man, who was his fate and his doom! Sometimes his blood froze… (5a).

К-407 • ПИТЬ/ВЫ́ПИТЬ ⟨СОСА́ТЬ, ВЫСА́СЫ-ВАТЬ/ВЫ́СОСАТЬ⟩ КРОВЬ *чью, из кого, у кого* all coll [VP; subj: human] to exploit s.o. cruelly, torment, oppress s.o. in every way possible: X сосёт кровь из Y-a ≃ **X sucks (out) Y's blood; X sucks the lifeblood out of Y; X sucks Y dry.**

«А фюрера ихнего [ungrammat = их] видел, Сталина?» – «Встречал, – говорю, – пару раз, в Баку и в Тифлисе. Он банки курочил [slang = грабил]… Неплохой был урка, но ссучился. Генсеком стал. Кровь из мужика пьёт…» (Алешковский 1). "Did you ever see their Führer, Stalin?" "Yeah, I've met him a couple of times," I said. "Once in Baku and once in Tiflis. He was holding up banks….He wasn't a bad crook, but he got out of the business. Became General Secretary. He…sucks the peasants' blood…" (1a). ♦ «Да помолчи ты, пожалуйста!», – поморщился Тимофей… «Я – помолчи! Я – помолчи! В своём-то доме помолчи? Вот как! Может, драться ещё будешь?.. Хватит! Попил ты моей кровушки…» (Абрамов 1). "Oh, please—just be quiet," said Timofei, wincing…."Me be quiet? Me be quiet? Be quiet in my own house? That's fine! Maybe you'd like a fight even?…That's enough. You sucked my lifeblood—" (1a).

К-408 • ПО́РТИТЬ КРОВЬ *кому;* **ПОПО́РТИТЬ ⟨ИС-ПО́РТИТЬ⟩ МНОГО ⟨СТО́ЛЬКО, СКОЛЬКО и т. п.⟩ КРО́ВИ** all coll [VP; subj: human or abstr] to bother, inconvenience, annoy s.o. greatly, cause problems for s.o.: X портит Y-у кровь ≃ **X causes Y (endless) trouble; X causes Y a lot of headaches; X causes Y (unnecessary) worry; [in limited contexts] X poisons Y's existence.**

«Ах, если бы как-нибудь вытянуть из него всё, что он знает! С каким наслаждением я бы потом его прикончил… Сколько он крови мне попортил…» (Стругацкие 2). "If only I could drag it out of him. Then it would give me great pleasure to finish him off. How much unnecessary worry he's caused me" (2a).

К-409 • ПО́РТИТЬ СЕБЕ́ КРОВЬ; ИСПО́РТИТЬ ⟨ПОПО́РТИТЬ⟩ СЕБЕ́ МНОГО ⟨СТО́ЛЬКО, СКОЛЬКО и т. п.⟩ КРО́ВИ all coll [VP; subj: human] to become distressed, annoyed, nervous etc: X портит себе кровь ≃ **X is getting himself (all) upset (over sth.); X is upsetting himself; X is getting irritated; X is getting into a state (over sth.); X is getting all shook up.**

К-410 • ПРОЛИВА́ТЬ ⟨ЛИТЬ⟩/ПРОЛИ́ТЬ КРОВЬ [VP; subj: human] **1.** ~ *за кого-что.* Also: **ПРОЛИВА́ТЬ ⟨ЛИТЬ⟩/ПРОЛИ́ТЬ СВОЮ́ КРОВЬ** to sacrifice o.s., be wounded or perish while fighting for s.o. or sth.: X проливал (свою) кровь (за Y-a) ≃ **X shed (his) blood (for Y); X poured out his blood (for Y).**

«Я счастлив, великий государь, что мог пролить кровь за своё отечество, и желал бы умереть за него» (Толстой 2). "I am happy, Your Majesty, that I was able to shed blood for my country, and I would like to die for her" (2b). ♦ «Арестовать его, подлеца! Мы кровь проливали, а он спасался по тылам!.. Берите его!»

(Шолохов 3). "Arrest him, the scoundrel! While we were shedding our blood he was skulking in the rear! Hold him!" (3a).

2. ~ *(чью, кого)* [obj: usu. pl] to wound, kill, put to death (many people): X пролил кровь Y-ов ≃ **X spilled the blood of Ys;** ‖ X пролил много крови ≃ **X was responsible for much bloodshed.**

Тот же механизм породил Марра, Лысенко и сотни тысяч подобных объединений, проливших слишком много крови (Мандельштам 2). It was the system that gave birth to Marr, Lysenko, and hundreds of thousands of lesser cliques of the same kind, all of them responsible for much bloodshed (2a).

К-411 • РАЗГОНЯ́ТЬ/РАЗОГНА́ТЬ КРОВЬ [VP; subj: human; often infin with надо, полезно etc] to increase one's blood circulation: X-у надо разогнать кровь ≃ **X needs to get the ⟨his⟩ blood moving ⟨going, flowing⟩.**

«Ты что – опять будешь устраивать Африку [в бане]?» – «Да, надо немножко кровь разогнать. У меня что-то ухо правое ломит – надуло, наверно, на реке» (Абрамов 1). "What's going on? Are you trying to turn this place [the bathhouse] into Africa again?" "Yep! Got to get the blood going a bit. My right ear's aching for some reason. Probably from the wind on the river" (1a).

К-412 • (ХОТЬ) КРОВЬ ИЗ НО́СА ⟨ИЗ НО́СУ, И́З НОСУ⟩ highly coll [(хоть +) NP; these forms only; adv; fixed WO] (in refer. to a demand or urgent need to do sth.) (sth. must be done) despite any difficulties or obstacles: **no matter what; even if it kills me ⟨you etc⟩; come hell or high water; by hook or by crook.**

Этот ответ значил: мне приказали – кровь из носу – провести заседание не откладывая… (Эткинд 1). This answer meant: "I've been ordered—by hook or by crook—to hold the meeting without delay…" (1a).

К-413 • КРО́ВЬЮ УМЫВА́ТЬСЯ/УМЫ́ТЬСЯ substand [VP; subj: human; fixed WO] (usu. of a person who is beaten in the face) to bleed profusely: X кровью умылся ≃ **X spit ⟨spouted⟩ blood; blood gushed from X's face ⟨mouth etc⟩.**

К-414 • МА́ЛОЙ КРО́ВЬЮ coll [NP_instrum; Invar; adv; fixed WO] (to attain, accomplish etc sth.) without enduring great losses, making major concessions, or exerting great effort: **shed(ding) hardly any blood; with few casualties; with small losses; (get off) cheap; on the cheap.**

[Воротынцев:] Ведь вы же двадцать четыре года кричали, что – не допустите, что – против любой комбинации, что на чужой территории, что малой кровью, а Гитлер один бил вас где хотели и как хотели… (Солженицын 9). [V.:] Haven't you been proclaiming for twenty-four years that you wouldn't let anyone pass; that you could resist any alliance, that you would fight on someone else's territory, that you would shed hardly any blood, while Hitler, all on his own, beat you as he pleased, where he pleased… (9a).

К-415 • НАЛИВА́ТЬСЯ/НАЛИ́ТЬСЯ КРО́ВЬЮ [VP; subj: human or лицо, шея etc; usu. pfv] to become red from a rush of blood (because of rage, extreme tension etc): X налился ⟨лицо и т. п. X-а налилось⟩ кровью ≃ **blood rushed to X's face; X got all red;** ‖ X-овы глаза налились кровью ≃ **X's eyes got (all) bloodshot; [in limited contexts; in refer. to rage] X had fire in his eyes.**

«Что-то не пойму я, – заговорил он [человек] весело и осмысленно. – Мне по матушке – нельзя. Плевать – нельзя. А от вас только и слышу: „Дурак, дурак". Видно, только профессорам разрешается ругаться в Ресефесере». Филипп Филиппович налился кровью и, наполняя стакан, разбил его (Булгаков 11). "I don't get it," he [the man] said ingenuously. "I mustn't swear. I mustn't spit. Yet all you ever do is call me names. I guess only professors are allowed to swear in the Russian Socialist Federated Soviet Republic." Blood rushed to Philip Philipovich's face. He filled a glass, breaking it as he did so (11b). ♦ «...Бывало, мы его [Азамата] вздумаем дразнить, так глаза кровью и нальются, и сейчас за книжал» (Лермонтов 1). "...Sometimes, we would start teasing him [Azamat], and then his eyes would get all bloodshot, and his hand would at once fly to his dagger" (1a).

К-416 • ПИСА́ТЬ/НАПИСА́ТЬ КРО́ВЬЮ (СЕ́РДЦА)
lit [VP; subj: human; usu. this WO] to write with sincerity and deep feeling about sth. through which one has suffered: X писал кровью сердца ≃ **X wrote with his heart's blood; X wrote straight from the heart.**

Мне показал этот список Д[омбровский], автор повести о нашей жизни, которая написана, как говорили в старину, «кровью сердца» (Мандельштам 1). This collection was shown to me by Dombrovski, the author of a book about our life which was written, as they used to say in the old days, "with his heart's blood" (1a).

К-417 • СМЫВА́ТЬ/СМЫТЬ КРО́ВЬЮ *что lit* [VP; subj: human]
1. often **смывать/смыть своей кровью** to redress sth. (usu. a disgrace etc brought upon o.s.) at the cost of one's life: X смоет Y своей кровью ≃ **X will redeem ⟨atone for⟩ Y with X's (own) blood; X will pay for Y with X's life.**

«Ларочка... Понимаешь ли ты, какой позор и как это затрагивает честь юнкерского мундира?.. Сходи к нему [Виктору Ипполитовичу]... попроси его... Ведь ты не допустишь, чтобы я смыл эту растрату своей кровью» (Пастернак 1). "Lara darling... You realize what this means to me, what a disgrace it is...the honor of my uniform is at stake. Go to see him [Victor Ippolitovich]...speak to him... You can't want me to pay for this with my life" (1a).

2. ~ *чьей, кого* [obj: usu. обида, оскорбление etc] to avenge (an insult, disgrace etc) by killing the offender: X смыл Y Z-овой кровью ≃ **X redeemed Y with Z's blood; X washed away Y by Z's blood.**

Такое оскорбление смывается кровью и только кровью оскорбителя (Искандер 5). Such an insult is washed away by the blood, and only by the blood, of the offender (5a).

К-418 • КРО́ХИ ⟨КРО́ШКИ⟩ С БА́РСКОГО ⟨С ГОСПО́ДСКОГО⟩ СТОЛА́ *lit* [NP; pl only; fixed WO] an insignificant material reward or benefit that s.o. receives from more wealthy, powerful etc people: **crumbs (that fall) from the masters' ⟨the master's⟩ table.**

Взглянуть правде в глаза трудно, а тем более участникам событий и добродушным свидетелям, которым тоже перепадают крохи с господского стола (Мандельштам 2). It is hard to look truth in the eye, whether you were an active participant in events or just a well-disposed onlooker receiving your share of crumbs from the master's table (2a).

< From the Bible (Matt. 15:27).

К-419 • НИ КРО́ШКИ; НИ КРО́ШЕЧКИ *both coll* [NP_gen; these forms only]
1. ~ *(чего)* нет, не осталось, не оставить и т. п. Also: **НИ КРО́ХИ** [subj/gen, quantif of subj/gen, or obj] (used in refer. to food, usu. food that crumbles) (there is, to leave etc) absolutely nothing: **not so much as a crumb ⟨a scrap, a drop, a teaspoonful⟩ etc); not one ⟨a⟩ morsel ⟨bite⟩.**

2. ~ не понять, не увидеть, не бояться и т. п. [adv (intensif)] not (to understand, see sth., get scared etc) at all: **not a ⟨one⟩ bit; not the least ⟨the slightest⟩ bit; not in the least ⟨the slightest⟩.**

Феня...сказала ему, уже ни крошечки не бояся за своё любопытство: «Руки-то какие у вас, Дмитрий Фёдорович, все-то в крови!» (Достоевский 1). ...Fenya, now not the least bit afraid of her curiosity, said to him: "But your hands, Dmitri Fyodorovich, they're all covered with blood!" (1a).

К-420 • ДЕ́ЛАТЬ/СДЕ́ЛАТЬ ⟨ДАВА́ТЬ/ДАТЬ⟩ КРУГ
coll [VP; subj: usu. human or collect] to go, travel somewhere by an indirect route (which takes longer than the direct route): X сделал круг ≃ **X took ⟨made⟩ a detour; X went ⟨took⟩ a roundabout way; X went ⟨took⟩ the long way (a)round.**

Григорий отвёл и посадил на коней две сотни, отошёл назад, стараясь, чтобы противник не определил его направления. Двадцать вёрст дали круга (Шолохов 3). Grigory withdrew the squadrons, got them mounted and rode back, trying to deceive the enemy as to the direction he was taking. They made a detour of twenty versts (3a). ♦ [Анна Петровна:] Как к вам ехать, Порфирий Семёныч? Через Юсновку? [Глаголев I:] Нет... Круг дадите, если поедете через Юсновку (Чехов 1). [А.Р.:] How do we reach your place, Mr. Glagolyev? Through Yusnovka? [G. Sr.:] No, that's the long way around (1b).

К-421 • ЗАКОЛДО́ВАННЫЙ КРУГ [NP; sing only; fixed WO]
1. (according to superstitious beliefs) a space made impenetrable to one's enemies by magical spells: **magic ⟨enchanted⟩ circle.**

2. *logic.* Also: **ПОРО́ЧНЫЙ КРУГ** an error in reasoning, when the premise is used to prove the conclusion, which, in turn, is used to prove the premise: **vicious circle.**

3. Also: **ПОРО́ЧНЫЙ КРУГ** a situation in which solving one problem creates an even more difficult problem, thus making ultimate resolution impossible: **vicious circle ⟨cycle⟩.**

«Надо подать проект, — подумал секретарь, — чтобы в каждом районе было два Учреждения. Тогда первое будет выполнять свои функции, а второе будет наблюдать, чтобы не пропало первое... А кто же будет наблюдать за другим Учреждением? Значит, нужно создать третье, а за третьим — четвёртое и так далее до бесконечности, но кто же тогда будет заниматься другими делами?» Получался какой-то заколдованный круг (Войнович 2). A resolution should be submitted, thought the Secretary, that there be two Institutions in each district. The first would carry out its usual functions and the second would keep an eye on the first so that it wouldn't disappear....But who's going to keep their eye on the second Institution? That means a third will have to be created, and a fourth for the third and so on, ad infinitum, and then who would be left to do anything else? It had turned into a vicious cycle (2a).

К-422 • НА КРУГ *coll* [PrepP; Invar; adv] as an approximate mean: **on (the ⟨an⟩) average.**

К-423 • возвраща́ться НА КРУ́ГИ СВОЯ́ *lit* [PrepP; Invar; adv; fixed WO] (to return) to its previous, normal state, condition: **(fall back) into place; (resume) its normal course; [in limited contexts] (drop ⟨fall⟩ back) into its rut.**

Всё суета сует и всяческая суета. Всё возвращается на круги своя (Максимов 2). Vanity of vanities, all is vanity. Everything falls back into place in the end... (2a). ♦ Скоро вся эта размазня кончится. И что останется от всей их болтовни? И всё вернётся на круги своя (Зиновьев 1). Soon all this mess will be over. And what'll be left of all their chatter? Everything will drop back into its rut (1a).

< From the Church Slavonic text of the Bible (Eccles. 1:6).

К-424 • ПО ВТОРО́МУ ⟨ТРЕ́ТЬЕМУ⟩ КРУ́ГУ *highly coll* [PrepP; these forms only; adv; fixed WO] (to do, try etc sth.) for the second or third time: **(have) another ⟨a second, a third⟩ go ⟨shot, crack⟩ (at sth.).**

«Я, говорит, Володичка, замуж собралась. Можно мне по второму кругу замуж выйти?» (Аржак 2). "Volodya," she says, "I was on the point of getting married. Is it all right for me to have a second go at marriage?" (2a).

К-425 • С КРУ́ГУ ⟨-а⟩ спиться *substand* [PrepP; these forms only; adv] (to become) an inveterate drunkard: **(become) a (hopeless) lush ⟨souse, drunk⟩**.

К-426 • В КРУЖО́К стричь, подстригать *кого и т. п.* [PrepP; Invar; adv] (to cut s.o.'s hair, have one's hair cut etc) in a straight line around the head: **(give s.o. ⟨get etc⟩) a bowl (hair)cut; (cut s.o.'s hair ⟨one's hair is cropped etc⟩) in peasant style.**

Тогда, к неописанному моему изумлению, увидел я среди мятежных старшин Швабрина, обстриженного в кружок и в казацком кафтане (Пушкин 2). Then, to my indescribable astonishment, I saw Shvabrin, his hair cut in peasant style and wearing a Cossack caftan, in the midst of the rebel elders (2b).

К-427 • КАК (ТАМ ⟨ТУТ⟩) НИ КРУТИ́ ⟨НИ ВЕРТИ́⟩ *coll* [subord clause; these forms only; fixed WO] regardless of from what perspective the fact in question is observed or regardless of s.o.'s reaction toward that fact (the fact itself is correct, reflects reality): **however ⟨no matter how, whichever way⟩ you look at it; whatever ⟨no matter what⟩ you do ⟨say⟩; there is no getting around it; like it or not.**

…Он понемножку начинал понимать, что такие люди, как Чернышевский, при ѕсех их смешных и страшных промахах, были, как ни верти, действительными героями в своей борьбе с государственным порядком вещей… (Набоков 1). …He began to comprehend by degrees that such uncompromising radicals as Chernyshevski, with all their ludicrous and ghastly blunders, were, no matter how you looked at it, real heroes in their struggle with the governmental order of things… (1a). ♦ «Как ни крути, [мы] сами виноваты» (Максимов 3). "Whichever way you look at it, we've only ourselves to blame" (3a). ♦ Как ни крути, говорили промеж собой довольные ибанцы [*nonce word*], а мы, ибанцы, единственные разумные существа во всей вселенной (Зиновьев 1). Whatever you say, the self-satisfied Ibanskians said to each other, we Ibanskians are the only intelligent life in the universe (1a). ♦ Ну, хорошо, нетяжёлая домашняя работа, понемногу готовка, магазины, но ведь, как ни крути, она [Нюра] психически неполноценна… (Трифонов 5). Well, fine, she [Nyura] could do some light housework—a little cooking and shopping—but still, there was no getting around the fact that she was mentally deficient (5a).

К-428 • КАК (ТАМ) НИ КРУТИ́СЬ ⟨НИ ВЕРТИ́СЬ⟩ *coll* [subord clause; these forms only; fixed WO] regardless of what one does (sth. cannot be avoided, changed etc): **no matter what you do ⟨one does⟩; no matter how (hard) you try ⟨one tries⟩; however much you try ⟨one tries⟩; try as you ⟨one⟩ might.**

«Ты огорчил барина!» – с расстановкой произнёс Илья Ильич и пристально смотрел на Захара, наслаждаясь его смущением. Захар не знал, куда деваться от тоски… «Эх, смерть нейдёт!» – подумал он, видя, что не избежать ему патетической сцены, как ни вертись (Гончаров 1). "You have grieved your master!" Oblomov spoke in a measured tone, fixing his gaze on Zakhar and enjoying his discomfort. Zakhar was so miserable he did not know what to do.…"Ah, I wish I were dead!" he thought, seeing that no matter how he tried, he would be unable to escape a "pathetic" scene (1b). ♦ [У меня] есть работа – не очень хорошая, но и не мерзкая… Да, вот с деньгами худо. Как ни крутись, а в зарплату не уложишься (Аржак 2). I've got a job—not a very good one, but not too bad either.…True, the money's not so good. However much you try, you can't make ends meet (2a).

К-429 • БРАТЬ/ВЗЯТЬ ПОД СВОЁ КРЫ́ЛЫШКО *кого coll* [VP; subj: human; usu. this WO] to offer s.o. care, protection, extend patronage to s.o.: **X взял Y-а под своё крылышко ≃ X took Y under X's wing; [in limited contexts] X gave Y a leg up.**

«Я познакомлю тебя с здешними барынями, я беру тебя под своё крылышко» (Тургенев 2). "I'll introduce you to the local young ladies; I'm taking you under my wing" (2d).

К-430 • ПОД КРЫ́ЛЫШКОМ ⟨ПОД КРЫЛО́М⟩ *чьим, (у) кого* быть₀, жить, держать *кого и т. п.*; ПОД КРЫ́ЛЫШКО ⟨ПОД КРЫЛО́⟩ *чьё, к кому* прятаться, пристраиваться *и т. п. all coll* [PrepP; these forms only; the resulting PrepP is subj-compl with copula (subj: human), obj-compl with держать (obj: human), or adv] under s.o.'s protecting influence, care, patronage: **under s.o.'s ⟨one's⟩ wing; under the tutelage of s.o.**

Он [граф] перевёл Петю из полка Оболенского в полк Безухова, который формировался под Москвою. Хотя Петя и оставался в военной службе, но при этом переводе графиня имела утешенье видеть хотя одного сына у себя под крылышком… (Толстой 6). He [the Count] got Petya transferred from Obolensky's regiment to Bezukhov's, which was in training near Moscow. Though Petya would remain in the army, this transfer would give the Countess the consolation of having at least one of her sons under her wing… (6a). ♦ Не злая по натуре, Нина Савоева совершила немало постыдного под крылом Гагкаева, этого районного Сталина… (Гинзбург 2). Not a vicious person by nature, Nina Savoeva had done many things to be ashamed of under the tutelage of Gavkaev [*sic*], the local Stalin… (2a).

К-431 • ОПУСКА́ТЬ/ОПУСТИ́ТЬ КРЫ́ЛЬЯ ⟨КРЫ́ЛЫШКИ *coll*⟩ [VP; subj: human] to lose one's vitality, energy, vigor: X опустил крылья ≃ **X lost his get-up-and-go.**

К-432 • ПОДРЕЗА́ТЬ/ПОДРЕ́ЗАТЬ ⟨ОБРЕЗА́ТЬ/ОБРЕ́ЗАТЬ, ПОДСЕКА́ТЬ/ПОДСЕ́ЧЬ, СВЯ́ЗЫВАТЬ/СВЯЗА́ТЬ⟩ КРЫ́ЛЬЯ *кому coll* [VP; subj: human or abstr] to make it difficult or impossible for s.o. to act, realize his potential (often by undermining his belief in himself): X подрезал крылья Y-у ≃ **person X clipped Y's wings.**

К-433 • РАСПРАВЛЯ́ТЬ/РАСПРА́ВИТЬ КРЫ́ЛЬЯ *lit* [VP; subj: human; fixed WO] to begin to manifest one's strengths, apply one's abilities in full measure, act independently: X расправил крылья ≃ **X spread ⟨tried⟩ his wings; X soared on his own.**

[author's usage] Рыба на зиму забивается на ямы, белка уходит в дремучие ельники, где полно шишки, птица отлетает в тёплые края, а почему он [Михаил] не может дать тяги? Почему он не развернёт свои крылья? Разве ему не двадцать лет? (Абрамов 1). Fish retreat to hollows for the winter; squirrels go to the dense fir forests where they will find plenty of pinecones; birds fly away to warmer climes. So why couldn't *he* [Mikhail] cut loose? Why shouldn't *he* spread his wings? After all, he was twenty years old, wasn't he? (1a).

К-434 • КАНЦЕЛЯ́РСКАЯ ⟨БУМА́ЖНАЯ, ЧЕРНИ́ЛЬНАЯ⟩ КРЫ́СА *coll, derog* [NP] a callous petty bureaucrat: **paper-pusher; paper shuffler; office drudge.**

К-435 • КРЫ́СЫ БЕГУ́Т С ТО́НУЩЕГО КОРАБЛЯ́ ⟨ПОКИДА́ЮТ ТО́НУЩИЙ КОРА́БЛЬ⟩ [saying] cowards or unworthy people desert their friends or a common cause in a time of trouble: ≃ **rats desert ⟨leave⟩ a ⟨the⟩ sinking ship.**

Однажды я рассказала ему, как к Настасье Васильевне приходил городовой с женой, и Павел Петрович сказал загадочно: «Крысы бегут с тонущего корабля»… И он объяснил, что в данном случае монархия, то есть самодержавие, — это корабль, а крысы — это те, кто догадывается, что он непременно потонет (Каверин 1). Another time I told him about the policeman coming with his wife to see Nastasya Vasilyevna, and Pavel Petrovich said cryptically: "The rats are leaving the sinking ship."…And he explained that, in this instance, the monarchy, that is to say the autocracy, was the ship and the rats were those who suspected that it was going to sink (1a).

< From the Russian translation of Shakespeare's *Tempest*, 1611.

К-436 • КРЫТЬ НЕЧЕМ *(кому)* coll [Invar; impers predic with быть∅] s.o. has no valid, convincing argument to offer as an objection to or refutation of some statement: (X-у) крыть нечем ≃ **X doesn't have a leg to stand on; there is nothing X can say; X has no (real) weapons to meet this argument;** [when used as an indep. sent to admit concession] **touché.**

«Не верю я, чтоб войсковое правительство спасло Дон! Какие меры применяются к тем частям, какие не желают вам подчиняться?.. Нечем вам крыть. А народ и фронтовые казаки за нас стоят» (Шолохов 3). "I don't believe the Army Government could save the Don! What measures are being taken against the units that don't want to obey you?…You haven't got a leg to stand on. The people and the frontline Cossacks are behind us!" (3a). ♦ «Мы по уши во лжи и лицемерии. Как же так? Как может такой человеческий материал в таких условиях создавать это самое, самое, самое…?» — «Одно дело — теория, другое — люди, исповедующие её и охраняющие», — говорю я неуверенно, ибо крыть тут нечем (Зиновьев 2). "We're up to our ears in lies and hypocrisy. How is this possible? How can it be that such human resources, working under such conditions, can create this thing which is the most this, the most that, that most everything…?" "Theory is one thing, and the people who preach it and defend it are another," I said, uncertainly, since I had no real weapons to meet this argument (2a).

К-437 • ПОД ОДНОЙ КРЫШЕЙ ⟨КРОВЛЕЙ⟩ *(с кем)* жить, находиться и т. п. [PrepP; these forms only; adv; fixed WO] (to live, be) in one building, house (with s.o.): **(live) under one ⟨the same⟩ roof; (share) the same premises ⟨roof⟩.**

«Что я разве друг его какой?.. или родственник? Правда, мы жили долго под одною кровлей… Да мало ли я с кем не жил?..» (Лермонтов 1). "I'm not a friend of his am I, or a relation? True, we lived a good while under the same roof—but then I've lived with plenty of different people in my time" (1c). "Yes, indeed, am I a friend of his or a relative? True, we shared the same roof for a long time, but then I have lived with all sorts of people" (1b). ♦ Из нашей комнаты было видно, как зажигаются окна в Доме Герцена — это собирался Союз писателей или Союз поэтов, раздельно существовавшие тогда под одной крышей (Мандельштам 2). …From the window of our apartment we could see the windows light up in the opposite wing of Herzen House whenever there was a meeting of the Union of Writers, or the Union of Poets; in those days these were separate organizations, though they shared the same premises (2a).

К-438 • ДАТЬ КРЮКУ coll [VP] **1.** Also: **ДАТЬ ⟨СДЕЛАТЬ⟩ КРЮК** [subj: human or collect] to go, travel somewhere by an indirect route (which takes longer than the direct route): X дал крюку ≃ **X took ⟨made⟩ a detour; X went ⟨took⟩ a roundabout way; X went ⟨took⟩ the long way (around ⟨round⟩);** [in limited contexts] **X went ⟨came⟩ (two kilometers ⟨a long way etc⟩) out of his way.**

Дав крюку, я завернул в Гнездниковский. Место опасности было оцеплено (Терц 2). Making a detour, I turned into Gnezdnikovsky Street. The danger zone had been cordoned off (2a). ♦ [Лыняев:] А то заставляете две версты крюку делать, заезжать к вам (Островский 5). [L.:] Now you have made me come out of my way a mile and a half, to see you (5a).

2. *obs* [subj: human] to make a slip, a blunder: X дал крюку ≃ **X made a gaffe; X slipped up;** [in refer. to speaking only] **X put his foot in his mouth ⟨in it⟩.**

К-439 • НА КРЮЧКЕ *у кого* быть∅, держать *кого* coll [PrepP; Invar; subj-compl with copula (subj: human) or obj-compl

with держать (obj: human)] (to be or fall) under another person's complete control (usu. from fear of exposure or blackmail), or (to gain) complete control over s.o. (usu. through threat of exposure or blackmail): X у Y-a ⟨Y держит X-а⟩ на крючке ≃ **X is ⟨Y has X⟩ under Y's thumb; Y has X on a string; Y has something on X; Y is holding sth. over X; Y has X on the hook;** [in limited contexts] **Y pulls the strings.**

«Радик, не связывайся с ним. Он какой-то полковник, мы тут все у него на крючке» (Аксёнов 6). "Radik, don't tangle with him. He's some kind of colonel; we're all under his thumb here" (6a). ♦ «…Я вовремя скумекал: если угроблю пахана, буду на крючке у Алика хлеще, чем он у меня» (Чернёнок 2). "…I had figured out in time that if I did the old guy in, Alik would have more on me than I did on him" (2a). ♦ «…Пистолет у меня забери». Сударь ответил: «Не-е. Ты у меня на крючке с этим пистолетом» (Семёнов 3). "…Take that pistol back." Squire replied: "No-o. I've got you on the hook with that pistol" (1a). ♦ …Ведь он [Сергеев] не может не думать, что ОСВАГ [политическая полиция] прослушивает лучниковские телефоны. Говоря так, он прямо «засвечивает» Таню, не оставляет ни малейшего сомнения у «осваговцев» в том, кто держит её на крючке (Аксёнов 7). Since he [Sergeev] must realize that OSVAG [the political police] has Luchnikov's phones tapped, he can only be doing one thing—purposely blowing Tanya's disguise, making it absolutely clear who is pulling the strings (7a).

К-440 • ПОПАДÁТЬСЯ/ПОПÁСТЬСЯ НА КРЮЧÓК coll [VP; subj: human] to yield to a temptation, enticement suggested by another person (who usu. wants sth. from one): X попался на крючок ≃ **X took ⟨swallowed⟩ the bait; X fell for it; person Y hooked X.**

К-441 • КСТÁТИ И НЕКСТÁТИ [AdvP; Invar; adv; fixed WO] regardless of whether or not it is suitable (for a particular moment, occasion etc): **in (season) and out of season; whether appropriately or not; be it appropriate or not;** [in limited contexts] **with or without need.**

В ряде критических статей он [Белинский] кстати и некстати касается всего, везде верный своей ненависти к авторитетам… (Герцен 2). In a series of critical articles he [Belinsky] touches in season and out of season upon everything, true everywhere to his hatred of authority… (2a). ♦ …Ко всему, что я ни делала, кстати и некстати присоединялась мысль об этой странной минуте — как под музыку, когда слушаешь, а сама думаешь о чём-то своём (Каверин 1). …To everything that I did was linked, whether appropriately or not, the thought of that strange moment, just as when you are listening to music and you think of something else (1a). ♦ Веселье… выдохлось: чёрненькая совсем ушла, а беленькая хозяйка непрестанно, кстати и некстати, и словно нечто подчёркивая, входила и выходила из комнаты (Битов 2). The gaiety…had gone flat: the dark girl had left altogether, while the light hostess came and went from the room incessantly, with or without need, and as if making some point (2a).

К-442 • КТО ГДЕ coll [usu. adv or indep. sent (often in response to an inquiry beginning with «Где» about several or many people); fixed WO] one person is in one place, others are in other places: **some here, some there; in various places.**

К-443 • КТО ⟨кого и т. п.⟩ КАК coll [usu. adv or indep. sent (often in response to an inquiry beginning with «Как» about several or many people)] some people do sth. one way, others another way: **that ⟨it (all)⟩ depends (on the person); each in a different ⟨in his own⟩ way; in various ways; everyone ⟨each one⟩ (does sth.) differently; it's different in each case ⟨with each person⟩;** [in limited contexts] **(it affects etc) different people differently; it doesn't mean the same thing to everybody; there are some who do ⟨are, have etc⟩.**

«Нигилист — это человек, который не склоняется ни перед какими авторитетами, который не принимает ни одного принципа на веру...» – «И что ж, это хорошо?» – перебил Павел Петрович. «Смотря как кому, дядюшка. Иному от этого хорошо, а иному очень дурно» (Тургенев 2). "A nihilist is a person who does not look up to any authorities, who does not accept a single principle on faith...." "Well, and is that a good thing?" Pavel Petrovich broke in. "It all depends, uncle. It may be good for some people and very bad for others" (2a). ♦ Сталин кивнул в сторону окна. «Ругают меня там?»... – «Кто как... – ответил Будягин. – Есть и ругают» (Рыбаков 2). Stalin nodded toward the window. "Are they cursing me out there?"..."There are bound to be some who do," Budyagin replied (2a).

К-444 • КТО ⟨кого и т. п.⟩ КАК, А... *coll* [a clause in a compound sent + Conj] others may act (think etc) otherwise, but (I, we etc)...: **do as you like but...; do ⟨say, think⟩ what you like but...; I don't know about anyone else, but...; what others think ⟨do⟩ is their (own) business but...**

«Вот что, станишники! Нам тут делать нечего. Надо уходить... Как вы, станишники?»... – «Нет уж, будем сидеть до конца»... – «Кому как, а наш взвод уходит!» (Шолохов 3). "Now listen to me, Cossacks! There's no point in our staying here. We've got to get away....How about it, Cossacks?"..."No, we'd better stay put."..."I don't know about anyone else, but our troop's leaving!" (3a). ♦ «...Кровь у всех одинаковая, сколько хошь [*ungrammat* = хочешь] лей, добра не будет. Крик один будет и беда, да такая, что и тыщу [*phonetic spelling of* тысячу] лет не расхлебать... Кто как, а я навоевался» (Максимов 3). [context transl] "...We all have the same blood. It doesn't matter how much you shed, no good can come of it. Nothing but chaos and misery, misery it'll take us a thousand years to get over....I, for one, have had my fill of fighting" (3a).

К-445 • КТО КОГО́ *coll* [sent; Invar; often used as a subord clause in a complex sent; fixed WO] who will turn out to be the winner: **who will win; who will have the upper hand; who will get the better of whom; who will get ⟨beat etc⟩ whom (in the end); who will come out on top.**

Пёстрая куча толстых людей справа от бочки, пёстрая куча – слева. А ну-ка! Кто кого?.. А ну-ка, кто кого перетянет?.. Тяни, тяни! (Федин 1). There was a motley crowd of fat people to the right of the barrel, a motley crowd to the left. Come on then! Who'll win?...Come on, who would out-tug whom?...Pull, pull! (1a). ♦ [Хлестаков:] ...Чиновники эти добрые люди: это с их стороны хорошая черта, что они мне дали взаймы... Ну-ка теперь, капитан! Ну-ка, попадись-ка ты мне теперь. Посмотрим, кто кого! (Гоголь 4). [Kh.:] ...They are good fellows, these officials. I mean, it was nice of them to have lent me all this money....Now, my dear captain, let me just come across you now, and we'll see who'll get the better of whom this time (4c). ♦ [Мышлаевский:] Ты ждёшь не дождёшься, чтобы Петлюра тебя по затылку трахнул? [Николка:] Ну, это ещё кто кого! (Булгаков 4). [M.:] Are you just sitting here waiting anxiously for Petlyura to bang you on the back of the head? [N.:] Well, we'll see who bangs whom! (4a).

К-446 • КТО́-КТО́ ⟨кого-кого и т. п.⟩, А... *coll* [NP + Conj; used as a restr marker] (used to single out one person or, occas., group among others) it is precisely the person specified who...: кто-кто, а X... ≃ **X of all people; others may not, but X...; if anybody..., X does ⟨is etc⟩; if anybody..., it is X; [in limited contexts] X...better than anyone; [when foll. by a clause with negated predic] X is the last man ⟨person⟩ (in the world) (to do sth. ⟨who would do sth.⟩); ∥ кого-кого, а X-а... ⟨кому-кому, а X-у... и т. п.⟩ ≃ if there's anyone..., it's X.**

«Помилуйте, – снисходительно усмехнувшись, отозвался профессор, – уж кто-кто, а вы-то должны знать, что ровно ничего из того, что написано в евангелиях, не происходило на самом деле никогда...» (Булгаков 9). "Oh, well," the professor responded with an indulgent smile. "You of all people should know that nothing that is told in the Gospels has ever really happened..." (9a). ♦ Уж кто-кто, а администратор хорошей гостиницы знает, что настоящие важные люди меньше, чем на «жигулях», не ездят (Войнович 1). Others may not, but a clerk in a good hotel knows that important people never drive anything less than a Zhiguli (1a). ♦ Кто-кто, а он-то знал, какой сейчас курорт у Трофима Лобанова (Абрамов 1). He knew better than anyone what kind of resort it was now at Trofim Lobanov's (1a). ♦ «...Нет, нет, поймите меня правильно! Кто-кто, а уж я-то не поклонник газетных штампов» (Аржак 1). "...No, no, don't misunderstand me. You know me, I'm the last man in the world to be impressed by newspaper clichés" (1a).

К-447 • КТО КУДА́ *coll* [Invar; fixed WO] **1.** [usu. adv or indep. sent (often in response to an inquiry beginning with «Куда» about several or many people)] some people (go, run etc) in one directon, others in other directions, (people go etc) to various places: **in different ⟨all⟩ directions; each (going) his own way; some (going) one way, some another; to all different places.**

Немцы оставили кинотеатр и с криками: «Спасайтесь! Крещатик взрывается!» – бросились бежать кто куда... (Кузнецов 1). The Germans now fled from the cinema, shouting, "Run for your lives! Kreshchatik is blowing up!" They ran in all directions... (1a). ♦ «Раз, – это было за Тереком, – я ездил с абреками отбивать русские табуны; нам не посчастливилось, и мы рассыпались кто куда» (Лермонтов 1). "One time – this happened beyond the Terek – I rode with the *abreks* to seize Russian horse herds; we had bad luck, and scattered, each his own way" (1a). ♦ «Айда по домам, старик». – «Ну уж это кто куда, – ответил Валя, – я человек молодой и свободный» (Семёнов 1). [context transl] "We might as well go on home, old man." "You go where you like," answered Roslyakov. "But I'm still young and free" (1a).

2. [adv] (the people in question do sth.) without agreement, cooperation, or coordination among themselves (may refer to singing and playing musical instruments): **everyone doing his own thing; [in limited contexts] (all) at sixes and sevens.**

К-448 • КТО (...) НИ...; КТО БЫ (...) НИ... [NP; used as subord Conj, concessive] it does not matter who: **no matter who; whoever.**

«Я буду у себя в комнате, – сказал он жене, вставая, – кто бы ни спрашивал, говори, что меня нет» (Искандер 5). "I'll be in my room," he told his wife as he got up. "No matter who asks, say I'm not here" (5a). ♦ «Кто бы она ни была – просто ли губернская львица, или «эманципе» вроде Кукшиной, только у ней такие плечи, каких я не видывал давно» (Тургенев 2). "Whoever she is – a provincial lioness or an *'émancipée'* like Madame Kukshin – anyhow she's got a pair of shoulders the like of which I haven't set eyes on for a long while" (2c).

К-449 • КТО ЧТО ⟨кому что, кто о чём и т. п.⟩ *coll* [NP; may be used as indep. sent in response to an inquiry beginning with «Что», «О чём» etc about several or many people; fixed WO] one person (does, has etc) one thing, another something else, it is different for each person: **that ⟨it⟩ depends (on the person); one person (has ⟨does etc⟩) this, another that; one does ⟨likes etc⟩ one thing, another – something else; some do ⟨like etc⟩ some things, others – other things; some liked one thing, some another; it's different in each case.**

«Что им понравилось на выставке?» – «Кому что». "What did they like at the exhibition?" "Some liked some things, others – other things." ♦ Верховые были одеты по-разному – кто в чём, и напоминали сразу и мужиков и солдат, точь-в-точь как красноармейцы сводного полка... (Федин 1). [context transl] The horsemen were in various dress – in what they had been able to find, and immediately reminded one of both muzhiks and soldiers, exactly like the Red soldiers of the composite regiment... (1a).

K-450 • НЕ КТО ИНО́Й, КАК... [NP; used as intensif Particle; foll. by NP (human, often a person's name); fixed WO] the named person himself: не кто иной, как X ≃ **none other than X; no one (else) but X; X and not someone else; X and no one else;** [in limited contexts] **(X and) X alone; X and only X.**

Оказалось... что «человечек» — не кто иной, как отставной приказный Боголепов... (Салтыков-Щедрин 1). It turned out...that the "little man" was none other than the retired clerk Deiformov... (1a). ♦ А вот приписка объясняет, почему Сталин для своего телефонного звонка выбрал не кого иного, как Пастернака (Мандельштам 1). ...It was the postscript at the end of his letter that explained why Stalin chose to telephone Pasternak and not someone else (1a). ♦ «...Помни, что если мать умрёт, не кто иной, как ты будешь виноват в этом» (Каверин 2). "...Remember, if our mother dies you alone will be to blame" (2a).

K-451 • ХОТЬ КТО ⟨кого и т. п.⟩ *highly coll* [NP; usu. obj; fixed WO] any person: **anyone (at all); whoever you want ⟨like⟩; anyone you like.**

Хоть кого спроси — тебе все скажут то же, что и я. Ask whoever you want—they'll tell you the same thing I did.

K-452 • НАБИВА́ТЬ/НАБИ́ТЬ КУБЫ́ШКУ; КЛАСТЬ/ПОЛОЖИ́ТЬ В КУБЫ́ШКУ деньги *both coll* [VP; subj: human] to accumulate money (keeping it at home, not investing it): X набил кубышку ≃ **X socked money away; X hoarded money; X stuffed his mattress full of money.**

K-453 • КУДА́ кому-чему ДО кого-чего ⟨ЗА кем⟩ *coll* [impers predic with быть∅; usu. pres; if indir obj is human, prep obj is also usu. human; if indir obj is abstr, prep obj is also usu. abstr etc] a person (or thing) significantly lags behind, falls short of another person or category of people (thing or category of things): куда X-у до Y-a ≃ **X cannot compare with Y; how can X compare with Y!; X is crude ⟨nothing, backward etc⟩ by comparison; X can't hold a candle to Y; Y is out of X's league; Y is in a different class than ⟨from⟩ X; X can't keep up with Y;** [in limited contexts] **X is no Y;** [in refer. to being unable to understand sth.] **Y is way over ⟨miles above⟩ person X's head.**

Когда-то я помнил эту теорию назубок. Изящная теория!! Куда до неё электродинамике! (Зиновьев 1). "There was a time when I knew this theory by heart. It was very elegant! Electrodynamics is crude by comparison!" (1a). ♦ Да куда мне за ней! Я даром что моложе, а не выстоять мне столько» (Гончаров 1). "...I'm afraid I can't keep up with her! I may be the younger one, but I can't stand as long as she can!" (1a). ♦ «Папа, ты герой». — «Нет, дочка, куда мне до героя. Вот у нас в роте был Петя Курочкин — это вот да, герой» (Абрамов 1). "Papa, you're a hero." "No, daughter. I'm no hero. Now there was a man called Petya Kurochkin in our outfit—*there* was a hero for you" (1a). ♦ «...Я очень рад, что вы занимаетесь естественными науками. Я слышал, что Либих сделал удивительные открытия насчёт удобрения полей...» — «Я к вашим услугам, Николай Петрович; но куда нам до Либиха! Сперва надо азбуке выучиться и потом уже взяться за книгу, а мы ещё аза в глаза не видали» (Тургенев 2). "I must say I...am very glad you are studying the natural sciences. I have heard that Liebig has made some astonishing discoveries to do with improving the soil...." "I'm at your service, Nikolai Petrovich; but Liebig is miles above our heads! One must learn the alphabet before learning to read, and we don't know the first letter yet" (2c).

K-454 • КУДА́ КАК... *coll, often iron* [Particle; Invar; foll. by AdjP (usu. short form or compar) or AdvP (which in some English equivalents may be replaced by a corresponding NP); fixed WO] very (much), to a great degree: куда как весело ⟨интересно и

т. п.⟩! ≃ **what could be more fun ⟨interesting etc⟩!; what fun ⟨how interesting etc⟩!;** [when used ironically only] **a lot of fun (that would be etc)!;** ‖ куда как умён ⟨независим и т. п.⟩ ≃ **(he etc is) so smart ⟨independent etc⟩; (he etc is) as smart ⟨independent etc⟩ as could be ⟨as they come⟩;** ‖ куда как лучше ⟨значительнее и т. п.⟩ ≃ **far ⟨a lot⟩ better ⟨more important etc⟩; what could be better ⟨more important etc⟩; much better ⟨more important etc⟩;** ‖ *Neg* куда как не глуп ⟨не юн и т. п.⟩ ≃ **far from stupid ⟨young etc⟩.**

[Катерина:] Ну, бери меня с собой, бери!.. [Кабанов:] Куда как весело с тобой ехать! (Островский 6). [Kat.:] Well, take me with you, take me!... [K.:] A lot of fun it would be to travel with you! (6a). ♦ Приедет [деревенская старуха], живёт и первое время куда как довольна. И готовит, и стирает, и внуков в школу снаряжает, да ещё и в церковь сходит, свечку за упокой души своего старика поставит (Войнович 1). She [the old country woman] arrived, lived in Moscow a while, and at first was as pleased as could be. She cooked, did the washing, outfitted her grandchildren for school, and went to church to light a candle for her late husband's soul (1a). ♦ «С с-сединой куда как л-лучше. Сейчас, говорят, с-седые мужчины в моду вошли» (Семёнов 1). "It's m-much better with g-grey hair. They say grey-haired m-men are in fashion now" (1a). ♦ «Советы и раньше уже были... — в иных случаях они тогда распоряжались куда как авторитетней и решительней, чем впоследствии, когда всё государство стало именоваться „советским"» (Копелев 1). "The soviets had existed earlier;...in some cases they handled things with much more authority and decisiveness than they did later, when the entire state was called 'soviet.'" (1a). ♦ ...Письмо было куда как не глупое и первый русский трезвый голос с Запада (Лимонов 1). ...It was a far from stupid letter and the first sober Russian voice in the West (1a).

K-455 • КУДА́ ТАМ ⟨ТУТ⟩!; ГДЕ (УЖ) ТАМ! *all coll* [Interj; these forms only; fixed WO] sth. is difficult or impossible to accomplish, the undertaking in question is futile, the effort in question did or will produce results opposite to those desired (often foll. by an explanation of why the attempt failed or what happened instead): **no way; not a chance; fat chance!; out of the question;** [in limited contexts] **far from it; what's the use?; not likely.**

«Твой ещё не проснулся?» — «Куды [*ungrammat* = куда] там, — засмеялась Нюра, — спит, как сурок. А чего?» — «Дело есть» (Войнович 2). "Your man up yet?" "Fat chance," laughed Nyura. "Sleeping like a log. What's the matter?" "I need to see him" (2a). ♦ Бабка понесла на базар какое-то барахло, простояла два дня подряд — куда там, никто не покупает, все только продают (Кузнецов 1). Grandmother took some stuff to the market and stood there two days in a row—but what was the use? Nobody was buying, everybody was selling (1a). ♦ «Вот у тебя по старому делу в 63 году Джилас шёл. Что это за штуковина?» — «Неужели даже вам [следователям КГБ] не дают почитать [конфискованные книги]? Тоже не доверяют?» — «Где там... Только и на прочитаешь, что на обыске отнимешь» (Буковский 1). "What about that book by Djilas that you were charged with in 1963? What sort of whatsit was it?" "Do you mean to say they don't let you [the KGB investigators] read them [confiscated books] either? Don't they trust you either?" "Not likely. All you get to read in my job is what you turn up in the searches" (1a).

K-456 • КУДА́ ⟨ГДЕ⟩ УЖ кому *coll* [Particle; foll. by infin; fixed WO] s.o. undoubtedly cannot do sth. (because of old age, poor health, inexperience, lack of training etc): куда уж X-у (сделать Y) ≃ **how (in the world) can X (be expected to) do Y?; how can you expect X to do Y?; there's no way X can do Y; X will never be able to do Y ⟨to handle it⟩; what chance does X have (of doing Y)?;** [in limited contexts] **X doesn't have what it takes; not in the state ⟨shape⟩ X is in; X is not up to that.**

Куда уж ему [Серёже], он ни разу не поцеловал девушки, а эти дьяволы опытны... (Гроссман 2). What chance did he have? He'd never kissed a girl in his life. And those devils were experienced... (2a). ♦ [Мелания:] Притворяется! Притворяется... [Ксения:] Ой ли? Где уж ему... (Горький 2). [M.:] He's pretending to be mad. Just pretending... [K.:] I'm not so sure. Not in the state he's in... (2a).

К-457 • ХОТЬ КУДА́ coll [AdvP; Invar; fixed WO] **1.** [subj-compl with copula (subj: any common noun) or nonagreeing modif] excellent, superior: **quite a...; first-rate; topnotch; great; fine; as good as they come;** [of a person only] **a fine figure of a man ⟨a woman** etc⟩; [when said proudly, yet with affected modesty, about o.s. or s.o. close to one] **not bad.**

Постепенно у Настёны разгладились ранние морщины на лице, налилось тело, на щеках заиграл румянец, осмелели глаза. Из недавнего чучела вышла невеста хоть куда (Распутин 2). Gradually Nastyona's premature wrinkles smoothed out, her body filled out, color came into her cheeks, and her eyes grew bolder. The recent scarecrow turned into quite a bride (2a). ♦ ...Хуже он [Котик] стал с прошлого года, когда его сделали заведующим кафедрой у себя в институте. С тех пор он стал как-то осторожней, потерял часть своей непосредственности... И всё-таки он и сейчас парень хоть куда... (Искандер 4). He [Kotik] began to deteriorate last year, when they made him head of a department at his institute. Since then he's become somehow more wary, lost some of his spontaneity....All the same, he's a great guy even now... (4a). ♦ «...Однако же я не вижу в нём ничего худого; парень хоть куда!» (Гоголь 5). "I see no harm in him, anyway: he is a fine fellow!" (5a).

2. [adv] (to do sth.) very well, excellently: **(be able ⟨fit⟩ to do sth.) with the best of them; (do) one hell of a job; splendidly; superbly;** [when said proudly, yet with affected modesty, about o.s. or s.o. close to one] **not badly.**

«Что говорят обо мне в Оренбурге?» – спросил Пугачёв, помолчав немного. «Да, говорят, что с тобою сладить трудновато...» Лицо самозванца изобразило довольное самолюбие. «Да! – сказал он с весёлым видом. – Я воюю хоть куда» (Пушкин 2). "What do they say about me at Orenburg?" asked Pugachev after a pause. "They say that it'll be difficult to get the better of you...." The pretender's face expressed satisfied vanity. "Yes!" he said gaily. "I don't fight badly" (2b).

К-458 • КУ́КИШ В КАРМА́НЕ (показывать кому); ФИ́ГА ⟨ДУ́ЛЯ⟩ В КАРМА́НЕ all highly coll, derog [NP; sing only; fixed WO] an expression of disagreement, censure, threat etc made in a cowardly manner, not to s.o.'s face: **thumbing one's nose at s.o. behind his back; giving s.o. the finger behind his back.**

В пятьдесят четвёртом году ко мне в руки попала первая самиздатская... тетрадка – поэма Твардовского «Тёркин на том свете». Многое сразу же запомнила наизусть, читала везде, и у Гидашей тоже. У них вместо радости, с которой встречали эти строки мои предшествующие слушатели, холодный душ: Агнеса олимпийски спокойная и олимпийски непогрешимая: «Что тебе тут нравится? Кукиши в кармане. Интеллигентская фронда» (Орлова 1). In 1954 the first *samizdat*...manuscript found its way into my hands: Tvardovsky's poem *Tyorkin in Hell*. I memorized a great deal of it at once and I [recited] it everywhere, at the Hidases as well. Instead of the joy with which my earlier listeners had greeted these verses, they expressed their cool indifference. With Olympian calm and Olympian infallibility Agnessa said: "What appeals to you here? He's just thumbing his nose behind their backs. Nothing but petty intellectual opposition" (1a).

К-459 • КУ́КИШ ⟨ФИ́ГА, ШИШ⟩ С МА́СЛОМ highly coll [NP; sing only; fixed WO] **1.** often получить, дать кому и т. п. кукиш ⟨фигу, шиш⟩ с маслом (to receive, give s.o. etc) absolutely nothing: **zilch; nil; nix; not a (frigging ⟨damn⟩)**

thing; [in refer. to s.o.'s having no money] **(be) really ⟨flat⟩ broke ⟨busted⟩.**

«Богатые, они всегда скупятся. Пять копеек на билет им жалко...» – «А может, у него в кармане шиш с маслом, – засмеялся парень в картузе. – Тогда я за него заплачу» (Паустовский 1). "Rich people are always stingy. They hate to waste five kopecks on a ticket...." "But maybe he's really broke," a young fellow in a cap said laughing. "In that case, I'll pay for him" (1b).

2. [usu. Interj] used to express flat denial, objection: **like hell (one will ⟨did** etc⟩); **no way; my ass; you ⟨he** etc⟩ **can kiss my ass; stuff it!**

«Вы, гражданин Шариков, говорите... несознательно. На воинский учёт необходимо взяться». – «На учёт возьмусь, а воевать – шиш с маслом», – неприязненно ответил Шариков... (Булгаков 11). "Citizen Sharikov, your words are...lacking in social consciousness. It is most essential to be registered in the military rolls." "I'll register, but if it comes to fighting, they can kiss..." Sharikov answered coldly... (11a).

К-460 • ЧЁРТОВА КУ́КЛА obsoles, highly coll, rude [NP] an expletive directed at s.o. (more often a woman, and often used in direct address): **wretch; damn fool.**

К-461 • МЕНЯ́ТЬ/ПРОМЕНЯ́ТЬ ⟨СМЕНЯ́ТЬ⟩ КУ-КУ́ШКУ НА Я́СТРЕБА obs, coll [VP; subj: human] to make a mistaken estimation and choose the worse of two bad options: X променял кукушку на ястреба ≃ **X chose the worse of two evils;** [in limited contexts] **X jumped out of the frying pan into the fire.**

К-462 • В КУЛА́К СВИСТЕ́ТЬ ⟨СВИСТА́ТЬ⟩ substand [VP; subj: human; usu. this WO] (having spent or squandered all one's money) to be penniless, experience need: X в кулак свистит ≃ **X is left without a penny to his name; X has to tighten his belt.**

К-463 • ЗАЖИМА́ТЬ/ЗАЖА́ТЬ В КУЛА́К ⟨В КУ-ЛАКЕ́⟩ кого-что coll [VP; subj: human; obj: often pl or collect] to hold a person, group of people etc in full submission, in a state of imposed obedience, oppress s.o.: X зажал Y-ов в кулак ≃ **X had ⟨kept⟩ Ys under X's thumb; X held ⟨had⟩ Ys in X's clutches; X had Ys in X's grip.**

К-464 • СМЕЯ́ТЬСЯ ⟨ПРЫ́СКАТЬ/ПРЫ́СНУТЬ, ХИХИ́КАТЬ⟩ В КУЛА́К coll [VP; subj: human] to laugh inwardly, secretly (occas. derisively): X смеялся в кулак ≃ **X was laughing in ⟨up⟩ his sleeve; X was giggling up his sleeve.**

«...[Голем] всё врал, улыбался и врал, с удовольствием врал, наслаждался, издевался надо мной, хихикал в кулак, когда я отворачивался, подмигивал сам себе...» (Стругацкие 1). "...He [Golem] was lying, smiling and lying, lying with the greatest enjoyment. He was laughing at me, giggling up his sleeve whenever I turned around and winking at himself..." (1a).

К-465 • СОБИРА́ТЬ/СОБРА́ТЬ ⟨СЖИМА́ТЬ/СЖАТЬ⟩ В КУЛА́К волю, силы и т. п. [VP; subj: human; usu. this WO] to summon all one's willpower, strength etc: X собрал в кулак волю ⟨силы⟩ ≃ **X mustered ⟨gathered⟩ all his willpower ⟨strength, courage** etc⟩.

К-466 • В КУЛАКЕ́ чьём, (у) кого быть₀, находиться; держать кого coll [PrepP; Invar; subj-compl with copula (subj: human or collect) or obj-compl with держать (obj: human or collect)] (to be, keep s.o. etc) in a state of submission, subjugation: X в кулаке у Y-а ≃ **X is under Y's thumb; X is in Y's grip ⟨clutches⟩; X is in Y's power;** ‖ Y держит X-а в кулаке ≃ **Y has ⟨keeps⟩ X under Y's thumb; Y keeps a tight rein on X.**

[Мария:] Смекалистые ваши мужички всех в кулаке держат, чтоб никто против них не пикнул (Салынский 1). [M.:] These crafty creatures have got everyone under their thumb and they won't let you make a murmur... (1a).

К-467 • **ВСЯК КУЛИ́К СВОЁ БОЛО́ТО ХВА́ЛИТ** [saying] everyone praises what is familiar, close, or dear to him (said in jest when a person speaks highly of the place where he lives, his job etc): ≃ **every bird likes its own nest (best); every cook praises his own broth.**

К-468 • **ЗА КУЛИ́САМИ** [PrepP; Invar; adv] **1.** behind the stage in a theater: **in the wings; backstage.**
 2. in a theatrical environment: **among theater people; in theatrical circles; in the theater community; among the theater crowd.**
 3. ~ (чего) covertly, clandestinely, nonofficially: **behind the scenes; in the wings; backstage; in the background.**
 У меня не было подвигов, я не действовала на сцене. Вся жизнь моя проходила за кулисами (Аллилуева 1). I have no great deeds to my credit; I've never been an actor on center stage. All my life was spent behind the scenes (1a). ♦ Претендент в комиссию не вошёл, но играл за кулисами первую скрипку (Зиновьев 1). Claimant was not a member of the commission, but played first fiddle in the wings (1a).

К-469 • беседы, говорить **В КУЛУА́РАХ** [PrepP; Invar; nonagreeing modif or adv] (in refer. to unofficial conversations, often of a political or social nature) (discussions, to discuss sth.) in well-informed, exclusive circles, not in public: **(talk ⟨conversations etc⟩) in the corridors ⟨the lobby, (the) back rooms⟩; back-room (conversations ⟨discussions etc⟩).**

К-470 • **ИЗ КУЛЬКА́ В РОГО́ЖКУ** substand [PrepP; Invar; adv; fixed WO] **1.** перебиваться ~ to live very poorly, suffer need, privations: X перебивается ~ ≃ **X barely makes ends meet ⟨scrapes by, keeps his head above water⟩; X has a hard time making ends meet; X lives from hand to mouth.**
 Теплякова — женщина тихая, многосемейная, вечно озабоченная... Без мужа живёт, тоже бабе приходится из кулька в рогожку переворачиваться (Тендряков 1). Teplyakova was a quiet woman with a large family and lots of worries....She had no husband, and had a hard time making ends meet (1a).
 2. попасть ~ (to go) from a bad situation to a worse one: **out of the frying pan into the fire.**

К-471 • **КУМ КОРОЛЮ́** coll [NP; Invar; fixed WO] **1.** [subj-compl with быть∅ (subj: human), usu. pres] one is successful, well-off, content with his life, and not dependent on anyone: X кум королю ≃ **X is doing fine for himself.**
 2. (жить) ~ [adv] (to live) very well, in prosperity: **(live) in clover; (live) high on ⟨off⟩ the hog; (live) like a king ⟨a queen⟩.**

К-472 • **ТВОРИ́ТЬ/СОТВОРИ́ТЬ ⟨СОЗДА́ТЬ⟩ СЕБЕ́ КУМИ́РА ⟨КУМИ́Р⟩ из кого-чего** lit [VP; subj: human; usu. pfv; often neg imper; fixed WO] to regard s.o. or sth. with great admiration, worship s.o. or sth.: X сотворил себе кумира из Y-a ≃ **X idolized Y; X put person Y on a pedestal; X deified ⟨hero-worshiped⟩ person Y.**
 < From the Bible (Ex. 20:4).

К-473 • **ЗА ЧТО КУПИ́Л, ЗА ТО И ПРОДАЮ́** [saying] I am just repeating what I have heard (said when a person repeats rumors or another person's words and therefore does not want to be held responsible for them, cannot vouch for their truthfulness etc): ≃ **I am only telling you ⟨passing on⟩ what I heard ⟨what they told me⟩; [in limited contexts] take it for what it's worth.**

[author's usage] «А ты-то это точно знаешь?»... — «Я почём купил, потом и продаю...» (Шолохов 4). "But do you know this for a fact?"..."I'm only telling you what I heard..." (4a). ♦ «...Иные там, с образом мыслей поблагороднее, так даже руки ему не хотели подать на первых порах: слишком уж стремительно в консерваторы перескочил... Повторяю: легенда. За что купил, за то и продал» (Достоевский 2). "...Some persons there, of a nobler cast of mind, did not even want to shake hands with him at first: he jumped over to the conservatives a bit too precipitously....I repeat: it's a legend. Take it for what it's worth" (2a).

К-474 • **КУПИ́ЛО ПРИТУПИ́ЛО ⟨ПРИТУПИ́ЛОСЬ⟩** (у кого) substand [VP_subj; past only; fixed WO] s.o. cannot buy sth. because he has too little or no money: (у Х-а) купило притупило ≃ **X's purse ⟨wallet⟩ is empty; X can't spend what he doesn't have.**

К-475 • **СТРИЧЬ КУПО́НЫ** [VP; subj: human] **1.** to live on the revenue earned by invested money: X стрижёт купоны ≃ **X lives off ⟨on⟩ his investments.**
 2. ~ с чего coll to gain from sth. one did earlier or receive recompense from s.o. in return for a previous favor: X стрижёт купоны с Y-ов ≃ **X is profiting from Ys; X reaps his reward(s).**
 «Теперь он [мой старший брат] купается в дерьме номенклатурной славы, стрижёт купоны с лент о счастливой жизни туземцев в эпоху социализма, а ваш покорный слуга всё ещё пребывает в состоянии бедной, но благородной праздности» (Максимов 2). [context transl] "Now he [my elder brother] is wallowing in official fame, pulling in a fortune from making films about how happy the natives are in the era of socialism, while your humble servant remains in a state of indigent yet noble idleness" (2a).

К-476 • **КАК КУР ВО́ ЩИ попа́сть(ся), угоди́ть** coll [как + NP; Invar; adv; fixed WO] (to find o.s. in or get into) unexpected trouble, an unpleasant situation: **(be ⟨end up etc⟩) in a jam ⟨a fix, hot water, a pickle⟩; (be ⟨wind up, find o.s. etc⟩) in a tight spot; (be) up the creek (without a paddle); (be ⟨wind up, find o.s. etc⟩) on ⟨in⟩ the hot seat.**

К-477 • **КУ́РАМ НА́ СМЕХ** coll [Invar; usu. subj-compl with быть∅ (subj: usu. это or abstr); fixed WO] sth. is completely senseless, absurd, absolutely unacceptable: это ~ ≃ **it would ⟨is enough to⟩ make a cat laugh; [in limited contexts] it's fantastic ⟨utter⟩ nonsense.**
 Если кто сомневается, можно хорошо убедить так: ваши опасения — курам на смех! (Солженицын 5). If anyone doubts it, we must argue along these lines: Your misgivings would make a cat laugh! (5a). ♦ «Колька Липатов — террорист! — захлебнулся от возмущения Алик. — Сволочи, вот сволочи! Да это же курам на смех!» (Чуковская 1). "Kolya Lipatov—a terrorist!" Alik was choking with indignation. "What scum they are, what utter scum! Why, it's fantastic nonsense!" (1a).

К-478 • **ЖИВ КУРИ́ЛКА!** coll, humor [sent; Invar; fixed WO] I am (you are etc) still alive, still have energy, can still do sth. well etc (used after s.o. has been long absent, has long shown little energy, not engaged in some activity etc): **he ⟨she⟩ is (still) alive and kicking; there's life in the old dog ⟨boy, gal⟩ yet.**
 [Анна Петровна:] Здоров он [Платонов]? [Трилецкий:] Он всегда здоров. Жив курилка! (Чехов 1). [A.P.:] Is he [Platonov] well? [T.:] He always is, there's life in the old dog yet (1b).
 < From an old Russian game in which a burning splinter («курилка») was passed around and the participants repeated «Жив Курилка» until it went out.

К-479 • **КАК ⟨БУ́ДТО, СЛО́ВНО, ТО́ЧНО⟩ КУ́РИЦА ЛА́ПОЙ писать** coll [как etc + NP; these forms only; adv;

fixed WO] (to write) illegibly: X пишет ~ ≃ X's **handwriting is (like) chicken scratching ⟨scratches⟩.**

К-480 • **КАК КУ́РИЦА С ЯЙЦО́М** носиться *с кем-чем coll* [как + NP; Invar; adv; fixed WP] (to show s.o. or sth.) excessive care and concern in an overzealous manner, (to pay) excessive attention to sth. insignificant: X носится с Y-ом ~ ≃ **X makes a big to-do over Y; X makes a great fuss over Y; X makes a big deal over ⟨of⟩ Y; X fusses over Y like a mother hen ⟨a hen with an egg⟩; X broods over Y like a hen over an egg.**

Он придумал какое-то пустяковое усовершенствование и теперь носится с ним как курица с яйцом. He came up with some insignificant improvement and now he's making a big to-do over it. ♦ «Объявляю тебе, что все вы, до единого, − болтунишки и фанфаронишки! Заведётся у вас страданьице − вы с ним как курица с яйцом носитесь!» (Достоевский 3). "I hereby declare to you that you're all, every last one of you, a crowd of windbags and show-offs! As soon as you come up against some pathetic little bit of suffering you fuss over it like a hen with an egg!" (3d).

К-481 • **(как) МО́КРАЯ КУ́РИЦА** *coll, rather derog* [NP; sing only; often subj-compl with copula (subj: human); fixed WO] **1.** a person who looks pitiful, downtrodden, depressed: **(be) a sorry sight; (look) like something the cat dragged in; (look) miserable.**

[Анна Петровна:] Прошлогодняя история... В прошлом году соблазнил и до самой осени ходил мокрой курицей, так и теперь... Дон-Жуан и жалкий трус в одном теле (Чехов 1). [A.P.:] Last year's business all over again. Last year you seduced some girl and the whole summer you went about looking miserable. The same thing's happening now. Don Juan and a pitiful coward rolled into one (1a). ♦ «Крепкоголовые» хихикали и надрывали животики, видя, как крикливый господин... превращался из гордого петуха в мокрую курицу (Салтыков-Щедрин 2). [context transl] The "die-hards" first sniggered and then nearly burst their sides laughing as they watched the clamourous gentleman...transform himself from a proud cock into a wet hen (2a).

2. a person lacking decisiveness, willpower, a person likely to be dominated by another: **wimp; milksop; jellyfish; pushover.**

К-482 • **СЛЕПА́Я КУ́РИЦА** *coll, usu. derog or condes* [NP; usu. sing; fixed WO] a shortsighted person, a person with poor eyesight: **(as) blind as a bat ⟨an owl⟩; [in limited contexts] gravel-blind; [said ironically] eagle eye.**

К-483 • **ВВОДИ́ТЬ/ВВЕСТИ́** *кого* **В КУРС** *чего,* often **дела** [VP; subj: human] to give s.o. information about sth. (often the latest developments in some matter) or familiarize s.o. with sth.: X ввёл Y-а в курс Z-а ≃ **X filled Y in on Z; X brought Y up-to-date on Z; X briefed Y on Z; [when acquainting s.o. with sth. new to him] X introduced Y to Z; X showed ⟨taught⟩ Y the ropes.**

[Анчугин:] Садись, Анна Васильевна, и слушай. Садитесь, граждане. *(Угарову)* Введи в курс (Вампилов 1). [A.:] Sit down, Anna Vasilyevna, and listen. Sit down, everybody. *(To Ugarov.)* Fill 'em in (1a). ♦ ...Дегтярёв с любопытством и некоторой жалостью смотрел, как я давлюсь, и вводил меня в курс дела (Кузнецов 1). Degtyarev, with curiosity and some pity, watched me stuff myself while he briefed me on his business (1a). ♦ Солдатов числился у них старшим. Он охотно ввёл Мишку в курс обязанностей... (Шолохов 4). Soldatov was the senior man there. He willingly introduced Mishka to his duties... (4a). ♦ Жили мы в камере дружно, без ссор, наши старики опекали нас, вводили в курс лагерного житья-бытья... (Марченко 1). We got along well in the cell, without quarrelling, and the old men watched over us, teaching us the ropes about how to make the best of camp life... (1a).

К-484 • **ВХОДИ́ТЬ/ВОЙТИ́ В КУРС** *чего,* usu. **дела** [VP; subj: human] to become familiarized with, comfortable doing sth. (usu. some job, occupation etc): X вошёл в курс Y-а ≃ **X became fully ⟨well-⟩ acquainted with Y; X learned the ropes; X got into the swim ⟨the swing⟩ of things ⟨it, Y⟩.**

Не успевал номер пятый... войти в курс дела, как его уже снимали и бросали на иную работу (Ильф и Петров 2). Hardly had the new inmate of No. 5 time to get into the swim of things when he was taken away and given some other job (2a). ♦ Отец устроился, вошёл, можно сказать, в курс, приобрёл специальность... (Рыбаков 1). Father had settled down on the job, got into the swing of it, become skilled... (1a).

К-485 • **ДЕРЖА́ТЬ КУРС ⟨ЛИ́НИЮ⟩** *на что media* [VP; subj: human or collect] to follow a specific policy aimed at achieving sth.: X держит курс на Y ≃ **X is working toward Y; X is striving to achieve Y.**

К-486 • **В КУ́РСЕ** *чего,* usu. **дела, быть**ø, **держать** *кого* [PrepP; Invar; subj-compl with copula (subj: human) or obj-compl with держать (obj: human)] (to be, keep s.o.) informed of the current condition of and latest developments in some matter, aware of the latest facts: X в курсе Z-а ≃ **X knows all about Z; X is up-to-date on Z; X is well-informed on Z; X is well-aware of Z ⟨of what is going on⟩; X knows what is going on; X is fully acquainted with Z; X is in the know; [in limited contexts] X keeps abreast of Z;** ‖ Y держит X-а в курсе Z-а ≃ **Y keeps X up-to-date on Z; Y keeps X informed ⟨posted⟩; Y keeps X abreast of Z.**

Было видно, что с Лёвой они уже всё обговорили, она [Аня] в курсе всего... (Рыбаков 1). It was clear enough that she [Anya] and Lyova had gone over the whole thing already, she knew all about it... (1a). ♦ Сидят на кухне в однокомнатной квартирке Ларисы... пьют кофе из болгарских чашечек и говорят о моём здоровье. Обе в курсе дела (Трифонов 5). They'd be sitting in Larisa's one-room apartment...drinking coffee from Larisa's Bulgarian demitasses and discussing my health. Both of them are up-to-date on the situation (5a). ♦ «...Он же − не в курсе, ничего не знает!» (Залыгин 1). "...He doesn't know what's going on. He doesn't know anything!..." (1a). ♦ Пьер начал рассказывать о самоуправстве комиссара. Секретарь его перебил: «Господин министр в курсе дела. Мы − социалисты и можем говорить откровенно...» (Эренбург 4). Pierre began to tell about the superintendent's arbitrary action. The secretary interrupted him. "Monsieur le Ministre is fully acquainted with the matter....We are Socialists and can talk frankly..." (4a). ♦ Лена Быстрова, которая была в курсе дела, в ответ на мой вопрос, о чём пойдёт речь, ответила загадочно: «И об этом»... (Каверин 1). Lena Bystrova, who was in the know, replied mysteriously when I asked her what our talk would be about: "About that, too..." (1a). ♦ Обсуждаемые вопросы − поставки зерна и мяса, улучшение и развитие животноводства − часть экономической политики партии, и он [Марк Александрович]... обязан быть в курсе всех её аспектов (Рыбаков 2). The questions that were debated − deliveries of grain and meat, improving and developing livestock − were all part of the Party's economic policy and...he [Mark Alexandrovich] was obliged to keep abreast of all its aspects (2a).

К-487 • денег **КУ́РЫ НЕ КЛЮЮ́Т** *(у кого) coll* [Invar; quantit predic (subj/gen: денег); fixed WO] (there is, one has) a lot of money: у X-а денег куры не клюют ≃ **X is rolling in money; X has money to burn; X is a real moneybags; X has more money than he knows what to do with.**

[Медведенко:] Вам хорошо смеяться. Денег у вас куры не клюют (Чехов 6). [M.:] It's all very well for you to laugh. You're rolling in money (6b). ♦ ...У Иннокентия Ивановича, всякий знал, денег куры не клюют, его так и звали: Иннокентий Карманович... (Распутин 2). ...Everyone knew Innokenty

Ivanovich had more money than he knew what to do with, and they all called him Innokenty Pockets... (2a).

К-488 • СТРО́ИТЬ КУ́РЫ *(кому) obs, humor* [VP; subj: human] to seek s.o.'s affections, flirt with s.o.: X строит куры Y-у ≃ **X is paying court to Y; X is offering his attentions to Y.**

«Как, неужели он и протопопше строил куры?» (Гоголь 3). "You don't say he's been paying court to the priest's wife?" (3d). ♦ «...[Ракитин] рассказал мне, что строит куры Хохлаковой...» (Достоевский 1). "...He [Rakitin] told me he was offering his attentions to Khokhlakov..." (1a).

< Partial loan translation of the French *faire la court.*

К-489 • (КАК) НА КУРЬЕ́РСКИХ *obs* [(как +) PrepP; these forms only; adv] very quickly, hurriedly: **swiftly; posthaste; promptly;** [in limited contexts] **make short work of sth.**

Наконец толстый [мужчина], послуживши богу и государю, заслуживши всеобщее уважение, оставляет службу, перебирается и делается помещиком, славным русским барином, хлебосолом, и живёт, и хорошо живёт. А после него опять тоненькие наследники спускают, по русскому обычаю, на курьерских всё отцовское добро (Гоголь 3). Finally, the fat man, after serving God and Tsar and earning general respect, retires from service, moves out of town, and settles down as a landowner, a hospitable Russian gentleman. And thus he lives, and lives well. And after him come his thin heirs, who promptly squander, Russian-style, the wealth he has accumulated (3e). In the end, after having served God and the Emperor and won general respect, the fat man resigns the service, goes to live on his estate, becomes a landowner, a fine Russian gentleman, a hospitable host, and lives on and lives well. After him, as is the Russian custom, his thin heirs make short work of their father's fortune (3a).

К-490 • КУСКА́ НЕДОЕДА́ТЬ *coll* [VP; subj: human] to deny o.s. food (for the sake of s.o. or sth.): X куска недоедает ≃ **X grudges himself every morsel of food; X grudges himself a crust of bread; X goes hungry.**

[Войницкий:] ...Мы, точно кулаки, торговали постным маслом, горохом, творогом, сами недоедали куска, чтобы из грошей и копеек собирать тысячи и посылать ему (Чехов 3). [V.:] ...Like kulaks, we sold vegetable oil, dried peas, cottage cheese, grudging ourselves every morsel of food, trying to save every little kopeck so we could send him thousands of rubles (3a).

К-491 • КУСО́К В ГО́РЛО ⟨В ГЛО́ТКУ⟩ НЕ ИДЁТ/ НЕ ПОЙДЁТ ⟨НЕ ЛЕ́ЗЕТ/НЕ ПОЛЕ́ЗЕТ⟩ *кому;* **В ГО́РЛО ⟨В ГЛО́ТКУ⟩ НЕ ИДЁТ/НЕ ПОЙДЁТ ⟨НЕ ЛЕ́ЗЕТ/НЕ ПОЛЕ́ЗЕТ⟩** *all coll* [VP_subj (variants with кусок) or VP with subj: a noun denoting some food (variants without кусок); if past, usu. impfv] s.o. cannot eat from exhaustion, nervousness etc: кусок ⟨X⟩ не идёт Y-у в горло ≃ **food ⟨X⟩ sticks ⟨gets stuck⟩ in Y's throat; it ⟨X⟩ won't go down (Y's throat); Y can't ⟨can hardly⟩ swallow X ⟨anything, a bite⟩; Y can't eat a thing.**

[Говорящий — мул] Нас [мула и ослика] пустили пастись во двор, но мне трава в горло не лезла, и я так уж, по привычке... ел её (Искандер 3). [The speaker is a mule] They turned us [the mule and the donkey] loose to graze in the yard, but I could hardly swallow, the grass stuck in my throat, and I just ate it out of habit (3a). ♦ ...Он [Михаил] не мог заставить себя притронуться к молоку. Не лезло ему молоко в горло... (Абрамов 1). ...Mikhail couldn't make himself touch the milk. It wouldn't go down his throat... (1b). ♦ После второго карцера мы совсем расхворались. Хлеб и баланда не лезли в горло (Гинзбург 1). After our second spell in the punishment block we both fell ill in good earnest. We could no longer swallow the bread and thin soup (1b). ♦ Стали люди разгавливаться [obs = разговляться], но никому не шёл кусок в горло, и все опять заплакали (Салтыков-Щедрин 1). The

people went to break their fast, but no one could eat a thing and they all began to cry again (1a).

К-492 • КУСО́К ХЛЕ́БА [NP; sing only; usu. obj; fixed WO] means of subsistence: **crust ⟨piece⟩ of bread; livelihood; means of support; bread and butter;** ‖ заработать на кусок хлеба ≃ **earn one's bread ⟨keep, livelihood⟩; earn a living;** ‖ думать ⟨беспокоиться⟩ о куске хлеба ≃ **worry about where the ⟨one's⟩ next meal is coming from; worry about putting bread on the table.**

«Итак, всё кончено, — сказал он [Дубровский] сам себе, — ещё утром имел я угол и кусок хлеба. Завтра должен я буду оставить дом, где я родился и где умер мой отец, виновнику его смерти и моей нищеты» (Пушкин 1). "So it's all over!" he [Dubrovsky] said to himself. "Only this morning I had a place to rest and a crust of bread to eat. To-morrow I must abandon the house where I was born, and where my father died, to the man who brought about his death and my beggary!" (1b). ♦ «Я не сделаю ни шага, пока вы не дадите мне возможность повидать сына. Он в школе. Остаётся на краю земли, один, без куска хлеба. Я должна поговорить с ним перед расставаньем...» (Гинзбург 2). "I won't take a step until you let me see my son. He's at school. He will be left behind out here at the end of the earth, all alone, with no means of support. I must talk to him before we are parted..." (2a). ♦ ...Меня не печатали и лишали куска хлеба ещё два года (до конца 1972), после чего власти, полагая, что я уже прочно стою на коленях, решили меня простить и даже издали одновременно две мои книги (Войнович 1). ...They stopped publishing me and kept me from earning a living for another two years, until the end of 1972. Then, assuming that they had me on my knees, the authorities decided to forgive me, and even published two of my books at the same time (1a).

К-493 • ЛА́КОМЫЙ КУСО́К ⟨КУСО́ЧЕК⟩ *coll* [NP; usu. sing; usu. this WO] s.o. or sth. tempting, alluring, attractive: **dainty ⟨tempting, mouth-watering⟩ morsel; tasty (little) morsel.**

[author's usage] [Варравин:] Этих случаев, сударь, веками дожидаются. Это всякому лакомый кус. Тут награды, кресты, чины (Сухово-Кобылин 3). [V.:] My God, man, people wait ages for just such opportunities. That'd be a dainty morsel for anyone. Think of the rewards, the medals, the honors (3a). ♦ Ведь если, положим, этой девушке да придать тысчонок двести приданого, из неё бы мог выйти очень, очень лакомый кусочек (Гоголь 3). Why, supposing the girl has a nice little dowry of two hundred thousand! That would certainly make her a very tasty little morsel (3a).

К-494 • ПРОНОСИ́ТЬ/ПРОНЕСТИ́ КУСО́К МИМО РТА *obs, coll* [VP; subj: human; often neg pfv fut] to fail to exploit an opportunity from which one might benefit, gain sth.: X пронёс кусок мимо рта ≃ **X let an opportunity pass him by; X passed up ⟨missed out on⟩ an opportunity; X let it slip by ⟨through his fingers⟩; X missed his chance; X missed the boat;** ‖ X кусок ⟨куска⟩ мимо рта не пронесёт ≃ **X will grab ⟨jump at⟩ the chance; X will seize the opportunity.**

Об издательско-то деятельности и мечтал Разумихин... «Иные издания дают теперь славный процент!.. И зачем, зачем мимо рта кусок проносить!» (Достоевский 3). It was publishing that Razumikhin had in mind...."Some books now make a wonderful profit!...And why, why miss the boat?" (3a).

К-495 • УРВА́ТЬ КУСО́К *coll, usu. disapprov* [VP; subj: human] to obtain or appropriate (usu. by rather unscrupulous means) a portion of some fortune, property etc: X урвал кусок ≃ **X got ⟨grabbed⟩ a piece of the pie; X got ⟨grabbed⟩ something for himself.**

К-496 • **В КУСТЫ́** (уходить, прятаться и т. п.) *coll* [PrepP; Invar; predic (with subj: human) or adv] to (try to) avoid doing sth. (taking responsibility for sth., participating in sth. potentially dangerous etc) out of cowardice, fear: X (уходит) в кусты ≃ **X chickens ⟨backs⟩ out; X slinks away; X runs for cover; X tries to hide; X looks for a way out;** [in limited contexts] **X dodges (sth.).**

[author's usage] [Гомыра:] По кустам он [Вася] никогда не прятался, друзей в беде не бросал (Вампилов 3). [G.:] He's [Vasia has] never chickened out of anything, never left a friend in the lurch (3a). ♦ Они за уважаемого [Иванько] только до тех пор, пока сила на его стороне. Чуть уважаемый качнулся, они — в кусты (Войнович 3). They were for their respected colleague [Ivanko] only as long as he had the power. As soon as he stumbled, they slunk away (3a). ♦ Шли молча; против моховского дома Иван Алексеевич, не выдержавший тошного молчания... сказал: «Нечего греха таить: с фронта пришли большевиками, а зараз [*regional* = сейчас] в кусты лезем!» (Шолохов 3). They walked on without speaking. As they were passing Mokhov's house, Ivan could bear the hateful silence no longer and...said, "You can't get away from it. We were Bolsheviks when we came home from the front, and now we're running for cover!" (3a). ♦ «Значит, вы ничем не хотите помочь партии. Разговор доходит до дела — и в кусты, так, что ли? Дерьмо вы, дерьмо собачье!» (Гроссман 2). "So you don't want to help the Party? Just when we get to the point, you try and hide. It's like that, is it? You're shit, real dogshit!" (2a). ♦ «Как я отвечу на такие вопросы? Неужто мой костюм даёт мне право на ответ? Он не даёт мне никаких особых прав, но лишь обязывает». — «Вот он и обязывает тебя не уходить в кусты от таких вопросов» (Аксёнов 6). "How can I answer such questions? Do you think my garb gives me the right to give you the answers? It gives me no special rights; it only places me under an obligation." "So it also places you under an obligation not to dodge questions like this" (6a).

К-497 • **СМОТРЕ́ТЬ ⟨ГЛЯДЕ́ТЬ⟩ В КУСТЫ́** *coll* [VP; subj: human] to try to avoid work, responsibility: X смотрит в кусты ≃ **X is trying to back ⟨duck⟩ out; X is trying to sneak out the back way; X is looking for a way out.**

К-498 • **ВАЛИ́ТЬ ⟨СВА́ЛИВАТЬ⟩/СВАЛИ́ТЬ ⟨МЕ-ША́ТЬ/СМЕША́ТЬ⟩ В (ОДНУ́) КУ́ЧУ** *кого-что coll, disapprov* [VP; subj: human; obj: often всех, всё] to mix, group different things or phenomena indiscriminately, failing to see their differences: X валит Y-ов в одну кучу ≃ **X lumps ⟨mixes, bunches⟩ Ys together; X puts Ys in the same bag ⟨basket⟩.**

[Воротынцев:] Вы по советским представлениям всех в одну кучу валите, кто только не большевик (Солженицын 9). [V.:] You, with your Soviet mentality, lump together everybody who's not a Bolshevik (9a). ♦ «Ты знаешь: нарисовал этот Евдокимов похабную карикатуру на декана...» — «Который её заслуживал? Ну, скажи, нет! Ты ведь сам его терпеть не можешь». Игорь невольно оглянулся на дверь. «Я — другое дело, — сказал он кисло. — Не вали, пожалуйста, всех в одну кучу...» (Ерофеев 3). "You know that Evdokimov drew a smutty caricature of the Dean...." "And he deserved it. Go on, deny it! You know you can't stand him yourself." Igor couldn't keep himself from glancing at the door. "What I think is something else entirely," he said in a sour voice. "Please don't put everyone in the same bag..." (3a).

Л

Л-1 • НЕ СЕ́МЕРО ПО ЛА́ВКАМ *у кого highly coll* [NP; Invar; the resulting phrase is usu. indep. sent; fixed WO] s.o. is not burdened with a large family needing support and care: у Х-а не семеро по лавкам ≃ **X doesn't have (too) many mouths to feed; X isn't saddled with a large brood.**

Л-2 • ПО ПЬЯ́НОЙ ЛА́ВОЧКЕ ⟨ПОД ПЬЯ́НУЮ ЛА́ВОЧКУ, ПО ПЬЯ́НКЕ, ПО ПЬЯ́НОМУ ДЕ́ЛУ⟩ *all highly coll* [PrepP; these forms only; adv; fixed WO] (in refer. to a person) in a state of intoxication: **when one is drunk ⟨pickled, in his cups⟩; when one has had one ⟨a few⟩ too many; when one has had too much to drink; in a drunken state.**

[Галина:] ...Бывал ли ты когда-нибудь в церкви? [Зилов:] Да. Раз мы заходили с ребятами. По пьянке. А ты? [Галина:] А я с бабушкой. За компанию (Вампилов 5). [G.:] Have you ever been to church? [Z.:] Yes. Looked in once with some of my mates, when we were drunk. Have you? [G.:] I went with my grandmother. To keep her company (5a). ♦ «Захочу, — говорит, — в два счёта повыгоняю вас с работы». Это он на деда и Сейдахмата. И то по пьяному делу (Айтматов 1). "If I have a mind to," he'd say, "I'll fire you all at one stroke." This was directed to grandfather and Seidakhmat. And pronounced when he was pickled (1b). ♦ [Брылов:] Ну, может, по пьянке баба ошиблась, не того [масла] купила (Солженицын 8). [B.:] Well, maybe my old woman made a mistake. Maybe she had one too many and bought the wrong kind of butter (8a). ♦ «Ну, а по пьяному делу, сама знаешь, мало ли чего можно сказать или сделать» (Войнович 5). "You know yourself the things you can say or do when you've had too much to drink" (5a). ♦ Среди них попадались славные малые, которые по пьяной лавочке умели рассказать много забавных историй... (Мандельштам 1). Among them there were some perfectly decent kids who in a drunken state would tell you [lots of] amusing tales... (1a). ♦ Друзей у него не было. Компании по пьяному делу он не водил — редко, разве что по большим праздникам, пропускал стопочку (Абрамов 1). [context transl] He had no friends. He did not indulge in drinking sessions — on rare occasions he would down a glass, but only on important holidays (1a).

Л-3 • ЗАКРЫВА́ТЬ/ЗАКРЫ́ТЬ ⟨ПРИКРЫВА́ТЬ/ПРИКРЫ́ТЬ⟩ ЛА́ВОЧКУ *highly coll* [VP; subj: human; usu. infin with надо, пора, пришлось etc or imper] (permanently or temporarily) to discontinue engaging in, or cause the discontinuance of, some activity, undertaking etc: пора закрывать лавочку ≃ **it's time to close ⟨shut⟩ up shop; it's time to call it quits;** [in limited contexts] **it's time to put up the shutters; it's time to put a stop to this ⟨to sth.⟩;** [in refer. to ending sth. for the day] **it's time to call it a day.**

Капитан насобачился делать печати. И дело пошло. Зарабатывали много... Потом они попали в облаву... Еле выкрутились... Так дальше не пойдёт, сказал Крикун. Эту лавочку надо прикрыть (Зиновьев 1). Captain found the knack of forging official stamps, and they were in business. They earned a great deal....But then they were picked up in a police raid....They only just got out of it...."We can't go on with this," said Bawler. "We'll have to shut up shop..." (1a). ♦ [Вася:] Ну, Гаврило Петрович, закрывай лавочку! Как Александра Николавна уедет, тебе больше не торговать! Баста! Калачом в театр не заманишь. Так ты и ожидай! (Островский 11). [V.:] Well, Gavril Petrovich, you might as well put up the shutters! When Alexandra Nikolavna goes away, there won't be any more business for you. *Basta!* You won't get them to the theatre for love or money — that's what *you're* soon going to find out! (11a). ♦ «Есть сигнал: к ним [в стройотряд] там один бродяга похаживает... тихую агитацию разводит, насчёт всемирного братства и равенства рассусоливает. В общем, анархия

вперемешку с поповщиной, прикрывать эту лавочку пора, только надо наверняка действовать» (Максимов 1). "We've heard on the grapevine that a tramp goes to see them [the construction brigade]....He keeps quietly propagandizing universal brotherhood and equality. All in all it's a mixture of anarchy and religious claptrap, and it's time to put a stop to their little racket, only we'll have to act firmly" (1a).

Л-4 • ПОЧИВА́ТЬ ⟨ПОКО́ИТЬСЯ *obs*⟩/ПОЧИ́ТЬ НА ЛА́ВРАХ *lit* [VP; subj: human; usu. this WO] to be satisfied with the accomplishments one has already achieved and not try to add to them: X почивает на лаврах ≃ **X rests on his laurels.**

[author's usage] [Дудукин:] Пора вам пользоваться своей славой, своими успехами, пора успокоиться на лаврах (Островский 3). [D.:] It is high time to enjoy your fame, to rest on your laurels (3a).

Л-5 • ЛА́ВРЫ чьи, кого НЕ ДАЮ́Т СПАТЬ ⟨ПОКО́Я⟩ *кому* [VP$_{subj}$; pres or past] s.o. experiences envy at another's success: лавры Х-а Y-у спать не дают ≃ **the thought of X's success is keeping Y awake nights ⟨at night⟩; Y can't stand the thought of X's success; the thought that X is successful ⟨has won etc⟩ is eating ⟨chewing⟩ Y up (inside).**

< Apparently, a modified loan translation from Latin or Greek. The Athenian statesman Themistocles (527?–460? B.C.) supposedly said, after Miltiades' brilliant victory over the Persians in the Battle of Marathon (490 B.C.), that he was "kept awake by the trophies of Miltiades" (Plutarch, *Life of Themistocles*, III, and Cicero, *Tusculan Disputations*, IV, 19 etc). Occasionally used in the form «Лавры Мильтиада не дают спать».

Л-6 • ПОЖИНА́ТЬ/ПОЖА́ТЬ ЛА́ВРЫ *lit* [VP; subj: human] to enjoy the honors brought by success (sometimes, success earned by another): X пожинает лавры ≃ **X wins ⟨gets⟩ the laurels; X reaps the rewards ⟨the benefits⟩; X takes the bows; X gets all the glory ⟨the credit, the acclaim⟩.**

Л-7 • ДЕ́ЙСТВОВАТЬ НА ДВА ЛА́ГЕРЯ [VP; subj: human or collect; the verb may take the final position, otherwise fixed WO] to serve two opposing sides at the same time (usu. for the sake of personal gain): X действует на два лагеря ≃ **X has a foot in each camp; X works both sides of the street.**

Л-8 • В ЛАД [PrepP; Invar] **1.** ~ *чему, с кем-чем* [Prep; the resulting PrepP is adv] corresponding exactly to (the beat, rate, rhythm etc of sth.): **in tune ⟨keeping, accord, harmony, concert⟩ with; in time with; to the rhythm of; at one with.**

«Была бы у меня эта книжечка, — сказала Лёлька, провожая меня до порога с малышом на руках, — я бы спать не ложилась — её читала! День и ночь бы читала, глаз бы не перевела!» Её речь звучала в лад со сказкой — это наново поразило меня (Чуковская 2). "Had I this little book," said Lyolka as she accompanied me to the door with the baby in her arms, "I would not go to bed, I would read it! Night and day I would read it without closing my eyes!" I was struck again how much her words sounded in tune with the fairy-tale (2a). ♦ ...Сами себе Андрей и Настёна виделись в этот укромный час не настоящими, чужими — настолько покаянно и тихо, смиряя всё вокруг, с полным прощением перед прощанием, отходил этот крутой, горячий день. И они в лад его смирению говорили тихо, почти шёпотом (Распутин 2). ...Andrei and Nastyona seemed unreal, strangers to themselves in this secluded hour — that was how funereally and quietly the abrupt, harsh, hot day departed, calming everything around them, with full forgiveness before its farewell. And they spoke softly, almost in a whisper, in keeping with the day's passing (2a). ♦ [Иван:] Быть может, настал час той славы, о которой мечтали вы с детства! Не уступите, не прозевайте... миллионы сердец бьются в лад с вами... (Олеша 6). [I.:] Perhaps now the hour has arrived of that glory of which you have been dreaming since childhood! Don't turn back, don't let the opportunity slip away; millions of hearts are beating in time with yours (6a).

2. [adv] together, in harmony, synchronously: **in unison; in concert; in tune; as one (man);** ‖ *Neg* не в лад ≃ **out of step ⟨tune, time⟩.**

Мы поздоровались с классом. Ребята ответили негромко, но в лад. We said hello to the class, and the kids responded softly, though in unison.

Л-9 • ИДЁТ/ПОШЛО́ НА ЛАД [VP; subj: usu. дело, less often дела, всё; fixed WO] things are going or are starting to go better than previously, well, without problems: дело идёт на лад ≃ **things have begun to go ⟨are going⟩ smoothly ⟨well, very nicely etc⟩; things have begun to improve ⟨are improving⟩; things have taken ⟨are taking⟩ a turn for the better; things are looking up; things are ⟨s.o.'s health is etc⟩ on the mend;** [in limited contexts] **(from here on in ⟨from now on etc⟩) it will be smooth sailing.**

[Городничий:] Ну, слава богу! Деньги взял. Дело, кажется, пойдёт теперь на лад (Гоголь 4). [Mayor:] Well, thank God, he took the money! Now I think everything will go smoothly (4f). [Mayor:] Phew! Thank God! He took the money. It'll be smooth sailing from now on (4d). ♦ [Кудряш:] Значит, у вас дело на лад идёт, коли сюда приходить велели (Островский 6). [K.:] Things must be going along very nicely if you've been told to come here (6c). ♦ Постепенно и на работе дела у него пошли на лад (Войнович 4). Even at work things began gradually improving for him (4a).

Л-10 • НА ОДИ́Н ⟨НА ТОТ ЖЕ⟩ ЛАД [PrepP; these forms only; fixed WO] **1.** [subj-compl with copula (subj: any count noun, pl)] (two or more people, things etc are) identical or very similar (to one another): **the same; alike.**

Все твои доводы на один лад. All your arguments are the same.

2. [adv; more often used with impfv verbs] identically or extremely similarly: **the same way; in the same manner; (come out etc) the same.**

Женщины пели все песни на один лад — медленно, заунывно. The women sang all the songs the same way—slowly and plaintively.

Л-11 • НА СВОЙ ЛАД; НА СВОЙ МАНЕ́Р *coll;* **НА СВОЙ САЛТЫ́К** *obs, coll* [PrepP; these forms only; adv; fixed WO] in a way specific to o.s. and corresponding to one's personality, tastes etc: **in one's own way; after ⟨in⟩ one's own fashion;** [in limited contexts] **the way one wants ⟨likes⟩.**

Бахут был мингрельцем и произносил его [Кязыма] имя на свой лад (Искандер 5). Bakhut was a Mingrelian and pronounced Kyazym's name in his own way (5a). ♦ Любовь в ней могла бы родиться; но Люсьен сделал всё, чтобы оттолкнуть Жаннет от себя... Трудно было понять его чувства: он и Жаннет любил на свой лад... (Эренбург 4). Love might have been awakened in her [Jeannette], but Lucien did everything to repel it....His feelings towards her were complex. He did love her after his own fashion... (4a). ♦ Первые дни я боялась, что Авдотья Никоновна станет всё переделывать на свой лад... (Каверин 1). For the first few days I was afraid that Avdotya Nikonovna would start changing everything round the way she wanted it... (1a).

Л-12 • ДЫША́ТЬ НА ЛА́ДАН *coll* [VP; pres or past; usu. 3rd pers] **1.** [subj: human] (of a mortally ill or old and feeble person) to be about to die: X дышит на ладан ≃ **X has one foot in the grave; X is on his last legs; X is breathing his last.**

...Почему-то в нём [Мите]... основалось убеждение, что этот старый развратитель, дышащий теперь на ладан, может быть, вовсе не будет в настоящую минуту противиться, если Грушенька устроит как-нибудь свою жизнь честно и выйдет за «благонадёжного человека» замуж (Достоевский 1). ...For some reason the conviction had settled in him [Mitya]...that this old profligate, now with one foot in the grave, might not be at all averse at the moment to Grushenka somehow arranging her life honorably and marrying "a trustworthy man" (1a). ♦ «Дышит на ладан, — возразил полковник. — Оставь его, Филюков. Можете оба идти» (Войнович 2). "He's breathing his last," retorted the colonel. "Leave him alone, Filiukov. You're both dismissed" (2a).

2. [subj: concr or collect] to be in the final period of existence, be about to stop functioning: X дышит на ладан ≃ **X is on its last legs; X is on the verge of collapse; X is in its last days; X is dying out.**

Второй — чистовой — экземпляр [«Шума времени»] кочевал по редакциям, и все отказывались печатать эту штуку, лишённую фабулы и сюжета, классового подхода и общественного значения. Заинтересовался Георгий Блок, двоюродный брат поэта, работавший в дышавшем на ладан частном издательстве (Мандельштам 2). The fair copy [of *Noise of Time*] went the rounds of various publishers who all rejected it, devoid as it was of plot, story, class consciousness, or any kind of social significance. The only person to show interest was Georgi Blok, the cousin of the poet, who worked for a private publishing firm already on its last legs (2a).

Л-13 • КАК ⟨БУ́ДТО, СЛО́ВНО, ТО́ЧНО⟩ НА ЛАДО́НИ ⟨НА ЛАДО́ШКЕ, НА ЛАДО́НКЕ *obs*⟩ *coll* [как etc + PrepP; these forms only] **1.** (видно, видеть *кого-что* и т. п.) ~ [adv or subj-compl with быть₀ (subj: usu. concr, often всё)] sth. is very clearly and distinctly visible, (to see s.o. or sth.) very clearly: **(be) in full ⟨plain⟩ view; (be ⟨stand⟩) open to view; (be as clearly visible) as if it were (spread out) on the palm of one's hand.**

Городок стоит открыто, как на ладони, кругом ни ветлы; где-то очень далеко, на самом краю неба, чернеется лесок (Достоевский 3). The town stands open to view; there is not a single willow tree around it; somewhere very far off, at the very edge of the sky, is the black line of a little forest (3c). ♦ По стеклянным ступеням мы поднялись наверх. Всё — под нами внизу — как на ладони... (Замятин 1). We ascended the glass stairs. Everything below was as clearly visible as if it were spread out on the palm of my hand (1a).

2. [subj-compl with быть₀ (subj: human or, less often, abstr)] everything about (a person, his life etc) is clear, evident, there is nothing secretive, hidden from view: X как на ладони ≃ **person X is an open book; (you can read person X) like a book; thing X is so ⟨absolutely⟩ clear ⟨transparent, plain⟩.**

...Ведь ты же знаешь все мои институтские штучки, ведь я у тебя весь как на ладони (Аксёнов 1). ...You know all my college-kid tricks, I'm an open book to you... (1a). ...Его безупречное притворство было как на ладони (Окуджава 2). ...His impeccable pretense was so transparent (2a).

3. ~ **выложить** *(кому) что,* **показать** *кому что* и т. п. [adv] (to tell, reveal sth. to s.o.) straightforwardly, clearly, and completely: **candidly; openly; concealing ⟨withholding, suppressing⟩ nothing.**

Л-14 • В ЛАДУ́ ⟨В ЛАДА́Х⟩ с кем **быть₀, жить** и т. п. *coll* [PrepP; these forms only; subj-compl with быть₀ (subj: human) or adv] (to be) friendly with s.o., have a good rapport with s.o.: X с Y-ом в ладу ≃ **X is on good ⟨friendly⟩ terms with Y; X gets along ⟨on⟩ (quite) well with Y; X gets along ⟨on⟩ fine with Y.**

[Беркутов:] Да мне бояться нечего: я здесь со всеми в ладу. Хоть ребячеств Лыняева и всей их компании я и не одобряю, а всё-таки не ссорюсь и с ними (Островский 5). [B.:] I'm not afraid of anything. I'm on good terms with everyone here. I don't approve of the childish behavior of Lynyayev and his associates, but still, I don't quarrel even with them (5a). ♦ «Да вот теперь у тебя власть—мужики: ты с ними в ладу и, конечно, их не обидишь, потому что они твои, тебе же будет хуже...» (Гоголь 3). "As it is, you have peasants under your power. You get along quite well with them, you won't hurt them, naturally, because they are your serfs, and hurting them would make things worse for you" (3c).

Л-15 • НЕ В ЛАДУ́ 〈НЕ В ЛАДА́Х〉 coll [PrepP; these forms only] **1.** ~ с кем [subj-compl with бытьθ (subj: human) or adv] one is in disagreement with s.o., has a strained relationship with s.o.: X не в ладу с Y-ом ≃ **X is at odds with Y; X is on the outs with Y; X is on bad 〈not on good〉 terms with Y; there's something wrong between X and Y; something is not right between X and Y; X does not get along 〈get on〉 with Y;** [in limited contexts] **X and Y just don't click.**

«Нет, он [Собакевич] с ними не в ладах», — подумал про себя Чичиков (Гоголь 3). "He [Sobakevich] must be at odds with them," Chichikov thought to himself (3c). ♦ ...Кузнец, который был издавна не в ладу с ним [с Чубом], при нём на то не отважится идти к дочке, несмотря на свою силу (Гоголь 5). ...The blacksmith, who had for a long time been on bad terms with him [Chub], would on no account have ventured, strong as he was, to visit the daughter when the father was at home (5a). ♦ По несчастью, татарин-миссионер был не в ладах с муллою в Малмыже (Герцен 1). Unfortunately, the Tatar missionary was not on good terms with the mullah at Malmyzho (1a). ♦ ...Я подумал: «Или вдовец, или живёт не в ладах с женой» (Шолохов 1). Either he's a widower, I decided, or there's something wrong between him and his wife (1c). ♦ С братьями по вере [пятидесятник] не в ладах. Слишком для них эксцентричен (Терц 3). He [the Pentecostalist] does not get on with his brethren in the faith—they find him too eccentric... (3a).

2. ~ с чем [subj-compl with бытьθ (subj: human)] one cannot understand or master sth., cannot learn how to use, apply etc sth.: X не в ладу с Y-ом ≃ **X is at odds 〈at variance〉 with Y; X is not (very) good at Y; X is not cut out for Y.**

«...Мне кажется, вы немножко не в ладах с русской грамматикой» (Войнович 3). "...It seems to me that you are somewhat at odds with Russian grammar" (3a).

3. rare ~ с чем [usu. var. не в ладу; subj-compl with бытьθ (subj: abstr or concr)] sth. is in discord with some other thing: X с Y-ом не в ладу ≃ **X is not in harmony 〈in tune〉 with Y; X and Y are at variance; X is not in sync with Y.**

Л-16 • НА ВСЕ ЛАДЫ́ повторять, твердить что, ругать кого и т. п. coll [PrepP; Invar; adv or, rare, nonagreeing post-modif; usu. used with impfv verbs; fixed WO] (to repeat sth., keep saying sth., swear at s.o. etc) in all possible ways, in every form imaginable: **in every possible way; with 〈in〉 all sorts of variations; (look at a matter 〈argue a point etc〉) from every (possible) angle 〈from all angles〉;** [in refer. to cursing only] **call s.o. every name in the book; curse s.o. up and down 〈up hill and down dale〉; curse a blue streak.**

Всё мёртво, только из всех углов несётся разнообразное храпенье на все тоны и лады (Гончаров 1). Everything was dead, except for the snoring that came in all sorts of tones and variations from every corner of the house (1a). ♦ Я знала, что вскоре после моего отъезда Репнин затосковал и вдруг исчез... Куда? Этот вопрос на все лады разбирался в зерносовхозе (Каверин 1). I knew that soon after my departure Repnin had become very depressed and then suddenly disappeared....Where had he gone? They had investigated this problem from every angle on the State Farm (1a). ♦ Загадка не давалась, как клад. На все лады перевёртывал он её... (Салтыков-Щедрин 2). The mystery remained unsolved. He tried to look at it from every possible angle... (2a). ♦ [Говорящий —

мул] Проклиная меня на все лады, он кое-как взобрался на меня, согнал ослика на тропу, и мы двинулись домой (Искандер 3). [The speaker is a mule] Cursing a blue streak, he somehow got up on me, drove the donkey back to the path, and we started for home (3a).

Л-17 • СКЛОНЯ́ТЬ НА ВСЕ ЛАДЫ́ кого-что coll [VP; subj: human; often 3rd pers pl with indef. refer.; the verb may take the final position, otherwise fixed WO] to mention s.o. or sth., speak about s.o. or sth. much and usu. disapprovingly: X-ово имя склоняли на все лады ≃ **X's name was bandied about.**

Л-18 • ЛА́ЗАРЯ ПЕТЬ/ЗАПЕ́ТЬ obsoles, disapprov [VP; subj: human; usu. impfv (often infin with хватит, перестань etc)] to pretend to be miserable and complain about one's fate in an attempt to move s.o. to pity: X пел Лазаря ≃ **X was moaning and groaning about his fate; X was playing on person Y's sympathies; X was playing Lazarus 〈the beggar, the pauper〉; X was pleading poverty.**

[Иванов:] А я-то, какой смешной болван! Православный народ смущаю, по целым дням Лазаря пою (Чехов 4). [I.:] And I—I'm just a ludicrous dolt! Day in and day out I go about upsetting decent people, playing Lazarus (4a). ♦ «Да полно тебе Лазаря петь», — перебил опять Базаров... «Лазаря петь! — повторил Василий Иванович. — Ты, Евгений, не думай, что я хочу... разжалобить гостя...» (Тургенев 2). "Now that's enough playing the beggar," Bazarov cut him short again...."Playing the beggar!" repeated Vasily Ivanovich. "Don't you take it into your head that I want to make our guest sorry for us..." (2e). "Come, that's enough of your pleading poverty," Bazarov interrupted him again...."Pleading poverty!" echoed the father. "Don't get the notion, Evgenii, that I want to win the sympathy of our guest..." (2d).

< From the Biblical parable about the beggar Lazarus (Luke 16:20–21).

Л-19 • НАОБУ́М ЛА́ЗАРЯ highly coll [AdvP; Invar; adv; fixed WO] without thinking sth. out, without considering sth. carefully: **recklessly; rashly; without using one's brains 〈head〉; without thinking; (just) any (which 〈old〉) way; (just) anyhow.**

На все убеждения Денисова не ездить [во французский лагерь] Петя отвечал, что он тоже привык всё делать аккуратно, а не наобум Лазаря, и что об опасности себе никогда не думает (Толстой 7). To all Denisov's efforts to dissuade him [from going to the French camp] Petya replied that he liked doing things with precision, not "just anyhow," and that he never thought of danger to himself (7a).

Л-20 • ДО ЛА́МПОЧКИ кому highly coll [PrepP; Invar; subj-compl with бытьθ (subj: any noun, often это, всё, всё это)] the person or thing in question does not matter at all to s.o.; does not interest s.o. in the least: X Y-у до лампочки ≃ **Y couldn't 〈could〉 care less about X; Y couldn't care a snap about X; Y doesn't 〈couldn't〉 give a damn 〈a hoot, a fig〉 about X; Y doesn't care at all (about X).**

[Алёна:] ...Мы же обречены ждать, ждать... [Нюша:] Хотя бы ради стариков. [Алёна:] Да старикам до лампочки. Это ты у нас чувствительная ко всякой ерунде (Панова 1). [A.:] ...We're doomed to wait and wait— [N.:] If only for the grandparents' sake... [A.:] They couldn't care less. It's you who worries about every little thing (1a). ♦ [Зилов:] ...Ты прекрасно знаешь, откуда у меня эта копейка. Но ты идёшь со мной, потому что тебе всё до лампочки, и откуда взялась моя копейка, на это тебе тоже наплевать... (Вампилов 5). [Z.:] ...You know full well where I got that kopeck. But you go with me because you don't give a damn and it's all one to you how I came by that kopeck... (5a). ♦ ...Аркадий ничем никому не угрожал: ни малейшим вмешательством, ни расспросами, самым обычным и естественным интересом:

«Ну, как вы тут живёте? Как тут у вас ладится?» Это всё Аркаше было до лампочки (Залыгин 1). ...Arkady was no threat to anyone: he didn't interfere in the least, didn't pester anyone with questions, not even the most normal and natural questions: "How's life here then? How are you getting on?" He didn't care at all (1a).

Л-21 • В ЛА́ПАХ ⟨В КОГТЯ́Х⟩ чьих, (у) кого **быть**₀, **оказаться, очутиться, держать** кого; **В ЛА́ПЫ ⟨В КО́ГТИ⟩** чьи, кого, (к) кому **попасть(ся)** all coll [PrepP; these forms only; subj-compl with copula (subj: human) or adv] (to be or end up) in s.o.'s power (may refer to one's being taken prisoner by s.o.): X в лапах у Y-а ≃ **X is in Y's clutches;** ‖ X попал в лапы (к) Y-у ≃ **X fell into Y's clutches.**

Половина с лишком мужиков была у него [Трифона Борисыча] в когтях, все были ему должны кругом (Достоевский 1). He [Trifon Borisich] had more than half of the peasants in his clutches, everyone was in debt to him (1a). ♦ «...Чего ты боишься?» — «Как чего боюсь, батюшка Кирила Петрович, а Дубровского-то; того и гляди попадёшься ему в лапы» (Пушкин 1). "What are you afraid of?" "What indeed, dear sir Kirila Petrovich! Dubrovskii, that's what! You can never tell when you might fall into his clutches" (1a). ♦ Несчастье заключалось в том, что в первые встречи «на частной квартире» они [люди, которых использовали в качестве агентов,] не отдавали себе отчёта, что навсегда и безвозвратно попадают в лапы к пресловутому учреждению (Мандельштам 2). [context transl] Their misfortunes always began with a failure to realize that after their first meeting in a "private apartment," they [people used as informants] would never again escape the clutches of the infamous institution behind it (2a).

Л-22 • (ХОДИ́ТЬ ⟨СТОЯ́ТЬ⟩) НА ЗА́ДНИХ ЛА́ПКАХ ⟨ЛА́ПАХ⟩ перед кем coll, derog [VP or PrepP (these forms only, subj-compl with быть₀); subj: human; the verb may take the final position, otherwise fixed WO] to fawn upon s.o., be obsequious (usu. in order to obtain sth. or out of fear of losing s.o.'s favor): X ходит перед Y-ом на задних лапках ≃ **X dances attendance on Y; X kowtows ⟨plays up⟩ to Y; X bows and scrapes to Y.**

Председатели колхозов на задних лапах перед ним [Егоршей], потому что пёс его знает, что он напоёт хозяину, когда останется с ним с глазу на глаз (Абрамов 1). Kolkhoz chairmen danced attendance upon him [Egorsha] since God knew what he would pass on to the Boss when he was with him eyeball to eyeball (1a).

Л-23 • ГУСИ́НЫЕ ЛА́ПКИ [NP; pl only; fixed WO] wrinkles in a fan-shaped cluster at the outer corners of the eyes: **crow's-feet (around s.o.'s eyes).**

Л-24 • (ПОДНИМА́ТЬ/ПОДНЯ́ТЬ) ЛА́ПКИ КВЕ́РХУ coll [VP or NP (Invar, usu. predic); subj: human; fixed WO] to admit defeat (without putting up any resistance, or already having ceased to resist): X (поднял) лапки кверху ≃ **X threw in the towel ⟨the sponge⟩; X cried uncle; X gave up (the fight); [in limited contexts] X was down for the count; X took it lying down.**

Тебя слегка покритиковали, а ты сразу же лапки кверху? A little criticism and you immediately throw in the towel?

Л-25 • СТАНОВИ́ТЬСЯ/СТАТЬ НА ЗА́ДНИЕ ЛА́ПКИ перед кем coll, disapprov [VP; subj: human; the verb may take the final position, otherwise fixed WO] to begin to take an obsequious attitude toward s.o., fawn upon s.o. (usu. in order to obtain sth.): X становится перед Y-ом на задние лапки ≃ **X begins to dance attendance on Y; X starts kowtowing ⟨playing up⟩ to Y.**

Л-26 • ЛА́ПТЕМ ЩИ ХЛЕБА́ТЬ coll [VP; subj: human; pres or past; fixed WO] to live in ignorance, be backward, uncultured:

X лаптем щи хлебает ≃ **X is a (country) bumpkin; X is a yokel ⟨a hayseed⟩.**

Л-27 • НЕ ЛА́ПТЕМ ЩИ ХЛЕБА́ТЬ coll [VP; subj: human; usu. pres; fixed WO] to understand things as well as others do, be as good, capable as others: X не лаптем щи хлебает ≃ **X knows a thing or two; X wasn't born yesterday; X knows his way around; X isn't just out of the trees; X knows which end is up.**

Воркута стоял в очереди за бандеролью и вот как загнёт в три этажа! Цензор, видно, решил показать, что тоже не лаптем щи хлебает, тоже кое-что умеет — и отозвался ещё похлеще (Марченко 1). He [Vorkuta] was lining up for printed packets when, all of a sudden he let loose a terrific hail of curses. The censor evidently decided to show that he wasn't born yesterday either and also knew a thing or two—and sent back an even bluer reply (1a). ♦ «Мы ведь там у себя [в провинции] тоже не лаптем щи хлебаем. Кое-что сами соображаем» (Зиновьев 2). "You know, even out in the provinces we're not just out of the trees; we're capable of understanding things for ourselves" (2a).

Л-28 • ЛА́ПТИ ПЛЕСТИ́ obs, substand [VP; subj: human] to do sth. clumsily, confusedly, incorrectly: X лапти плетёт ≃ **X makes a mess of it ⟨everything⟩; X does everything backward; X gets everything ⟨it all⟩ mixed up; X botches the job ⟨it, everything⟩ (up).**

Л-29 • НА ЛА́ПУ дать кому, взять и т. п. slang [PrepP; Invar; used as obj] (to give s.o. or accept) a bribe or bribes: X дал Y-у на лапу ≃ **X greased Y's palm;** ‖ X берёт на лапу ≃ **X takes ⟨accepts⟩ bribes; X won't refuse a bribe.**

«Ты... будешь в этой очереди стоять до второго пришествия или до тех пор, пока какому-нибудь нужному человеку на лапу не дашь» (Войнович 1). "You'll be on that waiting list until the Second Coming or until you grease the right person's palm" (1a).

Л-30 • СОСА́ТЬ ЛА́ПУ coll, occas. humor [VP; subj: human; often infin with придётся, должен etc] to eat skimpily due to having little or no means of subsistence: X-у придётся лапу сосать ≃ **X will have to tighten his belt ⟨to go hungry⟩; X will have to go ⟨do⟩ without (food).**

Л-31 • ВЕ́ШАТЬ/ПОВЕ́СИТЬ ⟨НАВЕ́ШИВАТЬ/НАВЕ́СИТЬ⟩ ЛАПШУ́ НА́ УШИ recent, coll [VP; subj: human; more often impfv] to (try to) fool, intentionally mislead s.o. by telling him lies, improbable stories: X вешает Y-у лапшу на уши ≃ **X dupes ⟨tries to dupe, suckers⟩ Y; X strings Y along; X takes Y for a ride; [in limited contexts] X takes Y for a sucker ⟨a fool⟩;** ‖ Neg Imper не вешай мне лапшу на уши ≃ **don't give me that baloney ⟨bull⟩; that's a bunch of baloney ⟨bull⟩.**

Л-32 • (А) ЛА́РЧИК ПРО́СТО ОТКРЫВА́ЛСЯ [sent; past or pres; fixed WO] some seemingly difficult problem turned out to have a simple solution, some seemingly inexplicable phenomenon turned out to have a simple explanation etc: **the explanation ⟨the solution, the answer (to the puzzle)⟩ was quite simple (after all); it was easy ⟨wasn't hard⟩ to figure out; the reason was (all) too obvious.**

«А ларчик просто открывался. Мы по душам говорили сегодня, и она сказала, что я её физически не удовлетворяю. Разрыв ещё не оформлен, на днях, наверное» (Шолохов 2). "The answer to the puzzle was quite simple after all. We had a heart-to-heart talk today and she told me I don't satisfy her physically. The break is not yet official, in a few days probably" (2a). ♦ Не странно ли, что судят тех, кто получил «контрабанду», но даже в свидетели не приглашают тех, кто её перевёз через границу.

Ларчик просто открывался: допроси хоть одного из этих иностранцев – он тут же доказал бы, что деньги разменял в Госбанке СССР, и этот зловещий фарс лопнул бы как мыльный пузырь (Ивинская 1). Was it not odd that those who had received these allegedly smuggled rubles were on trial, while the persons who had brought them across the frontier had not even been called as witnesses? The reason was all too obvious: if any of these foreigners had been questioned, he would immediately have been able to prove that he had obtained the rubles from the State Bank, and the whole wicked farce would have burst like a soap bubble (1a).

< From Ivan Krylov's fable "A Little Box" («Ларчик»), 1808.

Л-33 • ОДНА́ ЛА́СТОЧКА ВЕСНЫ́ НЕ ДЕ́ЛАЕТ [saying] isolated indications or the first signs of some phenomenon do not ensure its beginning or realization: **one swallow does not make a summer ⟨a spring⟩.**

«…Вот уже скоро сорок лет, как я наблюдаю эту тяжёлую болезнь, и впервые не узнал её. Вы совершили чудо. Но одна ласточка не делает весны. Будущее покажет» (Каверин 1). "I've been observing this grave illness for forty years now, and for the first time I've not been able to recognise it. You've performed a miracle. But one swallow doesn't make a summer. The future will show" (1a).

Л-34 • ПЕ́РВАЯ ЛА́СТОЧКА [NP; usu. subj-compl with copula, nom or instrum (subj: human, abstr, or concr); fixed WO] the earliest, very first indication of the approach of sth., the first member of a series to follow: **the first swallow (announcing the summer of sth.); the first sign ⟨the harbinger, the forerunner⟩ (of sth.).**

Рогозин сказал примерно следующее. Классики марксизма, а Ленин в особенности, были полными невеждами в области логики… С факультета Рогозина убрали, но не посадили… Судьба Рогозина… – одна из первых ласточек наступавшей либеральной эпохи (Зиновьев 2). What Rogozin said amounted roughly to this. The classics of Marxism, and Lenin in particular, were complete ignoramuses where logic was concerned.…Rogozin was expelled from the faculty, but left at liberty.…Rogozin's fate was one of the first swallows announcing the summer of the liberal period (2a).

Л-35 • ЛБОМ СТЕ́НУ ⟨СТЕ́НКУ, СТЕНЫ́⟩ НЕ ПРО-ШИБЁШЬ [saying] it is impossible, useless to oppose great force or the authorities (said when a person has to yield to circumstances and accept sth. imposed on him by those in power): ≃ **it's ⟨there's⟩ no use beating your head against a (brick) wall; you can't fight guns with sticks; you can't fight a howitzer with a peashooter.** Cf. **you can't fight city hall.**

Л-36 • НА ЛБУ НАПИ́САНО *у кого coll* [Invar; subj-compl with быть₀ (subj: usu. a clause), usu. pres; fixed WO] (sth., usu. a personality trait or s.o.'s profession, social status etc) is immediately visible, noticeable, apparent from a person's outward appearance: у Х-а на лбу написано ≃ **it's written all over X's face; X has it written all over him; you can tell it just by looking at X.**

[Саша:] Воды не попросит, папиросы не закурит без того, чтобы не показать своей необыкновенной честности. Ходит или говорит, а у самого на лбу написано: я честный человек! (Чехов 4). [S.:] He can't ask for a glass of water or light a cigarette without making a show of his extraordinary honesty. Whether he's talking to you or just walking about, it's written all over his face: I am an honest man (4a).

Л-37 • ОДНО́Й ЛЕ́ВОЙ *highly coll* [NP_{instrum}; Invar; adv; fixed WO] (to do sth.) without difficulty, quite easily: **just like that; without half trying; (be able to do sth.) with one hand tied behind one's back ⟨with one's eyes closed⟩.**

Разве это задача! Я такие задачи одной левой решаю. Some problem! I can solve this kind of thing with one hand tied behind my back.

Л-38 • ЛЕ́ГЧЕ ЛЁГКОГО *coll* [AdjP; Invar; subj-compl with copula (subj: usu. это or infin); fixed WO] it is very easy (to do sth.): это легче лёгкого ≃ **it's as easy ⟨simple⟩ as can be; it's (as) easy as pie ⟨as falling off a log⟩; it's the easiest thing in the world.**

Боясь связываться с вредной старухой, мои экзаменаторы не решились меня провалить, хотя сделать это было легче лёгкого: ведь я не владела искусством перебрасываться с преподавателями вопросами и ответами, словно теннисными мячами, и вполне могла перепутать все съезды… (Мандельштам 1). Afraid of antagonizing the difficult old lady, my examiners hesitated to fail me, though it would have been the easiest thing in the world: I had not mastered the art of bandying question-and-answer, like a tennis ball, with the lecturers, and I was quite capable of mixing up the Party Congresses (1a).

Л-39 • КАК ЛЁД [как + NP; Invar] **1.** (холодный, холоден) ~ [subj-compl with copula (subj: concr, often руки, ноги, пальцы etc) or modif] sth. is extremely cold: **(as) cold as ice; ice-cold; like ice.**

Наконец губы наши сблизились и слились в жаркий, упоительный поцелуй; её руки были холодны как лёд, голова горела (Лермонтов 1). At last our lips came close together and merged in an ardent rapturous kiss; her hands were as cold as ice, her brow was burning (1a).

2. (холоден) ~ [modif or, less often, subj-compl with copula (subj: human)] emotionally indifferent, uncaring: **(as) cold as ice.**

Узнав об отъезде Базарова, Павел Петрович пожелал его видеть и пожал ему руку. Но Базаров и тут остался холоден как лёд; он понимал, что Павлу Петровичу хотелось повеликодушничать (Тургенев 2). On learning that Bazarov was about to depart Pavel Petrovich asked to see him, and shook hands with him. But even now Bazarov remained as cold as ice; he realized that Pavel Petrovich wanted to play the magnanimous (2c).

Л-40 • ЛЁД ТА́ЕТ/РАСТА́ЯЛ [VP_{subj}; fixed WO] a feeling of tension, distrust, estrangement (between people) disappears: **the ice breaks; tension eases ⟨lets up⟩.**

Л-41 • ЛЁД ТРО́НУЛСЯ [VP_{subj}; this form only; usu. used as indep. sent; fixed WO] some long-awaited actions or changes in sth. have begun: **things are ⟨have started etc⟩ moving.**

В продолжение рассказа Остап несколько раз вскакивал и, обращаясь к железной печке, восторженно вскрикивал: «Лёд тронулся, господа присяжные заседатели! Лёд тронулся» (Ильф и Петров 1). During the account, Ostap jumped up several times and, turning to the iron stove, said delightedly: "Things are moving, gentlemen of the jury. Things are moving" (1a).

Л-42 • РАЗБИ́ТЬ ⟨СЛОМА́ТЬ⟩ ЛЁД [VP; subj: human; usu. past; fixed WO] to ease or remove tension, awkwardness, or formality in a social situation (by doing sth. friendly, starting up a friendly conversation etc): X разбил лёд ≃ **X broke the ice.**

Мне пришлось несколько раз встречаться с Цветаевой, но знакомства не получилось… Никто из нас не сумел сказать ни одного человеческого слова или, как говорили в старину, разбить лёд (Мандельштам 2). Though I met Tsvetayeva several times, we never really became friends.…Tsvetayeva and I were unable to say a human word to each other or—as they used to say in the old days—break the ice (2a).

Л-43 • РАСТОПИ́ТЬ ЛЁД [VP; subj: human; fixed WO] to ease tension, awkwardness, or formality (between people): X растопил лёд ≃ **X melted ⟨thawed⟩ the ice.**

[author's usage] Он почти представил, как он, Лёва, найдёт всё-таки, очень постепенно, очень тонко, подход к деду, ключ, растопит лёд обид и горя и, хотя на закате дней, деду улыбнётся любовь и очаг... (Битов 2). He [Lyova] could almost picture it: despite all, very gradually, very subtly, he would find an approach to Grandfather, a key, he would thaw the ice of resentment and woe, and, though in the sunset of his days, love and home would smile on Grandfather... (2a).

Л-44 • ЛЕЖМЯ́ ⟨ЛЁЖНЕМ⟩ ЛЕЖА́ТЬ *substand* [VP; subj: human] to lie (in bed) for a long time doing nothing productive: X лежмя лежит ≃ **X lies ⟨lounges⟩ around in bed (all day long** etc); [of a seriously ill person] **X is flat on his back; X is laid up.**

Л-45 • ЛЕЖА́ЧЕГО НЕ БЬЮТ [saying] mercy is or must be shown toward a person who is in trouble or who is suffering—he should not be caused further trouble: ≃ **(you) don't kick ⟨hit⟩ a man when he's down.**

Конечно, она [Ольга Васильевна] выставила свою досаду совершенно напрасно... Потому что — на него свалилась гора. Лежачего не бьют (Трифонов 3). Of course she [Olga Vasilievna] shouldn't have let her irritation show...because he really was in trouble and you don't hit a man when he's down (3a).

Л-46 • НЕ БЕЙ ЛЕЖА́ЧЕГО *highly coll* [VP_imper; Invar; usu. subj-compl with быть∅ (subj: работа, служба etc); fixed WO] some work is not hard, requires very little effort: работа — не бей лежачего ≃ **this is an easy ⟨a soft, a cushy⟩ job; this job is a piece of cake; this job is no sweat.**

Муж [Сони] — бывший лётчик, в отставке по болезни. Больно ударила его эта отставка, не мог примириться, что не у дел. Устроился по знакомству каким-то регистратором, работа... «не бей лежачего». А ему подавай дело — привычное, кипучее (Грекова 3). Her [Sonya's] husband was a former pilot, retired because of illness. That retirement had him hard. He couldn't live with the fact that he wasn't working. Through connections he got himself a kind of receptionist job, an easy, soft job. But he needed real work, his usual, tough work (3a).

Л-47 • ПЛО́ХО ЛЕЖИ́Т *highly coll* [VP; subj: usu. (всё,) что; usu. pres; used as a subord clause; usu. this WO] sth. is easily accessible and would be easy to appropriate, steal: **(anything) left lying around loose; (anything that) isn't carefully watched; (anything) within reach; (anything that) isn't nailed down.**

Все знали, что я не прочь украсть где что плохо лежит... (Лимонов 1). Everyone knew that I wasn't averse to stealing anything left lying around loose... (1a). ♦ «Помилуйте, да эти черкесы известный воровской народ: что плохо лежит, не могут не стянуть...» (Лермонтов 1). "Well, you see, it is a known fact that these Circassians are a bunch of thieves. They cannot help filching anything that is within reach..." (1a). "Well, you see these Circassians are a notoriously thievish race. They can't keep their hands off anything which isn't carefully watched" (1e).

Л-48 • напиться В ЛЁЖКУ *substand* [PrepP; Invar; adv (intensif)] (to get) very (drunk): **(get) smashed ⟨plastered, blitzed, bombed, sauced, pissed out of one's mind** etc⟩.

Л-49 • ЛЕЖА́ТЬ В ЛЁЖКУ *substand* [VP; subj: human] to be seriously, gravely ill, be confined to bed: X лежит в лёжку ≃ **X is flat on his back; X is laid up.**

Л-50 • УЛОЖИ́ТЬ ⟨ПОВАЛИ́ТЬ⟩ В ЛЁЖКУ *кого substand* [VP; subj: human or a noun denoting a strong alcoholic beverage] to make or get s.o. extremely drunk: X уложил Y-а в лёжку ≃ **X got Y dead drunk; X got Y smashed ⟨bombed, plastered** etc⟩; **person X made Y drink till Y passed out; person X made Y drink himself silly.**

Л-51 • (все, каждый) КОМУ́ (ТО́ЛЬКО) НЕ ЛЕНЬ *coll, occas. disapprov* [NP; these forms only; usu. nonagreeing modif (if все or каждый is ellipted, it is implied); fixed WO] any and every person who has the desire (to do sth.): **anyone ⟨everyone⟩ who feels like it; anyone ⟨everyone⟩ who wishes;** [in limited contexts] **just about everyone.**

Да, вот так быть за председателя колхоза, когда ты в то же время и главный подвозчик дров, и сена, и чёрт знает ещё чего. Каждый, кому не лень, глотку на тебя дерёт (Абрамов 1). Yes, that's what it was like to be acting *kolkhoz* Chairman when you were also the chief source of firewood and hay and heaven knows what else. Anyone who felt like it would give you a bawling out (1a). ♦ «Сколько уж тех раёв людям сулили, все кому не лень...» (Кузнецов 1). "How many times have people been promised Heaven on earth, by just about everyone!" (1a).

Л-52 • ДЕ́ТСКИЙ ⟨МЛАДЕ́НЧЕСКИЙ, РЕБЯ́ЧЕСКИЙ⟩ ЛЕ́ПЕТ *rather derog* [NP; sing only; subj-compl with copula (subj: usu. abstr)] naïve, immature, superficial ideas, writings etc: **childish prattle ⟨babbling⟩; infantile prattling.**

«Самые отважные дерзания Рембо — ребячий лепет по сравнению с тем, что делает Хлебников...» (Лившиц 1). "Rimbaud's most brazen audacities are like infantile prattling in comparison with what Khlebnikov is doing" (1a).

Л-53 • РАЗБИВА́ТЬСЯ/РАЗБИ́ТЬСЯ ⟨РАСШИ-БА́ТЬСЯ/РАСШИБИ́ТЬСЯ⟩ В ЛЕПЁШКУ *highly coll* [VP; subj: human; most often pfv fut] to make every effort, do everything possible to achieve sth. (or for s.o.'s sake): X в лепёшку разобьётся ≃ **X will do whatever it takes (to achieve sth.); X will knock himself out; X will bend over backward; X will go out of his way.**

Л-54 • ВНОСИ́ТЬ/ВНЕСТИ́ СВОЮ́ ЛЕ́ПТУ *во что rather elev; often humor in contempt. usage* [VP; subj: human] to do one's part in a shared effort: X внёс свою лепту в Y ≃ **X did his bit (for Y); X added ⟨contributed⟩ his mite to Y; X contributed his (small) share to Y; X made a ⟨his⟩ contribution to Y;** [in refer. to participation in a discussion etc] **X put in his two cents worth.**

Председатель Голубев сидел сейчас в кабинете и вносил свою лепту в общее большое бумажное дело (Войнович 2). At that very moment Golubev was sitting in his office doing his bit for the great cause of paper work (2a). ♦ «Как строители древних соборов, люди разных стран внесут свою лепту в дело созидания новой, лучшей Европы» (Эренбург 4). "Like the builders of the ancient cathedrals, the people of the various countries add their mite to the work of creating a new and a better Europe" (4a). ♦ Их уже не встретишь на Невском, тех пионеров... Их раскидало и расшвыряло, и они — выросли. Больше или меньше, но вносят они какой-нибудь службой лепту и в сегодняшний день (Битов 2). You won't encounter them on the Nevsky anymore, those pioneers... They were routed and sent flying—and they grew up. Whether more or less, they contribute their mite by some sort of service to the modern day as well (2a).

Л-55 • КТО В ЛЕС, КТО ПО ДРОВА́ [Invar; adv or indep. clause; fixed WO] (often in refer. to singing and playing musical instruments) (people do sth.) without coordination among themselves, without agreement, cooperation: **everyone doing his own thing; (all) at sixes and sevens;** [in limited contexts] **at cross-purposes; out of sync.**

«Ну-с...как бы вам описать эту симфонию наиболее популярно? Попробую. Итак, „ударили в смычки". Кто в лес, кто по дрова» (Катаев 3). "Now then—how shall I explain this symphony in the most popular manner? I shall try. Off go the violins! All at sixes and sevens" (3a).

Л-56 • ЛЕС ⟨ДРОВА́⟩ РУ́БЯТ – ЩЕ́ПКИ ЛЕТЯ́Т [saying] a major undertaking cannot be accomplished without errors, casualties etc (often used to justify the cost paid in lives during political purges etc): ≃ **you cannot make an omelet without breaking eggs; if you hew trees the chips must fly.**

Ведь именно люди двадцатых годов разрушили ценности и нашли формулы, без которых не обойтись и сейчас: молодое государство, невиданный опыт, лес рубят – щепки летят... Каждая казнь оправдывалась тем, что строят мир, где больше не будет насилия, и все жертвы хороши ради неслыханного «нового» (Мандельштам 1). It was, after all, these people of the twenties who demolished the old values and invented the formulas which even now come in so handy to justify the unprecedented experiment undertaken by our young State: you can't make an omelet without breaking eggs. Every new killing was excused on the grounds that we were building a remarkable "new" world in which there would be no more violence, and that no sacrifice was too great for it (1a). ♦ Одно распоряжение, которое... в этот доклад сделал Кутузов, относилось до мародёрства русских войск... «Пускай косят хлеба и жгут дрова на здоровье. Я этого не приказываю и не позволяю, но и взыскать не могу. Без этого нельзя. Дрова рубят – щепки летят» (Толстой 6). The only instructions he [Kutuzov]...added to the report concerned the looting by Russian troops....''Let them [the soldiers] cut down crops and burn wood to their heart's content! I do not order it, I do not permit it, but neither can I enforce punishment for it. It cannot be helped. If you hew trees the chips must fly'' (6a).

Л-57 • СМОТРЕ́ТЬ ⟨ГЛЯДЕ́ТЬ⟩ В ЛЕС coll [VP; subj: human; usu. pres] to long to leave one's residence or job because it has become tiresome: X в лес смотрит ≃ **X is looking for greener pastures; X can't ⟨can hardly⟩ wait to get out (of somewhere); X wants to split ⟨cut out⟩; X wants out.**

Л-58 • ТЁМНЫЙ ⟨ДРЕМУ́ЧИЙ⟩ ЛЕС для кого coll [NP; sing only; subj-compl with быть∅ (subj: abstr); may be used with pl subject; fixed WO] sth. is completely unfamiliar or totally incomprehensible (to s.o.): X для Y-а – тёмный лес ≃ **Y is completely in the dark (about X); X is Greek to Y; Y doesn't have a clue (about X).**

«Улики показывают, что в Новосибирске Степнадзе был, однако чем здесь занимался, пока – тёмный лес...» (Чернёнок 2). ''The evidence indicates that Stepnadze was in Novosibirsk. However, we haven't a clue as to what he was doing here...'' (2a).

Л-59 • ЧЕМ ДА́ЛЬШЕ В ЛЕС, ТЕМ БО́ЛЬШЕ ДРОВ [saying] the further events progress, the more unexpected difficulties and complications arise: ≃ **the further you get, the harder the going; things go from bad to worse.**

«Попервости-то [substand = сначала] было выговор объявили, а потом – дальше в лес, больше дров» (Гинзбург 1). ''First I got a reprimand, and then things went from bad to worse'' (1b).

Л-60 • СПУСКА́ТЬ/СПУСТИ́ТЬ С ЛЕ́СТНИЦЫ кого coll [VP; subj: human; usu. pfv] to force s.o. to leave one's house: X спустил Y-а с лестницы ≃ **X kicked ⟨threw, booted⟩ Y out of the house; X threw Y out (on his ear); [in limited contexts] X gave Y the bum's rush.**

[Нина:] Тебя надо гнать из дома... Тебя надо с лестницы спустить! (Вампилов 4). [N.:] You should be kicked out of the house...you ought to be thrown out on your ear! (4c).

Л-61 • КАК В (ТЁМНОМ) ЛЕСУ́ coll [как + PrepP; these forms only; subj-compl with copula (subj: human)] one is completely lacking in comprehension or understanding of sth.: X как в тёмном лесу ≃ **X is completely in the dark; X is all ⟨completely⟩ at sea; X is totally lost.**

Сочинения [Кирилл] писал посредственно, почерк ужасен, в математике соображал слабо... Английский язык? Ну, разве что. В детстве силой заставляли ходить в английскую группу... Но ведь только лексика, а в грамматике – как в лесу (Трифонов 5). His [Kirill's] school compositions were mediocre, his handwriting abominable, and he was weak in math....His knowledge of English? Well, that at least was something. When he was a child we had forced him to join an English language group....But even so, all he had was a large vocabulary. When it came to grammar, he was completely in the dark (5a). ♦ «Выслушайте же до конца, но только не умом: я боюсь вашего ума; сердцем лучше: может быть, оно рассудит, что у меня нет матери, что я была как в лесу...» (Гончаров 1). ''Hear me out, then, but not with your intellect – I'm afraid of your intellect – better with your heart; perhaps it will realize that I have no mother, that I was completely at sea...'' (1a).

Л-62 • СКО́ЛЬКО ЛЕТ, СКО́ЛЬКО ЗИМ! coll [formula phrase; Invar; fixed WO] (used upon meeting s.o. one has not seen for an extended period of time) we have not seen each other for a long time: **it's been ages!; it's (been) ages since I last saw you!; I haven't seen you for ages ⟨in a dog's age⟩!; (it's) been a long time, hasn't it?; long time no see.**

Лица, предназначенные для целования, движутся навстречу друг другу, изображая на лице нечто такое, что в великой ибанской [nonce word] литературе передаётся возгласом: ба, кого я вижу! Сколько лет, сколько зим!! Вот не чаял встретиться!!! (Зиновьев 1). The persons appointed to perform the kiss approach each other, their faces bearing an expression which in great Ibanskian literature is interpreted as ''Look who's here! It's ages since I last saw you! What a wonderful surprise!!!'' (1a). ♦ «Сергеич!..»... – «Сколько лет, сколько зим!» – «Вот гостя тебе из Москвы привёз» (Максимов 1). ''Sergeich!...''...''Haven't seen you out here for ages!'' ''I've brought you a visitor from Moscow'' (1a). ♦ [Подхалюзин:] А! Устинья Наумовна! Сколько лет, сколько зим-с! (Островский 10). [P.:] Ah, Ustinya Naumovna! Been a long time, hasn't it, ma'am? (10a). ♦ «Ты попробуй, зайди [в редакцию] часа в два». Я зашёл в два. «А! – закричал В.Б., – сколько лет, сколько зим!.. Пишите сейчас же рецензию!» (Довлатов 1). ''Try him [the editor] again, only this time drop by around two.'' And so I did. ''Aha!'' V.B. cried, ''Long time, no see!...Write your review right away!'' (1a).

Л-63 • СРЕ́ДНИХ ЛЕТ [NP_gen; Invar; nonagreeing modif or subj-compl with copula (subj: human); fixed WO] (a person who is) not young, but not yet old: **middle-aged.**

...Герой наш уже был средних лет и осмотрительно-охлаждённого характера (Гоголь 3). ...Our hero was already middle-aged and of cautious, tempered character (3d).

Л-64 • МНО́ГАЯ ⟨МНО́ГИЕ⟩ ЛЕ́ТА (желать кому) obs [NP; these forms only; usu. obj or indep. sent; fixed WO] (to wish s.o.) a long life and much happiness: **may you ⟨he etc⟩ have a long (and happy) life.**

< From a liturgical chant in the Russian Orthodox church.

Л-65 • ВЫСОКО́ ЛЕТА́ТЬ coll [VP; subj: human; usu. this WO] **1.** to occupy a prominent position in society: X высоко летает ≃ **X is flying ⟨riding⟩ high; X has made it big; X is a big shot.**

2. to behave arrogantly, have an excessively high opinion of o.s.: X высоко летает ≃ **X thinks that he is too good for everyone; X has a swelled head; X is full of himself.**

Л-66 • БА́БЬЕ ЛЕ́ТО [NP; sing only; fixed WO] warm days in early autumn: **Indian summer.**

Ноябрь был на редкость тёплый, настоящее бабье лето (Горенштейн 1). November was exceptionally warm, a real Indian summer (1a).

Л-67 • ЖИВА́Я ЛЕ́ТОПИСЬ *чего* [NP; sing only; often subj-compl with быть∅, считаться etc, nom or instrum (subj: human); fixed WO] a person who can clearly recall all the events that happened during his lifetime: **a living chronicle ⟨history book⟩.**

...Главным украшением прощального обеда должен был служить столетний старец Максим Гаврилыч Крестовоздвиженский... Идея пригласить к участию в празднике эту живую летопись нашего города, этого свидетеля его величия и славы, была весьма замечательна... (Салтыков-Щедрин 2). The chief ornament of the farewell dinner...was to be our centenarian Maxim Gavrilovich Krestovozdvizhensky....The idea of inviting this living chronicle of our town, this witness of its greatness and glory, to our celebration was indeed a most brilliant one... (2a).

Л-68 • КА́НУТЬ В ЛЕ́ТУ ⟨В РЕ́КУ ЗАБВЕ́НИЯ *obs*⟩ *lit* [VP; subj: abstr or human; fixed WO] to disappear completely, be forgotten forever: X канул в Лету ≃ **X was swallowed up by Lethe ⟨in the river of oblivion⟩; X sank into oblivion.**

«Так, понимаете, и слухи о капитане Копейкине канули в реку забвения, в какую-нибудь эдакую Лету, как называют поэты» (Гоголь 3). "It was thus, you understand, that the rumours about Captain Kopeikin were swallowed up in the river of oblivion, in this—er—Lethe, as the poets call it" (3a).

< From *Lethe* («Лета»), the name of a river in Hades. In classical mythology, those who drank the water of Lethe—also called "the river of oblivion" («река забвения»)—forgot the past.

Л-69 • ЛОВИ́ТЬ НА ЛЕТУ́ *что* [VP; subj: human; pres or past] **1.** Also: **СХВА́ТЫВАТЬ ⟨ХВАТА́ТЬ⟩ НА ЛЕТУ́ ⟨С ЛЁТУ⟩; ЛОВИ́ТЬ С ЛЁТУ** [obj: usu. всё, мысль etc; pres or past] to (be able to) understand, assimilate sth. (another's thoughts, ideas etc) quickly and easily: X ловит всё на лету ≃ **X picks things up quickly; X is quick to grasp things; X is quick to catch on (to things); X is quick on the uptake;** [in limited contexts] **X catches ⟨seizes⟩ everything on the wing.**

Итак, в дом ходит учитель Курас, у Иосифа есть способности, он всё схватывает на лету... (Рыбаков 1). So, the teacher [Kuras] would come to the house. Yosif was capable and picked things up quickly... (1a). ♦ Павел Николаевич... рад, что дочь выросла намного развитей его самого — опыта у неё недостаточно, но как же она всё на лету схватывает! (Солженицын 10). Pavel Nikolayevich was...glad that his daughter had grown up far more educated than himself. She hadn't had much experience yet, but she was so quick to catch on! (10a). ♦ Судя по тому, что Миха на лету ухватил мысль дяди Сандро, можно заключить, что он быстро одолел свою социальную тугоухость... (Искандер 3). Judging from the way Mikha seized Uncle Sandro's thought on the wing, we may conclude that he had quickly overcome his social deafness... (3a).

2. [obj: usu. слова, указания etc] to listen very attentively, trying to let nothing slip by: X ловит Y-овы слова ⟨каждое Y-ово слово⟩ на лету ≃ **X catches everything Y says; X hangs on Y's every word; X (makes sure he) doesn't miss what ⟨a single word that⟩ Y says.**

Дудырев привык к уважению в районе, к тому, что его слово ловят на лету (Тендряков 1). Dudyrev was used to respect in the district and to people hanging on his every word (1a).

Л-70 • НА ЛЕТУ́ [PrepP; Invar] **1.** [adv] during flight, while sth. or s.o. is still in the air: **on the fly; on the wing; in midair; in mid flight.**

Началось кормление. Александр Петрович вынул из сачка крупную ставриду и бросил её пеликану. Разинув свой чудовищный клюв, пеликан... на лету подхватил добычу (Искандер 3). The feeding began. Alexander Petrovich took a large horse mackerel from the net and threw it to the pelican. Opening its monstrous bill, the pelican caught it adroitly on the fly... (3a). ♦ Доктор ещё раз брезгливо оглядел комнату и сбросил с себя шубу... Штабс-капитан подхватил на лету шубу, а доктор снял фуражку (Достоевский 1). The doctor once again looked squeamishly around the room and threw off his fur coat....The captain caught the coat in midair, and the doctor took off his hat (1a).

2. [usu. adv or nonagreeing modif] (to do sth., sth. is carried out) in a hurried fashion (often during a brief encounter): **hurriedly; in a rush; for a brief moment; a quick ⟨brief, fleeting⟩** [NP].

Странное, необычное то было лето... Была радость у людей. Были свадьбы и скороспелая любовь на лету. И были плачи великие. От земли до неба. По тем, кто не вернулся с войны... (Абрамов 1). A strange, an unusual summer it was....There was rejoicing among the people. There were weddings and there were rushed, fleeting romances. And there was great weeping. From earth to heaven on high. For the ones who did not come home from the war (1a).

Л-71 • ДАТЬ ⟨ПОДДА́ТЬ⟩ ЛЕЩА́ *кому substand* [VP; subj: human] to strike or shove s.o. forcefully: X дал Y-у леща ≃ **X landed a good one; X smacked Y (but) good; X gave Y a swift kick.**

Л-72 • (как) ВЫ́ЖАТЫЙ ЛИМО́Н *coll* [NP; sing only; usu. subj-compl with быть∅ (subj: human)] **1.** a very tired, physically exhausted person: X как выжатый лимон ≃ **X is beat ⟨dead tired, done in, all in⟩; X is (as) limp as a (dish)rag.**

Дай маме отдохнуть — она как выжатый лимон. Let Mom rest—she's dead tired.

2. a person who has exhausted his creative talent: X выжатый лимон ≃ **X's creative juices have been sapped; X's creative energy has been spent; X is all washed-up; X is a has-been;** [of a writer, playwright etc] **X has written himself out.**

Л-73 • ИДТИ́/ПОЙТИ́ ПО ЛИ́НИИ ⟨ПО ПУТИ́⟩ НАИМЕ́НЬШЕГО СОПРОТИВЛЕ́НИЯ [VP; subj: human; the verb may take the final position, otherwise fixed WO] to choose the easiest course of action, avoiding difficulties, trouble: X идёт по линии наименьшего сопротивления ≃ **X takes ⟨follows, chooses⟩ the line ⟨the path, the course⟩ of least resistance.**

Л-74 • ПО ЛИ́НИИ *чего, какой* [PrepP; Invar; Prep; the resulting PrepP is adv or modif] **1.** in the sphere of sth.: **in the area ⟨field⟩ of; in relation to; along** [AdjP] **lines; as far as sth. is concerned; with regard ⟨respect⟩ to.**

По линии строительства у нас уже многое сделано. In the area of construction we have accomplished a great deal. ♦ Лёва не старался выдвинуться по общественной линии, т. е. избежал общественной работы, что в принципе просто соответствовало его склонности... (Битов 2). Lyova did not try to advance himself at the institute along social lines; i.e., he avoided community work, a policy that basically just suited his own inclination... (2a). ♦ ...Стоило бы ей [Ирине Викторовне] дать малейший повод, как тот же Строковский очень и очень заинтересовался бы ею не только по служебной линии (Залыгин 1). [context transl] ...If she [Irina Viktorovna] gave him the slightest encouragement Strokovsky himself would take a very lively interest in her, and not just a professional interest (1a). ♦ [Аким:] И вновь у тебя приличная жена и хорошая квартира. И по служебной линии всё в ажуре (Арбузов 3). [context transl] [A.:] Once again, you have a decent wife and a good flat. At work you're on velvet (3a).

2. in some organizations, organs: **in; by; through.**

Такие вопросы должны решаться по линии министерства. Such matters should be decided by the ministry.

Л-75 • ГНУТЬ СВОЮ́ ЛИ́НИЮ ⟨ГНУТЬ СВОЁ⟩ *coll;* **ВЕСТИ́ СВОЮ́ ЛИ́НИЮ** [VP; subj: human] to be extremely persistent in defending or maintaining one's position (in an argument or discussion), in insisting that one get what one wants (despite another's resistance), or in carrying out one's chosen line of action (despite some opposition): X гнул свою линию ≃ **X held ⟨stood⟩ his ground; X stuck to his guns; X stood firm ⟨fast⟩.**

...Александра Прокофьевна упорно гнула своё: «Нет, ваши доводы я нахожу несостоятельными» (Трифонов 3). ...Alexandra Prokofievna obstinately stuck to her guns. "No, I find your arguments unconvincing" (3a).

Л-76 • ОБДИРА́ТЬ/ОБОДРА́ТЬ ⟨ОБИРА́ТЬ/ОБОБРА́ТЬ, ОБЧИ́СТИТЬ, ОБЛУПИ́ТЬ⟩ КАК ЛИ́ПКУ *кого coll* [VP; subj: human; most often pfv] to ruin s.o. financially, rob s.o., take everything from s.o.: X ободрал Y-а как липку ≃ **X fleeced Y; X cleaned Y out; X took Y to the cleaners.**

В деревне же этот самый товарообмен шёл куда веселее, чем в городе, где человека обдирали как липку всяческие посредники, спекулянты и барышники... (Катаев 3). In the countryside this barter was much more lively than in the city, where people were mercilessly fleeced by all sorts of middlemen, profiteers and speculators... (3a).

Л-77 • ЛИСА́ ПАТРИКЕ́ЕВНА *coll, disapprov* [usu. sing; commonly used as vocative; both words capitalized] a sly flatterer (more often a woman): **sly fox ⟨devil⟩; crafty devil; slyboots.**

< The name of the fox in Russian folk tales.

Л-78 • КАК ⟨БУ́ДТО, СЛО́ВНО, ТО́ЧНО⟩ БА́ННЫЙ ЛИСТ пристать, привязаться, прилипнуть *(к кому) coll, disapprov* [как etc + NP; these forms only; adv (intensif); usu. used with pfv verbs; fixed WO] (to pester s.o., impose one's presence on s.o.) extremely irksomely, annoyingly, and unceasingly: **leech on to s.o.; be like a leech; be a regular pest.**

Л-79 • КАК (ОСИ́НОВЫЙ) ЛИСТ дрожать, трястись *coll* [как + NP; these forms only; adv (intensif); fixed WO] (to tremble) violently (out of fear, anxiety, from the cold etc): **(tremble ⟨shake, shake all over⟩) like a leaf.**

«„Это лошадь отца моего", — сказала Бэла, схватив меня за руку; она дрожала как лист...» (Лермонтов 1). "'That is my father's horse,' said Bela, clutching my arm; she was trembling like a leaf..." (1d). ♦ Она [Марья Кондратьевна] была как помешанная, передавал Алёша, и вся дрожала как лист (Достоевский 2). She [Maria Kondratievna] looked crazy, Alyosha went on, and was shaking all over like a leaf (2a).

Л-80 • С ЛИСТА́ играть, петь, переводить и т. п. [PrepP; Invar; adv] (to play, sing, translate etc) without previous rehearsal or study of the material: **on ⟨at⟩ sight;** ‖ чтение с листа ≃ **sight-reading;** ‖ перевод с листа ≃ **sight translation.**

Л-81 • ФИ́ГОВЫЙ ЛИСТО́К ⟨ЛИСТО́ЧЕК⟩ *lit* [NP; sing only; fixed WO] sth. meant to conceal what is considered unacceptable, shameful, unflattering etc: **fig leaf.**

Яша... пришивал ко всем отчётам фиговые листки оценок (Грекова 2). To every report he [Yasha] pins a fig leaf of evaluations (2a).

< From the Biblical account of how Adam and Eve made "aprons" from fig leaves to cover themselves after eating the forbidden fruit and realizing that they were naked (Gen. 3:7).

Л-82 • С ЛИХВО́Й вернуть, возместить *кому что*, окупиться и т. п. [PrepP; Invar; adv] with a surplus: **(pay s.o. back) with interest; (make sth. up to s.o.) handsomely; more**

than (makes up for etc sth.); [in limited contexts] **(pay s.o. back) with a vengeance.**

«Спасибо, ребята, — растроганно сказал Пантелей. — Вижу, что фронтовики... не забуду... верну с лихвой...» (Аксёнов 6). "Thanks, lads," said Pantelei, touched by such generosity. "I can see you're old frontline soldiers...won't forget. I'll pay it back with interest..." (6a). ♦ Эти нападения, конечно, могут выродиться в крайность, но ничего! — десятки жертв окупятся с лихвой, зато мы получим сотни опытных бойцов!.. (Солженицын 5). These attacks, of course, may degenerate into reckless extremism, but never mind! A few dozen casualties will be handsomely made up for if the party gains hundreds of experienced fighters (5a). ♦ «...Ужасные мучения, которые он [Чернышевский] переносил ради идеи, ради человечества, ради России, с лихвой искупают некоторую чёрствость и прямолинейность его критических взглядов» (Набоков 1). "...The fact that he [Chernyshevski] endured dreadful sufferings for the sake of his ideology, for the sake of humanity, for the sake of Russia, more than redeems a certain harshness and rigidity in his critical views" (1a).

Л-83 • НЕ ПОМИНА́Й(ТЕ) (меня ⟨нас⟩) ЛИ́ХОМ *coll* [VP$_{imper}$; usu. used as formula phrase; fixed WO] (usu. used as a request or wish made when parting with s.o. for an extended period of time) do not remember me (or us) badly: **don't think ill ⟨badly⟩ of me ⟨us⟩; remember me ⟨us⟩ kindly; think kindly of me ⟨us⟩.**

На другой день Аксинья, получив расчёт, собрала пожитки. Прощаясь с Евгением, всплакнула: «Не поминайте лихом, Евгений Николаевич» (Шолохов 4). The next day Aksinya was paid off and packed up her belongings. She gave a sob as she said goodbye to Yevgeny. "Don't think ill of me, Yevgeny Nikolayevich" (4a). ♦ [Маша:] Ну-с, позвольте пожелать вам всего хорошего. Не поминайте лихом (Чехов 6). [M.:] Well, I wish you all the best. Don't think badly of me (6a). ♦ «Я вашей работой доволен. И вы не поминайте нас лихом» (Рыбаков 1). "I've been very satisfied with your work. Remember us kindly" (1a). ♦ «Готово? Идём! — всполохнулся Митя. — ...Прощай, Пётр Ильич, не поминай лихом» (Достоевский 1). "Ready? Let's go!" Mitya got into a flutter. "...Farewell, Pyotr Ilyich, think kindly of me" (1a).

Л-84 • ЛИЦА́ НЕТ *на ком coll* [VP$_{subj/gen}$; pres or past] s.o. has become very pale, the expression on s.o.'s face has changed (usu. from extreme anxiety, fear etc): на X-е лица нет ≃ **X looks awful ⟨terrible, ghastly, terribly upset etc⟩; X is (as) pale ⟨white⟩ as a ghost; X is (as) white as a sheet; X is (as) pale as death; X doesn't look himself; X looks like death warmed over;** [usu. as a result of extreme fatigue] **X looks washed-out.**

[Косых:] Доктор, что это вы сегодня такой бледный? На вас лица нет (Чехов 4). [K.:] Doctor, why are you so pale today? You look awful (4a). [K.:] Why so pale today, Doctor? You look ghastly (4b). ♦ ...Лица на нём нет, сильно болен... (Солженицын 2). ...He looked terrible, he was very ill... (2a). ♦ Рассказывали, что на Никаноре Ивановиче лица не было, что он пошатывался, проходя, как пьяный, и что-то бормотал (Булгаков 9). It was said that Nikanor Ivanovich was pale as a ghost, that he swayed like a drunkard, and mumbled something indistinct (9a). ♦ И тут же появилась Фаина, и на ней не было лица. «Что с тобой?!» — воскликнул Лёва... (Битов 2). Faina reappeared instantly, pale as death. "What's the matter?" Lyova exclaimed... (2a). ♦ «Садчиков, я повторил тебе уже три раза — выполняй мои предписания... А потом отоспись — на тебе лица нет» (Семёнов 1). "Sadchikov, I've told you three times already—carry out your instructions....And then get some sleep, you look washed-out" (1a).

Л-85 • НЕВЗИРА́Я НА ЛИ́ЦА [PrepP; Invar; adv] without taking into consideration or being influenced by s.o.'s high position, title, social status etc: **without regard for rank; irrespective of rank; no matter who (s.o. is).**

Александр Петрович знал, что его при дворе считают чудаком за то, что он всегда, невзирая на лица, со всей откровенностью верноподданного высказывал свои мысли о средствах к спасению царя и государства российского (Искандер 3). He [Alexander Petrovich] knew that he was considered a crank at court because he always—without regard for rank, with all the candor of a loyal subject—spoke his thoughts on ways to save the czar and the Russian state (3a). ♦ «У нас лозунг: лифт для всех. Невзирая на лица» (Стругацкие 3). "Our slogan is 'elevators for everyone.' No matter who" (3a).

Л-86 • С ЛИЦА́ НЕ ВО́ДУ ПИТЬ [saying] physical attractiveness is not important (usu. said when choosing a plain-looking husband or wife): ≃ **beauty is only skin-deep; handsome is as handsome does; pretty is as pretty does; looks aren't everything.**

Муж у неё добрый, покладистый, а что некрасивый — так ведь с лица не воду пить. Her husband is kind and obliging. So what if he's unattractive—looks aren't everything.

Л-87 • СПАСТЬ С ЛИЦА́ *substand* [VP; subj: human; usu. past] to become thin in the face: X спал с лица ≃ **X's face became haggard ⟨drawn⟩; X's face looked pinched.**

Дети боранлинцев изнывали, томились, с лица спали, и некуда их было упрятать от духоты и изнуряющего зноя (Айтматов 2). The children at Boranly were miserable and tired, their faces drawn, and there was nowhere for them to escape from the oppressive, exhausting heat (2a).

Л-88 • СТЕРЕ́ТЬ ⟨СМЕСТИ́, СНЕСТИ́⟩ С ЛИЦА́ ЗЕМЛИ́ [VP; subj: human or collect; the verb may take the final position, otherwise fixed WO] **1.** ~ *что* to annihilate, destroy sth. completely, so that nothing is left of it: Х-ы стёрли Y с лица земли ≃ **Xs wiped Y off ⟨swept Y from⟩ the face of the earth; Xs wiped Y off the map; Xs razed Y to the ground; Xs blotted Y out.**

Это было маленькое и короткое по времени гетто. О нём не сохранилось письменных свидетельств, оно не фигурирует в официальных документах, просто оно было стёрто с лица земли (Рыбаков 1). It [the ghetto] was a little one, and it was shortlived. No written accounts of it have survived, it doesn't figure in official documents, it was simply wiped off the face of the earth (1a). ♦ ...Ратабон явился с великолепным и полностью разработанным проектом перестройки Лувра, причём для успешного хода этой работы необходимо снести с лица земли не только Малый Бурбон, но и прилегающую к нему церковь Сен-Жермен д'Оксерруа. Пол закачался под ногами у Мольера. «Значит, мы без предупреждения остаёмся на улице?» — спросил Мольер (Булгаков 5). ...Ratabon had come with a magnificent and fully detailed plan for the rebuilding of the Louvre, which required not only that the Petit Bourbon, but also the church of Saint-Germain-l'Auxerrois which adjoined it, be razed to the ground. The floor rocked under Molière's feet. "So we're being thrown out into the street without warning?" he asked (5a).

2. ~ *кого* to kill s.o. or exterminate some group of people: X сотрёт Y-a с лица земли ≃ **X will wipe Y off the face of the earth; X will do away with Y; X will rub out Y.**

Газеты были полны сообщениями о вредителях, саботажниках, уклонистах. «...Беспощадно карать!.. Стереть с лица земли!» (Рыбаков 2). The newspapers were full of attacks on wreckers and saboteurs and deviationists. "...Punish them mercilessly!...Wipe them off the face of the earth!" (2a). ♦ ...Казённые крестьяне сельца Вшивая-спесь... снесли с лица земли будто бы земскую полицию в лице заседателя, какого-то Дробяжкина... (Гоголь 3). The crown serfs of the hamlet of Vshivaya Spes' ["Lousy Pride"]...seemed to have done away with the local policemen in the person of a certain Drobiashkin, an assessor by rank... (3c).

Л-89 • В ЛИ́ЦАХ рассказывать, изображать *кого-что* и т. п. [PrepP; Invar; adv] (to tell about sth.) expressively, portraying s.o.'s manner of behavior and/or speech: [the idiom is translated together with the verb] **act sth. out; mimic ⟨imitate⟩ how ⟨the way⟩ s.o. speaks ⟨does sth.⟩.**

...Офицеры начинали хором петь песенку о начальнике станции... Офицеры разыгрывали эту песенку в лицах. Особенно хорош был пожилой полковник — «колонель» — с жёлтой бородкой, изображавший разъярённого начальника станции (Паустовский 1). ...The officers would begin to sing in chorus a song about a stationmaster....The officers acted out this song. The best of them all was an elderly colonel with a yellow beard who played the part of the infuriated stationmaster (1b). ♦ ...[Я] весело его [Эренбурга] высмеивала, изображая в лицах, как он меня поучает (Мандельштам 2). ...[I] made fun of him [Ehrenburg] to the others, mimicking the way he had tried to lecture me (2a).

Л-90 • В ЛИЦЕ́ *чьём, кого* [PrepP; Invar; Prep] as personified or represented by (s.o.): **in the person of; in s.o.'s person; in (s.o.); [in limited contexts] through (s.o.); in the form of.**

«Нашему доброму и чудному государю предстоит величайшая роль в мире... и он исполнит своё призвание задавить гидру революции, которая теперь ещё ужаснее в лице этого убийцы и злодея» (Толстой 4). "Our good and sublime sovereign is faced with undertaking the greatest role on earth...and he will fulfill his mission and crush the Hydra of revolution, which has become more dreadful than ever in the person of this assassin and miscreant" (4a). ♦ ...В лице Чернышевского был осуждён его — очень похожий — призрак; вымышленную вину чудно подгримировали под настоящую (Набоков 1). ...In Chernyshevski's person they condemned a phantasm closely resembling him; an invented guilt was wonderfully rigged up to look like the real one (1a). ♦ Я поступлю в институт и стану потом инженером или учителем. Но в моём лице люди потеряют великого путешественника (Казаков 2). All right, I'd finish the tenth class and enter the institute and become an engineer or a teacher. But in me they were losing a great explorer (2a). ♦ Сильвестр покачал головой. В его лице вся мировая джазовая общественность укоряла беспутного Саблера (Аксёнов 6). Silvester shook his head. Through him, jazz fans all over the world rebuked Sabler for his debauchery (6a). ♦ ...Первым делом надо было Вику прописать... Как ни облучала Вера [обаянием] начальника паспортного стола — не помогало. Письмо народной артистки Куниной тоже оказалось пустым номером. Пришлось вывести на позиции тяжёлую артиллерию в лице «очень ответственного» из номера люкс... (Грекова 3). ...First of all Vika had to be registered in her [Vera's] house....No matter how Vera sparkled at the director of the passport bureau it didn't help. A letter from People's Artist Kunina also didn't do the trick. She had to make use of heavy artillery in the form of a very important person staying in one of the luxury suites (3a). ♦ «...Вы его [сержанта] оскорбляете, называя идиотом. В его лице вы оскорбляете и те органы, которые он собой представляет (Войнович 2). [context transl] "...You insult him [the sergeant] by calling him an idiot. And when you insult him, you also insult those agencies which he represents" (2a).

Л-91 • ИЗМЕНИ́ТЬСЯ ⟨ПЕРЕМЕНИ́ТЬСЯ⟩ В ЛИЦЕ́ [VP; subj: human; usu. past; usu. this WO] **1.** Also: **МЕНЯ́ТЬСЯ В ЛИЦЕ́** to change the look on one's face quickly under the influence of some emotion: X изменился в лице ≃ **X changed his expression; X changed color; the expression on X's face changed; a (complete) change came over X's face ⟨expression⟩; X ⟨X's face⟩ turned ⟨went⟩ pale; ‖ Neg** X не изменился в лице ≃ **X's face betrayed no emotion.**

...Там, где наш брат призадумается и отшарахнется, он улыбнётся, не переменится в лице, не повысит голоса и — пойдёт далее без раскаяния и сомнения (Герцен 2). ...Where people like us would hesitate and shy away, he would smile and, without changing his expression or raising his voice, go forward remorseless and undoubting (2a). ♦ «Ты лжёшь, мерзавец! — вскричал я в бешенстве, — ты лжёшь самым бесстыдным образом». Швабрин переменился в лице. «Это тебе так не пройдёт», — сказал он… (Пушкин 2). "You're lying, scoundrel!" I exclaimed in a rage. "You're lying in the most shameless manner." Shvabrin changed color. "You are not going to get away with that," he said… (2a). ♦ Этот, казалось бы, простенький вопрос почему-то расстроил сидящего, так что он даже изменился в лице (Булгаков 9). This apparently simple question upset the man behind the desk so much that a complete change came over his expression (9b). ♦ «Вашего сына расстреляли немцы. Он просил передать вам колечко. Он говорил, что это его матери…» Ваше не изменился в лице (Эренбург 1). "The Germans have shot your son. He asked us to give you this ring. He said it was his mother's." Vacher's face betrayed no emotion (1a).

2. to have one's face change in appearance (becoming pale, thin etc as a result of illness, sadness, emotional upset etc): X изменился в лице ≃ **X's face changed ⟨lost⟩ color; X's face (was) changed; X's face became drawn ⟨haggard⟩.**

Дня три после ареста Мити Грушенька сильно заболела и хворала чуть не пять недель… Она сильно изменилась в лице, похудела и пожелтела, хотя вот уже почти две недели как могла выходить со двора (Достоевский 2). Some three days after Mitya's arrest, Grushenka had become quite ill and was sick for almost five weeks.…Her face was greatly changed, she had become thin and sallow, though for almost two weeks she had already been able to go out (2a).

Л-92 • НА ЛИЦЕ́ НАПИ́САНО *у кого* or *чьём coll* [subj-compl with быть$_\emptyset$ (subj: usu. a clause or abstr, often это, всё); usu. this form, but pl and other genders can be used; usu. pres or past; more often this WO] sth. (usu. a person's feelings, intentions, character type etc) is clearly visible from the person's facial expression: у X-а это на лице написано ≃ **it's written all over X's face.**

Они переглядывались между собой, когда к ним подкатил шпик (на лице которого было написано, что он шпик) и спросил, кого хоронят (Войнович 4). They exchanged glances again when they were approached by a spy (it was written all over his face) who asked them whose funeral it was (4a).

Л-93 • БРОСА́ТЬ/БРО́СИТЬ В ЛИЦО́ ⟨В ГЛАЗА́⟩ *кому что* [VP; subj: human] to address (sharp words, accusations, rebukes etc) directly to the person for whom they are intended, often displaying open defiance: X бросит Z в лицо Y-у ≃ **X will throw ⟨fling⟩ Z in Y's face.**

«…Ты, кажется, и не обратил внимания, как ты обидел Катерину Ивановну тем, что рассказал Грушеньке о том дне, а та сейчас ей бросила в глаза, что вы сами „к кавалерам красу тайком продавать ходили!"» (Достоевский 1). "…Mitya, you don't seem to have noticed how you offended Katerina Ivanovna by telling Grushenka about that day. And she immediately threw it in her face, that she 'went secretly to her gentlemen to sell her beauty'!" (1a). ♦ Байрон… сломился, но сломился, как грозный Титан, бросая людям в глаза своё презрение, не золотя пилюли (Герцен 2). Byron…was broken, but broken like a menacing Titan, flinging his scorn in men's faces and not troubling to gild the pill (2a).

Л-94 • В ЛИЦО́[1] *кому* говорить *что,* называть *кого чем,* смеяться, лгать и т. п. [PrepP; Invar; adv] (to say sth., call s.o. sth., laugh at s.o., lie to s.o. etc) openly, directly addressing the person involved: **(right ⟨straight⟩) to s.o.'s face; (tell s.o. sth.) face to face; (laugh) in s.o.'s face; [in refer. to lying] tell a bold-faced ⟨barefaced⟩ lie; lie through one's teeth.**

Она [Фанни Невская] — настоящая, с ней нельзя болтать, ей нельзя солгать, она заставляет говорить, как на исповеди. Она говорит в лицо то, что думает (Аллилуева 2). She [Fanny Nevskaya] was a real person. You couldn't just gossip with her, or lie to her. With her you spoke as if you were at confession. And she always said straight to your face what she thought (2a). ♦ Они лежали и говорили о чём придётся, точно обкладывая то самое главное, хрупкое и ломкое, что было сказано, мягкими оберегающими пустяками. Когда лежишь, легче вести такой разговор: можно, закрыв глаза, сказать то, что в лицо говорить не решишься… (Распутин 2). They lay and talked about anything that came to mind, bolstering the most important thing, delicate and fragile, with soft padding trifles. It's always easier to have a conversation like that when you're lying down: you can say things with your eyes closed that you could never say to someone's face… (2a).

Л-95 • В ЛИЦО́[2] знать *кого* [PrepP; Invar; adv] (to know s.o.) by his outward appearance (without being acquainted with him): X знает Y-а в лицо ≃ **X knows Y by sight; X knows what Y looks like; X would recognize Y.**

Митя хоть и знал этого купца в лицо, но знаком с ним не был и даже ни разу не говорил с ним (Достоевский 1). Though Mitya knew the merchant by sight, he was not acquainted with him and had never once spoken to him (1a). ♦ Вскоре Ольга Петровна знала уже всех в издательстве — и по фамилиям, и по должности, и в лицо: счетоводов, редакторов, техредов, курьерш (Чуковская 1). Soon Olga Petrovna knew everyone in the publishing house — their names, their jobs and what they looked like — ledger clerks, editors, technical editors, messengers (1a). ♦ Игорь Владимирович танцевал не так профессионально, как Лёвочка, но хорошо, на них [Игоря Владимировича и Варю] обращали внимание — он был известен, его знали в лицо (Рыбаков 2). Igor Vladimirovich danced very well, not as professionally as Lyova, but people watched as they [Igor Vladimirovich and Varya] danced. They recognized him (2a).

Л-96 • ЛИЦО́ ВЫ́ТЯНУЛОСЬ *у кого;* **ФИЗИОНО́МИЯ ВЫ́ТЯНУЛАСЬ** [VP$_{subj}$; usu. this WO] s.o.'s face assumed an expression of disappointment, distress, surprise (usu. caused by sth. unpleasant) etc: лицо у X-а вытянулось ≃ **X's face fell (in surprise ⟨bewilderment, disappointment etc⟩); [in limited contexts] X pulled ⟨put on⟩ a long face.**

Когда из пяти выпущенных мной пуль махальщики показали три попадания в головную мишень с четырёхсот шагов, лицо у ротного вытянулось от удивления… (Лившиц 1). When, out of the five bullets I spent, the signaller showed three bull's eyes at four hundred paces, the commander's face fell in surprise (1a). ♦ «Господа, — начал он всё в том же волнении, — эти деньги… я хочу признаться вполне… эти деньги были *мои*». У прокурора и следователя даже лица вытянулись, не того совсем они ожидали (Достоевский 1). "Gentlemen," he began in the same agitation, "the money…I want to confess completely…the money was *mine*." The prosecutor and the district attorney even pulled long faces: this was not at all what they expected (1a).

Л-97 • НА ОДНО́ ЛИЦО́ *coll* [PrepP; Invar; subj-compl with быть$_\emptyset$, казаться etc (subj: any count noun, pl); fixed WO] some people (things etc) are or seem to be identical in appearance to one another, devoid of individual distinctions: **(look ⟨seem to be⟩) (exactly) the same; (look) exactly alike; (be) as like as ⟨just like⟩ peas (in a pod).**

…Нюра же на первых порах начальников не различала, для неё они все были на одно лицо, как китайцы (Войнович 4). …Nyura could not tell one official from the other, they all looked the same to her, like Chinese (4a). ♦ Марсиян было человек двадцать, и все были, как мне тогда показалось, на одно лицо (Богданов 1). There were about twenty Martians, and my first impression was that they all looked exactly alike (1a). ♦ Напряжённо вглядываюсь в лица своих судей… Все на одно лицо, хотя один из них брюнет, другой убелён сединами (Гинзбург 1). I looked intently at the faces of my judges.…They were as like as peas, though one of the three was dark and another grey (1a).

Л-98 • ПОКАЗА́ТЬ СВОЁ (НАСТОЯ́ЩЕЕ ⟨И́СТИН-НОЕ⟩) ЛИЦО́ [VP; subj: human; the verb may take the final position, otherwise fixed WO] to reveal one's true nature, show one's true (usu. negative) character: X показал своё настоящее лицо ≃ **X showed his true colors; X showed his true ⟨real⟩ face.**

Л-99 • СОХРАНИ́ТЬ ЛИЦО́ [VP; subj: human; often infin after чтобы, пытаться etc] to avoid embarrassment, disgrace, or a humiliating loss of prestige: X пытался сохранить лицо ≃ **X tried to save face.**

Л-100 • ТЕРЯ́ТЬ/ПОТЕРЯ́ТЬ ЛИЦО́ [VP; subj: human; fixed WO] to suffer a loss of prestige, dignity, reputation, lose the respect of others: X потерял лицо ≃ **X lost face.**

Ещё не осмыслив глубины своего поражения, великий комбинатор допустил неприличную суетливость, о чём всегда вспоминал впоследствии со стыдом. Он настаивал, сердился, совал деньги в руки Александру Ивановичу и вообще, как говорят китайцы, потерял лицо (Ильф и Петров 2). Not yet realizing the full extent of his defeat, the great schemer permitted himself to make a scene which he always afterwards remembered with shame. He insisted, became angry, pushed the money into the hands of Alexander Ivanovich, and on the whole, as the Chinese say, lost face (2b).

Л-101 • ЛИЦО́М К ЛИЦУ́ [Invar; adv or, less often, subj-compl with copula (subj: human); fixed WO] **1. видеть** *кого* ~ (to be) very near to (some person who inspires fear, trepidation etc in one, or *by extension* death): (be ⟨find o.s.⟩) **face to face (with s.o. ⟨sth.⟩).**

Мысль увидеть императрицу лицом к лицу так устрашала её, что она с трудом могла держаться на ногах (Пушкин 2). The thought of finding herself face to face with the Empress frightened her so much that she could hardly stand on her feet (2a).

2. встретиться, столкнуться *с кем* и т. п. ~ (to meet up with s.o. etc) right up close: **come face to face with s.o.; meet s.o. face to face; run right into s.o.**

Поднявшись как-то ночью после смерти матери, она лицом к лицу столкнулась в сенях с отцом (Максимов 3). She had got up one night after her mother's death, and come face to face with her father in the hallway (3a).

3. стоять, столкнуться, соприкоснуться и т. п. *с чем* ~ (to be, find o.s. etc) facing (some problem, new phenomenon etc): **(be ⟨stand, come, find o.s.⟩) face to face (with sth.); [in refer. to difficulties only] (be) confronted head-on (with sth.).**

Я стоял лицом к лицу с невероятным явлением. Гумбольдтовское понимание языка как искусства находило себе красноречивейшее подтверждение в произведениях Хлебникова, с той только потрясающей оговоркой, что процесс, мыслившийся до сих пор как функция коллективного сознания целого народа, был воплощён в творчестве одного человека (Лившиц 1). I stood face to face with an extraordinary phenomenon. Humboldt's conception of language as an art form found a most eloquent confirmation in Khlebnikov's works – except that what had hitherto been understood as the function of the collective consciousness of a whole people was here incarnated in the work of a single man (1a).

Л-102 • НЕ УДА́РИТЬ ЛИЦО́М В ГРЯЗЬ *coll* [VP; subj: human or collect] to carry out some matter well, as it should be carried out, and thereby make a favorable impression on s.o. (often as a means of proving one's professional competence or in an attempt to show off): X не ударил лицом в грязь ≃ **X didn't disgrace himself; X didn't fall flat on his face; X refused ⟨was not⟩ to be outdone; X came through in good fashion ⟨with honor⟩; X didn't disappoint person Y.**

...Как всегда, наш город лицом в грязь не ударил, показал, что стоит на уровне века (Рыбаков 1). ...Once again our town didn't disgrace itself, but showed that it was living in the twentieth century (1a). ♦ [Балясников:] Смотри не ударь в грязь лицом, Блохин, я сообщил Виктоше, что ты величайший пельменный мастер (Арбузов 5). [В.:] Careful you don't fall flat on your face. I informed Viktosha you were the greatest expert on meat dumplings (5a). ♦ ...Шолохов рассказал о своём знакомстве с Трояновского – ныне советского посла в ООН, а я, чтобы не ударить лицом в грязь, о знакомстве с вдовой Литвинова – в прошлом наркома иностранных дел (Амальрик 1). He [Sholokhov] told me about his acquaintanceship with the wife of Oleg Troyanovsky, later the Soviet ambassador to the United Nations; and I, not to be outdone, told him of my acquaintanceship with the widow of Maxim Litvinov, the former People's Commissar of Foreign Affairs (1a). ♦ ...[Леонар Обри] взялся устроить великолепную мостовую перед театром. «Вы сами понимаете, ведь будут подъезжать кареты, господин Обри», – беспокойно потирая руки, говорил господин Мольер. Он вселил тревогу и в господина Обри, и тот не ударил лицом в грязь: мостовая вышла красивая и прочная (Булгаков 5). ...[Léonard Aubry] undertook to lay a most magnificent pavement before the theater. "You understand yourself, Monsieur Aubry, carriages will be driving up to the theater," Monsieur Molière said to him, rubbing his hands nervously. He infected Monsieur Aubry with his concern, and the latter did not disappoint him: the pavement turned out to be excellent (5a).

Л-103 • ПЕРЕД ЛИЦО́М *lit* [PrepP; Invar; the resulting PrepP is adv] **1.** ~ *кого-чего* in s.o.'s presence: **in front of; before.**

«Я, верховный главнокомандующий Корнилов, перед лицом всего народа объявляю, что долг солдата... и беззаветная любовь к родине заставили меня в эти тяжёлые минуты бытия отечества не подчиниться приказанию Временного правительства и оставить за собой верховное командование армией и флотом» (Шолохов 3). "I, the Supreme Commander-in-Chief Kornilov, declare before the whole nation that my duty as a soldier...and my unbounded love for the Motherland have compelled me in these grave minutes of the country's existence to ignore the order of the Provisional Government and retain the supreme command of the Army and Navy" (3a).

2. ~ *чего*, often **смерти** when faced by sth., directly before the approach of sth.: **in the face of; confronted with.**

...Началась первая мировая война, потом революция, и перед лицом таких великих событий никто уже не интересовался: сделали обрезание Якобу Ивановскому или не сделали (Рыбаков 1). ...It was soon the First World War, then the Revolution, and in the face of such great events nobody was interested in whether Jakob Ivanovsky was circumcised or not (1a). ♦ Монтень приводит примеры, когда люди перед лицом смерти с ничем непоколебимым самообладанием дают распоряжения о том, как поступить с их телом (Олеша 3). Montaigne cites examples of people confronted with death who, without any wavering of self-control, gave instructions for the disposal of their bodies (3a).

Л-104 • ПОВОРА́ЧИВАТЬСЯ/ПОВЕРНУ́ТЬСЯ ЛИЦО́М *к кому-чему* [VP; subj: human; often infin with должен, надо, нужно; fixed WO] to start paying attention to s.o. or sth., show a keen interest in s.o. or sth.: X должен повернуться лицом к Y-у ≃ **X should address the needs ⟨the problems etc⟩ of Y; [in limited contexts] X should move closer to Y.**

Центральный Комитет считал, что наука должна повернуться лицом к производству, ближе, тесней связаться с жизнью (Гроссман 2). The Central Committee considered that science must move closer to industry and become more integrated with real life (2a).

Л-105 • К ЛИЦУ́ *кому* [PrepP; Invar] **1.** [subj-compl with copula (subj: a noun denoting an item of clothing, a hairdo, jewelry, a facial expression etc) or adv; often neg] sth. befits s.o., makes him look more attractive: X Y-у не к лицу ≃ **X doesn't suit ⟨become⟩ Y; X doesn't look good on Y; X doesn't flatter Y;** ‖ одет(ый) к лицу ≃ **becomingly ⟨attractively⟩ dressed.**

«[Я] делаю ей походя комплимент: „Валентина Михайловна, какой на вас прекрасный жакет... Прекрасный, — повторяю, — жакет, и очень вам к лицу"» (Войнович 4). "[I] paid her an offhanded compliment—'Valentina Mikhailovna, what a pretty jacket you're wearing....It's beautiful and it suits you very well" (4a). ♦ О молодость! молодость!.. Ты как будто бы обладаешь всеми сокровищами вселенной, даже грусть тебя тешит, даже печаль тебе к лицу... (Тургенев 3). Oh youth, youth!...You seem to own all the treasures of the world; even sorrow amuses you, even grief becomes you... (3a). ♦ ...Сама Анна Дмитриевна была игрушечка — маленькая, худенькая, с свежим цветом лица, с хорошенькими маленькими ручками, всегда весёлая и всегда к лицу одетая (Толстой 2). ...Anna Dmitrievna herself was a *pretty toy*, small, thin, with a fresh complexion and pretty little hands, always gay and always becomingly dressed (2a).

2. [subj-compl with быть₀ (subj: abstr or infin); usu. neg] sth. is suitable, right for s.o., befits s.o.'s position: X ⟨делать X⟩ Y-у не к лицу ≃ **X ⟨doing X⟩ does not become ⟨suit⟩ Y; it is not fitting ⟨becoming⟩ for Y to do X; it is unseemly for Y to do X; X ill becomes Y.**

[Саша:] Пора уже тебе оставить выпивку и скандалы. Предоставь это тем здоровилам... Они молодые, а тебе всё-таки, старику, не к лицу, право... (Чехов 1). [S.:] ...It's time you gave up drinking and making scenes. Leave it to these hearty types. They're young, and it really doesn't suit an old man like you (1b). ♦ Восьмой [член правления], академик и герой труда, решил, что ему участвовать в этой склоке совсем не к лицу... (Войнович 3). The eighth [member of the board], an academician and Hero of Labor, decided that for him to participate in this squabble was not at all becoming... (3a). ♦ «Вчера вы изволили фокусы делать...» — «Я? — воскликнул в изумлении маг. — Помилосердствуйте. Мне это даже как-то не к лицу!» (Булгаков 9). "The other day, if you don't mind, it was your pleasure to perform some tricks..." "Tricks?" the magician exclaimed with astonishment. "Surely, you don't mean it! Such things would ill become me!" (9a).

Л-106 • **ПЕРЕХОДИ́ТЬ/ПЕРЕЙТИ́ НА ЛИ́ЧНОСТИ** *coll* [VP; subj: human; often neg imper] to make offensive remarks about s.o. in a presentation, conversation etc: X перешёл на личности ≃ **X got ⟨became⟩ personal; X brought personalities into it.**

Говори по существу, не надо переходить на личности. Stick to the point, no need to get personal.

Л-107 • **НЕ ЛИШЁН ⟨НЕ ЛИШЁННЫЙ⟩** *чего* [AdjP; the resulting phrase is subj-compl with copula (subj: any noun—short-form var.) or modif (long-form var.)] a person (thing etc) is not devoid of a certain (as specified) quality: X не лишён Y-а ≃ **X is not without (some) Y; there is some Y about person X ⟨in thing X⟩.**

Ваше замечание не лишено остроумия. Your remark is not without wit.

Л-108 • **ХВАТИ́ТЬ ЛИ́ШНЕГО ⟨ЛИ́ШНЕЕ⟩** *coll;* **ХВАТИ́ТЬ ЛИ́ШКУ** *highly coll* [VP; subj: human] **1.** to say or do sth. that goes beyond the accepted social limits, violates the rules of ordinary good behavior: X хватил лишнего ≃ **X went (a bit) too far; X carried ⟨took⟩ it too far.**

...Бахут его шутки не принял, он ринулся вперёд. «Ты всю жизнь лошадей любил больше, чем своих детей, ты чуть не умер, когда твоя [лошадь] Кукла порченая вернулась с перевала». — «Как видишь, не умер», — сказал Кязым. Он не любил, когда ему об этом напоминали. Бахут почувствовал, что хватил лишнее... (Искандер 5). ...Bakhut did not accept his joke, he plunged ahead. "All your life you've loved horses better than

your children. You nearly died when your Dolly came home from the pass ruined!" "As you see, I didn't die," Kyazym said. He disliked being reminded of that. Bakhut sensed that he had gone too far... (5a).

2. Also: **ХЛЕБНУ́ТЬ ⟨ПЕРЕЛОЖИ́ТЬ** *obs*⟩ **ЛИ́ШНЕЕ** *coll;* **ХЛЕБНУ́ТЬ ⟨ПЕРЕЛОЖИ́ТЬ** *obs*⟩ **ЛИ́ШКУ** *highly coll* to drink too much: X хлебнул лишку ≃ **X had one ⟨a few⟩ too many; X had ⟨took⟩ a drop too much.**

[Трилецкий:] Должно быть, именинником был... Хватил лишнее... (Чехов 1). [T.:] It must have been his birthday, he'd had a drop too much (1b). ♦ ...Не был он (по его выражению) и *врагом бутылки*, т.е. (говоря по-русски) любил хлебнуть лишнее (Пушкин 2). ...He was (as he himself put it) "no enemy of the bottle," that is (in plain Russian), he loved to take a drop too much (2a).

Л-109 • **НЕ ЛИ́ШНЕЕ ⟨НЕ ЛИ́ШНЕ⟩** [AdjP; subj-compl with быть₀ (subj: usu. infin or a clause) or obj-compl with находить, считать (1st var. only, obj: usu. deverbal noun or infin)] it would help, be useful (to do sth.): **it wouldn't be (such) a bad idea (to do sth.); it won't ⟨wouldn't⟩ hurt one (to do sth.); (there's) no harm in (doing sth.); it would be worthwhile (to do sth.); (sth.) is worth doing; it's ⟨it would be⟩ worth it (to do sth.); it wouldn't be out of place (to do sth.).**

[Нина:] Сначала думать надо, а потом уже с ума сходить! [Бусыгин:] Разве? Уж лучше наоборот. [Сарафанов:] ...По-моему, Володя прав. Думать, конечно, не лишнее, но... (Вампилов 4). [N.:] You must think first, and then go round the bend! [B.:] Really? Better the other way round. [S.:] I think Volodia's right. No harm in thinking, of course, but... (4a). ♦ «Запишите и про небо; это будет не лишним записать» (Достоевский 1). "Write that down about heaven, too; it's worth writing down" (1a).

Л-110 • **ПОЗВОЛЯ́ТЬ/ПОЗВО́ЛИТЬ СЕБЕ́ ЛИ́ШНЕЕ** [VP; subj: human; often neg; in the affirm лишнее takes the final position] **1.** to make expenditures one cannot afford: X не позволяет себе лишнего ≃ **X doesn't allow himself any extras; X lives within his means ⟨budget⟩; X doesn't exceed his budget.**

Мои сёстры живут скромно, не позволяют себе ничего лишнего. My sisters live modestly, not allowing themselves any extras.

2. Also: **СЛИ́ШКОМ МНО́ГО ПОЗВОЛЯ́ТЬ/ПО-ЗВО́ЛИТЬ СЕБЕ́** to go beyond the accepted limits or rules in one's behavior: X позволил себе лишнее ≃ **X went too far; X took liberties (with person Y).**

«Раиса Михайловна, я достал билеты на „Каренину"». Хана вздохнула. Слов нет, Фомичёв мил, не позволяет себе ничего лишнего, всегда хочет порадовать Раю. Ей скучно... Хана знает, что значит остаться без мужа (Эренбург 1). "Raya, I've got tickets for *Anna Karenina*." Hannah sighed. It couldn't be denied, Fomichev was a nice man, never took liberties; and Raya was lonely. Hannah knew what it was to be left without a husband (1a).

Л-111 • **СКАЗА́ТЬ ⟨СБОЛТНУ́ТЬ** *coll*⟩ **ЛИ́ШНЕЕ** [VP; subj: human] to say sth. one should not: X сказал лишнее ≃ **X said too much; X said the wrong thing; [in limited contexts] X made a slip of the tongue; X put his foot in his mouth ⟨in it⟩.**

Вступился Кривошлыков, опасаясь, как бы простоватый Подтёлков не сболтнул лишнего... (Шолохов 3). Fearing that Podtyolkov in his simplicity might say too much, Krivoshlykov intervened (3a). ♦ ...[Иван Иванович Поляшко был] полная противоположность Строковского: тяжелодум, упрямец, говорит и слушает сам себя — не сказал ли чего-нибудь лишнего? (Залыгин 1). He [Ivan Ivanovich Poliashko] was the very opposite of Strokovsky. Plodding, dogged, he listened to himself when he talked to make sure he didn't say the wrong thing (1a).

Л-112 • **С ЛИ́ШНИМ ⟨С ЛИ́ШКОМ** *coll*⟩ [PrepP; these forms only; used with a Num or quantit NP as nonagreeing modif] (used when expressing some amount of time, s.o.'s age, the size or quantity of sth. etc as an approximation rounded down to the nearest convenient figure) (the figure named) plus a small amount: **more than…; (a bit) over…; [Num]-odd; …or more; …and then some; …and some odd.**

Два с лишним года он [Бабий Яр] был запретной зоной, с проволокой под высоким напряжением… (Кузнецов 1). For more than two years it [Babi Yar] was a forbidden area, fenced off with high-tension wires… (1b). ♦ «Извини, что беспокою тебя, старина, но тут у меня объявилась дочка двенадцати с лишним лет, очень славная девочка, но мать у неё дура и отец тоже дурак…» (Стругацкие 1). "Sorry to bother you, old man, but I've got this daughter here. She's a bit over twelve, a terrific little girl, but her mother's a fool and her father's a fool too…" (1a). ♦ «…Разве я давно здесь?» — «Час с лишком» (Тургенев 3). "…Have I been here long?" "Over an hour" (3b). ♦ [Павлин:] Даже умственно зрелые люди утверждают, что царя надобно сместить, по неспособности его. [Булычов:] Двадцать лет с лишком способен был… (Горький 2). [P.:] Even mature minds assert that the tsar must be deposed on account of his incompetence. [B.:] He's been competent enough for twenty-odd years (2a). ♦ …На них [поминки] ухлопаны были чуть ли не десять рублей из двадцати с лишком, полученных от Раскольникова собственно на похороны Мармеладова (Достоевский 3). …Almost ten of the twenty and some odd rubles that Raskolnikov had given her [Katerina Ivanovna] for the actual funeral had been squandered on the [funeral] feast (3a).

Л-113 • ЛИШЬ БЫ (ТО́ЛЬКО)…; ТО́ЛЬКО БЫ…

1. [subord Conj; introduces a clause of purpose] for the purpose of (achieving sth. or, when used with a negation, preventing sth.; what is stated in the main clause usu. presents an extreme means of achieving the goal stated in the subord clause): **(in order) to…;** [when used with a negation] **(in order) to avoid (doing sth.).**

«[Исай Фомич] три года управлял большим имением…» — «Да можно ли положиться на него?» — «Честнейшая душа, не извольте беспокоиться! Он своё проживёт, лишь бы доверителю угодить» (Гончаров 1). "He [Isay Fomich] was the manager of a big estate for three years…" "But can he be relied on?" "Don't worry, he is as honest as they make 'em! He'd spend his own money to please the man who trusted him" (1a). ♦ «Её — эту Дёмину — у нас на заводе даже начальство за версту обходит, лишь бы не разговаривать» (Максимов 2). "Here at the shipyard even the bosses will go a mile out of their way to avoid having to talk to her [Dyomina]" (2a).

2. [subord Conj, condit] used to show that the truthfulness or realization of what is stated in the main clause is contingent upon the fulfillment of the condition stated in the subord clause; the fulfillment of this condition is considered desirable: **as ⟨so⟩ long as; if (only); provided that.**

…Мужикам, по их натуре, нужна любая техника, лишь бы она была новой, любая теория, лишь бы она сводила какие-нибудь концы с какими-нибудь другими концами… (Залыгин 1). By their nature they [men] needed any sort of science as long as it was new, any theory as long as it tied up one or two loose ends… (1a). ♦ [Венгерович I:] Всё можно узнать, лишь бы только желание было (Чехов 1). [V.:] Oh, one can find out everything if one wants to badly enough (1a).

3. [Particle] used to express a wish: **if only.**

Лишь бы только он доехал благополучно! If only he would arrive safely!

Л-114 • В ЛОБ [PrepP; Invar; adv] **1.** атаковать *кого,* наступать и т. п. ~ *mil* (to attack, advance etc) having the enemy immediately in front of o.s.: **(launch etc) a frontal ⟨head-on⟩ attack ⟨assault⟩; (attack) frontally ⟨head-on⟩.**

«В лоб на Вёшки они [красные] не пойдут…» (Шолохов 4). "They [the Reds] won't try a head-on attack on Vyoshenskaya…" (4a).

♦ Хотел Торопец ввести в заблуждение защитников Города, что он, Торопец, будет брать Город с его, Торопца, левого фланга (с севера), с предместья Куренёвки, с тем чтобы оттянуть туда городскую армию, а самому ударить в Город в лоб… (Булгаков 3). …Toropets wanted to fool the defenders of the City into thinking that he, Toropets, intended to assault the City from his left (the northern) flank, from the suburb of Kurenyovka, in order to draw the City's forces in that direction whilst the real attack on the City would be delivered frontally… (3a).

2. *nautical* (coming, blowing) from the direction in which a ship etc is headed: [of wind] **headwind;** [in limited contexts] **(sail) upwind; (sail) in the teeth of the wind;** [of waves] **beating head-on.**

3. говорить, спрашивать и т. п. ~ *coll* (to say, ask sth. etc) in a straightforward manner: **point-blank; directly; straight out; (come) right out (and say ⟨ask etc⟩ sth.).**

О нет, они [КГБ] не станут прямо так, в лоб, предлагать сотрудничество (Буковский 1). Oh no, they [the KGB] won't put it to you point-blank, suggesting you collaborate (1a). ♦ Тогда, не вставая, я спросил её прямо в лоб, где издательский экземпляр романа «В поисках радости» и почему она об этом ничего не сказала раньше (Терц 4). Then without getting up I asked her directly where the publisher's copy of *In Search of Joy* was and why she had said nothing about it before (4a). ♦ Очевидно, люди с трудом понимают замаскированные или даже слегка прикрытые высказывания. Им нужно, чтобы всё било прямо в лоб (Мандельштам 1). People evidently find it hard to understand anything that is camouflaged, or even just slightly veiled. They need to have everything said straight out… (1a).

Л-115 • ЗАБРИВА́ТЬ ⟨БРИТЬ⟩/ЗАБРИ́ТЬ ЛОБ ⟨ЛБЫ⟩ *кому;* **ЗАБРИ́ТЬ (ЛОБ) В СОЛДА́ТЫ ⟨В РЕ́КРУТЫ⟩** *all obs* [VP; subj: human; usu. pfv 3rd pers pl with indef. refer.] to conscript s.o. for military service: X-у забрили лоб ≃ **X was taken as a recruit; X was called up into the army ⟨the service⟩.**

[Слесарша:] …Мужу-то моему [городничий] приказал забрить лоб в солдаты… (Гоголь 4). [Locksmith's wife:] …He [the Mayor] ordered my husband, now, to be called up into the army… (4a).

Л-116 • ЛОБ В ЛОБ столкнуться, сойтись и т. п. *coll* [Invar; adv; fixed WO] (to meet, run into one another) right up close, facing each other: **(collide ⟨meet etc⟩) head-on; (run ⟨crash etc⟩) right into each other; (meet ⟨come etc⟩) face to face.**

…Стоило ему заступить в должность, как уже на другой день грянула беда: в самом исходе перегона Роща-Дубки лоб в лоб столкнулись два товарняка (Максимов 3). …Sure enough, the very day after he took up his duties, disaster struck. Two freight trains crashed head-on on the last lap of the Roshcha-Dubki run (3a).

Л-117 • МЕ́ДНЫЙ ЛОБ *highly coll, derog* [NP; fixed WO] a senselessly stubborn, dull-witted person: **blockhead; numskull; bonehead; fathead.**

Л-118 • ПОДСТАВЛЯ́ТЬ/ПОДСТА́ВИТЬ (СВОЙ) ЛОБ [VP; subj: human] to put o.s. in a dangerous position, in a position where one could be shot, severely punished etc: X подставил лоб ≃ **X made himself an open target; X presented himself as a target;** [in refer. to shooting only] **X risked having his brains blown out; X stood there waiting to be shot at.**

«Скверно! — решил он наконец, — скверно [, что будет дуэль], с какой стороны ни посмотри. Во-первых, надо будет подставлять лоб и во всяком случае уехать…» (Тургенев 2). "Yes, it's [dueling is] a bad business," he decided at last. "A bad business from whatever angle one looks at it. Firstly I risk having my brains blown out, and in any case I shall have to go away from here…" (2c). "It's [dueling is] a bad business!" he decided finally. "A bad business, whichever way you look at it. In the first place I'll have to stand there waiting to be shot at, and whatever happens I'll have to leave…" (2e).

Л-119 • ЧТО В ЛОБ, ЧТО ПО́ ЛБУ [saying] it makes no difference which of two available options is chosen because neither one is better or worse than the other: ≃ **(it's) six of one and half a dozen of the other; it's as broad as it is long.**

«Может, вместо Иванова назначить Сидорова?» – «Что в лоб, что по лбу: Сидоров ничуть не лучше». "Shall we appoint Sidorov instead of Ivanov?" "It's six of one and half a dozen of the other – Sidorov isn't any better."

Л-120 • ЛОВИ́ТЬ/ПОЙМА́ТЬ СЕБЯ́ на чём [VP; subj: human; prep obj: usu. на мысли (, что…) or на том, что…; fixed WO] to discover suddenly that one is thinking an unexpected thought, feeling an unexpected feeling etc: X поймал себя на Y-е ≃ **X caught ⟨found⟩ himself thinking ⟨feeling⟩ (Y ⟨that…⟩); X suddenly became aware that… ⟨aware of Y⟩; X suddenly realized that…**

Он [Базаров] ловил самого себя на всякого рода «постыдных» мыслях (Тургенев 2). He [Bazarov] caught himself thinking all kinds of "shameful" thoughts… (2f). ♦ …Будучи уже студентом и переживая свою первую и злосчастную любовь, поймал он себя однажды… на мысли, что он не родной сын своего отца (Битов 2). …One day, when he was already in college and suffering through his first and ill-starred love, he caught himself thinking…that he wasn't really his father's son (2a). ♦ …Антон неожиданно поймал себя на том, что мысли переключились к Алику Зарванцеву (Чернёнок 2). Anton suddenly found himself thinking about Alik Zarvantsev (2a). ♦ Тщетно понатужившись, он поймал себя на мысли, что жаждет непременно соригинальничать… (Ерофеев 4). Straining, but with no result, he suddenly became aware of his desire to come up with something completely original… (4a).

Л-121 • НА ЛОВЦА́ И ЗВЕРЬ БЕЖИ́Т [saying] (said when s.o. unexpectedly comes across a person he has been looking for or needs) you are or this is precisely the person I want to speak to, consult with etc at this moment: ≃ **just the person I need(ed) ⟨want(ed)⟩ to see;** [in limited contexts] **talk ⟨speak⟩ of the devil (and he appears ⟨will appear⟩).**

Л-122 • ЛО́ДЫРЯ ГОНЯ́ТЬ coll, disapprov [VP; subj: human; usu. this WO] to loaf, spend time idly: X лодыря гоняет ≃ **X spends his time goofing off; X twiddles his thumbs.**

Л-123 • ПРОКРУ́СТОВО ЛО́ЖЕ (чего) lit [NP; sing only; fixed WO] criteria, standards to which sth. is forcefully fitted or adapted (in order to produce conformity): **Procrustean bed; bed of Procrustes.**

< From the Greek legend about *Procrustes*, a robber who stretched or cut the legs of his victims to fit the length of his bed.

Л-124 • ПОД ЛО́ЖЕЧКОЙ болит, сосёт, щемит, холодеет и т. п. у кого coll [PrepP; Invar; adv] (to have a pain, spasm, feeling of hunger etc) in the upper part of the abdomen where it meets the chest: **in the pit of one's stomach.**

«Не знаю, что мне делать. Желудок почти не варит, под ложечкой тяжесть, изжога замучила, дыханье тяжело…» (Гончаров 1). "I don't know what to do. My digestion is bad, there's a heaviness in the pit of my stomach, and I am tortured by heartburn and shortness of breath" (1b).

Л-125 • ПОД ЛО́ЖЕЧКУ ударить кого coll; **ПОД ВЗДОХ ⟨ПОД ДЫХ⟩** substand [PrepP; these forms only; adv] (to hit s.o.) in the uppper part of the abdomen, esp. at the point where it meets the chest: **(hit ⟨punch etc⟩ s.o.) in the belly ⟨in the gut⟩.**

«Ишь чего захотел – простить», – выкрикнул некий лжечеловек из зала. Но другой, почти такой же, и всё-таки чуть получше, дал тому локтем под дых и громко сказал: «Заглохни, псина!» (Войнович 4). "Now look what he wants, us to forgive him," cried out a pseudo-human from the audience. Another one, almost the same but a bit better, elbowed him in the belly and said loudly: "Shut up, dog meat" (4a).

Л-126 • (ХОТЬ) ЛОЖИ́СЬ ДА ПОМИРА́Й substand [(хоть +) VP$_{imper}$; these forms only; usu. subord clause; fixed WO] (used to express hopelessness, despair) (the situation is so desperate that) there is no escape, death is the only way out for s.o.: **there's nothing (left) to do but lie down and die; there's nothing left but to lie down and die; you ⟨he etc⟩ might (just) as well lie down and die; life isn't worth living.**

[Лука:] Был он – бедный, жил – плохо… и когда приходилось ему так уж трудно, что хоть ложись да помирай, – духа он не терял… (Горький 3). [L.:] He was a poor man and had a hard life. Sometimes things got so bad it looked as if there was nothing left for him to do but lie down and die. But he didn't give up (3d).

Л-127 • ДОРОГА́ ЛО́ЖКА К ОБЕ́ДУ [saying] sth. is valuable only if it is available when needed: ≃ **slow help is no help; it's all in the timing;** [when used as a reproach in refer. to sth. done too late] **a day late and a ruble short.**

Л-128 • ЛО́ЖКА ДЁГТЮ В БО́ЧКЕ МЁДА ⟨-у⟩ [saying] sth. that spoils an otherwise good, satisfactory state of affairs (said in vexation when some insignificant but unpleasant thing spoils what is otherwise very good – a project, mood, impression etc): ≃ **a fly in the ointment.**

Л-129 • В ЛО́ЖКЕ ВОДЫ́ УТОПИ́ТЬ кого coll [VP; subj: human; usu. infin with рад, готов etc or fut; fixed WO] to cause s.o. great trouble without significant reason: X рад ⟨готов, пытается и т. п.⟩ Y-а в ложке воды утопить ≃ **X would love ⟨is ready etc⟩ to hang Y ⟨to have Y's neck⟩ for the slightest infringement ⟨offense⟩; X would use any ⟨the slightest⟩ excuse to do Y in; X would like nothing better than to see Y hang.**

Л-130 • БЛИ́ЗОК ⟨БЛИ́ЗКО⟩ ЛО́КОТЬ, ДА НЕ УКУ́СИШЬ [saying] sth. seems easy to do or obtain but is actually impossible to accomplish or get: ≃ **so near and yet so far.**

Хорошая семья. Крепкий корень. И если бы Егорша с такой семьёй породнился, может, он и сам бы немножко остепенился – повылезла бы из него лишняя дурь… Да нет, вздыхал Степан Андреянович, близко локоть, да не укусишь. Разве пойдёт такая девка за моего шалопая? (Абрамов 1). Good family.…Strong stock. And if Yegorsha should marry into such a family, maybe he might settle down a little and give up his wild and useless ways. But no, sighed Stepan Andreanovich, so near and yet so far. Would such a girl marry my black sheep? (1b).

Л-131 • КУСА́ТЬ ⟨СЕБЕ́⟩ ЛО́КТИ coll [VP; subj: human] to regret bitterly having made a mistake (that cannot be put right), having missed a chance (that may not come again) etc: X кусал (себе) локти ≃ **X could have kicked himself;** ‖ нечего локти кусать ≃ **it's no use ⟨there is no point (in)⟩ crying over spilt milk.**

[Володя:] Любишь ты её?.. Так в чём дело, дядя? Держи и не выпускай! Всю жизнь потом себе не простишь, увидишь!.. Потом локти будешь кусать, точно тебе говорю!.. (Рощин 1). [V.:] D'you love her?…Then what's wrong, chum? Hold on to her and never let her go! Otherwise you'll never forgive yourself as long as you live, mark my words!…You're going to kick yourself for this… (1b).

Л-132 • ОТРЕ́ЗАННЫЙ ЛОМО́ТЬ [NP; sing only; subj-compl with copula (subj: human), pres or past; fixed WO] **1.** a person (usu. a grown-up son or, less often, daughter) who no longer lives with his family, who has become independent and does not require support: X – отрезанный ломоть ≃ **X is on his own; X is ⟨has become⟩ his own man ⟨her own woman, his own master⟩; X has left the nest; X has cut loose.**

«Что делать, Вася! Сын – отрезанный ломоть. Он что сокол: захотел – прилетел, захотел – улетел...» (Тургенев 2). "What can we do, Vasya! Our son's his own master now. He's like a free bird of the skies: he wanted to come – came flying to us; wanted to go – and flew away" (2e).

2. a person who has dissociated himself from his milieu, from his traditional way of life, from his usual activity: X – отрезанный ломоть ≃ **X is cut off (from his country ⟨his milieu etc⟩);** [in limited contexts] **X is a lone wolf.**

...В Одессе он [Бунин] застрял: не хотел сделаться эмигрантом, отрезанным ломтём; упрямо надеялся на чудо – на конец большевиков, гибель советской власти и на возвращение в Москву под звон кремлёвских колоколов (Катаев 3). ...In Odessa he [Bunin] has stuck: he did not want to become an émigré, cut off from his country; he was stubbornly hoping for a miracle – for the Bolsheviks to be defeated, Soviet rule overthrown and his return to Moscow amid the triumphant ringing of the Kremlin bells (3a).

Л-133 • НА ЛО́НЕ ПРИРО́ДЫ lit [PrepP; Invar; adv; fixed WO] in the countryside, the forest, the fields etc: **in the bosom ⟨the lap⟩ of nature; close to nature.**

Человек-то лучше становится на лоне природы. И не так уже неприятен показался бы Александр Семёнович, как в городе (Булгаков 10). A man becomes better in the lap of nature. And even Alexander Semyonovich would not have seemed as unpleasant here as he had in the city (10a).

Л-134 • ВО ВСЕ ЛОПА́ТКИ удирать, бежать и т. п. [PrepP; Invar; adv; fixed WO] (to run away, race, gallop etc) very quickly, headlong: **(at) full tilt; for all one is worth; hell-for-leather; as fast as one can; as fast as one's legs will carry one; at top ⟨full⟩ speed.**

Он прискакал в Глупов, как говорится, во все лопатки... и едва вломился в пределы городского выгона, как тут же, на самой границе, пересёк уйму ямщиков (Салтыков-Щедрин 1). He galloped hell-for-leather, as they say, into Foolov...and no sooner had he overrun the borders than he flogged a bunch of coachmen, right then and there on the town common (1a). ♦ [Городничий:] Слушайте: вы побегите, да бегом во все лопатки, и снесите две записки... (Гоголь 4). [Mayor:] Listen, will you run, and I mean run, as fast as you can, and take two notes... (4b). ♦ Она [Гева] кинулась к кустам и ударила... по самой их гуще. В просвете торопливо мелькнуло округлое тело приручённого ею павлина, тёмным звёздным небом раскинулся хвост. Царственная птица удирала во все лопатки (Обухова 1). She [Heva] rushed toward the bushes and struck out at them. The rounded body of the peacock she had tamed burst out from among their stems. The tail spread open like a starry sky. The regal bird was scrambling away at top speed (1a).

Л-135 • КЛАСТЬ/ПОЛОЖИ́ТЬ ⟨УЛОЖИ́ТЬ⟩ НА (О́БЕ) ЛОПА́ТКИ кого [VP; subj: human; more often pfv; the verb may take the final position, otherwise fixed WO] **1.** in wrestling, to put s.o. flat on his back: X положил Y-а на обе лопатки ≃ **X pinned Y.**

2. coll to win a victory over s.o. (in an argument, contest etc): X положил Y-а на обе лопатки ≃ **X pinned Y to the mat; X laid ⟨put⟩ Y flat on his back; X beat Y (all) hollow.**

Он высмеял Топоркова за доклад, а затем... с профессиональной сноровкой уложил отца психоанализа на обе лопатки (Ерофеев 3). He ridiculed Toporkov's report and then...with professional aplomb, he pinned the father of psychoanalysis to the mat (3a). ♦

«На судебном процессе я уложил рвачей на лопатки, и они получили по заслугам» (Чернёнок 2). "At the trial I had those grabbers flat on their backs, and they got what they deserved" (2a).

Л-136 • ГРЕСТИ́ ⟨ЗАГРЕБА́ТЬ⟩ ЛОПА́ТОЙ деньги, золото, серебро coll [VP; subj: human] to make a lot of money: X гребёт деньги лопатой ≃ **X makes money hand over fist; X rakes in ⟨up⟩ the money; X makes big bucks.**

[Лапшин:] Они тут в Москве деньги-то лопатами гребут (Розов 2). [L.:] These Moscow folk, they make money hand over fist (2a). ♦ [Фома] Лесков рвал налево и направо: выколачивал пайки, топливо... что-то продавал, что-то выменивал, а в результате стол у них, и не по-военному сытный, не оскудевал. Петра Васильевича [Лашкова], правда, коробила эта не по их скромным нуждам предприимчивость напарника, он временами ворчал и нудился, хотя... молчал. Но когда тот заикнулся было о пассажирах-беженцах, с них, мол, лопатой грести можно, [Лашков] отказал наотрез... (Максимов 3). [Foma] Leskov stole things right and left: rustled up extra rations and fuel...sold this and swapped that, and as a result their larder was fuller than it should have been in wartime and never looked any worse than usual. True, his mate's resourcefulness, which far exceeded their modest needs, gave Pyotr Vasilievich [Lashkov] some qualms – he muttered and sulked occasionally, but he didn't speak up. Not until Foma started dropping hints about passengers – you could simply rake in the money from refugees, he said. Here Lashkov peremptorily refused (3a). ♦ «Построили санаторий, целебные воды, роскошный климат, деньги греби лопатой. Сюда из столицы ездили...» (Стругацкие 1). "We build the health resort – healing waters, superb climate – go rake up the money, it's yours. People used to come here from the capital" (1a).

Л-137 • ХОТЬ ЛО́ПНИ ⟨ТРЕ́СНИ⟩ substand [хоть + VP$_{imper}$; these forms only; subord clause] **1.** [usu. foll. by Conj «а» or «но» + imper сделай, выполни etc] despite any circumstances: **no matter what; come hell or high water.**

Он – человек, который знает, что ему надо. Вот выбрал меня и всё, хоть лопни, а будь его женой (Кожевников 1). He's a man who knows what he needs. So, he's chosen me. That's it, no matter what, I'll be his wife (1a).

2. despite whatever you do, however much effort you put into sth. (it is useless, futile): **no matter what you do; however hard you try; try as you might ⟨may⟩.**

...Бывают дни невезения, когда ни черта не клеится, хоть лопни (Трифонов 4). ...There were bad luck days when not a damn thing went right no matter what you did (4a).

Л-138 • ЧТОБ ТЫ ⟨он и т. п.⟩ ЛО́ПНУЛ ⟨ТРЕ́СНУЛ⟩!; ЧТОБ ТЕБЕ́ ⟨ему и т. п.⟩ ЛО́ПНУТЬ ⟨ТРЕ́СНУТЬ⟩! all substand, rude [sent; these forms only; fixed WO] an abusive phrase used to express one's anger, fury at s.o. or sth., one's wish that every kind of trouble befall s.o.: **blast ⟨damn, screw, to hell with⟩ you ⟨him, it etc⟩!;** [in limited contexts] **may you ⟨he etc⟩ be struck dumb!**

Проезжий... поглядывал в окно и посвистывал к великому неудовольствию смотрительши... «...Эк посвистывает, – чтоб он лопнул, окаянный басурман» (Пушкин 1). The traveler...looked through the window and whistled – an action that greatly annoyed the stationmaster's wife...."Ugh, he does whistle, may he be struck dumb, the damned infidel" (1a).

Л-139 • В ЛОСК substand [PrepP; Invar; adv (intensif)] **1.** ~ напиться, пьян и т. п. Also: **В ЛОСКУ́Т ⟨В ЛОСКУ́ТЫ́⟩** substand (to get or be) extremely (drunk): в лоск пьян ≃ **dead ⟨stinking, blind⟩ drunk; loaded to the gills; smashed ⟨plastered, bombed⟩ out of one's mind ⟨skull⟩.**

Все выступавшие были в лоскут пьяны, все мололи одно и то же... (Ерофеев 1). Everyone who delivered a speech was stinking drunk; they all ground on about one and the same thing... (1a). ♦ [Галина:] По-моему, я напилась... [Зилов:] Конечно. Пьяная в лоскуты (Вампилов 5). [G.:] I think I had too much to drink. [Z.:] Of course. You're blind drunk (5b). ♦ «Давно мы с тобой не пили, Лёха, — удовлетворённо похохатывал гость, — вернусь, напьёмся — нальёмся в драбадан». — «В доску!» — «В лоск!» (Максимов 1). "You and I haven't had a drink for ages, Lyonya," the visitor chuckled contentedly. "When I get back we'll get stuck in — we'll get drunk as lords!" "Completely plastered!" "Out of our skulls!" (1a).

2. totally, absolutely: **utterly; completely;** ∥ разориться ~ ≃ **go broke; be utterly ruined;** ∥ проиграться ~ ≃ **lose one's shirt;** ∥ износить что ~ ≃ **wear sth. out completely; wear sth. threadbare.**

Сел он играть с какими-то жуликами, — понятно, проигрался в лоск. He got into a game with some card sharks. It's no wonder he lost his shirt. ♦ Сапоги твои износились в лоск, пора покупать новые. Your boots are completely worn-out, it's time to buy new ones.

Л-140 • ТЁМНАЯ ЛОШÁДКА *coll* [NP; usu. sing; usu. subj-compl with copula (subj: human); fixed WO] a person, occas. an opponent or a competitor, whose true character, feelings, plans, abilities etc are unknown (in sports, often an athlete or team from whom one may expect surprises): **dark horse.**

Л-141 • КАК ЛОМОВÁЯ ЛÓШАДЬ работать [как + NP; nom only; adv] (to work) very hard (usu. doing heavy, tiring labor): **(be) a (real) workhorse; (work) like a horse ⟨a dog, a mule, a slave⟩.**

Л-142 • САДÍТЬСЯ/СЕСТЬ В ЛÝЖУ ⟨В КАЛÓШУ, В ГАЛÓШУ⟩ *coll* [VP; subj: human; more often pfv] to end up in a foolish, embarrassing position (because of failing to do sth. properly, making a blunder, revealing one's ignorance etc): X сел в лужу ≃ **X fell flat on his face; X made a fool ⟨an ass, a jackass⟩ of himself; X had ⟨ended up with⟩ egg on ⟨all over⟩ his face; X put his foot in it; X came a cropper; X looked ⟨appeared⟩ ridiculous; X looked ⟨ended up looking⟩ pretty stupid;** [in limited contexts] **X laid an egg; X got himself into a mess.**

Партийные идеологи с предсказанием сроков очень часто садятся в лужу. Никита Хрущёв обещал построить коммунизм за 20 лет, но теперь ясно видно, что он вряд ли будет построен и через 200 лет (Войнович 1). When making predictions about time, Party ideologists often fall flat on their faces. Nikita Khrushchev promised that Communism would be built in twenty years, but now it's clear that it can scarcely be built in two hundred (1a). ♦ [Сатин (*Барону, смеясь*):] Вы, ваше вашество, опять торжественно сели в лужу! Образованный человек, а карту передёрнуть не можете... (Горький 3). [S. (*to the Baron, laughing*):] Your Lordship has put your foot into it with a vengeance again. An educated man and doesn't even know how to cheat! (3e). ♦ [Муромский:] Посредь-то высшего общества не сесть бы в лужу. [Атуева:] И в лужу не сяду! (Сухово-Кобылин 2). [M.:] Make sure you don't come a cropper, with all of your high society looking on. [A.:] I won't come a cropper! (2a). ♦ «Его, чёрта, голыми руками не возьмёшь... Оперативников просить? А вдруг нет там никакого Цыганкова, а если и был, то второй раз на одно место не придёт? Значит, сядем в галошу, Лашков» (Максимов 3). "You won't catch that devil bare-handed....Maybe we ought to call the Criminal Investigation Squad? But what if it wasn't Tsygankov at all, or maybe he was there but won't come to the same place twice? We'd look pretty stupid, Lashkov" (3a). ♦ «Всё сгнило здесь, — думал Максим. — Ни одного живого человека. Ни одной ясной головы. И опять я сел в галошу, потому что понадеялся на кого-то или на что-то» (Стругацкие 2). "Everything is rotten here," thought Maxim. "There isn't one real man among them. Not a

single clear head. And I've gotten myself into a mess again because I relied on other people" (2a).

Л-143 • САЖÁТЬ/ПОСАДÍТЬ В ЛÝЖУ ⟨В КАЛÓШУ, В ГАЛÓШУ⟩ кого *coll* [VP; subj: human; more often pfv] to put s.o. in an awkward, ridiculous, foolish position: X посадил Y-а в лужу ≃ **X made a fool (out) of Y; X made Y look silly ⟨ridiculous⟩; X put Y on the spot; X tripped Y (up);** [in limited contexts] **X got ⟨put, plunked⟩ Y into a jam.**

Раздался дружный смех. Молодец Мёрзлый! Посадил секретаря [райкома] в лужу (Абрамов 1). Everyone laughed in unison. Good for you, Myorzly! You've plunked the Secretary [of the party District Committee] into a jam! (1a).

Л-144 • ОТ ЛУКÁВОГО *lit* [PrepP; Invar; subj-compl with быть∅ (subj: abstr, often всё, всё это)] (of a theory, idea, action, or phenomenon that s.o. does not understand and deems unnecessary) sth. is completely uncalled-for, bad, and potentially harmful: X — от лукавого ≃ **X is the work of the devil; X comes straight from the devil;** [in limited contexts] **X is evil.**

Всё, что не входило, не вмещалось в этот мир, в котором он вырос, выучился и по ступенькам дошёл до нынешнего положения, — было от лукавого (Гинзбург 2). Anything that did not form part of this world of his, to which he had been born, trained, and promoted step by step to his present position, was the work of the devil (2a).

< From the Bible (Matt. 5:37).

Л-145 • ПОД ЛУНÓЙ ⟨-ю⟩ [PrepP; these forms only; adv] in the world, on earth: **in this world; under the sun.**

Директор у нас был хороший, но увы, ничто не вечно под луной, — его сняли. Our director was a good man, but, alas, nothing in this world lasts forever: they fired him.

Л-146 • (как, будто, словно, точно) С ЛУНÝ СВАЛÍЛСЯ ⟨УПÁЛ⟩ *coll* [VP; subj: human; past only; usu. used in questions; usu. this WO] one does not know things that are obvious, known to everybody: ты что, с луны свалился? ≃ **where have you been all this time?; are you ⟨what are you,⟩ from another planet?**

«Приношу [плакат], а там...» — «Погоди, ради какого случая?» — «Ты что, с луны свалился? Ради Дня открытых убийств» (Аржак 1). "I took it [the poster] to them, and they..." "Wait a minute. In view of what occasion?" "Where have you been all this time? Public Murder Day, of course" (1a).

Л-147 • КАК ЛУНЬ седой, белый [как + NP; Invar; modif; may be used with pl subj] totally, absolutely (gray): **completely gray; (one's hair is) snow-white ⟨white as snow⟩.**

[Кречинский:] Смотришь, вот и старик отец идёт в комнату; седой как лунь, костылём подпирается... (Сухово-Кобылин 2). [K.:] Then into the room comes the aged father — hair white as snow, leaning on a crutch (2b).

Л-148 • ЛÝЧШЕ НЕ НÁДО *coll, approv* [Invar; usu. subj-compl with copula (subj: any common noun); fixed WO] sth. is extremely good, of very high quality, s.o. is excellent, entirely adept: **the best there is; couldn't be better; you couldn't ask for better ⟨a better...⟩.**

Мои друзья живут в прекрасном районе, квартира — лучше не надо. My friends live in a great neighborhood, and their apartment — you couldn't ask for better.

Л-149 • ЛÝЧШЕ ПÓЗДНО, ЧЕМ НИКОГДÁ [saying] it is better that sth. expected or desired happens late than not at all: **better late than never.**

Л-150 • ТЕМ ЛÝЧШЕ [AdvP; Invar; usu. indep. sent or predic (subj: a clause); fixed WO] that (outcome, state of affairs etc) is better, more desirable to or advantageous for s.o. (than another outcome or state of affairs might have been): **all ⟨so much⟩ the better; that's even better;** [in limited contexts] **(it ⟨that⟩ is) just as well.**

[Кашкина:] ...Ты не думай, что я про тебя ничего не знаю. Кое-что мне всё-таки известно. [Шаманов:] Тем лучше (Вампилов 2). [K.:] ...Don't think I don't know *anything* about you. A few things have come to my knowledge. [Sh.:] All the better (2a). ♦ «Если б вы знали, какая мучит меня забота!» — «Я всё знаю», — отвечал я... «Тем лучше: я не в духе рассказывать» (Лермонтов 1). "You've no idea how worried I am." "I know all about it," I replied.... "So much the better. I don't feel much like telling you" (1c).

Л-151 • ОСТАВЛЯ́ЕТ ЖЕЛА́ТЬ ЛУ́ЧШЕГО ⟨МНО́-ГОГО⟩ [VP; subj: usu. abstr; pres or past; fixed WO] sth. is unsatisfactory, not good enough, less than ideal: X оставляет желать лучшего ≃ **X leaves much ⟨a great deal⟩ to be desired; X falls short (of the mark); X doesn't fill the bill.**

«Я приму к сведению всё, что услышал сегодня, — объявил полицмейстер. — Ваш тон, сударь, оставляет желать лучшего, однако я обещаю лицам, уполномочившим вас, что разберусь...» (Стругацкие 1). "I will take everything into consideration," announced the police chief. "Your tone, sir, leaves much to be desired. However, I promise your superiors that I will look into the matter..." (1a). ♦ «Весьма обнадёживающе заявивший о себе ранее молодой поэт-колхозник Влад Самсонов из станицы Пластуновской, бросив семью и работу, ведёт богемный образ жизни, обивая пороги редакций со стихами, оставляющими желать много лучшего» (Максимов 2). "Vlad Samsonov, the peasant poet from the village of Plastunovskaya, whose early work was extremely promising, having abandoned his family and his work is now living a bohemian life and is pestering every editor in town with verses that leave a great deal to be desired" (2a).

Л-152 • НАВОСТРИ́ТЬ ЛЫ́ЖИ *(куда, откуда) highly coll* [VP; subj: human] to run away (or be about to run to or from some place): X навострил лыжи ≃ **X took ⟨was ready to take⟩ to his heels; X skipped out; X took ⟨was about to take⟩ off (for some place).**

«Дело известное, что мужик: на новой земле, да заняться ещё хлебопашеством, да ничего у него нет, ни избы, ни двора, убежит, как дважды два, навострит так лыжи, что и следа не отыщешь» (Гоголь 3). "You know perfectly well what a Russian peasant is like: settle him on new land and set him to till it, with nothing prepared for him, neither cottage nor farmstead, and, well, he'll run away, as sure as twice two makes four. He'll take to his heels and you won't find a trace of him" (3a).

Л-153 • НАПРАВЛЯ́ТЬ/НАПРА́ВИТЬ ЛЫ́ЖИ *куда highly coll* [VP; subj: human] to start off or be going in some direction: X направил лыжи в место Y ≃ **X headed (off) for place Y; X set off ⟨out⟩ for place Y; X took off for place Y.**

Л-154 • ЛЫ́КА ⟨-ом *obs*⟩ НЕ ВЯ́ЖЕТ *highly coll, disapprov* [VP; subj: human; fixed WO] one is so drunk that he cannot speak coherently: X лыка не вяжет ≃ **X (is so drunk that he) can't talk straight.**

Вот так, когда нам представляется сделать доброе дело, мы чувствуем, что слишком трезвы для него, а когда в редчайших случаях к нам обращаются за мудрым советом, оказывается, что именно в этот час мы лыка не вяжем (Искандер 5). So it goes—whenever it occurs to us to do a good deed, we feel we're too sober for it, but on the very rare occasion when we're consulted for wise advice, it turns out to be precisely the moment we can't talk straight (5a).

Л-155 • НЕ ВСЯ́КО(Е) ЛЫ́КО В СТРО́КУ [saying] not every error or fault should be held against the person who com-

mitted it (said to excuse a person who has made a blunder; also said as advice not to carp on trivial matters): ≃ **don't quibble over every trifle; everybody makes mistakes.**

< In old Russia, strips («строки») of bast («лыко») were used to make woven sandals. Not all bast was of good enough quality for use as strips.

Л-156 • СТА́ВИТЬ/ПОСТА́ВИТЬ ВСЯ́КОЕ ЛЫ́КО В СТРО́КУ *кому coll* [VP; subj: human] to blame s.o. for any and every mistake: X ставит Y-у всякое лыко в строку ≃ **X holds everything against Y; X blames ⟨sticks the blame on, pins the blame on⟩ Y for everything that goes wrong.**

[author's usage] «Русское дворянство, — говорил он, — виновато перед Россией, Евгения Николаевна, но оно умело её любить. В ту первую войну нам ничего не простили, каждое лычко поставили в строку, — и наших дураков, и оболтусов, и сонных обжор, и Распутина... и липовые аллеи, и беспечность, и чёрные избы, и лапти...» (Гроссман 2). "The Russian aristocracy," he would say, "may stand guilty before Russia, Yevgenia Nikolaevna, but they did at least love her. We were pardoned nothing at the time of that first War: our fools, our blockheads, our sleepy gluttons, Rasputin, our irresponsibility and our avenues of lime-trees, the peasants' huts without chimneys and their bast shoes—everything was held against us" (2a). ♦ [author's usage] «...Вы можете самого бога сбить с толку такими вопросами: где ступил, как ступил, когда ступил и во что ступил? Ведь я собьюсь, если так, а вы сейчас лыко в строку и запишете, и что ж выйдет? Ничего не выйдет!» (Достоевский 1). [context transl] "...You could confuse even God himself with such questions: where I stepped, how I stepped, when I stepped, what I stepped in? I'll get confused that way, and you'll pick up every dropped stitch and write it down at once, and what will come of it? Nothing will come of it!" (1a).

< See Л-155.

Л-157 • ЛЫ́КОМ ШИТ ⟨ШИ́ТЫЙ⟩ *coll* [AdjP; subj-compl with быть∅ (subj: human), pres only] one is unpolished, uneducated, uncultivated: X лыком шит ≃ **X is a ⟨country⟩ bumpkin ⟨a hick, a yokel⟩; X is cut from simple cloth;** [in limited contexts] **X was brought up in a barn.**

Л-158 • НЕ ЛЫ́КОМ ШИТ ⟨ШИ́ТЫЙ⟩ *coll* [AdjP; subj-compl with быть∅, оказаться (subj: human), pres or past, or detached modif (full form only)] one is as good as anyone else, is not lacking abilities, knowledge, manners etc: X не лыком шит ≃ **X is no ⟨country⟩ bumpkin ⟨no slouch, no hick, no yokel⟩; X is no ⟨nobody's⟩ fool; X wasn't born yesterday; X knows what's what.**

Дабы показать, что я тоже не лыком шит, я ответил, что оформился плотником, но это ненадолго, пока устроюсь в Москве, а вообще я, разумеется, не за тем сюда приехал, чтобы работать плотником (Войнович 5). To show him that I, too, was no bumpkin, I answered that I had been assigned the post of carpenter but that this was just for the interim until I had gotten myself settled in Moscow and, needless to say, I had not come here to work as a carpenter (5a). ♦ ...Защитник, тоже не лыком шитый, упирал на смягчающее слабоумие подсудимого (Терц 1). ...The defense counsel, who was also no fool, kept insisting on the extenuating feeblemindedness of the accused (1a). ♦ Слава Богу, пережили НЭП [новую экономическую политику], троцкистский заговор, бухаринскую оппозицию, космополитов и врачей-вредителей. Научились кой-чему, не лыком шиты (Буковский 1). Thank God, we've survived the NEP [New Economic Policy], the Trotskyist conspiracy, the Bukharinite opposition, the "rootless cosmopolitans," and the "doctor-wreckers." We've learned a thing or two along the way, we weren't born yesterday, you know (1a).

Л-159 • ИЗ ЛЮБВИ́ К ИСКУ́ССТВУ [PrepP; Invar; adv; fixed WO] (to do sth.) exclusively for the pleasure one derives from doing it rather than for the sake of achieving some goal: **(just) for the fun of it ⟨of the thing⟩; for the (sheer) love ⟨joy⟩ of it; for sheer pleasure.**

Никто из нас не носит носков, связанных бабушкой, но она продолжает вязать их из любви к искусству. None of us ever wears the socks Grandma knits, but she keeps on knitting them for the sheer joy of it.

Л-160 • НЕ ОТКАЖИ́(ТЕ) В ЛЮБЕ́ЗНОСТИ [VP$_{imper}$; these forms only; foll. by infin; fixed WO] a polite request: **(please) be so good ⟨kind⟩ (as to...).**

Не откажите в любезности сообщить мне результаты конкурса. Please be so kind as to let me know the results of the competition.

Л-161 • ЛЮ́БО-ДО́РОГО ⟨ЛЮ́БО-МИ́ЛО⟩ *coll* [AdvP; these forms only; usu. predic with быть$_\theta$ (impers or with subj: any common noun or infin)] (sth. is) very good, nice, (sth. is done, to do sth.) very well: **(be) a (real) treat; (be) marvelous ⟨lovely, a pleasure** etc⟩; ‖ любо-дорого посмотреть ≃ **(it's) a sight to see ⟨to behold⟩; (it's) a sight for sore eyes; (it's) a pleasure to look at ⟨to behold⟩; (it's) a (real) treat for the eyes.**

...[Егорша] кивнул на чулан, прислушиваясь к песне. «Райка, что ли, поёт?» – спросил Михаил. «Ага. Пойдём, я сейчас её выкупаю – любо-дорого!» (Абрамов 1). ...He [Egorsha] motioned toward the storeroom, from which singing could be heard. "That Raika singing?" asked Mikhail. "Yup. Come on. I'm going to give her a soaking. We're in for a treat!" (1a). ♦ «Теперь, вон, в столовой любо-дорого... На четыре гривенника ешь – не хочу...» (Максимов 3). "It's a real treat over there in the canteen nowadays....Eat as much as you like for a few coppers..." (3a).

Л-162 • ЛЮБО́ВЬ ЗЛА – ПОЛЮ́БИШЬ И КОЗЛА́ [saying] love cannot be rationalized, you may end up falling in love with a person whom others consider inappropriate for you: ≃ **beauty is in the eye of the beholder; love is blind.**

Л-163 • СТА́РАЯ ЛЮБО́ВЬ НЕ РЖАВЕ́ЕТ [saying] an old, deep feeling does not pass with time: ≃ **old loves are not easily forgotten.**

Л-164 • всё КАК У ЛЮДЕ́Й (*у кого, где*) *coll* [как + PrepP; Invar; subj-compl with быть$_\theta$ (subj: всё)] things are (or are done) the way they should be: **everything is (being done) as it should be; everything is (just) as ⟨the way⟩ it's supposed to be; everything is being done the way it's supposed to;** ‖ *Neg* всё не как у людей *disapprov* ≃ **everything is (being done) all wrong; nothing is the way it's supposed to be; nothing is being done the way it's supposed to.**

Виктор представил себе уютный вечерок: ...бутылка, шампанское шипит в фужерах, перевязанная ленточкой коробка шоколаду как адвокат, запакованный в крахмал, галстук бабочкой. Всё как у людей... (Стругацкие 1). Victor imagined a comfortable tête-à-tête:...a bottle, champagne fizzing in crystal glasses, a box of chocolates tied up with a ribbon, and the lawyer himself, all starched up and wearing a bow tie. Everything just as it's supposed to be... (1a).

Л-165 • ПОСПЕШИ́ШЬ – ЛЮДЕ́Й НАСМЕШИ́ШЬ [saying] when a person does sth. hastily, without careful consideration, planning etc, he is likely to end up failing, looking ridiculous etc: ≃ **haste makes waste.**

Л-166 • ВСЕ МЫ ЛЮ́ДИ, ВСЕ (МЫ) ЧЕЛОВЕ́КИ [saying] we all have deficiencies and weaknesses (said to excuse a person's shortcomings; also said charitably of human weaknesses in general): ≃ **we're only human; nobody's perfect.**

Л-167 • ВЫВОДИ́ТЬ/ВЫ́ВЕСТИ В ЛЮ́ДИ *кого* [VP; subj: human; more often pfv] to be actively involved in helping s.o. to achieve a secure or prominent position in society, in life: X вывел Y-a в люди ≃ **X set Y up in the world; X put ⟨set⟩ Y on Y's feet; X helped Y get on Y's feet.**

[Добротворский:] Ваш папенька... в люди меня вывел, я прежде очень маленький человек был (Островский 1). [D.:] Your papa...set me up in the world: before that I was a very insignificant man (1b). ♦ А там, гляди, устроится попрочнее, заслужит награду, ему комнатку дадут, и возьмёт он к себе кого-нибудь из братишек, чтобы и его в люди вывести (Мандельштам 1). He...would soon settle in a more permanent way, get some kind of award and a room to himself, after which he would invite one of his younger brothers to join him and help him get on his feet as well (1a).

Л-168 • ВЫХОДИ́ТЬ/ВЫ́ЙТИ ⟨ВЫБИВА́ТЬСЯ/ВЫ́-БИТЬСЯ⟩ В ЛЮ́ДИ [VP; subj: human; more often pfv] to achieve a prominent position in society, achieve success in life as a result of determined effort: X вышел в люди ≃ **X rose ⟨came up, moved up⟩ in the world; X made his way in the world; X made his way up (in the world); X became somebody; X got ahead in the world; X made something of himself; X made it;** [in limited contexts] **X worked his way up from...; X carved out a career for himself.**

«Ну что, Евгений, выходишь в люди, – бодро сказал Силаев. – Скоро вообще большим человеком будешь» (Войнович 5). "Well, Evgeny, you're moving up in the world," said Silaev heartily. "Pretty soon you'll be a big shot" (5a). ♦ «Вот уж эта [Татьяна] выбьется в люди» (Абрамов 1). "That one [Tatyana] will really make her way in the world" (1b). ♦ Про Алферова говорили, что он из захудалых казачьих офицеришек выбился в люди лишь благодаря своей жене – бабе энергичной и умной; говорили, что она тянула бездарного супруга за уши и до тех пор не давала ему дыхнуть, пока он, три раза срезавшись, на четвёртый всё же выдержал экзамен в академию (Шолохов 3). Alferov was said to have made his way up from being a lowly Cossack officer only thanks to his energetic and intelligent wife; she had dragged her dull-witted spouse out of his rut and never let him rest until, after three failures, he had passed the Academy entrance examination (3a). ♦ [Анастасия Ефремовна:] Мы думаем о том, чтобы ты в люди вышел, и считаться с твоими капризами больше не намерены! (Розов 1). [A.E.:] ...We want you to be somebody – so we don't intend to pay any attention to your whims (1a). ♦ Знаю я, как здесь фотографы десятилетиями вкалывают, выбиваясь в люди (Лимонов 1). I know how photographers knock themselves out for decades trying to make it here (1a). ♦ [author's usage] Из полковых писарей вылез Емельян Константинович [Атёпин] в люди, оттуда же принёс в семью затхлый душок подхалимства, заискивания (Шолохов 2). Atyopin had worked his way up from regimental clerk, and from his humble beginnings he brought to his family the fusty atmosphere of bootlicking and ingratiation (2a).

Л-169 • ЖИВУ́Т (ЖЕ) ЛЮ́ДИ! *coll* [Interj; these forms only; var. with же is more common; fixed WO] (said with a trace of envy or a mixture of envy and admiration when reacting to sth. desirable that another possesses, has the opportunity to do etc) some people are lucky: **some people know how to live; some people have it good; that's the life!** [in limited contexts] **the way some people live!**

Он нагнулся к туалетному столику, вытащил бутылку и стакан... «Ничего, если из одного стакана?» – «Это смотря что», – ответил Виктор и снова сел. «Шотландское... Устраивает?» – «Настоящее шотландское?» – «Настоящий скоч. Получайте». Он протянул Виктору стакан. «Живут же люди», – сказал Виктор и выпил (Стругацкие 1). He bent over to the night table and pulled out a bottle and a glass....Is it all right if we share a glass?" "It depends on what's in it," answered Victor and sat down again. "Scotch....Does that suit you?" "Real Scotch?" "The real thing. Allow me." He held out the glass to Victor. "Some people have it good," said Victor (1a).

Л-170 • **ИДТИ́/ПОЙТИ́ ⟨УЙТИ́⟩ В ЛЮ́ДИ** *obs* [VP; subj: human] to leave one's home in search of a job (usu. working for s.o. on whose premises one can reside): X пошёл в люди ≃ **X left home to earn his living; X went out to work as a live-in hired hand ⟨as a live-in domestic** etc⟩.

Двенадцати лет бабка пошла в люди, была прислугой, нянчила детей, потом стала прачкой (Кузнецов 1). At the age of twelve my grandmother went out to work; she looked after other people's children, worked as a domestic servant and then became a washerwoman (1b).

Л-171 • **ЛЮ́ДИ ДО́БРОЙ ВО́ЛИ** *media* [NP; pl only; fixed WO] (used by the Soviet media as a propagandistic cliché; used ironically by émigré writers) people striving for peace, for the good of the people: **people of good will.**

Ты себе не представляешь, Коля, до чего жестоки и тупы многие простые люди доброй воли (Алешковский 1). You have no idea how cruel and dense a lot of people of good will can be, Kolya (1a).

Л-172 • **НА́ ЛЮДИ ⟨НА ЛЮ́ДИ⟩** *coll* **выходить, показываться** и т. п.; **В ЛЮ́ДИ** *obs* [PrepP; these forms only; adv] (to go out, show o.s.) in society, in a public place: **(be) with people; (be) among ⟨around⟩ other people; (appear) in public; (go out etc to) see ⟨call on⟩ people.**

Душа её, взлетев и возликовав ещё на пашне, продолжала играть, просилась на люди, но что-то удерживало, наговаривало, что это не её день, не её победа, что она к победе никакого отношения не имеет (Распутин 2). Her soul, which had flown up and soared back in the fields, was still playing, begging to be with people, but something was holding her back, telling her that it wasn't her day, her victory, that she had nothing to do with the victory (2a). ♦ Несмотря на все эти причуды, другу его, Штольцу, удавалось вытаскивать его в люди... (Гончаров 1). Despite all these vagaries, his friend Stolz succeeded in dragging him out to see people... (1b).

Л-173 • **СВОИ́ ЛЮ́ДИ – СОЧТЁМСЯ** [saying] relatives, friends, people who are close will always be able to pay each other back, return a favor etc: ≃ **it's all among friends; it's all in the family; what's money ⟨a favor** etc⟩ **between friends?**

Л-174 • **ЖИТЬ ⟨СЛУЖИ́ТЬ⟩ В ЛЮ́ДЯХ** *obs* [VP; subj: human] to work for s.o. while residing on his premises: X жил в людях ≃ **X was a hired hand ⟨a live-in servant⟩; X was in the service of others.**

Л-175 • **НА ЛЮ́ДЯХ** *coll;* **В ЛЮ́ДЯХ** *obs* [PrepP; these forms only; adv or subj-compl with бывать, быть₀ etc (subj: human)] in the company of others: **in public; in company; in front ⟨in the presence⟩ of others ⟨of other people⟩; before other people; (be) among ⟨around⟩ (other) people.**

Теперь им совсем плохо, лежат пластом и до утра... на людях появиться не смогут (Стругацкие 3). Now they were quite ill, flat on their backs, and could not appear in public before morning (3a). ♦ Надя [Крупская]... в методичности, в бережливости не имеет равных. Она действительно нутром понимает... что каждый свободный франк – это лишняя длительность мысли и работы... И перед всем этим было бы непристойно революционеру стесняться на людях, что жена некрасива, или ума не выдающегося, или старше его на год... Для существования Ленина как политической личности союз с Крупской вполне достаточен и разумен (Солженицын 5). ...Nadya had no equal for orderliness and economy. She understood instinctively that every extra franc in hand meant extra time for thinking and working....In view of all this, it would ill become a revolutionary to be ashamed in company that his wife was far from beautiful, not outstandingly intelligent, and a year older than himself....For Lenin the politician, the union with Nadya was all that reason could require (5a). ♦ «...Дознано и доказано предварительным следствием, что подсудимый... всё время был на людях, а стало быть, не мог отделить от трёх тысяч половины и куда-нибудь спрятать в городе» (Достоевский 2). "...It has been determined and demonstrated by the preliminary investigation that the defendant...was constantly in the presence of other people, and therefore could not have separated half of the three thousand and hidden it somewhere in town" (2a). ♦ «...Ты вправе поступить с ним так, чтобы умалишённый Раймалы нас не позорил бы на людях...» (Айтматов 2). "...You've the right to proceed with him and take whatever steps are needed to prevent him from shaming us before other people" (2a). ♦ То ли оттого, что у тёти Маши муж был нелюдим, то ли это было свойством её собственной натуры, но тётя Маша любила бывать на людях (Искандер 3). Whether because Aunt Masha's husband was an unsociable person, or because it was a trait of her own nature, Aunt Masha loved to be among people (3a).

Л-176 • **ТЯНУ́ТЬ/ПОТЯНУ́ТЬ ЛЯ́МКУ** *coll* [VP; subj: human; usu. impfv] to be occupied for a long period of time with a difficult, unpleasant, monotonous task: X тянул лямку ≃ **X slaved ⟨toiled⟩ (away); X sweated it out; X performed ⟨was engaged in⟩ drudgery; X was ⟨remained⟩ in harness; X drudged;** [in limited contexts] **X sweated.**

Жерков после своего изгнания из главного штаба не остался в полку, говоря, что он не дурак во фронте лямку тянуть, когда он при штабе, ничего не делая, получит наград больше... (Толстой 4). After his dismissal from head-quarters Zherkov had not remained in the regiment, saying he was not such a fool as to slave at the front when he could get more rewards by doing nothing on the staff... (4b). ♦ Максим кончает пехотное училище, будет тянуть армейскую лямку (Рыбаков 2). ...Max was finishing infantry school and would sweat it out in the army (2a). ♦ ...При изменившихся обстоятельствах мне казалось невыносимым тянуть всё ту же лямку (Гинзбург 2). ...In the changed circumstances, it seemed insufferable to me to have to perform the same drudgery as before (2a). ♦ Отец его, боевой генерал 1812 года, полуграмотный, грубый, но не злой русский человек, всю жизнь свою тянул лямку, командовал сперва бригадой, потом дивизией... (Тургенев 2). His father, a general, who had seen active service in 1812, a coarse and uneducated Russian but not ill-natured, had been in harness all his life, commanding a brigade at first and then a division... (2a). His father, a general who had fought in 1812, a half-educated, coarse, but not ill-natured man, a typical Russian, had drudged all his life, first in command of a brigade, then of a division... (2b). ♦ «Нет, пускай послужит он в армии, да потянет лямку, да понюхает пороху, да будет солдат...» (Пушкин 2). "No, let him serve in the army, let him learn to sweat and get used to the smell of gunpowder, let him become a soldier..." (2a).

Л-177 • **ТОЧИ́ТЬ/ПОТОЧИ́ТЬ ЛЯ́СЫ ⟨БАЛЯ́СЫ⟩** *(с кем) highly coll* [VP; subj: human] to be occupied with idle chatter (often to the detriment of the matter at hand): X точит лясы (с Y-ом) ≃ **X is chewing the fat (with Y); X is shooting the breeze ⟨the bull⟩ (with Y); X is wagging his tongue.**

...За делом Алёша лясы не точил, знал прежде дело, а уж потом всё остальное... (Распутин 4). Alyosha never chewed the fat when there was work to be done, he did the work first and then whatever else he might have felt like... (4a). ♦ Вот мы с вами сидим, лясы точим и ноги чешем, а там, за окном, быть может... всему свету наступает конец... (Терц 6). Here we sit, you and I, wagging our tongues and scratching our heels, and who knows if there, outside the window...the whole world is coming to an end... (6a).

< «Лясы» or «балясы» were small, decorative columns used to adorn banisters. While making them, craftsmen entertained themselves by chatting with each other.

M

M-1 • МАГ И ВОЛШЕ́БНИК *usu. humor* [NP; usu. subj-compl with бытьө (subj: human); may be used as an exclamation; fixed WO] a person who does everything easily and adroitly, who performs exceptional deeds: **wonder-worker; miracle man ⟨worker⟩; sorcerer and magician.**

[source] [Расплюев:] Наполеон, говорю, Наполеон! великий богатырь, маг и волшебник! (Сухово-Кобылин). [R.:] A Napoleon, I tell you, a Napoleon! A great hero, a sorcerer and magician! (2a).

< From Aleksandr Sukhovo-Kobylin's *Krechinsky's Wedding* («Сва́дьба Крече́нского»), 1855.

M-2 • НА МАЗИ́ *highly coll* [PrepP; Invar; subj-compl with бытьө (subj: abstr, usu. всё, дело)] in a favorable state, condition, close to completion or realization: X на мази ≃ **X is going smoothly ⟨fine⟩; X is almost all set; X looks like a sure thing; X is practically in the bag.**

Ипполит Матвеевич внимательно поглядел на перильца, за которыми стояла чета. «Рождение? Смерть?» — «Сочетаться», — повторил мужчина в пиджаке... Девица прыснула. Дело было на мази (Ильф и Петров 1). Ippolit Matveyevich looked thoughtfully at the rail behind which the young couple were standing. "Birth? Death?" "Get married?" repeated the young man in the coat....The girl gave a giggle. Things were going fine (1a).

M-3 • КУДА́ МАКА́Р ТЕЛЯ́Т НЕ ГОНЯ́Л *coll* [subord clause; Invar; usu. used as adv; fixed WO] very far away, to a very remote, far-off place: **to the back of beyond; to the middle of nowhere; to the land of no return; to a ⟨some⟩ godforsaken place ⟨hole etc⟩ (miles from anywhere ⟨nowhere⟩).**

«Посмел бы возражать, завтра же отправили бы куда Макар телят не гонял. На урановые рудники» (Копелев 1). "If he dared argue, tomorrow he'd be shipped off to the back of beyond. To the uranium mines" (1a). ♦ ...Сев в кибитку, [Беневоленский] благополучно проследовал в тот край, куда Макар телят не гонял (Салтыков-Щедрин 1). ...Taking his seat in the carriage, [Benevolensky] drove safely off to that distant land of no return (1b). ♦ От такой бабы зависит его судьба! Сама небось только явилась из какого-нибудь Орехова-Зуева, а его, коренного москвича, готова заслать куда Макар телят не гонял (Рыбаков 2). This hag held his fate in her hands! She'd probably just got out of some dump in the sticks herself, but she was ready to send him, a native Muscovite, to some godforsaken hole miles from anywhere (2a).

M-4 • НА БЕ́ДНОГО МАКА́РА ВСЕ ШИ́ШКИ ВА́ЛЯТСЯ [saying] new troubles arise for an unfortunate person already burdened with many troubles: ≃ **when it rains, it pours; it never rains but it pours; trouble and I ⟨you etc⟩ are never far apart; trouble rides behind and gallops with me ⟨you etc⟩; (I ⟨you etc⟩ have) lots of luck and all of it bad;** [in limited contexts] **(I ⟨you etc⟩) can't win for losing; things are going from bad to worse.**

M-5 • ТАКИ́М МАКА́РОМ *highly coll* [NP_instrum; Invar; adv; fixed WO] **1.** in the following manner or fashion: **this way; this is how; like this;** ‖ таким же макаром ≃ **in the (exact) same way.**

Действовать тут надо таким макаром: сначала обсуди это дело у себя в отделе, а потом уже поговори с директором. This is how you should handle it: first discuss the matter in your department and then bring it up with the director.

2. that is the state of affairs (usu. used to sum up what had been previously said): **that's the way it is ⟨goes⟩; that's about the size of it; that's how things stand.**

[Жарков:] Вот, брат... таким макаром... Двух жизней не проживёшь, так хоть одну дожить не по-собачьи (Розов 4). [Zh.:] Well, that's about the size of it, mate....You can't live twice, so make sure the life you do live is a decent one (4a).

M-6 • МАЛ МАЛА́ МЕ́НЬШЕ *coll* [AdjP; Invar; usu. detached postmodif; fixed WO] **1.** (of many small children) all are very young—the oldest is young and the others even younger: **one smaller ⟨younger⟩ than the other; each (one) smaller ⟨younger⟩ than the next.**

«Ваш отец получает у нас всего семьдесят пять рублей месячных, а детей у него, кроме вас, ещё пять человек, мал мала меньше, — значит, вам скорей всего придётся всю жизнь прожить в бедности» (Бунин 1). "Your father only gets paid seventy-five roubles a month, and he has children, five apart from you, one smaller than the other—that means you're more than likely to spend your whole life in poverty" (1a). ♦ «Вдовой уже взял её, с троими детьми, мал мала меньше» (Достоевский 3). "When I married her she was already a widow with three children, each one smaller than the next" (3b). ♦ [Расположенский:] Было у него, сударыня ты моя, двенадцать дочерей — мал мала меньше (Островский 10). [R.:] He had twelve daughters, my dear lady—each younger than the next (10a).

2. (of many small objects) all are small—the largest is small and the others are even smaller: **one smaller than the other; each (one) smaller than the next.**

M-7 • ОТ МА́ЛА ДО ВЕЛИ́КА *coll* [PrepP; Invar; usu. nonagreeing postmodif; usu. used after все, все люди etc; fixed WO] **1.** everyone regardless of age, absolutely everyone: **young and old (alike); both young and old; from the youngest to the oldest; from the oldest to the youngest.**

Шёл [Прокофий] с ней за арбой с имуществом по хутору — высыпали на улицу все от мала до велика (Шолохов 2). As he [Prokofy] walked with her behind a wagon carrying all their belongings, the whole village, young and old, came out to watch (2a). ♦ [Мамаев:] Прежде, бывало, я у своих подданных во всякую малость входил. Всех поучал, от мала до велика (Островский 9). [M.:] Time was when I took up all the fine points with my—er—menials. Taught all of them, young and old alike (9b). ♦ ...Однажды часть галереи с одной стороны дома вдруг обрушилась... В доме сделался гвалт: все прибежали, от мала до велика... (Гончаров 1). One day...part of the balcony on one side of the house suddenly collapsed....There was a great commotion in the house: everyone, from the youngest to the oldest, rushed out... (1b).

2. every member (of a certain group, profession etc) regardless of his status, degree of talent etc: **(both) great and small; great and small alike.**

«Это и есть новое зрение, то самое, о котором вот уже пятьдесят лет говорят все художники от мала до велика» (Каверин 2). "It's the new vision which every artist, both great and small, has been talking about for the past fifty years" (2a).

M-8 • ПО МА́ЛЕНЬКОЙ *coll* [PrepP; Invar; adv] **1.** играть, ходить ~ (in refer. to a card game) (to play) for small amounts of money: **(play) for small stakes.**

2. выпить, пропустить ~ (to drink) a small amount of alcohol: **have (just) a drop; take a nip; wet one's whistle.**

Дядя Лазарь работал со мной на обувной фабрике, в ОТК, по-прежнему попивал, не валялся в канаве, но прикладывался *по маленькой*, без этой маленькой не мог работать...

(Рыбаков 1). Uncle Lazar worked with me at the factory, he still drank as before, not that you'd find him in a ditch, but he had to have a drop or he couldn't work... (1a). ♦ Что же это мы всё только разговариваем? Пора и пропустить по маленькой. Hey, why is it we're only talking? It's high time we wet our whistles.

M-9 • ПО МА́ЛЕНЬКОМУ; ПО МА́ЛОМУ ДЕ́ЛУ *both euph, highly coll;* **ПО ЛЁГКОМУ** *army slang* [PrepP; these forms only; adv; usu. used with хотеть, нужно, сходить etc] to urinate: **go ⟨do⟩ number one; take a leak; make water.**

«Вот это квас! Аж дух зашибает. Погоди, бабка, не уноси. Сейчас я сбегаю по малому делу, ещё выпью, а то уже некуда, под завязку» (Войнович 5). "That's kvass! Takes your breath away. Hold on, don't take it away. I'll run and take a leak and then I'll have some more. There isn't room for another drop in me right now" (5a).

M-10 • РАЗЛЮЛИ́ МАЛИ́НА *substand, approv* [NP; subj-compl with быть∅ (subj: usu. житьё, жизнь) or adv; also used as Interj; fixed WO] (sth. is) very good, wonderful, (sth. is going, is done etc) very well, wonderfully: **great; super(-duper); terrific.**

M-11 • МА́ЛО ЛИ [AdvP; Invar; adv or premodif] **1.** ~ **кто, что, где, когда, как, какой** и т. п. many different people, things, places, times, ways, kinds etc (and it may not be especially relevant what precisely they all are; in some contexts the speaker shifts the emphasis to this aspect of irrelevance, esp. when he is irritated by a question, sees no need to specify sth. etc): **all kinds ⟨sorts⟩ of people ⟨things, ways, places etc⟩; in all kinds ⟨sorts⟩ of ways ⟨places etc⟩; at all different times ⟨places etc⟩; all different kinds ⟨ways⟩; plenty of (different) people etc; lots ⟨any number⟩ of people etc; you never know ⟨who knows, (there's) no telling⟩ who ⟨what etc⟩; [with the emphasis on the unimportance of specifics] what difference does it make who etc?; it doesn't matter ⟨as if it matters, as if it could matter, what does it matter⟩ who etc; who cares what etc.**

Рассказывали, что таких лесов много за Красным Северным хребтом в стране варваров, но мало ли что рассказывают про страну варваров... (Стругацкие 4). There were rumors making the round that many such woods still existed beyond the Red Mountains, in the country of the barbarians—but there are all kinds of stories told about those barbarians, you know... (4a). ♦ Мало ли что с ней случалось в жизни: болезни, выздоровления, поездки, разные встречи, любовь... (Залыгин 1). All sorts of things had happened in her life: illnesses, recoveries, journeys, various meetings, love... (1a). ♦ «Ещё между собой придётся повоевать. Ты как думаешь?»... — «С кем воевать-то?» — «Мало ли с кем. Хотя бы с большевиками» (Шолохов 3). "There's still some fighting to be done among ourselves, don't you think?"..."Who have we got to fight?" "Plenty of people....The Bolsheviks, for instance" (3a). ♦ «Что я разве друг его какой?.. или родственник? Правда, мы жили долго под одною кровлей... Да мало ли с кем я не жил?..» (Лермонтов 1). "I'm not a friend of his am I, or a relation? True, we lived a good while under the same roof—but then I've lived with plenty of different people in my time" (1c). ♦ «А что ж бы я стал делать, если б не служил?» — спросил Судьбинский. «Мало ли что! Читал бы, писал...» — сказал Обломов (Гончаров 1). "But what should I do if I were not in the service?" asked Sudbinsky. "Lots of things! You could read, write..." said Oblomov (1a). ♦ Она попросила домашних окликнуть его, узнать, куда это он заторопился, но никто не стал окликать: мало ли куда человек идёт! (Искандер 4) She asked the others to hail him, find out where he was off to in such a hurry, but no one bothered: as if it could matter where the man was going! (4a). ♦ «Карамазов, скажите, я очень теперь смешон?» — «...Что такое смешон? Мало ли сколько раз бывает или кажется смешным человек?» (Достоевский 1). "Tell me, Karamazov, am I very ridiculous now?" "...What does it mean—ridiculous? What does it

matter how many times a man is or seems to be ridiculous?" (1a). ♦ «Ну, а по пьяному делу, сама знаешь, мало ли чего можно сказать или сделать» (Войнович 5). [context transl] "You know yourself the things you can say or do when you've had too much to drink" (5a).

2. ~ **кого-чего** [usu. in exclamations] a great deal: **many; lots of; plenty of; no end of; [in limited contexts] as if there weren't ⟨one didn't have etc⟩ enough...**

Да мало ли знает история вспышек простонародной безобразной ярости! (Солженицын 5). But history records many such obscene outbursts of mob fury! (5a). ♦ [Глаголев I:] Я тоже был другом вашего отца, Михаил Васильич! [Платонов:] Мало ли у него было друзей... (Чехов 1). [G. Sr.:] I, too, was your father's friend, Michael. [P.:] He had lots of friends... (1a). ♦ Можно иметь диплом и быть дубиной. Мало ли примеров! (Трифонов 1). One could have a degree and still be a fool. There were plenty of examples of that around! (1a). ♦ ...[Студент] взял целую связку серпантина и открыл оживлённый огонь. Его мишенью была девушка... Первая лента, достигшая цели, упала девушке на плечо. Она неторопливо скинула серпантин на землю. Мало ли здесь было серпантина! (Федин 1). ...[The student] took a whole bundle of streamers and opened brisk fire. His target was a girl....The first ribbon to reach its object fell on the girl's shoulder. Without haste she threw the ribbon on the ground. As if there weren't enough streamers here! (1a).

M-12 • МА́ЛО ЛИ ЧТО *coll* [Invar; fixed WO] **1.** [used in a rejoinder, usu. foll. by a predic that is a repetition of the predic from the interlocutor's preceding remark] it is inconsequential: **it ⟨that⟩ makes no difference; as if it matters (that ⟨what⟩...)!; it doesn't matter (that ⟨what⟩...); what of it?; so what?; so what if person X does ⟨has, is etc⟩?**

«Главное, улик никаких», — спокойно сказал исправник. «Как никаких, коли сами мальчики признались?» — «Мало ли что признались, а перед судьёй отопрутся, — там ведь их пороть не станут» (Сологуб 1). "The important thing is that we have no evidence," said the police chief quietly. "What do you mean 'no evidence' if the boys themselves confessed?" "That makes no difference—they might deny it in court, and there'd be no one to whip them there" (1a).

2. [usu. indep. sent] (s.o. takes a precautionary measure, acts in a cautious manner, prepares himself etc because) any number of things (usu. undesirable) might occur: **you never know; anything could happen.**

Катерине он советовал сбыть всё [всю картошку]... Но три куля Катерина всё-таки оставила — мало ли что! (Распутин 4). He suggested that Katerina sell all of hers [her potatoes].... But Katerina still kept three bags—you never know! (4a). ♦ У прохожих он узнал, что до закрытия магазина оставалось ещё больше часу, но он решил никуда не уходить, а дожидаться закрытия на этом месте. Мало ли что... Вдруг они вздумают закрыть свой магазин раньше времени (Искандер 4). From passersby he learned that it was still over an hour before the store closed, but he decided not to go anywhere, to wait right here. Anything could happen....What if they took it into their heads to close their store early (4a).

M-13 • МА́ЛО ТОГО́ [AdvP; Invar; sent adv (parenth); fixed WO] besides that, apart from that, further: **moreover; more than that; (and) what's more; (and) not only that; as if that were not enough.**

...Сам Николай Гаврилович [Чернышевский] был человек громадного, всестороннего ума, громадной творческой воли... Мало того, я утверждаю, что критик он был превосходный — вдумчивый, честный, смелый... (Набоков 1). ...Nikolai Gavrilovich Chernyshevski himself was a man with a vast, versatile mind, with enormous, creative willpower....Moreover I maintain that he was a superb critic—penetrating, honest, brave... (1a). ♦ Я допускаю, что Иосиф не случайно намекнул дедушке про Сарру… хотел избавиться от Сарры, но не хотел попадать в зависимость от дедушки и потому отдалённо намекнул ему про Сарру, знал, что дедушка поймёт самый отдалённый намёк. Дедушка понял. Мало того, проверил. И убедился, что Сарра знает о приходе Гриши… (Рыбаков 1). I reckon that Yosif's hint to grandfather about Sarah had been on purpose.…He wanted to get Sarah off his back, but he didn't want to be in debt to grandfather, so he gave him a remote hint, knowing that he would pick it up, which he did. More than that, grandfather did some checking up and was certain that Sarah knew about Grisha's visit (1a). ♦ …С первого же дня [отец] стал оказывать бабушке внимание и уважение, к которому в доме не привыкли, и это внимание и уважение само по себе звучало неким протестом. Мало того, отец заставил и мою мать относиться с уважением к бабушке… (Рыбаков 1). From the first day…he [father] showed concern and respect for grandmother, which nobody else was used to doing, and this attitude was something of a protest in itself. Not only that, father also compelled my mother to show respect to grandmother… (1a). ♦ Он [Фёдор Константинович] шёл по улицам, которые давно успели втереться ему в знакомство, — мало того, рассчитывали на любовь… (Набоков 1). He [Fyodor Konstantinovich] was walking along streets that had already long since insinuated themselves into his acquaintance—and as if that were not enough, they expected affection… (1a).

M-14 • МА́ЛО ТОГО́ ЧТО… (, ЕЩЁ И…) [coord Conj] apart from, in addition to: **not only…(but…); it is not enough that…(you ⟨he, it** etc⟩ **also…).**

…Перебежал на Запад скульптор Игорёха Серебро… Мало того что перебежал, ещё и снял штаны перед всем миром, и оказалось — не эллин, не бог, оказались под штанами замшелые ляжки старого стукача (Аксёнов 6). …The sculptor Igor Serebro had defected to the West.…And not only had he defected, but he had also stripped before the eyes of the whole world and revealed…not the figure of a Greek god but the hairy thighs of an old stool pigeon, a longtime secret informer for the KGB (6a). ♦ «Мало того что ты чуть не утопил мальчика из прекрасной семьи, — сердито говорил женский голос, — теперь ещё эта история, о которой говорит весь город!.. Расхлёбывай сам эту кашу» (Каверин 1). "It wasn't enough that you nearly drowned a boy of good family," said a woman's angry voice. "Now there has to be this affair, with the whole town talking about it.…You'll have to get out of this trouble by yourself" (1a). ♦ По какому-то дьявольскому стечению обстоятельств оказалось, что мой редактор пишет стихи. Мало того что он писал стихи, он ещё… выступал под псевдонимом… (Искандер 6). [context transl] By some freakish coincidence it turned out that the paper's editor-in-chief wrote poetry, and what was worse, published his verse under a pseudonym (6a).

M-15 • МА́ЛО ЧТО [Invar; subj or obj; fixed WO] a (very) small quantity or amount: **not (very) much (at all); (very) little; hardly anything;** [in limited contexts] **(very) few** [NPs]; **hardly any** [NPs].

Басню декламировали с выражением… пожалуй, в стиле Малого театра (хоть мы, будучи одесскими мальчиками, мало что о нём знали) (Олеша 3). We recited the fable with expression…perhaps even in the style of the Maly Theater (although being Odessa schoolboys, we didn't know very much about that) (3a). ♦ Нравственные поговорки бывают удивительно полезны в тех случаях, когда мы от себя мало что можем выдумать себе в оправдание (Пушкин 3). [context transl] Moral maxims are surprisingly useful on occasions when we can invent little else to justify our actions (3a).

M-16 • БЕЗ МА́ЛОГО coll; **БЕЗ МА́ЛА** substand [PrepP; these forms only; usu. used with a quantit NP as nonagreeing modif] a little less than (the amount, number etc named): **almost; just about; nearly; slightly less than; just under; a little short of; a bit less than; practically.**

…Он объяснил себе свои предчувствия так, что слишком давно ничего не писал «своего», уже без малого год, даже больше года. (Битов 2). …He explained his premonitions by telling himself that it was too long since he had written anything of his own, almost a year already, even more than a year (2a). ♦ «В чём же вы провинились?» — «Да не мы… Соседи. Нам заодно досталось…» — «А те что?» — «Да без малого все семь смертных грехов» (Пастернак 1). "What have you done?" "We didn't do anything, it was our neighbors; we got it too for good measure…" "And what crime had they committed?" "Just about all the seven deadly sins…" (1a). ♦ …Вот уже без малого двадцать лет [дочь] ходит за ним, кормит, обстирывает… (Максимов 3). …For nearly twenty years now [his daughter] had looked after him, fed him, washed his clothes… (3a). ♦ Без малого три месяца провалялся Андрей Гуськов в новосибирском госпитале (Распутин 2). Andrei [Guskov] languished in the hospital in Novosibirsk for just under three months (2a). ♦ Он именно, чуть ли не по пальцам, высчитал, что Митя, в первый приезд свой в Мокрое, за месяц почти пред катастрофой, не мог истратить менее трёх тысяч или «разве без самого только малого» (Достоевский 2). He calculated precisely, almost on his fingers, that during his first visit to Mokroye about a month before the catastrophe, Mitya could not have spent less than three thousand, or "maybe just a tiny bit less" (2a). ♦ [Бабакина:] Видано ли дело: первый заём стоит уж двести семьдесят, а второй без малого двести пятьдесят… (Чехов 4). [В.:] It's fantastic—they're up to two hundred and seventy roubles for the first draw and they're practically at two-fifty for the second (4b).

M-17 • СА́МАЯ МА́ЛОСТЬ coll [NP; fixed WO] **1.** ~ (чего) [subj or obj] a very small amount (of sth.): **a tiny ⟨the tiniest⟩ bit; just a tad; hardly any.**

2. [accus only; adv] to a small extent: **a tiny ⟨the tiniest⟩ bit; (just) barely; hardly at all.**

Она [Наталья] неотрывно глядела на Мятлева. Тёмные, глубокие, прекрасные её глаза немного пугали его, уж так, едва-едва, самую малость (Окуджава 2). She [Natalya] stared intently at Myatlev. Her dark, deep, lovely eyes frightened him—just barely, the tiniest…bit (2a).

M-18 • МА́ЛЫЕ МИ́РА СЕГО́ obs [NP; pl only; fixed WO] people of low social status: **the lowly (of this world); those of little importance.**

M-19 • ДО́БРЫЙ ⟨СЛА́ВНЫЙ⟩ МА́ЛЫЙ coll [NP; sing only; usu. subj-compl with бытьø, слыть etc (subj: human, male); fixed WO] a good, pleasant, well-meaning person (although, usu., in no way remarkable): **good ⟨nice, decent⟩ fellow ⟨man⟩; fine chap; regular guy.**

[Тузенбах:] По-видимому, [Вершинин] славный малый. Не глуп — это несомненно (Чехов 5). [T.:] [Vershinin] seems to be a nice fellow. Not stupid, that's certain (5a). ♦ Есть минуты, когда я понимаю Вампира!.. А ещё слыву добрым малым и добиваюсь этого названия (Лермонтов 1). There are times when I can understand the Vampire, and yet I still pass for a decent fellow and try my best to be thought so (1c). ♦ «Твой отец добрый малый», — промолвил Базаров… (Тургенев 2). "Your father's a nice man," said Bazarov… (2b).

M-20 • МА́ЛЬЧИК ДЛЯ БИТЬЯ́ [NP; fixed WO] a person blamed for the faults or misdeeds of others: **whipping boy; fall guy.**

M-21 • МА́ЛЬЧИК С ПА́ЛЬЧИК folk [NP; sing only; only мальчик declines; fixed WO] a tiny boy (in folk tales one who acts wisely and resourcefully): **boy as big as a thumb; boy the size of a thumb.** Cf. **Tom Thumb.**

Обо всём этом я думаю, когда дед рассказывает мне сказки. Он долго рассказывает. Разные есть — смешные есть, особенно про мальчика с пальчик по имени Чыпалак…

(Айтматов 1). I think about all this when grandfather tells me tales. He tells long, long ones. He has all kinds—funny ones, especially about the boy the size of a thumb called Chipalak... (1b).

M-22 • КАК ⟨БУ́ДТО, СЛО́ВНО, ТО́ЧНО⟩ МАМА́Й ПРОШЁЛ *highly coll* [как etc + VP_subj; these forms only; fixed WO] there is complete disorder, terrible devastation (in some place): **it's as if an army had marched through ⟨some place⟩; ⟨some place⟩ looks like a war zone; (it's) complete havoc ⟨in some place⟩; ⟨some place⟩ looks as if ⟨like⟩ it's been hit ⟨struck⟩ by a tornado.**

< From the name of the Tartar khan *Mamai,* who led a devastating invasion of Russia in the 14th cent.

M-23 • НА МАНЕ́Р *coll* [PrepP; Invar; adv]   **1.** ~ *какой* in a certain fashion (as specified), according to the fashion or custom of (some place or time): **in the [AdjP] fashion ⟨manner, style⟩; after the [AdjP] fashion ⟨manner⟩; à la;** ‖ на русский ⟨французский и т. п.⟩ манер ≃ **Russian-style ⟨French-style etc⟩.**

...Волос они на голове не носили ни хохлами, ни буклями, ни на манер чёрт меня побери, как говорят французы; волосы у них были или низко подстрижены, или прилизаны... (Гоголь 3). They did not wear their hair in a long forelock, nor in curls, nor in the devil-may-care style—as the French call it; they wore it short-cropped or slicked down... (3e). ♦ «Вот княгиня Лиговская... и с нею дочь её Мери, как она её называет на английский манер» (Лермонтов 1). "That's Princess Ligovskoj...and with her is her daughter Mary, as she calls her after the English fashion" (1a).

2. ~ *кого-чего* similar to, resembling s.o. or sth.: **like s.o. ⟨sth.⟩; in imitation of s.o. ⟨sth.⟩.**

Постепенно упорядочили свою деятельность внуки Карла Маркса, кропоткинцы, энгельсовцы и им подобные, за исключением буйной корпорации детей лейтенанта Шмидта, которую, на манер польского сейма, вечно раздирала анархия (Ильф и Петров 2). Little by little, the grandchildren of Karl Marx, the Kropotkinites, the Engelists, and their ilk organized their activity. The dissenters were the stormy "children of Lieutenant Schmidt," who, like the Polish *Sejm,* were eternally torn by anarchy (2a). ♦ ...[Три девушки] стали настраивать свои чонгури... Потом по знаку одной из них они [девушки] ударили по струнам — и полилась мелодия, которую они тут же подхватили голосами и запели на манер старинных горных песен без слов (Искандер 6). ...[The three girls] began tuning their *chonguris*....Then one of them gave a signal and they began to play. Their voices immediately took up the melody on the strings and they began singing in imitation of the mountaineer's old-fashioned song without words (6a). ♦ Я предложил ему свою комнату. Он не церемонился, даже ударил меня по плечу и скривил рот на манер улыбки (Лермонтов 1). [context transl] I offered him the use of my room; he made no pretense of ceremony, he even clapped me on the shoulder and twisted his mouth into the semblance of a smile (1a).

M-24 • МА́ННА НЕБЕ́СНАЯ [NP; sing only; fixed WO] sth. desired, much needed, long-awaited that s.o. receives (usu. unexpectedly): **manna from heaven.**

После этих посещений на нас вдруг свалилась манна небесная — меня пригласили в горжилотдел «для переговоров об улучшении квартирных условий» (Гинзбург 2). After these visits came manna from heaven: I was invited to the town housing department to "discuss an improvement in your accommodations" (2a).

< From the Bible (Ex. 16:31–35 et al.).

M-25 • ПИТА́ТЬСЯ МА́ННОЙ НЕБЕ́СНОЙ *coll, humor* [VP; subj: human; the verb may take the final position, otherwise fixed WO] to eat almost nothing: X питается манной небесной ≃ **X lives on air.**

Ты так похудела! Ты что, питаешься манной небесной? You've gotten so thin! What are you doing, living on air?

M-26 • КАК МА́ННЫ НЕБЕ́СНОЙ ждать *кого-чего,* жаждать *чего* и т. п. [как + NP; Invar; adv (intensif); fixed WO] (to wait for s.o. or sth.) with great impatience, desire, (to crave sth.) intensely: X ждёт Y-а как манны небесной ≃ **X is waiting for Y like manna from heaven; X (just) can't wait for Y; X is just ⟨simply⟩ dying for ⟨to get⟩ thing Y; X is yearning for thing Y.**

«Напиши в правительство». — «Хорошая идея, — усмехнулся Садчиков, — там ж-ждут моего письма, как манны небесной» (Семёнов 1). "Write to the government." "A good idea," grinned Sadchikov, "they're just waiting for my letter, like manna from heaven" (1a). ♦ [Глумов:] Ведь как ему растолкуешь, что мне от него ни гроша не надобно, что я только совета жажду, жажду, алчу наставления, как манны небесной (Островский 9). [G.:] How do you expect me to convince him that I don't want a penny of his, that all I want is his advice, that I'm simply dying to have him admonish me (9a).

M-27 • КАК ⟨БУ́ДТО, СЛО́ВНО, ТО́ЧНО⟩ ПО МАНОВЕ́НИЮ ⟨ПО МА́НИЮ *obs*⟩ ВОЛШЕ́БНОГО ЖЕЗЛА́ *lit;* **КАК ⟨БУ́ДТО, СЛО́ВНО, ТО́ЧНО⟩ ПО МАНОВЕ́НИЮ ВОЛШЕ́БНОЙ ПА́ЛОЧКИ** [как etc. + PrepP; these forms only; adv; usu. used with pfv verbs; fixed WO] very quickly, with ease, without difficulty: **(as if ⟨though⟩) with a wave of a ⟨one's⟩ magic wand; as if by magic.**

Она [Александрина] решила дождаться вечера, а дождавшись, торопливо побежала к Москве-реке... Но чья-то сильная рука помешала ей осуществить трагическое намерение. Человек, спасший её, оказался профессором медицины. Он дал ей выплакаться, девичье горе недолговечно, и вот перед ней, как по мановению волшебной палочки, открылась дивная страна... Он предложил Александрине поселиться в его доме, где у неё будет своя комната и все права члена семьи (Окуджава 2). She [Alexandrina] decided to wait for evening and then, when it came, ran to the Moscow River....But someone's strong hand kept her from realizing her tragic plan. The man who saved her was a professor of medicine. He let her have her cry—a young girl's sorrow is not long-lasting—and with the wave of a magic wand, a new world opened before her....He invited Alexandrina to live in his house, where she would have her own room and all the rights of a member of the family (2a).

M-28 • НАВОДИ́ТЬ/НАВЕСТИ́ (на себя) МАРАФЕ́Т *highly coll* [VP; subj: human] (more often of women) to make one's appearance neater or more attractive: X наводит на себя марафет ≃ **X is sprucing himself up; X is freshening up; woman X is fixing her face.**

Проснувшись... [Аркадий] переоделся в гражданское, навёл на себя всяческий блеск и марафет — и был таков (Залыгин 1). On waking...he [Arkady] changed into civilian clothes, spruced himself up and was gone (1a).

M-29 • ВЫ́СШЕЙ ⟨ПЕ́РВОЙ⟩ МА́РКИ *coll* [NP_gen; these forms only; nonagreeing postmodif; fixed WO] (usu. of some negative quality or phenomenon) to or of the highest degree: **of the first ⟨highest⟩ order; of the first water; of ⟨in⟩ the first degree; first-class [NP]; [in limited contexts] of the worst type.**

Насчёт газеты. Прямо завтра с утра: позвонить куда нужно, написать, свезти, безобразие вопиющее, вредительство высшей марки... (Трифонов 1). As far as the newspaper sketch was concerned, he must start in right away, the next morning. He should write it up, make phone calls wherever necessary, and deliver it in person. It was a crying shame, sabotage of the highest order... (1a). ♦ [Тамара:] А Гришка подонок оказался первой марки... (Панова 1). [T.:] And Grishka turned out to be a first-class rat... (1a).

M-30 • **ПОД МА́РКОЙ** *чего* [PrepP; Invar; Prep; the resulting PrepP is adv] (to do sth.) concealing one's true motives by adopting a false cover, acting in an insincere manner etc (as specified): **under the guise ⟨the pretext⟩ of.**

Сосед был человек неважнецкий. Комнату занял нахраписто после войны под маркой того, что инвалид (Трифонов 1). This neighbor was not a very nice man. He had seized his own one-room apartment right after the war, and rather highhandedly, under the guise of being a disabled veteran (1a).

M-31 • **ДЕРЖА́ТЬ ⟨ВЫДЕ́РЖИВАТЬ⟩ МА́РКУ** [VP; subj: human] to display the standards of behavior required by some group or specific to some category of people, thus maintaining the reputation of that group or confirming one's membership in that category of people: X держит марку ≃ **X keeps up appearances; X upholds his reputation (as...); [in limited contexts] X upholds the reputation ⟨the high standards⟩ of (some group etc).**

[Бакченин:] Я марку держу: бедные вы, говорю, вот я живу – как бог! Но тебе скажу откровенно: нехорошо так жить (Панова 1). [B.:] I keep up appearances: you poor fellows, I say, look how I live—like a god! But let me tell you frankly, my love, living like that is no good (1a).

M-32 • **ПОД МА́СКОЙ ⟨ПОД ЛИЧИ́НОЙ⟩** *кого-чего* [PrepP; Invar; Prep; the resulting PrepP is adv] hiding one's true identity, motives etc by pretending to be s.o. or sth. one is not: **under the guise ⟨the cover⟩ of; under ⟨behind, beneath⟩ a ⟨the⟩ mask of; disguised as; the cover of s.o. ⟨sth.⟩ conceals...**

...Я видел его только раз в моей жизни на большой дороге; следовательно, не могу питать к нему той неизъяснимой ненависти, которая, таясь под личиною дружбы, ожидает только смерти или несчастия любимого предмета, чтобы разразиться над его головою градом упрёков, советов, насмешек и сожалений (Лермонтов 1). ...I only saw him once, and that in passing, so I cannot feel for him that inexpressible hatred which lurks beneath the mask of friendship and waits only for the death or downfall of the other in order to shower him with reproaches, advice, taunts and regrets (1c). ♦ «Органами следствия установлено, что под личиной рядового Чонкина скрывался матёрый враг нашего строя, представитель высшей дворянской аристократии князь Голицын» (Войнович 4). "Our investigative organs have established that the cover of Private Chonkin concealed a sworn enemy of our way of life, a representative of the high court aristocracy, Prince Golitsyn" (4a).

M-33 • **НАДЕВА́ТЬ/НАДЕ́ТЬ (на себя) МА́СКУ ⟨ЛИЧИ́НУ⟩; НОСИ́ТЬ МА́СКУ ⟨ЛИЧИ́НУ⟩** *all rather lit* [VP; subj: human] to conceal one's true self, pretend to be s.o. or sth. one is not: X надевает (на себя) маску ≃ **X wears a mask; X plays a role ⟨a part⟩.**

M-34 • **СБРА́СЫВАТЬ/СБРО́СИТЬ (с себя) МА́СКУ; СНИМА́ТЬ/СНЯТЬ МА́СКУ ⟨ЛИЧИ́НУ⟩** *all rather lit* [VP; subj: human] to reveal who or what one really is, stop pretending: X сбросил маску ≃ **X took ⟨threw⟩ off his mask; X dropped the pretense.**

...Через день же [оппортунисты – руководители партии] собрали президиум партии и сбросили маску... Старый Грёйлих полез порочить всю цюрихскую партийную организацию... (Солженицын 5). They [the opportunist leaders of the party] called a meeting of the Presidium for the following day, and threw off their masks....Old Greulich stooped to defamation of the whole Zurich party organization... (5a). ♦ [Львов:] Полноте, кого вы хотите одурачить? Сбросьте маску (Чехов 4). [L.:] Enough of that! Whom are you trying to fool? Drop this pretense (4a).

M-35 • **СРЫВА́ТЬ/СОРВА́ТЬ ⟨СНИМА́ТЬ/СНЯТЬ⟩ МА́СКУ ⟨МА́СКИ⟩** *с кого all rather lit* [VP; subj: usu. human; often after надо, должен etc] to show who, what, or what kind of person s.o. really is: X сорвёт с Y-а маску ≃ **X will strip ⟨rip, tear⟩ off Y's mask; X will show Y for what Y really is.**

Полная измена Гримма... Всё упиралось в Гримма – и важно было сейчас не ошеломить его, разоблачить, сорвать маску (Солженицын 5). Grimm was an out-and-out traitor....He blocked their way completely: it was urgently necessary to ruin his reputation, expose him, strip off his mask (5a).

M-36 • **ПОДЛИВА́ТЬ/ПОДЛИ́ТЬ МА́СЛА В ОГО́НЬ** *coll* [VP; subj: human or abstr; the verb may take the final position, otherwise fixed WO] to intensify a feeling (often negative), a mood, s.o.'s interest in s.o. or sth. etc: X подлил масла в огонь ≃ **X added fuel to the fire ⟨the flames⟩; X poured oil on the fire ⟨the flames⟩; X fanned the flames.**

Теперь все были против него [Василия]. Теперь уж его никто не защищал, только подливали масла в огонь... (Аллилуева 1). Everyone...was against Vasily now. Not only did no one come forward in his defense, but everyone added fuel to the flames (1a). ♦ [Нина:] Давайте, давайте, оправдывайте его [Васеньку], защищайте. Если хотите, чтобы он совсем рехнулся... [Васенька:] Я с ума хочу сходить, понятно тебе? Сходить с ума и ни о чём не думать! И оставь меня в покое! (*Уходит в другую комнату.*) [Бусыгин (*Нине*):] Зачем же ты так? [Сарафанов:] Напрасно, Нина, честное слово. Ты подливаешь масло в огонь (Вампилов 4). [N.:] Go ahead, go ahead and agree with him [Vasenka], defend him. If you want him to go completely crazy.... [V.:] I want to go nuts, understand? Go nuts and not think about anything! So leave me alone! (*He goes into the other room.*) [B. (*to Nina*):] Why do you do that? [S.:] It's pointless, Nina, really. You're pouring oil on the fire (4b).

M-37 • **МА́СЛО МА́СЛЯНОЕ** [NP; fixed WO] the repetition of sth. already said in different words without clarifying anything: **(it's like saying) salt is salty ⟨water is wet etc⟩.**

M-38 • **КАК ⟨БУ́ДТО, СЛО́ВНО⟩ МА́СЛОМ ПО́ СЕРДЦУ ⟨ПО СЕ́РДЦУ⟩** *(кому) coll* [как etc + NP; these forms only; usu. impers predic or subj-compl with быть₀ (subj: abstr); fixed WO] sth. is very pleasant, delightful (for s.o.): X (Y-у) как маслом по сердцу ≃ **X makes Y's heart glad; X does Y's heart good; X makes Y feel good inside; [of spoken words only] X is (like) music to Y's ears.**

Люблю, когда моих детей хвалят, – это мне как маслом по сердцу. I love it when people praise my kids—it's like music to my ears.

M-39 • **КАК ПО МА́СЛУ** *идти, получаться, течь и т. п. coll* [как + PrepP; Invar; adv] (of affairs, undertakings etc) (to move along, proceed) very smoothly, without any difficulties or hindrances: **without a hitch; swimmingly; like clockwork; like a well-oiled machine; [in past contexts only] (things) could not have gone better.**

Пружины разбитого матраца кусали его, как блохи. Он не чувствовал этого. Он ещё неясно представлял себе, что последует вслед за получением ордеров, но был уверен, что тогда всё пойдёт как по маслу... (Ильф и Петров 1). The springs of the battered mattress nipped him like fleas, but he did not feel them. He still only had a vague idea of what would follow once the orders had been obtained, but was sure everything would go swimmingly (1a). ♦ [Кречинский:] Берегись старика; остальное пойдёт как по маслу... (Сухово-Кобылин 2). [K.:] Watch out for the old man. The rest will go like clockwork (2a). ♦ Этот генерал за короткий срок сделал головокружительную карьеру, потому что четыре года назад он носил ещё одну шпалу и командовал ротой. Но однажды ему крупно повезло... С тех пор дела его шли как по маслу (Войнович 2). The general had made a fabulous career for himself in a very short span of time. Four years before, he still wore only a single stripe and commanded a company. But then he had one great piece of luck....From then on, things could not have gone better for him (2a).

M-40 • В (О́БЩЕЙ) МА́ССЕ [PrepP; these forms only; adv; fixed WO] in the overwhelming majority of cases, the overwhelming majority (of some group is...): **most (of the)** [NP]; **on the ⟨as a⟩ whole; in the main; in the mass; for the most part; by and large.**

...Соколовы в массе своей трезвенники. Улыбки у них не встречишь (Коротюков 1). Most Sokolovs were teetotalers. They never smiled (1a). ♦ Мелькали гимназические шинели со светлыми пуговицами... но в массе преобладали солдатско-офицерские (Шолохов 3). An occasional gymnasium greatcoat with light-coloured buttons...was to be seen among them, but most of the column wore officers' and soldiers' greatcoats (3a). ♦ [Захар:] Среди рабочих есть очень любопытные фигуры, но в массе — я соглашаюсь — они очень распущенны... (Горький 1). [Z.:] There are some very interesting individuals among the workers, but taken in the mass, I agree, they're unruly and dissolute (1a).

M-41 • ВСЕХ ⟨ЛЮБЫ́Х, РА́ЗНЫХ⟩ МАСТЕ́Й [NP_gen; these forms only; nonagreeing postmodif; fixed WO] (people, often political opponents) of all or various groups, beliefs, trends etc: **of every stripe ⟨persuasion, hue⟩; of all denominations.**

«Разбитые наголову белобандиты всех мастей от Керенского до Деникина не успокоились...» (Войнович 4). "Utterly defeated, White Bandits of every stripe from Kerensky to Denikin did not settle down..." (4a).

M-42 • МА́СТЕР ⟨МАСТЕРИ́ЦА⟩ НА ВСЕ РУ́КИ coll, approv [NP; usu. subj-compl with copula (subj: human); more often var. with мастер (can be used of a woman); usu. this WO] a person who knows how to do many different things, usu. very well: X — мастер на все руки ≃ **X is a jack-of-all-trades; X is good at everything; X can turn his hand to anything.**

Ваня Бабичев был мастер на все руки. Сочинял он стихи и музыкальные пьески, отлично рисовал, множество вещей умел он делать... (Олеша 2). Young Ivan was a Jack-of-all-trades. He was good at composing verses and little musical plays, and at drawing. He could do many things (2a). ♦ Они могли пить водку до утра, разговаривать о футболе часами (а Рафику только того и надо!) и вообще были мастера на все руки (Трифонов 5). They could sit up drinking vodka all night and could talk about soccer for hours (what more could Rafik ask for!). In short, they were good at everything (5a). ♦ «...Батя мой мужик был хозяйственный, на все руки мастер: хоть веники, хоть ложки — всё умел и двух лошадей держал к тому же» (Максимов 2). "My father was a good craftsman, he could turn his hand to anything—making brooms, making spoons, he could do it all—and on top of that he kept two horses" (2a).

M-43 • ОДНО́Й ⟨(ОДНО́Й И) ТОЙ ЖЕ⟩ МА́СТИ; ПОД ОДНУ́ МАСТЬ all coll, usu. disapprov [NP_gen (variants with масти); PrepP (last var.); these forms only; usu. subj-compl with быть₀ (subj: human or concr); the last var. is used with pl subj; fixed WO] identical or very similar in some respect: [of people only] **(be) of the same stripe ⟨kind, sort⟩; (be) birds of a feather; (be) cut from the same cloth;** [of both people and things] **(be) much ⟨all⟩ the same.**

M-44 • В МАСТЬ кому-чему быть₀, прийтись; **К МА́СТИ; ПОД МАСТЬ** all obsoles, substand [PrepP; these forms only; subj-compl with copula (subj: human or abstr); often neg] to suit s.o. or sth., correspond to sth.: **(be) fitting; (be) in**

keeping with; [in limited contexts] **fill the bill;** Neg не в масть ≃ **not (be) s.o.'s style ⟨kind of thing⟩.**

...Лежали у него на столе цветные адриатические пейзажи, он был там в научной командировке и мне показать зачем-то. Ему самому это было крайне не в масть, нельзя придумать противоположней (Солженицын 2). On his desk he had some colored photographs of Adriatic scenery. He had been there on scientific business, and for some reason he decided to show them to me. It wasn't at all his style; in fact, it would be hard to think of anything more unlike him (2a).

M-45 • К ЕДРЁНОЙ МА́ТЕРИ ⟨БА́БУШКЕ⟩ иди, катись, послать кого и т. п. vulg [PrepP; these forms only; adv; fixed WO] an expletive used to express intense anger, irritation, contempt directed toward s.o., or a desire to be rid of s.o.: **go screw yourself;** [in limited contexts] **get the hell out of here!**

...Заместитель начальника полиции, точно исполняя приказ своего начальника, лично открыл камеру, в которой сидел дядя Сандро, и выпустил его, сказав при этом: «Катись к едрёной матери, пока сторож в сознании» (Искандер 3). ...The deputy chief of police, executing his chief's order with precision, personally opened the door to Uncle Sandro's cell and released him, saying, "Get the hell out of here while the watchman's still conscious" (3a).

M-46 • ВЫСО́КИЕ МАТЕ́РИИ lit [NP; pl only; fixed WO] intellectual topics for discussion: **lofty topics ⟨matters⟩; abstract matters ⟨arguments⟩.**

...Пора оставить высокие материи и попробовать сдвинуть с места сюжет (Искандер 4). It is time to abandon lofty topics...and try, despite all, to get the plot moving (4a). ♦ «Всё это верно... Однако футбол — не политика. И вообще, знаешь, не люблю я в высокие материи забираться. Это уж твоё прокурорское дело теории подводить» (Терц 7). "All that's true enough....But football isn't politics. And anyway, you know, I don't like getting too deep into abstract arguments. Theories are more in your line, you're the Prosecutor" (7a).

M-47 • БЛАГИ́М МА́ТОМ кричать, орать, вопить и т. п. highly coll [NP_instrum; Invar; adv (intensif); fixed WO] (to shout, yell etc) very loudly, furiously: X орал благим матом ≃ **X was yelling ⟨screaming⟩ at the top of his lungs ⟨voice⟩; X was yelling ⟨shouting, screaming⟩ his head off; X was screaming bloody murder; X was screaming ⟨yelling⟩ with all his might; X was screaming to high heaven.**

Дикий, отчаянный вопль донёсся оттуда. Потом увидели и самого Федьку. Бежит что есть мочи по пожне, кричит благим матом... (Абрамов 1). A wild, desperate wail had issued forth. Then they saw Fedka himself, running for all he was worth across the field, yelling at the top of his lungs (1a). ♦ «...Митрей взял кисть да мне по роже краской и мазнул... да и побёг [ungrammat = побежал], я за ним. И бегу... я за ним, а сам кричу благим матом...» (Достоевский 3). "...Mitrei took the brush and slapped some paint on my mug...and ran away, and I ran after him. So I was running after him, shouting my head off..." (3c). ♦ Нельзя кормить ночью. Светка орёт благим матом. Я креплюсь. Как мне хочется взять на руки этот комочек и покормить (Орлова 1). The child must not be fed at night. Sveta would scream bloody murder. I would be firm. How I wanted to take that little bundle in my arms and feed her (1a). ♦ «...Я пал в ноги ему и слёзно умолял; а он закричал благим матом: „Пошёл, пошёл!"» (Гончаров 1). "...I went down on my knees before him with tears in my eyes, but he yelled with all his might: 'Get out! Get out!'" (1b). ♦ Феня сидела со своею бабушкой, кухаркой Матрёной, в кухне, когда вдруг вбежал «капитан». Увидав его, Феня закричала благим матом (Достоевский 1). Fenya was sitting in the kitchen with her grandmother, the cook Matryona, when the "captain" suddenly ran in. Seeing him, Fenya screamed to high heaven (1a).

M-48 • ПО МА́ТУШКЕ ⟨ПО МА́ТЕРИ⟩ ругать(ся), обруга́ть *кого coll* [PrepP; these forms only; adv] (to curse, swear) using abusive, obscene words: **call s.o. unprintable names ⟨every name in the book⟩; swear like a trooper; swear obscenely; cuss ⟨curse, swear⟩ a blue streak.**

Изо дня в день разыгрывается на поверке потеха с Байгильдеевым. Никак он не может запомнить свою статью, по которой сидит уже девять лет.... «Байгильдеев!» – кричит вохровец по прозвищу Зверь... Он [Байгильдеев] трёт лоб... «Забыл статью... Опять забыл...» Зверь ругается по матушке (Гинзбург 2). Day in, day out at roll call we had the same comic scene with Baigildeev. He was quite incapable of remembering the article that had kept him inside for nine years...."Baigildeev!" shouted the guard who was called the Beast....He [Baigildeev] wiped his forehead...."I've forgotten the article...forgotten again...." The Beast called him unprintable names (2a). ♦ «В моём и Зины присутствии пёс (если псом, конечно, можно назвать) обругал профессора Преображенского по матери» (Булгаков 11). "In the presence of myself and Zina, the dog (if, indeed, one may use this designation) swore obscenely at Prof. Preobrazhensky" (11a).

M-49 • В ЧЁМ ⟨КАК⟩ МАТЬ РОДИЛА́ *highly coll* [these forms only; fixed WO] **1.** ~ оста́ться, оста́вить *кого и т. п.* [subj-compl with copula (subj: human), obj-compl with оставить etc (obj: human), or detached modif] (to remain, leave s.o. etc) without any clothes on: **in one's birthday suit; (as) naked as the day one was born; in the altogether; stark naked; in the buff; without a stitch of clothing (on); naked as a jaybird.**

«Ну, добежали [собаки] и в одну минуту спустили с меня всё моё рваньё. Остался в чём мать родила» (Шолохов 1). "They [the dogs] ran up to me, and in a moment they'd torn all my rags off me. I was left in my birthday suit" (1a). ♦ Нас голых, в чём мать родила, перед мытьём стригли в коридоре (Марченко 1). Naked as the day we were born, we had to wait there in the corridor to be shorn before going on to get washed (1a). ♦ Говорили о том, что был сеанс в Варьете, после коего все две тысячи зрителей выскочили на улицу в чём мать родила... (Булгаков 9). It was said that there had been a strange performance at the Variety Theater, after which the entire audience of two thousand persons ran out into the street stark naked... (9a).

2. ~ оста́вить, пусти́ть *кого и т. п.* [usu. obj-compl with оставить etc (obj: human)] (to leave s.o.) without money, without any means (usu. in contexts of robbing s.o., winning all s.o.'s money at cards, taking possession of all s.o.'s property by deceitful means etc): **without a penny to one's ⟨s.o.'s⟩ name.**

M-50 • ЁБ ТВОЮ́ ⟨ВА́ШУ⟩ МАТЬ; иди, катись, посла́ть *кого* К ЕБЁНЕ ⟨ЁБАНОЙ⟩ МА́ТЕРИ ⟨БА́БУШКЕ⟩ *absolute taboo* [these forms only; Interj or adv; fixed WO] a very strong expletive («ёб» is considered unprintable and is usu. replaced by dots in printed matter): **fuck your mother; fuck you; you motherfucking piece of shit.**

Дядя Сандро повернулся, и тот [его соперник] выстрелил. «...твою мать! – крикнул мой дядя Сандро сгоряча – если ты думаешь меня одной пулей уложить!» (Искандер 3). Uncle Sandro turned, and the shot rang out. "F—k your mother," Uncle Sandro screamed furiously, "if you think you can do me in with one bullet!" (3a).

M-51 • МАТЬ РОДНА́Я НЕ УЗНА́ЕТ *(кого) highly coll* [VP_subj; Invar; usu. subord clause after избить, отделать *кого* так, что...; fixed WO] (to beat s.o.) to the point where he is unrecognizable: **(beat s.o. so bad) his own mother wouldn't recognize him; (beat s.o.) to a pulp.**

M-52 • МА́ТЬ ТВОЮ́ ⟨его и т. п.⟩ ЗА́ НОГУ! *substand* [Interj; these forms only; fixed WO] a mild expletive expressing annoyance, indignation or surprise, delight: **(God) damn you ⟨him etc⟩!;** [annoyance only] **screw that ⟨him etc⟩!;** [surprise only] **well, I'll be damned ⟨a monkey's uncle⟩!**

«Ну, одно тебе скажу, Карась, молодцы большевики. Клянусь честью – молодцы... За что люблю – за смелость, мать их за ногу» (Булгаков 3). "...Well, I can tell you one thing, Karas – you have to hand it to those Bolsheviks. They really know their stuff....That's why I admire them – for their brazen impudence, God damn them" (3a). ♦ «Кончили, мать твою за ногу! – Сенька кричит. – Айда!» Носилки схватил – и по трапу (Солженицын 7). "Enough, damn it!" Senka shouted. "Time to be off!" He grabbed a handbarrow and away down the ramp (7c). ♦ ...Отсюда, с берега, казалось: человек идёт по воде. «Ты как Христос расхаживаешь», – сказал Егорша... «Христос, мать его за ногу!» – Михаил, выйдя из воды, с трудом разогнулся (Абрамов 1). From where Egorsha was on the bank, it looked like someone was walking on the water. "You look like Christ walking there," said Egorsha...."Christ? Screw that!" Mikhail had a hard time straightening up when he came out of the water (1a).

M-53 • МАТЬ ЧЕСТНА́Я! *highly coll* [Interj; Invar; fixed WO] used to express amazement, admiration, fear, irritation etc: **Mother of God!; Holy Mother!; heavens!; good Lord!; oh my God!**

[Мишка:] Погоди, а где я тебя прежде видел? Ну-ка, сними шапку... Мать честная, мой лучший друг... Тамарочка! (Арбузов 2). [M.:] Wait, where have I seen you before? Go on, take your hat off....Mother of God, my best friend, Tamara! (2a). ♦ «...А тут гляжу – мать честная – пехотка наша и справа и слева от грейдера по чистому полю сыплет, и уже мины рвутся по их порядкам» (Шолохов 1). "But then – Holy Mother! – I see our infantry to right and left of the road scattering over the open field, and mortars bursting fast and furious behind them" (1a).

M-54 • ПОКАЗА́ТЬ КУ́ЗЬКИНУ МАТЬ *кому highly coll* [VP; subj: human; most often 1st pers, fut or subjunctive (used as a threat); the verb may take the final position, otherwise fixed WO] to punish s.o. harshly: X покажет Y-у кузькину мать ≃ **X will fix Y's wagon; X will make it ⟨things⟩ hot for Y; X will show Y who's boss.**

«Эх, – дед даже застонал во тьме, – мне бы на такую-то гору взобраться [, как Сталин], я бы показал кой-кому кузькину мать!» (Максимов 2). "Ah" – here the old man actually groaned in the darkness – "now if I'd gotten to the top of the heap the way Stalin has, I'd show a few people who's boss" (2a).

M-55 • (ТА́К) ТВОЮ́ ⟨ВА́ШУ⟩ МА́ТЬ; МА́ТЬ ТВОЮ́ ПЕРЕМА́ТЬ; В БО́ГА ⟨ДУ́ШУ⟩ МАТЬ *all vulg* [Interj] an expletive expressing intense anger, resentment, frustration etc: **son of a bitch!; fuck you!; motherfucker(s)!; fucking ⟨motherfucking⟩ [NP].**

«Тьфу ты, мать твою так!» – товарищ Коба, рассердившись, плюнул ему в лицо (Войнович 5). "You son of a bitch!" Enraged, Comrade Koba spat in his face (5a). ♦ «Но кто такие? Неужели же Петлюра? Не может этого быть». – «...Я думаю, что это местные мужички – богоносцы достоевские!.. у-у... вашу мать!» (Булгаков 3). "But who were they? Surely they weren't Petlyura's men? It's impossible." "...I think they were some local peasants – Dostoevsky's 'holy Russia' in revolt. Ugh – motherfuckers..." (3a). ♦ «Техника, твою мать! Утильсырьё на колёсах туды твою растуды, на ней [машине] не ездить, а только орехи колоть, да и то не годится, мать твою перемать!» (Максимов 1). "Fucking technology! Scrap-iron on wheels, that's what this bugger is. It's no good for driving, you might try cracking nuts with it, though it probably wouldn't be any fucking good at that!" (1a).

M-56 • ОДНИ́М ⟨ЕДИ́НЫМ⟩ МА́ХОМ; С ОДНОГО́ ⟨ЕДИ́НОГО⟩ МА́ХУ; В ОДИ́Н MAX *all coll* [NP_instrum

(1st var.) or PrepP; these forms only; adv; more often used with pfv verbs; fixed WO] very quickly, without any pauses, and usu. in one motion: **in one fell swoop; with ⟨in, at⟩ one stroke; with a single movement; [in limited contexts] in one leap; with one ⟨a single⟩ blow; [with the emphasis on speed] in a flash; [in refer. to drinking] at one go; in one ⟨a single⟩ gulp.**

Когда я отмечаю своё неумение писать, то я имею в виду составление фразы. Мне очень трудно написать фразу одним, так сказать, махом, в особенности если фраза создаётся для определения каких-либо отвлечённых понятий (Олеша 3). When I mention my inability to write, I have in mind the composing of sentences. It is very difficult for me to write a sentence in one stroke, so to speak, especially if the sentence is intended to define an abstract idea (3a). ♦ ...Директор ресторана, вдруг почувствовав прилив смелости и творческой фантазии, дал ресторану название «Эллада», как бы единым махом отодвинув его на расстояние, недоступное для идеологических бурь (Искандер 4). ...The restaurant manager suddenly felt a surge of boldness and creative imagination and gave his restaurant the name Hellas, as if to remove it at one stroke beyond the range of ideological storms (4a). ♦ Он одним махом сдёрнул плед, прикрывающий Наденьку... (Ерофеев 3). With a single movement he jerked off the blanket covering her [Nadya]... (3a). ♦ Щедрый иностранец в один мах проскользнул через целый марш лестницы вниз... (Булгаков 9). In one leap the generous stranger had jumped down a whole flight of stairs... (9b). ♦ ...Иван в один мах выбрался из траншеи... (Максимов 3). ...Ivan scrambled out of the trench in a flash... (3a). ♦ Я в их годы делал так: вечером в четверг выпивал одним махом три с половиной литра ерша и ложился спать, не раздеваясь, с одной только мыслью: проснусь утром в пятницу или не проснусь? (Ерофеев 1). At their age I would do this: on Thursday evening I'd drink, all at one go, three and a half liters of beer and vodka mixed. I'd drink it and lie down to sleep without getting undressed and with one thought only—will I wake up on Friday or won't I? (1a). ♦ «„Что хочешь, то и говори", — отвечает [Алёша] и одним махом, как водку, выпивает свой компот и уходит к себе» (Искандер 5). "'Tell her whatever you want,' he [Alyosha] answers, and he downs his fruit compote in one gulp, like vodka, and goes to his room" (5a).

M-57 • ДАВА́ТЬ/ДАТЬ МА́ХУ coll [VP; subj: human; usu. pfv past; if impfv, usu. denotes a repeated action] to make an error in thinking or conduct: X дал маху ≃ **X blundered ⟨made a blunder⟩; X slipped up; X messed (it) up; X pulled a boner; [in limited contexts] X fell short of the mark; X let the chance slip by.**

«...Чем вы объясните, что за пятнадцать лет дети царя не выросли?" Тут помощники Большеусого растерялись, покраснели, побледнели, не знали, что сказать. Тут-то они докумекали, что втопыхах дали маху...» (Искандер 3). "How do you explain the fact that in fifteen years the czar's children haven't grown up?' The Big Mustache's aides were flustered, they turned red, turned white, didn't know what to say. Now they caught on that in their hurry they'd made a blunder..." (3a). ♦ «...Ну как его [Раскольникова] одного теперь пускать? Пожалуй, утопится... Эх, маху я дал!» (Достоевский 3). "...How could I let him [Raskolnikov] go off alone just now? Maybe he'll drown himself....Damn, I slipped up there!" (3a). ♦ Из-за полного своего невежества я особенного маху дал в пьесах (Солженицын 2). In my complete ignorance I had fallen particularly short of the mark in my plays (2a).

M-58 • С МА́ХУ coll [PrepP; Invar; adv] **1.** ~ бросить что, ударить кого и т. п. Also: **СО ВСЕГО́ МА́ХУ ⟨-а⟩** coll (to throw sth., hit s.o. etc) with great force: **with all one's might; as hard as one can; [in refer. to throwing sth.] fling ⟨hurl⟩ sth.**

Он подбежал к парню и с маху ударил его. He ran up to the guy and hit him with all his might. ♦ [Егорша] постоял под порогом, цыкнул слюной и вдруг со всего маха бросил на се-

рёдку избы глухаря (Абрамов 1). He [Egorsha] stood at the door, spat—Phthat!—and suddenly flung down a grouse into the middle of the floor... (1a).

2. Also: **СО ВСЕГО́ МА́ХУ ⟨-а⟩** coll (of a moving person, animal, vehicle etc) while moving or running very fast: **(while going ⟨running etc⟩) at full ⟨top⟩ speed; at a dead run.**

3. quickly, without contemplation: **right off (the bat); right away; straight off; [in limited contexts] off the top of one's head; on impulse; rashly.**

Дай мне подумать, я с маху ответить на такой вопрос не могу. Give me a second to think; I can't answer a question like this off the top of my head.

M-59 • КАК ЗАВЕДЁННАЯ МАШИ́НА; КАК ЗАВЕ-ДЁННЫЙ coll [как + NP; nom only; adv; 2nd var. is used of a person only; fixed WO] **1.** (one does sth., some enterprise operates etc) continually or practically all the time: **nonstop; without a break ⟨a letup⟩.**

2. (of a person) (one does sth.) in a monotonous, mechanical manner: **like an automaton ⟨a robot⟩; like a clockwork ⟨windup⟩ toy.**

M-60 • В МГНОВЕ́НИЕ ⟨-ье⟩ О́КА; В ОДНО́ МГНО-ВЕ́НИЕ ⟨-ье⟩ coll; **В ОДНО́ МГНОВЕ́НИЕ ⟨-ье⟩ О́КА** obsoles [PrepP; these forms only; adv; usu. used with pfv verbs; fixed WO] extremely quickly, instantaneously: **in the twinkling ⟨the wink⟩ of an eye; as fast as you can blink an eye; instantly; in a split second.**

Чуткий нос его [Ноздрёва] слышал за несколько десятков вёрст, где была ярмарка со всякими съездами; он уж в одно мгновенье ока был там... (Гоголь 3). His [Nozdryov's] sensitive nose could smell out a fair, an assembly, or a ball for miles around: and in the twinkling of an eye he was there... (3a). ♦ Она выпучила глаза на меня, и слёзы, как мне показалось, в мгновенье ока высохли на ней (Булгаков 12). Her eyes bulged at the sight of me and her tears, I noticed, dried up instantly (12a).

M-61 • ДЛЯ МЕ́БЕЛИ быть₀, находиться, сидеть и т. п. highly coll, disapprov [PrepP; Invar; subj-compl with copula (subj: human)] to be absolutely useless, not needed in some place where others are occupied, busy doing sth.: X (сидит) там для мебели ≃ **X is just for decoration; X sits around looking pretty.**

M-62 • МЕДВЕ́ДЬ ⟨СЛОН⟩ НА́ УХО НАСТУПИ́Л кому coll, usu. humor [VP_subj; these forms only; fixed WO] s.o. has absolutely no ear for music: X-у медведь на ухо наступил ≃ **X has a tin ear; X is tone-deaf; X can't carry a tune ⟨couldn't carry a tune in a bushel basket etc⟩.**

M-63 • СИДЕ́ТЬ НА МЕЛИ́; НА МЕЛИ́ быть₀, оказаться и т. п. both coll [VP (1st var.) or PrepP, Invar, subj-compl with copula (2nd var.); subj: human] to be (be left etc) with very little or no money: X сидит на мели ≃ **X is (almost ⟨practically, flat etc⟩) broke; X is (really) short of ⟨on⟩ cash; X is without ⟨does not have⟩ a kopeck ⟨a penny, a cent etc⟩ to his name; X is pressed for cash; X is (completely ⟨practically etc⟩) without means.**

Теперь мы сами удивлялись, куда ушли все деньги и почему мы сразу на мели (Гинзбург 2). And now we were ourselves astonished at where all the money had gone; all at once we were without means (2a).

M-64 • ПО МЕЛОЧА́М; ПО МЕ́ЛОЧИ [PrepP; these forms only; usu. adv or nonagreeing postmodif] **1.** in little amounts: **in small quantities ⟨amounts, sums⟩; small quan-**

tities ⟨amounts, sums⟩ of (sth.); ‖ должа́ть по мелоча́м ≃ **incur ⟨rack up** etc⟩ **small debts.**

[Подхалю́зин:] Отчего́ же э́то у вас ру́ки трясу́тся? [Рисположе́нский:] От забо́ты, Ла́зарь Елиза́рыч... [Подхалю́зин:] ...А я так полага́ю от того́, что бо́льно наро́д гра́бите... [Рисположе́нский:] Ла́зарь Елиза́рыч! Где нам гра́бить! Дели́шки на́ши ма́ленькие. Мы, как пти́цы небе́сные, по зёрнышку клюём. [Подхалю́зин:] Вы, ста́ло быть, бо́льше по мелоча́м? (Остро́вский 10). [P.:] Why do your hands shake? [R.:] From anxiety, Lazar Elizarych.... [P.:] ...I suppose it's because you're plundering people overmuch.... [R.:] ...Lazar Elizarych! How could I plunder anybody? My business is of a small sort. I'm like a little bird, picking up small grains. [P.:] You deal in small quantites, of course? (10b). ♦ Положе́ние Никола́я станови́лось ху́же и ху́же. Мысль о том, чтоб откла́дывать из своего́ жа́лованья, оказа́лась мечто́ю. Он не то́лько не откла́дывал, но, удовлетворя́я тре́бования ма́тери, должа́л по мелоча́м (Толсто́й 7). Nicholas's position became worse and worse. The idea of putting something aside out of his salary proved a dream. Not only did he not save anything, but to comply with his mother's demands he even incurred some small debts (7b).

2. usu. ко́е-что, ко́е-чего́ и т. п. ~ some unimportant, inconsequential matters: **(some) trifles ⟨trivial matters, little things⟩.**

Он мно́го ва́жного име́л сообщи́ть хозя́ину: что по́езд ещё не пришёл, но когда́ придёт, то не бу́дет не встре́чен, кто́-нибудь из соба́к обяза́тельно там карау́лит, что, в о́бщем, пока́ устро́ились на пе́рвое вре́мя и живу́т дру́жно, ну и ещё ко́е-чего́ по ме́лочи (Влади́мов 1). He had a great many important things to tell Master: that the train had not come yet, but that when it did come at least one of the dogs would certainly be on duty to meet it; that in general the dogs had settled down fairly well for the time being and were keeping together...and a few other more trivial matters (1a).

M-65 • РАЗМЕ́НИВАТЬ/РАЗМЕНЯ́ТЬ НА МЕ́ЛОЧИ ⟨НА (ВСЯ́КУЮ) МЕ́ЛОЧЬ, НА МЕ́ЛКУЮ МОНЕ́ТУ⟩ *что;* ТРА́ТИТЬ/ИСТРА́ТИТЬ ⟨РАСТРА́ТИТЬ⟩ ПО МЕ́ЛОЧИ ⟨ПО МЕЛОЧА́М⟩ [VP; subj: human] to expend (one's talent, abilities etc) on unimportant matters, waste (one's life): X разменя́л Y на ме́лочи ≃ **X threw away his Y; X frittered away his Y; X poured his Y down the drain;** [in limited contexts] **X wasted his Y on trifles.**

«...[Я] га́снул и тра́тил по ме́лочи жизнь и ум... Да́же самолю́бие — на что оно́ тра́тилось? Чтоб зака́зывать пла́тье у изве́стного портно́го? Чтоб попа́сть в изве́стный дом?.. И́ли я не по́нял э́той жи́зни, и́ли она́ никуда́ не годи́тся...» (Гончаро́в 1). "...[I was] fading out, wasting my mind, my life, on trifles....Even my self-respect—what was that wasted on? On ordering clothes from a famous tailor? On being invited to a celebrated house?...Either I failed to understand that life, or it was utterly worthless..." (1b).

M-66 • РАЗМЕ́НИВАТЬСЯ/РАЗМЕНЯ́ТЬСЯ НА МЕ́ЛОЧИ ⟨ПО МЕЛОЧА́М, НА (ВСЯ́КУЮ) МЕ́ЛОЧЬ, НА МЕ́ЛКУЮ МОНЕ́ТУ⟩ *coll* [VP; subj: human] **1.** to expend one's talent, abilities etc on unimportant matters, for nothing: X разменя́лся на ме́лкую моне́ту ≃ **X wasted ⟨squandered⟩ his talent ⟨his gifts** etc⟩ **on trifles; X frittered away his talent ⟨his life** etc⟩.

«Где же тут челове́к? Где его́ це́лость? Куда́ он скры́лся, как разменя́лся на вся́кую ме́лочь?» (Гончаро́в 1). "Where is the real man? Where is his integrity? Where has he hidden himself, and why is he squandering his gifts on trifles?" (1b).

2. to be occupied with unimportant, nonessential matters instead of things that are important: X разме́нивается на ме́лочи ≃ **X is ⟨gets⟩ caught up with matters of secondary importance.**

M-67 • САДИ́ТЬСЯ/СЕСТЬ НА МЕЛЬ *coll* [VP; subj: usu. human or collect; usu. pfv] to get into a very troublesome, difficult situation (usu. because of a lack of funds or other material resources): X сел на мель ≃ **X got into trouble; X got into a tight spot; X got into a fix ⟨a predicament, a bind⟩.**

M-68 • САЖА́ТЬ/ПОСАДИ́ТЬ НА МЕЛЬ *кого-что coll* [VP; subj: human; obj: human or collect; usu. pfv] to put s.o. (or some organization) in a very troublesome, difficult position (usu. because of a lack of funds or other material resources): X посади́л Y-а на мель ≃ **X got Y into trouble; X put Y in a tight spot; X put ⟨got⟩ Y into a fix ⟨a predicament, a bind⟩.**

M-69 • ВЕТРЯНА́Я МЕ́ЛЬНИЦА *highly coll, disapprov* [NP; sing only; usu. subj-compl with copula (subj: human) or obj-compl with называ́ть, счита́ть *кого* (obj: human)] a lightheaded, shallow person: **airhead; featherbrain.**

M-70 • СРАЖА́ТЬСЯ ⟨ВОЕВА́ТЬ⟩ С ВЕТРЯНЫ́МИ МЕ́ЛЬНИЦАМИ [VP; subj: human; the verb may take the final position, otherwise fixed WO] to expend one's strength, abilities uselessly, fighting imaginary or unimportant enemies or wrongs (while believing them to be real or important): X сража́ется с ветряны́ми ме́льницами ≃ **X tilts at windmills.**

[Ивано́в:] Был я молоды́м, горя́чим, и́скренним, неглу́пым... сража́лся с ветряны́ми ме́льницами, би́лся лбом об сте́ны... (Че́хов 4). [I.:] I used to be young, eager, sincere, intelligent....I tilted at windmills and banged my head against brick walls... (4b).

< From Miguel de Cervantes' novel *Don Quixote*, 1605 and 1615. In one of its episodes Don Quixote tilts at windmills, having taken them for giants.

M-71 • СА́МОЕ МЕ́НЬШЕЕ ⟨МА́ЛОЕ⟩ [AdjP; these forms only; used as a restr marker; fixed WO] not less than (the amount or thing named): **at least; at the very least; nothing short of.**

Ремо́нт да́чи вам обойдётся са́мое ме́ньшее в де́вять ты́сяч рубле́й. Renovating your dacha will cost you at least nine thousand roubles. ♦ Э́то ведь не шу́тка — самово́льно, вопреки́ райко́му снять челове́ка с лесозагото́вок. Са́мое ма́лое — строга́ч [*slang* = стро́гий вы́говор] обеспе́чен (Абра́мов 1). After all, it was no joke to go against the First Secretary and take someone off logging duty without authorization. At the very least you would be called on the carpet... (1a).

M-72 • В ПО́ЛНОЙ МЕ́РЕ [PrepP; Invar; adv; fixed WO] entirely: **fully; totally; completely; wholly; in full ⟨the fullest⟩ measure.**

Неизве́стно да́же, был ли он и́стинный революционе́р, то есть сознава́л ли в по́лной ме́ре зада́чи и це́ли [револю́ции] (Три́фонов 1). It wasn't even clear whether he had been a genuine revolutionary—that is, whether he had been fully aware of the goals and purposes of the revolution (1a). ♦ Черты́ лица́ его́ бы́ли лишены́ индивидуа́льности, хотя́ лицо́ его́ и бы́ло еди́нственным в своём ро́де и под како́й-либо привы́чный тип не подходи́ло, но — как бы сказа́ть? — оно́ и одно́ бы́ло типи́чно и не принадлежа́ло в по́лной ме́ре самому́ себе́ (Би́тов 2). His facial features were devoid of individuality; although his face was unique in its way and fitted no usual type, still—how should I put it?—even though one of a kind, it was typical and did not wholly belong to itself (2a). ♦ О́стрый и беспоко́йный умо́м челове́к, он на́чал свои́ заня́тия с изуче́ния знамени́тейшего филосо́фа дре́вности перипате́тика Аристо́теля и, изучи́в его́ в по́лной ме́ре, в тако́й же ме́ре его́ возненави́дел (Булга́ков 5). A keen and restless mind, he had begun his studies with the works of the most famous philosopher of antiquity, the peripatetic Aristotle, and, having studied him in the fullest measure, he came to detest him in the same measure (5a).

M-73 • НИ В КО́ЕЙ ⟨НИ В КАКО́Й⟩ МЕ́РЕ [PrepP; these forms only; adv; used with neg verbs; fixed WO] absolutely not: **in no way; not in any way whatever ⟨whatsoever⟩; by no means; not at all; not in the least.**

Один из бесчисленных злопыхателей, ненавидевших моего героя, утверждал много лет спустя, что в Орлеане всякий осёл может получить учёную степень, были бы только у него деньги. Однако это неверно. Осёл степени не получит, да и мой герой ни в какой мере не походил на осла (Булгаков 5). One of the innumerable slanderers who hated my hero asserted many years later that any ass could have received a learned degree in Orléans, provided he had money. This, however, is not true. An ass could not receive any degrees, nor did my hero resemble an ass in any way whatever (5a).

M-74 • ПО КРА́ЙНЕЙ МЕ́РЕ [PrepP; Invar; fixed WO]
1. Also: **ПО КРА́ЙНОСТИ** *obs, substand* [usu. sent adv (parenth)] to the extent of (what is stated), if nothing more: **at least; at any rate.**

«Дело заключается в следующем: хотя мы и не можем обнаружить — в данное время, по крайней мере, — каких-либо его [Га-Ноцри] поклонников или последователей, тем не менее ручаться, что их совсем нет, нельзя» (Булгаков 9). "The point is this: although we cannot find any of his [Ha-Nozri's] admirers or followers—at least at this time—no one can guarantee that there are none" (9a). ♦ «Вы поставлены, так сказать, у кормила общественного спокойствия, а с общественным спокойствием — по крайней мере, таково моё мнение — в сильной степени связано общественное благосостояние» (Салтыков-Щедрин 2). "You have been placed, as it were, at the helm of public security, and with public security,—this, at any rate, is my opinion, public well-being is inextricably bound up" (2a).

2. [adv; often used with a quantit NP] not less (and perhaps more) than: **at least; at the very least.**

Кирила Петрович гордился сим прекрасным заведением и никогда не упускал случая похвастаться оным перед своими гостями, из коих каждый осматривал его по крайней мере уже в двадцатый раз (Пушкин 1). Kirila Petrovich was proud of this superb establishment, and never let slip an opportunity to boast of it before his guests, all of whom had inspected it at least twenty times already (1b).

M-75 • ПО МЕ́НЬШЕЙ МЕ́РЕ [PrepP; Invar; fixed WO]
1. [sent adv (usu. parenth)] this much, if not more, being true: **to say the (very) least; to put it mildly ⟨gently, lightly⟩.**

«...Но при чём тут Чернышевский?» — «Упражнение в стрельбе», — сказал Фёдор Константинович. «Ответ по меньшей мере загадочный», — заметил инженер Керн... (Набоков 1). "...But what's the point of Chernyshevski?" "Firing practice," said Fyodor. "An answer which is, to say the least, enigmatic," remarked the engineer Kern... (1a). ♦ [Анна Петровна:] Нелюбезно провожать даму и всю дорогу говорить с нею только о своей честности! Может быть, это и честно, но по меньшей мере скучно (Чехов 4). [A.P.:] When you take a lady out, it's not very nice to keep on and on about how honest you are. Honest you may be, but you're also, to put it mildly, a bore (4b).

2. [adv; usu. used with a quantit NP] not less (and perhaps more) than: **at least; at the very least.**

Два с половиной часа! За это время наш Лопахин можно было обойти по меньшей мере три раза (Каверин 1). Two and a half hours! Why, in that time you could walk round our Lopakhin three times at least (1a). ♦ Итого восемь сотен по меньшей мере уплачено (Терц 8). All in all they must have paid eight hundred rubles at the very least (8a).

M-76 • ПО МЕ́РЕ *чего* [PrepP; Invar; Prep; the resulting PrepP is adv] **1.** (used to denote the gradual progression of an action expressed predominantly by a deverbal noun) in conjunction or proportion with (the action denoted by the deverbal noun): **as; as (sth.) progresses; (the...,) the...; in measure with; whenever.**

По мере уменьшения запаса угля мы стали топить всё реже и реже. As our stores of coal diminished, we turned on the heat less and less often. ♦ Рифмы по мере моей охоты за ними сложились у меня в практическую систему несколько карточного порядка (Набоков 1). As my hunt for them progressed, rhymes settled down into a practical system somewhat on the order of a card index (1a). ♦ В русском войске по мере отступления всё более и более разгорается дух озлобления против врага... (Толстой 6). The farther the Russian army retreats, the more intensely burns its animosity against the enemy... (6a). ♦ ...По мере приближения к Москве [Ростов] приходил всё более и более в нетерпение (Толстой 5). ...[Rostov] grew more and more impatient the nearer they got to Moscow (5a). ♦ Мать продолжала трепетать и мучиться, а Дарданелов по мере тревог её всё более и более воспринимал надежду (Достоевский 1). His mother went on trembling and suffering, and Dardanelov's hopes increased more and more in measure with her anxiety (1a). ♦ Она [жена Хабуга] тоже сидела сейчас на кухне и лущила в подол кукурузу, откуда по мере наполнения ссыпала её в таз (Искандер 3). She [Khabug's wife], too, sat in the kitchen now. She was shelling corn into her lap; whenever her skirt filled up she poured the corn into a pan (3a).

2. ~ **сил, надобности** и т. п. to the degree that (one's ability, strength etc allows, the situation demands etc): по мере сил ≃ **as much as one can; to the extent of one's abilities ⟨powers⟩; to the best of one's ability;** ‖ по мере надобности ≃ **as need dictates; if ⟨as⟩ need be.**

«Раз тюремщики вершат правое дело — твоя обязанность помогать им по мере сил» (Солженицын 3). "Since our jailers are in the right, it's your duty to help them as much as you can" (3a). ♦ ...Он [нарядчик] не заносчив и всегда рад по мере сил помочь политическим (Гинзбург 2). ...He [the work assigner] was not arrogant, and he was always glad to help politicals to the extent of his powers (2a). ♦ Работал инструментальщик без нормы, по мере надобности, а в основном по своему усмотрению (Гинзбург 2). The toolsetter worked without any fixed norm. He worked as need dictated, or rather, on the whole, as he thought fit (2a).

M-77 • ПО МЕ́РЕ ВОЗМО́ЖНОСТИ; ПО ВОЗМО́ЖНОСТИ; ПО СИ́ЛЕ ВОЗМО́ЖНОСТИ *lit* [PrepP; these forms only; sent adv (occas. parenth); fixed WO] to whatever degree is possible, one can etc: **to whatever extent (is) possible; to whatever extent one can; as far ⟨much etc⟩ as possible; as far as one can ⟨is able to⟩ (do so); as best (as) one can; to the best of one's ability ⟨abilities⟩.**

...Я избирал себе путь многолетнего молчания и скрытого труда. По возможности не делать ни одного общественного шага, дать себя забыть (о, если бы забыли!..) (Солженицын 2). ...I had chosen for many years ahead the way of silence and clandestine labor. As far as possible, I would not take a single public step. I would let people forget me (how I longed to be forgotten!) (2a). ♦ Мы не пишем фразу, она пишет себя, а мы лишь проясняем по силе возможности скрытый в ней, скопившийся смысл (Терц 3). We do not write a phrase—it writes itself, and all we do is to clarify, as far as we are able, the accumulated meaning concealed within it (3a). ♦ «Вы изволите говорить, что статья моя неясна; я готов её вам разъяснить, по возможности» (Достоевский 3). "You take the liberty of saying that my article is not clear; I'm quite prepared to explain it to you to the best of my ability" (3a).

M-78 • ПО МЕ́РЕ ТОГО́ КАК [subord Conj, correlative] while (some action is developing) and in proportion to (its development): **as; as (sth.) progresses; the..., the...**

По мере того как кортеж приближался, толпы глуповцев расступались и давали дорогу (Салтыков-Щедрин 1). As the cortege drew near, the crowds parted and the Foolovites made way (1a). ♦ «Постарайтесь любить ваших ближних деятельно и неустанно. По мере того как будете преуспевать в любви, будете убеждаться и в бытии бога, и в бессмертии души вашей» (Достоевский 1). "Try to love your neighbors actively and tirelessly. The more you succeed in loving, the more you'll be convinced of the existence of God and the immortality of your soul" (1a). ♦ По мере того как бричка близилась к крыльцу, глаза его делались веселее и улыбка раздвигалась более и более (Гоголь 3). The nearer the carriage drew to the front steps the merrier his eyes grew and the broader the smile (3a).

M-79 • МЕ́РЗОСТЬ ЗАПУСТЕ́НИЯ *obs, lit* [NP; sing only; fixed WO] a state of total ruin, waste, decay: **utter desolation ⟨devastation⟩.**

< From the Bible (Dan. 9:27).

M-80 • КАК СИ́ВЫЙ МЕ́РИН *highly coll* [как + NP; Invar; fixed WO] **1. врёт, брешет ~** [adv (intensif)] (one tells lies) shamelessly, unscrupulously: **(one lies) through ⟨in⟩ one's teeth; (one lies) like a trooper ⟨a rug⟩; (one is) an out-and-out ⟨a barefaced⟩ liar.**

«Вы понимаете, о чём я говорю?» – «Да откровенно говоря, нет...» – «...Фантастика всё это... Никакого удава в горах нет и никогда не было...» – «Постойте, постойте, – сказал я, – так, значит, Потапов врёт?» – «Значит, брешет наш Потапов как сивый мерин...» (Домбровский 1). "Do you see what I'm driving at?" "Well, to be quite honest, no I don't." "...The whole story is pure science-fiction. There is no boa-constrictor up in those hills and there never was...." "Just a minute," I said. "This means that Potapov must be lying." "Of course. Our Potapov is lying like a trooper..." (1a). ♦ Мы знали, что он врёт как сивый мерин, но Соне это было интересно... (Рыбаков 1). We knew he was an out-and-out liar, but Sonya found it interesting... (1a).

2. глуп, глупа ~ [modif] (stupid) to the extreme: **as dumb as an ox; as dumb ⟨stupid⟩ as they come.**

[Почтмейстер (*читает*):] «Оригиналы страшные. От смеху ты бы умер. Ты, я знаю, пишешь статейки; помести их в свою литературу. Во-первых: городничий – глуп, как сивый мерин...» (Гоголь 4). [Postmaster, *reads*:] "What oddballs! You'd die laughing. Why not put them into some of those sketches you write for the papers? Take the mayor—as dumb as an ox..." (4f).

M-81 • КАК МЁРТВОМУ ПРИПА́РКИ ⟨-а⟩ поможет, нужен и т. п. *coll* [как + NP; these forms only; adv (neg intensif); fixed WO] not at all (helpful), absolutely not (needed): **(need sth.) like a hole in the head; (need sth.) as much as a cat needs two tails; (be ⟨do s.o.⟩) no good at all.**

M-82 • В МЕ́РУ [PrepP; Invar] **1. ~ чего** [Prep; the resulting PrepP is adv] in accordance with: **to the extent of; within the limits of;** ‖ **в меру своих сил ⟨способностей, разумения⟩ ≃** [in refer. to exerting maximum effort] **as best one can; to the best of one's ability ⟨abilities⟩.**

«Знаменитый Логидзе тайну своих прохладительных напитков унёс с собой в могилу, – сказал Абесаломон Нартович, – я в меру своих скромных сил пытаюсь создать равноценный напиток» (Искандер 4). "The famous Logidze carried the secret of his soft drinks to the grave," Abesalomon Nartovich said. "To the extent of my modest abilities, I am trying to create a drink of equivalent worth" (4a). ♦ Мать сотворила глупость, но ведь написала правду... Значит, стыдиться за мать не нужно. Зачем стыдиться за несчастную женщину, которая терзается и не спит ночей из-за дочкиных неурядиц и пытается в меру своего разумения... Да ведь главное, главное: написала правду! (Трифонов 1). Granted, her mother had behaved foolishly, but what she had written was the truth, after all....So why should she feel shame for her mother? Why be ashamed of an unhappy woman who tormented herself and was unable to sleep at night because of her daughter's problems, a woman who tried as best she could to....Yes, and after all, the point was—the real point was that she had written the

truth! (1a). ♦ ...Я пытаюсь в меру своих сил раскрыть значительность эпического существования маленького народа (Искандер 3). ...I have attempted to reveal, to the best of my abilities, the significance of the epic existence of the little nation (3a).

2. ~ каков, как [modif or adv] (sth. is present) to a moderate, appropriate, or acceptable degree (used to express the speaker's opinion that sth. he considers positive is present to a sufficient degree, sth. he considers negative is not present to an excessive degree, or sth. about which he makes no value judgment is present to an average degree): **moderately; fairly; rather; reasonably.**

...Он [полковник] был в меру высок и в меру дороден... (Гинзбург 2). He [the Colonel] was moderately tall and moderately portly... (2a). ♦ ...Все веселились вовсю, танцевали под любошную, в меру модерновую музыку... (Залыгин 1). ...All were busy enjoying themselves dancing to some curious, fairly modern music... (1a). ♦ В вагоне было в меру накурено, прохладно (Шолохов 3). The carriage was rather smoky and cold (3a).

3. [adv] with temperance, within reasonable limits: **in moderation;** [in limited contexts] **not (taking ⟨carrying⟩ sth.) too far.**

...Всё делалось в меру, как того требуют обычаи и собственное желание (Искандер 3). Everything was done in moderation, as dictated by custom and personal inclination (3a). ♦ [Костылёв:] Ты что сказал? [Сатин:] Это я так... про себя... [Костылёв:] Смотри, брат! Шути в меру... да! (Горький 3). [K.:] What did you say? [S.:] I was just talking...to myself... [K.:] You be careful! Don't carry your jokes too far...I mean it! (3a).

M-83 • ЗНАТЬ МЕ́РУ [VP; subj: human; pres or past] (usu. in refer. to doing things that can be harmful, embarrassing etc when done excessively) to realize when one has reached a reasonable, sensible limit and be able to stop at that limit: X знает меру ≃ **X knows when to stop; X knows where to draw the line; X observes limits;** ‖ *Neg* X ни в чём не знает меры ≃ **X does everything without moderation.**

«А всё почему пьём?.. Я так считаю: пьём потому, что теперь такая необходимость появилась – пить»... – «Если бы меру знать, половины того, что она [выпивка] с нами творит, не было бы» (Распутин 3). "Why do we drink?...I reckon we drink because these days we have a need for it."..."If we knew when to stop, the stuff wouldn't do us half the damage it does" (3a). ♦ Главное, [Коля] знал меру, умел при случае сдержать себя самого, а в отношениях к начальству никогда не переступал некоторой последней и заветной черты, за которою уже проступок не может быть терпим, обращаясь в беспорядок, бунт и в беззаконие (Достоевский 1). Above all, he [Kolya] knew where to draw the line, could restrain himself when need be, and in relation to the authorities never overstepped that final and inscrutable limit beyond which a misdeed turns into disorder, rebellion, and lawlessness, and can no longer be tolerated (1a). ♦ «И всё-таки я не могу поверить в то, что величайшее явление в духовной жизни человечества есть просто чепуха... Надо же всё-таки знать меру» (Зиновьев 2). "All the same," I said, "I cannot believe that the greatest phenomenon of the spiritual life of mankind is just rubbish....We must observe some limits..." (2a). ♦ [Иванов:] ...Я спешил расходовать себя на одну только молодость, пьянел, возбуждался, работал; не знал меры (Чехов 4). [I.:] I lost no time in expending myself in my youth. I was overwrought, drank, worked, did everything without moderation (4a).

M-84 • НЕ В МЕ́РУ [PrepP; Invar; adv or modif] more than necessary, appropriate etc: **immoderately; excessively; beyond the accepted norm;** [as modif only] **too;** [as adv only] **too much; (go) too far (in sth.); exceed the limits (in doing sth.).**

С точки зрения науки, сказал Болтун, ругнув продавщицу за не в меру разбавленное водой пиво, следует говорить о причинах тех или иных явлений (Зиновьев 1). "From the scientific point of view," said Chatterer, after cursing the barmaid for having watered the beer beyond the accepted norm, "one must talk of the causes of certain manifestations" (1a). ♦ [Ведущий:] Вместо того чтобы спать, сохраняя здоровье, люди, беснуясь, нарушают режим: не в меру едят, пьют и ухаживают (Брагинский и Рязанов 1). [Narrator:] Instead of having a good night's sleep and keeping themselves healthy, people recklessly abandon all their regular habits: eat too much, drink too much, love too much... (1a).

M-85 • БЕЗ МЕ́РЫ [PrepP; Invar; adv] **1.** пить, курить и т. п. ~ (to drink, smoke etc) immoderately, consuming inordinate quantities: **far too much; far more than one should; to excess; excessively; without measure;** [in limited contexts] **excessive consumption (of sth.).**

«...Обращаю ваше внимание на кокаин, который вы... нюхаете без меры» (Пастернак 1). "...I must really draw your attention to your excessive consumption of cocaine" (1a).

2. любить *кого,* быть₀ влюблённым и т. п. ~ (to love s.o., be in love etc) to an extreme degree: **beyond (all) measure; (s.o.'s love) knows no end ⟨bounds⟩.**

[Лидочка:] Послушайте, Мишель; я хочу, чтоб вы меня ужасно любили... без меры... как я вас люблю (Сухово-Кобылин 2). [L.:] *Michel,* listen—I want you to love me terribly...beyond measure...the way I love you (2b).

M-86 • ПРИНИМА́ТЬ/ПРИНЯ́ТЬ МЕ́РЫ [VP; subj: human or collect] to carry out a series of actions (that should produce a certain result): **X принял меры ≃ X took (appropriate) measures ⟨steps⟩; X took action (on sth.); X did something (about it);** [in limited contexts] **X took (some) precautions.**

В Учреждение, возглавляемое капитаном Милягой, граждане почти всегда писали письма без обратного адреса... В таких письмах содержались обычно мелкие доносы... К чести Учреждения надо сказать, что оно принимало меры далеко не по каждому такому сигналу, иначе на воле не осталось бы ни одного человека (Войнович 2). Citizens almost always wrote letters to the Institution headed by Milyaga without a return address....As a rule, such letters contained petty denunciations....It must be said, to the Institution's credit, that very few such letters ever caused it to take measures; otherwise there would not have been a single person left free in the country (2a). ♦ Цель мероприятия — обнаружить тех, кто не одобряет его проведения, и принять меры (Зиновьев 1). The aim of the experiment was to detect those who did not approve of its being carried out and to take appropriate steps (1a). ♦ Дед заговорил вкрадчиво и мягко. Он сказал, что всё устроится по-хорошему. Если юноша тоскует, то надо, конечно, принять меры (Булгаков 5). The grandfather began to speak in mild, conciliatory tones. Everything, he said, would turn out for the best. If the young man was unhappy, then, of course, it was necessary to do something about it (5a). ♦ [Михаил:] Ну, завод закрыт. Но на всякий случай надо принять меры... (Горький 1). [M.:] Well, the factory's closed. But we'd better take some precautions, just in case (1b).

M-87 • СВЕРХ ⟨СВЫ́ШЕ⟩ (ВСЯ́КОЙ) МЕ́РЫ [PrepP; these forms only] **1.** Also: **ЧЕРЕЗ ⟨ЧРЕЗ⟩ МЕ́РУ** *obs* [modif] to a greater extent than is necessary, permissible, acceptable etc: **overly; excessively; exceedingly; more than one should.**

2. любить, ненавидеть и т. п. *кого* ~ [adv] (to love, hate s.o. etc) with extreme intensity: **beyond (all) measure; no end; (s.o.'s love ⟨hate etc⟩) knows no end ⟨bounds⟩;** [in limited contexts] **beyond all reason.**

Пётр Петрович [Лужин] презирал и ненавидел его [Лебезятникова] даже сверх меры, почти с того самого дня, как у него поселился... (Достоевский 3). ...Pyotr Petrovich despised and hated him [Lebezyatnikov], even beyond measure, and had done so almost from the very day he came to stay with him... (3c). ...He [Mr. Luzhin] had despised and hated him [Lebezyatnikov], beyond all reason even, almost from the very day he had moved in with him... (3a).

M-88 • ВЗЯТЬ ⟨РВАНУ́ТЬ *coll*⟩ С МЕ́СТА [VP; subj: human or a noun denoting a vehicle or a horse] to begin moving suddenly and with great speed from a complete stop: X взял с места ≃ **X tore ⟨sped, bolted⟩ off from a standing start;** [when it would be redundant to indicate that the motion is begun from a complete stop] **X tore ⟨sped, bolted⟩ off (down the road ⟨the track etc⟩).**

Володька сел за руль, дуднул, рванул с места (Аксёнов 3). Volodya climbed up behind the wheel, revved up the motor and tore off down the road (3a). ♦ ...Мелькало название станции — что-нибудь подмосковное: Особая, Маленковская, — и состав трогался дальше, стремительно рвал с места... (Битов 2). [context transl] ...There was a glimpse of the name of the station—Osobaya, Malenkovskaya, something near Moscow—and the train pulled out, yanked rapidly away... (2a).

M-89 • ЖИВО́ГО МЕ́СТА НЕТ ⟨НЕ ОСТА́ЛОСЬ⟩ *coll* [VP_{subj/gen}] **1.** ~ *на ком* s.o. is severely beaten, disfigured: на X-е живого места нет ≃ **X is beaten black-and-blue; X is black-and-blue all over; X is bruised from head to foot; X is beaten to a pulp.**

2. s.o. is so covered with dirt (tattoos etc) or sth. is so covered with filth (drawings, holes etc) that nothing of his or its original appearance remains: на X-е живого места нет ≃ **there isn't a clean ⟨clear etc⟩ spot ⟨place⟩ to be seen on X; there isn't a single ⟨isn't one⟩ patch on X where** [NP denoting the original surface] **is visible.**

...Воркута весь разрисован [татуировками], живого места нет ни на лице, ни на теле (Марченко 1). ...Vorkuta was absolutely smothered in tattoos, with not a clear place to be seen either on his face or body (1a). ♦ И ещё я знаю про Зенкова, что он любил красивые вещи. Вернее, не красивые, а изукрашенные. В музее хранится его портсигар из уральского камня. На нём не осталось живого места. Он весь в вензелях, образках, разноцветных жгуче-синих и розовых эмалях с картинками и видами (Домбровский 1). I also found that Zenkov loved beautiful things, or rather not beautiful but decorative things. His cigar-box made of uralite has been preserved in the museum. There is not a single patch on it where the stone is visible. It is covered in monograms, curlicues, pictures and views painted in hot pink and blue enamels (1a).

M-90 • МЕСТА́ НЕ СТОЛЬ ОТДАЛЁННЫЕ [NP; pl only; fixed WO] a distant place to which a person is sent as a form of punishment (in prerevolutionary Russia, usu. Siberia; now the idiom is used more broadly): **(a place of) exile ⟨banishment⟩; (exile s.o. to) distant provinces ⟨remote areas of the country⟩.**

Много лет прошло, прежде чем бывшего генерала вернули из мест не столь отдалённых... (Максимов 3). Many years went by before they allowed the ex-general to return from banishment... (3a). ♦ Даже чечено-ингуши и калмыки... на своей шкуре испытавшие мудрость сталинской национальной политики (они все были высланы Сталиным в места не столь отдалённые), — и те тоже очень возмущаются... (Ивинская 1). Even the Chechens, Ingush, and Kalmyks, who had experienced at first hand the wisdom of Stalin's policies toward the minorities (they were deported, men, women, and children, to remote areas of the country), joined in the chorus of indignation... (1a). ♦ Монархический орган «Восшествие» посвятил «Жизни Чернышевского» заметку, в которой указывалось, что всякий смысл и ценность разоблачения «одного из идеологических дядек большевизма» совершенно подрывается «дешёвым либеральничанием автора, всецело переходящего на сторону своего плачевного, но вредного героя, как только долготерпеливый Русский Царь наконец ссылает его в места не столь отдалённые» (Набоков 1). [context transl] The monarchist organ *The Throne* devoted to *The Life of Chernyshevski* a few lines in which it pointed out that any sense or value in the unmasking of "one of the ideological mentors of Bolshevism" was completely undermined by "the cheap liberalizing of the author, who goes wholly over to the side of his sorry, but pernicious hero as soon as the long-suffering Russian Tsar finally has him safely tucked away…" (1a).

M-91 • **НЕ НАХОДИ́ТЬ ⟨НЕ МОЧЬ НАЙТИ́⟩ (СЕБЕ́) МЕ́СТА** *(от чего)* *coll* [VP; subj: human] to be extremely worried, anxious, restless (often in fear for a loved one's safety, in anticipation of an important event etc): X не находил себе места (от волнения ⟨тревоги и т. п.⟩) ≃ **X was beside himself (with worry ⟨anxiety etc⟩); X couldn't find any peace; X nearly went out of his mind (with worry** etc**); X couldn't rest for worry ⟨worrying, fretting** etc⟩.

[Коля:] Ты что?! Мать места себе не находит… (Розов 2). [K.:] What do you think you're doing?! Mum's been beside herself with worry (2a). ♦ …Места себе не нахожу оттого, что прожил не свою, а какую-то вроде бы чужую жизнь (Зиновьев 1). "…I can't find any peace because it seems that I have been living someone else's life, not my own" (1a). ♦ …Когда была эта война, мама не находила себе места: отправят Генриха на Карельский перешеек… полезет в самое пекло и пропадёт (Рыбаков 1). When that war was going on, mother nearly went out of her mind; they'll send him [Genrikh] to the Karelian [Isthmus], she said…he'll get into the thick of the fighting and get himself killed (1a). ♦ С этим [с преступлениями] всё кончено, они с Сударем не могли себе найти места от стыда и раскаяния, они даже думали прийти и покаяться, попросить, чтобы их простили… (Семёнов 1). …This [their criminal activity] was all over now, he and Squire could not rest for shame and repentance, they had even thought of coming and owning up, of begging to be pardoned… (1a).

M-92 • **НЕ СОЙТИ́ МНЕ ⟨НАМ⟩ С (Э́ТОГО) МЕ́СТА!; (ЧТОБ) НЕ СОЙТИ́ ⟨НЕ ВСТАТЬ⟩ (МНЕ ⟨НАМ⟩) С (Э́ТОГО) МЕ́СТА!** *highly coll* [Interj; these forms only] an oath used by the speaker(s) to emphasize the truth of a statement: **may I ⟨we⟩ die on the spot (if…); may lightning strike me ⟨us⟩ (dead) (if…); may I ⟨we⟩ be rooted to the spot (if…).**

[Липочка:] Да вы все перед свадьбой так говорите, а там и обманете. [Подхалюзин:] С места не сойти, Алимпияда Самсоновна! Анафемой хочу быть, коли лгу! (Островский 10). [L.:] You all talk that way before the wedding; but afterwards you cheat us. [P.:] May I die on the spot, Olimpiada Samsonovna! Damnation blast me if I lie! (10b). ♦ Мне нравилось менять серебро у неё [кассирши], а не в автомате: то ахнешь… насчёт погоды, то пошутишь по адресу женского пола, а однажды, не сойти мне с этого места, я преподнёс ей гвоздику (Аксёнов 6). I like changing my silver with her [the cashier] instead of in a machine: You can grumble about the weather, or make jokes about the female sex, and once, may I be rooted to the spot if I'm lying, I gave her a carnation (6a).

M-93 • **НЕ СХОДЯ́ С МЕ́СТА** *coll* [Verbal Adv; Invar; adv; more often used with pfv verbs; fixed WO] **1.** immediately, without delay: **(right) on the spot;** [in past and future contexts only] **(right) then and there;** [in present contexts only] **(right) here and now.**

Требовалось тут же, не сходя с места, изобрести обыкновенные объяснения явлений необыкновенных (Булгаков 9). …He felt obliged to invent at once, right on the spot, some ordinary explanation for extraordinary events (9a). ♦ Да, взметнулась волна горя при страшном известии о Михаиле Александровиче. Кто-то суетился, кричал, что необходимо сейчас же, тут же, не сходя с места, составить какую-то коллективную телеграмму и немедленно послать её (Булгаков 9). A wave of grief surged up at the terrible news about Mikhail Alexandrovich. Someone fussed around shouting that they must all immediately, here and now, without delay compose a collective telegram and send it off (9b).

2. at one time, in one try: **in one go; at ⟨in⟩ one ⟨a single⟩ stroke; in a single breath ⟨gulp** etc⟩; **at ⟨in⟩ one fell swoop.**

Торт был такой вкусный, что я съел три куска не сходя с места. The cake was so good I ate three pieces at one go.

M-94 • **НЕТ МЕ́СТА** *кому-чему среди кого, где* [VP; impers; usu. pres] s.o. or sth. is rejected (by some group, in some organization, at some place) as being alien, harmful, sth. is regarded as intolerable: X-у нет места среди Y-ов ⟨в месте Z⟩ ≃ **there is no place ⟨room⟩ for X among Ys ⟨in place Z⟩; place Z has ⟨can have⟩ no room for (people ⟨things⟩ like) X; thing X is uncalled-for among Ys ⟨in place Z⟩.**

«…Предательству у нас нет прощения, а предателям нет и не должно быть места на нашей земле» (Войнович 4). "…We have no forgiveness for treason and there is no place for traitors in our land, nor should there be" (4a). ♦ «Ты тут демагогией не занимайся, тунеядец!.. На судно захотел, да? На сейнерах у нас сейчас таким, как ты, места нет, понял?» (Аксёнов 1). "Don't you pull any of your demagoguery on me, you parasite!…Took a notion to go on a ship, did you? No seiner of ours has room for the likes of you, understand?" (1a).

M-95 • **НИ С МЕ́СТА** *coll* [PrepP; Invar] **1.** [indep. sent] (used as a command) stand still, do not make the slightest movement: **don't move!; stay where you are!; stay put!; freeze!**

«Отрезвел я, когда они закрыли дверь кассы и длинный, вытащив наган, сказал: „Руки вверх, ни с места!"» (Семёнов 1). "I sobered up when they closed the door of the bank and the tall one pulled out a revolver and said: 'Hands up! Don't move!'" (1a).

2. [predic (subj: human, animal, or a noun denoting a vehicle)] to remain in the same position, not move from one's or its place: X — ни с места ≃ **X won't ⟨can't⟩ move an inch; X won't budge (an inch).**

«Ужасные бестии эти азиаты! Вы думаете, они помогают, что кричат? А чёрт их разберёт, что они кричат? Быки-то их понимают; запрягите хоть двадцать, так коли они крикнут по-своему, быки всё ни с места…» (Лермонтов 1). "They're terrific rogues, these Asiatics! You don't think their yelling helps much, do you? You can't tell what the devil they're saying. But the oxen understand them all right; hitch up twenty of the beasts if you wish and they won't budge once those fellows begin yelling in their tongue…" (1b).

3. [predic (subj: abstr or human)] (of work, matters etc) not to show any advancement, to be in the same state as previously: X ни с места ≃ **X is making no progress ⟨headway⟩; X is getting nowhere; there is ⟨person Y is making⟩ absolutely no progress with thing X; X is at a (complete) standstill.**

[Муромский:] …Пять месяцев я здесь живу… — а дело ни с места! (Сухово-Кобылин 1). [M.:] Here I am, five months already…and there's been absolutely no progress with the case! (1a).

M-96 • **С МЕ́СТА В КАРЬЕ́Р** *coll, occas. humor* [PrepP; Invar; adv; usu. used with verbs in the past tense; fixed WO] (to begin doing sth.) without delay, immediately: **right away; straightaway; at once; right off the bat; lose no time (in doing sth.); without wasting a moment ⟨a minute, a second⟩; in no time at all;** [in limited contexts] **(right) then and there.**

У таких [людей] любовь и спорт — одно и то же, вот он и начал брать очередной рекорд с места в карьер (Залыгин 1). To him and his type, love and sport were one and the same thing, and he lost no time in attacking the next record (1a). ♦ …По традиции, собрались [для встречи Нового года] около десяти… С места в карьер, все веселились вовсю, танцевали под любопытную, в меру модерновую музыку… (Залыгин 1). The guests arrived [to greet the New Year] at about ten, according to tradition.…Without wasting a moment, all were busy enjoying themselves dancing to some curious, fairly modern music… (1a). ♦ Юлька вбегает с шумом, с возгласами, с раскрытыми объятиями. С места в карьер отдаётся воспоминаниям (Гинзбург 2). Julia bounced in with cries of joy and open arms. In no time at all she was pouring out reminiscences (2a).

M-97 • **СДВИ́НУТЬ С МЕ́СТА** [VP; subj: human] **1.** ~ *кого* [often neg pfv fut, gener. 2nd pers sing не сдви́нешь] to rouse s.o. to act, do sth.: X-а с места не сдвинешь ≃ **you can't ⟨it's hard to⟩ get X going ⟨moving, started⟩.**

2. ~ *что* to set sth. in operation, in motion: X сдвинет Y с места ≃ **X will get Y going ⟨moving forward⟩; X will get things started; X will start ⟨get⟩ the ball rolling; X will get the show on the road;** [in limited contexts] **X will jump-start Y.**

Подобными размышлениями, однако, не сдвинешь с места повествование (Аксёнов 6). Reflections of this sort, however, will not get the narrative moving forward (6a).

M-98 • **СТА́ВИТЬ/ПОСТА́ВИТЬ ВСЁ НА СВОИ́ МЕСТА́ ⟨НА (СВОЁ) МЕ́СТО⟩** [VP; subj: usu. human or abstr] (in refer. to misunderstandings between people, jumbled ideas, facts taken out of context etc) to introduce clarity into a complex situation, explain it in a logical way, show the interconnection between different aspects of a matter etc: X поставил всё на свои места ≃ **X put everything in its rightful ⟨proper⟩ place; X sorted things ⟨it all⟩ out; X cleared things ⟨everything etc⟩ up;** [in limited contexts] **X set the record straight; X set things right.**

«История всё… поставит на своё место» (Солженицын 2). "History will put all things…in their rightful places" (2a). ♦ «У него не будет ничего своего. Он ничего не придумает, ничего не предпримет, — думал князь Андрей, — но он всё выслушает, всё запомнит, всё поставит на своё место, ничему полезному не помешает и ничего вредного не позволит» (Толстой 6). "He will put nothing forward of his own. He will devise nothing, undertake nothing," thought Prince Andrei, "but he will listen to everything, remember everything, put everything in its proper place, and will neither stand in the way of anything beneficial nor accede to anything detrimental" (6a). ♦ [author's usage] Только теперь ему [Андрею] стало ясно, что вся его жизнь укреплялась братом, его опытом, его силой, его авторитетом, наконец. Будь сейчас рядом Петёк, он моментально расставил бы всё по своим местам (Максимов 3). Only now did he [Andrei] realize how completely he relied on his brother, his brother's experience, his strength, and, of course, his authority. If only Pyotr were here, he'd sort it all out in a flash! (3a).

M-99 • всё **СТАНО́ВИТСЯ/СТА́ЛО ⟨ВСТА́ЛО⟩ НА СВОИ́ МЕСТА́ ⟨НА (СВОЁ) МЕ́СТО⟩** [VP; subj: всё; usu. pfv; usu. this WO] **1.** things are developing toward, have reached, or have gone back to a point where the situation is considered normalized, is as expected, desired etc: всё стало на свои места ≃ **everything fell into place ⟨sorted itself out⟩;** [when things return to their previous, normal state] **everything returned ⟨went back⟩ to normal; things got back on course ⟨track⟩.**

«Вы знаете, Оленька, — мягким кошачьим голосом говорила эта огромная заплывшая жиром туша, — разрешите мне показать этот роман вышестоящему лицу. Вполне возможно, всё станет на своё место» (Ивинская 1). "I tell you what, Olenka," she said in a soft, purring voice—she was a woman of enormous bulk, covered in rolls of fat—"let me show the novel to someone high up. It is quite possible that everything will then fall into place" (1a). ♦ …Она ясно осознала: у неё нет к нему любви, а есть только замешательство — в её жизнь неожиданно вторглась необыкновенный человек. И это замешательство надо преодолеть немедленно, не откладывая, и она отослала ему незаконченный портрет. Всё встало на свои места (Рыбаков 1). …She realized very clearly that she didn't love him, that her feelings were simply confused, because an unusual man had intruded into her life unexpectedly. This confusion had to be overcome

immediately, without delay, so she sent back the unfinished portrait. Everything returned to normal (1a).

2. (in refer. to s.o.'s understanding of the interconnection between various facts, phenomena etc) everything becomes clear and explainable: всё стало на свои места ≃ **everything fell into place.**

И вдруг всё стало на свои места. «Так вот что он имел в виду! — подумал Виктор про Голема. — Умные и все на подбор талантливые… Тогда что же это выходит? Тогда выходит, что они уже не люди. Зурзмансор мне просто баки забивал» (Стругацкие 1). And suddenly everything fell into place. "So that's what he has in mind!" Victor thought, remembering Golem. "Intelligent and talented, every single one of them. And what does it lead to? That they're not human anymore. Zurzmansor was just pulling the wool over my eyes" (1a).

3. (in refer. to the normalization of a person's visual perception of reality, temporarily distorted by dizziness, confusion etc) everything is again perceived by s.o. as it exists in reality: **everything returned ⟨went back⟩ to normal.**

M-100 • **НА МЕСТА́Х** [PrepP; Invar; adv] in the outlying regions, provincial organizations, institutions (as opposed to the central regions, organizations, institutions): **at the local level; in the provinces; locally.**

Ей [власти] требовались «на местах» точные и механизированные исполнители приказов… (Мандельштам 2). The sort of people now wanted down below, "at the local level," were efficient robots who automatically obeyed orders… (2a). ♦ По принятому у нас обычаю всякую кампанию принято поддерживать и развивать на местах (Искандер 3). The custom in our country is for every government campaign to be supported and developed in the provinces (3a).

M-101 • **ВСЁ НА (СВОЁМ) МЕ́СТЕ** *у кого highly coll, approv* [VP_subj with быть∅; usu. pres, rare past; fixed WO] (usu. of a woman) having an attractive physique, well-proportioned, well-built: у X-а всё на месте ≃ **X has everything in all the right places; X is really built.**

M-102 • **НА МЕ́СТЕ**[1] [PrepP; Invar] **1.** [adv] right there where sth. is happening: **on the spot; at the scene (of sth.).**

«…Неужели ты это тогда же так на месте и обдумал?» — воскликнул Иван Фёдорович вне себя от удивления (Достоевский 2). "…Can you possibly have thought of all that right there on the spot?" Ivan Fyodorovich exclaimed, beside himself with astonishment (2a).

2. [usu. subj-compl with быть∅, бывать etc (subj: human)] in the room or place where a person works and should be: X на месте ≃ **X is in (his office); X is at his desk ⟨station⟩;** [in limited contexts] **X is where he is supposed to be.**

Как раз именно полковник Добренький, которого никогда не бывает на месте, [лейтенанту] и нужен (Войнович 4). …It was precisely Colonel Dobrenky, who was never in, with whom he [the lieutenant] needed to speak (4a). ♦ Майор, против обыкновения, оказался на месте (Максимов 1). For once the major was in his office (1a). ♦ Разбирать конфликт должен заведующий… но его никогда нет на месте, целыми днями где-то пропадает… (Рыбаков 2). It was the manager's responsibility to straighten out problems…but he was never where he was supposed to be, he vanished for days at a time… (2a).

3. ~ *чьём, кого* [adv or subj-compl with copula (subj: human; subjunctive only)] (if s.o. were) in another person's situation: будь X ⟨если бы X был⟩ на месте Y-а ≃ **(if X were) in Y's place ⟨shoes, position⟩ (X would…);** [1st pers only] **if I were you.**

…Его лицо ничего не выражало особенного, и мне стало досадно: я бы на его месте умер с горя (Лермонтов 1). …His face did not express anything unusual, and this annoyed me; in his place, I would have died of grief (1a). …His face showed nothing in particular, and that annoyed me. If I'd been in his place, I'd have died of grief (1c). ♦ [Тригорин:] Я бы вот хотел хоть один час побыть на вашем месте, чтобы узнать, как вы думаете... [Нина:] А я хотела бы побывать на вашем месте. [Тригорин:] Зачем? [Нина:] Чтобы узнать, как чувствует себя известный талантливый писатель (Чехов 6). [Т.:] I'd like to be in your shoes, if only for an hour, to find out how you think... [N.:] And I should like to be in your shoes. [T.:] Why? [N.:] To find out how it feels to be a famous, gifted writer (6a). ♦ «А я бы на твоём месте, знаешь, что сделал? Для начала я перестал бы быть холуём при Иванько» (Войнович 3). "And in your position, you know what I would do? To start, I would stop toadying to Ivanko!" (3a). ♦ «...А я бы на вашем месте поостерёгся...» (Стругацкие 3). "I'd be worried if I were you" (3a).

4. уложить, убить, прихлопнуть и т. п. *кого* ~ *coll* [adv]. Also: **КЛАСТЬ/ПОЛОЖИТЬ НА МЕСТЕ** [VP; subj: human; usu. pfv; fixed WO] to kill s.o. outright, immediately: X уложил Y-а на месте ≃ **X killed Y on the spot; X killed Y where Y stood;** [in limited contexts] **X blasted Y on the spot.**

...Он пригласил к себе старшего помощника для объяснений и убил его на месте (Богданов 1). ...He summoned his assistant for an explanation and killed him on the spot (1a).

M-103 • НА МÉСТЕ²; НА СВОЁМ МÉСТЕ [PrepP; these forms only; subj-compl with copula (subj: human)] a person who is engaged in work or activities that suit his abilities, vocation: X на (своём) месте ≃ **X is the right man in the right place; X is the right man for the job; X is in his right ⟨proper⟩ place; X is right ⟨exactly⟩ where he belongs; X is in his element;** ‖ *Neg* X не на своём месте ≃ **X is the wrong man for the job; X is not in his right ⟨proper⟩ place; X is out of place ⟨out of his element⟩.**

Экспериментатором он быть не мог — только теоретиком, но здесь уж он был на месте (Грекова 2). He could not conduct experiments, he had to confine himself to theoretical work but here he was the right man in the right place (2a). ♦ ...Я думаю, генералом он был бы больше на месте, чем монахом... (Герцен 1). ...I think he would have been more in his right place as a general than as a monk... (1a).

M-104 • НА МÉСТЕ ПРЕСТУПЛÉНИЯ поймать, застать, накрыть *кого* и т. п. *often humor* [PrepP; Invar; adv; fixed WO] at the very moment when sth. reprehensible is being carried out: X-а поймали ~ ≃ **X was caught red-handed ⟨in the act⟩; X was discovered at the scene of the crime; X was caught with his hand in the cookie jar ⟨in the till⟩.**

[Осип:] В законе написано, что только тогда пойдёшь в Сибирь, когда на тебя обстоятельно докажут или на месте преступления поймают... (Чехов 1). [O.:] ...According to the law you can only be sent to Siberia if you're proved guilty or if you're caught red-handed (1a). ♦ Она [Мария] только на секунду остановилась и прошла в кухню. Кузьме стало противно и стыдно, будто эти деньги он украл у Марии и она застала его на месте преступления (Распутин 1). She [Maria] stopped for only an instant on her way to the kitchen, but her presence made Kuzma feel miserable and ashamed, as if he were stealing from her and she had caught him in the act (1a). ♦ Только что наконец застукав её [курицу] на месте преступления, если можно назвать преступлением высиживание собственных яиц, пусть даже в кустах бузины, поймав её за этим подпольным занятием, она [тётя Катя] согнала её с яиц... (Искандер 3). Having finally discovered her [the hen] just now at the scene of the crime — if hatching one's own eggs, even if in the elder bushes, can be called a crime — having caught her in this sub-rosa occupation, she [Aunt Katya] drove her off the eggs... (3a).

M-105 • НА ПУСТÓМ ⟨ГÓЛОМ⟩ МÉСТЕ [PrepP; these forms only; adv; fixed WO] **1.** ~ **начинать** to start sth. at the very beginning, from nothing: **(start) from scratch;** [in limited contexts] **(start) with a clean slate.**

[Бакченин:] Мне на голом месте начинать. Я должен быть свободен, чтоб заставить себя заниматься, заставить сидеть над книгами в Публичке, вообще переключиться с этой жизни на ту... (Панова 1). [B.:] I need to start with a clean slate. I have to be free in order to make myself work, to make myself sit over books in the public library, to switch over from this life to the one I want... (1a).

2. возникнуть, появиться и т. п. ~ [often neg] (usu. of a cultural phenomenon, school of thought etc) (to emerge, spring etc) in isolation from and not founded on any already existing (phenomenon, school of thought etc): **out of nowhere; in a vacuum; *in vacuo.***

...Много позже искусство христианской Европы строилось... не на пустом месте и не на греко-латинском фундаменте только, но на базе местных, древнеязыческих форм, чутких и восприимчивых к голосу новой эстетики именно соединением крайностей красоты и гротеска (Терц 3). ...The much later art of Christian Europe arose not *in vacuo* and not on Greco-Latin foundations alone but on the basis of ancient pagan forms of its own, which proved entirely consonant with the aesthetics of the new era for the very reason that they already combined the extremes of the beautiful and the grotesque (3a). ♦ И не всё у них [западных авторов] ошибочно. Есть кое-что заслуживающее внимания. Не на пустом же месте они вырастают, а на здоровом древе познания (Зиновьев 1). [context transl] And they [Western authors] are not always wrong. There is something there worthy of attention. They do not spring up like weeds in the desert; they are branches of the great and healthy tree of knowledge (1a).

3. *coll* without any cause: **for no apparent reason; for no reason at all;** ‖ *Neg* не на пустом месте ≃ **for good reason.**

Ссоры вспыхивали зря, на пустом месте... (Мандельштам 2). [context transl] Our squabbles were about nothing at all... (2a).

M-106 • НА РÓВНОМ МÉСТЕ *coll* [PrepP; Invar; adv; fixed WO] unexpectedly, for no apparent reason: **suddenly; all of a sudden; out of the blue; just; just like that; for no reason at all.**

Подполковник Лужин не относился к числу людей, не умеющих владеть собой, но когда ему на стол положили это сообщение в расшифрованном виде, он сказал: «Ого!.. Чудовищная удача!.. Чудовищная удача! И найти такое на ровном месте!» (Войнович 4). Lieutenant Colonel Luzhin was not to be numbered among those unable to control themselves, but when this communiqué had been deciphered and placed on his desk he said, "Oho!...A monstrous piece of luck....A monstrous piece of luck. And to find it just like that!" (4a).

M-107 • ПРОВАЛИ́ТЬСЯ (МНЕ) НА (ЭТОМ) МÉСТЕ; ЧТОБ МНЕ ПРОВАЛИ́ТЬСЯ НА (ЭТОМ) МÉСТЕ; ПРОВАЛИ́СЬ Я *all highly coll* [Interj; these forms only; fixed WO] an oath used by the speaker to emphasize the truth of a statement: **I swear it!; (I) swear to God!; honest to God!; may the earth swallow me up (right here) (if...); may I fall through the ground (if...); may lightning strike me (dead) (if...).**

«Знаешь, что я затеяла? Родить ребёнка». Вера обомлела. «Да что ты?! Врёшь!» — «Провалиться мне на этом месте» (Грекова 3). "Know what? I'm going to have a child." Vera was stunned. "Come on! That's not true." "Swear to God" (3a). ♦ [Бургомистр:] Я так, понимаешь, малыш, искренне привязан к нашему дракоше!.. Мне, понимаешь, даже, ну как тебе сказать, хочется отдать за него жизнь. Ей-богу правда, вот провалиться мне на этом месте! (Шварц 2). [Mayor:] You know, my dear boy, how sincerely I'm attached to our dear Dragon....Sometimes, do you know, I even feel as if I'd be ready to lay down my life for him. I swear by God that's true; may I fall through the ground if it's a lie (2a).

M-108 • СТОЯ́ТЬ ⟨ТОПТА́ТЬСЯ *coll*, ОСТАВА́ТЬСЯ⟩ НА (ОДНО́М) МЕ́СТЕ [VP; subj: human, collect, or abstr] (of a person or group) to act, do sth. ineffectively, not make progress; (of an abstract notion, often life, work etc) not to develop, not improve: X топчется на месте ≃ **X is making no headway; X is getting nowhere (fast); person X is spinning his wheels; person X is marking time; person X is on a treadmill; thing X is static ⟨at a standstill⟩.**

...Знаешь, чего нам не хватает? Движения. Мы топчемся на месте (Зиновьев 1). "...Do you know what we lack? We lack movement. We're just marking time" (1a).

M-109 • ТЁПЛОЕ ⟨ТЁПЛЕНЬКОЕ⟩ МЕСТЕ́ЧКО ⟨МЕ́СТО⟩ *coll* [NP; usu. subj or obj; fixed WO] a job that is lucrative or otherwise advantageous: **cushy job ⟨position⟩; soft job; comfortable (little) job.**

[Глумов:] Но и здесь можно добиться тёплого места и богатой невесты, – с меня и довольно (Островский 9). [G.:] But even here it should be possible to get a cushy job and a rich bride. That's all I want (9a). ♦ ...Пьер уже сбегал по лестнице, устланной малиновым ковром, сопровождаемый насмешливыми взглядами лакеев: «Не вышло у тебя с тёплым местечком!..» (Эренбург 4). ...Pierre was already running down the purple-carpeted stairway, under the mocking looks of the flunkeys: "So you didn't get your soft job!" (4a). ♦ Но даже уволенные и разжалованные бывшие эмведешники пристроились около оставшихся лагерей на тёпленьких местечках с солидным окладом (Марченко 1). But even those dismissed or demoted former MVD men managed to set themselves up in comfortable little jobs, with good rates of pay, in or around the remaining camps (1a).

M-110 • БОЛЬНО́Е МЕ́СТО (*чьё, для кого, кого, у кого*) [NP; sing only; usu. obj or compl of copula with subj: inanim; fixed WO] a very sensitive, vulnerable aspect (of s.o. or sth.); a matter that causes s.o. (or a group of people) feelings of grief, anxiety, resentment: **sore spot ⟨point⟩; sensitive ⟨tender, vulnerable⟩ spot;** [in limited contexts] **what troubles s.o. most;** ‖ задеть *кого* за больное место ≃ **touch ⟨hit⟩ a (raw) nerve; hit s.o. where it hurts (most) ⟨where it hurts him the most⟩.**

Сидящие на стульях, и на столах, и даже на двух подоконниках [литераторы]... серьёзно страдали от духоты... «А сейчас хорошо на Клязьме», – подудила присутствующих Штурман Жорж, зная, что дачный литературный посёлок Перелыгино на Клязьме – общее больное место (Булгаков 9). They [the writers] sat on chairs, on tables, and even on the two window sills...suffering extremely from lack of air...."It must be beautiful on the Klyazma," Pilot George egged on her colleagues, knowing that the vacation village of Perelygino on the Klyazma River was everybody's sore spot (9a). ♦ ...Что касается национальности, то отношение к ней... было больным его [Пастернака] местом. Не то чтобы он её стеснялся – этого не было. Но, являясь по духу глубоко русским поэтом, он терялся и не знал, что делать и что говорить, когда оказывалось, что его еврейское происхождение никогда не забывают и никогда не прощают (Ивинская 1). The matter of his origins...was a sore point with him [Pasternak]. It wasn't that he was embarrassed by them – there was no question of this. But as a Russian poet to the core of his being, he was at a loss what to do or say whenever he was brought up against the fact that his Jewish descent would never be forgotten or forgiven (1a). ♦ Одно она [свекровь] не хотела ей простить – то, что у Настёны не было ребятишек. Попрекать не попрекала, помня, что для любой бабы это самое больное место, но на сердце держала... (Распутин 2). The only thing she [the mother-in-law] could never forgive was that Nastyona had no children. She didn't rebuke her, remembering that for any woman that was the most sensitive spot, but she stored it away... (2a). ♦ [Маша:] Чего вы от него хотите? Чтобы он в гениях числился? Главные роли играл? Как вам не стыдно долбить его в больное место! (Розов 1). [M.:] What do you want of him? To

be a genius? To play only the leading roles? Aren't you all ashamed to keep hitting him where it hurts most! (1a).

M-111 • ЗЛА́ЧНОЕ МЕ́СТО *humor or iron* [NP; fixed WO except when used as VP$_{subj}$ with copula] a place where there is much drinking, indulgence in debauchery: **bawdy place; seedy hangout;** [in limited contexts] **bawdyhouse.**

«Хочу вас предупредить, девушка вы молодая, а место тут злачное» (Гинзбург 1). "What I wanted to say is that you had better watch out here. You're a young girl and this is a bawdy place" (1a).

M-112 • ЗНАТЬ СВОЁ МЕ́СТО *occas. derog* [VP; subj: human; often imper or infin with надо, должен etc; more often this WO] to act or behave in keeping with one's (usu. humble) position: X знает своё место ≃ **X knows his place;** ‖ *Imper* знай своё место ≃ **remember your place!; remember who you are!**

[Генерал:] Каждый должен знать своё место, вот что... (Горький 1). [General:] What I say is everybody must know his place (1a). ♦ «Помни, что ты дрянь; я принимаю тебя потому только, что нет никого лучше; а приехала какая-нибудь княжна Юзякина – ты знай своё место, стой у порога» (Гоголь 3). "Remember that you are rubbish and nothing else; I receive you because there is no one better around, but if some Princess Uzyakin is visiting me, you'd better remember your place and stand at the door" (3c). ♦ ...Офицер ударил Остапа наотмашь хлыстом поперёк лица и крикнул: «Знай своё место, мужик!» (Паустовский 1). ...The officer struck Ostap across the face with his whip, shouting "You lout! Remember who you are!" (1a).

M-113 • ИМЕ́ТЬ МЕ́СТО *lit* [VP; subj: abstr] **1.** to be, be present: X имел место ≃ **X existed; X had a ⟨its⟩ place.**

Некоторые довольно интеллигентные люди, замечая отдельные недостатки, которые всё ещё имеют место в нашей стране, думают: а что, если слегка потеснить большевиков, чтобы в дальнейшем, устранив эти недостатки, перестать их теснить? (Искандер 4). There are certain rather well-informed people who notice the isolated shortcomings that still exist in our country and think: What if we crowd the Bolsheviks a little, with the idea that we'll stop crowding them in the future, when we've eliminated these deficiencies? (4a). ♦ Она [наша публика] ещё не знает, что в порядочном обществе и в порядочной книге явная брань не может иметь места... (Лермонтов 1). It [our reading public] does not yet understand that obvious abuse can have no place in decent society and in decent books... (1d).

2. to happen: X имел место ≃ **X took place; X came to pass; X occurred;** [in limited contexts] **X was made ⟨done etc⟩.**

Главным развлечением в этом монотонном существовании была баня, которая, как говорится, имела место каждые десять дней (Максимов 2). The chief distraction in this monotonous existence was the bath, which took place every ten days (2a). ♦ ...Как сообщил впоследствии членам своего правления Председатель Турганов, 26 апреля 1973 года в кооперативе имел место очень прискорбный факт (Войнович 3). ...As Chairman Turganov subsequently informed the members of the board, on April 26, 1973, a most deplorable event occurred in the cooperative (3a). ♦ К счастью, все эти промахи имели место в самый разгар Феденькина либерализма и потому сошли Анне Григорьевне с рук довольно легко (Салтыков-Щедрин 2). Fortunately, all those blunders were made at the height of Fedenka's liberal phase and had for this reason no serious consequences for her [Anna Grigoryevna] (2a).

M-114 • МЕ́СТО ПОД СО́ЛНЦЕМ *lit* [NP; sing only; subj or obj; fixed WO] **1.** a visible position in society, among other people: **place in the sun.**

Глядя на них, мирно покуривающих у распахнутого окошка, Антонина позавидовала мужской доле. Сила мышц или знание ремесла уже обеспечивали им место под солнцем

(Максимов 3). Watching the men resting and smoking by the window, Antonina found herself envying their lot. Muscular strength, or knowledge of a craft, ensured them their place in the sun (3a).

2. the right to exist: **(have) a place in this world.**

М-115 • **МО́КРОЕ МЕ́СТО ОСТА́НЕТСЯ** *от кого;* **МО́КРОГО МЕ́СТА НЕ ОСТА́НЕТСЯ** *both highly coll* [VP$_{subj}$ or VP$_{subj/gen}$] (often used as a threat) s.o. will be completely destroyed, defeated, cruelly punished: от X-а мокрое место останется ≃ **(X will be beaten up so bad) there won't be anything left of him; X will be pulverized; person Y will make mincemeat out of X; person Y will wipe ⟨mop⟩ the floor with X; person Y will chew X up and spit him out.**

М-116 • **НА МЕ́СТО** *положить,* **поставить** *что* [PrepP; Invar; adv] (to put sth.) in the place where it should be: **(put sth.) in its (proper) place; (put sth.) back (in place); (put sth.) where it belongs.**

[Аркадий:] Положи [галстук] на место, слышишь? [Андрей:] Не кричи, отец занимается. Тихо! (Розов 1). [Arkady:] Put it [the necktie] back, do you hear?! [Andrei:] Don't shout. Father is working. Sh-h-h! (1a).

М-117 • **НЕ МЕ́СТО** *где,* often *здесь,* **тут** [NP; impers predic with быть$_{\theta}$; usu. pres] **1.** ~ *кому* it is inappropriate, wrong for s.o. to be in the place or among the people in question: Х-у здесь не место ≃ **this is not the place for X; this is no place for X.**

[Коршунов:] Погоди, Гордей Карпыч, не гони, что его [Любима] гнать! Пусть поломается, пошутит... [Гордей Карпыч:] Ему тут не место. Ступай вон! (Островский 2). [K.:] Wait a bit Gordey Karpych; don't turn him [Lyubim] out! Let him show off and make jokes.... [G.K.:] This isn't the place for him. Get out! (2a). ♦ [Львов:] Ну, зачем, спрашивается, вы привезли меня сюда, к этим коршунам? Не место тут для нас с вами! (Чехов 4). [L.:] And why, I should like to know, have you brought me here to this nest of vultures? This is no place for either of us (4a).

2. ~ *чему,* **что делать** [also used as subj-compl with быть$_{\theta}$ (subj: infin)] sth. (or doing sth.) is not appropriate in some place: здесь не место X-у ⟨делать X⟩ ≃ **this ⟨here⟩ is not the (proper) place for X ⟨to do X⟩; this is no place for X ⟨for doing X⟩.**

Тут не место распространяться о литературной деятельности младшего [из них]. Скажем только, что он был топорно груб и топорно наивен... (Набоков 1). This is not the place to enlarge upon the literary activities of the younger man. Let us merely say that he was uncouthly crude and uncouthly naïve... (1a). ♦ Здесь не место начинать об этой новой страсти Ивана Фёдоровича, отразившейся потом на всей его жизни: это всё могло бы послужить канвой уже иного рассказа, другого романа, который и не знаю, предприму ли ещё когда-нибудь (Достоевский 2). This is not the proper place to begin speaking of this new passion of Ivan Fyodorovich's, which later affected his whole life: it could all serve as the plot for another story, for a different novel, which I do not even know that I shall ever undertake (2a).

М-118 • **НЕ МЕ́СТО КРА́СИТ ЧЕЛОВЕ́КА, А ЧЕЛОВЕ́К МЕ́СТО** [saying] it is not a person's position at the workplace that is important, but the person's qualities, abilities etc: ≃ **the position ⟨job⟩ doesn't make the man, the man makes the position ⟨job⟩.**

М-119 • **О́БЩЕЕ МЕ́СТО** *lit, usu. disapprov* [NP; usu. obj or subj-compl with copula (subj: usu. это); fixed WO] a hackneyed expression, truism: **commonplace; platitude; worn-out phrase.**

Оригинальный, неповторимый... в музыкальном творчестве композитор оказался неискусным и вялым подражате-

лем общих мест символистской поэзии в искусстве словесном (Гладков 1). Uniquely original...as a composer, Scriabin the poet was revealed as an inept and jejune imitator of Symbolist commonplaces (1a). ♦ [Иванов:] Полюбил, разлюбил, не хозяин своим чувствам — всё это общие места, избитые фразы, которыми не поможешь... (Чехов 4). [I.:] Falling in love, falling out of love, not master of my feelings—all platitudes, trite phrases, which do not help... (4a).

М-120 • **ПУСТО́Е МЕ́СТО** *(для кого) coll, usu. derog* [NP; sing only; usu. subj-compl with быть$_{\theta}$ (subj: human) or obj-compl with считать *кого* и т. п. (obj: human); fixed WO] a person who does nothing beneficial, makes no worthwhile contribution (to some job, project etc), or who is of no significance (to s.o.): X (для Y-а) пустое место ≃ [in refer. to s.o.'s unsuitability for some job, lack of productivity etc] **X is useless; X is of no use to Y;** [in refer. to s.o.'s—often the speaker's—low estimation of or belittling attitude toward the person in question] **X is ⟨Y considers X⟩ a nonentity ⟨a nobody, a nothing⟩;** [in refer. to s.o.'s—often the speaker's—indifference toward, lack of caring about or respect for the person in question] **X means nothing (at all) to Y.**

«Никогда, слышишь, никогда в жизни не удастся тебе убедить Бланка, что то, что сегодня произошло, было ошибкой... Бланк — пустое место, но он знает теперь тебя. Он тебя *видел!*» (Битов 2). "You will never, do you hear, never in your life succeed in convincing Blank that what happened today was a mistake....Blank is a nobody, but he knows you now. He *saw* you!" (2a). ♦ Во всём ей чудились признаки небрежности. Оказывали ли ей повышенное внимание наезжавшие к Кологривовым знакомые, это значило, что к ней относятся как к безответной «воспитаннице» и лёгкой добыче. А когда её оставляли в покое, это доказывало, что её считают пустым местом и не замечают (Пастернак 1). [context transl] She suspected slights at every turn. If the Kologrivovs' friends were attentive to her she was sure that they regarded her as a submissive "ward" and an easy prey. If they left her alone, that proved that she did not exist for them (1a).

М-121 • **СВЯ́ТО МЕ́СТО ПУ́СТО НЕ БЫВА́ЕТ** [saying] there will always be someone to fill a vacancy: ≃ **nature abhors a vacuum; pedestals don't stay empty for long.**

Из Новосибирска меня отправили в Тайшет, там были огромные лагеря для 58-ой статьи. Но когда я туда приехал, оказалось, что там уже не осталось ни одного политического лагеря. Три дня назад ушёл последний спецэшелон в Мордовию. Свято место пусто не бывает: тайшетские лагеря сразу же стали заполняться бытовиками-уголовниками (Марченко 1). From Novosibirsk I was sent to Taishet, where there used to be enormous camps for politicals. But when I arrived there turned out to be not a single one left. Three days earlier the last special convoy had left for Mordovia. Nature abhors a vacuum, however, and the Taishet camps immediately began to fill with criminal cons (1a). ♦ Разумеется, погрома в литературе это [отказ Г. Свирского осудить роман В. Гроссмана «За правое дело»] не остановило. Свято место пусто не бывает (Свирский 1). Of course, that [Svirsky's refusal to condemn V. Grossman's novel *For a Just Cause*] didn't stop the literary pogrom. Pedestals don't stay empty for long (1a).

М-122 • **СЛА́БОЕ ⟨УЯЗВИ́МОЕ⟩ МЕ́СТО** *(чьё, кого-чего, у кого-чего)* [NP; fixed WO] s.o.'s most vulnerable area or shortcoming, or the weakest aspect of sth.: **weak spot ⟨point⟩; soft spot; chink (in s.o.'s armor).**

И ещё было много других замечательных указов. Но во всём архитектурной системе их он [Сталин] находил-таки последнее время одно слабое место — и постепенно зрел в голове его новый важный указ (Солженицын 3). There had been many other remarkable edicts. However, he [Stalin] still found one weak spot in the whole architectonic system, and gradually an important new edict was ripening in his mind (3a).

M-123 • СТА́ВИТЬ/ПОСТА́ВИТЬ НА (СВОЁ) МЕ́СТО *кого;* **УКА́ЗЫВАТЬ/УКАЗА́ТЬ** *кому* **ЕГО́ ⟨ЕЁ⟩ МЕ́СТО** [VP; subj: human] to point out to s.o. (usu. in an abrupt manner) that he is acting improperly, taking liberties etc; to remind s.o. of his low rank or position: X поставил Y-а на место ≃ X put Y in Y's place; X showed Y Y's place; X cut Y down to size; X pulled ⟨knocked⟩ Y off Y's high horse.

Нике в этих словах почудились какие-то шпильки. Ну, конечно, она [Надя] ставит его на место, напоминая ему, как он ещё мал (Пастернак 1). Nika thought there was a hidden barb in those words. Naturally, she [Nadia] was putting him in his place, reminding him he was a baby (1a).

M-124 • СТА́ВИТЬ/ПОСТА́ВИТЬ СЕБЯ́ НА МЕ́СТО *чьё, кого;* **СТАНОВИ́ТЬСЯ/СТАТЬ ⟨ВСТАТЬ⟩ НА МЕ́СТО** [VP; subj: human; 2nd var., usu. pfv imper] to (try to) imagine o.s. in someone else's situation: X поставил себя на место Y-а ≃ X put himself in Y's place ⟨shoes⟩.

«...Ты на минуту встань на моё место. Представь, что тебе приносят пулю и говорят: вот доказательство, что ты убил человека» (Тендряков 1). "...Put yourself in my place for a moment. Imagine that someone brings you a bullet, and says: 'Here is the evidence that you have killed a man'" (1a). ♦ Он поставил тут себя на место старого болвана-вохровца [= солдата вооружённой охраны], вообразил, как вдруг рушится перед ним выстроенный скудным умом логический мир... (Аксёнов 7). Putting himself in the old buzzard's shoes, he tried to picture what it would be like to have the logical world he had constructed with the meager resources of his brain crumble beneath him... (7a).

M-125 • У́ЗКОЕ МЕ́СТО *(чьё, кого, в чём)* [NP; often subj-compl with copula (subj: abstr or concr); fixed WO] the weakest, most vulnerable aspect of sth.: **weak ⟨trouble⟩ spot; weak link (in the chain).**

Санитарные условия на заводе — наше узкое место. Нужно ещё многое сделать. Sanitary conditions at the factory remain a trouble spot for us. Much still needs to be done.

M-126 • УСТУПА́ТЬ/УСТУПИ́ТЬ МЕ́СТО *чему* [VP; subj: abstr; fixed WO] to be supplanted by something else: X уступил место Y-у ≃ X gave way to Y; X was replaced by Y; X took a back seat to Y.

Наш герой горюет некоторое время, но вскоре его печаль уступает место весьма важной озабоченности, связанной с тем, что в Лондоне назначена коронация нового короля... (Олеша 3). Our hero grieves for a while, but soon his grief is replaced by extremely important concerns connected with the fact that in London has been fixed the coronation of the new king... (3a).

M-127 • ХЛЕ́БНОЕ МЕ́СТО ⟨МЕСТЕ́ЧКО⟩ *coll* [NP; usu. sing; fixed WO except when used as VP_subj with copula] a profitable, rewarding job: **lucrative ⟨plum, cushy⟩ job.**

Всё оказалось в нём [Чичикове], что нужно для этого мира: и приятность в оборотах и поступках, и бойкость в деловых делах. С такими средствами добыл он в непродолжительное время то, что называют хлебное местечко... (Гоголь 3). He [Chichikov] seemed to have everything that was necessary in that world: agreeable manners and turn of speech and a brisk way of dealing with business matters. By these means he obtained in a short time what is known as a lucrative job... (3a).

M-128 • К МЕ́СТУ ⟨У МЕ́СТА *obs*⟩ [PrepP; these forms only; adv or subj-compl with copula (subj: abstr)] fitting(ly), relevant(ly): **appropriate(ly); apt(ly); to the point; apropos.**

Однажды, во время обеда, после какого-то интересного, но довольно длинного Димкиного рассказа о ссылке, она, как ей тогда показалось, очень к месту привела прутковский афоризм... (Некрасов 1). One day, during dinner, after an interesting but lengthy story from Dimka about his exile, she had quoted—very appropriately, it had seemed to her at the moment—the "Prutkovian" aphorism... (1a). ♦ ...Он [Лакшин] прочно начитан в предшественниках, немало и к месту цитирует их (Солженицын 2). ...He [Lakshin] has a solid grounding in the works of his predecessors, and quotes them often and aptly (2a). ♦ ...Всё, что он говорил, было к месту (Айтматов 2). All that he said was to the point (2a).

M-129 • К МЕ́СТУ И НЕ К МЕ́СТУ [PrepP; Invar; adv; fixed WO] all the time, regardless of appropriateness: **in and out of season; whether (it is) relevant ⟨appropriate, apropos⟩ or not; even when nothing calls ⟨seems to call⟩ for it.**

«...Как всякий безграмотный человек, ты имеешь необъяснимое пристрастие к звучным иностранным словам, употребляешь их к месту и не к месту...» (Шолохов 5). "...Like any half-literate person, you have an inexplicable love of foreign words and use them in and out of season..." (5a). ♦ Видно, друзья по блату устроили ему однодневный пропуск. С тех пор он к месту и не к месту вспоминал об этом (Искандер 3). Evidently some friends had used influence to arrange a one-day pass for him. He was forever bringing it up, whether it was relevant or not (3a). ♦ [Варвара] ещё больше потолстела, стала к месту и не к месту по-старушечьи вздыхать, плакаться... (Распутин 3). [Varvara] had put on more weight, started snivelling and heaving old-maidenly sighs even when nothing seemed to call for them... (3a).

M-130 • НЕ К МЕ́СТУ ⟨НЕ У МЕ́СТА *obs*⟩ [PrepP; these forms only; adv or subj-compl with copula (subj: abstr)] unfitting(ly), irrelevant(ly): **inappropriate(ly); out of place; beside the point.**

Неловко ездить в автобусе и громко разговаривать «об умном». А Лёва как раз способен увлечься и что-нибудь такое брякнуть не к месту. Хотя, к чести его, могу добавить, что он легко краснеет (Битов 2). It's awkward having a loud "intelligent" conversation on the bus. And Lyova is just the kind to get carried away and blurt out something inappropriate. Although, to his credit, I can add that he blushes easily (2a). ♦ У Мити [Панина] Лёва совсем не к месту начинает читать стихи Мао Цзедуна (Орлова 1). At Panin's, Lev very inappropriately began to read the verses of Mao Tse-tung (1a). ♦ [Смельская:] Ах, оставьте, пожалуйста, ваши рассуждения! Ваша философия теперь не к месту (Островский 11). [S.:] Oh, please stop lecturing! Your philosophy is out of place just now (11a).

M-131 • МЕДО́ВЫЙ МЕ́СЯЦ [NP; fixed WO] **1.** [sing only] the initial, blissful stage of married life: **honeymoon.**

Он вспомнил медовый месяц и покраснел при этом воспоминании (Толстой 5). He remembered his honeymoon and blushed at the recollection (5a).

2. ~ *чего* the best period, zenith of sth.: **peak; heyday; golden days.**

M-132 • ПРЕЗРЕ́ННЫЙ МЕТА́ЛЛ *rather lit; humor or iron* [NP; sing only; usu. subj or obj] money, gold: **filthy lucre.**

M-133 • ПОД МЕТЁЛКУ ⟨ПОД МЕТЛУ́⟩ взять, забрать, очистить и т. п. *highly coll* [PrepP; these forms only; adv] (to take etc) absolutely everything, so that nothing is left: **(make) a clean sweep; clean (sth.) out; (get everything) down to the last bit ⟨grain etc⟩.**

«...[Ты] всей пропагандой в Кавкрайкоме командовал... сделал Кубань-матушку колхозной житницей, все сусеки [*regional* = закрома] под метёлку вычистил, ничего для родины не пожалел — ни себя, ни народа...» (Максимов 1). "...You were running propaganda throughout the Caucasus...you made all our mother Kuban a *kolkhoz* granary, you cleaned out all the peasant corn-bins, there was nothing you wouldn't have sacrificed for the motherland — yourself, the people..." (1a).

M-134 • НО́ВАЯ МЕТЛА́ ЧИ́СТО МЕТЁТ *often disapprov* [saying] a new supervisor puts his own, new order into effect and usu. is more carping, demanding than his predecessor: **a new broom sweeps clean;** [in limited contexts] **new lords, new laws.**

M-135 • ВЫМЕТА́ТЬ/ВЫ́МЕСТИ ЖЕЛЕ́ЗНОЙ МЕТЛО́Й *что media* [VP; subj: human or collect] to annihilate, eradicate sth. (some negative phenomenon, behavior etc): Х-ы должны вымести Y железной метлой ≃ **Xs must wipe ⟨blot, stamp⟩ Y out; Xs must obliterate ⟨put an end to⟩ Y.**

M-136 • НА РЫ́БЬЕМ МЕХУ́ *coll, humor* [PrepP; Invar; nonagreeing postmodif or subj-compl with бытьø (subj: a noun denoting an item of outer clothing); fixed WO] (sth. is) of no use to a person against the cold, of no warmth, often because it is worn-out: у Х-а пальто на рыбьем меху ≃ **X's coat has no warmth to it; X's coat offers no ⟨little⟩ protection from the elements; X's coat is no protection from the cold; X's coat is threadbare.**

M-137 • ВЛОЖИ́ТЬ МЕЧ В НО́ЖНЫ *elev* [VP; subj: human] to end a war or other serious discord: Х-ы вложили меч в ножны ≃ **Xs sheathed their swords; Xs buried the hatchet.**

M-138 • ДАМО́КЛОВ МЕЧ *висит над кем* or *над чьей головой;* **ПОД ДАМО́КЛОВЫМ МЕЧО́М** *бытьø, жить, ходить* и т. п. *all lit* [NP, sing only, usu. subj (1st var.); PrepP, Invar, subj-compl with copula (subj: human) or adv (2nd var.); fixed WO] danger, trouble that is constantly threatening s.o.: **sword of Damocles.**

...Всегда над головой его висел дамоклов меч — в любую минуту ему могли припомнить те анонимки (Эткинд 1). ...Always he lived under this sword of Damocles; at any time those anonymous letters could be held against him (1a).

< From the story of *Damocles,* courtier of the Syracusan tyrant Dionysius in classical mythology. At a banquet, Dionysius had Damocles seated under a sword suspended by a single hair to show him how precarious power and the ruler's happiness were.

M-139 • ПОДНИМА́ТЬ/ПОДНЯ́ТЬ МЕЧ *на кого, против кого;* **ОБНАЖА́ТЬ/ОБНАЖИ́ТЬ МЕЧ ⟨ПОДНИМА́ТЬ/ПОДНЯ́ТЬ ОРУ́ЖИЕ⟩** *(против кого) all elev* [VP; subj: human or collect] to start a war, an armed struggle against s.o.: X поднял меч на Y-а ⟨X обнажил меч⟩ ≃ **X took up the sword against Y; X took up arms against Y; X drew the sword; X unsheathed his sword.**

M-140 • НЕ МЕША́ЕТ ⟨НЕ МЕША́ЛО БЫ⟩ *(кому) coll* [VP; impers; these forms only; usu. foll. by infin] one should (do sth.), it would not be bad (to do sth.): не мешает ⟨не мешало бы⟩ (Х-у) сделать Y ≃ **it's not ⟨it wouldn't be⟩ a bad idea to do Y; it won't ⟨wouldn't⟩ hurt X to do Y; it wouldn't be a bad thing if X did Y ⟨for X to do Y⟩; it won't ⟨wouldn't⟩ do (X) any harm to do Y; it will ⟨would⟩ do X good to do Y; there's ⟨there would be⟩ no harm in doing Y.**

[Анна Петровна:] Я вам дам поесть! [Трилецкий:] Давно бы так. [Платонов:] Впрочем, не мешало бы... Который час? Я тоже голоден... (Чехов 1). [A.P.:] ...I'll give you something to eat. [T.:] And not a moment too soon. [P.:] It's not a bad idea, actually. What's the time? I'm starving too (1b). ♦ Он уже подходил к окончанию труда (а именно к рождению героя), когда Зина сказала, что не мешало бы ему развлечься... (Набоков 1). He was already approaching the end of his work (the hero's birth, to be precise) when Zina said it would not hurt him to relax... (1a). ♦

"Напиться бы", — сказал Митишатьев, мрачный от своей тройки. "А что, не мешало бы", — радостно сказал никогда не пивший Лёва и удивился (Битов 2). [context transl] "We should get drunk," Mitishatyev said, gloomy over his [grade of] 3. "Why not, it'll do us good," Lyova said gleefully, and felt surprised — he never drank (2a).

M-141 • МЕШКИ́ ПОД ГЛАЗА́МИ [NP; pl only; usu. subj or obj] puffy circles under the eyes: **bags under ⟨beneath⟩ one's ⟨s.o.'s⟩ eyes.**

Этот сутулый человек с длинным унылым носом, с мешками под глазами никогда ни с кем не вступал в разговоры, даже на приветствия обычно отвечал только кивком головы (Рыбаков 2). He was stooped and had a long, miserable nose with bags under his eyes. He never stopped to chat, and even when greeted, he would reply with no more than a nod of the head (2a).

M-142 • СИДЕ́ТЬ МЕШКО́М *на ком coll* [VP; subj: a noun denoting an item of clothing] (of a garment that is too large, wide etc) to fit poorly: X сидит на Y-е мешком ≃ **X is ⟨looks⟩ baggy on Y; X looks like a sack on Y; X hangs on Y.**

M-143 • ЗОЛОТО́Й ⟨ДЕ́НЕЖНЫЙ⟩ МЕШО́К *obs* [NP; sing only; usu. subj-compl with copula (subj: human)] very wealthy: X — золотой мешок ≃ **X is a moneybags; X is made of money ⟨rolling in money⟩.**

M-144 • МЕШО́К С СОЛО́МОЙ *highly coll, derog* [NP; sing only; usu. subj-compl with copula (subj: human); fixed WO] a sluggish, stupid, apathetic person: X — мешок с соломой ≃ **X is dense ⟨thick, slow-witted, dull-witted⟩; X is a clod ⟨a dolt⟩.**

M-145 • В МЕШО́ЧЕК (сварить) яйцо [PrepP; Invar; adv or nonagreeing postmodif] an egg cooked so that the yolk stays soft but the white gets hard: **(cook an egg ⟨an egg is cooked⟩) between hard and soft; semisoft; soft-boiled (egg) on the hard side.**

M-146 • МЕЩАНИ́Н ВО ДВОРЯ́НСТВЕ *lit, derog* [NP; sing only; fixed WO] an upstart, a person occupying a high position to which he has no rightful claim: **parvenu.**

< The title of a Russian translation of Molière's comedy *Le Bourgeois Gentilhomme,* 1670.

M-147 • В ОДИ́Н ⟨ЕДИ́НЫЙ⟩ МИГ [PrepP; these forms only; adv; used with pfv verbs] extremely quickly, instantaneously, in a very short span of time: **in a flash ⟨a wink, a jiffy, a trice, an instant, a split second⟩; in no time (flat); in a heartbeat;** [in limited contexts] **the next moment; overnight.**

Кот сделал судорожное глотательное движение горлом... и вдруг напряжённым, механическим голосом, но совершенно отчётливо произнёс, как человек, на чистейшем русском языке: «Мама»... Все в один миг оживились... (Катаев 2). The cat made a convulsive swallowing motion with its throat...and suddenly in a forced mechanical voice said, quite distinctly, like a human, in the purest Russian: "Mama."...In a flash everybody revived... (2a). ♦ ...[Алёша] пошёл в спальню, в бессилии прилёг на постель и в один миг заснул (Достоевский 1). ...He [Alyosha] went to the bedroom, lay exhausted on the bed, and the next moment was asleep (1a). ♦ [Лунц] всё рос да рос и уж совсем, видимо, стал считать себя неуязвимым, как вдруг в один миг оказался на краю пропасти (Буковский 1). Lunts...continued to grow and grow, and it seems that he had already come to regard himself as invulnerable, when suddenly, overnight, he found himself on the edge of an abyss (1a).

M-148 • С ⟨НА⟩ МИЗИ́НЕЦ *чего, often* **ума, способностей, власти** и т. п. *(у кого) coll* [PrepP; these forms only; usu.

quantit subj-compl with copula (subj/gen: usu. abstr)] (s.o. possesses) very little (intelligence, ability, power etc, as specified): **(have) hardly any** [NP]; **(have) almost ⟨next to⟩ no** [NP]; **(be) short on** [NP]; **(have) only a thimbleful of** [NP].

M-149 • НЕ СТО́ИТЬ *чьего* **МИЗИ́НЦА ⟨НО́ГТЯ,** *чьей* **ПОДМЁТКИ⟩** *coll* [VP; subj: human; usu. pres] to be worthless, extremely insignificant in comparison with someone else: X Y-ова мизинца не стоит ≃ **X isn't worth Y's little finger; X cannot hold a candle to Y; X isn't worthy of tying Y's shoelaces.**

«А по-моему, так вы, со всеми вашими достоинствами, не стоите мизинца этой несчастной девушки…» (Достоевский 3). "In my opinion you, with all your merits, are not worth this unfortunate girl's little finger…" (3a). ♦ «…Если хотите знать умного человека, так у нас действительно есть один, о котором, точно, можно сказать: умный человек, которого я и подмётки не стою» (Гоголь 3). "…If you really want to know an intelligent man, why, we actually have one such among us, of whom it may truly be said that he is an intelligent man, whose shoelaces I'm not worthy of tying" (3b).

M-150 • ПОД МИКИ́ТКИ *ударить, толкнуть кого substand* [PrepP; Invar; adv] (to strike, shove s.o.) in the lower part of the chest below the ribs: X ударил ⟨толкнул⟩ Y-а под микитки ≃ **X gave Y a poke in the ribs; X poked Y in the ribs ⟨the gut⟩.**

[Шабельский:] …Ваш этот тупой лекарь почувствовал бы себя… на седьмом небе, если бы судьба дала ему случай, во имя принципа и общечеловеческих идеалов, хватить меня публично по рылу и под микитки (Чехов 4). [Sh.:] …That dimwitted leech of yours…he'd be in seventh heaven if only fate would give him a chance—in the name of principle and humanitarian ideals—publicly to give me a rap in the snout or a poke in the ribs (4a).

M-151 • КАК МИ́ЛЕНЬКИЙ *coll* [как + AdjP; adv] **1.** [usu. nom; if used in nom, subj-controlled; if used in an oblique case, obj-controlled] (to do sth.) without resistance, not daring to object; (to do sth. to s.o.) without that person's daring to object: **like a good (little) boy ⟨girl⟩; like a lamb; without (daring to make) a whimper ⟨a peep⟩.**

«Вот уж на что Самохин, — сказал Ермошин, — а и тот не лучше нас. Приказали ему сдать дом к празднику — и он сдаст его как миленький, в каком бы состоянии этот дом ни был» (Войнович 5). "Take Samokhin," said Ermoshin, "Even he's no better than the rest of us. He's been ordered to turn over his building by the holiday and he'll do it like a good boy, no matter what condition it's in" (5a). ♦ «Утром она [жена] меня часа за два до работы на ноги подымет, чтобы я размялся. Знает, что на похмелье я ничего есть не буду, ну, достанет огурец солёный или ещё что-нибудь… нальёт гранёный стаканчик водки. „Похмелись, Андрюша, больше не надо, мой милый". Выпью, поблагодарю её без слов, одними глазами, поцелую и пошёл на работу как миленький» (Шолохов 1). "In the morning she'd [my wife would] get me up about two hours before work to give me time to come round. She knew I wouldn't eat anything after being drunk, so she'd get me a pickled cucumber or something like that, and pour me out a good glass of vodka—a hair of the dog, you know. 'Here you are, Andrei, but don't do it any more, dear.'…I'd drink it up, thank her without words, just with a look and a kiss, and go off to work like a lamb" (1c).

2. [nom only] (s.o. does sth., sth. is done) without any obstacles, difficulties: **(with) no problem; (with) no trouble at all; no sweat; easily.**

«У вас маленькая машина, мы все там не поместимся». — «Поместимся как миленькие!» "You've got a small car, all of us will never fit into it." "We'll fit—no sweat!"

M-152 • ВОТ (Э́ТО) МИ́ЛО! *coll, iron* [Interj; these forms only; fixed WO] used to express astonishment, indignation etc: **isn't that nice ⟨something⟩!; I like that!; I'll be darned!**

«Антон просил передать тебе, что не приедет». — «Вот это мило! Что ж он, не мог мне сам сказать?» "Anton asked me to tell you that he can't come." "Isn't that nice! Couldn't he have told me that himself?"

M-153 • МИ́ЛОСТИ ПРО́СИМ ⟨ПРОШУ́⟩ [VP; 1st pers only; fixed WO] a polite invitation (to visit, take part in conversation, refreshments etc): **please (stop by ⟨come in, have a seat etc⟩); [as an invitation to a guest to come in] welcome (to you); [as an invitation to come over and visit] you're welcome to come over ⟨come to our place, stop by etc⟩.**

«Вы графа Ильи Андреевича сын? Моя жена очень дружна была с вашею матушкой. По четвергам у меня собираются; нынче четверг, милости прошу ко мне запросто», — сказал губернатор, отпуская его (Толстой 7). "You are Count Ilya Andreyevich's son? My wife was a great friend of your mother's. We are at home on Thursdays—today is Thursday, so please come and see us without ceremony," said the Governor, as Nikolai took his leave (7a). ♦ [Ольга:] Господа, милости просим, пожалуйте завтракать (Чехов 5). [O.:] Please, gentlemen, lunch is served (5b). ♦ Пантелей Прокофьевич распахнул ворота, и брички одна за другой въехали на баз. С крыльца гусыней поплыла Ильинична… «Милости просим, дорогие сваточки!» (Шолохов 2). Pantelei threw open the gate and the wagons drove into the yard one after the other. Ilyinichna floated down from the porch like a mother goose…."Welcome to you, dear kinsmen!" (2a). ♦ «…На Беговую ко мне милости просим…» (Аксёнов 6). "…You're welcome to come to my place on Begovaya" (6a).

M-154 • МИ́ЛОСТИ ПРОШУ́ К НА́ШЕМУ ШАЛАШУ́ [saying] a humorous invitation to come and join a group of people (often when they are eating): ≃ **you're welcome to join us; [in limited contexts] welcome to our ⟨my⟩ humble abode.**

M-155 • ПО МИ́ЛОСТИ [PrepP; Invar; Prep; the resulting PrepP is adv] **1.** ~ *чьей, кого iron* because of s.o.'s fault: **thanks to; (all) because of; one has s.o. to thank for…; one can thank s.o. for…; one owes it (all) to s.o.**

[Иванов:] По вашей милости на свете скоро будут рождаться один только нытики и психопаты (Чехов 4). [I.:] Thanks to people like you, there'll soon be nothing but malcontents and psychotics born into the world (4a). ♦ [Глаголев 2:] По его милости я воротился с одной только зубочисткой! (Чехов 1). [G. Jr.:] Because of him I came back with nothing but my toothbrush (1a). ♦ «…По твоей милости перенёс я горя-то немало…» (Гончаров 1). "I can thank you for the trouble I've had…" (1b). ♦ «Я сына хотел на дантиста выучить, а где он — сын, а? И по твоей милости…» (Максимов 3). "I wanted to train my son to be a dentist, but where is he now, where's my son now, eh? I owe it all to you" (3a).

2. ~ *чьей, кого-чего obs* with the benefit of s.o.'s help or through some beneficial actions or means: **thanks to; by the kindness of s.o.; owing to.**

По милости Пугачёва, я имел добрую лошадь… (Пушкин 2). Thanks to Pugachev, I had a good horse… (2b). ♦ Печально простились мы с ним [Прудоном]… С тех пор я не видал его; в 1851 году, когда я, по милости Леона Фоше, приезжал в Париж на несколько дней, он был отослан в какую-то центральную тюрьму (Герцен 2). It was a mournful parting….Since then I have not seen him [Proudhon]: in 1851 when, by the kindness of Léon Faucher, I visited Paris for a few days, he had been sent away to some central prison (2a).

M-156 • ВКРА́ДЫВАТЬСЯ/ВКРА́СТЬСЯ ⟨ВТИ-РА́ТЬСЯ/ВТЕРЕ́ТЬСЯ⟩ В МИ́ЛОСТЬ *к кому, у кого*

[VP; subj: human; more often pfv] (to make an attempt) to attain s.o.'s favor (through crafty or artful means): X вкрался в милость к Y-у ≃ **X wormed himself ⟨his way⟩ into Y's good graces; X managed to get in good with Y; X ingratiated himself with Y.**

Он делал всё возможное, чтобы втереться в милость к начальству. He did everything he could to get in good with his bosses.

М-157 • ВХОДИ́ТЬ/ВОЙТИ́ ⟨ПОПАДА́ТЬ/ПО-ПА́СТЬ⟩ В МИ́ЛОСТЬ *чью, к кому, у кого rather obsoles* [VP; subj: human; more often pfv] to attain the favor, trust of s.o.: X вошёл в милость к Y-у ≃ **X got in Y's good graces; X gained ⟨won⟩ Y's favor ⟨confidence⟩; X gained ⟨won⟩ favor with Y.**

«Непостоянны сильные мира сего, — говорил Мольер Мадлене, — и дал бы я совет всем комедиантам. Если ты попал в милость, сразу хватай всё, что тебе полагается» (Булгаков 5). "How inconstant are the mighty of this world," Molière said to Madeleine. "And I would give this advice to all players: if you happen to win favor, seize everything you can at once" (5a).

М-158 • СДАВА́ТЬСЯ/СДА́ТЬСЯ НА МИ́ЛОСТЬ *кого,* usu. **победителя** [VP; subj: human or collect] to give in (to one's conqueror, enemy etc) unreservedly, making no demands and setting no conditions: X сдался на милость Y-а ≃ **X surrendered unconditionally (to Y); X surrendered himself to the mercies of Y; X threw himself upon the mercy of Y.**

...Накануне того дня, как ей уехать из санатория, Соискатель поднял руки вверх: «Сдаюсь! На милость победителя!» (Залыгин 1). ...On the eve of her departure from the sanatorium the Challenger put up his hands: "I surrender! Unconditionally!" (1a). ♦ Жилище Влада оказалось классической ловушкой, бежать было некуда, приходилось сдаваться на милость удачливого ловца (Максимов 2). Vlad's abode was a classic trap: there was no way of escape and he could only surrender himself to the mercies of his captor (2a). ♦ ...Ему [Сталину] трудно было поверить сейчас, что ровно пять лет назад, в эту же пору... Москва всерьёз готовилась сдаться на милость победителя... (Максимов 1). He [Stalin] could hardly believe now that exactly five years earlier, at this time of year, Moscow was seriously considering throwing herself upon the mercy of her conqueror... (1a).

М-159 • СДЕ́ЛАЙ(ТЕ) МИ́ЛОСТЬ; СДЕ́ЛАЙ(ТЕ) (ТАКО́Е) ОДОЛЖЕ́НИЕ *all old-fash, coll* [VP_imper; these forms only; usu. indep. clause; fixed WO] **1.** used to express a polite, sometimes persistent, entreaty (which is actually a demand in disguise): **(would you ⟨could you, please, do⟩) be so good ⟨kind⟩ as to; would ⟨will, could⟩ you please (do sth.); kindly (do sth.); do me a favor (and do sth.); do me the favor of (doing sth.); [in limited contexts] be a good fellow (and do sth.).**

«Пётр Петрович, сделайте милость, уйдите!» (Достоевский 3). "Mr. Luzhin, please be so kind as to leave!" (3a). ♦ «Сделайте одолжение, садитесь, — сказал он вдруг, — мне надо с вами поговорить» (Достоевский 3). "Do be so kind as to sit down," he said suddenly. "I have to talk to you" (3a). ♦ «Ваше благородие, сделайте мне такую милость, — прикажите поднести стакан вина...» (Пушкин 2) "Your Honour, be so good as to tell them to bring me a glass of wine..." (2b). ♦ [Лопахин:] Погодите, господа, сделайте милость, у меня в голове помутилось, говорить не могу... (Чехов 2). [L.:] Kindly wait a moment, ladies and gentlemen, my head is swimming, I can't talk... (2a). ♦ «Сделай милость, никогда *не смей* прикасаться к моим вещам», — сказал он... (Толстой 2). "Do me a favor, *don't dare* touch my things—ever," he said... (2b).

2. used to express polite assent to a request or proposition: **please do; go (right) ahead; (do) as you wish; very well; [in limited contexts] help yourself; you're welcome to it; be my guest.**

И если хочешь учиться, то, пожалуйста, сделай одолжение, учись на здоровье... (Рыбаков 1). ...You want to study? Then go ahead, study to your heart's content! (1a). ♦ «...Не позволите ли мне сказать, господа, всего одно слово этому несчастному человеку?..» — «Сделайте милость, Михаил Макарович», — ответил следователь... (Достоевский 1). "...Will you permit me, gentlemen, to say just one word to this unfortunate man?..." "As you wish, Mikhail Makarovich," the district attorney answered... (1a). ♦ «Ваше благородие, дозвольте вас прокатить по старой памяти?»... — «Что ж, сделай милость, поедем» (Шолохов 2). "Your Honour, allow me to drive you, for old time's sake?"..."Very well then, we'll go for a drive" (2a).

М-160 • СКАЖИ́(ТЕ) НА МИ́ЛОСТЬ [VP_imper; these forms only; fixed WO] **1.** *old-fash* [indep. clause] used when making a polite inquiry: **will ⟨would⟩ you please ⟨kindly⟩ tell me ⟨us⟩; would you mind telling me ⟨us⟩; (would ⟨could⟩ you) be so good ⟨kind⟩ as to tell me ⟨us⟩.**

[Лебедев:] Скажи на милость, за каким это лешим ты зачастил к Марфутке? (Чехов 4). [L.:] Will you please tell me why the devil you go to Marfutka's so often? (4a). ♦ «Григорий Пантелевич, ваше благородие, скажи на милость, «что это такое за животная [*ungrammat* = животное] у кадетов под орудиями?..» (Шолохов 5). "Grigory Panteleyevich, Your Honour, would you kindly tell us what breed of animal that was the Cadets had pulling their guns?..." (5a).

2. [sent adv (parenth)] used to add emphasis, often irony, to a statement or rhetorical question: **for heaven's ⟨goodness'⟩ sake; (who ⟨where etc⟩) in the world; (what ⟨where etc⟩) in God's name.**

«И, скажи на милость, откуда эта детская похвальба у меня взялась? Не утерпел-таки, сообщил [Ирине], что полковник обещал меня к награде представить...» (Шолохов 1). "For goodness' sake, where had I picked up that childish trick of bragging! All the same, I couldn't keep it to myself, I told her [Irina] the colonel had promised to recommend me for an award" (1a). ♦ «И чего только вы с ней связались, скажите на милость! Её — это Дёмину — у нас на заводе даже начальство за версту обходит, лишь бы не разговаривать» (Максимов 2). "What in God's name possessed you to tangle with Dyomina? Here at the shipyard even the bosses will go a mile out of their way to avoid having to talk to her" (2a).

3. [Interj] used to express one's surprise, bewilderment, dissatisfaction etc at s.o.'s statement, actions etc: **good heavens ⟨grief, gracious, Lord⟩!; (well,) I'll be darned!; how do you like that!; you don't say (so)!; well, what do you know!; well, I never!**

«...Я вёшенская, дедушка», — вспыхнув от радости, сказала Аксинья. — «Скажи на милость!» — воскликнул старик (Шолохов 5). "...I'm from Vyoshenskaya too, Grandad," Aksinya said, flushing with joy. "You don't say so!" the old man exclaimed (5a).

М-161 • ЯВИ́(ТЕ) ⟨СДЕ́ЛАЙ(ТЕ)⟩ БО́ЖЕСКУЮ МИ́-ЛОСТЬ *obs* [VP_imper; these forms only; indep. clause; usu. this WO] used to express an emphatic or humble request: **for heaven's ⟨God's, Christ's, pity's, mercy's⟩ sake; for the love of God.**

«Нет, уж вы, юноша, кокарду снимите, сделайте божескую милость» (Сологуб 1). "...No, you'd best take off the cockade, young man, for Heaven's sake" (1a).

М-162 • БО́ЖЬЕЙ МИ́ЛОСТЬЮ; ОТ БО́ГА *both coll* [NP_instrum or PrepP; these forms only; usu. nonagreeing postmodif] (of a person) gifted, naturally talented (in some area or field): **(one has) a God-given talent (for sth.); a natural-born [NP]; a born [NP]; [in limited contexts] (one is) a natural.**

Он блестящий врач, хирург милостью божьей. He is a brilliant doctor, a born surgeon.

М-163 • МИ́ЛЫЕ БРАНЯ́ТСЯ – ТО́ЛЬКО ТЕ́ШАТСЯ [saying] when people who love each other quarrel, their arguments are not serious, they will soon make up: ≃ **it's only a lover's quarrel ⟨tiff⟩; lovers' quarrels are soon mended; the quarrel of lovers is the renewal of love.**

Несколько зная язык, он [Васильев] писал статью начерно, оставляя пробелы, вкрапливая русские фразы и требуя от Фёдора Константиновича дословного перевода своих передовичных словец: ...чудеса в решете... пришла беда — растворяй ворота... милые бранятся — только тешатся... (Набоков 1). Having a smattering of the language, he [Vasiliev] wrote his article out in rough, with gaps and Russian phrases interspersed, and demanded from Fyodor a literal translation of the usual phrases found in leaders: ...wonders never cease...troubles never come singly...it's only a lover's tiff... (1a).

M-164 • С МИ́ЛЫМ РАЙ И В ШАЛАШЕ́ [saying] when you are with the one you love, you can be happy in any place, any living situation (even if less than ideal): ≃ **a cottage is a castle for those in love; love makes a cottage a castle.**

Через три дня они поженились. С милым рай и в шалаше. Ей было восемнадцать лет, ему двадцать. Поселились они в крохотной Димкиной комнатке на пятом этаже, которую он снимал, поссорившись с отцом, крупным инженером (Некрасов 1). Three days later they were married. A cottage is a castle for those in love. She was eighteen, he was twenty. They settled down in the minute fifth-floor room which Dimka had rented since quarreling with his father, a famous engineer (1a).

M-165 • КИ́СЛАЯ МИ́НА [NP; sing only; fixed WO] a displeased expression on one's face: **long ⟨wry⟩ face; sour expression;** ‖ Х сделал кислую мину ≃ **X made a wry face; X pulled a long face.**

Судья сидела, или сидел, или сидело за столом с кислой миной... (Аксёнов 6). The judge (he, she, or it) was sitting behind a table with a sour expression... (6a).

M-166 • В МИНИАТЮ́РЕ [PrepP; Invar; usu. nonagreeing modif] (some place, thing, event etc is similar to the place, thing, event etc named) except much smaller in size or scale: **a [NP] in miniature; a small-scale [NP]; a smaller ⟨tiny⟩ version of a [NP].**

Это очаровательный город, Париж в миниатюре. This is a charming city, a small-scale Paris.

M-167 • ДЕ́ЛАТЬ/СДЕ́ЛАТЬ ХОРО́ШУЮ ⟨ВЕСЁ-ЛУЮ⟩ МИ́НУ ПРИ ПЛОХО́Й ИГРЕ́ [VP; subj: human; usu. this WO] to mask one's annoyance, discontent, failure with the appearance of tranquillity, happiness: Х делает хорошую мину при плохой игре ≃ **X puts up a bold front; X puts a good face on things ⟨on a bad business⟩; X grins and bears it.**

Теперь же, ввязавшись в него [дело Синявского и Даниэля], [власти] делали хорошую мину при плохой игре, полностью игнорируя общественное мнение (Буковский 1). Once having blundered into it [the Sinyavsky and Daniel case], they [the authorities] put up a bold front to cover the stupidity of the Sinyavsky and Daniel arrests and totally ignored world public opinion (1a). ♦ Московское начальство было недовольно уродливым и глупым «делом Бродского», однако считало долгом, поддерживая своих провалившихся чиновников, делать хорошую мину при плохой игре (Эткинд 1). The Moscow leadership were dissatisfied with the ugly and stupid "Brodsky affair," but considered it their duty to support their blundering subordinates and put a good face on things (1a).

< The Russian idiom is a translation of the French *faire bonne mine à mauvais jeu.*

M-168 • ПОДВОДИ́ТЬ/ПОДВЕСТИ́ ⟨ПОДКЛА́ДЫ-ВАТЬ/ПОДЛОЖИ́ТЬ⟩ МИ́НУ ⟨МИ́НЫ⟩ *под кого coll* [VP; subj: human] to make trouble for s.o. stealthily, do a vile thing to s.o.; acting in secret, to undermine s.o.'s position at work

or in society: Х подложил мину под Y-а ≃ **X played a dirty trick on Y; X did a nasty thing to Y.**

M-169 • БЕЗ ПЯТИ́ МИНУ́Т *coll, humor* [PrepP; Invar; nonagreeing modif; foll. by a NP denoting a person's profession, position, post; fixed WO] a person who will soon become (a professional in the named field), begin (practicing the named profession), receive (the named rank or title) etc: **on the verge of becoming a [NP]; a step away ⟨one step⟩ from becoming a [NP]; a budding [NP]; a practically fully qualified [NP]; within inches ⟨an inch⟩ of becoming a [NP].**

На сцене хозяин дома Пётр Полуорлов, его сын Федя...; Валерик, бывший однокашник Полуорлова, а теперь без пяти минут доктор наук (Рощин 2). Present are the man of the house, Pyotr Eaglov; his son, Fedya...and Valerik, a former classmate of Eaglov's. Valerik is right on the verge of becoming a Doctor of Science (2a). ♦ Его судили за хранение иностранной валюты, какой-то литературы... Вот так и прибыл он к нам в бригаду без пяти минут англичанином (Марченко 1). He was tried for possessing foreign currency and some sort of printed matter....And so our gang acquired a practically fully qualified Englishman (1a).

M-170 • КАК ОДНА́ МИНУ́ТА пролететь, пройти [как + NP; Invar; adv; usu. used with pfv verbs; fixed WO] (of a period of time usu. defined by some event, occasion etc) (to pass) very quickly, unnoticeably: **(be over) before one knows it; (fly) right by.**

Мы так ждали лета, а оно пролетело как одна минута. We couldn't wait for summer, and then it was over before we knew it.

M-171 • МИНУ́ТА В МИНУ́ТУ; СЕКУ́НДА В СЕ-КУ́НДУ [NP; these forms only; adv; fixed WO] exactly, precisely at a fixed time: **to the minute; on the dot; right on time; at...sharp; on the nose.**

Ровно через две недели — минута в минуту — мы опять стояли на каменных плитах знакомой террасы... (Катаев 3). Exactly two weeks later — to the minute — we were again standing on the stone flags of that familiar veranda... (3a). ♦ Каждый гость мог записать в книгу, когда разбудить его завтра. Будили минута в минуту... (Грекова 3). Each guest could write in a book when he was to be awakened the next day, and the staff would wake him on the dot... (3a).

M-172 • В ДО́БРУЮ МИНУ́ТУ *obs* [PrepP; Invar; adv; fixed WO] when (a person is) in a good mood: **(catch s.o. when he is) in a good ⟨the right⟩ frame of mind; (catch s.o.) in the right mood ⟨at the right moment⟩.**

M-173 • В ⟨ОДНУ́⟩ МИНУ́ТУ [PrepP; these forms only; adv; fixed WO] instantaneously, very quickly: **immediately; at once; right away; in no time (flat); in a flash ⟨a jiffy, a wink, a moment, an instant, a heartbeat⟩.**

Читателей было, разумеется, гораздо больше, чем советчиков, и книги [Мандельштама] раскупались в одну минуту... (Мандельштам 2). There were of course many more readers than advisers, and M[andelstam]'s books were always sold out immediately... (2a). ♦ ...Я люблю скакать на горячей лошади по высокой траве, против пустынного ветра... Какая бы горесть ни лежала на сердце, какое бы беспокойство ни томило мысль, всё в минуту рассеется (Лермонтов 1). I love galloping through long grass on a fiery horse, with the desert wind in my face....Whatever sorrow weighs on the heart, whatever anxiety troubles the mind, it vanishes in a moment (1c).

M-174 • В ПЕ́РВУЮ МИНУ́ТУ [PrepP; Invar; adv; fixed WO] in the beginning: **at first; initially.**

В первую минуту я не понял, на что он намекает. At first I didn't understand what he was hinting at.

M-175 • **НА МИНУ́ТУ** ⟨**МИНУ́ТКУ** *coll*, **МИНУ-ТОЧКУ** *coll*, **МИГ, СЕКУ́НДУ, СЕКУ́НДОЧКУ** *coll*⟩ [PrepP; these forms only; adv; usu. used with pfv verbs] for a very short amount of time: **for a moment; for one (single) moment** ⟨**minute**⟩; **for a** ⟨**one**⟩ **brief moment; for a short time; not (for) more than a minute.**

«…Ты на минуту встань на моё место. Представь, что тебе приносят пулю и говорят: вот доказательство, что ты убил человека» (Тендряков 1). "…Put yourself in my place for a moment. Imagine that someone brings you a bullet, and says: 'Here is the evidence that you have killed a man'" (1a). ♦ Другие гости заходили не часто, на минуту, как первые три гостя… (Гончаров 1). Other visitors came seldom and only for a short time, as the first three visitors had done… (1a). ♦ «Ктой-то [*ungrammat* = кто это]?» — спросила Аксинья, натягивая на себя одеяло. «Это я». — «Я сейчас оденусь». — «Ничего. Я на минутку» (Шолохов 2). "Who's there?" Aksinya asked, pulling up the bedclothes. "It's me." "I'll get dressed." "Never mind that. I won't be more than a minute" (2a).

M-176 • **НИ НА МИНУ́ТУ** [PrepP; Invar; adv; used with negated verbs] not for the shortest amount of time: **not (even) for a minute** ⟨**a second**⟩; **not for one minute** ⟨**second**⟩; **not for a (single) moment; not for an instant; never (for a moment** ⟨**an instant**⟩); [with more than one subj] **neither…nor…for a minute** ⟨**a second, a moment, an instant**⟩.

Если появляется где-то поблизости жеребёнок, то мул старается ни на минуту от него не отходить… (Искандер 3). If a foal appears somewhere nearby, the mule tries not to leave his side even for a minute… (3a). ♦ Ни одна из нас ни на минуту не закрывала рта (Гинзбург 1). No one stopped talking for a second (1a). ♦ «…Я никогда, никогда не усомнился в главном. Понимаете, никогда, ни на минуту не усомнился» (Войнович 6). "…I never, never doubted the main thing. Never doubted it, not for one minute" (6a). ♦ Она была прелестная шестнадцатилетняя девочка, очевидно страстно его любящая (в этом он не сомневался ни на минуту) (Толстой 5). She was a charming girl of sixteen, and obviously was passionately in love with him (he did not doubt this for an instant) (5a). ♦ …Она женщина и ни на минуту не забывает об этом… (Залыгин 1). …She was a woman and never forgot it… (1a). ♦ …Ни усталость, ни скука не могли ни на минуту согнать с лица мягкость, которая была господствующим и основным выражением, не лица только, а всей души… (Гончаров 1). …Neither weariness nor boredom could for an instant erase the softness which was the predominant and essential expression, not only of his face but of his whole soul… (1b).

M-177 • **ОДНУ́ МИНУ́ТУ** ⟨**МИНУ́ТКУ, МИНУ́ТОЧКУ, СЕКУ́НДУ, СЕКУ́НДОЧКУ**⟩! *coll* [indep. sent; these forms only; fixed WO] a request to wait a little, stop etc: **just a moment** ⟨**a minute**⟩!; **one moment!; wait a minute!;** [in limited contexts] **wait for me** ⟨**us**⟩!

«Одну минуту, — сказал он, сверкнув золотыми зубами, — сейчас освобожусь» (Искандер 3). "Just a moment," he said, flashing his gold teeth. "I'm almost through" (3a). ♦ …Митя вдруг вскочил со стула. «Одну минуту, господа, ради бога одну лишь минутку; я сбегаю к ней…» (Достоевский 1). …Mitya suddenly jumped up from his chair. "One moment, gentlemen, for God's sake, just one moment; I'll run to her…" (1a). ♦ Должно быть, мы вышли из института одновременно, только я — из ворот, а Митя — из главного здания, потому что он вдруг оказался в двух шагах позади меня. «Одну минуту!» Я подождала, и мы пошли к площади Льва Толстого (Каверин 1). Mitya and I must have left the Institute at the same moment, I by the gate and he by the main building, because he suddenly appeared only a couple of steps behind me. "Wait for me!" I waited for him and we walked on together into Leo Tolstoy Square (1a).

M-178 • **СИЮ́ МИНУ́ТУ** ⟨**МИНУ́ТКУ, СЕКУ́НДУ**⟩ [NP$_{accus}$; these forms only; adv; fixed WO] **1.** immediately: **this (very) minute** ⟨**second, instant**⟩; **at once; right now.**

Филипп Филиппович навалился на дверь ванной, но та не поддавалась. «Открыть сию секунду!» (Булгаков 10). Philip Philippovich threw himself against the bathroom door, but it would not give. "Open up this very second!" (10a). ♦ [Любовь Андреевна:] Уходите, Яша, ступайте… [Яша:] Сейчас уйду. Сию минуту… (Чехов 2). [L.A.:] Go away, Yasha, run along. [Ya.:] I'm going, right away. This very instant (2a). ♦ …Тальберг сказал: «Нужно ехать сию минуту. Поезд идёт в час ночи…» (Булгаков 3). Talberg said: "I must go at once. The train leaves at one o'clock tonight…" (3a).

2. now, at this moment: **this minute** ⟨**second**⟩; **at this very moment.**

Какой-нибудь пустяк, 5.000 рублей, например, задатку, профессор может получить сию же минуту… (Булгаков 10). A trifling advance, say, five thousand rubles, can be placed at the professor's disposal at this very moment… (10a).

M-179 • **НИ МИНУ́ТЫ** ⟨**НИ СЕКУ́НДЫ**⟩ **не сомневаться, не колебаться, не думать** и т. п. [NP$_{gen}$; these forms only; used with negated verbs; usu. used with impfv verbs] not (to doubt sth., hesitate, assume sth. etc) even for the shortest moment: **not (for) a minute** ⟨**a moment, an instant**⟩; **without any** ⟨**a moment's**⟩ **(hesitation** ⟨**delay** etc⟩).

«Если я не подозревал в вас своего преемника, то вы не думали ни минуты, что я — ваш предшественник» (Федин 1). "As I didn't suspect my successor in you, so you didn't for a minute think that I had been your predecessor" (1a). ♦ …Законная власть ни минуты не сомневалась, что Козырь всегда оставался лучшею и солиднейшею поддержкой её (Салтыков-Щедрин 1). …The regime in power did not for a moment doubt that Hotspur had always been its best and most solid support (1a). ♦ «Это настоящий герой, о каком я мечтала девочкой… Я бы побежала за ним на край света. Ни секунды бы не думала!» (Дудинцев 1). "He is a real hero, the kind I dreamt of when I was a little girl….I would have followed him to the ends of the earth! I would not have hesitated an instant!" (1a).

M-180 • **С МИНУ́ТЫ НА МИНУ́ТУ** [PrepP; Invar; adv; fixed WO] (sth. will take place, s.o. will arrive etc) very soon, momentarily: **any minute** ⟨**moment, time**⟩ **now; any minute; at any moment.**

«Кстати, где она?» — «Ждём с минуты на минуту», — сказал Дон Рипат и, поклонившись, отошёл (Стругацкие 4). "By the way, where is she?" "We expect her any moment now," answered Don Ripat, who then bowed and walked away (4a).

M-181 • **МИР ПРА́ХУ** *чьему, кого lit* [indep. sent; Invar; fixed WO] (used as a wish to s.o. who has died) may s.o. lie peacefully: мир праху X-а ≃ **may X rest in peace; God rest X's soul.**

Так завершила свои дни пани Янжвецкая. Достойная, гордая оказалась женщина. Мир праху её! (Рыбаков 1). That's how Madame Yanzhvetska ended her days. She had been a proud and worthy woman, may she rest in peace (1a).

M-182 • **МИР ТЕ́СЕН** *coll* [usu. indep. sent; Invar; more often this WO] no matter where one is he may meet or hear about s.o. whom he knows or who is in some way connected with people or events in his past (often said when meeting an acquaintance unexpectedly): **it's a small world; small world!; the world is a small place.**

Эйдлин — известный китаист… И Сергей Сергеевич китаист, ученик Эйдлина. Кроме того, как вы помните, Сергей Сергеевич — личный друг Николая Т. Федоренко. А Николай Т. Федоренко тоже, кроме всего прочего, китаист. И если вы достанете сборник *Восемнадцать стихотворений* Мао Цзэ-дуна... то там вы прочтёте «перевод под редакцией Н. Федоренко и Л. Эйдлина». Вот как тесен мир! (Войнович 3). Eidlin is a well-known Sinologist. And Sergei Sergeevich is also a Sinologist, Eidlin's student. Besides that, as you remember, Sergei Sergeevich is a personal friend of Nikolai T. Fedorenko. And Nikolai T. Fedorenko is also, besides everything else, a Sinologist. If you look at *Eighteen Poems* by Mao Tse-tung...you will see "Translation edited by N. Fedorenko and L. Eidlin." Small world! (3a).

M-183 • ПЕРЕВЕРНУ́ТЬ ВЕСЬ МИР ⟨СВЕТ⟩ [VP; subj: human; usu. fut or infin with готов, решил etc] to do everything possible, make every effort (to achieve or obtain sth.): X перевернёт весь мир ≃ **X will move heaven and earth; X will accomplish ⟨do⟩ the impossible; X will turn the world upside down.**

...[Митя] решил перевернуть весь мир, если надо, но непременно эти три тысячи отдать Катерине Ивановне во что бы то ни стало *и прежде всего* (Достоевский 1). ...He [Mitya] decided to turn the whole world upside down, if need be, but to be sure to return the three thousand to Katerina Ivanovna at all costs and *before all else* (1a).

M-184 • УХОДИ́ТЬ/УЙТИ́ ⟨ПЕРЕСЕЛЯ́ТЬСЯ/ ПЕРЕСЕЛИ́ТЬСЯ, ОТБЫВА́ТЬ/ОТБЫ́ТЬ⟩ В ЛУ́ЧШИЙ ⟨В ИНО́Й, В ДРУГО́Й⟩ МИР *obs, elev* [VP; subj: human; usu. pfv] to die: X ушёл в лучший мир ≃ **X has gone to a better ⟨to the next⟩ world; X has left this world.**

Писатели, выступавшие в 1958 году на собрании, обещали роману «Доктор Живаго» место на свалке истории. С тех пор прошло двадцать семь лет. Давно умер создатель романа. Ушли в мир иной многие из его гонителей (Войнович 1). The writers who spoke out at the meeting in 1958 promised the author of *Doctor Zhivago* a place on the garbage dump of history. Since then, twenty-six years have passed, and the creator of the novel died quite some time ago. Many of his persecutors have gone to the next world as well (1a).

M-185 • ХУДО́Й МИР ЛУ́ЧШЕ ДО́БРОЙ ССО́РЫ [saying] usu. said when deciding not to allow strained relations to develop into a full-fledged conflict: ≃ **a bad peace is better than a good quarrel; better a bad peace than a good quarrel; a lean compromise is better than a fat lawsuit; a bad peace is better than a good victory.**

M-186 • НЕ ОТ МИ́РА СЕГО́ [PrepP; Invar; nonagreeing modif or subj-compl with быть∅ (subj: human), pres or past; fixed WO] a person who is a dreamer, who is not pragmatic or caught up in the worries of everyday life (and who may behave unusually and, occas., eccentrically): X не от мира сего ≃ **X is not of this world; X lives in a ⟨some⟩ dream world; X lives in another world; X is out of touch with reality.**

Он вспомнил про Полет. Вывезти её невозможно... Но как ей объяснить? Она не от мира сего... Будет плакать... (Эренбург 4). He remembered Paulette. It was impossible to take her with him....But how could he explain it to her? She was not of this world. She would only start to weep (4a). ♦ Один мой родственник, узнав о моих невзгодах, специально приехал из провинции ко мне, чтобы научить меня, как выйти из положения. «Пиши про Брежнева», — сказал он, считая, что я, как человек не от мира сего, сам додуматься до этой нехитрой мысли не мог (Войнович 1). Learning of my troubles, a relative of mine made a special trip from the provinces to advise me on how to get out of my situation. "Write about Brezhnev," he said, thinking that I lived in some dream world and was unable to come to that clever idea on my own (1a).

< From the Bible (John 18:36).

M-187 • ИДТИ́/ПОЙТИ́ НА МИРОВУ́Ю *coll* [VP; subj: human] **1.** *obs* to resolve a legal dispute without taking it to court: X и Y пошли на мировую ≃ **X and Y came to an agreement; X and Y settled it between ⟨among⟩ themselves; X and Y made a settlement;** [in limited contexts] **X and Y made an out-of-court settlement.**

«...Ты теперь вольный казак: затеешь следствие — законное дело! Небойсь [= небось], и немец струсит, на мировую пойдёт» (Гончаров 1). "...You're a free agent now: if you bring an action against him, it's perfectly legal. The German will probably get cold feet and come to an agreement" (1b).

2. *coll* to resolve a disagreement, dispute etc: X и Y пошли на мировую ≃ **X and Y made up ⟨made amends, made peace⟩.**

M-188 • ОДНИ́М МИ́РОМ МА́ЗАНЫ *coll, disapprov* [AdjP; subj-compl with быть∅ (subj: human, pl); usu. pres; fixed WO] the people in question are identical, similar to one another, have the same characteristics, esp. the same faults: X-ы ⟨X и Y, X-ы и Y-и⟩ одним миром мазаны ≃ **Xs ⟨X and Y, Xs and Ys⟩ are tarred with the same brush ⟨cast in the same mold, cut from the same cloth, birds of a feather⟩.**

«Принимай иди бригаду и помни, с кем дело имеешь, все они, сукины дети, одним миром мазаны...» (Максимов 1). "Go and find your brigade and don't forget who you're dealing with. They're all tarred with the same brush, the sons of bitches" (1a).

M-189 • С МИ́РОМ [PrepP; Invar; adv] **1. отпустить** *кого* ~ (to let s.o. go) peacefully, without punishment or pursuit: **(let s.o. go ⟨allow s.o. to go⟩) in peace; let s.o. off.**

...Началась заварушка. Подоспевшие милиционеры не смогли разобрать, кто виноват, и встали на сторону полковников... Их отпустили с миром, а студентов, на всякий случай, переписали (Зиновьев 1). A general brawl started. When the police arrived they couldn't tell who was guilty and joined in on the side of the colonels....They were allowed to go in peace, and the students' names were taken just in case (1a). ♦ «...Давай приезжай», — гудела трубка... «Я не смогу приехать, Александр Иванович... У меня срочная работа»... — «Ну, работай, чёрт с тобой!..» — сказал тесть [Игоря], вешая трубку. «Уф! Отпустил с миром!» (Ерофеев 3). "...Come on over," boomed the receiver...."I can't come over, Alexander Ivanovich....I've got a deadline."..."All right, do your work, the hell with you!..." he [Igor's father-in-law] said and hung up the phone. "Whew! He let me off..." (3a).

2. иди(те), поезжай(те), оставайся, оставайтесь ~ *obs* used to wish s.o. a pleasant trip; also used when taking leave of s.o. to wish him good fortune: [when wishing s.o. a pleasant trip] **go in peace; fare thee well;** [when taking leave] **the very best to you; be ⟨keep, stay⟩ well.**

M-190 • ИДТИ́ ⟨ХОДИ́ТЬ⟩/ПОЙТИ́ ПО́ МИРУ *coll;* **ИДТИ́ ⟨ХОДИ́ТЬ⟩/ПОЙТИ́ С СУМО́Й** *obsoles, coll;* **ДОХОДИ́ТЬ/ДОЙТИ́ ДО СУМЫ́** *obs* [VP; subj: human] to lead a beggarly life, ask for charity (usu. as a result of losing all one had): X пойдёт по миру ≃ **X will go begging; X will go out and beg; X will beg from door to door; X will beg for a living; X will be ⟨end up⟩ a beggar; X will be left a beggar; X will beg his bread.**

[Матрёна:] Маялась ты, маялась, сердечная, век-то свой с немилым, да и вдовой с сумой пойдёшь (Толстой 1). [M.:] Poor thing, all your life you've had to put up with a man you don't love and now when you're a widow you'll have to go begging (1c). ♦ [Золотуев:] Он [продавец] всё ему [ревизору] отдаст! Дом, машину, дачу! По миру пойдёт! (Вампилов 3). [Z.:] He'll [the salesman will] give him [the inspector] the lot! The house, the car, the cottage! He'll go out and beg! (3a). ♦ «...Где ей одной с такой ротой [с пятерыми детьми] справиться, не по миру же идти, в самом деле» (Максимов 3). "How can she manage a whole regiment of kids by herself? After all, she can't beg from door to door" (3a). ♦ Она писала, что ежели Николай не приедет и не возьмётся за дело, то всё имение пойдёт с молотка и все пойдут по миру (Толстой 5). She wrote that if he [Nikolai] did not come and take matters in hand their whole estate would be sold at auction and they would all be left beggars (5a).

M-191 • НА МИРУ́ ⟨НА ЛЮ́ДЯХ⟩ И СМЕРТЬ КРАСНА́ [saying] misfortunes are easier to bear when a person has his friends around him, or when he is with people who share a similar fate (formerly referred specifically to death): ≃ **misery loves company; company in distress makes (the) trouble less.**

M-192 • ПУСКА́ТЬ/ПУСТИ́ТЬ ПО́ МИРУ *кого coll;* **ПУСКА́ТЬ/ПУСТИ́ТЬ С СУМО́Й** *obsoles;* **ДОВОДИ́ТЬ/ДОВЕСТИ́ ДО СУМЫ́** *obsoles* [VP; subj: human; more often pfv] to ruin s.o., drive s.o. to penury: X пустит Y-а по миру ≃ **X will make a beggar (out) of Y; X will put Y in ⟨send Y to⟩ the poorhouse.**

«Благодетеля нашёл: немца! На аренду имение взял; вот погоди: он тебя облупит... Уж пустит по миру, помяни моё слово!» (Гончаров 1). "Found a benefactor, have you: a German! Leases your estate, does he? You just wait, he'll fleece you....He'll make a beggar of you, you mark my words!" (1b). ♦ «По миру нас пустит этот грех!» (Искандер 5). "This Greek will put us all in the poorhouse!" (5a).

M-193 • С МИ́РУ ПО НИ́ТКЕ *coll* [PrepP; Invar; adv; fixed WO] (in) small amounts from different sources: **(get) a little bit ⟨a little something⟩ from everybody; (get) a little (bit) from here and a little (bit) from there.**

«Они только что въехали в кооперативную квартиру, на мебель пока нет денег». — «Ничего, соберём им с миру по нитке». "They have just moved into a cooperative apartment and don't have any money right now for furniture." "Don't worry. We'll get them a little from here and a little from there."

< From the saying «С миру по нитке – голому рубашка». See M-194.

M-194 • С МИ́РУ ПО НИ́ТКЕ – ГО́ЛОМУ РУБА́ШКА ⟨РУБА́ХА⟩ [saying] small contributions from many people will give one person something substantial, significant (said when the aid of a group accomplishes sth. beyond the means or ability of one person alone): ≃ **many hands make light work; many a little makes a mickle.**

[author's usage] [Варравин:] Сделаем христианское дело; поможем товарищу – а?.. Нынче всё общинное в ходу, а с философской точки, что же такое община, как не складчина?.. [Четвёртый чиновник:] С миру по нитке – бедному рубашка (Сухово-Кобылин 3). [V.:] Let's do the Christian thing; let's help a comrade, shall we?...Nowadays everything communal is fashionable, and from a philosophical standpoint, what is a community if not a pooling of resources?... [4th Clerk:] Many a little makes a mickle (3a).

M-195 • ПО МНЕ¹ *highly coll* [PrepP; Invar; sent adv (parenth)] from my point of view: **if you ask me; to me; as far as I'm concerned; the way I see it; [in limited contexts] for all I care.**

Осетины шумно обступили меня и требовали на водку; но штабс-капитан так грозно на них прикрикнул, что они вмиг разбежались. «Ведь этакой народ, – сказал он: – и хлеба по-русски назвать не умеет, а выучил: „офицер, дай на водку!" Уж татары, по мне, лучше: те хоть непьющие...» (Лермонтов 1). The Ossetians vociferously besieged me, demanding money for vodka; but the captain shouted at them so fiercely that they dispersed in a moment. "You see what they are like!" he grumbled. "They don't know enough Russian to ask for a piece of bread, but they've learned to beg for tips: 'Officer, give me money for vodka!' To me the Tatars are better – they're tee-totalers at least..." (1b). ♦ «По мне, хоть вы все живите в пятикомнатных квартирах» (Войнович 3). "As far as I'm concerned, you can all live in five-room

apartments" (3a). ♦ «...По мне, его кобыла и с матерью – да будь они прокляты! – а я жеребца не дам обскакать!» (Шолохов 2). "...His mare and its mother can go to bloody hell for all I care, but I won't let him beat the stallion!" (2a).

M-196 • ПО МНЕ² ⟨ПО ТЕБЕ́ и т. п.⟩ *coll* [PrepP; subj-compl with бытьø, прийтись etc (subj: usu. abstr or, less often, human)] to be pleasing to me (you etc), be in accord with my (your etc) tastes, interests: X по мне ≃ **X is to my taste ⟨liking⟩; X suits me; X is my cup of tea ⟨my thing⟩; [in limited contexts] X is right for me; X is the one ⟨the [NP]⟩ for me;** ‖ *Neg* X не по мне ≃ **X doesn't sit too well with me; [in limited contexts] X grates on me.**

«Ну, для чего вы идёте на войну?» – спросил Пьер. – «Для чего? Я не знаю. Так надо. Кроме того, я иду... – Он остановился. – Я иду потому, что эта жизнь, которую я веду здесь, эта жизнь – не по мне!» (Толстой 4). "And why are you going to war?" asked Pierre. "Why? I don't know. Because I must. And besides, I'm going—" he paused. "I'm going because this life I am leading here – this life is – not to my taste" (4a). ♦ ...И то ему не так, и это не по нему. Что бы она ни сделала, всё было неладно (Распутин 3). Nothing was to his liking. Whatever she did displeased him (3a). ♦ ...Он [Чичиков] обратился к другому шкафу.... Всё книги философии... «Это не по мне»... (Гоголь 3). ...Chichikov turned to another bookcase....They were all books on philosophy.... "That's not my cup of tea"... (3a). ♦ [Ирина:] Надо поискать другую должность, а эта не по мне (Чехов 5). [I.:] I must try to find some other job, this one's not right for me (5d). ♦ [Фёкла:] ...Уж каких женихов тебе припасла!.. Первый, Балтазар Балтазарович Жевакин, такой славный, во флоте служил – как раз по тебе придётся (Гоголь 1). [F.:] ...What a bunch of gentlemen I've got for you!...First, Baltzazar Baltzazarovich Zhevakin, such a nice gentleman; he served in the navy – he's just the one for you (1c). ♦ ...Проходя однажды мимо МХАТа, я увидел объявление, что этому театру требуются рабочие сцены. Ну вот, решил я, эта работа... по мне (Войнович 1). One day, walking past the Moscow Art Theater, I noticed a sign saying that stage-set workers were needed. That's the job for me, I decided (1a). ♦ ...Вообще Пётр Петрович принадлежал к разряду людей, по-видимому чрезвычайно любезных в обществе... но которые, чуть что не по них, тотчас же и теряют все свои средства и становятся похожими скорее на мешки с мукой, чем на развязных и оживляющих общество кавалеров (Достоевский 3). Generally speaking, Pyotr Petrovich belonged to that category of people who appear extremely affable in company...but who, as soon as something grates on them, instantly lose all their resources and begin to seem more like sacks of flour than offhand and convivial cavaliers (3c).

M-197 • НИ МНО́ГО НИ МА́ЛО; НИ ⟨НЕ⟩ БО́ЛЬШЕ (И) НИ ⟨НЕ⟩ МЕ́НЬШЕ; НИ ⟨НЕ⟩ БО́ЛЕЕ (И) НИ ⟨НЕ⟩ МЕ́НЕЕ [these forms only; used as Particle; all variants are often foll. by как... when used prepositively, and variants with больше may be foll. by чем... as well; variants with больше and более have fixed WO] **1.** [usu. used with a quantit NP or a Num] exactly the amount indicated (often a sizable amount, quantity of sth.): **no more, no less (than); [in limited contexts] no less ⟨fewer⟩ than.**

Недели через две, когда уже вернулся он из отпуска в Москву, получил «Новый мир» среди дня распоряжение из ЦК: к утру представить ни много ни мало – 23 экземпляра повести. А в редакции их было три (Солженицын 2). Two weeks later, when he returned to Moscow from leave, *Novy Mir* received at midday an order from the Central Committee: submit no fewer than twenty-three copies by the following morning. The office had only three (2a).

2. precisely what is named (usu. used to emphasize that the person, phenomenon, place, action etc in question is in some way unexpected, surprising, extraordinary etc in the given circumstances): **no more, no less; …no less;** [when foll. by an anim noun only] **none other than;** [in limited contexts] **(the) [NP] himself ⟨itself⟩;** [when stressing the element of surprise, occas. flavored by indignation] **…of all people ⟨things, places⟩;** [when stressing the relative importance of sth.] **nothing less than ⟨short of⟩;** [when stressing the relative unimportance of sth.] **nothing more than.**

Никандров был крестьянским сыном, любил об этом говорить, любил это в себе, умел связать это с чем-то далёким и очень нужным для себя — ни больше ни меньше как с самой античностью… (Залыгин 1). Nikandrov was the son of a peasant, and he liked talking about it. It was something he liked about himself. He could establish a connection between it and something remote from it, but essential to him, with antiquity, no less (1a). ♦ Оказался он ни много ни мало в Париже. He turned up in Paris of all places. ♦ …Пронеслись слухи, что он не более не менее как миллионщик (Гоголь 3). …The rumor spread that he was nothing less than a millionaire (3e). ♦ Оказался этот вьюн ни больше ни меньше как лентой кардиограммы (Аксёнов 6). This eel turned out to be nothing more than a long paper printout of an electrocardiograph (6a). ♦ …Среди женщин в отделе информации… не было плакс и нытиков. И если уж слёзы — значит, ни много ни мало как ЧП [чрезвычайное происшествие] (Залыгин 1). [context transl] …Among the women [in the department]…there were no sissies or bleaters. If they did shed a tear, then it was a full-scale state of emergency (1a).

M-198 • НЕ МОГИ́ *substand, usu. humor* [VP_imper; this form only] used to discourage s.o. from doing sth.: **don't you dare (do sth.); don't even think (of doing sth.).**

M-199 • ПОСЛЕ́ДНИЙ ИЗ МОГИКА́Н; ПОСЛЕ́Д-НИЙ МОГИКА́Н [NP; fixed WO] the last representative of some trend, social group, political party, generation etc: **the last of the Mohicans.**

Последние могикане лефовского толка, которым сейчас уже за шестьдесят, продолжают прославлять двадцатые годы и удивляться новым читателям, ушедшим из-под их влияния (Мандельштам 1). The last of the Mohicans from LEF, who are now over sixty, continue to extol the twenties and shake their heads in wonderment at the young readers over whom they have lost all influence (1a).

< Title of the Russian translation of James Fenimore Cooper's novel *The Last of the Mohicans,* 1826 (translated 1833).

M-200 • БРА́ТСКАЯ МОГИ́ЛА [NP; fixed WO] a joint grave for many people who were killed in the same battle, died around the same time from the same cause etc: **common ⟨mass⟩ grave.**

…Теперь позаросли бурьяном высокие холмы братских могил, придавило их дождями, позамело сыпучим снегом (Шолохов 3). And now the high mounds of the common graves were overgrown with weeds, settled by rain, and canopied in drifting snow (3a).

M-201 • НАЙТИ́ (СЕБЕ́) МОГИ́ЛУ; НАЙТИ́ СМЕРТЬ ⟨(СВОЙ) КОНЕ́Ц, КОНЧИ́НУ⟩ *lit* [VP; subj: human or collect] to die, perish, be killed (usu. in refer. to death in battle, or accidental or unnatural death): X нашёл себе могилу ≃ **X met his death; X found his grave; X met his end ⟨fate, doom⟩.**

«…Лучшие дивизии врага и лучшие части его авиации уже разбиты и нашли себе могилу на полях сражения…» (Войнович 2). "…The enemy's best divisions and the best units of his air force have already been smashed and have found their graves on the field of battle…" (2a).

M-202 • РЫТЬ ⟨КОПА́ТЬ⟩ МОГИ́ЛУ *кому-чему* [VP; subj: human or collect] to work toward the destruction of s.o. or

sth.: X роет могилу Y-у ≃ **X is digging a grave for person Y ⟨the grave of thing Y⟩.**

[Болоснин:] …Роя могилу своей собственной империи, они [англичане] обманом обезоруживали нас и — отдавали большевикам! (Солженицын 9). [B.:] …While they [the English] were digging the grave of their own Empire, they disarmed us by deception and gave us up to the Bolsheviks (9a).

M-203 • РЫТЬ ⟨КОПА́ТЬ⟩ СЕБЕ́ МОГИ́ЛУ [VP; subj: human] to do sth. that will result in grave consequences for o.s.: X роет себе могилу ≃ **X is digging his own grave; X is driving nails into his own coffin.**

Тот, кто упрямится, будет сметён более хитрыми соперниками в борьбе за власть, но тот, кто делает эту уступку, неизбежно и парадоксально, против своей воли роет… себе могилу (Стругацкие 4). Those who resist will be swept away by cleverer rivals in the battle for power; those, on the other hand, who agree to make such concessions, will be digging their own graves against their own will—inescapably and paradoxically (4a).

M-204 • СВОДИ́ТЬ/СВЕСТИ́ ⟨ЗАГНА́ТЬ, УЛОЖИ́ТЬ *both coll*⟩ **В МОГИ́ЛУ** *кого* [VP; subj: human or abstr; usu. pfv fut or past] to cause s.o. to die a premature death (by burdening, worrying, harrassing etc him greatly): X сведёт Y-а в могилу ≃ **X will drive Y to an early grave; X will be the death of Y (yet).**

M-205 • СМОТРЕ́ТЬ ⟨ГЛЯДЕ́ТЬ⟩ В МОГИ́ЛУ ⟨В ГРОБ⟩ *coll* [VP; subj: human, usu. sing; pres or past] (of a sick or very old person) to be near the end of one's life, close to death: X в могилу смотрит ≃ **X has one foot in the grave; X is knocking at death's door; X is living on borrowed time.**

[Войницкий:] Моя старая галка, maman, всё ещё лепечет про женскую эмансипацию; одним глазом смотрит в могилу, а другим ищет в своих умных книжках зарю новой жизни (Чехов 3). [V.:] And my dear mother, the old chatterbox, still keeps burbling on about the emancipation of women. She's got one foot in the grave, but she still reads all those solemn pamphlets and thinks they'll lead her to a new life (3c).

M-206 • СХОДИ́ТЬ/СОЙТИ́ В МОГИ́ЛУ ⟨В ГРОБ⟩; ЛЕЧЬ В МОГИ́ЛУ ⟨В ГРОБ⟩; ЛОЖИ́ТЬСЯ/ЛЕЧЬ В ЗЕ́МЛЮ; УЙТИ́ В МОГИ́ЛУ ⟨В ЗЕ́МЛЮ⟩ *all rather elev* [VP; subj: human] to die: X сошёл в могилу ≃ **X went to his grave; X went to his final resting place; X went to (his) eternal rest; X laid his bones to rest; X lay in his grave;** [in limited contexts with subj: pl] **Xs died off.**

Несколько раз, со слезами на глазах, графиня говорила сыну, что теперь, когда обе дочери её пристроены, — её единственное желание состоит в том, чтобы видеть его женатым. Она говорила, что легла бы в гроб спокойною, ежели бы это было (Толстой 5). On several occasions, with tears in her eyes, the Countess had told her son that now that both of her daughters were settled, her only wish was to see him married. She said she could go to her grave content if this were accomplished (5a). ♦ [Лебедев:] Жениха бы ей лучше подыскала… [Авдотья Назаровна:] И найду! В гроб, грешница, не лягу, а её да Санечку замуж выдам!.. В гроб не лягу… (Чехов 4). [L.:] Better find her a husband. [A.:] I will, I will. I won't lay my sinful old bones to rest before I've found a husband for her and Sasha, that I won't (4b). [L.:] You'd do better to find her a husband. [A.:] Just see if I don't! Before this old sinner lies in her grave, I'll have her married, and Sanichka, too!…Yes, before I'm in my grave… (4a). ♦ …Убийцы и предатели находятся под верховной защитой, потому что они «ошибались» вместе со своим начальством. Постепенно они сойдут в могилы, а новые поколения выдвинут новые кадры убийц и предателей… (Мандельштам 2). All the killers and traitors…are under the highest protection because they "erred" together with those in authority over them. They will now gradually die off and a new generation will have no difficulty in finding its own murderers and informers... (2a).

M-207 • УНОСИ́ТЬ/УНЕСТИ́ ⟨С СОБО́Й⟩ В МО-ГИ́ЛУ *что* [VP; subj: human] to die without conveying sth. (usu. a secret or important message), without managing to accomplish sth.: X унёс с собой в могилу Y ≃ **X carried ⟨took⟩ Y to the grave (with him).**

«Знаменитый Логидзе тайну своих прохладительных напитков унёс с собой в могилу», – сказал Абесаломон Нартович... (Искандер 4). "The famous Logidze carried the secret of his soft drinks to the grave," Abesalomon Nartovich said (4a).

M-208 • ДО ⟨СА́МОЙ⟩ МОГИ́ЛЫ [PrepP; these forms only; adv or nonagreeing postmodif] to the end of one's life: **till the grave; to the ⟨one's very⟩ grave; to ⟨till⟩ one's dying day; till (the day) one dies; until death;** [as modif] **lifelong; everlasting.**

[Нароков:] Я всю жизнь поклонялся красоте и буду ей поклоняться до могилы... (Островский 11). [N.:] All my life I've worshipped beauty and I shall worship it till the grave... (11a). ♦ «...До могилы ты один останешься в моём сердце» (Пушкин 2). "...Till my dying day, you alone shall remain in my heart" (2b).

M-209 • НЕ МОГУ́ ЗНАТЬ *obs, now humor* [sent; Invar; fixed WO] (a respectful negative reply) I cannot answer because I do not know the answer: **that I wouldn't know (, sir); I wouldn't ⟨don't⟩ know, sir;** [in limited contexts] **that I daren't judge (, sir).**

«...Я его [щенка] вычёсывал». – «А отчего же блохи?» – «Не могу знать» (Гоголь 3). "I did comb him [the puppy] out, sir." "Why does he have fleas then?" "I wouldn't know, sir" (3c). ♦ «Что это значит? – закричал я в бешенстве. – Да разве он с ума сошёл?» – «Не могу знать, ваше благородие», – отвечал вахмистр (Пушкин 2). "What does this mean?" I shouted in a rage. "Has he lost his mind?" "That I daren't judge, Your Honour," answered the sergeant... (2a).

< Formerly used in the military as the negative reply of a subordinate to an officer of higher rank.

M-210 • БРАТЬ/ВЗЯТЬ МО́ДУ *highly coll* [VP; subj: human; often foll. by infin] to adopt a certain life style, habit etc (usu. a disagreeable one from the speaker's point of view), start doing sth. habitually: X взял моду делать Y ≃ **X took to doing Y; X got into the habit of doing Y; X picked up the habit of doing Y.**

Последнее время моя сестра взяла моду вставать после полудня. Lately my sister has taken to getting up after noon.

M-211 • С МОЁ ⟨С НА́ШЕ, С ТВОЁ, С ВА́ШЕ⟩ по-жить, испытать и т. п. *coll* [PrepP; these forms only; adv; used with pfv verbs] (to live) to the extent that I (we, you) have, (to experience) the number of things that I (we, you) have: поживи с моё ≃ **(when you've lived ⟨when you've been kicking around the world etc⟩) as long as I have; (when you've seen ⟨done etc⟩) as much as I have; (wait) till you're my age; (when you're as old) as me; (when you've been through) what I have;** ∥ *Neg* не с моё ⟨твоё⟩ ≃ **more than I ⟨you⟩ (have ⟨did etc⟩).**

[Золотуев:] Покрутись с моё, покувыркайся, тогда не будешь спрашивать, зачем людям деньги... (Вампилов 3). [Z.:] When you've been kicking around the world as long as I have, you won't be asking why people want money... (3a). ♦ Младший продавец, когда начали продавать мёд из запасной бочки, видно, кое о чём догадался... Шалико никак не мог решить – заткнуть ему рот парой тридцаток или не стоит унижаться? Не стоит, наконец решил он, пусть с моё поишачит, а потом будет в долю входить (Искандер 4). The junior salesman must have caught on when they began selling honey from the reserved

barrel....Shaliko could not decide: should he stop the man's mouth with a pair of thirty-ruble bills, or was it worth demeaning himself? It's not worth it, he decided finally; let him do as much scutwork as I did, and then he'll come into his share (4a). ♦ [Платонов:] Очень приятно, но... что же из этого следует? [Петрин:] Поживите с моё, душенька, так узнаете! (Чехов 1). [Platonov:] Very nice too, but where does it get us? [Petrin:] When you're as old as me, boy, you'll know (1b). ♦ «Я нанюхался пороху не с твоё!» (Шолохов 3). "I've seen a lot more action than you!" (3a).

M-212 • Е́ЛЕ МОЖА́ХУ ⟨-ом⟩ *obs, humor* [orig. VP; these forms only; fixed WO] **1.** [subj-compl with copula (subj: human) or adv] in a very drunken state: **staggering drunk; feeling no pain; three sheets to the wind.**

2. [adv] (to do sth.) with difficulty, almost not (be able to do sth.): **barely; only just.**

Зимнюю сессию он одолел «еле можахом», с хвостами, затевал разговор об академическом отпуске, даже пошёл без моего ведома в поликлинику, надеясь получить у врачей справку для отпуска, но там ему намылили шею (Трифонов 5). He had barely made it through the fall semester (as it was, he had a couple of incompletes) and was starting to talk about taking a leave of absence. Without my knowledge he had even gone to the policlinic, hoping to get a leave of absence on medical grounds; instead he had gotten a good scolding (5a).

< «Можаху» and «можахом» are the old forms of the 3rd and 1st person plural, respectively, of the imperfect tense.

M-213 • МО́ЖЕТ БЫТЬ [sent adv (parenth)] **1.** Also: **МО́ЖЕТ СТА́ТЬСЯ** *obs* [fixed WO] possibly: **perhaps; maybe; (it) could ⟨may⟩ be (that); (he ⟨she etc⟩) may ⟨might⟩ (perhaps); it is possible (that); (he ⟨she etc⟩) might just.**

Утешение же, а может быть, это и не утешением было, а чем-то другим – каким-то источником новых сил, – она стала находить в квартире Нюрка... (Залыгин 1). She began to find some comfort in Niurok's little flat...or perhaps it wasn't comfort at all, but something else, a kind of source of new strength (1a). ♦ В течение года, может быть двух, происходили столкновения, ссоры, драки, случилось даже убийство... (Федин 1). In the course of a year, maybe two, there occurred clashes, quarrels, fights, and even murder took place... (1a). ♦ Те [очевидцы], что остались, рассказывают по-разному, а некоторые и вовсе не помнят... Что касается меня, то я собрал в кучу всё, что слышал по данному поводу, и прибавил кое-что от себя, прибавил, может быть, даже больше, чем слышал (Войнович 2). Those [eyewitnesses] that are [left] tell all kinds of different stories and some can't remember anything at all....As for me, I've heaped up everything I heard on the subject and added a little something of my own as well, could be I even added more than I heard (2a). ♦ «За тобой я, может быть, пойду, а один не сдвинусь с места» (Гончаров 1). "I may, perhaps, follow you, but alone I shall not stir from this spot" (1b). ♦ В другое время и при других обстоятельствах подобные слухи, может быть, не обратили бы на себя никакого внимания... (Гоголь 3). At another time and under different circumstances such rumors might not have attracted attention (3c). At another time, under different circumstances, it is possible that these rumors wouldn't have had such an impact (3e). ♦ «Так если бы вы... Лягавому предложили вот то самое, что мне говорили, то, ой, может статься...» – «Гениальная мысль!» – восторженно перебил Митя (Достоевский 1). "So if you were to...make Lyagavy the same offer you made me, he might just..." "A brilliant idea!" Mitya interrupted ecstatically (1a).

2. used in sentences expressing urging, prompting etc (occas. in order to soften the categorical nature of the prompting): **perhaps; maybe; why not (do sth.); why don't you ⟨we etc⟩ (do sth.).**

Лёнька спросил: «Может быть, немного посидим?» – «Это ночью», – ответил Садчиков. «Ноги отваливаются» (Семёнов 1). Lyonka said: "Perhaps we can sit down for a while?" "Tonight," replied Sadchikov. "My legs are dropping off" (1a).

M-214 • **НЕ МО́ЖЕТ БЫ́ТЬ!; БЫ́ТЬ НЕ МО́ЖЕТ!** [Interj; these forms only] an exclamation expressing doubt of sth., distrust in sth., amazement bordering on incredulity: **impossible!; that couldn't ⟨can't⟩ be!; you don't say!; unbelievable!**

«Это далеко не простой кот. Это говорящий кот. Он умеет разговаривать». — «Не может быть!» (Катаев 2). "This is no ordinary cat. This is a talking cat. He can talk." "Impossible!" (2a). ♦ «А ты знаешь, что этот депутат не далее как вчера политическое убежище попросил?» — «Не может, — режиссёр говорит, — быть!» (Войнович 1). "Are you aware that this deputy only yesterday requested political asylum in the West?" "That can't be!" says the director (1a).

M-215 • **КАК МО́ЖНО...** [Invar; premodif; foll. by compar form of Adv; the resulting phrase is adv] to the utmost possible extent, exceedingly: **as [AdvP] as possible; as [AdvP] as one can.**

Я часто наводил разговор на «Господина из Сан-Франциско», желая как можно больше услышать от Бунина о том, как и почему написан им этот необыкновенный рассказ... (Катаев 3). I often worked the conversation round to *The Gentleman from San Francisco* because I wanted to hear as much as possible from Bunin about how and why he had written this amazing story... (3a). ♦ Она [Бэла] была без памяти. Мы изорвали чадру и перевязали рану как можно туже... (Лермонтов 1). She [Bela] was unconscious. We tore the veil into strips and bandaged the wound as tightly as we could (1b). ♦ «Вы ко мне с бумагами как можно реже ходите», — говорил он письмоводителю... (Салтыков-Щедрин 2). "Come to me with your papers as seldom as you can," he told his chief secretary... (2a). ♦ В доме дяди Сандро именитый гость был встречен прекрасно, а милая Катя так и летала, стараясь как можно лучше принять своего бывшего жениха (Искандер 5). [context transl] The distinguished guest met an excellent reception in Uncle Sandro's house, and sweet Katya simply flew, doing her utmost to entertain her former bridegroom (5a).

M-216 • **КАК (ЭТО) МО́ЖНО!; РА́ЗВЕ МО́ЖНО!** *coll* [Interj; these forms only; fixed WO] (used to express sharp disagreement, strong objection) that is utterly impossible, I cannot believe you could even suggest (say, think) such a thing: **(it's) out of the question; (it's) impossible!; no way!; [in limited contexts] how could I ⟨he etc⟩ (do that)!**

«Всё же [ты] не дал [жене] перекрасить черкеску», — напомнил дядя Сандро шутку Теймыра-головореза. «Как можно!» — сказал Аслан горделиво... (Искандер 5). "You haven't let her [your wife] dye your cherkeska," Uncle Sandro said, recalling the cutthroat Temyr's joke. "Impossible," Aslan said proudly... (5a). ♦ На другой день он содрогнулся при мысли ехать к Ольге: как можно! Он живо представил себе, как на него все станут смотреть значительно (Гончаров 1). The next day he shuddered at the thought of going to Olga's: how could he? He imagined everyone looking at him significantly (1b).

M-217 • **ДО МО́ЗГА КОСТЕ́Й** [PrepP; Invar; fixed WO]
1. [nonagreeing modif] (one is a certain type of person) entirely, in every way: **(a [NP]) to the (very) marrow of one's bones; (a [NP]) to the core; every inch (a ⟨the⟩ [NP]); (a [NP]) through and through; [in limited contexts] (an) out-and-out ([NP]).**

«Парамошина я знаю, пролетарий до мозга костей» (Максимов 3). "I know Paramoshin, he's a proletarian to the marrow of his bones" (3a).

2. [adv] to an extreme degree: **to the marrow of one's bones; to the bone ⟨the marrow, the core⟩; through and through;** ‖ **робеть и т. п. ~** ≃ **be scared out of one's wits.**

«Вот откуда пошло всё то, что случилось с Россией: декадентство, модернизм, революция, молодые люди, подобные вам, до мозга костей заражённые достоевщиной...» (Катаев 3). "That's where all that has happened to Russia now springs from, all the decadence, the modernism, the revolution, young people like yourself, infected to the bone with Dostoevskyism..." (3a). ♦ Решившись, с свойственною ему назойливостью, поехать в деревню к женщине, которую он едва знал... он всё-таки робел до мозга костей... (Тургенев 2). Having decided with characteristic impudence to repair to the country to pay a visit to a lady with whom he was barely acquainted...he was nevertheless scared out of his wits... (2c).

M-218 • **МОЗГА́ ЗА МОЗГУ́ ЗАХО́ДИТ/ЗАШЛА́** *у кого substand* [VP$_{subj}$; usu. impfv; usu. this WO] s.o. can no longer think coherently (often from excessively stressful, mentally taxing work, exhaustion etc): у X-а мозга за мозгу заходит ≃ **X can't think straight; X's brain is fried.**

M-219 • **ДАВА́ТЬ/ДАТЬ ПО МОЗГА́М** *кому highly coll* [VP; subj: human] to scold, curse s.o. rudely: X дал Y-у по мозгам ≃ **X lashed out at Y; X gave it to Y good; X settled Y's hash; X chewed ⟨bawled⟩ Y out.**

Оказывается, полчаса назад окончился худсовет и старик всем дал по мозгам — директору, заму, второму режиссёру! (Трифонов 1). It seemed that a meeting of the theater council had adjourned just half an hour ago and the old man lashed out at all of them—at the executive director and his assistant, and at the assistant artistic director! (1a).

M-220 • **ПОЛУЧА́ТЬ/ПОЛУЧИ́ТЬ ПО МОЗГА́М** *highly coll* [VP; subj: human] to be rudely scolded, reprimanded: X получил по мозгам ≃ **X got it good; X got ⟨caught⟩ it in the neck.**

«А знаешь, всё-таки жаль Евдокимова». — «Жаль, — согласился Игорь, — но он сам виноват [, что нарисовал карикатуру на декана]... У декана никто всё равно „профессора" не отобрал и не отберёт — хоть сто карикатур рисуй» — а Евдокимов крепко получил по мозгам, что и следовало ожидать с самого начала» (Ерофеев 3). "You know, it really is too bad about Evdokimov." "It is," agreed Igor, "but it's his own fault [that he drew a caricature of the Dean]....No one took away the Dean's full professorship and no one's going to take it away—not even if you do one hundred such cartoons!—and Evdokimov got it right in the neck, which could have been predicted" (3a).

M-221 • **ШЕВЕЛИ́ТЬ/ПОШЕВЕЛИ́ТЬ ⟨ШЕВЕЛЬНУ́ТЬ⟩ МОЗГА́МИ** *highly coll;* **ШЕВЕЛИ́ТЬ/ПОШЕВЕЛИ́ТЬ МОЗГО́Й** *substand;* **ВОРО́ЧАТЬ МОЗГА́МИ** *substand* [VP; subj: human; often infin with надо or нужно, or imper] to think hard (trying to understand, come up with etc sth.): пошевели мозгами ≃ **use your brain ⟨head, noodle etc⟩; set your mind to it; (you'd better) rack your brains; put on your thinking cap.**

«Никаких тебе забот — знай только шевели мозгами, думай, изобретай, совершенствуй, двигай науку и технику...» (Копелев 1). "No worries—just make sure to use your brain, think, invent, perfect, advance science and technology" (1a). ♦ «Ты что, первый раз на займе?» — спросил Ганичев. «После войны первый». — «То-то. А я на этих займах каждую весну. Знаю колхозную публику. Ты к нему в заулок, а он стрекача через поветь... Тут треба [*ungrammat* = нужно, требуется] пошевелить мозгой, а не с песнями вдоль деревни...» (Абрамов 1). "This is your first Loan, is it?" asked Ganichev. "First since the war." "Exactly. Well, I do these Loans every spring. I know these *kolkhoz* types. If you go in through the yard they give you the slip out the loft way....You've got to use your noodle here, not go marching through the village singing songs" (1a). ♦ «Знаете, вы довольно любопытную мысль сказали; я теперь приду домой и шевельну мозгами на этот счёт. Признаюсь, я так и ждал, что от вас можно кой-чему поучиться» (Достоевский 1). "You know, you've said a very interesting thought; I'll set my mind to it when I get home. I admit, I did suspect it would be possible to learn something from you" (1a).

M-222 • **ВПРАВЛЯ́ТЬ/ВПРА́ВИТЬ МОЗГИ́** *кому slang* [VP; subj: human or collect] to make s.o. behave more prudently, carefully by using severe measures: X вправил Y-у мозги́ ≃ **X set Y straight; X knocked some sense into Y's head; X put ⟨set⟩ Y right; X brought Y to his senses;** [in limited contexts] **X gave Y a thorough shaking-up.**

Стоя уже в дверях, Абарчук проговорил: «Я ещё приду к тебе... Я тебе вправлю мозги, теперь я буду твоим учителем» (Гроссман 2). Abarchuk was standing in the doorway when he finished. "I'll come and see you again. I'll put you right. I'll be your teacher now" (2a). ♦ Фиктивны выборы и в случае выборов братийных [*nonce word*, a play on партийных, "of the party"] органов. Хотя здесь порой и разгораются страсти, возникают конфликты, отводят намеченных кандидатов и выдвигают новых, это идёт в рамках дозволенного свыше. В противном случае строптивым вправляют мозги (Зиновьев 1). Elections to institutions of the Brotherhood are equally fictitious. Although in this case passions are sometimes aroused, although conflicts sometimes flare up, although the original candidates are sometimes removed from the ballot and replaced by new ones, this is all sanctioned from above. If there is any resistance, the obstinate ones get a thorough shaking-up (1a).

M-223 • **ДАВИ́ТЬ НА МОЗГИ́** *кому slang* [VP; subj: human; often neg imper] to try to force s.o. to relinquish his point of view and accept someone else's: X давит Y-у на мозги́ ≃ **X is trying to brainwash ⟨to sway⟩ Y; X is trying to change Y's mind.**

«Излагай и другие версии, другие точки зрения. И не мешай мне самому судить, выбирать. Не дави на мозги» (Копелев 1). "Tell me other versions, other points of view. And don't interfere with my making my own judgments and choices. Don't try to brainwash me" (1a).

M-224 • **КА́ПАТЬ НА МОЗГИ́** *(кому) slang, disapprov* [VP; subj: human] to assert sth. over and over to s.o., repeating it continually; to admonish s.o. endlessly: X ка́пает Y-у на мозги́ ≃ **X is (getting) on Y's back ⟨case⟩; X is pestering ⟨bugging⟩ Y.**

«Он тут... нам на мозги капает, а ты и вздыхаешь: вот, дескать, божий человек. А этот божий человек небось ряху наел» (Абрамов 1). "Here he is getting on our backs, and you just sigh and say, 'There's a simple man of God.' Well, this man of God managed to stuff his face pretty good" (1a).

M-225 • **КРУТИ́ТЬ/ЗАКРУТИ́ТЬ МОЗГИ́** *кому substand* [VP; subj: human] **1.** to (try to) deceive, confuse s.o.: X крутит Y-у мозги́ ≃ **X is trying to fast-talk Y; X is trying to put one over on Y; X is muddling ⟨addling⟩ Y.**

2. to cause s.o. to fall in love with one, win s.o.'s affections: X закрутил(а) мозги́ женщине/мужчине Y ≃ **X turned Y's head; X swept Y off her ⟨his⟩ feet.**

M-226 • **КУРИ́НЫЕ ⟨ЦЫПЛЯ́ЧЬИ⟩ МОЗГИ́** *(у кого) highly coll, derog* [NP; pl only] (s.o. has) limited mental capabilities, (is) unintelligent: **birdbrain ⟨pinhead, pea brain, lamebrain⟩; (s.o. is) birdbrained ⟨pinheaded, pea-brained, lamebrained⟩.**

M-227 • **МОЗГИ́ НАБЕКРЕ́НЬ ⟨НЕ НА МЕ́СТЕ, НЕ ТУДА́ ПОВЁРНУТЫ⟩** *у кого highly coll, derog* [VP$_{subj}$ with быть$_∅$, usu. pres; fixed WO] s.o. does not think rationally, is odd in his thinking: у X-а мозги́ набекрень ≃ **X's head is on backward; X's head isn't on straight; X is not playing with a full deck; X is a crackpot.**

«Владька, где там твой старый хрыч?.. Мать его в железку... мозги набекрень» (Максимов 2). "And what about that old fogey of yours, Vlad?...God damn him, the old crackpot" (2a).

M-228 • **ПРОМЫВА́ТЬ/ПРОМЫ́ТЬ МОЗГИ́** *кому coll* [VP; subj: human] **1.** [often 3rd pers pl with indef. refer.] to indoctrinate s.o. forcibly with political, social, religious etc beliefs that differ from or are contrary to his own: X-у промывают мозги́ ≃ **X is being brainwashed.** ○ **ПРОМЫ́ВКА МОЗГО́В** [NP; sing only; fixed WO] ≃ **brainwashing.**

2. to scold s.o. severely: X промыл Y-у мозги́ ≃ **X raked ⟨hauled⟩ Y over the coals; X took Y to task; X called Y on the carpet.**

...У Гангута как раз по приказу Комитета смыли фильм, на который потрачено было два года; как раз вызывали его на промывку мозгов в Союз, как раз не пустили на фестиваль в Канн... (Аксёнов 7). Gangut's latest film, a two-year project, had just been rejected by the censors; he had just been hauled over the coals by the Film Makers' Union; he had just been refused permission to go to Cannes... (7a).

M-229 • **ПУ́ДРИТЬ/ЗАПУ́ДРИТЬ МОЗГИ́** *кому slang* [VP; subj: human] to try to deceive or mislead s.o.: X пудрит Y-у мозги́ ≃ **X is bullshitting ⟨fast-talking⟩ Y; X is trying to dupe ⟨to con⟩ Y; X is throwing dust in Y's eyes; X is trying to muddle Y ⟨Y's brain⟩.**

Тотчас женский голос сердито выпалил: «Почему долго не открывал?!» Зарванцев что-то зашептал, но женщина, громко засмеявшись, оборвала его: «Не пудри мозги! Бабу, наверно, привёл?» (Чернёнок 1). Immediately a woman's voice shouted angrily: "Why did it take you so long?" Zarvantsev whispered something, but the woman, laughing noisily, cut him off. "Don't bullshit me! You must have a woman in here!" (1a). ♦ Пантюша слушал усмешливо и враждебно, тряс пальцем: «Да мы в школе эту историю читали. Зна-аем! Чего вы мне мозги пудрите? История, история...» (Трифонов 3). Pantyusha listened with a sarcastic, hostile sneer, and accompanied his objections with a furiously wagging finger: "We learned all about history in school. We know it all. Why are you trying to muddle me? History, history..." (3a).

M-230 • **НАСТУПА́ТЬ/НАСТУПИ́ТЬ НА (ЛЮБИ́МУЮ ⟨БОЛЬНУ́Ю⟩) МОЗО́ЛЬ** *кому coll* [VP; subj: human; usu. pfv past; if impfv, usu. infin with не надо, не стоит etc or neg imper] to mention sth. that bothers, hurts, or offends s.o. intensely: X наступил Y-у на любимую мозоль ≃ **X touched Y on a raw spot; X hit ⟨touched⟩ Y's sore spot; X hit ⟨touched⟩ a nerve.**

[Нина:] Ваша жизнь прекрасна! [Тригорин:] Что же в ней особенно хорошего?.. Вы, как говорится, наступили на мою самую любимую мозоль, и вот я начинаю волноваться и немного сердиться. Впрочем, давайте говорить (Чехов 6). [N.:] Your life must be wonderful! [T.:] Must it? What is there particularly good about it?...I'm afraid you've touched me on a raw spot, and I'm beginning to get worked up and a little cross. However, let's talk (6b).

M-231 • **ВА́ШИМИ ⟨ТВОИ́МИ⟩ МОЛИ́ТВАМИ** *old-fash, coll, humor* [NP$_{instrum}$; these forms only; usu. used as indep. sent; fixed WO] (used as an answer to a question about one's or s.o.'s health, state of affairs etc) everything is well: **can't complain; no complaints; not bad, thank you for asking.**

M-232 • **МОЛОДЕ́Ц ПРОТИВ ⟨СРЕДИ⟩ ОВЕ́Ц (, А ПРОТИВ МОЛОДЦА́ И САМ ОВЦА́)** [saying; often only the first half of the saying is used] some person is brave only when confronting those weaker, lower in rank etc than himself: ≃ **a lion among sheep (, a sheep among lions).**

M-233 • **МÓЛОДО-ЗÉЛЕНО** *coll, often condes or disapprov* [sent; Invar] s.o. is naïve, inexperienced in sth., lacking in seriousness because of his youth (said condescendingly when a person's behavior or words make his youth or inexperience obvious; also said to excuse youth's desire for fun): **(when) you're young, you're green; you're ⟨he's etc⟩ too young to know any better; you're ⟨he's etc⟩ young and green.**

Девушка молча вышла. Капитан [милиции] кивнул в её сторону и сказал: «Обижаются за профилактику, а потом сами прибегают и жалуются: „Изнасиловали! Ограбили!"»... — «Молодо-зелено», — сказал я (Искандер 6). The girl went out without saying a word. The [police] captain nodded in her direction and remarked: "They're offended when we take precautionary measures, and yet later on they themselves come running in to complain: 'He raped me! He robbed me!'"..."I suppose they're too young to know any better," I said (6a). ♦ [author's usage] Профессор снисходительно улыбнулся, давая понять, что студент ещё молод и зелен, и ему следует кое-что объяснить (Войнович 1). The professor smiled condescendingly, as if to say that the student was still young and green, and required enlightening (1a).

M-234 • **НЕ ПÉРВОЙ МÓЛОДОСТИ** [NP$_{gen}$; Invar; subj-compl with copula (subj: human) or nonagreeing postmodif; fixed WO] middle-aged, not young: **not ⟨no longer⟩ in one's first youth; not ⟨no longer⟩ (so) very young; past one's prime; getting on in years.**

Улыбка у неё открытая, обольстительная... красивая улыбка. Губы красивые. И женщина пикантная, пухленькая, лицо румяное, хотя не первой молодости (Трифонов 6). Her smile is open, alluring... A beautiful smile. Beautiful lips. A tasty morsel of a woman; chubby, a rosy complexion, though not in her first youth (6a). ♦ Дубков был маленький жилистый брюнет, уже не первой молодости... (Толстой 2). Dubkov was a small sinewy fellow with a dark complexion; he was no longer so very young... (2b).

M-235 • **ПО МÓЛОДОСТИ ЛЕТ** [PrepP; Invar; adv; fixed WO] as a result of a person's youth and insufficient experience: **because of (one's) youthful inexperience; being young and inexperienced ⟨naïve, immature⟩.**

M-236 • **ВТОРÁЯ МÓЛОДОСТЬ** [NP; fixed WO] **1.** a new surge of physical and spiritual forces that one feels at a mature age: **second youth; [in limited contexts] (whole) new lease on life.**

...Эти рисунки [Георгия Максимовича] выставлялись не раз, были репродукции, даже почтовые открытки, — и в жизни Георгия Максимовича наступил своего рода ренессанс, вторая молодость... (Трифонов 3). ...These drawings [by Georgii Maximovich] were exhibited several times, were reproduced in print and even made into postcards—and Georgii Maximovich underwent a kind of renaissance, a second youth... (3a).

2. widespread recognition, appreciation of sth. that for some period had fallen into oblivion: **renewed popularity; second heyday ⟨life⟩; [in limited contexts] (make) a comeback.**

Книга эта, пользовавшаяся большим успехом у современников, а потом на много лет забытая, сейчас живёт второй молодостью. This book, which enjoyed great success in its day and was then forgotten for many years, is now enjoying renewed popularity.

M-237 • **ИЗ МОЛОДЫ́Х ДА РÁННИЙ; МОЛОДÓЙ ДА РÁННИЙ** *both coll, often disapprov or humor* [PrepP or AdjP; usu. subj-compl with copula (subj: human), or detached modif; fixed WO] (of a person who gets ahead in some field or business at a young age, more often by behaving in a way that the speaker considers bad, deplorable, unacceptable etc) s.o. is young and moving ahead (too) fast and (too) aggressively: **X из молодых да ранний ⟨-яя⟩ ≃ X is a young upstart; X has come ⟨wants to go⟩ too far too fast; X is a brash young fellow ⟨young woman⟩; X is a young man ⟨a young woman⟩ in a hurry.**

...Имелись сведения, что он коллекционирует картины. И хотя точно никто не знал, какого характера работы он выбирает для своих коллекций, было подозрение, что он из молодых да ранний (Искандер 4). ...There were reports that he was collecting art. Although no one knew exactly what sort of work he was choosing for his collection, it was suspected that he was a brash young fellow (4a).

M-238 • **(ТÓЛЬКО) ПТИ́ЧЬЕГО МОЛОКÁ НЕТ ⟨НЕДОСТАЁТ, НЕ ХВАТÁЕТ⟩** *coll* [VP$_{subj/gen}$ or VP, impers; pres or past] there is everything that anyone could wish for, entirely enough, a complete abundance: **there is literally ⟨absolutely⟩ everything anyone could want; you name it, he's ⟨they've etc⟩ got it; there is everything under the sun.**

«Рос я, сами понимаете, в оранжерейных условиях, в доме только птичьего молока не было... я с детства не привык отказывать себе ни в чём» (Максимов 2). "I was raised, as you will appreciate, in hothouse conditions. At home there was literally everything that anyone could want....I grew up never having to refuse myself anything" (2a).

M-239 • **ОБЖЁГШИСЬ ⟨ОБЖЁГСЯ⟩ НА МОЛОКÉ, ДУ́ЕШЬ ⟨БУ́ДЕШЬ ДУТЬ⟩ И НÁ ВОДУ** [saying] a person who has experienced troubles, suffered failure etc becomes excessively cautious when similar circumstances arise again: ≃ **the scalded cat ⟨dog⟩ fears (even) cold water; once bitten, twice shy.**

[author's usage] «...Он далеко не глуп. Какие он мне давал полезные советы... особенно... насчёт отношений к женщинам». — «Ага! На своём молоке обжёгся, на чужую воду дует. Знаем мы это!» (Тургенев 2). "...He's far from being stupid. What useful advice he has given me, especially...especially in regard to relations with women." "Aha! a scalded cat fears cold water, we know that!" (2b).

M-240 • **МОЛОКÓ НА ГУБÁХ НЕ ОБСÓХЛО** *у кого;* **МÁТЕРИНО ⟨МАТЕРИ́НСКОЕ⟩ МОЛОКÓ НА ГУБÁХ НЕ ОБСÓХЛО** *all highly coll, often derog* [VP$_{subj}$; these forms only; fixed WO] s.o. is still very young, inexperienced, immature: у Х-а молоко на губах не обсохло ≃ **X is (still) wet behind the ears; X is (still) green ⟨a greenhorn⟩; X is barely out of diapers.**

«Не рано тебе наравне с мужиками пить? — не сдержался Василий. — ...Ещё молоко на губах не обсохло, а туда же. Что из тебя потом будет?» (Распутин 1). "Isn't it rather early for you to be taking a man-size drink?" said Vasily....."If you can drink like this while you're still wet behind the ears, what'll you do next?" (1a).

M-241 • **ВСÁСЫВАТЬ/ВСОСÁТЬ ⟨ВПИ́ТЫВАТЬ/ВПИТÁТЬ и т. п.⟩ С МОЛОКÓМ МÁТЕРИ** *что* [VP; subj: human; the verb may take the final position, otherwise fixed WO] to learn sth. well during one's earliest years: X всосал Y с молоком матери ≃ **X imbibed ⟨absorbed⟩ Y with his mother's milk; X drank Y in with his mother's milk; X learned ⟨was suckled on⟩ Y at his mother's breast; X was nurtured on his mother's milk with Y.**

Многих этому учат с детства. Для многих это — неоспоримые истины, воспринятые с молоком матери, и других они никогда не знали (Аллилуева 2). Many have been taught all this since childhood. For many these have been incontrovertible truths absorbed with their mother's milk: they have never known any others (2a). ♦ В них ещё говорит былой испуг и ужас перед разбушевавшейся стихией, хотя по возрасту большинство любителей порядка не могли в зрелом состоянии видеть стихию. Испуг они всосали с молоком матери (Мандельштам 2). These champions of order talk as they do because of the fear and horror once inspired in them by the elemental fury of popular revolution—though most of them were still at a tender age when it happened. They were suckled on fear of it at their mothers' breasts (2a). ♦ «…Она с молоком матери впитала любовь к труду, рабочая косточка…» (Орлова 1). "…She has been nurtured on her mother's milk with a love for work, she's a worker, body and soul" (1a).

M-242 • **С МОЛОТКА́** продать, пустить *что*, пойти *obs* [PrepP; Invar; usu. adv] (to sell sth., be sold) by public auction: **(bring sth. ⟨sth. went, sth. came⟩) under the hammer; (put sth. up ⟨be put up⟩) for auction; auction sth. ⟨be auctioned⟩ off; (be sold) at auction; [in limited contexts] (sell sth. ⟨be sold⟩) to the highest bidder.**

Она писала, что ежели Николай не приедет и не возьмётся за дело, то всё имение пойдёт с молотка и все пойдут по миру (Толстой 5). She wrote that if he [Nikolai] did not come and take matters in hand their whole estate would be sold at auction and they would all be left beggars (5a).

< At an auction a rap of the hammer («молоток») signifies that an item has been sold.

M-243 • **МЕЖДУ МО́ЛОТОМ И НАКОВА́ЛЬНЕЙ** *rather lit* [PrepP; Invar; subj-compl with copula (subj: human, collect, or abstr); fixed WO] in a difficult, dangerous situation when trouble threatens from both sides: **between a rock and a hard place ⟨spot⟩; between the devil and the deep blue sea.**

M-244 • **МОЛЧА́НИЕ – ЗНАК СОГЛА́СИЯ** [saying] when a person is silent, it implies that he agrees (usu. said when a question is left unanswered, which allows the assumption that the response is affirmative): ≃ **silence is a sign of consent; silence gives ⟨means⟩ consent.**

«Ольга, – сказал он, став перед ней на колени, – будь моей женой!» Она молчала… «Молчание?» – сказал он тревожно и вопросительно, целуя ей руку. «Знак согласия!» – договорила она тихо… (Гончаров 1). "Olga," he said, kneeling before her, "be my wife!" She said nothing.…"Silence?" he asked anxiously, as he kissed her hand. "Is a sign of consent," she said in a low voice… (1b).

M-245 • **ХРАНИ́ТЬ МОЛЧА́НИЕ** *lit* [VP; subj: human or collect; fixed WO] to be silent (usu. in a situation when some reaction is expected): X хранит молчание ≃ **X remains ⟨keeps⟩ silent; X maintains silence; X preserves his ⟨its⟩ silence.**

…Печать хранит молчание (это – для Запада, чтобы к травле не привлекалось внимание), а на закрытых собраниях и инструктажах ораторы по единой команде произносят многозначительно и уверенно любую ложь о неугодном человеке (Солженицын 2). …The press preserves its silence (for the benefit of the West—why draw attention to the witch hunt?), while speakers at public meetings and closed briefing sessions, obeying a single command, authoritatively and confidently utter any lie they please about the undesirable in question (2a).

M-246 • **ОБХОДИ́ТЬ/ОБОЙТИ́ ⟨ПРОХОДИ́ТЬ/ПРОЙТИ́** *rare*⟩ **МОЛЧА́НИЕМ** *что* [VP; subj: human or collect] to make no mention of sth. deliberately: X обошёл Y молчанием ≃ **X passed Y over ⟨over Y⟩ in silence.**

Тема эта неприятна, но обойти её молчанием я не могу, ибо в злонамеренно искажённых слухах она получила превратное толкование (Ивинская 1). This is not a pleasant matter, but I cannot pass it over in silence, if only on account of all the false and malicious rumors which circulated about it at the time (1a).

M-247 • **ИГРА́ТЬ В МОЛЧА́НКУ ⟨В МОЛЧА́НКИ⟩** *coll* [VP; subj: human] to keep silent, avoid conversation (occas. out of resentment, spite etc): X играет в молчанку ≃ **X is playing ⟨keeping⟩ silent; X isn't talking ⟨won't talk etc⟩; X**

won't say a word; [in limited contexts] **(it's as if) X has taken a vow of silence; X is playing dumb.** ○ **ИГРА́ В МОЛЧА́НКУ** [NP] ≃ **a game of silence.**

Поднявшись на второй этаж и подойдя к седьмому номеру, он [Фигурин] услышал внутри какой-то шум и приник ухом к двери. «Ну что, – услышал он звонкий голос, – будем играть в молчанку? Не выйдет! Если я захочу, у меня рыба заговорит!» (Войнович 4). Figurin walked up to the second floor. Hearing some sort of noise from inside [room number 7], he pressed his ear against the door. "What, are we going to play silent here?" said a ringing voice. "It won't work! I can make a fish talk if I want to!" (4a). ♦ «…Родился и вырос я в морально и физически здоровой среде. А тут разные фигли-мигли, интеллигентские штучки. По неделям в молчанки играем, даже обедаем порознь» (Терц 7). "…I was born and bred among people with healthy bodies and healthy minds. All this hocus-pocus, fancy intellectual stuff, it isn't my line. Sometimes we don't talk for weeks on end, we even have our meals apart" (7a). ♦ «Я с ним почти не общаюсь, так, шапочное знакомство». – «Общаться вам придётся волей-неволей, – возразил Алферов, – три года в молчанку не проиграешь, общение неизбежно» (Рыбаков 2). "I have very little to do with him. We're only on nodding terms." "You have to associate with him willy-nilly," Alferov objected. "You can't take a vow of silence for three years, so inevitably you'll associate with him" (2a). ♦ Садчиков изучающе разглядывал Сударя. Потом весело спросил: «Ну, в м-молчанку играть долго будем?» – «До конца» (Семёнов 1). Sadchikov inspected Squire closely. Then he asked cheerfully: "Well, will we be p-playing dumb for very long?" "To the end" (1a).

M-248 • **В ЛЮБО́Й МОМЕ́НТ** [PrepP; Invar; adv; fixed WO] at all times: **any time; always.**

Володя в любой момент готов помочь друзьям. Volodya is always ready to help his friends.

M-249 • **В МОМЕ́НТ** *highly coll*; **В ОДИ́Н МОМЕ́НТ** *coll* [PrepP; these forms only; adv] very quickly, immediately: **right away; in no time flat; at once; in a flash.**

Хочешь контрамарку в театр? Я тебе это в один момент устрою. Do you want a free ticket to the theater? I can get you one in no time flat.

M-250 • **ЛОВИ́ТЬ МОМЕ́НТ** [VP; subj: human; often imper or infin with надо, нужно etc] not to miss a favorable opportunity: X-у надо ловить момент ≃ **X should take advantage of it ⟨the opportunity⟩; X should seize the moment ⟨the opportunity⟩; X should jump at the chance.**

«Да, в меня здесь все влюбляются», – с угрюмым самохвальством сказал Передонов. «Ну, вот видишь, вот ты и лови момент», – убеждал Рутилов (Сологуб 1). "Yes, they're all in love with me around here," said Peredonov with sullen boastfulness. "Well there you are, and you should take advantage of it," pressed Rutilov (1a).

< A partial loan translation of the Latin *carpe diem*, which occurs in the odes of Horace (65–8 B.C.).

M-251 • **В ЧУЖО́Й МОНАСТЫ́РЬ СО СВОИ́М УСТА́ВОМ НЕ ХО́ДЯТ** [saying] when you are at some place other than your own home (office, country etc), you should follow the rules, order, customs that exist there: ≃ **when in Rome, do as the Romans do.**

M-252 • **ПОДВОДИ́ТЬ/ПОДВЕСТИ́ ПОД МОНАСТЫ́РЬ** *кого coll, occas. humor* [VP; subj: human; usu. pfv (often fut)] to cause s.o. or o.s. a great deal of trouble, put s.o. or o.s. in an extremely difficult situation (often unintentionally): X подведёт Y-а ⟨себя⟩ под монастырь ≃ **X will get Y ⟨himself⟩ into hot water ⟨into a jam, into a lot of trouble⟩; [in**

limited contexts] **X will do Y a bad turn; X will put Y ⟨X will be⟩ on the spot.**

«Эх, Ваня, Ваня... Придумал тоже коммунию... Подведёшь ты себя под монастырь, поздно окажется» (Максимов 1). "Oh, Vanya, Vanya....Some commune you've set up....You'll get yourself into a lot of trouble and it'll be too late" (1a). ♦ Работники скупки и домовой лавки, которые были ограблены... пришли в управление для того, чтобы опознать одного из грабителей. В кабинете у Садчикова посадили трёх парней [студентов университета]... Студенты всё время улыбались и весело переглядывались — это была их первая практика. Садчиков сказал: «Вы это, х-хлопцы, бросьте. Мы сейчас приведём т-того парня, так ему не до улыбок. Ясно? Вы его так сраз-зу под монастырь подведёте.» (Семёнов 1). The staff of the pawnshop that had been robbed...had come to headquarters in order to identify one of the thieves. Three [university] students...had been invited to Sadchikov's office. They smiled and looked at one another cheerfully the whole time—this was their first case. Sadchikov said: "Right, pack it up, l-lads. We're going to bring the other b-boy in now and he doesn't feel much like laughing. Got it? This way you'll p-put him on the spot right away" (1a). ♦ «Повезёшь моё письмо. Обыскивать вас не будут. Опустишь там в почтовый ящик, и всё». — «Подведёшь ты меня под монастырь», — говорю я (Зиновьев 2). [context transl] "So you can take out my letter. They'll never search you. All you've got to do is drop it in a postbox, and that's it." "Look — you're going to land me in jail," I said (2a).

M-253 • ХОДЯ́ЧАЯ МОНЕ́ТА [NP; sing only; usu. subj-compl with copula (subj: abstr); fixed WO] sth. that is widely prevalent, has become banal: **a commonplace; standard fare.**

M-254 • ПЛАТИ́ТЬ ⟨ОТПЛА́ЧИВАТЬ⟩/ОТПЛАТИ́ТЬ) ТОЙ ЖЕ МОНЕ́ТОЙ кому [VP; subj: human] to respond to s.o.'s actions, behavior by treating him in the same way (often in refer. to an offense, a hostile action etc): X отплатил Y-у той же монетой ≃ **X repaid Y ⟨paid Y back⟩ in his own coin ⟨in kind⟩; X gave Y a taste of Y's own medicine; X returned the compliment.**

Вы хотите мне отплатить тою же монетою, кольнуть моё самолюбие, — вам не удастся! (Лермонтов 1). You want to repay me in my own coin, to prick my vanity—you will not succeed (1a).

M-255 • ПРИНИМА́ТЬ/ПРИНЯ́ТЬ ЗА ЧИ́СТУЮ МОНЕ́ТУ что [VP; subj: human; usu. this WO] to accept sth. (often sth. that should be treated with skepticism, mistrust) as correct, true: X принял Y за чистую монету ≃ **X took Y at face value; X took Y in good faith.**

Дядя Сандро сразу заметил, что хозяин и его семьи ему обрадовались, хотя истинную причину этой радости он понял гораздо позже. Но тогда он её принял за чистую монету (Искандер 3). Uncle Sandro noticed immediately that the man and his family were glad to see him, although he did not understand the true reason for their gladness until much later. For the moment he took it at face value... (3a). ♦ Бирюков был далёк от мысли, чтобы всё, рассказанное Сипенятиным, принимать за чистую монету (Чернёнок 2). [context transl] Birukov was far from taking Sipeniatin's statements without a lot of salt (2a).

M-256 • МО́РЕ ПО КОЛЕ́НО⟨-а obs⟩ кому coll, often humor [NP; these forms only; usu. VP$_{subj}$ with быть$_\emptyset$; fixed WO] (used to characterize a brave, reckless person) nothing frightens s.o.: X-у море по колено ≃ **X is a daredevil; X is scared of nothing; X is a devil-may-care person ⟨man etc⟩; X feels equal to anything;** [in refer. to bravery induced by drinking] **X is full of drunken bravado.** Cf. **X is all Dutch courage.**

Он на всё и на всех плевал, всех крыл матом — и начальство и зэков, ему море было по колено (Марченко 1). He didn't give a damn about anything or anyone — he cursed the lot of them, admin and

cons alike, he was scared of nothing (1a). ♦ У меня уже шумело в голове, мне было море по колено, и я храбро пошёл к ней... (Катаев 2). There was a noise in my head. I was full of drunken bravado and I boldly went up to her room... (2a).

M-257 • РАЗЛИВА́ННОЕ МО́РЕ coll [NP: sing only] **1. ~ чего** an abundance (of wine, champagne, vodka etc. usu. at a party): **(the wine ⟨the champagne etc⟩ is) flowing like water ⟨like a fountain, in rivers, freely⟩.**

2. Also: РАЗЛИВНО́Е МО́РЕ obs a lively gathering where large amounts of alcohol are served: **drinking party; party where the wine ⟨the beer etc⟩ flows like water ⟨like a fountain, in rivers, freely⟩.**

[Миловзоров:] У них там пир горой, разливанное море. Тот говорит: «Со мной, господин Незнамов, выпьемте!» Другой говорит — со мной! (Островский 3). [M.:] ...The feasting is at its height, the wine is flowing in rivers. "Here, have a drink with me, Neznamov," says one; "No, with me," says another... (3a).

M-258 • МОРО́З ПО КО́ЖЕ ⟨ПО СПИНЕ́⟩ ПОДИРА́ЕТ ⟨ДЕРЁТ⟩/ПОДРА́Л ⟨ПРОДИРА́ЕТ/ПРОДРА́Л, ИДЁТ/ПОШЁЛ, ПРОХО́ДИТ/ПРОШЁЛ, ПРОБЕГА́ЕТ/ПРОБЕЖА́Л⟩ у кого (от чего) coll [VP$_{subj}$; usu. pres or past] s.o. experiences an unpleasant sensation, a chill runs through s.o.'s body from fright, strong fear, anxiety etc: у X-а пробежал мороз по коже (от Y-а) ≃ **a cold shiver ran down X's spine; Y sent cold shivers up ⟨down, running up and down⟩ X's spine; X's flesh ⟨skin⟩ crawled; X's flesh crept; Y made X's flesh crawl ⟨creep⟩; Y gave X the creeps.**

Он живо представил себе отсутствие себя в этой жизни... Всё вокруг преобразилось для него и показалось чем-то страшным и угрожающим. Мороз пробежал по его спине (Толстой 6). He pictured the world without himself....Everything around him underwent a sudden transformation and seemed to him sinister and menacing. A cold shiver ran down his spine (6a). ♦ [Кири:] У меня мороз по коже продирает при мысли о том, как явится на корабле эта толстая физиономия с рыжими бакенбардами (Булгаков 1). [K.:] My flesh creeps at the thought that that fat physiognomy with the red side whiskers will appear on his ship (1a). ♦ «...Он поднял голову и засмеялся... У меня мороз пробежал по коже от этого смеха...» (Лермонтов 1). "...He looked up and laughed....That laugh sent cold shivers running up and down my spine..." (1b).

M-259 • ЖДАТЬ У МО́РЯ ПОГО́ДЫ; СИДЕ́ТЬ У МО́РЯ И ⟨ДА⟩ ЖДАТЬ ПОГО́ДЫ all coll [VP; subj: human; often infin with приходится, не могу etc; usu. this WO] to wait for sth. passively, not undertaking any action: X ждёт у моря погоды ≃ **X sits around ⟨about⟩ waiting for things to take care of themselves ⟨for sth. to happen⟩; X is ⟨sits around⟩ waiting for the sun to shine.**

[Маша:] Безнадёжная любовь — это только в романах. Пустяки. Не нужно только распускать себя и всё чего-то ждать, ждать у моря погоды... (Чехов 6). [M.:] It's only in novels you read about unhappy love. It's nothing. The only sensible thing is not to brood over it, not to sit about waiting for something to happen (6b). ♦ Ещё троих [детей] старухе не пришлось похоронить — этих убила война... Ей всё время казалось, что она потеряла их сама, по своему недосмотру. Что она должна была делать, чтобы сохранить их, она не понимала и теперь, но что-то, наверно, делать надо было, а не сидеть сложа руки и не ждать у моря погоды (Распутин 3). The old lady had had no chance to bury the other three [children] — the ones the war had taken....She always felt that she had lost them herself, through her own negligence. To this day she had no idea what she ought to have done to keep them, but she felt sure she should have done something, and not just sat twiddling her thumbs and waiting for the sun to shine (3a).

M-260 • (И) МОСКВА́ НЕ СРА́ЗУ ⟨НЕ ВДРУГ⟩ СТРО́ИЛАСЬ [saying] any great undertaking starts out small, gradually gaining in scope: ≃ **Rome wasn't built in a day; an oak is not felled with one stroke; the longest journey begins with the first step.**

M-261 • МОСКВА́ ОТ КОПЕ́ЕЧНОЙ СВЕ́ЧКИ СГО-РЕ́ЛА ⟨ЗАГОРЕ́ЛАСЬ⟩ [saying] great troubles can result from insignificant things: ≃ **all it takes is a match to set a forest afire; a mighty fire begins with a straw; a penny candle set Moscow on fire.**

«Как? Вы не шутя думаете сладить, сладить с целым народом?» — «От копеечной свечи, вы знаете, Москва сгорела», — ответил Базаров (Тургенев 2). "What? Do you seriously think you can take on the whole nation?" "A penny candle, you know, set Moscow on fire," Bazarov responded (2c).

M-262 • МОСКВА́ СЛЕЗА́М НЕ ВЕ́РИТ [saying] tears, complaints, repentance etc will not arouse sympathy, cannot wash away or justify a wrongdoing, are useless: ≃ **Moscow doesn't believe in tears; tears won't help.**

«Физиономия у тебя больно бодрая». — «От характера». — «Ш-шутник». — «От положения. В моём положении только и шутить». — «В твоём положении плакать надо, Ромин». — «Москва слезам не верит» (Семёнов 1). "The expression on your face looks terribly cheerful." "That's my character." "You're a j-joker." "That's my situation. All one can do is joke in my situation." "In your situation you should be crying, Romin." "Moscow doesn't believe in tears" (1a).

M-263 • ДО МОСКВЫ́ НЕ ПЕРЕВЕ́ШАЕШЬ ⟨НЕ ПЕРЕВЕ́ШАТЬ⟩ кого-чего obs [these forms only; quantit subj-compl with быть∅ (subj/gen: usu. human, concr, or count abstr), pres only; fixed WO] very many, a great number of (people or things that, in most cases, the speaker considers useless): **a great deal of; more than you know what to do with.**

M-264 • ПЕРЕКИ́ДЫВАТЬ/ПЕРЕКИ́НУТЬ ⟨ПЕРЕ-БРА́СЫВАТЬ/ПЕРЕБРО́СИТЬ⟩ МОСТ откуда куда, от чего к чему, (из чего) во что, между чем [VP; subj: usu. human] to tie (two phenomena, time periods, movements etc) together (pointing out what unites them, showing the inherent similarities between them etc): X перебросил мост от Y-а к Z-у ≃ **X built ⟨threw etc⟩ a bridge across ⟨between⟩ Y and Z;** ‖ X перебросил мост в Z ≃ **X built a bridge into Z.**

Играя самого себя, вешая на гвоздь гороховое пальто, оправляя на себе полосатую кофту, закуривая папиросу, читая свои стихи, Маяковский перебрасывал незримый мост от одного вида искусства к другому... (Лившиц 1). In playing himself, in hanging up his cloak of buffoonery, in adjusting his striped jacket, in lighting up his cigarette and in reading out his verses, Maiakovsky threw an invisible bridge across the two art forms... (1a). ♦ Цивилизация Лаолы-Лиал, привнесённая на молодую планету, будет продолжаться во времени, и, может быть, именно тогда удастся, наконец, перекинуть мост в антимир? (Обухова 1). Transferred to a young planet, the civilization of Laola-Lyal would continue to exist in time. And then perhaps it would at last succeed in building a bridge into the antiworld (1a).

M-265 • ГРАНИ́ТЬ МОСТОВУ́Ю obs, highly coll [VP; subj: human] **1.** to walk much, for a long time over streets, roads etc (usu. covering a great distance, often when carrying out necessary errands): X гранил мостовую ≃ **X measured ⟨covered⟩ the versts ⟨the miles⟩ on foot; X tramped along; [in limited contexts] X trudged over the pavement.**

[Устинья Наумовна:] Ну, уж хлопотала, хлопотала я для тебя, Аграфена Кондратьевна, гранила, гранила мостовую-

то, да уж и выкопала жениха... (Островский 10). [U.N.:] Now, I've been bustling about, bustling about for you, Agrafena Kondratyevna; trudging, trudging over the pavement, and at last I've grubbed up a suitable man... (10b).

2. to roam or lounge about with nothing to do, be idle: X гранит мостовую ≃ **X is traipsing ⟨strolling⟩ about; X is hanging around doing nothing; X is lazing around (doing nothing).**

Должность у Козелкова была не мудрёная: выйти в двенадцать часов из дому в департамент, там потереться около столов и рассказать пару скандалёзных анекдотов, от трёх до пяти погранить мостовую на Невском... (Салтыков-Щедрин 2). Kozelkov's job as a civil servant was not what you might call an arduous one: he left home at noon for his office, spent a few hours there chatting amiably to other departmental chiefs and telling them a few smutty stories, from three to five he strolled about on the Nevsky Avenue... (2a).

M-266 • НАВОДИ́ТЬ/НАВЕСТИ́ МОСТЫ́ media [VP; subj: human (usu. pl) or collect; often infin with надо, пытаются etc] to establish contacts with the government of another country or with a certain organization, group etc: X-ы пытаются навести мосты ≃ **Xs are trying to build bridges; Xs are trying to establish relations ⟨contacts, ties⟩.**

M-267 • ОБРАСТА́ТЬ/ОБРАСТИ́ ⟨ЗАРАСТА́ТЬ/ЗА-РАСТИ́⟩ МО́ХОМ coll, disapprov [VP; subj: human] to become provincial, unsophisticated, backward: X оброс мохом ≃ **X became moss-grown; [in limited contexts] X fell ⟨lagged⟩ behind the times; X stopped changing with the times.**

«Я... того мнения, что для человека мыслящего нет захолустья. По крайней мере я стараюсь, по возможности, не зарасти, как говорится, мохом, не отстать от века» (Тургенев 2). "...I'm of the opinion that for an active-minded person there is no such thing as a godforsaken spot. At any rate I try my hardest not to become moss-grown, as they say, and keep abreast of the times" (2a).

M-268 • МОЧА́ В ГО́ЛОВУ УДА́РИЛА кому highly coll, derog [VP_subj; this form only; the verb may take the initial position, otherwise fixed WO] s.o.'s behavior, actions etc are foolishly illogical or abnormal: X-у моча в голову ударила ≃ **X is ⟨must be⟩ crazy ⟨off his rocker, off his nut, out of his mind⟩; X must have lost his wits ⟨his marbles⟩.**

Как? возмущался Марлен Михайлович. Даже без всякого классового сознания, без ненависти к победоносным массам, а только лишь из чистого любопытства гнусный аристократишка отвернул исторический процесс, просто моча ему в голову ударила (Аксёнов 7). How could it be? the young Marlen Mikhailovich would ask himself, bewildered. Without a drop of class consciousness, without a trace of hatred for the victorious masses, with no more than a morbid sense of curiosity, this ratty little aristocrat changed the course of world history. He must have been crazy, out of his mind (7a).

M-269 • ЖЕВА́ТЬ МОЧА́ЛКУ ⟨МОЧА́ЛО⟩ highly coll, disapprov [VP; subj: human] to repeat one and the same thing in a tedious and irksome manner: X жевал мочалку ≃ **X droned on and on; X repeated the same (old) stuff ⟨thing⟩ over and over again; X rehashed the same thing again and again.**

Доклад он сделал совсем неинтересный, опять мочалку жевал. His paper wasn't at all interesting; he just repeated the same thing over and over again.

M-270 • МО́ЧИ ⟨МО́ЧЕНЬКИ folk⟩ (чьей) НЕТ ⟨НЕ СТА́ЛО⟩ substand [VP_subj/gen; usu. foll. by infin] s.o. absolutely does not have the emotional or physical strength, endurance etc (to do or tolerate sth.): мочи (X-овой) нет ≃ **X can't take**

⟨bear, stand, face⟩ it ⟨this⟩ (anymore); **X can't take any more; X hasn't (got) the strength (to do ⟨tolerate etc⟩ sth.); X has (got) no strength left.**

«Если б она [жизнь] всё по голове гладила, а то пристаёт, как, бывало, в школе к смирному ученику пристают забияки: то ущипнёт исподтишка, то вдруг нагрянет прямо со лба и обсыплет песком... мочи нет!» (Гончаров 1). "...If it [life] just went on patting me on the head, but it keeps pestering me just as naughty boys pester a quiet boy at school, pinching him on the sly or rushing up to him and throwing sand in his face—I can't stand it anymore!" (1a). ♦ «...Мочи нет, — сказал Ильин... — И чулки, и рубашка, и под меня подтекло. Пойду искать приюта. Кажется, дождик полегче» (Толстой 6). "I can't stand this anymore," said Ilyin..."Stockings, shirt, everything—soaked through! I'm off to look for another shelter. The rain seems to have lessened" (6a). ♦ «Господи, да что же это!.. Неужто всегда так вот?.. Моченьки моей больше нету... Господи!»... — «Сейчас ляжешь, Люба, легче будет... Потерпи, Люба, потерпи, мать за доктором побежала...» (Максимов 1). "Lord, what's happening...Can it always be like this?...I can't take any more...Lord!"... "You can lie down now, Lyuba, you'll feel better....Hold on, Lyuba, just hold on. Your mother's gone for the doctor..." (1a). ♦ Аксинья, морщась, выжала юбку, подхватила на плечи мешок с уловом, почти рысью пошла по косе. Григорий нёс бредень. Прошли саженей сто, Аксинья заохала: «Моченьки моей нету!» (Шолохов 2). Aksinya, frowning, wrung out her skirt, heaved the sack of fish on to her shoulder and set off almost at a run. Grigory carried the net. After some two hundred yards Aksinya began to cry out. "Oh, I haven't the strength!" (2a). ♦ «Мочи моей нет, — сказал он вдруг решительно, обращаясь к фельдфебелю, — вели в госпиталь отослать, ломота одолела...» (Толстой 7). "I've got no strength left," he added with sudden resolution, turning to the sergeant-major. "Tell them to send me to the hospital; I'm aching all over" (7b). ♦ «Сменила б, слышь, меня на маленько... Спать хочется, мочи нет!» (Войнович 2). [context transl] "Listen, could you take my place for a little while...I'm so sleepy, I can't keep my eyes open" (2a).

M-271 • **ЧТО ЕСТЬ ⟨БЫ́ЛО⟩ МО́ЧИ ⟨СИ́ЛЫ, СИЛ⟩; ВО ВСЮ МОЧЬ; ИЗО ВСЕЙ МО́ЧИ** all coll [AdvP or PrepP; these forms only; adv (intensif); more often used with impfv verbs; fixed WO] **1.** (to do sth.) with the utmost possible exertion, intensity: **with all one's might; as hard as one can; for all one is worth.**

...Остервенясь, он раз десять сразу, из всей мочи, дёрнул в колокольчик (Достоевский 3). ...Enraged, he pulled at the bell with all his might about a dozen times (3b).

2. бежать, мчаться и т. п. ~ (to run, race etc) very fast: **at full ⟨top⟩ speed; (at) full tilt; for all one is worth; as fast as one can; as fast as one's legs can carry one.**

Он подбежал к нам, остановился, сопел — как воздушный насос — и не мог сказать ни слова: должно быть, бежал во всю мочь (Замятин 1). He rushed up to us, stopped, his breath hissing like an air pump, unable to say a word. He must have run at top speed (1a). ♦ Дикий, отчаянный вопль донёсся оттуда. Потом увидели и самого Федьку. Бежит что есть мочи по пожне, кричит благим матом... (Абрамов 1). A wild desperate wail had issued forth. Then they saw Fedka himself, running for all he was worth across the field, yelling at the top of his lungs (1a). ♦ «Беги что есть мочи туда, — кричал он ей вслед, — и не оглядывайся...» (Гончаров 1). "Run there as fast as you can," he shouted after her, "and don't look round..." (1a). ♦ Я обернулся к площади и увидел Максима Максимыча, бегущего изо всей мочи... (Лермонтов 1). I turned towards the square and saw Maxim Maximych running as fast as his legs could carry him (1c).

3. кричать, орать, гудеть и т. п. ~ (to shout, yell, blare etc) very loudly: **at the top of one's voice ⟨lungs⟩; with all one's ⟨its⟩ might; [of a radio, television etc] (at) full blast.**

...Здесь петухи пели иначе, чем в Атамановке, они здесь действительно пели, а не горланили что есть мочи, как в его родной деревне (Распутин 2). ...The roosters crowed differently here than they did in Atamanovka, singing instead of screaming at the top of their lungs (2a). ♦ Отец захохотал изо всей мочи и начал трепать сына по плечу так, что и лошадь бы не выдержала (Гончаров 1). His father burst out laughing with all his might and began patting his son's shoulders so vigorously that a horse would not have stood it... (1a). ♦ Гармошки... заскрежетали во всю мочь... (Владимов 1). The accordions were bellowing away at full blast... (1a).

M-272 • **ТРЯХНУ́ТЬ МОШНО́Й ⟨КАРМА́НОМ, КАЗ-НО́Й⟩** substand [VP; subj: human] to spend a great deal of money, usu. in order to flaunt one's wealth: **X тряхнул мошной** ≃ **X flashed his wallet; X (really) threw (his) money around; X shot the works.**

M-273 • **РАЗВЯ́ЗЫВАТЬ/РАЗВЯЗА́ТЬ МОШНУ́ ⟨КО-ШЕ́ЛЬ⟩** substand [VP; subj: human or collect] to spend, part with some money (usu. unwillingly): **X развязал мошну** ≃ **X loosened his purse strings; X pulled out his wallet.**

M-274 • **ЖИВЫ́Е ⟨ХОДЯ́ЧИЕ⟩ МО́ЩИ** coll [NP; these forms only; usu. used in refer. to one person; often subj-compl with copula (subj: human); fixed WO] a very thin, emaciated person: **a walking skeleton; [in limited contexts] a ghost of one's former self.**

M-275 • **ПОКРЫ́Т(О) МРА́КОМ НЕИЗВЕ́СТНОСТИ** lit, often humor [AdjP; subj-compl with copula (subj: abstr, often это or a clause); fixed WO] sth. is concealed, not made known: это покрыто мраком неизвестности ≃ **this is veiled in obscurity; this is hidden behind a veil of obscurity; this is shrouded in secrecy ⟨mystery⟩.**

M-276 • **МУДРЕНО́ ЛИ (, что...)** [Invar; subj-compl with бытьø (subj: usu. a clause, occas. infin); usu. the main clause in a complex sent foll. by a что-clause] is it astonishing, strange?: **is it any wonder ⟨surprise⟩ (that...)?; is it (really) surprising (that...)?; no wonder (that...).**

Мудрено ли, что красноречие не цветёт при таких поощрениях! (Герцен 2). Is it any wonder that eloquence does not flourish under encouragement of this kind? (2a). ♦ Таковы были эти «великие партии», лицом к лицу с которыми очутился Дмитрий Павлыч Козелков. Мудрено ли, что, с непривычки, он почувствовал себя в этом обществе и маленьким и слабеньким (Салтыков-Щедрин 2). These were the great parties with whom Dmitry Pavlych Kozelkov now found himself face to face. No wonder that, being unaccustomed to this sort of thing, he felt small and insignificant in their society (2a).

M-277 • **НЕ МУДРЕНО́ (, что...)** [Invar; subj-compl with бытьø (subj: usu. a clause, occas. infin); usu. the main clause in a complex sent foll. by a что-clause; may be used as an indep. sent] it is natural, completely understandable: **(it's) no wonder (that...); (it's) small wonder (that...); it's not surprising (that...); it comes as no surprise (that...); it's only natural (that...); you can see why...**

Дядя Митя был и старше-то отца всего лет на десять, а что без зубов — то не мудрено, рассуждал Лёва... (Битов 2). Uncle Mitya was only about ten years older than Father, and if his teeth were gone it was no wonder, Lyova reasoned... (2a). ♦ Впервые в жизни навстречу мне двинулась такая откровенная, смелая, поражающая своею меткостью ложь — не мудрено, что я растерялась (Каверин 1). It was the first time in my life that I had encountered such a blank, barefaced lie, so striking in its neatness; no wonder that I got confused (1a). ♦ Консилиум четырёх шарлатанов на сцене шёл под величайший смех публики, и не мудрено, что ненависть к Мольеру среди врачей достигла после представления «Любви-целительницы» необыкновенной степени (Булгаков 5). The consultation of the four charlatans on the stage provoked endless outbursts of laughter in the theater, and it is small wonder that hatred of Molière among the physicians reached unprecedented proportions (5a). ♦ «Всё взять от партии и не отдать ей ничего… вот, собственно, в двух словах, цель новой оппозиции. И не мудрено, что она… разлагается…» (Алешковский 1). "No, just take everything from the party and don't give anything back.…In a word, that's the new opposition's aim. You can see why…it degenerates…" (1a).

M-278 • МУДРЁНОГО НЕТ; ЧТО МУДРЁНОГО *both coll* [VP~subj/gen~ (1st var.); VP~subj~ with быть∅ (2nd var.)] there is nothing surprising about sth., it is entirely possible: **it's no wonder; that comes as no surprise; it's not surprising; it's only natural.**

«…Нет ничего мудрёного, что лица, получившие такое воспитание, оказываются неспособными выражать свои мысли связно и последовательно…» (Салтыков-Щедрин 2). "It is…no wonder that persons who have received such an education find it difficult to express their thoughts with any clarity or coherence…" (2a).

M-279 • НА ВСЯКОГО ⟨КАЖДОГО⟩ МУДРЕЦА ДОВОЛЬНО ПРОСТОТЫ [saying] even intelligent people can lack foresight, do stupid things: ≃ **even a wise man stumbles.**

[Глумов:] Вас возмутил мой дневник. Как он попал к вам в руки, я не знаю. На всякого мудреца довольно простоты (Островский 9). [G.:] You feel hurt because of what I said about you in my diary. I don't know how you got hold of it, but even a wise man stumbles (9a).

M-280 • НЕ ВЕЛИКА МУДРОСТЬ [NP; Invar; usu. subj-compl with быть∅ (subj: infin or a clause), pres only; fixed WO] sth. (or doing sth.) is not difficult, not hard: **no great feat; not that difficult; not that hard; no big deal; it doesn't take a genius (to do sth.).**

У меня выиграть не велика мудрость, ты вот попробуй с настоящими шахматистами сразиться. Beating me is no great feat, but just try taking on a real chess player.

M-281 • НЕ МУДРСТВУЯ ЛУКАВО *lit* [Verbal Adv; Invar; adv; fixed WO] (to do sth.) plainly, unaffectedly, without excessive pondering, speculation etc: **simply and unpretentiously; without unnecessary embellishment; without being ⟨trying to be⟩ too clever about it; without undue theorizing.**

[author's usage] «Знаю, что не веруется, – а вы лукаво не мудрствуйте; отдайтесь жизни прямо, не рассуждая…» (Достоевский 3). "I know belief [in God] doesn't come easily – but don't be too clever about it, just give yourself directly to life, without reasoning…" (3c).

< Words of the chronicler Pimen in Aleksandr Pushkin's tragedy *Boris Godunov* («Борис Годунов»), 1831.

M-282 • МУЖ И ⟨ДА⟩ ЖЕНА – ОДНА САТАНА [saying] a husband and wife have the same interests, desires etc: ≃ **like husband, like wife.**

M-283 • ДРУГАЯ ⟨ИНАЯ, НЕ ТА⟩ МУЗЫКА *highly coll, often humor* [NP; often subj-compl with быть∅ (subj: это); usu. this WO] (that is) something else entirely, entirely different: **another matter (altogether); a different ⟨an entirely different⟩ story ⟨thing⟩; a horse of a different color.**

M-284 • ПРОПАДАТЬ, ТАК С МУЗЫКОЙ! *highly coll* [sent; Invar; fixed WO] (said when a person embarks upon sth. risky) if s.o. is fated to suffer defeat, failure (even death), then he should do so in an impressive way (causing as much damage to the opposite side as possible): **if I am ⟨we are etc⟩ going to fail ⟨die etc⟩, I ⟨we etc⟩ should do it in style; if I am ⟨we are etc⟩ going to fail ⟨die etc⟩, I ⟨we etc⟩ want to go out in a blaze of glory.**

«Михаил Сидорович, задумал я большое дело, буду с вами о нём говорить. Пропадать, так с музыкой!» (Гроссман 2). "I've been thinking about something important, Mikhail Sidorovich. I need to talk to you. If we're going to die, I think we should do it in style" (2a).

M-285 • КЛАСТЬ/ПОЛОЖИТЬ ⟨ПЕРЕЛОЖИТЬ⟩ НА МУЗЫКУ ⟨НА НОТЫ⟩ *что* [VP; subj: human] to write music for some verses or text: X положил на музыку стихотворение Y ≃ **X set ⟨put⟩ poem Y to music.**

M-286 • МУКА МУЧЕНИЧЕСКАЯ [NP; sing only; fixed WO] very intense suffering or torture: **unbearable suffering; sheer torture; absolute misery ⟨torment⟩.**

M-287 • ПЕРЕМЕЛЕТСЯ – МУКА БУДЕТ [saying] things will smooth out, all troubles will pass (usu. said to encourage a person who is upset by what is happening, who is experiencing difficulties etc): ≃ **it will all come out in the wash; it will all come (out) right in the end; it will all work out in the end.**

…Николай принёс мне обед, и когда я разговорился с ним о том, что я наделал и что ожидает меня, он сказал: «Эх, сударь! Не тужите, перемелется – мука будет» (Толстой 2). …Nikolai brought me my dinner, and when I got into conversation with him about what I had done and what awaited me, he said: "Ah, master, don't brood about it, it will all come out in the wash" (2b). ♦ «Что ж так тревожиться, Илья Ильич? – сказал Алексеев. – Никогда не надо предаваться отчаянию: перемелется – мука будет» (Гончаров 1). "Why worry?" said Alexeyev. "A man must never give way to despair. It will all come right in the end" (1a).

M-288 • МУКИ ТАНТАЛА; ТАНТАЛОВЫ МУКИ *both lit* [NP; pl only; fixed WO (1st var.)] suffering caused by the knowledge that some desired object, goal is within reach yet unattainable: **the torments of Tantalus.**

До мельчайших подробностей помню день 1 сентября 1935 года, когда я, снятая партколлегией с преподавательской работы, заперлась в своей комнате, испытывая поистине танталовы муки (Гинзбург 1). I remember in the utmost detail the 1st of September 1935, when, having been dismissed from my teaching job, I shut myself up in my room and went through the torments of Tantalus (1a).

< In Greek mythology *Tantalus*, a king of Phrygia, was condemned by the gods for his crimes to sit chin-deep in water without ever being able to reach the food and drink that appeared in front of him.

M-289 • картошка В МУНДИРЕ ⟨В МУНДИРАХ⟩ [PrepP; these forms only; nonagreeing postmodif or adv] (potatoes cooked) unpeeled: **with the skin(s) on; in their skins ⟨jackets⟩.**

M-290 • НИ МУР-МУР *highly coll* [Invar; predic] **1.** [subj: human or animal] to be silent, not emit a sound: X – ни мур-мур ≃ **there hasn't been a peep ⟨a squeak⟩ out of X; X hasn't made a sound.**

Что-то у детей подозрительно тихо. Закрылись у себя в комнате час назад — и ни мур-мур. The kids are suspiciously quiet. They locked themselves in their room an hour ago, and there hasn't been a peep out of them since.

2. ~ *в чём* [subj: human] to understand, know absolutely nothing (about sth.): X в Y-е ни мур-мур ≃ **X doesn't know a damn(ed) thing about Y; X doesn't know beans ⟨the first thing⟩ about Y; X doesn't have the faintest ⟨foggiest⟩ idea about Y.**

Перегорели пробки, а сам я их починить не могу, я в этом деле ни мур-мур. The fuses blew, but I can't fix them. I don't know beans about that sort of thing.

М-291 • МУРА́ШКИ БЕ́ГАЮТ ⟨БЕГУ́Т⟩/ЗАБЕ́ГАЛИ ⟨ПО́ЛЗАЮТ, ПОЛЗУ́Т/ПОПОЛЗЛИ́, ПОБЕЖА́ЛИ, ПРОБЕЖА́ЛИ, ПОШЛИ́, ЗАПО́ЛЗАЛИ⟩ ПО СПИНЕ́ ⟨ПО ТЕ́ЛУ, ПО КО́ЖЕ⟩ (у кого) *coll* [VP$_{subj}$] s.o. feels a chill caused by fear, anxiety, the cold etc: у X-а мурашки бегают по спине ≃ **shivers run ⟨a chill runs⟩ up ⟨down, up and down⟩ X's spine; X has (got) shivers running up ⟨down, up and down⟩ his spine; it sends shivers up ⟨down, up and down⟩ X's spine; it gives X the creeps ⟨the shudders⟩; X feels tingles down his ⟨the⟩ spine; it makes X's skin crawl; it makes X's flesh creep.**

«Когда эта комната останется пустой, куда я... пойду поговорить о политике? У меня мурашки бегают по спине!» (Федин 1). "When this room is left empty, where shall I go...to talk politics? I've got shivers running up my spine!" (1a). ♦ «Легионеры! — каркнул он голосом, от которого у Гая пошли мурашки по коже. — Перед нами дело» (Стругацкие 2). "Legionnaires!" he bellowed in a voice that sent shivers up and down Guy's spine. "You have a job to do" (2a). ♦ «Я как подумаю, что я должен с ней вдвоём остаться, так у меня мурашки по спине бегают» (Эренбург 2). "When I think of having to stay alone with her, it gives me the shudders" (2a). ♦ И вместе с этим вопросом догадка и мурашки по спине: постой, да не мертвец ли это, поставленный на попа! (Искандер 4). And with this question a guess, and more tingles down the spine: Wait! Was this a dead man, propped upright? (4a).

М-292 • РАЗВОДИ́ТЬ МУРУ́ *slang* [VP; subj: human; often infin with хватит, перестань etc and in questions] to talk about, pay too much attention to, or devote too much time to insignificant matters: X муру разводит ≃ **X is wasting his time on that nonsense ⟨garbage⟩.**

М-293 • ДО БЕ́ЛЫХ МУХ *coll* [PrepP; Invar; adv; fixed WO] until the weather turns freezing and the snow begins to fall: **till the snow falls ⟨flies⟩; till the snowflakes fall.**

«Когда на Синельгу?» — заговорил Егорша... «Скоро». — «...Говорил — просись в кадру. Ну, ума нету — ишачь с бабами до белых мух» (Абрамов 1). "When do you leave for Sinelga?" asked Egorsha....“Soon.” "...I told you to ask for a permanent job. Well, if you don't have the gumption, you can just drudge away with the women till the snowflakes fall" (1a).

М-294 • КАК СО́ННАЯ МУ́ХА *coll* [как + NP; nom only; adv] languidly, unhurriedly: **like a sleepy fly.**

И в то утро она не дала мне спать... Потом мы, как сонные мухи... завтракали на веранде (Лимонов 1). Even that morning she wouldn't let me sleep....Then, like sleepy flies...we had breakfast on the veranda (1a).

М-295 • КАКА́Я МУ́ХА УКУСИ́ЛА кого *coll* [VP$_{subj}$; Invar; usu. used as a question or relative clause; fixed WO] s.o. is annoyed, angry, in a bad mood, behaving strangely without any apparent reason: какая муха укусила X-а? ≃ **what's bugging ⟨eating⟩ X?; what's got(ten) into X?; what's come over X?; what's with X?**

Однажды я неожиданно застал их в ожесточённом споре. Вся семья, включая старую бабку, спорила о Ленине... На следующий день зашёл я к ним опять — и опять застал их в споре о Ленине. Что за чёрт, какая их муха укусила? (Буковский 1). One day I was surprised to find the entire family, including the ancient grandmother, engaged in a violent argument about Lenin....The following day I saw them again, and again they were arguing about Lenin. What the devil had got into them? (1a).

М-296 • будто ⟨словно, точно⟩ МУ́ХА УКУСИ́ЛА кого *coll* [VP$_{subj}$; Invar; fixed WO] s.o. is acting so strangely that it seems as though sth. has suddenly happened to him: X-а будто муха укусила ≃ **something is ⟨must be⟩ bugging ⟨eating⟩ X; something has got(ten) into X; something has come over X.**

М-297 • СЛЫ́ШНО, КАК МУ́ХА ПРОЛЕТИ́Т *coll* [complex sent; fixed WO] there is absolute quiet: **you could hear ⟨have heard⟩ a pin drop.**

М-298 • БЕ́ЛЫЕ МУ́ХИ [NP; pl only; most often subj; fixed WO] very light flakes of snow that fall in early winter: **(the first) snowflakes (of winter); (the first) white flakes (of snow).**

М-299 • ДЕ́ЛАТЬ/СДЕ́ЛАТЬ ИЗ МУ́ХИ СЛОНА́ *coll, disapprov* [VP; subj: human; the verb may take the final position, otherwise fixed WO] to make sth. unimportant seem important, exaggerate sth.: X делает из мухи слона ≃ **X makes a mountain out of a molehill.**

...На пляже разгорелась дискуссия. Влад, услышав нападки [Ольги на Сергея], ринулся товарища защищать... [Рита] сказала, что Ольга по своему обыкновению делает из мухи слона (Трифонов 3). On the beach, when Vlad heard her [Olga] attacking him [Sergei], he rushed to his friend's defense....[Rita] said that Olga was, as usual, making a mountain out of a molehill (3a).

М-300 • ЕДЯ́Т ЕГО́ ⟨тебя и т. п.⟩ МУ́ХИ! *substand* [Interj; these forms only; fixed WO] used jocularly to express annoyance, surprise, reluctant admiration etc: **darn him ⟨you etc⟩!; doggone him ⟨you etc⟩!; well, ain't he ⟨you etc⟩ something!**

М-301 • КАК МУ́ХИ мрут, дохнут *highly coll* [как + NP; Invar; adv] (people die) in great numbers: **(drop) like flies.**

«И вы говорите, что у него, точно, люди умирают в большом количестве?» — «Как мухи мрут» (Гоголь 3). "Do you really mean that his people are dying in great numbers?" "They're dropping like flies" (3e).

М-302 • МУ́ХИ ДО́ХНУТ ⟨МРУТ⟩ *coll* [VP$_{subj}$; these forms only; fixed WO] it is unbearably boring (at some place): **you're bored to death ⟨to tears⟩; you climb the walls from boredom; you (could) die of boredom.**

«Пойдёшь со мной к Силиным?» — «Нет, я лучше телевизор посмотрю. У них всегда скука, мухи дохнут». "Are you coming to the Silins' with me?" "No, I'd rather watch TV. It's always so dull there—you could die of boredom."

М-303 • МУ́ХИ НЕ ОБИ́ДИТ *coll, approv* [VP; subj: human; usu. fut, occas. past; fixed WO] one is very gentle, inoffensive: X мухи не обидит ≃ **X wouldn't hurt ⟨harm⟩ a fly.**

«Ты видишь ли, я его [князя Андрея] давно знаю, и Машеньку, твою золовку, люблю. Золовки — колотовки, ну а уж эта мухи не обидит» (Толстой 5). "I have known him [Prince Andrei] a long time, you see, and I am very fond of Masha, your future sister-in-law. Sisters-in-law are troublemakers they say. But Masha wouldn't hurt a fly" (5a).

М-304 • ПОД МУ́ХОЙ *highly coll* [PrepP; Invar; usu. subj-compl with copula (subj: human)] in an intoxicated (usu. mildly intoxicated) state: X был под мухой ≃ **X was under the influence; X was (a little) tipsy ⟨high, tight⟩; X had ⟨had⟩ one ⟨a few⟩ too many; X was feeling good ⟨no pain⟩.**

Он же под мухой, ему нельзя садиться за руль. He's a little tipsy—he shouldn't be allowed behind the wheel. ♦ ...Блин кто-то под мухой на голову надел вместо кепки (Евтушенко 2). ...Someone who'd had one too many put a *blin* on his head instead of a cap (2a).

M-305 • как ⟨будто, словно, точно⟩ МУ́ХУ ПРОГЛОТИ́Л *coll, usu. humor* [VP; subj: human; past only; fixed WO] one looks displeased, has a sullen look: X точно муху проглотил ≃ **X has a sour puss; X looks like ⟨as if⟩ he has just eaten a lemon.**

M-306 • МУ́ХУ РАЗДАВИ́ТЬ ⟨ЗАШИБИ́ТЬ, ЗАДАВИ́ТЬ⟩ *obsoles, substand* [VP; subj: human; often infin with любит, хорошо бы, можно etc; fixed WO] to drink some alcohol: X любит муху раздавить ≃ **X likes to have a shot (of vodka etc); X likes to have a drop (of wine etc); X likes to have ⟨take⟩ a (little) nip.**

M-307 • БЕЗ МЫ́ЛА В ДУ́ШУ ЛЕЗТЬ/ВЛЕЗТЬ *highly coll, derog* [VP; subj: human, usu. sing; fixed WO] to (try to) gain s.o.'s favor or trust by cunning, flattery etc: X без мыла в душу лезет ≃ **X is falling all over himself to make s.o. like ⟨accept etc⟩ him; X is worming his way into s.o.'s good graces.**

M-308 • (весь) В МЫ́ЛЕ *highly coll* [PrepP; Invar; usu. subj-compl with copula (subj: human) or detached modif] very tired and sweaty from exertion: **covered ⟨dripping⟩ with sweat.**

M-309 • кого НА МЫ́ЛО! *highly coll, rude* [Interj; Invar] (a demand that s.o. who cannot handle a job or task be fired, expelled etc) out, away!: X-а на мыло! ≃ **get rid of X ⟨the bum⟩!; can X!; [in refer. to an athlete] send X to the showers!**

M-310 • ЧИТА́ТЬ/ПРОЧИТА́ТЬ МЫ́СЛИ чьи, кого [VP; subj: human] to know, be able to discern what another is thinking: X читает Y-овы мысли ≃ **X reads Y's mind ⟨thoughts⟩; X is a mind reader.**

...Я могу узнать время... например, рассматривая свою руку, усыпанную уже довольно крупными коричневыми пятнышками старости... и я вижу неотвратимое разрушение своего тела, и когда я протягивал ей свою руку, то подумал: «Без четверти вечность». Вероятно, она прочитала мои мысли, потому что сказала: «Сорок лет» — и ввела меня в свой дом (Катаев 2). ...I can get a sense of time...by looking, for example, at my hand, already covered with the large brown spots of old age, and thus actually seeing the relentless deterioration of my body. When I held out my hand to her, I thought "It's a quarter to eternity." She must have read my thoughts, because she said: "It's forty years." Then she led me into her house (2a).

M-311 • ЗА́ДНЯЯ МЫСЛЬ; often БЕЗ (ВСЯ́КОЙ) ЗА́ДНЕЙ МЫ́СЛИ ⟨БЕЗ (ВСЯ́КИХ) ЗА́ДНИХ МЫ́СЛЕЙ⟩ [NP, subj or obj (1st var.) or PrepP, adv (2nd var.); fixed WO] a secret intention, design: **ulterior ⟨hidden⟩ motive;** ‖ без всякой задней мысли ≃ **without any ulterior ⟨hidden⟩ motive(s) (whatsoever); without the slightest ⟨least⟩ ulterior motive; without the least hidden motive.**

Я тоже на неё [тётку] сильно обижался, даже не на окрик, а на то, что меня заподозрили в «нарочном», а я был совсем без задней мысли, никогда бы ничего не сделал назло или нарочно... (Битов 1). I, too, was terribly offended by her [Auntie]. Not for yelling at me, but for suspecting me of "doing it on purpose." when I hadn't the slightest ulterior motive and would never do anything

bad on purpose (1a). ♦ [Иван Фёдорович] наконец ему ответил, но не свысока-учтиво, как боялся ещё накануне Алёша, а скромно и сдержанно, с видимою предупредительностью и, по-видимому, без малейшей задней мысли (Достоевский 1). [Ivan Fyodorovich] answered at last, not with polite condescension, as Alyosha had feared the day before, but modestly and reservedly, with apparent consideration and, evidently, without the least ulterior motive (1a). ♦ И дальше [офицер] принимался рассказывать, как был на фронте и какие видел зверства. Говорил он всё это безо всякой задней мысли, вовсе не с тем, чтоб напугать меня или «перевоспитать», а просто по доброте душевной (Буковский 1). And then he [the officer] would start telling me about his experiences at the front and all the atrocities he had seen. He said all these things without the least hidden motive, not to scare me or "re-educate" me in any way, but simply out of the goodness of his heart (1a).

M-312 • НАВОДИ́ТЬ/НАВЕСТИ́ кого НА МЫСЛЬ (какую) [VP; subj: human or abstr; often foll. by a что-clause; usu. this WO] to suggest a certain idea to s.o., influence s.o. to think a certain way: X навёл Y-а на [AdjP] мысль ≃ **X put a [AdjP] thought ⟨idea⟩ into Y's head ⟨mind⟩;** ‖ X навёл Y-а на мысль, что... ≃ **X put the thought ⟨the idea⟩ into Y's mind that...; X prompted Y to think ⟨suggest, conclude etc⟩ that...; thing X gave rise to the thought that...; [in limited contexts] thing X led Y to the conclusion that...**

«Я говорю, — прогнусил [Азазелло], — что тебя хорошо было бы утопить». — «Будь милосерден, Азазелло, — ответил ему кот, — и не наводи моего повелителя на эту мысль» (Булгаков 9). "I say," drawled Azazello, "that you ought to be drowned." "Be merciful, Azazello," the cat replied, "and don't put such thoughts into my master's head" (9b). ♦ Новеллистичность поэзии Ахматовой навела Мандельштама на мысль, что её генезис нужно искать не в поэзии, а в русской психологической прозе (Мандельштам 2). It was this "novelistic" quality of Akhmatova's verse which prompted M[andelstam] to suggest that its genesis must be sought not in poetry at all, but in Russian psychological prose fiction (2a). ♦ ...Первым поводом его к отречению его от либерализма было появление гласных судов и земских управ. Это навело его на мысль, что существуют какие-то корни и нити, которые надобно разыскать и истребить... (Салтыков-Щедрин 2). ...The main reason why he had renounced his liberal faith was the institution of trials by jury and rural councils. This led him to the conclusion that there existed certain roots and threads which had to be found and destroyed (2a).

M-313 • РАСТЕКА́ТЬСЯ МЫ́СЛЬЮ ПО ДРЕ́ВУ *obs* [VP; subj: human; fixed WO] to speak about sth. at great length, with unnecessary details and irrelevant digressions: X растекается мыслью по древу ≃ **X's speech follows a circuitous path; X speaks in a circumlocutory manner.**

< From *The Tale of Igor's Campaign* («Слово о полку Игореве»), 12th cent., regarded as the greatest single piece of medieval Russian literature.

M-314 • СОБИРА́ТЬСЯ/СОБРА́ТЬСЯ С МЫ́СЛЯМИ [VP; subj: human] to regain control over one's thoughts and one's ability to concentrate on the matter at hand (often after having been frightened, having experienced some strong emotion etc): X собрался с мыслями ≃ **X collected ⟨gathered⟩ his thoughts.**

«А сейчас я... помолчу, соберусь с мыслями, попробую отогнать страхи» (Пастернак 1). "Now...I'll keep quiet and collect my thoughts and try to forget my anxieties" (1a).

M-315 • В МЫ́СЛЯХ называть, произносить и т. п. [PrepP; Invar; adv] (to say, name etc sth.) mentally: **in one's mind; inwardly; to oneself.**

В мыслях она произносила все те слова, которые не решалась ему сказать при встрече. In her mind she said everything that she couldn't bring herself to say to him in person.

M-316 • ДЕРЖА́ТЬ В МЫ́СЛЯХ [VP; subj: human] **1.** ~ *кого-что* to remember, think about s.o. or sth. constantly: X держит в мыслях Y-a ≃ **X keeps thinking about Y; X dwells on thing Y; X returns ⟨keeps returning⟩ to thoughts of Y.**

2. *Neg* **в мыслях не держать** *что* not (even) to have had some idea, the idea to do sth., or the intention of doing sth.: X Y-a (и) в мыслях не держал ≃ **it never (even) occurred to X (to do Y); X never (even) thought of doing Y; the thought ⟨Y⟩ never (even) crossed X's mind.**

«Я. Вы позволяете себе поучать меня... *Катакази.* Помилуйте, и в мыслях не держал» (Окуджава 2). *I:* You are permitting yourself to lecture me. *Katakazi:* Forgive me, it never even occurred to me (2a).

M-317 • И В МЫ́СЛЯХ ⟨В УМЕ́⟩ НЕТ *у кого чего* или *что (с)делать;* **В МЫ́СЛЯХ НЕ ИМЕ́ТЬ** *чего,* less often *кого* [VP; impers (1st var.) or with subj: human (2nd var.); pres or past; fixed WO] it is not and never was s.o.'s intent to do sth., some idea or the idea to do sth. never came into s.o.'s head: у X-a и в мыслях не было Y-a ⟨сделать Y⟩ ≃ **Y ⟨the thought of (doing) Y⟩ never (even) occurred to X; Y ⟨doing Y⟩ never (even) crossed X's mind; the thought (of doing Y) never entered X's mind; Y ⟨doing Y⟩ was the last thing that would (ever) enter X's mind; Y ⟨doing Y⟩ was the furthest thing from X's mind; X never (even) thought of Y ⟨doing Y⟩;** [in limited contexts] **X did not have the remotest intention of doing Y.**

«А Кухарский, по-твоему, кто?» — «Крыса-то? Русский, конечно», — сказал Лёва... «Еврей он, еврей. А Москвин, по-твоему, не еврей?» Лёва от души рассмеялся. «Ну уж ладно, Кухарский... Но — Москвин! Мы его, правда, все Мойшей звали. Но ведь это так, для смеха, ни у кого и в мыслях не было...» (Битов 2). "Tell me—what do you think Kukharsky is?" "You mean the Rat? Russian, of course," Lyova said....."He's a Jew, a Jew. And Moskvin, you think he's not a Jew?" Lyova laughed heartily. "Kukharsky—okay. But Moskvin! It's true we always called him Moshe. But that was nothing, a joke, it never crossed anyone's mind he was..." (2a). ♦ «Позволь и тебя спросить...: считаешь ты и меня, как Дмитрия, способным пролить кровь Езопа, ну, убить его, а?» — «Что ты, Иван! Никогда и в мыслях этого у меня не было!» (Достоевский 1). "...Let me ask you: do you consider me capable, like Dmitri, of shedding Aesop's blood, well, of killing him? Eh?" "What are you saying, Ivan! The thought never entered my mind!" (1a). ♦ Не отрицаю, мама была ревнивая, но не потому, что отец изменял ей — у него этого и в мыслях не было... (Рыбаков 1). My mother was a jealous woman, I wouldn't deny that, but not because father was unfaithful, that was the last thing that would ever enter his mind... (1a). ♦ ...Монтозье обнял его [Мольера] и в самых лучших выражениях стал благодарить его, заявляя, что ему лестно было служить оригиналом для портрета такого благородного человека, как Альцест... Интереснее всего то, что Мольер, создавая своего Альцеста, даже и в мыслях не имел герцога Монтозье (Булгаков 5). Montausier embraced him [Molière] with the warmest thanks, declaring that he was flattered to have been the model for the portrait of so noble a man as Alceste....The most interesting thing in all this was that, in creating his Alceste, Molière had never thought of Montausier at all (5a). ♦ «...В моих словах, кажется, ничего не было такого... у меня и в мыслях не было оскорбить вас... Простите меня» (Тургенев 3). "Surely there was nothing in my words that....I hadn't the remotest intention of insulting you....Please forgive me" (3b).

M-318 • НЕ МЫТЬЁМ, ТАК КА́ТАНЬЕМ *highly coll* [NP_{instrum}; Invar; adv; fixed WO] (to achieve or try to achieve sth.) by resorting to any means necessary, one way or another: **by hook or by crook; by fair means or foul;** [in limited contexts] **beg, borrow, or steal.**

«Они-то как раз и сделали так, что отменили тридцать лет моей жизни, вернув меня в прежнюю точку. Мол, это ошибка, что я жил эти тридцать лет так, как я их жил. А я их уже не проживу иначе. Не мытьём — так катаньем: не вышло отменить в тебе твою жизнь, посадив, отменим — отпустив» (Битов 2). "That's just what they did, they voided thirty years of my life, by returning me to the previous point. It's a mistake, they say, that I lived those thirty years the way I did. I'm not about to live them over again differently. By hook or by crook: it didn't work to void your life by putting you away, we'll void it by releasing you" (2a).

M-319 • НЕ МЫЧИ́Т, НЕ ТЕ́ЛИТСЯ *highly coll, rather rude* [VP; subj: human; usu. 3rd pers; pres only; fixed WO] one does not act in a situation where some action is necessary, expected of him etc: X не мычит (и) не телится ≃ **X is dragging his feet; X is hanging back;** [in limited contexts] **X is sitting on the fence.**

M-320 • ПОД МЫ́ШКОЙ ⟨ПОД МЫ́ШКАМИ⟩ *нести, держать что и т. п.;* **ПОД МЫ́ШКУ ⟨ПОД МЫ́ШКИ⟩** *класть, совать что и т. п.* [PrepP; these forms only; adv] (to carry, hold, put, tuck sth.) under the inner part of the upper arm: **under one's arm.**

Наконец отец взял под мышку свои чертежи и уехал работать на Горьковский автозавод (Кузнецов 1). Father at last gathered his blueprints under his arm and set off for a job at the Gorky Automobile Plant (1a).

M-321 • КАК МЫШЬ[1] *притаиться, затаиться и т. п. coll* [как + NP; Invar; usu. adv] (to hide, sit etc) very quietly: **(as) quiet as a mouse.**

В день, когда он [Мандельштам] сочинял эти стихи, я не догадалась, что он работает, потому что он лежал тихо, как мышь (Мандельштам 1). On the day he [Mandelstam] was composing this poem, I didn't realize he was working, because he was lying as quiet as a mouse (1a).

M-322 • КАК МЫШЬ[2] *мокрый coll* [как + NP; Invar; modif] extremely (wet): **sopping wet; drenched; soaked through; soaked (to the skin); (look) like a drowned rat.**

M-323 • КАК МЫШЬ НА КРУПУ́ *надулся, дуется coll* [как + NP; Invar; adv; fixed WO] (s.o. looks) offended, (is) dissatisfied with sth.: X дуется как мышь на крупу ≃ **X looks ⟨is⟩ sullen; X is sulking ⟨pouting, moping⟩; X is in a pout; X has pulled ⟨made⟩ a long face.**

«Ты погляди на него, он же никогда не улыбнётся. Всё время, как мышь на крупу, дуется» (Копелев 1). "Take a look at him, he never smiles. All the time, he's so sullen, always huffy" (1a).

M-324 • беден, нищ, КАК ЦЕРКО́ВНАЯ МЫШЬ ⟨КРЫ́СА⟩ *coll* [как + NP; Invar; modif; fixed WO] very, extremely (poor): **(as) poor as a church mouse.**

Служащий метро Обри был на редкость уродлив и нищ, как церковная крыса... (Эренбург 4). Aubry, a subway employee, was exceedingly ugly and poor as a church mouse (4a). ♦ [author's usage] Парень, должно быть, нищ, как монастырская крыса... (Аксёнов 12). The guy must be as poor as a church mouse... (12a).

M-325 • НА МЯКИ́НЕ НЕ ПРОВЕДЁШЬ *кого highly coll* [VP; neg pfv fut, gener. 2nd pers sing only; fixed WO] you cannot trick, outwit s.o.: X-a на мякине не проведёшь ≃ **you can't fool X; you have to get up pretty early in the morning to fool X; you can't pull the wool over X's eyes.**

«Реваз Давидович — умный человек. Его на мякине не проведёшь...» (Чернёнок 2). "Revaz Davidovich is a smart man. You can't fool him..." (2a).

< From the saying «Старого воробья на мякине не проведёшь» "He (she etc) is too old a bird to be caught with chaff"; see B-268. «Мякина» is the husks and stalks separated in the winnowing and threshing of grain and certain other crops.

M-326 • ПУ́ШЕЧНОЕ МЯ́СО [NP; fixed WO] soldiers considered as expendable war material: **cannon fodder.**

«Он [Сталин] ещё надеялся на массы, на классовую борьбу, на китайское пушечное мясо» (Копелев 1). "He [Stalin] still counted on the masses, on the class struggle, on the Chinese cannon fodder" (1a).

M-327 • С МЯ́СОМ вырвать, оторвать *что coll* [PrepP; Invar; adv] (to tear, rip a button, hook etc off) together with a piece of the material to which it is attached: **along with (some of) the material; taking a piece of the fabric with it.**

Н

Н-1 • **БИТЬ/ЗАБИ́ТЬ ⟨УДАРЯ́ТЬ/УДА́РИТЬ⟩ В НАБА́Т** *lit;* **БИТЬ НАБА́Т** *obs* [VP; subj: human; often infin with надо or imper] to draw general attention persistently to sth. alarming, to impending danger: X бьёт в набат ≃ **X sounds ⟨raises⟩ the alarm.**

Считая себя обязанным уберечь Россию от всеобщей, как он выражался устно, евреизации, а письменно – сионизации, Васька бил в набат, писал письма в ЦК КПСС, в Президиум Верховного Совета СССР, в Союз писателей, в Академию наук и в газеты (Войнович 6). Considering it his moral obligation to guard Russia from what he referred to in private as universal Hebraization (but in print, Zionization), Vaska sounded the alarm. He wrote letters to the Communist Party Central Committee, the Presidium of the Supreme Soviet of the USSR, the Writer's Union, the Academy of Sciences, and the newspapers (6a).

Н-2 • **БИТКО́М НАБИ́ТЬ** *что (кем-чем);* **БИТКО́М НАБИ́ТЬСЯ** *куда* [VP; subj: human; usu. past passive Part битком набит(ый)] (often refers to a large number of people in some place) to overfill some place (space, container etc): место X битком набито (Y-ами) ≃ **place X is filled ⟨full⟩ to overflowing ⟨to capacity⟩ (with Ys); X is packed tight (with Ys); place X is packed ⟨jammed⟩ to the rafters (with Ys); X is jammed full (of Ys); X is crammed ⟨crowded, jam-packed, bursting (at the seams)⟩ (with Ys); X is chock-full (of Ys).**

...[Пастернак] читал «Антония и Клеопатру». Небольшое помещение битком набито... (Гладков 1). ...[Pasternak] gave a reading of *Antony and Cleopatra.* The small room was packed tight with people... (1a). ♦ И вот мы в университетской аудитории. Это аудитория из небольших, она набита битком... (Олеша 3). And so there we were in the university lecture hall. It was one of the smaller ones, and it was jammed full... (3a). ♦ «Слыхали мы эти песни! Владимирская тюрьма битком набита, а вы всё о Промысле блажите» (Максимов 3). "We've heard all that before. Vladimir jail is crammed with prisoners and you go driveling on about Providence" (3a).

Н-3 • **НАБО́Р СЛОВ** [NP; sing only; fixed WO] a combination of words or phrases that the speaker considers to be devoid of meaning or substance: **mere ⟨empty⟩ verbiage; empty words.**

Н-4 • **ВО ВСЕЙ ⟨СВОЕ́Й⟩ НАГОТЕ́** представить, изобразить *что,* предстать *перед кем* и т. п. *lit* [PrepP; these forms only; adv or nonagreeing postmodif; своей can take the final position, otherwise fixed WO] (to present sth., portray sth., sth. appears etc) exactly as sth. is in reality, not positively embellished in any way: **unvarnished and unadorned; (paint sth.) in its true colors.**

Н-5 • **В НАГРА́ДУ** [PrepP; Invar; adv] as an expression of s.o.'s gratitude (for sth.), as recompense (for sth.): **in ⟨as a⟩ reward; as a token of s.o.'s appreciation; in thanks.**

Н-6 • **В НАДЕ́ЖДЕ** *на что;* **В НАДЕ́ЖДЕ (, что...)** [PrepP; Invar; the resulting PrepP is adv] wishing for and expecting sth.: **hoping for ⟨that, to⟩; with the hope that; in hopes that; in the hope of ⟨that⟩.**

«Я только умоляю вас, сударыня, меня выслушать, дайте мне только две минуты свободного разговора... Я ужасно спешу!..» – прокричал истерически Митя, почувствовав, что она сейчас опять начнёт говорить, и в надежде перекричать её (Достоевский 1). "I only beg you, madame, to listen to me, allow me just two minutes to speak freely....I'm in a terrible hurry!" Mitya shouted hysterically, feeling that she was about to start talking again and hoping to outshout her (1a). ♦ Они [молодые интеллигентные люди] несли куда следует стихи Мандельштама или доносы на сослуживца в надежде, что за это напечатают их собственные опусы или повысят их по службе (Мандельштам 1). They [young people of education] took copies of M[andelstam]'s verse to the police, or denounced colleagues in the hope of getting their own writings published, or of being promoted in their work (1a).

Н-7 • **ПИТА́ТЬ НАДЕ́ЖДУ ⟨-ы⟩** *(на что)* [VP; subj: human] to have a hope: X питает надежду (на Y) ≃ **X harbors ⟨cherishes, entertains⟩ the hope (that Y will happen); X hopes for Y.**

Инстинкт самосохранения был слишком силён, именно тот инстинкт, который заставляет осуждённого на казнь питать надежды, которым никогда не суждено сбыться (Салтыков-Щедрин 2). [context transl] His instinct for self-preservation was too strong, the same instinct which fills a man sentenced to death with hopes which are destined never to be fulfilled (2a).

Н-8 • **ВОЗЛАГА́ТЬ НАДЕ́ЖДЫ** *на кого-что* [VP; subj: human] to expect sth. good, favorable (from some person or thing): X возлагает надежды на Y-а ≃ **X places (his) hope in ⟨on⟩ Y; X sets ⟨pins, puts⟩ his hopes on Y; [in limited contexts] X's hope is that...**

Н. И. Грудинина вновь рассказала о том, как Бродский занимался в её семинаре молодых поэтов и какие надежды она возлагает на него... (Эткинд 1). N. I. Grudinina recounted once again how Brodsky had worked in her seminar for young poets and what hopes she had placed in him... (1a). ♦ «С ним [Мандельштамом] поступили очень милостиво: у нас и не за такое расстреливают»... Он [Винавер] тогда же предупредил меня, чтобы мы не возлагали лишних надежд на высочайшую милость: «Её могут отобрать, как только уляжется шум»... (Мандельштам 1). "He [Mandelstam] got off very lightly: people are shot for much less than that." At the same time he [Vinaver] warned me not to place too much hope in mercy from on high: "It might be withdrawn as soon as the fuss has died down," he said (1a). ♦ ...Они хотят показать Гитлеру, что в СССР есть политические силы... возлагающие на войну все свои надежды, чтобы свалить нынешнее руководство... (Рыбаков 2). ...*They* wanted Hitler to know that there were political forces in the U.S.S.R. that...were putting [all] their hopes on war to overthrow the present leadership... (2a). ♦ ...Мы возлагали все надежды на то, что арест [Мандельштама] вызван местью за пощёчину... Алексею Толстому (Мандельштам 1). ...Our main hope was that M[andelstam]'s arrest was indeed an act of vengeance for the slap in the face given to Alexei Tolstoi (1a).

Н-9 • **ПОДАВА́ТЬ (БОЛЬШИ́Е) НАДЕ́ЖДЫ** [VP; subj: human] to display great potential in some area: X подаёт (большие) надежды ≃ **X shows (great) promise; X is very promising;** ‖ подающий (большие) надежды ≃ **a (very) promising** [NP]; **a** [NP] **of (great) promise; [in limited contexts] an up-and-coming** [NP].

Тесть играл [в бильярд] лучше. Сказывалась многолетняя практика, а Игорь, по сравнению с Александром Ивановичем, был почти совсем новичок, хотя и подающий надежды (Ерофеев 3). His father-in-law was a better [billiards] player. He had many years of practice under his belt, and Igor, by comparison, was a novice, albeit a novice who showed promise (3a). ♦ ...Он как будто пренебрегал даже Ольгой-девицей, любовался только ею, как милым ребёнком, подающим большие надежды... (Гончаров 1). ...He seemed to ignore Olga as a girl and admired her merely as a charming child of great promise (1a).

H-10 • КТО ⟨КУДА⟩ НАДО *euph, coll* [NP or AdvP; used as subj., obj., or adv. depending on the first component; fixed WO] the person, people, or organization wielding influence or power in the area in question (often the authorities, the KGB etc): **(to etc) the right people ⟨place, quarters⟩; (to ⟨at etc⟩) the proper quarters.**

Когда профессор родился, подрядчик подмазал кого надо, профессора записали на покойного Ивановского... (Рыбаков 1). When the professor was born, this contractor bribed the right people and the professor was registered as [the late] Ivanovsky's son... (1a). ♦ У этого Учреждения создалась такая репутация, что оно всё видит, всё слышит, всё знает, и, если чего не так, оно уже тут как тут. Оттого и говорили в народе: будешь слишком умным, попадёшь Куда Надо; будешь много болтать, попадёшь Куда Надо (Войнович 2). This institution acquired the reputation of seeing everything, hearing everything, knowing everything, and, if something was out of line, the Institution would be there in a flash. For this reason people would say, If you're too smart, you'll end up in the Right Place; if you chatter too much, you'll end up in the Right Place (2a). ♦ ...Он не вылезал на тех или иных выгодных идеологических поветриях, чтобы выступить там со статьёй или речью лишь для того, чтобы всем стало видно и ясно, за что её автор и против чего он, и чтобы эта откровенная очевидность сразу была кем надо замечена и пошла данному автору на пользу (Битов 2). ...He didn't hop on board one or another advantageous ideological fad to come out with an article or a speech, just in order to make it visible and clear to everyone what the author was for and what against, and to get this candid obviousness noticed at once in the right quarters and make it work to that author's advantage (2a).

H-11 • НА́ДО ЖЕ!; ВЕДЬ НА́ДО ЖЕ!; (ВЕДЬ) Э́ТО ЖЕ НА́ДО!; НА́ДО ЖЕ ТАК! *all coll* [Interj; these forms only; fixed WO] used to express surprise, disbelief, displeasure etc: **what do you know!; wouldn't you know (it)!; good heavens!; well, I'll be!; you don't say!; well, fancy that!; (just) think of it!; who would have guessed ⟨thought it⟩!; [in limited contexts] what will they think of next!; of all people!; just my luck!**

[Себейкин:] Есть [водка]? [Вася:] Да что ты, полно! [Себейкин:] Надо же! Водка осталась! Когда это такое было-то! (Рощин 2). [S.:] Is there any [vodka] left? [V.:] C'mon, there's plenty! [S.:] What do you know! There's vodka left! When has that ever happened before? (2a). ♦ Взглянув на него [дядю Сандро], я почувствовал, что он мне порядочно надоел... И надо же — старый чёрт почуял дуновение моего робкого бунта (Искандер 4). Looking at him [Uncle Sandro], I became aware that I was good and sick of him....Wouldn't you know—the old devil got wind of my timid rebellion (4a). ♦ «А вы-то сами откуда?» — «С Улейкона», — ответили они. «Ну, братцы, — только и сказал я. С Улейкона пожаловали, надо же! (Аксёнов 1). "But now where are you from?" "Uleikon," they answered. "Well, brothers," was all I said. A visit from Uleikon—well I'll be! (1a). ♦ «Неужели до драки доходит?» — простодушно удивился Тэдди. «А ты думал! Напишут на тебя похвальную статью, что ты-де проникнут национальным самосознанием, идёшь искать критика, а он уже с компанией — и все молодые, задорные крепыши, дети президента...» — «Надо же», — сказал Тэдди сочувственно (Стругацкие 1). "Does it really come to blows?" asked Teddy innocently. "What did you think happens? They give you a good review, they say you're chock full of national self-awareness. You go to find the critic and he's already got his friends with him, and they're all hot-tempered musclemen, Sons of the President." "You don't say," sympathized Teddy (1a). ♦ «Надо же, — говорил мальчик, — я тогда был такой маленький, что бедной маме [оленихе] приходилось на колени становиться, чтобы я доставал до вымени» (Искандер 5). "Think of it," the boy would say, "I was so little then that poor Mama [Deer] had to kneel down for me to reach her udder" (5a). ♦ «У меня зубы хорошие, фарфоровые, с меня Аркаша Глотов за

них четыре сотни содрал...» Я смотрел на него с любопытством: надо же, всегда был такой запуганный, а тут размахался! (Войнович 6). "I have good porcelain teeth....Arkasha Glotov charged me four hundred rubles for them...." I looked at him with curiosity. Who would have thought it? He had always been so timid, yet here he was strutting, and clicking his teeth! (6a). ♦ Надо же! За арестантом, который тянет голодовку почти два месяца, нужен глаз да глаз: «склонен к побегу» (Марченко 2). What will they think of next! A prisoner who maintains a hunger strike for nearly two months must be closely watched, as he displays "tendencies to try to escape" (2a). ♦ Конечно, мысль мелькала у неё и раньше, но — не убедительно. Кто её в этой мысли убедил: Мансуров-Курильский! Надо же?! (Залыгин 1). Of course this thought had occurred to her before, but it hadn't seemed very convincing. And now who had convinced her of it but Mansurov-Kurilsky! Of all people! (1a). ♦ [Ирина:] Понимаете, мы договорились с ним встретиться сегодня в двенадцать часов у Главпочтамта. И надо же: как раз сегодня у нас сочинение (Вампилов 5). [I.:] You see, we agreed to meet at noon today by the main post office. And just my luck, today we had an essay to write (5a).

H-12 • ЧТО НА́ДО *highly coll* [Invar] **1.** [usu. subj-compl with copula (subj: human, concr, or abstr)] very good, excellent: **first-rate; topnotch; the best there is; you couldn't ask for better ⟨for a better [NP]⟩; a whiz-bang ([NP]); [in limited contexts] just what one needs.**

Через несколько минут мы были на шоссе. Сергей показывал класс — скорость была что надо! (Аксёнов 1). Within a few minutes we were on the highway. Sergei was showing his stuff—speed was just what we needed! (1a).

2. [adv] (to do sth.) very well, excellently: **superbly; wonderfully (well); incredibly; smashingly; [in limited contexts] (be) a hell of a [NP]; ‖ работать ~ ≃ (do) a hell of a job.**

Сергееву не жаль было потраченных денег: дом был построен что надо. Sergeev didn't regret the money he'd spent on building the house: it came out wonderfully.

H-13 • ПО КАЗЁННОЙ НА́ДОБНОСТИ *obs* [PrepP; Invar; adv or subj-compl with copula (subj: human); fixed WO] in conjunction with some official matters: **on official business.**

Я им объяснил, что я офицер, еду в действующий отряд по казённой надобности... (Лермонтов 1). I explained that I was an officer on my way to a line unit on official business... (1b).

H-14 • НЕ НАДЫ́ШИТСЯ *на кого;* **НЕ МО́ЖЕТ НАДЫША́ТЬСЯ** [VP; subj: human; 3rd pers only (1st var.); used in pres and past contexts] to love s.o. intensely and show him constant attention and caring: **X не надышится на Y-а ≃ X dotes on Y; X loves Y to distraction; Y is the apple of X's eye.**

[Жарков:] ...Работает [Ким] всегда честнее честного, на сына не надышится (Розов 4). [Zh.:] ...He [Kim] couldn't be more conscientious in his work, loves his son to distraction (4a). ♦ Вообще она [Анна Савишна] младшую дочку, наверно, больше любила. Зато Верочка — папина радость, отец на неё не надышится (Грекова 3). Because she pitied her, Anna Savishna probably loved her younger daughter more. But Vera was her father's joy, the apple of his eye (3a).

H-15 • ОДНО́ НАЗВА́НИЕ (, что...); (ОДНО́) ТО́ЛЬКО НАЗВА́НИЕ *all coll;* **ТО́ЛЬКО (ОДНА́) СЛА́ВА, что...** [NP; sing only; often the main clause in a complex sent; usu. this WO] (in refer. to the discrepancy between what s.o. or sth. is called and what he or it actually is) a person, thing, phenomenon etc does not fit his or its name: **s.o. ⟨sth.⟩ is a [NP] in name only; s.o. ⟨sth.⟩ doesn't deserve to be called a [NP]; (it's) not what you could call a real [NP]; [in limited contexts] only the name (of a [NP]) remains ⟨is left⟩.**

«Нынче мало ли французов этих побрали; а сапог... ни на одном настоящих нет, так, одно названье», — начал один из солдат новый разговор (Толстой 7). "Plenty of Frenchies taken today, but not what you could call a real pair of boots on a one of 'em," said a soldier, introducing a new topic of conversation (7a). ♦ «А слышь ты, Василиса Егоровна, — отвечал Иван Кузьмич, — я был занят службой: солдатушек учил». — «И, полно! — возразила капитанша, что солдат учишь: ни им служба не даётся, ни ты в ней толку не ведаешь» (Пушкин 2). [context transl] "But I was taken up with my service duties, Vassilissa Yegorovna," replied Ivan Kuzmich: "I was instructing my soldiers." "That'll do!" retorted the captain's wife. "It's all a lot of chatter about your instructing the soldiers; they're not fit for the Service and you don't know the first thing about it either" (2b).

Н-16 • КАК НАЗЛО́ *coll* [как + AdvP; Invar; adv; often parenth; fixed WO] (used to express annoyance, chagrin) unfortunately, as if meaning to thwart s.o.'s plans: **as (ill ⟨bad⟩) luck would have it; as if in spite; as if to spite s.o.**

Вот в таком виде встречаю я любовь мою, и, как назло, не на что положить пакет, чтобы броситься к ней на шею... (Битов 1). And that's the shape I'm in when I meet my beloved; and as luck would have it, there's no place to put my package down so that I can throw my arms around her... (1a). ♦ Он стал припоминать, чем бы подковырнуть Кязыма. Но, как назло, сейчас ничего не мог припомнить (Искандер 5). He began trying to remember some way of catching Kyazym out. But at the moment, as ill luck would have it, he couldn't remember a thing (5a). ♦ ...Мольер стал соображать, что делать и куда бежать, чтобы спасти пьесу. Было только одно лицо во Франции, которое могло исправить положение. Только у него можно было найти защиту в этом каверзном случае, но, увы, этого лица тогда, как назло, не было в Париже (Булгаков 5). ...Molière began to think of what could be done and where he might turn to save the play. There was but a single person in France who could save the situation. He alone could protect Molière in this nasty situation. But, alas, as if in spite, this person was away from Paris at the time (5a).

Н-17 • ТАК НАЗЫВА́ЕМЫЙ [AdvP; modif; fixed WO] **1.** called thus (used before a little-known, rarely used, or unusual word or phrase): **so-called; [in limited contexts] what is called.**

Не забудем, что летописец преимущественно ведёт речь о так называемой черни... (Салтыков-Щедрин 1). Let us not forget that the chronicler is speaking primarily of the so-called common people... (1a).

2. *derog* (used sarcastically to express the speaker's scornful attitude toward s.o. or sth.) incorrectly or undeservedly called thus: **so-called; [in limited contexts] what is called.**

Н-18 • ЧТО НАЗЫВА́ЕТСЯ *coll* [Invar; sent adv (parenth); fixed WO] as s.o. or sth. is commonly called, as is commonly said: **as they say; what one calls ⟨would call⟩...; what they call...; [in limited contexts] as the saying goes.**

«И что это за нелепая фигура! — скажете вы возмущённо. — Где тут пример для подрастающего поколения? И где автор увидел такого в кавычках героя?» И я, автор, прижатый к стенке и пойманный, что называется, с поличным, должен буду признаться, что нигде я его не видел, выдумал из своей головы и вовсе не для примера, а просто от нечего делать (Войнович 2). "What a sorry sight he makes!" you will say indignantly. "What kind of example is this for the younger generation? And just where has the author seen a quote unquote hero like this?" And I, the author, my back to the wall and caught, as they say, red-handed, will have to admit that I never saw him anywhere, that I thought him up with my own head, and not to use him as an example but simply to while away the time (2a). ♦ Эти ребята не знали многого, что знают их материковские ровесники. Они были, что называется, недоразвиты (Гинзбург 2). These children knew a lot less than their mainland counterparts. They were what one calls backward

(2a). ♦ Он понял уже, чем всё это кончится. Сердце её не выдержит борьбы, и она побежит за старым мужем, с которым прошли, что называется, «годы и вёрсты» (Аксёнов 6). He already knew how it would all end. Her heart would be unable to stand the struggle and she would run after her old husband, with whom she had passed so many "years of milestones," as the saying goes (6a). ♦ ...Задал Гладышев мерину вопрос, что называется, «на засыпку»... (Войнович 2). [context transl] ...[Gladishev] posed the gelding a question of the sort known as "stumpers" (2a).

Н-19 • ПО НАИ́ТИЮ (СВЫ́ШЕ) *lit* [PrepP; these forms only; adv; fixed WO] based on or guided by instinct, often in the form of a sudden insight: **intuitively; by intuition; in a flash of insight.**

А она к нему приближается, глядит на него и... по наитию... распознаёт, что человек-то совсем особенный, вовсе не такой, как все... (Залыгин 1). And here she was, drawing near, looking at him and, intuitively,...seeing that he was completely unlike everybody else... (1a).

Н-20 • НАЙТИ́ (САМОГО́) СЕБЯ́ [VP; subj: human; usu. this WO] to discover one's special role in life: **X нашёл себя ≃ X found himself; X found his calling; X found his purpose (in life).**

Был один из первых вечеров весны, когда, познакомившись с Мишо, она [Дениз] смутно почувствовала начало своего освобождения. А теперь осенний дождь стучал ночь напролёт о чердачное оконце. Нужны были все события этого лета, беседы с Мишо, долгие размышления, чтобы Дениз наконец-то нашла себя (Эренбург 4). It was on one of the early spring evenings after she [Denise] had first met Michaud that she vaguely felt the beginning of her emancipation. And now the autumn rain pattered all through the night on the little attic window. It had [taken] all the events of the summer, the conversations with Michaud, and long solitary reflections to help Denise to find herself at last (4a).

Н-21 • ПРО́СТО ⟨ПРЯ́МО, ВОТ, СУ́ЩЕЕ, ЧИ́СТОЕ, ЧТО ЗА⟩ НАКАЗА́НИЕ; НАКАЗА́НИЕ ГОСПО́ДНЕ(Е) ⟨БО́ЖЕСКОЕ, КАКО́Е-ТО⟩; НАКАЗА́НИЕ МНЕ *с кем-чем all coll* [Interj; these forms only; fixed WO] (used to express irritation, anger etc) s.o. or sth. is awfully troublesome: **what a nuisance ⟨a pain (in the neck)⟩!; (it's) a downright nuisance!; (it's) a real pain (in the neck)!; [in limited contexts] what did I ⟨we⟩ do to deserve this!**

[Ферапонт:] Пожарные, ваше высокородие, просят, позвольте на реку садом проехать. А то кругом ездиют, ездиют [*ungrammat* = ездят] — чистое наказание (Чехов 5). [F.:] The firemen, Your Honor, are asking permission to drive through the garden to the river. Otherwise they have to go round and round — a downright nuisance (5a). ♦ [Макарская:] А ну пусти! [Васенька:] Не пущу. [Макарская:] Я пожалуюсь твоему [отцу], ты достукаешься! [Васенька:] Почему ты кричишь? [Макарская:] Нет, это наказание какое-то (Вампилов 4). [M.:] C'mon, let me go! [V.:] I won't. [M.:] I'll complain to your father. You'll get it from him! [V.:] Why are you yelling? [M.:] What did I do to deserve this! (4b). ♦ «Служивого нашего встрел [*ungrammat* = встретил]? Вот наказание!» (Шолохов 4). [context transl] "Did you meet our old soldier? He's a terror, he is!" (4a).

Н-22 • С НАЛЁТА ⟨-у⟩ *coll* [PrepP; these forms only; adv] **1.** ~ удариться *обо что*, ударить *кого-что*, схватить *что* и т. п. Also: **С НАБЕ́ГА** (to bump into sth., kick s.o. or sth., grab sth. etc) while in full motion, without stopping (esp. when flying, running etc): **(fly ⟨run, crash etc⟩) right into (s.o. ⟨sth.⟩); [in refer. to very fast motion only] (at) full speed; (at) full tilt; [of birds etc only] in full flight; [esp. of birds, insects etc diving or plunging downward] swoop(ing) down on; with a swoop; swoop (and strike ⟨strike against, hit etc⟩ sth.).**

Проснувшаяся муха вдруг с налёта ударилась об стекло и жалобно зажужжала (Достоевский 3). An awakened fly suddenly swooped and struck against the window, buzzing plaintively (3c). A fly that had woken up suddenly swooped and beat against the windowpane, buzzing plaintively (3d).

2. ~ **понимать** *что,* **овладевать** *чем и т. п.* (to understand, master sth. etc) immediately, without encountering any difficulties: **in a flash; right away; right off the bat.**

Ему долго объяснять не надо, он всё с налёта понимает. You don't have to give him a long explanation, he picks up everything right off the bat.

3. *occas. disapprov* ~ **решать** *что,* **судить** *о чём и т. п.* (to decide, judge etc sth.) without due consideration or preparation: **on the spur of the moment; without stopping to think;** [in limited contexts] **rashly; on impulse.**

Н-23 • ТО́НКИЙ НАМЁК НА ТО́ЛСТОЕ ОБСТО-Я́ТЕЛЬСТВО ⟨НА ТО́ЛСТЫЕ ОБСТОЯ́ТЕЛЬ-СТВА⟩ *coll, iron or humor* [NP; fixed WO] a rather plain allusion to sth. evident: **subtle reference to a glaring fact; hint at the obvious.**

Редактор сказал, что его время ценится очень высоко. Но, хотя это был явно тонкий намёк на толстое обстоятельство, навязчивый посетитель не уходил. The editor said that his time was very valuable. However, even though this was clearly a subtle reference to a glaring fact, his irksome visitor did not leave.

Н-24 • НЕ НА ТОГО́ ⟨ТАКО́ГО⟩ НАПА́Л *highly coll;* **НЕ НА ТАКО́ВСКОГО НАПА́Л** *substand* [sent; past only; fixed WO] one (often the interlocutor) is underestimating the person with whom he is dealing (usu. the speaker): **you've ⟨they've etc⟩ picked the wrong person ⟨guy, gal etc⟩ (to fool around with); you ⟨they etc⟩ are messing with the wrong person ⟨guy, gal etc⟩;** [in limited contexts] **I'm not that sort (of person); you ⟨he etc⟩ mustn't take me for a fool.**

«Бандиты! — внутренне содрогнулся Иван Тимофеевич. — Сейчас начнут издеваться или просто зарежут. Нет, надо сразу показать, что не на того напали» (Войнович 4). "Cut-throats!" Ivan Timofeyevich shuddered inwardly. "Now they'll start picking on me or just kill me. No, I've got to show them right off they've picked the wrong guy" (4a). ♦ «Ну, меня... не застращаешь! Не на такого напали» (Эренбург 2). "You won't frighten me with that kind of thing!...I'm not that sort" (2a).

Н-25 • ПО НАПРАВЛЕ́НИЮ *к кому-чему;* **В НАПРАВ-ЛЕ́НИИ** *кого-чего или к кому-чему* [PrepP; these forms only; Prep; the resulting PrepP is adv] in a direction leading to: **toward; in the direction of; on the way ⟨road⟩ to; (headed) for.**

Пароход медленно плыл по направлению к пристани. The steamship moved slowly toward the dock.

Н-26 • НАПРА́ВО И НАЛЕ́ВО *coll* [AdvP; Invar; adv; usu. this WO] **1.** indiscriminately, (to) absolutely everyone: **right and left; left and right;** [in limited contexts] **on every side; on all sides.**

...К сирени Пётр Александрович относился почему-то не так бережно и ревниво, как ко многим цветам, разрешал ломать её, отсаживал кустами, дарил направо и налево... (Трифонов 1). For some reason...Pyotr Alexandrovich was less jealous and protective of his lilacs than of his many other flowers. He would transplant them from one place to another, allow others to cut off branches, and would himself give them away right and left... (1a). ♦ Многие до сих пор спрашивают меня, почему О. М[андель-штам] это сделал, то есть вступился за незнакомого человека в дни, когда расстреливали направо и налево (Мандель-штам 1). ...I am still always being asked why M[andelstam] did it — that is, why he intervened for a stranger at a time when people were being shot on every side (1a).

2. сорить деньгами, швырять деньгами *и т. п.* ~ (to spend money) recklessly, extravagantly: **(throw money around) right and left ⟨left and right⟩.**

[Иванов:] Веровал я не так, как все, женился не так, как все, горячился, рисковал, деньги свои, сам знаешь, бросал направо и налево... (Чехов 4). [I.:] My ideas were different from everyone else's, I married differently, I was hotheaded, took risks, threw my money around right and left... (4a).

Н-27 • ВОЗВОДИ́ТЬ/ВОЗВЕСТИ́ НАПРА́СЛИНУ *на кого coll* [VP; subj: human] to tell damaging or unflattering lies about s.o. (or o.s.), accuse s.o. (or o.s.) unjustly: X возвёл напраслину на Y-a ⟨на себя⟩ ≃ **X slandered ⟨maligned, vilified etc⟩ Y ⟨himself⟩; X made a false accusation against Y ⟨himself⟩; X gave Y a bum rap.**

[author's usage] [Беркутов:] Я долго говорил с Горецким и в город с ним ездил. Он тебя обманул. Ему понадобились деньги, он и сказал напраслину на себя (Островский 5). [B.:] I had a long talk with Goretsky, and drove to town with him....He deceived you. He needed the money, so he just made a false accusation against himself (5a). ♦ «...Директор, падло этакое, думал, что я с ним не здороваюсь, потому что осуждаю его за травлю морганистов — и упёк. А я просто не привык сволочам руку подавать. При чём тут Мендель — когда у него по роже видно, что — сволочь!.. Вот и возвёл на меня напраслину, говно!» (Битов 2). "...The director, what a stinking bastard, he thought I wasn't saying hello as a criticism of him for hounding the Morganists — and he got me sent up. I'm just not in the habit of shaking hands with scum. What's Mendel got to do with it, when you see by his ugly mug that he's scum! So he gave me a bum rap, the shit!" (2a).

Н-28 • НАПУСКА́ТЬ/НАПУСТИ́ТЬ НА СЕБЯ́ *что coll* [VP; subj: human; obj: usu. важность, строгость] to attempt purposely to display a certain characteristic or quality (usu. importance or strictness): X напускает на себя Y ≃ **X assumes an air of Y;** ‖ X напускает на себя важность ≃ **X puts on ⟨gives himself⟩ airs; X assumes an important air; X acts ⟨looks⟩ high-and-mighty; X acts snooty ⟨uppity, all-important⟩;** ‖ X напускает на себя строгость ≃ **X makes himself out to be strict; X tries to look strict.**

...К воротам дома подъехала принадлежавшая госпоже Хохлаковой карета. Штабс-капитан, ждавший всё утро доктора, сломя голову бросился к воротам встречать его. Маменька подобралась и напустила на себя важности (Достоевский 1). ...A carriage belonging to Madame Khokhlakov drove up to the gates of the house. The captain, who had been expecting the doctor all morning, madly rushed out to meet him. Mama pulled herself together and assumed an important air (1a).

Н-29 • НА ⟨ВО⟩ ВЕСЬ НАРО́Д *кричать, объявлять и т. п. obs* [PrepP; these forms only; adv; fixed WO] (to shout, announce sth.) publicly, so that everyone can hear it: **(shout sth.) from the housetops ⟨the rooftops⟩; (shout sth.) for all to hear; (tell) the whole world.**

[Городничий:] Всем объяви, чтобы все знали. Кричи во весь народ... (Гоголь 4). [Mayor:] Tell them all. Let them all know it. Shout it from the housetops! (4c).

Н-30 • ПРИ ВСЁМ ЧЕСТНО́М НАРО́ДЕ; ПРИ ⟨ВСЁМ⟩ НАРО́ДЕ; ПРИ ВСЕЙ ЧЕСТНО́Й КОМ-ПА́НИИ *all coll, often humor* [PrepP; these forms only; adv; fixed WO] publicly, in the presence of everyone: **for all to see ⟨to hear, to know⟩; in front of everyone ⟨of everybody, of the whole world⟩; in public.**

Ну, выпил я рюмку до прихода гостей, ну и что? Зачем говорить об этом сейчас, при всём честном народе? So I took a drink before the guests arrived, big deal. Why do you have to bring it up now, in front of everyone?

Н-31 • **КАК ⟨БУ́ДТО, СЛО́ВНО, ТО́ЧНО⟩ НА-РО́ЧНО** *coll* [как etc + AdvP; these forms only; adv; often parenth; fixed WO] (used to express annoyance, chagrin) unfortunately, as if intentionally to disrupt s.o.'s plans: **as ⟨ill ⟨bad⟩⟩ luck would have it; as if ⟨though⟩ on purpose; as if in spite; as if to spite s.o.**

Как нарочно, это случилось в ту самую пору, когда страсть к законодательству приняла в нашем отечестве размеры чуть-чуть не опасные... (Салтыков-Щедрин 1). As luck would have it, this happened at the time when the passion for lawmaking had assumed almost dangerous proportions in our fatherland (1a). ♦ Пробравшись в жилые покои, он, в темноте, прошёл в её спальню, в которой горела лампада. И, как нарочно, обе горничные её девушки ушли потихоньку без спросу, по соседству, на именинную пирушку... (Достоевский 1). Stealing into her apartments, he made his way through the darkness to her bedroom, where an icon lamp was burning. Her two maids, as if on purpose, had gone secretly, without asking permission, to a birthday party at a neighbor's house... (1a). ♦ [Анна Андреевна:] Экая досада! как нарочно, ни души! (Гоголь 4). [A.A.:] Oh, it's so annoying! Not a soul about—as if to spite me (4f).

Н-32 • **С НАСКО́КА ⟨-у⟩** [PrepP; these forms only; adv] **1.** while in full motion, without stopping (esp. when galloping, running etc): **(gallop ⟨run etc⟩) right into (sth.);** [in refer. to very fast motion only] **at full ⟨top⟩ speed; (at) full tilt; (at a) full gallop; at a dead run;** [esp. of a rider grasping, hitting etc s.o. or sth. while riding fast] **swoop(ing) down on.**

Лошадь с наскока врезалась в забор и сбросила всадника. The horse crashed into the fence at full tilt and sent its rider flying.

2. *coll, occas. disapprov* ~ **судить** *о чём*, **решать** *что*, и т. п. (to judge, decide etc sth.) without due consideration or preparation, without thinking it through: **(make) a rash judgment ⟨decision etc⟩; without stopping to think;** [in limited contexts] **at first glance; on impulse.**

Не суди с наскока. Этот конфликт сложнее, чем он кажется. Don't make a rash judgment! This conflict is more complicated than it seems. ♦ «В таком деле с наскоку не разберёшься» (Чернёнок 2). "In a case like this, you can't figure anything out at first glance" (2a).

Н-33 • **ВТОРА́Я НАТУ́РА** [NP; sing only; subj-compl with copula, nom or instrum (subj: usu. abstr or infin); fixed WO] sth. (or doing sth.) has become a deeply ingrained habit for, or characteristic tendency in, s.o.: **second nature.**

< From the saying «Привычка – вторая натура» ("Custom ⟨habit⟩ is a second nature"). See П-518.

Н-34 • **ШИРО́КАЯ НАТУ́РА ⟨ДУША́⟩** *coll* [NP; sing only; often subj-compl with copula, nom or instrum (subj: human); fixed WO] a person who is generous, magnanimous, does everything expansively, willingly shares what he has with others etc: **X — широкая натура ≃ X has a generous nature; X does things in a big way.**

Широкая натура, ей было... приятно, что я кормлю эту ораву... (Рыбаков 1). She had a generous nature, so she liked the fact that I was feeding the whole crowd (1a).

Н-35 • **ДЛЯ НАЧА́ЛА** *coll* [PrepP; Invar; adv] as a beginning, initially: **for a start; to start (with); for starters; as a starter; to begin with;** [in limited contexts] **one starts ⟨begins⟩ by (doing sth.).**

«Вот ваш бюджет – три миллиона. Для начала хватит?» (Аксёнов 12). "Here's your budget—three million. Will that be enough for a start?" (12a). ♦ ...Ему пришлось не сладко — кончался нэп, наступал государственный сектор. Для начала Алихану предложили расчленить кофейню-кондитерскую и свободно выбрать одно из двух: или кофейню, или кондитерскую (Искандер 3). ...Life was not sweet for him—the New Economic Policy ended, ...the state took over the economy. To start with, Ali Khan was ordered to separate the coffeehouse and bake shop and freely choose one of the two: either the coffeehouse or the bake shop (3a). ♦ «А я бы на твоём месте, знаешь, что сделал? Для начала я перестал бы быть холуём при Иванько» (Войнович 3). "And in your position, you know what I would do? To start, I would stop toadying to Ivanko!" (3a). ♦ «Ты представляешь себе, какой поднимется шум, когда кто-нибудь из них для начала преподнесёт читающей публике „Ревизора" или, на самый худой конец, „Евгения Онегина"!» (Булгаков 9). "Can you imagine the furore when one of them will, as a starter, present the reading public with an *Inspector General* or, if worst comes to worst, a *Yevgeny Onegin*?" (9a). ♦ ...Маг сказал: «Однако мы заговорились, дорогой Фагот, а публика начинает скучать. Покажи нам для начала что-нибудь простенькое» (Булгаков 9). ...The magician said, "That's enough talk from us, my dear Faggot—the audience is getting bored. Show us something simple to begin with" (9b). ♦ Не зная, чем его развлечь, я ему для начала рассказал о шахматном турнире, выигранном его любимым гроссмейстером Спасским (Войнович 6). Not knowing how to entertain him, I began by talking about the chess tournament, which had been won by his favorite grand master, Spassky (6a).

Н-36 • **БРАТЬ ⟨СВОЁ⟩ НАЧА́ЛО** *где, из чего* [VP; subj: река, дорога etc, the name of a river, road etc, or abstr; pres or past; usu. this WO] (of a river, road etc) to have its beginning, originate (in some place); (of a method, idea etc) to derive (from sth.): X берёт начало в месте ⟨около места и т. п.⟩ Y ≃ [of a river, road etc] **X begins ⟨originates⟩ in ⟨at, near etc⟩ place Y;** [of a river only] **X rises in ⟨springs from, flows from⟩ Y; X has its source ⟨origin⟩ in Y;** ‖ X берёт начало из Y-а ≃ [of a method, idea etc] **X arises ⟨stems, springs⟩ from Y; X has its source ⟨origin⟩ in Y; X goes back to Y.**

Волга берёт начало на Валдайской возвышенности. The Volga flows from the Valdai Hills. ♦ Новый уклад пользовался старыми представлениями и фразеологией, берущими своё начало ещё из дореволюционного становления большевистского крыла социал-демократической партии (Гроссман 2). ...It [this new social order] still made use of [notions and] phraseology that went back to the beginning of the twentieth century and the formation of the Bolshevik wing of the Social Democratic Party (2a).

Н-37 • **ВЕСТИ́ ⟨СВОЁ⟩ НАЧА́ЛО** *от кого-чего* [VP; subj: human (usu. pl), collect, or abstr; pres or past] (of a family) to originate (in some ancestor or ancestors); (of a phenomenon) to originate (in some phenomenon in the past): X ведёт ⟨своё⟩ начало от Y-а ≃ **X begins ⟨starts⟩ with Y; X derives from Y; thing X has its beginning(s) in Y;** [in refer. to a line of descent only] **family X descends from Y; family X traces its roots ⟨ancestry⟩ back to Y.**

Н-38 • **ДАВА́ТЬ/ДАТЬ ⟨КЛАСТЬ/ПОЛОЖИ́ТЬ⟩ НАЧА́ЛО** *чему* [VP; subj: human, abstr, or concr; more often pfv; usu. this WO] to initiate sth., be the source, beginning point of sth.: X дал начало Y-у ≃ **X started ⟨originated⟩ Y; thing X gave rise to Y;** [in limited contexts] **thing X was the starting point of Y.**

Его работы положили начало новому направлению в лингвистике. His works gave rise to a new school of linguistics.

Н-39 • **ХОРО́ШЕЕ ⟨ДО́БРОЕ⟩ НАЧА́ЛО ПОЛДЕ́ЛА ОТКАЧА́ЛО** [saying] a good start in some endeavor ensures a good outcome: ≃ **well begun is half done; the first blow is half the battle.**

Н-40 • ПОД НАЧА́ЛОМ *чьим, (у) кого* быть₀, работать, служить и т. п.; ПОД НАЧА́ЛО *чьё, кого, (к) кому* ⟨ПОД НАЧА́Л *чей, кого, (к) кому obs*⟩ попасть, поступить, отдать *кого* и т. п. [PrepP; these forms only; subj-compl with copula (subj: human or collect) or adv] (to be, work, serve, fall, be put etc) under s.o.'s supervision: **under s.o.'s authority** ⟨**control, direction**⟩; [in limited contexts] (**work** ⟨**serve**⟩) **under s.o.; (serve) under s.o.'s command; (be) under s.o.'s orders.**

«Слышно, земский суд к нам едет отдать нас под начал Кирилу Петровичу Троекурову...» (Пушкин 1). "We hear that the district court is going to put us under the authority of Kirila Petrovich Troyekurov..." (1a). ♦ Он часто хвастал: «Вот я буду инспектором. Вы тут киснуть будете, а у меня под началом два уезда будут. А то и три. Ого-го!» (Сологуб 1). "Yes," he often boasted, "I shall be an inspector. You'll be wasting away here, while I'll have two districts under my authority. And then perhaps three. Ho, ho, ho!" (1a). ♦ «...Я стал обидчивым, работая под твоим началом» (Семёнов 1). "I've grown sensitive working under your direction" (1a). ♦ Неужто не слыхали? Шестопалов. Квартирные вопросы решает. Я под его началом тринадцать лет прослужил (Терц 5). Never heard of him?...Shestopalov. Fellow who arbitrates housing problems. I worked under him for thirteen years (5a). ♦ Коптелов шепнул Лёве, что служил под началом Дмитрия Ивановича во время войны... (Битов 2). Koptelov whispered to Lyova that he had served under Dmitri Ivanovich's command during the war... (2a). ♦ [Дикой:] Что я, под началом, что ль, у кого? (Островский 6). [D.:] What, am I under somebody's orders, maybe? (6a).

Н-41 • ПО НАЧА́ЛЬСТВУ доносить, посылать *что* и т. п. *rather coll* [PrepP; Invar; adv] (to report, send sth. etc) to those in higher positions of authority, to a higher department: (**inform** ⟨**report to, report sth. to** etc⟩) **the authorities; (inform** ⟨**report to** etc⟩**) the** ⟨**one's**⟩ **higher-ups; (send a report** etc**) up the line.**

...Как человек обязательный, [штаб-офицер] телеграфировал о происшедшем случае по начальству... (Салтыков-Щедрин 1). [The state solicitor], as an obliging man, telegraphed the authorities regarding the incident... (1a). ♦ ...Выходит он на средину, а в руках бумага — форменное донесение по начальству. А так как начальство его было тут же, то тут же и прочёл бумагу вслух всем собравшимся... (Достоевский 1). ...He stepped into the middle of the room with a paper in his hand—a formal statement to the authorities. And since the authorities were right there, he read the paper right then to the whole gathering (1a).

Н-42 • НАЧИНА́ТЬ/НАЧА́ТЬ ИЗДАЛЕКА́ [VP; subj: human] to begin telling, relating sth. in an indirect, circuitous manner, not getting to the point immediately: X начал издалека ≃ **X began in a (somewhat) roundabout way; X started with something entirely unrelated.**

Дельце, о котором просил хозяин, касалось его сбежавшей жены. Начал он издалека, говоря, что он уже не мальчик, чтобы есть что попало и как попало, а человек в летах, и ему нужен человек, который мог бы приготовить и подать ему пищу (Искандер 4). The favor that [our host] Omar had requested concerned his runaway wife. He began in a roundabout way, saying that he was no longer a boy, to eat any old thing fixed any old way; he was a man getting on in years, he needed a person who could prepare and serve his food for him (4a). ♦ «Чем могу служить?» – спросил Персиков... Начал гость издалека, именно попросил разрешения закурить сигару, вследствие чего Персиков с большою неохотой пригласил его сесть. Далее гость произнёс длинные извинения по поводу того, что он пришёл поздно... (Булгаков 10). "What can I do for you?" Persikov asked....The guest began in a somewhat roundabout way. He begged permission to light his cigar, in consequence of which Persikov most reluctantly invited him to sit down. The guest proceeded to offer extended apologies for coming so late (10a).

Н-43 • НАЧИНА́Я С ⟨ОТ⟩ *кого-чего* [Prep; these forms only; the resulting PrepP is adv] beginning with s.o. or sth., or beginning at some date or time: **from...on up** ⟨**on down**⟩; **from...(down to); starting with** ⟨**from**⟩; [in refer. to dates, times etc] **since.**

Да они [учёные люди] и делаются учёными, считал он, начиная от всяких там писарей, именно для того, чтобы отойти от физической работы и от жизни под открытым небом (Искандер 4). That was why they [learned men] became learned, he believed, from all those wretched clerks on up: precisely in order to get away from manual labor and life under the open sky (4a). ♦ Все в доме и в деревне, начиная от барина, жены его и до дюжего кузнеца Тараса, — все трепещут чего-то в тёмный вечер... (Гончаров 1). Everyone in the house and in the village, from the master and the mistress down to the burly blacksmith Taras, quaked at something on dark nights... (1b). ♦ Начиная с 1968 года мне здесь неоднократно объясняли, что я поставил своё перо на службу каким-то разведкам... (Войнович 3). Since 1968...it had been repeatedly explained to me in this office that I had placed my pen at the service of some sort of intelligence agency... (3a).

Н-44 • МАМА́ЕВО НАШЕ́СТВИЕ [NP; sing only; fixed WO] large numbers of unwanted visitors, guests (who appear unexpectedly): **(like) a Mongol invasion** ⟨**horde**⟩.
    < See M-22.

Н-45 • И НА́ШИМ И ВА́ШИМ служить, угождать и т. п. *coll, disapprov* [NP_dat; indir obj or subj-compl with быть₀ (subj: human), pres or fut; fixed WO] (to serve, try to please etc) two different sides at the same time (in refer. to a person who, for selfish, mercenary reasons or from a lack of principles, is trying to oblige two people, groups etc that have different opinions, views, agendas): X служит и нашим и вашим ≃ **X serves two masters; X works for both sides; X works both sides of the street; X has a foot in both camps; X butters his bread on both sides; X runs with the hare and hunts with the hounds.**

«Что же, расстреливаешь братов [*ungrammat* = братьев]? Обернулся?.. Вот ты какой...» – Он, близко придвинувшись к Григорию, шепнул: «И нашим и вашим служишь? Кто больше даст?» (Шолохов 3). "So you're shooting your brothers? You've changed sides?...That's the kind of man you are." He stepped up close to Grigory and whispered, "Serving two masters? The highest bidder, eh?" (3a). ♦ [Белоботников:] И нарядчику не доверяйте, он и нашим и вашим (Солженицын 8). [B.:] And don't trust that work allocator....He works for both sides (8a). ♦ «...Буду опять его [журнал] издавать и непременно в либеральном и атеистическом направлении, с социалистическим оттенком, с маленьким даже лоском социализма, но держа ухо востро, то есть, в сущности, держа нашим и вашим и отводя глаза дуракам» (Достоевский 1). "...I will go on publishing it [the journal], most certainly with a liberal and atheistic slant, with a socialistic tinge, with even a little gloss of socialism, but with my ears open, that is, essentially, running with the hare and hunting with the hounds, and pulling the wool over the fools' eyes" (1a).

Н-46 • (КАК ⟨КАК БУ́ДТО, БУ́ДТО, СЛО́ВНО, ТО́ЧНО⟩) С НЕ́БА СВАЛИ́ТЬСЯ ⟨УПА́СТЬ⟩ *coll* [(как etc +) VP; usu. past; usu. this WO] **1.** [subj: human, abstr, or concr] to appear, occur unexpectedly, suddenly: X как с неба свалился ≃ **X appeared** ⟨**came**⟩ **(as if) out of the blue; X came** ⟨**sprang up**⟩ **(from) out of nowhere; X appeared** ⟨**came**⟩ **like a bolt from the blue.**
Среди всех этих толков и пересудов, вдруг как с неба упала повестка, приглашавшая именитейших представителей глуповской интеллигенции, в такой-то день и час, прибыть к

градоначальнику для внушения (Салтыков-Щедрин 1). Suddenly, amid all this talk and gossip, out of the blue came a notice summoning the most distinguished representatives of Foolov's intelligentsia to appear at such-and-such a day and hour at the town governor's for reprimand (1a). ♦ Когда мошенник Тартюф... уже торжествовал и разорил честных людей и когда, казалось, от него уже нет никакого спасения, всё-таки спасение явилось... Добродетельный полицейский офицер, свалившийся как бы с неба, не только в самый нужный и последний момент схватывает злодея, но ещё и произносит внушительный монолог... (Булгаков 5). When the swindler Tartuffe...was already on the verge of triumph, when he had ruined honest men and there seemed to be no escape from his clutches, rescue appeared....A virtuous police officer, who springs up from out of nowhere, not only arrests the hero at the last and most crucial moment, but also delivers a most instructive monologue... (5a).

2. [subj: human; most often 2nd pers] not to know things that are obvious, understood by all: ты что, с неба свалился? ≃ **where (on earth) have you been all this time?; did you fall out of the skies?; are you ⟨what are you,⟩ from another planet?; have you been living in a cave (all your life)?**

«Мы из оккупированной местности. Нам в городе прописки нету...» — «Вам сейчас сколько? Семнадцать? Девятнадцать? Так при немцах вам было восемь лет! Не больше! Столько, сколько Лёльке сейчас! — закричала я. — Какое же это может иметь значение?» Она не удостоила меня ответом. «А ты что, с неба свалилась? — выражала её спина. — Старая дура» (Чуковская 2). "...We're from occupied territory. They won't even give us permission to live in town...." "How old are you now? Seventeen? Nineteen? So when the Germans were here you were eight! Not more! As old as Lyolka is now!" I shouted. "How can that have any importance now?" She didn't deign to answer. "Where on earth have you been all this time, you old fool?" was what her back seemed to say (2a). ♦ «А „Кильдин", простите, что же, пришёл в Талый с острова Фиджи?» — «Прямым курсом из Марокко, — захотел корреспондент. — Да вы что, ребята, с неба свалились?» (Аксёнов 1). "And the *Kildin*? Pardon me, but what'd it do, come to Slush from the Fiji Islands?" "A steady course from Morocco," laughed the correspondent. "But what's with you guys, you fall out of the skies?" (1a). ♦ «...Я уверен, что наш советский доктор не мог, покрывая убийцу, взять деньги или ещё что-то. Вам это просто показалось». — «Я рассказал так, как я видел...» — «Да, да, — повторил космонавт, — вам это показалось. Там и начальник милиции был, так что ему нечего было бояться...» — «Да что он, с неба свалился!» — воскликнул по-абхазски молодой хозяин... (Искандер 4). "...I'm sure our Soviet doctor couldn't have taken money or anything else to cover up a murder. That was just your imagination." "I told it as I saw it...." "Yes, yes," the cosmonaut repeated, "it was your imagination. The police chief was there too, so he had nothing to fear—" "What is he, from another planet?" the young host exclaimed in Abkhazian... (4a).

3. [subj: concr or abstr] to be obtained, found unexpectedly, coming as a pleasant surprise: X (как) с неба упал ≃ **X appeared ⟨happened⟩ as if by magic; X came ⟨seemed to come⟩ out of the blue; X (just) landed ⟨fell⟩ in Y's lap; [in limited contexts] (it's as if ⟨though⟩) X fell from heaven ⟨the sky⟩.**

«Ну что бы с нами было теперь, Дуня, без этих трёх тысяч! Господи, точно с неба упали!» (Достоевский 3). "Where would we be now, Dunya, without those three thousand roubles! Lord, just as though they fell from heaven!" (3c).

H-47 • **СОЙТИ ⟨ПА́ДАТЬ/УПА́СТЬ⟩ С НЕ́БА НА ЗЕ́МЛЮ; СПУСКА́ТЬСЯ/СПУСТИ́ТЬСЯ (С НЕ́БА) НА ЗЕ́МЛЮ** [VP; subj: human; more often pfv; often infin with пора, надо etc or imper; usu. this WO] to free o.s. from illusions, come to a proper understanding of reality: сойди с неба на землю ≃ **come down to earth ⟨from the clouds⟩; get your head out of the clouds.**

[Лика (ласково):] Милый, мы уже не дети... пора спускаться на землю (Арбузов 4). [L. *(affectionately):*] My darling, we aren't children any more....It's time we came down to earth (4a). ♦ «На одной чаше весов вы — ссыльный контрреволюционер, на другой — председатель колхоза, он сила, власть, хозяин их судьбы. За кого они будут свидетельствовать? Спуститесь с небес, Панкратов, и правильно оцените своё положение» (Рыбаков 2). "So, on one side of the scales there's you, an exiled counterrevolutionary, and on the other side there's the chairman of the kolkhoz, the power, the authority, the keeper of their fate. For whom will they testify? Come down from the clouds, Pankratov, and try to evaluate your position realistically" (2a).

H-48 • **НА СЕДЬМО́М НЕ́БЕ быть₀, чувствовать себя** [PrepP; Invar; subj-compl with copula (subj: human) or adv; fixed WO] (to be, feel) boundlessly happy: **(be) in seventh heaven; (be) on cloud nine; (be) (sitting) on top of the world; (be) walking ⟨treading⟩ on air.**

[Шабельский:] А ваш этот тупой лекарь почувствовал бы себя... на седьмом небе, если бы судьба дала ему случай, во имя принципа и общечеловеческих идеалов, хватить меня публично по рылу и под микитки (Чехов 4). [Sh.:] But that dimwitted leech of yours...he'd be in seventh heaven if only fate would give him a chance—in the name of principle and humanitarian ideals—publicly to give me a rap in the snout or a poke in the ribs (4a).

H-49 • **ПРЕВОЗНОСИ́ТЬ/ПРЕВОЗНЕСТИ́ ⟨ВОЗНОСИ́ТЬ/ВОЗНЕСТИ́⟩ ДО НЕБЕ́С кого-что** *lit* [VP; subj: human] to praise s.o. or sth. excessively: X превозносил Y-а до небес ≃ **X was praising Y to the skies ⟨to high heaven⟩; X was lavishing ⟨showering⟩ praises on Y.**

[Жарков:] Где ты столько лет пропадал, когда меня и в газетах, и по радио до небес превозносили! (Розов 4). [Zh.:] Where were you hiding all those years when they were praising me to the skies in the newspapers and on the radio? (4a).

H-50 • **(КАК) НЕ́БО И ЗЕМЛЯ́** *coll* [(как +) NP; these forms only; subj-compl with быть₀ (subj: human, abstr, or concr, usu. pl); usu. this WO] (to be) not at all alike, complete opposites: X и Y — это (как) небо и земля ≃ **X and Y are like ⟨as different as⟩ heaven and earth; X and Y are like ⟨as different as⟩ day and night ⟨night and day⟩; there's a world of difference between X and Y.**

«Вот так жизнь и устроена, что рядом с Евгением Николаевичем живёт Петька Ларионов, а они друг дружке как небо и земля» (Распутин 1). "Funny thing: there's Evgeny Nikolaevich living next door to Piotr Larionov, and the two of them as different as heaven and earth" (1a). ♦ Скажу вам как специалист: на обувной фабрике склад готовой продукции и склад сырья — это небо и земля (Рыбаков 1). I'd like to say something, as an expert. In a shoe factory, the finished goods store and the raw material store are as different as day and night (1a).

H-51 • **КАК НЕ́БО ОТ ЗЕМЛИ́ отличаться** *coll* [как + NP; Invar; adv; fixed WO] (to differ) very much, sharply: X отличается от Y-а как небо от земли ≃ **X and Y are as different as heaven and earth ⟨as night and day⟩; X is the exact ⟨the very⟩ opposite of Y; X is poles apart from Y; X and Y are poles ⟨worlds⟩ apart.**

«Я не понимаю, отец, как с добрейшей душой, какая у тебя, и таким редким сердцем будешь принимать человека, который как небо от земли от тебя, о котором сам знаешь, что он дурён» (Гоголь 3). "I can't understand, father, how a man with a heart of gold like yours, a man as kind as you, can go on receiving a man who's the very opposite of you and who you yourself is a bad character" (3a). "I don't understand, father, that a man with a heart of gold like yours can go on receiving a person who is poles apart from you and whom you yourself know to be a bad character" (3d).

H-52 • **НЕ́БО КОПТИ́ТЬ; КОПТИ́ТЬ СВЕТ** *both coll, disapprov* [VP: subj: human] to live aimlessly, doing nothing useful: X небо коптит ≃ **X is wasting ⟨frittering⟩ his life away; X is idling away his life.** ○ **КОПТИ́ТЕЛЬ НЕ́БА** *obs* [NP] ≃ **idler; loafer.**

Так как уже не мало есть на белом свете людей, которые коптят небо, то почему ж и Тентетникову не коптить его? (Гоголь 3). …Since there are not a few people in the wide world who idle away their lives, why shouldn't Tentetnikov do the same? (3c). ♦ «А я бы их [душевнобольных] своим манером. Что им небо коптить без пользы?» (Максимов 3). [context transl] "I know how I'd deal with them [the mental patients]. Why should they clutter up the earth, when they're no use to anybody?" (3a).

H-53 • **НЕ́БО С ⟨В⟩ ОВЧИ́НКУ КА́ЖЕТСЯ/ПОКА-ЗА́ЛОСЬ** *кому highly coll* [VP_subj: usu. pfv; usu. this WO] (in refer. to a short-lived, intense sensation) s.o. experiences extreme fear, intolerable pain etc: X-у небо с овчинку показалось ≃ **X thought ⟨felt like⟩ he was going to die (on the spot); X felt as if the sky were about to come crashing down on his head ⟨on him⟩; X felt like the world was closing in on him;** [in refer. to fear only] **X was frightened ⟨scared⟩ out of his wits.**

«Струсил ты, признайся, когда молодцы мои накинули тебе верёвку на шею? Я чаю, небо с овчинку показалось…» (Пушкин 2). "You got scared, didn't you, when my lads threw the rope around your neck? Frightened out of your wits, weren't you?" (2a).

H-54 • **С НЕБОЛЬШИ́М** [PrepP; Invar; postmodif; usu. used after a Num or quantit NP] (used in making an approximate estimation of s.o.'s age, the size or quantity of sth. etc) with a small excess, slightly more than the amount just named: **a little over ⟨more than⟩; just over;** [Num]-**odd;** [in limited contexts] **…plus; …and then some;** [in refer. to time only] **a little past…**

Подумать только, лишь десять лет с небольшим проходит, и уже объяснять надо, как могло быть такое, как мог быть такой Лёва! (Битов 2). Just think, it's only been a little over ten years, and already we have to explain how such a thing could have happened, how there could be such a Lyova! (2a). ♦ Добрые кони в полчаса с небольшим пронесли Чичикова чрез десятивёрстное пространство… (Гоголь 3). In just over half an hour the excellent horses transported Chichikov over the seven miles… (3a).

H-55 • **МЕЖДУ НЕ́БОМ И ЗЕМЛЁЙ** *coll* [PrepP; Invar; adv or subj-compl with copula (subj: human); fixed WO] **1.** жить, пребывать и т. п. ~ to live without shelter, not to have permanent housing: X жил между небом и землёй ≃ **X lived ⟨was⟩ without a roof over his head; X was homeless.**

2. висеть, находиться и т. п. ~ to be in a state of uncertainty, be in an unsettled state: X висит между небом и землёй ≃ **X is (hanging ⟨sitting etc⟩) in limbo; X doesn't know where he stands.**

Кажется, мне хотелось, чтобы уже все… узнали, чтобы всё для всех стало ясно, чтобы я перестал висеть между небом и землёй (Аржак 2). It seems I wanted everyone to find out — wanted everything to come out into the open, so that I wouldn't have to go on hanging in this limbo (2a).

H-56 • **ПОД ОТКРЫ́ТЫМ НЕ́БОМ** [PrepP; Invar; adv or nonagreeing postmodif; fixed WO] outside of a building or shelter: **under the open sky; in the open air; out in the open; outdoors; out of doors;** [in limited contexts] **without shelter; without a roof over one's ⟨s.o.'s⟩ head.**

Да они [учёные люди] и делаются учёными, считал он, начиная от всяких там писарей, именно для того, чтобы отойти от физической работы и от жизни под открытым небом (Искандер 4). That was why they [learned men] became learned, he believed, from all those wretched clerks on up: precisely in order to get away from manual labor and life under the open sky (4a). ♦ …Немцы не хотят впускать в оккупированную зону беженцев. Пленных заставляют выполнять тяжёлые работы. Раненых держат под открытым небом (Эренбург 4). …The Germans were unwilling to let the refugees enter the occupied area. They were forcing the prisoners to carry on heavy labour and keeping the wounded out in the open (4a).

H-57 • **НЕ́БУ ЖА́РКО** *highly coll* [impers predic with быть∅, стать; often used as a subord clause after так…, что or такой…, что; fixed WO] s.o. does sth. in the most intense, energetic way possible (used to emphasize the highest degree of intensity of an action): **like you wouldn't believe; like gangbusters.**

H-58 • **В БЛАЖЕ́ННОМ НЕВЕ́ДЕНИИ** пребывать, находиться и т. п. *iron* [PrepP; Invar; adv or subj-compl with copula (subj: human); fixed WO] one knows nothing, does not suspect anything (about a problem or misfortune of which he should be aware): X пребывает в блаженном неведении ≃ **X is in a state of blissful ignorance; X lives in (a state of) blissful ignorance; X is ⟨lives⟩ in a fool's paradise.**

Жена ему открыто изменяет, а он пребывает в блаженном неведении. His wife is openly cheating on him, but he lives on in blissful ignorance.

H-59 • **ДО НЕВЕРОЯ́ТНОСТИ ⟨НЕВЕРОЯ́ТИЯ⟩** [PrepP; these forms only; usu. modif or adv (intensif)] extremely, to the highest degree: **incredibly; unbelievably; beyond belief; in the ⟨to an⟩ extreme.**

«…Оборок более не носят». — «Как не носят?» — «На место их фестончики». — «…Нехорошо, Софья Ивановна, если всё фестончики». — «Мило, Анна Григорьевна, до неверо-ятности…» (Гоголь 3). "…Flounces are out of fashion." "Out of fashion?" "Little festoons are coming in instead."…"It isn't pretty if it's festoons everywhere." "It's sweet, Anna Grigorievna, incredibly so…" (3c). ♦ …Глуповцы насеяли горчицы и персидской ромашки столько, что цена на эти продукты упала до невероятности (Салтыков-Щедрин 1). …The Glupovites sowed so much mustard and feverfew that their market price fell to an unbelievably low level (1b).

H-60 • **ХРИСТО́ВА НЕВЕ́СТА** *obs* [NP] **1.** a nun: **bride of Christ.**

2. a dead girl: **dead maiden.**

3. an aging woman who has never been married: **old maid.**

H-61 • **НЕВЕ́СТКЕ В ОТМЕ́СТКУ** *highly coll* [Invar; usu. adv; fixed WO] (to do sth.) in order to offend, embarrass etc s.o. who previously did the same to one; as an act of revenge: **(in order) to even the score; (in order) to give s.o. a taste of his own medicine; (in order) to get back at s.o.; (in order) to pay s.o. back in kind ⟨in his own coin⟩.**

Он опять вовремя не позвонил, и она решила — невестке в отместку — уйти из дому на весь вечер. Again he didn't call when he'd promised to, so she decided to even the score by going out for the whole evening.

H-62 • **НЕВЗИРА́Я НА** *кого-что* [Prep; Invar; the resulting PrepP is adv] regardless of (s.o. or sth.): **notwithstanding; in spite of; despite.**

Снилась ему широкая река… Над ней стоял тяжёлый пар, и все сотрудники института, невзирая на положение и возраст, должны были плыть через неё, для сдачи норм ГТО (Битов 2). He dreamed of a wide river.…A heavy vapor hung over it, and everyone at the institute, position and age notwithstanding, was supposed to swim across, in order to pass the Komsomol fitness test (2a).

Н-63 • НЕВЗИРА́Я НА ТО ЧТО *offic* [subord Conj, concessive] regardless of the fact that: **notwithstanding ⟨in spite of, despite⟩ the fact that.**

Н-64 • НЕВЗИРА́Я НИ НА ЧТО [PrepP; Invar; adv; fixed WO] despite everything, whatever the circumstances may be: **no matter what; in spite of everything; regardless; regardless of anything ⟨everything, what happens etc⟩.**

Как-то он [Иван] сказал писателю, чтобы тот перестал записывать и держал в уме свои жизненные наблюдения. Но тот ответил, что всё равно будет записывать, что бы Иван с ним ни сделал, пусть он его хоть побьёт, но он писатель и будет записывать, невзирая ни на что (Аксёнов 1). Once he [Ivan] told the writer to stop writing things down and to store his observations on life in his head. But this guy said he'd keep writing things down anyway, whatever Ivan did to him, even if Ivan beat him, he was a writer and would write things down no matter what (1a).

Н-65 • ВОТ ⟨ЧТО ЗА, Э́КА(Я), КАКА́Я⟩ НЕ́ВИДАЛЬ ⟨НЕВИДА́ЛЬЩИНА *obs*⟩! *coll, iron* [Interj; these forms only; fixed WO] there is nothing special, nothing extraordinary about s.o. or sth.: **aren't you ⟨isn't he etc⟩ a wonder!; what's so great about that!; big deal!;** [in limited contexts] **some prize!**

[Городничий] Фу ты, какая невидаль! Оттого, что ты шестнадцать самоваров выдуешь в день, так оттого и важничаешь? (Гоголь 4). [Mayor:] Ooh, aren't you a wonder! Swill down sixteen pots of tea a day — is that anything to put on airs about? (4b). ♦ «Замолчи, надоело слушать, как твой батя в семьдесят лет женился на молоденькой. Экая невидаль!» — сказала Шура... (Коротюков 1). "Oh, shut up. I'm sick and tired of hearing how your old man married some young thing at the age of seventy. What's so great about that?" Shura said... (1a). ♦ [Кочкарёв:] Эк невидаль жена! Без неё-то разве я не мог обойтись? (Гоголь 1). [K.:] Some prize — a wife! As if I couldn't manage without one (1b). ♦ [Домна Пантелеевна:] ...Какой-то купец полоумный серьги бирюзовые преподнёс... Очень нужно! Экая невидаль! (Островский 11). [context transl] [D.P.:] ...And those ear-rings that half-witted shopkeeper gave — a fat lot of good *they* were... (11a).

Н-66 • ОСКОРБЛЁННАЯ ⟨УГНЕТЁННАЯ⟩ НЕВИ́ННОСТЬ [NP; usu. obj or nonagreeing postmodif; fixed WO] a person who presents himself as one wrongly offended, insulted: **(put on airs of) injured ⟨wounded⟩ innocence; (portray o.s. as) an injured ⟨insulted⟩ innocent; (portray o.s. as) a victim ⟨an innocent victim⟩.**

Покритиковали тебя за дело, и нечего разыгрывать из себя оскорблённую невинность. They criticized you with good reason, so there's no need to put on airs of injured innocence.

Н-67 • ДО НЕВОЗМО́ЖНОСТИ [PrepP; Invar; adv (intensif) or modif] to the highest possible degree, above all measure: **extremely; to an ⟨in the⟩ extreme; exceedingly; unbelievably; incredibly.**

Дима был рассеян до невозможности и каждый раз, уходя в школу, забывал запереть входную дверь. Dima was incredibly absent-minded, and every morning when he went off to school he forgot to lock the front door.

Н-68 • НЕТ НЕДОСТА́ТКА *в ком-чём* [VP$_{subj/gen}$] some people (things etc) are present, available etc in sufficient quantity: **в X-ах нет недостатка ≃ there is no lack ⟨shortage⟩ of Xs.**

Несколько дней спустя состоялся бал у губернатора... Народу было пропасть, и в кавалерах не было недостатка... (Тургенев 2). A few days later the governor's ball took place....There were crowds of people and no lack of men for dancing-partners... (2c).

Н-69 • НЕЖДА́ННО-НЕГА́ДАННО появиться, наступить и т. п. *coll* [AdvP; Invar; adv; more often used with pfv

verbs] (to appear, arrive etc) suddenly, unexpectedly: **all of a sudden; (suddenly,) out of the blue; most unexpectedly.**

Вдруг, нежданно-негаданно, среди всех хлопот, ещё одно событие: приехал Таля, Виталий Петрович, санаторский знакомый (Грекова 3). Then, out of the blue, along with all these worries, something else happened. Talya arrived, Vitaly Petrovich... the man from the sanatorium (3a). ♦ Так вот-с, нежданно-негаданно появилась третья сила на громадной шахматной доске (Булгаков 3). Then suddenly, out of the blue, a third force appeared on the vast chessboard (3a). ♦ Так у Веры Платоновны Ларичевой нежданно-негаданно появилась дочь (Грекова 3). And so Vera Platonovna Laricheva most unexpectedly acquired a daughter (3a).

Н-70 • ТЕЛЯ́ЧЬИ НЕ́ЖНОСТИ *coll, often condes or derog* [NP; pl only; fixed WO] an excessive or inappropriate expression of tender feelings, sentimentality: **sloppy ⟨mushy⟩ sentimentality; sentimental slop.**

«...Примечаю, что в мальчике развивается какая-то чувствительность, сентиментальность, а я, знаете, решительный враг всяких телячьих нежностей, с самого моего рождения» (Достоевский 1). "...I noticed that a sort of tenderness, sensitivity, was developing in the boy, and, you know, I am decidedly the enemy of all sentimental slop, and have been since the day I was born" (1a).

Н-71 • НЕЗАВИ́СИМО ОТ *кого-чего* [Prep; Invar; the resulting PrepP is adv] without consideration of, not contingent upon (s.o. or sth.): **regardless of; irrespective of; independent(ly) of;** [in limited contexts] **no matter (who ⟨what etc⟩).**

Вмешиваться в литературу, поправлять ими писателей... или даже запрещать ими сочинённое могут все, кому не лень, независимо от уровня их компетенции (Войнович 1). Anyone who feels like it, regardless of his degree of competence, can intervene in literature, correct writers...or even ban their works (1a). ♦ ...Независимо от мер общих, он [Двоекуров], в течение нескольких лет сряду, непрерывно и неустанно делал сепаратные набеги на обывательские дома и усмирял каждого обывателя поодиночке (Салтыков-Щедрин 1). ...Irrespective of general measures, he [Duplicitov] made separate raids on the townsfolk's houses for several years running, continuously and tirelessly, and pacified each townsman individually (1a). ♦ Люди разделились на два лагеря: на уходящих и на остающихся. Первые, независимо от того, уходили ли они по доброй воле или по принуждению, считали себя героями (Лившиц 1). People were divided into two camps: those who were leaving and those who were staying behind. The former, independent of whether they were leaving of their own free will or by coercion, considered themselves to be heroes (1a). ♦ ...Почти независимо от его воли и несмотря на его нерешительность... он втягивается в заговор, имеющий целью овладение властью, и заговор увенчивается успехом (Толстой 7). ...Almost independently of his will, and despite his indecision...he is drawn into a conspiracy that aims at seizing power, and the conspiracy is crowned with success (7a). ♦ Каждый милиционер знает, что с водителя «Запорожца» можно содрать рубль всегда... Владелец «Волги»... может оказаться довольно важной персоной, его лучше и вовсе не трогать. А уж «Чайкам» и «Зилам» надо честь отдавать независимо от того, кто в них сидит (Войнович 1). Every policeman knows he can always squeeze a ruble out of the driver of a Zaporozhets....The person behind the wheel of a Volga could...prove important and is better left alone. Chaikas and Zils are to be saluted no matter who's inside (1a).

Н-72 • НЕЗАВИ́СИМО ОТ ТОГО́ ЧТО [subord Conj, concessive] without consideration of the fact that, not contingent upon the fact that: **regardless of (the fact that); irrespective of (the fact that);** [in limited contexts] **independent of (the fact that).**

Н-73 • **ЗА НЕИМЕ́НИЕМ** *кого-чего;* **ПО НЕИМЕ́НИЮ** *obs* [PrepP; these forms only; Prep; the resulting PrepP is *adv*] because of the absence of (s.o. or sth.): **for want ⟨lack⟩ of; lacking; in the absence of; there is no..., so...; having no ⟨not having any⟩...;** ∥ **за неимением лучшего** ≃ **for want of anything ⟨something⟩ better; lacking anything ⟨something⟩ better; for want of a better** [NP]; **lacking a better** [NP].

За неимением комнаты для проезжающих на станции, нам отвели ночлег в дымной сакле (Лермонтов 1). In the absence of a room for travelers at the post station, we were assigned night quarters in a smoky native hut (1a). ♦ Он был взяточник в душе... ухитрялся брать взятки, за неимением дел и просителей, с сослуживцев, с приятелей... (Гончаров 1). He was a bribe-taker at heart...and not having any official business with people, he contrived to take bribes from his colleagues and friends... (1a). ♦ [Дудукин:] ...В одно прекрасное утро его из дому совсем выгнали; тогда он пристал к какой-то бродячей труппе и переехал с ней в другой город. Оттуда его, за неимением законного вида, отправили по этапу на место жительства (Островский 3). [context transl] [D.:] One fine morning he was thrown out of the house altogether. He joined a troupe of strolling players and went with them to another town, but when it was discovered he had no passport he was sent home under police escort (3a).

Н-74 • **ДА́ЛЬШЕ НЕ́КУДА; ДА́ЛЬШЕ Е́ХАТЬ ⟨ИДТИ́⟩ НЕ́КУДА** *all coll* [these forms only; predic (impers or with subj: human, abstr, or a clause); may be used as a subord clause or indep. remark; fixed WO] some person (thing, the way sth. is done etc) is as bad as he or it could possibly be: X — дальше ехать некуда ≃ **X couldn't be worse; it's a case of the worst possible X; X gives (a) new meaning to the word "bad"; X is the worst ⟨the pits⟩; it ⟨thing X⟩ beats all ⟨everything⟩;** [when used as an indep. remark] **what next!**

Непосредственное начальство Филармона Ивановича вскочило, едва взгляд наивысшего начальства прикоснулся к нему, и быстро сказало, что вопрос ясен, поведение — дальше некуда... (Вахтин 1). Philharmon Ivanovich's immediate boss jumped up as the top boss's gaze passed over him and quickly said that this was clearly a case of the worst possible conduct... (1a). ♦ «Подтёлков твой — из каких? Вахмистр?.. Ого! Одних со мной чинов. Вот это так!.. Дожи́ли... Дальше некуда!» (Шолохов 3). "Your Podtyolkov—what is he? A sergeant-major?...Oho! The same rank as me. Well, well!...The things we've lived to see....What next!" (3a).

Н-75 • **КАК НЕЛЬЗЯ́...** *coll* [AdvP; Invar; modif; foll. by compar form of Adv; fixed WO] (used for maximum intensification of an adverb) exceedingly: как нельзя [compar AdvP] ≃ **as...as possible;** ∥ как нельзя лучше ≃ **as well as possible; as well as can ⟨could⟩ be; perfectly; in the best possible way; marvelously well; (it) couldn't be better;** ∥ как нельзя хуже ≃ **as bad(ly) as can ⟨could⟩ be; horribly; in the worst possible way; terribly bad; it couldn't be worse;** ∥ как нельзя больше ⟨более⟩ ≃ [with a verb] **completely; absolutely; fully; perfectly;** [in limited contexts] **as nearly as possible;** ∥ как нельзя более [AdjP or AdvP] ≃ **extremely; couldn't be ⟨have been⟩ more...; to the greatest degree; exceptionally.**

Все силы её [Наташи] с самого утра были устремлены на то, чтоб они все: она, мама, Соня — были одеты как нельзя лучше (Толстой 5). ...All her [Natasha's] energies had been directed to insuring that they all—herself, Mamma, and Sonya—should be as well dressed as possible (5a). ♦ «Я вижу, как вы развиваетесь после Каутского!» — взвизгливо и пожелтев, крикнул Филипп Филиппович. Тут он яростно нажал на кнопку в стене. — Сегодняшний случай показывает это как нельзя лучше!» (Булгаков 11). "I see how you are developing after Kautsky," Philip Philippovich screamed in a falsetto, his face turning yellow. He furiously pressed the button in the wall. "Today's case demonstrates it

perfectly" (11a). ♦ На другой день всё обделалось как нельзя лучше (Гоголь 3). The next day everything was arranged in the best possible way (3a). ♦ Жизнь Бунина в этих барских комнатах... как нельзя больше соответствовала моему представлению об аристократе, столбовом дворянине, российском академике, человеке безукоризненного вкуса (Катаев 3). Bunin's life in these lordly apartments...corresponded as nearly as possible to my conception of an aristocrat, a nobleman, a Russian Academician, a man of irreproachable taste (3a). ♦ ...Все трое как нельзя более довольны были друг другом (Гончаров 1). ...All three were extremely pleased with one another (1a). ...All three could not have been more pleased with one another (1b).

Н-76 • **КАК НЕЛЬЗЯ́ КСТА́ТИ** *coll* [AdvP; Invar; adv; may be used as indep. sent; fixed WO] at the most appropriate moment, very appropriately: **just at the right time; at the perfect time; perfect timing; just the thing ⟨the person⟩ I ⟨you⟩ need; the right thing at the right time; just in time.**

«Отец просил передать, что он вчера послал тебе денежный перевод». — «Как нельзя кстати». "Dad asked me to tell you that he sent you a money order yesterday." "Perfect timing!" ♦ Предложенный хозяйкой чай с бутербродами был как нельзя кстати: Виктор весь день ничего не ел. The tea and sandwiches that the hostess offered were just the right thing at the right time: Viktor hadn't eaten all day.

Н-77 • **НЕЛЬЗЯ́ НЕ...** [Invar; used as impers predic with бытьø; foll. by infin] one has to (do sth.): **one can't help but; one cannot but; one can't not; one can't help (doing sth.); it is impossible not to.**

Ваши доводы так убедительны, что с ними нельзя не согласиться. Your arguments are so convincing that one can't help but agree with them.

Н-78 • **В НЕМИ́ЛОСТИ** *у кого* бытьø; **ВПАДА́ТЬ/ВПАСТЬ ⟨ПОПАДА́ТЬ/ПОПА́СТЬ⟩ В НЕМИ́ЛОСТЬ** *к кому, у кого* [PrepP, Invar, subj-compl with бытьø (1st var.) or VP; subj: human] **1.** to be or become regarded by one's sovereign or superior with strong disapproval, scorn etc: X в немилости у Y-а ⟨X впал в немилость к Y-у⟩ ≃ **X is ⟨has fallen⟩ out of favor with Y; X is in disfavor ⟨disgrace⟩; X has fallen into disfavor (with Y); X has incurred Y's disfavor.**

[Дед Гришака] участвовал в турецкой кампании 1877 года, состоял ординарцем при генерале Гурко, попал в немилость и был отослан в полк (Шолохов 2). He [Grandad Grishaka] had taken part in the campaign against the Turks in 1877. At one time he had been orderly to General Gurko, but had fallen out of favor and been sent back to his regiment (2a). ♦ ...Мне приходилось встречать и таких, которые, как только я попал в немилость у советских властей, сразу перестали меня узнавать (Войнович 1). ...It was also my lot to encounter people who, as soon as I fell into disfavor with the Soviet authorities, immediately began pretending they did not know who I was (1a).

2. to lose, no longer enjoy s.o.'s amiable feelings toward one or favorable opinion of one: X в немилости у Y-а ⟨X впал в немилость к Y-у⟩ ≃ **X has lost Y's favor; X is ⟨has fallen⟩ out of favor with Y;** [in limited contexts] **X is ⟨has gotten⟩ in Y's bad books.**

...На тонком лице графа Малерского постоянно бродила какая-то недобрая улыбка; он действительно впал в немилость у Зинаиды и с особенным стараньем подслуживался старой княгине... (Тургенев 3). An unpleasant smile roved continually over Count Malevsky's thin features. The Count certainly had fallen out of favor with Zinaida and now waited diligently on the old princess... (3c).

Н-79 • **КАК НЕПРИКА́ЯННЫЙ** ходит, бродит, болтается и т. п. *coll* [как + AdjP; nom only; adv] (of a person) (one wanders, roams about etc) in a confused, bewildered manner, as if unsure of what he should do: **like a lost soul; as if one has lost his bearings.**

Митя забыл взять ключи и до возвращения родителей бродил по окрестным улицам как неприкаянный. Mitya forgot his keys and ended up roaming around the neighborhood like a lost soul until his parents got home.

Н-80 • ИГРА́ТЬ/ПОИГРА́ТЬ НА НЕ́РВАХ *чьих, (у) кого coll* [VP; subj: human] to irritate s.o. (often intentionally): X играет у Y-а на нервах ≃ **X is getting ⟨grating⟩ on Y's nerves.**

[Бусыгин:] Ты дрыхнул, а мы всю ночь играли друг у друга на нервах (Вампилов 4). [B.:] While you were snoozing we were getting on each other's nerves, all night long (4a).

Н-81 • ДЕ́ЙСТВОВАТЬ ⟨ПОДЕ́ЙСТВОВАТЬ⟩ НА НЕ́РВЫ *кому* [VP; subj: usu. human or abstr] to irritate, disturb s.o.: X действует Y-у на нервы ≃ **X gets ⟨grates⟩ on Y's nerves; X chafes Y's nerves; X gets under Y's skin; X has an effect on Y's nerves.**

Одна из машинисток, Зоя Викторовна, сильно действовала Ольге Петровне на нервы: ошибки чуть ли не в каждом слове, нахально курит и болтает во время работы (Чуковская 1). One of the typists, Zoya Viktorovna, really got on Olga Petrovna's nerves: she made a mistake in almost every word, smoked in an insolent manner and chattered all the time she was working (1a). ♦ Старик мой спокойно озирался и никак не показывал, что такое большое скопление эндурцев в одном месте действует ему на нервы (Искандер 3). My old man looked around calmly and gave no sign that such a big concentration of Endurskies in one place had any effect on his nerves (3a).

Н-82 • ТРА́ТИТЬ/ПОТРА́ТИТЬ НЕ́РВЫ *coll* [VP; subj: human; often infin with не надо, нечего etc or neg imper] to be nervous, wear o.s. out through excessive worry: X тратит нервы ≃ **X is (over)straining his nerves; X is expending (his) nervous energy;** ‖ нечего нервы тратить ≃ **save wear and tear on your nerves; give your nerves a rest.**

Обидней всего бесцельно тратить нервы и силу доводов не на конференции, не в брошюре, не в споре с важным партийным противником, а просто так, на губошлёпа, который и не думает серьёзно того, что говорит (Солженицын 5). Nothing was more vexatious than expending his nervous energy and his cogency in argument not at a conference, in a pamphlet, in debate with an important party opponent, but, for no good reason, on a lout who didn't even mean what he was saying (5a). ♦ «Ладно, ладно, милый, — затараторил он [Шикалов] скороговоркой. — Нечего зря шуметь, нервы тратить, пойди домой, отдохни, попей винца…» (Войнович 2). "All right there, all right," said Shikalov, unloosing a torrent of words. "No cause for a ruckus, save wear and tear on your nerves, go on home, take it easy, drink a little wine…" (2a).

Н-83 • ТРЕПА́ТЬ/ИСТРЕПА́ТЬ ⟨ПОТРЕПА́ТЬ, ПО́Р-ТИТЬ/ИСПО́РТИТЬ⟩ НЕ́РВЫ *coll* [VP; subj: usu. human] 1. ~ *кому*. Also: МОТА́ТЬ/ИЗМОТА́ТЬ ⟨ВЫ-МА́ТЫВАТЬ/ВЫ́МОТАТЬ⟩ НЕ́РВЫ *coll* to make s.o. very nervous, upset, worried etc: X треплет Y-у нервы ≃ **X makes Y a nervous wreck; X plays havoc with Y's nerves; X wears Y out (with his demands ⟨pestering etc⟩); X shatters Y's nerves.**

«…Вот они где у меня сидят, эти интуристы! — интимно пожаловался Коровьев, тыча пальцем в свою жилистую шею… — Приедет… и или нашпионит, как последний сукин сын, или же капризами все нервы вымотает: и то ему не так, и это не так!..» (Булгаков 9). "Those foreign tourists, I've got them up to here!" Koroviev complained confidentially, poking his fingers at his scrawny neck. "…They'll come and spy around, like sons of bitches, or

else they'll wear you out with their demands: this isn't right, and that isn't right!…" (9a).

2. ~ *(себе)* to be very nervous, wear o.s. out with excessive worry: X треплет себе нервы ≃ **X is becoming ⟨making himself⟩ a nervous wreck; X is wearing out his nerves.**

Зачем ты треплешь себе нервы из-за таких пустяков? Why make yourself a nervous wreck over such trifles? ♦ «…Это прямо стало невыносимым, с этими людьми какие угодно нервы испортишь!» (Платонов 1). [context transl] "It's become simply unbearable, the strongest nerves will wear out with these people!" (1a).

Н-84 • НЕСМОТРЯ́ НА *что* [Prep; Invar; the resulting PrepP is adv] notwithstanding: **despite; in spite of; regardless of;** ‖ несмотря на свой ум ⟨свой талант, своё богатство и т. п.⟩ ≃ **for all one's brains ⟨talent, wealth etc⟩; smart ⟨talented, rich etc⟩ as one is.**

…Дядя Сандро стал думать, но, несмотря на его изощрённый ум, на этот раз ничего не придумывалось (Искандер 3). Uncle Sandro began to think, but this time, despite his keen intellect, nothing came to him (3a). ♦ Несмотря на мерзкую погоду и слякоть, щегольские коляски пролетали взад и вперёд (Гоголь 3). In spite of the foul weather and the muddy roads, elegant carriages kept driving rapidly back and forth (3a). ♦ Несмотря на ум и талант, она не смогла сделать карьеры: характер помешал. For all her brains and talent she couldn't make a career for herself: her personality got in the way. ♦ …Кузнец, который был издавна не в ладах с ним [с Чубом], при нём ни за что не отважится идти к дочке, несмотря на свою силу (Гоголь 5). …The blacksmith, who had for a long time been on bad terms with him [Chub], would on no account have ventured, strong as he was, to visit the daughter when the father was at home (5a).

Н-85 • НЕСМОТРЯ́ НА ТО ЧТО [subord Conj, concessive] notwithstanding the fact that: **despite ⟨in spite of, regardless of⟩ the fact that; (even) though;** [in limited contexts] **ignoring the fact that.**

…Вопрос об изнеженности, инфантильности или физическом вырождении сам по себе отпадает, несмотря на то, что она [княгиня] была чистокровным потомком сванских князей (Искандер 3). …The question of her being effete, infantile, or physically degenerate simply does not arise, despite the fact that she [the princess] was a full-blooded descendant of the princes of Svanetia (3a). ♦ …Припоминалась осада Трои, которая длилась целых десять лет, несмотря на то что в числе осаждавших были Ахиллес и Агамемнон (Салтыков-Щедрин 1). …He could not help thinking about the siege of Troy which had lasted ten whole years—even though Achilles and Agamemnon had been on the side of the besiegers (1b). ♦ Анатоль не отпускал англичанина, и, несмотря на то, что тот, кивая, давал знать, что он всё понял, Анатоль переводил ему слова Долохова по-английски (Толстой 4). Anatole did not release him, and though he [the Englishman] kept nodding to show that he understood, Anatole went on translating Dolokhov's words into English (4b). ♦ «На каком же основании вы были так щедры к господину Ракитину?» — подхватил Фетюкович, несмотря на то что председатель сильно шевелился (Достоевский 2). "And on what grounds were you so generous to Mr. Rakitin?" Fetyukovich picked up, ignoring the fact that the judge was stirring uneasily (2a).

Н-86 • НЕСМОТРЯ́ НИ НА ЧТО [PrepP; Invar; adv; fixed WO] under any circumstances, despite all obstacles: **despite everything ⟨all⟩; in spite of everything; regardless; regardless of anything ⟨everything, what happens etc⟩; no matter what;** [in limited contexts] **against all (the) odds.**

Любой из них расхохотался бы, если б узнал, что человек в сползающих брюках и без единой театральной интонации, тот самый человек, которого к ним приводят под конвоем в любой час дня и ночи, не сомневается, несмотря ни на что, в своём праве на свободные стихи (Мандельштам 1). Any one of them would have laughed out loud at the idea that a man who could be brought before them under guard at any time of the day or night, who had to hold up his trousers with his hands and spoke without the slightest attempt at theatrical effects—that such a man might have no doubt, despite everything, of his right to express himself freely in poetry (1a). ♦ «Черта-то она отчасти карамазовская... жажда-то эта жизни, несмотря ни на что...» (Достоевский 1). "...It's a feature of the Karamazovs, to some extent, this thirst for life despite all..." (1a). ♦ ...Полюби мать Гайка, она ушла бы за ним на край света, несмотря ни на что и вопреки всему... (Рыбаков 1). ...If mother had loved Gaik she would have followed him to the ends of the earth, regardless and in spite of everything... (1a). ♦ Нещадно вырубаемая, истребляемая пожарами от чьих-то недотоптанных костров и дурацкими химическими опрыскиваниями... тайга всё же боролась за собственное существование, не сдавалась и, несмотря ни на что, оставалась прекрасной и великой (Евтушенко 1). Mercilessly hacked down, damaged by campfires that hadn't been put out properly, and by idiotic chemical sprays...the taiga nevertheless went on struggling for its very existence; it had not succumbed and it retained its beauty and strength no matter what (1a).

H-87 • К ⟨ПО⟩ НЕСЧА́СТЬЮ; НА НЕСЧА́СТЬЕ [PrepP; these forms only; sent adv (parenth)] regrettably, to s.o.'s misfortune etc: **unfortunately; unluckily; unhappily; alas.**

[Воротынцев:] ...У нас – не партия. К счастью или к несчастью, никогда не было партии (Солженицын 9). [V.:] We're not a party. Fortunately, or unfortunately, we never were a party (9a). ♦ К несчастью, вместо Лизы вошла старая мисс Жаксон, набелённая, затянутая [в корсет], с потупленными глазами... (Пушкин 3). Unhappily it was not Lisa, but Miss Jackson, powdered, corseted, with eyes downcast, who entered the room... (3b). ♦ Идеалом стала математическая логика, но, к несчастью, только на словах (Мандельштам 2). Their ideal was logic of a mathematical kind, though they only paid lip service to it, alas (2a).

H-88 • ДВА́ДЦАТЬ ДВА НЕСЧА́СТЬЯ coll, humor [NP; Invar; fixed WO] a person experiencing a long period of bad luck, a series of failures: **a walking catastrophe; [in limited contexts] trouble and he ⟨she etc⟩ are never far apart; an accident ⟨a disaster⟩ waiting to happen.**

[source] [Дуняша:] Человек он несчастливый, каждый день что-нибудь. Его так и дразнят у нас: двадцать два несчастья... (Чехов 2). [context transl] [D.:] ...He's an unlucky fellow: every day something happens to him. They tease him about it around here; they call him Two-and-twenty Troubles (2a).

< The nickname of a character in Anton Chekhov's play *The Cherry Orchard* («Вишнёвый сад»), 1903.

H-89 • А ТО НЕ́Т! substand [Interj; fixed WO] used to express the speaker's definitive positive reaction to a preceding question or statement: **of course!; surely!; sure thing!; certainly!; absolutely!; no doubt about it!; that's right!; [in limited contexts] I'm afraid so!; what else!**

«Я тебя устроила на работу». – «Как? Куда?» – «В гостиницу „Салют", дежурной по этажу». – «А я справлюсь?» – «А то нет!» (Грекова 3). "I've found you a job." "How?... Where?" "At the Hotel Salute, as a floor attendant." "Can I do it?" "Of course!" (3a). ♦ «Как же сказывали, Кутузов кривой, об одном глазу?» – «А то нет! Вовсе кривой» (Толстой 4). "Didn't they say Kutuzov was blind in one eye?" "That's right! Completely blind" (4a). ♦ «Ты думаешь, что внутри общества мы все и по-отдельности уже обанкротились?» – «А то нет!» (Аксёнов 6). "Do you think that by living within society each and every one of us is automatically bankrupt?" "I'm afraid so!" (6a). ♦ [Валентина:] Не ври, Павел. [Пашка:] Я вру? [Валентина:] А то нет. Ты меня испытываешь (Вампилов 2). [V.:] Don't lie, Pavel. [P.:] Me, lying? [V.:] What else. You're just testing me (2b).

H-90 • НЕТ И ⟨ДА⟩ НЕТ кого-чего coll [VP; subj/gen: usu. human, abstr, or concr; pres or past; often preceded by всё; fixed WO] (usu. of s.o. or sth. eagerly awaited) a person (thing, or phenomenon) has not appeared, come, been seen etc (yet): X-а нет и нет ≃ there's (still) no sign of X; X has not materialized; [in limited contexts] thing X has eluded person Y.

Мы ждём Петю с утра, а его всё нет и нет. We've been waiting for Petya since morning, but there's still no sign of him. ♦ ...Хотя он, старик, при ней и хотя он всё перетерпит ради дочери, счастья материнского ей всё нет да нет... (Айтматов 1). ...Although he, the old man, was with her and would endure everything for his own daughter's sake, the happiness of motherhood simply eluded her (1b).

H-91 • НЕТ КАК НЕТ кого-чего coll [VP; subj/gen: human, concr, or abstr; pres only; may be used in past, present, and future contexts; fixed WO] s.o. or sth. is already gone or has not appeared yet: X-а нет как нет ≃ X is nowhere to be found; X is nowhere in sight; there's no sign of X; [of a person or thing that is gone or ɔ.y] there's no sign of X; X has disappeared ⟨vanished⟩ (into thin air).

Его кто-то отвлёк, и он на секунду выпустил руку девочки. Оглянулся – а её нет как нет. Somebody distracted him and he let go of the little girl's hand for a moment. When he turned around, she was nowhere in sight.

H-92 • НЕТ-НЕТ ДА И...; НЕТ-НЕТ ДА ⟨И⟩... all coll [Particle; these forms only; fixed WO] periodically, sometimes, at irregular intervals: **from time to time; (every) once in a while; (every) now and then ⟨again⟩; every so often; occasionally; [in limited contexts] an occasional [NP].**

...Вращаясь в высоких кругах, Яконов нет-нет да и слышал подробности, недоступные печати (Солженицын 3). ...Moving as he did in high circles, Yakonov from time to time heard about details not available to the press (3a). ♦ Нюра, идя следом, нет-нет да и поглядывала украдкой на нового своего знакомого (Войнович 2). Every once in a while, as she followed behind him, Nyura would steal a glance at her new acquaintance (2a). ♦ «Буду вот твои сочинения читать, буду про тебя слышать ото всех, а нет-нет — и сам зайдёшь проведать, чего ж лучше?» (Достоевский 3). "I'll read your writings, I'll hear about you from everyone, and once in a while you'll stop by to see me yourself—what could be better?" (3c). "What I'll do is read your articles, and I'll also be hearing about you from everybody else, and now and again you'll come to see me yourself; what could be better?" (3a). ♦ Влад нет-нет да сходит туда, в тот двор, и теперь (Максимов 2). Even now Vlad still occasionally passes by and goes into that courtyard (2a). ♦ Самолёт всё ещё плыл над ватной пустыней, но в пустыне этой уже стали возникать просветы: нет-нет да блеснёт внизу ночное озеро или изгиб реки... (Аксёнов 6). The aircraft was still floating over a wilderness of cotton, but gaps were already starting to appear in that wilderness. Down below were occasional glints of nocturnal lake or the bend of a river... (6a).

H-93 • ДО НЕУЗНАВА́ЕМОСТИ [PrepP; Invar; adv] to the point where the person or thing in question cannot be recognized: **beyond recognition.**

За ним, натягивая подол рубахи на порванную штанину, гнётся Лагутин, третий – тамбовец Игнат, следующий – Ванька Болдырев, изменившийся до неузнаваемости, постаревший, по меньшей мере, на двадцать лет (Шолохов 3). Next to him stood Lagutin, leaning over to pull the hem of his vest over his torn trouser leg. The third was Ignat, the man from Tambov, and next to him was Vanka Boldyrev, who had changed beyond recognition and looked at least twenty years older (3a).

H-94 • НИКА́К НЕ́Т [sent; Invar; fixed WO] **1.** mil a negative reply to a question posed by s.o. of higher rank: **no, sir; certainly ⟨absolutely, of course⟩ not, sir; by no means, sir.**

...[Я] ещё раз, у одного из выходящих, спросил: «Это Усад, да?» А он (совсем неожиданно) вытянулся передо мной в струнку и рявкнул: «Никак нет!!» (Ерофеев 1). ...[I] again asked one of the passengers getting off: "This is Usad, right?" And (quite unexpectedly) he snapped to attention in front of me and bellowed: "No, sir!" (1a).

2. *obs* a respectful reply to some question (usu. by a person of low rank, status etc): **no, sir ⟨ma'am⟩; not at all, sir ⟨ma'am⟩; by no means (, sir ⟨ma'am⟩).**

«Господин профессор, — начал незнакомец приятным сиповатым голосом, — простите простого смертного, нарушившего ваше уединение». — «Вы репортёр?» — спросил Персиков... «Никак нет, господин профессор», — ответил толстяк (Булгаков 10). "Mr. Professor," the stranger began in a pleasant, slightly husky voice, "forgive an ordinary mortal who ventured to invade your privacy." "Are you a reporter?" asked Persikov.... "By no means, sir," replied the fat man (10a).

H-95 • БЕЗ НИКАКИХ *highly coll* [PrepP; Invar] **1.** [usu. the concluding clause in a compound sent; usu. used after a verb denoting a command that should be carried out] (used to emphasize the categorical nature of an order) no objection or discussion will be tolerated: **and no arguments ⟨back talk⟩; and that's that; and that's final; and I ⟨he etc⟩ won't take no for an answer; and I don't mean maybe; and no (ifs, ands, or) buts about it.**

Ну-ка, быстро за работу, без никаких! All right, hurry up and get to work, and no arguments!

2. [adv] freely, without waiting for an invitation, asking permission, or going through any formalities: **without ceremony; you don't need an invitation ⟨an excuse⟩.**

Мы всегда дома, заходите запросто, без никаких. We're always home, just drop in, you don't need an invitation.

H-96 • И НИКАКИ́Х! *coll* [Invar; usu. the concluding clause in a compound sent; usu. used after a verb denoting a command, decision etc that should be carried out] (used to emphasize the categorical nature of an order, the finality of a decision etc) no objection or discussion will be tolerated: **and no arguments ⟨back talk⟩; and that's that; and that's final; and that's the end of it; and I ⟨he etc⟩ won't take no for an answer; and I don't mean maybe; and I won't hear of anything else;** [when used as a command] **and no (ifs, ands, or) buts about it.**

[Сарафанов:] Володя! Я за то, чтобы ты у нас жил — и никаких (Вампилов 4). [S.:] Volodya! I want you to live with us and no arguments (4b). ♦ [Дергачёв (*грозно*):] Обслужить клиента, и никаких! (Вампилов 2). [D. (*threateningly*):] Serve the customer, and no back talk! (2b). ♦ [Зилов:] Вы будете пить за охоту — и никаких. А если нет, то зачем вы здесь собрались? (Вампилов 5). [Z.:] You're going to drink to duck-shooting, and that's the end of it. And if not, why did you come? (5a).

H-97 • КАК НИ́ТКА С ИГО́ЛКОЙ *coll* [как + NP; Invar; subj-compl with быть$_\varnothing$ (subj: human, pl); fixed WO] (usu. of two people) (we, you, they are) inseparable: **X и Y как нитка с иголкой ≃ X and Y are like each other's shadows; X and Y are like (Siamese) twins.**

H-98 • ШИ́ТО ⟨-ый и т. п.⟩ БЕ́ЛЫМИ НИ́ТКАМИ [AdjP; subj-compl with быть$_\varnothing$ (subj: usu. всё, это, всё это, or occas. abstr.) or (full-form only) modif (often detached); usu. this WO] (sth. is) poorly, clumsily concealed: **(that can be) easily seen through; obvious to anyone; poorly disguised; transparent;** [of a story, excuse etc] **(sth.) sounds shaky.**

«Слушай, может быть, тебе лучше явиться в Кежму, к Алферову? Заявишь, что шёл к нему просить перевести тебя к Фриде или Фриду к тебе. Тогда получится совсем по-другому: из района ты не ушёл, сам явился в Кежму». — «Шито бе-

лыми нитками», — поморщился Борис (Рыбаков 2). "Listen, maybe it would be best for you to show up in Kezhma and present yourself to Alferov. You can say you've come to ask him to transfer you to Freda or Freda to you. It will look quite different then: you wouldn't have gone outside the district, you'd have turned up in Kezhma." "It sounds shaky." Boris frowned (2a).

H-99 • ПО НИ́ТКЕ ⟨НИ́ТОЧКЕ⟩ разобрать, перебрать *что obs* [PrepP; these forms only; adv] (to analyze sth.) paying attention to even the smallest details: **down to the last detail; in great detail; (subject sth. to) minute scrutiny.**

H-100 • ДО (ПОСЛЕ́ДНЕЙ) НИ́ТКИ [PrepP; these forms only; adv] **1. промокнуть, вымокнуть** и т. п. ~ *coll* (to be, get etc) thoroughly wet: **X промок до нитки ≃ X was ⟨got⟩ soaked to the skin; X was ⟨got⟩ drenched ⟨soaked⟩ to the bone; X was ⟨got⟩ wet to the bone; X was ⟨got⟩ sopping ⟨soaking⟩ wet.**

В трёх верстах от станции*** стало накрапывать, и через минуту проливной дождь вымочил меня до последней нитки (Пушкин 3). Three versts from the posting-station at ***, a light drizzle began; a minute later it had changed to a driving rain and I was soaked to the skin (3b).

2. обобрать *кого*, **проиграть, пропить** и т. п. ~ *coll* (to rob, gamble away, spend on drinking etc) absolutely all the money one or s.o. has: **X обобрал Y-а ~ ≃ X robbed Y blind; X fleeced Y (down to Y's last kopeck ⟨penny etc⟩); X cleaned Y out;** ‖ **X проиграл всё ~ ≃ X gambled away everything down to the last kopeck ⟨penny etc⟩; X lost the shirt off his back;** ‖ **X пропил всё ~ ≃ X drank up every kopeck ⟨penny etc⟩ he had.**

Костю заметил Бейлис, главный бильярдист Москвы, ввёл в лучшие бильярдные, где обыгрывались «фраера», денежные провинциалы, командировочные с казёнными деньгами. С ними Костя был беспощаден, заманивал первым лёгким выигрышем, а потом раздевал до нитки (Рыбаков 2). He [Kostya] had been spotted by Beilis, the top billiards player in Moscow. Beilis took him to the best billiards halls, where they hustled freeloaders, moneyed provincials visiting Moscow on government funds. Kostya was merciless with them. He would con them by losing the first game and then fleece them down to their last kopeck (2a). ♦ [extended usage] «Англия и Франция навязали Германии Версаль, репарации, раздели до нитки, отобрали колонии...» (Рыбаков 2). [context transl] "England and France bound Germany hand and foot at Versailles, the reparations stripped her bare, they took her colonies..." (2a).

3. рассказать *что*, **разобрать(ся) в ком-чём, помнить** *что* и т. п. ~ *substand* (to tell, analyze, remember etc sth.) completely, thoroughly, including the small details: **(down) to the minutest ⟨the smallest, the tiniest, the last⟩ detail; in every detail.**

H-101 • (НИ ОДНО́Й) СУХО́Й ⟨ЖИВО́Й⟩ НИ́ТКИ НЕТ ⟨НЕ ОСТА́ЛОСЬ⟩ *на ком coll* [VP$_{subj/gen}$] s.o. has gotten thoroughly wet: **на X-е сухой нитки нет ≃ X is ⟨has gotten⟩ soaked to the skin; X is ⟨has gotten⟩ drenched to the bone; X is ⟨has gotten⟩ sopping ⟨soaking⟩ wet; there isn't a dry stitch ⟨spot⟩ on X.**

«Боги! — воскликнул Пилат, — да ведь на вас нет сухой нитки!» (Булгаков 9). "Gods!" exclaimed Pilate. "There's not a dry stitch on you!" (9b).

H-102 • НА ЖИВУ́Ю НИ́ТКУ *coll* [PrepP; Invar; adv; fixed WO] **1. сшить, сметать** *что* ~ to sew sth. together lightly, just so it holds together: **baste; tack; stitch together loosely.**

В то время как она [Наташа], надев смётанный на живую нитку ещё без рукавов лиф и загибая голову, гляделась в зеркало, как сидит спинка, она услыхала в гостиной оживлён-ные звуки голоса отца и другого, женского голоса... (Толстой 5). She [Natasha] had just put on a bodice that was basted together but still without sleeves, and was turning her head to see in the glass how it fitted, when she heard in the drawing room the animated sounds of her father's voice and another's—a woman's... (5a).

2. ~ **построить, сколотить, сделать** *что* (to build, make sth., put sth. together) carelessly, flimsily: **(build sth. ⟨put sth. together⟩) shoddily ⟨hastily, any old way, in a slipshod manner⟩; knock ⟨slap⟩ sth. together; haphazardly hook sth. together; jerry-build sth.**

Шагали, шагали и натолкнулись на занесённые снегом развалины – цель нашего путешествия – остатки кирпичного завода. Он был сотворён «на живую нитку», по-лагерному (Иоффе 1). We walked on and on and finally came upon the snow-covered ruins, the goal of our journey—the remains of the brickworks. It had been constructed in camp-style—hastily... (1a).

Н-103 • АРИА́ДНИНА НИТЬ; НИТЬ АРИА́ДНЫ *both lit* [NP; sing only; fixed WO] sth. that helps s.o. find a way out of a difficult situation or solve a difficult problem: **Ariadne's thread.**

< According to Greek myth, *Ariadne*, a daughter of Minos of Crete, gave Theseus a ball of thread, by which he traced his way out of the labyrinth.

Н-104 • ПУТЕВО́ДНАЯ НИТЬ *lit* [NP; sing only; often subj-compl with copula (subj: abstr); fixed WO] sth. that helps a person determine the best approach to a given situation, that serves as a guide in some matter: **guiding thread.**

...По тому инстинктивному чувству, которым один человек угадывает мысли другого и которое служит путеводной нитью разговора, Катенька поняла, что мне больно её равнодушие... (Толстой 2). ...By the instinctive feeling with which one human being guesses another's thoughts, and which serves as the guiding thread of conversation, Katya understood that her indifference hurt me (2a).

Н-105 • ПРОХОДИ́ТЬ ⟨ТЯНУ́ТЬСЯ⟩ КРА́СНОЙ НИ́ТЬЮ *через что, где lit* [VP; subj: abstr] to be fundamental to and pervade sth.: **X проходит красной нитью через Y ≃ X runs (like a thread) through Y; X is a central ⟨recurrent⟩ theme ⟨motif⟩ of ⟨in⟩ Y.**

...Его [Осноса] неверие в силу личности и преклонение перед силой организации... проходило красной нитью через всё, что он писал... (Амальрик 1). ...He [Osnos] lacked faith in the individual and showed deference to organizations. This trait ran like a thread through his writings... (1a).

Н-106 • ИЗ НИЧЕГО́ сделать, создать *что и т. п. coll* [PrepP; Invar; prep obj] (to make, create etc sth.) from nothing or from sth. insignificant: **from (next to) nothing; out of (next to) nothing.**

«Любовь к отцу, не оправданная отцом, есть нелепость, есть невозможность. Нельзя создать любовь из ничего, из ничего только бог творит» (Достоевский 2). "Love for a father that is not justified by the father is an absurdity, an impossibility. Love cannot be created out of nothing: only God creates out of nothing" (2a).

Н-107 • НИЧЕГО́ СЕБЕ́ *coll* [Invar; fixed WO] **1.** [adv] well enough (although usu. not extremely well): **not (so) badly; not too ⟨half⟩ badly; all right.**

[Наташа *(мельком глядится в зеркало, поправляется):*] Кажется, причёсана ничего себе... (Чехов 5). [N. *(she steals a glance at herself in the mirror and tidies herself up):*] My hair seems to be all right... (5c).

2. [subj-compl with copula (subj: any noun) or nonagreeing modif] quite good: **not (so) bad; not a bad [NP]; not too ⟨half⟩**

bad; **not bad at all;** [in refer. to appearance] **(quite) good-looking;** [as a positive response to a question about some quality, property etc] **quite.**

[Брат Сила:] Он ничего себе малый. Первоначально он мне не понравился, но теперь я вижу, что он добрый католик (Булгаков 8). [Brother Force:] He's not a bad fellow. At first I didn't like him, but now I see that he's a good Catholic (8a). ♦ Бунин несколько задержался на этом стихотворении... а затем наверху страницы поставил моим обгрызанным карандашом птичку, по-видимому означавшую, что стихи ничего себе, во всяком случае – «верные» (Катаев 3). Bunin paused for a while over this poem...and then with my chewed stump of pencil put a tick at the top of the page which seemed to indicate that the poem was not too bad, at any rate "true" (3a). ♦ ...[Ирунчик] была ничего себе женщина – в пропорциях и с фигурой, вполне пригодной для всего на свете: для верхней одежды, для дневного костюма, для вечернего платья, для купальника и т. д. (Залыгин 1). Irunchik was a good-looking woman, well proportioned, with a figure that could wear anything: an overcoat, a suit, an evening dress, a swim-suit, anything (1a). ♦ [Тузенбах:] [Вершинин] не глуп – это несомненно. Только говорит много. [Ирина:] Интересный человек? [Тузенбах:] Да, ничего себе... (Чехов 5). [T.:] [Vershinin] is not stupid, that's certain. Except that he talks a lot. [I.:] Is he an interesting person? [T.:] Yes, quite... (5c).

3. [nonagreeing modif] used to express the speaker's ironic reaction toward, indignation at, or disagreement with a stated or implied positive evaluation of s.o. or sth.: **some [NP]; [NP], indeed!; a fine [NP] (one is ⟨one has got etc⟩)!; [NP], my foot!**

«Почему [декан] Янсон не явился на разбор дела?» – «Болен». – «Болен... А где директор института?» Баулин пожал плечами. «Не пришла». – «Ничего себе организация», – усмехнулся Столпер... (Рыбаков 2). "Why hasn't Janson [the dean] turned up for the hearing?" "He's ill." "Ill. And what about the director of the institute?" Baulin shrugged his shoulders. "She didn't come." "Some organization!" Stolper sneered (2a). ♦ «...Разве ему недостаточно было пролистать нашу подшивку?» – спросил я. «А что такого, – сказал Автандил Автандилович, – подумаешь, два-три материала». Ничего себе два-три! Но я не стал затрагивать эту болезненную тему (Искандер 4). "...Wouldn't it have been enough for him to go through our files?" I asked. "But what's there?" Avtandil Avtandilovich said. "Imagine – two or three articles. Two or three, indeed! But I was not about to broach that painful subject (4a). ♦ ...Чуть в стороне – лежат тела убитых. Их снегом запорошило... Семь белых людей лежат и молчат... А мы вино пили. «Ничего себе командир, – говорю я Сашке, – сам напился и нам позволил» (Окуджава 1). A little way away are the bodies of the dead men. They are sprinkled with powdery snow....Seven white men lie in silence....And we were drinking wine. "A fine commander we've got," I say to Sashka. "Drinking like that and letting us drink, too!" (1a). ♦ «Он трёхнутый [*slang*], этот твой Прохор». – «Не „мой". Наш». – «Ничего себе „наш"... Он косых на десять нас с тобой дурит, не меньше» (Семёнов 1). "He's cracked, that Prokhor of yours." "Not 'mine.' Ours." "'Ours,' my foot....He's diddling us out of ten grand at least" (1a).

4. [Interj] used ironically to express indignation at, disapproval of, disagreement with etc sth.: **(just) great!; not bad!; well, well!; pretty good!; I like that!**

«Ты хоть спрашивала там кого? Нет? Ничего себе. Люди все в лес на месячник, а я пробежки по ночам делать...», – Михаил ещё говорил что-то в том же роде... (Абрамов 1). "Did you at least get someone's permission? No? Just great. Everybody's gone out to the forest for the Special Month and I'm running around in circles every night..." Mikhail went on a while in the same vein (1a). ♦ «У него, – продолжает Ленка, – все записи Окуджавы, Галича и Высоцкого. Книги Оруэла, Замятина, Солженицына»... – «Ничего себе, – говорю я. – Если узнают на факультете, влетит» (Зиновьев 2). "At home," Lenka continues, "he's got every recording of Okudzhava, Galich and Vysotsky. Books by Orwell, Zamyatin, Solzhenitsyn."..."Not bad," I say. "If they find out at the faculty, that'll be the end of him" (2a). ♦ «С каких это пор у нас воскресенье − и вдруг выходной?» − «Но майор сказал, что у нас сейчас нет срочной работы». Сологдин резко повернулся в сторону Еминой. «У *нас* нет срочной работы? − едва ли не гневно воскликнул он. − Ничего себе! У нас нет срочной работы!» (Солженицын 3). "Since when is Sunday a free day all of a sudden?" "But the major said we don't have any urgent work right now." Sologdin turned sharply toward Emina. "*We* have no urgent work?" he cried almost angrily. "Well, well! We have no urgent work!" (3a). ♦ «Ты в каком же классе?» − спросил он парнишку. «В восьмом». − «Ничего себе», − удивился Алтынник. Сам он кончил только семь классов (Войнович 5). "What grade are you in?" he asked the boy. "Eighth." "Pretty good," said Altinnik, impressed. He'd only gotten as far as the seventh himself (5a).

H-108 • **В НОВИ́НКУ** *кому coll* [PrepP; Invar; subj-compl with copula (subj: abstr or concr)] sth. is new and little known or completely unknown (to s.o.): X был Y-у в новинку ≃ **X was (something of) a novelty for ⟨to⟩ Y; X was new to Y; X was a new experience for Y.**

Мы слишком привыкли, что из спички вылетает огонь, а детям всё это в новинку. И что собаки лают, а петухи − поют… (Терц 3). We are more than accustomed to fire leaping out of a match, but for children it is something of a novelty − as are dogs barking and cocks crowing… (3a).

H-109 • **ПО НО́ВОЙ** *начинать, делать что и т. п. coll* [PrepP; Invar; adv] (to begin sth., do sth. etc) over again (sometimes differently than before): **start up again; (start) all over again; [in limited contexts] here we go again.**

Когда они храпят, кажется, что работают три перфоратора. Причём комедия: как один перестанет храпеть, так и второй прекращает и третий − стоп! А по новой начинают тоже одновременно (Аксёнов 1). When they snore, it's like three jackhammers going. And they do a comedy bit: as soon as one ceases to snore, the second one stops, and − *Cut!* − the third's out. And they start up again simultaneously, too (1a). ♦ [Сильва:] Всё. Пошли отсюда. [Бусыгин *(с досадой):*] Я остаюсь. [Сильва:] Ну вот, привет! Значит, всё по новой?.. Слушай, мне эта песня надоела (Вампилов 4). [S.:] That does it. Let's get out of here, I tell you. [B. *(pained):*] I'm staying. [S.:] Well, I like that! You mean we're gonna start all over again? Look I've had it − up to here! *(points to his neck)* (4c). [S.:] That'll do. Let's get going. [B. *(annoyed):*] I'm staying. [S.:] Well! That's news! Here we go again, eh?…You know, I've had enough of this game (4a).

H-110 • **ВОТ (ЕЩЁ) НО́ВОСТИ ⟨НО́ВОСТЬ⟩!; (ЭТО ЕЩЁ) ЧТО ЗА НО́ВОСТИ ⟨НО́ВОСТЬ⟩!** *all coll, disapprov* [Interj; these forms only; fixed WO] used to express unpleasant surprise, indignation etc in connection with sth. just heard, learned: **that's news to me!; that's a new one!; what next!; well, how do you like that!; well, you don't say!**

«Он говорит, что это его книга, а не твоя». − «Вот ещё новости!» "He says this is his book, not yours." "Well, how do you like that!"

H-111 • **БЕЗ ЗА́ДНИХ НОГ** [PrepP; Invar; fixed WO] **1. быть₀, остаться, вернуться** и т. п. ~ *highly coll.* Also: **БЕЗ НОГ** *coll* [subj-compl with copula (subj: human)] (to be, come back etc) exhausted, unable to move (because of walking, work etc): X был ~ ≃ **X was dead on his feet; X was dropping in his tracks; X was ready to drop; X was dead beat ⟨dead tired, dog-tired⟩; X was bushed ⟨worn out etc⟩; X had worn himself out; [in limited contexts] X was tuckered out.**

Дай ей отдохнуть немного, она вернулась домой без задних ног. Let her rest up a bit, she came home dead on her feet. ♦ …На похоронах из жильцов, званых на похороны… никто почти не был… Пётр Петрович Лужин, например, самый, можно сказать, солиднейший из всех жильцов, не явился… Не пришёл тоже и толстый подполковник (в сущности, ной штабс-капитан), но оказалось, что он «без задних ног» ещё со вчерашнего утра (Достоевский 3). …Of the lodgers that had been invited to the funeral…practically nobody had attended.…Pyotr Petrovich Luzhin, for example, the most respectable, one might say, of all the lodgers, had not put in an appearance.…A stout lieutenant colonel (in reality a retired second lieutenant) had not come either, but it turned out he had been "dead beat" since yesterday morning (3a). ♦ [Калошин:] Если бегать каждому в анкету заглядывать − без ног останешься (Вампилов 1). [K.:] If you had to run and check what everyone wrote on his registration form you'd wear yourself out… (1a).

2. *coll* **спать** ~ [adv] (to sleep) very soundly: X спит ~ ≃ **X is fast ⟨sound⟩ asleep; X is sleeping like a log; X is dead to the world.**

«Даже не шевельнулся, спит без задних ног» (Распутин 4). "He didn't even stir, he's fast asleep" (4a).

H-112 • **ВАЛИ́ТЬ ⟨СВА́ЛИВАТЬ/СВАЛИ́ТЬ⟩ С НОГ** *кого* [VP] **1.** Also: **СБИВА́ТЬ/СБИТЬ ⟨СШИБА́ТЬ/СШИБИ́ТЬ⟩ С НОГ** *coll*⟩ [subj: anim or удар, ветер etc; more often pfv] to knock s.o. to the ground: X свалил Y-a с ног ≃ **X knocked Y over ⟨off his feet⟩; X sent Y flying; X bowled Y over; X toppled ⟨felled⟩ Y; person X hurled Y to the ground; X laid Y low.**

Генералы и маршалы, как школьники на перемену, толпясь и чуть ли не сбивая друг друга с ног, ринулись в открытые двери (Войнович 4). Like schoolboys at recess the generals and the marshals dashed for the open doors, crowding together and almost knocking each other over (4a). ♦ Нержин, чуть не сбив с ног в полутёмном коридоре штаба… Наделашина, побежал в общежитие тюрьмы (Солженицын 3). In his rush to the prison dormitory Nerzhin almost knocked…Nadelashin off his feet in the dark corridor (3a). ♦ …И ядрёных… атаманцев умел Степан валить с ног ловким ударом в голову (Шолохов 2). That deft head-blow of Stepan's was powerful enough to fell…stalwart…men of the Ataman's Life Guards (2a). ♦ …Меня сшибли было с ног, но я встал и вместе с мятежниками вошёл в крепость (Пушкин 2). …I was hurled to the ground, but I got up again and entered the fortress with the rebels (2b).

2. [subj: abstr; occas. impers] (of illness, tiredness etc) to cause s.o. to lie down, fall sick; to weaken s.o., rob s.o. of his strength: X валит Y-a с ног ≃ **X knocks Y out; Y can barely ⟨hardly, scarcely⟩ stand up; X forces Y to take to his bed; Y is too tired ⟨ill, sick etc⟩ to move.**

Вспышка туберкулёза была настолько острой, что меня валило с ног (Мандельштам 2). My tuberculosis had suddenly got so bad again that I could scarcely stand up (2a). ♦ «Гришенька, это тиф!» − «Не болтай зря! Ничего не видно; лоб у тебя холодный, может, и не тиф», − утешал Григорий, но в душе был убеждён, что Аксинья заболела сыпняком, и мучительно раздумывал, как же поступить с ней, если болезнь свалит её с ног (Шолохов 5). "Grisha, darling, it's typhus." "Nonsense! There's no sign; your forehead's cool enough. It may not be that." Grigory tried to comfort her, but in his heart he was sure it was, and his brain was wrestling with the problem of what to do with her if she got too ill to move (5a).

H-113 • **ВАЛИ́ТЬСЯ/СВАЛИ́ТЬСЯ ⟨ПА́ДАТЬ⟩ С НОГ** *(от чего) coll* [VP; subj: human or, rare, animal; more often impfv] to be unable to stand on one's legs as a result of extreme fatigue, illness etc: X валился с ног ≃ **X was ready to drop ⟨to collapse⟩; X was dead on his feet; X could hardly stand ⟨stay⟩ on his feet; X was dropping ⟨collapsing⟩ (from exhaustion etc); X was dropping in his tracks; X was dead tired ⟨dog-tired⟩.**

[Зилов:] Нельзя так много работать. Мы не лошади. Я падаю с ног (Вампилов 5). [Z.:] It's no good working as hard as that. We're not cart-horses. I'm dead on my feet (5a). ♦ «...Почти все спят...» — «Они с ног валятся после вчерашней пьянки, их теперь не добудишься» (Шолохов 5). "...They're nearly all asleep." "They could hardly stay on their feet after yesterday's boozing, you won't wake them now" (5a).

H-114 • НЕ ЧУВСТВОВАТЬ ⟨НЕ СЛЫШАТЬ *coll*, **НЕ ЧУЯТЬ** *coll*⟩ **НОГ ПОД СОБОЙ** [VP; subj: human; pres or past] **1.** [usu. Verbal Adv не слыша, не чуя etc] to run very fast: X бежал, не чуя ног под собой ≃ **X was running at full speed ⟨at breakneck speed, (at) full tilt, as fast as his legs could carry him⟩;** ‖ X бегал, не чуя ног (под собой) ≃ **X was flying about.**

2. to be extremely tired, exhausted (from much walking, running, difficult labor etc): X ног под собой не слышал ≃ **X was ready to drop ⟨collapse⟩; X was dead on his feet; X was dropping in his tracks; X was dead tired;** [in limited contexts] **X was tuckered out.**

Весь день ей некогда было передохнуть, и к вечеру она ног под собой не чуяла. She didn't have a chance to take a break all day and by evening was ready to collapse.

3. to be very happy, be in ecstasy (over sth.): X ног под собой не чует ≃ **X is walking ⟨treading⟩ on air; X is beside himself (with joy etc).**

Прошло несколько окрыляющих мгновений, я шагал по дорожке сквера, не чувствуя под собой ног, и чем дольше я шёл, тем очевидней становилось моё спасение, и я двигался вперёд ликующими шагами (Искандер 4). Several encouraging instants went by. I strode down the garden path, treading on air. The longer I walked, the more obvious it became that I was safe, and I moved forward with exulting steps (4a).

H-115 • С НОГ НА ГОЛОВУ ставить, переворачивать *что*, **встать и т. п.** *coll* [PrepP; Invar; usu. adv; fixed WO] (in refer. to a state of affairs, s.o.'s understanding of sth. etc) (to present sth., sth. is perceived etc) as being opposite to what it is in reality, (to interpret sth., sth. is interpreted etc) as having a meaning opposite to what was intended: **(stand ⟨turn⟩ sth.) on its head; (stand ⟨turn⟩ sth.) upside down (on its head);** [in limited contexts] **(get ⟨have⟩ sth.) all backward; (put) the cart before the horse.**

Всё для Настёны перепуталось, всё сошло со своих мест и встало с ног на голову (Распутин 2). [For Nastyona] everything was mixed up, moved from its place and standing upside down on its head (2a).

H-116 • СБИВАТЬСЯ/СБИТЬСЯ С НОГ *coll* [VP; subj: human; usu. pfv past] to bustle about to the point of exhaustion (doing chores, looking for s.o. or sth. etc); to become exhausted (from bustling about doing chores, looking for s.o. or sth. etc): X с ног сбился ≃ **X ran his legs ⟨feet⟩ off; X was ready to drop ⟨collapse⟩; X wore ⟨knocked⟩ himself out; X ran himself ragged.**

На больших высотах небоскрёбов вдоль Бульвара 20 января с первыми лучами солнца появились красные и трёхцветные флаги... Царило радостное возбуждение... Полиция сбилась с ног, стараясь очистить главную улицу... (Аксёнов 7). Up and down the skyscrapers lining the Boulevard of the Twentieth of January the first rays of sun were joined by red flags and tricolors....The mood was one of joyous excitement....The police were running their legs off trying to clear [the main thoroughfare]... (7a). ♦ Рита говорила, что мы злостные бездельники, не помогаем ей, она с ног сбилась и теперь ещё мы хотим навьючить на неё больную домработницу (Трифонов 5). Rita responded that we were mean and lazy, that we didn't help her, that she wore herself out,

and now, to add insult to injury, we wanted to saddle her with a sick maid (5a).

H-117 • СО ВСЕХ НОГ бросить, кинуться, бежать и т. п. *coll* [PrepP; Invar; adv; fixed WO] (to take off, run) very rapidly, impetuously: **(at) full tilt; (at) full speed; like mad ⟨blazes⟩; headlong; as fast as one can ⟨could⟩; as fast as one's legs can ⟨could, would⟩ carry him;** [when the idiom and the verb are translated together] **take to one's heels; shoot off.**

...Пока он [лётчик] выполнял боевой разворот, Чонкин со всех ног кинулся к лесу (Войнович 4). ...By the time he [the pilot] had executed a battle turn, Chonkin was already dashing full speed for the safety of the nearby forest (4a). ♦ ...Дошло до Ревкина, что новый начальник интересуется и его, Ревкина, деятельностью тоже. Это было заметно по отношению к Ревкину его подчинённых, которые уже не улыбались ему приветливо, как раньше, и не кидались со всех ног исполнять его приказания (Войнович 4). ...Revkin learned that the new chief was interested in his, Revkin's, activities as well. This was evident in the way Revkin's subordinates related to him; they no longer smiled at him so affably and did not race headlong to execute his orders (4a). ♦ Капитан повернулся как по команде «кругом» и со всех ног бросился в казарму (Войнович 5). The captain wheeled around as if he had heard the command "About face!" and ran to the barracks as fast as his legs would carry him (5a). ♦ Обломов вдруг... вскочил на ноги и ринулся на Захара... Захар со всех ног бросился от него... (Гончаров 1). Oblomov suddenly jumped out of bed and rushed at Zakhar....Zakhar took to his heels... (1a). ♦ Разобрались. Вернулся [старший барака]. И вместе с надзирателем: «Первая! Вторая! Третья!..» Какую назовут пятёрку — со всех ног, и в барак (Солженицын 7). They finally lined up properly. He [the hut orderly] went back to his place, and shouted with the warder: "First five! Second! Third!" Each five shot off into the hut as its number was called (7c).

H-118 • У НОГ *чьих, кого* **быть₀, держать** *кого* **и т. п.** [PrepP; Invar; subj-compl with copula (subj: human or collect), obj-compl with держать etc (obj: human or collect), or adv] showing s.o. or having s.o. show one deep devotion, love, a willingness to serve etc: **(be ⟨sit⟩) at s.o.'s feet; (keep ⟨have etc⟩ s.o.) at one's feet.**

«Но разве могло быть иначе? — подумал он [Наполеон]. — Вот она, эта столица; она лежит у моих ног, ожидая судьбы своей» (Толстой 6). "But how could it be otherwise?" he [Napoleon] mused. "Here is this capital at my feet, awaiting its fate" (6a). ♦ «Тебе понравились однажды мои слёзы, теперь, может быть, ты захотел бы видеть меня у ног своих и так, мало-помалу, сделать своей рабой, капризничать, читать мораль...» (Гончаров 1). "You enjoyed seeing my tears once before, and now, perhaps, you would like to see me at your feet, so that little by little you could make me your slave, act capricious, moralize..." (1b).

H-119 • как, что, чего и т. п. чья ЛЕВАЯ НОГА ХОЧЕТ/ ЗАХОЧЕТ *coll* [VP_subj; these forms only; usu. subord clause; fixed WO] (what) a person feels inclined to do, (how) a person feels inclined to act etc (usu. in refer. to foolish, reckless behavior or arbitrary actions undertaken by a person who follows only his own whims): ...как ⟨что, когда и т. п.⟩ X-ова левая нога захочет ≃ **however ⟨what(ever), when(ever) etc⟩ X pleases; what(ever) ⟨however it, when(ever) it⟩ suits X's fancy; when(ever) the spirit moves X.**

«...В колхозе — как левая нога у начальства захочет. Захочет — даст, захочет — не даст. Иди в лес, серому волку жалуйся, вот и вся конституция» (Максимов 2). [context transl] "...In a kolkhoz everything depends on what sort of mood the bosses are in. If they feel like it, you'll get what's due to you—if they don't you won't. Go into the forest and complain to the wolves—that's all the law there is on a kolkhoz" (2a).

H-120 • НОГА́ ЗА́ НОГУ плестись, идти и т. п. [NP; Invar; adv; fixed WO] (in refer. to people, horses etc) (to go, move etc) very slowly: X плёлся ~ ≃ **X was dragging himself along; X was plodding ⟨trudging⟩ along; X was barely moving.**

H-121 • НОГА́ НА́ НОГУ (положить) [NP; Invar; usu. obj of положить; fixed WO] (of a person) (to put) one leg across the other (when sitting): X положил ~ ≃ **X crossed his legs;** ‖ положив ~ ≃ **with (one's) legs crossed; (one's) legs crossed; with crossed legs; cross-legged.**

Кязым сидел, положив нога на ногу и обхватив руками колено, глядя на огонь, слушал председателя (Искандер 5). Legs crossed, hands clasping his knee, Kyazym sat and stared at the fire as he listened to the chairman (5a).

H-122 • НОГА́ (человека) НЕ СТУПА́ЛА где, куда [VP_subj; Invar] (in refer. to a remote, desolate, uninhabited place) no one has ever been to or lived in (some place): нога человека не ступала в месте X ≃ **man has never ⟨no one has ever⟩ set foot in place X; man has never trod in place X.**

О, где вы, прелестные уголки, куда не ступала нога человека и где можно собирать гербарии? (Окуджава 2). Oh, where are you, you marvelous little corners where man has never trod and where one can gather herbs? (2a).

H-123 • ОДНА́ НОГА́ ЗДЕСЬ, (А) ДРУГА́Я ТАМ coll, occas. humor [sent; these forms only; fixed WO] (of a person) s.o. goes or runs somewhere and returns in a very short time, very quickly (often used as a command): **I ⟨he etc⟩ will be back ⟨will do sth.⟩ before you know it ⟨before you can turn around, in a flash, in a jiffy, in two shakes of a lamb's tail⟩.**

[author's usage] «Побегу, доложусь, дядя Коль, начальство порядок любит. Я бегом: одна нога там, другая – здесь» (Максимов 1). "I'll go and report, Uncle Kolya. The bosses like order. I shan't be long. I'll be back before you know it" (1a). ♦ «Иди тащи сюда свою роту». – «Я знал, Савва...» – «Иди, иди, а то раздумаю». – «Одна нога здесь, другая там...» (Максимов 2). "Go ahead and bring your horde in here." "I knew you would, Savva..." "Go on, before I change my mind." "I'll be back before you can turn around" (2a).

H-124 • ПОЛОЖИ́ТЬ что К НОГА́М чьим, кого ог кому lit [VP; subj: human or collect; usu. this WO] to place sth. in s.o.'s full possession or under s.o.'s complete control (usu. as an expression of admiration or a sign of total surrender): X положил к Y-овым ногам Z ≃ **X laid Z at Y's feet.**

«Каков мошенник! – воскликнула комендантша. – Что смеет ещё нам предлагать! Выйти к нему навстречу и положить к ногам его знамёна! Ах он собачий сын!» (Пушкин 2). "What a scoundrel!" exclaimed the captain's wife. "How does he dare propose such things to us! To meet him outside the fort and lay our flags at his feet! Oh, the son of a bitch!" (2a).

H-125 • ВВЕРХ ⟨КВЕ́РХУ⟩ НОГА́МИ coll [AdvP; these forms only; adv; fixed WO] **1.** [adv] держать, поставить, повесить, перевернуть что ~ (to hold, put, hang, turn sth.) so that the top part is on the bottom and the bottom part is on top: **upside down; bottom ⟨wrong⟩ side up.**

Среди совершенно непонятных для меня стихов, напечатанных вкривь и вкось, даже, кажется, кое-где вверх ногами... мне попался на глаза футуристический сборник «Садок судей»... (Катаев 3). Among these poems of which I could not understand a word, printed at all angles across the page, and sometimes even upside down...I came across a futurist collection called *A Stew of Judges*... (3a).

2. перевернуть что, перевернуться ~ и т. п. [obj-compl with перевернуть (obj: abstr or concr, often всё), or subj-compl with copula (subj: abstr or concr, often всё)] (in refer. to s.o.'s way of life, way of doing things, or, less often, the furnishings or objects in some place) (to bring sth., be brought etc) into a state of disorder, confusion: **(turn sth. ⟨everything etc⟩) upside down (on its head); (turn sth. ⟨everything etc⟩) on its head; (be ⟨end up, turn etc⟩) topsy-turvy.**

«...Доказано, что любовь – это состояние, зависящее от прилива крови к продолговатому мозгу, – серьёзно объяснил он. – И мне... не ясно, почему из-за этого факта, имеющего место в организме моего старшего брата, весь дом должен переворачиваться вверх ногами» (Каверин 1). "It has been proved," he observed seriously, "that...love is a condition which depends on the rush of blood to the *medulla oblongata*. And it's not at all clear to me why, because this is happening in the organism of my elder brother, the whole house has to be turned upside down" (1a). ♦ ...Все мысли в его голове перевернулись кверху ногами. И надо сказать, было от чего (Булгаков 9). All the thoughts in his head turned topsy-turvy. And, it must be said, with good reason (9a).

H-126 • ВЕРТЕ́ТЬСЯ ⟨ПУ́ТАТЬСЯ⟩ ПОД НОГА́МИ (у кого) coll [VP; subj: human] to annoy s.o. by one's presence, distract s.o. from what he is doing: X путается у Y-а под ногами ≃ **X is getting underfoot ⟨under Y's feet, in Y's way, in Y's hair⟩;** ‖ Neg Imper не вертись у Y-а под ногами ≃ **get ⟨keep, stay⟩ out of Y's way; get ⟨keep⟩ out from under Y's feet.**

Он всё время опасался, что кто-нибудь скажет: «А ты чего путаешься под ногами?» (Айтматов 1). He kept worrying that someone would say, "What are you doing here, getting under everybody's feet?" (1b). ♦ ...Из Ленинграда её [Ахматову] зимой выгоняли, чтобы она не путалась у Ирины Пуниной под ногами... (Мандельштам 2). ...[Akhmatova] was always ejected from the Punin apartment in Leningrad for the winter, to keep her out of Irina's way (2a).

H-127 • НОГА́МИ ВПЕРЁД (вынести кого) coll [AdvP; Invar; adv] dead (used to describe the position in which a person's body is carried, usu. out of some premises): **feet first.**

«А немец?» – «А немец вышел – ногами вперёд. Он ведь тогда тебе говорил: „Толик, воли мне не видать до конца жизни..." Здесь он и умер» (Марченко 1). "And the German?" "Yes, the German left," replied Ivan, "feet first. He told you, didn't he: 'I shall be here for the rest of my life, Tolik, I shan't be released...' Well, he died in here" (1a).

H-128 • В НОГА́Х кровати сидеть, стоять и т. п.; В НО́ГИ положить что и т. п. [PrepP; these forms only; adv] on or near the end of the bed opposite to the head: **at the foot of the ⟨one's, s.o.'s⟩ bed.**

...Все четверо потихоньку меня обсаживают – двое сели на стулья у изголовья, а двое в ногах (Ерофеев 1). ...All four of them quietly sat down around me, two on chairs at the head of the bed, and two at the foot... (1a).

H-129 • В НОГА́Х ПРА́ВДЫ НЕТ [saying] (usu. said when inviting s.o. to sit down) there is no need to stand – sit down: ≃ **take a load off your feet; give your feet a rest.**

Каждому, кто подходил, мы говорили: «Садись, товарищ, с нами – в ногах правды нет...» (Ерофеев 1). To everyone who came up, we said, "Sit down with us; take a load off your feet, comrade..." (1a).

H-130 • ВАЛЯ́ТЬСЯ ⟨ПОВАЛЯ́ТЬСЯ⟩ В НОГА́Х ⟨В НО́ЖКАХ⟩ coll у кого [VP; subj: human or collect; usu. impfv] to beg for sth. humbly: X валялся в ногах у Y-а ≃ **X threw himself at Y's feet; X fell ⟨lay prostrate⟩ at Y's feet; X groveled at Y's feet ⟨at the feet of Y⟩.**

Они стояли перед ним, лучшие его пастухи и гуртовщики, невозмутимые в своей правоте. Он неожиданно показался сам себе нашкодившим мальчишкой, и так-то ему вдруг захотелось, так захотелось поваляться у них в ногах, лишь бы они не бросили его среди этой проклятой снежной хляби, за сотни теперь вёрст от дому (Максимов 3). They stood before him, his best herdsmen and drovers, unshakable in their conviction that right was on their side. Suddenly he saw himself as a small boy who had misbehaved, and wanted, oh how desperately, to throw himself at their feet and beg them not to abandon him there in the middle of the infernal snow and slush, hundreds of miles from home (3a). ♦ Елисейково было повержено. Черкасово валялось у нас в ногах, Неугодово и Пекша молили о пощаде (Ерофеев 1). Eliseikovo was subdued. Cherkasovo lay prostrate at our feet; Neugodovo and Peksha begged for mercy (1a). ♦ Теперь, когда Вадим оказался с ним и нуждался в защите, не было на свете для Петра Васильевича преграды, какую он не сумел бы преодолеть, чтобы помочь внуку. Понадобится, он будет в ногах у местных властей валяться, но выхлопочет ему документы (Максимов 3). Now that Vadim was there and in need of protection, there was no obstacle on earth which Pyotr Vasilievich could not have overcome to help him [his grandson]. He would wangle papers for him, even if it meant groveling at the feet of the local powers-that-be (3a).

H-131 • ЕДВА́ ⟨Е́ЛЕ, ЧУТЬ, С ТРУДО́М⟩ ДЕР- ЖА́ТЬСЯ ⟨СТОЯ́ТЬ⟩ НА НОГА́Х; НА НОГА́Х НЕ ДЕРЖА́ТЬСЯ ⟨НЕ СТОЯ́ТЬ⟩ [VP; subj: human; usu. pres or past] to walk with difficulty (because of exhaustion, weakness, intoxication etc): X едва держится на ногах ≃ **X can hardly ⟨barely, scarcely⟩ stand on his feet; X can hardly ⟨barely, scarcely⟩ stand up (straight); X is having a hard time ⟨is experiencing some difficulty⟩ staying on his feet;** [in limited contexts] **X is almost dropping from fatigue; X is dead on his feet.**

[Ольга:] Я устала, едва на ногах стою... (Чехов 5). [O.:] I'm tired, I can barely stand on my feet... (5c). ♦ [author's usage] «Ну, веришь, Порфирий, [Раскольников] сам едва на ногах, а чуть только мы, я да Зосимов, вчера отвернулись – оделся и удрал потихоньку и куролесил где-то чуть не до полночи...» (Достоевский 3). "Would you believe it, Porfiry, he [Raskolnikov] could hardly stand up, but as soon as we—Zossimov and I—turned our backs yesterday, he got dressed and made off on the sly, and carried on somewhere till almost midnight..." (3c). ♦ Зурин поминутно мне подливал, повторяя, что надобно к службе привыкать. Встав из-за стола, я чуть держался на ногах... (Пушкин 2). Zurin kept filling my glass, repeating that I must get used to the ways of the Service. When I rose from the table, I could hardly stand up straight (2b). ♦ Договор был обмыт, и в сумерках, покидая контору, оба с трудом держались на ногах (Войнович 2). The agreement was sealed with a drink and when, at twilight, the two of them left the office, they were both experiencing some difficulty staying on their feet (2a). ♦ Главное было передохнуть и не ездить в Москву. Передышка нам была нужна как воздух. И психически сил не хватало на нищенство у довольно бедных людей, хотя по тем временам они казались богачами, и главное — потому что мы оба еле держались на ногах (Мандельштам 2). ...The main thing for us was to have a break from our journeys into Moscow. We needed this as much as air to breathe. We just had no heart anymore for the business of begging from people who were themselves quite poor— though by the standards of those times they seemed very well off. But even more to the point, we were almost dropping from fatigue (2a).

H-132 • НА НОГА́Х [PrepP; Invar; subj-compl with copula (subj: human), obj-compl with увидеть etc (obj: human), or adv]
1. in a standing position: **on one's feet; standing.**

Майор Мышин сидел в кресле, а Наделашина держал на ногах... (Солженицын 3). Major Myshin was seated in his arm-chair, and he kept Nadelashin standing... (3a).

2. awake and not in bed: X был на ногах ≃ **X was up (and about); X was ⟨had got(ten)⟩ out of bed.**

«В шесть чтобы был на ногах. Поедем к этому генералу» (Шолохов 5). "You've got to be up at six. We'll be going to see this general..." (5a). ♦ Пришёл Захар и, найдя Обломова не на постели, мутно поглядел на барина, удивляясь, что он на ногах (Гончаров 1). Zakhar came back and glared dully at his master, astonished that he should have got out of bed (1a). [context transl] Zakhar came back and stood gazing dully at his master, surprised at not finding him in bed (1b).

3. in motion, active and busy: **on one's feet; on the go.**

Он устал: с утра на ногах (Эренбург 2). He was tired. He had been on his feet all day (2a).

4. healthy, not sick: X был на ногах ≃ **X was up and about; X was on his feet.**

Ему [Твардовскому] Демичев сурово выговаривал, что не оказался он в нужную минуту на ногах: надо было ехать в Рим выбираться вице-президентом Европейской Ассоциации Писателей, не хотели там ни Суркова, ни Симонова (Солженицын 2). Demichev had harshly reprimanded him [Tvardovsky] for not being up and about when he was needed: he was supposed to go to Rome and be elected vice-president of the European Community of Writers; they didn't want either Surkov or Simonov (2a). ♦ Возчиком был Тимофей Лобанов, а какая же помощь от Тимофея? Замаялся человек брюхом — день на ногах да день лежит на нарах (Абрамов 1). The driver was Timofei Lobanov, and how could he be of any help? The man's gut was all out of whack; he'd be on his feet one day and flat on his back the next (1a).

5. (to be ill, combat illness) without taking to one's bed: **(stay) on one's feet.**

«Я вот, например, в больницах не лежу совсем. Должность не позволяет. На ногах болею» (Дудинцев 1). "I, for instance, do not use hospitals at all. My job won't allow me to. If I am ill, I stay on my feet" (1a).

H-133 • ПО́ЛЗАТЬ В НОГА́Х у кого; **ПО́ЛЗАТЬ НА КОЛЕ́НЯХ** перед кем [VP] **1.** [subj: human] to beg s.o. for sth. humbly, plead with s.o. for sth.: X ползал у Y-а в ногах ≃ **X crawled ⟨got⟩ on his knees before Y; X came crawling (on his knees) to Y; X begged Y on bended knee;** [in limited contexts] **X got down on his knees before Y.**

2. [subj: human or collect] to be servile, kowtow to s.o. (usu. s.o. in a position of authority, one's conqueror etc): X ползает на коленях перед Y-ом ≃ **X grovels to ⟨before⟩ Y; X crawls at Y's feet.**

H-134 • СТОЯ́ТЬ НА (СВОИ́Х ⟨СО́БСТВЕННЫХ⟩) НОГА́Х; КРЕ́ПКО ⟨ПРО́ЧНО, ТВЁРДО⟩ СТОЯ́ТЬ НА НОГА́Х [VP; subj: human, collect, or литература, искусство etc; usu. this WO] to be independent, well-established, not need any help or support: X стоит на своих ногах ≃ **person X stands on his own (two) feet; thing X stands on its own.**

«...Теперь ты твёрдо стоишь на ногах, но вспомни, как ты прибегала ко мне за советом...» (Эренбург 3). "...You stand firmly on your own feet today, but don't you remember how you used to run to me for advice?" (3a).

H-135 • НА ДРУ́ЖЕСКОЙ ⟨НА КОРО́ТКОЙ⟩ НОГЕ́ с кем держаться, находиться и т. п.; **НА ДРУ́ЖЕСКУЮ ⟨НА КОРО́ТКУЮ⟩ НО́ГУ** стать, сойтись с кем all coll [PrepP; these forms only; adv or subj-compl with copula (subj: human); fixed WO] (to have or enter into) a close, friendly relationship with s.o.: X на дружеской ноге с Y-ом ⟨X стал с Y-ом на дружескую ногу⟩ ≃ **X is ⟨got⟩ on friendly terms with Y; X is ⟨got⟩ on a friendly footing with Y; X is ⟨got⟩ in solid with Y; X is ⟨became⟩ friendly with Y.**

Они все были много моложе меня… но мы были на короткой ноге, вместе выпивали, играли в пинг-понг… (Аржак 2). They were all younger than me…but we were all on friendly terms, drinking together, playing table-tennis… (2a). ♦ …Все мои друзья были с ним на короткой ноге, и я с его друзьями (Аксёнов 1). …All my friends were in solid with him, and I with his friends (1a). ♦ [extended usage] Словно не решаясь открыть свою тайну в городе, где он со всеми булыжниками и кирпичами был на короткой ноге, Маяковский стремительно увёз меня в Сокольники (Лившиц 1). [context transl] Not wishing to disclose his secret in the city where he was on intimate terms with every cobblestone and every brick, Maiakovsky took me off to Sokolniki (1a).

Н-136 • НА ОДНОЙ НОГЕ сбегать, слетать и т. п. *highly coll* [PrepP; Invar; adv; fixed WO] (to run, go somewhere) extremely quickly (usu. used as a command): **in a flash ⟨a jiffy⟩;** [when used as a command] **make it quick ⟨snappy⟩.**

«Слушай, Самохин, — переходит на серьёзный тон начальник, — ты бы зашёл, поговорить надо». — «О чём?» — «Узнаешь. Не телефонный разговор». — «Хорошо. Сейчас обойду объект…» — «Ну давай, на одной ноге» (Войнович 5). "Listen, Samokhin," he [the boss] said, taking a more serious tone, "you ought to drop by. We need to have a little chat." "About what?" "You'll see. It's not something for the telephone." "All right. But right now I'm inspecting the building." "Go ahead, but make it quick" (5a).

Н-137 • НА РАВНОЙ НОГЕ *с кем* **стоять, держаться** и т. п. [PrepP; Invar; adv or subj-compl with copula (subj: human); fixed WO] (to be) of like standing, (to act with s.o.) as equals: X на равной ноге с Y-ом ≃ **X is on an equal footing with Y; X is on equal terms with Y;** [in limited contexts] **X talks to Y as an equal.**

Борис теперь был богатый человек, далеко ушедший в почестях, уже не искавший покровительства, но на равной ноге стоявший с высшими из своих сверстников (Толстой 6). Boris was now a rich man who had risen to high honors, and no longer sought patronage but was on an equal footing with the most distinguished men of his generation (6a).

Н-138 • НА РОДСТВЕННОЙ НОГЕ *с кем* **держаться** и т. п. [PrepP; Invar; usu. adv or subj-compl with copula (subj: human); fixed WO] (to behave toward s.o.) in a warm, casual way, as one would toward a relative: X держится с Y-ом на родственной ноге ≃ **X treats Y like ⟨as⟩ (one of the ⟨part of the⟩) family; X treats Y like close kin.**

«…Она [Пашенька], видя, что ты уже не студент, уроков и костюма лишился и что по смерти барышни ей нечего уже тебя на родственной ноге держать, вдруг испугалась…» (Достоевский 3). "…Seeing that you were no longer a student and no longer had any lessons or decent clothes, and that there was no longer any point in treating you like one of the family after the death of the young lady, she [Pashenka] suddenly got frightened…" (3a).

Н-139 • ПО НОГЕ [PrepP; Invar; subj-compl with copula (subj: a noun denoting footwear) or nonagreeing modif] of the correct size, comfortable on s.o.'s feet: X Y-у по ноге ≃ **X is the right ⟨my, your etc⟩ size; X fits (well);** ∥ *Neg* X Y-у не по ноге ≃ **X doesn't fit (right); X is too big ⟨small, tight⟩ for Y.**

…Семнадцатую путёвку принесла женщина в ватной солдатской теплушке, в больших, не по ноге, сапогах (Шолохов 3). A seventeenth warrant was brought by a woman in a soldier's wadded jacket and boots that were too big for her (3a).

Н-140 • БРАТЬ/ВЗЯТЬ НОГИ В РУКИ; НОГИ В РУКИ *both coll* [VP or PrepP (used as predic); subj: human; usu. imper; usu. foll. by a verb of motion which, if ellipted, is implied; fixed WO] to waste no time (and go, run etc someplace), hurry off (to some place): бери ноги в руки и (беги ⟨ступай и

т. п.⟩) в место X ≃ **hurry up (and go ⟨run etc⟩) to place X; hurry over to place X; get your butt in gear and go to place X; get to place X, now!;** ∥ (а ну-ка,) ноги в руки ≃ **get your butt in gear!; shake a leg!; get a move on!; make tracks!;** ∥ бери ноги в руки и марш ⟨беги и т. п.⟩ отсюда ≃ **get out of here, now!; hit the road!**

Отец сказал: «Нужно срочно связаться с семьёй Андрея, но у них не работает телефон. А ну-ка, бери ноги в руки — и к ним, скажи им об аварии». Father said, "I've got to get in touch with Andrei's family right away, but their telephone isn't working. Hurry over to their place and tell them about the accident."

Н-141 • БРОСИТЬСЯ ⟨КИНУТЬСЯ⟩ В НОГИ *кому* [VP; subj: human] to beg s.o. for sth. humbly, plead with s.o. for sth.: X брякнулся Y-у в ноги ≃ **X threw ⟨flung⟩ himself at Y's feet; X fell at Y's feet.**

Прачка Палашка, толстая и рябая девка, и кривая коровница Акулька как-то согласились в одно время кинуться матушке в ноги, винясь в преступной слабости и с плачем жалуясь на мусьё, обольстившего их неопытность. Матушка шутить этим не любила и пожаловалась батюшке (Пушкин 2). The washerwoman Palashka, a fat and pockmarked wench, and the one-eyed dairymaid Akulka somehow decided to throw themselves at my mother's feet at the same time, confessing to a reprehensible weakness and complaining in tears against the *mounseer*, who had seduced their innocence. My mother did not treat such things lightly, and complained to my father (2a).

Н-142 • ВСТАВАТЬ/ВСТАТЬ С ЛЕВОЙ ⟨НЕ С ТОЙ⟩ НОГИ; ВСТАВАТЬ/ВСТАТЬ ЛЕВОЙ НОГОЙ *all coll* [VP; subj: human] to be in a bad mood, in an irritable state (since awakening in the morning): X встал с левой ноги ≃ **X got up on ⟨got out of⟩ the wrong side of the bed; X got out of bed on the wrong side; X started the day off on the wrong foot.**

Н-143 • ЕДВА ⟨ЕЛЕ⟩ НОГИ ДЕРЖАТ ⟨НОСЯТ⟩ *кого* [VP_subj; usu. pres] s.o. is weak and can barely stand on his feet (from exhaustion, poor health, old age etc): X-а едва ноги держат ≃ **X's legs are about to give way; X can hardly ⟨barely, scarcely⟩ stand (up); X is about to drop;** [in limited contexts] **X is ready to drop in his tracks.**

Давай присядем где-нибудь отдохнуть, меня еле ноги держат. Let's sit down someplace and rest awhile. My legs are about to give way.

Н-144 • ЕЛЕ ⟨ЕДВА, НАСИЛУ, ЧУТЬ, С ТРУДОМ⟩ НОГИ ВОЛОЧИТЬ ⟨ПЕРЕДВИГАТЬ, ТАСКАТЬ, ТАЩИТЬ, ТЯНУТЬ⟩ *coll* [VP; subj: human; pres or past] to be barely able to walk (usu. from exhaustion, weakness, illness etc): X еле ноги волочил ≃ **X could hardly put one foot in front of the other; X could scarcely drag one foot after the other; X could scarcely ⟨barely⟩ drag himself along ⟨around⟩; X's legs would barely move.**

…Эти стихи он [Шаламов] писал, как и я, еле таская ноги, и наизусть, пуще всего таясь от обысков (Солженицын 2). …He [Shalamov] had written these poems as I had written mine, when he could scarcely drag himself along, committing them to memory because his main concern was to avoid discovery by the searchers (2a). ♦ …[Нюра] еле ноги таскала. Хотя ложились они рано, Чонкин ей спать не давал, будил по нескольку раз за ночь для своего удовольствия, да ещё и днём… (Войнович 2). …[Nyura] could barely drag herself around. Although she and Chonkin went to bed early, he wouldn't let her sleep, waking her up at least several times each night to take his pleasure, which he wanted in the daytime as well (2a). ♦ Выпили так много, что Ребров еле передвигал ноги (Трифонов 1). They had drunk so much that Rebrov's legs would barely move (1a).

H-145 • КЛА́НЯТЬСЯ/ПОКЛОНИ́ТЬСЯ В НО́ГИ ⟨В НО́ЖКИ *coll*⟩ [VP; subj: human] **1.** to beg for sth. humbly: X кланялся Y-у в ноги ≃ **X fell ⟨threw himself⟩ at Y's feet; X bowed down to Y; X begged Y on bended knee.**

Такие [люди] бывают везде и всюду, но у нас они получили право распределять воздух и хлеб. Если не поклониться в ноги уполномоченному в твоей области, подохнешь сразу... (Мандельштам 2). People such as these are found everywhere, but here they have been given the right to dispense the air we breathe and the bread we eat. Unless you are prepared to bow down to the person in charge of your particular field, you'll be a dead duck in no time at all... (2a). ♦ Рассказывал среди прочего Сабитжан, посмеиваясь, что те казахи да киргизы, которые в годы коллективизации ушли в Синьцзян, теперь снова возвращаются... Китайцы им такого показали, что бегут они оттуда... побросав всё имущество. В ноги кланяются, только пустите назад (Айтматов 2). Among other things, Sabitzhan was telling—and laughing the while—how these Kazakhs and Kirgiz who had left the country in the years of collectivization and gone to Sin'tsyan (Sinkiang) in China, were now coming here....The Chinese had treated them so badly that they had run away, leaving all their possessions behind them. Now they were begging on bended knee to be allowed to come back (2a).

2. to thank s.o. humbly and profusely: X Y-у в ноги поклонится ≃ **X will fall on ⟨to⟩ his knees in gratitude; X will go ⟨get⟩ down on bended knee ⟨on his knees⟩ and thank Y; X will bow down to ⟨before⟩ Y in gratitude.**

«Я думаю, что в ножки следовало бы поклониться Аристарху Платоновичу за то, что он из Индии [написал]...» — «Что это у нас всё в ножки да в ножки...» — вдруг пробурчал Елагин (Булгаков 12). "I think you should go down on bended knee and thank Aristarkh Platonovich for writing all the way from India..." "You're always telling people to get down on their knees..." Yelagin suddenly grumbled (12a). ♦ «Им бы самим у [Ивана] поучиться не грех, да за науку в ножки поклониться...» (Максимов 1). "It wouldn't be a bad idea for them to come and learn from him [Ivan] and bow down in gratitude to him..." (1a).

H-146 • КУДА́ НО́ГИ НЕСУ́Т/ПОНЕСУ́Т идти, брести и т. п. *coll* [subord clause (used as adv); usu. impfv (pres or past); fixed WO] (to go, walk) without a definite direction: **wherever one's feet take one.**

H-147 • НО́ГИ ЗАПЛЕТА́ЮТСЯ у кого *coll* [VP$_{subj}$; pres or past] s.o. walks with difficulty (from exhaustion): у X-а ноги заплетаются ≃ **X can hardly drag himself ⟨his feet⟩ along; X can hardly put one foot in front of the other ⟨drag one foot after the other⟩; X's legs are giving out.**

H-148 • НО́ГИ чьей ⟨НОГА́ чья obsoles⟩ НЕ БУ́ДЕТ где, у кого *coll*; ЧТОБ НОГИ́ чьей НЕ́ БЫЛО ⟨НЕ СТУПА́ЛО⟩ *coll*; ЧТОБ НОГА́ чья НЕ БЫЛА́ ⟨НЕ СТУПА́ЛА⟩ *obsoles, coll* [sent; these forms only; fixed WO] s.o. will never or must never visit a certain person or place (again) (usu. in refer. to a place formerly frequented): ноги X-овой не будет в месте Y ≃ **X will never set foot in place Y (again); X will never show his face in place Y (again); that's the last time X shows his face in place Y!; you ⟨they etc⟩ will never see X in place Y (again); ‖ чтоб ноги твоей не было в месте Y ≃ never ⟨don't you dare⟩ set foot in place Y (again); never ⟨you'd better not⟩ show your face in place Y (again); don't let me see ⟨catch (sight of)⟩ you in place Y (ever again); (you'd better) clear out of place Y.**

Я ушла из Союза писателей, написав Суркову письмо, что «ноги моей не будет в вашем грязном учреждении» (Мандельштам 2). When I left the premises of the Union of Writers...I wrote him [Surkov] a letter to say I would "never again set foot in your filthy institution" (2a). ♦ [Аким *(страшно рассердился)*:] А ну, вон отсюда, и чтоб ноги твоей не было больше в этом доме! (Арбузов 3). [A. *(terribly angry)*:] Now, get out! And never set foot in this house again! (3a). ♦ «Не остыл мужчин [*ungrammat* = мужний] след, а ты уже хвост набок!.. Ишь ты, курва, мало тебя били... Чтоб с нонешнего [*substand* = нынешнего] дня и ноги твоей на моём базу не ступало» (Шолохов 2). "Your husband barely out of the house and you go off on the loose!...You whore! You haven't been thrashed enough....From this day on, you don't dare set foot in my yard again" (2a). ♦ [Василиса *(Бубнову)*:] Чтобы ноги его [Алёшки] здесь не было! Слышишь? [Бубнов:] Я тут не сторож тебе (Горький 3). [V. *(to Bubnov)*:] Don't let me catch him [Alyoshka] here again, hear? [B.:] I'm not a watchdog (3d). ♦ «Вон, мерзавец! — закричал Обломов, бледный, трясясь от ярости. — Сию минуту, чтоб нога твоя здесь не была, или я убью тебя, как собаку!» (Гончаров 1). "Get out, you loathsome—" Oblomov was pale and trembling with rage. "Clear out of here this instant, or I'll kill you like a dog!" (1b).

H-149 • НО́ГИ НЕ ДЕ́РЖАТ кого [VP$_{subj}$; pres or past; usu. this WO] s.o. can barely stand or walk (because of exhaustion, illness, old age etc): X-а ноги не держат ≃ **X's legs won't ⟨refuse to⟩ support him; X's legs won't hold him up ⟨won't hold up under him⟩; X's legs are giving way; X is ready to drop in his tracks.**

«Ступайте домой, мсьё Вольдемар, почиститесь, да не смейте идти за мной — а то я рассержусь, и уже больше никогда...» Она не договорила своей речи и проворно удалилась, а я присел на дорогу... ноги меня не держали (Тургенев 3). "Go home, M'sieu Woldemar, and brush yourself, and don't you dare follow me, or I shall be angry and will never again—" She did not finish the sentence and walked rapidly away, while I sat down by the side of the road. My legs would not support me (3a). ♦ «Багратионский, меня ноги не держат. Догони эту падлу и дай ему по затылку», — попросил Пантелей (Аксёнов 6). "Bagrationsky, my legs won't hold me up. Chase after that bastard and give him a rabbit punch in the back of the neck," Pantelei begged (6a).

H-150 • пока НО́ГИ НО́СЯТ ⟨НЕСУ́Т⟩ кого *coll* [VP$_{subj}$; subord clause; usu. this WO] as long as a person has the strength to walk: пока X-а ноги носят ≃ **as long as X's legs can ⟨will⟩ carry him; as long as X is on his feet; as long as X can get about.**

H-151 • НО́ГИ ПОДКА́ШИВАЮТСЯ/ПОДКОСИ́ЛИСЬ у кого ⟨ОТКАЗА́ЛИ кому⟩ [VP$_{subj}$] s.o.'s legs lose their strength, become shaky, fail to support him because of intense alarm, fear, amazement etc: у X-а подкосились ноги ≃ **X's legs gave way (under him); X's legs buckled under him; X's legs wouldn't hold him up; X's legs refused to function; X's legs went weak; X went weak in the knees.**

...У неё [Сони] буквально подкосились ноги и она чуть не упала, когда я показал ей проспект «Библиотеки» (Мандельштам 2). ...Her [Sonia's] legs literally gave way and she nearly collapsed when I showed her the prospectus of the Library's forthcoming publications (2a). ♦ Радость [встречи с сыном] произвела в больном слишком сильное потрясение, он ослабел, ноги под ним подкосились... (Пушкин 1). The joy of seeing his son was too much of a shock for the sick man: he grew faint, his legs gave way under him... (1a). ♦ ...Его [Хвастищева] вдруг продрал озноб, и ноги неожиданно отказали ему... «что с тобой, Радик?» — «Пат, посмотри-ка — часы!» (Аксёнов 6). ...He [Khvastishchev] felt a sudden chill, and his legs unexpectedly refused to function...."What's the matter, Radik?" "Pat, look! A clock!" (6a).

H-152 • ПА́ДАТЬ/УПА́СТЬ ⟨ПАСТЬ obs⟩ В НО́ГИ кому ⟨К НОГА́М чьим, кого obs, НА КОЛЕ́НИ перед кем⟩ [VP; subj: human] to beg s.o. for sth. humbly (sometimes kneeling): X упал Y-у в ноги ≃ **X threw ⟨flung⟩ himself at Y's feet; X fell ⟨knelt⟩ at Y's feet; X went down on his knees before ⟨to⟩ Y.**

Я упаду ему в ноги, думает Смайльс Гендон, и попрошу у него защиты против моих обидчиков, лишивших меня наследства (Олеша 3). I shall fall at his feet, Miles Hendon thinks, and beg for his protection from those who have offended me and deprived me of my legacy (3a). ♦ «…Я пал в ноги ему и слёзно умолял; а он закричал благим матом: „Пошёл, пошёл!“» (Гончаров 1). "…I went down on my knees before him with tears in my eyes, but he yelled with all his might: 'Get out! Get out!'" (1b).

H-153 • ПОДНИМА́ТЬ ⟨ПОДЫМА́ТЬ⟩/ПОДНЯ́ТЬ ⟨СТА́ВИТЬ/ПОСТА́ВИТЬ⟩ НА́ НОГИ[1] [VP] 1. ~ кого [subj: human or nouns denoting a substance with a therapeutic effect] to cure s.o.: X поставил Y-а на ноги ≃ **X put ⟨got, set⟩ Y back on Y's feet.**

Мои приятели были воплощением здоровья, но материнский глаз нашёл в них какую-то перемену к худшему; обо мне же и говорить не приходится; меня сразу объявили заморышем, которого необходимо как можно скорее поставить на ноги (Лившиц 1). My friends were the picture of health, but the maternal eye saw a change for the worse in them; not to mention me—I was declared immediately to be a weakling who had to be put back on his feet as soon as possible (1a).

2. ~ кого [subj: human; more often last var.] to help s.o. become self-sufficient in life (usu. in refer. to rearing one's child): X поставил Y-а на ноги ≃ **X put ⟨set, got⟩ Y on Y's feet; X helped Y find Y's feet.**

[Ксения:] Ты — старый наш слуга, тебя батюшка мой на ноги поставил, ты обо мне подумай… (Горький 2). [K.:] You—you're an old servant of ours, my father put you on your feet—think about me… (2b). ♦ Много горьких жалоб услыхала тесная комната на седьмом этаже… То не хватало денег на ведёрко угля, и дети мёрзли, то протирались штанишки Жано, то надо было купить задачник Аннет. Она всё же поставила детей на ноги (Эренбург 4). Many bitter complaints were heard in the poky little room on the sixth storey….At times there was not enough money for a bucket of coal and the children froze; or else Jeannot's trousers were worn out or an exercise-book had to be bought for Annette. But she managed to set the children on their feet (4a). ♦ Он станет теперь совсем одинок. А у него теперь шестеро детей. И лавка на руках, и подымай на ноги всю ораву (Булгаков 5). [context transl] Now he would be altogether alone. And he had six children. And the shop was on his hands, and the upbringing of all the children (5a).

3. ~ что [subj: human or collect; obj: collect] to strengthen sth., make sth. more solid, independent, capable of functioning productively (again): X поставил Y на ноги ≃ **X put ⟨got, set⟩ Y (back) on Y's feet (again).**

«Это [генерал Корнилов] кристальной честности человек, и только он один в состоянии поставить Россию на ноги» (Шолохов 3). "He [General Kornilov] is a man of perfect integrity and he alone is capable of putting Russia on her feet again" (3a).

H-154 • ПОДНИМА́ТЬ ⟨ПОДЫМА́ТЬ⟩/ПОДНЯ́ТЬ ⟨СТА́ВИТЬ/ПОСТА́ВИТЬ⟩ НА́ НОГИ[2] [VP] 1. ~ кого-что [subj: human or a noun denoting a sound (variants поднимать ⟨подымать⟩/поднять only)] to awaken some person or group of people: X поднял Y-ов на ноги ≃ **X got ⟨woke⟩ Ys up; X roused Ys; X got Ys out of bed ⟨out of their beds⟩.**

«Заявляетесь ночью в пьяном виде, поднимаете на ноги весь дом, и у вас ещё хватает совести повышать на меня голос…» (Максимов 1). "You roll up drunk in the middle of the night, you wake up the whole house, and still you have the gall to raise your voice to me" (1a). ♦ Собаки залаяли. Значит, жена тревожит, поднимает боранлинцев на ноги (Айтматов 2). The dogs were barking…so evidently his wife was busy spreading the news and getting the people of Boranly out of their beds (2a).

2. ~ кого-что [subj: human; obj: human pl or collect; more often variants поднимать ⟨подымать⟩/поднять; usu. pfv fut] to make s.o. act energetically: X поднял Y-а на ноги ≃ **X**

roused Y; X got Y moving; [in limited contexts] **X had Y (out) doing sth.**

«Боже мой, без двадцати двенадцать! Мама, наверное, с ума сошла. Я обещала быть к ужину…» — «Может, всё-таки останешься?» — «Нет, что ты! Она подымет на ноги всю московскую милицию!» (Ерофеев 3). "Oh my God, it's twenty of twelve! Mama's probably crazy with worry. I promised to be home for supper…." "You don't think you could stay?" "No, it's out of the question! She'd have the whole Moscow police force out looking for me!" (3a).

3. ~ кого-что [subj: human or abstr; obj: human pl or collect; more often variants поднимать ⟨подымать⟩/поднять; usu. pfv] to agitate, disturb, arouse s.o. (usu. a group of people): X поднял на ноги Y-ов ≃ **X created a commotion among Ys; X stirred Ys up.**

Слух о мобилизации поднял всех на ноги. The rumor about mobilization stirred everyone up. ♦ Одиннадцатого октября, в тот самый день, когда в главной квартире всё было поднято на ноги известием о поражении Мака, в штабе эскадрона походная жизнь спокойно шла по-старому (Толстой 4). [context transl] On the eighth of October, the day when at headquarters all was in a turmoil over the news of Mack's defeat, the camp life of the officers in this squadron was quietly proceeding as usual (4a).

H-155 • ПРОТЯНУ́ТЬ ⟨ВЫ́ТЯНУТЬ⟩ НО́ГИ coll [VP; subj: human or animal] to cease living: X протянул ноги ≃ **X died;** [of a person only] **X turned up his toes; X gave up the ghost.**

«Вот он [Караман] и вытянул ноги, кое-как продержавшись пять лет» (Искандер 3). "He [Karaman] lasted five years, and now he's turned up his toes" (3a). ♦ «Вот тут мой и дом, и огород, тут и ноги протяну!» (Гончаров 1). [context transl] "This is my house and garden, right here, and this is where they'll lay me out!" (1b).

H-156 • СБИВА́ТЬСЯ/СБИ́ТЬСЯ С НОГИ́ ⟨С ША́ГА⟩; ТЕРЯ́ТЬ/ПОТЕРЯ́ТЬ НО́ГУ ⟨ШАГ⟩ [VP; subj: human] to step with the wrong foot while marching, having lost synchronization: X сбился с ноги ≃ **X fell ⟨got⟩ out of step.**

Навстречу ему [сотнику Листницкому] пламенно-рыжий бородач фельдфебель вёл солдата в караул. Он козырнул сотнику, не теряя ноги, ответил на вопрос и указал дом (Шолохов 2). A red-bearded sergeant-major came towards him [Lieutenant Listnitsky], marching a soldier to the guard-house. He saluted the lieutenant without getting out of step, answered his question, and pointed out the house (2a).

H-157 • СТАНОВИ́ТЬСЯ/СТАТЬ ⟨ВСТАВА́ТЬ/ВСТАТЬ, ПОДНИМА́ТЬСЯ/ПОДНЯ́ТЬСЯ⟩ НА́ НОГИ [VP] 1. [subj: human] to get well, be cured of an illness: X стал на ноги ≃ **X was back on his feet; X was on his feet again; X was up and about again.**

…Лёжа на носилках, на которых его выносили из Клуба писателей, Степан [Злобин] сказал мне…: «И неси свои материалы: какие есть. В палату. История антисемитизма… Молчать уж невмочь! Как встану на ноги, так…» Машина уехала (Свирский 1). As he lay on the stretcher carrying him out of the Writers' Union, Stepan [Zlobin]…said to me…"And bring any documents you've got with you to the hospital. Anything on the history of anti-Semitism….I can't keep quiet any longer! As soon as I'm on my feet again…" The ambulance drove away (1a).

2. [subj: human or collect; more often variants становиться/стать, вставать/встать] to become self-sufficient, independent: X встал на ноги ≃ **X got on his feet; X found his feet; X stood on his own (two) feet.**

Постепенно Люшка становилась на ноги. Приобулась, приоделась, вышла замуж за Егора, вступила в партию (Войнович 2). Gradually Lyushka got on her feet. She acquired shoes, some nice clothes; she married Egor; she joined the Party (2a).

♦ «Я хотела, чтобы ты защитился, встал на ноги» (Евтушенко 1). "I wanted you to get your thesis accepted, to stand on your own two feet" (1a).

3. [subj: collect] to gain strength, begin functioning productively, independently (again): X стал на ноги ≃ **X got (back) on its feet.**

«Отстраиваемся, значит?.. Это хорошо, пора стране на ноги вставать» (Максимов 1). "So reconstruction is proceeding?...That's good. It's time for the country to get back on its feet" (1a).

4. [subj: human or collect; more often variants становиться/стать, вставать/встать] to improve one's material situation: X стал на ноги ≃ **X got on ⟨to, onto⟩ his feet.**

«Дайте мне взаймы тысячу долларов, и, лишь только мы станем на ноги, я вам свято её верну» (Булгаков 2). "Lend me a thousand dollars. As soon as we get to our feet, I'll return it, I swear" (2a). ♦ Дед разорился, промотал всё состояние, играя в карты; снова поднялся было на ноги, но пожар слизал всё, и Сергею Платоновичу пришлось начинать сызнова (Шолохов 2). The grandfather, who had squandered one fortune at cards, was only just beginning to get back onto his feet again when the fire took everything, and Sergei Platonovich had to make a fresh start (2a).

H-158 • **УНОСИ́ТЬ/УНЕСТИ́ НО́ГИ** *coll* [VP; subj: human or animal; if pfv, usu. past (often after еле, едва, насилу); if impfv, often imper or infin with надо, пора, пришлось etc] to leave hurriedly, flee (usu. to escape danger): X унёс ноги ≃ **X cleared out; X took to his heels; X hightailed it (out of some place);** [with the focus on the outcome] **X got away with his skin; X got out in one piece;** ‖ X еле ⟨едва, насилу⟩ ноги унёс ≃ **X escaped ⟨got away⟩ by the skin of his teeth; X had a narrow escape; X had ⟨it was⟩ a close shave.**

Молодые люди, с которыми она знакомилась, танцевала и гуляла, все как один выявляли намерение — ...получить удовольствие и унести ноги (Солженицын 10). The young men she met all danced and went for walks with the same aim in mind:... have their fun and then clear out (10a). ♦ Она подняла крик и вырвала у меня газету. Покупка, яблоки или морковь, я уж не помню, рассыпались по тротуару. Я не стала ничего собирать и была рада, что удалось унести ноги (Мандельштам 2). She raised a great hue and cry and snatched the newspaper from me. The things I had wrapped in it—apples or carrots, I don't remember which—were scattered all over the pavement. I didn't wait to pick them up and was glad to get away with my skin (2a). ♦ [Кири:] Спасибо нужно сказать богам, что хоть ноги-то мы унесли (Булгаков 1). [K.:] We have to thank the gods that [at least] we got out in one piece (1a). ♦ Один единственный раз Мандельштам нарушил старый сговор и еле унёс ноги (Мандельштам 2). M[andelstam] broke the old agreement on this one solitary occasion and got away only by the skin of his teeth (2a). ♦ «Да вот хоть черкесы, — продолжал он, — как напьются бузы на свадьбе или на похоронах, так и пошла рубка. Я раз насилу ноги унёс...» (Лермонтов 1). "Yes, you take the Cherkesses," he continued, "they get drunk on their booze at a wedding or a funeral and that's when the slaughter starts. I had a narrow escape once..." (1d). ♦ Андрей Лучников тогда еле унёс ноги из горящего штаба венгерской молодёжи, кинотеатра «Корвин». Советская, читай русская, пуля сидела у него в плече (Аксёнов 7). Andrei Luchnikov had been caught in the flaming Corvina Cinema, headquarters of the new revolutionary youth movement. It was a close shave, and he had a Soviet—that is, Russian—bullet in his shoulder to prove it (7a).

H-159 • **ХРОМА́ТЬ НА О́БЕ НО́ГИ** *coll* [VP; usu. this WO] **1.** [subj: human] to have insufficient knowledge in some area, make significant errors: X хромает на обе ноги ≃ **X is floundering; X is weak ⟨shaky⟩ (in...).**

Мой племянник занимается неплохо по всем предметам, кроме математики: тут он хромает на обе ноги. My nephew does pretty well in all subjects except math: there he flounders.

2. [subj: abstr (often дисциплина, логика, методика etc)] (often of discipline, logic, methods etc) to be deficient, poor, bad: X хромает на обе ноги ≃ **X is in a sorry state;** [of logic or methods] **X is faulty ⟨flawed⟩.**

H-160 • **ЛЕ́ВОЙ НОГО́Й** *highly coll* [NP$_{instrum}$; Invar; adv; fixed WO] (to do sth.) in a negligent manner, poorly: **sloppily; shoddily; in a slipshod ⟨half-assed⟩ manner.**

H-161 • **НИ НОГО́Й** *coll* [NP$_{instrum}$; Invar; predic with subj: human; can be used in past, pres, and fut contexts or as a command] **1.** ~ *к кому, куда* not to visit s.o. or go somewhere at all: X к Y-у ни ногой ⟨в место Z⟩ ≃ [in present contexts] **X doesn't set ⟨never sets⟩ foot in Y's house ⟨in place Z etc⟩; X never crosses Y's threshold ⟨the threshold of Y's house, the threshold of place Z etc⟩; X keeps ⟨steers⟩ clear of Y ⟨Y's house, place Z etc⟩.**

«Мне сказывали, что в Риме наши художники в Ватикан ни ногой» (Тургенев 2). "I am told that in Rome our artists never set foot in the Vatican" (2c). ♦ «Вот только съезжу сегодня отобедаю — и ни ногой» (Гончаров 1). "I'll go and dine there to-day—and then I shall never cross the threshold of her house!" (1a). ♦ ...Всё больше таких мастаков *красилей* набирается: нигде не состоят, нигде не работают... И очень жена надежду таит, что вернётся Иван [из лагеря] и тоже в колхоз ни ногой, и тоже таким красилём станет (Солженицын 7). There were more of these master dyers all the time. They weren't on anybody's payroll, they had no regular job....His [Ivan's] wife's dearest hope was that when he got home [from the camp] he would keep clear of the kolkhoz and take up dyeing himself (7c).

2. ~ *откуда* never to leave some place: X из места Y ни ногой ≃ [in present contexts] **X never sets foot outside ⟨out of⟩ place Y.**

H-162 • **(СТОЯ́ТЬ) ОДНО́Й НОГО́Й В МОГИ́ЛЕ ⟨В ГРОБУ́⟩** *coll* [VP or NP$_{instrum}$ (used as subj-compl with быть$_ø$); subj: human; fixed WO with the verb movable] (of a seriously ill or very old person) to be nearing the end of one's life, be near death: X стоит одной ногой в могиле ≃ **X has one foot in the grave; X is at death's door.**

Голодный, холодный и бесправный, он ежедневно закапывал по десять-пятнадцать покойников, похоронил жену и сына и сам одной ногой стоял в могиле (Рыбаков 1). Hungry and cold, stripped of all rights, every day he was burying ten or fifteen dead, he buried his own wife and son, and he had one foot in the grave himself (1a).

H-163 • **СТАТЬ ТВЁРДОЙ НОГО́Й** *где lit* [VP; subj: human; usu. this WO] to gain a strong position, firmly settle (in some newly conquered territory): X стал твёрдой ногой в месте Y ≃ **X gained a firm foothold in place Y.**

H-164 • **С НОГОТО́К** *coll* [PrepP; Invar] **1.** [usu. nonagreeing postmodif] (of a person) very small: **tiny; teeny; pint-size.** Cf. **Tom Thumb.**

2. ~ *чего у кого, где* [quantit subj-compl with copula (subj/gen: concr or abstr)] (s.o. has) a very small amount of some quality (ability etc), (there is) very little of sth. (in some place): **(hardly) an ounce (of [NP]); almost ⟨next to⟩ no [NP]; hardly any [NP]; (be) short on [NP].**

Способностей у него с ноготок, но берёт усидчивостью. He has hardly an ounce of talent but makes up for it with tenacity.

H-165 • **ПОД НО́ГОТЬ взять, забрать, прибрать, подобрать** *кого substand* [PrepP; Invar; usu. obj-compl with взять etc (subj and obj: human)] (to get s.o.) under one's complete control: X прибрал Y-а под ноготь ≃ **X had ⟨got⟩ Y under X's thumb.**

H-166 • С ⟨ОТ⟩ МОЛОДЫ́Х ⟨МЛА́ДЫХ⟩ НОГТЕ́Й [PrepP; these forms only; adv; fixed WO] from the time a person is or was extremely young: **from ⟨since⟩ infancy; from the cradle; from ⟨since⟩ (early) childhood; from ⟨since⟩ one's earliest days; since one was knee-high.**

Юле, ещё с младых ногтей твёрдо усвоившей, что религия – опиум народа, невыносимо было слушать Антоновы разъяснения разницы между верой и суеверием (Гинзбург 2). Julia, who almost from the cradle had had it drummed firmly into her head that religion was the opium of the people, could not bear hearing Anton hold forth on the differences between faith and superstition (2a).

H-167 • К НО́ГТЮ (прижать, взять) *кого substand* [PrepP; Invar; adv or subj-compl with copula (subj: human or collect)] to deal with s.o. severely, sometimes going so far as to kill him: X прижмёт Y-а к ногтю ≃ [in refer. to punishment] **X will come down hard on Y;** [in refer. to killing] **X will blot ⟨wipe⟩ Y out; X will do away with Y.**

Если милиция его поймает, то всех нас к ногтю прижмут за то, что ему помогали. If the police catch him, they'll come down hard on us, too, for having helped him.

H-168 • В НО́ГУ *(с кем)* **идти, шагать, маршировать** и т. п.; **НОГА́ В НО́ГУ; ШАГ В ШАГ** [PrepP (1st var.); these forms only; adv; fixed WO] (of a person) (to go, march etc) in time with s.o.: X шёл в ногу с Y-ом ≃ **X kept ⟨walked, marched⟩ in step (with Y); X kept in stride;** ‖ *Neg* X шёл не в ногу с Y-ом ≃ **X walked ⟨marched, fell⟩ out of step ⟨out of stride⟩ with Y.**

«…Я шёл с нею рядом, стараясь идти в ногу, и, к удивлению моему, совершенно не чувствовал себя стеснённым» (Булгаков 9). "I walked side by side with her, trying to keep in step, and, to my utter amazement, did not feel in the least constrained" (9a). ♦ Друзья идут быстро, нога в ногу… (Федин 1). The friends are walking swiftly, in step… (1a).

H-169 • ВЗЯТЬ ⟨ДАТЬ⟩ НО́ГУ [VP; subj: human; often imper] to start or return to moving in rhythm with others when marching: возьми(те) ногу ≃ **keep ⟨get⟩ in step.**

H-170 • ИДТИ́ ⟨ШАГА́ТЬ⟩ В НО́ГУ *с кем-чем;* **ИДТИ́ ШАГ В ШАГ** [VP; subj: human or a noun denoting a branch of technology, school of thought etc] to progress at a pace equal to that of (another person, branch of technology etc, or the times in general): X идёт в ногу с Y-ом ≃ **X keeps up ⟨keeps pace⟩ with Y;** ‖ X идёт в ногу со временем ⟨с веком⟩ ≃ **X keeps ⟨is⟩ in step with the times.**

Методология науки, естественно, стремится идти в ногу с развитием конкретных наук… (Зиновьев 1). Naturally enough scientific methodology strives to keep up with the development of the concrete sciences… (1a). ♦ Единственная идеология, которой он поклоняется, – это максимальное удовлетворение личных потребностей… И тут он вовсе никакой не догматик и не ортодокс. Он идёт в ногу со временем… и приспосабливается к новым условиям (Войнович 3). The only ideology he worships is the maximum satisfaction of his personal needs.…And in this he is no dogmatist, no orthodox man. He's in step with the times, he…adapts himself to new conditions (3a).

H-171 • ЛЁГОК ⟨ЛЁГКИЙ⟩ НА́ НОГУ; СКОР ⟨СКО́РЫЙ⟩ НА́ НОГУ *all coll* [AdjP; subj-compl with copula, subj: human (all variants) or modif (variants with long-form Adj); fixed WO (variants with short-form Adj)] one walks (or, occas., runs) with a spirited step, quickly, and can keep going

for a long time without tiring: X лёгок на ногу ≃ **X is light on his feet; X is light-footed ⟨nimble-footed⟩.**

Ксюте бегать в школу приходилось далековато, но она была легка на ногу… (Евтушенко 2). Ksiuta had to run five versts to school every day but she was light on her feet… (2a).

H-172 • НА БО́СУ ⟨БОСУ́, БОСУ́Ю⟩ НО́ГУ [PrepP; these forms only; usu. adv or nonagreeing postmodif; fixed WO] (to wear shoes, boots etc) without stockings or socks: **(wear shoes etc) on one's bare ⟨sockless⟩ feet; (with) one's feet bare (in one's shoes etc).**

…Сандалии были рыночные, дешёвые и надеты на босу ногу (Катаев 3). …His sandals were a cheap pair from the market worn on his bare feet (3a). ♦ Фёдор Константинович проводил большую часть дня на тёмно-синей скамейке в сквере, без пиджака, в старых парусиновых туфлях на босу ногу, с книгой в длинных загорелых пальцах… (Набоков 1). Fyodor, in his shirt-sleeves and with sneakers on his sockless feet, would spend the greater part of the day on an indigo bench in the public garden, a book in his long tanned fingers (1a). ♦ Это человек, похожий на Христа, в потрёпанном пиджаке и туфлях на босу ногу (Лимонов 1). He is a Christlike man in a ragged suit jacket, his feet bare in his shoes (1a).

H-173 • НА ВОЕ́ННУЮ НО́ГУ [PrepP; Invar; adv or subj-compl with copula (subj: всё, хозяйство etc); fixed WO] in a military fashion: **on a military footing; in a military ⟨soldierly⟩ way; soldierly.**

«…У меня здесь всё по простоте, на военную ногу» (Тургенев 2). "…Everything here in my house is done in a plain way, on a military footing" (2b).

H-174 • НА НО́ВУЮ НО́ГУ поставить *что,* **пойти** и т. п. *obs* [PrepP; Invar; adv or, less often, subj-compl with copula (subj: usu. всё); fixed WO] (to make sth. function) differently from the way it did previously, in a more modern, improved manner; (to be) different from what it was previously, more modern, improved: **(set sth. up ⟨everything is set up, things start going etc⟩) in a new way.**

…Крестьянская реформа не только не застигла его [Быстрицына] врасплох, как других, но, напротив того, он встретил её во всеоружии и сразу сумел поставить своё хозяйство на новую ногу (Салтыков-Щедрин 2). [context transl] …The peasant reform did not catch him [Bystritsyn] unawares as it did the others. On the contrary, he was quite ready for it, meeting it fully armed, as it were, and he was able to reorganize his farm immediately in accordance with the new requirements of the time (2a).

H-175 • НА *какую* **НО́ГУ поставить, организовать** *что* [PrepP; Invar; usu. adv] (to organize, set up sth.) based on some approach, model, set of principles etc (as specified by the modifier): **on a [AdjP] basis ⟨footing⟩; in a [AdjP] manner.**

Другое дело было бы принять отдельную клинику и… всё поставить только на деловую ногу… (Солженицын 10). It would be a different matter to take over a separate clinic and put it all on a businesslike basis… (10b). ♦ Усадьба Лысых Гор была вновь отстроена, но уже не на ту ногу, на которой она была при покойном князе (Толстой 7). [context transl] The homestead at Bald Hills had been rebuilt, though not on the same scale as under the old Prince (7a).

H-176 • НА ХОЛОСТЯ́ЦКУЮ ⟨ХОЛОСТУ́Ю⟩ НО́ГУ жить *coll* [PrepP; these forms only; adv; fixed WO] (of a man) (to live) without the comforts characteristic of family life: **(live) like a (true ⟨typical⟩) bachelor; (lead ⟨live⟩) the bachelor life ⟨the life of a bachelor⟩.**

H-177 • НА ШИРО́КУЮ НО́ГУ *coll;* **НА БОЛЬШУ́Ю НО́ГУ** *obs* [PrepP; these forms only; adv; fixed WO] **1. жить,**

поставить *что* ~ и т. п. Also: **НА БА́РСКУЮ НО́ГУ** *obs* (to live, set up one's household etc) luxuriously, sparing no expense: **in grand ⟨high⟩ style; on a grand scale; [in limited contexts] he ⟨she etc⟩ really knows how to live!**

Её дом был поставлен на широкую ногу (Аллилуева 2). Her home was run in grand style (2a). ♦ [author's usage] «Что это вы оставили князя? Какой весёлый дом! На какую ногу поставлен!» (Гончаров 1). "Why have you given up the prince? It's such an amusing house! What a way they know how to live!" (1b).

2. организовать, поставить *что* и т. п. ~ (to organize, set up sth. etc) grandly, expansively, impressively etc: **on a grand ⟨large, big⟩ scale; in a big way.**

Всё пошло на большую ногу; закупка сахару, чаю, провизии, соленье огурцов, моченье яблок и вишен, варенье – всё приняло обширные размеры (Гончаров 1). Everything was done on a big scale: the buying of sugar, tea, and provisions, the pickling of cucumbers, the preserving of apples and cherries, jam-making—everything now assumed enormous proportions (1a). ♦ ...Суд будет через неделю и не в Чернигове, а здесь, у нас... и не наш народный суд, а выездная сессия областного суда. В общем, на широкую ногу, и результатов надо ждать самых скверных (Рыбаков 1). ...The trial was to take place in a week's time, not in Chernigov, but here, in our town...and it wouldn't be our own People's Court, but a session of the regional court assizes! In other words, it was going to be done in a big way, and we could expect the very worst possible outcome (1a). ♦ «Что-то многовато у Реваза Давидовича знакомых в вузах, не на широкую ли ногу он взяточничество поставил?» (Чернёнок 2). [context transl] "Revaz Davidovich seems to have too many friends in colleges. Could he be setting up a major bribery ring?" (2a).

Н-178 • НАСТУПА́ТЬ/НАСТУПИ́ТЬ НА́ НОГУ ⟨НА́ НОГИ⟩ *кому coll* [VP; subj: human] to offend s.o., infringe upon his sphere of interests, relate to him in an unacceptable manner etc: X наступил Y-у на ногу ≃ **X stepped on Y's toes;** ‖ X никому не позволит наступать себе на ногу ≃ **X won't let anyone push him around.**

[Миловидов:] ...[Я] пьяница, а благородный человек; на ногу себе наступить не позволю (Островский 8). [M.:] ...[I'm] a hard drinker—but a gentleman! I don't allow anyone to step on my toes! (8a).

Н-179 • ТЯЖЁЛ ⟨ТЯЖЁЛЫЙ⟩ НА́ НОГУ *coll* [AdjP; subj-compl with copula, subj: human (both variants) or modif (var. with long-form Adj); fixed WO (var. with short-form Adj)] one cannot walk long distances, one tires easily: X тяжёл на ногу ≃ **X's legs give out easily; X has trouble walking.**

Н-180 • (КАК ⟨СЛО́ВНО, ТО́ЧНО⟩) НОЖ В СЕ́РДЦЕ *кому coll* [(как etc +) NP; these forms only; subj-compl with быть∅ (subj: usu. abstr); fixed WO] extremely painful, hurtful for s.o. (in an emotional sense): **(it's) (like) a knife in s.o.'s heart; (it's) (like) a knife thrust into s.o.'s heart; (it's) (like) a stab in the heart; (it) cuts at s.o.'s heart; (sth. goes through s.o.) like a knife.**

«Вы должны поехать вместе со мной... завтра же... Если вы откажетесь, это будет мне нож в сердце...» (Лившиц 1). "You must go, together with me...tomorrow....If you refuse, it will be like a knife in my heart..." (1a). ♦ Добавлением к [моему] смятению было письмо от сына, пришедшее в Нью-Йорк через Швейцарию. Это был нож в самое сердце (Аллилуева 2). To add to my confusion, about this same time I received a letter from my son, which had reached New York via Switzerland. It was like a knife thrust straight into my heart (2a).

Н-181 • НОЖ В СПИ́НУ *кому, чью* [NP; sing only; usu. subj-compl with copula (subj: abstr); fixed WO] a traitorous act, traitorous conduct in dealing with s.o.: **stab in the back.**

«...Клеймим соглашение о перемирии, как нож в спину Парижу, который двое суток героически сражается против захватчиков...» (Эренбург 1). "We denounce the armistice as a stab in the back of Paris which has been heroically fighting the invaders two days and nights" (1a).

Н-182 • НОЖ О́СТРЫЙ *coll;* **НОЖ ВО́СТРЫЙ** *obs* [NP; sing only; subj-compl with быть∅ (subj: abstr); usu. pres; usu. this WO] extremely painful, upsetting for s.o.: **(like) a knife in s.o.'s heart.**

Н-183 • ПОД НОЖ пойти, пустить *что* [PrepP; Invar; subj-compl with copula (subj: a noun denoting printed materials)] (to be, have sth.) destroyed: **pulped; reduced to pulp.**

Это была борьба наследников, а пострадали люди и книга Ахматовой, которая пошла под нож (Мандельштам 2). It was all part of a struggle between the heirs to the throne, and people were sacrificed to it, as was Akhmatova's book—which was pulped (2a).

Н-184 • ТОЧИ́ТЬ НОЖ *на кого* [VP; subj: human or collect] **1.** Also: **ТОЧИ́ТЬ НОЖИ́** to prepare for an armed attack, for war: X-ы точат ножи на Y-ов ≃ **Xs are taking up arms against Ys; Xs are mustering their forces.**

2. *coll* to be planning to do sth. bad, dirty, evil to s.o.: X точит нож на Y-а ≃ **X has it in for Y; X is cooking up trouble for Y; X is plotting ⟨hatching a plot⟩ against Y.**

Н-185 • БЕЗ НОЖА́ РЕ́ЗАТЬ/ЗАРЕ́ЗАТЬ *кого highly coll* [VP; subj: human; usu. 2nd or 3rd pers; fixed WO] to put s.o. in an extremely difficult position: X Y-а без ножа зарезал ≃ **X put Y in a tight spot ⟨on the spot⟩; X got ⟨left, landed⟩ Y in a fix ⟨in a jam⟩.**

Н-186 • НА НОЖА́Х *с кем coll* [PrepP; subj-compl with быть∅ (subj: human); if there is no prep obj, subj: pl] one is on extremely hostile terms with s.o.: X с Y-ом на ножах ≃ **X and Y are at loggerheads ⟨at daggers drawn, at swords' points⟩; X is bitterly at odds with Y.**

...Коновницын нахмурился частью от головной усилившейся боли, частью от неприятной, пришедшей ему в голову мысли о том, как теперь взволнуется всё это гнездо штабных, влиятельных людей при этом известии, в особенности Бенигсен, после Тарутина бывший на ножах с Кутузовым... (Толстой 7). ...Konovnitsyn frowned—partly from an increased pain in his head and partly at the unpleasant thought that occurred to him, of how all that nest of influential men on the staff would be stirred up by this news, especially Bennigsen, who ever since Tarutino had been at daggers drawn with Kutuzov... (7b).

Н-187 • КО́ЗЬЯ НО́ЖКА *coll* [NP; subj or obj; fixed WO] a homemade, funnel-shaped cigarette: **hand-rolled ⟨handmade⟩ cigarette.**

Н-188 • ПОДСТАВЛЯ́ТЬ/ПОДСТА́ВИТЬ НО́ЖКУ ⟨НО́ГУ, ПОДНО́ЖКУ⟩ *кому;* **ДАВА́ТЬ/ДАТЬ ПОДНО́ЖКУ** *all coll* [VP; subj: human; more often pfv] **1.** to stick one's foot out so that s.o. stumbles over it: X подставил Y-у ножку ≃ **X tripped Y (up).**

[extended usage] Меня не любят вещи. Мебель норовит подставить мне ножку (Олеша 2). Things don't like me. Furniture tries to trip me up... (2a).

2. to harm s.o. intentionally and in an underhand way: X подставил Y-у ножку ≃ **X tripped Y up; [in limited contexts] X stabbed Y in the back.**

«Он добрый малый!» — сказал Обломов... «Такой обязательный, — прибавил Судьбинский, — и нет этого, знаешь, чтоб выслужиться, подгадить, подставить ногу, опередить...

всё делает, что может» (Гончаров 1). "He's a nice fellow," said Oblomov.... "So obliging," Sudbinsky added. "And, you know, never tries to curry favour, to make mischief, trip one up, get ahead of anyone – he does all he can for people" (1a). ♦ Теперь мне стало очевидно, что Барский, который всю дорогу завидовал мне и ревниво относился к каждой моей книге и статье, к каждой ссылке на мои работы, к каждому упоминанию моей фамилии, решил на сей раз использовать предоставившуюся ему возможность и подставить мне ножку (Зиновьев 2). ...Now I could see clearly that Barskiy, who had always been jealous of me and envious of every book or article I had written, of every quotation from my work, of every reference to my name, had decided on this occasion to take the opportunity to stab me in the back (2a).

Н-189 • КАК ⟨БУ́ДТО, СЛО́ВНО, ТО́ЧНО⟩ НОЖО́М ОТРЕ́ЗАЛО; КАК ОТРЕ́ЗАЛО *all coll* [как etc + VP; impers; these forms only; fixed WO] (in refer. to a relationship, friendship etc., or in refer. to some continuing action) sth. ceased abruptly: **(sth.) suddenly stopped ⟨ended⟩; (sth.) came to a sudden ⟨an abrupt⟩ halt; (s.o.) suddenly stopped doing sth.**

Раньше он часто звонил, а после этого разговора о политике – как ножом отрезало. He used to call all the time, but after that conversation about politics he suddenly stopped calling altogether.

Н-190 • КАК НОЖО́М ОТРЕ́ЗАЛ; КАК ОТРЕ́ЗАЛ *both coll* [VP; subj: human] to say sth. sharply, categorically, in a tone that does not permit objection: **X как ножом отрезал ≃ X said (sth.) brusquely ⟨flatly, with finality⟩.**

Но Константин Иванович... на этот раз даже головы в его [Влада] сторону не поднял, сказал, как отрезал: «Нету у тебя здесь ничего, уважаемый» (Максимов 2). This time, however... Konstantin Ivanovich did not even look up as Vlad walked in, and said brusquely: "Nothing for you here, my friend" (2a).

Н-191 • КАК ⟨СЛО́ВНО, ТО́ЧНО⟩ НОЖО́М РЕЗА-НУ́ТЬ ⟨РЕЗНУ́ТЬ *obs*, ПОЛОСНУ́ТЬ⟩ ПО́ СЕРДЦУ *кого;* **КАК ⟨СЛО́ВНО, ТО́ЧНО⟩ НОЖО́М РЕЗА-НУ́ТЬ ⟨РЕЗНУ́ТЬ *obs*, ПОЛОСНУ́ТЬ⟩; ПОЛОС-НУ́ТЬ ПО́ СЕРДЦУ** *all coll* [VP; subj: usu. abstr (often слова, известие, крик etc); often impers (last var., impers only)] to cause s.o. sudden intense emotional pain: **X как ножом резанул Y-а по сердцу ≃ X was like a knife in Y's heart;** ‖ **Y-а как ножом по сердцу полоснуло ≃ it was as if someone had thrust ⟨stuck⟩ a knife into Y's heart; it was as if someone had stabbed Y in the heart.**

[Анисья:] Веришь ли, тётушка, как сказали мне, что женить его, как ножом по сердцу полоснуло меня. Думаю, в сердце она у него (Толстой 1). [A.:] I tell you, Matryona, when I heard that he was going to be married, it was as if someone had stuck a knife into my heart. I can't help thinking that he's in love with her (1c).

Н-192 • ПОД НОЖО́М умереть, лежать, быть∅; **ПОД НО́Ж** ложиться, лечь [PrepP; these forms only; adv or subj-compl with copula (subj: human)] (to die) during surgery, (to be) in surgery etc: **(die ⟨be, go etc⟩) under the ⟨s.o.'s⟩ knife.**

«Вы изволите быть недовольным, что вас превратили в человека?.. Вы, может быть, предпочитаете снова бегать по помойкам?..» – «Да что вы всё попрекаете – помойка, помойка. Я свой кусок хлеба добывал. А если бы я у вас помер под ножом? Вы что на это выразите, товарищ?» (Булгаков 11). "Is it your pleasure to complain because you have been transformed into a man?...Perhaps you prefer to root around in garbage bins again?..." "Why are you throwing it up all the time – garbage and garbage. I came by my piece of bread honestly. And if I'd died under your knife. What will you say to that, comrade?" (11a).

Н-193 • (как) С НОЖО́М К ГО́РЛУ приставать, приступать (*к кому*) *highly coll* [PrepP; Invar; adv (intensif); fixed WO] (to bother s.o. by demanding or requesting sth.) persistently and obtrusively: **X пристаёт к Y-у с ножом к горлу ≃ X is badgering ⟨hounding, harrying⟩ Y; X is bugging Y to death; X is on Y's back ⟨case⟩ (to do sth.).**

Н-194 • НЕ ПО НОЗДРЕ́ *substand, rude* [PrepP; Invar; subj-compl with copula (subj: any noun)] not to appeal to s.o. at all, to vex s.o.: **X Y-у не по ноздре ≃ Y can't stand ⟨stomach⟩ X; Y thinks X is a pain in the ass.**

Н-195 • НОЛЬ ⟨НУЛЬ⟩ БЕЗ ПА́ЛОЧКИ (*для кого, перед кем*); **КРУ́ГЛЫЙ ⟨СОВЕРШЕ́ННЫЙ⟩ НОЛЬ** *all highly coll* [NP; sing only; usu. subj-compl with быть∅ (subj: human); fixed WO] a person who is considered by another or others to be of no value, worth nothing: **a big (fat) zero ⟨nothing⟩; absolutely worthless; a complete nonentity; less than nothing;** ‖ **X перед Y-ом ноль без палочки ≃ X is nothing (as) compared to Y; X isn't even in Y's league.**

«Вот тогда я поняла: первое для советской власти – план. Выполни план!.. Первое дело – государство. А люди – ноль без палочки» (Гроссман 1). "So then I understood: the most important thing for the Soviet government was the plan! Fulfill the plan!...The state comes first, and people are a big zero" (1a). ♦ «Кому он [Евдокимов] нужен? Круглый ноль!» (Ерофеев 3). "What use is he [Evdokimov] to anyone? A big fat nothing!" (3a). ♦ «Как учёный, он был совершенный ноль, но держался благодаря одной особе...» (Трифонов 2). "As a scholar he was a complete nonentity, but he kept his job thanks to a certain female person..." (2a). ♦ Раньше Кузьма Матвеевич думал, что он для Афродиты ничего, ноль без палочки, а тут ви-ишь, как убивается (Войнович 4). Kuzma Matveyevich had always thought he meant nothing to Aphrodite, less than nothing, and now just look at her grieving away (4a).

Н-196 • НОЛЬ ВНИМА́НИЯ (*на кого-что*); **НОЛЬ ВНИМА́НИЯ, ФУНТ ПРЕЗРЕ́НИЯ** *both coll* [NP; sing only; used as predic with subj: human; may be used with pl subj; fixed WO] to pay no attention to, completely disregard s.o. or sth. (sometimes in a pointed manner): **X на Y-а – ноль внимания ≃ X doesn't pay any ⟨the slightest ⟨bit of⟩⟩ attention to Y; X pays no heed to Y; X completely ignores Y; Y gets zero ⟨no⟩ attention (from X); [in limited contexts] X snubs Y.**

Пантелей входит в кабинет. Главный Жрец в исторической задумчивости медленно вращается на фортепианной табуретке. На Пантелея – ноль внимания (Аксёнов 6). Pantelei enters the office. Deep in historical reflection, the High Priest is slowly turning around on a revolving piano stool. He pays not the slightest attention to Pantelei (6a). ♦ «...Он почему-то только с её мужем ля-ля-ля, ля-ля-ля, а на неё ноль внимания» (Искандер 2). "...For some reason all he's doing is gabbing with her husband, and she's getting zero attention" (2a).

Н-197 • ПОД НОЛЬ ⟨НУЛЬ⟩ стричь *кого* [PrepP; these forms only; adv] (to cut, shave off s.o.'s hair) down to the scalp: **X постриг Y-а под ноль ≃ person X cut off all (of) Y's hair.**

Н-198 • ВЫКИ́ДЫВАТЬ/ВЫ́КИНУТЬ ⟨ОТКА́ЛЫ-ВАТЬ/ОТКОЛО́ТЬ, ВЫБРА́СЫВАТЬ/ВЫ́БРО-СИТЬ⟩ НО́МЕР ⟨НОМЕРА́⟩ *coll* [VP; subj: human, occas. жизнь; variants with номер usu. pfv, variants with номера usu. impfv] to do sth. unexpected, unusual, often ridiculous: **X выкинул номер ≃ X pulled a trick ⟨a stunt⟩; X sprang a surprise.**

...Спустя десять дней [жена Смолянова] Марта выкинула номер. Хотела из окна прыгнуть из новой квартиры на шестом этаже (Трифонов 1). Ten days later his [Smolyanov's] wife Marta had pulled a stunt of her own and had tried to jump out of the window of their new, sixth-floor apartment (1a).

H-199 • НО́МЕР ОДИ́Н *coll* [NP; sing only; usu. nonagreeing postmodif; fixed WO] **1.** (of a person) the most important, influential etc: [NP] **number one; main ⟨chief, principal** etc⟩ [NP].

После того, как меня сделали завотделом, я стал для Мышкина врагом номер один. After I was made head of the department, I became enemy number one for Myshkin.

2. проблема, обязанность, обязательство и т. п. ~ the most urgent, pressing, important etc (problem, duty, obligation etc): **number one** [NP]; **first and foremost** [NP]; **primary** [NP]; ‖ задача номер один ≃ **top priority.**

Близилась суровая зима, и обеспечить посёлок теплом было для строителей задачей номер один. A severe winter was on the way, and the builders' top priority was to provide heat for the settlement.

H-200 • ПУСТО́Й НО́МЕР *coll* [NP; sing only; subj-compl with copula, nom or instrum (subj: abstr or concr, often это); fixed WO] sth. is futile, will produce no results: X — пустой номер ≃ **X is a waste of time; X won't work ⟨help, do the trick** etc⟩; **X is useless.**

...Первым делом надо было Вику прописать... Как ни облучала Вера [обаянием] начальника паспортного стола — не помогало. Письмо народной артистки Куниной тоже оказалось пустым номером (Грекова 3). First of all Vika had to be registered in her [Vera's] house....No matter how Vera sparkled at the director of the passport bureau it didn't help. A letter from People's Artist Kunina also didn't do the trick (3a).

H-201 • (Э́ТОТ) НО́МЕР НЕ ПРОЙДЁТ ⟨НЕ ВЫ́Й-ДЕТ, НЕ УДА́СТСЯ⟩; Э́ТИ ШТУ́ЧКИ НЕ ПРОЙ-ДУ́Т; Э́ТО НЕ ПРОЙДЁТ *all coll* [sent; fixed WO] the plan (scheme etc) in question will not succeed, will not produce the desired result(s): **it ⟨this trick** etc⟩ **won't work; he ⟨you** etc⟩ **can't pull it off; he ⟨you** etc⟩ **won't get away with that; he ⟨you** etc⟩ **won't get by with that sort of game; nothing doing!**

Хлебовводов начал орать, что эти штучки не пройдут, что он деньги даром получать не желает и что он не позволит коменданту отправить коту под хвост четыре часа рабочего времени (Стругацкие 3). Khlebovvodov began shouting that these tricks would not work, that he did not wish to take money for nothing, and that he would not allow the commandant to flush four hours of work time down the tubes (3a). ♦ [author's usage] «А за что меня судить?» — «Я могу п-повторить ещё раз...» — «Не надо ваньку валять, — сказал Костенко... — у тебя только с Шрезелем такие номера проходили...» — «Я не понимаю, о чём вы говорите». — «З-значит, ты отказываешься давать показания?» (Семёнов 1). "But why will I be taken to court?" "I c-can repeat it for you...." "It's no good you playing the fool," said Kostyenko...."It was only with Schresel that you could get by with that sort of game...." "I don't know what you're talking about." "D-does that mean you refuse to give evidence?" (1a).

H-202 • НА ОДИ́ННАДЦАТОМ НО́МЕРЕ добираться, передвигаться и т. п.; **ОДИ́ННАДЦАТЫМ НО́МЕ-РОМ** *both coll, humor* [PrepP or NP~instrum~; these forms only; adv; fixed WO] (to get, go somewhere) on foot: **(on) one's own two feet ⟨pins⟩; (on) one's own two legs; under one's own power ⟨steam⟩; hoof ⟨foot⟩ it;** [in limited contexts] **on ⟨by⟩ shanks' mare.**

«Мамаша, — спросил Садчиков лифтёршу, — а у вас к-кабина вниз ходит?» — «Ещё чего! — ответила лифтёрша. — ...Только вверх, а оттеда [*ungrammat* = оттуда] — одиннадцатым номером» (Семёнов 1). "Dearie," said Sadchikov to the lift woman, "does your lift go down from here?" "Not on yer life!" replied the lift woman. "...Only up. Yer comes down on yer feet" (1a). ♦ ...Лукашину вдруг стало обидно за [уполномоченного райкома] Ганичева... Заём, налоги, хлебозаготовки, лес — всё уполномоченный! Тащись к дьяволу на кулички. В дождь, в мороз, в бездорожье. И хорошо бы на подводе, на машине, а то ведь и пёхом, на одиннадцатом номере (Абрамов 1). ...Suddenly Lukashin felt sorry for [the District Committee representative] Ganichev....Ganichev had to do it all: the Loan, the taxes, the grain procurements, the timber. He had to go to all sorts of godforsaken places. In the rain, in the cold, and when the roads were impassable. It wouldn't have been so bad if he had a cart or a car, but all he had were his own two pins (1a).

H-203 • В НО́РМЕ [PrepP; Invar; subj-compl with copula (subj: abstr, often всё, or human)] a person or thing is in his or its customary state: X в норме ≃ **X is ⟨seems⟩ normal; person X is his usual self.**

Не то чтобы я опьянел — сказалось, должно быть, долгое воздержание, — голова работала ясно, всё было в норме, кроме одного пункта, как в мире Кафки, где всё достоверно, кроме какого-нибудь одного обстоятельства: того, например, что Замза превратился в насекомое (Трифонов 5). Not that it made me drunk (here my previous long abstention must have played a role), for my head was functioning clearly and everything seemed normal except for one thing, as in Kafka, where everything is true to life except for one particular circumstance—Gregor Samsa's transformation into an insect, for example (5a).

H-204 • ВХОДИ́ТЬ/ВОЙТИ́ ⟨ПРИХОДИ́ТЬ/ПРИЙТИ́⟩ В НО́РМУ [VP; subj: abstr, often всё, or human; usu. pfv] to return to one's or its usual state: X вошёл в норму ≃ **X was ⟨went⟩ back to normal; X returned to normal.**

«Да, нам предстоит пережить несколько тяжёлых дней. А потом всё войдёт в норму...» (Эренбург 4). "Yes, the next few days will be critical for us. But afterwards everything will go back to normal" (4a). ♦ «Ну, что же, теперь лучше себя чувствуете?» — «Да, благодарю вас. Кажется, прихожу в норму» (Замятин 1). "Well, then, are you feeling better now?" "Yes, thank you. I think I am returning to normal" (1a). ♦ Чистый и прекрасный человек, он [Зощенко] искал связи с эпохой, верил широковещательным программам, сулившим всеобщее счастье, считал, что когда-нибудь всё войдёт в норму, так как проявления жестокости и дикости лишь случайность, рябь на воде, а не сущность, как его учили на политзанятиях (Мандельштам 2). [context transl] A wonderful, pure man, he [Zoshchenko] had always tried to find points of contact with the times he lived in. He believed in all the high-sounding schemes for universal happiness and thought that eventually everything would settle down—all the cruelty and savagery were only incidental, a temporary ruffling of the surface, not the essence, as we were always being told at political lectures (2a).

H-205 • С НО́РОВОМ *substand* [PrepP; Invar; nonagreeing modif or subj-compl with copula (subj: human or лошадь, мул etc)] self-willed, obstinate: **headstrong; willful;** [in limited contexts] **pigheaded;** [of a horse, mule] **restive; balky.**

H-206 • БРОСА́ТЬСЯ/БРО́СИТЬСЯ ⟨БИТЬ, УДА-РЯ́ТЬ/УДА́РИТЬ⟩ В НОС *(кому)* [VP] **1.** Also: **УДА-РЯ́ЕТ/УДА́РИЛО В НОС** *чем* [subj: a noun denoting smell; var. with *чем* impers] (of a sharp, unpleasant smell) to be sharply felt: X бросился (Y-у) в нос ≃ **X struck ⟨stung⟩ Y's nostrils; X assaulted the nose; Y was hit by the smell of X.**

Сейдахмат покачивался, улыбаясь сам себе. И когда он подошёл ближе, в нос [мальчику] ударил спиртной запах (Айтматов 1). He [Seidakhmat] swayed on his feet, smiling to himself. And when he came nearer, the smell of alcohol struck the boy's nostrils (1a).

2. *coll, often disapprov* [subj: abstr or concr] (to be intended) to attract attention, be striking: X бьёт (Y-у) в нос ≃ **X is glaring; X hits you in the face;** [in limited contexts] **X makes Y ⟨you, one⟩ sit up and take notice.**

Когда входишь к ним в дом, роскошь бьёт в нос. When you walk into their house, the luxuriousness of it hits you in the face. ♦ Он сшил себе новую пару платья и хвастался, что на днях откроет в Глупове такой магазин, что самому Винтергальтеру в нос бросится (Салтыков-Щедрин 1). He had a new suit made and boasted that any day now he would open such a store in Foolov that Winterhalter himself would have to sit up and take notice (1a).

H-207 • В НОС *говорить, произносить* и т. п. [PrepP; Invar; adv] (to speak, pronounce sth. etc) nasally: **(speak ⟨talk etc⟩) through one's nose.**

Не жаловали на Чёрной [лестнице]… аспирантов, в подражание декану говорящих немного в нос… (Ерофеев 3). The [Back] Stairway also had no use for the graduate students who talked through their noses in order to ape the Dean… (3a).

H-208 • ВÉШАТЬ/ПОВÉСИТЬ НОС *coll*; ВÉШАТЬ/ПОВÉСИТЬ НОС НА КВИ́НТУ *obs, coll* [VP; subj: human] to become upset, disheartened, dejected: X повесил нос ≃ **X was ⟨looked⟩ down in the mouth; X was down in the dumps; X was downhearted; X lost heart;** ‖ *Neg Imper* не вешай нос(а) ≃ **don't get so down in the mouth; keep your chin up.**

«Что нос повесил?» — спросил он (Кузнецов 1). "Why so down in the mouth?" he asked (1a). ♦ [Устинья Наумовна:] Что вы невеселы — носы повесили? (Островский 10). [U.N.:] What are you gloomy and down in the dumps for? (10b). ♦ [Боркин:] Господа, что же вы это в самом деле носы повесили? (Чехов 4). [B.:] Really, why so downhearted anyway, all of you…? (4b).

H-209 • ВОДИ́ТЬ ЗÁ НОС *кого coll, disapprov* [VP; subj: human] to deceive, delude s.o. intentionally, often by promising sth. and then not keeping one's promise: X водил Y-а за нос ≃ **X was leading Y on; X was leading Y up ⟨down⟩ the garden path; X was stringing Y along; X was taking Y for a ride; X was giving Y the runaround; X was misleading Y.**

[Ипполит:] Сегодня, Надя, в последний час старого года, я намерен поставить вопрос ребром. Хватить водить меня за нос! [Надя:] Чем ты недоволен? [Ипполит:] Своим холостым положением. И я предлагаю… [Надя (перебивает):] Сядь! (Брагинский и Рязанов 1). [I.:] Today, Nadya, in the last hour of the old year, I intend to put the question squarely. No more leading me on like this! [N.:] What's wrong? [I.:] My bachelor status. And I propose… [N. (interrupting):] Please, sit down (1a). ♦ О разведке у нас знают из кинофильмов. Служит под боком у Гитлера наш смельчак, одет с иголочки, побрит, надушен, водит за нос и Гиммлера, и Бормана, и Кальтенбруннера… (Рыбаков 1). People only know about intelligence from what they've seen in the movies. Our daring agent is operating right under Hitler's nose, dressed immaculately, clean-shaven and perfumed, leading Himmler, Bormann and Kaltenbrunner up the garden path… (1a). ♦ Если он скажет правду… тогда спросят: почему раньше увиливал? Чему верить? Зачем водите суд и следствие за нос? (Тендряков 1). If he were to tell the truth…then they would ask: Why did you deny this earlier? What are we to believe? Why are you trying to mislead the court? (1a).

H-210 • ВОРОТИ́ТЬ/ОТВОРОТИ́ТЬ НОС *от кого-чего highly coll*; ВОРОТИ́ТЬ/ОТВОРОТИ́ТЬ МÓРДУ ⟨РÓЖУ, РЫ́ЛО⟩ *substand, rude* [VP; subj: human] **1.** to stop looking at s.o. or sth. (usu. because one finds him or it disagreeable, unappealing etc): X воротит нос от Y-а ≃ **X turns away from Y.**

2. [impfv only] to regard s.o. or sth. with scorn: X воротит нос от Y-а ≃ **X turns up his nose at Y; X looks down his nose at Y; X has nothing but contempt for Y; [in limited contexts] X won't have anything to do with Y.**

В те благословенные времена советская молодёжь не воротила нос от советских же символов (Войнович 1). In those hallowed days, Soviet youth did not turn up its nose at Soviet symbols (1a). ♦ …Сердцем они [перечисленные мною писатели] новой власти не приняли, от политики партии и правительства в области литературы и искусства воротили нос, а сами ещё что-то писали в стол или старались удержать написанное в памяти… (Войнович 1). …In their hearts, they [the writers mentioned above] did not accept the new system, had nothing but contempt for Party and governmental policy in the arts and literature, and continued to write for the desk drawer or to memorize their works (1a).

3. to refuse s.o. or sth. with disdain: X воротит нос от Y-а ≃ **X turns up his nose at Y; X sniffs at Y.**

И женщины, те самые женщины, которые ещё недавно воротили нос от мяса, толпой сбились у прилавка… (Абрамов 1). And the women — the very same women who but a moment before had turned up their noses at this meat — came thronging around the counter (1a).

H-211 • ВЫСÓВЫВАТЬ/ВЫ́СУНУТЬ НОС *coll* [VP; subj: human; if impfv, usu. neg] **1.** ~ *откуда* to poke one's head just barely out of some place, just enough to see out: X высунул нос из места Y ≃ **X poked his nose out of place Y; X stuck ⟨poked⟩ his head out of place Y.**

…Ничто не ускользало от свежего, тонкого вниманья, и, высунувши нос из походной телеги своей, я глядел и на невиданный дотоле покрой какого-нибудь сюртука, и на деревянные ящики с гвоздями… с изюмом и мылом, мелькавшие из дверей овощной лавки… (Гоголь 3). …Nothing escaped my fresh, keen observation, and poking my nose out of my traveling cart, I would stare at a novel cut of a coat never seen before; at the wooden boxes filled with nails…or with raisins, or with soap — all glimpsed through the doors of grocery stores… (3c).

2. ~ *куда, откуда* [often neg pfv fut, gener. 2nd pers sing носа не высунешь; or pfv infin with нельзя, страшно etc] to leave the place one is in, go to some place (often with the implication that one abandons the protection of the place he is in and goes to an unsafe place, goes out into bad weather, exposes himself to danger etc): носа не высунешь ⟨нельзя нос высунуть⟩ (из дому ⟨на улицу⟩) ≃ **you can't poke your nose out ⟨outside (the house)⟩; you can't poke your nose out of doors ⟨out of the house etc⟩; you can't set foot out of doors ⟨out of the house etc⟩;** ‖ X не высовывал носа ≃ **X was sitting tight.**

Знаю я эти места, бывал и там. Сейчас там небось носа не высунешь, метёт! (Аксёнов 1). I know those parts, I've been up there. I bet right now it's snowing so hard there you can't poke your nose out (1a). ♦ …Нашему брату, хуторянину, высунуть нос из своего захолустья в большой свет — батюшки мои! — Это всё равно как, случается, иногда зайдёшь в покои великого пана: все обступят тебя и пойдут дурачить (Гоголь 5). …For a villager like me to poke his nose out of his hole into the great world is — merciful heavens! — just like what happens if you go into the apartments of some fine gentleman: they all come around you and make you feel like a fool… (5a). ♦ До самого генерального штаба ему не встретилось ни души… И хотя недавнее буйство, как показывал беглый осмотр, коснулось лишь нескольких улиц, все прочие горожане тоже сидели по норам и не высовывали носа. Верно, их распугал этот дальний грохот, теперь хорошо различимый (Терц 6). Not a soul did he meet all the way back to the H.Q. The recent violence, he now realised, had been confined to a few streets, but all the townsfolk — perhaps frightened by the distant rumbling which was growing louder — had crept into their lairs and were sitting tight (6a).

H-212 • ДЕРЖÁТЬ НОС ПО ВÉТРУ ⟨ПÓ ВЕТРУ⟩ *coll, disapprov* [VP; subj: human or collect] to adjust, accommodate o.s. to the circumstances by changing one's behavior, convictions etc unscrupulously: X держит нос по ветру ≃ **X follows**

⟨trims his sails to⟩ the prevailing winds; X goes as the wind blows; X tacks with the wind.

Толя при любом начальстве будет хорошо, он умеет держать нос по ветру. No matter who his boss is, Tolya will do fine: he knows how to trim his sails to the prevailing wind. ♦ Он [Вадим] удивительно умел держать нос по ветру, всегда тянулся к более сильным... (Рыбаков 2). Vadim was remarkably good at tacking with the wind, and he had always been drawn to stronger personalities (2a).

Н-213 • ЗАДИРА́ТЬ ⟨ДРАТЬ⟩/ЗАДРА́ТЬ ⟨ПОДНИ-МА́ТЬ/ПОДНЯ́ТЬ⟩ НОС (*перед кем*) *highly coll, disapprov* [VP: subj: human] to think too highly of o.s., behave arrogantly (toward s.o.): X задирает нос ≃ X puts on ⟨gives himself⟩ airs; X has his nose in the air; X has ⟨gets⟩ a swelled head; X acts high and mighty; [in limited contexts] there's no talking to X.

Егорша с первых слов начал задирать нос... Он, видите ли, отпускник, а не просто там на побывку после сплава домой пришёл, и потому намерен отдыхать культурно, ибо его здоровье – это уж не его здоровье, а здоровье рабочего класса (Абрамов 1). From his very first words Egorsha started putting on airs....You see, he was on official leave – not the same as mere time off at home after timber floating – and was therefore intending to relax in a civilized manner, since his health was not *his* health, but the health of the working class (1a).

Н-214 • НАТЯНУ́ТЬ ⟨НАСТА́ВИТЬ, НАКЛЕ́ИТЬ⟩ НОС *кому highly coll* [VP; subj: human] **1.** to deceive, dupe s.o.: X натянул Y-у нос ≃ X pulled a fast one on Y; X pulled the wool over Y's eyes.

2. to disgrace s.o. by having done sth. faster and better: X натянул Y-у нос ≃ X beat Y to it ⟨to the punch, to the draw⟩; X went Y one better.

Н-215 • НОС НЕ ДОРО́С *у кого highly coll* [VP_subj; Invar; fixed WO] s.o. is (still) not old and/or experienced enough (to do, undertake, handle etc sth.): у X-а (ещё) нос не дорос ≃ X is (still) wet behind the ears; X is (still) too green; X is (still) too young.

Начальник, улыбаясь, сказал Сергею, что ему требуются опытные электрики и что до такой работы у него, вчерашнего школьника, нос пока не дорос. Smiling, the boss said to Sergei that he needed experienced electricians, and that Sergei, just out of school, was too green for that kind of work. ♦ «Папа, можно посмотреть этот фильм?» – «У тебя ещё нос не дорос такие фильмы смотреть». "Dad, can I watch this movie?" "You're too young to watch this kind of movie."

Н-216 • ПОД НО́С ⟨ПО́Д НОС⟩ *бормотать, бубнить, бурчать и т. п. coll* [PrepP; these forms only; adv] (to mumble, mutter) very quietly, almost inaudibly: under one's breath; to oneself; [in limited contexts] into one's beard.

Работники Учреждения шли по утрам мимо Нюры и скрывались за этой таинственной дверью... Знакомым Нюра кивала головой и издалека кричала: «Эй, здравствуй!» Одни из них вздрагивали, недоуменно смотрели на Нюру и, пробурчав что-то себе под нос, двигались дальше (Войнович 4). The workers of the Institution walked past Nyura in the morning and then disappeared through that mysterious door....Nyura nodded to those she knew and shouted from a distance: "Hey, how are you?" Some of them would wince, look puzzled at Nyura, and having muttered something under their breath, keep moving (4a). ♦ Он шёл по уснувшей улице не спеша, мурлыча под нос старую тягучую песню (Семёнов 1). He walked unhurriedly down the sleeping street, humming an old plaintive tune to himself (1a). ♦ Начинаются занятия. Офицер бубнит себе под нос по конспекту...

(Марченко 1). The session begins. The officer mumbles into his beard, following his notes... (1a).

Н-217 • ПОКА́ЗЫВАТЬ/ПОКАЗА́ТЬ НОС ⟨НОСЫ́⟩ (*кому*) *obs, coll* [VP; subj: human] to make a derisive gesture, tease s.o. by spreading the fingers of one hand and touching the thumb to the tip of the nose, keeping the four fingers straight up: X показал Y-у нос ≃ X thumbed his nose at Y.

Н-218 • С ГУ́ЛЬКИН ⟨С ВОРОБЬИ́НЫЙ⟩ НОС *highly coll* [PrepP; these forms only] **1.** *кого-чего* ~ [quantit subj-compl with быть∅ (subj/gen: usu. abstr or subj: infin) or adv (quantif)] very little (more often in cases when the amount is considered inadequate): almost no; hardly any; (only) a little ⟨tiny⟩ bit; (just) a smidgen.

Работы там осталось с гулькин нос, мы за полчаса всё сделаем. There's hardly any work left; we'll have everything finished in half an hour.

2. [nonagreeing modif or subj-compl with copula (subj: concr or abstr)] very small (in size, amount etc): (teeny) tiny; negligible; minuscule; (amount to) a hairbreadth ⟨a hair's-breadth etc⟩.

«С чего вы цапаетесь-то? Никак не могу понять. Объясните? У вас и расхождения-то с гулькин нос!» (Залыгин 1). "What are you squabbling about? It makes no sense to me. Explain yourselves. Your differences amount to a hair's breadth" (1a).

Н-219 • СОВА́ТЬ/СУ́НУТЬ ПОД НОС ⟨В НОС⟩ *кому что highly coll* [VP; subj: human] to give, offer, show sth. to s.o. disrespectfully, rudely: X сунул Y Z-у в нос ≃ X shoved ⟨pushed, stuck⟩ Y under Z's nose; X shoved ⟨stuck⟩ Y in Z's face.

...Им [хозяйкам] в нос совали бумажку и говорили: «Видите, записано?!» (Рыбаков 1). Kusiel would shove the notes in their [the customers'] faces and say "Look, it's written down!" (1a).

Н-220 • СОВА́ТЬ/СУ́НУТЬ (СВОЙ) НОС *куда, во что,* often во всё, в чьи дела, не в своё дело, куда не следует, куда не просят и т. п.; **СОВА́ТЬСЯ/СУ́НУТЬСЯ СО СВОИ́М НО́СОМ** *all highly coll, disapprov* [VP; subj: human] to interfere, meddle in sth. in which one should not: X суёт свой нос в Y ⟨во всё, не в своё дело и т. п.⟩ ≃ X sticks his nose in(to) Y; X pokes his nose in where he has no business; X sticks ⟨pokes⟩ his nose where it doesn't belong ⟨where it isn't wanted⟩; || Neg Imper не суй нос в дела Z-а ⟨в чужие дела⟩ ≃ get your nose out of Z's ⟨other people's⟩ affairs; butt out of Z's ⟨other people's⟩ business.

«Советую не совать нос в мои обстоятельства, если вы не желаете спать в общей могиле с большевиками» (Паустовский 1). "I advise you not to stick your nose into my affairs unless you want to end up in a common grave with the Bolsheviks" (1b). ♦ [Нина:] А ты? Куда ты суёшь свой нос? Зачем? Почему ты сделал из него идиота? (Вампилов 4). [N.:] And you? Why did you stick your nose in? What for? Why did you make a fool out of him? (4b). ♦ Напоминание об отце [Влада], её муже, всякий раз выводило мать из равновесия... «Тот во всё нос совал, и этот туда же» (Максимов 2). Any reminder of her husband, Vlad's father, invariably threw Fedosya off balance....His father was always poking his nose in where he had no business, and now his son's doing the same" (2a). ♦ [Ведущий:] Эти лукашины – они во всё суют свой нос... (Брагинский и Рязанов 1). [context transl] [Narrator:] These Lukashins, they're born busy-bodies... (1a).

Н-221 • УТЕРЕ́ТЬ НОС *кому highly coll* [VP; subj: human] to outdo s.o., prove one's superiority in sth.: X утёр нос Y-у ≃ X showed Y up; X got the better of Y; X was one up on Y; X one-upped Y; [in limited contexts] X tweaked Y's nose.

Эх, многим бы нос утёр, показал бы, кто он есть! (Айтматов 1). Oh, he'd get the better of lots of people, he'd show them who he was (1b). ♦ «Печатается. Сотрудничает... С портретом. И уполномоченному нос утёр... Он теперь старше его по чину...» (Битов 2). "He gets published. A contributor...with his picture. And he's one up on the official—he outranks him now" (2a). ♦ Эти люди, думал Социолог, собираются здесь и образуют группы... без всякого принуждения... Здесь... можно воочию видеть социальность... Теперь-то он утрёт Им (тамошним социологам) нос... (Зиновьев 1). These people, thought Sociologist, gather here and form groups...without any compulsion.... "Here...we can see sociality as it is...." Now he would be able to tweak Their (the foreign sociologists') noses... (1a).

H-222 • УТКНУ́ТЬ НОС *во что;* **УТКНУ́ТЬСЯ НО́СОМ** *both coll* [VP; subj: human] to concentrate on sth., be completely absorbed in what one is doing: X уткнул нос в Y ≃ **X buried his nose ⟨head, face⟩ in Y; X had his nose ⟨head, face⟩ buried in Y;** [in limited contexts] **X was bent over Y.**

[Доктор:] Вы же видите, он не слушает меня. Он уткнулся носом в какие-то записки (Шварц 3). [Doctor:] You see he doesn't listen to me. He's buried his nose in some notes (3a). ♦ Мать сидит на диване... Подле неё сидит Настасья Ивановна да Пелагея Игнатьевна и, уткнув носы в работу, прилежно шьют что-то к празднику... (Гончаров 1). His mother was sitting on the sofa.... Beside her, bent over their work, sat Nastasya Ivanovna and Pelageya Ignatyevna, diligently sewing on something for a holiday... (1b).

H-223 • ИЗ-ПОД (СА́МОГО) НО́СА *чьего, (у) кого* ута́щить, унести, схватить *что,* увести *кого,* убежать и т. п. *highly coll* [PrepP; these forms only; adv] (to take, carry away some person or thing, escape etc) from very close proximity to s.o. (often taking advantage of s.o.'s carelessness, passivity etc): **(from) under s.o.'s (very) nose; from right under s.o.'s nose.**

Лучшие куски пищи ты выхватывал у гостей из-под носа и с возгласом «Это для вас!» подносил демонстративно Лиде, громоздя вокруг неё съедобную баррикаду (Терц 8). You grabbed the nicest tidbits from under the noses of the other guests and shouting "This is for you!" you ostentatiously offered them to Lida, building up a barricade of food all around her (8a). ♦ «Из-под носа дочь уводят... а ты, старый хрыч, глазами хлопаешь!» (Максимов 3). "Your daughter's being carried off under your very nose, and you don't lift a finger, you silly old devil" (3a).

H-224 • КОРО́ЧЕ ВОРОБЬИ́НОГО НО́СА *coll* [AdjP; Invar; subj-compl with бытьₒ; fixed WO] **1.** [subj: concr or abstr] (often of a story, essay etc that turns out shorter than expected) sth. is very brief: X короче воробьиного носа ≃ **X wouldn't have covered the back of a postage stamp; X is awfully short.**

[author's usage] О многом хотел рассказать дворник Штабелю, очень о многом, но, хоть и прошло столько лет, новости его оказались не длиннее воробьиного носа (Максимов 3). The yardman felt that he should have such a lot to tell Stabel, yet after all those years his news wouldn't have covered the back of a postage stamp (3a).

2. [subj: abstr] sth. is of short duration: X короче воробьиного носа ≃ **X is short-lived ⟨fleeting, short⟩.**

H-225 • НЕ ВИ́ДЕТЬ ДА́ЛЬШЕ СВОЕГО́ ⟨(СВОЕГО́) СО́БСТВЕННОГО⟩ НО́СА *coll, disapprov* [VP; subj: human; usu. pres; the verb may take the final position, otherwise fixed WO] to be narrow-minded, limited in one's outlook, fail to see the full scope of a situation: X не видит дальше своего носа ≃ **X doesn't ⟨can't⟩ see farther than the end of his (own) nose; X doesn't ⟨can't⟩ see beyond ⟨farther than⟩ his nose.**

[Астров:] Все они, наши добрые знакомые, мелко мыслят, мелко чувствуют и не видят дальше своего носа — просто-

напросто глупы (Чехов 3). [A.:] These good friends of ours all think their shallow little thoughts and have their shallow little feelings...not one of them can see farther than the end of his own nose. In fact they're just plain stupid (3c). ♦ Да, Терещенко дальше своего носа не видит, мелкий провинциальный адвокат, неспособен ухватить главное... (Рыбаков 1). Yes, Tereshchenko couldn't see beyond his nose, he was a petty provincial lawyer who couldn't grasp the main point... (1a).

H-226 • НЕ КАЗА́ТЬ ⟨НЕ ПОКА́ЗЫВАТЬ⟩/НЕ ПОКАЗА́ТЬ НО́СА ⟨-у⟩ *coll* [VP; subj: human; may be used without negation to convey the opposite meaning] **1.** ~ *(куда, к кому)* not to visit s.o. or go to some place: X (к Y-у) носа не кажет ≃ **X doesn't show his face (at Y's place); X keeps away (from Y).**

«...Мне на службу носа нельзя будет показать, я и так уже третий день не езжу» (Булгаков 11). "...I won't be able to show my face at the office. I haven't gone in for three days as it is" (11a).

2. ~ *откуда* not to leave or look out of some place or kind of lodging: X носа не показывал из места Y ≃ **X didn't poke his nose out ⟨outside, outside the house, outside (of) place Y⟩; X didn't poke his nose out of doors ⟨of the house etc⟩.**

В тот день под вечер ударил вдруг ветер сан-ташский, оттуда, с хребта поднебесного. Обрушился шквалом... Кое-как успели загнать скотину, убрать кое-что со двора, кое-как успели дров побольше наносить в дом. А потом уже и носа из дому не показывали (Айтматов 1). Towards evening of that same day, the San-Tash wind suddenly struck from up high on the mountain ridge which reached the sky. It whipped up into a tornado....Somehow, they managed to drive in the cattle and take in a few things from the yard; somehow they were able to carry an extra supply of firewood into the house. After this, no one poked his nose outside the house (1b). ♦ Он накрепко наказал Захару не сметь болтать с Никитой... а Анисье погрозил пальцем, когда она показала было нос из кухни и что-то хотела спросить Никиту (Гончаров 1). He gave strict orders to Zakhar not to chatter with Nikita...and when Anisya poked her nose out of the kitchen to ask Nikita something, he shook a finger at her in warning (1b).

H-227 • КЛЕВА́ТЬ ⟨ПОКЛЁВЫВАТЬ⟩ НО́СОМ *coll* [VP; subj: human; носом remains sing even when used with pl subj; fixed WO] (in refer. to a strong desire to sleep) to hang one's head, having dozed off for an instant: X клевал носом ≃ **X was ⟨kept⟩ nodding (off ⟨off to sleep⟩); X was ⟨kept⟩ nodding drowsily.**

А когда Павел Петрович доказывал, что лекарства нужны лишь для того, чтобы «пробудить природу от сна», ей неизменно представлялась старая дама в пенсне, вроде Агнии Петровны, которая клюёт носом на скамейке в саду... (Каверин 1). And when Pavel Petrovich said that medicine was necessary only in order to "rouse Nature from sleep," she invariably pictured to herself an old lady in pince-nez, like Agnia Petrovna, who was nodding on a bench in the garden... (1a). ♦ Мужчины спорили, галдели, дымили, допивали остатки... женщины клевали носом... (Трифонов 3). The men were still arguing at the tops of their voices, smoking, drinking the last of the liquor...while the women were nodding off (3a). ♦ В тот же вечер... дядя Сандро, посмеиваясь и то и дело кивая на жену, сидевшую тут же на отдельной скамейке, рассказал о том, что видел днём. (Кстати, кивки его в сторону жены имели двойной смысл: с одной стороны, он как бы призывал посмеяться над её предрассудками, а с другой стороны, обращал внимание слушателей на то, что она то и дело клевала носом) (Искандер 3). That night...Uncle Sandro kept chuckling and nodding toward his wife—who was sitting there too on a separate bench—as he recounted what he had seen that day. (Incidentally, the nods in his wife's direction had a dual meaning: on the one hand he invited his listeners to laugh at her superstitions, and on the other hand, he directed their attention to the fact that she kept nodding off to sleep) (3a). ♦ Брат дяди Сандро, поклёвывая носом, сидел у самогонного аппарата и следил, как по соломинке в бутылку стекает водка (Искандер 3). Uncle Sandro's brother was nodding drowsily as he sat by the still and watched the brandy drip through the straw into the bottle (3a).

H-228 • КРУТИ́ТЬ НО́СОМ *highly coll* [VP; subj: human; носом remains sing even when used with pl subj] to express dissatisfaction, disdain, reject sth. (sometimes in a capricious manner): X крутит носом ≃ **X is too picky ⟨finicky etc⟩; X turns up his nose (at sth.);** [usu. of children] **X is ⟨gets⟩ fussy.**

Я без работы уже год, и в моём положении крутить носом не приходится − нужно браться за любую работу. I've been out of work for a year already, and in my situation you can't be too picky − you've got to take any job you can find. ♦ В её возрасте пора перестать крутить носом при выборе жениха, чтобы не остаться старой девой. At her age, it's time to stop turning up her nose at every available man, or else she'll end up an old maid.

H-229 • НО́СОМ ⟨НОС⟩ К НО́СУ *coll* [these forms only; adv; fixed WO] **1.** ~ столкнуться, встретиться. Also: **НОС В НОС ⟨С НО́СОМ⟩** *obs* (to meet, run into one another) right up close, facing one another: **(bump into s.o.) nose to nose; (meet) face to face.**

Я едва успел сообразить, что случилось, как очутился нос с носом с лошадью… и с драгуном… (Герцен 2). I hardly had time to take in what was happening when I found myself nose to nose with a horse…and a dragoon… (2a). ♦ «Ну, а дальше сталкиваются оба эти мошенника на Шан-Зелизе, нос к носу…» (Булгаков 12). "Well, after that both rogues met face to face on the Champs Élysées" (12a).

2. увидеть *кого-что* и т. п. ~ (to see s.o. or sth.) at close proximity: **(see s.o. ⟨sth.⟩) up close; (be) face to face (with s.o. ⟨sth.⟩).**

H-230 • ПО́Д НОСОМ *у кого;* **ПОД ⟨ПЕРЕД⟩ СА́-МЫМ НО́СОМ** *all coll* [PrepP; these forms only; adv or subj-compl with copula (subj: concr or abstr)] right near s.o., in immediate proximity to s.o.: **(right) under s.o's (very) nose; staring s.o. in the face.**

Перед самым носом у тебя мелькают мощные подковы (Зиновьев 1). Right under your nose you can see those…great hooves pounding up and down (1a). ♦ Дома никто ничего не знал о случившемся, люди ничего не знали о том, что происходит у них под носом (Искандер 1). At home no one knew anything about what had happened; people didn't know anything about what was happening right under their very noses (1a).

H-231 • С НО́СОМ остаться, оставить *кого coll* [PrepP; Invar; subj-compl with остаться (subj: human) or obj-compl with оставить (obj: human); usu. used with pfv past] (to be left or leave s.o.) without sth. one or s.o. had hoped for or counted on: **(be left ⟨leave s.o.⟩) high and dry ⟨empty-handed, out in the cold, holding the bag⟩; (get) nothing for one's pains; (leave s.o.) with nothing to show for it.**

Он увлёкся Аней всерьёз, а она оставила его с носом и вышла замуж за другого. He fell hard for Anya, but she left him out in the cold and married someone else.

H-232 • ТЫ́КАТЬ/ТКНУ́ТЬ НО́СОМ *кого во что highly coll* [VP; subj: human] to point out in a rude manner sth. done poorly, carelessly in order to embarrass, humiliate, and/or edify s.o.: X тычет Y-а носом в Z ≃ **X rubs Y's nose in Z ⟨in it⟩.**

…Все те, кто не высказался столь определённо, начнут с радостью тыкать тебя носом в собственную определённость… (Битов 2). …All those who didn't express themselves so definitely will start gleefully rubbing your nose in your own definiteness… (2a).

H-233 • ХЛЮ́ПАТЬ/ХЛЮ́ПНУТЬ ⟨ШМЫ́ГАТЬ/ШМЫГНУ́ТЬ⟩ НО́СОМ *coll* [VP; subj: human] to draw air noisily in through the nose (usu. when crying, afflicted with a cold etc): X хлюпает носом ≃ **X sniffs ⟨snuffles, sniffles⟩.**

«Да ты не бойся, − сказал Витька, − я только так, чтоб ты отвязался…» Прохор всхлипнул и тяжело шмыгнул носом. «Ну брось… − попросил Витька. − Ну извини меня, если что не так» (Семёнов 1). "Don't be frightened," said Victor, "I only said it to make you leave me alone.…" Prokhor sobbed and sniffed heavily. "All right, pack it in…" begged Victor. "All right, I'm sorry if I was wrong" (1a). ♦ «Ну, как тут у вас победы праздновали? Шумно было?» − «Было. Всего было. И шуму было, и слёз было, и радости…» Анна хлюпнула носом… (Абрамов 1). "Well, how did you celebrate the victories here? Was it noisy?" "Yes. There was everything: noise, tears, joy.…" Anna sniffled… (1a).

H-234 • В НОСУ́ КОВЫРЯ́ТЬ *substand* [VP; subj: human] to idle, loaf about (usu. on the job): X в носу ковыряет ≃ **X sits around with his finger in ⟨up⟩ his nose; X lazes about; X sits on his butt ⟨duff⟩.**

H-235 • ЗАРУБИ́ТЬ (СЕБЕ́) НА НОСУ́ ⟨НА ЛБУ⟩ *coll* [VP; subj: human; usu. imper or infin with надо, следует etc; usu. this WO] (usu. used when reprimanding s.o. for sth. done wrong, warning s.o. against doing sth. etc) to understand sth. well, remember it, and keep it in mind to guide one's further actions: заруби(те) себе на носу ≃ **see ⟨make sure⟩ that you don't forget it; remember once and for all (that…); (you'd better) get it into your head (that…); don't you dare ⟨ever⟩ forget it!; you'd better remember!; tie a string around your finger if you have to, but remember this ⟨that…⟩.**

«Мы вам доверяем, но постольку-поскольку… Ваше предательство не скоро забудется. Пусть это зарубят себе на носу все, кто переметнулся осенью к красным…» (Шолохов 5). "We trust you, but only so far… Your treachery will not soon be forgotten. And those who went over to the Reds last autumn had better get that into their heads!" (5a). ♦ «Запомните и зарубите себе на носу, − он повысил голос и стал грозить пальцем, − у нас в Советском Союзе ни за что никого не сажают» (Войнович 4). "Tie a string around your finger if you have to, but remember this." He raised his voice and threatened her with one finger. "Here, in the Soviet Union, we do not put people in jail for no reason at all" (4a).

H-236 • НА НОСУ́ *coll* [PrepP; Invar; subj-compl with быть∅ (subj: usu. abstr)] sth. will happen (ensue etc) in the immediate future, very soon: X на носу ≃ **X is just ⟨right⟩ around the corner; X is close ⟨near⟩ at hand; X is almost here; X is (almost) on top of us ⟨upon us⟩; X is coming (up); it's almost (time for) X.**

«Нам надо, чтобы кузница сейчас дымила. Посевная на носу…» (Абрамов 1). "We need the smithy smoking away right now. The crop-sowing campaign is just around the corner" (1a). ♦ «Праздник на носу, жена велела продуктов купить» (Войнович 5). "The holiday's almost here and my wife wants me to do some shopping for her" (5a). ♦ [Лопахин:] И вишнёвый сад и землю необходимо отдать в аренду под дачи, сделать это теперь же, поскорее, − аукцион на носу! (Чехов 2). [L.:] The cherry orchard and the rest of the land must be leased out for summer cottages. You must act at once, without delay, the auction's almost on top of us (2c). ♦ [Сильва:] Да-да, надо ехать. У нас ведь там эта… сессия на носу (Вампилов 4). [S.:] Yes-yes, we have to leave. We've got those uh…exams coming up (4b). ♦ Незадолго до ареста, услыхав, М. М[андельштам] ведёт вольные разговоры с какими-то посторонними людьми, я напомнила: «Май на носу − ты бы поосторожнее!» (Мандельштам 1). Not long before his arrest, hearing M[andelstam] talk rather carelessly with some people we did not know, I said to him: "You'd better watch out − it's almost May!" (1a).

H-237 • НЕ ПО́ НОСУ *кому highly coll* [PrepP; Invar; subj-compl with быть₀ (subj: usu. abstr)] sth. is beyond s.o.'s ability (to do, get, handle, attain etc): X Y-у не по носу ≃ **X is too much for Y; X is out of Y's reach ⟨league⟩; Y doesn't have what it takes (to do ⟨attain etc⟩ X); [in financial contexts] X is beyond Y's means.**

H-238 • ЩЁЛКАТЬ/ЩЁЛКНУТЬ ⟨ДАВА́ТЬ/ДАТЬ, СТУ́КАТЬ/СТУ́КНУТЬ⟩ ПО́ НОСУ *кого coll;* УДАРЯ́ТЬ/УДА́РИТЬ ПО́ НОСУ *obs* [VP; subj: human or жизнь; usu. pfv] to reprimand or punish s.o. in such a way as to embarrass him, humble him, remind him of his inferior position, and/or ensure that he does not act similarly again: X щёлкнул Y-а по носу ≃ **X snapped his fingers in Y's face; X cut Y down to size; X rapped Y on the knuckles; [in limited contexts] X pulled ⟨knocked⟩ Y off Y's high horse.**

[Шпигельский:] Как я ни ломаюсь перед господами… по носу меня ещё никто не щёлкнул (Тургенев 1). [Sh.:] No matter how funny I appear in the presence of other people…no one ever dares to snap his fingers in my face (1e). ♦ «Господа! – сказал он, – …Печорина надо проучить! Эти петербургские слётки всегда зазнаются, пока их не ударишь по носу!» (Лермонтов 1). "Gentlemen!" he said. "…Pechorin must be taught a lesson. These Petersburg whipper-snappers get uppish until they're rapped on the knuckles" (1b).

H-239 • КАК ⟨СЛО́ВНО⟩ ПО НО́ТАМ разыгрывать(ся), идти *coll* [как etc + PrepP; these forms only; adv; fixed WO] (to do sth., bring sth. about, sth. proceeds) without difficulty, easily, as if by a previously conceived plan: всё было разыграно ~ ≃ **everything ⟨things⟩ went swimmingly ⟨superbly, smoothly, like clockwork⟩; everything went ⟨was carried off⟩ without a hitch.**

Задача перед Владом стояла нехитрая: отвлечь внимание старухи на себя, пока напарник будет шарить под её прилавком… Всё разыгрывалось, словно по нотам (Максимов 2). The job that Vlad had to do was not difficult: to distract the old woman's attention while his partner rifled her supplies under the counter….The operation went like clockwork (2a). ♦ У меня отлегло от души: всё понятно, конечно, Сергей страдает, но как ему приятно его страдание, как это всё отлично идёт, словно по нотам (Аксёнов 1). My heart lifted. I saw it all: sure Sergei was suffering, but how he was enjoying his suffering, how smoothly things were going, without a hitch (1a).

H-240 • ЧИТА́ТЬ/ПРОЧИТА́ТЬ НОТА́ЦИЮ ⟨МОРА́ЛЬ, ПРО́ПОВЕДЬ, НАСТАВЛЕ́НИЕ и т. п.⟩ *кому* [VP; subj: human] to reprove, admonish s.o., tell s.o. how to behave (usu. in a long-winded fashion): X прочитал Y-у нотацию ≃ **X lectured ⟨preached to⟩ Y; X preached ⟨gave⟩ Y a sermon; X gave Y a good talking-to; [in limited contexts] X moralized.**

…В отличие от Мальковой Дьяков не стал читать ему нотацию по поводу брата… (Рыбаков 1). Unlike Malkova, Dyakov did not lecture him about his brother… (1a). ♦ «Тебе понравились однажды мои слёзы, теперь, может быть, ты захотел бы видеть меня у ног своих и так, мало-помалу, сделать своей рабой, капризничать, читать мораль…» (Гончаров 1). "You enjoyed seeing my tears once before, and now, perhaps, you would like to see me at your feet, so that little by little you could make me your slave, act capricious, moralize…" (1b).

H-241 • (И) НЕ НОЧЕВА́Л *где, в чём coll* [VP; subj: abstr; past only] sth. is completely absent (in some place, literary work, piece of art work etc): X и не ночевал (в Y-е) ≃ **there isn't the slightest ⟨the least⟩ bit of X (in Y); there isn't the slightest trace ⟨hint⟩ of X (in Y); Y is totally lacking in X.**

И эту мазню вы называете живописью? Искусство тут и не ночевало. You call these smudges art? There's not the slightest trace of art in them.

H-242 • ДО́БРОЙ ⟨СПОКО́ЙНОЙ, ПОКО́ЙНОЙ *obs*⟩ НО́ЧИ [formula phrase; these forms only; also used as obj of желать/пожелать; fixed WO] used as a parting wish before one or s.o. goes to bed: **good night.**

Легко и порывисто бросилась она к нему, замерла подле кресла, осторожно дотронулась до пиджака, прошептала: «Покойной ночи» (Федин 1). Lightly and impetuously she dashed over to him, stood stock still beside the armchair, carefully touched his jacket and whispered: "Good night" (1a).

H-243 • НЕ К НО́ЧИ БУДЬ СКА́ЗАНО *coll;* НЕ К НО́ЧИ СКАЗА́ТЬ *obs, coll;* НЕ К НО́ЧИ БУДЬ ПОМЯ́НУТ *obs, coll* [parenth clause; these forms only; fixed WO] (of s.o. or sth. frightful, dangerous etc) it is better not to mention s.o. or sth.: **it would be better left unmentioned; I shouldn't even bring it up.**

H-244 • ВАРФОЛОМЕ́ЕВСКАЯ НОЧЬ *lit* [NP; sing only; fixed WO] the slaughter, annihilation of masses of (usually defenseless) people: **bloodbath; wholesale massacre ⟨slaughter⟩.**

< The phrase derives from, and originally referred to, a real historical event, the massacre of French Huguenots by Roman Catholic mobs on the night of Aug. 24, 1572, the eve of St. Bartholomew's Day.

H-245 • НА́ НОЧЬ *coll* [PrepP; Invar; adv] before a person goes to sleep, before bedtime: **before going to bed ⟨to sleep⟩; before turning in (for the night).**

Персиков около полуночи приехал на Пречистенку и лёг спать, почитав ещё на ночь какую-то английскую статью в журнале «Зоологический вестник», полученном из Лондона (Булгаков 10). Around midnight Persikov came home to Prechistenka and went to bed. Before going to sleep he read in bed an English article in the magazine *News of Zoology,* which he received from London (10b).

H-246 • НА́ НОЧЬ ГЛЯ́ДЯ идти, ехать, собраться и т. п. *coll* [Verbal Adv; Invar; adv; fixed WO] at a time of night considered by the speaker to be inappropriately late: **at this time of night; so late at night; at this (ungodly) hour; at such an ungodly hour; [in limited contexts] so near bedtime.**

…Вдруг звонок в дверь. Иду открывать, мысленно по дороге чертыхаясь: кого ещё там нелёгкая на ночь глядя принесла? (Войнович 1). …All of a sudden the doorbell rang. I went to the door, cursing on the way: Who the hell could it be at this time of night? (1a). ♦ [Сарафанов:] Что это вы, сосед, куда собрались на ночь глядя? (Вампилов 4). [S.:] What's the matter, neighbor, where are you going at this hour? (4b). ♦ «Ты куда это на ночь глядя волочишь гитару?» (Искандер 3). "Where are you off to with your guitar so near bedtime?" (3a).

H-247 • СВОЯ́ НО́ША НЕ ТЯ́НЕТ [saying] things that a person does or chooses to do for himself, his family etc do not seem burdensome, tiresome etc: ≃ **a burden of your own ⟨of your own choice, that you choose⟩ is not felt; your own burden doesn't hurt you; burdens you choose don't weigh you down.**

[Анна Петровна:] Ох, захлопоталась я нынче совсем, моченьки моей нет. Отдохнуть присесть. [Добротворский:] Что ж, свои ведь, сударыня, хлопоты. Своя ноша не тянет, говорится пословица (Островский 1). [A.P.:] I'm utterly worn out to-day, I haven't any more strength. Let's sit down and rest. [D.:] What of it, they're your own worries, madam. "Your own burden doesn't hurt you," says the proverb (1b). ♦ Чем дальше, тем чаще старуха отдыхала, прикладываясь мешком к близлежащим заборам. Однако ж, говорят, своя ноша не тянет (Войнович 2). The farther she went, the more often the old woman stopped to rest, leaning the sack against the nearest fence. However, as the saying goes, burdens you choose don't weigh you down (2a).

Н-248 • ПО НРА́ВУ *кому coll* [PrepP; Invar; subj-compl with быть∅, прийтись (subj: usu. abstr or human); more often neg] a person (phenomenon etc) is pleasing, appealing to s.o.: X Y-у по нраву ≃ X suits Y; X is to Y's liking; X is Y's cup of tea; Y took a fancy ⟨a shine⟩ to X; ‖ *Neg* X Y-у не по нраву ≃ X rubs Y the wrong way; Y has no taste for thing X; thing X goes against Y's grain; Y doesn't care for X.

...Физически *не может* советская власть выпустить на свободу хоть листик один, который им не по нраву (Солженицын 2). ...It is impossible, physically impossible, for the Soviet regime to release so much as a single sheet of paper that is not to its liking (2a). ♦ [У Риты] началось новое увлечение: прогулки пешие, на велосипеде, на лыжах – с Гартвигом... Гартвиг в шортах... скакал по кочкам... Рита, задыхаясь, поспешала за ним, а мне такая гонка была не по нраву (Трифонов 5). ...Now she [Rita] had a new diversion: excursions by foot, by bicycle, and on skis with Gartvig....There was Gartvig...leaping...from one knoll to another. And gasping for breath, Rita would go hurrying after him. As for me, I had no taste for such dashing around (5a).

Н-249 • (А) НУ́-КА *coll* [Interj; fixed WO] used (usu. with a command) to induce s.o. to action: **come on; all right now.**

А ну-ка успокойтесь! Come on, quiet down! ♦ Тётушка... достаёт таз, ставит его у наших ног и приказывает: «А ну-ка, ноги мыть!» (Искандер 4). Auntie...fetches a basin, sets it at our feet and orders, "All right now, wash your feet!" (4a).

Н-250 • НУ ДА́! *coll* [Interj; Invar; fixed WO] **1.** used to express agreement, affirmation, understanding etc in response to a question or statement: **yes, indeed; of course;** [in limited contexts] **why, so it is;** [usu. as an acknowledgment of a reminder] **oh, that.**

[Анна Андреевна:] ...Кто ж бы это такой был? [Марья Антоновна:] Это Добчинский, маменька. [Анна Андреевна:] Какой Добчинский?.. Совсем не Добчинский... [Марья Антоновна:] Право, маменька, Добчинский. [Анна Андреевна:] Ну вот: нарочно, чтобы только поспорить. Говорят тебе – не Добчинский. [Марья Антоновна:] ...Видите, что Добчинский. [Анна Андреевна:] Ну да, Добчинский, теперь я вижу (Гоголь 4). [А.А.:] Whoever could it be? [M.A.:] It's Mr Dobbin, Mummy. [A.A.:] Mr Dobbin indeed?...Certainly not Mr Dobbin.... [M.A.:] It's Mr Dobbin, Mummy, it really is. [A.A.:] There now, you said that deliberately, simply for the sake of argument. I tell you it is not Mr Dobbin. [M.A.:] ...You can see it is Mr Dobbin. [A.A.:] Why, so it is, it's Mr Dobbin. I can see now... (4b). ♦ «Кстати, – напомнил Ефим, – ты „Лавину" прочёл?» – «„Лавину"? – переспросил Баранов. – Что ещё за „Лавина"?» – «Мой роман. Который я тебе подарил на прошлой неделе». – «А, ну да», – сказал Баранов (Войнович 6). "And by the way," Yefim asked, "did you read *Avalanche*!?" "*Avalanche*. What's *Avalanche*?" "My novel. The one I gave you last week." "Oh, that," Kostya said (6a).

2. *iron* used to express disbelief, incredulity, objection etc: **oh (yeah), sure!; oh, right; of course; ..., my foot!**

[Фролов:] Получил назначение... В район. На селекционную станцию. [Колесов:] Подожди, на селекционную?.. У Маши, кажется, там родители? [Фролов:] Совпадение. [Букин:] Ну да, совпадение! Скрадывает мою жену. Очевидно (Вампилов 3). [F.:] I've been told where I'm going to work....Out of town. At the plant-breeding station. [K.:] Hang on, did you say the plant-breeding station? Isn't that where Masha's parents live? [F.:] Coincidence. [B.:] Oh yeah, sure – coincidence. He's stealing my wife. It's obvious (3a). ♦ [Васенька:] Встретимся завтра! Один раз!

На полчаса! На прощанье!.. [Макарская:] Ну да! От тебя потом не отвяжешься (Вампилов 4). [V.:] We'll meet tomorrow! Just once! For half an hour! For the last time!... [M.:] Oh, sure. And there'll be no getting rid of you afterwards (4a).

Н-251 • НУ И...!; НУ́ УЖ...! *both coll* [Interj; usu. foll. by a noun; fixed WO] used to express surprise, delight, displeasure, an ironic attitude etc: **what a [NP]; (that ⟨this⟩ is) some [NP]; that is ⟨you are etc⟩ (really) quite a [NP]; (now) that's ⟨here's, there's⟩ a [NP] (for you); (now) that's what I call (a real) [NP];** [in limited contexts] **(ugh ⟨wow⟩,) is it ⟨he etc⟩** [AdjP].

«Ну и местечко, – шёпотом, выдававшим душевный озноб, обронил он. – Могила» (Тендряков 1). "What a place," he said in a whisper, giving vent to the eerie feeling it gave him. "It's like a tomb" (1a). ♦ Ноги у Лёньки гудели. Он сидел неподвижно, не в силах пошевелиться. «Ну и работа у вас! – сказал он Садчикову. – ...Целый день на ногах – ужас!..» (Семёнов 1). Lyonka's legs throbbed painfully. He sat motionless, incapable of stirring. "Some job you've got!" he said to Sadchikov...."All day on your feet – it's terrible" (1a). ♦ «Ну и дед у тебя! – искренне подивился солдат. – Интересный дед. Только забивает он тебе голову всякой чепухой» (Айтматов 1). "That's some grandfather you have," said the soldier with genuine wonder. "A very interesting grandfather. Only he stuffs your head with all kinds of rubbish" (1b). ♦ «Ну и семейка, – говорю я. – Отец ортодоксальный марксист, один из ведущих теоретиков коммунизма. А дети почти диссиденты» (Зиновьев 2). "We really are quite a family," I say. "A father who's an orthodox Marxist, one of the leading communist theoreticians. And children who are almost dissidents" (2a). ♦ «Ну и сырость, надо было глотнуть перед уходом. Как только вернусь, сейчас же и глотну...» (Стругацкие 1). "Ugh, is it damp, should have taken a swig of something before I left. As soon as I get back, I'll have something" (1a).

Н-252 • НУ И НУ́!; АЙ ДА НУ́! *both coll* [Interj; these forms only; fixed WO] used to express surprise, delight, disapproval, reproach etc: **how do you like that!; well, I'll be (damned ⟨a monkey's uncle etc⟩)!; well now!; well, well (, well); well, what do you know!; well, I never!**

«Так вот ты... запер его [полицмейстера], беднягу, в сортирной кабинке, припёр дверцу метлой и не выпускал...» – «Серьёзно? – сказал Виктор. – Ну и ну. То-то он сегодня на меня весь день волком смотрит» (Стругацкие 1). "What happened...is that you backed him [the police chief] into the toilet. Then you barricaded the door with a broom and refused to let him out...." "No kidding," said Victor. "How do you like that? No wonder he's been giving me dirty looks all day" (1a). ♦ Уже вернувшись из-за границы, Фёдор Лиховидов укоренился в Пензе, при тамошнем генерал-губернаторе. В Каргине знакомые видели его фотографию и после долго покачивали головами, растерянно чмокали языками: «Ну и ну!..»... «С какими людьми дело водит, а?» (Шолохов 3). On his return from abroad Fyodor Likhovidov settled in Penza, at the residence of the Governor General. His acquaintances in Karginskaya once saw a photograph that caused much shaking of heads and astonished clicking of tongues. "Well, I'll be...!"..."The people he has to do with, eh?" (3a). ♦ Илья остановился, покачал головой. Ну и ну! Нашёл, о чём думать. Самое подходящее времечко выбрал, чтобы молодость вспомнить (Абрамов 1). Ilya stopped and shook his head. Well now! What a thing to be thinking about! Talk about choosing the very best time to hark back to the days of your youth! (1a). ♦ Прислушиваясь к разговорам Гронского, он только ухмылялся и крутил от восхищения головой: «Ну и ну!» (Паустовский 1). When he listened to Gronsky's conversation, he just grinned and shook his head in admiration, saying: "Well, well!" (1b). ♦ Вот он вернётся и не узнает её, встретив в НИИ-9, и скажет на «вы»: «Ирина Викторовна! Вы ли это? Что это вы разрисовали себя? Ну и ну!» (Залыгин 1). Soon he'd be back, he'd meet her in the institute, fail to recognize her immediately, and address her formally: "Irina

Viktorovna! It can't be you! What have you done with yourself? Well I never!" (1a).

H-253 • БОЛЬША́Я НУЖДА́ *highly coll* [NP; sing only; fixed WO] the act of moving one's bowels: (go ⟨do⟩) **number two; (do ⟨go do⟩) one's business.**

«С тех пор как ты поселился, мы никто ни разу не видели, чтобы ты в туалет пошёл. Ну, ладно, по большой нужде ещё ладно! Но ведь ни разу даже по малой... даже по малой!» (Ерофеев 1). "From the time you moved in we've not seen you go to the toilet once. OK, we're not speaking about number two. But not even number one, not even number one!" (1a).

H-254 • МА́ЛАЯ НУЖДА́ *highly coll* [NP; sing only; fixed WO] the act of urinating: (go ⟨do⟩) **number one; take a leak; make water.**

«С тех пор как ты поселился, мы никто ни разу не видели, чтобы ты в туалет пошёл. Ну, ладно, по большой нужде ещё ладно! Но ведь ни разу даже по малой... даже по малой!» (Ерофеев 1). "From the time you moved in we've not seen you go to the toilet once. OK, we're not speaking about number two. But not even number one, not even number one!" (1a). ♦ «Не знали, как быть. Дело, сам понимаешь, ответственное, а указания нет...» – ...«А ты, если по малой нужде идёшь, ширинку сам расстёгиваешь или тоже указания дожидаешь?» (Войнович 2). "We didn't know what to do. You know yourself this is a national matter, and there've been no instructions..."..."And when you go take a leak, do you unbutton your fly yourself or do you wait for instructions?" (2a).

H-255 • ЧТО ЗА НУЖДА́ (, что...) *obs* [Invar; often main clause in a complex sent; fixed WO] sth. is irrelevant: **what does it matter?; what of it?; it doesn't matter.**

Перечитывая эту страницу, я замечаю, что далеко отвлёкся от своего предмета... Но что за нужда?.. Ведь этот журнал пишу я для себя... (Лермонтов 1). On re-reading this page, I notice that I have strayed far from my subject....But what does it matter?...I write this journal for myself... (1a). Reading over this page I notice that I have digressed far from my subject. But what of it? For I am writing this journal for myself... (1b).

H-256 • НУЖДЫ́ МА́ЛО *кому (до чего) obs* [Invar; impers predic with быть$_\emptyset$; usu. pres] s.o. is indifferent to, not interested in or concerned about sth.: Х-у (до Y-а) нужды мало ≃ **X doesn't care (about Y); Y is of little ⟨no⟩ interest ⟨concern⟩ to X; what does X care (about Y)?**

H-257 • НУЖДЫ́ НЕТ *(кому) obs* [VP; impers; pres or past; usu. foll. by a что-clause; usu. this WO] it is unimportant to s.o. (that...): (Х-у) нужды нет (, что...) ≃ **it doesn't matter (to X); it's no matter (that...); it's nothing to X; it's of no concern to X (that...); X doesn't care (at all) (about...); it's all the same to X; never mind (about sth.).**

Обломову нужды... не было, являлась ли Ольга Корделией и осталась ли бы верна этому образу или пошла бы новой тропой и преобразилась в другое видение, лишь бы она являлась в тех же красках и лучах, в каких она жила в его сердце... (Гончаров 1). It did not matter to Oblomov whether Olga appeared as Cordelia and remained true to that image, or, following a new path, was transformed in another vision, so long as she appeared in the same colors in which she was enshrined in his heart... (1b). ♦ «Нужды нет, что он [бригадир] парадов не делает да с полками на нас не ходит», – говорили они... (Салтыков-Щедрин 1) "Tis no matter that he [the brigadier] don't have parades and march on us with regiments," they said... (1a). ♦ [Анна Андреевна:] ...Я просто видела в нём образованного светского, высшего тона человека, а о чинах его мне и нужды нет (Гоголь 4). [A.A.:] I saw in him simply an educated man of the world, a man of the highest society, and I don't care at all about his rank (4c).

H-258 • НУ́ЖЕН ТЫ ⟨он и т. п.⟩ МНЕ ⟨ему и т. п.⟩! *highly coll, iron* [Interj; fixed WO] used to express s.o.'s intense frustration with, disdainful attitude toward etc a person he wants nothing to do with: нужен X Y-у! ≃ **who needs X!; X is not worth it ⟨Y's time, the trouble⟩!**

Гриша рассвирепел. «Ты чо [*dial or phonetic spelling* = что], психованная, чо ли? И отец твой психованный, и ты... Нужна ты мне!» (Евтушенко 2). Grisha was furious. "Are you crazy? Your father is crazy, and so are you....Who needs you?" (2a). ♦ «Ты вот пооскорбляй меня...» – «Да кто тебя оскорбляет? Нужна ты мне!» (Распутин 1). [context transl] "All you're looking for's a chance to insult me." "Who's insulting you? As if I'd take the trouble" (1a).

H-259 • О́ЧЕНЬ ⟨КУДА́ КАК⟩ НУ́ЖНО (!) *coll, iron* [Interj or impers predic; these forms only; fixed WO] (used to express a scornful attitude toward sth., a contemptuous refusal of some suggestion, advice etc) it is completely unnecessary (to do sth.): **who needs that!; why bother!; what for!; why should I ⟨he etc⟩!; what need is there...?; I ⟨you etc⟩ don't want...; that's just what I need!; a lot of good that does!**

«Только вот чему я удивляюсь: как вы, с вашим умом, не видите, что делается вокруг вас?» – «А что же такое делается?» – подхватил я и весь насторожился. Доктор посмотрел на меня с каким-то насмешливым сожалением. «Хорош же и я, – промолвил он, словно про себя, – очень нужно это ему говорить» (Тургенев 3). "What I'm really surprised at, though, is how, with your intelligence, you can't see what is going on round you." "Why, what *is* going on?" I said, all ears. The doctor looked at me with a sort of mocking pity. "I'm a fine one too," he said, as though to himself. "Why should I be telling him this?" (3a). ♦ «Куда как нужно тратить лишние деньги и нанимать мусье, как будто и своих людей не стало!» (Пушкин 2). "What need is there to throw away money hiring this *mounseer*, as if there weren't enough of our own folk?" (2a). ♦ [Анна Петровна:] Зачем пришёл? [Осип:] Поздравить. [Анна Петровна:] Очень нужно! Проваливай! (Чехов 1). [А.Р.:] What did you come for? [O.:] I came to congratulate you, ma'am. [A.P.:] I don't want your congratulations. Clear out! (1a). ♦ [Полина Андреевна:] Жалко мне тебя, Машенька. [Маша:] Очень нужно! [Полина Андреевна:] Сердце моё за тебя переболело (Чехов 6). [P.A.:] I'm sorry for you, Mashenka. [M.:] A lot of good that does! [P.A.:] My heart aches for you (6a).

H-260 • СВОДИ́ТЬ/СВЕСТИ́ К НУЛЮ́ *что* [VP; subj: abstr or human] to reduce sth. to the point of having no importance, role, meaning etc at all: Х сводит Y к нулю ≃ **X reduces Y to nothing; thing X nullifies ⟨negates⟩ Y.**

H-261 • СВОДИ́ТЬСЯ/СВЕСТИ́СЬ К НУЛЮ́ [VP; subj: abstr] to be diminished to the point of having no importance, role, meaning etc at all: Х свёлся к нулю ≃ **X was reduced to nothing;** [in limited contexts] **X was (completely) lost.**

«В будущих войнах роль кавалерии сведётся к нулю» (Шолохов 2). "The role of the cavalry will be reduced to nothing in future wars" (2a). ♦ «...Мы должны жить так, точно всерьёз верим в свою свободу. Иначе сведётся к нулю вся прелесть этих расконвоированных дней и месяцев» (Гинзбург 2). "...We have to live as if we really believed in our freedom. Otherwise all the charm of those provisionally free days and months would be lost" (2a).

H-262 • НАЧИНА́ТЬ/НАЧА́ТЬ С НУЛЯ́ [VP; subj: human or collect] to begin doing sth. from the most rudimentary point, not using or relying on anything done or prepared earlier (occas. after a previous failed attempt): Х начал с нуля ≃ **X started from scratch; X started (all over again) from nothing ⟨from the beginning⟩.**

«Наша литература — это сконцентрированный душевный опыт народа, и пренебречь им – значит начинать с нуля...»

(Гладков 1). "Our literature is the concentrated spiritual experience of the nation, and to ignore it means to start all over again from nothing…" (1a).

Н-263 • **ПО НУТРУ́** *кому highly coll* [PrepP; Invar; subj-compl with copula (subj: usu. abstr or human); more often neg] to please s.o., appeal to s.o.: X Y-у ~ ≃ **X is to Y's liking; X is Y's cup of tea; X turns Y on; X goes over big with Y;** ‖ *Neg* X Y-у не по нутру ≃ **X rubs Y the wrong way; X doesn't sit too well with Y; X leaves Y cold ⟨flat⟩; thing X isn't Y's thing; [in limited contexts] thing X goes against Y's grain.**

…Говоря сравнительно, жить было всё-таки легко, и эта лёгкость в особенности приходилась по нутру так называемым смердам (Салтыков-Щедрин 1). …Comparatively speaking, life was still easy, and this ease was particularly to the liking of the so-called peasants (1a). ♦ *Словом, кому-то Сидоров пришёлся не по нутру… состряпали дело, написали фельетон, ошельмовали порядочных людей, десять человек, в том числе и моего отца (Рыбаков 1). In short, Sidorov had rubbed someone…the wrong way…the case was cooked up, and the article written to defame decent people, ten in all, including my father (1a).

Н-264 • **НЫ́НЕ И ПРИ́СНО; И НЫ́НЕ, И ПРИ́СНО (, И ВО ВЕ́КИ ВЕКО́В)** *both obs, lit* [AdvP; these forms only; adv; fixed WO] always: **now and forevermore ⟨forever⟩; now, in days to come, and to the end of time.**

Легко, что Твардовскому эта вещь не понравилась. Да если б дело кончалось тем, что «Новый мир» отклонял пьесу и предоставлял мне свободу с нею. Не тут-то было! Не так понимал Твардовский моё обещание и наше с ним сотрудничество ныне, и присно, и во веки веков (Солженицын 2). I can easily believe that Tvardovsky genuinely did not like the piece. There the matter should have ended—with *Novy Mir* rejecting the play and leaving me free to do what I liked with it. Nothing of the kind! That was not how Tvardovsky understood my promise and saw our collaboration now, in days to come, and to the end of time (2a).

< From the Russian Orthodox liturgical service.

Н-265 • **РАСПУСКА́ТЬ/РАСПУСТИ́ТЬ НЮ́НИ** *highly coll, disapprov* [VP; subj: human] **1.** to be or begin crying: X распустил нюни ≃ **X started ⟨was, burst out⟩ crying; X burst into tears; X turned on the tears ⟨the waterworks⟩.**

Хватит плакать! Крохотная царапина, а ты нюни распустил. Enough of your crying! A tiny little scratch and you turn on the waterworks.

2. to complain about sth. in an annoying manner, displaying a lack of resolve to right the situation about which one is complaining etc: X распускает нюни ≃ **X starts ⟨is⟩ whining ⟨sniveling, whimpering, bellyaching⟩.**

[Кабанов:] …Что я за несчастный такой человек на свет рождён, что не могу вам угодить ничем. [Кабанова:] Что ты сиротой-то прикидываешься! Что ты нюни-то распустил? (Островский 6). [K.:] Only what I'd like to know is what did I do to deserve it? Why can't I do anything to please you? [K-a:] Don't pretend to be such a poor helpless creature! What are you sniveling about? (6c). ♦ Вечером пришла Маша Смолина — весёлая, бодрая. «Ну вот, дорогая моя. Хватит распускать нюни. Я тебя устроила на работу» (Грекова 3). In the evening Masha Smolina came back,

cheerful, energetic. "Well now, my dear, stop whimpering. I've found you a job" (3a).

Н-266 • **(И) НЕ НЮ́ХАЛ** *чего coll* [VP; subj: human; past only] one is entirely unfamiliar with sth., has no knowledge of sth., has never experienced sth. etc (sometimes used as a condescending or scornful appraisal of a person with little or no experience in some area): X Y-а и не нюхал ≃ **X knows nothing about Y; X is ignorant of Y; [in limited contexts] X hasn't tasted Y.**

Сегодняшние националисты… и не нюхали Хомякова и славянофилов, которые отлично знали, что движущая сила — общество, а не государство, которому следует только осторожно поддерживать порядок и не душить общество (Мандельштам 2). …Our latter-day nationalists…are ignorant of Khomiakov and the other Slavophiles who all knew very well that society is the prime motive force, and that in keeping order the state should be careful not to stifle it (2a). ♦ …[Соня] носилась разгорячённая, суматошная, предовольная и готова была, кажется, приковать себя к этой квартире. А ведь тоже деревенская баба, с князьями да дворянами не возжалась [*nonstand* = не водилась], красивой жизни не нюхала, но… распушилась, откуда что и взялось? (Распутин 4). …[Sonya] raced around excited, animated, bustling, ever so happy and apparently ready to live forever in that apartment. And yet she was a country woman too, she didn't hang around with the princes and nobles, she hadn't tasted the good life, but…she took to it right away. Where did that come from? (4a).

Н-267 • **НЮ́ХОМ ЧУ́ЯТЬ ⟨ЧУ́ВСТВОВАТЬ⟩** *что;* **ЧУ́ЯТЬ НО́СОМ** *all coll* [VP; subj: human; fixed WO (var. with нюхом)] to be aware of, know, foresee sth. by intuition: X нюхом чует Y ≃ **X senses Y; X realizes ⟨knows⟩ instinctively (that…); X can tell (that…); X can tell by some sixth sense (that…); X feels it in his bones; X feels ⟨has a feeling⟩ in his bones (that…); [in refer. to trouble, danger, a scandal etc] X sniffs Y (ahead);** ‖ [1st pers sing only] нюхом чую ≃ **something tells me.**

Забулдыги, взяточники и развратники нюхом чуяли в ней [начальнице лагеря] что-то чужое и отскакивали от неё, как, говорят, отскакивает волк от хищников другой породы (Гинзбург 2). Debauchees, bribe takers, and rakes sensed something alien about her [the camp commandant] and recoiled from her, just as a wolf, so they say, will recoil from other predators (2a).

Н-268 • **У СЕМИ́ НЯ́НЕК ДИТЯ́ БЕЗ ГЛА́ЗУ** [saying] a matter suffers when several people are in charge of it (because each wants to handle it his own way, each expects s.o. else to handle it, or there is a general lack of coordination among those in charge): ≃ **too many cooks spoil the broth ⟨the soup⟩; everybody's business is nobody's business.**

Вскоре после манифеста семнадцатого октября задумана была большая демонстрация от Тверской заставы к Калужской. Это было начинание в духе пословицы «у семи нянек дитя без глазу» (Пастернак 1). Soon after the manifesto of October 17th several revolutionary organizations called for a big demonstration. The route was from Tver Gate to the Kaluga Gate at the other end of the town. But this was a case of too many cooks spoiling the broth (1a).

О

О-1 • **ПО́РТИТЬ/ИСПО́РТИТЬ (всю) ОБЕ́ДНЮ ⟨МУ́-ЗЫКУ⟩** *кому coll* [VP; subj: human or, less often, abstr] to hinder, harm s.o. in some matter, upset s.o.'s plans: X испортил Y-у всю обедню ≃ **X ruined things ⟨the whole thing⟩ for Y; X upset Y's ⟨the⟩ applecart; X spiked Y's guns; X cooked Y's goose; X screwed ⟨messed⟩ things up for Y.**

[Косых:] Вчера объявил маленький шлем на трефах, а взял большой. Только опять этот Барабанов мне всю музыку испортил!.. Покажи он, мерзавец, туза, я объявил бы большой шлем... (Чехов 4). [K.:] Yesterday I declared a little slam in clubs and got a grand slam. But once again friend Barabanov cooked my goose....If the swine had shown his ace I'd have declared a grand slam... (4b).

О-2 • **НЕ ОБЕРЁШЬСЯ** хлопот *(с кем-чем)*, **греха, стыда, сраму** и т. п. *coll* [VP; neg pfv fut, gener. 2nd pers sing only] there will be a great deal (of trouble with some person or matter), s.o. will feel a great degree (of shame with regard to some matter etc): хлопот (с X-ом) не оберёшься ≃ **there will be ⟨you'll have⟩ no end of trouble (with X); there will be ⟨you'll get involved in⟩ endless trouble (with X);** [in limited contexts] **person X is going to be trouble;** ‖ сраму не оберёшься ≃ **you won't know where to hide for shame;** ‖ страхов не оберёшься ≃ **your fear will know no bounds.**

Председатель тревожно прислушался к новым интонациям в голосе посетителя. «А вдруг припадочный? – подумал он. – Хлопот с ним не оберёшься» (Ильф и Петров 2). The chairman listened with anxiety to the new intonations in the voice of his visitor. "And suppose he's an epileptic," he thought. "There'll be no end of trouble with him" (2b). ♦ Он уж был не рад, что вызвал Захара на этот разговор. Он всё забывал, что чуть тронешь этот деликатный предмет, так и не оберёшься хлопот (Гончаров 1). He was sorry he had started the conversation with Zakhar. He kept forgetting that as soon as he touched on that delicate subject he got involved in endless trouble (1a). ♦ «Выходит, не успели построить дом, а он уже треснул»... «Это не трещина, – мрачно сказал я. – Это осадочный шов». Парень смутился, покраснел, но сказал очень строго: «Проверим, покажете потом проект». Я понял, что хлопот с ним не оберёшься (Войнович 5). "You've just finished the building and it's already cracking."..."That's not a crack," I growled. "It's a sedimentary seam." The young man was embarrassed and blushed, but he said very sternly: "We'll check it, and then you can show us your blueprint." I realized he was going to be trouble (5a). ♦ Неловкости, угрызений совести, стыда перед тётушкой и упрёков самой себе было тут, конечно, у Ирины Викторовны без конца и без края. Страхов – не оберёшься! (Залыгин 1). Naturally Irina Viktorovna did not do this without immense embarrassment, remorse, shame, and self-reproach. Her fear knew no bounds (1a).

О-3 • **В ОБИ́ДЕ** *на кого* [PrepP; Invar; subj-compl with быть₀ (subj: human); often neg] to feel annoyed, displeased with s.o., feel o.s. aggrieved: X на Y-а в обиде ≃ **X is offended (by Y's words ⟨by what Y did⟩ etc); X has taken offense ⟨umbrage⟩ at Y ⟨at Y's words etc⟩; X feels resentment toward Y; X resents Y's actions ⟨what Y did etc⟩; X is peeved at Y;** ‖ *Neg* X не будет на Y-а в обиде ≃ **X won't mind.**

...Молчал всесильный Парвус. Да он справедливо мог быть и в обиде. А не исключено: испытывал Ленина нервы, усилял свою позицию выжиданием (Солженицын 5). ...The all-powerful Parvus said nothing. Of course, he had every right to be offended. And it was quite possible that he was testing Lenin's nerves, and holding out to strengthen his own position (5a). ♦ Знаете, отец меня любил больше, чем меня любила мать. Не подумайте, что я на неё в обиде. Я очень любил маму, никакой обиды на неё не имел... (Рыбаков 1). He [Father] loved me more than mother did, you know. You mustn't think that I resented this. I loved mother very much and had no ill feelings at all towards her... (1a). ♦ «Ну, как обживаешься, солдат?» – обратился Подрезов к Илье. «Спасибо, товарищ секретарь. Не обижаюсь»... – «Значит, армия претензий к нам не имеет. Ну а у нас к армии претензия. Председатель на тебя в обиде» (Абрамов 1). "Well, getting used to being back home, soldier?" Podrezov asked Ilya. "Yes thanks, Comrade Secretary. I can't complain."..."So the army doesn't have any gripes with us. But we have a gripe with the army: the Chairwoman here is peeved at you" (1a). ♦ «...Ты – казак, вот и поедем со мной на поля... А Полюшка останется с бабкой домоседовать [*ungrammat* = домозедничать]. Она на нас в обиде не будет» (Шолохов 5). "You're a Cossack now, so come out into the fields with me....And Polyushka can stay at home with Granny. She won't mind" (5a).

О-4 • **НЕ В ОБИ́ДУ ⟨НЕ ВО ГНЕВ** *obs, lit*⟩ **БУДЬ СКА́ЗАНО** *(кому) coll* [these forms only; sent adv (parenth); fixed WO] offense should not be taken at what I said or am about to say: **no offense meant ⟨intended⟩; no harm meant; no insult intended; don't take it ⟨this⟩ the wrong way, but...; don't take this amiss, but...; no offense, but...**

«А вглядись-ка хорошенько: не узнаёшь ли меня?» – «Нет, не познаю. Не во гнев будь сказано, на веку столько довелось наглядеться рож всяких, что чёрт их и припомнит всех!» (Гоголь 5). "Well, have a good look: don't you know me?" "No, I don't know you. No offense meant: I've seen so many faces of all sorts in my day, how the hell can one remember them all?" (5a).

О-5 • **НЕ ДАВА́ТЬ/НЕ ДАТЬ В ОБИ́ДУ** *кого* [VP; subj: human or collect] not to allow s.o. to be injured, wronged in any way: X не даст Y-а в обиду ≃ **X will not let anyone harm ⟨hurt, insult etc⟩ Y; X will make sure ⟨see to it⟩ that no (possible) harm comes to Y; X will not see Y harmed ⟨insulted etc⟩; X will not let Y be ⟨allow Y to be⟩ hurt ⟨insulted etc⟩; X will not allow any harm to come to Y.**

«И давайте сразу договоримся: я вас в обиду не дам – только вы должны во всём меня слушаться» (Михайловская 1). "Let's have an understanding: I will not let anyone harm you, but you must do what I say" (1a). ♦ «...Детей они не дадут в обиду, непохоже это на них...» (Стругацкие 1). "...They won't let anyone hurt the children, it's not their style" (1a). ♦ «Я попрошу Алексея, чтобы тебя не дали в обиду» (Булгаков 3). "I shall ask Alexei to make sure that no possible harm comes to you" (3a). ♦ ...Стенка из тридцати одного западного писателя, выказав единство мировой литературы, объявила письмом в «Таймс», что в обиду меня не даст (Солженицын 2). ...Thirty-one Western writers had formed a solid wall, demonstrating the unity of world literature, and declared in a letter to the *New York Times* that they would not see me harmed (2a). ♦ «Если б я написала тебе всю правду, то ты, пожалуй бы, всё бросил и хоть пешком, а пришёл бы к нам, потому я и характер и чувства твои знаю, и ты бы не дал в обиду сестру свою» (Достоевский 3). "If I had written the whole truth, more than likely you would have thrown up everything and come to us, even if you had had to walk, for I know your character and sentiments, and you would not allow your sister to be insulted" (3a).

О-6 • **НЕ ДАВА́ТЬСЯ/НЕ ДА́ТЬСЯ ⟨НЕ ДАВА́ТЬ/НЕ ДАТЬ СЕБЯ́⟩ В ОБИ́ДУ** *(кому)* [VP; subj: human or collect] not to allow o.s. to be harmed, to know how to defend or protect o.s.: X себя в обиду не даёт ≃ **X stands ⟨knows how to**

stand⟩ up for himself; X can look after ⟨out for⟩ himself; X doesn't let anyone push him around.

[Арефьев *(входит)*:] Добрый вечер... Чего у вас — случилось что-нибудь? Поругались? Неужели уже поругались? [Бакченин:] Арефьев. Погуляй иди... [Арефьев:] Ну ладно... Приду, когда помиритесь. Ты мне только не обижай Олю... Не давайтесь ему, Оля, в обиду... Да вы крепкая, не дадитесь (Панова 1). [A. *(entering)*:] Good evening....What's wrong with you two? Something happen? Have an argument? Don't tell me you've already had an argument? [B.:] Arefyev, go take a walk.... [A.:] All right... I'll come back when you've made up. Only, don't you insult Olya on me....Stand up for yourself, Olya. Give it right back to him! You're a strong woman; don't give in (1a). ♦ Старуха не боялась за Люсю, верила, что она себя в обиду не даст — не такой она человек (Распутин 3). On Liusia's account she [the old lady] had nothing to fear. She knew Liusia could look after herself, she was that type (3a).

О-7 • БЕЗ ОБИНЯКО́В говорить, спрашивать и т. п. *coll;* **БЕЗ ⟨ВСЯ́КИХ⟩ ОКОЛИ́ЧНОСТЕЙ** *obs* [PrepP; these forms only; adv] (to speak or ask sth.) directly, openly, without allusiveness: **without beating around ⟨about⟩ the bush; in no uncertain terms; in so many words; not mincing (one's) words; pulling no punches;** [in limited contexts] **getting down to brass tacks; getting ⟨coming⟩ straight to the point.**

«Скажите, Карамазов, вы ужасно меня презираете? — отрезал вдруг Коля... — Сделайте одолжение, без обиняков» (Достоевский 1). "Tell me, Karamazov, do you despise me terribly?" Kolya suddenly blurted out...."Kindly tell me, without beating around the bush" (1a). ♦ Во дворе завхоз без обиняков предложил: «Может, погреемся, корреспондент? У меня есть. И омулёк найдётся» (Максимов 3). Out in the yard the bursar got down to brass tacks. "Well, Mr. Reporter, shall we warm ourselves up? I've got something. And there'll be a bit of salmon, too" (3a).

О-8 • ВИТА́ТЬ ⟨ПАРИ́ТЬ⟩ В ОБЛАКА́Х ⟨В ЭМПИ-РЕ́ЯХ *lit,* **МЕ́ЖДУ НЕ́БОМ И ЗЕМЛЁЙ⟩; УНО-СИ́ТЬСЯ В ОБЛАКА́ ⟨К ОБЛАКА́М⟩** [VP; subj: human] to be distanced, detached from reality (either by day-dreaming etc, or by viewing a situation unrealistically): X витает в облаках ≃ **X has ⟨is with⟩ his head in the clouds;** ‖ *Neg* X не витает в облаках ≃ **X has his feet (planted firmly) on the ground.**

«Витает он где-то там в своих эмпиреях, а его вдруг на землю спустят и спрашивают: а что вы, милейший, думаете относительно, скажем, левого уклонизма или правого оппортунизма?» (Войнович 4). "There he is with his head in the clouds, and suddenly they bring him back to earth and ask him: So, my good man, what are your thoughts regarding, say, leftist deviation or right-wing opportunism?" (4a). ♦ «Вот я вчера говорила с Кочкуровым, вы ведь знаете, он не витает в облаках» (Гроссман 2). "I was talking to Kochkurov yesterday. You know what he's like—he's certainly got his feet on the ground" (2a).

О-9 • СПУСТИ́ТЬСЯ С ОБЛАКО́В *coll* [VP; subj: human] **1.** Also: **СВАЛИ́ТЬСЯ ⟨УПА́СТЬ⟩ С ОБЛАКО́В** *coll* [often past after как, будто, словно, точно] to appear, arrive very suddenly: X как с облаков свалился ≃ **X appeared out of the blue ⟨out of nowhere, out of thin air⟩; it is as though X fell from the sky.**

2. [usu. infin with пора, нужно etc] to stop being out of touch with reality and start to live, think, look upon a situation etc realistically, practically: пора X-у спуститься с облаков ≃ **it's time for X to come down to earth ⟨to get his head out of the clouds⟩.**

О-10 • В О́БЛАСТИ чего [PrepP; Invar; Prep; the resulting PrepP is adv] in the (specified) sphere of (work, activity, human

interest etc): **in the area ⟨the field, the realm, the domain⟩ of; in;** [in limited contexts] **as far as...goes; where...is concerned.**

...В отличие от прочих областей общественности, в области кладбищенского дела старый режим прогнил, так сказать, не насквозь, а только частью... (Федин 1). ...Unlike other areas of public life, in the area of cemetery affairs the old regime was not rotten, so to speak, all through, but only partially... (1a). ♦ Власть есть совокупность воль масс, перенесённая выраженным или молчаливым согласием на избранных массами правителей. В области науки права... всё это очень ясно, но в приложении к истории это определение власти требует разъяснений (Толстой 7). Power is the collective will of the people transferred, by expressed or tacit consent, to their chosen rulers. In the domain of jurisprudence...it is all very clear; but when applied to history that definition of power needs explanation (7b). ♦ Рогозин сказал примерно следующее. Классики марксизма, а Ленин в особенности, были полными невеждами в области логики... С факультета Рогозина убрали, но не посадили... (Зиновьев 2). What Rogozin said amounted roughly to this. The classics of Marxism, and Lenin in particular, were complete ignoramuses where logic was concerned....Rogozin was expelled from the faculty, but left at liberty... (2a).

О-11 • ОТХОДИ́ТЬ/ОТОЙТИ́ ⟨УХОДИ́ТЬ/УЙТИ́⟩ В О́БЛАСТЬ ПРЕДА́НИЯ ⟨ПРЕДА́НИЙ, ВОСПО-МИНА́НИЙ⟩ *lit* [VP; subj: abstr; fixed WO] to cease to exist or be used, pass out of existence, disappear: X отошёл в область преданий ≃ **X is ⟨has become⟩ a thing of the past; X has passed into oblivion.**

О-12 • знать кого **КАК ОБЛУ́ПЛЕННОГО** *highly coll* [как + NP; obj-controlled; adv] (to know s.o.) very well: X знает Y-а как облупленного ≃ **X knows Y inside out ⟨through and through⟩.**

...Немца этого я знал как облупленного, равно как и он меня (Попов 1). I knew this German inside out, just like he knew me (1a).

О-13 • ОПТИ́ЧЕСКИЙ ОБМА́Н [NP; sing only; fixed WO] **1.** *special* a visually perceived image that represents the perceived object differently from the way it is in reality: **optical illusion.**

2. *lit* sth. that seems to be real but actually is not: **optical illusion; product of s.o.'s imagination.**

Мечте, загадочному, таинственному не было места в его душе. То, что не подвергалось анализу опыта, практической истины, было в глазах его оптический обман... (Гончаров 1). There was no room in his soul for a dream, for anything that was enigmatic and mysterious. He regarded everything that would not stand up to the analysis of reason and objective truth as an optical illusion... (1a).

О-14 • ПА́ДАТЬ/УПА́СТЬ В О́БМОРОК [VP; subj: human] to lose consciousness: X упал в обморок ≃ **X fainted (away); X fell in a (dead) faint; X fell into a swoon; X swooned; X passed out.**

Сам он, окончив речь свою, поспешно вышел и, повторяю, почти упал в другой комнате в обморок (Достоевский 2). He himself, having finished his speech, left hastily and, I repeat, nearly fainted in the next room (2a). ♦ [Наталья Петровна:] Берёзы не тают и не падают в обморок, как нервические дамы (Тургенев 1). [N.P.:] Birches do not melt and do not faint away like nervous ladies (1b). [N.P.:] Birch trees don't melt or fall into swoons like nervous ladies (1a).

О-15 • В ОБНИ́МКУ *coll* [PrepP; Invar; adv] **1.** ~ *(с кем)* **ходить, гулять** и т. п. (of persons, usu. two, walking, strolling etc) each having an arm around the shoulder or waist of the other (or those on either side of one): **with one's arm around s.o.; with one's arms (a)round each other ⟨one another⟩.**

[Женя:] Мама! Весь сыр-бор из-за того, что они шли в обнимку. Теперь все так ходят (Рощин 1). [Zh.:] Mother! All this fuss because they've been seen with their arms round each other. Everybody does that now (1b).

2. ~ **держать, брать** *что* (to hold, take hold of sth.) with both arms (around it): **(hold ⟨grab⟩ sth.) around the middle with one's arms; (have) both ⟨one's⟩ arms wrapped around sth.**

О-16 • БРАТЬ/ВЗЯТЬ В ОБОРО́Т ⟨В РАБО́ТУ⟩ *кого* *coll* [VP; subj: human; more often pfv] **1.** to put great pressure on s.o. in order to make him act as one desires: X взял Y-а в оборот ≃ **X turned ⟨put⟩ the heat on Y; X took Y in hand; X got after Y;** [in limited contexts] **X twisted Y's arm.**

Ту поэзию, которую заслуживают лишь немногие, обычно убивают или ещё хуже − поэта берут в оборот, запугивают и заставляют исправиться. Именно это сделали у нас с Заболоцким (Мандельштам 2). Poets "deserved" only by the few are generally killed off or − even worse − taken in hand and browbeaten into "mending their ways." This is what happened to Zabolotski (2a).

2. to reprimand, scold s.o. (for sth.): X взял Y-а в оборот ≃ **X took Y to task; X gave Y a (good) talking-to ⟨dressing-down⟩; X dressed Y down; X gave Y what for.**

О-17 • ПРИНИМА́ТЬ/ПРИНЯ́ТЬ *какой* **ОБОРО́Т** [VP; subj: abstr, often дело, события, всё это etc] (of a situation, events etc) to develop or change in a certain direction (as specified by the modifier): X принял дурной ⟨серьёзный, неожиданный и т. п.⟩ оборот ≃ **X took a bad ⟨serious, unexpected etc⟩ turn;** [with дурной, плохой etc only] **X took a turn for the worse.**

В его голосе чувствовалось и удивление, и беспокойство, что дело может принять неожиданный оборот... (Войнович 4). Surprise, and anxiety that things might take an unexpected turn, could be heard in his voice... (4a). ♦ «Будем надеяться, что дело вашего отца не примет дурного оборота...» (Рыбаков 1). "Let's hope your father's case doesn't take a turn for the worse" (1a).

О-18 • ПУСКА́ТЬ/ПУСТИ́ТЬ В ОБОРО́Т *что* [VP; subj: human; more often pfv] **1.** *special* ~ **деньги, капитал** to put (money) into commercial-industrial operations with the goal of receiving profits: X пустил деньги в оборот ≃ **X invested money.**

[3-й гость:] Процентные бумаги дают весьма немного дивиденда, а пускать деньги в оборот чрезвычайно опасно (Чехов 4). [Third Guest:] Interest-bearing securities yield exceedingly small returns, and to invest money is extraordinarily dangerous (4a).

2. *coll* to utilize sth.: X пустил Y в оборот ≃ **X made use of Y; X put Y to use; X used Y.**

«Когда же жить? − спрашивал он опять самого себя. − Когда же, наконец, пускать в оборот этот капитал знаний, из которых большая часть ещё ни на что не понадобится в жизни?» (Гончаров 1). "When am I to live?" he used to ask himself. "When shall I ever be permitted to make use of this store of knowledge, most of which will serve no purpose in my life?" (1b). ♦ [Хлестаков:] Разве из платья что-нибудь пустить в оборот? Штаны, что ли, продать? (Гоголь 4). [context transl] [Kh.:] Maybe I can raise some cash on my clothes? Sell my pants? (4f).

3. Also: **ВВОДИ́ТЬ/ВВЕСТИ́ В ОБОРО́Т; ПУСКА́ТЬ/ПУСТИ́ТЬ В ОБРАЩЕ́НИЕ** to bring sth. into general, widespread use: X ввёл Y в оборот ≃ **X started (using) Y; X put ⟨introduced⟩ Y into (widespread) circulation; X put Y into use.**

...Всё, что мог, он [Горький] уже совершил. Образец для подражания следующим поколениям соцреалистов − роман «Мать» − уже написал. Ленина и Сталина прославил. И свою знаменитую фразу «Если враг не сдаётся − его уничто-жают» уже пустил в обращение (Войнович 1). [context transl] He [Gorky] had already accomplished all he was capable of. He had already written *Mother*, the novel that would serve as the model for coming generations of socialist realists. He had sung the praises of Lenin and Stalin. And his most famous phrase "If the enemy does not surrender, he is wiped out" was already in circulation (1a).

О-19 • ГЛА́ВНЫМ О́БРАЗОМ [NP$_{instrum}$; Invar; adv or sent adv (occas. parenth); fixed WO] primarily, basically: **mainly; chiefly; essentially; for the most part; primarily; mostly;** [in limited contexts] **one's main object (in doing sth. is...).**

...Чехов, как большинство его современников, был чужд изобразительному искусству и понимал культуру главным образом как просвещение (Терц 3). ...Like most of his contemporaries, Chekhov was indifferent to the visual arts and understood culture mainly as education (3a). ♦ Полесов стоял в очередях главным образом из принципа. Денег у него не было, и купить он всё равно ничего не мог (Ильф и Петров 1). Polesov stood in line chiefly for reasons of principle. He had no money, so he could not buy anything, anyway (1a). ♦ В этот период я записывал более-менее подробно разговоры с ним [Пастернаком], т. е., конечно, главным образом то, что говорил он (Гладков 1). During this whole period I kept more or less detailed notes of my conversations with him [Pasternak] − mostly, of course, of what was said by him (1a). ♦ По иным донесениям из прошлого, он [Чернышевский] посетил Герцена главным образом для того, чтобы переговорить об издании «Современника» за границей... (Набоков 1). According to certain reports from the past his [Chernyshevsky's] main object in visiting Herzen was to discuss the publishing of *The Contemporary* abroad... (1a).

О-20 • КАКИ́М О́БРАЗОМ [NP$_{instrum}$; Invar; adv; fixed WO] in what manner: **how; in what way;** [in limited contexts] **by what means; the way (s.o. does sth. ⟨sth. happens⟩).**

«От меня зависит, как сложится ваша участь», − холодно произнёс обер-лейтенант. «Каким образом?» (Федин 1). "It depends on me how your future turns out," said the Ober-lieutenant coldly. "How?" (1a). ♦ ...[Известный советский критик] долго допытывался, когда и каким образом мне удалось вернуться из-за границы (Войнович 1). ...He [a well-known Soviet critic] went on and on, questioning me about when and by what means I had managed to return from abroad (1a). ♦ И по службе Мансуров кое-чего достиг − персональной машины, например, которой он был очень горд, надо было видеть, каким образом он в неё садился по утрам у подъезда своей квартиры... (Залыгин 1). In his job he [Mansurov] hadn't stood still either. He'd earned his own private car, of which he was very proud. It was a sight to see the way he got into it at the door [of his apartment building] every morning (1a).

О-21 • НЕ́КОТОРЫМ О́БРАЗОМ [NP$_{instrum}$; Invar; adv or modif; fixed WO] in some manner or measure: **in a ⟨some⟩ way; after a fashion; to some ⟨a certain⟩ extent ⟨degree⟩; somewhat.**

...Он ещё не может знать, не подозревает о существовании этих фактов, но эти факты тем не менее существуют сами по себе и существуют, некоторым образом, в его незнании (Битов 2). ...He cannot yet know about and does not suspect the existence of these facts, yet the facts nevertheless exist independently and also exist, after a fashion, in his ignorance (2a).

О-22 • НИКО́ИМ О́БРАЗОМ *coll*; **НИКАКИ́М О́БРАЗОМ** *obs* [NP$_{instrum}$; these forms only; adv; used with negated verbs; fixed WO] not under any circumstances, not at all: **in no way; by no means; not by any manner of means; not by a long shot; absolutely not;** [when used as an indep. remark] **(that's) (absolutely) impossible.**

И человек с искажённым от горя лицом вынужден был отказаться от своих попыток прорваться к повозкам, с которых уже сняли столбы. Эти попытки ни к чему не привели бы, кроме того, что он был бы схвачен, а быть задержанным в этот день никоим образом не входило в его план (Булгаков 9). And the man, his face contorted with grief, was compelled to abandon his attempts to break through to the carts, from which the posts had already been taken. These attempts would have resulted in nothing but his capture, and it was certainly in no way part of his plan to be arrested that day (9a). ♦ [Хлестаков:] Вы никак не можете мне помешать; никаким образом не можете; напротив того, вы можете принесть удовольствие (Гоголь 4). [Kh.:] You can't possibly disturb me, not by any manner of means; on the contrary, you can bring me happiness (4b).

O-23 • РА́ВНЫМ О́БРАЗОМ [NP$_{instrum}$; Invar] **1.** Also: **В РА́ВНОЙ МЕ́РЕ ⟨СТЕ́ПЕНИ⟩** *lit* [PrepP; modif; foll. by AdvP or AdjP] to an equal degree: **equally; just as.**

Великий комбинатор не любил ксендзов. В равной степени он отрицательно относился к раввинам, далай-ламам, муэдзинам, шаманам и прочим служителям культа (Ильф и Петров 2). The smooth operator didn't like Catholic priests. He took an equally dim view of rabbis, dalai lamas, popes, muezzins, medicine men, and other such ministers of religious worship (2a).

2. [sent adv] used to liken a statement to the preceding statement: **similarly; likewise; [in limited contexts] by the same token.**

«...Мы остереглись проговориться Петру Петровичу [Лужину] хоть о чём-нибудь из этих дальнейших мечтаний наших и, главное, о том, что ты будешь его компаньоном... Равным образом ни я, ни Дуня ни полслова ещё не говорили с ним о крепкой надежде нашей, что он поможет нам способствовать тебе деньгами, пока ты в университете...» (Достоевский 3). "...We have been careful not to let slip a word to Mr. Luzhin about any part of these dreams of ours for the future, and especially about you becoming his partner....Similarly, neither I nor Dunya has said a word to him yet about our confident hope that he will help us to supply you with funds while you are at the university" (3a).

O-24 • ТАКИ́М О́БРАЗОМ [NP$_{instrum}$; Invar; fixed WO] **1.** [adv] in the fashion or manner indicated or implied: **so; (in) this ⟨that⟩ way; thus; like this ⟨that⟩; in such a way.**

Дом стоял таким образом, что один конец веранды нависал над обрывом, поросшим непроходимыми зарослями ежевики и терновника (Искандер 3). The house was so situated that one end of the veranda hung over a precipice overgrown with impassable thickets of blackberries and blackthorn (3a). ♦ ...Он [Фердыщенко] преспокойно уселся на кочку и, покуривая из трубочки, завёл с землемерами пикантный разговор. Таким образом, пожирая Домашку глазами, он просидел до вечера... (Салтыков-Щедрин 1). ...He [Ferdyshchenko] calmly took a seat on a hummock, lit up his pipe, and started a risque conversation with the surveyors. Thus he sat, devouring Domashka with his eyes, until evening... (1a).

2. [sent adv (parenth)] used to introduce a deduction, conclusion: **thus; consequently; accordingly; hence; (and) so.**

«...Сейчас мы тебя отправим в камеру. Но имей в виду следующее: я скажу Сударю, что ты молчишь и, таким образом, берёшь на себя роль главаря банды» (Семёнов 1). "...We'll send you down to the cells now. But bear this in mind: I shall tell Squire that you're refusing to talk and are thus taking on the role of gang leader" (1a). ♦ «Я счастлив, что имею в настоящий момент возможность сообщить вам, что это поручение я в точности исполнил и, таким образом, вполне с вами расквитался» (Федин 1). "I am happy that I am now able to inform you that I carried out your mission to the letter and so we are completely quits" (1a).

O-25 • ПО О́БРАЗУ И ПОДО́БИЮ *чьему, кого obsoles* [PrepP; Invar; adv; fixed WO] patterned after s.o. or sth., using s.o. or sth. as an example: **in the image and likeness ⟨semblance⟩ of s.o. ⟨sth.⟩; in s.o.'s image and likeness; s.o.'s image ⟨likeness⟩.**

Повторяем: вся эта тяга к стиху, созданному по образу и подобию определённых социально-экономических богов, была в Чернышевском бессознательна... (Набоков 1). Let us repeat: all this leaning toward a line created in the image and likeness of definite socio-economic gods was unconscious on Chernyshevski's part... (1a). ♦ Мы вошли в аудиторию с твёрдой целью в ней основать зерно общества по образу и подобию декабристов и потому искали прозелитов и последователей (Герцен 3). We went into the lecture-room with the firm purpose of founding in it the nucleus of a society in the image and semblance of the Decembrists, and therefore we sought proselytes and adherents (2a). ♦ «Я думаю, что если дьявол не существует и, стало быть, создал его человек, то создал он его по своему образу и подобию». – «В таком случае, равно как и бога» (Достоевский 1). "I think that if the devil does not exist, and has therefore created him, he has created him in his own image and likeness." "As well as God, then" (1a). ♦ «И очень вам советую: подумайте, попытайтесь подумать, что вы можете дать детям. Поглядите на себя. Вы родили их на свет и калечите их по своему образу и подобию» (Стругацкие 1). "And I urge you: think, try to think of what you could do for the children. Look at yourselves. You gave them life, and you are deforming them in your own image" (1a).

< From the Bible (Gen. 1:26).

O-26 • ПО О́БРАЗУ ПЕ́ШЕГО ХОЖДЕ́НИЯ *obs, humor* [PrepP; Invar; adv; fixed WO] walking: **on ⟨by⟩ shanks' mare.**

O-27 • В ОБРЕ́З *(чего у кого)* [PrepP; Invar; subj-compl with copula (subj/gen: usu. a noun denoting time or money) or adv (quantif)] (there is, s.o. has etc) barely an adequate amount, no extra: **just ⟨barely⟩ enough; just barely enough; none ⟨no [NP]⟩ to spare; ‖ у X-а времени в обрез ≃ X is short of time; X doesn't have much time; X is pressed for time; there is no time to lose; time is short.**

[Алексей:] Помнишь, когда вы у нас жили, отца в армию взяли?.. Ну, не вернулся он... Денег – в обрез. Я и задумал подработать (Розов 1). [A.:] Do you remember, when all of you stayed with us? – they drafted Father into the army....Well, he never came back....Money – there was none to spare. So I decided to help out – do odd jobs after school (1a). ♦ ...Времени оставалось в обрез, через несколько часов отходил севастопольский поезд (Солженицын 1). ...There was no time to spare, the Sevastopol train would be leaving in a few hours (1a). ♦ «Дай другим своё дело спроворить, не отымай у их [*ungrammat* = них] время. У их его тоже в обрез» (Распутин 1). "Let others do their duty, don't take up their time. They're short of time too" (4a). ♦ Фаина считала, что [Ольге] нужно срочно искать мужа: «Не будь дурой. Сергея не вернёшь, а себя погубишь. Имей в виду, у тебя времени в обрез: год, два, потом пиши пропало» (Трифонов 3). Faina thought Olga should start looking for another husband at once: "Don't be a fool. You can't bring Sergei back, and you're destroying yourself. Bear in mind that you don't have much time – a year or two, and after that you can forget it" (3a). ♦ «Хотите взглянуть [на лагерь]?»... – «Разве что взглянуть, – неуверенно уступил он соблазну. – Только не задерживаться, времени у меня в обрез» (Максимов 1). "D'you want to take a look [at the camp]?"..."Well, we could have a look, I suppose," he said, succumbing to the temptation. "But we mustn't delay. I'm very pressed for time" (1a).

O-28 • НЕ ОБСЕ́ВОК В ПО́ЛЕ *substand* [NP; subj-compl with быть$_\emptyset$ (subj: human), pres only; used without negation to convey the opposite meaning; fixed WO] one is not a nonentity, not worse than others: **X не обсевок в поле ≃ X is not a nobody; X is no worse than anyone else; X is no slouch.**

O-29 • БРАТЬ/ВЗЯТЬ ПОД ОБСТРЕ́Л *кого-что* [VP; subj: human or collect] to (begin to) criticize s.o. or sth. harshly, sharply: X взял Y-а под обстрел ≃ **Y came under fire from X;**

X began attacking ⟨firing away at⟩ Y; X opened fire on Y; X blasted Y.

O-30 • **В ОБТЯ́ЖКУ** [PrepP; Invar; nonagreeing postmodif or adv] (a piece of clothing that) hugs the body, fits or is made to fit tightly: **close-fitting; snug-fitting.**

Московское платье оказалось превосходно: коричневые полуфрачки с бронзовыми пуговками были сшиты в обтяжку – не так, как в деревне нам шивали, на рост... (Толстой 2). Our Moscow clothes turned out to be superb: the brown dress coats had bronze buttons and were made close-fitting–not like they had been made in the country, with room for you to grow (2b).

O-31 • **(УДАРЯ́ТЬ ⟨БИТЬ** *rare*⟩**/УДА́РИТЬ) КАК ⟨БУ́ДТО, СЛО́ВНО, ТО́ЧНО⟩ О́БУХОМ ПО ГОЛОВЕ́** *coll* [VP or как etc + NP (subj-compl with быть∅); subj: usu. abstr; fixed WO] (of an unexpected piece of news, event etc) to shock s.o. greatly: X был (для Y-а) как обухом по голове ≃ X hit Y like a thunderbolt ⟨a bolt of lightning, a ton of bricks⟩; X was (like) a body blow (to Y); Y was stunned by X.

Оба эти подонка... стали давать против меня показания. Чего только они не врали!.. Вышел я от следователя как убитый... Будто обухом по голове была для меня вся эта история (Буковский 1). ...These two rats began giving evidence against me. The bullshit they talked!...I left the investigator's office poleaxed....This whole business had been a body blow (1a).

O-32 • **В ОБХО́Д** [PrepP; Invar; adv] **1.** ~ *(чего)* идти, двигаться и т. п. (to go, travel somewhere) by an indirect route (that takes longer than the direct route): **make a detour; go ⟨take⟩ a ⟨the⟩ roundabout way; go ⟨take⟩ the long way (around);** [in limited contexts] **skirt sth.**

...[Бородавкин] вынужден был отступить от горы с уроном. Пошли в обход, но здесь наткнулись на болото, которого никто не подозревал (Салтыков-Щедрин 1). ...[Wartkin] was forced to retreat from the mountain with casualties. They started to make a detour, but now they ran up against a swamp, the existence of which no one had suspected (1a).

2. ~ *кого-чего* идти, двигаться и т. п. *mil* (to go, maneuver) around the flank (of an opposing military unit): **outflank(ing).**

...Мюрат, желая загладить свою ошибку, тотчас же двинул свои войска на центр и в обход обоих флангов, надеясь ещё до вечера и до прибытия императора раздавить ничтожный, стоявший перед ним отряд (Толстой 4). Murat...anxious to make amends for his error, instantly moved his forces to attack the center and outflank both Russian wings, hoping before evening, and before the arrival of the Emperor, to crush the insignificant detachment facing him (4a).

3. ~ закона, правил и т. п. avoiding the observance of (the law, rules, regulations etc): **in contravention of the law ⟨the rules etc⟩; (by) going against ⟨skirting, getting around, sidestepping⟩ the law ⟨the rules etc⟩.**

4. ~ *кого* overlooking s.o.: **passing over s.o.**

Фалина назначили директором в обход Петрова, хотя Петров был гораздо опытнее его. In appointing Falin director, they passed over Petrov, even though Petrov was far more experienced.

O-33 • **НЕ ИМЕ́ТЬ НИЧЕГО́ О́БЩЕГО** *с кем-чем;* **НЕТ НИЧЕГО́ О́БЩЕГО** *у кого-чего с кем-чем* [VP, subj: usu. human or abstr (1st var.); VP_subj/gen (2nd var.)] not to be associated with or conditioned by s.o. or sth.: X не имеет ничего общего с Y-ом ≃ X has nothing to do with Y; thing X bears no relation to thing Y; thing X has no connection with thing Y; thing X isn't connected with thing Y.

Мерин сказал, что распределение людей по социальной иерархии не имеет ничего общего с умственными способностями (Зиновьев 1). Gelding said that the positions allocated to

people on the social ladder bore no relation to their intellectual capabilities (1a). ♦ Кроме этого чувства, поглощавшего её всю и мешавшего ей вникать в подробности планов мужа, в голове её мелькали мысли, не имеющие ничего общего с тем, что он говорил (Толстой 7). Besides this feeling, which absorbed her entirely and hindered her from following the details of her husband's plans, thoughts that had no connection with what he was saying flitted through her mind (7a).

O-34 • **В О́БЩЕМ** [PrepP; Invar; sent adv (often parenth)] generally speaking, considering everything together, taking everything important into consideration: **on the whole; by and large; all in all; all things considered; in general;** [in limited contexts] **in sum; taken as a whole;** [when summarizing] **in short; put simply.**

[Астров:] Переходим к третьей части: картина уезда в настоящем... От прежних выселков, хуторков, скитов, мельниц и следа нет. В общем, картина постепенного и несомненного вырождения... (Чехов 3). [A.:] Now let's go to the third section: a map of the district as it is today....There's not a trace of the settlements, farms, hermitages, water mills. On the whole it is a picture of gradual and unmistakable degeneration... (3a). ♦ Я спросил хозяев, не трудно ли им живётся. Они сказали, что, в общем-то, нелегко (Войнович 1). I asked our hosts if life was difficult for them. They said by and large it wasn't easy (1a). ♦ Вечером должны были идти в гости к Володе, моему кузену... Володя и Ляля относились к нам как будто дружески, но с какой-то внутренней настороженностью... В общем, родственники как родственники (Трифонов 5). That evening we were supposed to visit my cousin Volodya....Volodya and Lyalya were friendly though somewhat guarded in their relations with us....All in all, they were relatives like any other relatives (5a). ♦ В общем-то, лицо Мансурова было довольно красивым, особенно на первый взгляд... (Залыгин 1). Taken as a whole Mansurov's face was quite handsome, especially at first glance... (1a). ♦ Ух, дядя Митя веселился на свадьбе! Читал куплеты, разыгрывал с тёщей сценки, пел, плясал — в общем, был душой общества (Аксёнов 10). Oh, how Old Mitya enjoyed himself at the wedding! He recited couplets, acted scenes with his mother-in-law, sang and danced—in short, he was the life and soul of the party (10a).

O-35 • **В О́БЩЕМ И ЦЕ́ЛОМ** [PrepP; Invar; sent adv (often parenth); fixed WO] in general, in essence, without considering all the particulars, details: **on the whole; all in all; by and large; generally speaking.**

Проезжая сельсовет, они [члены комиссии] встретились с председателем [Тимуром Жванба] и посоветовали ему пока воздержаться от решительных мер, поскольку орех в общем и целом делает полезное нам дело (Искандер 3). Passing the village soviet, they [the commission members] encountered [the chairman] Timur Zhvanba and advised him to refrain from decisive measures for the time being, inasmuch as the walnut tree was doing something useful for us, on the whole (3a). ♦ ...Валерий Кирпиченко не обращал на него особого внимания. Понятно, фамилию эту знал и личность была знакомая — электрик Банин, но в общем и целом человек это был незаметный, несмотря на весь шум, который вокруг него поднимали по праздникам (Аксёнов 5). ...Kirpichenko never took much notice of him. He knew the name, of course, and he knew who the fellow was—Banin, the electrician—but by and large he didn't stand out in a crowd despite all the fuss kicked up about him on the big holidays (5a).

O-36 • **С РАСПРОСТЁРТЫМИ ОБЪЯ́ТИЯМИ** принимать, встречать *кого coll* [PrepP; Invar; adv; fixed WO] (to receive, welcome s.o.) warmly, cordially: **with open arms.**

С большим мастерством, с живостью изложения необыкновенной (её можно почти принять за сострадание), Странолюбский описывает его [Чернышевского] водворение на жительство в Астрахани. Никто не встречал его с распростёртыми объятиями… (Набоков 1). With great mastery and with the utmost vividness of exposition (it might almost be taken for compassion) Strannolyubski describes his [Chernyshevski's] installation in his Astrakhan residence. No one met him with open arms… (1a).

O-37 • В ОБЪЯ́ТИЯХ МОРФЕ́Я быть$_\theta$, находи́ться; В ОБЪЯ́ТИЯ МОРФЕ́Я ⟨К МОРФЕ́Ю⟩ пора́ и т. п. *old-fash, elev* [PrepP; these forms only; subj-compl with copula with subj: human (1st var.) or adv; fixed WO] (to be) asleep, (it is time to go) to sleep: **be in ⟨fall into⟩ the arms of Morpheus; be in the Land of Nod.**

Базаров начал зевать. «Я полагаю, пора путешественникам в объятия к Морфею», — заметил Василий Иванович (Тургенев 2). Bazarov began to yawn. "I suppose it is time for our travellers to fall into the arms of Morpheus," observed Vassily Ivanych (2c).

< *Morpheus* is the god of dreams in Greek mythology.

O-38 • ДУШИ́ТЬ/ЗАДУШИ́ТЬ В ОБЪЯ́ТИЯХ *кого* [VP; subj: human] to embrace s.o. firmly, with emotion: X душил Y-а в объятиях ≃ **X smothered Y with embraces.**

[Лидия:] Теперь уж, когда мне придёт в голову задушить тебя в своих объятиях, так я задушу (Островский 4). [L.:] And now, when I take it into my head to smother you with embraces, I'm going to do it (4a).

O-39 • ПО ОБЫКНОВЕ́НИЮ; ПО СВОЕМУ́ ОБЫКНОВЕ́НИЮ [PrepP; these forms only; sent adv (often parenth)] as is always the case, as s.o. or sth. always does: **as usual; as always; as is one's habit ⟨custom, wont, way⟩; [in limited contexts] one's ⟨its⟩ usual…**

[Павлин:] Газеты же, по обыкновению, лгут! (Горький 2). [P.:] The papers are lying, as usual (2a). ♦ Герой наш, по обыкновению, сейчас вступил с нею в разговор… (Гоголь 3). Our hero, as was his habit, immediately engaged her in conversation (3a). ♦ Несмотря на сложные личные обстоятельства, Ингурка, по своему обыкновению, упала в незамедлительный обморок любви к человеку… (Ахмадулина 1). In spite of the complex personal circumstances, Ingurka, as was her wont, fell into an instantaneous swoon of love…for the man (1a). ♦ «Скворцы» встрепенулись и, считая предмет исчерпанным, вознамерились было, по обыкновению, шутки шутить, но Собачкин призвал их к порядку… (Салтыков-Щедрин 2). The "starlings" stirred in their seats and, thinking the subject exhausted, were about to resume their usual occupation of exchanging jokes, but Sobachkin called them to order (2a).

O-40 • ПРОТИВ ОБЫКНОВЕ́НИЯ [PrepP; Invar; sent adv (often parenth)] in contrast to what is usually the case, what s.o. or sth. usually does etc: **contrary to usual; contrary to one's custom ⟨habit⟩; …which is quite unusual for s.o.; [in limited contexts] for once.**

Илья Ильич проснулся, против обыкновения, очень рано, часов в восемь (Гончаров 1). [Ilya Ilyich] Oblomov, contrary to his custom, had woken up very early—about eight o'clock (1a). ♦ До самого хутора Емельян, против обыкновения, не перекинулся с хозяином ни одним словом (Шолохов 3). Contrary to his habit, he [Yemelyan] did not exchange a single word with his master throughout the journey (3a). ♦ Майор, против обыкновения, оказался на месте (Максимов 1). For once the major was in his office (1a).

O-41 • ВМЕНЯ́ТЬ/ВМЕНИ́ТЬ В ОБЯ́ЗАННОСТЬ *кому что* или *что делать* [VP; subj: human] to obligate s.o. or o.s. to do sth.: X вменил Y-у ⟨себе⟩ в обязанность делать Z ≃ **X made it Y's ⟨X's⟩ duty to do Z; X imposed on Y ⟨on himself⟩ a duty to do Z; X considered it Y's ⟨X's⟩ obligation ⟨duty⟩ to do Z; X considered it an obligation ⟨a duty⟩ to do Z; [in limited contexts] X made it a requirement that Y do Z.**

Повторяю: я вменил себе в обязанность писать, ничего не утаивая (Замятин 1). I repeat: I have made it my duty to write without concealing anything (1a). ♦ Как когда-то ей самой Шунечка, она вменяла своим женщинам улыбку в обязанность, в служебный долг (Грекова 3). As Shunechka had done to her, she imposed on her women a duty to smile as part of their work (3a). ♦ Я знал, что отец почтёт за счастие и вменит себе в обязанность принять дочь заслуженного воина, погибшего за отечество (Пушкин 2). I knew that my father would consider it a blessing and an obligation to shelter the daughter of an honored warrior who had given his life for the fatherland (2a).

O-42 • ОТДЕЛЯ́ТЬ/ОТДЕЛИ́ТЬ ОВЕ́Ц ОТ КО́ЗЛИЩ *lit* [VP; subj: human; usu. this WO] to separate the good from the bad, the useful from the harmful (may refer to people): **separate the sheep from the goats; make a distinction between the sheep and the goats.**

…Именно люди двадцатых годов начали аккуратно отделять овец от козлищ, своих от чужих, сторонников «нового» от тех, кто ещё не забыл самых примитивных правил общежития (Мандельштам 1). It was the people of the twenties who first began to make a neat distinction between the sheep and the goats, between "us" and "them," between upholders of the "new" and those still mindful of the basic rules that governed human relations in the past (1a).

< From the Bible (Matt. 25:32).

O-43 • ОВЛАДЕВА́ТЬ/ОВЛАДЕ́ТЬ СОБО́Й; СПРАВЛЯ́ТЬСЯ/СПРА́ВИТЬСЯ С СОБО́Й [VP; subj: human; fixed WO] to overcome one's agitation, nervousness, distress etc and gain control of o.s.: X овладел собой ≃ **X recovered his self-control; X composed ⟨collected⟩ himself; X regained control of himself ⟨his composure⟩; X took himself in hand; X pulled himself together; X got a grip on himself.**

…Иван Фёдорович, по-видимому, совсем уже успел овладеть собой (Достоевский 2). …Ivan Fyodorovich had now apparently managed to regain control of himself (2a). ♦ Не дождавшись приглашения, Ефим сам придвинул стул, сел, поставил портфель на колени и, почти овладев собой, умильно посмотрел на Андрея Андреевича (Войнович 6). Without an invitation, then, Yefim pulled up a chair, sat down, put his attaché case on his lap, and, regaining some of his composure, smiled ingratiatingly at Andrey Andreevich (6a).

O-44 • ВСЯ́КОМУ ⟨КА́ЖДОМУ⟩ О́ВОЩУ СВОЁ ВРЕ́МЯ [saying] there is a proper time for all undertakings: ≃ **everything in its season; there's a (right) time for everything.**

O-45 • ЗАБЛУ́ДШАЯ ОВЦА́ ⟨ОВЕ́ЧКА⟩ *lit* [NP; usu. sing] a person who has strayed from a righteous way of life: **lost sheep; sheep that has gone astray.**

< From the Bible (Matt. 18:12, Luke 15:4-6).

O-46 • (ОДНА́) ПАРШИ́ВАЯ ОВЦА́ ВСЁ СТА́ДО ПО́РТИТ [saying] a bad person has a harmful effect on the group to which he belongs or creates a bad impression of the group he represents: ≃ **one rotten ⟨bad⟩ apple spoils the whole barrel; one scabby sheep infects the whole flock.**

O-47 • С ПАРШИ́ВОЙ ОВЦЫ́ ХОТЬ ШЕ́РСТИ КЛОК [saying] you might as well take whatever you can get from s.o., even though it is unsatisfactory etc, because you will not get anything better and you will be the one to lose out by refusing it (said with disdain about s.o. who produces sth. inferior, is inferior in some way etc): ≃ **even a mangy sheep is good for a little wool; something is better than nothing; half a loaf is better than none.**

«Чего надо-то?» – Богдашкин меня уже узнал, голос у него недовольный. «Ничего особенного. Бочку олифы». – «Олифы? – Богдашкин воспринимает это как личное оскорбление. – Вы её с хлебом, что ли, едите? Я тебе на прошлой неделе отправил две бочки. Больше нет... Алебастру немного могу дать, если хочешь». – «Чёрт с тобой, – соглашаюсь я, – давай алебастр. С паршивой овцы хоть шерсти клок» (Войнович 5). "What do you want?" said Bogdashkin, displeased, having recognized me. "Nothing special. A barrel of linseed oil." "Linseed oil?" Bogdashkin took this as a personal affront. "What do you do, put it on your bread or something? I sent you two barrels last week. There's no more....I can give you a little alabaster if you want." "The hell with you then," I agreed. "I'll take the alabaster. Even a mangy sheep's good for a little wool" (5a).

O-48 • ОВЧИ́НКА ВЫ́ДЕЛКИ НЕ СТО́ИТ [saying] the matter in question is not worth the time, energy, resources spent on it: ≃ **the game isn't worth the candle; it's more trouble than it's worth; it's not worth the trouble; it won't pay.**

Относись к своей работе как ко всякой работе, дающей средства существования, но не вкладывай в неё душу. Овчинка выделки не стоит (Зиновьев 2). Consider your work like any job that keeps you in food, but don't try to put your soul into it. The game isn't worth the candle (2a). ♦ ...Ведь для этой десятиминутной игры Брюсову пришлось выучить наизусть с полсотни трудных и плохо запоминающихся строк. Забава была в стиле десятых годов, но стоила ли овчинка выделки? (Мандельштам 2). ...For the sake of his ten minutes' fun, Briusov must have learned by heart at least fifty difficult and not very memorable lines. It was a practical joke very much in the style of the pre-Revolutionary years, but was it really worth all the trouble? (2a).

O-49 • ПОЛУЧА́ТЬ/ПОЛУЧИ́ТЬ ОГЛА́СКУ [VP; subj: abstr (often дело, история etc)] to become known to a lot of people: X получил огласку ≃ **X became widely known; X became public knowledge; [in limited contexts] X was publicized.**

Все знали... что дело это получило всероссийскую огласку, но всё-таки не представляли себе, что оно до такой уже жгучей, до такой раздражительной степени потрясло всех и каждого... (Достоевский 2). Everyone...knew that the case had been publicized all over Russia, but even so they never imagined that it had shaken all and sundry to such a burning, such an intense degree... (2a).

O-50 • ПОВОРА́ЧИВАТЬ/ПОВЕРНУ́ТЬ ⟨ПОВОРОТИ́ТЬ⟩ ОГЛО́БЛИ (НАЗА́Д) highly coll [VP; subj: human] **1.** rude when addressed to the interlocutor to set off back in the direction from which one came, leave some place (usu. with the implication that one has failed, or is about to fail, to accomplish what one set out to do): X повернул оглобли ≃ **X went back (where he came from); X (gave it up and) turned back; X turned back empty-handed; [in limited contexts] X turned tail.**

[Подхалюзин:] А то вон, что сватался за Алимпиаду Самсоновну, благородный-то, – и оглобли назад поворотил (Островский 10). [P.:] As for that noble's courting Olimpiada Samsonovna–why he's turned tail already (10b).

2. often disapprov to retreat from one's former position, renounce one's former convictions, go back on one's promise(s) etc: X повернул оглобли ≃ **X did ⟨made⟩ an about-face; X back-pedaled; X changed his tune.**

O-51 • БЕЗ ОГЛЯ́ДКИ coll [PrepP; Invar; adv] **1. бежать, убегать** и т. п. ~ (to run, run away etc) very quickly and without turning around to look behind one: **(fast and) without a backward glance; (fast and) without looking back; with abandon.**

Орозкул встал, подтянул штаны и, боясь оглянуться, затрусил прочь... Но Кулубек остановил его: «Стой! Мы тебе скажем последнее слово. У тебя никогда не будет детей. Ты

злой и негодный человек... Уходи — и чтобы навсегда. А ну быстрее!» Орозкул побежал без оглядки (Айтматов 1). Orozkul stood up, pulled up his trousers, and, afraid to glance back, ran away at a quick trot....But Kulubek stopped him: "Wait! We'll say to you one final word. You will never have any children. You are an evil and worthless man....Go from here–forever. Double quick!" Orozkul ran off without a backward glance (1a).

2. (to make a decision, set out upon a course of action etc) resolutely, without vacillation: **without looking back; without a backward glance; without any hesitation; without a second thought; without thinking twice.**

3. предаваться чему, делать что и т. п. ~ (to do sth.) unrestrainedly, forgetting all else, (indulge in sth.) without limiting o.s. etc: **unreservedly; without restraint ⟨reserve⟩; (give o.s.) completely (to sth.).**

4. любить кого, верить кому ~ (to love s.o.) to the greatest possible extent, (to trust s.o.) fully and completely: **without any reservations; without reservation; unreservedly; unconditionally.**

...Любить она [Кира] умела, как любят сейчас на Земле, – спокойно и без оглядки... (Стругацкие 4). Kyra was capable of true love, the way women on Earth would love–quiet and without any reservations (4a).

5. imprudently, without due consideration: **carelessly; recklessly; rashly; thoughtlessly; indiscriminately.**

Вместе с Ахматовой он [Мандельштам] выдумал игру: у каждого из них есть кучка талонов на признание поэтов, но она – жмот, сквалыга – свои талоны бережёт, а он истратил последний на старика Звенигородского и просит взаймы хоть один, хоть половинку... Она действительно свои талоны берегла, а в старости стала раздавать их без оглядки – направо и налево (Мандельштам 2). He [Mandelstam] and Akhmatova even invented a game: each of them had a certain number of tokens to be expended on the recognition of poets–but while she was tightfisted and hung on to her tokens for all she was worth, he spent his last one on old Zvenigorodski, and then had to beg her to "lend" him one, or even half of one....Having hoarded them up so jealously, in her old age Akhmatova began to hand out her tokens indiscriminately, right, left, and center (2a).

O-52 • С ОГЛЯ́ДКОЙ coll [PrepP; Invar; adv] (to do sth.) cautiously, warily: **looking over one's shoulder; with a perpetual glance over one's shoulder; with caution; discreetly; with care; circumspectly.**

Огромное большинство, миллионы людей, оплакивали Сталина и в рыданиях спрашивали друг друга: что же теперь будет? Другие радовались, но – молча, недоверчиво и с оглядкой. И лишь немногие рисковали выражать свою радость открыто (Ивинская 1). The vast majority, millions of people, wept for Stalin and asked each other through sobs: what will happen now? Others rejoiced–but in silence, furtively, and looking over their shoulders. Only very few were bold enough to give open expression to their joy (1a). ♦ Рассуждение о ямочках на щеках и тем более эпизод, связанный с биноклем, дядя Сандро передавал с оглядкой, чтобы тётя Катя этого не слышала (Искандер 5). The discussion of dimpled cheeks, and more especially the episode involving the binoculars, Uncle Sandro conveyed with care lest Aunt Katya hear (5a). ♦ ...Он [Штольц] начал решать... вопрос о том, может ли жить без него Ольга. Но этот вопрос не давался ему так легко. Он подбирался к нему медленно, с оглядкой, осторожно (Гончаров 1). ...He [Stolz] began wondering whether Olga could live without him or not. But that question was not so easy to answer. He approached it slowly, circumspectly, cautiously... (1a).

O-53 • ОГЛЯНУ́ТЬСЯ НЕ УСПЕ́ЕШЬ ⟨НЕ УСПЕ́ЕТ и т. п.⟩ (, как...) coll [VP; subj: human; often fut gener. 2nd pers sing не успеешь] (sth. will happen, take place etc) very quickly, almost immediately: **before you know it; before you have time to look around; before you can turn ⟨look⟩ around.**

Она сказала Андрею в тот разговор, когда он пристал с расспросами, что человек живёт на свете всего ничего. И верно, не успеешь оглянуться — жизнь прошла (Распутин 4). She had told Andrei when he was pestering her with questions that man lives almost no time at all. And it was true — before you knew it, life was over (4a). ♦ Быстро всё превращается в человеке: не успеешь оглянуться, как уже вырос внутри страшный червь, самовластно обративший к себе все жизненные соки (Гоголь 3). Everything in man is subject to a rapid metamorphosis; before you have time to look around, there has grown within him a terrible canker worm that has tyrannically diverted all his life sap toward itself (3c).

O-54 • МЕЖДУ ⟨МЕЖ⟩ ДВУХ ОГНЕЙ coll [PrepP; these forms only; usu. adv or subj-compl with copula (subj: human, collect, or, rare, abstr); fixed WO] (to be, find o.s.) in a difficult situation, when danger or trouble threatens from both sides: **between two fires; between a rock and a hard place; between the devil and the deep blue sea; caught in the cross fire.**

«Жена совершенно права. И без вас не сладко. Собачья жизнь, сумасшедший дом. Всё время меж двух огней...» (Пастернак 1). "My wife is quite right. Things are bad enough without you. It's a dog's life, a madhouse. I am caught between two fires" (1a). ♦ «Он [Андрей] оказался меж двух огней. Подозрение сверху и подозрение снизу...» (Аксёнов 12). "He's [Andrei is] caught between a rock and a hard place. Suspicion from above and suspicion from below..." (12a).

O-55 • ГОРИ́ ОГНЁМ кто-что; **ГОРИ́ (ОНО́) СИ́НИМ ⟨Я́СНЫМ⟩ ОГНЁМ ⟨ПЛА́МЕНЕМ⟩; ГОРИ́ (ОНО́ ⟨ВСЁ⟩) ПРА́ХОМ** all coll [Interj; these forms only; fixed WO] used to express indignation, resentment, annoyance: **to ⟨the⟩ hell with s.o. ⟨sth.⟩; I don't give a damn ⟨a hoot⟩ about s.o. ⟨sth.⟩; damn s.o. ⟨sth., it all⟩.**

...Возможность похотиться за живым умыкателем девушки вызвала в нём [Тенделе] прилив такого бескорыстного азарта, что он остался совершенно холоден к возможности получения патефона... «Гори огнём ваш патефон! – даже прикрикнул он на них. – Вы что, не видите, что творится?» (Искандер 3). The opportunity to go hunting for the live abductor of a maiden roused him [Tendel] to such unselfish fervor that he remained completely cold to the opportunity to acquire a phonograph....."To hell with your phonograph!" he even shouted at them. "Don't you see what's happening?" (3a).

O-56 • ДНЁМ С ОГНЁМ не найти, не найдёшь, не сыскать, не сыщешь, поискать и т. п. кого-что or чего coll [AdvP; Invar; adv; usu. used with infin or neg pfv fut, gener. 2nd pers sing не найдёшь etc; fixed WO] (of a person with remarkable qualities or qualifications, or a thing rarely come across or difficult to obtain) rare, almost impossible to find even when much effort is put into searching: Х-а ⟨такого or таких, как Х,⟩ днём с огнём не найдёшь ≃ Xs ⟨people like X, things like X⟩ are **hard to find ⟨(as) scarce as hen's teeth⟩; never in the world will you find another X ⟨another ([NP]) like X⟩; try as you may ⟨might⟩ you'll never find another X ⟨another ([NP]) like X⟩;** [in limited contexts] **person X is one in a million; you can't get thing X for love (n)or money.**

«Ну и бедна ж ты бедами, мать! Гляди, как Бог тебя милует. Днём с огнём таких поискать» (Пастернак 1). "Well, you are poor in sorrows, my dear. See how merciful God has been to you! Such as you are hard to find" (1a). ♦ «Баб-то, конечно, по военному времю [ungrammat = времени] много свободных, – размышлял счетовод, – да такую, как Зинаида, днём с огнём не найдёшь» (Войнович 4). Of course, there's lots of women around during wartime, reflected the bookkeeper, but ones like Zinaida are scarce as hen's teeth (4a). ♦ Днём с огнём не сыщешь другого

такого человека, который умел бы так держать себя в руках (Искандер 3). Never in the world will you find another man with the self-control that he has (3a).

O-57 • ИГРА́ТЬ ⟨ШУТИ́ТЬ⟩ С ОГНЁМ [VP; subj: human] to act imprudently, do things that may bring about dangerous consequences: Х играет с огнём ≃ **X is playing with fire; X is courting disaster; X is flirting with danger; X is inviting trouble.**

«...У людей такой отчаянной жизни иногда бывает желание поиграть с огнём и попытать судьбу» (Паустовский 1). "...People who live desperate lives often want to play with fire and tempt their fate" (1b).

O-58 • ОГНЁМ И МЕЧО́М покорить кого-что и т. п. lit [NP$_{instrum}$; Invar; adv; fixed WO] (to conquer, vanquish) brutally: **with fire and sword; ruthlessly; mercilessly; raining death on s.o.**

O-59 • ПРЕДАВА́ТЬ/ПРЕДА́ТЬ ОГНЮ́ что lit [subj: human or collect] to burn sth.: Х-ы предали Y огню ≃ **Xs set fire to Y; Xs torched ⟨put a torch to⟩ Y.**

Несколько троек, наполненных разбойниками, разъезжали днём по всей губернии, останавливали путешественников и почту, приезжали в села, грабили помещичьи дома и предавали их огню (Пушкин 1). Several troikas, filled with brigands, roamed the whole province in broad daylight, holding up travellers and mail-coaches, driving down into the villages and robbing and setting fire to the houses of the landowners (1b).

O-60 • ПРЕДАВА́ТЬ/ПРЕДА́ТЬ ОГНЮ́ И МЕЧУ́ кого-что lit [VP; subj: human or collect; obj: usu. землю, страну etc] to ravage sth. mercilessly, destroying and burning everything: Х-ы предали Y огню и мечу ≃ **Xs wreaked destruction upon Y; Xs laid Y waste with fire and sword; Xs reduced Y to rubble and ashes.**

«...Ты идёшь со своими сотнями, как Тарас Бульба... и всё предаёшь огню и мечу и казаков волнуешь. Ты остепенись, пожалуйста, пленных смерти не предавай, а направляй к нам» (Шолохов 4). "...You are riding with your squadrons like Taras Bulba...laying everything waste with fire and sword, and alarming the Cossacks. Steady up, please and stop putting prisoners to death; send them to us instead" (4a).

O-61 • попасть ИЗ ОГНЯ́ (ДА) В ПО́ЛЫМЯ [PrepP; these forms only; adv; fixed WO] (to get) out of one difficult situation, condition etc and (fall) into an equally difficult or more difficult one: ≃ **out of the frying pan (and) into the fire.**

Мы были остановлены караульными. На вопрос: кто едет? – ямщик отвечал громогласно: «Государев кум со своею хозяюшкою». Вдруг толпа гусаров окружила нас с ужасною бранью. «Выходи, бесов кум!» – сказал мне усатый вахмистр... Вахмистр повёл меня к майору. Савельич от меня не отставал, поговаривая про себя: «Вот тебе и государев кум! Из огня да в полымя...» (Пушкин 2). We were stopped by the sentries. To the challenge, "Who goes there?" our driver replied in a thunderous voice, "The Sovereign's trusty friend with his bride." Suddenly a throng of hussars surrounded us, swearing frightfully. "Get out of there, devil's trusty friend!" the sergeant said to me....The sergeant proceeded to conduct me to the major. Savelich followed right behind me, muttering to himself, "So much for the Sovereign's trusty friend! Out of the frying pan into the fire!" (2a).

O-62 • КАК ⟨ПУ́ЩЕ obs⟩ **ОГНЯ́** бояться кого-чего coll [как + NP; these forms only; adv (intensif)] (to fear s.o. or sth.) very intensely: Х боится Y-а как огня ≃ **X fears Y like the plague ⟨like the very devil⟩; X is scared stiff of Y; X lives in mortal fear of Y.**

Борис Григорьевич боялся её [Зайцеву] как огня. Зайцева была из тех администраторов, которые свою малую, временную власть над людьми воспринимают как великую, вечную (Грекова 3). Boris Grigorievich feared her [Zaitseva] like the plague. Zaitseva was of those administrators who perceive their limited temporary power over people as great and permanent... (3a). ♦ ...«Сергей Сергеич (это — директор всего предприятия, местный Хозяин) просил вас к такому-то числу заполнить вот эту анкету»... Может быть... Сергей Сергеевич вовсе о том не знает, но кто ж пойдёт проверять, когда Сергея Сергеевича самого боятся как огня? (Солженицын 10). ..."Sergei Sergeyevich" (he was the director of the entire enterprise, the Boss) "has asked you to fill out this form by such and such a date."...Sergei Sergeyevich might know nothing about all this—but who would dare to check it, when Sergei Sergeyevich was feared like the very devil (10b).

О-63 • НА ОГОНЁК к кому зайти, заглянуть, забежать coll [PrepP; Invar; adv] (to call on s.o.) while passing by his home, having seen by his lighted window(s) that he is home (occas. may refer to one's calling on s.o. at his office after hours etc): X зашёл к Y-у на огонёк ≃ **X saw Y's light(s) ⟨the light in Y's window⟩ and dropped in ⟨decided to drop in etc⟩.**

...[Михаил] хлопнул калиткой, топнул сапогами по мосткам... и первый раз не ползком, не на четвереньках, а как мужчина, с осевшей спиной поднялся на крыльцо... Он сказал: «Шёл мимо — давай, думаю, на огонёк...» (Абрамов 1). He [Mikhail] banged the gate, stamped his boots on the plank footpath...and for the first time went up to the porch, not crawling on all fours, but standing up straight like a man....He said, "I was just passing by and I saw the light in the window, so..." (1a). ♦ Вошёл Григорий Мелехов в наглухо застёгнутой шинели, бурый от мороза, с осевшей на бровях и усах изморозью. «Я на огонёк» (Шолохов 4). The man who entered was Grigory Melekhov, his greatcoat buttoned to the throat, his face ruddy from the cold, his brows and moustache rimed with frost. "I saw the light and decided to drop in" (4a).

О-64 • (ИДТИ́/ПОЙТИ́) В ОГО́НЬ И В ВО́ДУ за кого-что, за кем coll [VP or PrepP (used as predic); subj: human or collect; often used with готов; fixed WO] to perform selfless acts without hesitation, despite personal risk or danger (out of devotion to some person, cause etc): X готов за Y-а в огонь и в воду ≃ **X would go through fire and water for Y; X would go through hell and ⟨or⟩ high water for Y; X would go to hell and back for Y.**

...За каких-нибудь двадцать-тридцать минут Подрезов так накалил молодняк, что тот готов был ради него и в огонь, и в воду (Абрамов 1). ...Within twenty or thirty minutes, Podrezov had the young men so revved up that they were ready to go through fire and water for him (1a). ♦ «Мы с ним... вместе из окружения выходили. Да где там выходили, он меня на себе выволок. Я за ним... куда угодно, в огонь и в воду» (Максимов 1). "...We escaped from encirclement together. What am I saying, escaped, he carried me out on his back. I'd follow him...wherever you like, through hell or high water" (1a).

О-65 • ПРОЙТИ́ (СКВОЗЬ ⟨ЧЕРЕЗ, И⟩) ОГО́НЬ И ВО́ДУ ⟨ОГНИ́ И ВО́ДЫ⟩ (И МЕ́ДНЫЕ ТРУ́БЫ) coll [VP; subj: human; usu. past; the verb may take the final position, otherwise fixed WO] (of a person who, in the course of a difficult or complex life, has acquired vast life experience; occas. of a person with a tarnished reputation, undiscriminating sexual experiences etc) to experience, endure much: X прошёл огонь и воду (и медные трубы) ≃ **X has been ⟨gone⟩ through fire and water; X has survived fire and water; X has been through the mill ⟨through it all, through hell, through the wringer⟩; X has been there and back;** [in limited contexts] **there's nothing X doesn't know.**

Осталась она [при немцах] потому, что как пострадавшая от Советской власти ждала себе от немцев много хорошего и, пройдя огни и воды и медные трубы... решила, что и здесь не пропадёт (Рыбаков 1). She had stayed behind because she thought that, as someone who had suffered under Soviet rule, she could do well for herself with the Germans, and as she had already survived fire and water...she thought she would survive this, too (1a). ♦ Её [Одинцову] не любили в губернии... рассказывали про неё всевозможные небылицы, уверяли, что она помогала отцу в его шулерских проделках... «Прошла через огонь и воду», — говорили о ней (Тургенев 2). She [Madame Odintsov] was not popular in the province:...all sorts of impossible stories were invented about her: it was asserted that she had helped her father in his gambling escapades...."There's nothing she doesn't know," they said of her... (2c).

О-66 • С ОГОНЬКО́М coll [PrepP; Invar; adv] (to do sth.) with enthusiasm, animation: **with zest ⟨verve⟩.**

...А как работали, разве так, как теперь? С огоньком работали, с душой (Суслов 1). And how they worked, not at all like now! They worked with zest, with spirit (1a).

О-67 • ОГОРО́Д ГОРОДИ́ТЬ coll [VP; subj: human; usu. infin with для чего, стоит ли, не стоит, незачем etc; fixed WO] to undertake some bothersome and unnecessary matter: не надо было огород городить ≃ **I ⟨we etc⟩ shouldn't have started the whole thing ⟨bothered, made a fuss etc⟩ (in the first place);** ‖ зачем огород городить? ≃ **why go to the trouble ⟨make a fuss etc⟩?**

О-68 • В ОГОРО́ДЕ БУЗИНА́, А В КИ́ЕВЕ ДЯ́ДЬКА [saying] there is no logical connection between the various things s.o. is saying: ≃ **you're mixing apples and oranges.**

О-69 • КАК ОГУ́РЧИК (свежий) highly coll [как + NP; nom only; adv or subj-compl with быть∅ (subj: human)] completely healthy-looking: **(look ⟨be⟩) the picture of health; (be ⟨look⟩) fit as a fiddle.**

[author's usage] [Бургомистр:] Вспомните, кем я был при проклятом драконе? Больным, сумасшедшим. А теперь? Здоров как огурчик (Шварц 2). [B.:] Remember what I was like in the days of the accursed Dragon? I was sick, I was insane. But now I'm as fit as a fiddle (2b).

О-70 • ПО ОДЁЖКЕ ⟨ПО ПЛА́ТЬЮ⟩ ВСТРЕЧА́ЮТ, ПО УМУ́ ПРОВОЖА́ЮТ [saying; often only the first half of the saying is used] the first thing one notices when meeting s.o. is his outer appearance, but once one gets to know him it is his intelligence, personality etc that matters: ≃ **clothes count only for first impressions; looks ⟨appearances⟩ matter only upon first meeting; you are judged by appearances at first but by your mind later on;** [when only the first half is used] **people judge you by appearances; people treat you according to your clothes.**

[Виктория:] По одёжке, значит, встречаете? [Калошин:] А ты думала? На этой работе глаз — первое дело... [Виктория:] А что — одёжка? Есть большие люди, а одеваются скромно... (Вампилов 1). [V.:] You mean you treat all guests according to their clothes? [K.:] What do you think? In this job you don't get far without sharp eyes.... [V.:] What do clothes tell you? Plenty of important people dress modestly... (1a).

О-71 • ПО ОДЁЖКЕ ПРОТЯ́ГИВАЙ НО́ЖКИ [saying] live according to your means, in keeping with your income: ≃ **cut your coat according to your cloth; cut your coat to fit your cloth; put your hand no further than your sleeve will reach.**

«Где же я денег возьму? Ты знаешь, я в законный брак вступаю: две семьи содержать не могу, а вы с барином-то по одёжке протягивайте ножки» (Гончаров 1). "Where am I to get the money from? You know I am going to be married. I can't provide for two families, and you and your gentleman had better cut your coat according to your cloth" (1a). "Where do you think I can get the money? You know I'm getting married: I can't keep two families, so you and your fine gentleman must cut your coat to fit your cloth" (1b).

O-72 • (все) КАК ОДИ́Н ⟨ОДНА́⟩; КАК ОДИ́Н ЧЕЛОВЕ́К
[как + NP; these forms only; modif or adv; fixed WO] (of a group or crowd of people) absolutely everyone, excluding no one: **one and all; all to a man; all, without exception; every (last) one of us ⟨you, them⟩; (right) down to the last man;** [in refer. to everyone's voicing some common opinion, supporting s.o. or sth. etc in a unified manner] **as one man.**

…Все как один остались скорбно сидеть в своём классе, не поднимаясь в кабинет физики… (Битов 2). …One and all were still sitting mournfully in the classroom, not going up to the physics lab (2a). ♦ Женщины, стоявшие со мной в очереди, в разговоры старались не ввязываться. Все как одна утверждали, что их мужей взяли по ошибке и скоро выпустят… (Мандельштам 1). The women who stood in line with me tried not to get drawn into conversation. They all, without exception, said that their husbands had been arrested by mistake and would soon be released (1a). ♦ «И японцы, с которыми ты бражничаешь, все как один тоже разведчики, и крупные…» (Рыбаков 2). "And those Japanese you had a good time with, spies every last one of them, and big ones, too" (2a). ♦ «…Ночью по приказу командарма вся наша оборона, как один человек, ушла в порт грузиться на корабль» (Гроссман 2). "…That night the army commander had us all embark on board ship, right down to the last man" (2a). ♦ Все слушатели, как один, сказали, что роман мой напечатан быть не может по той причине, что его не пропустит цензура (Булгаков 12). They all said as one man that my novel was unprintable because it would never be passed by the censorship (12a).

O-73 • ОДИ́Н ЗА ВСЕХ, ВСЕ ЗА ОДНОГО́; ВСЕ ЗА ОДНОГО́, ОДИ́Н ЗА ВСЕХ
[saying] each person (within a certain group) supports, defends, and feels bound by friendship to the others: ≃ **all for one and one for all.**

«У них все за одного, один за всех. Знаешь, что у них на выпускном жетоне будет написано: „Счастье – в жизни, а жизнь – в работе"» (Каверин 1). "They're all for one and one for all. You know, the motto on their leaving certificates is: 'Happiness comes from life, and life from work'" (1a).

O-74 • ОДИ́Н ЗА ДРУГИ́М
[NP; fixed WO] each following the one in front of him or it: **one after another ⟨the other⟩; one by one.**

Опять шли гуськом тени одна за другой, всё шли, всё шли… (Салтыков-Щедрин 1). Again the shadows walked one after another in single file, kept walking, kept walking… (1a).

O-75 • ОДИ́Н К ОДНОМУ́[1] ⟨В ОДНОГО́, В ОДИ́Н⟩; ОДНА́ К ОДНО́Й ⟨В ОДНУ́⟩; ОДНО́ К ОДНОМУ́ ⟨В ОДНО́⟩
all coll, usu. approv [NP; these forms only; subjcompl with быть₀ (subj: human, animal, or concr, pl) or detached modif; fixed WO] (usu. in refer. to the physical features of some people, animals, or things) all are exceptional, or (when a particular quality is specified) all possess the positive quality in question to a great degree: **one better than the other ⟨the next⟩; first-class ⟨topnotch⟩, every one of them; all equally good; you won't find a better bunch ⟨group etc⟩; each ⟨one⟩ more [AdjP] than the next.**

[Нина:] А ты? Интересно работаешь? [Лёва:] Сверх! Чудом попал в самый интересный отдел… Там такие волшебные условия. И атмосфера… какая атмосфера!.. А главное – люди, Нина, какие у нас люди – один к одному! (Розов 4). [N.:] But what about you? Is your work interesting? [L.:] I should say!

By a miracle I managed to get into the most interesting department.…The conditions are so marvellous. And the atmosphere – what an atmosphere!…But the main thing, Nina, is the people there – first-class, every one of them (4a). ♦ Из какого мира явились эти шестеро, один к одному, здоровые и ладные парни? (Аксёнов 7). What world were they from, these six strapping lads, each more hale and hearty than the next? (7a).

O-76 • ОДИ́Н К ОДНОМУ́[2] (построить, скопировать, сделать и т. п. что) coll
[NP; Invar; adv; fixed WO] (to copy sth., build or make a replica of sth. etc) such that the copy or replica turns out to look precisely the same as the original: **(make ⟨build etc⟩) an exact replica ⟨carbon copy⟩ (of sth.); (make ⟨build etc⟩ sth.) exactly like (sth. else); (make things so that they come out) exactly alike.**

Сверх одного, по-настоящему стреляющего пистолета, были у нас две деревянные модели, которые я сделал с отцовского пистолета «ТТ» один к одному, миллиметр к миллиметру, и выкрасил в чёрную блестящую краску (Лимонов 1). In addition to one pistol that really fired, we had two wooden models that I had fashioned after my father's TT pistol, exactly like it, millimeter for millimeter, and painted a shiny black (1a).

O-77 • ОДИ́Н НА ОДИ́Н (с кем-чем)
[NP; Invar; fixed WO]
1. остаться (с кем-чем), поговорить (с кем) ~ и т. п. [subjcompl with copula (subj: human) or adv] (to remain with s.o. or sth., have a talk with s.o. etc) in private, without others: **alone (with s.o. ⟨sth.⟩); one on one.**

Я снова останусь один на один со своим героем… (Аржак 2). Again I'll remain alone with my hero… (2a).

2. биться, сражаться и т. п. ~ [adv] (to engage in combat, fight etc) without aid or support from others, without allies: **alone against s.o. ⟨sth.⟩; single-handed; all by o.s.;** [usu. when only two people are involved] **one on one; in single combat.**

Дедушка был один на один с десятком рассвирепевших ломовых извозчиков, которые готовы были своими ломами сделать из него котлету (Рыбаков 1). Grandfather was alone against ten infuriated wagon-drivers who intended to use their crowbars to turn him into mincemeat (1a). ♦ «…Если б мы оставили Францию одну – уже в этих бы днях её Германия разбила и повернулась бы на нас, – и нам пришлось бы один на один!» (Солженицын 1). "…If we had left France to fight alone the Germans would have smashed her by now and turned on us – and we would have had to face them single-handed!" (1a).

O-78 • ОДИ́Н-ОДИНЁХОНЕК ⟨-ОДИНЁШЕНЕК⟩; ОДНА́-ОДИНЁХОНЬКА ⟨-ОДИНЁШЕНЬКА⟩
all coll [AdjP; usu. nom; usu. subj-compl with copula (subj: human) or detached modif] absolutely and completely alone: **all alone; all by one's lonesome; all by o.s.**

Бывало, он меня не замечает, а я стою у двери и думаю: «Бедный, бедный старик! Нас много, мы играем, нам весело, а он – один-одинёшенек…» (Толстой 2). Sometimes he did not notice me and I would stand at the door and think. Poor, poor old man! There are lots of us, we can play and it's fun for us, but he – he's all alone… (2b). ♦ И этак проводил время, один-одинёшенек в целом мире, молодой… человек, сидень-сиднем, в халате и без галстука (Гоголь 3). And thus, all by his lonesome in the whole world, did a young man…pass his time, sitting like a bump on a log, a sloven in a dressing-gown and without a cravat (3b).

O-79 • В ОДИНО́ЧКУ
[PrepP; Invar; adv] **1.** separately, not with others, apart from others: **alone; by itself ⟨himself etc⟩; singly;** [in limited contexts; of people only] **in solitude.**

Выйдя из лесу, они увидели стоявший в одиночку дом. Coming out of the woods, they caught sight of a house standing by itself. ♦ Одно время начальник лагеря ещё такой приказ издал: никаким заключённым в одиночку по зоне не ходить

(Солженицын 7). At one time the camp commandant had given orders that zeks were not to walk about the camp singly (7c). ♦ Не любят русские люди мелочничать по углам, в одиночку, кустарным способом... Мы употребляем вино для усиления жизни и душевного разогрева, мы только жить начинаем, когда выпьем... (Терц 6). We Russians are not fond of tippling amateurishly, in solitude, each in his corner....What we drink for is to fire our souls and to feel we are alive. It's when we drink that we come to life... (6a).

2. by one's own efforts, without the participation of or help from others: **(all) alone; on one's own; by o.s.; single-handed(ly);** [in limited contexts] **go it alone; make one's own way ⟨do one's own thing⟩** etc⟩.

Ему не нужна поддержка начальства, ему не нужна любовь друзей, душевная общность с женой, он умеет воевать в одиночку (Гроссман 2). No, he didn't need the authorities' support, his friends' affection or his wife's understanding; he could fight on alone (2a). ♦ «Долго же вы от нас скрывались... И что же, так вот всё и действовали в одиночку?»... «Да, в одиночку» (Войнович 4). "You've been hiding from us a long time....Now tell us, were you acting alone all the time?"..."That's right, all alone" (4a). ♦ За обедом Марья Ивановна сказала Жене: «Евгения Николаевна, если разрешите, я могу пойти вместе с вами... Вдвоём как-то легче». Женя смутилась, ответила: «Нет, нет, спасибо большое, уж эти дела надо делать в одиночку» (Гроссман 2). While they were eating, Marya Ivanovna said to Yevgenia: "Let me go with you, Yevgenia Nikolaevna....It's always easier with someone else." Yevgenia looked very embarrassed. "No, no," she said, "but thank you very much. There are things one has to do on one's own..." (2a). ♦ По молодости он спешил двумя руками сворачивать горы в одиночку... (Солженицын 1). In his youth he had been in a hurry to move mountains single-handed (1a). ♦ ...Я не любил строй и в столовую или по утрам в уборную пробираться предпочитал в одиночку. Чаще всего эта операция мне удавалась, но... и я время от времени попадался (Войнович 5). ...I had no love for formation and preferred to make my own way to the mess hall or the latrine in the morning. Usually I was successful, but...I did get caught every once in a while (5a).

O-80 • ОДНО́ К ОДНОМУ́ coll [NP; Invar; indep. clause or subj-compl with бытьø (subj: всё), pres only; fixed WO] (this is a case in which) one trouble is coming right after another: **(it's) one thing after another; (it's) one thing ⟨trouble⟩ on top of another;** [in limited contexts] **it never rains but it pours; troubles never come singly.**

Тали надела на себя крепдешиновое платье... и, даже не высушив головы, кинулась к Маше. «Куда ты простоволосая, там чужие!» – крикнула тётя Катя... Тут тётя Катя обернулась к костру и увидела, что сброшенная слишком близко от огня рабочая одежда её дочки уже тихо тлеет и дымится... «Одно к одному»... (Искандер 3). Tali put on a crepe de chine dress...and dashed for Masha's without even drying her hair. "Where are you going with your hair down, there are other people there!" Aunt Katya shouted....Now Aunt Katya turned back to the fire and saw that her daughter's work clothes, thrown off too close to the fire, were quietly smoldering and smoking...."One thing after another"... (3a). ♦ [Василиса:] Гошка! (Плачет.) [Егор:] Ну... [Василиса:] Я боюсь. [Егор:] За Марию? [Василиса:] И за неё, и... ох, как всё одно к одному!.. За тебя тоже боюсь (Салынский 1). [V.:] Yegor! (Bursts into tears.) [Y.:] What's the matter? [V.:] I'm afraid. [Y.:] For Maria? [V.:] For her too and—oh, troubles never come singly. I'm afraid for you too (1a).

O-81 • все ДО ОДНОГО́ ⟨ДО ОДНО́Й, ДО ЕДИ́НОГО, ДО ЕДИ́НОЙ⟩ coll [PrepP; these forms only; modif] (all) excepting no one: **every last ⟨single⟩ one (of); every last ⟨single⟩** [NP]; **everyone ⟨all⟩ without exception; each and every one (of); one ⟨each⟩ and all; (all) to a man; all down to the last;**

all (right) down to the last one; [usu. in contexts of killing, being killed etc] **(all) (down) to the last man.**

...Вдруг... был прислан новый начальник, человек военный, строгий, враг взяточников и всего, что зовётся неправдой. На другой же день пугнул он всех до одного... (Гоголь 3). ...Suddenly... a new chief executive was sent; a military man, stern, a foe to all bribetakers and of all that is called wrongdoing. The very next day he threw a scare into every last one of those under him... (3b). ♦ «Поступаете опрометчиво, молодые люди. Через два дня здесь будет генерал Крымов. А мы вас всех запомним, до единого...» (Трифонов 6). "You're being hasty, young men. General Krymov will be here in two days, and we'll remember you all, every single one of you" (6a). ♦ «...Вы же знаете, что куры все издохли до единой». – «Ну так что из этого?» – завопил Персиков (Булгаков 10). "You know that every last chicken has died off?" "Well, what about it?" shrieked Persikov (10b). ♦ Я думаю даже, что и все дамы, все до единой, с таким нетерпением жаждавшие оправдания интересного подсудимого, были в то же время совершенно уверены в полной его виновности (Достоевский 2). I even think that the ladies, one and all, who yearned with such impatience for the acquittal of an interesting defendant, were at the same time fully convinced of his complete guilt (2a). ♦ Вообще во всей истории Глупова поражает один факт: сегодня расточат глуповцев и уничтожат их всех до единого, а завтра, смотришь, опять появятся глуповцы... (Салтыков-Щедрин 1). There is one striking fact about the whole history of Foolov: today the Foolovites would be dispersed and destroyed, all to a man, and lo, tomorrow the Foolovites would reappear... (1a). ♦ Я добросовестно прочитала вслух все переводы до одного... (Чуковская 2). I conscientiously read out all the translations down to the last... (1a). ♦ «Врёшь! Ты спала с ними [иностранцами]. Последний раз со шведом. Мы его знаем и всех, кто был до него, всех до единого» (Рыбаков 2). "That's a lie. You slept with them [foreigners]. The last time it was with the Swede. We know about him, and we know about all the others before him, right down to the last one" (2a).

O-82 • ПО ОДНОМУ́ [PrepP; Invar; adv] singly, not all together, following in succession: **one by one; one at a time;** [in limited contexts] **in single file.**

...Крушения не прекращались. Тогда-то и была создана комиссия... Уполномоченный особого отдела... вызывал их [членов комиссии] по одному и чуть не плакал, упрашивая их поторопиться. «Бросьте вы канитель разводить! Ясное дело – враг орудует» (Максимов 3). ...The crashes went on. At this point a commission of inquiry was set up....The representative of the security branch...called them [the members of the commission] in one by one and almost wept as he begged them to come to a verdict. "Stop dragging it out! It's clear enough—the enemy is at work" (3a). ♦ Альбом держат в кабинете Куненко, впускают туда по одному членов правления и запирают снаружи каждого на десять минут (Аксёнов 12). The album was kept in Kunenko's office, and they let in one member of the Union board at a time for ten minutes and locked the door from the outside (12a).

O-83 • НА СМЕ́РТНОМ ОДРЕ́ elev; **НА ОДРЕ́ СМЕ́РТИ** obs [PrepP; these forms only; adv, subj-compl with бытьø (subj: human), or obj-compl with найти, застать кого (obj: human); fixed WO] when s.o. is dying, in a state close to death: **on one's ⟨s.o.'s⟩ deathbed.**

Поздно, поздно переучивать человека на смертном одре (Абрамов 1). It's too late to re-educate a man, when he's on his deathbed (1a).

O-84 • БО́ЖИЙ ОДУВА́НЧИК coll, iron [NP; fixed WO] a very old, frail person (usu. said condescendingly, although not unkindly; more often of a woman): **(nice) little old lady ⟨man⟩; old granny ⟨grandpa⟩.**

O-85 • СВЕРХ ⟨ПРОТИВ⟩ (ВСЯ́КОГО) ОЖИДА́НИЯ ⟨(ВСЯ́КИХ) ОЖИДА́НИЙ⟩; ВОПРЕКИ́ (ВСЯ-

КОМУ) ОЖИДА́НИЮ ⟨(ВСЯ́КИМ) ОЖИДА́-НИЯМ⟩ [PrepP; these forms only; sent adv (parenth)] in spite of or exceeding what is expected: **contrary to (all) expectation(s); against all (one's) expectations.**

Митька лоснился сдерживаемой радостью. Торжество сквозило в каждом его движении. Сотник против ожидания показался Григорию нимало не сконфуженным... (Шолохов 2). Mitka was glistening with restrained joy. Triumph surged through every movement. Contrary to expectations, the lieutenant seemed not in the least put out... (2a). ♦ [Шмага:] Вчера у меня, сверх всякого ожидания, деньги завелись... (Островский 3). [context transl] [Sh.:] Yesterday, to my utter astonishment, I came into some money... (3a).

O-86 • **О́Й ЛИ?** *highly coll* [Interj; Invar] used in reaction to a statement to show that one doubts, disbelieves, is skeptical of, or does not entirely agree with it (in some cases surprise is expressed as well): **(oh,) really ⟨yeah⟩?; is that so?; you don't say (so)!; I'm not so sure (about that);** [in limited contexts] **is it ⟨do you, have they etc⟩?**

Нам так нужно, и мы в этом не виноваты. Не виноваты? Ой ли? (Аксёнов 6). That is what we need, and it is not our fault. Not our fault? Really? (6a). ♦ «...При большевиках кто будет у власти? Ты будешь, если выберут...» — «А сверху кто?» — «Опять же кого выберут. Выберут тебя — и ты будешь сверху». — «Ой ли? А не брешешь ты, Митрич?» (Шолохов 3). "...Under the Bolsheviks, who will get the power? You will, if you're elected..." "But who'll be at the top?" "Again it depends on who's elected. If they elect you, you'll be at the top." "Oh, yeah? Sure you're not kidding, 'Mit-rich?" (3a). ♦ [Вера:] В таком случае вы можете ему сказать... что я готова за него замуж выйти. [Шпигельский *(с радостным изумлением)*:] Ой ли? (Тургенев 1). [V.:] Then, you can tell him...that I am willing to marry him. [Sh. *(with joyful amazement)*:] You don't say so! (1a). ♦ [Мелания:] Притворяется он сумасшедшим. Притворяется... [Ксения:] Ой ли? (Горький 2). [M.:] He's pretending to be mad. Just pretending.... [K.:] I'm not so sure (2a). ♦ «Степанов [ребёнок]?» — «Твой». — «Ой ли?» (Шолохов 2). "Is it Stepan's [child]?" "It's yours." "Is it?" (2a).

O-87 • **НЕДРЕМА́ННОЕ О́КО** *iron* [NP; sing only] a vigilant observation (formerly often used in relation to political police, it has come to refer to censors, the KGB etc): **watchful ⟨vigilant⟩ eye; unslumbering ⟨unblinking⟩ eye.**

...[Посреди толпы] недреманным оком бодрствовал неустрашимый штаб-офицер (Салтыков-Щедрин 1). ...[Among the crowd] the intrepid staff-officer was keeping vigil with watchful eye (1a). ♦ [Портупея:] Ты, Марья, дурака не валяй! Ваши дела нам хорошо известны... Домком [домовой комитет] — око недреманное (Булгаков 7). [P.:] Don't play the fool, Manya! We know all about your goings on....The House Committee is an unslumbering eye (7a). ♦ «...Театр ещё хуже, чем литература. Там хоть видимость уединения, автономности, своего укромного уголка. А тут всё на виду, всё под недреманным оком, так сказать, любой спектакль может стать последним» (Максимов 2). "...The theater's even worse than the writing trade. As a writer you have at least the appearance of seclusion, a sense of autonomy, your own modest little niche. But in theater everything is on display, everything happens in front of an unblinking eye, so to speak, and every show may be the last" (2a).

O-88 • **О́КО ЗА О́КО (, ЗУБ ЗА ЗУБ)** *lit* [usu. indep. sent; fixed WO] an insult, injury is avenged in the same way, a punishment is as cruel as the crime: **an eye for an eye (and a tooth for a tooth).**

«Неужели, Юра, трудно понять, что если всегда „око за око", то кровь никогда не кончится» (Максимов 3). "Surely it isn't so hard to understand, Yura, that if it's always 'an eye for an eye' there'll never be an end to bloodshed" (3a).

< From the Bible (Ex. 21:24 et al.).

O-89 • **(ХОТЬ) ВИ́ДИТ О́КО, ДА ЗУБ НЕЙМЁТ** [indep. sent; fixed WO] the thing one strongly desires is or seems to be near, yet is not attainable: **so near and yet so far.**

< From Ivan Krylov's fable "Fox and the Grapes" («Лисица и виноград»), 1808.

O-90 • **О́ЛУХ ЦАРЯ́ НЕБЕ́СНОГО** *highly coll, derog, occas. humor* [NP; fixed WO] a very stupid, dull-witted person: **birdbrain; blockhead; half-wit; numskull.**

O-91 • **ТИ́ХИЙ О́МУТ** [NP; sing only; fixed WO] a quiet, secretive person who has the capacity for deep thoughts, emotional experiences, unexpected actions etc: **still waters (run deep).**

< From the saying «В тихом омуте черти водятся». See O-92.

O-92 • **В ТИ́ХОМ О́МУТЕ ЧЕ́РТИ ВО́ДЯТСЯ** [saying] a quiet, secretive person is capable of deeds that might seem unexpected of him: ≃ **still waters run deep.**

«Одинцова очень мила — бесспорно, но она так холодно и строго себя держит, что...» — «В тихом омуте... ты знаешь!» — подхватил Базаров (Тургенев 2). "Madame Odintsov is very charming—there is no doubt about that—but so cold and reserved that..." "Still waters...you know," put in Bazarov (2c). ♦ [author's usage] «Какой-то у ей [*ungrammat* = у неё, у Анфисы Петровны] в войну хахаль завёлся. Тут, говорят, был. Из фронтовиков... Родного муженька в отставку, а этого, значит, как его, ждёт...» — «Ну и ну!..» — «Смотри-ко, что в тихом-то омуте водится» (Абрамов 1). [context transl] "She [Anfisa Petrovna] got herself some lover-boy during the war. They say he lived here. One of the front-liners....She's given her better half the boot and is waiting for the other guy—what's his name." "Well, well, well!..." "You can never tell what's brewing in still waters" (1a).

O-93 • **СО ВСЕ́МИ ОНЁРАМИ** *obs* [PrepP; Invar; postmodif or subj-compl with бытьø (subj: abstr or concr); fixed WO] having, possessing, displaying etc every possible desirable feature (characteristic, aspect etc): **with all the trimmings; with everything one could possibly want; with the works.**

< «Онёр» (from the French *honneur*) was a high trump card in some card games.

O-94 • **ИЗ ДРУГО́Й ⟨НЕ ИЗ ТОЙ⟩ О́ПЕРЫ** *coll* [PrepP; these forms only; subj-compl with бытьø (subj: usu. это); fixed WO] sth. is not related to the matter at hand: это из другой оперы ≃ **that's another ⟨a different⟩ story; that's a different matter ⟨thing⟩.**

«А та девушка, с которой вы... которая вас... которую я...» — пробормотал Толя. «Это... совсем из другой оперы», — суховато ответил Гурченко... (Аксёнов 6). "And that girl, who you...who you...whom I..." mumbled Tolya. "That...is quite another story," Gurchenko answered curtly... (6a).

O-95 • **НЕ ПОДДАВА́ТЬСЯ ОПИСА́НИЮ** [VP; subj: abstr] to be so strong, exceptional, far beyond the limits of the ordinary that it cannot be described: X не поддаётся описанию ≃ **X beggars ⟨defies⟩ description; X is beyond description; words cannot describe ⟨express⟩ X.**

Действие смертей, и в особенности Суринамской жабы, на Персикова не поддаётся описанию (Булгаков 10). The effect of the deaths, especially that of the Surinam toad, upon Persikov defies description (10a). The effect of the deaths, especially that of the Surinam toad, on Persikov is beyond description (10b). ♦ Горе и ужас мадам Беломут не поддаются описанию (Булгаков 9). Words cannot describe the pain and distress which this caused Madame Belomut... (9b).

O-96 • ГО́РЬКИЙ О́ПЫТ; often наученный, прийти *к чему* ГО́РЬКИМ О́ПЫТОМ; убедиться НА (СВОЁМ) ГО́РЬКОМ О́ПЫТЕ [NP, sing only, or PrepP (adv); fixed WO] (through) difficult experiences: **(learn sth. by ⟨become wise from⟩) (one's) bitter experience; (find sth. out) the hard way; (learn sth. in) the school of hard knocks.**

«Вы меня понимаете?» — «Отлично понимаю, — серьёзно ответил Стравинский и, коснувшись колена поэта, добавил: — не волнуйтесь и продолжайте». — «Продолжаю, — сказал Иван, стараясь попасть в тон Стравинскому и зная уже по горькому опыту, что лишь спокойствие поможет ему... (Булгаков 9). "Do you understand me?" "I understand very well," Stravinsky answered seriously and, touching the poet's knee, he added: "Don't get upset. Continue please." "I will continue," said Ivan, trying to strike the same tone and knowing from bitter experience that only a calm approach could help him (9a).

O-97 • ОПЯ́ТЬ ДВА́ДЦАТЬ ПЯТЬ! *coll* [Interj; Invar; fixed WO] (in refer. to sth. tiresome, constantly repeated) again the same thing: **here we go again!; there you go again!; back to square one!; not again!; the same (old) thing ⟨question etc⟩ over and over (again)!**

«Я бы тебя выпорол, да вот дядя Илья не хочет. А за это ты нам с дядей Ильёй должна принести чего-нибудь закусить. Поняла?» — «Поняла». — «Ни холеры ты не поняла». — «Я мамке скажу, она даст». — «Опять двадцать пять. Опять она мамке скажет. Да ты без мамки-то не можешь, что ли?» (Распутин 3). "I'd give you a good spanking, but Uncle Ilia doesn't want me to. So in return you can bring me and Uncle Ilia something to eat. Got that?" "Yes." "Like hell you have." "I'll tell Mummy, and she'll give me something." "Here we go again! Telling Mummy again. Can't you do it without telling Mummy?" (3a). ♦ «Нет, — снова заупрямился старший, — и Сандро и кости отдавать вам будет многовато». — «Опять двадцать пять! — хлопнул милиционер себя по колену. — Мы же договорились?» (Искандер 3). "No," the elder relative said with renewed stubbornness. "That's too much, to let you have both Sandro and the bones." "Back to square one!" The policeman clapped his knee. "Did we make an agreement?" (3a).

O-98 • РАЗДЕ́ЛЫВАТЬ/РАЗДЕ́ЛАТЬ ⟨ОТДЕ́ЛЫВАТЬ/ОТДЕ́ЛАТЬ⟩ ПОД ОРЕ́Х *coll* [VP; subj: human; usu. pfv] **1.** ~ *кого* to scold s.o. severely, criticize s.o. mercilessly: X разделал Y-а под орех ≃ **X gave it to Y hot ⟨but good⟩; X gave Y a going-over ⟨a good dressing-down⟩; X cut ⟨picked⟩ Y to pieces; X let Y have it (with both barrels).**

Дело разбиралось в клубе, на собрании городской комсомольской ячейки. Я отлично помню Лёву на трибуне — разделал несчастного Зяму под орех (Рыбаков 1). The case was dealt with at the club at a meeting of the town Komsomol cell. I can remember Lyova on the platform perfectly, as he gave the wretched Zyama a going-over... (1a).

2. ~ *кого-что* [obj: usu. pl or collect] to defeat (the enemy, an athletic team, a competitor etc) overwhelmingly: X-ы разделали Y-ов под орех ≃ **Xs crushed ⟨routed, creamed, licked⟩ Ys; Xs made mincemeat out of Ys; Xs wiped ⟨mopped⟩ (up) the floor with Ys.**

3. ~ *что* to do sth. thoroughly, well: X разделал Y под орех ≃ **X did a splendid ⟨fine, crackerjack⟩ job (with ⟨on⟩ Y).**

O-99 • НА ОРЕ́ХИ достанется, попадёт, будет *кому (от кого)*, задать *кому coll*; НА КАЛАЧИ́ *obs* [PrepP; these forms only; adv] (s.o. will be scolded, punished, or to scold, punish s.o.) severely (occas. used in refer. to driving an opponent hard or being driven hard in a military conflict, athletic competition etc): X-у достанется на орехи (от Y-а) ⟨Y задаст X-у на орехи⟩ ≃ **X will (really) get it; X will be in for it; X will catch**

hell (for sth.); X will take ⟨get⟩ his lumps; Y will make it hot for X; Y will give X what for ⟨a going-over, a good dressing-down⟩; Y will let X have it (with both barrels).

«Я тоже шёпотом: „Любовник, что ли, скребётся?" — „Какой любовник? Реваз, кажется, раньше времени из поездки вернулся. Будет теперь мне на орехи — замучил старик проверками"» (Чернёнок 2). "I whisper back, 'Is that your lover scratching at the door?' 'What lover? I think Revaz is back from his trip earlier than planned. I'll really get it now — the old man is exhausting me with his suspicions'" (2a). ♦ [Лебедев:] Только смотри и виду не подавай, что у меня занял [деньги], храни тебя бог! А то достанется мне на орехи от кружовенного варенья! (Чехов 4). [L.:] Only mind you don't let on that you borrowed it [the money] from me — God help you — or Madame Gooseberry-Jam will make it hot for me! (4a). ♦ [Иванов:] Не знает об этом Дарвин, а то бы он задал вам на орехи! (Чехов 4). [I.:] It's a good job Darwin doesn't know, or he'd give you what for (4b).

O-100 • ЩЁЛКАТЬ КАК ОРЕ́ХИ ⟨ОРЕ́ШКИ⟩ *что coll* [VP; subj: human; obj: pl] to solve (problems, crossword puzzles etc) easily and quickly: X щёлкает Y-ы как орехи ≃ **X cracks ⟨solves⟩ Ys just like that; X breezes ⟨whizzes⟩ right through Ys; [in limited contexts] Ys are a snap ⟨as easy as pie⟩ for X.**

По части кроссвордов я с тобой соревноваться не могу, ты ведь щёлкаешь их как орехи. I can't compete with you when it comes to crossword puzzles — you whiz right through them.

O-101 • КРЕ́ПКИЙ ⟨ТВЁРДЫЙ⟩ ОРЕ́ШЕК ⟨ОРЕ́Х⟩ *coll* [NP; sing only] **1.** a person who is unbending, difficult to deal with, convince, subjugate etc: **tough cookie ⟨nut, customer⟩.**

«Напрасно вы упорствуете... Ответьте нам на один вопрос, и мы отпустим вас в камеру отдыхать. Так всё-таки кто же вас заслал в деревню Красное?» — «Кому надо, тот знает», — сказал Чонкин, отдуваясь. Словно кувалдой дали ему в подбородок... «Крепкий орешек», — потирая ушибленную руку, задумчиво сказал полковник (Войнович 4). "There's no point in resisting....Answer one question and we'll let you go rest in your cell. Who sent you to the village of Krasnoye?" "That's known by who's supposed to know," said Chonkin, panting. The next punch hit his chin like a sledgehammer....A tough nut," said the colonel pensively, rubbing his bruised hand (4a).

2. (of a matter, concept) difficult to understand, (of a problem) difficult to solve, (of an undertaking) difficult to accomplish, (of a fortress, city etc) difficult to capture etc: **tough ⟨hard⟩ nut to crack.**

O-102 • БРА́ТЬСЯ/ВЗЯ́ТЬСЯ ЗА ОРУ́ЖИЕ [VP; subj: human or collect] to begin an armed struggle: X-ы взялись за оружие ≃ **Xs took up arms; Xs went to war.**

Плохи времена, подумал дядя Сандро, если этот табачник взялся за оружие (Искандер 3). Times are bad, thought Uncle Sandro, if this tobacco grower has taken up arms (3a).

O-103 • НОСИ́ТЬ ОРУ́ЖИЕ [VP; subj: human; usu. infin after способный, уметь etc] (to be able, know how etc) to use arms and (be in adequate physical condition) to put that ability to use: X способен носить оружие ≃ **X is able to bear ⟨capable of bearing⟩ arms.**

На сходе постановили мобилизовать всех способных носить оружие, от шестнадцати до семидесяти лет (Шолохов 4). At a village meeting it was decided to mobilise everyone capable of bearing arms, from the age of sixteen to seventy (4a).

O-104 • СКЛА́ДЫВАТЬ/СЛОЖИ́ТЬ ОРУ́ЖИЕ [VP; subj: human or collect] **1.** Also: КЛАСТЬ/ПОЛОЖИ́ТЬ ⟨БРОСА́ТЬ/БРО́СИТЬ⟩ ОРУ́ЖИЕ to cease armed resistance, surrender: X-ы сложили оружие ≃ **Xs laid down (their) arms.**

«Русская армия под угрозой окружения с фланга и тыла сложила оружие» (Солженицын 1). "The Russian army laid down its arms under threat of encirclement from the flank and the rear" (1a).

2. to stop fighting for sth., abandon some course of action, admit defeat: X сложил оружие ≃ **X gave up (the fight ⟨the struggle etc⟩).**

Письмо с отказом, полученное Хлебцевичем на этот раз, было уже чрезвычайно резким и даже несколько угрожающим… Невероятно, но факт: Хлебцевич не сложил оружия и после этого (Владимиров 1). The letter rejecting his proposal which Khlebtsevich received this time was extremely abrupt and even threatening in character.…However unlikely it may seem in Soviet conditions, Khlebtsevich still did not give up even after this refusal (1a).

O-105 • БИТЬ *кого* ⟨**БОРО́ТЬСЯ** *с кем*⟩ **ЕГО́ ЖЕ** ⟨**ЕГО́ СО́БСТВЕННЫМ**⟩ **ОРУ́ЖИЕМ** [VP; subj: human; obj: usu. противника, врага etc] to achieve superiority over an opponent by employing his own arguments, methods etc: X бил Y-а его же оружием ≃ **X fought Y with Y's own weapon(s); X used Y's own weapons against him; X beat Y at Y's own game; X turned the tables on Y;** [in limited contexts] **fight fire with fire.**

…Пытаясь бороться с врагами их же оружием, то есть, в свою очередь, предавая их, так и не удавалось переиграть их, перещеголять в предательстве (Битов 2). …Although he tried to fight his enemies with their own weapon, that is, betrayed them in his turn, Lyova simply could not outplay them, outdo them in treachery (2a).

O-106 • БРЯЦА́ТЬ ⟨**ПОТРЯСА́ТЬ**⟩ **ОРУ́ЖИЕМ** *lit* [VP; subj: human or collect] to threaten with military action, attack; *by extension* to threaten with hostile actions: X-ы начали бряцать оружием ≃ **Xs began to brandish weapons ⟨to rattle their sabers⟩.** ◦ **БРЯЦА́НИЕ ОРУ́ЖИЕМ** [NP] ≃ **saber-rattling.**

«Это легко бряцать оружием, когда подписано перемирие» (Эренбург 1). "It's easy to brandish weapons when an armistice has been signed" (1a). ♦ Вы заметили некоторое изменение в тактике нашего уважаемого? Если он раньше действовал только с позиции силы, бряцал оружием и связями, то теперь через посредников передаёт своему сопернику положительные сведения о себе (Войнович 3). Have you noticed a certain change in our respected colleague's tactics? If before he acted only from a position of power, rattling his saber and his connections, he now sent his rival positive reports of himself through his intermediaries (3a).

O-107 • ПЕТЬ ⟨**ВОСКЛИЦА́ТЬ, ВОЗДАВА́ТЬ**⟩ **ОСА́ННУ** *кому-чему obs, lit* [VP; subj: human] to extol s.o.: X пел осанну Y-у ≃ **X sang hosannas to Y.**

O-108 • БУРИДА́НОВ ОСЁЛ *lit* [NP; sing only; fixed WO] an extremely indecisive person who is unable to choose between two equally desirable options: **Buridan's ass.**

< The idiom derives from the name of Jean *Buridan*, a French philosopher of the 14th cent., who wrote not about an ass but about a dog who, although dying of hunger, could not choose between two equidistant piles of food.

O-109 • КАК ОСЁЛ ⟨**МУЛ**⟩ **упрямый, упереться** *coll* [как + NP; nom only; adv] (to be) very stubborn, (to resist) strongly: **(as) stubborn as a mule; (balk) like a mule.**

Он был добр и человеколюбив, лечил бедных больных и крестьян даром, сам ходил в их конуры и избы и оставлял деньги на лекарство, но притом был и упрям как мул. Сбить его с его идеи, если она засела у него в голове, было невоз-

можно (Достоевский 2). He was kind and philanthropic, treated poor patients and peasants for nothing, visited their hovels and cottages himself, and left them money for medications, yet for all that he was stubborn as a mule. Once an idea had lodged itself in his head, it was impossible to shake it out of him (2a).

O-110 • ДАВА́ТЬ/ДАТЬ ОСЕ́ЧКУ *(в чём) coll* [VP; subj: human or abstr] (of a person) to make a blunder, do sth. foolish, (of a method, approach etc) to fail, go wrong: X дал осечку ≃ **person X goofed ⟨slipped up etc⟩; thing X went wrong ⟨fell flat, misfired etc⟩; (doing sth.) wasn't one of person X's better ⟨smarter⟩ moves ⟨ideas⟩; (doing sth.) wasn't a smart thing to do ⟨a smart move etc⟩; X missed the mark ⟨was wide of the mark etc⟩.**

Правда, в последние годы то ли под влиянием радиации, то ли ещё что, но негритянские гены, между нами говоря, стали не те. Осечки дают. Нет-нет да и появится смуглячок (Искандер 4). True, in recent years, whether under the influence of radiation, or whatever, Negro genes aren't what they used to be, just between us. They misfire. Every once in a while you get a little brown-skinned baby (4a). ♦ «Мне не надо было вкладывать деньги в этот кооператив». — «Да, тут ты дал осечку». "I shouldn't have invested money in that co-op." "Yeah, that wasn't one of your better moves."

O-111 • НАБИВА́ТЬ/НАБИ́ТЬ ОСКО́МИНУ *coll* [VP; usu. pfv] **1.** *(чем)* [subj: usu. human] to get an astringent sensation in one's mouth from sth. sour, tart (often unripe apples, berries etc): X набил оскомину (Y-ами) ≃ **X had a bitter taste in his mouth (from Ys); Ys left (X with) a bitter taste in X's mouth; Ys made X's mouth pucker; X set his teeth on edge (with Ys); Ys set ⟨put⟩ X's teeth on edge.**

«Они должны понять, что мы только можем проиграть, действуя наступательно…» — думал Кутузов. Он знал, что не надо срывать яблока, пока оно зелено. Оно само упадёт, когда будет зрело, а сорвёшь зелено, испортишь яблоко… и сам оскомину набьёшь (Толстой 7). "They must see," he [Kutuzov] thought, "that we can only lose by taking the offensive…" He knew the apple must not be picked while it is still green. It will fall of itself when ripe, but if you pick it unripe you spoil the apple…and set your teeth on edge (7a).

2. ~ *(кому)* [subj: usu. abstr] (of a statement, idea, procedure etc) to elicit an unfavorable reaction, cause s.o. to react negatively (by being or having been overused, often repeated, boring etc): X набил (Y-у) оскомину ≃ **X sets Y's teeth on edge; Y is ⟨has become⟩ sick and tired of X; Y is fed up with X;** ‖ набивший ⟨-ая, -ее⟩ оскомину анекдот ⟨фраза, клише и т. п.⟩ ≃ **hackneyed ⟨trite, tired old etc⟩ joke ⟨phrase etc⟩; cliché.**

«Парады, встречи, караулы — вся эта дворцовая служба набила мне оскомину» (Шолохов 2). "I am sick and tired of the whole business of service at court with its parades, receptions, changing of the guard and so on" (2a). ♦ Правда, среди набивших оскомину оборотов звучат и новые имена, новые… темы (Эткинд 1). It's true that among the tired old turns of phrase there are some new names and new…themes (1a).

O-112 • ВАЛАА́МОВА ОСЛИ́ЦА (ЗАГОВОРИ́ЛА) *lit* [NP (sing only) or VP_subj (usu. indep. clause)] a meek, quiet person who unexpectedly begins to protest sth. or express his opinion about sth.: **Balaam's ass (has begun to speak).**

«Ну, теперь тебе удовольствие будет, и именно на твою тему. Насмеёшься. У нас валаамова ослица заговорила, да как говорит-то, как говорит!» Валаамовою ослицей оказался лакей Смердяков (Достоевский 1). "Well, now you're going to have some fun, and precisely in your line. You'll laugh your head off. Balaam's ass, here, has started to talk, and what a talker, what a talker!" Balaam's ass turned out to be the lackey Smerdyakov (1a).

< From the Bible (Num. 22:27–28).

O-113 • **НА КАКО́М ОСНОВА́НИИ?** [PrepP; Invar; adv; fixed WO] why? with what justification?: **on what basis ⟨grounds⟩?; for what reason?; on account of what?**

«На каком основании я арестован?» (Семёнов 1). "…On what basis have I been arrested?" (1a). ♦ «На каком же основании вы были так щедры к господину Ракитину?» (Достоевский 2). "And on what grounds were you so generous to Mr. Rakitin?" (2a).

O-114 • **НА ОСНОВА́НИИ** *чего, каком;* **НА ОСНО́ВЕ** *чего, какой* [PrepP; these forms only; Prep; the resulting PrepP is adv] stemming, proceeding from sth., founded on sth.: **on the basis ⟨the strength⟩ of; on a [AdjP] basis; on the grounds of ⟨that…⟩; on [AdjP] grounds; based on.**

Генеральный план Платона Самсоновича… заключался в том, чтобы… на основании успехов козлотуризации нашего края окончательно утвердить общесоюзное название нового животного – козлотур… (Искандер 4). The overall plan outlined by Platon Samsonovich…was as follows:…on the basis of our successes in the goatibexation of Abkhazia, to establish *goatibex* as the All-Union name of the new animal once and for all… (4a). ♦ Фашизм пришёл к идее уничтожения целых слоёв населения, национальных и расовых объединений на основе того, что вероятность скрытого и явного противодействия в этих слоях и прослойках выше, чем в других группах или слоях (Гроссман 2). Fascism arrived at the idea of the liquidation of entire strata of the population, of entire nations and races, on the grounds that there was a greater probability of overt or covert opposition among these groupings than among others… (2a). ♦ Надо бы исписать десять листов для того, чтобы перечислить все те упрёки, которые делают ему [Александру I] историки на основании того знания блага человечества, которым пользу обладают (Толстой 7). It would take a dozen pages to enumerate all the reproaches leveled at him [Aleksandr I] by historians, based on their knowledge of what is good for humanity (7a).

O-115 • **ДО ОСНОВА́НИЯ** *разрушить что, истребить, потрясти кого-что и т. п.* [PrepP; Invar; adv] (to destroy some group of people, some phenomenon etc) completely, (to shock s.o.) profoundly etc: разрушить ⟨истребить⟩ ~ ≃ **totally ⟨utterly⟩ destroy ⟨ruin, annihilate⟩ s.o. ⟨sth.⟩; wipe out s.o. ⟨sth.⟩;** [in limited contexts] **raze ⟨level⟩ sth. (to the ground); destroy sth. to its ⟨the⟩ roots;** ‖ потрясти ~ ≃ **shake sth. to its foundations; shake s.o. badly.**

В обществе, в котором сильно развито религиозно-нравственное сознание, проповедник атеизма выступает как… враг мракобесия… Это – одно. И иное дело – общество, в котором до основания разрушено религиозно-нравственное сознание… (Зиновьев 2). In a society with a highly developed religious and moral conscience, the preacher of atheism can pass for…an enemy of obscurantism. That is one thing. Quite another is a society in which the religious and moral conscience has been totally destroyed… (2a). ♦ …Ошибка [Ивана] Грозного была не в том, что он казнил бояр, а в том, что мало казнил, не истребил четыре главных боярских рода до самого основания (Рыбаков 2). …Ivan's mistake was not that he punished them [the nobles], but that he didn't punish them enough, he did not destroy the four main noble clans right down to their roots (2a). ♦ Внутренняя борьба сотрясёт Россию до основания! (Солженицын 5). Internal struggles will shake Russia to its foundations (5a).

O-116 • **НЕ БЕЗ ОСНОВА́НИЯ** [PrepP; Invar; adv] not accidentally, having a rational cause: **not without (good) reason; with good reason.**

…[Хачик] всё заталкивал крупного мужчину поближе к мощному кактусу, а тот пугливо озирался, не без основания опасаясь напороться на него… (Искандер 5). …He [Khachik] kept jostling a big man closer to a mighty cactus, while the man looked back fearfully, afraid of running into it, and with good reason… (5a).

O-117 • **В ОСНОВНО́М** [PrepP; Invar; adv or sent adv (parenth)] **1.** (applicable) in more cases than not, (done) to a greater extent than not etc: **basically; mainly; in the main; for the most part; mostly; on the whole; by and large.**

«Товарищи прорабы, к празднику объект Самохина должен быть сдан. Если сдадим, годовой план по управлению будет в основном выполнен» (Войнович 5). "Comrade Supervisors, Samokhin's unit must be handed over by the holiday. If it is, the annual plan will be basically fulfilled" (5a). ♦ В жизни Лёвы Одоевцева, из тех самых Одоевцевых, не случалось особых потрясений – она, в основном, протекала (Битов 2). For Lyova Odoevtsev, of *the* Odoevtsevs, life had brought no special traumas; in the main, it had flowed along (2a). ♦ …В основном подписывались [под заявлением] охотно. Одни из чувства справедливости, другие из хорошего отношения к автору этих строк, третьи из ненависти к Турганову и Иванько (Войнович 3). …On the whole they signed [the petition] gladly. Some out of a sense of justice, others out of regard for the author, still others out of hatred for Turganov and Ivanko (3a).

2. predominantly: **mainly; mostly; primarily.**

[Гомыра:] А я с самого начала был против… [Репников:] Против чего? [Гомыра:] Против всего. В основном против женского персонала… (Вампилов 3). [G.:] Well, I was against it from the start…. [R.:] Against what? [B.:] Against everything. Mainly against female personnel… (3a). ♦ «…В институте я бываю очень редко, да и то прихожу в основном за стипендией» (Войнович 1). "…I'm rarely at the institute. I mostly go to pick up my scholarship funds" (1a).

O-118 • **ЗАКЛА́ДЫВАТЬ/ЗАЛОЖИ́ТЬ ОСНО́ВЫ ⟨ОСНО́ВУ, ФУНДА́МЕНТ⟩** *чего lit* [VP; subj: human or abstr] to set down the fundamental basis for, formulate the underlying principles of (a scientific discipline, artistic movement etc): X заложил основы Y-а ≃ **X laid the foundation ⟨the basis, the groundwork⟩ for Y; X paved the way for Y; thing X set the stage for Y.**

O-119 • **В ОСО́БЕННОСТИ** [PrepP; Invar; adv (used as restr marker) or sent adv] most of all: **in particular; particularly; especially; above all;** [after a negation] **certainly not.**

…Интересно отметить, что высшим женским свойством считалась тогда и продолжает считаться до сих пор степень лёгкости, с которой женщина обслуживает свой дом и особенно гостей. И давая оценку той или иной женщине или девушке, абхазцы вообще, а чегемцы в особенности, прежде всего ценят это качество (Искандер 5). …It is interesting to note that the highest feminine attribute was considered to be the degree of lightness with which a woman served her household and especially her guests. To this day, when appraising some woman or girl, Abkhazians in general and Chegemians in particular prize this quality above all (5a). ♦ Странная вещь сердце человеческое вообще, и женское в особенности! (Лермонтов 1). The human heart is a funny thing, particularly the heart of a woman (1c). ♦ В особенности тяжело было смотреть на город поздним вечером (Салтыков-Щедрин 1). The town was especially painful to see in the late evening (1a).

O-120 • **СЧАСТЛИ́ВО ОСТАВА́ТЬСЯ!** *coll* [formula phrase; Invar; fixed WO] used to wish those staying behind well when departing: **all the best; take care (of yourself);** [in limited contexts] **good luck (to you); lots of luck.**

…Подбежал весёлый солдат, прося огоньку в пехоту. «Огоньку горяченького в пехоту! Счастливо оставаться, землячки, благодарим за огонёк…» – говорил он, унося куда-то в темноту краснеющуюся головешку (Толстой 4). …A cheerful soldier ran up begging a little fire for the infantry. "A nice little hot torch for the infantry! Good luck to you, fellow countrymen. Thanks for the fire…" said he carrying away into the darkness a glowing stick (4b).

O-121 • **ОСТАВЛЯ́ТЬ/ОСТА́ВИТЬ ЗА СОБО́Й** [VP]
1. ~ *кого-что obsoles*. Also: **ОСТАВЛЯ́ТЬ/ОСТА́ВИТЬ ПОЗАДИ́ СЕБЯ́** *obsoles* [subj and obj: usu. human or collect, occas. a noun denoting the result of s.o.'s endeavors, creative efforts etc] to outdo, excel s.o. or sth.: X оставил за собой Y-a ≃ **X left Y far behind; X left Y in the dust; X surpassed ⟨outdistanced, outstripped⟩ Y.**

2. ~ *что* [subj: human] to retain sth. for o.s.: X оставил Y за собой ≃ **X kept Y (for himself); X reserved ⟨saved⟩ Y for himself; X set Y aside for himself.**

«…Скажите, что я, по обстоятельствам, не могу оставить квартиры за собой…» (Гончаров 1). "…Tell him that because of changed circumstances I cannot keep the flat…" (1a).

O-122 • *(кому)* **НИЧЕГО́ (ДРУГО́ГО) НЕ ОСТАЁТСЯ/ НЕ ОСТА́НЕТСЯ (, как…)** [VP_subj/gen; impers; if past, usu. impfv; if fut, usu. pfv; fixed WO (var. without другого)] there is only one possible course of action (left) for s.o. to take: X-у ничего не остаётся, как… ≃ **X has no (other) choice ⟨alternative⟩ but…; there is nothing (left) for X (to do) but…**

Ей читали их [письма] только по разу, а то и совсем не читали, в двух-трёх словах передавали то, что в них было, и всё, и старухе ничего не оставалось, как обходиться этой малостью (Распутин 3). These [letters] were read to her once only, if that. Often she got no more than a summary of the contents in two or three words, and she [the old lady] had no choice but to make do with this (3a). ♦ Инженеру [Хлебцевичу] ничего не оставалось после этого, как махнуть рукой и вернуться к своей работе, пока не выгнали и оттуда (Владимиров 1). There was nothing left for [the engineer] Khlebtsevich to do but give up the struggle and return to his own work until such time as he was thrown out of his job (1a).

O-123 • **ОСТАНО́ВКА ЗА** *кем-чем* [NP; Invar; the resulting phrase is VP_subj with быть∅] there is a delay because of s.o. or sth. (because s.o. or sth. is missing, unavailable etc): остановка за X-ом ≃ **the only ⟨the one⟩ thing stopping us ⟨them etc⟩ is X; the only thing holding us ⟨them etc⟩ up is X; the only difficulty ⟨problem, snag, hitch⟩ is X.**

[Ольга:] …Только растёт и крепнет одна мечта… [Ирина:] Уехать в Москву… Только вот остановка за бедной Машей. [Ольга:] Маша будет приезжать в Москву на всё лето, каждый год (Чехов 5). [О.:] …Just one dream grows stronger and stronger.… [I.:] To go to Moscow.…The one thing that stops us is poor Masha. [O.:] Masha will be coming to Moscow for the whole summer every year (5c).

O-124 • **БЕЗ ОСТА́ТКА** [PrepP; Invar; modif or adv; often after весь, целиком, полностью etc] entirely: **fully; completely;** ‖ отдаваться *чему* ~ ≃ **hold nothing back; withhold nothing ⟨not the slightest bit etc⟩;** ‖ исчезнуть ~ ≃ **vanish ⟨disappear⟩ without a trace.**

Я был весь, без остатка, поглощён рассматриванием спелого красного цветка… (Катаев 3). I became entirely absorbed in examining the ripe red flower… (3a). ♦ Ей покорялся один человек, всего лишь один, но зато целиком, без остатка, полностью. И этого для самоутверждения довольно (Чуковская 2). One person, just one person, had submitted to her unconditionally, completely and utterly. And this was enough for the assertion of her ego (2a). ♦ Он жил убеждённостью в нужности, необходимости своей работы, которой отдавался целиком, весь без остатка (Ерофеев 3). He lived by the conviction of the necessity of his work, to which he gave himself completely, withholding not the slightest bit (3a). ♦ С этой минуты исчез старый Евсеич, как будто его на свете не было, исчез без остатка… (Салтыков-Щедрин 1). And from that moment old Evseich vanished as though he had never been. He disappeared without a trace… (1b).

O-125 • **ЗАДАВА́ТЬ/ЗАДА́ТЬ ⟨ДАВА́ТЬ/ДАТЬ⟩ ОСТРА́СТКУ** *кому obs, coll* [VP; subj: human; usu. pfv] to frighten s.o. severely through harsh reprimands, threats, punishment etc with the goal of preventing him from acting in a reprehensible, undesirable etc manner: X задал Y-у острастку ≃ **X put the fear of God into Y; X gave Y a good scare; X instilled fear into Y.**

[Хлестаков:] О! Я шутить не люблю. Я им [чиновникам] всем задал острастку. Меня сам государственный совет боится (Гоголь 4). [Kh.:] Oh! I'm not one to play games! I put the fear of God into every last one of them [the officials]! Even the cabinet is scared stiff of me (4f).

O-126 • **ХОДИ́ТЬ ПО ОСТРИЮ́ ⟨ПО ЛЕ́ЗВИЮ⟩ НОЖА́** [VP; subj: human; the verb may take the final position, otherwise fixed WO] to take a great risk, do sth. that might have dangerous consequences for o.s.: X ходит по острию ножа ≃ **X is walking a tightrope; X is living ⟨sitting⟩ on a razor's edge; X is (skating) on thin ice.**

Работая одновременно на две разведки, он ходил по острию ножа: каждую минуту боялся разоблачения. Working simultaneously for two intelligence agencies, he was walking a tightrope: he lived in constant fear of exposure.

O-127 • **ХОТЬ ОТБАВЛЯ́Й** *кого-чего (у кого) coll* [хоть + VP_imper; Invar; quantit subj-compl with быть∅ (subj/gen: any common noun), more often pres; fixed WO] a large or excessive number or amount of (people, some type of person, things, some substance etc): X-ов (у Y-a) хоть отбавляй ≃ **there are ⟨Y has⟩ more than enough Xs; there are ⟨Y has⟩ plenty of Xs; there is ⟨Y has⟩ an abundance of Xs; there are ⟨Y has⟩ Xs galore; Y has enough and to spare of Xs; there is no end of Xs; there are Xs everywhere.**

«Лиха в нашем хозяйстве хошь [*ungrammat* = хоть] отбавляй; бедность, морковь одна да картошка» (Федин 1). "We've got more'n enough trouble in our farming; poverty, only carrots and potatoes" (1a). ♦ Добился… он [Митька] офицерского чина, да не так, как Григорий Мелехов, рискуя головой и бесшабашно геройствуя. Чтобы выслужиться в карательном отряде, от человека требовались иные качества… А качеств этих у Митьки было хоть отбавляй… (Шолохов 5). …[Mitka] had acquired officer's rank, and not like Grigory Melekhov, by risking his neck in reckless exploits. Meritorious service in a punitive detachment required other qualities.…And Mitka had enough and to spare of such qualities (5a). ♦ «А сюда, в Азию, уже по третьему кругу захожу, в первый раз ещё до войны был, место хлебное, фраеров – хоть отбавляй, жить можно» (Максимов 2). "This is my third time round on the trip to Asia. The first time was before the war, when there was plenty to eat, and suckers everywhere—you could really live in those days" (2a).

O-128 • **СДЕ́ЛАТЬ ОТБИВНУ́Ю** *из кого;* **СДЕ́ЛАТЬ (ОТБИВНУ́Ю) КОТЛЕ́ТУ** *both highly coll* [VP; subj: human] to beat s.o. severely: X сделает из Y-a отбивную ≃ **X will turn Y into mincemeat; X will make mincemeat out of Y; X will beat Y black and blue ⟨to a pulp⟩.**

Дедушка был один на один с десятком рассвирепевших ломовых извозчиков, которые готовы были своими ломами сделать из него котлету (Рыбаков 1). Grandfather was alone against ten infuriated wagon-drivers who intended to use their crowbars to turn him into mincemeat (1a). ♦ [Дудукин:] Вслед за этой обидой началось должное возмездие: из почтенного Мухобоева Незнамов сделал что-то вроде отбивной котлетки (Островский 3). [D.:] Well, such an insult had to be answered, and Neznamov made mincemeat out of Mukhoboyev (3a).

O-129 • **БИТЬ/ЗАБИ́ТЬ ОТБО́Й** *coll* [VP; subj: human; more often impfv] to relinquish a previous decision, plan, opinion etc: X бьёт отбой ≃ **X beats a retreat; X backs down ⟨out⟩; X changes his tune; X back-pedals;** [in limited contexts] **X pulls ⟨draws⟩ in his horns.**

Они [Аксёновы] прислали мне смятённое письмо, в котором... били отбой насчёт приезда Васи... Хотя за последние два года он донимал их своим своевольным поведением и они сами требовали, чтобы я взяла его к себе, но теперь, когда дело перешло в практическую плоскость, им стало страшно отпускать его в такой дальний путь (Гинзбург 2). They [the Aksyonovs] sent me an embarrassed letter in which they...changed their tune on the subject of Vasya. Although over the past two years he had almost worn them down with his wayward behavior and they themselves had demanded that I take him off their hands, now that it had become a practical possibility they were afraid to send him on such a long journey (2a).

O-130 • ДАВА́ТЬ/ДАТЬ ОТБО́Й [VP; subj: human] to hang up the telephone receiver: X дал отбой ≃ **X hung up (the phone); X rang off.**

O-131 • ОТБО́Я ⟨-ю⟩ НЕТ (у кого) от кого coll [VP, impers] there are more than enough or too many of a certain type or category of people: (у X-а) от Y-ов отбоя нет ≃ **X has no end of Ys; there is no end to the Ys;** [in limited contexts] **X has to beat (the) Ys off with a stick; X can't fight off the Ys; there is no coping with the Ys.**

...[Дедушка был] красавец, много разъезжал, привык к холостой жизни и, понимаете, к какой холостой жизни, от женщин у него отбоя не было... (Рыбаков 1). ...He [grandfather] was a very handsome man, who had travelled a lot and become accustomed to the bachelor life, and what a bachelor life! He'd had no end of women... (1a). ♦ [Фёдор:] Теперь: женский пол — опять то же... Какое количество у него их перебывало, так этого и вообразить не можно [ungrammat = нельзя]!.. Просто отбою нет (Сухово-Кобылин 2). [F:] And the fair sex—the same thing all over again....How many of them he's had, you couldn't even begin to imagine!...He can't fight them off (2b). ♦ Бабушка... была, как говорят, невероятно соблазнительна, настолько, что от поклонников не было отбоя... (Аллилуева 2). It is said that she [Grandmother] was unusually attractive, so that there was no coping with all her admirers (1a).

O-132 • ДО ОТВА́ЛА ⟨-у⟩ есть, наедаться, кормить кого coll [PrepP; these forms only; adv] (to eat or feed s.o.) to the point where one or s.o. can eat no more: **to the bursting point;** ‖ X наелся ~ ≃ **X gorged ⟨stuffed⟩ himself;** ‖ X накормил Y-а ~ ≃ **X stuffed Y with food; X stuffed Y to the limit.**

Совсем ещё недавно [Орозкул] сидел в гостях, пил кумыс, ел мясо до отвала (Айтматов 1). Just a short while ago he [Orozkul] had been sitting with friends, drinking *koumyss* and gorging himself on meat (1a). ♦ Они рассчитывали построить полный изм [nonce word = коммунизм] в ближайшие полгода и накормить изголодавшихся трудящихся до отвала (Зиновьев 1). They were counting on realising the total Ism [= Communism] in the next six months and stuffing the starving workers with food (1a).

O-133 • В ОТВЕ́Т [PrepP; Invar; adv] **1.** ~ (кому на что) (to say or write sth.) as a response to a question, a rejoinder to a remark etc: **in ⟨for⟩ answer; in response; in reply.**

Расхаживая по роскошным паркам, чуть тронутым августовской желтизной, госпожа де Кальвимон трогательно пожаловалась принцу на то, что в замке нет никаких развлечений. Принц в ответ сказал всё, что полагается говорить в таких случаях, то есть что желания госпожи являются для него законом... (Булгаков 5). Strolling through the magnificent parks, barely touched by the yellow of August, Madame de Calvimont complained to the Prince about the absence of any entertainments in the château. In reply, the Prince said everything that is commonly said on such occasions, namely that to him the lady's wishes were law (5a).

2. (to behave in some fashion) in reaction to sth.: **in reply; in response; in return; in ⟨for⟩ answer;** [in limited contexts] **one's answer is (to do sth.).**

...Я жалел князя и советовал ему взять отпуск и укатить в мою благословенную Грузию, но он лишь посмеивался в ответ... (Окуджава 2). I pitied the prince and recommended that he go on leave and come down to my beloved Georgia, but he merely laughed in reply... (2a). ♦ Александра Фёдоровна заметила устремлённый на неё взгляд мужа, исполненный участия и тепла, и постаралась незаметно улыбнуться ему в ответ (Окуджава 2). Alexandra Fyodorovna noticed her husband's gaze upon her, full of concern and warmth, and tried to smile secretly in return (2a). ♦ «У меня нет матери: она одна могла бы спросить меня, зачем я вижусь с тобой, и перед ней одной я заплакала бы в ответ...» (Гончаров 1). "I have no mother: she alone could have asked me why I saw you, and only in answer to her would I have cried..." (1a). ♦ «Держись за хвост моего мула, он тебя вынесет», — предложил Хабуг, но тот [председатель] в ответ только замотал головой, как бы отказываясь принимать помощь от единоличника (Искандер 3). "Grab hold of my mule's tail, he'll get you out," Khabug offered. The chairman's only answer was to shake his head as if he could not accept help from an independent farmer (3a).

O-134 • ДЕРЖА́ТЬ ОТВЕ́Т (перед кем, за что); **ДАВА́ТЬ ОТВЕ́Т** кому [VP; subj: human; usu. fut or infin (with придётся, умей etc)] to be accountable to s.o. for sth., (to be required or choose to) bear responsibility for sth. etc: X будет держать ответ (перед Y-ом за Z) ≃ **X will (have to) answer (to Y) for Z; X will be held responsible (to Y) for Z.**

«Я вам приказываю: ослобоните [*substand* = освободите] человека от смерти!.. Ответ... ответ будете держать!..» (Шолохов 3). "I order you to save that man from death!... You will have to answer for it!" (3b). ♦ Возможно, ещё придётся держать ответ в какой-нибудь инстанции за «срыв мероприятия». Это, впрочем, меньше всего меня пугало (Грекова 1). Perhaps I'll be held responsible to some higher-up or other for "undermining an organized activity." That was the least of my worries (1b).

O-135 • НИ ОТВЕ́ТА НИ ПРИВЕ́ТА от кого coll [NP_gen; Invar; used as subj/gen with не быть∅; fixed WO] no news, information, response has been received from s.o. (usu. s.o. who was expected to have kept in touch, answered an inquiry etc): от X-а ни ответа ни привета ≃ **there's been no word from X; person Y hasn't heard a word ⟨a thing⟩ from X.**

Он обещал писать, но пока ни ответа ни привета. He promised to write, but so far there hasn't been a word from him.

O-136 • В ОТВЕ́ТЕ (за кого-что) [PrepP; Invar; subj-compl with быть∅ (subj: human or collect)] one bears responsibility for s.o. or sth.: X в ответе за Y-а ≃ **X is responsible ⟨accountable⟩ (for Y); X has to answer for Y; X is answerable for Y.**

«...Я знать ничего не знаю... Ты и Затёртый были свидетелями, вы и в ответе!» (Гончаров 1). "...I know nothing about it....You and Zatyorty were the witnesses, you're responsible" (1b). ♦ «Понимаю, Танюша. Мне самой в Бутырках до смерти стыдно было перед Кларой. Немецкая коммунистка... Чудом вырвалась из гестапо. Всё мне казалось: я в ответе за то, что она в Бутырках» (Гинзбург 1). "Yes, Tanya, I understand. I felt desperately ashamed at Butyrki when I met Klara, the German Communist. She had escaped from the Gestapo by some miracle. I felt I was answerable for her being in Butyrki" (1b).

O-137 • ДЛЯ ОТВО́ДА ГЛАЗ coll [PrepP; Invar; adv or subj-compl with быть∅ (subj: usu. concr or abstr); fixed WO] in order to distract attention from sth., mislead s.o.: **as a diversionary move ⟨tactic, maneuver⟩; as a smoke screen; (in order) to divert attention from sth.;** [in limited contexts] **(using sth.) as a**

front; just to fool s.o.; ‖ X был для отвода глаз ≃ **X was a diversionary move** ⟨**tactic, maneuver**⟩; **X was a smoke screen;** [in limited contexts] **X was a front.**

В сетку для отвода глаз бросаете кусок мыла «Кармен»… но в секции детских игрушек берёте огромную резиновую рыбу, выпускаете из неё воздух, затычку прячете себе за щеку, а плоскую рыбу – себе под свитер (Аксёнов 6). As a diversionary move you throw into your basket a piece of Carmen brand soap… but in the children's toy section you pick up an enormous rubber fish, let the air out of it, then hide the plug in your mouth and the flattened fish under your sweater (6a). ♦ В указе говорилось о множестве жителей больших городов, которые состоят на работе для виду, для отвода глаз, а на самом деле занимаются тёмными махинациями… (Эткинд 1). The decree spoke of the large number of people living in large cities and taking on jobs for appearance' sake, to divert attention from their real and unsavory activities (1a). ♦ Кооператив… «важен для нас перед внешним миром, но мало значит внутри». То есть кооператив для отвода глаз, а на самом деле… «это наша альтернатива существующему строю» (Войнович 1). …A соор…"was important to us for the outside world but internally it had little meaning." In other words, the coop was a front; in fact, "it was our alternative to the existing system" (1a).

O-138 • БЕЗ ОТДА́ЧИ брать, занимать, давать *что coll* [PrepP; Invar; adv] (to take, borrow sth.) without planning to return it, (to give sth. to s.o.) without asking him to return it: [in refer. to taking, borrowing sth.] **never returning it** ⟨**them**⟩; **never intending to return it** ⟨**them**⟩; **with no intention of returning it** ⟨**them**⟩; [in refer. to money only] **with no intention** ⟨**notion**⟩ **of repaying it;** [in refer. to giving sth.] **for good; for keeps.**

Он был убеждён, что… он сотворён богом так, что должен жить в тридцать тысяч дохода и занимать всегда высшее положение в обществе. Он так твёрдо верил в это, что, глядя на него, и другие были убеждены в этом и не отказывали ему ни в деньгах, которые он, ни в высшем положении в свете, ни в деньгах, которые он, очевидно без отдачи, занимал у встречного и поперечного (Толстой 5). He believed that…God had created him to spend thirty thousand a year and always to occupy a prominent position in society. He was so firmly convinced of this that looking at him others were persuaded of it too, and refused him neither a leading place in society nor the money he borrowed right and left, obviously with no notion of repaying it (5a).

O-139 • ДЁШЕВО ⟨**ЛЕГКО́, СЧА́СТЛИВО**⟩ **ОТ-ДЕ́ЛАТЬСЯ** *coll* [VP; subj: human; more often past; fixed WO] to avoid or extricate o.s. from a disagreeable or dangerous situation without incurring significant trouble, losses, repercussions etc: X дёшево отделался ≃ **X got off** (**pretty** ⟨**so etc**⟩) **easy** ⟨**easily**⟩; **X got off lightly** ⟨**cheap(ly)**⟩.

«Феня, ради господа Христа нашего, скажи, где она?» – «Батюшка, ничего не знаю, голубчик Дмитрий Фёдорович, ничего не знаю…» – «Врёшь», – вскричал Митя… Он бросился вон. Испуганная Феня рада была, что дёшево отделалась, но очень хорошо поняла, что ему было только некогда, а то бы ей, может, несдобровать (Достоевский 1). "Fenya, for the sake of our Lord Jesus Christ, tell me where she is!" "My dear, I know nothing, dear Dmitri Fyodorovich, I know nothing…." "You're lying," roared Mitya….He dashed out. The frightened Fenya was glad to have gotten off so easily, but she knew very well that he simply had no time, otherwise it would have gone badly for her (1a). ♦ Он [дядя Сандро] ехал на грузовике вместе со своими земляками на какие-то большие похороны в селе Атары. Навстречу им мчался грузовик, возвращавший людей с этих же похорон… Машины столкнулись. К счастью, никого не убило, но было много раненых. Дядя Сандро сравнительно легко отделался, он вывихнул ногу и потерял один зуб (Искандер 3). He [Uncle Sandro] was riding in a truck with friends from home, on the way to a big funeral in the village of Atary. A truck bringing people back from the same funeral came hurtling toward them….The trucks collided. Luckily no one was killed, but many people were hurt. Uncle Sandro got off comparatively lightly: he dislocated his foot and lost one tooth (3a).

O-140 • В ⟨**ПО**⟩ **ОТДЕ́ЛЬНОСТИ** [PrepP; these forms only; adv or modif] singly, independently: **(taken) separately; individually.**

Все движения на свете в отдельности были рассчитанно-трезвы, а в общей сложности безотчётно пьяны общим потоком жизни, который объединял их (Пастернак 1). Every motion in the world taken separately was calculated and purposeful, but, taken together, they were spontaneously intoxicated with the general stream of life which united them all (1a). ♦ Кривошлыков протянул через стол заготовленный ультиматум Военно-революционного комитета, но Каледин, отстраняя бумагу движением белой ладони, твёрдо сказал: «Нет смысла терять время на ознакомление каждого члена правительства с этим документом в отдельности. Потрудитесь прочитать вслух ваш ультиматум» (Шолохов 3). Krivoshlykov held out the prepared text of the Military-Revolutionary Committee's ultimatum, but Kaledin brushed it aside with a white hand and said firmly, "There's no need for each member of the government to see this document separately. That would be a waste of time. Kindly read out your ultimatum" (3a).

O-141 • НЕ ДАВА́ТЬ НИ О́ТДЫХА ⟨**-у**⟩ **НИ СРО́КА** ⟨**-у**⟩ *кому obs, coll* [VP; subj: usu. human; the verb may take the final position, otherwise fixed WO] not to give s.o. any time or opportunity at all to rest, relax etc (by forcing him to work nonstop, pestering him continually etc): X не давал Y-у ни отдыха ни срока ≃ **X didn't give Y a moment's peace** ⟨**a moment's rest**⟩.

O-142 • НЕ ОТКАЖИ́(ТЕ) *что сделать* [formula phrase; these forms only] (used as part of a polite request) please agree (to do sth.): **(please) be so kind** ⟨**good**⟩ **(as to…).**

O-143 • НЕ ОТКАЖУ́СЬ; НЕ ОТКАЗА́ЛСЯ БЫ *coll* [VP; 1st pers fut or subjunctive only; often foll. by infin] I am (or we are) not averse to and would even quite enjoy (doing sth.): **I** ⟨**we**⟩ **wouldn't mind…; don't mind if I** ⟨**we**⟩ **do.**

«Чаю хотите?» – «Спасибо, не откажусь». "Would you like some tea?" "Thanks, don't mind if I do."

O-144 • БЕЗ ОТКА́ЗА действовать, работать [PrepP; Invar; adv] (of a machine, mechanism etc) (to work, run etc) very well, without problems: **(run) smoothly; (work** ⟨**run**⟩**) perfectly** ⟨**fine etc**⟩.

Хотя эти часы и старые, а работают без отказа. This watch may be old, but it runs perfectly.

O-145 • ДО ОТКА́ЗА *coll* [PrepP; Invar; adv] to the limit: набить ⟨забить, заполнить *что*, быть₀ набитым и т. п.⟩ ~ ≃ **fill sth.** ⟨**be filled, pack sth., be packed** etc⟩ **to capacity; fill sth.** ⟨**be filled** etc⟩ **to overflowing** ⟨**to bursting, to the bursting point, to the brim**⟩; **pack sth.** ⟨**be packed** etc⟩ **tight** ⟨**as tight as it will go**⟩; **cram sth.** ⟨**be crammed**⟩; [in refer. to a room, dwelling etc only] **pack sth.** ⟨**be packed**⟩ **to the rafters;** ‖ нажать *(на) что*, открутить, закрутить *что* ~ ≃ **(push** ⟨**press**⟩ **sth. down** etc) **all the way; (push** ⟨**press**⟩ **sth. down** etc) **as far as it will** ⟨**can**⟩ **go; (turn sth. on) full blast; (turn sth.) all the way on** ⟨**off**⟩.

Вокзал был полон, перрон забит людьми до отказа (Рыбаков 2). The station was crowded and the platform was packed to capacity (2a). ♦ …На хорах, на скамьях амфитеатра, вдоль боковых стен, в проходах и даже на эстраде… народа набилось «до отказа» (Лившиц 1). The choirs, the benches in the amphitheatre, the sides of the walls, the aisles, and even the stage...were filled "to overflowing" with people (1a). ♦ Все клетки-купе вагонзаков были забиты до отказа (Марченко 1). All the cages of the prison coaches were packed as tight as they would go (1a). ♦ Клуб был набит до отказа... (Рыбаков 1). The club was packed to the rafters (1a). ♦ ...[Таня] открутила до отказа все краны. В рёве воды разделась и встала перед зеркалом (Аксёнов 7). ...[Tanya] turned on the taps full blast. To the roar of the water she pulled off her clothes and picked herself up in front of the full-length mirror (7a).

О-146 • НЕЛЬЗЯ́ ОТКАЗА́ТЬ *кому в чём coll;* **НЕЛЬЗЯ́ ОТНЯ́ТЬ** *у кого что* or *чего obs;* **НЕ ОТКА́ЖЕШЬ** *кому в чём coll;* **НЕ ОТНИ́МЕШЬ** *что* or *чего у кого coll* [impers predic with быть∅, pres or past (variants with нельзя), or neg pfv fut, gener. 2nd pers sing (variants with не)] one cannot help but recognize, admit that s.o. has a certain quality: X-у нельзя отказать в Y-е ≃ **one cannot deny X Y; there's no denying that X has Y ⟨is** [AdjP]⟩**; you can't take that away from X; you can't say X is not** [AdjP].

Ему нельзя было отказать в недюжинной эрудиции, которая... могла покорить собеседника... (Ерофеев 3). One couldn't deny him the remarkable erudition with which he was able to overwhelm anyone he talked to... (3a). ♦ Ловко мы их [органы] обвели вокруг пальца, говорил Правдец своему Другу. Да, говорил Друг, это у нас не отнимешь! Тюремный опыт не пропал даром (Зиновьев 1). "We've really taken them [the secret police] for a ride," Truth-teller said to his Friend. "Yes," said Friend, "no-one can deny us that! Our prison experience has been of some use after all" (12a). ♦ «Что ты, не знаешь своей жены? Хозяйственная баба. Этого у неё не отнимешь. И уж если на то пошло, так с лесозаготовками у неё не хуже было, чем у других. А даже лучше» (Абрамов 1). "Don't you know your own wife? She's an efficient woman: that you can't take away from her. And while we're on the subject, her timber production was no worse than anyone else's. Better even" (1a).

О-147 • НИ В ЧЁМ СЕБЕ́ НЕ ОТКА́ЗЫВАТЬ [VP; subj: human] not to limit o.s. in anything, to live in grand style: X ни в чём себе не отказывает ≃ **X denies himself nothing; X does not refuse himself anything; X spares no expense to gratify his fancies ⟨desires** etc⟩; [in limited contexts] **X doesn't have to deny ⟨to refuse⟩ himself anything.**

Там у неё [Одинцовой] был великолепный, отлично убранный дом, прекрасный сад с оранжереями: покойный Одинцов ни в чём себе не отказывал (Тургенев 2). There she [Mme Odintsov] was mistress of a magnificent, excellently appointed house with a beautiful garden and conservatories: the late Odintsov had denied himself nothing (2e). There she [Mme Odintsov] had a magnificent, splendidly furnished house and a beautiful garden, with conservatories: her late husband had spared no expense to gratify his fancies (2b). ♦ ...Губернские дамы... всё-таки были не более как чиновницы, какие-нибудь председательши, командирши и советницы, родившиеся и воспитывавшиеся в четвёртых этажах петербургских казённых домов и только недавно, очень недавно, получившие понятие о комфорте и о том, что такое значит «ни в чём себе не отказывать» (Салтыков-Щедрин 2). ...Our provincial ladies...were after all only the wives and daughters of civil servants, a wife of some departmental president or of the commanding officer of the local garrison or of some councillor, all born and educated on some fourth story of a Petersburg government building, who had obtained their ideas of comfort only very recently, since it was only quite recently that they had really understood the meaning of the phrase, "not to have to deny oneself anything" (2a).

О-148 • ОТКА́ЗЫВАТЬ СЕБЕ́ *в чём* [VP; subj: human] to limit o.s. in sth.: X отказывает себе в Y-е ≃ **X denies himself Y.**

Их сердца наполнялись гордостью. Вот она, их страна, ударная бригада мирового пролетариата... Да, они живут по карточкам, отказывают себе во всём, зато они строят новый мир (Рыбаков 2). Their hearts swelled with pride. This was their country, the shock brigade of the world proletariat....True, they had ration cards and denied themselves everything, but they were building a new world (2a).

О-149 • НЕ ОТКЛА́ДЫВАЙ НА ЗА́ВТРА ТО, ЧТО МО́ЖНО ⟨МО́ЖЕШЬ⟩ СДЕ́ЛАТЬ СЕГО́ДНЯ [saying] (usu. said as advice to s.o. to overcome his laziness or reluctance to do sth.) do what you have to do right away: **don't put off till tomorrow what you can do today.**

О-150 • КАТИ́ТЬСЯ/ПОКАТИ́ТЬСЯ ПОД ОТКО́С [VP] **1.** Also: **ИДТИ́/ПОЙТИ́ ПОД ОТКО́С** [subj: usu. abstr, often дела, всё] to deteriorate sharply, collapse: X катится под откос ≃ **X is on the road to ruin; X is falling apart; X is going to pot ⟨to ruin⟩;** ‖ [of plans, s.o.'s career etc] X пошёл под откос ≃ **X got derailed.**

Боже мой, мне стало страшно, что жизнь моя вдруг пойдёт под откос! (Аксёнов 1). Suddenly I was terrified—my God, my life is about to get derailed! (1a).

2. [subj: human] to deteriorate morally: X покатился под откос ≃ **X went downhill ⟨wrong, astray⟩.**

О-151 • В ОТКРЫ́ТУЮ *действовать, говорить что, смеяться над кем-чем,* **врать** *и. т. п. coll* [PrepP; Invar; adv] (to act, speak etc) overtly, hiding nothing, (to laugh at s.o. or sth., lie etc) in an unconcealed manner: **openly;** ‖ действовать ~ ≃ **operate out in the open;** ‖ говорить ~ ≃ **speak candidly ⟨frankly, straight from the shoulder, outright** etc⟩; ‖ смеяться *над кем-чем* ~ ≃ **laugh out loud at s.o. ⟨sth.⟩; laugh one's head off (at s.o.'s expense);** ‖ врать ~ ≃ **lie through ⟨in⟩ one's teeth; tell bold-faced lies.**

...Он в открытую на худсовете выступал против смоляновской пьесы... (Трифонов 1). ...He had openly spoken out against Smolyanov's play at meetings of the theater council... (1a). ♦ «Остров наводнён агентурой. Си-Ай-Эй и Ка-Ге-Бэ действуют чуть ли не в открытую» (Аксёнов 7). "The Island is flooded with agents. The CIA and KGB operate quite out in the open..." (7a).

О-152 • БРАТЬ/ВЗЯТЬ НА О́ТКУП *что* [VP; subj: human] **1.** *obs* to receive exclusive rights to use or hold sth. in exchange for money: X взял на откуп Y ≃ **X farmed Y.**

2. *coll* to take for o.s. exclusive control over and responsibility for sth. (a project, assignment etc): X взял на откуп Y ≃ **X took over Y; X claimed Y (for himself).**

Мне не удастся поработать над этим проектом: его взял на откуп старший инженер. I'm not going to be able to work on that project: the senior engineer has claimed it.

О-153 • ОТДАВА́ТЬ/ОТДА́ТЬ НА О́ТКУП *что (кому)* [VP; subj: human] **1.** *obs* to give s.o. exclusive rights to use or hold sth. in exchange for money: X отдал Y на откуп ≃ **X farmed ⟨leased⟩ Y (out).**

[Боркин:] Еду сейчас к вам, а на реке у вас мужики с лозняка кору дерут. Отчего вы лозняк на откуп не отдадите? (Чехов 4). [B.:] As I was on my way here, I saw some peasants stripping the bark off your willow bushes along the river. Why don't you lease out those willow bushes? (4a).

2. *coll* to pass sth. (a project, assignment, responsibility for sth. etc) to s.o. such that he alone will handle it: X отдал Y на откуп

Z-у ≃ **X turned ⟨handed⟩ Y over to Z; X gave ⟨assigned, relegated etc⟩ Y to Z;** [in limited contexts] **X gave Z exclusive rights to Y.**

Производства новый директор не знал, работать не любил и всё руководство заводом фактически отдал на откуп главному инженеру. The new supervisor didn't know production, didn't like to work, and virtually turned over management of the factory to the chief engineer.

O-154 • НА ОТЛЁТЕ [PrepP; Invar] **1.** [adv or subj-compl with copula (subj: concr)] located at some distance away (from sth.), set apart: **off at a distance; (standing) off by itself.**

Мы пошли к дому, стоявшему на отлёте. We started walking toward the house standing off at a distance.

2. держать, нести *что* ~ [adv] (to hold, carry sth.) in one's hand(s) at a distance from one's body: **(hold sth. out) at arm's length; (hold ⟨carry⟩ sth.) in one's outstretched hand(s).**

Держа трость на отлёте, он учтиво поклонился дамам. Holding his cane out at arm's length, he courteously bowed to the ladies.

3. держаться ~ [adv] (of a person) (to remain) separate, isolated from others, not (to associate) with others: X держался на отлёте ≃ **X kept his distance ⟨maintained a distance⟩; X kept to himself; X kept ⟨held himself⟩ aloof.**

Он всегда держится на отлёте — не знаю, от застенчивости это или от самомнения. He always keeps aloof—I don't know if it's out of shyness or conceit.

O-155 • В ОТЛИЧИЕ ОТ *кого-чего* [PrepP; Invar; Prep; the resulting PrepP is adv] as distinct from: **unlike; in contrast to; as opposed to;** [in limited contexts] **as compared to.**

…[Щупов] не берёт взяток или берёт не со всех, в отличие от старого директора, который на том и погорел, что брал без разбору (Войнович 6). …[Shchupov] didn't take bribes, or at least he didn't take them indiscriminately—unlike the old director, whose downfall, indeed, had been that he took bribes from everyone (6a). ♦ Разговор шёл о том, что горные абхазцы, в отличие от долинных, более консервативны… (Искандер 3). The talk was about how the Abkhazian highlanders, as compared to the Abkhazian lowlanders, were more conservative… (3a).

O-156 • В ОТМЕСТКУ *(за что)* coll [PrepP; Invar; adv] (to do sth.) in redress (for an injury, insult etc): **in ⟨by way of⟩ revenge; in retaliation; to pay s.o. back; to get back at s.o.**

[Генерал Бетрищев] не любил всех, которые ушли вперёд его по службе… Больше всего доставалось его прежнему сотоварищу, которого считал он ниже себя и умом и способностями и который, однако же, обогнал его… В отместку язвил он его при всяком случае… (Гоголь 3). He [General Betrishchev] disliked everyone who had been promoted beyond his rank in the service.…He particularly singled out for attack a former comrade-in-arms of his, whom he considered to be his inferior in intelligence and abilities and who, nevertheless, had advanced faster in the service.…In revenge he taunted him at every opportunity… (3c). He [General Betrishchev] did not like those who rose above him in the service.…The man he attacked most of all was a former colleague whom he regarded as inferior to himself in intelligence and abilitites and who nevertheless had got ahead of him.…By way of revenge, he taunted him at every favorable opportunity… (3a). ♦ С пьяным упорством я противоречу Надеину в отместку за его слова о русских (Коротюков 1). I contradicted Nadein with drunken obstinacy to pay him back for what he had said about Russians (1a).

O-157 • В НЕКОТОРОМ ОТНОШЕНИИ; В НЕКОТОРЫХ ОТНОШЕНИЯХ [PrepP; these forms only; usu. sent adv; fixed WO] to a certain extent, from a certain point of view: **in certain ⟨some⟩ respects ⟨ways⟩; in a way; in a (certain) sense.**

В некоторых отношениях и судьба их была одинакова: оба женились по любви, оба скоро овдовели, у обоих оставалось по ребёнку (Пушкин 1). In certain respects, even fate had treated them similarly: both had married for love and soon lost their wives; and each was left with a child (1a). In certain ways, too, their destinies were similar: both had married for love, both had soon been widowed, and both had been left with an only child (1b).

O-158 • В ОТНОШЕНИИ *кого-чего;* **ПО ОТНОШЕНИЮ** *к кому-чему* [PrepP; these forms only; the resulting PrepP is adv] regarding: **in relation to; with respect ⟨regard⟩ to; concerning;** [in limited contexts] **in reference to;** ‖ вести ⟨держать⟩ себя по отношению *к кому* ≃ **behave ⟨act etc⟩ toward ⟨to⟩ s.o.**

Просто ей, как и всем в доме, надо было узнать, что делать с этой новостью, как вести себя дальше по отношению к Тали (Искандер 3). Like everyone else in the house, she simply had to find out what to do with this news, how to behave from now on in relation to Tali (3a). ♦ «Не скорость вызывает опьянение, а опьянение — есть скорость!» — провозгласил Лёва… Что-то есть точное в лёвином определении «опьянения», по крайней мере, в отношении самого Лёвы… (Битов 2). "Speed does not cause drunkenness. Drunkenness *is* speed!" Lyova proclaimed.…There is something exact about Lyova's definition of "drunkenness," at least with respect to Lyova himself (2a). ♦ …В отношении самого Мансурова как такового — последнее слово было за ней [Ириной Викторовной], а не за ним: ехать ли ему на курорт или не ехать, а если ехать — то когда; надевать тот или этот костюм на официальный приём; идти к врачу или не ходить… (Залыгин 1). …In anything concerning Mansurov personally she [Irina Viktorovna] always had the final say: whether he should go to a health resort or not, and if so, when; which suit he should wear for the coming official function; whether or not he should see a doctor… (1a). ♦ …Княжна Марья не переставая думала о том, как ей должно держать себя в отношении Ростова (Толстой 7). …Princess Marya never ceased thinking about how she ought to behave toward him [Rostov] (7a). ♦ Начальник штаба и раньше не отличался большой смелостью по отношению к вышестоящим командирам, но теперь, по причине глухоты, боялся их ещё больше, помня, что его в любое время могут уволить в запас (Войнович 2). [context transl] [The chief of staff] had never previously distinguished himself by great courage in dealing with his superiors and now, on account of his deafness, feared them all the more, knowing that at any moment they could transfer him to the reserves (2a).

O-159 • ВЫЯСНЯТЬ/ВЫЯСНИТЬ ОТНОШЕНИЯ *(с кем)* coll [VP; subj: human] to discuss and resolve the problem spots in an interpersonal relationship, air and get over mutual resentments: X и Y выясняют отношения ≃ **X and Y are sorting out ⟨clarifying⟩ their relationship;** ‖ X-у и Y-у надо выяснить отношения ≃ **X and Y must clear the air; X and Y need to have it out.**

«Семья тем и отличается от канцелярии, что в ней не ведутся протоколы и акты происшествий. Кроме того, выяснять отношения сейчас, а тем более прошлые отношения — поздно» (Залыгин 1). "The difference between a family and an office is that in a family you don't keep minutes and detailed records. Besides, it's too late now for us to sort out our relationship, let alone our past relationship" (1a). ♦ Рубин посмотрел на него скучающе. «Ты знаешь, почему лошади долго живут?» И после паузы объяснил: «Потому что они никогда не выясняют отношений» (Солженицын 3). Rubin looked at him vacantly. "Do you know," he asked, "why horses live a long time?" After a pause he explained: "Because they never go around clarifying their relationships" (3a).

O-160 • ВО ВСЕХ ОТНОШЕНИЯХ [PrepP; Invar; usu. modif; fixed WO] in all aspects: **in every respect ⟨way⟩; in all respects.**

«Ну, слушайте же, что такое эти мёртвые души», — сказала дама приятная во всех отношениях... (Гоголь 3). "Very well, then, listen to what sort of thing these dead souls are," said the lady who was agreeable in all respects... (3b).

O-161 • **ОТОРВИ́ ДА ⟨И⟩ БРОСЬ ⟨ВЫ́БРОСЬ⟩** *highly coll* [Invar; subj-compl with быть∅ (subj: human); fixed WO] (more often of a female) one is adroit, smart, daring: X – оторви да брось ≃ **X is one helluva ⟨hell of a⟩ gal ⟨guy⟩; X is quite a gal ⟨a guy⟩; X is a real firecracker ⟨dynamo⟩.**

O-162 • **КЛАСТЬ/ПОЛОЖИ́ТЬ ⟨НАКЛА́ДЫВАТЬ/ НАЛОЖИ́ТЬ⟩ ОТПЕЧА́ТОК ⟨ПЕЧА́ТЬ** *obsoles*⟩ **на кого-что; ОСТАВЛЯ́ТЬ/ОСТА́ВИТЬ ОТПЕЧА́ТОК ⟨ПЕЧА́ТЬ** *obsoles*⟩ **на ком-чём** [VP; subj: abstr; usu. pfv; usu. this WO] to leave a noticeable trace (on s.o. or sth.): X наложил отпечаток на Y-a ≃ **X left its ⟨a⟩ mark on Y; X left ⟨set⟩ its ⟨an⟩ imprint on Y; X had an ⟨its⟩ effect on Y; X set ⟨put, stamped⟩ a ⟨its⟩ seal on Y; Y was marked by X.**

Он [Захар] принадлежал двум эпохам, и обе положили на него печать свою (Гончаров 1). He [Zakhar] belonged to two different epochs, and each of them had left its mark on him (1a). ♦ ...Для всех шёл один двадцатый век, дымы Бабьих Яров стлались над миром, война колотила лучшую нашу пору — юность, и это было то общее, что наложило отпечаток на всю нашу жизнь (Кузнецов 1). ...We all lived in the same twentieth century; the smoke of the Babi Yars was spreading over the world, and the war was battering the best of our lives—our youth. This we shared, and it left an imprint on our lives forever (1a). ♦ Присутствие Ольги на всё в доме налагало свой отпечаток (Шолохов 4). Olga's presence had its effect on the whole household (4a). ♦ Предстоящий отъезд Аркадия наложил печать на семью Мансуровых, печать некоторой грусти, недоумения: ну, как это так — Аркашка, мальчишечка, несмышлёныш, и вдруг в армию? (Залыгин 1). Arkady's impending departure set a seal on the Mansurov family, a seal of a kind of sadness and uncertainty: how was it that a scatterbrained boy like Arkady could be off to the army? (1a). ♦ Власть «общего мнения» огромна, противиться ей гораздо труднее, чем думают, и на каждого из людей время кладёт свой отпечаток (Мандельштам 1). The power of the "general will" is enormous—to resist it is much harder than people think—and we are all marked by the times we live in (1a).

O-163 • **ДАВА́ТЬ/ДАТЬ ОТПО́Р** *кому-чему* [VP; subj: human or collect] **1.** to repulse s.o.'s attack: X-ы дали отпор Y-ам ≃ **Xs drove ⟨beat⟩ back Ys; Xs repelled Ys.**

«Бог милостив: солдат у нас довольно, пороху много, пушку я вычистил. Авось дадим отпор Пугачёву» (Пушкин 2). "The Lord is merciful: we have enough soldiers and plenty of powder, and I've cleaned out the cannon. With a little luck we'll drive back Pugachev" (2a).

2. to offer resistance to s.o.'s actions or words: X дал отпор Y-у ≃ **X fought back; X repulsed ⟨rebuffed⟩ Y.**

...В нас обоих его [Ваню] соблазнительно привлекало совершенно необычное для него критическое отношение к газетам, к официальной пропаганде... Иногда он всё же решался «давать отпор». Когда в разговоре о Демьяне Бедном я заметил, что тот ещё перед войной жестоко запивал, Ваня вспылил: «Этого не может быть! Старейший член партии!» (Копелев 1). ...What he [Vanya] found temptingly attractive about us both was our critical attitude, totally new to his experience, toward the newspapers and official propaganda....Sometimes he did muster his courage to "fight back." When in a conversation about the famous proletarian poet Demyan Bedny I noted that he had been a heavy drinker even before the war, Vanya howled: "That's impossible! One of the oldest members of the Party" (1a). ♦ ...Жена его всем своим обликом выразила готовность дать отпор явно приближающемуся, но ещё недостаточно приблизившемуся оскорблению её рода (Искандер 5). ...His wife's whole attitude expressed preparedness to repulse the obviously nearing, but as yet insufficiently near, insult to her clan (5a).

O-164 • **ОТРЫВА́ТЬ/ОТОРВА́ТЬ ОТ СЕБЯ́** *(что) coll* [VP; subj: human; usu. impfv] to sacrifice sth. one needs in order to give it to or share it with another: X отрывает от себя Y ≃ **X deprives himself (of Y); X shares what little he has (with s.o.); X shares his little bit of Y (with s.o.); X gives up Y (for someone else).**

O-165 • **НЕ ОТРЫВА́ЯСЬ смотреть, глядеть** *на кого-что,* **следить** *за кем-чем* [Verbal Adv; Invar; adv] (to look at s.o. or sth.) intently, constantly, without looking away: X не отрываясь смотрел на Y-a ≃ **X kept ⟨was⟩ staring at Y; X fixed his eyes ⟨had his eyes fixed⟩ on Y; X did not take his eyes off Y.**

...Борисов хлопнул [гипсовый бюст] Сталина по голове и затряс рукой от боли, но тут же выражение боли на его лице сменилось выражением смертельного страха... Он раскрыл рот и смотрел на Голубева не отрываясь, словно загипнотизированный. А тот и сам до смерти перепугался (Войнович 2). ...Borisov whacked [the plaster bust of] Stalin on the head, then shook his hand in pain. Instantly, the expression of pain on his face changed into one of mortal fear....He opened his mouth and stared at Golubev as if hypnotized. Golubev, meanwhile, was scared to death himself (2a).

O-166 • **В ОТРЫ́ВЕ** *от чего* [PrepP; Invar; the resulting PrepP is adv] separately (from sth.): **in isolation from;** [in limited contexts] **ignoring.**

Нельзя анализировать эту работу в отрыве от основных философских течений того времени. One can't analyze this work ignoring the basic philosophical movements of the time.

O-167 • **ДАВА́ТЬ/ДАТЬ ОТСТА́ВКУ** *кому coll* [VP; subj: human; more often female] to break off one's relationship with one's sweetheart or lover: X дала отставку Y-у ≃ **X dropped ⟨jilted, dumped⟩ Y; X gave Y the ax ⟨the boot, the heave-ho, the air, the gate⟩; X broke up with Y; X told Y to hit the road.**

O-168 • **ПОЛУЧА́ТЬ/ПОЛУЧИ́ТЬ ОТСТА́ВКУ** *coll* [VP; subj: human] to be rejected by one's sweetheart or lover: X получил отставку ≃ **X got jilted ⟨dumped⟩; X got the ax ⟨the boot, the heave-ho, the air, the gate⟩; X was told to hit the road.**

O-169 • **ЛИРИ́ЧЕСКОЕ ОТСТУПЛЕ́НИЕ** *lit, occas. humor* [NP; fixed WO] a divergence from the theme of a lecture, speech, story etc that allows the speaker or narrator to express some emotion: **lyrical digression.**

O-170 • **БЛИСТА́ТЬ (СВОИ́М) ОТСУ́ТСТВИЕМ** *lit, iron* [VP; subj: human, abstr, or concr] to be noticeably absent from somewhere, draw attention to o.s. or itself by being absent: X блистал своим отсутствием ≃ **X was conspicuous by his ⟨its⟩ absence; X was conspicuously absent.**

< Loan translation of the French *briller par son absence.* Original source: Tacitus (A.D. c55–c120), *Annals.* English source: Lord John Russell, *Speech to the electors of the City of London,* 1859.

O-171 • **ЗА ОТСУ́ТСТВИЕМ** [PrepP; Invar; the resulting PrepP is adv] **1.** ~ *кого* in connection with a person's temporary absence from a given place at a given time: **in the absence of.**

За отсутствием директора по всем вопросам нужно обращаться к его заместителю. In the absence of the director all problems should be addressed to his deputy.

2. ~ *кого-чего* in connection with the unavailability, complete absence of a person or thing: **for lack ⟨want⟩ of; in the absence of.**

...За отсутствием пристойной обуви я носила нелепые казанские сапожки с киевской ярмарки (Мандельштам 2). ...For want of proper shoes, I was wearing a grotesque pair of Kazan boots which I had bought at the Kiev fair... (2a).

O-172 • ОТДАВА́ТЬ/ОТДА́ТЬ ⟨ДАВА́ТЬ/ДАТЬ⟩ СЕБЕ́ ОТЧЁТ *в чём* [VP; subj: human; more often impfv; often foll. by в том, что; fixed WO] to comprehend, apprehend sth.: X отдаёт себе отчёт в том, что... ≃ **X realizes ⟨understands, knows, is aware⟩ that...;** || *Neg* X не отдаёт себе отчёта в том, что... ≃ **X has no idea...**

...Он [Пастернак], конечно, отдавал себе отчёт в том, что моим арестом дело не ограничится, что наступит день, когда начнётся лобовая травля, не оставляющая места никаким аргументам (Ивинская 1). ...He [Pasternak] realized, of course, that things would not end with my imprisonment, and that the day would come when the persecution against him would be launched head-on, in a form that would brook no argument (1a). ♦ Она вот ни разу не видела, чтобы пьяный приставал к милиционеру, значит, прекрасно отдаёт себе отчёт в том, что ему... можно и выгодно, а что — нет! (Залыгин 1). She'd never seen a drunkard pestering a policeman: that meant they knew perfectly well what they could do, what was worth trying, and what wasn't (1a). ♦ Письмо писала молодая сиделка. Руки её дрожали, она не отдавала себе отчёта в том, что делает... (Федин 1). A young nurse was writing a letter. Her hands were trembling and she was not aware of what she was doing... (1a). ♦ «Ты отдаёшь себе отчёт, что ты говоришь?» (Терц 7). "Have you any idea what you are saying?" (7a).

O-173 • НА ОТШИ́БЕ *coll* [PrepP; Invar] **1.** [adv, subj-compl with copula (subj: concr), or nonagreeing postmodif] set apart, quite a distance away (from some place): **at a distance from; far off; far away (from); way over ⟨out⟩ there;** [in limited contexts] **in a secluded ⟨remote⟩ spot ⟨place⟩; in an out-of-the-way place.**

Он и квартиру себе выбрал на отшибе нарочно, чтоб его не беспокоили в нерабочее время... (Солженицын 12). He had purposely chosen a billet far away from the station so that he would not be disturbed in his off-duty time... (12a). ♦ «Мати, вы чего там на отшибе? Первый раз на пожне?» То есть это означало: сколько ещё можно дуться? Давайте подходите сюда... (Абрамов 1). "Mama! What are you doing way over there? This your first harvest?" (Meaning, how much longer can we sulk? Come on over here...) (1a). ♦ Жил он [Камуг] немного на отшибе, поблизости от леса (Искандер 5). Kamug lived in a rather secluded spot, near the forest (5a).

2. держаться, чувствовать себя и т. п. ~ *(от кого)* [adv or subj-compl with бытьθ (subj: human)] (to be, choose to be etc) isolated, separate from others, (to feel) estranged: X (держится) на отшибе (от Y-ов) ≃ **X keeps aloof ⟨apart⟩ from Ys; X keeps his distance ⟨maintains a distance⟩; X keeps to himself;** || X чувствует себя на отшибе ≃ **X feels alienated ⟨cut off⟩.**

O-174 • В ОХА́ПКУ схватить *кого-что*, сгрести *кого* и т. п.; В ОХА́ПКЕ держать, нести *кого-что* и т. п. *both coll* [PrepP; these forms only; adv] (to take hold of, grab, hold, carry etc s.o. or sth.) with both arms around him or it: **(throw) one's arms around s.o. ⟨sth.⟩; (grab ⟨hold, carry⟩ etc s.o. ⟨sth.⟩) with both ⟨one's⟩ arms wrapped around him ⟨it etc⟩.**

Наконец, Зинаида схватила его в охапку и больше не выпустила (Терц 4). Finally Zinaida threw her arms around him and wouldn't let him go (4a).

O-175 • О́ХИ ДА ⟨И⟩ ВЗДО́ХИ *coll* [NP; pl only; fixed WO] complaints, lamentations: **moans and groans; moaning and groaning.**

Он вздыхал, проклинал себя, ворочался с боку на бок, искал виноватого и не находил. Охи и вздохи его достигли даже до ушей Захара (Гончаров 1). He sighed, cursed himself, turned from side to side, looked for someone to blame and could not find anyone. His moans and groans even reached Zakhar's ears (1a).

O-176 • ОХО́ТА ПУ́ЩЕ НЕВО́ЛИ [saying] when one does sth. willingly and for one's own pleasure it does not seem difficult, burdensome etc (said when a person undertakes sth. that others might consider unpleasant, too labor-intensive etc): ≃ **when you do something by choice ⟨for fun⟩ it doesn't seem hard; work you enjoy never feels too hard;** [in limited contexts] **a willing horse needs no spur.**

O-177 • В ОХО́ТКУ *substand* [PrepP; Invar] **1.** [adv] (to do sth.) willingly, enthusiastically: **gladly; with pleasure; (be) keen (on doing sth.);** || *Neg* не в охотку ≃ **(be) none too eager ⟨anxious⟩ (to do sth.).**

[Фирс:] Прежде у нас на балах танцевали генералы, бароны, адмиралы, а теперь посылаем за почтовым чиновником и начальником станции, да и те не в охотку идут (Чехов 2). [F.:] In the old days we used to have generals, barons, admirals dancing at our balls, but now we send for the post-office clerk and the stationmaster, and even they are none too eager to come (2a). [F.:] In the old days there were generals, barons, admirals dancing at our parties, and now we send for the post-office clerk and the stationmaster, and even they are none too anxious to come (2d).

2. ~ *кому* [usu. subj-compl with бытьθ (subj: concr, abstr, or infin)] sth. (or doing sth.) gives s.o. pleasure, a feeling of satisfaction: X Y-у в охотку ≃ **Y likes ⟨enjoys, fancies⟩ (doing) X; Y gets a kick out of (doing) X.**

«Думаю, дай достану [грибы], может, кому в охотку придутся. Кушайте, если нравятся» (Распутин 3). "So I thought I'd get them [the mushrooms] out, in case anybody fancied them. Help yourselves if you like them" (3a).

O-178 • В ОХО́ТУ *substand* [PrepP; Invar] **1.** [adv] as much as a person wants: **all one wants.**

2. ~ *кому* [subj-compl with бытьθ (subj: infin)] doing sth. is pleasant for s.o.: X-у делать Y в охоту ≃ **X likes doing Y; X does Y willingly.**

«...Я разобрала сегодня ваши чулки, — сказала она... — У вас некому разбирать, а мне в охоту» (Гончаров 1). "I've been sorting out your socks to-day," she said.... "You've got no one to sort them out, and I like doing it" (1a).

O-179 • ОТБИВА́ТЬ/ОТБИ́ТЬ ОХО́ТУ *у кого к чему* от *что делать coll* [VP; subj: abstr or human; more often pfv] to cause s.o. to lose the desire to do sth.: X отбил у Y-а охоту делать Z ≃ **X killed ⟨squelched⟩ Y's desire ⟨cured Y of the desire⟩ to do Z; X made Y lose interest in doing Z; X made Y lose Y's taste for doing Z; X discouraged Y's inclination to do Z.**

...Знакомство с русской историей могло бы давно отбить охоту искать какую-то руку справедливости, какой-то высший вселенский смысл в цепи русских бед... (Солженицын 2). An acquaintance with Russian history might long ago have discouraged any inclination to look for the hand of justice, or for some higher cosmic meaning, in the tale of Russia's woes... (2a).

O-180 • ОХУ́ЛКИ ⟨ПОХУ́ЛЫ⟩ НА́ РУКУ НЕ КЛАСТЬ ⟨НЕ ПОЛОЖИ́ТЬ⟩ *obs* [VP; subj: human; the verb may take the initial position, otherwise fixed WO] not to overlook one's own interests, not to fail to exploit an opportunity from which one might gain sth.: X охулки на руку не кладёт ≃

X doesn't let an opportunity pass him by; X doesn't pass up ⟨miss out on⟩ an opportunity; X doesn't lose sight of his own interests.

O-181 • **НА О́ЧЕРЕДИ** [PrepP; Invar; subj-compl with бытьø]
1. [subj: human] (to be) first in order of succession: X на очереди ≃ **X's turn is next; X is next (in line ⟨on the list etc⟩).**

Двоих из нашего отдела уже уволили, я на очереди. Two people from our department have already been fired, and I'm next on the list.

2. Also: **СТОЯ́ТЬ НА О́ЧЕРЕДИ** [VP; subj: human] to be included on a list (to receive sth.): X стоит на очереди ≃ **X is on a ⟨the⟩ waiting list.**

«Когда вам поставят телефон?» – «Кто знает? Мы уже год стоим на очереди». "When will you be getting a telephone?" "Who knows? We've been on the waiting list for a year now."

3. Also: **СТОЯ́ТЬ НА О́ЧЕРЕДИ** [VP; subj: abstr] (of a question, problem) (to be) urgent, demanding a quick resolution: на очереди стоит X ≃ **X is first on the agenda; X is ⟨has⟩ top priority; X demands immediate action; X is s.o.'s first priority ⟨most pressing concern⟩.**

O-182 • **ПО О́ЧЕРЕДИ** [PrepP; Invar; adv] **1.** in succession: **in turn; one after another ⟨the other⟩.**

Он по очереди обошёл всех обывателей, и хотя молча, но благосклонно принял от них всё, что следует (Салтыков-Щедрин 1). He made the rounds of all the townsfolk in turn and silently but graciously received from them all that was required (1a). ♦ [Человек] по очереди открыл замки (Федин 1). [The man] opened the locks, one after another (1a). ♦ На стене [летней уборной] справа, наколотые на гвоздик, висели квадратные куски газет. Чонкин срывал их по очереди и прочитывал... (Войнович 2). Squares of newspaper had been nailed to the wall [of the summer outhouse] on Chonkin's right. He tore them off one after the other and read them through... (2a).

2. alternately: **take ⟨taking⟩ turns; by turns.**

Персиков забыл и в течение полутора часа по очереди с Ивановым припадал к стеклу микроскопа (Булгаков 10). Persikov forgot his amoebas and for the next hour and a half took turns with Ivanov at the microscope lens (10a). ♦ Как мы с Таней болели! То вместе, то по очереди... (Набоков 1). What illnesses Tanya and I went through! Now together, now by turns... (1a).

O-183 • **В ПЕ́РВУЮ О́ЧЕРЕДЬ ⟨ГО́ЛОВУ** coll⟩ [PrepP; these forms only; adv or sent adv (often parenth); fixed WO] **1.** before (doing) anything else: **first of all; in the first place; first (off); the first thing (one does is...); (be) the first to...; (do sth.) first; (s.o.'s) first (job ⟨assignment etc⟩).**

«Уж коли ты такой большой начальник, то председателя-то в первую очередь менять надо...» – «Да, не мешало бы», – с ухмылкой протянул Михаил (Абрамов 1). "If you're such a big shot, then the Chairman should be the first to go..." "Yes, it wouldn't hurt." Mikhail smirked (1a). ♦ «Богдашкин, при распределении стройматериалов завтра в первую очередь учитывайте нужды Самохина» (Войнович 5). "Bogdashkin, when you're distributing building material tomorrow, take care of Samokhin's needs first" (5a). ♦ «...Сейчас надо утеплить машинный зал. Там три окна больших, их в первую очередь чем-нибудь забить» (Солженицын 7). "...Right now we must get the engine room warm. It's got three big windows, and your first job is to block them with something" (7c).

2. mainly: **most of all; above all.**

«Во-первых, ты уже начинал этот разговор, правда же? Много раз начинал. А во-вторых, это нужно всем нам, и в первую очередь твоей маме» (Трифонов 4). "In the first place, you began this conversation already didn't you? You started it many times. Secondly, this is necessary for all of us, most of all for your mama" (4a). ♦ ...Эта пепельница всегда мне напоминала

восточные стихотворения Бунина, и в первую очередь, конечно, «он на клинок дохнул...» (Катаев 3). ...This bowl reminded me of Bunin's eastern poems and, above all, of course, "he breathed upon the blade..." (3a).

O-184 • **В СВОЮ́ О́ЧЕРЕДЬ ⟨В СВОЙ ЧЕРЁД** obs⟩ [PrepP; these forms only; sent adv (often parenth); fixed WO] used to show that the action in question follows another action in series and is similar to that action in nature or effect: **in one's ⟨its⟩ turn; in turn;** [in limited contexts] **for one's part.**

...Они [амёбы] почковались... с молниеносной быстротой. Они разваливались на части в луче, и каждая из частей в течение 2 секунд становилась новым и свежим организмом. Эти организмы в несколько мгновений достигали роста и зрелости лишь затем, чтобы в свою очередь тотчас же дать новое поколение (Булгаков 10). ...The amoebas budded...with lightning speed. They split apart within the ray, and two seconds later each part became a new, fresh organism. In a few instants, these organisms reached their full growth and maturity, merely to produce new generations in their turn (10a). ♦ ...Имел он в виду вот что: замолви у меньшевиков за меня словечко, а я, в свою очередь, прикушу язык, что ты сюда приезжал с военной тайной (Искандер 3). What he had in mind was this: Put in a word for me with the Mensheviks, and I in turn will hold my tongue about your coming here with a military secret (3a). ♦ ...Ружьё есть ружьё, это не корыто, с ним расстаться он ни за какие пряники бы не смог. Настасья в свой черёд не захотела оставить прялку (Распутин 4). ...A gun's a gun and not a trough, and there was no way he could part with it. Nastasya for her part didn't want to leave her spinning distaff (4a).

O-185 • **СТА́ВИТЬ/ПОСТА́ВИТЬ НА О́ЧЕРЕДЬ** кого [VP; subj: human; usu. 3rd pers pl with indef. refer.] to include s.o. on a list (to receive sth.): X-а поставили на очередь ≃ **X ⟨X's name⟩ was put on a ⟨the⟩ waiting list.**

Нас поставили на очередь на квартиру. We were put on the waiting list for an apartment.

O-186 • **СТАНОВИ́ТЬСЯ/СТАТЬ ⟨ВСТАВА́ТЬ/ВСТАТЬ⟩ НА О́ЧЕРЕДЬ** [VP] **1.** ~ (на что) [subj: human] to include one's name on a list (to receive sth.): X стал на очередь ≃ **X put himself ⟨his name⟩ (down) on a ⟨the⟩ waiting list; X added his name to a ⟨the⟩ waiting list.**

Мы подумываем о покупке машины, уже стали на очередь. We're thinking about buying a car and have already put our name on the waiting list.

2. [subj: abstr] (of a question, problem) to become urgent, demanding a quick resolution: на очередь стал X ≃ **X became first on the agenda; X became top priority; X came to demand immediate action; X became s.o.'s first priority ⟨most pressing concern⟩;** [in limited contexts] **s.o.'s next concern was...**

Когда почва была достаточно взрыхлена учтивым обращением и народ отдохнул от просвещения, тогда, сама собой, стала на очередь потребность в законодательстве (Салтыков-Щедрин 1). When the ground had been sufficiently broken by courteous treatment, and when the people had had some respite from enlightenment, naturally, the next concern was for legislation (1b).

O-187 • **СМЕЖИ́ТЬ О́ЧИ** obs, elev; **СМЕЖИ́ТЬ ГЛАЗА́** obs [VP; subj: human] **1.** to fall asleep: X смежил глаза ≃ **X nodded ⟨drifted⟩ off; X slipped off to dreamland ⟨the land of dreams, the land of Nod⟩.**

2. to die: X смежил очи ≃ **X closed his eyes for the last time; X took his last sleep; X breathed his last.**

O-188 • **ДЛЯ ОЧИ́СТКИ СО́ВЕСТИ** [PrepP; Invar; adv; fixed WO] in order to avoid or eliminate feelings of remorse, guilt:

(in order) to clear ⟨appease⟩ one's conscience; for the sake of one's (own) conscience.

Кончилось тем, что Лена заставила его пообещать, что он завтра же с работы позвонит [тёще] Вере Лазаревне и мягко, деликатно... пригласит в Павлиново. Они, конечно, не приедут, потому что люди очень гордые. Но позвонить нужно. Для очистки совести (Трифонов 4). It ended with Lena making him promise that he'd call [his mother-in-law] Vera Lazarevna from work the next day, and gently, delicately...invite them to Pavlinovo. Of course, they wouldn't come, because they were very proud people. But he should call. To clear his conscience (4a). ♦ Мы обошли все этажи, и я предложил председателю и санинспектору посмотреть вторую секцию. Предложил я это просто для очистки совести, наверняка знал, что они откажутся (Войнович 5). We'd been on every floor when I proposed to Drobotun and the sanitation inspector that we take a look at the second section. This I did only for the sake of my own conscience, knowing they'd certainly refuse (5a).

O-189 • ВТИРА́ТЬ/ВТЕРЕ́ТЬ ОЧКИ́ *кому coll* [VP; subj: human; usu. impfv pres, past, or neg imper; if pfv, usu. infin with пытается, хочет, может etc] to (try to) mislead s.o. by presenting sth. in a false way that serves one's interests: X втирает Y-у очки ≃ **X pulls ⟨tries to pull⟩ the wool over Y's eyes; X puts ⟨tries to put⟩ something ⟨things⟩ over on Y; X tricks ⟨hoodwinks⟩ Y; X throws dust in Y's eyes; X fools ⟨tries to fool⟩ Y.**

Что уж говорить о тех, кто не имеет нашего опыта! Как легко, наверно, втирать им очки... (Гинзбург 2). And what of those who didn't have my experience? How easy it must be to pull the wool over their eyes... (2a). ♦ «Они, они! — козлиным голосом запел длинный клетчатый, во множественном числе говоря о Стёпе. — Вообще они в последнее время жутко свинячат. Пьянствуют, вступают в связи с женщинами, используя своё положение, ни черта не делают, да и делать ничего не могут, потому что ничего не смыслят в том, что им поручено. Начальству втирают очки!» (Булгаков 9). "They, they!" the lanky checkered character bleated like a goat, referring to Styopa in the plural. "Generally, they've been behaving like a dreadful swine lately. Drinking, having affairs with women on the strength of their position in the theater, not doing a stitch of work and really incapable of doing any, since they don't know the first thing about the job. Putting things over on their superiors!" (9a). ♦ История, как известно, фальсифицируется... и старшие поколения, пользуясь равнодушием младших, ловко втирают им очки (Мандельштам 2). And we

know only too well, history is constantly being falsified...and the older generation, exploiting the indifference of the young, cleverly hoodwinks them (2a).

O-190 • СМОТРЕ́ТЬ СКВОЗЬ РО́ЗОВЫЕ ОЧКИ́ *на кого-что* [VP; subj: human; usu. pres or past; the verb may take the final position, otherwise fixed WO] to idealize s.o. or sth., not notice his or its shortcomings: X смотрит на Y-а сквозь розовые очки ≃ **X sees ⟨looks at⟩ Y through rose-colored glasses.**

O-191 • ДАВА́ТЬ/ДАТЬ СТО ⟨ДЕ́СЯТЬ, ДВА́ДЦАТЬ и т. п.⟩ **ОЧКО́В ВПЕРЁД** *кому coll* [VP; subj: human; often pfv fut; the verb may take the final position, otherwise fixed WO] to surpass s.o. in sth. significantly: X Y-у даст сто очков вперёд ≃ **X will beat (out) Y hands down ⟨by a mile⟩; X will leave Y in the dust.**

«Это [стихи Влада] настоящее, это надолго! Он нашему Казимиру сто очков вперёд даст!» (Максимов 2). "This [Vlad's verse] is the real thing, it's classic stuff! He beats out Kazimir hands down!" (2a).

O-192 • КАК ОЧУМЕ́ЛЫЙ *бежит, несётся, мечется* и т. п. *highly coll* [как + AdjP; nom only; adv] (one runs, races, rushes about etc) in a crazed way, as if one has lost his mind: **like mad ⟨crazy⟩; like a madman ⟨a madwoman⟩; like one possessed.**

...Этот зажиточный негр и все его родственники как очумелые скакали по просёлочным дорогам на этой «Волге»... (Искандер 4). The prosperous Negro and all his relatives went right on racing around the country roads like mad in the Volga... (4a).

O-193 • КАК ОШПА́РЕННЫЙ *вскочил, выскочил* и т. п. *highly coll* [как + AdjP; nom only; adv] (to jump, run out etc) suddenly, swiftly: **as if (one had been) scalded; like a shot; like a bat out of hell.**

...Он вышел из-за стола и стал теснить Нюру к выходу... Отступая под его напором, Нюра пятилась до самой двери и, задом вышибя дверь, выскочила из неё как ошпаренная (Войнович 4). ...He came out from behind his desk and began to push Nyura toward the door....Yielding to his pressure, Nyura moved back over to the door, and knocking it open with her backside, she jumped through it as if she had been scalded (4a).

П

П-1 • НИ ПА́ВА НИ ВОРО́НА *obsoles, coll* [NP; subj-compl with быть∅, чувствовать себя etc (subj: human); fixed WO] a person who has drifted away from a certain group, milieu etc, yet has not become associated with another: X ни пава ни ворона ≃ **X is neither fish nor fowl; X is neither one thing nor the other.**

< From Ivan Krylov's fable "The Crow" («Воро́на»), 1825.

П-2 • СКЛОНЯ́ТЬ/ПРОСКЛОНЯ́ТЬ ВО ВСЕХ ПА-ДЕЖА́Х ⟨ПО ВСЕМ ПАДЕЖА́М⟩ *кого-что;* **СКЛО-НЯ́ТЬ И́МЯ** *чьё* ⟨**ИМЕНА́** *чьи*⟩ *all coll* [VP; subj: human; more often impfv; often 3rd pers pl with indef. refer.] to mention, speak about s.o. or sth. often, usu. with disapproval: X-a склоняли во всех падежах ≃ **X's name was bandied about.**

…На всех заседаниях, совещаниях, собраниях будут склонять наши имена (Зиновьев 2). Our names will be bandied about at every conference, meeting and assembly (2a).

П-3 • ДАЙ ЕМУ́ ПА́ЛЕЦ, ОН И ВСЮ РУ́КУ ОТКУ́-СИТ [saying] if you make a small concession to or do a favor for him (her etc), he (she etc) will demand even more: ≃ **give him ⟨her etc⟩ an inch and he'll ⟨she'll etc⟩ take a mile; given an inch he'll ⟨she'll etc⟩ take a yard; give ⟨offer⟩ him ⟨her etc⟩ a finger and he'll ⟨she'll etc⟩ grab your whole arm.**

[author's usage] [Захар:] Народ наш груб, он некультурен… и, если протянуть ему палец, он хватает всю руку… (Горький 1). [Zakhar:] Our people are coarse and uncultivated. If you offer them a finger they'll grab your whole arm (1b).

П-4 • НА БОЛЬШО́Й ПА́ЛЕЦ; НА БОЛЬШО́Й *both highly coll* [PrepP; these forms only] **1.** [adv] (sth. is done, one does sth.) very well, excellently: **superbly; splendidly; wonderfully; in fine fashion; like a pro.**

2. [subj-compl with быть∅ (subj: human, concr, or abstr) or, less often, nonagreeing modif] a person or thing is very good or excellent in qualities, condition etc: **first-rate; first-class; top-notch; super; A one; outstanding.**

«…Потом заеду к Дунярке… Вот, брат, как надо устраиваться! Квартирка из трёх комнат, свёкор – большая шишка… ходят по коврам… В общем, житуха у Дунярки на большой» (Абрамов 1). [context transl] "Then I'll pay a visit to Dunyarka….That's the way to live, brother! Three-room apartment—her father-in-law's a big cheese…the place is carpeted….All in all, Dunyarka has a great setup" (1a).

П-5 • ПА́ЛЕЦ ⟨ПА́ЛЬЦЕМ, ПА́ЛЬЦА *rare*⟩ **О ПА́ЛЕЦ НЕ УДА́РИТЬ** *(для кого-чего)* *coll, disapprov* [VP; subj: human; prep obj; usu. human or collect] not to undertake any action at all (may refer to a lack of effort in reaching some goal, an unwillingness to help s.o. needing one's assistance, or a lazy, unproductive way of spending time): X пальцем о палец не ударил (для Y-a) ≃ **X didn't lift a finger (to help Y); X didn't do a thing (for Y); X didn't make a move (to help Y);** [in refer. to an unproductive use of time only] **X goofed off.**

Анфиса вздохнула. Всем хорош у неё муженёк, а по дому палец о палец не ударит (Абрамов 1). Anfisa sighed. Her man was good in every way, but he didn't lift a finger around the house (1a).

П-6 • КАК ПА́ЛКА *худой, худ coll* [как + NP; Invar; modif (intensif)] (of a person) extremely (thin): **(as) thin as a rail ⟨a rake, a stick⟩.**

«Вообще, мне всегда было непонятно, почему женщины так падки на мышцы. Галочка, почему?» – «Мой муж худ

как палка». – «Ну, это, я думаю, вы его довели с вашей строптивостью» (Семёнов 1). "In general I could never understand why women are so partial to muscles. Why is it, Galina?" "My husband's as thin as a rake." "Well, I reckon you're the cause of that with your stubbornness" (1a).

П-7 • ПА́ЛКА О ДВУХ КОНЦА́Х [NP; sing only; subj-compl with быть∅, оказаться (subj: abstr, often это); fixed WO] (an action, policy, process etc that) has both positive and negative aspects and therefore is equally likely to bring about positive consequences as negative consequences: X – палка о двух концах ≃ **X is a double-edged ⟨two-edged⟩ sword; X could go either way; X can cut both ways.**

«[В статье] нового много выводят, да, кажется, идея-то о двух концах» (Достоевский 1). "There is much that is new in it [the article], but it seems the argument is two-edged" (1a).

П-8 • ПА́ЛКА ПЛА́ЧЕТ *по ком, по кому coll* [VP$_{subj}$] s.o. deserves to be punished, should be hit: по X-у палка плачет ≃ **X is asking for it; X is cruising for a bruising.**

«Митя, – сказал отец, – почему у тебя брюки опять порваны? Палка по тебе плачет!» "Mitya," said father, "why are your pants all ripped again? You're cruising for a bruising!"

П-9 • ВСТАВЛЯ́ТЬ ⟨СТА́ВИТЬ, СОВА́ТЬ⟩ ПА́ЛКИ В КОЛЁСА *кому coll, disapprov* [VP; subj: human] to (try to) hinder s.o. intentionally in some matter or in the realization of sth.: X вставляет Y-у палки в колёса ≃ **X puts spokes ⟨a spoke⟩ in(to) Y's ⟨the⟩ wheel; X throws a monkey wrench into the works; X upsets the ⟨Y's⟩ applecart; X trips ⟨tries to trip⟩ Y up; X spikes Y's guns.**

«Не нужно вставлять палки в колёса. Ведь стабильность правительства – единственный шанс мирного разрешения конфликта» (Эренбург 4). "There's no need to put spokes into our wheel. The stability of the Government is the only chance of a peaceful solution of the conflict" (4a). ♦ «Дай бог только, чтобы князь Кутузов, – сказала Анна Павловна, – взял действительную власть и не позволял бы *никому* вставлять себе палки в колёса – des batons dans les roues» (Толстой 6). "God grant that Prince Kutuzov assumes real power," said Anna Pavlovna, "and does not allow *anyone* to put a spoke in his wheel" (6a). ♦ «Исход предрешён в отрицательную сторону… Вот… посмотрите-ка, как эшелонировались войска!.. Вся эта железнодорожная сволочь вставляет нам палки в колёса» (Шолохов 3). "The scales are weighted against us….Look at the pattern of troop movements!…It's those damned railwaymen that are tripping us up" (3a).

< Loan translation of the French *mettre des batons dans les roues.*

П-10 • ИЗ-ПОД ПА́ЛКИ *coll* [PrepP; Invar; adv (usu. used with impfv verbs) or nonagreeing postmodif] (to do sth.) under duress, against one's desire: **under the lash ⟨the whip⟩; under (the) threat of punishment ⟨the stick⟩; under compulsion;** ‖ *Neg* не из-под палки ≃ **without any compulsion; of one's own free will.**

«Они все были мракобесы, большевикам служили из-под палки…» (Трифонов 6). "They were all obscurantists and served the Bolsheviks only under the lash" (6a). ♦ …Русскому правительству то-то и противно, что делается само собою. Всё надобно, чтоб делалось из-под палки… (Герцен 1). …Anything that is done of itself is distasteful to the Russian Government. Everything must be done under the threat of the stick… (1a). ♦ Не в первый раз Руслан наблюдал, как эти двуногие делают то, что им не нравится, и вовсе не из-под палки, – чего ни один зверь не стал бы делать

(Владимов 1). Many times Ruslan had noticed that humans often did things which they didn't like, and without any compulsion—something which no animal would ever do (1a).

П-11 • БРÓСИТЬ ⟨КИ́НУТЬ⟩ ПÁЛКУ *(кому) vulg* [VP; subj: human, male] to perform the sexual act: мужчина X бросил (женщине Y) палку ≃ **X stuck ⟨slipped⟩ it to Y; X screwed ⟨laid⟩ Y; X gave Y a (hot) rod.**

Сейчас, желая согреться, он притиснул к себе Таисию Рыжикову и пытался застегнуть у неё на спине пуговицы своего пальто. «Таська, я тебе сегодня палку брошу? Палку брошу?» — гнусавил он (Аксёнов 6). Right now, longing to warm himself, he had clasped Taisia Ryzhikova to his body and was trying to button up his overcoat behind her back. "Hey, Taska, shall I give you a hot rod today? How's about a hot rod?" he said in a nasal whine (6a).

П-12 • ПЕРЕГИБÁТЬ/ПЕРЕГНÝТЬ ПÁЛКУ *coll* [VP; subj: human] to do sth. to an excessive degree, past the point that is considered reasonable, acceptable etc: X перегнул палку ≃ **X went ⟨carried it⟩ to extremes; X went overboard ⟨too far⟩; X overstepped the mark; X overdid it; [in refer. to flattery] X laid it on too thick.**

«Скажите, серьёзно ли всё это? Не перегнули ли в этот раз палку Додичка и Володичка?» (Лившиц 1). "Tell me, is all this serious? Haven't Dodichka and Volodichka gone a bit too far?" (1a). ♦ Друзья Фуже на собрании радикальной фракции потребовали отставки правительства. Кокетливо улыбаясь, Тесса ответил: «Отставка правительства означает войну с нашим могущественным соседом»... От комиссии труда к Тесса явился Виар: «Я тебя недавно защищал на рабочем митинге... Ты перегнул палку. Правительство исключительно непопулярно» (Эренбург 4). At a meeting of the Radical Party, Fouget's friends demanded the resignation of the Government. Smiling jauntily, Tessa answered: "The resignation of the Government would lead to war with our powerful neighbour."...Villard called on Tessa on behalf of the Commission for Labour. "I defended you at a workers' meeting a few days ago," he said. "...You've laid it on too thick. The Government is more unpopular than ever" (4a).

П-13 • ПÁЛЬМА ПÉРВЕНСТВА *lit* [NP; sing only; fixed WO] full superiority (in some skill) or undisputed victory (in achieving sth. over one's opponent): **the palm (of supremacy);** ‖ пальма первенства принадлежала X-у ≃ **X bore ⟨carried off⟩ the palm;** ‖ X уступил Y-у ⟨Y отбил у X-а⟩ пальму первенства ≃ **X yielded the palm to Y; Y captured the palm.**

Отчасти это выглядело и как вручение пальмы первенства за лучший застольный рассказ (Искандер 4). It also looked a bit as if he were handing him the palm for the best dinner-table story (4a). ♦ «...Я согласен включить его в проект, поделить с ним лавры, отдать ему, наконец, пальму первенства» (Михайловская 1). "...I am ready to include him in the project, to share the laurels with him, even ready to give him the palm of supremacy" (1a). ♦ [author's usage] Вот тогда, после этого указания, мы сразу поняли, что пальму лунного первенства решено уступить американцам, а вскоре из бесед с сотрудниками Королёва я узнал подоплёку решения (Владимиров 1). [context transl] It was then, when we received those instructions, that we realised immediately that it had been decided to "yield" first place in the "moon race" to the Americans, and it was not long before I discovered from talks with Korolyov's colleagues what underlay the decision (1a).

< From an ancient Greek custom of awarding a palm branch to the winner of a competition.

П-14 • ВЫСÁСЫВАТЬ/ВЫ́СОСАТЬ ИЗ ПÁЛЬЦА *что coll, often disapprov* [VP; subj: human; more often pfv] to say or assert sth. that is not based on fact, that one creates in his mind: X высосал Y из пальца ≃ **X cooked ⟨dreamed, made⟩ up Y; X concocted Y; [in limited contexts] X pulled ⟨spun⟩ Y**

out of thin air; **X pulled Y out of a hat;** ‖ Y высосан из пальца ≃ **Y is a total ⟨complete⟩ fabrication.**

...Спустя месяц я вышла из [тюремной] больницы, допросы пошли своим чередом, хотя обвинения следователь [Семёнов] уже высасывал из пальца, очевидно нагоняя себе требуемые часы (Ивинская 1). ...After a month in the prison hospital, my interrogation was resumed and went on in the same old way—though Semionov, apparently trying to make up for lost time, now began to invent new accusations, spinning them out of thin air (1a). ♦ Я часто думал, почему в Союзе писателей так много бывших (и не только бывших) работников карательных служб. И понял: потому что они действительно писатели. Сколько ими создано сюжетов, высосанных из пальца! (Войнович 3). I often wondered why there were so many former (and not just former) punitive-service employees in the Writers' Union. And now I understand: because they really are writers. How many plots they've created, complete fabrications! (3a). ♦ Кто-то сдавленным шёпотом говорил рядом: «Они о людях, арестованных в тридцать седьмом году, сведения высасывают из пальца. Одной сказали: „Жив и работает", а она пришла во второй раз, и тот же дежурный ей дал справку — „Умер в тридцать девятом году"» (Гроссман 2). [context transl] One of the people near her said in a stifled whisper: "When it comes to people who were arrested in 1937, they just say whatever comes into their head. One woman was told: 'He's alive and working.' She came back a second time and the same person gave her a certificate saying that her husband had died in 1939" (2a).

П-15 • ОБВОДИ́ТЬ/ОБВЕСТИ́ ⟨ОБВЕРТÉТЬ, ОБВЕРНÝТЬ⟩ ВОКРÝГ ⟨КРУГÓМ⟩ ПÁЛЬЦА *кого coll* [VP; subj: human; more often pfv] to deceive s.o. skillfully, adroitly: X обвёл Y-а вокруг пальца ≃ **X took Y for a ride; X put ⟨slipped⟩ one over on Y; X bamboozled ⟨hoodwinked, duped etc⟩ Y; X pulled the wool over Y's eyes; [in limited contexts] X made Y look like an ass ⟨a fool, a jerk etc⟩; Y came out looking like an ass ⟨a fool, a jerk etc⟩.**

Ловко мы их [органы] обвели вокруг пальца, говорил Правдец своему Другу. Да, говорил Друг, это у нас не отнимешь! Тюремный опыт не пропал даром (Зиновьев 1). "We've really taken them [the secret police] for a ride," Truth-teller said to his Friend. "Yes," said Friend, "no-one can deny us that! Our prison experience has been of some use after all" (1a). ♦ «...И опять меня обвели вокруг пальца, я не знаю, как они это делают, но меня опять обвели вокруг пальца, и я опять дурак дураком, второй раз за этот день...» (Стругацкие 1). "And I came out of it looking like an ass again. I don't know how they do it, but I came out looking like an ass again, a real fool for the second time today" (1a).

П-16 • ПÁЛЬЦА ⟨ПÁЛЕЦ⟩ В РОТ НЕ КЛАДИ́ *кому coll* [VP$_{imper}$; these forms only; fixed WO] s.o. should be dealt with very carefully (because he is cunning, quick to take advantage of another's negligence or gullibility, cannot be trusted etc): X-у пальца в рот не клади ≃ **you have to be on your guard with X; X is not someone to mess around ⟨to trifle, to fool⟩ with; X is not (a man ⟨a woman⟩) to be trifled ⟨messed⟩ with; you can't ⟨I wouldn't etc⟩ trust X an inch.**

Меньшевикам очень хотелось к столу, но винтовки бросать не хотелось. Хозяина-то они не боялись, но уже поняли, что дяде Сандро пальца в рот не клади (Искандер 3). The Mensheviks very much wanted to sit down at the table but did not want to let go of their rifles. Although they were not afraid of the owner, they realized that Uncle Sandro was not to be trifled with (3a). ♦ «Что вы скажете насчёт Сноудена?» — «Я скажу вам откровенно, — отвечала панама, — Сноудену пальца в рот не клади» (Ильф и Петров 2). "...What do you think of Snowden?" "I tell you straight," replied the Panama, "I wouldn't trust him an inch" (2a).

П-17 • ПО ПÁЛЬЦАМ МÓЖНО ПЕРЕСЧИТÁТЬ ⟨ПЕРЕЧÉСТЬ, СОСЧИТÁТЬ, СЧЕСТЬ⟩ *кого-что* *coll* [VP; quantit impers predic with бытьø] (the people or things in question) are very few: Х-ов по пальцам можно пересчитать ≃ **you can count Xs on the fingers of one hand ⟨on your fingers⟩.**

Да и сегодня можно ещё по пальцам пересчитать примеры, когда литераторы отказывались бы публиковать свои произведения — не хочу вместо преследуемого, не хочу дать мерзавцу, стоящему во главе журнала, и т. д. (Орлова 1). Even today you could still count the examples on your fingers where writers would refuse to publish their works, saying "I don't want to do so in place of a person who is being persecuted, I won't give in to the villain who is at the head of the journal" and so forth (1a).

П-18 • **ПЛЫТЬ ⟨УПЛЫВА́ТЬ/УПЛЫ́ТЬ, УХОДИ́ТЬ/УЙТИ́⟩ МЕЖДУ ⟨МЕЖ⟩ ПА́ЛЬЦАМИ ⟨МЕЖДУ ПА́ЛЬЦЕВ, СКВОЗЬ ПА́ЛЬЦЫ⟩; ПРОХОДИ́ТЬ/ПРОЙТИ́ МЕЖДУ РУК** *all coll* [VP; subj: a noun denoting money, means] to be spent or wasted quickly and unnoticeably: Х уплыл между пальцами ≃ **X slipped through ⟨between⟩ Y's fingers.**

П-19 • **ПРОСКА́КИВАТЬ/ПРОСКОЧИ́ТЬ ⟨ПРОСКА́ЛЬЗЫВАТЬ/ПРОСКОЛЬЗНУ́ТЬ⟩ МЕЖДУ ПА́ЛЬЦАМИ ⟨МЕЖДУ ПА́ЛЬЦЕВ, МЕЖДУ РУК(А́МИ)⟩ *(у кого)*; ПРОСКА́КИВАТЬ/ПРОСКОЧИ́ТЬ СКВОЗЬ ПА́ЛЬЦЫ; УХОДИ́ТЬ/УЙТИ́ МЕЖДУ РУК** *all coll* [VP; subj: human or collect] to break away or escape adroitly: Х проскочил у Y-а между пальцами ≃ **X slipped through Y's fingers.**

«Вы со всею массою своею обрушились на несчастного Мортье при одной дивизии, и этот Мортье уходит у вас между рук? Где же победа?» (Толстой 4). "You with all your forces fall upon the unfortunate Mortier with his one division, and he slips through your fingers. Where's the victory?" (4a).

П-20 • **КАК СВОИ́ ПЯТЬ ПА́ЛЬЦЕВ знать *кого-что*** *coll* [как + NP; Invar; adv; fixed WO] (to know s.o. or sth.) very well: **(know sth.) like the back ⟨the palm⟩ of one's hand; (know s.o. ⟨sth.⟩) inside out.**

Слава спросил: «Город хорошо знаешь?» — «Как свои пять пальцев» (Чернёнок 1). Slava asked, "Do you know the city well?" "Like the back of my hand" (1a). ♦ Мы знали этот ручей как свои пять пальцев, мы в детстве запруживали его... и купались (Кузнецов 1). We knew the stream like the palms of our hands. In childhood we had dammed it to make ponds and...gone swimming in it (1a). ♦ «Микулицыных ваших знаю как свои пять пальцев» (Пастернак 1). "I know those Mikulitsyns of yours inside out" (1a).

П-21 • **ПА́ЛЬЦЕМ НЕ ТРО́ГАТЬ/НЕ ТРО́НУТЬ *кого*** *coll* [VP; subj: human; more often pfv; used without negation to convey the opposite meaning (often infin with verbs of prohibition); usu. this WO] not to cause s.o. any physical harm (by hitting, beating etc him): X Y-а пальцем не тронул ≃ **X didn't (so much as) lay a finger on Y; X never laid a finger ⟨a hand⟩ on Y; X didn't touch Y.**

Сыновей дедушка иногда избивал до полусмерти, но единственную дочь свою, Рахиль, как я уже говорил, ни разу пальцем не тронул (Рыбаков 1). Sometimes grandfather beat his sons till they were nearly half-dead, but he had never so much as laid a finger on his daughter, as I have already mentioned (1a). ♦ [Олег:] Не смей, не смей! Меня даже мама никогда пальцем не трогала! (Розов 2). [O.:] Don't you dare! Don't dare! Even mother never laid a finger on me! (2a).

П-22 • **ПА́ЛЬЦЕМ НЕ (ПО)ШЕВЕЛЬНУ́ТЬ ⟨НЕ ПОШЕВЕЛИ́ТЬ, НЕ ДВИ́НУТЬ⟩** *coll, disapprov* [VP; subj: human; used without negation to convey the opposite meaning] not

to make even the slightest effort (toward achieving some goal, helping s.o. etc): X пальцем не шевельнул ≃ **X didn't lift a finger; X didn't do a thing; X didn't make a (single) move.**

Незадолго до своего отъезда Хлебников пожаловался, что не хочет уезжать, но вынужден из-за отсутствия жилья... Хлебников согласился бы и на тёмный угол. Только никто ради него не пошевелил пальцем (Мандельштам 2). Not long before he went away, Khlebnikov complained that he didn't want to leave, but was forced to for lack of a roof over his head....Khlebnikov would have settled for any dark corner. Nobody, however, lifted a finger to help him (2a). ♦ Дело в том, что Тарантьев мастер был только говорить... но как только нужно было двинуть пальцем, тронуться с места — словом, применить им же созданную теорию к делу... — он был совсем другой человек: тут его не хватало... (Гончаров 1). The fact was that Tarantyev was proficient in nothing except talking...but the instant he was required to lift a finger, take a step, in other words, to apply his theories to any practical matter...he became an entirely different man, completely inadequate to the situation (1b). ♦ «В следующее воскресенье приходи, — сказал он мне на прощанье, — люди хотят отметить моё выздоровление». — «Клянусь богом, я пальцем не пошевелил ради этой бесстыжей затеи», — сказала тётя Катя... (Искандер 3). "Come over next Sunday," he said to me in farewell. "People want to celebrate my recovery." "I swear to God I'm not making a single move to help with this shameless plan," Aunt Katya said... (3a).

П-23 • **ПОКА́ЗЫВАТЬ ⟨УКА́ЗЫВАТЬ, ТЫ́КАТЬ⟩ ПА́ЛЬЦЕМ ⟨-ами⟩ *(на кого-что)*; ТЫ́КАТЬ ПА́ЛЬЦЕМ ⟨-ами⟩ *в кого* all coll, disapprov** [VP; subj and obj: human or collect] to censure s.o. (or some organization, group etc) openly, publicly, drawing general attention to the object of blame: X показывает пальцем на Y-а ≃ **X points a ⟨the, his⟩ finger at Y.**

В двадцатых годах все понемногу учили Мандельштама, в тридцатых на него показывали пальцами, а он жил, поплёвывая, в окружении дикарей и делал своё дело (Мандельштам 2). In the twenties everybody tried to reason with M[andelstam], but in the thirties they were already pointing their fingers at him; not concealing his distaste, he went on living among the barbarians and did what he had to do (2a).

П-24 • **ПОПАДА́ТЬ/ПОПА́СТЬ ПА́ЛЬЦЕМ В НЕ́БО** *coll, usu. humor or iron* [VP; subj: human; usu. pfv past] to give an answer, make a supposition etc that turns out to be incorrect, erroneous, absurd etc: X попал пальцем в небо ≃ **X was wide of the mark; X was way off (the mark); X was (way) out in left field.**

[Почтмейстер:] А что думаю? война с турками будет. [Аммос Фёдорович:] В одно слово! я сам то же думал. [Городничий:] Да, оба пальцем в небо попали! (Гоголь 4). [Postmaster:] What do I think? Why, there's going to be a war with the Turks. [A.F.:] Just what I said! I thought the same myself. [Mayor:] And both wide of the mark (4c).

П-25 • **ОБЖЕ́ЧЬ СЕБЕ́ ПА́ЛЬЦЫ ⟨РУ́КИ⟩ *на чём* coll** [VP; subj: human] to get in trouble or suffer loss or failure because of a miscalculation, one's foolishness etc: X обжёг себе пальцы на Y-е ≃ **X got burned (doing Y); X burned his fingers (by) doing Y; X had ⟨got⟩ his fingers burned.**

Сергеев уже обжёг себе пальцы на покупке краденого мотоцикла и больше ни о каких сделках, связанных с чёрным рынком, даже слышать не хотел. After getting burned buying a stolen motorcycle, Sergeyev didn't even want to hear about any more black-market deals.

П-26 • **ПРОПУСКА́ТЬ/ПРОПУСТИ́ТЬ СКВОЗЬ ПА́ЛЬЦЫ *что* coll** [VP; subj: human] **1.** (in refer. to sth.

reprehensible, offensive etc) to ignore sth. intentionally: X пропустил Y сквозь пальцы ≃ **X overlooked Y; X shrugged Y off; X let Y go (by).**

Он много прощал или, лучше, пропускал сквозь пальцы... (Герцен 1). He was ready to forgive much, or rather to overlook it... (1a).

2. Also: ПРОПУСКА́ТЬ/ПРОПУСТИ́ТЬ МИМО РУК *coll* (in refer. to a good opportunity, chance etc) to fail to take advantage of sth.: X пропустил Y сквозь пальцы ≃ **X let Y slip through his fingers; X let Y pass him by; Y slipped through X's fingers; X missed out on Y.**

П-27 • СМОТРÉТЬ/ПОСМОТРÉТЬ ⟨ГЛЯДÉТЬ/ПО-ГЛЯДÉТЬ⟩ СКВОЗЬ ПÁЛЬЦЫ *на что, rare на кого coll* [VP; subj: human or collect; usu. impfv; usu. this WO] (in refer. to s.o.'s reprehensible, illegal, annoying etc actions or behavior) intentionally not to react to sth., as if accepting it by allowing it to go on: X смотрит на Y сквозь пальцы ≃ **X turns a blind eye to Y; X closes ⟨shuts⟩ his eyes to Y; X looks the other way; X winks at Y; X deliberately overlooks Y; [in limited contexts] X takes a lenient view of Y; X doesn't check (up) on Y.**

«Неужели начальство не знает про эти тепловые ямы?» — «Отлично знает, но смотрит сквозь пальцы» (Аксёнов 6). "Surely the bosses at the top know about these heating tunnels, don't they?" "Of course they know, but they turn a blind eye to them" (6a). ♦ «...Он без разрешения ездил в Гольтявино. Возможно, я посмотрел бы на это сквозь пальцы, дело молодое, любовь и так далее. Но Гольтявино в ведении Дворцовской коменда-туры, а они на это сквозь пальцы смотреть не желают» (Рыбаков 2). "He went to Goltyavino without permission. I might have shut my eyes to it—young people, true love, and all that. But Goltyavino comes under the jurisdiction of the Dvorets commandant's office, and they are not prepared to shut their eyes to it" (2a). ♦ «Советская власть сквозь пальцы смотрит на возникновение Дальневосточной республики» (Пастернак 1). "They intend to form a Far Eastern republic, and the Soviet Government winks at it..." (1a). ♦ Единственная лазейка для склоки — соседский донос о непрописанном жилье, но начальство стало смотреть на это сквозь пальцы — время переменилось (Мандельштам 1). The only scope left for trouble-making is for a neighbor to denounce a tenant who lives without a permit, but the authorities have begun to take a lenient view of such cases. Times have changed (1a). ♦ «Это закрытая столовая... для сотрудников. Но на посторонних смотрят сквозь пальцы...» (Рыбаков 2). "This canteen is supposed to be reserved for employees, but they don't check up on outsiders" (2a).

П-28 • ПÁЛЬЧИКИ ОБЛИ́ЖЕШЬ ⟨-ете⟩ *coll* [VP; fut, gener. 2nd pers only; fixed WO] **1.** [indep. sent or predic (subj: a noun denoting some type of food, drink etc)] sth. is very tasty, appetizing: X — пальчики оближешь ≃ **X will make your mouth water; X is mouth-watering ⟨scrumptious⟩; you'll drool over X; X is finger-lickin' good.**

...Хотя главной их пищей была бульба-картофель, но из картофеля они готовили вкуснейшие блюда: бульба со шкварками, бульба с грибами, бульба с кислым молоком... А драники — картофельные оладьи с мёдом, сметаной или грибами — пальчики оближешь! (Рыбаков 1). ...Though their staple food was potatoes, they made them into the most delicious dishes, like potatoes with crackling, potatoes with mushrooms, potatoes with sour milk, and as for their potato fritters with honey, or sour cream, or mushrooms, we used to drool over them! (1a).

2. [indep. sent or predic (subj: usu. concr or human, female)] sth. is enticing, alluring; (of an attractive woman referred to in a conversation between men) some woman is very beautiful and desirable: X — пальчики оближешь ≃ **X will make your mouth water; you'll smack ⟨lick⟩ your lips (when you see X); X will make you lick your chops.**

«Рабинович-то твой у нас теперь обитает. Переселили. Ну и глаз у тебя, прокурор!.. Снайпер! Робин Гуд! Тиль Улен-шпигель!» Воровато оглядевшись, он [Скромных] почти уткнулся губами в прокурорскую шею. «Помнишь, намекал ты... ещё в сентябре? Я сразу догадался... Копнули мы поглубже и, говоря между нами, дельце получилось — пальчики оближешь» (Терц 7). "Your Rabinovich case has come my way. He's been turned over to us. I'll say you've got a good eye, Globov. You're a real sniper! A Robin Hood! A Tyll Eulenspiegel." Throwing a stealthy look over his shoulder, Skromnykh almost nuzzled the Prosecutor's neck. "Remember what you hinted at...as far back as September? I guessed what you were getting at at once. And now we've dug a little deeper: between you and me, we've got a case to make your mouth water" (7a). ♦ [Дулебов:] А я вам, вместо Негиной, выпишу актрису настоящую... Пальчики оближете (Островский 11). [D.:] And I'll send for a real actress to take Negina's place....You'll smack your lips when you see her (11a). ♦ «Гарнитур замечательный. Пальчики оближете. Впрочем, что вам объяснять! Вы сами знаете!» (Ильф и Петров 1). "It's a splendid suite. You'll lick your lips. Anyway, I don't need to tell you, you know yourself" (1a). ♦ «Такие, говорит, там шмары [*slang* = девушки] имеются — пальчики оближешь» (Абрамов 1). "He said they had skirts up there that'd make you lick your chops" (1a).

П-29 • БЕЗ ПÁМЯТИ *coll* [PrepP; Invar] **1.** [subj-compl with быть∅, лежать (subj: human)] one is, lies in a state of unconsciousness: X был без памяти ≃ **X was unconscious; X was out cold.**

«Когда дым рассеялся, на земле лежала раненая лошадь, и возле неё Бэла... Бедняжка, она лежала неподвижно, и кровь лилась из раны ручьями... Она была без памяти» (Лермонтов 1). "When the smoke had cleared, the wounded horse lay on the ground, and beside it lay Bela....Poor little thing, she was lying motionless, and blood poured out of her wound in streams....She was unconscious" (1a).

2. любить *кого-что,* **быть∅ влюблённым** *(в кого)* **увлечься** *кем-чем* и т. п. ~ [adv (intensif)] (to love s.o., be enamored of s.o. or sth.) very strongly, passionately: **(be) head over heels in love with s.o.; love s.o. madly ⟨to distraction⟩; (be) madly in love with s.o.; (be) crazy about s.o. ⟨sth.⟩.**

Целомудренный и застенчивый Николай... был без памяти влюблён в дочь управляющего одной из экономий (Ливиц 1). ...The chaste and shy Nikolai...was head over heels in love with the daughter of the manager of one of the estates (1a). ♦ Любил её Коля, простая душа, любил без памяти (Терц 5). Nicky loved her, the simple, decent fellow, loved her madly (5a). ♦ «Гостей множество, все они молоды, прекрасны, храбры, все без памяти влюблены в королеву» (Тургенев 3). "There are many guests. They are all young, beautiful, brave, and all are madly in love with the queen" (3b).

3. ~ *от кого-чего* [subj-compl with быть∅ (subj: human)] one is enraptured by s.o. or sth.: X был без памяти от Y-a ≃ **X was enchanted ⟨delighted, carried away⟩ by Y; X lost his head over person Y; X was ecstatic about thing Y; X was in raptures over Y; X was wild about Y.**

«По чести скажу вам: я до сих пор без памяти от вашего „Бригадира"» (Гоголь 5). "I tell you sincerely, I have not yet got over my delight at your *Brigadier*" (5a). ♦ В немного времени он [Чичиков] совершенно успел очаровать их. Помещик Манилов... был от него без памяти (Гоголь 3). It did not take him [Chichikov] long to charm both of them completely. Landowner Manilov...simply lost his head over Chichikov (3c).

4. бежать, нестись и т. п. ~ [adv] (of a person or animal) (to run, race etc) very fast, impetuously, not paying attention to anything around one: **like one possessed; like mad; at breakneck speed; like a bat out of hell.**

Пётр схватил конверт и без памяти помчался домой. Pyotr grabbed the envelope and raced home at breakneck speed.

П-30 • БЛАЖЕ́ННОЙ ⟨СВЕ́ТЛОЙ, НЕЗАБВЕ́ННОЙ⟩ ПА́МЯТИ *obs, lit* [NP_gen; these forms only; nonagreeing modif; foll. by a personal noun, often a person's name] (of a deceased person) remembered with respect and love: **of blessed ⟨hallowed, happy⟩ memory.**

«С блаженной памяти государя Петра Алексеевича история русской цивилизации принимает характер, так сказать, пионерный» (Салтыков-Щедрин 2). "...Beginning with Peter the Great, of blessed memory, the history of Russian civilization takes on a so to speak pioneering character" (2a). ♦ ...Между Крессе и Покленом произошёл серьёзнейший разговор. Передавать его не стану. Воскликну лишь: о светлой памяти Людовик Крессе! (Булгаков 5). ...A most serious conversation took place between Cressé and Poquelin. I shall not repeat it to you. I shall merely exclaim: Oh, Louis Cressé of hallowed memory! (5a).

П-31 • ВСПЛЫВА́ТЬ/ВСПЛЫ́ТЬ В ПА́МЯТИ *чьей, кого* [VP; subj: usu. abstr] to be recollected by s.o.: X всплыл в Y-овой памяти ≃ **X came back to Y; Y's mind returned to X; Y recalled X.**

Он долго не мог заснуть: в его памяти всплывала сцена на вокзале. It took him a long time to get to sleep: his mind kept returning to the events at the train station.

П-32 • ВЫЖИВА́ТЬ/ВЫ́ЖИТЬ ИЗ ПА́МЯТИ *coll* [VP; subj: human; more often pfv] to become forgetful because of old age, be unable to remember things: X выжил из памяти ≃ **X has lost his memory.**

П-33 • ВЫЧЁРКИВАТЬ/ВЫ́ЧЕРКНУТЬ ИЗ ПА́-МЯТИ *кого-что* [VP; subj: human; usu. pfv] to forget or make o.s. forget s.o. or sth., stop thinking about s.o. or sth.: X вычеркнул Y-а из памяти ≃ **X erased ⟨effaced⟩ Y from X's memory; X erased ⟨obliterated, blotted out⟩ all memory of Y; X excised Y from X's mind.**

Не хотелось больше этой боли, этой судороги, когда человек, на которого ты полагался, которого любил, вдруг малодушно предавал тебя и нужно было навсегда вычеркнуть его из памяти (Буковский 1). I could no longer face the pain and turmoil when a person you relied on and loved suddenly turned coward and betrayed you, and you had to excise him from your mind forever (1a).

П-34 • ДЕРЖА́ТЬ В ПА́МЯТИ *кого-что* [VP; subj: human] to retain s.o. or sth. in one's memory and/or constantly think of s.o. or sth.: X держит Y-а в памяти ≃ **X keeps Y in X's memory;** [in limited contexts] **X returns to thoughts of Y; X remembers Y.**

Старуха смотрела на Илью долго, до неловкой устали. Она искала в нём своего Илью, которого родила, выходила и держала в памяти, и то находила его в теперешнем, то опять теряла (Распутин 3). The old lady looked at Ilia until it was uncomfortable to do so any longer, searching for the Ilia she had brought into the world, raised, and kept in her memory, now finding him in the present Ilia, now losing him again (3a). ♦ Те [очевидцы], что остались, рассказывают по-разному, а некоторые и вовсе не помнят. Да, по правде сказать, и не такой это случай, чтоб держать его в памяти столько времени (Войнович 2). Those [eyewitnesses] that are [left] tell all kinds of different stories and some can't remember anything at all. Besides, to tell the truth, it was not the kind of incident you'd remember for that long a time (2a).

П-35 • НА ПА́МЯТИ *чьей, кого* [PrepP; Invar; the resulting PrepP is adv or subj-compl with быть_ø (subj: usu. abstr, human, or collect)] during s.o.'s lifetime, so that he himself has been a witness to sth. and remembers what happened at the time: на X-овой памяти ≃ **in ⟨within⟩ X's memory ⟨recollection⟩; X can recall ⟨remember⟩;** [in limited contexts] **in ⟨within⟩ living memory.**

Я думаю о своём роде, о его и своей судьбе... У нас было пять ветвей, все мужские. Четыре из них прекратились при моей жизни, на моей памяти (Федин 1). I think of my family, of its fate and my own... We had five branches, all male. Four of them came to an end during my lifetime, within my memory (1a). ♦ Саша никогда не думал, что в Советском Союзе есть ещё меньшевики и эсеры. Троцкисты — это уже на его памяти. Но эти? (Рыбаков 2). Sasha had never realized that there were still any Mensheviks or Socialist Revolutionaries left in the Soviet Union. Trotskyites he could remember. But the others? (2a).

П-36 • ПЕЧА́ЛЬНОЙ ⟨НЕДО́БРОЙ⟩ ПА́МЯТИ *lit* [NP_gen; these forms only; nonagreeing modif; often foll. by a personal or collect noun] (of the deceased who is) remembered disapprovingly; (of sth. that) once existed but then disappeared, leaving unpleasant memories: **of cursed memory; of ill repute; whom ⟨which⟩ no one cares to remember.**

П-37 • ПО ПА́МЯТИ *читать, рисовать, записывать что* и т. п. *coll* [PrepP; Invar; adv] (to recite, paint, write down etc sth.) without referring to the text, the original, or the source, but rather relying on one's recollection of it: **from memory.**

Тут Лёва написал ещё много отвлечённых от Тютчева страниц... Мы не можем восстановить по памяти, но там было несколько примечательно разумных страниц психологических обоснований... (Битов 2). Here without reference to Tyutchev, Lyova wrote a good many more pages....We can't re-create them from memory, but there were several remarkably judicious pages of psychological substantiation... (2a).

П-38 • ПО СТА́РОЙ ПА́МЯТИ [PrepP; Invar; adv; fixed WO] (to do sth.) because of pleasant or sentimental memories of times past (usu. related to an old friendship, an old love, or old traditions); (occas., to do sth.) as a result of a routine one followed in the past: **for old times' ⟨time's, memories'⟩ sake;** [in limited contexts] **by ⟨from⟩ force of habit; force of habit (makes s.o. do sth.); out of old habit.**

[Кай:] Появилась в половине одиннадцатого... Вся в снегу. «Приюти, говорит, по старой памяти — девочка в пути захворала...» (Арбузов 2). [K.:] She turned up at ten-thirty... She was covered with snow. "Take me in—for old times' sake," she said. "My little girl fell ill on the journey..." (2a). ♦ «Ваше благородие, дозвольте вас прокатить по старой памяти?» (Шолохов 2). "Your Honour, allow me to drive you, for old time's sake?" (2a). ♦ [Аннушка:] ...Вы меня любили прежде, — хоть по старой памяти скажите, отчего я вам опротивела (Островский 8). [A.:] You loved me once. For old memories' sake tell me why you despise me now! (8a). ♦ По старой памяти потянуло меня на Старую площадь (Зиновьев 2). Force of habit pulled me back to the Old Square (2a).

П-39 • РЫ́ТЬСЯ/ПОРЫ́ТЬСЯ ⟨КОПА́ТЬСЯ/ПОКО-ПА́ТЬСЯ⟩ В ПА́МЯТИ [VP; subj: human; more often pfv] to think concentratedly in an effort to remember or recall sth.: X порылся в памяти ≃ **X jogged his memory; X dug (down) deep into his memory.**

«Советую вам подумать, Панкратов... Мы вас щадим, поймите. И оцените. Покопайтесь в памяти, покопайтесь!» (Рыбаков 2). "I advise you to think seriously, Pankratov....We're being merciful with you, you must understand that. And you ought to appreciate it. Dig into your memory, dig deep!" (2a).

П-40 • В ПА́МЯТЬ *кого-чего* [PrepP; Invar; the resulting PrepP is adv] in honor of s.o. or sth., in order to preserve the memory of s.o. or sth.: **in memory of s.o. ⟨sth.⟩; in commemoration of sth.; to commemorate sth.**

Рядом справа был муж, которого она почему-то всегда называла Мансуровым, а иногда, то ли в насмешку, то ли в память давно минувших лет их островной жизни, — Мансуровым-Курильским (Залыгин 1). On her right was her husband, whom she habitually called Mansurov, but sometimes Mansurov-Kurilsky. This was half in fun and half in memory of the long-gone days when they lived on the Kurile Islands (1a). ♦ Так, я помню большой фейерверк в память гибели русского крейсера «Варяг» в японскую войну (Олеша 3). I remember, for example, a big fireworks display in commemoration of the loss of the heavy cruiser *Varangian* in the war with Japan (3a). ♦ «Я посадил дерево в память о том, что вы меня не любили» (Олеша 1). "I planted this tree to commemorate the fact that you didn't love me" (1a).

П-41 • ВЕ́ЧНАЯ ПА́МЯТЬ *кому* [indep. clause; fixed WO] a wish that the deceased always be remembered (usu. for his good deeds, noteworthy acts, great feats etc): вечная память X-у ≃ **may X's memory live ⟨on⟩ forever; may X never be forgotten; let us never forget X; let X be remembered forever.**

...Много девушек-связисток осталось в сталинградской земле, вечная им память! (Рыбаков 1). A lot of the girls in the signals were left behind in the soil of Stalingrad. May they never be forgotten (1a).

< The closing words of a funeral service.

П-42 • ВРЕЗА́ТЬСЯ/ВРЕ́ЗАТЬСЯ В ПА́МЯТЬ *кому, чью, кого* ⟨**В ПА́МЯТИ** *чьей*⟩ [VP; subj: usu. abstr or concr; usu. pfv] to be or become fixed firmly in s.o.'s memory: X врезался Y-у в память ≃ **X is ⟨has become⟩ etched (indelibly) in Y's memory ⟨mind⟩; X has etched itself into Y's memory ⟨mind⟩; X is ⟨has become⟩ engraved in Y's memory ⟨mind⟩; X is imprinted ⟨has imprinted itself⟩ on Y's memory ⟨mind⟩; X has stuck in Y's mind.**

Текстуально его слов я не помню, но смысл врезался мне в память... (Мандельштам 2). I do not remember the exact form of what he said but the sense is etched in my memory... (2a). ♦ «Так он говорил долго, и его слова врезались у меня в памяти...» (Лермонтов 1). "He went on like this for a long time, and his words became engraved in my memory" (1a). ♦ Случай этот сильно врезался в мою память (Герцен 1). This incident is vividly imprinted on my memory (1a). ♦ От скуки я разговорилась с крестьянской бабёнкой... «Ты чего за такого старого пошла? — спросила она... — Выдали что ли? А я себе сама взяла...» Дурацкий разговор врезался мне в память... (Мандельштам 1). To while away the time I got into a conversation with a peasant woman.... "What did you marry such an old 'un for?" she asked.... "Did they marry you off to him or something? I picked my man myself...." This absurd conversation has stuck in my mind... (1a).

П-43 • Е́СЛИ ПА́МЯТЬ НЕ ИЗМЕНЯ́ЕТ *кому* coll [subord clause; Invar; used in direct or indirect speech] used to indicate that although the speaker thinks that what he is about to say is correct, he might have remembered it incorrectly: если мне не изменяет память ≃ **if (my) memory doesn't fail ⟨deceive⟩ me; if (my) memory serves me correctly ⟨right⟩.**

П-44 • КОРО́ТКАЯ ПА́МЯТЬ (*у кого*); **ДЕ́ВИЧЬЯ ПА́МЯТЬ** coll **ДЫРЯ́ВАЯ** ⟨**КУ́РИНАЯ, ПТИ́ЧЬЯ** *obs*⟩ **ПА́МЯТЬ** coll [NP; usu. used as VP_subj with copula] (s.o. has) a bad memory, (is) forgetful: у X-а короткая память ≃ **X has a short ⟨a lousy etc⟩ memory; X has a head ⟨a brain, a memory⟩ like a sieve.**

Конечно, у западных учёных короткая память на русские фамилии... (Эткинд 1). Of course Western scholars have short memories for Russian surnames... (1a). ♦ «Одним словом, старик мог бы порассказать много интересного, если бы к концу

каждого столетия писал мемуары. Но Вечный Жид был неграмотен и... имел дырявую память» (Ильф и Петров 2). "In short, the old man could have described many interesting things had he written his memoirs at the end of each century. But the Wandering Jew was illiterate and...had a memory like a sieve..." (2a).

П-45 • НА ПА́МЯТЬ[1] знать, читать, цитировать и т. п. *что* coll [PrepP; Invar; adv] (to know, recite, quote etc sth.) without looking at the text, having memorized it beforehand: знать ⟨заучивать⟩ что ~ ≃ **know ⟨learn⟩ sth. by heart ⟨by rote⟩;** ‖ читать ⟨рассказывать, цитировать⟩ что ~ ≃ **recite ⟨narrate, quote⟩ sth. from memory.**

Все они чтили незабвенную память Н.М. Карамзина, любили Жуковского, знали на память Крылова... (Герцен 1). They all cherished the never-to-be-forgotten memory of N.M. Karamzin, loved Zhukovsky, knew Krylov by heart... (1a). ♦ За десять дней до приезда в Россию он [Маринетти] выпустил манифест... и теперь цитировал из него на память наиболее хлёсткие места (Лившиц 1). Ten days before his arrival in Russia, he [Marinetti] had published the manifesto...and now he quoted from memory its most trenchant passages (1a).

П-46 • НА ПА́МЯТЬ[2] давать, дарить, принимать *что* и т. п. coll [PrepP; Invar; adv] (to give or receive a gift) that is intended to remind the recipient in the future of s.o. or sth. special, dear etc to him in the past: **as a memento ⟨a souvenir, a keepsake, a remembrance⟩; to remember s.o. ⟨sth.⟩ by.**

«Пусть она [колода карт] останется у вас на память!» — прокричал Фагот (Булгаков 9). "Keep it [the deck of cards] as a memento!" cried Fagot (9a). ♦ Мне хотелось оставить ему что-нибудь на память, я снял небольшую запонку с рубашки и просил его принять её (Герцен 1). I wanted to leave him something as a souvenir. I took a little stud out of my shirt and asked him to accept it (1a). ♦ [Нина:] Я прошу вас принять от меня на память вот этот маленький медальон (Чехов 6). [N.:] I'd like you to have this little medallion as a keepsake (6b). ♦ ...Он [Чонкин] раскрыл свой вещмешок, переодел чистое бельё и стал рыться, перебирая своё имущество. В случае чего он хотел оставить Нюре что-нибудь на память (Войнович 2). ...Chonkin opened his knapsack, put on clean underwear, and then began rummaging through his possessions and sorting them out. In case anything happened, he wanted to leave Nyura something to remember him by (2a).

П-47 • НА СВЕ́ЖУЮ ПА́МЯТЬ записать, пересказать *что* и т. п. coll [PrepP; Invar; adv] (to write sth. down, retell sth. etc) while one still remembers it clearly, has not yet forgotten it: **while sth. is still fresh in one's memory ⟨mind⟩; before one forgets sth.**

Надо на свежую память записать эти анекдоты, а то забуду. I must jot down these jokes while they're still fresh in my memory, otherwise I'll forget them.

П-48 • ПРИВО́ДИТ НА ПА́МЯТЬ ⟨**НА УМ**⟩ *кому что* obs [VP; subj: usu. abstr] (some occurrence, situation, fact etc) causes s.o. to recall (some other occurrence, situation, fact etc): X приводит Y-у на память Z ≃ **X reminds Y of Z; X makes Y think of Z; X brings to mind Z; X brings back memories of Z; X calls Z to mind.**

Всегда бывает в январе несколько дней, похожих на весну — собственно, не то чтобы похожих на весну, а таких дней, которые вдруг приводят тебе на память облик весны (Олеша 3). In January there are always several springlike days, — actually, they don't so much resemble spring as suddenly remind you of what it is like (3a).

П-49 • ПРИХОДИ́ТЬ/ПРИЙТИ́ НА ПА́МЯТЬ *кому* [VP; subj: any noun] to be recollected by s.o.: Y-у пришёл на память X ≃ **Y recalled ⟨remembered⟩ X; X came back to Y; X came to mind.**

[450]

...При первом упоминании о Байбакове, всем пришло на память его странное поведение и таинственные ночные походы его в квартиру градоначальника... (Салтыков-Щедрин 1). ...At the mention of Baibakov everyone recalled his strange behaviour and his mysterious nocturnal visits to the governor's apartment... (1b). ...At the first mention of Dormousov, everyone remembered his strange behavior and his mysterious nocturnal expeditions to the town governor's apartment... (1a). ♦ Я думала о судьбе Сванидзе и Реденса... На память приходили опять послевоенные годы и мрачная зима 52–53 годов... (Аллилуева 2). I kept thinking of the fate of Svanidze and that of Redens....Again the postwar years and that grim winter of 1952–1953 came to mind... (2a).

П-50 • ПАН ИЛИ ПРОПА́Л; И́ЛИ ⟨ЛИ́БО⟩ ПАН, И́ЛИ ⟨ЛИ́БО⟩ ПРОПА́Л

[saying] (used to express a person's determination to risk everything in the hope of achieving success, obtaining sth. etc) either one will achieve all one wishes for, gain everything, or he will suffer total failure and lose everything: ≃ (it's) all ⟨neck⟩ or nothing; (it's) sink or swim; [in limited contexts] it will make me ⟨you etc⟩ or break me ⟨you etc⟩.

Рок, судьба, случай? Называйте как хотите... но то, что он, переведя дух, остановился именно перед нею [вывеской издательства], имело для него решающие последствия. Пан или пропал! (Максимов 2). Fate, destiny, chance? Call it what you like...but the fact that he stopped to catch his breath in front of that sign [the signboard of the publishing house] was to have decisive consequences. It was all or nothing (2a). ♦ [Купавина:] Чудо, как ты мила! Уж разве он [Лыняев] каменный, а то как бы, кажется... (В двери.) Тётя, прикажите обедать подавать. Да вот и Михайло Борисыч [Лыняев] идёт. [Глафира:] Подождите меня, я сейчас. Ну! Либо пан, либо пропал! (Островский 5). [K.:] It's wonderful how pretty you are! Unless he's [Lynyayev is] made of stone, then, seems to me... (At the door) Auntie, tell them to serve dinner. And here comes Mikhail Borisovich [Lynyayev]. [G.:] Wait for me; I'll be there right off. Well! Neck or nothing! (5a). ♦ В «поиске», когда захватывающая группа в пять-шесть человек кидается в немецкую траншею, вообще не до хитростей — тут уж либо пан, либо пропал, а подержишься, побережёшься, погубишь и себя, и всех (Распутин 2). When a party of five or six men throws itself at a German trench, there's no time for niceties anyway—it's all sink or swim, and if you hold back and try to cover yourself you'll destroy yourself and the others too (2a).

П-51 • ИДТИ́/ПОЙТИ́ ⟨ВЫХОДИ́ТЬ/ВЫ́ЙТИ⟩ НА ПАНЕ́ЛЬ

coll [VP; subj: human, female] to become a prostitute: X пошла на панель ≃ X became a streetwalker; X started turning tricks; X started ⟨took to⟩ selling herself (on the streets).

«Я с ней как с порядочной, а она меня обзывает, дрянь! Школу не успела кончить, уже на панель пошла, а меня обзывает!» (Рыбаков 2). "I spoke to her like a civilized woman, but she had to call me names, the slut! She hasn't even left school yet, and she's already turning tricks" (2a).

П-52 • СБИВА́ТЬ/СБИТЬ С ПАНТАЛЫ́КУ

кого highly coll [VP; subj: human or abstr] 1. Also: СБИВА́ТЬ/СБИТЬ С ПАХВЕ́Й obs to perplex s.o., throw s.o. into confusion: X сбил Y-а с панталыку ≃ X muddled ⟨befuddled⟩ Y; X got Y muddled ⟨rattled, flustered, all mixed up, all shook up⟩.

«Я, – говорил Персиков, – не могу понять вот чего: почему нужна такая спешность и секрет?» – «Вы, профессор, меня уже сбили с панталыку... вы же знаете, что куры все издохли до единой». – «Ну так что из этого? – завопил Персиков, – что же, вы хотите их воскресить моментально, что ли?» (Булгаков 10). "I cannot understand one thing," said Persikov. "Why is such rushing and secrecy necessary?" "You have already got me muddled, professor....You know that every last chicken has died off?" "Well, what about it?" shrieked Persikov. "Do you want to resurrect them instantly, or what?" (10b).

2. to induce s.o. to change his behavior for the worse, drive s.o. to do sth. wrong (by serving as a bad example or exerting some influence over him): X сбил Y-а с панталыку ≃ X led Y off the straight and narrow; X knocked Y off course; X led Y astray ⟨down the wrong path⟩.

П-53 • СБИВА́ТЬСЯ/СБИ́ТЬСЯ С ПАНТАЛЫ́КУ

highly coll [VP; subj: human; more often pfv] 1. Also: СБИВА́ТЬСЯ/СБИ́ТЬСЯ С ПАХВЕ́Й obs to become perplexed, not know what to do: X сбился с панталыку ≃ X got ⟨was⟩ muddled ⟨befuddled, rattled, flustered⟩; X got ⟨was⟩ all mixed up.

2. (often in refer. to moral deterioration) to change one's behavior for the worse: X сбился с панталыку ≃ X strayed from the straight and narrow; X got ⟨was⟩ knocked off course; X went astray ⟨wrong⟩; X went ⟨slid⟩ downhill.

Когда у человека наступает полоса невезения и он, как говорят, сбивается с панталыку, — кому какое дело! Вылезай сам (Трифонов 5). When you're overtaken by a streak of bad luck and are knocked off course, so to speak, who wants anything to do with you! It's your problem—you take care of it (5a).

П-54 • ПАНЫ́ ДЕ́РУТСЯ, А У ХЛО́ПЦЕВ ⟨ХОЛО́ПОВ⟩ ЧУБЫ́ ТРЕЩА́Т ⟨БОЛЯ́Т⟩

[saying] when those in power, the superiors, are in conflict, the common people, the subordinates, who suffer: ≃ the poor man always gets the blame; when (the) masters fall out, their men get the clout.

Несколько зная язык, он писал статью начерно, оставляя пробелы, вкрапливая русские фразы и требуя от Фёдора Константиновича дословного перевода своих передовичных словец: ...чудеса в решете... пришла беда — растворяй ворота... паны дерутся — у хлопцев чубы болят... (Набоков 1). Having a smattering of the language, he wrote his article out in rough, with gaps and Russian phrases interspersed, and demanded from Fyodor a literal translation of the usual phrases found in leaders: ...wonders never cease...troubles never come singly...the poor man always gets the blame... (1a). ♦ [author's usage] Штокман... обрисовал борьбу капиталистических государств за рынки и колонии. В конце его возмущённо перебил Иван Алексеевич. «Погоди, а мы-то тут при чём?» — ...«Ты не будь дитём [ungrammat = дитятею, ребёнком], — язвил Валет, — старая поговорка: „Паны дерутся, а у холопов чубы трясутся"» (Шолохов 2). Stokman described the struggle between the capitalist countries for markets and colonies. Before he could finish, Ivan interrupted indignantly, "But what has this got to do with us?"..."Don't talk like a kid," Knave sneered at Ivan. "You know the old saying, 'When masters fall out their men get the clout'" (2a).

П-55 • НЕ ПА́РА

кому [NP; Invar; subj-compl with быть∅ (subj: human); usu. pres] one does not suit s.o. in some respect, with regard to certain qualities (often in refer. to suitability for marriage in terms of social or financial status, age, appearance etc): X Y-у не пара ≃ X is not a (good) match for Y; X is not right ⟨not the right match⟩ for Y; X is no match ⟨mate⟩ for Y; X is not the man ⟨the woman⟩ for Y; [in limited contexts] X is not Y's equal; X is not meant for Y.

Наш замполит, капитан Сазонов, — типичный замполит, тупой, обрюзгший, с красной бычьей шеей и глазами навыкате, — был особенно ревнив... А она [его жена] — молоденькая, хрупкая, изящная, совсем ему не пара... (Буковский 1). Captain Sazonov, a typical commissar—stupid, flabby, with a red bull neck and bulging eyes—was the most jealous of all....She [his wife]—youthful, fragile, graceful—seemed not at all the right match for him... (1a). ♦ [Марья Андреевна:] Я искала любви, вы — интриги, побед. Мы с вами не пара (Островский 1). [M.A.:] I was looking for love, and you—for intrigues and conquests. You and I are no match, no match at all (1a). ♦ «Можете судить потому, до какой степени её бедствия доходили, что она [Катерина Ивановна], образованная и воспитанная, в фамилии известной, за меня согласилась пойти! Но пошла! Плача и рыдая, и руки ломая—пошла! Ибо некуда было идти»... Раскольникову [Катерина Ивановна] показалась лет тридцати, и действительно была не пара Мармеладову (Достоевский 3). "You can judge the degree of her privations from the fact that she [Katerina Ivanovna], so educated and cultivated and from a well-known family, consented to marry me! But she did! Weeping and sobbing and wringing her hands—she married me! For there was nowhere else to go."...She seemed to Raskolnikov to be about thirty, and truly was no mate for Marmeladov... (3a). ♦ «Я не богат, не чиновен, да и по летам совсем ему не пара...» (Лермонтов 1). "I am not rich, I don't hold high rank, and I'm certainly not his equal in years..." (1d).

П-56 • ПÁРА ПУСТЯКÓВ *(для кого)* coll [NP; sing only; subj-compl with copula, nom or instrum (subj: infin or abstr, often это); usu. pres; fixed WO] sth. or to do sth. is very easy: **child's play; a piece of cake; a cinch; (as) easy as pie; a snap; no sweat.**

Петя тебе починит утюг, для него это пара пустяков. Petya will fix your iron, that's a piece of cake for him.

П-57 • В ПÓЛНОМ ⟨ВО ВСЁМ, ПРИ ВСЁМ⟩ ПАРÁДЕ; ПРИ (ПÓЛНОМ) ПАРÁДЕ all coll [PrepP; these forms only; adv or subj-compl with бытьø (subj: human); fixed WO] in attractive (festive or official) clothing: **all dressed up; in full-dress uniform; in full regalia; dressed to kill; dressed to the nines; all decked out.**

«Я не при всём параде, так сказать, без галстука» (Грекова 3). "I'm not in full dress uniform, so to speak. No tie" (3a). ♦ [Нина:] *(Смотрит в окно.)* Васенька, иди полюбуйся. Наталья при всём параде (Вампилов 4). [N.:] *(Looking out of window.)* Vasenka, there's Natalia. Dressed to kill. Come and feast your eyes on her (4a).

П-58 • КОМÁНДОВАТЬ ПАРÁДОМ coll [VP; subj: human; fixed WO] to exercise control over everything, be the boss: X командует парадом ≃ **X runs the (whole) show; X is in charge; X calls the shots;** [of a woman who controls her husband and makes all the decisions] **X wears the pants (in the family).**

Сильной личностью считалась мать, командовала парадом она, властная, категоричная, неуступчивая... (Рыбаков 1). Mother seemed to have the stronger personality, she was the one in charge, authoritative, assertive, unyielding... (1a).

< From *The Golden Calf* («Золотой телёнок»), by Ilya Ilf and Evgeny Petrov, 1931, ch. 2.

П-59 • ПОД ПАРÁМИ [PrepP; Invar] **1.** [subj-compl with бытьø, стоять etc (subj: паровоз, пароход)] (a locomotive or ship is) ready to set out (upon some course): X стоял ~ ≃ **X was under steam; X had steam up.**

2. *substand* [adv or subj-compl with бытьø (subj: human)] in a drunken state (more often a slightly drunken one): X был под парами ≃ **X was (a little) fuzzy ⟨tipsy, high, tight⟩; X had had a few.**

П-60 • НА ВСЕХ ПАРÁХ [PrepP; Invar; adv] **1.** ~ идти, мчаться и т. п. (of a train, ship etc) (to go, race) at full capacity: **under a full head of steam; at full steam ⟨throttle⟩; full steam ⟨speed⟩ ahead;** [of a ship or boat] **under full sail.**

...[Коля] предложил, что он, ночью, когда придёт одиннадцатичасовой поезд, ляжет между рельсами ничком и пролежит недвижно, пока поезд пронесётся над ним на всех парах

(Достоевский 1). ...[Kolya] offered to lie face down between the rails that night when the eleven o'clock train came, and to lie there without moving while the train passed over him at full steam (1a).

2. ~ лететь, мчаться, нестись и т.п. *(куда)* coll. Also: **НА ВСЕХ ПАРУСÁХ** (to race, run toward some place or, when used figuratively, advance toward some goal) with great speed, with the utmost effort: **under full sail; at full ⟨top⟩ speed; at full throttle; full speed ahead.**

Главное то, что у меня объявился свой капитал, а потому и пустился я жить в своё удовольствие, со всем юным стремлением, без удержу, поплыл на всех парусах (Достоевский 1). The chief thing was that I had come into my own money, and with that I threw myself into a life of pleasure, with all the impetuousness of youth, without restraint, under full sail (1a).

3. *coll.* Also: **НА ВСЕХ ПАРУСÁХ** (to do sth.) very quickly: **on the double; in short order; posthaste.**

П-61 • В ПÁРЕ *с кем* coll [PrepP; Invar; adv] (in refer. to two people) (to do sth.) with someone else in a coordinated, cooperative fashion: **together; team up (with s.o.);** [in limited contexts] **as a team;** [often in tennis, badminton etc] **(be) partners (with s.o.); (play) doubles (with another team** etc).

Когда мы, в блокадную зиму, пилили с ней [тёткой] в паре дрова... она, пятидесятилетняя, точно так сердилась на меня, пятилетнего, как сейчас (Битов 1). During the winter of the blockade of Leningrad, when she [Auntie] and I were sawing wood together...she, fifty years old, lost her temper at me, a five-year-old, in exactly the same way as now (1a). ♦ «Мы с ним в паре играли утром в теннис против уругвайца и ирландца» (Аксёнов 7). "We played doubles this morning with a Uruguayan and an Irishman" (7a).

П-62 • ПÉРВЫЙ ПÁРЕНЬ НА ДЕРÉВНЕ ⟨НА СЕЛÉ⟩ coll, iron or humor [NP; sing only; subj-compl with бытьø, nom or instrum (subj: human) or obj-compl with считать кого etc (obj: human)] a man who stands out among a small group (often a group of which the speaker has a low opinion; often used in refer. to a man's popularity among a group of women): **cock of the walk ⟨the village⟩; king of the hill;** [in limited contexts] **a big fish ⟨frog⟩ in a little ⟨small⟩ pond.**

Им [офицерским жёнам] тоже скучно в тесном офицерском посёлке, расположенном обычно рядом с лагерем, вдали от больших населённых пунктов. Развлечений никаких, даже кино нет... Одна надежда — завести роман в лагере с зэком помоложе. Разумеется, избраннику завидует весь лагерь, и он ходит гоголем — первый парень на деревне (Буковский 1). They [the officers' wives] too found life boring, for in the cramped officers' quarters, which were unusually situated next to the camp and far away from any population centers, there were no amusements, not even a movie....Their only distraction was to start a romance with one of the young cons in the camp. Of course, the entire camp would be green with envy at the lucky fellow, and he would strut like a bantam—the cock of the village (1a).

П-63 • ДЕРЖÁТЬ ПАРИ́ [VP; subj: human; often foll. by a что-clause] **1.** ~ *(с кем, на что, в чём)* to stake or pledge sth. on the outcome of a yet undecided matter, usu. in return for a similar pledge by another or others: X держал пари (с Y-ом) (что...) ≃ **X made a bet ⟨a wager⟩ (with Y) (that...); X bet ⟨wagered⟩ (that...).**

[Шабельский:] Я с ним пари дорогой держал, что, как приедем, Зюзюшка сейчас же начнёт угощать нас кружовенным вареньем... (Чехов 4). [Sh.:] I made a bet with him on the way here that as soon as we arrived Zyuzyushka would start serving the gooseberry jam... (4a). ♦ Готов держать пари, сказал Учитель, что, если под землёй люди уцелели, они развили цивилизацию, являющуюся точной копией нашей (Зиновьев 1). "I'm prepared to bet," said Teacher, "that if people have survived under the ground they will have developed a civilisation which is an exact copy of ours" (1a).

2. держу пари [this form only] I assure you, I am ready to swear that...: **I (will) bet ⟨wager⟩ (that...); I'm ready to bet ⟨wager⟩ (that...).**

«Знаешь ли что? – сказал я ему, – я пари держу, что она не знает, что ты юнкер...» (Лермонтов 1). "Do you know what?" I said to him, "I bet she does not know that you are a cadet..." (1a). "You know what," said I, "I'll wager she does not know you are a cadet..." (1b).

П-64 • С ЛЁГКИМ ПА́РОМ! *coll* [formula phrase; Invar; fixed WO] a greeting to s.o. who just took a bath, often at a public bathhouse: **hope you enjoyed your bath!; hope you had a good bath!**

[Лукашин:] Я понимаю, ванна в каждой квартире – это правильно, это удобно, это цивилизация. Но процесс мытья, который в бане звучит как торжественный обряд, в ванне – просто смывание грязи. И хорошие поздравительные слова – с лёгком паром – они же к ванне неприменимы: какой может быть в ванне пар? [Александр:] Ты прав, баня очищает (Брагинский и Рязанов 1). [L.:] Yes, having your own bathroom, it's the proper thing, I know. It's convenient, it's civilisation. But having a good steam in the public baths is a ritual. At home it's just a matter of getting the dirt off. And that traditional greeting people give you when you come home from the baths – "I hope you enjoyed your bath!" It just doesn't apply to home bathing. What kind of steam can you get in a bathroom! [A.:] You're right, the bathhouse is a place of purification... (1a).

П-65 • ЗАДАВА́ТЬ/ЗАДА́ТЬ ПА́РУ *кому highly coll* [VP; subj: human; usu. pfv] to scold or rebuke s.o. severely: **X задал Y-у пару ≃ X let Y have it (with both barrels); X gave Y hell; X gave Y what for; X bawled ⟨chewed⟩ Y out.**

П-66 • НА ПА́РУ *(с кем) coll* [PrepP; Invar; adv] (in refer. to two people) (to do sth.) with someone else: **together; the two of us ⟨you, them⟩; team up (with s.o.).**

...Мы с Боликом пошли на пару в кинотеатр на Крещатике на «Праздник святого Иоргена» (Кузнецов 1). So Bolik and I went off together to the cinema on the Kreshchatik to see a funny film called *St. Jorgen's Day* (1b). The two of us, Bolik and I, went to the movie theater on Kreshchatik to see *St. Jorgen's Day* (1a).

П-67 • НА ПА́РУ СЛОВ *позвать, вызвать кого и т. п.;* НА ДВА СЛО́ВА; НА ПОЛСЛО́ВА *all coll* [PrepP; these forms only; adv; fixed WO] (to call, invite etc s.o.) for a brief conversation: ты мне нужен ⟨можно тебя (попросить), пойдём-ка и т. п.⟩ ≃ **I need ⟨I must have, can I have etc⟩ a word (or two) with you; I'd like to have a couple of words ⟨a few words⟩ with you; let's (go ⟨go and⟩) talk (for) a bit.**

Тальберг... глянул на часы и неожиданно добавил: «Елена, пойдём-ка на пару слов...» Елена торопливо ушла вслед за ним на половину Тальбергов в спальню... (Булгаков 3). Talberg...glanced at his watch and added unexpectedly: "Elena, I must have a word with you in our room...." Elena hastily followed him out into the bedroom in the Talbergs' half of the apartment... (3a). ♦ «Тогда другая просьба. С разрешения Ларисы Фёдоровны мне вас на два слова, и, если можно, с глазу на глаз» (Пастернак 1). "In that case, with Larisa Feodorovna's permission I should like to have a couple of words with you, if possible alone" (1a). ♦ «Пойдём-ка на пару слов, Люба», – позвал Егор (Шукшин 1). "Let's go talk for a bit, Lyuba," said Egor (1a).

П-68 • ПОД ПА́РУ *кому coll* [PrepP; Invar; the resulting PrepP is subj-compl with бытьø (subj: human)] one suits s.o. in some

respect or with regard to certain qualities (often in refer. to how a spouse or potential spouse is suited for his or her mate in terms of social status, age, appearance etc): X Y-у под пару ≃ **X is a good match for Y; X and Y are well matched ⟨suited⟩; X and Y make a good couple.**

[Шпигельский:] ...Мы друг другу нравимся. И в других отношениях мы тоже под пару (Тургенев 1). [Sh.:] ...We like each other. And in other respects too we are well matched (1a). [Sh.:] ...We like each other, and in other regards we are also well suited (1b).

П-69 • СКАЗА́ТЬ ПА́РУ ТЁПЛЫХ СЛОВ *кому coll, often humor* [VP; subj: human] to scold, reprimand s.o. with harsh words: X скажет Y-у пару тёплых слов ≃ **X will give Y a piece of X's mind; X will tell Y a thing or two; X will have a few choice words for Y; Y is (really) going to hear it from X.**

П-70 • КВАСНО́Й ПАТРИОТИ́ЗМ *lit* [NP; fixed WO] unquestioning dedication to, and indiscriminate praise of, everything native, even outmoded life styles, manners, and traditions: **blind patriotism; jingoism; [in limited contexts] hurrah patriotism; tub-thumping nationalism.**

«И, знаешь, в моем сознании с царских времён анти-семитизм связан с квасным патриотизмом людей из Союза Михаила Архангела» (Гроссман 2). "And one thing – ever since the time of the Tsars I've associated anti-Semitism with the jingoism of people from the Union of Michael the Archangel" (2a).

< From Prince Pyotr Vyazemsky's *Letters from Paris* («Письма из Парижа»), 1827. Vyazemsky coined the phrase «квасной патриотизм» to convey the meaning of the French phrase *du patriotisme d'antichambre*. The popular Russian beverage "kvass" («квас») was known in Europe.

П-71 • (И) МЫ ПАХА́ЛИ *coll* [sent; these forms only; may be used of one person or several people; fixed WO] said mockingly of a person who claims to have helped in some work but actually did little or nothing: **he ⟨she etc⟩ was a big help!; some ⟨big⟩ help he ⟨she etc⟩ was!; [in limited contexts] we worked hard, didn't we?**

«Тимченко утверждает, что работал вместе с вами над проектом». – «Он-то? И мы пахали! Да он ровно ничего не сделал». "Timchenko insists he worked on this project with you." "Him? Some help he was! He did absolutely nothing."

< From Ivan Dmitriev's fable "The Fly" («Муха»), 1803.

П-72 • (И) НЕ ПА́ХНЕТ *чем coll* [VP; impers; pres or past] sth. is completely absent (and there are no indications that it will appear): X-ом и не пахнет ≃ **there isn't (even) a trace ⟨a hint, a sign⟩ of X.**

То они в Загорск, то в Суздаль, то на Святые Горы. И всё поближе к монахам, к старине... Нет, конечно, никакой верой в настоящем смысле тут и не пахло, а вот как: томление духа... И даже, пожалуй, мода (Трифонов 5). Sometimes they went to Zagorsk, sometimes to Suzdal, and sometimes to Svyatye Gory. Ever closer to the monks and to antiquity....No, in this case, of course, there wasn't even a trace of faith in the real sense of the word, but rather a certain spiritual weariness....Perhaps too, it was even a question of fashion (5a).

П-73 • ПЛО́ХО ⟨НЕХОРОШО́⟩ ПА́ХНЕТ *coll* [VP; subj: abstr; pres or past; fixed WO] sth. seems suspicious, does not bode well: X плохо пахнет ≃ **X smells fishy; there's something fishy about X; X doesn't smell right; I smell a rat.**

[Атуева:] Этот маркёр... такой игрок на бильярде, что, может, первый по всему городу... и играет он с одним важным, очень важным лицом... Этот теперь маркёр во время игры-то всякие ему... историйки и подпускает, да вдруг и об деле каком ввернёт, – и, видите, многие лица через этого маркёра успели. [Нелькин:] Ну, нет, Анна Антоновна, — это что-то нехорошо пахнет (Сухово-Кобылин 1). [А.:] ...This marker...is perhaps the best billiard player in the whole city....He happens to play billiards with one important, one very important person....Now when they play, this marker tells him all kinds of little stories and this way can raise some important issue when he wants. There are a number of people who've made out very well on account of this marker. [N.:] Anna Antonovna, it just doesn't smell right to me (1a).

П-74 • **НА ПАЯ́Х** *(с кем)* [PrepP; Invar; adv, subj-compl with быть∅ (subj: human), or nonagreeing modif] (to undertake some venture) collaboratively, contributing funds and/or labor to it: **go shares on sth.; share sth.; (do sth.) jointly ⟨as partners⟩; (be in sth.) together;** ‖ на равных паях ≃ **(a venture ⟨sth. is undertaken etc⟩) with equal shares; (undertake sth.) in equal shares;** [when there are exactly two participants] **with ⟨in⟩ half shares.**

Со Ставровыми Пряслины жили коммуной, считай, всю войну... Они держали на паях корову, сообща заготовляли сено, дрова, выручали друг дружку едой (Абрамов 1). Throughout the war...the Pryaslins and the Stavrovs had lived as a little commune: they shared a cow, laid in hay and firewood together and helped each other out with food (1a). ♦ «...Да вы-то, господин Лужин, чего же? Ведь это ваша невеста... И не могли же вы не знать, что мать под свой пенсион на дорогу вперёд занимает? Конечно, тут у вас общий коммерческий оборот, предприятие на обоюдных выгодах и на равных паях, значит, и расходы пополам...» (Достоевский 3). "...But you, Mr. Luzhin, what about you? She's your bride... Can you possibly be unaware that her mother is borrowing money on her pension for the journey? Of course, you've set up a joint commercial venture here, a mutually profitable enterprise, and with equal shares, so the expenses should also be divided equally..." (3c).

П-75 • **НАЖИМА́ТЬ/НАЖА́ТЬ НА ВСЕ ПЕДА́ЛИ** *coll;* **НАЖИМА́ТЬ/НАЖА́ТЬ (НА) ВСЕ ПРУЖИ́НЫ** *obs, coll* [VP; subj: human] to make every effort and exploit every available possibility (in order to attain sth. or achieve some goal): Х нажимает на все педали ≃ **X is pulling out all the stops; X is giving it his all ⟨everything he's got⟩; X is going all out; X is doing his utmost;** [in refer. to one's use of personal influence or connections to obtain sth.] **X is pulling strings ⟨wires⟩.**

Чтобы получить выгодный государственный заказ, Панкин нажимал на все педали: звонил знакомым чиновникам, давал взятки и даже пригласил влиятельную секретаршу замминистра в ресторан. In order to get a profitable government contract, Pankin pulled out all the stops: he called some officials he knew, greased a few palms, and even invited the deputy minister's influential secretary out to dinner.

П-76 • **(КАК БУ́ДТО ⟨СЛО́ВНО, ТО́ЧНО⟩) ПЕЛЕНА́ ПА́ДАЕТ/УПА́ЛА ⟨СПАДА́ЕТ/СПА́ЛА⟩ (С ГЛАЗ** *чьих*); **(КАК БУ́ДТО ⟨СЛО́ВНО, ТО́ЧНО⟩) ПОКРО́В ПА́ДАЕТ/УПА́Л ⟨СПАДА́ЕТ/СПАЛ⟩ (С ГЛАЗ** *чьих)* all *lit* [VP_subj; usu. pfv] s.o. suddenly becomes aware of the truth and realizes that he had been mistaken: пелена упала с Х-овых глаз ≃ **(it's as if) the scales fell from X's eyes; (it's as if) a blindfold had been taken from X's eyes.**

П-77 • **В ПЕЛЁНКАХ** *coll* [PrepP; these forms only; subj-compl with copula or adv] **1.** [subj: human] in one's infancy: **in the cradle; in diapers;** [in limited contexts] **when one was wetting his diapers.**

2. Also: **В КОЛЫБЕ́ЛИ** *lit* [subj: abstr] in an embryonic state, in its initial period of development: **in its infancy; in its earliest stages of development; in the earliest stages of its development.**

П-78 • **ВЫХОДИ́ТЬ/ВЫ́ЙТИ ИЗ ПЕЛЁНОК** *coll* [VP; usu. pfv; subj: human] to become an adult (old enough to make one's own decisions, run one's own life etc): Х вышел из пелёнок ≃ **X is (all) grown up; X is a big boy ⟨girl⟩ (now); X isn't a kid ⟨a baby⟩ anymore.**

Митя давно уже вышел из пелёнок, а ты с ним по-прежнему разговариваешь как с маленьким. Mitya's been grown up for a long time, but you still talk to him as if he were a kid.

П-79 • **С ⟨ОТ⟩ ПЕЛЁНОК** *coll;* **С ⟨ОТ⟩ ПЕЛЁН** *obs;* **С ⟨ОТ⟩ КОЛЫБЕ́ЛИ** *lit* [PrepP; these forms only; adv] from an extremely early age: **from the cradle; from the day one was born; from one's (very) infancy; from one's earliest childhood; while still in diapers.**

Идеология вдалбливалась в нас с пелёнок. Некоторые в неё поверили искренне. Другие относились, как к религии, со смесью веры и сомнения... (Войнович 1). Ideology was drummed into our heads from the day we were born. Some of us were sincere in our beliefs. Others approached ideology with a mixture of belief and doubt, the way people approach religion... (1a). ♦ «Я спрашиваю: о чём люди — с самых пелёнок — молились, мечтали, мучились?» (Замятин 1). "I ask you: what did people—from their very infancy—pray for, dream about, long for?" (1a). ♦ Коля был сыном известного мелюзеевского часовщика. В Мелюзееве его знали с пелёнок (Пастернак 1). Kolia, the son of a well-known Meliuzeievo clockmaker, had been a familiar figure in Meliuzeievo from his earliest childhood (1a).

П-80 • **СНИМА́ТЬ/СНЯТЬ ПЕ́НКИ** *(с чего) coll, disapprov* [VP; subj: human or collect; usu. impfv] to take for o.s. the benefits from or the best part of sth. (usu. without having earned it or having any right to it; often in cases where one benefits from another's labor): Х снимает пенки ≃ **X laps up the cream; X skims the cream (off Y);** [in cases where one benefits from another's labor only] **X reaps the benefits.**

«Собаку Савранских будут снимать в телерекламе». — «Они неплохо устроились: собака будет работать, а Савранские — снимать пенки!» "The Savranskys' dog is going to be in a TV commercial." "Not a bad setup: the dog will work and the Savranskys will reap the benefits!" ♦ «Совершенно ясно, что некоторое время мы продержимся впереди автопробега, снимая пенки, сливки и тому подобную сметану с этого высококультурного начинания» (Ильф и Петров 2). [context transl] "It is perfectly clear that for a certain time we shall keep ahead of the auto race, skimming the heavy cream, the light cream, and the other densities of cream that this highly cultured enterprise may yield (2a).

П-81 • **С ПЕ́НОЙ У РТА** *доказывать, утверждать что, спорить* и т. п. [PrepP; Invar; adv; used with impfv verbs; fixed WO] (to assert sth., argue etc) vehemently, passionately: **with fervor ⟨zeal⟩; heatedly; aggressively; furiously.**

«Дементьев сильно эволюционировал за десять лет». — «Да где ж эволюционировал, если с пеной у рта бился против „Ивана Денисовича"?» (Солженицын 2). [context transl] "Dementyev has developed a lot in the last ten years." "How can you say that when he fought tooth and nail against *Ivan Denisovich*?" (2a).

П-82 • **КАК ПЕНЬ** *стоять, сидеть* и т. п. *highly coll, disapprov, rude when used in direct address* [как + NP; Invar; adv; may be used with pl subj] (to stand, sit etc somewhere) not saying or doing anything, not showing any interest in or understanding of what is going on etc: Х стоял ⟨сидел⟩ как пень ≃ **X was standing ⟨sitting⟩ (there) like a dummy.**

П-83 • **ПЕНЬ БЕРЁЗОВЫЙ** *highly coll, rude* [NP; sing only; fixed WO] a dull-witted, dumb person: **blockhead; numskull; dolt.**

П-84 • **ЧЕРЕЗ ПЕНЬ КОЛО́ДУ ⟨ПЕНЬ-КОЛО́ДУ⟩** *coll, disapprov* [PrepP; these forms only; adv; usu. used with impfv verbs; fixed WO] **1. делать, рассказывать** и т. п. *что* ~ (to do sth.) negligently, carelessly, or (to narrate, tell etc sth.) in an irregular fashion: **any old ⟨which⟩ way; haphazardly; in a slipshod manner;** [in limited contexts] **stumble (along);** [in refer. to narrating a story etc only] **stumble over.**

Новые рабочие оказались ленивыми и неквалифицированными: всё, что им поручалось, они делали через пень колоду. The new workers turned out to be lazy and incompetent: they did everything assigned to them in a slipshod manner.

2. идти, развиваться ~ (of the way some work, project, enterprise etc is going) in an uneven fashion, not as smoothly, quickly, or efficiently as desired: **limp (along).**

П-85 • **ПЕНЯ́ТЬ НА СЕБЯ́** [VP; subj: human; usu. imper пеняй(те) or пусть пеняет ⟨пеняют⟩; fixed WO] (usu. used in the imperative as a warning or threat that if the person in question does not do what he should, what he is ordered to etc, he will have to bear the consequences) to be solely at fault (for the outcome): пеняй(те) на себя ≃ **you ⟨you'll⟩ have only yourself to blame; you can only blame yourself.**

«Если каким бы то ни было образом вы знаете и укажете нам, где он [государственный кредитный билет] теперь находится, то, уверяю вас честным словом, и беру всех в свидетели, что дело тем только и кончится. В противном же случае принуждён буду обратиться к мерам весьма серьёзным, тогда... пеняйте уже на себя-с!» (Достоевский 3). "If by any manner of means you know and are able to tell us where it [the state credit bill] now is, then I give you my word of honour, and summon those present as witnesses, that I shall let the matter end there. If such is not the case, then I shall have no option but to resort to measures of a thoroughly serious nature, and then...you will have only yourself to blame!" (3d).

П-86 • **ВОЗРОДИ́ТЬСЯ ИЗ ПЕ́ПЛА** *lit, elev* [VP; subj: concr] (of sth. that has been destroyed, burned, pillaged etc) to reappear in its former condition: X возродился из пепла ≃ **X rose from the ashes.**

Роман Булгакова [«Мастер и Маргарита»] вышел как бы из небытия, возродился из пепла, подтверждая тем самым главную надежду автора, что рукописи не горят (Войнович 1). Bulgakov's novel [*The Master and Margarita*] seemed to return from oblivion, to rise from the ashes, thereby confirming the author's principal hope—that manuscripts don't burn (1a).

П-87 • **ВЫХОДИ́ТЬ/ВЫ́ЙТИ ИЗ-ПОД ПЕРА́** *чьего, кого lit* [VP; subj: a noun denoting a written piece] to be written by s.o.: X вышел из-под пера Y-а ≃ **X issued ⟨came, flowed⟩ from Y's pen.**

Все эти награды он [Федин] получил лишь многократно доказав, что как писатель он полностью кончился и из-под его пера никогда не выйдет ни одной живой строчки (Войнович 1). He [Fedin] was presented all those awards only after demonstrating many times over that he was utterly finished as a writer and that a single living line would never issue from his pen (1a).

П-88 • **НЕ ТЫ ⟨я, он** и т. п.**⟩ ПЕ́РВЫЙ, НЕ ТЫ ⟨я, он** и т. п.**⟩ ПОСЛЕ́ДНИЙ** [sent; fixed WO] you are (I am etc) not the only person in the world who has ever gone through, or will ever go through, the experience in question (often used to console s.o. or o.s. during a painful or unpleasant experience): **you're ⟨I'm, he's etc⟩ not the first and you ⟨I, he etc⟩ won't be the last.**

Она согласилась на аборт ради него... Всё на свете повторяется и будет повторяться миллион раз, не она первая, не она последняя, обычное женское дело (Рыбаков 2). She agreed to have an abortion for his sake....Everything in life repeats itself and will go on repeating itself a million times over, she wasn't the first and wouldn't be the last, it was a normal female thing (2a).

П-89 • **НЕТ ПЕРЕВО́ДА** *кому-чему highly coll* [VP; impers] certain categories of people (types of animals, kinds of objects etc) are available in large numbers or quantities: X-ам нет перевода ≃ **there's no end to the Xs; there's no lack of Xs; there's an abundance of Xs.**

П-90 • **ПЕРЕЖИВА́ТЬ/ПЕРЕЖИ́ТЬ (САМОГО́) СЕБЯ́** [VP; usu. pfv] **1.** *lit* [subj: human] (of a person who had a great impact on society, intellectual life etc) to retain significance and be remembered after death: X переживёт себя ≃ **X will live on (in people's memories); X will not be forgotten.**

2. [subj: human or abstr] (of a person) to lose significance during one's own lifetime; (of an idea, method etc) to become dated: X пережил себя ≃ **X has outlived his ⟨its⟩ usefulness; X has had his ⟨its⟩ day; person X has become a has-been; thing X has become passé.**

П-91 • **ПЕРЕКАТИ́-ПО́ЛЕ** *coll* [NP; usu. subj-compl with бытьø (subj: human)] a person who is prone to constantly changing his place of residence or work: **rolling stone.**

«Наших товарищей предупредили, что Еврейская лига обороны хочет устроить беспорядки, постарается сорвать митинг», — сказала Кэрол усмехаясь, испытующе погилядывая на нас с Александром. Мне-то что, я перекати-поле, я русский украинец, есть во мне осетинская кровь и татарская, я только и ищу приключений, а вот Александр — еврей... (Лимонов 1). "Our comrades have been warned that the Jewish Defense League wants to start a riot, they're going to try and break up the meeting," Carol said with a grin, glancing searchingly at Alexander and me. What did I care, I was a rolling stone, a Russian Ukrainian; I had both Ossetian and Tatar blood in me, all I sought was adventure. But Alexander was a Jew... (1a).

< From the name of a desert plant ("tumbleweed") that breaks off at the root when mature and is blown about by the wind.

П-92 • **КРИЧА́ТЬ НА ВСЕХ ПЕРЕКРЁСТКАХ** *(о ком-чём) coll* [VP; subj: human] to say or tell sth. repeatedly, insistently, and for all to hear: X кричал (об Y-е) на всех перекрёстках ≃ **X shouted about Y from the rooftops ⟨from the housetops, on every street corner⟩; X shouted from the rooftops ⟨the housetops etc⟩ that...; X broadcast (the fact) that...**

«Мы оба считаем, что об этом надо кричать на всех перекрёстках, а когда доходит до дела, вдруг вспоминаем о дисциплине и принимаемся послушно играть на руку всем этим вождистам, либералам, просветителям...» (Стругацкие 2). "Both you and I believe that it must be shouted from the rooftops; but when it comes time to act, we suddenly remember about discipline and play docilely into the hands of our great leaders, those outstanding liberals, those pillars of enlightenment" (2a).

П-93 • **ПЕРЕЛА́МЫВАТЬ/ПЕРЕЛОМИ́ТЬ СЕБЯ́** [VP; subj: human; more often pfv, esp. pfv infin with хотел, пытался, не мог etc] **1.** to compel o.s. to act in a different fashion, change one's conduct, habits etc: X не может переломить себя ≃ **X cannot force himself to change ⟨to act differently⟩; X cannot change his (own) nature.**

2. to suppress, conquer some feeling, mood: X переломил себя ≃ **X overcame ⟨mastered⟩ his emotions; X got a grip on himself; X got hold of himself; X restrained himself.**

Сочувствую вашему горю, но всё же вам надо переломить себя и вернуться к работе. I sympathize with your sorrow, but all the same, you've got to get a grip on yourself and go back to work.

П-94 • **БРАТЬ/ВЗЯТЬ В ПЕРЕПЛЁТ** *кого coll* [VP; subj: human] to force s.o. to act as one desires by putting pressure on him, reprimanding him etc: X взял Y-а в переплёт ≃ **X got tough with Y; X cracked down on Y; X came down hard on Y.**

За два месяца до соревнований тренер взял нас в переплёт и тренировал нас по восемь часов в день. Starting two months before the competition, the coach got tough with us and made us train eight hours a day.

П-95 • ПОПАДА́ТЬ/ПОПА́СТЬ В ПЕРЕПЛЁТ ⟨В ПЕРЕДЕ́ЛКУ, В ПЕРЕДРЯ́ГУ⟩; БЫВА́ТЬ/ПОБЫВА́ТЬ В ПЕРЕПЛЁТЕ ⟨В ПЕРЕПЛЁТАХ, В ПЕРЕДЕ́ЛКЕ, В ПЕРЕДЕ́ЛКАХ, В ПЕРЕДРЯ́ГЕ, В ПЕРЕДРЯ́ГАХ⟩ all coll [VP; subj: human; usu. past] to find o.s. in a difficult, unpleasant, or dangerous situation: X попал в переплёт ≃ **X got ⟨ran⟩ into trouble; X landed in trouble; X got into a scrape ⟨a mess⟩; X got ⟨was⟩ in a jam ⟨a fix⟩; X was ⟨ended up⟩ in a tight spot ⟨corner⟩.**

Больше всего он [Зенкевич] боится чужих. После ареста Мандельштама в 38 году он встретил меня на улице и напал за то, что я пускала в дом «чужих». Чужими оказались биологи во главе с Кузиным. Они тоже гневались на меня, считая, что Кузин попал в переплёт оттого, что встречался у нас с подозрительными людьми вроде Зенкевича (Мандельштам 2). He [Zenkevich] feared strangers like the plague. After M[andelstam]'s arrest in 1938, we happened to meet on the street, and he took me to task for letting "strangers" come to see us. By this he meant the biologist Kuzin and his friends. (These were also angry with me, thinking Kuzin had landed in trouble through meeting suspect people like Zenkevich at our apartment) (2a). ♦ «За Клавдию Лукьяновну не беспокойся. Она... бывала и не в таких переплётах» (Рыбаков 2). "Don't worry on her [Klavdya's] account....She's been in worse scrapes than this" (2a). ♦ «Скажи, — Дудырев приподнялся на локте, повернувшись к Семёну, — ты вот во всяких переделках бывал, шестьдесят медведей свалил, случалось тебе... испугаться до беспамятства?» (Тендряков 1). "Tell me," Dudyrev asked Simon, leaning over to him on his elbow, "you've been in a tight corner many a time—after all you've brought down sixty bears—have you ever lost your head from fright?" (1a).

П-96 • С ПЕРЕПО́Я ⟨-ю⟩ highly coll [PrepP; these forms only; adv] as a result of or after heavy drinking: **(being) dead drunk; (after) having gotten drunk; (being) in a drunken state; (being) hung over.**

П-97 • ЧЁРТОВА ПЕ́РЕЧНИЦА highly coll, rude [NP; usu. sing; usu. used as vocative or appos] an abusive expression (now used more frequently of or in addressing a shrewish old woman): **old hag ⟨bag, witch, shrew, fart⟩.**

П-98 • ВОЗВОДИ́ТЬ/ВОЗВЕСТИ́ В ПЕРЛ СОЗДА́НИЯ что obs, elev [VP; subj: human] to present or transform sth. in such a way as to make it outstanding, exceptionally beautiful etc: X возвёл Y в перл создания ≃ **X transformed Y into a pearl ⟨a gem, a jewel⟩ of creation; X turned ⟨transformed⟩ Y into a work of art.**

...Много нужно глубины душевной, дабы озарить картину, взятую из презренной жизни, и возвести её в перл созданья... (Гоголь 3). ...Great spiritual depth is required to illumine a picture drawn from ignoble life and transform it into a pearl of creation... (3a).

П-99 • БО́ЙКОЕ ПЕРО́ (у кого) [NP; sing only; usu. VP$_{subj}$ with быть$_\emptyset$ or obj of иметь] (s.o. has) the ability to write easily and well: у X-а бойкое перо ≃ **X wields a clever pen; X has a lively pen.**

«Тут он немножко кольнул вас. Но сознайтесь, какое бойкое перо» (Гоголь 3). "Here he has a go at you a little. But you must admit he wields a clever pen!" (3a). "That's a slight dig at you. But you must confess that he has a lively pen!" (3d).

П-100 • БРА́ТЬСЯ/ВЗЯ́ТЬСЯ ЗА ПЕРО́ [VP; subj: human; fixed WO] to begin or begin trying to write sth.: X взялся за перо ≃ **X put pen to paper; X took up his pen; X took to writing (sth.).**

Я не берусь за перо, ставя себе задачу написать «антисоветское» или «советское». Я пишу своё (Марченко 2). In putting pen to paper I do not aim to write anything "anti-Soviet" or "Soviet." I write my own way (2a). ♦ Тут редакция посылала записку за запиской, требуя оригинала, и закабалённый литератор со скрежетом зубов брался за перо и писал те ядовитые статьи... которые так поражали читателей (Герцен 2). Then the publishers sent note after note demanding copy, and the enslaved writer, grinding his teeth, took up his pen and wrote the venomous articles...which so impressed their readers (2a). ♦ После возвращения из Союза он [Лучников] нашёл газету свою не вполне благополучной. По-прежнему она процветала и по-прежнему тираж раскупался, но, увы, она потеряла тот нерв, который только он один и мог ей дать... Вернувшись в газету, Андрей Лучников прежде всего сам взялся за перо (Аксёнов 7). After his return from the Soviet Union he [Luchnikov] found his paper in a less than satisfactory state. Business was booming, all right, and his readers were every bit as loyal, but it had lost the life that he and only he was able to give it....To remedy the situation, Luchnikov took to writing more of the paper himself (7a).

П-101 • ВЛАДЕ́ТЬ ПЕРО́М [VP; subj: human] to have the ability to write skillfully and eloquently: X владеет пером ≃ **X wields a skillful pen; X is a master of the pen ⟨of the written word⟩; X has a mastery of the pen.**

[Крутицкий:] Коли хочешь приносить пользу, умей владеть пером (Островский 9). [K.:] If you want to be useful, you must know how to wield a skillful pen (9c). ♦ «Совершенно справедливо изволили выразить, ваше превосходительство: истинно преполезный человек; может побеждать даром слова и владеет пером» (Гоголь 3). "You have expressed yourself most aptly, Your Excellency. Yes, indeed, a most useful man. He has the gift of words and a mastery of the pen" (3d).

П-102 • ПОД ПЕРО́М чьим, кого [PrepP; Invar; the resulting PrepP is adv] when described by s.o., in s.o.'s written works: **when written about ⟨when penned⟩ by s.o.; (coming) from the pen of s.o.; in s.o.'s writing(s); in the writings of s.o.**

И эти старые, изношенные пугала из гегелизма правой стороны пришлось-то мне ещё раз увидеть под пером Прудона! (Герцен 2). And to think that I should meet these old, shabby bogeys from right-wing Hegelianism in the writings of Proudhon! (2a).

П-103 • ЧТО НАПИ́САНО ПЕРО́М, ТОГО́ НЕ ВЫ́РУБИШЬ ТОПОРО́М [saying] when some statement has been put in writing (and read by others), it cannot be changed (said when great importance is attributed to what has been written): ≃ **that which is written with a pen cannot be cut out with an ax(e); a written word cannot be hewn out with an ax(e); a word that has been written down cannot be cut out with an ax(e); the written word remains.**

«Всё, что на бумаге, это уже не личное слово. Что написано пером, того не вырубить топором» (Айтматов 2). "Once a thought is down on paper, it's no longer personal. That which is written with a pen cannot be cut out with an axe" (2a). ♦ Произнесённое метко, всё равно что писаное, не вырубливается топором. А уж куда бывает метко всё то, что вышло из глубины Руси... (Гоголь 3). A neatly uttered word is like a word that has been written down and that, according to the Russian proverb, cannot be cut out with an axe. And how wonderfully apt are the sayings that come out of the depths of Russia... (3a).

П-104 • ПЕРСО́НА ГРА́ТА [NP; only персона declines; fixed WO] a diplomatic representative whose candidacy is approved by the government of the country where he will be accredited; *by extension* a person who is fully accepted and trusted by those in the circles in question: **persona grata**.

«Я вам назову десяток имён римских вольноотпущенников, которые стали потом персонами грата» (Гинзбург 2). "I can quote you a dozen examples of released Roman slaves who later became personae gratae" (2a).

< Transliteration of the Latin *persona grata*. Often written in its Latin form.

П-105 • **ПЕРСО́НА НОН ГРА́ТА** [NP; only персона declines; fixed WO] a diplomatic representative who is declared untrustworthy by the government of the country where he is accredited; *by extension* a person who is not accepted or trusted by those in the circles in question: **persona non grata**.

< Transliteration of the Latin *persona non grata*. Often written in its Latin form.

П-106 • **СО́БСТВЕННОЙ ПЕРСО́НОЙ** [NP$_{instrum}$; Invar; nonagreeing postmodif] personally, oneself: **in person; in the flesh; …himself ⟨herself⟩**; [in limited contexts] **(as) big ⟨large⟩ as life**.

При виде Лучникова он [человек] поднялся. Это был генерал барон фон Витте собственной персоной (Аксёнов 7). The man stood up as Luchnikov got out of the car. It was General von Witte in person (7a).

П-107 • **один, одна, одни КАК ПЕРСТ** [как + NP; Invar; modif of один etc] **1.** (one is) completely alone, without family, relatives: **(all) alone (in the world); without kith or kin**.

[Золотуев:] Давай-ка ты ко мне… Я ведь один, ты знаешь. Один как перст (Вампилов 3). [Z.:] Why don't you come with me… I'm alone, you know. All alone (3b). ♦ «…[Илюше] всего девять лет-с, один как перст…» (Достоевский). "…He's [Ilyusha is] only nine years old, alone in the world…" (1a).

2. (one is) in a state of complete solitude: **(all) alone; alone as can be; all by oneself**.

«Беспредельная, вихрям открытая равнина. И мы одни как перст. Нас за ночь снегом занесёт, к утру не откопаемся» (Пастернак 1). "Just think! – alone on a boundless, wind-swept plain! If we were snowed under in the night we couldn't dig ourselves out in the morning!" (1a).

П-108 • **ПЕРСТ СУДЬБЫ́ ⟨РО́КА, ПРОВИДЕ́НИЯ, БО́ЖИЙ, СВЫ́ШЕ⟩** *obs, lit* [NP; sing only; fixed WO] divine forces (that preordain and actualize a crucial, deciding event in s.o.'s life): **the finger of fate; the finger ⟨the hand⟩ of God; fate**.

«Он просто шёл, глядя прямо перед собой круглыми, преданными глазами, и – всё, а перст судьбы указывал вдруг на него, и его вызывали в отдел кадров или в партком» (Ерофеев 3). "He just kept on looking straight ahead with those wide-open, dedicated eyes of his, and that was all, when suddenly the finger of fate pointed to him, and they called him into the Cadres Office or into the Party Committee" (3a). ♦ «…Если он убил теперь не меня, а только отца своего, то, наверное, потому, что тут видимый перст божий, меня охранявший…» (Достоевский 1). "…If he hasn't killed me now, but only his father, it is most likely because the hand of God is obviously protecting me…" (1a).

< «Перст божий» comes from the Bible (Ex. 8:19, 31:18).

П-109 • **ПРИНАДЛЕЖА́ТЬ ПЕРУ́** *кого, чьему lit* [VP; subj: a noun denoting a written piece; fixed WO] to be written by s.o., be the product of s.o.'s literary efforts: X принадлежит перу Y-a ≃ **X came ⟨issued, flowed⟩ from Y's pen**.

Зная, что Карл Иваныч любил списывать стишки, я стал потихоньку рыться в его бумагах и в числе немецких стихотворений нашёл одно русское, принадлежащее, должно быть,

собственно его перу (Толстой 2). Knowing that Karl Ivanich liked to copy verses, I began going through his papers on the sly and among a number of German poems found one in Russian that must have come from his own pen (2b).

П-110 • **ЗАДАВА́ТЬ/ЗАДА́ТЬ ПЕ́РЦУ** *кому highly coll* [VP] **1.** Also: **ЗАДАВА́ТЬ/ЗАДА́ТЬ ⟨ПОКА́ЗЫВАТЬ/ПОКАЗА́ТЬ⟩ ФЕ́ФЕРУ ⟨ПФЕ́ФЕРУ⟩** *obs, coll* [subj: human] to reprimand s.o. harshly, take severe disciplinary measures: X задаст Y-у перцу ≃ **X will make it hot for Y; X will give it to Y good; X will show ⟨fix⟩ Y; X will give Y hell ⟨what for⟩; X will chew Y out**.

[Городничий:] …Теперь же я задам перцу всем этим охотникам подавать просьбы и доносы (Гоголь 4). [Mayor:] …I'll show 'em, I'll show all those who fell over themselves to lodge complaints and denunciations against me (4c).

2. [subj: human or collect] to defeat s.o. overwhelmingly (usu. a military adversary): X-ы задали Y-ам перцу ≃ **Xs routed ⟨crushed, clobbered⟩ Ys; Xs ran Ys into the ground**.

П-111 • **В БЕ́ЛЫХ ПЕРЧА́ТКАХ** [PrepP; Invar; adv; usu. used with negated verbs] (to do sth.) cautiously, trying to avoid cruel, severe, or unethical measures: **(one ⟨you⟩ can't do sth.) without getting one's ⟨your⟩ hands dirty; (one ⟨you⟩ can't do sth.) without taking one's ⟨your⟩ gloves off**.

Оправдывая террор, они постоянно повторяли: «Не надо бояться крови! Революцию нельзя делать в белых перчатках!» Justifying the terror, they never tired of repeating, "Don't shrink from bloodshed! You can't make revolutions without getting your hands dirty!"

П-112 • **БРОСА́ТЬ/БРО́СИТЬ ПЕРЧА́ТКУ** [VP; subj: human] **1.** ~ *кому obs* to challenge s.o. to a duel: X бросил перчатку Y-у ≃ **X threw ⟨flung⟩ down the gauntlet ⟨the glove⟩ (to Y)**.

2. ~ *кому-чему lit* [obj: usu. human or collect] to challenge s.o. to sth. (often a contest): X бросил Y-у перчатку ≃ **X threw ⟨flung⟩ down the gauntlet ⟨the glove⟩**.

Где, в каком углу современного Запада найдёте вы такие группы отшельников мысли, схимников науки, фанатиков убеждений, у которых седеют волосы, а стремленья вечно юны? Где? Укажите – я бросаю смело перчатку… (Герцен 2). Where, in what corner of the Western world of to-day, will you find such groups of anchorites of thought, of ascetics of learning, of fanatics of conviction, whose hair is turning grey but whose enthusiasms are for ever young? Where? Point to them. I boldly throw down the glove… (2a).

П-113 • **ПОДНИМА́ТЬ/ПОДНЯ́ТЬ ПЕРЧА́ТКУ** [VP; subj: human] **1.** *obs* to accept a challenge to a duel: X поднял перчатку ≃ **X took ⟨picked⟩ up the gauntlet ⟨the glove⟩**.

2. to accept a challenge to enter into a contest with s.o.: X поднял перчатку ≃ **X took ⟨picked⟩ up the gauntlet ⟨the glove⟩; X took up the challenge**.

Оказалось, то, что мы принимали за описку или даже ошибку, было ложной, вредной, но всё-таки системой взглядов, а с системой надо бороться, и мы подымаем перчатку, брошенную из-за хребта (Искандер 6). It turns out that what we assumed to be a slip of the pen or a simple confusion of terms was actually the false and harmful manifestation of a whole system of beliefs. And since it is always the system itself one might fight, we hereby take up the gauntlet flung down from beyond the mountains (6a).

П-114 • **ЧИ́СТИТЬ/ПОЧИ́СТИТЬ ПЁРЫШКИ** *coll* [VP; subj: human, usu. female; usu. impfv] to spend time making o.s. look pretty: X чистит пёрышки ≃ **X is preening her feathers; X is primping (herself)**.

Чистить пёрышки — Варино любимое занятие, она может часами сидеть перед зеркалом. Preening her feathers is Varya's favorite pastime. She can sit in front of the mirror for hours.

П-115 • ПÉСЕНКА ⟨ПÉСНЯ⟩ СПÉТА *чья coll* [VP$_{subj}$ with быть$_\emptyset$; fixed WO] s.o.'s career, success, well-being, or life has ended or is about to end (usu. as a result of unfavorable circumstances): X-ова песенка спета ≃ **X's song is over ⟨has ended⟩; X is finished ⟨done for⟩; X's number ⟨time⟩ is up; it's all over for X;** [in limited contexts] **X's goose is cooked; X has had it ⟨his day⟩.**

«Но армия?.. Что станет с армией?» — «Армия может возродить Францию. А если нет?.. Тогда её песенка спета. Лет на сто...» (Эренбург 4). "But the Army?" said Picard. "What will happen to the Army?" "The Army can regenerate France. And if not? Well, then her song is over. For a hundred years..." (4a). ♦ При такой разрухе, какая царила на дороге, сторожка могла оказаться пустой и развалённой. В таком случае песенка его будет спета... (Максимов 3). The whole route was in such a state of chaos that the hut might very well be deserted and in ruins. In that case he was done for... (3a). ♦ «Твой отец добрый малый, — промолвил Базаров, — но он человек отставной, его песенка спета» (Тургенев 2). "Your father's a good man," said Bazarov, "but he's old-fashioned, he's had his day" (2c).

П-116 • СТРÓИТЬ/ПОСТРÓИТЬ НА ПЕСКÉ ⟨НА ПЕСЦÉ *obs*⟩ *(что)* [VP; subj: human] (usu. in refer. to a plan, project, theory etc) to base sth. on unreliable facts, approaches etc: X строит Y на песке ≃ **X builds Y on sand ⟨on shaky ground, on a shaky foundation⟩;** [in limited contexts] **doing sth. is making bricks without straw.**

...Оказывалось, что Бородавкин поспел как раз кстати, чтобы спасти погибавшую цивилизацию. Страсть строить на «песце» была доведена в нём почти до исступления (Салтыков-Щедрин 1). ...It turned out that Wartkin had arrived just in time to save a perishing civilization. In him, the passion to build on sand amounted almost to a frenzy (1a).

< From the Bible (Matt. 7:26–27).

П-117 • ИЗ ПÉСНИ СЛÓВА НЕ ВÝКИНЕШЬ [saying] you should tell the whole (oftentimes unpleasant) truth without leaving out any part that makes you feel ashamed, may offend the listener(s) etc: ≃ **there is no escaping ⟨avoiding, getting around⟩ the truth; there is no getting away from it; there is no escaping ⟨avoiding⟩ it; you have to tell it like it is; the whole truth must be told.**

Впоследствии, перечитав вещь, он ужаснётся её местечковой сентиментальности, многословию и профессиональному убожеству, но из песни слова не выкинешь, именно ей дано было сыграть решающую в его судьбе роль... (Максимов 2). On re-reading it much later he was to be appalled by its small-town sentimentality, its prolixity and literary mediocrity, but there is no getting away from it—this particular book was to play a decisive role in his destiny... (2a).

П-118 • ТЯНÝТЬ ⟨ПЕТЬ⟩ ОДНÝ И ТУ ЖЕ ПÉСНЮ *coll* [VP; subj: human] to repeat very often or incessantly the same opinion, judgment etc: X тянет одну и ту же песню ≃ **X keeps singing the same song; X keeps harping on the same string ⟨thing, subject⟩; X keeps repeating the same thing over and over; X keeps playing the same tune.**

Два месяца пытаюсь добиться от директора ответа, а он всё тянет одну и ту же песню: ждите, вопрос ещё не решён. I've been trying to get an answer from the director for two months now, but he keeps playing the same tune: you've got to wait, nothing has been decided yet.

П-119 • ДÓЛГАЯ ⟨ДЛИ́ННАЯ⟩ ПÉСНЯ *coll* [NP; sing only; usu. subj-compl with быть$_\emptyset$ (subj: usu. infin, a clause, or это), usu. pres; more often this WO] sth. that cannot be done or told quickly, that requires an extended period of time for its completion: это долгая песня ≃ [of undertakings] **that ⟨it⟩ will be a long-drawn-out process; that ⟨it⟩ will drag out ⟨on⟩ a long time;** [of narration] **that's ⟨it's⟩ a long story.**

«...Ты расскажи, как это тебя из части отпустили?» — «Это — песня длинная, после расскажу», — уклончиво ответил Прохор... (Шолохов 5). "...Tell me...how was it you got permission to leave your unit?" "That's a long story, I'll tell you later," Prokhor replied evasively... (5a).

П-120 • ЛЕБЕДИ́НАЯ ПÉСНЯ ⟨ПЕСНЬ⟩ *чья, кого lit* [NP; sing only; usu. this WO] the last (and often most significant) act or work of a writer, artist etc, the last expression of his talent: **swan song.**

Я честно обещал покончить с писательской страстью, от которой мы все так долго страдали. И непременно покончу, как только напишу последнюю вещь — свою лебединую песнь (Терц 4). I had honestly promised to end the writing craze from which we had all suffered so long. And I definitely do intend to finish with it as soon as I've written my last work—my swan song (4a).

< From a popular belief that a swan sings only once in its lifetime—as it is dying.

П-121 • СТÁРАЯ ⟨ПРÉЖНЯЯ, ВСЁ ТА ЖЕ⟩ ПÉСНЯ *coll, usu. rather derog* [NP; sing only; fixed WO] sth. that has already been said or done repeatedly: **the same old story ⟨song, tune⟩.**

[Армандо:] А ты как? Женишься на своей Лауре. Старая песня, чёрт её побери (Погодин 1). [A.:] So, what will you do? You'll marry your Laura. Same old story, goddamn it (1a).

П-122 • КАК ПЕСÓК МОРСКÓЙ; КАК ⟨ЧТО⟩ ПЕСКÝ МОРСКÓГО *кого-чего* [как + NP; these forms only; adv (var. with песок) or quantit subj-compl with copula, subj/gen: any common noun (var. with песку); fixed WO] (to increase) to large amounts; (some people or things are) available in large numbers or quantities: **(multiply etc) like the sands of the sea; (be ⟨become⟩) as numerous as the sands of the sea.**

«...Показания умножились, как песок морской!» (Достоевский 2). "...The evidence has multiplied like the sands of the sea!" (2a).

< From the Bible (Gen. 22:17, 41:49 et al.).

П-123 • ПЕСÓК СЫ́ПЛЕТСЯ *(из кого) coll* [VP$_{subj}$; pres only; usu. this WO] s.o. is very old, decrepit, and near the end of his life: из X-а песок сыплется ≃ **X is on his last legs.**

«Каков он из себя? Очень стар?» — «Лет восемьдесят». — «Однако же и движется, бодр?..» — «Песок сыплется...» (Гоголь 3). "...What does he look like? Is he very old?" "About eighty." "But he can still move about, eh? He's in good health, isn't he?..." "He's on his last legs" (3a).

П-124 • ПРОТИРÁТЬ/ПРОТЕРÉТЬ ⟨ПРОДИРÁТЬ/ПРОДРÁТЬ, ПРОБИРÁТЬ/ПРОБРÁТЬ⟩ С ПЕСÓЧКОМ ⟨С ПЕСКÓМ⟩ *кого highly coll* [VP; subj: human] to reprimand s.o. severely: X протрёт Y-а с песочком ≃ **X will let Y have it (but good); X will rake Y over the coals; X will tear Y to shreds; X will chew Y out.**

П-125 • В ПЕТЛÉ ⟨В ПÉТЛЕ⟩ оказаться, очутиться и т. п.; В ПЕТЛЮ́ ⟨В ПÉТЛЮ⟩ попасть и т. п. [PrepP; these forms only; subj-compl with copula (subj: human) or adv] (to find o.s., wind up etc) in a hopeless, desperate situation: X оказался в петле ≃ **X had a noose around his neck; X was trapped.**

П-126 • **МЕТА́ТЬ ПЕ́ТЛИ** *obs, coll* [VP; subj: human] to confuse and/or deceive s.o. intentionally: X мечет петли ≃ **X weaves a tangled web; X weaves a web of deceit.**

П-127 • **ЛЕЗТЬ/ПОЛЕ́ЗТЬ В ПЕ́ТЛЮ** [VP] **1.** [subj: human] to expose o.s. knowingly to serious danger; to get o.s. into serious trouble: X лезет в петлю ≃ **X puts ⟨sticks⟩ his head in a ⟨the⟩ noose; X risks his neck; X puts his head on the (chopping) block.**

[Свадебный ужин в общежитии. Букин и Маша (жених и невеста), гости.] [Букин:] Я уверен, что впоследствии ты его [Гомыру] полюбишь. [Маша:] ...Почему я его должна полюбить? [Букин:] Но ведь он мне друг, не просто так... И, видишь ли, сейчас ему кажется, что я лезу в петлю. [Маша:] В петлю? А ты что на это скажешь? [Букин:] Я? Лезу и радуюсь. *(Целует её.)* (Вампилов 3). [The wedding feast at the dormitory. Bukin and Masha (the bride and groom), guests.] [B.:] I'm sure you'll get to like him [Gomyra] later. [M.:] ...Why should I get to like him? [B.:] But he's my friend, he's not just anyone....And, you see, at the moment he thinks I'm putting my head in a noose. [M.:] A noose? And what do you think? [B.:] Me? I'm happy to put my head in it *(Kisses her.)* (3a).

2. ~ *кому coll* [impfv infin only; used as impers predic (may be used with остаётся, впору etc)] used to express despair when faced with a hopeless situation, or extreme frustration when one ends up in a desperate predicament: X-у (остаётся) в петлю лезть ≃ **X feels absolutely desperate; X might ⟨may⟩ as well go (and) hang himself.**

П-128 • **НАДЕВА́ТЬ/НАДЕ́ТЬ ⟨НАКИ́ДЫВАТЬ/НАКИ́НУТЬ⟩ ПЕ́ТЛЮ ⟨ПЕТЛЮ́⟩ НА СЕБЯ́ ⟨СЕБЕ́ НА ШЕ́Ю, НА ШЕ́Ю *кому*⟩** [VP; subj: human] to create an extremely difficult, hopeless situation for o.s. or another: X надел петлю на себя ⟨Y-у на шею⟩ ≃ **X put a noose around his ⟨Y's⟩ neck; X stuck his (own) neck ⟨Y's neck⟩ in the ⟨a⟩ noose; X slipped a noose on himself ⟨on Y⟩.**

Да вот что: не потому ли Парвус так и старается, чтоб именно – Ленина замарать с собою вместе? Вот такой индивидуально-семейной поездкой накинуть петлю – а потом и в руки взять? а потом и условия диктовать – как революцию вести? (Солженицын 5). Perhaps that was it: perhaps Parvus was going to so much trouble simply so that Lenin would be tarred with the same brush? Perhaps Parvus had arranged this individual and family journey to slip a noose on him and then take him in hand? Dictate conditions, tell him how to conduct the revolution? (5a).

П-129 • **ХОТЬ В ПЕ́ТЛЮ ЛЕЗЬ ⟨ПОЛЕЗА́Й⟩** *coll* [хоть + VP_imper; these forms only; usu. subord clause; fixed WO] (used to express despair, one's inability to find a way out of a difficult, hopeless situation) one feels absolutely desperate: **one might ⟨may⟩ as well go (and) hang o.s.; one could hang ⟨kill⟩ o.s.**

[Один из купцов:] Такого городничего никогда ещё... не было. Такие обиды чинит, что описать нельзя. Постоем совсем заморил, хоть в петлю полезай (Гоголь 4). [Merchant:] Never before...has there been such a Prefect. The outrages that he commits are quite indescribable. His billeting has been the ruin of us—we may as well go and hang ourselves (4b). ♦ «Что я делала?.. А, да. Я в тот вечер, помнится, психанула. Мотала я бинты, и вдруг такая тоска на меня навалилась, как головная боль, хоть в петлю» (Стругацкие 1). "What was I doing? Oh, I know. That was the evening I broke down. I'd been rolling bandages, and then this incredible despair came over me, like a headache, I could have killed myself" (1a).

П-130 • **ЖА́РЕНЫЙ ПЕТУ́Х НЕ КЛЕВА́Л/НЕ КЛЮ́НУЛ** *кого highly coll* [VP_subj; used without negation to convey the opposite meaning; when used without negation, usu. pfv; when used with negation, usu. impfv] s.o. has not yet encountered real difficulties or ordeals in life: X-а жареный петух не клевал ≃ **X has never even had a taste of trouble; X has never been through hard times; X has never had to struggle; X has had it easy; X doesn't know anything about life;** ‖ X-а жареный петух клюнул ≃ **X came upon ⟨fell upon, got hit with⟩ hard times.**

«Слушай ты, мыслитель... тебя ещё, видно, жареный петух в задницу не клевал, так я устрою: каждый клевок девять грамм, понял?» (Максимов 1). "Listen, philosopher....If you don't know anything about life yet, then I'll teach you, and each lesson will have nine grams of lead in it, is that clear?" (1a).

П-131 • **КРА́СНЫЙ ПЕТУ́Х** *coll, rather folk* [NP; usu. sing; fixed WO] arson: **torching.**

П-132 • **ПУСКА́ТЬ/ПУСТИ́ТЬ ⟨ПОДПУСКА́ТЬ/ПОДПУСТИ́ТЬ⟩ (КРА́СНОГО) ПЕТУХА́** *(кому, по чему, на что) coll* [VP; subj: human] to commit arson: X пустил красного петуха Y-у ≃ **X put Y's house ⟨Y's estate etc⟩ to the torch; X set fire to Y's house ⟨Y's estate etc⟩; X set Y's house ⟨Y's estate etc⟩ on fire; X put a match ⟨a light⟩ to Y's house ⟨Y's estate etc⟩;** ‖ X пустил красного петуха по деревне ⟨по поместью и т. п.⟩ ≃ **X put the village ⟨the estate etc⟩ to the torch; X set fire to the village ⟨the estate etc⟩; X set the village ⟨the estate etc⟩ on fire; X put a match ⟨a light⟩ to the village ⟨the estate etc⟩.**

Лежал [на кладбище] прадед Ардабьева, сосланный когда-то со Владимирщины за «красного петуха», подпущенного помещику (Евтушенко 1). Here [in the cemetery] lay Ardabiev's great-grandfather, exiled at some time from Vladimir province for setting fire to his landlord's estate (1a). ♦ «Рас-сх-ходис-сь, говорю, с-слыш-шите?» Тогда в ответ резнуло криком: «Петуха, что ль, пустить по дачке, а?» (Федин 1). "Break it up, I say, d'you hear?" Then a shout in reply: "Well, maybe we'll put a light to the house, eh?" (1a).

П-133 • **ПУСКА́ТЬ/ПУСТИ́ТЬ ⟨ДАВА́ТЬ/ДАТЬ⟩ ПЕТУХА́** *coll* [VP; subj: human or голос (var. with давать/дать only); more often pfv] having strained one's vocal cords on a high note (while singing, shouting, or speaking in a high voice), to emit a squeaking sound: X пустил петуха ≃ **X's voice broke ⟨cracked⟩; X let out a squeak.**

...На более высокой и пронзительной ноте брала она следующий куплет песни, и казалось, сейчас сорвётся и даст петуха, но не срывалась (Войнович 4). ...At the highest and most piercing note she began the second couplet of the song and it seemed that any moment her voice would catch and break, but it did not (4a).

П-134 • **С ПЕТУХА́МИ** *coll* [PrepP; Invar; adv] **1.** ложиться, засыпать ~ (to go to bed) very early in the evening: **(go to bed) with the chickens ⟨the sun⟩.**

Не звони ему так поздно: он обычно ложится спать с петухами. Don't call him so late at night: he usually goes to bed with the sun.

2. вставать, просыпаться ~ *coll* (to rise, wake up) before daybreak or very early in the morning: **with the cock's crow; at cockcrow; with the chickens ⟨the sun⟩; with the birds; at the crack ⟨the break⟩ of dawn.**

...В лагере мы жили в конюшне, на другой её половине – соседи-лошади... Ложимся с курами, встаём с петухами (Иоффе 1). ...In one of the camps we lived in the stables, horses were our neighbors in the other half....We went to bed with the hens and rose at cockcrow (1a).

П-135 • **ДО (ПÉРВЫХ ⟨ВТОРЫ́Х, ТРÉТЬИХ⟩) ПЕ-ТУХÓВ** *coll* [PrepP; these forms only; adv] **1.** ~ **сидеть, говорить** и т. п. Also: **ДО ПÓЗДНИХ ПЕТУХÓВ** *obs* (to stay up, keep talking etc) very late into the night or until the break of day: **till (first ⟨second, third⟩) cockcrow; till the cock crows; till cock's crow; till the small hours; till the wee hours (of the morning); till daybreak ⟨dawn⟩.**

«Мы у него проиграли в вист вместе с прокурором и председателем палаты до самых поздних петухов...» (Гоголь 3). "We played whist in his house together with the prosecutor and the president till cockcrow" (3d). "We played whist at his house with the public prosecutor and the president of the court till the small hours" (3a). ♦ Комиссия засиживалась до третьих петухов, но сколько-нибудь вразумительного объяснения [причины аварий] так и не находила (Максимов 3). Though the commission's meetings dragged on till dawn, they still couldn't find anything like a plausible explanation [for what caused the crashes] (3a).

2. вставать, просыпаться ~ (to rise, wake up) very early in the morning, while it is still dark: **before cockcrow ⟨the cock's crow⟩; before dawn ⟨daybreak⟩.**

< From the method of telling time based on the crowing of roosters. Traditionally first cockcrow, «первые петухи», is the earliest cockcrow after midnight; second cockcrow, «вторые петухи», is sometime after first cockcrow and before daybreak; and third cockcrow, «третьи петухи», is right at daybreak.

П-136 • **ПОСЛЕ ПÉРВЫХ ⟨ВТОРЫ́Х, ТРÉТЬИХ⟩ ПЕТУХÓВ возвращаться, приходить** и т. п. *coll* [PrepP; these forms only; adv] (to return, come etc) very late at night or very early in the morning: **in the wee ⟨small⟩ hours (of the morning); after (first ⟨second, third⟩) cockcrow; after the cock's crow.**

...В ночь [Дарья] куда-то исчезла и вернулась только после первых петухов (Шолохов 5). That night she [Darya] took herself off somewhere and returned only after first cockcrow (5a).

< See П-135.

П-137 • **НÉ БЫЛО ПЕЧÁЛИ, (ТАК) ЧÉРТИ НА-КАЧÁЛИ** [saying; often only the first half of the saying is used] this new problem, trouble, complication etc is very annoying, aggravating, and I have more than enough problems without it: ≃ **that's the last thing I ⟨we etc⟩ need!; just what I ⟨we etc⟩ need!; as if I ⟨we etc⟩ didn't have enough problems ⟨enough to do, enough to worry about⟩ already ⟨as it is⟩!**

«Экзамен опять перенесли». — «Ну вот, не было печали». "They've postponed the exam again." "Oh, great, that's the last thing I need!"

П-138 • **КАКÁЯ ⟨ЧТО ЗА⟩ ПЕЧÁЛЬ** *кому highly coll* [indep. clause; fixed WO] it does not concern s.o. (and there is no reason why s.o. should be interested in it): X-у какая печаль ≃ **what's that got to do with X?; what business is that of X's?; what's it to X?; that's no business of X's; that's none of X's business.**

[Подхалюзин:] ...Зачем это вы к нам больно часто повадились? [Устинья Наумовна:] А тебе что за печаль! (Островский 10). [P.:] ...Why do you come here to us so confoundedly often? [U.N.:] What's that to you? (10b). [P.:] ...Why is it you're in the habit of coming here so much? [U.N.:] Why, that's no business of yours! (10a).

П-139 • **КÁ́ИНОВА ПЕЧÁТЬ; ПЕЧÁТЬ КÁИНА; КÁИНОВО КЛЕЙМÓ** *all lit* [NP; sing only] an imprint or external sign of criminality: **the mark of Cain.**

...В генеральской прессе, более верной идеям партии, чем сама партия, разъяснили армейским политрукам, что: «Но-белевская премия [присуждённая Солженицыну] есть каинова печать за предательство своего народа» (Солженицын 2). ...The generals' press, which is more faithful to the ideas of the Party than the Party itself, explained...for the benefit of political officers in the army that "the Nobel Prize [awarded to Solzhenitsyn] is the mark of Cain for betraying his people" (2a).

< From the Bible (Gen. 4:15).

П-140 • **ЗА СЕМЬЮ́ ПЕЧÁТЯМИ (храниться, находиться** и т. п.) *lit* [PrepP; Invar; adv, subj-compl with copula (subj: usu. abstr), or nonagreeing postmodif] (to be, remain etc) beyond the scope of s.o.'s comprehension, completely inaccessible to s.o.: **sealed with seven seals; under lock and key; behind seven veils.**

Если бы знать, куда дело загнётся! Но Глебов всегда был в чём-то туг и недальновиден. Сложные ходы, которые потом обнаружились, были для него тайной за семью печатями (Трифонов 2). If only he had known where it would all lead! But in some things Glebov was a little slow-witted, somewhat lacking in foresight. To him, the complex situation in which he was later embroiled remained a mystery sealed with seven seals (2a). ♦ Лихэ — увлечённая, деловитая, готовая вышутить любой порыв чувствительности, но неизменно правдивая и надёжная, — продолжала оставаться его женой. Таинственным существом за семью печатями! (Обухова 1). Likhé, busy, absorbed, ever ready to mock any emotional impulse but invariably truthful and reliable, remained his wife. A mysterious being behind seven veils! (1a).

< (?) From the Bible (Rev. 5:1).

П-141 • **ВСÉМИ ПЕЧЁНКАМИ ненавидеть, презирать** *кого-что* и т. п. *substand* [NP_{instrum}; Invar; adv (intensif); fixed WO] (to hate, despise etc s.o. or sth.) very intensely: **more than anything ⟨anyone⟩ (in the world); with all one's guts; with a (purple) passion; [in limited contexts] hate s.o.'s guts.**

Свою соседку Дарья ненавидит всеми печёнками и никогда не упускает возможности сделать ей какую-нибудь гадость. Darya hates her neighbor with a passion and never misses a chance to do something nasty to her.

П-142 • **СИДÉТЬ В ПЕЧЁНКАХ** *у кого highly coll, rude* [VP; subj: any noun] to be extremely annoying, aggravating etc to s.o.: X сидит у Y-а в печёнках ≃ **Y has had it up to here with X; Y is fed up with X; Y is sick to death of X.**

[Хороших:] У меня этот твой ремонт в печёнках уже сидит (Вампилов 2). [Kh.:] ...I'm fed up with these repairs (2a). ♦ Толпа баб и мужиков ругалась и посылала куда следует терпение, сидевшее у них в печёнках (Мандельштам 2). This crowd of working folk went on swearing and cursing about "patience"—they were sick to death of it... (2a).

П-143 • **ОТ ПÉЧКИ начинать, делать** *что coll* [PrepP; Invar; adv] (to do sth.) over, starting from the beginning: **(start) from square one; (be) back to square one; (start) from scratch; (go) back to the drawing board; (start ⟨do sth.⟩) all over again.**

...Хотя нас вправе упрекнуть (уже упрекнули), что мы способны рассказывать лишь всё по порядку, «от печки», мы считаем это правильным, то есть иначе не можем (Битов 2). Although people are within their rights to reproach us (they already have) for being capable of telling things only in order, "from square one," we consider this correct; i.e., we can't do it any other way (2a).

П-144 • **ПÉЧКИ-ЛÁВОЧКИ** *substand* [NP; pl only] **1.** trifles, unimportant things: **this and that; nothing in particular.**

«О чём вы с ней говорили?» — подозрительно спросил Паниковский. «Так, ни о чём, печки-лавочки», — ответил Остап (Ильф и Петров 2). "What were you talking about?" Panikovsky asked suspiciously. "Oh, this and that," Ostap replied (2a).

2. (to engage in) empty talk: **(engage in) idle chatter; (be) chattering ⟨gabbing, chitchatting, yakking etc⟩; chatter away.**

Хватит печки-лавочки разводить, пора за дело приниматься. Quit your yakking, it's time to get down to work.

3. ~ *у кого с кем* a close acquaintanceship: **buddy-buddy relationship; getting chummy (with s.o.).**

П-145 • ТАНЦЕВА́ТЬ ОТ ПЕ́ЧКИ *coll* [VP; subj: human] to begin at the beginning, from the simplest point, and follow the usual routine: X танцует от печки ≃ **X starts ⟨takes it⟩ from step one ⟨square one⟩;** [in limited contexts] **X starts over ⟨goes through it again⟩ from the beginning; X takes it from the top ⟨starts over⟩ again; X starts all over; X goes back to the drawing board ⟨to square one⟩; it's back to the old drawing board!**

Аудитория была совсем не подготовлена, и лектору пришлось танцевать от печки и объяснять самые элементарные вещи. The audience didn't have a clue about the subject of the talk, and the speaker had to take it from square one, spelling out the basics.

П-146 • В ПИ́КУ *кому* сделать, сказать *что coll* [PrepP; Invar; the resulting PrepP is adv] (to do or say sth.) in order to annoy s.o.: **(just ⟨in order⟩) to spite ⟨irritate, pique⟩ s.o.; (in order) to get a rise out of s.o.; (in order) to get under s.o.'s skin; (in order) to get s.o.'s goat.**

Безусловно, эти назначения санкционированы. Вероятно, сделаны даже по прямому указанию Сталина для «выкорчёвывания остатков оппозиции» в пику ему, Кирову, — не хочешь делать сам, сделаем без тебя... (Рыбаков 2). These appointments had undoubtedly been approved. Probably they had been made on Stalin's instructions to "root out the remains of the opposition" and to spite Kirov: you won't do it yourself, so we'll do it for you (2a). ♦ ...Как ни непонятно казалось, что без него будет тот бал, который гусары должны были дать панне Пшаздецкой в пику уланам, давававшим бал своей панне Боржозовской, — он знал, что надо ехать из этого ясного, хорошего мира куда-то туда, где всё было вздор и путаница (Толстой 5). ...Inconceivable as it seemed that the ball the hussars were giving in honor of Panna Przazdzieska (to pique the Uhlans, who had given a ball for Panna Borzozowska) would take place without him—he knew he must leave this bright, pleasant world to go where everything was absurd and a muddle (5a).

П-147 • ЗОЛОТИ́ТЬ/ПОЗОЛОТИ́ТЬ ПИЛЮ́ЛЮ *lit;* **ПОДСЛАСТИ́ТЬ ПИЛЮ́ЛЮ** [VP; subj: human] to make an unpleasant thing somewhat more tolerable for s.o.: X позолотил пилюлю ≃ **X sugared ⟨sugarcoated, sweetened, coated, gilded⟩ the pill; X sweetened the medicine.**

Он [Маяковский] был очень строг со мной, как и со всеми, высказывал своё мнение о моих вещах, если они ему не нравились, не золотя пилюли: «Читал ваш рассказ. Никогда подобной скуки не читал!» (Олеша 3). He [Mayakovsky] was very strict with me, just as he was with everybody, and outspoken in his opinion of those things of mine he didn't like, never sugaring the pill. "I read your story. I've never read anything so boring!" (3a). ♦ Байрон... сломился, но сломился, как грозный Титан, бросая людям в глаза своё презрение, не золотя пилюли (Герцен 2). Byron... was broken, but broken like a menacing Titan, flinging his scorn in men's faces and not troubling to gild the pill (2a). ♦ Начинать прямо с разгрома было неловко. Я решил подсластить пилюлю и сказать для разгона что-нибудь позитивное (Войнович 6). I could not begin right off with a devastating blow. Better to sweeten the medicine first by saying something positive (6a).

П-148 • ПОДНОСИ́ТЬ/ПОДНЕСТИ́ ⟨ПРЕПОДНО-СИ́ТЬ/ПРЕПОДНЕСТИ́⟩ ПИЛЮ́ЛЮ ⟨-и⟩ *кому* [VP; subj: human] to say or do sth. unpleasant, offensive, hurtful etc to

s.o.: X поднёс Y-у пилюлю ≃ **X got Y where it hurts; X gave Y a bitter pill to swallow.**

П-149 • ПРОГЛОТИ́ТЬ ⟨СЪЕСТЬ⟩ ПИЛЮ́ЛЮ [VP; subj: human] to endure an offense or insult without protest: X проглотил пилюлю ≃ **X swallowed ⟨pocketed⟩ the insult ⟨the dig etc⟩; X just took it; X took it lying down.**

П-150 • ГО́РЬКАЯ ПИЛЮ́ЛЯ; ПИЛЮ́ЛЯ ГОРЬКА́ *both lit* [NP; sing only; VP$_{subj}$ with copula (2nd var.)] sth. unpleasant or painful for s.o. (that s.o. must accept, come to terms with etc): **a bitter pill (for s.o.) (to swallow).**

«Я наконец сказал ей [матери], что вы, мол, меня понять не можете; мы, мол, принадлежим к двум различным поколениям. Она ужасно обиделась, а я подумал: что делать? Пилюля горька — а проглотить её нужно» (Тургенев 2). "At last I said to her, 'Of course, you cannot understand me: we belong to two different generations,' I said. She was dreadfully offended but I thought to myself, 'It can't be helped. It is a bitter pill but she must swallow it'" (2c).

П-151 • ВАЛТАСА́РОВ ПИР ⟨ВАЛТАСА́РОВО ПИР-ШЕСТВО⟩ *obs, lit* [NP; sing only] a carefree existence in the face of danger, inevitable ruin: **Belshazzar's feast.**
< From the Bible (Dan. 5).

П-152 • ЛУКУ́ЛЛОВ(СКИЙ) ПИР [NP] a rich, lavish feast: **Lucullan feast.**
< From *Lucullus*, a Roman general famous for lavish feasts.

П-153 • ПИР ГОРО́Й *coll;* **ПИР НА ВЕСЬ МИР** *coll, rather folk* [NP; sing only; usu. subj or obj; fixed WO] a festive celebration with copious amounts of food and drink: **a feast of feasts; a lavish ⟨sumptuous, real⟩ feast ⟨banquet⟩; a feast fit for a king; a feast such as the world has never seen.**

Началась почти оргия, пир на весь мир (Достоевский 1). What began then was almost an orgy, a feast of feasts (1a). ♦ Всё время их пребывания на барском дворе шёл пир горой у прислуги... (Герцен 1). All the time they stayed in the master's courtyard the servants kept up a sumptuous banquet... (1a).

П-154 • ВОТ КАКИ́Е ПИРОГИ́ *coll* [sent; Invar; fixed WO] (used to round off a story) that is what the situation is (more often in refer. to sad circumstances, a distressing situation etc): **that's how it is; that's the situation ⟨the deal, the story etc⟩.**

Стал он выпивать, сначала — понемногу, потом — всё больше и больше, а теперь его за пьянство с работы уволили. Вот какие пироги... He started hitting the bottle—only a little at first, but then more and more—and now they've fired him for drunkenness. That's the story.

П-155 • В ЧУЖО́М ПИРУ́ ПОХМЕ́ЛЬЕ [NP; fixed WO] a trouble for s.o. brought about by the fault of another or others: **pay(ing) with a hangover for the feasting of others;** [in limited contexts] **(be) a scapegoat for someone else.**

«Вот что случилось: Азамат вбежал туда в разорванном бешмете, говоря, что Казбич хотел его зарезать. Все выскочили, схватились за ружья — и пошла потеха... „Плохое дело в чужом пиру похмелье, — сказал я Григорью Александровичу, поймав его за руку, — не лучше ли нам поскорее убраться?"» (Лермонтов 1). "Here's what had happened: Azamat had burst in, his *beshmet* torn, saying that Kazbich had wanted to cut his throat. Everybody dashed out, grabbed their rifles—and the sport began!...'It is no fun to pay with a hangover for the feasting of others,' said I to Pechorin, catching him by the arm. 'Hadn't we better clear out at once?'" (1a). ♦ Суд-то будет, уж спросят о пуле, начнут при народе пытать. Нет пули — и шабаш! Не хочет он принимать во чужом пиру похмелье (Тендряков 1). There was bound to be a trial and then they would ask him about the bullet in front of everybody....But there was no bullet, and that's all there was to it. He was not going to be a scapegoat for anybody! (1a).

П-156 • НЕ ПРО МЕНЯ́ ⟨тебя и т. п.⟩ ПИ́САНО ⟨-ы⟩ *highly coll* [predic (impers or with subj: abstr or concr, often это); fixed WO] to be beyond my (your etc) understanding: это не про меня писано ≃ **this is (way) above ⟨over⟩ my head; this is too deep for me; this is beyond ⟨outside⟩ my ken.**

Я и не пытаюсь разобраться в этих компьютерных программах — не про меня писано. I don't even try to understand these computer programs—they're way over my head.

П-157 • КАК ⟨БУ́ДТО, СЛО́ВНО, ТО́ЧНО⟩ ПО ПИ́САНОМУ *coll* [как etc + PrepP; these forms only; adv] **1.** говорить, рассказывать и т. п. ~ (to talk, tell a story etc) glibly, fluently, smoothly: **like ⟨as if⟩ reading (from ⟨out of⟩) a book ⟨a script⟩.**

«Давно ли слова не могла сказать, и вот, пожалуйста, вовсю разговорилась. Прямо как по-писаному чешешь» (Распутин 3). "A moment ago you couldn't get a word out, and now look at you rattling away! Like you was reading a book!" (3a).

2. идти, происходить и т. п. ~ (to go, proceed etc) as expected, as it is supposed to, without any complications: **without a hitch; like clockwork; according to script ⟨plan⟩; just as it should.**

В глупой, ребячьей наивности он предполагал, что достаточно вернуться домой, сменить шинель на зипун, и всё пойдёт как по-писаному: никто ему слова не скажет... и будет он жить да поживать мирным хлеборобом и примерным семьянином (Шолохов 5). Foolishly as a child he had thought he could just come home, change his army greatcoat for a ploughman's homespun and everything would go according to plan; no one would say a word against him...and he would live the life of a peaceful farmer and perfect family man (5a). ♦ ...Лошади, чуя близкий дом... пошли свежо, шибко. Встречавшиеся казаки кланялись, с базов и из окон куреней из-под ладоней глядели бабы... Всё шло гладко, как по-писаному (Шолохов 3). The horses, sensing that home was near, stepped out spiritedly....Passing Cossacks bowed their heads. Women shaded their eyes and looked out of the houses and the yards....Everything was just as it should be (3a).

П-158 • КАК ПИТЬ ДАТЬ ⟨ДАСТ, ДАДУ́Т *both obs*⟩ *coll* [как + VP; these forms only; usu. used as adv; usu. used with verbs in pfv fut or, less often, subjunctive; fixed WO] (used to emphasize that an action will occur, a situation will be etc precisely as predicted or stated) certainly, without a doubt: **(that's) for (dead) sure ⟨certain⟩; as sure as sure can be; (there are) no two ways about it; no doubt ⟨question⟩ about it; you can count on ⟨be sure of⟩ that.**

«Нет, взять надо, а то её [водки] завтра, если получку привезут, как пить дать не будет. Я знаю, у нас тут это так» (Распутин 3). "We must get it [vodka] today, or it won't be there tomorrow if the wages come in, that's for dead certain. That's the way it is here" (3a). ♦ «Ах, полковник, вы не знаете женщин. Ведь пойдёт, как пить дать — пойдёт» (Терц 2). "But, Colonel, you don't understand women. She *will* go, she will go, as sure as sure can be" (2a). ♦ ...Он [местный нарядчик], вроде, обдуманно сел [в тюрьму] «вовремя и по отличной бытовой статье». Промешкай он со своей хозяйственной махинацией до тридцать седьмого [года], подсунули бы ему, как пить дать, террор или вредительство (Гинзбург 2). ...He [the local work assigner] had, as it were, deliberately got himself put away "in good time and on an excellent nonpolitical charge." Had he missed the boat with his economic machinations and left them until '37, he would have found himself—no doubt about it—up on a charge of terrorism or sabotage (2a). ♦ «Будешь у нас мотористом... Восемь бумаг в месяц,

работа — не бей лежачего...»... Может, действительно, плюнуть на всё, на все эти студии и сценарии, и пойти к нему? «Ладно, подумаю. Вот завалят мне сценарий...» — «Завалят, как пить дать» (Некрасов 1). "You could get a job with us as a mechanic....Eight hundred a month, and it's not hard work...." ...Perhaps, Vadim thought, he really should say to hell with it all, the studios and scenarios, and go work with Romka. "All right, I'll think it over. If they turn down my scenario...." "They'll turn it down, you can count on that" (1a). ♦ «Хотите пари? Коллективу строителей Лозунга дадут Ленинскую премию. Как пить дать, дадут!» (Зиновьев 2). [context transl] "Do you want a bet? They'll give the people who built the Slogan the Lenin Prize. It's as good as done" (2a).

П-159 • ПИШИ́ ПРОПА́ЛО *coll* [indep. clause; Invar; fixed WO] (if sth. mentioned in the immediately preceding context comes about or has come about, then) failure, loss is inevitable: **it's hopeless; that's the end; it's as good as lost ⟨done for⟩; you can forget it; you ⟨we etc⟩ might as well write sth. ⟨s.o.⟩ off as a (total) loss;** [in limited contexts] **you ⟨we etc⟩ have had it.**

Фаина считала, что [Ольге] нужно срочно искать мужа: «Не будь дурой. Сергея не вернёшь, а себя погубишь. Имей в виду, у тебя времени в обрез: год, два, потом пиши пропало» (Трифонов 3). Faïna thought Olga should start looking for another husband at once: "Don't be a fool. You can't bring Sergei back, and you're destroying yourself. Bear in mind that you don't have much time—a year or two, and after that you can forget it" (3a). ♦ ...Есть вещи, которых дамы не простят никому, будь он кто бы то ни было, и тогда прямо пиши пропало! (Гоголь 3). ...There are things ladies never forgive anyone, whatever he may be, and then he might just as well be written off as a loss (3e).

П-160 • СИДЕ́ТЬ НА ПИ́ЩЕ ⟨ВКУША́ТЬ ОТ ПИ́ЩИ⟩ СВЯТО́ГО АНТО́НИЯ *obs, lit, often humor* [VP; subj: human] to live in a half-starved condition: X сидит на пище святого Антония ≃ **X lives on air ⟨on next to nothing⟩; X is on starvation rations;** [in limited contexts] **X is fasting for the sins of mankind.**

< From the name of the Christian ascetic *St. Anthony* of Thebes, who lived on roots and grasses in the desert.

П-161 • ДАВА́ТЬ/ДАТЬ ПИ́ЩУ *чему, для чего* [VP; subj: abstr or human] to contribute to an increase in (s.o.'s curiosity, interest in sth. etc) or to the dissemination of (rumors, gossip etc): X дал пищу Y-у ≃ **X sowed ⟨nourished, invited, aroused, gave rise to⟩ Y; X gave (person Z) ammunition for Y;** [in refer. to rumors, gossip] **X set tongues wagging; X sets rumors flying.**

Я спросила его [Абдуллина], что мне делать: оставаться в партии на таком положении, когда у тебя не хотят принимать взносов? Или положить билет на стол, дав этим новую пищу обвинениям? (Гинзбург 1). I asked Abdullin what I should do: stay in the party although my dues were being refused, or turn my card in and thereby invite fresh accusations (1a). ♦ На другой день весть о пожаре разнеслась по всему околотку. Все толковали о нём с различными догадками и предположениями... Вскоре другие вести дали другую пищу любопытству и толкам (Пушкин 1). News of the fire spread throughout the neighborhood the next day. Everybody talked about it, offering different guesses and suppositions....Soon other reports aroused curiosity and gave rise to gossip (1a). ♦ Ксана на приставания Иосифа не отвечала, но городок маленький, южный, всё на виду, все видят, как Иосиф вяжется к Ксане, и этот факт... даёт пищу судам и пересудам... (Рыбаков 1). Ksana didn't respond to his passes, but it was a small town in the south, where everything is out in the open, everyone could see that Yosif was trying to get involved with her...giving ammunition for gossips and rumour-mongers... (1a). ♦ [Павел Михайлович:] Ты позволяешь себе какие-то глупейшие, мальчишеские выходки, домой не ходишь, заводишь в городе роман, даёшь пищу сплетне... (Погодин 1). [P.M.:] You pull some of the stupidest, little-boy pranks, don't go home, have an affair in town, set rumors flying… (1a).

П-162 • МÉЛКО ПЛÁВАТЬ *coll, rather derog* [VP; subj: human; pres or, rare, past; fixed WO] **1.** to lack sufficient ability, knowledge, experience etc to do sth. (usu. to accomplish sth. significant): X мелко плавает ≃ **X doesn't have what it takes (for sth.); X is not the right caliber (for sth.); X is out of ⟨beyond⟩ his depth (in sth.).**

2. to be considered insignificant by the speaker (usu. because of one's minor official position or low social status): X мелко плавает ≃ **X is a ⟨one of the⟩ small fry; X is a nobody ⟨a nonentity⟩;** ‖ *Neg* X не из мелко плавающих ≃ **X isn't just anybody.**

[Войницев:] Отчего ты с ним редко беседуешь? Это человек не из мелко плавающих, малый развитой и слишком нескучный! (Чехов 1). [N.:] …Why do you avoid him? He's not just anybody, you know. He's a most intelligent fellow, and far from boring (1a).

П-163 • НА ЗÁДНЕМ ПЛÁНЕ быть₀; **НА ЗÁДНИЙ ПЛАН** отойти, отодвинуть *что и т. п.* [PrepP; these forms only; subj-compl with быть₀ (subj: usu. abstr or human) or adv] (to occupy, fade to etc) an unimportant, insignificant position: X — на заднем плане ≃ **X is in the background; thing X is low on person Y's list of priorities;** ‖ X отошёл ⟨был отодвинут⟩ на задний план ≃ **X receded ⟨was pushed⟩ into the background; X took ⟨had to take⟩ a back seat.**

Политика отодвинула в нём [Сталине] все другие человеческие интересы на задний план — и так было всю жизнь (Аллилуева 2). Politics pushed all other human interests into the background, and it remained that way all his [Stalin's] life (2a).

П-164 • ПЕРЕМЕНИ́ТЬ ⟨СМЕНИ́ТЬ⟩ ПЛАСТИ́НКУ *recent, highly coll, rude when used in direct address* [VP; subj: human; often imper] to move on to a new subject of conversation: X переменил пластинку ≃ **X changed the subject ⟨the topic⟩; X switched topics.**

Послушай, сколько можно говорить об одном и том же! Перемени пластинку! Listen, how long can you go on talking about the same thing! Change the subject!

П-165 • ЛЕЖÁТЬ ПЛАСТÓМ ⟨КАК ПЛАСТ⟩ *coll* [VP; subj: human] (usu. of a person who is sick or very tired) to lie completely immobile: X лежит пластом ≃ **X is flat on his back.**

Теперь им совсем плохо, лежат пластом и до утра… на людях появиться не смогут (Стругацкие 3). Now they were quite ill, flat on their backs, and could not appear in public before morning (3a).

П-166 • СТОЯ́ТЬ НА ПЛАТФÓРМЕ *чего, какой media, rather offic* [VP; subj: human; fixed WO] to adhere to certain views, to a certain teaching or movement: X стоит на платформе Y-а ≃ **X is a supporter of Y; X stands for Y;** ‖ X стоит на иной платформе ≃ **X is in a different camp; X is of a different school of thought.**

«Не важно, верите вы в бога или нет… Точно так же не имеет значения – монархист вы или учредиловец, или просто казак, стоящий на платформе самостийности» (Шолохов 5). "It doesn't matter whether you believe in God or not….Nor does it matter whether you're a monarchist or a supporter of the Constituent Assembly, or simply a Cossack who stands for self-government" (5a).

П-167 • БЕРЕГИ́ ⟨ПЛÁТЬЕ СНÓВУ, А⟩ ЧЕСТЬ СМÓЛОДУ [saying] (used as advice to young people) value

your honor and good name from your youth (just as you ought to take care of clothing when it is new): ≃ **(take care of your clothes while they're still new,) cherish your honor from a tender age.**

«Служи верно, кому присягнёшь; слушайся начальников; за их лаской не гоняйся; на службу на напрашивайся; от службы не отговаривайся; и помни пословицу: береги платье снову, а честь смолоду» (Пушкин 2). "Serve faithfully the Sovereign to whom you swear allegiance; obey your superiors; don't curry favor with them; don't volunteer for duty, but don't shirk it either; and remember the proverb, 'Take care of your clothes while they're still new; cherish your honor from a tender age'" (2a).

П-168 • ХОТЬ ПЛАЧЬ *coll* [хоть + VP_imper; Invar; usu. subord clause; fixed WO] (used to express despair at one's inability to find a way out of a terrible situation) this is unbearably upsetting, depressing etc: **it's enough to make you cry; I ⟨you⟩ could (just) cry; I ⟨you⟩ could scream.**

«Разное [я] в жизни испытала; вашего брата — мужиков — должна бы уж хорошо знать. А вот влюбилась, хоть плачь, хоть головой об стенку…» (Копелев 1). "I've seen a lot in life; I should know you men well by know. But I'm in love; I could cry, beat my head against the wall" (1a).

П-169 • ПЛЕВÁТЬ Я ХОТÉЛ ⟨*less often* **хочу** *и т. п.*⟩ *на кого-что substand* [VP_subj; subj: human; usu. past (хотел etc) which may be used in pres contexts; fixed WO] (used to express one's absolute indifference to or disdain for s.o. or sth.) I am (you are etc) not at all interested in or concerned about s.o. or sth.: плевать X хотел на Y-а ≃ **X couldn't ⟨could⟩ care less about Y; what does X care about ⟨for⟩ Y; X doesn't give a damn ⟨a hoot, a tinker's damn, a rap, a shit etc⟩ about Y; to hell with Y;** [in limited contexts] **you ⟨he etc⟩ can stuff Y.**

«…Мы плевать хотели на марксизм и монархизм, на Возрождение и на Идею Общей Судьбы!» (Аксёнов 7). "What do we care for Marxism or monarchism, the resurrection of Holy Russia or the Idea of a Common Fate?" (7a). ♦ «Перестань. Товарищ может плохое подумать». – «Плевать!.. – Люсьена, зажмурясь, икнула. – Плевать я хотела, Алик, что обо мне подумают…» (Чернёнок 1). "Stop it. The comrade will think badly of us." "I don't give a damn!" Lusya squinted and burped. "I don't give a damn, Alik, what people think of me…" (1a). ♦ «…Штраф… с меня сдерут, этого не миновать. Чтобы полиция да потеряла случай содрать с человека штраф… А, плевать я хотел… По крайней мере, душу отвёл…» (Стругацкие 1). "They'll fine me, there's no getting out of it. The police would hardly lose the opportunity to collect a fine. Oh, I don't give a shit….At least I got it off my chest" (1a). ♦ [Галина:] Я опоздаю на поезд. [Зилов:] Плевать я хотел на этот поезд (Вампилов 5). [G.:] I'll miss my train. [Z.:] To hell with your train! (5a). ♦ [Зилов:] Кого вы тут обманываете? И для чего? Ради приличия?.. Так вот, плевать я хотел на ваши приличия. Слышите? Ваши приличия мне опротивели (Вампилов 5). [Z.:] Who are you trying to fool? And why bother? For the sake of decency?…You can stuff your decency. Do you hear? I'm sick to death of your decency (5a).

П-170 • ОТДЕЛЯ́ТЬ/ОТДЕЛИ́ТЬ ПЛÉВЕЛЫ ОТ ПШЕНИ́ЦЫ *lit* [VP; subj: human; the verb may take the final position, otherwise fixed WO] to separate what is valuable from what is worthless: X отделил плевелы от пшеницы ≃ **X separated ⟨sifted⟩ the wheat ⟨the grain⟩ from the chaff.**

< From the Bible (Matt. 13:24–30).

П-171 • ПЛЕВКÁ НЕ СТÓИТ *highly coll* [VP; pres or past] **1.** *derog* [subj: human] one is completely lacking merit, value: X плевка не стоит ≃ **X is worthless ⟨trash⟩.**

[463]

2. [subj: abstr or concr] sth. is very insignificant, not worth paying attention to: X плевка не стоит ≃ **X isn't worth worrying (your head) about.**

П-172 • **ПЛЕТÉНИЕ СЛОВÉС** *lit* [NP; sing only; fixed WO] a loquacious, pretentious style (of speaking or writing that usu. hides a lack of content): **verbal pyrotechnics.**

Что вам сказать о его лекции? Плетение словес, но никакой глубины. What can I say about his lecture? All verbal pyrotechnics and no real substance.

П-173 • **ПЛÉТЬЮ НЕ ВЫ́ШИБЕШЬ** *что из кого highly coll* [VP; neg pfv fut, gener. 2nd pers sing only; fixed WO] it is impossible to make s.o. relinquish the habit, idea, prejudice etc in question: из X-а Y плетью не вышибешь ≃ **you couldn't beat ⟨thrash⟩ Y out of X (with a whip ⟨a stick⟩).**

[Маврикий:] Чёрт знает, до шести лет казалось забавным, что он называет меня Маврушкой. А теперь плетью не вышибешь (Солженицын 11). [M.:] Damn it, until he was six it was amusing to hear him call me Maury. But now you couldn't thrash it out of him with a whip (11a).

П-174 • **ПЛÉТЬЮ ÓБУХА НЕ ПЕРЕШИБЁШЬ** [saying] it is useless to oppose great force or fight a more powerful opponent (said when a person is forced to accept sth. that has been imposed by a stronger party, resign himself to circumstances): ≃ **you can't chop wood with a penknife; you can't fight guns with sticks; you can't fight a howitzer with a peashooter; there's no arguing with a big fist.**

...К донкихотам и донкихотству у него был особый личный счёт... Они опровергали мудрость, которой он жил все годы: ...плетью обуха не перешибёшь... (Орлова 1). He had his own particular and personal estimation of the Don Quixotes and their tilting at windmills....They were denying the wisdom whereby he had lived all those years:...you can't chop wood with a penknife (1a). ♦ «Надо в чём-то уступить советской власти!.. Плетью обуха не перешибёшь» (Солженицын 2). "...You must make some concessions to the Soviet regime....You can't fight a howitzer with a peashooter" (2a).

П-175 • **С ПЛЕЧ ⟨С РУК** *obs*⟩ **ДОЛÓЙ** *coll* [these forms only; predic (impers or with subj: abstr); can be used in past, pres, and fut contexts; fixed WO] (in refer. to freeing o.s. from certain obligations, concerns, usu. upon conclusion of the matter in question) there is no need to worry about sth., burden o.s. with sth. anymore: (X) с плеч долой ≃ [in past contexts] **X ⟨it⟩ was off person Y's shoulders ⟨back, mind⟩; Y got X ⟨it⟩ off his back.**

Странная мысль пришла ему вдруг: встать сейчас, подойти к Никодиму Фомичу и рассказать ему всё вчерашнее, всё до последней подробности... «Не обдумать ли хоть минуту? – пронеслось в его голове. – Нет, лучше и не думая, и с плеч долой!» (Достоевский 3). A strange thought suddenly came to him: to get up now, go over to Nikodim Fomich, and tell him all about yesterday, down to the last detail....“Shouldn't I at least think it over for a moment?” raced through his head. “No, better do it without thinking, just to get it off my back!” (3c).

П-176 • **СБРÁСЫВАТЬ/СБРÓСИТЬ ⟨СВÁЛИВАТЬ/ СВАЛИ́ТЬ, СКИ́ДЫВАТЬ/СКИ́НУТЬ, СТРЯХИ́ВАТЬ/СТРЯХНУ́ТЬ⟩ С ПЛЕЧ** *что coll* [VP; subj: human; usu. pfv] to free o.s. of some burden: X сбросил Y с плеч ≃ **X got Y off his back ⟨shoulders⟩; X got rid of Y; X got Y out of the way;** [in limited contexts] **X shed ⟨cast off, shook off⟩ the burden of...**

«Я, по правде сказать, буду очень рад свалить с своих плеч это неприятное дело» (Герцен 2). "...To tell you the truth, I shall be very glad to get this unpleasant affair off my shoulders" (2a). ♦ Первое время своего приезда Николай был серьёзен и даже скучен.

Его мучила предстоящая необходимость вмешаться в эти глупые дела хозяйства, для которых мать вызвала его. Чтобы скорее свалить с плеч эту обузу, на третий день своего приезда он сердито... пошёл с нахмуренными бровями во флигель к Митеньке и потребовал у него *счёты всего* (Толстой 5). At first after his return home Nikolai was pensive and even bored. He was worried by the imminent necessity of going into the stupid business matters for which his mother had summoned him home. To be rid of this burden as quickly as possible, on the third day after his arrival, angry and scowling...he marched off to Mitenka's lodge to demand *an accounting of everything* (5a). ♦ [author's usage] ...Он [Чичиков] сам в себе чувствовал желание скорее как можно привести дела к концу; ...всё-таки приходила мысль, что души не совсем настоящие и что в подобных случаях такую обузу всегда нужно поскорее с плеч (Гоголь 3). ...Chichikov felt an urge to get the business over as quickly as possible;...for the thought that the souls were not quite genuine did occur to him now and then and brought with it the desire to shed the burden of impending formalities without any delay (3c).

П-177 • **СВÁЛИВАТЬСЯ/СВАЛИ́ТЬСЯ С ПЛЕЧ** *чьих, кого* [VP; subj: abstr (usu. обуза, тяжесть, ноша etc); more often pfv] (of a burden, usu. an unwanted one) to cease being s.o.'s concern, responsibility etc: X свалился с Y-овых плеч ≃ **X fell from Y's shoulders; Y was free of X.**

Он ждал, что лицо Аксиньи будет отмечено волнением, но когда коляска, резко шурша, поравнялась с воротами и он с дрожью в сердце взглянул направо и увидел Аксинью, – его поразило лицо её, сдержанно-весёлое, улыбающееся. У него словно тяжесть свалилась с плеч, он успокоился, кивнул на приветствие (Шолохов 4). He had expected Aksinya's face to betray her emotion, but when the carriage swept in through the gate and he glanced at her in trepidation, he was struck by the calm and smiling cheerfulness of her expression. A huge weight fell from his shoulders and he nodded a greeting (4a).

П-178 • **СПИ́ХИВАТЬ/СПИХНУ́ТЬ С ПЛЕЧ ⟨С ШÉИ⟩** *что highly coll* [VP; subj: human] to rid o.s. of sth. burdensome, unpleasant: X спихнул Y с плеч ≃ **X got Y off X's back; X got Y over (and done) with.**

Сергей понимал, что серьёзного разговора с деканом не избежать, и хотел поскорее спихнуть с плеч это неприятное дело. Sergei understood that there was no getting around a serious conversation with the dean, and he wanted to get it over with as soon as possible.

П-179 • **С ПЛЕЧÁ**[1] *отвечать, осуждать* и т. п. *coll* [PrepP; Invar; adv] (to answer, condemn s.o. or sth. etc) right away, without thinking: **(condemn ⟨judge, reject⟩) out of hand; (answer) rashly; (decide) on the spur of the moment.**

[author's usage] ...Решено было, что Капа расскажет ей о письме Миная, о Родичеве и Гузуне всё, как оно есть... Как она воспримет эту историю?.. Не осудит ли с беззаботного плеча? (Солженицын 10). It had been decided that Kapa should tell her about Minai's letter and the whole truth about Rodichev and Guzun....How would she react?...Mightn't she condemn them thoughtlessly, out of hand? (10a).

П-180 • **С ПЛЕЧÁ**[2] *чьего coll* [PrepP; Invar; the resulting PrepP is a nonagreeing postmodif or subj-compl with быть∅ (subj: a noun denoting a piece of clothing)] (a piece of clothing that) belonged to, was worn by another: **a hand-me-down (from s.o.); from ⟨part of⟩ s.o.'s wardrobe; once ⟨at one time⟩ s.o.'s;** ‖ со своего плеча ≃ **from one's own wardrobe; off one's own back.**

Чемодан внесли кучер Селифан... и лакей Петрушка, малый лет тридцати, в просторном поддержанном сюртуке, как видно, с барского плеча... (Гоголь 3). The trunk was brought in by the joint efforts of Selifan the coachman…and the valet Petrushka, a fellow of thirty or so, wearing a very loose, well-worn coat, evidently a hand-me-down from his master… (3e). The trunk was brought in by Selifan, the coachman…and Petrushka, the valet, a fellow of about thirty, wearing a shabby loose frock coat (apparently at one time his master's)… (3c). ♦ Эта Ира чем-то так очаровала всемогущую Гридасову, что та снабдила её чистым паспортом, одела с ног до головы в одежду со своего плеча и на свой счёт отправила на материк (Гинзбург 2). Ira had somehow cast such a spell on the omnipotent Gridasova that the latter had provided her with a perfectly clean passport, given her a complete set of clothing from her own wardrobe, and paid for her passage back to the mainland (2a). ♦ «Ваше благородие! Отец наш вам жалует лошадь и шубу с своего плеча…» (Пушкин 2). "Your Honor, the Tsar Our Father is sending you as a present this horse and a fur coat off his own back" (2a).

П-181 • С ЧУЖО́ГО ПЛЕЧА́ *coll* [PrepP; Invar; nonagreeing postmodif or subj-compl with быть₀ (subj: a noun denoting a piece of clothing); fixed WO] (a piece of clothing) worn formerly by another, usu. not the right size for the person wearing it: **a hand-me-down (jacket ⟨dress** etc**⟩); a secondhand (jacket ⟨dress** etc**⟩); (a jacket ⟨dress** etc**⟩) off someone else's back; someone else's castoff(s); other people's castoffs;** [in limited contexts] **a borrowed (jacket ⟨dress** etc**⟩).**

…Пришёл кособокий мужичок в пиджаке с чужого плеча… (Трифонов 6). A lopsided fellow came along wearing a hand-me-down jacket… (6a). ♦ Даже… костюм, туфли и шляпа — были куплены в комиссионном магазине и при всей своей превосходной доброте имели изъян — это были вещи не свои, не родные, с чужого плеча (Ильф и Петров 2). Even the…suit, hat, and shoes…were bought in a second-hand shop, and despite their excellent quality, they suffered from the one defect that they were not his but off someone else's back (2a). ♦ Всё на девчонке не впору, с чужого плеча, с чужой ноги: большие валенки, большой, не по росту, засаленный, с оборванными пуговицами ватник, большой чёрный платок, повязанный крест на крест, так, что узел приходится впереди, чуть повыше колен (Чуковская 2). Nothing the little girl was wearing fitted her. Her clothes were other people's castoffs. She had on large felt boots, a grease-stained padded jacket with the buttons torn off and a large black shawl fastened cross-wise so that the knot came in front, a little higher than the knees (2a). ♦ Они вошли в дом. И тут только, после пережитых минут глубокого волнения, Бунчука вновь стало тяготить пальто с чужого плеча, — оно стесняло, давило под мышками, путало каждое движение (Шолохов 3). They went into the house. And only then, after those first minutes of emotion, did Bunchuk again feel uncomfortable in the borrowed overcoat. It was too tight, he felt cramped under the arms, afraid to move (3a).

П-182 • СО ВСЕГО́ ПЛЕЧА́ ударять, бить и т. п. [PrepP; Invar; adv; fixed WO] (to strike, hit etc s.o. or sth.) with a powerful, sweeping movement of one's whole arm: **with a full swing of the ⟨one's⟩ arm; straight from the shoulder.**

Иван махнул топором со всего плеча и вместо сухой ветки срубил всю яблоньку. Ivan swung the ax straight from the shoulder, and instead of chopping the dead branch off the little apple tree, he took down the whole thing.

П-183 • ЗА ПЛЕЧА́МИ [PrepP; Invar] **1.** ~ чьими, у кого [the resulting PrepP is subj-compl with быть₀, остаться etc (subj: abstr) or obj-compl with иметь (obj: abstr)] sth. is part of a person's past experience: X у Y-а за плечами ≃ **X is behind Y; Y has X behind him; Y has X under Y's belt;** [of sth. unpleasant whose consequences are still felt] **X is still around Y's neck.**

Я совсем не хочу сказать, что была такая уж умная, но за моими плечами был печальный опыт лагеря… (Ивинская 1). I am far from wanting to claim I was being all that farsighted, but I had the sad experience of the camp behind me… (1a). ♦ «В Москву меня

не пустят. Значит, опять скитаться, да ещё с пятьдесят восьмой [статьёй Уголовного кодекса] за плечами» (Рыбаков 2). "They won't let me go back to Moscow, so it'll mean wandering around again, and with Article Fifty-eight [of the Criminal Code] still around my neck" (2a).

2. ~ (у кого) [subj-compl with быть₀, стоять etc (subj: abstr)] (usu. of sth. unwelcome, dangerous; often of death) sth. is impending, about to happen: X за плечами ≃ **X is (close) at hand; X is not far off; X is just around the corner.**

Страшный, кровавый бой, не предсказывавший ничего доброго, был за плечами (Герцен 2). A fearful, bloody conflict, foreboding nothing good was at hand (2a).

П-184 • ПОЖИМА́ТЬ/ПОЖА́ТЬ ПЛЕЧА́МИ [VP; subj: human] to raise and lower one's shoulders as a sign that one does not understand sth., know the answer to some question etc: X пожал плечами ≃ **X shrugged (his shoulders).**

Филипп Филиппович… вгляделся в Шарикова и спросил: «Позвольте узнать, что вы можете сказать по поводу прочитанного». Шариков пожал плечами. «Да не согласен я» (Булгаков 11). Philip Philipovich…stared at Sharikov and asked: "What comment can you make on what you've read?" Sharikov shrugged. "I don't agree" (11b).

П-185 • ВИСЕ́ТЬ ⟨СИДЕ́ТЬ⟩ НА ПЛЕЧА́Х (у) кого *highly coll* [VP; subj: human or collect] to follow close behind s.o. and be about to overtake s.o.: X висел у Y-а на плечах ≃ **X was right on top of Y; X was (right) on Y's heels ⟨tail⟩.**

Он бежал не оглядываясь, но чувствовал, что те парни висят у него на плечах. He ran without looking back but could feel that the other guys were right on his heels.

П-186 • ВЫНОСИ́ТЬ/ВЫ́НЕСТИ ⟨ВЫВОЗИ́ТЬ/ВЫ́-ВЕЗТИ⟩ НА (СВОИ́Х ⟨СО́БСТВЕННЫХ⟩) ПЛЕ-ЧА́Х ⟨НА СЕБЕ́ *coll*, **НА СВОЁМ** or **НА СО́Б-СТВЕННОМ ГОРБУ́** *coll*⟩ что [VP; subj: human] (in refer. to something burdensome, difficult) to cope with sth. independently, without anyone's help: X вынесет Y на своих плечах ≃ **X will bear the responsibility ⟨the burden** etc**⟩ of Y all alone ⟨all by himself⟩; X will shoulder the responsibility for Y all by himself; X will bear the responsibility for Y on his (own) shoulders; X will do ⟨take care of** etc**⟩ Y single-handed(ly) ⟨by himself⟩.**

Он никогда не острил бесцельно, ради красного словца. Он делал это по заданиям юмористических журналов. На своих плечах он выносил ответственнейшие кампании, снабжал темами для рисунков и фельетонов большинство московских сатирических журналов (Ильф и Петров 1). He never made them [jokes] without reason, just for the effect. He made them to order for humorous journals. On his shoulders he bore the responsibility for highly important campaigns, and supplied most of the Moscow satirical journals with subjects for cartoons and humorous anecdotes (1a). ♦ И после такой жизни на него [Захара] вдруг навалили тяжёлую обузу выносить на плечах службу целого дома! (Гончаров 1). And after such a life, he [Zakhar] was suddenly burdened with the heavy task of doing the work of a whole household single-handed! (1a).

П-187 • ЛЕЖА́ТЬ НА ПЛЕЧА́Х чьих, (у) кого; **НА ПЛЕЧА́Х** [VP or PrepP (Invar, used as subj-compl with быть₀); subj: abstr] to be s.o.'s (usu. burdensome) responsibility, demanding much time, work, care etc from s.o.: X лежит на Y-овых плечах ≃ **X rests ⟨lies, is** etc**⟩ on Y's shoulders; X rests ⟨falls⟩ on Y.**

Хозяйство, забота о детях, о больной матери — всё лежало на её плечах. Running the household, looking after the children and her ailing mother—everything rested on her shoulders.

П-188 • **НА ПЛЕЧА́Х** (y) *кого* ворваться, вступить *куда,* идти и т. п. [PrepP; Invar; the resulting PrepP is adv] (to follow) right behind (a retreating enemy); (to enter into a city, town etc) right behind (the enemy who failed to defend it and retreated into it): **right ⟨hot⟩ on s.o.'s heels ⟨tail⟩; (right) on top of s.o.; (closely) pursuing s.o.**

Два полка были сметены и бежали, бросая оружие. На плечах их шёл полк немецких гусар (Шолохов 2). The two regiments were mown down and fled, abandoning their arms. They were pursued by a regiment of German hussars (2a).

П-189 • **ВЗВА́ЛИВАТЬ/ВЗВАЛИ́ТЬ** *что* **НА ПЛЕ́ЧИ** *чьи, кого, кому* [VP; subj: human] (in refer. to burdensome tasks, work, concerns etc) to make some person responsible for sth., make some person handle sth.: X взвалил Y на Z-овы плечи ≃ **X burdened Z with Y; X placed ⟨laid⟩ Y on Z's shoulders; X heaped ⟨piled⟩ Y on(to) Z's shoulders;** ‖ X взвалил Y себе на плечи ⟨на свои плечи⟩ ≃ **X shouldered ⟨took on⟩ Y.**

...Он [Никандров] к её непониманию прибавил ещё и своё собственное: проблемы Чертёжников и Конструкторов, вопрос о личном КПД [коэффициенте полезного действия], если на то пошло — об античности, да мало ли чего он...неизменно взваливал на её плечи? (Залыгин 1). ...To her imperfect understanding he [Nikandrov] had added his own: his problems of draughtsmen and designers, the question of his personal performance coefficient, the question of antiquity, if it came to that, and many other problems which he invariably heaped on to her shoulders (1a). ♦ С того самого злополучного дня, с той самой минуты, когда ему пришлось нежданно и негаданно взвалить на свои плечи тяжкий груз забот, он понял, что все подчинённые ему люди и даже те, что от него независимы, что вообще люди, вообще человечество оценивает и будет оценивать его впредь в первую очередь... по тому, каким он предстанет перед ним (Окуджава 2). From that infamous day, from the very minute, when he had unexpectedly to shoulder the heavy burden of responsibility, he had realized that all the people subordinate to him and even all the people dependent on him, that people in general—humanity—judged and would judge him first and foremost...by the way he presented himself to them... (2a). ♦ [Марк:] Говорю тебе откровенно: я не люблю её, она не любит меня. Ты знаешь, я взвалил себе на плечи что-то непосильное, измучился с ней (Розов 3). [М.:] I can tell you frankly: I don't love her, she doesn't love me. You know, I took on a burden that's more than I can carry, have worn myself out with her (3a).

П-190 • **ЛОЖИ́ТЬСЯ/ЛЕЧЬ ⟨СВА́ЛИВАТЬСЯ/СВА-ЛИ́ТЬСЯ** *coll*⟩ **НА ПЛЕ́ЧИ** *чьи, кого, кому* [VP; subj: abstr; usu. pfv] (of sth. burdensome) to become the object of s.o.'s concern, become s.o.'s responsibility: X лёг на Y-овы плечи ≃ **X fell ⟨rested⟩ on Y's shoulders; Y was burdened with X.**

Долгие годы она вела хозяйство, воспитывала детей, во всём старалась угодить своенравной свекрови. Вся тяжесть полевых работ ложилась на её худые плечи (Шолохов 5). Year after year she had run the farm, brought up the children, and done all she could to please her harsh-tempered mother-in-law. All the burden of the field work rested on her thin shoulders (5a). ♦ Это была фотография Нины Георгиевны в ту пору, когда она вышла из тюрьмы. В подполье она показала себя смелой и беззаветно преданной. Потом на её плечи легли заботы о больном муже, о детях (Эренбург 1). It was a photograph of [Nina Georgievna] at the time she was released from prison. While working underground she displayed courage and selfless devotion. Later she was burdened with the care of her sick husband and her children (1a).

П-191 • **ПЕРЕКЛА́ДЫВАТЬ/ПЕРЕЛОЖИ́ТЬ** *что* **НА ПЛЕ́ЧИ** *чьи, кого, кому* [VP; subj: human or collect] to shift (the blame, responsibility etc for sth.) to another person, thereby freeing o.s. from it: X перекладывает Y на Z-овы плечи ≃ **X shifts Y (on)to Z ⟨(on)to Z's shoulders⟩; X puts Y on Z.**

«Каждый платит за своё». — «Нет, за кровь платят все! Поэтому мы — евреи — обязаны нести ношу своей национальной ответственности сами, а не перекладывать-таки её на плечи других» (Максимов 3). "Each man pays his own personal debt." "Not for bloodshed—everybody pays for that. So we Jews must share the burden of our national responsibility and not try to shift it onto other people's shoulders" (3a). ♦ Да, «моя вина», и я не могу оставаться равнодушной, когда её перекладывают на плечи самого близкого мне человека (Ивинская 1). Yes, it was my fault, and I cannot remain indifferent when the blame is put on the man who was dearer to me than anybody else (1a).

П-192 • **ПЛЕЧО́М ⟨ПЛЕЧО́⟩ К ПЛЕЧУ́; ПЛЕЧО́ В ⟨О⟩ ПЛЕЧО́** [these forms only; adv] **1.** идти, стоять, сидеть и т. п. ~ (to go, stand, sit etc) alongside s.o.: **shoulder to shoulder; side by side.**

Потом он по-солдатски поправил ногу и пошёл плечом к плечу с monsieur Перси (Федин 1). Then he got into step like a soldier and walked shoulder to shoulder with Monsieur Percy (1a).

2. жить, работать, бороться и т. п. ~ (to live, work, fight etc) together, as like-minded people: **shoulder to shoulder; side by side; cheek by jowl.**

«Я человек широких взглядов, я вполне могу представить себе, что когда-нибудь стану работать с вами плечом к плечу...» (Стругацкие 4). "I am a man of broad views, and I can well imagine that some day we will work together, standing shoulder to shoulder..." (4a).

П-193 • **ПО ПЛЕЧУ́** *кому coll* [PrepP; Invar; nonagreeing modif or subj-compl with быть∅, оказаться (subj: usu. abstr, often дело, работа, задача etc)] (sth. is) within the range of s.o.'s abilities, achievable by or understandable to s.o.: X Y-у по плечу ≃ **X is within Y's grasp ⟨reach⟩; Y is capable of doing ⟨handling etc⟩ X; Y can handle ⟨do etc⟩ X; Y is equal to the task ⟨the work, the job etc⟩;** ‖ *Neg* X Y-у не по плечу ≃ **X is too big ⟨much⟩ for Y; Y is out of his depth in ⟨with⟩ X; X is beyond Y; X is over Y's head; Y is not up to X.**

Для творческой личности, говорит Неврастеник самому себе, самая большая трагедия — невозможность сделать дело, которое, как чувствует личность, ей по плечу (Зиновьев 1). For a creative person, said Neurasthenic to himself, the greatest tragedy is not to be able to do what he believes himself capable of (1a). ♦ «Рано, раненько мы возгордились, не по плечу задачку взяли» (Максимов 3). "We were a bit too hasty with our damned pride, we took on something too big for us" (3a). ♦ Многие хотели бы видеть его, Кирова, на посту Генсека — ему это не нужно, не по плечу, он не теоретик, он практик революции (Рыбаков 2). A lot of people would like to see him, Kirov, in the post of general secretary, but he didn't want it, he wasn't up to it. He wasn't a theoretician, he was one of the practical organizers of the Revolution (2a).

П-194 • **ПОХЛО́ПЫВАТЬ ПО ПЛЕЧУ́** *кого coll* [VP; subj: human] to relate to s.o. in an overly familiar, patronizing way: X похлопывает Y-а по плечу ≃ **X pats Y on the head; X treats Y condescendingly.**

То, что вы занимаете более высокую должность, ещё не даёт вам права похлопывать меня по плечу. Just because you have a more important job than I do doesn't give you the right to pat me on the head.

П-195 • **ЗАПРЕ́ТНЫЙ ПЛОД** *lit* [NP; sing only; fixed WO] sth. tempting, desirable, but prohibited: **forbidden fruit.**

Я даже секретные материалы перестал просматривать. Сначала было интересно. Всё-таки запретный плод. Потом я убедился, что это такая же серость и скукота, как и всё то, что публикуется официально (Зиновьев 1). "I've even stopped looking at secret documents. It was interesting at first, forbidden fruit after all. But eventually I realised that it was all as drab and tedious as everything that is published officially…" (1a).

< From the Biblical account (Gen. 2:16–17) involving the tree of the knowledge of good and evil, whose fruit God forbade Adam and Eve to eat.

П-196 • **ПОЖИНА́ТЬ/ПОЖА́ТЬ ПЛОДЫ́** *(чего) lit;* **ВКУША́ТЬ/ВКУСИ́ТЬ ПЛОДЫ́** *elev* [VP; subj: human] to enjoy the results (or, in ironic usage, face the unpleasant repercussions) of sth. done, accomplished, achieved: X пожинает плоды Y-a ≃ **X reaps the fruit(s) ⟨the benefits⟩ of Y; X reaps his reward;** [in refer. to unpleasant repercussions only] **X reaps the consequences of Y; X has to live with the consequences of Y;** ‖ X пожинает плоды чужого труда ≃ **X reaps the fruit(s) of another's labor(s); X reaps where he hasn't sown.**

[Глумов:] Вы видите, что мне некогда, год я должен сердобольно ухаживать за больной, а потом могу пожинать плоды трудов своих… (Островский 4). [G.:] You see, I haven't any time to lose. For a year I must watch over my invalid tenderly, but afterwards I can reap the fruits of my labors… (4a). ♦ Явившись тогда с визитом к Раскольникову, он вошёл с чувством благодетеля, готовящегося пожать плоды и выслушать весьма сладкие комплименты (Достоевский 3). When paying a visit to Raskolnikov that time he had gone there feeling like a benefactor, prepared to reap his reward and to listen to a series of extremely sweet compliments (3a). ♦ «Вы видите, когда нужно действовать решительно и твёрдо, правительство ограничивается полумерами… Что же… будет время — пожнут плоды своей политики полумер» (Шолохов 3). "As you see, when firm and resolute action is needed, the government confines itself to half-measures….Well, the time will come when they will reap the consequences of their policy of half-measures" (3a). ♦ Он и тогда это понимал, и тогда почувствовал, что совершил ошибку, теперь пожинает её плоды (Рыбаков 2). He'd realized it then—but now he was having to live with its consequences (2a).

< The variant вкушать/вкусить плоды is related to the Biblical «вкушать плоды дел своих», "eat the fruit of their doings" (Isa. 3:10).

П-197 • **КАТИ́ТЬСЯ/ПОКАТИ́ТЬСЯ ⟨ПОКАТИ́ТЬ, ИДТИ́/ПОЙТИ́⟩ ПО НАКЛО́ННОЙ ПЛО́СКОСТИ** *lit;* **КАТИ́ТЬСЯ/ПОКАТИ́ТЬСЯ ПО СКО́ЛЬЗКОЙ ДОРО́ЖКЕ** *coll* [VP; subj: human] to decline rapidly in a moral and spiritual sense: X катится по наклонной плоскости ≃ **X is sliding ⟨going⟩ downhill; X has gone wrong;** [in limited contexts] **X will ⟨is going to⟩ end up in the gutter.**

Она говорила себе: — А если бы она была замужем? Чем бы это отличалось?.. Как ему не стыдно валяться в ногах у неё и умолять: «Так не может продолжаться. Подумай, что я с тобой сделал. Ты катишься по наклонной плоскости. Давай откроем матери. Я женюсь на тебе» (Пастернак 1). What if she were married, she asked herself, what difference would it make?…How can he not be ashamed to grovel at her feet and plead with her? "We can't go on like this. Think what I have done to you! You will end up in the gutter. We must tell your mother. I'll marry you" (1a).

П-198 • **ВО ПЛОТИ́** *lit* [PrepP; Invar; usu. nonagreeing postmodif] in bodily form: **in the flesh.**

«Эта… девица – это дочка моя-с, Нина Николаевна-с, забыл я вам её представить – ангел божий во плоти…» (Достоевский 1). "This…girl here—she's my daughter, sir, Nina Nikolaevna, I forgot to introduce her to you—is God's angel in the flesh…" (1a).

П-199 • **ВХОДИ́ТЬ/ВОЙТИ́ В ПЛОТЬ И КРОВЬ** *чью, кого* [VP; subj: abstr] (of an attitude, mode of behavior etc) to become fixed in s.o., become a permanent part of s.o.'s life, personality etc: X вошёл в плоть и кровь Y-a ≃ **X became second nature to Y; X became (a) part of Y.**

Ужаснее всего это несокончаемое притворство и двуличие, входящее в плоть и кровь советского человека уже со школьной скамьи (Аллилуева 2). The ugliest feature of Soviet life was the endless dissimulation and double-facedness infused into the Soviet people from their schoolroom days, so that it became almost second nature (2a).

П-200 • **ОБЛЕКА́ТЬ/ОБЛЕ́ЧЬ В ПЛОТЬ (И КРОВЬ)** *что;* **ОБЛЕКА́ТЬ/ОБЛЕ́ЧЬ ПЛО́ТЬЮ (И КРО́ВЬЮ)** *all lit* [VP; subj: human] to express sth. (an idea, artistic concept etc) in a concrete, definite form: X облёк Y в плоть и кровь ≃ **X gave form and substance to Y; X brought Y to life.**

П-201 • **ОБЛЕКА́ТЬСЯ/ОБЛЕ́ЧЬСЯ В ПЛОТЬ (И КРОВЬ); ОБЛЕКА́ТЬСЯ/ОБЛЕ́ЧЬСЯ ПЛО́ТЬЮ (И КРО́ВЬЮ)** *all lit* [VP; subj: abstr] (of an idea, artistic concept etc) to acquire a concrete, definite form: X облёкся в плоть и кровь ≃ **X took a tangible ⟨discernible etc⟩ form; X came ⟨sprang⟩ to life ⟨into being⟩.**

П-202 • **ПЛОТЬ ОТ ПЛО́ТИ (И КРОВЬ ОТ КРО́ВИ ⟨И КОСТЬ ОТ КО́СТИ⟩); КОСТЬ ОТ КО́СТИ; КРОВЬ ОТ КРО́ВИ** *all elev* [NP; these forms only; usu. subj-compl with быть₀ or appos; may be used with pl subj; WO within the плоть…, кровь…, and кость… components is fixed, but the components as units may be transposed] **1.** ~ *чьей, кого.* Also: **ПЛОТЬ И КРОВЬ** *чья, кого* [subj: human] (in refer. to a blood relationship) s.o.'s own child: **s.o.'s (own) flesh and blood; (the) flesh of s.o.'s flesh (and bone of s.o.'s bone).**

«Божественный и святейший старец! – вскричал он, указывая на Ивана Фёдоровича. – Это мой сын, плоть от плоти моей, любимейшая плоть моя!» (Достоевский 1). "Divine and most holy elder!" he cried, pointing at Ivan Fyodorovich, "this is my son, the flesh of my flesh, my own dear flesh!" (1a).

2. ~ *кого-чего, чьей.* Also: **ПЛОТЬ И КРОВЬ** *кого-чего, чья* [subj and obj: human or collect; if obj: human, usu. pl] a person (or group of people) that is related ideologically, spiritually etc to a group or movement that came before and is therefore viewed as its ideological heir(s): **flesh and blood of s.o. ⟨sth.⟩; flesh of the flesh (and blood of the blood) of s.o. ⟨sth.⟩.**

Почему же… они так быстро капитулировали?.. А загадки никакой нет. Просто они плоть от плоти и кровь от крови этого общества (Зиновьев 1). …Why did they capitulate so quickly?…But there's really no mystery about it. They are simply the flesh and blood of this society (1a). ♦ Бердяев, плоть от плоти символистов, в конце жизни предпочитал литературу девятнадцатого века, но продолжал считать начало века периодом расцвета (Мандельштам 2). By the end of his life Berdiayev, who was flesh of the flesh of the Symbolists, came to prefer the literature of the nineteenth century, but he continued to regard the beginning of the present century as a time of revival (2a).

П-203 • **ПЛЮ́НУТЬ И ⟨ДА⟩ РАСТЕРЕ́ТЬ** *substand* [VP; fixed WO] **1.** [subj: human; usu. imper] (in refer. to sth. that the speaker considers not worth s.o.'s or, occas., one's own time or attention) to disregard sth. completely, not pay any attention to sth.: плюнь и разотри ≃ **pay it no mind; forget it; don't trouble yourself about it.**

2. [infin only; used as subj-compl with быть₀ (subj: usu. abstr)] sth. is unimportant, insignificant, not worth worrying about: X – плюнуть и растереть ≃ **X is no big deal ⟨thing⟩;**

X is not even worth talking about; X doesn't amount to a hill of beans.

Не относитесь серьёзно к Колиным жалобам. Все его проблемы – плюнуть да растереть. Don't take Kolya's complaints seriously. None of his problems are even worth talking about.

П-204 • ПЛЮ́НУТЬ НЕ́ГДЕ ⟨НЕ́КУДА⟩ *highly coll* [these forms only; usu. impers predic with быть∅] some place is so full of people or things that there is absolutely no free space: **one can hardly ⟨barely⟩ move ⟨breathe⟩; there's barely ⟨scarcely, hardly⟩ room to move ⟨to breathe⟩; there's no room to spit; there isn't room to swing a cat.**

…[Моя бабушка] родилась и выросла в селе Деремезна Обуховского уезда, в проклятущей халупе, где, как и в дедовой семье, некуда было плюнуть из-за детей (Кузнецов 1). …[My grandmother] was born and grew up in the village of Deremezna in the Obukhov district in a godforsaken old shack, with scarcely room to move because of all the children (1b).

П-205 • КУДА́ НИ ПЛЮНЬ *substand* [subord clause; Invar; fixed WO] everywhere, all around: **wherever you look ⟨turn⟩; everywhere you look ⟨turn⟩.**

«…У нас музыкой заправляют евреи… Да, да, это все знают. Куда ни плюнь, какой-нибудь Ойстрах или Гилельс…» (Копелев 1). "…The Jews are running our music. Yes, everyone knows that. Wherever you look, there's some Oistrakh or Gilels" (1a).

П-206 • НА ПОБЕГУ́ШКАХ *coll* [PrepP; Invar] **1.** [subj-compl with быть∅, находиться (subj: human), obj-compl with держать (obj: human), or nonagreeing postmodif of мальчик, девочка] one performs minor services, small tasks for s.o.; (to have s.o.) perform minor services, small tasks for one: X (у Y-a) на побегушках ≃ **X runs errands (for Y); X fetches and carries (for Y); X does (all) the legwork for Y; X is an errand boy ⟨girl⟩; X is a gofer;** ‖ Y держит X-a на побегушках ≃ **Y keeps X running errands; Y has made an errand boy ⟨an errand girl, a gofer⟩ out of X;** ‖ мальчик ⟨девочка⟩ на побегушках ≃ **errand boy ⟨girl⟩; gofer.**

И после такой жизни на него [Захара] вдруг навалили тяжелую обузу выносить на плечах службу целого дома! Он и служи барину, и мети, и чисть, он и на побегушках! (Гончаров 1). And after such a life, he [Zakhar] was suddenly burdened with the heavy task of doing the work of a whole household single-handed! He had to look after his master, sweep and clean, and run errands! (1a). ♦ Тут старуха стала ругаться, что Скороход не чтит абхазские обычаи, по которым старого человека надо уважать, а не держать его на побегушках (Искандер 5). Now the old woman began to scold, saying that Highspeed didn't revere Abkhazian custom, according to which an old person must be respected and not be kept running errands (5a). ♦ У редактора был денщик, мальчик на побегушках, некий Орлов (Довлатов 1). He [the editor] had a kind of batman or errand boy named Orlov (1a).

2. ~ *у кого* [the resulting PrepP is subj-compl with быть∅, состоять, or is under s.o.'s influence or control, fulfills s.o.'s desires, whims without question: X у Y-a на побегушках ≃ **X is at Y's beck and call; X is at Y's service; X waits on Y hand and foot.**

Дома всем заправляют жена и тёща, он у них на побегушках. His wife and mother-in-law run everything at home: he's at their beck and call.

П-207 • ПИ́РРОВА ПОБЕ́ДА *lit* [NP; sing only; fixed WO] a victory in which the victor's losses are so great that they outweigh or overshadow any gain: **Pyrrhic victory.**

< From the name of King *Pyrrhus* of Epirus, who defeated the Romans in 279 B.C. but at such great cost that he exclaimed, "One more such victory and Pyrrhus is undone."

П-208 • ПОБЕДИ́ТЕЛЕЙ НЕ СУ́ДЯТ *lit* [sent; fixed WO] if a person achieves success or is victorious no one criticizes his means or methods (even if they are unscrupulous): **victors need never explain; success is never blamed.**

< Attributed to Catherine the Great.

П-209 • ДАВА́ТЬ/ДАТЬ ⟨ДЕ́ЛАТЬ/СДЕ́ЛАТЬ⟩ ПОБЛА́ЖКУ ⟨-и⟩ *кому coll;* **ДАВА́ТЬ/ДАТЬ ПОТА́ЧКУ** *obs, coll;* **ДАВА́ТЬ/ДАТЬ ПОВА́ДКУ** *obs, substand* [VP; subj: usu. human] to react to sth. (s.o.'s undesirable, underhanded etc behavior or action) mildly, be lenient with s.o.: X дал Y-у поблажку ≃ **X let Y get away with it; X gave Y a break; X made an allowance ⟨allowances⟩ for Y; X went ⟨took it⟩ easy on Y; X made a concession to Y; X showed Y indulgence; X let Y have Y's (own) way; X let Y take liberties with…;** ‖ *Neg* X не даёт Y-у поблажек ≃ **X doesn't let Y have an easy time of it; X is tough on Y.**

…Дедушка сам работал не разгибая спины и от других требовал того же, никому… не давал поблажки: ни сыновьям, ни внукам, ни подмастерьям, ни зятю… (Рыбаков 1). Grandfather himself worked without let-up and he demanded the same of the others. He made no allowances for anybody, neither his sons and grandsons, nor his workmen, nor his son-in-law… (1a). ♦ Рано или поздно так случалось со всеми [собаками]. Одни теряли чутьё или слепли от старости, другие слишком привыкали к своим подконвойным и начинали им делать кое-какие поблажки, третьих – от долгой службы – постигало страшное помрачение ума, заставлявшее их рычать и кидаться на собственного хозяина (Владимов 1). Sooner or later it happened to all of them [the dogs]. Some lost their "nose" or went blind from old age; others got too familiar with the prisoners and began to make little concessions to them; others, from overlong service, were afflicted by a terrible clouding of the mind which made them growl and attack their own masters (1a). ♦ А если я… желал, чтоб эти взносы делались не по принуждению, то опять-таки не затем, чтоб дать поблажку непросвещённой и грубой черни… (Салтыков-Щедрин 2). And if…I further desired that the peasants should not be made to pay up by force, it was again not because I sought in any way to show any indulgence to the ill-mannered and ignorant mob… (2a). ♦ [Бурмистр:] Какие ж мои окаянства? Что потачки вам не даю, вот вас всех злоба за что… (Писемский 1). [Bailiff:] What are my abominations? Because I don't let you have your own way – that's why all of you are angry! (1a). ♦ «А это на что похоже, что вчера только восемь фунтов пшена отпустила, опять спрашивают… А я пшена не отпущу… Нет, я потачки за барское добро не дам. Ну виданное ли это дело – восемь фунтов?» (Толстой 2). "And what sort of game is this? Only yesterday I let them have eight pounds of rice and now they're asking for more!…I'm not giving you any more rice.…No, I'm not letting anybody take liberties with the master's things. Well, who ever heard of such a thing – eight pounds?" (2b). ♦ Буйная имеет десять лет… Два сына сидят в уголовных лагерях на севере. Она работает вовсю, висит на доске лагерных ударников. Её обязанность – никому не давать поблажки (Ивинская 1). Buinaya was serving a ten-year sentence.…Her two sons were in camps for common criminals in the North. She worked for all she was worth and was always being commended as a "shock worker" on the camp's bulletin board. It was her job not to let anyone have an easy time of it (1a).

П-210 • МАМА́ЕВО ПОБО́ИЩЕ *occas. humor* [NP; sing only; fixed WO] **1.** a heated, uncontrolled, and often violent quarrel or fight (in which one side clearly defeats the other): **brawl; fracas.** Cf. **donnybrook.**

2. large-scale layoffs, dismissals, expulsions etc: **mass firings ⟨expulsions etc⟩;** ‖ X устроил мамаево побоище ≃ **X purged the place ⟨the department etc⟩.**

Новый управляющий устроил настоящее мамаево побоище: уволил двух своих заместителей, заменил почти всех начальников отделов и вынудил главного инженера уйти на пенсию. The new director purged the place: he fired two of his assistant directors, replaced almost all of the department heads, and forced the chief engineer into retirement.

< From the name of the Tartar khan *Mamai,* defeated by the Russians in 1380 on the Kulikovo Field.

П-211 • женщина, девица и т. п. ЛЁГКОГО ПОВЕДЕ́НИЯ *euph* [NP_{gen}; Invar; nonagreeing postmodif; fixed WO] a woman who enters into chance, short-lived relations with men: **woman of easy virtue; easy woman.**

П-212 • С КЕМ ПОВЕДЁШЬСЯ, ОТ ТОГО́ И НАБЕ-РЁШЬСЯ [saying; occas. only the first half of the saying is used] you unwittingly adopt the views, habits of a person with whom you socialize or are on friendly terms: ≃ **he who ⟨that⟩ lies down with dogs gets up with fleas; he who ⟨that⟩ lives with a cripple learns how to limp; you cannot touch pitch without being defiled;** [when only the first half of the saying is used] **it's catching.**

[Леонидик:] Он любит тебя. Он сам сказал мне это. [Лика:] Ого!.. Берёшь пример с настоящего мужчины? [Леонидик:] С кем поведёшься... (Арбузов 4). [Leonidik:] He loves you. He told me. [Lika:] Oh! So you're behaving like a real man! [Leonidik:] It's catching... (4a).

П-213 • НА ПОВЕ́РКУ [PrepP; Invar; usu. sent adv] (used when emphasizing that the real nature of s.o. or sth., when allowed to reveal itself and/or when inspected more closely, differs from what it appears to be at first) in actuality: **in (actual) fact; actually; in reality;** ‖ на поверку оказалось ⟨вышло и т. п.⟩, что... ≃ **on closer inspection it turned out that...**

«Конечно, образован, толковый инженер, способен придумывать и выдумывать. Но поверхностен... Свою ограниченность называет сосредоточенностью, целеустремлённостью. А на поверку просто боится растеряться, боится разносторонних исследований...» (Копелев 1). "Of course, he's an educated, sensible engineer, he's capable of thinking and inventing....He's superficial....He calls his limitations concentration, direction. But actually he's just afraid of getting sidetracked, afraid of multi-faceted research..." (1a). ♦ «...Надо очень чётко и честно определять людские поступки, и тогда то, что нам кажется глупостью, может на поверку оказаться либо преступлением, либо узкомыслием» (Семёнов 1). "...One must weigh people's actions extremely carefully and honestly, so that what to us looks like stupidity may turn out on closer inspection to be either narrow-mindedness or a crime" (1a).

П-214 • КАК ⟨КУДА́⟩ НИ ПОВЕРНИ́(ТЕ) ⟨НИ ПОВОРОТИ́(ТЕ) *obsoles*⟩ *coll* [subord clause; these forms only; fixed WO] no matter which assumption you make or which approach you take: **whichever way you look at it; no matter how ⟨which way⟩ you look at it.**

Словом, куда ни повороти, [Чичиков] был очень порядочный человек (Гоголь 3). In short, whichever way you looked at it, he [Chichikov] was a man of utmost respectability and honesty (3a).

П-215 • ПОВЕРНУ́ТЬСЯ ⟨ПОВОРОТИ́ТЬСЯ *obs*⟩ НЕ́ГДЕ; НЕ ПОВЕРНЁШЬСЯ; НЕ ПОВЕРНУ́ТЬСЯ *all coll* [these forms only; impers predic with быть_{∅} (variants with infin) or neg pfv fut, gener. 2nd pers sing; var. не повернуться can be used as quantit subj-compl with быть_{∅} (subj/gen: людей, народу etc)] some place is so full of people or things that there is no free space: **there's no room to move ⟨to turn around⟩; one can hardly ⟨barely⟩ move ⟨breathe⟩; there's hardly ⟨barely, scarcely⟩ room to move ⟨to breathe⟩; there isn't room to swing a cat.**

Квартира так заставлена мебелью, что повернуться негде. The apartment is so full of furniture there's no room to turn around.

П-216 • СКОЛЬЗИ́ТЬ ПО ПОВЕ́РХНОСТИ (чего) *often disapprov* [VP; subj: human] to have only a superficial idea about some matter, not delve deeply into the essence of sth.: X скользит по поверхности (Y-a) ≃ **X skims ⟨scratches⟩ the surface (of Y); X does not go below the surface (of Y); X does not get to the heart of the matter ⟨the question etc⟩.**

Сначала создаётся впечатление, что автор изучил проблему глубоко, но, вчитавшись в статью, понимаешь, что он лишь скользит по поверхности. At first you get the impression that the author has thoroughly explored the problem, but when you read the article carefully you see that he has just skimmed the surface.

П-217 • ВСПЛЫВА́ТЬ/ВСПЛЫТЬ НА ПОВЕ́РХНОСТЬ; ВСПЛЫВА́ТЬ/ВСПЛЫТЬ ⟨ВЫПЛЫ-ВА́ТЬ/ВЫ́ПЛЫТЬ⟩ НАРУ́ЖУ [VP; subj: usu. abstr] to emerge (suddenly), be revealed, become clear (may refer to sth. reprehensible that s.o. wishes to hide): X всплыл на поверхность ≃ **X surfaced; X came out; X came ⟨rose, sprang etc⟩ to the surface; X came up; X came to light;** [of sth. reprehensible] **X leaked out.**

...Стали всплывать на поверхность подозрительные Венечкины финансовые отчёты, фальшивые командировки... (Аксёнов 12). ...Various suspicious things began to surface: [Venechka] Probkin's financial reports, faked business trips... (12a). ♦ Неожиданные для неё самой – сила жизни, надежды на счастье всплыли наружу и требовали удовлетворения (Толстой 7). To her own surprise the life force and the hope of happiness rose to the surface and demanded to be satisfied (7a). ♦ ...Их [стукачей] заверяли, что их деятельность никогда не выплывет наружу, не станет явной (Мандельштам 1). ...They [the informers] were always assured that nothing about their activities would ever leak out or become public knowledge (1a).

П-218 • ПОВЕ́СТКА ДНЯ [NP; sing only; fixed WO] **1.** Also: ПОРЯ́ДОК ДНЯ a list of questions or subjects for discussion at a meeting; *by extension* an informal list or plan of things to be done, addressed etc: **agenda; order ⟨business⟩ of the day;** [in limited contexts, extended usage only] **schedule of events.**

Согласно повестке дня, за Крамовым должен был выступить какой-то профессор Горский... (Каверин 1). According to the agenda, a certain Professor Gorsky was due to speak after Kramov... (1a). ♦ [extended usage] Вопрос, почему Строковский держит Поляшко в институте, да ещё на первых ролях, никогда не сходил с повестки дня кулуарных разговоров (Залыгин 1). [context transl] A constant theme of corridor gossip was why Strokovsky kept Poliashko at the institute and in a key position (1a).

2. на повестке дня быть_{∅}, стоять; ставить *что* на повестку дня; снимать *что* с повестки дня (to be, be made etc) a priority: **(be on ⟨put sth. on, take sth. off⟩) the agenda; (be) the order of the day.**

Нет, стоп! – сказал район. Берись-ка сперва за заём. Эта кампания на повестке дня (Абрамов 1). "Halt!" said the District Committee. First take care of the Loan – that was the campaign on the agenda (1a). ♦ «Вы, русские, – странный народ... Готовы до бесконечности спорить о вещах и вопросах, которые в цивилизованном мире давно решены и сняты, как у вас говорят, с повестки дня...» (Максимов 2). "You Russians are a strange people....You are prepared to argue endlessly about things which in the civilized world have long since been resolved and have been, as you put it, taken off the agenda..." (2a).

П-219 • С ПОВИ́ННОЙ приходить, являться и т. п.; С ПОВИ́ННОЙ ГОЛОВО́Й [PrepP; these forms only; subj-compl with copula (subj: human) or, rare, nonagreeing postmodif] (to come to s.o., show up etc) conceding that one is guilty and often repenting of one's wrongdoing, crime etc: **confess(ing) ⟨acknowledge, acknowledging⟩ one's guilt; confess and plead guilty; with an admission of one's guilt; owning up (to one's guilt ⟨crime etc⟩); [in limited contexts] (come) cap ⟨hat⟩ in hand; [usu. of a criminal] turn o.s. in; give o.s. up (and plead guilty).**

На вопросы же, что именно побудило его явиться с повинною, [Раскольников] отвечал, что чистосердечное раскаяние (Достоевский 3). And to the question of what precisely had prompted him to come and confess his guilt, he [Raskolnikov] answered directly that it was sincere repentance (3c). ♦ «Я до тех пор не намерен ехать в Покровское, пока не вышлете Вы мне псаря Парамошку с повинною...» (Пушкин 1). "I do not intend to come to Pokrovskoe until you send me your kennelman Paramoshka with an admission of his guilt..." (1a). ♦ Самым употребительным в его лексиконе было слово «нельзя». Нельзя то, нельзя это. Нельзя вообще ничего. Но дети росли, и мир с каждым следующим днём становился для них шире и выше его «нельзя». И они уходили, а он оставался в злорадной уверенности в их скором возвращении с повинной (Максимов 3). The most frequently used word in his vocabulary was "don't." Don't do this, don't do that. In fact, don't do anything. But his children got bigger, and with every day that passed their world got higher and wider than his "don'ts." Away they went, and he was left with the spiteful assurance that they would soon be back, cap in hand (3a). ♦ «Вы не хотите принять во внимание, что я явился с повинной» (Войнович 4). "You won't take into consideration that I've turned myself in" (4a). ♦ «Что, ежели [казаки] одумаются и пойдут с повинной?» — не без тревоги подумал Иван Алексеевич... (Шолохов 3). "What will happen if they [the Cossacks] change their minds and give themselves up?" Ivan wondered with some alarm... (3a).

П-220 • ПРИНОСИ́ТЬ/ПРИНЕСТИ́ ПОВИ́ННУЮ
(ГО́ЛОВУ *obs*) (*кому*) [VP; subj: human] to acknowledge one's guilt, usu. expressing repentance: X принёс повинную ≃ **X (humbly) confessed his guilt; [in limited contexts] X came cap ⟨hat⟩ in hand; [usu. of a criminal] X gave himself up; X turned himself in.**

...Увидев, что правда на стороне головотяпов, [кособрюхие] принесли повинную (Салтыков-Щедрин 1). Only when they [the Skewbellies] saw that right was on the side of the Knockheads did they give themselves up (1a).

П-221 • ДАВА́ТЬ/ДАТЬ ⟨ПОДАВА́ТЬ/ПОДА́ТЬ⟩ ПО́ВОД (*кому*) (*к чему, что делать*) [VP; subj: human or abstr (слова, поведение etc)] to cause s.o. to act or think in a specific way: X даёт (Y-у) повод (к Z-у ⟨делать Z⟩) ≃ **X gives Y reason (to do Z); X gives Y cause ⟨grounds⟩ for Z ⟨to do Z⟩; X arouses Z in Y.**

«...Каких же последствий вы опасаетесь?» — «В гимназии разврат начнётся», — сказал Передонов. Хрипач нахмурился и сказал: «Вы слишком далеко заходите. Всё, что вы мне до сих пор сказали, не даёт мне ни малейшего повода разделять ваши подозрения» (Сологуб 1). "What consequences are you afraid of?" "Depravity will begin in the gymnasium," said Peredonov. Khripach frowned. "You go too far," he said. "Nothing that you have said to me so far gives me the slightest cause to share your suspicions" (1a). ♦ Наконец, случайно выяснилось, что девушка, подавшая повод к сложным Лариным чувствованиям, — сестра Коки, и Ларины соображения не имели под собой никакой почвы (Пастернак 1). ...Finally Lara learned that the girl who had aroused such complicated feelings in her was the young man's sister and that her suspicions had been groundless (1a).

П-222 • ДЕРЖА́ТЬ НА КОРО́ТКОМ ПОВОДКЕ́ *кого*
coll [VP; subj: human; the verb may take the final position, otherwise fixed WO] (often in refer. to relations between spouses)

to keep s.o. in subordination, not letting him freely exercise his will or act on his own initiative: X держал Y-а на коротком поводке ≃ **X kept Y on a short leash; X kept a tight rein on Y.**

Это только кажется, что Игорь даёт жене полную свободу — на самом деле он держит её на коротком поводке. It just looks like Igor gives his wife absolute freedom; in reality he keeps her on a short leash.

П-223 • ИДТИ́/ПОЙТИ́ НА ПОВОДУ́ *у кого;* ХОДИ́ТЬ НА ПОВОДУ́; НА ПОВОДУ́ *all coll* [VP or PrepP (Invar, used as subj-compl with быть₀); subj: human] to submit fully to s.o., not act on one's own initiative: X идёт на поводу у Y-а ≃ **X lets Y lead X by the nose; X follows Y's tastes ⟨every whim etc⟩; X lets Y ⟨allows Y to⟩ push X around; X lets himself ⟨allows himself to⟩ be run by Y; [in limited contexts] X listens to Y.**

Секс, порнография и насилие — вот что пользуется неизменным успехом на западном книжном рынке. «Мы, — замечает с горечью мистер Гопкинс, — вынуждены идти на поводу у читателя» (Войнович 3). Sex, pornography, rape—that's what enjoys invariable success in the Western book market. "We are forced," Mr. Hopkins remarks bitterly, "to follow the readers' tastes" (3a). ♦ «Ну да... — задумчиво сказал Слава. — Это всё, конечно, бабы... Эх, эти бабы! Ну, конечно, я представляю теперь всё несколько иначе... Но Солженицын не пошёл бы у баб на поводу...» (Ивинская 1). "Yes, I see..." Slava said thoughtfully. "It was all because of women, naturally....God, these women! Well, of course, that gives me a rather different picture....But Solzhenitsyn would never have allowed himself to be run by women..." (1a). ♦ Киров обнял и поцеловал Орджоникидзе, обнял и поцеловал Зинаиду Гавриловну, дружески строго сказал ей: «Не ходи у него на поводу, заставляй лечиться» (Рыбаков 2). Kirov embraced and kissed first Ordzhonikidze and then his wife. "Don't listen to him," he admonished her as a friend. "Make him get treatment" (2a).

П-224 • ПО ПО́ВОДУ [PrepP; Invar; Prep; the resulting PrepP is usu. adv] 1. ~ *кого-чего* in refer. to s.o. or sth., with respect to s.o. or sth.: **concerning; regarding; about; in ⟨with⟩ regard to; in connection with; apropos of; [in limited contexts] on; over; on the subject of; [as part of an indep. remark, often preceded by это] it has to do with...; [as part of an indep. remark, often preceded by что-то, что-нибудь etc] something (having) to do with...**

Председатель, обратившись к подсудимому, спросил: не имеет ли он чего заметить по поводу данных показаний? (Достоевский 2). The judge, addressing the defendant, asked whether he had anything to say concerning the present testimony (2a). ♦ ...В отличие от Мальковой Дьяков не стал читать ему нотации по поводу брата, видимо, уже осведомлён на этот счёт (Рыбаков 2). Unlike Malkova, Dyakov did not lecture him about his brother. He had evidently been informed on that score (2a). ♦ «Я решился обеспокоить вас, сударыня, по поводу общего знакомого нашего Дмитрия Фёдоровича Карамазова» (Достоевский 1). "I have ventured to trouble you, madame, in connection with our mutual acquaintance Dmitri Fyodorovich Karamazov" (1a). ♦ Это не столько *записки*, сколько *исповедь*, около которой, по поводу которой собрались там-сям схваченные воспоминания из *Былого*, там-сям остановленные мысли из *Дум* (Герцен 1). These are not so much notes as a confession, round which, *à propos* of which, have been assembled memories snatched from here and there in the *Past,* and ideas from my *Thoughts,* which here and there have remained behind (1a). ♦ Филипп Филиппович... вгляделся в Шарикова и спросил: «Позвольте узнать, что вы можете сказать по поводу прочитанного?» Шариков пожал плечами. «Да не согласен я» (Булгаков 11). Philip Philipovich...stared at Sharikov and asked: "What comment can you make on what you've read?" Sharikov shrugged. "I don't agree" (11b). ♦ По поводу незадачливого брата дяди Сандро долго смеялись...

(Искандер 3). They had a good long laugh over Uncle Sandro's luckless brother... (3a). ♦ «Что вас привело к нам?» — «Самсонов». — «Лёнка?» — «Леонид?» — «Да». — «Что-нибудь по поводу собаки?» (Семёнов 1). "What brings you here?" "Samsonov." "Lyonka? Leonid?" "Yes." "Something to do with the dog?" (1a).

2. ~ *чего* for the reason specified: **because of; on account of.**

Его прооперировали в срочном порядке по поводу аппендицита. He had an emergency operation on account of appendicitis.

П-225 • ПОВОРО́Т НА СТО ВО́СЕМЬДЕСЯТ ГРА́ДУСОВ *media or coll* [NP; sing only; usu. this WO] a sudden reversal of s.o.'s attitude, position, opinion etc: **about-face; flip-flop; 180-degree turn; (turn around) 180 degrees.**

Тут, наконец, до Марлена Михайловича дошло: вот она — главная причина сегодняшнего высокого совещания. Обеспокоены «поворотом на 180 градусов», перепугались, как бы не отплыл от них в недосягаемые дали Остров Крым, как бы не отняли того, что давно уже считалось личной собственностью (Аксёнов 7). In a flash Marlen Mikhailovich realized what the meeting was for. They were upset by the aboutface, concerned that the Island of Crimea would float out of their reach, that they would be robbed of what they had long considered their due (7a). ♦ И ежели у какой бабы и было ещё намерение повздыхать о прошлом, а заодно и Анфису Петровну добрым словом помянуть, то после его [Михаила] выкрика поворот на сто восемьдесят градусов (Абрамов 1). If any of the women had had half a mind to sigh for the past and to have a kind word for Anfisa Petrovna, then after his [Mikhail's] attack they turned around one hundred eighty degrees (1a).

П-226 • ЛЕ́ГЧЕ ⟨ПОЛЕ́ГЧЕ⟩ НА ПОВОРО́ТАХ! *highly coll, impol* [imper sent; these forms only; fixed WO] (used as a warning or threat) be more careful of what you do, say etc: **(you'd better) watch what you're saying ⟨doing⟩!; (you'd better) watch your tongue ⟨step⟩!; tone it down (a bit)!; go easy.**

«Вы вор!» — «Легче на поворотах! Я ведь могу на вас в суд подать за клевету». "You're a thief!" "You'd better watch what you're saying! I could take you to court for slander." ♦ Каждый раз, когда сын говорит мне, что ему предстоит объяснение с женой, я всегда даю один и тот же совет: «Легче на поворотах». Every time my son tells me he needs to clear the air with his wife, I give him one and the same piece of advice: Go easy.

П-227 • ПОВТОРЕ́НЬЕ – МАТЬ УЧЕ́НЬЯ [saying] the way to master sth. is by constantly repeating or practicing it: ≃ **practice makes perfect; it's dogged that does it.**

П-228 • В ТРИ ПОГИ́БЕЛИ ⟨В ДУГУ́, В ТРИ ДУГИ́⟩ согну́ться, скорчиться и т. п. *coll* [PrepP; these forms only; adv; fixed WO] (to bend, stoop down etc) very low (often because of pain): X согнулся в три погибели ≃ **X bent double;** [when caused by pain only] **X doubled up.**

Согнувшись в три погибели, она пыталась сдвинуть с места свою перегруженную тележку (Зиновьев 2). She was bent double trying to heave her overloaded cart (2a). ♦ Тут Запятаев согнулся в три погибели, схватился за живот и мелко затрясся, словно в припадке (Войнович 4). Zapyataev doubled up and clutched his stomach, trembling slightly as if having a fit (4a).

П-229 • ПОГИ́БЕЛИ ⟨ПРО́ПАСТИ⟩ на кого-что НЕТ! *substand, rude* [these forms only; the resulting phrase is used as Interj] used to express indignation, annoyance at s.o. or sth.: погибели на X-а нет! ≃ **(God) damn X!;** [in limited contexts] **X will be the death of me!; will I ⟨we⟩ never be rid of X!**

Григорий с досадой сказал: «Ты, бабушка, лучше дай косу...» Старуха сурово глянула на Григория и отвернулась. «Ступай сам возьми, она, никак, под сараем висит»... Когда [Григорий] проходил мимо старухи, [он] отчётливо слышал,

как та проговорила: «Погибели на вас, проклятых, нету!» К этому ещё не привыкать Григорию. Он давно видел, с каким настроением встречают их жители хуторов (Шолохов 5). Grigory said irritably, "You'd better give me that scythe, Granny...." The old woman looked hard at Grigory and turned away. "Go and get it yourself. It must be hanging up in the shed."...As he [Grigory] walked past the woman, [he] distinctly heard her say, "Will we never be rid of you, spongers!" This was nothing new for Grigory. He had long been aware of the attitude to them in the villages (5a).

П-230 • КАК (Я) ПОГЛЯЖУ́ *coll* [VP$_{subj}$; these forms only; sent adv (parenth); fixed WO] as it appears to me, as can be deduced (from sth.): **as far as I can see ⟨tell⟩; it looks ⟨seems⟩ to me; as I see it; by the look of it;** [in limited contexts] **I see.**

Помахав руками, что должно было, по-видимому, означать утреннюю зарядку, Росляков сказал: «Слава, ты чувствуешь, какой здесь воздух?» — «Дымный, — сказал Костенко, — не будь идеалистом». — «Ты чёрствый человек, старина». — «А ты сегодня что-то слишком, как я погляжу, радостный» (Семёнов 1). Waving his arms about, which, evidently, was supposed to serve him as morning exercises, Roslyakov said: "Slava, can you smell the air here?" "Smoggy," said Kostyenko, "don't be an idealist." "You're a hard man, oldster." "And you're a bit too cheerful as far as I can see" (1a). ♦ «Ого! Ну, теперь хватит! Погутарили — и хватит. Обое [*ungrammat* = оба] вы горячие, как погляжу... Ну, не сошлись, и не надо, об чём [*ungrammat* = о чём] толковать?» (Шолохов 5). "Oho! That's enough! You've had your little chat. You're both firebrands, by the look of it....If you can't agree, never mind. What's the good of quarreling?" (5a). ♦ «Так ты, негодяй, для спасения моей души стараешься?» — «Надо же хоть когда-нибудь доброе дело сделать. Злишься-то ты, злишься, как я погляжу!» — «Шут!» (Достоевский 2). "So, you scoundrel, you're troubling yourself over the salvation of my soul?" "One needs to do a good deed sometimes, at least. But I see you're angry with me, really angry!" "Buffoon!" (2a).

П-231 • ДЕ́ЛАТЬ ПОГО́ДУ *coll* [VP; subj: human, concr, or abstr, usu. pl; often neg] to have the deciding influence on sth., be of primary importance: Х-ы делают погоду ≃ **Xs have ⟨play⟩ the leading ⟨key, crucial⟩ role (in sth.);** [of people only] **Xs carry ⟨have⟩ weight;** [in limited contexts] **Xs call the shots ⟨the tune⟩;** [in refer. to the moral, intellectual etc atmosphere in some organization, within some group etc] **Xs create the climate;** ‖ Neg Х-ы не делают погоды ≃ **Xs don't count; Xs cut no ice.**

У нас отсутствуют нравственные принципы и традиции, по которым какая-то влиятельная категория лиц отдаёт предпочтение действительно более ценным и талантливым продуктам творчества... Лишь единицы оказываются способными противостоять этой ситуации. А они не делают погоды (Зиновьев 1). "We lack any moral principles or traditions under which some influential group of people would give priority to any really worthwhile and talented creative products....There are only a few isolated individuals who are able to withstand this situation. And they don't create the climate" (1a). ♦ Среди людей, крутившихся тогда у Маяка [*coll* = площади Маяковского], много ещё было всякого рода неомарксистов и неокоммунистов, однако они уже не делали погоды. Эта тенденция отмирала, уходила в прошлое... Власти давно не считались с авторитетами, вывешенными на партийном фасаде, а исходили из своих конъюнктурных соображений (Буковский 1). Among the people circulating in Mayakovsky Square at that time were a lot of neo-Marxists and neo-Communists of various kinds, but they no longer counted. That tendency was dying out and receding into the past....The authorities had long since ceased to take note of the prophets displayed on the party façade and were guided by considerations of their own self-interest (1a).

П-232 • НЕМНО́ГО ⟨ЧУТЬ⟩ ПОГОДЯ́; НЕМНО́ГО СПУСТЯ́ *coll* [Verbal Adv (variants with погодя) or PrepP (last var.); these forms only; adv; fixed WO] after a short period of time, soon: **a little (while) later; in a short ⟨little⟩ while; in a bit.**

Ливень стал утихать, ветер разогнал тучи, и немного погодя на небе снова засияло солнце. The downpour began to let up, the wind dispersed the clouds, and in a short while the sun shone again in the sky.

П-233 • **ПОГРЕБА́ТЬ/ПОГРЕСТИ́ СЕБЯ́ ЗА́ЖИВО ⟨В ЧЕТЫРЁХ СТЕНА́Х⟩** [VP; subj: human; more often pfv] to renounce life and society, lead the life of a hermit: X погрёб себя заживо ⟨в четырёх стенах⟩ ≃ **X turned his back on the world; X shut himself away; X confined himself within four walls.**

П-234 • **И ПОДА́ВНО** coll [AdvP; Invar; used as Particle; fixed WO] (used to show that what was said to be true of some person, thing, action etc in the preceding context is) even more true (of the person, thing, action etc stated in conjunction with the idiom): **even more; so much the more (so); all the more;** [with negated verb] **certainly...not; so much the less; there's no way...**

«Уходи, Виктор, и не показывайся мне больше на глаза, не доводи до краю, если мне своей жизни не жалко, то твоей и подавно...» (Максимов 1). "Go away, Viktor, and don't let me ever set eyes on you again. Don't push me too far. If my own life is unimportant to me, then so much the more so is yours..." (1a). ♦ [Кабанова:] ...Тебя [жена] не станет бояться, меня и подавно. Какой же это порядок-то в доме будет? (Островский 6). [K.:] If she isn't afraid of you she certainly won't be afraid of me. What sort of order will there be in the house? (6d). [K.:] If she has no fear of you, so much the less she'll have of me. And then what kind of order will there be in the house? (6a). ♦ «Докторская нам не светит, а в Академию и подавно мы никогда не попадём» (Зиновьев 2). [context transl] "We haven't got much chance of a doctorate, and it's not even worth thinking about the Academy" (2a).

П-235 • **НЕ ПОДА́РОК; НЕ ПОДА́РОЧЕК** both coll [NP; these forms only; subj-compl with быть∅] **1.** [subj: human] a person who is not easy to have dealings with: X — не подарок ≃ **X is no prize; X is tough ⟨no fun⟩ to deal with; X is no gift to mankind ⟨humanity⟩; X is no pushover; X is a tough customer;** [in limited contexts] **X is going to be trouble.**

Стёпа был хорошо известен в театральных кругах Москвы, и все знали, что человек этот — не подарочек. Но всё-таки то, что рассказывал администратор про него, даже и для Стёпы было чересчур (Булгаков 9). Styopa had a reputation in Moscow theatrical circles, and everybody knew that the man was no gift to humanity. Nevertheless, what the house manager was telling about him was too much even for Styopa (9a).

2. [subj: abstr or infin] sth. (or doing sth.) is unpleasant, undesirable: X — не подарок ≃ **X isn't what I ⟨you⟩ would call luck ⟨fun⟩; X isn't my ⟨our⟩ idea of fun ⟨of fun and games, of a good time⟩; X is no picnic.**

«Родители уехали, а меня оставили с младшими братьями. Это, я тебе скажу, не подарок!» — «Я тебе сочувствую». "My parents are out of town and I'm stuck watching my little brothers. I tell you, it's not what you'd call fun!" "You have my sympathy."

П-236 • **ПОДА́РОК С НЕ́БА** coll [NP; sing only] sth. unexpected and very much desired: **godsend; stroke of fortune; like pennies from heaven.**

«Она умна, — повторил он, — мила, образованна, на нашего брата и не посмотрит. Ах... — прибавил он, вдруг обращаясь ко мне, — вот чудесная мысль, поддержите честь вятского общества, поволочитесь за ней... ну, знаете, вы из Москвы, в ссылке, верно, пишете стихи — это вам с неба подарок» (Герцен 1). "She is intelligent," he repeated, "nice, cultured....She won't look at fellows like us. Ah..." he added, suddenly turning to me, "there's a happy thought; you must keep up the honour of Vyatka society and get up a flirtation with her....Why, you are from Moscow, you know, and in exile; no doubt you write verses. She's a godsend for you" (1a).

П-237 • **С ПОДА́ЧИ** чьей, кого coll [PrepP; Invar; the resulting PrepP is adv] acting in accordance with s.o.'s suggestion, idea, recommendation: **on s.o.'s advice; at s.o.'s suggestion; on a tip from s.o.; (it was) s.o.'s idea (that...).**

Я решил с Васиной подачи написать об этом инциденте в редакцию местной газеты. I decided at Vasya's suggestion to write a letter to the editor of the local paper about this incident.

П-238 • **(КАК ⟨БУ́ДТО, СЛО́ВНО, ТО́ЧНО⟩) НА ПОДБО́Р** coll, often approv [(как etc) + PrepP; these forms only; usu. subj-compl with copula (subj: human, animal, or concr, pl), modif, or detached modif (variants with как etc); fixed WO] (usu. in refer. to positive physical qualities; when no particular quality is specified, implies generally positive features) (the people, animals, or things in question are) all equally exceptional, or all in possession of the specified quality to an equally high degree: **they look as if they were handpicked ⟨specially chosen⟩; the pick of the crop ⟨the lot etc⟩; first-rate ⟨first-class, topnotch etc⟩ (, every single one of them); a choice ⟨first-rate etc⟩ selection; as pretty ⟨good-looking etc⟩ as they come; one prettier ⟨better-looking etc⟩ than the next; pretty ⟨good-looking etc⟩, every single one of them.**

Мать была из низовских, из-под Братска, где цокают и шипят... На Ангаре всего несколько деревень с таким выговором и с красивым, как на подбор, рослым и работящим народом, особенно женщинами... (Распутин 2). His mother came from near Bratsk where they all talked in that strange, lisping way. There were only a few villages along the Angara with pronunciation like hers and with such hardworking, handsome people, who looked as if they were handpicked, particularly the women... (2a). ♦ На баскетбол [в лагере] собирается множество болельщиков, играют классные команды литовцев, латышей, эстонцев, — ребята как на подбор, молодые, рослые, ловкие (Марченко 1). The basketball always used to attract large numbers of spectators: there were high class teams of Lithuanians, Latvians and Estonians, lads who were the pick of the camp, young, tall and agile (1a). ♦ [Агафья Тихоновна:] Что ж они, дворяне? [Фёкла:] Все как на подбор. Уж такие дворяне, что ещё и не было таких (Гоголь 1). [A.T.:] But who are they—noblemen? [F.:] Every one of them, a choice selection. And such noblemen, there's never been the like (1a). ♦ И вдруг всё стало на свои места. «Так вот что он имел в виду! — подумал Виктор про Голема. — Умные и все на подбор талантливые... Тогда что же это выходит? Тогда выходит, что они уже не люди. Зурзмансор мне просто баки забивал» (Стругацкие 1). And suddenly everything fell into place. "So that's what he has in mind!" Viktor thought, remembering Golem. "Intelligent and talented, every single one of them. And what does it lead to? That they're not human anymore. Zurzmansor was just pulling the wool over my eyes" (1a).

П-239 • **НИЧЕГО́ НЕ ПОДЕ́ЛАЕШЬ ⟨НЕ ПОПИ́ШЕШЬ⟩** coll⟩ [sent; these forms only; fixed WO] there is no way out of some unpleasant situation or difficult circumstance, so you must reconcile yourself to the way things are: **there's nothing to be done about it; there's nothing you ⟨I etc⟩ can do (about it); it can't be helped; there's no help for it; you ⟨I etc⟩ can't help it; there's no way around it; resign yourself ⟨I have to resign myself etc⟩ to it.**

[Шарлемань:] Не надо, успокойся. Не плачь... Тут уж ничего не поделаешь (Шварц 2). [Ch.:] Oh, don't! Do calm yourself! Don't cry! There's nothing we can do... (2a). ♦ [Ирина:] Мама в Москве погребена. [Ольга:] В Ново-Девичьем... [Маша:] Представьте, я уж начинаю забывать её лицо. Так и о нас не будут помнить. Забудут. [Вершинин:] Да. Забудут. Такова уж судьба наша, ничего не поделаешь (Чехов 5). [I.:] Mother is buried in Moscow. [O.:] In the Novo Devichy.... [M.:] Imagine, I'm already beginning to forget her face. Just as we won't be remembered either. They'll forget us. [V.:] Yes. They'll forget us. Such is our fate, it can't be helped (5c). ♦ Все добрые дела Рафика надо хорошо помнить. Это нудно, но ничего не поделаешь, входит в правила игры (Трифонов 5). ...You had to keep all of Rafik's good deeds constantly in mind. This was tiresome, but there was no way around it, it was simply one of the rules of the game (5a).

П-240 • ЧТО (ЖЕ) ПОДЕ́ЛАЕШЬ; ЧТО (ЖЕ) ПОДЕ́ЛАТЬ ⟨ДЕ́ЛАТЬ⟩ all coll [sent; these forms only; used as indep. clause; fixed WO] you must reconcile yourself to the way things are (because there is nothing you can do to change them): **what can you ⟨we etc⟩ do?; you ⟨I etc⟩ can't help it; there's no help for it; it can't be helped.**

Года три назад, когда с деньгами было особенно туго, да и Кирилл подрос, решили с [домработницей] Нюрой расстаться. Ну, что делать: из месяца в месяц задалживаем [ей] зарплату! (Трифонов 5). About three years ago, when we were in particularly bad financial straits and Kirill, of course, was no longer a child, we decided to part with [our maid] Nyura. Well, what else could we do? From one month to the next we were behind in her pay! (5a). ♦ Всё время, что Кира Георгиевна провела в Киеве, дней пять или шесть, она чувствовала себя странно. Родное и в то же время чуждое... Чужим показался и Крещатик. Он стал шире, торжественнее, с одной стороны появился красивый бульварчик из каштанов, но, что поделаешь, старый и в общем не очень-то красивый Крещатик с его дребезжащими трамваями и гранитной мостовой был куда ей милее (Некрасов 1). During Kira Georgievna's entire stay in Kiev—five or six days—she felt strange. It was her native city and at the same time it was alien....The Kreshchatik was also strange and alien. It was broader, more impressive, on one side was a beautiful little avenue of chestnut trees, but—she couldn't help it—although the old Kreshchatik with its cobbles and rattling streetcars was not really very beautiful, it was far, far dearer to her heart (1a). ♦ Кажется, я повторяюсь, слишком часто упоминая верхний ярус этого ресторана. Но что делать, в нашем городе так мало осталось уютных мест... (Искандер 5). I'm repeating myself, I think, mentioning the upper deck of this restaurant too often. But there's no help for it, we have so few cozy spots left in our city... (5a). ♦ «Сколько рабочих ваш завод теряет каждую осень, когда в деревне начинается уборка?» — спрашивает он. «Что ж поделаешь? Видно, иначе нельзя» (Распутин 1). "How many workers does your factory lose every autumn when they're sent to help the farmers gather in the crops?" he asked. "Can't be helped. Apparently there's no other way out" (1a).

П-241 • НИЧЕГО́ НЕ ПОДЕ́ЛАТЬ с кем-чем; **НИЧЕГО́ НЕЛЬЗЯ́ ⟨не могу́ и т. п.⟩ ПОДЕ́ЛАТЬ** all coll [predic; impers or with subj: human (var. with не могу etc)] it is impossible to make s.o. behave correctly, make sth. work right, or, in refer. to o.s., regulate one's own thoughts, feelings etc: X не может ничего с Y-ом поделать ⟨с Y-ом ничего нельзя поделать⟩ ≃ **X can't handle ⟨cope with⟩ Y; X can't get anywhere with Y; X can't do anything ⟨a thing⟩ with Y; there's no coping with Y; X can't control person Y;** ‖ X не может ничего с собой поделать ≃ **X can't control ⟨cope with⟩ his feelings ⟨emotions etc⟩; X can't help it; X can't do anything ⟨a thing⟩ with himself.**

...Варя выбрала этот путь ещё в школе: мальчишки, губная помада, тряпки. Нина и тогда ничего не могла с ней поделать, ничего не может сделать и сейчас (Рыбаков 2). ...Varya had chosen her life while still at school. She had gone out with lots of boys, used lipstick, spent all her money on clothes. Even then Nina had been unable to control her, and she certainly couldn't now (2a). ♦ Садчиков ничего не мог с собой поделать. Он не мог сейчас думать ни о чём другом, кроме как об убитом парне (Семёнов 1). Sadchikov could not do a thing with himself. He could not think of anything else at the moment except the dead man (1a).

П-242 • ПОДЖИ́ЛКИ ТРЯСУ́ТСЯ/ЗАТРЯСЛИ́СЬ (у кого от чего) coll [VP_subj; usu. this WO] s.o. experiences great fear, anxiety, trepidation etc: у X-а затряслись поджилки ≃ **X was shaking in his shoes ⟨boots⟩; X's knees were shaking; X went weak in the knees.**

«Я так взволновалась! — воскликнула Маргарита, — это случилось так неожиданно». — «Ничего в этом нет неожиданного», — возразил Азазелло, а Коровьев завыл и заныл: «Как же не взволноваться? У меня у самого поджилки затряслись!» (Булгаков 9). "I had such a shock!" exclaimed Margarita, "it happened so unexpectedly!" "There was nothing unexpected about it," Azazello objected, and Koroviev whined, "Of course she was shocked. Why, even I was shaking in my shoes!" (9b).

П-243 • (ВОТ) ПОДИ́ (Ж) ТЫ!; (ВОТ) ПОДИ́ Ж!; (А ⟨ДА⟩) ВОТ ПОДИ́ (Ж) ТЫ! all coll [Interj; these forms only; fixed WO] used to express surprise, disbelief, bewilderment etc (upon encountering, realizing, or learning of the occurrence of sth. unexpected; the var. поди ты usu. expresses strong surprise, amazement): **what do you know!; just think ⟨imagine⟩!; just think of it!; who would have thought (it)!; if that don't beat all!; well I'll be!; [in limited contexts] Good Lord, fancy...!; (just) look at him ⟨her etc⟩.**

«Да как это он ещё жив по сю пору? Поди ты, ещё не умер! Ну, слава богу!» (Гончаров 1). "How is it he's still alive? Just think of it, not dead yet! Well, thank God!..." (1b). ♦ ...На первом же собрании бабы завопили в один голос: «Лу-ка-ши-на!» Толку из этого вопля, казалось тогда, никакого не будет, ибо всем давно известно, что такие дела не тут, не в деревенском клубе, бывшей церкви, решаются, а немножко повыше... А вот поди ты: услыхали, видно, бабий вопль наверху (Абрамов 1). At the very first meeting, the women yelled in unison, "Lu-u-ka-shin for chairman!" It looked then as if the yelling would be of no use whatever, for it was known long ago to everyone that such affairs are decided not in the village club—a former church—but a bit higher up....But who would have thought it! Upstairs, they apparently did hear the women's yell (1b).

П-244 • КАК ПОДКО́ШЕННЫЙ упал, свалился, рухнул и т. п. coll [как + AdjP; nom only; adv] (of a person) (one fell, dropped etc) in a single motion, as if dead: X упал ~ ≃ **X dropped on the spot; X collapsed as if he had been shot ⟨cut down⟩; X fell to the ground as though mown down.**

Укороченное тело Жикина дёрнулось, и самодельная тележка, к которой он был приторочен ремнями, с размаху ударила вертухая по ногам чуть ниже колен. Тот рухнул как подкошенный... (Войнович 4). ...Zhikin's abbreviated body gave a twitch and his homemade cart, to which he was strapped with belts, struck the other guard full force just below the knee. The guard collapsed as if he'd been shot... (4a). ♦ Вне себя от ярости, Дмитрий размахнулся и изо всей силы ударил Григория. Старик рухнулся как подкошенный... (Достоевский 1). Beside himself with rage, Dmitri swung and hit Grigory with all his strength. The old man collapsed as if he had been cut down... (1a). ♦ Я глядел на неё [Зинаиду] — и... живо воображал себе, как она вдруг, в припадке неудержимой печали, ушла в сад и упала на землю, как подкошенная (Тургенев 3). I looked at her [Zinaida], and...conjured a vivid image of how, suddenly, in a paroxysm of ungovernable grief, she had walked into the garden and fallen to the ground as though mown down (3b).

П-245 • НЕ ПОДМА́ЖЕШЬ — НЕ ПОЕ́ДЕШЬ [saying] if you do not give a bribe, you will not get what you want, nothing will be done for you: ≃ **wheels don't run without oil; you have to grease s.o.'s palm to make things happen; no silver, no servant; you get along by going along.**

«Добывайте командировку, — говорил ему носильщик в белом фартуке. — Надо каждый день наведываться. Поезда теперь редкость, дело случая. И само собой разумеется... (носильщик потёр большой палец о два соседних)... Мучицы там или чего-нибудь. Не подмажешь — не поедешь» (Пастернак 1). "You must get a priority," a porter in a white apron told him. "Then you must come every day to ask if there is a train. Trains are rare nowadays, it's a question of luck. And of course" (he rubbed two fingers with his thumb) "a little flour or something....Wheels don't run without oil, you know..." (1a).

П-246 • КАК ⟨КАК БУ́ДТО, БУ́ДТО, СЛО́ВНО, ТО́ЧНО⟩ ПОДМЕНИ́ЛИ *кого-что coll* [VP; 3rd pers pl with indef. refer. only; obj: usu. human or collect] (in refer. to s.o.'s personality, behavior, appearance etc) a drastic change came over s.o.: Х-а словно подменили ≃ **X became a different person ⟨man, woman⟩; X changed completely;** [in refer. to a positive change only] **X became ⟨was like⟩ a new man ⟨woman** etc⟩.

Григория будто подменили на войне. Он весь как-то размяк, раздался вширь, у него даже волос поредел... (Абрамов 1). Grigory had become a different person during the war; he was sort of soft now. He had spread out, and his hair had [even] thinned... (1a). ♦ Исподволь наблюдая за Деменским, Бирюков подметил характерную деталь: как только разговор зашёл о Степнадзе, Юрия Павловича будто подменили (Чернёнок 1). Observing Demensky, Birukov noted a characteristic detail: as soon as the conversation touched on Stepnadze, Yuri Pavlovich became a different man (1a). ♦ [Линевский:] Был парень как парень... И вдруг что-то с ним сделалось. Как подменили! (Панова 1). [L.:] He was an all-right fellow....And then suddenly something happened to him. He changed completely! (1a). ♦ [author's usage] «По субботам тебя как будто подменяют. Это от предчувствия свиданья» (Федин 1). "On Saturdays you're like a new man. That's from your anticipation of a date" (1a).

П-247 • В ПОДМЁТКИ НЕ ГОДИ́ТСЯ ⟨НЕ СТА́НЕТ *obs*⟩ *кому-чему coll, rather derog* [VP; subj: human, abstr, or concr; pres or past only (1st var.); fut only (2nd var.)] (used when contrasting two people, things etc either on a general basis or with regard to a specific quality) one person or thing is so much worse than the other that they cannot even be compared: X Y-у в подмётки не годится ≃ **X cannot hold a candle to Y; X doesn't come close to Y; person X isn't fit to tie person Y's shoelaces ⟨bootlaces⟩; person X isn't fit to shine person Y's shoes;** [in limited contexts] **person Y has more [NP] in his little finger than person X has in his whole body; (there's) absolutely no comparison.**

Конечно, есть люди, может быть, красивее Сони, у них длинные косы, голубые глаза, какие-нибудь особенные ресницы, но всё это ерунда. Потому что они Соне в подмётки не годятся (Трифонов 2). Naturally there are girls who are maybe prettier than Sonya, who have long braids, blue eyes and long eyelashes, but none of that matters. Because not one of them can hold a candle to Sonya (2a). ♦ [Бобчинский:] А я так думаю, что генерал-то ему [Хлестакову] в подмётки не станет! (Гоголь 4). [B.:] And I, sir, think a general isn't fit to tie his [Khlestakov's] bootlaces! (4c). ♦ «Эх, Любка, ты ведь и не знаешь, что я к тебе завтра утром приеду. Розка — зараза, в подмётки не годится. Маникюр сделала и думает, что царица» (Семёнов 1). "Ah, Lyubka, you don't even know that I'm coming to see you tomorrow morning. Rosa's a bitch—absolutely no comparison. Had a manicure and thinks the world of herself" (1a).

П-248 • ПОДНИМА́Й ⟨ПОДЫМА́Й⟩ ВЫ́ШЕ ⟨ПОВЫ́ШЕ⟩! *coll* [VP_imper; these forms only; fixed WO] (usu. used in response to an inquiry or guess regarding the status, worth etc of s.o. or sth.) you have underestimated and should have assumed

better, s.o. or sth. is of higher status, greater worth etc than you think: **don't sell me ⟨him, it etc⟩ short; guess ⟨try⟩ again; I'm ⟨he is etc⟩ a notch ⟨a peg, a step⟩ or two higher than that;** [in limited contexts] **keep going.**

«Ты всё там же, по-прежнему замдиректора?» — «Поднимай выше, я теперь директор». "Are you still working there as the deputy director?" "Guess again—I'm the director now."

П-249 • ПОДО́БНО ТОМУ́ КАК [subord Conj; introduces a compar clause] in the same way that: **just as; the way...**

«Писать стихи надо каждый день, подобно тому как скрипач или пианист непременно должен каждый день без пропусков по нескольку часов играть на своём инструменте. В противном случае ваш талант неизбежно оскудеет, высохнет, подобно колодцу, откуда долгое время не берут воду» (Катаев 3). "One must write poetry every day, just as a violinist or a pianist must play every day on his instrument for several hours without fail. If not, your talent will stagnate and run dry, like a well from which no water is drawn" (3a). ♦ Я так думаю, что в течение множества лет, пользуясь безграмотностью моих земляков, мир разбазаривал чегемские идеи, подобно тому, как древние римляне беспощадно вырубали абхазский самшит (Искандер 5). Over the years, I think, the world has taken advantage of my countrymen's illiteracy to squander Chegemian ideas, the way the ancient Romans ruthlessly felled Abkhazian boxwood (5a).

П-250 • НИЧЕГО́ ПОДО́БНОГО! *coll* [Interj; Invar; fixed WO] (used by the speaker to express his firm denial of or disagreement with sth.) that is positively not so: **nothing of the kind ⟨sort⟩!; no such thing!; absolutely not!; not on your life!; far from it.**

Михаил... думал: шутит Иван Дмитриевич. Петра Житова хочет разыграть. Ничего подобного! (Абрамов 1). Mikhail thought that Ivan Dmitrievich was joking, that he wanted to tease Pyotr Zhitov. Nothing of the kind! (1a). ♦ Маргарита побледнела и отшатнулась. «...Вы хотите меня арестовать?» — «Ничего подобного», — воскликнул рыжий... (Булгаков 9). Margarita paled and edged away. "...Have you come to arrest me?" "Nothing of the sort!" exclaimed the man with red hair (9b). ♦ Хотя бы [Аркадий сказал] одно слово в том смысле, что служба в армии — дело серьёзное, но что он постарается держаться. Ничего подобного!.. Отец, мать, бабушка и четыре девочки только и слышали о том, какие мелодии он разучит на саксофоне в ближайшем будущем (Залыгин 1). He [Arkady] might have said something to the effect that army service was no joking matter, but that he would do his best, but he didn't say a word about it. Far from it. All his father, mother, grandmother, and the four girls heard from him was what tunes he'd soon be learning for the saxophone (1a).

П-251 • И ТОМУ́ ПОДО́БНОЕ, may be abbreviated in writing to и. т. п. *lit* [NP; sing only; fixed WO] (used at the end of a list to indicate that more objects or phenomena could be included) and other similar things: **and so on; and so forth (and so on); and the ⟨such⟩ like; et cetera; etc.; and things of that sort; and more of the same; and more to that effect.**

Колотилось сердце, и набегали всякие слова, злые, справедливые, которые не были сказаны. А почему Милютина, которая в театре без году неделя?.. — и так далее и тому подобное (Трифонов 1). Her heart was pounding, and all of the just and nasty things that she had left unsaid came rushing to mind. And why should Milyutina, who was completely new in the theater?...—and so forth and so on (1a). ♦ Все чиновники говорили о ненадёжности войск, о неверности удачи, об осторожности и тому подобном (Пушкин 2). All the officials spoke about the unreliability of our troops, the uncertainty of success, the need for caution, and the like (2a). ♦ «Народ не может жить без святынь, — рассуждал Джамхух, — вера в главную святыню порождает множество малых святынь, необходимых для повседневной жизни: святыню материнства, святыню уважения к старшим... и тому подобное» (Искандер 5). "A people cannot live without holding some things sacred," Jamkhoukh argued. "Faith in a great thing engenders the many lesser ones necessary for daily life: the sacredness of motherhood, the sacredness of respect for elders…and things of that sort" (5a). ♦ [Надзиратель] ушёл, пришёл с дежурным офицером: «Выходи! Почему безобразничаешь? Карцера захотел? На этап не отправим», – и тому подобное (Марченко 2). He [the guard] went away and came back with the duty officer. "Come on out! What are you cuttin up for? You want the punishment cell? We won't ship you out of here…" And more to that effect (2a).

П-252 • **ПОДОБРУ́-ПОЗДОРО́ВУ ⟨ПОДОБРУ́ ДА ПОЗДОРО́ВУ⟩** *coll* [AdvP; these forms only; adv; fixed WO] **1.** жить, поживать, добраться *куда* и т. п. ~ *obs* (to live, be living, make one's way to some place etc) without problems or difficulties: **(just ⟨perfectly⟩) fine;** [in refer. to how a person is doing at a given moment only] **(be) quite well;** [in refer. to traveling only] **(get somewhere) safe and sound ⟨without mishap⟩.**

2. уйти, убраться ~ (to leave some place, go away) voluntarily and at a prudent time, while the situation is still calm (before a scandal erupts, sth. dangerous happens, or one is forced to leave): **while the going ⟨the getting⟩ is good; while there's still time; while one is still in one piece; before it's too late.**

[Скотинин:] Да эдак и до меня доберутся… Уберусь же я отсюда подобру-поздорову (Фонвизин 1). [S.:] If they'll keep this up they'll get to me also.…I'd better get out of here while the going's good (1a). ♦ *(Кречинский в глубокой задумчивости водит пальцем туда и сюда и произносит неясные слова. Расплюев следит за ним.)* [Расплюев:] Уберусь я от него подобру-поздорову… (Сухово-Кобылин 2). *(Krechinsky deep in thought wags his index finger and mutters to himself, Rasplyuev watching.)* [R.:] I better beat it while there's still time and I'm still in one piece (2a). ♦ Многих, которые не успели умереть, выгнали за неблагонадёжность, других отдали под суд; самые счастливые были те, которые… убрались подобру да поздорову в благоприобретенные углы (Гончаров 1). Many of those who had survived were dismissed as unreliable, others had been brought to trial; the luckiest were those who…retired, before it was too late, to their well-feathered nests (1b).

П-253 • **ДАВА́ТЬ/ДАТЬ ПОДПИ́СКУ** *coll* [VP; subj: human; often foll. by infin or a что-clause; often neg] to promise sth. firmly, commit o.s. to do sth.: X подписки не давал ≃ **X didn't solemnly swear (to do sth.); X didn't sign a declaration promising (to do sth.); X didn't sign any paper saying (that he would do sth.).**

При рождении я не давал подписки одобрять всё то, что они натворили (Зиновьев 1). I didn't sign a declaration the day I was born promising to approve of everything they do (1a).

П-254 • **В ПОДПИ́ТИИ** *coll* [PrepP; Invar; usu. subj-compl with быть∅, приходить etc (subj: human)] in a drunken state: **drunk; under the influence; feeling one's liquor.**

Он рассказал жене и дочери случай, который они обе знали ещё с довоенных времён, – Сталин ночью появился в метро, он был в лёгком подпитии, сел рядом с молодой женщиной, спросил её: «Чем бы я вам мог помочь?» (Гроссман 2). He told [his wife and daughter] a story they had all known even before the war. One night Stalin appeared in the metro, slightly drunk, sat beside a young woman, and asked: "What can I do for you?" (2a).

П-255 • **ПОДРУ́ГА ЖИ́ЗНИ** *obsoles, now usu. humor* [NP; sing only; fixed WO] wife: **companion on the road of life; partner to share one's ⟨s.o.'s⟩ life (with).**

[Яичница:] …Служу коллежским асессором, любим начальниками, подчинённые слушаются, недостаёт только

одного: подруги жизни (Гоголь 1). [Omelet:] …I am a collegiate assessor, beloved by my superiors, obeyed by my subordinates. I lack only a companion on the road of life (1b). ♦ «У вас всё есть… одного только недостаёт». – «Чего?»… – «Подруги жизни, – сказал Чичиков. – …Право, Андрей Иванович, вам бы очень не мешало жениться» (Гоголь 3). "You've got everything…only one thing's lacking." "What?"…"A partner to share your life," said Chichikov.…"Honestly, my dear fellow, it would not be a bad thing at all if you got married" (3a).

П-256 • **ПО́ДСТУПА ⟨-у⟩ НЕТ** *к кому obsoles, coll* [VP; impers; fixed WO] it is impossible to address, speak with, or gain access to s.o. (because he is angry, arrogant, occupies an important position etc): к X-у подступа нет ≃ **there's no getting near ⟨talking to, approaching⟩ X; X is impossible to approach; X is totally unapproachable ⟨inaccessible⟩; you can't get near ⟨within ten feet of⟩ X;** [in limited contexts] **you'd be afraid to go ⟨get⟩ near X.**

П-257 • **НЕ ⟨НЕЛЬЗЯ́, СТРА́ШНО⟩ ПОДСТУПИ́ТЬСЯ; НЕ ПОДСТУ́ПИШЬСЯ** *all coll* [VP; impers predic with быть∅ (variants with подступиться) or neg pfv fut, gener. 2nd pers sing (last var.); these forms only] **1.** к чему ~ sth. is too expensive for s.o. to be able to afford: к X-у не подступиться ≃ **X is out of (my ⟨your⟩ etc) reach; X is beyond my ⟨your⟩ etc means; X is too much ⟨rich⟩ for my ⟨your⟩ etc pocket(book).**

Квартиры в этом районе стоят так дорого, что не подступишься. Apartments in this neighborhood are so expensive, they're out of our reach.

2. к кому ~ it is impossible to address or gain access to s.o. (because of his importance, high position, arrogance etc): к X-у не подступиться ≃ **you can't get near ⟨within ten feet of⟩ X; there's no getting near ⟨talking to, approaching⟩ X; X is impossible to approach; X is totally unapproachable ⟨inaccessible⟩;** [in limited contexts] **you'd be afraid to go ⟨get⟩ near X.**

Чернов теперь такой важный – не подступишься. Раньше я запросто заходил к нему в кабинет, а теперь надо у секретарши записываться. Chernov has gotten to be such a big shot that you can't get near him. I used to just drop by his office and see him, but now you've got to make an appointment through his secretary.

П-258 • **КТО БЫ МОГ ПОДУ́МАТЬ!; КТО БЫ ПОДУ́МАЛ!** *both coll* [sent; these forms only; used as Interj or indep. clause foll. by a что-clause; fixed WO] it is hard to believe (that the situation has turned out this way), no one could ever have predicted (that things would turn out this way): **who would (ever) have thought?; who could have imagined?; it's hard to believe!; I never would have guessed!; (just) imagine!;** [used as Interj only] **what do you know!; imagine that!; incredible!**

[Сарафанов:] Нина! У меня никакого сомнения! Он твой брат!.. Боже мой… Ну кто бы мог подумать? (Вампилов 4). [S.:] Nina! I don't have any doubts at all! He's your brother!…My God.…Well, who would ever have thought? (4b). ♦ …Кто бы мог подумать, что Варвара не одна дома? А она таки действительно была не одна – с Анисьей Лобановой (Абрамов 1). Who could have imagined that Varvara would not be alone in the house? But in fact, she was not alone; she was with Anisya Lobanova (1a).

П-259 • **ПОДУ́МАТЬ ТО́ЛЬКО!; (НЕТ,) ТЫ ⟨вы⟩ ТО́ЛЬКО ПОДУ́МАЙ ⟨-те⟩!** *all coll* [sent; these forms only; used as Interj or indep. clause; fixed WO] this is absolutely amazing, totally unexpected, hard to believe (sometimes said ironically, often accompanied by naming the cause of one's surprise): **just think ⟨imagine⟩!; imagine (that ⟨it⟩)!; (just) think**

of it!; would ⟨can⟩ you believe it!; fancy ⟨look at⟩ that!; the very idea (of it)!

Иван только горько усмехался про себя и размышлял о том, как всё это глупо и странно получилось. Подумать только! Хотел предупредить всех об опасности, грозящей от неизвестного консультанта, собирался его изловить, а добился только того, что попал в какой-то таинственный кабинет... (Булгаков 9). Ivan merely grinned bitterly to himself, reflecting on how stupidly and strangely things had turned out. Just think! He wanted to warn everyone of the danger from the unknown consultant and to catch him, but all he achieved was to be brought to this mysterious room... (9a). ♦ Кто вступал через эту арку? Войска Елизаветы Петровны? Этого я не видел, хотя эти сроки очень сжаты. Подумать только, я родился через семьдесят девять лет после смерти Наполеона! (Олеша 3). Who marched under that arch? The troops of Elizaveta Petrovna? That I didn't see, although these periods are very close together. Just imagine, I was born a mere seventy-nine years after the death of Napoleon! (3a). ♦ У Севки трое детей. Подумать только (Войнович 5). Sevka has three children. Imagine that (5a). ♦ У него и дом-то нашего сарая плоше, а он ещё и флюгер на крышу поставил, подумать только — флюгер! (Соколов 1). His house is worse than our shed, but to top things off he put a windvane on his roof, just think of it—a windvane! (1a). ♦ Подумать только! Симонов, автор длинных, скучных, неряшливо написанных романов, не признавал в Зощенко прозаика (Войнович 1). Think of it! Simonov, the author of long, boring, sloppily written novels, not recognizing Zoshchenko as a prose writer (1a).

П-260 • И НЕ ПОДУ́МАЮ ⟨-ешь и т. п.⟩ coll [VP; subj: human; fixed WO] (used as a response to a suggestion, request etc) I will not (do sth.), I do not intend to (do sth.): **no way (would I do sth.); no chance; nothing doing!;** [usu. when the speaker is wounded, insulted, or outraged by the interlocutor's suggestion] **I wouldn't dream ⟨think⟩ of it ⟨of doing such a thing etc⟩.**

«Ты был неправ, извинись». — «И не подумаю». "You were wrong, apologize." "No way." ♦ Съезд открылся ровно через десять минут после того, как мы заняли чьи-то чужие кресла... [Машка] стала писать знакомым студентам анонимные записки, глупые, но довольно смешные. «Кто это?» — спросила она, когда Митя, которого я до сих пор не видела, появился на эстраде... Я ответила: «Доктор Львов». — «Ты его знаешь?». — «Немного»... — «Давай напишем ему... А потом ты нас познакомишь». — «И не подумаю». — «Не познакомишь?». — «Да нет, могу познакомить, но зачем же писать?» (Каверин 1). The Congress began exactly ten minutes after we had taken somebody else's seats....[Mashka] began to write anonymous notes to students she knew. It was silly, but quite funny. "Who's that?" she asked, when Mitya, whom I hadn't seen until then, appeared on the dais...."Dr. Lvov," I replied. "Do you know him?" "A little.."..."Let's write to him....Then later on you'll introduce me to him." "I wouldn't think of doing such a thing." "What, you won't introduce me?" "Why, yes, perhaps, but why should I write to him?" (1a).

П-261 • НА ПОДХВА́ТЕ (у кого) coll [PrepP; Invar; subj-compl with бытьø (subj: human)] one performs minor services, small tasks for s.o.: X (у Y-a) на подхвате ≃ **X runs errands (for Y); X fetches and carries (for Y); X does (all) the legwork for Y; X is an errand boy ⟨girl⟩; X is a gofer.**

На новой работе он первое время был на подхвате, ничего важного ему не поручали. At first in his new job he was only an errand boy; they didn't entrust him with anything important.

П-262 • ЛЁГОК ⟨ЛЁГКИЙ⟩ НА ПОДЪЁМ coll [AdjP; subj-compl with copula (subj: human) or modif (long-form var. only)] **1.** a person who is ready to go anywhere at any time: X лёгок на подъём ≃ **X is always ready to get up and go; X can**

⟨will⟩ go at the drop of a hat; [in limited contexts] **X is always ready to pack up and go.**

Он молод, лёгок на подъём, ему ничего не стоит переехать на новое место. He is young and always ready to pack up and go; moving to a new place is nothing to him.

2. a person who readily undertakes or engages in various activities, who is quick to seize the opportunity to participate in sth.: X лёгок на подъём ≃ **X is ready and willing; X is quick off the mark.**

...Есть роды, где часто рождаются мудрые, а есть роды, где часто рождаются хитрые, и есть роды, лёгкие на подъём... (Искандер 5). There were clans where the wise were often born, and there were clans where the sly were often born, and there were clans that were quick off the mark... (5a).

П-263 • ТЯЖЁЛ ⟨ТЯЖЁЛЫЙ⟩ НА ПОДЪЁМ coll [AdjP; subj-compl with copula (subj: human) or modif (long-form var. only)] **1.** a person who is inactive, does not move about readily, does not like to go out anywhere: X тяжёл на подъём ≃ **X is hard to get moving; it's hard to get X off his derrière ⟨rear end etc⟩; X is slow-moving ⟨sluggish⟩.**

Он тяжёл на подъём, его даже в кино трудно вытащить. It's hard to get him off his derrière, even to go to the movies.

2. a person who gets down to work on things slowly and with great reluctance: X тяжёл на подъём ≃ **X has a hard time getting going ⟨started⟩; X is a slow starter; X is slow at the gate; X is slow off the blocks ⟨the mark⟩.**

Он тяжёл на подъём, но если уж возьмётся за что-нибудь, то делает добросовестно. He's a slow starter, but when he finally gets down to something he does it conscientiously.

П-264 • ДОБРО́ ПОЖА́ЛОВАТЬ! [formula phrase; Invar; fixed WO] a greeting to a person who is arriving, or an invitation to come in or, occas., to come over: **welcome (to you); please come in; come right in;** [as an invitation to come over and visit] **you're welcome to come over ⟨come to our place, stop by etc⟩.**

Увидав Алпатыча, он подошёл к нему. «Добро пожаловать, Яков Алпатыч» (Толстой 6). He caught sight of Alpatych and went up to him. "Welcome, Yakov Alpatych" (6a). ♦ «А, Пётр Андреич! — сказал он, увидя меня, — добро пожаловать!» (Пушкин 2). "Ah, Petr Andreich," said he, as he saw me, "come right in" (2a).

П-265 • КАК ⟨БУ́ДТО, СЛО́ВНО, ТО́ЧНО⟩ НА ПОЖА́Р бежать, мчаться и т. п. coll [как etc + PrepP; these forms only; adv; fixed WO] (to run, race) very fast, headlong, rushing madly: **as if (going) to a fire; like mad ⟨hell, the devil⟩; (ride ⟨go⟩) hell-for-leather ⟨hellbent⟩;** ‖ не беги как на пожар ≃ **where's the fire?**

Затем ещё одна делегатка — Анфиса Петровна. Эта прискакала верхом, как на пожар. «Ох, всё думала — опоздаю» (Абрамов 1). Then another delegate arrived: Anfisa Petrovna. Galloping along on horseback, as if to a fire. "Oof! I kept thinking I'd be late" (1a).

П-266 • НЕ НА ПОЖА́Р (кому) coll [PrepP; Invar; impers predic] there is no reason for s.o. to hurry: (X-у) не на пожар ≃ **X is not going to a fire; X is in no rush ⟨hurry⟩; what's the rush ⟨the hurry⟩?; there's no rush ⟨hurry⟩;** [in limited contexts] **where's the fire?**

«Остановите троллейбус!» — крикнул Арон Маркович... «Да не кричите вы! — рассердился водитель. — Будет остановка, и выйдете. Нечего панику пороть. Не на пожар!» (Семёнов 1). "Stop the bus!" cried Aron Markovich...."Stop shouting!" said the driver angrily. "There'll be a bus stop soon and then you can get out. There's no need to get in a panic. You're not going to a fire!" (1a).

П-267 • **ПОЖИВЁМ – УВИ́ДИМ** [saying] time will show how things will turn out (said when a person does not have sufficient basis to judge sth. or does not want to express his opinion on sth. that is unclear at present and will become obvious only in the future): ≃ **we shall see (what we shall see); (only) time will tell; wait and see; we'll see what happens.**

При всей его дикости, письмо [письмо-донос трёх литераторов в партийные органы] вызвало чуткую реакцию наверху. Требования «подлинных советских ленинградцев» были частично удовлетворены... Директора [Дома Маяковского] попросту сняли. Был также изменён состав комиссии по работе с молодыми литераторами... Единственное, чего не удалось добиться авторам письма, – так это привлечения молодых литераторов к уголовной ответственности. А впрочем, поживём – увидим (Довлатов 1). ...Despite its crudeness, this letter [a denunciation submitted to the Party Organs by three writers] evoked a sympathetic response from the higher-ups. The demands of the "genuine Soviet Leningraders" were satisfied in part....The director [of Mayakovsky House] was simply removed from office. The staff of the commission that worked with young writers was also changed....The only thing that the authors of the letter didn't manage to accomplish was the institution of criminal proceedings against the young writers. However, we shall see what we shall see (1a). ♦ [Зилов:] Утиная охота – это вещь... [Галина:] Ну скажи, убил ты что-нибудь хоть раз? Признайся! Ну хотя бы маленькую, ну хоть вот такую *(показывает на пальце)* птичку? [Кузаков:] Ну что ты ему показываешь? Он в такую *(показывает обеими руками)* не попадает, а ты что хочешь? *(Все смеются.)* [Зилов:] Ладно, ладно. Поживём – увидим (Вампилов 5). [Z.:] It's a fine thing, duck-shooting.... [G.:] Well, have you ever shot anything? Even once? Own up! Even a tiny little bird, even this big? *(Showing length on one finger.)* [K.:] What's that you're showing him? He couldn't hit one this big, *(Showing with both hands)* let alone that little thing. *(All laugh.)* [Z.:] All right, all right. Wait and see (5a).

П-268 • **С ВА́ШЕГО ПОЗВОЛЕ́НИЯ ⟨РАЗРЕШЕ́НИЯ⟩** [these forms only; sent adv (parenth); fixed WO] **1.** used to add politeness to a statement, sometimes a statement of intent: **if you'll allow ⟨permit⟩ me (to ask ⟨say so etc⟩); if I may (say so etc); with your permission.**

...[Чичиков] изъявил готовность принять на себя обязанность платить подати за всех крестьян, умерших такими несчастными случаями. Предложение, казалось, совершенно изумило Плюшкина... «Как же, с позволения вашего, чтобы не рассердить вас, вы за всякий год берётесь платить за них?..» (Гоголь 3). ...He [Chichikov] expressed his readiness to pay the taxes on the peasants lost in such painful circumstances. The offer seemed to stun Plewshkin...."Now, if you'll allow me to ask – and I haven't the least wish to offend you – I'd like to know...are you taking it upon yourself to pay the tax for them every year?" (3e). ♦ [Кудимов *(наливает всем шампанского)*:] С вашего разрешения – за вас, за наше знакомство (Вампилов 4). [K. *(Pouring champagne for everyone)*:] With your permission – to you, to our meeting (4b).

2. used to add sarcastic politeness to a statement (often one of a shocking, offensive etc nature) or to a response (usu. when responding to a question whose answer is obvious): **if you please.**

Там остановились вдруг среди толпы и уставились вглубь [кафе] «Куполи» два белоснежных животных – коза и лама... «Это ещё что такое?» – вскричал Огородников. «Коза и лама, с вашего позволения» (Аксёнов 12). Suddenly two snow-white animals stopped in the crowd and stared into the café – a nanny goat and a llama...."And what's this!?" cried Ogorodnikov. "A goat and a llama, if you please" (12a).

П-269 • **С ПОЗВОЛЕ́НИЯ СКАЗА́ТЬ** [Invar; sent adv (parenth); usu. precedes the word or phrase to which it refers; fixed WO] **1.** (an apologetic expression warning the listener that sth. rude, pointed, not quite proper will be said next) I apologize for what I am about to say: **pardon ⟨if you don't mind⟩ my saying so; if I may say so; if I may be so bold.**

«В нашем полку был поручик, прекраснейший и образованнейший человек, который не выпускал изо рта трубки не только за столом, но даже, с позволения сказать, во всех прочих местах» (Гоголь 3). "In our regiment there was a lieutenant, a truly fine and well-educated man, who never let a pipe out of his mouth, not only at table but, pardon my saying so, in all other places" (3c).

2. used by the speaker to express his negative, disdainful attitude toward s.o. or sth., his opinion that s.o. or sth. does not deserve his or its name: **so-called; if I ⟨you⟩ could (even) call it ⟨him etc⟩ that; if such it ⟨he etc⟩ may be called.**

«Горько и обидно, что какие-то слизняки правят страной. Безволие, слабохарактерность, неумение, нерешительность, зачастую простая подлость – вот что руководит действиями этого, с позволения сказать, „правительства"» (Шолохов 3). "It is a bitter shame that the country should be ruled by such worms. Lack of will, lack of character, of ability, of resolution, and even downright treachery – these are the qualities that determine the actions of this 'government,' if such it may be called" (3a).

П-270 • **Е́СЛИ ПОЗВО́ЛИТЕ** [these forms only; sent adv (parenth); fixed WO] used to add politeness to a statement of intention and, at the same time, request the interlocutor's consent: **if you don't mind; if it ⟨that⟩ would be all right; if I may; if you'll permit ⟨allow⟩ me.**

Я, если позволите, позвоню в Москву. I'm going to call Moscow, if that would be all right. ♦ «Много, много испытал я на своём веку. Вот, например, если позволите, я вам расскажу любопытный эпизод чумы в Бессарабии» (Тургенев 2). "I have had many, many experiences in my life. For example, if you will allow me, I will tell you a curious episode of the plague in Bessarabia" (2b).

П-271 • **НЕ ПОЗДОРО́ВИТСЯ** *кому coll* [VP; impers; usu. fut or subjunctive] (usu. used as a threat or warning) very unpleasant things, troubles are awaiting s.o. (often because of his wrongdoing): Х-у не поздоровится ≃ **X is (really) going to get ⟨to catch⟩ it; X will be in big trouble; X will get what's coming to him; X will be in for it; X is going to have it rough; there will be hell ⟨the devil⟩ to pay.**

Если Родионов начнёт давать правдивые показания, то многим городским руководителям не поздоровится. If Rodionov starts giving truthful testimony, quite a few city officials are going to be in big trouble.

П-272 • **С ЧЕМ ВАС И ПОЗДРАВЛЯ́Ю ⟨-ем⟩** *coll, iron or humor* [sent; these forms only; fixed WO] an expression of congratulations to s.o. on account of sth. unpleasant, unenviable (some failure, trouble, nuisance etc): **lucky you!; aren't *you* the lucky one(s)!; (isn't that) just great!; (oh,) congratulations!**

«Нам пришлось съехаться со свекровью». – «С чем вас и поздравляю». "We had to move in with my mother-in-law." "Lucky you!"

П-273 • **СТАНОВИ́ТЬСЯ/СТАТЬ ⟨ВСТАТЬ⟩ В ПО́ЗУ** [VP; subj: human] **1.** ~ *(какую)*. Also: **ПРИНИМА́ТЬ/ПРИНЯ́ТЬ ПО́ЗУ** [more often pfv] to assume a purposely affected stance, usu. in order to make an impression on s.o.: X принял позу ≃ **X struck ⟨assumed⟩ a pose ⟨an attitude⟩.**

...Какой-то несостоявшийся артист, встав в позу, читал с выражением поэму Маяковского «Хорошо» (Войнович 4). ...Some failed actor, striking a pose, was reciting Mayakovsky's poem "It's Good" with genuine emotion (4a). ♦ Чичиков попробовал, склоняя голову несколько набок, принять позу... (Гоголь 3). Bending his head a little to the side, Chichikov tried to assume a pose... (3d). ♦ В это время дамы отошли от колодца и поравнялись с нами. Грушницкий успел принять драматическую позу с помощью костыля и громко отвечал мне по-французски... (Лермонтов 1). At this point the ladies moved away from the well and came level with us. Grushnitski had time to assume a dramatic attitude with the help of his crutch, and loudly answered me in French... (1a).

2. ~ *кого, какую lit* to adopt the traits and mannerisms of a type of person one is not and try to create for o.s. the reputation of being that type of person: X становится в позу Y-a ≃ **X assumes ⟨takes on⟩ the role of a [NP]; X strikes the pose of a [NP]; X acts ⟨plays⟩ the part of a [NP]; X makes himself out to be a [NP].**

Тактические соображения не раз заставляли бывшего партаппаратчика Демидова становиться в позу демократа. More than once tactical considerations forced former apparatchik Demidov to assume the role of a democrat.

3. ~ *кого, какую,* often **в позу обиженного, оскорблён-ного** etc to act as if one were the victim of some great offense, displaying one's hurt (or feigned hurt) in an exaggerated manner: X становится в позу обиженного ≃ **X assumes an offended ⟨injured etc⟩ air; X strikes an injured ⟨a wounded⟩ pose; X acts offended ⟨injured, wounded etc⟩; X takes great offense.**

Илье показалось, что его родители были недостаточно любезны с его невестой. Он стал в позу обиженного и перестал звонить им. It seemed to Ilya that his parents weren't nice enough to his fiancée. He took great offense and stopped calling them.

П-274 • ПОИ́ТЬ И КОРМИ́ТЬ ⟨ПОИ́ТЬ-КОРМИ́ТЬ⟩ *кого highly coll* [VP; subj: human; fixed WO] to support s.o., have s.o. as one's dependent: X поил и кормил Y-a ≃ **X fed and kept Y.** ○ **ПОЙЛЕ́Ц И КОРМИ́ЛЕЦ ⟨ПОЙЛЕ́Ц-КОРМИ́ЛЕЦ, ПОЙЛИ́ЦА И КОРМИ́ЛИЦА, ПОЙ-ЛИ́ЦА-КОРМИ́ЛИЦА⟩** *obs* [NP] ≃ **breadwinner.**

«А сколько мои родители престарелые получают – это тебе известно, товарищ Ганичев? Нет? А кто их поит-кормит? Давай обсудим и этот вопрос...» (Абрамов 1). "And how much do my aged parents get? Do you happen to know *that,* Comrade Ganichev? No? And who feeds them and keeps them? Let's discuss that matter" (1a). ♦ «Кормилец ты наш и поилец, куды [*ungrammat* = куда] ж ты от нас уходишь!» (Войнович 4). "You, our breadwinner, where are you leaving us for?" (4a).

П-275 • ДАЛЕКО́ ПОЙТИ́ ⟨УЙТИ́ rare⟩ *coll, approv or iron* [VP; subj: human; usu. this WO] to achieve great success, a high position in life, or attain great results in sth. (when used ironically refers to success achieved through unethical means or in criminal circles): X далеко пойдёт ≃ **X will go far; X will go a long way.**

Маргарита Антоновна гордилась Вериным возвышением, как лично своей заслугой: «Я говорила, вы далеко пойдёте! У меня на это нюх!» (Грекова 3). Margarita Antonovna was proud of Vera's promotion, took personal credit for it, remarking, "I said you'd go far! I've got a flair for that!" (3a). ♦ ...Таланты у него налицо. Как он здорово обошёл самого господина Ней! Подстроил референции. Может быть, подговорил и служащего в банке. Да, этот тип далеко пойдёт! (Эренбург 2). His talent had been proved. How thoroughly he had taken in M. Ney himself! He had forged references: perhaps he had bribed the bank clerk. Yes, that type would go a long way (2a).

П-276 • ПОКА́ ЧТО *coll* [AdvP; Invar; adv; fixed WO] **1.** at the present time, regardless of what may happen later: **for the time being; for the present; for the moment; for now; right now (s.o. ⟨sth.⟩ still...).**

«Видите, какой я радостный? Это потому, что у меня всё впереди. А пока что мне вполне достаточно одного острова из группы Курильских островов, вас, милые жители этого острова, избушки на курьих ножках да милой жены!» (Залы-

гин 1). "See how happy-go-lucky I am? That's because I've got everything before me. But for the moment I'm perfectly content with what I've got now: one island in the Kurile Chain; you, my dear islanders; a hut on wobbly stilts, and a pretty wife" (1a). ♦ Дом, который я строю, почти готов к сдаче. Вот он стоит за забором пока что пустой, с потемневшими от дождя стенами из силикатного кирпича (Войнович 5). The building I'm constructing will soon be ready to hand over. Right now it still stands empty behind the fence, its silicate brick walls darkened by the rain (5a).

2. concurrently with (the action, activity etc mentioned in the preceding context): **in the meantime; meanwhile; during all this.**

...Полгода понадобилось «Крохоткам», чтобы достичь Европы, – для того же, чтоб о случившемся доложили вверх по медлительным нашим инстанциям... – ещё 8 месяцев... А пока что произошла «малая октябрьская» – сбросили Никиту [Хрущёва] (Солженицын 2). ...If it had taken the "Miniatures" six months to reach Europe, it took another eight months for a report on this event to make its way upward through the various levels of our dilatory bureaucracy. In the meantime, the "Little October Revolution" had taken place: Khrushchev had been thrown overboard (2a). ♦ ...Митишатьев произвёл столько шуму, словно ввалилась с морозу большая компания... Готтих пока что тихо снял пальто, повесил его куда положено – на вешалку... (Битов 2). ...Mitishatyev made as much noise as if a large group had come bursting in from the cold....Gottich, during all this, had quietly taken off his coat and hung it where it belonged – on the coatrack... (2a).

3. up to and including the present: **so ⟨thus⟩ far; as yet; as of now; up till now;** [with a negated predic only] **yet.**

Опыты эти пока что реальных результатов не давали, хотя некоторые характерные признаки пукса [гибрида картофеля с помидором] стали уже проявляться: листья и стебли на нём были вроде картофельные, зато корни точь-в-точь помидорные (Войнович 2). So far these experiments had not produced any actual results, although certain characteristics of the PATS [a hybrid of the potato and the tomato] had started to appear: the leaves and stems were potato-like, while the roots were letter-perfect tomato (2a). ♦ Он наобещал нам много, но пока что ничего не сделал. He has promised us a lot, but so far hasn't done anything. ♦ «А что, жена уже родила?» – спросил он. «Нет, она пока что не родила» (Войнович 3). "What, did your wife give birth already?" he asked. "No, she hasn't yet" (3a).

П-277 • ПОКА́ЗЫВАТЬ/ПОКАЗА́ТЬ СЕБЯ́ [VP; subj: human, collect, or animal; more often pfv] to demonstrate one's (usu. positive) qualities, abilities in full measure: X покажет себя ≃ **person X will show (you ⟨them⟩) who he is; X will show (you ⟨them⟩) what he is capable of ⟨what he can do⟩; X will show (you ⟨them⟩) what kind of man ⟨woman etc⟩ he ⟨she⟩ is; X will show (you ⟨them⟩) the stuff he is made of;** [of a person only; with an emphasis on one's desire to make a positive impression on s.o.] **X will show himself in the best possible light; X will put his best foot forward;** ∥ X умеет показать себя ≃ [in limited contexts] **X knows how to sell himself.**

«Попробуй он слегка верхушек какой-нибудь науки... [он] ещё, пожалуй, скажет потом: «Дай-ка себя покажу! Да такое выдумает мудрёное постановление, что многим придётся солоно...» (Гоголь 3). "If a man like that acquires a smattering of some science...he may even say to himself, 'I'll show them who I am,' and invent such a sage law that many people will smart for it..." (3c). ♦ Грузинское гостеприимство... исключительно, за месяц мы почти не имели возможности тратить свои деньги. Конечно, в этом есть желание «показать себя»... (Амальрик 1). The famous Georgian hospitality...is unique. During our month there, we had almost no occasion to spend our own money. Naturally, the desire to put one's best foot forward plays a large part in this... (1a). ♦ «Таких, как он, мастеров у нас – раз-два и обчёлся. А он ещё и умеет показать себя, вовремя поддакнуть начальству» (Копелев 1).

"You can count masters like him here on the fingers of one hand. And he knows how to sell himself, when to toady" (1a).

П-278 • ВОЗВОДИ́ТЬ/ВОЗВЕСТИ́ ПОКЛЁП на кого
[VP; subj: human] to tell lies about s.o. (or o.s.), accuse s.o. (or o.s.) falsely: X возвёл поклёп на Y-а ⟨на себя⟩ ≃ X made a false accusation against Y ⟨himself⟩; X slandered ⟨slurred⟩ Y ⟨himself⟩.

[Арина Пантелеймоновна:] Да ведь она [Фёкла] лгунья, мой свет. *(Те же и Фёкла.)* [Фёкла:] Ан нет, Арина Пантелеймоновна, грех вам понапрасну поклёп возводить (Гоголь 1). [A.:] But she's [Fiokla is] a liar, you know, my love. *(Enter Fiokla.)* [F.:] Oh no, Arina Panteleimonovna, it's...bad of you to slander me for nothing (1c).

П-279 • НА ПОКЛО́Н ⟨С ПОКЛО́НОМ *obs*⟩ к кому
идти, ходить, ехать и т. п. [PrepP; these forms only; adv]
1. *obs* (to come to s.o.) expressing one's devotion, deference: X пошёл на поклон к Y-у ≃ X went to pay his respects ⟨homage⟩ to Y.

Он избрал филологический факультет. Мать ходила на поклон к профессорам, дабы их задобрить... (Набоков 1). He chose the philological faculty. His mother went to pay her respects to the professors in order to cajole them... (1a).
2. *coll* (to address s.o.) with a humble request, asking for help, patronage etc: X пойдёт на поклон к Y-у ≃ X will go begging to Y; X will come to Y cap ⟨hat⟩ in hand; X will go to Y to seek favor.

В Москву он [Маленков] ни разу не ездил «на поклон» и «прощения» не просил (Аллилуева 2). He [Malenkov] never once came to Moscow to seek favor, nor did he ever beg forgiveness (2a).

П-280 • КЛАСТЬ ПОКЛО́НЫ *obs* [VP; subj: human] to bend
toward the ground (often down low, usu. when praying): X клал поклоны ≃ X bowed (to the ground).

По всей церкви слышно было, как казак Свербигуз клал поклоны (Гоголь 5). All over the church one could hear the Cossack Sverbiguz bowing to the ground (5a). ♦ Однажды вечером, когда старая графиня, вздыхая и кряхтя... клала на коврике земные поклоны вечерней молитвы, её дверь скрипнула и... вбежала Наташа (Толстой 5). One night when the old Countess...knelt sighing and groaning on a rug and bowing to the floor in prayer, her door creaked and Natasha...ran in (5a).

П-281 • НА ПОКО́Е *obsoles* [PrepP; Invar; subj-compl with
быть∅, жить etc (subj: human)] (to be, live) at rest, not working (because of advanced age): **in retirement.**

П-282 • ОСТАВЛЯ́ТЬ/ОСТА́ВИТЬ В ПОКО́Е кого-что
[VP; subj: human; obj: more often human] to cease disturbing s.o. or sth., stop pestering s.o.: X оставил Y-а в покое ≃ X left person Y in peace; X left ⟨let⟩ Y alone; X did not bother person Y anymore; X let Y be.

Я не опасен вам нисколько — и оставьте меня в покое (Солженицын 2). I am not the least bit dangerous to you, so leave me in peace (2a). ♦ [Нина:] Давайте, давайте, оправдывайте его [Васеньку], защищайте. Если хотите, чтобы он совсем рехнулся... [Васенька:] Я с ума хочу сходить, понятно тебе? Сходить с ума и ни о чём не думать! И оставь меня в покое! *(Уходит в другую комнату.)* (Вампилов 4). [Nina:] Go ahead, go ahead and agree with him [Vasenka], defend him. If you want him to go completely crazy.... [Vasenka:] I want to go nuts, understand? Go nuts and not think about anything! So leave me alone! *(He goes into the other room.)* (4b). ♦ «Баранов, — застонал Ефим, — оставь меня в покое. Ты же знаешь, что я по утрам работаю» (Войнович 6). "Kostya," Yefim groaned, "please let me alone. You know I work in the mornings" (6a). ♦ «Оставь его [мальчика] в покое, Тоня, — попросил доктор. — Не мучь его и не расстраивайся

сама» (Пастернак 1). "Let him [the boy] be, Tonia," the doctor said. "Don't bother him, and don't upset yourself" (1a).

П-283 • ВЕ́ЧНЫЙ ПОКО́Й *lit* [NP; sing only] **1.** peace after
death: **eternal rest; everlasting peace.**

«Ты, великий, если ты есть, прости нас и прими захоронение раба твоего Казангапа с милостью, и, если он того заслуживает, определи его душу на вечный покой» (Айтматов 2). "You, oh great one, if You exist, forgive us and in your mercy accept the burial of your Kazangap and, if he deserved it, grant his soul everlasting peace" (2a).
2. ~ кому [the resulting phrase is used as indep. sent] let the deceased be at peace: **may he ⟨she⟩ rest in peace; God rest his ⟨her⟩ soul.**

П-284 • НА ПОКО́Й [PrepP; Invar] **1.** (кому) пора, надо,
можно и т. п. ~ [adv (with the infin implied)] (it is time to, one should, one can etc) go to sleep: (X-у) пора на покой ≃ **(it's) time (for X) to turn in ⟨to get some rest, to get some sleep⟩; now to bed; (it's) time for bed.**

[Любовь Андреевна:] Кофе выпит, можно на покой (Чехов 2). [L.A.:] Well, I've finished my coffee. Now to bed (2b).
2. уйти, удалиться, пора и т. п. ~ [adv] to stop working (at one's job) because of advanced age: X ушёл на покой ≃ **X retired; X went into retirement;** ‖ X-у пора на покой ≃ **X should retire; it's time X retired;** [in limited contexts] **X is overdue for retirement.**

...Конферансье ушёл на покой и начал жить на свои сбережения, которых, по его скромному подсчёту, должно было хватить ему на пятнадцать лет (Булгаков 9). ...The master of ceremonies retired and went to live on his savings, which, according to his modest calculations, should last him for fifteen years (9a). ♦ Обо всём переговорили — о критиках, о главреже [главном режиссёре], которому давно на покой пора, освободить место... (Трифонов 1). ...They had discussed everything there was to discuss, including the critics and the theater's artistic director, who should have retired long ago and allowed someone else to take over (1a). ♦ «Легионы ведёт седой римский воин, изрубленный в боях. Ему уже пора на покой, но он всё-таки хочет познать неведомое» (Домбровский 1). "...The legions are commanded by a grizzled Roman warrior, scarred in battle. He's overdue for retirement but he still wants to discover the unknown" (1a).
3. пора, можно и т. п. ~ [adv (with the infin implied)] (it is time for s.o.) to die: X-у пора на покой ≃ **X's time has come (to die).**

Смерть не страшила старуху: она давно свыклась с мыслью, что пора на покой. Death didn't frighten the old woman: she had long been used to the idea that her time had come.

П-285 • ПОКО́НЧИТЬ С СОБО́Й; ПОКО́НЧИТЬ
(СЧЁТЫ) С ЖИ́ЗНЬЮ *lit;* ПОКО́НЧИТЬ (ЖИЗНЬ) САМОУБИ́ЙСТВОМ [VP; subj: human] to kill o.s.: X покончил с собой ≃ **X committed suicide; X took his (own) life; X did away with himself; X finished himself off.**

Оставшись одна, Соня тотчас же стала мучиться от страха при мысли, что, может быть, действительно он покончит самоубийством (Достоевский 3). Left alone, Sonya immediately began to be tormented by fear at the thought that he might indeed commit suicide (3c). ♦ «...Так как подсудимый уверяет, что убил [отца] не он, то, стало быть, должен был убить Смердяков... Вот, вот, стало быть, откуда произошло это „хитрое" и колоссальное обвинение на несчастного, вчера покончившего с собой идиота!» (Достоевский 2). "...The defendant insists it was not he who killed his father, so Smerdyakov must have killed him....Here, here then is the source of this 'cunning' and colossal accusation against the unfortunate idiot who yesterday took his own life!" (2a). ♦ [Кавалеров:] Вы хотите, чтобы всё было полезно, а я хочу быть бесполезным. Взять, например, и покончить с собой (Олеша 6). [K.:] You want everything to be useful, but I want to be useless. For example, I might just finish myself off (6a).

П-286 • **ПОКОРИ́ТЕЛЬ ⟨ПОКОРИ́ТЕЛЬНИЦА⟩ СЕР- ДЕ́Ц** *humor or iron* [NP; fixed WO] a person who enjoys success with members of the opposite sex: **conqueror of women's ⟨men's⟩ hearts; heartbreaker;** [of a man only] **lady-killer; ladies' ⟨lady's⟩ man; heartthrob; Romeo;** [of a woman only] **siren; femme fatale.**

...Почти все дамы, по крайней мере огромнейшее большинство их, стояли за Митю и за оправдание его. Может быть, главное, потому, что о нём составилось представление как о покорителе женских сердец (Достоевский 2). ...Almost all the ladies, at least the great majority of them, favored Mitya and his acquittal. Mainly, perhaps, because an idea had been formed of him as a conqueror of women's hearts (2a).

П-287 • **НЕ ДАВА́ТЬ ПОКО́Я ⟨-ю⟩** *кому* [VP; subj: human or abstr] to disturb, worry s.o. unremittingly: X не даёт Y-у покоя ≃ **X gives Y no peace ⟨rest⟩; X doesn't give Y a moment's peace ⟨rest⟩; person X doesn't ⟨won't⟩ leave ⟨let⟩ Y alone (for a second ⟨a moment etc⟩); X haunts Y.**

В первые дни Семён опасался, что Митягин покою не даст — каждый день будет приходить и жаловаться (Тендряков 1). For the first few days Simon feared that Mityagin would give him no peace — that he would come round every day and whine (1a). ♦ [Софья Егоровна:] Вы как-то странно смотрите [на меня]... преследуете... Точно шпионите!.. Вы не даёте мне покоя... (Чехов 1). [S.E.:] You have this odd way of looking [at me]...and follow me about—as if you were spying on me....You won't leave me alone... (1b). ♦ ...В Сибири, где одни лиственницы да якуты слушали его, ему не давал покоя образ «эстрады» и «залы»... (Набоков 1). ...In Siberia, where his only listeners were the larches and the Yakuts, he was haunted by the image of a "platform" and a "lecture hall"... (1a).

П-288 • **НЕ ЗНАТЬ ⟨НЕ НАХОДИ́ТЬ/НЕ НАЙТИ́ (себе), НЕ ВИ́ДЕТЬ⟩ ПОКО́Я ⟨-ю⟩** [VP; subj: human] to be in a nervous state, experience constant anxiety: X не знает покоя ≃ **X knows no peace; X is unable to find peace of mind.**

[Дом] много раз перестраивали, по плану отца. Должно быть, он просто не находил себе покоя... То ему не хватало солнца, то нужна была тенистая терраса; если был один этаж — пристраивали второй, а если их было два — то один сносили... (Аллилуева 1). My father had it [the house] rebuilt over and over again. Probably he was just unable to find peace of mind....Either there was too little sunshine for him or it needed a terrace in the shade. If there was one floor it needed two, and if there were two, well, better tear one down (1a).

П-289 • **ПОД ПОКРО́ВОМ** *чего*, often **ночи, темноты** [PrepP; Invar; the resulting PrepP is adv] masked by sth., using sth. as concealment, as a disguise: **under cover ⟨a cloak, a veil, a blanket⟩ of; hidden by a shroud of; under the guise of.**

П-290 • **НА ОДИ́Н ПОКРО́Й; ОДНОГО́ ПОКРО́Я** *both coll* [PrepP or NP_gen; these forms only; usu. subj-compl with copula (subj: human, concr, or abstr, pl), adv (1st var.), or nonagreeing modif; fixed WO] (two or more people, things etc are) very similar or identical to one another in some respect (esp. in regard to shortcomings): (все) X-ы ⟨X-ы и Y-и и т. п.⟩ на один покрой ≃ **Xs ⟨Xs and Ys⟩ are all alike;** [of people only] **Xs ⟨Xs and Ys⟩ are (all) cut from the same cloth; Xs ⟨Xs and Ys⟩ are cast in the same mold; Xs ⟨Xs and Ys⟩ are birds ⟨all⟩ of a feather; Xs ⟨Xs and Ys⟩ are (all) of the same ilk;** [of things only] **Xs are all done ⟨written etc⟩ in the same style.**

«Кажется, я имел случай изучить эту породу людей — их столько к тебе ходит, — все на один покрой» (Толстой 2). "I think I've had occasion enough to get to know this breed by now — so many of them come to you — and they're all of a feather" (2b).

П-291 • **СТА́РОГО ПОКРО́Я** *obs* [NP_gen; Invar; nonagreeing modif; fixed WO] a person who has old-fashioned ways, adheres to old-fashioned ideas and beliefs etc: **of the old school ⟨stamp⟩.**

Они поцеловались, по старому русскому обычаю, трое-кратно...: барин был старого покроя (Гоголь 3). They kissed each other thrice according to the old Russian custom: the gentleman was of the old school (3d).

П-292 • **ПОКУШЕ́НИЕ ⟨ПОПЫ́ТКА⟩ С НЕГО́Д- НЫМИ СРЕ́ДСТВАМИ** *rather lit* [NP; sing only; fixed WO] an attempt to do sth. without sufficient resources, means etc (with the implication that it is doomed to fail): **exercise in futility; fruitless exercise; futile ⟨hopeless⟩ attempt.**

Когда Костя начал звонить Алле каждый день и посылать ей цветы, все думали, что это покушение с негодными средствами. Но не прошло и трёх месяцев, как она вышла за него замуж. When Kostya started calling Alla every day and sending her flowers, everyone thought it was an exercise in futility. But before three months were up, she had married him.

П-293 • **СИ́ЛЬНЫЙ ПОЛ** [NP; sing only; fixed WO] men: **the stronger ⟨sterner⟩ sex.**

П-294 • **СЛА́БЫЙ ⟨НЕ́ЖНЫЙ, ПРЕКРА́СНЫЙ⟩ ПОЛ** [NP; sing only; fixed WO] women: **the fair ⟨weaker⟩ sex.**

Главною его слабостью была страсть к прекрасному полу; нередко за свои нежности получал он толчки, от которых охал по целым суткам (Пушкин 2). His main weakness was a passion for the fair sex; his amorous advances frequently earned him raps and knocks that would make him groan for days (2a).

П-295 • **ОДИ́Н В ПО́ЛЕ НЕ ВО́ИН** [saying] a person undertaking or trying to carry out sth. alone encounters endless difficulties, has trouble coping, cannot do everything himself: ≃ **one's as good as none; one body is nobody; one man can't win a war;** [in limited contexts] **there is strength in numbers.**

П-296 • **ПО́ЛЕ БРА́НИ** *elev;* **ПО́ЛЕ ЧЕ́СТИ** *obs, elev;* **ПО́ЛЕ БИ́ТВЫ ⟨СРАЖЕ́НИЯ, БО́Я⟩** [NP; only поле сражения can be used in pl; fixed WO] the territory on which a battle takes place: **field of battle; battlefield; battleground.**

...Едва ли не в эту самую эпоху сложилась знаменитая пословица: шапками закидаем! — которая впоследствии долгое время служила девизом глуповских подвигов на поле брани (Салтыков-Щедрин 1). The famous saying "It's in the bag!"—which afterwards served for a long time as the motto for Foolovian exploits on the field of battle — must have arisen in this period (1a). ♦ «Ужасно то, что красота есть не только страшная, но и таинственная вещь. Тут дьявол с богом борется, а поле битвы — сердца людей» (Достоевский 1). "The terrible thing is that beauty is not only fearful but also mysterious. Here the devil is struggling with God, and the battlefield is the human heart" (1a).

П-297 • **ПО́ЛЕ ЗРЕ́НИЯ** *чьё, кого* [NP; sing only; fixed WO] **1.** the area or expanse perceived by the eye: **field ⟨range⟩ of vision; visual field;** ‖ в поле зрения ≃ **in sight; within view.**

Четыре орудия поочерёдно слали снаряды туда, за поваленные ряды пшеницы, но, сверх Григорьева ожидания, орудийный огонь не внёс заметного замешательства в цепи красных, — они отходили неспешно, организованно и уже выпадали из поля зрения сотни, спускаясь за перевал в балку (Шолохов 4). The four guns, one after the other, sent their shells across the swathes of wheat, but to Grigory's surprise the artillery fire caused no noticeable confusion in the Red lines. They fell back in an unhurried, orderly fashion and disappeared from the squadron's field of vision into a ravine (4a).

2. (in refer. to a person's being in, disappearing from, removing himself from etc) s.o.'s area of interest, concern, attention etc: X держал Y-а в поле зрения ⟨не упускал Y-а из поля зрения⟩ ≃ **X kept track of Y; X kept an eye ⟨kept tabs⟩ on Y;** ‖ X упустил Y-а из поля зрения ≃ **X lost touch with Y; X lost track of Y; X fell out of touch with Y;** ‖ Y исчез из X-ова поля зрения ≃ **Y stopped communicating (with X) altogether; Y stopped writing ⟨calling⟩ (X) altogether; Y fell out of touch with X; Y dropped out of sight.**

Родственники Марата по материнской линии, оказывается, всё время держали его в поле своего зрения... (Искандер 2). Marat's relatives on his mother's side, it turned out, constantly kept an eye on him... (2a).

П-298 • **ПОЛИ́ТИКА КНУТА́ И ПРЯ́НИКА** [NP; fixed WO] tactics combining (the threat of) punishment and (the promise of) reward: **carrot-and-stick policy.**

Правительства всегда и везде проводят политику кнута и пряника. Кнут вы получили. Теперь ждите пряник (Зиновьев 1). "Governments always and everywhere have used carrot and stick policies. You've had your share of the stick. Now you're waiting for a bit of carrot to come your way" (1a).

< This phrase became commonly used in Russian after the publication of *The Golden Calf* («Золотой телёнок»), by Ilya Ilf and Evgeny Petrov, 1931 (ch. 12).

П-299 • **С ПОЛИ́ЧНЫМ** поймать, задержать *кого*, попасться и т. п. [PrepP; Invar; adv] (to catch s.o., be caught etc) at the scene of a crime with indisputable evidence: X поймал Y-а с поличным ≃ **X caught Y red-handed; X caught Y in the act (of doing sth.);** [in refer. to stealing only] **X caught Y with Y's hand in the cookie jar ⟨in the till⟩.**

Полковник Емышев... украл двести казённых рублей, но, пойманный с поличным, вынужден был их вернуть и уйти с работы... (Войнович 3). Colonel Emyshev stole two hundred rubles of state funds, but, caught red-handed, he was forced to return them and leave work... (3a). ♦ Уже неподалёку от румынской территории, в какой-то зажиточной деревушке, Чубатый ухитрился выкрасть из амбара с меру ячменя. Хозяин поймал его с поличным... (Шолохов 3). In a prosperous little village not far from the Romanian border Curly managed to steal a peck of barley from a barn. The owner caught him in the act... (3a).

П-300 • **НА́ШЕГО ⟨В НА́ШЕМ⟩ ПОЛКУ́ ПРИ́БЫЛО** *coll* [sent; these forms only; fixed WO] (in refer. to a group or type of people sharing a common cause, belief etc) with this addition or these additions there are more of us now, there is an increase in people like us: **our ranks have grown ⟨swelled⟩; our numbers have grown ⟨increased⟩; that's a gain for our side; there is a new recruit ⟨there are new recruits⟩ to our ranks;** [in limited contexts] **reinforcements have arrived.**

[Беркутов:] Разумеется, я душою всегда буду с вами, в вашей партии. [Мурзавецкая:] Ну, так мы тебя и запишем; значит, нашего полку прибыло (Островский 5). [B.:] Of course, I shall always be in sympathy with you; one of your party. [M.:] Well, then, we'll register you; that means a gain for our side (5a).

П-301 • **ДА И ПО́ЛНО** *obs, coll* [Invar; usu. the concluding clause in a compound sent; fixed WO] used to add emphasis and a note of finality to the word or phrase with which it is used (that word or phrase itself generally summarizes what came before): **and that's all there is to it; and that's the ⟨a⟩ fact; in a word.**

«А вот у хрыча Черевика нет совести, видно, и на полшеляга: сказал да и назад... Ну, его и винить нечего, он пень, да и полно» (Гоголь 5). "But it seems that old grumbler Cherevik has not a half pint of conscience: he gave his word, but he has taken it back....Well, it is no good blaming him: he is a blockhead and that's the

fact" (5a). ♦ ...Рознь да галденье пошли пуще прежнего: опять стали взаимно друг у друга земли разорять, жён в плен уводить, над девами ругаться. Нет порядку, да и полно (Салтыков-Щедрин 1). ...The dissension and ruckus started up worse than ever: they began mutually ravaging each other's lands again, taking wives into captivity, and outraging virgins. In a word—no law and order (1a).

П-302 • **ОТ ПОЛНОТЫ́ ДУШИ́ ⟨СЕ́РДЦА, ЧУ́ВСТВ(А)⟩** [PrepP; these forms only; adv] from an excess of emotion: **from ⟨out of⟩ the fullness of one's heart; from (a) fullness of heart; from a plenitude ⟨an abundance⟩ of feeling.**

[Городничий:] У меня уж такой нрав: гостеприимство с самого детства; особливо если гость просвещённый человек. Не подумайте, чтобы я говорил это из лести. Нет, не имею этого порока, от полноты души выражаюсь (Гоголь 4). [Mayor:] That's my disposition, hospitable from my childhood, especially if the guest is a man of culture. Don't think I'm saying this in flattery: no, I haven't that vice; I am expressing myself out of the fullness of my heart (4d). ♦ Я схватил её руку и долго не мог вымолвить ни одного слова. Мы оба молчали от полноты сердца (Пушкин 2). I seized her hand and for a long time could not utter a single word. We both kept silent from a fullness of heart (2a). ♦ ...Товарищ Сталин пошёл перед строем и стал совать каждому свою сморщенную ладошку для пожатия... Дрынов с перепугу несколько перестарался. Великий вождь поморщился от боли и вскинул на Дрынова подозрительный взгляд. Но моментально понял, что генерал сделал это не из террористических побуждений, а от полноты чувств... (Войнович 4). Comrade Stalin walked in front of the formation and began thrusting his wrinkled hand toward each man to shake....Out of fear Drinov overdid the handshake. The great leader grimaced in pain and cast a suspicious glance at Drinov. But he at once understood that the general had not done it with any terroristic motives but from a plenitude of feeling... (4a).

П-303 • **ДРАЖА́ЙШАЯ ПОЛОВИ́НА** *obs, humor;* **МОЯ́ ⟨твоя, его, её⟩ ПОЛОВИ́НА** *humor* [NP; fixed WO] a wife or, rarely, a husband as viewed in relation to her or his spouse: **one's better half.**

П-304 • **ВХОДИ́ТЬ/ВОЙТИ́ В ПОЛОЖЕ́НИЕ** *чьё, кого* [VP; subj: human; often pfv imper or infin with надо, стараться etc; fixed WO] to identify o.s. with another, understand his problems, situation, motives etc and relate to him with full attention and empathy: войди(те) в X-ово положение ≃ **put yourself in X's place ⟨position, shoes⟩; put yourself in the position ⟨place⟩ of X; try to see X's side of it; try to understand X's position; look at it from X's perspective ⟨point of view, position⟩.**

«Выхожу на службу, продал быков — коня справил, а его взяли и забраковали... Порченый, говорят, на ноги... „Войдите, — говорю, — в положение, что у него ноги как у призового жеребца, но ходит он петушиной рысью"... проходка у него петушиная". Нет, не признали» (Шолохов 2). "When I was due for service, I had to sell my oxen and buy myself a horse. And then they go and reject it....His legs are no good, they says. 'Put yourself in my place,' I says. 'He's got legs like a prize stallion, it's just his walk....He struts like a young cock.' But no, they wouldn't have him" (2a). ♦ «Ну, если я тебе обещал [жениться], я готов, Людмила, пожалуйста... но и ты войди в моё положение, пожалей меня. Я ведь, Людмила, ещё молодой, я хочу учиться, повышать свой кругозор. Зачем тебе губить молодую жизнь?» (Войнович 5). "All right, if I promised [to marry] you, I'm ready, Ludmilla, but please...put yourself in my position, take pity on me. You know I'm still young, Ludmilla, I want to study and broaden my horizons. What do you need to ruin a young life for?" (5a). ♦ [Нина *(Полине Андреевне):*] Отказать Ирине Николаевне, знаменитой артистке!.. Просто невероятно! [Полина

Андреевна *(в отчаянии)*:] Что я могу? Войдите в моё положение: что я могу? (Чехов 6). [Nina *(To Pauline)*:] To refuse Irina Nikolaevna, the famous actress!…It's simply unbelievable! [Pauline *(in despair)*:] What can I do? Put yourself in my shoes, what can I do? (6d). [Nina *(to Polina Andreyevna)*:] To refuse Irina Nikolayevna, the famous actress!…It's simply unbelievable! [Polina Andreyevna *(in despair)*:] What can I do? Look at it from my position: what can I do? (6c). ♦ Илья Ильич [Обломов] думал, что начальник до того входит в положение своего подчинённого, что заботливо расспросит его: каково он почивал ночью, отчего у него мутные глаза и не болит ли голова? (Гончаров 1). Oblomov had thought that a superior was so eager to put himself in the place of his subordinate that he would inquire carefully how he had slept, why he was bleary-eyed, and whether he had a headache (1a).

П-305 • **ЛО́ЖНОЕ ПОЛОЖЕ́НИЕ** [NP; sing only; fixed WO] an uncomfortable situation: **awkward ⟨embarrassing, false⟩ position.**

«[Вы] поступили неправильно… поставили сержанта Токареву в ложное положение, но, принимая во внимание, что вы боевой офицер, я это дело прекращаю…» (Рыбаков 1). "You acted improperly.…You placed Sergeant Tokareva in a false position, but in view of the fact that you're a combat officer, I'm closing the case" (1a).

П-306 • **ПИ́КОВОЕ ПОЛОЖЕ́НИЕ** *highly coll* [NP; sing only; fixed WO except when used as VP$_{subj}$ with copula] a difficult, troublesome situation: **sticky ⟨tough, tricky⟩ situation; (person X is in) a mess ⟨a tight spot, a bind, a pickle⟩.**

«Она [Лиля] потребовала книгу стихов Блока с автографом. „Но как же я это сделаю, если я с Блоком, в сущности, даже не знаком. Тем более — футурист, а он — символист…" — „Это ваше дело". Положение пиковое, но если Лиличка велела… о чём тут может быть речь?..» (Катаев 3). "…What she [Lilya] wanted was a signed copy of Blok. 'But how can I do that when I don't even know Blok properly? Specially as I'm a futurist and he's a symbolist…' 'That's your business.' Well, I was in a tough spot, but if that was what Lilichka wanted.…That was that" (3a).

П-307 • **ПОЛОЖЕ́НИЕ ВЕЩЕ́Й** [NP; sing only; usu. subj or obj] the situation, circumstances: **the state of affairs; the lay of the land; the way things are;** [often after каково] **how things are; how the land lies.**

«Я понимаю, тебе очень тяжело. Но я хочу, чтобы ты ясно представила себе положение вещей» (Рыбаков 2). "I know it's very hard for you, but I want you to have a clear understanding of the way things are" (2a).

П-308 • **ПОЛОЖЕ́НИЕ ХУ́ЖЕ ГУБЕРНА́ТОРСКОГО** *obsoles, coll, humor* [VP$_{subj}$ with быть$_{\emptyset}$; usu. pres; fixed WO] the situation is extremely unpleasant, difficult etc: **this is ⟨things are in⟩ a fine mess; it's about as bad as it can get; s.o. is up the creek (without a paddle).**

< According to academician Viktor Vinogradov, «губернатор» is an old term from horse-breeding jargon for a male horse that was used to excite a mare before she was mated with a stallion of good breeding. He points out, though, that 19th-cent. writers assumed the phrase to be based on the office of a "governor," the common meaning of «губернатор».

П-309 • **СПАСА́ТЬ/СПАСТИ́ ПОЛОЖЕ́НИЕ** [VP; subj: human; more often pfv past] to set right or smooth over a difficult, uncomfortable, tense etc situation or find a way of getting o.s. or another out of such a situation: X спас положение ≃ **X remedied the situation; X saved the day;** [in limited contexts] **X found ⟨gave person Y⟩ a way out ⟨an escape hatch⟩.**

В гостиной явно нарастало напряжение. Спорящие, казалось, готовы были броситься друг на друга, но тут вбежал плачущий ребёнок, отвлёк внимание и тем спас положение. The tension in the living room was clearly building. It seemed as if those arguing were about to lash out at one another, when suddenly a child ran in crying, diverting everyone's attention and thus saving the day.

П-310 • **В ПОЛОЖЕ́НИИ** *euph;* **В ИНТЕРЕ́СНОМ ПОЛОЖЕ́НИИ** *obsoles, euph* [PrepP; these forms only; subj-compl with быть$_{\emptyset}$ (subj: human, female); fixed WO] one is pregnant: X в (интересном) положении ≃ **X is in the ⟨a⟩ family way; X is expecting; X is with child.**

Пишу в какую-то инстанцию письмо. Показываю одному из своих доброжелателей, вижу — он недоволен. «Ну зачем вы пишете в требовательном тоне? Просите. Расскажите, что вы из рабочих… что жена в положении…» (Войнович 3). I wrote a letter to some office; I showed it to one of my well-wishers and saw that he was not pleased. "Why do you write in a demanding tone? Request. Tell them you're from the working class…that your wife is expecting…" (3a).

П-311 • **ВЫХОДИ́ТЬ/ВЫ́ЙТИ ИЗ ПОЛОЖЕ́НИЯ** [VP; subj: human; more often pfv] to find a means of escape from a situation that is difficult, unpleasant, awkward etc: X вышел из положения ≃ **X found a way out (of the situation); X found an escape hatch; X got out of the ⟨his⟩ situation; X extricated himself from the predicament; X remedied the situation;** ‖ X умело ⟨с честью и т. п.⟩ вышел из незавидного ⟨неловкого и т. п.⟩ положения ≃ **X emerged deftly ⟨with honor etc⟩ from an unenviable ⟨embarrassing etc⟩ situation.** ○ **ВЫ́ХОД ИЗ ПОЛОЖЕ́НИЯ** [NP] ≃ **way out.**

И самое неприятное в их состоянии было то, что, кажется, в этот раз им *самим* [секретариату Союза писателей] предложили выходить из положения… — а вот *этого* они не умеют, за всю жизнь они ни одного вопроса никогда не решили *сами* (Солженицын 2). And the worst of it was that this time it had apparently been left to *them* [the secretariat of the Writers' Union] to find a way out of the situation…and *that* was just the sort of thing they couldn't do; they had never solved a problem for themselves in all their lives (2a). ♦ Один мой родственник, узнав о моих невзгодах, специально приехал из провинции ко мне, чтобы научить меня, как выйти из положения (Войнович 1). Learning of my troubles, a relative of mine made a special trip from the provinces to advise me on how to get out of my situation (1a). ♦ Она [тётушка Хрисула] имела в виду, что, даже поймав осквернённый инжир, Деспина могла с честью выйти из этого положения, просто перебросив этот инжир ей, тётушке Хрисуле (Искандер 5). She [Auntie Chrysoula] meant that even after catching the defiled fig, Despina could have remedied the situation honorably, simply by throwing the fig to her, Auntie Chrysoula (5a). ♦ Я ещё раз перечитал письмо. Ну что ж… Пожалуй, оно как раз кстати. Удобный выход из положения (Войнович 5). I read the letter one more time. How about that, it seemed to have come just in the nick of time. An easy way out (5a).

П-312 • **ДО ПОЛОЖЕ́НИЯ РИЗ** [PrepP; Invar; fixed WO] **1.** напиться, пьян и т. п. ~ *coll* [adv (intensif) or modif] (to get or be) extremely (drunk): X напился ~ ≃ **X was ⟨got⟩ dead ⟨blind, stone⟩ drunk; X drank himself under the table ⟨into a stupor⟩.**

…До положения риз [Платон] не напивался… (Грекова 3). …[Platon] never got dead drunk… (3a). ♦ И этого секретаря… удалось заполучить однажды на дачу к нашим знакомым в Снегири — там он надрался до положения риз, всем надоел… (Трифонов 5). We subsequently managed to get this secretary out to the dacha of some friends of ours in Snegiri, where he proceeded to get stone drunk and to antagonize absolutely everyone (5a).

2. *obs* [adv (intensif)] to an extreme degree: **(do sth.) to the limit; (love ⟨hate⟩) terribly; (fight) to the finish.**

[Глагольев 2:] Правду ли говорят, что она... любит деньги до положения риз? (Чехов 1). [G. Jr.:] Is it true that she loves money? I mean, terribly? (1a). ♦ «Ах, Аркадий! Сделай одолжение, поссоримся раз хорошенько — до положения риз, до истребления» (Тургенев 2). [context transl] "Oh, Arcadii! Do me a favor: let's have an honest-to-goodness quarrel for once — till we're both laid out cold, till we exterminate each other" (2d).

П-313 • КАК ПОЛОТНÓ ⟨СКÁТЕРТЬ⟩ бледный, белый, побледнеть [как + NP; these forms only; modif or adv (intensif)] (to be, turn) very (pale): **(as) white ⟨pale⟩ as a sheet.**

Малов, бледный как полотно, сделал отчаянное усилие овладеть шумом и не мог; студенты вскочили на лавки (Герцен 1). Malov, white as a sheet, made a desperate effort to control the uproar but could not; the students jumped on to the benches (1a). ♦ Борисов сел. Шевчук продолжал стоять бледный как полотно (Войнович 4). Borisov sat down. Shevchuk continued to stand, pale as a sheet (4a).

П-314 • РАСКЛÁДЫВАТЬ/РАЗЛОЖИ́ТЬ ПО ПÓЛОЧКАМ ⟨ПО ПÓЛКАМ⟩ что coll [VP; subj: human; obj: материал, явления, идеи, often всё] to arrange sth. according to a well-thought-out system, in strict order: X разложил Y по полочкам ≃ **X organized ⟨categorized⟩ Y; X sorted Y out; X put Y in order; X arranged Y systematically.**

Каким образом мы, полгода назад употреблявшие слово «футуризм» лишь в виде бранной клички, не только нацепили её на себя, но даже отрицали за кем бы то ни было право пользоваться этим ярлыком? Сыграла ли тут роль статья Брюсова в «Русской мысли», где он... разложил по полкам весь оказавшийся у него в руках, ещё немногочисленный к тому времени материал наших сборников?.. (Лившиц 1). How was it that we, who six months before had used the word "Futurism" only as a term of abuse, had not only appropriated it for ourselves, but denied anyone [else] the right to use the label? Had Briusov's article in *Russian Thought* played a role in the matter? In the article Briusov...had categorized all the material in our miscellanies (which was not very much)... (1a).

П-315 • НА ПОЛПУТИ́ ⟨НА ПОЛДОРÓГЕ⟩ остановиться, бросить что и т. п. [PrepP; these forms only; adv] (to come to a stop) in the middle of sth., not having achieved the desired result; (to give up some undertaking, activity etc) in the middle, without bringing it to completion: **(stop ⟨abandon sth.⟩) halfway ⟨midway⟩; (stop ⟨quit⟩) halfway through; (leave sth.) half-finished.**

Что я мог сказать Марату? Что рок никогда не останавливается на полпути, а всегда до конца доводит свой безжалостный замысел? (Искандер 2). What could I say to Marat? That Fate never stops halfway, but always carries its pitiless design to the end! (2a). ♦ Разбираемая книга служила ему [Белинскому] по большей части материальной точкой отправления, на полдороге он бросал её и впивался в какой-нибудь вопрос (Герцен 2). The book he [Belinsky] was reviewing usually served him as a starting-point, but he abandoned it halfway and plunged into some other question (2a).

П-316 • ЗАВОДИ́ТЬСЯ/ЗАВЕСТИ́СЬ С ПОЛУОБОРÓТА ⟨С ПОЛ-ОБОРÓТА, С ОДНОГÓ ОБОРÓТА⟩ *highly coll* [VP; subj: human] to become easily angered, lose one's self-control quickly, react temperamentally to criticism: X завёлся с пол-оборота ≃ **X went off half-cocked; X flew off the handle;** ‖ X всегда заводится с пол-оборота ≃ **X is quick to fly off the handle; X has a short fuse.**

Ведь я знаю: искренним или фальшивым выглядит собеседник, тактичен он или хам, заводится с пол-оборота или проявляет терпимость, — всё равно всё это ложь, ложь и лицемерие (Марченко 2). I know that, regardless of how sincere or hypocritical the official may look, whether he is tactful or uncouth, whether he goes off half-cocked or keeps his cool — it is all a lie anyway — a lie and a sham (2a).

П-317 • С ПОЛУСЛÓВА ⟨С ПОЛСЛÓВА coll⟩ понимать кого-что, схватывать что [PrepP; these forms only; adv; more often used with impfv verbs] (of a person) (to understand s.o. or sth., grasp sth.) at once, from the first words spoken, from just a hint: X понимает всё ~ ≃ **X picks up on everything ⟨understands everything, gets the point⟩ at a word ⟨right away etc⟩;** ‖ X понимает Y-а ~ ≃ **X catches person Y's meaning at once ⟨right away etc⟩; X understands person Y immediately ⟨right away etc⟩;** ‖ X и Y понимают друг друга ~ ≃ **X and Y don't need to spell everything out.**

Да, её муж стар и не очень красив, у него лысина, брюшко, но с ним легко и просто, он всё понимает с полуслова... (Некрасов 1). Yes, her husband was old and not very good-looking, he was bald, he had a paunch, but life with him was easy and simple; he understood everything at a word... (1a). ♦ «...Лучше бы он [старик] совсем не говорил. Путается, хочет всё объяснить... То ли дело эти молодые немочки, всё с полуслова понимают...» (Искандер 5). "...He [the old man] would have done better not to talk at all. He kept getting tangled up....The girls were a different story, they picked up on everything right away..." (5a). ♦ Мы понимали друг друга с полуслова, давая об этом знать специальным сигналом, что тоже ускоряло наше общение, сокращая слова (Гинзбург 1). We no longer needed to spell everything out. We had a special sign to show that we had understood, so we could use abbreviations and save time (1a).

П-318 • НА ПОЛУСЛÓВЕ ⟨НА ПОЛСЛÓВЕ coll⟩ замолчать, остановиться, оборвать кого и т. п. [PrepP; these forms only; adv; more often used with pfv verbs] (of a person) (to cease talking, interrupt s.o. etc) at the very start or in the middle of a conversation, speech etc: X замолчал ~ ≃ **X stopped ⟨broke off, checked himself⟩ in midsentence ⟨in midword, in midflow, in midspeech, in the middle of a sentence, in the middle of a word⟩;** ‖ X оборвал Y-а ~ ≃ **X cut Y off (in midsentence ⟨in midword, in the middle of a sentence, in the middle of a word⟩); X cut Y short (in the middle of what Y was saying ⟨in the middle of Y's speech etc⟩).**

Говорили все трое, и все трое замолкли на полуслове, как только я появился в дверях... (Искандер 5). All three were talking, and all three stopped in midsentence as soon as I appeared in the doorway... (5a). ♦ Было это осенью 1937 года, в разгар арестов и расстрелов. Говорил он [Пастернак] один, а я молчал, смущённый неожиданной горячностью его монолога, который он вдруг оборвал чуть ли не на полуслове (Гладков 1). This was in the autumn of 1937, at the height of the arrests and executions. He [Pasternak] talked while I listened, embarrassed by the unexpected vehemence of his diatribe, until he suddenly checked himself almost in mid-sentence (1a). ♦ «Брешешь ты всё», — сказал Николай Курзов, стоявший от Плечевого справа. Плечевой споткнулся на полуслове, посмотрел на Николая... сверху вниз... и, подумав, сказал: «Брешет собака. А я говорю. А ты свою варежку закрой...» (Войнович 2). "Horseshit!" said Nikolai Kurzov, who was standing to Burly's right. Burly stumbled in mid-speech, gave Nikolai the once-over...then paused for a moment to think, and said: "Horseshit comes from a horse. And I'm no horse. So shut your trap..." (2a). ♦ Мы считаем вслух, но я вдруг обрубил на полуслове и стою, разинув рот... (Замятин 1). We calculate aloud, but I break off in the middle of a word and stand there, gaping... (1a). ♦ Лёва чуть не плакал: что сделали с человеком! Но сдержался, заговорил о другом, сильно издалека... Дед прервал Лёву на полуслове (Битов 2). Lyova all but wept: what had they done to the man! But he contained himself and started talking about something else, in a very roundabout way....Grandfather cut Lyova short (2a).

П-319 • ДО ПОЛУСМЕ́РТИ [PrepP; Invar; adv (intensif) or modif] intensely, to a very high degree: избить *кого* ~ ≃ **beat s.o. half ⟨almost⟩ to death; beat s.o. till he is (nearly) half-dead; beat s.o. to within an inch of his life;** ‖ испугать *кого* ~ ≃ **scare s.o. (half) to death; scare the wits ⟨the living daylights⟩ out of s.o.;** ‖ испугаться ~ ≃ **be scared (half) to death; be scared stiff ⟨out of one's wits⟩;** ‖ устать ⟨измучиться⟩ ~ ≃ **be ⟨get⟩ dead tired; be ready to drop.**

Бездетность-то и заставляла Настёну терпеть всё... Лишь однажды, когда Андрей, попрекая её, сказал что-то совсем уж невыносимое, она... ответила, что неизвестно ещё, кто из них причина — она или он, других мужиков она не пробовала. Он избил её до полусмерти (Распутин 2). And it was barrenness that made Nastyona bear it all....Only once, when Andrei, berating her, said something completely unbearable, she replied that it wasn't clear yet whose fault it was—hers or his, since she hadn't tried other men yet. He beat her half to death (2a). ♦ Долго драгуны не могли освободить окровавленного, до полусмерти избитого фабричного (Толстой 6). It was a long time before the dragoons could extricate the bleeding youth, beaten almost to death (6b). ♦ Сыновей дедушка иногда избивал до полусмерти, но единственную дочь свою, Рахиль, как я уже говорил, ни разу пальцем не тронул (Рыбаков 1). Sometimes grandfather beat his sons till they were nearly half-dead, but he had never so much as laid a finger on his daughter, as I have already mentioned (1a). ♦ «Помните жандармского полковника Стрельникова? Тоже работал без перчаток: писал фальшивые признания вместо забитых им до полусмерти революционеров» (Гроссман 2). "Do you remember Strelnikov, the political-police chief? He didn't wear kid gloves either. He had revolutionaries beaten up till they were half-dead and then wrote out false confessions..." (2a). ♦ Сударь помнил, как отец, загнав его в угол, избил до полусмерти (Семёнов 1). Squire remembered how his father would drive him into a corner and beat him to within an inch of his life (1a).

П-320 • ИЗ-ПОД ПОЛЫ́ *coll* [PrepP; Invar; adv] **1.** продавать, покупать, торговать ~ (in refer. to the illegal sale or purchase of sth.) (to sell, buy sth., trade) secretly, stealthily: **(from) under the counter; on the black market.**

Ибанцы [*nonce word*] обожают иностранцев... И всё иностранное ибанцы тоже любят. Во-первых, потому, что оно дороже и достать его труднее. Доставать-то приходится из-под полы втридорога, во-вторых, в иностранном сам себя чувствуешь чуть-чуть иностранцем и чуть-чуть за границей (Зиновьев 1). [The] Ibanskians adore foreigners....And the Ibanskians love everything foreign. First of all because foreign goods are dearer and harder to find. They have to come from under the counter at three times the price. Secondly, if you're wearing foreign clothes you feel just a little bit foreign, just a little bit as if you were abroad (1a). ♦ Жители Савёлова работали на заводе, а кормились рекой — рыбачили и из-под полы продавали рыбу (Мандельштам 1). The inhabitants of Savelovo worked mainly at the nearby factory, but they got a livelihood from the river by catching fish and selling it on the black market (1a).

2. (to do sth.) furtively, secretly: **in secret; under cover; on the sly;** [in limited contexts] **underhanded(ly); underhand.**

Мы видели её [статью] однажды на кафедре, уже жёлтую, с потрёпанными ушами... Она там хранилась, по-видимому, как беспрецедентный случай. Ею гордились, не перечитывая, и кое-кому, из-под полы, показывали (Битов 2). We saw it [the article] once at the department, already yellow and dog-eared. It was apparently being preserved there as an unprecedented case. They were proud of it, although they didn't reread it, and they showed it to a few people on the sly (2a). ♦ Роман [«Доктор Живаго»] в рукописи

несколько лет ходил в Москве по рукам, официально обсуждался в наших редакциях... В чём же был криминал? Всё делалось не тайком, не из-под полы, а открыто... (Гладков 1). The novel [*Doctor Zhivago*] had been circulating in Moscow in manuscript copies for several years; it had been officially under consideration by Soviet publishers....What, then, was so criminal in Pasternak's case? There was nothing secretive or underhand here; it was all done quite openly... (1a).

П-321 • ИЗ ПОЛЫ́ В ПОЛУ́ дать, передать, получить *что obs, coll* [PrepP; Invar; adv; fixed WO] (in buying and selling, to give or receive sth.) right to or from another with no intermediary: **personally; in person; directly.**

П-322 • В ПО́ЛЬЗУ *чью, кого-чего* [PrepP; Invar; the resulting PrepP is adv] **1.** (often in refer. to the outcome of a trial, vote, sports competition etc) with the result favoring some person or group: **in favor of s.o. ⟨sth.⟩; in s.o.'s favor; to s.o.'s advantage;** [in limited contexts] **favorable to s.o.**

«Ну что ты беспокоишься, — сказал он. — Собрание решило в твою пользу, значит, всё в порядке» (Войнович 3). "Well, what are you worried about?" he said. "The assembly decided in your favor, that means everything's all right" (3a). ♦ Матч закончился со счётом 3:0 в нашу пользу. The final score of the game was 3–0 in our favor. ♦ ...Она [Агафья Матвеена] ужасно изменилась, не в свою пользу. Она похудела... Глаза у ней впали (Гончаров 1). She [Agafya Matveyevna]...had changed terribly, and not to her advantage. She had grown thinner....Her eyes were sunken (1a).

2. so that s.o. or sth. will benefit or profit: **in favor of s.o. ⟨sth.⟩; for the sake ⟨the benefit⟩ of s.o. ⟨sth.⟩; for s.o.'s benefit; in the interests of s.o. ⟨sth.⟩; in ⟨on⟩ behalf of s.o. ⟨sth.⟩.**

[Войницкий:] Имение это не было бы куплено, если бы я не отказался от наследства в пользу сестры, которую горячо любил (Чехов 3). [V.:] ...This estate would not have been bought if I hadn't given up my share in the inheritance in favor of my sister, whom I loved dearly (3b). ♦ Наша публика похожа на провинциала, который, подслушав разговор двух дипломатов, принадлежащих к враждебным дворам, остался бы уверен, что каждый из них обманывает своё правительство в пользу взаимной, нежнейшей дружбы (Лермонтов 1). Our reading public is like some country bumpkin who hears a conversation between two diplomats from opposing courts and goes away convinced that each is betraying his government for the sake of an intimate mutual friendship (1c). Our public resembles a provincial who, upon overhearing the conversation of two diplomats belonging to two warring Courts, is convinced that each envoy is betraying his government in the interests of a most tender mutual friendship (1a). ♦ «...Призывал я вас, через Андрея Семёновича, единственно для того только, чтобы переговорить с вами о сиротском и беспомощном положении вашей родственницы, Катерины Ивановны... и о том, как бы полезно было устроить в её пользу что-нибудь вроде подписки, лотереи или подобного» (Достоевский 3). "...I summoned you, through Andrei Semyonovich, for the sole purpose of discussing with you the orphaned and helpless situation of your relative, Katerina Ivanovna...and how useful it would be to organize something like a subscription, a lottery, or what have you, for her benefit" (3c).

3. in defense of, backing s.o. or sth. (some measure, opinion etc): **in support ⟨favor⟩ of s.o. ⟨sth.⟩;** [in limited contexts] **(be disposed ⟨be inclined, incline etc⟩) toward sth.**

Публика начала даже склоняться в пользу того мнения, что вся эта история есть не что иное, как выдумка праздных людей... (Салтыков-Щедрин 1). The assemblage even began to incline toward the opinion that this whole incident was no more than the fabrication of idle people... (1a).

4. расположить *кого* в свою пользу ог в пользу *чью, кого* to evoke a favorable attitude toward o.s. or s.o.: [of a person] X расположил Y-а в свою пользу ≃ **X gained ⟨won⟩ Y's support ⟨favor⟩; X won Y over; X got into Y's good books**

⟨good graces⟩; ‖ Y расположен в X-ову пользу ≃ **Y is well-disposed toward X; Y looks favorably upon X; X is in Y's good books** ⟨**good graces**⟩; ‖ X расположил Y-а в Z-ову пользу ≃ **X gained** ⟨**won**⟩ **Z the support of Y; X made Y look favorably upon Z; X helped Z get into Y's good books** ⟨**good graces**⟩; ‖ [of a person's qualities] X-ова скромность ⟨откровенность и т. п.⟩ располагает в его пользу ≃ **X's modesty** ⟨**frankness etc**⟩ **produces a favorable impression;** ‖ Neg X-ово упрямство ⟨бахвальство и т. п.⟩ не располагает в его пользу ≃ **X's obstinacy** ⟨**bragging etc**⟩ **works against him.**

Помочь тебе может только Семён Михайлович. Поговори с ним, постарайся расположить его в свою пользу. The only one who can help you is Semyon Mikhailovich. Talk to him, and try to win his support. ♦ Её манера вести себя не располагает в её пользу: она слишком заносчива и самоуверенна. The way she behaves works against her: she's too arrogant and self-assured.

П-323 • **В ПО́ЛЬЗУ БЕ́ДНЫХ** coll, iron [PrepP; Invar; adv, nonagreeing modif (of разговор, занятие etc), or subj-compl with copula (subj: abstr, often всё); fixed WO] (to do sth.) uselessly, producing no positive, constructive results; **useless (talk, work etc); sth. is useless: (do sth.) in vain; (do sth.** ⟨**sth. is**⟩**) to no avail; (sth. is) an exercise in futility; futile** ([NP]); [of talk only] **(nothing but) palaver; a lot of hot air.**

Городской совет с утра до вечера обсуждает, как улучшить жизнь горожан, но всё это разговоры в пользу бедных: у городских властей нет денег. The municipal council discusses from morning till night how to improve citizens' lives, but all their talking is an exercise in futility: the city government is penniless.

П-324 • **ГОВОРИ́ТЬ** ⟨**СВИДЕ́ТЕЛЬСТВОВАТЬ**⟩ **В ПО́ЛЬЗУ** чью, кого-чего [VP; subj: abstr] to serve as evidence of the positive qualities of s.o. or sth.: X говорит в пользу Y-а ≃ **X speaks well of Y; X is to person Y's credit;** ‖ Neg X не говорит в пользу Y-а ≃ [in limited contexts] **X does nothing to improve Y's reputation** ⟨**the reputation of Y**⟩.

Она [аристократия] существовала, оказалось, лишь в своей классовой принадлежности, у неё не было идеи... У неё ничего не оказалось, когда у неё отняли принадлежность к классу. И то, что не все были враги, тоже не говорит в её пользу (Битов 2). They [the aristocrats] turned out to have existed only in their class affiliation, they lacked an idea....There was nothing left to them when their class affiliation was taken away. Nor does it speak well of the aristocracy that they were not all enemies (2a). ♦ Короче, то, что у Якоба мать немка, говорит только в его пользу (Рыбаков 1). In a nutshell, the fact that Jakob's mother was a German was only to his credit (1a). ♦ ...Уж одно то, что она [жимолость] подделывалась под голубицу и не имела своего чистого вида, не говорило в пользу этой жимолости (Распутин 4). ...The fact that it [honeysuckle] pretended to look like bilberry and didn't have its own appearance did nothing to improve its reputation (4a).

П-325 • **НА ПО́ЛЬЗУ** кому-чему [PrepP; Invar; subj-compl with быть∅, идти etc (subj: abstr or concr)] sth. is beneficial for some person or thing: X (идёт) Y-у ~ ≃ **X is good for Y; X does Y good; X helps Y; X is** ⟨**works out**⟩ **to Y's advantage; Y benefits from X;** [in limited contexts] **it's for Y's own good.**

«Фрукты полезны, вино сухое... Пей, ешь — всё на пользу будет» (Рыбаков 2). "...The fruit is good, and dry wine....Eat and drink, it's all good for you" (2a). ♦ ...Пиво Ефим, конечно, пьёт и пьёт много, в этом он себе не отказывает, и пей, пей, Фима, если тебе на пользу (Аксёнов 6). ...Yefim, of course, drank beer and drank a lot of it—he never deprived himself of this—so OK, drink, Yefim, drink, if it does you good (6a). ♦ «...Какая бы чума на нашу голову ни свалилась, а эндурцам, глядишь, всё на пользу» (Искандер 5). "No matter what plague lands on us, it works out to the Endurskies' advantage" (5a). ♦ Кто-то сказал, что он прекрасно

выглядит, Лёва, и что воздержание на пользу не одному Толстому (Битов 2). Someone said that he looked wonderful, Lyova did, and that Tolstoy wasn't the only one to benefit from abstinence (2a). ♦ ...Наташка молодец. Правда, она держит Антона под каблуком. Но это ему на пользу (Зиновьев 2). ...Natasha is wonderful. It's true she keeps Anton under her thumb, but it's for his own good (2a).

П-326 • **ПОЛЮБИ́ТЕ НАС ЧЁРНЕНЬКИМИ, А БЕ́ЛЕНЬКИМИ ВСЯ́КИЙ ПОЛЮ́БИТ** [saying] accept, appreciate, love us just as we are, with our shortcomings because we cannot and/or do not want to change: ≃ **take us as you find us; take us as we are; accept us for what we are.**

П-327 • **ОДНОГО́** ⟨**ТОГО́ ЖЕ, СВОЕГО́, НА́ШЕГО** и т. п.⟩ **ПО́ЛЯ Я́ГОДА** ⟨**Я́ГОДЫ, Я́ГОДКИ**⟩ coll [NP; subj-compl with быть∅ (subj: human); pres only; fixed WO] (in refer. to personality traits, behaviors etc, often negative ones) s.o. is very similar to another (named or implied) person; two or more persons are very similar to each other: X и Y одного поля ягоды ≃ **X and Y are birds of a feather; X and Y are two of a kind; X and Y are tarred with the same brush; X and Y are cast in the same mold; X and Y are of the same ilk** ⟨**stripe**⟩; ‖ Neg X — не нашего поля ягода ≃ **X is cast in a different mold (from us); X is of a different breed (from us); X is a bird of a different feather (from us).**

Понимает она хоть капельку Ирунчика или нисколько? Одного они с нею поля ягоды или с разных планет? (Залыгин 1). Had she an ounce of understanding for Irunchik, or none at all? Were they birds of a feather, or were they from different planets? (1a). ♦ [Платонов:] Это подобие твоё; разница только в том, что он умней тебя... Одного поля ягоды... (Чехов 1). [P.:] ...He's the same as you, except for having more sense....You're both tarred with the same brush... (1b). ♦ [Антонина Николаевна:] Я с удовольствием вышла бы замуж за богатого, честного человека, но где такой? Они — не нашего поля ягода (Розов 3). [A.N.:] I would be delighted to marry a rich, honest man, but where is there one? They are birds of a different feather from us (3a).

П-328 • **ПОМАТРО́СИЛ И БРО́СИЛ** highly coll [VP; subj: human, male (usu. omitted); more often past; fixed WO] a man has had a short and casual affair with a woman and then left her: **you've** ⟨**he's**⟩ **had your** ⟨**his**⟩ **fun, and now it's good-bye; love 'em and leave 'em; use them and lose them.**

«Так, Лашков, так, Вася, — отчеканила она. — Так. Выходит, о шкуре своей печёшься? А я как?.. Как я? Поматросил и бросил. Наше вам, мол, с кисточкой? Спасибо, Вася, только временить и ждать тебя я не собираюсь» (Максимов 3). "All right, Lashkov, all right, Vasilii," she said slowly and distinctly. "Right. So you're worried about your own skin, are you? And what about me?...What about me? You've had your fun, and now it's good-bye and good luck? Thanks, Vasilii, but I won't be hanging around to wait for you..." (3a).

П-329 • **И ПОМИ́НА** ⟨**-у**⟩ **нет** о ком-чём obs [NP_{gen}; these forms only; used as subj/gen] **1.** (s.o. or sth. is) not discussed or referred to at all in conversation: об X-е и помину не было ≃ **X was not even mentioned** ⟨**made mention of**⟩; **no mention was made of X; not a word was said about X.**

...Опять Анисья заговорила носом, что «она в первый раз от хозяйки слышит о свадьбе, что в разговорах с ней даже помину не было, да и свадьбы нет, и статочное ли дело?» (Гончаров 1). ...Again Anisya's nose proclaimed that this was the first time she had ever heard the landlady speak of a wedding; that it had never even been mentioned between them; and there was no wedding, was there, and how could such a thing be possible? (1b).

2. (s.o. or sth. is) completely absent, entirely missing, nonexistent etc: об X-е и помину не было ≃ **there was no sign of X; there was not even ⟨not so much as⟩ a hint ⟨a trace etc⟩ of X.**

П-330 • ПОМИНА́Й КАК ЗВА́ЛИ *coll* [Invar; predic or indep. clause; usu. follows one or more predicates having the same subj; used in pres, past, and future contexts; fixed WO] **1.** ~ *(кого)* [impers or with subj: human] s.o. died, perished or will die, perish: (X-а) поминай как звали ≃ [in past contexts] **that was the end of X; that was the end of the road (for X); it was all over (for X).**

«…Или, может, и сам [ты], лёжа на полатях, думал, думал, да ни с того ни с другого заворотил в кабак, а потом прямо в прорубь, и поминай как звали» (Гоголь 3). "Or perhaps you took to brooding lying at night on your bunk over the oven, and then suddenly, for no reason whatsoever, after a stop at a tavern, headed straight for the river, jumped into a hole in the ice, and that was the end of you" (3c). ♦ «Пора положить конец всему: пропадай душа, пойду утоплюсь… и поминай как звали!» (Гоголь 5). "It's time to put an end to it all. Damn my soul, I'll go and drown myself…and it will all be over!" (5a).

2. Also: **МИ́ТЬКОЙ ЗВА́ЛИ** *substand* [impers or with subj: human (both variants) or animal (var. with поминай only)] s.o. disappeared and has not been seen since, or will disappear and not be seen again: X ушёл ⟨уехал и т. п.⟩ и поминай как звали ≃ **X left ⟨took off etc⟩ and that's the last we ⟨I etc⟩ ever saw of him; X left etc and we ⟨I etc⟩ haven't seen him since; X left ⟨disappeared etc⟩, never to return ⟨never to be seen again, never to be heard of again⟩; X left ⟨disappeared etc⟩ and was never heard of again.**

После смерти матери Михаил уехал из родной деревни — и поминай как звали. After his mother's death Mikhail left his native village, never to return.

3. [used as a clause] (in refer. to sth. mentioned in the preceding context that has been lost, stolen, borrowed etc) sth. was never seen again or will never be seen again: [in past contexts] **(and) that's the last we ⟨I etc⟩ (ever) saw of it; (and) we ⟨I etc⟩ never saw it again; (and) we ⟨I etc⟩ haven't seen it since; it disappeared without a trace; [in limited contexts] it had vanished into thin air.**

«Дай, Захар, фрак, не упрямься!» — «Не дам! — холодно отвечал Захар. — Пусть прежде они принесут назад жилет да нашу рубашку… Взяли вот этак же на именины, да и поминай как звали…» (Гончаров 1). "Don't be obstinate, Zakhar, bring the coat." "I won't!" Zakhar answered coldly. "Let him first return your waistcoat and shirt….He borrowed them to go to a birthday party and we've never seen them since" (1a). ♦ На другой день хватился — нет топора. Обыскал всё — нет, поминай как звали (Распутин 2). …The next day he noticed that the ax was gone. He searched everywhere—it was gone, vanished into thin air (2a).

П-331 • (И) В ПОМИ́НЕ нет, не осталось *кого-чего (где, у кого) coll* [PrepP; these forms only; adv] (s.o. or sth. is) completely absent, entirely missing etc: X-а и в помине не было ≃ **there was no sign of X; there was not even ⟨not so much as⟩ a hint ⟨a trace⟩ of X; there was no ⟨not the slightest⟩ hint ⟨trace⟩ of X; [in limited contexts] there wasn't even a mention of X; [in refer. to a specific character trait] person Y didn't possess ⟨have⟩ any X at all; [in refer. to a false account, invented story etc] person Y made it ⟨things⟩ up out of thin air.**

Впервые чувство отщепенства зародилось у Мандельштама в двадцатые годы. В ранних стихах его нет и в помине… (Мандельштам 2). The feeling that he was an outsider first came to M[andelstam] in the twenties.…There is no sign of it in his early verse (2a). ♦ Естественно, что никаких шашлыков здесь и в помине не было… (Попов 1). Naturally there wasn't even a hint of

any shashlik here (1a). ♦ К тому времени у неё и в помине не было любви к Григорию (Абрамов 1). …By then she was feeling not so much as a hint of love for Grigory (1a). ♦ Хватаю справочник Союза писателей, открываю на нужную букву: Иванович, Ивантер, Ивасюк, нет здесь Иванько и в помине (Войнович 3). I grabbed the directory of the Writers' Union, opened to the necessary letter: Ivanovich, Ivanter, Ivasyuk, not even a mention of Ivanko here (3a). ♦ Как это ни странно, Б. Л. [Пастернак] относился к нему [критику Т.] снисходительно. Он приписывал Т. какую-то непонятную ему сложность и особого рода тонкость, чего не было и в помине (Гладков 1). Strange to say, Pasternak took a lenient view of [the critic] T., crediting him with some peculiar kind of unfathomable depth and subtlety which in actual fact he did not possess at all (1a).

П-332 • ЛЁГОК ⟨ЛЁГКИЙ⟩ НА ПОМИ́НЕ *coll* [AdjP; subj-compl with быть₀, subj: human (usu. short-form var.) or detached modif (long-form var.); fixed WO] s.o. appears suddenly (and usu. unexpectedly) just as or right after he is mentioned or thought of: **speak ⟨talk⟩ of the devil.**

[Каретников:] А ну-ка, почему-ка Свидерского нет? Ему бы надлежало быть… *(В калитку входит Свидерский Леонид Казимирович…)* Лёгок на помине! (Арбузов 1). [K.:] And why isn't Svidersky here? He should be among those present….*(Leonid Svidersky enters by the garden gate…)* [K.:] Talk of the devil! (1a).

П-333 • НЕ ПО́МНИТЬ СЕБЯ́ (от радости, от счастья, от ярости, от боли и т. п.) *coll;* **СЕБЯ́ НЕ СЛЫ́ШАТЬ** *obs* [VP; subj: human] to be gripped by intense emotion, not be in control of one's behavior, actions etc (as the result of great joy, passion, pain etc): X не помнил себя (от Y-а) ≃ **X was beside himself (with Y); X forgot himself; X didn't know ⟨had no idea⟩ what he was doing; X got carried away; X got ⟨was⟩ out of control; X lost control of himself.**

Мария Вениаминовна долго играла Шопена; Б. Л. [Пастернак] был особенно возбуждён музыкой, глаза его блестели. А я себя не помнила от счастья (Ивинская 1). Maria Veniaminovna played Chopin for a long time. B.L. [Pasternak] was particularly affected by the music and his eyes shone. I was beside myself with happiness (1a). ♦ …Виктор тоже закричал, не помня себя от ужаса при мысли о том, что сейчас произойдёт (Стругацкие 1). Victor also started to shout, forgetting himself in horrified awareness of what was about to happen (1a). ♦ «Хотят вывести, что брат сумасшедший и убил в помешательстве, себя не помня, — тихо улыбнулся Алёша, — только брат не согласится на это» (Достоевский 2). "They want to establish that my brother is crazy and killed in a fit of madness, not knowing what he was doing," Alyosha smiled quietly, "only my brother won't agree to it" (2a). ♦ …Предводитель вошёл уже в ярость и не помнил себя (Салтыков-Щедрин 1). …The marshal was already rabid and out of control (1a).

П-334 • ВЫБРА́СЫВАТЬ/ВЫ́БРОСИТЬ НА ПОМО́ЙКУ *кого-что highly coll* [VP; subj: human] to rid o.s. of an unwanted person or thing, usu. in a harsh manner: X выбросил Y-а на помойку ≃ **X relegated Y to the ash heap ⟨pile⟩; X dumped ⟨ditched⟩ Y; X threw ⟨tossed, kicked⟩ Y out; [in refer. to firing] X sacked person Y; X gave person Y the boot ⟨the sack, the ax⟩.**

Мне больно, что он так опустился. Он мой старый друг, а старых друзей не выбрасывают на помойку. It hurts me to see how he's let himself go. He's an old friend, and you don't relegate old friends to the ash heap.

П-335 • ВОДИ́ТЬ ⟨ДЕРЖА́ТЬ⟩ НА ПОМОЧА́Х *кого* [VP; subj: human] to control and, often, overprotect s.o., not giving him the freedom to act independently: X водит Y-а на помочах ≃ **X keeps Y on a (short) leash; X won't let Y fly on**

his own; **X won't let Y become his own person;** [of a woman dominating her husband, son etc] **X has ⟨keeps⟩ Y tied to her apron strings.**

Слушай, твоему сыну уже за тридцать, а ты всё его на помочах держишь. Он без тебя шагу ступить не может. Listen, your son is already over thirty, and still you keep him tied to your apron strings. He can't make a move without you.

< «Помочи» are straps used to support a toddler under the arms when he or she is learning to walk.

П-336 • ХОДИ́ТЬ НА ПОМОЧА́Х у кого; **НА ПОМО-ЧА́Х** [VP or PrepP (Invar, used as subj-compl with быть₀); subj: human] to submit to the wishes or leadership of another because of one's own lack of confidence, independence etc: X ходит у Y-а на помочах ≃ **X is on Y's leash;** [of a man dominated by his wife, mother etc] **X is tied to Y's apron strings.**

< See П-335.

П-337 • ПРИ ПО́МОЩИ ⟨С ПО́МОЩЬЮ⟩ чего [PrepP; these forms only; Prep; the resulting PrepP is adv] with the aid of (sth.): **using; with the help of.**

В это время дамы отошли от колодца и поравнялись с нами. Грушницкий успел принять драматическую позу с помощью костыля и громко отвечал мне по-французски… (Лермонтов 1). At this point the ladies moved away from the well and came level with us. With the aid of his crutch Grushnitsky struck a dramatic pose and answered me loudly in French… (1c).

П-338 • (ВОТ) Э́ТО Я ПОНИМА́Ю! coll [Interj; these forms only; fixed WO] (used to express approval, delight, encouragement etc) that is wonderful, this is an outstanding (person, accomplishment etc): **you can't beat that ⟨this⟩!; that's ⟨this is⟩ great!; (now) that's ⟨this is⟩ what I call…!**

«Сегодня у нас на десерт будет наполеон». — «Вот это я понимаю!» "Today for dessert we're having napoleons." "That's what I call dessert!"

П-339 • ДЛЯ ПО́НТА slang, orig. camp slang [PrepP; Invar; adv] for effect, in order to produce an impression on those watching: **for show; (in order) to show off; (in order) to make a splash.**

«Антонина Валерьяновна, не вы ли у меня взяли лупу? Нельзя ли попросить на минутку?» Лупа была ему абсолютно не нужна… но делалось это… для понта, и Нержин внутренне хохотал… (Солженицын 3). "Antonina Valeryanovna, was it you who took the magnifying glass? Could I please have it a moment?" He had absolutely no need of the magnifying glass…but this was done…for show, and Nerzhin laughed inwardly… (3a).

П-340 • НИ ЗА ПОНЮ́ШКУ ⟨ПОНЮ́Х⟩ ТАБАКУ́ пропасть, погибнуть, погубить кого etc highly coll [PrepP; these forms only; adv; more often used with pfv verbs] (to die, be killed, have one's career destroyed etc, or to kill s.o., destroy s.o.'s career etc) purposelessly, futilely, needlessly: **(all) for naught ⟨for nothing⟩; in vain; to no purpose; for no (good) reason.**

И там… на песке жгли костёр. Смолянов говорил, что там ютится шпана, ходить опасно. Вот если сейчас спуститься вниз — свободно прирежут, ни за понюх табаку (Трифонов 1). Down on the sand…someone had lighted a campfire. Smolyanov told her that this was a gathering place for various criminal types and that the area was unsafe. And if they were to venture down there right now, somebody might knife them—just like that, for no good reason (1a).

П-341 • С ПОНЯ́ТИЕМ substand [PrepP; Invar; nonagreeing postmodif or subj-compl with быть₀ (subj: human or animal)] knowledgeable, competent, clever: X (парень) с понятием ≃ **X has plenty ⟨a lot⟩ on the ball; X is no dummy; X is (really)**

smart; **X is a smart [NP]; X knows his onions;** [in limited contexts] **X is a man ⟨a women etc⟩ with ideas.**

Карько — конь с понятием. Самый трудный перевал… просадил без остановки (Абрамов 1). Blacky is a smart horse. The hardest pass…he made without a stop (1a). ♦ [Большов:] …Он малый с понятием, да и капиталец есть (Островский 10). [B.:] He's a youngster with ideas; and besides, he has a little money (10a).

П-342 • НЕ ИМЕ́ТЬ ПОНЯ́ТИЯ (о чём or что…, где…, зачем… и т. п.) coll [VP; subj: human] not to know (some fact) or not to have any knowledge (in some area): X не имел понятия ≃ **X had no idea; X didn't have ⟨hadn't⟩ the slightest ⟨the foggiest⟩ (idea ⟨notion⟩); X didn't have a clue; X was clueless;** ‖ X не имеет понятия об Y-е ≃ **X doesn't know a thing about Y; X is clueless when it comes to Y;** ‖ [when used as a response only] понятия не имею! ≃ **beats me!; you got me!; don't ask me!**

Он [отец Алексей] сел за зелёный стол с умеренным изъявлением удовольствия и кончил тем, что обыграл Базарова на два рубля пятьдесят копеек ассигнациями: в доме Арины Власьевны и понятия не имели о счёте на серебро… (Тургенев 2). He [Father Alexei] took his seat at the card-table with a moderated show of pleasure and ended by winning from Bazarov two and a half roubles in paper money: in Arina Vlassyevna's house they had no idea of how to reckon in silver… (2c). ♦ Я стал её [девушку] искать. Я знал, что я её увижу, а что дальше будет — понятия не имел (Искандер 6). I began to look for her [the girl]. Although I knew that I would eventually find her, I hadn't the slightest idea what would happen after that (6a).

П-343 • КАКО́В ПОП, ТАКО́В И ПРИХО́Д [saying] as a leader behaves, so do his subordinates, followers etc ≃ **judge the flock by its priest; like priest, like people; like master, like man.**

«А что ты делал в моём саду?» — «Малину крал», — отвечал мальчик с большим равнодушием. «Ага, слуга в барина, каков поп, таков и приход…» (Пушкин 1). "What were you doing in my garden?" "I was stealing raspberries," the boy replied with great equanimity. "Aha! Like master, like servant. Judge the flock by its priest" (1b).

П-344 • КОМУ́ ПОП, КОМУ́ ПОПАДЬЯ́, А КОМУ́ ПОПО́ВА ДО́ЧКА; КТО ЛЮ́БИТ ПОПА́, (А) КТО ПОПАДЬЮ́, (А) КТО ПОПО́ВУ ДО́ЧКУ both obs [saying; often only the first half of the saying is used] people enjoy different things, everyone has his own taste: ≃ **every man to his taste; each to his own taste; there is no accounting for tastes; one man's meat is another man's poison.**

«На вкусы нет закона: кто любит попа, а кто попадью, говорит пословица» (Гоголь 3). "Every man to his taste; what's one man's meat is another man's poison, as the proverb has it" (3b).

П-345 • НА ПОПА́ поставить что, **стать** highly coll [PrepP; Invar; adv] (usu. of or in refer. to oblong objects) (to put sth., stand etc) in a vertical position: поставить что на попа ≃ **set sth. (up) on end; set ⟨stand⟩ sth. (up) on its end; upend sth.; stand sth. up; stand ⟨prop, place⟩ sth. upright;** ‖ стать на попа ≃ **stand ⟨stay⟩ upright.**

Сологдин проследил, как младшина [here ≃ младший лейтенант] завёл Нержина в штаб, потом поправил чурбак на попа и с таким ожесточением размахнулся, что не только развалил его на две плахи, но ещё вогнал топор в землю (Солженицын 3). Sologdin watched as the junior lieutenant led Nerzhin into the staff building; then he set the piece of wood up on end and struck it so violently that he not only split it in two but drove the ax into the ground (3a). ♦ «Баллон с кислородом надо поднять на четвёртый этаж…» Баллоны лежали возле подъезда в грязи. Я поднял с земли щепку, поставил баллон на попа и очистил его немного (Войнович 5). "The oxygen cylinder has to be hoisted up to the fourth floor...." The cylinders were lying in the mud near the entrance. I upended the cylinder, then picked up a piece of wood from the ground and used it to scrape off some of the mud (5a). ♦ И вместе с этим вопросом догадка и мурашки по спине: постой, да не мертвец ли это, поставленный на попа! (Искандер 4). And with this question a guess, and more tingles down the spine: Wait! Was this a dead man, propped upright? (4a).

П-346 • ПÉРВЫЙ ПОПÁВШИЙСЯ ⟨ПОПÁВШИЙ

substand⟩ [AdjP (used as modif) or NP; fixed WO] whatever person or thing happens to be closest by, soonest available, easiest to reach, most readily obtainable etc: **the first [NP] (that) one comes across; the first [NP] one sees ⟨meets, runs into, can get one's hands on etc⟩; the first [NP] one happens to see ⟨to meet, to come across etc⟩; the first [NP] that comes to hand; the first [NP] who ⟨that⟩ turns up; the first [NP] to come along; the first available [NP];** [of sth. recalled, thought of] **the first [NP] that comes to mind.**

«Какую газету тебе купить?» — «Да первую попавшуюся». "What newspaper should I buy you?" "Oh, the first you come across." ♦ ...[Пьер] взял первую попавшуюся с полки книгу (это были Записки Цезаря) и принялся, облокотившись, читать её из середины (Толстой 4). ...[Pierre] took from the shelf the first book that came to hand (it was Caesar's *Commentaries*), and, propping his head on his elbow, commenced reading it from the middle (4a).

П-347 • ПОПАДÁТЬ/ПОПÁСТЬ ⟨ПОПАДÁТЬСЯ/ ПОПÁСТЬСЯ *obs*⟩ ВПРОСÁК *coll* [VP; subj: human; fixed WO] to end up in an uncomfortable, embarrassing, disadvantageous situation because of one's mistake or one's ignorance of sth.: X попал впросак ≃ **X put his foot in it ⟨in his mouth⟩; X made a gaffe ⟨a blunder⟩; X made a fool of himself.**

Мне захотелось спросить, зачем Катыку отличаться хоть чем-нибудь от других, но, чтобы не попасть впросак, я промолчала (Каверин 1). I would have liked to ask why Katyk wanted to make himself different from the others in some way, but I kept quiet for fear I should put my foot in it (1a).

< Originally, «попадать в просак». «Просак» was a machine used for making ropes. Workers' clothes often got drawn into it, thus putting them in an awkward, potentially dangerous position.

П-348 • ГДЕ ⟨КУДÁ⟩ ПОПÁЛО *coll;* ГДЕ ⟨КУДÁ⟩ НИ ПОПÁЛО *obs, substand;* ГДЕ ⟨КУДÁ⟩ ПРИ-ДЁТСЯ [AdvP; these forms only; adv; fixed WO] in or to any place, not one specifically or carefully chosen (when said critically, expresses the speaker's opinion that not selecting carefully is negligent, unacceptable etc): **wherever (one happens to be ⟨sth. ends up etc⟩); anywhere (one wants ⟨feels like etc⟩); anywhere at all; it doesn't matter (where); any old place;** [often when said critically] **just anywhere; God knows where;** ‖ разбежаться ⟨побежать и т. п.⟩ куда попало ≃ **scatter ⟨run etc⟩ in all (different) directions; scatter ⟨run etc⟩ every which way.**

...В моё время... люди изданные на Западе книги не только у себя дома, на семь замков запершись, читали, а где попало, в том числе и в общественном транспорте (Войнович 1). ...In my time...people did not read books published in the West only at home with every lock on every door locked, but indulged wherever they happened to be, even on public transportation (1a). ♦ Первое время Илья совал бумаги куда придётся... А потом увидел — надо наводить порядок, иначе запутаешься (Абрамов 1). At first Ilya had shoved his papers any old place....But then he realized that he needed to organize things or there'd be a muddle (1a). ♦ Домой приходишь только поесть, грубишь матери, ночуешь где попало! Безобразие! You come home only to eat, you're rude to your

mother, and you spend the nights God knows where! This is outrageous! ♦ Один отчаянный, испуганный крик первого увидавшего казаков француза — и всё, что было в лагере, неодетое, спросонков бросило пушки, ружья, лошадей и побежало куда попало (Толстой 7). One desperate, terrified cry from the first French soldier to catch sight of the Cossacks, and the men in the camp, half-dressed and half-asleep, ran in all directions, abandoning cannons, muskets, and horses (7a).

П-349 • КАК ПОПÁЛО *coll;* КАК НИ ПОПÁЛО *obs, substand;* КАК ПРИДЁТСЯ [AdvP; these forms only; adv; fixed WO] in any way, not paying particular attention to how, and, often, not paying attention to the quality of the results of the action (usu. said critically to express the speaker's opinion that the action should have been carried out more diligently, with more care, and that the result should have been better): **any which ⟨old⟩ way; haphazardly; carelessly;** [in limited contexts] **at random;** [when said critically only] **God knows how.**

Одевается [Гартвиг] как попало. Чаще всего он появлялся в нашем доме в каких-то полутуристских-полуспортивных обносках... (Трифонов 5). He [Gartwig] dresses any which way. Most of the time he appeared at our apartment in some sort of old gym or hiking clothes... (5a). ♦ Дельце, о котором просил хозяин, касалось его сбежавшей жены. Начал он издалека, говоря, что он уже не мальчик, чтобы есть что попало и как попало, а человек в летах, и ему нужен человек, который мог бы приготовить и подать ему пищу (Искандер 4). The favor that [our host] Omar had requested concerned his runaway wife. He began in a roundabout way, saying that he was no longer a boy, to eat any old thing fixed any old way; he was a man getting on in years, he needed a person who could prepare and serve his food for him (4a). ♦ Бились крепко всю ночь, бились не глядя, а как попало... Только когда уже совсем рассвело, увидели, что бьются свои с своими... (Салтыков-Щедрин 1). They fought hard all night, fought without looking, haphazardly....Only when it was broad daylight did they see they were fighting their own... (1a). ♦ У двери [Ленин] натянул тяжёлое пальто, насадил котелок как попало, побрёл (Солженицын 5). At the door he [Lenin] pulled on his heavy overcoat, carelessly crammed on his bowler hat, and shuffled off (5a). ♦ Отделы карательных органов использовали своих агентов по назначению, а не как попало (Мандельштам 2). The various departments of the security services used their agents according to their qualifications, not just at random (2a).

П-350 • КАКÓЙ ПОПÁЛО *coll;* КАКÓЙ НИ ПОПÁЛО *obs, substand;* КАКÓЙ ПРИДЁТСЯ [AdvP; modif; fixed WO] any one, not one specifically or carefully chosen (when said critically, expresses the speaker's opinion that not selecting carefully is negligent, unacceptable etc): **whichever (one) (s.o. sees first ⟨s.o. wants etc⟩); whichever (one) comes to hand; any one ⟨kind⟩ (at all); it doesn't matter (which one ⟨what kind⟩);** [often when said critically] **just any one ⟨kind⟩; God knows what kind.**

«Какую сковородку взять?» — «Какую попало». "Which frying pan should I use?" "Whichever one comes to hand." ♦ «Почему бы тебе не одолжить велосипед у своего брата?» — «Потому что мне нужен гоночный велосипед, а не какой попало!» "Why not borrow your brother's bike?" "Because I need a racing bike, not just any kind of bike!"

П-351 • КОГДÁ ПОПÁЛО *coll;* КОГДÁ НИ ПОПÁЛО *obs, substand;* КОГДÁ ПРИДЁТСЯ [AdvP; these forms only; adv; fixed WO] at any time, not one specifically or carefully chosen (when said critically, expresses the speaker's opinion that not selecting carefully is negligent, unacceptable etc): **whenever (one feels like it ⟨one gets around to it, one happens to think of it, it's convenient etc⟩); anytime (one wants etc); it doesn't**

matter (when); [usu. when said critically] **just anytime; God knows when** ⟨**at God knows what hour** etc⟩.

«Я всегда встаю в семь утра. А ты?» – «А я – когда попало, мне ведь на работу ходить не нужно». "I get up at seven o'clock every morning. How about you?" "I get up whenever I feel like it; after all, I don't have to go to work." ♦ Скажи своим друзьям, чтобы они перестали звонить когда попало. Звонят ночью, спать не дают. Tell your friends to stop calling you at God knows what hour. They phone in the middle of the night and won't let us sleep.

П-352 • **КТО ПОПА́ЛО** *coll;* **КТО НИ ПОПА́ЛО** *obs, substand;* **КТО ПРИДЁТСЯ** [NP; fixed WO] any person, not one specifically or carefully chosen (when said critically, expresses the speaker's opinion that not selecting carefully is negligent, unacceptable etc): **whoever (happens to be available** ⟨**happens to be there** etc⟩**); who(m)ever (s.o. sees first** ⟨**s.o. can find** etc⟩**); anyone** ⟨**anybody**⟩ **(s.o. can find** ⟨**who happens to be there** etc⟩**); it doesn't matter (who);** [in limited contexts] **anyone and everyone; (ask** ⟨**punish** etc⟩ **people) at random;** [usu. when said critically] **just anyone** ⟨**anybody**⟩**; God knows who.**

«Как же так? – спросила Вика. – Ты пришла с нами, а танцуешь с кем попало» (Рыбаков 2). "What are you doing?" Vika asked. "You came here with us, but you're dancing with anyone who asks you" (2a). ♦ «...Народ какой-то пошёл слабонервный. И чего они нас [КГБ] боятся? Мы же кого попало не хватаем, а только по ордеру» (Войнович 2). "People's nerves are starting to go. Why are they so afraid of us [the KGB]? We just don't grab anybody we bump into, there's got to be a warrant" (2a). ♦ «... Мне это отделение известно! Там кому попало выдают паспорта!» (Булгаков 9). "I know this department—they issue passports to anyone and everyone" (9a). ♦ Террор в том и заключается, что берут кого попало для острастки оставленных на воле (Мандельштам 2). The whole point of terror is that people are arrested at random in order to instill fear into everybody else (2a).

П-353 • **ОТКУ́ДА ПОПА́ЛО** *coll;* **ОТКУ́ДА НИ ПОПА́ЛО** *obs, substand;* **ОТКУ́ДА ПРИДЁТСЯ** [AdvP; these forms only; adv; fixed WO] from any place, not one specifically or carefully chosen (when said critically, expresses the speaker's opinion that not selecting carefully is negligent, unacceptable etc): **from wherever (one can get it** ⟨**one wants** etc⟩**); from anywhere** ⟨**anyplace**⟩ **(one wants** ⟨**one can get it** etc⟩**); from anywhere** ⟨**anyplace**⟩ **at all; it doesn't matter where from** ⟨**from where**⟩**; from any old place;** [usu. when said critically] **from just anywhere; from God knows where.**

«...Я, видишь ли, любитель и собиратель некоторых фактиков и, веришь ли, записываю и собираю из газет и рассказов, откуда попало, некоторого рода анекдотики...» (Достоевский 1). "...You see, I'm an amateur and collector of certain little facts; I copy them down from newspapers and stories, from wherever, and save them—would you believe it?—certain kinds of little anecdotes" (1a).

П-354 • **ЧТО ПОПА́ЛО** *coll;* **ЧТО НИ ПОПА́ЛО** *obs, substand;* **ЧТО ПРИДЁТСЯ** [NP; fixed WO] anything, not sth. specifically or carefully chosen (when said critically, expresses the speaker's opinion that not selecting carefully is negligent, unacceptable etc): **whatever (comes to hand** ⟨**is handy** etc⟩**); anything (one can get hold of** ⟨**that comes to hand** etc⟩**); it doesn't matter (what); any old thing;** [in limited contexts] **anything and everything; (take** ⟨**use** etc⟩ **things) at random;** [with verbs of speaking] **(say** etc**) whatever** ⟨**anything that**⟩ **comes to mind; whatever comes** ⟨**pops**⟩ **into s.o.'s head;** [usu. when said critically] **just anything; God knows what.**

...Наиболее отважные и сильные жители местечка снабжены особыми бляхами с соответствующим номером, чтобы в случае пожара не метаться, не хватать что попало, а

бежать к месту бедствия со своим инструментом (Искандер 3). ...The town's bravest and strongest inhabitants were provided with special nameplates with corresponding numbers, so that in the event of a fire they would not cast about, seizing whatever came to hand, but would run to the scene of the disaster with their own implements (3a). ♦ Случалось, брали фотоаппарат со вспышкой и... снимали перепуганных, оглушённых любовников, наспех чем попало прикрывших свою срамоту (Ерофеев 3). Sometimes they brought a camera [with a flash] and would snap pictures of the dumbfounded, panic-stricken lovers trying to cover themselves with whatever was handy (3a). ♦ Недалеко от Доброго огромная толпа оборванных, обвязанных и укутанных чем попало пленных гудела говором, стоя на дороге подле длинного ряда отпряжённых французских орудий (Толстой 7) Near Dobroe an immense crowd of tattered prisoners buzzing with talk, and wrapped and bandaged in anything they had been able to get hold of, were standing in the road beside a long row of unharnessed French guns (7b). ♦ Дельце, о котором просил хозяин, касалось его сбежавшей жены. Начал он издалека, говоря, что он уже не мальчик, чтобы есть что попало и как попало, а человек в летах, и ему нужен человек, который мог бы приготовить и подать ему пищу (Искандер 4). The favor that [our host] Omar had requested concerned his runaway wife. He began in a roundabout way, saying that he was no longer a boy, to eat any old thing fixed any old way; he was a man getting on in years, he needed a person who could prepare and serve his food for him (4a). ♦ ...Он [Чернышевский] делал вид, что несёт что попало, ради одной пустой и тёмной болтовни, — но в полосах и пятнах слов, в словесном камуфляже, вдруг проскакивала нужная мысль (Набоков 1). ...Chernyshevski would pretend he was chattering about anything that came to mind, just for the sake of incoherent and vacant prattle—but suddenly, striped and spotted with words, dressed in verbal camouflage, the important idea he wished to convey would slip through (1a).

П-355 • **ТЫ** ⟨**он** и т. п.⟩ **У МЕНЯ́ ПОПЛЯ́ШЕШЬ** ⟨**-ет** и т. п.⟩ *coll* [VP_subj; fut only; usu. this WO] (used as a threat) I will punish you (him etc), make things difficult for you (him etc): **X у меня попляшет** ≃ **I'll give X what for; I'll give it to X (good); X'll get** ⟨**catch**⟩ **it from me; I'll teach X a lesson he'll never forget; I'll get X for it** ⟨**this, that**⟩**.**

Не могу даже описать, что дальше было с Ефимом. Он вскакивал, бегал по комнате, размахивал руками, бормотал что-то вроде того, что кто-то у него теперь попляшет... (Войнович 6). It's difficult to describe what happened next. Yefim kept jumping up, running around the room and waving his arms, and muttering something to the effect that now he would give that so-and-so what for (6a).

П-356 • **ПОПЫ́ТКА НЕ ПЫ́ТКА (, А СПРО́С НЕ БЕДА́)** [saying; usu. only the first half of the saying is used] one can go ahead and try sth., nothing bad will happen (said when it is considered worthwhile to try sth., even if success is not guaranteed): ≃ **(there's) no harm in trying; it wouldn't** ⟨**won't**⟩ **hurt to try; nothing ventured, nothing gained.**

П-357 • **(ИДТИ́/ПОЙТИ́) НА ПОПЯ́ТНЫЙ** ⟨**НА ПОПЯ́ТНУЮ, НА ПОПЯ́ТНЫЙ ДВОР** *obs*⟩ *coll* [VP or PrepP (these forms only, used as predic); subj: human] to retreat from a decision made earlier, go back on an agreement, retract consent already given etc: X (пошёл) на попятный ≃ **X backed out** ⟨**off, down**⟩**; X went back (on his word** ⟨**promise**⟩**); X back-pedaled** ⟨**backtracked**⟩**; X beat a hasty retreat.**

Видят головотяпы, что вор-новотор кругом на кривой их объехал, а на попятный уж не смеют (Салтыков-Щедрин 1). The Knockheads saw that Thief-Among-Thieves had bamboozled them, but they didn't dare back out (1a). ♦ ...Никто всерьёз эти слова не принял: где же председателю колхоза свою дорогу торить? Хорошо уж и то, что слова не побоялся сказать. И Михаил тут не был исключением. Он был тоже уверен, что за ночь Лукашин одумается, пойдёт на попятный, — и кто укорит его за это? (Абрамов 1). …No one took what he said seriously: how could a *kolkhoz* Chairman blaze his own trail? It was enough that he had even dared to open his mouth. And Mikhail thought no differently. He too was sure that Lukashin would think better of it by the next day and back down. And who would blame him? (1a). ♦ «Ну вот видишь, вот уж и нечестно с твоей стороны: слово дал, да и на попятный двор» (Гоголь 3). "There, you see, that's not fair of you: you have given me your word of honor, and now you are going back on it" (3c).

П-358 • **ДО КАКИ́Х ⟨КОТО́РЫХ⟩ ПОР** [PrepP; these forms only; adv; fixed WO] **1.** until what time, for how much more time: **(for) how long; until ⟨till⟩ when; how much longer;** [in limited contexts] **when (will one stop doing sth.).**

[Анна Петровна:] Скажите: до каких пор будут ненавидеть меня отец и мать? (Чехов 4). [A.P.:] Tell me: how long will my father and mother go on hating me? (4a). [A.P.:] Tell me, when will my mother and father stop hating me? (4b). ♦ «Отпустите, ради Христа… Измотались все, тоской изошли… До каких же пор?.. Господи!.. Неужели не отпустите?» (Шолохов 3). "Let us go, for Christ's sake….We've had as much as we can stand….How much longer?….God almighty!….Won't you let us go?" (3a).

2. *coll* (in refer. to s.o.'s reading, memorizing etc sth.) up to what point: **up to where ⟨what page, what part etc⟩; how far (one has gotten ⟨read up to etc⟩).**

Когда я спросил его, до каких пор он прочитал конспект, он сказал, что ещё даже не начинал его. When I asked him how far he had gotten in reading that abstract, he said he hadn't even started it.

П-359 • **ДО СИХ ПО́Р ⟨ДО́ СИХ ПОР⟩** [PrepP; these forms only; adv; fixed WO] **1.** Also: **ДО СЕЙ ПОРЫ́; ПО СЮ ПО́РУ** *both obs* until the present time: **to this day; until ⟨till, up till, up to⟩ now; to date; thus ⟨so⟩ far; up to the present day ⟨time⟩; hitherto; heretofore; still; (as) yet;** [in limited contexts] **even now;** [with negated predic] **never.**

«До сих пор, как вспомню, не могу удержаться от смеха» (Войнович 4). "To this day when I think of it I can't help laughing" (4a). ♦ До сих пор он покойно жил, никого не боялся, любому и каждому мог без опаски смотреть в глаза (Тендряков 1). Up till now he had lived quietly, fearing no one, and able to look any man straight in the eye (1a). ♦ …Если сказать правду, до сих пор никаких иных отношений с женщинами, кроме заочных, у него [Алтынника] не было (Войнович 5). …If the truth be told, thus far Altinnik's relations with women had been confined to the mail (5a). ♦ «А тут на днях налог принесли». — «Налог?» — Михаил озадаченно посмотрел на мать. До сих пор налоги обходили их стороной (Абрамов 1). "Then there's that tax thing they brought around the other day." "Taxes?" Mikhail gave his mother a puzzled look. So far, taxes had passed them by (1a). ♦ «…Слушайте, я буду читать: „Только что вышедшая книга стихов до сих пор неизвестного автора, Фёдора Годунова-Чердынцева, кажется нам явлением столь ярким, поэтический талант автора столь несомненен". Знаете что, оборвём на этом…» (Набоков 1). "…Listen to this—I'm going to read it to you: 'The newly published collection of poems by the hitherto unknown author Fyodor Godunov-Cherdyntsev strikes one as such a brilliant phenomenon, and the poetic talent of the author is so indisputable…' You know what, I shan't go on…" (1a). ♦ [Елена:] Сказал, что приедет утром, а сейчас девять часов, и его нет до сих пор (Булгаков 4). [E.:] He said he'd come in the morning, but it's nine o'clock right now, and he still isn't here (4a). ♦ Обед этот в семейном и дружеском кругу человека, которым он так восхищался, прежде очень интересовал князя Андрея, тем более что до сих пор он не видал Сперанского в его домашнем быту; но теперь ему не хотелось ехать (Толстой 5). The prospect of this dinner in the intimate home circle of the man he so greatly admired had seemed very interesting to Prince Andrei, especially as he had not yet seen Speransky in his domestic surroundings, but now he had lost all desire to go (5a). ♦ До сих пор я

не знаю, как назвать это состояние… В нём не было ни капли восторженности. Наоборот, оно приносило покой и отдых (Паустовский 1). Even now I don't know what to call this mood….There was not a trace of exaltation in it. On the contrary, it brought peace and quiet (1b). ♦ «Удивительное дело, — размышлял Остап, — как город не догадался до сих пор брать гривенники за вход в Провал» (Ильф и Петров 1). "What a remarkable thing," mused Ostap, "that the town has never thought of charging ten kopeks to see the Drop…" (1a).

2. (in refer. to s.o.'s reading, memorizing etc sth.) up to this place: **up to here; up to this point; this far; this much.**

Я ещё не кончил статью, прочитал только до сих пор. I haven't finished the article yet. I've only read up to here.

П-360 • **ДО ТЕХ ПОР** [PrepP; Invar; adv; fixed WO] until that time: **until ⟨till, up till⟩ then; till ⟨up to⟩ that moment; thus far.**

Фёдор Павлович ложился по ночам очень поздно, часа в три, в четыре утра, а до тех пор всё, бывало, ходит по комнате или сидит в креслах и думает (Достоевский 1). Fyodor Pavlovich went to bed very late, at about three or four o'clock in the morning, and until then would pace around the room or sit in his armchair and think (1a). ♦ Это был страшный момент моей жизни: смерть на пороге освобождения и гибель всего написанного, всего смысла прожитого до тех пор (Солженицын 2). This was a dreadful moment in my life: to die on the threshold of freedom, to see all I had written, all that gave meaning to my life thus far, about to perish with me (2a). ♦ …[В общежитии] горячей воды… ванной или душа не было. Но всё-таки условия по сравнению с теми, которые мне пришлось испытать до тех пор, были вполне приличными (Войнович 1). [context transl] …[In the hostel] there was…no hot water, no bath or shower. But after the conditions in which I had been living, these were entirely decent (1a).

П-361 • **ДО ТЕХ ПОР ПОКА́** [subord Conj, temporal] up to the time when (the action in process ceases or the state in question changes): **as ⟨so⟩ long as;** [in limited contexts] **(up) to the point where;** [after a negated predic] **until.**

Он сказал, что войны наши с Бонапартом до тех пор будут несчастливы, пока мы будем искать союзов с немцами и будем соваться в европейские дела… (Толстой 5). He said that our wars with Bonaparte would be disastrous so long as we sought alliances with the Germans and meddled in European affairs… (5a). ♦ Про Алферова говорили, что он из захудалых казачьих офицеришек выбился в люди лишь благодаря своей жене — бабе энергичной и умной; говорили, что она тянула бездарного супруга за уши и до тех пор не давала ему дыхнуть, пока он, три раза срезавшись, на четвёртый всё же выдержал экзамен в академии (Шолохов 3). Alferov was said to have made his way up from being a lowly Cossack officer only thanks to his energetic and intelligent wife; she had dragged her dull-witted spouse out of his rut and never let him rest until, after three failures, he had passed the Academy entrance examination (3a).

П-362 • **ДО ТЕХ ПОР ПОКА́ НЕ** [subord Conj, temporal] up to the time when (sth. happens): **until; (up) until the time when ⟨that⟩;** [in limited contexts] **until after.**

«Скажи ему, что он не уедет отсюда до тех пор, пока не вылечит мне девчонку!..» (Шолохов 2). "Tell him he won't leave here until he cures the girl for me!…" (2a). ♦ …Его коллега Н. скрылся в неизвестном направлении и не появлялся до тех пор, пока сбор подписей не был закончен… (Войнович 3). …His colleague N. disappeared and didn't reappear until after the collection of signatures was completed… (3a).

П-363 • **С КАКИ́Х ⟨КОТО́РЫХ⟩ ПОР** [PrepP; these forms only; adv; fixed WO] from what time: **since when.**

«Да у вас по контракту нанята квартира?» — спросил Алексеев, оглядывая комнату с потолка до полу. «Да, только срок контракту вышел; я всё это время платил помесячно... не помню только, с которых пор» (Гончаров 1). "Have you got a lease?" inquired Alekseyev, surveying the room from floor to ceiling. "Yes, but it has expired, and I've been paying the rent by the month ever since....I've forgotten since when" (1b).

П-364 • С НЕ́КОТОРЫХ ПОР [PrepP; Invar; adv; fixed WO] beginning from a certain unspecified time, from a certain point in time: **for ⟨quite⟩ some time (now); for ⟨quite⟩ a while (now);** [in limited contexts] **a while ago.**

«С некоторых пор мне страшно смотреть на женское бельё», — сказал я ей (Лимонов 1). "I've been terrified to look at women's underwear for some time," I told her (1a). ♦ Он сказал, что с некоторых пор перестал ходить туда. He said he had stopped going there a while ago.

П-365 • С ТЕХ ПОР; С ТОЙ ПОРЫ́ [PrepP; these forms only; adv; fixed WO] beginning with the specified moment or period of time: **ever since; since then ⟨that time etc⟩; from then ⟨that time etc⟩ on; after that.**

[Говорящий — мул] Примерно через месяц рана на моей спине совсем зажила, и старик мой оседлал меня и поехал в село Атары. С тех пор мы с ним неразлучны... (Искандер 3). [The speaker is a mule] After about a month, when the wound on my back had healed completely, my old man saddled me and went to the village of Atary. He and I have been inseparable ever since... (3a). ♦ «Ты бы подстригся, молодец», — сказал он [Шунечка] однажды. Вовус поглядел непочтительно... С тех пор он больше для Шунечки не существовал (Грекова 3). "You ought to get a haircut, young fellow," he [Shunechka] once said. Vovus looked at him scornfully....From that time on he ceased to exist for Shunechka (3a). ♦ ...К осени [Прокофий] увёл на новое хозяйство сгорбленную иноземку-жену... С той поры редко видели его в хуторе, не бывал он и на майдане (Шолохов 2). ...By autumn he [Prokofy] was able to take his bowed foreign wife to her new home....After that he was seldom seen in the village and never came to the village meetings (2a).

П-366 • С ТЕХ ПОР КАК [subord Conj, temporal] from the time that, in the period following the time when: **(ever) since; since ⟨from⟩ the time (that);** [in limited contexts] **after.**

С тех пор, как я живу и действую, судьба как-то всегда приводила меня к развязке чужих драм... (Лермонтов 1). Ever since I began to live and act, fate has somehow associated me with the denouement of other people's tragedies... (1b). ♦ Прошло несколько дней с тех пор, как исчезло ведомство капитана Миляги, но в районе никто этого не заметил (Войнович 2). Several days had passed since Captain Milyaga's department had vanished, but nobody in the district seemed to notice (2a). ♦ «С тех пор как ты поселился, мы никто ни разу не видели, чтобы ты в туалет пошёл» (Ерофеев 1). "From the time you moved in we've not seen you go to the toilet once" (1a).

П-367 • С Э́ТИХ ПОР; С Э́ТОЙ ПОРЫ́ [PrepP; these forms only; adv; fixed WO] beginning with this or that moment or period of time (as specified): **ever since; since then ⟨that time etc⟩; from then ⟨that time etc⟩ on; from that ⟨this⟩ moment on.**

...Среди мирных подпольных фабрик Эндурска появилась сверхподпольная трикотажная фабрика, выпускающая изделия из «джерси» и работающая на японских станках... В один прекрасный день в Эндурске сгорел подпольный склад [, принадлежавший конкурентам этой трикотажной фабрики,] с огромным запасом временно законсервированных нейлоновых кофточек... С этих пор лекторы Эндурска и Мухуса с немалым успехом используют эту историю как наглядный пример, подтверждающий тезис о хищническом характере частнособственнического развития... (Искандер 3). ...Among the peaceful underground factories of Endursk, there had appeared a supersecret knitting mill which turned out articles made of jersey and used Japanese machines....One fine day the underground warehouse in Endursk [owned by the competitors of that knitting mill] burned down, and with it a huge stock of nylon blouses....Ever since, the lecturers of Endursk and Mukhus have used this story with considerable success as a graphic example supporting the proposition that the development of private ownership is rapacious in character... (3a). ♦ ...Глуповцам это дело не прошло даром. Как и водится, бригадирские грехи прежде всего отразились на них. Всё изменилось с этих пор в Глупове (Салтыков-Щедрин 1). This affair was not without consequence for the Foolovites....As usual, the brigadier's sins were visited first of all upon them. From that time on, everything was changed in Foolov (1a).

П-368 • НА ПЕ́РВЫХ ПОРА́Х [PrepP; Invar; adv; fixed WO] during the initial period (of some activity, process, s.o.'s stay somewhere etc): **at ⟨in⟩ the (very) beginning; at first; at the start ⟨the outset⟩; in the early days; early on.**

Одам инстинктивно боялся перемен... Убежав из племени, совершив поступок грандиозный и революционный, он пытался тотчас как бы забыть начисто об этом и жить как можно более похоже на то, как жилось ему раньше. На первых порах он стал даже более косным, чем был прежде (Обухова 1). Odam instinctively feared any changes....Having left the tribe, having committed a stupendous, revolutionary act, he tried, as it were, to forget it as completely as he could and live as much as possible as he had lived before. In the beginning, he had even become more rigid in his ways than he had been before (1a). ♦ Я до того испугался неожиданного появления отца, что даже на первых порах не заметил, откуда он шёл и куда исчез (Тургенев 3). I was so frightened by my father's unexpected appearance that at first I did not even notice whence he had come or where he went (3c). ♦ «Не могу врать...» – «Надо научиться»... Но на первых порах я была не очень понятливой ученицей... (Гинзбург 1). "Well, I can't tell lies." "Then you had better learn, hadn't you?"...At the start I showed little talent... (1a). ♦ ...Когда [мать] была недовольна отцом, то молчала. На первых порах это, наверно, мучило отца... (Рыбаков 1). When she [mother] was displeased with father, she fell silent. In the early days this must have tormented him... (1a).

П-369 • В СА́МОЙ ⟨ВО ВСЕЙ⟩ ПОРЕ́; В ПОРЕ́ *all obs, coll* [PrepP; these forms only; nonagreeing modif or subj-compl with бытьø (subj: human); fixed WO] at the point in one's life when one is most vigorous, attractive etc: X в самой поре ≃ **X is in the (very) prime of life; X is in his prime;** [mainly of a woman] **X is in full bloom.**

[Вера:] Разве в его лета ещё женятся? [Наталья Петровна:] Да что ты думаешь? Сколько ему лет? Ему пятидесяти лет нету. Он в самой поре (Тургенев 1). [V.:] At his age, do men still marry? [N.P.:] What do you think? How old is he? He isn't fifty yet. He is in the very prime of life (1b). ♦ [Пелагея Егоровна:] Она теперь девушка в самой поре... (Островский 2). [P.E.:] She's a maid in full bloom... (2b).

П-370 • НЕ ПОЯВЛЯ́ТЬСЯ ⟨НЕ ПОКА́ЗЫВАТЬСЯ⟩ НА ПОРО́Г *coll* [VP; subj: human] not to come to s.o.'s home for a long time (because one has quarreled with s.o., is too busy, no longer wants to see s.o. etc): X не появляется на порог ≃ **X never visits Y; X never comes ⟨goes⟩ to see Y;** [in limited contexts] **X doesn't set foot in ⟨show his face at⟩ Y's house ⟨home etc⟩.**

Мы с Максимом поссорились, с тех пор он не появляется на порог. Maksim and I had a falling-out, and he hasn't shown his face at my house since.

П-371 • НЕ ПУСКА́ТЬ/НЕ ПУСТИ́ТЬ НА ПОРО́Г *кого coll* [VP; subj: human] not to allow s.o. into one's house: X не пустит Y-а на порог ≃ **X won't let Y set foot in X's house ⟨home etc⟩; X won't let Y in the door (of his house etc); X won't**

have Y in X's home; X won't allow Y over X's threshold; X won't let Y (so much as) cross X's threshold.

«А дочь свою и не думай приводить к нам. На порог не пущу...» (Айтматов 1). "And don't have any ideas about taking your daughter in with us. I won't let her set foot in here..." (1b). ♦ ...Мать [Тани] упёрлась и твердила одно: Игорь — авантюрист, он хочет проникнуть в наш круг... Я его больше на порог не пущу (Ерофеев 3). ...[Tanya's mother] persisted and kept repeating the same thing: Igor was a shady character; he was trying to get into their circle....She just wouldn't have him in their home one more time (3a). ♦ Отец Зины, Оскар Григорьевич Мерц, умер от грудной жабы в Берлине четыре года тому назад, и немедленно после его кончины Марианна Николаевна вышла замуж за человека, которого Мерц не пустил бы к себе на порог... (Набоков 1). Zina's father, Oscar Grigorievich Mertz, had died of angina pectoris in Berlin four years ago, and immediately after his death Marianna Nikolavna [sic] had married a man whom Mertz would not have allowed over his threshold... (1a). ♦ Эти товарищи — управители наши, Юриных родителей на порог не пускают (Рыбаков 2). ...The comrades, the bosses and managers...wouldn't let Yuri's parents so much as cross their threshold... (2a).

П-372 • ПЕРЕСТУПА́ТЬ/ПЕРЕСТУПИ́ТЬ ⟨ПЕРЕХОДИ́ТЬ/ПЕРЕЙТИ́, ПЕРЕША́ГИВАТЬ/ПЕРЕШАГНУ́ТЬ⟩ (ЧЕРЕЗ) ПОРО́Г чей, чего, какой [VP; subj: human or, rare, чья нога; often neg or infin with verbs of prohibition] to appear at s.o.'s house, office etc or enter some place: X не переступит Y-ова порога ⟨порога места Z⟩ ≃ X will not cross ⟨step across⟩ the threshold ⟨the threshold of place Z⟩; X will not cross ⟨step across⟩ the threshold of Y's house ⟨office etc⟩; X will not set foot in Y's home ⟨office etc⟩.

«Можешь покупать этот дом, но ни я в него ни ногой, ни ты никогда не переступишь порога моего дома!» (Искандер 3). "You can buy this house, but I will never set foot in it, nor will you ever cross the threshold of my house!" (3a). ♦ Надеялся я, что никогда больше не переступлю этого порога... (Войнович 3). I had hoped I would never step across that threshold again... (3a). ♦ «Извольте вон идти! и чтоб нога ваша не смела переступить моего порога!» — сказала она ему, указывая дверь (Герцен 1). "Kindly leave my house and don't dare to set foot in it again," she said, pointing to the door (1a).

П-373 • ОТМЕТА́ТЬ/ОТМЕСТИ́ С ПОРО́ГА что coll [VP; subj: human] to reject sth. without discussing it, without listening to all the available information and supporting arguments: X отмёл с порога Y-овы аргументы ⟨возражения и т. п.⟩ ≃ X dismissed Y's arguments ⟨objections etc⟩ out of hand; X dismissed Y's arguments ⟨objections etc⟩ without hearing Y out.

Не отметай с порога его аргументы, выслушай его. Don't dismiss his arguments out of hand, hear him out.

П-374 • С ПОРО́ГА ляпнуть, выпалить что и т. п. highly coll [PrepP; Invar; adv] (to say sth., break the news etc) immediately upon one's arrival at some place: right away; immediately; right off the bat.

Во всём человек хладнокровный и рассудительный, вот с этой только бабьей манерой Капа никогда не могла расстаться: если что новое — хорошее ли, плохое, обязательно ляпнуть с порога (Солженицын 10). Kapa was a cool and reasonable person except for one feminine habit which she could do nothing about: whenever there was news, good or bad, she immediately let the cat out of the bag (10a).

П-375 • У ПОРО́ГА [PrepP; Invar; subj-compl with быть∅, стоять (subj: abstr)] near, soon to come: X у порога ≃ X is close ⟨near⟩ at hand; X is on the doorstep; X is just (a)round the corner; X is (knocking) at s.o.'s ⟨the⟩ door.

Зима уже стояла у порога. Winter was already close at hand.

П-376 • НА ПОРО́ГЕ lit [PrepP; Invar] 1. ~ чего [the resulting PrepP is adv or subj-compl with copula (subj: human or collect)] in the period or stage immediately preceding sth.: on the threshold ⟨the verge, the brink⟩ of; ∥ на пороге смерти ≃ at death's door.

Абрам Менделевич стал ему рассказывать, что мы находимся «на пороге открытия новой науки»... (Копелев 1). Abram Mendelevich began telling him that we were "on the threshold of discovering a new science..." (1a). ♦ [Андрей:] Итак, Кавалеров, мы находимся на пороге великих событий (Олеша 6). [A.:] So, Kavalerov, we're on the verge of great things, eh? (6a).

2. [subj-compl with быть∅, стоять (subj: abstr)] very near, very soon to come: X на пороге ≃ X is very close ⟨near⟩ at hand; X is right on the doorstep; X is just (a)round the corner; X is (knocking) at s.o.'s ⟨the⟩ door.

Потеплело, растаял снег — весна была на пороге. It got warmer and the snow melted—spring was just around the corner.

П-377 • ОБИВА́ТЬ/ОБИ́ТЬ ⟨ПООБИВА́ТЬ/ПООБИ́ТЬ rare⟩ ПОРО́ГИ (чьи) ⟨ПОРО́Г (чей)⟩ (чего, у кого, где); ОБИВА́ТЬ/ОБИ́ТЬ ⟨ПООБИВА́ТЬ/ПООБИ́ТЬ rare⟩ ВСЕ ПОРО́ГИ ⟨ВЕСЬ ПОРО́Г⟩ (у кого, где) all coll [VP; subj: human; usu. impfv] (usu. in refer. to trying to obtain sth. important for one's job or career from one's superior(s) or some organization(s); may refer to a person trying to get a job, a man trying to gain the affection of a woman etc) to go to some place(s) repeatedly, persistently requesting sth.: X обивает пороги ≃ X beats down doors; ∥ X обивает Y-ов порог ≃ X haunts ⟨hangs around⟩ Y's door(way); ∥ X обивает пороги редакций ⟨школ и т. п.⟩ ≃ X haunts the door(way)s of various editorial ⟨principals' etc⟩ offices; X haunts (the) editors' ⟨(the) principals' etc⟩ offices; X runs from one editorial ⟨principal's etc⟩ office to another; X pesters every editor ⟨principal etc⟩ (in town).

«Я, конечно, напишу...» — «Напишу! Ты весь в этом. Не писать надо, а ехать, лично просить, пороги обивать!» (Стругацкие 1). "Of course I'll write—" "You'll write! That's just like you. It's not writing you have to do, you have to go there, ask in person, beat down doors" (1a). ♦ Статейки эти... быстро пошли в ход, и уж в этом одном молодой человек оказал всё своё практическое и умственное превосходство над тою многочисленною, вечно нуждающеюся и несчастною частью нашей учащейся молодёжи обоего пола, которая в столицах... с утра до ночи обивает пороги разных газет и журналов... (Достоевский 1). These little articles...were soon in great demand; and even in this alone the young man demonstrated his practical and intellectual superiority over that eternally needy and miserable mass of our students of both sexes who, in our capitals, from morning till night...haunt the doorways of various newspapers and magazines... (1a). ♦ [Тригорин:] Такой любви я не испытал ещё... В молодости было некогда, я обивал пороги редакций, боролся с нуждой... (Чехов 6). [T.:] I have never known a love like that....In my youth there wasn't time, I was always haunting the editors' offices, fighting off poverty... (6a). [T.:] I have never known a love like that. As a young man, I never had time; I was too busy running from one editorial office to another, trying to earn a living (6b). ♦ «Весьма обнадёживающе заявивший о себе ранее молодой поэт-колхозник Влад Самсонов из станицы Пластуновской, бросив семью и работу, ведёт богемный образ жизни, обивая пороги редакций со стихами, оставляющими желать много лучшего» (Максимов 2). "Vlad Samsonov, the peasant poet from the village of Plastunovskaya, whose early work was extremely promising, having abandoned his family and his work is now living a bohemian life and is pestering every editor in town with verses that leave a great deal to be desired" (2a).

П-378 • ДЕРЖА́ТЬ ПО́РОХ СУХИ́М *lit* [VP; subj: human, usu. pl, or collect] (of soldiers, an army etc) to be prepared to defend one's country (cause etc) at any moment: X-ы держат порох сухим ≃ **Xs keep their powder dry.**

< Attributed to Oliver Cromwell, addressing his troops as they prepared to cross a stream or river before battle, possibly the Battle of Edgehill in Oct. 1642. The reference is presumably to gunpowder, which would be useless if wet.

П-379 • ЕСТЬ ЕЩЁ ПО́РОХ В ПОРОХОВНИ́ЦАХ [sent; Invar; fixed WO] in spite of a person's advanced age, he is still active, full of energy, able to accomplish things etc (used by the speaker to express surprise or admiration when an old person accomplishes sth. he was not expected to be able to do; also, used by an old person himself to express satisfaction upon accomplishing sth., or to reassure those who question his abilities): **there is life in the old dog ⟨boy, girl⟩ yet; one still has a lot of steam.**

< From Nikolai Gogol's *Taras Bulba* («Тарас Бульба»), the revised version of 1842.

П-380 • ТРА́ТИТЬ ⟨ИЗВОДИ́ТЬ⟩ ПО́РОХ даром, зря, попусту и т. п. *(на что)* coll [VP; subj: human] to waste energy in vain, for nothing, say or argue sth. in vain: X даром тратит порох ≃ **X is wasting his time ⟨his breath⟩; X is wasting steam.**

«Ты болен?» — спросил его на другой день один из пулемётчиков. — «Нет». — «А что ж ты? Тоскуешь?» — «Нет». — «Ну, давай закурим. Её [Анну], браток, теперь не воротишь. Не трать на это дело пороху» (Шолохов 3). "Are you ill?" one of the machine-gunners asked him the next day. "No." "What's up then? Missing her [Anna]?" "No." "Well, let's have a smoke. You can't bring her back now, mate. It's no good wasting steam on that" (3a).

П-381 • (НИ) СИНЬ ⟨СИ́НЯ⟩ ПО́РОХА нет, не осталось, не оставить и т. п. *obs* [NP_gen; these forms only; subj or obj; fixed WO] (there is, there remained, to leave etc) absolutely nothing: **nothing at all; not a single thing; absolutely nil;** [in limited contexts] **not a single one.**

П-382 • ПО́РОХА ⟨-у⟩ НЕ ВЫ́ДУМАЕТ coll [VP; subj: human; 3rd pers fut only; fixed WO] one is ordinary, unimaginative, not very gifted: X пороха не выдумает ≃ **X won't set the world on fire; X is no bright light ⟨no genius, no worldbeater⟩.**

Пороха Фомичёв не выдумает, но он трудолюбив, услужлив и честен. Fomichov won't set the world on fire, but he's hard-working, obliging, and honest.

П-383 • ПА́ХНЕТ/ЗАПА́ХЛО ПО́РОХОМ [VP; impers] war is imminent: **there is a smell of gunpowder in the air; things smell of gunpowder; war is in the air.**

«Когда порохом запахло, когда [Сталин] почуял опасность, так вспомнил про Россию, про русских полководцев и про Александра Невского...» (Копелев 1). "When things smelled of gunpowder, when he [Stalin] sensed danger, he remembered Russia, and Russian military leaders, and Alexander Nevsky..." (1a).

П-384 • НЮ́ХАТЬ/ПОНЮ́ХАТЬ ⟨НАНЮ́ХАТЬСЯ⟩ ПО́РОХУ ⟨-а⟩ coll [VP; subj: human; often neg] to participate in fighting a war, be in battle(s): X понюхал пороху ≃ **X has smelled ⟨tasted⟩ gunpowder; X has seen combat ⟨action⟩; X knows the smell of gunpowder;** [in limited contexts] **X has gotten used to the smell of gunpowder.**

«На этот раз отстоять вас [от мобилизации] не удастся. Страшная нехватка военно-медицинского персонала. Придётся вам понюхать пороху» (Пастернак 1). "I can't stop them [from drafting you] this time. There's a terrible shortage of medical personnel. You'll be smelling gunpowder before long" (1a). ♦ «Я нанюхался пороху не с твоё!» (Шолохов 3). "...I've seen a lot more action than you!" (3a). ♦ «Нет, пускай послужит он в армии, да потянет лямку, да понюхает пороху, да будет солдат...» (Пушкин 2). "No, let him serve in the army, let him learn to sweat and get used to the smell of gunpowder, let him become a soldier..." (2a).

П-385 • ПО́РОХУ ⟨-а⟩ НЕ ХВАТА́ЕТ/НЕ ХВАТИ́ЛО *у кого* coll [VP; impers; often used with infin] s.o. does not have the courage, energy, will etc to accomplish sth.: у X-а пороху не хватает ≃ **X hasn't got the guts ⟨the stomach, the gumption, the stamina, the strength⟩ (to do sth.); X hasn't got it in him (to do sth.); X doesn't have what it takes.**

Рита... сказала, что боится за себя, за то, что не хватит пороха ухаживать за больной... (Трифонов 5). ...Rita went on to say that she was worried on her own account, that she wouldn't have the strength to take care of a sick person... (5a).

П-386 • СТЕРЕ́ТЬ ⟨ИСТЕРЕ́ТЬ⟩ В (МЕ́ЛКИЙ) ПОРО́ШОК *кого* coll [VP; subj: human or collect; often pfv fut, used as a threat] (in refer. to killing s.o., or ruining s.o.'s career, social standing etc) to deal with s.o. harshly or destroy s.o.: X сотрёт Y-а в порошок ≃ **X will make mincemeat of Y; X will pulverize Y; X will grind Y to ⟨into⟩ dust; X will grind Y into the dust; X will be utterly ruthless with Y.**

Каждый дом, квартира... деревня, не говоря уж о городах и областях, получили своего верховода (сначала их было по несколько, потом один брал верх), который распоряжался, инструктировал, отдавал приказания и обязательно грозил стереть сопротивляющегося в порошок (Мандельштам 2). Every house, apartment, and village, not to mention every town and province, had its little tyrant (at first there would be several, until a single one took over), who gave orders and instructions, threatening always to "make mincemeat" of anyone who resisted (2a). ♦ В бесчисленных кабинетах меня уговаривали, умоляли снять свою подпись [с писем в защиту нескольких писателей], мне льстили, мне угрожали, обещали стереть меня в порошок (Войнович 1). In an endless succession of offices I was urged and entreated to withdraw my signature [from letters in defense of several writers]. I was flattered, threatened—they promised to grind me to dust (1a). ♦ Все понимали, что если Королёв жертвует собой (а состояние его здоровья было всем известно), то он сотрёт в порошок всякого, кто нерасторопностью или просто неполным напряжением сил задержит подготовку хоть на минуту (Владимиров 1). They all understood that if Korolyov was sacrificing himself (and everybody knew about the state of his health) he would be utterly ruthless with anyone who through slackness or failure to make a real effort held up the preparations even by a minute (1a).

П-387 • ЖИВО́Й ПОРТРЕ́Т *кого* coll [NP; sing only; usu. subj-compl with copula, nom or instrum (subj: human)] (in refer. to physical appearance) one is an exact likeness (of someone else): **the living image of; the spitting ⟨spit and⟩ image of; a carbon copy of; the very picture of.**

Этот мальчик — живой портрет отца. That boy is the spitting image of his father.

П-388 • В СА́МУЮ ПО́РУ coll [PrepP; Invar; usu. subj-compl with copula; fixed WO] **1.** ~ *(кому)* [subj: concr, abstr, or infin; occas. used as nonagreeing modif] sth. is timely, sth. happens at the appropriate time, exactly when wanted, needed etc: **(it's ⟨this would be** etc⟩) **just the right time ⟨just the right moment, the perfect time, the perfect moment⟩; at just the right time ⟨just the right moment, the perfect time, the perfect moment⟩; (sth.) couldn't have come at a better time;** ‖ X-у было бы в самую пору сделать Y ≃ **this would be a perfect time for X to do Y; this would be just the time for X to do Y.**

Сама же Людмила Афанасьевна и подвела его [Орещенкова] к этому рассуждению рассказом о сыне. И так как с сыном оставалось не решено, то ей бы в самую пору сейчас слушать и думать, как это всё отнести к сыну (Солженицын 10). He [Oreshchenkov] had embarked on this topic because of Lyudmila Afanasyevna's own talk of her son. Since she was having trouble with her son, this would be just the time for her to hear this and ponder how to apply it to her son's case (10b).

2. ~ *кому* **быть$_\emptyset$, прийтись** и т. п. [subj: a noun denoting footwear, an item of clothing etc] sth. is exactly s.o.'s size: X Y-у в самую пору ≃ **X is just Y's size; X is just the right size for Y; X fits Y perfectly; X is a perfect fit; it's as if X were made to measure.**

Сапоги были девочке в самую пору. The boots were just the girl's size.

П-389 • В ТУ ПО́РУ *obs* [PrepP; Invar; adv; fixed WO] at the time or moment in the past specified by the context: **at that time.**

…В ту пору он у нас слишком уж даже выделанно напрашивался на свою роль шута, любил выскакивать и веселить господ, с видимым равенством, конечно, но на деле совершенным пред ними хамом (Достоевский 1). …At that time he was even overzealously establishing himself as a buffoon, and loved to pop up and amuse the gentlemen, ostensibly as an equal, of course, though in reality he was an absolute boor beside them (1a).

П-390 • ОБ Э́ТУ ПО́РУ *obs, substand* [PrepP; Invar; adv; fixed WO] at or by the present time or moment, or at or by the specified time or moment in the past: **at ⟨by⟩ this time; [in past contexts] at ⟨by⟩ that time.**

«Так вы передадите ему, что я вас просил?» — кланяясь и уходя, говорил Обломов. «Вот через полчаса они сами будут... Об эту пору они всегда приходят...» (Гончаров 1). "Then you will tell him what I said, won't you?" asked Oblomov, bowing and going to the door. "In half an hour he'll be here....He's always home by this time" (1b).

П-391 • КРУГОВА́Я ПОРУ́КА [NP; sing only] **1.** joint responsibility of all members of a group for the actions of the group as a whole or the actions of its individual members: **mutual ⟨collective⟩ responsibility; responsibility for each other; mutual guarantee.**

«Ну, насчёт общины, — промолвил он, — поговорите лучше с вашим братом. Он теперь, кажется, изведал на деле, что такое община, круговая порука, трезвость и тому подобные штучки» (Тургенев 2). "Well, so far as the commune is concerned," he said, "you'd better talk with your brother about it. I think he has now learned by experience what the commune is: mutual responsibility, sobriety, and all that kind of thing" (2f). ♦ Дворянство обязывало. Разумеется, так как его права были долею фантастические, то и обязанности были фантастические, но они делали известную круговую поруку между равными (Герцен 2). Noble rank had its obligations. Of course, since its rights were partly imaginary, its obligations were imaginary too, but they did provide a certain mutual guarantee between equals (2a).

2. mutual support and concealment (often among participants in improper or criminal matters): **covering (up) for each other ⟨one another⟩; vouching for each other ⟨one another⟩.**

Нам трудно понять и расценить действия этих людей [следователей]... Несомненно только одно: всякий замкнутый, изолированный круг развивается, подобно блатарям, по своим законам и вопреки интересам общества в целом. Такой круг... соблюдает круговую поруку (до поры до времени), хранит тайны, избегает общения с посторонними, а иногда по непонятным причинам уничтожает друг друга (Мандельштам 2). It was hard for us to interpret the actions of these people [the investigators]....But there is no doubt that, like any other isolated, exclusive caste—the professional criminals, for example—

they lived by their own laws, contemptuous of the interests of society as a whole. Closed societies of this kind…cover up for each other (as long as it suits them), guard their secrets, avoid contact with outsiders, and sometimes, for obscure reasons, engage in mutual destruction (2a). ♦ Среди арестантов — переносчиков станка успела возникнуть круговая порука, преступный сговор (Солженицын 3). The prisoners who had carried the lathe had evolved the successful technique of vouching for one another—criminal collusion (3a).

П-392 • НА ПОРУ́КИ взять, отдать, выпустить *кого* [PrepP; Invar; adv] responsibility (taken by a person, group, or organization) for s.o.'s, usu. an offender's, good behavior: X взял Y-а ~ ≃ **X stood surety for Y; X took ⟨accepted⟩ responsibility for Y; X took Y on probation;** ‖ Y-а выпустили ~ ≃ **Y was granted ⟨released on⟩ probation.**

Дзержинский ещё не отступился от старого стиля. Он принял О. М[андельштама] запросто и предложил взять брата на поруки (Мандельштам 1). Dzerzhinski had not yet given up the old ways. He received M[andelstam] in simple fashion and suggested he stand surety for his brother... (1a). ♦ …Отголоском чьей-то тревоги за участь заключённых прозвучало письмо Каледина, адресованное генералу Духонину... в котором он настоятельно просил Корнилова и остальных арестованных на поруки (Шолохов 3). …An echo of someone's concern for the fate of the prisoners came in the shape of a letter from Kaledin to General Dukhonin…in which Kaledin offered to accept responsibility for Kornilov and other arrested generals (3a). ♦ Обыск в квартире, где жил Константин Назаренко, 1935 года рождения, холостой, без определённых занятий, судимый в 1959 году за хулиганство и взятый на поруки коллективом производственных мастерских ГУМа, где он работал в то время экспедитором, ничего не дал (Семёнов 1). A search of the flat inhabited by Konstantin Nazaryenko, born 1935, bachelor, of no fixed occupation, sentenced in 1959 for disorderly conduct and taken on probation by the production workers' collective of the State Universal Stores, where he worked as a filing clerk, gave no results (1a). ♦ Дядя был исключён из партии, снят с должности завгара [заведующего гаражом], осуждён на год за злостное хулиганство, однако взят на поруки из уважения к фронтовым и трудовым заслугам... (Евтушенко 2). Uncle was expelled from the party, fired from his job as head of the garage, and sentenced to a year in jail for malicious hooliganism. However, he was granted probation in view of his wartime and labor record (2a).

П-393 • ДО ПОРЫ́ ДО ВРЕ́МЕНИ; ДО ПОРЫ́ *obs* [PrepP; these forms only; adv; fixed WO] for the meantime, until a moment when the situation changes, some opportunity arises etc: **for the time being; for the present; for a time; [in limited contexts] until the right time; until the time is right; until such time as s.o. ⟨sth.⟩ is needed; as long as it suits (s.o.); for now.**

Никаких работ, связанных с ракетами, этим людям до поры до времени не поручали (Владимиров 1). For the time being they were not given any work connected with rockets (1a). ♦ Как было уже сказано, он поддерживал ровный огонь своей репутации, и до поры это даже отдавало игрой, почти искусством... (Битов 2). As has already been said, he maintained the steady flame of his reputation, and for a time this even smacked of a game, almost an art... (2a). ♦ «С той поры, как только началась позиционная война, казачьи полки порассовали по укромным местам и держат под спудом до поры до времени» (Шолохов 3). "Ever since this positional warfare started, the Cossacks have been tucked away in safe corners and are being kept under wraps until such time as they are needed" (3a). ♦ Нам трудно понять и расценить действия этих людей [следователей]... Несомненно только одно: всякий замкнутый, изолированный круг развивается, подобно блатарям, по своим законам и вопреки интересам общества в целом. Такой круг... соблюдает круговую поруку (до поры до времени)... (Мандельштам 2). It was hard for us to interpret the actions of these people [the investigators]….But there is no doubt that, like any other isolated, exclusive caste—the professional criminals, for example—they lived by their own laws, contemptuous of the interests of society as a whole. Closed societies of this kind…cover up for each other (as long as it suits them)… (2a).

П-394 • ДЛЯ ПОРЯ́ДКА ⟨-y⟩ *coll* [PrepP; these forms only; adv or subj-compl with бытьθ (subj: abstr)] for the observance of form: **for appearance' ⟨form's, propriety's⟩ sake; for the sake of appearances ⟨convention, propriety⟩; as a formality;** [in limited contexts] **(just) to do things properly ⟨right⟩.**

По коридору бегают надзиратели, гремят ключами, заглядывают в глазок. «Не спать, не спать, в карцер захотели?» — это Озерову и Шорохову, больше для порядка (ведь они дремлют сидя, а не лёжа) (Марченко 1). The warders were running along the corridor, rattling their keys and looking into the peepholes: "No more sleep, no more sleep, is it the cooler you want?" This was addressed to Ozerov and Shorokhov, but more for form's sake than anything else; they were dozing sitting up and not lying down (1a). ♦ Сам он не выпил во все это время ни одной капли вина и всего только спросил себе в вокзале чаю, да и то больше для порядка (Достоевский 3). He himself had not drunk a drop of wine the whole time, but had only ordered some tea in the vauxhall, and even that more for propriety's sake (3c). ♦ У нас было тоже восемь лошадей (прескверных), но наша конюшня была вроде богоугодного заведения для кляч; мой отец их держал отчасти для порядка и отчасти для того, чтоб два кучера и два форейтора имели какое-нибудь занятие… (Герцен 1). We also had eight horses (very poor ones), but our stable was something like an almshouse for broken-down nags; my father kept them partly for the sake of appearances and partly so that the two coachmen and the two postillions should have something to do… (1a). ♦ Для порядка поговорили сначала о культурно-массовой и спортивной работе, а потом перешли к кардинальному вопросу повестки дня… (Аксёнов 1). For the sake of propriety they talked about the mass-culture and sports programs first, and then turned to the cardinal question on the agenda… (1a).

П-395 • В ПОЖА́РНОМ ПОРЯ́ДКЕ *coll, often humor* [PrepP; Invar; adv] urgently, fast, very quickly: **on the double; as quickly ⟨soon⟩ as possible; in short order; in no time flat; posthaste.**

Отчёт мне приходится писать в пожарном порядке: завтра приедет ревизор, времени остаётся меньше суток. I've got to write the report in no time flat: the inspector's coming tomorrow, and there's less than twenty-four hours left.

П-396 • В ПОРЯ́ДКЕ[1]; В ПО́ЛНОМ ПОРЯ́ДКЕ [PrepP; these forms only] **1.** ~ бытьθ, оказаться, содержаться, содержать *что* и т. п. [subj-compl with copula (subj: usu. concr) or obj-compl with содержать etc (obj: usu. concr)] (to be, keep sth. etc) in proper condition or order: X в (полном) порядке ≃ **X is in (good ⟨perfect⟩) order; X is perfectly in order; X is in good shape;** [in limited contexts] **X is (working ⟨running etc⟩) fine.**

Он [комиссар] повернулся к журналистам. «Ваши документы»… — «У нас документы в полном порядке, товарищ комиссар» (Паустовский 1). He [the commissar] turned to the journalists. "Your documents."…"Our documents are completely in order, Comrade Commissar" (1b). ♦ Машина никак не заводилась. Мы проверили батарею, но батарея была в порядке. The car just wouldn't start. We checked the battery, but it was fine.

2. [subj-compl with copula (subj: human)] one is well, in good physical or psychological condition, not experiencing difficulties etc: X в порядке ≃ **X is all right ⟨OK⟩; X is doing fine; X is in (perfectly) good shape.**

«Скажи, Фима, ты вообще-то в порядке?» — он положил руку на плечо старому товарищу (Аксёнов 12). "Tell me, Fima,

are you all right in general?" He put his hand on his old friend's shoulder (12a). ♦ «Он был в полном порядке, когда они разошлись, — у неё совесть перед ним чиста» (Гроссман 2). "…He was doing fine when they separated—she's got nothing to feel guilty about" (2a). ♦ «Сама ты, чувиха, пропащий человек! Мы с Академиком в полном порядке!» (Аксёнов 6). "You're the one who's lost, kid! Academician and I are in perfectly good shape" (6a).

3. всё ~ *(у кого) (с кем-чем)* [subj-compl with copula (subj: всё)] everything is satisfactory, things are going smoothly, without problems: у X-а всё в порядке ≃ **everything is all right ⟨(just) fine⟩ (with X); things are going fine (for X); everything is in order;** ‖ у X-а всё в порядке с Y-ом ≃ **as far as thing Y goes ⟨is concerned⟩, X is doing fine ⟨is in good shape, is all right⟩;** ‖ *Neg* у X-а с Y-ом не всё в порядке ≃ **X has a problem ⟨some problems⟩ with Y ⟨in thing Y⟩.**

«Ничего, Любаша!.. Всё будет в порядке!.. Вы у меня будете жить хорошо» (Шукшин 1). "Don't worry, Lyubasha!… Everything will turn out all right!…You'll have a good life with me…" (1a). ♦ «Всё в порядке?» — «Всё в порядке», — …ответила Варя… (Рыбаков 2). "Everything all right?" he asked. "Yes, everything's fine," Varya answered… (2a). ♦ С жадностью начал он расспрашивать этих женщин, не заметили ль они чего вчера вечером. Те очень хорошо понимали, о чём он разузнаёт, и разуверили его вполне: никого не было, ночевал Иван Фёдорович, «всё было в совершенном порядке» (Достоевский 1). Greedily he began inquiring of the women whether they had noticed anything the previous evening. They knew very well what he was trying to find out and reassured him completely: no one had come, Ivan Fyodorovich had spent the night there, "everything was in perfect order" (1a). ♦ За такой стиль, конечно, надо убивать, но… я промямлил, что по части стиля у него всё в порядке, хотя есть некоторые шероховатости… (Войнович 6). For such writing a man should be shot. But…I mumbled that as far as style went, he was in good shape, though there were a few rough spots… (6a). ♦ «Ты же знаешь, я не секретарь Союза писателей, не член партии и с пятым пунктом у меня не всё в порядке» (Войнович 6). "You know I'm not a secretary of the Writers' Union. I'm not a Party member. And I have a slight problem in the ethnic origin area" (6a). ♦ «С обжираловкой у вас всё в порядке, — объявил старший великан, — посмотрим, как у вас с опиваловкой» (Искандер 5). [context transl] "You're all set on trenchering," the eldest giant announced. "Let's see how you are on swilling" (5a).

П-397 • В ПОРЯ́ДКЕ[2] *чего off* [PrepP; Invar; Prep; the resulting PrepP is adv] **1.** in the capacity or function of, serving as: **by way of; as.**

Комитет постановил в порядке наказания исключить эту спортсменку из сборной команды страны. As punishment, the committee decided to remove the athlete from the national team.

2. following sth., in accordance with sth.: **in keeping with; because it is part of; in the course of.**

Лабазов сказал, что стихи он читает только в порядке служебных обязанностей (Эренбург 1). Labazov said he read poems only because it was part of his duties (1a). ♦ Персональное дело — это такое дело, когда большой коллектив людей собирается в кучу, чтоб в порядке внутривидовой борьбы удушить одного из себя сдуру, по злобе или же просто так (Войнович 4). A personal case is when a large human group closes ranks in the course of an interspecific struggle, to suffocate one of its members, out of sheer foolishness, out of malice, or for no reason at all (4a).

П-398 • В ПОРЯ́ДКЕ ВЕЩЕ́Й [PrepP; Invar; subj-compl with copula (subj: abstr, often это, всё это); fixed WO] some happening (behavior etc) is usual, natural, normal: это ~ ≃ **it's in the nature of things; it's (in) the (natural) order of things; it's quite ⟨only⟩ natural; that's the way things go ⟨happen⟩;** [in limited contexts] **that's ⟨it's⟩ as it should be.**

Но, думал Григорий Иванович, если Алексей будет у меня всякий день, то Бетси должна же будет в него влюбиться. Это в порядке вещей. Время всё сладит (Пушкин 3). But, thought Grigorii Ivanovich, if Aleksei started coming over every day, Liza would be bound to fall in love with him. That was in the nature of things: time is the best matchmaker (3a). ♦ "...Теперь вы мне доскажете вашу историю про Бэлу; я уверен, что этим не кончилось". — "А почему ж вы так уверены?"... — "Оттого, что это не в порядке вещей..." (Лермонтов 1). "Now you will finish your story about Bela. I'm sure it didn't end there." "And why are you so sure?" "Because it isn't in the order of things..." (1d). ♦ С Варварой гости, как всегда, обращались цинично и неуважительно; ей казалось это в порядке вещей (Сологуб 1). The guests, as always, treated Varvara cynically and disrespectfully, but this seemed only natural to her (1a). ♦ Подруги ссорятся, мирятся, это в порядке вещей... (Рыбаков 1). Friends quarrel and make up, that's the way things go (1a). ♦ [Дорн:] Если в обществе любят артистов и относятся к ним иначе, чем, например, к купцам, то это в порядке вещей (Чехов 6). [D.:] If actors are liked in society and treated differently from—shall I say?—tradespeople, it's as it should be (6b).

П-399 • В ПОРЯДКЕ ЖИВОЙ ОЧЕРЕДИ (обслуживать *кого,* продавать *что* и т. п.) *coll* [PrepP; Invar; adv; fixed WO] (to serve, sell to etc customers) in the order in which they come: **first come, first served; on a first-come, first-served basis; (people will be served ⟨waited on etc⟩) in the order in which they come.**

Над кассой висело объявление: «Билеты продаются в порядке живой очереди». A sign hung over the ticket window: "Tickets are sold on a first-come, first-served basis."

П-400 • В РАБОЧЕМ ПОРЯДКЕ [PrepP; Invar; adv; fixed WO] (to solve some problem, settle some question etc) while continuing to engage in one's normal work duties, in the framework of the normal work routine, without taking any special measures: **along the way; as one goes; in the regular ⟨normal etc⟩ course of (one's) work.**

«Не будем терять времени, — сказал главный инженер, закрывая совещание, — завтра утром начинаем монтаж. Вопросы техники безопасности будем решать в рабочем порядке». "Let's not waste time on this now," said the chief engineer, ending the meeting. "Tomorrow we'll start installing the equipment, and decide questions regarding safety measures as we go."

П-401 • СВОИМ ПОРЯДКОМ идти, пойти, делать *что* и т. п. *coll* [NP_{instrum}; Invar; adv; fixed WO] in the normal, expected manner (in some cases, with events occurring in their usual succession): **(go ⟨go on⟩) as usual ⟨as always, the same as usual, the same as always, just as before⟩; take ⟨resume, pursue⟩) its normal ⟨usual⟩ course;** [in limited contexts] **(be) business as usual.**

Прошло около двух недель. Жизнь в Марьине текла своим порядком: Аркадий сибаритствовал, Базаров работал (Тургенев 2). About a fortnight passed. Life at Maryino pursued its normal course: Arkady gave himself up to luxurious living and Bazarov worked (2c).

П-402 • ЯВОЧНЫМ ПОРЯДКОМ ⟨ПУТЁМ⟩ [NP_{instrum}; these forms only; adv; fixed WO] (to do sth.) without receiving authorization beforehand: **without advance permission;** [in limited contexts] **just go ahead and do sth.**

П-403 • ПО ПОРЯДКУ (рассказывать, описывать *что* и т. п.) [PrepP; Invar; adv] (to tell a story, describe sth. etc) presenting things in a logical sequence (and, in the case of a story, in the order in which events occurred): **in (its ⟨the⟩ proper)**

order; in sequence; step by step; (recount etc sth.) in the order in which sth. happened; ‖ *Neg* не ~ ≃ out of order.

...Хотя нас вправе упрекнуть (уже упрекнули), что мы способны рассказывать лишь всё по порядку, «от печки», мы считаем это правильным, то есть иначе не можем (Битов 2). Although people are within their rights to reproach us (they already have) for being capable of telling things only in order, "from square one," we consider this correct; i.e., we can't do it any other way (2a). ♦ «...Мне нужно сесть с тобой рядом и рассказать всё по порядку» (Федин 1). "I've got to sit down beside you and tell you everything in its proper order" (1a). ♦ «Расскажи только в подробности, как ты это сделал. Всё по порядку. Ничего не забудь» (Достоевский 2). "Just tell me in detail how you did it. Step by step. Don't leave anything out" (2a). ♦ Митя хоть и засуетился, распоряжаясь, но говорил и приказывал как-то странно, вразбивку, а не по порядку (Достоевский 1). Though Mitya began bustling about, making arrangements, he spoke and gave commands somehow strangely, at random and out of order (1a). ♦ Теперь в Москве большинство моих знакомых живут в отдельных благоустроенных квартирах со всеми удобствами. А вот когда-то... Впрочем, расскажу по порядку. Я приехал в Москву в пятьдесят шестом году (Войнович 1). [context transl] The majority of the people I know in Moscow live in comfortable apartments with all the conveniences. Nevertheless, there was a time... But I should start at the beginning. I arrived in Moscow in 1956 (1a).

П-404 • ПРИЗЫВАТЬ/ПРИЗВАТЬ К ПОРЯДКУ *кого* [VP; subj: human; often pfv infin with надо, пора etc] to make s.o. stop doing sth. objectionable, wrong, or illegal: **X призвал Y-а к порядку ≃ X got Y in line; X set Y straight; X put ⟨kept⟩ Y in Y's place;** [at a meeting, public gathering, at court] **X called Y to order.**

«Скворцы» встрепенулись и, считая предмет исчерпанным, вознамерились было, по обыкновению, шутки шутить, но Собачкин призвал их к порядку... (Салтыков-Щедрин 2). The "starlings" stirred in their seats and, thinking the subject exhausted, were about to resume their usual occupation of exchanging jokes, but Sobachkin called them to order (2a).

П-405 • ПРИВОДИТЬ/ПРИВЕСТИ В ПОРЯДОК *что* [VP; subj: human] to arrange sth. in an organized fashion: **X привёл Y в порядок ≃ X put ⟨set⟩ Y in order; X brought order to Y;** [in limited contexts] **X neatened ⟨tidied⟩ up Y;** ‖ [in refer. to putting scattered or misplaced things where each of them belongs] **X привёл Y-и в порядок ≃ X put Ys in place ⟨in their proper places⟩;** ‖ **X привёл свои мысли в порядок ≃ X composed his thoughts.**

«Господин сотник, что это за чёрт? Приведите свой взвод в порядок» (Шолохов 2). "What the devil are you doing, Lieutenant! Put your troop in order!" (2a). ♦ Сенатор, возвратившись в Россию, принялся приводить в порядок своё имение... (Герцен 1). The senator, on his return to Russia, proceeded to set his estate in order... (1a). ♦ [Брудастый] назначен был впопыхах и имел в голове некоторое особливое устройство, за что и прозван был «Органчиком». Это не мешало ему, впрочем, привести в порядок недоимки, запущенные его предместником (Салтыков-Щедрин 1). [Wolfbound] was appointed in haste and had in his head a certain peculiar device, because of which he was nicknamed Music Box. This did not prevent him, however, from bringing order to the tax arrears, which had been neglected by his predecessor (1a). ♦ Отпарывая черенки, он аккуратно складывал [табачные] листья, как складывают деньги, и, может быть, получал от этого не меньше удовольствия, чем торговец, приводящий в порядок шальную выручку, или удачливый игрок (Искандер 5). As he ripped out the stems he stacked the [tobacco] leaves neatly the way one stacks money, and perhaps he took no less pleasure in this than a tradesman neatening up an easy profit, or a lucky gambler (5a). ♦ Княжна Марья остановилась на крыльце, не переставая ужасаться перед своею душевною мерзостью и старThe flabby face with its unhealthy, greyish skin, the puffy eyelids, the lackluster eyes. It was as though he had just woken up after a binge and стараясь привести в порядок свои мысли, прежде чем войти к нему [отцу] (Толстой 6). Princess Marya lingered on the porch, still horrified at her own spiritual infamy and trying to compose her thoughts before going to her father (6a).

П-406 • ПРИВОДИ́ТЬ/ПРИВЕСТИ́ СЕБЯ́ В ПОРЯ́-ДОК [VP; subj: human] to neaten one's appearance: X привёл себя в порядок ≃ X tidied ⟨spruced⟩ himself up; X freshened (himself) up; [in limited contexts; of a woman only] X привела себя в порядок ≃ X fixed her makeup.

Помятое лицо с нездоровой сероватой кожей, припухшие веки, мутные глаза. Он как будто только что проснулся после попойки и ещё не успел привести себя в порядок (Лившиц 1). The flabby face with its unhealthy, greyish skin, the puffy eyelids, the lackluster eyes. It was as though he had just woken up after a binge and had not yet managed to tidy himself up (1a). ♦ Очевидно, уже после того, как [Поликарпов] смотался с нами в Переделкино, он успел привести себя в порядок (Ивинская 1). It was clear that after our trip out to Peredelkino, he [Polikarpov] had managed to freshen himself up… (1a).

П-407 • ЧТО ПОСЕ́ЕШЬ, ТО И ПОЖНЁШЬ [saying] the way you treat others is the way you will be treated: ≃ **as ye sow, so shall ye reap; as you do unto others, so they will do unto you;** [in limited contexts] **you have made your bed, now (you must) lie in ⟨on⟩ it.**

«Господи… – трясясь от негодования, причитала мать [Влада]. – …Ты скоро вгонишь меня в гроб раньше времени, негодяй!.. Сил моих больше нет!» Тётка, сурово поджав губы, молчала. Её неприязнь к Владу уравновешивалась сейчас торжеством над золовкой: мол… что посеешь, то и пожнёшь (Максимов 2). "Lord…" his [Vlad's] mother wailed, shaking with indignation. "…You'll drive me to an early grave, you little horror!…I've reached the end of my tether!" His aunt, her lips pressed sternly together, said nothing. Her dislike of Vlad was now equalled by the sense of triumph over her sister-in-law:…as ye sow, so shall ye reap (2a).

П-408 • ДО ПОСИНЕ́НИЯ кричать, орать, спорить, зубрить *что* и т. п. *highly coll* [PrepP; Invar; adv; usu. used with impfv verbs] (to shout, yell, argue, cram for an exam etc) very intensely for a long period of time, until one is very tired or very tired of doing it (occas. with the implication that one's efforts fail to produce the desired results): **(do sth.) till one is about to drop ⟨till one drops⟩; (do sth.) till one can't do it anymore; (do sth.) to the point of exhaustion ⟨till one is exhausted⟩;** [with verbs of speech only] **till ⟨until⟩ one is blue in the face.**

«Как твой дед проводит время?» – «Спорит с соседом о политике до посинения». "How does your grandfather spend his time?" "He argues about politics with his neighbor till they're both blue in the face."

П-409 • ПОСЛА́ТЬ (КУДА́) ПОДА́ЛЬШЕ *кого;* **ПОСЛА́ТЬ КУДА́ СЛЕ́ДУЕТ** *all highly coll* [VP; subj: human; the verb may take the final position, otherwise fixed WO] to tell s.o. to stop bothering one and go away: X послал Y-a подальше ≃ **X told Y to go to hell ⟨to blazes⟩; X told Y where to go ⟨to head⟩; X told Y to get lost; X sent Y on Y's way.**

«…Если мы не найдём общего языка, если вы меня пошлёте сейчас подальше, я и это пойму, поверьте…» (Аксёнов 7). "If we, shall we say, fail to find a common language, if you tell me to go to blazes, I'll understand, believe me" (7a). ♦ «…Конечно, в гражданской жизни такого положения не бывает, потому что там каждый человек отработал свои восемь часов на производстве, считает себя уже свободным, и если какой инженер или мастер прикажет ему что-нибудь, так он может послать его куда подальше и правильно сделает» (Войнович 2). "…Of course in civilian life such a situation is impossi-ble because there, after a person's put in his eight hours at the factory, he can think of himself as a free man, and if some engineer or foreman orders him to do anything, he can just tell him where to go and he'd be right to do it" (2a). ♦ В сопровождении работницы иностранной комиссии Союза писателей входит мистер Гопкинс… Будь это какой-нибудь болгарин или другой социалистический брат, так его можно бы послать подальше. Но за мистером Гопкинсом международная разрядка и конвертируемая валюта (Войнович 3). Accompanied by a worker from the foreign office of the Writers' Union, Mr. Hopkins enters….If he were a Bulgarian or some other brother in socialism, he [Ivanko] could send him on his way. But behind Mr. Hopkins there is international détente and convertible foreign currency (3a).

П-410 • ДО ПОСЛЕ́ДНЕГО [PrepP; Invar] **1. биться, сражаться** и т. п. ~ [adv] (to fight, struggle, continue doing sth. etc) as long as one's strength lasts, exerting every effort, and, in military contexts, to the point of sacrificing one's life: **to the last; to the bitter end; to the (very) end;** [in limited contexts] **to the last man.**

А что, правда: остаться [в России] и биться до последнего? И будь что будет? (Солженицын 2). What, then, should I do? Stay on [in Russia] and fight to the last? Come what may? (2a). ♦ Старуха и сама до последнего возилась со скотом, уж и двигаться как следует не могла, а всё хваталась за подойник… (Распутин 3). The old lady herself had looked after cattle to the bitter end. Even when she could hardly walk she would still pick up her pail and set off… (3a).

2. usu. **всё до последнего** [postmodif] all (of sth.) without exception: **absolutely (everything); every last (thing ⟨detail etc⟩).**

Он ничего от неё не утаил, рассказал всё до последнего. He held nothing back; he told her every last detail.

П-411 • ВХОДИ́ТЬ/ВОЙТИ́ В ПОСЛО́ВИЦУ ⟨В ПО-ГОВО́РКУ⟩ [VP; subj: usu. abstr; usu. pfv] (usu. of some quality manifest in a person or thing to a very high degree) to become widely known, commonly referred to: X вошёл в послови-цу ≃ **X is ⟨has become⟩ proverbial ⟨legendary⟩.**

Одним из первых был взят директор туберкулёзного ин-ститута профессор Аксянцев, старый член партии. Следом за ним ректор университета Векслин, чья безоглядная предан-ность партии вошла в Казани в поговорку (Гинзбург 1). One of the first [to be arrested] was Professor Aksyantsev, an old Party member and the head of the Tuberculosis Institute. The next to go was the rector of the university, Vekslin, whose selfless devotion to the Party was proverbial (1b).

П-412 • СЛЕЧЬ В ПОСТЕ́ЛЬ [VP; subj: human] to become so sick that one has to stay in bed: X слёг в постель ≃ **X took to his bed; X fell ill (and took to his bed); X was ⟨became⟩ bedridden.**

Его мать так огорчилась тайным браком, что слегла в постель и умерла… (Герцен 2). His mother was so chagrined at the secret marriage that she took to her bed and died… (2a). ♦ «А не боялся, что я не спала ночь, бог знает что передумала и чуть не слегла в постель?» – сказала она, поводя по нём испытую-щим взглядом (Гончаров 1). "But you weren't afraid of my spend-ing sleepless nights, thinking God knows what, and almost falling ill?" she asked, scrutinizing his face (1b).

П-413 • ПОСТО́ЛЬКУ, ПОСКО́ЛЬКУ [subord Conj, correlative] to the extent that: **insofar ⟨in so far⟩ as.**

[Серебряков:] …Я стар, болен и потому нахожу своевременным регулировать свои имущественные отно-шения постольку, поскольку они касаются моей семьи (Чехов 3). [S.:] I'm old and ill, so it seems to me high time to put my property and affairs in order in so far as they affect my family (3c).

П-414 • ПОСТО́ЛЬКУ-ПОСКО́ЛЬКУ *coll* [AdvP; Invar; adv] (in refer. to a person) (to do sth.) not in full measure (may refer to s.o.'s having only a limited knowledge of sth., doing a job without exerting maximum effort, being unwilling to trust another fully etc): **to some degree; up to a point; only so far; not put a lot of effort into (doing sth.).**

«Мы вам доверяем, но постольку-поскольку... Ваше предательство не скоро забудется...» – «Ну, и мы вам послужим постольку-поскольку!» – с холодным бешенством подумал... Григорий (Шолохов 5). "We trust you, but only so far.... Your treachery will not soon be forgotten...." "Then we'll serve you only so far," Grigory reflected with cold fury... (5a). ♦ Немецкий язык мне нравится меньше, чем французский, поэтому я и занимаюсь им постольку-поскольку. I don't like German as much as French, so I don't put a lot of effort into studying it. ♦ [Вадим:] Галя, я из детского возраста вырос и, если считаю, что в моей будущей профессии какие-то школьные науки не будут иметь значения, могу заниматься ими постольку-поскольку (Розов 1). [context transl] [V.:] Look, I have outgrown my childhood, and if I am convinced that in my chosen profession I'll have no use for certain school subjects, I have the right to be less serious about them (1a).

П-415 • **ПОСТОЯ́ТЬ ЗА СЕБЯ́** *coll* [VP; subj: human; often infin with уметь, мочь, готов etc] to defend o.s. against attack, opposition, criticism etc: X умеет постоять за себя ≃ **X can ⟨knows how to⟩ stand ⟨stick⟩ up for himself; X can look after ⟨take care of⟩ himself; [in limited contexts] X is man ⟨woman⟩ enough to stand ⟨stick⟩ up for himself ⟨herself⟩.**

Мне нравилась наивная девушка, которая за себя постоять умела... (Герцен 1). I liked the simple-hearted girl who knew how to stand up for herself... (1a). ♦ «Не связывайся, Фатима. Сама за себя постою» (Пастернак 1). "Don't you meddle in this, Fatima, I can look after myself" (1a). ♦ Мальчики в училище дразнили Иосифа: отец не мог постоять за себя (Рыбаков 2). The boys in school [teased Josef], saying that his father hadn't been man enough to stand up for himself (2a).

П-416 • **(НАШ) ПОСТРЁЛ ВЕЗДЕ́ ПОСПЕ́Л** [saying] said (either disapprovingly or, less often, humorously and approvingly) of an enterprising, clever person who is involved in everything, and who learns of and acts on new developments before others do: ≃ **he ⟨she⟩ has a finger in every pie; he ⟨she⟩ beats everyone to the punch; he ⟨she⟩ gets in on everything.**

«Хорош мальчик! Вдруг из отцовских сорока сделал тысяч триста капиталу, и в службе за надворного перевалился, и учёный... Пострел везде поспел!» (Гончаров 1). "Oh, he's a fine fellow! He suddenly turns a capital of forty thousand into three hundred thousand, manages to become a court councilor and a man of learning....He has a finger in every pie" (1b).

П-417 • **НА ПОСЫ́ЛКАХ** (*у кого*) *obsoles, coll* [PrepP; Invar; subj-compl with copula (subj: human) or obj-compl with держать (obj: human)] one performs minor services, small tasks for s.o. (to have s.o.) perform minor services, small tasks for s.o.: X у Y-а на посылках ≃ **X runs errands for Y; X is Y's errand boy ⟨girl⟩; X fetches and carries for Y.**

[Шелавина:] Так болтается где-то, у начальника на посылках, должно быть (Островский 3). [Sh.:] He puts in hours somewhere – probably running errands for his chief (3a). ♦ «Так, видно, этот Кирила Петрович у вас делает что хочет?» – «И вестимо, барин: ...исправник у него на посылках» (Пушкин 1). "So evidently this Kirila Petrovich does just what he likes in these parts?" "Aye, so he does, young master:...the police superintendent is his errand boy" (1a).

П-418 • **ВГОНЯ́ТЬ/ВОГНА́ТЬ В ПОТ** *кого coll* [VP; subj: human] **1.** [usu. impfv] (often in refer. to physical labor) to compel s.o. to work a lot and very intensely: X вгонял Y-а в пот ≃ **X worked Y hard ⟨into the ground⟩; X made Y work very hard; X pushed Y to the limit; X drove Y hard ⟨relentlessly⟩.**

До сдачи проекта оставались считанные дни, и Нефедов не только сам работал по шестнадцать часов в сутки, но вгонял в пот даже самых ленивых своих подчинённых. There were precious few days left before the project was due, and not only did Nefedov himself work sixteen hours a day, he pushed even the laziest of his workers to the limit.

2. to cause s.o. to feel extremely agitated, disquieted etc: X вогнал Y-а в пот ≃ **X made Y very nervous; X got Y all nervous; X made Y sweat; X threw Y into a panic.**

П-419 • **ПРОЛИВА́ТЬ/ПРОЛИ́ТЬ ПОТ** *coll*; **ПРОЛИ́ТЬ СЕМЬ ПОТО́В** *coll*; **УМЫВА́ТЬСЯ ПО́ТОМ** *substand* [VP; subj: human] to work until exhausted: X проливает пот ≃ **X sweats and slaves ⟨strains⟩; [in limited contexts] X lives by the sweat of his brow.**

[author's usage] «Я всю жисть [*substand* = жизнь] работал... потом омывался...» (Шолохов 4). "I've worked hard all my life, sweating and straining" (4a). ♦ [Софья Егоровна:] Мы будем людьми, Мишель! Мы будем есть свой хлеб, мы будем проливать пот, натирать мозоли... (Чехов 1). [S.E.:] We'll be decent people, Michael. We shall eat our own bread. We shall live by the sweat of our own brows. We shall have calloused hands (1a).

П-420 • **ДО КРОВА́ВОГО ПО́ТА** работать и т. п. *coll* [PrepP; Invar; adv; fixed WO] (in refer. to physically taxing work) (to work) to the point of complete exhaustion: X работал ~ ≃ **X worked till he sweated blood; X worked till he dropped.**

П-421 • **ДО СЕДЬМО́ГО ⟨ДЕСЯ́ТОГО⟩ ПО́ТА** работать, трудиться и т. п. *coll* [PrepP; these forms only; adv; fixed WO] (more often in refer. to physical labor) (to work) until one is extremely tired, fatigued: X работал до седьмого пота ≃ **X worked himself into the ground; X worked himself into a lather; X sweated his guts out working.**

П-422 • **В ПО́ТЕ ЛИЦА́** работать, трудиться и т. п.; **В ПО́ТЕ ЛИЦА́ СВОЕГО́** *obs, elev* [PrepP; these forms only; adv; fixed WO] (to work) with great zeal, applying all one's strength and energy: **by the sweat of one's brow.**

[Ирина:] Человек должен трудиться, работать в поте лица, кто бы он ни был... (Чехов 5). [I.:] Man must work, he must toil by the sweat of his brow, no matter who he is... (5a).

< From the Bible: "In the sweat of thy face shalt thou eat bread..." (Gen. 3:19).

П-423 • **БЛУЖДА́ТЬ ⟨БРОДИ́ТЬ⟩ В ПОТЁМКАХ** *coll* [VP; subj: human] to try to understand sth. or find the correct solution to some problem without having the necessary experience or information: X блуждает в потёмках ≃ **X is (groping ⟨fumbling⟩) in the dark.**

«Ты нам всё по совести рассказывай!» – «Мы тут в потёмках блукаем [*Ukrainian* = блуждаем]» (Шолохов 3). "Tell us the truth." "We're all in the dark here" (3b).

П-424 • **В ПОТЁМКАХ** *coll* [PrepP; Invar; subj-compl with copula (subj: human)] one is completely uninformed about a specific situation or occurrence, is lacking knowledge or understanding of a specific subject etc: X был в потёмках ≃ **X was in the dark; X was lost ⟨at a loss, at sea⟩.**

Спасибо, что вы мне рассказали правду о том, что произошло. Всё это время я была в потёмках. Thank you for telling me the truth about what happened. All this time I was in the dark.

П-425 • **ДО ПОТЕ́РИ СОЗНА́НИЯ** *coll* [PrepP; Invar; adv; fixed WO] to an extremely high degree: **like mad ⟨crazy⟩;** ‖

зубрить ~ ≃ **cram till one drops; study to the point of exhaustion;** ‖ злить ⟨раздражать⟩ *кого* ~ ≃ **vex ⟨irritate⟩ s.o. no end;** ‖ устать ~ ≃ **be dead tired ⟨dog-tired⟩;** ‖ влюбиться (*в кого*) ~ ≃ **fall madly in love (with s.o.); fall head over heels for s.o.;** ‖ изумить *кого* ~ ≃ **throw s.o. for a loop; bowl s.o. over; shock ⟨surprise⟩ the hell out of s.o.**

П-426 • **ЧЬЯ ПОТЕ́РЯ, МОЯ́ НАХО́ДКА** *coll, cliché* [sent; Invar; fixed WO] (said, usu. by children, when finding sth.; usu. the person who finds the lost object does not show anyone what he has found) the person who finds a lost thing has the right to keep it: **finders keepers (, losers weepers).**

П-427 • **КАК ⟨БУ́ДТО, СЛО́ВНО, ТО́ЧНО⟩ ПОТЕ́-РЯННЫЙ** **ходить, броди́ть, гляде́ть** и т. п. *coll* [как etc + AdjP; nom only; adv] (to walk around, wander etc) in an unsettled, distressed, confused state, (to look) unsettled, distressed, confused: **like a lost soul; like a man ⟨a woman⟩ distraught;** [in limited contexts] **with a lost look; out of one's senses.**

На жилищных – стояли ряды бараков... громадных, длинных, одинаковых бараков. Попадались палатки. Попадались землянки. Тоже большие и тоже одинаковые. Она бродила среди них как потерянная (Катаев 1). At the habitation sectors stood rows of barracks...huge, long barracks, all alike; occasionally, tents; occasionally, sod huts – also large and also all alike. She wandered among them like a lost soul (1a). ♦ Купцы и сидельцы (их было мало), как потерянные, ходили между солдатами, отпирали и запирали свои лавки и сами с молодцами куда-то выносили свои товары (Толстой 6). The shopkeepers and their assistants (of whom there were but few) moved about among the soldiers like men distraught, unlocking their shops, locking them up again, and themselves, together with their shopboys, carrying off armloads of their own goods (6a). ♦ Соня остановилась в сенях у самого порога, но не переходила за порог и глядела как потерянная, не сознавая, казалось, ничего... (Достоевский 3). Sonya stood in the entryway, just at the threshold but not crossing it, with a lost look, unconscious, as it seemed, of everything... (3c). ♦ «Заметьте, он над Григорием трудится, обтирает ему платком голову и, убедясь, что он мёртв, как потерянный, весь в крови, прибегает опять туда, в дом своей возлюбленной...» (Достоевский 2). "Notice, he takes trouble over Grigory, he wipes his head with a handkerchief, and, convinced that he is dead, he runs, out of his senses, all covered with blood, there, to the house of his sweetheart..." (2a).

П-428 • **ПОШЛА́ ПОТЕ́ХА!** *highly coll* [sent; fixed WO] some boisterous, impetuous action began: **(then) the fun ⟨the excitement, the trouble⟩ began; (and) the fun was on; (then) all hell broke loose;** [in limited contexts] **and the sport began.**

«Через две минуты уж в сакле был ужасный гвалт... Все выскочили, схватились за ружья... Крик, шум, выстрелы...» (Лермонтов 1). "Two minutes later a terrific uproar broke out in the hut....Everybody rushed out and went for their rifles – and the fun was on! There was screaming and shouting and shots were fired..." (1b). "Two minutes later, there was a terrible uproar indoors....Everybody dashed out, grabbed their rifles – and the sport began! There was shouting, noise, rifle shots..." (1a).

П-429 • **СЕМЬ ⟨ДЕ́СЯТЬ⟩ ПОТО́В СГОНЯ́ТЬ/СО-ГНА́ТЬ ⟨СПУСКА́ТЬ/СПУСТИ́ТЬ⟩** *coll* [VP; subj: human; usu. pfv; usu. this WO] **1.** ~ *с кого* to wear out, exhaust s.o. with hard work: X с Y-а семь потов сгонит ≃ **X will work Y till Y drops; X will work Y to the point of exhaustion ⟨into the ground⟩; X will make Y sweat blood.**

Семь потов сгоню, но сделаю из тебя настоящего мастера. I'll work you into the ground, but I'll make a real master craftsman of you.

2. (usu. in refer. to physical labor or athletics) to expend an enormous amount of effort: X семь потов спустил ≃ **X knocked himself out; X did sth. till he dropped; X sweated blood.**

Когда Харламов начал полнеть, он стал тренироваться ежедневно, сгоняя на каждой тренировке по семь потов. When Kharlamov began to put on weight, he started working out every day, and would knock himself out at each training session.

П-430 • **СЕМЬ ⟨ДЕ́СЯТЬ⟩ ПОТО́В СОШЛО́** *с кого coll* [VP~subj~; usu. this WO] s.o. made a tremendous effort, exerted an enormous amount of energy, exhausted himself (in accomplishing sth.): с X-а семь потов сошло ≃ **X sweated blood; X knocked himself out; X did sth. till he dropped.**

«Однажды у нас пропала лошадь... Часа два шли мы по её следу, пока не увидели её на таком выступе, откуда она сама спуститься не могла... Семь потов с нас сошло, пока мы её оттуда выволокли и пригнали обратно» (Искандер 3). "One time one of our horses got lost....We followed the tracks for two hours until we saw him on a ledge he couldn't get down from by himself....We sweated blood dragging him out of there and driving him back" (3a).

П-431 • **отдать на ПОТО́К И РАЗГРАБЛЕ́НИЕ** *что;* **предать ПОТО́КУ И РАЗГРАБЛЕ́НИЮ** *что both obs, lit* [NP; fixed WO] complete destruction and widespread looting (of some place, country etc): X-ы отдали Y на поток и разграбление ≃ **Xs surrendered Y to be ravaged and plundered ⟨pillaged and ruined⟩;** ‖ X-ы предали Y потоку и разграблению ≃ **Xs ravaged and plundered ⟨pillaged and ruined⟩ Y.**

< In Old Russia «поток» was a punishment that allowed for the property of the punished person or group to be plundered.

П-432 • **С ПОТОЛКА́ взять, сказать** *что coll* [PrepP; Invar; adv] (to say, claim etc sth.) without any factual basis, evidence etc: X взял Y ~ ≃ **X got Y (from) out of the blue; X pulled Y from out of nowhere; X pulled ⟨made up⟩ Y out of thin air; Y came out of thin air; X was talking through his hat; X got ⟨came up with⟩ Y off the top of X's head.**

В передовой его [редактора Ермолкина] всегда интересовали не тема, не содержание, не, скажем, стиль изложения, его интересовало только, чтобы слово «Сталин» упоминалось не меньше двенадцати раз... Почему он взял минимальным это число, а не какое другое, просто ли с потолка или чутьё подсказывало, сказать трудно, но было именно так (Войнович 4). It was never the editorial's theme, content, or, shall we say, its expository style which interested him [Editor Ermolkin]; all that interested him was that the word "Stalin" be mentioned no less than twelve times....Why he selected this as the minimum and not some other amount, whether he got it from out of the blue or was following some hint, is difficult to say, but in any case, that was how it was (4a).

П-433 • **ПЛЕВА́ТЬ В ПОТОЛО́К** *coll* [VP; subj: human] to idle, do absolutely nothing: X плюёт в потолок ≃ **X goofs off; X loafs; X twiddles his thumbs; X sits around on his butt.**

Варвара жаловалась на сына: «Не знаю, что с ним делать. Работать не хочет, целыми днями плюёт в потолок». Varvara complained about her son: "I don't know what to do with him. He doesn't want to work, and he spends whole days goofing off."

П-434 • **ПО́ТОМ И КРО́ВЬЮ добывать** *что* **доставаться** и т. п. *coll* [NP~instrum~; Invar; adv; fixed WO] at the cost of great effort, much work etc: **(achieve sth. by ⟨cost s.o. etc⟩) a lot of blood and sweat ⟨blood, sweat, and tears⟩; (achieve ⟨get⟩ sth.) by one's own sweat and blood.**

[Варравин:] Состояние?! – А что, вы как думаете, – оно мне даром пришло – а? Потом да кровью пришло оно мне! (Сухово-Кобылин 1). [V.:] Fortune?! What, do you think I got mine for nothing? Well? I got it by my own sweat and blood! (1a).

П-435 • ПОТОМУ́ ЧТО ⟨КАК *substand*⟩; **ОТТОГО́ ЧТО** [subord Conj; introduces a clause of reason] for the reason that: **because; as; for; since.**

«Третий закон: спишь с начальством – не показывай вида, потому как начальники меняются…» (Максимов 3). "Third Commandment: If you sleep with the boss, don't make it so obvious, because bosses come and go" (3a). ♦ «Я стал читать, учиться – науки также надоели; я видел, что ни слава, ни счастье от них не зависят нисколько, потому что самые счастливые люди – невежды…» (Лермонтов 1). "I began to read and to study, but wearied of learning too; I saw that neither fame, nor happiness depended on it in the slightest, for the happiest people were the ignorant…" (1b).

П-436 • ДО ПОТО́ПА *coll, usu. humor or iron* [PrepP; Invar; adv] very long ago: **way back when; before the flood.**

«Посмотри, что я нашла в бабушкином сундуке!» – «Такие платья, должно быть, до потопа носили». "Look what I found in Grandma's old trunk!" "They must have worn dresses like that way back when."

< Referring to the Biblical account of the Deluge (Gen. 7, 8).

П-437 • С ⟨СО ВСЕ́МИ⟩ ПОТРОХА́МИ *highly coll* [PrepP; these forms only; adv; usu. used with pfv verbs] in full, completely, with everything there is: **lock, stock, and barrel; body and soul; hook, line, and sinker; bag and baggage;** ‖ **продать** *кого* **со всеми потрохами** ≃ **sell s.o. out; sell s.o. down the river.**

Сговориться с Лурье мне было нетрудно, ибо сговариваться, правду сказать, было не о чем: я без колебаний отдавал ему на съедение всего Баха с потрохами… (Лившиц 1). I had no problem in reaching an agreement with Lourié because to tell the truth, there was nothing to reach an agreement about. I could safely leave Bach, lock, stock and barrel to his mercy… (1a). ♦ К несчастью, то, что у нас обозначается компромиссом, есть нечто иное. Пойти на компромисс равносильно тому, чтобы запродать себя с потрохами (Мандельштам 2). Unfortunately, "compromise" in this country means something different from elsewhere – namely, selling yourself body and soul (2a).

П-438 • ДО (СА́МЫХ) ПОТРОХО́В промёрзнуть, промо́кнуть, потрясти́ *кого и т. п. highly coll* [PrepP; these forms only; adv; used with pfv verbs] very thoroughly, extremely: **промёрзнуть** ~ ≃ **get chilled to the bone ⟨to the marrow, right through⟩;** ‖ **промокнуть** ~ ≃ **get soaked to the skin; get soaked through; get drenched to the bone;** ‖ **потрясти** ~ ≃ **shock the hell out of s.o.**

День был холодный, и мы промёрзли до самых потрохов. It was a cold day, and we got chilled to the bone.

П-439 • ПРОДАВА́ТЬ/ПРОДА́ТЬ ЗА ⟨ПРОМЕНЯ́ТЬ НА⟩ ЧЕЧЕВИ́ЧНУЮ ПОХЛЁБКУ *кого-что;* **ПРОДАВА́ТЬСЯ/ПРОДА́ТЬСЯ ЗА ЧЕЧЕВИ́ЧНУЮ ПОХЛЁБКУ** *all lit, derog* [VP; subj: human; usu. pfv; the verb may take the final position, otherwise fixed WO] to betray s.o. or some important cause for a meager reward, out of petty self-interest: X продал Y-а за чечевичную похлёбку ≃ **X sold Y for a mess of pottage.**

…Врачу в лагере труднее, чем всем прочим смертным, сохранить душу живую, не продать за чечевичную похлёбку совесть, жизнь тысяч товарищей (Гинзбург 1). …[In camp], it was harder for a doctor than for anyone else to keep his integrity and resist selling the lives of thousands of his fellow-prisoners for a mess of pottage (1a).

< From the Biblical account (Gen. 25: 29–34) of how Esau sold his birthright to his brother Jacob for a pottage of lentils.

П-440 • С ПОХО́ДОМ взвесить, продать *highly coll* [PrepP; Invar; adv or nonagreeing modif (when used with a quantit NP)] (to weigh sth. out, sell sth.) adding a small surplus (for no extra charge): **giving s.o. a little extra for good measure; a generous** [quantit NP]; **(weigh sth. out etc) generously; (give ⟨sell⟩ s.o.)** [quantit NP] **and then some; (be) far from stingy (in weighing out sth.).**

Приятно покупать мёд на пасеке. Пасечник не только мёдом угостит, но и взвесит с походом. It's nice to buy honey at an apiary. The beekeeper not only treats you to some honey, but, when weighing out your purchase, gives you a little extra for good measure.

П-441 • НА КОГО́ ⟨НА ЧТО⟩ ПОХО́Ж *coll* [AdjP; subj-compl with быть∅, стать (subj: human, usu. pers pronoun); fixed WO] (of a person who looks sloppy, unhealthy, frozen etc) s.o. looks worse than usual and/or worse than he should: на кого X похож! ≃ **what a state X is in!; X looks a sight!; what a sight X is!; just look at X!**

Митя, на кого ты похож! Где ты так выпачкался? Mitya, just look at you! Where did you get so dirty?

П-442 • НА ЧТО Э́ТО ПОХО́ЖЕ? *coll* [sent (with быть∅); usu. pres or fut; fixed WO] (used to express indignation, resentment, reproach etc) what kind of behavior or action is this?: **whoever heard (of) the like?; whoever heard of such a thing?; what (sort of game) is this?; what do you ⟨they etc⟩ think you ⟨they etc⟩ are doing?; [in limited contexts] what will ⟨did⟩ it look like?; what sort of situation is this ⟨would that be etc⟩?**

[Городничий:] А, Степан Ильич, скажите ради бога, куда вы запропастились? На что это похоже? (Гоголь 4). [Mayor:] Ah, Stepan Ilyich! Say, for God's sake, where've you been hiding out? Whoever heard the like! (4d). ♦ «А это на что похоже, что вчера только восемь фунтов пшена отпустила, опять спрашивают… А я пшена не отпущу» (Толстой 2). "And what sort of game is this? Only yesterday I let them have eight pounds of rice and now they're asking for more!…I'm not giving you any more rice" (2b). ♦ Михаилу вдруг нестерпимо стыдно стало и за себя и за Егоршу… На что это похоже? Пришли, уселись за стол и давай отчитывать старика (Абрамов 1). Suddenly Mikhail felt unbearably ashamed, for himself and for Egorsha….What did it look like? They arrive, sit down at his table and start lecturing the old guy (1a). ♦ Ну, представьте себе… если грешники в аду начнут права качать – на что это будет похоже? (Буковский 1). Well, I ask you, what would it be like if the sinners in hell suddenly started shouting for their rights – what sort of situation would that be? (1a).

П-443 • НЕ ПОХО́ЖЕ *на кого coll* [AdjP; Invar; subj-compl with быть∅ (subj: infin or это)] doing sth. is not typical, characteristic of s.o.: это не похоже на X-а ≃ **that's unlike ⟨not like⟩ X; that's not the X I know; that's out of character for X.**

[Варвара Капитоновна:] Никому ничего не сказать. Так не похоже на Борю (Розов 3). [V.K.:] Not telling anybody anything. That's not like Borya (3a).

П-444 • ПОХО́ЖЕ (НА ТО), ЧТО… *coll* [these forms only; impers predic with быть∅; fixed WO] apparently, evidently: **it looks like; it looks as if; (it's) as if; it seems that.**

Похоже на то, что он на меня нынче смотрит только лишь как на лидера группы… (Аксёнов 12). It looks as if he sees me now as only the leader of the new group… (12a). ♦ В Москве шли холодные дожди, похоже было на то, что лето уже прошло и не вернётся… (Бунин 1). Cold rain was falling in Moscow, as if summer were already over and would not return… (1a).

П-445 • **(ЭТО) НИ НА ЧТО НЕ ПОХО́ЖЕ!** *coll* [usu. indep. sent; fixed WO] (used to express indignation, anger, or a sharply negative attitude toward some action or occurrence) this is very bad, no good at all: **this is (absolutely) unheard of!; I've never seen ⟨heard (of)⟩ anything like it!; that's ⟨it's⟩ beyond anything ⟨everything⟩!; it's unthinkable!; this is outrageous; this is (just) too much.**

«Ну, сколько тут, говори скорей!» — «Да вот мяснику восемьдесят шесть рублей пятьдесят четыре копейки»... — «Ну, ещё кому?» — говорил Илья Ильич... «Ещё сто двадцать один рубль восемнадцать копеек хлебнику да зеленщику». — «Это разорение! Это ни на что не похоже!» — говорил Обломов, выходя из себя (Гончаров 1). "Well, what does it come to? Be quick, tell me!" "Well—for the butcher, eighty-six rubles, fifty-four kopecks."..."Well, who else do we owe?" asked Ilya Ilych...."A hundred and twenty-one rubles, eighteen kopecks to the baker and the greengrocer." "That's devastating! Absolutely unheard of!" exclaimed Oblomov, beside himself (1b). ♦ «...Это ни на что не похоже; хоть бы ты побранил свою жену. Что это? Как сумасшедшая без тебя. Ничего не видит, не помнит...» (Толстой 7). "...I never saw anything like it; you really must give your wife a good scolding! She is like one possessed without you. No eyes for anything, forgets everything" (7a). ♦ ...[Я] подкрался к окну... Говорили обо мне... «Господа!.. это ни на что не похоже; Печорина надо проучить!» (Лермонтов 1). ...[I] crept up to the window.....They were talking about me...."Gentlemen...I've never heard anything like it. We must teach Pechorin a lesson!" (1d). ♦ «Право, как вообразишь, до чего иногда доходит мода... ни на что не похоже!» (Гоголь 3). "Really, when one imagines to what lengths fashion will go at times...it's beyond anything!" (3b). ♦ «...Это ни на что не похоже! Половина людей разбежалась» (Толстой 6). "...This is outrageous! Half of the men have bolted!" (6a).

П-446 • **ВОЗДУ́ШНЫЙ ПОЦЕЛУ́Й (послать кому)** [NP; usu. obj; fixed WO] a gesture used to represent a kiss, made by moving one's hand toward one's lips and then in the direction of s.o.: **X послал Y-у воздушный поцелуй ≃ X blew Y a kiss.**

Статный австрийский офицер со спортсменской выправкой шёл под конвоем на вокзал. Ему улыбнулись две барышни, гулявшие по перрону. Он на ходу очень ловко раскланялся и послал им воздушный поцелуй (Шолохов 2). A fine-looking Austrian officer with the bearing of an athlete was being taken under guard to the station building. Two young ladies strolling along the platform smiled at him. He managed a very neat bow without stopping and blew them a kiss (2a).

П-447 • **ИУ́ДИН ПОЦЕЛУ́Й; ИУ́ДИНО ЛОБЗА́НИЕ; ПОЦЕЛУ́Й ИУ́ДЫ** *all lit, derog* [NP; fixed WO] betrayal hypocritically concealed by outward friendliness: **Judas kiss; kiss of Judas.**

< From the Bible (Matt. 26:48–49, Mark 14:44–45, Luke 22:47–48).

П-448 • **ПО́ЧВА ⟨ЗЕМЛЯ́⟩ УХО́ДИТ/УШЛА́ ⟨УСКОЛЬЗА́ЕТ/УСКОЛЬЗНУ́ЛА, УПЛЫВА́ЕТ/УПЛЫЛА́⟩ ИЗ-ПОД НОГ** *чьих, (у) кого;* **ПО́ЧВА КОЛЕ́БЛЕТСЯ/ЗАКОЛЕБА́ЛАСЬ ПОД НОГА́МИ** *чьими, у кого* [VP_subj] s.o.'s position is becoming extremely tenuous, unstable, s.o. is losing confidence in himself, in his chances to achieve success in sth.: почва уходит у X-a из-под ног ≃ **the ground is giving way ⟨is slipping (out) from⟩ beneath X's feet; the ground is giving way under X; the rug is being pulled out from under X.**

...Когда последний огонёк Узловска исчез за срезом оконного проёма и сырая темнота вплотную приникла к стеклу, он почувствовал, что земля уходит у него из-под ног (Максимов 3). ...When he had watched from his carriage window as the last light [of Uzlovsk] disappeared and the damp darkness pressed in against the glass, he had felt that the ground was giving way beneath his feet (3a). ♦ [author's usage] В чаду своих занятий и увлечений Пьер, однако, по прошествии года начал чувствовать, как та почва масонства, на которой он стоял, тем более уходила из-под его ног, чем твёрже он старался стать на ней (Толстой 5). Amid the hurly-burly of his activities, however, before the year was out Pierre began to feel as though the more firmly he tried to rest upon the ground of Freemasonry on which he had taken his stand, the more it was giving way under him (5a).

П-449 • **НА ПО́ЧВЕ** *чего, какой* [PrepP; Invar; Prep; the resulting PrepP is adv] by reason of sth., as a consequence of sth.: **on the grounds of; on account of; because of; due ⟨owing⟩ to; (resulting) from.**

На почве вызовов [в политическую полицию] у людей развились две болезни: одни подозревали во всяком человеке стукача, другие боялись, что их примут за стукача (Мандельштам 1). Because of this system of "interviews [with the secret police]," people developed two kinds of phobia—some suspected that everybody they met was an informer, others that they might be taken for one (1a). ♦ Сам он говорил, что на него нашло затмение на почве выпивки... (Искандер 3). He himself said that his head had been befuddled from drink (3a). ♦ На почве разницы в этих привилегиях иногда такие неприятности случаются, что иной раз задумаешься, может, этих привилегий лучше и совсем не иметь (Войнович 1). [context transl] Differences in privileges are sometimes grounds for such problems that you might think better not to have those privileges at all (1a).

П-450 • **СТОЯ́ТЬ НА ТВЁРДОЙ ⟨РЕА́ЛЬНОЙ⟩ ПО́ЧВЕ; ИМЕ́ТЬ (ТВЁРДУЮ) ПО́ЧВУ ПОД НОГА́МИ** *all lit* [VP; subj: human] to be in a secure position, have a basis allowing one to feel secure: X стоит на твёрдой почве ≃ **X is (standing) on solid ⟨firm⟩ ground; X has a firm footing.**

Получив постоянную работу, Карпов ощутил, что стоит на твёрдой почве. Once he got a steady job, Karpov felt that he was on solid ground.

П-451 • **ВЫБИВА́ТЬ/ВЫ́БИТЬ ⟨ВЫШИБА́ТЬ/ВЫ́ШИБИТЬ⟩ ПО́ЧВУ ИЗ-ПОД НОГ** *чьих, (у) кого* [VP; subj: human or, less often, abstr] to undermine s.o.'s sense of security, undercut s.o.'s plans, arguments etc, make precarious s.o.'s position in life or in some situation etc: X выбил у Y-a почву из-под ног ≃ **X cut the ground (out) from under Y ⟨Y's feet⟩;** [often in refer. to withholding or withdrawing support from s.o.] **X pulled the rug out from under Y;** [usu. in refer. to undercutting s.o.'s arguments in a debate, negotiations etc] **X left Y without a leg to stand on.**

Разрешив банкам обмен денег, правительство выбило почву из-под ног спекулянтов валютой. By permitting banks to change money, the government cut the ground out from under speculators in hard currency.

П-452 • **ЗОНДИ́РОВАТЬ/ПОЗОНДИ́РОВАТЬ ⟨ПРОЗОНДИ́РОВАТЬ⟩ ПО́ЧВУ** *lit* [VP; subj: human] to (try to) find out about sth. beforehand (usu. in order to determine ahead of time the chances for success): X зондирует почву ≃ **X tests ⟨explores⟩ the ground; X tests the waters; X sounds ⟨feels, checks⟩ out the possibilites; X puts out feelers.**

По прибытии нашем в роту нас медленно ощупывали, заранее стараясь определить, какое количество жизненных благ можно от нас получить... Мы, со своей стороны, тоже зондировали почву... (Лившиц 1). When one of us arrived in the company, they mentally felt us over, trying to predetermine the number of earthly blessings which they could extract from us....For our part we also explored the ground... (1a).

< The Russian idiom is apparently a loan translation of the French *sonder le terrain.*

П-453 • ИМЕ́ТЬ ПОД СОБО́Й ПО́ЧВУ *(какую)* lit [VP; subj: abstr (подозрение, опасение, заключение etc); usu. neg] (of a suspicion, apprehension, conclusion etc) to have a rational basis: X имеет под собой почву ≃ **X is grounded in fact; X is well-founded ⟨well-grounded⟩; X has a firm ⟨solid⟩ basis;** ‖ *Neg* X не имеет под собой почвы ≃ **X is groundless ⟨ungrounded, unfounded, without foundation⟩; there is no basis for X.**

Наконец... выяснилось, что девушка, подавшая повод к сложным Лариным чувствованиям, – сестра Коки, и Ларины соображения не имели под собой никакой почвы (Пастернак 1). ...Finally Lara learned that the girl who had aroused such complicated feelings in her was the young man's sister and that her suspicions had been groundless (1a). ♦ ...Я думаю, что утверждение некоторых очевидцев, что скот села Анхара, проявляя массовое ясновиденье, предсказывал бой, не имеет под собой серьёзной научной почвы (Искандер 3). ...I do not think there is any serious scientific basis for the claim of some eyewitnesses that the livestock of the village of Ankhara displayed mass clairvoyance and foretold the battle (3a).

П-454 • ПОДГОТА́ВЛИВАТЬ/ПОДГОТО́ВИТЬ ⟨РАСЧИЩА́ТЬ/РАСЧИ́СТИТЬ и т. п.⟩ ПО́ЧВУ *для чего* lit [VP; subj: human or abstr] to prepare the conditions that allow for sth.: X подготовил почву для Y-а ≃ **X prepared ⟨laid⟩ the ground for Y; X prepared ⟨paved⟩ the way for Y; X set the stage for Y.**

[author's usage] Понятие «развитие», очевидно, прочно связалось с позитивистами – Контом, Стюартом Миллем и всеми теми, кого читали и чтили люди поколения его [Мандельштама] матери, и он пробил у нас почву для марксизма (Мандельштам 1). For him [Mandelstam], the concept of "development" was evidently firmly associated with the positivists—Comte, Stuart Mill and others, read and revered by people of his mother's generation, who had prepared the way for Marxism (1a).

П-455 • ПРОЩУ́ПЫВАТЬ/ПРОЩУ́ПАТЬ ⟨НАЩУ́ПЫВАТЬ/НАЩУ́ПАТЬ⟩ ПО́ЧВУ *(для чего)* coll [VP; subj: human] to (try to) find out what the situation is, what the circumstances are (usu. in order to see whether they are conducive to the realization of one's goals): X прощупывает почву ≃ **X is testing the waters; X is putting out feelers; X is feeling ⟨checking⟩ out the situation; X is getting the lay of the land; X is exploring ⟨testing⟩ the ground;** [in limited contexts] **X is sounding ⟨feeling⟩ person Y out.**

Он хочет выяснить, поддержим ли мы его, поэтому и задаёт столько вопросов. Прощупывает почву. He wants to find out whether or not we'll support him, that's why he's asking so many questions. He's testing the waters.

П-456 • ТЕРЯ́ТЬ/ПОТЕРЯ́ТЬ ПО́ЧВУ ⟨ЗЕ́МЛЮ⟩ ПОД НОГА́МИ ⟨ИЗ-ПОД НОГ, ПОД СОБО́Й⟩ [VP; subj: human] to lose one's sense of security, lose confidence in o.s. etc (often as a result of having lost one's social position, job etc): X потерял почву под ногами ≃ **the ground slipped (out) from ⟨gave way⟩ beneath X's feet; X felt the ground slipping (out) from ⟨giving way⟩ beneath his feet; X felt the ground slipping (out) from under his feet; X felt the ground slipping away (from) under him ⟨his feet⟩.**

Красивая роль руководителя народного чувства так понравилась Растопчину, он так сжился с нею, что... необходимость оставления Москвы без всякого героического эффекта застала его врасплох, и он вдруг потерял из-под ног почву, на которой стоял, и решительно не знал, что ему делать (Толстой 6). The illustrious role of leader of popular feeling so delighted Rostopchin, and he had grown so accustomed to it, that the necessity of...surrendering Moscow with no heroic display of any kind

took him unawares, and he suddenly felt the ground slipping away from under him and was utterly at a loss to know what to do (6a).

П-457 • ПОЧЁМ ЗРЯ́ ругать, бранить *кого,* ругаться, лупить, бить *кого,* врать и т. п. *highly coll* [AdvP; Invar; adv (intensif); usu. used with impfv verbs; fixed WO] (to berate s.o., swear, beat s.o., lie etc) to an extreme degree, to the utmost extent: ругать ⟨бранить и т. п.⟩ *кого* ~ ≃ **curse s.o. for all one is worth; curse ⟨chew⟩ s.o. out; abuse s.o. in every way one can;** ‖ ругаться ⟨браниться⟩ ~ ≃ **turn the air blue; curse ⟨cuss⟩ a blue streak; curse for all one's worth;** ‖ бить *кого* ~ ≃ **give s.o. a good beating ⟨thrashing⟩; beat s.o. black and blue;** ‖ врать ~ ≃ **lie like a rug.**

...В середине лета Константин Иванович пал духом, клянёт правительство почём зря (Трифонов 6). ...By midsummer Konstantin Ivanovich had grown despondent and was cursing the government for all he was worth (6a). ♦ ...Старший политрук, начав кричать, никак не мог остановиться, он крестил Чонкина почём зря, говоря, что вот, мол, к чему приводит политическая незрелость и потеря бдительности... (Войнович 2). Having started shouting, the senior politruk was unable to stop. He chewed Chonkin out, saying that this was what political immaturity and loss of vigilance can lead to... (2a). ♦ Тут ещё соседи из двух таких же деревянных домиков портили дело: тоже строчили заявления, собирали подписи. Но они-то наоборот – торопились ломаться, ругали Петра Александровича почём зря (Трифонов 1). To add to his troubles, two of Pyotr Alexandrovich's neighbors who lived in wooden houses just like his own began scribbling letters of petition and gathering signatures. But they, by contrast, were trying to speed up the demolition process and abused Pyotr Alexandrovich in every way they could (1a).

П-458 • ПОЧЁТ И УВАЖЕ́НИЕ *obsoles* [formula phrase; Invar; fixed WO] a salutation upon meeting: **good day ⟨morning, evening, afternoon⟩; how do you do; greetings; my compliments.**

П-459 • В ПОЧЁТЕ *(у кого, где)* [PrepP; Invar; subj-compl with быть∅; prep obj: usu. pl or collect] **1.** [subj: human] one enjoys the respect of s.o. (usu. some group, community etc): X ~ (у Y-ов) ≃ **Ys hold X in high esteem ⟨regard⟩; X is held in high esteem ⟨regard⟩ (by Ys); X is highly regarded ⟨esteemed, respected⟩ (by Ys);** ‖ *Neg* X (у Y-ов) не ~ ≃ **X is viewed with disfavor (by Ys); Ys don't think much of X; X doesn't get much respect (from Ys).**

Специалисты высокого класса у нас в почёте. We hold first-rate specialists in high esteem. ♦ «Гришка-то непочтительный, поганец. Надысь [*regional* = на днях] иду из церкви, встретился со мной и не поздравствовался. Старики ноне [*obs* = нынче] не дюже [*substand* = очень] в почёте...» (Шолохов 2). "Grishka is a disrespectful young scoundrel. I passed him coming home from church the other day and the scalawag didn't even say good morning. Old folk don't get much respect nowadays" (2a).

2. [subj: abstr] sth. is considered worth practicing, a worthwhile undertaking, is respected, supported, recognized: X ~ (у Y-ов) ≃ **X is well-regarded ⟨highly regarded⟩ (by Ys); X is popular ⟨enjoys (much) popularity⟩ (with Ys);** [in limited contexts] **X has an honored part to play;** ‖ *Neg* X (у Y-ов) не ~ ≃ **Ys don't think much of X; X is looked down upon (by Ys).**

Огромное значение имело бы исследование количества доносов по периодам и распределение доносителей по возрасту. Существенно также качество и стиль доноса. К сожалению, социологические исследования у нас не в почёте (Мандельштам 2). A study of the number of denunciations by periods and by age of their authors would have enormous importance. The question of their quality and style would also repay investigation. But, alas, sociological studies are not well regarded in this country (2a). ♦ «Ошибки у нас бывают, – ещё Ленин говорил, не ошибается тот, кто ничего не делает, — но на ошибках учимся, критика и самокритика у нас в почёте...» (Максимов 1). "We do make mistakes, of course. Only those who do nothing make no mistakes, as Lenin said. But we learn from our mistakes. Criticism and self-criticism have an honoured part to play here..." (1a).

П-460 • МОЁ ⟨НАШЕ⟩ ПОЧТЕ́НИЕ¹ (кому); НИЖА́Й-ШЕЕ ПОЧТЕ́НИЕ all obsoles [formula phrase; these forms only; fixed WO] a salutation used upon meeting or parting: [upon meeting] **good day ⟨morning, evening, afternoon⟩; my respects; my compliments; greetings!; how do you do;** [when parting] **(my) regards; good day (to you); have a good ⟨pleasant⟩ day.**

«М-маё п-пачтенье [phonetic spelling = моё почтенье]!» — вскричал вдруг знакомый голос. Раскольников задрожал. Пред ним стоял Порох; он вдруг вышел из третьей комнаты (Достоевский 3). "M-my c-compliments, sir!" a familiar voice suddenly exclaimed. Raskolnikov gave a shudder. Before him stood Gunpowder; he had suddenly come out of the third room (3d). "Gr-r-reetings!" a familiar voice cried out suddenly. Raskolnikov shook. There stood Gunpowder; he walked out suddenly from the third room (3c). ♦ [Городничий:] Желаю здравствовать! [Хлестаков:] Моё почтение... (Гоголь 4). [Mayor:] How do you do, Sir! [Kh.:] My respects... (4b). ♦ [Сахатов:] Да, да. Моё почтение! (Уходит с лёгким поклоном.) (Толстой 3). [S.:] Good day to you, then. (Gives a small bow, and turns to go) (3b).

П-461 • МОЁ ПОЧТЕ́НИЕ² obsoles [NP; Invar] **1.** approv [usu. subj-compl with быть∅ (subj: any common noun)] sth. is absolutely amazing, unbelievable: X — моё почтение ≃ **X is really something!; X is (really) something else!; X is like nothing you've ever seen ⟨tasted etc⟩ before;** [in limited contexts] **I take off my hat to X.**

«...Признаюсь, не люблю я также винтовок черкесских; они как-то нашему брату неприличны, — приклад маленький, того и гляди нос обожжёт... Зато уж шашки у них — просто моё почтение!..» (Лермонтов 1). "I must say, I also do not like Circassian rifles. Somehow, they don't seem to be suitable for the likes of us: the butt is so small you have to be careful not to get your nose burnt....But then, those swords they have—ah, they're really something!" (1a). "I must admit I don't like the Cherkess rifles either; they are a bit inconvenient for the likes of us; the butt is so small that unless you watch out you may get your nose scorched....Their sabres now are a different matter—I take my hat off to them!" (1b).

2. obsoles, iron [Interj or subj-compl with быть∅ (subj: usu. infin); pres only] (used to express one's refusal to do sth., usu. sth. unpleasant, that is proposed, suggested, or requested by another) I absolutely will not do it: **thanks, but no thanks!; no way!**

Ехать в такой ливень на другой конец города? Нет уж, моё почтение! Go all the way across town in a downpour like this? Thanks, but no thanks!

П-462 • С ПОЧТЕ́НИЕМ быть∅ у кого, **явиться к кому** и т. п. obs [PrepP; Invar; adv] (to visit s.o.) as an expression of one's high regard for him: X был с почтением у Y-а ≃ **X paid his respects to Y.**

Весь следующий день посвящён был визитам; приезжий отправился делать визиты всем городским сановникам. Был с почтением у губернатора... Потом отправился к вице-губернатору, потом был у прокурора... (Гоголь 3). All the next day was devoted to calls. The newcomer set out on a round of visits to all the high officials in town. He paid his respects to the Governor....Then [he] called on the Vice-Governor, on the Public Prosecutor... (3c).

П-463 • С СОВЕРШЕ́ННЫМ ⟨СОВЕРШЕ́ННЕЙ-ШИМ, ГЛУБО́КИМ, НИЖА́ЙШИМ⟩ ПОЧТЕ́-НИЕМ; ПРИМИ́ТЕ УВЕРЕ́НИЯ В СОВЕРШЕ́Н-НОМ ⟨СОВЕРШЕ́ННЕЙШЕМ⟩ ПОЧТЕ́НИИ all obs [formula phrase; these forms only; fixed WO] (a polite closing formula in a letter to s.o.) with an expression of my great respect for you: **respectfully yours; with deepest respect.**

П-464 • ПОЧТИ́ ЧТО coll [AdvP; Invar; modif or adv; fixed WO] nearly: **almost; all but; practically; virtually;** [in limited contexts] **hardly.**

«У нас хоть нелепо рубить голову брату потому только, что он стал нам брат и что на него сошла благодать, но, повторяю, у нас есть своё, почти что не хуже. У нас историческое, непосредственное и ближайшее наслаждение истязанием битья» (Достоевский 1). "Though for us it's absurd to cut our brother's head off only because he's become our brother and grace has descended upon him, still, I repeat, we have our own ways, which are almost as good. We have our historical, direct, and intimate delight in the torture of beating" (1a). ♦ Писатели его [Лукина] ценили за то, что он, умея составлять бумаги, сам не лез в писатели, а мог бы, потому что в своём жанре равных себе не знал и вообще был почти что гений (Войнович 6). The writers appreciated Lukin because despite his skill with forms, he did not try to be a writer himself. But he could have been, because in the genre of forms he knew no equal, in fact the man was practically a genius (6a). ♦ «Читал?» — спросил Меркулов, с комическим испугом бросая листок... «Помилуйте, ваше благородие! Да я почти что неграмотный!» (Шолохов 3). "Did you read this?" Merkulov asked, dropping the sheet in a comic display of fright...."Beg pardon, Your Honour! I can hardly read" (3a).

П-465 • Е́СЛИ (УЖ) НА ТО ПОШЛО́; Е́ЖЕЛИ ⟨КО́ЛИ, КОЛЬ⟩ (УЖ) НА ТО ПОШЛО́ all coll [subord clause; these forms only; уж may take the initial position, otherwise fixed WO] since the topic has been raised, I would like to say...; the topic under discussion prompts me to say... (occas. the statement in question expresses sth. that the speaker refrained from saying earlier but now feels a responsibility or desire to interject; occas. it presents a contrast with a previous statement or with a commonly held idea, belief etc): **since ⟨while, now that⟩ we're on the subject ⟨the topic⟩; speaking of that;** [in limited contexts] **for that matter; come to think of it; come to that.**

«Что ты, не знаешь своей жены? Хозяйственная баба. Этого у неё не отнимешь. И уж если на то пошло, так с лесозаготовками у неё не хуже было, чем у других. А даже лучше» (Абрамов 1). "Don't you know your own wife? She's an efficient woman: that you can't take away from her. And while we're on the subject, her timber production was no worse than anyone else's. Better even" (1a). ♦ ...Как же измучит его отвращением крохотный угорёк под ухом раскрасивейшей Альбины, когда он, лишь только погаснет этот сладкий и такой не вечный миг, отрывается от неё всем своим существом и разглядывает со стороны. Нет ничего некрасивей красивой женщины, если вы её не любите, если уж на то пошло (Битов 2). ...How he will be tormented by his revulsion at the teeny little blackhead under very, very beautiful Albina's ear, as soon as this sweet and so uneternal instant fades and with his whole being he tears himself away to study her from a distance. For that matter, there is nothing uglier than a beautiful woman if you don't love her (2a). ♦ Нет, Нюрок — не учитель! Если на то пошло, у Ирины Викторовны никогда не было учителя, не нашлось во всём белом свете. Одни только советники, консультанты, наставники, вожатые, воспитатели, тренеры, инструкторы, секретари и председатели, а учителя — ни одного! (Залыгин 1). No, Niurok was no teacher. Come to think of it, Irina Viktorovna had never had a teacher. She'd never found one in all the world. Only advisers, consultants, mentors, guides, trainers, instructors, secretaries, and chairmen—never a teacher (1a).

П-466 • ЗАТКНУ́ТЬ ЗА ПО́ЯС ⟨ЗА́ ПОЯС obsoles⟩ кого coll, approv [VP; subj: human; usu. fut] to surpass or be superior

[503]

to another or others in some area or with regard to some quality: X Y-а заткнёт за пояс ≃ **X will ⟨can⟩ outshine ⟨outdo, beat⟩ Y; X will ⟨can⟩ run circles ⟨rings⟩ around Y; X is a damn(ed) sight more intelligent ⟨beautiful etc⟩ than Y; X is twice as smart ⟨talented etc⟩ as Y; [in limited contexts] X will put Y to shame.**

«...С ней живёт холостой брат: голова, не то, что вот эта, что тут в углу сидит, — сказал он, указывая на Алексеева, — нас с тобой за пояс заткнёт!» (Гончаров 1). "Her unmarried brother lives with her. He's a clever fellow, not like that chap in the corner there," he said, pointing to Alexeyev. "He's a damn sight more intelligent than you or I" (1a). ♦ «Я поставлю полные баллы во всех науках тому, кто ни аза не знает, да ведёт себя похвально; а в ком я вижу дурной дух да насмешливость, я тому нуль, хотя он Солона заткни за пояс!» (Гоголь 3). "I shall give full marks in all subjects to the boy who, even if he does not know his ABC[s], behaves properly; but if I see a wrong and scoffing spirit in anyone, I shall give him a nought, though he be twice as wise as Solon!" (3d).

П-467 • КЛА́НЯТЬСЯ/ПОКЛОНИ́ТЬСЯ В ПО́ЯС

(кому) [VP; subj: human] **1.** *obs* to make a low bow before s.o.: X поклонился Y-у в пояс ≃ **X bowed at ⟨from⟩ the waist (to Y); X bowed low to Y.**

«За оговор и за злобу мою простите». — «Бог простит», — ответил Раскольников, и как только произнёс это, мещанин поклонился ему, но уже не земно, а в пояс... (Достоевский 3). "Forgive me for slandering you and for having such evil thoughts." "God will forgive you," replied Raskolnikov, and as soon as he said it, the furrier bowed again, but not to the floor this time, merely at the waist... (3a). ♦ Лошади поскакали; народ на улице останавливался и кланялся в пояс. Пугачёв кивал головою на обе стороны (Пушкин 2). The horses set off at a gallop; the people in the street stopped and bowed from the waist. Pugachev nodded to them right and left (2a).

2. to express deep gratitude: X поклонится Y-у в пояс ≃ **X will bow down to the ground to Y.**

А может, Лизка и права, подумал вдруг Михаил. Может, и надо было спасибо [Анфисе] сказать... Нет, голубушка, мысленно сказал Михаил и стиснул зубы... Ты суд надо мной да над Варварой устроила, а я принародно в пояс тебе кланяться? (Абрамов 1). Maybe Lizka was right, Mikhail suddenly thought. Maybe they should have thanked her [Anfisa]....No, my dear, thought Mikhail, gritting his teeth....You make an example of Varvara and me, and you expect me to bow down to the ground to you in front of everyone? (1a).

П-468 • удар, бить НИ́ЖЕ ПО́ЯСА

coll [AdvP; Invar; usu. nonagreeing postmodif or adv; fixed WO] (of an action, remark etc) (sth. that is) unfair, cowardly, or unsporting; (do sth.) against the rules of fairness, justice: удар ~ ≃ **a blow ⟨a hit⟩ below the belt; low blow; cheap shot; ‖ бить ~ ≃ hit below the belt.**

Карикатура была совершенно правильная... Но в такой момент, когда повсюду открыто говорили о восстановлении норм, это был удар ниже пояса (Зиновьев 1). The cartoon was completely accurate...But at a time when everyone everywhere was talking openly about the re-establishment of legality and democracy, it was a blow below the belt (1a).

П-469 • ВСТУПА́ТЬ/ВСТУПИ́ТЬ ⟨ВХОДИ́ТЬ/ВОЙТИ́⟩ В СВОИ́ ПРАВА́

[VP; subj: abstr] to manifest itself in full measure, at full strength: X вступил в свои права ≃ **X came into its own; X appeared in full force; X asserted itself; X burst forth.**

На гумнах на минуту приостанавливалась работа... а потом снова начинали глухо погромыхивать на токах каменные катки, понукали лошадей и быков мальчишки-погонычи, гремели веялки, трудовой день вступал в свои неотъемлемые

права (Шолохов 5). For a minute the work on the threshing floors would cease...and then the stone rollers would resume their thudding, the boy drivers would urge on the horses and oxen, the winnowers would clatter, and the working day would come into its own again (5a). ♦ [author's usage] Опухоль, на которую он сперва досадовал, потом боялся её, теперь вошла в права — и уже не он, а она решала, что же будет (Солженицын 10). The tumor, which he had first complained of as an annoyance, and then feared, now asserted itself; it was no longer he deciding what would happen, it was the tumor (10b).

П-470 • КАЧА́ТЬ ПРАВА́ *slang, orig. camp and prison slang*

[VP; subj: human] to demand that the law, the rules etc be observed, demand that one be given or allowed sth. that is (or that he considers) his by right: X качал права ≃ **X stuck ⟨stood⟩ up for his rights; X pushed ⟨shouted⟩ for his rights.**

Паёк этих тысячу не одну переполучал Шухов в тюрьмах и в лагерях, и хоть ни одной из них на весах проверить не пришлось, и хоть шуметь и *качать права* он, как человек робкий, не смел, но всякому арестанту и Шухову давно понятно, что, честно вешая, в хлеборезке не удержишься (Солженицын 7). Shukhov had had thousands of these rations in prisons and camps, and though he'd never had a chance to weigh a single one of them on a scale and he was always too shy to stick up for his rights, he and every other prisoner had known a long time that the people who cut up and issued your bread wouldn't last long if they gave you honest rations (7a). ♦ Ну, представьте себе... если грешники в аду начнут права качать — на что это будет похоже? (Буковский 1). Well, I ask you, what would it be like if the sinners in hell suddenly started shouting for their rights—what sort of a situation would that be? (1a).

П-471 • НА ПРАВА́Х кого

[PrepP; Invar; the resulting PrepP is adv] **1.** in the position of: **as; in the capacity of.**

Михаил на правах хозяина первый поднял рюмку... (Распутин 3). Mikhail, as host, raised his glass first... (3a).

2. utilizing the rights, privileges etc specific to one's position: **exercising one's rights as; as; on the strength of (being a [NP] ⟨having done sth. etc⟩).**

Юный негодяй был влюблён в княгиню и тоже торчал у неё день и ночь, кажется, на правах соседа или дальнего родственника со стороны мужа (Искандер 3). The young reprobate was in love with the princess and had also been hanging around her day and night, exercising his rights as a neighbor, I believe, or a distant relative on the husband's side (3a). ♦ В годы либерализации он стал появляться у должностных лиц, иногда на правах человека, который неоднократно встречался с ними за столом, а иногда просто входил к ним с административными предложениями (Искандер 3). In the years of the liberalization he began calling on officials, sometimes on the strength of his having met them repeatedly at the table, sometimes simply walking in with administrative suggestions (3a).

П-472 • НА ПТИ́ЧЬИХ ПРАВА́Х жить, существовать и

т. п. *coll* [PrepP; Invar; adv; fixed WO] (to be, live etc somewhere) without sanction, authorization, stability, or the guarantee of permanence: **without any right (to be there); (live) on sufferance.**

«Человек он странный, больной... Часто днём ему надо прилечь, а где он тут может? Он говорит: если б хоть свой угол, хоть маленькая верандочка...» — «Ну и?.. Что дальше?» — «Он говорит: больше сил нет. На птичьих правах... Понимаешь, он на пределе...» (Трифонов 6). "He's a strange, sick man. He often needs to have a rest during the day, and where can he here? He says if only he had his own corner or a little veranda...." "So? What else?" "He says he can't bear it anymore. This living on sufferance....Do you understand? He's at the end of his tether" (6a).

П-473 • НА РА́ВНЫХ ПРАВА́Х [PrepP; Invar; adv or subj-compl with бытьø (subj: human); fixed WO] (to do sth.) sharing equal status with another or others, (to be) of equal status with another or others: **on an equal footing; on the same footing; on equal terms; as an equal; (be) equal.**

«Прежде так купцы писали: честь имеем сообщить, что в наш торговый дом на равных правах вошёл Иван Иваныч Сидоров» (Федин 1). "Once merchants used to write: We have the honor to inform you that Ivan Ivanich Sidorov has entered our firm on an equal footing" (1a). ♦ «Пока мы с вами на равных правах. Вы командуете дивизией, и я тоже. И пока вы на меня не шуми-те...» (Шолохов 5). "At present we're equal. You command a division and so do I. So for the present you'd better not shout at me..." (5a).

П-474 • (ВЕЛИ́КАЯ) СЕРМЯ́ЖНАЯ ПРА́ВДА iron or humor in contemp. usage [NP; sing only; fixed WO] the truth (which, it was formerly believed, could be found among plain folk): **(great) homespun truth.**

Дружбу Нержина с дворником Спиридоном Рубин и Со-логдин благодушно называли «хождением в народ» и поис-ками той самой великой сермяжной правды, которую ещё до Нержина тщетно искали Гоголь, Некрасов, Герцен, славя-нофилы, народники, Достоевский, Лев Толстой и, наконец, Васисуалий Лоханкин (Солженицын 3). Nerzhin's friendship with the janitor Spiridon was referred to by Rubin and Sologdin as "going to the people." In their view, Nerzhin was seeking that same great homespun truth which before his time had been sought in vain by Gogol, Nekrasov, Herzen, the Slavophiles, the "People's Will" revolutionaries, Dostoevsky, Lev Tolstoi, and, last of all, Vasisualy Lokhankin (3a).

< This phrase became popular in its ironic usage after the publication of *The Golden Calf* («Золотой телёнок»), by Ilya Ilf and Evgeny Petrov, 1931, ch. 13.

П-475 • И ТО́ ПРА́ВДА coll [sent; Invar; fixed WO] (used to express agreement with the interlocutor, or, occas. with one's own thought or statement) that is correct: **it's ⟨that's, 'tis⟩ true (enough); (that's) quite right;** [when expressing agreement with the interlocutor only] **you're right; you've got a point (there).**

«...Мы к нему всей душой, а он послал нас искать князя глупого!»... – «Что же!.. нам глупый-то князь, пожалуй, ещё лучше будет! Сейчас мы ему коврижку в руки: жуй, а нас не замай!» – «И то правда» (Салтыков-Щедрин 1). "We went to him in all good faith, and he sent us to seek a foolish prince!"..."What of that!...Might be, a foolish prince'd be better yet! We hand him some gingerbread–'Chaw away, and leave us be!'" "Tis true" (1a). ♦ «Сам ты рассуди, – отвечал я ему, – можно ли было при твоих людях объявить, что дочь Миронова жива. Да они бы её загрызли. Ничто её бы не спасло!» – «И то правда», – сказал, смеясь, Пугачёв (Пушкин 2). "Judge for yourself," I answered him: "could I have declared in front of your men that Captain Mironov's daughter was still alive? They would have torn her to pieces. Nothing would have saved her!" "That's true enough!" said Pugachev, laughing (2b).

П-476 • НЕ ПРА́ВДА ЛИ? coll [Invar; usu. used to form a question out of an affirm or neg statement; may be in the initial position; fixed WO] (what I said or am about to say) is correct, is it not?: **isn't that so ⟨right, true⟩?; don't you agree?; am I right?;** [after an affirm statement] **don't you think (so)?; isn't it?; don't ⟨haven't, aren't etc⟩ you ⟨they etc⟩?;** [after a neg statement] **is it?; do ⟨have, are etc⟩ you ⟨they etc⟩?;** [when used in the initial position] **isn't it true that...?**

«Положение становится неловким. Разрешить его мог бы только полицейский чиновник, не правда ли?» (Федин 1). "The situation is becoming awkward. It could be saved only by a police official, isn't that so?" (1a). ♦ В самом деле, в том, чтобы дожить до старости, есть фантастика. Я вовсе не острю. Ведь я мог и не дожить, не правда ли? (Олеша 3). In reaching old age there really is something fantastic. I'm quite serious. You see, I might not have lived, isn't that right? (3a). ♦ «...Какая отвратительная, однако же, харя, не правда ли?» (Достоевский 1). "What a disgusting mug, by the way, don't you agree?" (1a). ♦ [Хлестаков:] Ведь это не столица. Не правда ли, ведь это не столица? [Почтмейстер:] Совершенная правда (Гоголь 4). [Kh.:] After all, it's not the capital. Am I right–it's not the capital? [Postmaster:] Quite right, sir (4f). ♦ [Колесов:] Живописный уголок, не правда ли? (Вампилов 3). [K.:] A picturesque corner, don't you think? (3a). ♦ «А посмотрите это: не правда ли, очень мило?» (Гонча-ров 1). "And have a look at this. Very charming, isn't it?" (1a). ♦ [Репников:] Веселиться они ещё не разучились, не правда ли? (Вампилов 3). [R.:] They haven't forgotten how to have a good time, have they? (3a). ♦ «...Вы оставили письмо в келье, и это меня ободрило: не правда ли, вы потому оставили его в келье, что предчувствовали, что я буду требовать назад письмо, так чтобы не отдавать его?» (Достоевский 1). "...You left the letter in your cell, and that encouraged me: isn't it true that you left it in the cell because you anticipated that I would demand the letter back, so that you wouldn't have to give it back?" (1a).

П-477 • ПРА́ВДА ГЛАЗА́ КО́ЛЕТ [saying] it is unpleasant to hear the disagreeable truth (said when a person tries to object to fair, just criticism): ≃ **the truth hurts; the truth tastes bitter; nothing hurts like the truth; it stings because it's true.**

[Клава:] Ты мне тут обиды не строй! Правда-то глаза колет!.. (Рощин 2). [K.:] Don't make like you're insulted! The truth hurts, doesn't it!... (2a). ♦ [author's usage] «Помощниками Де-никина нас величают... А кто же мы? Выходит, что помощники и есть, нечего обижаться. Правда-матка глаза заколола...» (Шолохов 4). "They call us accomplices of Deni-kin....And what are we? That's just what we are. So why get huffy about it? It stings because it's true" (4a).

П-478 • ТВОЯ́ ⟨ВА́ША⟩ ПРА́ВДА obsoles, coll [NP; these forms only; used as indep. clause] you are correct: **you're (quite) right; right you are; what you say is right ⟨true⟩; true enough.**

«Насчёт него [Ильи], твоя правда, брат, клеймо на нём, печать каинова, не жилец он...» (Максимов 3). "As for him [Ilya], you are right, brother, he has the brand on him, the mark of Cain; he is not long for this world" (1a). ♦ [Муромский:] Да Ар-датовский уезд в Нижегородской губернии. [Расплюев:] В Нижегородской? Как в Нижегородской?.. [Кречинский:] Да нет! их два... [Расплюев:] Один-то Ардатов в Нижегород-ской, а другой – в Симбирской. [Муромский:] Извините, извините, ваша правда (Сухово-Кобылин 2). [M.:] But the Ardatov district is in the province of Nizhni-Novgorod. [R.:] Nizhni-Novgorod? How could it be in Nizhni-Novgorod?... [K.:] Why, of course–there are two of them... [R.:] One Ardatov in Nizhni-Novgorod, and another one in Simbirsk. [M.:] Forgive me, my fault, you're quite right (2b). ♦ [Пологий:] ...Конечно, ваша правда, я человек маленький, жизнь у меня мелкая... (Горький 1). [P.:] What you say is right–I'm a small man and my life is a trivial one... ♦ «А что, коньячку не выпьешь?..» – «Нет, не надо, благодарю. Вот этот хлебец возьму с собой, коли дадите... А коньяку и вам бы не пить», – опасливо посоветовал он, вглядываясь в лицо старика. «Правда твоя...» (Достоев-ский 1). "Say, how about a little cognac?..." "No, no, thank you. But I'll take this bread with me, if I may....And you'd better not have any cognac either," he advised cautiously, looking intently into the old man's face. "True enough..." (1a).

П-479 • ЧТО ПРА́ВДА, ТО ПРА́ВДА coll [sent; Invar; fixed WO] (used to express agreement or to emphasize the accuracy of a statement) that really is so: **what's true is true; the truth is the truth; that's true; there's no denying it; how very true.**

«...Наши барыни, как соберутся, так и передерутся!» – ответил хозяин. «...Какие ты вещи говоришь!» – обиделась супруга его. «Ну, уж извини меня, Татьяна Михайловна! а что правда, то правда!» (Салтыков-Щедрин 2). "...Our ladies start quarreling as soon as they get together!" their host replied...."...What a thing to say!" his wife said in a hurt voice. "Pardon me, Tatyana Mikhailovna, but the truth is the truth!" (2a). ♦ [Дулебов:] Какая публика? Гимназисты, семинаристы, лавочники, мелкие чиновники! Они рады все руки себе отхлопать, по десяти раз вызывают Негину, а уж ведь они, канальи, лишнего гроша не заплатят. [Домна Пантелевна:] Что правда, то правда, ваше сиятельство (Островский 11). [D.:] What audiences? Schoolboys, shopkeepers, divinity students, petty officials? They'll applaud anything, they'll call Negina back ten times, but you know the rascals won't pay a kopek extra. [D.P.:] That's true, your Highness (11a). ♦ Привык к Людмиле, присушился, что правда, то правда (Трифонов 1). He had gotten used to Liudmila, had become attached to her—there was no denying it (1a).

П-480 • (всеми, всякими, разными и т. п.) **ПРА́ВДАМИ И НЕПРА́ВДАМИ** [NP_instrum; Invar; adv; fixed WO] not hesitating to employ any (often unscrupulous) methods: **by hook or by crook; by fair means or foul; one way or another; go(ing) to any length(s).**

У Иры Егеровой было 50 рублей. Её отец, известный в Казани профессор строительного института, какими-то правдами и неправдами добился передачи их дочке (Гинзбург 1). Ira had fifty roubles which her father, a professor at the institute of civil engineering, had managed, by hook or by crook, to get to her (1a). ♦ Лошадей [Григорий] стал подготавливать к короткому, но стремительному пробегу ещё две недели назад: вовремя поил их... всеми правдами и неправдами добывал на ночёвках зерно, и лошади его выглядели лучше, чем у всех остальных... (Шолохов 5). He [Grigory] had started grooming his horses for a short but fast gallop two weeks before. He watered them regularly....By fair means or foul he obtained grain for them at night and his horses looked better than any of the others... (5a). ♦ В пристрастном освещении Клыкачёва Степанов предстал человеком кляузным, скрытным, всеми правдами и неправдами выращивающим трёх сыновей (Солженицын 3). In Klykachev's prejudiced view, Stepanov was a furtive slanderer who would go to any lengths to fix things for his three sons (3a).

П-481 • **ПО ПРА́ВДЕ** говорить, сказать, ответить и т. п. *coll* [PrepP; Invar; adv] (to say sth., answer etc) sincerely, openly: **(tell) the truth; (tell ⟨say etc⟩ sth.) in all honesty; (tell sth. ⟨respond etc⟩) honestly ⟨truthfully, frankly⟩.**

«Одно, что тяжело для меня, — я тебе по правде скажу, André, — это образ мыслей отца в религиозном отношении» (Толстой 4). "The only thing that is hard for me—I'll tell you the truth, Andrei—is Father's attitude to religion" (4a).

П-482 • **ПО ПРА́ВДЕ ГОВОРЯ́ ⟨СКАЗА́ТЬ⟩; ПРА́ВДУ ГОВОРЯ́ ⟨СКАЗА́ТЬ⟩** *all coll* [these forms only; sent adv (parenth); usu. this WO (last var.)] (used to emphasize the truthfulness or correctness of a statement) speaking candidly, frankly: **to tell (you) the truth; if the truth be told; truth to tell; to be (quite) honest ⟨frank⟩.**

«По правде сказать, я даже не знаю толком, где эта Финляндия. Но говорят, что там чертовски холодно. Если пошлют наших, они замёрзнут...» (Эренбург 4). "To tell you the truth," he said, "I don't even know exactly where Finland is. But they say it's damned cold up there. If our men are sent there, they'll freeze to death" (4a). ♦ Верстах в трёх от Кисловодска... есть скала, называемая *Кольцом*... Многочисленная кавалькада отправилась туда посмотреть на закат солнца сквозь каменное окошко. Никто из нас, по правде сказать, не думал об солнце (Лермонтов 1). About two miles from Kislovodsk...there is a rock called The Ring....A great cavalcade set off for it to see the sun set through the little stone window. To tell the truth, none of us was thinking about the sun (1d). ♦ «...Она [твоя невеста] же тебя просто умыкнула! По правде сказать, тебя бы надо было посадить на лошадь с женским седлом!» (Искандер 5). "She [your bride] abducted *you!* Truth to tell, it's you we should put on the horse with the woman's saddle!" (5a).

П-483 • **СМОТРЕ́ТЬ ⟨ГЛЯДЕ́ТЬ, ВЗГЛЯНУ́ТЬ⟩ ПРА́ВДЕ В ГЛАЗА́ ⟨В ЛИЦО́⟩** [VP; subj: human or collect; often infin with надо, нужно, будем etc] to see things or evaluate facts as they really are, look at things clearly, soberly: надо смотреть правде в глаза ≃ we ⟨you etc⟩ **must look the truth (straight) in the eye; we ⟨you etc⟩ must face (up to) the truth; we ⟨you etc⟩ must look the facts in the face; we ⟨you etc⟩ must face (the) facts; we ⟨you etc⟩ must face up to reality; we ⟨you etc⟩ must confront the truth; [in limited contexts] let's ⟨you might as well etc⟩ face it.**

[Трофимов:] Продано ли сегодня имение или не продано — не всё ли равно? С ним давно уже покончено, нет поворота назад... Надо хоть раз в жизни взглянуть правде прямо в глаза (Чехов 2). [T.:] Whether or not the estate is sold today—does it really matter? That's all done with long ago; there's no turning back... At least once in one's life one ought to look the truth straight in the eye (2a). ♦ «Нас казаки предали, не пошли за нами и не пойдут. Надо иметь мужество и смотреть правде в глаза, а не обольщаться дурацкими надеждами» (Шолохов 5). "The Cossacks have betrayed us. They didn't follow us then and they won't now. You've got to have the courage to face the truth, not comfort yourself with vain hopes (5a). ♦ Глянем правде в глаза. Его [мой роман] никто не читал (Булгаков 12). ...No one, let's face it, had read it [my novel] (12a).

П-484 • **РЕ́ЗАТЬ ⟨ГОВОРИ́ТЬ и т. п.⟩ ПРА́ВДУ-МА́ТКУ (В ГЛАЗА́)** *substand;* **РЕ́ЗАТЬ ПРА́ВДУ В ГЛАЗА́** *coll* [VP; subj: human] to express o.s. openly, confront s.o. with the truth: X режет правду-матку ≃ **X speaks straight from the shoulder; X tells the truth to your face; X gives it to you straight; X tells it like it is; X calls a spade a spade.**

Она любила «резать правду-матку», не признавала «никаких экивоков» и «сантиментов с сахаром» (Гинзбург 2). She loved to "call a spade a spade," scorned all "quibbles" and "sugary sentiments" (2a).

П-485 • **ПО ВСЕМ ПРА́ВИЛАМ** [PrepP; Invar; adv; fixed WO] in the accepted, proper, accustomed manner: **by ⟨according to, following⟩ (all) the rules; by ⟨according to⟩ the book; following ⟨according to⟩ procedure; the way it's supposed to be done ⟨handled etc⟩.**

Помощнику городового пристава тотчас же поручили набрать штук до четырёх понятых и по всем правилам, которых уже я здесь не описываю, проникли в дом Фёдора Павловича и следствие произвели на месте (Достоевский 1). The assistant police chief was immediately ordered to round up as many as four witnesses, and, following all the rules, which I am not going to describe here, they penetrated Fyodor Pavlovich's house and carried out an investigation on the spot (1a).

П-486 • **ПО ВСЕМ ПРА́ВИЛАМ ИСКУ́ССТВА** [PrepP; Invar; adv; fixed WO] (to do sth.) very skillfully, in masterly fashion: **using ⟨drawing upon⟩ all the secrets ⟨the tricks⟩ of the trade; (do sth.) like a pro; have (got) it down to a fine art ⟨a science⟩.**

Подсиживать своих сотрудников он умеет! Он это делает по всем правилам искусства. He really knows how to scheme against his coworkers! He has it down to a science.

П-487 • **НЕ В** *чьих* **ПРА́ВИЛАХ** [PrepP; Invar; the resulting PrepP is subj-compl with быть₀ (subj: abstr, often это, or infin); usu. pres or past] sth. is in contradiction with s.o.'s values, standards etc: X не в Y-овых правилах ≃ **X is ⟨goes⟩ against Y's principles.**

[Негина:] Я не желаю получать подарков, это не в моих правилах (Островский 11). [N.:] …I don't want to receive gifts; it's against my principles (11a).

П-488 • **КАК ПРА́ВИЛО** [как + NP; Invar; sent adv (parenth)] commonly, almost always: **as a (general) rule; usually; generally;** [in limited contexts] **typically.**

…Своих лучших работниц Андриолли умел ценить… Тем более что, как правило, они попусту не беспокоили его ненужными просьбами (Войнович 5). Andriolli knew how to value his best workers.…All the more so since, as a rule, they didn't pester him with useless requests (5a). ♦ …[Нина] решительная была, и её решения, как правило, оказывались верными… (Рыбаков 1). …She [Nina] was decisive and…her decisions were generally the right ones… (1a).

П-489 • **ПОЛОЖИ́ТЬ ⟨ПОСТА́ВИТЬ, ВЗЯТЬ⟩ (СЕБЕ́) ЗА ПРА́ВИЛО; ПОЛОЖИ́ТЬ ⟨ПОСТА́ВИТЬ, ВЗЯТЬ⟩ (СЕБЕ́) ПРА́ВИЛОМ** [VP; subj: human; foll. by infin] to make it one's principle, custom (to do sth.): X поставил себе за правило (делать Y) ≃ **X made it a rule (to do Y); X made a point (of doing Y).**

Главный, по-видимому, поставил себе за правило соглашаться со всем и радоваться всему, что бы ни говорили ему окружающие, и выражать это словами «славно, славно…» (Булгаков 9). The chief had evidently made it a rule to agree with everything and to rejoice in everything his companions said to him, and to express this with the words, "Fine, fine…" (9a).

П-490 • **ПО ПРА́ВУ**[1] [PrepP; Invar; adv] justifiably, deservedly: **by right(s); rightly; rightfully; (have) every right (to do sth.); legitimately.**

Они хотят только привилегий, которые, как они думают, принадлежат им по праву (Зиновьев 1). "They want only the privileges which they believe are theirs by right" (1a). ♦ …Мои крупицы [слова и выражения из моих рукописей], даже в искажённом виде, помогли ему быстро сделать блистательную карьеру, и теперь без зазрения совести он потреблял плоды славы, которые по праву принадлежали мне одному (Терц 4). …The crumbs from my table [words and expressions from my manuscripts], even in distorted form, had helped him rapidly to achieve a brilliant career, and now, without any qualms of conscience, he was consuming the fruits of glory which by rights belonged to me alone (4a). ♦ Кязым по праву считался одним из самых умных людей Чегема (Искандер 5). Kyazym was rightly considered to be one of the smartest men in Chegem (5a). ♦ Умел Александр Иванович держаться достаточно твёрдо, знал, когда казнить, а когда миловать, и мог по праву этим гордиться (Ерофеев 3). Alexander Ivanovich knew the fine art of keeping to a steady course; he knew when to punish and when to forgive and had every right to be proud of this knowledge (3a).

П-491 • **ПО ПРА́ВУ**[2] [PrepP; Invar; the resulting PrepP is adv] **1.** ~ *кого* utilizing the prerogatives or entitlements specific to one's position: **exercising one's rights as; as; on the strength of (being a [NP]); it is one's privilege as (s.o.'s [NP]).**

По праву родственника тесть вмешивается во все наши дела. Exercising his rights as a family member, my father-in-law interferes in all our affairs. ♦ «Хорошо, что ты приехал, Сергей Миронович», – говорил Сталин, усаживаясь по праву хозяина во главе стола… (Рыбаков 2). As the host Stalin sat at the head of the table. "I'm glad you came, Sergei Mironovich" (2a). ♦ Потом… потом, по праву и обязанности жениха, он привезёт невесте подарок… (Гончаров 1). Then…then it would be his privilege and his duty, as Olga's fiancé, to bring her a gift (1b).

2. ~ *чего* owing to sth., because of sth.: **by right ⟨virtue⟩ of; on the strength of.**

…[Харлампо] отрицательным движением головы показывал, что он не собирается таким коварным путём овладеть любимой девушкой. Возможно, тут сказывалась его затаённая под лавиной унижений гордость, его уверенность, что он, столько прождавший, в конце концов, законным путём получит то, что принадлежит ему по праву любви (Искандер 5). …[Harlampo] shook his head again to show that he had no intention of using such guile to possess the girl he loved. This may have been his pride showing through, buried though it was under an avalanche of humiliations – his conviction that in the end, having waited so long, he would receive by legal means what belonged to him by right of love (5a).

П-492 • **ОТПРАВЛЯ́ТЬ/ОТПРА́ВИТЬ К ПРА́ОТЦАМ** *кого obs, lit* [VP; subj: human; usu. pfv; usu. this WO] to kill s.o.: X отправил Y-а к праотцам ≃ **X sent Y to kingdom come ⟨to the great beyond, to meet Y's Maker⟩.**

П-493 • **ОТПРАВЛЯ́ТЬСЯ/ОТПРА́ВИТЬСЯ К ПРА́ОТЦАМ** *obs, lit* [VP; subj: human; usu. pfv; usu. this WO] to die: X отправился к праотцам ≃ **X joined his ancestors ⟨forefathers⟩; X went to the great beyond; X met his Maker.**

[author's usage] [Епиходов:] Долголетний Фирс, по моему окончательному мнению, в починку не годится, ему надо к праотцам (Чехов 2). [E.:] The venerable Fiers, according to my conclusive opinion, is not worth mending, he ought to join his forefathers (2a).

П-494 • **ОТРЯСТИ́ ⟨ОТРЯХНУ́ТЬ⟩ ПРАХ** *чего* **ОТ ⟨С⟩ (СВОИ́Х) НОГ** *lit* [VP; subj: human] to break with sth. decisively and forever, renounce sth.: X отряхнул прах Y-а от своих ног ≃ **X shook the dust of Y from ⟨off⟩ his feet.**

Таким было её возвращение на эту планету, в прежний мир, прах которого, ей казалось, она уже давным-давно отряхнула со своих ног (Залыгин 1). Such was her return to this planet, to the world whose dust she thought she had long since shaken off her feet (1a).

< From the Bible (Matt. 10:14, Mark 6:11 et al.).

П-495 • **ПОВЕРГА́ТЬ/ПОВЕ́РГНУТЬ ⟨ПРЕВРАЩА́ТЬ/ПРЕВРАТИ́ТЬ, ОБРАЩА́ТЬ/ОБРАТИ́ТЬ⟩ В ПРАХ** *кого-что obs, lit* [VP; subj: usu. human, collect, or, rare, abstr] to eradicate, put an end to the existence of s.o. or sth.: X поверг Y-а в прах ≃ **X reduced thing Y to ashes ⟨to dust⟩; X completely destroyed ⟨annihilated, obliterated⟩ Y.**

П-496 • **ПОВЕРГА́ТЬСЯ/ПОВЕ́РГНУТЬСЯ В ПРАХ** *obs, lit* [VP] **1.** [subj: usu. human] to collapse and die: X повергся в прах ≃ **X fell down dead.**

2. ~ *перед кем* [subj: human or collect] to yield completely to s.o., showing one's full submission, admitting utter defeat: X повергся в прах перед Y-ом ≃ **X prostrated himself before Y.**

П-497 • **ПРЕВРАЩА́ТЬСЯ/ПРЕВРАТИ́ТЬСЯ ⟨ОБРАЩА́ТЬСЯ/ОБРАТИ́ТЬСЯ⟩ В ПРАХ** *lit* [VP; subj: usu. collect, concr, or abstr] to cease to exist, be eradicated: X превратился в прах ≃ **X turned ⟨was reduced⟩ to dust;** [in limited contexts] **X was reduced to ashes; X was completely destroyed ⟨annihilated, obliterated⟩.**

Я знала теперь, что, сколько бы ни пытался грешный, жестокий человек утвердить свою власть на земле, рано или поздно правда восторжествует и былая слава превратится в прах (Аллилуева 2). Now I knew that no matter how much sinful, cruel man might strengthen his power on earth, sooner or later Truth would triumph and the past glory would turn to dust (2a).

П-498 • **ИДТИ́/ПОЙТИ́ ⟨РАССЫПА́ТЬСЯ/РАССЫ́-ПАТЬСЯ, РАЗЛЕТА́ТЬСЯ/РАЗЛЕТЕ́ТЬСЯ, ЛЕ-**

ТЕ́ТЬ/ПОЛЕТЕ́ТЬ⟩ ПРА́ХОМ [VP; more often pfv]
1. [subj: abstr (надежды, планы, дела, жизнь etc, often всё), ог заведение, предприятие etc; more often this WO] (of hopes, plans, affairs, s.o.'s life etc, or an establishment, a business etc) to collapse totally, suffer failure: X пошёл прахом ≃ **X went to rack and ruin; X went down the tube(s); X went ⟨fell⟩ to pieces;** [in limited contexts] **X went to the dogs; X went up in smoke;** [of plans, hopes etc only] **X came to nothing ⟨to naught⟩.**

Говорят, именно в тот год дела его пошли прахом (Искандер 3). They say that his affairs went to rack and ruin that year (3a). ♦ «Обидно, Сергей Платонович!.. Обидно, что не придётся поглядеть, как распотрошат ваши капиталы и вас вспугнут из тёплого гнёздышка... Всё же, знаете, приятно будет видеть, как всё пойдёт прахом» (Шолохов 3). "It's such a shame, Sergei Platonovich!...Such a shame that I shan't live to see your capital done away with and you flushed out of your cosy little nest....After all, you know, it would be nice to see everything go up in smoke" (3a).

2. [subj: a quantit NP denoting a period of time] to pass without yielding hoped-for results: X пойдёт прахом ≃ **X will go ⟨be⟩ (all) for nothing ⟨naught⟩; X will count for nothing; X will go down the drain.**

...Сделай я что-нибудь политически скандальное, меня начисто выметут из ибанской [nonce word] истории. Двадцать лет труда пойдёт прахом (Зиновьев 1). ...If I do anything politically scandalous I'll simply be swept out of the history of Ibansk. Twenty years of work will go for nothing (1a).

П-499 • ПРЕВОЗМОГА́ТЬ/ПРЕВОЗМО́ЧЬ ⟨ПЕРЕСИ́ЛИВАТЬ/ПЕРЕСИ́ЛИТЬ⟩ СЕБЯ́ [VP; subj: human] to gain control of one's feelings, conquer some desire, force o.s. to disregard an oppressive emotional or physical state etc: X превозмог себя ≃ **X took himself in hand; X took ⟨got⟩ hold of himself; X overcame his nervousness ⟨apathy, fear etc⟩; X mastered his feelings; X conquered his fear ⟨distaste etc⟩;** [in limited contexts] **X made an effort (and did sth.).**

Ему лень было встать и умыться, — сказывалась нажитая за дорогу усталость. Пересилив себя, он встал, позвал вестового (Шолохов 3). He felt too lazy to get up and wash. The effects of the journey were beginning to tell. Making an effort, he rose and called his batman (3a).

П-500 • ПРЕВОСХОДИ́ТЬ/ПРЕВЗОЙТИ́ (САМОГО́) СЕБЯ́ [VP; subj: human; usu. pfv] to do sth. better than before or better than could have been expected: X превзошёл самого себя ≃ **X surpassed ⟨outdid⟩ himself;** [in limited contexts] **X exceeded my ⟨our, everybody's etc⟩ expectations.**

Ответы диктовал Тюфяев, он превзошёл себя в этом деле (Герцен 1). Tyufyayev dictated the answers; he surpassed himself on this occasion (1a).

П-501 • ПРЕВЫ́ШЕ ВСЕГО́ lit [AdvP; Invar; fixed WO]
1. любить, ценить, ставить кого-что и т. п. [adv] (to love, value, appreciate etc s.o. or sth.) to a greater extent than (one loves, values, appreciates etc) all others: **more than anyone ⟨anything⟩; most of all.**

Превыше всего он ценил в людях порядочность и умение держать слово. What he valued more than anything in people was their decency and their ability to be true to their word.

2. [subj-compl with copula (subj: usu. abstr or collect)] sth. is more important (to s.o.) than anything else: **(be) most important (of all); (come) before all else;** [in limited contexts] **(be ⟨have⟩) top priority.**

«Только тут я сообразил, что меня обманули. Объегорили подло, мелко, предательски. У кого на моём месте не опустились бы руки, но я человек долга, долг для меня превыше всего» (Максимов 2). "It was only then that I realized I had been cheated. I had been basely, pettily, treacherously swindled. Anyone in my place would have given up the struggle, but I am a man of duty; with me, duty comes before all else" (2a).

П-502 • ДО ПРЕДЕ́ЛА какой, каков [PrepP; Invar; modif] very, extremely: **utterly; exceedingly; absolutely; completely; to the highest ⟨the nth⟩ degree.**

Всегда поглощённый какими-нибудь идеями, Уманский был рассеян до предела (Гинзбург 2). Umansky was always absorbed in some idea to the exclusion of everything else, and he was utterly absent-minded (2a). ♦ У него маленькая, сухая змеиная голова. Уши мелки и подвижны. Грудные мускулы развиты до предела... Он кровный донец (Шолохов 4). He had a small, lean snake-like head. His ears were neat and mobile. His chest muscles were developed to the highest degree....He was a Don thoroughbred (4a).

П-503 • НА ПРЕДЕ́ЛЕ [PrepP; Invar; subj-compl with бытьø] **1.** [subj: нервы, терпение, силы etc] s.o.'s nerves are stressed, patience is tried, strength is depleted to the utmost degree (such that s.o. feels that he is about to break down, lose control etc): **(be) about to give out; (be) at the breaking point; (be) strained to the limit; (be) stretched to their ⟨its⟩ limit.**

От всех этих неприятностей у него началась бессонница, нервы его были на пределе. All these troubles had given him insomnia, and his nerves were at the breaking point.

2. [subj: human] one is extremely irritated, upset etc and is about to break down: X на пределе ≃ **X is at the breaking point; X can't take any more; X has reached ⟨is at⟩ the end of his rope ⟨tether⟩; X has (about ⟨just about⟩) had it.**

«Человек он странный, больной... Часто днём ему надо прилечь, а где он тут может? Он говорит: если б хоть свой угол, хоть маленькая верандочка...» — «Ну и?.. Что дальше?» — «Он говорит: больше сил нет. На птичьих правах... Понимаешь, он на пределе...» (Трифонов 6). "He's a strange, sick man. He often needs to have a rest during the day, and where can he here? He says if only he had his own corner or a little veranda...." "So? What else?" "He says he can't bear it anymore. This living on sufferance....Do you understand? He's at the end of his tether" (6a).

П-504 • ПОД ПРЕДЛО́ГОМ чего, каким [PrepP; Invar; Prep; the resulting PrepP is adv] putting forward sth. as one's ostensible reason, intention, goal etc (for undertaking the action in question): **on ⟨under⟩ the pretext of.**

Под предлогом серебряной свадьбы Граубе, Генрих Иванович, пригласил к себе на квартиру четырёх сослуживцев... (Терц 8). On the pretext of celebrating his silver wedding anniversary, Genrikh Ivanovich Graube invited four colleagues...to his apartment... (8a).

П-505 • ДЕ́ЛАТЬ/СДЕ́ЛАТЬ ПРЕДЛОЖЕ́НИЕ кому [VP; subj: human, male] to ask (a woman) to become one's wife: X сделал предложение женщине Y ≃ **X proposed to Y; X asked for Y's hand in marriage.**

...Кто такой я и кто такая она? Я сапожник... А она актриса... Как в таких условиях я мог сделать ей предложение? (Рыбаков 1). ...What was I and what was she? I was a shoemaker...whereas she was an actress....How could I possibly propose to her in those circumstances? (1a).

П-506 • НА КАКО́Й ПРЕДМЕ́Т? [PrepP; Invar; adv; fixed WO] why?: **what for ⟨about⟩?; for what reason ⟨purpose⟩?**

«Иван Петрович, вас вызывает начальство». — «Вы не знаете, на какой предмет?» "Ivan Petrovich, the boss wants to see you." "Do you know what for?"

П-507 • **НА ПРЕДМЕ́Т** *чего rather offic* [PrepP; Invar; Prep; the resulting PrepP is adv] with the aim of: **for ⟨with⟩ the purpose of; with the object of; for; in order to.**

Я пригласил вас на предмет обсуждения вашего патента. I invited you here for the purpose of discussing your patent.

П-508 • **НА Э́ТОТ ⟨ТОТ, СЕЙ⟩ ПРЕДМЕ́Т** *obs, now humor* [PrepP; these forms only; adv; fixed WO] about this (or that), for this (or that), in this (or that) case: **concerning ⟨regarding, as regards, in regard to⟩ this ⟨that⟩; on this ⟨that⟩ score; to this ⟨that⟩ end.**

П-509 • **ПРЕДОСТАВЛЯ́ТЬ/ПРЕДОСТА́ВИТЬ СА-МОМУ́ СЕБЕ́** *кого* [VP; subj: human; usu. pfv passive Part предоставлен(ный) or 3rd pers pl with indef. refer.] **1.** to leave s.o. to do for himself and to act at his own discretion (may be said approvingly or disapprovingly): X был предоставлен самому себе ≃ **X was (left) on his own; X was left to fend for himself; X was left to his own devices ⟨resources⟩; X was allowed to do as he liked ⟨pleased⟩.**

Он был... доволен, что снова предоставлен самому себе (Стругацкие 2). ...He was relieved to be on his own again (2a). ♦ За столом Антонину уже ждали. Ей мгновенно очистили место, пододвинули хлебницу и, предоставляя её самой себе, занялись едой (Максимов 3). At the table everybody was waiting for Antonina. They instantly cleared a space, pushed over the bread basket, then left her to fend for herself and busied themselves with their food (3a). ♦ Женщины будили в ней нездоровое любопытство, и она — тогда ещё угловатый и застенчивый подросток, — предоставленная самой себе, росла, как в лесу куст дикой волчьей ягоды (Шолохов 2). The women awakened an unhealthy curiosity in her while she was still only a shy and gawky adolescent and, left to her own devices, she grew up like a bush of wild spurge in the forest (2a). ♦ «Вот нынешнее воспитание! Ещё за границей... этот молодой человек предоставлен был самому себе, и теперь в Петербурге, говорят, он такие ужасы наделал, что его с полицией выслали оттуда» (Толстой 4). "That's what comes of a modern education....It seems that while he was abroad this young man was allowed to do as he liked, and now in Petersburg I hear he has been doing such terrible things that he has been expelled by the police" (4b).

2. *usu. disapprov* (usu. in refer. to children, patients etc) to leave s.o. unsupervised: X предоставлен самому себе ≃ **X is left unattended; X is left on his own ⟨by himself⟩.**

П-510 • **ПО ПРЕИМУ́ЩЕСТВУ** *rather lit* [PrepP; Invar; adv or modif] chiefly, basically: **mainly; primarily; mostly; for the most part; predominantly.**

...Он, с самой той могилки, стал по преимуществу заниматься «божественным»... (Достоевский 1). ...Ever since that little grave, he had mainly concerned himself with "the divine"... (1a). ♦ Что касается до внутреннего содержания «Летописца», то оно по преимуществу фантастическое... (Салтыков-Щедрин 1). As concerns the *Chronicle*'s subject matter, it is for the most part fantastical... (1a). ♦ Близость Сенной, обилие известных заведений и, по преимуществу, цеховое и ремесленное население, скученное в этих серединных петербургских улицах и переулках, пестрили иногда общую панораму такими субъектами, что странно было бы и удивляться при встрече с иною фигурой (Достоевский 3). The proximity of the Haymarket, the abundance of certain establishments, a population predominantly of craftsmen and artisans, who clustered in these central Petersburg streets and lanes, sometimes produced such a motley of types in the general panorama that to be surprised at meeting any sort of figure would even have been strange (3c).

П-511 • **В ПРЕТЕ́НЗИИ** *на кого* [PrepP; Invar; subj-compl with быть∅ (subj: human); often neg] one is (or feels) offended by s.o., is displeased with s.o.: X на Y-а не в претензии ≃ **X doesn't bear Y a grudge; X doesn't bear a grudge against Y; X doesn't hold ⟨have⟩ a grudge ⟨anything⟩ against Y; X doesn't harbor any bad feelings toward Y; X doesn't resent Y.**

«Вы продолжаете шутить... Но после любезной готовности, оказанной вами, я не имею права быть на вас в претензии...» (Тургенев 2). "You still persist in jesting....But after the courteous disposition you have evinced I have no grounds for bearing a grudge..." (2a). ♦ [Кречинский:] Я человек прямой: дело объяснится просто, и никто из нас на вас в претензии не будет (Сухово-Кобылин 2). [K.:] I am a straightforward person. The matter will be cleared up and no grudges held (2a). ♦ «Пришлось вас побеспокоить, Маргарита Николаевна и мастер, — заговорил Воланд после некоторого молчания, — но вы не будьте на меня в претензии» (Булгаков 9). "We had to trouble you, Margarita Nikolayevna and Master," said Woland after a silence. "But don't resent me for it" (9a).

П-512 • **ПРИБАВЛЕ́НИЕ СЕМЕ́ЙСТВА** *coll, often humor* [NP; sing only; usu. subj or obj; fixed WO] the birth of a child in a family: **addition to the ⟨s.o.'s⟩ family; new arrival in the family.**

У вас, я слышал, прибавление семейства. Мальчик или девочка? I heard you've got an addition to the family. Is it a boy or a girl?

П-513 • **КЛАСТЬ/ПОЛОЖИ́ТЬ С ПРИБО́РОМ** *на кого-что vulg* [VP; subj: human] to reject s.o. or sth. with disdain: X кладёт на Y-а с прибором ≃ **X couldn't ⟨doesn't⟩ give a shit ⟨a good goddamn⟩ about Y; X spits on Y; ‖ X положил на Y-а с прибором ≃ X told person Y to eat shit ⟨go to hell⟩; X told person Y to head in ⟨where to go⟩; ‖ я кладу на тебя ⟨на него и т. п.⟩ с прибором ≃ shit on you ⟨him, it etc⟩; screw you ⟨him, it etc⟩; to hell with you ⟨him, it etc⟩; he etc can eat shit (for all I care).**

«Пей степенно, ты же в офицерском чине». — «Я на этот чин кладу с прибором!» (Шолохов 5). "Drink with dignity, man, you've got officer's rank, ye know." "Shit on that rank!" (5a).

П-514 • **С ПРИВЕ́ТОМ**[1] *highly coll* [PrepP; Invar; nonagreeing modif or subj-compl with copula (subj: human)] odd, having rather bizarre ideas and/or behaviors, slightly crazy: X — (парень) с приветом ≃ **X is a little touched (in the head); X is an oddball; X has a few screws loose; X is a bit daffy; X has bats in his belfry.**

П-515 • **С ПРИВЕ́ТОМ**[2] *highly coll* [PrepP; Invar; predic; subj: human; introduced by Conj «и»; used after one or more predicates having the same subject] (in refer. to one's leaving, abandoning, or foresaking some person, place, job etc in an abrupt manner, without giving any explanation, fulfilling one's obligations etc) one's association, contact, dealings etc (with s.o. or sth.) are over: **(and) that's the end of it; (and) he ⟨she etc⟩ calls it quits; (and) it's "so long" (forever); (and) some person ⟨place, job etc⟩ is history; (and) he ⟨she etc⟩ runs in the opposite direction; (and) he ⟨she etc⟩ takes off.**

Он девушек меняет, как перчатки: погуляет денёк-другой и — с приветом. He changes girls the way he changes clothes: he goes out with a girl for a day or two and then calls it quits. ♦ [extended usage] «А кто за каждую копейку дрожит, у того их [денег] не будет». — «Как же не будет, если он их не бросает зря на ветер, не пропивает, как ты?» — «А так. Они [деньги] поймут, что он жмот, и — с приветом!» (Распутин 1). "A person who counts every kopeck'll never have money." "Why won't he if he doesn't throw it away and doesn't drink it up like you do?" "Well, he won't, I tell you. Money'll see he's stingy and run in the opposite direction" (1a).

П-516 • ПРИВОДИ́ТЬ/ПРИВЕСТИ́ В СЕБЯ́ *кого* [VP; subj: usu. human or abstr; more often pfv] **1.** to bring s.o. out of an unconscious state: X привёл Y-а в себя ≃ **X brought Y (a)round ⟨to⟩; X restored Y ⟨brought Y back⟩ to consciousness; X revived Y.**

Она была без памяти. Мы... перевязали рану как можно туже; напрасно Печорин целовал её холодные губы — ничто не могло привести её в себя (Лермонтов 1). She was unconscious. We...tied the wound as tightly as we could; Pechorin kissed her cold lips without response—nothing could bring her around (1d). She was unconscious. We...bandaged the wound as tightly as we could. In vain Pechorin kissed her cold lips; nothing could bring her back to consciousness (1b).

2. to bring s.o. back to a normal state of attention, composure etc (may refer to a person who is temporarily upset, lost in thought, fantasizing etc): X привёл Y-а в себя ≃ **X brought Y back to reality; X brought Y to Y's senses; X snapped ⟨brought⟩ Y out of it;** [in limited contexts] **X calmed Y down.**

Он глубоко задумался, и даже громкий стук в дверь не привёл его в себя. He was lost in thought, and even a loud knock at the door didn't snap him out of it.

П-517 • НЕ ПРИВЫКА́ТЬ *(кому)* coll; **НЕ ПРИВЫ-КА́ТЬ СТАТЬ** substand [these forms only; impers predic with бытьø; usu. pres; fixed WO] s.o. is accustomed to sth., sth. is not novel for s.o.: X-у не привыкать ≃ **X is used to it; it's nothing new to ⟨for⟩ X; it's not new to X.**

Григорий с досадой сказал: «Ты, бабушка, лучше дай косу...» Старуха сурово глянула на Григория и отвернулась. «Ступай сам возьми, она, никак, под сараем висит». ... Когда [Григорий] проходил мимо старухи, [он] отчётливо слышал, как та проговорила: «Погибели на вас, проклятых, нету!» К этому было не привыкать Григорию. Он давно видел, с каким настроением встречают их жители хуторов (Шолохов 5). Grigory said irritably, "You'd better give me that scythe, Granny...." The old woman looked hard at Grigory and turned away. "Go and get it yourself. It must be hanging up in the shed."...As he [Grigory] walked past the woman, [he] distinctly heard her say, "Will we never be rid of you, spongers!" This was nothing new for Grigory. He had long been aware of the attitude to them in the villages (5a).

П-518 • ПРИВЫ́ЧКА — ВТОРА́Я НАТУ́РА [saying] a longtime behavior that has become routine for or customary to s.o. is so much a part of him that it is hard to change or alter it: ≃ **custom ⟨habit⟩ is a second nature; old habits die hard;** [when used to justify one's actions] **(one did sth.) from ⟨out of⟩ force of habit.**

П-519 • ВХОДИ́ТЬ/ВОЙТИ́ В ПРИВЫ́ЧКУ *(чью, у кого)* [VP; subj: abstr or infin] to become habitual, routine: X вошёл (у Y-а) в привычку ≃ **X became (a) habit (with Y); X became a matter of course (for Y).**

Беспартийных никто... не заставляет высказываться. А партийный или комсомолец обязан выступать и — вошло уже в привычку, думая одно, говорить вслух другое (Аллилуева 2). People not belonging to the Party...were not called upon to express an opinion; but Party members and Komsomols were in duty bound to stand up and express themselves. It had become a habit with them to express one opinion aloud while convinced of something quite different (2a). ♦ Заставляйте себя делать упражнения каждое утро, пока это не войдёт в привычку. Make yourself exercise every morning until it becomes a matter of course.

П-520 • ДЕРЖА́ТЬ НА ПРИ́ВЯЗИ *кого* coll [VP; subj: human] to restrict s.o.'s independence, not allow s.o. to act on his own initiative: X держит Y-а на привязи ≃ **X keeps Y on a (short) leash; X keeps Y in leading strings; X keeps a tight rein on Y.**

Добрая душа Михеич. Не он — Настёне в эти годы пришлось бы совсем худо. Семёновна готова держать её на привязи... (Распутин 2). Mikheyich was a kind soul....If not for him, Nastyona's life would have been miserable all those years. Semyonovna was ready to keep her on a leash... (2a).

П-521 • В ПРИДА́ЧУ [PrepP; Invar; used as Particle or sent adv] in addition to (what has been named): **to boot; as well; on top of that; thrown in; into the bargain; for good measure.**

«Кулак, кулак! — подумал про себя Чичиков, — да ещё и бестия в придачу!» (Гоголь 3). "A tightfisted fellow and a low-down beast to boot," Chichikov thought to himself (3c). ♦ «Всего мне довелось увидеть на своём веку: и сумы, и тюрьмы, с войной в придачу» (Максимов 1). "I've seen all kinds of things in my life: begging and prisons and the war as well" (1a). ♦ «Представьте себе, Соня, что вы знали бы все намерения Лужина заранее, знали бы (то есть наверно), что через них погибла бы совсем Катерина Ивановна, да и дети; вы тоже, в придачу (так как вы себя ни за что считаете, так *в придачу*)» (Достоевский 3). "Imagine, Sonya, that you'd known in advance exactly what Luzhin had planned to do, and known (for a certainty, I mean) that it would cause the total ruin of Katerina Ivanovna and her children; and of yourself, too, into the bargain (since you don't attach any value to yourself, let it be *into the bargain*)" (3d).

П-522 • С ПРИ́ДУРЬЮ coll [PrepP; Invar; nonagreeing modif or subj-compl with copula (subj: human)] **1.** slightly stupid: **a bit dense ⟨silly⟩; a bit weak in the head; not too bright.**

[Городничий:] Не извольте гневаться, ваше превосходительство, она [моя жена] немного с придурью... (Гоголь 4). [Mayor:] I do beseech Your Excellency not to be annoyed. She's [my wife is] a little bit silly... (4b).

2. Also: **С ДУ́РЬЮ** highly coll eccentric, having bizarre ideas, slightly mad: **a bit touched (in the head); not quite right (in the head); a bit odd ⟨off⟩; slightly nuts ⟨crazy, daft⟩; one of those weird types; an odd bird ⟨duck, sort⟩.**

Иленька был добрый, очень честный и весьма неглупый молодой человек, но он был то, что называется малый с дурью... (Толстой 2). Ilinka was a kind, very honorable, and not in the least stupid young man, but he was what was called a bit touched... (2b). ♦ «Но к чему так громко? Старик услышит, обидится». — «Ничего он не услышит... А и услышит, не возьмёт в толк, — с придурью» (Пастернак 1). "But don't talk so loud. You don't want to hurt the old man's feelings." "He won't hear anything....And if he did, he wouldn't understand—he's not quite right in the head" (1a). ♦ «Видал, — кивнул вслед матери Мозговой, — она у меня особенная, с придурью: её всю жизнь безменом по лбу, а она ко всем со скатертью...» (Максимов 1). "D'you see?" Mozgovoy nodded as his mother moved away. "She's a bit odd. All her life she's been beaten over the head, but still she comes out offering hospitality" (1a).

П-523 • СКВОЗЬ ⟨ЧЕРЕЗ⟩ ПРИ́ЗМУ *чего* смотреть, глядеть, оценивать и т. п. lit [PrepP; these forms only; the resulting PrepP is adv] (to look at, appraise etc sth.) from a specific point of view, taking into account certain factors: **through the prism of.**

Профессор рассматривал творчество современных художников сквозь призму своих весьма консервативных представлений о прекрасном. The professor looked at the work of modern artists through the prism of his extremely conservative notions of what is beautiful.

П-524 • ПОДАВА́ТЬ/ПОДА́ТЬ ПРИ́ЗНАКИ ЖИ́ЗНИ [VP; often neg] **1.** [subj: human] to give some indication that one is alive: X не подавал признаков жизни ≃ **X showed ⟨gave⟩ no sign(s) of life.**

Один эсэсовец наткнулся на Дину, и она показалась ему подозрительной. Он посветил фонариком, приподнял её и стал бить. Но она висела мешком и не подавала признаков жизни (Кузнецов 1). An SS man stumbled on Dina and thought her suspicious for some reason. He turned his flashlight on her, raised her up and struck her savagely, but she hung limp, showing no sign of life (1a). ♦ Они [противники] лежали в грязи и все, кроме рыжего, не подавали признаков жизни (Войнович 2). They [the enemies] were all lying in the mud now and, with the exception of the one with the red hair, gave no signs of life (2a).

2. [subj: human or collect] to be or become noticeably active, actively involved in (the activity specified or implied): X не подавал признаков жизни ≃ **X gave ⟨showed⟩ no sign(s) of life; X didn't make his presence known ⟨felt⟩.**

…[Жена Серго] тихонечко стушевалась где-то в углу комнаты, между кроватью и шкафом, до самого конца не подавая оттуда признаков жизни (Максимов 1). …[Sergo's wife] melted quietly away into a corner of the room between the bed and the cupboard, giving no sign of life until the very end (1a). ♦ С Садовой сообщали, что проклятая квартира опять подала признаки жизни в ней (Булгаков 9). It was reported from Sadovaya that the infernal apartment was again showing signs of life (9a).

П-525 • ПРИЗНА́ТЬСЯ СКАЗА́ТЬ *obs, coll;* **НА́ДО ⟨НУ́ЖНО⟩ ПРИЗНА́ТЬСЯ** [these forms only; sent adv (parenth); fixed WO] speaking honestly, I must say frankly: **I ⟨we⟩ must admit; to tell (you) the truth; truth to tell; if the truth be told; to be (perfectly ⟨quite⟩) honest; frankly (speaking);** [in limited contexts] **I ⟨we⟩ must ⟨have to⟩ confess.**

[Анна Петровна:] Нравится ли он [твой жених] тебе? Признаться сказать, скоренько дело-то сделали… (Островский 1). [A.P.:] Do you like him [your fiancé]? I must admit the thing was done pretty quickly (1b). ♦ «Да, мне пора!» — произнёс он, взявшись за шляпу. «А чайку?» — «Нет, уж чайку пусть лучше когда-нибудь в другое время». — «…Я, признаться сказать, не охотник до чаю: напиток дорогой, да и цена на сахар поднялась немилосердная» (Гоголь 3). "Yes, it's time I went!" he said, reaching for his hat. "And what about tea?" "No thank you, sir, I'd rather have a cup of tea with you some other time." "…To tell you the truth, I don't really care for tea very much myself: it's an expensive beverage and, besides, the price of sugar has gone up cruelly" (3a).

П-526 • ПРИКАЗА́ТЬ ⟨ВЕЛЕ́ТЬ⟩ ДО́ЛГО ЖИТЬ [VP; usu. past] **1.** [subj: human] to die: X приказал долго жить ≃ **X went to his final ⟨eternal⟩ rest; X passed away ⟨on⟩; X took leave of ⟨departed⟩ this world; X breathed his last.**

Одним утром Матвей взошёл ко мне в спальню с вестью, что старик Р. «приказал долго жить» (Герцен 1). One morning Matvey came into my bedroom with the news that old R— "had passed away" (1a). ♦ «Каледин… приказал долго жить» (Шолохов 3). "Kaledin has passed on" (3a).

2. *coll, often humor* [subj: collect, concr, or abstr] to cease to exist or function: X приказал долго жить ≃ **X died (out); X went out of existence; X is no more.**

Мне нужно купить новый компьютер — мой приказал долго жить, а мне нужно закончить срочную работу. I have to buy a new computer: mine died, and I've got an urgent project to finish up. ♦ Этот журнал больше не издаётся. Он просуществовал три года и приказал долго жить. That magazine is no longer published. It survived for three years then went out of existence.

П-527 • НА ПРИКО́ЛЕ [PrepP; Invar; usu. subj-compl with copula] **1.** *nautical* [subj: a noun denoting a ship, a vessel] sth. is secured by cables, anchors etc: X на приколе ≃ **X is moored; X is ⟨lies⟩ at anchor.**

2. [subj: a noun denoting a car, a piece of machinery, equipment] sth. is inactive, not in operation: X (стоит) на приколе ≃ **X is idle ⟨laid up, not in use⟩.**

«Райкомовская легковуха [*substand* = легковая машина] зимой на приколе — не сидеть же тебе сложа руки» (Абра-

мов 1). "The District Committee jalopy is laid up in the winter, and you can't just sit twiddling your thumbs" (1a).

П-528 • ИЗ-ПОД ПРИЛА́ВКА торговать, продавать и т. п. *coll* [PrepP; Invar; adv] (in refer. to the illegal sale or purchase of sth. in a store) (to sell, buy etc sth.) secretly, stealthily: **under the counter.**

Через некоторое время ему предложили прекратить продажу в кофейне горячительных напитков, одновременно расширив ассортимент прохладительных. Алихан согласился, но схитрил, продолжая из-под прилавка продавать горячительные напитки (Искандер 3). After a while he was ordered to discontinue the sale of hard liquor in the coffeehouse and at the same time broaden his assortment of soft drinks. Ali Khan consented, but dissembled, continuing to sell hard liquor under the counter (3a).

П-529 • БЕСПЛА́ТНОЕ ПРИЛОЖЕ́НИЕ *coll* [NP; sing only; obj or subj-compl with copula (subj: human or concr); fixed WO] an unwanted person (or thing) that accompanies a welcome or expected person (or thing) and must be tolerated: **"(added) bonus"; an extra; (as) part of the package ⟨the deal⟩;** [in limited contexts] **fifth wheel; "fringe benefit."**

Если ты собираешься приглашать Антона, то приготовься к тому, что он приведёт с собой в качестве бесплатного приложения всю свою компанию. If you're planning on inviting Anton, be prepared to have him bring his whole gang along as an "added bonus."

П-530 • БРАТЬ/ВЗЯТЬ ПРИМЕ́Р *с кого* [VP; subj: human] to do sth. as another or others do it, emulate s.o.: X взял пример с Y-a ≃ **X followed Y's example; X took ⟨used⟩ Y as an example; X took a lesson ⟨his cue⟩ from Y; X took a leaf ⟨a page⟩ from ⟨out of⟩ Y's book; X took ⟨followed⟩ Y's lead; X modeled ⟨patterned⟩ himself after Y;** [in limited contexts] **X followed suit.**

«Она [ваша книга] знакомит нас с настоящими героями, с которых хочется брать пример» (Войнович 6). "It [your book] acquaints us with real heroes, whose example we want to follow" (6a). ♦ …Тут брехня на брехне, всё шиворот-навыворот. Егорша передовой… Егорша новый… С Егорши пример надо брать… (Абрамов 1). …This was one piece of garbage after another, everything turned topsy-turvy. Egorsha the progressive….Egorsha the New Man….One should take Egorsha as an example… (1a). ♦ «Вон бери пример, здесь старуха одна едет, она за всю жизнь ни разу на своего старика не крикнула. А вы чуть чего — и гавкать» (Распутин 1). "You ought to take a lesson from that old lady in our compartment. She's never yelled at her old man in her life, not once, and you—you start yapping at the slightest excuse" (1a).

П-531 • НЕ В ПРИМЕ́Р *coll* [PrepP; Invar] **1.** ~ *кому-чему* [the resulting PrepP is adv; a person may be contrasted only with a person, an object only with an object etc] in contrast to (and usu. better than) s.o. or sth., not as s.o. or sth.: **unlike; not like;** [in limited contexts] **as distinct from; the same cannot be said of ⟨for⟩.**

…Мы были сначала в полном отчаянии — где взять здесь, в тайге, новые шприцы? А потом Погребной с ветпункта выручил. У него, оказывается, большой запас был, не в пример нам (Гинзбург 2). We had despaired at first of finding any new needles out in the taiga; but then Pogrebnoy, from the veterinary station, had come to our rescue. Unlike us, as it turned out, he had a large stock of needles (2a). ♦ «Вот, не в пример тебе, с каким форсом свадьбу потомкам справляет!» (Максимов 3). "And here he is marrying his descendants off in high old style, not like you!" (3a). ♦ [Верка] была глубоко принципиальной взяточницей. Взяв что-нибудь, она честно расплачивалась. Не в пример многим другим (Гинзбург 1). …Verka was a high-principled looter who was scrupulous about giving value for goods taken. The same could not be said of most of her colleagues (1a).

2. [premodif; foll. by compar form of Adj or Adv, more often denoting a positive quality] considerably (better, more interesting etc): **(ever so) much; (by) far; incomparably; a great deal; a lot.**

[Василий:] Известно, вы не как другие. [Телятев:] Лучше? [Василий:] Не в пример (Островский 4). [V.:] You aren't at all like the rest. [T.:] Am I better? [V.:] Ever so much (4a). [V.:] You ain't like the rest of 'em, sir. [T.:] Better, eh? [V.:] Much better, sir (4b). ♦ В первый раз свободно вздохнули глуповцы и поняли, что жить «без утеснения» не в пример лучше, чем жить «с утеснением» (Салтыков-Щедрин 1). For the first time the Foolovites drew free breath and realized that to live "without oppression" was far better than to live "with oppression" (1a). ♦ ...Мой Бопре очень скоро привык к русской настойке и даже стал предпочитать её винам своего отечества, как не в пример более полезную для желудка (Пушкин 2). ...He [Beaupré] soon grew accustomed to homemade Russian vodka, eventually even preferring it to the wines of his homeland as a drink incomparably better for the stomach (2a). ♦ «...Он не в пример меня глупее. Сколько денег просвистал без всякого употребления-с» (Достоевский 1). "...He's a lot stupider than me. He's blown so much money, and for nothing, miss" (1a).

П-532 • ПОДАВА́ТЬ/ПОДА́ТЬ ⟨ПОКА́ЗЫВАТЬ/ПО-КАЗА́ТЬ⟩ ПРИМЕ́Р кому [VP; subj: human or collect] to behave in such a way as to be an example for others: X подаёт пример Y-у ≃ **X serves as an example to Y; X sets an example ⟨a standard⟩ for Y; X is ⟨serves as⟩ a role model for Y.**

[Ликки:] Личным мужеством твоим ты должен показать пример гвардейцам! (Булгаков 1). [L.:] You must set an example for the guardsmen with your own bravery! (1a).

П-533 • ДЛЯ ПРИМЕ́РА [PrepP; Invar; adv] in order to deter others (from doing the action in question or anything similar): **as an example to others ⟨to the others, to the rest etc⟩.**

Узнав, что девятиклассники зло подшутили над учителем физики, директор школы решила во что бы то ни стало найти зачинщиков и для примера строго наказать их. When she learned that some ninth-graders had played a dirty trick on their physics teacher, the principal decided to do whatever it took to find out the instigators and then to punish them severely as an example to the others.

П-534 • К ПРИМЕ́РУ; К ПРИМЕ́РУ СКАЗА́ТЬ ⟨ГО-ВОРЯ́⟩ coll [these forms only; sent adv (parenth); fixed WO] as an illustration (of the point in question): **for example; for instance; as an example.**

[Золотуев:] Покрутись с моё, покувыркайся, тогда не будешь спрашивать, зачем людям деньги... Знаю я, к примеру, случай один, старичка одного знаю... Хочешь, расскажу? (Вампилов 3). [Z.:] When you've been kicking around the world as long as I have, you won't be asking why people want money....For example, I know of one case: there's this old man....Shall I tell you about it? (3a). ♦ «У меня есть о чём вспомнить. Разве вы, Андрей Васильевич, слышали когда-нибудь, к примеру, о Ледовом походе?» (Максимов 3). "I've got plenty to look back on. Have you ever heard, for instance, of the Icy March, Andrei Vasilievich?" (3a). ♦ Каждое событие, происходящее сейчас в России, должно рассматриваться с точки зрения борения двух этих течений. Возьмём, к примеру, одно из самых примечательных: эмиграция евреев... (Аксёнов 7). Every aspect of life in Russia today must be examined in the light of these two forces. Let us take one of the most noteworthy of recent events as an example. We have in mind the emigration of the Jews... (7a).

П-535 • ДУРНЫ́Е ПРИМЕ́РЫ ЗАРАЗИ́ТЕЛЬНЫ ⟨ДУРНО́Й ПРИМЕ́Р ЗАРАЗИ́ТЕЛЕН⟩ [saying] s.o.'s misbehavior provokes others to act in a similar manner: ≃ **bad habits ⟨deeds⟩ are contagious ⟨catch on⟩; misbehavior is con-** tagious ⟨catches on⟩; **monkey see, monkey do;** [in limited contexts] **it's catching.**

П-536 • ИМЕ́ТЬ ⟨ДЕРЖА́ТЬ⟩ НА ПРИМЕ́ТЕ кого-что [VP; subj: human] to have noticed s.o. or sth. and usu. to maintain an ongoing interest in him or it, keep one's attention on him or it, factor him or it into one's plans etc: X держит Y-а на примете ≃ **X is keeping Y in mind; X has his eye on Y;** [in limited contexts] **X knows ⟨happens to know⟩ (of) Y.**

Ему будет очень приятно работать со мной в клопиной подкомиссии, он давно меня держит на примете, он вообще всегда держит на примете нашу чудесную, талантливую мо-лодёжь (Стругацкие 3). He would be very happy working with me in the bedbug subcommittee, he had long had me in mind, and in general he always had our wonderful, talented youth in mind (3a).

П-537 • НА ПРИМЕ́ТЕ у кого быть, быть∅, иметься [PrepP; Invar; subj-compl with copula (subj: human, collect, concr, or count abstr)] a person (thing etc) has been noticed by s.o., brought to the attention of s.o. etc, and usu. is the object of his ongoing interest, attention, plans etc: у Y-а есть на примете один ⟨такой и т. п.⟩ X ≃ **Y has an ⟨a certain, one⟩ X in mind; Y has his eye on an X ⟨a certain X, one X (that...) etc⟩; Y knows of an ⟨one etc⟩ X; there's this one ⟨a certain⟩ X who(m) ⟨that⟩ Y has his eye on (who ⟨that⟩...);** ‖ (этот) X у Y-а давно на примете ≃ **Y has had an ⟨his⟩ eye on (this ⟨that⟩) X for (quite) some time ⟨for quite a while (now) etc⟩.**

[Отрадина:] А не разбогатею, так, может быть, и без приданого добрый человек возьмёт. Как ты думаешь? У меня такой есть на примете (Островский 3). [O.:] Well, if I don't get rich perhaps some good man will have me anyway. Don't you think he might? I have a certain person in mind (3a). ♦ «В Ташкент махнём... Там у меня есть кой-чего на примете» (Максимов 2). "We'll go to Tashkent. Got my eye on a job there" (2a). ♦ Несколько раз, со слезами на глазах, графиня говорила сыну, что теперь... её единственное желание состоит в том, чтобы видеть его жена-тым... Потом говорила, что у неё есть прекрасная девушка на примете, и выпытывала его мнение о женитьбе (Толстой 5). Several times the countess, with tears in her eyes, told her son that now...her only wish was to see him married....Then she told him she knew of a splendid girl, and tried to discover what he thought about marriage (5b). ♦ «За Фоминым будем смотреть, он у нас давно на примете, только едва ли и Фомин отважится на выступление» (Шолохов 5). "We'll watch Fomin, we've had an eye on him for some time, but I shouldn't think even Fomin would risk any action" (5a).

П-538 • БРАТЬ/ВЗЯТЬ НА ПРИМЕ́ТУ кого-что [VP; subj: human] to notice s.o. or sth., pay special attention to s.o. or sth.: X возьмёт Y-а на примету ≃ **X will take notice ⟨note⟩ of Y; X will keep an eye on Y; X will make a mental note of thing Y.**

П-539 • ПО ПРИНАДЛЕ́ЖНОСТИ отправить, передать что и т. п. offic [PrepP; Invar; adv] (to dispatch, transmit etc sth.) to where it belongs: **to the proper ⟨right⟩ party ⟨quarter, place etc⟩.**

В отделе перевозки Сергееву сказали, что передадут до-ставленный им пакет по принадлежности. In the shipping de-partment they told Sergeev that they'd pass on to the proper quarter the package he had delivered.

П-540 • ИЗ ПРИ́НЦИПА [PrepP; Invar; adv] because of one's commitment to some idea, belief etc: **on principle; as a matter of principle; for reasons of principle; out of principle.**

Он [Серёжа] продолжал ходить к Васину. Теперь делал это из упрямства и из принципа (Трифонов 3). Sergei continued to visit Vasin, doing so now out of obstinacy, as a matter of principle (3a). ♦ Полесов стоял в очередях главным образом из принципа. Денег у него не было, и купить он всё равно ничего не мог (Ильф и Петров 1). Polesov stood in line chiefly for reasons of principle. He had no money, so he could not buy anything, anyway (1a).

П-541 • **В ПРИ́НЦИПЕ** [PrepP; Invar; adv] with regard to the essence, the basic nature of sth.: **in principle; in theory; in general; generally; basically.**

Нам кажется, что во второй части Лёва будет более реален, зато он живёт в максимально нереальном мире. В первой же части куда реальнее был окружающий мир, зато Лёва в нём совершенно нереален, бесплотен. Не значит ли это, что человек и реальность разлучены в принципе? (Битов 2). It seems to us that Lyova will be more real in part two, but he lives in a maximally unreal world. In part one the world around him was much more real, but there Lyova was utterly unreal, incorporeal. Does this mean that man and reality have been severed in principle? (2a). ♦ Она училась радоваться не только в принципе — это легко и просто... она радовалась и деталям, и прямо-таки микроскопическим подробностям своего совместного существования с Рыцарем... (Залыгин 1). She schooled herself to rejoice not only in theory — that was easy....She rejoiced at the practical details, the tiny, microscopic details of her life with her Knight... (1a). ♦ Лёва не старался выдвинуться по общественной линии, т.е. избежал общественной работы, что в принципе просто соответствовало его склонности... (Битов 2). Lyova did not try to advance himself at the institute along social lines; i.e., he avoided community work, a policy that basically just suited his own inclination... (2a).

П-542 • **СБО́КУ ПРИПЁКА ⟨-у⟩; СБО́КУ-ПРИПЁКУ** *both highly coll* [AdvP; these forms only; fixed WO] **1.** [adv or subj-compl with copula (subj: usu. human or concr)] entirely unneeded, superfluous, not belonging (to the matter, event, or group in question): X был сбоку припёка ≃ **X was totally unnecessary ⟨entirely out of place etc⟩; person X was an appendage ⟨extra baggage, a fifth wheel⟩.**

Мы собрались на аэродроме. Я говорю: «Мы»! Уж я-то был сбоку припёка, случайно прихваченный человечек (Олеша 2). We gathered at the airfield. I say "we," but I myself was just an appendage, somebody brought along by sheer chance (2a). ♦ «За кладбищем я её зарывать не буду. Она мне не сбоку-припёку, а родная сноха» (Шолохов 5). [context transl] "I'm not going to bury her outside the cemetery. She's not just a stray that wandered in from somewhere, she's my own daughter-in-law" (5a).

2. сказать, сделать *что* ~ *obs* [adv] (to say or do sth.) rashly, without sufficient basis or obvious reason: **out of the blue; all of a sudden.**

[Подколёсин:] Ну, да как же ты хочешь, не поговоря прежде ни о чём, вдруг сказать сбоку-припёку: сударыня, дайте я на вас женюсь! (Гоголь 1). [P.:] Well, how do you expect me, without any previous introduction, to say to her suddenly, out of the blue, "Young lady, let's get married" (1a).

П-543 • **В ПРИРО́ДЕ ⟨НАТУ́РЕ** *obs*⟩ **ВЕЩЕ́Й** [PrepP; these forms only; subj-compl with copula (subj: abstr, often это, это всё); fixed WO] some happening (behavior etc) is natural, normal, expected: X в природе вещей ≃ **X is in the nature ⟨the order⟩ of things.**

«Енюшка, Енюшка», — раздался трепещущий женский голос. Дверь распахнулась, и на пороге показалась кругленькая, низенькая старушка... Пухлые её ручки мгновенно обвились вокруг его [Базарова] шеи, голова прижалась к его груди, и всё замолкло. Только слышались её прерывистые всхлипыванья... «Ну да, конечно, это всё в натуре вещей», — промолвил Василий Иваныч... (Тургенев 2). "Yevgeny darling, Yevgeny," came a quavering woman's voice. The door was thrown open, revealing on the threshold a round little old lady....Her plump little arms instantly went round his [Bazarov's] neck, her head was pressed to his breast and everything around was hushed. All that could be heard were her broken sobs...."Well, yes, of course, it's all in the nature of things," said Vassily Ivanich... (2a).

П-544 • **ОТ ПРИРО́ДЫ** [PrepP; Invar; modif or adv] by innate characteristics: **by nature; naturally; from birth; born** [AdjP or NP]; [in limited contexts] **nature gives ⟨grants⟩ s.o. sth.**

...Белокурые волосы, вьющиеся от природы, так живописно обрисовывали его бледный, благородный лоб... (Лермонтов 1). ...His fair hair, wavy by nature, framed, so picturesquely, his pale, noble brow... (1a). ♦ Я засветил серную спичку и поднёс её к носу мальчика: она озарила два белые глаза. Он был слепой, совершенно слепой от природы (Лермонтов 1). I lit a sulphur match and brought it close to the lad's very nose; it illuminated two white eyes. He was blind, totally blind from birth (1a). ♦ И так человеку от природы дано стремление уйти от праха, от уничтожения, от небытия через серьёзное дело жизни (Искандер 3). And so nature grants man the drive to escape from dust, annihilation, nonexistence, by means of a serious lifework (3a).

П-545 • **В ⟨ЗА⟩ ОДИ́Н ПРИСЕ́СТ** *coll* [PrepP; these forms only; adv; fixed WO] (to do sth.) all at one time, during one (usu. short) period of time: **at ⟨in⟩ one sitting; at a single sitting; at a stretch; at ⟨in⟩ one go.**

В тот день, при закатывающемся солнце, она прочла пришедшей паре мою книгу «Мы — национальный герой» на английском языке, благо манускрипт состоял из кусочков, и её можно было прочесть в один присест (Лимонов 1). As the sun went down that day, she read my book *We Are the National Hero* to the visiting couple, in English; since the manuscript consisted of short pieces, it could be read in one sitting (1a). ♦ Я сказал ему, что большое и сложное по содержанию стихотворение, вернее, маленькая поэма, кажется написанной одним дыханием, в один присест, залпом (Гладков 1). I said that the poem, long and complex though it was, seemed to have been written at one go, at a single sitting, without pausing for breath (1a).

П-546 • **С ПРИСТРА́СТИЕМ**[1] осматривать, проверять и т. п. [PrepP; Invar; adv] (to examine, check etc sth.) very thoroughly, paying particular attention to detail (often, looking for faults): **painstakingly; captiously; (go over sth.) with a fine-tooth(ed) comb.**

В конце смены мастер с пристрастием осмотрел каждую деталь, сделанную молодым рабочим, и остался доволен результатом. At the end of the shift the foreman painstakingly examined every part the young worker had made and was satisfied with the results.

П-547 • допрос, допрашивать **С ПРИСТРА́СТИЕМ**[2] [PrepP; Invar; nonagreeing postmodif or adv] **1.** *obs* (an interrogation, to interrogate s.o.) with the application of torture: **with (the use of) torture; under torture.**

Преступника изловили и стали допрашивать с пристрастием... (Салтыков-Щедрин 1). They nabbed the offender and began interrogating him under torture... (1a).

2. *usu. humor* thorough, captious (questioning), (to question s.o.) thoroughly, painstakingly etc: допрос ~ ≃ **third degree; (thorough ⟨painstaking etc⟩) cross-examination;** ‖ допрашивать ~ ≃ **give s.o. the third degree; cross-examine; grill.**

Денщик, допрошенный с пристрастием, повторил то же самое... (Искандер 3). Under cross-examination the orderly repeated the story... (3a).

П-548 • **ПРИ́СТУПУ ⟨-a⟩ НЕТ** *obs, coll* [VP; impers] **1.** ~ *к кому* it is impossible to address, speak with, or gain access to s.o. (because of his important position, bad mood, quick temper etc): **к X-у приступу нет** ≃ **there's no approaching ⟨getting near, talking to⟩ X; you cannot get near ⟨within ten feet of⟩ X; X is impossible to approach; X is totally unapproachable ⟨inaccessible⟩;** [in limited contexts] **you don't dare get near ⟨close to⟩ X.**

[Тарелкин:] Что же с Муромским-то делать? [Варравин:] Приказал; вы его нрав знаете. [Тарелкин:] Однако это всегда в ваших руках было. [Варравин:] И приступу нет (Сухово-Кобылин 1). [T.:] But what's to be done with Muromsky? [V.:] The prince gave an order—and you know his temper. [T.:] But the case was always in your hands. [V.:] There's no approaching him further on the matter (1a). ♦ [Скотинин:] Ба! Да ты весельчак. Давеча я думал, что к тебе приступу нет (Фонвизин 1). [S.:] Yeah, you're a real joker. Not long ago I used to think a fellow couldn't get near you (1b).

2. ~ *к чему* it is impossible (for s.o.) to buy, acquire sth. because of its high cost: **к X-у приступу нет** ≃ **X is beyond person Y's means;** [in limited contexts] **X is priced out of the market ⟨out of reach⟩.**

П-549 • ПРИСУ́ТСТВИЕ ДУ́ХА [NP; sing only; fixed WO] the ability to remain levelheaded, in command of one's thoughts and actions (esp. under stressful, dangerous etc circumstances): **presence of mind; composure;** ‖ сохранять присутствие духа ⟨не терять присутствия духа⟩ ≃ **remain ⟨be⟩ calm and collected; maintain one's composure.**

[Надежда Антоновна:] Я надеюсь, что у тебя достанет присутствия духа выслушать меня хладнокровно (Островский 4). [N.A.:] I hope that you will have enough presence of mind to listen calmly to what I have to tell you… (4a). ♦ По ночам я кричала. В ту зиму я начала кричать страшным нечеловеческим криком… А О. М[андельштам] упорно не терял присутствия духа и продолжал шутить (Мандельштам 1). That winter I began shouting in my sleep at night. It was an awful, inhuman cry.…But M[andelstam] was as calm and collected as ever, and went on joking to the end (1a). ♦ Привязав лошадь у Нюриной калитки, председатель Голубев поднялся на крыльцо. Нельзя сказать, чтобы он при этом сохранял полное присутствие духа, скорее наоборот, он входил в Нюрин дом, испытывая примерно такое волнение, как входя к первому секретарю райкома (Войнович 2). Chairman Golubev tied his horse to Nyura's gate and climbed up to the porch. It cannot be said he maintained complete composure; quite the contrary, he was entering Nyura's house with the same sort of trepidation he'd experienced when going in to see the First Secretary of the District Committee (2a).

< Loan translation of the French *présence d'esprit*.

П-550 • ПРИ́ТЧА ВО ЯЗЫ́ЦЕХ *lit* [NP; sing only; usu. subj-compl with copula (subj: human or abstr); fixed WO] a subject of general conversation, mockery, gossip etc: **the talk of the town ⟨village, office etc⟩; (some place is) abuzz with the story (of s.o. ⟨sth.⟩);** [in limited contexts] **the scandal of the neighborhood.**

Их скандальный развод стал притчей во языцех. Their scandalous divorce has become the talk of the town.

< From the Bible (Deut. 28:37): "And thou shalt become an astonishment, a proverb, and a byword, among all nations whither the Lord shall lead thee." «Во языцех» is the Church Slavonic form of the locative plural of «язык».

П-551 • СО́ЛОНО ПРИХО́ДИТСЯ/ПРИШЛО́СЬ ⟨ДОСТА́ЛОСЬ⟩ *кому coll* [VP; impers] s.o. is faced with a difficult situation (often one that results in some kind of suffering, punishment, defeat etc): **X-у солоно придётся** ≃ **X will have his fair share of troubles; X will have it rough; X is in for it ⟨for hard times, for a rough ride⟩;** [in limited contexts] **X will be in a pickle; X will smart for it.**

…Молодому человеку в первые его два года в университете пришлось очень солоно, так как он принуждён был всё это время кормить и содержать себя сам и в то же время учиться (Достоевский 1). …For his first two years at the university the young man found himself in a pickle, since he was forced all the while both to feed and keep himself and to study at the same time (1a). ♦ «Попробуй он слегка верхушек какой-нибудь науки… [он] ещё, пожалуй, скажет потом: „Дай-ка себя покажу!" Да такое выдумает мудрое постановление, что многим придётся солоно…» (Гоголь 3). "If a man like that acquires a smattering of some science…he may even say to himself, 'I'll show them who I am,' and invent such a sage law that many people will smart for it…" (3c).

П-552 • ТУ́ГО ⟨КРУ́ТО⟩ ПРИХО́ДИТСЯ/ПРИ-ШЛО́СЬ *кому coll* [VP; impers] s.o. finds himself in a difficult situation (often in refer. to having to work very hard to make a living, learn sth., accomplish sth. etc): **X-у туго придётся** ≃ **things will be difficult ⟨rough, tight etc⟩ for X; X will have a hard ⟨rough, tough etc⟩ time; X will have it rough ⟨tough⟩; X will have his share of troubles; X is in for a rough time ⟨a rough ride⟩;** [in refer. to financial hardships only] **X will be hard up.**

Уходя из дома, она [Людмила] не взяла с собой кружку, не взяла хлеба; казалось, что она всю дорогу не будет ни есть, ни пить. Но на пароходе… ей мучительно захотелось есть, и Людмила поняла, что ей круто придётся (Гроссман 2). She [Lyudmila] hadn't brought a mug or even any bread; she had thought she wouldn't want to eat or drink during the journey. On the steamer, however, she had felt desperately hungry…and had realized that things were going to be difficult (2a). ♦ У самой Аны детей не было. Зато у её трёх братьев и двух сестёр было в общей сложности 44 ребёнка… Ана сказала, что… большинство из них, вырастая, хотят иметь высшее образование, и её братьям и сёстрам приходится туго — им нужно много работать, чтобы дети имели высшее образование (Лимонов 1). Ana herself had no children. But all in all her three brothers and two sisters had forty-four children.…Ana said that…most of them, as they grew up, wanted to have a higher education, and things were tight for her brothers and sisters—they had to work very hard so that the children could have more education (1a). ♦ Советский паспорт, советское гражданство… Сколько возвышенных слов сочинено о том, какая честь быть гражданином СССР. Честь, конечно, большая, но туго приходится тем, кто пытается от неё отказаться (Войнович 1). A Soviet passport, Soviet citizenship.…How many exalted words have been written about the honor it is to be a citizen of the USSR. It is, of course, a great honor, but anyone who tries to renounce it is in for a rough time (1a). ♦ Сначала им [табачнику Коле и его жене Даше] пришлось довольно туго, но потом, во времена нэпа, персидский коммерсант снова открыл свою кофейню-кондитерскую, на этот раз осторожно назвав её «Кейфующий пролетарий». Он взял в долю бывшего табачника… (Искандер 3). At first they [the tobacco merchant Kolya and his wife Dasha] were rather hard up. Then, during the era of the New Economic Policy, the Persian merchant opened his coffeehouse and bake shop again—this time cautiously naming it the Idle Proletariat—and took on the former tobacco merchant as partner… (3a).

П-553 • ПРИХОДИ́ТЬ/ПРИЙТИ́ В СЕБЯ́ [VP; subj: human] **1.** to return to a conscious state (after having been unconscious) or to a fully alert state (after having been very drunk, very drowsy etc): **X пришёл в себя** ≃ [in refer. to returning to consciousness] **X came to his senses; X came to (himself); X came (a)round; X regained consciousness;** [after being drunk] **X sobered up;** [after drowsiness] **X roused himself; X brightened ⟨perked⟩ up again.**

«Около десяти часов вечера она пришла в себя; мы сидели у постели…» (Лермонтов 1). "Around ten at night she came to; we were sitting by her bed…" (1a). ♦ Отогревшись у мельничного костра, Харлампо пришёл в себя… (Искандер 5). When he was warmed up beside the mill fire, Harlampo regained consciousness… (5a).

2. [more often pfv] to come out of a state of intense nervousness, fright, worry, surprise etc, settle down: X пришёл в себя ≃ **X calmed down; X recovered (from a shock** etc**); X pulled himself together; X regained his composure; X was ⟨became⟩ himself ⟨his old self⟩ again; X felt more like himself (again); X came to his senses; X got over it ⟨the shock** etc⟩.

Весь ещё во власти раздражения, он мало-помалу приходил в себя (Максимов 3). He was still in the grip of his irritation, but gradually calmed down (3a). ♦ …Почтенные представители долго ещё не могли прийти в себя от удивления (Салтыков-Щедрин 2). …The worthy representatives did not recover from their surprise for some time (2a). ♦ Рвацкий меня изумил, а я Рвацкого испугал… когда я объяснил, что пришёл подписать договор с ним на печатание моего романа в издаваемом им журнале. Но тем не менее он быстро пришёл в себя… (Булгаков 12). If Rvatsky astonished me, I clearly terrified Rvatsky…when I explained that I had come to sign a contract with him for my novel which was going to be printed in the magazine he published. However, he quickly pulled himself together… (12a). ♦ Егор тараторил, а сам, похоже, приходил пока в себя — гость был и вправду нежданный (Шукшин 1). Egor chattered on while making an effort to regain his composure: the guest was indeed most unexpected (1a). ♦ Оставшись один, он [Голубев] немного пришёл в себя и стал раскладывать лежавшую на столе груду бумаг (Войнович 2). Left alone, Golubev began to feel more like himself and started to arrange the heap of papers on his desk (2a).

3. to overcome one's fatigue by taking a short rest: X пришёл в себя ≃ **X caught his breath; X rested up;** [in limited contexts] **X got his bearings.**

Я устал с дороги. Дай мне в себя прийти, а потом поговорим. I'm tired from the trip. Let me catch my breath, and then we'll talk. ♦ …Войдя в избу, Михаил поставил на пол плетёную из бересты корзину… «Самовар ставить или баню затоплять?» — спросила она [мать]. «Погоди маленько. Дай в себя прийти» (Абрамов 1). When he got inside, Mikhail put down his birch-bark basket.…"Shall I put on the samovar or heat up the bathhouse?" she [his mother] asked. "Wait a bit. Give me some time to get my bearings" (1a).

П-554 • ПРИХОДИ́ТЬСЯ/ПРИЙТИ́СЬ КСТА́ТИ [VP; subj: concr, abstr, or, rare, human; usu. pfv] to turn out to be needed, appropriate etc and/or to come about, appear at the right moment: X пришёлся кстати ≃ **X came at the perfect time; X couldn't have come at a better time; X was just what one needed (at the ⟨that⟩ moment); thing X came in handy; thing X couldn't have been more timely.**

Перевод, присланный родителями, пришёлся кстати, так как Оле даже нечем было заплатить за квартиру. The money order her parents sent was just what Olya needed, because she didn't even have money to pay the rent.

П-555 • БРАТЬ/ВЗЯТЬ НА ПРИЦЕ́Л ⟨НА МУ́ШКУ coll⟩ **кого-что** [VP; subj: human] **1.** to aim a weapon at s.o. or sth.: X взял Y-а на мушку ≃ **X took aim at Y; X got ⟨had⟩ Y (lined up) in X's sights; X drew a bead on Y.**

Лейтенант скомандовал взять на прицел два окна с правой стороны дома. The lieutenant ordered his men to take aim at two windows on the right side of the house.

2. to direct one's attention to s.o. or sth., pay special attention to s.o. or sth.: X возьмёт Y-а на прицел ≃ **X will keep an eye on Y; X will take note of Y.**

Гроссмейстер заметил незаурядные способности рыжего мальчика и взял его на прицел. The grand master noticed that the red-haired boy had remarkable talent and started keeping an eye on him.

П-556 • ДА́ЛЬНИЙ ⟨ДАЛЁКИЙ⟩ ПРИЦЕ́Л [NP; sing only; fixed WO] a far-reaching plan, project etc: **distant aim in view; long-range goal;** ‖ с дальним прицелом ≃ **with an eye toward the future; with a long-range goal in mind.**

Ну, а если уж вспоминать, так в разное время бывали и ещё какие-то, в общем-то, довольно милые Добровольцы, они её [Ирину Викторовну] встречали, провожали, сопровождали… Но всё это — корректно и бескорыстно, без дальнего прицела (Залыгин 1). Having once started reminiscing she [Irina Viktorovna] recalled that there'd also been a number of quite likable Volunteers at various times. They'd met her and accompanied her here and there.…All this was done correctly and with no thought of gain, without any…distant aim in view (1a).

П-557 • ПО ПРИЧИ́НЕ чего [PrepP; Invar; Prep; the resulting PrepP is adv] owing to: **because of; on account of; by reason of; the reason being.**

Когда их обмундировывали, на складе не хватило шинелей и бойцам выдали зимние маскхалаты, которые были использованы по причине плохой погоды (Войнович 2). When they were being outfitted, there had not been enough overcoats at the depot and the soldiers had been issued winter camouflage cloaks, which they were now using because of the bad weather (2a). ♦ Мне Абесаломон Нартович всегда нравился за свой талант рассказчика и балагура… Я ему тоже, мне кажется, нравился… Во мне, я думаю, он всегда ценил поклонение своему дару, развернуть который он не мог по причине своего служебного положения (Искандер 4). I have always liked Abesalomon Nartovich for his talent as a storyteller and entertainer.…He liked me too, I think.…What he valued in me, I think, was my admiration for his gift, which he could not develop on account of his official position (4a). ♦ [Телегин:] Жена моя бежала от меня на другой день после свадьбы с любимым человеком по причине моей непривлекательной наружности (Чехов 3). [Т.:] My wife ran away with the man she loved the day after our wedding, the reason being my unprepossessing appearance (3a).

П-558 • ДО ВТОРО́ГО ПРИШЕ́СТВИЯ [PrepP; Invar; adv; fixed WO] for a very long time, endlessly, forever: **until the Second Coming; till doomsday; till kingdom come.**

«Ты… будешь в этой очереди стоять до второго пришествия или до тех пор, пока какому-нибудь нужному человеку на лапу не дашь» (Войнович 1). "You'll be on that waiting list until the Second Coming or until you grease the right person's palm" (1a).

< From the Christian doctrine of Christ's future return to earth.

П-559 • ПРО́БА ПЕРА́ [NP; sing only; fixed WO] s.o.'s first attempt at writing a literary work: **test of the pen;** [in limited contexts] **literary debut; beginner's exercise; first effort.**

Упорнее всего Твардовский и редакция добивались: а что у меня есть ещё?.. Пробегая мои похороненные от 1948-го года пласты, я выбирал, что ж им назвать. Едучи сюда, я не готовился ничего больше открывать, но что-то было надо, трудно было убедить их, что «Иван Денисович» написан как первая проба пера (Солженицын 2). The question to which Tvardovsky and his colleagues most persistently returned was: "What else have you to offer?…" Mentally running through the layers secreted over the years since 1948, I selected things I could mention to them. On my way there, I had meant to reveal nothing else, but I couldn't keep it up: it would have been difficult to convince them that *Ivan Denisovich* was a beginner's exercise (2a).

П-560 • КАК ПРО́БКА глуп(ый) coll [как + NP; Invar; modif (intensif)] extremely (stupid): **(as) dumb ⟨dense, thickheaded⟩ as they come; (as) dumb as an ox.**

«Как тебе понравился Зоин муж?» — «Хорош собой, но глуп как пробка». "How did you like Zoya's husband?" "He's good-looking, but dumb as they come."

П-561 • ПРО́БКОЙ ⟨КАК ПРО́БКА⟩ ВЫ́ЛЕТЕТЬ ⟨ВЫ́СКОЧИТЬ⟩ *откуда coll* [VP; subj: human] to run or walk out of some place very quickly, headlong: X пробкой вылетел из места Y ≃ **X dashed ⟨flew, came flying⟩ out of place Y like a shot; X shot out of place Y (like a rocket).**

Поняв, что отец в плохом настроении, Дима пробкой вылетел из комнаты. Realizing that his father was in a bad mood, Dima shot out of the room.

П-562 • НА ПРО́БУ взять, дать *что* и т. п. [PrepP; Invar; adv] (to take, give etc sth.) for examination, trial, or appraisal: **as a sample; on trial; to try ⟨test⟩.**

А. Т. [Твардовский] дал ему [Лебедеву, советнику Хрущёва] на пробу только четверть романа, сказав: «Первая часть. Над остальными работает» (Солженицын 2). А. Т. [Tvardovsky] gave him [Lebedev, Khrushchev's adviser] only a quarter of the novel as a sample, telling him, "This is Part One. He's working on the rest" (2a). ♦ «Видели это?» — спросил он, показывая руку, как вылитую в перчатке. «Что это такое?» — спросил Обломов в недоумении. «А новые *lacets*!.. Это только что из Парижа. Хотите, привезу вам на пробу пару?» (Гончаров 1). "Have you seen this?" he asked, holding up one hand in a well-fitting glove. "What is it?" asked Oblomov, puzzled. "The new *lacets* [*Fr* = laces]!...Brand new—from Paris. Shall I bring you a pair to try?" (1b).

П-563 • ПРО́БУ ⟨-ы⟩ СТА́ВИТЬ НЕ́ГДЕ ⟨НЕ́КУДА⟩ *(на ком) highly coll* [these forms only; impers predic with быть∅] (of a person who displays a high degree of the specified, usu. negative, quality or is involved in some disreputable activity) s.o. is a complete, absolute (scoundrel, cheat etc): на X-е пробу ставить негде ≃ **X is as bad ⟨rotten etc⟩ as they come; X is a downright ⟨an out-and-out, a shameless, a notorious⟩** [NP].

Все они жулики, пробу ставить негде. They're all a bunch of cheats—as bad as they come. ♦ Он мгновенно перестроился на деловой тон. «Условия вы, ребята, знаете. Решайте, берёмся или нет?» После недолгого молчания первым откликнулся Альберт Гурьяныч. Лениво позёвывая, он сказал: «Тебе видней, бригадир. Только на этом Карасике, сам знаешь, пробы ставить негде: обманет и не кашлянёт» (Максимов 3). [context transl] His voice changed immediately and became businesslike. "You know the conditions, boys. Make up your minds, shall we take it on or not?" After a brief silence, the first response came from Albert Guryanich. "You know best, foreman," he said, yawning lazily. "But that Karasik, as you know yourself, is a double-crossing bastard. He'll swindle us as soon as look at us" (3a). ♦ Тут он помчался в Росфото, весь оставшийся вечер колобродил там от стола к столу, торчал в баре, рассказывая брежневские анекдоты завзятым стукачам, и девочку подклеил — пробы негде ставить, известную всем сотрудницу Виолетту (Аксёнов 12). [context transl] He rushed over to Rosfoto, the Photographers' Club, and spent the rest of the evening table-hopping, hanging around the bar, telling Brezhnev jokes to inveterate stoolies, and then picked up a girl—everyone's fingerprints all over her, the well-known plant Violetta (12a).

П-564 • ВЫ́СШЕЙ ⟨ВЫСО́КОЙ, ЧИ́СТОЙ⟩ ПРО́БЫ [NP_{gen}; these forms only; nonagreeing modif; fixed WO] (s.o. or sth.) embodying the type or quality specified to the highest possible degree: **of a high ⟨the highest⟩ order; of the first water; of the highest caliber; first-rate; first-class;** [of a positive type or quality only] **sterling** [NP].

Николай Иванович был часовщиком высшей пробы: он мог починить любые часы — даже такие, с которыми не могли справиться другие мастера. Nikolai Ivanovich was a watchmaker of the highest caliber: he could repair any watch, even the ones that other masters were unable to fix. ♦ Этот на вид приличный человек оказался мошенником высшей пробы. This respectable-looking man turned out to be a first-class scoundrel.

П-565 • НИ́ЗШЕЙ ⟨НИ́ЗКОЙ⟩ ПРО́БЫ *derog* [NP_{gen}; these forms only; nonagreeing modif; fixed WO] (of a person's professional qualifications, ethical standards etc, or of the quality of a work of literature, art etc) of very low quality, base, devoid of merit etc: **of the worst ⟨lowest, basest⟩ type ⟨kind, sort⟩.**

Это не поэт, а версификатор низкой пробы. He's no poet; he's a rhymster of the worst sort.

П-566 • ДА́ЛЬНИЕ ⟨ДО́ЛГИЕ⟩ ПРО́ВОДЫ — ЛИ́ШНИЕ СЛЁЗЫ [saying] if a person spends a long time saying good-bye to s.o. or seeing s.o. off, he is sure to become upset: ≃ **long partings mean a lot of tears; the longer the good-bye ⟨the goodbye, the leave-taking⟩, the more the tears.**

Григорий... попрощался с родными... «Ну, дальние проводы — лишние слёзы. Прощайте!» — дрогнувшим голосом сказал Григорий и подошёл к коню (Шолохов 5). Grigory...said goodbye to his family.... "Well, long partings mean a lot of tears. Goodbye!" Grigory said with a quiver in his voice, and walked to his horse (5a). ♦ [Кабанов:] Прощайте, маменька! *(Кланяется.)* [Кабанова:] Прощай! Дальние проводы — лишние слёзы (Островский 6). [K-ov:] Good-bye Mama! *(He bows.)* [K-ova:] Good-bye. The longer the leave-taking, the more the tears. (6d).

П-567 • В ПРОДОЛЖЕ́НИЕ *чего* [PrepP; Invar; Prep; the resulting PrepP is adv] throughout the duration, continuance of sth.: **during; throughout; all through; for; in the course of; for ⟨over⟩ the space of;** || в продолжение всего дня ⟨целого года и т. п.⟩ ≃ **all day ⟨year etc⟩ long.**

В продолжение ужина Грушницкий шептался и перемигивался с драгунским капитаном (Лермонтов 1). During the supper Grushnitski kept whispering and exchanging winks with the Captain of Dragoons (1a). All through supper Grushnitsky was whispering and exchanging winks with the dragoon captain (1c). ♦ У него как раз к этому сроку иссякли все... не прерывавшиеся в продолжение стольких лет его доходы от подачек Фёдора Павловича (Достоевский 1). Just at that time he had exhausted all his income from Fyodor Pavlovich's handouts, which...had continued nonstop for so many years (1a). ♦ В продолжение года, во время которого я вёл уединённую, сосредоточенную в самом себе, моральную жизнь, все отвлечённые вопросы о назначении человека... уже представились мне... (Толстой 2). In the course of the year during which I led a solitary moral life, turned in upon myself, I was already confronted by all the abstract questions concerning man's destiny... (2b). ♦ Войска авангарда расположились впереди Вишау, в виду цепи неприятельской, уступавшей нам место при малейшей перестрелке в продолжение всего дня (Толстой 4). The troops of the vanguard were stationed before Wischau within sight of the enemy line, which all day long had yielded ground to us at the least skirmish (4a).

П-568 • НЕ ПРОДОХНЁ́ШЬ; НЕ ПРОДОХНУ́ТЬ; ПРОДОХНУ́ТЬ НЕЛЬЗЯ́ *all coll* [VP; neg pfv fut, gener. 2nd pers sing не продохнёшь or impers predic with быть∅ (variants with продохнуть)] it is impossible to breathe (in some place because the air is stuffy, there is a bad smell etc): **you ⟨one⟩ can hardly breathe; it's hard to breathe; there isn't a breath of (fresh) air (in some place).**

Ну и накурили они здесь — не продохнёшь. Well, they certainly smoked their fill of cigarettes here—you can hardly breathe.

П-569 • НА ПРОИЗВО́Л СУДЬБЫ́ бросить, оставить, покинуть *кого* [PrepP; Invar; adv; fixed WO] (to leave, abandon s.o.) unattended, without help or support: **(leave s.o.) to ⟨at⟩ the mercy of fate; (abandon s.o.) to the mercy ⟨the whims, the vagaries⟩ of fate; (leave s.o.) to his fate.**

«Не уходите к партизанам, — сказал Штальбе, — в лесу вы погибнете от холода и голода, партизаны не принимают евреев, бросают их в лесу на произвол судьбы» (Рыбаков 1).

"Don't go to the partisans," Stalbe told them. "You'll die of cold and hunger in the forest, the partisans don't accept Jews, they'll leave you in the forest to the mercy of fate" (1a). ♦ ...Собака, которая привязана к будке, находится даже в более выгодном положении, её хотя бы кормят только за то, что она собака, а его, Ивана, оставили на произвол судьбы и, неизвестно, собираются забрать или нет (Войнович 2). ...Even a dog tied to a doghouse was better off than Chonkin because it, at least, gets fed because it's a dog, while he, Ivan [Chonkin], had been abandoned to the whims of fate—who knew if they had any intention of ever coming to get him? (2a). ♦ Князь Василий имел вид человека, отягчённого делами, усталого, измученного, но из сострадания не могущего, наконец, бросить на произвол судьбы и плутов этого беспомощного юношу, сына всё-таки его друга, après tout, и с таким огромным состоянием (Толстой 4). He [Prince Vasily] had the air of a man oppressed by business, weary, harassed, but who, out of compassion, was unable to abandon to the vagaries of fate and the designs of rogues this helpless youth, the son, after all, of his friend and the possessor of such an enormous fortune into the bargain (4a). ♦ Елена поднимает голову на часы и спрашивает: «Неужели, неужели они оставят нас на произвол судьбы?» (Булгаков 3). Elena looked up at the clock and asked: "Surely, surely they won't just leave us to our fate?" (3a).

П-570 • **КАК ПРО́КЛЯТЫЙ работать, заниматься** и т. п. *highly coll* [как + AdjP; nom only; adv (intensif)] (to work, study etc) without rest and exerting great effort: **like mad; like the dickens; like one possessed; (study) one's brains out.**

Вдруг Рита сказала: «Между прочим, дорогие друзья, хотя Герасим Иванович отличный преподаватель, но прежде всего Кирка помог себе сам. Он занимался как проклятый. Совершенно как проклятый» (Трифонов 5). Suddenly Rita broke in, "By the way, dear friends, although it's true that Gerasim Ivanovich is an excellent teacher, Kirka got in [the institute] thanks to his own efforts more than anything else. He studied like mad, he really did" (5a).

П-571 • **ДАВА́ТЬ/ДАТЬ ⟨ДЕ́ЛАТЬ/СДЕ́ЛАТЬ⟩ ПРО́-МАХ ⟨ПРОМА́ШКУ⟩** *coll* [VP; subj: human] to do or say the wrong thing because of bad judgment, a mistake etc: X дал промах ≃ X slipped up; X made a slip ⟨a blunder, a (big) mistake⟩; X tripped ⟨got tripped⟩ up; X put his foot in it ⟨in his mouth⟩; [in limited contexts] X missed his chance.

«Но уж тогда разрешите — я ещё разик у вас надымлю. Или мне выйти?» (Выйти ему?! Прозрачно! Понял, что промах дал, теперь хочет смыться.) «Нет-нет, курите здесь. Я люблю табачный дым» (Солженицын 12). "Well, in that case, may I have another smoke here? Or should I step outside?" (Go outside?! How blatant. He realises he's made a slip, so now he wants to clear off.) "No, no. Smoke here. I like tobacco smoke" (12a). ♦ Он [царь Николай] не думал, что род учителей может оказаться таким гордым. И тут он дал промашку (Искандер 5). He [Czar Nicholas] didn't think a clan of teachers could be so proud. That was a big mistake (5a). ♦ О чём бы разговор ни был, он всегда умел поддержать его: ...трактовали ли касательно следствия, произведённого казённою палатою, — он показал, что ему не безызвестны и судейские проделки; было ли рассуждение о биллиардной [*obs* = бильярдной] игре — и в биллиардной игре не давал он промаха... (Гоголь 3). Whatever topic the conversation turned upon, he could always keep it up:...if they mentioned an investigation conducted by the Revenue Office, he showed that he was not ignorant of judicial trickery, if they conversed about the game of billiards, he would not be tripped up here either... (3c).

П-572 • **(малый, парень** и т. п.) **НЕ ПРО́МАХ** *coll* [NP; Invar; nonagreeing postmodif or, less often, subj-compl with бытьø (subj: human)] a bright, clever person who lets no opportunity slip by, who knows how to look after his interests: X малый не промах ≃ X is no ⟨nobody's⟩ fool; X is pretty smart; X is a smart cookie; X knows what's what; X knows his way around;

X is a sharp man ⟨woman etc⟩; you can't fool ⟨put anything over on⟩ X.

«...Чего ты боишься?» — «Как чего боюсь, батюшка Кирила Петрович, а Дубровского-то; того и гляди попадёшься ему в лапы. Он малый не промах, никому не спустит...» (Пушкин 1). "What are you afraid of?" "What indeed, dear sir Kirila Petrovich! Dubrovskii, that's what! You can never tell when you might fall into his clutches. He's nobody's fool: he doesn't let people off lightly..." (1a). ♦ «Папенька-то ваш меня спрашивал: „Как это, говорит, ещё не вставал?" Я, знаете, не промах: голова изволит болеть, с утра-с жаловались...» (Герцен 1). "Your papa was asking me, 'How is it,' says he, 'he is not up yet?' I was pretty smart. I said, 'His honour's head aches; he complained of it from early morning...'" (1a). ♦ «Ты сама баба не промах, — сказал он ей, отделяя ей тысяч с восемь, — сама и орудуй...» (Достоевский 1). "You're a sharp woman," he said to her, giving her about eight thousand roubles, "you'll make out for yourself..." (1a). ♦ «Да вот товарищ Борщёв, — сказал он с лёгким сарказмом, — предлагает мне вместе с ним отстраниться от активной деятельности, уйти во внутреннюю эмиграцию». Но Борщёв был тоже парень не промах. «Дурак ты!» — сказал он, поднимаясь и расправляя грудь. — Я тебя только пощупать хотел, чем ты дышишь» (Войнович 5). "Comrade Borshchev here," he said with a touch of sarcasm, "was just suggesting that he and I abandon our political activities and join the inner emigration." But you couldn't put anything over on Borshchev either. "You fool!" he said, rising and smoothing his chest. "I only wanted to feel you out and see what makes you tick" (5a).

П-573 • **ГДЕ НА́ША НЕ ПРОПАДА́ЛА ⟨ГДЕ НА́ШЕ НЕ ПРОПАДА́ЛО⟩!** [saying] said when s.o. (usu. the speaker himself) is about to undertake sth. that either involves risk or is not sensible, well-advised: ≃ **I'll take that risk ⟨that chance⟩!; I'll risk it!; I've ⟨you've etc⟩ got nothing to lose; what do I ⟨you etc⟩ have to lose!; nothing ventured, nothing gained!; we ⟨you⟩ only live once; (there's) no harm in trying!; what the hell!; here goes nothing!**

«...Почему бы не попотчевать гостя, только тебе, Паша, довольно бы, мне не жалко, да ведь назавтрева [*ungrammat* = завтра] опять головой мучиться будешь». — «Ладно, мать, — добродушно отмахнулся тот, — мечи на стол, где наша не пропадала!» (Максимов 1). "There's no reason why I shouldn't get the guest a drink, only you, Pasha, have probably had enough. It's not that I grudge you, but you'll just go around with a sore head tomorrow." "All right, Mother," he shrugged it off good-naturedly, "let's have what we've got on the table. I'll take that chance!" (1a). ♦ [Маша:] Выпью рюмочку винца! Эх ма... где наша не пропадала! (Чехов 5). [M.:] I'll have a little glass of wine. Why not...we only live once! (5a).

П-574 • **НЕ ПРОПАДЁТ** *за кем coll* [VP; impers; this form only] **1.** Also: **НЕ ЗАРЖАВЕ́ЕТ** *за кем highly coll* [fut or subjunctive] what was borrowed or spent will be reimbursed, returned by s.o.: за X-ом не пропадёт ≃ **X will pay person Y back; X will make it up to person Y; X will get it back to person Y; (the money etc) will be safe in X's hands; X will make it good.**

У меня тоже попросил пятёрку один знакомый парень, шофёр из партии Айрапета. «За мной не заржавеет», — сказал он (Аксёнов 1). Someone I knew asked me for a five-spot, too—a driver from Airapet's party. "I'll get it back to you," he said (1a). ♦ «Ну, когда дадут [ссуду], тогда и расплатишься. Я тебя торопить не буду. Я знаю, ты человек надёжный, за тобой не пропадёт» (Распутин 1). "Well, when you get it [the loan] you can pay me back. I won't press you. I know you can be trusted. It'll be safe in your hands" (1a).

2. s.o. will respond to another's actions or behavior by treating him in the same way (often in refer. to an offense, injury etc; often used by the speaker as a threat): за мной не пропадёт ≃ **I'll pay him ⟨her etc⟩ back (in kind);** [in refer. to harm, injury etc] **I'll**

[517]

pay him ⟨her etc⟩ **back with interest; I'll give him ⟨her etc⟩ a taste of his ⟨her etc⟩ own medicine; I'll get even with ⟨get back at⟩ him ⟨her etc⟩.**

То, что вы сделали — это предательство. Я вам этого не забуду и не прощу. За мной не пропадёт. What you did is treachery. I won't forgive and forget. I'll get back at you for it.

П-575 • **ПРОПАДИ́ ты ⟨он, она, оно (всё), они (все), всё⟩ ПРО́ПАДОМ; ПРОПАДИ́ТЕ вы (все) ПРО́ПАДОМ; ПРОПАДА́Й всё ПРО́ПАДОМ** *all coll* [Interj; these forms only; fixed WO] used to express extreme displeasure with, or annoyance, irritation at, s.o. or sth.: пропади X пропадом! ≃ **to hell ⟨to blazes⟩ with X!; person X can go to hell ⟨to blazes⟩!; person X can drop dead!; damn X ⟨it all⟩!; blast it!; the devil take X!**

…Во всём виновата Зоя… если бы не она, я бы и думать не стал об этом проклятом Дне убийств. Какое мне дело до него?.. Да пропади они пропадом! (Аржак 1). …It was all Zoya's fault. If it hadn't been for her I wouldn't have given that damned Murder Day a second thought. Why should it concern me? To hell with it… (1a). ♦ «Ах, жизнь артиста! Фраки, манишки, овации, медали, репортёры! Тьфу! Пропади всё это пропадом!» (Семёнов 1). "Oh, the life of a musician! Tailcoats, cuffs, ovations, medals, reporters! Pah! To blazes with the lot of it!" (1a). ♦ …В это время Силач, разговаривая с Джамхухом, узнал, куда он идёт, и попросился идти с ним. «А как же жена?» — спросил Джамхух. «Да пропади она пропадом со своими курами», — отвечал Силач… (Искандер 5.) Strongman, meanwhile, conversing with Jamkhoukh, had learned where he was going and asked to go with him. "What about your wife?" Jamkhoukh asked. "She can just go to hell, and her chickens with her," Strongman replied (5a).

П-576 • **ЧЁРТОВА ПРО́ПАСТЬ ⟨ГИ́БЕЛЬ** *obs*⟩ **(кого-чего)** *highly coll* [NP; sing only; usu. obj or subj; quantif; fixed WO] very many, a huge amount: **one ⟨a⟩ hell of a lot (of); a ton ⟨tons⟩ (of); piles ⟨heaps⟩ of.**

«Будь только на твоей стороне счастие, ты можешь выиграть чёртову пропасть» (Гоголь 3). "…If luck's on your side, you can win a hell of a lot" (3a).

П-577 • **НА ПРОПО́Й ДУШИ́** *obs, humor* [PrepP; Invar; adv; fixed WO] (in refer. to money given to s.o. to buy alcohol) for drinking: **so (that) s.o. can (go) drown his sorrows ⟨troubles⟩.**

П-578 • **ПРОПИСА́ТЬ ПРОПО́РЦИЮ** *кому obs, sub-stand, rare* [VP; subj: human] to give s.o. a whipping, a thrashing: X пропишет Y-у пропорцию ≃ **X will tan Y's hide; X will beat ⟨knock⟩ the tar out of Y; X will let Y have it; X will give Y a hiding ⟨a (good) licking⟩.**

П-579 • **КАК В ПРО́РВУ** *highly coll* [как + PrepP; Invar; adv or subj-compl with быть∅ (subj: usu. a noun denoting money, efforts etc)] (usu. in refer. to appreciable amounts of money, energy etc spent on sth.) sth. is completely wasted, has no perceptible results: **it's money ⟨a lot of effort etc⟩ down the drain ⟨the tubes⟩; [in limited contexts] (it's) like throwing it ⟨sth.⟩ down a well ⟨into a bottomless pit⟩.**

«…Им сто твоих зарплат не хватит, дели — не дели, всё равно не насытишь, как в прорву…» (Иоффе 1). "You could pay them a hundred times over, share everything you've got with them, and they'd never be satisfied. It's like throwing it down a well!" (1a).

П-580 • **КАК ИЗ ПРО́РВЫ** *highly coll* [как + PrepP; Invar; adv] in large amounts, in abundance: **in an endless stream; as if they ⟨it⟩ would never end ⟨stop⟩.**

Неприятности сыпались на меня как из прорвы. Troubles rained down on me in an endless stream.

П-581 • **НЕТ ⟨НЕСТЬ⟩ ПРОРО́КА В ОТЕ́ЧЕСТВЕ СВОЁМ ⟨В СВОЁМ ОТЕ́ЧЕСТВЕ⟩** *lit* [sent; fixed WO] a great, outstanding person is recognized and accepted by everyone except those closest to him—his own countrymen, associates, family etc; *by extension* may refer to a remarkable idea, invention etc: **a prophet is not without honor, save in his own country; a man is not a prophet in his own country.**

…Мне пришёл в голову вопрос: почему Дмитрий… имевший всегда перед глазами милую, любящую Софью Ивановну, вдруг страстно полюбил непонятную Любовь Сергеевну… Видно, справедливо изречение: «Нет пророка в отечестве своём» (Толстой 2). …It occurred to me to ask myself: why was it that Dmitri…who had the sweet loving Sofya Ivanovna constantly before his eyes, why had he fallen passionately in love with the incomprehensible Lyubov Sergeyevna?… Clearly there is truth in the saying that a prophet is not without honor, save in his own country (2b).

< From the Bible (Matt. 13:57, Mark 6:4 et al.).

П-582 • **ПОСЛЕ́ДНЕЕ ПРОСТИ́** *послать, сказать кому obs, lit* [NP; usu. obj; fixed WO] (to say, send s.o.) a final parting word, (to say) good-bye forever: **(say ⟨send⟩) a ⟨one's⟩ last ⟨final⟩ farewell; (say) one's last good-bye ⟨good-by⟩.**

«Неужели у вас нет друзей, которым бы вы хотели послать своё последнее прости?..» (Лермонтов 1). "Have you no friends you'd like to send a last farewell?" (1c). ♦ Настало время сказать последнее прости городу Бишофсбергу (Федин 1). The time has come to say our last good-by to the city of Bischofsberg (1a).

П-583 • **ПРО́СТО ТА́К** [AdvP; Invar; usu. adv; usu. this WO] without having any special reason, aim, or intention: **for no reason (at all); for no good ⟨particular⟩ reason; without a reason; without any particular aim in mind; (just) for the sake ⟨the fun, the hell⟩ of it; just because (one feels like it); [in limited contexts] just (do sth.).**

Персональное дело — это такое дело, когда большой коллектив людей собирается в кучу, чтоб в порядке внутривидовой борьбы удушить одного из себе подобных сдуру, по злобе или же просто так (Войнович 4). A personal case is when a large human group closes ranks in the course of an interspecific struggle, to suffocate one of its members, out of sheer foolishness, out of malice, or for no reason at all (4a). ♦ Настроение нам испортили пьяные ребята. Они прицепились к нам просто так, от нечего делать… (Зиновьев 2). Our good mood was ruined by some young drunks. They began to pester us for no good reason because they'd nothing better to do… (2a). ♦ Затащив Ефима в кабинет, он его сердечно обнял и даже похлопал по спине и огорошил вопросами… «Как Кукуша? Надеюсь, у Тишки в аспирантуре всё в порядке? У меня… внук тоже аспирант. В институте кинематографии. Замечательный парень. — Да, извини… ты ведь не просто так ко мне пришёл. Наверное, какое-то дело» (Войнович 6). …Drawing Yefim into the office, he embraced him heartily, even slapped him on the back, and peppered him with personal questions…. "How's Kukusha? Everything's all right with Tishka at graduate school? My grandson's a graduate student, too….At the film institute. A remarkable lad….But forgive me," he said, "you didn't come to see me for no reason. You must have some business matter to discuss" (6a). ♦ Всерьёз он не рассчитывал ни с кем из этих заочниц встретиться и вёл всю эту переписку просто так, от нечего делать (Войнович 5). He did not seriously count on ever meeting any of his pen pals and carried on these correspondences just to while away the time, without any particular aim in mind (5a). ♦ «Тали, — спросил он, увидев её, — тебя за чем-нибудь прислали?»… —«Нет, — сказала она, — я просто так…» (Искандер 3). "Tali," he asked when he saw her, "did they send you for something?"…"No," she said, "I just came" (3a). ♦ [Митька] не просто так-таки пришёл, а сватать дочь его Елизавету (Шолохов 2). [context transl] …He [Mitka] had come not to pay just a casual call, but to ask Liza's hand in marriage (2a).

П-584 • **ПРÓЩЕ ПРОСТÓГО** *coll* [AdjP; Invar; subj-compl with copula (subj: usu. infin or это); fixed WO] doing sth. is very easy, very simple: это ⟨сделать X⟩ ~ ≃ **it's as easy as pie (to do X); it's ⟨doing X is⟩ as easy as one, two, three ⟨as can be⟩; nothing could be simpler ⟨easier⟩ than doing X; it's ⟨doing X is⟩ the easiest ⟨simplest⟩ thing in the world ⟨on earth⟩.**

«Дураку понятно, Сивого засудить проще простого: ...у [его] мамаши сумку потерпевшей изъяли...» (Чернёнок 2). "Even a fool can see that it's as easy as pie to put Vasya Sivy away:...the victim's purse was found at his mother's..." (2a). ♦ «Ну, с талантами, знаете ли, расправляться проще простого» (Войнович 4). "But, you know, nothing could be simpler than making short work of talented people" (4a). ♦ ...Она не посмела отпроситься у брата. В другое бы время проще простого: сбегаю на часик в клуб, ладно? А сегодня язык не поворачивается (Абрамов 1). ...She could not get up the courage to ask her brother's permission. At any other time it would be the simplest thing in the world: I'm going over to the club for an hour, okay? But today she could not work up the nerve (1a). ♦ Была для Митьки несложна и пряма жизнь... Голоден — можно и должно украсть...; износились сапоги — проще простого разуть пленного немца... (Шолохов 3). For Mitka life was straight and uncomplicated....If he was hungry, he could and should steal...; if his boots were worn out, the simplest thing on earth was to take a pair off a German prisoner... (3a).

П-585 • **(О) СВЯТÁЯ ПРОСТОТÁ!** [Interj; these forms only; often used when responding to the interlocutor's statement, suggestion etc] how naïve you are (he is etc): **(oh,) blessed innocence; oh holy simplicity!**

«Значит, надо обязательно обманывать кого-то?» — «О святая простота!» — говорит Юрка... (Михайловская 1). "Does that mean that deception is necessary?" "Oh, blessed innocence," says Yuri... (1a).

< The Russian phrase is a loan translation of the Latin *sancta simplicitas*. The use of the Latin phrase in this meaning is attributed to Jan Hus (John Huss), a Bohemian religious reformer (1370?–1415).

П-586 • **ПРОСТОТÁ ХÝЖЕ ВОРОВСТВÁ** [saying] an excess of naïveté leads to trouble, causes problems: **simplicity is worse than robbery ⟨thievery⟩.**

...Я навсегда усвоил себе несколько бунинских рекомендаций: такт, точность, краткость, простота, но разумеется, — и Бунин это подчёркивал много раз, — он говорил не о той простоте, которая хуже воровства, а о простоте как следствии очень большой работы над фразой, над отдельным словом... (Катаев 3). I...resolved to be guided always by Bunin's recommendations concerning tact, precision, brevity and simplicity, but, as Bunin often emphasized, he was talking not about that simplicity which, as the saying goes, is worse than robbery, but about the simplicity that comes from intensive work on a phrase or a particular word... (3a).

П-587 • **ПО ⟨В⟩ ПРОСТОТÉ ДУШÉВНОЙ ⟨ДУШИ́, (СВОЕГÓ) СÉРДЦА** *obs*⟩; **ПО ПРОСТОТÉ СЕРДÉЧНОЙ** [PrepP; these forms only; adv; fixed WO] out of a lack of sophistication, because of one's trusting nature: **in the simplicity of one's soul ⟨heart⟩; in one's naïveté ⟨innocence⟩; naïvely.**

Они в простоте души понимали и приводили в исполнение единственное употребление капиталов — держать их в сундуке (Гончаров 1). In the simplicity of their souls they understood and practiced only one method of handling capital — that of keeping it in a chest (1b). ♦ ...Их [женщин] столько раз называли ангелами, что они в самом деле, в простоте душевной, поверили этому комплименту... (Лермонтов 1). ...They [women] have been called angels so often that in their innocence they have actually come to believe it... (1d). ♦ «Анатолий Овчинников напросился проводить меня после спектакля... По простоте душевной впустила в квартиру и до трёх часов не могла выпроводить» (Чернёнок 2). "Anatoly Ovchinnikov asked to take me home after the opera....I naïvely let him into the apartment and couldn't get him out until three" (2a).

П-588 • **БЕЗ ПРÓСЫПА ⟨-у⟩** *highly coll* [PrepP; these forms only] **1.** спать, дрыхнуть ~ [adv] (to sleep) soundly and without waking up (usu. for a long time): **(sleep) like a log; (sleep) [Num] hours straight.**

«Ну, брат, ты дрыхнешь, как пожарник в рейхстаге: вторые сутки без просыпу» (Алешковский 1). "Well, bud, I'd say you've been snoozing like a fireman at the Reichstag. Forty-eight hours straight" (1a).

2. пить, пьянствовать ~ [adv] (to drink alcohol) constantly, never sobering up: **(be drunk) all the time; (drink) nonstop.**

Возник вопрос: какую надобность мог иметь градоначальник в Байбакове, который, кроме того что пил без просыпа, был ещё и явный прелюбодей? (Салтыков-Щедрин 1). The question arose, What need could the town governor have of Dormousov, who in addition to being drunk all the time was also an overt adulterer? (1a).

3. *rare* пьян ~ [modif (intensif)] extremely (drunk): **dead ⟨blind⟩ drunk; stewed ⟨lit, tanked⟩ to the gills; drunk as a skunk.**

П-589 • **НЕ ПРОСЫХÁТЬ** *substand* [VP; subj: human; usu. pres or past] to drink alcohol all the time, always be drunk: X не просыхает ≃ **X never dries out ⟨sobers up⟩; X drinks nonstop.**

«...[Владимир] в сельпо оформился шофёром... Так с того дня у Симки и сидит в закутке, нарядов нет, не просыхает...» (Аксёнов 3). "...He [Vladimir] signed on as a driver at the village general store....But since then he's been on a binge over at Simka's hole-in-the-wall. There are no orders to fill and he won't sober up" (3a).

П-590 • **В ПРОТИВОВÉС** *кому-чему lit* [PrepP; Invar; Prep; the resulting PrepP is adv] unlike and in opposition to s.o. or sth.: **in contrast to; as distinct from.**

«События требуют работать с уверенностью и отрадным сознанием исполняемого долга, когда знаешь, что Круг — верховный выразитель воли Дона — тебе доверяет, когда, в противовес большевистской распущенности и анархии, будут установлены твёрдые правовые нормы» (Шолохов 4). "Events demand that I should work with confidence and a joyful sense of performing my duty, a sense that I can have only when I know that the Council—the supreme expression of the will of the Don—trusts me, when in contrast to Bolshevik dissipation and anarchy there are firmly established legal standards" (4a).

П-591 • **НА ПРОТЯЖÉНИИ** *чего* [PrepP; Invar; Prep; the resulting PrepP is adv] over a certain (as specified) period of time or throughout the duration of sth.: **over; in ⟨over⟩ the course of; over a period of; during (the course of); [in limited contexts] within a span of; throughout; for.**

В давние, описываемые автором времена повсеместно существовало некое Учреждение, которое было не столько военным, сколько воинственным. На протяжении ряда лет оно вело истребительную войну против собственных сограждан, и вело с непременным успехом (Войнович 2). In the bygone times described by the author, there existed everywhere a certain Institution, which was not so much military as militant. Over the years it waged a crippling war against its own citizens and waged it with unfailing success (2a). ♦ Были ли случаи на протяжении двух тысячелетий, когда свобода, человечность пользовались антисемитизмом как средством своей борьбы? Может быть, и были, но я не знаю таких (Гроссман 2). In the course of two millennia, have there ever been occasions when the forces of freedom and humanitarianism made use of anti-Semitism as a tool in their struggles? Possibly, but I do not know of them (2a). ♦ Когда на протяжении десяти суток в Польше было взято двенадцать крепостей и занято двадцать восемь городов, над Бишофс-бергом плавало облако копоти от факелов и лампионов (Федин 1). When, within a span of ten days, twelve fortresses were taken and twenty-eight towns occupied in Poland, a cloud of soot hung over Bischofsberg from the torches and lanterns (1a).

П-592 • ПРОФЕ́ССОР КИ́СЛЫХ ЩЕЙ *highly coll* [NP; usu. sing; often used as Interj; fixed WO] used to express an ironic or humorous attitude toward a person who makes a pretense of having considerable knowledge, but, in the speaker's opinion, has little or none; when said of a real professor, used to underscore what the speaker considers a lack of professional qualifications, academic expertise etc: **some expert he 〈she〉 is!**; [of a real professor] **fine kind of professor 〈scholar etc〉 he 〈she〉 is!**

Ох, и поиздевалась же она надо мной: мол, профессор, а анкету правильно заполнить не может! Профессор кислых щей! (Зиновьев 2). Oh, and then she had a really good go at me. Look at you, a professor, and you can't even fill a form in properly! Fine kind of professor you are! (2a).

П-593 • С ПРОХЛА́ДЦЕЙ 〈-ем〉 *coll* [PrepP; these forms only; adv] **1.** (to do sth.) unhurriedly, without zeal, enthusiasm etc: **halfheartedly; at a leisurely pace; without making much effort; taking one's time.**

«Хорошего сварщика из Павла не получится, — сказал мастер. — Профессию нашу он не любит, работает с прохлад-цей». "Pavel will never make a good welder," said the foreman. "He doesn't like our trade and works halfheartedly."

2. относиться *к кому-чему* — (to relate to s.o. or sth.) indifferently: X относится к Y-у ~ ≃ **X is cool toward person Y; X is not particularly fond of Y; thing Y doesn't particularly appeal to X.**

П-594 • НЕ ДАВА́ТЬ/НЕ ДАТЬ ПРОХО́ДА 〈-у〉 *кому coll* [VP; subj: human; usu. impfv; if pfv, fut only] to bother s.o. incessantly with endless requests, nagging etc: X Y-у прохода не даёт ≃ **X gives Y no peace; X doesn't give Y a moment's 〈a minute's〉 peace; X doesn't leave 〈never leaves〉 Y alone; X pesters Y; X is after Y all the time; X never lets up (on Y); X won't let Y be; Y can't get rid of X; Y can't get X off Y's back.**

«Ах, какая пыль!.. Ты и здесь хочешь такой же беспорядок завести: пыль, паутину? Нет, извини, я не позволю! И так Ольга Сергеевна мне проходу не даёт: „Вы любите, говорит, сор"» (Гончаров 1). "Oh, what dust!...Do you intend to have the same disorder here—dust, cobwebs? No, I shall not permit it. As it is, Olga Sergeyevna gives me no peace: 'You must like dirt,' she says" (1b). ♦ Старик отсутствовал неделю, именно про эту неделю мать говорила, что отец не давал ей прохода, а отец — что она расставляла ему силки и капканы (Рыбаков 1). He [the old man] was away for a week, and it was during that week that mother said father wouldn't leave her alone, and father said he kept setting traps for him (1a). ♦ [Кабанов:] Вот видишь ты, вот всегда мне за тебя достаётся от маменьки!.. Проходу не даёт — всё за тебя (Островский 6). [K.:] There now, you see the way I keep on catching it from Mama over you....[She] never lets up—all on your account (6d). ♦ «Он мне проходу не давал, ухаживал с утра до вечера» (Рыбаков 1). "I couldn't get rid of him, he followed me around from morning till night" (1a).

П-595 • ПРОХО́ДА 〈-у〉 НЕТ *coll* [VP; impers] **1.** ~ (*кому от кого-чего*) s.o. is constantly bothered by another, cannot rid himself of another or of another's badgering, ridicule etc: X-у от Y-а прохода нет ≃ **Y doesn't give X a moment's peace; X can't get rid of Y; X can't find refuge from Y;** ‖ прохода от Y-а нет ≃ **there's no getting rid of Y; there's no end to Y's nagging**

〈pestering etc〉; ‖ X-у прохода нет ≃ **X doesn't have a moment's peace; X doesn't have any peace at all.**

[Таня:] ...Всякий пристаёт; хоть бы Григорий Михайлыч, проходу от него нету (Толстой 3). [T.:] ...Every man is after me. Take Grigori Mikhailych, for example—there's no getting rid of him (3a). ♦ «Мне скоро проходу не будет. Все пальцем показывают» (Абрамов 1). "Soon I won't have any peace at all. Everyone's pointing a finger at me" (1a).

2. ~ *от кого disapprov* there are a great number of, too many (people of a certain type): от X-ов прохода нет ≃ **there are tons of Xs; we 〈you, they〉 are swamped 〈overrun〉 with Xs.**

Везде одни бюрократы, прохода от них нет. There are bureaucrats everywhere—we're swamped with them.

П-596 • НЕ ПРОХО́ДИТ/НЕ ПРОШЁЛ ДА́РОМ [VP; subj: usu. count abstr] **1.** ~ (*для кого*) [more often pfv past] some event (period of time etc) produces certain results, has certain consequences, brings about certain changes etc: X не прошёл (для Y-а) даром ≃ **X was not in vain 〈not for nothing, not for naught〉; X left its mark (on Y); [in limited contexts] Y hasn't wasted X; X has been of some use.**

...Долгая привычка спать на казённом диване не прошла даром... (Войнович 4). ...His old habit of sleeping on the office couch had left its mark (4a). ♦ ...Я понял, что годы, когда мы не виделись, не прошли для моего друга даром, он уже вполне овладел новым, передовым и единственно правильным миро-воззрением... (Войнович 1). I realized that my friend had not wasted the years in which we hadn't been seeing each other. He had acquired a new, progressive world view, the only correct one... (1a). ♦ [author's usage] Ловко мы их [органы] обвели вокруг пальца, говорил Правдец своему Другу. Да, говорил Друг, это у нас не от-нимешь! Тюремный опыт не пропал даром (Зиновьев 1). "We've really taken them [the secret police] for a ride," Truth-teller said to his Friend. "Yes," said Friend, "no-one can deny us that! Our prison experience has been of some use after all" (1a). ♦ [2-й (гуляющий):] Уж ты помяни моё слово, что эта гроза даром не пройдёт... Либо уж убьёт кого-нибудь, либо дом сгорит... (Островский 6). [context transl] [Second Stroller:] Mark my words, this storm won't pass without doing some damage....It'll either kill someone or set a house on fire (6c).

2. ~ *кому*. Also: **ТАК НЕ ПРОХО́ДИТ/НЕ ПРОШЛО́** [subj: often это or это дело, эти слова etc; usu. pfv fut; var. with так has fixed WO] s.o.'s reprehensible action (words etc) will definitely result in unpleasant consequences or punishment for him: X 〈это〉 Y-у даром не пройдёт ≃ **Y won't get away with X 〈it〉; Y will (have to) pay for X 〈it, this〉; Y will not get off scot-free; X will not be without consequence (for Y); [in limited contexts] X will not be easily forgotten.**

«Ты лжёшь, мерзавец! – вскричал я в бешенстве, – ты лжёшь самым бесстыдным образом». Швабрин переменился в лице. «Это тебе так не пройдёт», – сказал он... (Пушкин 2). "You're lying, scoundrel!" I exclaimed in a rage. "You're lying in the most shameless manner." Shvabrin changed color. "You are not going to get away with that," he said... (2a). ♦ Из слов его я заметил, что про меня и княжну уж распущены в городе разные дурные слухи: это Грушницкому даром не пройдёт (Лермонтов 1). I could tell by what he had said that diverse malicious rumours had been spread all over town about the Princess and myself: Grushnitsky will have to pay for this! (1b). ♦ ...Глуповцам это дело не прошло даром (Салтыков-Щедрин 1). This affair was not without consequence for the Foolovites... (1a). ♦ [Курчаев:] Если мои по-дозрения оправдаются, так берегитесь! Такие вещи даром не проходят (Островский 9). [K.:] If what I suspect is true, you'd better look out. Such things are not easily forgotten (9a).

П-597 • ПРОХОДИ́ТЬ/ПРОЙТИ́ МИ́МО [VP; more often pfv; if impfv, often imper; fixed WO] **1.** ~ (*кого-чего*) [subj: human or collect] (often in refer. to negative phenomena, facts) to disregard s.o. or sth., not pay attention to sth., remain uninvolved: X прошёл мимо Y-a ≃ **X ignored Y; X passed Y over ⟨by⟩; X chose not to see Y; [in limited contexts] X overlooked Y; X pretended Y didn't exist.**

«Если бы эту брошюру написал рядовой историк, то можно было бы пройти мимо: историки могут ошибаться... Но ведь эту брошюру написал не рядовой историк, а один из руководителей партии и государства» (Рыбаков 2). "If an ordinary historian had written it [this pamphlet], one could have ignored it. Historians often make mistakes....But this pamphlet was not written by an ordinary historian, it was written by one of the leaders of the Party and state" (2a).

2. ~ *кого* [subj: abstr (often горе, беда etc)] to be overlooked or disregarded by s.o. (may refer to a person's lack of emotional involvement with regard to another's pain, grief etc): X прошёл мимо Y-a ≃ **X slipped by ⟨past⟩ (Y); X passed Y by unnoticed; Y didn't notice X; Y remained unaffected by X; [in refer. to s.o.'s lack of emotional involvement] X left Y unmoved ⟨cold⟩; Y remained indifferent to X.**

...Несмотря на то, что все начальники отделов кадров только тем и занимаются, что вчитываются в анкеты, выискивая несоответствия и изъяны в биографии сотрудников того или иного учреждения, иногда самые невероятные нелепости проходят мимо их бдительного ока (Войнович 1). ...Despite the fact that all personnel managers do nothing but pore over questionnaires seeking out inconsistencies and flaws in the biographies of employees of one institution or another, the most incredible absurdities do sometimes slip past their watchful eyes (1a).

3. ~ *кого-чего* [subj: human] (often in refer. to not recognizing a potential spouse) having failed to recognize the merits, worth etc of s.o. or sth., to pay no attention to, not follow up on etc s.o. or sth. and thereby lose him or it: X прошёл мимо Y-a ≃ **X passed Y by; X let Y slip through X's fingers.**

«А если хочешь знать правду, так я и тебя научил любить его [Обломова]... Без меня ты бы прошла мимо его, не заметив» (Гончаров 1). "And if you want to know the truth, it was I who taught you to love him [Oblomov]....If it hadn't been for me you would have passed him by without noticing him" (1b). ♦ «Чуть было не прошёл мимо великого начинания». «А что, если бы прошли?» – говорил я. «Не говори», – отвечал Платон Самсонович и снова вздрагивал (Искандер 6). "To think that I almost let this great undertaking slip through my fingers!" "Well, and what if you had?" I would ask. "Don't even suggest such a thing," he would answer, wincing once again (6a).

4. ~ *чего* [subj: human] not to address or discuss (some problem, question etc): X прошёл мимо Y-a ≃ **X passed over Y in silence; X made no mention of Y; X didn't touch (on ⟨upon⟩) Y.**

Докладчика критиковали за то, что он прошёл мимо основной проблемы – финансирования проекта. The speaker was criticized for not touching upon the fundamental problem—how to finance the project.

П-598 • **И ПРО́ЧЕЕ (И ПРО́ЧЕЕ) ⟨И ПРО́ЧАЯ (И ПРО́ЧАЯ)** *obs*⟩, may be abbreviated in writing to **и пр. (и пр.)** or **и проч. (и проч.)** [NP; these forms only] (used at the end of a list to indicate that more objects or phenomena could be included) and other similar things: **and so on (and so forth ⟨on⟩); and so forth (and so on); and the like; and such like; and things of that sort; and more to that effect; et cetera; etc.**

На дело Карамазовых, как оказалось потом, он [председатель суда] смотрел довольно горячо, но лишь в общем смысле. Его занимало явление, классификация его, взгляд на него как на продукт наших социальных основ, как на характеристику русского элемента, и проч., и проч. (Достоевский 2). He [the presiding judge] took, as it turned out later, a rather passionate view of the Karamazov case, but only in a general sense. He was concerned with the phenomenon, its classification, seeing it as a product of our social principles, as characteristic of the Russian element, and so on and so forth (2a).

П-599 • **МЕ́ЖДУ ПРО́ЧИМ** [PrepP; Invar; fixed WO]
1. сказать, заметить и т. п. ~ [adv] (to say, mention etc sth.) without making it sound overly important, without putting special emphasis on it: **casually; in passing; [in limited contexts] (s.o.'s response sounds etc) casual.**

Лет через сто мы знаем, кто был настоящий учёный в наше время и что действительно ценного было открыто... Но это я сказал так, между прочим (Зиновьев 1). In a hundred years we shall know who in our time were real scientists and what was discovered of real value....But I'm just saying that in passing (1a). ♦ Лёва угощал и, симулируя беспечность: о том, о сём, – всё подбирался к цели. И когда, наконец, не узнавая свой голос, сразу выдав себя с головой (хотя все силы его были направлены, чтобы вопрос был безразличен и между прочим), всё-таки задал его, то неповторимая улыбочка вдруг подёрнула губы Митишатьева... (Битов 2). He [Lyova] bought the drinks and all the while—feigning unconcern, talking of this and that—kept sneaking up on his goal. When at last, not recognizing his own voice, betraying himself at once (though he bent every effort to make his question indifferent and casual)—when he did ask it, Mitishatyev's lips suddenly twitched in an inimitable little smile... (2a).

2. [sent adv (parenth)] in connection with or in addition to what has been said: **by the way; apropos of that; incidentally; come to think of it.**

Какая печальная история, юноша, как понятны мне ваши чувства, чувства ученика, потерявшего любимого учителя. Что-то похожее было, между прочим, и в моей жизни (Соколов 1). What a sad story, lad, how well I understand your feelings, the feelings of a student who has lost his favorite teacher. Something similar happened, by the way, in my own life (1a). ♦ «Это вы меня напугали своим рассказом... А, между прочим, говорят, что здесь действует какая-то местная банда» (Стругацкие 1). "You frightened me with your story. Incidentally, they say there's some sort of local gang operating here" (1a).

П-600 • **НЕ ПРОЧЬ** *coll* [Invar; subj-compl with быть∅ (subj: human); usu. foll. by (pfv) infin] s.o. has no objections to, and would even rather enjoy (doing sth.): X не прочь сделать Y ≃ **X doesn't ⟨wouldn't⟩ mind (doing) Y; X is not averse ⟨opposed⟩ to (doing) Y.**

Даже сосед, кажется, не прочь сегодня поддержать беседу (Михайловская 1). It seems that even the neighbor wouldn't mind joining in the conversation today (1a). ♦ Так же, как и остальные, Петро не прочь был пограбить, поругать начальство, пожалеть пленного... (Шолохов 4). Like any of the others, Petro was not averse to a little looting, to cursing his superiors or to sparing the life of a prisoner... (4a).

П-601 • **ОТХОДИ́ТЬ/ОТОЙТИ́ ⟨УХОДИ́ТЬ/УЙТИ́, КА́НУТЬ⟩ В ПРО́ШЛОЕ** [VP; subj: abstr] no longer to exist or be current: X отошёл в прошлое ≃ **X is ⟨has become⟩ a thing of the past; X is all in the past; X is ⟨has become⟩ ancient history; X has passed into history; X has disappeared into the past.**

Теперь, после тридцать девятого [года], деятельность этих людей уже, вроде бы, отошла в прошлое (Гинзбург 2). In the post-1939 period the activity of these people had, it seemed, become a thing of the past (2a). ♦ Больше пятнадцати лет она [Тваржинская] была объектом насмешек нашей институтской прогрессивной молодёжи. Но время это ушло в прошлое (Зиновьев 2). For more than fifteen years she [Tvarzhinskaya] was the butt of all the sarcasm of the progressive young people of our institute, but that is now all in the past (2a).

П-602 • **ПРОШУ́ ⟨про́сим⟩ ЛЮБИ́ТЬ И ⟨ДА⟩ ЖА́ЛО-ВАТЬ** *obs* [formula phrase; these forms only; fixed WO] I (we) ask that you show s.o. favor, pay attention to s.o. (used when introducing s.o. —or, less often, o.s. —to another person): **please give him ⟨her, them⟩ a warm welcome!; please make him ⟨her, them⟩ feel welcome; I hope you will ⟨we shall⟩ become ⟨be⟩ (good) friends.**

«А это, — прибавила она, обращаясь ко мне и указывая поочерёдно на гостей, — граф Малевский, доктор Лушин, поэт Майданов… Прошу любить да жаловать» (Тургенев 3). "And these," she added, turning to me and pointing to each one of her guests in turn, "are Count Malevsky, Dr. Lushin, the poet Maydanov….I hope you will all be good friends" (3a). ♦ [Лыняев:] Вот и хорошо, соседи будем. Прошу любить да жаловать (Островский 5). [L.:] That's nice. We'll be neighbors. I hope we shall be good friends, too (5a).

П-603 • **ПРОШУ́ ПОКО́РНО**[1]; **ПОКО́РНЕЙШЕ ПРОШУ́** *both obs* [formula phrase; these forms only; often foll. by infin] (used when addressing s.o. with a polite request, invitation etc) I kindly request that you…: **(please) be so kind as to (do sth.); I should be greatly obliged if you would (do sth.); I beg of you (to do sth.); I humbly beg you (to do sth.).**

[Агафья Тихоновна:] Прошу покорнейше садиться (Гоголь 1). [A.T.:] Please be so kind as to sit down (1a). ♦ «Прошу покорно передать доверенность другому лицу (писал сосед), а у меня накопилось столько дела, что, по совести сказать, не могу как следует присматривать за вашим имением» (Гончаров 1). "I should be greatly obliged," wrote the neighbor, "if you would transfer your power of attorney to someone else, as I have such an accumulation of business that, to be quite frank, I am unable to look after your estate properly" (1b). ♦ «Покорнейше прошу», — сказал Петух, взявши Чичикова под руку и вводя его во внутренние покои (Гоголь 3). "I beg of you to come in," said he [Petuh], taking Chichikov by the arm and leading him into the inner chambers (3b). ♦ «Покорнейше прошу – оцепите всех этих граждан, сделайте обыск и проверьте у них документы» (Паустовский 1). "I humbly beg you—cordon off all these citizens, search them, check their documents" (1b).

П-604 • **ПРОШУ́ ПОКО́РНО!**[2] *coll* [Interj; Invar; fixed WO] used to express bewilderment, indignation, surprise colored by indignation etc: **if you please; how do you like that!; just imagine!; think of it!; I ask you!; would ⟨can⟩ you believe it?**

«Прошу покорно, Ольга, девочка! По ниточке, бывало, ходила. Что с ней?» (Гончаров 1). "A child, if you please, a little girl who used to be at my beck and call! What is the matter with her?" (1b). ♦ «Уж не гордится ли, чего доброго, эта глупая немка тем, что она… из милости согласилась помочь бедным жильцам? Из милости! Прошу покорно!» (Достоевский 3). "Was she proud, by any chance, that stupid German woman, of the fact that she…had helped her poor lodgers out of the goodness of her heart? Out of the goodness of her heart! I ask you!" (3a).

П-605 • **НА ПРОЩА́НИЕ** [PrepP; Invar; adv] right before or while parting company with s.o.: **at ⟨in⟩ parting.**

…Я приуныл, считая, что навсегда провалился в глазах Бунина и хорошего поэта из меня не выйдет, тем более что на прощание он не сказал мне ничего обнадёживающего (Катаев 3). …I felt despondent at the thought that I had failed in the eyes of Bunin and would never make a good poet, particularly since he had nothing encouraging to say to me in parting (3a).

П-606 • **ПРОШУ́ ПРОЩЕ́НИЯ** *coll* [formula phrase; Invar; fixed WO] used to attract s.o.'s attention when addressing him; also used as a polite form of requesting s.o.'s tolerance, forgiveness etc for a minor infraction, for one's troubling him for assistance etc: **I beg your pardon; excuse me; pardon me.**

«Прошу прощения! я, кажется, вас побеспокоил. Пожалуйста, садитесь сюда! Прошу!» (Гоголь 3). "I beg your pardon. I believe I've inconvenienced you. Please, be seated! Here, I beg you!" (3c).

П-607 • **(ХОТЬ) ПРУД ПРУДИ́** *кого-чего,* rare *кем-чем coll* [хоть + VP_imper; these forms only; subj-compl with copula (subj/gen: any common noun) or adv (quantif); fixed WO] (s.o. has or in some place there is) a surplus or a lot of (people or things): X-ов у Y-а ⟨в месте Z⟩ хоть пруд пруди ≃ **person Y has more Xs than he knows what to do with; place Z is swarming ⟨crawling⟩ with Xs; there are scores of Xs in place Z; Xs are as plentiful as fish in the sea in place Z; person Y has Xs in spades ⟨Xs galore, Xs enough and to spare⟩; there are Xs in spades ⟨Xs galore, Xs enough and to spare⟩ in place Z.**

…В докладной записке для Теоретика он писал, что известность Мазилы на Западе имеет скорее политический характер, так как художников таких на Западе пруд пруди (Зиновьев 1). …In a brief report to Theoretician he wrote that Dauber's fame in the West was largely political, because the West had more artists like him than they knew what to do with (1a). ♦ «Видите, та жирная… стерва? У неё в каждом ушке ценности, особняк можно купить. Посмотрите на её лапы! А таких теперь пруд пруди» (Зиновьев 2). "You see that fat old cow?…Each of her earrings is worth a mansion. And look at her paws! There are scores of people like her these days" (2a). ♦ Руководил отделом [сельского хозяйства] Платон Самсонович. Не следует удивляться его имени. У нас таких имён хоть пруд пруди (Искандер 6). The paper's agricultural section was headed by Platon Samsonovich. If one wonders at the name, I should point out that in our region such names were as plentiful as fish in the sea (6a). ♦ «Да таких колхозниц и колхозников у нас хоть пруд пруди» (Абрамов 1). "If it's *kolkhozniki* like her you're talking about, we've got them in spades" (1a).

П-608 • **ВО ВСЮ ПРЫТЬ бежать, мчаться, нестись, скакать** и т. п. *coll* [PrepP; Invar; adv; fixed WO] (to run, race etc) very fast, at maximum speed: **at top ⟨full⟩ speed; (at) full tilt; as fast as one can; as fast as one's legs can carry one; [in refer. to horses] at (a) full gallop.**

Увидев сторожа, мальчишки пустились во всю прыть в разные стороны. Catching sight of the guard, the boys took off in all directions as fast as their legs could carry them.

П-609 • **ОТКУ́ДА ПРЫТЬ ВЗЯЛА́СЬ** (у кого) *coll* [VP_subj; past only; usu. used as indep. clause; usu. this WO] (in refer. to s.o.'s sudden display of vigor, nerve etc) what is the source of this unexpected energy, strength, readiness to do sth. etc?: откуда у X-а прыть взялась? ≃ **where did X get this sudden burst ⟨charge⟩ of energy?; where did X get the spunk ⟨the pluck, the gumption, the pep⟩ (, I wonder)?**

[author's usage] Откуда только взялось прыти? Он вскочил и отбежал в середину бойлерной (Аксёнов 6). Where did he get this sudden burst of energy? He jumped to his feet and ran into the middle of the boiler room (6a). ♦ Когда я в тот же день вечером рассказал Дмитрию своё приключение с Колпиковым… он удивился чрезвычайно. «Да это тот самый! — сказал он, — можешь себе представить, что этот Колпиков известный негодяй, шулер, а главное трус, выгнан товарищами из полка за то, что получил пощёчину и не хотел драться. Откуда у него прыть взялась?» (Толстой 2). When I told Dmitri that same evening about my adventure with Kolpikov…he was extremely surprised: "Oh, so that's the one!" he said. "Just imagine, that Kolpikov's a notorious rogue and card-sharp, but the main thing is he's a coward and was drummed out of his regiment by his comrades because his face was slapped and he wouldn't fight. Where did he get the spunk, I wonder?" (2b).

П-610 • **ИГРА́ТЬ В ПРЯ́ТКИ ⟨В ЖМУ́РКИ⟩** *с кем coll* [VP; subj: human] to hide the truth by being evasive and/or pretending not to know it: X играет с Y-ом в прятки ≃ **X is playing games ⟨hide-and-seek⟩ with Y;** [in limited contexts] **X is beating around the bush.** ○ ИГРА́ В ПРЯ́ТКИ ⟨В ЖМУ́РКИ⟩ [NP] ≃ **hide-and-seek.**

«Ну, в прятки нам с вами играть или говорить открыто?» — «Конечно, открыто» (Семёнов 1). "Well, shall we play hide-and-seek with you or speak openly?" "Openly, of course" (1a). ♦ Первый раз в жизни выступал он перед такой ответственной аудиторией... Он начал с того, что здесь все коммунисты и поэтому в прятки играть нечего (Войнович 4). It was the first time in his career that he had ever spoken in front of such an important audience....He began by saying that they were all Communists and so there was no need to beat around the bush (4a).

П-611 • ПСУ́ ⟨СОБА́КЕ, КОБЕЛЮ́ *rude*, КО́ШКЕ, КОТУ́⟩ ПОД ХВОСТ (выбросить, выкинуть *что* и т. п.; пойти́ и т. п.) *highly coll* [PrepP; these forms only; adv or subj-compl with copula (subj: abstr, often всё); fixed WO] (in refer. to or of time, money, energy, work etc) (to spend sth., waste sth., be wasted etc) for nothing, to no purpose: **(go) to waste; (flush sth.) ⟨go etc⟩ down the tube(s) ⟨the drain, the toilet⟩; (be) shot to hell; (be) a goddamn(ed) waste of time ⟨money, energy etc⟩.**

Хлебовводов начал орать, что... он не позволит коменданту отправить коту под хвост четыре часа рабочего времени (Стругацкие 3). Khlebovvodov began shouting that...he would not allow the commandant to flush four hours of work time down the tubes (3a). ♦ «Значит, все решения Двадцатого съезда выброшены коту под хвост?» (Аксёнов 12). "Does that mean that all the decisions of the Twentieth Congress are shot to hell?" (12a). ♦ «Что с тобой?» — спросил я. «Сволочи, — ответил он. — Работал, работал, а всё псу под хвост» (Аржак 1). "What's the matter?" I asked. "Those bastards," he replied. "I worked and worked, and it was all a goddamned waste of time" (1a).

П-612 • РА́НО ПТА́ШЕЧКА ЗАПЕ́ЛА, КАК БЫ КО́ШЕЧКА НЕ СЪЕ́ЛА [saying] it is too early to rejoice, things may end up badly: ≃ **laugh before breakfast and you'll cry before supper.**

П-613 • РА́ННЯЯ ПТА́ШКА *coll, approv* [NP; often subj-compl with быть∅ (subj: human); usu. this WO] a person who gets up early in the morning: **early bird; early riser.**

П-614 • ЖЕЛТОРО́ТЫЙ ПТЕНЕ́Ц *occas. condes or derog* [NP; obj, appos, or subj-compl with copula, nom or instrum (subj: human)] a very young, naïve, inexperienced person: **greenhorn; tenderfoot; pup; (one is) (still) wet behind the ears.**

У нас тут народ опытный, ты рядом с ними — желторотый птенец. Our people are experienced; compared to them, you're still wet behind the ears.

П-615 • ВА́ЖНАЯ ПТИ́ЦА *coll* [NP; more often sing; often subj-compl with copula, nom or instrum (subj: human); fixed WO] a person who has a high, important post, great authority etc: **big shot ⟨wheel⟩; heavy hitter; bigwig;** [when used sarcastically as Interj, usu. after подумаешь, тоже мне etc] **isn't he ⟨isn't she, aren't we⟩ a hotshot!; some big shot ⟨heavy hitter etc⟩ (he ⟨she⟩ is)!**

[Таня:] Хозяин дачи важный человек? [Колесов:] Да, он важная птица (Вампилов 3). [T.:] Is the owner of this place someone important? [K.:] Yes, he's a big shot (3b). ♦ Серёжа как-то сказал, посмеиваясь: «А наш Гена действительно стал важной птицей» (Трифонов 3). At some point Sergei had said with a chuckle, "Our Gena has really become a big wheel..." (3a).

П-616 • ВИДНА́ ПТИ́ЦА ПО ПОЛЁТУ; ВИ́ДНО ⟨ВИДА́ТЬ⟩ ПТИ́ЦУ ⟨СО́КОЛА⟩ ПО ПОЛЁТУ *usu.*

disapprov [saying] you can tell by a person's behavior, actions, looks, and/or deeds what kind of person he is: ≃ **we know ⟨can tell⟩ a bird by its flight; the bird is known by his note ⟨his song⟩; you can tell a leopard by its spots.**

[author's usage] «Вы, я знаю, привыкли к роскоши, к удовольствиям, но и великие мира сего не гнушаются провести короткое время под кровом хижины». — «Помилуйте, — возопил Аркадий, — какой же я великий мира сего! И к роскоши я не привык». — «Позвольте, позвольте, — возразил с любезной ужимкой Василий Иванович. — Я хоть теперь и сдан в архив, а тоже потёрся в свете — узнаю птицу по полёту» (Тургенев 2). "You, I know, are accustomed to luxury and enjoyment, but even the great ones of this world would not disdain to spend a short time under a cottage roof." "Good heavens," protested Arkady, "as though I were one of the great ones of this world! And I'm not accustomed to luxury either." "Pardon me, pardon me," Vassily Ivanych retorted with a polite simper. "Though I'm a back number now, I have knocked about the place in my time — I know a bird by its flight" (2c).

П-617 • ВО́ЛЬНАЯ ПТИ́ЦА ⟨ПТА́ШКА *coll*⟩ [NP; more often sing; often subj-compl with copula, nom or, rare, instrum (subj: human); usu. this WO] a person who has no constraints on his actions, who can do whatever he wants to: **(as) free as a bird ⟨as the wind⟩; free man ⟨woman⟩; one's own master.**

...Виолет не могла нарадоваться: отец сиял... «С сегодняшнего дня я вольная птица» (Эренбург 4). ...Violette was unable to contain her joy; her father was radiant....“From today I'm as free as a bird," he said (4a). ♦ [Борис:] Что обо мне-то толковать! Я вольная птица. Ты-то как? (Островский 6). [B.:] Why talk about me! I'm a free man. What's it like for you? (6a).

П-618 • жить КАК ПТИ́ЦА ⟨ПТИ́ЧКА⟩ НЕБЕ́СНАЯ [как + NP; nom only; adv; fixed WO] (to live) without worrying about the future, free of responsibility and obligations: **be ⟨live⟩ carefree as a (little) bird; be ⟨live⟩ without a care in the world; (be) happy-go-lucky.**

П-619 • ПТИ́ЦА ВЫСО́КОГО ПОЛЁТА *coll* [NP; often subj-compl with copula, nom or instrum (subj: human)] an influential person who occupies a prominent position in society: **big shot; big wheel; bigwig; big gun; heavy hitter; (be) flying high.**

[Городничий:] ...Какие мы с тобою теперь птицы сделались! а, Анна Андреевна? Высокого полёта... (Гоголь 4). [Mayor:] ...We've turned into a fine pair. Eh, Anna Andreyevna? We're flying high now... (4f).

П-620 • ПТИ́ЦА НИ́ЗКОГО ⟨НЕВЫСО́КОГО⟩ ПОЛЁТА; НЕВЕЛИКА́ ПТИ́ЦА *all coll, condes or rather derog* [NP; usu. subj-compl with copula, variants with полёта — nom or instrum, last var. — nom only (subj: human)] a person whose social status, position at work, rank etc is low, or is considered by the speaker to be low: **small fry; small potatoes; little fish; (being a [NP] etc is) no big deal.**

«Игорь днями мне заявил: „Третий секретарь — подумаешь, невелика птица“» (Гроссман 2). "Igor said to me the other day, 'Third secretary — that's no big deal'" (2a).

П-621 • СИ́НЯЯ ПТИ́ЦА *lit* [NP; sing only; fixed WO] sth. that embodies the concept of happiness for s.o.: **bluebird of happiness.**

< The Russian phrase is a translation of the title of Maurice Maeterlinck's play *L'Oiseau bleu*, which premiered at the Moscow Art Theater in Sept. 1908.

П-622 • ПТИ́ЦЫ ОДНО́ГО́ ПОЛЁТА *coll* [NP; pl only; subj-compl with быть∅ (subj: human, pl); fixed WO] two or more people are very similar in some respect (with regard to views, status, qualities, behavior etc; often in refer. to negative qualities, reprehensible behavior etc): X и Y птицы одного полёта ≃ **X and Y are birds of a feather; X and Y are two of a kind; X and Y are tarred with the same brush; X and Y are cast in the same mold; X and Y are of the same ilk ⟨stripe⟩.**

П-623 • ИГРА́ТЬ ⟨РАБО́ТАТЬ coll⟩ НА ПУ́БЛИКУ [VP; subj: human] to behave consciously in an unnatural or not entirely appropriate manner in order to make a certain impression on those observing: X играл на публику ≃ **X played to his ⟨an⟩ audience; X kept ⟨had⟩ one eye on the gallery; X put on a show (for s.o.).**

П-624 • ЗАСТЁГНУТ(ЫЙ) НА ВСЕ ПУ́ГОВИЦЫ [AdjP; detached modif (var. with long-form Part) or subj-compl with copula with subj: human (both variants); fixed WO] (one is) official, cool, stern (in his manner of conduct): **(be) stiff ⟨standoffish, starchy⟩.**

П-625 • ПУД ⟨МНО́ГО, КУЛЬ⟩ СО́ЛИ СЪЕСТЬ с кем **coll** [VP; subj: human; often infin with надо] having had extensive (usu. close) contact with s.o., to understand him and his character thoroughly: X с Y-ом пуд соли съел ≃ **(having spent so much time with Y,) X knows ⟨has gotten to know⟩ Y really well; X has spent years ⟨a lot of time⟩ with Y (and knows him very well); X has eaten the proverbial peck of salt with Y.**

«Ты видел Зиновьева и Каменева только на трибунах съездов, я с ними пуд соли съел...» (Рыбаков 2). "You've only seen Zinoviev and Kamenev on the platform at congresses, whereas I've spent years with them..." (2a).
< From the saying «Чтобы узнать человека, надо с ним пуд соли съесть» ("A man must eat a peck of salt with his friend before he knows him"). See Ч-54.

П-626 • ОТ ПУ́ЗА есть, наесться, давать **что** и т. п. **substand** [PrepP; Invar; adv] (to eat, allow s.o. to eat etc) until one (or s.o.) is completely satiated, satisfied, can eat no more: наесться ~ ≃ **eat a bellyful; eat one's fill; fill one's belly; eat as much as one wants; eat till one is stuffed;** ∥ накормить кого ~ ≃ **feed s.o. as much as s.o. wants ⟨can eat⟩; feed s.o. till s.o. is stuffed;** [in limited contexts] **fill ⟨stuff⟩ s.o.'s belly.**

...Дядя Сандро поручал мне, если я к нему приходил в сезон, только собирать фрукты. «Можешь есть от пуза», — говорил он... (Искандер 3). ...Uncle Sandro merely commissioned me to pick fruit if I came to him in season. "You can eat a bellyful," he would say... (3a). ♦ «А япошки сытые... Им от пуза дают» (Гинзбург 2). "The Japs, though, are well fed....They're allowed to eat their fill" (2a). ♦ «Хавай [substand = ешь], харч казённый, зато от пуза» (Максимов 2). "Help yourself—it's only prison food, but there's as much as you want" (2a). ♦ Человечество было бедным и прокармливало себя трудясь... Оно могло, подголадывая, накормить «от пуза» несколько там князей и церковников... (Битов 2). Man was poor and fed himself by laboring....By going slightly hungry he could fill the bellies of a few princes and churchmen... (2a).

П-627 • ДУ́ТЫЙ ПУЗЫ́РЬ coll, derog [NP; sing only; often subj-compl with быть∅ (subj: human); fixed WO] a person who has, in the speaker's opinion, an exaggeratedly positive reputation in his field, profession etc: X — дутый пузырь ≃ **X is a fake ⟨a phony, a sham⟩; X is made too much of.**

П-628 • ЛО́ПНУТЬ КАК МЫ́ЛЬНЫЙ ПУЗЫ́РЬ coll [VP; subj: abstr (план, затея, надежда etc); fixed WO] (of a plan, undertaking, hope etc) to fail or fall through completely: X

лопнул как мыльный пузырь ≃ **X fell ⟨went⟩ to pieces; X went up in smoke; X burst like a soap bubble.**

...Допроси хоть одного из этих иностранцев — он тут же доказал бы, что деньги разменял в Госбанке СССР, и этот зловещий фарс лопнул бы как мыльный пузырь (Ивинская 1). ...If any of these foreigners had been questioned, he would immediately have been able to prove that he had obtained the rubles from the State Bank, and the whole wicked farce would have burst like a soap bubble (1a).

П-629 • МЫ́ЛЬНЫЙ ПУЗЫ́РЬ coll, disapprov [NP; sing only; often subj-compl with copula, nom or instrum (subj: human); fixed WO] a person who seemed impressive, but actually turned out to be insignificant, worthless: **soap bubble; empty vessel.**

[Войницкий:] Я обожал этого профессора... Я гордился им и его наукой, я жил, я дышал им!.. Вот он в отставке, и теперь виден весь итог его жизни: после него не останется ни одной страницы труда, он совершенно неизвестен, он ничто! Мыльный пузырь! (Чехов 3). [V.:] I worshipped that professor....I was proud of him, proud of his learning, it was the breath of life to me....Now he has retired, and the sum total of his life can be seen: not one page of his work will survive him, he is absolutely unknown, he is nothing! A soap bubble! (3a).

П-630 • ПУ́ЛЕЙ ⟨СТРЕЛО́Й⟩ ВЫЛЕТА́ТЬ/ВЫ́ЛЕТЕТЬ откуда **coll** [VP; subj: human; usu. pfv] to run or walk out of some place very quickly, headlong: X пулей вылетел из места Y ≃ **X shot out of place Y; X dashed ⟨flew etc⟩ out of place Y like a shot.**

На доклад секретарши Сурков пулей вылетел из кабинета. Он кинулся ко мне и спросил, кем я прихожусь Мандельштаму (Мандельштам 2). As soon as his secretary told him [Surkov] I was there, he shot out of his office, raced up to me and asked how I was related to M[andelstam] (2a).

П-631 • ОТЛИВА́ТЬ ⟨ЛИТЬ⟩/ОТЛИ́ТЬ ПУ́ЛИ ⟨ПУ́ЛЮ⟩ highly coll [VP; subj: human; variants with пули are usu. impfv, variants with пулю are usu. pfv] **1.** to lie shamelessly, brazenly: X пули отливает ≃ **X is spinning yarns; X is giving ⟨telling⟩ person Y cock-and-bull stories; X is telling tall tales; X is piling it on.**

И наврёт совершенно без всякой нужды: вдруг расскажет, что у него была лошадь какой-нибудь голубой или розовой шерсти и тому подобную чепуху, так что слушающие, наконец, все отходят, произнёсши: «Ну, брат, ты, кажется, уж начал пули лить» (Гоголь 3). And he would tell these lies utterly without any need for it: he would suddenly say that he had once had a light-blue or pink horse or some other nonsense of the kind, so that his listeners finally would move away from him, saying, "Well, brother, you seem to be giving us another of your cock-and-bull stories" (3c). ♦ [Городничий:] Прошу посмотреть, какие пули отливает! И старика-отца приплёл! (Гоголь 4). [Mayor:] Listen to him pile it on! He's even dragged in his father! (4f).

2. to say or do sth. unusual, unexpected, often funny: X пули отливает ≃ **X is cutting up; X is pulling (some) funny business.**

П-632 • ПУСКА́ТЬ/ПУСТИ́ТЬ (СЕБЕ́) ПУ́ЛЮ В ЛОБ coll [VP; subj: human; usu. pfv; the verb may take the final position, otherwise fixed WO] to commit suicide by shooting o.s.: X пустил себе пулю в лоб ≃ **X put a bullet through his head ⟨his brain⟩; X put a gun to his head; X blew his brains out.**

«У нас, я помню, один подполковник тоже ожидал полковничьей папахи, а когда не дали, пустил себе пулю в лоб» (Войнович 6). "I remember we had a lieutenant colonel who was expecting a hat too—a colonel's *papakha*. When they didn't give him one, he put a bullet through his head" (6a). ♦ [Львов:] Если он хоть один вечер проведёт дома, то с тоски пулю себе пустит в лоб (Чехов 4). [L.:] If he spent [even one] evening at home he'd get so bored he'd blow his brains out (4b).

П-633 • **ХОТЬ ПУ́ЛЮ В ЛОБ** *coll* [хоть + NP; Invar; usu. subord clause (often introduced by что) or Interj; fixed WO] used to express despair when one finds o.s. in such a difficult, hopeless situation that one feels like killing o.s.: **I ⟨he feels like he etc⟩ might as well put a bullet through my ⟨his etc⟩ head ⟨brain⟩; I ⟨he feels like he etc⟩ might as well shoot myself ⟨himself etc⟩ (and be done with it).**

[Иванов:] Что же со мною?.. Откуда во мне эта слабость? Что стало с моими нервами?.. Просто хоть пулю в лоб!.. (Чехов 3). [I.:] What's the matter with me?…Where does my weakness come from? What's happened to my nerves?…I might as well shoot myself and be done with it (4b).

П-634 • **КУЛЬМИНАЦИО́ННЫЙ ПУНКТ** *чего*; **КУЛЬМИНАЦИО́ННАЯ ТО́ЧКА** *both lit* [NP; sing only; fixed WO] the climax, acme of sth.: **high point; culmination; peak.**

П-635 • **ПО ПУ́НКТАМ; ПУНКТ ЗА ПУ́НКТОМ** **объяснять, рассказывать** и т. п. [these forms only; adv; fixed WO] (to explain, tell etc sth.) in detail and in a logical sequence: **point by point; step by step; item by item.**

Присяжные совещались ровно час… Помню, как присяжные вступили в залу. Наконец-то! Не привожу вопросов по пунктам, да я их и забыл (Достоевский 2). The jury deliberated for exactly an hour.…I remember how the jury filed into the courtroom. At last! I omit giving the questions point by point, besides I've forgotten them (2a).

П-636 • **ПУП ЗЕМЛИ́** [NP; sing only; often subj-compl with copula (subj: usu. human or collect); may be used with pl subj; fixed WO] (said sarcastically of s.o. who considers himself or is considered) more important than everyone else, above all the rest, better than the rest: X считает, что он пуп земли ≃ **X thinks he's the center ⟨the hub⟩ of the universe; X thinks he's God's gift to the world ⟨to mankind⟩; X thinks the world revolves around him;** ‖ X считает, что Y — пуп земли ≃ **X thinks the sun rises and sets on ⟨on⟩ Y.**

«Конечно, у него ужасный характер. Эгоист, воображает, что он — пуп земли. Но он знающий, опытный врач» (Копелев 1). "Of course, he does have a terrible personality. He's an egoist, he thinks he's the center of the universe. But he's a knowledgeable, experienced doctor" (1a).

П-637 • **ПУСКА́ТЬСЯ/ПУСТИ́ТЬСЯ ⟨БРОСА́ТЬСЯ/ БРО́СИТЬСЯ, КИДА́ТЬСЯ/КИ́НУТЬСЯ⟩ НАУ-ТЁК** *coll* [VP; subj: human or animal] to take off, fleeing from s.o. or sth. (danger, pursuers etc): X пустился наутёк ≃ **X took to his heels; X turned tail (and ran); X dashed away; X made a run for it.**

Два волка неожиданно выскочили из ольшаника, и все лошади и ослы бросились наутёк (Искандер 3). Two wolves suddenly sprang out of an alder thicket, and all the horses and donkeys took to their heels (3a). ♦ …Заслышав родную речь, сперва летим, как безумные, на её звук: «Вы русские?» И тут же, опомнившись и даже не дослушав ответа, сломя голову кидаемся наутёк (Войнович 1). …Hearing our own language we first run like madmen toward the sound, saying: "Are you Russian?" But then at once we come to our senses and, without waiting for an answer, dash away as fast as our feet will carry us (1a).

П-638 • **ПЕРЕЛИВА́ТЬ ⟨ПЕРЕСЫПА́ТЬ** *obs*⟩ **ИЗ ПУСТО́ГО В ПОРО́ЖНЕЕ** *coll, disapprov* [VP; subj:

human; fixed WO] to spend time unproductively, occupying o.s. with unnecessary, useless activities or carrying on empty, pointless conversations: X переливает из пустого в порожнее ≃ **X is milling the wind ⟨pouring water through a sieve, beating the air⟩;** [in refer. to empty conversations only] **X is shooting the breeze; X is engaged in idle chatter.**

[Войницкий:] Человек ровно двадцать пять лет читает и пишет об искусстве, ровно ничего не понимая в искусстве… Двадцать пять лет читает и пишет о том, что умным давно уже известно, а для глупых неинтересно: значит, двадцать пять лет переливает из пустого в порожнее (Чехов 3). [V.:] …A man lectures and writes about art for exactly twenty-five years, and understands exactly nothing about it.…Twenty-five years lecturing and writing about what intelligent people already know and stupid people aren't interested in—which means twenty-five years of milling the wind (3a).

П-639 • **ПУСТЬ ⟨ПУСКА́Й⟩ СЕБЕ́; ПУСТЬ ⟨ПУС-КА́Й⟩ ЕГО́ ⟨ЕЁ, ИХ⟩** [Particle; these forms only; often foll. by a finite verb form; fixed WO] (used to express the speaker's indifference to, acceptance of, or consent to another's action) one may do or continue to do sth.: **let him ⟨her, them⟩ (do sth. ⟨keep doing sth.⟩).**

«Услышат… хозяйка подумает, что я в самом деле хочу уехать…» — «Ну, так что ж? Пусть её думает!» (Гончаров 1). "They may hear you.…My landlady may think…that I really mean to go away." "Well, what of it? Let her!" (1b). ♦ Те, что раньше знали дядю Сандро, но теперь завидовали, проходили, делая вид, что не замечали его. Но дядя Сандро на них не обижался, пусть себе идут, всем не угодишь своим возвышением (Искандер 3). Those who had known Uncle Sandro before, but now envied him, walked on by, pretending not to notice him. But Uncle Sandro did not take offense: Let them go about their business, you can't please everyone by being moved up (3a).

П-640 • **ПУСТЬ ТА́К** *coll* [sent; Invar; fixed WO] used to express concession, agreement etc: **maybe so; could be; you ⟨he etc⟩ may be right ⟨may have a point there⟩; perhaps you're ⟨he is etc⟩ right;** [when replying to a statement that contains a negation] **maybe not.**

«Да, ты возьмёшь меня: вдвоём мы сделаем всё. Один ты не сумеешь, не захочешь!» — «Пусть так; но ты расстроишься и, может быть, надолго» (Гончаров 1). "You will take me: together we can do everything. You won't be able to do it alone—you won't, you may not!" "You may be right; but you will be upset, and perhaps for a long time" (1b). ♦ «Ты не сможешь её переубедить». — «Пусть так, но я хочу попробовать». "You won't be able to make her change her mind." "Maybe not, but I want to try."

П-641 • **ПУТЁВКА В ЖИЗНЬ** *rather lit or media* [NP; sing only; often obj of давать/дать; fixed WO] sth. (an institution, organization, s.o.'s support etc) that helps a person to begin functioning independently and successfully, sth. (s.o.'s professional approval, backing etc) that helps (a project, undertaking etc) to be implemented, adopted, developed etc: **(give s.o. ⟨sth.⟩) a start in life.**

П-642 • **БЕЗ ПУТИ́ бранить, ругать** *кого* и т. п. *obs, substand* [PrepP; Invar; adv] (to scold, berate s.o.) without any reason or justification: **for no reason at all; for nothing.**

П-643 • **НА ЛО́ЖНОМ ПУТИ́ ⟨НА ЛО́ЖНОЙ ДО-РО́ГЕ⟩ быть₀, стоять, находиться; НА ЛО́ЖНЫЙ ПУТЬ ⟨НА ЛО́ЖНУЮ ДОРО́ГУ⟩ стать; ПО ЛО́Ж-НОМУ ПУТИ́ ⟨ПО ЛО́ЖНОЙ ДОРО́ГЕ⟩ идти** [PrepP; these forms only; subj-compl with copula (subj: human or collect) or adv; fixed WO] (in refer. to the course one is following in one's investigation, research, life etc; when in refer. to the course of one's life, implies moral deterioration) one is going or has started going amiss, on a faulty, incorrect etc course: X стоит на ложном пути ≃ **X is on ⟨has taken⟩ the wrong track ⟨path⟩; X is on ⟨has gotten on⟩ a false track ⟨path⟩; X has gone astray.**

Он и не думал сомневаться в самом масонстве, но подозревал, что русское масонство пошло по ложному пути и отклонилось от своего источника (Толстой 5). He never thought of doubting Freemasonry itself, but suspected that Russian Masonry had got onto a false track and had deviated from its original principles (5a).

П-644 • НА ПЛОХО́М ⟨ДУРНО́М⟩ ПУТИ́ ⟨НА ПЛОХО́Й or ДУРНО́Й ДОРО́ГЕ or ДОРО́ЖКЕ⟩ быть₀, стоя́ть; НА ПЛОХО́Й ⟨ДУРНО́Й⟩ ПУТЬ ⟨НА ПЛОХУ́Ю or ДУРНУ́Ю ДОРО́ГУ or ДОРО́ЖКУ⟩ стать [PrepP; these forms only; subj-compl with copula (subj: human) or adv; fixed WO] one is leading or has begun to lead an improper, disreputable life style, one is behaving or has begun to behave reprehensibly: X стоит на плохом пути ≃ **X is going ⟨sliding⟩ downhill;** ‖ X пошёл по дурному пути ≃ **X went wrong ⟨astray⟩.**

П-645 • НА ПРА́ВИЛЬНОМ ПУТИ́ ⟨НА ПРА́ВИЛЬНОЙ ДОРО́ГЕ⟩ быть₀, стоя́ть; НА ПРА́ВИЛЬНЫЙ ПУТЬ ⟨НА ПРА́ВИЛЬНУЮ ДОРО́ГУ⟩ стать, вы́йти; ПО ПРА́ВИЛЬНОМУ ПУТИ́ ⟨ПО ПРА́ВИЛЬНОЙ ДОРО́ГЕ⟩ идти́ [PrepP; these forms only; subj-compl with copula (subj: human) or adv; fixed WO] (in refer. to the course one is following in one's research, investigation, life etc; when in refer. to the course of one's life, implies moral virtue, upstandingness etc) one is going or has started to go on the correct, proper etc course: X на правильном пути ≃ **X is on the right track ⟨on a good path⟩; X has taken the correct path ⟨course⟩; X is doing the right thing;** [when contrasting s.o.'s present behavior with his former behavior] **X has mended his ways.**

[Бусыгин:] Папа, о чём ты грустишь? Людям нужна музыка, когда они веселятся и тоскуют. Где ещё быть музыканту, если не на танцах и похоронах? По-моему, ты на правильном пути (Вампилов 4). [B.:] What are you looking so sad about, Dad? People need music when they're happy and when they're sad. Where's a musician's place, if not at dances and funerals? I reckon you're doing the right thing (4a).

П-646 • НА ПУТИ́ к чему [PrepP; Invar; Prep; the resulting PrepP is adv] moving toward the specified goal, developing in the specified direction: **on the path to; on a path leading to; heading toward.**

«Многим пришлось пережить мучительную ломку на пути к политической зрелости...» (Войнович 4). "Many of us had to experience an agonizing spiritual crisis on the path to political maturity..." (4a).

П-647 • НА ХОРО́ШЕМ ПУТИ́ ⟨НА ХОРО́ШЕЙ ДОРО́ГЕ⟩ быть₀, стоя́ть; НА ХОРО́ШИЙ ПУТЬ ⟨НА ХОРО́ШУЮ ДОРО́ГУ⟩ стать, вы́йти; ПО ХОРО́ШЕМУ ПУТИ́ ⟨ПО ХОРО́ШЕЙ ДОРО́ГЕ⟩ идти́ [PrepP; these forms only; subj-compl with copula (subj: human) or adv; fixed WO] one is leading or has begun to lead a respectable, reputable life style, one is behaving or has begun to behave upstandingly, in a morally virtuous manner: X на хорошем пути ≃ **X is on the right track ⟨on a good path⟩;** [when contrasting s.o.'s present behavior with his former behavior] **X has mended his ways.**

«Ну теперь, после такого вашего признания, я верую, что вы искренни и сердцем добры. Если не дойдёте до счастия, то всегда помните, что вы на хорошей дороге, и постарайтесь с неё не сходить» (Достоевский 1). "Well, now, after such a confession from you, I believe that you are sincere and good at heart. If you do not attain happiness, always remember that you are on a good path, and try not to leave it" (1a).

П-648 • НЕИСПОВЕДИ́МЫ ПУТИ́ ГОСПО́ДНИ *lit* [sent; неисповедимы may take the final position, otherwise fixed WO] things that happen in life are determined by God or, as some see it, fate etc and therefore are unpredictable and often impossible to understand: **mysterious are the ways of the Lord; the ways of the Lord are inscrutable ⟨unfathomable, unknowable⟩; God ⟨the Lord⟩ moves in mysterious ways; the will of heaven ⟨God⟩ is mysterious and not easily discovered; life is mysterious ⟨unpredictable⟩.**

[author's usage] «Из всех неисповедимых путей Господа, наверное, самый неисповедимый привёл тебя в полувымершую семью московских мастеровых из бывших крестьян, к девочке, почти подростку, с которой ты зачал родословную новой фамилии, гремучего симбиоза славянских и библейских кровей» (Максимов 2). "Of all the mysterious ways of the Lord, perhaps the most inscrutable was that which brought you into this half-extinct Moscow working-class family of erstwhile peasants, to marry a girl, still almost a child, with whom you founded a new branch of the family tree, a fierce symbiosis of Slavic and Hebraic blood..." (2a).

< Cf. the Bible, "How unsearchable are His [God's] judgments, and His ways past finding out!" (Rom. 11:33).

П-649 • ПУТИ́ ⟨ДОРО́ГИ⟩ чьи, кого РАСХО́ДЯТСЯ/ РАЗОШЛИ́СЬ [VP_subj] contact or close relations with s.o. are ending (because of a dissimilarity of views, interests etc): наши пути разошлись ≃ **our ways parted; our paths diverged; we went our separate ways; we reached the parting of the ways; we parted company; we drifted apart.**

...Я полагал себя марксистом... а Митя из истового православного стал ещё более истовым католиком. Но всё же общего, объединяющего нас, казалось, было больше, чем разногласий. И старая арестантская дружба словно бы стала ещё крепче. А в семидесятых годах [наши] пути разошлись (Копелев 1). ...I considered myself a Marxist...and Mitya had changed from a fervent Russian Orthodox to a more fervent Catholic. But we still seemed to agree more than disagree. And the old prison friendship seemed to become even stronger. In the seventies, however, our paths diverged (1a). ♦ «Романтик сказал бы: я чувствую, что наши дороги начинают расходиться, а я просто говорю, что мы друг другу приелись» (Тургенев 2). "A romanti[ci]st would say: I feel that we have reached the parting of the ways, but I merely say that we are fed up with each other" (2a).

П-650 • СБИВА́ТЬ/СБИТЬ С ПУТИ́ ⟨С ПУТИ́ И́СТИННОГО, С ПУТИ́ И́СТИНЫ, С ДОРО́ГИ⟩ кого *disapprov* [VP; subj: human] to induce s.o. to change his behavior for the worse, incite s.o. to do wrong: X сбивает Y-а с пути ≃ **X leads Y astray; X tempts Y to abandon the straight and narrow.**

Мало того что он сам законченный алкоголик — он и других с пути сбивает. Not only is he himself an inveterate drinker, but he leads others astray as well.

П-651 • СБИВА́ТЬСЯ/СБИ́ТЬСЯ С ПУТИ́ ⟨С ДОРО́ГИ⟩ [VP; subj: human] **1.** to become lost: X сбился с дороги ≃ **X lost his way ⟨bearings⟩; X got lost.**

«Кто стучит?..» — «Приезжие, матушка, пусти переночевать», — произнёс Чичиков. «...Здесь тебе не постоялый двор, помещица живёт». — «Что ж делать, матушка: видишь, с дороги сбились. Не ночевать же в такое время в степи» (Гоголь 3). "Who's knocking?..." "We are travelers, my good woman; put us up for the night," said Chichikov. "...This is not an inn; a lady landowner lives here." "What are we to do, my good woman? We got lost. We can't spend the whole night in the open steppe, can we?" (3c).

2. *disapprov.* Also: **СБИВА́ТЬСЯ/СБИ́ТЬСЯ С ПУТИ́ И́СТИННОГО ⟨И́СТИНЫ⟩** to begin to follow a disreputable life style, lean toward wrong persuasions, be headed for sth. bad: X сбился с пути ≃ **X went astray; X strayed from the true path ⟨from the straight and narrow, from the path of righteousness⟩; X slipped from the right path.**

Я выкрикивала именно те могущественные банальности, которые могли тронуть её сердце. О материнских слезах... О том, что чужой ребёнок никому не нужен... И о том, что сирота может сбиться с пути... (Гинзбург 2). I found myself shouting out precisely the powerful clichés that could move her heart. A mother's tears....Nobody wants someone else's child....An orphan can so easily go astray... (2a). ♦ Уже тогда, в 1833 году, *либералы* смотрели на нас исподлобья, как на сбившихся с дороги (Герцен 1). Even then, in 1833, the Liberals looked at us askance, as having strayed from the true path (1a). ♦ Он, видите ли, сжалился, он, прославленная личность, пожалел несчастного, сбившегося с пути молодого человека (Олеша 2). [context transl] You see, he took pity on me. He, the exalted public figure, has taken pity on a wayward young man (2a).

П-652 • **СТАНОВИ́ТЬСЯ/СТАТЬ ⟨ВСТАТЬ, СТОЯ́ТЬ⟩ ПОПЕРЁК ПУТИ́ ⟨ДОРО́ГИ⟩ кому, у кого; СТАНОВИ́ТЬСЯ/СТАТЬ ⟨ВСТАТЬ, СТОЯ́ТЬ⟩ НА ПУТИ́ чьём ⟨НА ДОРО́ГЕ чьей⟩, (у) кого coll** [VP; subj: human] to impede, hamper s.o.'s progress (usu. toward the attainment of some goal) intentionally: X стал Y-у поперёк пути ≃ **X got ⟨stood, was⟩ in Y's way; X stood in the way of Y; X blocked Y's path; Y's growth ⟨advancement, promotion etc⟩ is blocked by X.**

[Христофор:] Правильно — встал он на нашем пути, проклятый Лепёшкин. Ну и пусть (Арбузов 5). [K.:] It's true, that damned Lepyoshkin got in our way. Never mind (5a). ♦ «Ну как, — спрашивает лифтёрша, — этот-то [высокопоставленный чиновник Иванько] всё ещё к вам пристаёт?» — «Да нет, вроде отстал». — «Это ж надо какой!.. Съездил в Америку, набрался американского духа... Это хорошо, что у нас советская власть. Всё ж таки можно правды добиться»... Если бы всесильный Иванько встал на пути нашей прекраснодушной лифтёрши (а он бы не постеснялся), я не убеждён, что её вера в любимую власть осталась бы непоколебленной (Войнович 3). "Well," asked the elevator lady, "is he [Ivanko, a high-ranking official] still pestering you?" "Guess not, he apparently gave up." "What a character, that one!...He went to America, picked up those American ways....It's a good thing we've got the Soviet regime. We can still get at the truth...." If the all-powerful Ivanko stood in the way of our pure-souled elevator lady (and he would not be ashamed to), I am not convinced that her faith in the beloved regime would remain steadfast (3a). ♦ «...На пути их [молодых коммунистов] роста, их продвижения стоят старые зиновьевские кадры, которые, естественно, двигают *своих*...» (Рыбаков 2). "...Their [the young Communists'] own growth and progress is being blocked by the old Zinovievite establishment, who naturally advance their own people..." (2a).

П-653 • **СЧАСТЛИ́ВОГО ⟨ДО́БРОГО⟩ ПУТИ́!; СЧАСТЛИ́ВЫЙ ПУТЬ!; ДО́БРЫЙ ПУТЬ!; ПУТЬ ДО́БРЫЙ!** *all coll* [formula phrase; these forms only; variants with пути are also used as obj of желать/пожелать; fixed WO] a wish for a successful trip, journey to a person who is leaving: **have a good ⟨safe, nice⟩ trip!; have a safe journey!; bon voyage!; Godspeed ⟨good speed⟩ (to you)!; [in limited contexts] good luck!**

«Прощайте, Пётр Андреич, сокол наш ясный!.. Счастливый путь, и дай бог вам обоим счастия!» (Пушкин 2). "Farewell, Petr Andreich, my brave falcon!...Have a safe journey, and may God grant happiness to you both!" (2a). ♦ «Доброго вам пути, раз вы спешите» (Искандер 5). "Goodspeed to you, if you're in a hurry" (5a). ♦ «Чайку хотите?» — «Хочу, только времени нет. До свиданья». — «Доброго пути» (Семёнов 1). "Feel like a cup of tea?" "Yes, but I've no time. Goodbye." "Good luck" (1a).

П-654 • **В ДО́БРЫЙ ПУТЬ!** [formula phrase; Invar; fixed WO] used to wish s.o. success, prosperity, usu. before beginning some important undertaking or setting out on a trip: **good luck (to you)!; the best of luck!; all the best!; I wish you luck!; [as a wish for a successful trip only] have a good ⟨safe, nice⟩ trip; have a safe journey!; Godspeed ⟨good speed⟩ (to you)!**

П-655 • **ДЕРЖА́ТЬ ПУТЬ куда coll, rather folk** [VP; subj: human; often used in questions] to move in the direction of (some place): X держал путь в место Y ≃ **X was headed ⟨bound⟩ for place Y; X was heading for place Y; X was making ⟨wending⟩ his way to place Y; X was off to place Y;** ‖ X держал путь дальше (через лес и т. п.) ≃ **X traveled ⟨continued⟩ on (through the woods etc).**

«Куда, бабуля, путь держишь?» — «В город, милок, в город...» (Войнович 4). "Where are you headed, old woman?" "To town, dearies, to town" (4a). ♦ «Путники, куда путь держите?» — спросил Джамхух (Искандер 5). "Travelers, where are you bound for?" Jamkhoukh asked (5a). ♦ Вот сговорились новые приятели, чтоб не разлучаться и путь держать вместе (Гоголь 5). So the new friends agreed not to part, but to travel on together (5a).

П-656 • **ЗАКА́ЗЫВАТЬ/ЗАКАЗА́ТЬ ПУТЬ ⟨ДОРО́ГУ, (ВСЕ) ПУТИ́⟩ кому куда coll** [VP; subj: human; often passive short-form Part путь заказан etc] to deny s.o. access to a certain place, make it impossible for s.o. to go to that place: X заказал Y-у путь в место Z ≃ **X shut the doors (of place Z) to Y (forever); X barred Y from place Z;** ‖ Y-у в место Z ⟨к X-у⟩ пути заказаны ≃ **place Z is barred ⟨off limits⟩ to Y; X's door ⟨the door to place Z⟩ is shut to Y; Y is not welcome ⟨not allowed⟩ in place Z ⟨at X's place, in X's office etc⟩.**

Он сидел здесь, куда обычному лагернику путь был заказан, он курил и беседовал — да с кем ещё! — с самим Главным хозяином (Владимов 1). He was sitting there, in a place that was strictly off limits to ordinary prisoners, smoking and talking with—of all people!—the Chief Master himself (1a).

П-657 • **НАПРАВЛЯ́ТЬ/НАПРА́ВИТЬ ПУТЬ ⟨СТОПЫ́ obs, lit, ШАГИ́ obs⟩ куда, к кому-чему** [VP; subj: human] to move in the direction of (some place, s.o.'s home, or some person): X направляет свой путь в место Z ≃ **X directs his steps toward Z; X makes ⟨wends⟩ his way toward Z; X is headed for Z;** ‖ X направляет свой путь к Y-у ≃ **X directs his steps toward Y; X makes ⟨wends⟩ his way toward Y; X goes up to Y.**

Наконец Козелков явился весь радостный и словно даже светящийся. Он прямо направил стопы к баронессе... (Салтыков-Щедрин 2). Kozelkov arrived at last, looking almost radiant with happiness. He went straight up to the baroness... (2a).

П-658 • **НАСТАВЛЯ́ТЬ/НАСТА́ВИТЬ ⟨НАПРАВЛЯ́ТЬ/НАПРА́ВИТЬ, ОБРАЩА́ТЬ/ОБРАТИ́ТЬ⟩ НА ПУТЬ И́СТИНЫ ⟨И́СТИННЫЙ⟩ кого lit, often iron in contemp. usage** [VP; subj: human] to point out repeatedly to s.o. the right way to do sth. (often in refer. to living a respectable life), induce s.o. to change his behavior for the better etc: X наставил Y-а на путь истины ≃ **X set ⟨put⟩ Y on the right path ⟨track⟩; X set Y on ⟨turned Y onto⟩ the path of truth; [in**

refer. to life style only] **X set Y on the path of righteousness; X set ⟨put⟩ Y on the straight and narrow.**

Обе тётушки души в ней [Вике] не чаяли. Каждая по-своему наставляла её на путь истинный... (Грекова 3). Both "aunties" adored her [Vika]. Each in her own way tried to set Vika on the right path... (3a). ♦ У меня всегда в ушах жалоба Достоевского в письме к жене накануне пушкинской речи: «Они пришли руководить меня»... Передовые молодые люди пришли наставить Достоевского на путь истины, он почему-то не внял... (Мандельштам 2). I often recall the complaint Dostoyevski made in a letter to his wife on the eve of his Pushkin speech: "They have come to instruct me...." The progressive young people of the day had come to set him on the path of truth, but for some reason he did not listen... (2a). ♦ «Что же, обратил грешницу? — злобно засмеялся он Алёше. — Блудницу на путь истины обратил?» (Достоевский 1). "So you converted a sinful woman?" he laughed spitefully to Alyosha. "Turned a harlot onto the path of truth?" (1a).

П-659 • **ОБРАТИ́ТЬСЯ НА ПУТЬ И́СТИНЫ ⟨И́СТИННЫЙ⟩** *obs* [VP; subj: human] to return to a proper, righteous way of life or form of behavior: X обратился на путь истины ≃ **X got back on the right path ⟨track⟩; X returned to the path of truth ⟨of righteousness⟩; X returned to ⟨got back on⟩ the straight and narrow.**

В это время обратились на путь истины многие из прежних чиновников и были вновь приняты на службу (Гоголь 3). At this time many of the officials employed formerly returned to the path of righteousness and were accepted back into service (3c).

П-660 • **ОКО́ЛЬНЫЙ ⟨ОБХОДНО́Й⟩ ПУТЬ;** often **действовать, идти** и т. п. **ОКО́ЛЬНЫМ ⟨ОБХОДНЫМ⟩ ПУТЁМ** or **ОКО́ЛЬНЫМИ ⟨ОБХОДНЫМИ⟩ ПУТЯ́МИ** [NP; fixed WO] an indirect and, in some cases, cunning, underhanded approach to achieving some goal or end: **roundabout way ⟨approach⟩.**

П-661 • **ПОСЛЕ́ДНИЙ ПУТЬ** [NP; sing only; fixed WO] s.o.'s burial procession: **s.o.'s final ⟨last⟩ journey.**

...Провожая Казангапа в последний путь... об этом [об этой истории] неотступно думал Едигей (Айтматов 2). ...Accompanying Kazangap on his last journey, Yedigei spent most of the time recalling that story (2a).

П-662 • **СТАНОВИ́ТЬСЯ/СТАТЬ ⟨ВСТАВА́ТЬ/ВСТАТЬ, ВСТУПА́ТЬ/ВСТУПИ́ТЬ⟩ НА ПУТЬ** *чего, какой* [VP; subj: human or collect; indir obj: abstr; fixed WO] to begin to act in a certain way (as specified), pursue a certain course of action: X вступил на путь Y-а ≃ **X took ⟨embarked on, set out on⟩ the path of Y;** [in limited contexts] **X took up the ⟨a⟩ life of Y;** ‖ X вступил на [AdjP] путь ≃ **X took ⟨embarked on, set out on⟩ a [AdjP] path.**

Позже, когда председатель Тимур Жванба стал на путь прямого мошенничества, на не слишком громкие укоры своей совести он, бывало, злорадно отвечал, что у Маркса тоже кое-какие несоответствия имеются... (Искандер 3). Later on, when Chairman Timur Zhvanba took up the life of an outright swindler, he stilled the none-too-loud reproaches of his conscience with the malicious reply that there were some inconsistencies in Marx, too... (3a). ♦ Сообщая об этом по инстанции, Васька понимал, на какой опасный путь он вступил... (Войнович 6). Reporting all this to the authorities, Vaska understood how dangerous was the path he had embarked on (6a).

П-663 • **В ПУХ И (В) ПРАХ; В ПУХ** *both coll* [PrepP; these forms only; adv (intensif); fixed WO] **1.** Also: **В ПРАХ** *coll* completely, utterly, thoroughly: разбить ⟨разгромить⟩ *кого-что* ~ ≃ **wipe s.o. ⟨sth.⟩ out; tear s.o. ⟨sth.⟩ to pieces; demolish ⟨destroy⟩ s.o. ⟨sth.⟩; crush and defeat s.o. ⟨sth.⟩;**

beat s.o. ⟨sth.⟩ (all) hollow; ‖ разругать ⟨раскритиковать, разнести⟩ *кого-что* ~ ≃ **tear s.o. ⟨sth.⟩ to shreds; pick s.o. ⟨sth.⟩ to pieces; smash s.o. ⟨sth.⟩ to smithereens;** ‖ разругаться *с кем* ~ ≃ **have a bad falling-out with s.o.;** ‖ проиграться ⟨разориться⟩ ~ ≃ **lose one's shirt; lose everything one has; be cleaned out; be completely ruined;** ‖ обыграть *кого* ~ ≃ **clean s.o. out; ruin s.o. completely.**

«Тут, главное, можно осадить и в прах разбить торжествующего романиста подробностями, теми самыми подробностями, которыми всегда так богата действительность...» (Достоевский 2). "Here, above all, the triumphant novelist can be brought up short and demolished by details, those very details in which reality is always so rich..." (2a). ♦ «Вы не читали мой последний роман?.. Прочтите, получите огромное удовольствие. Между прочим, я там их разнёс в пух и прах, сказал всё, что я о них думаю». — «О ком? О них?» — шёпотом переспрашивает собеседник. «Именно о них, — громко настаивает первый. — Я имею в виду американских империалистов» (Войнович 1). "You haven't read my latest novel?...Read it. It'll give you enormous pleasure. By the way, I smash them to smithereens in that book, I say everything I think of them." "About whom? Them?" whispers the first man. "That's right, them," the second man insists loudly. "The American imperialists" (1a). ♦ ...[Локтев] кончил тем, что проигрался в прах и принуждён был поселиться в деревне, где, впрочем, скоро умер... (Тургенев 2). ...[Loktev] wound up by losing his shirt gambling and was driven to settling in the country, where he died soon afterward... (2d). ♦ [Косых:] Всю ночь провинтили и только что кончили... Проигрался в пух... (Чехов 4). [K.:] We played vint all night, only just finished... Lost everything I had... (4a). ♦ «А я, брат, с ярмарки. Поздравь: продулся в пух!» (Гоголь 3). "I've come from the fair, my dear fellow. Congratulate me, I've been cleaned out!" (3a). ♦ Несколько дней спустя дошла до нас новая весть: на заседании какой-то высокой инстанции Иванько в пух и прах разгромил готовившийся к печати сборник... Турганова (Войнович 3). [context transl] Several days later, a new piece of news reached us: at a meeting of some high board, Ivanko completely wrecked the chances of the Turganov collection...that was being prepared for publication (3a).

2. разодеться, расфрантиться, нарядиться и т. п. ~ (to dress) very smartly, splendidly: **(be) dressed to kill ⟨to the hilt, to the nines⟩; (dress) in one's finest; (be dressed) in all one's finery; (be) all decked out; (be) all dressed up.**

...[Амалия Ивановна] была вся разодета хоть и в траур, но во всё новое, в шёлковое, в пух и прах, и гордилась этим (Достоевский 3). ...She [Mme Lippewechsel] was all dressed up and although in mourning, everything she wore was new and silken; she was in all her finery and proud of it (3a).

П-664 • **ПУХ И ⟨ДА⟩ ПЕ́РЬЯ ЛЕТЯ́Т/ПОЛЕТЯ́Т** *(от кого)* *coll* [VP_subj; usu. pres or pfv fut] s.o. gets soundly defeated (in an argument, quarrel etc): от Х-а пух да перья полетят ≃ **X will take a beating; X will get his lumps; X will get the stuffing knocked out of him.**

П-665 • **НИ ПУ́ХА (тебе ⟨вам⟩) НИ ПЕРА́** *coll* [formula phrase; Invar; also used as obj of желать/пожелать; fixed WO] (a wish for success, luck in sth.) may things go well for you: **good luck!; break a leg!; (wish s.o. the) best of luck.**

«Сегодня в Тарасовке на загородном филиале стадиона со вторым „Спартаком" играем. В семь часов. Хочешь — приезжай». — «Я за Любкой еду»... «Ну, пока», — сказал Алик. «Пока. Ни пуха тебе ни пера» (Семёнов 1). "We're playing Spartak Reserves today at the suburban stadium in Tarasovka. At seven o'clock. You can come along if you want to." "I'm going to fetch Lyubka."..."Well, so long," said Alec. "So long. Good luck..." (1a). ♦ «Ни пуха ни пера!» [Нина Львовна] пыталась перекрестить [чтеца] (Ерофеев 4) "Break a leg!" She [Nina Lvovna] tried to make the sign of the cross over him [the actor] (4a). ♦ Выйдя в столовую, все трое что-то такое друг другу сказали, что-то выпили, посидели молча, поговорили об Аркашке, пожелали ему ни пуха ни пера – год-то был для него выпускной (Залыгин 1). In the dining-room the three of them exchanged a few words, drank a little, sat in silence, talked a little about Arkady and wished him the best of luck – he'd be leaving school this year (1a).

< Originally a wish of luck to a hunter setting out after wild fowl. The use of the negative (i.e., «ни пуха ни пера» – "neither fluff nor feathers") was based on the superstition that openly wishing success would jinx the hunt.

П-666 • ИЗ ПУ́ШКИ ⟨ПУ́ШЕК⟩ ПО ВОРОБЬЯ́М СТРЕЛЯ́ТЬ ⟨ПАЛИ́ТЬ, БИТЬ⟩ [VP; subj: human] to waste a lot of strength, energy on sth. that does not require or justify such effort (and yields insignificant results): X стреляет из пушки по воробьям ≃ **X is using a cannon to kill ⟨scatter⟩ sparrows; X is swatting a fly with a sledgehammer; X is cracking a nut with a sledgehammer; X is shooting squirrels with an elephant gun.**

Зачем тратить столько тяжеловесных доказательств на такую незначительную идею? Зачем стрелять из пушки по воробьям? Why waste so many weighty arguments on such an insignificant idea? Why swat a fly with a sledgehammer?

П-667 • КАК ИЗ ПУ́ШКИ явиться, быть готовым и т. п. *coll* [как + PrepP; Invar; adv; usu. used after another adv indicating a point in time] (to come, be ready etc) right on time, exactly at the specified time: **on the dot; on the button.**

Собираемся в шесть, всем быть как из пушки. We'll meet at six – everyone be there on the dot.

П-668 • ПУ́ШКОЙ НЕ ПРОШИБЁШЬ ⟨НЕ ПРО-БЬЁШЬ⟩ *coll* [VP; neg pfv fut, gener. 2nd pers sing only; fixed WO] **1.** there are a great number of people (in some place): X-ов в месте Y – пушкой не прошибёшь ≃ **there is an army of Xs in place Y; there are tons ⟨scores etc⟩ of Xs in place Y.**

2. ~ *кого.* Also: **ИЗ ПУ́ШКИ НЕ ПРОШИБЁШЬ ⟨НЕ ПРОБЬЁШЬ⟩** *coll* (in refer. to s.o.'s stubbornness, unwillingness etc to do sth.) you cannot convince or influence s.o. (to do sth.): X-а пушкой не прошибёшь ≃ **X can't be budged.**

П-669 • БРАТЬ/ВЗЯТЬ НА ПУ́ШКУ ⟨НА БО́ГА *rare*⟩ *кого highly coll* [VP; subj: human; more often impfv] to (try to) deceive s.o., represent a situation in a false manner (usu. in order to get sth. from s.o.; occas. resorting to threats, intimidation): X берёт Y-а на пушку ≃ **X is trying to trick ⟨con, bluff⟩ Y; X is taking Y for a ride; X is pulling ⟨trying to pull⟩ the wool over Y's eyes; X is trying to put ⟨slip⟩ something over on Y; X is trying to trap Y; X is laying a trap for Y;** [in limited contexts] **X is trying to browbeat ⟨to bully⟩ Y.**

«Никакого наркотика ты не получишь, – сказал Костенко. – Это раз. Подписи нам твои не нужны. Это два. И показания – тоже. Это три. Понял?» – «Ты меня на пушку не бери...» (Семёнов 1). "You won't get any dope from us," said Kostyenko. "That's number one. We don't need your signature on anything. That's number two. And we don't need a statement. That's number three. Got it?" "Don't try to pull the wool over my eyes..." (1a). ♦ «Кто был у мамаши?» – «После вас – Звонкова». – «...Чего она припёрлась?» – «Вы ведь ей звонили». Почти минуту Сипенятин сидел остолбенело. Затем, сглотнув слюну, криво усмехнулся: «На пушку берёшь, инспектор?» (Чернёнок 2). "Who was at my mother's?" "After you, Zvonkova." "...What did she come over for?" "You called her." For a minute Sipeniatin sat in stunned silence. Then, swallowing hard, he smiled crookedly. "Are you trying to trap me, inspector?" (2a).

П-670 • В ПЫЛУ́ сражения, битвы, спора и т. п. [PrepP; Invar; the resulting PrepP is adv] at the most intense moment (of a fight, quarrel etc): **in the heat of; at the height of.**

Кто-то кого-то в пылу споров толкнул, у кого-то кровь из носа вышибли... (Шолохов 3). In the heat of argument someone pushed someone else and someone else drew blood from somebody's nose... (3a).

П-671 • С ПЫ́ЛУ, С ЖА́РУ *coll* [PrepP; Invar; nonagreeing modif, subj-compl with copula or obj-compl with подать etc (subj or obj: a noun denoting baked, cooked, fried etc food)] freshly baked, just cooked, roasted, fried etc and still very hot: **sizzling ⟨piping, steaming⟩ hot; straight from the oven ⟨the pot etc⟩; hot off the stove ⟨the griddle, the fire⟩.**

Перед камином в пентхаузе [у Лучникова] в тот вечер собралось семь или восемь друзей, одноклассников. Они ели шашлыки, доставленные с пылу, с жару из подвалов «Курьера»... (Аксёнов 7). Seven or eight of his classmates had come together that evening before the fire in Luchnikov's penthouse. They were eating shish kebab delivered sizzling hot from the *Courier*'s basement kitchens... (7a). ♦ [author's usage] «Замёрз? А мы ждали: щи горячие, прямо с пылу» (Шолохов 3). "Are you frozen? We've been waiting for you. The soup's all ready and piping hot" (3a).

П-672 • ПУСКА́ТЬ/ПУСТИ́ТЬ ПЫЛЬ В ГЛАЗА́ *кому coll* [VP; subj: human] to represent o.s. or one's affairs in a falsely advantageous light (by boasting, exaggerating, doing sth. flashy etc) in an attempt to fool others: X пускает Y-у пыль в глаза ≃ **X is trying to impress Y (with...); X is trying to pass himself off as rich ⟨important etc⟩ (in front of Y);** [in refer. to speaking only] **X is spinning Y a fine yarn; X is laying it on thick (to Y);** [only when the surrounding context makes it clear that what is displayed does not reflect the true state of affairs] **X is showing ⟨trying to show⟩ off (to Y); X is making ⟨trying to make⟩ a splash; X is putting ⟨trying to put⟩ on the dog; X is dazzling ⟨trying to dazzle⟩ Y; X is cutting ⟨trying to cut⟩ a swath.**

Петрушка пустил Григорию пыль в глаза своею бывалостью в разных местах; Григорий же осадил его сразу Петербургом, в котором Петрушка не был (Гоголь 3). Petrushka tried to impress Grigory with having been in all sorts of places, but Grigory at once floored him with Petersburg, a place Petrushka had never visited (3a). ♦ [author's usage] [Хлестаков:] ...Они меня принимают за государственного человека. Верно, я вчера им подпустил пыли (Гоголь 4). [Kh.:] ...They have taken me for someone of great importance in the government. I must have spun them a fine yarn yesterday (4c). ♦ ...На свадьбе его сына впервые в нашем городе появился автомобиль, специально выписал его из Чернигова или из Гомеля, не знаю уж откуда, любил пустить пыль в глаза (Рыбаков 1). At his son's wedding the first automobile in town made its appearance, specially ordered from Chernigov, or Gomel, I'm not sure which – anyway, he loved to show off (1a). ♦ Изредка, в большие праздники, любил Сергей Платонович пустить пыль в глаза: созывал гостей и угощал дорогими винами, свежей осетровой икрой... лучшими закусками (Шолохов 2). Occasionally, at festival time Sergei Platonovich liked to make a splash. He would give a party and treat his guests to expensive wines, fresh sturgeon caviar...and other delicacies (2a). ♦ [Леонид:] Она молоденькая, хорошенькая, ей хочется повертеться, пустить пыль в глаза другим, это молодость, чепуха! Пройдёт! (Розов 2). [L.:] She's young, pretty, she wants to show off, dazzle people. It's just youth, nonsense. It'll pass! (2a).

П-673 • ПЫЛЬ СТОЛБО́М *где* [Invar; usu. VP$_{subj}$ with быть$_\theta$; fixed WO] some place is full of noise, uproar, disorder, turmoil: в месте X пыль столбом ≃ **there is pandemonium in place X; all hell has broken loose in place X; place X is a three-ring(ed) circus.**

П-674 • НЕ ПЫ́ЛЬНАЯ работа (у кого) *highly coll* [AdjP; fem sing only; subj-compl with быть∅ (subj: работа)] work that does not demand a great expenditure of effort: у X-а работа не пыльная ≃ **X has a cushy job; X doesn't have a tough job; X's job is a cinch** ⟨**a piece of cake, no sweat**⟩.

Вообще у них, у этих астрономов, работа, как мне показалось, не пыльная (Аксёнов 1). It struck me that on the whole they do not have a tough job, these astronomers (1a).

П-675 • СЕМИ́ ⟨СЕМЬ *rare*⟩ ПЯ́ДЕЙ ⟨ПЯДЕ́Й *obsoles*, ПЯДЕ́НЬ *obs*, ПЯДЕ́НЕЙ *obs*⟩ ВО ЛБУ́ *coll* [NPgen or NP; these forms only; usu. subj-compl with быть∅, subj: human (var. with семи); var. with семь is used as subj with быть∅ or obj of иметь; usu. condit будь кто семи пядей во лбу; fixed WO] one is very intelligent, quick-witted, has remarkable abilities: будь X семи пядей во лбу ≃ **be X** ⟨**even if X were**⟩ **a genius** ⟨**a real brain, the smartest man in the world**⟩; **be X** ⟨**even if X were**⟩ **(as) wise as an owl** ⟨**(as) shrewd as a fox, (as) wise as Solomon, (as) smart as a whip**⟩.

[Чугунов:] Будь ты хоть семи пядей во лбу, да коли законов не знаешь... [Павлин:] Понимаю я-с (Островский 5). [Ch.:] You can be as wise as an owl, but if you don't know the law... [P.:] I understand, sir (5b). ♦ «Кто из моих людей смеет обижать сироту? – закричал он. – Будь он семи пядень во лбу, а от суда моего на уйдёт» (Пушкин 2). "Who among my men dares mistreat an orphan?" he cried. "Be he as shrewd as a fox, he won't escape my judgment!" (2a).

< «Пядь» is an old unit of length equal to the distance between the tips of the thumb and the index finger when they are extended.

П-676 • ДО ПЯТ *coll* [PrepP; Invar; usu. nonagreeing modif] (of a skirt, dress, coat etc) very long, almost reaching the ground: **down to one's ankles; ankle-length.**

П-677 • АХИЛЛЕ́СОВА ПЯТА́ ⟨ПЯ́ТКА⟩ чья, кого-чего, у кого *lit* [NP; sing only; fixed WO] a point or area that is particularly weak or vulnerable: **Achilles heel.**

Отсутствие ясно сознанной цели – вот ахиллесова пята всех администраторов, получавших воспитание у Дюссо... (Салтыков-Щедрин 2). The absence of a clearly defined purpose is the Achilles heel of every administrator educated at Dusseau's... (2a).

< From the Greek legend of *Achilles*, whose heel was the only vulnerable point on his body.

П-678 • ПО ПЯТА́М [PrepP; Invar; adv] **1.** идти, следовать, гнаться и т. п. ~ чьим, кого, за кем (to follow, race after s.o.) closely, persistently: **(follow** ⟨**be**⟩**) on** ⟨**at**⟩ **s.o.'s heels; (follow s.o.) closely; (follow close behind s.o.; dog s.o.'s footsteps; [in limited contexts] tail s.o.**

Путь французов был неизвестен, и потому, чем ближе следовали наши войска по пятам французов, тем больше они проходили дороги (Толстой 7). The road the French would take was unknown, and therefore the more closely our troops followed on their heels the more ground they had to cover (7a). ♦ «Ваше высокопреосвященство, что же это вы тут богослужение устроили? Драпать надо! Корпус идёт за нами по пятам!..» (Булгаков 2). "Your Eminence, what's the idea of this sacred service now? We've got to clear out! The Reds are on our heels!.." (2a). ♦ Левее маршрута 80-й дивизии передвигались 283-й Павлоградский и 284-й Венгровский полки 71-й дивизии. По пятам за ними шёл полк уральских казаков... (Шолохов 3). On their [the 80th Division's] left the 283rd Pavlograd and the 284th Węgrów regiments of the 71st Division were also on the march, closely followed by a regiment of Urals Cossacks... (3a). ♦ «Я пойду вперёд, – продолжала Низа, – но ты иди по моим пятам, а отделись от меня» (Булгаков 9). "I'll go first," Niza went on, "but don't follow close behind me, go separately" (9b). ♦ ...Какие-то

подозрительные личности шли по пятам, куда бы мы ни шли (Ивинская 1). ...Wherever we went, our footsteps were dogged by suspicious-looking characters (1a).

2. ходить ~ за кем not to leave s.o., to stay close to s.o. all the time, annoying, irritating him with one's presence: **(be** ⟨**follow**⟩**) on** ⟨**at**⟩ **s.o.'s heels; follow s.o. around; breathe down s.o.'s neck.**

[Макарская:] ...Я хочу, чтобы ты меня больше не ждал, не следил за мной, не ходил по пятам. Потому что из этого ничего не выйдет... (Вампилов 4). [M.:] ...I don't want you to wait for me anymore, or follow me, or be on my heels all the time. Because nothing's going to come of all this... (4b). ♦ «Прошлой зимой мы капремонт [капитальный ремонт] пансионата делали, а этот дедуга, как надсмотрщик, за нами по пятам ходил» (Чернёнок 1). "Last winter we did major repairs on the hotel, and the old man followed us around and 'supervised'" (1a). ♦ «Сволочь, – любезно сказал Лучников. – Сволочь пайковая. Ты полагаешь, что я должен быть паинькой, когда за мной ходят по пятам ваши псы?!» (Аксёнов 7). "Bastard," said Luchnikov affectionately. "Kremlin-bought bastard. So I'm supposed to act like a good little boy while your hit men breathe down my neck!" (7a).

П-679 • ЛИЗА́ТЬ ПЯ́ТКИ ⟨НО́ГИ, САПОГИ́, РУ́КИ⟩ кому, у кого *highly coll, derog* [VP; subj: human] to fawn on, cringe and grovel before s.o.: X лижет пятки Y-у ≃ **X licks Y's boots** ⟨**shoes, feet**⟩.

[extended usage] [Нелькин:] Разве все они [честные люди] должны кланяться силе, лизать сапоги у насилия? (Сухово-Кобылин 1). [N.:] Must all of them [honest people] submit to force, and lick the boots of oppression? (1a).

П-680 • НАСТУПА́ТЬ/НАСТУПИ́ТЬ НА ПЯ́ТКИ кому *coll* [VP; usu. impfv] **1.** [subj: human, collect, or animal] to be following s.o. very closely and be about to come even with him: X наступал Y-у на пятки ≃ **X was hard on Y's heels; X was (close) at Y's heels; X was close behind Y; X was catching up with** ⟨**to**⟩ **Y.**

Его преследователям удалось сократить расстояние, они уже наступали ему на пятки. His pursuers managed to close in on him—they were already at his heels.

2. [subj: human or collect] to be about to reach a skill level equal to another's in some activity: X наступает Y-у на пятки ≃ **X is catching up with** ⟨**to**⟩ **Y; X is gaining on Y; X is close behind Y; X** ⟨**X's work, X's performance** etc⟩ **is becoming as good as Y** ⟨**Y's**⟩**; X is right** ⟨**close**⟩ **at Y's heels; X is hard on Y's heels.**

П-681 • ПОКА́ЗЫВАТЬ/ПОКАЗА́ТЬ ПЯ́ТКИ *coll* [VP; subj: human] to run away, flee: X показал пятки ≃ **X showed a clean pair of heels; X took to his heels.**

Мы хотели было тут и расположиться со своими лекарствами, но вдруг из какого-то подъезда выскочил милиционер и побежал к нам по туннелю, заливисто свистя... Мы улепетнули от стража, показали ему... пятки (Аксёнов 6). We were about to settle down and spread out our supply of medication then and there, when suddenly a policeman leaped out of a doorway and ran down the tunnel toward us, loudly blowing his whistle....We bolted and showed this guardian of the law a clean pair of heels (6a).

П-682 • СМА́ЗЫВАТЬ/СМА́ЗАТЬ ⟨ПОДМА́ЗЫВАТЬ/ПОДМА́ЗАТЬ, НАМА́ЗЫВАТЬ/НАМА́ЗАТЬ⟩ ПЯ́ТКИ ⟨СА́ЛОМ⟩ *highly coll* [VP; subj: human, often pl] to run away, flee (often from an enemy): X-ы смазали пятки салом ≃ **Xs greased their heels; Xs took to their heels; Xs took flight; Xs headed for the hills; Xs beat a hasty retreat.**

[Мышлаевский:] И пойду, и буду служить. Да! [Студзинский:] Почему?! [Мышлаевский:] А вот почему! Потому! Потому что у Петлюры, вы говорили, сколько? Двести тысяч! Вот эти двести тысяч пятки салом подмазали и дуют при одном слове «большевики» (Булгаков 4). [М.:] And I'll go, and I'll serve. Sure! [S.:] Why? [M.:] Here's why! Because! Because Petlyura has—how many did you say?—two hundred thousand! And here these two hundred thousand have greased their heels and faded away just on the mention of the word "Bolsheviks" (4b).

П-683 • **ТО́ЛЬКО ПЯ́ТКИ СВЕРКА́ЮТ/ЗАСВЕРКА́ЛИ** *(у кого) coll* [VP_subj; often after помчался, понёсся и т. п.; if a verb of motion is not present, it is implied] s.o. runs away very quickly: у Х-а ⟨Х помчался и т. п.,⟩ только пятки засверкали ≃ X took off like greased lightning; X was ⟨took⟩ off like a shot; X showed a clean pair of heels; X took to his heels (out of there).

Когда ребята увидели сторожа, у них только пятки засверкали. When the kids caught sight of the guard they took off like greased lightning.

П-684 • **СЕМЬ ПЯ́ТНИЦ НА НЕДЕ́ЛЕ** *у кого coll, often disapprov* [NP; Invar; used as VP_subj with быть∅, usu. pres or past; fixed WO] s.o. often, easily, and sometimes irresponsibly changes his mind, opinions, plans etc: у Х-а семь пятниц на неделе ≃ X says ⟨does⟩ one thing one day ⟨minute⟩ and another the next; with X it's one thing one day and something else the next; one minute X says ⟨does⟩ something, the next minute—something else altogether; X is as fickle as they come; [in limited contexts] X blows hot and cold (about ⟨over⟩ sth.); rain before seven, clear ⟨fine⟩ before eleven.

[Липочка:] Ах, если бы вы знали, Лазарь Елизарыч, какое мне житьё здесь! У маменьки семь пятниц на неделе... (Островский 10). [L.:] Oh, if you knew, Lazar Elizarych, what my life here is like! Mamma says one thing one day, and another the next... (10b).

П-685 • **БЕ́ЛОЕ ПЯТНО́** [NP; often pl; fixed WO] **1.** often ~ на ка́рте, на земле́ an unmapped or unexplored territory: blank; blank spot (on the map); uncharted area.

Казалось бы, наша планета исследована вдоль и поперёк, и всё же на её карте ещё есть белые пятна. It would seem that our planet has been studied inside out, and yet there are still uncharted areas on the map.

2. ~ (в чём) an unexplored problem, undecided question: blank; unsolved problem; gap in one's knowledge (of sth.).

Несмотря на большие успехи, достигнутые в последние годы, в вирусологии пока есть белые пятна. Despite great advances made over the past few years, there are still blanks in the field of virology.

П-686 • **РОДИ́МОЕ ПЯТНО́** [NP; fixed WO] **1.** a spot, blemish on a person's skin that was there at birth: birthmark.

2. ~ чего a remnant of sth.: mark; vestige.

Сегодня, чем старше человек, тем прочнее в него въелись «родимые пятна» прошлой эпохи (Мандельштам 2). Nowadays, the older a man is, the more he bears the marks of the past (2a).

П-687 • **ТЁМНОЕ ⟨ЧЁРНОЕ⟩ ПЯТНО́** [NP; fixed WO] a shameful, discreditable action, mode of behavior etc (usu. in s.o.'s past): black spot ⟨mark⟩; blemish; [in limited contexts] blot on s.o.'s escutcheon.

Чтобы такой человек и не присосался к правящей партии, это казалось мне совершенно невероятным. Если он этого не сделал, значит, были серьёзные причины... Моральных преград для вступления в партию у него, разумеется, нет и быть не могло. Значит, в его биографии были какие-то тёмные пятна, которые и партия считает тёмными (Войнович 3). That such a person had not attached himself to the ruling party seemed completely incredible to me. If he did not do so, it meant there were serious reasons....He did not have, and could not have had, of course, any moral objections to joining the Party. That meant there were black spots on his record that even the Party considered black (3a).

П-688 • **С ПЯ́ТОГО НА ДЕСЯ́ТОЕ** *coll* [PrepP; Invar; adv; fixed WO] **1.** рассказывать, перескакивать ~ и т. п. Also: **ПЯ́ТОЕ ЧЕРЕЗ ДЕСЯ́ТОЕ** *coll* (to tell, recount sth.) in a disorganized, nonsequential manner: (jump ⟨skip⟩) from one point ⟨thing⟩ to another; (tell sth.) in a mixed-up ⟨confused, jumbled etc⟩ way.

Что ты перескакиваешь с пятого на десятое? Начни сначала и изложи всё последовательно и детально. Why do you keep jumping from one thing to another? Start over and tell everything in order, with all the details.

2. Also: **ЧЕРЕЗ ПЯ́ТОЕ НА ДЕСЯ́ТОЕ** *coll* (to do sth.) in a careless, disorderly fashion: in a slipshod manner ⟨fashion⟩; any old way; poorly; sloppily.

Дочка наша учится хорошо, а сын — с пятого на десятое, больше футболом интересуется. Our daughter does well in school, but our son does poorly. He's more interested in soccer.

3. ~ понима́ть, знать и т. п. Also: **ИЗ ПЯ́ТОГО В ДЕСЯ́ТОЕ** *coll* (to understand, know etc) a little bit, only certain parts of sth.: (to understand ⟨know⟩) bits and pieces; (understand) snatches (here and there).

«Ты всё понимаешь, когда смотришь французские фильмы?» — «Честно говоря, с пятого на десятое». "When you watch French films, do you understand everything they say?" "To tell you the truth, I only catch bits and pieces."

П-689 • **ПЯ́ТОЕ-ДЕСЯ́ТОЕ** *coll* [NP; sing only] (used, usu. after то и сё, instead of a detailed enumeration) various things: this and that; one thing and another; this, that, and the other; lots ⟨a number⟩ of things.

[Гаев:] В четверг я был в окружном суде, ну, сошлась компания, начался разговор о том о сём, пятое-десятое... (Чехов 2). [G.:] On Thursday I was in the district court, well, a group of us gathered together and began talking about one thing and another, this and that... (2a). ♦ Конечно, обидно: маловато успел. Со стороны может показаться, что вовсе не так. Я и то, и это, пятое, десятое. Но уж я-то знаю, что чепуха (Трифонов 5). It was humiliating, of course. I had accomplished very little. From an outsider's point of view it might not appear that way. I've done this, that, and a number of things. But I myself know how little it has all amounted to (5a).

П-690 • **ПОД ПЯТО́Й** *чьей, (у) кого* быть∅, находи́ться, жить и т. п. [PrepP; Invar; the resulting PrepP is usu. subj-compl with copula (subj: human or collect) or adv] (to be, live etc) under s.o.'s control, domination, yoke: under s.o.'s heel ⟨thumb⟩; under the heel ⟨the thumb⟩ of s.o.; in s.o.'s power.

В доме он был всегда под пятой у женщин — у сестёр, у жены (Аллилуева 2). At home he had always been under the thumb of women—his sisters, his wife (2a).

Р

Р-1 • РАБ БОЖИЙ *obs* [NP; usu. sing; usu. this WO] **1.** a person as a subject of God: **God's creature; God's servant; servant of God ⟨of our Lord⟩.**

«Помянем раба Божия Фому. Царство ему Небесное!» (Максимов 3). "Let's drink to the memory of God's servant Foma. May he rest in peace!" (3a). ♦ «Человек не раб Божий, но и не царь природы – обе формулировки одинаково нелепы...» (Горенштейн 1). "Man is not a servant of God, but neither is he the lord of nature. The two formulas are equally absurd..." (1a).

2. *iron or humor* simply a human being (usu. used in refer. to a person who has to submit to s.o.'s will, to some circumstances etc): **God's servant.**

[Расплюев:] Свезут тебя... в Преображенскую и посадят тебя, раба божия, на цепуру (Сухово-Кобылин 2). [R.:] They'll take you...to the madhouse and keep you, God's servant, on a chain... (2a).

Р-2 • ЕГИПЕТСКАЯ РАБОТА; ЕГИПЕТСКИЙ ТРУД *both obs* [NP; sing only] very hard, exhausting labor: **slave labor; backbreaking labor.**

< From the Biblical account of the hard labor the Israelites were forced to do while enslaved in Egypt (Ex. 1–2).

Р-3 • РАБОТА ⟨ДЕЛО⟩ НЕ ВОЛК ⟨НЕ МЕДВЕДЬ⟩, В ЛЕС НЕ УЙДЁТ ⟨НЕ УБЕЖИТ⟩ [saying] the work in question (or any work) is not so urgent that it cannot be put off: ≃ **the work isn't going anywhere; the work will still be there (tomorrow);** [in limited contexts] **don't do today what you can put off till tomorrow.**

Р-4 • РАБОТАТЬ НАД СОБОЙ [VP; subj: human; usu. this WO] to try to better o.s. in some area (by adding to one's credentials, furthering one's education etc): X работает над собой ≃ **X is improving ⟨trying to improve⟩ himself; X is working (hard) at self-improvement; X is broadening his horizons.**

«Желание работать над собой и постоянное воспоминание о вас, фрейлейн Мари, не покидают меня...» (Федин 1). "The desire to improve myself, and the constant memory of you, Fräulein Marie, never leave me..." (1a).

Р-5 • ГОРЕТЬ НА РАБОТЕ *coll, often humor or iron* [VP: subj: human] to devote o.s. completely to one's work, sparing no effort: X горит на работе ≃ **X lives for (his) work; X is married to his job ⟨work, career⟩.**

«Да перестань же ты, Марлен, всё время думать о делах, – одёрнул себя Кузенков. – ...Тебе ли уподобляться замшелым «трезорам», которые, по тогдашнему выражению, «горели на работе», а проку от которых было чуть, одна лишь кровь и пакость. Ты современный человек» (Аксёнов 7). Can't you ever stop thinking about work? said Kuzenkov to himself reproachfully.... You don't want to be like the moss-backed old guard that lived for work and got nothing in return but blood, sweat, and tears. You're a man of the present (7a).

Р-6 • РАВНО КАК (И) *lit* [subord Conj, compar] used to liken two persons, phenomena etc: **just as ⟨like⟩; as well as.**

«Я вышел из штаба последним ровно в полдень, когда с Печерска показались неприятельские цепи». – «Ты – герой, – ответил Мышлаевский, – но надеюсь, что его сиятельство, главнокомандующий, успел уйти раньше... Равно как и его светлость, пан гетман... его мать...» (Булгаков 3). "I was the last to leave headquarters, exactly at noon, when the enemy's troops appeared in Pechorsk." "You're a hero," said Myshlaevsky, "but I hope that his excellency, the commander-in-chief managed to get away sooner. Just like his highness, the Hetman of the Ukraine...the son of a bitch..." (3a). ♦ ...В этих глазах, равно как и в очертании прелестных губ, было нечто такое, во что, конечно, можно было брату его влюбиться ужасно... (Достоевский 1). ...In those eyes, as well as in the outline of her lovely lips, there was something that his brother certainly might fall terribly in love with... (1a).

Р-7 • НА РАВНЫХ говорить, держать себя *с кем*, работать, разговор *и т. п.* [PrepP; Invar; adv, nonagreeing modif, or subj-compl with copula (subj: usu. human)] (to speak, conduct o.s., work etc with s.o.) as one equal with another or as if one were equal to another (in terms of age, position, social status etc); (a conversation is held, discussion takes place etc) with all parties being equal or treating each other as equals: **as equals; as if ⟨though⟩ we ⟨you, they⟩ were equals; on equal terms; on an equal footing ⟨basis⟩.**

Зачем сблизился с Тимофеем? Зачем поехал с ним на сенокос? От них надо подальше, а он раскис, держался на равных... (Рыбаков 2). Why did he have to get to know Timofei? Why had he gone haymaking with him? He ought to have kept himself at a distance, whereas he had relaxed, he'd behaved as if they were equals... (2a). ♦ Его [императора] крайне забавляло, что она [девушка] не догадывалась вовсе, с кем имеет дело, и держала себя с ним на равных (Окуджава 2). He [the emperor] was vastly amused that she [the girl] had no idea who he was and behaved as though they were equals (2a). ♦ [Валя:] Да почему он мне должен что-то давать? Почему нельзя на равных?.. (Рощин 1). [V.:] But why does he have to give me something? Why can't we be on equal terms?... (1b). ♦ «Мы не умеем сотрудничать на равных, мы умеем приручать...» (Горенштейн 1). "We don't know how to work together on an equal basis, we know how to tame..." (1a).

Р-8 • ПРИ ПРОЧИХ РАВНЫХ [PrepP; Invar; sent adv; fixed WO] provided that all other facts or circumstances taken into consideration make no difference: **other ⟨all⟩ things being equal.**

Два издательства проявляют интерес к моей книге. При прочих равных я, пожалуй, предпочёл бы «Аврору». Two publishers have shown interest in my book. All things being equal, I would probably prefer Aurora.

Р-9 • (И) САМ НЕ РАД; НЕ РАД *all coll* [AdjP; subj-compl with бытьθ (subj: human); often foll. by a что-clause] one regrets sth. that happened through one's own fault or with one's participation: X и сам был не рад ≃ **X could have kicked himself (for having done sth.); X was none too happy with himself (for having done sth.); X wished (that) he hadn't (done sth.).**

Я и сам не рад, что последовал совету Никиты. I could kick myself for having followed Nikita's advice. ♦ Глебов был уж не рад, что затеял разговор (Трифонов 2). Glebov wished that he had not started the conversation (2a).

Р-10 • МАЛО РАДОСТИ *(кому от кого-чего) coll* [Invar; impers predic or subj-compl with бытьθ (subj: infin)] sth. (or doing sth.) is unpleasant (for s.o.), it is not pleasurable (for s.o. to be in another's company): X-у от Y-а ⟨X-у делать Y⟩ мало радости ≃ **doing Y is no treat ⟨fun⟩ (for X); it's no ⟨not much⟩ fun doing ⟨to do⟩ Y; X doesn't get much pleasure out of (doing) Y; thing Y doesn't thrill X; doing Y is not X's favorite thing (in the world).**

«Конечно, мало радости сидеть круглый год в бюро, но что поделаешь…» (Михайловская 1). "Of course, it's not much fun sitting around all year in a division office, but what can I do" (1a).

Р-11 • С КАКО́Й РА́ДОСТИ? *highly coll* [PrepP; Invar; adv; fixed WO] why, for what reason?: **why on earth?; what (in the world) for?;** [in limited contexts; as a sarcastic response to an undesirable request, order etc] **to what do I ⟨we etc⟩ owe the honor of…?**

«С какой радости я сюда пришла? – думала Катя. – Знала ведь, что будет скучно». "Why on earth did I come here?" thought Katya. "After all, I knew I'd be bored." ♦ «Сейчас приду, – думал Николай, и перво-наперво: „Беги, Тимоша, за пол-литром". А он мне: „С какой это радости мне за пол-литром бечь [*ungrammat* = бежать]?"» (Войнович 5). "I'll go and see him right now," thought Nikolai. "First, I'll tell him: Go and get half a liter, Timosha. And he'll say: And to what do I owe the honor of running out for half a liter?" (5a).

Р-12 • ВЕЛИКА́ РА́ДОСТЬ! *coll, iron* [Interj; Invar; fixed WO] used to reject a suggestion or express dissatisfaction, displeasure etc: **what a thrill!; what a joy!; won't ⟨wouldn't⟩ that be fun!; I can hardly wait!**

[Сатин:] …Женись на Василисе… хозяином нашим будешь… [Пепел:] Велика радость! (Горький 3). [S.:] …You could marry Vassilissa—become our landlord— [P.:] I can hardly wait! (3b).

Р-13 • НЕ В РА́ДОСТЬ *кому coll* [PrepP; Invar; subj-compl with быть∅ (subj: abstr or, rare, human); can be used without negation to convey the opposite meaning] some thing (or, occas., person) does not give s.o. satisfaction, does not bring s.o. joy or happiness: X Y-у не в радость ≃ **thing X holds no joy ⟨pleasure⟩ for Y; Y doesn't enjoy X; Y doesn't get any pleasure out of X.**

Р-14 • ОДНА́ РА́ДОСТЬ В ГЛАЗУ́ *у кого folk* [NP; sing only; fixed WO] s.o.'s only consolation: **s.o.'s only comfort; the only good ⟨comforting⟩ thing for s.o.**

Р-15 • С РА́ДОСТЬЮ *coll* [PrepP; Invar; adv] willingly, readily: **gladly; with pleasure; eagerly; (one would be) glad ⟨happy⟩ (to do sth.).**

Р-16 • НА РА́ДОСТЯХ ⟨РА́ДОСТИ⟩ *coll* [PrepP; these forms only; adv] thanks to or because of one's elevated mood (on the occasion of a joyful event): **in one's joy ⟨rejoicing⟩; from sheer joy; in celebration; to celebrate; elated (, one does sth.).**

Обыкновенно или чиновник умирал, или государь – и тогда наследник на радостях прощал долги (Герцен 2). Usually either the official died or the Tsar did, and then in his rejoicing the heir forgave the debts (2a). ♦ «Постой-ка, угощу тебя», – бессвязно бормотала она, доставая из сундука хранившуюся с давнишних пор бутылку самогона. Прохор присел, разгладил усы. «Ты-то выпьешь со мной на радостях?» – спросил он (Шолохов 5). "Just a minute, I've got something here for you…" she mumbled, rummaging in the chest for a bottle of home-brew that she had been keeping for many a long day. Prokhor sat down and stroked his moustache. "You'll have one with me to celebrate, won't you?" he asked (5a).

Р-17 • ВХОДИ́ТЬ/ВОЙТИ́ ⟨ПРИХОДИ́ТЬ/ПРИЙТИ́, ВПАДА́ТЬ/ВПАСТЬ⟩ В РАЖ *coll* [VP; subj: human] to become so angry or excited that one cannot control o.s.: X вошёл в раж ≃ **X got all worked up; X blew his cool;** [in refer. to anger only] **X got hot under the collar; a fit of rage overcame X.**

Спорить с Виктором бесполезно: он входит в раж и начинает на всех кричать. It doesn't pay to argue with Victor. He gets all worked up and starts yelling at everyone. ♦ [Ефим] вернулся к машинке и, впав в некий раж, стал быстро-быстро стучать по клавишам, не соображая, что пишет (Войнович 6). …When he [Yefim] returned to the typewriter, a fit of rage overcame him and he began banging away at the keys without stopping to think (6a).

Р-18 • В КОТО́РЫЙ РАЗ [PrepP; Invar; adv; fixed WO] (s.o. does sth., sth. happens) one more time after too many times (often used to convey irritation): **for the umpteenth time; once more ⟨again⟩; yet again;** [in limited contexts] **how many times.**

«Смена времён года – в который раз! Сколько можно!» (Битов 2). "The changing of the seasons—for the umpteenth time! Not again!" (2a). ♦ Кузьма устраивается поудобнее и в который раз пытается уснуть (Распутин 1). He [Kuzma] huddled under the blanket and tried once more to fall asleep (1a). ♦ …Потеряв голову, опозорясь с нобелевской церемонией, власти прекратили публичную травлю и в который раз по несчастьи стёкшихся против них обстоятельств оставили меня на родине и на свободе (Солженицын 2). …Having panicked, and disgraced themselves over the Nobel ceremony, the authorities stopped hounding me publicly and, circumstances having conspired so unhappily against them, were forced yet again to leave me in my native land and at large (2a). ♦ «Светлана, а почему бы вам не написать воспоминания? Ведь вам есть что рассказать!» Опять! Наверно, все сговорились; в который раз приходится слышать эти слова (Аллилуева 2). "Svetlana, why don't you write your memoirs? You have so much to say!" Again! They must have all got together on the subject—how many times have I heard those words! (2a).

Р-19 • В СА́МЫЙ РАЗ *coll* [PrepP; Invar; usu. subj-compl with copula; fixed WO] **1.** [subj: concr, abstr, or infin] sth. is timely, sth. happens at the appropriate time: **(it's) just the right time; (at) just the right moment; (at) the perfect time; perfect timing.**

[Весёлый:] А не спеть ли нам ребята? По-моему, в самый раз (Вампилов 3). [Cheerful:] Why don't we sing something, eh? I think this is just the right time for it (3a).

2. ~ *(кому)* [subj: abstr, human, concr, or infin] a person or thing is exactly what is needed or what s.o. wants, needs etc: **just right; just the thing; just what person Y needs;** [when used as indep. sent] **that's it; that's the way ⟨the ticket⟩.**

«Друзья мои, – сказал он, – ушедшие ушли, а мы давайте займём места за этим столом. Если они вернут нашу девочку в целости – пиршество будет в самый раз. Если не вернут – будем считать этот стол поминальным» (Искандер 3). "My friends," he said, "those who have gone are gone, and as for us, let us take our places at these tables. If they bring our girl back safe and sound—the feast will be just the thing. If they don't—we'll count this as the funeral table" (3a). ♦ «Раечка, Лёвушка, спасибо, дорогие. Сикстинская – это в самый раз! Очень я ей обрадовалась» (Орлова 1). "Raya and Lev, thank you, my dears. Raphael's Madonna was just what I needed! I was overjoyed with her" (1a).

3. ~ *(кому)* [subj: a noun denoting footwear, an item of clothing etc] sth. fits s.o. exactly as it should: X Y-у в самый раз ≃ **X is just Y's size; X fits (Y) perfectly ⟨well⟩; X is a perfect fit; X fits (Y) like a glove; it's as if X were made to measure;** [in limited contexts] **there's a good fit now.**

Француз, видимо, боялся, чтобы пленные, смотревшие на него, не засмеялись, и поспешно сунул голову в рубашку… «Вишь, в самый раз», – приговаривал Платон, обдёргивая рубаху (Толстой 7). He [the Frenchman] was evidently afraid that the prisoners looking on would laugh at him, and thrust his head into the shirt hurriedly…. "See, it fits well!" Platon kept repeating, pulling the shirt straight (7b). He [the Frenchman] was evidently afraid that the prisoners looking on would laugh at him, and hastily thrust his head into the shirt…. "There's a good fit now!" Platon kept saying, pulling the shirt down (7a).

Р-20 • ВОТ ТЕБЕ́ ⟨ТЕ⟩ (И) РА́З!; ВОТ ТЕБЕ́ ⟨ТЕ⟩ (И) НА́!; ВОТ ТАК ТА́К! *all coll* [Interj; these forms only; fixed

WO] used to express surprise, disappointment, bewilderment, frustration etc (usu. in reaction to some unexpected circumstance, occurrence etc): **well, I never!; how do you like that!; good Lord!; (well,) what do you know!; (well,) how about that!; holy mackerel!; that's ⟨this is⟩ a fine ⟨pretty⟩ kettle of fish!; well, I'll be (darned ⟨damned⟩)!; who'd have thought it!; (well,) well, well;** [in limited contexts] **that's a good one; did ⟨were etc⟩ you ⟨they etc⟩ now?**

[Кочкарёв:] Зачем же откладывать? Ведь ты согласен? [Подколёсин:] Я? Ну, нет... я ещё не совсем согласен. [Кочкарёв:] Вот тебе на! Да ведь ты сейчас объявил, что хочешь (Гоголь 1). [K.:] Why put it off? You do agree, don't you? [P.:] I? Well, no...I'm not quite agreed yet. [K.:] Well, I never! But you just now said that you wanted to (1a). ♦ «Вчерась обещал на ей [*ungrammat* = ней] жениться, а теперь и нос в сторону». – «Кто? Я обещал?» – ещё больше удивился Иван. «Я, что ли?» – «Вот тебе на!» – Алтынник подпёр голову рукой и задумался (Войнович 5). "Yesterday you promised to marry her and now you turn your nose up at her." "Who, me? I promised?" Altinnik's surprise grew even greater. "That's a fine kettle of fish!" Altinnik propped his head on his hand and lost himself in thought (5a). ♦ [Городничий:] К нам едет ревизор. [Аммос Фёдорович:] Как ревизор? [Городничий:] Ревизор из Петербурга, инкогнито. И ещё с секретным предписаньем. [Аммос Фёдорович:] Вот те на! (Гоголь 4). [Mayor:] A government inspector is on his way. [A.F.:] A government inspector?... [Mayor:] From Petersburg, incognito! And with secret instructions to boot! [A.F.:] Well I'll be! (4f). ♦ [Сотрудник НКВД] Дьяков передал ему ряд людей, с которыми *работал*, среди них и Вику Марасевич. Вот тебе и на! Вот так новость! И Вика, значит... (Рыбаков 2). [NKVD agent] Dyakov handed over to him a number of people he had been *working* with, and among them was Vika Marasevich. Well, well, well, what a surprise! That meant that Vika... (2a). ♦ «Что это за критик Латунский?» – спросил Воланд, прищурившись на Маргариту... Маргарита ответила, краснея: «Есть такой один критик. Я сегодня вечером разнесла всю его квартиру». – «Вот тебе и раз! А зачем же?» – «Он, мессир, – объяснила Маргарита, – погубил одного мастера» (Булгаков 9). "What's this about Latunsky?" inquired Woland, frowning at Margarita....Margarita replied, blushing, "He's a critic. I wrecked his apartment this evening." "Did you now! Why?" "Because, Messire," Margarita explained, "he destroyed a certain master" (9b).

Р-21 • ИНО́Й ⟨ДРУГО́Й⟩ РАЗ [NP; these forms only; adv; fixed WO] periodically, at unfixed intervals: **sometimes; now and then; occasionally; on occasion; at times.**

Если Лёва и обращал иной раз внимание на женщин, то только как бы с точки зрения Фаины, только на тех, кого Фаина могла бы счесть своими соперницами... (Битов 2). If Lyova did sometimes notice women, he noticed them only from Faina's standpoint, noticed only those whom Faina might look upon as her rivals... (2a). ♦ Дед купил его [школьный портфель] в заезжей автолавке. Автолавка, объезжая с товарами скотоводов в горах, заглядывала иной раз и к ним на лесной кордон в Сан-Ташскую падь (Айтматов 1). Grandfather bought it [the schoolbag] from the visiting store truck, which made the rounds of the cattle breeders in the mountains and occasionally looked in on the forest post in the San-Tash Valley (2a). ♦ Сердце у него было довольно мягкое, но речь весьма самоуверенная, а иной раз чрезвычайно даже заносчивая... (Достоевский 3). His heart was fairly soft but he spoke with great self-confidence and even, at times, with extraordinary arrogance... (3a).

Р-22 • КАЖИ́ННЫЙ РАЗ НА Э́ТОМ (СА́МОМ) МЕ́СТЕ *coll, humor* [sent; fixed WO] every time some trouble, embarrassment etc occurs the circumstances are the same: **one gets stuck in the same place ⟨spot⟩ every time; and they say, "Lightning never strikes in the same place twice!"**

< From Ivan Gorbunov's story "At the Post Station" («На почтовой станции»), 1875. «Кажинный» is a substandard variant of «каждый».

Р-23 • КАК РА́З [Invar] **1.** *coll* [usu. adv] timely, at the appropriate time: **(at) just the right moment; (it's) just the right time; just in time; right on time; perfectly timed; perfect timing.**

«Я не рано пришёл? – «Нет, как раз». "I'm not too early?" "No, perfect timing."

2. *кому* ~ *coll* [subj-compl with copula (subj: a noun denoting footwear, a piece of clothing etc)] sth. fits s.o. exactly as it should: **X Y-у как раз ≃ X fits Y perfectly ⟨just right⟩; X is a perfect fit;** [in limited contexts] **X is just right for Y; X fits (Y) like a glove.**

Продавщица с феноменальной скоростью завязала концы шнурка – и тронула носок башмака двумя пальцами. «Как раз!» – сказала она. «Новые всегда немножко...» – продолжала она поспешно, вскинув карие глаза. – «Конечно, если хотите, можно подложить косок под пятку. Но они – как раз, убедитесь сами!» (Набоков 1). With phenomenal speed the salesgirl tied the lace ends and touched the tip of the shoe with two fingers. "Just right," she said. "New shoes are always a little..." she went on rapidly, raising her brown eyes. "Of course if you wish, we can make some adjustments. But they fit perfectly, see for yourself!" (1a). ♦ «Надевай, милая, мою синюю юбку. Она тебе... как раз будет» (Шолохов 2). "Put on my blue skirt, dear. It'll be just right for you..." (2a).

3. ~ *кому, для кого coll* [intensif Particle] (a person or thing is) suitable, appropriate for s.o.: **(suit s.o.) just right; (be) just right (for s.o.); (be) just the (right) thing (for s.o.); (be) just the (right) one (for s.o.); (be) perfect (for s.o.); (suit s.o.) to a T ⟨a tee⟩.**

Когда совсем подошли к острову, стали видны ветряная мельница, прекрасная старинная изба, амбарные постройки – всё пустое, неподвижное, музейное. Агеев усмехнулся. «Как раз для меня», – пробормотал он... (Казаков 1). When they came right to the island, they saw a windmill and a beautiful ancient farmhouse with its outbuildings and barns – all empty and without a sign of life, like pieces in a museum. Ageyev grinned. "Just the right thing for me," he muttered... (1a). ♦ [Фёкла:] ...Уж каких женихов тебе припасла!.. Первый, Балтазар Балтазарович Жевакин, такой славный, во флоте служил – как раз по тебе придётся (Гоголь 1). [F.:] What a bunch of gentlemen I've got for you!...First, Baltazar Baltazarovich Zhevakin, such a nice gentleman; he served in the navy – he's just the one for you (1c). [F.:] ...What gentlemen I've got in store for you!...First, there's Baltazar Baltazarovich – just marvelous. A navy man. He'll suit you to a tee (1b).

4. [intensif Particle] (used to emphasize the word or phrase to which it refers) namely (the person, thing, place etc): **exactly; precisely; just; the very; right (when ⟨then etc⟩).**

...В то время я как раз и был самым молодым работником редакции (Искандер 4). ...That is exactly what I was at the time – the youngest member of the editorial staff (4a). ♦ Если бы она написала мужу ещё в войну: так и так, мол, встретила человека... ей бы не в чем было упрекнуть себя... Но как раз вот этого-то она и не сделала. Не хватило духу. Пожалела (Абрамов 1). If she had written to her husband during the war to say, well, to say that she had met someone...she would have had nothing to reproach herself with....But that was precisely what she had not done. She hadn't had the heart. She had taken pity on him... (1a). ♦ Водку в буфете принесла ему высокая рыжая официантка. «Гениальная баба!» – пробормотал Агеев, восхищённо и жадно провожая её взглядом. А когда она опять подошла, он сказал: «...Вы как раз то, что я искал всю жизнь» (Казаков 1). A tall waitress with red hair brought him his vodka. "What a girl," Ageyev muttered, his eyes following her with greedy pleasure, and when she came up to him again he said: "...You're just what I've been looking for all my life" (1a). ♦ ...Его невольно отрезвляла какая-нибудь её интонация, смешок, веяние тех определённых духов, которыми почему-то душились как раз те женщины, которым он нравился... (Набоков 1). ...He was involuntarily sobered by a certain intonation of hers, her little laugh, the smell of that certain scent which somehow was always used by the very women who liked him... (1a).

5. [intensif Particle] (used to emphasize that sth. will happen, should be done etc) differently from the way stated, suggested etc: **quite the contrary; s.o. ⟨sth.⟩ is ⟨does, will etc⟩ in fact...; actually.**

«Ничего из этой затеи не получится». — «А вот как раз получится». "Nothing's going to come out of this venture." "Quite the contrary, something *will* come out of it."

6. *obs* [intensif Particle] (it is) probable (that sth. will happen): **s.o. ⟨sth.⟩ is very likely to...; it is quite likely ⟨probable⟩ that...; s.o. ⟨sth.⟩ may very well...; [in limited contexts] it doesn't take much to...**

«Да, вишь, какая погода: как раз собьёшься с дороги» (Пушкин 2). "...But you see what the weather's like: it doesn't take much to lose your way" (2a).

Р-24 • **КА́К-ТО РАЗ; (РАЗ) КА́К-ТО** *coll* [AdvP; these forms only; adv] at one time in the past: **once; on one occasion.**

[Городничий:] Раз как-то случилось, забавляя детей, выстроил будку из карт... (Гоголь 4). [Mayor:] Once, merely to amuse the children, I built a house of cards... (4f).

Р-25 • **ЛИ́ШНИЙ РАЗ** [NP; Invar; adv; fixed WO] one extra, additional time: **one more time; once more ⟨again⟩; (yet) again.**

Дядя Сандро лишний раз убедился, что здесь установлен строгий контроль за трупами... (Искандер 3). Uncle Sandro was once more made aware that bodies were kept under strict control here... (3a).

Р-26 • **НЕ РАЗ** [NP; Invar; adv] a few, several, or multiple times: **more than once; time and (time) again; many a time; many times.**

«Ты в России-то бывал?» — «Бывал, — говорю, — не раз» (Алешковский 1). "Have you ever been to Russia?" "Yep," I said. "More than once" (1a). ♦ «А лошадь его славилась в целой Кабарде, — и точно, лучше этой лошади ничего выдумать невозможно. Недаром ему завидовали все наездники и не раз пытались её украсть, только не удавалось» (Лермонтов 1). "As for his horse, it was famous in all Kabarda, and indeed, you couldn't think of a better horse. The horsemen all around had very good reason to envy him, and time and again they tried to steal the animal, but in vain" (1b). ♦ Ирина Викторовна вышла из троллейбуса, обогнула ограду и тоже подошла к Огню и Могиле. Она видела и то и другое не раз, но теперь всматривалась в прозрачную яркость и в синеву огня с особым вниманием...(Залыгин 1). Irina Viktorovna got out of the bus, stepped round the barrier and approached the flame and the tomb. She had seen both many times before, but now she looked into the bright transparent blue of the flame with special attention... (1a).

Р-27 • **РАЗ В ГОД ПО ОБЕЩА́НИЮ** *coll* [Invar; adv; fixed WO] very seldom: **once in a blue moon; (every) once in a great while.**

Р-28 • **РАЗ В РА́З** [Invar; adv] **1.** идти, двигаться ~ *obs, coll, rare* (to go, move) in the same rhythm: **in step; in sync; in time.**

2. (рас)считать ~ *substand* (to calculate) exactly: **to the kopeck ⟨penny⟩; precisely.**

Р-29 • **РАЗ-ДВА́ ⟨ОДИ́Н-ДВА́, ОДИ́Н-ДРУГО́Й, РА́З-ДРУГО́Й⟩ (ДА) И ОБЧЁЛСЯ** *кого-чего coll* [Invar;

quantit subj-compl with быть₀ (subj/gen: any count noun); fixed WO] the people or things in question are extremely few: X-ов раз-два и обчёлся ≃ **there are no more than one or two ⟨two or three, a couple of⟩ Xs; you can count Xs on the fingers of one hand.**

«Именем Нестора не всякому разрешают клясться», — услышал дядя Сандро из-за дверей. «Таких в Абхазии раз-два и обчёлся», — уточнил другой земляк дяди Сандро... (Искандер 3). "Not everyone is allowed to swear by the name of Nestor," Uncle Sandro heard from behind the door. "Not more than one or two people in Abkhazia," another loyal Chegemian said, making it more specific... (3a). ♦ «А много ли у меня было женщин? Раз-два и обчёлся» (Зиновьев 2). "And how many women have I had? You can count them on the fingers of one hand" (2a).

Р-30 • **РАЗ-ДВА́ ⟨РАЗ-РА́З⟩ И ГОТО́ВО** *coll* [usu. indep. clause; fixed WO] sth. is done or can be done very quickly and efficiently, without any trouble: **one, two, three (and it's done ⟨over, in the bag⟩); it will be ⟨was⟩ done in no time (flat); it will be ⟨was⟩ done just like that.**

Что ты мучаешься с зубом? Пойди к зубному врачу, он тебе вырвет зуб — раз-два и готово. Why are you suffering with your tooth? Go to the dentist and he'll pull it out—one, two, three and it's done.

Р-31 • **РАЗ ЗА РА́ЗОМ** [Invar; adv; fixed WO] **1.** repeatedly, many times in succession: **over and over (again); again and again; time and (time) again; time after time.**

Раз за разом возвращалась Алла к мысли об эмиграции, но не находила в себе сил принять окончательное решение. Alla returned time and again to the thought of emigrating, but couldn't find it in herself to make a final decision.

2. successively: **in a row; one after ⟨following⟩ the other ⟨another⟩; in succession.**

Раз за разом на улице прозвучали три выстрела. Three shots rang out on the street, one after another.

Р-32 • **РАЗ (И) НАВСЕГДА́** [AdvP; these forms only; adv; more often used with pfv verbs; fixed WO] once and forever, irrevocably: **once and for all; for good.**

Так заманчиво — раз и навсегда избавиться от нищеты и преступности, от горя и страданий (Буковский 1). It is so alluring—to escape from poverty and crime, grief and suffering once and for all (1a).

Р-33 • **РАЗ НА РАЗ НЕ ПРИХО́ДИТСЯ** *coll* [sent; pres only; fixed WO] things, conditions etc do not repeat themselves, they are different every time: **it's never the same twice; things are not always the same; [when comparing a less successful attempt, outcome etc with a more successful one] it can't be perfect every time.**

«Тут всегда такая хорошая рыбалка?» — «Ну, раз на раз не приходится». "Is the fishing here always this good?" "Well, it's never the same twice." ♦ «Осудят его?» — спросил Костенко. «Какой судья попадётся, — сказал Садчиков. — Раз на раз не приходится» (Семёнов 1). "Will he be convicted?" asked Kostyenko. "It depends on which judge he gets," said Sadchikov. "Things are not always the same" (1a).

Р-34 • **РАЗ ОТ РА́ЗУ ⟨-а⟩** [these forms only; adv; often used with compar form of Adv] with every new repetition, every new occurrence: **each ⟨every⟩ time.**

Он выступил в нескольких шахматных турнирах — раз от разу всё лучше. He competed in several chess tournaments and did better and better each time. ♦ Повторялось это и в следующие дни, но внимательный наблюдатель мог заметить, что раз от разу собак приходило всё меньше... (Владимов 1). [context transl] The same scene was repeated on the following days, but an attentive observer might have noticed that day by day fewer dogs came... (1a).

P-35 • РАЗ ПЛЮ́НУТЬ *(кому)* *highly coll* [Invar; usu. subj-compl with бытьø (subj: usu. infin or это); fixed WO] doing sth. is very easy, requires very little effort (from s.o.): (Y-у) сделать X – раз плю́нуть ≃ **doing X is a cinch ⟨a snap, a breeze, nothing, no sweat, as easy as pie⟩ (for Y); doing X is a piece of cake (for Y); (there's) nothing to it ⟨to doing X⟩; doing X is as easy (for Y) as falling off a log.**

Ему любую алгебраи́ческую зада́чу реши́ть – раз плю́нуть. Solving any algebra problem is a cinch for him. ♦ «...В связи... с отравле́нием атмосфе́ры... зара́зу ликвиди́ровать и учреди́ть в отдалённой ме́стности. Годи́тся?» – ...«Молоде́ц, – сказа́л бургоми́стр. – Голова́...» – «Ерунда́, – сказа́л Роше́пер. – Раз плю́нуть...» (Струга́цкие 1). "In view of the poisoning of the atmosphere...the germs are to be liquidated and reestablished in a remote province. How's that?"..."Good boy," said the burgomaster. "What a mind...." "Peanuts," said Rosheper. "Nothing to it" (1a).

P-36 • СА́МЫЙ РАЗ *substand* [NP; Invar; usu. subj-compl with бытьø (subj: infin); fixed WO] (the moment of speech or the time specified is) an ideal time or moment for doing sth.: **just the (right) time; the ⟨a⟩ perfect time ⟨moment⟩; there couldn't be a better time.**

P-37 • СЕМЬ РАЗ ПРИМЕ́РЬ ⟨ОТМЕ́РЬ⟩, (А) ОДИ́Н (РАЗ) ОТРЕ́ЖЬ [saying] before you do or decide sth. important, think it over carefully, plan well, take all the necessary precautions etc (because once sth. is done there is no undoing it): ≃ **look before you leap; better ⟨it's better to be⟩ safe than sorry.**

P-38 • С РАЗБЕ́ГА ⟨-y⟩ [PrepP; these forms only; adv] while running, having gained speed, while in full motion: **at a run; from a running start;** [in refer. to very fast motion only] **at a dead run.**

На э́тот призы́в выхо́дит из толпы́ па́рень и с разбе́га броса́ется в пла́мя (Салтыко́в-Щедри́н 1). [context transl] At this appeal a lad came forward from the crowd, took a running leap and hurled himself into the flames (1a).

P-39 • НЕ РАЗБЕРИ́-ПОЙМЁШЬ ⟨-ПОЙМИ́, -БЕРИ́⟩ *substand* [VP; these forms only] it is impossible to understand, make sense of (a situation): **who (the hell) knows?; you don't know what to make of it; you can't make head(s) or tail(s) of it; you can't figure it out.**

Нау́тро разъе́хались все, кро́ме Русла́на, кото́рый уже́ с неде́лю торча́л на да́че: то ли он рабо́ту домо́й, то ли заведе́ние тако́е... что посеща́ть не ну́жно, а денежки пла́тят. Не разбери́-поймёшь... (Три́фонов 6). The next morning they all departed except Ruslan, who had been hanging around the dacha for a week. Hard to tell whether he was on vacation, whether he had brought work home or whether...he could collect his pay without having to go in. Who knows? (6a).

P-40 • РАЗБИ́ТЬ ⟨РАЗГРОМИ́ТЬ⟩ НА́ГОЛОВУ *кого* [VP; subj: human (usu. pl) or collect] to defeat s.o. overwhelmingly: X-ы разби́ли Y-ов наголову ≃ **Xs routed ⟨wiped out, crushed, utterly defeated etc⟩ Ys.**

Он [Григо́рий] знал, что при пе́рвом же серьёзном столкнове́нии с какой-либо регуля́рной кавалери́йской ча́стью Кра́сной А́рмии они [ба́нда Фоми́на] бу́дут разгро́млены наголову. И всё же оста́лся подру́чным у Фоми́на... (Шо́лохов 5). He [Grigory] knew they [Fomin's band] would be routed in their first encounter with any regular cavalry unit of the Red Army. But still he stayed on as Fomin's righthand man... (5a). ♦ «Разби́тые

наголову белобанди́ты всех масте́й от Ке́ренского до Дени́кина не успоко́ились...» (Войно́вич 4). "Utterly defeated, White Bandits of every stripe from Kerensky to Denikin did not settle down..." (4a).

P-41 • РАЗБО́ЙНИК С БОЛЬШО́Й ДОРО́ГИ [NP; fixed WO] a scoundrel, crook, thief: **highway robber; bandit.**

«О, разбо́йник с большо́й доро́ги. На похме́лку у сы́на кни́ги вору́ет...» (Черне́нок 2). "Oh, what a highway robber. He steals his son's books for something to drink..." (2a).

P-42 • БЕЗ РАЗБО́РА ⟨-y⟩ [PrepP; these forms only; adv] without making distinctions between various people or things, choosing at random: **indiscriminately; without discrimination; without picking or choosing.**

Расстре́ливали и свои́х и чужи́х без разбо́ру (Манде́льштам 2). They were always shooting friend and foe indiscriminately (2a). ♦ «...Когда́ бог ука́зывает ей [Богома́тери] на прогвождённые ру́ки и но́ги её сы́на и спра́шивает: как я прощу́ его́ мучи́телей, — то она́ вели́т всем святы́м, всем му́ченикам, всем а́нгелам и арха́нгелам пасть вме́сте с не́ю и моли́ть о поми́ловании всех без разбо́ра» (Достое́вский 1). "...When God points out to her [the Mother of God] the nail-pierced hands and feet of her Son and asks: 'How can I forgive his tormentors?' she bids all the saints, all the martyrs, all the angels and archangels to fall down together with her and plead for the pardon of all without discrimination" (1a).

P-43 • С РАЗБО́РОМ [PrepP; Invar; adv] showing preference for certain people or things over others: **discriminately; selectively; (be) choosy (about sth.);** [in limited contexts] **pick and choose.**

Попа́сть в э́тот коопера́тив тру́дно, туда́ принима́ют с разбо́ром. It's difficult to get into that cooperative; they're choosy about whom they accept.

P-44 • К ША́ПОЧНОМУ РАЗБО́РУ прийти́, яви́ться, попа́сть и т. п. *coll* [PrepP; Invar; adv; fixed WO] (to arrive, appear etc) at the very end or conclusion of sth.: **when ⟨(just) as, not...till⟩ the show is over; when it's all over (but the shouting); when ⟨as⟩ things are coming to a close; when everybody is leaving ⟨is getting ready to leave⟩; at the tail end (of a party ⟨a meeting etc⟩).**

На́ши посети́тели монастыря́ к обе́дне... не пожа́ловали, а прие́хали ро́вно к ша́почному разбо́ру (Достое́вский 1). Our monastery visitors did not...appear at the liturgy, but arrived just as the show was over (1a). ♦ «Отправля́ю тебя́ пе́рвым парохо́дом...» — «Выхо́дит, про́чие к ша́почному разбо́ру поспе́ют?» (Макси́мов 1). "I'm sending you in the first ship..." "Does that mean the others won't get there till the show is over?" (1a). ♦ «Пойдём к све́тлой зау́трене». — «Иди́те, я по́сле [*ungrammat* = по́сле] приду́». — «К шапо́шному [*phonetic spelling*] разбо́ру?» (Шо́лохов 2). "Come with us to the morning service." "I'll come along later." "When it's all over?" (2a). ♦ Мы о́чень опозда́ли на совеща́ние — пришли́ к ша́почному разбо́ру, когда́ обсужде́ние ва́жных вопро́сов бы́ло зако́нчено. We were really late for the meeting. We arrived when things were coming to a close and all the important questions had already been discussed.

P-45 • РА́ЗВЕ ЧТО ⟨ТО́ЛЬКО, ЛИШЬ, ВОТ⟩ **1.** [Particle] except for, or possibly except for (the specified thing, person, event etc): **except (perhaps ⟨maybe⟩);** [in limited contexts] **but only.**

«Мы про́чно засе́ли там в желе́зном до́те. Желе́зный – так мы его́ называ́ли, ду́мали, нас ничто́ отту́да не вы́шибет. Ра́зве что – прика́з захвати́ть го́род» (Миха́йловская 1). "We sat there secure in an iron pillbox. We called it iron because we thought nothing could get us out of it, except perhaps an order to seize the city"

(1a). ♦ Друзей у него не было. Компании по пьяному делу он не водил — редко, разве что по большим праздникам, пропускал рюмочку (Абрамов 1). He had no friends. He did not indulge in drinking sessions—on rare occasions he would down a glass, but only on important holidays (1a). ♦ «Нет, так не пойдёт! Желаете счастья зятю и дочери, а сами не пьёте», — упрекнул Кокетай засмущавшегося деда Момуна. «Ну разве что за счастье, я что ж», — заторопился старик (Айтматов 1). [context transl] "No, no, that will not do! You toast to the happiness of your daughter and your son-in-law and then don't drink yourself," Koketay reproached the embarrassed Momun. "Well, if it's to happiness, sure…" he mumbled hurriedly (1a).

2. [subord Conj; restr-concessive] except, or possibly except, in the named situation, set of circumstances etc: **except ⟨perhaps ⟨maybe⟩⟩ when ⟨if, that⟩; [in limited contexts] unless.**

«…Я из квартиры не выеду, ни под каким нажимом. Разве что меня вместе с беременной женой вынесут на руках» (Войнович 3). "…I will not move out of that apartment under any sort of pressure. Except maybe if they carry me and my pregnant wife out in their arms" (3a). ♦ «…Тайно, по ночам приторговывает рабами наш князь. Но торгует он рабами из чужеземных народов. Ну разве что иногда его люди прихватят зазевавшегося эндурца» (Искандер 5). "Our prince does trade in slaves secretly, at night. But the slaves he sells are from foreign nations. Well, except that his men occasionally catch an unwary Endursky" (5a).

Р-46 • (ВОТ) И ВЕСЬ РАЗГОВОР ⟨СКАЗ⟩; ВОТ (ТЕБЕ́ ⟨ВАМ⟩) И ВЕСЬ РАЗГОВОР ⟨СКАЗ⟩ *all coll* [usu. indep. clause; these forms only; fixed WO] (used to emphasize that the preceding statement has exhausted, concluded the topic) there is nothing more to talk about, this is the end of the conversation: **and that's that; that's all there is to it; case closed.**

Являются два полиция, приказывают отцу следовать за ними. Куда? В комендатуру… Отец пытается отговориться… но полицаи ничего не желают знать — приказано доставить Ивановского в комендатуру, и весь разговор! (Рыбаков 1). Two policemen turned up and told father to come with them. Where to? To the commandant's.…Father tried to talk himself out of it…but the police wouldn't have any of it, they'd been ordered to deliver Ivanovsky to the commandant, and that was that! (1a). ♦ «Что я скажу людям-то? Спросят, куда делась, — что я говорить буду?»… — «Скажи, что ничего не знаешь, вот и весь сказ» (Шолохов 5). "…What shall I tell people? What shall I say when they ask what's become of you?" "Say you don't know and that's all there is to it" (5a).

Р-47 • ДРУГОЙ РАЗГОВОР *coll* [NP; sing only; subj-compl with быть∅ (subj: usu. это, occas. any noun or a clause); fixed WO] that changes (or would change) the situation (entirely): **that's another ⟨a different⟩ story (altogether); that's (quite) another ⟨a different⟩ matter; that's different ⟨something else altogether⟩; [in fut and condit clauses] things ⟨everything, it⟩ will ⟨would⟩ be different.**

[Говорящий — кот] «Я напудрил усы, вот и всё. Другой разговор был бы, если б я побрился! Бритый кот — это действительно уж безобразие, тысячу раз готов признать это» (Булгаков 9). [The speaker is a cat] "I powdered my whiskers, that's all! It would be different if I had shaved! A shaven tom would indeed be outrageous, I agree a thousand times" (9a).

Р-48 • ПЕРЕВОДИ́ТЬ/ПЕРЕВЕСТИ́ РАЗГОВОР НА ДРУГОЕ ⟨НА ДРУГУ́Ю ТЕ́МУ⟩ [VP; subj: human] to drop a topic and begin talking about sth. different: X перевёл разговор на другое ≃ **X changed the subject.**

Открывай планету, называй её собственным именем, определяй физические характеристики… [Школьники] будут взирать на тебя с почтительностью, но учитель при встрече спросит только: «Ты всё ещё в ГСП [Группе Свободного Поиска]?»» — и переведёт разговор на другую тему… (Стру-гацкие 2). Discover a planet, name it after yourself, determine its physical characteristics.…[The school kids] would gaze at you in awe. But your old teacher would ask only: "Are you still with the IRU [Independent Reconnaissance Unit]?" Then he'd change the subject… (2a).

Р-49 • РАЗГОВО́Р КОРО́ТКИЙ *у кого с кем;* ШУ́ТКИ КОРО́ТКИЕ ⟨КО́РОТКИ⟩ *all coll* [VP_subj with быть∅; fixed WO (var. with short-form Adj)] (may refer to dealing with one person, a group of people, people of a given type etc) s.o. deals with another or others in an abrupt and decisive manner, not wasting time on conversations or explanations: у X-а с Y-ом разговор короткий ≃ **X takes swift action with Y; X takes quick, firm action with Y; X doesn't waste ⟨mince⟩ words with Y.**

«С прогульщиками у меня разговор короткий, — сказал декан. — За шесть пропущенных без уважительных причин занятий снимаю со стипендии». "I take swift action with students who cut classes," said the dean. "Six cuts without a good reason, and I pull your stipend."

Р-50 • ЧТО ЗА РАЗГОВО́Р!; КАКО́Й (МО́ЖЕТ БЫТЬ) РАЗГОВО́Р!; О ЧЁМ РАЗГОВО́Р ⟨РЕ́ЧЬ⟩! *all coll* [Interj; these forms only; fixed WO] (often used in answer to a question, request etc) it is completely understood and agreed to, certainly: **of course!; it ⟨that⟩ goes without saying; what question can there be?; [in limited contexts] (there's) no need to even ask.**

«Это [генерал Корнилов] кристальной честности человек, и только он один в состоянии поставить Россию на ноги… Какой может быть разговор? Всякий порядочный человек за Корнилова!» (Шолохов 3). "He [General Kornilov] is a man of perfect integrity and he and he alone is capable of putting Russia on her feet again.…What question can there be? Every decent person is bound to support Kornilov" (3a).

Р-51 • И РАЗГОВО́РА ⟨-у⟩ НЕТ ⟨БЫТЬ НЕ МО́ЖЕТ⟩ *(о чём) coll* [VP; impers; pres only; fixed WO] **1.** sth. is impossible, ruled out altogether: об X-е и разговора быть не может ≃ **X is out of the question; there is ⟨can be⟩ no question of X; [in limited contexts] that isn't even up ⟨a matter⟩ for discussion.**

Главный инженер сказал мне, что о том, чтобы перевести меня на работу в Москву, и разговора быть не может. «Вы нужны нам здесь». The chief engineer told me that my being transferred to Moscow was out of the question. "We need you here."

2. yes, certainly: **no question!; (what a question ⟨what are you talking about⟩,) of course one will ⟨can etc⟩!; (but,) of course!**

«Ты думаешь, он справится?» — «И разговору нет!» "Do you think he can manage?" "What a question! Of course he can!"

Р-52 • БЕЗ ВСЯ́КИХ РАЗГОВО́РОВ; БЕЗ ВСЯ́КОГО РАЗГОВО́РА *both coll* [PrepP; these forms only; adv; fixed WO] **1.** (to do sth.) without raising any objections: **without any arguments; [in direct address] and no arguments ⟨back talk⟩; and no ifs, ands, or buts; [in limited contexts] and I don't want to hear any back talk.**

Вам дали приказ — вот и выполняйте без всяких разговоров. You were ordered to do something, so do it—and no arguments.

2. (to do sth. to s.o.) quickly and decisively, without wasting time on discussion, explanations etc: **without wasting words; wasting no time on talk; [in limited contexts] without (even) giving s.o. time to object ⟨explain (himself) etc⟩.**

Когда Антон в третий раз опоздал на работу, бригадир уволил его без всяких разговоров. The third time Anton was late to work, the foreman fired him without even giving him time to object.

P-53 • **С РАЗГО́НА** ⟨-у⟩ [PrepP; these forms only; adv] while in full motion, having gained speed: [of a means of transportation] **(while) barreling along; (while going ⟨moving** etc⟩**) at full ⟨high⟩ speed; (while going) full tilt;** [of a person or animal] **at a dead run.**

Маши́на с разго́на вре́залась в сара́й. The car slammed into the shed at high speed.

P-54 • **В РАЗГО́НЕ** *coll* [PrepP; Invar; subj-compl with copula (subj: human or a noun denoting a means of transportation, pl)] some people are not in their offices, workplaces etc, but out doing things (taking care of small tasks, attending meetings etc); some trucks (buses etc) are not in their garages or parking lots, but out being used (making deliveries, running their routes etc): X-ы в разго́не ≃ [of people] **Xs are out on ⟨running⟩ errands; Xs are running about ⟨around⟩; Xs are tied up elsewhere;** [of means of transportation] **Xs are in use; Xs are (out) on the road.**

Никого́ из мои́х помо́щников сейча́с нет: все в разго́не. None of my assistants are here now—they're all out on errands.

P-55 • **НЕ РАЗГО́НИШЬСЯ** *coll* [VP; neg pfv fut, gener. 2nd pers sing only] (used in refer. to the impossiblity of undertaking or implementing sth. under the existing circumstances, with the available funds etc) only very little can be done: **you can't do much; there isn't much you can do; you can't get anywhere ⟨very far⟩.**

Ей прихо́дится эконо́мить, на её зарпла́ту не разго́нишься. She has to cut corners because you can't get very far on her salary.

P-56 • **С ⟨СО ВСЕГО́⟩ РАЗМА́ХА** ⟨-у⟩ [PrepP; these forms only; adv] **1.** with great power or momentum: **with all one's might; hard; as hard as one can; full force.**

По́сле э́того он поверну́лся к ма́льчику... и с разма́ху си́льно шлёпнул его́ ладо́нью по голове́ (Искандер 5). After that he turned to the boy...and slapped his head with all his might (5a). ♦ Укоро́ченное те́ло Жи́кина дёрнулось, и самоде́льная теле́жка, к кото́рой он был приторо́чен ремня́ми, с разма́ху уда́рила вертуха́я по нога́м чуть ни́же коле́н. Тот ру́хнул как подко́шенный... (Войнович 4). ...Zhikin's abbreviated body gave a twitch and his homemade cart, to which he was strapped with belts, struck the other guard full force just below the knee. The guard collapsed as if he'd been shot... (4a).

2. while already in motion, having gained speed: [of a vehicle] **(while) barreling along; (while going ⟨moving⟩** etc⟩**) at full ⟨high⟩ speed; (while going) (at) full tilt; (while going) full throttle;** [of a person or animal] **at a dead run.**

Са́нки с разма́ху налете́ли на пень, и мы все вы́валились в снег. The sled barreled into the tree stump at full tilt, and we all fell off into the snow.

P-57 • **С РАЗМА́ХОМ** [PrepP; Invar; adv] to a great degree or measure, impressively, grandly: **on a grand ⟨large⟩ scale; in a big way;** [in limited contexts] **think ⟨plan** etc⟩ **big.**

Но пре́жде чем де́лать моде́ли, нужна́ тео́рия. Бу́дут разраба́тывать математи́ческий аппара́т. Пойду́т симпо́зиумы, конгре́ссы и т. п. Создаду́т институ́ты. Де́лать, как говори́тся, так по-большо́му! У нас всё с разма́хом де́лается (Зиновьев 1). "But before you make your models, you have to have a theory. So they'll have to develop a conceptual mathematical scheme. There'll be conferences and congresses and so on. Institutes will be founded. If the thing's going to be done at all, it had better be done on a grand scale. We always think big" (1a).

P-58 • **БОЛЬША́Я РА́ЗНИЦА** [NP; sing only; subj-compl with быть∅ (subj: э́то, infin, or subord clause or clauses); fixed WO] some circumstance (action etc) is entirely different from another previously mentioned circumstance (action etc): э́то больша́я ра́зница ≃ **there's ⟨it makes⟩ a big difference.**

Ты согласи́лся перейти́ в друго́й отде́л сам, а меня́ заста́вили. Э́то больша́я ра́зница. You *agreed* to transfer to another department, but I was *forced* to transfer—there's a big difference.

P-59 • **КАКА́Я РА́ЗНИЦА** *(кому)?* [NP; Invar; usu. indep. clause; fixed WO] does it really make any difference?: **what's the difference?; what difference does it (really) make?; what do I ⟨you** etc⟩ **care?;** [in limited contexts] **isn't it all the same anyway?**

Ири́на Ви́кторовна то́тчас вы́гнала Мишеля́ из ко́мнаты № 475, причём, бу́дто бы оговори́вшись, назвала́ его́ Анато́лем... Он возмути́лся, а Ири́на Ви́кторовна сказа́ла ему́, махну́в руко́й: «Да ну, не всё ли равно́? Мише́ль, Анато́ль — кака́я ра́зница?» (Залыгин 1). Irina Viktorovna lost no time in driving Michel out of Room 475. In a deliberate slip of the tongue she called him Anatole....He bridled, but Irina Viktorovna simply waved her hand and said, "Come on! What does it matter? Michel or Anatole—what's the difference?" (1a). ♦ ...В су́щности, кака́я ра́зница, на два́дцать лет ра́ньше ли, по́зже ли роди́лся и у́мер Держа́вин?.. (Терц 3). ...What difference does it really make whether Derzhavin died twenty years earlier or later than he did?... (3a). ♦ Ах, кака́я тебе́ ра́зница, кто он... не всё ли равно́! (Битов 2). Oh, what do you care who it was—what does it matter! (2a).

P-60 • **ДВЕ БОЛЬШИ́Е РА́ЗНИЦЫ** *highly coll* [NP; pl only; subj-compl with быть∅ (subj: any two common nouns, infinitives, or clauses), usu. pres; fixed WO] two people (things, or phenomena, or two groups of people, things, or phenomena) are totally different, defy comparison: X и Y — две больши́е ра́зницы ≃ **there is a big ⟨great⟩ difference between X and Y; there is a world of difference between X and Y; thing X and thing Y are two very ⟨totally⟩ different things.**

«Она́ [Варва́ра] и мои́ сёстры — э́то... две больши́е ра́зницы. Бо́йкие бары́шни, живы́е... Да и молоды́е, — са́мая ста́ршая втро́е моло́же твое́й Варва́ры» (Сологуб 1). "She [Varvara] and my sisters? Listen here...there is a great difference between them. They [my sisters] are lively young ladies, full of pep....And they are young, why, the very oldest is three times younger than your Varvara" (1a).

P-61 • **РА́ЗНЫЕ РА́ЗНОСТИ** *coll* [NP; sing rare; fixed WO] (often of various topics of conversation) very diverse things, phenomena: **all kinds ⟨sorts⟩ of things ⟨goods** etc⟩**; this and that; various (and sundry) things;** [in limited contexts] **everything under the sun.**

Стару́шки люби́ли посиде́ть на со́лнышке, поговори́ть о ра́зных ра́зностях. The old women loved to sit in the sun and talk about various and sundry things. ♦ Вади́м рассужда́л о ра́зных ра́зностях, переска́кивал с оправда́ния Дими́трова на постано́вку «Мёртвых душ» во МХА́Те, с «но́вого ку́рса» Рузве́льта на смерть Лунача́рского в Менто́не (Рыбаков 2). Vadim was holding forth on everything under the sun, jumping from the Reichstag fire to the new production of *Dead Souls* at the Moscow Arts, from Roosevelt's New Deal to the death of Lunacharsky in Menton (2a).

P-62 • **РА́ЗОМ ⟨ТО⟩ ГУ́СТО, РА́ЗОМ ⟨ТО⟩ ПУ́СТО** [saying] there is either a lot of sth. or none at all: ≃ **(it's) feast or famine; (it's) either feast or famine ⟨a feast or a famine⟩.**

P-63 • **ЧТОБ ТЕБЯ́ ⟨ЕГО́ и т. п.⟩ РАЗОРВА́ЛО!; ЧТОБ ТЕБЯ́ ⟨ЕГО́ и т. п.⟩!** *all highly coll, rude* [Interj; these forms only; fixed WO] (used to express one's anger, indignation at s.o.) may terrible things happen to you: чтоб тебя́ разорва́ло! ≃ **damn ⟨darn, blast⟩ you!; (you can) go to hell!; the ⟨to⟩ hell with you!; the devil take you!; may you burn ⟨fry⟩ in hell!**

Соба́ки с раздира́ющим ду́шу ви́згом бро́сились на него́ [медве́дя] и отскочи́ли... «Ах, чтоб тебя́!» — с бо́лью кри́кнул Семён (Тендряков 1). The dogs flung themselves at the bear with earsplitting yelps, but fell back at once. "Damn you," Simon shouted with exasperation (1a). ♦ «Захар!» — кликнул Обломов. «О, чтоб вас там!»… (Гончаров 1). "Zakhar!" Oblomov called. "Oh, the devil take you!"… (1a).

P-64 • **ХОТЬ (ПОПОЛА́М) РАЗОРВИ́СЬ** *coll* [хоть + VP_{imper}; these forms only; fixed WO] **1.** [usu. subord clause] whatever you do, however much you try, you cannot attain the desired result: **no matter how hard you try; try as you might; try as hard as you like; knock yourself out.**

Асеев записал слова Есенина: «Никто тебя знать не будет, если не писать лирики: на фунт помолу нужен фунт навозу — вот что нужно. А без славы ничего не будет, хоть ты пополам разорвись — тебя не услышат» (Гладков 1). Aseyev wrote down his [Yesenin's] remarks word for word: "If you don't write lyrics, no one will ever know you: for every pound of flour, you need a pound of dung. Without fame, you won't get anywhere, try as hard as you like — no one will listen" (1a).

2. [usu. impers predic] (used when s.o. has to do several things at once, be in several places at the same time) it is very difficult for s.o. to cope with all the things he has to do simultaneously: **I have ⟨he has etc⟩ only got two hands (, after all); there is only one of me ⟨him etc⟩.**

«Хозяйство, дети — всё на мне, — жаловалась Мария, — всё приходится самой делать. Хоть разорвись…» "It's all on my shoulders," Maria complained, "the housework, the kids. I have to do everything myself, and I've only got two hands, after all."

P-65 • **В РАЗРЕ́ЗЕ** *чего, каком* [PrepP; Invar; the resulting PrepP is adv] (when looked at) from the indicated perspective, in the indicated respect: **in a [AdjP] light ⟨way⟩; from a [AdjP] angle.**

Ваша точка зрения мне ясна. Теперь давайте посмотрим на эту проблему в другом разрезе. I understand your point of view, but now let's look at this problem from another angle.

P-66 • **НИ РА́ЗУ НЕ…** [Invar; adv] not at any time, not on any occasion: **never (once); (never,) not once; not a single time.**

…Надо отдать ему должное, ни разу в жизни он ещё не был так тонок, точен, чуток — так умён (Битов 2). …To give him his due, he had never in his life been so subtle, exact, sensitive — so intelligent (2a). ♦ Митя хоть и знал этого купца в лицо, но знаком с ним не был и даже ни разу не говорил с ним (Достоевский 1). Though Mitya knew the merchant by sight, he was not acquainted with him and had never once spoken to him (1a). ♦ «Вон бери пример, здесь старуха одна едет, она за всю жизнь ни разу на своего старика не крикнула» (Распутин 1). "You ought to take a lesson from that old lady in our compartment. She's never yelled at her old man in her life, not once…" (1a).

P-67 • **(И) РАД БЫ В РАЙ, ДА ГРЕХИ́ НЕ ПУС-КА́ЮТ** [saying] s.o. (usu. the speaker) would like to do sth., but cannot for reasons beyond his control: ≃ **I would if I could (, but I can't so I won't ⟨shan't⟩).**

[author's usage] «Документы?» Паспорт свой Влад подавал уже безо всякой надежды. И действительно, слегка полистав серую книжицу, кадровик безо всякого выражения обронил: «Не пойдёт… Рад бы в рай, да, сам понимаешь, начальство мне оформление твоё не санкционирует…» (Максимов 2). [context transl] "Papers?" Vlad handed over his passport, but without hope. As he had expected, having flipped through the gray booklet the man gave it back with an expressionless face and said: "No good.…Myself, I'd be happy to take you on, but you know how it is: my boss would never allow you to sign on…" (2a).

P-68 • **РАЙ ЗЕМНО́Й** [NP; sing only; usu. this WO] a beautiful place where one can feel happy and at peace: **paradise ⟨heaven⟩ on earth; (a real) paradise.**

P-69 • **КАК РАК** **красный, покраснеть** *coll* [как + NP; Invar; adv (intensif)] (to be, grow) very (red in the face): **(be ⟨turn⟩) (as) red as a beet ⟨a lobster⟩; (turn ⟨flush⟩) beet red; (blush) furiously ⟨scarlet, beet red⟩.**

…Агеев выскочил за Громовым в зону красный как рак (Марченко 1). …When Ageyev scrambled out into the zone behind Gromov he was as red as a beet (1a). ♦ Увидев Наташу, Николай Иванович обомлел. Несколько справившись с собою, весь красный как рак, он объявил, что счёл долгом поднять рубашечку, лично принести её… (Булгаков 9). At the sight of Natasha, Nikolay Ivanovich was petrified. Then he collected himself a little and, red as a lobster, declared that he had deemed it his duty to pick up the shift and return it personally… (9a). ♦ «А знаете, Авдотья Романовна, вы сами ужасно как похожи на вашего брата, даже во всём!» — брякнул он вдруг, для себя самого неожиданно, но тотчас же, вспомнив о том, что сейчас говорил ей же про брата, покраснел как рак… (Достоевский 3). "You know, Miss Raskolnikov, you're terribly like your brother — in everything!" he blurted out all of a sudden, surprising even himself, and then at once, remembering what he had just said to her about her brother, he turned as red as a lobster… (3a).

P-70 • **КАК РАК НА МЕЛИ́** **сидеть, оказаться и т. п.** *coll* [как + NP; Invar; adv or subj-compl with copula (subj: human); fixed WO] (to be, find o.s.) in a very difficult position: **in a tight spot; in a (real) jam ⟨fix, pickle, pinch⟩; up the creek (without a paddle).**

P-71 • **КОГДА́ ⟨ПОКА́⟩ РАК (НА ГОРЕ́) СВИ́СТНЕТ** *highly coll* [subord clause; adv] in the very distant future if at all, probably never: **when hell freezes over; on a cold day in hell ⟨in July⟩; when pigs fly; when ⟨not until⟩ the cows come home.**

«Как ты думаешь, когда он вернёт деньги?» — «Когда рак свистнет». "When do you think he'll pay me back?" "When hell freezes over."

P-72 • **ЗНАТЬ, ГДЕ РА́КИ ЗИМУ́ЮТ** *coll* [VP; subj: human; pres or past; only знать conjugates; fixed WO] to be clever, sometimes sly, and know how to act to one's own advantage: **X знает, где раки зимуют ≃ X knows the score ⟨what's what, his way around⟩; X knows how to look out for himself ⟨for number one⟩; X knows on which side his bread is buttered.**

P-73 • **ПОКАЗА́ТЬ, ГДЕ РА́КИ ЗИМУ́ЮТ** *кому coll* [VP; subj: human; most often 1st pers, fut; only показать conjugates; fixed WO] (often used as a threat) to make things very unpleasant for s.o. (by punishing him, proving him wrong, showing one's superiority etc): **X покажет Y-у, где раки зимуют ≃ X will show Y a thing or two ⟨what's what, what X can do⟩; X will give Y something to remember X by; Y will know better when X is through ⟨done⟩ with him.**

«Ничего, Иосиф! — воскликнул Ворошилов, потрясённый тем, что вождь не только понимает его обиды, но и ставит их рядом со своими, — ты им ещё покажешь, где раки зимуют…» (Искандер 3). "Never mind, Iosif!" Voroshilov exclaimed, electrified by the fact that the Leader not only understood his hurt feelings but placed them on a level with his own. "You'll show them a thing or two" (3a). ♦ В его голосе звучало такое искреннее убеждение, такая несомненная решимость, что мне невольно пришло на мысль: да, если этот человек не попадёт под суд, то он покажет, где раки зимуют! (Салтыков-Щедрин 2). There was such sincere conviction in his voice, such indomitable resolution in every word he uttered, that I couldn't help thinking, "Ah, if this man's lucky enough to escape being put on trial, he'll certainly show them what's what!" (2a).

P-74 • **УЗНА́ТЬ, ГДЕ РА́КИ ЗИМУ́ЮТ** *coll* [VP; subj: human; usu. 2nd or 3rd pers, fut; only узнать conjugates; fixed

WO] **1.** to (begin to) experience serious difficulties, misfortune: X узнает, где раки зимуют ≃ **X will find out what real trouble is** ⟨**what tough sledding is all about**⟩; **X will get a taste of real hardship** ⟨**trouble**⟩; **X is in for a rough ride.**

2. (used as a threat or warning) to be punished severely: X узнает, где раки зимуют ≃ **X will get what's coming to him; person Y will give X something to remember Y by; person Y will show X a thing or two** ⟨**what's what**⟩.

«Руки у меня связаны, — горько жаловался он [градоначальник] глуповцам, — а то узнали бы вы у меня, где раки зимуют!» (Салтыков-Щедрин 1). "My hands are tied," he [the governor] complained bitterly to the Glupovites. "Otherwise I'd give you something to remember me by!" (1b).

Р-75 • ДЕРЖА́ТЬ СЕБЯ́ В РА́МКАХ ⟨В ГРАНИ́ЦАХ *obs*⟩ **(ПРИЛИ́ЧИЯ)** [VP; subj: human] to conduct o.s. in a restrained, correct manner, not go beyond the accepted rules in one's behavior: X держит себя в рамках (приличия) ≃ **X does not overstep his bounds** ⟨**limits**⟩; **X does not overstep the bounds of propriety; X keeps himself (with)in (certain) bounds; X stays within (certain) limits.**

«По-моему, — сказал Виктор, — у культурных людей гораздо больше оснований напиваться, чем у некультурных». — «Возможно, — согласился Павор. — Однако культурный человек обязан держать себя в рамках» (Стругацкие 1). "In my opinion," said Victor, "civilized people have far more reason to get drunk than uncivilized ones." "Possibly," said Pavor. "Except that a civilized person is obliged to keep himself in certain bounds" (1a).

Р-76 • ПО РАНЖИ́РУ [PrepP; Invar; adv] **1.** *obs* (of people) in ascending or descending order based upon height, size: **according to height** ⟨**size**⟩; **in size order** ⟨**order of size**⟩; **by height** ⟨**size**⟩.

И дед принялся рассказывать хорошо известную мальчику историю, как выстроили их, трудармейцев, привезённых с разных концов страны, в длиннющий строй по ранжиру, и оказалось, что киргизы почти все в самом конце... (Айтматов 1). And grandfather fell to telling the story, well known to the lad, of how they, the labour-soldiers who'd been transported there from various corners of the country, were set out in a long, long line according to height. It turned out that the Kirghizians were almost all at the very end... (1b).

2. in order based on seniority, rank, or significance: **according to rank** ⟨**seniority, status**⟩; **by rank** ⟨**seniority**⟩; **in order of importance; in accordance with their** ⟨**our, your**⟩ **importance** ⟨**status** etc⟩.

Ну что ж... пора выстроить по ранжиру должностных лиц, вступивших по такому ерундовому делу на путь прямого нарушения... советских законов (Войнович 3). Well, now it's time...to arrange in order of importance the public servants who, over such a trivial matter, headed toward direct violation of Soviet law... (3a). ♦ ...Не только герои, но и писатели строго расставлены по ранжиру. Секретарь Союза писателей СССР считается писателем лучшим, чем секретарь Союза писателей РСФСР, а тот, в свою очередь, ценится выше секретаря областной или городской писательской организации (Войнович 1). It is not only heroes, but also writers, who are ranked in strict accordance with their importance. The secretary of the Soviet Writers' Union is considered a better writer than the secretary of the Russian Writers' Union, who in turn enjoys greater esteem than the secretaries of a province or municipal writers' organization (1a).

Р-77 • РА́НО И́ЛИ ПО́ЗДНО [AdvP; Invar; adv; fixed WO] (sth. will certainly happen, come to pass etc) sometime in the future: **sooner or later; in the end; ultimately.**

Тайное рано или поздно становится явным, говорит Мазила (Зиновьев 1). "Sooner or later secrets become widely known," said Dauber (1a).

Р-78 • БЕРЕДИ́ТЬ/РАЗБЕРЕДИ́ТЬ (ста́рую ⟨душе́вную, серде́чную⟩) РА́НУ *чью, кого, кому, в ком;* **БЕРЕДИ́ТЬ/РАЗБЕРЕДИ́ТЬ РА́НЫ** [VP; subj: human or abstr] to hurt s.o. by saying or doing sth. that is particularly painful to him: X бередит Y-ову рану ≃ **X is rubbing salt in Y's** ⟨**the**⟩ **wound; X is twisting a** ⟨**the**⟩ **knife in Y's wound;** ‖ X разбередил Y-ову старую рану ≃ **X rubbed salt in Y's old wound; X reopened Y's (old) wound(s).**

...К нему подсаживается совершенно посторонний человек и сразу, сам того не зная, начинает дымящуюся рану его сердца (Салтыков-Щедрин 2). ...A complete stranger sits down beside him and immediately, without being aware of it himself, begins to twist a knife in his open wound (2a). ♦ Он... мирно и с сочувствием расспрашивал об отношениях с женой, не бередя моих ран, а так, как бы между прочим (Лимонов 1). In a peaceful and sympathetic way he inquired about my relationship with my wife, not to reopen my wounds, he just asked, as if in passing (1a).

Р-79 • РАСПОЛОЖЕ́НИЕ ⟨СОСТОЯ́НИЕ⟩ ДУ́ХА *rather lit* [NP; sing only; fixed WO] a temporary disposition, state of one's feelings: **frame ⟨state⟩ of mind; mood; spirits; humor.**

А Чичиков в довольном расположении духа сидел в своей бричке, катившейся давно по столбовой дороге (Гоголь 3). As for Chichikov, he was in a contented frame of mind, sitting in his britska, which had for some time been rolling along the highroad (3c). ♦ Я приехал в довольно миролюбивом расположении духа, но всё это начинало меня бесить (Лермонтов 1). I had arrived in a fairly peaceable state of mind, but all this was beginning to annoy me (1a). ♦ «Ты сегодня в дурном расположении духа?» — «Да». — «Жаль...» (Федин 1). "You're in a bad mood today?" "Yes." "A pity..." (1a). ♦ В хорошем расположении духа Гитлер лёг спать (Войнович 4). Hitler went to bed in excellent spirits (4a). ♦ Однажды он [отец] пришёл ко мне в добром расположении духа, чего с ним давно не бывало... (Тургенев 3). One day Father came to me in a good humor—a mood I had not known him to be in for a long time (3c). ♦ Старик находился в хорошем расположении духа после дообеденного сна (Толстой 4). The old gentleman was in excellent humor after his nap (4a).

Р-80 • В РАСПОРЯЖЕ́НИИ *чьём, кого-чего* **бытьø, находи́ться; В РАСПОРЯЖЕ́НИЕ** *чьё, кого-чего* **поступа́ть, дава́ть, получа́ть** *кого-что* и т. п. [PrepP; these forms only; the resulting PrepP is subj-compl with copula with subj: human, concr, or count abstr (1st var.) or adv (2nd var.)] (to be or be placed under s.o.'s control, give or receive sth. etc) for use as s.o. sees fit: **at s.o.'s disposal ⟨service⟩; at the disposal (of s.o. ⟨sth.⟩); for s.o.'s use;** ‖ явиться в *чьё* распоряжение ≃ **present o.s. for duty (to s.o.).**

В первых числах августа смотритель получил приказ откомандировать Кошевого в распоряжение станичного правления (Шолохов 4). ...In the early days of August the overseer received orders to put Koshevoi at the disposal of the stanitsa authorities (4a).

Р-81 • РАСПРА́ВА КОРО́ТКАЯ ⟨КОРОТКА́⟩ *у кого (с кем);* **РАСЧЁТ КОРО́ТКИЙ** *all coll* [VP$_{subj}$ with бытьø; fixed WO (var. with short-form Adj)] s.o. takes quick and decisive punitive action (with another or others) (may refer to a one-time action or to the way s.o. generally treats a specific person or type of person): у X-а с Y-ом расправа будет короткая ≃ **X will make short work of Y; with X, justice will be swiftly executed; with X, retribution will be swift;** ‖ у X-а с такими, как Y, расправа короткая ≃ **X makes short work of people like Y; X has a quick way of handling ⟨dealing with⟩ people like Y; with X, justice is quickly executed; with X, retribution is swift.**

У него [батюшки] расправа была коротка. Он тотчас потребовал каналью француза. Доложили, что мусье давал мне свой урок. Батюшка пошёл в мою комнату. В это время Бопре спал на кровати сном невинности... Батюшка за ворот приподнял его с кровати, вытолкал из дверей и в тот же день прогнал со двора... (Пушкин 2). With him [my father], justice was swiftly executed. He instantly sent for that rogue, the Frenchman. He was informed that "Monsoo" was giving me my lesson. My father went up to my room. At that moment Beaupré was on the bed, sleeping the sleep of the innocent....My father lifted him off the bed by his collar, pushed him out of the door and banished him from the premises that very same day... (2b).

P-82 • НА РАСПУ́ТЬЕ; НА ПЕРЕПУ́ТЬЕ [PrepP; these forms only; subj-compl with copula (subj: human), adv, or non-agreeing modif] to be undecided, not know how to act at a time when one must make a decision: **(be) in a quandary;** [in refer. to a crucial decision only] **(be ⟨stand⟩) at a ⟨the⟩ crossroads.**

Новое поколение писателей романов не пишет, но оно стоит на распутье, потому что мысль не созревает... (Мандельштам 2). The new generation of prose writers has renounced the novel, but they are in a quandary because no new ideas have crystalized... (2a).

P-83 • В РАССРО́ЧКУ покупать, продавать *что* и т. п. [PrepP; Invar; adv] (to buy or sell sth., paying for it or receiving payment) on a gradual basis: **on an ⟨the⟩ installment plan; in installments; on time.**

На телевизор у нас деньги есть, а мебель придётся купить в рассрочку. We have the money for a TV, but we'll have to buy furniture on the installment plan.

P-84 • ДЕРЖА́ТЬ НА (ПОЧТИ́ТЕЛЬНОМ ⟨ИЗВЕ́СТ-НОМ⟩) РАССТОЯ́НИИ *кого;* **ДЕРЖА́ТЬ В ПОЧТИ́-ТЕЛЬНОМ ⟨ИЗВЕ́СТНОМ⟩ ОТДАЛЕ́НИИ** *rare* [VP; subj: human] to keep s.o. from becoming too close to or friendly with oneself: **X держит Y-а на (почтительном) расстоянии ≃ X keeps Y at arm's length ⟨at a (respectable) distance⟩; X doesn't let Y get too close.**

У Рины знакомых здесь было не меньше, чем у Кости. Компанейская, со всеми ладила, но умела держать людей на расстоянии (Рыбаков 2). Rina knew as many people as did Kostya. A companionable girl, she was on good terms with everyone, but she also knew how to keep people at arm's length (2a).

P-85 • ДЕРЖА́ТЬСЯ НА (ПОЧТИ́ТЕЛЬНОМ ⟨ИЗ-ВЕ́СТНОМ⟩) РАССТОЯ́НИИ *от кого;* **ДЕРЖА́ТЬСЯ В ПОЧТИ́ТЕЛЬНОМ ⟨ИЗВЕ́СТНОМ⟩ ОТДАЛЕ́-НИИ** *rare* [VP; subj: human] to avoid becoming too close to or friendly with s.o.: **X держится от Y-а на (почтительном) расстоянии ≃ X keeps his ⟨a safe, a respectable⟩ distance from Y; X steers clear of Y; X gives Y a wide berth.**

После одной кулачной истории я держался от него на расстоянии (Довлатов 1). After one incident of fisticuffs I learned to keep my distance from him... (1a).

P-86 • ТЕПЛИ́ЧНОЕ ⟨ОРАНЖЕРЕ́ЙНОЕ⟩ РАСТЕ́-НИЕ; ТЕПЛИ́ЧНЫЙ ЦВЕТО́К *usu. disapprov* [NP; sing only; usu. this WO] a spoiled, overprotected person who is ill-suited for life (as a result of his upbringing, way of life etc): **hothouse flower.**

Её невестка оказалась тепличным растением: не умеет ни готовить, ни убирать. It turns out that her daughter-in-law is a hothouse flower: she can neither cook nor clean.

P-87 • РАСТИ́ НАД СОБО́Й *highly coll, humor or iron* [VP; subj: human; fixed WO] to work, make an effort to improve one's standing, status, cultural level etc: **X растёт над собой ≃ X is working ⟨trying⟩ to improve ⟨to better⟩ himself;** [in limited contexts] **X is trying to get culture;** [of o.s., in response to the interlocutor's remark, praise etc] **we're trying; we're doing our best ⟨the best we can, what little we can⟩.**

...Вот посмотрите, за один только год сколько скопил полных собраний, не у каждого потомственного интеллигента найдёшь... Может, вы думаете, дорогая, что я эти книжки-то солю? Читаю, дорогая, вникаю, даже делаю выписки. Постоянно приходится расти над собой, жизнь подсказывает (Аксёнов 12). [context transl] "...Take a look, think how many complete collections I got in just one year, not every hereditary intellectual would have so many....Maybe you think I just salt these books away, darling? I read them, darling, delve, even take notes. You have to keep growing, life tells you that" (12a).

P-88 • ВЫВОДИ́ТЬ/ВЫ́ВЕСТИ ⟨ПУСКА́ТЬ/ПУ-СТИ́ТЬ, СПИ́СЫВАТЬ/СПИСА́ТЬ⟩ В РАСХО́Д *кого coll* [VP; subj: human] to execute s.o. by shooting him: **X вывел Y-а в расход ≃ X liquidated ⟨shot⟩ Y; X did away with Y; X finished Y off.**

«Привезли вчера дюжину абреков, — продолжал добродушный чекист, — похоже — пустят в расход...» (Искандер 3). "They brought in a dozen abreks [rebel outlaws] yesterday," the good-natured Chekist went on. "Looks like they're going to liquidate them" (3a).

P-89 • ВВОДИ́ТЬ/ВВЕСТИ́ В РАСХО́Д(Ы) ⟨В ИЗ-ДЕ́РЖКИ⟩ *кого;* **ВВОДИ́ТЬ/ВВЕСТИ́ ⟨ВГОНЯ́ТЬ/ВОГНА́ТЬ⟩ В УБЫ́ТОК** *coll* [VP; subj: human or abstr] to cause s.o. to spend money: **X ввёл Y-а в расход ≃ X put Y to expense; X put Y out of pocket; X caused Y expense;** [in limited contexts] **person X ran up Y's bill ⟨tab etc⟩.**

«Сегодня...Лиза ввела меня в непредвиденный расход. Ей до зарезу захотелось пообедать в хорошем ресторане и купить себе шёлковые чулки» (Шолохов 2). "Today...Liza put me to an unexpected expense. She suddenly had an irresistible desire to dine at a good restaurant and buy herself a pair of silk stockings" (2a). ♦ «...Мы оба женимся, я на твоей бывшей невесте, а ты на этой... как её?» — «Шазине?!»... — «Да, — сказал дядя Сандро неумолимо... — Твои родственники ждут тебя с невестой, а получится, что ты ввёл их в расходы ради того, чтобы женить своего друга» (Искандер 5). "We're both getting married, I to your former bride and you to this—what's her name?" "Shazina?!"..."Yes," Uncle Sandro said relentlessly...."Your relatives are expecting you with a bride, and it will look as if you've put them out of pocket to get your friend married" (5a). ♦ ...Платить придётся Игорю Владимировичу, неудобно его вводить в большие расходы (Рыбаков 2). ...Igor Vladimirovich would be paying and it would be embarrassing to run up a big bill (2a).

P-90 • БРАТЬ/ВЗЯТЬ РАСЧЁТ *coll* [VP; subj: human] to leave one's job: **X взял расчёт ≃ X quit (his job); X packed it in.**

...Я с этого вторника не работаю у вас, беру расчёт (Соколов 1). ...As of this Tuesday I'm not working there any more, I'm quitting (1a).

P-91 • ПРИНИМА́ТЬ/ПРИНЯ́ТЬ ⟨БРАТЬ/ВЗЯТЬ⟩ В РАСЧЁТ *кого-что* [VP; subj: human or collect] to consider s.o. or sth. in one's calculations, estimations, plans etc: **X принимает в расчёт Y-а ≃ X takes Y into consideration; X gives consideration to Y; X takes thing Y into account; X takes account of thing Y; X makes allowances for Y; X allows for thing Y; X bears it in mind (that...);** [in limited contexts] **X gives some weight to thing Y; X has person Y in mind;** ‖ *Neg* X не принимает Y-а в расчёт ≃ **X ignores Y.**

Кагановича, Ворошилова, Андреева, Шверника никто серьёзно в расчёт не принимал. Микоян умудрялся быть в мире со всеми… (Аллилуева 2). No one gave Kaganovich, Voroshilov, Andreyev, Shvernik any serious consideration. Mikoyan somehow managed to live in peace with them all… (2a). ♦ «Вы можете в Москве за два дня сделать дело, честное слово! Вы верите мне?..» – «Надо принять в расчёт дорогу!» (Федин 1). "You can do your business in Moscow in two days, take my word for it! D'you believe me?…" "The journey has to be taken into account!" (1a). ♦ …Лишняя жилплощадь – это лишняя уборка, тоже надо принять в расчёт (Залыгин 1). More space meant more cleaning – that had to be borne in mind (1a). ♦ Одной из главных причин «кампании петиций» была вера, что власти примут в расчёт общественное мнение и, по крайней мере, проявят гибкость… (Амальрик 1). One of the chief reasons for the petition campaign was the belief that the authorities would give some weight to this show of public opinion and at least evince some flexibility (1a). ♦ Секретарь тут лишь для проформы, его можно в расчёт не принимать (Зиновьев 1). "Secretary's only there for the sake of appearances; you can ignore him" (1a).

Р-92 • В РАСЧЁТЕ¹ *(с кем) coll* [PrepP; Invar; subj-compl with быть₀ (subj: human)] not obliged or indebted to s.o. in any way: X с Y-ом в расчёте ≃ **X and Y are even; X is (all) square with Y; X doesn't owe Y ⟨Y doesn't owe X⟩ a thing;** [in refer. to money only] **X doesn't owe Y ⟨Y doesn't owe X⟩ a kopeck ⟨a penny, a cent⟩.**

Р-93 • В РАСЧЁТЕ² *на что* or *(на то,) что…; С РАСЧЁТОМ* [PrepP; these forms only; the resulting PrepP is adv] expecting, anticipating, or hoping for sth. or that sth. will come to pass: **in anticipation of; with the expectation of ⟨that⟩; counting on ⟨upon⟩; banking on (the fact that); figuring that; in the hope that.**

Его [Михаила] удивил яркий свет в своей избе, который он увидел ещё от задних воротец. Не иначе как зажгли новую… лампу, которую он купил нынешней весной в расчёте на хорошие перемены в жизни (Абрамов 1). He [Mikhail] was surprised by the bright light in his house, which he noticed from the back gate. They must have lit the new…lamp that he had bought that spring in anticipation of changes for the better (1a). ♦ [Репников:] Да понимаешь ли ты, что этот прохвост пришёл сюда в расчёте, что ты ему поможешь? (Вампилов 3). [R.:] Do you realize that scoundrel came here counting on you to help him? (3b). ♦ …[Строители] станут планировать жильё с расчётом на эти бараки. Раз стоят [бараки], – значит, жить можно, мало ли что некрасиво и неудобно – не до жиру, быть бы живу (Тендряков 1). [context transl] …[The builders] would take these barracks into account in planning future housing needs. Since they [the barracks] were already there, they would argue, people might as well stay in them, in spite of the fact that they were ugly and inconvenient: beggars couldn't be choosers (1a).

Р-94 • РВАТЬ И МЕТАТЬ *coll* [VP; subj: human; fixed WO] (of s.o. who has a higher social status, holds a higher position, or is older than the person who provokes his reaction) to yell, swear, and/or gesticulate wildly in anger, indignation etc (the cause of which is usu. indicated in the context): X рвёт и мечет ≃ **X is ranting and raving; X is (going) mad with rage; X is blowing his top ⟨stack⟩.**

Нет, у неё другая новость: Твардовский уже четвёртый день меня ищет, рвёт и мечет… (Солженицын 2). No, she had brought another piece of news. Tvardovsky had been trying to find me for four days, and was ranting and raving… (2a). ♦ «…[Галиуллин] при имени Стрельникова рвёт и мечет…» (Пастернак 1). "…He [Galiullin] goes mad with rage at the sound of Strelnikov's name" (1a).

Р-95 • ГДЕ ТОНКО, ТАМ И РВЁТСЯ [saying] when misfortune strikes, it strikes the weakest part or member of some specified or implied whole, or, occas., it damages the whole by

striking the weakest part or member: ≃ **the thread breaks where it is weakest; where it is weakest, there the thread breaks; the weakest fruit drops earliest to the ground; the weak have the worst;** [often in refer. to a situation in which the weakest member of a group is jeopardizing, or has the potential to jeopardize, the group as a whole] **a chain is only as strong as its weakest link.**

Р-96 • ПЕРЕСЧИТАТЬ (все) РЁБРА ⟨КОСТИ⟩ *кому highly coll* [VP; subj: human; often fut or subjunctive] to beat s.o. severely: X Y-у все рёбра пересчитает ≃ **X will break ⟨bust⟩ Y's ribs ⟨legs etc⟩; X will beat the living daylights ⟨the tar, the stuffing⟩ out of Y.**

«На старичишке решила зло сорвать… Ты бы в городе кой-кому рёбра пересчитала бы…» (Искандер 4). "Had to take it out on a wretched old man….If you were going to break anyone's ribs, it should have been someone in the city" (4a).

Р-97 • РЕВМЯ РЕВЕТЬ *coll* [VP; subj: human] to cry very hard and loudly: X ревмя ревел ≃ **X cried his eyes out; X howled ⟨bawled⟩ for all he was worth.**

…Они [ребята] ловили меня, обхватывали за колени, ревмя ревели, приговаривая: «Евгеничку Семёновну опять на этап»… (Гинзбург 2). …They [the children] caught me, clung to me, howled for all they were worth, and chanted: "Our Eugenia Semyonovna is off to camp again!" (2a).

Р-98 • РЕДКО ⟨хоть РЕДКО⟩, ДА МЕТКО *говорить и т. п. coll* [AdvP; these forms only; adv; fixed WO] (to speak, say sth.) rarely, but always getting to the heart of the matter: **talk ⟨speak⟩ little but say much; be short on words but long on meaning.**

Человек он был замкнутый, но неглупый. Говорил редко, да метко. He was a private person, but quite intelligent. He spoke little but said much.

Р-99 • В РЕДКОСТЬ [PrepP; Invar] **1.** *obs* [adv] very infrequently: **hardly ever; rarely.**

2. ~ *(кому, у кого, для кого, где) coll* [subj-compl with быть₀ (subj: concr, count abstr, human, or infin)] some type of person (thing, phenomenon etc) is rare, seldom encountered: Х-ы (для Y-а ⟨в месте Z⟩) в редкость ≃ **Xs ⟨people/things like X⟩ are a rarity (for Y ⟨in place Z⟩); Xs are not at all common (in place Z); Xs are rare occurrences (in place Z); Y doesn't see Xs ⟨people/things like X⟩ very often.**

Такие засухи в наших местах в редкость. Droughts of this sort are not at all common in our region.

Р-100 • МУЗЕЙНАЯ РЕДКОСТЬ [NP; fixed WO] **1.** a rare and very valuable object of art or historical relic: **museum piece; collector's item; rare specimen.**

2. *humor or iron* [often subj-compl with copula (subj: concr, human, or abstr)] an object, phenomenon, or type of person that is rarely encountered (because the object is outdated, the phenomenon is a thing of the past, the type of person is highly unusual etc): **rare specimen; antique; museum piece; relic; artifact.**

[Вера:] Вы хороший муж. Прямо – музейная редкость (Вампилов 5). [V.:] You're a good husband. Really a rare specimen (5b).

Р-101 • НА РЕДКОСТЬ [PrepP; Invar] **1.** [modif (intensif)] extremely, to an extent rarely encountered: **exceptionally; uncommonly; unusually; most; extraordinarily; exceedingly;** [in limited contexts] **a rare** [NP].

Ноябрь был на редкость тёплый, настоящее бабье лето (Горенштейн 1). November was exceptionally warm, a real Indian summer (1a). ♦ Мой спутник оказался очень услужливым и на редкость молчаливым стариком (Искандер 3). The old man proved to be a very obliging and uncommonly taciturn traveling companion (3a). ♦ ...Он нашёл вместо Фаины лишь маленькое, на редкость ласковое письмо. Она ушла (Битов 2). ...He found, instead of Faina, only a short, unusually affectionate letter. She was gone (2a). ♦ Пожалуй, единственное преимущество его состояло в том, что он не боялся уронить себя в чьих-то глазах... В этом смысле Момун, сам того не подозревая, был на редкость счастливым человеком (Айтматов 1). Perhaps his only advantage was that he never feared losing face with others....In this respect, Momun, without suspecting it himself, was extraordinarily fortunate (1a). ♦ Служащий метро Обри был на редкость уродлив... (Эренбург 4). Aubry, a subway employee, was exceedingly ugly... (4a).

2. [adv (intensif)] excellently, highly satisfactorily, as happens rarely: **extremely well;** ‖ знать своё дело ~ ≃ **really know one's business ⟨stuff⟩; know one's business ⟨stuff⟩ inside and out; know all the ins and outs (of sth.);** ‖ удаться ~ ≃ **turn ⟨come⟩ out perfectly ⟨great etc⟩; be as good as they come; be a great success;** ‖ нам ~ повезло ≃ **we (really) lucked out; we had a rare stroke of luck; we were extremely lucky.**

Однажды мне на редкость повезло. Меня повезли на допрос не ночью, как обычно, а среди белого дня. И, выходя из ворот дома Васькова [тюрьмы], я увидела своего Васю... Вот он, жив-здоров и неплохо выглядит (Гинзбург 2). One day I had a rare stroke of luck. I was taken along to the interrogation not, as usual, at night but in broad daylight. As I emerged from the gates of [the prison called] Vaskov's House I caught a glimpse of my Vasya....There he was, alive and well, and looking reasonably fit (2a).

3. [subj-compl with copula (subj: concr, abstr, or human) or nonagreeing modif] a thing (phenomenon, or, less often, person) is of remarkable quality, of a quality rarely encountered: **X был на редкость ≃ X was exceptional ⟨outstanding, beyond compare⟩; X was exceptionally good ⟨beautiful etc⟩.**

...Георгины в эту осень вышли на редкость, хоть в Женеву на выставку... (Трифонов 1). The dahlias were exceptionally beautiful that fall—good enough to put on exhibit in Geneva... (1a).

Р-102 • **ХУ́ЖЕ ⟨ПУ́ЩЕ⟩ ГО́РЬКОЙ РЕ́ДЬКИ** *coll* [AdjP or AdvP; these forms only; fixed WO] **1. надоесть, осточертеть** *кому* ~ . Also: **КАК ГО́РЬКАЯ РЕ́ДЬКА** *coll* [adv (intensif)] (to annoy, vex s.o.) a great deal, to an intolerable extent: X надоел Y-y ~ ≃ **Y is sick and tired ⟨sick to death, really sick⟩ of X; Y is totally ⟨thoroughly⟩ fed up with X; Y has had it up to here with X.**

[Трилецкий:] Или вот что, Мишель... Говорю тебе раз навсегда. Меня не трогай! Надоел ты мне пуще горькой редьки своими поучениями! (Чехов 1). [T.:] Look here, Michael, once and for all, will you leave me alone? I'm sick and tired of you and your lectures (1b). ♦ Домой не хотелось. Дом с верной супругой... опостылел хуже горькой редьки (Аксёнов 12). He didn't feel like going home. He was really sick of home and his wife (12a). ♦ [author's usage] За каждыми пустяками он [полячок] поминутно прибегал к самой Катерине Ивановне, бегал даже отыскивать её в Гостиный двор, называл её беспрестанно: «Пани хорунжина», и надоел ей наконец как редька... (Достоевский 3). He [the little Pole] came running to Katerina Ivanovna for every trifle, even ran to look for her in the Gostiny Arcade, kept calling her "pani chorunżina," until at last she got thoroughly fed up with him... (3c).

2. ~ *для кого, кому* [subj-compl with быть∅ (subj: abstr)] sth. is intolerable (for s.o.): X для Y-а ~ ≃ **X is more than Y can take ⟨bear, stand⟩; X turns Y's stomach; Y finds X unbearable.**

«Да ты вникнул ли хорошенько, что значит переехать — а?..» — «И так не вникнул!» — смиренно отвечал Захар, готовый во всём согласиться с барином, лишь бы не доводить дела до патетических сцен, которые были для него хуже горькой редьки (Гончаров 1). "Have you really grasped what it means to move—hah?..." "I guess, I haven't," Zakhar replied humbly, ready to agree with anything to avoid another of those "pathetic" scenes, which he found unbearable (1b).

Р-103 • **КАК РЕ́ЗАНЫЙ** кричать, орать *highly coll* [как + AdjP; nom only; adv (intensif)] (to scream) loudly, wildly: **(scream) like a banshee; (scream) bloody murder.**

Р-104 • **ТЯНУ́ТЬ РЕЗИ́НУ** *highly coll* [VP; subj: human] **1.** to act extremely slowly, procrastinate in dealing with s.o. or sth.: X тянет резину ≃ **X is dragging things ⟨it⟩ out; X is dragging his feet ⟨heels⟩; X is stalling; X is holding it ⟨things, person Y etc⟩ up.**

«Лучше сразу порвать, — говорит, — всё равно я жениться не могу, а чего резину тянуть» (Искандер 5). "It's better to make a clean break," he says. "I can't marry her anyway, why drag it out" (5a). ♦ [Шаламов (по телефону):] Что там у вас? Когда будет машина?.. Мне всё равно, но если ехать, значит, нечего тянуть резину, уже одиннадцатый час... (Вампилов 2). [Sh. (into the telephone):] What's going on there? When will I have a car?...It makes no difference to me, but if I'm going, then there's no use stalling, it's already after ten... (2b). ♦ «Ну, как там у нас? Пустили третий цех?» — «Нет ещё». — «Почему?» — «Техника безопасности резину тянет» (Аксёнов 8). "Well, how are things back home? Have you got the third shop going?" "Not yet." "Why?" "The Industrial Safety Board is holding it up" (8a).

2. to be slow with one's reply: X тянет резину ≃ **X is stalling; X is dragging things ⟨this business etc⟩ out;** ‖ Neg Imper не тяни резину ≃ **out with it; spit it out.**

«А ты что ответил?» — «А я... сразу не отвечаю, тяну резину...» (Копелев 1). "What did you say?" "...I don't answer right away, I drag things out..." (1a). ♦ [Следователь] сел, раскрыл Сашино дело. «Так, Панкратов... Подумали вы над тем, что я вам советовал?» — «Да, подумал. Но я не знаю, о чём идёт речь». — «Хотите резину тянуть?» — «Я не знаю, о каких контрреволюционных разговорах вы говорили в прошлый раз» (Рыбаков 2). ...[The investigator] sat down and opened Sasha's file. "So, Pankratov. Have you thought about my advice to you?" "Yes, I have, but I still don't know what it's all about."..."Are you going to try to drag this business out?" "I don't know what counterrevolutionary conversations you meant last time" (2a).

Р-105 • **В РЕЗУЛЬТА́ТЕ** [PrepP; Invar] **1.** [sent adv] consequently: **as a result ⟨a consequence⟩; result in...**

...Много полицейских было переброшено для охраны станции и в железнодорожный посёлок, как «заражённый партизанами», в результате охрана гетто ослабла... (Рыбаков 1). ...A lot of police were transferred to guard duty at the station and the railway settlement as a place "infected by partisans" and, as a result, security in the ghetto weakened... (1a). ♦ Он понял, что час триумфа уже наступил и что триумф едва ли не будет полнее, если в результате не окажется ни расквашенных носов, ни свороченных на сторону скул (Салтыков-Щедрин 1). He realized that the hour of triumph was already upon him, and that triumph would almost be fuller if it did not result in bloodied noses or dislocated cheekbones (1a).

2. ~ *чего* [Prep; the resulting PrepP is adv] caused by or proceeding from sth.: **as a result ⟨a consequence⟩ of; stemming from.**

...В результате взрыва погибли тысячи ни в чём не повинных людей... (Войнович 1). ...Thousands of innocent people were killed as a result of the explosion... (1a).

Р-106 • **ВЫХОДИ́ТЬ/ВЫ́ЙТИ ИЗ-ПОД РЕЗЦА́** *чьего, кого* [VP; subj: a noun denoting a piece of sculpture; usu. pfv] to be sculpted, carved by s.o.: X вышел из-под резца Y-а ≃ **X was fashioned by Y's chisel; X was chiseled by Y.**

P-107 • **МОЛО́ЧНЫЕ РЕ́КИ И КИСЕ́ЛЬНЫЕ БЕ-РЕГА́; МОЛО́ЧНЫЕ РЕ́КИ, КИСЕ́ЛЬНЫЕ БЕ-РЕГА́** *folk poet* [NP; pl only; fixed WO] an idyllic place or a life of ease and plenty in such a place: **(life in) a ⟨the⟩ land of milk and honey; (life in) a land flowing with milk and honey.**

Молферма... Самое слово звучало для эльгенских узников как обозначение волшебной страны. Молочные реки, кисельные берега... (Гинзбург 2). The dairy farm...the very words sounded to Elgen inmates like the designation of a fairy kingdom. A land flowing with milk and honey... (2a).

< The phrase often occurs in Russian folk tales. «Кисель с молоком» ("a gelatinous fruit dessert served with milk") used to be popular among peasants. The phrase may have been influenced by the Bible (Ex. 3:8).

P-108 • **СТА́ВИТЬ/ПОСТА́ВИТЬ НА РЕ́ЛЬСЫ** *что media* [VP; subj: human or collect] **1.** ~ *чего, какие.* Also: **ПЕРЕВОДИ́ТЬ/ПЕРЕВЕСТИ́ НА РЕ́ЛЬСЫ** *media* [obj: промышленность, экономику, завод, страну etc] (in refer. to an industry, the economy, a factory, a country etc) to set sth. going on a specific course (of development): X поставил Y на рельсы Z-а ≃ **X got Y headed toward ⟨in the direction of⟩ Z;** ‖ X ставит Y на [AdjP] рельсы ≃ **X is restructuring Y along [AdjP] lines; X is getting Y headed in a [AdjP] direction; X is converting Y to a [AdjP] system ⟨footing etc⟩; X is putting ⟨placing⟩ Y on a [AdjP] footing.**

Правительство переводит экономику на рельсы свободного предпринимательства. The government is converting the economy into a free enterprise system.

2. to set sth. up, put sth. into operation: X поставил Y на рельсы ≃ **X got Y going ⟨on its feet⟩; X set Y in motion.**

P-109 • **СТАНОВИ́ТЬСЯ/СТАТЬ НА РЕ́ЛЬСЫ** [VP] **1.** ~ *чего, какие.* Also: **ПЕРЕХОДИ́ТЬ/ПЕРЕЙТИ́ НА РЕ́ЛЬСЫ** *all media* [subj: usu. collect (завод, страна, промышленность, экономика etc)] (of a factory, a country, an industry, the economy etc) to start moving along a specific course (of development): X стал на рельсы Y-а ≃ **X set out on the ⟨a⟩ path of Y; X started heading toward ⟨in the direction of⟩ Y;** ‖ X стал на [AdjP] рельсы ≃ **X set out on a [AdjP] path; X started heading in a [AdjP] direction; X was converted to a [AdjP] system ⟨footing⟩; X took a [AdjP] line; X switched over to a [AdjP] footing.** ○ **ПЕРЕХО́Д НА РЕ́ЛЬСЫ** *чего, какие* [NP] ≃ **taking a [AdjP] line ⟨approach etc⟩; switching over to a [AdjP] footing.**

«Наверху готовятся большие перемены... Имеется в виду переход на более демократические рельсы, уступка общей законности, и это дело самого недалёкого будущего» (Пастернак 1). "Big changes are being planned at the top....What they have in mind is to take a more democratic line, make a concession to legality, and this will come about quite soon" (1a). ♦ На дворе лейтенант Филиппов занимался с личным составом строевой подготовкой... В обычное время на строевую подготовку времени никак не хватало. Всегда было слишком много работы. А тут в короткий период перехода на военные рельсы выдался свободный денёк (Войнович 2). Down in the courtyard Lieutenant Filippov was busy drilling the staff....In normal times there was never enough time for drill. There was always too much work to do. But now, in this short period of transition when they were switching over to a wartime footing, a free day had turned up (2a).

2. *obs* [subj: human, collect, or abstr; often neg] to reach a stage when one progresses or sth. develops at a fast pace and unimpeded: X ещё не стал на рельсы ≃ **X hasn't taken off yet; X isn't in (high) gear yet.**

P-110 • **ДЕШЕ́ВЛЕ ПА́РЕНОЙ РЕ́ПЫ (купить, продать** *что) obsoles, coll;* **ДЕШЕ́ВЛЕ ГРИБО́В** *coll* [AdjP or AdvP; adv or subj-compl with copula (subj: concr or animal); fixed WO] (to buy or sell sth.) very inexpensively; sth. is very inexpensive: **dirt cheap; (be) a real steal ⟨bargain⟩; (go etc) for practically ⟨next to⟩ nothing; (be sold etc) for a song.**

P-111 • **ПРО́ЩЕ ПА́РЕНОЙ РЕ́ПЫ** *highly coll* [AdjP; subj-compl with copula (subj: usu. abstr or infin); fixed WO] sth. is extremely simple: X проще пареной репы ≃ **X is (as) easy as pie; X is a snap ⟨a cinch, a breeze, a piece of cake, duck soup⟩; X is (as) simple as can be.**

«...Дверь на замке. У меня — отмычка в кармане. Знакомый замок открыть проще пареной репы» (Чернёнок 2). "...The door is locked. I have a pick in my pocket. It's a snap to undo a familiar lock" (2a).

P-112 • **НЕ МО́ЖЕТ БЫТЬ И РЕ́ЧИ** *о чём;* **(И) РЕ́ЧИ БЫТЬ НЕ МО́ЖЕТ** *all coll* [VP; impers; pres or past; if pres, usu. used to reject categorically some idea, suggestion, offer etc] sth. is so impossible that it is not even worth talking about, sth. is ruled out altogether: об X-е не может быть и речи ≃ **X is (entirely) out of the question; there is ⟨can be⟩ no question of X; [in limited contexts] I ⟨he etc⟩ won't even hear of X.**

О том, чтобы Мольера хоронить по церковному обряду, не могло быть и речи. Грешный комедиант умер без покаяния и не отрёкшись от своей осуждаемой церковью профессии... (Булгаков 5). Burying Molière with the appropriate Church rites was out of the question. The sinful comedian died without a last confession and without repudiating his profession, which was condemned by the Church (5a). ♦ ...Если фамилия самого автора состоит в списке запрещённых к упоминанию, то о публикации его книги, какого бы содержания она ни была, не может быть и речи (Войнович 1). ...If the author himself is one of those whose names are on the forbidden list, the publication of his book, no matter what its contents, is entirely out of the question (1a). ♦ «Вот ваша рукопись, — вдруг проговорил Васильев, насупив брови и протягивая ему папку. — Берите. Никакой речи не может быть о том, чтобы я был причастен к её напечатанию» (Набоков 1). "Here's your manuscript," said Vasiliev suddenly, knitting his brows and handing him the folder. "Take it. There can be no question of my being party to its publication" (1a). ♦ «Мой муж говорит, что вам нужна только хорошая квартира, ни о какой квартире Бажовой не может быть даже и речи...» (Войнович 3). "My husband says that you want only a really good apartment, that you won't even hear of Bazhova's apartment" (3a).

P-113 • **ВЕСТИ́ РЕЧЬ** *к чему,* often **к тому, что...** [VP; subj: human] to have some goal or end in mind when saying sth.: к чему X ведёт речь? ≃ **what is X getting ⟨driving⟩ at?;** ‖ X ведёт речь к тому, что... ≃ **what X is getting ⟨driving⟩ at is that...**

P-114 • **РЕЧЬ ⟨ДЕ́ЛО⟩ ИДЁТ** *о ком-чём* [VP_subj; fixed WO] what is involved here is...: речь идёт об X-е ≃ **it is a question ⟨a matter⟩ of X; the matter ⟨the question⟩ concerns ⟨involves⟩ X.**

[Михаил *(волнуется)*:] ...Давайте говорить серьёзно. Речь идёт о деле, а не о справедливости... (Горький 1). [M. *(agitated)*:] ...Can't we talk seriously? It's a question of good business practice, not of justice... (1b). ♦ «Вот это, господа присяжные, я называю уликой! Вот тут уж я знаю, вижу, осязаю деньги и не могу сказать, что их нет или не было. Так ли в настоящем случае? А между тем ведь дело идёт о жизни и смерти, о судьбе человека» (Достоевский 2). "This, gentlemen of the jury, is what I call evidence! Here I know, I see, I touch the money, and I cannot say that it does not or never did exist. Is that so in the present case? And yet it is a matter of life and death, of a man's fate" (2a). ♦ Полицейские были довольны, что узнали, кто раздавленный. Раскольников назвал и себя, дал свой адрес и всеми силами, как будто дело шло о родном отце, уговаривал перенести поскорее бесчувственного Мармеладова в его квартиру (Достоевский 3). The policemen were pleased to learn the trampled man's identity. Raskolnikov gave his own name too, and his address, and did his very utmost, as if it were his own father involved, to persuade them to take the unconscious Marmeladov back as quickly as possible to his own apartment (3a). ♦ «...Ради бога, не откажите мне в моей просьбе: дело идёт о счастии всей моей жизни» (Пушкин 2). [context transl] "...For the love of God, please do not refuse my request: the happiness of my whole life is at stake" (2a).

P-115 • **СОЛОМО́НОВО РЕШЕ́НИЕ** [NP; usu. sing; fixed WO] an unusually wise decision or judgment: **a decision ⟨a judgment⟩ worthy of Solomon.**

< From the Bible (based on the parable in I Kings 3:16–28).

P-116 • **РЕШЕНО́ И ПОДПИ́САНО** coll [AdjP; subj-compl with быть∅ (subj: это or всё это, often omitted; pres only; fixed WO] this is definitively decided, not subject to change: **(it's) signed, sealed, and delivered; (it's) signed and sealed; it's final ⟨definite, (all) settled⟩; (it's) a done deal.**

[Соня:] Сами вы пейте, если это вам не противно, но, умоляю, не давайте пить дяде. Ему вредно. [Астров:] Хорошо. Мы не будем больше пить. Я сейчас уеду к себе. Решено и подписано (Чехов 3). [S.:] You can drink, if it doesn't disgust you, but, I implore you, don't let my uncle drink. It's bad for him. [A.:] Very well. We won't drink any more. I was just leaving. Signed and sealed (3a).

P-117 • **ЗА РЕШЁТКОЙ** быть∅, сидеть, оказаться; **ЗА РЕШЁТКУ** сесть, посадить кого и т. п. both coll [PrepP; these forms only; subj-compl with copula (subj: human) or obj-compl with посадить etc (obj: human)] (to be, end up, put s.o. etc) in prison: X сидит за решёткой ≃ **X is behind bars; X is in jail;** ‖ X-а бросили за решётку ≃ **X was put ⟨they put X⟩ behind bars; X was thrown ⟨they threw X⟩ in jail.**

Потом [заместитель министра] Севастьянов повёл Осколупова и Яконова к себе и угрозил, что обоих их загонит за решётку... (Солженицын 3). Then [Deputy Minister] Sevastyanov took Oskolupov and Yakonov to his office and threatened to put them both behind bars... (3a).

P-118 • **ПОЕ́ХАЛ В РИ́ГУ** old-fash, euph, highly coll [VP; subj: human; usu. past] to vomit, usu. as a result of excessive intoxication: X поехал в Ригу ≃ **X puked; X tossed his cookies; X lost his lunch ⟨supper etc⟩; X kissed the porcelain god.**

< (?) Apparently based on phonetic similarity of the words «Рига» (a city name) and «срыгнуть» ("to vomit").

P-119 • **РИСК – БЛАГОРО́ДНОЕ ДЕ́ЛО** [saying] said (often in jest) to justify a person's intention to undertake sth. risky: ≃ **nothing ventured, nothing gained; you never know until you try.**

P-120 • **ГНУТЬ/СОГНУ́ТЬ ⟨СКРУТИ́ТЬ, СВЕРНУ́ТЬ⟩ В БАРА́НИЙ РОГ** кого; **ГНУТЬ/СОГНУ́ТЬ В ДУГУ́ ⟨В ТРИ ДУГИ́, В ТРИ ПОГИ́БЕЛИ⟩** all coll [VP; subj: usu. human; var. with рог—more often pfv; variants with в дугу, в три дуги—more often impfv; the verb may take the final position, otherwise fixed WO] to force s.o. to submit to one's will by means of oppression, cruel treatment, coercion etc: X Y-а в бараний рог согнул ≃ **X bent ⟨twisted⟩ Y to X's will; X made Y knuckle under; X beat Y into submission;** [in limited contexts] **X knocked Y into a cocked hat;** ‖ X гнёт Y-а в дугу ≃ **X tyrannizes Y; X rides roughshod over Y.**

[author's usage] «Так-то, — ехидно посмеивался Орозкул про себя, — приполз, упал мне в ноги. Ух, нет у меня большей

власти, не таких бы крутил в бараний рог!» (Айтматов 1). "So," Orozkul grinned inwardly. "Crawled over, eh? Groveling at my feet. Ah, if only I had more power—I'd twist some bigger fellows to my will" (1a). ♦ «Да вы сознаёте, что происходит в России? — спрашивает Шура. — Или мы мировую буржуазию в бараний рог, или она нас» (Трифонов 6). "Are you aware of what is happening in Russia?" asks Shura. "Either we make the world bourgeoisie knuckle under or they'll do it to us" (6a). ♦ «А вот погоди! Я вас ужо в бараний рог согну!» (Салтыков-Щедрин 2). "You wait! I'll knock you into a cocked hat!" (2a).

P-121 • **РОГ ИЗОБИ́ЛИЯ** lit [NP; sing only; fixed WO] an inexhaustible source of sth.: **horn of plenty; cornucopia;** ‖ сыпаться ⟨литься и т. п.⟩ как из рога изобилия ≃ **pour down (on s.o.) as if from a horn of plenty ⟨as if from a cornucopia⟩; rain down (on s.o.) in a never-ending stream.**

...Рог изобилия опрокинулся над Мавринским институтом: импортные и советские радиодетали, аппаратура, мебель; техническая библиотека...; заключённые специалисты, вызванные из лагерей; лучшие оперуполномоченные и архивариусы... наконец, особая железная охрана (Солженицын 3). ...The horn of plenty had emptied its bounty on the Mavrino Institute: imported and Soviet-made radio parts, equipment, furniture, a technical library..., prisoner specialists pulled out of camps, the very best security officers and file supervisors...and finally a special, iron-hard corps of guards (3a).

< From Greek mythology.

P-122 • **НАСТАВЛЯ́ТЬ ⟨СТА́ВИТЬ⟩/НАСТА́ВИТЬ РОГА́** кому coll [VP] **1.** [subj: human, female] to be unfaithful to one's husband: X наставила Y-у рога ≃ **X cuckolded Y; X made a cuckold of Y.**

[Галина:] Куда я еду, к кому — тебе это всё равно. И не делай вида, что это тебя волнует. Тебя давно уже ничего не волнует... У тебя нет сердца... [Зилов (трясёт её):] А у тебя, дрянь такая, у тебя есть сердце? А? Где оно?.. [Галина:] Пусти меня... [Зилов:] Ах, ты торопишься... Я понимаю, тебе не терпится наставить мне рога... (Вампилов 5). [Galina:] It makes no difference to you where I'm going or who I'm going to see. And don't pretend you care. You haven't cared about anything for ages....You've no heart.... [Zilov (shaking her):] And what about you, you bitch? Have you got a heart? Have you? Where is it?... [Galina:] Let me go!... [Zilov:] Oh, of course. You're in a hurry... You can't wait to make a cuckold of me... (5a).

2. [subj: human, male] to take a man's wife as one's lover (thus humiliating, offending that man): X наставил Y-у рога ≃ **X cuckolded Y; X fooled around with Y's wife.**

P-123 • **ОБЛА́МЫВАТЬ/ОБЛОМА́ТЬ ⟨СЛОМА́ТЬ, СЛОМИ́ТЬ⟩ РОГА́** кому highly coll [VP; subj: human; usu. pfv] to curb s.o.'s actions, suppress s.o., force s.o. to submit: X Y-у обломал рога ≃ **X brought Y to heel; X put Y in Y's place.**

P-124 • **ПО РОГА́М** prison and camp slang [PrepP; Invar; usu. nonagreeing postmodif] removal of the rights of citizenship: **disfranchisement; disenfranchisement.**

«Вот я шестой год [в заключении] разменял. Имею... пятнадцать наличными и пять по рогам» (Копелев 1). "Now I've just finished my sixth year [of imprisonment]. I have fifteen years plus five of disenfranchisement" (1a).

P-125 • **СТА́ВИТЬ РОГА́ТКИ** кому-чему coll [VP; subj: human or collect; obj: usu. human or collect] to (try to) impede s.o.'s efforts to accomplish sth., hinder an undertaking deliberately: X ставит Y-у рогатки ≃ **X is tripping ⟨trying to trip⟩ Y up; X is upsetting ⟨trying to upset⟩ Y's applecart; X is putting hurdles ⟨obstacles⟩ in Y's way; X is getting in the way of thing Y.**

Власти постоянно ставят рогатки коммерческим предприятиям: то ссуды не дают, то налоги повышают. The government is constantly putting hurdles in the way of commercial enterprises: one minute it refuses them loans, the next it raises their taxes.

P-126 • ВСЯ́КОГО ⟨РА́ЗНОГО, РАЗЛИ́ЧНОГО⟩ РО́ДА [NP_gen; these forms only; nonagreeing modif; fixed WO] of all sorts: **all kinds ⟨sorts, types⟩ of; of all kinds; of every kind ⟨sort⟩; any kind ⟨sort, type⟩ of.**

[Грекова:] Вы так привыкли к разного рода резкостям, что мои слова едва ли будут вам в диковинку... (Чехов 1). [G.:] You're so used to all kinds of rudeness, I doubt if what I say will surprise you at all (1b). ♦ Собственно говоря, именно Октябрь и привил ему начальную тягу ко всякого рода машинам... (Аксёнов 12). It was actually October who infected him with a passion for all sorts of machinery... (12a). ♦ Это была знакомая мещанская ненависть ко всякого рода чудачествам, отклонениям от нормы, преувеличениям (Искандер 2). It was the familiar bourgeois hatred for any kind of eccentricity, exaggeration, or departure from the norm (2a).

P-127 • ИЗ РО́ДА В РОД [PrepP; Invar; adv; fixed WO] from one generation to the next, by heritage: **from generation to generation; generation after generation; for generations; through (the) generations.**

«Это умение очень тонкое, которое из рода в род передаётся» (Каверин 1). "It's a very subtle skill, handed down from generation to generation" (1a). ♦ Предки Иконникова со времён Петра Великого были из рода в род священниками (Гроссман 2). Since the days of Peter the Great, generation after generation of his [Ikonnikov's] ancestors had been priests (2a). ♦ В антресолях — из рода в род повелось у Попковых и Ордыниных — девичья часть, живут дочери (Пильняк 1). In the attic, in the maids' quarters, live the daughters—this has been the custom with the Popkovs and Ordinins for generations (1a).

P-128 • ОСО́БОГО РО́ДА [NP_gen; Invar; nonagreeing modif; fixed WO] of a distinctive, singular type: **a special ⟨particular⟩ type ⟨kind⟩ of.**

Он с значительным видом сиживал в кабинете за этим чтением, сперва возложенным на себя как обязанность, а потом сделавшимся привычным занятием, доставлявшим ему особого рода удовольствие... (Толстой 7). He would sit in his study with a grave air, reading—a task he first imposed upon himself as a duty, but which afterwards became a habit affording him a special kind of pleasure... (7b). ♦ [Васильков:] ...Я с вами откровенно буду говорить; у меня особого рода дела... (Островский 4). [V.:] ...I'll speak openly with you. I have a particular kind of business... (4a).

P-129 • СВОЕГО́ РО́ДА [NP_gen; Invar; nonagreeing modif; fixed WO] to a certain extent, from a certain standpoint: **in a sense; in a way; in one's ⟨its⟩ (own) way; a kind ⟨a sort⟩ of; of a sort; of sorts; something of a...**

...Они [московские славянофилы] должны были сомкнуть свои ряды и высказаться при появлении «Письма» Чаадаева и шуме, который оно вызвало. «Письмо» Чаадаева было своего рода последнее слово, рубеж (Герцен 2). ...They [the Moscow Slavophiles] had had to close their ranks and take a definite stand on the appearance of Chaadayev's *Letter* and the commotion it caused. That *Letter* was in a sense the last word, the limit (2a). ♦ Этические построения Чернышевского — своего рода попытка построить всё тот же перпетуум-мобиле, где двигатель-материя движет другую материю (Набоков 1). Chernyshevski's ethical structures are in their own way an attempt to construct the same old "perpetual motion" machine, where matter moves other matter (1a). ♦ Дядя Сандро любил прогуливаться с камчой, но не потому, что стремился оседлать ближнего. Здесь была своего рода военная хитрость, самооборона (Искандер 3). That Uncle Sandro liked to stroll with his quirt was not due to any striving to subdue his neighbor. It was a sort of military stratagem, a self-defense (3a). ♦ «Я имел настолько свинства в душе и своего рода честности, чтоб объявить ей [Марфе Петровне] прямо, что совершенно верен ей быть не могу. Это признание привело её в исступление, но, кажется, моя грубая откровенность ей в некотором роде понравилась...» (Достоевский 3). "I had enough swinishness in my soul, and honesty of a sort, to announce to her [Marfa Petrovna] straight off that I could not be completely faithful to her. This admission drove her into a frenzy, but I think she in some way liked my crude frankness..." (3c).

P-130 • ТАКО́ГО ⟨ПОДО́БНОГО⟩ РО́ДА [NP_gen; these forms only; nonagreeing modif; fixed WO] of a comparable type, nature, quality, degree etc: **such; of this ⟨that, a similar⟩ kind ⟨type, sort⟩; this ⟨that⟩ kind ⟨type, sort⟩ of; like this ⟨that⟩; similar; [in limited contexts] of this nature.**

«Это самый развращённый и погибший в пороках человек, из всех подобного рода людей!» (Достоевский 3). "He is the most depraved and vice-ridden man of all the men of that type in existence!" (3a). ♦ Автор должен признаться, что весьма завидует аппетиту и желудка такого рода людей (Гоголь 3). The author must admit that he is quite envious of the appetite and digestion of this sort of people (3c). ♦ В нём [Пьере], хотя он и не отдавал себе отчёта, уничтожилась вера и в благоустройство мира, и в человеческую, и в свою душу, и в бога... Прежде, когда на Пьера находили такого рода сомнения, — сомнения эти имели источником собственную вину... (Толстой 7). Though he [Pierre] was not even aware of it, his faith in the right ordering of the universe, in humanity, in his own soul, and in God, had been destroyed....When similar doubts had assailed him in the past they had arisen from his own wrongdoing... (7a). ♦ Подобного рода свидетельств у меня... очень много... (Салтыков-Щедрин 2). I possess a great deal of evidence of this nature... (2a).

P-131 • В НЕ́КОТОРОМ РО́ДЕ [PrepP; Invar; usu. nonagreeing modif or adv; fixed WO] to a certain degree, in some respect: **in a ⟨some⟩ way; in a certain sense; a kind ⟨sort⟩ of; of sorts; something of a [NP]; to some ⟨a certain⟩ extent; after a fashion; in a manner (of speaking).**

Быть принятым в салоне графини Безуховой считалось дипломом ума... секретари посольства, и даже посланники, поверяли ей дипломатические тайны, так что Элен была сила в некотором роде (Толстой 5). To be received in the Countess Bezukhova's salon was regarded as a diploma of intellect....Secretaries of the embassy, and even ambassadors, confided diplomatic secrets to her, so that in a way Hélène was a power (5b). ♦ «Я имел настолько свинства в душе и своего рода честности, чтоб объявить ей [Марфе Петровне] прямо, что совершенно верен ей быть не могу. Это признание привело её в исступление, но, кажется, моя грубая откровенность ей в некотором роде понравилась...» (Достоевский 3). "I had enough swinishness in my soul, and honesty of a sort, to announce to her [Marfa Petrovna] straight off that I could not be completely faithful to her. This admission drove her into a frenzy, but I think she in some way liked my crude frankness..." (3c). ♦ «Но любишь ли ты меня?» — «То, что говорю, и есть в некотором роде объяснение в любви», — ответил Фёдор Константинович. «Мне мало „некоторого рода"» (Набоков 1). "But do you love me?" "What I am saying is in fact a kind of declaration of love," replied Fyodor. "A 'kind of' is not enough" (1a). ♦ Я стал в некотором роде знаменитостью... (Катаев 3). I had become something of a celebrity... (3a). ♦ ...Там из окна выглядывает, в некотором роде, сёмга эдакая, вишенки по пяти рублей штучка, арбуз-громадище... — словом, на всяком шагу соблазн такой, слюнки текут... (Гоголь 3). ...He'd catch sight of a huge salmon staring out of the window at him, in a manner of speaking, lovely cherries at five roubles apiece, an enormous watermelon...—in short, such temptation at every step that his mouth watered... (3a).

P-132 • В СВОЁМ РО́ДЕ [PrepP; Invar; nonagreeing modif; fixed WO] to a certain extent and in a way specific to the person, thing, or phenomenon in question: **in one's ⟨its⟩ (own) way.**

«Какой я вам коллега, — буркнул я. — Я художник». — «И я художник, — подхватил он. — Художник в своём роде» (Аржак 2). "What do you mean 'colleague'?" I growled. "I'm an artist." "So am I," he said. "An artist in my own way" (2a). ♦ Борис Евгеньевич Ермолкин был замечательный в своём роде человек (Войнович 4). Boris Evgenevich Ermolkin was, in his way, a remarkable man (4a). ♦ «Знаешь, в одном монастыре есть одна подгородная слободка, и уж всем там известно, что в ней одни только „монастырские жёны" живут... Я там был, и, знаешь, интересно, в своём роде разумеется...» (Достоевский 1). "You know, there's one monastery that has a little village nearby, and everybody around knows that only 'monastery wives' live there....I was there, and, you know, it's interesting — in its own way of course..." (1a). ♦ Поездка оказалась в своём роде увеселительной... (Мандельштам 2). The journey proved to be quite a joy ride in its way (2a).

P-133 • В Э́ТОМ ⟨ТАКО́М⟩ РО́ДЕ [PrepP; these forms only; usu. nonagreeing modif; often after что-то, нечто, что-нибудь etc; fixed WO] somewhat similar (to what has been mentioned in the preceding context): **(something) like that; (something) of the ⟨this, that⟩ kind ⟨sort⟩; (something) to that effect; (something) of that nature; (something) along that line ⟨those lines⟩;** [in limited contexts] **in a similar ⟨in the same⟩ vein.**

«Вопросник. Беру словечко на вооружение. Кратко и точно. У вас, наверное, есть ещё в таком роде, вы ж газетный работник» (Иоффе 1). "'Questionnaire.' I'm going to adopt this word. Brief and exact. You probably have a few more like that — after all, you are a journalist" (1a). ♦ «...Твоя Лимфа-Д — это струящаяся душа, что ли, нечто в этом роде...» (Аксёнов 6). "...That Lymph-D of yours is liquid soul or something like that" (6a). ♦ Что-то не помнится, чтобы появление пишущей машинки в какой-то степени было предсказано, как это бывает с другими чудесами в этом роде (Олеша 3). Somehow I don't seem to recall that the emergence of the typewriter was in any way foreshadowed, as is the case with other miracles of that kind (3a). ♦ ...[Мадлена] сочинила роман под названием «Клелия (Римская история)»... К первому тому его была приложена такая прелесть, как аллегорическая Карта Нежности, на которой были изображены Река Склонности, Озеро Равнодушия... и прочее в этом роде (Булгаков 5). ...[Madeleine] composed a novel she titled *Clélie, A Roman Story*....The first volume included so delectable an appendix as an allegorical Map of Tenderness, containing a River of Propensity, a Lake of Indifference...and so on in the same vein (5a).

P-134 • ЕДИ́НСТВЕННЫЙ В СВОЁМ РО́ДЕ [AdjP; modif or subj-compl with copula, nom or instrum (subj: any common noun); fixed WO] inimitable, singular: **the only one ⟨[NP]⟩ of its ⟨his etc⟩ kind; one of a kind; in a class by itself ⟨himself etc⟩; unique.**

Кто он был, этот безумный человек, единственный в своём роде писатель в мировой литературе?.. (Олеша 3). Who was he, that mad person, the only writer of his kind in world literature?.. (3a). ♦ Увлекающийся Стеклов называет «ликующим гимном любви» это единственное в своём роде произведение, — напоминающее скорее всего добросовестнейший доклад (Набоков 1). The easily carried-away Steklov refers to this unique production (reminding one most of all of an extremely conscientious business report) as "an exultant hymn of love" (1a).

P-135 • НЕ РОДИ́СЬ КРАСИ́ВЫМ ⟨КРАСИ́В⟩, А РОДИ́СЬ СЧАСТЛИ́ВЫМ ⟨СЧАСТЛИ́В⟩ [saying] a person who is born lucky is more fortunate than a person who is born beautiful: ≃ **it is luck, not looks, that counts.**

P-136 • НЕ ПО́МНЯЩИЙ РОДСТВА́ [AdjP; modif]
1. *obs* (a person) without a family (said of a person who does not

have a family or who refuses to provide information about his family): **without any roots; not knowing one's roots; without (kith or) kin.**

[Незнамов:] ...Что же я за фигуру буду представлять из себя? Бродяга, не помнящий родства, и человек без определённых занятий! (Островский 3). [N.:] What will become of me then — a tramp without kith or kin or a worthy occupation? (3a).

2. Also: ИВА́Н, НЕ ПО́МНЯЩИЙ РОДСТВА́ (a person) who has broken with the environment in which he was raised and has become indifferent to or even scornful of it: **denying one's roots ⟨origins⟩.**

< Originally a legal term in old Russia applied to vagrants who had no passports.

P-137 • БЕЗ РО́ДУ, БЕЗ ПЛЕ́МЕНИ; БЕЗ РО́ДУ И (БЕЗ) ПЛЕ́МЕНИ [PrepP; these forms only; nonagreeing modif or subj-compl with бытьø (subj: human); fixed WO]
1. *obs* lowly, from a socially disadvantaged background: **of low ⟨humble⟩ birth; of humble origin; of low ⟨mean⟩ parentage.**

2. without family or loved ones: **without (kith or) kin; without kinfolk ⟨kindred⟩; alone in the world; all alone.**

Заигрались они [дети], не заметили, как зашли глубоко в чащу. А когда услышали шум и крики побоища и кинулись назад, то не застали в живых ни отцов, ни матерей своих, ни братьев, ни сестёр. Остались дети без роду, без племени (Айтматов 1). In the excitement of their game, they [the children] had gone deeper and deeper into the thickets. Hearing the din and noise of the attack, they rushed back, but found nobody alive — neither their fathers, nor their mothers, nor their brothers and sisters. The children remained without kith or kin (1a).

P-138 • НА РОДУ́ НАПИ́САНО *кому, у кого coll* [AdjP; subj-compl with бытьø (subj: infin or a clause); usu. this WO] sth. is predestined, preordained for s.o.: X-у на роду написано ≃ **X is destined ⟨fated⟩ to...; that ⟨it⟩ is X's fate ⟨destiny⟩; it was X's fate ⟨destiny⟩ from birth; (that's the way) it was meant to be; it was in the cards;** [in limited contexts] **that's the way nature meant it to be;** [in refer. to troubles, misfortunes etc] **X is doomed ⟨was doomed from the day he was born⟩ to...**

«Ведь есть, право, этакие люди, у которых на роду написано, что с ними должны случаться разные необыкновенные вещи» (Лермонтов 1). "...After all, some people are fated to have unusual things happen to them" (1c). ♦ Пусть уж одна Нинка пропадает. Так уж, видно, ей на роду написано (Гинзбург 1). Let Nina alone suffer, if that was to be her fate (1b). ♦ «А если сторож умрёт?» — спросил принц, стараясь постигнуть психологию поступка молодого аборигена. «Значит, так у него на роду написано», — ответил дядя Сандро... (Искандер 3). "And if the watchman dies?" the prince asked, trying to grasp the psychology of what the young aborigine had done. "Well, it was in the cards," Uncle Sandro replied (3a). ♦ «Баба у человека должна быть одна, так ему на роду написано» (Максимов 2). "A man should have one woman, that's the way nature meant it to be" (2a). ♦ ...Видно, всем добрым начинаниям 1848 года было на роду написано родиться на седьмом месяце и умереть прежде первого зуба (Герцен 2). ...It seems that all the good projects of the year 1848 were doomed to be born in their seventh month and to die before cutting their first tooth (2a).

P-139 • НИ РО́ДУ НИ ПЛЕ́МЕНИ нет *у кого, не иметь coll* [NP_gen; Invar; used as subj/gen or obj; fixed WO] (s.o. has) no family or loved ones: **(s.o. has) neither kith nor kin; (s.o. has) no kinfolk ⟨kindred⟩; (s.o. is) alone in the world.**

P-140 • ОТ РО́ДУ [PrepP; Invar; used as a restr marker]
1. used with a quantifier to denote s.o.'s age (the idiom may be omitted in translation): [Num] **years of age;** [Num] **years ⟨months etc⟩ old.**

Скончался он [мой отец], когда было мне всего лишь два года от роду, и не помню я его вовсе (Достоевский 1). He [my father] died when I was only two years old, and I do not remember him at all (1a). ♦ Между тем 17 ноября 1861 г., имея двадцать пять лет от роду, Добролюбов скончался (Набоков 1). Meanwhile, on November 17, 1861, at twenty-five years of age, Dobrolyubov died (1a). ♦ Это был человек лет тридцати двух-трёх от роду, среднего роста, приятной наружности... (Гончаров 1). He was a man of about thirty-two or three, of medium height and pleasant appearance... (1a).

2. coll throughout one's entire life: **in (all) one's life**; [when used with a negated verb only] **never in all one's born days.**

«Вы счастливы в игре», – сказал я Вуличу... «В первый раз от роду», – отвечал он... (Лермонтов 1). "You've got gambler's luck," I said to Vulich. "For once in my life," he said... (1c). ♦ «Этакого дурака я ещё от роду не видывал...» (Гоголь 3). "I've never met a fool like that in all my life," said Chichikov (3a). "Never in all my born days have I seen such a fool" said Chichikov (3b).

P-141 • ПО РОЖДЕ́НИЮ [PrepP; Invar; usu. sent adv or non-agreeing modif] **1.** by descent: **by birth ⟨parentage, extraction, lineage⟩; (person X comes) from a line ⟨a family⟩ of** [NPs].

Но при всех своих достоинствах товарищ Дзержинский был барин по рождению... И при всех своих достоинствах товарищ Дзержинский, надо сказать, не лишён был некоторого позёрства... (Рыбаков 2). For all his qualities, Comrade Dzerzhinsky had been an aristocrat by birth....And for all his qualities, it had to be said, Comrade Dzerzhinsky was not entirely free of posturing... (2a).

2. with regard to one's birthplace: **by birth; (person X) was born in...**

По рождению я москвич, но всю жизнь живу в Петербурге. I'm a Muscovite by birth, but I've lived in St. Petersburg all my life.

P-142 • ОСТА́ЛИСЬ РО́ЖКИ ДА НО́ЖКИ *от кого-чего coll* [VP_subj; the verb may take the final position, otherwise fixed WO] practically nothing is left of s.o. or sth.: **от X-а остались рожки да ножки ≃ only bits and pieces (of X) remained ⟨were left⟩; virtually ⟨next to⟩ nothing was left of X;** [in limited contexts] **nothing was left of animal/person X but the bones and the beak.**

Мать, Анна Савишна, поселилась у Ларичевых с тех пор, как в одну из вёсен полой водой смыло под обрыв старую хату... «Ремонтировать бесполезно», – сказал Ларичев и... распорядился: «Взять вещи, какие остались, маму – к нам». Анна Савишна что-то говорила про «инструмент» – пианино... Александр Иванович её высмеял – от «инструмента» остались рожки да ножки. Мать покорилась (Грекова 3). Anna Savishna had moved in with the Larichevs one spring when the flood waters had washed the old house over the cliff...."No use fixing it," Larichev had said. "Take whatever is left, she's coming to live with us." Anna Savishna said something about the "instrument," the upright piano....Alexander Ivanovich made fun of her—only bits and pieces of the instrument remained—and Anna Savishna gave in (3a). ♦ Вдруг раздался треск, отломились сразу обе передние ножки. Забыв друг о друге, противники принялись терзать ореховое кладохранилище... Спинка отлетела, отброшенная могучим порывом... Через пять минут стул был обглодан. От него остались рожки да ножки (Ильф и Петров 1). Suddenly there was a crack and both front legs broke off simultaneously. Forgetting about one another, the opponents began tearing the walnut treasure-chest to pieces....The back was torn off with a mighty tug....Five minutes later the chair had been picked clean. Bits and pieces were all that was left (1a). ♦ «...Швондер и есть самый главный дурак. Он не понимает, что Шариков для него ещё более грозная опасность, чем для меня. Ну, сейчас он всячески старается натравить его на меня, не соображая, что если кто-нибудь, в свою очередь, натравит Шарикова на самого Швондера, то от него останутся только рожки да ножки!» (Булгаков 11). "...Shvonder is the biggest fool of all. He doesn't see that Sharikov is much more of a threat to him than he is to me. Right now he's doing all he can to turn Sharikov against me, not realizing that if someone in his turn sets Sharikov against Shvonder himself, there'll soon be nothing left of Shvonder but the bones and the beak" (11b).

P-143 • КАКО́ГО РОЖНА́ *substand, rude* [NP_gen; Invar; fixed WO] **1.** ~ **надо, нужно, не хватает** *кому* и т. п. [obj] what is it (that s.o. needs or that is lacking for s.o.): **what the hell ⟨in hell, the blazes, in blazes, the devil⟩ does s.o. want ⟨need⟩?**

[Рита:] Уж [если] твой Валя им нехорош – не знаю, какого ещё рожна надо! (Рощин 1). [R.:] If your Valia isn't good enough for them—I don't know what the hell they need! (1a).

2. [adv] why, what for: **why on earth ⟨the hell, in hell, in blazes, the devil⟩?; what the hell ⟨in blazes, the devil⟩ for?**

P-144 • ПЕРЕ́ТЬ/ПОПЕРЕ́ТЬ ПРОТИВ РОЖНА́ *substand;* **ПРАТЬ ПРОТИВ РОЖНА́** *obs* [VP; subj: human; often neg pfv fut, gener. 2nd pers sing не попрёшь] to undertake sth. that is risky or destined to fail (usu. in cases when one resists some much greater force, incontestable authority etc): **против рожна не попрёшь ≃ why fight a losing battle?;** [in refer. to one's opposition to some prevailing opinion, movement etc] **why swim against the tide?; why swim upstream?**

Каким образом мы, полгода назад употреблявшие слово «футуризм» лишь в виде бранной клички, не только нацепили её на себя, но даже отрицали за кем бы то ни было право пользоваться этим ярлыком? Сыграла ли тут роль статья Брюсова в «Русской мысли»?.. Или, окинув хозяйским оком создавшееся положение, решил смекалистый Давид [Бурлюк], что против рожна не попрёшь, что упорствовать дальше, отказываясь от навязываемой нам клички, значило бы вносить только лишний сумбур в понятия широкой публики и... оттолкнуть её от себя (Лившиц 1). How was it that we, who six months before had used the word "Futurism" only as a term of abuse, had not only appropriated it for ourselves, but denied anyone [else] the right to use the label? Had Briusov's article in *Russian Thought* played a role in the matter?...Or did clever David [Burliuk] cast a proprietary eye round the real situation and decide that we couldn't swim against the tide, that to reject a name which had been foisted upon us would only make the public more confused and antagonistic? (1a).

< «Рожон» *(obs)* is a pointed stake.

P-145 • ЛЕЗТЬ ⟨ИДТИ́⟩/ПОЛЕ́ЗТЬ НА РОЖО́Н *coll;* **ПЕРЕ́ТЬ/ПОПЕРЕ́ТЬ НА РОЖО́Н** *substand* [VP; subj: human] to undertake sth. risky, potentially dangerous: X лезет на рожон ≃ **X is taking a (big) risk; X is sticking his neck out; X is going out on a limb; X is risking his neck;** [in refer. to rash behavior] **X is acting recklessly ⟨foolhardily⟩; X is asking ⟨begging⟩ for trouble;** ‖ *Neg Imper* не лезь на рожон ≃ **play it ⟨things⟩ safe; don't take any chances.**

«Ты, я считаю, с самого начала повёл это дело неправильно. Полез на рожон, стал угрожать» (Войнович 3). "I think that you conducted this affair improperly from the very beginning. Went out on a limb, used threats" (3a). ♦ [Андрей] Гуськов знал, что на рожон он не полезет и последних дуростей делать не станет, и надеялся, что, как бы ни повернулось дело, успеет скрыться (Распутин 2). Andrei [Guskov] knew that he wouldn't ask for trouble and he wouldn't do anything too stupid, and he hoped that no matter how things turned out, he would manage to get away (2a).

< See P-144.

P-146 • КО́РЧИТЬ/СКО́РЧИТЬ ⟨СТРО́ИТЬ/СО-СТРО́ИТЬ, ДЕ́ЛАТЬ/СДЕ́ЛАТЬ⟩ РО́ЖУ *(какую, кому)*; **КО́РЧИТЬ ⟨СТРО́ИТЬ, ДЕ́ЛАТЬ⟩ РО́ЖИ**

(какие, кому) all highly coll; **СКРО́ИТЬ РО́ЖУ (какую)** substand [VP; subj: human; var. with рожу is usu. pfv; var. with рожи is usu. impfv] to grimace, distort one's facial expression (in order to show one's dislike of or dissatisfaction with s.o. or sth., amuse or frighten s.o. etc): X скорчил (Y-y) рожу ≃ **X made a face (at Y); X pulled a face;** ‖ X строил смешные ⟨весёлые, глупые, страшные⟩ рожи ≃ **X was making funny ⟨comic, silly, terrible etc⟩ faces.**

[Лука Лукич:] Вот ещё на днях, когда зашёл было в класс наш предводитель, он скроил такую рожу, какой я никогда ещё не видывал (Гоголь 4). [L.L.:] Only the other day when our marshal of nobility came into the classroom he made a face the like of which I never saw before! (4c). ♦ «Ах ты, бедняга ты мой! Изжога, говоришь, одышка, соболезную...» — бормотал сочувственно, а сам, глядя в зеркало, строил весёлые рожи (Трифонов 1). "Oh, dear, you poor man! Heartburn, you say, and shortness of breath—well, I *am* sorry," he mumbled sympathetically, while at the same time making comic faces at himself in the mirror (1a).

Р-147 • РО́ЖУ КРИВИ́ТЬ/СКРИВИ́ТЬ substand [VP; subj: human] to distort one's facial expression (showing disgust, dissatisfaction, or contempt for s.o. or sth.): X рожу скривил ≃ **X made a puss; X screwed up his face.**

Р-148 • В РО́ЗНИЦУ продавать, покупать что [PrepP; Invar; adv] (to sell or buy sth.) as individual units or in small quantities: **retail; by the piece.**

Это не магазин, а склад, здесь ничего в розницу не продают. This isn't a store, it's a warehouse. Nothing is sold by the piece here.

Р-149 • НЕТ РО́ЗЫ БЕЗ ШИПО́В [saying] anything that is attractive or good also has its bad side: ≃ **(there's) no rose without a thorn; (there are) no roses without thorns; every rose has its thorn.**

Р-150 • В РО́ЛИ кого-чего, какой [PrepP; Invar; Prep; the resulting PrepP is adv or subj-compl with copula (subj: human or collect)] in the capacity of: **in the role of; in a [AdjP] role; (using s.o. ⟨sth.⟩) as.**

«Там, внизу [на Земле], льётся кровь, — сказал я, — а здесь вчерашний работник в роли спокойного созерцателя». — «Кровь льётся там ради лучшего будущего», — отвечал Нэтти (Богданов 1). "Back there [on Earth] blood is being spilled," I said, "yet here stands yesterday's revolutionary in the role of a calm observer." "Blood is being shed for the sake of a better future," replied Netti (1a). ♦ «А в милицию его за бульдога надо было обязательно водить?» — «Это глупость. Меня здесь не было, понимаете? А завуч решила его припугнуть». — «Что, милиция в роли огородного чучела?» (Семёнов 1). "Did you really have to take him to the police over a bulldog?" "It was silly, really. I wasn't here, you see. And the director of studies decided to give him a fright." "Oh, using the police as a sort of scarecrow?" (1a).

Р-151 • ВЫХОДИ́ТЬ/ВЫ́ЙТИ ИЗ РО́ЛИ [VP; subj: human] to stop pretending (that one is a certain type of person), stop affecting a certain quality, emotion etc: X вышел из роли ≃ **X abandoned ⟨his⟩ role; X relinquished his role;** ‖ *Neg* X не выходил из роли ≃ **X remained in character.**

Я старался понравиться княгине, шутил, заставляя её несколько раз смеяться от души; княжне также не раз хотелось похохотать, но она удерживалась, чтоб не выйти из принятой роли... (Лермонтов 1). I did my best to charm the old princess, told jokes and made her laugh heartily several times; her daughter too wanted to laugh more than once, but she suppressed the desire so as not to abandon the role she [had] assumed... (1b). ♦ Красивая роль руководителя народного чувства так понра-

вилась Растопчину, он так сжился с нею, что необходимость выйти из этой роли, необходимость оставления Москвы без всякого героического эффекта застала его врасплох... (Толстой 6). The illustrious role of leader of popular feeling so delighted Rostopchin, and he had grown so accustomed to it, that the necessity of relinquishing it and surrendering Moscow with no heroic display of any kind took him unawares... (6a).

Р-152 • НЕ ИГРА́ТЬ (НИКАКО́Й) РО́ЛИ [VP; subj: usu. abstr, often это] to be insignificant: X не играет никакой роли ≃ **X is of no importance; X is of no consequence (at all); X is unimportant ⟨inconsequential⟩; X hardly matters; X doesn't mean a thing;** [in limited contexts] **X is beside the point.**

«Смотри, все ведущие идеологические посты заняли наши люди». — «Это не играет роли. Они... будут действовать в силу обстоятельств, а не в силу личных симпатий и антипатий...» (Зиновьев 2). "Look, all the important posts went to our people." "That's of no consequence at all....They'll act according to circumstances, not because of any personal sympathies or antipathies..." (2a). ♦ Кто позавидует Ахматовой, которая не смела слова произнести у себя в комнате и только пальцем показывала на дырочку в потолке, откуда осыпалась на пол кучка штукатурки. Был там установлен подслушиватель или нет, роли не играет (Мандельштам 2). What reason was there to envy Akhmatova, who did not dare utter a word in the privacy of her own room and used to point to the hole in the ceiling from which a little pile of plaster had fallen on the floor? Whether or not there was actually a listening device is beside the point... (2a).

Р-153 • ВХОДИ́ТЬ/ВОЙТИ́ В РОЛЬ [VP; subj: human] **1.** to (begin to) portray a character in a play, movie etc naturally and convincingly, transform o.s. into that character: X вошёл в роль ≃ **X got into his role ⟨part⟩; X got into character; X got the feel of his part; X grew into his role.**

2. ~ кого, чью, какую to (begin to) conduct o.s. in accordance with one's position or function in a given situation, milieu etc: X вошёл в роль Y-a ≃ **X got ⟨fell, grew⟩ into the role of Y; X assumed the role of Y; X played the ⟨his⟩ role of Y; X adapted to his role as Y;** ‖ X снова вошёл в роль Y-a ≃ **X resumed his role of Y.**

Евгений Устинович мешал ему входить в новую роль тридцатилетнего молодого человека (Дудинцев 1). ...[Evgeni Ustinovich] hampered him in playing his new role of young man of thirty (1a). ♦ При слове «пустыня» воображение Феденьки, и без того уже экзальтированное, приобретало такой полёт, что он, не в силах будучи управлять им, начинал очень серьёзно входить в роль погубителя Навозного. Ангел смерти, казалось ему, парит над нечестивым городом... (Салтыков-Щедрин 2). At the word "desert" Fedenka's imagination, already in a state of high exaltation, soared aloft so high that, unable to control it any longer, he began quite seriously to assume the role of Navozny's destroyer. The Angel of Death, it seemed to him, was already spreading his wings over the doomed city (2a). ♦ ...Мансуров-Курильский снова вошёл в роль по части ценных указаний, хотя и высказывал их в более лояльной форме... (Залыгин 1). ...Mansurov-Kurilsky resumed his role of order-giver, although he was fairer about it now... (1a).

Р-154 • ВЫДЕ́РЖИВАТЬ/ВЫ́ДЕРЖАТЬ РОЛЬ (кого, какую) [VP; subj: human; more often pfv] not to deviate from one's chosen or outlined mode of conduct: X выдержал роль (Y-a) ≃ **X kept up his role (as Y); X played his part ⟨the part of Y⟩ to the end; X did not depart from his role as Y ⟨from the role of Y⟩;** ‖ *Neg* X не выдержал роли ≃ **X failed to keep up his role.**

«Я совсем не могла обедать, — сказала она. — Я думала, что не выдержу эту страшную роль до конца» (Каверин 2). "I could eat nothing at dinner," she said. "I thought I should never endure playing this ghastly part to the end" (2a). ♦ «Что, если это мираж, и я во всём ошибаюсь, по неопытности злюсь, подлой роли моей не выдерживаю?» (Достоевский 3). "What if it's a mirage, what if I'm completely mistaken, get angry on account of my inexperience, and fail to keep up my vile role?" (3c). ♦ Потом взошёл мой отец. Он был бледен, но старался выдержать свою бесстрастную роль. Сцена становилась тяжела. Мать моя сидела в углу и плакала (Герцен 1). [context transl] Then my father came up. He was pale but tried to maintain his studied indifference. The scene was becoming painful. My mother sat in the corner, weeping (1a).

P-155 • **ИГРА́ТЬ ПЕ́РВУЮ РОЛЬ** *coll* [VP; subj: human] to be the most important, influential, or noticeable person: X играет первую роль ≃ **X is number one; X plays ⟨has⟩ the key role; X plays the leading role.**

Ася привыкла всегда и везде играть первую роль и не могла примириться с тем, что на новой работе она всего лишь рядовой сотрудник. Asya was used to being number one always and everywhere, and couldn't accept the fact that at her new job she was just another employee.

P-156 • **ИГРА́ТЬ/СЫГРА́ТЬ РОЛЬ** [VP] **1.** ~ *какую (в чём)* [subj: human, collect, or abstr] to have a certain (as specified) meaning, significance, influence etc: X играет [AdjP] роль (в Y-e) ≃ **X plays a [AdjP] role ⟨part⟩ (in Y); [in limited contexts, with большую, огромную etc] X is very ⟨enormously etc⟩ important.**

Володину было лестно играть такую значительную роль при таком выдающемся событии в жизни такого почтенного лица (Сологуб 1). Volodin was flattered to play such a significant role in such an important moment in the life of such a respected person (1a). ♦ ...Когда случается провожать старого или встречать нового начальника, то я всегда при этом играю видную роль (Салтыков-Щедрин 2). ...Whenever we have to bid farewell to one of our chiefs, or extend a loyal welcome to a new one, I always play an important part in these proceedings (2a). ♦ ...Андрей однажды сказал мне: «Для Мити внешняя сторона играет огромную роль» (Каверин 1). ...Andrei had said to me one day: "The outward appearance of things is enormously important for Mitya" (1a).

2. [subj: human, collect, or abstr; used without a modif; impfv only] to be of considerable significance: X играет роль ≃ **X plays a leading ⟨an important⟩ role ⟨part⟩; X really matters ⟨counts⟩; X has ⟨exerts⟩ influence.**

...Вероятно, Станкевичу говорили о том, что он... может занять в обществе почётное место, что он призван, по богатству и рождению, играть роль... (Герцен 2). ...Stankevich had probably been told that...he could occupy an honourable position in society, that he was called by wealth and birth to play an important part... (2a).

3. ~ *кого-чего* [subj: human, collect, or abstr] to be or act in the capacity of s.o. or sth.: X играл роль Y-a ≃ **X played the part ⟨the role⟩ of Y.**

Воспитанный полуиностранным воспитаньем, он хотел сыграть в то же время роль русского барина (Гоголь 3). Although his education had been half foreign, he wanted at the same time to play the part of a Russian landed gentleman (3d). ♦ ...С той поры сколько раз уже я играл роль топора в руках судьбы! (Лермонтов 1). How often since then have I played the role of an axe in the hands of fate! (1b).

4. ~ *(кого, rare чего, какую)*. Also: **РАЗЫ́ГРЫВАТЬ/РАЗЫГРА́ТЬ РОЛЬ** [subj: human] to pretend to be what one is not, act unnaturally: X играет роль ≃ **X is playing a role ⟨a part⟩; X is putting on an act; X is acting a part; X is playacting;** ‖ *Neg* X не играл (никакой) роли ≃ **X adopted no pose.**

«Наконец давнишнее желание моего сердца свершилось!» — повторил он и остановился, чтобы перевести дух. Я понял, что старик играет роль... (Салтыков-Щедрин 2). "At last my dearest wish has come true!" he repeated and stopped to take breath. I realized that the old fellow was acting a part... (2a). ♦ Кутузов никогда не говорил... о жертвах, которые он приносит отечеству, о том, что он намерен совершить или совершил: он вообще ничего не говорил о себе, не играл никакой роли, казался всегда самым простым и обыкновенным человеком... (Толстой 7). Kutuzov never talked of...the sacrifices he was making for the fatherland, or of what he meant to or had done: in general he said nothing about himself, adopted no pose, always appeared to be the simplest and most ordinary of men... (7a).

P-157 • **ПОМЕНЯ́ТЬСЯ РОЛЯ́МИ** *(с кем)* [VP; subj: human (pl if there is no prep obj), collect, or abstr] to exchange places (with another person, group, or phenomenon): X и Y поменялись ролями ⟨X поменялся ролями с Y-ом⟩ ≃ **X and Y have traded ⟨switched, swapped⟩ roles ⟨places⟩; X and Y have exchanged roles; X has traded ⟨switched, swapped⟩ roles ⟨places⟩ with Y; the roles are reversed; X's and Y's roles have been reversed; [in limited contexts] the shoe is on the other foot; X has turned the tables on Y.**

[author's usage] Старый князь с сыном как бы переменились ролями после кампании 1805 года. Старый князь, возбуждённый деятельностью, ожидал всего хорошего от настоящей кампании; князь Андрей, напротив... видел одно дурное (Толстой 5). The old Prince and his son seemed to have exchanged roles after the campaign of 1805. The father, stimulated by his activity, expected the best results from the new campaign, while Prince Andrei on the contrary...saw only the dark side (5a). ♦ А! господин Грушницкий! ваша мистификация вам не удастся... мы поменяемся ролями: теперь мне придётся отыскивать на вашем бледном лице признаки тайного страха (Лермонтов 1). Ah, Grushnitsky, your ruse won't work. The roles will be reversed—it'll be I who studies your pale face for the marks of hidden fear (1c).

P-158 • **НА ВТОРЫ́Х РОЛЯ́Х** [PrepP; Invar; subj-compl with copula (subj: human) or obj-compl with держать (obj: human); fixed WO] (to be or keep s.o.) in a position of secondary importance: **(play) a supporting role; (be ⟨keep s.o.⟩) in a subordinate position.**

И хотя со временем бабушка освоилась с хозяйством и с семьёй, но она так и осталась на вторых ролях (Рыбаков 1). ...And although in time she [Grandmother] learned to cope with the house and the family, she always played a supporting role (1a).

P-159 • **НА ПЕ́РВЫХ РОЛЯ́Х** [PrepP; Invar; subj-compl with copula (subj: human) or obj-compl with держать (obj: human); fixed WO] (to be or keep s.o.) in an important, influential position: **(play) a key role; (be ⟨keep s.o.⟩) in a key position ⟨role⟩.**

Вопрос, почему Строковский держит Поляшко в институте, да ещё на первых ролях, никогда не сходил с повестки дня кулуарных разговоров (Залыгин 1). A constant theme of corridor gossip was why Strokovsky kept Poliashko at the institute and in a key position (1a).

P-160 • **КРУТИ́ТЬ/ЗАКРУТИ́ТЬ ⟨ПОКРУТИ́ТЬ⟩ РОМА́Н ⟨ЛЮБО́ВЬ⟩** *с кем highly coll* [VP; subj: human] to have an amorous relationship with s.o.: X крутит роман с Y-ом ≃ **X has something ⟨a thing⟩ going with Y; X is fooling around with Y.**

P-161 • **МА́КОВОЙ РОСИ́НКИ ⟨НИ (МА́КОВОЙ) РОСИ́НКИ, НИЧЕГО́⟩ ВО РТУ НЕ́ БЫЛО** *(у кого) coll* [VP_{subj/gen}; past only] s.o. has not eaten anything at all: у X-а маковой росинки во рту не было ≃ **X hasn't had ⟨touched, eaten⟩ a thing; X hasn't eaten a bite ⟨a scrap of food⟩; X hasn't had a (single) bite (to eat); X hasn't had a morsel of food; X has had nothing whatsoever.**

«Я измучена, даже есть не могу, хотя с утра во рту ни маковой росинки» (Свирский 1). "I'm exhausted, I can't swallow a thing, although I haven't eaten a scrap of food all day" (1a). ♦ [Астров:] Возился я целый день, не присел, маковой росинки во рту не было... (Чехов 3). [A.:] I was on the go all day—didn't so much as sit down or have a bite to eat... (3c). [A.:] I was on the move all day, didn't sit down or have a morsel of food... (3a). ♦ ...Семён, разбудив старуху, наскоро перекусил — больше суток маковой росинки не было во рту... (Тендряков 1). Simon woke up his wife and had a bite to eat—he had had nothing whatsoever for more than twenty-four hours... (1a).

Р-162 • НИ (МА́КОВОЙ) РОСИ́НКИ не дать *кому,* **не получить** и т. п. *coll* [NP$_{gen}$; these forms only; fixed WO] (to give, get etc) absolutely nothing: **not a (blessed) thing;** [in refer. to food or drinks only] **not a drop** ⟨**a morsel, a bite to eat**⟩.

[Баян:] ...До свадьбы задатком стакан и ни росинки больше, а работу выполнят, тогда хоть из горлышка (Маяковский 1). [Oleg Bard:] I'll give them one glass in advance before the wedding and not a drop more. When they've done their job, they can drink straight out of the bottle, if they like (1a).

Р-163 • (НИ) НА МА́КОВУЮ РОСИ́НКУ *coll* [PrepP; these forms only; adv (intensif); used with negated predic; fixed WO] (not even) in the smallest amount or to the smallest degree: **(not) at all; (not) a** ⟨**one**⟩ **bit.**

Лгун он, ему на маковую росинку нельзя верить. He's a liar, don't believe him one bit.

Р-164 • ПОЗВОЛЯ́ТЬ/ПОЗВО́ЛИТЬ (СЕБЕ́) РО́С- КОШЬ [VP; subj: human; foll. by infin] to treat o.s. to sth. expensive, extravagant, or beyond what is really necessary: X позволил себе роскошь (сделать Y) ≃ **X permitted** ⟨**allowed**⟩ **himself the luxury of (doing Y).**

Восемнадцать лет как Майер — мастер, но всё ещё не может позволить себе роскоши отоплять все комнаты своей мансарды... (Федин 1). Maier had been a foreman eighteen years, but he still could not permit himself the luxury of heating all the rooms of his mansard... (1a).

Р-165 • В РОСТ¹ [PrepP; Invar; nonagreeing modif or adv] (of a portrait, photograph etc, or to paint, photograph etc s.o.) capturing the entire figure: портрет ⟨фотография и т. п.⟩ Х-а в рост ≃ **a full-length portrait** ⟨**photograph** etc⟩ **of X;** ‖ написать портрет Х-а в рост ≃ **paint a full-length portrait of X;** ‖ сфотографировать Х-а в рост ≃ **take a full-length picture of X; photograph X full-length.**

«Ты вот что, Аркадий, ты первым делом, как надену форму, — пришли нам фото. Понял?» — ...«В рост фото или в рост и ещё — анфас?» (Залыгин 1). "You know what, Arkady? As soon as you get into uniform, send us a photo, first thing. Okay?"..."A full-length shot, or one full-length and one head-and-shoulders?" (1a).

Р-166 • В РОСТ² давать, отдавать, пускать деньги [PrepP; Invar; adv] (to lend money) on the condition that the borrower pay for the use of the borrowed money: **(lend money) on interest; (lend money and) charge interest.**

Жила она уединённо, питаясь скудною пищею, отдавая в рост деньги... (Салтыков-Щедрин 1). She lived in seclusion, on a meager diet, lending money on interest... (1a).

Р-167 • ВО ВЕСЬ РОСТ; В ПО́ЛНЫЙ РОСТ [PrepP; these forms only] **1. (в)стать, стоять, подниматься, вытягиваться** и т. п. ~ [adv] (to raise o.s. up, stretch o.s. out etc) to a fully straight position, (to hold o.s.) erect: **stand up** ⟨**draw o.s. up, rise**⟩ **to one's full height; (stretch out) full length.**

Он поднялся во весь рост и с криком: «За родину! За Сталина! Ура!» — размахивая пистолетом, побежал навстречу танкам (Войнович 4). He drew himself up to his full height and yelled: "For the motherland! For Stalin! Hurrah!" Brandishing his pistol, he began running straight for the tanks (4a). ♦ С этой минуты настойчивый взгляд Ольги не выходил из головы Обломова. Напрасно он во весь рост лёг на спину, напрасно брал самые ленивые и покойные позы — не спится, да и только (Гончаров 1). From that moment Olga's persistent gaze haunted Oblomov. In vain did he stretch out full length on his back, in vain did he assume the laziest and most comfortable positions—he simply could not go to sleep (1a).

2. [nonagreeing modif or adv] (of a portrait, photograph etc, or to paint, photograph etc s.o.) capturing the entire figure: портрет ⟨фотография и т. п.⟩ Х-а во весь рост ≃ **a full-length portrait** ⟨**photograph** etc⟩ **of X;** ‖ написать портрет Х-а во весь рост ≃ **paint a full-length portrait of X;** ‖ сфотографировать Х-а во весь рост ≃ **take a full-length picture of X; photograph X full-length.**

На стене висел портрет хозяйки дома во весь рост. On the wall there was a full-length portrait of the lady of the house.

3. ~ вставать, подниматься и т. п. [adv] (usu. of a question, problem, threat etc) (to arise, present itself etc) in all its seriousness or urgency: **(arise etc) in all its magnitude** ⟨**immensity**⟩; **(assume) its true, overwhelming proportions** ⟨**dimensions**⟩; [in limited contexts] **in full measure.**

Это его всегдашнее бессилие что-либо знать о Фаине снова подступило в полный рост... (Битов 2). Again his everlasting powerlessness to know anything about Faina came over him in full measure... (2a).

4. *lit* [adv] (of a people, a hero, death etc) displaying to the utmost extent one's or its great might, importance etc: **(tower) to one's** ⟨**its**⟩ **full height; (rise) to one's** ⟨**its**⟩ **full stature; (arise) in all one's greatness.**

...К самой войне все участники прежней относились пренебрежительно: и размах, и силы, и потери — всё в сравнении с германской войной было игрушечно. Одна лишь чёрная смерть, так же, как и на полях Пруссии, вставала во весь свой рост, пугала и понуждала по-животному оберегаться (Шолохов 4). All those who had taken part in the previous war treated this one with scorn; the scale, the forces involved, the losses were all of toylike dimensions compared with the war against the Germans. Only death was the same as on the fields of Prussia, ever towering to its full height and frightening men into defending themselves like animals (4a).

Р-168 • РОСТ В РО́СТ [Invar; detached modif or subj-compl with copula (subj: human, pl); fixed WO] (usu. of tall people) equally tall: **(exactly) the same height; the exact same height.**

Ребята в нашей баскетбольной команде как на подбор: рост в рост. The guys on our basketball team look as if they were handpicked: they are exactly the same height.

Р-169 • ПО РО́СТУ *(кому)* [PrepP; Invar; nonagreeing modif or subj-compl with copula (subj: a noun denoting an item of clothing)] in correspondence with a person's size: **(just) s.o.'s** ⟨**the right**⟩ **size;** ‖ *Neg* не по росту ≃ **not s.o.'s size; the wrong size;** ‖ большой ⟨маленький⟩, не по росту ≃ **too big** ⟨**small**⟩ **(for s.o.).**

По безлюдному отрезку улицы двигались навстречу мне две фигуры — мужская и женская. Мужская была неестественно расширившаяся от шубы явно не по росту... (Олеша 3). Two figures, a man's and a woman's, were moving toward me along a deserted section of street. The man's figure was rendered unnaturally broad by a fur coat manifestly the wrong size... (3a). ♦ Большая, не по росту шинель висела на нём, как кафтан на бахчевном чучеле (Шолохов 3). His greatcoat was too big for him and hung like a robe on a scarecrow (3a).

P-170 • **(ОДНИ́М ⟨ЕДИ́НЫМ⟩) РО́СЧЕРКОМ ПЕРА́** погубить *кого-что,* решить *что,* уволить *кого* и т. п.; **ПО ОДНОМУ́ ⟨ЕДИ́НОМУ⟩ РО́СЧЕРКУ ПЕРА́** [NP$_{instrum}$ or PrepP; these forms only; adv; fixed WO] (usu. used to characterize actions that result in undesirable consequences) (to destroy s.o. or sth., decide sth., fire s.o. etc) abruptly, without due deliberation, simply by signing a mandate: **with one ⟨a single⟩ stroke of the pen; at a ⟨one⟩ stroke of the pen.**

Решения принимаются быстро, и там, где зимой раздумывают, взвешивают, обсуждают, летом решают одним росчерком пера (Михайловская 1). Decisions are made quickly, and whereas in the wintertime they think about it, weigh it, discuss it, in summer the decisions are made with one stroke of the pen (1a).

P-171 • **В РОТ НЕ БРАТЬ** *coll* [VP; subj: human] **1.** ~ *чего* to refrain totally from eating certain foods or drinking certain beverages: X Y-а в рот не берёт ≃ **X never touches ⟨eats, drinks, goes near⟩ Y; X won't touch ⟨eat, drink, go near⟩ Y; X stays away from Y; X steers clear of Y;** [in refer. to alcohol only] **X won't touch a drop (of Y); X never lets Y pass ⟨touch⟩ his lips; X is a teetotaler.**

«...[Штольц] ухи терпеть не может, даже стерляжьей не ест; баранины тоже в рот не берёт» (Гончаров 1). "He [Stolz] can't bear fish soup—not even sturgeon, and he never touches mutton" (1b). ♦ [Фёкла:] ...И такой купец трезвый, совсем не берёт хмельного в рот... (Гоголь 1). [F.:] ...Such a sober man he is, too; never touches a drop... (1a). ♦ Женившись, он в рот не брал водки. Раньше-то пил много (Семёнов 1). Once he was married he didn't touch a drop of vodka. Before he had been a heavy drinker (1a).

2. usu. *ничего* ~ not to eat or drink anything: X ничего в рот не брал ≃ **X hasn't touched a thing ⟨a bite⟩; X hasn't had anything ⟨a thing⟩ (to eat or drink); X hasn't had a bite to eat.**

P-172 • **В РОТ НЕ ВОЗЬМЁШЬ; В РОТ НЕЛЬЗЯ́ ВЗЯТЬ** *coll* [VP; these forms only; neg pfv fut, gener. 2nd pers sing (1st var.) or impers predic with быть∅ (2nd var.)] sth. is extremely unpalatable, not suitable for eating: **you don't dare touch it; you can't eat it; it's inedible ⟨not fit to eat⟩.**

Мясо так подгорело, что в рот нельзя взять. This meat is so burnt you can't eat it.

P-173 • **ВО ВЕСЬ РОТ** [PrepP; Invar; adv] **1.** улыбаться, зевать и т. п. ~ *coll* (to smile) very widely, (to yawn) with one's mouth open wide: **(grin) from ear to ear; (smile) nice and wide; (have) a broad grin (on one's face); (grin) showing all one's teeth; (give) a big yawn.** Cf. **(grin) like a Cheshire cat.**

«Вы совсем не волнуетесь?» – спросил Рейл с удивлением. «Нет!» – сказала я, чувствуя, что улыбаюсь, что хочу улыбаться во весь рот... (Аллилуева 2). "Aren't you nervous?" Rayle asked in some surprise. "Not at all." And I found myself smiling. I felt like grinning from ear to ear... (2a). ♦ «Открываю дверцу, пропускаю красулечку, а она мне во весь рот улыбается» (Искандер 2). "I open the door, let the peach in, and the whole time she's smiling nice and wide to me" (2a). ♦ На правом фланге резерва возвышался Максим и опять улыбался во весь рот (Стругацкие 2). Maxim, with a broad grin on his face again, towered above the backup team's right flank (2a). ♦ «Зачем это письмо? К чему я не спал всю ночь, писал утром?..» Он зевнул во весь рот (Гончаров 1). "Why did I send that letter? Why didn't I sleep all night and why did I write it in the morning?..." He gave a big yawn (1a).

2. кричать, орать ~ *highly coll* (to yell) very loudly: **(shout) one's head off; (shout) at the top of one's voice ⟨lungs⟩.**

P-174 • **ДЕРЖА́ТЬ РОТ НА ЗАМКЕ́** *coll;* **РОТ НА ЗАМО́К** *coll;* **РОТО́К НА ЗАМО́К** *rather folk* [VP; subj:

human (1st var.), often imper; NP, usu. used as imper (variants without держать); fixed WO (2nd and 3rd variants)] to keep quiet, keep a secret, not blab sth.: держи рот на замке ≃ **keep your mouth ⟨trap⟩ shut; button your lip; keep a lid on it.**

«Ты, Самохин, слушать – слушай, да только помалкивай... что видел, что слышал – военная тайна, роток на замок, как говорится, ясно?» (Максимов 1). "You, Samokhin, listen if you like, but keep it to yourself....Whatever you see or hear is a military secret. Keep your trap shut, as they say, is that clear?" (1a).

P-175 • **ЗАМА́ЗЫВАТЬ/ЗАМА́ЗАТЬ РОТ** *кому (чем)* *highly coll* [VP; subj: human] to force s.o. to keep silent about sth. (generally by using bribery or flattery): X замазал Y-у рот (Z-ом) ≃ **X kept Y from talking (by means of Z); X shut Y up ⟨silenced Y⟩ (with Z);** [in refer. to bribery only] **X bought Y off ⟨bought Y's silence⟩; X gave ⟨paid⟩ Y hush money.**

Продавец против заведующей не пойдёт, она ему взяткой рот замазала. The salesman won't say anything against the manager—she silenced him with a bribe.

P-176 • **ЗАТЫКА́ТЬ/ЗАТКНУ́ТЬ ⟨ЗАКРЫВА́ТЬ/ЗАКРЫ́ТЬ, ЗАЖИМА́ТЬ/ЗАЖА́ТЬ⟩ РОТ** *кому highly coll* [VP; subj: human] to force s.o. to be silent, prevent s.o. from speaking or voicing his opinion: X заткнул рот Y-у ≃ **X shut Y up; X shut ⟨stopped⟩ Y's mouth; X gagged ⟨silenced⟩ Y; X muzzled Y; X put a muzzle on Y.**

«А теперь если ты, скажем, ошибаешься, а я хочу тебя поправить, говорю тебе об этом словами, а ты меня не слушаешь, даже рот мне затыкаешь – так что мне делать? Палкой тебя по голове?» (Солженицын 3). "Let's say you make a mistake and I want to correct you. I speak to you about it, and you don't listen to me, you even shut me up. Well, what am I supposed to do? Beat you over the head?" (3a). ♦ Младший продавец, когда начали продавать мёд из запасной бочки, видно, кое о чём догадался... Шалико никак не мог решить – заткнуть ему рот парой тридцаток или не стоит унижаться? (Искандер 4). The junior salesman must have caught on when they began selling honey from the reserved barrel....Shaliko could not decide: should he stop the man's mouth with a pair of thirty-ruble bills, or was it worth demeaning himself? (4a). ♦ «Володя, чтобы не было недоразумений. Я разделяю линию партии. Будем держать свои взгляды при себе. Ни к чему бесполезные споры». – «У меня там более нет желания дискутировать со сталинскими подголосками, – высокомерно ответил Володя, – но уж раз вы меня сюда [в ссылку] загнали, то рот не заткнёте» (Рыбаков 2). "Volodya, just so there won't be any misunderstandings, I want you to know that I accept the Party line. Let's keep our views to ourselves. No need to have pointless arguments." "I haven't the slightest desire to debate with Stalinist yes-men," Volodya had replied haughtily. "But since you put me here, don't try to gag me as well" (2a). ♦ Помню, как... вмешался Твардовский: «Дайте ей сказать, я хочу понять – что произошло; что вы ей рот затыкаете?» (Ивинская 1). I remember that Tvardovski tried to intervene on my behalf: "Let her speak. I want to understand what happened. Why do you want to muzzle her?" (1a).

P-177 • **ЛИ́ШНИЙ РОТ** *coll* [NP; fixed WO] a person who cannot provide for himself and is a burden to those who have to feed and keep him: **extra mouth to feed.**

И без того обездоленная слухами о своём классовом происхождении, совесть его окончательно замолкла и в распрях его страстей уже не принимала никакого участия, как бедная родственница, лишний рот, незаметно устраивалась где-нибудь в уголке, чтобы не слишком попадаться на глаза... (Искандер 3). His conscience, which had already been harassed and impoverished anyway by rumors about its class origin, was silenced for good and took no sides in the feuding among his passions—like a poor female relative, an extra mouth to feed, who fixes herself up in some out-of-the-way corner lest she invite too much attention... (3a).

P-178 • **НА ЧУЖО́Й РОТ ПУ́ГОВИЦЫ НЕ НА-ШЬЁШЬ** [saying] you cannot force others to be silent (said when gossip or rumors about a person are being circulated): ≃ **people will talk; you ⟨one⟩ can't stop people from talking.**

«На днях покровский пономарь сказал на крестинах у нашего старосты: полно вам гулять; вот ужо приберёт вас к рукам Кирила Петрович. Микита кузнец и сказал ему: и, полно, Савельич, не печаль кума, не мути гостей...; да ведь на чужой рот пуговицы не нашьёшь» (Пушкин 1). "Just the other day the sacristan from Pokrovskoe said at a christening held at our elder's house: 'The good times are over: you'll see what it's like when Kirila Petrovich takes you in hand.' Mikita the blacksmith answered him. 'Enough of that, Savelich,' he says, 'don't sadden the godfather, don't upset the guests....' But people will talk" (1a).

P-179 • хлопот, забот и т. п. **ПО́ЛОН РОТ** *у кого coll* [Invar; quantit subj-compl with быть$_\emptyset$ (subj/gen: хлопот, забот etc), usu. pres; fixed WO] s.o. has very many (obligations, cares etc): у X-а хлопот ~ ≃ **X has his hands full;** [in limited contexts] **X is up to his neck ⟨ears⟩ in jobs ⟨work etc⟩; X has too much on his plate;** ‖ у X-а своих ⟨и без того⟩ забот полон рот ≃ **X has enough to do ⟨handle etc⟩ as it is; X has enough to worry about without you ⟨all this etc⟩.**

С потьминской пересылки меня направили в 10-ый лагерь... У новичка в лагере хлопот полон рот: надо найти место в бараке, получить койку, тюфяк, подушку, одеяло, постельные принадлежности, форменную спецовку для работы... (Марченко 1). From the Potma transit prison I was directed to camp number ten....A novice in camp is up to his ears in jobs. First he has to find himself a place in a hut and get himself a cot, straw mattress, pillow, blanket and bedding, and regulation overalls for work... (1a). ♦ И вправду, Фома, внезапно возникнув в купе, поспешил выручить главного: «Пошли, Валентина, пошли... У Петра Васильевича своих забот полон рот... Видишь, кругом документация...» (Максимов 3). Sure enough, Foma had suddenly materialized in the compartment and hastened to his boss's rescue. "Come on, Valentina, come on....Pyotr Vasilievich has got enough to worry about without you....Documents all over the place, see?..." (3a).

P-180 • **РАЗЕВА́ТЬ/РАЗИ́НУТЬ РОТ ⟨РТЫ⟩** *highly coll;* **РАСКРЫВА́ТЬ/РАСКРЫ́ТЬ ⟨ОТКРЫВА́ТЬ/ОТ-КРЫ́ТЬ⟩ РОТ ⟨РТЫ⟩** *coll* [VP; subj: human] **1.** to begin to speak, say sth., express one's opinion etc: X рот разинул ≃ **X opened his mouth;** ‖ *Neg* [in cases where one or more speakers monopolize the conversation] X не мог рта раскрыть ≃ **X couldn't get a word in edgewise.**

«Кто там смел рот разинуть», — сказал грозно исправ-ник... (Пушкин 1). "Who was it dared open his mouth over there?" asked the superintendent menacingly (1a).

2. to get distracted from what one should be doing or paying attention to at the given moment: X разинул рот ≃ **X was napping ⟨spacing out⟩;** ‖ чего рот разинул? ≃ **why are you standing ⟨sitting etc⟩ there with your mouth open?; why are you standing ⟨sitting etc⟩ there gaping?;** ‖ *Neg Imper* не разевай рот! ≃ **wake up!; get with it!**

3. to be utterly amazed and show one's amazement: X рот разинул ≃ **X's mouth fell open; X's jaw dropped (in amazement); X gasped; X gaped with open mouth;** [in limited contexts] **X was knocked ⟨thrown⟩ for a loop;** ‖ X стоял разинув рот ≃ **X stood there with his mouth open.**

[Расплюев:] А сколько ты мне, например, говорит, Иуда, дашь денег под это детище?.. Того так и шелохнуло, и рот разинул... (Сухово-Кобылин 2). [R.:] And how much would you give me, Judas, he says, on this little trinket? That stirred him so, his mouth fell open (2b). ♦ ...Недоимок накопилось такое множество, что местный казначей, заглянув в казённый ящик, разинул рот... (Салтыков-Щедрин 1). ...Such an amount of taxes went uncollected that when the local treasurer looked into the treasury cash-box, his jaw dropped in amazement... (1b). ♦ И бабка, и тётка Бекей, и Гульджамал с дочкой — все стояли бы разинув рты. Где это видано, чтобы голова была человечья, а тело рыбье! (Айтматов 1). And grandma, and Aunt Bekey, and Guldzhamal with her daughter would all stand gaping with open mouths. Who has ever seen a creature with a human head and the body of a fish! (1a). And old grandma, Aunt Bekai and Guljamal with her daughter—they'd all stand there with their mouths open. Who's ever heard of such a thing?—a person's head on a fish's body (1b).

4. [often pfv Verbal Adv with слушать] to become totally absorbed in listening to s.o.: X слушал раскрыв рот ≃ **X listened open-mouthed ⟨with open mouth, with his mouth wide open⟩.**

Коротеев... любит пощеголять своими знаниями, ему лестно, что Лена слушает его раскрыв рот... (Эренбург 3). Dmitry [Koroteyev] was...fond of showing off his knowledge, it flattered him to have Lena listening to him open-mouthed (3a). ♦ «Смотри, как девчоночке голову задуряет! А она рот раскрыла, дура, и слушает [*regional* = слушает]» (Свирский 1). "See how she's turning that girl's head! And there she stands with her mouth wide open drinking it all in, the fool!" (1a).

P-181 • **РАЗЖЁВЫВАТЬ/РАЗЖЕВА́ТЬ И В РОТ КЛАСТЬ/ПОЛОЖИ́ТЬ** *(что) кому coll* [VP; subj: human; usu. pfv] to explain sth. to s.o. in the simplest and most detailed way possible: X разжевал Y и Z-у в рот положил ≃ **X spelled Y out for Z; X spoon-fed Y to Z.**

P-182 • **РАССТЕГНУ́ТЬ РОТ ⟨ГЛО́ТКУ⟩** *substand, rude* [VP; subj: human] **1.** to begin to talk, chatter, sing, swear etc: X рот расстегнул ≃ **X opened his mouth ⟨trap, big mouth, big fat mouth, big yap⟩ etc⟩.**

2. ~ *кому* to force s.o. to start talking, singing etc: X Y-у рот расстегнёт ≃ **X will make Y open his mouth;** [in limited contexts] **X will force ⟨squeeze⟩ it out of Y.**

P-183 • **РОТ ДО УШЕ́Й** *(у кого) coll* [NP; fixed WO] **1.** a large mouth: **whale ⟨cavern⟩ of a mouth.**

2. s.o. is laughing or smiling in such a manner that his mouth seems to stretch all the way to his ears: (у X-а) ~ ≃ **X is grinning from ear to ear.** Cf. **X is grinning like a Cheshire cat.**

P-184 • **СМОТРЕ́ТЬ ⟨ГЛЯДЕ́ТЬ⟩ В РОТ** *кому coll* [VP; subj: human] **1.** to watch, usu. hungrily and with envy, while another eats: X Y-у в рот смотрит ≃ **X stares (hungrily) at Y's mouth; X watches Y's every bite.**

Костанжогло не любил, чтобы лакеи слушали господские разговоры, а ещё более, чтобы глядели ему в рот в то время, когда он ест (Гоголь 3). ...[Kostanzhoglo] did not like to have the flunkies listening to the masters' talk and, still more, he disliked having them staring at his mouth every time he took a bite (3b).

2. to listen to s.o. very attentively, eagerly: X смотрит Y-у в рот ≃ **X hangs on Y's every word; X listens spellbound (to Y); X listens to Y with rapt attention.**

Алёша и Саня приезжали к нам в Москву. Тогда у нас сразу в квартире становилось тесно, а мои дети смотрели Алёше в рот, потому что он так занимательно рассказывал (Аллилуева 2). Alyosha and Sanya sometimes came to stay with us in Moscow. Our apartment would immediately become very crowded and my children would hang on Alyosha's every word, for he had an entrancing way of telling stories (2a). ♦ ...Она ему в рот смотрела, что бы он ни говорил... Она всё как бы ждала (это Лёва прекрасно чувствовал), чтобы он напомнил о том вечере... (Битов 2). She listened spellbound no matter what he said....She seemed to keep waiting (Lyova was well aware of this) for him to remind her of the other evening... (2a).

P-185 • ЗОЛОТА́Я РО́ТА *obsoles, coll* [NP; the collect noun рота – sing only; fixed WO] derelicts: **bums; tramps; hobos.**

«…Сюда всё больше шпана, рвачи, золотая рота за длинным рублём налетела…» (Максимов 1). "…Most of the people we get here these days are riff-raff, rabble, tramps on the lookout for easy money" (1a).

P-186 • НА ЧУЖО́Й ⟨НА ВСЯ́КИЙ⟩ РОТО́К НЕ НА-КИ́НЕШЬ ПЛАТО́К [saying] you cannot make others be silent (said when gossip or rumors about a person are being circulated): ≃ **you ⟨one⟩ can't stop people from talking; people will talk.**

«Про меня в городе всякий вздор мелют, — угрюмо говорил Передонов, — чего и не было, наплетут». — «На чужой роток не накинешь платок, — сказал хозяин, — а впрочем, в наших палестинах, известно, кумушкам что и делать, как не язычки чесать» (Сологуб 1). "They're spreading all sorts of non-sense about me in the town," said Peredonov sullenly, "and they make up things that never happened." "You can't stop people from talking," said the host, "and besides, it is well known that the scandalmongers in our provincial Palestines have nothing to do but wag their tongues" (1a).

P-187 • МИМО РТА ПРОШЛО́ ⟨ПРОЛЕТЕ́ЛО⟩ *coll* [VP; subj: abstr (usu. omitted); these forms only] sth. evaded s.o.: мимо рта прошло ≃ **person X didn't get it; it passed person X by; person X missed out on it.**

P-188 • (так и) ТА́ЕТ ВО РТУ *coll* [VP; subj: a noun denoting some food, esp. sth. baked; usu. pres or past] sth. is very delicious: X (так и) тает во рту ≃ **X melts in your mouth; X is scrumptious ⟨divine, out of this world⟩.**

Гречневая каша с грибами и жареным луком так и таяла во рту. The buckwheat kasha with mushrooms and fried onions was out of this world.

P-189 • РУБА́ХА-ПА́РЕНЬ *highly coll* [NP; sing only; obj, appos, or subj-compl with copula (subj: human, male)] a sociable, easygoing, friendly and open person: **regular guy; outgoing fellow; happy-go-lucky sort (of fellow ⟨of guy⟩); hail-fellow well met ⟨hail-fellow-well-met⟩.**

[Сатин:] Я, брат, молодой – занятен был!.. Рубаха-парень… плясал великолепно, играл на сцене, любил смешить людей… славно! (Горький 3). [S.:] You know, friend, when I was young I was pretty entertaining!…An outgoing fellow…I danced terrifically, did some acting, liked to make people laugh….It was great! (3a). ♦ Овчинников производил двоякое впечатление. С одной стороны – это был рубаха-парень… с другой – амурные похождения и постоянные выпивки Анатолия Николаевича… были так густо переплетены, что он, наверное, и сам не мог разобраться, где говорит правду, а где сочиняет (Чернёнок 1). Ovchinnikov made an ambiguous impression. On the one hand, he was a hail-fellow-well-met….On the other hand, the amorous adventures and constant drinking of Anatoly Nikolaevich were such a part of him that probably he himself couldn't tell anymore when he was telling the truth and when he was lying (1a).

P-190 • СВОЯ́ РУБА́ШКА ⟨РУБА́ХА⟩ БЛИ́ЖЕ К ТЕ́ЛУ [saying] one's own well-being (or the well-being of those dear to one) is more important than other people's interests (when said of o.s., usu. used to justify one's actions; when said of another, usu. used disapprovingly): ≃ **charity begins at home; self loves itself best; self comes first; people look out for number one; people look out for their own skins first; men value their own skins more than those ⟨that⟩ of others.**

…Ни один из его клевретов – ни Бунина, ни Кулешов, ни Козловский – не подняли руку в его защиту. Почему? А потому что своя рубашка ближе к телу. Они за уважаемого только до тех пор, пока сила на его стороне (Войнович 3). …Not one of his minions – not Bunina, not Kuleshov, not Kozlovsky – raised a hand in his defense. Why not? Why, because charity begins at home. They were for their respected colleague only as long as he had the power (3a). ♦ [author's usage] Просил раненый Степан: «Братцы! Не дайте пропасть! Братцы! Что ж вы меня бросаете!..» – но брызнула тут по проволоке пулемётная струя, и уползли казаки. «Станишники! Братцы!» – кричал вслед Степан, – да где уж там – своя рубашка, а не чужая к телу липнет (Шолохов 3). The wounded man had begged, "Brothers! Don't leave me to my death! How can you, brothers!" But a burst of machine-gun fire had splashed over the wire and the Cossacks made off. Stepan's imploring cry had followed them, but men value their own skins more than that of others (3a).

P-191 • В ОДНО́Й РУБА́ШКЕ ⟨БЕЗ РУБА́ШКИ⟩ остаться, оставить *кого obsoles, coll* [PrepP; these forms only; subj-compl with остаться (subj: human) or obj-compl with оставить (obj: human)] (to be brought or bring s.o. to) a state of financial ruin, (to reduce s.o. or be reduced to) poverty: X оставил Y-а в одной рубашке ≃ **X left Y with nothing but the shirt on Y's back; X took Y to the cleaners; ‖ X остался в одной рубашке ≃ X was left with nothing but the shirt on his back; X lost his shirt; X got taken to the cleaners.**

Эти шулера обыграли его дочиста, в одной рубашке оставили. Those card sharks cleaned him out, left him with nothing but the shirt on his back.

P-192 • РОДИ́ТЬСЯ В РУБА́ШКЕ ⟨В СОРО́ЧКЕ⟩ *coll, occas. humor* [VP; subj: human; usu. past] to be lucky: X родился в рубашке ≃ **X was born under a lucky star; X was born lucky.** Cf. **have the luck of the Irish.**

«Может быть, вы в сорочке родились, если это вам так сойдёт» (Солженицын 2). "If you get away with this, you must have been born under a lucky star" (2a).

< According to popular belief a baby born with a caul («в рубашке», «в сорочке») will succeed in everything he or she does.

P-193 • ДО (ПОСЛЕ́ДНЕЙ) РУБА́ШКИ спустить, про-играть(ся), отдать *что и т. п. obsoles, coll* [PrepP; these forms only; usu. adv or postmodif; fixed WO] (to lose, give up etc) absolutely everything: X спустил всё до последней рубашки ≃ **X lost ⟨gave up, pawned etc⟩ everything down to his last shirt; X lost his shirt.**

[Нелькин:] Вам больше делать нечего: отдавайте!!. Отдавайте, Пётр Константинович, отдавайте всё; – до рубашки!.. (Сухово-Кобылин 1). [N.:] There's nothing more you can do: give them what they want!!…Give them everything, Pyotr Konstantinovich, everything – down to your last shirt!… (1a).

P-194 • НАДЕВА́ТЬ/НАДЕ́ТЬ СМИРИ́ТЕЛЬНУЮ РУБА́ШКУ ⟨РУБА́ХУ⟩ *на кого* [VP; subj: human; often 3rd pers pl with indef. refer.] to put a stop to s.o.'s disruptive, objectionable behavior: X наденет на Y-а смирительную рубашку ≃ **X will straitjacket ⟨shackle⟩ Y; X will bring Y to heel;** [in limited contexts] **X will muzzle Y.**

P-195 • СНИМА́ТЬ/СНЯТЬ (ПОСЛЕ́ДНЮЮ) РУ-БА́ШКУ *с кого coll* [VP; subj: human; usu. pfv] to ruin s.o., reduce s.o. to poverty: X с Y-а последнюю рубашку снимет ≃ **X will take Y's last penny; X will clean Y out; X will send Y to the poorhouse.**

P-196 • СНЯТЬ (С СЕБЯ́) ПОСЛЕ́ДНЮЮ РУБА́ШКУ ⟨РУБА́ХУ⟩ *(для кого)*; ОТДА́ТЬ (С СЕБЯ́) ПОСЛЕ́Д-НЮЮ РУБА́ШКУ ⟨РУБА́ХУ⟩ *(кому) all coll* [VP; subj:

human; often infin with готов] (to be willing) to share what little one has: X готов последнюю рубашку снять с себя для Y-а ≃ **X would give Y the shirt off X's back; X would share his last penny with Y.**

«Ведь, наверное, когда-нибудь кому-нибудь ты помог, протянул руку, вытащил кого-нибудь из воды или огня или последнюю отдал рубаху?» (Войнович 4). "You must have helped somebody some time, lent a hand, pulled somebody out of the water or from a fire, or given someone the shirt off your back?" (4a).

P-197 • ПЕРЕЙТИ́ РУБИКО́Н *lit* [VP; subj: human] to make an important decision that cannot be reversed and that determines the course of future events: X перешёл Рубикон ≃ **X crossed ⟨passed⟩ the Rubicon.**

Я встряхнулся. Я снова выпятил челюсть и решительно двинулся к двери прямо. Эдик шёл рядом со мной. «Рубикон перейдён!» — заявил я и пнул дверь ногой (Стругацкие 3). I got myself together. I stuck out my jaw again and resolutely strode toward the middle door. Eddie walked next to me. "The Rubicon is crossed!" I announced and kicked the door (3a).

< From the name of the river *Rubicon,* which Julius Caesar crossed in 49 B.C., thus starting the civil war that changed the history of Rome.

P-198 • РУБИ́ТЬ СПЛЕЧА́ *coll* [VP; subj: human; more often pres, neg imper, or infin with нельзя, не надо, не стоит etc] **1.** to speak directly, bluntly, without regard for anyone or anything: X рубит сплеча ≃ **X speaks straight from the shoulder ⟨straight out⟩; X shoots from the hip; X calls a spade a spade; X doesn't mince words; X tells it like it is.**

И в своих показаниях, и в письмах, и на суде, и в сделанных после суда заявлениях оба держались по-разному: Якир рубил сплеча, как бы сознавая, что терять ему уже нечего, Красин... подводил подо всё определённую философию (Амальрик 1). Each behaved somewhat differently from the other, however, in his recantation, in letters, in court, and in issuing statements after the trial. Yakir, as though realizing that he had nothing to lose, spoke straight out. But Krasin...attributed his actions to a well-defined philosophy (1a). ♦ Французские рефюжье, с своей несчастной привычкой рубить сплеча и всё мерить на свою мерку, сильно упрекали Кошута за то, что он... в речи, которую произнёс в Лондоне с балкона Mansion House, с глубоким уважением говорил о парламентаризме (Герцен 3). The French refugees, with their unfortunate habit of calling a spade a spade and measuring everything by their own standard, made it a great reproach against Kossuth that...in the speech delivered in London from the balcony of the Mansion House, [he] had spoken with deep respect of the parliamentary system (3a).

2. to act in an impetuous and rash manner, not troubling o.s. to think things over: X рубит сплеча ≃ **X acts recklessly ⟨impulsively, on impulse⟩; X leaps before he looks; X goes off half-cocked;** ‖ *Neg Imper* не руби сплеча ≃ **look before you leap; don't do anything hasty ⟨rash⟩.**

«Подозреваю, что записи в бухгалтерских книгах подделал Кузнецов. Нужно срочно принять меры». — «Не руби сплеча. Подожди, пока у тебя будут доказательства». "I suspect it was Kuznetsov who falsified the records in the account books. We must take immediate action." "Look before you leap. Wait until you have some evidence."

P-199 • НЕ ИМЕ́Й СТО РУБЛЕ́Й, (А) ИМЕ́Й СТО ДРУЗЕ́Й [saying] it is better to have many friends than to have much money (said when friends and acquaintances come to a person's aid in a time of trouble; occas. said when a friend does a person a great favor): ≃ **where your friends are, there your riches are; they are rich who have true friends;** [in limited contexts] **it's always good to have a friend in court.**

P-200 • БИТЬ РУБЛЁМ *кого coll* [VP; subj: human or collect; often infin with надо, следует, можно etc] to penalize s.o. financially for failing to work up to the required standard, for working poorly or making mistakes: X бьёт Y-а рублём ≃ **X docks Y ⟨Y's pay⟩.**

P-201 • ДЛИ́ННЫЙ РУБЛЬ; usu. ехать, гнаться, охотиться и т. п. **ЗА ДЛИ́ННЫМ РУБЛЁМ** *coll, often disapprov* [NP (sing only) or PrepP (Invar); usu. prep obj; fixed WO] a large amount of money earned quickly and easily: **(make) a fast buck; (make ⟨earn⟩) big money ⟨bucks⟩; (chase after ⟨be on the lookout for⟩) easy money; (chase) the big bucks ⟨money⟩.**

«Мы с Доменико, кореш у меня там был, итальянец, в Аргентину намыливались за длинным рублём...» (Аксёнов 6). "I had a pal called Domenico, an Italian, and we were...on our way to Argentina to make a fast buck" (6a). ♦ «...Подался милёнок мой за длинным-то рублём на стройку пятилетки да и сгинул там безо всякого поминания...» (Максимов 2). "...My fellow went off to earn big money on a construction site for the Five-Year-Plan, and he just vanished there without a trace..." (2a). ♦ «...Сюда всё больше шпана, рвачи, золотая рота за длинным рублём налетела...» (Максимов 1). "...Most of the people we get here these days are riff-raff, rabble, tramps on the lookout for easy money" (1a). ♦ [Василиса:] ...За полтора года, пока ты гонялся за длинным рублём, я... я вышла замуж (Салынский 1). [V.:] ...In the past year and a half while you've been chasing the big money, I...I got married (1a).

P-202 • РУГА́ТЕЛЬСКИ РУГА́ТЬ *кого coll* [VP; subj: human; fixed WO] to curse s.o. profusely: X ругательски ругал Y-а ≃ **X cursed Y out; X cursed Y up one side and down the other; X cursed Y up and down.**

Если случалось, что он приносил домой не всю зарплату, жена его ругательски ругала. If he ever brought home less than his entire wages, his wife would curse him up one side and down the other.

P-203 • В РУЖЬЁ! *mil* [PrepP; Invar] **1.** стать, встать и т. п. ~ [subj-compl with copula (subj: human pl or a noun denoting a unit of ground forces)] (to get) in formation with weapons in hand: X-ы стали в ружьё ≃ **Xs came to arms ⟨to the ready⟩; Xs prepared for combat ⟨for battle⟩.**

Роте была дана команда стать в ружьё. The company was given the order to prepare for battle.

2. поставить, поднять *кого-что* ~ [obj-compl with поставить, поднять (obj: human or a noun denoting a unit of ground forces)] (to bring) to a state of military preparedness: X поднял Y-ов в ружьё ≃ **X placed Ys on combat ⟨battle⟩ alert; X called Ys to arms.**

По сигналу тревоги капитан поднял роту в ружьё. When the alarm was sounded, the captain placed his company on combat alert.

3. [indep. sent] used as a command to make ready for battle: **to arms!**

Кто-то заливисто и испуганно кричал возле дверей: «В ружьё!.. В ружьё!..» (Шолохов 3). Someone shouted wildly at the door, "To arms!...To arms!" (3a).

4. стоять ~ *obs* [subj-compl with стоять (subj: human, usu. pl, or a noun denoting a unit of ground forces)] (to be) in a state of battle readiness: **on alert; at the ready; under arms; ready for battle.**

Мы пошли на вал... Там уже толпились все жители крепости. Гарнизон стоял в ружьё (Пушкин 2). We made our way to the rampart....All the inhabitants of the fortress were already crowded there. The garrison was under arms (2b).

P-204 • **ПОД РУЖЬЁ** *mil* [PrepP; Invar] **1. поставить, призвать** *кого и т. п.* ~ [obj-compl with поставить etc (obj: human pl or collect)] (to call s.o. up) for military service: X поставил Y-ов под ружьё ≃ **X called Ys to active duty ⟨service⟩; X placed Ys under arms; X called Ys to arms.**

Когда началась война, всех запасников призвали под ружьё. When the war started, all reservists were called to active duty.

2. поставить *кого obs* [obj-compl with поставить (obj: human or collect)] (in refer. to a soldier in the Imperial army) (to punish a soldier by) making him stand for a certain period of time fully armed and in full marching gear: X-а поставили под ружьё ≃ **X was ordered to stand punishment in full combat gear.**

P-205 • **ПОД РУЖЬЁМ** *mil* [PrepP; Invar] **1. быть∅, находиться** *и т. п.* ~; **держать** *кого* ~ [subj-compl with copula or obj-compl with держать (subj and obj: human, usu. pl, or collect)] (to be or have s.o.) mobilized: **under arms; armed and ready.**

2. стоять ~ [subj-compl with стоять (subj: human or collect)] (to be) in a state of battle readiness: **on alert; at the ready; under arms; ready for battle.**

3. стоять ~ [subj-compl with стоять (subj: human or collect)] (of a soldier in the Imperial army) (to stand) for a certain period of time fully armed and in full marching gear as a form of punishment: X стоял под ружьём ≃ **X stood punishment in full combat gear.**

P-206 • **БЕЗ РУК!** *coll* [indep. sent; Invar] (used as a command) do not touch (me, him, her): **(keep your) hands off!**

P-207 • **ВÁЛИТСЯ ИЗ РУК** (*у кого*) *coll* [VP; subj: всё, работа, дело etc; usu. pres or past] everything (or some work, project etc) is coming out badly for s.o. because he lacks the appropriate mood, cannot concentrate on what he is doing etc: (у X-а) всё ⟨работа⟩ валится из рук ≃ **X can't do anything right; X can't do the simplest thing; X's work isn't coming out right; X is making a mess of everything; X can't put his mind to anything ⟨to his work⟩.**

Я изнывал в отсутствие Зинаиды: ничего мне на ум не шло, всё из рук валилось, я по целым дням напряжённо думал о ней... (Тургенев 3). In Zinaida's absence I pined: I could not concentrate; I could not do the simplest thing. For whole days I did nothing but think intensely about her (3b). ♦ [extended usage] «Вот вам тема для диссертации — что такое монополия, почему всё валится у неё из рук и чем она отличается от настоящего коллектива» (Дудинцев 1). "There's a theme for a thesis if you like: what is the nature of a monopoly, and why does it make a mess of everything it undertakes, and in what respect does it differ from a genuine collective?" (1a).

P-208 • **ВЫПУСКÁТЬ/ВЫ́ПУСТИТЬ ИЗ РУК** [VP; subj: human] **1.** ~ *что* [often neg] to part with sth., give sth. away: X не выпустит Y из рук ≃ **X won't let Y out of his hands; X won't let go of Y; X won't let Y go; X won't give Y up.**

Павел Иванович как-то особенно не любил выпускать из рук денег. Если ж настояла крайняя необходимость, то всё-таки, казалось ему, лучше выдать деньги завтра, а не сегодня (Гоголь 3). Pavel Ivanovich somehow had a particular aversion to letting money out of his hands. Even if there was an urgent necessity to do so, it still seemed to him that it would be better to pay the money tomorrow and not today (3c).

2. ~ *кого-что* to allow s.o. or sth. that is available to one to escape one, fail to make use of or avail o.s. of sth., s.o.'s services etc: X выпустил Y из рук ≃ **X let Y slip through his fingers; X let Y slip ⟨pass him⟩ by; X failed to take advantage of thing Y.**

Тебе предлагали квартиру в центре Москвы за полцены, и ты отказался? Как ты мог выпустить из рук такую возможность! They offered you an apartment in the center of Moscow for half price and you turned it down? How could you let an opportunity like that slip through your fingers?

P-209 • **ИЗ ВТОРЫ́Х ⟨ТРÉТЬИХ⟩ РУК** *сведения, информация; узнать, получить, купить что* [PrepP; these forms only; nonagreeing modif or adv; fixed WO] (to get information, find sth. out, buy sth. etc) through an intermediary or intermediaries, not directly (from the original source, owner etc): **secondhand; at second ⟨third⟩ hand; through a third party.**

Я передаю рассказ, полученный мною из вторых, точнее, из третьих рук... (Мандельштам 2). ...I have the story at second, or, rather, at third hand... (2a).

P-210 • **ИЗ ПÉРВЫХ РУК** *сведения, информация; узнать, получить, купить что* [PrepP; Invar; nonagreeing modif or adv; fixed WO] (to get information, find sth. out, buy sth. etc) without an intermediary, directly (from the original source, owner etc): [in refer. to information] **firsthand; at first hand; (straight) from the horse's mouth;** [in refer. to purchasing sth.] **straight from the owner.**

«Когда тронемся, неизвестно, может, через час, а может, через месяц...» — «Тронемся в восемнадцать ноль-ноль... Не пяль глаза, у меня сведения из первых рук» (Максимов 3). "There's no knowing when we'll get away from here....It may be an hour and it may be a month." "We'll be off at eighteen hundred hours....No need to stare like that. I've got firsthand information" (3a).

P-211 • **ИЗ РУК В РУ́КИ** [PrepP; Invar; adv; fixed WO] **1. передавать, отдавать** *что кому и т. п.* (to deliver, give sth. to s.o. etc) directly: X отдал Y-у Z ~ ≃ **person X handed Z over to Y (in person); person X handed Z in (in person); person X delivered Z into Y's hands;** [in limited contexts] **Y got Z direct from the source.**

Теперь он... смело шёл Куда Надо (правда, с чёрного всё-таки хода) и передавал написанное из рук в руки (Войнович 4). Now he...went bravely to the Right Place (though he did make use of the rear entrance) to hand in what he had written (4a). ♦ «Здравствуй, брат мой Иван, получил твоё письмо... из рук в руки...» (Максимов 1). "Hail, my brother Ivan! I have received your letter....It was delivered into my hands" (1a). ♦ ...Строительный материал, как мы знаем, был получен меньшевиками не по каким-то там казённым поставкам, а свеженьким, из рук в руки (Искандер 3). ...As we know, the Mensheviks had not procured their building materials through any official supply channels but fresh, direct from the source (3a).

2. ходить, переходить, передаваться ~ (to pass, be passed) from one person to another, from some people to others: X передаётся из рук в руки ≃ **X passes ⟨is passed⟩ from hand to hand; X is passed around; X goes ⟨is passed⟩ from one person to another ⟨to the next⟩; X makes the rounds;** [in limited contexts] **X changes hands.**

«От кого ж бы это? — задумчиво говорил Обломов, рассматривая адрес. — Рука как будто знакомая, право!» И письмо пошло ходить из рук в руки (Гончаров 1). "Who could it be from?" mused Oblomov, examining the address. "The handwriting looks familiar...it really does!" The letter was passed from hand to hand (1b). ♦ В описанной уже выше баньке за семью печатями «Курьер» со статьёй «Ничтожество» переходил из рук в руки (Аксёнов 7). Back in the bathhouse-behind-the-seven-locks outside Moscow the issue of the *Courier* containing the "Nonentity" article was making the rounds (7a). ♦ В Одессу же вместо немцев пришли их победители... и на юге начался почти двухлетний период, в течение которого власть переходила из рук в руки раз шесть, а то и больше... (Катаев 3). The Germans in Odessa had now been replaced by their conquerors...and in South Russia there now began a period of almost two years in which power changed hands six times if not more... (3a).

P-212 • ИЗ РУ́К ВОН *coll* [PrepP; Invar; fixed WO] **1.** ~ **плохой, плохо, скверный, скверно и т. п.** [modif (intensif)] (used to emphasize the highest degree of some negative quality or characteristic) very, extremely (bad, poorly): **incredibly ⟨terribly, hopelessly, outrageously⟩ (bad ⟨poorly⟩);** [when the equivalent incorporates the AdjP or AdvP that follows] **as bad as (bad) can be; couldn't be (any) worse; terrible ⟨-bly⟩; awful(ly); wretched(ly); abominable ⟨-bly⟩;** ‖ **дела** *(чьи, кого)* **из рук вон плохи ⟨обстоят из рук вон плохо⟩ ≃** [in limited contexts] **things have hit ⟨fallen to⟩ rock bottom (for s.o.);** [often in refer. to a gravely ill person] *s.o.* **is in a (very) bad way.**

Стихи, разумеется, были из рук вон плохи... (Максимов 2). His poems were, of course, incredibly bad... (2a). ♦ ...Сталин говорил с ним грубо, упрекал Берию в том, что руководимая им служба работает из рук вон плохо... (Войнович 4). ...Stalin had spoken harshly to him..., reproaching Beria that his organization could not be doing any worse... (4a). ♦ Нет, конечно, сомнения, что Бородавкин мог избежать многих весьма важных ошибок. Так, например, эпизод, которому летописец присвоил название «слепорода», – из рук вон плох (Салтыков-Щедрин 1). There is, of course, no doubt that Wartkin could have avoided many great errors. Thus, for example, the episode on which the chronicler conferred the name Bornblind—that was awful (1a). ♦ ...[Ефим] спросил, что я думаю об общем построении романа, о том, *как* это написано. Написано это было, как всегда, из рук вон плохо... (Войнович 6). ...[Yefim] asked what I thought of the overall structure of the novel, and of the *writing*. The writing, as always, was abominable (6a). ♦ Из всего выходило, что дела Андрея из рук вон плохи... (Максимов 3). What it all came to was that Andrei was in a very bad way... (3a). ♦ Воспитание его было поставлено из рук вон плохо... (Стругацкие 4). [context transl] His education had been grossly neglected... (4a).

2. это (же ⟨уж, совсем и т. п.⟩) ~ ! [Interj] this is entirely unacceptable, cannot be tolerated: **that's ⟨this is⟩ (really) too much!; that's the limit!; that's ⟨this is⟩ unthinkable ⟨beyond anything⟩!**

Снял мой полицейский офицер сапоги... «Вытрясите их и вычистите». – «Это из рук вон!» (Герцен 2). My police-officer took off the boots. "Knock the dirt off and polish them." "That's really too much!" (2a). ♦ «Что ты, писал, назначил время?» – «Ничего не писал». – «Помилуй, братец, да что же мы с тобой сделаем? Это из рук вон, это белая горячка!» (Герцен 1). "Have you written? Have you fixed a time?" "I have written nothing." "Upon my word, my boy, but what are we to do with you? It's beyond anything, it's raving madness!" (1a).

P-213 • КАК БЕЗ РУК *без кого-чего coll* [как + PrepP; Invar; usu. subj-compl with copula (subj: human)] one is unable to cope, incapable of doing anything without s.o. or sth.: **X без Y-а как без рук ≃ X is lost ⟨helpless⟩ without Y.**

Меня сняли с работы. «Без всякого объяснения причин», – взволнованно сообщала мне моя заведующая [заведующая детским садом]... «Как без рук остаёмся», – продолжала сокрушаться она... (Гинзбург 2). I was dismissed from my job. "Without any explanation," as my kindergarten head told me. She was very upset about it...."We'll be lost without you," she went on (2a). ♦ После поездки в район за телом Тимофея Лобанова Михаил Пряслин больше трёх недель не вставал с постели: горячка. И он, Лукашин, без него как без рук (Абрамов 1). After his trip to the district for Timofei Lobanov's body, Mikhail Pryaslin didn't get out of his bed for over three weeks: fever. Lukashin was...helpless without him (1b).

P-214 • НЕ ВЫПУСКА́ТЬ ИЗ РУК *что, чего coll* [VP; subj: human] (in refer. to an activity associated with what is specified by the object) to be very immersed in and do a lot of a certain activity: **X не выпускает Y ⟨Y-а⟩ из рук ≃ X doesn't let Y out of X's hand; X never puts Y down; X always has Y in X's hand.**

С пятнадцати лет [Егорша] топор из рук не выпускает (Абрамов 1). He [Egorsha] hadn't let his ax out of his hand since the age of fifteen (1a).

P-215 • НЕ ВЫПУСКА́ТЬ ИЗ РУК ОРУ́ЖИЯ ⟨МЕЧА́ *obs⟩ lit* [VP; subj: human, usu. pl] to be vigilant, prepared for battle at any moment: **Х-ы не выпускают из рук оружия ≃ Xs (always) have one hand on their swords; Xs are armed and ready.**

P-216 • НЕ ПОКЛАДА́Я РУК *работать, трудиться и т. п.* [Verbal Adv; Invar; adv; used with impfv verbs; fixed WO] (to work, do sth.) diligently, without stopping: **nonstop; without respite ⟨a break, a moment's rest⟩; without taking a moment off; tirelessly;** [equivalents incorporate the verb] **one's hands are never still for a moment; one keeps his nose to the grindstone.**

Лара работала не покладая рук и была счастлива (Пастернак 1). She [Lara] worked without respite and was happy (1a). ♦ [Кузьмин:] Обещаю вам работать не покладая рук за двоих, за десятерых (Розов 3). [K.:] I promise you to work tirelessly, to do the work of two, of ten (3a). ♦ «...Много ли может, по-вашему, бедная, но честная девица честным трудом заработать?.. Пятнадцать копеек в день, сударь, не заработает, если честна и не имеет особых талантов, да и то рук не покладая работавши!» (Достоевский 3). "How much, in your opinion, can a poor but honest girl earn by honest labor?...Not even fifteen kopecks a day, sir, if she is honest and has no special talents, and then only if her hands are never still for a moment" (3c).

P-217 • ОТБИВА́ТЬСЯ/ОТБИ́ТЬСЯ ОТ РУК *coll* [VP; subj: human; usu. pfv past] to cease obeying s.o., submitting to s.o.'s authority; (often of children) to begin behaving willfully: **X отбился от рук ≃ X is ⟨has gotten⟩ out of hand ⟨out of control⟩; X is ⟨has gotten to be⟩ (quite) unmanageable.**

«Деспина!» – предупреждала её тётушка Хрисула и, обращаясь к тете Нуце, говорила, что Деспина здесь в Чегеме совсем отбилась от рук, ошалев от встречи с Харлампо (Искандер 5). "Despina!" Auntie Chrysoula warned. Turning to Aunt Noutsa, she would say that Despina had gotten completely out of hand here in Chegem, she'd been unbalanced by her meeting with Harlampo (5a). ♦ «Поживи-ка у нас: который год дожди, на полях всё погнило, дети от рук отбились...» (Стругацкие 1). "Try living with us: how many years has this rain been coming down, everything's rotted in the fields, the children are out of control" (1a). ♦ ...[Павел Петрович] заговорил о хозяйстве и о новом управляющем, который накануне приходил к нему жаловаться, что работник Фома... (Тургенев 2). ...[Pavel Petrovich] began to talk about farming and the new bailiff who had come to him the day before with a complaint about Foma, a farm-hand who...was quite unmanageable (2c).

P-218 • С РУК *покупать, доставать что, продавать, продажа и т. п. coll* [PrepP; Invar; adv or nonagreeing postmodif] (to buy, obtain, sell sth. etc) independently, outside of an established store or trading network: **directly; privately;** [in limited contexts] **on the black market.**

В букинистических магазинах этот хлам, по-моему, не продаётся. Доставала с рук... (Трифонов 5). I don't think they sell such rubbish in secondhand bookstores; she must have obtained them from certain individuals directly... (5a). ♦ Никогда отец не ворчал, если деньги шли на то, чтоб хорошо одевалась Алла. Доставали вещи с рук... (Солженицын 10). Her father had never grumbled if money was spent on dressing Alla well. They got things on the black market... (10a). ♦ Торговал он с рук разной, необходимой в казачьем обиходе рухлядью… и два раза в год ездил в Воронеж, будто за товаром, а на самом деле доносил, что в станице пока-де спокойно и казаки нового злодейства не умышляют (Шолохов 2). [context transl] He traded in various odds and ends that were of use to Cossacks…and twice a year he travelled to Voronezh ostensibly to replenish his stocks, but actually to report that the stanitsa was calm and the Cossacks were not plotting any fresh mischief (2a).

Р-219 • **С РУК НÁ РУКИ сдавать, передавать** *кого-что (кому)* [PrepP; Invar; adv; fixed WO] (to give s.o. or sth.) straight to s.o., (to place s.o. or sth.) right in s.o.'s custody: X сдал Y-a ~ Z-y ≃ **X handed ⟨gave⟩ Y directly to Z; X handed Y over (personally) to Z.**

Мы проговорили чуть не до утра. Я проводил Антона домой и передал его с рук на руки Наташе (Зиновьев 2). We went on talking until just before dawn. I walked Anton home and handed him over to Natasha (2a). ♦ Мама сдала его [Васю] Нине Константиновне с рук на руки… (Гинзбург 2). Mother had handed him [Vasya] over personally to Nina Konstantinovna… (2a).

Р-220 • **СБЫВÁТЬ/СБЫТЬ С РУК** *coll* [VP; subj: human] **1.** ~ *что.* Also: **СПУСКÁТЬ/СПУСТИ́ТЬ С РУК** *coll* to sell sth. (often sth. that is hard to sell): X сбыл Y с рук ≃ **X got Y off X's hands; X got rid of Y.**

«Ну, жинка, а я нашёл жениха дочке!» — «Дурень, дурень!.. Где ж таки ты видел, где ж таки ты слышал, чтобы добрый человек бегал теперь за женихами? Ты подумал бы лучше, как пшеницу с рук сбыть…» (Гоголь 5). "Well, wife, I have found a husband for my daughter!" "You are a fool—a fool!…Whoever has seen, whoever has heard of such a thing as a decent man running after husbands at a time like this? You had much better be thinking how to get your wheat off your hands" (5a).

2. ~ *кого-что* [often pfv infin with хотеть, стараться, рад etc] to rid or free o.s. of s.o. or sth. burdensome, needless: X сбыл Y-a с рук ≃ **X got Y off X's hands; X got rid of Y; X got person Y out of X's hair.**

«Тебе бы только [ребёнка] с рук сбыть, бабка называется!» — разъярилась Клавдия (Трифонов 2). "You just want to get the child off your hands. Call yourself a grandmother!" said Klavdia in fury (2a). ♦ «Когда ты его дурноеда сбудешь с рук?.. У самих хлеба осталось — кот наплакал, а ты его, чёрта горбатого, содержишь, кормишь каждый день» (Шолохов 5). "When will you get rid of this sponger?…We've got precious little grain left for ourselves, and you keep that hunchbacked devil here, feeding him every day" (5a).

Р-221 • **СМОТРÉТЬ ⟨ГЛЯДÉТЬ⟩ ИЗ РУК** *чьих, кого obs* [VP; subj: human] to act the way another wants one to, not independently: X смотрит из Y-овых ⟨из чужих⟩ рук ≃ **X does as Y pleases ⟨as others please⟩.**

Р-222 • **СХОДИ́ТЬ/СОЙТИ́ С РУК** [VP] **1.** ~ *кому coll* [subj: abstr, often всё (это), это] not to result in punishment for s.o.: X сошёл Y-y с рук ≃ **Y got away with X; Y got off ⟨away⟩ scot-free; X had no ⟨serious ⟨negative etc⟩⟩ consequences for Y; Y didn't get into (any) trouble for X;** || *Neg* X не сойдёт Y-y с рук ≃ **Y will pay dearly for X.**

Возможно, мне всё это сошло бы с рук, если б не одна деталь (Искандер 6). Perhaps I might even have gotten away with my indiscretion, had it not been for one small detail (6a). ♦ [Кушак:] Если вы думаете, что теперь им всё сойдёт с рук, — вы ошибаетесь (Вампилов 5). [K.:] If you think they're going to get off scot free now, you're mistaken (5b). ♦ Пока он крал, делал всякие сделки и махинации да набивал себе карман, никто его не трогал, всё ему с рук сходило (Буковский 1). While he was stealing, fixing deals and other illicit operations, and filling his pockets, nobody touched him and he got away scot-free (1a). ♦ К

счастию, все эти промахи имели место в самый разгар Феденькина либерализма и потому сошли Анне Григорьевне с рук довольно легко (Салтыков-Щедрин 2). Fortunately, all these blunders were made at the height of Fedenka's liberal phase and had for this reason no serious consequences for her [Anna Grigoryevna] (2a). ♦ …Все эти вольнодумства ему с рук сходили, потому что Самсон Самсонович пользовался почётом у самого Государя (Терц 6). …He never got into trouble for any of his peccadilloes because he was held in esteem by the Emperor himself (6a). ♦ «Он на Ивана Купала по ночам в лесу один шатается: к ним [немцам], братцы, он не пристаёт. Русскому бы не сошло с рук!..» (Гончаров 1). "He's not afraid of walking in the woods alone on St John's Eve. All that means nothing to Germans. A Russian would have paid dearly for it!" (1a).

2. ~ *как obs* [subj: usu. count abstr] (of some matter, undertaking etc) to transpire or come out (as specified, usu. well): X сошёл с рук [AdvP] ≃ **X passed ⟨came, went⟩ off [AdvP].**

…Хозяин, оставшись один, усталый, бросается на софу и благодарит небо за то, что вечер сошёл с рук без неприятностей (Герцен 2). …The host as soon as he is alone throws himself exhausted on the sofa and thanks heaven that the evening has passed off without unpleasantness (2a). ♦ …Дело сошло с рук благополучно. С остальными тузами и чиновниками оно пошло ещё легче (Салтыков-Щедрин 2). The whole thing went off satisfactorily. With the other bigwigs and civil servants it went off even better (2a).

3. *obs, substand* [subj: concr] to be gotten rid of through selling: X сошёл с рук ≃ **X was sold; X was off person Y's hands.**

Р-223 • **УСКОЛЬЗÁТЬ/УСКОЛЬЗНУ́ТЬ ИЗ РУК** *чьих, кого* [VP] **1.** [subj: human or collect] to avoid capture successfully after almost having been caught: X ускользнул из рук Y-a ≃ **X slipped through Y's fingers; X slipped away from Y.**

2. [subj: abstr or concr] not to be, or to discontinue to be, available to, attainable by etc s.o.: X ускользает из рук Y-a ≃ **X is slipping out of Y's hands ⟨grasp⟩; X is slipping through Y's fingers; X is slipping away from Y.**

Тренер отчётливо видел, что победа ускользает из их рук. The coach saw clearly that victory was slipping out of their grasp.

Р-224 • **УХОДИ́ТЬ/УЙТИ́ ИЗ РУК** *чьих, кого* [VP] **1.** [subj: concr] to discontinue being in s.o.'s possession or at s.o.'s disposal: X ушёл из Y-овых рук ≃ **X slipped away from Y; X slipped out of Y's hands ⟨grasp⟩.**

2. [subj: usu. human] to liberate o.s. from s.o. who has the power to control one, dictate one's future etc: X ушёл из рук Y-a ≃ **X slipped out of Y's hands; X slipped through Y's fingers; X escaped ⟨got away⟩ from Y.**

«Что я, в самом деле, за дурак, стою тут и греха набираюсь! Назад!» — и набожный кузнец опрометью выбежал из хаты. Однако ж чёрт, сидевший в мешке и заранее уже радовавшийся, не мог вытерпеть, чтобы ушла из рук его такая славная добыча. Как только кузнец опустил мешок, он выскочил из него и сел верхом ему на шею (Гоголь 5). "What a fool I am, really. I am standing here and preparing to sin! Back!…" And the pious blacksmith ran headlong out of the hut. But the devil, sitting in the sack and already gloating over his prey, could not endure letting such a glorious capture slip through his fingers. As soon as the blacksmith put down the sack the devil skipped out of it and straddled his neck (5a).

Р-225 • **БОЛЬШÁЯ РУКÁ** *obsoles, coll* [NP; sing only; fixed WO] a person who is influential by virtue of his position: **big wheel; very important person ⟨VIP⟩; (one who) carries a lot of weight.**

Р-226 • **ЛЁГКАЯ РУКÁ** *у кого coll, approv* [NP; sing only; usu. VP_subj with copula, pres or past] s.o. has skill, ability, and/or luck that makes him successful in what he undertakes: y X-a лёгкая рука ≃ **X has a magic touch;** [in limited contexts] **X is clever (at sth.);** [in refer. to financial success] **X has the Midas touch.**

У Веры была лёгкая рука на полноту, умела так скроить, чтобы скрыть изъяны фигуры (Грекова 3). Vera was clever at dealing with stoutness, at cutting fabric to hide the defects of a figure (3a).

P-227 • НЕ РУКА́ *кому obs* [NP; Invar; subj-compl with быть₀ (subj: usu. infin)] **1.** doing sth. is not suited to s.o.'s plans, purposes, tastes etc: делать X Y-у не рука ≃ **it doesn't suit Y to do X;** [in limited contexts] **it is inconvenient for Y to do X.**

[Митя:] …Я к другому-то месту и не пойду. [Гуслин:] Отчего же не пойдёшь? Вот у Разлюляевых жить хорошо — люди богатые и добрые. [Митя:] Нет, Яша, не рука! (Островский 2). [M.:] …I won't go to another place. [G.:] Why won't you go? There at the Razlyulyayevs' it's very nice—the people are rich and kind. [M.:] No, Yasha, that doesn't suit me! (2a).

2. doing sth. is not to s.o.'s advantage: делать X Y-у не рука ≃ **it is not in Y's (best) interests to do X; it wouldn't serve Y's (best) interests to do X.**

3. doing sth. is improper, unbefitting for s.o.: делать X Y-у не рука ≃ **it is unbecoming ⟨not right⟩ for Y to do X; it doesn't suit Y to do X.**

P-228 • ПРА́ВАЯ РУКА́ *чья, кого, у кого* [NP; sing only; subj-compl with copula, nom or instrum (subj: human) or appos; fixed WO] a person of great value and usefulness to s.o., s.o.'s most trusted assistant: X — правая рука Y-a ≃ **X is Y's right hand ⟨arm⟩; X is Y's right-hand man ⟨woman⟩.**

[Соня:] Илья Ильич — наш помощник, правая рука (Чехов 3). [S.:] Ilya Ilyich is our helper, our right hand (3a). ♦ Особенно выделялся чех по имени Антон, любимец и правая рука Радомского (Кузнецов 1). Especially distinguished was a Czech named Anton, Radomski's favorite and his right-hand man (1a).

P-229 • РУКА́ НАБИ́ТА *чья, у кого (в чём, на чём) coll* [VP_subj with быть₀] s.o. has skill, experience, or mastery in sth.: у X-a (в Y-e) рука набита ≃ **X is a practiced hand (at Y); X is an old hand (at Y).**

P-230 • РУКА́ НЕ ДРО́ГНЕТ *чья, у кого coll* [VP_subj; usu. fut; often used with the infin of another verb] s.o. has enough determination, resolve (to do sth., often sth. cruel or harmful to another person): у X-a рука не дрогнет ≃ **X's hand won't shake ⟨tremble⟩; X won't shrink from (doing sth.); X won't hesitate (to do sth.).**

Вот сила — Сталин! Его потому и зовут хозяином. Его рука ни разу не дрогнула, в нём не было интеллигентской дряблости Бухарина (Гроссман 2). Stalin…was a man of true strength. It wasn't for nothing he was known as "the boss." His hand had never trembled—he had none of Bukharin's flabby intellectuality (1a). ♦ «…Не приставай больше, завтра же рапорт на фронт подам, не останусь я здесь, а не отпустят, руки на себя наложу, застрелюсь… Уходи, Виктор, и не показывайся мне больше на глаза, не доводи до краю, если мне своей жизни не жалко, то твоей и подавно, у меня рука не дрогнет. Уходи!» (Максимов 1). "…Stop pestering me. Tomorrow I'll request a transfer to the front, I shan't stay here; and if they don't let me go, I'll lay hands on myself, I'll shoot myself….Go away, Viktor, and don't let me ever set eyes on you again. Don't push me too far. If my own life is unimportant to me, then so much the more so is yours; I wouldn't hesitate. Go away!" (1a).

P-231 • РУКА́ НЕ ПОДНИМА́ЕТСЯ ⟨НЕ ПОДЫ-МА́ЕТСЯ⟩/НЕ ПОДНЯЛА́СЬ *у кого coll* [VP_subj; used

without negation, usu. in questions, to convey the opposite meaning] **1.** ~ *на кого* s.o. lacks the resolve to hit, beat, or kill another: у X-a на Y-a рука не поднимается ≃ **X can't bring himself to hit ⟨kill etc⟩ Y; X doesn't have the heart ⟨doesn't have it in him⟩ to hit ⟨kill etc⟩ Y; X can't lift a hand against Y.**

«…Когда забирали его в плен, можно было бы кокнуть, а уж после как-то рука у меня не подымалась…» (Шолохов 5). [context transl] "…When we captured him, I could have cut him down, but afterwards somehow I couldn't do it in cold blood…" (5a).

2. Also: **РУКА́ НЕ НАЛЕГА́ЕТ/НЕ НАЛЕГЛА́** *obs* [used with the infin of another verb] s.o. lacks the resolve (to do sth.): у X-a рука не поднимается сделать Y ≃ **X can't bring himself to do Y; X doesn't have the heart ⟨the courage⟩ to do Y.**

…Обезображивать такого красавца, как [верблюд] Каранар, — прокалывать ему ноздри… — [у Едигея] рука не поднималась (Айтматов 2). …To spoil such a handsome beast as [the camel] Karanar—to pierce his nostrils….Yedigei could not bring himself to do that (2a).

P-232 • РУКА́ О́Б РУКУ [Invar; adv] **1.** идти, ходить, гулять и т. п. ~ *(с кем)*. Also: **О́Б РУКУ; РУКА́ В РУ́КУ** *obs;* **РУКА́ С РУКО́Й** *obs* (to walk with s.o.) with interlocking arms or holding hands: **arm in arm; hand in hand.**

Он поднялся со скамеечки, и мы втроём, рука об руку, пошли вдоль улицы Первого мая (Стругацкие 3). He got up from the bench and the three of us went down First of May Street arm in arm (3a). ♦ Товарищ Голосов — молодой человек, и стоит ли говорить о том, что в его годы не зазорно показаться на улице рука об руку с девушкой? (Федин 1). Comrade Golosov was a young man, and is it worth mentioning that at his age there was nothing to be ashamed of in appearing on the street hand in hand with a girl? (1a).

2. жить, работать *(с кем)* и т. п. ~. Also: **РУКА́ В РУ́КУ** *obs;* **РУКА́ С РУКО́Й** *obs* (to live, work etc) together, as associates, as comrades: **hand in hand; shoulder to shoulder;** [in limited contexts] **hand in ⟨and⟩ glove.**

Его [Гладышева] разговоры насчёт замечательного гибрида невесты ещё терпели и соглашались даже на то, чтобы вдвоём, рука об руку, нести сквозь жизнь бремя научного подвига, надеясь, впрочем, что дурь эта у Гладышева со временем пройдёт сама по себе (Войнович 2). The girls would put up with his [Gladishev's] discourses on his remarkable hybrid and would even agree to work hand in hand with him and share the burden of his scientific crusade, meanwhile hoping that given time this foolishness would pass from Gladishev by itself (2a). ♦ «Рука с рукой мы пойдём в бой против тех, кто порабощал трудящихся в течение целых столетий!» (Шолохов 3). "Shoulder to shoulder we will go into action against those who have been enslaving the working people for centuries!" (3a).

3. идти ~ *с чем* (to be) connected, closely related (to sth.): **(go) hand in hand (with sth.).**

В его творчестве теория шла рука об руку с практикой… (Лившиц 1). In his creative work theory went hand in hand with practice (1a).

P-233 • РУКА́ РУ́КУ МО́ЕТ [saying] two parties cover for or assist each other in certain matters (which are, or are considered by the speaker to be, dishonest, reprehensible, undesirable etc): ≃ **one hand washes the other; you scratch my back and I'll scratch yours; you ⟨they etc⟩ all look after each other ⟨one another⟩; honor among thieves.**

«…Все они зажиточные. Каждый имеет свой домик, свою бабу со всяким удовольствием… Половина из них баптисты. Сам хозяин [завода] — проповедник у них, ну, и рука руку моет…» (Шолохов 2). "…They're all comfortably off. Every one of them has his own house, his wife, and all they could wish for….Half of 'em are Baptists. The owner [of the factory] himself is a preacher, so they all look after each other…" (2a). ♦ «Ты что, лавочку здесь собрал? Рука руку моет, да? По тюрьме соскучился? Ты мне арапа не заправляй, не таких обламывали!» (Максимов 3). "So you've got a gang of crooks here? Honor among thieves? Can't wait to go to prison, is that it? I'm warning you, don't try to take me for a ride, we've had tougher ones than you to handle" (3a).

< Loan translation of the Latin *manus manum lavat*.

P-234 • СВОЯ́ РУКА́ ВЛАДЫ́КА [saying] the person in question is in a position to do as he sees fit or deems necessary because he is fully in charge of sth. (often said critically when a person acts arbitrarily, willfully, or in a stubborn manner): ≃ **I'm ⟨he's etc⟩ the boss; what I say ⟨he says etc⟩ goes; [in limited contexts] I'm ⟨he's etc⟩ in the driver's seat ⟨in the saddle⟩; I rule ⟨he rules etc⟩ the roost; I call my ⟨he calls his etc⟩ own shots; my ⟨his etc⟩ word is law.**

Наш директор ни с кем не считается, действует по принципу «Своя рука владыка». Our director does exactly as he pleases, acting on the principle "What I say goes."

P-235 • СИ́ЛЬНАЯ РУКА́ (у кого где) coll [NP; sing only; fixed WO] an influential patron: **friend in high places; friend at court; s.o. to pull strings for one.**

P-236 • ТВЁРДАЯ РУКА́ (у кого) [NP; sing only] a decisive person who is able to bend others to his will, keep things under control etc: **(someone ⟨a person etc⟩ with) a strong ⟨firm⟩ hand.**

Положение у нас на заводе тяжёлое. Чтобы исправить его, нужна твёрдая рука. Things at the factory are in a critical state. In order to correct them we need someone with a firm hand.

P-237 • ТЯЖЁЛАЯ РУКА́ у кого coll [NP; sing only; usu. VP_subj with copula] **1.** s.o. delivers hard blows when hitting another: у Х-а тяжёлая рука ≃ **X has a heavy hand.**

«Бью его теперь, что неделя. А рука тяжёлая у меня» (Солженицын 6). "I beat him every week now. And I've got a heavy hand" (6a).

2. a person who brings failure to any endeavor in which he engages: у Х-а тяжёлая рука ≃ **X is bad luck; X is a jinx.**

P-238 • В РУКА́В смеяться, хихикать и т. п. coll [PrepP; Invar; adv] (to laugh) inwardly, to o.s.: **(laugh) up ⟨in⟩ one's sleeve.**

Игорь [Серебро] был автором знаменитой галереи портретов под лаконичным названием «Отцы». Это были портреты отечественной аристократии: доярка, металлург, партработник, хлопковод, генерал, писатель... Никакого гротеска, иронии... идеальная бронза, фотографически точные портреты, придраться невозможно, но... люди, знающие Серебро, а таких по Москве было немало, хихикали в рукава и перемигивались — вот, мол, паноптикум, вот, мол, воткнул им Серебро, пусть на себя посмотрят... (Аксёнов 6). Igor [Serebro] was the creator of a famous series of busts that went by the laconic general title of *Fathers*. These were portraits of typical representatives of the Soviet aristocracy: a milkmaid, a metalworker, a Party official, a cotton grower, a general, a writer. There was nothing grotesque about them, nothing ironic...nothing but ideal bronze, photographically exact portraits to which no one could possibly object. But...people who knew Serebro, and there were quite a few of them around Moscow, laughed up their sleeves and exchanged winks. "What a collection! Serebro has really stuck the knife into them, now let them look at themselves" (6a).

P-239 • ЗАСУЧИ́В РУКАВА́ взяться за что, работать и т. п. coll [Verbal Adv; Invar; adv; fixed WO] (of a person) (to get to work, to work etc) diligently, energetically: засучив рукава, Х взялся ⟨принялся⟩ за дело ⟨работу и т. п.⟩ ≃ **X rolled up his sleeves and got down to work ⟨to the job etc⟩; X buckled ⟨knuckled⟩ down to work.**

...Появился у неё [у отсталой страны] Великий Царь. Увидел он отставание и решил прекратить это безобразие. Засучив рукава, он взялся за дело и прорубил окно в Европу (Зиновьев 1). ...Then a Great Tsar appeared [in the backward land]. He saw the backwardness all around him, and he decided it had to stop. So he rolled up his sleeves, got down to work, and opened up a window on Europe (1a). ♦ Ольга Васильевна сказала, что паники, собственно, нет, [Сергею] надо спокойно всё обдумать, учесть замечания, переделать, что необходимо и с чем ты внутренне согласен, — словом, взяться засучив рукава, но не поддаваться слабости (Трифонов 3). Olga said that there was, in fact, no panic; what Sergei had to do was to think it all over calmly, to take note of the adverse comments, to revise whatever was necessary and whatever, in his own view, was genuinely in need of revision—in other words, to roll up his sleeves and get down to the job but *not* give way to weakness (3a).

P-240 • СПУСТЯ́ РУКАВА́ coll, disapprov [Verbal Adv; Invar; adv; more often used with impfv verbs] (to do sth.) carelessly, haphazardly, without an honest attempt: **any old way; in a slipshod manner; sloppily; halfheartedly; slapdash; lazily.**

«Другие люди к работе относятся спустя рукава, лишь бы день до вечера, а Федоша... для него, понимаете, семья на втором месте, а на первом работа» (Войнович 4). "Other people work any old way, just put in their time, but Fedosha...for him, you see, the family is second, work comes first" (4a). ♦ «Все боялись халтурить, симулировать, работать спустя рукава» (Копелев 1). "Everyone was afraid to goof off, or pretend, or work in a slipshod manner" (1a).

< «Спустя» is the old form of the short active participle of the verb «спустить»; the corresponding modern form is the perfective verbal adverb «спустив».

P-241 • ДЕРЖА́ТЬ В ЕЖО́ВЫХ РУКАВИ́ЦАХ ⟨БРАТЬ/ВЗЯТЬ В ЕЖО́ВЫЕ РУКАВИ́ЦЫ⟩ кого coll [VP; subj: human; the verb may take the final position, otherwise fixed WO] to keep or assume strict control over s.o., subjugate, oppress s.o.: Х держит Y-а в ежовых рукавицах ≃ **X keeps a tight rein on Y; X keeps Y in an iron grip; X rules Y with an iron hand ⟨fist, rod⟩; X rules Y with a rod of iron; X controls Y with a heavy hand; [in limited contexts] X runs a tight ship; X holds Y in a mailed fist.**

По правде сказать, он [Мандельштам] держал меня в ежовых рукавицах, а я побаивалась его, но виду не показывала и всё пыталась не то чтобы соскользнуть, но ускользнуть хоть на часок (Мандельштам 2). To tell the truth, he [Mandelstam] kept a very tight rein on me, and indeed I was rather frightened of him, but I did not show it and kept trying not so much to escape as to slip away for an hour or so (2a). ♦ Больной Самсонов... подпал... под сильное влияние своей протеже, которую сначала было держал в ежовых рукавицах и в чёрном теле... (Достоевский 1). The ailing Samsonov...fell...under the strong influence of his protégée, whom he had at first kept in an iron grip, on a short leash... (1a). ♦ [Руководитель] держал жену в ежовых рукавицах и, путешествуя по джунглям общепита, звонил ей, проверяя, дома ли она (Евтушенко 2). ...He [the leader] ruled [his wife] with an iron hand. As he traveled through the jungles of gastronomy, he telephoned home to make sure she was there (2a). ♦ «...Мужики Чичикова пьяницы...» — «Нужно... чтоб он держал их в ежовых рукавицах, гонял бы их за всякий вздор...» (Гоголь 3). "...Chichikov's serfs are drunkards...." "He should rule them with a rod of iron, punish them for every trifle" (3a). ♦ «...Он распечатал письмо и стал читать его вполголоса, делая свои замечания... „Теперь о деле... К вам моего повесу"... гм... „держать в ежовых рукавицах"...» (Пушкин 2). "...He broke the seal and started reading the letter under his breath, making comments as he read on....'And now, turning to business... my rascal to your care'... hmm... 'hold him in a mailed fist'" (2a).

Р-242 • ЕЖО́ВЫЕ РУКАВИ́ЦЫ *coll* [NP; pl only; fixed WO] very strict, oppressive treatment: **iron hand ⟨fist, rod, rule⟩; rod of iron; tight rein; mailed fist.**

В то время ещё ничего не было достоверно известно ни о коммунистах, ни о социалистах, ни о так называемых нивелляторах вообще. Тем не менее нивелляторство существовало, и притом в самых обширных размерах. Были... нивелляторы «бараньего рога», нивелляторы «ежовых рукавиц» и проч. и проч. (Салтыков-Щедрин 1). At that time nothing was yet known for certain about either communists, socialists, or so-called levelers in general. Nevertheless, leveling existed, and on a very vast scale. There were...levelers of "knuckling under," levelers of "the rod of iron," and so forth (1a).

Р-243 • БИТЬ ⟨УДАРЯ́ТЬ/УДА́РИТЬ⟩ ПО РУКА́М *old-fash, coll* [VP; subj: human, usu. pl] to come to an agreement, usu. sealing it by shaking hands: X и Y ударили по рукам ≃ **X and Y struck a bargain ⟨made a deal⟩;** [when a handshake accompanies or replaces a spoken agreement] **X and Y shook (hands) on it.**

Потом татары поталалакают по-своему, набавят, княгиня сбавит, ударят по рукам... (Пильняк 1). Then the Tatars will gabble in their own language, increase the amount, the Princess will reduce it, they'll strike a bargain... (1a). ♦ «„Дьявол, а не женщина... только я вам даю моё честное слово, что она будет моя..." Я покачал головою. „Хотите пари?" — сказал он, — через неделю!" — „Извольте!" — Мы ударили по рукам и разошлись» (Лермонтов 1). "A demon, not a woman!...Only I give you my word of honor that she will be mine...' I shook my head. 'Would you like to bet?' he said. 'In a week's time!' 'Agreed!' We shook hands on it and parted" (1a).

Р-244 • ГУЛЯ́ТЬ ПО РУКА́М *coll* [VP; subj: concr] to be passed from one person to another (for inspection, familiarization): X гуляет по рукам ≃ **X is passed ⟨handed⟩ around; X is passed from hand to hand; X is going ⟨making⟩ the rounds.**

Всем хотелось рассмотреть шкатулку, и она пошла гулять по рукам. Everyone wanted to examine the little box, so it was passed around.

Р-245 • ДАВА́ТЬ/ДАТЬ ПО РУКА́М *кому coll* [VP; subj: human; more often pfv] to reprimand or punish s.o., thereby bringing a decisive, abrupt end to s.o.'s actions: X дал Y-у по рукам ≃ **X gave Y a slap on the wrist; X rapped Y's knuckles.**

«Брось свои институтские штучки. Я тебе не позволю, я тебе дам по рукам!» (Аксёнов 1). "Quit your college-kid tricks. I won't let you, you'll get your knuckles rapped" (1a).

Р-246 • ПО РУКА́М! *coll* [PrepP; Invar; usu. indep. sent] (said when two parties make a deal or reach an agreement) let us consider the matter decided (and shake hands to finalize it): **it's ⟨let's call it⟩ a deal!; let's shake (hands) on it!;** [in questions] **shall we shake (hands) on it?; shall we call it a deal?**

«А пойдёшь за меня?» — «Ещё погожу. Вот семьдесят стукнет, честное слово, выйду». — «Значит, по рукам?» (Грекова 3). "So will you marry me?" "I'll still wait. When I'm seventy I'll marry you." "Shake on it?" (3a). ♦ «А согласны ли вы, — сказал он вслух, — погостить у брата денька два? Иначе он меня не отпустит». — «С большим удовольствием. Хоть три». — «Ну, так по рукам! Едем!» (Гоголь 3). "And will you agree," he said aloud, "to stay two days at my brother's? Otherwise he won't let me go." "With the greatest pleasure. Even three if you like." "Well, in that case, let's shake hands on it! We're going!" (3c). ♦ «Так что ж, матушка, что ли?» — говорил Чичиков (Гоголь 3). "Well, my dear lady, shall we call it a deal?" Chichikov was saying (3c).

Р-247 • ПОЛУЧА́ТЬ/ПОЛУЧИ́ТЬ ПО РУКА́М *coll* [VP; subj: human; more often pfv] to be reprimanded or punished, and be forced to discontinue some action: X получил по рукам ≃ **X got his hand ⟨wrist⟩ slapped; X got his knuckles rapped; X got a rap on ⟨over⟩ the knuckles.**

«Мы вам здесь клуб Петёфи устроить не дадим! Здесь вам не Венгрия! По рукам получите, господин Пантелей!» (Аксёнов 6). "We won't let you start a seditious Petöfi-style Writers' Club here! This isn't Hungary, you know! You'll get a rap over the knuckles, Mr. Pantelei!" (6a).

Р-248 • ПРИБИРА́ТЬ/ПРИБРА́ТЬ К РУКА́М [VP; subj: human; usu. pfv] **1.** ~ *кого* to make s.o. submit to o.s. (esp. when trying to make him change his behavior): X прибрал Y-а к рукам ≃ **X took Y in hand; X gained the upper hand (over Y).**

«На днях покровский пономарь сказал на крестинах у нашего старосты: полно вам гулять; вот ужо приберёт вас к рукам Кирила Петрович. Микита кузнец и сказал ему: и, полно, Савельич, не печаль кума, не мути гостей...; да ведь на чужой рот пуговицы не нашьёшь» (Пушкин 1). "Just the other day the sacristan from Pokrovskoe said at a christening held at our elder's house: 'The good times are over: you'll see what it's like when Kirila Petrovich takes you in hand.' Mikita the blacksmith answered him. 'Enough of that, Savelich,' he says, 'don't sadden the godfather, don't upset the guests....' But people will talk" (1a). ♦ Была у него хозяйка, да вот он, видно, не сумел прибрать её к рукам... (Искандер 4). He had a wife, but he must have failed to gain the upper hand over her... (4a).

2. ~ *что disapprov* (in refer. to sth. that one has no right to) to appropriate sth., take sth. into one's possession willfully: X прибрал Y к рукам ≃ **X got ⟨laid⟩ his hands on Y; X seized Y;** [in refer. to power, a business etc] **X took over Y (completely); X secured Y;** [in refer. to power only] **X took hold of Y;** [in refer. to money, goods etc only] **X helped himself to Y;** [in limited contexts] **X pocketed ⟨swiped⟩ Y.**

[author's usage] Взято было тут же тысяча пятьсот человек пленных, тридцать восемь орудий, знамёна и, что важнее всего для казаков, лошади, сёдла, одеяла и различные предметы. Со всем этим надо было обойтись, прибрать к рукам пленных, пушки, поделить добычу... (Толстой 7). Fifteen hundred prisoners and thirty-eight guns were taken on the spot, besides standards and, most important to the Cossacks, horses, saddles, horsecloths, and the like. All this had to be dealt with, the prisoners and guns secured, the booty divided... (7a).

Р-249 • ПУСКА́ТЬ/ПУСТИ́ТЬ ПО РУКА́М *что* [VP; subj: human] to cause sth. to pass from one person to another: X пустил Y по рукам ≃ **X circulated Y from hand to hand; X passed Y around; X passed Y (on) to other people;** ‖ Y пустили по рукам ≃ **Y was passed from hand to hand.**

Прежде чем передать эту книжку издателю, я пустил её по рукам... (Войнович 3). Before turning this book over to be published, I circulated it from hand to hand... (3a). ♦ ...Я переписала их [письма] для Ахматовой, а она, не спросясь, пустила по рукам (Мандельштам 2). ...I copied them [the letters] out for Akhmatova and she passed them to other people without telling me... (2a).

Р-250 • СВЯ́ЗЫВАТЬ ⟨ВЯЗА́ТЬ⟩/СВЯЗА́ТЬ ⟨СКО́ВЫВАТЬ/СКОВА́ТЬ, СПУ́ТЫВАТЬ/СПУ́ТАТЬ⟩ ПО РУКА́М И (ПО) НОГА́М *кого;* СВЯ́ЗЫВАТЬ/СВЯЗА́ТЬ РУ́КИ *кому* [VP; subj: human or abstr; the verb may take the final position, otherwise fixed WO] to deprive s.o. of the freedom to act as he wishes, restrict s.o.'s actions: X связывает Y-а по рукам и (по) ногам ≃ **X ties ⟨binds⟩ Y hand and foot; X ties Y's hands.**

«Я, право, — говаривала, например, m-me Прово, — на месте барыни просто взяла бы да и уехала в Штутгарт...» — «Разумеется, — добавляла Вера Артамоновна, — да вот что связало по рукам и ногам», — и она указывала спичками чулка на меня (Герцен 1). "If I were in the mistress's place," Madame Proveau would say, for instance, "I would simply go straight back to Stuttgart...." "To be sure," Vera Artamonovna would assent, "but that's what ties her, hand and foot," and she would point with her knitting-needle towards me (1a). ♦ «Господи, мы же вас и связали! Да вы опомнитесь, Пётр Петрович, это вы нас по рукам и по ногам связали, а не мы вас!» (Достоевский 3). "Lord, and it's we who bound you! Come to your senses, Pyotr Petrovich; it is you who have bound us hand and foot, and not we you!" (3c). ♦ «Мне тоже многое не нравится, Александр Васильевич, — сказал Румата. — Мне не нравится, что мы связали себя по рукам и ногам самой постановкой проблемы» (Стругацкие 4). "There are lots of things I don't like either, Alexander Vassilievich," said Rumata. "For instance, I don't like the fact that we have tied our own hands, the way we have set up our problem here" (4a).

P-251 • ХОДИ́ТЬ/ПОЙТИ́ ПО РУКА́М¹ [VP; subj: concr, often a noun denoting a written or printed work; more often impfv; fixed WO] to be passed from one person to another: X ходил по рукам ≃ X was passed from hand to hand; X was passed ⟨handed⟩ around; X was going ⟨making⟩ the rounds; X (was) circulated.

Тогда же я прочла «Разговоры со Сталиным» Милована Джиласа. Австралийское издание этой книги... кто-то привёз в Москву, и она ходила по рукам (Аллилуева 2). It was at this time that I read Milovan Djilas' *Conversations with Stalin*. Someone had brought to Moscow the Australian version of this book, and it was passed from hand to hand (2a). ♦ Ходили по рукам полемические сочинения, в которых горчица есть былие [= былье], выросшее из тела девки-блудницы... (Салтыков-Щедрин 1). Polemical compositions were handed around, explaining that mustard was a green which grew from the body of a fornicatress... (1a). ♦ [Твардовский] боялся другого, он ещё с лета угрожающе выпытывал, не ходит ли роман по рукам? (Солженицын 2). [Tvardovsky's] fears were quite different. That summer he had begun asking menacingly whether the novel was going the rounds (2a). ♦ Роман «Доктор Живаго» в рукописи несколько лет ходил в Москве по рукам, официально обсуждался в наших редакциях... (Гладков 1). The novel [*Doctor Zhivago*] had been circulating in Moscow in manuscript copies for several years; it had been officially under consideration by Soviet publishers... (1a).

P-252 • ХОДИ́ТЬ/ПОЙТИ́ ПО РУКА́М² *coll* [VP; subj: human, female; usu. pfv] to have sexual relations with one man after another: X пошла по рукам ≃ X began ⟨has been⟩ sleeping around; X went ⟨has been going⟩ from one man to another; [in limited contexts] X began ⟨has been⟩ living off men.

«Мать, говорит, воровка, по магазинам промышляет, а она сама с пятнадцати по рукам пошла, но разденется, есть на что посмотреть!» (Максимов 1). "She said her mother's a thief, goes around stealing from shops, and that she herself has been living off men since she was fifteen, but when she took her clothes off, she was something to look at!" (1a).

P-253 • БРАТЬ/ВЗЯТЬ ⟨ЗАБРА́ТЬ⟩ ГО́ЛЫМИ РУКА́МИ *кого-что coll* [VP; subj: human; often neg pfv fut, gener. 2nd pers sing не возьмёшь; the verb may take the final position, otherwise fixed WO] to capture, win sth. or overcome s.o. without difficulty: X возьмёт Y-а голыми руками ≃ X will seize ⟨capture, take⟩ Y barehanded ⟨with X's bare hands⟩; X will win ⟨beat Y⟩ hands down; [often in refer. to a sports competition] X will trounce Y; X will blow Y away; ‖ Neg Y-а голыми руками не возьмёшь ≃ [in refer. to a cunning person] you can't put anything over on Y; you can't outsmart ⟨outmaneuver⟩ Y.

Участковый сидел у раскалённой добела времянки в комнате дворника, отогревал посиневшие руки и хрипло раздумывал вслух: «Его, чёрта, голыми руками не возьмёшь... Оперативников просить?» (Максимов 3). The block sergeant sat by the white-hot, portable stove in the yardman's room, trying to warm his blue hands and hoarsely thinking aloud. "You won't catch that devil bare-handed....Maybe we ought to call the Criminal Investigation Squad?" (3a). ♦ [Пепел:] Нас, ярославских, голыми руками не сразу возьмёшь... Горький 3). [P.:] You can't take a man from Yaroslavl with your bare hands (3c).

P-254 • ГО́ЛЫМИ РУКА́МИ ⟨ГО́ЛОЙ РУКО́Й⟩ *coll* [NP_instrum; these forms only; adv; fixed WO] (to do or make sth.) without the use of weapons, tools etc: with one's bare hands; barehanded.

«Из штрафных лагерей я попал в самый ужасный... Снежное поле под открытым небом, посередине столб, на столбе надпись „Гулаг 92 Я Н 90" и больше ничего... В мороз голыми руками жердинник ломали на шалаши» (Пастернак 1). "We got sent to...the worst of the penal camps....An open snow field with a post in the middle and a notice on it saying: 'GULAG 92 Y. N. 90' – that's all there was....We broke saplings with our bare hands in the bitter cold, to get wood to build huts" (1a).

P-255 • ОБЕ́ИМИ РУКА́МИ ПОДПИ́СЫВАТЬСЯ/ ПОДПИСА́ТЬСЯ *под чем coll* [VP; subj: human; the verb may take the initial position, otherwise fixed WO] to agree with, support sth. readily and completely: X обеими руками подписывается под Y-ом ≃ X is all for Y; X supports Y all the way; X couldn't agree more with Y; X supports ⟨agrees with, is behind⟩ Y one hundred percent; X agrees wholeheartedly with Y.

Я обеими руками подписываюсь под вашим решением. I support your decision one hundred percent.

P-256 • ОТБИВА́ТЬСЯ РУКА́МИ И НОГА́МИ *(от чего);* **УПИРА́ТЬСЯ/УПЕРЕ́ТЬСЯ РУКА́МИ И НОГА́МИ** *both coll* [VP; subj: human; the verb may take the final position, otherwise fixed WO] to refuse categorically (to do, accept, agree to etc sth.): X отбивается (от Y-а) руками и ногами ≃ X resists (Y) with all he's got; X fights ⟨it ⟨Y⟩⟩ tooth and nail; X fights tooth and nail against Y; [in limited contexts] X wants no part of it ⟨Y⟩.

Ивана хотят сделать старостой группы, а он отбивается руками и ногами. They want to put Ivan in charge of the group, but he's resisting with all he's got. ♦ «Уж как ни упирайтесь руками и ногами, мы вас женим!» (Гоголь 3). "You can fight tooth and nail against it but we'll marry you off just the same!" (3c).

P-257 • РАЗВОДИ́ТЬ/РАЗВЕСТИ́ РУКА́МИ *coll* [VP; subj: human; more often past] to be unpleasantly shocked, bewildered, and show that one does not know what to do, how to react etc: X развёл руками ≃ X was at a loss (to know what to do ⟨how to react etc⟩); X shrugged his shoulders (in bewilderment ⟨perplexity etc⟩); X threw up ⟨spread⟩ his hands (in bewilderment ⟨perplexity etc⟩); X was dumbfounded ⟨nonplussed etc⟩.

...О. М[андельштам] спросил, почему сейчас заболевают после нескольких дней внутренней тюрьмы, хотя раньше просиживали по многу лет в крепости и выходили здоровыми. Врач только развёл руками (Мандельштам 1). M[andelstam] then asked him why it was that people got into this state [i.e., became ill] after a few days in prison, whereas in the old days prisoners spent years in dungeons without being affected like this. The doctor only shrugged his shoulders (1a). ♦ [Войницкий:] Дайте себе волю хоть раз в жизни, влюбитесь поскорее в какого-нибудь водяного по самые уши — и бултых с головой в омут, чтобы герр профессор и все мы только руками развели! (Чехов 3).

[V.:] Let yourself go for once in your life, fall head over heels in love with some water-sprite, and plunge headlong into the deep, so that the *Herr* Professor and all of us just throw up our hands! (3a). ♦ «Так где же он?» – «Нету», – отвечал бухгалтер, всё более бледнея и разводя руками (Булгаков 9). "Where is it, then?" "It's not here," replied the bookkeeper, growing more and more pale and spreading his hands in perplexity (9a). ♦ «Уж если вы... недоумеваете, как за границу ваше произведение попало, позвольте уж и нам руками развести...» (Аксёнов 12). [context transl] "If you have no idea how your work got abroad, then we can only join you in your bewilderment..." (12a).

P-258 • **РУКА́МИ И НОГА́МИ** быть$_\emptyset$ за, поддерживать *кого-что coll* [NP$_{instrum}$; Invar; adv; fixed WO] (to be in favor of, support s.o. or sth.) fully, very strongly: **one ⟨a⟩ hundred percent; all the way; (be) all for (sth.); lock, stock, and barrel.**

«Этот термин „советская власть" стал неточно употребляться. Он означает: власть депутатов трудящихся, *только* их одних, *свободно* ими избранную и *свободно* ими контролируемую. Я – руками и ногами за такую власть!..» (Солженицын 2). "The term 'Soviet regime' has come to be used imprecisely. It should mean government by the soviets, by representatives of the toilers and by no one else, freely elected by the toilers and freely controlled by them. I am a hundred percent in favor of such a government!..." (2a).

P-259 • **С ПУСТЫ́МИ РУКА́МИ** приходить, возвращаться, уходить и т. п. *coll* [PrepP; Invar; adv; fixed WO] bringing or having gained nothing: **(return ⟨leave, come etc⟩) empty-handed; (leave ⟨go back etc⟩) with nothing to show for one's efforts;** ‖ *Neg* не с пустыми руками ≃ **not (come) with one's hands hanging ⟨empty⟩; [in limited contexts] not (come ⟨arrive etc⟩) unprepared.**

«„Я не попаду, – говорю, – уйдут маралы, второй раз не вернутся. А нам с пустыми руками не стоит возвращаться"» (Айтматов 1). "'I'll miss,' I said to him. 'The deer will get away and won't come back again. And we cannot return empty-handed, you know that'" (1a). ♦ ...Я решился разъяснить хотя бы те основные пункты помпадурской деятельности, которые настолько необходимы для начинающего помпадура, чтобы он, приезжая на место, являлся не с пустыми руками (Салтыков-Щедрин 2). ...I made up my mind to elucidate at least those fundamental principles of pompadour activity, an understanding of which is so essential to any pompadour who is new to his job, so that he should not arrive unprepared at the place of his appointment (2a).

P-260 • **С РУКА́МИ И (С) НОГА́МИ; С РУКА́МИ-НОГА́МИ** *coll* [PrepP; these forms only; adv; fixed WO] **1.** (выдавать, разоблачать *кого,* отдавать, брать *что* и т. п.) ~ (to give s.o. away, expose s.o., give s.o. sth., take sth. etc) entirely, fully: **completely; altogether; totally; lock, stock, and barrel.**

Рецензия анонимная, но нетрудно догадаться, кто её написал: злобный тон и полное отсутствие объективности выдают автора с руками и ногами. The review was anonymous, but it's not hard to guess who wrote it: the spiteful tone and complete lack of objectivity give the author away completely. ♦ «...Этакую-то драгоценность, этакой факт... я вам так, с руками и с ногами, и выдал, я-то, следователь! И вы ничего в этом не видите?» (Достоевский 3). "...I let you have such a precious thing, such a fact...just like that, lock, stock, and barrel – I, an investigator! And you see nothing in it?" (3c). ♦ «Аркадий Иванович, помните, на сумке Холодовой следы растворителя масляной краски... Не отпечатки ли пальцев им ликвидировали?» – «Возможно, но для этого проще было применить одеколон, – ответил Дымокуров. – Почему возник такой вопрос?» – «Кажется, в деле замешан Алик Зарванцев». – «Логично ли? Пользуясь растворителем, художник, как говорится, с руками и ногами выдаёт себя» (Чернёнок 2). [context transl] "Arkady Ivanovich, do you remember there were turpentine traces on Kholodova's purse? Could it have been used to obliterate fingerprints?" "Perhaps, but it would have been easier to use cologne," Dymokurov replied. "Why?" "I think that Alik Zarvantsev is mixed up in this." "Is that logical? Using turpentine when you're an artist is like signing a confession" (2a).

2. eagerly, willingly: **with (great) pleasure; gladly; (be) more than happy to (do sth.); (be) thrilled ⟨delighted⟩ to (do sth.); I'd ⟨he'd etc⟩ love to.**

«Как ты насчёт того, чтобы перейти к нам на работу?» – «С руками и ногами!» "How would you feel about coming to work for us?" "I'd love to!"

P-261 • **С РУКА́МИ ОТОРВА́ТЬ** *coll* [VP; subj: human; usu. fut, 3rd pers pl with indef. refer. оторвут; fixed WO] **1.** *что* ~ to buy or take sth. eagerly: Х-ы с руками оторвут ≃ **Xs will be snatched ⟨snapped⟩ (right) up; Xs will be grabbed up; they will snatch Xs right out of person Y's hands; Xs will sell ⟨go⟩ like hot cakes.**

Отвези цветы на рынок – их там с руками оторвут. Take the flowers to the market – they'll sell like hot cakes.

2. *кого (где)* ~ to take s.o. (as an employee, spouse etc) readily: Х-а с руками оторвут ≃ **they'll snatch ⟨snap⟩ X (right) up; they'll grab X in a minute ⟨in a second⟩; they'll take X just like that; they're crying out for someone like X.**

Таких нападающих, как ты, у них в команде нет, тебя там с руками оторвут. They don't have any forwards like you on the team – they'll snatch you right up.

P-262 • **С РУКА́МИ РВАТЬ** *что coll* [VP; subj: human; obj: a noun (concr pl or mass) denoting some merchandise; often 3rd pers pl with indef. refer. рвут; fixed WO] to buy up sth. quickly, eagerly: Х-ы Y-и с руками рвут ≃ **Xs are grabbing ⟨snatching, snapping⟩ Ys (right) up; Ys are selling ⟨going⟩ like hot cakes.**

«Что, бабка, солёные огурцы хорошо продаются?» – «С руками рвут!» "So, lady, how are your pickles selling?" "People are grabbing them up!"

P-263 • **СВОИ́МИ РУКА́МИ; (СВОИ́МИ) СО́БСТВЕННЫМИ РУКА́МИ** [NP$_{instrum}$; these forms only; adv; fixed WO] (to do sth.) oneself, through one's own actions, work, efforts etc: **with one's own hands.**

...Он завёл штат младших редакторов, постепенно продвигая их в старшие, которые точили, шлифовали и подпиливали каждую фразу, каждое слово, каждый оборот, приводя их к прилично-му среднему уровню. У них кружилась голова от мысли, что они собственными руками делают литературу (Мандельштам 2). ...He created a special staff of junior editors, gradually promoting them to senior status, who polished, filed, and honed every sentence, every word and turn of phrase, until all manuscripts were reduced to the same presentably average level. The thought that they were creating literature with their own hands fairly made their heads spin... (2a).

P-264 • **УХВАТИ́ТЬСЯ ⟨СХВАТИ́ТЬСЯ⟩ ОБЕ́ИМИ РУКА́МИ** *за что* [VP; subj: human; obj: usu. предложение, возможность, шанс etc; the verb may take the final position, otherwise fixed WO] to accept (an offer, proposal etc) or take advantage of (an opportunity, chance etc) immediately, eagerly, and enthusiastically: X ухватился за это предложение ⟨за этот шанс⟩ обеими руками ≃ **X jumped at the chance ⟨the opportunity⟩; X seized the opportunity; X grabbed at the offer ⟨the opportunity, the chance etc⟩.**

P-265 • **ЧУЖИ́МИ РУКА́МИ** *coll, usu. disapprov* [NP$_{instrum}$; Invar; adv; usu. used with impf verbs; fixed WO] (often in refer. to matters in which one does not want to be openly involved) (to get sth. done) by having another or others do it for one, by using his or their time, efforts etc: **getting someone else to do it ⟨for one⟩; getting someone else to do one's dirty work; letting ⟨making etc⟩ someone else (actually) do it for one; making someone do all the work; using someone else as a cat's-paw.**

«Директор был в отпуске. А Геннадий Витальевич этот вопрос решать категорически не хотел». – «Геннадий Витальевич не хотел? Про Геннадия Витальевича можете мне не рассказывать. Он-то как раз хотел [уволить Сергея] больше всех, но только – чтоб чужими руками» (Трифонов 3). "The director was on vacation. And Gennadii Vitalevich Klimuk most definitely didn't want to make the decision." "Gennadii Vitalevich didn't want to? Don't talk to me about Gennadii Vitalevich. More than any of the others he wanted to get rid of Sergei—but only if someone else would actually do it" (3a).

P-266 • ЧУЖИ́МИ РУКА́МИ ЖАР ЗАГРЕБА́ТЬ *coll, disapprov* [VP; subj: human; usu. infin used with a finite form of привыкнуть, хотеть, любить etc] to use the product of another's labor to one's own advantage: X привык чужими руками жар загребать ≃ **X is accustomed to reaping the fruit of someone else's labor; X is accustomed to reaping where he hasn't sown; X is accustomed to making ⟨letting etc⟩ others do all the dirty work (for him); X is accustomed to using others as a cat's-paw.**

«...При царе... вашими руками на войне жар загребали. Загребают и при Керенском...» (Шолохов 3). [context transl] "Under the tsar they...used you to grab the spoils of war. They're still grabbing under Kerensky..." (3a).

P-267 • В НАДЁЖНЫХ ⟨ХОРО́ШИХ⟩ РУКА́Х быть₀, находиться и т. п.; **В НАДЁЖНЫЕ ⟨ХОРО́ШИЕ⟩ РУ́КИ** попасть, передать *что* и т. п. [PrepP; these forms only; usu. subj-compl with copula (subj: concr or abstr); fixed WO] (to be, end up etc) in the care of a dependable, trustworthy person, group, or organization: X в надёжных ⟨хороших⟩ руках ≃ **X is in reliable ⟨good⟩ hands;** ‖ X попал в надёжные ⟨хорошие⟩ руки ≃ **X ended up in reliable ⟨good⟩ hands.**

«Передай моему другу Автандилу Автандиловичу, что пропаганда козлотура в надёжных руках» (Искандер 6). "Tell my friend Avtandil Avtandilovich that the promotion of the goatibex is in reliable hands" (6a). ♦ «В ваших руках судьба моего клиента, в ваших руках и судьба нашей правды русской. Вы спасёте её, вы отстоите её, вы докажете, что есть кому её соблюсти, что она в хороших руках!» (Достоевский 2). "In your hands is the fate of my client, in your hands is also the fate of our Russian truth. You will save it, you will champion it, you will prove that there are some to preserve it, that it is in good hands!" (2a).

P-268 • В ОДНИ́Х РУКА́Х [PrepP; Invar; adv or subj-compl with copula (subj: concr pl or abstr); fixed WO] in the possession or under the control of one individual: **in the hands of one person.**

Опасно, когда большая власть сосредоточена в одних руках. It's dangerous when a great deal of power is in the hands of one person.

P-269 • В РУКА́Х *чьих, у кого, каких* быть₀, находиться и т. п. [PrepP; Invar; the resulting PrepP is usu. subj-compl with copula] **1.** [subj: human or жизнь, судьба etc] a person (his life etc) is entirely subject to s.o., under s.o.'s complete control: X у Y-а в руках ≃ **X is in Y's hands ⟨power⟩; person X is at the mercy of Y; thing X lies ⟨is, rests⟩ in Y's hands.**

Страшная мысль мелькнула в уме моём: я вообразил её [Машу] в руках у разбойников (Пушкин 2). A terrible thought passed through my mind: I imagined her [Masha] in the hands of the marauders (2a). ♦ Он дал ей почувствовать, что судьба её детей

в его руках... (Герцен 1). ...He gave her to understand that her children's future lay in his hands... (1a).

2. [subj: concr or abstr] sth. is in s.o.'s possession, at s.o.'s disposal: X у Y-а в руках ⟨в Y-овых руках⟩ ≃ **X is in Y's hands; Y has possession of X; X belongs to Y;** [in limited contexts] **Y has hold of X.**

Все архивы были в его руках (Аллилуева 2). All the archives had been in his hands (2a). ♦ Инициатива... в эти дни была в руках у немцев (Гроссман 2). The initiative at this time belonged to the Germans (2a). ♦ «У неё в руках один документ есть, собственноручный, Митенькин, математически доказывающий, что он убил Фёдора Павловича». – «Этого быть не может!» – воскликнул Алёша (Достоевский 2). "She has hold of a document, in Mitenka's own hand, which proves mathematically that he killed Fyodor Pavlovich." "That can't be!" Alyosha exclaimed (2a).

3. в наших ⟨ваших, его и т. п.⟩ руках [subj: abstr, often всё] (of a decision or the outcome of sth.) sth. is dependent upon s.o., exclusively determined by s.o.: X в Y-овых руках ≃ **X is in Y's hands; X is (entirely) up to Y; it's in Y's power to decide...**

[Зилов:] ...Жизнь идёт, но мы с тобой – у нас с тобой всё на месте. Во всяком случае, у меня к тебе всё в целости-сохранности. Как шесть лет назад... [Галина:] Ничего у нас не осталось. [Зилов:] Да нет, всё в порядке. А если что не так, мы всё можем вернуть в любую минуту. Хоть сейчас. Всё в наших руках (Вампилов 5). [Z.:] Life moves on, but you and I haven't changed. At least my feelings for you are just as they were six years ago.... [G.:] There's nothing left. [Z.:] No, no, everything's fine. If something's not quite right, we can bring it all back any time we like. Right now, if you like. It's up to us entirely (5a).

P-270 • ГОРИ́Т В РУКА́Х *чьих, у кого coll, approv* [VP; subj: дело, работа, всё; pres or past] some work is being done efficiently and well by s.o., or everything s.o. does is done efficiently and well by him: у X-а работа горит в руках ≃ **X is doing a ⟨one⟩ heck of a job; X is doing a bang-up job;** ‖ у X-а всё горит в руках ≃ **X makes everything look easy; everything ⟨whatever⟩ X does comes out just fine.**

Поправит столбик, отойдёт с прищуренным глазом, посмотрит и радуется сам на себя: вот, дескать, какой я мастер – за что ни возьмусь, всё в руках горит (Войнович 2). He straightened out a post, then took a few steps back; his eyes narrowed; what he saw gave him great joy—what a master I am, thought Chonkin, whatever I try my hand at comes out just fine (2a).

P-271 • ДЕРЖА́ТЬ В РУКА́Х *кого-что* [VP; subj: human; obj: human or collect] to keep s.o. in subjugation, exercise control over s.o.: X держит Y-а в руках ≃ **X keeps ⟨has⟩ Y (well) in hand; X keeps Y under X's thumb; X has Y under X's control.**

И он [командир полка] умел держать в руках отчаянных воздушных лейтенантов (Гроссман 2). And he [the commander of a fighter squadron] knew how to keep [the] wild young pilots under his thumb (2a).

P-272 • ДЕРЖА́ТЬ СЕБЯ́ В РУКА́Х [VP; subj: human; often infin (used with умеет, надо etc) or imper] to maintain one's self-possession, not give in to an emotional outburst: X держал себя в руках ≃ **X kept himself in hand; X controlled himself; X used ⟨exercised⟩ self-control; X kept a grip on himself; X kept his cool;** ‖ X умеет держать себя в руках ≃ **X has self-control.**

Моя мать была вспыльчива, но, когда надо, умела держать себя в руках... (Рыбаков 1). Mother had a fiery temper, but when she had to she knew how to control herself... (1a). ♦ ...Таков мой старик. Ни один человек в мире не умеет так себя в руках держать, как он (Искандер 3). ...That's my old man. Not another man in the world has the self-control that he has (3a).

P-273 • **НА РУКА́Х** [PrepP; Invar] **1.** ~ *у кого, чьих, кого* **быть**$_\emptyset$, **остаться** и т. п. [the resulting PrepP is usu. subj-compl with copula (subj: human, or a noun denoting an enterprise, area of activity etc)] a person (or thing) is, remains etc in s.o.'s charge, requiring s.o.'s supervision: у Y-а ~ X ≃ **X is on Y's hands; Y has X on Y's hands; person X is in Y's care; Y has X to look after.**

«А Николай Васильевич редко бывает в институте?» — «Николай Васильевич? Очень редко. У него на руках другой институт» (Каверин 1). "Does Nikolai Vasilyevich often come to the Institute?"..."Nikolai Vasilyevich? Very rarely....He has another Institute on his hands" (1a). ♦ «А что Маша, капитанская дочка?» Я отвечал, что она осталась в крепости на руках у попадьи (Пушкин 2). "But what happened to Masha, the captain's daughter?" I replied that she remained at the fort, in the care of the priest's wife (2a). ♦ ...Старшего сына Сташенка, Андрея, в августе четырнадцатого призвали в армию, и жена его, Ксана, осталась с грудным ребёнком на руках... (Рыбаков 1). ...The eldest Stashenok boy, Andrey, was called up in August 1914, leaving his wife, Ksana...with a small baby to look after... (1a).

2. ~ *у кого* **быть**$_\emptyset$, **иметься** и т. п. [the resulting PrepP is subj-compl with copula (subj: concr)] sth. is possessed, held by s.o. at a specific moment: X у Y-а ~ ≃ **X is in Y's possession; Y has X on ⟨in⟩ hand; Y has X on ⟨with⟩ him; Y has X (on his person).**

«Если лицо это вас действительно приглашало [в США], то у вас на руках должно быть от него какое-то приглашение...» (Войнович 1). "If he [this person] really invited you [to the United States], you should have the invitation from him in hand..." (1a). ♦ В половине первого Костя позвонил и сказал, что билеты у него на руках... (Рыбаков 2). At twelve-thirty Kostya called and said he had the tickets (2a).

3. **быть**$_\emptyset$, **оказаться** ~ [subj-compl with copula (subj: usu. a noun denoting a library book, journal etc)] sth. is on loan, temporarily borrowed from the library: **(be) out; (be) out on loan; (be) checked ⟨charged⟩ out.**

«К сожалению, Сименон сейчас весь на руках» (Чернёнок 2). "Unfortunately, all the Simenon is out right now" (2a). ♦ Нет, никогда «Прокажённая» не оказывалась в библиотеке. Она всё была на руках (Олеша 3). No, *The Leper Woman* never did turn up at the library, it was always out on loan (3a).

4. **умереть** ~ *чьих, (у) кого* [the resulting PrepP is adv] (to die) in the presence of s.o. (often s.o. who had been caring for the dying person): **(die) in s.o.'s arms;** [used when s.o. does not want the responsibility of looking after the deceased, is afraid of the consequences of the person's death etc] **(die) on s.o.'s hands.**

И он испытал дух под вопли старухи, на руках у слесаря Пушкина (Битов 2). He departed this life, to the wails of the old woman, in the arms of Pushkin the locksmith (2a). ♦ В разгар приступа я слышу, как тётушка в другой комнате разговаривает с дядей. Она говорит, чтобы он поехал в деревню, где тогда жила моя мать, и привёз её сюда. Дядя говорит, что это излишне, что не стоит беспокоить мою маму. Тётушка возражает и говорит, как бы я не умер на их руках (Искандер 4). At the height of the attack I hear my aunt and uncle talking in the next room. She says he should ride to the village where my mother is staying and fetch her. Uncle says that's unnecessary, there's no point alarming my mother. Auntie protests and says what if I died on their hands (4a).

P-274 • **НОСИ́ТЬ НА РУКА́Х** *кого coll* [VP; subj: human or collect] to value s.o. very highly, admire s.o., feel devoted to s.o., grant s.o.'s every desire etc: X носит Y-а на руках ≃ **X adores Y; X worships the ground Y walks on; X thinks the world of Y;** [usu. in refer. to the attitude of an adult, esp. a parent, toward a child] **X dotes on Y;** [in limited contexts] **X spoils ⟨coddles⟩ Y;** [usu. in refer. to a husband's attitude toward his wife] **X waits on Y hand and foot;** [usu. in refer. to one's respect for another's intelli-

gence, skill etc] **X has (put) Y on a pedestal; X idolizes Y;** ∥ X-ы носят Y-а на руках ≃ [usu. in refer. to the admiration of a group of people for a celebrity] **Xs lionize Y; Y is the darling of Xs; Xs make much ⟨a fuss⟩ of Y.**

Живёт [Женя] в Москве, муж большой человек, старше её на двадцать лет, разумеется, её обожает, прямо на руках носит (Грекова 3). She [Zhenya] was living in Moscow. Her husband was an important person, twenty years older than she, and of course adored her, worshiped the ground she walked on (3a). ♦ «А уж чтоб вот так с тобой быть — и не надеялся, не смел. Это-то за что мне привалило? За одно за это... я должен тебя на руках носить» (Распутин 2). "But I never dreamed that I would be with you like this, I didn't dare dream. Why was I granted this? For this alone...I [should] wait on you hand and foot" (2a). ♦ Он [Павел Петрович] с детства отличался замечательною красотой... он не мог не нравиться... Его носили на руках, и он сам себя баловал, даже дурачился, даже ломался; но и это к нему шло (Тургенев 2). From childhood he [Pavel Petrovich] had been distinguished by exceptional good looks;...he could not fail to please....He was generally made much of and he also indulged himself, even played the fool, even cultivated a certain affectation of manner; but this also suited him (2e). ♦ Они так полюбили его, что он не видел средств, как вырваться из города; только и слышал он: «Ну недельку, ещё одну недельку поживите с нами, Павел Иванович!» — словом, он был носим... на руках (Гоголь 3). They had grown so fond of him that he could think of no way of escaping from the town. All he heard was: "Come, stay another week with us, just one more week, dear Mr Chichikov!" In short, they made a fuss of him... (3a).

P-275 • **ПО РУКЕ́** [PrepP; Invar; subj-compl with copula (subj: concr) or nonagreeing modif] **1.** (of gloves, mittens) of the correct size, comfortable on s.o.'s hands: X Y-у по руке ≃ **X is the right ⟨my, your etc⟩ size; X fits (well);** ∥ *Neg* X Y-у не по руке ≃ **X doesn't fit (right); X is too big ⟨small, tight⟩ for Y.**

2. (of a pen, tool etc) of a suitable size, weight, shape etc for s.o.'s hand: X Y-у по руке ≃ **X is comfortable (to write ⟨work etc⟩ with); X fits Y's hand; X sits well in Y's hand; X feels good (to Y ⟨in Y's hand⟩).**

P-276 • **БОЛЬШО́Й ⟨ПЕ́РВОЙ⟩ РУКИ́** *obsoles, coll* [NP$_{gen}$; these forms only; nonagreeing modif] possessing or exhibiting a high degree of a specific quality: **of the first water ⟨order, magnitude⟩; first-class; first-rate; darn good.**

[Бодаев:] Только вы с ним поосторожнее, он плут большой руки (Островский 7). [B.:] You had better be on your guard with him; he's a knave of the first water (7a). ♦ «Кто ты есть такой, Лашков? Полжизни наганом промахал, а теперь: „Ваши билетики, граждане!" А Витька мой — мастер-лекальщик первой руки, не тебе... чета» (Максимов 3). "Who d'you think you are, Lashkov? You spend half your life waving a revolver at people, and now it's 'tickets, citizens, please!' Victor's a craftsman, a first-class template-maker, so he's a cut above you" (3a).

P-277 • **БРАТЬ/ВЗЯТЬ В РУ́КИ** *кого* [VP; subj: human; obj: human or collect; more often pfv] to bring s.o. under one's control, make s.o. obey: X взял Y-а в руки ≃ **X took Y in hand; X brought Y into line.**

Вера знала, что выходит замуж за пьяницу и гуляку, но надеялась взять его в руки. Vera knew she was marrying a drunk and a playboy, but she hoped she'd be able to bring him into line.

P-278 • **БРАТЬ/ВЗЯТЬ В (СВОИ́) РУ́КИ** *что* [VP; subj: human or collect] to take upon o.s. the leadership or direction of sth., take responsibility for sth.: X взял Y в свои руки ≃ **X took Y ⟨the matter etc⟩ into his own hands; X took charge ⟨control⟩ of Y;** ∥ X взял инициативу в свои руки ≃ **X took the initiative;** ∥ X взял власть в (свои) руки ≃ **X took power into his (own) hands.**

Зная ход суда над Синявским и Даниэлем, я мог предвидеть, что судьи и прокурор постараются не дать мне говорить, будут обрывать свидетелей и вообще постараются взять всё в свои руки (Буковский 1). Knowing how the trial of Sinyavsky and Daniel had been conducted, I foresaw that the judge and the prosecuting counsel would try to prevent me from speaking, would interrupt the witnesses, and do all they could to take the proceedings into their own hands (1a). ♦ Надо было взять разговор в свои руки, а тогда его можно будет самой и кончить… (Залыгин 1). She felt she had to take control of the conversation, so that she would be able to end it… (1a). ♦ На этот раз инициативу взял в свои руки Лукашин. Пётр Житов выслушал его не перебивая… (Абрамов 1). This time Lukashin took the initiative. Pyotr Zhitov heard him out, not interrupting (1b).

Р-279 • БРАТЬ/ВЗЯТЬ СЕБЯ В РУ́КИ [VP; subj: human, more often pfv; fixed WO] to regain control of one's feelings, mood, or actions (usu. after a shock, when suppressing one's extreme reaction, emotional outburst etc, or when attempting to become more focused, goal-oriented): X взял себя в руки ≃ X **took himself in hand; X got a grip on himself; X got (a) hold of himself; X pulled himself together; X got control of himself.**

…Виктор стоял, стиснув в кулаке записки, и чувствовал себя болваном, и знал, что красен, что вид имеет растерянный и жалкий, но он взял себя в руки, сунул записки в карман и спустился со сцены (Стругацкие 1). Victor stood, crumpling the notes in his hand, feeling like an idiot. He knew that he was red in the face, that he looked lost and pathetic, but he took himself in hand, stuffed the notes into his pocket, and left the stage (1a). ♦ Я не могу позволить им убить себя. Я должен жить. Я спрячусь, забаррикадируюсь, я пересижу у себя в комнате. Я не хочу умирать. Не хо-чу!.. Стоп! Надо взять себя в руки (Аржак 1). I couldn't let them kill me! I must live. I'll go into hiding, I'll barricade myself, I'll sit it out in my own room. I don't want to die. *I do not want to…* Stop! I must get a grip on myself (1a). ♦ Чувствую, что меня всё время заносит, а остановиться не могу. Надо сейчас же взять себя в руки и немедленно вернуться в строгие рамки сюжета (Искандер 4). I keep feeling myself getting carried away, and I can't stop. I must get hold of myself immediately and return forthwith to the strict framework of the plot (4a). ♦ На минуту меня охватывает панический ужас. А вдруг они меня зовут сейчас не в Бутырки, а в подвал? В знаменитый Лефортовский подвал, где расстреливают под шум заведённых тракторов… Невообразимым усилием воли… беру себя в руки (Гинзбург 1). For a second I panicked. Suppose it was not to Butyrki they were taking me, but to the cellars? The famous Lefort cellars where…they used the noise of tractor engines to drown that shooting….It took an unbelievable effort to pull myself together (1a).

Р-280 • В ОДНИ́ РУ́КИ *coll* [PrepP; Invar; prep obj; fixed WO] **1. продавать, отпускать** и т. п. *что* (used in cases when any one individual is not allowed to buy or receive more than a limited amount of some type of food or goods) (to sell, give out etc a certain amount of sth.) per person: **(to) a customer; per customer; apiece.**

Ну, там, конечно, эта… ну, давка, и народ волнуется, кричат: «Без очереди не пускайте! В одни руки больше одной ёлки не выдавайте!» и выбирать не дают (Войнович 1). Of course…the place is packed with people, all excited and shouting, You have to take your turn! One tree to a customer! And they don't let you pick it (1a).

2. передавать, отдавать и т. п. *что* ~ (often in refer. to power, authority over sth. etc) (to give, hand over etc the whole of sth.) to a single organization, group, or individual: **into the hands of one organization 〈group, person〉; to one organization 〈group, person〉.**

Р-281 • В СО́БСТВЕННЫЕ РУ́КИ вручить, отдать *кому что coll* [PrepP; Invar; usu. nonagreeing modif or prep obj; fixed WO] (to present or deliver sth. to s.o.) directly: **right to s.o.; into s.o.'s (own) hands.**

«Кому вы отдали телеграмму?» — «Ивану Петровичу в собственные руки». "Who did you give the telegram to?" "I gave it right to Ivan Petrovich."

Р-282 • В ТРЕ́ТЬИ РУ́КИ передавать *что*, **переходить** и т. п. [PrepP; Invar; prep obj; fixed WO] (to give sth. over, be passed etc) to a person (or an organization) not directly involved in the matter at hand: **to a third party; to someone else.**

Ещё плохо зная нравы западных корреспондентов, я дал ответ [«Литературной газете»] через корреспондента гамбургской газеты «Ди Вельт», а он… отдал в третьи руки… (Солженицын 2). I still did not know the ways of the Western newsmen very well, and I replied [to *Literaturnaya Gazeta*] through the correspondent of the Hamburg newspaper *Die Welt*, but he passed it on to someone else… (2a).

Р-283 • В ЧУЖИ́Е РУ́КИ попадать, отдавать *что* и т. п. [PrepP; Invar; prep obj; fixed WO] (to end up going, be given etc) to a person or persons who are not members of the family, group etc in question: **into strange hands; to (perfect) strangers; to a (perfect) stranger.**

Бедное его достояние могло отойти от него в чужие руки — в таком случае нищета ожидала его (Пушкин 1). His meagre property was likely to pass into strange hands—in which case beggary awaited him (1b).

Р-284 • ГРЕТЬ/ПОГРЕ́ТЬ 〈НАГРЕВА́ТЬ/НАГРЕ́ТЬ〉 РУ́КИ *(на чём, около чего) coll, disapprov* [VP; subj: human] to make a profit for o.s. through some dishonest means: X нагрел руки (на Y-е) ≃ **X lined his pockets 〈purse〉 (from Y); X feathered his nest.**

«Заметов человек чудеснейший». — «И руки греет». — «Ну, и руки греет, и наплевать!» (Достоевский 3). "Zametov's a really excellent fellow." "And lines his pockets." "Well, so he lines his pockets, who cares?" (3a).

Р-285 • ДЕРЖА́ТЬ РУ́КИ ПО ШВАМ [VP; subj: human; the verb may take the final position, otherwise fixed WO] **1. Also: СТОЯ́ТЬ 〈ВЫТЯ́ГИВАТЬ/ВЫ́ТЯНУТЬ** и т. п.〉 **РУ́КИ ПО ШВАМ** to stand erect with one's arms extended downward at the sides of one's body (generally when standing at attention): X стоял 〈вытянул〉 руки по швам ≃ **X stood with his hands at his sides; X held his arms at his sides; X dropped his hands 〈arms〉 to his sides; [in limited contexts] X stood to 〈at〉 attention.**

Шура стоял руки по швам, бледный… (Шукшин 1). Shura was standing there with his hands at his sides, his face white… (1a).

2. ~ *при ком, перед кем* to be extremely deferential, obedient to s.o., act in a humble, proper manner in his presence (out of fear of this person, respect for his professional reputation, standing etc): X при Y-е держит руки по швам ≃ **X stands at attention 〈snaps to attention〉 in Y's presence.**

Нашего директора школы все боятся — при нём даже самые отпетые хулиганы держат руки по швам. Everyone is afraid of the principal of our school—even the biggest rowdies snap to attention in his presence.

Р-286 • ДЛИ́ННЫЕ РУ́КИ *у кого coll* [NP; pl only; usu. VP$_{subj}$ with copula] **1.** (in refer. to a person or organization) s.o. or sth. has so much power, influence etc that it is impossible to hide from or escape him or it: у X-а длинные руки ≃ **X has a long reach.**

«Впрочем, вы можете уйти, но у нас, предупреждаю, длинные руки!» (Ильф и Петров 1). "You can leave, by the way, but I warn you, we have a long reach" (1a).

2. s.o. is thievish, prone to steal: у Х-а длинные руки ≃ **X is light-fingered ⟨sticky-fingered⟩; X has sticky fingers.**

P-287 • ДЫРЯ́ВЫЕ РУ́КИ *у кого coll* [NP; pl only; usu. VP$_{subj}$ with быть$_\theta$] s.o. is clumsy, drops and/or breaks everything he touches: у Х-а дырявые руки ≃ **X is ⟨X's fingers are⟩ all thumbs; X is butterfingered ⟨a butterfingers⟩; X has butterfingers; X has two left hands.**

...Разве стала бы я огорчаться подобными мелочами, если бы в лаборатории хоть что-нибудь получалось? Если бы Петя, застенчиво улыбаясь, не спрятал от меня стеклянный колпак от микроскопа — я била посуду. Если бы красивая, гордая ассистентка не сказала Николаю Васильевичу, думая, что я не услышу: «Никогда ничего не выйдет. Дырявые руки!» (Каверин 1). ...Would I have been depressed by such trifles if I'd managed to achieve [at least] something in the laboratory? If Petya, smiling shyly, had not hidden the glass cover of the microscope from me in the cupboard? (I had broken some glassware.) Or if the handsome, proud woman assistant had not told Nikolai Vasilyevich, thinking that I wasn't listening...: "Nothing will ever come of her. All her fingers are thumbs" (1a).

P-288 • ЗАБИРА́ТЬ/ЗАБРА́ТЬ В РУ́КИ [VP; subj: human; more often pfv] **1.** ~ *кого* to bring s.o. under one's control, subject s.o. to one's power or will: Х забрал Y-а в руки ≃ **X took Y in hand; X had Y under his thumb.**

«Иная барышня только от того и слывёт умною, что умно вздыхает; а твоя за себя постоит, да и так постоит, что и тебя в руки заберёт...» (Тургенев 2). "Some young ladies have the reputation of being intelligent because they can sigh cleverly; but your young lady can hold her own, and do it so well that she'll take you in hand also..." (2c).

2. ~ *что* to assume authority, power over sth.: Х забрал Y в руки ≃ **X took ⟨got⟩ (full) control of Y; X took over Y.**

[Глафира:] ...Между тем [я] понемногу забираю в руки... всё ваше хозяйство... (Островский 5). [G.:] ...Meanwhile, little by little, I'm getting full control of...all your domestic affairs (5a).

P-289 • ЗОЛОТЫ́Е РУ́КИ *approv* [NP; pl only] **1.** ~ *у кого* [VP$_{subj}$ with copula] s.o. is very skilled in his craft or in everything he attempts to do with his hands: у Х-а золотые руки ≃ **X is good ⟨clever⟩ with his hands; X can do anything with his hands; X has golden ⟨great⟩ hands.**

...У Санагиной были поистине золотые руки и по-мужицки хитрый, первозданный ум (Ивинская 1). Very clever with her hands, Sanagina had the cunning of a peasant, and a natural intelligence (1a). ♦ ...Дом Ильи был одним из самых благополучных в деревне: хозяин вернулся с войны, и совершенно целёхонек... и руки золотые у мужика... (Абрамов 1). ...Ilya's home was one of the happiest in the village. The master had returned from the war all in one piece...and the man could do anything with his hands (1b).

2. [subj-compl with быть$_\theta$ (subj: human), postmodif, or indep. sent; if used as subj-compl, usu. preceded by another subj-compl; fixed WO] a person who is very skilled in his craft or in everything he attempts to do with his hands: **a real ⟨true⟩ master (of one's craft); a wonder with one's hands; (s.o. has) golden hands!**

За что Максим ни возьмётся, сделает лучше всех. Золотые руки. No matter what Maksim sets out to make, he does it better than anyone. He's a wonder with his hands. ♦ Но знаете ли вы, что самое гадкое в стукачах и доносчиках? Вы думаете то плохое, что есть в них? Нет! Самое страшное — то хорошее, что есть в них... Какие среди них есть даровитые поэты, музыканты, физики... какие среди них умельцы слесаря, плотники, те, о которых народ с восхищением говорит — золотые руки (Гроссман 1). But do you realize the most loathsome thing about stool pigeons and informers? Do you think it is the evil that is in them? No, not at all; the most awful thing is the good that is in them....What

talented poets are to be found among them, and musicians, and physicists, and what talented lathe operators, too, and carpenters, the kind of whom people exclaim with delight: "Golden hands!" (1a).

3. ~ *(чьи, кого)* [subj or obj; fixed WO] the ability to do or make sth. very skillfully: **skillful ⟨clever, golden⟩ hands; golden touch.**

И когда идёшь, скажем, по улице Горького (бывшая Торговая) и видишь пышные деревянные ансамбли... то понимаешь: это всё Зенков — его душа, его золотые руки, его понятия о красоте (Домбровский 1). And when you walk, for instance, down Gorky Street (which used to be Commercial Street) and you see those gorgeous wooden buildings...you realise that this is a faithful expression of Zenkov himself: his soul, his golden touch, his sense of beauty (1a).

P-290 • ИГРА́ТЬ В ЧЕТЫ́РЕ РУКИ́ *(с кем)* [VP; subj: human; if there is no obj, subj: dual] (of two people) to play the piano as a team: Х и Y играют в четыре руки ≃ **X and Y play duets (on the piano).**

Супруги жили очень хорошо и тихо: они почти никогда не расставались, читали вместе, играли в четыре руки на фортепьяно, пели дуэты... (Тургенев 2). The young couple lived very happily and peacefully; they were scarcely ever apart; they read together, sang and played duets together on the piano... (2b).

P-291 • ЛОМА́ТЬ РУ́КИ ⟨ПА́ЛЬЦЫ⟩ [VP; subj: human] to twist one's hands together as an expression of deep grief, despair, or severe agitation: Х ломал руки ≃ **X wrung his hands.**

Час спустя Павел Петрович уже лежал в постели с искусно забинтованною ногой. Весь дом переполошился; Фенечке сделалось дурно. Николай Петрович втихомолку ломал себе руки, а Павел Петрович смеялся, шутил, особенно с Базаровым (Тургенев 2). An hour later Pavel Petrovich was reposing in bed with a skilfully bandaged leg. The whole house was in a turmoil. Fenichka came over faint. Nikolai Petrovich wrung his hands in silence while Pavel Petrovich continued to laugh and joke, especially with Bazarov... (2c).

P-292 • МАРА́ТЬ ⟨ПА́ЧКАТЬ⟩ РУ́КИ *(об кого, обо что, чем) coll* [VP; subj: human; usu. infin used with нечего, зачем, не хочет(ся) etc.] to take part in sth. that is or is considered reprehensible, unworthy, demeaning: Х-у не хотелось рук марать (об Y-а) ≃ **X didn't want to dirty ⟨soil⟩ his hands (on person Y ⟨with thing Y, in thing Y etc⟩); X didn't want to get his hands dirty (being involved with person Y ⟨doing thing Y etc⟩).**

«Только не бейте меня!» Садчиков засмеялся. «Д-да кто об тебя р-руки станет марать?» (Семёнов 1). "But don't beat me!" Sadchikov laughed. "W-what? Who's going to d-dirty their hands on you?" (1a). ♦ *(Шмага за дверью: «Бить не будешь?»)* [Незнамов:] Да не буду, очень мне нужно об тебя руки марать! (Островский 3). *(Shmaga's voice: You won't touch me?)* [N.:] I wouldn't soil my hands (3a).

P-293 • МОЗО́ЛИТЬ РУ́КИ [VP; subj: human] to work very hard (usu. physically): Х мозолит руки ≃ **X works ⟨wears⟩ his fingers to the bone.**

P-294 • НА ВСЕ РУ́КИ *coll, approv* [PrepP; Invar; subj-compl with copula (subj: human) or nonagreeing postmodif] a person who knows how to do everything: Х был на все руки ≃ **X was a jack-of-all-trades; X was good at everything; X could turn his hand to anything.**

P-295 • НА́ РУКИ [PrepP; Invar; adv] **1.** выдать, раздать *кому что* ~ (to deliver or distribute sth.) straight to s.o.: Х выдал Y Z-у на руки ≃ **X handed Y to Z; X gave ⟨handed⟩ Y to Z directly.**

«Как с радиоактивным золотом?» – спросила она. «Всё-таки обещают. Может быть, на днях дадут, – так же собранно и сумрачно говорил он. – Но ведь это, оказывается, не на руки, это ещё будут пересылать служебным порядком» (Солженицын 10). "How are things with the radioactive gold?" she asked. "They're making promises still. Perhaps they'll give it to us in the next few days." He was speaking in his usual intense, somber manner. "But it seems they don't give it *to* you directly, they have to send it through official channels" (10a).

2. получить ~ *что* to receive sth. and have it in one's possession: **(have sth.) in (one's) hand; (get ⟨receive⟩ sth. from s.o.) in person.**

Она не заплатит ему ни копейки до тех пор, пока не получит ордер на руки (Трифонов 4). She wouldn't pay him a kopek until she had the order in her hand (4a).

3. отдать *кого* ~ *кому obs, coll* (to give a person over) into s.o.'s custody, keeping: **X отдал Y-а на руки Z-у ≃ X entrusted Y to Z's care; X put Y in Z's charge.**

С пятилетнего возраста отдан я был на руки стремянному Савельичу, за трезвое поведение пожалованному мне в дядьки (Пушкин 2). At the age of five I was entrusted to the care of the groom Savelich, appointed to be my personal attendant in recognition of his sober conduct (2a).

Р-296 • НАКЛА́ДЫВАТЬ/НАЛОЖИ́ТЬ НА СЕБЯ́ РУ́КИ [VP; subj: human; usu. pfv] to end one's life by suicide: **X наложил на себя руки ≃ X laid hands on himself; X did away with himself; X did himself in; X took his own life; X died by his own hand; X committed suicide.**

Было велено не трогать её [тётю Катю], но из уважения к семье и роду издали следить, чтобы она не наложила на себя руки (Искандер 3). People were ordered not to touch her [Aunt Katya], but, out of respect for family and clan, to watch from a distance lest she lay hands on herself (3a). ♦ «Вчера умереть готова была. Если бы не Гульджамал, наложила бы руки на себя» (Айтматов 1). "Yesterday I was ready to die. If it wasn't for Guldzhamal, I would have done myself in" (1a). ♦ «Вы, Лев Львович, человек праведной жизни, скажите мне, можно ли раба Божьего, руки на себя наложившего, отмолить?» (Максимов 3). "You are a righteous man, Lev Lvovich. Tell me, is it possible by prayer to save the soul of a servant of God who has taken his own life?" (3a).

Р-297 • НЕ БРАТЬ В РУ́КИ *что, чего coll* [VP; subj: human] (in refer. to an activity that involves sth. held in or used by the hand) not to engage in some activity at all (either for a specified period of time or in general): **X Y-а в руки не берёт ≃ X hasn't touched ⟨never touches⟩ Y; X hasn't gone ⟨never goes⟩ near Y.**

[Городничий:] Я карт и в руки никогда не брал; даже не знаю, как играть в эти карты (Гоголь 4). [Mayor:] I've never touched a card in my life; I don't even know how card-games are played (4b). ♦ «Посмотри-ка, Анисьюшка, что струны-то целы, что ль, на гитаре-то? Давно уже в руки не брал...» (Толстой 5). "Anisya, go and see if the strings of my guitar are all right. I haven't touched it for a long time" (5b). ♦ [Муромский:] ...Нелькин карт в руки не берёт (Сухово-Кобылин 2). [M.:] ...Nelkin never goes near cards (2b).

Р-298 • НЕ С РУКИ́ *кому* [PrepP; Invar; subj-compl with быть∅; used without negation to convey the opposite meaning] **1.** [subj: infin] (in refer. to actions that require the use of a tool, instrument, weapon etc) it is difficult or impossible for s.o. to do sth. (because he is holding the tool etc that he is using in an uncomfortable position): делать X Y-у не с руки ≃ **it is uncomfortable ⟨difficult⟩ for Y to do X; Y cannot do X; [in limited contexts] Y is out of position ⟨Y isn't positioned right⟩ to do ⟨for⟩ X.**

Опусти пилу пониже, мне не с руки держать её так высоко. Lower the saw a little bit. It's uncomfortable for me to hold it up so

high. ♦ Австриец бежал вдоль решётки, Григорию не с руки было рубить, он, перевесившись с седла, косо держа шашку, опустил её на висок австрийца (Шолохов 2). The Austrian was keeping close to the railing and Grigory was out of position for a slash. Leaning out of his saddle he held the sabre at an angle and let it fall on the Austrian's temple (2a).

2. [subj: infin or abstr, often это] the given time or circumstances are not appropriate, convenient etc for s.o. to do sth.: делать X Y-у не с руки ≃ **it is inconvenient for Y to do X; it's not a good idea for Y to do X; [in refer. to an inopportune moment] X is coming at the wrong time ⟨at a bad time⟩; it's not the right ⟨a good⟩ time for Y to do X; [in limited contexts] Y cannot spare the time to do X.**

Так было с Францией – вдруг [Сергей] сказал, что исчезло всякое желание ехать: «Мне сейчас не с руки» (Трифонов 3). ...He [Sergei] had decided against the trip to France. He suddenly announced that he had lost all desire to go: "I can't spare the time right now" (3a).

3. [subj: usu. abstr or infin] sth. is not acceptable or agreeable to s.o.: X ⟨делать X⟩ Y-у не с руки ≃ **X ⟨doing X⟩ doesn't suit ⟨appeal to⟩ Y; it doesn't suit ⟨appeal to⟩ Y to do X.**

«Я не поеду», – решительно заявил Митька. «Ты что? – Христоня нахмурился... – Отбиваешься от своих? Не с руки?» (Шолохов 3). "I won't go," Mitka said decidedly. "What's the idea?" Khristonya frowned....."Are you breaking away from your own pals? Don't they suit you now?" (3a). ♦ «Меня и в город зовут, да не с руки мне там, и соблазна много» (Максимов 3). [context transl] "I've had offers in the town, but it isn't really what I'm looking for, and there would be too many temptations" (3a).

Р-299 • ОБАГРЯ́ТЬ/ОБАГРИ́ТЬ РУ́КИ КРО́ВЬЮ ⟨В КРОВИ́⟩ *(кого) lit* [VP; subj: human] to commit murder or participate in a murder or execution: X обагрил руки кровью (Y-а) ≃ **X bloodied his hands; X has (Y's) blood on his hands; X stained his hands with Y's blood; X's hands are bloodstained ⟨stained with (Y's) blood⟩.**

«...Пусть на минуту и я соглашусь с обвинением, что несчастный клиент мой обагрил свои руки в крови отца. Это только предположение, повторяю, я ни на миг не сомневаюсь в его невинности...» (Достоевский 2). "...Suppose for a moment that I, too, agreed with the prosecution that my unfortunate client stained his hands with his father's blood. This is only a supposition, I repeat, I do not doubt his innocence for a moment..." (2a).

Р-300 • ОПУСКА́ТЬ/ОПУСТИ́ТЬ РУ́КИ *coll* [VP; subj: human; more often pfv] to become disheartened and lose the desire or ability to act: X опустил руки ≃ **X lost heart ⟨hope⟩ (and gave up); X gave up (in despair).**

И даже когда Алтынник перестал отвечать на её письма и перестал их читать и, не читая, вкладывал в конверт и отправлял назад доплатным, Людмила не отчаялась, не опустила руки, а продолжала писать с завидной настойчивостью (Войнович 5). And even when Altinnik stopped answering her letters and ceased even to read them, returning them unread and postage due, Ludmilla did not despair or lose heart but continued to write with enviable persistence (5a). ♦ Надо сказать, что вдова отца протоиерея Савватия Дроздова, скончавшегося в 26 году от антирелигиозных огорчений, не опустила рук, а основала замечательнейшее куроводство (Булгаков 10). It must be said that the widow of Father Savvaty Drozdov, who had passed away in 1926 of antireligious woes, did not give up, but started some most remarkable chicken breeding (10b).

Р-301 • ОТ РУКИ́ *писать, переписывать и т. п.* [PrepP; Invar; adv] (to write etc) by using one's hand (as opposed to a typewriter, computer etc): **(write sth. ⟨write sth. out etc⟩) by hand; (write sth.) in longhand; (be) handwritten; ‖ переписать** ~ ≃ **copy sth. out.**

Видимо, этот знак на машинке был повреждён, и машинистка ставила запятые от руки (Чернёнок 1). Apparently the machine's comma didn't work and the typist had inserted them by hand (1a). ♦ Ну, не всё ли равно, напечатан рассказ в типографии или написан от руки в детской тетради (Некрасов 1). What difference does it make whether a story has been set in type or simply written in longhand in a child's exercise book? (1a). ♦ «Оценку поставим сейчас или потом сами напишем?» – «Давай сейчас, – сказал Дроботун. – Чтобы не от руки» (Войнович 5). "Should we type in the rating now or will you write it in after?" "Let's do it right now," said Drobotun. "So it won't have to be handwritten" (5a). ♦ ...Я переписывала её [«Четвёртую прозу»] от руки столько раз, что запомнила наизусть (Мандельштам 1). ...I copied it ["Fourth Prose"] out so many times that I remember it word for word (1a).

Р-302 • ОТСО́ХНИ (У МЕНЯ́) РУ́КИ И НО́ГИ!; ОТСО́ХНИ У МЕНЯ́ РУКА́!; ЧТОБ У МЕНЯ́ РУ́КИ (И НО́ГИ) ОТСО́ХЛИ!; ПУСТЬ ⟨ПУСКА́Й⟩ У МЕНЯ́ РУКА́ ОТСО́ХНЕТ! all substand [main clause in a complex sent, or indep. sent; often foll. by a clause introduced by если, коли etc; these forms only] (an oath used to assure the interlocutor that the speaker did or did not do, or will or will not do, what is stated in the surrounding context) may terrible things happen to me if I...: **may I be forever damned (if...)**; **may my hand wither and drop off (if...)**.

[Пепел:] Пускай у меня рука отсохнет, коли я тебя трону!.. (Горький 3). [P.:] May my hand wither and drop off if ever I lift it against you! (3e).

Р-303 • ПЛЫТЬ ⟨ПРОСИ́ТЬСЯ, ИДТИ́⟩ В РУ́КИ (кому) [VP; subj: usu. concr or abstr; the subj is often foll. by the pronoun сам] (of money, material possessions, career opportunities etc) to be readily available (to s.o.) and obtainable with little or no effort: X плывёт Y-у в руки ≃ **X is falling ⟨dropping⟩ into Y's lap**; **X is begging Y to grab it**.

[author's usage] Цель всей жизни была достигнута. Свечной заводик в Самаре сам лез в руки (Ильф и Петров 1). His life ambition was achieved. The candle factory in Samara was falling into his lap (1a). ♦ Что значит быть красивой, – всё само... плывёт в руки (Рыбаков 2). That's what being beautiful meant. Everything just dropped into your lap (2a). ♦ [Глумов:] Богатство само прямо в руки плывёт; прозевать такой случай будет и жалко, и грех... (Островский 9). [G.:] Here is a fortune just begging me to grab it; a sin and a shame to let it slip through my fingers (9b).

Р-304 • ПО́Д РУКИ держать, брать, вести кого [PrepP; Invar; adv] (two people support, take, lead s.o.) holding his arms from either side: **by the ⟨both⟩ arms**; **(support s.o.) under the arms**; **(grasp s.o.) by the elbows**.

...Присутствующие женщины подхватили под руки это побледневшее, встрёпанное, мокрое, рыдающее создание и, окружив плотным кольцом, повели утешать и обсушивать (Окуджава 2). ...The women hoisted the pale, ruffled, wet, weeping creature by the arms and, surrounding her, took her away to dry and comfort her (2a). ♦ Им стали встречаться раненые. Одного, с окровавленною головой, без шапки, тащили двое солдат под руки (Толстой 4). They commenced meeting the wounded. One, with a bloody head and no cap, was being dragged along by two soldiers who supported him under the arms (4a). ♦ Наконец Пугачёв встал с кресел и сошёл с крыльца в сопровождении своих старшин. Ему подвели белого коня, украшенного богатой сбруей. Два казака взяли его под руки и посадили на седло (Пушкин 2). At last Pugachev rose from the armchair and came down from the porch, accompanied by his chiefs. His white horse with its richly ornamented harness was brought to him. Two Cossacks grasped him by the elbows and lifted him into the saddle (2a). ♦ Увезли деда Максима: на берег его вели под руки, своим ходом дед идти не мог (Распутин 4). [context transl] They took away Grandpa Maxim: they

held him up and walked him to the shore, he couldn't get there on his own (4a).

Р-305 • ПОПАДА́ТЬ(СЯ)/ПОПА́СТЬ(СЯ) В РУ́КИ чьи, кого, (к) кому [VP] **1.** [subj: usu. concr] to happen to come into s.o.'s possession: X попал Y-у в руки ≃ **X fell ⟨found its way⟩ into Y's hands**; **X ended ⟨wound⟩ up in Y's hands**; [in limited contexts] **X came Y's way**; **Y came upon X**.

Однажды мне попала в руки книга Шеллера-Михайлова... (Олеша 3). Once a book by Scheller-Mikhaylov fell into my hands... (3a). ♦ В пятьдесят четвёртом году ко мне в руки попала первая самиздатская... тетрадка – поэма Твардовского «Тёркин на том свете» (Орлова 1). In 1954 the first samizdat...manuscript found its way into my hands: Tvardovsky's poem *Tyorkin in Hell* (1a). ♦ Оказывается, что королю тотчас после представления [«Блистательных возлюбленных»] попала в руки только что написанная трагедия Расина «Британник»... (Булгаков 5). It turned out that, immediately after the first performance [of *The Magnificent Lovers*], the King came upon a newly written tragedy by Racine, *Britannicus*... (5a).

2. [subj: human or collect] to end up under s.o.'s control, authority: X попал в руки к Y-у ≃ **X fell into Y's hands**; ‖ [used as a threat] X ещё попадётся мне в руки ≃ **I'll get X yet**.

[Голубков:] Белые уезжают. Нам надо бежать с ними, иначе мы опять попадём в руки к красным (Булгаков 2). [G.:] The Whites are leaving. We must go with them, or we'll fall into the hands of the Reds again (2a).

Р-306 • ПРИЛОЖИ́ТЬ РУ́КИ к кому-чему coll [VP; subj: human; often infin with надо, хочется, некому etc] to attend to s.o. or sth. in a serious, thorough way: X-у надо приложить руки к Y-у ≃ **X must give Y the attention Y deserves**; ‖ некому руки приложить к Y-у ≃ **there's no one to take care of Y ⟨to tend (to) Y⟩**.

Сад запущенный, а руки к нему приложить некому. The garden is a mess, and there's no one to give it the attention it deserves.

Р-307 • ПРОСИ́ТЬ ⟨ИСКА́ТЬ⟩ РУКИ́ чьей, кого obs [VP; subj: human, male] to approach (a woman or her parents, guardian etc) with a proposal of marriage: X просит руки женщины Y ≃ **X asks for ⟨seeks⟩ Y's hand (in marriage)**.

«Вы влюблены в меня?» – перебила его Наташа. – «Да, влюблён, но, пожалуйста, не будем делать того, что сейчас... Ещё четыре года... Тогда я буду просить вашей руки» (Толстой 4). "Are you in love with me?" Natasha broke in. "Yes, I am, but— Please, we mustn't do that—what you just— In another four years—then I will ask for your hand" (4a). ♦ [Анна Андреевна:] Знаешь ли ты, какой чести удостоил нас Иван Александрович? Он просит руки нашей дочери (Гоголь 4). [A.A.:] Are you aware of the honor His Excellency is conferring on us? He's asking for our daughter's hand in marriage (4f).

Р-308 • ПРОХОДИ́ТЬ/ПРОЙТИ́ ЧЕРЕЗ РУ́КИ чьи, кого [VP; subj: human (often pl), concr (if count, usu. pl), or abstr] (of legal cases, money managed by s.o., patients cared for by medical personnel, students trained by teachers etc) to be handled, dealt with, or in the charge of s.o. for some finite period of time: X-ы прошли через руки Y-а ≃ **Xs passed through Y's hands ⟨through the hands of Y⟩**; [in limited contexts] **Xs passed ⟨went⟩ through Y's office**.

Позвольте, товарищи, вдруг вылез некто Щавский, вечный «друг молодёжи», через руки которого... и Огородников прошёл, а позже и Охотников, а сейчас уже и Штурмин, вечный председатель комиссии по работе с молодыми (Аксёнов 12). "Allow me, comrades," said Comrade Shchavski, the eternal "friend of youth," the eternal chairman of the commission on work with young photographers, through whose hands Ogo had passed, and later Alexei Okhotnikov, and more recently Shturmin

(12a). ♦ [Надежда Антоновна:] Он имел видное и очень ответственное место; через его руки проходило много денег... (Островский 4). [N.A.:] He had a very prominent and responsible position, a great deal of money passed through his hands... (4a).

P-309 • **РАБО́ЧИЕ РУ́КИ** [NP; pl only, may refer to one person; usu. this WO] people who work (more often those who perform physical or unskilled labor): **worker(s); working hands; manpower; labor;** ‖ в месте X не хватает рабочих рук ≃ **place X is short-handed.**

По тем временам достать справку об увольнении из совхоза, где каждые рабочие руки числились на вес золота, было делом нелёгким... (Максимов 2). To obtain a release permit from a state farm in those days, when every worker was worth his weight in gold, was not an easy matter... (2a). ♦ Подлинно нечего было писать старому Листницкому о своей жизни, текла она, по-старому однообразная, неизменная, лишь рабочие руки поднялись в цене да ощущался недостаток в спиртном (Шолохов 2). It was true enough that the old Listnitsky had nothing to write about his life. It dragged along in its old rut, as monotonous and unchanging as ever. Perhaps the only difference was that the cost of labour had risen and there seemed to be a shortage of liquor (2a).

P-310 • **РАЗВЯ́ЗЫВАТЬ/РАЗВЯЗА́ТЬ РУ́КИ** кому [VP; subj: human, collect, or abstr; more often pfv] to give s.o. complete freedom of action by releasing him from his previous commitments, obligations, ties etc: X развязал Y-у руки ≃ **X untied ⟨freed⟩ Y's hands.**

Теперь ЧКГБ имеет против меня полный судебный букет (по их кодексу, разумеется) – и это только развязало мне руки, я стал идеологически экстерриториален! (Солженицын 2). Now the KGB had a whole bouquet of criminal charges to pin on me (according to their legal code, of course), yet this had only untied my hands, given me ideological extraterritoriality! (2a). ♦ [Лидия:] Застрелитесь, пожалуйста, поскорей!.. Вы мне развяжете руки, и уж в другой раз я не ошибусь в выборе или мужа, или... ну, сами понимаете кого (Островский 4). [L.:] Shoot yourself, do, and be quick about it!...You'll free my hands, and the next time I won't make a mistake when I choose a husband, or a... Well, you know yourself what I mean (4a).

P-311 • **РАЗВЯ́ЗЫВАТЬ/РАЗВЯЗА́ТЬ СЕБЕ́ РУ́КИ** [VP; subj: human; more often pfv] to gain complete freedom of action by liberating o.s. from one's previous commitments, obligations, ties etc: X развязал себе руки ≃ **X freed himself ⟨set himself free⟩;** [in limited contexts] **X was free to do as he pleased ⟨liked etc⟩.**

Я рассказала, как Глафира Сергеевна потребовала, чтобы Агния Петровна немедленно переехала в Москву, разумеется, чтобы развязать себе руки (Каверин 1). I told him how Glafira Sergeyevna had demanded that Agnia Petrovna should immediately move to Moscow, for the purpose, of course, of leaving her free to do as she liked (1a).

P-312 • **РАСПУСКА́ТЬ/РАСПУСТИ́ТЬ РУ́КИ** coll [VP; subj: human] **1.** to hit or beat s.o.: X руки распустил ≃ **X used ⟨let loose with⟩ his fists (on person Y); X punched ⟨beat up etc⟩ person Y.**

2. (usu. of a man) to touch s.o. in a sexual manner, displaying one's erotic desire for that person: X распускает руки ≃ **X can't keep his hands to himself; X is (too) free with his hands.**

P-313 • **РУ́КИ В БРЮ́КИ** ходить, слоняться и т. п. highly coll [Invar; usu. adv; fixed WO] (to be) idle, doing nothing: **(walk ⟨stand etc⟩ around) with one's hands in one's pockets; (be ⟨sit somewhere etc⟩) twiddling one's thumbs.**

Как тебе не стыдно! Все работают, а ты стоишь руки в брюки. You should be ashamed of yourself! Everyone else is working and you're standing around twiddling your thumbs.

P-314 • **РУ́КИ ВВЕРХ!** [sent; Invar; fixed WO] (used as a command, usu. when a person holding a weapon orders another to offer no resistance) raise your hands: **hands up!; hands in the air!; stick 'em up!**

«Отрезвел я, когда они закрыли дверь кассы и длинный, вытащив наган, сказал: „Руки вверх! Ни с места!"» (Семёнов 1). "I sobered up when they closed the door of the bank and the tall one pulled out a revolver and said: 'Hands up! Don't move!'" (1a).

P-315 • **РУ́КИ ЗАГРЕБУ́ЩИЕ (, ГЛАЗА́ ЗАВИДУ́ЩИЕ)** у кого highly coll, derog [NP; pl only; often VP_subj with быть∅] a greedy person who strives to get or grab hold of much: у X-а руки загребущие (, глаза завидущие) ≃ **X has (greedy ⟨big⟩ eyes and) an itching ⟨itchy⟩ palm.**

P-316 • **РУ́КИ КО́РОТКИ ⟨КОРОТКИ́⟩** (у кого) coll [VP_subj with быть∅ (pres only), оказаться (past only); often used with the infin of another verb; fixed WO] s.o. does not have the right, authority, or influence to do sth. (used—often as a response in a dialogue—to state that the person or organization threatening to harm the speaker or another person will not be able to carry out the threat): (у X-а) руки коротки (сделать Y) ≃ **X's reach is (too) short; X's arm isn't long enough; X doesn't have the power ⟨X is powerless⟩ (to do Y);** [in limited contexts] **(just) let X try (to do Y);** ‖ [when used in direct address] руки (у тебя ⟨у вас⟩) коротки! ≃ **just try it!; just you try!**

«Вы знаете, что он помогает бургомистру упечь вас под суд?» – «Догадываюсь». – «Это вас не волнует?» – «Нет. Руки у них коротки. То есть, у бургомистра руки коротки, и у суда» (Стругацкие 1). "You know that he's helping the burgomaster haul you into court?" "I guessed as much." "That doesn't bother you?" "No. His reach is short. That is to say, the burgomaster's. Also the court's" (1a). ♦ В мрачном взгляде Баулина Саша почувствовал предостережение. Но этот взгляд только подхлестнул его. От чего предостерегает? Снова исключат? Руки коротки! (Рыбаков 2). Baulin's sullen look was a signal to Sasha not to go too far. Instead, it only spurred him on. What was Baulin warning him about? Were they going to expel him again? Let them try! (2a).

P-317 • **РУ́КИ-КРЮ́КИ ⟨РУ́КИ КАК КРЮ́КИ⟩** у кого coll [NP; these forms only; VP_subj with быть∅; usu. pres] s.o. is awkward, clumsy, and drops everything: у X-а руки-крюки ≃ **X is ⟨X's fingers are⟩ all thumbs; X is butterfingered ⟨a butterfingers⟩; X has butterfingers.**

P-318 • **РУ́КИ НЕ ДОХО́ДЯТ/НЕ ДОШЛИ́** (у кого до кого-чего or что сделать) coll [VP_subj; may be used without negation to convey the opposite meaning; usu. this WO] s.o. cannot find the time to turn his attention to or focus on some person, matter etc: у X-а руки не доходят до Y-а ≃ **X never gets around to Y; X never has time for Y; X never has a ⟨the⟩ chance to do thing Y; X never gets down to thing Y;** ‖ у X-а не до всего доходят руки ≃ **X can't manage ⟨cope with⟩ everything (at the same time).**

Говорят, что он собирался как-нибудь на досуге почитать написанное Ермолкиным, но то забывал, то руки не доходили... (Войнович 4). They say that he intended to read what Ermolkin had written when he had time to spare, but either forgot or never got around to it (4a). ♦ Не до всего доходили руки старика, посев уменьшился, а про остальное уж и говорить нечего (Шолохов 3). The old man could not cope with everything; he had even reduced his sowings, not to mention other things (3a).

P-319 • **РУ́КИ НЕ ОТВА́ЛЯТСЯ ⟨НЕ ОТСО́ХНУТ⟩** у кого highly coll [VP_subj; fut only; may be used without negation to convey the opposite meaning; usu. this WO] it will not overstrain, exhaust, or harm s.o. to do sth.: у X-а руки не отвалятся ≃ **it won't kill ⟨hurt⟩ X (to do sth.).**

...Они вдвоём взялись за работу — к столу с внутренней стороны кнопками пришпиливали денежные бумажки... «Неудобно, — сказала Ванда, — понадобится бумажка, нужно стол переворачивать». — «И перевернёшь, руки не отвалятся, — сипло ответил Василиса, — лучше стол перевернуть, чем лишиться всего» (Булгаков 3). ...They set to work together, pinning banknotes to the underside of the table with thumbtacks.... "It's going to be inconvenient," said Wanda. "Every time I want some money I shall have to turn the dining-room table over." "So what, it won't kill you," replied Vasilisa hoarsely. "Better to have to turn the table over than lose everything" (3a).

Р-320 • **РУ́КИ ОПУСКА́ЮТСЯ/ОПУСТИ́ЛИСЬ** *у кого coll* [VP_subj] s.o. becomes disheartened and loses the desire or ability to act or work at sth.: у X-а опускаются руки ≃ **X is losing heart ⟨hope⟩ (and giving up); X is giving up (the struggle ⟨the fight⟩ etc); X feels like giving up ⟨quitting, throwing in the towel⟩.**

Другой, видя проявление зла, чувствует его бесконечную связь с мировым злом, и у него опускаются руки от понимания, что вместо отрубленной ветки зла вырастет другая или даже многие (Искандер 4). The other, seeing a manifestation of evil, is aware of its infinite interconnections with universal evil and loses heart at the realization that if he chops off one branch of evil, another, or even many, will grow in its place (4a). ♦ «Только тут я сообразил, что меня обманули. Объегорили подло, мелко, предательски. У кого на моём месте не опустились бы руки...» (Максимов 2). "It was only then that I realized I had been cheated. I had been basely, pettily, treacherously swindled. Anyone in my place would have given up the struggle..." (2a). ♦ «Обсуждение? Мы вас щадили... Зачем вам? Актёры... люди бестактные, грубые, скажут какую-нибудь неприятность — вы полгода работать не сможете, руки опустятся» (Трифонов 1). [context transl] "An official discussion? We wanted to spare you....What would you gain from it? Our actors...are rude, tactless people. They might say something unpleasant—and there you'd be, so discouraged that you wouldn't be able to get back to work for six months" (1a).

Р-321 • **РУ́КИ ОТВА́ЛИВАЮТСЯ/ОТВАЛИ́ЛИСЬ** *у кого coll* [VP_subj; usu. impfv] s.o. is very tired from working with his arms: у X-а руки отваливаются ≃ **X's arms are falling ⟨ready to fall⟩ off.**

Р-322 • **РУ́КИ ПО ШВАМ!** *mil* [sent; Invar; fixed WO] (used as a command) assume the military posture of attention: **attention!**

Р-323 • **РУ́КИ ПРОЧЬ** *от кого-чего!* [sent; Invar; fixed WO] (often used as a slogan) do not interfere in sth. or in the affairs of s.o.: руки прочь от X-а! ≃ **hands off X!**

«Ты должен изменить направление „Курьера"... Я же не говорю тебе о коренном изменении, о повороте на 180 градусов... Несколько негативных материалов о Союзе... Пойми, несколько таких материалов, и твои друзья смогут... тогда говорить: „Курьер" — это независимая газета Временной Зоны Эвакуации, руки прочь от [редактора] Лучникова» (Аксёнов 7). "You could change the politics of the *Courier*....I don't mean anything basic; I don't mean an about face....Just a few negative fillers about the Soviet Union....Try to understand, Andrei. All it will take is a few short pieces and your friends will be able...to say, 'The *Courier* is an independent newspaper of the Provisional Evacuation Zone. Hands off [the editor] Luchnikov'" (7a).

Р-324 • **РУ́КИ ЧЕ́ШУТСЯ/ЗАЧЕСА́ЛИСЬ** *у кого coll;* **РУ́КИ ЗУДЯ́Т** *highly coll* [VP_subj; usu. pres or past] **1.** ~ *(на кого)* s.o. wants very much to have a fight, beat s.o. up etc: у X-а чешутся руки (на Y-а) ≃ **X is spoiling ⟨itching⟩ for a fight; X is itching ⟨dying⟩ to get ⟨lay⟩ his hands on Y.**

[Расплюев:] Уж очень у меня на этого Попугайчикова руки чешутся; потому, подлец, всякую совесть потерял... Вы ему приказывать изволили, а он смеётся (Сухово-Кобылин 3). [R.:] ...I've been just itching to lay my hands on that Popugaychikov. That's because the good-for-nothing's lost all sense of responsibility....You order him to do something and he just laughs (3a).

2. ~ *(что сделать* or *на что)* s.o. wants very much to do sth. or start doing sth.: у X-а руки чешутся сделать Y ≃ **X is itching ⟨dying⟩ to do Y; X's hands are itching to do Y; [in limited contexts] X is champing at the bit.**

А если высокое и низкое в человеке сочетается? Тогда своеобразие образа заключается именно в этом причудливом сочетании, и у писателя чешутся руки обязательно сохранить его (Искандер 4). And if the high and the low are combined in one man? Then the uniqueness of the image lies precisely in this capricious combination, and the writer itches to preserve it without fail (4a). ♦ Режиссёру понравилась пьеса молодого автора, и у него чесались руки скорее приступить к репетициям. The director liked the young author's play and was champing at the bit to begin rehearsals.

Р-325 • **С ЛЁГКОЙ РУКИ́** *чьей, кого coll* [PrepP; Invar; the resulting PrepP is adv; fixed WO] prompted by or patterned upon s.o.'s successful initiative or action (which has served as a catalyst for other similar actions): с лёгкой руки X-а... ≃ **following X's example; X set the example; X started ⟨set⟩ the ball rolling (by doing sth.).**

...С лёгкой руки Клавки Стригуновой [бабы] раздевались до голых грудей, с отчаянным и разбойным видом выступали перед мужиками... (Распутин 4). ...Following Klavka Strigunova's...example, the women stripped down to bare breasts, stepping out in front of the men with a daring and dashing air... (4a). ♦ С лёгкой руки Кульбина, в совершенстве постигшего искусство зазывания, в программу наворачивали всё, что ни набредало на ум. Отвечать за соответствие тезисов фактическому содержанию лекции не приходилось, ибо после первых фраз... из зала доносились негодующие реплики, свистки, бранные возгласы, превращавшие дальнейшую часть доклада в сплошную импровизацию (Лившиц 1). Kulbin, who really knew how to attract an audience, set the ball rolling by throwing into the programme anything which came into his head. There was no need to worry about whether the actual content of the lecture corresponded to the theses set out because after the first few phrases...such indignant repartees, cat-calls and shouts and abuse came from the audience that the rest of the lecture had to be improvised (1a).

Р-326 • **СКЛА́ДЫВАТЬ/СЛОЖИ́ТЬ РУ́КИ** [VP; subj: human] (having become disheartened, having lost hope in achieving success) to cease to act: X сложил руки ≃ **X threw up his hands; X gave up; X quit.**

[author's usage] К такому способу существования сразу привыкнуть нельзя, и человек долго барахтается, пока не решит сложить ручки и покориться судьбе (Мандельштам 2). Such an existence takes some getting used to, and one may flounder about for a long time before giving up and bowing to fate (2a).

Р-327 • **СЛОЖА́ РУ́КИ** *сидеть,* less often *ждать, стоять и т. п. coll* [Verbal Adv; Invar; adv; fixed WO] (to be) idle, inactive (usu. when the situation requires some decisive, energetic action): **(be) sitting on one's hands; (be sitting around ⟨about⟩) twiddling one's thumbs; (be sitting around) doing nothing; (be sitting) idly by.**

«Та-ли!» — кричала она, как бы выплёскивая из рыданий имя дочери. «А-а-а», — рыданьем отвечали женщины со двора тёти Маши, как бы говоря ей: и мы скорбим с тобой, и мы, как видишь, не сидим сложа руки (Искандер 3). "Ta-li!" she shouted, casting up her daughter's name from a wave of sobs. "A-a-ah," the women sobbed in reply from Aunt Masha's yard, as if to tell her: We too grieve with you, and as you see, we're not sitting on our hands (3a).

♦ Лизка — молодчага, не сидела сложа руки. Пока он [Михаил] ходил за житом, она заново подтопила печь... (Абрамов 1). Lizka was splendid; she hadn't been sitting around twiddling her thumbs. While he [Mikhail] was out getting the barley she had gotten the stove hot again (1a). ♦ «А не думаете ли вы, Елена Станиславовна, что нам нужно продолжать работу?.. Нельзя сидеть сложа руки!» (Ильф и Петров 1). "Don't you think we ought to carry on without them, Elena Stanislavovna?…We can't sit around doing nothing" (1a).

< «Сложа» is the old form of the short active participle of the verb «сложить»; the corresponding modern form is the perfective verbal adverb «сложив».

P-328 • СРЕ́ДНЕЙ РУКИ́ [NP_gen; Invar; nonagreeing modif]
1. (a person or thing that is) not in any way outstanding: **ordinary; average; run-of-the-mill; mediocre; a pretty mediocre (sort of…); of a ⟨the⟩ middling sort; second-rate.**

«„Дай, думает, зайду в ресторанчик, перекушу". Видит — огни. Чувствует, что где-то не в центре, всё, по-видимому, недорого. Входит. Действительно, ресторанчик средней руки» (Булгаков 12). "'I'll go to some little restaurant,' he thought, 'and have a bite to eat.' He saw a brightly lit restaurant and because it was away from the center he felt it ought not to be too expensive. So in he went and it was, in fact, a pretty mediocre sort of restaurant" (12a). ♦ Свидригайлов в этой комнате был как у себя и проводил в ней, может быть, целые дни. Трактир был грязный, дрянной и даже не средней руки (Достоевский 3). …Svidrigailov seemed at home in this room and spent, perhaps, whole days in it. The tavern was dirty, wretched, not even of a middling sort (3c). ♦ …Привычки дурно воспитанного барича средней руки остались в нём на всю жизнь… (Герцен 3). …He retained the habits of an ill-bred landowner of the middling sort all his life… (3a).

2. neither rich nor poor: **of moderate means.**

Если б над Англией не тяготел свинцовый щит феодального землевладения… если б она, как Голландия, могла достигнуть для всех благосостояния мелких лавочников и небогатых хозяев средней руки, — она успокоилась бы на мещанстве (Герцен 3). If England were not weighed down by the leaden shield of feudal landlordship…if, like Holland, she could achieve for everyone the prosperity of small shopkeepers and of *patrons* of moderate means, she would settle down quietly in her pettiness (3a).

P-329 • УКОРА́ЧИВАТЬ/УКОРОТИ́ТЬ РУ́КИ кому *highly coll* [VP; subj: human; usu. pfv] to force s.o. to stop acting aggressively, fighting, beating another etc: X укоротит Y-у руки ≃ **X will settle Y's hash; X will bring Y to heel.**

P-330 • УМЫВА́ТЬ/УМЫ́ТЬ РУ́КИ [VP; subj: human; usu. this WO] to refuse to accept responsibility for some matter, withdraw from participation in sth. (usu. in order to avoid unpleasant consequences): X умывает руки ≃ **X washes his hands of it ⟨of thing Y⟩.**

«Война проиграна!.. Мы теперь можем умыть руки: мы сделали всё, что могли. Как говорили римляне, пускай другие сделают лучше» (Эренбург 4). "The war is lost!…We can now wash our hands of it all. We've done all we could. As the Romans used to say: 'Let others do better'" (4a).

< From the Biblical account of Pontius Pilate's words at the trial of Jesus (Matt. 27:24).

P-331 • ЖИВО́Й РУКО́Й *obs, coll;* **ЖИВЫ́М МАНЕ́РОМ** *obsoles, substand* [NP_instrum; these forms only; adv] (to do sth.) very quickly, promptly: **in no time (flat); in a jiffy; in a flash.**

P-332 • КАК ⟨БУ́ДТО, СЛО́ВНО, ТО́ЧНО⟩ РУКО́Й СНЯЛО́ что (с кого) *coll* [VP; impers; fixed WO] (in refer. to an illness, fatigue, emotions etc that) disappeared or passed immediately and completely: X как рукой сняло ≃ **X just vanished; X vanished without a trace; X vanished in a trice; X vanished at once; X was suddenly gone.**

«Ты… ты… всё приняла вчера?» — спросил я диким голосом. «Всё, батюшка милый, всё, — пела бабочка сдобным голосом, — дай вам бог здоровья за эти капли… полбаночки — как приехала, а полбаночки — как спать ложиться. Как рукой сняло…» (Булгаков 6). "You…you…you mean to say you drank all this yesterday?" I asked, appalled. "All of it, sir, all of it," said the woman in her comfortable, sing-song voice. "And God bless you for it…half the bottle when I got home and the other half when I went to bed. The pain just vanished…" (6a). ♦ Мимо парикмахерской, всё так же ощупывая палочкой дорогу перед собой, шёл Саня-слепой, тот самый, который встретился мне в первый день на десятом [в 10-ом лагере] два с лишним года назад. Всё приподнятое настроение как рукой сняло. Чему я, дурак, радуюсь?! Ведь это всё та же Мордовия… (Марченко 1). Tapping his way past the barber's shop with a stick came Blind Sanya, that same Sanya I had met on my first day in camp ten, just over two years ago. My exalted mood vanished in a trice. What was I feeling so pleased about, idiot? I was still in Mordovia, wasn't I… (1a). ♦ Забылся Григорий на заре, но вскоре проснулся, поднял со стола отяжелевшую голову. Лихачёв сидел на соломе… В [его] глазах светилась такая мёртвая тоска, что у Григория сон будто рукой сняло (Шолохов 4). Grigory dozed off at dawn, but soon awoke and lifted his heavy head from the table. Likhachov was sitting on the straw.…There was such mortal anguish in his eyes that Grigory's drowsiness vanished at once (4a).

P-333 • МАХНУ́ТЬ РУКО́Й (на кого-что) *coll* [VP; subj: human; fixed WO] to cease attending to s.o. or sth., cease expending time, effort etc on s.o. or sth. upon realizing that one's efforts are futile: X махнул на Y-а рукой ≃ **X gave up on Y; X gave Y up as a hopeless case ⟨cause⟩; X gave thing Y up as hopeless ⟨as lost, for lost⟩; X gave up the struggle;** ‖ X махнул на себя рукой ≃ **X stopped caring (about himself); X stopped taking care of himself.**

[Аннунциата:] …Государь махнул рукой на дела управления. Первые министры с тех пор стали сами сменять друг друга. А государь занялся театром (Шварц 3). [А.:] …The King gave up on this business of running things. Since then the Prime Ministers themselves have done the replacing of each other. And the King took up the theater (3a). ♦ …[Николай Петрович] должен был, подобно брату Павлу, поступить в военную службу; но он переломил себе ногу в самый тот день, когда уже прибыло известие об его определении, и, пролежав два месяца в постели, на всю жизнь остался «хроменьким». Отец махнул на него рукой и пустил его по штатской (Тургенев 2). …[Nikolai Petrovich] was destined, like his brother Pavel, to take up a military career; but he broke his leg on the very day that news was received that he had been accepted for the army and, having lain in bed for two months, was left with a slight limp which remained with him for the rest of his life. His father gave him up as a hopeless case and permitted him to take up a civilian career (2e). ♦ [Мелузов:] А если я перестану учить, перестану верить в возможность улучшать людей или малодушно погружусь в бездействие и махну рукой на всё, тогда покупайте мне пистолет, спасибо скажу (Островский 11). [M.:] And if I *do* stop teaching, stop believing in the possibility of improving people, or pusillanimously sink into idleness and give up everything for lost, *then* buy me a revolver and I'll thank you! (11a). ♦ Инженеру [Хлебцевичу] ничего не оставалось после этого, как махнуть рукой и вернуться к своей работе, пока не выгнали и оттуда (Владимиров 1). There was nothing left for Khlebtsevich to do but give up the struggle and return to his own work until such time as he was thrown out of his job (1a). ♦ …Заметней всех изменилась Луиза, похудела, ссутулилась, и платье на ней было такой чудовищной пошлости и дешевизны, что Ольга Васильевна ужаснулась: женщина махнула на себя рукой! (Трифонов 3). …The most noticeable change had occurred in Louisa; she had grown much thinner, she had a pronounced stoop and the dress she wore was so appallingly tasteless and cheap that Olga was horrified: the woman had so obviously stopped caring (3a).

P-334 • **ПОД РУКО́Й**[1]; **ПОД РУКА́МИ** *both coll* [PrepP; these forms only; adv or subj-compl with copula (subj: usu. human or concr)] (of or in refer. to things, often household items that are located in convenient places so that one can easily use them; of or in refer. to people who stay or are kept nearby s.o., ready to help him, carry out his orders etc) (a person or thing is) very close by, easily accessible: **(close ⟨near⟩) at hand; on hand; within easy ⟨arm's⟩ reach; at one's ⟨s.o.'s⟩ side ⟨elbow⟩; (readily) available; right there;** [of or in refer. to things only] **handy; at one's ⟨s.o.'s⟩ fingertips.**

Мужчине всегда в некоторой степени свойственно желание попетушиться, а тут ещё под рукой такая штучка, как револьвер, почему же не схватить его, если для этого нужно только открыть ночной столик? (Олеша 3). It's always, to a certain extent, the nature of a man to want to ride the high horse, and when a thing like a revolver is close at hand, why not grab it, especially if all one has to do is open the night table? (3a). ♦ ...По-видимому, распорядитель пира не считал, что веселью пришёл конец, и он, как опытный тамада, всегда имел под рукой верное средство для того, чтобы вдохнуть жизнь в замирающее застолье (Катаев 2). ...The *tamada* evidently decided it was not yet time to end the party, and like the experienced master of ceremonies he was, he had at hand a sure means of breathing life into the expiring company (2a). ♦ Ежели у человека есть под руками говядина, то он, конечно, охотнее питается ею, нежели другими, менее питательными веществами... (Салтыков-Щедрин 1). If a man has beef on hand, then of course he lives on that more willingly than on other less nourishing substances... (1a). ♦ Он отдал распоряжение шофёру. Он приказал референту сообщить в Департамент, что господин прокурор занят... Никого не принимать, отключить телефон и вообще убираться к дьяволу с глаз долой, но так, впрочем, чтобы всё время оставаться под рукой (Стругацкие 2). He gave instructions to his chauffeur and ordered his assistant to inform the department that the prosecutor was occupied. "Don't admit anyone, disconnect the phone. Go to the devil, get out of my sight, but stay within easy reach" (2a). ♦ «Я поглотил кучу книг и приобрёл уйму знаний, чтобы быть полезным ей и оказаться под рукой, если бы ей потребовалась моя помощь» (Пастернак 1). "For her sake I devoured piles of books and absorbed a great mass of knowledge, to be available to her if she asked for my help" (1a). ♦ «Вы дилетант». Сейчас можно признаться, что тогда я не знал и этого слова. И не имея под рукой словаря иностранных слов, не посмел возражать (Войнович 5). "You're a dilettante." Now I can admit that at the time I had no idea what that word meant, and with no dictionary of foreign words handy, I did not dare object (5a).

P-335 • **ПОД РУКО́Й**[2] *кого;* **ПОД РУКА́МИ** [PrepP; these forms only; adv] when worked on, refined, crafted etc by s.o.: **in the hands of; under the hand(s) of.**

Под рукой мастера кусок теста превращается в произведение кулинарного искусства. In the hands of a great chef a lump of dough turns into a work of culinary art.

P-336 • **ПОД РУКО́Й**[3] **⟨-ю⟩** *чьей, (у) кого obsoles, coll* [PrepP; these forms only; subj-compl with copula (subj: usu. human or collect)] a person (or group) is under s.o.'s authority or direction, is totally subjugated to s.o.: X под рукой у Y-a ≃ **X is under Y's command ⟨rule, control, thumb⟩; Y controls X.**

P-337 • **ПОД РУКО́Й**[4] **⟨-ю⟩** *obs* [PrepP; these forms only; adv] (to do or say sth.) concealing it from others, without the knowledge of others: **secretly; in secret; stealthily; by stealth; discreetly.**

Ему [помощнику градоначальника] предстояло одно из двух: или немедленно рапортовать о случившемся по начальству и между тем начать под рукой следствие, или же некоторое время молчать и выжидать, что будет (Салтыков-Щедрин 1). He [the assistant town governor] had two choices: either to report the occurrence to the authorities at once, and secretly begin an investigation in the meantime; or else to keep quiet for a while and see what would happen (1a). ♦ «Собираются на обед, на вечер, как в должность, без веселья, холодно, чтоб похвастать поваром, салоном, и потом под рукой осмеять, подставить ногу один другому» (Гончаров 1). [context transl] "If they meet at a dinner or a party, it is just the same as at their office—coldly, without a spark of gaiety, to boast of their chef or their drawing-room, and then to jeer at each other in a discreet aside, to trip one another up" (1a).

P-338 • **РУКО́Й НЕ ДОСТА́НЕШЬ ⟨НЕ ДОСТА́ТЬ⟩** *(кого) coll* [VP; neg pfv fut, gener. 2nd pers sing (1st var.) or impers predic with быть∅ (2nd var.); these forms only; fixed WO] s.o.'s high position or status makes him hard to reach, gain access to etc (may imply that s.o.'s high position allows him to act reprehensibly with impunity): X-a рукой не достанешь ≃ **you can't get near ⟨within ten feet of⟩ X; X is (totally) inaccessible.**

P-339 • **РУКО́Й ПОДА́ТЬ** *coll* [VP; infin only; usu. impers predic; less often, subj-compl with copula; fixed WO] **1.** ~ *(от чего до чего)* [when used as subj-compl, subj: a geographical name or a noun denoting a specific site or location] (some place is) very close by, a short distance away: (от X-a) до Y-a рукой подать ≃ **it's (just) a stone's throw (from X) to Y; Y is (just ⟨within⟩) a stone's throw from X; Y is ⟨it's⟩ (just) a stone's throw away; Y is within spitting distance of X.**

«Поедем к ореху, а там и до Сандро рукой подать», — сказал Махты (Искандер 3). "Let's go to the walnut tree, it's just a stone's throw from there to Sandro's," Makhty said (3a).

2. ~ *(до чего)* [when used as subj-compl, subj: a noun denoting an important event, holiday, season, month etc] some event (holiday etc) is very near in time, soon to come: до X-a рукой подать ≃ **X is close ⟨near⟩ at hand; X is just around the corner.**

До праздников рукой подать, пора начинать готовиться. The holidays are just around the corner. It's time to start preparing for them.

P-340 • **ХОДИ́ТЬ/ПОЙТИ́ С ПРОТЯ́НУТОЙ РУКО́Й** [VP; subj: human] to seek alms: X ходит с протянутой рукой ≃ **X begs; X panhandles.**

Магазины исчезли. Карточки еле отоваривались, и беглецам, чтобы не умереть с голоду, только оставалось, что ходить с протянутой рукой — только никто не подавал, потому что и горожане были нищими, — или грабить (Мандельштам 2). For refugees the only thing left, unless they were to die of hunger, was to roam the streets and beg—not that the townspeople had anything to give—or to steal (2a).

P-341 • **ЩЕ́ДРОЙ РУКО́Й** *раздавать, давать что* и т. п. [NP_instrum; Invar; adv; fixed WO] (to give, give out etc sth.) generously, without begrudging s.o. sth.: **with an unsparing hand; with a lavish hand; openhandedly; without skimping; (provide) liberally (for sth.).**

Не стану в подробности описывать, как удалось тогда Ивану Фёдоровичу достигнуть цели и пристроить мужика в части, с тем чтобы сейчас же учинить и осмотр его доктором, причём он опять выдал и тут щедрою рукой «на расходы» (Достоевский 2). I will not describe in detail how Ivan Fyodorovich then managed to achieve his goal and get the peasant installed in the police station and have him examined immediately by a doctor, while he once again provided liberally "for the expenses" (2a).

P-342 • РУ́КОПИСИ НЕ ГОРЯ́Т [sent; fixed WO] it is impossible to destroy good literature, good literature will live on despite oppression and find its way to the reader: **manuscripts don't burn.**

[source] «...Я сжёг его [роман] в печке». – «Простите, не поверю, – ответил Воланд, – этого быть не может. Рукописи не горят» (Булгаков 9). "I burned it [the novel] in the stove." "Forgive me, but I won't believe it," said Woland. "This cannot be, manuscripts don't burn" (9a). ♦ Роман Булгакова [«Мастер и Маргарита»] вышел как бы из небытия, возродился из пепла, подтверждая тем самым главную надежду автора, что рукописи не горят (Войнович 1). Bulgakov's novel [*The Master and Margarita*] seemed to return from oblivion, to rise from the ashes, thereby confirming the author's principal hope—that manuscripts don't burn (1a).

< From Mikhail Bulgakov's novel *The Master and Margarita* («Мастер и Маргарита», ch. 24), written in the late 1940s and published in 1966–67.

P-343 • ЗАПУСКА́ТЬ/ЗАПУСТИ́ТЬ РУ́КУ ⟨ЛА́ПУ⟩ *во что, куда coll, disapprov* [VP; subj: human] to steal, appropriate sth. belonging to another (usu. the public or the government): X запустил руку в Y ≃ **X put ⟨stuck⟩ his hand ⟨paw⟩ into person Z's pocket; X had his hand in the till; X helped himself to Y.**

«Труслив ты стал, кум! Затёртый не первый раз запускает лапу в помещичьи деньги, умеет концы прятать» (Гончаров 1). "You're too easily scared, brother. This isn't the first time Zatyorty has stuck his paw into a landowner's pocket. He knows how to cover his tracks" (1b).

P-344 • ИГРА́ТЬ/СЫГРА́ТЬ НА́ РУКУ *кому coll* [VP; subj: usu. human or collect] to help s.o. (usu. an adversary) or further sth. (usu. the cause of an adversary) by one's actions, often without being aware of doing so: X играет на руку Y-у ≃ **X is playing into the hands of Y ⟨into Y's hands⟩.**

«Мы оба считаем, что об этом надо кричать на всех перекрёстках, а когда доходит до дела, вдруг вспоминаем о дисциплине и принимаемся послушно играть на руку всем этим вождистам, либералам, просветителям...» (Стругацкие 2). "Both you and I believe that it must be shouted from the rooftops; but when it comes time to act, we suddenly remember about discipline and play docilely into the hands of our great leaders, those outstanding liberals, those pillars of enlightenment" (2a).

P-345 • ИМЕ́ТЬ РУ́КУ *где;* (СВОЯ́) РУКА́ ЕСТЬ ⟨ИМЕ́ЕТСЯ⟩ *у кого, где all coll* [VP with subj: human (var. with руку) or VPsubj (variants with рука)] to have an influential friend, patron etc in some place who is willing to help one: X имеет руку в месте Y ≃ **X has connections in ⟨at⟩ place Y; X has a contact ⟨contacts⟩ in ⟨at⟩ place Y.**

«Вам написал аудитор просьбу, – продолжал Тушин, – и надо подписать, да вот с ним и отправить. У них, верно (он указал на Ростова), и рука в штабе есть. Уж лучше случая не найдёте» (Толстой 5). "The auditor wrote out a petition for you," continued Tushin, "and you ought to sign it and send it off with this gentleman. No doubt he" (indicating Rostov) "has connections on the staff. You won't find a better opportunity" (5a).

P-346 • НА ЖИВУ́Ю РУ́КУ *obs, coll* [PrepP; Invar; adv; fixed WO] (to do sth.) hurriedly and not very thoroughly: **(throw sth. together ⟨whip sth. up etc⟩) hastily ⟨in a hurry⟩; (do sth.) slapdash.**

P-347 • НА́ РУКУ *кому coll* [PrepP; Invar; the resulting PrepP is subj-compl with copula (subj: abstr, often это)] sth. is advantageous for s.o., conducive to the realization of s.o.'s plans, inten-

tions: X Y-у на руку ≃ **X suits ⟨serves⟩ Y; X serves Y's purposes; X is to Y's advantage ⟨benefit⟩; X is just what ⟨the thing⟩ Y wants ⟨needs⟩;** [in limited contexts] **X plays into the hands of Y ⟨into Y's hands⟩; Y profits by X.**

[Зилов:] Признавайтесь, вам обоим это на руку. Разве нет?.. (Вампилов 5). [Z.:] Admit it, this way suits you both, doesn't it?... (5a). ♦ Он подолгу доказывал себе, что затея маршала ему на руку... (Эренбург 4). He kept telling himself that the marshal's scheme was to his advantage... (4a). ♦ ...Козы были куплены, но потом стали поступать жалобы, что некоторые козлотуры проявляют хладнокровие по отношению к козам. По этому поводу редактор поставил вопрос об искусственном осеменении коз, но Платон Самсонович стал утверждать, что такой компромисс на руку нерадивым хозяйственникам (Искандер 6). ...No sooner had the goats been purchased than our paper began receiving complaints to the effect that some of the goat-ibexes were acting very coolly toward the females. This prompted our editor to suggest the possibility of artificial insemination, but Platon Samsonovich was firmly opposed to the idea, insisting that such a compromise would only play into the hands of the lazier chairmen (6a).

P-348 • НА́ РУКУ НЕЧИ́СТ; НЕЧИ́СТЫЙ НА́ РУКУ *coll, disapprov* [AdjP; subj-compl with copula, subj: human (both variants), or detached modif (2nd var.)] one is inclined to steal or swindle: X на руку нечист ≃ **X is sticky-fingered ⟨light-fingered, itchy-fingered⟩; X has itchy ⟨sticky⟩ fingers;** [of a cardplayer] **X cheats (at cards); X is a cardsharp(er).**

[Большов:] Вспомни то, Лазарь, сколько раз я замечал, что ты на руку нечист! (Островский 10). [B.:] Think back, Lazar, how many times I saw how light-fingered you were! (10a).

P-349 • НА СКО́РУЮ РУ́КУ *coll* [PrepP; Invar; adv; more often used with pfv verbs; fixed WO] (to do sth.) hurriedly, without spending much time on it, not as thoroughly as it could or should be done: **hastily; in a hurry; in a rough-and-ready fashion; slapdash; (do) a rush job (on sth.);** [equivalents incorporate the verb] **slap sth. together ⟨throw sth. together, cobble sth. together, whip sth. out etc⟩ hastily ⟨in a hurry⟩; give sth. a lick and a promise;** ‖ построить ⟨сколотить и т. п.⟩ ~ **jerry-build sth.;** ‖ перекусить ⟨перехватить и т. п.⟩ ~ ≃ **grab a quick bite (to eat);** ‖ приготовить поесть ~ ≃ **whip up sth.;** ‖ написать *что* ~ ≃ **whip off sth.;** [usu. in refer. to a short piece of writing, a letter etc] **tear ⟨dash⟩ off sth.**

Дождь лил ливнем, и Ростов с покровительствуемым им молодым офицером Ильиным сидел под сороженным на скорую руку шалашиком (Толстой 6). The rain was falling in torrents, and Rostov, with a young officer named Ilyin, a protégé of his, was sitting in a hastily rigged-up shelter (6a). ♦ «К февралю она [установка, идентифицирующая голоса] будет готова?» – «К февралю? Вы что – смеётесь? Если для отчёта, на скорую руку да на долгую муку – ну, что-нибудь... через полгодика» (Солженицын 3). "Will it [the voice identifier] be ready by February?" "By February? Are you joking? If it's a question of slapping something together in a hurry and regretting it later, well then—in half a year" (3a). ♦ Пришлось вместе с профессором Португаловым и приват-доцентом Ивановым и Борнгартом анатомировать и микроскопировать кур в поисках бациллы чумы и даже в течение трёх вечеров на скорую руку написать брошюру «Об изменениях печени у кур при чуме» (Булгаков 10). He had to work with Professor Portugalov and Assistant Professors Ivanov and Bornhart, dissecting and microscoping chickens in search of the plague bacillus. He even hastily whipped out a pamphlet in three evenings, "On the Changes in Chicken Kidneys as a Result of the Plague" (10a). ♦ [Клавдия Васильевна:] Я поставлю чайник. [Леночка:] Нет, нет! Что-нибудь на скорую руку. У нас, кажется, ещё ветчина есть (Розов 2). [K.:] I'll put the kettle on. [L.:] No, please, don't bother. Just a quick bite. I think we've still got some ham left (2a).

Р-350 • НА ШИРО́КУЮ РУ́КУ устроить *что obs, coll*
[PrepP; Invar; adv; fixed WO] (to set up or organize sth.) grandly, impressively, sparing no expense: **in grand style; on a grand ⟨large, big⟩ scale; lavishly; in a big way.**

Ему [графу Ростову] было поручено от клуба устройство торжества для Багратиона, потому что редко кто умел так на широкую руку, хлебосольно устроить пир... (Толстой 5). He [Count Rostov] was entrusted with the arrangements for the fete for Bagration because few men knew how to plan a banquet as lavishly and hospitably as he... (5a).

Р-351 • НАБИВА́ТЬ/НАБИ́ТЬ РУ́КУ *(в чём, на чём) coll*
[VP; subj: human; more often pfv] to become skillful, experienced in sth.: X набил руку в Y-е ≃ **X got the knack ⟨the hang⟩ of Y; X got a grasp ⟨a handle, a grip⟩ on Y; X became versed in Y; X caught on;** [in limited contexts] **X learned his trade.**

Переводить мне приходилось много. Но скоро я набил руку и легко перевыполнял норму... (Копелев 1). I had a lot to translate. But soon I got a handle on it and easily overfulfilled my quotas... (1a). ♦ В три-четыре недели он уже так набил руку в таможенном деле, что знал решительно всё... (Гоголь 3). In three or four weeks he had become so perfectly versed in the affairs of the customs that he knew absolutely everything about them... (3a).

Р-352 • НАКЛА́ДЫВАТЬ/НАЛОЖИ́ТЬ РУ́КУ; НАКЛА́ДЫВАТЬ/НАЛОЖИ́ТЬ ЛА́ПУ *coll* [VP; subj: human or collect] **1.** ~ на что to appropriate sth., take sth. into one's possession willfully: X наложил руку на Y ≃ **X got ⟨laid⟩ his hands on Y; X seized Y.**

При жизни Борис Иванович был очень одинок, но после его смерти нашлось немало желающих наложить руку на его имущество. During his lifetime Boris Ivanovich was very much alone, but after his death there was no shortage of people wanting to lay their hands on his property. **2.** ~ на кого-что [obj: human or collect] to subject s.o. to one's authority or will, take control of s.o. or sth.: X наложил руку на Y-а ≃ **X got Y under X's control; X took hold of Y.**

Р-353 • ОТДАВА́ТЬ/ОТДА́ТЬ РУ́КУ *obs* [VP; subj: human] **1.** ~ чью кому to agree to allow a suitor to marry s.o. (one's daughter, niece etc): X отдал Y-у руку женщины Z ≃ **X gave Y woman Z's hand.**

[Хлестаков:] Если вы не согласитесь отдать руки Марьи Антоновны, то я чёрт знает что готов (Гоголь 4). [Kh.:] If you don't agree to give me Marya Antonovna's hand, why God only knows what I'll do (4a). **2.** ~ кому. Also: ОТДАВА́ТЬ/ОТДА́ТЬ РУ́КУ И СЕ́РДЦЕ *obs* [subj: female] to agree to become s.o.'s wife: X отдала руку (и сердце) Y-у ≃ **X gave Y her hand (in marriage); X gave Y her hand and heart.**

Р-354 • ПОД ВЕСЁЛУЮ РУ́КУ *obs, coll* [PrepP; Invar; adv; fixed WO] (to do sth.) when in a cheerful frame of mind: **when (one is) in a (very) good ⟨merry etc⟩ mood; when (one is) in good humor ⟨in high spirits⟩.**

В тот же вечер, за ужином, стряпчий, под весёлую руку, рассказывал посетителям клуба о необыкновенном казусе, случившемся с помпадуром (Салтыков-Щедрин 2). The same evening, at supper, the lawyer, being in a very merry mood, told the members of the club about the extraordinary adventures of the pompadour (2a).

Р-355 • ПОД ГОРЯ́ЧУЮ РУ́КУ сделать, сказать *что*, попасться, подвернуться *(кому)* и т. п. *coll* [PrepP; Invar; adv; fixed WO] (to say or do sth. when one is, run into s.o. when he is etc) in an angry mood, highly and visibly displeased, dissatisfied

etc: **in a (fit of) temper; in (a fit of) anger; when (one is) angry ⟨steamed (up), fuming, peeved, hot under the collar, in a huff etc⟩;** ‖ X попался Y-у ~ ≃ **X ran into Y when Y was angry ⟨steamed etc⟩;** ‖ не попадайся Y-у ~ ≃ **steer clear of Y when Y is angry ⟨steamed etc⟩.**

...Молчали, не обижались бабы. Даже самые языкатые из них, способные, казалось, под горячую руку переговорить самого чёрта, лишь горько усмехались в ответ из-под сдвинутых к самым бровям платков (Максимов 3). ...The women stood in silence and didn't take offense. Even the most shrewish among them, who could talk the devil's hind leg off when they were in a temper, only smiled back ruefully from under their headscarves (3a). ♦ За долгую свою жизнь похоронил Иван Кузьмич много собак, и Чарли, пожалуй, окажется той собакой, которая переживёт его и будет ждать его возвращения из смерти. А ведь случалось, пинал его Иван Кузьмич под горячую руку (Евтушенко 2). In his long life Ivan Kuzmich had buried many dogs, but Charlie would probably be the dog that outlived him and would wait for him to return from the dead. Yet sometimes Ivan Kuzmich kicked him in anger (2a).

Р-356 • ПОД ПЬЯ́НУЮ РУ́КУ *substand* [PrepP; Invar; adv; fixed WO] (to say or do sth. when one is, run into s.o. when he is etc) in a state of intoxication: **in a drunken state; when (one is) drunk ⟨smashed, sloshed, stewed, under the influence etc⟩;** ‖ X попался Y-у ~ ≃ **X ran into Y when Y was drunk ⟨smashed etc⟩;** ‖ не попадайся Y-у ~ ≃ **steer clear of Y when he's drunk ⟨smashed etc⟩.**

Р-357 • ПО́Д РУКУ¹ ⟨ПОД РУ́ЧКУ *coll*⟩ взять, держать *кого*, идти, гулять и т. п. [PrepP; these forms only; adv] (to take, support, walk with etc s.o.) holding s.o.'s arm at the elbow or bending one's arm through the crook of his: X взял Y-а ~ ≃ **X took Y's arm; X took Y by the arm; X linked his arm through Y's; X linked arms with Y;** ‖ X и Y взяли друг друга ~ ≃ **X and Y linked arms;** ‖ X держал Y-а ~ ≃ **X was holding Y by the arm;** [in limited contexts] **X was on Y's arm;** ‖ X и Y шли ⟨гуляли⟩ ~ ≃ **X and Y were walking ⟨strolling⟩ arm in arm.**

Востоков деликатно взял её под руку (Аксёнов 7). Vostokov gently took her arm... (7a). ♦ Каримов взял Штрума под руку. «Виктор Павлович, вы заметили, самая невинная вещь у Мадьярова выглядит как обобщение?» (Гроссман 2). Karimov took Viktor by the arm. "Victor Pavlovich, have you noticed that the most innocent remark of Madyarov's somehow sounds like a generalization?" (2a). ♦ Несколько раз княжна под ручку с матерью проходила мимо меня, сопровождаемая каким-то хромым старичком... (Лермонтов 1). Several times the young princess passed nearby on her mother's arm, accompanied by a lame old man (1a). ♦ До марта 1953 года можно было всегда видеть Маленкова и Берия гуляющими под руку (Аллилуева 2). Until March 1953 one could always see Malenkov and Beria walking arm in arm (2a).

Р-358 • ПО́Д РУКУ² говорить *coll, disapprov* [PrepP; Invar; adv; often used with neg imper не говори(те)] (to make an ill-timed remark, often offering unsought advice) when s.o. is busy doing sth., thus distracting him: не говори под руку ≃ **quit kibitzing!; don't distract me when I'm trying to do something; don't distract me by talking;** [in limited contexts] **don't speak until ⟨unless⟩ (you're) spoken to.**

На рыбалку я тебя больше не возьму — только мешаешь, всё время что-нибудь под руку говоришь. I'm not taking you fishing anymore—you only get in the way, and always distract me by talking.

Р-359 • ПОД СЕРДИ́ТУЮ РУ́КУ сделать, сказать *что*, попасться, подвернуться *(кому)* и т. п. *coll* [PrepP; Invar; adv; fixed WO] (to say or do sth. when one is, run into s.o. when he is etc) in an angry mood, highly and visibly displeased, dissatisfied etc: **in (a fit of) anger; when (one is) angry ⟨steamed (up), fuming, peeved, hot under the collar, in a huff** etc⟩; ‖ X попался Y-у ~ ≃ **X ran into Y when Y was angry ⟨steamed** etc⟩; ‖ не попадайся Y-у ~ **steer clear of Y when Y is angry ⟨steamed** etc⟩.

[Дудукин:] Его любили, с ним обращались хорошо, хотя не без того чтобы под сердитую руку не попрекнуть его незаконным происхождением (Островский 3). [D.:] They loved him and were good to him, although when angry they were apt to taunt him with his illegitimate birth (3a).

Р-360 • ПОДАВА́ТЬ/ПОДА́ТЬ РУ́КУ *кому* [VP; subj: human] **1.** to clasp s.o.'s hand when greeting, parting with, or congratulating him: X подал Y-у руку ⟨X и Y подали друг другу руки⟩ ≃ **X shook Y's hand ⟨X and Y shook hands, X shook hands with Y⟩.**

«...Иные там, с образом мыслей поблагороднее, так даже руки ему не хотели подать на первых порах: слишком-де уж стремительно в консерваторы перескочил...» (Достоевский 2). "...Some persons there, of a nobler cast of mind, did not even want to shake hands with him at first: he jumped over to the conservatives a bit too precipitously..." (2a).

2. to extend one's hand or arm to s.o. as an offer of help: X подал Y-у руку ≃ **X offered Y his hand ⟨arm⟩; X held out his hand ⟨arm⟩ to Y.**

Дойдя до середины комнаты, она пошатнулась; я вскочил, подал ей руку и довёл её до кресел (Лермонтов 1). When she reached the middle of the room she swayed; I leapt to her side, offered her my arm and led her to an armchair (1b).

Р-361 • ПОДНИМА́ТЬ ⟨ПОДЫМА́ТЬ⟩/ПОДНЯ́ТЬ РУ́КУ [VP; subj: human] **1.** ~ *на кого* to (try to) harm s.o. physically (may refer to hitting, beating, killing etc): X поднял руку на Y-а ≃ **X raised his hand against ⟨to⟩ Y; X lifted his hand against Y; X tried to hit ⟨strike, kill** etc⟩ **Y; X hit ⟨struck, killed** etc⟩ **Y.**

«Я надеялась, что вы будете благодарны... за попечения и труды его, что вы будете уметь ценить его заслуги, а вы, молокосос, мальчишка, решились поднять на него руку» (Толстой 2). "I had hoped that you would be grateful...for his care and labors, that you would know how to value his services, but you, you milksop, you brat, decided to raise your hand against him" (2b). ♦ [Кавалеров:] Андрей Петрович, я поднял на вас руку... и не могу... судите меня... накажите... (Олеша 6). [K.:] Andrei Petrovich, I tried to kill you...but I can't...put me on trial...punish me... (6a).

2. ~ *на кого-что* to criticize openly and express strong disapproval of some person, idea, policy, school of thought etc: X поднял руку на Y-а ≃ **X came ⟨spoke⟩ out against Y; X took a stand against Y; X decried Y.**

...На него [Ленина] никогда не подымали руки — на трибуне. В выступлениях. Никогда не опровергали публично... Разве что по ошибке (Свирский 1). ...No one spoke out against him [Lenin] from public platforms, in speeches. No one ever rejected him in the open...except sometimes by mistake (1a).

Р-362 • ПОЛОЖА́ ⟨less often ПОЛОЖИ́В(ШИ)⟩ РУ́КУ НА́ СЕРДЦЕ *сказать, ответить, утверждать* и т. п. [Verbal Adv; these forms only; adv; often used with imper; fixed WO] (to say sth., respond, declare sth. etc) absolutely sincerely: **hand on ⟨upon⟩ heart; with one's hand on ⟨upon⟩ one's heart; in ⟨with⟩ all sincerity; in all honesty; [in limited contexts] cross my heart (and hope to die).**

«Я полагаю с своей стороны, положив руку на сердце: по восьми гривен за душу — это самая красная цена!» (Гоголь 3). "I, for my part, would offer eighty kopecks per soul. Hand upon heart,

this is the top price" (3c). ♦ Положа руку на сердце, я утверждаю, что подобное извращение глуповских обычаев было бы не только не полезно, но даже положительно неприятно (Салтыков-Щедрин 1). With my hand on my heart, I declare that such a distortion of Foolovian customs would be not only pointless but even positively unpleasant (1a). With all sincerity I assert that such a distortion of the habits of the Glupovites would not only be useless, but even positively disagreeable (1b).

< «Положа» is the old form of the short active participle of the verb «положить»; the corresponding modern form is the perfective verbal adverb «положив».

Р-363 • ПОПАДА́ТЬ(СЯ)/ПОПА́СТЬ(СЯ) ⟨ПОДВЁР-ТЫВАТЬСЯ, ПОДВОРА́ЧИВАТЬСЯ/ПОДВЕР-НУ́ТЬСЯ⟩ ПО́Д РУКУ *(кому)* [VP; subj: usu. concr or human; more often past; more often this WO] to turn up, happen to be proximate, be found by chance: X попался Y-у под руку ≃ **Y happened to come across X; Y happened upon X; person X happened along;** ‖ [used as obj] всё, что подвернулось ⟨всех, кто подвернулся⟩ Y-у под руку ≃ **everything ⟨everybody, anything, anyone⟩ Y could get ⟨lay⟩ his hands on; everything ⟨anything⟩ that came to hand; everything ⟨everyone** etc⟩ **within reach; everything ⟨everyone** etc⟩ **that comes within Y's reach;** ‖ первое, что подвернулось Y-у под руку ≃ **the first thing that came to hand; the first thing Y laid his hand(s) on; the first thing Y's hand happened to light upon; the first thing Y could get ⟨lay⟩ his hands on.**

...Через несколько дней ему под руку попался всё тот же шахматный журнальчик [«8 x 8»], он перелистал его, ища недостроенных мест, и, когда оказалось, что всё уже сделано, пробежал глазами отрывок в два столбца из юношеского дневника Чернышевского... (Набоков 1). ...A few days later he happened to come across that same copy of [the chess magazine] 8×8; he leafed throught it, looking for unfinished bits, and when all the problems turned out to be solved, he ran his eyes over the two-column extract from Chernyshevski's youthful diary... (1a). ♦ Тогда фашисты стали хватать всех, кто подвернулся под руку на Крещатике, сажали в машины и отправляли в Бабий Яр (Кузнецов 1). The fascists began to seize everybody on Kreshchatik they could lay their hands on; they put them in trucks and sent them off to Babi Yar (1a). ♦ Он читал и читал всё, что попадалось под руку, и читал так, что, приехав домой, когда лакеи ещё раздевали его, он, уже взяв книгу, читал... (Толстой 5). He read and read, anything that came to hand, so that coming home at night he picked up a book even while his valets were still taking off his clothes... (5a). ♦ По призванию... он был вор. Он крал, словно находясь в каком-то вдохновенном трансе. Крал нагло, открыто, жадно всё, что попадалось ему под руку (Максимов 2). ...By vocation he was a thief. When he stole, he did so as though in a kind of inspired trance. He stole impudently, openly and greedily everything that came within his reach (2a). ♦ Видно, что повар руководствовался более каким-то вдохновеньем и клал первое, что попадалось под руку: стоял ли возле него перец — он сыпал перец, капуста ли попалась — совал капусту... (Гоголь 3). Evidently the cook was guided mostly by inspiration and put into the pot the first thing he laid his hand on. If a pepper shaker happened to be close by, he put in pepper; if it was cabbage, in went the cabbage (3c). It was obvious that the cook was guided by some kind of inspiration and put in the first thing that his hand happened to light upon: if pepper happened to be near, he put in some pepper, if cabbage turned up, he shoved in cabbage... (3a).

Р-364 • ПРЕДЛАГА́ТЬ/ПРЕДЛОЖИ́ТЬ РУ́КУ (И СЕ́РДЦЕ) *кому old-fash* [VP; subj: human, male] to ask s.o. to become one's wife: X предложил женщине Y руку (и сердце) ≃ **X offered Y his hand (in marriage); X offered Y his hand and heart.**

Аптекарь был в Ревеле; там он познакомился с какой-то молодой девушкой и предложил ей руку... (Герцен 1). The dispenser was away in Reval; there he made the acquaintance of a young girl and offered her his hand... (1a). ♦ ...[Одинцов] влюбился в неё и предложил ей руку. Она согласилась быть его женой... (Тургенев 2). ...He [Odintsov] fell in love with her and offered her his hand in marriage. She consented to become his wife... (2e). ♦ [Шпигельский:] Протобекасов приезжает, волочится, влюбляется, наконец предлагает руку и сердце (Тургенев 1). [Sh.:] [Protobekasov] arrives, flirts, falls in love, and finally offers his hand and heart (1a).

P-365 • ПРИЛОЖИ́ТЬ РУ́КУ¹ к чему, под чем obs [VP; subj: human] to put one's signature on a document or paper: X приложил руку к Y-у ≃ X set his hand to Y; X signed Y; X signed on the dotted line; [in limited contexts] Y was signed by X's own hand.

«К сему показанию явный прелюбодей Василий Иванов Байбаков руку приложил» (Салтыков-Щедрин 1). "To this deposition I, Overt Adulterer Vasily Ivanov Dormousov, have set my hand" (1a). ♦ Затем следовали изъявления преданности и подпись: «Староста твой, всенижайший раб Прокофий Вытягушкин собственной рукой руку приложил» (Гончаров 1). There followed expressions of devotion and the signature: "Your steward and most humble serf, Prokofy Vytyagushkin, signed by his own hand" (1b).

P-366 • ПРИЛОЖИ́ТЬ РУ́КУ² ⟨РУ́КИ⟩ (к чему) coll, disapprov [VP; subj: human; obj: abstr, often это, or a clause introduced by к тому, что ⟨чтобы⟩] to be involved in sth. (usu. of a reprehensible nature): X приложил руку (к Y-у) ≃ X had a hand ⟨a part⟩ in Y; X helped Y to come about; X helped to bring Y about; [in limited contexts] X had a finger in the pie.

Я поражаюсь Елизавете. Ей 21 год. Когда она успела так разложиться? Что у неё за семья, как она воспитывалась, кто приложил руку к её развитию? (Шолохов 2). I am astounded at Liza. She is twenty-one. When did she have time to become so depraved? What kind of family has she got, how was she brought up, who had a hand in her development? (2a). ♦ В Воронеже хозяева охотно пускали на свою площадь ссыльных. Над ссыльными всегда висела угроза, что их вышлют в более глухое место, и, в случае конфликта, хозяин мог приложить к этому руку (Мандельштам 1). In Voronezh the most favored tenants were exiles. Since they were always under threat of being forced to move to some remoter place, the owner of the room they rented could always, in case of conflict, help this to come about (1a). ♦ Народный фронт победил на выборах; к этой победе приложил руку и Дессер (Эренбург 4). The Popular Front had won a victory in the elections and Desser had helped to bring it about (4a).

P-367 • ПРОТЯ́ГИВАТЬ/ПРОТЯНУ́ТЬ РУ́КУ (ПО́-МОЩИ) кому; ПОДАВА́ТЬ/ПОДА́ТЬ РУ́КУ ПО́-МОЩИ all lit [VP; subj: human] to help s.o. when he is going through a difficult time: X протянул Y-у руку помощи ≃ X extended ⟨lent, held out, reached out, stretched out⟩ a helping hand (to Y); X stretched ⟨held, reached⟩ out his hand to Y; [in limited contexts] X lent (Y) a hand.

«...[Я] перечёл письма Иосифа Алексеевича, вспомнил свои беседы с ним и из всего вывел то, что я не должен отказывать просящему и должен подать руку помощи всякому, тем более человеку, столь связанному со мною...» (Толстой 5). "...[I] re-read Joseph Alexeevich's letters and recalled my conversations with him, and deduced from it all that I ought not to refuse a suppliant, and ought to reach out a helping hand to everyone—especially to one so closely bound to me..." (5b). ♦ «Протяните руку падшему человеку... Любите его, помните в нём самого себя и обращайтесь с ним, как с собой, — тогда я... склоню перед вами голову...» (Гончаров 1). "...Stretch out your hand to the fallen man....Love him; see yourself in him, and treat him as you would yourself—then I will...bow down before you" (1b).

P-368 • ПРОТЯНУ́ТЬ РУ́КУ к чему coll [VP; subj: human] to attempt to seize s.o.'s property: X протянул руку к Y-у ≃ X tried to get his hands on Y; X grabbed at Y; X tried to move in on Y.

P-369 • СКОР ⟨СКО́РЫЙ⟩ НА́ РУКУ coll [AdjP; subj-compl with copula, subj: human (both variants), or modif (var. with long-form Adj); fixed WO] **1.** quick to harm or punish s.o. by striking him (with one's hand, a belt etc): **quick with one's fists; quick to use the strap ⟨the belt, the rod⟩;** [of a parent] **quick to hit ⟨spank, smack, whack, wallop etc⟩ one's child ⟨kids etc⟩.**

Иван Петрович был скор на руку: узнав о драке, он сразу же отколотил Павлика, а потом уж стал разбираться, кто прав, кто виноват. Ivan Petrovich was quick to hit his kids: when he heard about the fight, he immediately whacked Pavlik and only then began looking into who was right and who was wrong.

2. quick in one's work, in making decisions, in accomplishing things etc: **(one) gets things done ⟨can do sth. etc⟩ in no time flat; (one) makes ⟨can make⟩ short work of sth.**

Палатку у нас всегда разбивает Инна, так как она скора на руку. Inna's the one who always pitches our tent because she can do it in no time flat.

P-370 • СХВАТИ́ТЬ ⟨ПОЙМА́ТЬ⟩ ЗА́ РУКУ кого coll [VP; subj: human; often 3rd pers pl with indef. refer. or neg pvf fut, gener. 2nd pers sing не схватишь ⟨не поймаешь⟩] to catch s.o. at a moment when he is doing sth. reprehensible: X-а схватили за руку ≃ X was caught red-handed; X was caught in the act; X was caught with his hand in the till ⟨the cookie jar⟩.

P-371 • ТЯЖЁЛ ⟨ТЯЖЁЛЫЙ⟩ НА́ РУКУ coll [AdjP; subj-compl with copula, subj: human (both variants), or modif (var. with long-form Adj)] (one) delivers hard blows when hitting another: **(have) a heavy hand; (be) heavy-handed.**

P-372 • БЕЗ РУЛЯ́ И БЕЗ ВЕТРИ́Л lit [PrepP; Invar; adv, nonagreeing modif, or subj-compl with быть∅ (subj: human); fixed WO] one lacks direction, a specific goal in life, one does sth. in an unfocused manner, not working toward a clear goal: **like a ship without a rudder; rudderless and without sails; (flounder ⟨live, proceed etc⟩) without aim or direction.**

< From Mikhail Lermontov's *The Demon* («Демон»), 1829–39.

P-373 • ПОДХОДИ́ТЬ/ПОДОЙТИ́ ⟨ПРИКЛА́ДЫ-ВАТЬСЯ/ПРИЛОЖИ́ТЬСЯ⟩ К РУ́ЧКЕ чьей, кого; ПОДХОДИ́ТЬ/ПОДОЙТИ́ К РУКЕ́ all obs [VP; subj: human] to approach s.o. and kiss his or her hand as a sign of gratitude, good will, congratulations etc, or kiss a woman's hand upon meeting: X подошёл к Y-овой ручке ≃ X came ⟨went⟩ up to Y and kissed her ⟨his⟩ hand; X came ⟨went⟩ up to kiss Y's hand ⟨the hand of Y⟩; X kissed Y's hand; X carried ⟨raised⟩ woman Y's hand to his lips.

Пётр... не подошёл к ручке барича, а только издали поклонился ему... (Тургенев 2). Pyotr...had not come up to kiss the young master's hand but had merely bowed to him from a distance... (2e). ♦ Ротный портной, вооружённый тупыми своими ножницами, резал у них [гарнизонных солдат] косы. Они, отряхиваясь, подходили к руке Пугачёва... (Пушкин 2). The tailor of the platoon, armed with his blunt scissors, was snipping off their [the garrison soldiers'] locks. They shook their clipped hair off and went up to kiss the hand of Pugachev... (2a). ♦ Она поднялась с дивана, на котор=ом сидела; Чичиков не без удовольствия подошёл к её ручке (Гоголь 3). She rose from the sofa on which she had been sitting. Chichikov carried her hand to his lips, not without a certain amount of pleasure (3c).

Р-374 • ДО РУ́ЧКИ дойти, довести *кого-что* и т. п. *highly coll* [PrepP; Invar; adv; more often used with pfv verbs] (usu. of or in refer. to a person, a group, or a sphere of human activity) (to reach, drive s.o. or sth. to etc) a hopeless, desperate state: X дошёл ~ ≃ **person X reached ⟨was at⟩ the end of his rope ⟨tether⟩; person X reached the end of the line; person X was at the breaking point; thing X was in shambles; thing X was in (a state of) total disarray; thing X was a complete mess;** ‖ Y довёл X-а ~ ≃ **person Y pushed person X to the limit ⟨to the breaking point⟩; person Y made a mess of thing X; person Y reduced thing X to a state of total disarray; [in limited contexts] Y drove person X off the deep end.**

[Шаманов:] …Тогда мне было всё равно. Так всё равно, что я даже не почувствовал, что я дошёл до ручки (Вампилов 2). [Sh.:] Then, I didn't even care. I cared so little I didn't even realize I'd reached the end of the line (2b). ♦ Древесный вспомнил главрежа [главного режиссёра] с Солянки. Даже его довели до ручки, проклятые! Теперь театр, последний оплот Шестидесятых, конечно, рухнет… (Аксёнов 12). Drevesny thought of the director of the Solyanka. They drove even him off the deep end, the bastards! Now the theater, the last bastion of the sixties, will collapse, of course… (12a).

Р-375 • ДЕ́ЛАТЬ/СДЕ́ЛАТЬ РУ́ЧКОЙ *(кому)* *obs, now humor or iron* [VP; subj: human; more often pfv] to move one's hand in s.o.'s direction as a greeting, salutation: X сделал (Y-у) ручкой ≃ **X waved (to Y); X waved his hand at Y; X waved hello ⟨good-bye⟩ to Y;** [when addressing small children] сделай Y-у ручкой ≃ **wave bye-bye to Y.**

Из-за поворота выкатил встречный «ЗИЛ» Жорки Борбаряна… «Э-и-ей, дядя Митя!» – крикнул Жорка, высовывая голову из окна… Дядя Митя только успел ему сделать ручкой (Аксёнов 10). From round a bend Zhorka Borbaryan's Zil came at them.…"Heh-e-eh, Old Mitya!" Zhorka shouted, sticking his head out of the window.…Mitya had time only to wave (10a).

Р-376 • ПОЗОЛОТИ́ТЬ РУ́ЧКУ ⟨РУ́КУ⟩ *(кому)* *obsoles* [VP; subj: human] **1.** *substand* to pay a fortune-teller: X позолотил Y-у ручку ≃ **X crossed Y's palm (with silver).**

2. *usu. humor in contemp. usage* to give s.o. a bribe: X позолотил Y-у руку ≃ **X greased Y's palm; X paid Y off.**

Р-377 • В ТРИ РУЧЬЯ́ *coll* [PrepP; Invar; adv (intensif); fixed WO] ~ плакать, рыдать и т. п.; слёзы льются, текут ~ ; пот катится, льёт и т. п. ~ (of a person) (to cry or sweat) profusely, copiously: X (за)рыдал ~ ≃ **X cried his eyes out; X cried ⟨sobbed⟩ his heart out; X cried buckets ⟨a river⟩ (of tears); X cried his head off; (the) tears streamed ⟨came streaming⟩ out of X's eyes ⟨down X's face⟩;** [pfv only] **X turned on the waterworks;** ‖ пот катился с X-а ~ ≃ **sweat ⟨perspiration⟩ was streaming down X's face; X was dripping (wet) with sweat ⟨perspiration⟩; X was drenched ⟨soaked⟩ with sweat.**

А ещё какую-то минуту спустя она уже утешала плачущую, в три ручья заливающуюся слезами Татьянку, которую, подталкивая, ввели в избу двойнята (Абрамов 1). And a minute or two later, she was comforting Tatyanka, whom the twins were nudging forward into the house and who was sobbing her little heart out (1a). ♦ «…Я открыла глаза, смотрю: она, моя голубушка, сидит на постели, сложила вот этак ручки, а слёзы в три ручья так и текут» (Толстой 2). "…I opened my eyes and looked: there she was, the darling, sitting on the bed with her hands

clasped so, and the tears came streaming out of her eyes" (2b). ♦ «…Смотри, отец мой, насчёт подрядов-то: если случится муки брать ржаной или гречневой, или круп, или скотины битой, так уж, пожалуйста, не обидь меня». – «Нет, матушка, не обижу», – говорил он, а между тем отирал пот, который в три ручья катился по лицу его (Гоголь 3). "…My dear sir, about those government contracts, if you should be wanting rye or buckwheat flour or any cereals or slaughtered animals, mind you don't forget me." "No, of course I won't forget you, ma'am," he said, wiping away the perspiration that was streaming down his face (3a).

Р-378 • БИ́ТЬСЯ КАК РЫ́БА ОБ ЛЁД *coll* [VP; subj: human] to strive in vain to cope with one's low standard of living, work very hard to survive: X бьётся как рыба об лёд ≃ **X struggles to keep his head above water ⟨to keep body and soul together⟩; X (barely) ekes out a living; X struggles desperately; X struggles for survival.**

Р-379 • КАК РЫ́БА нем, молчать *coll* [как + NP; Invar; adv (intensif)] (to be silent) in a persistent manner: **be ⟨remain⟩ (as) mute as a fish.**

[Крутицкий:] Он не болтун?.. [Мамаев:] Ни-ни-ни! Только прикажите, будет нем как рыба (Островский 3). [K.:] He's not a windbag, is he?… [M.:] Not at all, not at all.…Only say the word and he'll be as mute as a fish (3a).

Р-380 • КАК РЫ́БА В ВОДЕ́ быть₀, чувствовать себя *(где, в чём, с кем)* *coll* [как + NP; Invar; adv or subj-compl with copula (subj: human); fixed WO] (to be, feel) totally at ease (in the specified surroundings, with the specified area of knowledge, in s.o.'s company etc): **(be) in one's element; (be ⟨feel⟩) right at home; (be ⟨feel⟩) as much at home as a fish in water; (feel) perfectly comfortable.**

Сопровождаемые толпою любопытных, поражённых оранжевой кофтой… мы стали прогуливаться. Маяковский чувствовал себя как рыба в воде. Я восхищался невозмутимостью, с которой он встречал устремлённые на него взоры (Лившиц 1). Accompanied by a crowd of curious people struck by the orange jacket…we started to stroll about. Maiakovsky was in his element. I admired the imperturbability with which he encountered the stares (1a). ♦ Конечно, [Гартвиг] не преминул блеснуть учёностью, вспомнил Сократа, перипатетиков и прочую древность, где, видно, чувствовал себя как рыба в воде (Трифонов 5). Naturally he [Gartvig] didn't miss the opportunity to show off his erudition, making references to Socrates, the Peripatetics, and other figures of antiquity, with whom he obviously felt as much at home as a fish in water (5a). ♦ …В бесчинстве оголтелой семьи Ивлевых Вера чувствовала себя как рыба в воде (Грекова 3). …Vera felt perfectly comfortable with the happy-go-lucky Ivlev family and its wild behavior (3a).

Р-381 • НИ РЫ́БА НИ МЯ́СО *coll, usu. disapprov, occas. derog* [NP; Invar; usu. subj-compl with copula (subj: usu. human); fixed WO] ordinary, undistinguished, devoid of striking characteristics: X – ни рыба ни мясо ≃ **X is lackluster ⟨colorless, run-of-the-mill⟩;** [with the emphasis on one's lack of decisiveness] **X is wishy-washy;** [in refer. to the vagueness of one's position] **X is neither fish (, flesh,) nor fowl; X is neither fish, flesh ⟨fowl⟩, nor good red herring.**

О Сипенятине и Люсе Пряжкиной Нина «понятия не имела», Овчинникова назвала «трепачом-нахалом», Алика Зарванцева определила как «ни рыба ни мясо»… (Чернёнок 2). Nina "had no idea" about Sipeniatin and Lusya Priazhkina, called Ovchinnikov "an obnoxious bum," defined Alik Zarvantsev as "neither fish nor fowl…" (2a). ♦ «…Если забастовка не кончится, я закрываю завод». – «Не думаю, чтобы ваше предложение было принято». Пьер, обычно порывистый, восторженный, был сух. Дессер почувствовал неприязнь. «Зачем сердиться?

Я – капиталист, этим сказано всё. Рабочие по-своему правы. А вы?.. Вы ни рыба ни мясо» (Эренбург 4). "If the strike isn't called off, I'll shut down the factory." "I don't think your proposition will be accepted." Usually impulsive and enthusiastic, Pierre was now curt. Desser at once sensed his hostility. "Why get angry?" he said. "I'm a capitalist. That tells you everything. The workers are right in their way. But you, you're neither fish, fowl, nor good red herring..." (4a).

P-382 • РЫ́БА С ГОЛОВЫ́ ГНИЁТ ⟨ВОНЯ́ЕТ, ТУ́ХНЕТ⟩ [saying] decay, corruption, disorder etc in a given environment or group begins with those in positions of authority: **a fish stinks ⟨rots⟩ from the head; a fish always stinks from the head downward(s); a fish begins to stink at the head.**

«Вот папа, например... он не может себе этого представить. Он не может представить, до какой степени разложения дошла наша армия... Самовольно уходят с позиций, грабят и убивают жителей, убивают офицеров, мародёрствуют... Невыполнение боевого приказа – теперь обычная вещь». – «Рыба с головы гниёт»... (Шолохов 3). "Father here, for example – he simply can't imagine it. He can't imagine to what extent our army has disintegrated....They leave their positions in defiance of orders, rob and kill civilians, murder their own officers, go about marauding....Refusal to obey orders is the usual thing nowadays." "A fish rots from the head"... (3a).

P-383 • РЫБА́К РЫБАКА́ ВИ́ДИТ ИЗДАЛЕКА́ [saying] people who have similar characteristics or interests quickly recognize one another and find a common language (said in jest, often disapprovingly, when a similarity in character traits or similar interests form the basis for a quick friendship or mutual understanding): ≃ **birds of a feather flock together; it takes one to know one.**

P-384 • КАК РЫ́БКЕ ⟨РЫ́БЕ⟩ ЗО́НТИК нужен *highly coll* [как + NP; these forms only; adv (neg intensif)] completely unnecessary, of no use to s.o.: **(be as much use to s.o.) as an umbrella to a duck; (need sth.) like ⟨as⟩ a duck needs an umbrella.**

P-385 • НЕ УЧИ́ РЫ́БУ ПЛА́ВАТЬ [saying] a person who is expert at what he does has no need of another's advice: ≃ **fish do not need to be taught how to swim.**

P-386 • Я ⟨ты, он и т. п.⟩ РЫ́ЖИЙ *coll* [VP$_{subj}$ with быть$_\emptyset$, pres only; usu. in questions or neg] (said sarcastically, often with aggravation, when one is left out, ignored, not treated as well as the other etc) I am (you are etc) worse than the others: что я, рыжий? ≃ **what am I, chopped liver?**

P-387 • С РЫ́ЛА (брать, получать *что* и т. п.) *substand, rude* [PrepP; Invar; prep obj] (to take, get etc sth.) from each person: **from every ⟨damn ⟨stinking, bloody⟩⟩ one of us ⟨you, them⟩; out of every ⟨damn ⟨stinking, bloody⟩⟩ one of us ⟨you, them⟩; a head; apiece.**

P-388 • КУВШИ́ННОЕ РЫ́ЛО *obs or substand* [NP; fixed WO] an ugly face that juts forward; *by extension* a person who has such a face: **jug snout; juglike snout.**

[source] Иван Антонович, казалось, имел уже далеко за сорок лет; волос на нём был чёрный, густой; вся середина лица выступала у него вперёд и пошла в нос, словом, это было то лицо, которое называют в общежитье кувшинным рылом (Гоголь 3). He [Ivan Antonovich] looked considerably over forty; his hair was black and thick, while the central part of his face jutted forward and ran mostly into nose – in short, his was a face that in common usage is called a "jug snout" (3c). ♦ Природа при рождении одарила его кувшинным рылом (Сухово-Кобылин 1). At his birth nature endowed him with a juglike snout (1a).

< From Nikolai Gogol's *Dead Souls* («Мёртвые души»), vol. I, 1842.

P-389 • НА РЫ́ЛО (приходится давать *что* и т. п.) *substand, rude* [PrepP; Invar; prep obj] each (gets), (to give) to each person: **for ⟨to⟩ every ⟨damn ⟨stinking, bloody⟩⟩ one of us ⟨you, them⟩; a head; apiece.**

P-390 • РЫ́ЛОМ НЕ ВЫ́ШЕЛ *substand, rude* [VP; subj: human; past only] **1.** (*для кого-чего*) ~. Also: **РО́ЖЕЙ ⟨МО́РДОЙ⟩ НЕ ВЫ́ШЕЛ** *substand, rude* one is too bad-looking (to be s.o.'s romantic interest, participate in some activity etc): X рылом не вышел ≃ **X is too ugly (for s.o. ⟨sth.⟩);** [when used as a rejoinder] **not with a mug ⟨a puss⟩ like X's!; not with X's looks!; with a mug ⟨a puss⟩ like X's?**

«Эй, чернявая, айда с нами, – не пожалеешь!» – «Девушки, вы – подружки?» – «Или не видишь, Сёма, ясно – подружки». – «Тогда пусть берут меня в игрушки». – «Ты, Сёма, рылом не вышел» (Максимов 3). "Hey, you with the black hair, come for a walk with us – you won't be sorry!" "Hallo, girls – are you two playmates?" "'Course they're playmates, Syoma, anybody can see that." "I'd like to be their plaything, then." "What, with a mug like yours, Syoma?" (3a).

2. [often used with infin of another verb] one is not fit or qualified for sth., does not meet the necessary criteria for doing sth. (because of his low social status, inferior position etc): X рылом не вышел ≃ **X isn't good enough (to do Y ⟨for thing Y⟩); X has no business (doing Y); (doing Y) is not for the likes of X.**

P-391 • НЕ ПО РЫ́ЛУ *кому substand, rude* [PrepP; Invar; subj-compl with быть$_\emptyset$ (subj: infin); pres only] doing sth. is wrong, improper, unbefitting for s.o. (because of his insufficient income, low status etc): не по рылу X-у делать Y ≃ **X has no business doing Y; who is X to do Y?; doing Y is not for the likes of X.**

P-392 • РЫ́ЛЬЦЕ В ПУХУ́ ⟨В ПУШКУ́⟩ *у кого coll* [NP; these forms only; VP$_{subj}$ with быть$_\emptyset$; fixed WO] s.o. is implicated in sth. reprehensible, dishonorable: у X-а рыльце в пушку ≃ **X has (obviously) been at the jam pot ⟨the cookie jar⟩; (it's clear that) X is a party to it.**

< From Ivan Krylov's fable "Fox and Marmot" («Лисица и Сурок»), 1813.

P-393 • БЫ́ЛИ КОГДА́-ТО И МЫ РЫСАКА́МИ [sent; fixed WO] (said when a person is recalling his youth, happier days, and his youthful derring-do) there was a time when we, too, were young and in our prime: **we too had our hour of glory; we too were young and daring once.**

< From Aleksei Apukhtin's poem "A Team of Bays" («Пара гнедых»), 1895. The original line has «вы» (rather than «мы»).

P-394 • НА РЫСЯ́Х; НА ВСЕХ РЫСЯ́Х [PrepP; these forms only; adv; fixed WO] **1.** ~ ехать, идти и т. п. Also: **НА ПО́ЛНЫХ РЫСЯ́Х** (of a horse or a horse and its rider) (to move) at a gait between a walk and a canter in speed: **(go) at a trot;** ‖ на всех ⟨полных⟩ рысях ≃ **at a full ⟨fast⟩ trot.**

Он тронул лошадь, скомандовал и в то же мгновение, услыхав за собой звук топота своего развёрнутого эскадрона, на полных рысях, стал спускаться к драгунам под гору (Толстой 6). He touched the horse, gave the command, and at the same instant, hearing the hoofbeats of his squadron deployed behind him, rode at a full trot down the hill toward the dragoons (6a).

2. ~ бежать, мчаться, нестись и т. п. Also: **ВО ВСЮ РЫСЬ** *all highly coll* (of a person) (to run, race etc) at a relatively rapid or quite rapid pace (depending on the verb of motion used in conjunction with the idiom): **at a good ⟨fast, quick** etc⟩ **pace; at a good clip;** [the equivalent incorporates the verb of motion] trot (off ⟨down the street etc⟩).

…Когда мы подъехали к хвосту очереди, из-за угла выскочил парень с двумя пакетами апельсинов и на рысях помчался к парадному входу — обмывать, значит, это дело (Аксёнов 1). …As we drove up to the line a guy with two bags of oranges popped out from around the corner and trotted off toward the front entrance—to celebrate his purchase, I guess (1a).

P-395 • РЫ́ЦАРЬ БЕЗ СТРА́ХА И УПРЁКА *lit, elev* [NP; usu. sing; fixed WO] a courageous man with high morals: **knight without fear and without reproach ⟨blemish⟩; daring and irreproachable;** *chevalier sans peur et sans reproche.*

[author's usage] Захару было за пятьдесят лет. Он был уже не прямой потомок тех русских Калебов, рыцарей лакейской, без страха и упрёка, исполненных преданности к господам до самозабвения, которые отличались всеми добродетелями и не имели никаких пороков (Гончаров 1). Zakhar was over fifty years old. He was not one of those direct descendants of the Russian Calebs, knights of the servants' hall, without fear, without reproach, endowed with every virtue, immune to every vice, and replete with selfless devotion to their masters (1b). ♦ Рыцарь без страха и упрёка, географ шёл… против всех с открытым забралом, разгневанно (Соколов 1). …Daring and irreproachable, the geographer moved openly against everyone, infuriated (1a).

< Loan translation of the French *chevalier sans peur et sans reproche*, a description in contemporary chronicles of the French knight Pierre Terrail, Seigneur de Bayard (1473–1524).

P-396 • РЫ́ЦАРЬ ПЕЧА́ЛЬНОГО О́БРАЗА *lit, usu. said with good-natured irony* [NP; more often sing; fixed WO] a person who is magnanimous and idealistic, but very naïve and impractical: **knight of the rueful ⟨doleful⟩ countenance.**

< From an appellation given to Don Quixote in Miguel de Cervantes's novel of that title, 1605.

P-397 • талия В РЮ́МОЧКУ [PrepP; Invar; nonagreeing postmodif] (a waist that is) very slender: **wasp ⟨waist⟩.**

P-398 • ПРОПУСКА́ТЬ/ПРОПУСТИ́ТЬ РЮ́МОЧКУ ⟨СТАКА́НЧИК, СТО́ПОЧКУ, ЧА́РОЧКУ⟩ *all old-fash, coll* [VP; subj: human] to drink a glass or small amount of liquor: X пропустил рюмочку ≃ **X had ⟨took⟩ a nip; X downed ⟨tossed down⟩ a glass; X had a shot (of liquor).**

Друзей у него не было. Компании по пьяному делу он не водил — редко, разве что по большим праздникам, пропускал стопочку (Абрамов 1). He had no friends. He did not indulge in drinking sessions—on rare occasions he would down a glass, but only on important holidays (1a).

P-399 • ИЗ РЯ́ДА ⟨-у⟩ ВОН *coll* [PrepP; these forms only; fixed WO] **1.** [modif (intensif)] extremely, unusually: **extraordinarily; exceptionally; uncommonly; incredibly.**

Лето было из ряду вон дождливое. Summer was incredibly rainy.

2. [subj-compl with copula (subj: abstr)] very unusual, remarkable: X — из ряда вон ≃ **X is (quite) out of the ordinary; X is exceptional ⟨extraordinary⟩.**

Этот случай был, конечно, из ряда вон (Гинзбург 2). This was, of course, an exceptional case (2a).

3. [subj-compl with быть₀ (subj: это); used as Interj] used to express resentment, indignation etc: **it's outrageous!; it's an outrage!; that's ⟨this is⟩ (really) too much!**

Вчера Петя опять сбежал с уроков и пошёл с мальчишками в кино. Это уж из ряда вон! Petya cut classes again yesterday and went to the movies with his buddies. This is really too much!

P-400 • ИЗ РЯ́ДА ВОН ВЫХОДЯ́ЩИЙ [AdjP; modif or subj-compl with copula (subj: usu. abstr, occas. concr or human); often postmodif of нечто, что-нибудь, ничего etc; usu. this WO] very unusual, outstanding in some way, strikingly different from other (phenomena, things, or people in its or his group, category etc): **(quite) out of the ordinary; exceptional; extraordinary; no everyday** [NP]; [in limited contexts] **unprecedented.**

…Боже упаси тебя сделать что-нибудь из ряда вон выходящее или, страшно подумать, выдающееся!.. Тогда обнаружится, что любой желающий может провалить твою работу [книгу] или, по крайней мере, задержать на неопределённый срок под любым предлогом (Зиновьев 1). …God help you if you produce something out of the ordinary or, horror of horrors, outstanding!…You will discover that anybody, no matter who, can sink your book, or at least freeze it on any pretext for an indefinite time… (1a). ♦ Подобно древнему Соломону, изрекавшему в острые моменты жизни своё «и это пройдёт», наша бабушка, выслушав сообщение о каком-нибудь из ряда вон происшествии, обычно говорила: «Такое-то уже было…» (Гинзбург 1). Just as, we are told, King Solomon observed at moments of crisis, "This too will pass," so Grandmother, on being told of some extraordinary event, would usually say: "Yes, it's happened before…" (1b). ♦ …Ресторан зажил своей обычной… жизнью и жил бы ею до закрытия… если бы не произошло нечто, уже совершенно из ряду вон выходящее… (Булгаков 9). …The restaurant resumed its customary life and would have gone on peacefully until closing time…had it not been for an utterly unprecedented occurrence… (9a).

P-401 • В ПЕ́РВЫХ РЯДА́Х *кого-чего* идти, находиться и т. п. *rhet, media* [PrepP; Invar; adv or subj-compl with copula (subj: human or collect)] (to be) among the leaders in sth. (some field, movement etc): **(be) in the front ranks ⟨the vanguard⟩; (be) at the forefront.**

В нашей гимназии в каждом классе было по два отделения — первое и второе. Первое отделение считалось аристократическим, второе — демократическим… Вражда между первым и вторым отделениями никогда не затихала. Она выражалась в взаимном презрении. Но раз в год, осенью, происходила традиционная драка между первыми и вторыми отделениями… Почти всегда в первых рядах победителей был гимназист с задорным вздёрнутым носом — будущий писатель Михаил Булгаков (Паустовский 1). Every class in our high school was divided into two groups, the first and the second. The first section was considered to be aristocratic, the second democratic….The enmity between the first and second sections never died down. It was usually expressed in mutual contempt. But once a year, in the autumn, it produced a traditional battle between the first and second sections of all the classes….Almost always in the front ranks of the conquerors was a high school boy with a perky, turned-up nose—the future writer Mikhail Bulgakov (1b).

P-402 • РЯ́ДОМ С *кем-чем* [AdvP; Invar; Prep; the resulting PrepP is adv] **1.** in close proximity to: **next to; alongside (of);** [in limited contexts] **next door to.**

Рядом с нашей школой есть бассейн. There is a swimming pool next to our school.

2. when placed side by side (with s.o. or sth.) and observed in relation to him or it: **next to; in comparison with; (as) compared with ⟨to⟩.**

[Шервинский:] Вы красивая, умная, как говорится, интеллектуально развитая… А он рядом с вами — вешалка, карьерист, штабной момент (Булгаков 4). [Sh.:] You are beautiful, intelligent, intellectually developed, as they say….And compared to you he's a coat rack, a careerist, a headquarters nothing (4a).

3. at the same time as, together with: **along with.**

Когда я узнал Никиту поближе, я понял, что рядом с детской наивностью в нём живёт трезвая расчётливость. When I got to know Nikita better, I understood that along with his childlike naïveté he had sober common sense.

P-403 • **В РЯДУ́** *кого-чего* [PrepP; Invar; the resulting PrepP is adv] in the class or group of: **among(st); in ⟨among⟩ the ranks of.**

Ему принадлежит почётное место в ряду создателей современной офтальмологии. He occupies a place of honor among the founders of modern ophthalmology.

P-404 • **СОМКНУ́ТЬ РЯДЫ́** *rhet or elev* [VP; subj: human pl or collect] to unite, join forces in order to achieve a common goal (often implies overcoming petty differences in the process): X-ы сомкнули ряды ≃ **Xs closed ranks.**

Они [московские славянофилы] должны были сомкнуть свои ряды и высказаться при появлении «Письма» Чаадаева и шуме, который оно вызвало. «Письмо» Чаадаева было своего рода последнее слово, рубеж (Герцен 2). ...They [the Moscow Slavophiles] had had to close their ranks and take a definite stand on the appearance of Chaadayev's *Letter* and the commotion it caused. That *Letter* was in a sense the last word, the limit (2a).

C

C-1 • **САДИ́ТЬСЯ/СЕСТЬ ВЕРХО́М** *на кого coll* [VP; subj: human] taking advantage of s.o.'s gentleness or weak will, to make him submit to one's will, carry out one's wishes: X сядет на Y-а верхом ≃ **X will walk all over Y; X will boss ⟨push⟩ Y around; X will order Y about ⟨around⟩;** [in limited contexts] **X will twist Y (a)round X's little finger.**

Алёша робкий, боязливый, на него кто угодно может сесть верхом. Alyosha is shy and timorous; anyone can walk all over him. ♦ Он имел о себе самое высокое мнение; тщеславие его не знало границ... а со всем тем... всякий несколько опытный чиновник садился на него верхом (Тургенев 2). He had the highest opinion of himself; his vanity knew no bounds....But for all that...any less experienced civil servant could twist him round his little finger (2e).

C-2 • **ростом В КОСУ́Ю СА́ЖЕНЬ** *coll* [PrepP; Invar; nonagreeing modif; fixed WO] (usu. of a man) a very tall person: **a giant (of a man); (a) stalwart (man).**

< From the name of an old unit of measure: the distance from the tip of the toes on one foot to the tip of the index finger on the opposite hand when that arm is raised straight into the air.

C-3 • **КОСА́Я СА́ЖЕНЬ В ПЛЕЧА́Х** *coll* [NP; sing only; detached modif or subj-compl with быть∅ (subj: human)] (usu. of a man) a person with large, muscular shoulders: **broad-shouldered; (with) big broad shoulders; (one has) broad shoulders.**

[Варравин:] Ну, а к девочке-то и подделался один франт, некто Кречинский, молодчина, косая сажень в плечах... (Сухово-Кобылин 1). [V.:] Well, some dandy, a certain Krechinsky, good-looking, big broad shoulders, wormed his way into the girl's good graces (1a).

< See C-2.

C-4 • **ЗАГИБА́ТЬ/ЗАГНУ́ТЬ САЛА́ЗКИ** *кому substand* [VP; subj: human] **1.** *obs* to raise and push s.o.'s legs toward his head with great force while he is lying on his back, thereby causing him great pain: X загнул Y-у салазки ≃ **X bent Y into a pretzel.**

2. to punish s.o. severely, deal with s.o. harshly: X загнёт Y-у салазки ≃ **X will fix ⟨get⟩ Y (good); X will fix Y's wagon; X will settle Y's hash.**

Тихон исподлобья окинул Штабеля с ног до головы, как бы прикидывая, во сколько обойдётся ему драка с дюжим австрийцем, потом коротко переглянулся с братом, тот хмуро кивнул, и они двинулись прочь, и лишь с порога парадного Тихон пьяно погрозил: «Я тебе, немецкая морда, ещё загну салазки!» (Максимов 3). Tikhon sullenly looked him [Stabel] up and down, calculating how much a fight with the sturdy Austrian might cost him, then exchanged a brief glance with his brother, who nodded equally sullenly. They moved away, and had reached the front door before Tikhon uttered his drunken threat. "I'll settle your hash, you ugly German bastard!" (3a).

C-5 • **САМ НЕ СВОЙ** *coll* [AdjP; usu. sing; subj-controlled; detached modif or subj-compl with copula (subj: human); fixed WO] one has lost his composure, is not acting as he usually does (under the influence of a strong emotion—usu. grief, worry, occas. joy, excitement etc): X сам не свой ≃ **X is not himself; X is beside himself (with worry ⟨grief, joy etc⟩).**

Первые недели и даже месяцы после ареста Вадима Киля ходила сама не своя (Некрасов 1). During the first weeks, even months, after Vadim's arrest Kilia was not herself (1a). ♦ По инсти-туту мгновенно распространилась весть, что «Эс-Пе» (кличка Королёва среди сотрудников) приехал «сам не свой» (Владимиров 1). The word went around the institute in a flash that 'S.P.' (as he was known by his colleagues) had been beside himself when he returned (1a).

C-6 • **САМ ПО СЕБЕ́** [AdjP; fixed WO] **1.** [usu. modif] (of a person, thing, phenomenon etc) considered as a separate entity, with a focus on his or its intrinsic qualities, apart from related circumstances, events etc: **in (and of) oneself ⟨itself⟩;** [in limited contexts] **in one's ⟨its⟩ own right;** [when it modifies a deverbal noun or a clause] **the very fact of (doing sth.); the mere fact that...**

Мне было неловко видеть её [бабушки] печаль при свидании с нами; я сознавал, что мы сами по себе ничто в её глазах, что мы ей дороги только как воспоминание... (Толстой 2). I was embarrassed to see her [Grandmother's] sorrow at the sight of us; I realized that in ourselves we were nothing in her eyes, that we were dear to her only as a reminder... (2b). ♦ «Сама по себе затея написать книжку о выдающемся деятеле шестидесятых годов ничего предосудительного в себе не содержит» (Набоков 1). "In itself the idea of writing a book about an outstanding public figure of the sixties contains nothing reprehensible" (1a). ♦ Для Анны Николаевны пролетарская этика была священна сама по себе... (Богданов 1). To Anna Nikolaevna, proletarian ethics were sacred in and of themselves... (1a). ♦ В конце концов я узнал, что Иванько Сергей Сергеевич, 1925 года рождения: а) родственник бывшего председателя КГБ Семичастного; б) ближайший друг бывшего представителя СССР в Организации Объединённых Наций... Николая Т. Федоренко; в) сам по себе тоже большая шишка (Войнович 3). In the end, I learned that Ivanko, Sergei Sergeevich, born 1925, was: a. A relative of the former director of the KGB, Semichastny. b. A close friend of Nikolai T. Fedorenko, the former Soviet representative to the United Nations... c. A big shot in his own right (3a). ♦ На избирательных участках стоят, правда, задёрнутые шторами кабинки для «тайного» голосования... но даже сам по себе заход в эту кабинку будет кем-нибудь отмечен, и в досье совершившего этот «антиобщественный» поступок гражданина появится соответствующая отметка (Войнович 1). The polling places do...have booths with blinds that can be closed for casting a "secret" ballot....But the very fact of entering the booth will be noted in the dossier of the citizen committing that "antisocial" act (1a). ♦ Основное обвинение отец решительно отверг, но то, что он не сгрёб Лёву за шиворот и не вышвырнул тут же из кабинета, само по себе было очень примечательно (Битов 2). Father emphatically rejected the main accusation, but the mere fact that he didn't scoop Lyova up by the scruff of the neck and fling him right out of the study was very noteworthy (2a).

2. расти, жить и т. п. ~ [adv] (of a child) (to grow up) without receiving any attention, care, guidance etc from one's parents or guardians, (of an adult) (to live) having little or no contact with the person or people with whom one lives: **on one's own;** [in limited contexts] **live one's own life.**

Родители были всегда заняты, и мальчик фактически рос сам по себе. The boy's parents were always busy, so actually he grew up on his own. ♦ У них с отцом [у Андрея с отцом] не существовало каких-то особых отношений — ни плохих, ни хороших, каждый... жил сам по себе (Распутин 2). He [Andrei] and his father had no special relationship—it wasn't bad, it wasn't good, each lived his own life (2a).

3. быть∅, существовать, жить и т. п. ~ [subj-compl with copula (subj: human, abstr, or concr) or adv; when used with two subjects, the idiom is repeated with each of them; often used in two clauses connected by contrastive Conj «а»] some thing (phenomenon etc) is separate from, exists separately from a connected thing (phenomenon etc); some person (or group) lives, works etc individually, apart from some other person (or group): **(all) by o.s. ⟨itself⟩; on one's ⟨its⟩ own; independently (of s.o. ⟨sth.⟩);** [of things, phenomena etc only] **(be) a separate entity ⟨separate entities⟩;** ‖ [when both subjects are specified] X сам по себе, а Y сам по себе ≃ [of people] **X went X's way and Y went Y's;** [of things] **X is one thing and Y is another.**

[Липочка:] Так смотрите же, Лазарь Елизарыч, мы будем жить сами по себе, а они [тятенька и маменька] сами по себе (Островский 10). [L.:] Then, look here, Lazar Elizarych, we'll live by ourselves, and they'll [mama and daddy will] live by themselves (10a). ♦ ...Он [Лёва] ещё не может знать, не подозревает о существовании этих фактов, но эти факты тем не менее существуют сами по себе и существуют некоторым образом в его незнании (Битов 2). ...He [Lyova] cannot yet know about and does not suspect the existence of these facts, yet the facts nevertheless exist independently and also exist, after a fashion, in his ignorance (2a). ♦ «Ты, Илья Никанорыч, не подумай чего, наше дело — сторона, мы люди маленькие... Ванька сам по себе, а я сам по себе, у меня к евонным [*ungrammat* = его] затеям никакого касательства» (Максимов 1). "Ilya Nikanorych, please don't get the wrong idea. We're not mixed up in this, we're just simple people!...Vanka went his way and I went mine. I had nothing to do with what he was up to" (1a). ♦ Жизнь у него [Обломова] была сама по себе, а наука сама по себе (Гончаров 1). For him [Oblomov] life was one thing and learning another (1b). ♦ «...У вас на заводе работает инженер с высшим образованием и имеет в своём подчинении 10-12 чел. Он может приказать им что-нибудь только по работе, а после работы или во время выходного дня они ему уже не подчиняются и могут делать, что хотят, как говорится, ты сам по себе, а я сам по себе» (Войнович 2). [context transl] "...At the factory you have an engineer with a higher education, with some ten to twelve men under him. He can order them to do anything at work, but after work or on their days off they're not subordinate to him any more and they can do whatever they want—as the saying goes, you're your own boss and I'm mine" (2a).

4. действовать, происходить и т. п. ~ [adv] (of a person) (to act) on one's own initiative, not influenced by anyone's suggestions, without interference; (of a thing, event etc) (to happen, proceed etc) without any outside influence or interference: **(all) by o.s. ⟨itself⟩; of one's ⟨its⟩ own accord; of one's ⟨its⟩ own volition; on one's ⟨its⟩ own.**

«Да где ж это видано, чтобы народ сам по себе собирался без всякого контроля со стороны руководства?» (Войнович 2). "Who ever heard of people assembling all by themselves, without any control on the part of the leadership?" (2a). ♦ Привычные словосочетания притупляли ощущение горя, уводили сознание в сторону, и вскоре язык Килина болтал уже что-то сам по себе, как отдельный и независимый член организма (Войнович 2). The familiar word patterns dulled his sense of grief, distracted his mind, and soon Kilin's tongue was babbling away all by itself, like a separate and independent part of his body (2a). ♦ Глаза были похожи на два неестественно голубых, светящихся шарика, подвешенных в воздухе над рулём пустой машины, которая идёт без водителя, сама по себе (Евтушенко 1). They were like two unnaturally blue shiny balloons, suspended in mid-air over the steering wheel of an empty car, which moved along of its own accord without a driver (1a). ♦ ...Ему надо только придумать первую фразу, а там дальше дело пойдёт само по себе (Войнович 6). [context transl] He had only to put together the first sentence, and after that the book would write itself (6a).

C-7 • САМ СОБОЙ ⟨-ю⟩ [AdjP; subj-controlled; adv; more often used with pfv verbs; fixed WO] **1.** (to happen, occur etc) without any outside influence or interference: **(all) by itself; on one's own; of itself; of its own accord ⟨volition⟩; automatically.**

Дойдя на Севере до Архангельска... [куриный] мор остановился сам собой по той причине, что идти ему дальше было некуда, — в Белом море куры, как известно, не водятся (Булгаков 10). Having reached Archangel...in the North, the [chicken] plague stopped by itself, for the reason that there was nowhere for it to go—as everybody knows, there are no hens in the White Sea (10b). ♦ Про кампанию оппозиции забудут, и она задохнётся сама собой (Зиновьев 1). "The campaign for protest will be forgotten and it'll wither away on its own" (1a). ♦ Князь Андрей, точно так же как и все люди полка, нахмуренный и бледный, ходил взад и вперёд по лугу... Делать и приказывать ему нечего было. Всё делалось само собою. Убитых оттаскивали за фронт, раненых относили, ряды смыкались (Толстой 6). Prince Andrei, pale and depressed like everyone else in the regiment, paced up and down from one border to another on the meadow....There were no orders to be given, nothing for him to do. Everything happened of itself. The dead were dragged back from the front, the wounded carried away, and again the ranks closed up (5a). ♦ Мнили, что во время этой гульбы хлеб вырастет сам собой, и потому перестали возделывать поля (Салтыков-Щедрин 1). They imagined that while this gaiety was going on, the corn would grow of its own accord, and they gave up tilling the fields (1b). ♦ «Нож», — крикнул Филипп Филиппович. Нож вскочил ему в руки как бы сам собой... (Булгаков 11). "Knife," cried Philip Philippovich. The knife leaped into his hands as of its own volition... (11a). ♦ О его сборничке так никто и не написал, — он почему-то полагал, что это само собою сделается, и даже не потрудился разослать редакциям... (Набоков 1). His book of poems did not get any reviews after all (somehow he had assumed it would happen automatically and had not even taken the trouble of sending out review copies...) (1a).

2. ~ **додумался** *до чего,* **добился** *чего* и т. п. *obsoles* (one came up with an idea or solution, achieved sth. etc) independently, without anyone's help: **(all) by o.s.**

[Городничий:] О, я знаю вас: вы если начнёте говорить о сотворении мира, просто волосы дыбом поднимаются. [Аммос Фёдорович:] Да ведь сам собою дошёл... (Гоголь 4). [Mayor:] Oh I know you. When you start spouting your crazy theories of the Creation, it's enough to make a man's hair stand on end. [A.F.:] But I arrived at it all by myself... (4f).

C-8 • САМИ́М СОБО́Й быть, оставаться [NP; these forms only; subj-compl with copula (subj: human); var. with быть is used in past and fut only] (to be, remain) the way one is by nature (in terms of character, outlook etc), (to behave) in one's customary manner: X был ⟨оставался⟩ ~ ≃ **X was ⟨remained⟩ himself; X was ⟨remained⟩ true to himself.**

Дайте мне в этой стране остаться самой собою — это единственное, что я прошу у Свободы (Аллилуева 2). Let me remain myself in this country. This is the only thing I ask of Freedom (2a).

C-9 • САМО́ СОБО́Й ⟨-ю⟩ РАЗУМЕ́ЕТСЯ; САМО́ СОБО́Й ⟨-ю⟩ *all coll* [these forms only; sent adv (parenth), main clause in a complex sent, or indep. sent (used as affirm response); fixed WO] certainly; it is so apparent, expected that there is hardly any need even to mention it; that is the way things are supposed to go or be: **it ⟨that⟩ goes without saying; naturally; of course; needless to say; obviously; it ⟨that⟩ stands to reason.**

Само собой разумеется, что есть общая установка, определяющая развитие всей науки на данном историческом этапе (Зиновьев 1). It goes without saying that there is a general directive defining the development of all science for the given historical period (1a). ♦ Сейчас Кузьма Кузьмич возвращался с очередного районного совещания, и разговор, само собой, зашёл о лесозаготовках (Абрамов 1). Right now Kuzma Kuzmich was on his way back from a District Committee meeting, so naturally the conversation turned to logging (1a). ♦ ...Само собою, после того, как контракт был предъявлен, дальнейшие выражения удивления были бы просто неприличны (Булгаков 9). ...Of course, after the contract was presented, further expression of astonishment would have been improper (9a). ♦ Само собою разумеется, что сегодняшняя казнь оказалась чистейшим недоразумением — ведь вот же философ, выдумавший столь невероятно нелепую вещь вроде того, что все люди добрые, шёл рядом [с прокуратором], следовательно, он был жив (Булгаков 9). Needless to say, today's execution turned out to have been a sheer misunderstanding, for the philosopher, who had invented the incredibly absurd idea that all men were good, walked by his [the Procurator's] side; hence, he was alive (9a). ♦ «Здесь всегда жили абхазы, убыхи, гениохи, картвелы, мегрелы, греки и люди многих других племён. Ну, и эндурцы, само собой» (Искандер 5). "There have always been Abkhaz, Ubykhs, Geniokhs, Kartveli, Mingrelians, Greeks and people of many other tribes living here. Oh, and Endurskies, obviously" (5a).

С-10 • ПУСКА́ТЬ/ПУСТИ́ТЬ НА САМОТЁК дело, всё *coll, usu. disapprov* [VP; subj: human or collect] to let some matter or work develop spontaneously, without any concrete plan: X пустил дело на самотёк ≃ **X let things ⟨matters⟩ take their course; X let things develop as they might; X let things run themselves.**

«У нас там Комитета по спорту вовсе нет. Всё пущено на самотёк» (Аксёнов 7). "We have no Sports Commission whatsoever. We let things take their course" (7a). ♦ «Вообще-то, с этой конференцией в Западном Берлине непорядок. Ника Буренин всё пустил на самотёк» (Аксёнов 12). "In general, that conference in West Berlin is a shambles. Burenin is letting the whole thing run itself" (12a).

С-11 • НЕ В СВОЙ СА́НИ НЕ САДИ́СЬ [saying; other finite forms and infin are also used] do not undertake sth. that is more than you can manage: ≃ **don't bite off more than you can chew; don't try to do something ⟨things⟩ you're not fit for.**

[author's usage] «Я вижу, образование у неё небольшое». — «Какое там образование — грамотёшка! С таким образованием только получку считать, а не казённые деньги. Я ей сколько раз говорил: не лезь не в свои сани. Работать как раз некому было, ей и уговорили» (Распутин 1). "She doesn't seem to have had much of an education." "Education? You're joking. Can't do much more than count her pay, let alone the till. How many times did I tell her: don't try to do something you're not fit for. But there was nobody else to take the job and they talked her into it" (1a).

С-12 • ЛЮ́БИШЬ ⟨ЛЮБИ́⟩ КАТА́ТЬСЯ, ЛЮБИ́ И СА́НОЧКИ ВОЗИ́ТЬ [saying] you have to pay for your pleasures (with work, time, or money): ≃ **if you want to dance, you have to pay the piper; no pain, no gain; no sweat, no sweet.**

С-13 • РАЗВОДИ́ТЬ/РАЗВЕСТИ́ ⟨УДАРЯ́ТЬСЯ/УДА́РИТЬСЯ В⟩ САНТИМЕ́НТЫ *coll* [VP; subj: human] to display extreme, unnecessary sensitivity, tender emotions etc: X разводит сантименты ≃ **X is sentimentalizing; X is getting ⟨being⟩ overly sentimental; X is getting mushy.**

С-14 • ДВА САПОГА́ (—) ПА́РА *coll* [NP; Invar; used as indep. sent or as subj-compl with бытьø (subj: human, dual); pres only; fixed WO] the two people in question are similar with regard to personality traits, behaviors etc (which are usu. negative, undesirable): X и Y — два сапога пара ≃ **X and Y are a real pair; X and Y are cast in the same mold; X and Y are (like) two peas in a pod; two shoes make a pair.**

«Вы как с Петрухой-то вот с Катерининым не смыкнулись?.. Он такой же. Два сапога — пара» (Распутин 4). "How come you haven't gotten together with Katerina's Petrukha?...He's just like you. Two shoes make a pair" (4a).

С-15 • САПОГИ́ ВСМЯ́ТКУ *obs, coll* [NP; Invar; subj-compl with бытьø (subj: это, may be omitted); fixed WO] foolishness, senseless talk, reasoning etc: **stuff and nonsense; (a lot ⟨a bunch⟩ of) garbage ⟨rubbish, baloney⟩; a pile of rubbish; (a lot of) hogwash; tommyrot; balderdash; moonshine.**

[Кречинский (*отирает лицо и пробегает письмо*):] Мой тихий ангел... милый... милый сердцу уголок семьи... м... м... м... нежное созвездие... чёрт знает, какого вздору!.. Чёрт в ступе... сапоги всмятку и так далее (Сухово-Кобылин 2). [K. (*wipes his face and quickly peruses the letter*):] My gentle angel...family haven so dear to the heart...hm...mm...hm...tender constellation...devil knows what nonsense!...gibberish, balderdash, tommyrot, and the like (2b). ♦ Какая же причина в мёртвых душах? Даже и причины нет. Это, выходит, просто: белиберда, сапоги всмятку! Это просто чёрт побери!.. (Гоголь 3). But what reason could there be in dead souls? None whatsoever. It was all...absurdity, moonshine! It was simply...oh, the Devil take it all!... (3c).

С-16 • САПОГИ́-СКОРОХО́ДЫ; СЕМИМИ́ЛЬНЫЕ САПОГИ́ *both folk* [NP; pl only] (in fairy tales) magic boots that quickly carry the wearer great distances: **seven-league boots.**

С-17 • ПОД САПОГО́М чьим, (у) кого бытьø, жить и т. п.; **держать** кого *coll* [PrepP; Invar; subj-compl with copula (subj: human or collect) or obj-compl with держать (obj: human or collect)] (to be, live) under s.o.'s power; (to keep s.o.) under one's power: X был ~ у Y-а ≃ **X was under Y's heel ⟨yoke, control, thumb⟩;** ‖ Y держит X-а ~ ≃ **Y keeps ⟨has⟩ X under Y's yoke ⟨control, thumb⟩.**

С-18 • КАК САПО́ЖНИК ⟨-и⟩ *highly coll, disapprov* [как + NP; nom only] **1.** [adv] (to do sth.) very poorly or clumsily: играть в теннис ⟨в шахматы и т. п.⟩ как сапожник ≃ **play a rotten ⟨lousy, pathetic etc⟩ game of tennis ⟨chess etc⟩; play tennis etc like a klutz;** ‖ ездить верхом ⟨играть на скрипке и т. п.⟩ как сапожник ≃ **be a lousy ⟨rotten, terrible, hopeless etc⟩ rider ⟨violinist etc⟩;** ‖ переводить как сапожник ≃ **be a lousy ⟨bungling, awkward etc⟩ translator.**

С ним скучно играть в теннис: он играет как сапожник. It's boring to play tennis with him—he plays like a klutz.

2. пьян(ый), напиться, нарезаться и т. п. ~ [modif or adv (intensif)] (to be, get etc) very (drunk): **(be ⟨get⟩) drunk as a skunk ⟨as a sailor, as a fiddler⟩.**

3. ругаться, материться ~ [adv (intensif)] (to swear) vehemently: X ругался ~ ≃ **X swore like a trooper ⟨a stevedore, a truckdriver⟩; X cursed ⟨cussed⟩ a blue streak; X turned the air blue; X cursed up hill and down dale.**

Она курила длинные иностранные сигареты, которые доставала по блату... пила водку, пела похабные частушки и вообще материлась как сапожник (Войнович 6). She smoked long foreign cigarettes that she got through her connections...drank vodka, sang bawdy songs, and swore like a trooper (6a).

С-19 • САПО́ЖНИК (ВСЕГДА́ ⟨ХО́ДИТ⟩) БЕЗ САПО́Г [saying] a person whose skill and expertise serve others well often neglects, or is unable, to use his talents to provide for himself and/or his family: ≃ **all cobblers go barefoot; the shoemaker's children are ill-shod; the shoemaker's child goes barefoot; there is none worse shod than the shoemaker's wife; the tailor's wife is worst clad; a needle clothes people, yet is itself naked.**

С-20 • ТИ́ХОЙ СА́ПОЙ *coll, often disapprov* [NP_instrum; Invar; adv; more often used with impfv verbs; fixed WO] (to act, try to attain sth.) by stealth, secretly: **on the sly; on the quiet; on the q.t.; surreptitiously.**

Они [мои сторонники] меня всё время учат: «Тише, тише, вы всё не так делаете, вы нам только мешаете, вы уж лучше помолчите». Они считают, что всё надо делать тихой сапой (Войнович 3). They're [my supporters are] always telling me, "Calm down, calm down, you do everything wrong, you only get in our way, you'd better shut up." They think everything should be done on the sly (3a). ♦ …[Золотарёв] тихой сапой дрался не на жизнь, а на смерть за каждую пядь своего места под солнцем, расталкивая локтями близстоящих, а иногда и перешагивая через них… (Максимов 1). [context transl] …[Zolotarev] began a surreptitious life-and-death struggle for every inch of his place in the sun, elbowing those near him aside and sometimes stepping over them… (1a).

< «Сапа» (from French *sape*) is a hidden ditch or tunnel dug toward the enemy's lines and used for surprise attack.

С-21 • НЕ СА́ХАР 〈НЕ МЁД〉 *(кому с кем* or *где) coll* [NP; these forms only; subj-compl with быть∅ (subj: human, abstr, or infin) or impers predic with быть∅ (var. with *кому с кем* or *где*)] s.o. (sth., being with s.o. etc) is unpleasant, disagreeable, difficult: X — не сахар ≃ [of a person] **X is no prize 〈no angel, no gem〉**; [of life, work, doing sth. etc] **X is no fun 〈no bed of roses, no picnic〉**; **X isn't all milk and honey**; [in limited contexts] **X is no lump of sugar 〈no piece of candy〉**; ‖ X-у с Y-ом не сахар ≃ **being with Y is no fun 〈no bed of roses, no picnic〉 for X.**

«Наверное, я тоже был не сахар. Наверное, я и сейчас не сахар, но тогда я пил ещё больше, чем сейчас…» (Стругацкие 1). "No doubt I wasn't any prize myself. No doubt I'm still no prize, but in those days I drank even more than I do now…" (1a). ♦ Видно, что её [женщины-следователя] работа для неё — утомительный источник зарплаты и только… Да и подопечные её — не сахар, должно быть (Марченко 2). It was clear that her [the woman interrogator's] work was simply an exhausting way to earn an income, and nothing more….And those charges were not exactly angels, no doubt (2a). ♦ Кирпичный завод и на воле-то не сахар, а тем более в лагере (Марченко 1). A brick factory even in normal conditions is no bed of roses, and in the camps it is even worse (1a). ♦ Неужели все наши цели сводятся к тому, чтобы уподобить ибанский [*nonce word*] образ жизни западному? Ведь кое в чём мы их опередили. Да и на Западе жизнь не сахар (Зиновьев 1). Surely our objectives cannot be reduced to an attempt to establish an imitation of the Western way of life in Ibansk? Apart from anything else there are some areas where we are ahead of them. And anyway life isn't all milk and honey in the West either (1a). ♦ «А вообще, Люба… жизнь армейская, конечно, не сахар» (Войнович 2). "Naturally, Lyuba, all things considered…army life is no lump of sugar" (2a).

С-22 • СА́ХАР МЕДО́ВИЧ *obs* [NP; sing only; often subj-compl with copula (subj: human); fixed WO] an excessively sweet and courteous (albeit not necessarily sincere) person: **(one is) all sugar and honey; (one is) sickeningly sweet.**

С-23 • КТО КУДА́, А Я В СБЕРКА́ССУ *coll* [sent; Invar; fixed WO] you are free to do whatever you want, but I am going where I want or have to go (may be used as a pretext for breaking away from a group): **you can do as you please 〈like〉, but I'm off 〈gone, out of here, off to…〉; you can do what you want 〈like〉, but I must be off 〈going〉.**

«Ну, ребята, кто куда, а я в сберкассу, — надо в деревню сходить». — «Прощальный визит — пошли!» (Гроссман 2). "Well, my friends, *you* can do as you please, but I'm off to the village." "A parting visit? Let's go then!" (2a).

< Valentin Kataev, in *The Grass of Oblivion* («Трава забвенья»), 1967, attributes this phrase to the poet Vasily Lebedev-Kumach.

С-24 • В СБО́РЕ быть∅, оказаться, застать *кого* [PrepP; Invar; subj-compl with copula (subj: human or collect) or obj-compl with застать (obj: human or collect)] (of people who are expected to be somewhere) gathered, in attendance: Х-ы были в сборе ≃ **Xs were there 〈here, assembled, present〉; Xs had assembled.**

…Он [дядя Сандро] быстро направился к дому тёти Маши. Там уже почти все были в сборе… (Искандер 3). …He [Uncle Sandro] hastily set out for Aunt Masha's house. Almost everyone was already there… (3a). ♦ [Букин:] Вот, все в сборе. Вас только и не хватало (Вампилов 3). [B.:] Look, everyone's here. You were the only one missing (3a). ♦ По вечерам, возвращаясь с поля, Михаил частенько слышит ликующие голоса своих братьев в сосняке за деревней… Сегодня, к его немалому удивлению, вся семья была в сборе (Абрамов 1). Returning from the field in the evenings, Mikhail would often hear the exultant voices of his brothers in the pine forest back of the village….Today, though, to his considerable surprise, the whole family was assembled (1a). ♦ Созванные на совещание генералы были в сборе (Шолохов 3). The generals summoned to the conference had all assembled (3a).

С-25 • БРИЛЛИА́НТОВАЯ 〈АЛМА́ЗНАЯ〉 СВА́ДЬБА [NP; usu. this WO] a seventy-fifth wedding anniversary celebration: **diamond (wedding) anniversary; diamond wedding.**

С-26 • ЗОЛОТА́Я СВА́ДЬБА [NP; usu. this WO] a fiftieth wedding anniversary celebration: **golden (wedding) anniversary; golden wedding.**

Должен вам сказать, что в наших местах серебряные и золотые свадьбы не праздновали (Рыбаков 1). I should explain that silver and golden weddings were not normally celebrated in our part of the world (1a).

С-27 • СЕРЕ́БРЯНАЯ СВА́ДЬБА [NP; usu. this WO] a twenty-fifth wedding anniversary celebration: **silver (wedding) anniversary; silver wedding.**

Под предлогом серебряной свадьбы Граубе, Генрих Иванович, пригласил к себе на квартиру четырёх сослуживцев… (Терц 8). On the pretext of celebrating his silver wedding anniversary, Genrikh Ivanovich Graube invited four colleagues…to his apartment… (8a).

С-28 • (КАК) НА МАЛА́НЬИНУ СВА́ДЬБУ наварить, напечь и т. п. *coll, humor* [(как +) PrepP; these forms only; adv (quantif); fixed WO] (to prepare) a great deal (of food): **(cook 〈make〉) enough for an army 〈enough to feed an army〉.**

С-29 • ДО СВА́ДЬБЫ ЗАЖИВЁТ *coll, humor* [sent; Invar; often preceded by ничего, не плачь, не огорчайся etc; fixed WO] it will soon pass, it is not worth getting upset about (often said as a consolation to s.o. experiencing minor pain or distress): **you're 〈he's etc〉 going to be just fine; you'll 〈he'll etc〉 live 〈survive〉; you'll 〈he'll etc〉 get over it; you'll 〈he'll etc〉 soon be right as rain.**

«Тебе нелегко будет сообщить им [родителям] это известие [об отъезде]. Они всё рассуждают о том, что мы через две недели делать будем». — «Нелегко. Чёрт меня дёрнул сегодня подразнить отца… Он очень сконфузился, а теперь мне придётся вдобавок его огорчить… Ничего! До свадьбы заживёт» (Тургенев 2). "You're not going to find it easy to break it [the news of your leaving] to them [your parents]. They are always discussing what we are going to do in two weeks' time." "No, it won't be easy. The Devil got into me today to annoy Father….He was quite overcome, and now I shall have to disappoint him into the bargain. Never mind! He'll get over it" (2e). ♦ [Лопахин:] Помню, когда я был мальчонком лет пятнадцати, отец мой… ударил меня по лицу кулаком, кровь пошла из носу… Любовь Андреевна…

подвела меня к рукомойнику, вот в этой самой комнате, в детской. «Не плачь, говорит, мужичок, до свадьбы заживёт...» (Чехов 2). [L.:] I remember when I was a lad of fifteen and my father...punched me in the face and made my nose bleed....Lyuba Ranevsky...brought me over to the wash-stand here in this very room, the nursery as it was. "Don't cry, little peasant," she said. "You'll soon be right as rain" (2c).

C-30 • НА СВА́ЛКЕ ИСТО́РИИ быть$_\emptyset$, оказаться, место и т. п.; НА СВА́ЛКУ ИСТО́РИИ выбросить, выкинуть *кого-что* и т. п. [PrepP; these forms only; subj-compl with copula (subj: human, collect, or abstr), nonagreeing postmodif (of место), or adv; fixed WO] (to end up in, be in, relegate s.o. or sth. to etc) historical oblivion: **on ⟨to⟩ the ash ⟨rubbish, garbage, junk⟩ heap of history; in ⟨to⟩ the garbage dump ⟨the junk bin, the dustbin⟩ of history.**

«Процесс бездушного отношения к эволюции преступления нами развенчан полностью, а пресловутая презумпция невиновности выкинута на свалку истории...» (Алешковский 1). "We've totally eliminated investigation's indifference to the evolution of a crime, and we've thrown the notorious assumption of innocence on the garbage heap of history..." (1a).

C-31 • НИ СВАТ НИ БРАТ *кому*; НИ КУМ НИ СВАТ *both coll* [NP; sing only; subj-compl with быть$_\emptyset$ (subj: human); pres only; usu. this WO] one is not s.o.'s close friend or relative and not of any concern or interest to s.o.: X Y-у — ни сват ни брат ≃ **X is no one to Y; X is neither kith nor kin to Y; who is X to Y anyway?**

[author's usage] «Почему, собственно, я так взволновался из-за того, что Берлиоз попал под трамвай? — рассуждал поэт. — В конечном счёте, ну его в болото! Кто я, в самом деле, кум ему или сват?» (Булгаков 9). "Properly speaking, why did I get so upset when Berlioz fell under the streetcar?" the poet argued. "In the final analysis, to blazes with him! What am I to him—kith or kin?" (9a).

C-32 • ПЕРЕЕ́ЗЖАЯ СВА́ХА *coll* [NP; usu. sing] a person who often changes his place of residence: **bird of passage; nomad.**

C-33 • К ВА́ШЕМУ ⟨ТВОЕМУ́⟩ СВЕ́ДЕНИЮ *coll, occas. impol* [PrepP; these forms only; sent adv (parenth); fixed WO] so that you are aware (of sth.): **for your information ⟨enlightenment⟩; just so you know; you might want to know; you might as well know; I would like to inform you.**

«Вставай, Капарин. Гость у нас. Это наш человек — Мелехов Григорий, бывший сотник, к твоему сведению» (Шолохов 5). "Get up, Kaparin. We have a guest. This is our man—Melekhov, Grigory—a former lieutenant, for your information" (5a).

C-34 • ПРИНИМА́ТЬ/ПРИНЯ́ТЬ К СВЕ́ДЕНИЮ *что* [VP; subj: human or collect; more often pfv; usu. this WO] to consider sth., allow for sth. when making a judgment or decision: X принял к сведению Y ≃ **X took Y into consideration ⟨account⟩; X bore ⟨kept⟩ Y in mind;** ‖ примите ⟨прошу принять⟩ к сведению ≃ [when used in an official context] **(please) be advised.**

Конечно, сказать, что я это [мещанскую ненависть жены Марата ко всякого рода чудачествам] заметил и принял к сведению, было бы неточно. Я в самом деле это заметил, но тогда подумал, что... это мне показалось (Искандер 2). Of course, it would be imprecise to say that I noticed this [Marat's wife's bourgeois hatred for any kind of eccentricity] and took it into account. I did in fact notice it, but at the time I thought I was imagining things (2a). ♦ [Шмага:] Гришка погиб для нашего общества!.. [Коринкина:] Что, его сглазили, что ли? [Шмага:] Сглазили,

[Коринкина:] Кто же? [Шмага:] Приезжая знаменитость... [Коринкина:] Миловзоров, это надо принять к сведению (Островский 3). [Sh.:] Grisha's done for as far as our set is concerned.... [K.:] He must be under a spell. [Sh.:] He is; oh, that he is! [K.:] Whose spell? [Sh.:] The visiting eminence.... [K.:] That's something to bear in mind, Milovzorov (3a). ♦ Ему очень понравилось, как Иван Дмитриевич срезал Петра Житова. Твёрдо и в то же время не обидно. Дескать, учти, любезный. Я сразу понял, что ты за гусь. Каждое дело вспрыскивать — вот ты из каких. А этого у меня не будет. Прошу принять к сведению (Абрамов 1). He was very pleased with the way Ivan Dmitrievich had cut Pyotr Zhitov off. Firmly and at the same time without causing offense. As if saying, "Look out, my dear fellow. I've got your number, all right. You're the kind who likes to lubricate every occasion, and I won't stand for it. Please be advised" (1a).

C-35 • ДОВОДИ́ТЬ/ДОВЕСТИ́ ДО СВЕ́ДЕНИЯ *чьего* или *кого, что* или *о чём usu. offic* [VP; subj: human or collect; usu. this WO] to notify s.o. of sth.: X довёл до сведения Y-а Z ≃ **X brought Z to Y's attention ⟨to the attention of Y, to Y's knowledge⟩; X apprised ⟨advised, informed⟩ Y of Z.**

«...Я уполномочен довести до вашего сведения, что в случае нового задержания наших грузов вы будете иметь дело с генералом Пфердом» (Стругацкие 1). "...I have instructions to bring to your attention that if our goods should be detained a third time you will be dealing directly with General Pferd" (1a). ♦ «Сущность Вашей телеграммы Временному правительству доведена до моего сведения» (Шолохов 3). "The gist of your telegram to the Provisional Government has been brought to my knowledge" (3a).

C-36 • НЕ ПЕ́РВОЙ СВЕ́ЖЕСТИ *coll* [NP$_{gen}$; Invar; subj-compl with copula or nonagreeing modif; fixed WO] **1.** [subj: a noun denoting a food product] not as fresh as it could or should be: X был ~ ≃ **X wasn't very ⟨particularly⟩ fresh; X was going bad; X was starting to spoil;** [of milk, cream etc] **X had turned;** [of bread, a cake etc] **X was pretty stale.**

Не покупай это мясо: оно не первой свежести. Don't buy this meat—it's going bad.

2. [subj: a noun denoting an item of clothing, piece of linen etc] having been worn or used since its last washing, sth. is less than totally clean: X был ~ ≃ **X was not completely ⟨quite, very⟩ clean ⟨fresh⟩; X had already been worn ⟨used, slept in etc⟩.**

На Васе были помятые брюки и рубашка не первой свежести. Vasya had on wrinkled pants and a shirt that had already been worn.

3. [subj: анекдот, новости, информация etc] an anecdote (joke, some news, information etc) is not the most recent: [of an anecdote or joke only] **stale; (that's) an old one ⟨a chestnut⟩; that one has been around for a while;** [of news, information etc only] **old (news); nothing new;** [in limited contexts] **(information etc that s.o.) already knows ⟨has known for quite a while etc⟩.**

Анекдот, рассказанный Геннадием, оказался не первой свежести и никого не насмешил. The anecdote Gennady told was an old one and didn't make anyone laugh.

4. [subj: human] (often of a person, more commonly a woman, who tries to appear younger than he or she actually is) one no longer is or no longer looks very young: **not exactly in the first flush ⟨the first blush, the prime⟩ of youth; not exactly in the flower of (one's) youth; no youngster;** [in limited contexts] **no spring chicken.**

Несмотря на искусство гримёра, было видно, что актриса уже не первой свежести. Despite the makeup artist's skill, it was obvious that the actress wasn't exactly in the first flush of youth.

C-37 • СВЕ́РХУ ДО́НИЗУ [AdvP; Invar; adv; fixed WO] **1.** entirely, completely: **from top to bottom.**

«Осмотреть помещение кооператива сверху донизу. Перетряхнуть все лари, заглянуть под прилавки» (Пастернак 1).

"Have the shop searched from top to bottom. Turn everything inside out, and see that you look under the counters" (1a).

2. from the highest ranking members to those at the lowest level: **from top to bottom.**

В жизни работника той службы, к которой принадлежал капитан [Миляга], бывают тревожные моменты, когда торжествует Законность. За время своей карьеры Афанасию Миляге дважды пришлось пережить подобную неприятность. Оба раза шерстили всех сверху донизу, но Миляге удалось уцелеть и даже продвинуться по службе... (Войнович 2). In the life of those who serve the Institution there are sometimes moments of anxiety when legality triumphs. In the space of his career Afanasy Milyaga had twice to experience that particular unpleasantness. Both times, everyone from top to bottom had been sheared away, but both times Milyaga managed to come out in one piece and even to advance in the service... (2a).

С-38 • ВСЯК СВЕРЧОК ЗНАЙ СВОЙ ШЕСТОК; ЗНАЙ СВЕРЧОК СВОЙ ШЕСТОК [saying] do not overstep the limits of your authority (said to or about a person who is behaving in a way inappropriate to his position or is interfering in someone else's affairs): ≃ **stay on your own side of the fence; the cobbler should ⟨let the cobbler⟩ stick to his last; mind your own business.**

[Аграфена Кондратьевна:] Опомнись! [Большов:] Знай сверчок свой шесток! Не твоё дело! (Островский 10). [А.К.:] Recollect yourself! [B.:] Stay on your own side of the fence! This is none of your business! (10a). ♦ [Кочкарёв:] Не смыслишь ничего, не мешайся. Знай сверчок свой шесток – убирайся! (Гоголь 1). [K.:] You don't understand anything. Don't interfere. The cobbler should stick to his last. Clear off! (1a).

С-39 • БÉЛЫЙ ⟨БÓЖИЙ⟩ СВЕТ, often НА (ВСЁМ) БÉ-ЛОМ СВÉТЕ, ВО ВСЁМ БÉЛОМ СВÉТЕ, ПО БÉЛУ ⟨БÉЛОМУ⟩ СВÉТУ rather folk poet [NP; sing only; usu. this WO] the world around us, life in all its manifestations: **this ⟨the⟩ world; the (whole) wide world; the wide, wide world; the great wide world.**

Что же это делается на белом свете? (Булгаков 11). What's happening in this world? (11a). ♦ Он [мальчик] не знал... что его ждут новые события в его маленькой жизни, что наступит день, когда он останется один на всём белом свете... (Айтматов 1). He [the lad]...didn't know that new events in his young life awaited him, that a day would come when he'd remain alone in the whole wide world... (1b). ♦ Так как уже не мало есть на белом свете людей, которые коптят небо, то почему ж и Тентетникову не коптить его? (Гоголь 3). ...Since there are not a few people in the wide world who idle away their lives, why shouldn't Tentetnikov do the same? (3c). ♦ Я бросил ответный взгляд [на Гудзия], этого было достаточно, чтобы почувствовать, что ты сейчас не один на белом свете (Свирский 1). I looked back at him [Gudzy]—and it was enough to make me realize that I wasn't alone in the wide, wide world anymore (1a). ♦ ...Моряк тут же принялся рассказывать о всяких своих странствиях по белу свету в качестве механика какого-то сухогруза (Войнович 1). ...He [the merchant seaman] set at once to telling us about his wanderings through the great wide world as a mechanic on board a freighter that hauled dry cargo (1a).

С-40 • В БÉЛЫЙ СВЕТ КАК В КОПÉЕЧКУ выстрелить, палить и т. п. coll, rare [PrepP; Invar; adv; fixed WO] (to shoot) without aiming: **(shoot) at random; (fire) a random shot ⟨random shots⟩.**

С-41 • ВЫВОДИ́ТЬ/ВЫ́ВЕСТИ НА СВЕТ БÓЖИЙ кого-что [VP; subj: usu. human; the verb may take the final position, otherwise fixed WO] (in refer. to some wrongdoing, plotting, illegal operation etc or the person or people involved in it)

to make sth. public, expose s.o. or sth.: X вывел Y-а на свет божий ≃ X blew the whistle on Y; X unmasked Y; X brought thing Y out into the open; X took the wraps off thing Y; X blew the lid off thing Y.

С-42 • ВЫВОЗИ́ТЬ/ВЫ́ВЕЗТИ В СВЕТ кого obs, now humor [VP; subj: human; obj: usu. female; in extended contempt. usage may have obj: inanim] to take s.o. (usu. a young woman) to social gatherings, balls etc sponsored and attended by an established society in order to introduce her to that established society: X вывез женщину Y в свет ≃ X brought woman Y out (into society).

С-43 • ВЫЕЗЖА́ТЬ/ВЫ́ЕХАТЬ В СВЕТ obs [VP; subj: human, more often female; usu. impfv] to (begin to) attend social gatherings, balls etc sponsored by an established society: X выезжает в свет ≃ X is coming out (into society); X is entering the social scene; X is making his ⟨her⟩ debut ⟨début⟩ (in society).

«...Любочка ведь скоро должна выезжать в свет. С этакой belle-mère не очень приятно, она даже по-французски плохо говорит...» (Толстой 2). "...Lyubochka will have to come out very soon. It's not very nice with a belle mère like that: she even speaks bad French..." (2b). "...Lyuba will soon be making her début in society. With a stepmother like that it won't be very pleasant. She doesn't even speak French properly..." (2c).

С-44 • ВЫПЛЫВА́ТЬ/ВЫ́ПЛЫТЬ ⟨ВСПЛЫВА́ТЬ/ВСПЛЫ́ТЬ и т. п.⟩ НА СВЕТ БÓЖИЙ coll; ВЫСТУ-ПА́ТЬ/ВЫ́СТУПИТЬ НА СВЕТ БÓЖИЙ obsoles, coll [VP; subj: usu. abstr; the verb may take the final position, otherwise fixed WO] (usu. of some wrongdoing, plotting, illegal operation etc) to become or be made public knowledge, become known, exposed: X выступил на свет божий ≃ X came to light; X surfaced.

С-45 • ВЫПУСКА́ТЬ/ВЫ́ПУСТИТЬ В СВЕТ что [VP; subj: human or collect; obj: a noun denoting a book, journal etc] to issue (a book, periodical etc) in printed copies for sale or distribution: X выпустил Y в свет ≃ X published ⟨printed, brought out⟩ Y; Y saw the light of day. ○ ВЫ́ПУСК В СВЕТ [NP; sing only; fixed WO] ≃ publication; printing.

...Фёдор Константинович вспомнил: [это] Буш, два с половиной года тому назад читавший в кружке свою пьесу. Недавно он её выпустил в свет... (Набоков 1). ...Fyodor remembered: it was Busch, who two and a half years ago had read his play at that literary circle. Recently he had published it... (1a). ♦ Так, прежде чем выпустить в свет книгу о геологах (пусть это будет даже роман), издательство направляет её в геологическое ведомство, о пограничниках – в КГБ, о революционерах – в Институт марксизма-ленинизма и т. д. (Войнович 1). Before a book about geologists, even if it's a novel, can see the light of day, the publisher sends it to the Department of Geology; if it's about border guards, to the KGB; if it's about revolutionaries, to the Institute of Marxism-Leninism, and so forth (1a).

С-46 • ВЫХОДИ́ТЬ/ВЫ́ЙТИ В СВЕТ [VP; subj: a noun denoting a book, journal etc] to be produced and offered to the public: X вышел в свет ≃ X came out; X was published; X appeared in print; X saw the light of day. ○ ВЫ́ХОД В СВЕТ [NP; sing only; fixed WO] ≃ publication; printing.

«Сама по себе затея написать книжку о выдающемся деятеле шестидесятых годов ничего предосудительного в себе не содержит. Ну, написал, ну, вышла в свет, – выходили в свет и не такие книги» (Набоков 1). "In itself the idea of writing a book about an outstanding public figure of the sixties contains nothing reprehensible. One sits down and writes it – fine; worse books than that have come out" (1a). ♦ «...Вместо фразы: „На этот вопрос заведующая иностранным отделом, понятно, никакого ответа дать не могла" – машинистка напечатала: „Заведующая иностранным отделом Попятна"... – и так далее. Ну, что же можно было сделать? Номер-то уж вышел в свет» (Домбровский 1). "...Instead of the sentence: 'To these questions the librarian in charge of the foreign section naturally could give no reply,' the typesetter had written, 'The librarian in charge of the foreign section, Natralova...' and so on. What could I do? The issue was already on the newsstands" (1a).

C-47 • ИЗВЛЕКА́ТЬ/ИЗВЛЕ́ЧЬ НА СВЕТ (БО́ЖИЙ) *что* [VP; subj: human] **1.** to draw out sth. hidden, forgotten about, or unused from the place where it has been located: X извлёк на свет божий Y ≃ **X took ⟨pulled⟩ Y out; X dug Y up ⟨out⟩.**

Открыв шкатулку, дед извлёк на свет божий пожелтевший конверт. Opening the case, Grandfather took out a yellowed envelope.

2. to reveal sth., make known sth. that was long hidden (usu. a secret, a piece of information etc): X извлёк на свет божий Y ≃ **X brought Y to light; X brought Y out into the open.**

C-48 • НА СВЕТ (БО́ЖИЙ) НЕ ГЛЯДЕ́Л ⟨НЕ СМОТРЕ́Л⟩ БЫ *obsoles, coll, rather folk* [VP; subj: human, usu. я (implied); subjunctive only] nothing is dear to me, I have no desire to go on living: **I feel life isn't worth living (anymore); I feel there's nothing to live for (anymore).**

C-49 • НА ЧЁМ СВЕТ СТОИ́Т ругать, бранить, поносить *кого*, ругаться и т. п. *coll* [Invar; adv (intensif); more often used with impfv verbs; fixed WO] (to reprimand s.o., swear at s.o., curse etc) with great intensity: распекать ⟨бранить⟩ и т. п. *кого* ~ ≃ **give s.o. a good tongue-lashing; lay s.o. out in lavender; rake ⟨haul⟩ s.o. over the coals;** ‖ ругать ⟨поливать⟩ и т. п. *кого* ~ ≃ **call s.o. every name ⟨all the names⟩ in the book; swear at s.o. for all one is worth; curse s.o. up (hill) and down (dale);** ‖ ругаться ~ ≃ **curse ⟨cuss⟩ a blue streak; swear like a trooper ⟨the devil⟩; turn the air blue; curse up (hill) and down (dale).**

«...Узнал я вдруг... что подполковником нашим недовольны... что враги его готовят ему закуску. И впрямь приехал начальник дивизии и распёк на чём свет стоит» (Достоевский 1). "...I suddenly learned...that there was some dissatisfaction with regard to our colonel...that his enemies were arranging a little surprise for him. And indeed the division commander came and hauled him over the coals" (1a). ♦ «Это когда они [женщины] ругаются с нами, думают, что мы им не нужны. Разойдётся и... поливает на чём свет стоит» (Распутин 1). "It's when we quarrel the women think they can get along without us. Call us all the names in the book" (1a). ♦ «Пушкина [новый пациент] ругает на чём свет стоит и всё время кричит: „Куролесов, бис, бис!" – говорил гость, тревожно дергаясь (Булгаков 9). "He [the new patient] swears at Pushkin for all he's worth and keeps shouting, 'Kurolesov, encore, encore!'" the guest said, twitching anxiously (9a). ♦ А потом покойный начальник службы движения Егоркин, стуча кулаком по столу, честил его на чём свет стоит: «Под трибунал захотел, Лашков! У меня не засохнет!» (Максимов 3). Next comes Yegorkin, the traffic manager, long since dead, banging his fist on the table and cursing him up hill and down dale. "Asking for a tribunal you are, Lashkov! I shan't forget it in a hurry!" (3a). ♦ [Борис:] Папе звонили! [Варвара Капитоновна:] Сейчас придёт. [Марк:] Ругался в трубку на чём свет (Розов 3). [B.:] Did you call Papa? [V.K.:] He'll be here in a minute. [M.:] He swore like a trooper over the phone (3a).

C-50 • НЕ БЛИ́ЖНИЙ ⟨НЕ БЛИ́ЗКИЙ, НЕ БЛИ́ЗОК⟩ СВЕТ *coll* [NP; these forms only; usu. subj-compl with быть∅ (subj: a geographical name, a noun denoting a place or

destination, or infin); fixed WO] very far (from some place or from where the speaker is): **far away ⟨off⟩; a long way off ⟨away, from here etc⟩; not right next door.**

«Гостя тебе привёз, Санёк, – заметно заискивая, сообщил тому парень, – из...Москвы». – «Ну». – «Не ближний свет, понимаешь?» (Максимов 1). "I've brought you a visitor, Sanyok," said the boatman with a noticeably ingratiating tone. "He's from Moscow...." "Well." "It's not right next door, you know" (1a).

C-51 • НИ СВЕТ НИ ЗАРЯ́ встать, проснуться, разбудить *кого*, уехать, прийти и т. п. *coll* [NP; Invar; adv; fixed WO] (to get up, wake up, wake s.o. up, leave, arrive etc) very early in the morning, before daybreak: **at an ungodly ⟨unearthly⟩ hour; (well) before dawn ⟨sunup⟩; at the crack of dawn; when the sun is barely ⟨hardly⟩ up.**

Князю стали нашёптывать. В один прекрасный день он уехал в многодневный охотничий поход, но неожиданно, ни свет ни заря, вернулся на следующий день и застал Щащико у себя в спальне (Искандер 3). People began to whisper to the prince. One fine day he left for a protracted hunting trip, but he returned the next day unexpectedly, at an ungodly hour, and caught Shashiko in his bedroom (3a). ♦ На следующее утро он [Хлебников] ни свет ни заря пришёл ко мне, и мы в четверть часа составили воззвание... (Лившиц 1). The next morning he [Khlebnikov] came by at an unearthly hour and within fifteen minutes we had composed an appeal (1a). ♦ Выехал он [Григорий] ни свет ни заря. Лежал впереди путь в сто тридцать пять вёрст, и дорога была каждая минута (Шолохов 2). He [Grigory] set off in the morning well before dawn. He had a distance of one hundred and thirty-five versts to cover and every minute was precious (2a). ♦ На другой день, ни свет ни заря, Лиза уже проснулась. Весь дом ещё спал (Пушкин 3). Liza awoke the next morning at the crack of dawn. The rest of the house was still asleep (3b). ♦ [Хороших:] Не видите? Ни свет ни заря уже запузыривают (Вампилов 2). [Kh.:] Can't you see? The sun's barely up and they're already tying one on (2b).

C-52 • ОТПРАВЛЯ́ТЬ/ОТПРА́ВИТЬ НА ТОТ СВЕТ *кого coll* [VP; subj: human; usu. pfv; the verb may take the final position, otherwise fixed WO] to kill s.o.: X отправил Y-а на тот свет ≃ **X did Y in; X finished ⟨knocked, bumped⟩ Y off; X dispatched Y (to the next world).**

«Ты что, на тот свет хочешь отправить меня?» – орал Орозкул на тестя (Айтматов 1). "What are you trying to do – finish me off?" Orozkul screamed at his father-in-law (1b). ♦ «В Омске я должен был отправить его [Реваза Давидовича] на тот свет» (Чернёнок 2). "I was supposed to bump him [Revaz Davidovich] off in Omsk" (2a). ♦ [Платонов:] Убить, значит, пришёл! [Осип:] Так точно... [Платонов (дразнит):] Так точно... Какое нахальство, чёрт побери! Он пришёл отправить меня на тот свет... (Чехов 1). [P.:] So you've come to murder me? [O.:] Yes sir. [P. *(imitating him):*] "Yes sir." What damned cheek! He's come to dispatch me to the next world (1b).

C-53 • ОТПРАВЛЯ́ТЬСЯ/ОТПРА́ВИТЬСЯ НА ТОТ СВЕТ *coll, occas. humor* [VP; subj: human; usu. pfv; often pfv past with чуть не; the verb may take the final position, otherwise fixed WO] to die: X отправился на тот свет ≃ **X went to the next ⟨a better⟩ world; X left ⟨departed⟩ this world; X departed for a better world; X gave up the ghost.**

Женитьба его ничуть не переменила, тем более что жена скоро отправилась на тот свет, оставивши двух ребятишек, которые решительно ему были не нужны (Гоголь 3). Marriage did not change him at all, especially since his wife had soon departed for a better world, leaving behind two children, for whom he had absolutely no use (3c). ♦ [Ирина:] Паренёк совсем был готов... на тот свет отправиться... (Розов 3). [I.:] The fellow was all set...to give up the ghost... (3a).

C-54 • ПОЯВЛЯ́ТЬСЯ/ПОЯВИ́ТЬСЯ ⟨ЯВЛЯ́ТЬСЯ/ ЯВИ́ТЬСЯ *obs*⟩ НА СВЕТ [VP; usu. pfv] **1.** [subj: human] to be brought into life: X появился на свет ≃ **X came into the ⟨this⟩ world; X was born.** ○ ПОЯВЛЕ́НИЕ НА СВЕТ [NP; fixed WO] ≃ **s.o.'s appearance in the world; s.o.'s entrance ⟨advent⟩ into the world; s.o.'s birth.**

«Это страшный человек. Это оборотень, который явился на свет только упущением божьим. Я врач, но мне не стыдно признаться, что при случае я охотно умертвил бы его» (Стругацкие 4). "He's a hideous person, a monster who came into this world only because of some divine oversight. I am a physician, but I'm not ashamed to admit that I would kill him if I only had an opportunity to do so" (4a). ♦ Нельзя ли отсюда вывести, что дети, не успевшие вдосталь пожить, для восстановления равенства отправлялись не в землю, но специальным рейсом — прямой дорогой — через дерево — на небо, с тем чтобы скорейшим образом снова появиться на свет?.. (Терц 3). May this have meant that children, since they had not had time for a full life, were despatched by way of compensation, not into the earth, but by a direct, privileged route—via the tree—to heaven, in order to be born once again as quickly as possible?... (3a). ♦ У них [герра и фрау Урбах] дети. Тот мальчик, появлением на свет которого был неожиданно осчастливлен герр Урбах, и девочка по имени Мари (Федин 1). They [Herr and Frau Urbach] had children. That little boy with whose appearance in the world Herr Urbach was unexpectedly blessed, and a little girl named Marie (1a). ♦ Едва ли кто-нибудь, кроме матери, заметил появление его [Алексеева] на свет, очень немногие замечают его в течение жизни... (Гончаров 1). It is doubtful if anyone except his mother noticed his [Alexeyev's] advent into the world, and indeed very few people are aware of him while he lives... (1a).

2. [subj: usu. concr or count abstr] (usu. of a literary work, painting, sculpture etc, or of a document, testimony, accusation etc) to come into existence, be created, produced, brought out: X появился на свет ≃ **X appeared ⟨emerged⟩; X saw the light of day;** [of a work of literature, art etc only] **X was born;** [of a document, testimony etc only] **X came to light.** ○ ПОЯВЛЕ́НИЕ НА СВЕТ [NP; fixed WO] ≃ **the emergence (of sth.); the appearance (of sth.).**

...Что ни говори, не приди в голову Чичикову эта мысль [купить мёртвые души], не явилась бы на свет сия поэма (Гоголь 3). ...Say what you like, if this idea [to buy dead souls] had not occurred to Chichikov, this epic poem would never have seen the light of day (3a).

C-55 • ПРОИЗВОДИ́ТЬ/ПРОИЗВЕСТИ́ НА СВЕТ *кого* [VP; subj: human or, rare, animal, female; more often pfv] to bear a child: X произвела на свет Y-a ≃ **X brought Y into the world; X gave birth to Y.**

«...Любить шалопая только за то, что ты сама произвела его на свет, — это нехорошо, это даже низко!» (Залыгин 1). "...It's bad, base even, to love a scapegrace simply because you brought him into the world" (1a). ♦ Врачи предупреждали, что вторые роды убьют её. Всё же она забеременела вновь... И [она] и младенец Виктор выжили; а в декабре 58 года она вновь чуть не умерла, производя на свет третьего сына, Мишу (Набоков 1). The doctors warned them that a second child would kill her. Still, she became pregnant anew....Both [she] and the infant Victor survived; and in December, 1858, she again almost died, giving birth to a third son, Misha (1a).

C-56 • ПРОЛИВА́ТЬ/ПРОЛИ́ТЬ ⟨БРОСА́ТЬ/БРО́СИТЬ⟩ СВЕТ *на что lit* [VP; subj: human or abstr; fixed WO] (in refer. to sth. mysterious or hard to comprehend) to make sth. clear, understandable: X проливает свет на Y ≃ **X sheds ⟨casts⟩ light on Y; thing X throws light on Y; X clarifies Y.**

Словом, находки [оперативников] были типичными для пригородного места и ни малейшего света на загадочную смерть Пряжкиной не проливали (Чернёнок 2). Basically their [the detectives'] finds were typical of a suburban area and shed no light at all on the mysterious death of Priazhkina (2a). ♦ Сочинение это проливает... свет не только на внутреннюю, но и на внешнюю политику помпадуров... (Салтыков-Щедрин 2). This work throws light not only on the external, but also on the internal policies of the pompadours... (2a).

C-57 • СВЕТ ⟨МИР⟩ НЕ БЕЗ ДО́БРЫХ ЛЮДЕ́Й [saying] (said when a person receives help from s.o., usu. in a time of need) there really do exist kindhearted people who voluntarily help others: ≃ **there are still some good people ⟨a few kind folk⟩ in the world ⟨in this world, on this earth⟩.**

«Без мужа-то как обходишься?» Она [женщина] повернулась к Григорию лицом. На смуглых скулах её заиграл румянец, в глазах вспыхнули и погасли рыжеватые искорки. «Ты про что это?» — «Про это самое». Она сдвинула с губ платок, протяжно сказала: «Ну, этого добра хватает! Свет не без добрых людей...» (Шолохов 5). "But how d'you make out with no husband?" She [the woman] turned to face Grigory. A flush played on her brown cheeks and tiny reddish sparks flared and died in her eyes. "What are you getting at?" "What d'you think?" She pulled the kerchief away from her lips and drawled, "Oh, there's plenty of *that!* There's still a few kind folk in the world..." (5a).

C-58 • СВЕТ НЕ КЛИ́НОМ ⟨КЛИ́НОМ НЕ⟩ СОШЁЛСЯ *на ком-чём;* ЗЕМЛЯ́ НЕ КЛИ́НОМ СОШЛА́СЬ *all coll* [VP$_{subj}$; past only; used without negation to convey the opposite meaning; fixed WO] a certain person, thing, place etc is not the only one acceptable or desirable—there are other people, things, places etc that are just as good: на X-е свет не клином сошёлся ≃ **X is not the only [NP]; the world is bigger than thing X; place X is not the only [NP] where the sun shines;** [usu. used to console s.o. who has been rejected by the person he or she loves] **there are (plenty of) other fish in the sea; there are plenty of other pebbles on the beach; person X is not the only pebble on the beach;** ‖ на X-е свет клином сошёлся ≃ **X is everything ⟨the whole world⟩ (to person Y); (person Y thinks ⟨you'd think⟩) the sun rises and sets on X; person X is person Y's one and only.**

[Хорьков:] ...Но я боюсь, что она [Марья Андреевна] мне откажет. [Хорькова:] Ах, боже мой! Свет-то не клином сошёлся — найдём другую (Островский 1). [M.Kh.:] But I'm afraid she'll [Marya Andreyevna will] turn me down. [A.Kh.:] Oh, good Lord! Look here, she's not the only girl in the world. We'll find another (1a). ♦ Из двух мест я уже ушёл «по собственному желанию». Можно бы уйти и отсюда — на этом городе свет клином не сошёлся — но мне уже надоело скитаться (Войнович 5). I have already left two jobs "of my own accord." Maybe I'll leave this one, too. This isn't the only town where the sun shines; but I'm tired of this rootless life (5a). ♦ Если она не ответит мне и на это письмо, то всё — вычеркну тогда её из своей личной жизни. Дам ей понять, что на ней свет клином не сошёлся... (Аксёнов 1). If she didn't answer this letter either, then that was it—I'd cross her out of my personal life. I'd give her to understand that there were other fish in the sea... (1a). ♦ [Фёдор Иванович:] ...Марк — для него свет клином на музыке сошёлся... (Розов 3). [F.I.:] ...To Mark music is the whole world... (3a). ♦ «Мамочка, где мои очки?!» Нина строго нахмурилась: «Чего психуешь? Можно подумать, свет клином на твоих очках сошёлся...» (Чернёнок 2). "Mama, where are my glasses?" Nina glowered at him. "What's the matter with you? You'd think the sun rises and sets on your glasses..." (2a).

C-59 • СВЕТ ⟨МИР⟩ НЕ ПРОИЗВОДИ́Л *кого-чего;* СВЕТ НЕ ВИДА́Л ⟨НЕ ВИ́ДЕЛ, НЕ ВИ́ДЫВАЛ⟩ *all coll* [VP$_{subj}$; these forms only; usu. used in a subord clause after такой... какого ⟨каких⟩; fixed WO] (in refer. to a high degree of

[589]

a certain, generally negative, human quality) such as has never before existed: **the likes of which the world has never known; the world has never known such a [NP]; the biggest ⟨greatest etc⟩ [NP] the world has ever known ⟨produced⟩; like ⟨such as⟩ you've never seen; you've never seen anything like him ⟨her etc⟩; the biggest ⟨worst etc⟩ [NP] on earth.**

Когда знакомые хвалили характер Николая Андреевича, Мария Павловна, глядя на мужа весёлыми сердитыми глазами, говорила: «Пожили бы с ним под одной крышей, вы бы узнали чудного Коленьку: деспот, псих, а эгоист такой, какого свет не видел» (Гроссман 1). His [Nikolai Andreyevich's] acquaintances praised his character now and then, but when they did, Mariya Pavlovna, with her gay and angry eyes fixed on her husband, would exclaim: "You think he's so wonderful. You ought to live with him and then you would find out all about him: Kolya, the despot, the psychopath, an egoist the likes of which the world has never known" (1a). ♦ Он [Захар] иногда, от скуки, от недостатка материала для разговора или чтоб внушить более интереса слушающей его публике, вдруг распускал про барина какую-нибудь небывальщину... Или объявит, что барин его такой картёжник и пьяница, какого свет не производил... (Гончаров 1). [Sometimes,] out of boredom, or lacking material for a conversation, or simply to arouse the interest of his audience, he [Zakhar] would suddenly unfold some cock-and-bull story about his master....Or he would announce that his master was the greatest gambler and drunkard the world had ever known... (1b). ♦ [Кочкарёв:] ...[Дом невесты] не только заложен, да за два ещё процента не выплачены. Да в сенате есть ещё брат, который тоже запускает глаза на дом; сутяги такого свет не производил... (Гоголь 1). [K.:] Not only is it [the young lady's house] mortgaged, the interest hasn't been paid for two years. And there's a brother in the Senate who's got his eye on the property—a shyster; you've never seen anything like him (1b). ♦ «...Он [председатель палаты] только что масон, а такой дурак, какого свет не производил» (Гоголь 3). "...He [the President of the Court of Justice] may be a freemason, but he's the biggest fool on earth" (3a).

C-60 • СВЕТ ОЧЕ́Й *чьих* ⟨**ЖИ́ЗНИ** *чьей*⟩ *elev* [NP; often vocative; fixed WO] a dear, deeply loved person: **apple of s.o.'s eye; light of s.o.'s life; [in limited contexts] s.o.'s one and only.**

C-61 • СВЕТ ПОМЕ́РК В ГЛАЗА́Х *чьих, (у) кого lit* [VP$_{subj}$; past only; usu. this WO] everything has become disagreeable, distasteful to s.o.: свет померк в Х-овых глазах ≃ **the light went out in ⟨of⟩ X's life; X felt he had nothing (left) to live for; there was nothing for X to live for (anymore).**

C-62 • ТОТ СВЕТ [NP; fixed WO] the afterworld as opposed to this world: **the next ⟨the other⟩ world; the world beyond; the (great) beyond; the other side.**

«Жаба у меня, — сказал Николай Александрович глуховато... Если бы не вы — быть бы мне на том свете» (Чуковская 2). "I've got angina," said Nikolai Aleksandrovich in a rather hollow voice. "...If it weren't for you I would be in the next world now" (2a). ♦ «На ногах? А мне говорили: Мишка на тот свет собрался...» (Абрамов 1). "You're up? And they told me you were making tracks for the other world" (1a). ♦ Родители встретили нас, будто мы явились с того света (Мандельштам 2). [context transl] My parents welcomed us as though we had come back from the dead (2a).

C-63 • УВИ́ДЕТЬ СВЕТ [VP] **1.** [subj: human] to be brought into life: Х увидел свет ≃ **X came into the world; X was born.**

2. [subj: a noun denoting a book, journal etc] to be produced and offered to the public: Х увидит свет ≃ **X will see the light of day; X will be published ⟨brought out⟩; X will come out; X will appear in print.**

...[Твардовский] не просто порицал пьесу [«Олень и шалашовка»], не просто говорил о ней недоброжелательно, но

предсказывал, что пьеса не увидит света... (Солженицын 2). ...[Tvardovsky] not only condemned the play [*The Love Girl and the Innocent*], not only spoke of it with hostility, but *prophesied* that it would never see the light of day... (2a).

3. *rare* [subj: human] to be freed of adversity and suffering: Х увидит свет ≃ **X will breathe easy ⟨easily, freely⟩.**

C-64 • ЧУТЬ СВЕТ встать, проснуться, разбудить *кого,* уехать, прийти и т. п. *coll;* **ЧЕМ СВЕТ** *obs* [AdvP; these forms only; adv; fixed WO] (to get up, wake up, wake s.o. up, leave, arrive etc) very early, when it is just beginning to get light in the morning: **at daybreak; at dawn; at the crack of dawn; at first light; (get up) with the sun.**

«...Медлить нечего. Ступай готовить Машу в дорогу. Завтра чем свет её и отправим...» (Пушкин 2). "...We've no time to lose: go and get Masha ready for the journey. We'll send her off at daybreak tomorrow..." (2a). ♦ ...Чуть свет Момун переправился верхом на тот берег (Айтматов 1). ...Momun crossed to the opposite bank on horseback at the crack of dawn (1b). ♦ «Завтра, ребята, чуть свет выезжать на пост». — «Куда?» — ...«В местечко Любов» (Шолохов 2). "Tomorrow, lads, we'll be on the road at first light." "Where to?"...."A place called Lubow" (2a). ♦ [Ирина:] Как хорошо быть рабочим, который встаёт чуть свет и бьёт на улице камни... (Чехов 5). [I.:] Oh, how wonderful it must be to be a laborer who gets up with the sun and breaks stones by the roadside... (5b).

C-65 • Э́ТОТ СВЕТ [NP; fixed WO] earthly existence as opposed to that after death: **this world ⟨life⟩; the world of the living.**

«...Я буду помнить, что на этом свете нельзя ждать награды, что на этом свете нет ни чести, ни справедливости» (Толстой 4). "I shall always remember that in this world one can expect no reward, that in this world there is neither honor nor justice" (4a).

C-66 • СВЕ́ТА (БЕ́ЛОГО ⟨БО́ЖЬЕГО⟩) НЕ ВИ́ДЕТЬ *coll* [VP; subj: human] **1.** to have no opportunity to rest and relax (because one is burdened by an excessive work load, serious concerns etc): Х света белого не видит ≃ **X is snowed ⟨plowed⟩ under (with work); X is buried under a pile of work; X doesn't have a chance ⟨a moment⟩ to breathe.**

2. to experience excruciating pain: Х света белого не видел ≃ **X was racked by pain; X was going through (the agonies of) hell.**

C-67 • СВЕ́ТА ⟨-у⟩ (БО́ЖЬЕГО) НЕВЗВИ́ДЕТЬ [VP; subj: human] to experience intense pain, fear, anger etc: Х света невзвидел ≃ [in refer. to pain] **X saw stars; X nearly passed out;** [in refer. to fear] **X was scared out of his wits; X was scared (half) to death;** [in refer. to anger] **X went blind with rage.**

«...Он и начал руку в плече прощупывать своими тонкими пальцами, да так, что я света невзвидел» (Шолохов 1). "...He began to poke his thin fingers around my shoulder so hard that I saw stars" (1b). ♦ Какой-то сволочной, под сибирского деланный, кот-бродяга вынырнул из-за водосточной трубы и, несмотря на вьюгу, учуял краковскую [колбасу]. Пёс Шарик свету невзвидел при мысли, что богатый чудак, подбирающий раненых псов в подворотне, чего доброго, и этого вора прихватит с собой... (Булгаков 11). A mangy stray tom, pretending to be Siberian, dived out from behind a drainpipe; he had caught a whiff of the sausage despite the storm. [The dog] Sharik went blind with rage at the thought that the rich eccentric who picked up wounded mutts in gateways might take it into his head to bring along that thief as well... (11a).

C-68 • СЖИВА́ТЬ/СЖИТЬ ⟨СГОНЯ́ТЬ/СОГНА́ТЬ *obs⟩* **СО СВЕ́ТА ⟨СО́ СВЕТУ, СО СВЕ́ТУ⟩** *кого coll* [VP; subj: human or collect; more often pfv] to torment, oppress s.o. intensely, causing him great suffering and sometimes even bringing about his premature death: X сживёт Y-a со света ≃ **X will hound ⟨nag, plague⟩ Y to death; X will be the death of Y; X will drive Y to an early grave; X will bother the life out of Y.**

…В Союзе писателей распределили, говорят, 15 экземпляров [книги Булгакова] среди членов секретариата (почему-то они охотятся не за книгами друг друга, а за Булгаковым, которого… сжили со свету) (Войнович 3). …In the Writers' Union, they say, fifteen copies [of Bulgakov's volume] were distributed among the members of the Secretariat (for some reason they don't want each other's books, but Bulgakov's, a man they hounded to death) (3a). ♦ «Ты его [моего мужа] не знаешь. Он только перед чужими такой тихонький. Он меня со свету сживёт, если девочка [родится]» (Аржак 3). "You don't know him [my husband]. He's only nice when other people are there. If I had a girl he'd nag me to death" (3a). ♦ …Не только что книгу зарезать, а и автора сжить со свету ему [Иванько] не доставит большого труда (Войнович 3). …Not only can [Ivanko] shoot down a book but without great difficulty can be the death of the author as well (3a). ♦ [Кабанова:] И пойдут детки-то по людям славить, что мать ворчунья, что мать проходу не даёт, со свету сживает (Островский 6). [K.:] So off go the children, spreading it about that Mother is a grumbler, that Mother won't leave them alone, that she's bothering the life out of them (6d).

С-69 • **В РО́ЗОВОМ ⟨РА́ДУЖНОМ⟩ СВЕ́ТЕ** видеть, представлять *кого-что* и т. п.; **В РО́ЗОВОМ ЦВЕ́ТЕ** [PrepP; these forms only; adv; more often used with impfv verbs; fixed WO] (to see, imagine s.o. or sth., interpret sth. etc) in an idealized form, as better than he or it actually is: **(see s.o. ⟨sth.⟩) through rose-colored glasses; (have) a rosy outlook (on sth.); (paint sth.) in a rosy hue; (things) look ⟨seem⟩ rosy to s.o.**

Я ожидал вёрстку. Жизнь представлялась в розовом свете (Довлатов 1). I was waiting for my stories to be run off at the printer's. Life seemed rosy (1a).

С-70 • **В СВЕ́ТЕ**¹ *чего lit* [PrepP; Invar; Prep; the resulting PrepP is adv] from a certain position, proceeding from a particular view of sth.: **in (the) light of; from the standpoint ⟨the point of view⟩ of.**

…Поскольку ему сейчас надо было рассказать деду что-то об отце, отцу — о сыне, да ещё в свете всякой душевной тонкости по «растоплению льда», он начал… выбирать, что сказать и чего не сказать… (Битов 2). Since he must now tell Grandfather something about Father, tell father about son — and what is more, in the light of all manner of emotional subtlety, because of the "thawing of the ice" — he became…busy choosing what to say and what not to say… (2a).

С-71 • **В СВЕ́ТЕ**² *каком* видеть, представлять, изображать *кого-что* и т. п. [PrepP; Invar; the resulting PrepP is adv; more often used with impfv verbs] (to see, present, portray s.o. or sth.) in a way that emphasizes a certain (as specified by the modifier) aspect of him or it: в выгодном ⟨невыгодном, мрачном, ином, ложном и т. п.⟩ свете ≃ **in a favorable ⟨bad, gloomy, different, false etc⟩ light;** ‖ в истинном свете ≃ **(see sth.) in its true light; (see) s.o.'s true colors; (see sth.) in its true colors;** ‖ в наилучшем свете ≃ **in the best possible light.**

…Я в таком выгодном свете выставил её поступки и характер, что она поневоле должна была простить мне моё кокетство с княжной (Лермонтов 1). …[I] portrayed her actions and character in so favourable a light that she could not but forgive me my flirtation with the Princess (1b). ♦ «Появись у нас литература такого масштаба, и московская жизнь представилась бы совсем в ином свете» (Зиновьев 2). "If only we had a literature on that level, Moscow life would appear in quite a different light" (2a). ♦ В то время, когда возник «Тартюф», итальянцы сыграли фарс «Скарамуш-отшельник», в котором в крайне отрицательном

свете был изображён монах (Булгаков 5). At the time of *Tartuffe's* appearance, the Italians presented their farce *Scaramouche the Hermit*, in which a monk was shown in an extremely unfavorable light (5a). ♦ …Она написала несколько романов, из которых в одном, под названием «Скиталица Доротея», изобразила себя в наилучшем свете (Салтыков-Щедрин 1). She also wrote several novels, in one of which, *Dorothea the Pilgrim*, she portrayed herself in the best possible light (1b).

С-72 • **НЕ ЗНАТЬ, НА КАКО́М СВЕ́ТЕ** *coll* [VP; subj: human; fixed WO] to be in a state of confusion, be unable to think clearly because of having too much work to do, too many cares etc: X не знает, на каком он свете ≃ **X doesn't know if he is coming or going; X doesn't know which end is up (anymore); X doesn't know whether he is (standing) on his head or on his heels.**

С-73 • **НЕ СВЕ́ТИТ** *кому highly coll* [VP; subj: abstr, concr, or infin; occas. impers; pres or past] s.o. has little or no possibility or hope of obtaining or doing sth.: X Y-у не светит ≃ **Y hasn't got a chance (in hell) of doing ⟨getting etc⟩ X; Y hasn't got much (of a) chance of doing etc X; there's no way in the world ⟨in hell⟩ Y will get ⟨will (be able to) do etc⟩ X.**

«Докторская нам не светит, а в Академию и подавно мы никогда не попадём» (Зиновьев 2). "We haven't got much chance of a doctorate, and it's not even worth thinking about the Academy" (2a).

С-74 • **ТО́ЛЬКО И СВЕ́ТУ ⟨-a⟩ В ОКО́ШКЕ ⟨В ОКНЕ́⟩ (у кого); (ВЕСЬ ⟨ОДИ́Н⟩) СВЕТ В ОКО́ШКЕ** (у кого, для кого) *all coll* [usu. main clause (with быть₀) in a complex sent, foll. by a что-clause (1st var.); NP (2nd var.); fixed WO] (a person, group etc is) s.o.'s sole joy, consolation: у X-а только и свету в окошке, что Y ≃ **Y is X's all ⟨everything⟩; person Y is the (only) light of X's life; Y is everything ⟨all⟩ X has (in life); Y is all X lives for; Y is ⟨means⟩ all the world to X.**

«А по правде, так весь свет в окошке у меня теперь здесь» (Максимов 3). "Anyway, to tell the truth, all I live for now is right here" (3a).

С-75 • **ДО (СКО́РОГО) СВИДА́НИЯ; ДО СКО́РОГО** *coll* [formula phrase; these forms only] a farewell salutation: **good-bye ⟨goodbye, good-by⟩; bye; I'll ⟨we'll⟩ be seeing you; see you later; (I'll ⟨we'll⟩) see you soon; till we meet again; till (the) next time.**

«На днях вы ко мне придёте по вызову, как свидетель. Мы ещё вспомним эту беседу. До свидания» (Тендряков 1). "In a day or two I shall summon you officially as a witness. We shall then come back to what we're talking about now. Goodbye" (1a). ♦ «Фёдор Васильевич, выпишите, пожалуйста, гражданина Бездомного в город. Но эту комнату не занимать, постельное бельё можно не менять. Через два часа гражданин Бездомный опять будет здесь… До скорого свидания!» (Булгаков 9). "Fyodor Vasilievich, please sign out citizen Homeless. He may go back to town. But keep his room open, and there is no need to change the bedding. Citizen Homeless will be back here inside two hours….See you soon!" (9a). ♦ «Ну, до свидания», — сказал князь Андрей, протягивая руку Тушину. «До свидания, голубчик», — сказал Тушин… (Толстой 4). "Well, till we meet again," he [Prince Andrei] said, holding out his hand to Tushin. "Good-bye, my dear boy," said Tushin (4a).

С-76 • **СО СВИДА́НЬИЦЕМ ⟨СВИДА́НИЕМ⟩** *coll* [PrepP; these forms only; usu. used as indep. sent] the first toast offered at an informal get-together of acquaintances, relatives etc who have not seen each other for a considerable period of time: **here's to our reunion.**

Трясущимися руками он разлил непочатую ещё четвертинку в два стакана и один из них пододвинул брату: «Со свиданьицем...» (Максимов 3). With shaky hands he poured a still untouched quarter into two glasses and pushed one over to his brother. "Here's to our reunion..." (3a).

С-77 • СВИНЕ́Ц НА ДУШЕ́ ⟨НА́ СЕ́РДЦЕ, НА СЕ́РДЦЕ⟩ *у кого* [VP$_{subj}$ with быть$_\emptyset$] s.o. is depressed, burdened by troubles, sadness etc: у X-а на душе свинец ≃ **X's heart is heavy; X feels weighed down; there is a weight on X's heart.**

С-78 • КАК ⟨БУ́ДТО, СЛО́ВНО, ТО́ЧНО⟩ СВИН-ЦО́М НАЛИТА́ ⟨налито, налиты⟩ [как etc + AdjP; nom only; subj-compl with быть$_\emptyset$ (subj: голова, руки, ноги, тело etc)] s.o. has a feeling of heaviness (in his head, arms, legs, whole body etc): голова как свинцом налита ≃ **s.o.'s head is ⟨feels⟩ like lead.**

Утром Нина с трудом встала: всё тело было словно свинцом налито. Nina had difficulty getting up in the morning—her whole body felt like lead.

С-79 • ЛЕЧЬ СВИНЦО́М НА́ ДУШУ ⟨НА́ СЕ́РДЦЕ, НА СЕ́РДЦЕ⟩ *кому rather elev* [VP; subj: abstr; the verb may take the final position, otherwise fixed WO] to make s.o. depressed, despondent: X лёг свинцом на душу Y-у ≃ **X made Y heartsick; X weighed heavily on Y's heart.**

С-80 • ПОДКЛА́ДЫВАТЬ/ПОДЛОЖИ́ТЬ СВИНЬЮ *кому coll, disapprov* [VP; subj: human; usu. pfv] to do a vile thing to s.o., make trouble for s.o. surreptitiously: X подложил Y-у свинью ≃ **X did Y dirt; X played a dirty ⟨nasty⟩ trick on Y; X double-crossed Y.**

А сейчас разве это изм [*nonce word* = коммунизм]? Каждый гоношит обмануть, урвать, наябедничать, подложить свинью, свалить на другого... (Зиновьев 1). "See what we've got at the moment. You can't call that the Ism [= Communism]. Everyone doing their best to cheat, to steal, to inform, to do other people dirt, to dodge responsibility..." (1a). ♦ ...Говорили, что Строковский когда-то подложил серьёзную свинью Поляшко, а теперь хотел бы загладить вину (Залыгин 1). It was said that Strokovsky had once double-crossed Poliashko and now wanted to make amends (1a).

С-81 • КАК СВИНЬЯ́ пить, напиться, пьян и т. п. *coll, derog* [как + NP; nom only; adv (intensif) or modif] (to drink) excessive, enormous (quantities of alcohol), (be, become) extremely, disgustingly (drunk): **(drink) like a pig; (be) drunk as a skunk; (get) stinking drunk.**

«Все ценные люди России, все *нужные* ей люди — все пили, как свиньи» (Ерофеев 1). "All worthwhile people in Russia, all the necessary people, they all drank, they drank like pigs" (1a). ♦ Какая респектабельность, какой этикет, когда господа офицеры по любому поводу и без всякого повода напивались, как свиньи... (Рыбаков 1). Who needed respectability and etiquette when the gentlemen-officers got themselves stinking drunk on any excuse, or none at all... (1a).

С-82 • КАК СВИНЬЯ́ В АПЕЛЬСИ́НАХ разбираться, понимать, смыслить *в чём coll, often derog* [как + NP; Invar; adv (neg intensif); fixed WO] (to understand) absolutely nothing (with regard to sth.): X разбирается в Y-е ≃ **X doesn't know beans ⟨the first thing, a blasted thing, a blessed thing⟩ about Y; X knows as much about Y as a pig about pineapples.**

В живописи наш начальник разбирается как свинья в апельсинах: посмотрите, какую мазню он повесил у себя в кабинете. Our boss doesn't know the first thing about art: just look at the piece of junk he has hanging in his office.

С-83 • СВОДИ́ТЬ/СВЕСТИ́ НА НЕТ *что* [VP; subj: human or abstr; more often pfv] to reduce sth. to the point of having no importance, role, meaning etc at all: X свёл Y на нет ≃ **X reduced Y to nought ⟨nothing⟩; thing X brought Y to nought ⟨nothing⟩; thing X nullified ⟨negated⟩ Y.**

Не такие мы дураки, чтобы дать неудачнику при помощи рассеянной улыбки смазать свою неудачу, свести её на нет, растворить её, как говорится, в море коллегиальности (Искандер 3). We are not such fools as to let a failure slur over his failure by means of a distracted smile—reduce it to nought, dissolve it, so to speak, in the sea of collectivity (3a). ♦ Есть бо́льшие грехи, чем обычные и свойственные всем людям, и они-то губительно влияют на дар художника и сводят его дар на нет (Мандельштам 2). There are...sins greater than the ordinary ones common to everyone, and it is these which can have a calamitous effect on an artist's gift and reduce it to nothing (2a).

С-84 • БРАТЬ/ВЗЯТЬ СВОЁ [VP] **1.** [subj: human; usu. pfv] to achieve one's desired, established aim (when in conflict with another person or when struggling against adverse circumstances): X возьмёт своё ≃ **X will succeed ⟨prevail, win out⟩; X will get ⟨have⟩ his way; [in limited contexts] X's turn ⟨day, moment⟩ will come; X will get back at person Y; X will take his revenge.**

«Дождались станишники [*phonetic spelling* = станичники] своего часа. И уж они, будьте покойны, они своё возьмут» (Максимов 3). "This is just what the Cossacks have been waiting for. They'll take their revenge, don't you worry" (3a).

2. [subj: a noun denoting a season, natural phenomenon etc] to manifest itself fully: X возьмёт своё ≃ **X will come into its own.**

...Весна брала своё. Всё кругом золотисто зеленело... (Тургенев 2). ...Spring was coming into its own. All around him was the gold and verdure of spring... (2a).

3. [subj: abstr] to render its typical effect, dominate, usu. in an evident manner: X брал своё ≃ **X was making itself felt; X was having its way; X was claiming its own; X was prevailing; [usu. of old age, illness etc] X was taking its toll; X was telling (on person Y); X was catching up (with person Y); [of age only] person Y was feeling his age; [of disease only] X was overpowering person Y.**

Так жила тётя Маша со своими богатырскими дочерями — бедно, вольно, неряшливо. Дети и сама она питались чем попало, но могучая природа брала своё, и все они выглядели румяными, сильными, довольными (Искандер 3). Thus Aunt Masha lived with her herculean daughters—poor, free, and slovenly. The children, and she herself, lived from hand to mouth, but mighty nature had its way and all of them looked rosy, strong, and content (3a). ♦ «...Слышу, патер в дырочку [исповедальни] ей [девушке] назначает вечером свидание, а ведь старик — кремень, и вот пал в одно мгновение! Природа-то, правда-то природы взяла своё!» (Достоевский 2). "...I heard the priest arranging a rendezvous with her [the girl] for that evening through the hole [of the confessional booth]; the old man was solid as a rock, but he fell in an instant! It was nature, the truth of nature, claiming its own!" (2a). ♦ ...Молодость брала своё: горе Наташи начало покрываться слоем впечатлений прожитой жизни, оно перестало такою мучительною болью лежать ей на сердце, начинало становиться прошедшим, и Наташа стала физически оправляться (Толстой 6). ...Youth prevailed: Natasha's grief began to be submerged under the impressions of daily life and ceased to weigh so heavily on her heart; it gradually faded into the past, and she began to recover physically (6a). ♦ Он был уже так слаб от двенадцати [уколов], уже [врачи] качали головами над его анализами крови, — а надо было выдержать ещё столько же? Не мытьём, так катаньем болезнь брала своё (Солженицын 10). He was so weak from the twelve [injections] he had had—already they [the doctors] were shaking their heads over his blood count—might he really have to endure the same number again? By hook or by crook the disease was overpowering him (10a).

C-85 • ПОСТА́ВИТЬ ⟨НАСТА́ИВАТЬ/НАСТОЯ́ТЬ⟩ НА СВОЁМ [VP; subj: human or collect] to (try to) gain one's objective, (try to) succeed in doing sth. in the way one prefers, despite opposition: X поставил на своём ≃ X got ⟨had⟩ his (own) way; X had it ⟨things⟩ his (own) way; X insisted on having it ⟨things⟩ his (own) way; X won out.

[Михаил:] А великолепно чувствуется, когда поставишь на своём! (Горький 1). [M.:] It makes you feel fine to have things your own way! (1c). ♦ Его [Михаила] удивил яркий свет в своей избе... [Он] заглянул в окошко. Степан Андреянович сидит за столом, Илья Нетёсов, Егорша — серебром переливаются молнии на кожаной куртке. Так, так, подумал Михаил. Сваты. Егорша решил на своём настоять... (Абрамов 1). He [Mikhail] was surprised by the bright light in his house....[He] peeped in at the window. Stepan Andreyanovich was sitting at the table, along with Ilya Netyosov and Egorsha—the zipper on his leather jacket giving off a silvery gleam. So that's it, thought Mikhail. Matchmakers. Egorsha decided to insist on having his way (1a). ♦ [extended usage] «От судьбы, Настёна, никуда не уйдёшь... Она на своём поставит» (Распутин 2). "You can't get away from destiny, Nastyona....It will win out" (2a).

C-86 • СТОЯ́ТЬ ⟨УПЕРЕ́ТЬСЯ coll⟩ НА СВОЁМ [VP; subj: human or collect] to continue to defend one's views, beliefs etc, refuse to change one's opinions: X стоит на своём ≃ X stands ⟨holds⟩ his ground; X won't budge ⟨give in⟩; X sticks to his guns; [in limited contexts] X sticks to ⟨by⟩ what he said.

...Сколько [жалобщики] его ни уговаривали, он твёрдо стоял на своём (Искандер 4). ...Despite their [the plaintiffs'] best efforts to win him over, he firmly stood his ground (4a). ♦ Ему [сапожнику] объясняли, что своим поведением он наносит урон социалистической родине и рабочему классу, но он стоял на своём (Мандельштам 2). They said he [the cobbler] was letting down the Socialist motherland and the working class, but he would not budge (2a). ♦ «В 1937 году, когда был процесс по делу Якира, Тухачевского и других, среди писателей собирали подписи под письмом, одобряющим смертный приговор. Пришли и ко мне. Я отказался подписать... Меня начали уламывать, я стоял на своём» (Ивинская 1). "In 1937, at the time of the trial of Yakir, Tukhachevski, and others, the writers were asked to put their signature to a statement endorsing the death sentence. They came to try and get mine as well. I refused to give it....They tried to put pressure on me, but I wouldn't give in" (1a).

C-87 • ОСТАВА́ТЬСЯ/ОСТА́ТЬСЯ ПРИ СВОИ́Х coll [VP; subj: human; more often pfv] 1. (in refer. to gambling) to end up with neither a loss nor a profit: X остался при своих ≃ X broke even.

2. not to experience any change as a result of some developments, to remain in the same position, circumstances as before: X останется при своих ≃ X will neither win nor lose; everything will remain the same for X.

C-88 • СВОЯ́ СВОИ́Х НЕ ПОЗНА́ША [saying] said when, because of some confusion, an ally is mistaken for an enemy: ≃ he ⟨you etc⟩ didn't recognize (one of) his ⟨your etc⟩ own; he ⟨you etc⟩ couldn't tell (a) friend from (a) foe.

В первый же день он [Саша] сказал: «Володя, чтобы не было недоразумений. Я разделяю линию партии. Будем держать свои взгляды при себе. Ни к чему бесполезные споры». — «У меня тем более нет желания дискутировать со сталинскими подголосками, — высокомерно ответил Володя, — но уж раз вы меня сюда [в ссылку] загнали, то рот не заткнёте». Саша улыбнулся. «Я вас сюда не загонял, меня самого загнали». — «Своя своих не позна́ша» (Рыбаков 2). On the very first day, he [Sasha] said: "Volodya, just so there won't be any misunderstandings, I want you to know that I accept the Party line. Let's keep our views to ourselves. No need to have pointless arguments." "I haven't the slightest desire to debate with Stalinist yes-men," Volodya had replied haughtily. "But since you put me here [in exile], don't try to gag me as well." Sasha smiled. "It wasn't me who sent you here. I've been sent here too, you know." "They don't recognize their own, do they?" (2a).

< From the Church Slavonic text of the Bible (John 1:10–11).

C-89 • В СВЯЗИ́ с чем [PrepP; Invar; Prep; the resulting PrepP is adv] by reason of: because of; in view of; in connection with; in light of; owing to; as a result of; on the grounds of; [in limited contexts] (and) hence; [when a deverbal noun is translated by a verb] now that; since; ‖ в связи с этим ≃ as a result (of this).

«...В связи с некоторыми обстоятельствами ведущим работникам института нужно будет заполнить вот эту анкету» (Гроссман 2). "...In view of various circumstances senior members of staff are being asked to fill in this questionnaire here" (2a). ♦ ...Вспоминалась ему [Гипатову] первая практика — в горах, на строительстве рудника, куда Назаренко не поехал, достав справку о временной нетрудоспособности в связи с гипотонией (Семёнов 1). ...He [Gipatov] recalled their first practice trip—to the mountains where a mine was being built—on which Nazaryenko did not go, having obtained a certificate to say that he was temporarily excused from work on the grounds of low blood pressure (1a). ♦ Время было глухое, так как короля не было в Париже, в связи с чем отбыли и многие знатные люди (Булгаков 5). The season was dull, since the King was away from Paris, and hence many of the nobles were also absent (5a). ♦ ...Как водится, наши заглядывали в лица местных эндурцев, чтобы установить, как они намерены вести себя в связи с таким необыкновенным возвышением (Искандер 5). As usual, our folks went around peering into the faces of the local Endurskies to determine how they intended to behave, now that they had been so extraordinarily elevated (5a).

C-90 • ХОТЬ СВЯТЫ́Х ⟨ВОН⟩ ВЫНОСИ́ ⟨НЕСИ́, УНОСИ́⟩ obsoles, coll [хоть + VP$_{imper}$; these forms only; usu. subord clause, often introduced by что; fixed WO] (sth. is) intolerable, appalling, embarrassing, or repulsive to the eyes or ears: (it ⟨this [NP] etc⟩ is) enough to make the saints blush; such a [NP] ⟨so [AdjP]⟩ that the saints would blush; (it ⟨this [NP] etc⟩ is) enough to make a preacher ⟨the saints⟩ swear; (it ⟨this [NP] etc⟩ is) enough to try the patience of a saint.

Был он чудак... шутник, враль. Бывало, такого наврёт, хоть святых выноси (Грекова 3). He was an oddball, a joker, a liar. Sometimes he could invent such lies that the saints would blush... (3a).

C-91 • СВЯТА́Я СВЯТЫ́Х (чего) elev, rhet [NP; Invar; fixed WO] 1. a well-protected place inaccessible to the uninitiated: the holy of holies; the inner sanctum; the sanctum sanctorum.

...Конструкторскими делами всё больше занимался... Янгель, которого перевезли в Москву вместе с группой других немецких инженеров и допустили в «святая святых» — в ракетный институт (Владимиров 1). ...[Yangel] took over more and more of the designing work. He had been brought to Moscow along with a group of other German engineers and had been admitted to the "holy of holies"—the missile institute (1a). ♦ Фишер соответствующим жестом пояснил своему спутнику, что вот теперь тот — в «святая святых», в таком, можно сказать, убежище свободного духа, где производится неподцензурный альбом «Скажи изюм!»... (Аксёнов 12). With an appropriate gesture Fisher made it clear to his companion that now he was in the inner sanctum, in what might be termed the refuge of the free spirit, where the uncensored album Say Cheese! was being produced... (12a).

2. sth. very dear, sacred: the holy of holies; [in limited contexts] the sacrosanct ⟨hallowed etc⟩ principle.

В условиях нашей системы коллектив – это чуть ли не святая святых (Войнович 3). Under our system, the collective is practically the holy of holies (3a).

< Originally, the inner chamber of the Temple in Jerusalem, which only the chief priest was allowed to enter.

C-92 • **ДАВА́ТЬ/ДАТЬ СДА́ЧИ** ⟨-у⟩ *(кому)* coll [VP; subj: human] to return (a blow, an insult etc) similar to the one received: X дал (Y-у) сдачи ≃ **X paid Y back in kind ⟨in Y's own coin⟩; X hit (Y) back; X struck back; X gave back blow for blow; X gave as good as he got.**

Какая-то стерва толкнула меня в бок и меня же обругала. А я растерялся и не успел дать сдачи (Зиновьев 2). Some old cow rammed her elbow in my side and then bawled me out on top of it. And I was so taken aback that I didn't even manage to pay her back in her own coin (2a). ♦ Что с тобой будет, малышка?.. Сумеешь ли ты выстоять, приспособиться и научиться давать сдачи? (Зиновьев 2). What's going to happen to you, little girl?…Will you be able to hold out, to adapt yourself and learn to give back blow for blow? (2a).

C-93 • **ПОЛУЧА́ТЬ/ПОЛУЧИ́ТЬ СДА́ЧИ** coll [VP; subj: human] to be repaid (for a blow, an insult etc) with a similar one: X получил сдачи ≃ **X was ⟨got⟩ paid back in kind ⟨in his own coin⟩; X got back blow for blow.**

C-94 • **СДЕ́ЛКА С СО́ВЕСТЬЮ** [NP; fixed WO] an action undertaken by one that defies one's convictions and that one tries to justify to o.s. (usu. on some flimsy grounds): **a deal ⟨a compromise etc⟩ with one's conscience;** ‖ пойти на сделку с совестью ≃ **make a deal ⟨a bargain⟩ with one's conscience; compromise one's conscience.**

C-95 • **СДЕ́РЖИВАТЬ/СДЕРЖА́ТЬ СЕБЯ́** [VP; subj: human; more often pfv] to refrain from displaying some emotion or performing some action: X сдержал себя ≃ **X restrained ⟨checked⟩ himself; X managed to keep himself in check; X managed to control himself.**

«Вы отказываетесь выполнить моё приказание?» – с видимым усилием сдерживая себя, хрипло спросил Фицхалауров. «Да». – «В таком случае потрудитесь сейчас же сдать командование дивизией!» (Шолохов 5). "Do you refuse to obey my order?" Fitzhelaurov asked hoarsely, restraining himself with an obvious effort. "Yes." "In that case kindly hand over command of the division!" (5a). ♦ Потом он [Терещенко] вдруг говорит: «Ваша мать была в своё время очень красивой девушкой». И опять ехидно улыбается: мол, такая была красавица, но пренебрегла им, Терещенко, вышла за неудачника и вот по собственной глупости попала в такую ужасную историю. Меня это взорвало… но в такой ситуации нельзя давать волю чувствам, надо сдерживать себя… (Рыбаков 1). Suddenly he [Tereshchenko] said, "In her time your mother was a very beautiful girl." Again he gave me his malicious grin, as though to say, such a pretty girl could have had a happy life, but she had spurned him and married a failure and now through her own stupidity she had landed in this terrible mess. I thought I would explode…but in a situation like that, you can't give vent to your feelings, you must control yourself… (1a).

C-96 • **К СЕБЕ́** [PrepP; Invar; adv] **1.** in the direction of the doer: **toward;** [as a sign on doors etc] **pull.**

2. пойти, уйти и т. п. ~ (to go) to the place where one lives, works, is staying etc: X пошёл к себе ≃ **X went to his room ⟨to his office, home etc⟩.**

«„…Что сказать, если Грета спросит о тебе?" – „Что хочешь, то и говори", – отвечает [Алёша] и одним махом, как водку, выпивает свой компот и уходит к себе» (Искандер 5). "'What should I tell Greta if she asks about you?' 'Tell her what you

want,' he [Alyosha] answers, and he downs his fruit compote in one gulp, like vodka, and goes to his room" (5a). ♦ [Платонов:] Не пойду я к себе… На дворе дождь… Тут лягу (Чехов 1). [P.:] I'm not going home. It's raining. I'll lie down here (1a).

C-97 • **НЕ В СЕБЕ́** coll [PrepP; Invar; subj-compl with быть∅ (subj: human)] **1.** one is in a state of severe emotional upset, has lost his composure: X не в себе ≃ **X is in a bad way ⟨in bad shape⟩; X has been thrown off balance;** [in limited contexts] **X is not in his right mind.**

«Я вижу, ты не в себе, чувак. Лучше бы дома сидел» (Аксёнов 6). "I can see you're in a bad way, kid. You should have stayed at home" (6a). ♦ «Знаешь наших-то [из миномётной]?» – «Знаю, знаю, – говорит он, – всех знаю… Всех [убило]. Подчистую. Один я остался»… – «Врёшь ты все!» – «Ты его не слушай, – говорит сестра, – он ведь не в себе» (Окуджава 1). "Do you know our men [from the mortar battery]?" "Yes, I know them," he says. "I know them all….The lot of them. Wiped clean out. I'm the only one left…." "You're lying. It's all lies!…" "Don't listen to him," says the nurse. "He's not in his right mind" (1a).

2. one is not in his usual frame of mind, feels different than usual: X не в себе ≃ **X is not (quite) himself; X is out of sorts.**

[Андрей:] Я всю ночь не спал и теперь немножко не в себе, как говорится (Чехов 5). [A.:] I haven't slept all night, and now I'm not quite myself, as they say (5a).

C-98 • **НЕ ПО СЕБЕ́** *кому* [PrepP; Invar; impers predic with быть∅, становиться, делаться] **1.** s.o. feels indisposed, weak: X-у не по себе ≃ **X is not feeling well ⟨(quite) right⟩; X is feeling sick ⟨poorly⟩; X is not feeling himself; X is under the weather; X is out of sorts.**

Лёве вдруг не по себе… Тошнотворное чувство овладевает им (Битов 2). Lyova suddenly felt sick….A sense of nausea gripped him… (2a).

2. ~ *(от чего)* s.o. feels tense, apprehensive, embarrassed etc (because of unsettling surroundings, fear, an unpleasant foreboding, awkwardness in a social situation etc): X-у было не по себе ≃ **X was ⟨felt⟩ ill at ease; X was ⟨felt⟩ (very) uneasy; X was uptight;** [usu. in refer. to an unpleasant foreboding, fear] **X was upset ⟨disturbed, distressed⟩; X didn't feel (quite) right; X was ⟨grew⟩ worried;** [usu. in refer. to social awkwardness] **X felt uncomfortable; X didn't feel ⟨wasn't⟩ at home;** [in limited contexts] **X was not himself; X was ⟨felt⟩ self-conscious.**

Приёмник выплёвывал непонятные и от этого ещё более страшные слова. Гитлер лаял, как старый волк. Жолио стало не по себе… (Эренбург 4). The loud-speaker spat out the unintelligible words that sounded for this very reason all the more terrible. Hitler barked like an old wolf. Joliot felt very uneasy (4a). ♦ Припав к отцовскому плечу, она шёпотно запричитала: «Папаня, родненький… Как же вы тут без меня будете?..» Николай, переминаясь с ноги на ногу, стоял сбоку, затравленно поглядывая в их сторону, и по всему видно было, что ему тоже не по себе (Максимов 3). She hid her head in her father's shoulder, and tearfully whispered, "Daddy, dearest Daddy…how will you manage without me?"…Nikolai stood to one side, shifting from foot to foot, looking at them like a hunted animal, and it was obvious that he too was upset (3a). ♦ И всё-таки не по себе ей было, всё не шёл у ней из головы этот проклятущий след от папоротниковой ветки на нежной ноге её девочки, повыше колена (Искандер 3). Still, she did not feel right, her mind kept going back to the accursed mark from the fern frond on her little girl's tender leg, above the knee (3a). ♦ «В лесу, наверно, совсем страшно», – думал мальчик, прислушиваясь к звукам за окнами. Ему стало не по себе, когда вдруг стали доноситься какие-то смутные голоса, выкрики какие-то (Айтматов 1). "It must be very frightening in the woods," the boy thought, listening to the sounds outside the window. He grew worried when he suddenly heard muffled voices and cries (1a). ♦ «Располагайтесь, это теперь ваш дом». Слово «ваш» он произнёс с тем особым ударением, от которого всем вдруг стало немного не по себе... (Максимов 3). "Make yourself at home—it's your home now." He pronounced the word "your" with a particular emphasis that made them all suddenly feel uncomfortable... (3a). ♦ Люди вроде Орсини сильно действуют на других, они нравятся своей замкнутой личностью, и между тем с ними не по себе... (Герцен 2). Men like Orsini have a powerful influence on others: people are attracted by their reserved nature and at the same time are not at home with them... (2a).

С-99 • ПО СЕБЕ́ [PrepP; Invar] **1. найти, выбрать** *кого-что* ~ *coll* [usu. nonagreeing modif] (to find, choose s.o. or sth.) coinciding with one's taste, of one's preference, commensurate with one's abilities, status etc: **to one's liking; who ⟨that⟩ suits one; suitable** [NP].

Бабушка говорила: «Будет несчастной та женщина, на которой Иосиф женится». Но, представьте, он женился очень удачно, отхватил жену по себе... (Рыбаков 1). Grandmother said, "It'll be an unhappy woman that Yosif marries." Yet, can you imagine, he actually married very well, he picked out a wife who really suited him... (1a). ♦ «...Видеть его [Бориса] таким близким с тобой может повредить тебе в глазах других молодых людей, которые к нам ездят, и, главное, напрасно мучает его. Он, может быть, нашёл себе партию по себе, богатую...» (Толстой 5). "...To see him [Boris] so intimate with you may injure you in the eyes of other young men who visit us, and above all, it torments him for nothing. He may already have found a suitable and wealthy match..." (5b).

2. оставить ~ *что*, usu. *какую* **память** [adv] (to leave sth. to those who remain) after one's departure or death: **leave behind; leave s.o. with.**

...Все [градоначальники], как бурные, так и кроткие, оставили по себе благодарную память в сердцах сограждан, ибо все были градоначальники (Салтыков-Щедрин 1). ...All [the Town Governors], both the stormy and the mild, left behind in the hearts of their fellow citizens a thankful memory, for all were Town Governors (1a).

С-100 • ПРИ СЕБЕ́ быть, быть₀, иметь, держать *что* и т. п.; **С СОБО́Й** [PrepP; these forms only; subj-compl with copula (subj: concr) or obj-compl with держать (obj: concr)] sth. is in s.o.'s immediate possession, (to have, keep sth.) in one's immediate possession: **on ⟨with⟩ one ⟨s.o.⟩; on one's ⟨s.o.'s⟩ person.**

«...У тебя партбилет с собой?» — «...Завсегда [substand = всегда], как положено, в левом кармане» (Войнович 2). "...Do you have your party card on you?" "...As always, right where it belongs, in my left pocket" (2a). ♦ «У вас нет с собой никаких документов?» — «С собой нет, я позабыл» (Федин 1). "Don't you have any papers with you?" "With me no, I forgot" (1a).

С-101 • ВНЕ СЕБЯ́ *(от чего)* [PrepP; Invar; usu. subj-compl with быть₀ (subj: human)] one is in an extremely excited or irritated state: вне себя (от злости ⟨гнева и т. п.⟩) ≃ **beside o.s. (with anger ⟨rage etc⟩); furious; fit to be tied; seething with anger ⟨fury⟩; fuming; purple with rage;** ‖ вне себя от радости ⟨счастья⟩ ≃ **beside o.s. with joy; wild with joy; jumping up and down for joy;** ‖ вне себя от испуга ⟨страха⟩ ≃ **scared stiff ⟨out of one's wits⟩.**

Вне себя от ярости, Дмитрий размахнулся и изо всей силы ударил Григория. Старик рухнулся как подкошенный... (Достоевский 1). Beside himself with rage, Dmitri swung and hit Grigory with all his strength. The old man collapsed as if he had been cut down... (1a). ♦ Я — вне, вне себя, что не могу тотчас же ехать в Скандинавию! (Солженицын 5). I am furious, absolutely furious that I cannot come to Scandinavia immediately! (5a). ♦ Он присоединился к конвенции вне себя от злости (Ильф и Петров 2). He joined the convention, seething with fury (2a). ♦

Завтра уезжают мои хозяева, и от радости я вне себя: *вне себя*, — очень приятное положение, как ночью на крыше (Набоков 1). Tomorrow my landlord and landlady are going away and I am beside myself with joy: *beside myself*—a very pleasant situation, like on a rooftop at night (1a).

С-102 • ИЗ СЕБЯ́ *substand* [PrepP; Invar; usu. modif] (usu. of a person) with regard to outward features, characteristics: X из себя [AdjP] ≃ **in appearance, X is [AdjP]; X is [AdjP]-looking; X looks [AdjP];** [of an attractive person] **X is a real ⟨not a bad⟩ looker; X is not bad (at all);** ‖ X из себя симпатичный ⟨некрасивый и т. п.⟩ ≃ [in limited contexts] **X is nice ⟨not much etc⟩ to look at;** ‖ какой ⟨каков⟩ X из себя? ≃ **what does X look like?**

Мося из себя такой: лицо — скуластый глиняный кувшин; щегольская батумская кепка; ...глаза быстрые, неистовые, воровские (Катаев 1). In appearance, Mosya was something like this: his face—an earthen pitcher with prominent cheek-bones; then a dashing Batoum cap;...quick frantic, thievish eyes (1a). ♦ ...[Я] осталась при доме, работал на обувной фабрике мастером... Парень молодой, из себя ничего, к тому же из армии, не сопляк какой-нибудь... (Рыбаков 1). ...[I] stayed at home, working at the shoe factory as a craftsman....At twenty-one I wasn't bad looking, I had been in the army and was no milksop... (1a). ♦ «...Он [казак] из себя ничего. Только седых волос много, и усы вон почти седые» (Шолохов 5). "...He's [the Cossack is] not a bad looker. Too much grey hair though, and his moustache is nearly all grey too" (5a). ♦ «Вообще, конечно, Нюрка — баба справная и видная из себя, но и я ведь тоже ещё молодой, обсмотреться надо сперва что к чему...» (Войнович 2). "Of course Nyura's a good girl and nice to look at, but, you know, I'm still a young guy, gotta have a look around first, see what's what..." (2a). ♦ «Тебе чего, милок?» — «Зинку». — «А фамилиё [ungrammat = фамилия]?» — «Фамилия?.. Забыл вроде...» — «А из себя какая?» (Максимов 2). "What d'you want, dear?" "Zinka." "What's her last name?" "Her last name?...I...I seem to have forgotten it...." "What does she look like?" (2a).

С-103 • ОТ СЕБЯ́ [PrepP; Invar; adv] **1.** in the direction away from the doer: **away from;** [as a sign on doors etc] **push.**

Уважаемый тянет ручку двери — не поддаётся. Тянет сильнее — никакого эффекта. Да что за чёрт!.. Он тянет ручку двумя руками. Спокойно. Никакой истерики. Надо взять себя в руки. Здесь что-то написано: «От себя» (Войнович 3). Our respected colleague pulls on the door handle—it doesn't give. He pulls harder—no effect. What the devil!...He pulls the handle with both hands. Easy, no hysterics. You must get control of yourself. There's something written here....It says PUSH (3a).

2. говорить ~ to speak on one's own behalf, communicate one's own ideas, views, convictions: **(speak) for o.s.; (express ⟨voice⟩) one's own opinion;** [in limited contexts] **speak on one's own.**

«Вы хотите сказать от себя — вы ничего не можете сказать от себя. Вы только от лица той же власти сказать можете» (Битов 2). "You want to speak on your own—you can't speak a word on your own. You can speak only in the name of that same regime" (2a).

С-104 • ПРО СЕБЯ́ [PrepP; Invar; adv] **1. говорить, бормотать, напевать** и т. п. ~ (to say sth., mutter, hum etc) quietly, in a barely audible manner: **(mutter sth. ⟨say sth., swear etc⟩) under one's breath; (talk ⟨mutter sth., murmur etc⟩) to o.s.; mutter ⟨murmur etc⟩ sth. (to o.s.).**

«Ну пошло!» — ругнулся про себя Едигей (Айтматов 2). "Here we go," Yedigei muttered under his breath... (2a). ♦ «Береги силы!» — прибавил тихо, почти про себя, Штольц в ответ на её страстный порыв (Гончаров 1). "Conserve your strength!" he [Stolz] added softly, almost to himself, in answer to her passionate outburst (1b). ♦ Я взглянул на Савельича; старик крестился, читая про себя молитву (Пушкин 2). I glanced at Savelich: the old man was crossing himself and muttering a prayer (2a).

2. ~ **думать, признавать, улыбаться** и т. п. (to think sth., admit sth., smile etc) without any outward expression or indication: **to o.s.; inwardly; privately; secretly.**

…В эту самую минуту один миллион двести пятьдесят тысяч взрослых женщин обсуждали покрой своего платья… ещё двадцать два миллиона сто сорок восемь тысяч – вслух и про себя думали о том, из чего и как приготовить обед… (Залыгин 1). …At this very moment one million, two hundred and fifty thousand grown-up women were discussing the cut of a dress….Another twenty-two million, one hundred and forty-eight thousand were thinking to themselves or thinking aloud what to cook for dinner… (1a). ♦ …[Я] с совершеннейшей ясностью убедился в том, что инструментарий в ней [больнице] богатейший. При этом с тою же ясностью я вынужден был признать (про себя, конечно), что очень многих блестящих девственно инструментов назначение мне вовсе не известно (Булгаков 6). …[I] was left in no doubt whatever that it [the hospital] was generously equipped. With equal certainty I was forced to admit (inwardly, of course) that I had no idea what very many of these shiny, unsullied instruments were for (6a). ♦ «Повсюду только и слышишь: графомания, графомания. Другим словом – бездарно. А я говорю им – не вслух конечно, а про себя, в своей сокровенной душе говорю: – Подите вы все к чёртовой матери!» (Терц 4). "All you hear everywhere is 'graphomania, graphomania.' A mediocrity, in other words. But I tell them (not aloud of course, but privately, in the secret parts of my soul): 'To hell with the lot of you!'" (4a).

С-105 • У СЕБЯ [PrepP; Invar; subj-compl with copula (subj: human) or adv] in the place where one lives, works, is staying etc: X у себя ≃ **X is in his room ⟨in his office, (at) home** etc⟩; [usu. of one's being in his office] **X is in.**

[Анна Петровна:] Где Софья? [Войницев:] Должно быть, у себя… (Чехов 1). [А.P.:] Where's Sophia? [V.:] In her room, I suppose (1a). ♦ «А вы, пожалуй, зайдите к Сергею Леонидовичу, – сказал Маревин. – Поговорите с ним. Зайдите, зайдите сейчас же! Он у себя, я знаю» (Трифонов 1). "And perhaps you should drop in on Sergei Leonidovich," said Marevin. "Discuss the matter with him. Go and see him, go and see him right now. I happen to know that he's in his office" (1a). ♦ «Владимир Адольфович у себя?» – «У себя», – нахально отвечает она [секретарша] (Попов 1). "Is Vladimir Adolfovich in?" "He's in," she [the secretary] answers snidely (1a).

С-106 • НЕ СЕГÓДНЯ-ЗÁВТРА; НЕ НЫ́НЧЕ-ЗÁВТРА both coll [AdvP; these forms only; adv; used with fut (usu. pfv) verbs] imminently: **any day (now); any time (now); (at) any moment (now); very soon;** [in limited contexts] **(in) no more than a day or two.**

«Я не хочу пугать тебя, но временами у меня ощущение, будто не сегодня-завтра меня арестуют». – «Сохрани Бог, Юрочка. До этого, по счастью, ещё далеко» (Пастернак 1). "I don't want to worry you, but occasionally I have the feeling that they might arrest me any day." "God forbid, Yurochka. It hasn't come to that yet, fortunately" (1a). ♦ «…Не сегодня-завтра начнётся оттепель – переправить через Дон не только артиллерию, но и конницу будет невозможно…» (Шолохов 3). "The thaw will be here any day now….It'll be impossible to bring artillery or even cavalry across the Don" (3a). ♦ «Испанцы не сегодня-завтра выступят» (Эренбург 4). "The Spaniards are going to make a move very soon" (4a). ♦ Когда окончательно стало ясно, что старуха не сегодня-завтра отойдёт, Михаил пошёл на почту и отбил брату и сёстрам телеграммы – чтобы приезжали (Распутин 3). When it finally became apparent that she [the old lady] had no more than a day or two to live, Mikhail went to the post office and sent telegrams to his brother and his sisters, telling them to come (3a).

С-107 • ВЫБИВÁТЬ/ВЫ́БИТЬ ⟨ВЫШИБÁТЬ/ВЫ́ШИБИТЬ⟩ ИЗ СЕДЛÁ кого coll [VP; subj: usu. abstr, occas. human; often passive Part выбит] to deprive s.o. of a certain position in life, emotional stability, confidence in sth. etc: X выбил Y-а из седла ≃ **X cut the ground ⟨knocked the props⟩ (out) from under Y; X threw Y off balance;** ‖ Y выбит из седла ≃ **Y has lost his footing;** [in limited contexts] **Y is battered by life.**

С-108 • БÁРХАТНЫЙ СЕЗÓН [NP; sing only; fixed WO] the autumn months (September, October) in the south of Russia (the best time for vacations): **the warm autumn season; the warm ⟨pleasant⟩ southern autumn.**

С-109 • НЕ СЕКРÉТ (для кого) [NP; sing only; subj-compl with быть∅ (subj: usu. abstr or a clause), pres only] sth. is well-known (to s.o.): X (для Y-а) не секрет ≃ **X is no secret (to Y); X is no news to Y.**

…Не секрет, что иные фотографы смотрели на него [Венечку Пробкина] косо… (Аксёнов 12). It was no secret that some photographers looked askance at him [Venechka Probkin]… (12a).

С-110 • СЕКРÉТ ПОЛИШИНÉЛЯ [NP; sing only; fixed WO] a secret that actually is known to all: **open secret; widely known secret.**

< Loan translation of the French secret de polichinelle.

С-111 • НЕ ДÉЛАТЬ СЕКРÉТА ⟨ТÁЙНЫ⟩ из чего [VP; subj: human] not to conceal sth.: X не делает секрета из Y-а ≃ **X makes no secret ⟨X doesn't make a secret⟩ of Y; X is open about Y; X doesn't try to hide Y;** [in limited contexts] **X makes no bones about Y.**

Михаил не делал секрета из своих планов. Mikhail didn't make a secret of his plans. ♦ Тоня не делает секрета из того, что хочет разбогатеть. Tonya makes no bones about her desire to get rich.

С-112 • В СЕКРÉТЕ [PrepP; Invar] **1.** [adv] (to do sth.) concealing it from others: **in secret; secretly; in secrecy; stealthily.**

Он с упоением помышлял, в глубочайшем секрете, о девице благонравной и бедной (непременно бедной), очень молоденькой, очень хорошенькой, благородной и образованной, очень запуганной… (Достоевский 3). In deepest secret he had dreamed rapturously of a maiden who was both virtuous and poor (she had to be poor), who was both very young and very pretty, and who was respectable, well-educated and very timid… (3a). ♦ «Как раз пред тем, как я Грушеньку пошёл бить, призывает меня в то самое утро Катерина Ивановна и в ужасном секрете, чтобы покамест никто не знал… просит меня съездить в губернский город и там по почте послать три тысячи Агафье Ивановне, в Москву…» (Достоевский 1). "Just before I went to give Grushenka a beating, that very morning, Katerina Ivanovna sent for me and, in terrible secrecy, so that for the time being no one would know…she asked me to go to the provincial capital and from there post three thousand roubles to Agafya Ivanovna in Moscow…" (1a).

2. держать что ~ [obj-compl with держать (obj: abstr, often идею, план etc)] (in refer. to an idea, plan etc) (to keep sth.) concealed: X держал Y в секрете ≃ **X kept Y (a) secret; X kept Y to himself ⟨under wraps, under his hat⟩; X kept quiet ⟨didn't breathe a word⟩ about Y.**

«Как только полк отзовут, мы строго покараем всех нарушителей дисциплины, и в частности тех красноармейцев, которые говорили сообщённое вами сейчас… Надо принять срочные меры по локализации этой опасности. Прошу вас держать в секрете наш разговор» (Шолохов 4). "As soon as the regiment is taken out of line we'll crack down on all infringers of discipline and particularly those who said what you've just reported....Urgent measures must be taken to localise this danger. Please, keep our conversation secret" (4a).

C-113 • ПО СЕКРЕ́ТУ сказать, сообщить и т. п.; **ПОД СЕКРЕ́ТОМ** [PrepP; these forms only; adv] with the understanding that what is said will remain confidential: **in secret; in (strict ⟨strictest⟩) confidence; secretly; confidentially; privately.**

«Скажу вам, Marie, по секрету: мы все, сколько нас ни есть, мы все немножко нигилисты...» (Салтыков-Щедрин 2). "Let me tell you something in secret, Marie. Every one of us, however many there are of us, every one of us is a bit of a nihilist" (2a). ♦ Наташа была очень больна, и как Марья Дмитриевна под секретом сказала ему [Пьеру], она в ту же ночь, как ей было объявлено, что Анатоль женат, отравилась мышьяком, который она тихонько достала (Толстой 5). Natasha was very ill, as Marya Dmitrievna told him [Pierre] in confidence, having poisoned herself the night she learned that Anatol was married, with some arsenic she had procured by stealth (5a). ♦ Лена Будягина со слов Юры Шарока под большим секретом сказала ей, что в институте, где учился Саша, существовала антисоветская организация... (Рыбаков 2). According to Lena Budyagina, who reported what Yuri Sharok had told her in strict confidence, there had been an anti-Soviet organization at Sasha's institute (2a). ♦ ...Однажды он под секретом, потребовав сохранения тайны, показал Рите медицинскую справку... (Трифонов 3). [context transl] One day, under an oath of secrecy, he showed Rita a medical certificate... (3a).

C-114 • НИ К СЕЛУ́ НИ К ГО́РОДУ coll [PrepP; Invar; adv or, less often, subj-compl with copula (subj: замечание, выступление etc); fixed WO] (to say or do sth.) that is inappropriate at the given moment, that is completely unassociated with what is being said or done: **(totally ⟨completely etc⟩) out of place; apropos of nothing; out of the blue; without rhyme or reason; totally inappropriate** [NP]; [adv only] **for no apparent reason; for no reason at all; irrelevantly; at an utterly inappropriate moment.**

Он однажды пошёл гулять со мною по Нескучному саду, был очень добродушен и любезен, сообщал мне названия и свойства различных трав и цветов и вдруг, как говорится, ни к селу ни к городу, воскликнул, ударив себя по лбу: «А я, дурак, думал, что она [Зинаида] кокетка!» (Тургенев 3). One day he went for a walk with me in the Neskoochny Park, was very amiable and friendly, told me the names and properties of various herbs and flowers, and suddenly, as they say, "out of the blue," cried, striking himself on the forehead, "And I, fool that I am, thought she [Zinaida] was a flirt" (3a). ♦ Позже, когда в литературных кругах стало известно о случившемся [о том, что Пастернак отдал рукопись романа итальянскому издателю], писатель К., разговаривая с Алей Эфрон, вдруг расхохотался, казалось бы ни к селу ни к городу: «Представляю себе их х-хари, когда они об этом узнают: то-то забегают!» (Ивинская 1). In the days when it had already become known in literary circles what had happened [that Pasternak had given his novel to an Italian publisher], the writer K., while talking with Ariadna Efron, suddenly burst out into laughter, apparently for no reason at all, and then said: "I can just imagine the look on their fat faces when they get to know about it: how they will fuss!" (1a). ♦ «Я — историк, — подтвердил учёный и добавил ни к селу ни к городу: — Сегодня вечером на Патриарших [прудах] будет интересная история!» (Булгаков 9). "I am a historian," confirmed the scholar, and added irrelevantly, "There will be a most interesting occurrence at the Patriarchs' Ponds this evening!" (9a). ♦ ...В течение нескольких дней [Василий Иванович], ни к селу ни к городу, всё твердил: «Ну, это дело девятое!»... (Тургенев 2). ...For several days on end he [Vasily Ivanovich] kept repeating at utterly inappropriate moments "Well, that's no very great matter!..." (2e).

C-115 • КАК СЕЛЬДЕ́Й В БО́ЧКЕ (набилось) кого где; **КАК СЕ́ЛЬДИ В БО́ЧКЕ (набились)** both coll [как + NP; these forms only; usu. quantit subj-compl with copula, subj: human (the 1st var. is used with subj/gen), or adv (quantif); fixed WO] some people are crowded in some place that is too small to accommodate them: X-ов в месте Y было как сельдей в бочке ≃ **Xs were packed (together) like sardines in ⟨into⟩ place Y.**

Он [поезд] состоял... из здоровенных четырёхосных пульманов, и в каждом зэки, как сельди в бочке (Марченко 1). This [train]...consisted of big, strong, eight-wheeled cars into which the cons were packed like sardines (1a).

C-116 • В СЕМЬЕ́ НЕ БЕЗ УРО́ДА [saying] in every family or group there is a member who stands out from the rest in a negative way (or, when used ironically or humorously, in a positive way): ≃ **there's a black sheep in every flock ⟨family⟩; there's one in every crowd ⟨family etc⟩; there's a ⟨one⟩ rotten ⟨bad⟩ apple (in every barrel); there's always one bad apple; there's always one.**

«Даже и коммунисты — и те перегрызлись между собой». — «Не клевещите, Марченко! Коммунисты — в едином строю!» — «А китайцы? Албанцы? А раскол во многих компартиях?» — «Что китайцы! В семье не без урода» (Марченко 1). "Even the communists have fallen out among themselves." "Don't speak such slander, Marchenko! Communists form a united front." "What about the Chinese? And the Albanians? And the splits in all sorts of communist parties?" "What about the Chinese! There's a black sheep in every family" (1a). ♦ Говорят, что многие известные люди откликнулись на предложение газеты дать в печати достойную отповедь этому отщепенцу... Но в семье, как говорится, не без урода. Говорят, что один известный деятель... позволил себе усомниться (Войнович 4). They say that many well-known people responded to the newspaper's offer to give this turncoat the rebukes he deserved in print....But, as the saying goes, there's always one bad apple. There was talk that a certain well-known figure...permitted himself to doubt (4a).

C-117 • КРАПИ́ВНОЕ СЕ́МЯ obs, derog [NP; often refers to a group; fixed WO] an inferior, corrupt bureaucrat or group of bureaucrats: **pettifogger(s); shyster(s); pack of shysters.**

[Попугайчиков:] Ну ты, гнида, где расписаться? [Ванечка (подаёт ему перо):] Вот-с вам, Флегонт Егорыч, — вот и пёрышко — мы вам, сударь, в лучшем виде, Флегонт Егорыч-с! Сделайте милость... Флегонт Егорыч. [Попугайчиков:] Ишь, крапивное семя!.. (Сухово-Кобылин 3). [P.:] Well, nit, where do I sign? [V. (handing him a pen):] Here you are, Flegont Egorych, Sir—Here's a pen. Everything'll be just fine, Sir! Be so kind...Flegont Egorych.... [P.:] There, you pack of shysters! (3a).

C-118 • СМОТРЕ́ТЬ СЕНТЯБРЁМ obsoles, coll, humor [VP; subj: human] to look sullen, morose, unhappy: X смотрит сентябрём ≃ **X has a long face on; X looks glum ⟨down in the mouth, down in the dumps⟩.**

C-119 • ПО СЕ́НЬКЕ (И) ША́ПКА [saying] what the person in question receives or has received is appropriate, fair, and he does not deserve better: ≃ **he ⟨she etc⟩ got his ⟨her etc⟩ just deserts; he ⟨she etc⟩ got (just) what he ⟨she etc⟩ deserved; it serves him ⟨her etc⟩ right.**

C-120 • ПОД СЕ́НЬЮ lit [PrepP; Invar; the resulting PrepP is adv] **1. ~** чего under the cover of sth.: **in the shadow ⟨shade⟩ of; in ⟨under, inside⟩ the shelter of.**

Дорога идёт извиваясь между кустарниками, опускаясь в небольшие овраги, где протекают шумные ручьи под сенью высоких трав... (Лермонтов 1). ...The road winds through patches of scrub and drops into small ravines where roaring streams flow in the shade of tall grass (1c). ♦ Как хорошо, как спокойно ей здесь [в женском монастыре], под сенью этих мирных стен!.. Она готова по целым дням болтать с молодыми монашками... (Салтыков-Щедрин 2). How wonderful everything was there [in the nunnery], inside the shelter of those peaceful walls!...She was ready to go on talking forever with the young nuns (2a).

2. ~ *кого-чего obs* under the patronage of s.o., protected by s.o. or sth.: **under the protection of (s.o. ⟨sth.⟩); under (s.o.'s) care.**

С-121 • БОЛЬШО́ГО СЕ́РДЦА ⟨БОЛЬШО́Й ДУШИ́⟩ человек [NP$_{gen}$; these forms only; nonagreeing modif; fixed WO] (a person who is) responsive to the needs, troubles of others, sincere, giving: **(have) a big heart; (be) bighearted; (a man ⟨a woman⟩) with a big heart.**

«...Воробьянинов, Ипполит Матвеевич, батюшка ваш, царство ему небесное, большой души был человек...» (Ильф и Петров 1). "...Vorobyaninov, Ippolit Matveyevich, your father, God rest his soul, was a man with a big heart..." (1a).

С-122 • ВЫРЫВА́ТЬ/ВЫ́РВАТЬ ИЗ СЕ́РДЦА ⟨ИЗ ДУШИ́⟩ *кого-что lit* [VP; subj: human] to force o.s. to make an emotional break with s.o. or sth. dear to one's heart: X вырвал Y-а из сердца ≃ **X wrenched ⟨ripped, tore etc⟩ Y out of X's heart.**

С-123 • ОТ ВСЕГО́ СЕ́РДЦА желать *кому чего* or чтобы..., благодарить *кого*, поздравлять *кого*, сочувствовать *кому*, советовать *кому* и т. п. [PrepP; Invar; adv or, rare, nonagreeing modif; fixed WO] in a sincere, enthusiastic, completely frank manner: **(thank s.o. ⟨congratulate s.o., wish s.o. sth. etc⟩) from the (very) bottom of one's heart; (thank s.o. ⟨wish s.o. sth., empathize with s.o., rejoice etc⟩) with all one's heart (and soul); (one's congratulations ⟨thanks etc⟩ come) straight ⟨right⟩ from the heart; [as modif] heartfelt (thanks ⟨wishes etc⟩).**

«Мы действительно должны помогать немцам...от всего сердца!..» (Эренбург 4). "We really must help the Germans...with all our heart and soul!" (4a). ♦ Несомненно, Хемингуэй с его критикой богатых, с его любовью от всего сердца к бедным, с его органическим непризнанием расизма является одним из передовых писателей Америки (Олеша 3). Undoubtedly Hemingway, with his criticism of the rich, his heartfelt love for the poor, and his organic rejection of racism, is one of America's leading writers (3a).

С-124 • ОТ ДО́БРОГО СЕ́РДЦА [PrepP; Invar; adv; fixed WO] with good motives: **with good ⟨the best (of)⟩ intentions; mean(ing) well; with ⟨having⟩ s.o.'s best interests at heart.**

[Городничий:] А вот вам, Лука Лукич, так, как смотрителю учебных заведений, нужно позаботиться особенно насчёт учителей... Один из них... никак не может обойтись, чтобы, взошедши на кафедру, не сделать гримасу... [Лука Лукич:] Вот ещё на днях, когда зашёл было в класс наш предводитель, он скроил такую рожу, какой я никогда ещё не видывал. Он-то её сделал от доброго сердца, а мне выговор: зачем вольнодумные мысли внушаются юношеству (Гоголь 4). [Mayor:] It is you, my dear Khlopov, who, as Inspector of Schools, must keep an eye on the teachers....One of them...always makes faces when he goes to his desk.... [L.L.:] Only the other day when our marshal of nobility came into the classroom he made a face the like of which I never saw before! He did it with the best intentions, but I was reprimanded: why do I permit the boys' minds to be corrupted by godless ideas? (4c).

С-125 • ОТ ЧИ́СТОГО СЕ́РДЦА [PrepP; Invar; adv or, less often, subj-compl with быть$_ø$ (subj: abstr); fixed WO] **1.** ~ поздравлять *кого*, желать *кому* (*чего* or чтобы...), жалеть *кого*, сочувствовать *кому*, смеяться и т. п. (expressing one's

feelings, emotions) absolutely sincerely: **(congratulate s.o. ⟨wish s.o. sth. etc⟩) right ⟨straight⟩ from the heart; (congratulate s.o. ⟨wish s.o. sth. etc⟩) from the bottom of one's heart; (wish s.o. sth. ⟨pity s.o. etc⟩) with all one's heart; (wish s.o. sth. ⟨sympathize with s.o. etc⟩) wholeheartedly; (laugh) heartily; (do sth.) with a pure heart; (a wish ⟨one's laughter etc⟩ is) perfectly genuine; [of sympathy only] express one's heartfelt sympathy for s.o.**

[Суходолов:] Как мальчик, от чистого сердца я и сказал ей, что пришёл без всякого дела, ничего мне не надо, ни за чем (Погодин 1). [S.:] Like a little boy, I told her straight from my heart that I had come on no business at all, I didn't need anything, I had come for *no special reason* (1a). ♦ Марья Ивановна так просто рассказала моим родителям о странном знакомстве моём с Пугачёвым, что оно не только не беспокоило их, но ещё заставляло часто смеяться от чистого сердца (Пушкин 2). Maria Ivanovna had related my strange acquaintance with Pugachev so innocently that it not only did not worry my parents, but even made them laugh heartily (2a). ♦ «Мой идеал — войти в церковь и поставить свечу от чистого сердца, ей-богу так. Тогда предел моим страданиям» (Достоевский 2). "My ideal is to go into a church and light a candle with a pure heart—by God, it's true. That would put an end to my sufferings" (2a). ♦ «Я вспомнил случай... Случай на одном юбилее... Отмечали какое-то „летие" одного старого, доброго, хорошего художника. Его все любили. По очереди подымались на трибуну, читали адреса, говорили речи, обнимали старика, целовали. И, ей-Богу, всё это было от чистого сердца» (Некрасов 1). "I remember one case....It occurred at an anniversary celebration....It was in honor of an old, kindhearted, good artist. Everyone liked him. One after another these people climbed up onto the platform, read out their congratulations, made their speeches, embraced and kissed the old man. And, by God, all this was perfectly genuine" (1a).

2. ~ советовать *кому*, предлагать *кому* (*что, что сделать*), дарить *кому что* и т. п. with the best motives, for s.o.'s benefit: **(give s.o. advice ⟨offer s.o. sth., give s.o. sth. etc⟩) from ⟨out of⟩ the (sheer) goodness of one's heart; (s.o.'s advice ⟨offer, gift etc⟩ is ⟨comes⟩) right ⟨straight⟩ from the heart; (give s.o. advice etc) having s.o.'s (best) interests at heart; [in refer. to giving s.o. unwelcome advice that will ultimately benefit him] (tell s.o. to do sth.) for his own good.**

Искренне желая мне помочь, он [секретарь сельского райкома] предложил мне переделать конец повести... Его советы были от чистого сердца... (Войнович 1). Sincerely wishing to help me, he [the secretary of a rural district committee] proposed that I rewrite the ending [of the novella]....His advice came from the goodness of his heart... (1a). ♦ «Езжай-ка ты поскорей домой... Это я тебе — от чистого сердца. Понятно? В наши дела незачем вам мешаться. Понял?» (Шолохов 5). "You'd better go home as soon as you can....I mean it for your own good. Understand? It's no use meddling in our affairs. Get me?" (5a).

С-126 • ОТЛЕГЛО́ ОТ СЕ́РДЦА ⟨НА СЕ́РДЦЕ, ОТ ДУШИ́, НА ДУШЕ́ *obsoles*⟩ *у кого coll*; **ОТОШЛО́ ОТ СЕ́РДЦА** *obs* [VP; impers] a calm settled over s.o., a feeling of alarm, anxiety left s.o.: у X-а отлегло от сердца ≃ **X was ⟨felt⟩ (greatly) relieved; X felt a sense of relief; X's heart lifted ⟨lightened, grew lighter⟩; it was a load off X's mind; a weight was lifted from X; a sense of inner calm came over X.**

Он [Обломов] и не глядя видел, как Ольга встала с своего места и пошла в другой угол. У него отлегло от сердца (Гончаров 1). He [Oblomov] could see without looking that Olga had got up from her seat and walked to another end of the room. He felt greatly relieved (1a). ♦ «Ребята, — сказал я... — сейчас капитан Курасов проговорился, кто нас предаёт. Это последний человек, и фамилия его стоит последней в нашем списке»... Все молчали. Я посмотрел на Яхонтова... Наконец, Генка Денисов спросил, явно волнуясь: «Яшка, это правда?» Все замерли… «Правда», – тихо ответил Яшка, и у меня отлегло от сердца (Войнович 5). "Hey, guys," I said.…"Captain Kurasov just let slip who's been squealing on us. He's just about the lowest thing you could imagine and his name is just about the lowest on the list at roll call.".…No one said a word. I looked over at Yakhontov.…Finally, Genka Denisov, clearly upset, asked: "Yashka, is it true?" Everyone froze.… "It's true," answered Yashka softly, and I felt a sense of relief (5a). ♦ Катя заулыбалась, глядя на Танаку, и у меня почему-то немного отлегло от души с его приходом (Аксёнов 1). Looking at Tanaka, Katya began to smile, and for some reason my heart lifted a little with his arrival (1a). ♦ «Владимир Николаевич, как вы думаете о себе, вы советский человек?» У меня немного отлегло от сердца. Если они ещё не решили, советский я или не советский, значит, может, и расстреляют не сразу (Войнович 1). "Do you consider yourself a good Soviet, Vladimir Nikolaevich?" My heart lightened a little. If they hadn't decided yet whether I was a good Soviet or not, that meant they might not put me in front of a firing squad right away (1a). ♦ Когда прошение было прочитано и закрестовано, то у всех словно отлегло от сердца (Салтыков-Щедрин 1). When the petition had been read and marked with Xs, they all felt as if a weight had been lifted from them (1a).

C-127 • ОТРЫВА́ТЬ/ОТОРВА́ТЬ ОТ СЕ́РДЦА [VP; subj: human] 1. ~ что to force o.s. to part with, give up sth. dear to one: X оторвал Y от сердца ≃ X ripped ⟨tore⟩ Y from X's heart.

[Ребров] трамваем поехал на Башиловку. Нужно было взять несколько книг, которые давно уже оторвал от сердца, мысленно свыкся: продать (Трифонов 1). …He [Rebrov] set off by streetcar to Bashilov Street. He needed to pick up some books which he was planning to sell, having torn them from his heart long ago and already adjusted himself to their absence (1a).

2. ~ кого to break one's emotional ties to s.o.: X оторвал Y-а от сердца ≃ X tore ⟨shut⟩ Y out of X's heart; X closed his heart to Y.

«…Я, Ксюша, всё никак тебя от сердца оторвать не могу… Сам я наполовину седой сделался, сколько годов промеж нами пропастью легли… А всё думается о тебе» (Шолохов 4). "…I still can't tear you out of my heart, love.…I'm half grey, we've been parted for so many years now.…But I still think of you" (4a).

C-128 • В СЕРДЦА́Х сказать, крикнуть, швырнуть что, схватить что, толкнуть кого-что и т. п. coll; С СЕ́РД-ЦЕМ obsoles [PrepP; these forms only; usu. adv; more often used with pfv past verbs] (to say sth., shout, hurl sth., grab sth., push s.o. or sth. etc) in an outburst of anger: in a fit of anger ⟨temper⟩; angrily; heatedly; in one's anger; furiously; [in limited contexts] vehemently; ‖ сказать ⟨ответить и т. п.⟩ в сердцах ≃ [in limited contexts] snap (at s.o.).

«…Не говорил ли [Дмитрий Фёдорович] когда при вас… или как-нибудь мельком, или в раздражении, – хватил вдруг Николай Парфёнович, – что намерен посягнуть на жизнь своего отца?» – …«Несколько раз поминал, всегда в сердцах» (Достоевский 1). "…Did he [Dmitri Fyodorovich] ever say before you…somehow in passing, or in irritation," Nikolai Parfenovich suddenly struck, "that he intended to make an attempt on his father's life?"…"He mentioned it several times, always in a fit of anger" (1a). ♦ Мужики орали во всю глотку, в сердцах швыряли на пол пачки билетиков… (Аксёнов 6). Shouting at the top of their lungs, the men angrily threw down wads of betting slips onto the floor… (6a). ♦ «…Зачем же вы мне этого не объявили прежде? Зачем из пустяков держали?» – сказал с сердцем Чичиков (Гоголь 3). "…Why didn't you tell me about that before? Why did you keep me here for nothing?" Chichikov exclaimed heatedly (3d). ♦ …[Верблюд Каранар] выражал своё недовольство, – свирепо разевая зубатую пасть, вопил время от времени… Едигей в сердцах накричал на Каранара: «Ты чего орёшь?..» (Айтматов 2). …He [the camel Karanar] was showing his displeasure by baring his teeth and now and again howling.…In his anger,

Yedigei…shouted at Karanar, "What are you making all that din for?…" (2a). ♦ «Сегодня тебя ждать?» – «Я позвоню». – «Завтра днём?» – «Ч-что ты, Г-галочка!» – «До свиданья, – сказала она, – всего тебе хорошего». Садчиков в сердцах швырнул трубку на рычаг и вышел из комнаты, хлопнув дверью (Семёнов 1). "Shall I wait up for you tonight?" "I'll give you a ring." "Tomorrow afternoon?" "C-come on now, Galya!" "Goodbye," she said, "and the best of luck to you." Sadchikov threw the receiver furiously on to its rest and left the room, slamming the door behind him (1a). ♦ Лизка сказала с сердцем: «Загребайте отсюда. Всё равно и это сено когда-нибудь надо сгребать» (Абрамов 1). Lizka snapped, "Start raking over here. This hay will have to be gathered up sometime anyway" (1a).

C-129 • БОЛЬШО́Е СЕ́РДЦЕ (у кого) [NP; sing only; fixed WO] a person (by extension a people) with the capacity to experience intense feeling, empathy, show kindness: (have) a big heart; (a man ⟨a woman⟩) with a big heart; (be) bighearted.

C-130 • ВЫМЕЩА́ТЬ/ВЫ́МЕСТИТЬ СЕ́РДЦЕ на ком-чём [VP; subj: human] to let out one's anger by shouting at, hurting etc an innocent person (or animal), or by striking, breaking etc some object: X выместил сердце на Y-е ≃ X vented his anger ⟨resentment⟩ on Y; X took it ⟨his anger⟩ out on Y.

Всё своё горькое сердце вымещала она [Андронова] на курах и петухах, ради которых, впрочем, готова была работать круглые сутки (Гинзбург 2). She [Andronova] vented all her resentment on the hens and cocks, but was none the less ready to work for them right around the clock (2a).

C-131 • ДЕРЖА́ТЬ ⟨ИМЕ́ТЬ⟩ СЕ́РДЦЕ на кого substand [VP; subj: human] to have or harbor a feeling of dislike, ill will toward s.o. (for sth. bad that he has said or done): X держал сердце на Y-а ≃ X bore ⟨nursed⟩ a grudge against Y; X held something ⟨it⟩ against Y; X had hard feelings toward Y; X was angry with ⟨at⟩ Y.

Дуняшка, провожая его [Григория] на новое жительство, всплакнула. «Братушка, не держите на меня сердца, я перед вами не виноватая», – сказала она, умоляюще глядя на брата (Шолохов 5). Dunyashka wept when she saw him [Grigory] off to his new home. "Don't hold it against me, brother. It's not my fault," she said, looking up at him imploringly (5a). ♦ «Не держи на меня сердца, я сам по себе хочу, чтобы как у людей: кто как, а я навоевался» (Максимов 3). "Don't be angry with me, I want to go on my own way, like everyone else. I, for one, have had my fill of fighting" (3a).

C-132 • ОТДАВА́ТЬ/ОТДА́ТЬ СЕ́РДЦЕ кому elev [VP; subj: human, usu. female; usu. pfv] to love or fall in love with s.o.: X отдала сердце Y-у ≃ X gave ⟨lost⟩ her heart to Y.

Почувствовав в ней [богатой госпоже] любовь великую, сделал он ей изъяснение в любви и начал склонять её выйти за него замуж. Но она отдала уже своё сердце другому, одному знатному не малого чина военному… (Достоевский 1). Feeling great love for her [the wealthy lady], he made her a declaration of his love, and tried to persuade her to marry him. But she had already given her heart to another man, an officer of noble birth and high rank… (1a).

C-133 • ОТКРЫВА́ТЬ/ОТКРЫ́ТЬ СЕ́РДЦЕ (кому) lit [VP; subj: human] 1. to make a declaration of love (to s.o.): X открыл сердце женщине Y ≃ X opened his heart to Y; X declared his love to Y.

[Подколёсин:] Да зачем же мне оставаться здесь? Ведь я всё уже сказал, что следует. [Кочкарёв:] Стало быть, сердце ей ты уже открыл? (Гоголь 1). [P.:] But why should I stay here? I've already said everything that was necessary. [K.:] You mean, you've already opened your heart to her? (1a).

2. to reveal openly one's emotions and innermost thoughts: X открыл сердце Y-у ≃ **X opened his heart ⟨his soul⟩ to Y; X bared his soul to Y.**

С-134 • ПОКОРЯ́ТЬ/ПОКОРИ́ТЬ СЕ́РДЦЕ *чьё, кого* [VP; subj: usu. human] to infatuate s.o., cause s.o. to fall in love with one: X покорил сердце Y-а ≃ **X won Y's heart; X won the affection of Y; X won Y over.**

[extended usage] Шарик-пёс обладал каким-то секретом покорять сердца людей (Булгаков 11). The dog Sharik possessed some secret which enabled him to win people's hearts (11b).

С-135 • СЕ́РДЦЕ ЗАКА́ТЫВАЕТСЯ/ЗАКАТИ́ЛОСЬ *у кого (от чего) obs* [VP$_{subj}$; usu. pfv] s.o. feels as if his heart has momentarily stopped beating (from extreme fear): у X-а сердце закатилось ≃ **X's heart skipped ⟨missed⟩ a beat; X's heart stood still.**

С-136 • СЕ́РДЦЕ ЗАМИРА́ЕТ/ЗА́МЕРЛО ⟨ЁКАЕТ/ЁКНУЛО *coll*⟩ *(у кого)*; ДУША́ ЗАМИРА́ЕТ/ЗА́МЕРЛА; ДУХ ЗАМИРА́ЕТ/ЗА́МЕР [VP$_{subj}$] s.o. feels as if his heart has momentarily stopped beating (from fear, alarm, sudden foreboding, surprise, a sudden thrill etc): у X-а замерло сердце ≃ **X's heart missed ⟨skipped⟩ a beat; X's heart stood still.**

Что-то необъяснимое есть в этой реке: всякий раз, когда взгляд встречает её водную поверхность, замирает сердце (Аллилуева 2). There is about this river something inexplicable: every time the eye meets its watery surface, the heart skips a beat (2a). ♦ Они [мой старик и его знакомый] долго оставались в кухне, и я сильно волновался от неизвестности. Но вот они вышли из кухни и стали подходить ко мне, и сердце у меня замерло (Искандер 3). They [my old man and his acquaintance] stayed in the kitchen a long time, and the uncertainty made me violently nervous. But now they came out of the kitchen and started over to me, and my heart stood still (3a).

С-137 • СЕ́РДЦЕ ЗАХО́ДИТСЯ/ЗАШЛО́СЬ *(у кого) coll* [VP$_{subj}$] s.o. feels as if his heart has stopped beating entirely (from nervousness, fear, ecstasy etc): у X-а сердце зашлось ≃ **X's heart stood still; X's heart almost stopped beating.**

С-138 • СЕ́РДЦЕ КРО́ВЬЮ ОБЛИВА́ЕТСЯ/ОБЛИ-ЛО́СЬ *чьё, у кого (от чего)* [VP$_{subj}$; usu. impfv] s.o. feels intense anxiety, deep emotional pain etc (often in response to another's suffering): у X-а сердце кровью обливается ≃ **X's heart bleeds (for person Y); it ⟨sth.⟩ makes X's heart bleed; X's heart goes out (to person Y).**

«Я стою у окна и смотрю на это пепелище — и сердце моё обливается кровью» (Битов 2). "I stand by the window and look at these ashes—and my heart bleeds" (2a). ♦ «Может, наконец, воевать начнём, а то не война, а сплошные поддавки, только людей гробим. И каких людей!.. Сердце кровью обливается!» (Максимов 1). "Maybe we're really going to start fighting at last. So far we seem to have been playing to lose—only burying people. And what people!...It makes your heart bleed!" (1a).

С-139 • СЕ́РДЦЕ НЕ КА́МЕНЬ [saying] (one fulfills another's request, does sth. to make another happy, makes concessions to another etc because) despite one's reluctance to oblige s.o., one has feelings and cannot help but be responsive, compassionate: ≃ **a man's heart isn't made of stone; one doesn't have a heart of stone.**

«На днях...въезжает на санях во двор, по воде и грязи больной крестьянин... Отказываюсь принять. „Не взыщи, милый, перестал этим заниматься...“... „Помоги. Кожею скудаем [*regional* = болеем]. Помилосердствуй...“» Что де-

лать? Сердце не камень... „Раздевайся“» (Пастернак 1). "The other day...a sick peasant drove his sleigh into the yard through the mud and slush. I refused to examine him. 'I've given up practicing,' I said....'Help me. My skin is bad. Have pity on me....' What could I do? I don't have a heart of stone. I told him to undress" (1a).

С-140 • СЕ́РДЦЕ ОТХО́ДИТ/ОТОШЛО́ *(у кого)* [VP$_{subj}$] s.o. ceases to worry about or be irritated by sth.: сердце (у X-а) отошло ≃ **X calmed ⟨settled⟩ down.**

«Ночью то погладишь его [сынишку] сонного, то волосёнки на вихрах понюхаешь, и сердце отходит, становится мягче, а то ведь оно у меня закаменело от горя» (Шолохов 1). [context transl] "At night, I can stroke him [the little boy] while he's sleeping, I can smell his curls. It takes some of the pain out of my heart, makes it a bit softer. It had just about turned to stone, you know" (1c).

С-141 • СЕ́РДЦЕ ПА́ДАЕТ/УПА́ЛО ⟨ОБРЫ-ВА́ЕТСЯ/ОБОРВА́ЛОСЬ or ОБОРВАЛО́СЬ, ОТРЫ-ВА́ЕТСЯ/ОТОРВА́ЛОСЬ or ОТОРВАЛО́СЬ⟩ *у кого*; ОБОРВАЛО́СЬ ⟨ОТОРВАЛО́СЬ⟩ В СЕ́РДЦЕ ⟨В ГРУДИ́⟩ *у кого* [VP$_{subj}$, usu. pres or past (1st group); VP, impers, usu. past (2nd group)] s.o. feels as if his heart has momentarily stopped beating (from fear, alarm, sudden foreboding, disappointment etc): у X-а упало сердце ≃ **X's heart skipped ⟨missed⟩ a beat; X's heart jumped; (s.o. ⟨sth.⟩) nearly gave X heart failure;** [usu. in refer. to disappointment] **X's heart sank.**

«А вечером, только спать собралась, — звонок. Сердце оборвалось» (Чернёнок 2). "And that night, just when I was about to go to sleep, the phone rings. My heart jumped" (2a). ♦ «О Николае Васильевиче слышала?» — «Нет. А что?» — «Избран членом Украинской Академии наук». — «Фу! У меня уж сердце упало!» (Каверин 1). "You've heard about Nikolai Vasilyevich?" "No. What?" "He's been elected to the Ukrainian Academy of Sciences." "Well, now! You nearly gave me heart failure" (1a).

С-142 • СЕ́РДЦЕ *(чьё, у кого)* ⟨ДУША́ *(чья, у кого)*⟩ РАЗРЫВА́ЕТСЯ (НА ЧА́СТИ) *(от чего)*; СЕ́РДЦЕ ⟨ДУША́⟩ РВЁТСЯ НА ЧА́СТИ *coll* [VP$_{subj}$] s.o. feels deep emotional suffering (in empathy for another's pain, or in response to his own misfortune): у X-а сердце разрывается на части ≃ **X's heart is breaking (with pity ⟨compassion etc⟩); X's heart is breaking ⟨torn⟩ in two (with pity ⟨compassion etc⟩); X's heart aches (for s.o.); X's heart goes out to ⟨bleeds for⟩ s.o.**

«В тот день, когда ты так сурово уехал... сердце разрывалось на части» (Чернёнок 1). "That day when you left so angrily...my heart was breaking" (1a). ♦ «Тут у [меня] самого от жалости к ней сердце на части разрывается, а тут она с такими словами» (Шолохов 1). "My heart was already torn in two with pity for her, and then she goes and says a thing like that!" (1a).

С-143 • СКРЕПЯ́ СЕ́РДЦЕ *coll* [Verbal Adv; Invar; adv; fixed WO] with great unwillingness: **reluctantly; (much) against one's will; grudgingly; grit(ting) one's teeth;** [in limited contexts] **swallow(ing) one's objections.**

«Он делает это, скрепя сердце, преодолевая мучительные сомнения и колебания» (Каверин 1). "He does this reluctantly, overcoming doubts and hesitations which torment him" (1a). ♦ ...В начале зимы мужики скрепя сердце повезли картофель в центральные ямы (Герцен 1). ...At the beginning of winter the peasants, much against their will, took the potatoes to the central pits (1a). ♦ «Без тебя не будет никаких происшествий, а надо, чтобы были происшествия. Вот и служу скрепя сердце, чтобы были происшествия, и творю неразумное по приказу» (Достоевский 2). "Without you there would be no events, and there must be events. And so I serve grudgingly, for the sake of events, and I do the unreasonable on orders" (2a).

< «Скрепя» is the old form of the short active participle of the verb «скрепить»; the corresponding modern form is the perfective verbal adverb «скрепив».

C-144 • НОСИ́ТЬ ПОД СЕ́РДЦЕМ *кого obs* [VP; subj: human, female] to be pregnant: X носила Y-а ⟨ребёнка⟩ под сердцем ≃ **X carried Y ⟨a child⟩ under her heart; X was with child.**

На шестом месяце, когда скрывать беременность было уже нельзя, Аксинья призналась Григорию. Она скрывала, боясь, что Григорий не поверит в то, что его ребёнка носит она под сердцем… (Шолохов 2). Aksinya told Grigory of her pregnancy only in her sixth month, when it could no longer be concealed. She had kept it from him for fear that he would not believe it was his child she was carrying under her heart (2a).

C-145 • С ЛЁГКИМ СЕ́РДЦЕМ; С ЛЁГКОЙ ДУШО́Й [PrepP; these forms only; usu. adv; fixed WO] feeling good, relieved, with a positive attitude etc: **with a light heart; lightheartedly.**

«Уж кого-кого, а тебя на свадьбу позову». Григорий шутливо хлопнул сестру по плечу и с лёгким сердцем пошёл с родного двора (Шолохов 5). "Don't worry, I'll invite you to the wedding if I invite anyone!" Grigory patted his sister's shoulder jokingly and left his father's house with a light heart (5a). ♦ «…Новому человеку позволительно стать человеко-богом.» – и, уж конечно, в новом чине, с лёгким сердцем перескочить всякую прежнюю нравственную преграду прежнего раба-человека, если оно понадобится» (Достоевский 2). "…The new man is allowed to become a man-god…and of course, in this new rank, to jump lightheartedly over any former moral obstacle of the former slave-man, if need be" (2a).

C-146 • С ТЯЖЁЛЫМ СЕ́РДЦЕМ [PrepP; Invar; usu. adv] in a depressed state, feeling unhappy, upset: **with a heavy heart.**

Оформляю, плачу в кассу что положено и возвращаюсь домой с тяжёлым сердцем: дело попало в плохие руки, и виноват я, никто другой (Рыбаков 1). I signed the papers, paid the bill and went home with a heavy heart. The case had got into the wrong hands, and nobody was to blame but myself (1a).

C-147 • С УПА́ВШИМ СЕ́РДЦЕМ [PrepP; Invar; adv; fixed WO] in a very frightened, alarmed state: **with one's heart in one's mouth ⟨boots⟩; overcome by fear.**

C-148 • С ЧИ́СТЫМ СЕ́РДЦЕМ [PrepP; Invar; adv; fixed WO] with complete candor or sincerity, with good intentions: **with an open ⟨a sincere⟩ heart.**

C-149 • ПРИНИМА́ТЬ/ПРИНЯ́ТЬ (БЛИ́ЗКО) К СЕ́РДЦУ *что* [VP; subj: human; if imper, only neg impfv] to react to sth. with great sensitivity, be deeply affected by sth. (usu. used in situations when one sympathizes deeply with another's misfortune or reacts to sth. more intensely than is warranted): X принимает Y (близко) к сердцу ≃ **X takes Y (right ⟨very much etc⟩) to heart.**

«Я бы очень желал не так живо чувствовать и не так близко принимать к сердцу всё, что ни случается» (Гоголь 3). "I wish I did not feel so keenly and did not take everything that happens so much to heart" (3a). ♦ Голубева этот разговор страшно заинтересовал. И он принял его близко к сердцу (Войнович 2). Golubev found this conversation terribly interesting. And he took it right to heart (2a).

C-150 • СЕ́РДЦУ НЕ ПРИКА́ЖЕШЬ [saying] you cannot force yourself to fall in or out of love with s.o.: ≃ **the heart has a will of its own; one can't tell one's heart what to feel; the heart has reasons that reason does not understand.**

«…О Мишке Кошевом с нонешнего [*regional* = нынешнего] дня и думать позабудь»… – «Вы, братушка, знаете? Сердцу не прикажешь!» (Шолохов 5). "…Forget Mishka Koshevoi and never think of him again."…"Surely you should know, brother? We can't tell our hearts what to feel!" (5a).

C-151 • ЗОЛОТА́Я СЕРЕДИ́НА [NP; sing only; fixed WO] a middle position, policy etc that falls between extremes: **the golden mean; happy medium.**

«Есть золотое правило: не лезь в первые, не оставайся последним. Потому что спереди бьют в лоб, а сзади пинают в крестец. Спокойнее всего посередине. Потому и называется – золотая середина» (Копелев 1). "There's a golden rule: don't push to be first and don't be left last. Because in front they hit you in the forehead and behind they kick you in the ass. It's best in the middle. That's why they call it the golden mean" (1a).

< Loan translation of the Latin *aurea mediocritas*, used by Horace (65–8 B.C.).

C-152 • СЕРЕДИ́НКА НА ПОЛОВИ́НКУ ⟨НА ПОЛОВИ́НКЕ⟩; СЕРЕДИ́НА НА ПОЛОВИ́НУ ⟨НА ПОЛОВИ́НЕ⟩; СЕРЁДКА НА ПОЛОВИ́НКУ ⟨НА ПОЛОВИ́НКЕ, НА ПОЛОВИ́НУ, НА ПОЛОВИ́НЕ⟩ *all coll* [NP; these forms only; fixed WO] **1.** [usu. subj-compl with copula (subj: any noun)] a person (a thing etc) does not possess the distinguishing characteristics of either of the two (expressed or implied) extremes, is somewhere in the middle: [when the two extremes are specified by the preceding context] **neither this nor that; neither one nor the other; something ⟨somewhere⟩ in between;** [when used in refer. to a qualitative evaluation] **ordinary; just average; middling; run-of-the-mill; commonplace.**

Тебе могут говорить разное, умное и глупое и серёдка на половинку… (Аксёнов 1). People may tell you different things, wise and foolish and neither one nor the other… (1a). ♦ [Таня:] Думаете, очень из себя хороши? [Григорий:] А что, неприятен? [Таня:] Так, ни приятен, ни неприятен, а серёдка на половину (Толстой 3). [T.:] Think you're beautiful, do you? [G.:] What—ugly, am I? [T.:] Not ugly. Not handsome. Just average (3b).

2. [adv] neither poorly nor well, in a mediocre fashion: **(only) so-so; not great; fair to middling.**

Экзамены Саша сдал серединка на половинку. Sasha did only so-so on his exams.

C-153 • НА ПО́ЛНОМ СЕРЬЁЗЕ *говорить, отвечать, спрашивать и т. п. highly coll* [PrepP; these forms only; adv] (to speak, answer, ask sth. etc) completely seriously, without joking: **in all seriousness;** [equivalents incorporate the verb of speaking] **be dead ⟨totally⟩ serious;** [in limited contexts] **mean business; mean it.**

Я тебе говорю на полном серьёзе: не связывайся с этими спекулянтами, это может плохо кончиться. I'm dead serious: don't get mixed up with those speculators—you could end up in a lot of trouble.

C-154 • ВА́ША СЕСТРА́ *coll* [NP; sing only; subj or obj; fixed WO] (you and) women similar to you: **(all) you women ⟨girls, gals⟩; (you and) women ⟨girls, gals⟩ like you; (you and) the likes of you;** [in limited contexts] **your brand ⟨type, sort etc⟩ of woman.**

[Никита:] Эх! С вашей сестрой разговаривать, никаких резонов не понимают; уйди, говорю, до худа доведёшь (Толстой 1). [N.:] No use talking with girls like you; they won't listen to reason. Clear out, I tell you, or you'll make me do something bad (1b).

C-155 • НА́ША СЕСТРА́ *coll* [NP; sing only; subj or obj; fixed WO] (we or I and) women similar to us or me: **we women; (all) us**

women ⟨**girls, gals**⟩; women ⟨**girls, gals**⟩ **like us** ⟨**me**⟩; **the likes of us**; [in limited contexts] **our brand** ⟨**type, sort** etc⟩ **of woman**.

[Варвара:] ...Её [калитку] маменька запирает на замок, а ключ прячет. Я его унесла, а ей подложила другой, чтоб не заметила. На, вот... *(Подаёт ключ.)* Если увижу [Бориса], так скажу, чтоб приходил к калитке... [Катерина:] Не надо! Не надо!.. Вот так-то и гибнет наша сестра-то (Островский 6). [V.:] ...Mama keeps it [the gate] locked and hides the key away, but I found it and put another in its place so she wouldn't notice. Here it is, the key to the gate.... *(Holds it out.)* If I see him [Boris] I will tell him to come to the gate.... [K.:] I don't want it! Take it away! That's how we women come to a bad end (6b). ♦ [Бакченин:] Не помнишь наши первые встречи? Нашу последнюю встречу? [Шеметова:] Фронтовой эпизод. Мало ли что случается с нашей сестрой (Панова 1). [B.:] Don't you remember when we were first together? The last time we met? [Sh.:] A wartime story. Lots of things happen to us women (1a).

C-156 • **ВСЕМ СЁСТРА́М ПО СЕРЬГА́М** [saying] (usu. in refer. to reprimands, criticism etc) absolutely everyone gets something: ≃ **no one is left out** ⟨**spared**⟩; **everyone gets what he deserves** ⟨**what is coming to him**⟩; [in limited contexts] **he** ⟨**she** etc⟩ **gives everyone a hard time** ⟨**a piece of his/her mind, a beating** etc⟩.

[author's usage] И вот кабы не Анфиса Петровна — ставь крест на всей затее с сенокосом. А Анфиса Петровна всем по серьге выдала (Абрамов 1). So if it hadn't been for Anfisa Petrovna, he [Mikhail] could have kissed the whole harvest idea goodbye. But Anfisa Petrovna had given them all a piece of her mind (1a).

C-157 • **ПОЙМА́ТЬ В СВОЙ СЕ́ТИ** *кого obsoles* [VP; subj: human, usu. female] to make s.o. fall in love with one: X поймала Y-а в свои сети ≃ **X snared** ⟨**hooked, roped in** etc⟩ **Y**.

C-158 • **ПОПАДА́ТЬ(СЯ)/ПОПА́СТЬ(СЯ) В СЕ́ТИ** *(чьи, кого* или *чего) coll* [VP; subj: human; usu. pfv] **1.** to fall in love with s.o., be captivated by s.o., give in to s.o.'s charm: X попал в сети Y-а ≃ **X fell for Y**; **X fell under Y's spell**.

Не буду скрывать, что я незаметно попал в небрежные сети его [Тенгиза] обаяния (Искандер 3). I must admit that without noticing it I fell under the spell of his [Tengiz's] offhand charm (3a).

2. to be drawn into sth. reprehensible or illegal (usu. as a result of another's skillful exploitation of one's weaknesses): X попал в сети Y-а ≃ **X fell into** ⟨**got caught in**⟩ **Y's web** ⟨**trap**⟩.

Директор магазина и его окружение — это шайка мошенников, и очень жаль, что вы попали в их сети. The store manager and his people are a bunch of crooks—too bad you've fallen into their web.

C-159 • **РАССТАВЛЯ́ТЬ/РАССТА́ВИТЬ СЕ́ТИ** *кому coll* [VP; subj: human] **1.** [subj: usu. female] to try to make s.o. fall in love with one: X расставила сети Y-у ≃ **X tried to snare** ⟨**hook, rope in** etc⟩ **Y**.

2. to try to hinder or ruin s.o. by using cunning or ruses: X расставляет Y-у сети ≃ **X is setting a trap for Y**; **X is spinning a web for** ⟨**to snare**⟩ **Y**; **X is spreading a net for** ⟨**to snare**⟩ **Y**; **X is digging a pit** ⟨**a hole**⟩ **for Y to fall into**.

C-160 • **УКАТА́ЛИ** ⟨**УХОДИ́ЛИ, УМЫ́КАЛИ**⟩ **СИ́ВКУ** ⟨**БУ́РКУ**⟩ **КРУТЫ́Е ГО́РКИ** [saying] a hard life, old age, and/or hardships have sapped a person's strength and made him weak, sick, or apathetic: ≃ **he** ⟨**she**⟩ **is not the man** ⟨**the woman**⟩ **he** ⟨**she**⟩ **used to be; the old gray mare ain't what she used to be**.

Боль в сердце становилась всё горячее. На лбу у него [Григория] выступила испарина. Он сошёл с крыльца, испуганно

прижимая к левой стороне груди ладонь, подумал: «Видно, укатали сивку крутые горки...» (Шолохов 5). The pain in his [Grigory's] heart had grown more intense. Perspiration broke out on his forehead. He walked down the steps, pressing his hand to his left side in fright and telling himself he was not the man he used to be (5a).

C-161 • **ВО́Т ГДЕ СИДИ́Т** *у кого coll* [VP; subj: any noun; pres only; fixed WO] a person (a situation etc) has caused s.o. so much irritation, annoyance, frustration etc that he cannot tolerate that person or situation any longer (usu. accompanied by a motion of the hand toward the neck): X у Y-а вот где сидит ≃ **Y has had it up to here** ⟨**with X**⟩; **Y has got X up to here; Y is fed up** ⟨**with X**⟩; **Y has had about all he can take** ⟨**stand**⟩ **of X**.

«Вот они где у меня сидят, эти интуристы!» — интимно пожаловался Коровьев... (Булгаков 9). "I can tell you I'm fed up with these foreign tourists," complained Koroviev confidentially (9b).

C-162 • **СИ́ДНЕМ** ⟨**СИДМЯ́** *obs*⟩ **СИДЕ́ТЬ** *coll* [VP; subj: human] **1.** to spend all one's time in a seated position because one is physically unable to walk: X сиднем сидит ≃ **X just** ⟨**only**⟩ **sits**.

2. to spend a long uninterrupted period of time seated while doing sth. that requires one to sit (i.e., writing, reading etc): X сиднем сидит ≃ **X sits (for hours** ⟨**days** etc⟩ **on end) (doing sth.)**.

3. *usu. disapprov* to sit and be inactive when some action is expected or required of one: X сиднем сидит ≃ **X just sits (there** ⟨**here, around** etc⟩**) on his butt** ⟨**duff, backside** etc⟩; **X sits (there** ⟨**here** etc⟩**) like a bump on a log**.

...Удивил Лизку возчик, который сиднем сидел в стороне. Надрывайтесь, рвите, мужики, жилы, а мне и горюшка мало (Абрамов 1). Lizka was amazed to see the driver sitting on his backside, apart from the others. Bust your guts, boys, knock yourselves out! I could care less (1a).

4. *often disapprov* to have a physically inactive life style, lead a physically inactive life: X сиднем сидит ≃ **X sits around all day** ⟨**all the time** etc⟩; **X just sits around; X sits like a bump on a log; X sits around on his butt** ⟨**backside, duff** etc⟩ **(all the time)**.

5. to spend a long uninterrupted period of time in one place (usu. some room, building etc), not going out of or away from that place: X сиднем сидит в месте Y ≃ **X never leaves place Y; X has holed himself up in place Y; X stays put in place Y**.

C-163 • **СИ́КОСЬ-НА́КОСЬ** *highly coll* [AdvP; Invar; adv or subj-compl with copula (subj: usu. всё)] **1.** (of numerous disorderly lines made when writing, drawing, stitching etc) (to do sth., be done) in an irregular or disorderly fashion, (to go) unevenly, in different directions: **every which way**; [in limited contexts] **all askew; crisscrossing (in all directions)**.

2. (to do sth., sth. is done, everything is done) poorly, carelessly, not the way it should be done: **in a half-assed** ⟨**lousy, slipshod** etc⟩ **manner; (do) a half-assed job (of it); (do sth.) any which** ⟨**old**⟩ **way (not giving a damn how it turns out)**; ‖ делать всё ~ ≃ **make a mess of** ⟨**botch up, mess up, screw up** etc⟩ **everything one does**; ‖ всё ~ ≃ **what a (bloody** ⟨**rotten** etc⟩**) mess!; this is a** ⟨**one**⟩ **big mess**; [in limited contexts] **everything is at sixes and sevens**.

Что моему брату ни поручи, он всё делает сикось-накось. No matter what you ask my brother to do, he does a half-assed job of it.

C-164 • **ВЫБИВА́ТЬСЯ/ВЫ́БИТЬСЯ ИЗ СИЛ** [VP] **1.** [subj: human or animal] to get extremely tired, weak from work, intense physical exertion, or tension: X выбился из сил ≃ **X had no strength left; X's strength gave out** ⟨**was gone**⟩; **X was (all) worn-out; X was ready to drop**.

[Соня:] Я работаю одна, совсем из сил выбилась... (Чехов 3). [S.:] I'm the only one that works, and I have no strength left (3d). ♦ [Косуля], несмотря на две полученные пули, проволокла его [Адгура] по глубокому снегу метров десять, но тут выбилась из сил и рухнула (Искандер 3). ...In spite of the two bullets it had taken, it [the roebuck] dragged him [Adgur] ten meters through the deep snow, but then its strength gave out and it crashed to the ground (3a). ♦ Я взвалил тяжеленную корзину на плечо... и потопал. Уже выбился из сил, едва дойдя до Сирецкой (Кузнецов 1). I swung the heavy basket to my shoulder...and trudged off. My strength was gone by the time I reached Syretskaya Street (1a).

2. [subj: human; impfv only; usu. foll. by чтобы + infin] to apply all one's efforts toward attaining or accomplishing sth.: X выбивается из сил ≃ **X does his utmost; X goes all out; X knocks himself out;** [in limited contexts] **X goes out of his way; X bends over backward.**

«Мы выбиваемся из сил, чтоб всё шло как можно тише и глаже...» (Герцен 2). "We do our very utmost that everything shall go as quietly and smoothly as possible..." (2a). ♦ В купе Остап по-прежнему выбивался из сил, чтобы понравиться компании. И он достиг того, что студенты стали считать его своим (Ильф и Петров 2). In the compartment, Ostap continued to go all out to amuse the gathered company. He was finally accepted by the students as one of them (2a). ♦ «От тебя же никакого проку. Я одна из сил выбиваюсь, не могу ничего. Я для неё [дочери] нуль...» (Стругацкие 1). "You're no help. I'm knocking myself out all alone, and I can't get anywhere. To her [our daughter] I'm nothing, a zero..." (1a).

C-165 • ВЫ́ШЕ СИЛ *чьих* [PrepP; Invar; subj-compl with copula (subj: abstr)] doing sth. is beyond s.o.'s strength, impossible for s.o.: X выше Y-овых сил ≃ **X is too much (for Y) to bear; X is more than Y can handle ⟨take etc⟩.**

Совершенно бесспорно, что задача, которая была на меня возложена, оказалась выше моих сил (Богданов 1). It is patently evident that the task entrusted to me was more than I could handle (1a).

C-166 • ИЗ ПОСЛЕ́ДНИХ СИЛ *coll* [PrepP; Invar; adv; usu. used with impfv verbs; fixed WO] using whatever small amount of strength, power etc that remains (in s.o. or sth.): **with one's ⟨its⟩ last ounce ⟨bit⟩ of strength; with what is left of one's strength; with all (the strength) one has left.**

«Ветер, снег, не видать ничего. Машина воет, плачет, как живая. Из последних сил взбирается» (Айтматов 1). "The wind, the snow—you couldn't see a thing. The lorry howled and cried like it was alive. It inched forward with its last ounce of strength" (1b). ♦ Старик заколебался, кому же дать первому. Помедлив несколько томительных секунд, он вылил воду в скотское долблёное корыто... Пленные из последних сил бросились к корыту (Шолохов 4). The old man did not know who to give the first drink. After a few agonising seconds, he poured the water into the wooden cattle trough....With what was left of their strength, the prisoners threw themselves on it (4a). ♦ ...Стрельба и канонада не только не ослабевали, но усиливались до отчаянности, как человек, который, надрываясь, кричит из последних сил (Толстой 6). [context transl] ...The roar of cannons and musketry, far from abating, had increased furiously, like a man exerting himself to the utmost to put forth one final, desperate cry (6a).

C-167 • ИЗО ВСЕХ СИЛ [PrepP; Invar; adv (intensif); fixed WO] **1.** ~ трудиться, стараться, сопротивляться, сдерживаться и т. п. Also: **ИЗО ВСЕЙ СИ́ЛЫ** (of a person or, occas., an animal) (to work, try to do sth., resist, restrain o.s. etc) very intensely, with great force, effort etc; (of a natural phenomenon) (to manifest itself) to a maximum degree: **with all one's might ⟨strength⟩; as hard as one can; as best (as) one can; for all one is worth; trying one's hardest ⟨best⟩; doing one's utmost**

⟨**best**⟩; **giving it everything ⟨all⟩ one's got ⟨one has⟩; making every ⟨an all-out⟩ effort;** [in limited contexts] **with might and main; straining every muscle (in one's body);** [of a natural phenomenon] **full force.**

Мальчик изо всех сил стал вырываться из рук охотника... (Искандер 5). The little boy tried with all his might to break free from the hunter's grasp... (5a). ♦ Высокий белобровый австриец... почти в упор выстрелил в Григория с колена. Огонь свинца опалил щёку. Григорий повёл пикой, натягивая изо всей силы поводья (Шолохов 2). A tall fair-browed Austrian...fired almost point-blank at Grigory from a kneeling position. The heat of the molten lead scorched Grigory's cheek. He aimed his lance and reined in with all his strength (2a). ♦ Стук продолжался. Иван хотел было кинуться к окну; но что-то как бы вдруг связало ему ноги и руки. Изо всех сил он напрягался как бы порвать свои путы, но тщетно (Достоевский 2). The knocking continued. Ivan wanted to rush to the window; but something seemed suddenly to bind his legs and arms. He was straining as hard as he could to break his bonds, but in vain (2a). ♦ Котов с большим трудом вырвал для меня перевод. Отдел сопротивлялся изо всех сил... (Мандельштам 2). With great difficulty Kotov managed to get some translating work for me. The members of the department concerned resisted for all they were worth... (2a). ♦ Карасик изо всех сил старался выглядеть, как всегда, уверенным и властным, но получалось это у него не без натуги и смущения (Максимов 3). Karasik was trying his hardest to look as self-assured and authoritative as ever, but he could not avoid showing a certain strain and embarrassment (3a). ♦ Упираясь рогами в кузов, Рогатая мать-олениха выкатывала машину с возом сена на гору. Мальчик помогал ей, старался изо всех сил (Айтматов 1). Pressing her horns into the body of the truck, the Horned Mother Deer pushed the truckload of hay up the mountain. The boy helped her, straining every muscle (1a).

2. бежать, мчаться, нестись и т. п. ~ (to run, race etc) very fast, at maximum speed: **at top ⟨full⟩ speed; (at) full tilt; as fast as one can; as fast as one's legs can ⟨will⟩ carry one; for all one is worth.**

3. кричать, орать и т. п. ~. Also: **ИЗО ВСЕЙ СИ́ЛЫ** (of a person, an animal, or an apparatus that produces or transmits sounds) (to shout, yell, blast etc) very loudly: **at the top of one's voice ⟨lungs⟩; with all one's ⟨its⟩ might; (at) full blast.**

Покисен закричал изо всех сил: «Вы с ума сошли?» (Федин 1). Pokisen cried at the top of his lungs: "Have you gone crazy?" (1a).

C-168 • НАБИРА́ТЬСЯ/НАБРА́ТЬСЯ СИЛ [VP; subj: human] to become stronger (often replenishing one's strength after intense exertion, an illness etc): X набрался сил ≃ **X gained strength; X built up his strength;** [after an illness, injury etc] **X regained his strength; X got his strength back.**

Так олениха стала выкармливать младенца, который быстро рос и набирался сил на добром оленьем молоке (Искандер 5). So the doe began to raise the baby, who quickly grew and gained strength on the good deer's milk (5a). ♦ [Эльза:] Возьмите ещё масла... [Ланцелот:] Да, да, я возьму. Мне нужно набраться сил (Шварц 2). [E.:] Please help yourself to some more butter.... [L.:] Yes, yes, I will take some more. I must build up my strength (2a).

C-169 • СИЛ НЕТ¹ (*у кого*) (терпеть, смотреть *на кого-что* и т. п.); **СИЛ моих НЕТ** *both coll* [VP; impers; pres or past] it is impossible for s.o., beyond s.o.'s strength (to tolerate, look at etc s.o. or sth.): у X-а сил нет ≃ **X can't bear ⟨endure, stand⟩ it ⟨to do sth.⟩; X can't take it ⟨doing sth.⟩; X can hardly bear it ⟨to do sth.⟩;** [in limited contexts] **X has reached ⟨is at⟩ the end of his tether ⟨his rope⟩.**

И вдруг старик упал на колени и, вздевая руки, застонал...: «Возьми меня, забери меня, горемычного! Только дай ей дитя! Сил моих нет глядеть на неё... Пожалей нас...»

(Айтматов 1). Suddenly the old man fell to his knees and, raising up his arms, he groaned....“Take me, receive me, wretched as I am. Only give her a child. I can't bear to look at her....Have pity on us” (1b). ♦ «Господи, за что же мне это такое наказание?» — трясясь от негодования, причитала мать [Влада]. — ...Ты скоро вгонишь меня в гроб раньше времени, негодяй!.. Сил моих больше нет!» (Максимов 2). “Lord, what have I done to deserve this punishment?” his [Vlad's] mother wailed, shaking with indignation. “...You'll drive me to an early grave, you little horror!...I've reached the end of my tether!” (2a). ♦ Не хватало рук для жатвы: соседний однодворец... надул самым бессовестным образом; свои бабы заламывали цены [за работу] неслыханные... «Сил моих нет!» — не раз с отчаянием восклицал Николай Петрович (Тургенев 2). There was a shortage of hands for the harvesting—a neighbor who was a landowner in a small way...had rooked him in a most conscienceless manner; his own peasant women were extorting unheard of wages....“I'm at the end of my rope!” Nikolai Petrovich had cried out in despair on more than one occasion (2d).

C-170 • СИЛ НЕТ[2]; СИЛ НЕТ, КАК ⟨ДО ЧЕГО и т. п.⟩ хочется, нравится, надоело и т. п. all coll [these forms only; usu. a clause in a compound or complex sent used as adv (intensif); usu. this WO] (some desire, emotion etc) is extremely intense, overwhelming; (s.o. wants, likes, is tired of etc sth.) to an extreme, overwhelming degree: сил нет, как хочется ≃ **s.o. is dying for sth.; s.o. has a craving ⟨a hankering⟩ for sth.;** ‖ сил нет, как нравится ≃ **s.o. is crazy about sth.; s.o. is bananas over sth.; s.o. would jump at the chance (to do sth.);** ‖ сил нет, до чего надоело ≃ **s.o. is sick to death ⟨sick and tired⟩ of sth.; s.o. is fed ⟨has had it⟩ up to here with sth.; s.o. is fed to the gills with sth.**

Сил нет, как хочется закурить. I'm dying for a cigarette.

C-171 • НЕЧИ́СТАЯ СИ́ЛА coll; **НЕЧИ́СТЫЙ ДУ́Х** obs [NP; sing only; subj or obj] an evil being, a demon or demons: **the devil; the devil's brood; evil forces ⟨spirits⟩; the powers of darkness.**

«...Кто-то неведомый, но весьма энергичный выхватывал у нас из-под носа и переправлял за пределы королевства самых важных, самых отпетых и отвратительных преступников. Так ускользнули от нас: безбожный астролог Багир Киссэнский; преступный алхимик Синдра, связанный, как доказано, с нечистой силой и с ируканскими властями...» (Стругацкие 4). “Some unknown but extremely energetic person snatched away from right under my nose all the most important, incorrigible and detestable criminals and abducted them across the border. This way many have gotten away, as for instance the godless astrologer Bagir Kissenski; the criminal alchemist Synda, who, it has been definitely proven, was in alliance with the devil's brood as well as with the Irukanian potentates...” (4a). ♦ Не хотите икону, убеждения не позволяют? — обойдёмся простой репродукцией... От нечистой силы, от дурного глаза тоже хорошо помогает (Терц 5). You say you don't want an icon; your convictions don't permit it? Then we'll manage with a simple reproduction....It also gives good protection against the powers of darkness and the evil eye (5a).

C-172 • РАБО́ЧАЯ СИ́ЛА [NP; sing only, usu. refers to more than one person; fixed WO] people who work (more often, those who perform physical or not highly skilled labor): **manpower; workers; labor;** ‖ в месте X не хватает рабочей силы ≃ **place X is short-handed.**

[Угаров:] Где работаете? [Хомутов:] ...Агроном я! [Анчугин:] Агроном? [Хомутов:] Агроном... [Анчугин:] Колхоз, конечно, миллионер? [Хомутов:] Миллионер, да... [Анчугин:] Рабочей силы, конечно, не хватает? [Хомутов:] Рабочей силы?.. Да, не хватает (Вампилов 1). [U.:] What do you do? [Kh.:] ...I'm an agronomist. [A.:] An agronomist? [Kh.:] Yes.... [A.:] On a filthy-rich collective farm, naturally. [Kh.:] It's rich, yes.... [A.:] Short-handed, naturally? [Kh.:] Yes, it's a bit short (1a).

C-173 • С НА́МИ КРЕ́СТНАЯ СИ́ЛА! obs, coll [Interj; Invar; usu. this WO] an exclamation made by superstitious people when frightened or amazed: **Lord ⟨God⟩, help us ⟨me⟩!; heaven help us ⟨me⟩!; may the Lord God protect us ⟨me⟩!; Lord, have mercy (up)on us ⟨me⟩!**

Поп и попадья крестились, услыша, что Пугачёву известен их обман. «С нами сила крестная!» — говорила Акулина Памфиловна (Пушкин 2). The priest and his wife both crossed themselves when they heard that Pugachev had found out about their deception. “May the Lord God protect us!” said Akulina Pamfilovna (2a). ♦ «С нами крестная сила! Какие ты страсти говоришь!» — проговорила старуха, крестясь (Гоголь 3). “Lord have mercy upon me, what dreadful things you say!” said the old woman crossing herself (3a).

C-174 • СИ́ЛА СОЛО́МУ ЛО́МИТ [saying] the power, authority etc of another or others compels a person to submit (said when s.o. feels helpless, defenseless before a force greater than himself and has to yield to it): ≃ **might makes ⟨goes before⟩ right; a straw must break in a strong hand.**

И вот... приезжает к нему [Твардовскому] молодой, полный сил, блеска и знаний заместитель и говорит: надо уступить, сила солому ломит (Солженицын 2). And lo and behold: his young deputy, so full of vigor and brilliance and knowledge...comes to Tvardovsky and tells him: You must give way; a straw must break in a strong hand (2a).

C-175 • ВСЕ́МИ СИ́ЛАМИ стараться, стремиться, хотеть, поощрять и т. п. [NP$_{instrum}$; Invar; adv; fixed WO] (to try, strive to do sth., encourage s.o. etc) in any way one can, exerting every possible effort: **(try) with all one's might; (do) everything in one's power (to...); (do) everything (humanly) possible (to...); (do) all one can; (try) as hard as one can; (do) one's utmost; (do ⟨try⟩) one's (very) best (to...); [in limited contexts] (fight) tooth and nail.**

Бесплодные сожаления о минувшем, жгучие упрёки совести язвили его [Обломова], как иглы, и он всеми силами старался свергнуть с себя бремя этих упрёков... (Гончаров 1). Fruitless regrets for the past and the stinging reproaches of conscience pricked him [Oblomov] like needles, and he tried with all his might to throw off the burden of this censure... (1b). ♦ С тех пор, как заболел несчастный Иса, и до этих дней все родственники, и в особенности старый Хабуг, всеми силами помогали его семье (Искандер 3). Up to this point, ever since the unfortunate Isa had fallen ill, all the relatives, and old Khabug in particular, had done everything in their power to help his family (3a). ♦ «...Не верю! Не могу верить!» — повторял озадаченный Разумихин, стараясь всеми силами опровергнуть доводы Раскольникова (Достоевский 3). “I don't believe it! I can't believe it!” Razumikhin repeated, perplexed, trying as hard as he could to refute Raskolnikov's arguments (3b). ♦ Юрий Андреевич лёг ничком на койку, лицом в подушку. Он всеми силами старался не слушать оправдывавшегося Ливерия... (Пастернак 1). Yurii Andreievich lay down flat on his bunk, his face in his pillow, doing his utmost not to listen to Liberius justifying himself... (1a).

C-176 • НИКАКИ́МИ СИ́ЛАМИ не заставить, не удержать, не остановить кого-что и т. п. [NP$_{instrum}$; these forms only; adv; used with negated verbs; fixed WO] not by any means or methods can (s.o. be forced to do sth., be kept from doing sth. etc): **no power on earth ⟨no power in the world, nothing in the world⟩ (can stop s.o. from doing sth. ⟨stop sth. from happening etc⟩); there's no way (one can make s.o. do sth. ⟨stop sth. from happening etc⟩); there's nothing one ⟨anyone⟩ can do (to make s.o. do sth. ⟨stop sth. from happening etc⟩).**

[author's usage] [Катерина:] А уж коли очень мне здесь опостынет, так не удержат меня никакой силой (Островский 6). [K.:] ...If things get too unbearable for me, no power on earth will be able to keep me here (6c). ♦ «Если б гром загремел тогда, камень упал бы надо мной, я бы всё-таки сказал. Этого никакими силами удержать было нельзя...» (Гончаров 1). "If a thunderbolt had struck me at that moment, or stone had fallen on me, I still should have said it! No power in the world could have stopped me!" (1b).

C-177 • СОБИРА́ТЬСЯ/СОБРА́ТЬСЯ С СИ́ЛАМИ [VP; subj: human] **1.** [if pfv, often infin with надо, нужно etc] to gather one's strength (before doing sth. difficult, after having been ill etc): X соберётся с силами ≃ **X will summon ⟨muster, regain⟩ his strength; X will recharge his batteries; X will get his ⟨a⟩ second wind; X will rally (and do sth.); X will rally his strength ⟨his energy etc⟩.**

[Прокурор] сделал новое волевое усилие, чтобы двинуть ногой, но она была неподвижна... Он решил передохнуть, собраться с новыми силами, усыпить бдительность организма (Войнович 4). ...He [the prosecutor] made another effort of the will to make his leg move, but it remained motionless....He decided to catch his breath, summon new strength, and lull the body's vigilance (4a). ♦ ...Сам я, живой человек, смотрел на эту сцену откуда-то сбоку и свысока, и я тоже плакал и кричал во весь голос, чтобы они подождали со мною прощаться, потому что, может быть, я соберусь ещё с силами и встану (Терц 2). ...I was still alive and I was looking down at the scene from somewhere on the side, and I cried as well, and shouted at the top of my voice, telling them to wait, because I might still rally and get up (2a).

2. [more often pfv, esp. past or Verbal Adv собравшись] to make up one's mind to do sth., overcoming fear, timidity, uncertainty etc: X собрался с силами ≃ **X summoned ⟨gathered, mustered⟩ his strength ⟨courage⟩; X braced himself; X took ⟨got⟩ hold of himself;** [in limited contexts] **X pulled himself together.**

Найман-Ана осталась на месте, присела на корточки, всхлипывая... и так сидела, не поднимая головы. Потом собралась с силами, пошла к сыну, стараясь сохранить спокойствие (Айтматов 2). Naiman-Ana remained where she was and squatted down, sobbing...and not raising her head. Then she gathered her strength and walked over to her son, trying to keep calm (2a). ♦ Нужно было дать ответ Гастону Руа... Лансье собрался с силами и сказал: «Хорошо» (Эренбург 1). He [Lancier] had to give Gaston Roy an answer....Lancier pulled himself together and said: "All right" (1a).

C-178 • НЕ В СИ́ЛАХ [PrepP; Invar; used without negation to convey the opposite meaning] **1.** [subj-compl with copula (subj: usu. human, collect, animal, or мозг, сердце etc) or part of detached modif; usu. used with infin] a person (a group of people etc) does not have the capability to do sth. (because of inadequate physical or emotional strength, a lack of means, low status etc): X не в силах делать Y ≃ **X lacks ⟨doesn't have⟩ the strength ⟨the power⟩ to do Y; X cannot ⟨is (quite) unable to⟩ do Y; X is incapable of doing Y; Y is more than X can handle ⟨take, bear⟩; Y is too much for X; X is powerless to do Y; X doesn't have it in him to do Y; Y is beyond X's power ⟨capability⟩; X is not strong enough to do Y.**

Илюша болезненно ему улыбался, всё ещё не в силах сказать слова. Коля вдруг поднял руку и провёл для чего-то своею ладонью по волосам Илюши (Достоевский 1). Ilyusha kept smiling wanly, still unable to say a word. Kolya suddenly reached out and for some reason stroked Ilyusha's hair with his hand (1a). ♦ Когда день полон грохота и человек по уши погружён в котёл войны, он не в силах понять, увидеть свою жизнь... (Гроссман 2). When a man is plunged up to his neck into the cauldron of war, he is quite unable to look at his life and understand anything... (2a). ♦ Ноги у Лёньки гудели. Он сидел неподвижно, не в силах пошевелиться (Семёнов 1). Lyonka's legs throbbed painfully. He sat motionless, incapable of stirring (1a). ♦ В конце 1936 года Коган, переведённый к тому времени в Ярославль, бросился под поезд, не в силах больше переносить ожидания ареста (Гинзбург 1). At the end of 1936 Kogan, by then transferred to Yaroslavl, found the daily expectation of arrest more than he could bear and threw himself under a train (1b). ♦ «...Его внимание не в силах сосредоточиться на чём-нибудь одном...» (Катаев 3). "...It is too much for his mind to concentrate on one thing" (3a). ♦ Они [чегемские старцы] как бы осознают, что происходящее должно было быть ими остановлено, но понимая, что не в силах ничего сделать, они чувствуют гнёт вины за собственное молчание, осквернённость своей духовной власти (Искандер 5). They [the elders of Chegem] seem to recognize that they should have stopped what is happening, and though they realize that they are powerless to do anything, they feel oppressed by guilt for their own silence, the defilement of their spiritual authority (5a).

2. не в моих ⟨твоих и т. п.⟩ силах [subj-compl with copula (subj: infin or abstr)] sth. (or doing sth.) is beyond the limits of s.o.'s physical strength, ability, competence etc: (с)делать X не в Y-овых силах ≃ **Y cannot do X; Y lacks ⟨doesn't have⟩ the power to do X; (doing) X is beyond Y's power ⟨capability⟩; X is more than Y can do ⟨handle⟩; Y is powerless to do X.**

«Юрий Андреевич, будьте умницей, выйдите на минуту к мадемуазель, выпейте воды, голубчик, и возвращайтесь сюда таким, каким я вас привыкла и хотела бы видеть. Слышите, Юрий Андреевич? Я знаю, это в ваших силах. Сделайте это, я прошу вас» (Пастернак 1). "Yurii Andreievich...do be sensible, go off to Mademoiselle for a minute, have a drink of water and come back, please, as I've always known you till now and as I want you to be. Do you hear, Yurii Andreievich? I know you can do it. Please do it, I beg you" (1a). ♦ «Свободу вы у меня давно отняли, а вернуть её не в ваших силах, ибо её нет у вас самого» (Солженицын 3). "You took my freedom away long ago, and you don't have the power to return it because you don't have it yourself" (3a). ♦ «Скоро тут произойдёт невообразимая свалка. Предотвратить её не в наших силах» (Пастернак 1). "There will be an unimaginable mess here soon; it's beyond our power to avert it" (1a).

C-179 • В СИ́ЛЕ[1] [PrepP; Invar; subj-compl with бытьₒ (subj: human)] **1.** one has strength, energy, is able-bodied: X был в силе ≃ **X was strong and healthy; X was hale and hearty;** [in limited contexts] **X was in his prime.**

Вспоминал [Едигей] те дни, когда они с Казангапом были молоды и в силе... (Айтматов 2). He [Yedigei] recalled those days when Kazangap and he had been young and in their prime (2a).

2. one has authority, holds an important position: X в силе ≃ **X wields ⟨has, is in⟩ power; X has influence;** [in limited contexts] **X has clout;** ‖ X в большой силе ≃ **X has ⟨is of⟩ (great) influence.**

Попасть на трибуну для Канарейкина большая удача. Об этом напечатают в газетах. Пойдёт слух, что Канарейкин ещё в силе (Зиновьев 2). It was a great personal triumph for Kanareikin to be allowed to speak. The newspapers would report it. There would be a rumour that Kanareikin still wielded power (2a). ♦ Ему [Петру Петровичу] надо было только поскорей и немедленно разузнать: что и как тут случилось? В силе эти люди или не в силе? Есть ли чего бояться собственно ему, или нет? (Достоевский 3). He [Pyotr Petrovich] needed only to find out at once and quickly what went on here, and how. Did these people have any power, or did they not have any power? Was there anything for him to fear personally, or was there not? (3c). ♦ ...Князь Андрей возобновил старые знакомства, особенно с теми лицами, которые, он знал, были в силе и могли быть нужны ему (Толстой 5). ...Prince Andrei looked up old acquaintances, especially with those whom he knew to be in power and whose aid he might need (5a). ♦ «Зачем ты не сказал, что он [немец] в силе?» (Гончаров 1). "Why didn't you tell me he [the German] had influence?" (1a). ♦ «Кто это?» — «Лазарев — чиновник особых поручений при министре и в большой силе» (Герцен 1). "Who is that?"..."Lazarev, a clerk of special commissions and of great influence with the Minister" (1a).

С-180 • **В СИ́ЛЕ²** [PrepP; Invar; subj-compl with бытьø, оставаться (subj: закон, приказ, приговор etc) or obj-compl with оставлять (obj: закон, приказ, приговор etc)] (of or in refer. to a law, an order, a verdict etc) sth. is effective, is to be obeyed: оставаться ~ ≃ **(be ⟨remain⟩) in force; (be ⟨remain⟩) in effect; (be) valid; stand; apply;** ‖ оставлять ~ ≃ **uphold sth.; let sth. stand.**

Человеческие законы цивилизации кончились. В силе были зверские (Пастернак 1). The laws of human civilization were suspended. The jungle law was in force (1a). ♦ Всё выражение его лица говорило ей, что утренний разговор им не забыт, что решенье его осталось в прежней силе и что только благодаря присутствию гостей он не говорит ей этого теперь (Толстой 5). The whole expression of his face told her that he had not forgotten the morning's talk, that his decision remained in force, and only the presence of visitors hindered his speaking of it to her now (5b). ♦ О деле Норвегова кое-где узнали, прошли демонстрации, но приговор остался в силе (Соколов 1). Here and there people learned about the Norvegov case, there were demonstrations, but the sentence remained in force (1a). ♦ «Ну, пока поверим [вам]. Но предупреждение моё остаётся в силе» (Солженицын 3). "Well, we'll believe you for now. But my warning still stands" (3a).

С-181 • **СО СТРА́ШНОЙ СИ́ЛОЙ** highly coll [PrepP; Invar; adv (intensif); fixed WO] very (strongly, intensively, much, loudly etc): **like mad; like crazy;** ‖ врать ~ ≃ **lie like a rug;** ‖ ругаться ~ ≃ **cuss a blue streak; swear like a trooper;** ‖ упираться ⟨сопротивляться⟩ ~ ≃ **resist with all one's might ⟨with everything one's got⟩; resist for all one is worth;** ‖ храпеть ~ ≃ **snore like a chain saw ⟨a buzz saw⟩;** ‖ везёт кому ~ ≃ **s.o. is lucky as hell;** ‖ рваться куда, к чему ~ ≃ **try for all one is worth; do one's damnedest;** ‖ кому хочется что сделать ~ ≃ **s.o. wants to do sth. so bad he can taste it;** ‖ солнце палит ~ ≃ **the sun beats down mercilessly;** ‖ цены растут ~ ≃ **prices are skyrocketing.**

Начальство хочет перевести меня в другой отдел, а я упираюсь со страшной силой. My boss wants to transfer me to a different department, but I'm resisting for all I'm worth.

С-182 • **В ПО́ЛНУЮ СИ́ЛУ** работать [PrepP; Invar; adv; fixed WO] (to work) at maximum level: **to ⟨at⟩ one's ⟨its⟩ full capacity; to capacity; at one's full potential.**

«На воле голова редко бывает занята одной работой... Значит, на воле инженер не может работать в полную силу» (Копелев 1). "On the outside [i.e., when not in prison], your head is rarely concerned only with work....So, that means that on the outside an engineer can't work to his full capacity..." (1a).

С-183 • **В СИ́ЛУ¹** чего [PrepP; Invar; Prep; the resulting PrepP is adv] by reason of: **because of; owing to; as a result of; in view of; on account of;** [in limited contexts] **on the strength of;** ‖ в силу привычки ≃ **by force of habit;** ‖ в силу обстоятельств ≃ **in accordance ⟨keeping⟩ with (the) circumstances; according to (the) circumstances;** [in limited contexts] **by force of circumstances.**

«Вернувшись домой, я вымылся в ванной и стал дожидаться отца. Но он пришёл поздно, и в силу некоторых домашних причин я ему рассказывать ничего не стал, чтобы ещё больше не нервировать» (Семёнов 1). "When I returned home I washed in the bathroom and waited for my father. But he returned late and because of certain family matters I did not tell him anything, in order not to worry him any more" (1a). ♦ А что происходит реально в силу особенностей системы, в которой принято решение [повысить уровень науки]? (Зиновьев 1). But what really happens in view of the peculiarities of the system within which the decision [to raise the level of science] is taken? (1a). ♦ ...Она рассеянно смотрела на него [Мансурова], в силу давно

выработанной многолетней привычки почти ничего не слыша и почти всё запоминая... (Залыгин 1). ...She would look at him [Mansurov] absent-mindedly, by force of long habit remembering almost everything while hardly hearing anything (1a). ♦ «Смотри, все ведущие идеологические посты заняли наши люди». – «Это не играет роли. Они... будут действовать в силу обстоятельств, а не в силу личных симпатий и антипатий...» (Зиновьев 2). "Look, all the important ideological posts went to our people." "That's of no consequence at all....They'll act according to circumstances, not because of any personal sympathies or antipathies..." (2a). ♦ «Нельзя ли к этому придраться?»... «Если бы, например, ваше превосходительство могли... достать от вашего соседа запись или купчую, в силу которой владеет он своим имением, то конечно...» (Пушкин 1). [context transl] "Couldn't we make a case out of that?"..."If, for instance, Your Excellency could...obtain from your neighbor the record or deed that entitles him to his estate, then, of course..." (1a).

С-184 • **В СИ́ЛУ²** obs [PrepP; Invar; adv] having to exert great effort and almost not succeeding: **hardly; barely; with difficulty.**

...В силу, в силу перетащились они [гости] на балкон и в силу поместились в креслах (Гоголь 3). ...They [the guests] could hardly drag themselves over to the balcony, were barely able to sink into the armchairs (3c).

С-185 • **В СИ́ЛУ ТОГО́ ЧТО** lit [subord Conj; introduces a clause of reason] by reason of the fact that: **because; owing to the fact that; as a result of the fact that; in view of the fact that; on account of the fact that.**

С-186 • **ВО ВСЮ СИ́ЛУ** [PrepP; Invar; adv (intensif)] exerting great power, with great intensity: **with all one's ⟨its⟩ might; full force.**

У него не хватило ума понять, что если уж бить, так бить во всю силу (Зиновьев 1). He didn't have the sense to understand that if you are going to strike people, you must strike them with all your might (1a).

С-187 • **ВХОДИ́ТЬ/ВОЙТИ́ В СИ́ЛУ** [VP] **1.** Also: **ВСТУПА́ТЬ/ВСТУПИ́ТЬ В (ЗАКО́ННУЮ) СИ́ЛУ** [subj: закон, постановление, приговор etc] to become legal, effective: X вступил в силу ≃ **X took ⟨went into⟩ effect; X went ⟨came⟩ into force;** [in limited contexts] **X became law.**

Довольно много людей было отправлено в Бабий Яр за голубей. Дело в том, что приказ [уничтожить всех голубей] вступил в силу буквально на следующий день, не все успели даже прочесть его в газете (Кузнецов 1). Quite a few people were sent to Babi Yar because of their pigeons. This was because the order [to destroy all pigeons] went into effect on the very next day, and many people did not even get to see it in the newspaper (1a).

2. [subj: human] to assume an influential position or fortify one's position (in society, the workplace, a political movement etc): X вошёл в силу ≃ **X gained power ⟨influence⟩; X established himself; X came into his own.**

Мольер и Люлли – композитор, входивший всё больше в славу и силу при дворе, – получили приказ сочинить смешную комедию с музыкой для шамборских празднеств... (Булгаков 5). Molière and Lully, who was steadily gaining fame and influence at Court, were commanded to compose an amusing comedy set to music for the Chambord entertainments... (5a). ♦ То самое Женевское озеро разделяло их [Ленина и Инессу], только оно, ещё незнакомых, когда он, входя в силу, принимал делегатов II-го съезда... (Солженицын 5). Lake Geneva again, nothing more, had been between them [Lenin and Inessa], before they had known each other, when he was beginning to come into his own, receiving delegates to the Second Congress... (5a).

3. obs [subj: human or concr] (of a person recovering from an illness, or of growing bushes, trees etc, particularly those bearing fruit) to become robust, gain vitality: X вошёл в силу ≃ [of a person] **X regained 〈got back〉 his strength; X was on the mend 〈on the upswing〉;** [of a bush, tree etc] **X got big 〈became lush etc〉.**

С-188 • ЗАБИРА́ТЬ/ЗАБРА́ТЬ 〈БРАТЬ/ВЗЯТЬ *obsoles, substand〉* **СИ́ЛУ** [VP] **1.** Also: **ЗАБИРА́ТЬ/ЗАБРА́ТЬ ВЛАСТЬ** [subj: human] to become powerful, influential: X забрал силу ≃ **X gained power 〈influence〉.**

2. [subj: usu. пожар, огонь etc] to become stronger, intensify: X взял силу ≃ **X gained strength; X increased 〈spread, flared up〉.**

...Вот в стороне блеснула ещё светлая точка, потом её закрыл густой дым, и через мгновение из клубов его вынырнул огненный язык; потом язык опять исчез, опять вынырнул — и взял силу (Салтыков-Щедрин 1). ...Somewhere else another point flashed, then was hidden by thick clouds of smoke, and in an instant a flaming tongue surfaced from the clouds; then the tongue disappeared again, surfaced again—and gained strength (1a).

С-189 • НАБИРА́ТЬ/НАБРА́ТЬ СИ́ЛУ 〈-ы〉 [VP; subj: usu. collect or abstr] to become more powerful, intensify: X набирает силу ≃ **X is gathering strength 〈force〉; X is gaining (in) strength; X is growing more powerful; X is growing stronger.**

«...Технократический аппарат ему [Орджоникидзе] предан. Но предан до поры до времени, предан, пока набирает силу. А вот когда они наберут силу, они обойдутся без товарища Орджоникидзе!» (Рыбаков 2). "...The technocratic staffs are loyal to him [Ordzhonikidze]. But they are loyal only for the time being, only while they are gathering strength. And once they have gathered that strength, they will do without Comrade Ordzhonikidze!" (2a). ♦ Индустрия смерти набирала силу, и надо было готовиться к обороне, обороне с пустыми руками, в которой они погибнут, но погибнут с честью (Рыбаков 1). The death industry was gathering force and the people had to prepare to defend themselves, to defend themselves with their bare hands, to die in the act, but to die with honour (1a). ♦ ...Мы сами помогали — молчанием или одобрением — сильной власти набирать силу и защищаться от хулителей... (Мандельштам 1). ...Either by silence or consent we ourselves helped the system to gain in strength and protect itself against its detractors... (1a).

С-190 • НЕ ПОД СИ́ЛУ *кому* [PrepP; Invar; subj-compl with copula (subj: abstr or infin); used without negation to convey the opposite meaning] **1.** Also: **НЕ ПО СИ́ЛАМ** [occas. used as nonagreeing postmodif] sth. is beyond the limits of s.o.'s physical strength or beyond his abilities, competence etc: X Y-у не под силу ≃ **X is beyond Y's power 〈strength, capacity (to understand), reach〉; X is not in 〈within〉 Y's power; X is more than Y can do 〈deliver, handle〉; Y doesn't have what it takes (to do X); X is too much for Y; Y lacks the strength 〈the ability〉 (to do X);** [in limited contexts] **Y is not competent at X;** ‖ X Y-у под силу ≃ **Y has the strength 〈the ability, the power〉 to do X; Y can do 〈handle〉 X; Y has it in him 〈has what it takes〉 to do X;** [in limited contexts] **Y is competent at X; X is within Y's means.**

«До сих пор я не понимал себя, я задавал себе задачи, которые мне не по силам...» (Тургенев 2). "Up till now I did not understand myself, I set myself tasks beyond my capacity..." (2c). ♦ Сейчас, задним числом, я думаю, что у кагебешников даже и шанса не было не сдаться. Вопрос о моём отъезде был решён на каких-то верхах, мне недоступных. И нарушить решение верхов им было не под силу (Войнович 1). Now, with hindsight, I think the KGB had no choice but to give in. The question of my leaving the country had been decided high up, on levels to which these men had no access. It was not in their power to violate such a decision (1a). ♦ На одно мгновение смысл существования опять открывался Ларе. Она тут, — постигала она, — для того, чтобы

разобраться в сумасшедшей прелести земли и всё назвать по имени, а если это будет ей не по силам, то из любви к жизни родить себе преемников, которые это сделают вместо неё (Пастернак 1). For a moment she [Lara] rediscovered the purpose of her life. She was on earth to grasp the meaning of its wild enchantment and to call each thing by its right name, or, if this were not within her power, to give birth out of love for life to successors who would do it in her place (1a). ♦ ...Иногда в голове возникают изумительные проекты, но чувствуешь, что тебе не под силу протолкнуть их через соответствующие учреждения (Искандер 4). Sometimes an amazing scheme will come to you, but you are aware that you don't have what it takes to push it through the appropriate channels (4a). ♦ ...[Я] взвалил его [баллон] на плечо... Пройдя первые десять ступенек, я понял, что слишком много взял на себя. Лет пять назад я мог пройти с таким баллоном втрое больше, теперь это было мне не под силу (Войнович 5). ...I hefted the cylinder up on my shoulder....After the first ten steps I realized that I'd bitten off more than I could chew. Five years ago I could have carried a cylinder like that three times as far, but now it was too much for me (5a). ♦ Путь Хлебникова был для меня запретен. Да и кому, кроме него, оказался бы он под силу? (Лившиц 1). For me the path chosen by Khlebnikov was a forbidden one. And who, apart from him, would have found the strength to pursue it? (1a). ♦ «Давайте найдём себе дело по силам. К примеру, преферанс» (Распутин 1). "Let's turn to something we're more competent at—a game of preference, for instance" (1a). ♦ «Вопрос обсуждаемого романа — чего стоит человеку социализм и под силу ли цена?» (Солженицын 2). "The question in the novel we are discussing is: What does socialism cost, and is the price within our means?" (2a).

2. sth. is very difficult or impossible for s.o. to do (because he lacks decisiveness, does not dare to, cannot overcome his sluggishness etc): X Y-у не под силу ≃ **Y just can't 〈get himself to 〈make himself etc〉〉 do X; Y is incapable of doing X; there is no way Y can do X;** [in limited contexts] **Y can't bear the thought of doing X.**

[Мандельштам] не мог отделить мою судьбу от своей... Мою любовь к живописи... он сразу забрал себе и так же решил поступить с Шекспиром. Ведь любить врозь означает отделиться друг от друга — это было ему не под силу (Мандельштам 2). ...He [Mandelstam] could make no distinction between my life and his own....He had immediately taken over my love of painting...and decided on the same policy with regard to Shakespeare. Loving different things was the same as separating, and he just could not bear the thought (2a).

С-191 • ЧЕРЕЗ СИ́ЛУ [PrepP; Invar; adv] (to do sth.) unwillingly, pushing o.s. to overcome some barrier (exhaustion, pain, fear, animosity, nervousness etc): **with (a) great 〈(an) obvious, (a) tremendous〉 effort; with great 〈the utmost〉 difficulty; forcing o.s. (to do sth.); making an effort (to do sth.);** [in refer. to physical barriers] **straining o.s.;** [in refer. to emotional barriers] **in a reluctant manner; (doing sth.) costs s.o. an effort.**

Лошадь опять стала, сторожко пофыркивая, но вконец обозлённый Мелентьев остервенело рванул вожжи: «Пошла, паскуда-а!..». Та через силу сделала шаг, другой... (Максимов 3). The horse stopped again, snorting with apprehension. Melentiev could no longer control his rage, and tugged furiously at the reins. "Get on with you. You rotten sod...." With a great effort the horse took one step, then another... (3a). ♦ [Лаборантка] спросила через силу: «Аристарх Аполлинариевич, а правда, что вы?..» — «Вздор!» — вскричал он (Аксёнов 6). ...With an obvious effort, she [the lab assistant] asked, "Aristarkh Appolinarievich, is it true that you—" "Nonsense!" he shouted (6a). ♦ Он должен был что-то крикнуть, потому что крик подкатился к горлу — но вместо крика ткнул в спину извозчика и выдавил из горла через силу: «Гони!» (Федин 1). He should have cried out, because a cry had risen in his throat...but instead of crying out he prodded the cabby in the back and with a tremendous effort forced from his throat: "Drive on!" (1a). ♦ «Как ты обманул меня! Разве я поехала бы без тебя? О, я знаю, я знаю, ты это сделал через силу, ради моего воображаемого блага. И тогда всё пошло прахом» (Пастернак 1). "How you deceived me! Would I ever have gone without you? Oh, I know, I know, you forced yourself to do it, you thought it was for my good. And after that everything was ruined" (1a). ♦ «Там этот пришёл... твой», – сказал он [Петро] по своей привычке как бы нехотя, через силу (Шукшин 1). "He showed up again here...your..." Petro broke off, speaking in his customary reluctant manner (1a). ♦ «Здоров, Андрюха», – бодрое радушие давалось ему явно через силу (Максимов 3). "Good to see you, Andrei, lad." His brisk friendliness obviously cost him an effort (3a).

С-192 • НАДРЫВА́ТЬ/НАДОРВА́ТЬ ⟨ПОДРЫВА́ТЬ/ ПОДОРВА́ТЬ⟩ СИ́ЛЫ чьи [VP; subj: usu. abstr] to exhaust s.o. utterly and for a long time: X надорвал Y-овы силы ≃ X **sapped (all) Y's strength; X drained all of Y's strength; X totally drained Y;** [in limited contexts] **X broke Y's health.**

[author's usage] Последние недели, проведённые Наташей в комнате матери, надорвали её физические силы (Толстой 7). Those weeks spent in her mother's room had completely broken Natasha's health (7a).

С-193 • ОТ СИ́ЛЫ [PrepP; Invar; used as a restr marker (with a quantit NP or Num denoting a relatively small quantity)] not more than, at the highest calculation: **at most; at the (very) most; at the (very) outside; maximum; tops;** [in limited contexts] **at best; a mere** [NP].

«...Сколько [вы] могли бы убить? Одного, двух, трёх, ну десяток от силы» (Войнович 4). "...How many could you have killed? One, two, three, a dozen at most" (4a). ♦ «...Мы предлагаем с завтрашнего дня установить к-круглосуточное дежурство и патрулирование по центральным улицам города...» – «Ладно. День, от силы два побродите» (Семёнов 1). "We propose to establish, as from tomorrow, round-the-clock observation and patrol of the city's central streets...." "Okay. Walk around for a day – or two at the most" (1a). ♦ На завтрак мне давали пять копеек... Разумеется, это было мало – пять копеек. Мало потому, что начинало хотеться есть к первой перемене... На ней уже покупалось, скажем, яблоко. На второй перемене съедали, скажем, бублик. К большой перемене... уже ничего не оставалось... От силы, как говорится, оставалась копейка на стакан чаю... (Олеша 3). I was given five kopecks for lunch....Obviously, however, five kopecks wasn't very much. It wasn't much because I was always hungry by the first break....And so I bought, say, an apple. On the second break, I bought a roll. By the lunch break...I had nothing left....I'd managed at the outside, as they say, to save only a kopeck for a glass of tea (3a). ♦ «Это я для себя только так решил. Думаю, до сорока годов доживу, ну, до сорока пяти от силы, и хватит. А то это, знаешь, всё ходи, мучайся. То поясницу ломит, то ревматизм на погоду болит» (Войнович 5). "This is just how I worked it out for myself. I figure I'll live to forty, forty-five tops, and that's it. After that, just walking around can be hell. Either your back's killing you or the weather's making your rheumatism ache" (5a).

С-194 • СИ́ЛЬНЫЕ МИ́РА СЕГО́ [NP; pl only; fixed WO] people of prominent social status, the most influential, powerful people in society: **the mighty ⟨the powerful (ones), the great ones⟩ of this world; the high and mighty; the powers that be.**

«Непостоянны сильные мира сего, – говорил Мольер Мадлене, – и дал бы я совет всем комедиантам. Если ты попал в милость, сразу хватай всё, что тебе полагается» (Булгаков 5). "How inconstant are the mighty of this world," Molière said to Madeleine. "And I would give this advice to all players: if you happen to win favor, seize everything you can at once" (5a). ♦ Всякое великое искусство нуждается в покровительстве со стороны сильных мира сего... (Зиновьев 1). "Every great art needs the protection of the powerful ones of this world..." (1a). ♦ При этой погоде все сильные мира сего одеты, как в униформу, в серый габардин

(Гинзбург 2). In such weather all the great ones of this world were dressed – as if it were a uniform – in gray gabardine (2a).

С-195 • ЛУ́ЧШЕ СИНИ́ЦА В РУКА́Х ⟨В РУ́КИ⟩, ЧЕМ ЖУРА́ВЛЬ В НЕ́БЕ; НЕ СУЛИ́ ЖУРАВЛЯ́ В НЕ́БЕ, А ДАЙ СИНИ́ЦУ В РУ́КИ [saying] a less-than-ideal object, opportunity etc that a person already possesses or has available to him is preferable to a better object, opportunity etc that he may never (be able to) get: ≃ **a bird in the hand is worth two in the bush; better an egg today than a hen tomorrow; one today is worth two tomorrows.**

С-196 • СИНИ́ЦА В РУКА́Х coll [NP; sing only] a less-than-ideal object, opportunity etc that a person already possesses or has available to him (and which therefore is preferable to a better object, opportunity etc that he may never get): **the proverbial bird in the hand; a (real ⟨an actual⟩) bird in the hand.**

Итак, он давно бы хотел в таможню, но удерживали текущие разные выгоды по строительной комиссии, и он рассуждал справедливо, что таможня, как бы то ни было, всё ещё не более как журавль в небе, а комиссия уже была синица в руках (Гоголь 3). And so he had long been longing to get into the Customs, but had been held back by sundry current benefits accruing from the Building Commission, and he had reasoned, justly enough, that the Customs was, after all, no more than the proverbial two birds in the bush whereas the Building Commission was an actual bird in the hand (3b).

< From the proverb «Лучше синица в руках, чем журавль в небе». See С-195.

С-197 • КАЗА́НСКАЯ ⟨-ий⟩ СИРОТА́ coll, rather derog [NP; usu. sing] a person who pretends to be unhappy, helpless, offended etc in order to gain s.o.'s compassion: **sympathy seeker;** ‖ X прикидывается казанской сиротой ⟨X строит из себя казанскую сироту⟩ ≃ **X is moaning and groaning about his fate; X is playing on s.o.'s sympathies ⟨feelings⟩; X is making himself out to be a pitiful thing ⟨a poor soul⟩; X is playing the beggar ⟨the victim⟩.**

[author's usage] [Войницев:] Не к лицу вам, милостивый государь, мой бывший друг, это казанское сиротство! Я понимаю вас! Вы ловкий подлец! Вот кто вы! (Чехов 1). [V.:] It doesn't suit you at all, my dear sir, my ex-friend, to try to play on our feelings. I can see through you. A cunning scoundrel, that's what you are! (1a).

< Initially referred to Tartar princes who, after the subjugation of Kazan (capital of the Tartar empire) by Ivan the Terrible in 1552, tried to get more concessions and gratuities by moving the tsar to pity when they appeared at his court.

С-198 • ОТ СИХ (И) ДО СИХ [PrepP; these forms only; adv; fixed WO] (to read sth., do a job, carry out an order etc) within the strict boundaries of what is assigned (usu. used sarcastically with the implication that by doing so one demonstrates a lack of initiative, intellectual curiosity etc): **from here to here ⟨there⟩;** [in limited contexts] **within precise limits; from point A to point B (and no further).**

...В их головах не укладывается, чтобы парень без образования, вроде меня, сам читал Ленина или что-нибудь ещё. Они сами-то его читали «от сих до сих» (Марченко 1). ...Their minds couldn't contain the idea of an uneducated fellow like me actually reading Lenin – or anything else for that matter. They themselves had read only "from here to here" (1a). ♦ Это же вдуматься: земля – тюрьма, кругом запреты, всё нормировано от сих до сих, всё разгорожено и перегорожено, ходи только так, живи только так (Кузнецов 1). When you came to think of it, the whole world was a prison: restrictions on all sides; everything laid down within precise limits; everything concreted up and divided off: you can go only here, live only like this... (1b).

C-199 • НИЧЕГО́ НЕ СКА́ЖЕШЬ *coll* [Invar; sent adv (parenth) or indep. remark; fixed WO] (used to confirm the truth of what is being stated) that is absolutely true, indeed: **there's no denying it; you ⟨one⟩ can't deny it; there's no getting away from it; there's no doubt about it;** [in limited contexts] **what can you say?**

[Афанасий:] Мысли верные, ничего не скажешь... (Розов 1). [A.:] Your ideas are good, there's no denying it (1a). ♦ «...Мне надо выговориться. Не с Лушей же, она тут же перебьёт и сама начнёт говорить. И друзей у меня как-то нет... То есть есть, и хорошие даже, ничего не скажешь, но начнёшь с ними говорить, и через минуту, глядишь, мусор какой-то начинается — что кто где написал или сказал, и что было у художников на последнем пленуме, и где достать краски» (Некрасов 1). "...I feel I've got to talk. Not with Lusha—she would interrupt and start to talk herself. And I don't seem to have any friends....That's not right, I do have friends, good friends too, I can't deny it, but you begin to talk to them and right away some sort of nonsense begins—who wrote or said what where, what happened at the last artists' plenum, where to get paints" (1a). ♦ «Как [Костенко] жену аттестует, а? Скромность украшает человека, ничего не скажешь...» (Семёнов 1). "What a testimonial he's [Kostyenko's] giving his wife, eh? Modesty enhances a man, there's no getting away from it..." (1a). ♦ Несколько дней спустя дошла до нас новая весть: на заседании какой-то высокой инстанции Иванько в пух и прах разгромил готовившийся к печати сборник... Турганова. Ничего не скажешь. Друзья познаются в беде (Войнович 3). Several days later, a new piece of news reached us: at a meeting of some high board, Ivanko completely wrecked the chances of the Turganov collection...that was being prepared for publication. What can you say? You know who your friends are when times are bad (3a).

C-200 • СКА́ЖЕШЬ ТО́ЖЕ *highly coll* [Interj; 2nd or 3rd pers only; fixed WO] used to express the speaker's skeptical or sarcastic attitude toward another's statement, his belief that what another has said or asked is impossible, absurd, absolute nonsense: **you've got to ⟨you must⟩ be kidding!; what are you talking about!; don't give me that!; you don't say!;** [in limited contexts] **come off it!**

Разнообразные сведения, получаемые в этих беседах, вызывали у нашего хозяина то радостное изумление: «Ишь ты!», то скептические возгласы: «Скажешь тоже!» (Гинзбург 2). The varied information acquired in these conversations would elicit from him [our host] either a pleasurably astonished "What do you know!" or a skeptical "You don't say!" (2a).

C-201 • НЕ СКАЖИ́(ТЕ) *coll* [indep. sent; these forms only] (used to express an objection to or disagreement with what the interlocutor has said) you are not quite correct: **I don't know about that; I'm not (so) sure (about that); I wouldn't be so sure (about that); don't be so sure; I wouldn't say that.**

Заговорили о немцах... «У них в общем [патрульные] пары не так крепки». — «Ну, не скажи» (Гроссман 2). The conversation turned to the Germans...."Their patrols don't stick together like we do." "I don't know about that" (2a). ♦ [Лукашин:] Ну, а я представитель самой консервативной профессии. [Надя:] Не скажите. Мы с вами можем соревноваться (Брагинский и Рязанов 1). [L.:] Well, I'm a member of the most conservative profession there is. [N.:] Don't be so sure. We can offer you some competition there (1a).

C-202 • СКАЖИ́(ТЕ) ПОЖА́ЛУЙСТА *coll* [Interj; these forms only; fixed WO] used to express one's surprise (which may be colored by irony), bewilderment, discontent, indignation etc at s.o.'s statement or actions: **you don't say!; fancy that!; (well,) I'll be darned!; well, I never!; well, what do you know!; for heaven's ⟨goodness'⟩ sake!; how do you like that!; do tell!; is that so!; really!; good heavens ⟨grief, gracious⟩!; for crying**

out loud!; [in limited contexts] **aren't we (picky ⟨touchy, clever** etc⟩)!**

«Ну, веришь, Порфирий, [Раскольников] сам едва на ногах, а чуть только мы, я да Зосимов, вчера отвернулись — оделся и удрал потихоньку и куролесил где-то чуть не до полночи, и это в совершеннейшем, я тебе скажу, бреду!.. Замечательнейший случай!» — «И неужели в *совершеннейшем бреду?* Скажите пожалуйста!» (Достоевский 3). "Well, would you believe it, Porfiry, he [Raskolnikov] could hardly stand on his feet, but as soon as we turned our backs—Zosimov and me, that is—he got dressed and sneaked out and was fooling around somewhere till almost midnight. And all this, I tell you, while he was utterly delirious! A most remarkable case!" *"Utterly delirious?* You don't say!" (3b). ♦ [Городничий:] ...Говорил, что застрелится. «Застрелюсь, застрелюсь» — говорит. [Многие из гостей:] Скажите пожалуйста! (Гоголь 4). [Mayor:] He was positively terrifying, he said he was going to shoot himself, "I'll shoot myself, I'll shoot myself," says he. [Many guests:] Fancy that! (4b). ♦ [Беркутов:] ...Сейчас один молодой человек сам сознался, что наделал фальшивых векселей. [Чугунов *(качая головой)*:] Скажите пожалуйста, какие дела творятся на белом свете! (Островский 5). [В.:] ...A certain young man has just confessed that he's been forging notes. [Ch. *(shaking his head)*:] Do tell! What things people do in this world! (5a). ♦ [Анна Петровна:] Надо с вами поговорить как следует... Вот только не знаю, с чего начать... [Платонов:] Не начать ли мне, Анна Петровна? [Анна Петровна:] Ведь вы околёсную понесёте, Платонов, когда начнёте! Скажите пожалуйста! Он сконфузился! (Чехов 1). [A.P.:] ...It's time we had a proper talk....Only I don't know how to start.... [P.:] Shall I start then? [A.P.:] You'll only talk a lot of rot if you do. Good grief, the man's embarrassed (1b). ♦ «Вложи шашку в ножны! И пошутить с тобой нельзя, что ли? Скажи пожалуйста, строгий какой! Чисто девочка шестнадцати годов...» (Шолохов 5). "Put your sabre back! Can't I even have a little joke with you? Oh, aren't we touchy! Just like a girl of sixteen..." (5a).

C-203 • СКА́ЗАНО — СДЕ́ЛАНО [saying] said when a person's decision or intention is immediately carried out, when a person can be counted on to do, without delay, what he says he will do: ≃ **no sooner said than done; it's as good as done.**

Обеденный перерыв был на носу, и Леонид Николаевич решил быстренько смотаться домой, закусить там на скорую руку и привезти шефу подарок. Сказано — сделано (Аржак 3). It was almost the lunch-break, so Leonid decided to dash home, grab a bite there and then bring the gift back to his chief. No sooner said than done (3a).

C-204 • (ДА) И ТО́ СКАЗА́ТЬ *coll* [these forms only; sent adv (parenth); precedes the statement with which it is used; fixed WO] used for emphasis with a statement that corroborates, explains, justifies etc sth. previously stated: **after all;** [in limited contexts] **and with good reason; (and) well one might.**

«Вам трудно, да всё же вы дома; а они — видите, до чего они дошли, — сказал он [Кутузов], указывая на пленных. — Хуже нищих последних... И то сказать, кто же их к нам звал? Поделом им...» (Толстой 7). "...It is hard for you, but still you are at home while they—you see what they have come to," he [Kutuzov] said, pointing to the prisoners. "Worse off than our poorest beggars....But after all, who asked them here? Serves them right..." (7b). ♦ Парк, молодая красавица, ресторан на воде, рубль нищему — такое злачное количество другой жизни ослепило и Лёву, и он пошёл домой, раздавленный. И то сказать, — время ещё было тяжёлое... (Битов 2). A park, a beautiful young woman, a restaurant on the water, a ruble for a beggar—such a lush quantity of other life dazzled Lyova, too, and he went home overwhelmed. Well he might; times were still hard... (2a).

C-205 • КАК СКАЗА́ТЬ *coll* [indep. sent or clause; Invar; fixed WO] **1.** Also: КА́К ТЕБЕ ⟨ВАМ⟩ СКАЗА́ТЬ *coll* (used to express the speaker's hesitation or inability to answer a question confidently and specifically) it is hard for me to answer that precisely: **how should ⟨shall, can⟩ I put it?; how can I explain?; let's put it this way; let me see; [in limited contexts] I don't know if I'd say that.**

[Кручинина:] Вас любил кто-нибудь? [Незнамов:] Как вам сказать... Настоящим образом нет... (Островский 3). [K.:] Has no one ever loved you? [N.:] Hm, how shall I put it? Not really (3a). ♦ «Ну что?» — положив трубку, она [прокурор] смотрит на меня с улыбкой, не предвещающей ничего хорошего. — Значит, въехали самовольно в чужую квартиру?» — «Да как вам сказать, — бормочу я, понимая заранее, что все объяснения лишни. — Не совсем в чужую и не совсем самовольно» (Войнович 3). "Well, then." Putting down the phone, she [the Public Prosecutor] looks at me with a smile that portends no good. "So, you moved into someone else's apartment without authorization." "How can I explain?" I mumble, knowing in advance that all explanations are superfluous. "Not exactly someone else's and not exactly without authorization" (3a). ♦ Ревкину показалось, что Голубев сказал не «с бабой», а «с бандой». «И большая у него [Чонкина] банда?» — поинтересовался он. «Да как сказать... — замялся Голубев, вызывая в своём воображении образ Нюры... — вообще-то порядочная» (Войнович 2). ...It seemed to Revkin that Golubev had not said "girl" but "gang." "And how big is his [Chonkin's] gang?" inquired Revkin. "Now let me see..." Golubev hesitated, summoning up Nyura's image in his mind. "...Pretty good-sized on the whole" (2a). ♦ Вконец раздобревший хозяин кинулся было в магазин за добавкой, но гость решительно перевернул свой стакан вверх дном: «Я... пас». — «Что так?» — «Папашка не любит, когда посреди работы». — «Строг?» — «Да как сказать. Строг не строг, а порядок любит» (Максимов 3). Completely mellowed by now, he wanted to run to the shop for fresh supplies, but his guest resolutely turned his glass upside down. "I pass..." "How's that?" "The old man doesn't like it in the middle of a job." "So he's strict?" "I don't know if I'd say that. He isn't exactly strict, but he likes things to be proper" (3a).

2. often это ⟨ещё⟩ ~ (used by the speaker to express his disagreement with or objection to the preceding statement) I cannot agree with that: **I wouldn't say that; I wouldn't exactly put it that way; I wouldn't put it quite that way; I beg to differ (with you); that's what you think ⟨he thinks etc⟩; [in limited contexts] that's stretching a ⟨the⟩ point (a bit).**

«Задание несложное». — «Это как сказать, в нём есть свои трудности». "The assignment isn't that hard." "That's what you think — it has its difficulties." ♦ Ну, а насчёт мягкости приговора, так это ещё как сказать (Марченко 2). To say that the sentence was mild is stretching a point (2a).

C-206 • КСТА́ТИ СКАЗА́ТЬ ⟨ГОВОРЯ́⟩ [these forms only; sent adv (parenth); fixed WO] in connection with or in addition to what was said: **incidentally; by the way; by the bye; come to think of it.**

Многими чегемцами было замечено, что парень этот своими глубоко запавшими глазами и большими часами кировского завода на широком запястье, носимыми поверх рукава рубахи, сильно смущает девушек округи... Кстати говоря, кроме часов в те годы, как знак власти, начинали входить в моду чесучовые кителя (Искандер 3). It was noted by many Chegemians that this young man with the deep-sunken eyes and the big Kirov watch on his thick wrist (he wore the watch over his shirtsleeve) created quite a stir among the neighborhood girls.... Incidentally, besides watches, another item that began to come into fashion in those years as a mark of power was the tussah tunic of military cut (3a).

C-207 • ЛЕГКО́ СКАЗА́ТЬ coll [Invar; usu. indep. sent or clause; fixed WO] (used to object to a suggestion to do sth. difficult) suggesting it is easy, doing it is far more difficult: **(that's)**

easier said than done; (it's) easy (for you ⟨him etc⟩) to say; (it's) easy enough to say; if only ⟨I wish⟩ it were that easy.

[Нина:] И что случилось? [Бусыгин:] Влюбился. [Нина:] В кого? [Бусыгин:] Как тебе сказать... Она принадлежит другому. [Нина:] Отбей. У тебя должно получиться. [Бусыгин:] Легко сказать (Вампилов 4). [N.:] What happened? [B.:] I fell in love. [N.:] Who with? [B.:] How shall I put it?...She belongs to another. [N.:] Win her over. You shouldn't have any trouble. [B.:] Easier said than done (4a). ♦ ...Легко сказать — вывезти сено. А кто его будет вывозить? (Абрамов 1). It's easy to say "haul out the hay." But who will there be to haul it? (1b). ♦ «Самое главное, абсолютно забудь про их погоны и чины. Обращайся с ними как с обычными учениками...» Легко сказать! А каково рвать прочные, устоявшиеся условные рефлексы! (Гинзбург 2). "The one important thing is to forget all about their epaulettes and ranks. Address them as you would normal pupils..." Easy enough to say! But it's not so easy breaking firmly established conditioned reflexes! (2a).

C-208 • ЛУ́ЧШЕ ⟨ВЕРНЕ́Е, ПРО́ЩЕ, ТОЧНЕ́Е⟩ СКАЗА́ТЬ coll [these forms only; sent adv (parenth); fixed WO] (used to indicate that the speaker is about to modify or present more accurately what he has just said) it would be more correct to phrase it this way: **better (to say); (to put it) more precisely.**

...Иван Фёдорович принял было в Смердякове какое-то особенное вдруг участие, нашёл его даже очень оригинальным. Сам приучил его говорить с собою, всегда, однако, дивясь некоторой бестолковости или, лучше сказать, некоторому беспокойству его ума... (Достоевский 1). ...Ivan Fyodorovich had suddenly taken some special interest in Smerdyakov, found him even very original. He got him accustomed to talking with him, always marveling, however, at a certain incoherence, or, better, a certain restiveness in his mind... (1a). ♦ Они вышли из врат и направились лесом. Помещик Максимов, человек лет шестидесяти, не то что шёл, а, лучше сказать, почти бежал сбоку, рассматривая их всех с судорожным, невозможным почти любопытством (Достоевский 1). They went out the gate and through the woods. The landowner Maximov, a man of about sixty, was not so much walking but, more precisely, almost running alongside, staring at them all with contorted, almost impossible curiosity (1a).

C-209 • МО́ЖНО СКАЗА́ТЬ [Invar; sent adv (parenth); fixed WO] it is possible, reasonable, acceptable to phrase sth. the way the speaker has phrased or is about to phrase it: **one ⟨you⟩ might ⟨could⟩ say; [in limited contexts] what one ⟨you⟩ might call; what could ⟨might⟩ be called ⟨termed⟩.**

...Правдивость рассказчика нужна самому рассказчику прежде всего, это форма его борьбы с собственным распадом, можно сказать, божественный эгоизм собственного бытия (Искандер 3). ...The storyteller's veracity is necessary first of all to the storyteller himself. It is a form of his struggle against his own disintegration; it is, one might say, the divine egoism of his own being (3a). ♦ «Пусть видят все, весь Петербург, как милостыни просят дети благородного отца, который всю жизнь служил верою и правдой и, можно сказать, умер на службе» (Достоевский 3). "Let everybody see, let the whole of St. Petersburg see these children begging for alms, although they had a respectable father who gave a lifetime of true and faithful service and even died, you might say, in harness" (3a). ♦ Михаилу, можно сказать, повезло. Берег обрывистый, старая развесистая черёмуха над плёсом, так что ни малейшей тени (Абрамов 1). You could say that Mikhail was lucky. The bank was steep and there was a big old bird-cherry tree spreading over that stretch of river, so there was not the slightest shadow (1a). ♦ Фишер соответствующим жестом пояснил своему спутнику, что вот теперь тот в «святая святых», в таком, можно сказать, убежище свободного духа, где производится неподцензурный альбом «Скажи изюм!»... (Аксёнов 12). With an appropriate gesture Fisher made it clear to his companion that now he was in the inner sanctum, in what might be termed the refuge of the free spirit, where the uncensored album *Say Cheese!* was being produced… (12a).

C-210 • **НЕЛЬЗЯ́ СКАЗА́ТЬ, чтобы…** [main clause in a complex sent; Invar; fixed WO] it would be incorrect, unjustified to state that…: **one ⟨you⟩ cannot ⟨could not⟩ say (that)…; s.o. ⟨sth.⟩ cannot be ⟨could not have been⟩ said to…; it cannot ⟨could not⟩ be said ⟨claimed⟩ (that)…; it can hardly be said (that)…; [in limited contexts] not that…**

Нельзя сказать, чтоб предводитель отличался особенными качествами ума и сердца… (Салтыков-Щедрин 1). One could not say that the marshal was notable for any special qualities of the mind or heart… (1a). ♦ Привязав лошадь у Нюриной калитки, председатель Голубев поднялся на крыльцо. Нельзя сказать, чтобы он при этом сохранял полное присутствие духа, скорее наоборот, он входил в Нюрин дом, испытывая примерно такое волнение, как входя к первому секретарю райкома (Войнович 2). Chairman Golubev tied his horse to Nyura's gate and climbed up to the porch. It cannot be said he maintained complete composure; quite the contrary, he was entering Nyura's house with the same sort of trepidation he'd experienced when going in to see the First Secretary of the District Committee (2a). ♦ Нельзя сказать, чтоб утро пропадало даром в доме Обломовых. Стук ножей, рубивших котлеты и зелень в кухне, долетал даже до деревни (Гончаров 1). It could not be said that the morning was wasted in the Oblomov house. The clatter of knives chopping meat and vegetables in the kitchen was heard as far as the village (1b). ♦ «Обстановка на фронте, товарищ Мелехов, на нынешний день такова: красные удерживают Усть-Медведицкую… Обдонские высоты заняты ими. Ну, и позиции их — нельзя сказать, чтобы были неприступные, но… довольно-таки трудные для овладения» (Шолохов 5). "The situation at the front, Comrade Melekhov, as of today's date is as follows. The Reds are holding Ust-Medveditskaya….They command the high ground along the Don. Not that their positions are impregnable but they're going to be rather difficult to capture" (5a).

C-211 • **НЕ́ЧЕГО СКАЗА́ТЬ** *coll* [Invar; fixed WO] **1.** [Interj] used to express displeasure with, indignation at, or an ironic attitude toward s.o., sth., or, occas., o.s. (used in conjunction with a word or phrase expressing a positive evaluation to emphasize that this word or phrase is used ironically): **(a fine ⟨nice, brilliant** etc⟩ [NP]), **I must say!; (a fine ⟨nice, brilliant** etc⟩ [NP]), **indeed ⟨to be sure⟩!; some** [NP] **(he ⟨that** etc⟩ **is)!**

«Поздравляю, господин исправник. Ай да бумага! По этим приметам немудрено будет вам отыскать Дубровского. Да кто же не среднего роста, у кого не русые волосы, не прямой нос да не карие глаза!.. Нечего сказать, умные головушки приказные» (Пушкин 1). "I congratulate you, Mr Chief of police. What a document! It'll be easy to trace Dubrovsky from such a description! Who is not of medium height? Who has not got fair hair – or a straight nose, or brown eyes?…I must say, these officials are clever fellows!" (1b). ♦ Хорош, нечего сказать! Опять двойку принёс – уже вторую на этой неделе. You're a fine one indeed! This is the second "D" you've brought home this week. ♦ «Хорош, нечего сказать! хорош мальчик!.. Отец на одре лежит, а он забавляется, квартального на медведя верхом сажает. Стыдно, батюшка, стыдно!» (Толстой 4). "A fine fellow, to be sure! A fine fellow!…His father is on his deathbed, and he amuses himself by mounting a policeman on a bear. For shame, sir, for shame!" (4a).

2. *obs* [usu. sent adv (parenth)] (used to confirm the truth and indisputable nature of what is being stated) truly, without question: **there's no denying it; you ⟨one⟩ cannot deny it; [in limited contexts] and ⟨make⟩ no mistake (about it).**

«Что будет — то будет, — сказала попадья, — а жаль, если не Владимир Андреевич будет нашим господином. Молодец, нечего сказать» (Пушкин 1). "What will be, will be," said the priest's wife. "But it'll be a pity if Vladimir Andreyevitch does not become our master. He is a fine young man, and no mistake" (1b).

C-212 • **ТАК СКАЗА́ТЬ** [Invar; sent adv (parenth); fixed WO] if one may say it in such a way (used to tone down the phrasing of a statement or to indicate its impreciseness): **so to speak; as it were; one ⟨you⟩ might say; what one ⟨you⟩ might call…; in a manner of speaking.**

«Хочешь, Лёва, я тебе, от всей души, совет дам? Так сказать, одно правило подскажу. „Правило правой руки Митишатьева"… „Если человек кажется дерьмом — то он и есть дерьмо"» (Битов 2). "Want me to give you some advice, Lyova, from the bottom of my heart? Let me suggest a rule, so to speak. Mitishatyev's Right-Hand Rule: 'If a man seems to be a turd, he *is* a turd'" (2a). ♦ …Он уже потому чувствовал себя беззащитным перед демагогами, что последние, так сказать, считали его своим созданием и в этом смысле действовали до крайности ловко (Салтыков-Щедрин 1). …He felt himself defenceless against the demagogues because they saw in him, as it were, their own creation, and in this respect they had acted extremely cleverly (1b). ♦ Конечно, и Васькин за это время преуспел. Но — с большим отставанием и в меньших масштабах [, чем я], на задворках, так сказать (Зиновьев 2). Of course, during the same period Vaskin, too, came to succeed. But he was very much behind me, on a lower scale – forced, one might say, to take a back seat (2a).

C-213 • **ЧТО́БЫ НЕ СКАЗА́ТЬ…** [Invar; used as Conj; fixed WO] used to introduce a harsher phrasing of what has just been stated, or to introduce a word (compar form of Adv) indicating that the speaker could have phrased his statement more harshly: **(and) you could even (go so far as to) say; (and) it wouldn't even be stretching it to say;** ‖ ~ **больше ⟨хуже и т. п.⟩** ≃ **to say the least; to put it mildly ⟨lightly⟩.**

Михаил вёл себя нечестно, чтобы не сказать просто подло. Mikhail acted dishonestly – you could even say downright meanly. ♦ «В этом государстве, чтобы не сказать хуже, вы единственный, кого мне не противно целовать…» (Окуджава 2). "In this kingdom, to put it mildly, you are the only person it does not disgust me to kiss" (2a).

C-214 • **СКА́ЗКА ПРО БЕ́ЛОГО БЫЧКА́** *coll, usu. disapprov* [NP; usu. sing; fixed WO] a topic that is brought up or returned to incessantly, or the raising of or return to the same topic incessantly: **(it's) the same old story ⟨thing, stuff, song** etc⟩; **(s.o. brings up** etc⟩ **the same thing all over again.**

«А где… она [Таньчора], где? Почему её тут нету?» — «Опять „где она". Сказка про белого бычка у нас с тобой, мать, получается» (Распутин 3). "Well, where is she [Tanchora]… eh? Why ain't she here?" "Here we go again. You keep coming back to the same old song, Mum" (3a).

C-215 • **СКО́РО СКА́ЗКА СКА́ЗЫВАЕТСЯ, ДА ⟨А⟩ НЕ СКО́РО ДЕ́ЛО ДЕ́ЛАЕТСЯ** [saying; traditional refrain in folk tales] some matter, job etc may be described quickly, but takes much time to accomplish: ≃ **(it's) easier said than done.**

[Кулигин:] Судятся-судятся [купцы] здесь, да в губернию поедут… Скоро сказка сказывается, да не скоро дело делается: водят их, водят, волочат их, волочат… (Островский 6). [K.:] There's trial after trial here, and they [the merchants] even take it to the provincial capital….But it's easier said than done: they lead them on, and on, and drag it out and out… (6a).

C-216 • **НИ В СКА́ЗКЕ СКАЗА́ТЬ, НИ ПЕРО́М ОПИСА́ТЬ** *folk poet* [Invar; predic (impers or with subj: any common noun); fixed WO] (used to describe the highest degree of some quality, characteristic, attribute etc) a person, thing etc is too extraordinary to be described: **(mere) words cannot (begin to) describe it; one ⟨you⟩ couldn't begin to describe it (with words); (some person or thing is) more [AdjP] than words can tell ⟨say⟩.**

«Я видел, как они [американцы] Германию разделывали. Ни в сказке сказать, ни пером описать... Летели сотни-тысячи в два, три слоя» (Копелев 1). "I saw them [the Americans] deal with Germany. You couldn't begin to describe it. Hundreds and thousands flew in two or three formations" (1a). ♦ ...Она [няня] нашёптывала ему [Обломову] о какой-то неведомой стороне... где никто ничего круглый год не делает, а день-деньской только и знают, что гуляют всё добрые молодцы, такие, как Илья Ильич, да красавицы, что ни в сказке сказать, ни пером описать (Гончаров 1). ...[Oblomov's nurse] was whispering a fairystory to him about some wonderful country...where no one did a stroke of work all the year round, and fine fellows, like Oblomov, and maidens more beautiful than words can tell did nothing but enjoy themselves all day long (1a).

С-217 • БА́БЬИ ⟨БА́БУШКИНЫ⟩ СКА́ЗКИ *coll, rather derog* [NP; pl only; fixed WO] fables, nonsense: **old wives' tales.**

«Бог с тебя спросит, Иван». — «Никакого Бога нету... Бабьи сказки» (Максимов 2). "You'll answer for it to God, you know." "There ain't no God... Old wives' tales" (2a).

С-218 • РАССКА́ЗЫВАТЬ СКА́ЗКИ *(кому) coll* [VP; subj: human] to tell s.o. invented, fabricated, concocted stories: X рассказывает (Y-у) сказки ≃ **X is spinning yarns; X is telling (fish) stories; X is telling tall tales; X is telling ⟨giving, handing⟩ Y cock-and-bull stories; X is handing Y a line;** [in limited contexts] **X is giving Y a song and dance; X is making it up;** ‖ *Neg Imper* не рассказывай сказки ≃ **don't give me that.** Cf. **tell it to the marines.**

[author's usage] «Не кипятись, Варвара! Я никогда не вру». — «Врёшь! Врёшь! Это кому ты сказки-то сказываешь?» (Абрамов 1). "Don't get worked up, Varvara. I never lie to you." "Liar! Liar! Who are you telling stories to?" (1a). ♦ «И каждому из нас отлично понятно, что именно ты хотел сказать этими своими словами... А теперь будешь нам сказки рассказывать, он, мол, не в этом смысле» (Войнович 4). "Everyone here understands full well just what you meant by those words....And now, you're going to hand us some cock-and-bull story about what you meant and didn't mean" (4a). ♦ [Шмага:] ...Я убеждал Гришку отправиться в трактир «Собрание весёлых друзей»... [Дудукин:] Отказался? Неужели? [Коринкина:] Да это он сказки рассказывает (Островский 3). [Sh.:] ...I tried to convince Grisha to set out with me for the Merrymen Tavern.... [D.:] You mean to say he refused? Is it possible? [K.:] Don't listen to him, he's just making it up (3a).

С-219 • НА (ВСЁМ ⟨ПО́ЛНОМ⟩) СКАКУ́ [PrepP; these forms only; adv] **1.** while galloping: на скаку ≃ **at a gallop; as one is galloping (along);** ‖ на всём скаку ≃ **at (a) full gallop; (gallop) at full tilt.**

«Вот наконец мы были уж от него [Казбича] на ружейный выстрел... Смотрю: Печорин на скаку приложился из ружья... „Не стреляйте! — кричу я ему, — берегите заряд; мы и так его догоним"» (Лермонтов 1). "Well, at last we got within rifle range of him [Kazbich]....I looked and saw Pechorin take aim at full gallop. 'Don't fire!' I cried to him. 'Save your shot, we'll catch up with him anyway'" (1a). ♦ Воротца на задворках были открыты, и Михаил на всём скаку влетел в заулок (Абрамов 1). The gate around back was open, and Mikhail galloped into the yard at full tilt (1a).

2. ~ остановить лошадь, остановиться to stop a horse suddenly, come to an abrupt halt: **rein in a horse from a full gallop (to a sudden halt); pull up a horse abruptly ⟨short⟩ (from a full gallop); come ⟨bring one's horse⟩ to a sudden halt.**

С-220 • СО ШКО́ЛЬНОЙ ⟨С УНИВЕРСИТЕ́ТСКОЙ и т. п.⟩ СКАМЬИ́ [PrepP; these forms only; fixed WO] **1.** [subj-compl with быть₀ (subj: human) or adv] one has just fin-

ished high school or college: X − (только что) со школьной ⟨с университетской⟩ скамьи ≃ **X is right ⟨just, fresh⟩ out of school ⟨college⟩.**

2. [adv] from the time of one's study in school (or college): **from one's school ⟨schoolroom, classroom, university, college⟩ days.**

Ужаснее всего это нескончаемое притворство и двуличие, входящее в плоть и кровь советского человека уже со школьной скамьи (Аллилуева 2). The ugliest feature of Soviet life was the endless dissimulation and double-facedness infused into the Soviet people from their schoolroom days, so that it became almost second-nature (2a).

С-221 • СКА́ТЕРТЬЮ ДОРО́ГА ⟨ДОРО́ЖКА⟩ (кому) *coll* [indep. sent; these forms only; fixed WO] **1.** *obs* a wish for a good journey: **I wish you ⟨him etc⟩ Godspeed ⟨godspeed⟩; (may) God speed you ⟨him etc⟩ (on your ⟨his etc⟩ way); Godspeed to you ⟨him etc⟩!;** [in direct address only] **Godspeed!**

[Феклуша:] Что делаешь, милая? [Глаша:] Хозяина в дорогу собираю... [Феклуша:] Надолго, милая, едет? [Глаша:] Нет, не надолго. [Феклуша:] Ну, скатертью ему дорога! (Островский 6). [F.:] What's that you're busy at now? [G.:] Getting my master's clothes ready for his journey... [F.:] Will he be gone long, my dear? [G.:] No, not long. [F.:] I wish him godspeed, that I do (6b).

2. go away or let s.o. go away (used as a wish to be free of s.o. or as a scornful dismissal of s.o.): **good riddance.**

[Надя:] Тогда уйду я! [Лукашин:] Скатертью дорога! (Брагинский и Рязанов 1). [N.:] I'll go myself then! [L.:] Good riddance! (1a).

С-222 • СКА́ЧКА С ПРЕПЯ́ТСТВИЯМИ *coll, humor* [NP; fixed WO] an undertaking, process etc that does not progress smoothly, that constantly meets with difficulties: **uphill battle;** [in limited contexts] **obstacle course.**

[Дорн (стараясь отворить левую дверь):] Странно. Дверь как будто заперта... Скачка с препятствиями (Чехов 6). [D. (trying to open the door on left):] Extraordinary! The door seems to be locked....An obstacle course! (6b).

С-223 • (НЕТ) НИ СКЛА́ДУ НИ ЛА́ДУ *в чём highly coll* [VP_subj/gen; fixed WO] sth. lacks logic, order, sth. is done without coordination etc: в X-е ни складу ни ладу ≃ **there is no rhyme or reason to X.**

На каждом объекте люди с бору да сосенки, во всём ни складу ни ладу... (Иоффе 1). People are chosen at random to do certain jobs, no rhyme or reason to it at all (1a).

С-224 • НА СКЛО́НЕ ЛЕТ ⟨ДНЕЙ, ЖИ́ЗНИ⟩ [PrepP; these forms only; adv; fixed WO] when one is old: **in one's declining ⟨later⟩ years; in one's old age; in the twilight ⟨the winter⟩ of one's life.**

Пьер Корнель не знает, что на склоне лет он будет рад, когда мальчишка примет к постановке его пьесу и заплатит ему, постепенно беднеющему драматургу, деньги за эту пьесу (Булгаков 5). Pierre Corneille does not know that in his declining years he will be happy when this boy accepts his play for production and pays him, a playwright gradually sinking into poverty, money for the play (5a). ♦ Это советский пешеход-физкультурник, который вышел из Владивостока юношей и на склоне лет у самых ворот Москвы будет задавлен тяжелым автокаром, номер которого так и не успеют заметить (Ильф и Петров 2). He's a hiker who left Vladivostok as a young man and who, in his old age, will be run over at the very gates of Moscow by a large truck, the number of which no one will have a chance to catch (2a).

С-225 • В СКО́БКАХ сказать, заметить, прибавить, упомянуть и т. п. [PrepP; Invar; adv] (to note, add, say etc sth.)

incidentally, as an aside from the main topic: **parenthetically; in parentheses ⟨parenthesis⟩**.

Заметим в скобках и мельком, что Пётр Ильич был довольно-таки красивый молодой человек, и сам это знал о себе (Достоевский 1). Let us note parenthetically in passing that Pyotr Ilyich was quite a handsome young man, and was aware of it himself (1a). ♦ …Она казалась гораздо моложе своих лет, что бывает почти всегда с женщинами, сохранившими ясность духа, свежесть впечатлений и честный, чистый жар сердца до старости. Скажем в скобках, что сохранить всё это есть единственное средство не потерять красоты своей даже в старости (Достоевский 3). …She looked much younger than her years, something that nearly always happens to women who keep the lucidity of their spirit, the freshness of their perceptions, and an honest, pure warmth of heart until old age. Let us observe in parenthesis that the retention of all these things is the only means by which one may avoid losing one's looks even when one is old (3d).

С-226 • ВЫНОСИ́ТЬ/ВЫ́НЕСТИ ЗА СКО́БКИ *что lit*
[VP; subj: human] to separate a certain question, problem, occurrence etc from the context in which it belongs: X вынес Y за скобки ≃ **X took Y out of context; X isolated Y;** [in limited contexts] **Y was torn from ⟨out of⟩ (its) context.**

«Тезис личной судьбы — вот что ты не хочешь учесть в своих рассуждениях. На протяжении всех культур — греческой, египетской, европейской — он казался вынесенным за скобки, свободным от законов истории» (Каверин 2). "The thesis of personal destiny — that's what you leave out of account in your deliberations. In the course of every culture — Greek, Egyptian, European, it appears to have been torn out of its context and has not been subject to the laws of history" (2a).

С-227 • ВО ВЕСЬ СКОК *лететь, пустить лошадь и т. п.*
[PrepP; Invar; adv; fixed WO] (of a horse) (to race along) as fast as possible; (of a person) (to make one's horse go) as fast as possible: **(race along ⟨go⟩) at (a) full gallop; (put one's horse) to a full gallop; (go ⟨make one's horse go⟩) flat out.**

Ростов пустил лошадь во весь скок, для того чтоб уехать с дороги от этих кавалеристов… (Толстой 4). Rostov put his horse to a full gallop to get out of their [the cavalry men's] way… (4a).

С-228 • СКО́ЛЬКО (…) НИ…; СКО́ЛЬКО БЫ (…) НИ… [subord Conj, concessive] regardless of how great a number of times (one does or attempts sth.) or regardless of how great a quantity of sth. (exists, is in s.o.'s possession etc) (the desired result will not be achieved): **however much; no matter how much ⟨how often, how many times etc⟩; as much as;** ‖ сколько ни пытайся ≃ **try as you might; however ⟨no matter how⟩ hard you try; despite all s.o.'s efforts;** ‖ [when used with NP] **no matter how much** [NP] **⟨how many** [NPs]**⟩; it doesn't matter how much** [NP] **⟨how many** [NPs]**⟩.**

…Сколько ей [Марье] ни толкуй — не понимает, что по нынешним временам учение — основа жизни (Абрамов 1). However much you explain it to her [Marya], she doesn't understand that today learning is the foundation of life (1b). ♦ Признаюсь, сколько я ни старался различить вдалеке что-нибудь наподобие лодки, но безуспешно (Лермонтов 1). I must confess that however hard I tried to make out something like a boat in the distance, I had no success (1d). ♦ …Сколько его [Цурцумия] ни уговаривали, он твёрдо стоял на своём (Искандер 4). …Despite their best efforts to win him [Tsurtsumia] over, he firmly stood his ground (4a).

С-229 • ДО СКОНЧА́НИЯ ВЕ́КА ⟨МИ́РА *obs*⟩ *coll*
[PrepP; these forms only; adv; fixed WO] (usu. in refer. to sth. unpleasant, undesirable) (to do sth., continue etc) forever, eternally: **till the end of time.**

С-230 • ВСЕМ СКО́ПОМ *coll* [NP$_{instrum}$; Invar; adv; fixed WO] (of people) (to do sth.) together, jointly: **in ⟨as⟩ a group; as one man ⟨person⟩.**

Если же коллектив всем скопом набрасывался на одного своего члена… — такой коллектив по понятиям людей и выше Степанова был *здоровый* (Солженицын 3). If the collective as one man attacked one of its members…that collective — according to the notion shared by people even higher than Stepanov — was *healthy* (3a).

С-231 • МИРОВА́Я СКОРБЬ *lit, iron* [NP; sing only; fixed WO] extreme pessimism, disillusionment with life: **world-weariness;** *Weltschmerz*.

С какой-то точки зрения стукачи мало чем отличаются от наших либеральных друзей. Они по крайней мере не изображают из себя мировую скорбь (Зиновьев 1). "From a certain point of view informers aren't very different from our liberal friends. And at least they don't pretend to be suffering from world weariness" (1a).

С-232 • СКОРЕ́Е ВСЕГО́ [AdvP; Invar; usu. sent adv; fixed WO] very probably, the probability is great (that…): **most likely ⟨probably⟩; in all likelihood ⟨probability⟩; chances are; more likely (than not).**

…Он мне говорил, что был когда-то эсером, за это и пострадал. Я в это не верил тогда и сейчас думаю, что сидел он скорее всего по уголовному делу… (Войнович 5). …He told me that it was once having been a member of the Socialist Revolutionary Party which had caused him so much grief. I didn't believe it then, and now I think that he'd most likely been in prison on criminal charges (5a). ♦ …Ягов теперь заключил, что Парвус надувал германскую империю, никакой революции реально не готовил, а взятые миллионы скорее всего положил себе в карман (Солженицын 5). …Jagow now concluded that Parvus had been deceiving the German Reich all along, that he had never seriously tried to bring about a revolution, that he had most probably simply pocketed the millions given to him (5a). ♦ …Небольшого ума требует, взглянув на всё, понять, что выигрыш тут мал и временен и всё совершенно вилами по воде писано: выигрыш ли ещё это, — а скорее всего, что и нет… (Битов 2). …It doesn't take much intelligence to realize, all things considered, that the gain here is small and temporary and it's still up in the air whether it *is* a gain, more likely it's not… (2a).

С-233 • ЗАМЫКА́ТЬСЯ/ЗАМКНУ́ТЬСЯ ⟨УХОДИ́ТЬ/УЙТИ́, ПРЯ́ТАТЬСЯ/СПРЯ́ТАТЬСЯ⟩ В СВОЮ́ СКОРЛУПУ́ [VP; subj: human; usu. this WO] to stand aloof from one's surroundings, isolate o.s. from the world around one: X замкнулся в свою скорлупу ≃ **X retreated ⟨withdrew⟩ into his shell; X retreated into himself.**

«…Считай я, например, того, другого, третьего за преступника, ну зачем, спрошу, буду я его раньше срока беспокоить, хотя бы я и улики против него имел-с?.. Ведь засади его не вовремя, — хоть я бы и был уверен, что это *он,* — так ведь я, пожалуй, сам у себя средства отниму к дальнейшему его обличению, а почему? А потому что я ему, так сказать, определённое положение дам, так сказать, психологически его определю и успокою, вот он и уйдёт от меня в свою скорлупу: поймёт наконец, что он арестант» (Достоевский 3). "…Suppose I think, for example, that this man or that or somebody else is a criminal; now, why, I ask you, should I bother him too soon, even if I had evidence against him, eh?…Suppose I lock him up too soon, even though I'm absolutely positive it's *him;* well, then, more than likely I'm depriving myself of the means to incriminate him further. Why so? Because I'm giving him, so to speak, a definite status, yes; I'm defining him, so to speak, psychologically, and putting his mind at rest, and then he'll go away from me and retreat into his shell — he'll realize, at last, that he's a suspect" (3a). ♦ В эпохи насилия и террора люди прячутся в свою скорлупу и скрывают свои чувства, но чувства эти неискоренимы, и никаким воспитанием их не уничтожить (Мандельштам 1). In periods of violence and terror people retreat into themselves and hide their feelings, but their feelings are ineradicable and cannot be destroyed by any amount of indoctrination (1a).

С-234 • ВЫХОДИ́ТЬ/ВЫ́ЙТИ ИЗ СВОЕЙ СКОРЛУПЫ́ [VP; subj: human; usu. this WO] to begin to open o.s. up to the world around one, stop cutting o.s. off from one's surroundings: X вышел из своей скорлупы ≃ **X came out of his shell.**

Вокруг столько интересного, а ты живёшь, как отшельник. Пора тебе выйти из своей скорлупы. The world is filled with so many interesting things, and yet you live like a hermit. It's time for you to come out of your shell.

С-235 • КОЛЬ СКО́РО *lit;* **КАК СКО́РО** *obs* [subord Conj] **1.** [condit; used with verbs in the indicative] considering that: **as long as; since.**

«Пролетарский поэт и восхищался стихами контрика? И никто не донёс?.. Не смею сомневаться, коль скоро вы настаиваете. Но я дивлюсь, дивлюсь!» (Копелев 1). "A proletarian poet enjoying the poetry of a 'contra'? And no one denounced him?...I don't dare doubt you, since you insist. But I am amazed, amazed!" (1a).

2. *rare* [temporal] used to show that the situation or action presented in the main clause immediately follows the situation or action presented in the subordinate clause: **as soon as; just as; hardly ⟨scarcely, just⟩...when; the moment ⟨the minute⟩...; no sooner...than.**

Грушницкого страсть была декламировать: он закидывал вас словами, как скоро разговор выходил из круга обыкновенных понятий... (Лермонтов 1). Grushnitski's passion was to declaim; he bombarded you with words as soon as the talk transcended the circle of everyday notions... (1a). ♦ ...Князь Андрей скакал в почтовой бричке, испытывая чувство человека, долго ждавшего и, наконец, достигшего начала желаемого счастия. Как скоро он закрывал глаза, в ушах его раздавалась пальба ружей и орудий, которая сливалась со стуком колёс и впечатлением победы (Толстой 4). ...Prince Andrei sped along in a post chaise, enjoying the feelings of a man who had at last begun to attain a long-desired happiness. The moment he closed his eyes, there echoed in his ears the sound of gunfire mingled with the rattle of wheels and the sensations of victory (4a). ♦ Несмотря на то, что положение французского войска и его численность были неизвестны русским, как скоро изменилось отношение, необходимость наступления тотчас же выразилась в бесчисленном количестве признаков (Толстой 7). Though the condition and numerical strength of the French army were unknown to the Russians, this change had no sooner occurred than the need for attacking manifested itself in countless signs (7a).

С-236 • СКРЕ́ЖЕТ ЗУБО́ВНЫЙ; often СО СКРЕ́ЖЕТОМ ЗУБО́ВНЫМ *both lit* [NP, subj or obj (1st var.); PrepP, Invar, adv (2nd var.); usu. this WO] hatred, malice; (one does sth.) extremely unwillingly, hating what he has to do, having to overcome internal resistance: скрежет зубовный ≃ **gnashing ⟨clenching, grinding⟩ of one's teeth;** ∥ со скрежетом зубовным ≃ **gnashing ⟨clenching, grinding⟩ one's teeth.**

[author's usage] «...Я ушёл с убеждением, что существо это [Смердяков] решительно злобное, непомерно честолюбивое, мстительное и знойно завистливое. Я собрал кой-какие сведения: он ненавидел происхождение своё, стыдился его и со скрежетом зубов припоминал, что „от Смердящей произошёл"» (Достоевский 2). "...I left convinced that he [Smerdyakov] was a decidedly spiteful being, enormously ambitious, vengeful, and burning with envy. I gathered some information: he hated his origin, was ashamed of it, and gnashed his teeth when he recalled that he was 'descended from Stinking Lizaveta'" (2a).

< From the Bible (Matt. 8:12).

С-237 • ВТОРА́Я СКРИ́ПКА [NP; sing only; fixed WO] a person who occupies a secondary or subordinate position in sth.: **second fiddle; number two.**

«Мой второй старик, Фриц, тоже старательный... Но он у Вальтера вторая скрипка — подсобник...» (Копелев 1). "My other old man, Fritz, is also assiduous...but he's Walther's second fiddle, an assistant" (1a).

С-238 • ПЕ́РВАЯ СКРИ́ПКА [NP; sing only; fixed WO] a person who occupies the leading, predominant position in sth.: **number one; the number-one person; the pivotal ⟨key⟩ player; the top man ⟨woman⟩.**

С-239 • ИГРА́ТЬ ВТОРУ́Ю СКРИ́ПКУ [VP] **1.** [subj: human] to play the second violin part (in an orchestra or ensemble): X играет вторую скрипку ≃ **X plays second violin.**

2. ~ *(в чём)* [subj: usu. human or collect] to have a secondary or less important position (as compared to another person or group), be of secondary importance: X играет вторую скрипку ≃ **X plays second fiddle (to s.o.); X takes a back seat (to s.o.); X is number two.**

С-240 • ИГРА́ТЬ ПЕ́РВУЮ СКРИ́ПКУ [VP] **1.** [subj: human] to play the first violin part (in an orchestra or ensemble): X играет первую скрипку ≃ **X plays first violin.**

2. ~ *(в чём)* [subj: usu. human or collect] to occupy the leading, predominant position in sth.: X играет первую скрипку ≃ **X plays the leading role; X is number one; X is the pivotal ⟨key⟩ player; X is the top man ⟨woman⟩.**

С-241 • СО СКРИ́ПОМ идти, протекать, делать *что* и т. п. *coll* [PrepP; Invar; adv; more often used with impfv verbs] (in refer. to an undertaking, project etc) (to progress, do sth. etc) very slowly, impeded by difficulties along the way: **plod(ding) ⟨inch(ing)⟩ along; meet(ing) with all kinds of difficulties; with setbacks at every step; (progress) painfully slowly; it's slow going (all the way).**

Никто не мог понять... почему одних (меньшую часть) всё же выпускают из лагеря, хоть и со скрипом... а других, наоборот, загоняют в эту страшную категорию людей, оставляемых в лагере «до особого распоряжения» (Гинзбург 2). [context transl] No one could understand...why some—the minority—were released grudgingly...but still released; while others were consigned to the fearful category of those held in camps "pending special orders" (2a).

С-242 • НЕЛА́ДНО ⟨НЕСКЛА́ДНО, ХУ́ДО⟩ СКРО́ЕН, ДА КРЕ́ПКО ⟨ПЛО́ТНО⟩ СШИТ *coll* [AdjP; subj-compl with быть∅ (subj: human); pres or past; fixed WO] one is clumsily built and awkward, but strong and sturdy: X неладно скроен, да крепко сшит ≃ **X is poorly cut, but strongly sewn; X is badly cut, but strongly stitched together.**

Как взглянул он [Чичиков] на его [Собакевича] спину, широкую, как у вятских, приземистых лошадей, и на ноги его, походившие на чугунные тумбы, которые ставят на тротуарах, не мог не воскликнуть внутренно: «Эк наградил-то тебя бог! Вот уж точно, как говорят, неладно скроен, да крепко сшит!..» (Гоголь 3). After a glance at his [Sobakevich's] back, as broad as that of a thick-set Percheron horse from Vyatka, and at his legs, resembling the stumpy cast-iron pillars that are placed along sidewalks for displaying theater bills, he [Chichikov] could not help exclaiming inwardly, "Truly God has endowed you bountifully! Here is one who, as they say, is badly cut but strongly stitched together!..." (3c).

С-243 • ДАВА́ТЬ/ДАТЬ СЛАБИНУ́ *highly coll* [VP; subj: human] to yield (to s.o.'s requests, usu. out of a desire not to offend him); to back down from a stand one has taken, be insufficiently firm: X дал слабину ≃ **X showed weakness; X gave in.**

Иногда я пытался как-нибудь отбрыкаться [от чтения его рукописи]. «Ну зачем тебе моё мнение? Ты же знаешь, что от критики я отошёл...» Он в таких случаях пугался, смущался и пытался меня уверить, что ни на какую печатную критику и не надеется, ему достаточно только моего высокоавторитетного устного мнения. И, конечно, я всегда давал слабину (Войнович 6). Sometimes I tried to get out of it [reading his manuscript]. "Why do you want my opinion? You know I quit criticism...." Then, blushing, he would assure me that he wasn't asking for an actual review—just my highly authoritative verbal opinion. And of course I always gave in (6a).

C-244 • СЛА́ВА БО́ГУ *coll* [NP; Invar; fixed WO] **1.** [subj-compl with copula (subj: any common noun, often всё), adv, or indep. sent used in response to «Как дела?» etc] sth. is (things are) going well, without problems: **all right; (just) fine; pretty good; well and good;** [when used as indep. sent in response to «Как дела?»] **very well, thank you.**

У нас всё слава Богу, жаловаться не на что. Things are going just fine with us—no complaints. ♦ [Ислаев *(...оборачивается ко входящему Беляеву)*:] А... это вы! Ну... ну, как можете? [Беляев:] Слава богу, Аркадий Сергеич (Тургенев 1). [I. *(...turns to Beliayev, who has just entered)*:] Oh, it's you...well, how goes it? [B.:] Very well, thank you, Arkady Sergeych (1d).

2. [sent adv (parenth)] fortunately: **thank God ⟨goodness, heaven, the Lord⟩.**

Мой старик презирает этого Карамана, а всё-таки едет на его оплакивание... Но, слава богу, дом этого Карамана оказался недалеко (Искандер 3). My old man scorns this Karaman, but still he goes to his wake....But, thank God, this Karaman's house turned out to be nearby (3a). ♦ Меня лечил полковой цирюльник, ибо в крепости другого лекаря не было, и, слава богу, не умничал (Пушкин 2). The regimental barber—there was no other doctor in the fortress—treated my wound, and thank heaven, he did not try to be too clever (2b). ♦ «Сообщаю вам, что наш Гришка чудок не отдал богу душу, а сейчас, слава богу, находится живой и здоровый...» (Шолохов 2). "...I have to inform you that our Grisha nearly gave up the ghost, but that now, thank the Lord, he's alive and well..." (2a).

3. Also: **СЛА́ВА ТЕБЕ́ ⟨ТЕ** *substand*⟩ **ГО́СПОДИ** *coll* [Interj] used to express happiness, relief, or satisfaction on the occasion of sth.: **thank God ⟨heavens, goodness⟩; I'm happy ⟨glad⟩ (to hear it).**

Иван Николаевич покосился недоверчиво [на врача], но всё же пробурчал: «Слава те господи! Нашёлся наконец один нормальный среди идиотов...» (Булгаков 9). Ivan Nikolayevich looked at him [the doctor] distrustfully out of the corner of his eye; nevertheless he muttered: "Thank God! At last there is one normal man among all those idiots..." (9a). ♦ «Аппетит у меня хороший, — сказала Женя, — ...волнения на нём не отражаются». — «Ну, и слава Богу», — сказала Людмила Николаевна и поцеловала сестру (Гроссман 2). "Yes, I've got a good appetite. Nothing affects that...." "I'm glad to hear it," said Lyudmila, giving her sister a kiss (2a).

C-245 • ВО СЛА́ВУ *кого-чего lit* [PrepP; Invar; the resulting PrepP is adv or nonagreeing postmodif] for the praise and honor of s.o. or sth.: **to the glory of; for the greater glory of; in glorification of; glorifying.**

«Действие у меня в Испании, в Севилье, в самое страшное время инквизиции, когда во славу божию в стране ежедневно горели костры...» (Достоевский 1). "My action is set in Spain, in Seville, in the most horrible time of the Inquisition, when fires blazed every day to the glory of God..." (1a). ♦ ...Люди, принявшие эту доктрину, честно поработали во славу новой морали... (Мандельштам 1). ...The people who accepted this doctrine worked

sincerely for the greater glory of the new morality... (1a). ♦ ...Под гром рукоплесканий Лакоба выпил свой бокал. И не успел замолкнуть этот гром во славу скромности вождя, как в дверях появился повар в белом халате... (Искандер 3). [context transl] ...To the thunder of applause, Lakoba drained his glass. Before this thundering glorification of the Leader's modesty had stopped, the cook came through the door in his white apron... (3a).

C-246 • НА СЛА́ВУ *coll* [PrepP; Invar; adv or subj-compl with copula (subj: usu. concr or abstr)] very well, remarkably; great, remarkable: **beautiful(ly); wonderful(ly); wonderfully well; splendid(ly); glorious(ly); magnificent(ly);** [in limited contexts] **famously; (do) a wonderful job; most enjoyable ⟨-ably⟩;** ‖ X удался ~ ≃ **X was a smash ⟨a hit⟩; X was a big ⟨tremendous, immense⟩ success;** ‖ справить свадьбу ⟨день рождения и т. п.⟩ ~ ≃ **celebrate a wedding ⟨a birthday etc⟩ in a big way;** [in limited contexts] **make an occasion of one's ⟨s.o.'s⟩ wedding ⟨birthday etc⟩.**

День направлялся на славу; в добрый день выпало старикам уезжать с Матёры (Распутин 4). The day promised to be beautiful; the weather was good on the day the old people had to leave Matyora (4a). ♦ День разгулялся на славу (Абрамов 1). It had turned out to be a splendid day (1a). ♦ ...Она взялась накрыть стол, доставить бельё, посуду и проч. и приготовить на своей кухне кушанье... Действительно, всё было приготовлено на славу... (Достоевский 3). ...She had undertaken to set the table and obtain a tablecloth and crockery, etc., and to prepare the food in her kitchen....And indeed everything had been done wonderfully well... (3a). ...She undertook to lay the table, to provide linen, dishes, and so on, and to prepare the food in her kitchen....Indeed, everything was done up famously... (3c). ♦ Мастерская сверкала... немыслимой чистотой. Панкратиха поработала на славу (Некрасов 1). The studio gleamed with an...impossible cleanliness. Pankratikha had done a wonderful job (1a). ♦ ...Вечер получился на славу. Все были в приподнятом настроении... (Айтматов 2). ...It was a most enjoyable evening. Everyone was in good spirits... (1a). ♦ Ёлка удалась на славу. Да это и не трудно было (Гинзбург 2). The New Year's concert was an immense success, which was not all that hard to achieve (2a). ♦ Комиссар был гостеприимен, любил людей... И он захотел справить свадьбу на славу, как справляют этот праздник в степи, на просторе, под небом (Федин 1). The commissar was hospitable, he liked people....And he wanted to make an occasion of his wedding, as is done in the steppes, out in the open, under the open sky (1a).

C-247 • НЕ СЛА́ДКО *кому coll* [Invar; usu. impers predic with copula or subj-compl with copula (subj: infin)] (in refer. to s.o.'s life, the way things in general are going for s.o. etc) sth. is unpleasant, difficult for s.o.: X-у (приходится) не сладко ≃ **life is not sweet ⟨easy, a bowl of cherries⟩ for X; life is no picnic ⟨party⟩ for X; things are bad ⟨rough⟩ for X; X is not having an easy time (of it);** [in limited contexts] **it ⟨doing sth.⟩ is hard on X.**

Он [Коля] добился своего — Даша осталась с ним. Но и ему пришлось не сладко — кончался нэп, наступал государственный сектор (Искандер 3). He [Kolya] got what he wanted—Dasha remained with him. But life was not sweet for him—the New Economic Policy ended, the state took over the economy (3a). ♦ Прямо напротив нас живёт Настя, бывшая колхозница из-под Харькова. Во время войны её, тогда молодую девушку, немцы угнали в Германию. После войны домой не вернулась. Здесь ей было не сладко, но и на родину ехать не решилась (Войнович 1). Nastya, a former collective-farm worker from outside Kharkov, lives right across from us. During the war, when she was a young girl, the Germans deported her to work in Germany. She didn't return to the Soviet Union after the war. Life wasn't easy for her here; even so, she couldn't bring herself to return to her native land... (1a). ♦ «Жена совершенно права. И без вас не сладко. Собачья жизнь, сумасшедший дом. Всё время меж двух огней...»

(Пастернак 1). "My wife is quite right. Things are bad enough without you. It's a dog's life, a madhouse. I am caught between two fires" (1a). ♦ ...Сквозь мятые, подмоченные дождём строки письма ощутимо дышала горькая грусть. Не сладко, видно, и Петру вливалась служба (Шолохов 2). ...The crumpled, rain-blurred lines of the letter were tinged with a bitter sadness. Evidently Petro was not having an easy time [in the army] either (2a). ♦ «Пересудов людских ты боишься... Что они тебе?.. Не людей — себя слушай. Ты знаешь, как было. Что ни перед кем ты не виноватая... Этим себя охраняй, этим спасайся, этим. Конечно, не сладко тебе придётся» (Распутин 2). "You're afraid of people's judgment....What do you care!...Don't listen to people—listen to yourself. You know what really happened: that you're not to blame before anyone....Guard yourself, save yourself with those thoughts. Of course, it'll be hard on you" (2a).

C-248 • СЛÁДУ ⟨-а⟩ НЕТ с кем-чем coll [VP; impers; prep obj: human or collect] it is impossible to cope (with s.o. or sth.): с Х-ом сладу нет ≃ **there is nothing I ⟨he etc⟩ can do with X; I ⟨he etc⟩ can't do anything with X; there is no dealing with X; X is impossible ⟨unmanageable⟩; person X is ⟨gets⟩ out of hand.**

...Случилось одно небольшое происшествие в станционной парикмахерской. Решили подстричь ребят. А когда очередь дошла до Эрмека, тут поднялся такой крик и плач, что сладу не было никакого с мальчишкой (Айтматов 2). ...There had been one small incident in the local hairdressers. They had decided to get the children's hair cut. And when it had come to Ermek's turn, he set up such a great display of shouting and tears, that there was nothing they could do with the boy (2a). ♦ «А этот, — она снисходительно кивнула в сторону мальчишки... — совсем от рук отбился, никакого сладу с ним нет. Был бы отец, научил бы уму-разуму...» (Максимов 1). "But as for him," she gave a contemptuous nod in the direction of the boy..., "he's got completely out of hand, I can't do anything with him. If his father was here he'd knock some sense into him..." (1a). ♦ На террасе татарского дома, где мы спали на положенном на пол тюфяке, он [Мандельштам] долго заедал меня, что ему пришлось целый час искать меня, что я своей глупостью срываю ему работу, что со мной нет сладу и что я никогда не поумнею... (Мандельштам 2). On the veranda of the Tartar house (where we slept on a mattress laid on the floor) he [Mandelstam] went on at me a long time about how he had spent a whole hour trying to find me, about how hard I was making it for him to do his work—I had got quite out of hand and would never learn any sense (2a).

C-249 • (И) СЛÉД ПРОСТЫ́Л ⟨ПРОПÁЛ⟩ coll [VP_subj; these forms only; fixed WO] **1.** кого-чего ~ (of a person, animal, or vehicle) s.o. or sth. abruptly disappeared (when of a person, by hiding or running off), making it seem as if he or it had never been in the place in question at all: Х-а и след простыл ≃ **X vanished without a trace; X vanished ⟨disappeared⟩ into thin air; all trace of X vanished ⟨disappeared⟩; [in limited contexts] X was long gone; person X beat it ⟨flew the coop, took off⟩.**

Думаю, что козы — самые хитрые из всех четвероногих. Бывало, только зазеваешься, а их уже и след простыл... (Искандер 6). I think goats are the most cunning of all four-legged creatures. I had only to let my mind wander a moment and sometimes they would vanish without a trace... (6a). ♦ Потребовал Бородавкин к себе вероломного жида, чтоб повесить, но его уж и след простыл... (Салтыков-Щедрин 1). Wartkin summoned the perfidious Jew in order to hang him, but he had disappeared into thin air... (1a). ♦ ...Едва я на миг отвернулся, как на пустом месте уже снова стоял знакомый розовый куст, а девушки и след простыл (Катаев 2). ...I only had to turn away for a moment for the familiar pink bush to reappear in this empty space, while all trace of the girl had disappeared (2a). ♦ Он [старик] повернулся, чтобы снова ухватить к себе за рукав длинноволосого, в джинсах и с портфельчиком, врага, но того, оказывается, уже и след простыл

(Аксёнов 7). ...He [the old man] swirled around to recapture the enemy, but the enemy—long hair, jeans, attaché case, and all—had in the interim flown the coop (7a).

2. чего ~ (of lost, stolen etc objects) sth. disappeared and cannot be found or gotten back: Х-а и след простыл ≃ [present contexts] **X is nowhere to be found ⟨seen⟩; there is no sign of X (anywhere); (it's as if) X vanished into thin air.**

Вчера я забыла на работе сумку. Вернулась с полдороги — а её и след простыл. Yesterday I forgot my pocketbook at work, and when I went back for it, it was nowhere to be found.

C-250 • НАПАДÁТЬ/НАПÁСТЬ ⟨ПОПАДÁТЬ/ПО-ПÁСТЬ obsoles⟩ **НА СЛЕД** чей, кого-чего [VP; subj: human or collect; more often pfv] to uncover information or leads that allow one to follow or find s.o. (usu. a fugitive, a missing person, or s.o. who does not want his whereabouts known) or to find sth. (often a stolen object, an object whose location is being kept secret etc): X напал на след Y-а ≃ **X picked up the scent (of person Y); X got on the track ⟨trail⟩ of Y; X picked up Y's trail; X came upon evidence of thing Y.**

Эсэсовцы свирепствовали на станции, пытаясь обнаружить пособников налёта... Гестаповцам удалось напасть на след. Во время допросов и пыток кто-то назвал имя Андрея Сташенка (Рыбаков 1). The Gestapo went on the rampage at the station in their efforts to find the accomplices.... [They] managed to pick up the scent. Under interrogation and torture, someone mentioned Andrey Stashenok (1a). ♦ Вероятно, он [Сунгуров] очень хорошо знал местность, ему удалось уйти от офицера, но на другой день жандармы попали на его след (Герцен 1). Probably he [Sungurov] knew the locality well. He succeeded in getting away from the officer, but next day the gendarmes got on his track (1a). ♦ «Русские через какого-то японца из Токио напали на мой след, но их сведения обо мне пока что слишком расплывчаты» (Войнович 4). "Via some Japanese from Tokyo, the Russians have picked up my trail, but their information concerning me is still too vague" (4a).

C-251 • НЕ СЛЕД (кому) substand [Invar; impers predic with быть_ø; used with infin] s.o. must not (do sth.), it is inadvisable (to do sth.): не след (Х-у) делать Y ≃ **X shouldn't do Y; X ought not to do Y; it wouldn't be right (for X) to do Y.**

«М-да, не всякие штаны лучше бабьей юбки. Вот что не след забывать, мальчик» (Абрамов 1). "Mm-m-m. Not every pair of trousers is better than a woman's skirt. That's something you shouldn't forget, boy" (1b). ♦ За дверью послышались... голоса про больницу и что здесь не след беспокоить напрасно (Достоевский 3). Outside the door...voices were raised about the hospital, and how one ought not to disturb people unnecessarily (3c).

C-252 • СЛЕД ⟨СЛÉДОМ⟩ В СЛЕД за кем идти [NP; these forms only; adv; fixed WO] (to walk) right behind s.o., stepping where he has stepped: **(follow) in s.o.'s tracks; (tread) on s.o.'s heels; [in limited contexts] in single file.**

...Лашков, посожалев, тронул своей дорогой, а когда заканчивал круг, снова встретил ветеринара, за которым всё так же, след в след, плёлся уже знакомый ему цыган (Максимов 3). Lashkov regretfully rode on his way and, as he was finishing his rounds, met the vet with the now familiar gypsy still treading on his heels (3a).

C-253 • БЕЗ СЛЕДÁ пройти, исчезнуть и т. п. [PrepP; Invar; adv] (of some emotion, phenomenon etc) (to pass or disappear) completely, leaving nothing behind: **without (leaving) a trace.**

Орозкул засопел и всхлипнул. Жалость и злоба душили его. Жалко ему было, что жизнь пройдёт без следа, и разгоралась в нём злоба к бесплодной жене (Айтматов 1). Orozkul sniffled and gave a sob. Pity and anger choked him. Pity for himself, regret that his life would pass without leaving a trace, and mounting anger at his barren wife (1a). ♦ Величавая дикость прежнего времени исчезла без следа... (Салтыков-Щедрин 1). The majestic savagery of former times disappeared without a trace (1a).

C-254 • **НЕТ И СЛЕДА́** *(от) чего;* **НЕ ОСТА́ЛОСЬ И СЛЕДА́** *от чего* [VP$_{subj/gen}$] it is as if sth. never existed or was present; sth. is entirely absent: (от) Х-а нет и следа ≃ **there is no ⟨not a⟩ trace (left) of X; X has vanished without a trace; X no longer exists.**

...Кутузов обратился к князю Андрею. На лице его не было и следа волнения. Он с тонкою насмешливостью расспрашивал князя Андрея о подробностях его свидания с императором... (Толстой 4). ...He [Kutuzov] turned to Prince Andrei. There was not a trace of agitation on his face. With delicate irony he questioned him about the details of his interview with the Emperor... (4a). ♦ [Астров:] Переходим к третьей части: картина уезда в настоящем... От прежних выселков, хуторков, скитов, мельниц и следа нет (Чехов 3). [A.:] Now let's go to the third section: a map of the district as it is today....There's not a trace of the settlements, farms, hermitages, water mills (3a). [A.:] Now let's move on to part three, a picture of the district as it is today....The old hamlets, farmsteads, hermitages and mills have vanished without a trace (3c). ♦ Теперь от прошлой Юзовки не осталось следа. На её месте вырос благоустроенный город (Паустовский 1). The Yuzovka I knew no longer exists. Today there is a prosperous industrial city in its place (1a).

C-255 • **ПО ГОРЯ́ЧИМ ⟨СВЕ́ЖИМ⟩ СЛЕДА́М; ПО ГОРЯ́ЧЕМУ ⟨СВЕ́ЖЕМУ⟩ СЛЕ́ДУ** [PrepP; these forms only; adv] **1.** ~ *(чьим, кого)* идти и т. п. (to chase) closely after a person or animal: X идёт по горячим следам (Y-а) ≃ **X is hot on Y's trail ⟨heels⟩; X is (right) on Y's tail.**

«Вам повезло, — говорил Остап своему спутнику. — Вы присутствуете при смешном событии — Остап Бендер идёт по горячему следу» (Ильф и Петров 2). "You're in luck," Ostap remarked to his companion. "You're present on an amusing occasion — Ostap Bender hot on the trail" (2a).

2. ~ *(чего)* immediately following some event: **while the trail is still warm ⟨hot⟩; hot on the heels of; (immediately afterwards,) while sth. is still fresh.**

...Ошибку эту, впрочем, можно объяснить тем, что события описывались «Летописцем», по-видимому, не по горячим следам, а несколько лет спустя (Салтыков-Щедрин 1). ...This error, however, can be explained by the fact that the events were apparently described by the *Chronicle* not while the trail was still warm but several years later (1a). ♦ «Начался трудовой, организационный период» — писал я по горячим следам событий в «Записках о гражданской войне» (Катаев 3). "The working, organizational period began," I wrote hot on the heels of events in my *Notes on the Civil War* (3a). ♦ Есть только один момент для осмысления происходившего — по горячим следам, когда ещё сочится кровь... (Мандельштам 2). In fact, the only possible moment at which to make proper sense of events is immediately afterwards, while they are still fresh, before the blood has congealed... (2a).

C-256 • **СЛЕ́ДОМ ЗА** *кем-чем* [AdvP; Invar; Prep; the resulting PrepP is adv] immediately following (s.o. or sth.) in time or space: **(right) after; (right) behind.**

И опять ему снилась какая-то чертовщина. Бабка Наталья... протягивала ему горсть мятых вишен... А потом покойный начальник службы движения Егоркин... честил его на чём свет стоит... Следом за Егоркиным выплыла из небытия собственная его — Лашкова — свадьба... (Максимов 3). Once again all hell was let loose in his dreams. Granny Natalya...offered him a handful of dried [*sic*] cherries....Next comes Yegorkin, the traffic manager, long since dead...cursing him up hill and down dale....After Yegorkin, his own wedding floated up from oblivion... (3a). ♦ Не успели обыватели оглянуться, как из

экипажа выскочил Байбаков, а следом за ним в виду всей толпы очутился точь-в-точь такой же градоначальник, как и тот, который, за минуту перед тем, был привезён в телеге исправником! (Салтыков-Щедрин 1). Before the townsfolk could look around, out of the carriage jumped Dormousov, and behind him, in full view of the crowd, appeared a town governor who was the spit and image of the one the commissioner had brought by cart the moment before! (1a).

C-257 • **КАК СЛЕ́ДУЕТ** *coll* [как + VP; Invar; adv] in the right way or to the fullest extent possible: **properly; as ⟨the way⟩ one should; as ⟨the way⟩ one is supposed to; (do sth.) right ⟨the way it should be done, really well⟩; (sth. is done) as it should be; as well as one should;** [in limited contexts] **really; good and proper;** ‖ избить *кого* ~ ≃ **beat the hell out of s.o.; beat ⟨pound⟩ the stuffing out of s.o.;** ‖ обругать *кого* ~ ≃ **call s.o. every name in the book.**

О, они не умеют как следует стрелять! (Федин 1). Oh, they don't know how to shoot properly! (1a). ♦ «...У меня накопилось столько дела, что, по совести сказать, не могу как следует присматривать за вашим имением» (Гончаров 1). "I have so great an accumulation of business that, to be quite frank, I cannot look after your estate as I should" (1a). ♦ [Репников:] Да ведь ты его [Колесова] не знаешь как следует. А если он совсем не тот, за кого себя выдаёт?.. (Вампилов 3). [R.:] ...But you don't really know him [Kolesov]. What if he's not at all what he pretends to be?... (3b). ♦ Они осторожно, чтобы не побеспокоить остальных, вытащили его [руководящего товарища] из-за стола и во дворе измолотили как следует (Искандер 3). Circumspectly, so as not to alarm the other people there, they dragged him [the highly placed comrade] away from the table, and in the yard they pounded the stuffing out of him (3a).

C-258 • **ЗАМЕТА́ТЬ/ЗАМЕСТИ́ СЛЕДЫ́ ⟨СЛЕД⟩** *(чего)* [VP; subj: human; if pfv, often infin with надо, хотеть etc or after чтобы] to hide or destroy evidence of one's involvement in sth. reprehensible: X заметает следы ≃ **X covers (up) his tracks; X hides his tracks;** ‖ X заметает следы Y-а ≃ **X covers up the ⟨all⟩ traces of Y.**

В краткий период безначалия... он [Козырь], с изумительною для глуповца ловкостью, перебегал от одной партии к другой, причём так искусно заметал следы свои, что законная власть ни минуты не сомневалась, что Козырь всегда оставался лучшею и солиднейшею поддержкой её (Салтыков-Щедрин 1). In the short period of anarchy...he [Hotspur] switched from one party to another with an adroitness amazing in a Foolovite, covering his tracks so skillfully that the regime in power did not for a moment doubt that Hotspur had always been its best and most solid support (1a). ♦ Именно с помощью такой анкеты Русанову удалось добиться разводов нескольких женщин, мужья которых находились в заключении по 58-й статье. Уж как эти женщины заметали следы, посылали посылки не от своего имени, не из этого города или вовсе не посылали — в этой анкете слишком строго стоял частокол вопросов, и лгать дальше было нельзя (Солженицын 10). With its [the questionnaire's] help Rusanov had succeeded in making several women divorce their husbands, who were imprisoned under Article 58. However cleverly the women hid their tracks, sent off their parcels under different names and from different towns, or even sent no parcels at all, the net of questions woven by this form was so fine that further lying became impossible (10a).

C-259 • **ДО СЛЁЗ** [PrepP; Invar; modif or adv (intensif)] **1.** to a very high degree: **extremely; really;** ‖ *кому* обидно ~ ≃ **s.o. is frustrated to the point of tears; s.o. is so upset ⟨frustrated etc⟩ he could cry; s.o. is so frustrated ⟨annoyed etc⟩ he could scream;** [in limited contexts] **s.o. could just cry ⟨scream⟩!** ‖ обижаться ~ ≃ **be offended to the point of tears; be deeply offended;** ‖ *кому* ~ хочется *чего* или *что* (с)делать ≃ **s.o.**

desperately wants (to do) sth.; s.o. wants (to do) sth. so badly he can taste it; s.o. has a burning desire for sth. ⟨to do sth.⟩; ‖ кому ~ жаль кого ≃ (seeing some person in such a state etc) is enough to make you want to cry; s.o. feels desperately ⟨incredibly⟩ sorry for some person; s.o. is so sorry for some person that he could cry ⟨weep⟩; ‖ тронуть кого ~ ≃ move s.o. to tears; ‖ ~ какой ≃ extremely ⟨ever so⟩ [AdjP].

Когда мы, в блокадную зиму, пилили с ней [тёткой] в паре дрова... она, пятидесятилетняя, точно так сердилась на меня, пятилетнего, как сейчас. Она обижалась на меня до слёз в споре, кому в какую сторону тянуть... (Битов 1). During the winter of the blockade of Leningrad, when she [Auntie] and I were sawing wood together...she, fifty years old, lost her temper at me, a five-year-old, in exactly the same way as now. She was offended to the point of tears by an argument about who was supposed to pull in which direction (1a). ♦ С близкого поля, которое растекалось по обе стороны дороги прямо от истока слободы, тянуло зацветающей гречихой. На душе у Петра Васильевича стало вдруг так мирно и благостно, что ему захотелось, до слёз захотелось туда, в этот запах, в этот давным-давно забытый сквозной простор... (Максимов 3). From a nearby field which welled up at the edge of the settlement and flowed along both sides of the road there came a scent of buckwheat in flower. Pyotr Vasilievich suddenly felt blissfully at peace, and wanted desperately to go in that direction — into that scent, into those long-forgotten boundless spaces... (3a). ♦ ...Ему всё-таки до слёз жалко было князя Андрея, жалко было его гордости (Толстой 5). ...He could have wept, so sorry was he for Prince Andrei and his wounded pride (5a). ♦ Сцена эта может показаться очень натянутой, очень театральной, а между тем через двадцать шесть лет я тронут до слёз, вспоминая её... (Герцен 1). This scene may strike others as very affected and theatrical, and yet twenty-six years afterwards I am moved to tears as I recall it... (1a).

2. ~ смеяться, хохотать (to laugh) very hard: **laugh until ⟨till, so hard⟩ one cries; laugh till tears flow ⟨come⟩; laugh till tears run down one's face ⟨cheeks⟩.**

Я иногда даже хохочу. И тот, в зеркале, хохочет. Я хохочу до слёз. И тот, в зеркале, плачет (Олеша 3). Sometimes I even laugh. And the one in the mirror laughs. I laugh until I cry. And the one in the mirror cries too (3a).

C-260 • **ОБЛИВА́ТЬСЯ ⟨ЗАЛИВА́ТЬСЯ, УМЫ-ВА́ТЬСЯ** coll⟩ **СЛЕЗА́МИ** [VP; subj: human] to cry hard, inconsolably: X обливался слезами ≃ **X shed floods ⟨buckets⟩ of tears; the tears streamed down X's face; X wept bitter tears;** [in refer. to a repeated action only] **X used to burst into tears (whenever ⟨every time** etc⟩...).

Я сел в кибитку с Савельичем и отправился в дорогу, обливаясь слезами (Пушкин 2). I got into the wagon with Savelich and set out on my journey, shedding floods of tears (2a). ♦ [extended usage] «Мордой его [пса] потычьте в сову, Филипп Филиппович, чтобы он знал, как вещи портить». И начинался вой. Пса, прилипшего к ковру, тащили тыкать в сову, причём пёс заливался горькими слезами и думал: «Бейте, только из квартиры не выгоняйте!» (Булгаков 11). "Poke his [the dog's] snout into the owl, Philip Philippovich, let him know how to spoil things." And a wild howling broke out. The dog, who clung to the rug, was dragged to have his nose poked at the owl, and he wept bitter tears, praying, beat me, but don't kick me out of here (11a). ♦ ...Чернышевский признавался, что поэзия сердца всё же милее ему поэзии мысли, и обливался слезами над иными стихами Некрасова (даже ямбами!), высказывающими всё, что он сам испытал... (Набоков 1). ...Chernyshevski, who confessed that poetry of the heart was even dearer to him than poetry of ideas, used to burst into tears over those of Nekrasov's verses (even iambic ones!) which expressed everything he himself experienced... (1a).

C-261 • **СЛЕЗА́МИ ГО́РЮ НЕ ПОМО́ЖЕШЬ** [saying] crying and getting upset will not remedy the situation, so cheer up (said in an attempt to raise the spirits of a hurt, disappointed etc

person): ≃ **crying won't help ⟨get you anywhere, solve anything⟩;** [in limited contexts] **it's ⟨there's⟩ no use crying over spilt ⟨spilled⟩ milk.**

[author's usage] «Не кричи, Натальюшка. Слезой тут не поможешь. Бог даст, живых-здоровых увидим» (Шолохов 5). "Don't cry, Natalya, dearie. Tears won't help. God grant we'll see them all again safe and sound" (5a). ♦ [author's usage] «Ну что ж! — сказал Чичиков... — Плачем горю не пособить...» И вот решился он сызнова начать карьер [obs = карьеру] (Гоголь 3). "Oh, well!" said Chichikov... "...No use crying over spilt milk...." And so he resolved to begin his career anew... (3b).

C-262 • **В СЛЕЗА́Х** [PrepP; Invar; usu. subj-compl with copula (subj: human) or detached modif; often preceded by весь] one is crying: **(one is) in tears.**

Алёша вышел весь в слезах... Глубокое, бесконечное сострадание вдруг охватило и измучило его мгновенно (Достоевский 2). Alyosha walked out all in tears....Deep, infinite compassion suddenly took hold of him and at once tormented him (2a).

C-263 • **УТОПА́ТЬ В СЛЕЗА́Х** obs [VP; subj: human] to cry inconsolably: X утопал в слезах ≃ **X was drowning in his tears; X was crying uncontrollably.**

C-264 • **СО СЛЕЗО́Й** говорить, сказать что и т. п. coll [PrepP; Invar; adv] (to speak, say sth. etc) as if one were about to cry, plaintively: **tearfully.**

C-265 • **ПУСКА́ТЬ/ПУСТИ́ТЬ ⟨ПРОЛИ́ТЬ, РОНЯ́ТЬ/ПРОРОНИ́ТЬ⟩ СЛЕЗУ́** coll [VP; subj: human; more often pfv] to cry (from emotion, in an attempt to gain sympathy, in order to produce an effect etc): X пустил слезу ≃ **X shed a tear; X shed (a few) tears; X let fall a tear; X turned on the tears ⟨the waterworks⟩.**

Мне говорила Люба [Эренбург], что Фадеев был холодным и жестоким человеком, что вполне совместимо с чувствительностью и умением вовремя пустить слезу (Мандельштам 1). Liuba [Ehrenburg] has told me that Fadeyev was a cold and cruel man — something quite compatible with emotionalism and the ability to shed a tear at the right moment (1a). ♦ ...Молодец баба! Терентия убили в прошлом году, а кто слыхал от неё стон?.. Слезу пускать да реветь — это каждый умеет. А ты вот попробуй рот скалить, когда у тебя сердце кровью обливается (Абрамов 1). She was some terrific gal! Her Terenty had been killed the year before, but who had heard her moaning?...Shedding tears and howling — anyone can do that. But just you try to grin and bear it when your heart's bleeding (1a). ♦ Он [человек-дятел] пригорюнился, пустил слезу, потом встрепенулся и сделал бурную попытку уговорить хозяина совершить благородный акт восточного гостеприимства и подарить ему говорящего кота (Катаев 2). He [the human woodpecker] began to mope, and let fall a tear, then he perked up and made a vigorous attempt to persuade the host to perform a noble act of oriental hospitality by giving him the talking cat (2a).

C-266 • **СЛА́Б(ЫЙ) НА СЛЕЗУ́ ⟨НА СЛЁЗЫ⟩** coll [AdjP; subj-compl with copula (subj: human) or detached modif (variants with long-form Adj only)] one cries often and usu. without any real reason: X слаб на слезу ≃ **X is easily moved to tears; tears come to X too easily; it doesn't take much to make X cry.**

Он высморкался, рукавом чекменька раздавил щекотавшую щёку слезу, подумал: «Старею, видно. Слабый на слезу стал...» (Шолохов 2). He blew his nose, smeared away a tear that was tickling his cheek with the sleeve of his coat, and thought to himself, "I must be getting old. The tears come too easily..." (2a).

C-267 • **ГЛОТА́ТЬ СЛЁЗЫ** [VP; subj: human] to try to refrain from crying: X глотал слёзы ≃ **X was swallowing his tears; X was fighting back (the) tears; X was trying to hold back (the) tears.**

Словно что-то оборвалось внутри Григория… Внезапно нахлынувшие рыдания потрясли его тело, спазма перехватила горло. Глотая слёзы, он жадно ждал, когда запевала начнёт… (Шолохов 5). Something seemed to snap inside Grigory.…A sudden fit of sobbing shook his body and a spasm seized his throat. Swallowing his tears, he waited eagerly for the [song-]leader to begin again (5a).

С-268 • КРОКОДИ́ЛОВЫ ⟨КРОКОДИ́ЛЬИ *coll*⟩ СЛЁЗЫ (лить, проливать) [NP; pl only; usu. this WO] (used sarcastically or mockingly) (to shed) insincere tears, (to make) a false display of pity or sorrow: **(shed) crocodile tears.**

«С чувством гнева и возмущения, — говорится в статье, — узнали мы о чёрном предательстве некоего Голицына, бывшего князя… Теперь, изобличённый с поличным, этот… князь будет лить крокодиловы слёзы и каяться» (Войнович 4). [The article said:] "It was with a sense of anger and indignation that we learned of the black treachery of a certain Golitsyn, a former prince.…Now, caught red-handed, this…prince will cry crocodile tears and repent" (4a).

< According to an old belief crocodiles weep while eating their prey.

С-269 • ЛИТЬ ⟨ПРОЛИВА́ТЬ/ПРОЛИ́ТЬ, РОНЯ́ТЬ⟩ СЛЁЗЫ [VP; subj: human] to cry (sometimes profusely): X проливал слёзы ≃ **X shed tears; X cried hard;** [in limited contexts] **the floodgates opened;** ‖ X лил горькие ⟨горючие⟩ слёзы ≃ **X wept bitter tears.**

[Жители Глупова] поздравляли друг друга с радостью, целовались, проливали слёзы, заходили в кабаки, снова выходили из них и опять заходили (Салтыков-Щедрин 1). They [the inhabitants of Glupov] joyfully congratulated each other, kissed, and shed tears. They went into the taverns, came out, and went back in again (1b). ♦ …На четвёртый день [Григорий] уехал в район. Да не один, а с Варварой Иняхиной… Сколько она [Анфиса] слёз тогда пролила! И из-за чего? Из-за того, что бабы на каждом перекрёстке судачат да языком чешут (Абрамов 1). …On the fourth day he [Grigory] had left for the district center. Not alone but with Varvara Inyakhina.…Then the floodgates had opened! But why?…It was because of those women tittle-tattling and gabbing on every corner (1a).

С-270 • НЕ ПРОРОНИ́ТЬ СЛЕЗЫ́ ⟨(НИ) СЛЕ-ЗИ́НКИ⟩ *coll* [VP; subj: human] to refrain from crying, remaining unmoved or indifferent: X не проронил слезы ≃ **X didn't shed ⟨let fall⟩ a (single) tear.**

С-271 • ОСУША́ТЬ/ОСУШИ́ТЬ СЛЁЗЫ *lit* [VP; more often pfv] **1.** ~ *чьи, кому* [subj: human or abstr] to console, calm s.o. who is crying: X осушил Y-овы слёзы ≃ **X dried Y's tears;** notion X was a source of consolation to Y.

2. Also: **ОСУША́ТЬ/ОСУШИ́ТЬ СВОИ́ СЛЁЗЫ** *lit* [subj: human] to cease crying: X осушил (свои) слёзы ≃ **X dried his tears ⟨eyes⟩.**

…Вдруг слёзы побежали по её бледному лицу. Князь… нахмурился. «Пошла, пошла, пошла, — сказал Кирила Петрович, — осуши свои слёзы и воротись к нам веселёшенька» (Пушкин 1). Suddenly tears began to run down her pale face. The Prince frowned.…"Go on, off with you!" said Kirila Petrovitch. "Go and dry your tears and come back your usual merry self" (1b).

С-272 • ОТОЛЬЮ́ТСЯ СЛЁЗЫ *чьи кому coll* [VP_subj; fut only] a person who inflicts pain on another will eventually be punished for it, will suffer for it: отольются Y-у X-овы слёзы ≃ **Y will (have to) pay for X's tears ⟨for what Y did to X⟩.**

< From the sayings «Отольются волку овечьи слёзки ⟨слёзы⟩» ("the wolf will pay for the sheep's tears") and «Ото-льются ⟨отзовутся⟩ кошке мышкины слёзки» ("the cat will pay for the mouse's tears").

С-273 • СНИМА́ТЬ/СНЯТЬ СЛИ́ВКИ (с чего) coll, *disapprov* [VP; subj: human or collect; usu. impfv] to take the best part of sth. for o.s. (usu. in cases where one's position gives one both first access to sth. and the opportunity to exploit the system to one's own advantage): X снимает сливки (с Y-а) ≃ **X laps up the cream; X skims the cream (off Y); X skims the choicest morsels ⟨the best bits** etc⟩ **(for himself).**

…Либералы печатали статью за статьёй, книгу за книгой… Ездили на конгрессы, симпозиумы, коллоквиумы. Организовывали лаборатории, кафедры, институты. Фигурировали в газетах и журналах. Красовались по телевизору. В общем, снимали сливки (Зиновьев 1). …The liberals published article after article, book after book.…They went to congresses, conferences, symposiums. They organised faculties, laboratories, institutes. Their names were constantly in the papers and magazines. They paraded themselves on television. In short, they were lapping up the cream (1a). ♦ «Совершенно ясно, что некоторое время мы продержимся впереди автопробега, снимая пенки, сливки и тому подобную сметану с этого высококультурного начинания» (Ильф и Петров 2). [context transl] "It is perfectly clear that for a certain time we shall keep ahead of the auto race, skimming the heavy cream, the light cream, and the other densities of cream that this highly cultured enterprise may yield" (2b).

С-274 • БЕЗ ЛИ́ШНИХ ⟨ДА́ЛЬНИХ⟩ СЛОВ ⟨РАЗГО-ВО́РОВ⟩ *coll* [PrepP; these forms only; adv] (to do sth.) immediately, without wasting time on discussion or argument: **without wasting words ⟨one's breath⟩; without another word;** [in limited contexts] **without further ado.**

В конце коридора его [поручика] уже ждут — два затхлых человека из тени. Неприятно усмехаясь, они загораживают дорогу и предлагают поговорить. Поручик без лишних слов принимается их бить и одерживает неожиданно лёгкую победу (Стругацкие 1). At the end of the corridor, the two moldy figures from the shadows are lying in wait for him [the lieutenant]. Snickering unpleasantly, they bar his path and propose a little chat. Without wasting his breath, the lieutenant starts beating them up. His victory is unexpectedly easy (1a).

С-275 • ДВУХ СЛОВ СВЯЗА́ТЬ не мочь, не уметь и т. п. *coll* [VP; infin subj-compl with не мочь, не уметь (subj: human)] to be unable to speak or express one's thoughts coherently (because of nervousness, shock, embarrassment etc, or because of one's poor mastery of the spoken language): X двух слов связать не мог ≃ **X couldn't put ⟨string⟩ two words together; X couldn't get out a coherent sentence; X couldn't say anything ⟨could say nothing⟩ coherent (at all).**

…[Чичиков] отправился тут же к председателю палаты, но председатель палаты так смутился, увидя его, что не мог связать двух слов… (Гоголь 3). …[Chichikov] set out immediately to see the Director of the Revenue Office. But the Director of the Revenue Office was thrown into such confusion at the sight of him that he could say nothing coherent at all… (3c).

С-276 • С ЧУЖИ́Х СЛОВ знать, рассказывать, говорить *что* и т. п. [PrepP; Invar; usu. adv; fixed WO] (to know, say etc sth.) on the basis of the account(s) of others: **(know) from what others have told one; (report ⟨repeat** etc⟩**) what others have said; (relate sth.) based on what ⟨on stories⟩ one has heard from another ⟨others⟩;** [in limited contexts] **(know) from a secondhand ⟨thirdhand⟩ account.**

Всё это я, конечно, рассказываю с чужих слов, может быть, в действительности это было не совсем так… (Рыбаков 1). Of course, I'm only reporting what others have said, maybe things weren't quite like that (1a).

C-277 • СЛОВ ⟨-а⟩ НЕТ¹; СПÓРУ ⟨-а⟩ НЕТ *all coll* [these forms only; indep. clause used as sent adv (parenth); foll. by another statement, often introduced by contrastive Conj «но»; fixed WO] (used to emphasize that the statement it modifies is, in fact, true, even though a statement to follow will detract from or contrast with it) that is definitely true, there is no reason to doubt it: **there's no denying ⟨disputing⟩ it; it can't be denied; (there's) no question ⟨doubt⟩ about it ⟨that⟩; there's no question ⟨doubt⟩ that...; (there are) no two ways about it; it's beyond dispute (that...); that's for sure.**

«Это [реальное развитие мира в сторону коммунизма] — грандиозный процесс, слов нет. Меня лишь интересует, что он с собой несёт фактически, а не на лозунгах и в демагогии...» (Зиновьев 2). "It [the actual evolution of the world toward communism] is a grandiose process; there's no denying it. But what interests me lies in just what it really offers, not in its slogans and its demagogy..." (2a). ♦ [Астров:] Она [Елена Андреевна] прекрасна, спора нет, но... ведь она только ест, спит, гуляет, чарует всех нас своею красотой — и больше ничего (Чехов 3). [A.:] She [Helen] *is* beautiful, there's no question about that, but—let's face it, she does nothing but eat, sleep, go for walks and enchant us with her beauty. That's all (3c). ♦ [author's usage] [Муаррон:] Отец — пристойная личность, нет слов, но не ревнив, как сатана, и характера ужасного (Булгаков 8). [M.:] Father is a decent sort, no doubt about that, but he's as jealous as Satan, and he has a terrible personality (8a). ♦ Спору нет, Раскольников успел уже себя и давеча слишком скомпрометировать, но до *фактов* всё-таки ещё не дошло... (Достоевский 3). It was beyond dispute that Raskolnikov had already managed to compromise himself too much during this scene, but nevertheless they still had not come down to *facts*... (3a).

C-278 • СЛОВ ⟨-а⟩ НЕТ² (, как, до чего и т. п.) *coll* [these forms only; main or subord clause in a complex sent; used as intensif] (s.o. or sth. is) such as cannot be described or expressed in words: **I can't tell you (how ⟨what⟩...); words fail me; (s.o. ⟨sth.⟩ is) incredibly ⟨unbelievably, indescribably⟩ [AdjP]; (s.o. ⟨sth.⟩ is) beyond description; (s.o. ⟨sth.⟩ is) [AdjP] beyond belief.**

Вот это пирог! Слов нет, как вкусно! What a pie! It's incredibly delicious!

C-279 • СО СЛОВ *кого* ⟨С *чьих* СЛОВ⟩ знать, говорить, рассказывать *что* и т. п. [PrepP; these forms only; adv] (to know, say etc sth.) based on s.o.'s oral communication: **(hear ⟨find out, learn⟩) from s.o.; (know ⟨tell⟩ sth.) based on s.o.'s account; (relate ⟨report etc⟩) what s.o. has told one; (know sth.) from what s.o. has told one; [in limited contexts] (be) told by s.o.**

Вскоре... в гетто снова пришёл дядя Гриша и в подробностях рассказал об акции, рассказал со слов спасшихся мужчин, примкнувших к отряду Сидорова... (Рыбаков 1). Soon...Uncle Grisha turned up in the ghetto again and gave a detailed account of the action, having heard it from those who had escaped and joined Sidorov's unit... (1a). ♦ ...Впоследствии со слов Азалии Митрофановны стало известно, что предсмертное заявление состояло из одной фразы... (Войнович 4). ...It was subsequently learned from Azalia Mitrofanovna that the suicide note consisted of a single sentence... (4a). ♦ Со слов мужа она всё знала о Григории... (Шолохов 5). From what her husband had told her she knew all about Grigory... (5a).

C-280 • БРАТЬ/ВЗЯТЬ (СВОИ) СЛОВА ⟨(СВОЁ) СЛОВО⟩ ОБРАТНО ⟨НАЗАД⟩ *coll* [VP; subj: human] to renounce what one has said, admit that sth. one has said is wrong: X взял (свои) слова обратно ≃ **X took back ⟨retracted⟩ what he said; X took back his words; X took it (all) back; [in limited contexts] X had to eat his words.**

«...Я беру свои слова обратно: когда-то я говорила, что ты одна такая на десять тысяч женщин. Так вот: не на десять, а на сто тысяч» (Залыгин 1). "I take back what I said.... I said once that you were one woman in ten thousand. I was wrong. You're one in a hundred thousand, not ten thousand" (1a). ♦ «...Вы сказали мне такие слова: подло и тому подобное, которые я... никому не позволю»... — «Что ж, вам нужно удовлетворение?» — насмешливо сказал Пьер. «По крайней мере вы можете взять назад свои слова» (Толстой 5). "...You have used such words to me—base, and so on—which...I don't permit anyone to use."..."Is it satisfaction you want?" said Pierre mockingly. "At least you can retract what you said" (5a). ♦ «Гражданин подполковник, вы не имеете права оскорблять моих близких. Я настаиваю, чтобы вы взяли свои слова обратно!» (Копелев 1). "Citizen Lieutenant Colonel, you do not have the right to insult my family. I insist that you take back your words!" (1a).

C-281 • ВЗВÉШИВАТЬ/ВЗВÉСИТЬ СВОИ́ СЛОВА́; ВЗВÉШИВАТЬ/ВЗВÉСИТЬ КА́ЖДОЕ СЛÓВО [VP; subj: human; often imper] to consider carefully what one is about to say before saying it: X взвешивал свои слова ≃ **X weighed his words (carefully); X weighed (his) every word; X weighed every word he said; X chose his words carefully.**

...[Министр] сдавленно сказал: «Бобынин! Я прошу вас — взвесьте ваши слова» (Солженицын 3). The minister said in a constrained voice, "Bobynin, I'm asking you to weigh your words carefully" (3a). ♦ «Мне не нужно знать, — придушенным, злым голосом отозвался Пилат, — приятно или неприятно тебе говорить правду. Но тебе придётся её говорить. Но, говоря, взвешивай каждое слово, если не хочешь не только неизбежной, но и мучительной смерти» (Булгаков 9). "I am not interested," Pilate spoke in a choked, angry voice, "whether you find it pleasant or unpleasant to speak the truth. You shall have to speak it. But as you do, weigh every word if you want to avoid not only an inevitable, but an agonizing death" (9a). ♦ «Я познакомлю тебя с людьми. Положение, которое они занимают, ко многому обязывают. Тебе придётся взвешивать свои слова» (Рыбаков 2). "I'm going to be introducing you to people. The positions they hold carry a lot of responsibility. You are going to have to weigh every word you say around them" (2a).

C-282 • ГЛОТА́ТЬ СЛОВА́ [VP; subj: human; often Verbal Adv глотая; usu. this WO] to speak inarticulately, failing to pronounce the ends of words distinctly: X глотает слова ≃ **X swallows ⟨chokes off⟩ his words.**

Когда он волнуется, он говорит быстро, глотает слова. When he gets nervous he speaks quickly and swallows his words.

C-283 • ЛИША́ТЬ/ЛИШИ́ТЬ СЛÓВА *кого* [VP; subj: human] (usu. of a person who chairs a meeting, conference etc) to force s.o. to stop speaking before he has finished what he wanted to say: X лишил Y-а слова ≃ **X took the floor away from Y; X cut Y off ⟨short⟩; [in limited contexts] X silenced Y.**

...Не пора ли лишить слова бишофсбергских бюргеров и рассказать обо всём с присущим нам бесстрастием? (Федин 1). ...Is it not time to silence the Bischofsberg burghers and relate all with our customary impartiality? (1a).

C-284 • НЕ ГОВОРЯ́ ХУДÓГО ⟨ДУРНÓГО⟩ СЛÓВА [Verbal Adv; these forms only; adv; fixed WO] (to do sth.) not having said anything about it or given any advance notice: **without (saying ⟨uttering⟩) a word; without saying anything ⟨a thing⟩; without a word of warning.**

«Тот [немецкий автоматчик], какой впереди колонны шёл, поравнялся со мною и, не говоря худого слова, наотмашь хлыстнул меня ручкой автомата по голове» (Шолохов 1). "When the one [the German submachine-gunner] at the head of the column came alongside of me, he struck me full force on the head with the butt of his gun, without saying a word" (1b). ♦ Тут его [Рабиновича] двое молодцов, не говоря худого слова, хватают, руки за спину крутят и запихивают в серый автомобиль (Войнович 1). There he [Rabinovich] was grabbed by two hulking guys, who, without a word of warning, twisted his arms behind his back and shoved him into a gray car (1a).

С-285 • НЕ ДА́ВШИ СЛО́ВА, КРЕПИ́СЬ, А ДА́ВШИ, ДЕРЖИ́СЬ; ДА́ВШИ СЛО́ВО, ДЕРЖИ́СЬ, А НЕ ДА́ВШИ, КРЕПИ́СЬ [saying] either be true to your word or do not make promises: ≃ **don't make promises you can't keep.**

С-286 • НЕ ПРОРОНИ́ТЬ НИ СЛО́ВА ⟨(НИ) СЛОВЕ́ЧКА coll⟩ [VP; subj: human] **1.** not to say anything: X не проронил ни слова ≃ **X didn't say a word ⟨a thing⟩; X didn't utter a (single) word; X said nothing ⟨not a word⟩; X didn't open his mouth;** ‖ X не проронил Y-у ни слова (о Z-е) ≃ **X didn't breathe a word about Z to Y;** ‖ не проронив ни слова [Verbal Adv] ≃ **without (saying ⟨uttering⟩) a word.**

Бирюков, слушая старушку, не проронил ни слова (Чернёнок 1). Biriukov, listening to the woman, didn't utter a word (1a). ♦ Она [Ахматова] добилась приёма у Енукидзе. Тот внимательно её выслушал и не проронил ни слова (Мандельштам 1). She [Akhmatova] managed to get an interview with Yenukidze, who listened to her carefully but said not a word (1a). ♦ Она вспомнила о заложенном жемчуге, о серебре, о салопе и вообразила, что Штольц намекает на этот долг; только никак не могла понять, как узнали об этом, она ни слова не проронила не только Обломову об этой тайне, даже Анисье... (Гончаров 1). She remembered the pawned string of pearls, the silver, and the fur coat, and imagined that Stolz was referring to that debt, only she could not understand how he had got to know of it, for she had never breathed a word about it not only to Oblomov, but even to Anisya... (1a). ♦ Маковкина посмотрела на размашистый почерк и, не проронив ни слова, положила листок в папку (Чернёнок 1). Makovkina looked at the scrawled handwriting and without a word put the paper in her briefcase (1a).

2. not to let anything s.o. says pass by one unheard, to make sure one hears everything: X не проронил ни слова ≃ **X didn't miss a word; X didn't miss anything ⟨a thing⟩ (person Y said).**

Они [студент и молодой офицер] стали говорить о Лизавете... Раскольников не проронил ни одного слова и зараз всё узнал: Лизавета была младшая, сводная (от разных матерей) сестра старухи, и было ей уже тридцать пять лет (Достоевский 3). They [the student and the young officer] began talking about Lizaveta....Raskolnikov did not miss a word and at once learned everything: Lizaveta was the old woman's younger half sister (they had different mothers) and was thirty-five years old (3c). ♦ [author's usage] ...Он [Николенька] хотел быть учёным, умным и добрым, как Пьер. В присутствии Пьера на его лице было всегда радостное сияние... Он не проранивал ни одного слова из того, что говорил Пьер... (Толстой 7). ...He [Nikolenka] wanted to be learned, wise, and kind like Pierre. In Pierre's presence his face was always radiant with happiness....He never missed anything Pierre said... (7a).

С-287 • НИ СЛО́ВА ⟨НИ ПОЛСЛО́ВА coll⟩ [NP_{gen}; these forms only] **1.** ~ не говорить кому, не понимать и т. п. [obj] (to say, understand etc) absolutely nothing: **not a (single) word; not so much as a word; not a thing; not (understand) a bit (of what s.o. says** etc).

...Тут же ни слова не сказано о том, что это – о нас, сказал Мазила (Зиновьев 1). "There isn't a word here that says it's all about us," observed Dauber (1a). ♦ Они впервые стояли рядом – зять и свояк. За столом они не сказали друг дружке ни слова (Абрамов 1). For the first time they stood side by side – brothers-in-law. At the table they had not spoken a single word to each other (1b). ♦ «...Ни я, ни Дуня ни полслова ещё не говорили с ним [Петром Петровичем] о крепкой надежде нашей, что он поможет нам

способствовать тебе деньгами, пока ты в университете...» (Достоевский 3). "...Neither Dunya nor I have as yet said so much as a word to him [Pyotr Petrovich] on the subject of our fervent hope that he'll help us to supply you with money while you're still in university..." (3d).

2. ~ (кому о чём) [predic (subj: human); usu. used as imper, occas. used in past or fut contexts] do not say anything about sth. (to s.o. or to anyone), one did not or will not say anything about sth. (to s.o. or to anyone): Imper Y-у ⟨никому⟩ о Z-е ни слова ≃ **don't breathe ⟨say, utter⟩ a word about Z to Y ⟨to anyone⟩;** ‖ X ни слова ≃ [in past contexts] **X didn't say ⟨utter⟩ a word; X said nothing.**

«...И ни полслова никому о том, что ты меня видел в Москве» (Герцен 1). "...And don't breathe a word to anyone about having seen me in Moscow" (1a). ♦ «...Так что прошу вас – никому ни слова и полнейший секрет!..» (Булгаков 9). "...I must ask you not to say a word about it to anyone...it must be a total secret..." (9a).

3. ~ от кого [subj/gen] there have been no letters or any other type of communication from s.o.: от X-а – ни слова ≃ **there has been no word from X; I haven't ⟨he hasn't etc⟩ heard a word ⟨a thing⟩ from X.**

От Нины уже два месяца ни слова, я очень беспокоюсь. I haven't heard a word from Nina for two months already and I'm awfully concerned.

С-288 • ОТ СЛО́ВА ДО СЛО́ВА помнить, пересказывать, переписывать, читать что и т. п. [PrepP; Invar; adv; fixed WO] (to remember, relate, copy, read etc sth.) completely, in full: **every word (of sth.); from beginning to end; word for word.**

Девушка трудящаяся и вполне предана советской власти. Работает прекрасно, прямо-таки лучше всех – это раз. Политически грамотная – это два. Она не то что Ольга Петровна, она дня не пропустит, чтобы не прочитать «Правду» от слова до слова (Чуковская 1). The girl was a hard worker and absolutely loyal to the Soviet regime. For one thing, she worked excellently, better than any of them. And then, she was politically aware. Not like Olga Petrovna. She never let a day pass without reading *Pravda* from beginning to end (1a). ♦ «Поручили выпустить стенгазету, – продолжала Нина. – Она [Варя] пошла в соседний класс и списала там номер от слова до слова, даже фамилии поленилась изменить» (Рыбаков 2). "They were told to make a wall newspaper," Nina went on. "So, she [Varya] goes into the neighboring classroom and copies theirs – word for word, and she was even too lazy to change the names" (2a).

С-289 • ОТ СЛО́ВА К СЛО́ВУ [PrepP; Invar; adv; used with impfv verbs; fixed WO] as the discussion or conversation develops: **with every word.**

Слушая Савранского, я от слова к слову всё больше убеждалась, что он именно тот человек, который нам нужен. Listening to Savransky, I grew more convinced with every word that he was exactly the man we needed.

С-290 • С ПЕ́РВОГО СЛО́ВА ⟨С ПЕ́РВЫХ СЛОВ⟩ понять, объявить, заметить что и т. п. [PrepP; these forms only; adv; more often used with pfv verbs; fixed WO] (to realize, announce, notice etc sth.) immediately, from the moment one or s.o. begins speaking: **from one's ⟨s.o.'s⟩ (very) first words; at s.o.'s first words; right at the outset (of the conversation etc); the minute one ⟨s.o.⟩ opens one's ⟨his⟩ mouth.**

Егорша с первых слов начал задирать нос... Он, видите ли, отпускник, а не просто там на побывку после сплава домой пришёл, и потому намерен отдыхать культурно, ибо его здоровье – это уже не его здоровье, а здоровье рабочего класса (Абрамов 1). From his very first words Egorsha started putting on airs....You see, he was on official leave – not the same as mere time off at home after timber floating—and was therefore intending to relax in a civilized manner, since his health was not *his* health, but the health of the working class (1a). ♦ ...Он заметил с первых же слов её, что она в каком-то сильном возбуждении, может быть очень в ней необычайном, — возбуждении, похожем почти даже на какой-то восторг (Достоевский 1). ...He noticed at her first words that she was in some great excitement, perhaps quite unusual for her—an excitement even almost resembling a sort of rapture (1a).

С-291 • СЛО́ВА НЕ ДОБИ́ТЬСЯ *от кого, у кого* [VP; subj: human; often neg pfv fut, gener. 2nd pers sing не добьёшься or infin; used without negation with нельзя, не могу etc] to be unable to get s.o. to speak, take part in a conversation, answer a question etc: от Х-а слова нельзя добиться ≃ **you ⟨one⟩ cannot get a word out of X; you ⟨one⟩ cannot get X to say a word.**

«...Бывало, по целым часам [от Печорина] слова не добьёшься, зато уж иногда как начнёт рассказывать, так животики надорвёшь со смеха» (Лермонтов 1). "...Sometimes you couldn't get a word out of him [Pechorin] for hours on end, but when he occasionally did start telling stories you'd split your sides laughing" (1b).

С-292 • СЛОВА́ НЕ ИДУ́Т С ЯЗЫКА́ *у кого* [VPsubj; pres or past; usu. this WO] s.o. is unable or lacks the resolve to say sth. (because he is embarrassed, nervous, afraid of unpleasant repercussions, afraid of upsetting the interlocutor etc): у Х-а слова не идут с языка ≃ **X cannot bring himself to utter a word; X cannot get a word out of his mouth; X cannot get the words to come out; X is incapable of uttering a word; X is tongue-tied.**

Он [Обломов] припал к её руке лицом и замер. Слова не шли более с языка (Гончаров 1). He [Oblomov] pressed his face to her hand and fell silent. He could not bring himself to utter another word (1a). He [Oblomov] pressed his face to her hand and fell silent, incapable of uttering another word (1b).

С-293 • СЛО́ВА НЕ СКАЖИ́ *кому*; **СЛО́ВА СКАЗА́ТЬ НЕЛЬЗЯ́** *coll* [VP; these forms only; imper used as impers predic (1st var.); impers predic with быть∅ (2nd var.); fixed WO (1st var.)] it is absolutely impossible to say, express sth. to s.o. because of his quick temper, impatience, importance etc: Х-у слова не скажи ≃ **there's no talking to X; there's no approaching ⟨getting near⟩ X.**

«Вам уж и слова сказать нельзя. Важные стали» (Распутин 3). "There's no talking to you at all now you're up on your high horse" (3a).

С-294 • ПО СЛОВА́М *чьим, кого* [PrepP; Invar; the resulting PrepP is sent adv (usu. parenth)] **1.** as was stated by s.o.: по Х-овым словам ≃ **according to X; as X put it; X said; as X told it; by X's (own) account;** ‖ по словам всех ≃ **by all accounts.**

В пересыльном лагере, по словам Казарновского, был ларёк, где продавали табак и, кажется, сахар (Мандельштам 1). According to Kazarnovski, the transit camp had a shop where they apparently sold tobacco and sugar (1a). ♦ Раньше, по его [дяди Сандро] словам, между гневом властей и хватанием за пистолет гораздо больше времени проходило и всегда можно было что-нибудь сообразить (Искандер 3). In the old days, as he [Uncle Sandro] put it, you had much more time between the anger of the authorities and the seizing of a pistol, and you could always think of something (3a). ♦ Сейчас он [Мыльников] рассказывал Ефиму о своей недавней поездке в Лондон... По его словам, он имел в Лондоне бурный успех (Войнович 6). Now he [Mylnikov] was telling Yefim about his recent trip to London....He had been, he said, a howling success in London (6a). ♦ Старый Тендел стал рассказывать историю своей женитьбы... По словам Тен-

дела, это случилось в дни его далёкой молодости, когда он ещё не выдурился (Искандер 5). Old Tendel began to tell the tale of how he got married....As Tendel told it, it had happened in the days of his distant youth, when he hadn't yet outgrown folly (5a).

2. according to s.o.'s opinion: по Х-овым словам ≃ **in X's opinion ⟨view⟩; to X's mind ⟨way of thinking⟩.**

Сам я этой статьи не читал, но, по словам рецензента, в ней нет ни одной свежей мысли. I didn't read the article myself, but in the reviewer's opinion there isn't a single original idea in it.

С-295 • БРОСА́ТЬСЯ СЛОВА́МИ ⟨ОБЕЩА́НИЯМИ⟩ *coll* [VP; subj: human] to speak or make promises irresponsibly: X бросается словами ⟨обещаниями⟩ ≃ **X makes irresponsible ⟨careless, reckless etc⟩ statements; X makes idle ⟨empty⟩ promises;** ‖ *Neg* X словами не бросается ≃ **X means what he says; X is true to his word.**

Рабочие говорили: «Наш Анри словами не бросается...» Его любили за суровость, преданность, за большую душевную чистоту (Эренбург 1). The workers said: "Our Henri means what he says." They loved him for his sternness, devotion, and sterling honesty (1a).

С-296 • ДРУГИ́МИ ⟨ИНЫ́МИ⟩ СЛОВА́МИ [NPinstrum; these forms only; usu. sent adv (parenth); fixed WO] phrased in a different way: **in other words; to put it differently ⟨another way⟩; [in limited contexts] that is to say.**

Теперь он [Фёдор] читал как бы в кубе, выхаживая каждый стих... Другими словами, он, читая, вновь пользовался всеми материалами, уже однажды собранными памятью для извлечения из них данных стихов... (Набоков 1). Now he [Fyodor] read in three dimensions, as it were, carefully exploring each poem....In other words, as he read, he again made use of all the materials already once gathered by his memory for the extraction of the present poems... (1a). ♦ «Ну что ж, товарищи, — оглядев присутствующих, сказал Ревкин. — Начнём, пожалуй». Закрыли двери, отключили все телефоны, и началось закрытое, то есть тайное от других, или, говоря иными словами, подпольное заседание (Войнович 4). "Well, then, comrades," said Revkin with a glance that took in everyone, "I guess we should begin." They closed the doors and disconnected all the telephones. A closed meeting began—that is, one kept secret from others, or to put it another way, an underground session (4a).

С-297 • ИГРА́ТЬ СЛОВА́МИ ⟨В СЛОВА́⟩ [VP; subj: human] **1.** to use words in a witty manner based on the substitution of one word (or meaning) for another: X играл словами ≃ **X was playing on words; X was making plays on words; X was punning ⟨making puns⟩.** ○ **ИГРА́ СЛОВА́МИ ⟨В СЛОВА́⟩** [NP; sing only] ≃ **play on words.**

2. to speak evasively, using imprecise, ambiguous language: X играл словами ≃ **X was giving (person Y) a lot of double-talk; X was double-talking (person Y); X was hedging.** ○ **ИГРА́ СЛОВА́МИ ⟨В СЛОВА́⟩** [NP; sing only] ≃ **double-talk.**

С-298 • ПОСЛЕ́ДНИМИ СЛОВА́МИ *бранить, ругать кого, ругаться и т. п. coll* [NPinstrum; Invar; adv; fixed WO] (to abuse s.o. verbally, curse etc) using indecent, highly offensive words: **(curse ⟨berate etc⟩ s.o.) in the choicest ⟨vilest, foulest, crudest (possible)⟩ language; (curse s.o. ⟨swear at s.o. etc⟩) for all one is worth.**

Ругаясь последними словами, поплёвывая на асфальт, все трое стали говорить о ней [Ирине Викторовне]: какая у неё грудь, какие ноги... (Залыгин 1). ...All three started talking about her [Irina Viktorovna], cursing in the choicest language and spitting on the asphalt: what breasts she had, what legs... (1a). ♦ Константин Иванович то восхваляет правительство, то поносит последними словами (Трифонов 6). Konstantin Ivanovich alternately extols the government and abuses it in the foulest language (6a).

♦ Утром прибежала текстильщица, та самая, которой я накануне вечером так испугалась. Она заплакала и последними словами крыла сукиных детей (Мандельштам 1). In the morning the woman textile worker I had been so afraid of the evening before came to me and wept, cursing the "sons of bitches" for all she was worth (1a).

С-299 • **СВОИ́МИ СЛОВА́МИ** рассказывать, пересказывать, передавать *что* и т. п. [NP$_{instrum}$; Invar; adv; fixed WO] (to tell, recount etc sth.) not word for word, but conveying the main thought, the basic content: **in one's own words.**

Вот что я слышал в детстве о Джамхухе — Сыне Оленя и теперь своими словами пересказываю здесь (Искандер 5). That is what I heard in childhood about Jamkhoukh, Son of the Deer, and have retold here in my own words (5a).

С-300 • **В ДВУХ ⟨В НЕ́СКОЛЬКИХ⟩ СЛОВА́Х** рассказывать, объяснять *что* и т. п. *coll* [PrepP; these forms only; adv or sent adv (parenth); fixed WO] (to tell, explain etc sth.) concisely and simply: **in a word; in two ⟨a few⟩ words; in short; in a nutshell; briefly; in brief;** [in limited contexts] **(be) brief;** [when used as a request or command] **make it brief.**

«Всё взять от партии и не отдать ей ничего... — вот, собственно, в двух словах, цель новой оппозиции» (Алешковский 1). "...Just take everything from the party and don't give anything back....In a word, that's the new opposition's aim" (1a). ♦ «Соблаговолите выслушать, сударыня, только полминуты, и я в двух словах разъясню вам всё», — с твёрдостью ответил Перхотин (Достоевский 1). "Be so good, madame, as to listen for only half a minute, and I shall explain everything in two words," Perkhotin answered firmly (1a). ♦ «Рассказывай же про себя — что и как ты?» — «О, мы там качнули дело!.. Вели организационную и политическую работу... да разве всё это расскажешь в двух словах?» (Шолохов 3). "Tell me about yourself. How are you? What have you been doing?" "Oh, we made things hum there!...We were doing organisational and political work....But how can I tell you in a few words?" (3a). ♦ «...В двух словах, — упирая на каждое слово, проговорил опять отец Паисий, — по иным теориям, слишком выяснившимся в наш девятнадцатый век, церковь должна перерождаться в государство...» (Достоевский 1). "In short," Father Paissy said again, stressing each word, "according to certain theories, which have become only too clear in our nineteenth century, the Church ought to be transforming itself into the state..." (1a). ♦ ...Всё это она [тётя Катя] с такими подробностями рассказывала позднее, а когда прибежал дядя Сандро, она ему только в двух словах изложила суть дела... (Искандер 3). ...She [Aunt Katya] told the whole story in such detail only later. When Uncle Sandro ran up she gave it to him in a nutshell... (3a). ♦ [Лопахин:] Сейчас уеду, некогда разговаривать... ну, да я в двух-трёх словах (Чехов 2). [L.:] I'm just leaving and there isn't time to say much. Anyway, I'll be brief (2c).

С-301 • **НА СЛОВА́Х** [PrepP; Invar] **1.** ~ рассказать, передать, доложить *что* и т. п. [adv] (to tell, recount, report etc sth.) in spoken form: **(recount sth. ⟨relay a message etc⟩) orally ⟨verbally⟩; (give) an oral ⟨a verbal⟩ report ⟨account⟩ (of sth.);** [in some contexts the idiom may be omitted in translation].

Решено было послать донесение в штаб. Для этого избран толковый офицер, Болховитинов, который, кроме письменного донесения, должен был на словах рассказать всё дело (Толстой 7). ...It was decided to send a dispatch to the staff. An able officer, Bolkhovitinov, was chosen for the purpose; besides the written report, he was to give a verbal account of the whole affair (7a).

2. *often disapprov* [adv or subj-compl with быть$_\emptyset$ (subj: это, всё это)] (s.o. states, proclaims etc sth.) insincerely, not supporting or intending to support his words by actions (the opposition between what is stated and what exists in reality is either overtly expressed, usu. by a clause beginning with на деле, or implied):

in words; [in limited contexts] **pay lip service to;** [as subj-compl only] **just talk.**

[Марья Андреевна:] Иван Иваныч, вы меня любите? [Милашин:] Люблю, Марья Андреевна, ей-богу, люблю!.. Я для вас готов жизнью пожертвовать. [Марья Андреевна:] Должно быть, на словах только? Я целый час прошу вас уйти, а вы всё ни с места (Островский 1). [M.A.:] Ivan Ivanych, do you love me? [M.:] I love you, Marya Andrevna, really and truly I love you....I'm ready to sacrifice my life for your sake. [M.A.:] Only in words, no doubt? I've begged you a whole hour to leave, but you haven't moved one inch (1a). ♦ ...Если нам дана эта жизнь, в ней должен быть смысл, хотя все поколения, с которыми я встретилась в жизни, начисто снимали этот вопрос... Идеалом стала математическая логика, но, к несчастью, только на словах (Мандельштам 2). If this life was given to us, it must have a meaning, although the very idea was dismissed out of hand by everybody, young and old, whom I have ever known in my lifetime....Their ideal was logic of a mathematical kind, though they only paid lip service to it, alas (2a).

С-302 • **ЛОВИ́ТЬ/ПОЙМА́ТЬ НА СЛО́ВЕ ⟨НА́ СЛОВЕ, НА СЛОВА́Х⟩** *кого coll* [VP; subj: human] **1.** [usu. pres, 1st pers sing] to accept s.o.'s statement as sincere and true, and act in accordance with what he said: ловлю тебя ⟨вас⟩ на слове ≃ **I'll take you at your word; I'm going to take what you said ⟨your offer, your promise etc⟩ at face value;** [in limited contexts] **I'll take you up on your ⟨the⟩ offer.**

[Вася:] Папа... только что ты приглашал меня заходить почаще... [Я] ловлю тебя на слове (Арбузов 3). [V.:] Papa, you've asked me to come and see you more often. I'll take you at your word (3a).

2. [often neg imper] to interpret incorrectly what s.o. says or attribute to his words an unintended meaning based on his ambiguous wording, contradictory phrasing, or slip(s) of the tongue (one's misconstrual is usu. intentional and purposeful): *Neg Imper* не ловите меня на слове ≃ **don't read into my words ⟨into what I said etc⟩ something that isn't ⟨wasn't⟩ there; don't take me ⟨what I said etc⟩ too literally; don't misinterpret ⟨misconstrue⟩ what I said ⟨I'm saying etc⟩;** ‖ X поймал Y-а на слове ≃ [in refer. to a breach in logic] **X caught Y.**

Юмор должен проникнуть на все собрания, на все конференции, на все пленумы, на все съезды. Нет, меня на слове не поймаете, деловая часть не отменяется. Но все доклады, например, на съездах будут пронизаны юмором (Искандер 4). Humor must penetrate all meetings, all conferences, all plenary sessions, all congresses. No, don't take me too literally, the working sessions won't be abolished. But all the reports at the congresses, for example, will be shot through with humor (4a). ♦ «Я думаю, что если дьявол не существует и, стало быть, создал его человек, то создал он его по своему образу и подобию». — «В таком случае, равно как и бога». — «...Ты поймал меня на слове, пусть, я рад» (Достоевский 1). "I think that if the devil does not exist, and man has therefore created him, he has created him in his own image and likeness." "As well as God, then." "...So you caught me, but let it be, I'm glad" (1a).

С-303 • **НА ЧЕ́СТНОМ СЛО́ВЕ** держаться *coll, humor* [PrepP; Invar; subj-compl with держаться (subj: concr, usu. пуговица, крючок, брюки etc, or abstr); fixed WO] (of a button, a hook, s.o.'s pants etc) (to hang, be held) precariously, not securely; (of a venture, an undertaking etc) (to be) in a precarious state, liable to end badly: **(be) hanging by a thread;** [of a button etc only] **(be) about (ready) to fall off ⟨down⟩; (be) practically ⟨almost⟩ falling off ⟨down⟩;** [of a venture etc only] **(be) likely to fall through ⟨to fail etc⟩;** [in limited contexts] **(things are) touch-and-go.**

Смотри, не потеряй пуговицу, она держится на честном слове. Be careful not to lose that button—it's about ready to fall off. ♦ Подполковник Горчаков был в ночной рубашке, в рейтузах, державшихся на честном слове, и в галошах на босу ногу (Лившиц 1). Lieutenant-Colonel Gorchakov was dressed in a night-shirt, in riding breeches which were almost falling down and in galoshes on his bare feet (1a).

С-304 • СПАСИ́БО НА ДО́БРОМ СЛО́ВЕ *coll* [formula phrase; Invar; fixed WO] an expression of gratitude for a word of approval, encouragement etc: **thanks for the kind word; thank you for your ⟨those⟩ kind words.**

«А знаешь, – сказал он [Михаил], – здоровому-то мужику теперь тяжельше... Ей-богу! Я пацаном был — мне легче было...» Илья как-то поспешно, словно боясь этого разговора, сунул ему руку, сказал: «Ладно, Михаил. Спасибо на добром слове» (Абрамов 1). "You know," he [Mikhail] said, "nowadays it's harder for a grown man. Really and truly! When I was just a kid, it was easier for me." As if afraid of this conversation, Ilya hastily thrust out his hand to Mikhail and said, "Okay, Mikhail. Thank you for those kind words" (1a).

С-305 • ЗАМО́ЛВИТЬ СЛОВЕ́ЧКО ⟨СЛО́ВО, СЛОВЦО́⟩ *(кому за кого* or *о ком) coll* [VP; subj: human] to speak well of s.o. to a person who is in an influential position, petition on s.o.'s behalf: X замолвил (Y-у) словечко за Z-a ≃ **X put in a ⟨good⟩ word for Z (with Y); X spoke with Y on Z's behalf.**

...Имел он [хозяин] в виду вот что: замолви у меньшевиков за меня словечко, а я в свою очередь прикушу язык, что ты сюда приезжал с военной тайной (Искандер 3). What he [the host] had in mind was this: Put in a word for me with the Mensheviks, and I in turn will hold my tongue about your coming here with a military secret (3a). ♦ «Я хотел, ma tante, просить вас, чтоб вы замолвили за меня словечко князю», — опять начал Козелков (Салтыков-Щедрин 2). "I wanted to ask you, *ma tante*," Kozelkov tried again, "to put in a good word for me with the prince" (2a).

С-306 • БРАТЬ/ВЗЯТЬ СЛО́ВО¹ [VP; subj: human] to speak on one's own initiative at a meeting, conference etc: X взял слово ≃ **X took the floor; X spoke.**

«Я протестую, – сказал Фарфуркис. – Во-первых, товарищ представитель снизу нарушил здесь все правила ведения заседания, взял слово, которое ему никто не давал, и вдобавок ещё превысил регламент» (Стругацкие 3). "I protest," said Farfurkis. "First of all, comrade representative from below violated all the rules of order for the meeting, took the floor, which no one had given him, and went over the time limit, on top of it" (3a). ♦ Пастернак берёт слово трижды, но говорит ещё более хаотично, чем обычно (Гладков 1). Pasternak spoke three times, but in an even more disorganized way than usual (1a).

С-307 • БРАТЬ/ВЗЯТЬ СЛО́ВО² *с кого* [VP; subj: human] to have s.o. promise or assure one of sth.: X взял слово с Y-a ≃ **X made Y promise ⟨swear⟩.**

Он [Пастернак] поздравляет и отдаёт мне экземпляр пьесы, взяв слово, что я верну его ему... (Гладков 1). He [Pasternak] congratulated me and gave me back the play, after making me promise to return it... (1a). ♦ ...Бабушка взяла с дяди Миши слово ничего не говорить родным (Рыбаков 1). ...[Grand-mother] made Misha swear not to tell the others a word (1a). ♦ ...Взяв с Пьера честное слово молчать обо всём, что он узнает, Марья Дмитриевна сообщила ему, что Наташа отказала своему жениху без ведома родителей... (Толстой 5). [context transl] ...Having exacted from Pierre his word of honor that he would not repeat anything she told him, Marya Dmitrievna informed him that Natasha had broken her engagement with Prince Andrei without her parents' knowledge... (5a).

С-308 • В ОДНО́ СЛО́ВО [PrepP; Invar; adv; fixed WO] **1.** ~ сказать, подумать и т. п. *coll* (in refer. to words said by or thoughts occurring to two or more people at the same time) (to say, think etc sth.) simultaneously: [in refer. to speaking] **in one voice; as one man;** [in refer. to thinking] **(we ⟨you and I etc⟩ are) thinking the exact same thing;** [as indep. remark] **my words ⟨thoughts⟩ exactly; (that's) just what I said ⟨was saying, thought, was thinking⟩; you ⟨he etc⟩ took the words (right) out of my mouth.**

[Почтмейстер:] А что думаю? Война с турками будет. [Аммос Фёдорович:] В одно слово! Я сам то же думал (Гоголь 4). [Postmaster:] What do I think? Why, there's going to be a war with the Turks. [A.F.:] Just what I said! I thought the same myself (4c).

2. ~ говорить, утверждать *substand* (to say or repeat) the same thing (usu. incessantly): **(tell s.o.) the same thing again and again ⟨over and over⟩; (keep on saying) the same (old) thing; (give s.o.) the same old story.**

С-309 • ВЕ́РИТЬ/ПОВЕ́РИТЬ НА́ СЛОВО *(кому)* [VP; subj: human] to accept s.o.'s statement as being true without confirmation of the facts: X поверил Y-у на слово ≃ **X took Y's word for it; X took the word of Y; X took on trust ⟨on faith⟩ what Y said.**

«Что вы мне предъявляете? И с кем я вообще имею честь беседовать?» — «Вам документы показать или... поверите на слово?» (Семёнов 1). "What are you charging me with? And anyway, to whom have I the honour of speaking?" "Would you like to see the documents or will you take our word for it?" (1a). ♦ И ведь полиция не сама со мной расправлялась, она предпочла это руками профессоров и писателей. Однако ни те, ни другие доказательств не потребовали и не получили — они поверили на слово полицейским следователям (Эткинд 1). Indeed the police did not deal with me themselves, they preferred to act through the professors and writers. Neither the professors nor the writers, however, either demanded or obtained any proof—they simply took the word of the police investigators (1a).

С-310 • ДАВА́ТЬ/ДАТЬ СЕБЕ́ СЛО́ВО [VP; subj: human] to decide firmly (to do sth.): X дал себе слово ≃ **X promised himself; X made a promise to himself; X vowed ⟨swore⟩ to himself; X made himself a vow ⟨a promise⟩; X vowed (to do sth.).**

Направляясь в мурьёвскую глушь, я, помнится, ещё в Москве давал себе слово держать себя солидно (Булгаков 6). Back in Moscow, when I found out that I was to go to remote Muryovo, I had promised myself that I would behave in a dignified manner (6a). ♦ С тех пор как его любимая лошадь Кукла, во время войны мобилизованная для доставки боеприпасов на перевал, вдруг сама вернулась домой, до смерти замученная, со стёртой спиной, а главное, он был в этом абсолютно уверен, со сломленным духом, с навсегда испорченными скаковыми качествами, он дал себе слово никогда не заводить лошадей (Искандер 5). Ever since his beloved horse Dolly had been mobilized during the war to deliver military supplies to the pass, and had suddenly come home by herself, deathly tired, with her back raw, and, most importantly—he was absolutely sure of this—with her spirit broken, her racing qualities forever ruined, he had made himself a vow never to raise horses (5a). ♦ «Отчего вы не служите в армии?» — «После Аустерлица! — мрачно сказал князь Андрей. — Нет, покорно благодарю, я дал себе слово, что служить в действующей русской армии я не буду» (Толстой 5). "Why aren't you serving in the army?" "After Austerlitz!" said Prince Andrei somberly. "No, thank you; I vowed never again to go on active service in the Russian army" (5a).

С-311 • ДАВА́ТЬ/ДАТЬ СЛО́ВО¹ *(кому);* **ПРЕДО-СТАВЛЯ́ТЬ/ПРЕДОСТА́ВИТЬ СЛО́ВО** [VP; subj: human] to allow s.o. to speak (usu. at a meeting, conference etc): X дал слово Y-у ≃ **X gave Y the floor; X let Y have the floor; X gave Y the opportunity ⟨the chance⟩ to speak; X called on ⟨upon⟩ Y to speak.**

Хочешь высказаться, тяни повыше руку, заметят — дадут слово, не то что в Союзе писателей (Войнович 3). You want to express yourself, just raise your hand, they'll notice you and give you the floor, not like in the Writer's Union (3a). ♦ [Гомыра *(поднимается, идёт к Фролову)*:] Вася, дай слово мне (Вампилов 3). [G. *(getting up and going to Frolov)*:] Vasya, let me have the floor (3b). ♦ Затем предоставлено было слово самому подсудимому. Митя встал, но сказал немного (Достоевский 2). Then the defendant himself was given the opportunity to speak. Mitya stood up, but said little (2a). ♦ Дроздов дал слово мне, и я ответила, что от всей души благодарю за советы (Каверин 1). Drozdov called on me to speak and I replied that I was deeply grateful for the advice (1a).

С-312 • ДАВА́ТЬ/ДАТЬ СЛО́ВО² [VP; subj: human] **1.** ~ *(кому)* [usu. foll. by infin or a что-clause] to make a promise to s.o., assure s.o. of sth. or guarantee sth. with an oath: X дал (Y-у) слово ≃ **X gave ⟨pledged⟩ his word (to Y); X promised (Y).**

Василиса Егоровна принудила его во всём признаться, дав ему слово не рассказывать о том никому (Пушкин 2). Vassilissa Yegorovna forced him to tell her everything, after giving her his word that she would not say a word of it to anyone (2b). ♦ «...Дай мне слово никогда не охотиться на оленей!» (Искандер 5). "...Pledge me your word never to hunt deer!" (5a).

2. *obsoles* [subj: usu. female] to agree to marry s.o.: X дала слово Y-у ≃ **X pledged to marry Y.**

С-313 • ДЕРЖА́ТЬ/СДЕРЖА́ТЬ (СВОЁ) СЛО́ВО [VP; subj: human] to fulfill one's promise: X сдержал слово ≃ **X kept his word ⟨promise⟩; X was true to his word; X was as good as his word; X made good on his promise;** ‖ *Neg* X не сдержал слова ≃ **X went back on his word; X failed to keep his word; X broke his promise.**

Бенгальский сдержал слово и никому не сказал, что гейшею был наряжен мальчик (Сологуб 1). Bengal'sky kept his word and didn't tell anyone that the geisha was a disguised boy (1a). ♦ [Глаголев 1:] Софья Егоровна, милейший мой друг, дала мне слово, что в четверг вы все будете у меня... [Войницев:] Мы и сдержим это слово (Чехов 1). [G. Sr.:] Sonya promised you'd all come over to my place on Thursday, old friend.... [V.:] We'll be as good as our word... (1b).

С-314 • ЖИВО́Е СЛО́ВО [NP; sing only] **1.** *lit* oral speech as opposed to written matter: **the living word; living speech.**

...Может быть, в сей же самой повести почуются иные, ещё доселе небранные струны, предстанет несметное богатство русского духа, пройдёт муж, одарённый божескими доблестями, или чудная русская девица, какой не сыскать нигде в мире, со всей дивной красотой женской души, вся из великодушного стремления и самоотвержения. И мёртвыми покажутся пред ними все добродетельные люди других племён, как мертва книга перед живым словом (Гоголь 3). ...Perhaps in this very narrative, chords until now unplayed will resound, chords that will convey the infinite wealth of the Russian spirit, and perhaps there'll emerge a man endowed with supernatural virtues or a divine Russian maiden unequaled in the world in the spiritual beauty of her feminine soul, filled to the brim with generosity and abnegation. And the virtuous people of all other tribes will appear dead to us, as a book is dead compared to the living word... (3e).

2. (usu. of oral discourse) discourse containing fresh, interesting thoughts that excite the listener: **thought-provoking words; stimulating speech; fresh idea(s).**

С-315 • ЗАКИ́ДЫВАТЬ/ЗАКИ́НУТЬ СЛО́ВО ⟨СЛОВЕ́ЧКО, СЛОВЦО́⟩ *obs* [VP; subj: human] **1.** ~ *(кому о чём).* Also: **ЗАПУСКА́ТЬ/ЗАПУСТИ́ТЬ СЛОВЕ́ЧКО** [usu. pfv] to make a passing remark about or allude to sth.: X закинул словечко (Y-у о Z-е) ≃ **X mentioned Z (to Y); X dropped (Y) a hint about Z.**

[1-й мужик:] А ты помни, как он [Василий Леонидыч] слово закинул, чтоб мяту сеять? [2-й мужик:] Как же, мяту сей, вишь. Ты попытай-ка, горбом поворочай — запросишь мяты небось... (Толстой 3). [First Peasant:] And remember how he [Vasili Leonidych] mentioned sowing mint?... [Second Peasant:] Sure, raise mint! He should try and do a little work—he wouldn't be so fast to talk about mint (3a).

2. *(кому о ком* or *за кого)* [pfv only] to speak well of s.o. to a person in an influential position, petition on s.o.'s behalf: X закинул (Y-у) словечко за Z-а ≃ **X put in a (good) word for ⟨regarding⟩ Z (with Y); X spoke with Y on Z's behalf.**

[Пётр:] Тятенька таки о тебе словечко закинул, а она ему напрямки: «просватана» (Островский 7). [P.:] Dad had just started putting in a word regarding you, when she came out flat with: "She's engaged" (7a).

С-316 • КРЕ́ПКОЕ СЛО́ВО ⟨СЛОВЦО́⟩ *coll* [NP; sing only; fixed WO] a profane word or expression: **strong ⟨off-color⟩ language; unprintable name; swearword; curse word.**

«Что ж ты врёшь?» — говорит капитан-исправник с прибавкою кое-какого крепкого словца (Гоголь 3). "Why are you lying?" says the police captain with the addition of some strong language (3a). ♦ «Чей ты?» — говорит капитан-исправник, ввернувши тебе при сей верной оказии кое-какое крепкое словцо (Гоголь 3). "Who do you belong to?" asks the captain of police, taking advantage of the occasion to call you a few unprintable names (3a).

С-317 • ЛОВИ́ТЬ КА́ЖДОЕ СЛО́ВО чьё *coll* [VP; subj: human; the verb may take the final position, otherwise fixed WO] to listen to s.o. very attentively, trying to let nothing he says slip by: X ловит каждое Y-ово слово ≃ **X hangs on Y's every word; X catches everything Y says; X tries not to miss a single word (that) Y says.**

Вчерашний трудолюбивый затворник, не читающий газет, превратился в модную и сенсационную фигуру. За ним [Пастернаком] охотились иностранные корреспонденты, ловившие каждое его слово (Гладков 1). The hard-working recluse who never read the newspapers had become almost overnight a sensational, much sought-after figure. He was pursued by foreign journalists who hung on his every word (1a).

С-318 • НО́ВОЕ СЛО́ВО в чём [NP; sing only; often subj-compl with copula, nom or instrum (subj: concr or abstr); fixed WO] the most recent, original, major achievement in some sphere of science, technology, or culture that significantly moves the field forward: **a (major) breakthrough; a (giant) step forward; a major advance; groundbreaking work ⟨a groundbreaking discovery etc⟩;** ‖ сказать новое слово в интерпретации ⟨понимании и т. п.⟩ чего ≃ **add new dimensions to the interpretation ⟨the understanding etc⟩ of sth.; lift the interpretation ⟨the understanding etc⟩ of sth. to a higher level ⟨to new heights⟩.**

Ваша последняя работа — это новое слово в иммунологии. Your latest work is a major advance in immunology. ♦ Своей постановкой «Горя от ума» Товстоногов сказал новое слово в прочтении грибоедовской пьесы. Through his staging of *Woe From Wit*, Tovstonogov added new dimensions to the interpretation of Griboedov's play.

С-319 • ПЕ́РВОЕ СЛО́ВО в чём [NP; sing only; subj-compl with copula, nom or instrum (subj: concr or abstr); fixed WO] the very beginning (of a project, some work etc): **(be ⟨mark⟩) the beginning of sth.; (be) the start ⟨the starting point⟩ of sth.**

C-320 • ПОД ЧЕСТНОЕ СЛОВО дать, одолжить *что* и т. п. [PrepP; Invar; adv; fixed WO] (to give, lend etc sth.) relying on s.o.'s honesty and his promise to return it: **on s.o.'s word of honor; on s.o.'s word alone; on trust.**

«Главное... заиметь личную дружбу с милицией. Когда было собрание, на котором меня принимали в партию, я был посажен на пятнадцать суток за мелкое хулиганство. Так меня под честное слово выпустили» (Зиновьев 2). "The main thing...is to make personal friends of the police. On the day of the meeting when I was to be admitted to the party, I was put inside for [fifteen] days for a breach of the peace. Well, I was released simply on my word of honour" (2a). ♦ Борис одолжил мне деньги под честное слово, расписку взять не захотел. Boris lent me money on trust — he didn't want to take an IOU.

C-321 • ПОМЯНИ(ТЕ) ⟨ПОПОМНИ(ТЕ)⟩ МОЁ СЛОВО; ПОМЯНИ(ТЕ) ⟨ПОПОМНИ(ТЕ)⟩ МЕНЯ *all coll* [VP$_{imper}$; these forms only; usu. a clause in a compound sent; fixed WO] you can be sure that what I am saying is true or will come to pass: **(you) mark my words; take my word for it.**

Помяните моё слово, эта ошибка ещё даст о себе знать роковым образом (Зиновьев 1). Mark my words, this mistake will have fateful consequences in the future (1a).

C-322 • ПОСЛЕДНЕЕ СЛОВО¹ *чего* [NP; sing only; fixed WO] the most novel, recent innovation in science, technology, art, fashion etc: **the last word; the latest (thing); the most up-to-date** [NP]; [in limited contexts] **the most advanced** [NP]; ‖ в месте X всё оборудовано по последнему слову техники ≃ **place X is equipped with all the latest technology; everything in place X is state-of-the-art.**

Снимок с последней вещи Пикассо. Его лишь недавно привезла из Парижа Экстер. Последнее слово французской живописи (Лившиц 1). It's a photograph of Picasso's latest painting. Exter had just brought it from Paris. The last word in French painting (1a).

C-323 • ПОСЛЕДНЕЕ СЛОВО² [NP; sing only; fixed WO] **1.** the final and decisive point (in an argument, discussion etc) or the final decision or conclusive judgment (in some matter): **the last word; the final word ⟨say⟩.**

Получается впечатление, что упрямый Чернышевский как бы желает иметь последнее слово в споре... (Набоков 1). One gets the impression that the stubborn Chernyshevski wants to have the last word in the quarrel... (1a). ♦ ...В отношении самого Мансурова... — последнее слово было за ней [Ириной Викторовной], а не за ним: ехать ли ему на курорт или не ехать, а если ехать — то когда; надевать тот или этот костюм на официальный приём; идти к врачу или не ходить... (Залыгин 1). ...In anything concerning Mansurov...she [Irina Viktorovna] always had the final say: whether he should go to a health resort or not, and if so, when; which suit he should wear for the coming official function; whether or not he should see a doctor... (1a).

2. the defendant's statement made directly prior to the pronouncement of the verdict: **concluding statement; final plea.**

...Я твёрдо знал, что не только следствие от меня ничего не услышит, легче умру; что не только суда не признаю, отвод ему дам в начале, весь суд промолчу, лишь в последнем слове их прокляну; — но уверен я был, что и низменному тюремному положению наших политических не подчинюсь (Солженицын 2). I...knew for certain that not only would the interrogators get nothing at all out of me (I would die first), not only would I refuse to recognize the court, ignore it from the start, remain silent throughout (except for the curse I would put on them in my concluding statement) — I was quite sure, too, that in jail I would not accept the humiliations to which Soviet political prisoners are subjected (2a). ♦ В последнем слове я сказал [суду], что испытываю чувство безнадёжности, тем, что я говорю, просто пренебрегают, — если меня осуждают за слова, то должны принимать мои слова

всерьёз (Амальрик 1). In my final plea, I told the court I was nearly overcome by a feeling of hopelessness when I realized that everything I said was simply ignored; that if I was to be judged by what I said, then what I said should be taken seriously (1a).

C-324 • ПРАВО СЛОВО *substand* [Invar; sent adv (parenth); fixed WO] (used by the speaker to emphasize the truth of a statement) what I am saying is really true: **no fooling; honest(ly); I mean it; (up)on my word.**

«Любочку зря ты обидел, она прямо как ягодка — красавица, глаз с неё не свесть [*obs* or *substand* = свести]. Был бы помоложе — отбил бы, право слово, Витёк...» (Семёнов 1). "It was silly of you to offend your Lyubka, she's a real peach — a beauty, impossible to take one's eyes off her. If I was younger I'd cut you out there, honest I would, Victor..." (1a). ♦ «Обозники приехали. С ними папаша ваш, Григорий Пантелевич». — «Ну?! Будет брехать!» — «Право слово» (Шолохов 4). "The transport men have arrived. Your father's with them, Grigory Panteleyevich." "No?! Tell us another one!" "I mean it" (4a). ♦ [Разлюляев:] А после праздника женюсь!.. Право слово, женюсь! (Островский 2). [R.:] And after the holidays I shall marry! — Upon my word I shall marry! (2a).

C-325 • СКАЗАТЬ СВОЁ СЛОВО *(в чём)* [VP; subj: human, collect, or abstr; more often fut] to act in such a way as to influence (some course of events, the development of some situation etc): X скажет своё слово ≃ **X will make his ⟨its⟩ presence felt; X will have an impact ⟨a notable impact etc⟩ (on sth.);** [with subj: abstr only] **X will have its say.**

[Звонцов:] Общественные силы организуются закономерно и скоро скажут своё слово (Горький 2). [Z.:] The social forces are rallying systematically and will soon have their say (2a).

C-326 • СЛОВО В СЛОВО повторять, пересказывать, запоминать *что* и т. п.; ДО СЛОВА [NP or PrepP; these forms only; adv; fixed WO] (to repeat, recount, memorize etc sth.) precisely: **(repeat ⟨memorize etc⟩ sth.) word for word; (repeat ⟨copy etc⟩ sth.) verbatim; (remember ⟨recall etc⟩) every word (of sth.).**

Я просто списываю — слово в слово — то, что сегодня напечатано в Государственной Газете... (Замятин 1). I shall simply copy, word for word, the proclamation that appeared today in the *One State Gazette*... (1a).

C-327 • СЛОВО ЗА СЛОВО *coll* [Invar; adv or indep. clause] **1.** ~ (разговориться, познакомиться, расспросить и т. п.) (to get to talking) in a gradual, natural manner, with each participant's remarks eliciting a response from the other; (to get to know s.o., question s.o. etc) in a gradual, natural manner in the course of a conversation: [in past contexts] **one word ⟨thing⟩ led to another; as the conversation progressed (one got to know s.o. ⟨asked s.o. sth. etc⟩); little by little (one got to talking with s.o. ⟨convinced s.o. of sth. etc⟩).**

Да, так встретились [дед и запорожец]. Слово за слово, долго ли до знакомства? Пошли калякать, калякать так, что дед совсем уже было позабыл про путь свой (Гоголь 5). So they [Grandad and a Dnieper Cossack] met. One word leads to another, it doesn't take long to make friends. They fell to chatting and chatting, so that Grandad quite forgot about his journey (5a). ♦ [Кашкина:] Как это вы вдруг... разговорились? [Шаманов *(насмешливо)*:] Да так, очень просто. Я сделал ей комплимент, она... Да, вот так, слово за слово... (Вампилов 2). [K.:] How come you two suddenly started...talking? [Sh. *(Mockingly)*:] Oh, it was very simple. I paid her a compliment, and she....And then, one thing led to another (2b). ♦ ...Слово за слово, [Пидорка] уговорила старуху идти с собою (Гоголь 5). ...Little by little, she [Pidorka] persuaded the old hag to go home with her (5a).

2. ~ (рассориться, разругаться и т. п.) [usu. used with pfv verbs] (to quarrel, have an argument with s.o. etc) with increasing intensity: **one word provoked another; one hard ⟨harsh⟩ word brought another; one thing led to another; (the argument became more heated ⟨one became more brash etc⟩) with every word.**

...Ребров потерял равновесие. Слово за слово – и все, будто только того и ждали, закрутились в эту воронку (Трифонов 1). ...He [Rebrov] lost his self-control. One word provoked another, and this seemed to be all that was needed for the volcano to erupt (1a). ♦ «Разозлившись на то, что мать и сестра не хотят, по его наветам, со мною рассориться, он [Лужин], слово за слово, начал говорить им непростительные дерзости» (Достоевский 3). "Angry that my mother and sister did not want to quarrel with me over his calumny, he [Luzhin] became more unpardonably rude to them with every word" (3c).

С-328 • СЛО́ВО НЕ ВОРОБЕ́Й, ВЫ́ЛЕТИТ – НЕ ПОЙМА́ЕШЬ [saying] words that are said cannot be taken back: ≃ **spoken words are like flown birds – neither can be recalled; a word spoken is past recalling; words once spoken you can never recall; a word too much cannot be recalled; what is said cannot be unsaid.**

Потом, уже в эмиграции, в конце жизни, Бунин вычеркнул мистиков, богоискателей, поэтов, эстетов [из своего стихотворения]... Но я не признаю этой самоцензуры. Что написано – написано. Слово не воробей (Катаев 3). Later as an emigré, towards the end of his life, Bunin deleted the mystics, god-seekers, poets and aesthetes [from his poem].... But I do not accept this self-censorship. What is written is written. What is said cannot be unsaid (3a).

С-329 • СЛО́ВО – СЕРЕБРО́, МОЛЧА́НИЕ – ЗО́-ЛОТО [saying] it is better to be silent than to say something you will regret later: ≃ **speech is silver, silence is golden; speech is (of) silver, silence is gold; words are silver and silence is gold; [in limited contexts] silence is golden; a shut mouth catches no flies.**

«...Ничего и не надо рассказывать. Обо всём самое лучшее молчок теперь... Это истина вечная. Слово серебро, а молчание золото» (Пастернак 1). "...Don't start telling anything at all. It's better to keep your mouth shut....Speech is of silver, silence is gold. That has always been true" (1a).

С-330 • ЧЕ́СТНОЕ СЛО́ВО [NP; sing only; usu. sent adv (parenth); fixed WO] (used to emphasize the truth of a statement) I am really telling the truth: **word of honor; (up)on my honor ⟨word⟩; honest to goodness ⟨to God⟩; honest; I swear (it); [in limited contexts] take my word for it; really.**

[Кай:] Растерялся я... Честное слово. Совершенно растерялся (Арбузов 2). [K.:] I lost my head. Word of honour. I completely lost my head (2a). ♦ «Если бы не дети, честное слово, Едигей, не стала бы я жить сейчас» (Айтматов 2). "If it wasn't for the children, on my honour, Yedigei, I wouldn't go on living" (2a). ♦ «Аксакал, я тебя так люблю! Честное слово, аксакал, как отца родного» (Айтматов 1). "Aksakal, I love you. Honest I do, like my own father" (1a). ♦ [Зоя:] ...Вы вошли ко мне как статуя... Я, мол, светская дама, а вы – портниха... [Алла:] Зоя Денисовна, это вам показалось, честное слово (Булгаков 7). [Z.:] ...You came in to me like a statue....As if to say, "I'm a society lady, but you're a dressmaker..." [A.:] Zoya Denisovna, it just seemed that way to you, I swear it! (7a). ♦ «Вы можете в Москве в два дня сделать дело, честное слово!» (Федин 1). "You can do your business in Moscow in two days, take my word for it!" (1a). ♦ [Нина:] Давайте, давайте, оправдывайте его [Васеньку], защищайте. Если хотите, чтобы он совсем рехнулся... [Васенька:] Я с ума хочу сходить, понятно тебе? Сходить с ума и ни о чём не думать! И оставь меня в покое! (*Уходит в другую комнату.*)

[Бусыгин *(Нине)*:] Зачем же ты так? [Сарафанов:] Напрасно, Нина, честное слово. Ты подливаешь масло в огонь (Вампилов 4). [Nina:] Go ahead, go ahead and agree with him [Vasenka], defend him. If you want him to go completely crazy.... [Vasenka:] I want to go nuts, understand? Go nuts and not think about anything! So leave me alone! *(He goes into the other room.)* [Busygin *(to Nina)*:] Why do you do that? [Sarafanov:] It's pointless, Nina, really. You're pouring oil on the fire (4b).

С-331 • ВЛАДЕ́ТЬ СЛО́ВОМ ⟨ДА́РОМ СЛО́ВА⟩ [VP; subj: human; the verb may take the final position, otherwise fixed WO] to possess the ability to speak and write expressively, eloquently: X владеет словом ≃ **X has a way with words; X is good ⟨expert⟩ with words; X is a master of the spoken ⟨written⟩ word; [in limited contexts] X has a silver tongue ⟨is silver-tongued⟩.**

«Главный дар поэта – его воображение. Богатое, бурное, стремительное воображение – именно этим отличались Маяковский и Есенин от множества отлично владевших словом непоэтов» (Гладков 1). "A poet's main gift is imagination. A rich, boisterous, unruly imagination is what distinguished Mayakovski and Yesenin from all the non-poets who were merely expert with words" (1a).

С-332 • ЗА СЛО́ВОМ В КАРМА́Н НЕ ЛЕ́ЗЕТ ⟨НЕ ЛА́-ЗИТ, НЕ ХО́ДИТ *obs*⟩**/НЕ ПОЛЕ́ЗЕТ** *coll, often approv* [VP; subj: human; infin without negation is used with не привык, не надо etc] one is quick to respond in a discussion, conversation, argument etc: X за словом в карман не лезет ≃ **X is never at a loss for words ⟨for something to say⟩; X never has to search for words; X doesn't lack for words; X (always) has a ready answer; [in limited contexts] X is fast on the comeback.**

Движения его были смелы и размашисты; говорил он громко, бойко и почти всегда сердито... Никогда в карман за словом не ходил и вообще постоянно был груб в обращении со всеми, не исключая и приятелей (Гончаров 1). His gestures were bold and sweeping; he spoke loudly, glibly, and almost always angrily....He was never...at a loss for words, and generally rude to everyone, not excluding his friends... (1b). ♦ Слыхала, слыхала она [Лизка] от этого злыдня кое-что и похлестче – за словом Егорша в карман не лез (Абрамов 1). It was true that she [Lizka] had heard nastier words from that stinker before – Egorsha was never at a loss for something to say (1a). ♦ «Ваш муж держится [на суде] замечательно, за словом в карман не лезет!» (Амальрик 1). "Your husband is bearing up very well [at the trial]. He certainly doesn't lack for words!" (1a). ♦ «...Что это у тебя за дела такие спешные проявились? Прознать можно?» – «Всё будете знать – раньше времени помрёте». Дарья, как и всегда, за словом в карман не лазила... (Шолохов 5). "...What's bitten you all of a sudden? Can't we know?" "If you know everything you'll die before your time." As usual Darya had a ready answer... (5a).

С-333 • НЕ ОБМО́ЛВИТЬСЯ СЛО́ВОМ ⟨НИ (ЕДИ́-НЫМ) СЛО́ВОМ, НИ СЛОВЕ́ЧКОМ⟩ *(о ком-чём)* *coll* [VP; subj: human] to refrain totally from mentioning s.o. or sth.: X ни единым словом не обмолвился (об Y-е) ≃ **X didn't say a word ⟨a thing⟩ (about Y); X didn't mention Y at all; X didn't utter ⟨breathe⟩ a word (about Y).**

После какой-то рюмки, однако, Виктор вспомнил, что Ирма ни словом не обмолвилась о его диком поведении у перекрёстка (Стругацкие 1). After an indefinite number of drinks Victor remembered that Irma had not breathed a word about his dreadful behavior at the crossroads (1a).

С-334 • ОДНИ́М СЛО́ВОМ ⟨СЛО́ВОМ СКАЗА́ТЬ *obs, coll*⟩ [these forms only; sent adv (parenth); fixed WO] (used to introduce a summary of what has been stated or to replace part of a narration that the speaker is omitting) briefly: **in a word; in short; in brief;** [in limited contexts] **to make a long story short.**

[Тригорин:] Тороплюсь кончить повесть, а затем ещё обещал дать что-нибудь в сборник. Одним словом – старая история (Чехов 6). [T.:] I'm in a hurry to finish a story, and I've promised to give something else to an anthology. In short – the same old thing (6c). ♦ После этого небольшого лирического отступления он продолжал свой рассказ. Одним словом, они просидели за столом остаток ночи – пили вино и доедали барана (Искандер 3). After this small lyric digression he went on with his story. In brief, they sat at the table the rest of the night – drank wine and finished up the sheep (3a).

C-335 • **ПЕРЕКИ́НУТЬСЯ ⟨ПЕРЕБРО́СИТЬСЯ, ПЕРЕМО́ЛВИТЬСЯ⟩ СЛО́ВОМ ⟨СЛОВЕ́ЧКОМ, СЛОВЦО́М, ДВУМЯ́ СЛОВА́МИ⟩** (с кем) coll; **ПЕРЕБРО́СИТЬ ⟨ПЕРЕКИ́НУТЬ obs⟩ СЛО́ВО ⟨СЛОВЕ́ЧКО⟩** с кем substand [VP; subj: human; if there is no obj, subj: pl (variants with reflexive verbs)] to speak with s.o. briefly, make a few remarks back and forth: X перекинулся словом с Y-ом ⟨X и Y перекинулись двумя словами⟩ ≃ **X exchanged a word ⟨a few words⟩ with Y; X had a quick word with Y.**

Этап, этап... На этот раз одиночный, так что даже словом переброситься не с кем (Гинзбург 2). One forced march and then another. This time I was all on my own, so there was no other prisoner even to exchange a word with (2a). ♦ Дело было именно в том, чтобы был непременно *другой* человек, старинный и дружественный, чтобы в больную минуту позвать его, только с тем чтобы всмотреться в его лицо, пожалуй переброситься словцом... (Достоевский 1). The thing precisely was that there should be *another* man, ancient and amicable, who could be summoned in a morbid moment, so that he could look him in the face and perhaps exchange a few words... (1a). ♦ Сходил Иван [Лёвушкин] на соседнюю стройку пару раз, перекинулся словом с мастерами, постоял у одного-другого за подручного, – и радуйся, Отто Штабель! – двинулось вверх его жильё от ловкой лёвушкинской руки (Максимов 3). Ivan Lyovushkin went over to a nearby building site once or twice, had a quick word with the bricklayers, did a bit of laboring for one or another, and Otto Stabel was the beneficiary – his home rose steadily under Lyovushkin's clever hands (3a).

C-336 • **ПОМИНА́ТЬ/ПОМЯНУ́ТЬ НЕДО́БРЫМ СЛО́ВОМ** кого-что [VP; subj: human; often neg imper] to say or think negative, bad things about s.o. or sth. when recalling him or it: X поминает Y-а недобрым словом ≃ **X thinks ill ⟨badly⟩ of Y; X thinks ⟨speaks⟩ unkindly of Y; X has a harsh word to say about Y; X doesn't have a good word ⟨thing⟩ to say about Y.**

[author's usage] Он поднял стакан в сторону Андреева: «Павел Андреевич, не вспоминай меня плохим словом» (Гроссман 2). He turned to Andreyev and raised his glass. "Don't think badly of me when I'm gone!" (2a). ♦ Ровно в полночь все двенадцать литераторов покинули верхний этаж и спустились в ресторан. Тут опять про себя недобрым словом помянули Михаила Александровича... (Булгаков 9). Exactly at midnight all twelve writers left the upper floor and descended to the restaurant. Here each one again thought unkindly to himself of Mikhail Alexandrovich... (9a). ♦ Почти каждый день приходилось отрывать быков и лошадей от работы и посылать в станицу. Выпрягая из косилок лошадей, не один раз недобрым словом поминали старики затянувшуюся войну (Шолохов 5). Nearly every day horses and oxen had to be taken off work and sent to the stanitsa. As they unharnessed the horses from the reapers the old men had many a harsh word to say about this never-ending war (5a).

C-337 • **К СЛО́ВУ**[1] пришлось, пришёлся и т. п. coll [PrepP; Invar; adv or sent adv (parenth)] (s.o. says sth. because) it seems appropriate, comes to mind, is suggested by the course of the conversation: к слову пришлось ≃ **it ⟨he etc⟩ (just) happened to come up (in conversation ⟨in the conversation etc⟩); since ⟨now that, as long as⟩ I'm ⟨we're etc⟩ on the subject ⟨topic⟩ (of...); it fits in with what I'm ⟨we're etc⟩ talking about.**

«...Я упомянула о своём состоянии только потому, что к слову пришлось» (Тургенев 2). "I only mentioned my fortune because it happened to come up" (2e). ♦ ...[Щащико] всё говорил, если приходилось к слову, что истинное счастье – это жить у себя дома, работать у себя в поле и спать в своей постели (Искандер 3). [context transl] ...[Shashiko] kept saying, whenever he got the chance, that true happiness was to live in your own home, work in your own field, and sleep in your own bed (3a).

C-338 • **К СЛО́ВУ**[2]; **К СЛО́ВУ СКАЗА́ТЬ ⟨ГОВОРЯ́⟩** [these forms only; sent adv (parenth); fixed WO] as an aside or additional comment connected to or suggested by the topic at hand: **by the way; by the bye; incidentally;** [in limited contexts] **come to think of it; I should mention (that...).**

...С той стороны реки паром уже приближался. К слову сказать, сколько я ни напрягал свой ум, а у меня, слава богу, есть что напрягать, я никак не мог понять, какая сила движет паром поперёк реки (Искандер 3). ...The ferry was already drawing near from the other side of the river. By the way, no matter how hard I strain my mind, and thank God I do have a mind to strain, I cannot understand what force moves the ferry across the river (3a). ♦ «Выехав на упомянутое заседание, каковое, к слову говоря, и назначено-то вчера не было, Аркадий Аполлонович отпустил своего шофёра у здания акустической комиссии...» (Булгаков 9). "When he went to the meeting – which, incidentally, was never scheduled to take place yesterday – Arkady Appolonovich dismissed his chauffeur at the Acoustics Commission..." (9b). ♦ Постоянная слежка тётушки Хрисулы за целомудрием Дестины была предметом всевозможных шуток и подначек обитателей Большого Дома и их гостей... К слову сказать, тётушка Хрисула была невероятная говорунья. По этому поводу обитатели Большого Дома отмечали, что рот её хоть так, хоть этак, но обязательно должен работать (Искандер 5). Auntie Chrysoula's constant watch over Destina's chastity was the object of all kinds of joking and needling from the inhabitants of the Big House and their guests....I should mention that Auntie Chrysoula was an incredible chatterbox. In this connection the inhabitants of the Big House observed that if it wasn't one thing it was the other – her mouth had to be working (5a).

C-339 • **ДЛЯ ⟨РАДИ⟩ КРА́СНОГО СЛОВЦА́** говорить, острить и т. п. coll, occas. disapprov [PrepP; these forms only; adv; fixed WO] (to say sth.) in an attempt to show how witty, clever etc one is, in order to show off in conversation: **just for (the) effect; (just) to create an impression;** [in limited contexts] **just to be witty; for (its) eloquence alone; to make it sound good.**

Она нисколёшенько не верила Егоршиным сказкам насчёт коровы. Сбрехнул, для красного словца сказал (Абрамов 1). She did not believe Egorsha's yarn about the cow one little bit. He was fibbing; he'd said it just for effect (1a). ♦ Он [Авессалом] никогда не острил бесцельно, ради красного словца. Он делал это по заданиям юмористических журналов (Ильф и Петров 1). He [Absalom] never made them [jokes] without reason, just for the effect. He made them to order for humorous journals (1a). ♦ Не нужно на них сердиться, они наивные, добрые, очень добрые... только вот дурачества иногда говорят, глупости, ради красного словца (Трифонов 1). There was no need to get angry with them. They were naïve and goodhearted, terribly goodhearted....It was just that they sometimes said dumb, stupid things, just to be witty (1a). ♦ Пушкин как-то сказал: «Гений и злодейство несовместны»... И чем больше я думаю о литературе и судьбах писателей, тем больше убеждаюсь, что сказано это было не для красного словца (Войнович 1). Pushkin once said: "Genius and crime are incompatible."...The more I think about literature and the fates of various writers, the more I am convinced that Pushkin did not make that statement for its eloquence alone (1a). ♦ «„Хоть мы идём и разными путями, но я глубокий поклонник вашего таланта. Даже если хотите — ученик. Ваш и Хлебникова. Хлебников гений. Вы до известной степени тоже". Ну, тут он [Блок] для красного словца немножко загнул...» (Катаев 3). "Though we are following different paths, I am a profound admirer of your talent. Perhaps even a pupil. Yours and Khlebnikov's. Khlebnikov is a genius. So, to some extent, are you.' But here he [Blok] stretched a point to make it sound good..." (3a).

С-340 • КРА́СНОЕ СЛОВЦО́ [NP; sing only; fixed WO] a witty word or phrase that produces an effect on the listeners: **clever ⟨scintillating⟩ remark; apt remark;** [in limited contexts] **flash of wit; quip; one-liner;** [usu. *disapprov*] **(mere) rhetoric.**

Первый удар я намечал — письмо министру внутренних дел — ударить их о *крепостном праве*... (Не красное словцо, действительно таково: крепостное) (Солженицын 2). The first blow I had planned was my letter to the Minister of the Interior, in which I flung the word "serfdom" in their faces....(This was not mere rhetoric—serfdom is the only word for it) (2a).

С-341 • В О́БЩЕЙ СЛО́ЖНОСТИ [PrepP; Invar; adv or sent adv; fixed WO] in sum: **altogether; (all) in all; in toto; all told; taken together.**

У самой Аны детей не было. Зато у её трёх братьев и двух сестёр было в общей сложности 44 ребёнка... (Лимонов 1). Ana herself had no children. But all in all her three brothers and two sisters had forty-four children... (1a). ♦ Все движения на свете в отдельности были рассчитанно-трезвы, а в общей сложности безотчётно пьяны общим потоком жизни, который объединял их (Пастернак 1). Every motion in the world taken separately was calculated and purposeful, but, taken together, they were spontaneously intoxicated with the general stream of life which united them all (1a).

С-342 • (как) СЛОН В ПОСУ́ДНОЙ ЛА́ВКЕ *coll* [NP; sing only; adv (when used after как only) or subj-compl with быть₀ (subj: human); fixed WO] one is clumsy, awkward: **(be ⟨move etc⟩ like) a bull in a china shop.**

С-343 • СЛОНА́ НЕ ПРИМЕ́ТИТЬ [VP; subj: human; usu. past; fixed WO] not to notice the most important, significant thing: **слона-то X и не приметил ≃ X overlooked the obvious.** Cf. **visit Rome and not notice the Pope.**

< From Ivan Krylov's fable "The Sightseer" («Любопытный»), 1814.

С-344 • КАК ⟨ЧТО⟩ СЛОНУ́ ДРОБИ́НА ⟨ДРОБИ́НКА⟩ (кому) *coll* [как etc + NP; these forms only; subj-compl with быть₀ (subj: concr, usu. a noun denoting a small quantity of food or drink); fixed WO] sth. is insufficient in quantity for s.o.: X (Y-у) ~ ≃ **X is like buckshot to an elephant; X is a drop in the bucket (for Y);** [of food only] **X is not enough to make a dent in Y's appetite; X isn't enough to fill a cavity;** [of a drink only] **X is not enough to wet Y's whistle.**

...Тоненько закрученные сигаретки джойнтов он купил, раскрутил, смешал с обычным сигарным табаком и курил... Конечно, было понятно теперь, почему марихуана не действовала на него, он жаловался на это всё время. «Это же как слону дробина, курить-то нужно именно эту тоненькую, уже готовую сигаретку, ни с чем не смешивая» (Лимонов 1). ...He bought joints that had been rolled into nice slim cigarettes, unrolled them, mixed them with ordinary cigar tobacco, and then smoked them. Now it was clear, of course, why marijuana didn't affect him; he was always complaining about it. "That's like buckshot to an elephant. You're supposed to smoke that nice slim ready-made cigarette without mixing it with anything" (1a).

С-345 • СЛОНЫ́ ⟨СЛОНО́В⟩ СЛОНЯ́ТЬ *obs, substand, disapprov* [VP; subj: human; fixed WO] to walk about without reason or aim: **X слоны слонял ≃ X was roaming ⟨wandering⟩ around (aimlessly).**

С-346 • ВАШ ⟨ТВОЙ⟩ ПОКО́РНЫЙ СЛУГА́; ВАШ ПОКО́РНЕЙШИЙ СЛУГА́ [NP; sing only; fixed WO]
1. *obs* [formula phrase] a courteous closing to a letter: **your obedient ⟨humble⟩ servant.**

«Имею честь быть ваш покорный слуга. Ив. Головин» (Герцен 3). "I have the honour to be your obedient servant, Ivan Golovin" (3a). ♦ «Ну, что нового у вас [в канцелярии]?» — спросил Обломов. «Да много кое-чего: в письмах отменили писать „покорнейший слуга", пишут „примите уверение"»... (Гончаров 1). "Well, any news at the office?" asked Oblomov. "Yes, all sorts of things. We don't sign letters now, 'Your humble servant,' but: 'Accept our assurance of'" (1a).

2. used when the speaker wants to avoid saying «я», «меня» etc: **yours truly; your obedient ⟨faithful, humble⟩ servant.**

[Филипп:] Дорогие друзья! Много лестных тостов было сегодня произнесено в честь создания института биокибернетики... в честь получения профессорского звания вашим покорным слугой (Солженицын 11). [Ph.:] Dear friends! Many flattering toasts have been drunk today in honor of the founding of our new Institute of Biocybernetics...in honor of the professorship granted to your obedient servant (11a). ♦ А вот уж это — ваш покорный слуга... автор поэмы «Москва — Петушки»... (Ерофеев 1). And here we have your faithful servant...author of the poem *Moscow to the End of the Line*... (1a).

3. *obs* [indep. sent or subj-compl with быть₀ (subj: я), pres only] I am ready to do anything you want me to, to help you in any way: **(I am) at your service; I am your humble servant.**

...По дороге от барского дома показались две женщины и человек в белой шляпе, шедшие к офицерам. «В розовом моя, чур не обивать!» — сказал Ильин, заметив решительно подвигавшуюся к нему Дуняшу... «Что, моя красавица, нужно?» — сказал Ильин, улыбаясь. «Княжна приказала спросить, какого вы полка и как ваша фамилия?» — «Это граф Ростов, эскадронный командир, а я ваш покорный слуга» (Толстой 6). ...Two women and a man in a white hat appeared on the road leading from the big house, coming toward the officers. "The one in pink is mine, so keep off!" said Ilyin, catching sight of Dunyasha resolutely advancing toward them...."What do you want, my pretty one?" asked Ilyin with a smile. "The Princess sent me to ask your regiment and your name." "This is Count Rostov, squadron commander, and I am your humble servant" (6a).

С-347 • СЛУГА́ ДВУХ ГОСПО́Д *rather derog* [NP; sing only; fixed WO] a person who tries to please simultaneously two persons, groups etc with opposite viewpoints, goals etc: **servant of two masters.**

По какому-то неопределимому признаку Юрий Андреевич вообразил, что Комаровский завёл в эту минуту речь именно о нём... о том как он человек ненадёжный («слуга двух господ» — почудилось Юрию Андреевичу), что неизвестно, кто ему дороже, семья или Лара, и что Ларе нельзя на него положиться... (Пастернак 1). Something made Yurii Andreievich feel that just then Komarovsky was speaking about him, saying something to the effect that he should not be trusted ("serving two masters," he thought he heard), that it was impossible to tell if he were more attached to Lara or to his family, that Lara must not rely on him... (1a).

< The title of the Russian translation of Carlo Goldoni's play *Il servitore di due padroni*, 1745; of Biblical origin (Matt. 6:24, Luke 16:13).

С-348 • СЛУГА́ ПОКО́РНЫЙ *iron* [NP; sing only; usu. used as indep. sent; fixed WO] (used to express refusal or disagreement) no, I do not want to: **thank you very much; thanks a million; thanks, but no thanks.**

[Мышлаевский:] Спереди красногвардейцы, как стена, сзади спекулянты и всякая рвань с гетманом, а я посредине? Слуга покорный! Нет, мне надоело изображать навоз в проруби. Пусть мобилизуют! (Булгаков 4). [M.:] In front the Red Guards like a wall, behind the speculators and all kinds of trash with the Hetman,—and in between—me? Thank you very much! No, I'm sick and tired of playing the dung in the ice hole. Let them mobilize me! (4a). ♦ «...Нет, я категорически против „Колизея", — гремел на весь бульвар гастроном Амвросий. — Не уговаривай меня, Фока!» — «Я не уговариваю тебя, Амвросий, — пищал Фока. — Дома можно поужинать». — «Слуга покорный, — трубил Амвросий, — представляю себе твою жену, пытающуюся соорудить в кастрюльке в общей кухне дома порционные судачки а натюрель! Ги-ги-ги!..» (Булгаков 9). "No, no, I categorically oppose the Coliseum," the gourmet Amvrosy thundered across the entire boulevard. "Don't try to persuade me, Foka!" "I'm not trying to persuade you, Amvrosy," squeaked Foka. "A man can dine at home too." "Thanks a million," boomed Amvrosy. "I can imagine your wife trying to cook perch au naturel in a saucepan in the communal kitchen at home! He-he-he!..." (9a).

С-349 • **НЕ В СЛУ́ЖБУ, А В ДРУ́ЖБУ** [PrepP; Invar; indep. clause or adv; fixed WO] (said when asking s.o. to render a service) out of kindness rather than a sense of duty: **do s.o. a favor (and do sth.); (do sth.) as a (special) favor; you're not obliged to but I'd be much obliged if you did.**

...Если вечером все сидели на веранде, а Харлампо в это время находился на кухне, кто-нибудь потихоньку просил Деспину якобы не в службу, а в дружбу принести что-нибудь из кухни... (Искандер 5). ...If they were all sitting on the veranda in the evening and Harlampo was in the kitchen, someone would quietly ask Despina to do her a favor and fetch something from the kitchen... (5a). ♦ Втроём они в два приёма опорожнили бутылку, и Храмов, выудив из пиджака красненькую, протянул её Ивану: «Иван Никитич, не в службу, как говорят, а в дружбу... я бы и сам, но боюсь — не дойду... пустая бутылка стала наводить на меня тоску...» (Максимов 3). When the three of them had emptied the bottle in two rounds, Khramov fished a ten out of his jacket and held it out to Lyovushkin. "Ivan Nikitich, you know what they say—you're not obliged to but I'd be much obliged if you did....I'd go myself only I'm afraid I'd never make it....This empty bottle has begun to depress me" (3a).

С-350 • **СОСЛУЖИ́ТЬ СЛУ́ЖБУ** [VP] **1.** ~ кому-чему (какую) [subj: human] to have done sth. that benefits s.o. or sth., is useful to s.o. or sth.: X сослужил службу Y-у ≃ **X did ⟨rendered, occasioned⟩ Y a service; X did person Y a favor; X did person Y a good turn.**

[Мурзавецкая:] Как по-твоему, кому ты должен служить: мне или ей? [Чугунов:] Никому, кроме вас, благодетельница. [Мурзавецкая:] Вот и сослужи своей благодетельнице службу великую, избавь её от заботы! Ведь иссушил меня племянничек-то. [Чугунов:] Ничего-с, можно-с, не извольте беспокоиться (Островский 5). [M.:] In your opinion, whom ought you to serve, me or her? [Ch.:] No one but you, my benefactress. [M.:] Then do your benefactress a great service; save her from anxiety. You know my nephew has been a vexation to me. [Ch.:] Don't worry; it can be done. Please don't be uneasy (5a). ♦ Если бы отделённый Фёдор Лепендин болел дольше, то, может быть, он и сослужил бы ещё какую-нибудь службу науке (Федин 1). If Private Lependin had been ill longer he might perhaps have occasioned still further service to science (1a).

2. сослужить свою службу [subj: concr or collect] (of an object) to fulfill its function, (of a group, organization etc) to fulfill its mission (usu. with the implication that the object or group in question has exhausted its usefulness): X сослужил свою службу ≃ **X has served its purpose; X has done its job.**

[author's usage] Этот аппарат уже отслужил свою службу и больше в таком виде ему [Сталину] не нужен, ему нужен другой аппарат... (Рыбаков 2). This organization had served its purpose and had no further use in its present form; he [Stalin] needed a new one... (2a).

3. usu. **сослужить** какую (usu. **хорошую, неплохую, плохую, недобрую** etc) **службу** кому-чему [subj: usu. concr or abstr] to have had a certain (a positive, a harmful etc) effect on s.o. or sth.: X сослужил Y-у хорошую службу ≃ **X was (really) helpful to Y; X stood Y in good stead;** ‖ X сослужил Y-у плохую службу ≃ **X did Y a disservice; X did Y harm;** [in limited contexts] **X did Y more harm than good.**

Даже лёгкий намёк на знакомство [с Мятлевым] мог сослужить ей [Лавинии] дурную службу... (Окуджава 2). Even the slightest hint that they [Myatlev and Lavinia] might be acquainted could do her a disservice... (2a).

С-351 • **СТА́ВИТЬ/ПОСТА́ВИТЬ** что **НА СЛУ́ЖБУ** кому-чему lit or media [VP; subj: human; fixed WO] to apply sth. (one's talents, discoveries etc) or dedicate sth. (one's life, work etc) to furthering some cause or serving some person's or organization's interests: X поставил Y на службу Z-у ≃ **X placed Y at the service of Z.**

Начиная с 1968 года мне здесь [в кабинете генерала Ильина] неоднократно объясняли, что я поставил своё перо на службу каким-то разведкам... (Войнович 3). Since 1968...it had been repeatedly explained to me in this [General Ilin's] office that I had placed my pen at the service of some sort of intelligence agency... (3a).

С-352 • **АБСОЛЮ́ТНЫЙ СЛУХ** music [NP; fixed WO] the ability to sing any named note or identify any heard pitch without relying on a surrounding musical context, an instrument etc: **absolute ⟨perfect⟩ pitch.**

[extended usage] Дядя Сандро был рад, что остановил выбор на этом доме, что ему не изменило его тогда ещё только брезжащее чутьё на возможности гостеприимства, заложенные в малознакомых людях. Впоследствии беспрерывными упражнениями он это чутьё развил до степени абсолютного слуха, что отчасти позволило ему стать знаменитым в наших краях тамадой... (Искандер 3). Uncle Sandro was happy that his choice had fixed on this house, that his already sensitive nose for the possibilities of finding hospitality among people he barely know had not betrayed him. In later years, with continuing practice, he developed this sense to the point of absolute pitch. It was largely responsible for his becoming a celebrated tamada, or toastmaster, in our part of the world... (3a).

С-353 • **НА СЛУХ** [PrepP; Invar; adv] **1.** воспринимать, различать, определять и т. п. ~ (to perceive, distinguish, recognize etc sth.) by only listening: **by ear.**

«Я [стихи] на слух не воспринимаю... Литература, понимаете, дело интимное, она непосредственного глаза требует» (Максимов 2). "I can't take it [poetry] in by ear. Literature is a sensitive business, you know. The eye is essential" (2a).

2. петь, играть ~. Also: **ПО СЛУ́ХУ** (to sing or play sth.) without referring to printed music: **by ear.**

[Беневоленский:] ...Он на фортепьянах всё, что вам угодно, самоучкой играл, по слуху... (Островский 1). [B.:] ...He could play anything, whatever you liked, on the piano. He taught himself and played by ear (1a).

С-354 • **ПРЕВРАЩА́ТЬСЯ/ПРЕВРАТИ́ТЬСЯ ⟨ОБРАЩА́ТЬСЯ/ОБРАТИ́ТЬСЯ⟩ В СЛУХ** [VP; subj: human or collect; fixed WO] to listen very attentively: X превратился в слух ≃ **X was ⟨became⟩ all ears ⟨attention⟩; X was ⟨became⟩ completely absorbed in listening; X listened ⟨began to listen⟩ with rapt ⟨undivided⟩ attention.**

«Ну, слушайте же, что такое эти мёртвые души», — сказала дама приятная во всех отношениях, и гостья при таких словах вся обратилась в слух; ушки её вытянулись сами собою, она приподнялась, почти не сидя и не держась на диване... (Гоголь 3). "Well, let me tell you what these dead souls are," said the lady agreeable in all respects, and at these words her visitor was all attention: her ears seemed to prick up of their own accord, she raised herself so that she was hardly touching the sofa at all... (3a). ♦ ...[Он] глухо покашлял, снова заговорил, и я весь превратился в слух (Шолохов 1). ...He cleared his throat and began to talk. And I was completely absorbed in listening (1a).

С-355 • ПО СЛУ́ХАМ [PrepP; Invar] **1.** ~ знать, узнавать *что* ~ [adv] (to know, find out sth.) from the conversations or words of others: **through hearsay; through the grapevine; from rumors.**

2. [sent adv (usu. parenth)] according to rumors, stories etc that are being circulated: **rumor has it; it is rumored; by all accounts; [in limited contexts] ...or so they say.**

Старуха, не будь дура, отнесла записку [Сталина] не на склад, а в музей Революции, где получила такую сумму, что купила под Москвой домик, коровку, ушла с работы и, по слухам, до сих пор возит молоко на Тишинский рынок (Войнович 5). The old woman, no fool, did not take the note [written by Stalin] to the storehouse but to the Museum of the Revolution, where she sold it for enough money to buy herself a little house near Moscow and a cow; she quit her job, and rumor has it that to this day she's still bringing in milk to sell at Tishinsky market (5a). ♦ ...По слухам, такие челюсти делают специально для космонавтов... (Зиновьев 1). ...It was rumoured that these jaws had been specially made for the cosmonauts... (1a). ♦ Двурушник, по слухам, получил приличный гонорар за что-то, так что деньги у него наверняка были (Зиновьев 1). By all accounts Double-dealer had just received a very healthy fee for something so he almost certainly had some cash (1a).

С-356 • СЛУ́ХОМ ⟨СЛУ́ХАМИ⟩ ЗЕМЛЯ́ ПО́ЛНИТСЯ [saying] news or gossip spreads everywhere (said when a person does not want to specify how or from whom he learned sth., but rather alludes to the fact that it is widespread): ≃ **things get around; news spreads like wildfire; it came through the grapevine; bad news travels fast; [said ironically] good news travels fast.**

«Лучше скажите, каким вас ветром занесло? Больше года тут, и всё не могли собраться, удосужиться?» — «Откуда вы знаете?» — «Слухами земля полнится» (Пастернак 1). "Better tell me what brought you here. You've been around more than a year and you never found a moment to come till now." "How do you know?" "Things get around" (1a). ♦ Да я, впрочем, не спорить пришёл, а, узнав про вторую беду твою, пришёл утешить, потолковать с другом...» — «Какую такую беду?!» — «Да ведь Ивану-то Васильевичу пьеска не понравилась, — сказал Ликоспастов, и глаза его сверкнули, — читал ты, говорят, сегодня?» — «Откуда это известно?!» — «Слухом земля полнится», — вздохнув, сказал Ликоспастов... (Булгаков 12). "Still, I didn't come here to argue. When I heard about your bit of bad luck I came over to cheer you up, have a talk..." "What bit of bad luck?!" "Ivan Vasilievich didn't like your play," said Likospastov, his eyes shining. "You read it to him today, didn't you?" "How do you know?" "Oh, the grapevine, you know..." said Likospastov with a sigh... (12a).

С-357 • НИ СЛУ́ХУ НИ ДУ́ХУ (нет) *о ком-чём, от кого* coll [NP_gen; Invar; fixed WO] there has been no news of s.o. or sth. (for an indicated or implied period of time, or since an indicated or implied moment): об Х-е ⟨от Х-а⟩ ни слуху ни духу ≃ **there has been neither hide nor hair of person X; there has been neither sight nor sound of person X; there has been no word from person X ⟨of X⟩; I haven't ⟨he hasn't etc⟩ heard a word** ⟨a thing⟩ **about X ⟨from person X⟩; not a word has been heard about X; (there has been) no sign ⟨not a sign⟩ of X.**

Глуповцы торжествовали. Но, несмотря на то что внутренние враги были побеждены и польская интрига посрамлена, атаманам-молодцам было как-то не по себе, так как о новом градоначальнике всё ещё не было ни слуху ни духу (Салтыков-Щедрин 1). The Foolovites celebrated. But despite the fact that their internal enemies had been conquered and the Polish intrigue disgraced, the bold atamans were still not quite themselves, since there was neither hide nor hair of a new town governor (1a). ♦ ...В положении Чонкина было что-то такое, что не давало ему жить спокойно, а именно то, что оставили его вроде бы на неделю, но неделя эта прошла, а из части ни слуху ни духу, никаких дальнейших распоряжений (Войнович 2). ...There was something in Chonkin's situation which gave him no peace—namely, that he was supposed to have been left there for a week, the week had already passed, and there had been no word from his unit, no further instructions (2a). ♦ До пасхи о войне не было ни слуху ни духу... (Шолохов 3). Not a word was heard about war right up to Easter... (3a). ♦ «Я своего заказа жду два месяца, и о нём ни слуху ни духу» (Булгаков 10). "I've waited for my order for two months—and not a sign of it" (10a).

С-358 • В ДА́ННОМ СЛУ́ЧАЕ [PrepP; Invar; sent adv; fixed WO] in the given instance: **in this case ⟨instance⟩; on this occasion; in the present case; in the case in question ⟨at hand⟩.**

«Смотрите! – вдруг закричал он в восторге. – Продают квас! Вот здорово!» Действительно, далеко в перспективе улицы можно было разглядеть жёлтую цистерну с квасом, окружённую толпой. Девочка посмотрела и презрительно пожала плечами. «Вовсе не квас, а керосин», – сказала она... Это мог быть, конечно, и керосин, который развозили в подобных же цистернах, но в данном случае это был действительно квас (Катаев 2). "Look," he shouted suddenly with joy. "They're selling kvas! Super!" True enough, in the distance at the end of the street you could make out a yellow tank surrounded by a crowd. The girl also looked and shrugged with contempt. "It's not kvas at all, it's kerosene," she said....It might well have been kerosene, which was sold in tanks like this, but on this occasion it was in fact kvas (2a). ♦ Если я сказал, что я сделаю то-то и то-то, я должен это сделать. А уж в данном случае тем более (Войнович 1). If I've said I'll do something, I should do it. Especially in the case at hand... (1a).

С-359 • В КРА́ЙНЕМ СЛУ́ЧАЕ [PrepP; Invar; usu. sent adv (often parenth); fixed WO] in case of extreme need, when there is no other option or solution: **if worst comes to worst; if (the) worse comes to (the) worst; at (the) worst; as a last resort; [in limited contexts] in a pinch.**

«Сиди дома. В крайнем случае, если пойдёшь к Борису... Не качай головой, я знаю» (Терц 2). "Stay at home. If worst comes to worst and you go to Boris's—don't shake your head; I know" (2a). ♦ «...Очень хорошо, что вы согласились включить в наш план новые темы, Татьяна Петровна». – «Вы думаете?» – «В крайнем случае, потеряем полгода» (Каверин 1). "...It's very good that you've agreed to include those new subjects in our plan, Tatyana Petrovna." "You think so?" "At the worst, we'll lose six months" (1a). ♦ В милицию не заявляли, чтобы не напоминать властям о человеке, хотя и прописанном и не судившемся, но в современном понимании далеко не образцовом. Наводить милицию на его след решили лишь в крайнем случае (Пастернак 1). They did not report him as missing to the police. Although he was registered and had no police record, it was better not to draw the attention of the authorities to a man who, by the standards of the day, lived anything but an exemplary life. They decided not to put them on his track except as a last resort (1a). ♦ «...Вы должны выбрать, кто вам дороже – Чонкин или советская власть». Нюра смотрела на него полными слёз глазами. Она не знала, почему обязательно выбирать, почему в крайнем случае нельзя совместить то и другое (Войнович 4). "...You should make up your mind what is dearest to you—Chonkin or the Soviet government." Nyura looked over at him with tear-filled eyes. She did not know why she was obliged to choose, why, in a pinch, there wasn't room enough for them both, Chonkin and the Soviet government (4a).

С-360 • В ЛУ́ЧШЕМ СЛУ́ЧАЕ [PrepP; Invar; usu. sent adv (parenth); fixed WO] under the most favorable circumstances: **at best.**

На свои заграничные гонорары Мыльников купил себе экспортную «Волгу» (другие писатели в лучшем случае ездили на «Жигулях»)... (Войнович 6). On his foreign royalties Mylnikov had bought himself an export-grade Volga (other writers drove Zhigulis, at best)... (6a).

С-361 • В ЛЮБО́М СЛУ́ЧАЕ [PrepP; Invar; sent adv; fixed WO] regardless of which of two or more options, possible circumstances etc is realized, is valid etc: **in any case; whatever the case;** [in limited contexts] **either way; in either case; whatever the truth.**

Я не знаю, влюблена она в Мишу, в Петю или в Сашу. В любом случае она влюблена не в тебя. I don't know whether she's in love with Misha, Petya, or Sasha. In any case, she's not in love with you. ♦ Решай сам, поедешь ты со мной или нет. Я еду в любом случае. Make up your mind whether you are coming with me or not. I'm going either way. ♦ В Лёве всё приподнялось навстречу счастью — скажи сейчас Митишатьев, что глупо, несправедливо, напрасно приревновал его Лёва — бросился бы, расцеловал, расплакался и — в любом случае! — поверил бы! (Битов 2). Lyova's whole being rose to meet happiness. Were Mitishatyev to say that Lyova had been foolishly, unfairly, needlessly jealous, he would fall upon him, smother him with kisses, burst into tears and—whatever the truth!—he would believe! (2a).

С-362 • В ПРОТИ́ВНОМ СЛУ́ЧАЕ [PrepP; Invar; sent adv; fixed WO] if the opposite of what is needed, expected, demanded etc should happen: **otherwise; elsewise; or else; if not; failing which; if such is not the case.**

...Они [глуповцы] выстроились в каре перед присутственными местами и требовали к народному суду помощника градоначальника, грозя в противном случае разнести и его самого, и его дом (Салтыков-Щедрин 1). ...They [the Glupovites] formed themselves in a square outside the government offices and demanded that the deputy governor be handed over for trial, otherwise they would tear him and his house apart (1b). [context transl] ...They [the Foolovites] formed up in a square before the government offices and summoned the assistant town governor to a people's court, threatening to smash up both him and his house in the event of noncompliance (1a). ♦ «Писать стихи надо каждый день, подобно тому как скрипач или пианист непременно должен каждый день без пропусков по нескольку часов играть на своём инструменте. В противном случае ваш талант неизбежно оскудеет, высохнет, подобно колодцу, откуда долгое время не берут воду» (Катаев 3). "One must write poetry every day, just as a violinist or a pianist must play every day on his instrument for several hours without fail. If not, your talent will stagnate and run dry, like a well from which no water is drawn" (3a). ♦ «Если каким бы то ни было образом вы знаете и укажете нам, где он [государственный кредитный билет] теперь находится, то, уверяю вас честным словом, и беру всех в свидетели, что дело тем только и кончится. В противном же случае принуждён буду обратиться к мерам весьма серьёзным, тогда... пеняйте уже на себя-с!» (Достоевский 3). "If by any manner of means you know and are able to tell us where it [the state credit bill] now is, then I give you my word of honour, and summon those present as witnesses, that I shall let the matter end there. If such is not the case, then I shall have no option but to resort to measures of a thoroughly serious nature, and then...you will have only yourself to blame!" (3d). ♦ Разбойник объявлял о своём намерении немедленно идти на нашу крепость; приглашал казаков и солдат в свою шайку, а коман-

диров увещевал не сопротивляться, угрожая казнью в противном случае (Пушкин 2). [context transl] The impostor declared his intention to march on our fort immediately; he invited the Cossacks and soldiers to join his band and admonished the commanders not to offer any resistance on pain of death (2a).

С-363 • В СЛУ́ЧАЕ¹ быть∅; В СЛУ́ЧАЙ попасть (у кого) both obs [PrepP; these forms only; subj-compl with copula (subj: human)] (to be, end up) under the patronage of an influential person: X попал в случай ≃ **X was ⟨found himself, ended up⟩ in Y's good graces; X gained Y's favor;** [in limited contexts] **X became ⟨was⟩ a court favorite ⟨a favorite of the tsar's etc⟩.**

«Подойди, подойди, любезный! Я и отцу-то твоему правду одна говорила, когда он в случае был, а тебе-то и бог велит» (Толстой 4). "Come on, come closer, my dear! I used to be the only one to tell that father of yours the truth in the days when he was a court favorite, and now it's my sacred duty to do the same for you" (4a).

С-364 • В СЛУ́ЧАЕ² чего [PrepP; Invar; Prep (used with abstr, often deverbal, nouns); the resulting PrepP is adv] if sth. should happen, come about etc: **in case of; in case...; in the event of ⟨that...⟩;** [in limited contexts] **if there is ⟨are⟩ any...; if it becomes a question of;** ‖ в случае необходимости ⟨нужды etc⟩ ≃ **if need be.**

«...В случае нападения запирайте ворота да выводите солдат» (Пушкин 2). "...In case of an attack lock the gates and assemble the men" (2a). ♦ «Я думал, что в случае войны мы забудем все раздоры...» (Эренбург 4). "I thought that in the event of war we'd forget all our dissensions" (4a). ♦ «В случае невозможности Вашего личного присутствия, просим дать доверенность члену семьи...» (Войнович 3). "In the event that your personal attendance is impossible, we ask you to give power of attorney to a member of your family..." (3a). ♦ «Ведь в случае новых потрясений казаки Первого и Четвёртого полков перестреляют своих офицеров...» (Шолохов 3). "If there's any fresh upheavals, the Cossacks of the 1st and 4th regiments will shoot their officers to a man" (3a). ♦ Он пишет обширнейшие циркуляры, в которых призывает, поощряет, убеждает, надеется, а в случае нужды даже требует и угрожает (Салтыков-Щедрин 2). He writes circulars of enormous length in which he makes appeals, holds out an encouraging hand, uses persuasion, expresses hope and, if need be, threatens (2a).

С-365 • В СЛУ́ЧАЕ ЧЕГО́ coll [PrepP; Invar; sent adv (often parenth); fixed WO] if some trouble should occur or need should arise: **if something ⟨anything⟩ happens ⟨should happen⟩; in case ⟨in the event that⟩ something ⟨anything⟩ happens; if anything crops up; if something ⟨anything⟩ goes ⟨should go⟩ wrong; if need be; in the event of trouble; if there's any trouble.**

«Всё [ордера на мебель] в порядке. Где что стоит — всё известно. На корешках все адреса прописаны и собственноручная подпись получателя. Так что никто, в случае чего, не отопрётся» (Ильф и Петров 1). "They're [the orders for furniture are] all in order. You know where each item is. All the counterfoils have the addresses on them and also the receiver's own signature. So no one can back out if anything happens" (1a). ♦ ...Он [Чонкин] раскрыл свой вещмешок, переодел чистое бельё и стал рыться, перебирая своё имущество. В случае чего он хотел оставить Нюре что-нибудь на память (Войнович 2). ...Chonkin opened his knapsack, put on clean underwear, and then began rummaging through his possessions and sorting them out. In case anything happened, he wanted to leave Nyura something to remember him by (2a). ♦ «Не спеши! Давай подпустим ближе. Их только двенадцать человек. Разглядим их как следует, а в случае чего можно и ускакать» (Шолохов 5). "Don't be in such a hurry! Let 'em come a bit nearer. There're only a dozen. We'll have a proper look at 'em and we can still get away if need be" (5a). ♦ «Дашь ему документ — найду твою собаку. Не дашь — не буду искать...» — «Дядя Сандро, как я могу», — заныл внук Тендела... «Чего ты боишься?.. Он в случае чего скажет, что в колхозе достал...» (Искандер 4). "You give him the document—I'll find your dog. You don't—I won't look." "Uncle Sandro, how can I," Tendel's grandson whined.... "What are you afraid of?...If there's any trouble he'll say he got it at a kolkhoz" (4a).

С-366 • В ТАКО́М ⟨Э́ТОМ⟩ СЛУ́ЧАЕ; В ТАКО́М РА́ЗЕ *substand* [PrepP; these forms only; sent adv; fixed WO] given such a situation, under the given circumstances: **in that case; if that's the case; then;** [in limited contexts] **if so.**

[Бутон:] Мэтр, вы сами... палашом повалили свечку. [Мольер:] Врёшь, бездельник! [Риваль:] Он прав. Вы задели свечку шпагой... [Мольер:] Так я повалил? Гм... Почему же, в таком случае, я на тебя кричал? (Булгаков 8). [B.:] Maître, you yourself...knocked over that candle with your broadsword. [M.:] You're lying, you loafer! [R.:] He's right. You caught the candle with your sword.... [M.:] So I knocked it over? Me? Hm....In that case, why was I screaming at you? (8a). ♦ «Я думаю, что если дьявол не существует и, стало быть, создал его человек, то создал он его по своему образу и подобию». — «В таком случае, равно как и бога» (Достоевский 1). "I think that if the devil does not exist, and man has therefore created him, he has created him in his own image and likeness." "As well as God, then" (1a).

С-367 • В (ТОМ) СЛУ́ЧАЕ Е́СЛИ ⟨Е́ЖЕЛИ coll⟩ [subord Conj, condit] if it should happen that: **if; in case; in the event that;** [in limited contexts] **supposing.**

Жилец приказал Анфисе, преданной и давней домашней работнице Анны Францевны, сказать, в случае если ему будут звонить, что он вернётся через десять минут... (Булгаков 9). The lodger told Anfisa, Anna Frantzevna's devoted servant of many years, to say that if anybody rang him up he would be back in ten minutes (9b).

С-368 • В ХУ́ДШЕМ СЛУ́ЧАЕ [PrepP; Invar; usu. sent adv; fixed WO] under the least favorable circumstances: **at (the) worst.**

...Эти [бывшие марксисты и атеисты], преданные идеалам, с принципиальной прямотой могли в лучшем случае обрушить на вас град цитат, а в худшем и вытащить на собрании, не пожалев ни ближайшего друга, ни любимого учителя, ни папу, ни маму (Войнович 1). ...Those [former Marxists and atheists] devoted to ideals and firm in their principles could rain quotations down on you at best and, at worst, drag you out in front of a meeting, with no mercy for a close friend, a favorite teacher, a father, or a mother (1a). ♦ ...Баба Дуня широко распространила свой сон, будто её курица Клашка родила козла с четырьмя рогами, однако знатоки толковали данное видение как безобидное; в худшем случае, рассуждали, — к дождю (Войнович 2). [context transl] ...Granny Dunya had been spreading word about the dream she had in which her hen Klashka had given birth to a goat with four horns. The experts, however, had judged the vision in question to be harmless; the worst it could mean, in their opinion, was rain (2a).

С-369 • ВО ВСЯ́КОМ СЛУ́ЧАЕ [PrepP; Invar] **1.** [usu. adv; used with verbs in the fut or with надо, следует, пора etc] without fail, given any circumstances (the action in question will or should be carried out or come about): **in any case ⟨event⟩; one way or another ⟨the other⟩; whatever happens.**

...Ему [Бородавкину] незачем было торопиться, так как можно было заранее предсказать, что предприятие его во всяком случае окончится успехом... (Салтыков-Щедрин 1). ...He [Wartkin] had no reason to hurry, since he could predict beforehand that his venture would in any case end in success... (1a). ♦ «Скверно! — решил он наконец, — скверно, с какой стороны ни посмотри. Во-первых, надо будет подставлять лоб и во всяком случае уехать...» (Тургенев 2). "It's a bad business!" he decided finally. "A bad business, whichever way you look at it. In the first place I'll have to stand there waiting to be shot at, and whatever happens I'll have to leave..." (2e).

2. [used as Particle; often parenth; usu. placed before the word or phrase modified] used in conjunction with a word or phrase that qualifies or restricts the preceding statement: **at least; at any rate; in any case;** [in limited contexts] **anyway.**

Я неудачник. Во всяком случае так считает моя мама (Войнович 5). I'm a failure. Or at least my mother considers me one (5a). ♦ «Не нужно нам никакой квартиры, — сказал Дмитриев задыхающимся голосом. — Не нужно, понятно тебе? Во всяком случае, *мне* не нужно» (Трифонов 4). "We don't need any apartment at all," said Dmitriev in a choked voice. "We don't need it, you understand? In any case *I* don't need it" (4a). ♦ ...Никто у него в семье не был [в 1937 году] посажен или убит и палачей — явных, во всяком случае, — не определялось (Аксёнов 12). ...No one in his family had been imprisoned or killed [in 1937] and there were no executioners—obvious ones, anyway—recruited from among his kin (12a).

3. [sent adv (parenth)] regardless of the circumstances described in the preceding context, often regardless of which of the described options is correct or valid: **in any case ⟨event⟩; at any rate; at ⟨in⟩ all events; whatever the case.**

От Коровьева и Бегемота несло гарью, рожа Бегемота была в саже, а кепка наполовину обгорела. «Салют, мессир», — прокричала неугомонная парочка... «Очень хороши», — сказал Воланд... «Во всяком случае, мы явились, мессир, — докладывал Коровьев, — и ждём ваших распоряжений» (Булгаков 9). Koroviev and Behemoth reeked of smoke, Behemoth's face was sooty, and his cap badly singed. "Salute, Messire!" cried the irrepressible pair.... "A fine pair," said Woland. "In any case, we've come, Messire," reported Koroviev, "and we are waiting for your orders" (9a). ♦ «Значит, он миллионер?» — «Во всяком случае, за расходами не стоит» (Войнович 3). "Then he's a millionaire?" "At any rate, he doesn't spare expense" (3a). ♦ Возможно, он [архитектор Ш.] сам спровоцировал запрет барельефа. Возможно, сразу согласился. Возможно, не очень энергично отстаивал. Во всяком случае, теперь сотрудничество с тобой повредило бы его положению и карьере (Зиновьев 1). "Probably he [the architect S.] provoked the banning of the bas-relief himself. Probably he was the first to agree to it. Probably he defended it without any great conviction. At all events, working with you would have damaged his professional position" (1a). ♦ Знал ли он [Маяковский] о моём восторженном отношении к нему? Во всяком случае, между нами порой среди той или иной собравшейся группы литераторов устанавливался бессловесный контакт... (Олеша 3). Was he [Mayakovsky] aware of my rapturous regard for him? Whatever the case, from time to time, at one gathering of literary people or another, a tacit understanding was established between us... (3a).

С-370 • НИ В КО́ЕМ ⟨КАКО́М⟩ СЛУ́ЧАЕ; НИ В КО́ЕМ ⟨КАКО́М⟩ РА́ЗЕ *substand* [PrepP; these forms only; adv; used as indep. sent in response to a question or suggestion, or to intensify the preceding negated statement; fixed WO] under no conditions or circumstances: **not on any account; not ⟨never⟩ under any circumstances;** [in limited contexts] **not for anything; not for one moment; not on your life; in no way; (there's) no way; there isn't the slightest chance; (that's) out of the question; certainly not; (no,) of course not.**

«...Идите на площадь и скажите старшинам, чтобы ни в коем случае оружие казакам не сдавали!» (Шолохов 4). "Go to the square and tell the sergeants-major not to surrender their weapons to the Cossacks on any account!" (4a). ♦ Присутствие Бланка и Готтиха раскаляло беседу... То, что ни в коем случае не предназначалось для ушей Готтиха, кричалось на ухо Бланку, а то, что не годилось для ушей Бланка, хором вшёптывалось Готтиху (Битов 2). The presence of Blank and Gottich raised the conversation to fever pitch.... Anything not meant under any circumstances for Gottich's ears was shouted in Blank's ear, and anything not fit for Blank's ears was whispered in unison in Gottich's (2a).

♦ «Скажите, Максудов, а ваш роман пропустят?» — «Ни-ни-ни! — воскликнул пожилой литератор, — ни в каком случае!» (Булгаков 12). "Tell me, Maxudov, do you think your novel will get past the censor?" "Never, never, never," cried the elderly writer; "never, under any circumstances" (12a). ♦ «Ни в коем случае не допускаю мысли, — говорил негромко Афраний, — о том, чтобы Иуда дался в руки каким-нибудь подозрительным людям в черте города» (Булгаков 9). "I cannot believe for one moment," said Aphranius in a low voice, "that Judas would have allowed himself to be caught by any ruffians within the city limits" (9b). ♦ [Репников:] Включите свет. [Колесов:] Ни в коем случае! (Вампилов 3). [R.:] Turn on the light. [K.:] Not on your life! (3a). ♦ ...В его обязанности ни в коем случае не входило извещать директора комедиантов о тех перестройках, которые намечает в королевских зданиях архитектор короля (Булгаков 5). ...It was in no way a part of his duties to notify the director of the players concerning the Royal Architect's plans for reconstructions of the King's buildings (5a). ♦ Кто лидер? Хмырь? Учитель? Ни в коем случае... (Зиновьев 1). "Who'll be the leader? Bloke? Teacher? No way!..." (1a). ♦ Тогда её [статью] можно было напечатать без всякого для них риска. Теперь она не пройдёт ни в коем случае (Зиновьев 1). At that time this piece could have been published without the slightest risk to them. Now, there isn't the slightest chance of it seeing the light of day (1a). ♦ «Так вы сделаете это?» — тихо спросила Маргарита. «Ни в коем случае», — ответил Воланд (Булгаков 9). "So you will do it?" Margarita asked quietly. "Certainly not," said Woland (9a).

С-371 • ПРИ СЛУ́ЧАЕ *coll* [PrepP; Invar; adv]   **1.** when or if needed: **if ⟨when⟩ the occasion requires (sth. ⟨that...⟩); as required; if ⟨when⟩ necessary; if ⟨when⟩ need be; if ⟨when⟩ one has to.**

...Она [княгиня] отлично ездила верхом, неплохо стреляла, а при случае могла выдоить даже буйволицу (Искандер 3). ...She [the princess] was an excellent rider, not a bad shot, and when the occasion required it, she could even milk a buffalo (3a). ♦ Главное, [Коля] знал меру, умел при случае сдержать себя самого, а в отношениях к начальству никогда не переступал некоторой последней и заветной черты, за которою уже проступок не может быть терпим, обращаясь в беспорядок, бунт и в беззаконие (Достоевский 1). Above all, he [Kolya] knew where to draw the line, could restrain himself when need be, and in relation to the authorities never overstepped that final and inscrutable limit beyond which a misdeed turns into disorder, rebellion, and lawlessness, and can no longer be tolerated (1a).

2. when or if circumstances are favorable or appropriate: **given the opportunity ⟨the chance⟩; when ⟨if, as⟩ (the) opportunity arises; when ⟨if, as⟩ (the) opportunity presents itself; when ⟨if⟩ one has an ⟨the⟩ opportunity; when ⟨if⟩ one has the chance.**

Егорша любил при случае выдать себя за начальника... (Абрамов 1). ...Given the opportunity, Egorsha liked to pass himself off as a manager... (1a). ♦ [Чекисты] приглашали людей обычно не на Лубянку, а на специально содержавшиеся с этой целью квартиры. Отказывающихся держали там часами, бесконечно долго, предлагая «подумать». Из вызовов тайны не делали: они служили важным звеном в системе устрашения, а также способствовали проверке гражданских чувств — упрямцев брали на заметку и при случае с ними расправлялись (Мандельштам 1). They [the Chekists] generally invited people for these interviews not to the Lubianka, but to apartments specially allotted for the purpose. The uncooperative were kept for hours on end and urged to "think again." No secret was made of all this—it was an important element in the general system of intimidation, as well as being a good way of testing a person's "loyalty." The stubborn became marked men and were "dealt with" as opportunity arose (1a). ♦ «Это страшный человек. Это оборотень, который явился на свет только упущением божьим. Я врач, но мне не стыдно признаться, что при случае я охотно умертвил бы его»

(Стругацкие 4). "He's a hideous person, a monster who came into this world only because of some divine oversight. I am a physician, but I'm not ashamed to admit that I would kill him if I only had an opportunity to do so" (4a).

С-372 • НА ВСЯ́КИЙ ПОЖА́РНЫЙ СЛУ́ЧАЙ *coll* [PrepP; Invar; adv; fixed WO] as a precautionary measure, usu. in case an urgent need should arise: **just in case; just to be absolutely ⟨doubly, extra etc⟩ sure; as a safety net;** [in limited contexts] **in case of trouble ⟨of dire need etc⟩.**

...Они [Лёшка и Константин] говорили до позднего вечера, а когда закрылись Сандуновские бани, взяли они Соломона Моисеевича, чтобы стоял на шухере [*slang* = настороже], и заграничный браунинг на всякий пожарный случай, унесённый Лёшкой с поля сражения во время Великой Отечественной войны, и пошли, не мешкая, к тому месту, где была припасена их квартирка со всеми удобствами (Терц 1). ...They [Lyoshka and Konstantin] talked until late at night, and when the Sandunovsky baths closed they took Solomon Moiseyevich along as look-out man, along with a Browning revolver (just in case of trouble) which Lyoshka had removed from the field of battle during the [Great Patriotic] war, and set off without delay to the place where that little apartment that had everything was waiting (1a).

С-373 • НА ВСЯ́КИЙ СЛУ́ЧАЙ [PrepP; Invar; adv or sent adv (often parenth); fixed WO] as a precautionary measure, usu. in order to be prepared for the possibility of sth. unexpected or for possible necessity: **just in case; (just) to be on the safe side; just to be ⟨make⟩ sure; (just) to be ⟨to play it⟩ safe; (just) for safety's sake; as a precaution;** [in limited contexts] **it might come in handy.**

Боль прошла совершенно, я поднялся со скамейки и двинулся по аллее. Хотелось дойти до колодца и набрать в кувшин воду на всякий случай (Трифонов 5). Now the pain was completely gone. I got up from the bench and started down the pathway. I wanted to get a pitcherful of water from the well, just in case (5a). ♦ Дома все озабоченно обсуждали, что делать с продуктами... Дед был готов на казнь, только не сдавать. «Это они [немцы] пугают!»... Никто ничего не вернул и не сдал [немцам]. Но на всякий случай дед спрятал продукты в сарае под сено (Кузнецов 1). There was a worried discussion at home as to what to do about our food supplies....Grandfather was ready to face execution rather than give any of it up. "They're [the Germans are] just trying to scare us!"...No one returned or delivered anything [to the Germans], but, to be on the safe side, Grandfather hid our food under the hay in the shed (1a). ♦ Я на всякий случай уточнил у мальчишки моих лет: «В Германию облава?» (Кузнецов 1). Just to be sure I checked with a boy of my own age: "Is this a round-up for Germany?" (1b). ♦ «Ты, конечно, знаешь, зачем я тебя вызвал?» После разговора с Ермошиным я догадывался, но на всякий случай сказал, что не знаю (Войнович 5). "Of course you know why I called you in?" I had some idea after my talk with Ermoshin, but just to play it safe, I said I didn't know (5a). ♦ Я помню, сказал Учитель, мы в школе играли в конституцию. Тогда... все взрослые играли в неё. Сочинили и мы свою конституцию. И деньги свои выпустили. На деньгах на всякий случай написали: на эти деньги ничего купить нельзя (Зиновьев 1). "I remember," said Teacher, "that when I was at school we played at constitutions. It's the game that all the grown-ups were playing at the time. We used to draw up our own constitution and we issued our own money. Just for safety's sake we wrote on the notes: Nothing can be bought with this money" (1a). ♦ На всякий случай, для профилактики, икону можно повесить. Пусть это вас не смущает: я привык, в деревне воспитывался. Предрассудки эти в народной среде очень распространены (Терц 5). As a precaution against all eventualities you can hang up an ikon. Don't let that embarrass you—I'm used to it, having been brought up in the country. These superstitions are very common among the country folk (5a).

C-374 • **НА КРА́ЙНИЙ СЛУ́ЧАЙ** оставить, приберечь *кого-что*, отложить, припрятать *что* и т. п. *coll* [PrepP; Invar; adv; fixed WO] (to put sth. aside, save sth. etc) in case an urgent need should arise, (to save one's opportunity to approach s.o., ask s.o. for a favor etc) until an urgent need arises: отложить *что* ~ ≃ **put sth. aside in case of an emergency;** ‖ оставить *кого-что* ~ ≃ **leave ⟨keep⟩ s.o. ⟨sth.⟩ as a last resort; use s.o. ⟨sth.⟩ only as a last resort.**

Оставим Спекулянтку на крайний случай, сказал Учитель. А пока обойдём старых друзей, если это слово сохранило здесь какой-то смысл (Зиновьев 1). "Let's keep Speculatress as a last resort," said Teacher. "First let's go round to all my old friends, if the word still has any meaning" (1a).

C-375 • **НА ПЕ́РВЫЙ СЛУ́ЧАЙ** [PrepP; Invar; adv or sent adv; fixed WO] **1.** as a first (action, step toward some goal etc), as a start: **to start ⟨begin⟩ with; for starters ⟨openers⟩.**

[Таня:] Куда вы меня приглашаете? [Колесов:] На свадьбу. На первый случай я приглашаю вас на свадьбу (Вампилов 3). [T.:] What are you inviting me to? [K.:] A wedding. To start with, I'm inviting you to a wedding (3a). ◆ «Делать нечего, видно, мне вступиться в это дело да пойти на разбойников с моими домашними. На первый случай отряжу человек двадцать, так они и очистят воровскую рощу...» (Пушкин 1). "It seems that there's nothing for it but for me to take a hand in this affair, and go after the brigands with my own people. To begin with, I'll arm twenty men and have the copse set free of brigands" (1b).

2. for the initial period of time (that sth. is in effect, sth. is being undertaken, s.o. is doing sth. etc): **for the first little while ⟨bit⟩;** [in limited contexts] **for now; for the time being.**

«Ваших, то есть мамашу и сестрицу, жду с часу на час... Приискал им на первый случай квартиру...» (Достоевский 3). "I'm expecting your people, that is your mama and sister, at any moment now....I've found them rooms for the time being—" (3a).

C-376 • **НА СЛУ́ЧАЙ** [PrepP; Invar] **1.** ~ *чего* [Prep; used with abstr nouns; the resulting PrepP is adv] if sth. should happen, come about etc: **in the event of ⟨that...⟩; in case of; in case...;** [in limited contexts] **(so as) to be prepared for.**

...У жены мелькали иногда кое-какие мысли, имущественные и квартирные предположения на случай смерти мужа... (Солженицын 10). ...The wife had had a few fleeting thoughts about the property and apartment in the event of her husband's death... (10b). ◆ ...Дядя Сандро думает, что же будет, если Щащико поверит этому негодяю [Омару]?.. А если тот на случай дурного исхода вот так же, как и он, Сандро, предупредил своего брата и тот сейчас прячется в лесу? Не перестреляют ли они все друг друга? (Искандер 3). ...Uncle Sandro thought, What will happen if Shashiko believes this son of a bitch [Omar]?...And if Omar, just like me, has warned his brother in case of an evil outcome, and now the brother's hiding in the woods? Will they all shoot each other? (3a). ◆ «С Овчинниковым все жильцы нашего дома знакомы. Безотказный он на случай срочного ремонта» (Чернёнок 1). [context transl] "All the residents of our building know him [Ovchinnikov]. He never refuses to do an emergency repair" (1a).

2. *obs* [adv] accidentally, without being planned: **by chance ⟨happenstance⟩; (s.o. ⟨sth.⟩) happens to...; fortuitously.**

[Городничий:] Так сделайте милость, Иван Кузьмич: если на случай попадётся жалоба или донесение, то без всяких рассуждений задерживайте (Гоголь 4). [Mayor:] Mr. Pry [Ivan Kuzmich], will you do me one kindness: if a complaint or report should happen to come in, have no compunction in holding it up (4b).

C-377 • **НА (ТОТ) СЛУ́ЧАЙ Е́СЛИ** [subord Conj, condit, with the additional meaning of purpose] so as to be prepared if: **(just) in case...**

Я... купил два карандаша на случай, если потеряю ручку, и перочинный ножик, чтобы точить карандаши (Искандер 6). ...[I] picked up...two pencils (just in case I should lose my pen) and a penknife with which to sharpen them (6a).

C-378 • **СЛУ́ЧАЙ ПРИВЁЛ** *coll;* **СУДЬБА́ ПРИВЕЛА́** [VP~subj~] it happened that s.o. had the occasion (to do sth.): **(s.o.) got the chance ⟨the opportunity⟩ (to do sth.).**

[Хлестаков:] ...Страх хотелось бы с ним ещё раз сразиться. Случай только не привёл (Гоголь 4). [Kh.:] ...I was crazy to have another go at him, but I didn't have the opportunity (4d).

C-379 • **ПО СЛУ́ЧАЮ** [PrepP; Invar] **1.** ~ *чего* [Prep; the resulting PrepP is usu. adv] by reason of (sth.), resulting from (certain conditions): **on account of; because of; owing to;** [in limited contexts] **on the occasion of;** [when used with a noun denoting a holiday, festive event] **(in order) to commemorate ⟨to celebrate, to mark⟩ (sth.).**

«Мы им помощь везли по случаю землетрясения» (Аксёнов 3). "We shipped them supplies on account of the earthquake" (3a). ◆ «...Во всех пяти этажах уборные закрыты по случаю аварии водопроводной сети...» (Катаев 1). "...The lavatories have been closed on all five floors because of a break in the water system..." (1a). ◆ Пётр Житов был в загуле — от него так и разило сивухой. Первые два дня он пил по случаю майских праздников, потом подошли похороны Трофима Лобанова, — и как же было не почтить память старика? (Абрамов 1). Pyotr Zhitov was on a binge, and he reeked of vodka. For the first two days he had drunk to commemorate the May celebrations. Then came Trofim Lobanov's funeral—how could he not honor the old man's memory? (1a). ◆ По случаю приезда московских племянников в гости к деду съехалась почти поголовно вся родня (Максимов 2). Almost the entire clan descended upon the house to mark the visit of their Moscow cousins (2a).

2. ~ **купить, приобрести, достать** *что* и т. п. [adv] (to buy, acquire etc sth.) taking advantage of an opportunity, as the result of a favorable coincidence: **by (a lucky) chance; by happenstance;** [in limited contexts] **chance (up)on sth.; happen (up)on sth.; stumble (up)on ⟨across⟩ sth.**

...Наверное, Потёртый думал о том, как ему легко, по случаю, достался этот красавец-пёс, могучий и склонный к верности, которого и воспитывать не надо и который... будет ему спутником и защитой (Владимов 1). The Shabby Man, no doubt, was thinking how easily, by what a lucky chance he had acquired this handsome dog, strong and naturally loyal, who needed no training and who...would be his companion and defender (1a).

C-380 • **ПО ТАКО́МУ ⟨Э́ТОМУ⟩ СЛУ́ЧАЮ** [PrepP; these forms only; sent adv; fixed WO] since the circumstances are such (as they have just been described), as a consequence of (what has just been stated): **that being the case; in view of that ⟨of what you have just said⟩ etc⟩;** [in refer. to a previously mentioned holiday, festive event] **to mark the occasion.**

[Шмага:] Я подозреваю, что у вас есть намерение угостить нас, первых сюжетов, завтраком; по этому случаю вы мне дадите денег... (Островский 3). [Sh.:] I suspect that you intend treating us, the leading actors of our company, to lunch. That being the case, you forward the cash... (3a).

C-381 • **НЕ УПУСКА́ТЬ/НЕ УПУСТИ́ТЬ СЛУ́ЧАЯ** *coll* [VP; subj: human] to make use of favorable circumstances (and do sth.): X не упустит случая сделать Y ≃ **X won't let slip ⟨won't lose⟩ the opportunity to do ⟨of doing⟩ Y; X won't let the opportunity to do Y pass him by.**

«...Не только никаких Тихоновых и большинства Союза [писателей] нет для меня и я их отрицаю, но я не упускал случая открыто и прямо заявлять. И они, разумеется, правы, что в долгу у меня не остаются» (Гладков 1). "...Not only do Tikhonov and his like as well as most other members of the Union of Writers no longer exist for me, not only do I deny them, but I also lose no opportunity of saying so openly and plainly. And they, of course, are quite right to pay me back in kind" (1a).

C-382 • **ОТ СЛУ́ЧАЯ К СЛУ́ЧАЮ** [PrepP; Invar; adv; used with impfv verbs; fixed WO] (one does sth., sth. happens) irregularly, the occasions being separated by variable intervals of time: **(only) on occasion; (only ⟨just⟩) once in a while; from time to time; every so often; (only) off and on ⟨on and off⟩; sporadically.**

Моя сестра живёт далеко, мы обе очень заняты, вот и видимся от случая к случаю. My sister lives far away and we're both really busy, so we end up seeing each other only once in a while.

C-383 • **ГДЕ ⟨РА́ЗВЕ⟩ Э́ТО СЛЫ́ХАНО?** coll [indep. clause; these forms only; usu. foll. by infin or a чтобы-clause; fixed WO] (used to express indignation over or a strongly negative attitude toward some action or occurrence) this is unacceptable, unreasonable, outrageous: **whoever ⟨who's ever⟩ heard of such a thing ⟨of anything like it⟩?; it's (simply) unheard of.**

«Как?! – удивились чегемцы, – ты никогда не видел человека, а сам разговариваешь с нами, да ещё на нашем абхазском языке? Разве это слыхано?» (Искандер 5). "What!" the Chegemians marveled. "You've never seen a person, but you're talking to us, and in our Abkhazian language at that? Who ever heard of such a thing?" (5a).

C-384 • **СЛЫ́ХОМ НЕ СЛЫХА́ТЬ** coll [VP; fixed WO] **1.** ~ о ком-чём, про что. Also: **СЛЫ́ХОМ НЕ СЛЫХИ́ВАТЬ** coll [subj: human] not to have any knowledge or information about s.o. or sth.: X слыхом не слыхал об Y-е ≃ **X has never heard of Y; X knows nothing about Y; X doesn't have the faintest idea ⟨the slightest idea, the foggiest (notion)⟩ (who person Y is ⟨what thing Y is etc⟩); [usu. in response to a question] X doesn't have a clue.**

«Эта Светлана, о которой я слыхом не слыхивала до позавчерашнего дня, ждёт ребёнка от Сергея» (Трифонов 3). "This Svetlana, whom I had never heard of until the day before yesterday, is expecting Sergei's child" (3a).

2. ~ кого rare [infin only; impers predic with быть₀] s.o. is absent altogether, has disappeared: X-а слыхом не слыхать ≃ **there is no ⟨not a⟩ sign ⟨trace⟩ of X; X is nowhere to be found.**

C-385 • **РАСПУСКА́ТЬ/РАСПУСТИ́ТЬ СЛЮ́НИ** highly coll [VP; subj: human] **1.** to be or begin crying: X распустил слюни ≃ **X started crying ⟨blubbering, boohooing, bawling⟩; X turned on the tears ⟨the waterworks⟩; X burst into tears.**

...Я разревелся от злости... Когда Наталья Савишна увидала, что я распустил слюни, она тотчас же убежала... (Толстой 2). ...I howled with rage....When Natalya Savishna saw that I was crying she immediately ran away (2b).

2. to complain about sth. in an annoying, self-pitying manner, displaying a lack of resolve to right the situation about which one is complaining etc: X распускает слюни ≃ **X starts ⟨is⟩ whining ⟨whimpering, sniveling⟩.**

Да ведь это пустяк, даже и неприятностью назвать нельзя, а ты уже и слюни распустил. It's no big deal – you can't even really call it trouble, and yet you're already whining.

3. to become excessively sentimental, exaggeratedly emotional about sth., thus producing an objectionable impression: X распускает слюни ≃ **X is getting mushy ⟨gushy⟩; [often in refer. to sexual attraction] X is starting to drool.**

«Пол-Фосфатки её [Катю] любит и треть всего побережья, и даже на Улейконе я знаю нескольких парней, которые сразу же распускают слюни, как только речь заходит о ней» (Аксёнов 1). "Half of Phosphate loves her [Katya], and a third of the whole seaboard, and even in Uleikon I know a bunch of guys who start to drool as soon as you mention her" (1a).

C-386 • **ГЛОТА́ТЬ СЛЮ́НКИ** coll [VP; subj: human] to look with desire at sth. alluring (yet inaccessible): X глотает слюнки ≃ **X's mouth waters; thing Y makes X's mouth water; X drools (over thing Y); X looks on longingly ⟨hungrily, enviously⟩.**

Смотрю на их новую машину и слюнки глотаю. Мне бы такую! When I look at their new car my mouth waters. If only I could own one like that!

C-387 • **СЛЮ́НКИ ТЕКУ́Т/ПОТЕКЛИ́** (у кого) coll [VP_subj] **1.** s.o. wants some food or drink that he sees or smells so much that saliva is building up in his mouth: у X-а слюнки текут ≃ **X's mouth is watering; thing Y makes X's mouth water.**

Пройдёт ли мимо Милютинских лавок: там из окна выглядывает, в некотором роде, сёмга эдакая, вишенки по пяти рублей штучка, арбуз-громадище... – словом, на всяком шагу соблазн такой, слюнки текут... (Гоголь 3). Every time he went past the Milyutinsky stores he'd catch sight of a huge salmon staring out of the window at him, in a manner of speaking, lovely cherries at five roubles apiece, an enormous water-melon...—in short, such temptation at every step that his mouth watered... (3a). ♦ Она выложила телячьи отбивные на сковородку, по кухне распространился запах вкусной ресторанной пищи. Галя, усмехаясь, заметила: «Ишь, как пахнет... Слюнки текут...» (Рыбаков 2). She laid the veal chops [from the restaurant] in the hot frying pan and the communal kitchen was permeated with their delicious aroma. Galya observed with a smirk, "Goodness, how those smells make your mouth water!" (2a).

2. ~ (от чего, при виде кого-чего, при мысли о ком-чём и т. п.) seeing (thinking of etc) some desirable, alluring person or thing elicits in s.o. a strong desire for him or it: у X-а слюнки текут (от Y-а ⟨при виде Y-а и т. п.⟩) ≃ **X's mouth is watering; (seeing ⟨thinking of etc⟩ Y) makes X's mouth water; X wants Y so badly he can taste it; X is dying to get Y; [in limited contexts] X is drooling (over); just seeing ⟨thinking of etc⟩ Y is enough to make X's mouth water.**

«У них слюнки потекут, когда они увидят её [машину]...» (Олеша 2). "Their mouths will water when they see it [the machine]" (2a). ♦ «Приходит к старику патеру блондиночка, норманочка, лет двадцати... Красота, телеса... – слюнки текут» (Достоевский 2). "A girl comes to an old priest, a blonde, from Normandy, about twenty years old. Beautiful, buxom...enough to make your mouth water" (2a). ♦ «Я эту самую мысль прокурору в опросе моём не то что ясно сказал, а, напротив, как будто намёком подвёл-с... так у господина прокурора от этого самого намёка моего даже слюнки потекли-с...» (Достоевский 2). "In my interrogation, I told this same thought to the prosecutor, not quite clearly, but, on the contrary, as if I were leading him to it by a hint...and Mr. Prosecutor even started drooling over that same hint of mine, sir..." (2a).

C-388 • **НЕ СМЕ́Й(ТЕ)** [VP_imper; these forms only; foll. by infin] used to forbid s.o. categorically (to do sth.): **don't you dare; [in limited contexts] you wouldn't dare (do ⟨to do⟩ sth.)!; don't even think about (doing sth.)!**

[Несчастливцев:] Ты у меня не смей острить, когда я серьёзно разговариваю (Островский 7). [N.:] Don't you dare to joke when I'm talking seriously (7a).

C-389 • **БРАТЬ/ВЗЯТЬ НА СЕБЯ́ СМЕ́ЛОСТЬ** [VP; subj: human; foll. by the infin (more often pfv) of another verb; fixed WO] to dare (to say or do sth.): X берёт на себя смелость (сделать Y) ≃ **X takes the liberty of doing Y; X is ⟨makes⟩ so bold as to do Y; X makes bold to do Y; X presumes to do Y.**

«P. S. Я взял на себя смелость... отправить к вам несколько проб». Образчики эти были в полубутылках, на которых он собственноручно надписывал не только имя вина, но и разные обстоятельства из его биографии... (Герцен 3). "P.S.—I have taken the liberty of despatching to you...a few samples." These samples were in half-bottles on which he had inscribed with his own hand not only the name of the wine but various circumstances from its biography... (3a). ♦ Небритый брал на себя смелость сомневаться в белом цвете белых [шахматных фигур] (Ерофеев 2). The unshaven one used to be so bold as to doubt the whiteness of the white [chess] pieces (2a). ♦ Все три стихотворения абсолютны по форме и поэтической выраженности. Именно поэтому он берёт на себя смелость, не вдаваясь в обсуждение развития поэтических форм, сравнить их по *содержанию*... (Битов 2). All three poems are perfect in form and poetic expression. Precisely for this reason, without getting into a discussion of the development of their poetic forms, he has made bold to contrast them in *content*... (2a).

С-390 • СМЕ́ЛОСТЬ ГОРОДА́ БЕРЁТ [saying] bold people succeed at what they attempt to do: ≃ **fortune favors the bold** ⟨**the brave, the daring**⟩; [in limited contexts] **faint heart never won fair lady.**

С-391 • ДО́ СМЕ́РТИ [PrepP; Invar] **1.** убить *кого*, убиться ~ [adv (intensif)] used to emphasize the finality and fatal result of the action: **kill s.o.** ⟨**o.s.**⟩ **dead.**

2. [adv (intensif) or modif] to an extreme degree: напугать ⟨испугать, перепугать⟩ *кого* ~ ≃ **scare** ⟨**frighten**⟩ **s.o. to death; scare** ⟨**frighten**⟩ **s.o. out of his wits; scare the (living) daylights out of s.o.; give s.o. the fright of his life; scare the pants off s.o.;** ‖ напугаться ⟨испугаться, перепугаться⟩ ~ ≃ **be scared** ⟨**frightened**⟩ **to death; be scared** ⟨**frightened**⟩ **out of one's wits; be scared stiff** ⟨**silly**⟩; ‖ ~ надоел ⟨наскучил⟩ *кому* ≃ **s.o. is sick to death of him** ⟨**it** etc⟩; **s.o. is sick and tired of him** ⟨**it** etc⟩; **s.o. is fed up to here (with him** ⟨**it** etc⟩); ‖ скучно *кому* ~ ≃ **s.o. is bored to death** ⟨**to tears, out of his mind, stiff**⟩; **s.o. is dying of boredom;** ‖ ~ хотеть ⟨~ хочется *кому*⟩ ≃ **one** ⟨**s.o.**⟩ **is (just) dying (to get** ⟨**do**⟩ **sth.);** ‖ ~ не хотеть ⟨~ не хочется *кому*⟩ ≃ **one** ⟨**s.o.**⟩ **would (almost) rather die (than do sth.);** ‖ ~ любить *кого* ≃ **love s.o. to death** ⟨**to distraction**⟩; **be crazy about s.o.;** ‖ ~ не любить *что* ⟨*что делать*⟩ ≃ **loathe (doing) sth.; not be able to stand (doing) sth.; have a mortal aversion to (doing) sth.;** ‖ ~ устать ⟨измучиться⟩ ≃ **be dead** ⟨**deathly**⟩ **tired; be dead beat;** ‖ заговорить *кого* ~ ≃ **talk s.o. to death; talk s.o.'s ear off.**

«Нянечка до смерти напугана случившимся» (Чернёнок 2). "The nurse's aide is frightened out of her wits by what happened" (2a). ♦ Правда, и Зина, когда уже кончилось, болтала, что в кабинете, у камина, после того как Борменталь и профессор вышли из смотровой, её до смерти напугал Иван Арнольдович (Булгаков 11). It's true, also, that when everything was over, Zina babbled that Ivan Arnoldovich [Bormenthal] had given her the fright of her life in the office after he and the professor had left the examination room (11a). ♦ ...Борисов хлопнул [гипсовый бюст] Сталина по голове и затряс рукой от боли, но тут же выражение боли на его лице сменилось выражением смертельного страха... Он раскрыл рот и смотрел на Голубева не отрываясь, словно загипнотизированный. А тот и сам до смерти перепугался. (Войнович 2). ...Borisov whacked [the plaster bust of] Stalin on the head, then shook his hand in pain. Instantly, the expression of pain on his face changed into one of mortal fear....He opened his mouth and stared at Golubev as if hypnotized. Golubev, meanwhile, was scared to death himself (2a). ♦ К числу мелких литературных штампов Бунин... относил, например, привычку ремесленников-беллетристов того времени своего молодого героя непременно называть «студент первого курса»... «До смерти надоели все эти литературные сту-

денты первого курса», — говорил Бунин (Катаев 3). Among the minor literary clichés Bunin...included, for example, the hack-writer's habit in those days of describing his hero as a "first-year student."..."I am sick to death of all these literary first-year students," Bunin would say (3a). ♦ [Серафима:] Турку до смерти русского студня хочется, а не может на русском говорить (Эрдман 1). [S.:] The Turk was just dying to get some of the Russian meat-jelly but couldn't speak any Russian (1a). ♦ Даже по ушам его шапки было видно, что он до смерти не хочет ехать (Булгаков 6). The very earflaps of his hat told me that he would almost rather die than go (6a). ♦ С тех пор как его любимая лошадь Кукла, во время войны мобилизованная для доставки боеприпасов на перевал, вдруг сама вернулась домой, до смерти замученная... он дал себе слово никогда не заводить лошадей (Искандер 5). Ever since his beloved horse Dolly had been mobilized during the war to deliver military supplies to the pass, and had suddenly come home by herself, deathly tired...he had made himself a vow never to raise horses (5a). ♦ «Дядя Сандро, может, и смог бы её перепить, да ведь она его сначала заговорит до смерти, а там уж и перепьёт!» (Искандер 5). "Maybe Uncle Sandro could outdrink her, but she'll talk him to death first and then she'll outdrink him!" (5a).

С-392 • ПРИ́ СМЕ́РТИ быть₀, лежать, находиться [PrepP; Invar; subj-compl with copula (subj: human)] one is in critical condition, is about to die: X лежит при смерти ≃ **X is at death's door; X is near death; X is dying; X is on his deathbed.**

«[Михаил] мужика в лес гонит, а тот уж при смерти...» (Абрамов 1). "He [Mikhail] forces a man out to the forest when he's at death's door..." (1a). ♦ [Муаррон:] Госпожу Мадлену Бежар вы забыли? Да? Она при смерти... (Булгаков 8). [M.:] Have you forgotten Madame Madeleine Béjart? Yes? She is near death... (8a). ♦ «Да кто это? Как фамилия?» — «Самый наш жених бывший, князь Болконский! — вздыхая, отвечала горничная. — Говорят, при смерти» (Толстой 6). "But who is it? What is his name?" "Our one-time betrothed, Prince Bolkonsky!" sighed the maid. "They say he is dying" (6a). ♦ Только на четвёртый день прибило Настёну к берегу недалеко от Карды. Сообщили в Атамановку, но Михеич лежал при смерти, и за Настёной отправили Мишку-батрака (Распутин 2). On the fourth day Nastyona floated up near Karda. They sent word to Atamanovka, but Mikheyich was on his deathbed and they sent Mishka the hired hand for Nastyona (2a).

С-393 • РА́НЬШЕ ⟨ПРЕ́ЖДЕ⟩ СМЕ́РТИ НЕ ПОМРЁШЬ ⟨НЕ УМРЁШЬ⟩ [saying] a person dies when he is fated to, not earlier: ≃ **nobody dies before his time.**

«Остров объявлен на военном положении...» Затем, проследив за метаниями хозяйки, [кадровик] брезгливо поморщился: «Раньше смерти не помрёшь, Самохина, не суетись...» (Максимов 1). "Martial law has been declared over the island...." Then watching Fyodor's mother rushing about the room, he [the personnel officer] winced with disgust: "Why the hurry, Samokhina? Nobody dies before their time" (1a).

С-394 • СМОТРЕ́ТЬ ⟨ГЛЯДЕ́ТЬ⟩ СМЕ́РТИ В ГЛАЗА́ ⟨В ЛИЦО́⟩ *elev* [VP; subj: human] **1.** to be exposed to mortal danger (while engaged in battle, chasing an armed criminal etc): X смотрел в глаза смерти ≃ **X looked death in the face; X stood face to face with death.**

«Мы — коммунисты — всю жизнь... всю кровь свою... капля по капле... отдавали делу служения рабочему классу... угнетённому крестьянству. Мы привыкли бесстрашно глядеть смерти в глаза!» (Шолохов 4). "We Communists have given our whole lives...all our blood...drop by drop...to the cause of serving the working class...the oppressed peasantry. We are used to looking death fearlessly in the face" (4a).

2. to be about to die: X смотрел смерти в глаза ≃ **X was staring death in the face; X was at death's door; X was on the brink of death.**

С-395 • **КАК СМЕРТЬ** бледный, побледнеть [как + NP; Invar; adv (intensif) or modif] (to be, turn) very pale: **(as) pale as death; deathly pale; (as) white ⟨pale⟩ as a sheet; (as) pale ⟨white⟩ as a ghost.**

«Знаешь, что случилось?» — сказали мне в один голос три офицера, пришедшие за мною; они были бледны как смерть. «Что?» — «Вулич убит» (Лермонтов 1). "Do you know what's happened?" the three officers who had come for me said to me in chorus; they were as pale as death. "What?" "Vulic has been killed" (1b). ♦ «...Он хочет увезти губернаторскую дочку»... Приятная дама, услышав это, так и окаменела на месте, побледнела, побледнела, как смерть... (Гоголь 3). "...He wants to elope with the governor's daughter."...On hearing it the agreeable lady was petrified, she went as white as a sheet... (3d).

С-396 • **ПЕРЕД СМЕРТЬЮ НЕ НАДЫШИШЬСЯ** [saying] you cannot do at the last moment what you did not do before, when there was more time: ≃ **you can't make up for lost time; it's too late for that now.**

Перед трудными экзаменами Маша обычно занималась всю ночь, хотя и понимала, что перед смертью не надышишься. Before hard exams Masha typically studied all night, even though she knew that you can't make up for lost time.

С-397 • **СВОЕЙ СМЕРТЬЮ** умереть [NP$_{instrum}$; Invar; adv; fixed WO] (to die) from natural causes: X умер своей смертью ≃ **X died a natural death;** [in limited contexts] **X died in his bed;** ‖ *Neg* X умер не своей смертью ≃ **X died a violent death; X met with a violent end;** [in limited contexts] **X was cut off in his prime.**

Двоекуров, Семён Константиныч, штатский советник и кавалер... Умер в 1770 году своею смертью (Салтыков-Щедрин 1). Dvoekurov, Semen Konstantinych. State Councillor and knight of an order....Died in 1770 of natural causes (1b).

С-398 • **(ТОЛЬКО) ЗА СМЕРТЬЮ ПОСЫЛАТЬ** кого coll [VP; these forms only; impers predic; the verb always takes the final position] (used to express irritation at the long absence of s.o. who was sent on an errand) when he (she etc) goes on an errand, you have to wait an extremely long time for him (her etc) to return: Х-а только за смертью посылать ≃ **you could grow old waiting for X (to get back ⟨to do the simplest little errand etc⟩); it takes X forever (and a day) to do the simplest of errands; X is slower than molasses (in January).**

Где ты столько времени ходишь? Тебя только за смертью посылать! Where have you been all this time? You're slower than molasses in January!

С-399 • **ДВУМ СМЕРТЯМ ⟨ДВУХ СМЕРТЕЙ⟩ НЕ БЫВАТЬ, А ОДНОЙ НЕ МИНОВАТЬ** [saying] the inevitable is going to happen whether or not one takes a risk (said to encourage a person who is about to undertake a risky venture, or to justify one's own decision to undertake such a venture): ≃ **you ⟨a man⟩ can only die once (and you'll ⟨he'll⟩ die one day anyway); a man can die but once; one cannot die twice.**

«Городок у нас хоть и старинный, а маленький, работать негде, парни после армии домой не едут, вот девчата наши и наладились в Игарку вербоваться... Я сперва не хотела, очень уж боязно, говорят, пьянка там большая и ночь долгая, да где наша не пропадала, двух смертей не бывать, одной не миновать, нынче вот собралась...» (Максимов 2). "This town of ours is old, but it's so small there isn't much work. After they've done their time in the army the boys never come back here, so the girls have taken to going to Igarka to look for jobs....I didn't want to go at first, I was too frightened. People said there was an awful lot of hard drinking there, and the nights are long, but in the end I thought 'nothing venture, nothing gain,' you can only die once and you'll die one day anyway, why not give it a try? So now I'm on my way there" (2a).

С-400 • **НЕ СМЕТЬ ДОХНУТЬ** coll ⟨**ДЫХНУТЬ** substand⟩ [VP; subj: human] to be extremely afraid (of s.o.) or nervous (about sth.) and usu. not move (for fear of drawing s.o.'s attention to one, making sth. go wrong etc): X не смел дохнуть ≃ **X didn't dare (to) breathe; X didn't dare (to) move a muscle.**

Новый учитель был так строг, что ученики при нём дохнуть не смели. The new teacher was so strict that the students didn't dare to move a muscle in his presence.

С-401 • **(И) СМЕХ И ГРЕХ ⟨ГОРЕ⟩** coll [indep. clause; these forms only; fixed WO] sth. is both amusing and sad, is ridiculous and pathetic at the same time: **you don't know whether to laugh or cry; it makes you want to laugh and cry (at the same time); it's (both) funny and sad at the same time.**

Посмотрите на эту актрису. Ну разве можно в пятьдесят лет играть Джульетту? И смех и грех! Just look at that actress. Really, how can you possibly play Juliet at fifty years of age? It's funny and sad at the same time!

С-402 • **КАК ⟨БУДТО, СЛОВНО, ТОЧНО⟩ НА СМЕХ** coll [как etc + PrepP; these forms only; adv] as if intentionally to ridicule s.o.: **as if out of spite; as if to mock s.o.**

Последовал экономический кризис... В это же время, словно на смех, вспыхнула во Франции революция, и стало всем ясно, что «просвещение» полезно только тогда, когда оно имеет характер непросвещённый (Салтыков-Щедрин 1). An economic crisis ensued....At that same time, as if out of spite, revolution flared up in France, and it became clear to all that "enlightenment" was useful only when it had an unenlightened character (1a). ♦ ...После моего отъезда старейшины города Цюриха узнали, что я вовсе не русский граф, а русский эмигрант и... что я человек нерелигиозный и открыто признаюсь в этом. Последнее они вычитали в ужасной книжке *Vom andern Ufer,* вышедшей, как на смех, у них под носом, из лучшей цюрихской типографии (Герцен 2). ...After I had gone away the elders of the town of Zürich learnt that I was not a Russian Count at all but a Russian *émigré* and...that I was a man without religion and openly admitted the fact. This last they learned from an awful little book, *Vom andern Ufer*, which, as though to mock them, had been issued under their very noses by the best firm of publishers in Zürich (2a).

С-403 • **ПОДНИМАТЬ ⟨ПОДЫМАТЬ⟩/ПОДНЯТЬ НА СМЕХ** кого-что coll [VP; subj: human] to make s.o. or sth. an object of ridicule: X поднял Y-а на смех ≃ **X made fun of Y; X made a laughingstock of Y; X made Y a laughingstock; X had a laugh at person Y's expense;** [in limited contexts] **X started jeering at Y;** [when ridiculing s.o.'s suggestion, comment etc] **X laughed Y down.**

...Он [Антонович] слышал, что Надя просила выдать ей папку с несекретной перепиской Лопаткина и что ей отказали. Во время работы комиссии он осторожно заговорил об этом, и Урюпин, громко хохоча, поднял его на смех. Антонович знал, что в папке не только свобода — вся жизнь Дмитрия Алексеевича (Дудинцев 1). ...He [Antonovich] had heard that Nadia had asked for the file with Lopatkin's non-secret correspondence to be handed over to her, and that this had been refused. While the commission had been at work, he [Antonovich] had cautiously referred to this, and Uriupin, laughing loudly, had made fun of him. Antonovich knew that that file held, not only Lopatkin's liberty, but his whole life's work (1a). ♦ «Я поделился своим открытием лишь с одним человеком — с моим коллегой Мишечкиным. Он меня поднял на смех, назвал это научным мистицизмом...» (Евтушенко 1). "I shared my discovery with only one man, my colleague Mishechkin. He made a laughing stock of me and called it all 'scientific mysticism'" (1a). ♦ «Весь тот день [Илюша] мало со мной говорил, совсем молчал даже... А в тот-то именно день мальчишки и подняли его на смех в школе...» (Достоевский 1). "All that day he [Ilyusha] hardly spoke to me, he was even quite silent....And it was precisely that day when the boys started jeering at him in school…" (1a). ♦ …По бульвару на большой скорости пронеслись полдюжины броневиков-амфибий с горящими фарами и воющими сиренами… В кафе «Марсово поле» некий иностранец предположил, что подразделение мчалось «брать» Совет Министров. Его подняли на смех (Аксёнов 7). …Half a dozen amphibious armored cars sped down the center of the road, their headlights glaring red and sirens going full blast.…A foreigner in the Café Champs de Mars suggested they might be off to "take" the Council of Ministers. He was laughed down (7a).

C-404 • ПРО́СТО ⟨ПРЯ́МО⟩ СМЕХ (ОДИ́Н) *coll*; (ПРО́СТО ⟨ПРЯ́МО⟩) СМЕХ ОДИ́Н *coll*; СМЕХ ДА И ТО́ЛЬКО *coll*; (ПРО́СТО ⟨ПРЯ́МО⟩) ОДНА́ СМЕХОТА́ *substand*; СМЕХОТА́ ДА И ТО́ЛЬКО *substand* [usu. indep. sent; usu. this WO] it is laughable, ludicrous: **it's hilarious ⟨hysterical, ridiculous, (simply) absurd, a (sheer) farce, a joke, a riot⟩; it's enough to make a cat laugh.**

[Кабанова:] …Гостей позовут, посадить не умеют, да ещё, гляди, позабудут кого из родных. Смех да и только! (Островский 6). [K.:] …They invite guests, don't know how to seat them, or even, think of it! leave out one of the family. It's simply absurd! (6a). ♦ У большинства политических [заключённых] десятилетка, многие с высшим образованием, с кандидатскими диссертациями… Смех один, когда отрядный, повторяющий, как попугай, чужие слова, не умеющий разобраться даже в собственных записях, проводит с ними политбеседу на уровне четвёртого класса школы (Марченко 1). The majority of the [political] prisoners have completed high school, many of them [have] also had a higher education and have doctoral dissertations to their name.…It's sheer farce when the company officer, repeating somebody else's words parrot-fashion and unable to make head or tail of his own notes, conducts a political discussion with them on the level of class four [fourth grade] in school (1a). ♦ [Зинаида Савишна:] Как он, бедный, ошибся!.. Женился на своей жидовке и так, бедный, рассчитывал, что отец и мать за нею золотые горы дадут, а вышло совсем напротив… [Бабакина:] Господи, да и достаётся же теперь ей от него! Просто смех один (Чехов 4). [Z.S.:] The poor man made a ghastly mistake—marrying that wretched Jewess and thinking her parents would cough up a whacking great dowry. It didn't come off.… [B.:] And now he gives her a terrible time, God knows—it's enough to make a cat laugh (4b).

C-405 • СМЕ́ХА РА́ДИ *coll*; ДЛЯ СМЕ́ХУ ⟨-а⟩ *coll*; НА́ СМЕХ *coll*; ДЛЯ ХО́ХМЫ *highly coll* [PrepP; these forms only; adv] in order to amuse o.s. (and others), in jest: **(just) for fun; (just) for the fun of it; (just) for ⟨as⟩ a joke ⟨a laugh⟩; (just) for kicks.**

«Была бы я царевна, — певуче, по-бабьи, сказала она, — я не была бы злая… Я не отнимала бы у него эту дудочку, я бы только дунула в неё разок — так, для смеху… Я бы его [пастуха], который мне дудочку принёс, жалела…» (Чуковская 2). "Were I a princess," she said in singsong voice, like a peasant woman telling a fairy story, "I would not be wicked…I would not have taken his pipe away from him, I would have blown on it once—just for fun.…I would have had pity on the shepherd-boy who brought me the pipe…" (2a). ♦ Взял дед свои [карты] в руки — смотреть не хочется, такая дрянь, хоть бы на смех один козырь (Гоголь 5). Grandad picked up his [cards]—he couldn't bear to look at them, they were such trash; they could have at least given him one trump just for the fun of it (5a). ♦ Я сам один раз для хохмы пустил такой слушок про Претендента (Зиновьев 1). "Once, just for a joke, I started a rumour like that about Claimant" (1a). ♦ «Раз, для смеха, Григорий Александрович обещался ему [Азамату] дать червонец, коли он ему украдёт лучшего козла из отцовского стада» (Лермонтов 1). "Once, for a laugh, Grigory promised to give him [Azamat] ten rubles if he would steal the best goat from his father's flock" (1d).

C-406 • ПОКА́ТЫВАТЬСЯ ⟨КАТА́ТЬСЯ, ВАЛЯ́ТЬСЯ⟩/ПОКАТИ́ТЬСЯ СО́ СМЕХУ ⟨ОТ СМЕ́ХА, С ХО́ХОТУ, ОТ ХО́ХОТА⟩ *all coll* [VP; subj: human or collect] to laugh hard: **X покатился со смеху ≃ X rolled ⟨rocked, roared⟩ with laughter; X laughed his head off; X split ⟨burst⟩ his sides laughing; X fell down laughing; X was convulsed with laughter; X busted a gut laughing; (sth.) made X roll ⟨rock, roar⟩ etc) with laughter.**

«Он очень нервный мальчик, — говорит мать… и добавляет шёпотом: — У него случается ночное недержание…» Но все всё слышат, и весь перрон покатывается от смеха, указывает на меня пальцами… (Арканов 2). "He's a very nervous child," my mother says…and adds in a whisper, "He sometimes wets the bed." But they all hear it, all of it, and the whole platform rolls with laughter, and they all point their fingers at me… (2a). ♦ Как только Ткач пугливо взглядывал на меня, я начинал пристально смотреть на которое-нибудь из его ушей. А однажды, когда он сидел на скамейке, я подошёл сзади и ощупал его ухо. Бедняга оглянулся, увидел меня и обомлел. Он закрыл уши ладонями, перебежал к своей койке и долго сидел на ней, не решаясь отнять руки от головы. Вся камера покатывалась со смеху… (Марченко 1). As soon as I caught Tkach's fearful glance upon me I would begin to stare at one or the other of his ears; and once, when he was sitting on the bench, I came up behind him and tweaked his ear. The poor fellow glanced round, caught sight of me and turned to stone. He clapped his hands over his ears, ran to his bunk and for a long time remained sitting there, unable to bring himself to lower his hands from his head. The whole cell rocked with laughter (1a). ♦ [Лукашин:] И знаете, если мы встретимся с вами, ну, когда-нибудь, случайно, и вспомним всё это, мы будем покатываться со смеху… (Брагинский и Рязанов 1). [L.:] One day, you know, if we happen to meet again and remember all this, we'll simply laugh our heads off (1a). ♦ «Хочешь свеженький анекдотик? Со смеху покатишься…» (Чернёнок 1). "You want to hear the latest joke? You'll fall down laughing" (1a). ♦ Он рассказывал мне армейские анекдоты, от которых я со смеху чуть не валялся, и мы встали из-за стола совершенными приятелями (Пушкин 2). He told me anecdotes of army life that made me roll with laughter; by the time we got up from the table we were bosom friends (2a).

C-407 • УМИРА́ТЬ/УМЕРЕ́ТЬ ⟨ПОМИРА́ТЬ/ПОМЕРЕ́ТЬ⟩ СО́ СМЕХУ *coll*; ЛО́ПНУТЬ ⟨ТРЕ́СНУТЬ, ПОДЫХА́ТЬ/ПОДО́ХНУТЬ⟩ СО́ СМЕХУ ⟨ОТ СМЕ́ХА⟩ *highly coll* [VP; subj: human or collect; if pfv past, usu. after чуть не] to laugh without restraint, laugh to the point of exhaustion: **X умрёт со смеху ≃ X will die laughing; X will split ⟨burst⟩ his sides laughing; X will roll ⟨rock, roar⟩ with laughter; X will bust a gut laughing; X will be in stitches.**

«Ещё одно слово о „Фантомах", и я лопну от смеха…» (Ерофеев 1). "One more word about Phantoms and I'll die laughing" (1a). ♦ «Поверите ли, ваше превосходительство, — продолжал Ноздрёв, — как сказал он [Чичиков] мне: „Продай мёртвых душ", я так и лопнул со смеху» (Гоголь 3). "Will you believe it, Your Excellency," Nozdrev continued, "when he [Chichikov] said to me, 'Sell me some dead souls,' I simply split my sides laughing" (3b). ♦ Тётя Маруся чуть не лопнула со смеха, когда выяснилось, что я не понимаю значения популярного среди вольного населения глагола «отоварить» (Гинзбург 2). Aunt Marusya almost burst her sides laughing upon discovering that I was ignorant of the meaning of the phrase "to trade in," much in use among the free population (2a). ♦ Сейдахмат что-то громко рассказывал. Сидевшие смеялись его словам. «Ну и что дальше?» — «Рассказывай!» — «Нет, слушай… ты повтори ещё раз», — чуть не умирая от смеха, просил Орозкул… (Айтматов 1). Seidakhmat was loudly telling some story. The others laughed at his words. "And what happened then?" "Go on!" "No…tell it again," Orozkul begged, rolling with laughter (1a).

C-408 • УМОРИ́ТЬ СО́ СМЕХУ *кого coll* [VP; subj: human] to make s.o. laugh hard, to the point of exhaustion: X уморит Y-а со смеху ≃ **X will have Y in stitches; X will make Y die laughing; X will make Y laugh so hard Y will cry;** [in limited contexts] **Y is going to die laughing.**

[Добротворский:] Ах вы, проказник!.. Будет вам проказничать-то, уморили со смеху! Поцелуемтесь (Островский 1). [D.:] Oh, you joker, you....Enough of your silly jokes, now. I'm going to die laughing. Kiss me (1a).

C-409 • СМЕШИ́НКА В РОТ ПОПА́ЛА *(кому) coll* [VP$_{subj}$; Invar] s.o. cannot stop laughing, keeps on laughing with no apparent reason: X-у смешинка в рот попала ≃ **X has (got) the giggles; X has a laughing fit.**

(Снова хохочут. Маша заливается.) [Валентин:] Машка, перестань!.. Ну, смешинка в рот попала! (Рощин 1). *(They laugh again. Masha is in fits.)* [V.:] Masha stop it! You've got the giggles! (1b).

C-410 • ДО СМЕШНО́ГО [PrepP; Invar; modif or adv (intensif)] extremely, to an excessive degree: **to the point of absurdity; absurd(ly); ridiculous(ly); to ridiculous lengths.**

«...Согласитесь, Павел Петрович, что поединок наш необычаен до смешного. Вы посмотрите только на физиономию нашего секунданта» (Тургенев 2). "...You must admit, Pavel Petrovich, that our duel is unusual to the point of absurdity. Just look at our second's countenance" (2c). ♦ ...Он успешно выступал на собраниях и откровенно, на глазах у живого завуча, правда, до смешного похожего на дореволюционного интеллигента, метил на его место и был близок к цели (Искандер 3). ...He made some successful speeches at meetings and openly set his sights on the principal's job—in full view of the existing principal, who did in truth bear an absurd resemblance to a prerevolutionary intellectual—and came close to getting it (3a). ♦ В «Новом мире» с первой же минуты получения рукописи «[Ракового] корпуса» из неё сделали секретный документ, так определил Твардовский. Они боялись, что рукопись вырвется, *пойдёт*, остерегались до смешного: не дали читать... в собственный отдел прозы! (Солженицын 2). As soon as the manuscript of *Cancer Ward* arrived at *Novy Mir*, it became a secret document, on Tvardovsky's instructions. In their fear that it [the manuscript] would slip its leash and "go the rounds," they carried their precautions to ridiculous lengths: they wouldn't even show it to the staff of their own prose department! (2a).

C-411 • НЕ СМИГНУ́В(ШИ) *сказать, ответить и т. п. coll* [Verbal Adv; these forms only; adv] (to say sth., answer a question etc) without getting confused or embarrassed (usu. in situations when the speaker knowingly makes a false statement): **without batting an eye ⟨an eyelid, an eyelash⟩; without hesitation.**

Хотя всем присутствующим ложь его была очевидна, Женька продолжал врать не смигнувши, надеясь отсрочить наказание за разбитое окно. Although it was clear to everyone there that Zhenka was lying, he continued doing so without batting an eye, hoping to delay his punishment for breaking the window.

C-412 • БЕСПЛО́ДНАЯ СМОКО́ВНИЦА [NP; sing only] **1.** an infertile woman: **(a woman) as barren as the proverbial fig tree.**

2. a person whose activity brings no results: X — бесплодная смоковница ≃ **X is (like) barren ground.**

< From the Bible (Matt. 21:19).

C-413 • чёрный КАК СМОЛЬ [как + NP; Invar; modif (intensif)] very black and shiny (usu. of hair, a mustache, whiskers etc): **jet-black; pitch-black; coal-black.**

Волоса его, недавно чёрные как смоль, совершенно поседели... (Пушкин 2). His hair, jet-black only a short while before, had turned entirely gray... (2a). ♦ Это был среднего роста, очень

недурно сложённый молодец с полными, румяными щеками, с белыми как снег зубами и чёрными как смоль бакенбардами (Гоголь 3). He was a young fellow of medium height, of excellent build, with full rosy cheeks, snow-white teeth, and pitch-black whiskers... (3a).

C-414 • СМОТРЕ́ТЬ ⟨ГЛЯДЕ́ТЬ⟩ В О́БА *coll* [VP; subj: human; usu. infin (with надо, нужно etc) or imper] **1.** ~ *(за кем-чем).* Also: СЛЕДИ́ТЬ В О́БА *coll;* СМОТРЕ́ТЬ ⟨ГЛЯДЕ́ТЬ⟩ В О́БА ГЛА́ЗА *coll* (in refer. to visual observation) to watch s.o. or sth., or look for s.o. or sth., very attentively: [when the person or thing is in sight] смотри за Y-ом в оба ≃ **watch Y closely ⟨carefully⟩; keep an eye ⟨a watchful eye, a close watch⟩ on Y;** ‖ [when looking for a person or thing that is not yet in sight] смотри в оба, чтобы не пропустить поворот ⟨не проехать въезд на шоссе и т. п.⟩ ≃ **keep an eye out for the turn ⟨the entry onto the highway etc⟩; keep your ⟨both⟩ eyes peeled for the turn ⟨the entry onto the highway etc⟩; keep your eye open for the turn ⟨the entry onto the highway etc⟩;** [in limited contexts] **look sharp (now).**

«Теперь мне в оба глядеть, — строго добавил он. — Чуть только [цыплята] начнут вылупливаться, сейчас же мне дать знать» (Булгаков 10). "Look sharp now," he added sternly. "The moment they [the chicks] begin to hatch, let me know at once" (10a).

2. ~ *за кем-чем* [prep obj: human or collect] to keep s.o. or sth. under one's close, general observation: смотри за Y-ом в оба ≃ **watch Y (especially) closely ⟨carefully⟩; keep an eye ⟨a watchful eye, a close watch⟩ on Y.**

Выступал там и Васькин. И называл имена тех, за кем надо смотреть в оба (Зиновьев 2). Vaskin was one of the speakers. And he named certain people who had to be specially closely watched (2a).

3. to be watchful, cautious, vigilant (in order to avoid danger, prevent an unpleasant occurrence, protect one's interests etc): смотри в оба ≃ **keep your ⟨both⟩ eyes open; be on your guard; be on the lookout; watch out; don't let your guard down; be careful.**

Поневоле начинаю волноваться. Вокруг освобождающейся квартиры что-то происходит, плетутся какие-то интриги. На каждом шагу встречаю доброжелателей, которые предупреждают. «Вам надо смотреть в оба, вы должны бороться». Почему бороться и с кем? (Войнович 3). Against my will, I began to get worried. Something was going on with that vacant apartment, intrigues were being spun. At every step I was meeting well-wishers who forewarned me. "You have to keep your eyes open, you should put up a fight." Why fight, and who with? (3a). ♦ Он всех одолеет, надо только смотреть в оба и не поддаваться (Сологуб 1). He would be victorious over everyone. It was necessary only to keep both eyes open and not to yield (1a).

C-415 • СМОТРЕ́ТЬ ⟨ГЛЯДЕ́ТЬ⟩ ВОН *coll* [VP; subj: human] to want and be ready to leave or get out of some place: X смотрит вон ≃ **X is looking to clear out; X is looking ⟨ready⟩ to split; X is anxious to leave ⟨get out⟩.**

«Холодно, что ли, в комнате или пахнет нехорошо, что вы так и смотрите вон?» (Гончаров 1). "Are you cold here or is there a bad smell in the room that you're so anxious to get out?" (1a).

C-416 • СМОТРЕ́ТЬ ⟨ГЛЯДЕ́ТЬ⟩ КО́СО *на кого-что coll* [VP; subj: human] to regard s.o. or sth. suspiciously, unfavorably, hostilely: X смотрит косо на Y-а ≃ **X looks askance at Y; X frowns (up)on Y; X takes a dim view of Y.**

...Не секрет, что иные фотографы смотрели на него [Венечку Пробкина] косо... (Аксёнов 12). It was no secret that some photographers looked askance at him [Venechka Probkin]... (12a).

C-417 • СМОТРЕ́ТЬ ⟨ГЛЯДЕ́ТЬ⟩ НЕ́ НА ЧТО *coll, disapprov* [VP; infin only; predic with быть$_{ø}$ (impers or with subj: human, animal, or concr); usu. pres; usu. this WO] (usu. used to express dissatisfaction, a scornful attitude etc toward s.o. or sth.) some person, animal, or thing is too unattractive (small, lacking in some area etc) even to merit attention: (X —) смотреть не на что ≃ **X isn't (even) worth a second look; X is nothing ⟨not much⟩ to look at; X is too ugly ⟨small, dinky etc⟩ (even) to bother with;** [in limited contexts] **there's nothing ⟨there isn't anything⟩ to look at;** [of an animal or thing only] **X isn't worth the space it takes up ⟨the money one paid for it etc⟩; X isn't (even) worth having.**

Другой раз попадётся такой [мужик], что и смотреть не на что: кривой, горбатый, деньги пропивает, жену и детей бьёт до полусмерти (Войнович 2). Sometimes you might get one [a man] that's not much to look at—blind in one eye, hunchbacked, drinks away his money, beats his wife and children half to death (1a). ♦ [Пашка:] Когда я отсюда уезжал, ты вот *(показывает)* была. Совсем пацанка, я и не смотрел на тебя... Да и смотреть не на что было... (Вампилов 2). [P.:] When I left this place you were this high. *(He indicates.)* Nothing but a kid, and I never even looked at you....And there wasn't anything to look at either... (2b). ♦ Серафима Платоновна всем расхваливает свою новую мебель, а там и смотреть не на что. Serafima Platonovna brags to everybody about her new furniture, but it's not worth the space it takes up.

С-418 • СМОТРЕ́ТЬ ⟨ГЛЯДЕ́ТЬ⟩ СВЕ́РХУ ВНИЗ *на кого;* СМОТРЕ́ТЬ ⟨ГЛЯДЕ́ТЬ⟩ СВЫСОКА́ [VP; subj: human; usu. this WO] to regard s.o. with condescension, scorn: X смотрит на Y-а сверху вниз ≃ **X looks down on Y; X looks down his nose at Y.**

По-кавказски укоренённо презирая русских и всё русское вообще, он [Сталин] жаждал выглядеть со стороны чистокровным русским, чтобы по праву смотреть свысока на инородцев... (Максимов 1). For all his deep-rooted Caucasian contempt for Russians and everything Russian, he [Stalin] still wanted outsiders to take him for a full-blooded Russian, so as to have the right to look down on foreigners... (1a).

С-419 • СМОТРЕ́ТЬ ⟨ГЛЯДЕ́ТЬ⟩ СНИ́ЗУ ВВЕРХ *на кого* [VP; subj: human; usu. this WO] to regard s.o. with admiration, reverence: X смотрит на Y-а снизу вверх ≃ **X looks up to Y.**

Олеся смотрела на Лёву, как и я, снизу вверх. Она выросла в простой семье, мать её была домашней хозяйкой, и бабушки её и золовки тоже были при доме, и Олеся тянулась за Лёвой... хотела учиться, хотела работать, быть самостоятельной... (Рыбаков 1). Like me, she [Olesya] looked up to Lyova. She had grown up in a simple family, with her mother who ran the house, and her grandmother and sisters-in-law, and she tried to keep up with Lyova...she wanted to study, to work, to be independent (1a).

С-420 • КУДА́ (ТО́ЛЬКО) СМО́ТРИТ; ЧТО ⟨ЧЕГО́⟩ СМО́ТРИТ *all coll* [VP; subj: human or collect; pres or past] why does one take no action against, pay no attention to (some reprehensible, undesirable etc action or those who are carrying it out)?: куда смотрит X? ≃ **what is X thinking of?; what is X doing (when he should be taking action ⟨measures etc⟩)?;** [in limited contexts] **where is X?**

«Где они там живут?» — ...быстро и нервно спросил Павла Воронцов. «В бараке». — «В бараке?! Барак стоит?!.. — Воронцов даже затрясся и кинулся к окну... — А ты... ты, Павел Миронович, куда смотрел? Как позволил?» (Распутин 4). "Where are they living over there?" Vorontsov asked quickly and nervously...."In the shack." "In the shack? The shack is standing?!..." Vorontsov shook and ran to the window...."And you...you, Pavel Mironovich, what were you thinking of? How could you let them?" (4a). ♦ Люди кричали: «Безобразие! Куда смотрит милиция?! Милицию сюда!» (Семёнов 1). People shouted: "Scandalous! Where are the police? Get the police!" (1a).

С-421 • СМОТРИ́(ТЕ) У МЕНЯ́! *coll* [imper sent; these forms only] (used to express a warning or threat) stop doing or do not do reprehensible things or else I will punish you: **don't you dare (, you hear me)!; (you'd better) watch out ⟨watch it, watch your step⟩!; mind what I say!**

«Сидоркин, вы там опять в шахматы режетесь?» — «Никак нет!» — рявкает Сидоркин и нагло ест начальство глазами. «Смотрите у меня» (Войнович 5). "Sidorkin, are you playing chess over there?" "Of course not!" barked Sidorkin, devouring the chief with his impudent eyes. "Don't you dare, you hear me!" (5a).

С-422 • СМОТРЯ́ КТО ⟨ЧТО, КАКО́Й, КА́К, ГДЕ́, КУДА́, КОГДА́, СКО́ЛЬКО⟩ [NP, AdjP, or AdvP, depending on the 2nd component; fixed WO] contingent upon who, what, what kind etc: **it depends (on) who ⟨what, what kind, how, where, when, how much, how many⟩ etc⟩.**

[Шеметова:] Нелепость, безумие — так играть своей жизнью, когда конец завиднелся! [Бакченин:] Какой конец? [Шеметова:] Войне конец... [Бакченин:] Когда началось, многие тоже говорили — от силы год. Я лично так считал... И что такое год? Величина в высшей степени относительная. И полгода относительная. И день. И минута... Одна длина у минуты в Казани, другая — у разведчика на вражьей полосе... Так что «скоро конец» — это смотря для кого... (Панова 1). [Sh.:] It's stupidity, madness to risk your life like that when the end is in sight. [B.:] What end? [Sh.:] The end of the war.... [B.:] When it started, lots of people said: At most, a year. I thought so myself. And what's a year? A highly relative quantity. And six months, too. And a day. And a minute....A minute has one amount of time in it in Kazan, but a different amount for a scout in enemy territory. So "the end is in sight" depends on who for... (1a). ♦ «Умерла Клавдия Ивановна», — сообщил заказчик. «Ну, царствие небесное, — согласился Безенчук. — Преставилась, значит, старушка... Старушки, они всегда преставляются... Или богу душу отдают, — это смотря какая старушка. Ваша, например, маленькая и в теле, — значит, преставилась. А например, которая покрупнее да похудее — та, считается, богу душу отдаёт...» (Ильф и Петров 1). "Claudia Ivanovna's dead," his client informed him. "Well, God rest her soul," said Bezenchuk. "So the old lady's passed away. Old ladies pass away...or they depart this life. It depends who she is. Yours, for instance, was small and plump, so she passed away. But if it's one who's a bit bigger and thinner, then they say she has departed this life..." (1a).

С-423 • СМОТРЯ́ ПО *чему* [Prep; Invar; the resulting PrepP is adv] as conditioned by: **depending ⟨it depends⟩ on; contingent (up)on.**

«Мы поедем завтра в лес?» — «Смотря по погоде». "Are we going to the woods tomorrow?" "It depends on the weather."

С-424 • В ПО́ЛНОМ СМЫ́СЛЕ СЛО́ВА [PrepP; Invar; nonagreeing modif; fixed WO] (one is a certain type of person, sth. is a certain type of thing or phenomenon etc) entirely, in every way: **(a [NP]) in the fullest ⟨full, true⟩ sense of the word.**

[Утешительный:] [Аркадий Андреевич Дергунов] игру ведёт отличную, честности беспримерной... люди у него воспитанны, камергеры, дом — дворец, деревня, сады, всё это по аглицкому [*obs* = английскому] образцу. Словом, русский барин в полном смысле слова (Гоголь 2). [U.:] He [Arkady Andreievich Dergunov] is a first-rate player, of exemplary honesty;...his servants are refined people, perfect gentlemen, his house is a regular palace, his estate, his parks are all in the English style; in fact he is a Russian gentleman in the fullest sense of the word (2b). ♦ Угрюм-Бурчеев был прохвост [*used here in its obsolete meaning*] в полном смысле этого слова. Не потому только, что он занимал эту должность в полку, но прохвост всем своим существом, всеми помыслами (Салтыков-Щедрин 1). Gloom-Grumblev was a hangman in the full sense of the word. Not only because he occupied this post in the regiment, but a hangman in his whole being, all his thoughts (1a).

С-425 • В СМЫ́СЛЕ [PrepP; Invar; Prep; the resulting PrepP is adv] **1.** ~ *чего, каком* in relation to sth., in a certain respect: **with regard to; as for; as far as...goes 〈is concerned〉; in terms of; from the...point of view; in the sense of 〈that...〉;** ‖ в этом смысле ≃ **in this 〈that〉 sense 〈regard, respect, way〉;** ‖ в некотором смысле ≃ **in a certain sense 〈way〉.**

Тоталитарные идеологии создают тоталитарные режимы — в этом смысле коммунизм ничем не отличается от фашизма (Аллилуева 2). Totalitarian ideologies create totalitarian regimes, and in this sense Communism doesn't differ in any way from Fascism (2a). ♦ Вбежав в избу, она [Нюра] первым делом обратила внимание на крышку подпола, но в этом смысле всё было в порядке... (Войнович 2). The first thing Nyura did in the hut was to check the cellar door, but everything was fine in that respect... (2a). ♦ Я бы даже сказал, что высшие руководители в некотором смысле ещё бесправнее рядовых советских граждан. Они не только обязаны неукоснительно соблюдать все правила и ритуалы, принятые в их среде, не только живут в постоянном страхе друг перед другом, но и от самих привилегий отказаться не могут (Войнович 1). I'd even say that in a certain sense the higher leaders have fewer rights than the average Soviet citizen. They are not only obliged to observe rigorously all the rules and rituals of their milieu, they not only live in constant fear of each other, but also they cannot refuse the privileges that are theirs (1a).

2. ~ *кого-чего* in a specific capacity: **as.**

«Как понимать ваши слова — в смысле просьбы?» — «В смысле приказа, с вашего позволения!» "How am I to take what you said—as a request?" "As an order, if you please!"

С-426 • СО СНА [PrepP; Invar; adv] (having) just awakened or (being) not fully awake: **(still) half-asleep; (only) half-awake; not quite awake;** [in limited contexts] **(being) (still) too sleepy.**

Со сна я не мог понять, что отцу нужно. Only half-awake, I couldn't understand what Father wanted. ♦ Начали собираться к чаю: у кого лицо измято...; тот належал себе красное пятно на щеке и висках; третий говорит со сна не своим голосом (Гончаров 1). The company began to assemble for tea; one had a crumpled face...; another had a red spot on the cheek and on the temple; a third was still too sleepy to speak in his natural voice (1a).

С-427 • СНАРУ́ЖИ МИ́ЛО, А ВНУТРИ́ ГНИ́ЛО [saying] what is attractive on the outside can actually be fundamentally bad, worthless etc (used to emphasize that one should not judge people and things by their outward appearances): ≃ **fair without but foul within; a prize apple can have a worm inside.**

С-428 • (И) ВО СНЕ́ НЕ СНИ́ЛОСЬ/НЕ ПРИ-СНИ́ТСЯ *кому;* **(И) НЕ СНИ́ЛОСЬ/НЕ ПРИ-СНИ́ТСЯ** *all coll* [VP; subj: abstr or a clause; usu. impfv past, pfv fut, or pfv subjunctive] sth. is so unusual, extraordinary that s.o. would never have expected or imagined it: X Y-у и (во сне) не снился ≃ **Y never 〈even〉 dreamed of X; X is beyond Y's wildest dreams 〈imagination〉.**

Искусство одержимо таким чувством реального, какое и не снилось людям практической жизни (Терц 3). Art is possessed by a sense of reality never dreamed of by "practical" people (3a). ♦ [Иванов:] Клялся [Сарре] в вечной любви, пророчил счастье, открывал перед её глазами будущее, какое ей не снилось даже во сне (Чехов 4). [I.:] I swore to love her [Sarah] for ever, told her how happy we'd be, offered her a future beyond her wildest dreams (4b).

С-429 • КАК ПРОШЛОГО́ДНИЙ СНЕГ нужен *кому,* **интересует** *кого* и т. п. *coll* [как + NP; Invar; adv (neg intensif); fixed WO] some person or thing is not at all necessary or

of interest to s.o.: X нужен Y-у ~ ≃ **Y doesn't need X in the least; X is of absolutely no use to Y;** ‖ X интересует Y-а ~ ≃ **X doesn't interest Y in the least; Y doesn't give a hoot about X.**

С-430 • КАК 〈БУ́ДТО, СЛО́ВНО, ТО́ЧНО〉 СНЕГ НА́ ГО́ЛОВУ (свалиться, явиться и т. п.) *coll* [как etc + NP; these forms only; adv (more often used with pfv verbs) or subj-compl with быть∅ (subj: abstr); fixed WO] (to appear, arrive, happen etc) totally unexpectedly, suddenly: **like a bolt from the blue; out of the blue; out of a clear blue sky; out of nowhere.**

И вот Витбергу, как снег на голову, — разрешение возвратиться в Москву или Петербург (Герцен 1). And behold, like a bolt from the blue, comes permission for Vitberg to return to Moscow or Petersburg (1a). ♦ «Явился, голубчик... И опять как снег на голову» (Стругацкие 2). "So, my friend, you've turned up out of the blue again" (2a).

С-431 • ЗИМО́Й СНЕ́ГА 〈СНЕ́ГУ〉 НЕ ВЫ́ПРО-СИШЬ *у кого coll, disapprov* [VP; neg pfv fut, gener. 2nd pers sing only] s.o. is very stingy, excessively frugal: у X-а зимой снега не выпросишь ≃ **asking X to lend 〈give〉 you (sth.) is like trying to get blood from 〈out of〉 a stone; X wouldn't give away snow in winter.**

Просить у Панкратова взаймы деньги — пустая трата времени: у него зимой снега не выпросишь. Asking Pankratov for a loan would be a waste of time—it'd be like trying to get blood from a stone.

С-432 • ЗАСНУ́ТЬ 〈УСНУ́ТЬ〉 ВЕ́ЧНЫМ 〈МОГИ́ЛЬ-НЫМ, ПОСЛЕ́ДНИМ〉 СНОМ *lit;* **ПОЧИ́ТЬ ВЕ́Ч-НЫМ 〈НЕПРОБУ́ДНЫМ〉 СНОМ** *obs, lit* [VP; subj: human] to die: X заснул вечным сном ≃ **X went to his eternal rest 〈to his final resting place〉.**

В последние пять лет из нескольких сот душ не умер никто, не то что насильственною, даже естественною смертью. А если кто от старости или от какой-нибудь застарелой болезни и почил вечным сном, то там долго после того не могли надивиться такому необыкновенному случаю (Гончаров 1). In the past five years not one of the several hundred inhabitants had died even a natural death, to say nothing of a violent one. When anyone went to his eternal rest, either from old age or chronic illness, they could not help marveling at such an extraordinary event (1b).

С-433 • МЁРТВЫМ 〈МЕРТВЕ́ЦКИМ〉 СНОМ спать, заснуть, уснуть *coll* [NP_{instrum}; these forms only; adv; fixed WO] (to sleep, fall asleep) very soundly: X спал 〈заснул〉 мёртвым сном ≃ **X was dead to the world; X was 〈fell〉 dead asleep; X was in 〈fell into〉 a deep sleep; X was 〈fell〉 sound asleep; X was 〈went〉 out like a light.**

...[Больной Григорий Васильевич] вытерся весь с помощью супруги водкой с каким-то секретным крепчайшим настоем, а остальное выпил... и залёг спать. Марфа Игнатьевна вкусила тоже и, как непьющая, заснула подле супруга мёртвым сном (Достоевский 1). ...With his wife's help he [the sick Grigory Vasilievich] had rubbed himself all over with some secret, very strong infusion made from vodka, and had drunk the rest... after which he lay down to sleep. Marfa Ignatievna also partook, and, being a nondrinker, fell into a dead sleep next to her husband (1a). ♦ [Евгения:] Я пойду лягу, будто сплю мёртвым сном, ты тоже схоронись где-нибудь (Островский 8). [E.:] I'll go and lie down, as if I were sound asleep. And you go hide somewhere or other (8a).

С-434 • НИ СНОМ НИ ДУ́ХОМ не виноват *в чём,* не причастен *к чему,* не знает, не ведает *о чём coll* [NP_{instrum}; Invar; adv (intensif); fixed WO] one is absolutely and completely not guilty of, involved in, knowledgeable about etc sth.: X ~ не виноват (в Y-е) ≃ **X is not at all guilty (of Y); X is not at all to blame (for Y);** ‖ X ~ не причастен к Y-у ≃ **it ⟨Y⟩ has nothing whatever ⟨whatsoever⟩ to do with X;** ‖ X ~ не ведает об Y-е ≃ **X doesn't know a (single) thing about Y; X has never (even) heard of Y.**

Николай Васильевич [Ганчук] был в тот день не в духе, мрачноват и вовсе ничего не замечал… Глебов подумал: уж не его ли присутствие мешает разговору? Шепнул Соне: уехать? Соня замотала головой. «Ни в коем случае! Он чем-то расстроен. Ты здесь ни сном ни духом» (Трифонов 2). Nikolai Vasilievich [Ganchuk] was out of sorts that day, gloomy and unaware of anything around him….Glebov wondered whether the Ganchuks felt unable to talk freely because he was there. He whispered to Sonya: "Should I go?" Sonya shook her head. "No, of course not. He's just worried about something. It's nothing whatever to do with you" (2a).

C-435 • СНОМ ПРА́ВЕДНИКА ⟨ПРА́ВЕДНИЦЫ, ПРА́ВЕДНЫХ⟩ спать, заснуть, уснуть *often humor* [NP_instrum; these forms only; adv; fixed WO] (to sleep, fall asleep) soundly, peacefully: X спит сном праведника ≃ **X is sleeping the sleep of the just ⟨the blessed⟩.**

«Успокойся, ничего с ней [Любой] не сделается, спит сном праведницы…» (Максимов 1). "Calm down, nothing's happened to her [Lyuba]. She's sleeping the sleep of the just…" (1a). ♦ [Григорий] приходил, и Фёдор Павлович заговаривал о совершеннейших пустяках и скоро отпускал, иногда даже с насмешечкой и шуточкой, а сам, плюнув, ложился спать и спал уже сном праведника (Достоевский 1). Grigory would come, and Fyodor Pavlovich would begin talking about perfect trifles, and would soon let him go, sometimes even with a little joke or jibe, and would spit and go to bed himself, and sleep the sleep of the blessed (1a).

C-436 • СПАТЬ ВЕ́ЧНЫМ ⟨МОГИ́ЛЬНЫМ, НЕПРО-БУ́ДНЫМ, ПОСЛЕ́ДНИМ⟩ СНОМ; ПОЧИВА́ТЬ ВЕ́ЧНЫМ СНОМ *all obs, lit* [VP; subj: human; the verb may take the final position, otherwise fixed WO] to be dead: X спит вечным сном ≃ **X has gone to his eternal rest ⟨to his final resting place⟩.**

C-437 • НА СНОСЯ́Х ⟨НА СНО́СЕ obs⟩ *substand* [PrepP; these forms only; usu. subj-compl with быть₀ (subj: human, female)] one is in the last month of pregnancy: X на сносях ≃ **X is almost ⟨(just) about⟩ due; X is near her time.**

«Вот у меня жена на сносях, так что ей, значит, так вот в трухлявом бараке дитю [ungrammat = дитя] пролетария и на свет выносить?..» (Максимов 3). "My wife here is near her time. I mean to say, she can't bring a proletarian kid into the world in some moldering old barracks, can she?" (3a).

C-438 • КАК ⟨ЧТО⟩ СОБА́К НЕРЕ́ЗАНЫХ *кого (у кого, где)* *highly coll, derog* [как etc + NP; these forms only; quantit subj-compl with copula (subj/gen: human); fixed WO] very many: X-ов у Y-а ⟨в месте Z⟩ ~ ≃ **Y has more Xs than he knows what to do with ⟨than he can handle⟩; Y has Xs coming out of his ears; Xs are a dime a dozen in place Z; there are more Xs in place Z than you can ⟨could⟩ shake a stick at; place Z is crawling ⟨teeming⟩ with Xs.**

C-439 • (всех) СОБА́К ВЕ́ШАТЬ/НАВЕ́ШАТЬ ⟨ПОНА-ВЕ́ШАТЬ⟩ *на кого coll, disapprov* [VP; subj: human] to accuse s.o. of or blame s.o. for (some particular thing or everything bad that happens), usu. unfairly: X собак вешает на Y-а ≃ **X blames Y for sth. ⟨everything⟩; X pins ⟨sticks⟩ sth. ⟨everything⟩ on Y; X jumps ⟨is always jumping⟩ all over Y; X lands ⟨is always landing, is always coming down⟩ on Y.**

C-440 • ВОТ ГДЕ ⟨В ЧЁМ⟩ СОБА́КА ЗАРЫ́ТА; ВОТ ТУТ ⟨ТУТ-ТО, ЗДЕСЬ, В Э́ТОМ⟩ И ЗАРЫ́ТА

СОБА́КА *all coll* [sent; these forms only; used also as subord clause after знать, понимать etc (when 1st var. is used, вот is omitted)] (usu. used to emphasize that the preceding context explains the main reason behind sth., or to express the speaker's sudden understanding of sth.) in this (that etc) lies the essence of the matter, the reason for sth.: **(so) that's what it's all about ⟨what's going on, what lies at the bottom of it etc⟩; (so) that's the crux ⟨the heart⟩ of the matter; [in limited contexts] there's ⟨herein lies etc⟩ the rub.**

«Вот где собака зарыта!» — воскликнул он, когда узнал, что на место уволенного без видимой причины Онуфриева принята племянница нашего директора. "So that's what's going on!" he exclaimed when he found out that the director's niece had taken over Onufriev's job after he was fired without apparent cause.

< The Russian idiom is the translation of the German *Da liegt der Hund begraben.*

C-441 • КА́ЖДАЯ ⟨ВСЯ́КАЯ, ЛЮБА́Я⟩ СОБА́КА *(знает кого-что, скажет что и т. п.)* *highly coll, derog* [NP; sing only; fixed WO] each person (in some place, group etc) (knows s.o. or sth., will say sth. etc): **absolutely everybody ⟨everyone⟩; each and every person; everybody and his uncle ⟨brother⟩.**

Алик на нашей улице пятнадцать лет живёт, его тут каждая собака знает. Alik has been living on our block for fifteen years, and absolutely everyone knows him.

C-442 • КАК СОБА́КА *highly coll* [как + NP; Invar; adv (intensif)] (in refer. to a person) extremely, to a very high degree: X устал ~ ≃ **X is dog-tired ⟨dog weary, dead tired⟩;** ‖ X голоден ⟨проголодался⟩ ~ ≃ **X is hungry as a wolf ⟨a bear⟩; X is so hungry he could eat a horse;** ‖ X замёрз ~ ≃ **X is frozen through; X is chilled to the bone ⟨to the marrow⟩;** ‖ X зол ~ ≃ **X is mad as hell ⟨as the dickens, as the devil⟩; X is absolutely livid; X is fuming ⟨furious⟩.**

Я пришла с работы усталая как собака. Мальчишки — ну, конечно! — играли в шахматы. Это какая-то мужская болезнь. Я сказала: «…Опять эти дурацкие шахматы! Как долго это будет продолжаться?» (Грекова 1). I came home [from work] dog-tired. The boys, of course, were playing chess. Seems to be some kind of male disease. "…Again those stupid chess pieces! How long is this going to go on?" (1a). ♦ Он был голоден как собака — с утра ничего не ел (Абрамов 1). …He was as hungry as a wolf, having eaten nothing all day (1a). ♦ Было поздно. Метро уже не работало. И мы с Тамарой полчаса ловили такси… Тамара была злая как собака (Зиновьев 2). It was late and the metro was no longer running. It took Tamara and me half an hour to get a taxi….Tamara was absolutely livid (2a).

C-443 • (КАК) СОБА́КА НА СЕ́НЕ *coll, disapprov* [(как +) NP; often subj-compl with copula (var. with как—nom only, var. without как—nom or instrum, subj: human); fixed WO] a person who neither uses sth. himself nor lets others use it: **(like) a dog in the manger.**

< From the saying «Как собака на сене (лежит): (и) сама не ест и другим не даёт» ("Like a dog in a manger: he doesn't eat and he won't let others eat"). Original source: Aesop's fable.

C-444 • КАК СОБА́КА ПА́ЛКУ *любить кого-что coll, iron* [как + NP; Invar; adv (neg intensif); fixed WO] not (to like s.o. or sth.) at all: **(like sth.) about as much as a dog likes (getting) a beating; (like s.o. ⟨sth.⟩) about as much as a cat likes water; (love s.o. ⟨sth.⟩) as a horse loves the whip.**

«…Мигулин что большевиков, что беляков любит одинаково: как собака палку!» (Трифонов 6). "Migulin doesn't care whether it's Bolsheviks or Whites, he loves them all just the same: as a horse loves the whip!" (6a).

С-445 • НИ ОДНА́ СОБА́КА *highly coll* [NP; sing only] absolutely nobody: **no one at all; not one ⟨a single⟩ person; not a single ⟨living⟩ soul; not a soul.**

«Прибегай, Настёна. Я буду ждать. Но только чтоб ни одна собака тебя не углядела» (Распутин 2). "Come to me, Nastyona. I'll be waiting. But be sure that not a living soul sees you" (2a).

С-446 • КАК СОБА́КЕ ПЯ́ТАЯ НОГА́ нужен *кому highly coll, rude* [как + NP; Invar; adv (neg intensif); fixed WO] a person or thing is not at all needed by s.o.: X нужен Y-у ~ ≃ **Y needs X like (he needs) a hole in the head.**

Прислали мне двух помощников − ничего не умеют делать. Мне такая помощь нужна как собаке пятая нога. They sent me two assistants who don't know how to do anything. I need that kind of help like I need a hole in the head.

С-447 • СВОИ́ СОБА́КИ ГРЫЗУ́ТСЯ ⟨ДЕРУ́ТСЯ⟩, ЧУЖА́Я НЕ ПРИСТАВА́Й ⟨НЕ ПОДХОДИ́⟩ [saying] do not get involved in sth. that is not your affair (said when an outsider gets involved in a quarrel between close friends, spouses, relatives etc, thus putting himself in an awkward situation): ≃ **mind your own business; keep your nose out of it; don't poke your nose where it doesn't belong; this is our ⟨their⟩ fight, keep out of it; it's ⟨this is⟩ none of your business.**

«За что ты мальчика тиранишь?» − спросил Тиверзин, протискавшись сквозь толпу. «Свои собаки грызутся, чужая не подходи», − отрезал Худолеев (Пастернак 1). "Why do you tyrannize the boy?" asked Tiverzin, elbowing his way through the crowd. "It's none of your business," Khudoleiev snapped (1a).

С-448 • СОБА́КУ СЪЕСТЬ на чём, в чём *coll, approv* [VP; subj: human; usu. past (with resultative meaning), Part, or Verbal Adv; usu. this WO] to gain much experience, acquire substantial knowledge in some field through a lot of practice: X на Y-е собаку съел ≃ **X knows Y inside out; X is an expert at ⟨in⟩ Y; X knows the tricks of the trade; X is a past master at ⟨in⟩ Y; [in limited contexts] X is an old hand ⟨pro⟩ at Y; X has Y down pat ⟨cold⟩.**

[Мерещун:] Так вот, если вы хотите производительность труда − я вам человека нашёл... Деловой, требовательный, в производстве собаку съел. Он вам дело поставит... (Солженицын 8). [M.:] Listen, if you want to increase productivity, I've found just the man....He's efficient, he's demanding, and he knows productivity inside out. He'll fix it for you just like that (8a). ♦ ...Позднее мы узнали, что в это время уже начинался процесс изъятия первого «слоя» в самом НКВД... Под некоторых следователей уже «подбирали ключи», и они, съевшие собаку на делах такого сорта, смутно чувствовали это (Гинзбург 1). Later we were to learn that the purge of the NKVD itself had already begun....A number of interrogators had already been singled out, and, as experts in such matters, they were dimly aware of this (1b). ♦ «Вы бы хоть со мной заранее посоветовались. В этом-то деле я собаку съел» (Дудинцев 1). "You would have done better to consult me first, as this is something I am a past master in" (1a).

С-449 • ИДТИ́/ПОЙТИ́ ПРОТИВ (своей) СО́ВЕСТИ; поступать, делать что **ПРОТИВ (своей) СО́ВЕСТИ** [VP, subj: human (1st var.); PrepP, Invar, adv (2nd var.)] to act against one's moral principles, convictions: X пошёл против совести ≃ **X went ⟨acted⟩ against his conscience; X compromised his convictions ⟨his standards⟩.**

«Я жду, что вы поможете мне, как когда-то я помог вам... Я понимаю, что это против вашей совести. Но разве я отпустил вас из Шенау не против своей совести?» (Федин 1). "I expect you to help me as I once helped you....I understand that it goes against your conscience. But didn't I also go against my conscience in releasing you from Schönau?" (1a).

С-450 • НА СО́ВЕСТИ чьей, кого, у кого лежать, быть₀, иметься и т. п. [PrepP; Invar; the resulting PrepP is subj-compl with copula (subj: usu. abstr)] sth. is (remains etc) morally burdensome to s.o., a source of guilt, regret etc (usu. in refer. to a reprehensible or unethical action, a promise s.o. failed to fulfill etc): X лежит на Y-овой совести ≃ **X is ⟨weighs, lies⟩ on Y's conscience.**

«Уголовная кличка „Вася Сивый". Привлекался за хулиганство, карманные и квартирные кражи, за угон частных автомашин, мотоциклов. Словом, на Васиной совести много всякой всячины» (Чернёнок 1). "His underground name is Vasya Sivy. He's been arrested for hooliganism, holdups, break-ins, car and motorcycle theft. In a word, there's a lot on Vasya's conscience" (1a). ♦ ...Вспоминая времена нашей юности... я не помню ни одной истории, которая осталась бы на совести, которую было бы стыдно вспомнить (Герцен 1). Recalling the days of our youth...I do not remember a single incident which would weigh on the conscience, which one would be ashamed to think of (1a).

С-451 • ПО СО́ВЕСТИ[1] [PrepP; Invar] **1.** ~ **жить, поступать** и т. п. [adv or, less often, subj-compl with copula (subj: abstr)] (to live, act etc) in an upstanding manner, the way one should: **according to one's conscience; honest(ly); decent(ly); conscientious(ly); in good conscience; honorable ⟨honorably⟩.**

«Я рад за вас − вы поступили по совести» (Гроссман 2). "I'm glad for you−you've acted according to your conscience" (2a). ♦ ...Надо отдать должное Варваре: честно, по совести вела она хлебные дела все эти трудные годы (Абрамов 1). ...You had to give Varvara her due: throughout all those difficult years she had managed the grain supplies honestly and conscientiously (1a). ♦ Председатель начал было с того, что он [Иван Фёдорович] свидетель без присяги, что он может показывать или умолчать, но что, конечно, всё показанное должно быть по совести, и т. д., и т. д. (Достоевский 2). The presiding judge began by saying that he [Ivan Fyodorovich] was not under oath, that he could give evidence or withhold it, but that, of course, all testimony should be given in good conscience, etc., etc. (2a). ♦ А может, Лизка и права, подумал вдруг Михаил. Может, и надо было спасибо сказать. Ведь всё-таки, ежели рассудить по совести, заслужила (Абрамов 1). [context transl] Maybe Lizka was right, Mikhail suddenly thought. Maybe they should have thanked her. After all, to be fair, she did deserve it (1a).

2. ~ **сказать, признаться** и т. п. *coll.* Also: **ПО ЧИ́СТОЙ СО́ВЕСТИ** *coll* [adv] (to say, admit etc sth.) sincerely, openly: **(tell ⟨say etc⟩ sth.) in all honesty; (tell ⟨admit etc⟩ sth.) honestly ⟨truthfully, frankly⟩; be (quite) frank; (tell) the truth.**

[Соня:] Скажи мне по совести, как друг... Ты счастлива? (Чехов 3). [S.:] Tell me in all honesty, as a friend−are you happy? (3b). ♦ «Скажи по совести, Илья: как давно с тобой не случалось этого?» (Гончаров 1). "Tell me honestly, Ilya, how long is it since such a thing has happened to you?" (1b). ♦ [Маша:] Я вам по совести: если бы он [Константин] ранил себя серьёзно, то я не стала бы жить ни одной минуты (Чехов 6). [M.:] I'll be quite frank with you; if he [Konstantin] had hurt himself badly, I wouldn't have gone on living another minute (6b). ♦ «Ты нам всё по совести рассказывай!» − «Мы тут в потёмках блукаем [*Ukrainian* = блуждаем]» (Шолохов 3). "Tell us the truth." "We're all in the dark here" (3b).

С-452 • ПО СО́ВЕСТИ[2]; **ПО СО́ВЕСТИ ГОВОРЯ́ ⟨СКАЗА́ТЬ, ПРИЗНА́ТЬСЯ⟩** *all coll* [these forms only; sent adv (parenth)] speaking openly, if one is to speak honestly: **in (all) conscience; in all honesty ⟨sincerity⟩; frankly (speaking); to be truthful; to be (quite) frank ⟨honest⟩; to tell (you) the truth.**

«Всю эту психологию мы совсем уничтожим, все подозрения на вас в ничто обращу, так что ваше преступление вроде помрачения какого-то представится, потому, по совести, оно помрачение и есть» (Достоевский 3). "We'll completely destroy all this psychological stuff and I'll bring all suspicions of you to nought, so that your crime will appear to be the result of a kind of blackout, because in all conscience that's what it was" (3a). ♦ «...Но, по совести, какие мы с вами поэты? Бунин — вот кто настоящий поэт» (Катаев 3). "...But, to be quite frank, are we really poets? Bunin now—there's a real poet" (3a).

C-453 • СÓВЕСТИ ХВАТÁЕТ/ХВАТИ́ЛО у кого coll
[VP; impers; usu. foll. by infin] s.o. is not ashamed to do sth. (unscrupulous, rude, brazen etc): у X-а хватает совести (с)делать Y ≃ **X has the impudence ⟨the effrontery, the nerve, the gall⟩ to do Y;** ‖ как у X-а совести хватает? ≃ **has X no shame?**

Выпроводив его [стукача], О. М[андельштам] всякий раз говорил: «Теперь, конечно, он больше не придёт»... Ему казалось, что у парня не хватит совести снова прийти в дом, где его разоблачили... (Мандельштам 1). Every time M[andelstam] threw him [the police spy] out, he said: "That's the end, he won't turn up again." He just couldn't believe that the man would have the impudence to come back being so thoroughly exposed (1a). ♦ «Заявляетесь ночью в пьяном виде, поднимаете на ноги весь дом, и у вас ещё хватает совести повышать на меня голос...» (Максимов 1). "You roll up drunk in the middle of the night, you wake up the whole house, and still you have the gall to raise your voice to me" (1a). ♦ Руслан Павлович. Хам, алкоголик... Ходит по дачам, просит по трояку, по пятёрке в долг... похмелиться... И как совести хватает? Ведь инженер, с высшим образованием... (Трифонов 6). Ruslan Pavlovich. A lout and an alcoholic. Goes around the dachas asking for a loan of three, five rubles to go for a dose of the hair of the dog. Has the man no shame? After all, he's an engineer; he has higher education (6a).

C-454 • ИМÉЙ(ТЕ) ⟨ПОИМÉЙ(ТЕ)⟩ СÓВЕСТЬ; ПОИМÉЛ БЫ ТЫ ⟨он и т. п.⟩ СÓВЕСТЬ; СÓВЕСТЬ ИМÉТЬ ⟨ЗНАТЬ⟩ НÁДО all highly coll
[usu. indep. sent] be reasonable (used to urge s.o. either to do what the speaker wants him to do or to stop doing sth. the speaker considers undesirable, reprehensible etc): **have a heart; have you no shame?; you ⟨he etc⟩ ought to be ashamed of yourself ⟨himself etc⟩.**

«А вон-то, вот-то! Ещё один пароход!» Пароход этот — плот с сеном — плыл сверху... «Да ведь это, никак, наши», — сказала Варвара... Бабы заволновались. Пристать к пекашинскому берегу в половодье можно только в одном месте — у глиняного отлогого спуска, там, где сейчас стоял «Курьер». «Отваливай! — разноголосо закричали они капитану [«Курьера»]. — ...Поимей совесть» (Абрамов 1). "Over there! Over there! There's another steamer!" The "steamer"—a raft laden with hay—was heading downstream...."Hey! It looks like our lads," said Varvara....The women became agitated. At spring flood time, it was possible to come alongside the Pekashino bank at one spot only: the clayey incline where the *Kurier* was now at anchor. "Push off! Push off!" they cried out to the captain [of the *Kurier*]. "...Have a heart!" (1a).

C-455 • НА СÓВЕСТЬ работать, стараться и т. п. coll
[PrepP; Invar; adv] (to work, try to do sth. etc) well, conscientiously: **(try) hard ⟨in earnest, for all one is worth⟩; do one's best; give it everything one's got; make an honest effort;** ‖ сделано ⟨построено⟩ ~ ≃ **made ⟨built⟩ to last.**

Майор старался на совесть, забивал наручники рукояткой пистолета. Руку заломило так, что я чуть не взвыл (Марченко 1). The major was out to do his best and hammered the handcuffs tight with the butt of his pistol. My wrist was twisted so tightly that I almost whimpered (1a). ♦ «Неужто и компот дают [в лагере]?»... — «Это где какой начальник. Один голодом морит, а другой, если хочет, чтобы план выполняли, и накормит тебя, и оденет потеплее, только работай на совесть» (Войнович 2). "They

actually serve compote in there [the camp]?"...."Depends on your boss. One'll starve you to death, another one, if he wants to fulfill the plan, will feed you and dress you warm, as long as you give it everything you've got, that's all" (2a). ♦ ...Кто-то выстрелил в дверь, и она треснула. Посыпались тяжёлые удары прикладов. Дверь закачалась. «На совесть строили», — восхищённо сказал всё тот же охрипший голос (Паустовский 1). Someone fired a shot and the door cracked. It was pounded with rifle-butts. It swayed on its hinges. "Made to last!" the same hoarse voice said admiringly (1a). ♦ Родимцев, прищурившись, оглядел попрысканного одеколоном и напудренного Крымова, удовлетворённо кивнул и сказал: «Что ж, гостя побрил на совесть. Теперь меня давай обработай» (Гроссман 2). [context transl] Narrowing his eyes, Rodimtsev looked Krymov over—he had by now been thoroughly sprinkled with powder and eau-de-cologne—and nodded with satisfaction. "Well, you've certainly done a good job on our guest. Now you can give me the once-over" (2a).

C-456 • ПОРÁ ⟨НÁДО⟩ (И) СÓВЕСТЬ ЗНАТЬ coll
[sent] (used to express disapproval of, dissatisfaction with etc the previously mentioned activity or way of spending time) it is time to stop doing sth.: **shame on me ⟨you etc⟩; I ⟨you etc⟩ should be ashamed of myself ⟨yourself etc⟩; enough of this!; I ⟨you etc⟩ should listen to my ⟨your etc⟩ conscience.**

Пробило половина десятого, Илья Ильич встрепенулся. «Что ж это я в самом деле? — сказал он вслух с досадой, — надо совесть знать: пора за дело!» (Гончаров 1). The clock struck half past nine and Ilya Ilych gave a start. "Now, what am I doing?" he said aloud, in annoyance. "Enough of this! Time to set to work!" (1b). ♦ Михаил оглянулся, услыхал шорох сухих листьев. Лизка. Идёт по промежку и руками размахивает: радость какая-то. «Чего вернулась?» — «А, ладно. Нахожусь ещё по кинам [ungrammat = кино]. Надо... и совесть знать. Верно?» (Абрамов 1). Hearing the rustle of dry leaves, Mikhail looked around. Lizka was walking along the field verge waving her hands and looking pleased about something. "Why've you come back?" "It doesn't matter. Plenty of other chances to go to the movie. I should listen to my conscience...right?" (1a).

C-457 • ПОТЕРЯ́ТЬ СÓВЕСТЬ ⟨ВСЯ́КУЮ СÓВЕСТЬ, (ПОСЛÉДНИЕ) ОСТÁТКИ СÓВЕСТИ⟩ all coll, disapprov or humor
[VP; subj: human or animal] to behave reprehensibly, unconscionably without feeling guilty or embarrassed: X потерял всякую совесть ≃ **X has no shame ⟨conscience⟩; X has lost all sense of shame ⟨of decency⟩.**

Час ночи, а твоих друзей ещё нет? Совсем совесть потеряли! It's one a.m. and your friends still aren't here? They have no shame!

C-458 • СÓВЕСТЬ ЗÁЗРИЛА (кого) obs, coll
[VP_subj] s.o. was (or will be) ashamed of himself: (X-а) совесть зазрила ≃ **X's conscience bothered ⟨pricked⟩ him; X had a pang ⟨a twinge⟩ of conscience.**

[Бакин:] ...Я думал, что вы меня на дуэль вызовете. [Мелузов:] Дуэль? Зачем? У нас с вами и так дуэль, постоянный поединок, непрерывная борьба. Я просвещаю, а вы развращаете... Вот и давайте бороться... И посмотрим, кто скорее устанет. Вы скорее бросите своё занятие; в легкомыслии немного привлекательного; придёте в солидный возраст, совесть зазрит (Островский 11). [B.:] ...I thought you'd challenge me to a duel? [M.:] Duel! What for? You and I *have* a duel, a constant duel, an endless battle. I enlighten, you deprave....So let's fight on...and we'll see who tires the quicker. You'll chuck *your* occupation first; there's nothing permanently attractive in frivolity; when you grow old your conscience will prick you... (11a).

C-459 • ПРИМИРИ́ТЬСЯ ⟨ПОМИРИ́ТЬСЯ⟩ СО СВОÉЙ СÓВЕСТЬЮ
[VP; subj: human; usu. this WO] to rid o.s. of feelings of shame (by repenting or making amends for some

wrongdoing): X примирился со своей совестью ≃ **X made peace with his conscience.**

C-460 • **С ЧИ́СТОЙ СО́ВЕСТЬЮ** [PrepP; Invar; fixed WO] **1.** [adv] (to do sth.) without feelings of guilt (often after having atoned for a wrongdoing, accomplished what was required of one etc): **with a clear ⟨an untroubled⟩ conscience.**

Если бы меня спросили — что вы помните о времени работы в «Пароходстве», я с чистой совестью ответил бы — ничего (Булгаков 12). If someone had asked me what I remembered of the time I worked on the *Shipping Gazette*, I would have replied with a clear conscience—nothing (12a).

2. человек, люди ~ [nonagreeing postmodif] (a person or persons who are) completely honest, with nothing weighing on his conscience or their consciences: **(a man ⟨a woman etc⟩) with a clear conscience; (people) with clear consciences.**

C-461 • **СО СПОКО́ЙНОЙ СО́ВЕСТЬЮ** [PrepP; Invar; adv; fixed WO] (to do sth.) feeling fully justified for and correct in what one is doing, without any feelings of guilt or self-reproach: **with a clear ⟨an untroubled, a peaceful⟩ conscience; without a qualm of conscience; without feeling (the least bit) guilty.**

…[Он] искренне презирал подлецов и дурных людей и с спокойною совестью высоко носил голову (Толстой 5). …[He] felt genuine contempt for wrongdoers and scoundrels, and with a clear conscience held his head high (5a). ♦ «Ты слишком честен и неглуп для того, чтобы мог со спокойной совестью пресмыкаться. Этой черты не было ни у кого из нашей фамилии» (Шолохов 2). "You are too honest and intelligent to be able to kowtow with an untroubled conscience. No member of our family ever had that proclivity" (2a).

C-462 • **СОВЕ́Т ДА ⟨И⟩ ЛЮБО́ВЬ (вам, им)** *obsoles, folk poet* [formula phrase; these forms only; usu. this WO] a wish for a happy life to those who are entering marriage: **I wish you ⟨them⟩ every happiness; I wish you ⟨them⟩ peace and happiness; best wishes for a happy life together; may you ⟨they⟩ live happily ever after.**

(*Саша шепчет Платонову на ухо.*) [Платонов:] Ах, чёрт возьми! Вот память-то! Что же ты раньше молчала? Сергей Павлович! [Войницев:] Что? [Платонов:] А он и молчит! Женился и молчит!.. (*Кланяется.*) Совет да любовь, милый человек! (Чехов 1). (*Sasha whispers in Platonov's ear.*) [Platonov:] Damnation! What a memory—why didn't you tell me before? Sergey! [Sergey:] Yes? [Platonov:] He's struck dumb too. Gets married and doesn't breathe a word….(*Bows*) I wish you every happiness, man (1b). ♦ «Возьми себе свою красавицу; вези её куда хочешь, и дай вам бог любовь да совет!» (Пушкин 2). "Take your beautiful one, go with her where you want, and may God grant you peace and happiness!" (1a). ♦ [Авдотья Назаровна:] Они будут жить да поживать, а мы глядеть на них да радоваться. Совет им и любовь… (Чехов 4). [A.N.:] They'll have their bit of fun and we'll enjoy watching them. May they live happily ever after (4b).

C-463 • **СОДО́М И ГОМО́РРА ⟨ГОМО́РР⟩** [NP; sing only; fixed WO] **1.** a place where debauchery and drunkenness reign: **Sodom and Gomorrah.**

…Союз писателей, не принявший когда-то Цветаеву, проклявший Замятина, презревший Булгакова, исторгнувший Ахматову и Пастернака, представлялся мне из подполья совершенным Содомом и Гоморрой, теми ларёшниками и менялами, захламившими и осквернившими храм, чьи столики надо опрокидывать, а самих бичом изгонять на внешние ступени (Солженицын 2). …The Writers' Union, which in its day had refused membership to Tsvetayeva, anathematized Zamyatin, treated Bulgakov with contempt, ostracized Akhmatova and Pasternak, seen from the underground was a veritable Sodom and Gomorrah, or a rabble of hucksters and moneychangers littering and defiling the tem-

ple, whose stalls must be overturned and they themselves scourged and driven into the outer porch (2a).

2. total disorder, confusion: **complete ⟨utter, total⟩ chaos; pandemonium.**

< From the Biblical account of the ancient cities of Sodom and Gomorrah, which were destroyed by fire and brimstone from heaven because of the sins of their inhabitants (Gen. 19:24–25).

C-464 • **К СОЖАЛЕ́НИЮ; К БОЛЬШО́МУ ⟨ВЕЛИ́КОМУ, ГЛУБО́КОМУ⟩ СОЖАЛЕ́НИЮ** [these forms only; sent adv (parenth)] to one's or s.o.'s misfortune: **unfortunately; unluckily; unhappily; I'm afraid; worse luck; alas.**

[Репников:] А кто вы здесь такой, извините?.. [Букин:] Как кто? Жених… к сожалению… (Вампилов 3). [R.:] Sorry, but who are you?… [K.:] How do you mean "who"? The bridegroom…unfortunately (3a). ♦ Огромное значение имело бы исследование количества доносов по периодам и распределение доносителей по возрасту. Существенно также качество и стиль доноса. К сожалению, социологические исследования у нас не в почёте (Мандельштам 2). A study of the number of denunciations by periods and by the age of their authors would have enormous importance. The question of their quality and style would also repay investigation. But, alas, sociological studies are not well regarded in this country (2a).

C-465 • **ДОВОДИ́ТЬ/ДОВЕСТИ́** *что* **ДО СОЗНА́НИЯ** *чьего, кого* [VP; subj: human] to explain sth. to s.o. so that he understands it fully: X довёл Y до сознания Z-a ≃ **X made Y clear ⟨plain⟩ to Z; X got Y across to Z; X brought Y home to Z.**

C-466 • **ДОХОДИ́ТЬ/ДОЙТИ́ ДО СОЗНА́НИЯ (чьего, кого)** [VP; subj: usu. abstr] (of the essence, the real meaning of sth.) to become clear to s.o., be understood by s.o.: X дошёл до сознания (Y-a) ≃ **X sank in; X registered (with Y).**

Вале пришлось перечитать письмо матери несколько раз, пока суть его дошла до её сознания: её родители разводятся. Valya had to read her mother's letter several times before its message sank in: her parents were getting a divorce.

C-467 • **ВЫЖИМА́ТЬ/ВЫ́ЖАТЬ ⟨ВЫСА́СЫВАТЬ/ВЫ́СОСАТЬ⟩ СО́КИ ⟨СОК, ВСЕ or ПОСЛЕ́ДНИЕ СО́КИ⟩** *из кого;* **ЖАТЬ ⟨ТЯНУ́ТЬ, СОСА́ТЬ⟩ СОК ⟨СО́КИ⟩** *all coll, disapprov* [VP; subj: human; more often impfv] to exploit s.o. cruelly, oppress s.o. in all possible ways: X выжимает соки из Y-a ≃ **X sucks the lifeblood (out) of Y; X sucks the life out of Y; X squeezes the last drop of life ⟨blood⟩ out of Y; X bleeds Y dry ⟨white⟩; [in limited contexts] X milks Y dry; X squeezes Y to the last drop.**

«Преступление? Какое преступление?.. То, что я убил гадкую, зловредную вошь, старушонку процентщицу, никому не нужную, которую убить сорок грехов простят, которая из бедных сок высасывала, и это-то преступление?» (Достоевский 3). "Crime? What crime?…My killing a loathsome, harmful louse, a filthy old moneylender woman who brought no good to anyone, to murder whom would pardon forty sins, who sucked the lifeblood of the poor, and you call that a crime?" (3d). ♦ «[Саня] тоже зуб на Реваза имеет. Он из неё пять лет соки тянул» (Чернёнок 2). "She's [Sanya has] got it in for Revaz, too. He bled her dry for five years" (2a). ♦ …Деньги платят не за работу, а за то, чтобы ты жал соки из зэков (Марченко 1). …You were paid not for the work you did but for squeezing cons to the very last drop (1a).

C-468 • **ГОЛ КАК СОКО́Л** *coll* [AdjP; Invar; subj-compl with copula (subj: human, male); fixed WO] one is extremely poor: X гол как сокол ≃ **X is (as) poor as a church mouse; X doesn't have a kopeck ⟨a penny⟩ to his name.**

…Троекуров часто говаривал Дубровскому: «Слушай… Андрей Гаврилович: коли в твоём Володьке будет путь, так отдам за него Машу; даром что он гол как сокол» (Пушкин 1). Kirila Petrovich often said to Dubrovskii, "Listen…Andrei Gavrilovich: if your Volodka grows into a sensible lad, I'll let him marry Masha; never mind if he's poor as a church mouse" (1a).

C-469 • В (СА́МОМ ⟨ПО́ЛНОМ⟩) СОКУ́ coll [PrepP; these forms only; subj-compl with бытьø (subj: human) or nonagreeing modif] one is at the point in life when one's health and vigor are at their peak: **in the prime of (one's) life; in one's prime.**

«Да кто же мужчины носят корсет? – возражала Варвара, – никто не носит». – «Верига носит», – сказал Передонов. «Так Верига – старик, а ты, Ардальон Борисыч, слава богу, мужчина в соку» (Сологуб 1). "Whoever heard of a man wearing a corset," retorted Varvara. "No one wears one." "Veriga does," said Peredonov. "But Veriga's an old man, while you, Ardal'on Borisych, are thank God, in the prime of life" (1a).

C-470 • ВАРИ́ТЬСЯ В СО́БСТВЕННОМ СОКУ́ coll [VP; subj: human] to live, work etc alone or within a very small circle of people, often being deprived of the opportunity to confer with others or benefit from their experience: X варится в собственном соку ≃ X is left to his own resources; X is cut off from his colleagues ⟨fellow [NPs] etc⟩.

После окончания института молодой врач попал в маленькую сельскую больницу, где он варился в собственном соку, не имея возможности ни с кем посоветоваться. After graduating from medical school the young doctor ended up in a small country hospital, where he was left to his own resources, without anyone to consult with. ♦ В больнице теперь были новые правила: всех иностранцев перевели на один этаж, чтобы изолировать от «отечественных» больных. Только выходившие гулять в сад могли перекинуться словом с русским. Это раздражало иностранцев, варившихся в собственном соку (Аллилуева 2). [context transl] The hospital had new rules now: all foreigners had been moved to one floor, so as to isolate them from "native" patients. Only those who went for walks in the garden could exchange a few words with Russians. This annoyed the foreigners, who got tired of each other's company (2a).

< Apparently a loan translation (but with a different sense) of the French *cuire dans son jus* or the English "to stew in one's own juice." Both the French and the English idioms mean "to suffer the unpleasant consequences of one's own foolish actions."

C-471 • НАСЫ́ПАТЬ СО́ЛИ НА ХВОСТ кому highly coll [VP; subj: human or collect] **1.** to do sth. vile, underhanded to s.o., create trouble for s.o.: X насыпал Y-у соли на хвост ≃ X did something nasty ⟨mean, lowdown etc⟩ to Y; X did Y dirt; X screwed Y.

2. (the only thing one can do is) to feel anger and helplessness (because the act in question is irrevocable and/or the person who carried it out has left): теперь X может Y-у только соли на хвост насыпать ≃ now all X can do is curse Y from afar.

«Она уехала, не заплатив за квартиру, и я не знаю её нового адреса». – «Да, теперь ты можешь только соли ей на хвост насыпать». "She left without paying the rent and I don't know her new address." "Well, all you can do now is curse her from afar."

C-472 • ЗАЛИВА́ТЬСЯ/ЗАЛИ́ТЬСЯ ⟨РАЗЛИВА́ТЬСЯ, ПЕТЬ/ЗАПЕ́ТЬ⟩ СОЛОВЬЁМ coll, often humor or iron [VP; subj: human; usu impfv] to speak eloquently and with enthusiasm (usu. trying to impress s.o., win s.o. over to one's side etc): X заливался соловьём ≃ X warbled ⟨trilled away⟩ like a nightingale; X sang like a bird.

Эфрос разливался соловьём, доказывая, что без взаимной поддержки сейчас не прожить (Мандельштам 2). Efros trilled away like a nightingale, impressing upon us that, as things now were, we should survive only if we stuck together (2a).

C-473 • СОЛОВЬЯ́ БА́СНЯМИ НЕ КО́РМЯТ [saying] words should be supplemented and supported by sth. more tangible (usu. said by a host when interrupting a conversation in order to invite his guests to the table for food and drinks; *by extension* used to stress that talking is of little help when an object, service etc is being sought): ≃ **fine words do not make full stomachs; fine ⟨fair⟩ words butter no parsnips;** [in limited contexts] **actions speak louder than words.**

[author's usage] «А теперь, я надеюсь, Арина Власьевна, что, насытив своё материнское сердце, ты позаботишься о насыщении своих дорогих гостей, потому что, тебе известно, соловья баснями кормить не следует» (Тургенев 2). "…And now, Arina Vlas'evna, I hope that having satiated your motherly heart you'll make ready to satiate our dear guests, for as you know fine words do not make full stomachs" (2e). "And now, Arina Vlasyevna, I hope that your maternal heart having had its fill, you will see about filling our dear guests, for, you know, fair words butter no parsnips" (2a).

C-474 • ХВАТА́ТЬСЯ/СХВАТИ́ТЬСЯ ЗА СОЛО́МИНКУ coll [VP; subj: human; more often impfv] to resort to obviously ineffectual measures in a desperate attempt to save o.s. or find a way out of a difficult situation: X хватается за соломинку ≃ X grasps ⟨clutches, catches⟩ at a straw ⟨at straws⟩.

«…Он спрашивает… почему я до сих пор не в партии. Не знаю, как отвечать, что-то мямлю, а он опять улыбается и сам подсказывает: „Считаете себя недостойным?" – „Да-да, – хватаюсь я за эту соломинку, – именно недостоин", – (Войнович 4). "Then he asked…: why hadn't I joined the Party yet? Not knowing what to answer, I mumbled something; he smiled again and supplied the answer himself: 'You consider yourself unworthy?' 'That's right,' I grasped at the straw. 'That's right, unworthy'" (4a). ♦ О, как ему всё это надоело! А между тем он всё-таки спешил к Свидригайлову; уж не ожидал ли он чего-нибудь от него нового, указаний, выхода? И за соломинку ведь хватаются! (Достоевский 3). Oh, how tired he was of all that! Yet here he was hurrying to see Svidrigailov; might it not be that he was hoping for something *new* from him, some hint, some way out? Like a man clutching at straws? (3d).

< From the saying «Утопающий хватается (и) за соломинку» ("A drowning man will grasp ⟨clutch, catch⟩ at a straw"). See У-149.

C-475 • АТТИ́ЧЕСКАЯ СОЛЬ lit [NP; sing only; fixed WO] subtle, delicate wit or an elegant joke: **Attic salt ⟨wit, humor⟩.**

< From *Attica*, the name of a region in ancient Greece famous for the wit of its inhabitants. Attic Greek became the standard language of classical Greek literature in the 5th and 4th cents. B.C.

C-476 • СОЛЬ ЗЕМЛИ́ lit [NP; sing only; usu. subj-compl with copula, nom or instrum (subj: human or collect, sing or pl) or objcompl with считать etc (obj: human or collect, sing or pl); fixed WO] a person or group of people whose character, moral qualities etc are considered to be extremely upstanding, worthy; the best, most valuable part of society: **the salt of the earth.**

Комсомольцы [в двадцатые годы] ещё чувствовали себя солью земли, но сознавали, что следует подсолониться культурой (Мандельштам 2). At that time [in the twenties] its [the Komsomol's] members still thought themselves the salt of the earth, though they recognized the need to pick up a smattering of "culture" (2a).

< From the Bible (Matt. 5:13).

C-477 • СЫ́ПАТЬ СОЛЬ НА РА́НЫ чьи ⟨РА́НУ чью⟩ [VP; subj: human] to say or do sth. that intensifies s.o.'s feelings of injury, embarrassment etc: X сыпал соль на Y-ову рану ≃ **X rubbed salt in(to) Y's ⟨the⟩ wound; X rubbed it in.**

C-478 • БРАТЬ/ВЗЯТЬ ПОД СОМНЕ́НИЕ *что* [VP; subj: human, collect, or abstr; usu. this WO] to question, challenge sth. (usu. some theory, evidence etc): X берёт под сомне́ние Y ≃ **X casts doubt on Y; X calls Y into question.**

...Великий Лев Толстой совершенно спокойно, не считаясь ни с чем, подверг уничтожающей критике самого Шекспира, взявши под сомнение не только ценность его мыслей, но и просто-напросто высмеяв его как весьма посредственного – точнее, никуда не годного – сочинителя (Катаев 3). ...The great Leo Tolstoy...quite calmly and without regard for anything or anyone, had subjected Shakespeare himself to annihilating criticism, not only casting doubt on the value of his ideas but simply ridiculing him as an extremely mediocre, or rather, perfectly useless scribbler (3a).

C-479 • НЕ ПОДЛЕЖИ́Т СОМНЕ́НИЮ [VP; subj: abstr, often это or a clause] sth. is unquestionable, is undoubtedly true, cannot be refuted: X не подлежит сомнению ≃ **X is indisputable ⟨incontestable, irrefutable, undeniable, incontrovertible⟩; X is not open to doubt;** [in limited contexts] **there is no doubt ⟨question⟩ about it; there is no doubt ⟨question⟩ about the fact that...**

Этот анекдот, которого верность не подлежит ни малейшему сомнению, бросает... свет на характер Николая (Герцен 1). This anecdote, the truth of which is not open to the slightest doubt, throws...light on the character of Nicholas (1a). ♦ Не подлежит сомнению, что ещё год-другой – и молодой фон Витте стал бы командующим ВСЮРа [Вооружённых Сил Юга России]... (Аксёнов 7). [context transl] Another year or so and young General von Witte would doubtless have been named commander in chief of the armed forces of South Russia... (7a).

C-480 • БЕЗ ⟨ВНЕ⟩ (ВСЯ́КОГО) СОМНЕ́НИЯ [PrepP; these forms only; sent adv (parenth)] indisputably, unquestionably: **no doubt; undoubtedly; doubtless(ly); surely.**

Старец Зосима был лет шестидесяти пяти, происходил из помещиков, когда-то в самой ранней юности был военным и служил на Кавказе обер-офицером. Без сомнения, он поразил Алёшу каким-нибудь особенным свойством души своей (Достоевский 1). The elder Zosima was about sixty-five years old, came from a landowning family, had been in the army back in his very early youth, and served in the Caucasus as a commissioned officer. No doubt he struck Alyosha by some special quality of his soul (1a).

C-481 • КАК ⟨БУ́ДТО, СЛО́ВНО, ТО́ЧНО⟩ СКВОЗЬ СОН помнить, слышать, представлять *что* и т. п. [как etc + PrepP; these forms only; adv] (to remember, hear sth. etc) not altogether clearly, not quite distinctly: **as (if) in a dream ⟨a trance⟩; vaguely.**

Я ещё, как сквозь сон, помню следы пожара, оставшиеся до начала двадцатых годов... (Герцен 1). I still remember, as in a dream, the traces of the fire, which remained until early in the 'twenties... (1a).

C-482 • НА СОН ГРЯДУ́ЩИЙ [PrepP; Invar; adv; fixed WO] before going to bed: **before ⟨at⟩ bedtime; before one goes to sleep ⟨to bed⟩; as one is falling asleep;** [in limited contexts] **bedtime** [NP]; ‖ почитать *кому* (*что*) ~ ≃ **read s.o. a bedtime story; read to s.o. before bed ⟨at bedtime⟩;** [in limited contexts] **read s.o. to sleep.**

[Трилецкий:] Вот он сидит, наш великий мудрец и философ! Сидит настороже и с нетерпением ожидает добычи: кому бы нотацию прочесть на сон грядущий? (Чехов 1). [T.:] There he sits, our great sage and philosopher. Always on the look out. Waiting impatiently for his prey: whom to regale with a lecture before bedtime (1a). ♦ Иногда, на сон грядущий, она позволяла себе помечтать. Вот её назначают старшим администратором... (Грекова 3). Sometimes as she was falling asleep she let herself dream: she was being appointed senior administrator (3a). ♦ Кто подаст [сибаритам] куда-то запропастившуюся табакерку или поднимет упавший на пол платок?.. Кто почитает книжку на сон грядущий и поможет заснуть? (Гончаров 1). Who would hand them [sybarites] the snuffbox they mislaid, or pick up the handkerchief they dropped?...Who would read them to sleep at bedtime? (1b).

C-483 • СЕДЬМО́Й ⟨ДЕСЯ́ТЫЙ и т. п.⟩ СОН СНИ́ТСЯ *кому*; **СЕДЬМО́Й ⟨ДЕСЯ́ТЫЙ и т. п⟩ СОН ВИ́ДЕТЬ** *all coll* [VP$_{subj}$ (1st var.); VP, subj: human (2nd var.); the verb may take the initial position, otherwise fixed WO] s.o. has been sleeping soundly for a long time: X-у седьмой сон снится ≃ **X has been dead to the world ⟨sleeping like a log, sleeping like a baby, (fast) asleep⟩ for hours ⟨for quite a while⟩.**

«Сейчас... 12 часов, для нас с тобой это детское время, а позвонить сейчас простому человеку, такому, как эта девица, – значит обидеть её. Да она давно видит пятый сон» (Лимонов 1). "...It's twelve o'clock. The night is young for you and me, but it would be an insult to go calling up an ordinary person like that girl. She's been asleep for hours" (1a).

C-484 • СКВОЗЬ СОН слышать, чувствовать *что* [PrepP; Invar; adv] (to hear, feel sth.) while one is sleeping: **in one's sleep.**

Сквозь сон Андрей слышал неясный шум, отдельные восклицания, но, проснувшись утром, так и не мог понять, приехал ли ночью дядя Миша или ему это только приснилось. In his sleep Andrei heard some indistinct noises and isolated remarks, but when he woke up in the morning he couldn't figure out if Uncle Misha had arrived or if it was all a dream.

C-485 • СОН В РУ́КУ *coll* [sent; Invar; fixed WO] a dream is subsequently enacted in real life: **the dream comes true; my ⟨your etc⟩ dream was prophetic.**

Судьба, будто продолжая наяву недавний сон в самолёте, настигла его [Золотарёва] здесь, в этом лагерном зимовье... «Сон в руку», – сглотнул он жаркую горечь в горле (Максимов 1). As if continuing in his waking moments the dream he [Zolotarev] had had recently on the plane, fate had caught him here, in this prison cabin....“The dream comes true.” He swallowed the searing bitterness that rose to his throat (1a). ♦ Ночью хмельному Лашкову снился сон... Он идёт по Сокольникам с Грушей под руку... Пробуждаясь, [Лашков] со злым недоумением подумал: «К чему бы это?» Потом рассудил для себя приятнее: «Может, сон-то в руку?» И ещё, но уже не без кокетливого сожаления: «Вроде, на ущербе жизнь твоя холостяцкая, Вася?» (Максимов 3). Lashkov, slightly drunk, had a dream that night. He and Grusha were walking arm in arm through Sokolniki Park....[Lashkov] awoke, irritable and perplexed. What did it mean? Then he put the most flattering interpretation he could on it. Maybe it was prophetic? Vasilii, my boy, he commiserated with himself coyly, it looks as though your bachelor days are nearly over (3a).

C-486 • ЧТО СЕЙ СОН ЗНА́ЧИТ ⟨ОЗНАЧА́ЕТ⟩? *obs, now humor* [sent; these forms only; fixed WO] (used in refer. to some unusual or unexpected occurrence, action etc) how is this to be understood?: **what does this mean?; what is this supposed to mean?**

< A paraphrase of a line from Aleksandr Pushkin's poem "The Bridegroom" («Жених»), 1827: «Что ж твой сон гласит?» ("Well then, what was your dream about?"). In the poem the line refers to a dream; later the phrase came to refer to real events.

C-487 • ПРИНИМА́ТЬ/ПРИНЯ́ТЬ ⟨БРАТЬ/ВЗЯТЬ⟩ В СООБРАЖЕ́НИЕ *что obs* [VP; subj: human or collect] to include (some facts, circumstances etc) in one's deliberations (when making a decision, plans, a judgment etc): X принял в соображение Y ≃ **X took Y into consideration ⟨account⟩; X considered Y.**

«Но ведь не убил же его [отца], ведь спас же меня ангел-хранитель мой — вот этого-то вы и не взяли в соображение...» (Достоевский 1). "But I didn't kill him [my father], my guardian angel saved me—that's what you haven't taken into consideration..." (1a). ♦ «...Прошу вас, моя почтеннейшая, принять в соображение, что никакое здание, хотя бы даже то был куриный хлев, разом не завершается!» (Салтыков-Щедрин 1). "...Dear Madam, I beg you to consider—that no building, not even a chicken-run, is ever built all at once" (1b).

С-488 • НИ С ЧЕМ НЕ СООБРА́ЗНЫЙ ⟨СООБРА́-ЗЕН⟩ lit [AdjP; modif (var. with long-form Adj only) or subj-compl with copula (subj: abstr); fixed WO] (sth. is) senseless, illogical: (sth. is) utterly absurd ⟨nonsensical⟩; (sth. is) absolutely ridiculous ⟨ludicrous⟩; (sth. is) completely preposterous; (sth.) makes no sense; [in limited contexts] (s.o.'s words ⟨thoughts etc⟩) are incongruous.

Что касается до внутреннего содержания «Летописца», то оно по преимуществу фантастическое и по местам даже почти невероятное в наше просвещённое время. Таков, например, ни с чем не сообразный рассказ о градоначальнике с музыкой (Салтыков-Щедрин 1). As concerns the *Chronicle's* subject matter, it is for the most part fantastical, and even, in places, nearly incredible to us in our enlightened epoch. Such, for example, is the utterly nonsensical tale of the town governor with the music (1a). ♦ Никто в доме не знал о предположенном побеге... Но Марья Гавриловна сама в беспрестанном бреду высказывала свою тайну. Однако ж её слова были столь несообразны ни с чем, что мать, не отходившая от её постели, могла понять из них только то, что дочь её была смертельно влюблена во Владимира Николаевича и что, вероятно, любовь была причиною её болезни (Пушкин 3). Nobody in the household knew about the intended elopement....It was only Maria Gavrilovna who revealed her secret in her continual state of delirium. Her words, however, were so incongruous that her mother, who never for a moment left her bedside, could make out only that Masha was fatally in love with Vladimir Nikolaevich, and that her love was probably the cause of her illness (3a).

С-489 • В СООТВЕ́ТСТВИИ С чем [PrepP; Invar; Prep; the resulting PrepP is adv] in agreement with (sth.): in accordance with; according to; in line with; in keeping with; in compliance with; in conformity with; as per.

Мы жили в полное своё удовольствие, каждый в соответствии со своими склонностями (Катаев 2). We lived just as we pleased, each of us in accordance with his taste (2a). ♦ ...[Комиссия] обязана наблюдать, чтобы правление вершило свои дела в соответствии с волей большинства пайщиков... (Войнович 3). ...[The committee is] charged with seeing to it that the board manages its affairs according to the will of the majority of the shareholders... (3a).

С-490 • СОПЛЁЙ ПЕРЕШИБЁШЬ ⟨кого⟩; СОПЛЁЙ ПЕРЕШИБИ́ТЬ МО́ЖНО both substand, derog [VP; neg pfv fut, gener. 2nd pers sing (1st var.) or impers predic with быть∅ (2nd var.); fixed WO] s.o. looks weak, feeble, as if he could easily be beaten in a physical conflict: X-а соплёй перешибёшь ≃ you could knock X down just by looking ⟨sneezing⟩ at him; you could knock X down ⟨split X in half etc⟩ with a ⟨one⟩ good sneeze; a ⟨one⟩ good sneeze could knock X down.

«Гляжу, рядом с вахтой офицерья навалом и все — навытяжку, а посреди них сидит себе на стульчике, покуривает плюгавенький такой шибздик [slang = недоросток] в полковничьей папахе, соплёй перешибёшь» (Максимов 1). "All around the guard-room there were crowds of officers and all of them were standing to attention, and in the middle, sitting smoking on a little stool, is a puny little runt in a colonel's coat. You could have knocked him down just by looking at him" (1a).

С-491 • РАСПУСКА́ТЬ/РАСПУСТИ́ТЬ СО́ПЛИ highly coll, rude [VP; subj: human] 1. not to wipe one's running nose: X распустил сопли ≃ X let his nose drip ⟨run⟩.

2. to whimper, complain in a whimpering manner (and often give up what one is trying to do): X распускает сопли ≃ X whines ⟨snivels⟩; X sits around ⟨here, there⟩ whining ⟨sniveling⟩.

Надо действовать, ребята, а не сопли распускать. Если только ныть и жаловаться друг другу — толку не будет. We've got to take action, guys, and not sit here sniveling. We won't get anywhere by just whining and complaining to each other.

С-492 • НА СОПЛЯ́Х highly coll, rude [PrepP; Invar] 1. ~ дотягивать, тянуть и т. п. [adv] (to operate an automobile, airplane etc) on a fuel supply that is almost exhausted: (drive ⟨run⟩) on empty; (drive ⟨run⟩) on fumes.

2. держится, построено, сделано ~; сделать что и т. п. ~ [adv or subj-compl with copula (subj: usu. concr)] sth. is built (sth. is done, to do sth. etc) poorly, sth. is flimsily put together: jerry-built; sloppily (built ⟨done⟩); just thrown together; just hanging together; almost ⟨practically⟩ falling down ⟨falling apart⟩.

Лодку сделали на соплях — вот она и затонула сразу же после спуска на воду. The boat was jerry-built so it sunk the minute it hit the water.

С-493 • В СОПРОВОЖДЕ́НИИ [PrepP; Invar; Prep; the resulting PrepP is adv] 1. ~ кого-чего in the company of s.o., with s.o. along: accompanied by; [in limited contexts] escorted by.

2. ~ чего (in refer. to a musical performer or performers) supported by (an instrument, ensemble etc): to the accompaniment of; accompanied by.

С-494 • ВЫНОСИ́ТЬ/ВЫ́НЕСТИ СОР ИЗ ИЗБЫ́ coll [VP; subj: human; often impfv infin with зачем, не надо, не стоит etc] to divulge arguments, squabbles etc occurring within one's family or a narrow circle of friends, coworkers etc: зачем выносить сор из избы ≃ why wash ⟨air⟩ your dirty linen ⟨laundry⟩ in public?; why tell tales out of school?; why expose your dirty laundry to the public gaze?

«Жена настаивала, чтобы я прямо звонил генеральному прокурору. Вероятно, так и следовало бы сделать, но мне, откровенно говоря, не хотелось выносить сор из избы...» (Войнович 6). "My wife told me to phone the prosecutor general immediately. That's probably what I should have done. But, frankly, I didn't want to wash our dirty linen in public" (6a).

С-495 • СО́РОК СОРОКО́В чего obs [NP; fixed WO] a very large number of sth.: countless; a multitude of; numerous; a host of.

«Все мы исповедуем христианский закон прощения обид и любви к ближнему — закон, вследствие которого мы воздвигли в Москве сорок сороков церквей, а вчера засекли кнутом бежавшего человека...» (Толстой 5). "We all profess the Christian law of forgiveness of injuries and love for our neighbor—the law in honor of which we have built countless churches in Moscow—but yesterday a deserter was whipped to death with the knout..." (5a).

< From the now archaic word «сорокъ», an old unit of count in Russia. Originally, «сорокъ» was a shirt used as a bag that held forty sable pelts, a full set for a fur coat.

С-496 • ЗАЛА́ДИЛА ⟨ЗАТВЕРДИ́ЛА⟩ СОРО́КА Я́КОВА (ОДНО́ ПРО ВСЯ́КОГО) [saying] said to or of a person who repeats sth. again and again: ≃ you're ⟨he's etc⟩ like the proverbial magpie ⟨like the magpie in the proverb⟩ who

keeps repeating (one and) the same thing over and over (again); you keep ⟨he keeps etc⟩ harping on the same string.

«Два рублика», — сказал Чичиков. «Эк право, затвердила сорока Якова одно про всякого, как говорит пословица; как наладили на два, так не хотите с них и съехать. Вы давайте настоящую цену!» (Гоголь 3). "Two roubles," said Chichikov. "Really, my dear sir, you're just like the magpie in the proverb who keeps repeating one and the same thing over and over again. You've got those two roubles on the brain and you can't get rid of them. Give me your real price" (3a).

C-497 • КАК СОРÓКА трещать, болтать и т. п. *coll* [как + NP; nom only; adv] (to talk) loudly, quickly, and too much: **(chatter away) like a magpie; (talk) without coming up for air;** [in limited contexts] **(talk) a mile a minute; (talk) a blue streak.**

Под хохот публики легкомысленные жёны обманывали ворчливых дураков-мужей, и фарсовые сводницы-кумушки тарахтели как сороки (Булгаков 5). To the wild laughter of the audience, frivolous wives deceived their grumbling, stupid husbands, and comic bawds chattered away like magpies (5a).

C-498 • СОРÓКА НА ХВОСТÉ ПРИНЕСЛÁ *coll* [sent; Invar; usu. this WO] the source of the information in question is unknown or will not be disclosed (usu. used as a humorous or evasive answer to the question "How do you know that?"): **a little bird(ie) told me.**

C-499 • ПÉРВЫЙ СОРТ *coll, approv* [NP; Invar; subj-compl with быть₀ (subj: any common noun), nonagreeing modif, or adv; fixed WO] superb, remarkable: **first-rate; first-class; top-notch; second to none; grade A; couldn't be better.**

[Гурмыжская:] Иван Петрович, хорошо это письмо написано? [Восьмибратов:] Первый сорт-с! (Островский 7). [G.:] Ivan Petrovich, is that letter written well? [V.:] First-rate! (7a). ♦ «Этакое богатое тело! — продолжал Базаров, — хоть сейчас в анатомический театр». — «Перестань, ради бога, Евгений!..» — «Ну, не сердись, неженка. Сказано — первый сорт. Надо будет поехать к ней» (Тургенев 2). "Such a magnificent body!" continued Bazarov. "Just perfect for the anatomical theatre." "Stop it, for goodness' sake, Yevgeny!..." "Come now, don't be angry, tenderfoot. I mean she's first-class. We must go and visit her" (2e).

C-500 • ЗАБЛУДÍТЬСЯ В ТРЁХ СÓСНАХ *coll, disapprov* [VP; subj: human] to fail to cope with a simple task, undertaking etc (e.g., to lose one's way in an uncomplicated place, get confused doing sth. easy etc): X заблудился в трёх соснах ≃ **(easy as it was ⟨although it was simple** etc⟩,**) X got lost ⟨(all) mixed up, (all) screwed up** etc⟩; [in refer. to losing one's way only] **X got lost in broad daylight;** ‖ X может заблудиться в трёх соснах ≃ **X could put two and two together and get three.**

«Теперь эту кнопку нажимать?» — «Да нет, не эту, а ту. Опять ты в трёх соснах заблудился». "Now I push this button?" "No, not that one—this one. You've gotten all mixed up again."

C-501 • В СОСТОЯ́НИИ [PrepP; Invar; subj-compl with copula (subj: any common noun, usu. human or collect); used with infin] a person (a group etc) has the ability, authority etc (to do sth.): X в состоянии сделать Y ≃ **X can ⟨is able to⟩ do Y; X is capable of doing Y; doing Y is within X's capacity ⟨power⟩;** ‖ *Neg* X не в состоянии делать Y ≃ **X is (quite) unable to do Y; X is incapable of doing Y; doing Y is beyond X's capacity; doing Y is not within X's power;** [usu. in refer. to one's physical or mental health] **person X is in no shape ⟨condition⟩ to do Y.**

«...Вот что счастливо, это то, что вы сами, лично, в состоянии будете передать теперь в Москве, тётушке и Агаше, всё моё положение...» (Достоевский 1). "...What is for-

tunate is that you yourself, personally, will now be able to tell auntie and Agasha, in Moscow, of my whole situation..." (1a). ♦ «...[Генерал Корнилов] кристальной честности человек, и только он один в состоянии поставить Россию на ноги» (Шолохов 3). "He [General Kornilov] is a man of perfect integrity and he and he alone is capable of putting Russia on her feet again" (3a). ♦ «...Я двух дней не в состоянии прожить ни с кем в одной комнате, о чём знаю из опыта» (Достоевский 1). "...I am incapable of living in the same room with anyone even for two days, this I know from experience" (1a). ♦ Он был не в состоянии думать о своих делах, хозяйственных распоряжениях... (Пушкин 1). ...He was in no shape to take care of his affairs or manage his estate... (1a). He was in no condition to think about his affairs or the running of his estate... (1b).

C-502 • НИ ПОД КАКИ́М СÓУСОМ *coll* [PrepP; Invar; adv; used with negated verbs; fixed WO] one will (or would) absolutely and positively not (do sth.): **not under any circumstances; not for anything; no matter what;** [in limited contexts] **no way.**

Отсрочки мы тебе не дадим. Ни под каким соусом. Даже и не проси. We're not going to give you an extension, no matter what. Don't even bother asking.

C-503 • ПОД СÓУСОМ каким, каким-нибудь, этим и т. п. *coll* [PrepP; Invar; the resulting PrepP is adv] (to present sth.) in the way specified (often disguising or concealing one's true intentions, the true state of affairs etc): под каким соусом ≃ **under what guise; in what way;** [in limited contexts] **under what pretext;** ‖ под каким-нибудь ⟨тем или иным⟩ соусом ≃ **under some guise (or other); some way or other;** [in limited contexts] **using some pretext (or other); using some excuse (or other);** ‖ под этим соусом ≃ **under this guise; in this way;** [in limited contexts] **under this pretext; using this as an excuse.**

«...Тебя из списка авторов [проекта] выкинут под каким-нибудь соусом» (Зиновьев 1). "...They'll remove your name from the list of artists and designers under some pretext or other" (1a).

C-504 • МÉЛКАЯ СÓШКА *coll, usu. rather derog or condes* [NP; usu. sing; often subj-compl with copula (subj: human); fixed WO] a person or people occupying a low social or professional position: **small fry; small potatoes; tiny cog(s) (in the machine ⟨in the wheel, in some department, in an organization** etc⟩**).**

«Странно. Начальник — и вдруг занимается такой мелкой сошкой, как я» (Семёнов 1). "That's queer. Fancy a boss suddenly taking an interest in small fry like me" (1a). ♦ «Послушай-ка, — сказали они, — ты это брось». — «Что „брось"?..» — я изумился и чуть привстал. «Брось считать, что ты выше других... что мы мелкая сошка...» (Ерофеев 1). "Listen, you," they said. "Cut it out." "Cut out what?" I said with surprise, sitting up. "Cut out thinking that you're better than anyone else. That we're small potatoes..." (1a). ♦ ...Корытов — всего лишь мелкая сошка в аппарате ЦК (Зиновьев 2). ...Korytov was only a tiny cog in the Central Committee machine (2a).

C-505 • СПАСÁЙСЯ, КТО МÓЖЕТ [imper sent; Invar; fixed WO] (when a group of people is in a dangerous situation) each person must look after himself rather than depend on help from another: **every man for himself;** [in limited contexts] **run for your life ⟨for it⟩!**

Такие эпохи порождают только индивидуализм, основанный на принципе «спасайся, кто может», а совсем не чувство личности (Мандельштам 2). Times such as these breed only individualism based on the principle "every man for himself," not a true sense of one's own worth (2a).

C-506 • И НА ТÓМ СПАСИ́БО; СПАСИ́БО И НА ÉТОМ *both coll* [sent; these forms only; usu. this WO] although sth. (often some outcome) may not be entirely satisfactory, it does have at least some positive aspect(s) (as indicated) that the concerned person appreciates or should appreciate: **that's (at least) something to be thankful for; that's something, at least; one should ⟨must⟩ be thankful ⟨grateful⟩ at least for that; thanks for that, anyway;** [in limited contexts] **and one is lucky to get that (much).**

…Нелепо мне ходить по Москве с переводчиком. Стучать на меня бессмысленно, секретов-то нету, это вы знаете. Спасибо и на этом (Аксёнов 7). I feel ridiculous with an interpreter on my heels. Why spy on me? What's the point? You know I have no secrets. "That's something at least" (7a). ♦ Он [Виктор] поглядел вдоль бетонки. До перекрёстка шесть километров и от перекрёстка до города — километров двадцать… Тут он заметил, что дождь ослабел. «И на том спасибо», — подумал он (Стругацкие 1). He [Victor] looked down the road. Four miles till the cross roads and thirteen miles from there to town…He suddenly noticed that the rain had died down. "Thanks for that, anyway," he thought (1a). ♦ [Лопахин:] Сколько она пришлёт? Тысяч сто? Двести? [Любовь Андреевна:] Ну… Тысяч десять-пятнадцать, и на том спасибо (Чехов 2). [L.:] How much is she sending? A hundred thousand roubles? Two hundred thousand? [Mrs. Ranevsky:] Oh, about ten or fifteen thousand, and we're lucky to get that much (2c).

С-507 • СПА́СУ ⟨-а⟩ НЕТ *substand;* **СПАСЕ́НИЯ НЕТ** *coll* [VP; impers] **1.** ~ *от кого-чего.* Also: **СПА́СУ НЕ СТА́ЛО** *substand* it is impossible to avoid or rid o.s. of s.o. or sth. tiresome or bothersome: от Х-а спасу нет ≃ **there's no escaping X; you can't get away from ⟨get rid of⟩ X.**

Они [Михаил и Дунярка] шли по проспекту Павлина Виноградова и молчали. Люди — нету спасенья от людей. Спереди, с боков, сзади (Абрамов 1). They [Mikhail and Dunyarka] walked in silence along Pavlin Vinogradov Prospekt. People—there was no escaping people—in front, behind, on all sides (1a).

2. [used as intensif] it is impossible to tolerate sth., overcome some desire etc: **it's more than person X can stand ⟨take⟩; it's enough to drive person X crazy ⟨wild, nuts etc⟩; person X will die (if he doesn't do ⟨get etc⟩ sth.).**

«Дай закурить. Спасу нет, хочу курить, а у меня кончились» (Распутин 1). "Give me a smoke. I'll die if I don't smoke and I'm out of cigarettes" (1a).

3. [used as intensif] (some quality is present or manifested) to a very high degree: **incredibly; unbelievably;** [in refer. to a negative quality only] **unbearably.**

С-508 • СБИВА́ТЬ/СБИТЬ СПЕСЬ ⟨ГО́НОР⟩ с кого или **кому; СБИВА́ТЬ/СБИТЬ ФОРС** *coll;* **СШИБА́ТЬ/ СШИБИ́ТЬ СПЕСЬ ⟨ФОРС⟩** *highly coll* [VP; subj: human] to make s.o. (who is overconfident, arrogant etc) less sure of himself, cause him to become more humble: X сбил с Y-а спесь ≃ **X deflated Y's ego; X took ⟨brought, knocked⟩ Y down a peg (or two); X took Y down a notch; X cut Y down to size.**

…[Александра Прокофьевна] называла его Гешей, как в старину, всячески сшибала с него спесь (Трифонов 3). …[Alexandra Prokofievna] called him Gesha as she did in the old days, and did everything she could to deflate his ego (3a). ♦ «Я вас ненавижу, товарищ Бабичев. Это письмо пишется, чтобы сбить вам спеси» (Олеша 2). "I hate you, Comrade Babichev. I'm writing this letter to bring you down a peg" (2a).

С-509 • НЕ К СПЕ́ХУ *coll* [PrepP; Invar; used without negation to convey the opposite meaning] **1.** [subj-compl with copula (subj: дело, работа etc) or adv] some matter (job etc) is not pressing, need not be taken care of immediately: X не к спеху ≃ **X isn't urgent; X can ⟨will⟩ wait; there's no hurry ⟨rush⟩;** ‖ X к спеху ≃ **X is needed ⟨wanted⟩ in a hurry;** [as adv] **urgently.**

«Я своих гусар не могу жертвовать. Трубач! Играй отступление!» Но дело становилось к спеху. Канонада и стрельба, сливаясь, гремели справа и в центре… (Толстой 4). "I cannot sacrifice my hussars. Bugler! Sound the retreat!" But matters were becoming urgent. The mingled sound of cannon and musketry thundered on the right and in the center… (4a). ♦ …Кузнецы, как водится, были отъявленные подлецы и, смекнув, что работа нужна к спеху, заломили ровно вшестеро (Гоголь 3). …[The blacksmiths] were plain blackguards, as usual, and realizing that the work was needed in a hurry, charged him six times the regular price (3c).

2. *кому* ~ [impers predic with быть₀] s.o. is not rushing, is not pressed for time: Х-у не к спеху ≃ **X is in no hurry ⟨rush⟩; there's no hurry ⟨rush⟩; X can wait.**

[Аристарх:] Если вы, извиняюсь, здесь что-нибудь делали, ради Бога, пожалуйста, продолжайте. [Семён:] Ничего-с. Мне не к спеху (Эрдман 1). [A.:] If you, I beg your pardon, were doing something, by all means continue, please do. [S.:] Oh, that's all right. I'm in no hurry (1a). ♦ «Извините, — сказал он парикмахеру. — Как-нибудь в другой раз… Не к спеху… В другой раз…» (Айтматов 2). "Forgive us," he said to the hairdresser, "it'll have to be some other time….There's no hurry. Another time will do" (2a).

С-510 • НЕ СПЕША́ [Verbal Adv; Invar; adv] (to do sth.) without rushing: **unhurriedly; at a leisurely pace; leisurely.**

Он шёл по уснувшей улице не спеша, мурлыча под нос старую тягучую песню (Семёнов 1). He walked unhurriedly down the sleeping street, humming an old plaintive tune to himself (1a). ♦ …Это были два чудаковатых субъекта, которые… встречались на площади Коллективизации и не спеша прогуливались по улице Поперечно-Почтамтской от площади до колхозного рынка и обратно (Войнович 2). …These two were somewhat eccentric types who…would meet on Collectivization Square and leisurely stroll down Post Office Cross Street to the kolkhoz market and back (2a).

С-511 • ЗА СПИНО́Й ⟨-ю⟩ [PrepP; these forms only] **1.** ~ *(чьей, у кого)* [adv or subj-compl with copula (subj: concr or abstr)] (in refer. to spatial relations, usu. distance covered during a trip) sth. is already past: **behind s.o.**

К вечеру большая часть пути осталась у нас за спиной. By evening the greater part of the journey was behind us.

2. ~ *(чьей, кого, у кого)* [adv or subj-compl with copula (subj: usu. abstr)] sth. is part of a person's past experience: X остался у Y-а за спиной ≃ **X is behind Y; Y has X behind him; Y has been through X; Y has X under Y's belt.**

Он завидовал им [бойцам, вырвавшимся из вражеского окружения,] и готов был, кажется, принять на себя даже некоторую их небезупречность, чтоб только знать, что за его спиной тоже — бои, обстрелы, переправы (Солженицын 12). He envied them [soldiers who had escaped from enemy encirclement] and would have been prepared to share their somewhat tarnished reputation if only he could say that he had been through the same fighting, shellfire, and river crossings that they had (12a).

3. жить, сидеть и т. п. ~ *чьей, (у) кого coll, often disapprov* [adv or subj-compl with copula (subj: human)] one is under s.o.'s care, protection: X живёт ~ у Y-а ≃ **X depends on Y for support; X is Y's dependent; X has Y to take care of X; X lives off Y;** ‖ X живёт за чужой спиной ≃ **X has someone else to take care of him; X lives off someone else.**

4. ~ *чьей, (у) кого disapprov* [adv] without s.o.'s knowledge, secretly: **behind s.o.'s back.**

Кукуша складывала в папку какие-то бумаги и удалялась, а кто и что судачил там за спиной, её не очень-то волновало (Войнович 6). Kukusha would throw some papers into a folder and leave. What people said behind her back did not greatly concern her (6a).

С-512 • **СТОЯ́ТЬ ЗА СПИНО́Й** *чьей, (у) кого* [VP; subj: human] to direct and support s.o.'s actions secretly: за Y-овой спиной стоит X ≃ **X is behind Y.**

Ревкин понял, что Ермолкину и тем, кто стоит за его спиной, пора показать характер (Войнович 4). Revkin realized that it was time to show some muscle to Ermolkin and those behind him (4a).

С-513 • **ГНУТЬ СПИ́НУ**[1] *(на кого) coll;* **ЛОМА́ТЬ СПИ́НУ** *coll;* **ГНУТЬ 〈ЛОМА́ТЬ〉 ГОРБ** *coll;* **ГНУТЬ ХРЕБЕ́Т** *substand* [VP; subj: human] to work, labor to the point of exhaustion, wear o.s. out with hard, usu. menial, work (usu. in an attempt to earn enough money to live on, often with the implication that one is being exploited by s.o.): X гнёт спину ≃ **X is breaking his back; X is working his fingers to the bone; X is working his tail off.**

…Орозкул ненавидит свою жизнь… Эта жизнь для таких, как Расторопный Момун. Ему-то что надо, Момуну? Сколько живёт, столько и горб гнёт изо дня в день, без отдыха. И в жизни ни один человек не был у него в подчинении… (Айтматов 1). …Orozkul hated his life.…It was a life for people like Efficacious Momun. What did he need for himself, that Momun? As long as he lived he'd break his back day after day without a breather. In his whole life, he never had anyone under him… (1b).

С-514 • **ГНУТЬ СПИ́НУ**[2] **〈ШЕ́Ю〉** *перед кем coll;* **ГНУТЬ ХРЕБЕ́Т** [VP; subj: human] to act in a servile manner, fawn on s.o.: X гнёт спину перед Y-ом ≃ **X kowtows to Y; X cringes before Y; X bows and scrapes to 〈before〉 Y; X falls all over Y.**

С-515 • **ПОКА́ЗЫВАТЬ/ПОКАЗА́ТЬ СПИ́НУ** *(кому) coll* [VP] **1.** [subj: human] to turn away from s.o., showing one's reluctance to speak with him or one's disdain for him (may imply walking away from him as well): X показал (Y-у) спину ≃ **X turned his back on Y; X turned his back and walked away; X turned away (from Y); X showed his back to Y.**

Первые же слова Егорши: «Здорово, невеста!» — …полымем одели её [Лизкины] щёки. Но она не растерялась: «Проваливай! Чего здесь не видал?»… «Проваливай, говорю! Нечего тебе тут делать», — ещё строже сказала Лизка и, недолго думая, показала спину (Абрамов 1). Egorsha's first words—"Hi there, fiancée!"—…brought a blush to her [Lizka's] cheeks. But she did not lose her head. "Get lost! What do you want around here?"…"Get lost, I tell you! There's nothing here for you," said Lizka more sternly, and without further ado she turned her back on him (1a). ♦ Развернувшись чисто по-воински, через левое плечо, Козлов показал гостям спины, скрылся в кабинете и в два оборота ключа отгородил себя от своего будущего соседа раз и навсегда (Максимов 3). With a soldierly, left-about turn, Kozlov showed his back to his guests, vanished into his study, and with two turns of the key shut himself off once and for all from his future neighbor (3a).

2. Also: **ПОКА́ЗЫВАТЬ/ПОКАЗА́ТЬ ТЫЛ** *obs, coll* [subj: human or collect] to run away, quickly retreat (often from the enemy): X показал (Y-у) спину ≃ **X turned tail (on Y); X beat a 〈hasty〉 retreat; X made tracks 〈a quick exit〉; X cleared out in a hurry.**

С-516 • **ПРЯ́ТАТЬСЯ/СПРЯ́ТАТЬСЯ ЗА** *чью* **СПИ́НУ 〈ЗА ЧУЖУ́Ю СПИ́НУ, ЗА ДРУГИ́Х〉** *coll, usu. derog* [VP; subj: human] to avoid taking responsibility or answering for sth. by letting another take the blame or responsibility: X прячется за Y-ову 〈за чужую〉 спину ≃ **X hides behind Y's 〈someone else's〉 back; [in limited contexts] X lets Y take the rap 〈the heat〉.**

«Мне легче будет, если я отвечу за свою вину, чем спрячусь за чью-то спину» (Тендряков 1). "I would rather take my share of the blame than hide behind someone else's back" (1a).

С-517 • **НЕ РАЗГИБА́ТЬ СПИНЫ́** *coll* [VP; subj: human] to work without respite: X не разгибает спины ≃ **X works without a break 〈without letup〉; X works nonstop.**

С-518 • **НЕ РАЗГИБА́Я СПИНЫ́** *работать, трудиться* и т. п. *coll* [Verbal Adv; Invar; adv] (to work, labor) without respite: **without a break; without letup; nonstop.**

[Тесть Игоря] отдохнул немножко… а кто уж в отдыхе действительно нуждался, так это именно он, работавший не разгибая спины… (Ерофеев 3). He [Igor's father-in-law] had rested up a bit, and if anyone needed some relaxation, it was him. He worked…without a break (3a). ♦ …Дедушка сам работал не разгибая спины и от других требовал того же… (Рыбаков 1). Grandfather himself worked without letup and he demanded the same of the others (1a).

С-519 • **СПИТ И ВИ́ДИТ** *(что);* **СПИТ И ВО СНЕ ВИ́ДИТ** *both coll* [VP; subj: human; often foll. by a что-, как-, or когда-clause; usu. pres; fixed WO] one wants sth. very much, longs for sth.: X спит и видит Y ≃ **X dreams of getting 〈doing〉 Y; X is dying 〈itching, aching〉 to do 〈to get〉 Y; X's heart's desire is to do 〈to get〉 Y; X can't wait for Y 〈to do Y〉.**

Ради того, чтобы скопить на мотоцикл, мужик будет ходить в последних штанах…; он спит и видит себя с мотоциклом, и на заплатки на штанах ему наплевать (Распутин 1). A *muzhik* would walk about in ragged trousers so as to save up money for a motorcycle. What did he care about patches when his heart's desire was to own a motorcycle? (1a). ♦ «…Сплю и вижу тот день, когда этот комбинат станет, рабочий класс вокруг него поселится» (Тендряков 1). "I can't wait for the day when the factory over there gets started and there'll be workers living all around" (1a).

С-520 • **ПОСЛЕ́ДНЯЯ 〈ПЯ́ТАЯ, ДЕСЯ́ТАЯ〉 СПИ́ЦА В КОЛЕСНИ́ЦЕ** *coll, condes or rather derog* [NP; usu. sing; usu. subj-compl with быть∅ (subj: human); fixed WO] one is very insignificant with respect to position, status, role in sth. etc: **a mere 〈tiny〉 cog in the machine 〈the wheel〉; (just) a cog in the wheel; low man on the totem pole.**

Он дал нам понять, что у себя на работе он не последняя спица в колеснице. He made it clear to us that at work he was not low man on the totem pole.

С-521 • **КАК СПИ́ЧКА** *(худой, тощий* и т. п.*) coll* [как + NP; Invar; modif (intensif)] extremely (skinny): **(as) (thin 〈spindly etc〉) as a matchstick 〈a rail〉; (one is) a toothpick.**

Старшая девочка, лет девяти, высокенькая и тоненькая как спичка…́ стояла в углу подле маленького брата… (Достоевский 3). The elder daughter, about nine, stood in the corner by the side of her small brother. She was rather tall, and spindly as a matchstick… (3b).

С-522 • **СПЛОШЬ И 〈ДА〉 РЯ́ДОМ** *coll* [AdvP; these forms only; adv; used with impfv verbs; fixed WO] very frequently: **time and again; over and over again; all the time; (very) often.**

[Бакченин:] Сплошь да рядом, чтоб вы знали, выигрывает отчаянный, а осторожный пропадает (Панова 1). [B.:] Time and again, let me tell you, the daredevil gets through where the cautious man gets caught (1a). ♦ Город ***, куда отправились наши приятели, состоял в ведении губернатора из молодых, прогрессиста и деспота, как это сплошь да рядом случается на Руси (Тургенев 2). The town for which our friends had set out was under the jurisdiction of a governor of the youngish variety, a progressive fellow and, at the same time, a despot—a phenomenon which occurs over and over again in our land of Russia (2d).

C-523 • ОЛИМПИ́ЙСКОЕ СПОКО́ЙСТВИЕ *lit* [NP; fixed WO] complete calm, imperturbability: **Olympian calm.**

Завидую его самообладанию. Когда мы спорим, я обычно злюсь, а он сохраняет олимпийское спокойствие. I envy his self-possession. When we argue, I usually get angry, while he maintains an Olympian calm.

< From Mount *Olympus* in Greece, the name of the abode of the gods in Greek mythology.

C-524 • НА СПОР *coll;* **НА ПАРИ́** [PrepP; these forms only; adv] (to do sth.) so as to fulfill the terms of a bet in order to win that bet: **on a bet ⟨a wager⟩.**

Ходила легенда, что Вахтанг однажды на спор выпрыгнул в море из окна бильярдной (Искандер 5). Legend had it that Vakhtang, on a bet, had once dived into the sea from the billiard room window (5a).

C-525 • (НУ) Я́ ВАС ⟨ТЕБЯ́⟩ СПРА́ШИВАЮ! *coll* [Interj; these forms only; fixed WO] used to express strong surprise at, displeasure with etc a person's actions or words: **(well,) I ask you.**

«Нет, это что такое за безобразие, я тебя спрашиваю... В выходные льёт дождь!» (Ерофеев 3). "Now what kind of a disgrace is this, I ask you? Rain on a holiday!" (3a).

C-526 • БЕЗ СПРО́СА ⟨-у⟩ *coll* [PrepP; these forms only; adv] (to do sth.) without having asked for the consent of the person in charge (at work—one's superior, at home—one's parents etc): **without asking (permission ⟨for s.o.'s permission etc⟩); without (s.o.'s) permission ⟨leave⟩.**

...Обе горничные её девушки ушли потихоньку без спросу, по соседству, на именинную пирушку, случившуюся в той же улице (Достоевский 1). Her two maids...had gone secretly, without asking permission, to a birthday party at a neighbor's house on the same street (1a). ♦ ...Распоряжаться без спроса хлебниковским именем не имел права никто (Лившиц 1). Nobody had the right to use Khlebnikov's name without permission (1a).

C-527 • ИЗ-ПОД СПУ́ДА извлечь, вынуть *что* и т. п. [PrepP; Invar; adv] (to take out etc sth.) retrieving it after it had been forgotten about or hidden away: **dig up ⟨out⟩ sth.; pull out sth.**

Для того чтобы очистить официальную историю гражданской войны от искажений и лжи, историкам нужно извлечь из-под спуда хранящиеся в архивах свидетельства очевидцев и тщательно изучить их. In order to purge the official history of the Civil War of distortions and lies, historians must dig eyewitness accounts out of the archives and study them carefully.

C-528 • ПОД СПУ́ДОМ держать *что,* лежать, оставаться и т. п.; **ПОД СПУД** класть *что obs* [PrepP; these forms only; subj-compl with copula (subj: usu. concr or abstr, occas. human or collect), obj-compl with держать etc (obj: usu. concr or abstr, occas. human or collect), or adv] (to keep sth., be, remain) concealed, stored away (for later use or because one does not want it known about): **under wraps; hidden (away).**

«С той поры, как только началась позиционная война, казачьи полки порассовали по укромным местам и держат под спудом до поры до времени» (Шолохов 3). "Ever since this positional warfare started, the Cossacks have been tucked away in safe corners and are being kept under wraps until such time as they are needed" (3a). ♦ Я когда-то читала заветную повестушку Зенкевича, написанную после гибели Гумилёва... Он хранит рукопись под спудом и никому её не показывает (Мандельштам 2). I once read a manuscript written by Zenkevich after the death of Gumilev....He now keeps his manuscript hidden away and never shows it to anyone (2a).

C-529 • НЕ ДАВА́ТЬ/НЕ ДАТЬ СПУ́СКУ ⟨-a⟩ *кому coll* [VP; subj: human] to make no allowances for s.o., not let s.o.'s acts, misdeeds, or offenses go unpunished: X не даёт спуску Y-у ≃ **X doesn't give Y a break; X gives Y no quarter;** [in limited contexts] **X lets Y have it (when X has the chance).**

«...Я за производство болею, никому спуску не даю» (Копелев 1). "...I worry about production. I don't give anyone a break" (1a). ♦ «Мы с ним всю войну дружили. Это был великолепный лётчик и прекрасный товарищ... Он очень гордый парень был и в воздухе никому спуска не давал, но и мандраж этот перед начальством у него был» (Искандер 5). "He and I were buddies all through the war. A magnificent pilot and an excellent comrade....He was a very proud guy and gave no quarter to anyone in the air, but he got the shakes in front of big shots" (5a). ♦ Он [Мишка-сын] работал с Галибутаевым на одном производстве... То спросит какую-нибудь гадость, то толкнёт... Гонял его. Галибутаев... спуску тоже не давал. Баш на баш (Попов 1). He [Sonny Mishka] worked at the same factory as Galibutayev....One minute he'd be asking Galibutayev some filthy question, the next he'd be shoving him....Always after him....But he [Galibutayev] would also let Sonny Mishka have it, when he got the chance. Tit for tat (1a).

C-530 • СПУ́ТНИК ⟨СПУ́ТНИЦА⟩ ЖИ́ЗНИ *old-fash, lit* [NP; fixed WO] one's (or s.o.'s) spouse: **partner (in life); life partner; life's companion ⟨life-companion⟩.**

«Любовь к будущему спутнику жизни, к мужу, должна превышать любовь к брату», — произнёс он сентенциозно... (Достоевский 3). "Love for one's future partner in life, one's husband, ought to exceed love for one's brother," he pronounced sententiously... (3a). "Love for one's future life-companion, a future husband, ought to exceed the love for one's brother," he pronounced sententiously... (3c). ♦ «Я прочту объявление. Слушайте: „Немецкий солдат из хорошей семьи, потерявший на войне ногу и вследствие этого брошенный своей невестой, ищет в спутницы жизни товарища по несчастью"» (Федин 1). "I'll read an announcement....Listen: 'A German soldier of good family, having lost a leg in the war and as a consequence of this abandoned by his fiancée, seeks a fellow unfortunate as his life's companion'" (1a).

C-531 • НЕ ИДТИ́ В СРАВНЕ́НИЕ ⟨НИ В КАКО́Е СРАВНЕ́НИЕ⟩ *с кем-чем;* **НЕ ПОДДАВА́ТЬСЯ НИКАКО́МУ СРАВНЕ́НИЮ; НЕ ВЫДЕ́РЖИВАТЬ (НИКАКО́ГО) СРАВНЕ́НИЯ** [VP; subj: any noun; the verb may take the final position, otherwise fixed WO] to be so different from someone or something else that no comparison can be drawn (often because one of the people, things etc is far superior to the other): X не идёт ни в какое сравнение с Y-ом ≃ **X can't compare with Y; X is in no way comparable to Y; there's no comparing X and Y; X is nothing compared with ⟨to⟩ Y; X is nothing in comparison with Y.**

...Девушка не шла ни в какое сравнение с Фаиной... (Битов 2). ...The girl couldn't compare with Faina... (2a). ♦ До этого Сталин был за границей только в Таммерфорсе и Стокгольме. Но те съезды не шли ни в какое сравнение с лондонским, где собралось более трёхсот делегатов... (Рыбаков 2). Until then, Stalin had been abroad only to Party meetings in Tammerfors and Stockholm. But they had been nothing compared to the London congress, where more than three hundred delegates had gathered... (2a).

C-532 • ПО СРАВНЕ́НИЮ *с кем-чем;* **В СРАВНЕ́НИИ** [PrepP; these forms only; Prep; the resulting PrepP is adv] when (a person, thing etc is) compared with (another person, thing etc): **(as) compared with ⟨to⟩; in comparison with ⟨to⟩;** [in limited contexts] **by comparison;** [when comparing s.o. or sth. to someone or something else previously encountered] **after...**

Должно быть, слова в старину читались медленнее и про-износились значительнее. По сравнению с позднейшей убори-стой печатью, на странице помещалось мало знаков (Терц 3). In the old days people probably read much more slowly and put much greater meaning into words. Compared to the very close print of a later age, there were fewer letters to a page (3a). ♦ ...В эту минуту Наполеон казался ему столь маленьким, ничтожным челове-ком в сравнении с тем, что происходило теперь между его душой и этим высоким, бесконечным небом с бегущими по нём облаками (Толстой 4). ...At that moment Napoleon seemed to him such a small, insignificant creature compared with what was taking place between his soul and that lofty, infinite sky with the clouds sailing over it (4a). ♦ Нужно сказать, что все события, сопро-вождавшие выход предыдущих пьес Мольера, решительно померкли по сравнению с тем, что произошло немедленно после премьеры «Школы жён» (Булгаков 5). It must be said that, whatever incidents attended the presentation of Molière's previous plays, they dimmed to insignificance in comparison with the things that transpired after the premiere of *The School for Wives* (5a). ♦ Тесть играл [в бильярд] лучше. Сказывалась многолетняя прак-тика, а Игорь, по сравнению с Александром Ивановичем, был почти совсем новичок, хотя и подающий надежды (Еро-феев 3). His father-in-law was a better [billiard] player. He had many years of practice under his belt, and Igor, by comparison, was a novice, albeit a novice who showed promise (3a). ♦ ...[В общежитии] горячей воды... ванной или душа не было. Но всё-таки условия по сравнению с теми, которые мне пришлось испы-тать до тех пор, были вполне приличными (Войнович 1). ...[In the hostel] there was...no hot water, no bath or shower. But after the conditions in which I had been living, these were entirely decent (1a).

С-533 • ПРОДА́ТЬ ⟨ПРЕДА́ТЬ⟩ ЗА ТРИ́ДЦАТЬ СРЕ́БРЕНИКОВ *кого lit* [VP; subj: human; the verb may take the final position, otherwise fixed WO] to betray s.o. out of base, mercenary considerations: X продал Y-а за тридцать сребре-ников ≃ **X sold ⟨betrayed⟩ Y for thirty pieces of silver.**

< From the Bible (Matt. 26:15).

С-534 • ТРИ́ДЦАТЬ СРЕ́БРЕНИКОВ *lit* [NP; fixed WO] payment received for betraying s.o. (out of base, mercenary con-siderations): **thirty pieces of silver.**

Именно показания [его] жены [Риммы] дали основание для вынесения ему смертного приговора. За всё это Римма получила тридцать сребреников реальных, в виде постоян-ных передач, и тридцать — иллюзорных, в виде обещаний дать ей... не тюрьму, не лагерь, а только ссылку, да ещё всего на три года (Гинзбург 1). It was the evidence supplied by his wife [Rimma] which had sent him to his death. She was rewarded with thirty genuine pieces of silver in the form of permission to get any number of parcels, and thirty false ones—a promise she would not be sent to prison or to camp, but only into exile, and only for a maximum of three years at that (1b).

< See С-533.

С-535 • В СРЕ́ДНЕМ [PrepP; Invar; adv or sent adv] as an approximate mean: **on (the ⟨an⟩) average;** [in limited contexts] **(there is) an average of...; average.**

...Комиссия закончила работу и выяснила, что в среднем на каждое жилое строение Бишофсберга приходилось по 9$\frac{1}{37}$ флага... (Федин 1). ...The commission had completed its work and announced that there was an average of 9$\frac{1}{37}$ flags on every inhabited structure in Bischofsberg... (1a). ♦ ...Как только Кукуша ушла, [Ефим] посуду помыл и — к столу, чтобы написать за день свои четыре страницы, такая у него в среднем дневная норма (Войнович 6). When Kukusha leaves, he [Yefim] washes the dishes and goes to his desk to write his four pages—his daily average (6a).

С-536 • НЕ ПО СРЕ́ДСТВАМ [PrepP; Invar] **1.** ~ *жить, одеваться* и т. п. [adv] (to live, dress etc) spending more money

than one's salary or income allows: X живёт ~ ≃ **X lives beyond his means; X exceeds his means; X spends more than he can afford.**

Поначалу он долго, с ненужными подробностями, расска-зывал биографию, затем стал жаловаться, как дурно влиял на него живущий не по средствам дядя... (Чернёнок 2). At first he gave his biography at length, sparing no details, then began com-plaining what a bad influence his uncle, who lived beyond his means, was on him... (2a).

2. ~ *кому* [subj-compl with copula (subj: usu. concr or infin)] sth. costs more than s.o. can pay: X Y-у ~ ≃ **X is more than Y can afford; X is out of Y's reach ⟨price range⟩.**

С-537 • ДА́Й(ТЕ) СРОК *coll* [imper sent; these forms only; fixed WO] wait for some time to pass (and sth. will be accom-plished, will happen): **give me ⟨him etc⟩ time; just (you) wait; (you) wait a bit; wait a little bit.**

«Ну, сколько ж это будет всего, считай!» — говорил Илья Ильич и сам начал считать. Захар делал ту же выкладку по пальцам. «...Ну, сколько у тебя? Двести, что ли?» — «Вот погодите, дайте срок!» — говорил Захар, зажмуриваясь и ворча (Гончаров 1). "What does it come to altogether—add it up," said Ilya Ilych, and he himself began figuring. Zakhar made his calculations on his fingers. "...What do you make it? Two hundred, isn't it?" "Wait a minute, give me time!" said Zakhar, screwing up his eyes and muttering (1b). ♦ «...В одном я с тобой не согласный». — «В чём это?» — «В том, что я пробка. Это я у вас — пробка, а вот погоди, дай срок, перейду к красным, так у них я буду тяжелей свинца» (Шолохов 5). "...There's one thing I don't agree with you about." "What is it?" "That I'm a blockhead. I may be one while I'm with you, but just you wait. One day I'll go over to the Reds, and then I'll be sharp as steel" (5a). ♦ Когда мне было лет пять-шесть и я очень шалил, Вера Артамоновна говаривала: «Хорошо, хорошо, дайте срок, погодите, я всё расскажу княгине, как только она приедет» (Герцен 1). When I was five or six years old and very naughty, Vera Artamonovna used to say: "Very well, very well, you wait a bit, I'll tell the princess everything as soon as she comes" (1a). ♦ [Таня:] Послать его [Семёна] вам? [2-ой мужик:] Чего посылать-то. Дай срок. Успеем! (Толстой 3). [T.:] Should I send him [Semyon] to you? [Second Peasant:] Why send him now? Wait a little bit. There'll be plenty of time later! (3a).

С-538 • ДЕ́ЛАТЬ/СДЕ́ЛАТЬ СТА́ВКУ *на кого-что* [VP; subj: human] to rely on some person (thing, character trait etc) to produce some desired result, put one's hopes in s.o. or sth. with an aim toward a certain goal: X делает ставку на Y-а ≃ **X counts ⟨banks⟩ on Y; X puts his trust in Y; X gambles ⟨puts his chips⟩ on Y;** [in limited contexts] **X stakes his all on thing Y; X hitches his (own) fortune to person Y.**

О. М[андельштам], человек абсолютно жизнерадостный, никогда не искал несчастья, но и не делал никакой ставки на так называемое счастье (Мандельштам 1). Nobody was so full of the joy of life as M[andelstam], but though he never sought unhappi-ness, neither did he count on being what is called "happy" (1a). ♦ ...На него [Кирова] теперь делают они главную свою ставку, так же как в своё время делали ставку на товарища Сталина, чтобы устранить Троцкого (Рыбаков 2). ...He [Kirov] was the only one they were banking on now, just as they had once banked on Comrade Stalin as a means of getting rid of Trotsky (2a). ♦ «Отдайте письмо!» — выбросила она [начальница лагеря] мне в лицо сквозь свои длинные зубы. Конечно, можно бы сказать: не знаю, может, выронили? Но я почему-то делаю ставку на пристрастие начальницы к честности (Гинзбург 2). "Hand back the letter!" she [the camp commandant] hissed at me through her long teeth. I could, of course, have said, "I don't know anything about it—perhaps you dropped it." But for some reason I put my trust in her passion for honesty (2a). ♦ Судя по тому, что Миха на лету ухватил мысль дяди Сандро, можно заключить, что он бы-стро одолел свою социальную тугоухость... Да и вообще, если подумать, была ли свойственна социальная тугоухость человеку, который первым из абхазцев не только сделал ставку на свиней, но и первым догадался перегонять их осенью в каштановые и буковые урочища? (Искандер 3). Judging from the way Mikha seized Uncle Sandro's thought on the wing, we may conclude that he had quickly overcome his social deafness....And if you think about it, was social deafness generally characteristic of the man who was the first Abkhazian not only to gamble on pigs but also to think of driving them to chestnut and beech groves in the fall? (3a). ♦ ...Он [Юрий] решил полностью провести задуманный план. Суть его состояла в том, чтобы притвориться несчастным. Нет, на её [Марины] жалость Юрий не рассчитывал, он делал ставку на лесть — это гораздо вернее. Всякой женщине лестно, что из-за неё страдают... (Терц 7). He [Yury] made up his mind to carry out the whole of his plan. The main point was to pretend to be unhappy. Not that he counted on her [Marina's] pity — he staked his all on the effects of flattery, which he believed to be the surer means. Any woman would feel flattered at being the cause of suffering... (7a).

С-539 • КАК СТА́ДО БАРА́НОВ идти, двигаться, следовать *за кем и т. п. derog* [как + NP; adv; fixed WO] (to go, move, follow s.o. etc) as an unorganized crowd and blindly, without thinking: **like (a flock of) sheep; like (a herd of) cattle.**

С-540 • ВО ЧТО́ БЫ ТО НИ СТА́ЛО [Invar; adv or, less often, nonagreeing modif; usu. used with pfv infin (and a word expressing need, determination, intent etc) or with pfv fut; fixed WO] (used to express the necessity for sth., or the determination, desire etc of a person or group to accomplish sth.) regardless of what obstacles might arise or how difficult the undertaking might turn out to be: **whatever ⟨no matter what⟩ the cost; at all costs; no matter what; cost what it might; (do) whatever it takes;** [in limited contexts] **come what may.**

Она сидела на перилах веранды, озарённая солнцем, сильная девушка, и ни капли не скрывала своего намерения во что бы то ни стало выжить (Искандер 3). She sat on the veranda railing, a strong young woman illuminated by the sun, and made no secret of the fact that she intended to survive, whatever the cost (3a). ♦ Батальонный командир Фабр получил приказ: защищать город во что бы то ни стало (Эренбург 4). Fabre, the commander of the battalion, had been given orders to defend the town at all costs (4a). ♦ Путь [в гимназию] был обставлен ритуалами, пронизан суеверием, заклятиями. Так, например, следовало не пропустить некоторых плиток на тротуаре, во что бы то ни стало ступить на них... Иначе в гимназии могли бы произойти несчастья — получение двойки или что-нибудь в этом роде (Олеша 3). That route [to school] was surrounded with rituals and run through with superstitions and incantations. Thus, for example, I couldn't omit certain sidewalk squares, but had to step in them no matter what...lest something unfortunate happen to me at school, such as getting a bad mark or something like that (3a). ♦ Претендент понял, что ему представился шанс. И решил во что бы то ни стало стать Директором (Зиновьев 4). Claimant understood that he now had a great opportunity. And he decided to become Director cost what it might (1a). ♦ И сейчас [в военное время] бабка решила во что бы то ни стало на пасху печь кулини (Кузнецов 1). And now, though it was wartime, my grandmother decided that, come what may, she was going to bake Easter cakes (1b).

С-541 • СТА́ЛО БЫТЬ [Invar; sent adv (often parenth); can be preceded by coord Conj («и», «а») or used (with раз, если, коли etc) as part of a correlative subord Conj, usu. resultative; fixed WO] accordingly: **then; so; therefore; it follows that; consequently; hence;** [in limited contexts] **which means; you mean...?; does that mean...?; apparently; must** [+ infin].

«...На мой вопрос, не выплачивались ли кому деньги во дворце Каифы, мне сказали категорически, что этого не было». — «Ах так? Ну, что же, не выплачивались, стало быть, не выплачивались» (Булгаков 9). "When I asked whether anyone had been paid at Kaiyapha's palace, I received a categorical denial." "Ah, so? Well, then, if no one was paid, then no one was paid" (9a). ♦ [Сатин *(собирая карты)*:] Ты, Асан, отвяжись... Что мы — жулики, тебе известно. Стало быть, зачем играл? (Горький 3). [S. *(collecting the cards)*:] Cut the nagging, Asan....You know damned well we're cheats. So why did you play? (3a). ♦ «Я думаю, что если дьявол не существует и, стало быть, создал его человек, то создал он его по своему образу и подобию» (Достоевский 1). "I think that if the devil does not exist, and man has therefore created him, he has created him in his own image and likeness" (1a). ♦ «Много у нас всякого шуму было! — рассказывали старожилы. — Многие даже в Сибирь через это самое дело ушли!» — «Стало быть, были бунты?» (Салтыков-Щедрин 1). "We had quite a to-do!" recounted the old-time residents. "...There were many even went to Siberia thanks to this thing!" "You mean there were rebellions?" (1a). ♦ «Вчера слышал про вас оттуда. — Он показал на потолок. — Стало быть, там вас знают». — «Видно, знают», — сказал Ефим не без гордости (Войнович 6). "Yesterday I heard about you from *there*." He pointed to the ceiling. "Apparently you are known there." "Apparently," Yefim said, not without pride (6a). ♦ «Зараз [*regional* = сейчас, только что] разведка вернулась, говорят, что бугор пустой. Стало быть, Журавлёв потерял нас, а то бы он теперь на хвосте висел» (Шолохов 5). "Our patrol has just come in, they say there's no one on the hill. Zhuravlyov must have lost us or he'd be on our tail right now" (5a).

С-542 • (И) СТАР И МАЛ ⟨МЛАД⟩; (И) СТА́РЫЙ И МА́ЛЫЙ *all coll* [NP; usu. subj (all variants) or obj (last var.); fixed WO] everyone, without regard to age: **(the) young and (the) old; old and young ⟨young and old⟩ alike.**

...Давно надо было свозить её [жену] на станцию вставить эти самые металлические зубы, теперь все, и стар и млад, ходят с такими... (Айтматов 2). He should have taken her [his wife] to the town long ago to have some of those metal teeth fitted. Everyone wore them now, young and old (2a).

С-543 • РАД СТАРА́ТЬСЯ [predic; subj: human; fixed WO] **1.** *obs, mil* [1st pers only (subj omitted)] a soldier's (or soldiers') acknowledgment of commendation in the old army: **at your command, sir!; thank you, sir!**

2. *obsoles, coll* [1st pers only] (used to express the speaker's or speakers' willingness to make every possible effort to please s.o., usu. the interlocutor) I (or we) will try very hard to please you: **I'll ⟨we'll⟩ do my ⟨our⟩ best.**

3. usu. а ты ⟨он и т. п.⟩ (и) рад стараться *coll, humor or iron* [pres only] to engage in an activity to a greater extent than is permitted or expected: а X рад стараться ≃ **but ⟨and⟩ X goes overboard; but X doesn't know when to stop; but X goes ⟨carries it⟩ too far.**

Я Мите разрешила только попробовать торт, а он рад стараться — добрую половину съел. I gave Mitya permission just to taste the cake, but he went overboard and ate a good half of it.

С-544 • ПО СТАРИ́НКЕ *coll* [PrepP; Invar; adv] **1.** ~ жить, одеваться и т. п. Also: **ПО СТАРИНЕ́** (to live, dress etc) according to the tastes or customs of a former time: **(in) the old-fashioned way; as in (the) olden days; in the old style.**

Комната притаилась, по старинке убранная прожившей в этом доме полжизни нянькой (Федин 1). The room remained hushed, furnished in the old style by Nanny who had lived half her life in it (1a).

2. (to do sth., usu. one's job) using old, outdated methods: **the way it was done in the old(en) days; (in) the old-fashioned way;** [in limited contexts] **the way they did it in the good old days.**

Когда надо было что-нибудь сосчитать, бабушка делала это по старинке, на счётах. When something had to be calculated, Grandma did it the old-fashioned way: on an abacus.

C-545 • **ТРЯХНУ́ТЬ СТАРИНО́Й** *coll* [VP; subj: human; more often this WO] to undertake the same thing(s) or do sth. in the same manner as one did earlier, usu. in one's youth: X тряхнёт стариной ≃ **X will revive ⟨relive, bring back⟩ a bit of the past; X will go back for a taste of the past ⟨the good old days etc⟩; X will go back to the good old days ⟨to his youth etc⟩;** [in limited contexts] **X will go back to his old trade ⟨hobby etc⟩; X will rake ⟨dredge⟩ up the old skills.**

…Ребров предложил скинуться, по трёшке, купить пару бутылок, сырку, колбаски. А он знает тут неподалёку отличное местечко. Мы так и сделали – решили тряхнуть стариной, как выразился Безымянный («Давненько не пил из горла!») (Зиновьев 2). …Rebrov proposed that we each chip in three roubles and buy a couple of bottles and some cheese and sausage. And he knew just the place near by. So that's what we did—decided, as Nameless put it, to go back to the good old days ("it's quite a while since I drank straight from the bottle") (2a). ♦ «Ведь я, ты знаешь, от [врачебной] практики отказался, а раза два в неделю приходится стариной тряхнуть… Докторов здесь совсем нет» (Тургенев 2). "You see, as you know I've retired from my [medical] practice, but two or three times a week I still have to rake up the old skills.…There are no doctors round here…" (2e).

C-546 • **КТО СТА́РОЕ ПОМЯ́НЕТ ⟨ВСПОМЯ́НЕТ⟩, ТОМУ́ ГЛАЗ ВОН** [saying] past offenses should be forgiven and forgotten: ≃ **let bygones be bygones.**

[Купавина:] Я очень жалею, Меропа Давыдовна, что подала вам повод к неудовольствию. [Мурзавецкая:] Кто старое помянет, тому глаз вон (Островский 5). [K.:] I'm sorry, Meropia Davydovna, that I gave you cause for displeasure. [M.:] Let bygones be bygones (5b).

C-547 • **НА СТА́РОСТИ ЛЕТ** [PrepP; Invar; adv; fixed WO] when one gets old: **in one's old age;** [in limited contexts] **with old age; late in life; when one is getting on in years;** [when used by or of an old person to emphasize that the action in question does not befit s.o. of that age] **at my ⟨your etc⟩ age.**

«Ого! – сказал восхищённый Остап. – Полный архив на дому!» – «Совершенно полный, – скромно ответил архивариус. – Я, знаете, на всякий случай… Коммунхозу он не нужен, а мне на старости лет может пригодиться…» (Ильф и Петров 1). "Oho!" exclaimed the delighted Ostap. "A full set of records at home." "A complete set," said the record keeper modestly. "Just in case, you know. The communal services don't need them and they might be useful to me in my old age" (1a). ♦ «Почему я сам кличу на себя беду? Одурел на старости лет, ум отшибло» (Айтматов 1). "Why do I keep calling misfortune on myself? Have I gone daffy with old age and lost my wits?" (1a). ♦ «Что ж мне, лгать, что ли, на старости лет?» – оправдывался Захар (Гончаров 1). "You don't expect me to go around telling lies at my age, do you?" Zakhar protested (1b).

C-548 • **СТА́РОСТЬ НЕ РА́ДОСТЬ** [saying] (said with regret, and sometimes in jest, when a middle-aged or older person thinks or talks about his age and the effects it has on his health, physical strength etc; may be said by a young person as a joke) being or getting old is difficult and unpleasant: ≃ **it's no fun getting ⟨to get⟩ old; old age is no fun; getting old is no picnic ⟨no fun⟩;** [in limited contexts] **I'm ⟨he's etc⟩ not as young as I ⟨he etc⟩ used to be.**

[Матрёна:] …На старости лет кто пожалеет. Старость не радость (Толстой 1). [M.:] …In your old age who's going to feel sorry for you? It's no fun to get old (1a). ♦ Ноги у Петра Васильевича сделались ватными. Трясущимися руками отодвинув щеколду, он растерянно бормотал перед запертой дверью: «Сейчас, Вадя… Сейчас… Вот старость не радость… Руки не слушаются…» (Максимов 3). Pyotr Vasilievich's legs went weak. He released the catch with trembling fingers, and mumbled through the open door without knowing what he was saying. "Coming, Vadya…coming.…Not as young as I used to be.…Hands won't do what I want" (3a).

C-549 • **И НА СТАРУ́ХУ БЫВА́ЕТ ПРОРУ́ХА** [saying] even an experienced person can err, blunder (said to excuse the mistakes or negligence of a person from whom such things are not expected): ≃ **even a wise man stumbles; we all make mistakes; anyone can make a mistake; even the best of us ⟨them etc⟩ can slip up; to err is human.**

«Да, вы ошиблись. И на старуху бывает проруха…» (Ильф и Петров 2). "Yes, you were wrong. We all make mistakes…" (2a). ♦ «Ошибки были», – быстро сказал Хлебоввводов. «Люди не ангелы. И на старуху бывает проруха» (Стругацкие 3). "There have been mistakes," Klebovvodov said quickly. "People are not angels. Anyone can make a mistake" (3a). ♦ [author's usage] «…Дудырев охотится уже много лет». – «Мало ли что, и на старуху иной раз находит проруха». – «Согласен. Может случиться всякое…» (Тендряков 1). "…Dudrev's been going out hunting for many years." "What of it? Even the best of hunters can slip up." "I agree—anything can happen…" (1a).

C-550 • **С КАКО́Й СТА́ТИ?** [PrepP; Invar; adv; fixed WO] for what reason? (often used in questions to express the speaker's bewilderment, annoyance etc): **why (on earth)?; what for?; why (on earth) should…?;** [in limited contexts] **what is the point (of…)?; what reason (does one have to…)?**

«Я боюсь, останься… Тебя убьют». – «…С какой стати меня убивать? Они меня все боятся» (Стругацкие 4). "I am afraid. Stay here.…They'll kill you!" "…Why should they kill me? They're all afraid of me…" (4a). ♦ «Я не знаю даже, дадут ли нам утром пожрать. Боюсь, что опять не дадут: с какой стати?» (Стругацкие 2). "I don't even know if we'll get grub tomorrow morning. I'm afraid we won't get anything more. Why on earth should they feed us now?" (2a). ♦ «Скажите, с какой же стати вы надеялись, что я отыщу Жучку?..» (Достоевский 1). "Tell me, what reason did you have to hope that I would find Zhuchka?…" (1a).

C-551 • **НИ СТА́ТЬ НИ СЕ́СТЬ** *(где)* *coll* [Invar; impers predic with бытьø; fixed WO] some place is so crowded or small that there is no space left unoccupied, no room to move about freely: (в месте X) ни стать ни сесть ≃ **(place X is so crowded ⟨cramped, tiny etc⟩ that) there is hardly any room to breathe ⟨to turn around⟩; there is no elbow room (in place X).**

В аудиторию набилось столько народу, что ни стать ни сесть. So many people were crammed into the auditorium that there was hardly any room to breathe.

C-552 • **НИ СТАТЬ НИ СЕСТЬ НЕ УМЕ́ТЬ** *coll, disapprov* [VP; subj: human; не уметь may take the initial position, otherwise fixed WO] not to conduct o.s. properly in society out of a lack of good breeding, to lack good manners: X ни стать ни сесть не умеет ≃ **X's manners are atrocious; X is a (total) boor; X doesn't know the first thing about behaving in society; X is uncultured ⟨uncouth⟩; X acts like a real bumpkin.**

C-553 • **ПОД СТАТЬ** *coll* [PrepP; Invar] **1.** ~ *кому* [subj-compl with copula (subj: human) or nonagreeing modif] one is well-suited for s.o. with regard to certain qualities (skills, experience, personality etc): X Y-у ~ ≃ **X is a good ⟨perfect⟩ match for Y; X is (just) right for Y; X and Y are well ⟨perfectly⟩ matched.**

Она и ещё что-то думала вокруг этого, а вокруг этого оказался Мансуров-Курильский, человек, безусловно, бесталанный, но, в общем-то, не плохой и, следовательно, по всем статьям под стать ей самой… (Залыгин 1). Her thoughts turned around this question and lighted upon Mansurov-Kurilsky, a talentless man if ever there was one, but not a bad man, all in all, and therefore in every respect a good match for her (1a).

2. ~ *чему* [subj-compl with copula (subj: usu. abstr) or nonagreeing modif] sth. corresponds with something else: X ~ Y-y ≃ **X matches Y; X jibes ⟨is in keeping⟩ with Y; X and Y agree; X is as [AdjP] as Y.**

Собачья погода была прямо под стать дяди-Митиному собачьему настроению (Аксёнов 10). The foul weather exactly matched Old Mitya's foul mood (10a). ♦ Дни тянулись медленно, в химерах и воспоминаниях, в невесёлых, под стать погоде, думах о предстоящей жизни в лагере (Максимов 2). The days dragged slowly by, days spent in daydreams and memories, and in thoughts, cheerless as the weather, about the prospects of life in a prison camp (2a).

3. ~ *кому-чему* [subj-compl with copula (subj: human or abstr) or nonagreeing modif] a person (or thing) resembles another person (or thing): X ~ Y-y ≃ **X is like ⟨similar to⟩ Y; X is similar (in nature) to Y.**

...Отец [Сергея] когда-то был крупный работник, но так никуда и не вылез, мать — домашняя юристка с принципами и запросами, и он сам им под стать (Трифонов 3). ...His [Sergei's] father had once been an outstandingly able man; yet he had never made it to the top; his mother was a nonpracticing lawyer with principles and high standards — and Sergei was similar in nature to both of them (3a).

4. ~ *кому* [subj-compl with быть₀ (subj: infin); often neg] it is fitting, decent (for s.o. to do sth.): делать X Y-у не под стать ≃ **doing X does not befit ⟨suit, become⟩ Y; it isn't right ⟨appropriate, proper, suitable, seemly⟩ for Y to do X.**

C-554 • ОСО́БЬ ⟨ОСО́БАЯ⟩ СТАТЬЯ́ *coll* [NP; sing only; usu. subj-compl with быть₀ (subj: any noun); fixed WO] a person (thing, matter etc) is totally different from and not to be considered with others: **(quite) a different story ⟨matter⟩; another matter (altogether); a horse of a different color; a case apart.**

И, наконец, остаюсь я — руководитель авторского коллектива. Но это — особая статья (Зиновьев 2). And finally there is me — the head of the entire collective of authors. But that is quite a different story (2a). ♦ ...Старичок с бородой, который на чёрной доске в столовой висит, над сервантом, один велит: добро делайте. Ну, и как с ним, с добром? Нельзя ей [Рите] было с работы уходить. Потому что если нет людей вокруг — и добро делать некому... Но Гартвиг — то особь статья. О каком же добре речь! (Трифонов 5). ...That old fellow with the beard who looks out from the ancient ikon hanging in the dining room, above the buffet, commands only one thing: to do good. Well, and what about that, what about goodness? She [Rita] should never have stopped working. For if there's no one around you, there's no one for whom you can do good....But Gartvig — that was another matter. Doing good had no relevance for him! (5a).

C-555 • ПО ВСЕМ СТАТЬЯ́М [PrepP; Invar; adv or nonagreeing modif; fixed WO] with regard to everything, every point of consideration: **in all respects; in every respect; in every way; on all counts.**

Она и ещё что-то думала вокруг этого, а вокруг этого оказался Мансуров-Курильский, человек, безусловно, бесталанный, но, в общем-то, не плохой и, следовательно, по всем статьям под стать ей самой... (Залыгин 1). Her thoughts turned around this question and lighted upon Mansurov-Kurilsky, a talentless man if ever there was one, but not a bad man, all in all, and therefore in every respect a good match for her (1a). ♦ «Да, Лазарь Михалыч, сдал ты, я вижу, по всем статьям сдал, а ведь каким орлом по уезду летал, сколько кровей контре пустил, куда всё девалось!» (Максимов 2). "Yes, Lazar, I can see you have really given up — in every way. But when I think what a tiger you once were, how much counter-revolutionary blood you shed! What's become of the Lazar I once knew?" (2a).

C-556 • КАК СТЁКЛЫШКО *coll* [как + NP; Invar; adv (intensif) or subj-compl with быть₀] **1.** (чистый) ~ [subj: concr] very clean: **spick-and-span; spotless; clean as a whistle.**

2. (чистый, чист) ~ [subj: human или анкета] (of a person or his record) morally blameless: X чист как стёклышко ≃ **person X ⟨X's record⟩ is (as) clean as the proverbial whistle; X is irreproachable; X's record is unblemished ⟨impeccable, spotless⟩; X is (as) pure ⟨white⟩ as the driven snow; X is purer ⟨whiter⟩ than the driven snow.**

Он [Ефим] устремил свой взгляд на директора, давая ему понять, что ему нечего, совершенно нечего скрывать от органов, он перед ними как стёклышко чист (Войнович 6). ...[Yefim] fastened his gaze on the director, giving him to understand that he had nothing, absolutely nothing, to hide from the security system, that he was clean as the proverbial whistle (6a). ♦ До ареста бедняга считал себя «чистым как стёклышко», но на первом же допросе у него подкашивались ноги, потому что он чувствовал себя безнадёжно скомпрометированным связью с преступником. Сознание это лишало его способности к самозащите и сопротивлению... (Мандельштам 2). Before his arrest the poor devil may have thought himself purer than the driven snow, but at his first interrogation he would begin to quake in his shoes and feel hopelessly compromised by his contact with a criminal. The mere awareness of this deprived him of the will to defend himself and resist... (2a).

3. (трезв, трезвый) ~ [subj: human] absolutely sober: **(as) sober as a judge.**

[Гомыра:] Маша, мне надо с тобой поговорить. [Маша:] Тебе?.. Со мной? [Гомыра:] Конфиденциально. Я абсолютно трезвый, прошу заметить... Я трезв как стёклышко (Вампилов 3). [G.:] Masha, I have to talk to you. [M.:] You?...To me? [G.:] Confidentially. And may I point out that I'm completely sober....I'm sober as a judge (3a).

C-557 • МЯ́ГКО СТЕ́ЛЕТ, ДА ЖЁСТКО СПАТЬ *coll, disapprov* [VP; subj: human; usu. pres; fixed WO] one (often a boss or supervisor) is outwardly gentle and courteous, but in reality is very firm, deals with people severely etc: X мягко стелет, да жёстко спать ≃ **X has ⟨is⟩ an iron fist ⟨hand⟩ in a velvet glove.**

Два советника казённой палаты чуть не поссорились между собою, рассуждая о том, будет ли Козелков дерзок на язык или же будет «мягко стлать, да жёстко спать» (Салтыков-Щедрин 2). Two councillors of the provincial Treasury nearly came to blows over the question of whether Kozelkov would be overbearing in his speech or whether he would have "an iron hand in a velvet glove" (2a). ♦ [author's usage] «Тут до тебя много перебывало, все на фронт загремели, у этого майора не забалуешься, мягко стелет, да жёстко просыпаться» (Максимов 1). [context transl] "There have been lots of others here before you and they've all ended up at the front in no time at all. Our major's a hard master, he gives you a soft bed and a harsh awakening" (1a).

C-558 • В СТЕ́ЛЬКУ пьян(ый), напиться и т. п. *highly coll;* **КАК СТЕ́ЛЬКА** *obs, highly coll* [PrepP (1st var.); как + NP (2nd var.); these forms only; modif or adv (intensif)] one is or gets very drunk: **drunk as a skunk ⟨a lord, a fiddler⟩; completely smashed ⟨plastered, pie-eyed, soused, sauced, sozzled etc⟩; pissed out of one's mind.**

Участкового споить не удалось, так как он с утра был в стельку пьян (Зиновьев 1). They weren't able to get the Fuzz drunk because he had been completely sozzled since dawn (1a). ♦ Ты погляди, он же пьян в стельку. И спит (Зиновьев 1). "You can see he's pissed out of his mind and sound asleep" (1a).

C-559 • И У СТЕН ЕСТЬ ⟨БЫВА́ЮТ⟩ У́ШИ; (И) СТЕ́НЫ ИМЕ́ЮТ У́ШИ [saying] one can be overheard because another or others might be listening surreptitiously, even the most secret conversations may become known to others: ≃ **(even) the walls have ears.**

C-560 • КИТА́ЙСКАЯ СТЕНА́ *lit* [NP; sing only; fixed WO] an impenetrable barrier that completely isolates s.o. or sth. from s.o. or sth. else (often from the rest of the world): **Chinese wall.**

Этот милый юноша… уже тогда считался членом семьи. Он один сумел пробить брешь в китайской стене, отделявшей Бурлюков от всего мира… (Лившиц 1). This nice young man…was then already regarded as a member of the family. He was the only one who managed to make a breach in the Chinese wall which separated the Burliuks from the whole world (1a).

< From *Great Wall of China*, the name given to the ancient system of fortifications between China and Mongolia.

C-561 • СТЕНА́ В СТЕ́НУ; СТЕНА́ ОБ СТЕ́НУ ⟨ОБ СТЕНУ⟩; СТЕ́НКА В ⟨ОБ⟩ СТЕ́НКУ *coll* [NP; these forms only; adv; fixed WO] **1. находиться, стоять** и т. п. **~ с чем** (of a building) (to be located) very close by and usu. immediately adjacent to (another building): **right next door (to sth.); right alongside sth.; in the immediate neighborhood (of sth.).**

Наш дом легко найти: он стоит стенка в стенку с новой больницей. Our house is easy to find: it's right next door to the new hospital.

2. жить ~ с кем (of a person) (to live) in a room or apartment sharing a common wall with s.o., or (to live) in a house adjacent to s.o. else's: **one door down ⟨over⟩; right next door; in the next room ⟨apartment, house⟩; in the room ⟨apartment etc⟩ adjoining s.o.'s room ⟨apartment etc⟩; on the other side of s.o.'s wall ⟨of the wall from s.o.⟩.**

«Сам я живу от жильцов. Софья Семёновна живёт со мною стена об стену, тоже от жильцов» (Достоевский 3). "I'm subletting from tenants. Sofya Semyonovna lives on the other side of my wall; she also sublets from tenants" (3c).

C-562 • В ЧЕТЫРЁХ СТЕНА́Х сидеть, жить и т. п. [PrepP; Invar; adv] **1.** (to spend all or almost all of one's time) in one's home or a certain building: **(be ⟨live⟩) within these ⟨those, one's own⟩ four walls.**

[Домна Пантелевна:] Измучилась я в театре-то: жара, духота, радёхонька, что выкатилась. [Матрёна:] Да вестимо, летнее дело в четырёх стенах сидеть… (Островский 11). [context transl] [D.P.:] That theatre wore me out; it was so hot and stuffy I was glad to come away. [M.:] It's a shame to be cooped up in summer (11a).

2. (to live) like a recluse, associating little or not at all with others and spending all one's time inside: **(stay ⟨be buried, hole o.s. up⟩) within these ⟨those, one's own⟩ four walls.**

[Войницкий:] Двадцать пять лет я вот с этой матерью, как крот, сидел в четырёх стенах… (Чехов 3). [V.:] For twenty-five years I have sat here with this mother, buried like a mole within these four walls… (3a).

C-563 • ПРИПИРА́ТЬ/ПРИПЕРЕ́ТЬ ⟨ПРИЖИ-МА́ТЬ/ПРИЖА́ТЬ⟩ К СТЕ́НКЕ ⟨К СТЕНЕ́⟩ кого *all coll* [VP; subj: human; more often pfv] by using irrefutable facts and conclusive arguments, to make it impossible for s.o. to deny sth. or defend his own position in an argument, debate etc: X припёр Y-а к стенке ≃ **X pinned ⟨nailed etc⟩ Y to the wall; X had ⟨got⟩ Y (up) against the wall; X drove ⟨backed⟩ Y into a corner;** ‖ **припёртый к стенке ~ (with) one's back against ⟨to⟩ the wall.**

«Ты знаешь: нарисовал этот Евдокимов похабную карикатуру на декана… Вёл он себя в высшей степени трусливо, сначала отнекивался, отрицал *авторство* и только тогда признался, когда доказательствами к стене приперли» (Ерофеев 3). "You know that Evdokimov drew a smutty caricature of the

Dean.…He behaved in a most cowardly fashion; first he tried to get out of it, he denied authorship, and only when they nailed him to the wall with proof did he admit to it" (3a). ♦ «…Когда из Новосибирска отчалили?» — «Двадцать первого после обеда». — «Где предыдущие две ночи ночевали?» Выражение лица Овчинникова стало таким, словно при жеребьёвке ему показали две спички и надо было определить, какая из них счастливая. Совершенно неожиданно он расхохотался: «Сдаюсь, шеф! Припёр ты меня к стенке. У Люси Пряжкиной две ночи провёл» (Чернёнок 2). "…When did you leave Novosibirsk?" "On the twenty-first, after lunch." "Where did you spend the two nights before that?" Ovchinnikov looked as if he had to choose the lucky matchstick out of several. Then, totally unexpectedly, he laughed. "I give up, chief! You've got me against the wall. I spent two nights with Lusya Priazhkina" (2a). ♦ С его обострённой логикой насчёт Фаины он быстро припёр её к стенке, и она, с неожиданной, мучительной лёгкостью, созналась во всём (Битов 2). His sharpened logic where Faina was concerned quickly drove her into a corner, and with unexpected, excruciating readiness, she confessed all (2a).

C-564 • СТА́ВИТЬ/ПОСТА́ВИТЬ К СТЕ́НКЕ ⟨К СТЕНЕ́⟩ кого *coll* [VP; subj: human] to execute s.o. by shooting him: X поставит Y-а к стенке ≃ **X will have ⟨put, stand⟩ Y up against a wall; X will have Y face the firing squad; X will have Y shot;** ‖ [with obj: pl] X поставит Y-ов к стенке ≃ **X will line Ys up against the wall (and shoot them ⟨have them shot⟩).**

Все жали Мыслителю руку и говорили, что он проявил большое мужество, вычеркнув из статьи такие обвинения в адрес Клеветника, за которые раньше ставили к стенке (Зиновьев 1). Everyone shook Thinker by the hand and remarked on his courage in removing from the article about Slanderer the kind of observations that in the past would have been enough to get him shot (1a). ♦ [Баев:] Был огонь на колокольне? [Паисий:] Что вы, что вы! Какой огонь? [Баев:] Огонь мерцал! Ну, ежели я что-нибудь на колокольне обнаружу, я вас всех до единого… к стенке поставлю! (Булгаков 2). [B.:] Was there a light in the bell tower? [P.:] What do you mean? What light? [B.:] There was a flickering light! Just wait, if I find anything in the bell tower, I'll line you up against the wall, to the last one of you!… (2a).

C-565 • КАК ОБ ⟨В⟩ СТЕ́НКУ ⟨ОБ СТЕ́НУ, О́Б СТЕНУ, В СТЕ́НУ⟩ ГОРО́Х ⟨ГОРО́ХОМ⟩; КАК ОТ СТЕ́НКИ ⟨ОТ СТЕНЫ́⟩ ГОРО́Х; ЧТО СТЕНЕ́ ⟨СТЕ́НКЕ⟩ ГОРО́Х *all coll, disapprov* [как + PrepP or что + NP; these forms only; usu. subj-compl with copula (subj: abstr, often всё, infin, or a clause); fixed WO] all requests (orders etc) are ignored, disregarded by s.o.; all attempts to persuade s.o. to do sth. or to change his mode of behavior produce no results, have no effect on s.o.: **(it's) like beating ⟨banging⟩ your ⟨one's⟩ head against the wall ⟨a wall, a brick wall, a stone wall⟩; (it's) like talking to the wall ⟨a brick wall⟩; you might as well beat ⟨bang⟩ your head against a wall ⟨a brick wall, a stone wall⟩; you might as well talk to the wall ⟨a wall, a brick wall⟩.**

Обо всём этом ему [Наделашину] говорилось тогда же. Но Наделашину сколько ни говори — всё как об стенку горох (Солженицын 3). He [Nadelashin] had been told about it at the time. But no matter how often one spoke to Nadelashin, it was like beating one's head against a stone wall (3a). ♦ «Пробовал я договориться с этим Големом — как об стену горох…» (Стругацкие 1). "I tried to come to an agreement with this Golem. It's like talking to a brick wall" (1a). ♦ «Осторожно. Скользко тут. Сколько раз говорила, чтобы не выливали помоев перед дверью, — как об стену горох» (Пастернак 1). "Careful—it's slippery. I don't know how many times I've told them not to throw the slops out of the door—might as well talk to a wall" (1a).

C-566 • ВСТАВА́ТЬ/ВСТАТЬ ⟨СТАНОВИ́ТЬСЯ/ СТАТЬ⟩ СТЕНО́Й [VP] **1. ~ за кого-что** [subj: human (usu. pl) or collect] to stand united behind and strongly support, defend s.o. or sth.: X-ы встали стеной за Y-а ≃ **Xs stood up for Y; Xs made a stand for Y; Xs gave their full support ⟨backing⟩ to Y; Xs stuck by Y.**

Чернова хотели уволить, но рабочие встали за него стеной. They wanted to fire Chernov, but the workers stood up for him.

2. [subj: human] to take (and maintain) a strong unyielding position on some matter: X встал стеной ≃ **X took a (firm) stand; X put his foot down; X stood his ground.**

...Кончились приданые деньги. Пришлось продать граммофон... Скоро проели и граммофон. Платон продал кровать... Скоро прожили и кроватные деньги. Платон замахнулся было на швейную машину, но тут уж Анна Савишна встала стеной: «Не отдам!» (Грекова 3). ...The dowry ran out and they [Platon and Anna Savishna] had to sell the gramophone....Soon they had run through that money, and Platon sold [the bed]....Soon they had gone through the money from the bed, and Platon was about to go after the sewing machine. But here Anna Savishna stood her ground...."I won't give it up!" (3a).

С-567 • КАК ЗА КА́МЕННОЙ СТЕНО́Й жить, чувствовать себя и т. п. *coll* [как + PrepP; Invar; adv or subj-compl with copula (subj: human); fixed WO] to live, feel that one is) under s.o.'s reliable protection or patronage: (one is ⟨feels⟩) **safe with s.o.; (one lives) as safely as behind a stone wall; (in s.o., one has) a good solid wall to protect one; with s.o., one is ⟨feels⟩ protected ⟨shielded etc⟩ from everything.**

[Нина:] Сегодня я вас познакомлю. Он [мой жених] хороший парень. [Бусыгин:] Я представляю. Наверно, он большой и добрый... Волевой, целеустремлённый. В общем, за ним ты — как за каменной стеной (Вампилов 4). [N.:] I'll introduce you [to my fiancé] tonight. He's a nice fellow. [B.:] I can imagine. He's probably big and kind-hearted....Strong-willed, highly motivated. In general, you'll be safe with him (4b). ♦ «Нина — женщина от земли. Её не столько интересует мужчина, сколько хозяин в доме, за спиной которого можно жить, как за каменной стеной» (Чернёнок 2). "Nina is an earthy woman. She's not as interested in a man so much as in a master of the house behind whose back she can live as safely as behind a stone wall" (2a). ♦ [Лукашин:] Уже тридцать два... (*Задумчиво.*) А семьи всё нет. Ну, не складывалось... Не повезло. И вдруг появляется Ипполит, положительный, серьёзный... хороший... С ним спокойно, надёжно... За ним как за каменной стеной. Он ведь, наверно, выгодный жених (Брагинский и Рязанов 1). [L.:] Thirty-two... (*Thoughtfully.*) And you still haven't a family. Well, things didn't work out....Just bad luck. And suddenly Ippolit appears, a positive, serious person....A good person....Life with him would be safe, peaceful, steady....A good solid wall to protect you. Yes, he looks like a fine prospective husband (1a).

С-568 • СТОЯ́ТЬ СТЕНО́Й [VP] **1.** ~ *за кого-что* [subj: human (usu. pl) or collect] to stand united behind and strongly support, defend s.o. or sth.: X-ы стояли стеной за Y-а ≃ **Xs stood (firmly) behind Y; Xs stood up for Y; Xs gave their full support ⟨backing⟩ to Y.**

...За Караваева стеной стояли интеллигенция [Брянска] и рабочие арсенала (Паустовский 1). ...The Bryansk intellectuals as well as the workers at the Arsenal stood firmly behind him [Karavayev] (1a).

2. [subj: human] to be firm, unyielding in one's position on some matter: X стоял стеной ≃ **X stood ⟨held⟩ his ground; X stood firm ⟨fast⟩; X stuck to his guns.**

[author's usage] Рахиль стояла как стена: ни в какую Швейцарию она не поедет, ей и здесь хорошо... (Рыбаков 1). Rachel stood her ground. She wasn't going to go to any Switzerland, she liked it here (1a).

С-569 • ЛЕЗТЬ/ПОЛЕ́ЗТЬ НА СТЕ́НУ ⟨НА́ СТЕНУ, НА СТЕ́НКУ⟩ *highly coll* [VP; subj: human] to become

extremely irritated, annoyed, furious: X полез на стенку ≃ **X went up the wall; X got (all) worked ⟨riled⟩ up; X got mad ⟨saw red etc⟩; [in limited contexts] X started climbing (up) the wall(s); X went haywire.**

Когда я сказал боссу, что я не согласен с его решением, он полез на стенку и стал кричать на меня. When I told the boss that I didn't agree with his decision, he went up the wall and started yelling at me. ♦ Два дня нас не покорми — мы сами не свои, мы на стенку лезем (Солженицын 10). If we're not fed for two days we go out of our minds, we start climbing up the wall (10a).

С-570 • ДО́МА (И) СТЕ́НЫ ПОМОГА́ЮТ [saying] a person feels more sure of himself, performs better etc in his home or usual, familiar surroundings than he does in an unfamiliar setting: ≃ **everything is easier at home; it helps to be in your own territory ⟨in your own home, on your own turf etc⟩; [usu. in sporting contexts] one has the home court ⟨field etc⟩ advantage.**

С-571 • В ВЫ́СШЕЙ СТЕ́ПЕНИ [PrepP; Invar; intensif; fixed WO] **1.** [modif] very, excessively, to the greatest possible extent: **extremely; in ⟨to⟩ the highest degree; in the extreme; highly; utterly; extraordinarily; most; nothing if not; [in limited contexts] deeply (offended ⟨sorry etc⟩); shamelessly (crude ⟨exaggerated etc⟩).**

...Вёл он [Хряк] себя в этой в высшей степени выгодной для себя ситуации крайне глупо (Зиновьев 1). ...In this extremely advantageous situation for himself, he [Hog] has behaved with extreme stupidity (1a). ♦ «...Я вижу, что вы искренни в высшей степени, а потому вы и правы...» (Достоевский 1). "...I see that you are sincere in the highest degree, and therefore you are right..." (1a). ♦ Правдец — интеллигент в высшей степени, хотя о нём нельзя сказать, что он высокообразованный человек... (Зиновьев 1). "Truth-teller is an intellectual to the highest degree, although it cannot be said that he is a highly educated man..." (1a). ♦ ...[Мадлена] сочинила роман под названием «Клелия (Римская история)»... Роман был галантен, фальшив и напыщен в высшей степени (Булгаков 5). ...[Madeleine] composed a novel she titled *Clélie, A Roman Story*....The novel was elegant, false, and pompous in the extreme (5a). ♦ «Этот поступок, то есть именно присвоение чужих трёх тысяч рублей, и, без сомнения, лишь временное... поступок этот, на мой взгляд по крайней мере, есть лишь в высшей степени поступок легкомысленный...» (Достоевский 1). "...This action—namely, that is, the appropriation of another person's three thousand roubles, and, no doubt, only temporarily—this action, in my opinion at least, is simply a highly thoughtless action..." (1a). ♦ ...Назначение Микаладзе было для глуповцев явлением в высшей степени отрадным (Салтыков-Щедрин 1). ...The appointment of Mikaladze was...a most happy event for the Glupovites (1b). ...Mikaladze's appointment was nothing if not gratifying for the Foolovites (1a). ♦ Обломов поклонился иронически Захару и сделал в высшей степени оскорблённое лицо... «С глаз долой!» — повелительно сказал Обломов, указывая рукой на дверь (Гончаров 1). He [Oblomov] made a mocking bow to Zakhar and looked deeply offended...."Out of my sight!" Oblomov commanded, pointing to the door (1b). ♦ Повторяю: всё это [рассказы иностранцев о России] в высшей степени преувеличено и до бесконечности невежественно... (Салтыков-Щедрин 2). All this [foreigners' portrayals of Russian life], I repeat, is not only shamelessly exaggerated, but also reveals a quite abysmal ignorance of the conditions in our country (2a).

2. ~ *наплевать, начхать на кого-что* и т. п. [adv] not (to care about sth.) at all, (be) completely (indifferent to sth.): X-у ~ наплевать на Y-а ≃ **X couldn't ⟨could⟩ care less (about Y); X doesn't give a hoot ⟨a damn⟩ about Y.**

С-572 • НЕ В ТУ СТЕПЬ (заехал, понесло *кого* и т. п.) *coll, usu. humor* [PrepP; Invar; adv or subj-compl with быть∅ (subj:

human)] (one said) sth. that is not relevant to the theme of the conversation, or that goes beyond what is considered acceptable under the given circumstances: X не в ту степь заехал ≃ **X went too far; X was wide of the mark; what X said was off the wall ⟨out of line⟩.**

[author's usage] По бесстрастному лицу помощника Марлен Михайлович понял, что в этот момент он слегка пережал, прозвучал слегка — не-совсем-в-ту-степь, но ему как-то уже было всё равно (Аксёнов 7). The blank face of the Important Personage's assistant told him [Marlen Mikhailovich] that this time he had gone a bit too far, but by now he was past caring (7a).

С-573 • СТЕ́РПИТСЯ, СЛЮ́БИТСЯ [saying] when you give yourself time to get used to people, things etc that you do not initially like, you find that you (can) grow to like them (said to comfort and reassure a person who has to act against his wishes; sometimes said to a person entering into marriage without love): ≃ **you'll grow to like him ⟨her, it etc⟩ with time ⟨in time, after a time⟩; you'll like him ⟨her, it etc⟩ once you get used to him ⟨her, it etc⟩; love comes with habit ⟨with time⟩; you'll learn to love him ⟨like it etc⟩;** [in limited contexts] **marry first, and love will follow.**

«А ты, мой батюшка, — продолжала она, обращаясь ко мне, — не печалься, что тебя упекли в наше захолустье. Не ты первый, не ты последний. Стерпится, слюбится» (Пушкин 2). "And you, my good sir," she continued, turning to me, "you mustn't grieve at being sent to this god-forsaken place. You are not the first, and you won't be the last. You will grow to like it after a time" (2b). ♦ «...Намерен я тебя женить». — «На ком это, батюшка?» — спросил изумлённый Алексей. «На Лизавете Григорьевне Муромской...» — «Воля ваша, Лиза Муромская мне вовсе не нравится». — «После понравится. Стерпится, слюбится» (Пушкин 3). "...I intend to get you a wife." "Who would that be, father?" asked the astonished Aleksei. "Lizaveta Grigorevna Muromskaia...." "That's all very well, but I don't like Liza Muromskaia in the least." "You'll grow to like her later. Love comes with time" (3a).

С-574 • СТИХ НАХО́ДИТ/НАШЁЛ ⟨НАПАДА́ЕТ/ НАПА́Л, НАКАТИ́Л⟩ на кого coll [VP$_{subj}$] **1.** ~ **какой, что делать** s.o. is overtaken by a specific mood or by a strong desire to do sth.: на X-а нашёл философский ⟨меланхолический, ностальгический и т. п.⟩ стих ≃ **a philosophical ⟨melancholy, nostalgic etc⟩ mood came over X; X was in a philosophical ⟨melancholy, nostalgic etc⟩ mood;** ∥ на X-а нашёл стих делать Y ≃ **X felt ⟨got⟩ the urge to do Y; X was in the mood to do Y.**

Человек, говорил он, никогда не примирится со смертью... Она улыбалась, слыша такие его речи за ужином и в постели, когда на него вдруг находил стих курить и философствовать (Трифонов 3). Man, he used to say, is never reconciled with death....She used to smile when she listened to him holding forth in this vein at dinner or in bed, at moments when he would suddenly feel the urge to smoke and philosophize (3a).

2. s.o. is overcome with a desire to do something extravagant, outrageous: на X-а стих нашёл ≃ **something came over X; something possessed X; X was seized by a (silly ⟨crazy etc⟩) whim.**

Николаю потом, когда он вспомнил об этом порыве ничем не вызванной, необъяснимой откровенности, которая имела, однако, для него очень важные последствия, казалось (как это и всегда кажется людям), что так, глупый стих нашёл... (Толстой 7). Afterward, when he [Nikolai] recalled this outburst of unsolicited, inexplicable frankness, which nevertheless had very important consequences for him, it seemed to him (as it seems to everyone in such instances) that he had been seized by a silly whim... (7a).

С-575 • В СВОЕ́Й СТИХИ́И быть$_\emptyset$, чувствовать себя и т. п. [PrepP; Invar; subj-compl with copula (subj: human); fixed WO] (to be, feel that one is) in a situation or surroundings in which one can thrive, in which one feels comfortable, competent, able to function most efficiently etc: X был в своей стихии ≃ **X was in his element; X felt ⟨was⟩ right at home.**

Я ещё вся — там [в Новосибирске], там я читала специальный курс лекций, посвящённый американской литературе. Была в своей стихии (Орлова 1). My mind was still there [in Novosibirsk]. I was giving a special course of lectures devoted to American literature. I was in my element (1a).

С-576 • НА ВСЕ СТО highly coll [PrepP; Invar; fixed WO] **1. верить кому, соглашаться с кем, поддерживать кого** и т. п. ~; **быть$_\emptyset$ каким** ~. Also: **НА ВСЕ СТО ПРОЦЕ́Н-ТОВ** coll [adv or nonagreeing modif] (to believe, agree with, support etc s.o.) fully; (be) absolutely...: **(agree with ⟨support etc⟩ s.o.) one ⟨a⟩ hundred percent; (believe ⟨agree with etc⟩ s.o.) completely (and utterly); (support s.o. etc) to the hilt;** [as modif only] **complete; total; through and through.**

«Ты права, дочка, на все сто процентов», — решил Сафронов (Платонов 1). "You are right, girl, one hundred percent," Safronov decided (1a). ♦ «А вы соглашаетесь с вашим собеседником?» — осведомился неизвестный, повернувшись вправо к Бездомному. «На все сто!» — подтвердил тот... (Булгаков 9). "And do you agree with your friend?" inquired the unknown man, turning to Bezdomny on his right. "A hundred percent!" affirmed the poet... (9b). ♦ ...Он [Марлен Михайлович] был действительно своим в верховном учреждении, на все сто своим... (Аксёнов 7). He [Marlen Mikhailovich] was completely at home with them [the upper echelons], completely and utterly... (7a).

2. approv [nonagreeing modif; the resulting phrase is subj-compl with copula (subj: any common noun or a person's name)] (a person, thing etc is) of the highest merit, extremely good: **excellent; first-rate; A 1 ⟨A-1⟩; of the first order; topnotch.**

...Виктор Колтыга — парень на все сто. Разве он виноват, что ростом вышел лучше, чем я, и возрастом солидней, и профессия у него земная? Морякам в любви никогда не везло (Аксёнов 1). ...Victor Koltyga is an A-1 guy. Is it his fault that he grew more than I did, and he's a more respectable age, and he has a job on land? Sailors have never been lucky in love (1a).

3. [adv] (to do sth., sth. is done, sth. turns out) very well: **(do) a first-rate ⟨first-class, bang-up etc⟩ job; s.o. couldn't do sth. better ⟨be a better [NP]⟩; sth. couldn't have been ⟨have turned out, have been done etc⟩ better.**

С-577 • НА ТОМ СТОИ́М; НА ТОМ СТОЯ́ЛИ, СТОИ́М И СТОЯ́ТЬ БУ́ДЕМ both coll [VP; subj: мы, usu. omitted; usu. used as indep. sent in response to the interlocutor's statement, or to reinforce one's own statement; occas. used in the 2nd and 3rd pers; fixed WO] this is in accordance with my (or our) principles, this is how I (or we) think things should be: **I ⟨we⟩ wouldn't have it any other way.**

«У вас в ресторане всегда самые изысканные блюда». — «На том стоим! Дорожим своей репутацией». "Your restaurant always has the most exquisite dishes." "We wouldn't have it any other way! We pride ourselves on our reputation."

С-578 • НЕ СТО́ИТ coll [formula phrase; Invar] a polite reply to an expression of gratitude: **don't mention it; not at all; it's nothing; my pleasure; no problem.**

«Это замечание ваше ещё даже остроумнее давешнего...» — «Благодарю-с...» — «Не стоит-с...» (Достоевский 3). "This remark of yours is even more apt than the one before." "Thank you." "Don't mention it..." (3a). "That remark was even wittier than your last one..." "Thank you, sir..." "Not at all, sir..." (3d).

C-579 • НИЧЕГО́ НЕ СТО́ИТ (кому) coll [VP; impers or with subj: это or pfv infin; 3rd pers sing only; pres or past; fixed WO] it is not difficult (for s.o. to do sth.): X-у ничего не стоит сделать Y ≃ **doing Y is ⟨would be⟩ the easiest thing in the world (for X); nothing could ⟨would⟩ be easier (for X) than to do Y; X can ⟨could⟩ (very) easily do Y; it would be a trifling matter for X to do Y; it's ⟨it would be⟩ no trouble at all for X to do Y; it would cost X nothing to do Y; it would take nothing for X to do Y; [in limited contexts] X would think nothing of doing Y.**

Не задала я Чечановскому и другого вопроса: почему он обращается ко мне, а не к Мандельштаму. Ведь он бывал у нас, и ему ничего не стоило поговорить с Мандельштамом (Мандельштам 2). There was something else I did not ask Chechanovski: Why was he telling me this instead of M[andelstam] directly? He was always coming to see us, and nothing would have been easier than to mention it to M[andelstam] himself (2a). ♦ В приведённой песне святой намекает, что ему ничего не стоило бы победить русских, уничтожив Владикавказ и Санкт-Петербург... (Терц 3). In the song quoted above the saint is hinting that it would be a trifling matter for him to defeat the Russians by destroying Vladikavkaz and St. Petersburg... (3a). ♦ «...Мне ничего не стоит дать вам свою визитную карточку, и вас напечатают в любом толстом журнале... но лучше не надо. Подождите» (Катаев 3). "...It would cost me nothing to give you my card and you would be published in any of the big monthlies...but better not. Wait a while" (3a). ♦ «Если вы не знаете, что такое Лужин, я вам скажу: это чудовище... Этому дяденьке ничего не стоит перестрелять хоть тысячу человек одновременно» (Войнович 4). "If you don't know what Luzhin is like, I'll tell you—a monster....He would think nothing of having a thousand men shot in one day" (4a).

C-580 • СТО́ИТ ТОГО́ coll [VP; subj: any common noun or a person's name; pres or past] a person (or thing) deserves the effort, time, money etc (as specified by the preceding context) spent on him (or it): X стоит того ≃ **X is worth it ⟨the effort⟩; X is worthy of it; thing X is worth my ⟨your etc⟩ while ⟨time⟩; [in limited contexts] it's for a worthy ⟨good⟩ cause.**

«Да, психологией русского преступления займутся, может быть, когда-нибудь первенствующие умы, и наши и европейские, ибо тема стоит того» (Достоевский 2). "Yes, perhaps some day the foremost minds both here and in Europe will consider the psychology of Russian crime, for the subject is worthy of it" (2a).

C-581 • ЧЕГО́-НИБУДЬ ДА СТО́ИТ coll [VP; subj: any common noun; pres only; fixed WO] a person or thing is of some importance: X чего-нибудь да стоит ≃ **X is (worth) something; X counts for something; X carries some weight; X has some value.**

...На нём [Павле Петровиче] была его обычная светлая шляпа, вся в небольших дырочках, будто изъеденная молью или многократно пробитая ревизорским компостером, а на самом деле дырочки были пробиты на фабрике, чтобы у покупателя, а в данном случае у Павла Петровича, в жаркие времена года не потела голова. А кроме того, думали на фабрике, тёмные дырочки на светлом фоне — это всё-таки что-нибудь да значит, чего-нибудь да стоит, это лучше, чем ничего, то есть лучше с дырочками, чем без них, решили на фабрике (Соколов 1). ...He [Pavel Petrovich] had on his usual light cap, all covered with little holes, as if eaten by a moth or repeatedly punched by a ticket-checker's punch, but in reality the holes had been put in at the factory so that the buyer's head, in this case, Pavel Petrovich's, would not get sweaty during the hot times of the year. And moreover, they thought at the factory, dark holes on a light background—that did mean something, it was worth something, it was better than nothing, that is, better with holes than without them, or so they thought at the factory (1a). ♦ «...Третий год головой хожу, так моё слово у господ горожан чего-нибудь да стоит» (Соло-

губ 1). "...This is my third term as mayor, so my word counts for something among the townspeople" (1a).

C-582 • (один...) ЧЕГО́ СТО́ИТ coll [VP; subj: any noun; pres or past; fixed WO] the person, thing, circumstance etc in question (which is cited as one of the factors producing the overall effect, result etc described in the preceding context) would be sufficient by himself or itself to produce the described effect, result etc: один X чего стоит ≃ **X alone is enough to...; look at X alone!**

«Редко где найдётся столько мрачных, резких и странных влияний на душу человека, как в Петербурге. Чего стоят одни климатические влияния!» (Достоевский 3). "Rarely will you find so many gloomy, harsh and strange influences at work on a man's soul as you will in St. Petersburg. Look at the influence of climate alone!" (3a).

C-583 • ЧТО́ ⟨ЧЕГО́⟩ кому СТО́ИТ coll [VP; impers; pres or past; fixed WO] (used to emphasize, sometimes with irony, condescension etc, how very easy it would be for s.o. or o.s. to carry out some action or fulfill some request; also used to reproach s.o. or o.s. for not having done sth.) it would not require much effort (for s.o. to do sth.): что X-у стоит ≃ **that's not too much to ask; that's not asking (too) much; it would be easy enough (for X to do sth.); what would it cost X (to do sth.)?; it wouldn't cost X anything ⟨would cost X nothing⟩ (to do sth.); [in refer. to o.s.] no problem ⟨sweat⟩.**

«Сходи к нему, чего тебе стоит, попроси его...» (Пастернак 1). "Go to see him, that's not too much to ask, speak to him..." (1a). ♦ «А может, ещё выпьем?» — «Эт-то можно», — сказал Готтих. «Только надо сбегать, а?» — «Сами бегайте». — «Ты же всё равно хотел уйти — всё равно выйдешь на улицу — так что тебе стоит?» (Битов 2). "Maybe we should have another [drink]?" "Can do," Gottich said. "Only you have to go out for it, okay?" "Go yourself." "You wanted to leave anyway—you're going out anyway—so what will it cost you?" (2a). ♦ «Что вам стоит сказать слово государю, и он [Борис] прямо будет переведён в гвардию», — просила она. «Поверьте, что я сделаю всё, что могу, княгиня», — отвечал князь Василий... (Толстой 4). "It would cost you nothing to say a word to the Emperor—and he [Boris] would be transferred to the Guards at once," she pleaded. "Believe me, Princess, I shall do all I can," replied Prince Vasily... (4a).

C-584 • ХОТЬ СТОЙ, ХОТЬ ПА́ДАЙ coll [Invar; usu. indep. or subord clause; fixed WO] used to express the speaker's ironic reaction to sth. absurd, ridiculous, shocking etc: **it beats all; (it's) truly unbelievable; [in limited contexts] I ⟨he etc⟩ (just) couldn't believe my ⟨his etc⟩ ears ⟨eyes⟩.**

Иван на собрании такую глупость сморозил, что хоть стой, хоть падай. At the meeting Ivan came out with such a stupid remark—I couldn't believe my ears.

C-585 • СТО́ЙКА СМИ́РНО; ПО СТО́ЙКЕ СМИ́РНО стоять, вытягиваться и т. п. [NP or PrepP (Invar, adv); fixed WO] (to stand in, come to etc) the position of attention: **(stand) at attention; (come ⟨snap⟩) to attention.**

«А что это она [учительница химии] позволяет себе так со мной говорить? Она, наверное, не представляет себе, кто я такой. Да я в нашем районе могу любого директора школы вызвать к себе в кабинет, поставить по стойке „смирно", и он будет стоять хоть два часа» (Войнович 1). "What gives her [the chemistry teacher] the right to talk to me like that? She must have no idea who I am. In our district, I can call any school principal into my office, have him stand at attention, and keep him standing there for two hours" (1a).

C-586 • КРУ́ГЛЫЙ СТОЛ; встреча, совещание и т. п. ЗА КРУ́ГЛЫМ СТОЛО́М media [NP or PrepP (used as non-agreeing modif); fixed WO] a meeting (a conference etc) at which all participants have an equal opportunity to speak, present their views, and engage in discussion: **round table; round-table discussion** ⟨**meeting**⟩.

Потом я встречался с Рогозиным в редколлегии нашего журнала. Мы устроили «круглый стол» на тему: «Психическое, физиологическое, логическое». Пригласили видных специалистов (Зиновьев 2). Later I met Rogozin on the editorial board of our journal. We had organised a round-table discussion on "the Psychic, the Physiological and the Logical." We invited a number of leading specialists (2a).

C-587 • ЛОЖИ́ТЬСЯ/ЛЕЧЬ НА СТОЛ [VP; subj: human] to undergo an operation: X-у придётся лечь на стол ≃ **X will have to have surgery** ⟨**to be put on the operating table, to go on the operating table, to go under the knife**⟩.

«А операция – невозможна?» (Он спрашивал «невозможна?», – но больше всего боялся именно лечь на стол. Как всякий больной, он предпочитал любое другое долгое лечение) (Солженицын 10). [context transl] "Is an operation impossible?" (He was asking if it was "impossible," but he feared the operating table most of all. Like any patient, he preferred any other, prolonged treatment) (10b).

C-588 • ПИСА́ТЬ В СТОЛ ⟨**В Я́ЩИК**⟩ *coll* [VP; subj: human] to write literary works, knowing that they will not pass censorship and be published: X пишет в стол ≃ **X writes for the desk drawer.**

А потом времена пошли куда вольнее: русские писатели не писали больше *в стол*, а всё печатали, что хотели… (Солженицын 2). Much freer times followed. Russian writers no longer wrote "for the desk drawer" but could publish whatever they liked… (2a).

C-589 • ПОД СТОЛ ПЕШКО́М ХО́ДИТ *coll, humor* [VP; subj: human; pres or past; if pres, 3rd pers only; the verb always takes the final position] one is a young, small child: X под стол пешком ходит ≃ **X is knee-high to a grasshopper; X is (only) this high** [accompanied by a hand movement indicating the child's approximate height – at waist level or lower]; **X can walk under tables without bending over.**

«Ты меня слушай, Красюк, ты ещё под стол пешком ходил, когда я уже в органах работал…» (Максимов 1). "Listen to me Krasyuk, when I started working for the Organs you could still walk under tables without bending over" (1a).

C-590 • САДИ́ТЬСЯ/СЕСТЬ ЗА ОДИ́Н СТОЛ *media* [VP; subj: human] to begin negotiations in order to come to an agreement: X и Y сели за один стол ≃ **X and Y sat down at the bargaining** ⟨**negotiating**⟩ **table.**

C-591 • СТОЛБНЯ́К НАПА́Л ⟨**НАШЁЛ**⟩ *на кого coll* [VP_subj] s.o. cannot move (usu. out of fear, horror): на X-а столбняк напал ≃ **X froze (on the spot); X became rooted to the spot; X stood stock-still; X was paralyzed with fear.**

C-592 • СТОЯ́ТЬ СТОЛБО́М ⟨**КАК СТОЛБ**⟩ *coll* [VP; subj: human] to stand unmoving, usu. with a vacant look on one's face: X стоял столбом ≃ **X stood motionless** ⟨**stock-still**⟩; **X stood there like a dummy** ⟨**a statue**⟩; **X stood as if rooted to the spot;** [in limited contexts] **X stood (there) gaping.**

C-593 • ПРИГВОЖДА́ТЬ/ПРИГВОЗДИ́ТЬ ⟨**ПРИКО́ВЫВАТЬ/ПРИКОВА́ТЬ** и т. п.⟩ **К ПОЗО́РНОМУ СТОЛБУ́** *кого rather lit* [VP; subj: human; usu. this WO] to make s.o. an object of public condemnation: X пригвоздит Y-а к позорному столбу ≃ **X will put** ⟨**have**⟩ **Y in the pillory; X will pillory Y.**

Хотелось мне… поговорить с ним [Гарибальди] о здешних интригах и нелепостях, о добрых людях, строивших одной рукой пьедестал ему и другой привязывавших Маццини к позорному столбу (Герцен 3). …I wanted to have a talk with him [Garibaldi] about the intrigues and absurdities here, about the good people who with one hand were setting up a pedestal for him, and with the other putting Mazzini in the pillory (3a). ♦ [author's usage] Ах, поганые оппортунисты, подлейшие мерзавцы, ну, подождите, мы вас пристегнём к позорному столбу! (Солженицын 5). Filthy opportunists, sneaking scoundrels – just wait, we'll have you in the pillory! (5a). ♦ «История всё разберёт. Потомство пригвоздит к позорному столбу бурбонов комиссародержавия и их чёрное дело» (Пастернак 1). "History will tell the truth. Posterity will pillory the Bourbons of the commissarocracy together with their dirty deeds" (1a).

< Originally referred to the punishment of a criminal who was tied to a post («столб») in a public square so that everyone would see him.

C-594 • ГЕРКУЛЕ́СОВЫ ⟨**ГЕРКУЛЕ́СОВСКИЕ**⟩ **СТОЛБЫ́** ⟨**СТОЛПЫ́**⟩ *(чего) lit* [NP; pl only; fixed WO] the maximum level (of sth.): **the utmost limit (of sth.); the farthest** ⟨**upper**⟩ **limits (of sth.); the ultimate (in sth.).**

«…Дело Главлита охранять военную и государственную тайну, а не… вмешиваться в литературную ткань произведения… (Аплодисменты. Возгласы с мест: „Верно… Правильно…".) Это вмешательство достигло ныне геркулесовых столпов глупости» (Свирский 1). "…The job of Glavlit is to preserve state and military secrets, not…to interfere in the creative process." (Applause. Shouts from the hall: "That's true, that's right!") "This interference has now reached the farthest limits of stupidity" (1a).

< Originally, the name of the two high points of land (the *Pillars of Hercules*) on either side of the Strait of Gibraltar believed to be "the limits of the earth." According to Greek legend the Pillars were raised by Hercules.

C-595 • НА СТОЛЕ́ лежать, быть_ø, застать *кого и т. п.* [PrepP; Invar; subj-compl with copula (subj: human) or obj-compl with застать etc (obj: human)] (of a dead person) prepared for burial: **(be** ⟨**find s.o. etc**⟩**) laid out.**

C-596 • ВАВИЛО́НСКОЕ СТОЛПОТВОРЕ́НИЕ *rather lit, disapprov* [NP; sing only] total confusion, disorder: **pandemonium; chaos; bedlam; uproar.**

< From the Biblical story of the building of the *Tower* («столпа творение») *of Babel* (Gen. 11:1–9).

C-597 • НЕ СТО́ЛЬКО… СКО́ЛЬКО… [Conj, correlative] (one thing, quality etc) to a lesser degree than (another): **not so much…as…; less…than…**

…Он не столько переживал сейчас из-за ног, сколько из-за сапог. Ноги – что. На ногах новая кожа вырастет, а вот на сапогах не вырастет (Абрамов 1). …He was not so much worried about his feet as about his boots. His feet – so what? New skin would grow on his feet, but not on his boots (1a). ♦ Явились даже опасные мечтатели. Руководимые не столько разумом, сколько движениями благодарного сердца, они утверждали, что при новом градоначальнике процветёт торговля… (Салтыков-Щедрин 1). There were even some dangerous day-dreamers, who, moved less by reason than by the stirrings of a grateful heart, declared that under the new governor trade would flourish… (1b).

C-598 • НИ ⟨И⟩ (ВОТ) НА СТО́ЛЬКО ⟨СТО́ЛЕЧКО⟩; И ВОТ СТО́ЛЬКО *coll* [PrepP or AdvP; these forms only; adv (intensif); used with negated verbs] not even a small amount or to a small extent: **not a ⟨one little, the least little⟩ bit; not a whit; not ⟨none⟩ at all; no [NP] at all;** [when indicating a small amount with one's fingers] **not even that ⟨this⟩ much.**

«Очевидно, мы с вами разно понимаем вопросы чести». — «Это потому, что у вас её не осталось и вот столько!» (Шолохов 5). "Apparently we have different conceptions of honour." "That's because you haven't one little bit of it left!" (5a). ♦ «Стреле-то вот ни на столечко не поверил, сами изволили видеть!» (Достоевский 3). "I didn't believe in that thunderbolt the least little bit, you saw that for yourself!" (3a). ♦ «Ну вот уж здесь, — сказал Чичиков, — ни вот на столько не солгал», — и показал большим пальцем на своём мизинце самую маленькую часть (Гоголь 3). "This time," said Chichikov, "I haven't lied even that much," and he pointed with his thumb to the tip of his little finger (3a).

С-599 • ИДТИ́ ⟨СЛЕ́ДОВАТЬ⟩/ПОЙТИ́ ПО СТО-ПА́М *чьим, кого lit;* **ИДТИ́/ПОЙТИ́ ПО СЛЕДА́М** [VP; subj: human] to follow after s.o. in doing sth., looking to him as an example: X пошёл по стопам Y-а ≃ **X followed in the footsteps of Y ⟨in Y's footsteps⟩; X followed Y's example ⟨lead⟩; X followed suit.**

Я невольно увлекался его [Володиными] страстями; но был слишком горд, чтобы идти по его следам, и слишком молод и несамостоятелен, чтобы избрать новую дорогу (Толстой 2). I involuntarily got drawn into his [Volodya's] crazes; but I was too proud to follow in his footsteps and too young and dependent to choose a new path for myself (2a). ♦ «Ваша выходка напоминает каннибальское времяпровождение нашего старичья! Я уверен, что они даже в настоящую минуту дуют водку и занимаются расшибанием кому-нибудь головы в клубе — неужели вы хотите идти по стопам их!» (Салтыков-Щедрин 2). "Your disgraceful behaviour reminds me of the cannibal pastimes of our elders! I'm sure that even now, at this very moment, gentlemen, they're consuming gallons of vodka and having a fine time breaking the head of some poor devil at the club! Do you want to follow their example?" (2a).

С-600 • ПОВЕРГА́ТЬ/ПОВЕ́РГНУТЬ К СТОПА́М ⟨К НОГА́М⟩ *чьим* or *кого obs, lit* [VP; usu. this WO] **1.** ~ *кого* [subj: usu. human] to cause a person to become totally submissive to oneself or another; (of o.s.) to become totally submissive, and show homage to another: X поверг Y-а к своим стопам ≃ **X brought Y to X's feet;** ‖ X поверг себя к Z-овым стопам ≃ **X bowed down to Z; X prostrated himself before Z; X knelt before Z ⟨at Z's feet⟩.**

...[Ольга] любовалась, гордилась этим поверженным к ногам её, её же силою, человеком! (Гончаров 1). ...She [Olga] gazed with admiration and pride at this man whom she brought to her feet by her own power (1b).

2. ~ *что* [subj: human or collect] to present sth. to s.o. as a sign of one's dependence on or submissiveness to that person, or as an offering when requesting sth. of that person: X поверг Y к ногам Z-а ≃ **X laid Y at Z's feet;** [in refer. to a banner, standard etc] **X lowered Y at Z's feet.**

Когда на бале Кутузов, по старой екатерининской привычке, при входе государя в бальную залу велел к ногам его повергнуть взятые знамёна, государь неприятно поморщился и проговорил слова, в которых некоторые слышали: «старый комедиант» (Толстой 7). When, in accordance with the custom of Catherine's time, Kutuzov ordered the captured standards to be lowered at the Emperor's feet as he entered the ballroom, the Emperor made a wry face and muttered something, which some people understood as "the old comedian" (7a).

С-601 • ПРИПАДА́ТЬ/ПРИПА́СТЬ К СТОПА́М *чьим, кого obs, elev* [VP; subj: human] to implore, beg s.o. for sth. humbly: X припал к стопам Y-а ≃ **X fell ⟨threw himself⟩ at Y's feet; X prostrated himself before Y.**

С-602 • ОБОРО́ТНАЯ ⟨ОБРА́ТНАЯ, ДРУГА́Я⟩ СТО-РОНА́ МЕДА́ЛИ [NP; sing only; usu. obj or subj; fixed WO] the opposite, usu. negative, darker side of sth.: **the other ⟨the flip⟩ side of the coin.**

«Чему же верить? Первой ли легенде — порыву ли высокого благородства, отдающего последние средства для жизни и преклоняющегося пред добродетелью, или оборотной стороне медали, столь отвратительной?» (Достоевский 2). "What are we to believe, then? The first legend—the impulse of a lofty nobility giving its last worldly means and bowing down before virtue, or the other side of the coin, which is so repugnant?" (2a).

С-603 • ЗЕВА́ТЬ ПО СТОРОНА́М *coll* [VP; subj: human] to stare with a blank expression (at s.o. or sth., or randomly): X зевает по сторонам ≃ **X gawks ⟨gapes⟩ at s.o. ⟨at sth., all over the place etc⟩; X stands around ⟨sits there etc⟩ gaping ⟨gawking⟩.**

...На седьмом году правления Фердыщенку смутил бес... Начал требовать, чтоб обыватели по сторонам не зевали, а смотрели в оба... (Салтыков-Щедрин 1). ...In the seventh year of his administration Ferdyshchenko was troubled by a demon....He began to demand that the townsfolk not stand around gaping but keep their eyes peeled... (1a).

С-604 • СМОТРЕ́ТЬ ⟨ГЛЯДЕ́ТЬ, ОЗИРА́ТЬСЯ и т. п.⟩ ПО СТОРОНА́М [VP; subj: human] to glance around, look at what surrounds one: X глядел по сторонам ≃ **X gazed about; X looked (a)round (in all directions); [in limited contexts] X was rubbernecking.**

...Слобода безмолвствовала, словно вымерла. Вырывались откуда-то вздохи, но таинственность, с которою они выходили из невидимых организмов, ещё более раздражала огорчённого градоначальника. «Где они, бестии, вздыхают?» — неистовствовал он, безнадёжно озираясь по сторонам... (Салтыков-Щедрин 1). ...The settlement lay silent, as if deserted. There were breathing sounds coming from somewhere, but the mysterious way they issued from unseen bodies irritated the chagrined governor still more. "Where are they breathing, the rogues?" he raged, gazing hopelessly about... (1a). ...The suburb was silent as the dead. From somewhere came a sound of sighing, but the mysterious way in which these sighs escaped from unseen beings increased still more the annoyance of the exasperated town-governor. "Where are these swine who are sighing?" he raged, looking hopelessly round in all directions... (1b). ♦ «...Посмотри-ка по сторонам. Ничего не замечаешь?» Пробкин тут же и увидел «скорую помощь» у грязного забора. «Опять она?» — «Вот именно...» (Аксёнов 12). "Just look around. Notice anything?" Probkin immediately saw the "ambulance" by the dirty fence. "Again?" "Precisely" (12a).

С-605 • В СТОРОНЕ́ [PrepP; Invar] **1.** ~ *(от кого-чего)* [adv or Prep (the resulting PrepP is adv)] at a relatively small distance away (from s.o. or sth.), somewhat set apart (from s.o. or sth.): **some distance away (from); (off ⟨away⟩) to one side; somewhat removed (from).**

В стороне от дома был небольшой сарай. There was a small barn some distance away from the house. ♦ Вернулся... старик Мочёнкин, стоял в стороне хмурый, строго наблюдал (Аксёнов 3). Old Mochenkin returned....Standing to one side, he frowned and observed everything with a critical eye (3a). ♦ Она понимала, почему брат хочет устроить её возле печи. Тут теплее и в стороне (Абрамов 1). She understood why her brother wanted to get her settled in beside the stove. It was warmer there, and somewhat removed (1a).

2. [adv or subj-compl with copula (subj: concr)] sth. is located far off, in a distant, isolated place: **in a remote place; in a secluded spot; far away from everything.**

Постоялый двор... находился в стороне, в степи, далече от всякого селения... (Пушкин 2). This wayside inn...was in a remote place, in the middle of the steppe, far from any habitation... (2a).

3. ~ (от кого) **держаться** и т. п. [the resulting PrepP is subj-compl with copula (subj: human or animal)] (to remain) separate, isolated from others, not (to associate) with others: X держится в стороне (от Y-ов) ≃ **X keeps his distance (from Ys); X remains ⟨holds himself⟩ aloof (from Ys).**

Я с самого начала говорил, что революция достигает чего-нибудь нужного, если совершается в сердцах, а не на стогнах. Но уж раз начали без меня – я не мог быть в стороне от тех, кто начал (Ерофеев 1). From the very first, I said that revolution achieves something essential when it occurs in the heart and not in the town square. But once they began it without me, I could not remain aloof from those who began it (1a).

4. ~ (от кого-чего) **держаться, стоять, оставаться** и т. п. Also: **В СТОРО́НКЕ** coll [the resulting PrepP is subj-compl with copula (subj: human)] (to remain) uninvolved with s.o. or in sth., not to participate in sth.: X остаётся в стороне ≃ **X stays ⟨remains⟩ on the sidelines; X keeps ⟨stays⟩ out of it;** [in limited contexts] **X remains aloof.**

«Я на тебя всё взваливаю, взваливаю, а сам... в сторонке, ты одна обязана колотиться» (Распутин 2). "I keep heaping things on you and then I remain on the sidelines, leaving you to struggle with all the responsibility" (2a). ♦ «Я вообще считаю, что военных надо держать в стороне. Глупо с ними советоваться» (Эренбург 4). "...As a general rule, my opinion is that military men must be kept out of it. It's folly to take their advice" (4a). ♦ Я подозреваю, что мужу её [княгини], мирному абхазскому князю, приходилось терпеть более грубые формы её деспотического темперамента. Так что он на всякий случай старался держаться в сторонке (Искандер 3). [context transl] I suspect that her [the princess's] husband, a peaceable Abkhazian prince, was forced to bear cruder expressions of her despotic temperament. So, just in case, he tried to keep out of range (3a).

5. ~ **оставаться, оказываться** и т. п. Also: **В СТОРО́НКЕ** coll [subj-compl with copula (subj: abstr or human)] (to be) disregarded, unnoticed, not included: X остался в стороне ≃ **X was ignored ⟨passed over, left out⟩.**

«О редкостях [в статье] расписали много, а работа коллектива библиотеки осталась в стороне» (Домбровский 1). "A great deal was said [in the article] about rare books but all the library staff's good work was ignored" (1a). ♦ «Когда я была на заводе, я это почувствовала... Они могут нас считать своими, любить, баловать, но вот придёт минута, и мы окажемся в сторонке» (Эренбург 4). "When I was at the factory, I had this feeling. I thought: 'They may consider us to be on their side, they may like us and spoil us, but there'll come a moment when we'll find ourselves left out'" (4a).

С-606 • НА СТОРОНЕ́ [PrepP; Invar] **1.** ~ чьей, кого-чего [the resulting PrepP is subj-compl with copula (subj: abstr)] sth. works for or is to the advantage of s.o. or sth.: X на стороне Y-a ≃ **X is on Y's side ⟨the side of Y⟩; X is in Y's favor;** [of power, the advantage in sth. etc] **Y has X.**

Я думал, что все права не только юридические, но и моральные настолько на моей стороне, что меня сразу же все поддержат... (Войнович 3). I thought that all rights, not only legal, but moral, were so much on my side that I would be given immediate support... (3a). ♦ К середине матча стало ясно, что перевес на нашей стороне. Toward halftime it became obvious that things were in our favor. ♦ ...Ни один из его клевретов – ни Бунина, ни Кулешов, ни Козловский – не подняли руку в его защиту. Почему? А потому что своя рубашка ближе к телу. Они за уважаемого только до тех пор, пока сила на его стороне (Войнович 3). ...Not one of his minions – not Bunina, not Kuleshov, not Kozlovsky – raised a hand in his defense. Why not? Why, because charity begins at home. They were for their respected colleague only as long as he had the power (3a).

2. ~ чьей, кого-чего [subj-compl with copula (subj: human or collect) or adv] one supports s.o. or sth., expresses his solidarity with s.o.: X на стороне Y-a ≃ **X is on Y's side ⟨the side of**

Y⟩; **X is ⟨stands⟩ behind Y; X has taken Y's side ⟨the side of Y⟩.**

Собрание в основном было на моей стороне... (Войнович 3). The assembly was basically on my side (3a). ♦ Гассенди был всей душой на стороне гениального физика Галилея, которого заставили... отречься от его убеждения, что Земля движется (Булгаков 5). Gassendi was heart and soul behind the brilliant physicist Galileo, who had been compelled...to renounce his conviction that the earth moved (5a).

3. ~ **работать, делать** что [adv] (to do sth.) not where one is supposed or expected to do it, but somewhere else (may refer to moonlighting, extramarital affairs etc): **on the side; elsewhere; away from home ⟨from s.o.⟩; somewhere (else).**

Слух ходит, что ты какими-то тёмными делишками на стороне занимаешься (Зиновьев 1). "There are rumours that you've got yourself involved in some dirty little deals on the side" (1a). ♦ ...Она [труппа] однажды явилась во главе с Шарлем Лагранжем и сообщила Мольеру, что ввиду того, что он соединяет с необыкновенными способностями честность и приятное обращение, труппа просит его не беспокоиться: актёры не уйдут искать счастья на стороне, какие бы выгодные предложения им ни делали (Булгаков 5). ...One day his [Molière's] players came to him, headed by Charles La Grange, and assured him that, in view of his fairness and kindness, as well as his extraordinary talents, he had nothing to worry about—they would not leave to seek their fortunes elsewhere no matter how tempting the offers they received (5a). ♦ [Бакченин:] Дети растут на стороне — по сути дела чужие... [Панова:] [В.:] The children are growing up away from me—are actually strangers to me... (1a). ♦ [Ксения:] Чего я от него [Егора] не терпела! Дочь прижил на стороне да посадил на мою шею (Горький 2). [К.:] The things I've had to stand from him! Brought in a bastard daughter from somewhere and burdened me with her (2b).

С-607 • ОСТАВЛЯ́ТЬ/ОСТА́ВИТЬ В СТОРОНЕ́ что [VP; subj: human; fixed WO] not to pay attention to or remark upon sth. (usu. sth. offensive): X оставил Y в стороне ≃ **X let Y pass ⟨go⟩; X disregarded ⟨ignored⟩ Y.**

С-608 • ОБХОДИ́ТЬ/ОБОЙТИ́ СТОРОНО́Й ⟨СТО-РО́НКОЙ⟩ кого-что [VP] **1.** [subj: human or collect] intentionally not to come into contact with some person or go to some place: X обходит Y-a стороной ≃ **X avoids Y; X gives a wide berth to Y.**

Оплакивая погибшие шестидесятые, он блуждал по остаткам декады и дом своего старого друга старался обходить стороной (Аксёнов 6). Lamenting the lost sixties, he had wandered among the remnants of the decade and tried to avoid the house of his old friend (6a).

2. [subj: usu. abstr] not to affect, touch, have an impact on s.o. or sth.: X обошёл Y-a стороной ≃ **X passed Y by;** ‖ Neg X не обошёл Y-a стороной ≃ [in limited contexts] **X left its mark on Y.**

«А тут на днях налог принесли». – «Налог?» — Михаил озадаченно посмотрел на мать. До сих пор налоги обходили их стороной (Абрамов 1). "Then there's that tax thing they brought around the other day." "Taxes?" Mikhail gave his mother a puzzled look. So far, taxes had passed them by (1a). ♦ Новое гуманистическое время не обошло стороной и ипподромный верзошник [slang = уборная]: кабинки спилили чуть ли не до пупа... (Аксёнов 6). The new age of humanism has also left its mark on the men's room at the racetrack: The cubicle walls have been sawn off almost down to navel height... (6a).

С-609 • БРАТЬ/ВЗЯТЬ ⟨ПРИНИМА́ТЬ/ПРИНЯ́ТЬ⟩ СТО́РОНУ чью, кого-чего; **СТАНОВИ́ТЬСЯ/СТАТЬ ⟨ВСТАВА́ТЬ/ВСТАТЬ⟩ НА СТО́РОНУ** [VP; subj and indir obj: human or collect] to support s.o. (or some group), express one's solidarity with s.o.: X взял сторону Y-a ≃ **X took Y's side ⟨the side of Y⟩; X sided with Y; X backed Y up; X stood up alongside Y; X stood by Y; X defended Y; X stood up for Y; X made common cause with Y.**

...Он с самого начала подозревал, что Надька примет сторону Евдокимова (Ерофеев 3). ...He had expected from the start that Nadya would take Evdokimov's side (3a). ♦ ...Слуга Григорий, мрачный, глупый и упрямый резонёр, ненавидевший прежнюю барыню Аделаиду Ивановну, на этот раз взял сторону новой барыни, защищал и бранился за неё с Фёдором Павловичем почти непозволительным для слуги образом (Достоевский 1). ...The servant Grigory, a gloomy, stupid, and obstinate pedant, who had hated his former mistress, Adelaida Ivanovna, this time took the side of the new mistress, defended her, and abused Fyodor Pavlovich because of her in a manner hardly befitting a servant... (1a). ♦ «...Жалкая кучка его [подсудимого] приспешников не решилась открыто встать на его сторону» (Войнович 4). "...His [the defendant's] pitiful band of cohorts could not bring themselves to stand up alongside him" (4a). ♦ [author's usage] ...В сущности виконт готов был стать на сторону какого угодно убеждения или догмата, если имел в виду, что за это ему перепадёт лишний четвертак (Салтыков-Щедрин 1). ...In actuality the Vicomte was ready to defend any conviction or dogma whatsoever if he thought it might bring him an extra twenty-five kopecks (1a).

C-610 • В СТО́РОНУ [PrepP; Invar] **1.** ~ *кого-чего, чью* [Prep; the resulting PrepP is adv] facing, moving, pointing etc toward s.o. or sth.: **in the direction of s.o. ⟨sth.⟩; in s.o.'s direction; toward s.o. ⟨sth.⟩; s.o.'s way; (look) at s.o. ⟨sth.⟩;** [in limited contexts] **face sth.**

Капарин глянул в сторону... Фомина и Чумакова... (Шолохов 5). Kaparin glanced in the direction of Fomin and Chumakov (5a). ♦ Дети её, милые дети, обнимали меня, целовали и плакали. И только мой старик не посмотрел на меня, и я старался не смотреть в его сторону... (Искандер 3). Her children, sweet children, hugged me, kissed me, and cried. Only my old man didn't look at me, and I tried not to look in his direction... (3a). ♦ Близился полдень, и пахарь уже настораживал слух в сторону дома, что вот-вот жена его должна позвать обедать, да и быкам пора передохнуть (Искандер 4). It was getting near noon, and the plowman had an ear cocked toward the house: any minute now his wife would be calling him to dinner, and besides it was time to rest the oxen (4a). ♦ ...[Юра] даже не смотрел в сторону мясного... (Аксёнов 1). Yura...hadn't even looked at the meat dish... (1a).

2. ~ *от кого-чего* [Prep; the resulting PrepP is adv] in a direction leading from s.o. or sth.: **away from s.o. ⟨sth.⟩.**

Тропинка вела в сторону от дома. The path led away from the house.

3. отойти, отозвать *кого и т. п.* ~ [adv] (to step, move etc) a short distance away (from some person, group etc), (to ask s.o. to move) a short distance away (from the person or group he is with, usu. so one can talk to him): **(move ⟨step, pull s.o., call s.o.** etc⟩) **aside.**

...Из куреня прибежала Лукинична... Она отозвала мужа в сторону. «Наталья пришла!..» (Шолохов 2). ...Lukinichna came running from the house....She called her husband aside. "Natalya has come back!..." (2a). ♦ Отзови директора в сторону и скажи ему об аварии. Pull the director aside and tell him about the accident.

4. (уходить, отходить) ~ [adv or predic (subj: human)] to avoid taking responsibility for or participating in sth.: X (уходит) в сторону ≃ **X steps ⟨moves⟩ aside (from sth.);** [in limited contexts] **X stands aside (from sth.); X moves ⟨fades⟩ into the background.**

В той ситуации, которая складывалась тогда во всех социально значимых сферах нашей жизни, чётко обозначились два лагеря. Один лагерь составляли мракобесы и реакционеры... Другой лагерь составляли все те, кто был против мракобесов и реакционеров... И были ещё единицы, которые с самого начала понимали: надо уйти от всего этого в сторону... (Зиновьев 1). In the situation at that time in all socially significant spheres of our life, two camps could be clearly distinguished. One of them consisted of obscurantists and reactionaries....The other camp was made up of all those who were against obscurantists and reactionaries....And there were, too, some isolated beings who had realised from the very beginning that they must stand aside from all this... (1a).

5. [predic; impers] one neglects to do or avoids doing sth. for a time: **put sth. off; hold off on sth.**

Нина всё время по танцулькам бегает, а учёбу — в сторону. Nina's always going out dancing, and as for her studies—she puts them off.

6. [predic; impers] doing sth. or s.o.'s involvement with sth. should be stopped: **away with...; no more...; that's enough...**

[Глумов:] Эпиграммы в сторону! Этот род поэзии, кроме вреда, ничего не приносит автору (Островский 9). [G.:] Away with epigrams! That kind of poetry brings nothing but trouble to the author (9a).

7. (сказать, произнести) ~ [adv] (to say sth.) turning away from one's listener so that he does not hear: **aside; (make) an aside.**

[Городничий:] Я карт и в руки никогда не брал; даже не знаю, как играть в эти карты... Как можно, чтобы такое драгоценное время убивать на них. [Лука Лукич (в сторону):] А у меня, подлец, выпонтировал вчера сто рублей (Гоголь 4). [Mayor:] I've never touched a card in my life; I don't even know how those card-games are played....How can people waste such valuable time on them? [L.L. (aside):] Cad! He won a hundred roubles off me yesterday (4b).

8. уводить (разговор), отвлекаться, уходить ~ [adv] to digress in conversation: X ушёл в сторону ≃ **X got off the subject; X went ⟨got⟩ off on a tangent; X strayed from the point ⟨the subject⟩; X got off (the) track; X got sidetracked.**

Простите, мы, кажется, отвлекаемся в сторону (Зиновьев 1). "Forgive me, we seem to be getting off the subject" (1a). ♦ Эти встречи я мог бы описать по записям очень подробно, но тем ушёл бы в сторону, да наверно это уже сделали или сделают другие, без меня (Солженицын 2). [context transl] I could give a very detailed description of these meetings from my notes, but that would be a digression, and in any case, others have probably done it already, or will do it (2a).

C-611 • ДЕРЖА́ТЬ СТО́РОНУ ⟨РУ́КУ *obs*⟩ *чью, кого* [VP; subj: human or collect] to be s.o.'s supporter, share s.o.'s views, express one's solidarity with s.o.: X держал сторону Y-a ≃ **X was on Y's side ⟨the side of Y⟩; X took Y's side; X supported Y ⟨Y's side⟩; X sided with Y; X backed Y (up); X stood by Y; X was for Y.**

Дмитрий Алексеевич и не подозревал того, что майор Бадьин на процессе всё время держал его сторону и даже написал по делу особое мнение (Дудинцев 1). Lopatkin had never dreamed that during his trial Major Badyin had been on his side the whole time, and had even written a dissenting opinion about the case (1a). ♦ Всегда тёща держала его сторону в спорах с женой, и кормила хорошо, и внуков приучала уважать батьку (Аксёнов 10). His mother-in-law had always taken his side in quarrels with his wife, fed him well too, and taught her grandsons to respect Dad (10a). ♦ Из двенадцати [членов правления] сторону Иванько с самого начала активно держали четверо... (Войнович 3). Of the twelve [members of the board], four actively supported Ivanko's side from the very beginning... (3a). ♦ Степан Андреянович [Лизку] не обманет... всегда во всяком деле держал её сторону (Абрамов 1). Stepan Andreyanovich would not deceive her [Lizka]....He had always stood by her in everything (1a). ♦ [Глаголев 1:] Крестьяне держали сторону генерала, а мы...сторону Василия Андреича [Платонова]... (Чехов 1). [G. Sr.:] The villagers on the jury backed the general, and the rest of us…were for old Mr. Platonov (1b).

C-612 • НА́ СТО́РОНУ [PrepP; Invar; adv] **1. работать ~** *obs* (to work) for, under someone else: **on the side; elsewhere; away from home.**

2. продавать, сбывать что ~ *coll* (to sell sth.) illegally, outside of authorized channels: **on the side; under the counter ⟨the table⟩; [in limited contexts] on the black market.**

Директора магазина давно подозревали в том, что часть товаров он сбывает на сторону. They have suspected for a long time that the store manager has been selling some goods on the side.

C-613 • СМОТРЕ́ТЬ НА́ СТО́РОНУ *coll* [VP; subj: human, more often male] to seek out extramarital affairs: X смотрит на сторону ≃ X has a roving ⟨wandering⟩ eye; [in limited contexts] X tomcats around.

C-614 • ТЯНУ́ТЬ СТО́РОНУ ⟨РУ́КУ obs⟩ чью, кого *coll* [VP; subj: human or collect] to support s.o., share s.o.'s views, express one's solidarity with s.o.: X тянет сторону Y-а ≃ X is on Y's side ⟨on the side of Y⟩; X takes Y's side; X sides with Y; X backs Y (up).

C-615 • НА ВСЕ ЧЕТЫ́РЕ СТО́РОНЫ идти, убираться, отпустить кого и т. п. *coll* [PrepP; Invar; adv; fixed WO] (to go, let s.o. go etc) to any place that one or s.o. desires: **anywhere one ⟨s.o.⟩ likes; wherever one ⟨s.o.⟩ wishes ⟨wants, chooses, pleases etc⟩;** ‖ *Imper* катись на все четыре стороны *rude* ≃ **get the hell out of here; go wherever you damn well please.**

«Ступай себе на все четыре стороны и делай что хочешь. Завтра приходи со мною проститься, а теперь ступай себе спать…» (Пушкин 2). "Go wherever you want, and do what you like. Come and say good-bye tomorrow; and now go to bed…" (2a). ♦ Оправдают их присяжные – бог с ними совсем, пусть идут на все четыре стороны (Герцен 3). If the jury acquit them, we have nothing more to say to them; let them go wherever they choose (3a). ♦ Мне позвонили из отдела прозы журнала, чтоб я быстро, не мешкая, забрал свой роман «Ленинский проспект» и катился на все четыре стороны (Свирский 1). I got a phone call from the prose department to ask me to come around quickly and retrieve the manuscript of my novel *Leninsky Prospekt* and then get the hell out of there (1a).

C-616 • С ОДНО́Й СТОРОНЫ́… С ДРУГО́Й СТО-РОНЫ́ ⟨С ДРУГО́Й⟩ [these forms only; sent adv (parenth); fixed WO] used in contrasting two facts, phenomena etc: **on the one hand…on the other (hand).**

Чтоб это [впечатление, которое произвёл Чичиков на дам,] сколько-нибудь изъяснить, следовало бы сказать многое о самих дамах, об их обществе, описать, как говорится, живыми красками их душевные качества; но для автора это очень трудно. С одной стороны, останавливает его неограниченное почтение к супругам сановников, а с другой стороны… с другой стороны, просто трудно (Гоголь 3). In order to explain it [the impression Chichikov made upon the ladies] to any extent it would be necessary to say a great deal about the ladies themselves, about their social life – to describe, as they say, in vivid colors their spiritual endowments; but this is very difficult for the author. On the one hand he is restrained by his boundless respect for the wives of high officials; on the other hand – it is simply too difficult (3c).

C-617 • СО ⟨С obs⟩ СВОЕ́Й СТОРОНЫ́ [PrepP; these forms only; sent adv (parenth); fixed WO] as regards one's participation in sth., contribution to sth., opinion etc: **for one's part; as ⟨so⟩ far as one is concerned.**

По прибытии нашем в роту нас медленно ощупывали, заранее стараясь определить, какое количество жизненных благ можно от нас получить… Мы, со своей стороны, тоже зондировали почву… (Лившиц 1). When one of us arrived in the company, they mentally felt us over, trying to predetermine the number of earthly blessings which they could extract from us.…For our part we also explored the ground… (1a). ♦ «Я, с своей стороны, принял себе за правило: быть справедливым – и больше ничего!» (Салтыков-Щедрин 2). "So far as I'm concerned, I've made it a strict rule to be just and nothing more" (2a).

C-618 • СО СТОРОНЫ́ [PrepP; Invar] **1. ~ кого-чего** [Prep; the resulting PrepP is adv] moving, coming, or issuing from some person, place, location etc: **from the direction of.**

Ему в голову не могло прийти, что у них гости и что ржание коня доносится со стороны микулицынского крыльца, из сада (Пастернак 1). It never occurred to him that they had guests or that the neighing came from the direction of Mikulitsyn's house (1a).

2. ~ смотреть, наблюдать, видно и т. п. [adv] (to look at s.o. or sth., be visible etc) from some distance away: **from a distance.**

На солнечном пригреве, на камне, ниже садовой скамейки, сидел Костоглотов… И даже не видно было со стороны, чтобы плечи его поднимались и опускались от дыхания (Солженицын 10). Kostoglotov was sitting in a sunny spot on a stone below a garden bench.…From a distance one could not even see his shoulders rising and falling as he breathed… (10a).

3. ~ смотреть (на кого-что), судить, казаться и т. п. [adv] (to look at, judge etc s.o. or sth.) from the point of view of one who is not directly involved in the matter at hand, (to appear a certain way) to s.o. who is not directly involved in the matter at hand: **(look at s.o. ⟨sth.⟩) from the outside; from an outsider's perspective ⟨point of view⟩; from an outside viewpoint; (as) seen from the outside; [in limited contexts] as an outsider; to an outsider ⟨a bystander⟩ (sth. might look ⟨seem etc⟩); (view sth.) with (great) detachment; (take) a detached view.**

Конечно, обидно: маловато успел. Со стороны может показаться, что вовсе не так. Я и то, и это, пятое, десятое. Но уж я-то знаю, что чепуха (Трифонов 5). It was humiliating, of course. I had accomplished very little. From an outsider's point of view it might not appear that way. I've done this, that, and a number of things. But I myself know how little it has all amounted to (5a). ♦ В том-то и дело, что если рассказать с некоторой правдивостью любую жизнь со стороны и хотя бы отчасти изнутри, то картинка наша будет такова, что этот человек дальше жить не имеет ни малейшей возможности (Битов 2). That's just the point, that if we tell the story of any life with a degree of truthfulness, from an outside viewpoint and at least partially from within, then the picture will be such that the man hasn't the slightest chance of living on (2a). ♦ …Она [жена Огарёва] сама сказала мне впоследствии, что сцена эта показалась ей натянутой, детской. Оно, пожалуй, и могло так показаться со стороны; но зачем же она смотрела со стороны?.. (Герцен 2). …She [Ogaryov's wife] told me herself afterwards that this scene had struck her as affected and childish. Of course it might strike one so looking on at it as an outsider, but why was she looking on at it as an outsider? (2a). ♦ Шли они [Костенко и Росляков] не быстро и не медленно, весело о чём-то разговаривали, заигрывали с девушками… Со стороны могло показаться, что два бездельника просто-напросто убивают время (Семёнов 1). They [Kostyenko and Roslyakov] walked neither quickly nor slowly, talking gaily about something, flirting with the girls.…To a bystander they might have looked like a couple of idlers simply killing time (1a). ♦ Он [Эренбург] на всё смотрел как бы со стороны – что ему оставалось делать после «Молитвы о России»? – и прятался в ироническое всепонимание (Мандельштам 2). He [Ehrenburg] seemed to view everything with great detachment – what else could he do after his *Prayer for Russia*? – and took refuge in a kind of ironical knowingness (2a).

4. человек, люди и т. п. ~ [nonagreeing postmodif] a person (or people) not belonging to the group, organization etc in question: **from ⟨on⟩ the outside; outsider(s).**

[666]

«Какая баба!.. Ей бы и быть председателем. И на хрена нам кого-то со стороны искать» (Абрамов 1). "What a woman!... If only she could be Chairwoman, and the hell with searching for one on the outside" (1a). ♦ В деревне не хватало мужчин, и председателю пришлось нанять рабочих со стороны. There weren't enough men in the village, so the chairman had to hire outsiders.

5. ~ *кого, чьей* [Prep; the resulting PrepP is adv] used to denote a person or group of people with whom an action or statement originates: **for ⟨on⟩ s.o.'s part; on the part of; [in limited contexts] of s.o.; by s.o.**

[Бутон:] Так что вы говорите, милостивый государь? Что наш король есть самый лучший, самый блестящий король во всём мире? С моей стороны возражений нет (Булгаков 8). [B.:] So what are you saying, dear sir? That our king is the very best, the most brilliant king in the whole world? For my part I have no objections (8a). ♦ ...Тут было много и простодушия со стороны Мити, ибо при всех пороках своих это был очень простодушный человек (Достоевский 1). ...There was much simple-heartedness on Mitya's part, for with all his vices this was a very simple-hearted man (1a). ♦ «Да где ж это видано, чтобы народ сам по себе собирался без всякого контроля со стороны руководства?» (Войнович 2). "Who ever heard of people assembling all by themselves, without any control on the part of the leadership?" (2a). ♦ «...Примите в соображение, что ошибка возможна ведь только со стороны первого разряда, то есть „обыкновенных" людей...» (Достоевский 3). "...You must take into consideration the fact that a mistake can be made only by a member of the first class, that is, by the 'ordinary' people..." (3a).

6. ~ *кого, чьей* [Prep; the resulting PrepP is adv] used to denote a person or group of people whose action, behavior, statement etc is characterized or evaluated: **(how generous ⟨it's not nice, that's not fair etc⟩) of s.o. (to do sth.).**

Это очень плохо с его стороны — оставить нас наедине. Никогда не ожидал я от него такого предательства! (Казаков 2). That's not nice of him—to leave us alone. I never expected such treachery from him (2a). ♦ «Ну вот видишь, вот уж и нечестно с твоей стороны: слово дал, да и на попятный двор» (Гоголь 3). "There, you see, that's not fair of you: you have given me your word of honor, and now you are going back on it" (3c).

7. ~ *чего, какой* [Prep; the resulting PrepP is adv] in a certain respect (as specified by the context): **from the standpoint ⟨the vantage point⟩ of; from the point of view of; from a [AdjP] standpoint ⟨point of view⟩.**

«Стригуны» молчали; они понимали, что слова Собачкина очень последовательны и что со стороны логики под них нельзя иголки подточить (Салтыков-Щедрин 2). The "colts" were silent; for they realized that Sobachkin's words were very logical and that, from the point of view of pure logic, they were absolutely unassailable (2a).

8. ~ *кого, чьей, какой* [Prep; the resulting PrepP is adv] used to indicate a line of familial descent: **on (one's ⟨the⟩ father's ⟨mother's, husband's, wife's etc⟩) side.**

Юный негодяй был влюблён в княгиню и тоже торчал у неё день и ночь, кажется, на правах соседа или дальнего родственника со стороны мужа (Искандер 3). The young reprobate was in love with the princess and had also been hanging around her day and night, exercising his rights as a neighbor, I believe, or a distant relative on the husband's side (3a).

С-619 • НЕ СТОЯ́ТЬ/НЕ ПОСТОЯ́ТЬ за ценой, за деньгами и т. п. *coll* [VP; subj: human; most often pfv fut] to be willing to pay generously for sth.: X за ценой ⟨за деньгами⟩ не постоит ≃ **money ⟨price⟩ is no object with X; X won't quibble ⟨argue⟩ over the price (of sth.); X will spare no expense; X will pay anything (for sth.).**

«...А за деньгами он не постоит. — Коровьев оглянулся, а затем шепнул на ухо председателю: — Миллионер!» (Булгаков 9) "Money's no object with him." Koroviev looked around, then whispered into the chairman's ear, "A millionaire!" (9a). ♦ «Значит, он миллионер?» — «Во всяком случае, за расходами не стоит» (Войнович 3). "Then he's a millionaire?" "At any rate, he doesn't spare expense" (3a).

С-620 • СТОЯ́ТЬ ВЫ́ШЕ [VP; subj: human; fixed WO] **1.** ~ *кого* to surpass s.o. (in achievements, abilities etc): X стоит выше Y-а ≃ **X is superior to Y; X is better than Y (in sth.); X outclasses Y.**

Он [Володя] во всём стоял выше меня: в забавах, в учении, в ссорах, в умении держать себя... (Толстой 2). He [Volodya] was superior to me in everything: in games, in studies, in quarrels, and in his ability to comport himself well... (2b).

2. ~ *чего.* Also: **СТАТЬ ВЫ́ШЕ** to ignore sth. (usu. sth. petty, banal), considering it unworthy of one's attention: X стоит выше Y-а ≃ **X is ⟨rises⟩ above Y; Y is beneath X.**

...Перед лицом смерти надо стать выше всяких обид (Рыбаков 1). ...In the face of death you have to be able to rise above any grudge (1a). ♦ [Филипп:] Ты знаешь, Ал... Когда истина открыта не нами, она что-то теряет из своей привлекательности. [Алекс:] Фил, надо стать выше этого! (Солженицын 11). [Ph.:] You know, Al....When truth is discovered by someone else, it loses something of its attractiveness. [A:] Phil, you need to rise above that! (11a).

С-621 • СТОЯ́ТЬ НАВЫ́ТЯЖКУ [VP; subj: human] to stand very straight with one's hands at one's sides: X стоял навытяжку ≃ **X stood at attention.**

С-622 • НА СТРА́ЖЕ стоять, быть₀ и т. п.; **НА СТРА́ЖУ** встать, стать [PrepP; these forms only; subj-compl with copula (subj: human or collect); usu. this WO] **1.** (to be, start etc) guarding s.o. or sth. (in a physical sense), watching to be sure that he or it is not harmed, stolen etc: X стоит на страже ≃ **X is on guard; X is on guard ⟨sentry⟩ duty; X is standing guard ⟨sentry⟩.**

2. ~ *чего elev, occas. iron* (to be, start etc) protecting, securing sth. (some cause, idea, one's or s.o.'s interests etc): X стоит на страже Y-а ≃ **X stands guard over (the interests of) Y; X (safe)guards (the interests of) Y.**

Можно сказать, что в поведении Камуга с женой стихийно, в зачаточной форме проявилась идея диктатуры пролетариата, стоящего на страже интересов трудящейся земли (Искандер 5). You might say that Kamug's behavior toward his wife exhibited in elemental, rudimentary form the idea of the dictatorship of the proletariat, standing guard over the interests of the toiling earth (5a). ♦ Господин Альфред Ней сейчас выполняет ещё более высокую работу: как солдат Великой Армии, среди этой дикой страны, он стоит на страже прекрасной Франции! (Эренбург 2) M. Alfred Ney was doing even finer work. Here, in this savage country, he was safeguarding the interests of his beautiful France, like a soldier of the Grande Armée (2a).

С-623 • ПОД СТРА́ЖЕЙ ⟨ПОД КАРАУ́ЛОМ *obs*⟩ находиться, содержаться, быть₀, держать *кого* [PrepP; these forms only; subj-compl with copula (subj: human) or obj-compl with держать (obj: human)] (to be) imprisoned, (to keep s.o.) in confinement: X находится ⟨X-а держат⟩ под стражей ≃ **X has been placed ⟨is being held⟩ under arrest; X has been placed ⟨is being kept⟩ under guard; X is (being held) in custody; person Y has got ⟨is keeping⟩ X locked up; X has been locked up.**

«В настоящее время преступник захвачен и содержится под стражей...» (Войнович 4). "At the present time, the criminal has been captured and is being held under arrest..." (4a). ♦ Перед отправкой арестованных в гостиницу «Метрополь», где они должны были содержаться под стражей, Алексеев с глазу на глаз о чём-то в течение двадцати минут беседовал с Корниловым… (Шолохов 3). Before sending them [the arrestees] to the Hotel Metropole, where they were to be kept under guard, Alexeyev spoke confidentially with Kornilov for about twenty minutes (3a). ♦ «Скажи, братец, какую девушку держишь ты у себя под караулом?» (Пушкин 2). "Tell me, brother, who is this young girl you've got locked up here?" (2b).

C-624 • БРАТЬ/ВЗЯТЬ ПОД СТРА́ЖУ ⟨ПОД КАРА́УЛ *obs*⟩ *кого* [VP; subj: human; often 3rd pers pl with indef. refer.; usu. this WO] to incarcerate s.o.: X-а взяли под стражу ≃ **X was taken into custody; X was arrested ⟨apprehended⟩; X was placed under guard.**

Когда Садчикову рассказали про звонок из прокуратуры — требуют взять под стражу Лёньку Самсонова, — он хлопнул по столу папкой так, что подскочила телефонная трубка (Семёнов 1). When Sadchikov was told about the call from the Public Prosecutor's office and the demand that Lyonka Samsonov be taken into custody, he banged his desk with a file so hard that the telephone receiver fell off (1a). ♦ Неделю назад был взят под стражу третий бухгалтер, когда обнаружилось, что из сейфа исчезло сто тысяч рублей (Искандер 5). The third bookkeeper had been taken into custody a week ago, after the discovery that a hundred thousand rubles had disappeared from the safe (5a).

C-625 • ВПИСА́ТЬ НО́ВУЮ СТРАНИ́ЦУ *во что lit or media* [VP; subj: human or abstr; usu. this WO] to discover or accomplish sth. outstanding (in some area of life, field of science, or branch of culture): X вписал новую страницу в Y ≃ **X wrote a new page ⟨chapter⟩ in Y; X broke new ground in Y.**

C-626 • ОТКРЫВА́ТЬ/ОТКРЫ́ТЬ НО́ВУЮ СТРАНИ́ЦУ *в чём lit or media* [VP; subj: human or abstr; usu. this WO] to start a new trend, movement, school of thought etc in some area or field: X открыл новую страницу в Y-е ≃ **X opened a new page ⟨chapter⟩ in Y.**

Я часто наводил разговор на «Господина из Сан-Франциско», желая как можно больше услышать от Бунина о том, как и почему написан им этот необыкновенный рассказ, открывший — по моему мнению — совершенно новую страницу в истории русской литературы… (Катаев 3). I often worked the conversation round to *The Gentleman from San Francisco* because I wanted to hear as much as possible from Bunin about how and why he had written this amazing story, in my opinion opening an entirely new page in the history of Russian literature… (3a).

C-627 • НА СВОЙ ⟨СО́БСТВЕННЫЙ⟩ СТРАХ И РИСК *coll;* **НА СВОЙ ⟨СО́БСТВЕННЫЙ⟩ СТРАХ** *obs* [PrepP; these forms only; adv; usu. this WO] (to do sth. that involves risk, danger, the possibility of negative repercussions for o.s. etc) taking full responsibility for the outcome upon o.s.: **at one's own risk.**

…Беспрерывно отгибая вниз непослушную манишку, [Паниковский] поведал Балаганову о серьёзнейшем опыте, который он проделал на свой страх и риск (Ильф и Петров 2). …Incessantly straightening out his recalcitrant dickey, [Panikovsky] told Balaganov of an important experiment he had carried out at his own risk (2a).

C-628 • НЕ ЗА СТРАХ, А ЗА СО́ВЕСТЬ *работать, трудиться, служить* и т. п. [PrepP; Invar; adv; more often used with impfv verbs; fixed WO] (to work, labor etc) applying all one's energy to what one is doing; (to serve) loyally and well: **with total dedication ⟨devotion⟩; with a strong sense of duty; very conscientiously;** [often ironic] **with zeal.**

…Оказавшись наверху… [Кублицкий-Пиоттух] стал исполнять свой долг не за страх, а за совесть… (Аксёнов 7). Once in office…he [Kublitsky-Piottukh] set about fulfilling his obligations with a strong sense of duty… (7a).

C-629 • СТРА́ХА РА́ДИ ИУДЕ́ЙСКА *lit* [PrepP; Invar; adv; fixed WO] (to do sth.) with a servile attitude, driven by one's fear of the authorities, of those in a position to affect one's destiny: **out of fear of the powers that be.**

Если и был он [психоневролог] осведомителем КГБ, может быть, ещё с лагеря, то «страха ради иудейска»… (Амальрик 1). If he [the psychoneurologist] was a KGB informer—and perhaps he had been since his days in camp—it was out of fear of the powers that be (1a).

< From the Biblical account of Joseph of Arimathea, who "for fear of the Jews" hid the fact that he was a disciple of Jesus (John 19:38).

C-630 • У СТРА́ХА ГЛАЗА́ ВЕЛИКИ́ [saying] when a person fears sth., he imagines there is danger where, in reality, there is none: ≃ **the eyes of fear see danger everywhere; the fear's greater than the reason for it; fear closes the ears of the mind; fear always exaggerates (things).**

Стаднюк встретил его [Игоря] радушно… А ещё совсем недавно… всего час назад, замышлял ему здесь разнос. «Впрочем, — мелькнуло у Игоря, — у страха глаза велики. Замышлял ли?» (Ерофеев 3). Stadniuk had given him [Igor] a cordial reception.…And to think that just a little while ago, not more than an hour ago, he had expected Stadniuk to really give it to him. They do say that fear always exaggerates, thought Igor. Maybe I just imagined it all? (3a).

C-631 • В СТРА́ХЕ (БО́ЖИЕМ *or* **БО́ЖЬЕМ)** *держать, воспитывать кого* и т. п. [PrepP; these forms only; adv; fixed WO] (to keep, raise s.o.) in a state of total submission by punishing him severely without cause and/or making him deathly afraid of punishment: X держал Y-а ~ ≃ **X put the fear of God in ⟨into⟩ Y;** ∥ X воспитывал Y-а ~ ≃ **X brought Y up in the fear of God.**

Жену он держал в страхе Божьем… (Максимов 1). He put the fear of God into his wife… (1a). ♦ «Вот об этой-то последней, *пьяной*, рюмке [водки] и намерен я беседовать с вами. Где, в каком притоне… человек находит сию пагубную для него рюмку? Дома он не найдёт её, ибо здесь его остановит заботливая рука жены, умоляющие взоры воспитанных в страхе божием детей…» (Салтыков-Щедрин 2). "It is about this last, *drunken*, glass that I intended to talk to you now. Where, in what den of iniquity…does a man find this last fatal glass? He will not find it at home, for there the solicitous hand of his wife will stop him, not to mention the imploring eyes of his children, brought up in the fear of God…" (2a).

C-632 • ПОД СТРА́ХОМ *чего* [PrepP; Invar; the resulting PrepP is adv] at the risk of incurring a specified penalty: **under (the) threat of; on ⟨under⟩ pain of.**

Ему [Марку Крысобою] прокуратор приказал сдать преступника начальнику тайной службы и при этом передать ему распоряжение прокуратора о том, чтобы… команде тайной службы было под страхом тяжкой кары запрещено о чём бы то ни было разговаривать с Иешуа или отвечать на какие-либо его вопросы (Булгаков 9). He [Mark Rat-Killer] was ordered by the Procurator to turn the criminal over to the chief of the secret service, and to relay the Procurator's command that…the soldiers of the secret service detachment be forbidden, under threat of severe punishment, to speak with Yeshua about anything, or to answer any of his questions (9a). ♦ …Если ребята под страхом расстрела искали в лесу бомбы и гранаты, под угрозой расстрела приносили их в гетто, то, как вы понимаете, не для игр они это делали (Рыбаков 1). If the children had gone in search of bombs [and grenades] in the woods on pain of shooting, and had brought them back into the ghetto, also on pain of shooting, you can be sure it wasn't because they were playing games (1a).

C-633 • ДАВА́ТЬ/ДАТЬ ⟨ЗАДАВА́ТЬ/ЗАДА́ТЬ⟩ СТРЕКАЧА́ ⟨СТРЕЧКА́⟩ *highly coll, usu. humor* [VP; subj: human or animal; more often pfv] to run away quickly (usu. in order to escape danger, pursuit etc): X дал стрекача ≃ **X took to his heels (out of some place); X made tracks; X made off; X bolted (from some place); X hightailed it; X made a run for it; X beat a hasty retreat;** [in limited contexts] **X gave s.o. the slip.**

Александр Иванович не стал мешкать, бросил прощальный взгляд на потрескавшийся фундамент электростанции… и задал стрекача (Ильф и Петров 2). Alexander Ivanovich lost no time, cast a farewell glance at the crumbling foundation of the electric power station…and took to his heels (2b). ♦ То, что жеребёнок наклонился к гусыне, страшно не понравилось одному гусаку. Гусак, вытянув шею, как змея, ринулся на жеребёнка. Бедняга от неожиданности так перепугался, что вспрыгнул на месте на всех четырёх ногах, а потом развернулся и дал стрекача к матери (Искандер 3). There was one gander who was greatly displeased that the colt bent down to the goose. Stretching its neck like a snake, the gander charged at the colt. The poor thing took such a fright that he leapt up with all four feet off the ground, and then turned and bolted for his mother (3a). ♦ Видно, пока головорез Теймыр возился с этой полонянкой… девушки успели далеко уйти или вообще дали стрекача (Искандер 5). While the cutthroat Temyr fussed around with this first captive…the girls had evidently walked way ahead or given him the slip completely (5a).

C-634 • СТРЕ́ЛОЧНИК ВИНОВА́Т; ВСЕГДА́ ВИНОВА́Т СТРЕ́ЛОЧНИК *both coll* [sent (with быть∅)] (said with sarcasm) when sth. ends in failure, meets with difficulties etc, it is (always) someone occupying a low position who gets blamed: **the little guy ⟨man⟩ (always) gets the blame; they (always) blame the little guy ⟨man⟩.**

C-635 • СТРО́ИТЬ ИЗ СЕБЯ́ *кого-что coll, usu. disapprov* [VP; subj: human] to try to make others perceive one in a certain way (which is usu. contrary to, or does not reflect, one's true nature, character): X строит из себя Y-а ≃ **X poses ⟨tries to pose⟩ as Y; X makes himself out to be Y; X tries to pass for Y; X passes ⟨tries to pass⟩ himself off as Y.**

[Платонов:] Я пропадаю, совсем пропадаю, моя дорогая! Угрызения совести, тоска, хандра… [Анна Петровна:] Не терплю я этих романических героев! Что вы строите из себя, Платонов?.. Хандра, тоска, борьба страстей… (Чехов 1). [P.:] I'm going completely to the dogs, darling, what with my pangs of conscience, misery, depressions…. [A.P.:] I loathe these romantic heroes. What are you trying to pose as?…Depression, misery, the battleground of passions… (1b).

C-636 • ВВОДИ́ТЬ/ВВЕСТИ́ В СТРОЙ *что offic, media* [VP; subj: human; obj: usu. a noun denoting an industrial unit; often 3rd pers pl with indef. refer.] to make sth. functional, operational: X-ы ввели в строй Y ≃ **Xs put Y into operation ⟨into service⟩; Xs put Y in commission.**

Новую гидроэлектростанцию ввели в строй два месяца назад. The new hydroelectric power plant was put into service two months ago.

C-637 • ВСТУПА́ТЬ/ВСТУПИ́ТЬ ⟨ВХОДИ́ТЬ/ВОЙТИ́⟩ В СТРОЙ *offic, media* [VP; subj: usu. a noun denoting an industrial unit] to become functional, operational: X вступил в строй ≃ **X was put into operation ⟨into service⟩; X went into operation.**

C-638 • ПРОГОНЯ́ТЬ/ПРОГНА́ТЬ СКВОЗЬ СТРОЙ *кого obs* [VP; subj: human; often 3rd pers pl with indef. refer.] (in refer. to a form of punishment in the Imperial army) to make an offender pass between two columns of soldiers who beat him with

sticks: X-а прогнали сквозь строй ≃ **X was made to ⟨had to⟩ run the gauntlet.**

Военный суд приговорил его [Полежаева] прогнать сквозь строй; приговор послали к государю на утверждение (Герцен 1). The court-martial condemned him [Polezhayev] to run the gauntlet; the sentence was despatched to the Tsar for confirmation (1a).

C-639 • ЧИТА́ТЬ/ПРОЧИТА́ТЬ МЕЖДУ СТРОК ⟨СТРО́ЧЕК, СТРОКА́МИ, СТРО́ЧКАМИ⟩ [VP; subj: human; more often impfv; fixed WO] to (be able to) deduce the underlying meaning of what s.o. says by guessing at what has not been directly expressed: X читал между строк ≃ **X read between the lines.**

Написанные четыре года назад к другу, который понимает и читает между строк, эти слова, брошенные в открытый, бурный, жадный мир, часто не понимавший и не желавший понять, летели назад, в другом звучании, в искажённом значении… (Аллилуева 2). Written four years earlier to a friend who knew how to read between the lines, these words, flung into a wide-open, wild, greedy world, which often could not or did not wish to understand, were flying back at me with a different sound, a distorted meaning… (2a).

C-640 • ПРИКА́ЗНАЯ СТРОКА́ *obs, derog* [NP; sing only; fixed WO] a petty bureaucrat: **pettifogger.**

C-641 • НЕ В СТРО́КУ (отвечать, говорить и т. п.) *obs* [PrepP; Invar; adv or subj-compl with copula (subj: всё, слова etc)] (to say sth., give an answer that is etc) inappropriate, inopportune, irrelevant: **off the point; out of place.**

C-642 • ВЫВОДИ́ТЬ/ВЫ́ВЕСТИ ИЗ СТРО́Я *кого-что* [VP; if obj: human, subj is usu. abstr (болезнь, неудача etc) or concr (пуля, мина etc); if obj: concr (завод, станок etc), subj is usu. human or abstr; more often pfv] to render s.o. or sth. unable to carry out his or its function (in refer. to a person—unable to work or serve in the military; in refer. to a factory, machine etc—inoperative): X вывел Y-а из строя ≃ **X put Y out of commission ⟨action⟩; X disabled ⟨incapacitated, sidelined⟩ person Y; X put thing Y out of operation.**

…Одно только никак не укладывалось у Лёши в голове — зачем отцу нужно было выводить из строя эту самую печь? Неужели он думал, что вместе с этой печью рухнет всё советское государство? (Войнович 2). …There was just one thing Lyosha found difficult to accept—why had his father wanted to put that particular furnace out of commission? Could he really have thought the loss of this one furnace would cause the entire Soviet state to collapse? (2a). ♦ …Ничтожный осколок вывел его [фон Шенау] из строя, и сразу лазареты, лечебницы, курорты, консилиумы… (Федин 1). …A mere splinter had put him [von Schönau] out of action, and right away sick-bays, hospitals, resorts, consultations… (1a). ♦ Вратарь, единственный из всех, охал по поводу того, что ранение вывело его из строя (Гроссман 2). The goalkeeper was the only one to complain about being temporarily disabled (2a).

C-643 • ВЫХОДИ́ТЬ/ВЫ́ЙТИ ⟨ВЫБЫВА́ТЬ/ВЫ́БЫТЬ⟩ ИЗ СТРО́Я [VP; subj: human or concr (завод, станок etc)] to become unable to carry out one's or its function (of a person—unable to work or serve in the military; of a factory, machine etc—inoperative): X вышел из строя ≃ **X was (put) out of commission ⟨action⟩; person X became disabled ⟨incapacitated⟩; person X was sidelined; thing X stopped functioning ⟨working⟩; thing X ground to a halt;** [in limited contexts] **thing X broke down; thing X was ⟨went⟩ on the blink.**

«Председателю должны были сказать вы, а вы ему не сказали, и в результате аппарат вышел из строя» (Рыбаков 2).

"You were the one who ought to have told the manager, but you didn't, and as a result the machine is out of action" (2a). ♦ Возможно, она [княгиня] его [юного негодяя] не прогоняла, потому что он подхлёстывал дядю Сандро на всё новые и новые любовные подвиги. А может, она его держала при себе на случай, если дядя Сандро внезапно выйдет из строя (Искандер 3). Possibly she [the princess] refrained from banishing him [the young reprobate] because he spurred Uncle Sandro to ever more inventive feats of love. Or perhaps she kept him around just in case Uncle Sandro suddenly became disabled (3a). ♦ За двадцать лет редеют леса, оскудевает почва. Самый лучший дом требует ремонта. Турбины выходят из строя (Трифонов 5). In twenty years forests thin out and the soil becomes depleted. Even the best house requires repairs. Turbines stop functioning (5a). ♦ Я думаю, если дело протянулось бы несколько дольше и вся тюрьма включилась бы в эту работу, то советская бюрократическая машина просто вышла бы из строя... (Буковский 1). I think that if the business had continued a little longer and involved everyone in the prison, the Soviet bureaucratic machine would have simply ground to a halt... (1a).

С-644 • СНИМА́ТЬ/СНЯТЬ СТРУ́ЖКУ *с кого highly coll* [VP; subj: human] to reprimand, criticize, scold s.o. severely: X снимет с Y-а стружку ≃ **X will give Y a dressing-down ⟨a talking-to, the business, a hard time⟩; X will bawl ⟨chew⟩ Y out.** Cf. **read s.o. the riot act.**

«Комендант прикатил, стружку за план снимать будет» (Максимов 2). "The commandant's arrived. He's come to give me a hard time because we're behind with the delivery plan" (2a).

С-645 • СЛА́БАЯ СТРУНА́ ⟨СТРУ́НКА⟩ *чья, кого* [NP; fixed WO] the most vulnerable part of a person's character, a sensitivity or character flaw that can easily be used by another to his own advantage: **a ⟨s.o.'s, one's⟩ weak ⟨vulnerable⟩ spot; a ⟨s.o.'s, one's⟩ weakness; a ⟨s.o.'s, one's⟩ foible;** [in limited contexts] **a ⟨the⟩ chink in s.o.'s ⟨one's⟩ armor;** ‖ играть на слабых струнах *чьих, кого* ≃ **play on s.o.'s weaknesses.**

Он довольно остёр; эпиграммы его часто забавны, но никогда не бывают метки и злы: он никого не убьёт одним словом; он не знает людей и их слабых струн... (Лермонтов 1). He is rather witty and his epigrams are frequently amusing but never pointed or malicious; he does not annihilate a person with one word. He knows neither people nor their foibles... (1b).

С-646 • В СТРУНЕ́ *держать кого coll* [PrepP; Invar; objcompl with держать (obj: human)] (to be) strict with, impose strict rules of conduct on s.o. (or o.s.): X держит Y-а ⟨себя⟩ ~ ≃ **X keeps a tight rein on Y ⟨on himself⟩; X keeps Y ⟨himself⟩ in check ⟨in line⟩; X keeps Y ⟨himself⟩ in hand.**

[Аркадина:] Я, милая, держу себя в струне, как говорится, и всегда одета и причёсана *comme il faut* (Чехов 6). [A.:] Yes, my dear, I keep myself in hand, as they say. I'm always dressed, and my hair is always *comme il faut* (6a).

С-647 • ХОДИ́ТЬ ПО СТРУ́НКЕ ⟨В СТРУ́НКУ *obs*⟩ *(у кого, перед кем);* **ХОДИ́ТЬ ПО НИ́ТОЧКЕ** *(у кого) all coll* [VP; subj: human] to obey some person fully and unquestioningly (usu. because one fears him) or to obey the rules at some place fully and unquestioningly (usu. because one is afraid of the superior, supervisor etc and the possible negative consequences of unacceptable behavior): X (у Y-а) по струнке ходит ≃ **(with ⟨for⟩ Y,) X toes the line ⟨the mark⟩; X is on his best behavior (with ⟨for⟩ Y);** [in limited contexts] **X is at Y's beck and call.**

[Буланов:] Я вам не Раиса Павловна; у меня все по струнке будете ходить, а то и марш со двора (Островский 7). [B.:] I am not like Raisa Pavlovna; with me you will all have to toe the mark or get fired (7a). ♦ «Вот Наталья Афанасьевна, дай ей бог всего хорошего, моего Ванюшку согласилась у себя поместить...» — «Будет шалить вместе с Владей, — угрюмо сказал Пере-

донов — ещё дом сожгут». — «Не посмеет! — решительно крикнул Мурин. — Вы, матушка Наталья Афанасьевна, за это не беспокойтесь: он у вас по струнке будет ходить» (Сологуб 1). "Natal'ya Afanas'evna, God bless her, has agreed to room my Vaniushka...." "He'll get into trouble with Vladya, and they'll burn the house down," said Peredonov morosely. "He wouldn't dare!" declared Murin with conviction. "Don't you worry about that, my dear Natal'ya Afanas'evna. He'll be on his best behavior" (1a). ♦ «Прошу покорно, Ольга, девочка! По ниточке, бывало, ходила. Что с ней?» (Гончаров 1). "A child, if you please, a little girl who used to be at my beck and call! What is the matter with her?" (1b).

С-648 • В СТРУ́НКУ ⟨В СТРУ́НУ⟩ *вытянуться, выпрямиться и т. п.* [PrepP; these forms only; adv] **1.** (of a person) (to assume) the posture of attention: **(come ⟨snap⟩) to attention; (stand) at attention.**

...Когда подъехали к остановке и дверь растворилась, я не удержался и спросил ещё раз, у одного из выходящих, спросил: «Это Усад, да?» А он (совсем неожиданно) вытянулся передо мной в струнку и рявкнул: «Никак нет!!» (Ерофеев 1). ...As we were approaching another stop and the doors started to open, I couldn't resist, and again asked one of the passengers getting off: "This is Usad, right?" And (quite unexpectedly) he snapped to attention in front of me and bellowed: "No, sir!" (1a). ♦ ...Указывая Пфейферше на вытянувшихся в струнку пожарных и полицейских солдат... [Грустилов] сказал: «Видя внезапное сих людей усердие, я в точности познал, сколь быстрое имеет действие сия вещь, которую вы, сударыня моя, внутренним словом справедливо именуете» (Салтыков-Щедрин 1). He [Melancholov] pointed out the policemen and firemen standing at attention...and said to Mme Pfeifer, "When I saw the unexpected zeal of these men, I knew precisely how rapid an effect there would be from this thing which you, madam, have justly named the inner word" (1a).

2. (of an animal running fast) (to run straight ahead,) one's body appearing to be stretched out parallel to the ground: **(run) flat-out.**

С-649 • ЗАДЕВА́ТЬ/ЗАДЕ́ТЬ ⟨(ЗА)ТРО́НУТЬ⟩ (ЗА) ЧУВСТВИ́ТЕЛЬНУЮ ⟨БОЛЬНУ́Ю⟩ СТРУНУ́ *(чью, кого) obsoles* [VP; subj: human or abstr] to mention (usu. in conversation) a topic or issue that is particularly sensitive and painful for s.o.: X задел больную струну Y-а ≃ **X struck a sensitive chord; X touched ⟨hit⟩ a ⟨Y's⟩ sore spot; X struck ⟨hit⟩ a nerve.**

С-650 • ВЛИВА́ТЬ/ВЛИТЬ ⟨ВНОСИ́ТЬ/ВНЕСТИ́⟩ ЖИВУ́Ю ⟨СВЕ́ЖУЮ⟩ СТРУЮ́ *во что lit or media* [VP; subj: abstr or human; usu. pfv] to enliven sth., make it more interesting: X внёс свежую струю в Y ≃ **X breathed new life into Y; X livened up Y.**

С-651 • СИДЕ́ТЬ МЕЖДУ ДВУХ СТУ́ЛЬЕВ ⟨МЕЖДУ ДВУМЯ́ СТУ́ЛЬЯМИ⟩ *disapprov* [VP; subj: human; often infin with нельзя] to be in a state of indecision, unable or unwilling to make a choice (often in refer. to choosing a side, point of view etc; in political contexts, usu. refers to unprincipled behavior): X сидит между двух стульев ≃ **X is sitting on the fence;** [in limited contexts] **X is a fence-sitter.**

«Этот случай должен показать, что нельзя быть двуликим Янусом и сидеть между двух стульев» (Эткинд 1). "This case should be a lesson to us that one must not act like a two-faced Janus, sitting on the fence..." (1a).

С-652 • СТЫД НЕ ДЫМ, ГЛАЗА́ НЕ ВЫ́ЕСТ [saying] shame can be endured and does no lasting harm: ≃ **a little shame won't hurt you.**

Ни вероисповедания, ни образа правления эти племена не имели... Заключали союзы, объявляли войны, мирились, клялись друг другу в дружбе и верности, когда же лгали, то прибавляли «да будет мне стыдно», и были наперёд уверены, что «стыд глаза не выест» (Салтыков-Щедрин 1). These tribes had neither religion nor any form of government....They concluded alliances, declared wars, made peace, swore friendship and fidelity to one another, and when they lied they added, "Shame on me!" and were sure ahead of time that "a little shame won't hurt you" (1a).

C-653 • **НИ СТЫДА́ НИ СО́ВЕСТИ НЕТ** *у кого, в ком coll, disapprov;* **НЕТ СТЫДА́ В ГЛАЗА́Х** *у кого obs, substand, disapprov* [VP$_{subj/gen}$; pres only; fixed WO (1st var.), fixed WO with нет movable (2nd var.)] s.o. conducts himself dishonorably and feels and/or exhibits no remorse: ни стыда ни совести у Х-а нет ≃ **X has no conscience (at all); has X ⟨have you⟩ no shame (at all)?; X should ⟨ought to⟩ be ashamed of himself.**

[Угаров:] Анна Васильевна, голубушка! Спаси. Дай три рубля до завтра. [Васюта *(быстро)*:] Нет, нет. Не дам. Ни стыда у вас, ни совести! (Вампилов 1). [U.:] Anna Vasilyevna, dear Anna Vasilyevna! Save us. Lend us three rubles till tomorrow. [V. *(quickly)*:] Oh no. Nothing doing. Have you no shame at all? (1a).

C-654 • **СГОРА́ТЬ/СГОРЕ́ТЬ СО ⟨ОТ⟩ СТЫДА́** *coll* [VP; subj: human; often impfv Verbal Adv сгорая; if pfv—often subjunctive or past with чуть не] to experience intense shame, embarrassment: X сгорал со стыда ≃ **X was burning (up) with shame; X was dying ⟨nearly died⟩ of shame; X was embarrassed to death; X was bitterly ashamed of himself.**

[extended usage] Зина повела его [пса] гулять на цепи... Пёс шёл как арестант, сгорая от стыда... (Булгаков 11). Zina took him [the dog] walking on the chain....He walked like a convict, burning up with shame (11a). ♦ [Иванов:] Перед тобою стоит человек, в тридцать пять лет уже утомлённый, разочарованный, раздавленный своими ничтожными подвигами; он сгорает со стыда... (Чехов 4). [I.:] You see a man exhausted at the age of thirty-five, disillusioned, crushed by his own pathetic efforts, bitterly ashamed of himself... (4b).

C-655 • **К СТЫДУ́ СВОЕМУ́ ⟨МОЕМУ́ и т. п.⟩** [these forms only; sent adv (parenth)] used to express dissatisfaction with one's own or another's blameworthy behavior or actions: **to my ⟨his etc⟩ shame ⟨embarrassment, chagrin⟩; [in limited contexts] I'm ⟨he was etc⟩ ashamed ⟨embarrassed⟩ to say...**

К стыду своему, я всё ещё не умею плавать. I'm ashamed to say that I still don't know how to swim.

C-656 • **ПОКА́ СУД ДА ДЕ́ЛО** *coll* [subord clause; Invar; fixed WO] while sth. is happening, until such time as circumstances clarify themselves, in the intervening time: **in the meantime; while ⟨until⟩ things sort themselves out; while this is (still) in the works; while this is (still) going on; meanwhile; [in limited contexts] for the time being.**

«Захватишь узлы, и вот что, Филат, присматривай тут [за домом], пожалуйста, пока суд да дело» (Пастернак 1). "Take the bundles over. And keep an eye on the house, Filat, until things sort themselves out" (1a). ♦ [Кот:] Умоляю вас — вызовите его [дракона] на бой. Он, конечно, убьёт вас, но пока суд да дело, можно будет помечтать перед очагом, о том, как случайно или чудом, так или сяк, не тем, так этим, может быть, как-нибудь, а вдруг и вы его убьёте (Шварц 2). [Cat:] Do challenge him [the Dragon], I implore you. He will kill you, of course, but while it's all going on I shall be able to dream in front of the fire of how, perchance, by some accident or some miracle, in this way or that way, somehow or other, you might kill him (2b). ♦ «Донат! Донат! Вещи снеси вот, пока суд да дело, в пассажирский зал, в ожидальную» (Пастернак 1). "Donat! Donat! Take these things into the waiting room for the time being" (1a).

C-657 • **ШЕМЯ́КИН СУД** [NP; sing only; fixed WO] an unfair trial: **unjust ⟨biased⟩ trial.** Cf. **kangaroo court.**

< Apparently from *Shemyaka*, the name of an arbitrary and casuistic judge in a satirical old Russian tale.

C-658 • **НА НЕТ И СУДА́ НЕТ** [saying] used to express resignation to, but not dissatisfaction with, the absence of sth., s.o.'s refusal to do sth. etc: ≃ **if s.o. doesn't ⟨can't, hasn't etc⟩, then s.o. doesn't ⟨can't, hasn't etc⟩; if it hasn't come ⟨didn't happen etc⟩, it hasn't (come) ⟨didn't (happen)⟩ etc⟩; if that's the way it is ⟨s.o. feels about it etc⟩ then there's nothing to be done about it; so be it; what cannot be cured must be endured.**

[Кочкарёв:] Да ведь вы слышали, у ней приданого ничего нет. [Жевакин:] На нет и суда нет (Гоголь 1). [K.:] But you must have heard. She's got no dowry. [Zh.:] If she hasn't, then she hasn't (1a). ♦ «Сегодня вас не ждали, батюшка, говядинки не привезли», — промолвил Тимофеич... «И без говядинки обойдёмся, на нет и суда нет» (Тургенев 2). "They didn't expect you today, master, and the beef's not come," announced Timofeyich...."We'll manage without the beef, if it's not there, it's not" (2e).

C-659 • **СУДА́ НЕТ** *на кого* [VP; impers] **1.** *obs* it would be unfair to criticize s.o. for his actions (because, although in other cases such actions might be considered reprehensible, in this case the circumstances justify them): на Х-а суда нет ≃ **no one can blame X; who could blame X?**

2. *coll* [usu. Interj] used to express indignation at s.o. who acts disgracefully or contemptibly and deserves to be severely punished (yet manages to avoid punishment): суда на Х-а нет! ≃ **hanging's too good for X!**

«Марью опять муж бьёт! Суда на него нет, на пьяницу!» — кричала Вера. "Marya's husband is beating her again! Hanging's too good for that drunkard!" cried Vera.

C-660 • **СУДИ́ТЬ ДА ⟨И⟩ РЯДИ́ТЬ** *(о ком-чём);* **СУДИ́ТЬ-РЯДИ́ТЬ** *all old-fash, coll* [VP; subj: human, often pl] to discuss s.o. or sth. thoroughly, in detail: Х-ы судили да рядили ≃ **Xs were hashing and rehashing everything ⟨some question etc⟩; Xs were hashing ⟨thrashing⟩ things ⟨it⟩ out; Xs were talking it ⟨things, everything⟩ over; ‖ Х-ы судили и рядили об Y-е ≃ Xs were hashing out ⟨thrashing out, hashing and rehashing⟩ thing Y ⟨person Y's situation etc⟩; Xs were talking over thing Y ⟨person Y's behavior etc⟩.**

Лизка была в боковушке. Такой уж порядок: пока судят да рядят старшие, девка в стороне (Абрамов 1). Lizka was in the side room. That was the custom: while her elders were thrashing things out, the girl kept away to one side (1a).

C-661 • **СУ́ДЫ ДА ⟨И⟩ ПЕРЕСУ́ДЫ** *coll, disapprov* [NP; pl only; fixed WO] unkind talk or stories: **gossip and rumors.**

Ксана на приставания Иосифа не отвечала, но городок маленький, южный, всё на виду, все видят, как Иосиф вяжется к Ксане, и этот факт... даёт пищу судам и пересудам... (Рыбаков 1). [context transl] Ksana didn't respond to his passes, but it was a small town in the south, where everything is out in the open, everyone could see that Yosif was trying to get involved with her...giving ammunition for gossips and rumour-mongers... (1a).

C-662 • **НЕ СУДЬБА́** *(кому-чему)* [NP; subj-compl with быть₀ (subj: infin, often omitted); usu. pres] fortune decrees that sth. is not to happen or be accomplished: не судьба Х-у делать Y ≃ **it is not destined that X do Y; it's not X's destiny ⟨fate⟩ to do Y; X is not destined ⟨fated⟩ to do Y; it is not (meant) to be; it is not in the cards; [when used without an infin, as an indep. remark] fate willed ⟨ordained⟩ otherwise.**

[Телегин:] Значит, Марина Тимофеевна, не судьба им жить тут. Не судьба... (Чехов 3). [T.:] It means, Marina Timofeevna, that it's not their fate to live here. Not their fate... (3d). ♦ «Всё кончено!» — отвечал я и отдал ей батюшкино письмо... Прочитав, она возвратила мне письмо дрожащею рукою и сказала дрожащим голосом: «Видно, мне не судьба... Родные ваши не хотят меня в свою семью» (Пушкин 2). "It's all over!" I answered, handing her my father's letter....Having read the letter, she returned it to me with a trembling hand and said in a faltering voice: "Evidently, fate has ordained otherwise....Your parents do not wish to receive me into their family" (2a).

C-663 • КАКИ́МИ СУДЬБА́МИ? *coll* [NP$_{instrum}$; Invar; usu. used as a formula phrase; fixed WO] (an exclamation made at an unexpected encounter) why are you here? —I am very surprised to see you: **what brings you here?; fancy meeting you here; what are you doing here?;** [in limited contexts] **how did you end up in our institute ⟨get on our team etc⟩?**

А хозяин уже спешил встретить гостя, источая... радуше и сердечность: «Пётр Васильевич! Какими судьбами?» (Максимов 3). His host was already hurrying to meet him, oozing cordiality. "Pyotr Vasilievich! What brings you here?" (3a). ♦ «Ба, ба, ба! — вскричал он вдруг, расставив обе руки при виде Чичикова. — Какими судьбами?» (Гоголь 3). "Hullo, hullo, hullo!" he exclaimed suddenly, flinging wide his arms at the sight of Chichikov. "Fancy meeting you here!" (3a). ♦ «А... Владимир Георгиевич, вы какими судьбами в наш взвод?» (Шолохов 3). "Ah, Vladimir Georgievich, how did you get into our platoon?" (3a).

C-664 • ОБИ́ЖЕННЫЙ ⟨ОБИ́ЖЕН, ОБОЙДЁН-НЫЙ⟩ СУДЬБО́Й [AdjP; modif (variants with long-form Part) or subj-compl with быть$_∅$, subj: human, pres or past (var. with short-form Part); usu. this WO (variants with long-form Part)] unlucky: **wronged by life; unfortunate.**

Какое ему было дело до этого дурацкого портфеля, до этого брошенного родителями мальчишки, племянника жены, если сам он был так обижен судьбой, если бог не дал ему сына собственного, своей крови, в то время как другим дарит детей щедро, без счёта?.. (Айтматов 1). What did he care about that stupid schoolbag, about that brat abandoned by his parents, when he himself was so wronged by life, when God didn't see fit to grant him a son of his own, his own flesh and blood, while others were blessed with all the children they could want (1a). ♦ Тётя Глаша, хоть и бедная и обиженная судьбой, никогда ничего у Нюры не просила и, наоборот, сама, как могла, старалась Нюру ободрить (Трифонов 5). Although she was poor and unfortunate, Aunt Glasha had never asked anything of Nyura, but on the contrary had herself tried as best she could to cheer Nyura up (5a).

C-665 • ИСКУША́ТЬ ⟨ИСПЫ́ТЫВАТЬ⟩ СУДЬБУ́ ⟨ПРОВИДЕ́НИЕ *lit*⟩ [VP; subj: human; often neg imper or infin with нельзя, не надо, не следует etc] to do sth. that seems or is excessively risky, likely to bring harm to oneself: X искушает судьбу ≃ **X tempts fate;** [in limited contexts] **X flies in the face of fortune ⟨providence⟩.**

«...Кажется (я боюсь искушать судьбу), кажется, мы попытаемся прилететь в Москву (во Внуково) в воскресенье 8-го» (Ивинская 1). "I think—I am afraid of tempting fate—I think we shall try to fly back to Moscow (Vnukovo) on Sunday the 8th" (1a).

C-666 • ОТ СУДЬБЫ́ НЕ УЙДЁШЬ [saying] you cannot avoid your destiny: ≃ **there's no escaping ⟨flying from⟩ fate; you can't escape your fate.**

[Василиса:] Убили! Мужа моего... вот кто убил! Васька убил! Я — видела!.. Что, Вася, мил друг? От судьбы — не уйдёшь... Полиция! Абрам... свисти! (Горький 3). [V.:] [He] killed him! Killed my husband....There's who did it! Vaska killed him! I saw it!...So, Vasya, honey? There's no escaping fate....Police! Abram...blow your whistle! (3a). ♦ [Агафья Тихоновна:] Везде, куды [*ungrammat* = куда] ни поворочусь, везде так вот и стоит Иван Кузьмич [Подколёсин]. Точно правда, что от судьбы никак уйти нельзя (Гоголь 1). [A.T.:] Wherever I turn I see Mr. Podkolyosin. How true it is that you can't escape your fate (1b).

C-667 • СУ́ДЯ ПО *чему* [Prep; Invar; the resulting PrepP is adv] on the basis of sth.: **judging by ⟨from⟩; by;** ‖ судя по всему ≃ **to ⟨from⟩ all appearances; (judging) by all appearances; apparently; by all indications.**

«Четверостишие принадлежит поэту Николаю Рубцову. Судя по почерку, переписано оно рукой мужчины» (Чернёнок 1). "The verse belongs to the poet Nikolai Rubtsov. Judging by the handwriting, it was copied by a man" (1a). ♦ «Тебе надо подкрепиться, судя по лицу-то. Сострадание ведь на тебя глядя берёт. Ведь ты и ночь не спал, я слышал, заседание у вас там было» (Достоевский 1). "By the looks of you, you need fortifying. What a sorry sight! You didn't sleep last night, so I hear, you had a meeting" (1a). ♦ ...По достоверным сведениям, красные никого из мирных жителей не трогали и, судя по всему, даже и не помышляли о мщении (Шолохов 5). ...According to reliable information the Reds had not touched any civilians and, to all appearances, had no vengeful intentions (5a). ♦ Там стояла табуретка, на ней — тазик с мутной водой и влажная тряпка, которой, судя по всему, мыли снаружи оконные стёкла (Чернёнок 1). There was a stool out there and on it a pan of murky water and a wet rag, which, apparently, was used for washing windows (1a). ♦ Дело в том, что дядя Сандро влюблён в невесту своего друга, и она, судя по всему, тоже в него влюблена (Искандер 5). The trouble is that Uncle Sandro is in love with his friend's bride, and by all indications she is in love with him too (5a).

C-668 • СУ́ДЯ ПО ТОМУ́ ЧТО [subord Conj; introduces a clause of reason] based on the fact that: **judging by ⟨from⟩ the fact that...; from the fact that...;** [in limited contexts] **judging from the way (s.o. did sth. ⟨sth. happened⟩).**

...Судя по тому, что он [Лакоба] и Сталин несколько раз бросали взгляд в его сторону, дядя Сандро, сладко замирая, почувствовал, что говорят о нём (Искандер 3). ...From the fact that he [Lakova] and Stalin glanced in his direction several times, Uncle Sandro sensed, with sweetly fluttering stomach, that they were talking about him (3a). ♦ Судя по тому, что Миха на лету ухватил мысль дяди Сандро, можно заключить, что он быстро одолел свою социальную тугоухость... (Искандер 3). Judging from the way Mikha seized Uncle Sandro's thought on the wing, we may conclude that he had quickly overcome his social deafness... (3a).

C-669 • СУЕТА́ СУЕ́Т (И ВСЯ́ЧЕСКАЯ СУЕТА́) *lit* [sent; often only the first half is used; fixed WO] the matter in question is totally insignificant, trivial, devoid of any value: **vanity of vanities (, all is vanity).**

«...Я скорее соглашусь, кажется, лаять на владыку, чем косо взглянуть на Кирила Петровича...» — «Суета сует, — сказал священник, — и Кирилу Петровичу отпоют вечную память, всё как ныне и Андрею Гавриловичу, разве похороны будут побогаче да гостей созовут побольше, а богу не всё ли равно!» (Пушкин 1). "For my part I'd sooner affront the bishop than look askance at Kirila Petrovich...." "Vanity of vanities," said the priest. "One day the burial service will be read over Kirila Petrovich, just as it was over Andrei Gavrilovich this morning; only perhaps the funeral will be more sumptuous and more people will be invited, but isn't it all the same to God?" (1a).

< From the Bible (Eccles. 1:2).

C-670 • РУБИ́ТЬ ⟨ПОДРУБА́ТЬ⟩ СУК, НА КОТО́-РОМ СИДИ́ШЬ *coll* [VP; subj: human; usu. 2nd or 3rd pers] to do sth. that will bring harm or trouble upon o.s.: X рубит сук, на котором сидит ≃ **X is cutting his own throat; X is sawing the branch he's sitting on;** [in limited contexts] **X is cutting off his nose to spite his face.**

[author's usage] Александр слышал наш спор. После работы он спросил меня: «А вы понимаете, что рубите ветку, на которой сидите? Начальство не любит, когда ему доказывают, что оно темнит и выдаёт говно за золото...» (Копелев 1). Aleksandr had overheard our argument. After work he asked me: "Do you realize that you're sawing the branch you're sitting on?

The bosses don't like to be shown that they're gold-bricking and passing shit off as gold" (1a).

С-671 • КЛАСТЬ/ПОЛОЖИ́ТЬ ПОД СУКНО́ *что,* usu. заявле́ние, про́сьбу, жа́лобу и т. п. [VP; subj: human] to postpone making a decision on some matter, not address or act on (an application, request, complaint etc): X положи́л Y под сукно́ ≃ **X shelved ⟨pigeonholed, tabled⟩ Y; X put Y in(to) cold storage; X put Y on the back burner.**

«Тала́нтливых учёных назнача́ть администра́торами с кру́пным окла́дом. Все без исключе́ния изобрете́ния принима́ть... и класть под сукно́. Ввести́ драко́новские нало́ги на ка́ждую това́рную и произво́дственную нови́нку...» (Струга́цкие 1). "Talented scientists should be turned into highly paid administrators. All inventions are to be accepted and then shelved....Draconic taxes should be extracted for all commercial or industrial innovations" (1a).

С-672 • ДЕРЖА́ТЬ ПОД СУКНО́М *что,* usu. заявле́ние, про́сьбу, жа́лобу и т. п. [VP; subj: human] to delay taking action on (an application, request, complaint etc): X де́ржит Y под сукно́м ≃ **X has shelved ⟨pigeonholed, tabled⟩ Y; X has ⟨is keeping⟩ Y in cold storage ⟨on the back burner⟩.**

«Почему́ вы кричи́те?» — «Потому́ что вы де́ржите моё заявле́ние под сукно́м уже́ бо́льше ме́сяца!» "Why are you yelling?" "Because you've had my application in cold storage for over a month now!"

С-673 • ЛЕЖА́ТЬ ПОД СУКНО́М [VP; subj: заявле́ние, про́сьба, жа́лоба etc] (of an application, request, complaint etc) not to be given any attention, not be processed: X лежи́т под сукно́м ≃ **X has been shelved ⟨pigeonholed, tabled⟩; X is (being kept) in cold storage ⟨on the back burner⟩.**

С-674 • СУМА́ ПЕРЕМЁТНАЯ *coll, derog* [NP; sing only; often subj-compl with copula, nom or instrum (subj: human) or appos] a person who easily changes his convictions, changes sides: **turncoat; double-crosser; (double-crossing) traitor.**

«Атама́ны-молодцы́! Где же я вам его́ [градонача́льника] возьму́, коли он на ключ за́перт!» — угова́ривал толпу́ объя́тый тре́петом чино́вник, вы́званный собы́тиями из администрати́вного оцепене́ния. — Но волне́ние не унима́лось. «Врёшь, перемётная сума́!» — отвеча́ла толпа́... (Салтыко́в-Щедри́н 1). "Chieftains, bold atamans—where shall I get him [the town governor] for you if he's all locked up!" The fear-stricken official, summoned by events from his administrative torpor, attempted to sway the multitude....But the agitation did not abate. "You lie, turncoat!" replied the crowd (1a). ♦ По лёгкой поспе́шности, с како́й майо́р не гля́дя наложи́л утверди́тельную резолю́цию, его́ [Фёдора] осени́ло, что тому́ о нём с Поли́ной давно́ всё изве́стно. «Но́сов, — запозда́ло догада́лся он, — сума́ перемётная!» (Макси́мов 1). The haste with which the major, without looking at him [Fyodor], wrote out a note expressing his agreement made him realize that he had long known all about Fyodor and Polina. "Nosov," he realized too late, "the double-crossing traitor!" (1a).

С-675 • КРУ́ГЛАЯ ⟨КРУ́ГЛЕНЬКАЯ⟩ СУ́ММА [NP; sing only] a large, significant amount (of money): **a tidy sum; a pretty penny; a small fortune.**

В профко́ме [институ́та] возни́кли тури́стские путёвки во Фра́нцию, оди́ннадцать дней, шесть дней Пари́ж, пять — Марсе́ль, Ни́цца и про́чее, мечта́ жи́зни сто́имостью в кру́гленькую су́мму (Три́фонов 3). The committee of the institute's staff association had been given a number of travel vouchers for a trip to France of eleven days, six in Paris and five in Marseilles, Nice, and so on—the dream of a lifetime, and costing a tidy sum (3a).

С-676 • В СУ́ММЕ [PrepP; Invar; adv or sent adv] when everything is added together: **altogether; all in all; in total.**

В су́мме у нас бы́ло о́коло пяти́ ты́сяч рубле́й. All in all we had about five thousand rubles.

С-677 • НИЧТО́ЖЕ СУМНЯ́ШЕСЯ ⟨СУМНЯ́СЯ⟩ *obs, lit; now iron or humor* [these forms only; adv or sent adv (parenth); fixed WO] (one does sth.) unhindered by doubts, with no reservations, without vacillating (occas. implies that the doer is not afraid of offending s.o., of doing sth. unethical etc): **without a moment's hesitation; without wavering.**

< From the Church Slavonic text of the Bible (James 1:6).

С-678 • ПОД СУРДИ́НКУ ⟨-ой *obs*⟩ *coll* [PrepP; Invar; adv] **1.** sounding at reduced volume: **mutedly; (sound) muted; softly; quietly; low.**

[author's usage] В ко́мнате послы́шалось храпе́нье, снача́ла ти́хое, как под сурди́ной, пото́м гро́мче... (Гончаро́в 1). Suddenly there was a sound of snoring in the room, at first gentle, as though muted, then growing louder... (1b).

2. covertly, clandestinely: **secretly; in secret; on the quiet ⟨q.t.⟩; quietly; on the sly.**

Обвенча́ться под сурди́нку в Москве́ бы́ло не легко́... (Ге́рцен 2). To marry on the quiet in Moscow was not easy... (2a). ♦ ...Ка́менскую трепа́ла прифронтова́я лихора́дка... В частя́х шли перевы́боры кома́ндного соста́ва. Под сурди́нку уезжа́ли из Ка́менской каза́ки, не жела́вшие войны́ (Шо́лохов 3). Kamenskaya was in a frontline fever of activity....New unit commanders were being elected. The Cossacks opposed to war were leaving quietly (3a).

С-679 • КАК СУРО́К спать [как + NP; nom only; adv] (to sleep) very soundly: **(sleep) like a log ⟨a baby⟩.**

Он шёл домо́й и, уходя́, спеши́л загляну́ть на больно́го [Раско́льникова]. Разуми́хин донёс ему́, что тот спит, как суро́к (Достое́вский 3). He was about to go home and was going to look in on the patient before he went. Razumikhin told him Raskolnikov was sleeping like a log (3b).

С-680 • ПО СУ́ТИ (ДЕ́ЛА) [PrepP; these forms only; sent adv (usu. parenth); fixed WO] **1.** if the basic aspects of the matter in question are considered: **in essence; essentially; in effect; to ⟨for⟩ all intents and purposes.**

«Кра́йне ва́жная зада́ча — практи́чески привле́чь рабо́чих к управле́нию [произво́дством]... Э́тому, по су́ти, посвящена́ и вся моя́ рабо́та» (Сви́рский 1). "The most important task we have is to find a practical way of involving the workers [in the management of production]....That essentially is what my work is all about..." (1a). ♦ Опроки́нулась теле́га рома́новской мона́рхии, зали́тая кро́вью и гря́зью... По су́ти э́то и есть нача́ло всео́бщей вели́кой гражда́нской войны́, к кото́рой мы призыва́ли... (Солжени́цын 5). Awash in blood and mud, the cart of the Romanov monarchy is overturned....This is in effect the beginning of that great universal civil war to which we have long summoned you... (5a).

2. in reality: **actually; in (actual) fact; in actuality; in point of fact; as a matter of fact.**

Ка́к-то смягчи́лся в па́мяти прокля́тый бесо́вский кот, не пуга́ла бо́лее отре́занная голова́, и, поки́нув мысль о ней, стал размышля́ть Ива́н о том, что, по су́ти де́ла, в кли́нике о́чень неплохо́, что Страви́нский у́мница и знамени́тость и что име́ть с ним де́ло чрезвыча́йно прия́тно (Булга́ков 9). The memory of the damned infernal tom had softened, the severed head no longer frightened him, and, abandoning his preoccupation with it, Ivan began to reflect that, actually, the hospital was not so bad, that Stravinsky was clever and famous, and extremely pleasant to deal with (9a).

С-681 • СУТЬ ДЕ́ЛА [NP; sing only; fixed WO] the main point, most important aspect etc of some matter: **the heart ⟨the crux, the essence, the gist⟩ of the matter.**

[Учёный:] Наконец-то мы подошли к самой сути дела (Шварц 3). [Scholar:] At last we've come to the real crux of the matter (3a). ♦ Поскольку здесь всего в избытке, то все потребности удовлетворяются, и… Вот в этом-то и состоит суть дела (Зиновьев 1). Since we have more than enough of everything, all needs are satisfied and….That is the essence of the matter (1a).

C-682 • БЕЗ СУЧКА́ БЕЗ ЗАДО́РИНКИ; БЕЗ (СУЧКА́ И) ЗАДО́РИНКИ

all coll [PrepP; these forms only; usu. adv; fixed WO] (sth. is carried out, proceeds etc) easily and smoothly, without complications, very well: **without a hitch; like clockwork.**

Не вернись я с юга – их [КГБ] операция прошла бы без задоринки… (Солженицын 2). If I hadn't come back from the south, their [the KGB's] operation would have gone off without a hitch (2a).

< From the speech of carpenters and joiners. «Задоринка» is a snag on the surface of a smoothly planed board.

C-683 • НИ СУЧКА́ НИ ЗАДО́РИНКИ

coll [NP_gen; Invar; usu. subj/gen or obj; when used in a чтоб(ы)-clause after a command, the clause functions as adv; fixed WO] (there is, to find etc) not a single mistake, imperfection (in sth.): **(there is) not a flaw; (it is) a flawless ⟨perfect⟩ job; (sth. is) flawless ⟨perfect⟩; (sth. is done) flawlessly ⟨perfectly, precisely as it should be done** etc⟩; [in refer. to the cleanliness of sth.] **(sth. is) spick-and-span.**

< See C-682.

C-684 • ПО СУЩЕСТВУ́

[PrepP; Invar] **1.** ~ говорить, замечание и т. п. [adv, nonagreeing modif, or subj-compl with copula (subj: критика, замечание etc)] (to say sth., a remark is etc) relevant, (to speak) relevantly: **to the point; pertinent(ly); germane(ly); (a comment ⟨question** etc⟩ **that) gets to the heart of the matter; apropos;** ‖ *Neg* не по существу ≃ **beside the point; off the subject.**

«Переживаете, да?.. Но ведь критика была по существу» (Аксёнов 1). "You're taking it hard, aren't you?…But the criticism was very much to the point" (1a).

2. Also: ПО СУЩЕСТВУ́ ГОВОРЯ́; В СУ́ЩНОСТИ (ГОВОРЯ́) [sent adv (parenth)] if the basic aspects of the matter in question are considered: **in essence; essentially; in effect; to ⟨for⟩ all intents and purposes.**

Странно, что существует на виду, так сказать, у всех стиль Толстого с его нагромождением соподчинённых придаточных предложений (вытекающие из одного «что» несколько других «что», из одного «который» несколько следующих «которых»). По существу говоря, единственно встречающийся в русской литературе по свободе и своеобразной неправильности стиль (Олеша 3). It's strange that Tolstoy's style with its piling up of coordinate clauses (several "that's" ensuing from a single "that"; several subsequent "whiches" issuing from a single "which") exists, so to speak, in plain view of everybody. In essence, it is the only style in Russian literature characterized by freedom and by a peculiar impropriety (3a).

3. Also: ПО СУЩЕСТВУ́ ГОВОРЯ́; В СУ́ЩНОСТИ (ГОВОРЯ́) [sent adv (parenth)] in reality: **actually; in (actual) fact; in actuality; in point of fact; as a matter of fact.**

Не в первый раз уже Ирина Викторовна убеждалась в том, что Южно-Американский Вариант, по существу, перестал быть для неё вариантом… (Залыгин 1). Not for the first time it was borne in upon Irina Viktorovna that the South American Variant had in fact ceased to be a variant for her (1a). ♦ …В сущности, виконт готов был стать на сторону какого угодно убеждения или догмата, если имел в виду, что за это ему перепадёт лишний четвертак (Салтыков-Щедрин 1). …In actuality the Vicomte was ready to defend any conviction or dogma whatsoever if he thought it might bring him an extra twenty-five kopecks (1a). ♦ В

сущности, пострадал один Платон Самсонович, первый проповедник козлотура, — его снизили в должности (Искандер 4). In point of fact, the only one who suffered was Platon Samsonovich, the first to advocate the goatibex: he was demoted (4a). ♦ В сущности говоря, разбор всякой книги нелеп и бесцелен… (Набоков 1). As a matter of fact, the analysis of *any* book is awkward and pointless… (1a).

C-685 • СХОДИ́ТЬ/СОЙТИ́ НА НЕТ

[VP] **1.** [subj: usu. concr or голос, звук etc] to get smaller and smaller, softer and softer until it becomes invisible or inaudible: X сошёл на нет ≃ **X trailed off; X faded away ⟨diminished⟩ (to nothing);** [of a visible object only] **X disappeared;** [of a sound only] **X died away.**

Иди по этой тропинке примерно полкилометра. В том месте, где тропинка сходит на нет, посмотри направо – и ты увидишь озеро. Follow the path about half a kilometer. At the spot where it trails off, look to your right and you'll see the lake.

2. [subj: usu. abstr, occas. human] to lose all significance: X сошёл на нет ≃ **X came to naught; X fizzled (out); X petered ⟨died⟩ out; X disappeared from the scene.**

…Начатая было в областной газете кампания быстро сошла на нет (Грекова 3). …The campaign, which had been begun in the local newspaper, quickly fizzled (3a).

C-686 • ПОЯВЛЯ́ТЬСЯ/ПОЯВИ́ТЬСЯ ⟨ВЫСТУ-ПА́ТЬ/ВЫ́СТУПИТЬ, ЯВЛЯ́ТЬСЯ/ЯВИ́ТЬСЯ obsoles⟩ НА СЦЕ́НУ

[VP; subj: human, concr, or, occas., abstr] to appear (somewhere), arrive: X появился на сцену ≃ **X appeared ⟨arrived⟩ on the scene; X entered (up)on the scene; X made an appearance.**

Когда очередь дошла до варенья, Аркадий, не терпевший ничего сладкого, почёл, однако, своею обязанностью отведать от четырёх различных, только что сваренных сортов… Потом явился на сцену чай со сливками, с маслом и кренделями… (Тургенев 2). When the jams appeared, Arkady, who could not endure anything sweet, none the less considered it his duty to taste the four different kinds, only just made….Then tea, with cream and butter and cracknels, appeared on the scene… (2f). ♦ Не стало интимных вечеров, замолкли либеральные разговоры, на сцену… выступила внутренняя политика… (Салтыков-Щедрин 2). There were no more intimate evenings, liberal talks were banned, internal policy made its appearance… (2a).

C-687 • УСТРА́ИВАТЬ ⟨ДЕ́ЛАТЬ⟩ СЦЕ́НУ ⟨-ы⟩ кому; УСТРО́ИТЬ ⟨СДЕ́ЛАТЬ⟩ СЦЕ́НУ

[VP; subj: human; pfv is used with sing сцену only] to express one's intense dissatisfaction with s.o.'s behavior directly to him in a loud and emotional manner, demanding an explanation: X устроил Y-у сцену ≃ **X made a scene (with Y); X blew up at Y.**

[Захар:] Вот ты утром привела к столу этого Грекова… Я его знаю, он очень развитой парень, — однако тебе не следовало из-за него устраивать тёте сцену (Горький 1). [Z.:] Look how you brought Grekov to the table this morning….I know him, he's a very bright lad, but all the same you shouldn't have made a scene with your aunt on his account (1a).

C-688 • СХОДИ́ТЬ/СОЙТИ́ СО СЦЕ́НЫ

[VP] **1.** [subj: human] (of an actor) to end one's career: X сошёл со сцены ≃ **X retired from the stage.**

2. [subj: пьеса, опера etc; often neg impfv] (of a play, opera etc) to cease being performed: X сошёл со сцены ≃ **X is not staged ⟨put on⟩ anymore; X is no longer produced ⟨performed⟩;** ‖ *Neg* X не сходит со сцены много лет ≃ **X has been running ⟨playing⟩ for many years.**

3. [subj: human or, rare, abstr] to cease to be influential, significant in some area, stop one's activity in some area: X сошёл со сцены ≃ **X disappeared ⟨passed⟩ from the scene; X faded**

out of the picture; **X faded into the background;** [in limited contexts] **X left the** [AdjP] **scene.**

Сторонники этой теории давно сошли со сцены. Proponents of this theory passed from the scene long ago. ♦ Хрущёв в своё время пытался демократизировать партию и ввёл в устав пункт о постоянной сменяемости высших партийных кадров. Это и стало одной из причин его собственного падения. Свергнув Хрущёва, его преемники этот неприятный им пункт из устава немедленно вычеркнули. И сами себя обрекли на то, что сойти с политической сцены с почётом можно только умерев на посту (Войнович 1). At one point, Khrushchev tried to democratize the Party and introduced a rule to the effect that top Party people were interchangeable. This was one of the causes of his own downfall. Having overthrown Khrushchev, his successors immediately had that unpleasant rule stricken from the books. In so doing, they doomed themselves to leave the political scene honorably only by dying at their posts (1a).

4. *obs* [subj: human] to die: **X сошёл со сцены** ≃ **X passed on ⟨away⟩.**

С-689 • МЕЖДУ СЦИ́ЛЛОЙ И ХАРИ́БДОЙ *lit* [PrepP; Invar; subj-compl with copula (subj: human or collect); fixed WO] one is (or finds o.s.) in a situation in which dangers, troubles etc threaten from both sides, and avoidance of one increases the probability of being harmed by the other: **between Scylla and Charybdis.**

< From the classical Greek myth about two monsters that inhabited either side of a narrow sea passage between Italy and Sicily.

С-690 • НА СЧА́СТЬЕ *coll* [PrepP; Invar] **1.** (дать, подарить *что кому* и т. п.) ~ [adv] (to give sth. to s.o.) so that it will bring him good fortune: **for (good) luck; as a good-luck charm.**

Нина подарила мне на счастье своё кольцо. Nina gave me her ring as a good-luck charm.

2. ~ *(чьё)* [sent adv (parenth)] by favorable chance: **fortunately (for s.o.); luckily (for s.o.).**

…Хотя все уже знали о приезде начальства, но решительно не могли в себе преодолеть мучительной инерции бездействия… Симочки, на её счастье, на работе не было – она отгуливала переработанный день… (Солженицын 3). …Though everyone now knew about the arrival of the committee, they were still unable to overcome the tormenting inertia of inaction…. Simochka, fortunately for her, was not on duty; she had the day off in return for the extra day she had worked… (3a). ♦ В Карду [Настёна и уполномоченный] приехали засветло, магазин, на счастье, был открыт (Распутин 2). They [Nastyona and the representative] got to Karda before dark and the store, luckily, was open (2a).

С-691 • СЧА́СТЬЕ ТВОЁ ⟨его и т. п.⟩ *coll* [NP; nom only; usu. the main clause in a complex sent (foll. by a что-clause)] it is fortunate for you (him etc) that…: **(it's) lucky for you ⟨him** etc⟩ **(that)…; you're ⟨he's** etc⟩ **lucky (that…).**

«Хороша, очень хороша! – сказала Марья Дмитриевна. – В моём доме любовникам свиданья назначать!.. Счастье его, что он от меня ушёл; да я найду его» (Толстой 5). "A fine girl, very fine!" said Marya Dmitrievna. "Making assignations with lovers in my house!"…"It's lucky for him that he escaped me, but I'll find him!" (5a). ♦ «Тише ори… всех погубишь, чёрт сопливый. Слышишь, Штрезенские рыщут – шастают… Вот они. Замри… Ну, твоё счастье… Прошли мимо» (Пастернак 1). "Not so loud. You'll give us all away, you devil. Can't you hear – Strese's crowd are prowling up and down….There they are. Don't breathe….Lucky for you they've gone by…" (1a).

С-692 • К СЧА́СТЬЮ (чьему, для кого); **ПО СЧА́СТЬЮ** [PrepP; these forms only; sent adv (parenth)] by favorable chance: **fortunately (for s.o.); luckily (for s.o.).**

«Я не хочу пугать тебя, но временами у меня ощущение, будто не сегодня-завтра меня арестуют». – «Сохрани Бог, Юрочка. До этого, по счастью, ещё далеко» (Пастернак 1). "I don't want to worry you, but occasionally I have the feeling that they might arrest me any day." "God forbid, Yurochka. It hasn't come to that yet, fortunately" (1a). ♦ Большая часть из них [путевых записок], к счастию для вас, потеряна, а чемодан, с остальными вещами, к счастию для меня, остался цел (Лермонтов 1). The greater part of them [the notes on my travels], luckily for you, has been lost; while the valise with its other contents, luckily for me, remains safe (1a).

С-693 • НЕ́ БЫЛО БЫ СЧА́СТЬЯ, ДА НЕСЧА́СТЬЕ ПОМОГЛО́ [saying] said when something pleasant comes about as a result of trouble or misfortune: ≃ **every cloud has a silver lining; it's a blessing in disguise;** [in limited contexts] **it's an ill wind that blows no good.**

«Отстраиваемся, значит?.. Это хорошо, пора стране на ноги вставать». – «Не было бы счастья, да несчастье помогло, – невесело усмехнулся обкомовец и тут же заторопился с разъяснениями: – Сами бы мы не потянули… спасибо эмведе порадело своим контингентом [заключённых], у них людей хватает» (Максимов 1). "So reconstruction is proceeding?…That's good. It's time for the country to get back on its feet." "Every cloud has a silver lining," the secretary grinned morosely, and immediately explained: "We wouldn't have got it done ourselves…but fortunately the MVD helped us out with a contingent [of camp inmates]. They never run short of men" (1a).

С-694 • ПОПЫТА́ТЬ СЧА́СТЬЯ ⟨СЧА́СТЬЕ⟩ *coll* [VP; subj: human; often infin with можно, надо, хочет, решил etc] to attempt sth., hoping for success: **X хочет попытать счастья** ≃ **X wants to try his luck.**

[Гаев:] Хорошо бы получить от кого-нибудь наследство… хорошо бы поехать в Ярославль и попытать счастья у тётушки-графини. Тётка ведь очень, очень богата (Чехов 2). [G.:] It would be good to receive a legacy from someone…good to go to Yaroslavl and try our luck with our aunt, the Countess. She is very, very rich, you know (2a).

С-695 • НЕ СЧЕСТЬ ⟨НЕ СОСЧИТА́ТЬ⟩ (кого-чего); **НЕ СОЧТЁШЬ** *all coll* [VP; these forms only; infin is used as impers predic with бытьø; all variants are used as quantit subj-compl (subj: a clause or subj/gen: concr or count abstr)] the people (things etc) in question are so numerous that they cannot be counted: **X-ов не счесть** ≃ **there is no end to (the) Xs; Xs are innumerable ⟨countless⟩; there are more Xs than you can count.**

Сколько бы ещё свалилось на неё [Ирину Викторовну] утренних и вечерних заданий-нарядов – не счесть! (Залыгин 1). She'd [Irina Viktorovna would] receive even more orders of the day, morning and evening – there'd be no end to them (1a).

С-696 • В СЧЁТ *чего* [PrepP; Invar; Prep; the resulting PrepP is adv] **1.** (some money, goods etc are given or received) as part of (eventual full payment for some item, full reimbursement for s.o.'s work, settlement of a debt etc): **against; toward; to be applied against ⟨toward⟩; to be counted toward.**

Вот 20 рублей в счёт платы за магнитофон. Here's twenty rubles toward the tape recorder. ♦ Он [старый Хабуг] сказал, что отделяет Харлампо тридцать коз в счёт его будущей работы (Искандер 5). [context transl] He [old Khabug] said that he would set Harlampo up with thirty goats, to be repaid with future work (5a).

2. (some work is done, action is carried out etc) as part of or contributing to (a larger obligation, plan, design etc that is yet to be fulfilled): **toward.**

План на этот год мы уже выполнили, сейчас работаем в счёт будущего года. We've already fulfilled this year's plan — now we're working toward next year's. ♦ [Маленькие изуверы с командирскими нашивками на рукавах] били всех и всякого по поводу и без повода, в счёт будущего, авансом, для острастки (Максимов 2). [context transl] They [the little fanatics with officers' badges on their sleeves] would beat up anyone with and without reason, as an advance on future punishment and for sheer intimidation (2a).

C-697 • ГА́МБУРГСКИЙ СЧЁТ *lit* [NP; sing only; fixed WO] the objective evaluation of the worth of a person or his work (independent of his status, rank, popularity etc): **honest ⟨objective⟩ rating.**

[Розенцвейг] хорошо знал гамбургский счёт в литературе. Ведь именно он напористо пробивал книги Грина и Хемингуэя — не первым, не бросаясь на амбразуру, но тогда, когда ещё было множество препятствий на пути этих писателей (Орлова 1). [context transl] He [Rozenzweig] knew what was what in literature. He was the one who energetically promoted the books of Greene and Hemingway. He wasn't the first and he didn't throw himself into the line of fire, but nevertheless he did so when there was a multitude of obstacles in the path of these writers (1a).

< The title of a collection of articles by Viktor Shklovsky (1928), this phrase (literally, "The Hamburg Reckoning") refers to annual wrestling competitions that were supposedly once held in Hamburg. These long and grueling contests, which took place behind closed doors in order to be unaffected by bet-driven cheating, showed who the true champions were. Shklovsky used the phrase to rate contemporary writers.

C-698 • ЗА СВОЙ СЧЁТ [PrepP; Invar] **1.** Also: **НА СВОЙ СЧЁТ; ЗА ⟨НА⟩ СО́БСТВЕННЫЙ СЧЁТ** [adv] so as to be paid for by o.s.: **(do sth.) at one's own expense; (pay for sth.) out of one's own pocket; (pay for sth.) o.s.**

Это чудовищно несправедливо, говорит Мазила. Я — художник. Моё законное право побывать в музеях Франции и Италии... Я хочу поехать туда за свой счёт. Никаких преступлений я не совершал... И меня не пускают (Зиновьев 1). "It's monstrously unjust," said Dauber. "I am an artist. It is my legal right to visit museums in France and Italy....I want to travel at my own expense. I haven't committed any crimes....And yet they won't let me go" (1a). ♦ «Я бы постоянную сиделку за свой счёт пригласила, — мне говорят, и это нельзя?» (Солженицын 10). "...I'd be ready to pay for a permanent nurse out of my own pocket. But they tell me that's not allowed either" (10a). ♦ Эта Ира чем-то так очаровала всемогущую Гридасову, что та снабдила её чистым паспортом, одела с ног до головы в одежду со своего плеча и на свой счёт отправила на материк (Гинзбург 2). [context transl] Ira had somehow cast such a spell on the omnipotent Gridasova that the latter had provided her with a perfectly clean passport, given her a complete set of clothing from her own wardrobe, and paid for her passage back to the mainland (2a).

2. отпуск ~ [nonagreeing modif] time off from work during which one does not receive pay: **leave ⟨leave of absence⟩ without pay; unpaid leave ⟨leave of absence⟩; leave of absence at one's own expense.**

Надо быть сумасшедшим, чтобы в такое время прийти в отдел кадров и просить отпуск за свой счёт (Михайловская 1). One would have to be insane to ask for leave-without-pay right now (1a). ♦ Отец взял отпуск за свой счёт и поехал с Килей в Москву (Некрасов 1). Her father took a leave of absence at his own expense and accompanied Kilia to Moscow (1a).

C-699 • ЗА СЧЁТ¹ *чей, кого-чего, какой* [PrepP; Invar; the resulting PrepP is adv] so as to be subsidized, financed by s.o. (or

some organization): **at s.o.'s ⟨sth.'s⟩ expense; at the expense of s.o. ⟨sth.⟩; on s.o.'s ⟨sth.'s⟩ money ⟨funds⟩; s.o. ⟨sth.⟩ pays for...;** ∥ за государственный ⟨за казённый⟩ счёт ≃ **at government ⟨the government's, state, the state's, public⟩ expense; on ⟨with⟩ government money ⟨funds⟩;** ∥ за счёт ресторана ⟨кафе и т. п.⟩ ≃ **on the house.**

Если я завтра умру, от меня ничего не останется. Меня похоронят за счёт профсоюза (Войнович 5). If I die tomorrow, no trace of me will remain. I'll be buried at my union's expense... (5a). ♦ «Стыдно сказать... за Фросин счёт выпиваю» (Чернёнок 2). "I'm ashamed to admit that I'm drinking on Frosya's money" (2a). ♦ «Товарищ Худобченко остался мной очень доволен, собрал совещание, хвалил меня, ставил другим в пример, и дело, как обычно, закончилось большой пьянкой за казённый, разумеется, счёт» (Войнович 4). "Comrade Khudobchenko was quite pleased with me. He called a meeting, praised me, held me up as an example to the others, all of which ended, as usual, in a big drinking bout, at state expense of course" (4a). ♦ Забрали его санитары и сами похоронили, за казённый счёт (Суслов 1). The orderlies took him and buried him themselves, at public expense (1a). ♦ «И потом я замечаю, что комендант развёл у себя в Колонии любимчиков и прикармливает их там за государственный счёт» (Стругацкие 3). "And then, I notice that the commandant has developed favorites within the colony and is feeding them on government funds" (3a). ♦ «Напиши ты ему [бургомистру] эту статью, и всё в порядке... Давай я тебе по этому поводу налью за счёт заведения» (Стругацкие 1). "Write him [the burgomaster] his article and everything'll be all right....For that I'll give you a drink on the house" (1a).

C-700 • ЗА СЧЁТ² *чего* [PrepP; Invar; Prep; the resulting PrepP is adv] **1.** because of sth., as a consequence of sth.: **owing to; thanks to; due to; owe sth. to;** [in limited contexts] **accounted for by.**

...Такие, как я, прыгают через ступеньки и возносятся за счёт «личных способностей», вызывая раздражение у всех — и у своих, и у чужих (Зиновьев 2). ...Those like me skip some steps and rise thanks to their "personal capacities," which irritates everyone, both their friends and their enemies (2a). ♦ Взвешивание [пса] дало неожиданный результат — вес 30 кило, за счёт роста (удлинения) костей (Булгаков 11). Weighing-in [the dog] produced unexpected results: weight 30 kilograms, accounted for by growth (lengthening) of bones (11a).

2. (sth. is done, accomplished etc in one area) by s.o.'s giving up sth. (in another area): **at the expense ⟨cost⟩ of; by sacrificing (sth.).**

Веранду пристроили к дому за счёт одной из комнат. They added a porch onto the house by sacrificing one of the rooms.

C-701 • ЗАКРЫВА́ТЬ/ЗАКРЫ́ТЬ СЧЁТ [VP] **1.** [subj: human] (of a depositor) to withdraw all one's money from the bank: X закрыл счёт ≃ **X closed (out) his account.**

2. [subj: банк, сберегательная касса] (of a bank) to halt the payment of money on a depositor's account: X закрыл счёт ≃ **X stopped payment.**

3. [subj: human] to make one's final payment (to a municipal organization for the use of one's apartment, utilities etc) and thereby discontinue one's access to these services (usu. before moving to a new residence): X закрыл счёт ≃ **X closed (out) his account; X settled his account.**

В связи с переездом нам нужно закрыть счёт в домоуправлении. Since we're moving we need to settle our account with the building management.

C-702 • ЗНАТЬ СЧЁТ ДЕНЬГА́М *coll* [VP; subj: human] to be prudent in managing one's money (esp. hard-earned money), not to spend money needlessly, recklessly: X знает счёт деньгам ≃ **X knows the value of money ⟨a dollar⟩.**

Отец не скупой, но счёт деньгам знает. Father's not stingy, but he knows the value of money.

С-703 • НА СЧЁТ¹ *чей, кого-чего, какой* [PrepP; Invar; the resulting PrepP is adv] so as to be subsidized, financed by s.o. (or some organization): **at s.o.'s ⟨sth.'s⟩ expense; at the expense of s.o. ⟨sth.⟩; on s.o.'s ⟨sth.'s⟩ money ⟨funds⟩; s.o. ⟨sth.⟩ pays for...;** ‖ **на казённый счёт** ≃ **at government ⟨the government's, state, the state's, public⟩ expense; on ⟨with⟩ government money ⟨funds⟩.**

Я, например, учился на счёт Коммерческого собрания, был его стипендиатом (Олеша 3). I, for example, studied at the expense of the Commerce Club; I was its stipendiary (3a). ♦ Таким образом, дядю Сандро на казённый счёт, на казённой машине отправили в Ткварчели... (Искандер 3). Thus Uncle Sandro, at government expense, in a government car, was sent to Tkvarcheli... (3a).

С-704 • НА СЧЁТ² *чей, кого* [PrepP; Invar; the resulting PrepP is adv] in relation to s.o., regarding s.o.: **about; concerning; referring to; on s.o.'s account;** [of a remark, criticism etc] **aimed ⟨pointed⟩ at;** [of a mocking comment, unkind joke etc] **at s.o.'s expense.**

Я ещё ни одной женщины не обидел всерьёз, а всё потому, что не разрешал им строить иллюзии на свой счёт... (Аржак 1). I've never really hurt a woman up to now, and that's only because I've never let them have any illusions about me (1a). ♦ [Беляев:] ...Мне невозможно будет... теперь, с вами обеими... [Вера:] О, на мой счёт не беспокойтесь! (Тургенев 1). [B.:] ...It would be impossible for me...now...with you both... [V.:] Oh, don't trouble yourself on my account! (1a). ♦ Княжна меня решительно ненавидит; мне уже пересказывали две-три эпиграммы на мой счёт, довольно колкие, но вместе очень лестные (Лермонтов 1). The young princess definitely hates me: people have already reported to me two or three epigrams aimed at me, fairly caustic, but at the same time very flattering (1a). ♦ «Елизавета ведёт себя недостойно: всё время она злословит на мой счёт, иногда очень грубо» (Шолохов 2). "Liza's conduct is deplorable. She keeps making cutting remarks at my expense, and sometimes they are very rude" (2a).

С-705 • НА ⟨ЗА⟩ ЧУЖО́Й СЧЁТ *жить, есть, пить* и т. п. [PrepP; these forms only; adv; fixed WO] (to live, eat, drink etc) on another's or others' means, money: **at someone else's expense; at others' ⟨other people's⟩ expense; at the expense of others;** [in refer. to eating, drinking etc only] **on someone else's tab;** [in refer. to living only] **live ⟨sponge⟩ off other people ⟨someone else⟩.**

На мою голову Тамурка вспомнила, что у меня приближается день рождения. «Надо отметить как следует...» Я всеми силами отнекивался... но не устоял под напором Тамурки и соратников из отдела, которым захотелось выпить и пожрать за чужой счёт (Зиновьев 2). To my dismay Tamurka remembered that my birthday was drawing near. "We must celebrate it properly...." I tried to resist in every possible way...but I had to give way to the pressure from Tamurka and my colleagues in the department, who were very keen on the idea of eating and drinking at someone else's expense (2a). ♦ Чего же ещё? Хотите к тому же за чужой счёт или за свой (безразлично) за границу ездить? (Зиновьев 1). "What more do you want? You want on top of that to travel at others' expense (or at your own, it makes no difference) to a foreign country?" (1a). ♦ [Трофимов:] ...Ваша мать, вы, дядя уже не замечаете, что вы живёте... на чужой счёт... (Чехов 2). [T.:] ...Your mother, you yourself, and your uncle no longer realize that you are living...at other people's expense... (2b).

С-706 • НА Э́ТОТ СЧЁТ [PrepP; Invar; prep obj; fixed WO] with respect to the matter in question: **on this ⟨that⟩ score ⟨point, matter⟩; concerning this ⟨that, it, this matter etc⟩; about this ⟨that, it, this matter etc⟩; in that regard.**

«Отдел информации и библиографии — моё детище, и он должен быть самым красивым. Пока его возглавляет Мансурова — у меня нет на этот счёт никаких опасений» (Залыгин 1). "The data and bibliography department is my baby and it's got to be the most beautiful. As long as Mansurova's in charge of it I've no worries on that score" (1a). ♦ Он по-прежнему жил с родителями и пока женат не был. Мама гадала на этот счёт безуспешно (Битов 2). He lived as before with his parents and was not yet married. Mama speculated on this point without success (2a). ♦ На цыган фашисты охотились, как на дичь. Я нигде ничего не встречал официального на этот счёт, но ведь на Украине цыгане подлежали такому же немедленному уничтожению, как и евреи (Кузнецов 1). The fascists hunted Gypsies as if they were game. I have never come across anything official concerning this, yet in the Ukraine the Gypsies were subject to the same immediate extermination as the Jews (1a). ♦ «Она ни в чём, ни в чём не виновата!.. Нельзя ли, не можете ли мне сказать: что вы с нею теперь сделаете?» — «Решительно успокойтесь на этот счёт, Дмитрий Фёдорович, — тотчас же и с видимою поспешностью ответил прокурор, — мы не имеем пока никаких значительных мотивов хоть в чём-нибудь обеспокоить особу, которою вы так интересуетесь» (Достоевский 1). "She is guilty of nothing, nothing!...Won't you, can't you tell me what you're going to do with her now?" "You can be decidedly reassured in that regard, Dmitri Fyodorovich," the prosecutor replied at once, and with obvious haste. "So far we have no significant motives for troubling in any way the person in whom you are so interested" (1a). ♦ «Знаете, вы довольно любопытную мысль сказали; я теперь приду домой и шевельну мозгами на этот счёт. Признаюсь, я так и ждал, что от вас можно кой-чему поучиться» (Достоевский 1). [context transl] "You know, you've said a very interesting thought; I'll set my mind to it when I get home. I admit, I did suspect it would be possible to learn something from you" (1a).

С-707 • НЕ В СЧЁТ; НЕ ИДТИ́ В СЧЁТ *both coll* [PrepP, Invar, subj-compl with copula (1st var.) or VP; subj: any noun] a person (a thing etc) is not or should not be taken into consideration: X не в счёт ≃ **X doesn't count.**

[Говорящий — мул] Несколько раз навстречу нам показывались верховые... О том, что нас ни один всадник не обогнал, не может быть и разговоров, я бы этого никогда не позволил. Мой старик меня любит не только за плавный ход, но также за очень бодрый шаг. Ну, разумеется, если кто-нибудь пустится сзади галопом, он нас опередит. Но это не в счёт (Искандер 3). [The speaker is a mule] Several times men on horseback came toward us....There could be no question of any horseman passing us from behind; I'd never allow it. My old man loves me not only for my smooth gait but also for my very brisk pace. Well, of course, if someone starts off at a gallop, he'll leave us behind. But that doesn't count (3a).

С-708 • ОТКРЫВА́ТЬ/ОТКРЫ́ТЬ СЧЁТ [VP] **1.** [subj: human] (of a depositor) to start an account at a bank: X открыл счёт ≃ **X opened an account.**

2. ~ *кому* [subj: банк, сберегательная касса] (of a bank) to accept s.o. as a customer: X открыл счёт Y-у ≃ **X established ⟨opened, set up⟩ an account (for Y).**

3. *sports* [subj: human or collect] to make the first score, be first on the scoreboard in some game or competition: X открыл счёт ≃ **X scored the first point; X opened the scoring.**

4. ~ *чему* [subj: human or collect; indir obj: pl] to achieve one's first combat success (by shooting down one's first enemy plane, blowing up one's first enemy tank etc): X открыл счёт Y-ам ≃ **X scored ⟨shot down, disabled, got, bagged etc⟩ his first Y.**

С-709 • ОТНОСИ́ТЬ/ОТНЕСТИ́ *что* **ЗА ⟨НА⟩ СЧЁТ** *кого-чего* [VP; subj: human] to interpret sth. as being caused by sth. else: X относит Y за счёт Z-a ≃ **X attributes ⟨credits⟩ Y to Z; X puts Y down to thing Z.**

Признаться, Федины объяснения несколько успокоили меня. Эдик же, напротив, впал в подавленное состояние. Эта подавленность удивляла меня, я относил её целиком за счёт того, что Эдик всегда был человеком чистой науки, далёким от всяких там входящих и исходящих, от дыроколов и ведомостей (Стругацкие 3). I must admit that Fedya's explanations had calmed me somewhat. But Eddie had become depressed. I was surprised by his depression, but I attributed it completely to the fact that Eddie had always been a man of pure science far removed from lost shipments, paper punching, and expense forms (3a). ♦ Я ещё не видел её [мою пьесу] на сцене, а уже получил за неё высшую награду — его [Пастернака] одобрение. Даже если большую часть отнести на счёт его доброжелательности и дружеской снисходительности, то и того, что останется, вполне достаточно, чтобы чувствовать себя безмерно счастливым (Гладков 1). I have not yet seen it [my play] put on the stage, but I have already received the highest accolade: his [Pasternak's] approval. Even allowing that most of it must be put down to his generosity and kindhearted indulgence, it is still more than enough to make me feel boundlessly happy (1a). ♦ То, что Дьяков женат на Ревекке, Юра относил за счёт его собственной неприглядности (Рыбаков 2). [context transl] Yuri thought Dyakov must have married Rebecca because he was so unattractive himself (2a).

С-710 • ПРЕДЪЯВЛЯ́ТЬ/ПРЕДЪЯВИ́ТЬ СЧЁТ *кому-чему (за что)* [VP; subj: usu. human or collect] to make known certain charges against s.o. or sth. (often some political, literary etc trend or school of thought): X предъявил Y-у счёт ≃ **X presented a claim ⟨a bill⟩ to Y.**

Идеализируя уходящий образ жизни, возможно, мы, сами того не сознавая, предъявляли счёт будущему. Мы ему как бы говорили: «Вот что мы теряем, а что ты нам даёшь взамен?» (Искандер 3). We may not recognize it, but in idealizing a vanishing way of life we are presenting a bill to the future. We are saying, "Here is what we are losing; what are you going to give us in exchange?" (3a).

С-711 • ПРИНИМА́ТЬ/ПРИНЯ́ТЬ НА СВОЙ СЧЁТ *что* [VP; subj: human or collect] to perceive, interpret sth. (usu. a remark, inference, action etc that may be offensive or unpleasant) as pertaining to o.s.: X принял Y на свой счёт ≃ **X took Y personally ⟨as aimed at himself⟩; X took Y to apply to X; X thought Y was aimed at ⟨meant for, intended for⟩ him;** [in limited contexts] **X thought Y was ⟨done ⟨said⟩⟩ on his account.**

...Неврастеник сказал, что Кис напрасно принимает карикатуру на свой счёт (Зиновьев 1). ...Neurasthenic said it was foolish [for Puss] to take the caricature personally (1a). ♦ Он не мог отвязаться от застрявшего в ушах гулкого крика: «Позор!» — и не мог забыть той секунды, когда он принял этот крик на свой счёт (Федин 1). He could not get rid of that loud shout echoing in his ears: "Shame!"—and could not forget the moment when he had taken this shout to apply to him (1a). ♦ [Городничий:] Конечно, если он [учитель] ученику сделает такую рожу, то оно ещё ничего... но... если он сделает это посетителю — это может быть очень худо: господин ревизор или другой кто может принять это на свой счёт (Гоголь 4). [Mayor:] Now, of course, if he [the teacher] makes faces like that at one of the boys, it doesn't matter....But what if he should do the same thing to a visitor? It might lead to all sorts of very unfortunate consequences. The Government Inspector or some other official might think it was meant for him (4c). ♦ [Войницев:] Ты плачешь? [Софья Егоровна:] Не принимайте этих слёз на свой счёт! (Чехов 1). [V.:] You're crying? [S.E.:] Don't think these tears are on your account (1a).

С-712 • ПРОХА́ЖИВАТЬСЯ/ПРОЙТИ́СЬ ⟨ПРОЕЗ-ЖА́ТЬСЯ/ПРОЕ́ХАТЬСЯ⟩ НА СЧЁТ *чей* ⟨**ПО А́Д-РЕСУ** *чьему, кого,* **НАСЧЁТ** *кого-чего*⟩ *all coll* [VP; subj: human] to speak of s.o. or sth. in a mocking or disapproving tone,

speak ill of s.o.: X прохаживался на Y-ов счёт ≃ **X was taking stabs ⟨potshots, swipes⟩ at person Y; X was running person Y down; X was poking fun at Y; X was making sport of person Y; X was making fun of Y.**

С-713 • ТЕРЯ́ТЬ/ПОТЕРЯ́ТЬ СЧЁТ *(кому-чему)* [VP; subj: human; more often pfv] not to have kept track of or not to be able to count the number of people, things etc in question because their number is so great: X потерял счёт (Y-ам) ≃ **X lost count (of Ys).**

[Лебедев:] Лет тридцать я тебя старухой знаю... [Авдотья Назаровна:] И счёт годам потеряла... (Чехов 4). [L.:] You've been an old woman ever since I've known you—for the last thirty years. [A.N.:] I've lost count of the years... (4a).

С-714 • БЕЗ СЧЁТА ⟨**-у**⟩ *(кого-чего)*; **БЕЗ ЧИСЛА́** [PrepP; these forms only; adv (quantif) or quantit subj-compl with copula (subj/gen: human, concr, or abstr)] in large quantity, very many: **lots (of); an untold amount ⟨quantity⟩ (of); countless; without number; more than one can count;** [in limited contexts] **all one could (ever) want.**

[Митя] поднял тогда цыган целый табор (в то время у нас закочевавший), которые в два дня вытащили-де у него, у пьяного, без счёту денег и выпили без счёту дорогого вина (Достоевский 1). He [Mitya] had roused a whole camp of gypsies that time (they were in our neighborhood then), who in two days, while he was drunk, relieved him of an untold amount of money and drank an untold quantity of expensive wine (1a). ♦ Какое ему было дело до этого дурацкого портфеля, до этого брошенного родителями мальчишки, племянника жены, если сам он был так обижен судьбой, если бог не дал ему сына собственного, своей крови, в то время как другим дарит детей щедро, без числа?.. (Айтматов 1). What did he care about that stupid schoolbag, about that brat abandoned by his parents, when he himself was so wronged by life, when God didn't see fit to grant him a son of his own, his own flesh and blood, while others were blessed with all the children they could want (1a).

С-715 • В ДВА СЧЁТА *coll* [PrepP; Invar; adv; usu. used with pfv verbs; fixed WO] (to do sth.) very quickly, without delay, at once: **in no time (flat); in no time at all; in a jiffy ⟨a wink, a flash⟩; one-two-three; in two shakes of a lamb's tail.**

...В первых числах августа смотритель получил приказ откомандировать [Мишку] Кошевого в распоряжение станичного правления. Мишка собрался в два счёта, сдал казённую экипировку, в тот же день навечер выехал домой (Шолохов 4). ...In the early days of August the overseer received orders to put [Mishka] Koshevoi at the disposal of the stanitsa authorities. Mishka was ready in no time, handed in the equipment that had been issued to him, and by evening on the same day was on his way home (4a). ♦ Ведь от такой работы ежедневной свихнёшься в два счёта (Трифонов 6). Doing that kind of work every day you'd go batty in no time flat (6a). ♦ Давайте совместными усилиями, как когда-то бывало, поналяжем и попробуем разок крутануть колесо истории. Вы только верните нам Лёню Тихомирова, царя, волю, как её? — энергию эту самую дайте, и мы вам снова в два счёта построим коммунизм... (Терц 6). Why don't we pool our efforts once again, and have a really good try and give the wheel of history one more turn? All you have to do is give us back our Lenny Makepeace, our Tsar, our will, our—energy—or whatever you call it—and we'll build you communism once again in no time at all... (6a). ♦ «Ты где пропадаешь? — грозно окликнул он Сейдахмата. — Гость тут дрова рубит, — кивнул он на шофёра, коловшего поленья, — а ты песни поёшь». — «Ну, это мы в два счёта», — успокоил его Сейдахмат, направляясь к шофёру (Айтматов 1). "Where've you been?" he called menacingly to Seidakhmat. "Our guest over here is splitting firewood"—he nodded towards the driver, who was working away at some logs—"and you're singing songs." "Ah, we'll take care of that in a jiffy," Seidakhmat mollified him and headed towards the driver (1b). ♦ [Железнодорожник] едет довольный, говорил — вызвали к министру; наверно, рассчитывает на повышение. А вот произойдёт крушение, в два счёта снимут, это бесспорно (Эренбург 3). [The railway engineer] sits there [in the train] smirking, says he's summoned by his Ministry, must be counting on promotion. And suppose there is a railway accident—one-two-three and out you go, no nonsense about that (3a).

C-716 • ДЛЯ РО́ВНОГО СЧЁТА [PrepP; Invar; adv; fixed WO] in order to bring a sum or quantity to a round number (usu. the nearest multiple of 10, 50, 100 etc): **to make it even; to round it off; in round figures ⟨numbers⟩.**

«Сколько тебе надо?» — «Шестьсот девяносто с чем-то рублей, скажем для ровного счёта семьсот», — немного замявшись, сказал Родя (Пастернак 1). "How much do you need?" "Six hundred and ninety odd rubles. Say seven hundred in round figures," he [Rodia] added after a slight pause (1a).

C-717 • НЕ ЗНАТЬ СЧЁТА ДЕНЬГА́М *coll* [VP; subj: human] to have a lot of money and usu. to spend it recklessly, frivolously: X не знает счёта деньгам ≃ **X has more money than he can count ⟨than he knows what to do with⟩; X has money to throw around ⟨to burn⟩.**

«Вообразите себе молодость, ум, красоту... громкое имя, деньги, которым не знал он счёта и которые у него никогда не переводились» (Пушкин 3). "Picture in your mind youth, intelligence, good looks...an exalted name, and money, more than he could count, in an inexhaustible supply..." (3a).

C-718 • В КОНЕ́ЧНОМ ⟨ПОСЛЕ́ДНЕМ⟩ СЧЁТЕ [PrepP; these forms only; adv or sent adv (parenth); fixed WO] as a final result or when some final result is examined: **in the final analysis ⟨reckoning⟩; in the end; in the long run ⟨haul⟩; when all is said and done; ultimately.**

Вот какая страшная отвлечённость получилась в конечном счёте из «материализма»! (Набоков 1). Look what a terrible abstraction resulted, in the final analysis, from "materialism"! (1a). ♦ «Ты историю изучай, да о сегодняшнем дне помни. Мы что строим и уже построили? То-то. Значит, в конечном счёте, понимаешь — в конечном! — правильно делали наши предки. Справедливо» (Терц 7). "Study your history but don't forget the present day. Think of what we are building! Well, there you are—In the final reckoning, if you see what I mean—ultimately—our ancestors were right. What they did was just" (7a).

C-719 • СБРА́СЫВАТЬ/СБРО́СИТЬ ⟨СКИ́ДЫВАТЬ/ СКИ́НУТЬ, СНИМА́ТЬ/СНЯТЬ⟩ СО СЧЕТО́В ⟨СО СЧЁТОВ, СО СЧЁТА⟩ *кого-что* [VP; subj: human; often impfv infin with нельзя, не надо, не следует etc] to leave s.o. or sth. out of one's considerations, and/or exclude s.o. or sth. as a possibility: X сбросит Y-а со счетов ≃ **X will discount ⟨dismiss, ignore, write off, forget⟩ Y; X will rule ⟨count⟩ out Y.**

Как легко сбрасывается со счёта обретённое в голоде, в лишениях сокровище — великий двадцатилетний опыт масс! (Иоффе 1). How easily the great twenty years' experience of the masses, this great treasure of theirs, obtained in the face of hunger and deprivations, was discounted! (1a). ♦ Случаи индивидуальных и даже групповых действий тебе известны. Их нельзя сбрасывать со счёта. Они своё дело делают (Зиновьев 1). You already know of cases of individual and even collective actions. They cannot be ignored. They have their effect (1a).

C-720 • КРУ́ГЛЫМ СЧЁТОМ [NP$_{instrum}$; Invar; adv; fixed WO] expressed as a round number (usu. the nearest multiple of 10, 50, 100 etc): **in round figures ⟨numbers⟩; rounded off.**

C-721 • РО́ВНЫМ СЧЁТОМ[1] [NP$_{instrum}$; Invar; adv; used with a Num or quantit NP; fixed WO] **1.** precisely (as many, much, long etc as stated): **exactly; ...to the day ⟨year, ruble etc⟩.**

Было бы тягостным недоразумением и шло бы вразрез с прямыми намерениями автора, если бы полемика с прошлым о прошлом, проходящая через эту книгу, была истолкована как желание оживить литературное движение, скончавшееся ровным счётом восемнадцать лет назад (Лившиц 1). It would be an onerous misunderstanding and would go against the author's immediate intentions, if the polemics with the past about the past which run through this book, were to be interpreted as a wish to resurrect a literary movement which died exactly eighteen years ago (1a).

2. merely: **only; just; no more than; but.**

До зарплаты ещё целая неделя, а у меня осталось ровным счётом два рубля. It's still a whole week till payday, and I have only two rubles left.

C-722 • РО́ВНЫМ СЧЁТОМ[2] **ничего** *coll* [NP$_{instrum}$; Invar; modif; fixed WO] altogether, completely (nothing): **absolutely nothing; nothing at all; not a (single) thing.**

[Нюша:] Я вас предупреждаю — из этого не получится ровным счётом ничего (Панова 1). [N.:] I warn you that absolutely nothing will come of this (1a). ♦ [Шаманов:] ...Моё выступление ничего не изменит. Ничего ровным счётом (Вампилов 2). [Sh.:] ...My testimony now isn't going to change a thing. Not a thing (2b). ♦ Деменский заговорил как будто откровенно, но к предыдущим своим показаниям ровным счётом ничего не добавил (Чернёнок 1). Demensky started talking in what seemed to be a frank way, but he didn't add a single thing to his previous statements (1a).

C-723 • НА СЧЕТУ́[1] [PrepP; Invar] **1.** ~ *(у кого)* [subj-compl with быть$_\emptyset$ (subj: any count noun); if subj: sing, it is usu. preceded by каждый] every person (or thing) is taken into consideration, is important, valued, significant: (у Y-а) каждый X на счету ≃ **every X counts (for Y); every X is precious (to Y); every X means something ⟨a lot, a great deal⟩ (to Y).**

...Кто-то выпустил Абдула, он, кажется, не покусал никого, но напугал сильно и одежду порвал. Лёвке-то что, а у Антона всякая тряпочка была на счету (Трифонов 2). One of them let Abdul off the leash, and although he didn't actually bite anyone, he gave the victims a bad fright and tore their clothes. This didn't bother Lev too much, but to Anton every scrap of clothing was precious (2a).

2. ~ *(у кого)* [subj-compl with быть$_\emptyset$ (subj: human, often pl, or collect)] a person or group is kept under observation (often by s.o. in a position of authority who believes that that person or group has done sth. illegal, reprehensible etc): все X-ы на счету (у Y-а) ≃ **all Xs are monitored by Y; Y keeps tab(s) ⟨an eye⟩ on all Xs; Y keeps track of all Xs; all Xs live ⟨fall⟩ under the watchful eye of Y.**

Мать Лены хотела поскорее выдать дочь замуж, и все потенциальные женихи были у неё на счету. Lena's mother wanted to marry her off as soon as possible and kept track of all eligible young men. ♦ Городок у нас маленький, все наркоманы на счету у милиции. Our town is small, and all the drug addicts live under the watchful eye of the militia.

3. ~ *чьём, (у) кого* [subj-compl with быть$_\emptyset$ (subj: count abstr or concr, usu. pl) or obj-compl with иметь (obj: count abstr or concr, usu. pl)] (s.o. has the specified achievements or, occas., undesirable actions) as part of his past experience: у X-а на счету много Y-ов ≃ **X has many Ys under his belt; X has many Ys to his name ⟨his credit⟩; X has racked up ⟨accumulated etc⟩ a lot of Ys.**

У Дмитрия на счету больше ста изобретений. Dmitry has more than one hundred inventions under his belt.

С-724 • НА СЧЕТУ́² *каком (у кого)* [PrepP; Invar; the resulting PrepP is subj-compl with copula (subj: human)] one is looked upon, perceived in the way specified: X на хорошем ⟨плохом и т. п.⟩ счету (у Y-а) ≃ **X is in good ⟨bad etc⟩ standing (with Y); X is in Y's good ⟨bad⟩ books; X is well ⟨ill⟩ thought of (by Y); X has a good ⟨bad etc⟩ reputation.**

В активистках в университете она не состояла, но была на хорошем счету (Мандельштам 2). Though not an activist at the university, she was nevertheless in good standing (2a). ♦ «А ты спроси у отрядного, что надо делать, чтобы быть на хорошем счету» (Марченко 1). "And you ask the company commander what one has to do in order to be in his good books" (1a). ♦ Во всё время пребывания в училище был он на отличном счету... (Гоголь 3). All the time he was at school he was well thought of... (3a).

С-725 • ПО БОЛЬШО́МУ СЧЁТУ *usu. media* [PrepP; Invar; fixed WO] **1.** ~ судить, оценивать и т. п. [adv or sent adv (parenth)] applying the strictest criteria, demands: **(judge s.o.) by the highest ⟨strictest⟩ standards ⟨criteria⟩; (evaluate s.o.) using the highest ⟨strictest⟩ standards ⟨criteria⟩.**

2. ~ (жить, работать и т. п.) [adv or subj-compl with copula (subj: abstr, often всё)] (to live, work etc) in a highly moral fashion: **in keeping with ⟨according to⟩ the highest standards.**

С-726 • СЧЁТУ ⟨-а⟩ НЕТ *кому-чему coll;* НЕТ ⟨НЕСТЬ *obs*⟩ ЧИСЛА́ [VP; impers] some people (things etc) are present or exist in very great or infinite numbers: X-ам счёту нет ≃ **there are innumerable ⟨countless, myriad⟩ Xs; there is no counting ⟨no end to⟩ the Xs; there are more Xs than one can count.**

...Находившийся перед ним [Чичиковым] узенький дворик весь был наполнен птицами и всякой домашней тварью. Индейкам и курам не было числа... (Гоголь 3). ...The small yard outside was full of birds and all sorts of domestic creatures. There were innumerable chickens and turkey hens... (3e). ...He [Chichikov] saw that the narrow yard was teeming with fowl and every kind of domestic animal. There was no counting the turkeys and hens... (3d).

С-727 • ПОКО́НЧИТЬ ⟨КО́НЧИТЬ⟩ (ВСЕ) СЧЁТЫ *с кем-чем* [VP; subj: human] to cease to have dealings with some person, group, or organization, or to cease to be involved in or occupied by sth.: X покончил счёты с Y-ом ≃ **X severed all ties with Y; X is through ⟨finished⟩ with Y; X parted company with Y; [in limited contexts] X called it quits with Y.**

С этими людьми я больше не имею дела, все мои счёты с ними покончены. I don't have dealings with those people anymore—I've severed all ties with them.

С-728 • СВОДИ́ТЬ/СВЕСТИ́ СЧЁТЫ *с кем* [VP; subj: human; more often this WO] **1.** to make a (mutual) settlement of financial accounts with s.o., pay s.o. what one owes him: X свёл счёты с Y-ом ≃ **X squared accounts with Y; X settled (up) accounts with Y; X settled up with Y; X paid up (what he owed Y).**

2. [more often impfv (pres or infin with не будем, не надо etc)] to take revenge for an offense or injury: X свёл счёты с Y-ом ≃ **X settled a score with Y; X got even with Y; X got back at Y; X paid Y back; X settled accounts (with Y).**

Давыдов стал кричать, что никакой он не еврей и никакой не партизан, а Пузенко сводит с ним личные счёты (Кузнецов 1). Davydov shouted that he was no Jew, and no partisan either, but that Puzenko was merely settling a personal score with him (1a). ♦ Марфа Гавриловна ему [Худолееву] отказала... Худолеев запил и стал буянить, сводя счёты со всем светом, виноватым, как он был уверен, в его нынешних неурядицах (Пастернак 1). ...Marfa Gavrilovna rejected him [Khudoleiev]....Khudoleiev took to drink and rowdiness, trying to get even with a world which was to

blame, so he believed, for all his misfortunes (1a). ♦ В разгар «культурной революции» был момент: многие такие, как он [Ма Хун], поверили, что удастся свести счёты с властями (Буковский 1). At the height of the "cultural revolution" there was a moment when many like him [Ma Hun] thought they'd have a chance to settle accounts with the regime (1a).

С-729 • ЧТО ЗА СЧЁТЫ! *coll* [sent; Invar; fixed WO] (used as a friendly response to s.o.'s statement indicating that he wants to return a favor) I am (or we are) not paying attention to such trifles and neither should you: **who's counting?; who's keeping score?**

«Позвольте мне заплатить за билеты». — «Вы платили в прошлый раз, сегодня моя очередь». — «Что за счёты!» "Let me pay for the tickets." "You paid last time, now it's my turn." "Who's counting?"

С-730 • НА СЪЕДЕ́НИЕ *кому* оставить, отдать *кого,* остаться и т. п. *coll, often humor* [PrepP; Invar; adv] (to leave s.o., be left etc) completely under some person's power, helpless to act against that person's will: X отдал Y-а на съедение Z-у ≃ **X put ⟨left⟩ Y at the mercy of Z; X left Y to Z's mercy; X left Y to be victimized by Z.**

Сговориться с Лурье мне было нетрудно, ибо сговариваться, правду сказать, было не о чем: я без колебаний отдавал ему на съедение всего Баха с потрохами... (Лившиц 1). I had no problem in reaching an agreement with Lourié because to tell the truth, there was nothing to reach an agreement about. I could safely leave Bach, lock, stock and barrel to his mercy... (1a). ♦ «Так это должно быть! — думал князь Андрей, выезжая из аллеи лысогорского дома. — Она, жалкое невинное существо, остаётся на съедение выжившему из ума старику. Старик чувствует, что виноват, но не может изменить себя» (Толстой 6). "It had to be so!" thought Prince Andrei, as he drove out of the avenue of Bald Hills. "She, poor innocent creature, is left to be victimized by an old man who has outlived his wits. The old man feels he is guilty but cannot change" (6a).

С-731 • СЪЕСТЬ ЖИВЬЁМ *кого coll* [VP; subj: human; often fut] to reprimand or punish s.o. severely: X съест Y-а живьём ≃ **X will eat Y alive; X will have Y's head (on a platter).**

С-732 • БЛУ́ДНЫЙ СЫН *lit* [NP; sing only; fixed WO] a person who leaves his parents' home (*by extension* his collective, social group etc) in search of sth. new and better, but later returns to what he had left (often repentant of what he has done): **prodigal son.**

[Мишка] хотел уже пугануть штабного [, который его расспрашивал,] печёным словом, но в этот момент вошёл Штокман. «Блудный сын!.. Что ты его, товарищ, распытываешь? Да ведь это же наш парень!» (Шолохов 4). He [Mishka] was about to give the clerk [who was interrogating him] the rough edge of his tongue, when the door opened and Stokman entered. "Why, it's our prodigal son!...What are you interrogating him for? He's one of our lads!" (4a). ♦ [extended usage] Блудная дочь вернулась к родным осинам. Говорят, сразу по возвращении пошла она [Светлана Аллилуева] к Кремлёвской стене поклониться папиному праху и оставила у могилы его цветы (Войнович 1). ...The prodigal daughter revisited her native aspen trees for a time. They say that the minute Svetlana [Alliluyeva] returned home, she went straight to the Kremlin wall to pay respects to her father's ashes and to put flowers by his grave (1a).

< From the Biblical parable (Luke 15:11–32).

С-733 • КУ́РИЦЫН СЫН *obs, highly coll, humor* [NP] a mild expletive (often used as vocative) in refer. to a man: **son of a gun.**

С-734 • СУ́КИН СЫН *highly coll* [NP] **1.** *rude.* Also: ВРА́ЖИЙ, ЧЁРТОВ, СОБА́ЧИЙ *obs*⟩ СЫН *highly* *coll, rude* [pl: сукины, собачьи etc дети (all variants) or сукины сыны́ (var. with сукины only)] an expletive (often used as vocative) in refer. to a man: **son of a bitch; s.o.b.; bastard; swine.**

«Почему сорван график?.. Отвечайте, или я вас всех, не отходя от кассы, перестреляю, сукины сыны!» (Алешковский 1). "Who interrupted the schedule?…You tell me, or I'll blow your brains out right here, you s.o.b.s! (1a). ♦ …Ведь он, сукин сын, не позволял вдове и копейки тратить на дочерей… (Рыбаков 1). You know, that swine wouldn't give the widow a penny to spend on the girls… (1a).

2. *rather humor* [usu. sing] an extremely familiar and slightly indecorous yet not unkind way to address or refer to s.o.: **son of a gun.**

С-735 • МА́МЕНЬКИН СЫНО́К ⟨СЫНО́ЧЕК⟩ *coll,*
disapprov or iron [NP; often subj-compl with copula, nom or instrum (subj: human, male); fixed WO] an effeminate, spoiled, and inept boy or young man: **mama's boy; mother's darling; sissy; mollycoddle.**

[Володя:] До войны я что знал? Дом да школу… Ну, стадион ещё. В общем — маменькин сынок был… (Розов 3). [V.:] What did I know before the war? Home, and school….And sports, too. I was just a mama's boy… (3a).

С-736 • КАК ⟨СЛО́ВНО⟩ СЫР В МА́СЛЕ КАТА́ТЬСЯ
coll [VP; subj: human; the verb may take the initial position, otherwise fixed WO] to live in complete prosperity: X как сыр в масле катается ≃ X is ⟨lives⟩ in clover; X lives in the lap of luxury; X lives off ⟨on⟩ the fat of the land; X lives high off ⟨on⟩ the hog.

…Только одна Варвара всё равно стала бы жаловаться, если бы даже каталась как сыр в масле… (Распутин 3). Varvara was the only one who would find cause for complaint even if she lived in the lap of luxury (3a).

С-737 • откуда, из-за чего и т. п. СЫР-БО́Р ЗАГОРЕ́ЛСЯ ⟨ГОРИ́Т⟩; (ВЕСЬ) СЫР-БО́Р (ЗАГОРЕ́ЛСЯ) *из-за*
кого-чего, от кого-чего all coll [VP_subj] (why has, it is unclear why etc) some event, commotion, trouble etc occurred: **(that's) what ⟨who⟩ sparked the whole thing; (that's) what set the fur flying; (that's) what set the whole thing off; (that's ⟨person X is⟩) the cause of all the trouble; (that's) what touched off the whole ruckus; (that's) what all the commotion was about; (that's ⟨person X is⟩) the reason for the whole upheaval; (that's) what caused ⟨hence etc⟩ all the fuss.**

«„Но ты же угрожал ему [майору] пистолетом, — говорит он, — ты понимаешь, куда он это может повернуть“. — „А мы скажем, что он врёт, — отвечаю я, — скажем, что он сам хотел остаться с бабами и от этого весь сыр-бор“» (Искандер 5). "'But you threatened him [the major] with a pistol,' he says. 'You realize what he can make this sound like.' 'And we'll say he's lying,' I answer. 'We'll say he wanted to stay with the women himself and that's what sparked the whole thing'" (5a). ♦ Только потом, много позже, рассказал Михаил, из-за чего сыр-бор загорелся (Абрамов 1). Only later, much later, did Mikhail tell her what had set the fur flying (1a). ♦ …А эти-то, из-за которых весь сыр-бор, беспрепятственно выезжают в Палестину для укрепления враждебного государства… (Аксёнов 6). …And those other ones, who are the cause of all the latest trouble, can emigrate to Palestine without hindrance in order to strengthen a hostile state… (6a). ♦ А потом, добавил Михаил, возвращаясь к тому, из-за чего загорелся сыр-бор, может, Евсей Тихонович вовсе и не за себя хочет получить пенсию, а за детей? (Абрамов 1). And besides, Mikhail added, returning to the subject which had touched off the whole ruckus,

maybe it wasn't because of himself that Evsei Tikhonovich felt entitled to the pension, but because of his children (1a). ♦ Вот опять нам пришло на ум уотергейтское дело. Кто из нас, следивших за его перипетиями по передачам зарубежного радио, не приходил в изумление! Боже мой, из-за чего весь сыр-бор? Президент величайшей страны собирался кого-то подслушать. Всего-навсего (Войнович 3). Once again the Watergate affair comes to mind. Who among us, following his peripeteia on the foreign radio broadcasts, was not amazed? My heavens, what was all the commotion about? The President of the greatest country on earth wanted to eavesdrop on someone. That's all there was to it (3a). ♦ Восторгаясь Еленой Прекрасной, как-то запамятовали, что она дочь Зевса, и поэтому сыр-бор загорелся: кому владеть? (Терц 3). In their admiration for Helen of Troy people somehow leave out of account that she was the daughter of Zeus—hence all the fuss about who was to possess her (3a).

< «Сыр» is the old short-form adjective, used instead of the contemporary long-form adjective «сырой».

С-738 • РАЗВОДИ́ТЬ/РАЗВЕСТИ́ СЫ́РОСТЬ *coll, often*
humor [VP; subj: human; often impfv (neg imper or infin with хватит, нечего etc)] to cry: X развёл сырость ≃ **X turned on the waterworks ⟨the tears⟩;** || *Neg Imper* не разводи ⟨хватит разводить⟩ сырость ≃ **turn off the waterworks;** [in limited contexts] **quit blubbering.**

[Лебедев:] Ну, все заревели! Квартет! Да будет вам сырость разводить! Матвей!.. Марфа Егоровна!.. Ведь этак и я… я заплачу… (Чехов 4). [L.:] There, now, everyone's bawling! A quartet! That's enough. Turn off the waterworks! Matvei!…Marfa Egorovna!…If you keep it up, I…I'll start crying, too… (4a). ♦ И вдруг Лизка охнула, пала на скамейку и расплакалась… Егорша в нерешительности остановился… «Ладно, — сказал он, неприязненно глядя на неё, — хватит сырость разводить» (Абрамов 1). Then suddenly she [Lizka] groaned, slumped onto the bench and burst into tears….Egorsha stopped in indecision. …"Okay," he said, looking at her with hostility. "Quit blubbering" (1a).

С-739 • СЫ́ТЫЙ ГОЛО́ДНОГО НЕ РАЗУМЕ́ЕТ
[saying] one who has everything he needs, is perfectly comfortable etc does not understand the plight of those who live in need, are suffering etc: ≃ **the well-fed don't understand the hungry; he that is warm thinks all so.**

[author's usage] «…Какой живой ещё Н.Н.! Слава богу, здоровый человек, ему понять нельзя нашего брата, Иова многострадального; мороз в двадцать градусов, он скачет в санках, как ничего… с Покровки… а я благодарю создателя каждое утро, что проснулся живой, что ещё дышу. О… о… ох! недаром пословица говорит: сытый голодного не понимает!» (Герцен 1). "What a lively fellow N.N. still is! Thank God, he's a healthy man and cannot understand a suffering Job like me; [it's twenty degrees below zero], but he dashes here all the way from Pokrovka in his sledge as though it were nothing…while I thank the Creator every morning that I have woken up alive, that I am still breathing. Oh…oh…ough…! It's a true proverb; the well-fed don't understand the hungry!" (1a).

С-740 • СЫЧО́М ⟨КАК СЫЧ⟩ ГЛЯДЕ́ТЬ ⟨СМО-
ТРЕ́ТЬ, СИДЕ́ТЬ⟩ *coll* [VP; subj: human] to have a dour look on one's face, look sullen: X сычом глядел ≃ **X looked glum ⟨gloomy⟩; X looked down in the mouth ⟨in the dumps⟩.**

С-741 • СЫЧО́М ⟨КАК СЫЧ⟩ ЖИТЬ *coll* [VP; subj:
human] to live in solitude, isolation: X живёт как сыч ≃ **X lives like a hermit ⟨a recluse⟩.**

Т

T-1 • ТА́БЕЛЬ О РА́НГАХ [NP; sing only; fixed WO]
1. [табель is fem] the hierarchical system of military, civil, and court ranks introduced by Peter I: **Table of Ranks.**

Возникавшие вопросы вовсе не относились до табели о рангах (Герцен 1). The problems that were arising amongst us had no reference whatever to the Table of Ranks (1a).

2. [табель is masc or fem] a system of ranking in an institution or within some group of people: **hierarchy; rules ⟨order⟩ of precedence; rules of rank; pecking order.**

Во всяком месте своя табель о рангах... (Грекова 3). Every organization has its own hierarchy (3a). ♦ Обсуждение пошло дальше с претензией на некоторую спонтанность, но в то же время и с соблюдением неписаной табели о рангах (Аксёнов 12). The discussion continued with pretensions to spontaneity, but at the same time following unwritten rules of rank (12a). ♦ Одновременно со мной болел Вишневский, и только поэтому я узнала, что существуют новые лекарства, которые могли значительно ускорить моё выздоровление. Но и лекарства распределяются у нас по табели о рангах (Мандельштам 1). [context transl] Vishnevski happened to be in the hospital at the same time, and it was from him that I learned of the existence of new drugs which would have helped me recover much more quickly. But even the medicine you get depends on your status (1a).

T-2 • ВО́Т ТАК...! *coll* [Particle; Invar; foll. by NP; fixed WO] used in exclamations to express the speaker's ironic, condescending, scornful etc attitude toward s.o. or sth., or to express his opinion that the person or thing in question does not deserve to be called by a certain name (as specified by the NP that follows): **what a [NP]!; nice [NP]!; [NP], my foot!; some [NP] (one is)!; one calls himself a [NP]!**

«У вас, конечно, большой опыт. Я вас хотел спросить: по какому это признаку можно узнать, любишь человека или нет?» Вот так вопрос! Придётся отвечать (Грекова 1). "You've got great experience, and I want to ask you, what are the signs by which one can tell whether one does or doesn't love someone?" Nice question! I had to answer... (1b). ♦ Вот так садовод! Грушу от яблони отличить не может! Some gardener! He can't tell a pear tree from an apple tree!

T-3 • ЗА ТА́К *highly coll* [PrepP; Invar; adv] **1.** Also: **ЗА (ОДНО́) СПАСИ́БО** *coll* (to get, receive etc sth.) without having to pay for it, (to render a service, give s.o. sth etc) without receiving any pay in return: **for nothing; for free; free of charge; [in limited contexts] (just) give sth. away.**

И вам она предлагает [прочитать «Архипелаг Гулаг»] не за так, а за то, что вы, ознакомившись с отдельными абзацами насчёт генерала Власова, напишете в газету отклик, разумеется, не положительный (Войнович 3). And she offers it [The Gulag Archipelago] to you, not for nothing, but so that, after you get acquainted with the special paragraphs on General Vlasov, you'll write a statement for the newspaper—an unfavorable one, of course (3a). ♦ «Достань мне вина [here = водки] и курева». — «Курева я достать не могу». — «Хрен с ним, вина достань» — «За спасибо водку не дают» (Рыбаков 1). "Get me vodka and something to smoke." "A smoke I can't get." "Bugger the tobacco, get me the vodka." "They don't give it away, you know" (1a).

2. ~ пропасть, погибнуть и т. п. (in refer. to a person) (to perish, be killed etc) to no purpose, futilely: **for nothing; for naught; in vain.**

Не такой он дурак, чтобы за так пропасть. He's not so stupid as to die in vain.

T-4 • И ТА́К [Particle; Invar] anyhow, even without (doing what is specified in the preceding context): **as it is; anyway; [in limited contexts] already.**

[Сарафанов:] Как? Ты хочешь уехать?.. Прямо сегодня? Сейчас? [Бусыгин:] Да, папа. Мы и так задержались (Вампилов 4). [S.:] What? You want to go?...Today? This minute? [B.:] Yes, Dad. We've stayed too long as it is (4a). ♦ ...Коля собственноручно заколотил дверь, ведущую во двор, и велел Даше не открывать парадной двери незнакомым людям, пока не посмотрит на них с балкона. «Я и так всегда на балконе», — сказала Даша (Искандер 3). ...Kolya personally boarded up the door to the courtyard and ordered Dasha not to open the front door until she had looked from the balcony to see who was there. "I'm always on the balcony anyway," Dasha said (3a). ♦ На его лице появилось выражение надменности и самодовольства. Царственно он сунул руку в боковой карман, где лежат документы. «Не трудитесь, — сказал я ему, — я и так вижу, кто вы такой» (Войнович 1). [context transl] His face assumed a smug and arrogant expression. With a regal gesture, he stuck his hand into the pocket containing his ID. "Don't bother," I said. "I don't need that to know who you are" (1a).

T-5 • И ТАК ДА́ЛЕЕ, may be abbreviated in writing to **и т. д.** [AdvP; Invar; fixed WO] (used at the end of an enumeration to indicate that the list has not been exhausted, that it could be continued to include similar objects or phenomena) and other similar things: **and so forth (and so on); and so on; et cetera; etc.; [in limited contexts] and the ⟨such⟩ like; and more of the same; and all that; and more to that effect.**

...Она сказала то, что говорила всегда: что она никуда не поедет, не ударит пальцем о палец и так далее (Каверин 1). ...She said what she always said: that she would take no steps, she would not lift a finger, and so forth (1a). ♦ «Надо подать проект, — подумал секретарь, — чтобы в каждом районе было два Учреждения. Тогда первое будет выполнять свои функции, а второе будет наблюдать, чтобы не пропало первое... А кто же будет наблюдать за другим Учреждением? Значит, нужно создать третье, а за третьим — четвёртое и так далее до бесконечности...» (Войнович 2). A resolution should be submitted, thought the Secretary, that there be two Institutions in each district. The first would carry out its usual functions and the second would keep an eye on the first so that it wouldn't disappear....But who's going to keep their eye on the second Institution? That means a third will have to be created, and a fourth for the third and so on, ad infinitum... (2a). ♦ Председатель начал было с того, что он [Иван Фёдорович] свидетель без присяги, что он может показывать или умолчать, но что, конечно, всё показанное должно быть по совести, и т. д., и т. д. (Достоевский 2). The presiding judge began by saying that he [Ivan Fyodorovich] was not under oath, that he could give evidence or withhold it, but that, of course, all testimony should be given in good conscience, etc., etc. (2a). ♦ «...Он без разрешения ездил в Гольтявино. Возможно, я посмотрел бы на это сквозь пальцы, дело молодое, любовь и так далее. Но Гольтявино в ведении Дворцовой комендатуры, а они на это сквозь пальцы смотреть не желают» (Рыбаков 2). "He went to Goltyavino without permission. I might have shut my eyes to it—young people, true love, and all that. But Goltyavino comes under the jurisdiction of the Dvorets commandant's office, and they are not prepared to shut their eyes to it" (2a).

T-6 • (И) ТА́К И СЯ́К *coll* [AdvP; these forms only; fixed WO] **1.** [adv or predic (subj: human)] (to do or try to do sth.) in various ways: **this way and that; first one way, then another; in all different ways.**

Редкие стрелы дождя, утратившего и строй, и вес, и способность шуметь, невпопад, так и сяк вспыхивали на солнце (Набоков 1). Stray arrows of rain that had lost both rhythm and weight and the ability to make any sound, flashed at random, this way and that, in the sun (1a).

2. Also: **ТА́К-СЯ́К** [adv] not especially well but bearably, tolerably: **so-so; passably; fair to middling.**

«Каково торгует ваша милость?» – спросил Адриян. «Э-хе-хе, – отвечал Шульц, – и так и сяк. Пожаловаться не могу» (Пушкин 3). "How's Your Honor's business?" asked Adrian. "Oh, well," answered Schulz, "so-so. I can't complain" (3a). ♦ Остальной персонал отеля относится ко мне так-сяк (Лимонов 1). The rest of the hotel staff treat me passably (1a).

3. Also: **ТА́К-СЯ́К** [subj-compl with copula (subj: any common noun)] a person (thing, place etc) is not especially good but is bearable, tolerable, such that one can accept him (or it): **X и так и сяк ≃ X is not so bad; X is not that bad; X is satisfactory ⟨acceptable⟩; X will do.**

[Себейкин:] Шашлычная ещё так-сяк, у нас там возле артели стекляшку построили... (Рощин 2). [S.:] A shashlik place isn't so bad. They built one near our shop, all made of glass... (2a). ♦ [Ихарев:] Балык, кажется, не того, а икра ещё так и сяк (Гоголь 2). [I.:] The salmon's not up to scratch, but the caviar's satisfactory (2a).

Т-7 • (И) ТА́К И Э́ТАК ⟨Э́ДАК⟩; (И) ТА́К И ТА́К *all coll* [AdvP; these forms only; fixed WO] **1.** [adv or predic (subj: human)] (to do or try to do sth.) in various ways: **this way and that; in all different ways; first one way, then another;** [in limited contexts] **(try ⟨do⟩) everything (one can).**

[Расплюев:] Как взял он [Кречинский] это дело себе в голову, как взял он и дело, кинул так и этак... (Сухово-Кобылин 2). [R.:] As soon as the idea came to his [Krechinsky's] mind, he turned it over this way and that... (2b). ♦ Принц Ольденбургский так и эдак его [нашего представителя] уламывал, но ничего не получилось (Искандер 4). Prince Oldenburgsky tried to talk him [our spokesman] into it, first one way, then another, but he got nowhere (4a). ♦ Чем, скажите мне, выводить пятна с одежды? Я пробовал и так и эдак... (Булгаков 12). Will somebody please tell me how to get stains out of clothes? I tried everything (12a).

2. [adv] regardless of (what one does, how events develop etc): **anyway; anyhow; in any case ⟨event⟩; at any rate; one way or another;** [when there are only two possible outcomes, options etc] **either way.**

Невероятно, но факт – проспали! Придётся теперь ехать в Ленинград, сдавать билеты... Впрочем, самому ему, как Лёва тут же рассудил, это только на руку: ведь, так и так, он не мог бы поехать... (Битов 2). Incredible, but a fact – they had overslept! Now they would have to go to Leningrad and turn in their tickets....Then again, as Lyova decided on the spot, this was just as well for him personally: he couldn't go anyway, of course... (2a). ♦ «Вот что, ребятишки... ломать [дом] так и так придётся: противопожарная безопасность» (Максимов 3). "Well, boys, here it is. You'll have to pull some of it [the house] down in any case. Fire regulations" (3a). ♦ «Вечером со сватами приду, – объявил Егорша. – Чего тут канитель разводить? Ты войди в моё положение. Мне так и этак жениться надо» (Абрамов 1). "This evening I'm coming over with the matchmakers," announced Egorsha...."Why drag it out? Put yourself in my position. One way or another I'm going to have to get married" (1a). ♦ Хотя мельница была в трёх километрах от деревни на дне ущелья, он [Кунта] не чувствовал большой разницы – что самому тащить [кукурузу], что с осликом тащить. И так и идти (Искандер 4). Although the mill was three kilometers from the village at the bottom of a ravine, he [Kunta] did not see much difference – lug it [his corn] himself, tramp beside a donkey, either way he would have to walk (4a).

Т-8 • НЕ ТА́К ЛИ? *coll* [Invar; used to form a question out of an affirm or neg statement; fixed WO] (what I said) is correct, is it

not?: **isn't that so ⟨right, true⟩?; (am I) right?; don't you agree?;** [after an affirm statement] **don't you think (so)?; isn't ⟨doesn't etc⟩ it?; don't ⟨haven't, aren't etc⟩ you ⟨they etc⟩?;** [after a neg statement] **is it?; do ⟨have, are etc⟩ you ⟨they etc⟩?**

«Вам нужна земля, не так ли?» (Гоголь 3). "You need land, isn't that so?" (3b). ♦ «...За космической гранью неминуемо нужно признать божественную силу. Не так ли?» (Гроссман 2). "Beyond a cosmic boundary, we have to admit the presence of a divine power. Right?" (2a). ♦ «Ведь обидеться иногда очень приятно, не так ли?» (Достоевский 1). "It sometimes feels very good to take offense, doesn't it?" (1a).

Т-9 • НЕ ТА́К ЧТОБ(Ы) (очень, слишком и т. п.) какой, как *coll* [Particle; these forms only] (used to express mild negation) not especially, not overly...: **not very ⟨really, particularly⟩...; not (all) that...; not too...;** [in limited contexts] **not what you would call...**

«Я туда [в институт] поступил ещё перед войной. Не так чтоб особенный интерес был. Но там броню давали...» (Копелев 1). "I had started there [at the institute] before the war. Not that I was particularly interested. But they gave a military deferment" (1a). ♦ В бричке сидел господин, не красавец, но и не дурной наружности, ни слишком толст, ни слишком тонок; нельзя сказать, чтоб стар, однако ж и не так чтобы слишком молод (Гоголь 3). The gentleman in the carriage was not handsome, but neither was he particularly bad-looking; he was neither too fat, nor too thin; he could not be said to be old, but he was not too young, either (3a). ♦ ...Дела в колхозе шли плохо. То есть не так чтобы очень плохо, можно было бы даже сказать – хорошо, но с каждым годом всё хуже и хуже (Войнович 2). ...Things at the kolkhoz were going poorly. Not what you would call very poorly, you could even say things were going well, except that they were getting worse and worse every year (2a).

Т-10 • НИ ЗА ТА́К *substand* [PrepP; Invar; adv] to no purpose at all: **for nothing; for naught; for no reason; in vain.**

«Гражданин полковник! Я слишком ничтожен, никому неизвестен. Я не хотел отдать свою свободу ни за так» (Солженицын 3). "Citizen Colonel! I am too unimportant, no one knows me. I didn't want to give my freedom away for nothing –" (3a).

Т-11 • (НУ) ТАК ЧТО́ Ж(Е) *coll* [sent; fixed WO] **1.** (used in response to the interlocutor's statement to show that the speaker does not consider it very important, of particular consequence) what is so important about that?: **(so ⟨well,⟩) what of it?; so what?**

«Услышат... хозяйка подумает, что я в самом деле хочу уехать...» – «Ну, так что ж?» Пусть её думает!» (Гончаров 1). "They may hear you....My landlady may think...that I really mean to go away." "Well, what of it? Let her!" (1b). ♦ [Смельская:] За мной очень ухаживает князь. [Негина:] Так что ж! Уж это твоё дело (Островский 11). [S.:] The prince is paying me a lot of attention. [N.:] What of it? That's your business (11a).

2. used to induce the interlocutor to begin or continue speaking, or to encourage him to get to the point: **so...?; so tell me ⟨us⟩...; then what?; go on.**

Ну так что же, будешь запираться дальше или скажешь всю правду? So, are you going to continue insisting you're not guilty or are you going to tell us the truth?

Т-12 • РАЗ ТА́К *coll* [subord clause; Invar; often preceded by Conj «а»; fixed WO] inasmuch as matters are the way they are described in the preceding context: **that being the case; that being so; since that's the way it is ⟨one feels about it etc⟩; in that case;** [in limited contexts] **if that's the way it is ⟨one feels about it etc⟩.**

У нас отсутствуют нравственные принципы и традиции, по которым какая-то влиятельная категория лиц отдаёт предпочтение действительно более ценным и талантливым продуктам творчества. А раз так, снижается число лиц, живущих с учётом того, что справедливая оценка их творчества возможна (Зиновьев 1). "We lack any moral principles or traditions under which some influential group of people would give priority to any really worthwhile and talented creative products. And since that's the way it is, the number of people who have any hope of being judged by any fair assessment of their creative abilities is declining all the time" (1a). ♦ [Колесов:] Куда же вы собрались? Неужели в театр?.. Всё ясно. Куда — вы этого сами ещё не знаете. А раз так, то идёмте со мной (Вампилов 3). [К.:] Where, then, are you planning to go? Not to the theatre?…I get it. You still don't know yourself. In that case, come with me (3b). ♦ …Она [девушка] мне уже мерещилась. Чуть-чуть, но всё-таки. А раз человек мерещится, можно быть спокойным — сам найдётся. Раз так, подумал я, значит, я излечился от старой болезни (Искандер 6). …By now she [the girl] was fixed in my mind. And once a person is fixed in your mind, however slightly, you can be sure that somehow, somewhere your paths will cross. Well, I thought to myself, if this is the way I feel about this girl, I must finally be cured of the old one (6a).

Т-13 • ТАК ВОТ *coll* [Invar; usu. parenth; fixed WO] used to indicate a transition from one part of a story to the next, or to introduce an unexpected piece of information, a summary of what has been said etc: **well then; (and) so; thus.**

Старый Тендел стал рассказывать историю своей женитьбы… По словам Тендела, это случилось в дни его далёкой молодости, когда он ещё не выдурился. Тут гости прервали его рассказ дружным смехом, выражая этим смехом уверенность, что он ещё и до сих пор не выдурился… Так вот, продолжал Тендел, в те дни, когда он ещё не выдурился, пришлось ему кутить в одном доме в селе Кутол (Искандер 5). Old Tendel began to tell the tale of how he got married….As Tendel told it, it had happened in the days of his distant youth, when he hadn't yet outgrown folly. Here the guests interrupted his story with friendly laughter, their laughter expressing the conviction that even to this day he hadn't yet outgrown folly….Well then, Tendel went on, in those days, when he hadn't yet outgrown folly, he happened to go carousing at a certain house in the village of Kutol (5a). ♦ Тут кум-комедиант позволил себе сказать следующее: «Так вот, ваше величество, я хотел всеподданнейше испросить разрешение на представление „Тартюфа"». Изумление поразило кума-короля (Булгаков 5). At this point the comedian permitted himself to say the following words: "And so, Your Majesty, I wish most humbly to beg your permission to present *Tartuffe*." The king was stunned (5a). ♦ «…Я беру свои слова обратно: когда-то я говорила, что ты одна такая на десять тысяч женщин. Так вот: не на десять, а на сто тысяч» (Залыгин 1). [context transl] "I take back what I said. I said once that you were one woman in ten thousand. I was wrong. You're one in a hundred thousand, not ten thousand" (1a).

Т-14 • ТАК ЕГО́ ⟨её, их⟩! *coll* [Interj; these forms only; fixed WO] an exclamation of encouragement directed toward a person or persons who are punishing s.o., disciplining s.o., beating s.o. (up) etc: **let him ⟨her, them⟩ have it!; give it to him ⟨her, them⟩ good!; that's giving it to him ⟨her, them⟩!; [in refer. to verbal reprimands only] that's telling him ⟨her, them⟩!**

Т-15 • ТА́К ЖЕ КАК (И)… [correlative Conj] along with: **just as; as well as; [in limited contexts] (just) like; also.**

Человеку дано стать палачом, так же как и дано не становиться им. В конечном итоге выбор за нами (Искандер 3). Man is given the choice of becoming a hangman, just as he is given the choice of not becoming one. In the final analysis, the choice is ours (3a). ♦ Принцы и маркизы были пансионерами лицея, имели свою собственную прислугу, своих преподавателей, отдельные часы для занятий, так же как и отдельные залы (Булгаков 5). Princes and marquises were boarders at the lycée, with their own servants, their own instructors, their own separate hours of study, as well as their own separate classrooms (5a). ♦ Пётр Петрович Коновницын, так же как и Дохтуров… пользовался репутацией человека весьма ограниченных способностей и сведений… (Толстой 7). Like Dokhturov, he [Pyotr Petrovich Konovnitsyn] had the reputation of being a man of very limited ability and knowledge… (7a). ♦ Азазелло… одетый, как и Воланд, в чёрное, неподвижно стоял невдалеке от своего повелителя, так же как и он не спуская глаз с города (Булгаков 9). Azazello…dressed in black like Woland, stood motionless not far from his master, his eyes also fixed on the city (9a).

Т-16 • ТА́К И [intensif Particle; Invar; fixed WO] **1.** used to emphasize the intensive, energetic nature of some action or the intensity of some feeling: **positively; simply;** [may be translated by an intensifier specific to the context, or in conjunction with the Russian verb by a stronger English verb].

Комья земли так и выпрыгивали из-под мотыги Харлампо… (Искандер 5). Clods of earth positively flew from under Harlampo's hoe… (5a). ♦ «На диоскурийском базаре, — начал Джамхух, — где бывает очень много народу… в толпе так и шныряют карманщики» (Искандер 5). "At the Dioscurias bazaar," Jamkhoukh began, "where there are a great many people…the crowd simply crawls with pickpockets" (5a). ♦ Снег так и валил (Пушкин 2). The snow was falling thick and fast (2a). ♦ «А сирень всё около домов растёт, ветки так и лезут в окна, запах приторный» (Гончаров 1). "Lilac always grows close to houses, the branches thrust themselves in at the windows, the smell is so cloying" (1a). ♦ Меня это взорвало, мне так и хотелось съездить по его бритой роже, но в такой ситуации нельзя давать волю чувствам, надо сдерживать себя… (Рыбаков 1). I thought I would explode, I wanted to smash his ugly mug so much, but in a situation like that, you can't give vent to your feelings, you must control yourself… (1a). ♦ Митя же, заслышав вопль её, так и задрожал… (Достоевский 1). Mitya, hearing her wail, shuddered all over… (1a).

2. used for emphasis with verbs denoting actions that occur quickly, unexpectedly: **just; simply.**

…Он [Бородавкин] явился в Глупов и прежде всего подвергнул строгому рассмотрению намерения и деяния своих предшественников. Но когда он взглянул на скрижали, то так и ахнул (Салтыков-Щедрин 1). …He [Wartkin] arrived in Foolov and began by subjecting the plans and actions of his predecessors to a strict examination. But when he looked at the annals he simply gasped (1a).

3. used in response to a confirmation of one's or s.o.'s supposition, guess etc: **just as I ⟨he etc⟩ thought ⟨said etc⟩; I thought so!; I (just) knew it!; I ⟨he etc⟩ knew it all along; I ⟨he etc⟩ thought ⟨said, knew etc⟩ as much.**

Накануне вечером ему позвонил по телефону Ландесман, и Штрум ему сказал, что ничего не получается с его оформлением. «Я так и предполагал», — сказал Ландесман… (Гроссман 2). The previous evening, Landesman had phoned; Viktor had told him of his failure to secure his nomination. "Just as I expected!" Landesman had said… (2a). ♦ «Вы художники? Я так и знал!» (Федин 1). "Are you artists? I knew it!" (1a). ♦ «Я так и знала, что вы так ответите» (Достоевский 1). "I just knew you'd say that" (1a). ♦ «Кстати, он кто, этот Савелий?» — «Прораб», — осторожно сказал Ефим. «Так я и думал» (Войнович 6). "This Savely, by the way — what is he?" "A construction boss," Yefim said warily. "I thought as much" (6a).

4. [used with a pfv verb] used to express disagreement with some statement or strong skepticism that some action will take place: **there's no way…!; as if s.o. would (actually) do sth.; you've got to be kidding if you think…!; [in limited contexts] fat chance!**

«Я попросил Аркадия привезти мне книги». — «Так он тебе и привезёт! Нашла кого просить!» "I asked Arkady to bring me the books." "As if he'd actually bring them to you! You sure picked the right person to ask!"

5. [used with a negated verb] used for emphasis when stating that sth. never occurred, was never completed etc: [equivalents incorporate the negation] **(one) never (really ⟨actually⟩) did…**; [in limited contexts] **not once did (one ever).**

Ответа на заявление я так и не получил (Марченко 1). And I never did get a reply to my protest (1a). ♦ Так [я] за всю войну и не увидел, чтобы подбили самолёт (Искандер 6). In fact, not once during the course of the war did I ever see one of these planes put out of action (6a).

6. used to emphasize that an action takes place in an unobstructed manner: **just; simply.**

Т-17 • ТА́К И НА́ДО ⟨НУ́ЖНО⟩ *кому coll* [indep. clause; these forms only; fixed WO] it is what s.o. really deserves (as a punishment etc): **так Х-у и надо** ≃ **(it) serves X right; that's what X deserves; X had it coming (to him); X was asking for it.**

«Сумасшедший, ведь ты убил его [Фёдора Павловича]!» — крикнул Иван. «Так ему и надо! — задыхаясь, воскликнул Дмитрий. — А не убил, так ещё приду убить» (Достоевский 1). "Madman, you've killed him [Fyodor Pavlovich]!" shouted Ivan. "Serves him right!" Dmitri cried, gasping. "And if I haven't killed him this time, I'll come back and kill him" (1a). ♦ [Гетман:] Что вы такое говорите? Отбыл с дежурства?.. Значит, бросил дежурство? У вас тут происходит, в конце концов? *(Звонит по телефону.)* Комендатура?.. Дать сейчас же наряд… Наряд на квартиру к моему адъютанту корнету Новожильцеву, арестовать его и доставить в комендатуру. Сию минуту. [Шервинский *(в сторону)*:] Так ему и надо! (Булгаков 4). [Н.:] What are you saying? Left his duty-post?…I.e. he abandoned his post? What's really going on here? *(He calls up on the telephone.)* Commandant's?…Give me a detail immediately.…A detail to the apartment of my adjutant, Cornet Novozhiltsev, arrest him and take him to the commandant's. Immediately. [Sh. *(aside)*:] That's what he deserves! (4a).

Т-18 • ТА́К И ТА́К (МОЛ ⟨ДЕ́СКАТЬ⟩); ТА́К-ТО И ТА́К-ТО *all coll* [Invar; sent adv (parenth)] used to indicate that what one is about to say repeats or conveys what was said by o.s. or another at an earlier time; when used with a verb of speaking, adds colloquial flavor to the verb and reinforces that one is repeating words spoken earlier: **he says ⟨I said etc⟩; he says, well, he says that ⟨I said, well, I said that… etc⟩; he says ⟨I said etc⟩, you know (, that)…; he goes ⟨I went etc⟩; (go to see s.o. ⟨write to s.o. etc⟩) to say, well, to say (that)…**

Если бы она написала мужу ещё в войну: так и так, мол, встретила человека… ей бы не в чем было упрекнуть себя… Но как раз вот этого-то она и не сделала. Не хватило духу. Пожалела (Абрамов 1). If she had written to her husband during the war to say, well, to say that she had met someone…she would have had nothing to reproach herself with.…But that was precisely what she had not done. She hadn't had the heart. She had taken pity on him… (1a).

Т-19 • ТА́К ИЛИ ИНА́ЧЕ [AdvP; Invar; fixed WO] **1.** [adv] in this or another manner, in some way: **in some way or another;** [in limited contexts] **in one form ⟨capacity etc⟩ or another.**

Это есть действие по отношению к… другим индивидам, так или иначе затрагивающее их интересы (Зиновьев 1). It is an action directed towards…other individuals which, in some way or another, affects their interests (1a). ♦ За двадцать лет, что я прожил с Ритой, не было, наверное, ни одной недели, чтобы я так или иначе не касался мыслями этой темы (Трифонов 5). During the whole twenty years that I had lived with Rita, there probably had not been a single week when this thought had not crossed my mind in one form or another (5a).

2. [sent adv (usu. parenth)] whatever the circumstances or situation was or may be, regardless of other (often adverse) circumstances: **at any rate; in any event; anyway; be that as it may;** [in limited contexts] **somehow or other.**

Возможно, вмешательство дяди Сандро в эту знаменитую игру… с точки зрения содержателей европейских игорных домов и покажется недопустимым давлением на психику игрока, я всё-таки склонен считать поступок дяди Сандро исторически прогрессивным. Так или иначе он помог сохранить имущество Коли Зархиди, которое, за исключением настенного зеркала, проломанного буфета и других мелочей, полностью перешло в руки советской власти (Искандер 3). From the standpoint of the keeper of a European gambling house, Uncle Sandro's intervention in this famous game…may seem like impermissible pressure on a gambler's psyche. Nevertheless, I am inclined to view Uncle Sandro's deed as historically progressive. At any rate, he helped preserve Kolya Zarhidis' property, which, with the exception of the wall mirror, the broken sideboard, and other trifles, passed intact into the hands of the Soviet authorities (3a). ♦ Теперь… мне кажется странным, что эта дешёвая «серия Синема — чудо XX века» так увлекла меня, что я… начала думать о театре. Но может быть, эта мысль забрела в мою голову значительно раньше — в тот день, когда, играя героиню Анну, я выходила на сцену?.. Так или иначе, но она явилась, эта чудесная мысль, и что ни день, то всё с большей уверенностью принялась распоряжаться моею душой (Каверин 1). Now…it seems strange to me that this cheap series, *The Cinema: Miracle of the Twentieth Century*, should have carried me away to such an extent that…I began to think about the theatre. Perhaps, though, the idea had entered my head considerably earlier, that day when, playing the heroine Anna, I had gone out on to the stage.…Anyway, this wonderful idea appeared and then with every passing day took command of my heart with greater confidence (1a). ♦ Весной началась кампания по сокращению штатов, и я попал под неё… Чтобы замаскировать свою пристрастность ко мне, редактор сократил вместе со мной нашу редакционную уборщицу, хотя сократить следовало двух наших редакционных шофёров… Так или иначе, сокращение состоялось… (Искандер 6). A drive to cut back on personnel was launched that same spring, and I became one of its victims.…To avoid being accused of any bias in relation to me, he [the editor] also fired our staff cleaning lady. Actually, he should have fired the two staff chauffeurs.…Be that as it may, the staff reduction took place… (6a). ♦ Во время одного довольно незначительного застолья, что было особенно обидно, дядя Сандро почувствовал себя плохо. Он почувствовал, что сердце его норовит остановиться. Но он не растерялся. Он ударил себя кулаком по груди, и оно снова заработало, хотя не так охотно, как прежде… Так или иначе, по словам очевидцев, в ту ночь у него хватило мужества и сил в качестве тамады досидеть за столом до утра (Искандер 3). During a certain supper party—to add insult to injury, it was rather a minor one—Uncle Sandro had begun to feel unwell. He felt his heart trying to stop. But he did not get flustered. He struck himself on the chest with his fist, and his heart started working again, although not so willingly as before.…Somehow or other, according to eyewitnesses, he had the courage and strength that night to sit at the table as tamada [toastmaster] until morning (3a).

Т-20 • ТА́К КАК [subord Conj; introduces a clause of reason] for the reason that: **since; (inasmuch) as; because.**

Многие очевидцы этого утра теперь утверждают, что скот села Анхара предчувствовал начало боя, хотя с достоверностью этого утверждения трудно согласиться… Так как голодный скот, находясь взаперти, всегда даёт о себе знать, теперь трудно установить, в самом деле он предчувствовал кровопролитие или нет (Искандер 3). Many eyewitnesses now claim that the livestock of the village of Ankhara had a premonition the battle would begin that morning, although this claim is hard to authenticate.…Since hungry animals who find themselves penned up always make themselves heard, it is difficult to establish now whether they actually had a premonition of bloodshed or not (3a). ♦ Научная ценность её [книги] невелика, так как почти все её идеи в той или иной форме обсуждались в западной литературе такого рода (Зиновьев 2). The scientific value of the book was minimal, as almost all its ideas had already been discussed in some form or other in Western literature of a similar kind (2a). ♦ ...О некоторых предметах я имел ещё весьма смутное представление, так как ничем, кроме римского права и отчасти гражданского, не занимался (Лившиц 1). ...I had only a very vague idea about some of the subjects because, apart from Roman law and to some extent civil law, I did not study anything (1a).

T-21 • ТА́К ЛИ, СЯ́К ⟨Э́ТАК⟩ ЛИ; ТА́К ИЛИ СЯ́К; ХОТЬ ТА́К, ХОТЬ СЯ́К ⟨Э́ТАК⟩ *all coll* [AdvP; these forms only; adv] by some means or other: **somehow (or other); one way or another ⟨the other⟩.**

[Кот:] Умоляю вас – вызовите его на бой. Он, конечно, убьёт вас, но пока суд да дело, можно будет помечтать, развалившись перед очагом, о том, как случайно или чудом, так или сяк... может быть, как-нибудь, а вдруг и вы его убьёте (Шварц 2). [Cat:] Do challenge him, I implore you. He will kill you, of course, but while it's all going on I shall be able to dream in front of the fire of how, perchance, by some accident or some miracle...somehow or other, one way or another, you might kill him (2b). ♦ К слову сказать, тётушка Хрисула была невероятная говорунья. По этому поводу обитатели Большого Дома отмечали, что рот её хоть так, хоть этак, но обязательно должен работать (Искандер 5). [context transl] I should mention that Auntie Chrysoula was an incredible chatterbox. In this connection the inhabitants of the Big House observed that if it wasn't one thing it was the other – her mouth had to be working (5a).

T-22 • ТА́К НА ТА́К *highly coll* [AdvP; Invar; adv] **1. менять, обменивать** *что* ~ (to exchange) one for another without additional payment: **(make) an even swap ⟨trade, exchange⟩.**

«Откуда у тебя велосипед?» – «Поменялся с соседом: я ему – магнитофон, а он мне – велосипед. Так на так». "Where did you get a bicycle from?" "I traded with my neighbor: I gave him a cassette player and he gave me this bike. An even swap."

2. in equal portions, in equal quantities: **(in) equal parts; in equal measure.**

Смешай молотый кофе и цикорий так на так. Mix equal parts of ground coffee and chicory.

3. получается, выходит ~ (it works out) so that one thing compensates for another: **it all evens out; one (thing) offsets ⟨counterbalances⟩ the other; one (thing) makes up for the other.**

T-23 • ТАК НЕ́Т (ЖЕ) *coll* [these forms only; used as Conj (contrastive-concessive); fixed WO] used to connect two statements, the former of which shows what the speaker thinks should be done and the latter of which shows what is done in reality (which contradicts the speaker's opinion, evaluation etc): **but no; but not him ⟨her etc⟩.**

«Вы бы здесь потрудились – так нет, за границу сбежать хотели» (Марченко 1). "You should get down to some hard work here, but no, you want to run abroad instead" (1a).

T-24 • ТА́К СЕБЕ *coll* [AdvP; Invar; fixed WO] **1.** [adv] in a mediocre way, neither well nor poorly: **so-so; fair to middling.**

Ноздрёв приветствовал его по-дружески и спросил: каково ему спалось? «Так себе», – отвечал Чичиков весьма сухо (Гоголь 3). Nozdryov greeted him in a very friendly fashion and asked him whether he had slept well. "So-so," Chichikov replied rather dryly (3a).

2. [subj-compl with copula (subj: any common noun) or non-agreeing modif] mediocre, undistinguished: **so-so; nothing special; (quite) ordinary; nothing out of the ordinary; not much of a [NP]; nothing ⟨not much⟩ to write home about.**

Есть род людей, известных под именем: люди так себе, ни то ни сё... (Гоголь 3). There is a type of man who is described as "so-so," neither one thing nor the other... (3a). ♦ Коньяк был так себе и стоил шесть пенсов дороже, чем в лавке (Герцен 3). The brandy was nothing special and cost sixpence more than at the shops (3a). ♦ [Отрадина:] Значит, хорош собой? [Шелавина:] Ну, нельзя сказать; так себе (Островский 3). [О.:] Then he must be handsome. [Sh.:] I wouldn't say so; quite ordinary looking (3a). ♦ Родственник был так себе, десятая вода на киселе, но он был в числе тех, кому принц помогал (Искандер 3). He wasn't much of a relative, a cousin ten times removed, but he was among those whom the prince helped (3a). ♦ Конь был трофеем, им можно было похвалиться: и статью взял, и резвостью, и проходкой, и строевой выправкой. А вот седло было под Кошевым – так себе седлишко. Подушка потёрта и залатана, задняя подпруга – из сыромятного ремня, стремена – в упорно не поддающейся чистке, застарелой ржавчине (Шолохов 4). The horse was a trophy and was something to show off; its height, speed, gait and military bearing were all admirable. But Koshevoi's saddle was not much to write home about. The seat was worn and patched, the rear girth was a strip of rawhide, and the stirrups had a stubborn coating of rust that would not come off (4a).

3. *obs* [usu. adv] without any apparent reason, with no definite purpose: **(one) just (does sth.).**

T-25 • ТА́К-ТО (ОНО́) ТА́К, НО ⟨А, ДА⟩... *coll* [a clause in a compound sent + Conj; fixed WO] (used when the speaker basically agrees with what has just been stated but wants to qualify it, single out an exception, voice an objection to a specific point etc) all of this is correct, true, but...: **that's all well and good, but...; that's all very well, but...; that may (very well) be true, but...; that may (well) be, but...**

Пиши, что в голову взбредёт. А в Органах сами разберутся, какими методами ты руководствовался. Так-то оно так, сказал Двурушник. Но мне бы не хотелось идти дорогой Правдеца (Зиновьев 1). "Just write what passes through your mind. The secret police will work out for themselves the methods you've used." "That's all very well," said Double-dealer. "But I don't want to go the same way as Truth-teller" (1a). ♦ «Для них [хозяев] для всех авторитет возможен только на страхе. Значит: дави, сажай, стреляй!..» – «Так-то оно так, но с международным положением считаться надо» (Копелев 1). "For all of them [the bosses] the only possible authority is based on fear. That means: suppress, send up, shoot!..." "That may be, but you have to take the international situation into account" (1a).

T-26 • ТА́К ТО́ЛЬКО *coll* [AdvP; Invar; adv; fixed WO] without special need, reason or without a definite goal, intention: **just; merely.**

...Она [Соня] часто приходила на госпитальный двор, под окна, особенно под вечер, а иногда так только, чтобы постоять на дворе минутку и хоть издали посмотреть на окна палаты (Достоевский 3). ...She [Sonia] would come often to the hospital yard and stand beneath the windows, especially in the evening, sometimes merely to stand in the yard for a moment and look at the windows, even if only from a distance (3b).

T-27 • ТАК ТО́ЧНО [indep. sent; Invar; fixed WO] (used as an affirmative response to a question or to corroborate the interlocutor's statement; common in the military; usu. used when addressing a person of a higher status or rank) yes, that is correct: **that's right; yes, he does ⟨they are etc⟩; indeed it is ⟨he does etc⟩; yes, sir ⟨madam, ma'am etc⟩; [in response to a question with neg predic] no, sir ⟨madam, ma'am etc⟩; [in military usage] yes, sir!**

«Вы, наверное, из штаба фронта, товарищ подполковник?» – «Так точно», – ответил Даренский... (Гроссман 2). "Are you from Front HQ, comrade Lieutenant-Colonel?" "That's right," said Darensky (2a). ♦ «Ну, как, опомнились? Свои-то оказались лучше большевиков?» – «Так точно, ваше благородие!» (Шолохов 5). "Well, have you come to your senses? So your own people turned out to be better than the Bolsheviks, did they not?" "Yes, they did, Your Honour!" (5a). ♦ «Вы, верно, едете в Ставрополь?» — «Так-с точно... с казёнными вещами» (Лермонтов 1). "You'll be going to Stavropol, I expect?" "Yes, sir.... Carrying government property" (1c). ♦ «Какой же из тебя будет казак, ежели ты наймитом таскаешься? Отец, отделяя тебя, разве ничего не дал?» — «Так точно, ваше превосходительство, не дал» (Шолохов 2). "What kind of Cossack will you make if you hire yourself out like this? Did your father not give you anything when you left home?" "No, Your Excellency, he didn't" (2a).

Т-28 • ТА́К ЧТО [subord Conj, resultative] with the result or consequence that: **so; and so; hence; therefore; consequently;** [in limited contexts] **so that.**

Коммунизм идеологический изложен в обширнейшей марксистской литературе, так что говорить на эту тему, казалось, нет надобности (Зиновьев 2). Communism is ideologically set out in the immense literature of Marxism, so it might seem that there is little need to say anything on the subject (2a). ♦ Пушечку Коля держал в руке пред всеми, так что все могли видеть и наслаждаться (Достоевский 1). Kolya held the cannon up in his hand before them all, so that they could all see and delight in it (1a).

Т-29 • ТА́К ЧТО́БЫ ⟨ЧТОБ⟩ [subord Conj; introduces a clause of purpose] in order that: **so as to; so that.**

Как только кто-нибудь начинал кричать, чтобы его отпустили, на нём мгновенно повисали три-четыре человека, так, чтобы всем ясно было — не отпускают парня, а то наделал бы он делов (Искандер 3). As soon as someone began shouting to be turned loose, three or four men instantly hung on him so as to make clear to everyone that they would not turn the fellow loose, or he'd make trouble (3a).

Т-30 • ТО ТА́К, ТО СЯ́К ⟨ТА́К, Э́ТАК⟩ all coll [AdvP; these forms only; adv; fixed WO] in various ways: **this way and that; first one way, then another ⟨the other⟩; first like this, then like that; now one way, now another ⟨the other⟩.**

Кончеев медленно и осторожно взял с этажерки, у которой сидел, большую книгу (Фёдор Константинович заметил, что это альбом персидских миниатюр) и, всё так же медленно поворачивая её то так, то сяк на коленях, начал её тихо и близоруко рассматривать (Набоков 1). Koncheyev slowly and carefully took a large volume from the bookshelf near which he was sitting (Fyodor noticed that it was an album of Persian miniatures), and just as slowly turning it this way and that in his lap, he began to glance through it with myopic eyes (1a).

Т-31 • ХОТЬ ⟨ХОТЯ́⟩ БЫ И ТА́К coll [indep. sent; these forms only; fixed WO] (used in response to some statement) although what has just been stated is true, there is nothing special or bad about it, there is no reason to exaggerate its importance etc: **so what(!); what of it(!).**

«Инквизитор твой не верует в бога, вот и весь его секрет!» — «Хотя бы и так!» (Достоевский 1). "Your Inquisitor doesn't believe in God, that's his whole secret!" "What of it!" (1a).

Т-32 • КАК ТАКОВО́Й lit [как + AdjP; modif; fixed WO] viewed as an independent person or entity, separate from all other (people, things, circumstances etc): **as such; per se; in and of itself.**

По тому, как Кораблёв налил рюмку... было видно, что он пьёт профессионально... У Веры заныло внутри. Пьянство как таковое на её пути ещё не встречалось (Грекова 3). The way Korablev poured out the glass...made it clear that he was a most experienced drinker. Vera shuddered inside. She had never run into drunkenness as such (3a). ♦ ...В отношении самого Мансурова как такового — последнее слово было за ней [Ириной Викторовной], а не за ним: ехать ли ему на курорт или не ехать, а

если ехать — то когда; надевать тот или этот костюм на официальный приём; идти к врачу или не ходить... (Залыгин 1). [context transl] ...In anything concerning Mansurov personally she [Irina Viktorovna] always had the final say: whether he should go to a health resort or not, and if so, when; which suit he should wear for the coming official function; whether or not he should see a doctor... (1a).

Т-33 • ТАКО́Й-СЯКО́Й ⟨ТАКО́Й И СЯКО́Й⟩ coll, usu. humor; **ТАКО́Й-СЯКО́Й (СУХО́Й) НЕМА́ЗАНЫЙ ⟨НЕМА́ЗАНЫЙ СУХО́Й⟩** substand, occas. humor; [AdjP; usu. subj-compl with быть₀ (subj: human, pres only) or detached modif; fixed WO] used in place of a detailed, usu. negative, assessment of a person's character when addressing or referring to that person: **you ⟨that, the⟩ (old) so-and-so;** [in limited contexts] **you ⟨that, the⟩ (old) son of a gun.**

«Мать отправляет свою дочь отца искать — ага. „Иди, — говорит, — в забегаловку, опять он, такой-сякой, наверно, там". Он, понятное дело, там...» (Распутин 3). "Mum sends her daughter out to find Dad. 'Look in the boozer,' she says. 'That's where he'll be, the old so-and-so.' Sure enough, he's there..." (3a).

Т-34 • ТАКО́Й-ТО (И ТАКО́Й-ТО) [AdjP; modif] used in lieu of a word or words denoting the exact name, number, quality etc in question (to show that the speaker is intentionally not providing the specifics): [NP] **so-and-so; such and such a** [NP].

Ученик такой-то, позвольте мне, автору, снова прервать ваше повествование. Дело в том, что книгу пора заканчивать: у меня вышла бумага (Соколов 1). Student so-and-so, allow me, the author, to interrupt your narrative again. The thing is that it's time to end the book: I'm out of paper (1a). ♦ ...Трудно было бы узнать накануне и наверно... что завтра, в таком-то часу, такая-то старуха, на которую готовится покушение, будет дома одна-одинёхонька (Достоевский 3). ...It would be difficult to find out for sure the day before...that on the following day, at such and such a time, such and such an old woman whom he planned to assassinate would be home and all alone (3a).

Т-35 • С ТА́КОМ substand, humor [PrepP; Invar; usu. nonagreeing modif] (of some food, dish, baked goods etc) without any sauce, dressing, filling etc: **(just) plain.**

Мать замесила тесто, а начинить было нечем, вот и получились пирожки с таком. Mother mixed the dough, but there was nothing to fill it with, so she ended up with plain pirozhki.

Т-36 • В ТАКТ (чему) [PrepP; Invar; adv] in accordance with the rhythm of sth.: **in time with ⟨to⟩; keeping time with ⟨to⟩; in rhythm to ⟨with⟩;** [in refer. to marching, walking etc] **fall ⟨get⟩ into step with;** ‖ Neg не в такт ≃ **out of time ⟨sync, step⟩ with.**

Она [мама] кивала головой в такт своим словам (Рыбаков 2). She [mother] nodded her head in time with her words (2a). ♦ «Как, как, как стихи-то Марина, как стихи, как? Что на Геракова написал: „Будешь в корпусе учитель..." Скажи, скажи», — заговорил Кутузов, очевидно собираясь посмеяться. Кайсаров прочёл... Кутузов, улыбаясь, кивал головой в такт стихов [the use of the genitive is dated] (Толстой 6). "Those verses...those verses of Marin's...how do they go, eh? The lines he wrote about Gerakov: 'Thou, preceptor to the corps...' Recite them, recite them!" he said, obviously prepared to laugh. Kaisarov recited the lines. Kutuzov smiled and nodded his head in rhythm to the verses (6a). ♦ Листницкий шёл, непроизвольно улыбаясь, норовя шагать в такт голосам (Шолохов 3). A smile came involuntarily to Listnitsky's lips and he tried to fall into step with the beat of the song (3a).

Т-37 • ЗАРЫВА́ТЬ/ЗАРЫ́ТЬ ТАЛА́НТ (В ЗЕ́МЛЮ) [VP; subj: human] to leave one's abilities undeveloped or underdeveloped, not make use of one's talent: X зарыл свой талант ≃ **X wasted his talent(s) ⟨abilities⟩; X let his talent(s) ⟨abilities⟩ go to waste.**

< From the Biblical parable about a man who buried his money («талант») in the earth, rather than put it to good use (Matt. 25: 14–30). «Талант» (from the Greek *talanton*) was a unit of money in ancient Greece, Palestine, etc.

Т-38 • **ТА́М И ТУ́Т** ⟨**СЯ́М** old-fash, **ЗДЕ́СЬ**⟩; **ТУ́Т** ⟨**ЗДЕ́СЬ**⟩ **И ТА́М** all coll [AdvP; these forms only; adv; fixed WO] in various places, in many places: **here and there; here, there, and everywhere; all over (the place); [in limited contexts] hither and yon.**

В одном месте пели песни, в другом ругались; там и сям кричали: караул! (Салтыков-Щедрин 2). In one place songs resounded, in another raucous voices were raised in heated argument, here and there people shouted, "Help!" (2a). ♦ …Некоторые вольнолюбцы… потому свои мысли вольными полагают, что они у них в голове, словно мухи без пристанища, там и сям вольно летают (Салтыков-Щедрин 1). …Certain Freedom-lovers… suppose their thoughts free because they fly freely hither and yon in their heads, like houseflies without a *pied-à-terre* (1a).

Т-39 • **ТАМ** ⟨**ВЕЗДЕ́**⟩ **ХОРОШО́, ГДЕ НА́С НЕТ** [saying] (said, often ironically, in response to a statement that things are better elsewhere) it always seems that things are better someplace other than where you are: ≃ **the grass is always** ⟨**always seems, always looks**⟩ **greener on the other side (of the fence** ⟨**the hill**⟩**).**

«Скажите, отчего, даже когда мы наслаждаемся, например, музыкой, хорошим вечером… отчего всё это кажется скорее намёком на какое-то безмерное, где-то существующее счастие, чем действительным счастием, то есть таким, которым мы сами обладаем? Отчего это? Или вы, может быть, ничего подобного не ощущаете?» – «Вы знаете поговорку: „Там хорошо, где нас нет"», – возразил Базаров… (Тургенев 2). "Tell me why it is that even when we are enjoying music, for instance, or a fine evening…it all seems an intimation of some measureless happiness existing apart somewhere rather than actual happiness—such, I mean, as we ourselves are in possession of? Why is it? Or perhaps you have no feelings like that?" "You know the saying, 'The grass is always greener…'" replied Bazarov (2b).

Т-40 • **НЕ В СВОЕ́Й ТАРЕ́ЛКЕ быть**₀, **бывать, чувствовать себя** coll [PrepP; Invar; subj-compl with copula (subj: human) or adv; occas. used without negation to convey the opposite meaning; fixed WO] **1.** (to be) in an unpleasant, negative state of mind, (to feel) worse than one usu. does: X не в своей тарелке ≃ **X is** ⟨**feels**⟩ **out of sorts; X isn't (quite) himself; X doesn't feel (quite) (like) himself; [in limited contexts] X is in a foul** ⟨**bad**⟩ **mood.**

«Мне и его [Алёшу] жалко. Он с тех пор замкнулся, так и ходит весь чёрный. А между тем нас никуда не тянут. И я думаю: майор оказался лучше, чем мы ожидали. Через пару дней подхожу к Алексею. „Слушай, – говорю, – ты видишь, майор оказался лучше, чем мы думали. Раз до сих пор не капнул, значит, пронесло. Я же вижу, ты не в своей тарелке"» (Искандер 5). "I felt sorry for him [Alyosha], too. He had withdrawn into himself, he went around looking positively black. Meanwhile, they hadn't hauled us in. I thought, the major's turned out better than we expected. A couple of days later I went to Alyosha. 'Listen,' I said, 'you see the major's turned out better than we thought. If he hasn't squealed by now, then it's blown over. But I can see you're out of sorts'" (5a).

2. (often in refer. to social situations) to feel anxious, not relaxed, and (in the case of social situations) as if one does not belong in the given milieu, company etc: X не в своей тарелке ≃ **X feels** ⟨**is**⟩ **ill at ease; X feels uneasy** ⟨**uncomfortable, out of place**⟩; **X is out of his element; ‖ X в своей тарелке ≃ X is in his element; X feels (perfectly) at home.**

…Вдруг все взглянули на него, один господин в лорнет. «Кто это?» – тихо спросила Сонечка. «Илья Ильич Обло-

мов!» – представила его Ольга. Все пошли до дома пешком. Обломов был не в своей тарелке… (Гончаров 1). Suddenly they all…looked at him, one gentleman peering through a lorgnette. "Who is that?" Sonya asked softly. "Ilya Ilych Oblomov," Olga introduced him. They all walked to Olga's house. Oblomov felt uncomfortable… (1b). ♦ Там [на мысу Херсонес], в одной из крохотных бухточек, готовились к побегу четверо молодых людей… Впрочем, их было пятеро – в побеге участвовал и новорождённый Арсений… Энергии Бен-Ивана хватало на всех пятерых. Он чувствовал себя в своей тарелке, побег был его стихией (Аксёнов 7). There [, at Cape Kherson], in one of the many tiny bays, two couples…were planning their escape. Actually there were five of them: the newborn Arseny was in on it as well….Ben-Ivan had enough energy for the five of them. He was in his element: escapes were his specialty… (7a). ♦ Патрику Тандерджету чрезвычайно понравился «Мужской клуб», он сразу почувствовал себя здесь в своей тарелке (Аксёнов 6). Patrick Thunderjet greatly loved the Men's Club; he immediately felt at home there (6a).

< Translation of the French *ne pas être dans son assiette.*

Т-41 • **ЛЕТЕ́ТЬ/ПОЛЕТЕ́ТЬ В ТАРТАРАРЫ́** coll [VP; subj: usu. abstr, often всё, occas. concr] (usu. of some plans, matters, s.o.'s life etc) to move toward a state of collapse or be totally ruined: X полетел в тартарары ≃ **X went down the drain** ⟨**the tube(s)**⟩; **X went to hell** ⟨**to the dogs**⟩; **X fell apart** ⟨**to pieces**⟩.

Помимо указательных, Мансуров как-то незаметно-незаметно, а присвоил себе ещё и запретительные функции… Ему даже казалось, что если он перестанет запрещать – завтра же всё рухнет, полетит в тартарары, вся семья погибнет… (Залыгин 1). On top of his instructional functions Mansurov had in some imperceptible way arrogated to himself the right of veto….It actually seemed to him that if he once stopped forbidding things everything would crumble into ruins the next day, everything would fall to pieces, the family would perish (1a).

Т-42 • **ПРОВАЛИ́ТЬСЯ В ТАРТАРАРЫ́** coll [VP; subj: human; often infin with готов, рад, лучше бы etc] (one is ready, would like, wants etc) to disappear completely, get away from where he is (because he is so embarrassed, uneasy, ashamed etc): X готов провалиться в тартарары ≃ **X wishes the earth would swallow him up** ⟨**the earth would open up and swallow him**⟩; **X wishes he could** ⟨**X is ready to**⟩ **sink through the floor.**

Сидя спиной к двери, он почему-то уверил себя, в эту минуту, что его провал, его позор, его поражение происходят у неё на глазах, в её присутствии, и от этого готов был провалиться сейчас в тартарары, раствориться в воздухе, слинять, улетучиться, не существовать вовсе (Максимов 2). Sitting with his back to the door he somehow managed to convince himself at that moment that his failure, his shame and defeat were happening before her eyes, in her presence, and because of this he was ready to sink through the floor, dissolve into thin air, vanish, evaporate, cease to exist (2a).

Т-43 • **РАЗВОДИ́ТЬ ТА́РЫ-БА́РЫ** ⟨**ТА́РЫ ДА БА́РЫ, ТА́РЫ-БА́РЫ-РАСТАБА́РЫ**⟩ (с кем) highly coll [VP; subj: human] to engage in empty conversation, idle chatter: X и Y разводят тары-бары ≃ **X and Y are shooting the breeze** ⟨**the bull**⟩; **X and Y are chewing the fat** ⟨**the rag**⟩; **X and Y are wagging their tongues** ⟨**chins**⟩.

Т-44 • **ТА́РЫ-БА́РЫ** ⟨**ТА́РЫ ДА БА́РЫ, ТА́РЫ-БА́РЫ-РАСТАБА́РЫ**⟩ all highly coll [NP; fixed WO] empty conversation, idle chatter: **tittle-tattle; chitchat; chitter chatter; [when trying to get sth. from s.o., occas. in a relationship between the sexes] sweet talk; sweet-talking.**

Егорша решил: обстановка неподходящая. В избу к себе Раечку не затащишь, на маслозаводе постоянно вертятся люди, надо, видно, на природу выходить. Листочки, кустики, то-сё, тары-бары-растабары — растает (Абрамов 1). Egorsha decided it was the surroundings that were not conducive. Raechka would not let herself be dragged off to his place, and there was a constant mob of people at the dairy. So obviously she would have to be taken out into the wide-open spaces. The leaves, the bushes, this and that, a little sweet-talking—she'd melt! (1a).

T-45 • ДАВА́ТЬ/ДАТЬ ⟨ЗАДАВА́ТЬ/ЗАДА́ТЬ⟩ ТА́СКУ *кому substand* [VP] **1.** [subj: human] to hit s.o. repeatedly (usu. while holding him by the hair): X дал Y-у таску ≃ **X grabbed Y by the hair and punched the crap ⟨the hell etc⟩ out of him; X beat the tar ⟨the crap etc⟩ out of Y.**

2. [subj: human (usu. pl) or collect] to cause s.o. (usu. a hostile army, the enemy) great losses, overwhelm or defeat s.o.: X-ы дали Y-ам таску ≃ **Xs crushed ⟨routed, clobbered⟩ Ys; Xs gave Ys a good ⟨real etc⟩ thrashing ⟨beating etc⟩.**

...[Фёдор Карлович] похвастался тем, что он был рекрутом под Ватерлоо и что немцы дали страшную таску французам (Герцен 1). ...[Fedor Karlovich bragged] of having been a recruit at Waterloo, and of the Germans having given the French a terrible thrashing (1a).

T-46 • ВСЯ́КОЙ ⟨КА́ЖДОЙ⟩ ТВА́РИ ПО ПА́РЕ *где coll, humor* [NP_gen; these forms only; fixed WO] (in refer. to a heterogeneous group of people or, less often, animals in which various types are represented) there are a few of each type (in some place): **all sorts ⟨kinds⟩ of people ⟨animals⟩; some of every type; people ⟨animals⟩ of every possible kind ⟨sort⟩; (people) of every stripe.**

< From the Biblical story of Noah's Ark (Gen. 6:19–20).

T-47 • ЧТО ТВОЙ... *obsoles* [AdjP; modif; fixed WO] a genuine person or thing of the given type: **a real ⟨regular, veritable⟩ [NP].**

T-48 • ВО́Т ТЕБЕ ⟨ВАМ⟩! *coll* [Interj; these forms only; fixed WO] take the punishment you deserve (often said while dealing a blow): **take *this,* and *that!;* take *this* ⟨*that*⟩!**

T-49 • ВО́Т ТЕБЕ И... *coll* [Interj; Invar; fixed WO] used to express one's surprise (usu. unpleasant) that s.o. or sth. turned out to be very different than expected; or used to express one's dissatisfaction that sth. anticipated either does not take place at all or turns out worse than expected: **so much for...; that's ⟨there's⟩ a [NP] for you; there goes your [NP]; some [NP].**

Собрались мы в лес по грибы, а тут дождь пошёл. Вот тебе и грибы! We were just about to leave for the woods to pick mushrooms when suddenly it started to rain. So much for mushroom picking! ♦ «Полянкин оказался прекрасным бизнесменом: он уже разбогател в своём кооперативе». — «Вот тебе и бывший партийный функционер!» "Polyankin turned out to be quite a businessman: he has already made a fortune off his cooperative." "There's a former party functionary for you!" ♦ Сколько Настёна помнила, никогда в эту пору так не заметало. Вот тебе и весна — март покатился под горку (Распутин 2). As long as Nastyona could remember, it never snowed like this at this time of the year. Some spring—and March was almost over (2a).

T-50 • НА́ ТЕБЕ! *coll* [Interj; Invar; often preceded by и, и вдруг, и вот, а тут etc; fixed WO] used to express surprise or dissatisfaction on the occasion of sth. unexpected: **wouldn't you know (it)!; look at him ⟨it etc⟩!; now look!; now ⟨then⟩ this!; [in limited contexts] bang!**

«И чего на него нашло такое? Никому никогда не перечил, тише воды, ниже травы был — и на тебе вдруг!» (Айтматов 1). "What's come over him? He never crossed anyone, always quiet as a mouse, and now—look at him" (1a). ♦ [Сильва:] Чёртов ветер! Откуда он сорвался? Такой был день и — на тебе! (Вампилов 4). [S.:] Damn that wind! Where did it come from? It was such a nice day and now look! (4b). [S.:] Bloody wind! Where did it come from? Such a fine day—and now this! (4a). ♦ [Сарафанов:] Жили в одном дворе, тихо, мирно, и вдруг — на тебе! Сдурел, уезжать собирается (Вампилов 3). [S.:] We all lived here as good neighbors, quietly, peacefully, and suddenly—bang! He loses his head, and he's all ready to leave home (3a).

T-51 • (ДА ⟨А⟩) НУ́ ТЕБЯ ⟨*его и т. п.*⟩! *coll* [Interj; these forms only; fixed WO] **1.** used to express one's dissatisfaction with s.o.'s statement(s) or action(s) (occas. used when the speaker pretends to be annoyed): **oh, you ⟨him etc⟩!; you're ⟨he's etc⟩ impossible ⟨unbelievable, incorrigible, hopeless, too much⟩!; [in limited contexts] that's enough from you!**

(Влетает Маша). [Валентин:] Маша? Ты что? [Маша *(с ходу):*] Да ну их! Совсем уж! Детям до шестнадцати [не разрешается], детям до шестнадцати [не разрешается]! (Рощин 1). *(Masha rushes in...)* [V.:] Masha! Back already? [M. *(furiously):*] Oh, *them!* It's too much! Children under sixteen not admitted! Children under sixteen not admitted! (1a). ♦ [Анастасия Ефремовна:] Где пепельница? [Андрей:] Вадим взял. [Анастасия Ефремовна:] Я же просила не трогать! Из неё окурки выковыривать трудно. [Андрей:] Сама говорила — для гостей. Да ну тебя! (Розов 1). [A.E.:] What did you do with the ash tray? [A.:] Vadim is using it. [A.E.:] Didn't I ask you not to touch it? It's hard to clean the cigarette butts out of it. [A.:] You said yourself that it was for guests! Oh, you're impossible! (1a).

2. used to express intense irritation with s.o. or sth. and usu. the speaker's desire to be entirely rid of him or it: **get lost!; to ⟨the⟩ hell with you ⟨him etc⟩; (oh,) go to hell!; the devil take you ⟨him etc⟩.**

«[Мы с женой] разошлись, я сразу поехал». — «А почему?» — «Без понятия она, не понимала меня. Поэтому... Ну её!.. На свете баб много» (Распутин 1). "[My wife and I have] parted. I up and left." "What for?" "She's dumb, didn't understand me. That's why....Oh, to hell with her!...There's lots of other women in the world" (1a). ♦ Друг мой прочитал договор и, к великому моему удивлению, рассердился на меня. «Это что за филькина грамота?..» — спросил он меня. «Да ну вас!» — вскричал я... (Булгаков 12). My friend read the contract and to my great astonishment lost his temper with me. "This is nothing but a useless scrap of paper!..." he shouted...."Oh, go to hell!" I shouted... (12a).

T-52 • СПАДА́ТЬ/СПАСТЬ С ТЕ́ЛА *substand* [VP; subj: human or, rare, animal] to grow thin: X спал с тела ≃ **X got thin ⟨skinny⟩; [in limited contexts] person X lost ⟨dropped⟩ weight.**

T-53 • В ТЕ́ЛЕ *substand* [PrepP; Invar; subj-compl with copula (subj: human) or nonagreeing modif] one is of a heavy build: **plump; on the heavy ⟨plump⟩ side; fleshy; (have) some meat on one.**

«Умерла Клавдия Ивановна», — сообщил заказчик. «Ну, царствие небесное, — согласился Безенчук. — Преставилась, значит, старушка... Старушки, они всегда преставляются... Или богу душу отдают, — это смотря какая старушка. Ваша, например, маленькая и в теле, — значит, преставилась. А например, которая покрупнее да похудее — та, считается, богу душу отдаёт...» (Ильф и Петров 1). "Claudia Ivanovna's dead," his client informed him. "Well, God rest her soul," said Bezenchuk. "So the old lady's passed away. Old ladies pass away...or they depart this life. It depends who she is. Yours, for instance, was small and plump, so she passed away. But if it's one who's a bit bigger and thinner, then they say she has departed this life..." (1a). ♦ [Фёкла:] [Балтазар Балтазарович] говорит, что ему нужно, чтобы невеста была в теле... (Гоголь 1). [F.:] He [Baltazar Baltazarovich] says he must have a young lady on the plump side...

(1c). [F.:] [Baltazar Baltazarovich] says he needs a bride with some meat on her (1b).

T-54 • ДЕРЖА́ТЬ В ЧЁРНОМ ТЕ́ЛЕ *кого coll* [VP; subj: human; the verb may take the final position, otherwise fixed WO] to treat s.o. severely, be unduly strict with s.o. etc (may refer to forcing s.o. to work excessively, providing a dependent person with only minimal subsistence, depriving s.o. of pleasure, treating s.o. as greatly inferior to o.s. etc): X держит Y-a в чёрном теле ≃ X ill-treats Y; X is very hard on Y; X treats Y shabbily; X makes Y's life miserable; [in limited contexts] X keeps Y on short rations; X holds Y down; X keeps Y on a short leash.

Казачьи офицеры... держались в чёрном теле, движение по службе было слабым... (Шолохов 3). The Cossack officers were...treated shabbily, promotion was slow... (3a). ♦ [author's usage] «Я думал их в чёрном теле попридержать и довести их, чтоб они на меня как на провидение смотрели, а они вон!..» (Достоевский 3). "I just wanted to keep them on short rations for a bit, so that they'd look upon me as a savior, but now look at them!..." (3a). ♦ Их [мещан] держала аристократия в чёрном теле...; освобождённые, они... ввели свой порядок (Герцен 2). They [the *petits bourgeois*] had been held down by the aristocracy...; set free, they...established their own régime... (2a). ♦ Больной Самсонов... подпал... под сильное влияние своей протеже, которую сначала было держал в ежовых рукавицах и в чёрном теле... (Достоевский 1). The ailing Samsonov...fell...under the strong influence of his protégée, whom he had at first kept in an iron grip, on a short leash... (1a).

T-55 • ВИСЕ́ТЬ ⟨ПОВИ́СНУТЬ⟩ НА ТЕЛЕФО́НЕ *coll* [VP; subj: human] to talk on the telephone at length (and frequently), or be talking on the telephone: X всегда висит на телефоне ≃ X is always ⟨forever⟩ on the phone; X monopolizes ⟨hogs⟩ the phone; X never gets off the phone; X spends days ⟨hours etc⟩ on the phone; ‖ «Где X?» — «Висит на телефоне». ≃ "Where is X?" "On ⟨tying up⟩ the phone."

«Наш „Иван Иванович" две ночи висел на телефоне, чтобы получить это разрешение...» (Аксёнов 6). "The KGB man in charge of our party had spent two whole nights on the phone to Moscow to wangle me that permission..." (6a). ♦ [Бабушка:] Он висит на телефоне и звонит на аэродром, а ему отвечают одно и то же: [самолёт] опаздывает... Ему говорят «опаздывает», а он не знает что думать (Панова 1). [Grandmother:] He's still on the phone, calling the airport, and they keep telling him the same thing: [the plane is] delayed....They keep telling him "delayed," and he doesn't know what to think (1a).

T-56 • ЗОЛОТО́Й ⟨ЗЛАТО́Й⟩ ТЕЛЕ́Ц *lit* [NP; sing only; usu. this WO] money, riches as the object of pursuit: **the golden calf.**

< From the Biblical account of the golden calf made by Aaron and worshiped as an idol by the Jews during their wanderings in the desert (Ex. 32).

T-57 • ВХОДИ́ТЬ/ВОЙТИ́ В ТЕ́ЛО *old-fash, coll* [VP; subj: human] to gain weight, become heavier: X вошёл в тело ≃ X fattened up; X filled out.

Позже Баграт говорил, что именно тогда у него мелькнула и тут же забылась мысль, что хорошо бы эту девчонку забрать домой, вымыть её как следует, дать попастись, не выпуская со двора, чтобы немного вошла в тело, а потом жениться на ней (Искандер 1). Bagrat said later that that was when the thought flashed through his mind—and was promptly forgotten—that it would be nice to take this little girl home, give her a good scrubbing, have her graze a while without letting her out of the yard so that she'd fatten up a bit, and then marry her (3a). ♦ «Это правда, — спросил старый Хабуг... — что эти не любят, чтобы девочки замуж выскакивали, пока не войдут в тело?» (Искандер 3). "Is

it true," old Khabug asked..."that They don't like girls to rush into marriage before they fill out?" (3a).

T-58 • А МЕ́ЖДУ ТЕ́М [coord Conj, usu. contrastive] in opposition to what has been stated: **(and) yet; nevertheless.**

Можно подумать, что доктор Вальтер благополучнейший частно-практикующий доктор... А между тем Антон Яковлевич Вальтер сидит уже десять лет, с тридцать пятого (Гинзбург 2). It would have been easy to take Dr. Walter for a highly successful private practitioner....And yet Anton Yakovlevich Walter had spent ten years inside [the camps], since '35 (2a). ♦ ...Казалось бы, что тут... кроме отчаяния, ничего уже более для него [Мити] не оставалось; ибо где взять вдруг такие деньги, да ещё такому голышу, как он? А между тем он до конца всё то время надеялся, что достанет эти три тысячи... (Достоевский 1). ...It would seem that...nothing was left for him [Mitya] but despair; for how could one suddenly come up with so much money, especially such a pauper as he? Nevertheless, to the very end he kept hoping that he would get the three thousand... (1a).

T-59 • ВМЕ́СТЕ С ТЕ́М [AdvP; Invar; usu. sent adv (occas. parenth.); usu. used after Conj «и», «но», «но и»; fixed WO] in addition to or along with what has been stated (a contrast may be implied): **at the same time;** [in limited contexts] **at once; also;** [only when a contrast is implied] **(and) yet.**

На остальных же, бывших в распивочной, не исключая и хозяина, чиновник смотрел как-то привычно и даже со скукой, а вместе с тем и с оттенком некоторого высокомерного пренебрежения... (Достоевский 3). The clerk was regarding the other people in the bar, including the proprietor, with a kind of familiarity and even boredom, and at the same time with a hint of haughty disdain... (3a). ♦ Во всякой книге предисловие есть первая и вместе с тем последняя вещь... (Лермонтов 1). The foreword is at once the first and the last thing in any book... (1b). ♦ Ленин... писал: Сталин капризен. Но вместе с тем он терпелив, настойчив и задуманное *всегда* доводит до конца (Рыбаков 2). Lenin had written that Stalin was capricious. But he was also patient and persistent, and he always carried his intentions through to the end (2a).

T-60 • МЕ́ЖДУ ⟨МЕЖ *obs*⟩ ТЕ́М [PrepP; these forms only; sent adv] during the intervening period of time: **in the meantime; meanwhile.**

Возвратясь с Сенной, он [Раскольников] бросился на диван и целый час просидел без движения. Между тем стемнело... (Достоевский 3). Returning from Sennaya Square, he [Raskolnikov] flung himself on the couch and sat there a whole hour without moving. In the meantime it grew dark... (3a). On returning from the Haymarket, he [Raskolnikov] flung himself on his couch and sat there a whole hour without moving. Meanwhile it grew dark (3b).

T-61 • МЕ́ЖДУ ⟨МЕЖ *obs*⟩ ТЕ́М КАК [subord Conj, usu. contrastive] used to juxtapose two actions, phenomena etc (occas. introduces the additional meaning of simultaneity or concession): **while; whereas;** [in limited contexts] **at the same time as; (and) meanwhile.**

...Она [Лиза] Алексея ещё не видала, между тем как все молодые соседки только об нём и говорили (Пушкин 3). ...She [Liza] had not had a chance to meet him [Aleksei], while all her young neighbors could speak of nothing but him (3a). ♦ ...Акмеизм наощупь подыскивал себе тяжеловесные корреляты в живописи, между тем как я, вырвавшись из плена сухих абстракций, голодным летом четырнадцатого года переживал запоздалый рецидив фрагонаровской весны... (Лившиц 1). ...Acmeism groped for ponderous correlates in painting; and meanwhile I, who had broken loose from the prison of dry abstractions, experienced the belated return of a Fragonard spring in the hungry summer of 1914... (1a).

T-62 • **ПЕРЕД ТЕ́М КАК** [subord Conj, temporal] previously to the time when: **before.**

Перед тем, как случиться всей этой истории, я спокойно писал своего *Чонкина*... (Войнович 3). Before this whole thing happened, I was peacefully writing my *Chonkin*... (3a).

T-63 • **С ТЕ́М ЧТОБЫ** [subord Conj; introduces a clause of purpose] with the purpose of: **in order to ⟨that⟩; so that; so as to; with the intention ⟨the aim⟩ of; [in limited contexts] with the idea that; intending to; (in order) to.**

И прежде чем нам удастся продолжить, нам придётся пересказать всю нашу историю заново, с тем чтобы уяснить, чем же она казалась герою, пока он в ней был жив (Битов 2). Before we succeed in continuing our story, we will have to tell it all over again, in order to get a clear idea how it seemed to the hero while he was alive in it (2a). ♦ Нестор Аполлонович... велел сейчас же снарядить человека в Чегем, чтобы тот выяснил, откуда там появились верблюды, и, если можно, пригнал их в Кенгурск с тем, чтобы потом перегнать их в Мухус... (Искандер 3). Nestor Apollonovich...ordered that a man be dispatched to Chegem at once to ascertain how the camels got there and, if possible, drive them to Kengursk, so that someone could then drive them on to Mukhus... (3a). ♦ Победав и выпив немножко лишнего венгерского, Ростов, расцеловавшись с помещиком... по отвратительной дороге, в самом весёлом расположении духа, поскакал назад, беспрестанно погоняя ямщика, с тем чтобы поспеть на вечер к губернатору (Толстой 7). After dining and drinking a little too much Hungarian wine, Rostov embraced the landowner...and in the best of spirits galloped back over abominable roads, continually urging on the driver so as to be in time for the Governor's soirée (7a). ♦ «Убей её [старушонку] и возьми её деньги, с тем чтобы с их помощию посвятить потом себя на служение всему человечеству и общему делу: как ты думаешь, не загладится ли одно, крошечное преступленьице тысячами добрых дел?» (Достоевский 3). "Kill her [the old woman] and take her money, with the aim of devoting yourself later, with its aid, to the service of humanity and the common good: what do you think, won't one little crime be wiped out by these thousands of good deeds?" (3a). ♦ Квартиры у него сначала не было, и он попытался её нанять в этом посёлке с тем, чтобы попозже выбить себе участок и построить здесь собственный дом (Искандер 3). At first he did not have an apartment, and he tried to rent one in this neighborhood with the idea that he would later wangle an allotment for himself and build his own house here (3a). ♦ Купчиха Кондратьева, одна зажиточная вдова, даже так распорядилась, что в конце ещё апреля завела Лизавету к себе, с тем чтоб её и не выпускать до самых родов (Достоевский 1). The widow of the merchant Kondratiev, a wealthy woman, even arranged it all so that by the end of April she had brought Lizaveta to her house, intending to keep her there until she gave birth (1a). ♦ В конце января княжна Марья уехала в Москву, и граф настоял на том, чтобы Наташа ехала с нею, с тем чтобы посоветоваться с докторами (Толстой 7). At the end of January, Princess Marya left for Moscow, and the Count insisted on Natasha's going with her to consult the doctors (7a).

T-64 • **ТЕМ БО́ЛЕЕ ⟨ПА́ЧЕ** *obs*⟩ [these forms only; usu. sent adv; fixed WO] (used to single out a statement or part of a statement and thus emphasize its importance) what was said to be true of some person, thing, action etc in the preceding context is even more true of the person, thing, action etc in question: **especially; particularly; even ⟨only, still⟩ more so; the more so; [in limited contexts] all the more; more especially; [when the preceding context contains a negation] much less; still less; let alone; [in limited contexts] certainly not...**

Она всегда робела в подобных случаях и очень боялась новых лиц и новых знакомств, боялась и прежде, ещё с детства, а теперь тем более... (Достоевский 3). She always felt shy on such occasions and was very afraid of new faces and new acquaintances; she had been afraid before, but was even more so now... (3a). ♦

...В иных случаях, право, почтеннее поддаться иному увлечению, хотя бы и неразумному, но всё же от великой любви происшедшему, чем вовсе не поддаться ему. А в юности тем паче, ибо неблагонадёжен слишком уж постоянно рассудительный юноша и дешева цена ему... (Достоевский 1). ...In certain cases, really, it is more honorable to yield to some passion, however unwise, than not to yield to it at all. Still more so in youth, for a young man who is constantly too reasonable is suspect and of too cheap a price... (1a). ♦ Его ухаживание за Викой всех бесит? Прекрасно! Тем более он будет ухаживать за ней (Рыбаков 2). If his flirting with Vika was going to get everyone mad, let it! He'd flirt with her all the more! (2a). ♦ Рассуждение о ямочках на щеках и тем более эпизод, связанный с биноклем, дядя Сандро передавал с оглядкой, чтобы тётя Катя этого не слышала (Искандер 5). The discussion of dimpled cheeks, and more especially the episode involving the binoculars, Uncle Sandro conveyed with care lest Aunt Katya hear (5a). ♦ ...Уходя из семьи, Платон Самсонович не собирался обзаводиться новой семьёй или тем более любовницей (Искандер 6). Platon Samsonovich was not...leaving his family in order to acquire a new one, much less a mistress (6a). ♦ Прекратились разногласия между партиями, сословиями, народностями — осталась одна великая Россия! Могли мы ждать этого недавно?.. Вот так мы сами не знаем себя, а Россию тем более (Солженицын 1). Wrangling between parties, classes, nationalities had stopped, and what was left was one great Russia! Could anyone have expected this even a little while ago?...How little we know ourselves—and we know Russia still less (1a). ♦ «Ты — замужем, он — женат. Ты ведь не бросишь своего Курильского, тем более — Аркашку. Никандров тоже не бросит семью» (Залыгин 1). "You're both married. You won't leave your Kurilsky, let alone Arkady. And Nikandrov won't leave his family either" (1a).

T-65 • **ТЕМ БО́ЛЕЕ ЧТО** [subord Conj; introduces a clause of reason] particularly for the reason that: **especially since ⟨because, as⟩; (all) the more so since ⟨because⟩; the more so as; particularly as.**

Парижане зачитывались им [романом], а для дам он стал просто настольной книгой, тем более что к первому тому его была приложена такая прелесть, как аллегорическая Карта Нежности... (Булгаков 5). The novel was enormously popular among the Parisians, and to the ladies it became virtually a bible, especially since the first volume included so delectable an appendix as an allegorical Map of Tenderness... (5a). ♦ ...Своих лучших работниц Андриолли умел ценить и считал своей обязанностью проявлять к ним внимание. Тем более что, как правило, они попусту не беспокоили его ненужными просьбами (Войнович 5). Andriolli knew how to value his best workers and considered it his duty to give them his attention. All the more so since, as a rule, they didn't pester him with useless requests (5a). ♦ Многие из «высших» даже лиц... ставили себе в первейшую обязанность, все до единого, глубочайшую почтительность и деликатность во всё время свидания, тем более что здесь денег не полагалось... (Достоевский 1). Even many "higher" persons...considered it their foremost duty—to a man—to show the deepest respect and tactfulness throughout the audience, the more so as there was no question of money involved... (1a). ♦ «Забудьте же это, — продолжал он, — забудьте, тем более, что это неправда...» (Гончаров 1). "Please forget it," he added. "Forget it, particularly as it wasn't true—" (1b).

T-66 • **ТЕМ НЕ МЕ́НЕЕ** [Invar; usu. coord Conj, contrastive, or sent adv (parenth); often preceded by «и», «но», or «а»] however, despite (the circumstances, facts etc presented in the preceding context): **nevertheless; nonetheless; all ⟨just⟩ the same; still and all; even so; [when the idiom is translated in conjunction with the preceding clause] although ⟨though⟩...**

«...Хотя мы и не можем обнаружить — в данное время, по крайней мере, — каких-либо его [Иешуа] поклонников или последователей, тем не менее ручаться, что их совсем нет, нельзя» (Булгаков 9). "...Although we have not been able—at least not at present—to find any followers or disciples of his [Yeshua's], we nevertheless cannot be certain that he had none" (9b). ♦ [«Запорожец»] глох в самых неудачных местах. То во время обгона на узкой дороге, то на железнодорожном переезде. Но тем не менее, мы на нём всю Прибалтику исколесили (Войнович 1). It [our Zaporozhets] would conk out in the most inconvenient of places: at railroad crossings or while passing on narrow roads. All the same, we traveled throughout the Baltic states in it (1a). ♦ Будучи полностью обеспечен и копиркой, и лентами для машинок, и даже финской бумагой, Ефим, тем не менее, протолкался к Серафиме Борисовне... (Войнович 6). Though he was fully stocked with carbons, typewriter ribbons, and even Finnish paper, Yefim elbowed his way to Serafima Borisovna... (6a).

T-67 • ТЕМ СА́МЫМ [Invar; adv; fixed WO] by doing or saying that (which is specified in the preceding context): **thereby; thus; in that way;** [may be omitted in transl].

Целых два дня брат его уговаривал прийти в милицию и тем самым показать, что ему нечего бояться, что он никакого участия в этом убийстве не принимал (Искандер 3). For two whole days his brother tried to persuade him to go to the police, thereby proving that he had nothing to fear, that he had taken no part in the murder (3a). ♦ Выставив против меня превосходящие силы, Иванько утверждал, что, выступая против него, я тем самым выступаю против советской власти (Войнович 1). Bringing overwhelming forces to bear on me, Ivanko claimed that in acting against him, I was acting against the Soviet authorities (1a).

T-68 • ОТ ⟨С⟩ ТЕМНА́ ДО ТЕМНА́ coll [PrepP; these forms only; adv; fixed WO] from early morning till evening: **from dawn to ⟨till⟩ dusk; from sunrise to ⟨till⟩ sunset; from sunup to ⟨till⟩ sundown.**

«...Как я по чужим людям за пятнадцать копеек стирала от темна до темна, — он это помнит?» (Кузнецов 1). "...Does he remember how I washed clothes for strangers from dawn to dusk for fifteen kopeks?" (1a).

T-69 • УСТРА́ИВАТЬ/УСТРО́ИТЬ ⟨ДЕ́ЛАТЬ/СДЕ́ЛАТЬ⟩ ТЁМНУЮ кому slang [VP; subj: human, usu. pl] to beat s.o. up under circumstances that do not allow the victim to see his attackers—usu. in the dark, or covering the victim's head with a blanket or his eyes with a blindfold: X-ы устроили Y-у тёмную ≃ **Xs jumped ⟨blindsided⟩ Y and beat him up; Xs beat Y up in the dark.**

T-70 • В ТЕ́МПЕ coll [PrepP; Invar; adv] (to do sth.) very quickly and energetically: **on the double; in short order; in a jiffy; promptly; posthaste.**

[Валентин:] Маш! Ты бы заканчивала всё в темпе, и тогда... [Маша:] Можно гулять?.. Ура!.. (Рощин 1). [V.:] Mash! Why don't you finish in short order, and then.... [M.:] And then I can go out! Hurray! (1a).

T-71 • В ТЕНИ́ [PrepP; Invar] **1.** оставаться, быть∅, держаться, находиться и т. п. ~; держать, оставлять и т. п. кого ~ [subj-compl with copula (subj: human) or obj-compl with держать etc (obj: human)] (to remain, be, be kept, keep s.o. etc) in a position, capacity etc where one or s.o. is not noticed, not conspicuous, does not attract attention etc: **(remain ⟨be, keep s.o. etc⟩) in the shadows ⟨in the background⟩;** [in limited contexts] **keep a low profile; lie low.**

«Вы, улучшенцы, и так почти двадцать лет держали Васькиных в тени. Теперь их время наступает» (Зиновьев 2). "After all, you improvers have kept the Vaskins in the shadows for almost twenty years. Now their time is about to come" (2a). ♦ Так создавались книги — одна за другой — и авторы входили в программы учебных заведений, наших и зарубежных, а редактор... пребывал в тени, был невидимкой (Мандель-

штам 2). This is how books were turned out, one after the other, winning their authors a place in school and university curricula, both here and abroad—while all the time...the editors remained hidden from view in the background (2a). ♦ Когда под слободой Солонкой Филиппов увёл офицеров, Петро остался. Смирный и тихий, постоянно пребывающий в тени, во всём умеренный, вместе с полком пришёл он в Вёшенскую (Шолохов 4). When Filippov went off with the other officers at Solonka, Petro stayed behind. Quiet and submissive, always keeping in the background, moderate in all things, he rode into Vyoshenskaya with the regiment (4a).

2. оставаться, оставлять что и т. п. ~ [subj-compl with copula (subj: abstr) or obj-compl with оставлять (obj: abstr)]: (to remain, keep sth.) concealed, withheld, unknown (to s.o.): X остался ~ ≃ X was kept (a) secret; X was kept under wraps; X was ⟨remained⟩ a mystery; X was ⟨remained⟩ veiled in secrecy; ‖ Y оставил X ~ ≃ Y kept X a secret; Y kept X under wraps; Y veiled X in secrecy; [in limited contexts] Y shed no light on X.

...Эта сторона жизни его [Евпраксеина] осталась совсем в тени (Войнович 4). ...That part of his [Evpraksein's] life had always been a total mystery (4a).

T-72 • ОСТАВЛЯ́ТЬ/ОСТА́ВИТЬ В ТЕНИ́ кого [VP; subj: human] to surpass, outdo s.o.: X оставил в тени Y-а ≃ **X outshone ⟨overshadowed, upstaged, eclipsed⟩ Y; X ran rings ⟨circles⟩ around Y; X left Y far behind.**

Новый год они встречали в компании актёров. Олег был в ударе и оставил в тени всех признанных остряков. They saw in the New Year in the company of actors. Oleg was in top form and upstaged all the acknowledged wits.

T-73 • БРОСА́ТЬ/БРО́СИТЬ ⟨НАВОДИ́ТЬ/НАВЕСТИ́, КИДА́ТЬ/КИ́НУТЬ, НАБРА́СЫВАТЬ/НАБРО́СИТЬ⟩ ТЕНЬ [VP] **1.** ~ на кого-что [subj: human or abstr] to raise doubts about the respectability of s.o. or sth.: X бросает тень на Y-а ≃ **X casts (a shadow of) suspicion on Y; person X casts aspersions on Y; X casts a shadow on thing Y;** [in limited contexts] **thing X reflects badly on Y; X taints ⟨tarnishes⟩ person Y's reputation ⟨name etc⟩.**

[Тальберг:] Ты женщина умная и прекрасно воспитана. Ты прекрасно понимаешь, как нужно держать себя, чтобы не бросить тень на фамилию Тальберг (Булгаков 4). [T.:] You are an intelligent woman of excellent upbringing. You understand quite well how you must conduct yourself so as not to cast a shadow on the Talberg name (4a).

2. ~ на что, usu. на чьи отношения, дружбу и т. п. obs [subj: abstr] (in refer. to a friendship, relationship etc) to affect sth. adversely: X бросил тень на Y ≃ **X cast a shadow ⟨a pall⟩ on Y; X clouded Y.**

T-74 • КАК ТЕНЬ ходить, идти, следовать за кем, преследовать кого и т. п. [как + NP; Invar; adv] (to walk behind s.o., follow s.o. etc) unceasingly: X ходит за Y-ом как тень ≃ **X follows ⟨pursues⟩ Y like a shadow; X dogs Y's footsteps.**

[Саша:] ...Раньше, когда вы преследовали его, как тень, и мешали ему жить, вы были уверены, что исполняете свой долг, что вы честный человек (Чехов 4). [S.:] ...Before that, when you were pursuing him like a shadow and interfering with his life, you were convinced that you were fulfilling your duty, that you were an honest man (4a).

T-75 • НАВОДИ́ТЬ/НАВЕСТИ́ ТЕНЬ НА ПЛЕТЕ́НЬ; НАВОДИ́ТЬ/НАВЕСТИ́ ТЕНЬ (НА Я́СНЫЙ ДЕНЬ) all coll [VP; subj: human; more often impfv (neg imper or infin with нечего, хватит, зачем etc); the verb may take the final position, otherwise fixed WO] to muddle (sometimes deliberately) some clear issue or matter, present it differently than it is in reality, often in order to confuse or delude s.o.: X наводит тень (на плетень) ≃ **X is confusing ⟨clouding, fogging, obscuring⟩ the issue; X is confusing the matter ⟨matters⟩;** [in limited contexts] **X is fooling person Y.**

«Понимаешь ты это, что я сражаюсь за идею?» – «...Ты мне не наводи тень на плетень. Я тебе не мальчик! Тоже, нашёлся идейный! Самый натуральный разбойник ты, и больше ничего» (Шолохов 5). "Don't you realise, you fool, that I'm fighting for an idea!" "...You can't fool me! I wasn't born yesterday! Fighting for an idea, are you! You're nothing but an out-and-out brigand" (5a).

T-76 • ОДНА́ ТЕНЬ ОСТА́ЛАСЬ *от кого;* **ОСТА́ЛАСЬ (ТО́ЛЬКО) ТЕНЬ** *all coll* [VP~subj~; usu. past] s.o. has become very thin, pale, and, in most cases, looks sickly: от X-а одна тень осталась ≃ **X is only ⟨but⟩ a shadow of his former self; X has wasted away to nothing; X is ⟨has become⟩ skin and bones.**

T-77 • ОТХОДИ́ТЬ/ОТОЙТИ́ ⟨УХОДИ́ТЬ/УЙТИ́, ОТСТУПА́ТЬ/ОТСТУПИ́ТЬ⟩ В ТЕНЬ [VP; subj: human or abstr] to lose one's or its significance, move to a secondary position: X отошёл в тень ≃ **X retreated ⟨fell back⟩ into the shadows; X faded into the background; thing X became obscured.**

T-78 • ТЕНЬ ПА́ДАЕТ/(У)ПА́ЛА ⟨ЛОЖИ́ТСЯ/ЛЕГЛА́⟩ на кого-что [VP~subj~] doubts are raised about the respectability of s.o. or sth.: тень падает на X-а ≃ **(a shadow of) suspicion falls on X; a shadow falls on person X's name ⟨reputation⟩.**

[author's usage] Что же это обозначает? А то, что акт 1643 года содержит в себе ложные сведения и, следовательно, ровно ничего не стоит. А раз так, то густая тень подозрения падает и на эту таинственную, ещё не окрещённую девочку (Булгаков 5). What can this mean? It means that the document of 1643 contains false information and, hence, is quite worthless. And if this is so, then a dense shadow of suspicion falls also upon this mysterious, still unbaptized girl (5a). ♦ Она не хочет, чтобы на отца падала хоть какая-нибудь тень (Аллилуева 1). She doesn't want the least little shadow to fall on my father's name (1a).

T-79 • ИСПЫ́ТЫВАТЬ ТЕРПЕ́НИЕ чьё [VP; subj: human] to annoy, irritate s.o. very much: X испытывает Y-ово терпение ≃ **X is trying ⟨is wearing out⟩ Y's patience.**

[Иванов:] О боже мой! Анюта, испытывать так терпение... (Чехов 4). [I.:] God, to try one's patience like this, Anna— (4b).

T-80 • ТЕРПЕ́НИЕ И ТРУД ВСЁ ПЕРЕТРУ́Т [saying] with patience and persistent work one can overcome all obstacles (said to encourage a person who is faced with a difficult undertaking, challenging task etc): ≃ **little strokes fell great oaks; perseverance overcomes all things; patience wins the day; he that can have patience can have what he will; they that have patience may accomplish anything.**

T-81 • ТЕРПЕ́НИЕ ЛО́ПАЕТСЯ/ЛО́ПНУЛО чьё, (у) кого coll [VP~subj~; more often pfv] one cannot (or could not) endure any more aggravation (and is about to, or did, react by shouting, getting visibly angry, taking severe measures etc): у X-а лопнуло терпение ≃ **X's patience gave ⟨ran⟩ out; X ran out of patience; X lost his ⟨all⟩ patience; X's patience wore thin; X's patience was exhausted; X had had it.**

«Словом, всё шло ничего, пока...» – «Пока что?» – «Пока не лопнуло терпение» (Грекова 3). "Well, everything was OK, until..." "Until what?" "Until I ran out of patience" (3a). ♦ «...Тот

нахал, вообразите, развалился в кресле и говорит, улыбаясь: „А я, говорит, с вами по дельцу пришёл потолковать". Прохор Петрович вспылил...: „Я занят!" А тот, подумайте только, отвечает: „Ничем вы не заняты..." А? Ну, тут уж, конечно, терпение Прохора Петровича лопнуло, и он вскричал: „Да что ж это такое?"» (Булгаков 9). "...Then, if you please, that impudent creature stretched out in his chair and said with a smile, 'I've come to have a chat with you on a little matter of business.' Prokhor Petrovich snapped at him.... 'I'm busy,' to which the beast said, 'You're not busy at all.' How d'you like that? Well, of course, Prokhor Petrovich lost all patience then and shouted, 'What is all this?'" (9b). ♦ «Я его [верблюда] недавно прогнал, терпение моё лопнуло, так он сегодня прибрёл. Едва ноги приволок» (Айтматов 2). "Not long ago, I drove him [the camel] off—my patience was exhausted. Today he staggered home again. He could hardly drag his legs behind him" (2a).

T-82 • ТЕРЯ́ТЬ/ПОТЕРЯ́ТЬ ТЕРПЕ́НИЕ coll; ВЫХОДИ́ТЬ/ВЫ́ЙТИ ИЗ ТЕРПЕ́НИЯ [VP; subj: human] to become extremely angry: X потерял терпение ≃ **X lost (his ⟨all⟩) patience (with s.o. ⟨sth.⟩);** [in limited contexts] **X lost his temper.**

...Кончилось тем, что Рита, потеряв терпение, тайно от меня сама позвонила Рафику и встретилась с ним (Трифонов 5). ...In the end, having lost all patience with me, she [Rita] went ahead and called Rafik on her own and secretly arranged to meet with him (5a). ♦ «Эк её [старуху], дубинноголовая какая!» – сказал про себя Чичиков, уже начиная выходить из терпения (Гоголь 3). "Blast her [the old lady], what a blockhead!" Chichikov exclaimed inwardly, already beginning to lose his temper (3d).

T-83 • ВООРУЖА́ТЬСЯ/ВООРУЖИ́ТЬСЯ ⟨ЗАПАСА́ТЬСЯ/ЗАПАСТИ́СЬ⟩ ТЕРПЕ́НИЕМ; НАБИРА́ТЬСЯ/НАБРА́ТЬСЯ ТЕРПЕ́НИЯ [VP; subj: human] to (try to) be very patient: X вооружился терпением ≃ **X armed ⟨girded⟩ himself with patience; X prepared himself to be patient;** ‖ *Imper* запасись терпением ≃ **you must ⟨have to⟩ be patient.**

«Вооружитесь терпением. Приедет государь, я могу вам дать честное слово, что его монаршая милость вас не оставит» (Гоголь 3). "Arm yourself with patience. I give you my word of honour that as soon as the Emperor arrives, his Majesty won't let you go without conferring some favour upon you" (3a). ♦ «...Вашу телеграмму из Канска могли переврать, ваше первое письмо почему-либо до вашей матушки не дошло, значит, она получила только второе письмо и ответ ждите ещё через месяц-полтора. Наберитесь терпения, мой друг» (Рыбаков 2). "They might have garbled your cable [from Kansk] and your first letter to your dear mother may never have got there for any number of reasons, so she only got your second letter and you'll have to wait for an answer another month or six weeks. You'll have to be patient, my friend" (2a).

T-84 • ВЫВОДИ́ТЬ/ВЫ́ВЕСТИ ИЗ ТЕРПЕ́НИЯ кого coll [VP; subj: human or abstr; more often pfv; if impfv, often neg imper] to irritate s.o. greatly, make s.o. very angry: X вывел Y-а из терпения ≃ **X tried ⟨exhausted, wore out⟩ Y's patience; X made Y lose Y's patience; X drove Y out of (all) patience; X exasperated Y;** [in limited contexts] **X made Y lose Y's temper.**

[Мамаева:] Послушайте, вы меня выведете из терпения, мы с вами поссоримся (Островский 9). [M.:] You are trying my patience, sir; you and I are going to quarrel (9b). ♦ Новый градоначальник [города Глупова]... поставил себе задачею привлекать сердца исключительно посредством изящных манер... Только однажды, выведенный из терпения продолжительным противодействием своего помощника, он дозволил себе сказать: «Я уже имел честь подтверждать тебе, курицыну сыну»... (Салтыков-Щедрин 1). The new town-governor...set out to win the Glupovites' hearts by the single means of elegant manners....Only once, when his patience was exhausted by the persistent contrariness of his assistant, did he allow himself to say: "I have already had the honour of telling you, you swine..." (1b). ♦ Она [жена Энгельсона] не могла пропустить ни одного случая, чтоб не кольнуть меня самым злым образом... Наконец булавочные уколы в такое время, когда я весь был задавлен болью и горем, вывели меня из терпения (Герцен 2). ...She [Engelson's wife] could not let slip any chance for having a spiteful dig at me....Finally these pin-pricks, at a time when I was utterly crushed by grief and distress, drove me out of all patience (2a). ♦ «Фрейлейн, — говорила мисс Рони провинившейся воспитаннице, — вы ошибаетесь, если думаете, что, выведенная из терпения, я отошлю вас к родителям» (Федин 1). [context transl] "Fräulein," Miss Ronny would say to a guilty pupil, "you are mistaken if you think that I shall send you back to your parents out of exasperation" (1a).

T-85 • **ТЕРПЕ́ТЬ НЕ МОГУ́** ⟨не можешь и т. п.⟩ *кого-что, делать что coll* [VP; subj: human; pres or past; only могу conjugates; fixed WO] I (you etc) strongly dislike s.o. or sth., I (you etc) absolutely cannot tolerate s.o. or sth.: X терпеть не может Y-а ≃ **X can't bear ⟨stand, stomach⟩ Y ⟨doing thing Y⟩; thing Y turns X's stomach; X hates ⟨loathes⟩ Y ⟨doing thing Y⟩; X hates person Y's guts; X cannot endure Y.**

«...[Штольц] ухи терпеть не может, даже стерляжьей не ест; баранины тоже в рот не берёт» (Гончаров 1). "He [Stolz] can't bear fish soup—not even sturgeon, and he never touches mutton" (1b). ♦ «Терпеть не могу таких имён: Валерик, Виталик, Владик, Алик...» (Грекова 1). "I can't stand those diminutives: Valerik, Vitalik, Vladik, Alik..." (1b). ♦ «Вы, на мой вкус, здесь лишний; я вас терпеть не могу, я вас презираю...» (Тургенев 2). "To my taste, your presence here is superfluous; I cannot endure you; I despise you..." (2b).

T-86 • **НЕ́ЧЕГО ТЕРЯ́ТЬ** *кому coll* [Invar; impers predic with быть∅] s.o. might as well venture sth., take some risk because the possible negative consequences are not that serious, because his situation could not get any worse etc: X-у нечего терять ≃ **X has nothing to lose.**

«Мы любили друг друга», — прошептал, роняя голову на грудь, Самсик. «С иностранной подданной?»... Ужас пронзил Самсика. Да ведь действительно она иностранная подданная!.. Да, теперь он уличён и терять больше нечего. «Угу, с иностранной подданной», — прошептал он (Аксёнов 6). "We loved each other," Samsik whispered, dropping his head on his chest. "You loved a *foreigner*?"...Fear gripped Samsik. It was true—she was a foreign citizen!...Yes, he was found out now and had nothing more to lose. "Uh-huh, I loved a foreigner," he whispered (6a).

T-87 • **ТЕРЯ́ТЬ/ПОТЕРЯ́ТЬ СЕБЯ́** [VP; subj: human] **1.** to lose one's individual personality traits under the influence of others or one's surroundings: X потерял себя ≃ **X lost his individuality.**

Сашины родители боялись, что в армии, в казарменной обстановке, он потеряет себя. Sasha's parents feared that in the army, in barracks life, he would lose his individuality.

2. *obsoles, coll* [pfv only] to lose one's composure, self-control: X потерял себя ≃ **X lost his temper; X blew up; X lost his head.**

3. *obs* [subj: female; pfv only] to fail to preserve one's chastity: X потеряла себя ≃ **X lost her virginity ⟨her virtue⟩.**

T-88 • **В ТЕСНОТЕ́, ДА НЕ В ОБИ́ДЕ** [saying] even though some place is crowded, no one objects (or would turn others away) because everyone is friendly: ≃ **the more the merrier; there is always room for (one) more; where there is room in the heart, there is room in the house.**

Он познакомил меня со всеми своими друзьями... Мы заняли столик в столовой и расселись вокруг в тесноте, да не в обиде (Аксёнов 1). He introduced me to all his friends....We took a table in the Lighthouse and crowded in around it, the more the merrier... (1a).

T-89 • **(СДЕ́ЛАН ⟨ИСПЕЧЁН⟩) ИЗ ДРУГО́ГО ⟨НЕ ИЗ ТОГО́⟩ ТЕ́СТА; (СДЕ́ЛАНЫ ⟨ИСПЕЧЕНЫ́⟩) ИЗ РА́ЗНОГО ТЕ́СТА** *all coll* [AdjP or PrepP; subj-compl with быть∅ (subj: human); last var.—pl only; the Part сделан etc may take the final position, otherwise fixed WO] one is totally dissimilar from another or others in his views, character, life style etc, or two or more people are totally dissimilar from one another in their views, characters, life styles etc: X (сделан) из другого теста (, чем Y) ≃ **X is cut from a different cloth (than Y); X is cast in a different mold (than Y); X is a breed apart ⟨of a different breed⟩;** [in limited contexts] **X is made of different stuff (than Y); X is of (quite) a different stripe (from Y); X is in a different category (than Y).**

И я снова должна была осознавать, что все простые человеческие радости не про меня. Ко мне не приедут. Мне *не положено.* Я из другого теста (Гинзбург 2). Thus I was reminded all over again that all the ordinary human joys were not for me. There was no one to visit me. *It was not within my rights.* I was in a different category (2a).

T-90 • **(СДЕ́ЛАНЫ ⟨ИСПЕЧЕНЫ́⟩) ИЗ ОДНО́ГО ⟨ИЗ ТОГО́ ЖЕ, ИЗ ОДНОГО́ И ТОГО́ ЖЕ⟩ ТЕ́СТА** *all coll* [AdjP or PrepP; subj-compl with быть∅ (subj: human, pl); the Part сделаны etc may take the final position, otherwise fixed WO] two or more people are very similar in their views, characters, life styles etc: X и Y (сделаны) из одного теста ≃ **X are Y are cut from the same cloth; X and Y are cast in the same mold; X and Y are made the same ⟨made of the same stuff⟩; X and Y are of the same breed ⟨ilk, stripe⟩.**

«А тут ещё это проклятье — демократическое воспитание: эгалите, фратэрните, все люди — братья, все из одного теста...» (Стругацкие 1). "And then this damned democratic upbringing: *égalité, fraternité,* all men are brothers, we're all made the same" (1a). ♦ Сталин не знал Европы, презирал партийных интеллигентов — эмигрантов, кичливых всезнаек, сделанных из того же теста, что и западные рабочие лидеры... Он вёл в России жизнь подпольщика, его ссылали, он бежал, скрывался, а они жили за границей, в безопасности, почитывали, пописывали, становились известными (Рыбаков 2). Stalin didn't know Europe...and despised the émigré Party intellectuals—they were conceited know-it-alls of the same stripe as the Western labor leaders....While Stalin had been living the life of an underground activist, sent into exile, escaping, and going into hiding, they had been living abroad in perfect safety, doing a bit of reading, a bit of writing, and becoming famous (2a).

T-91 • **ГЛУХА́Я ТЕТЕ́РЯ ⟨ГЛУХО́Й ТЕ́ТЕРЕВ⟩** *highly coll, usu. derog* [NP; 2nd var.—sing only, used in refer. to a man only; usu. subj, obj, or vocative] a person (usu. an old person) who hears poorly: [in refer. to a man only] **deaf old coot;** [in refer. to a woman only] **deaf old bag;** [in limited contexts; in refer. to either a man or a woman] **(s.o. who is) stone-deaf ⟨deaf as a post⟩; (s.o. who) can't hear a bloody thing.**

T-92 • **ЛЕНИ́ВАЯ ТЕТЕ́РЯ** *highly coll, derog or humor* [NP; usu. subj, obj, or vocative] a very lazy person: **lazybones; sluggard;** [in limited contexts] **goof-off.**

T-93 • **СО́ННАЯ ТЕТЕ́РЯ** *highly coll, derog or humor* [NP; usu. subj, obj, or vocative] a person who likes to sleep excessively: **slugabed.**

T-94 • **В ТЕЧЕ́НИЕ** *чего* [PrepP; Invar; Prep; the resulting PrepP is adv] **1.** for the specified period of time: **for;** [in limited contexts] **over a period of; over ⟨in⟩ the course of.**

«Рука с рукой мы пойдём в бой против тех, кто порабощал трудящихся в течение целых столетий!» (Шолохов 3). "Shoulder to shoulder we will go into action against those who have been enslaving the working people for centuries!" (3a). ♦ В течение года, может быть двух, происходили столкновения, ссоры, драки, случилось даже убийство... (Федин 1). In the course of a year, maybe two, there occurred clashes, quarrels, fights, and even murder took place... (1a).

2. over the duration of (some activity, event, occasion etc): **during; throughout; all through; [in limited contexts] over ⟨in⟩ the course of;** ‖ в течение всего дня ⟨всего прошлого года, всего следующего месяца и т. п.⟩ ≃ **all day (long) ⟨all last year, all the following year⟩ etc.**

Едва ли кто-нибудь, кроме матери, заметил появление его на свет, очень немногие замечают его в течение жизни... (Гончаров 1). It is doubtful if anyone except his mother was aware of his entrance into the world; few noticed him during his lifetime... (1b). ♦ В течение всего его градоначальничества глуповцы не только не садились за стол без горчицы, но даже развели у себя довольно обширные горчичные плантации для удовлетворения требований внешней торговли (Салтыков-Щедрин 1). Throughout his governorship the Foolovites not only did not sit down to table without mustard, but even cultivated rather extensive mustard plantations to satisfy the requirements of foreign trade (1a). ♦ Он в течение всего спора сидел как на угольях и только украдкой болезненно взглядывал на Аркадия (Тургенев 2). He had been sitting on tenterhooks all through the dispute, now and again stealing pained glances at Arkady (2a). ♦ До самого вечера и в течение всего следующего дня Василий Иванович придирался ко всем возможным предлогам, чтобы входить в комнату сына... (Тургенев 2). Till late that evening and all the following day Vassily Ivanych seized on every possible pretext to go into his son's room... (2c).

3. inside the limits of (the specified period of time): **within; in the space of.**

Берман, узнав об этом деле, разъярился и проявил столько энергии, что в течение десяти дней Мухин был судим трибуналом и приговорён к расстрелу (Гроссман 2). Berman was furious; he pursued the case with such furious energy that within ten days Mukhin had appeared before a tribunal and been sentenced to be shot (2a).

T-95 • С ТЕЧЕ́НИЕМ ВРЕ́МЕНИ [PrepP; Invar; adv; fixed WO] after some time has passed, or in conjunction with the passing of time: **in ⟨with⟩ time; after a time; in the course of time; as time goes ⟨went⟩ by; with the passage of time.**

С течением времени обойщик добился ещё одного звания — камердинера его величества короля Франции (Булгаков 5). In time the upholsterer attained yet another title—that of Valet to His Majesty, the King of France (5a). «...Я усматриваю, что наше общество продолжает коснеть всё в том же бездействии, в каком я застал его и в первое время по приезде моём в Навозный край. А именно: путей сообщения не существует, судоходство в упадке, торговля преследует цели низкие и неблагородные... К сему, с течением времени, присоединились: процветание кабаков и необыкновенный успех сибирской язвы» (Салтыков-Щедрин 2). "I must state that our society continues to stagnate in the same state of inactivity in which I found it on my arrival in the Navozny province. To be more precise, there are no means of communication, navigation is in a state of complete decay, trade is pursuing base and dishonourable ends....To this have been added in the course of time the great increase in the number of public houses and the quite extraordinary success achieved by anthrax!" (2a).

T-96 • ПЛЫТЬ ПО ТЕЧЕ́НИЮ usu. disapprov [VP; subj: human; fixed WO] to live or act as circumstances dictate, passively going along with whatever happens: X плывёт по течению ≃ **X drifts with the current ⟨the tide⟩.**

Сдерживал меня в моем «хотении» не Достоевский, а Мандельштам. Он не позволял мне плыть по течению и следовать последней моде жестокого и ничтожного века (Мандельштам 2). The only restraining influence on me came not from Dostoyevski, but from M[andelstam]. It was he who stopped me from drifting with the current and aping the latest fashion of our cruel and tawdry age (2a).

T-97 • ПЛЫТЬ ⟨ИДТИ́/ПОЙТИ́⟩ ПРОТИВ ТЕЧЕ́НИЯ usu. approv [VP; subj: human] to live or act in an independent, energetic fashion, in defiance of prevailing views, ideas etc: X плывёт против течения ≃ **X swims ⟨paddles, goes⟩ against the current ⟨the tide⟩.**

...Он [дядя] был потомком землепроходцев, и ему нравилось плыть против течения. Он выстроил дом для своей пассии, как крепость свободы своего духа (Евтушенко 2). ...Uncle had descended from a long line of explorers and liked paddling against the current. He built a house for his lover, and it stood as his monument to freedom of the spirit (2a).

T-98 • ТИПУ́Н НА ЯЗЫ́К кому coll [indep. sent; Invar; fixed WO] an unkind wish addressed to s.o. who says sth. inappropriate, meanspirited etc: типун тебе на язык ≃ **may your tongue fall off (for saying that); bite your tongue.**

...Егор в это время ковылял по другой стороне улицы и зло и беспомощно косил на Настасью глазом: опять, блажная, типун ей на язык, рассказывает про него сказки (Распутин 4). ...Meanwhile Egor would be hobbling along on the other side of the street, angrily and helplessly squinting at Nastasya: the feeble-minded woman was at it again, may her tongue fall off, telling fairy tales about him (4a). ♦ «Она [мама] страшно боится, что я завалю последний экзамен». — «Вдруг, правда, завалите?» Девушка сердито блеснула очками: «Типун вам на язык!» (Чернёнок 1). "She [Mother] is terribly worried that I'll flunk the last of my exams." "What if you really do?" The girl's bespectacled eyes flashed angrily. "Bite your tongue!" she said (1a).

T-99 • ВЫХОДИ́ТЬ/ВЫ́ЙТИ В ТИРА́Ж [VP; subj: human] **1.** to become unfit for sth., cease working or functioning productively in one's capacity: X вышел в тираж ≃ **X was (ready to be) put out to pasture; X was ⟨became⟩ a back number; X lost his usefulness; X became deadwood.**

«Хелло, Арси, — бормотал в трубке старый развратник, — похоже на то, что мы с тобой ещё не вышли в тираж». — «Поздравляю, — сухо сказал Арсений Николаевич. — На меня твои успехи совершенно не распространяются» (Аксёнов 7). "Hello, Arsy," came the voice of the old reprobate through the receiver. "Looks like we don't have to be put out to pasture yet, the two of us." "Congratulations," said Arseny Nikolaevich curtly, "but your prowess has nothing to do with me" (7a). ♦ Радуясь за неё [дочь], он в глубине души ревновал её к Николаю, постепенно заместившему отца в сердце дочери: «В тираж выходишь, Лашков, скоро совсем никому не будешь нужен» (Максимов 3). He was glad for her [his daughter], but deep down he felt jealous of Nikolai, who had gradually replaced her father in his daughter's heart. "You're a back number, Lashkov. Soon nobody will want you" (3a). ♦ Лучников обнимал за зябкие плечики Лору Лерову, одну из тех увядающих «букетиков», что украшали недавний праздник «Курьера». Десяток лет назад — звезда Москвы, манекенщица Министерства лёгкой промышленности, поочерёдная любовница дюжины гениев, сейчас явно выходила в тираж (Аксёнов 7). [context transl] Luchnikov had his arm around the unprotected shoulders of Lora Lerova, one of the fading nosegays who had adorned the *Courier* brunch. Ten or twelve years ago—the toast of Moscow, star model for the Ministry of Light Industry, mistress of a dozen geniuses; now—Miss Passée (7a).

2. obs [usu. pfv] to die: X вышел в тираж ≃ **X left this world; X passed away ⟨on⟩.**

T-100 • СПИ́СЫВАТЬ/СПИСА́ТЬ ⟨СДАВА́ТЬ/ СДАТЬ⟩ В ТИРА́Ж *кого* [VP; subj: human; often infin (after пора, надо, хотеть etc) or 3rd pers pl with indef. refer.] to dismiss s.o. permanently, recognizing that he is unfit for some activity (usu. in refer. to a person unfit to fulfill his responsibilities at work): X-а списали в тираж ≃ **X was put out to pasture.**

С работой наш бухгалтер уже не справляется, сказывается возраст. Пора списать его в тираж. Our accountant's age is telling on him, he can't handle the work any more. It's time to put him out to pasture.

T-101 • В ТИСКА́Х быть∅, находиться, держать *кого-что* и т. п.; В ТИСКИ́ попасть, взять *кого-что* и т. п. [PrepP; these forms only; usu. subj-compl with copula (subj: human or collect) or obj-compl with держать etc (obj: human or collect)] **1.** *mil* used in refer. to the envelopment of enemy forces from two sides: X-ы оказались в тисках ≃ **Xs were outflanked;** ‖ Y-и взяли X-ов в тиски ≃ **Ys outflanked Xs.**

2. (to be) oppressed by s.o. or (to be) in a very difficult, trying situation; (to keep s.o.) in a state of complete submission, subjugation: X (находится) в тисках у Y-а ⟨попал в тиски к Y-у⟩ ≃ **X is in ⟨fell into⟩ Y's clutches;** ‖ Y держит X-а в тисках ≃ **Y has X in a vise; Y has a tight ⟨viselike⟩ grip on X; Y has X in Y's clutches ⟨grasp, grip⟩.**

Обломов понял, в какие тиски попал он, когда всё, что присылал Штольц, стало поступать на уплату долга, а ему оставалось только небольшое количество денег на прожиток (Гончаров 1). Oblomov realized what a vise he was in when he saw that everything Stolz sent him went to pay his debt, leaving him little to live on (1b).

T-102 • ТИШЬ ДА ⟨И⟩ ГЛАДЬ (ДА ⟨И⟩ БО́ЖЬЯ БЛАГОДА́ТЬ) *coll, occas. iron* [NP; sing only; fixed WO] (usu. of a quiet, carefree life) total peace, serenity: **peace and quiet ⟨tranquillity⟩.**

Николай Николаевич глядел в переулок и вспоминал прошлогоднюю петербургскую зиму, Гапона, Горького, посещение Витте, модных современных писателей. Из этой кутерьмы он удрал сюда, в тишь да гладь первопрестольной, писать задуманную им книгу (Пастернак 1). Nikolai Nikolaevich stood gazing into the distance. He thought of his last winter in Petersburg—Gapon, Gorky, the visit to Prime Minister Witte, modern, fashionable writers. From that bedlam he had fled to the peace and quiet of the ancient capital to write the book he had in mind (1a).

T-103 • А ТО́ [Invar] **1.** Also: (А) НЕ ТО́ [coord Conj, connective-contrastive; introduces a clause with the verb in fut or subjunctive] used to introduce a clause indicating what will happen (would happen, or would have happened) if the order, intention etc contained in the preceding clause is not (were not, or had not been) carried out; or used to introduce a clause indicating what would occur (would have occurred) if the situation in the preceding clause were (had been) different: **or else; or; otherwise;** [in limited contexts] **if not.**

«А ты тут лучше не ходи и не путайся под ногами, а то и тебя возьмём как соучастницу» (Войнович 4). "And you better stop coming here and getting under our feet or else we'll pick you up, too, as an accessory" (4a). ♦ «Лучше я отсюду от него, – сказал Тимур, шумно вставая, – а то этот человек доведёт меня до преступления!» (Искандер 5). "I'd better sit somewhere else," Timur said, noisily getting to his feet, "or this man will drive me to a crime!" (5a). ♦ «Руки у меня связаны, – горько жаловался он [градоначальник] глуповцам, – а то узнали бы вы у меня, где раки зимуют!» (Салтыков-Щедрин 1). "My hands are tied," he [the governor] complained bitterly to the Glupovites, "Otherwise I'd give you something to remember me by!" (1b). ♦ «Обижаешь ста-

руху. Я ведь тебя ещё маленькую в колыске [*Ukrainian* = в колыбели] качала. Ты уж лучше пусти, не то закричу» (Войнович 2). [context transl] "You're insulting an old woman. You know, I used to rock you in your cradle. Better let me go before I start shouting" (2a).

2. [subord Conj; introduces a clause of reason] for the reason that: **because;** [may be omitted in transl].

«И сейчас ещё говорит, но только всё меньше и меньше, так что пользуйтесь случаем, а то он скоро совсем умолкнет» (Булгаков 11). "He still speaks, but less and less. I would suggest you take advantage of the moment, because he'll soon grow silent altogether" (11a). ♦ [Аркадина:] Костя, закрой окно, а то дует (Чехов 6). [A.:] Kostya, shut the window, it's drafty (6c).

3. *substand.* Also: (А) НЕ ТО́ *substand* [coord Conj, disjunctive] used to indicate an alternative: **or; or even ⟨maybe⟩.**

[Рисположенский:] Да вы мне ещё полторы тысячи должны... Давайте деньги, а то документ (Островский 10). [R.:] You still owe me fifteen hundred rubles....Give me the money, or a note for it (10b).

4. [coord Conj, contrastive] used to indicate that the state of affairs expressed by the statement that follows is, in the speaker's opinion, abnormal, bad, or contrary to the way it should be, whereas the state of affairs expressed by the preceding context reflects the way things should be: **but (instead ⟨on the contrary⟩); rather than; instead (of); while instead; as it is.**

«Ты уж меня выручи, старика, Вить. В последний раз, а? Вить? Чего молчишь?» – «Не буду выручать, Архип Иваныч. Завязал». – «...Чего тебе завязывать-то? Если б ты какой бандит... был, а то – трудяга, шофёр» (Семёнов 1). "Do me a favour, Vic, do it for an old man. For the last time. Eh, Vic? Why don't you say something?" "I won't do you a favour, Arkhip Ivanich. I've quit." "What's the matter, Vic....It would be different if...you had been some sort of crook, but you're a hard worker, a driver" (1a). ♦ «Не хочется мне это делать». – «Ты бы так и говорил, а то придумываешь всякие отговорки». "I don't feel like doing this." "Then why didn't you say so instead of making up all kinds of excuses?" ♦ [Анна Петровна:] Как бы папенька-то твой не мотал без памяти, так бы другое дело было, а то оставил нас почти ни с чем (Островский 1). [A.P.:] If only your papa hadn't spent his money like water, then everything'd be different. As it is, he left us almost nothing at all (1a).

5. Also: А НЕ ТО́ *coll* [Particle; usu. foll. by imper or subjunctive] used to express mild inducement or an invitation to do sth.: **do [+ a positive imper]; why not; why don't you.**

6. *coll* [Particle; usu. foll. by imper; often used with пожалуй] used to introduce an expression of agreement with some suggestion after an initial refusal or vacillation: **(or) well, perhaps ⟨maybe⟩; or perhaps; well, actually, maybe; well, all right.**

[Анна Ивановна:] Что ж это они не идут, соколы-то наши?.. Не сходить ли за ними? [Любовь Гордеевна:] Нет, не надо. А то, пожалуй, сходи. (*Обнимает её.*) Сходи-ка, Аннушка (Островский 2). [A.I.:] What could be keeping them, our young gallants? Perhaps I ought to go for them? [L.G.:] Oh, no, don't. Or perhaps... (*hugs her*). Yes, do go, Anna (2b).

7. *coll, impol* [Particle] obviously, of course (used with interrogative pronouns or adverbs as an affirmative response to a question): **what ⟨who, where etc⟩ else; who else's.**

«Это твоя книга?» – «А то чья же?» "Is this your book?" "Who else's?"

T-104 • А ТО́ И [coord Conj, disjunctive or connective-disjunctive] used to introduce an alternative (usu. one that is more intense or goes further than the preceding element): **or (perhaps) even; (and sometimes) even; and even; if not...; or else...**

[Доктор:] ...Волноваться-то очень незачем. [Барыня:] Да ведь как же? Полную дезинфекцию надо. [Доктор:] Нет, что ж полную, это дорого слишком, рублей триста, а то и больше станет. А я вам дёшево и сердито устрою (Толстой 3). [Doctor:] ...There's no reason to get very excited. [A.P.:] What do you mean? There'll have to be a complete disinfection. [Doctor:] No, why a complete disinfection? That's too expensive. That could run to some three hundred rubles, or even more. I'll fix you one that's cheap and effective (3a). ♦ За последнее десятилетие выяснилось, что тайное становится явным... Для этого нужно только время — десяток лет или ещё полстолетия, а то и столетие (Мандельштам 2). In the last decade we have seen how "nothing is hidden that shall not be known"....All that is needed is time—ten years, or fifty, or perhaps even a hundred (2a). ♦ ...Определять подлинность достижений в сферах человеческого духа – дело довольно сложное. Иногда на это уходили годы, а то и столетия (Войнович 5). The definition of authenticity of achievements in various fields of human creative endeavor would...be a rather difficult task. In fact, this has sometimes taken years, if not centuries (5a). ♦ В то время было или казалось, а то и делали вид, что было, временное равновесие сил (Искандер 3). At that time there was, or seemed to be, or else they pretended there was, a [temporary] balance of power (3a).

T-105 • (ВОТ) ТО́-ТО И ОНО́ ⟨ОНО́-ТО⟩; (ВОТ) ТО́-ТО (ОНО́) И ЕСТЬ *all coll* [Interj; used as indep. sent or main clause in a complex sent (usu. foll. by a что-clause); these forms only; fixed WO] this/that is the important factor, the essential thing (used to emphasize that what has just been said or is about to be said is the central issue, the most important aspect of the matter in question): **that's just it ⟨the thing, the point⟩; that's the whole point;** [in limited contexts] **(and) that's the problem ⟨the trouble⟩; you've put your finger on it; my point exactly; that's just my point;** [when foll. by a что-clause] **the thing is...; the (whole) point is...; my point is...;** [in limited contexts] **the problem ⟨the trouble⟩ is...**

«...А не подождать ли тебе вечера, чтобы по темноте выехать? Главное, через совхоз незамеченным проехать. А не то, если засекут...» — «Оно-то верно, — заколебался Кокетай. — Да долго ждать до вечера. Выедем потихоньку. Поста ведь нет на дороге, чтобы проверить нас?.. Случайно если наткнёшься на милицию или на кого ещё...» — «То-то и оно!» — пробурчал Орозкул... (Айтматов 1). "...It might be best if you don't start out back till evening. Let it get darker. The main thing is to get past the Soviet farm without attracting attention. If they find out..." "You're right enough." Koketay was undecided. "But it's a long wait till evening. We'll start out slowly. After all, there's no patrol post on the road to check us. Unless you accidentally run into the police or someone like that...." "That's just it," mumbled Orozkul... (1a). ♦ Поставил один унитаз, хочется поставить второй, а куда? Вот то-то и оно-то... (Войнович 3). He puts in one toilet; then he wants to put in another. But where? And that's the problem (3a). ♦ «Я бы про него [Панкратова] сказал так: любил командовать, быть первым». — «То-то и оно...» (Рыбаков 2). "I would put it this way: he [Pankratov] liked giving orders, and he wanted to be in charge." "You've put your finger on it..." (2a).

T-106 • И ТО́ **1.** Also: **ДА ⟨НО⟩ И ТО́** [coord Conj, connective] used to emphasize that the second of the statements it joins further restricts, narrows, or makes extreme the first statement (which is itself unusually restricted, narrow, or extreme): **and then only; and even then; and (even) that.**

...Вино подавалось у нас только за обедом, и то по рюмочке... (Пушкин 2). ...With us, wine was only served at dinner, and then only one glass each... (3b). ♦ Сам он не выпил во всё это время ни одной капли вина и всего только спросил себе в вокзале чаю, да и то больше для порядка (Достоевский 3). He himself had not drunk a drop of wine the whole time, but had only ordered some tea in the vauxhall, and even that more for propriety's sake (3c). ♦ Первая неудача заключалась в том, что сын мельника достал, и то с большим трудом, только одну лошадь, которую одолжил ему сосед (Искандер 3). The first

failure was that the miller's son obtained—and that with great difficulty—only one horse, which a neighbor lent him (3a).

2. [coord Conj, contrastive] used to show that the statement it introduces is unexpected, illogical, strange etc considering the information presented in the preceding statement: **(and) still...;** [in limited contexts] **and even (he ⟨she etc⟩)...**

Другого графолога звали Веров... Он мне сказал, что если ему дадут даже листок, напечатанный на пишущей машинке, то он и то определит характер печатавшего. Сказал также, что по почерку он может определить не то что характер, а сколько у человека комнат в квартире (Олеша 3). Another graphologist was called Verov....He told me that if he were given only a typewritten sheet, he would still be able to determine the writer's personality. He said that he could not only determine personality by handwriting, but even how many rooms the person had in his apartment (3a). ♦ Катя очень хорошо водит машину, и то она решила, что в такую пургу лучше остаться дома. Katya's a very good driver, and even she decided it was better to stay home in such a snowstorm.

3. [intensif Particle] used to emphasize that the immediately preceding element justifies, exemplifies, or supports particularly well what is stated in the preceding context: **even.**

[Говорящий – мул] Там, в городе, одни люди хватают других людей и отправляют в холодный край, название которого я забыл. А иногда просто убивают. А за что — никто не знает... Я одного не пойму, почему все эти люди, прежде чем их схватят, никуда не бегут... Я и то в своё время сбежал от злого хозяина и пришёл к своему старику. И ничего — обошлось (Искандер 3). [The speaker is a mule] Down there, in the city, some people are seizing other people and sending them off to a cold country, I forget the name of it. And sometimes they just kill them. No one knows what for....One thing I'll never understand is why all those people don't run away somewhere before they get caught....Even I, in my time, once ran away from a bad master to come to my old man. And nothing happened—it turned out all right (3a). ♦ Пирог оказался очень вкусным — я и то не смогла устоять. The pie ended up being really good—even I couldn't resist.

4. *substand* [Particle] used as, or as part of, an affirmative answer to or a confirmation of some preceding statement: **oh, yes; yes ⟨yup, aye etc⟩ (...), that's ⟨'tis⟩ true; indeed.**

«Ноги с пару зашлись». — «Вот прошлогодняя копна, может, погреешься?» — «И то. Покуда до дому дотянешь, помереть можно» (Шолохов 2). "My legs are numb with cold." "There's an old haystack. Couldn't you get warm in there?" "Oh, yes. Or I'll be dead before we get home" (2a). ♦ [Анисья:] Да ты заходи, самовар поставим, чайком душеньку отведёшь. [Матрёна (садится):] И то уморилась, миленькие (Толстой 1). [А.:] But come in and we'll get the samovar ready. You'll feel better after a cup of tea. [M. (sitting down):] Aye, I'm tired out, that's true (1c). ♦ Не бойся, дядя Митя, я не стану этого делать, не стану я переваливать свой груз на твои слабенькие, дохленькие плечи, не стану подвергать я тебя опасности унижения от собственного бессилия... я поберегу тебя... Почти так говорил себе Лёва... И то, надо отдать ему должное, ни разу в жизни не был так тонок, точен, чуток — так умён (Битов 2). Don't worry, Uncle Mitya, I won't do it, I will not dump my burden on your weak little sickly shoulders, not will I subject you to the danger of being humiliated by your own helplessness...I'll look after you....Lyova was talking to himself almost this way....Indeed, to give him his due, he had never in his life been so subtle, exact, sensitive—so intelligent (2a).

T-107 • НА ТО́ И; НА ТО́ [PrepP; these forms only; usu. adv; often foll. by a чтобы-clause] used when emphasizing that the given statement expresses the main function (job, role) or characteristic feature of s.o. or sth.: **(after all,) that's what a [NP] is for ⟨does⟩; (after all,) that's what [NPs] are for ⟨do⟩; that ⟨it⟩ is what is to be expected (of a [NP] ⟨in some place etc⟩);** [in limited contexts] **the job of a [NP] is to...; (as a [NP],) that's your**

⟨his etc⟩ **job** ⟨**department**⟩; **that's what** [NP] **is about; the** [NP], **being the** [NP],…

Правда, пожары в Гаграх, как в турецкой бане, случались крайне редко, но на то и санитарные меры (Искандер 3). Admittedly, fires were as rare in Gagra as in a Turkish bath, but that's what public safety measures are for (3a). ♦ Комиссар почувствовал свою вину за то, что в госпитале умирают люди. До приезда [Людмилы] Шапошниковой его это не тревожило, на то и госпиталь во время войны (Гроссман 2). The commissar felt guilty because men were dying in his hospital. Until Lyudmila's visit this had never disturbed him: it was what was to be expected in a military hospital (2a). ♦ «Душегуб ты…» – «Это какой же я душегуб?» – «Истинный! Кто Петра убил? Не ты?» – «Я… А ежели б Петро меня поймал, что бы он сделал?.. Он бы тоже меня убил… На то она и война» (Шолохов 5). "You're a murderer…" "Me? A murderer?" "Indeed, you are! Who killed Petro? Wasn't it you?" "Yes….Suppose Petro had caught me, what would he have done?…He'd have killed me the same….That's what war's about" (5a). ♦ …Царь на то и царь, чтобы, не останавливаясь, ехать к своему почётному месту (Искандер 5). The czar, being the czar, rides to his place of honor without stopping (5a).

Т-108 • НЕ ТО ЧТО… А… [coord Conj, correlative] **1.** Also: **НЕ ТО ЧТОБ(Ы)… (НО ⟨А⟩…); НЕ ТО ЧТО… НО…** [variants with чтобы are more common] used to indicate that of the two given ways of expressing, describing, explaining etc sth., the second is more accurate, precise etc: **not so much…as ⟨but⟩…; not exactly…but…; it's not so much…as…; it's not so much that…but…; it's not so much a matter of…, but rather…; it's not exactly…but;** [in limited contexts] **though one ⟨it⟩ is not exactly…**

Всегда бывает в январе несколько дней, похожих на весну – собственно, не то чтобы похожих на весну, а таких дней, которые вдруг приводят тебе на память облик весны (Олеша 3). In January there are always several springlike days, – actually, they don't so much resemble spring as suddenly remind you of what it is like (3a). ♦ Они вышли из врат и направились лесом. Помещик Максимов, человек лет шестидесяти, не то что шёл, а лучше сказать, почти бежал сбоку, рассматривая их всех с судорожным, невозможным почти любопытством (Достоевский 1). They went out the gate and through the woods. The landowner Maximov, a man of about sixty, was not so much walking but, more precisely, almost running alongside, staring at them all with contorted, almost impossible curiosity (1a). ♦ «Отец мой один из замечательнейших людей своего века. Но он становится стар, и он не то что жесток, но он слишком деятельного характера» (Толстой 5) "My father is one of the most remarkable men of his time. But he's growing old, and though he is not exactly cruel, he has too vigorous a nature" (5a).

2. Also: **НЕ ТО ЧТО…; …(А) НЕ ТО ЧТО; …(А) НЕ ТО ЧТОБЫ** [variants with что are more common] used in a two-part statement in which the element directly following не то что or не то чтобы is more pertinent to the speaker and the other element, an exaggeration, is used for reinforcement: **not only… (, but…);** [when, in translation, the element introduced by не то что etc follows the other, more extreme, element] **let alone; not to mention; to say nothing of; much less.**

[Говорящий – мул] «„Сейчас никому нельзя доверять. Даже собственному мулу не доверяй своих мыслей!" Ну уж такой глупости я от Самуила никак не ожидал. Я не то чтобы предать своего хозяина, я жизнь готов за него отдать» (Искандер 3). [The speaker is a mule] "'You mustn't confide in anyone now. Don't even confide your thoughts to your own mule!' Now, I never expected to hear such foolishness from Samuel. I not only wouldn't betray my master, but would lay down my life for him" (3a). ♦ У Гудзя генеральский авторитет, но он безволен, трусоват, видимо необразован… Была бы воля Ершова, он генералу Гудзю полком не доверил бы командовать, не то что корпусом (Гросс-

ман 2). General Gudz had the authority of his rank, but he was weak-willed, cowardly and obviously uneducated….If it had been up to him, Yershov wouldn't have trusted Gudz with a regiment, let alone a whole corps (2a). ♦ [Миловзоров:] Шмага, ты не видал Незнамова? Будет он на репетиции? [Шмага:] Кто же его знает! Я не нянька его. [Миловзоров:] Вы, кажется, такие неразрывные были. [Шмага:] …И мужья с жёнами расходятся, а не то что друзья (Островский 3). [M.:] Shmaga, have you seen Neznamov? Will he be at rehearsal today? [Sh.:] How should I know? I'm not his nurse-maid. [M.:] I thought you two were inseparable. [Sh.:] …Even husbands and wives part company, to say nothing of friends (3a). ♦ «Взял март у апреля два дня и нагнал такую погоду, что по нужде не выйдешь из-под крыши, а не то чтобы стадо вывести» (Искандер 3). "March took two days from April and brewed up some weather that was so bad you wouldn't set foot out of doors for a call of nature, much less lead the flock out" (3a).

Т-109 • НИ ТО́ НИ СЁ coll, usu. disapprov [NP; Invar; usu. this WO] **1.** [subj-compl with быть∅, оказаться (subj: human) or nonagreeing modif] a person or thing that lacks distinguishing characteristics or features, that is mediocre: **neither this nor that; neither one thing nor the other; nothing out of the ordinary; run-of-the-mill; nondescript;** [in limited contexts] **betwixt and between.**

…В одном звуке этого слова [миллионщик]… заключается что-то такое, которое действует и на людей подлецов, и на людей ни то ни сё, и на людей хороших, – словом, на всех действует (Гоголь 3). …The mere sound of the word ["millionaire"]…contains something that affects people of all descriptions: the ones who are scoundrels, the ones who are neither this nor that, and those who are really good – in short, it affects everybody (3c). ♦ Есть род людей, известных под именем: люди так себе, ни то ни сё… (Гоголь 3). There is a type of man who is described as "so-so," neither one thing nor the other… (3a).

2. rare [adv] in a mediocre way, neither well nor poorly, neither positively nor negatively etc: **so-so; fair to middling.**

«Как твой сын учится?» – «Ни то ни сё». "How is your son doing in school?" "Fair to middling."

3. rare [often used as an indep. remark] used to relay one's own or someone else's previous or expected noncommittal response to a question, suggestion etc: **neither yes nor no; one remains noncommittal; one doesn't give (s.o.) any definite answer.**

Т-110 • ПОКА́ ТО́ ДА СЁ coll [subord clause; Invar; fixed WO] while something is slowly developing or being carried out: **in the meantime; meanwhile; while this is happening ⟨going on⟩.**

Ждать обеда придётся долго. Давайте перекусим, пока то да сё. Dinner won't be ready for quite a while. Let's have a snack in the meantime.

Т-111 • ТО́ БИШЬ obsoles, coll [subord Conj; introduces an appos clause] used by the speaker to clarify a preceding remark or correct his mistake: **or rather; that is; I mean.**

«…Господин сочинитель, то бишь студент, бывший то есть, денег не платит, векселей надавал, квартиру не очищает, беспрерывные на них поступают жалобы, а изволили в претензию войти, что я папироску при них закурил!» (Достоевский 3). "…Mr. Writer here – I mean student – that is, former student – won't pay up, handed out IOU's, won't get out of his room, is getting constant complaints made against him and then complained, if you please, when I lit up a cigarette in his presence!" (3a).

Т-112 • ТО ДА СЁ; (И) ТО И СЁ; ТО-СЁ, often **говорить, думать** и т. п. **О ТОМ (И) О СЁМ** all coll [NP; usu. obj; fixed WO] (to talk, chat, think etc about) various things, all kinds of things (usu. used instead of enumerating various topics, circumstances, matters etc): **this and that; this, that, and the**

other thing; one thing and another; [in limited contexts] **(occupy o.s. with 〈engage in etc〉) small talk; and all that.**

«Я угостила его [генерала] чем бог послал, разговорились о том о сём, наконец и о Дубровском» (Пушкин 1). "I treated him [the general] to whatever was in the house, and we talked about this and that, mentioning at last Dubrovskii, too" (1a). ♦ Что делать в потёмках? Стали разговаривать о том о сём. Она рассказывала про своего отца... И я стал рассказывать про свою жизнь (Трифонов 5). We had to do something, sitting there in the dark, and so we began talking about one thing and another. She told me about her father....Then I began telling her about my life (5a). ♦ [Дуняша (прислушивается):] Вот, кажется, уже едут. [Лопахин (прислушивается):] Нет... Багаж получить, то да сё... (Чехов 2). [D. (listens):] It sounds as if they're coming. [L. (listening):] No, they're not. There's the luggage to be got out and all that (2c).

Т-113 • ТÓ ЕСТЬ [Invar] **1.** [coord Conj; introduces an appos] stating sth. again using different words, reiterating sth. using a different formulation (sometimes stating it more specifically): **that is; in other words; that is to say; i.e.; (or) to put it another way; meaning;** [in limited contexts] **or.**

Затем был прочитан список лиц, вызванных к судебному следствию, то есть свидетелей и экспертов (Достоевский 2). Then a list of persons called for questioning in court—that is, of witnesses and experts—was read (2a). ♦ «Игорь вырос в Париже, сын эмигранта, то есть человека, пострадавшего от революции...» (Рыбаков 2). "Igor grew up in Paris, the son of an émigré, in other words someone who suffered from the Revolution..." (2a). ♦ Покой был известного рода; ибо гостиница была тоже известного рода, то есть именно такая, как бывают гостиницы в губернских городах... (Гоголь 3). The room was of the familiar sort, for the inn too was of the familiar sort, that is to say, the sort of inn that is to be found in all provincial towns... (3a). ♦ Лёва не старался выдвинуться по общественной линии, т. е. избежал общественной работы... (Битов 2). Lyova did not try to advance himself at the institute along social lines; i.e., he avoided community work... (2a). ♦ «Знаешь что: Грушенька просила меня: „Приведи ты его (тебя то есть), я с него ряску стащу"» (Достоевский 1). "You know, Grushenka said to me: 'Bring him over (meaning you), and I'll pull his little cassock off'" (1a). ♦ До Коряжска было шестьдесят пять километров, то есть часа два езды с учётом местных дорог и без учёта странностей Володиного характера (Аксёнов 3). It was about 65 kilometers to Koryazhsk, or a two hour drive if you take into consideration the condition of local roads and ignore the peculiarities of Volodya's personality (3a).

2. [coord Conj; introduces an appos] stating sth. more correctly, slightly correcting and specifying what has just been said: **or rather; or to put it more precisely 〈accurately〉;** [in limited contexts] **I mean; that's not right.**

Искусство нагло, потому что внятно. То есть: оно нагло для ясности (Терц 3). Art is insolent because it is so clear. Or rather, it is insolent in order to make itself clear (3a). ♦ «Только едва он коснулся двери, как она вскочила, зарыдала и бросилась ему на шею. — Поверите ли? я, стоя за дверью, также заплакал, то есть, знаете, не то чтоб заплакал, а так — глупость!» (Лермонтов 1). "But barely had he touched the door, than she jumped up, burst into sobs and threw herself on his neck. Would you believe it? As I stood behind the door, I, too, began to cry; I mean, you know, it was not really crying, it was just—oh, silliness!" (1a). ♦ «...Мне надо выговориться. Не с Лушей же, она тут же перебьёт и сама начнёт говорить. И друзей у меня как-то нет... То есть есть, и хорошие даже, ничего не скажешь, но начнёшь с ними говорить, и через минуту, глядишь, мусор какой-то начинается — что кто где написал или сказал, и что было у художников на последнем пленуме, и где достать краски» (Некрасов 1). "...I feel I've got to talk. Not with Lusha—she would interrupt and start to talk herself. And I don't seem to have any friends... That's not right, I do have friends, good friends too, I can't deny it, but you begin to talk to

them and right away some sort of nonsense begins—who wrote or said what where, what happened at the last artists' plenum, where to get paints" (1a).

3. coll [Particle; used with как or before как это; if the preceding remark contains an interrogative adverb or pronoun, this adverb or pronoun, or the word or phrase to which the speaker reacts, is repeated] used to express bewilderment, displeasure etc in response to the interlocutor's words: **what do you mean!; what are you saying!;** [in limited contexts] **you can't be serious; what's this?**

...[Нюрок] обратила к Ирине Викторовне свои чудные глаза: «Страшно!» — «То есть как это?» — «Да очень просто! Очень страшно, и больше ничего!» (Залыгин 1). ...[Niurok] turned her wonderful eyes to Irina Viktorovna and said, "I was scared." "What do you mean?" "Just what I say. I was really scared. That's all" (1a). ♦ «А мы не негры, — сказал хозяин, улыбаясь своей характерной улыбкой и кивая на остальных негров, — мы — абхазцы». — «То есть как? Отрекаетесь?» — стал уточнять принц... (Искандер 4). "We aren't Negroes," the host said, smiling his characteristic smile and nodding at the other Negroes. "We're Abkhazians." "What's this? Are you renouncing—?" The prince began trying to pin him down... (4a).

4. obs, highly coll [Particle] used to increase the emotional intensity of a statement: **really.**

Т-114 • ТÓ ЛИ... ТÓ ЛИ...; НЕ ТÓ... НЕ ТÓ... [coord Conj, disjunctive] used when citing two (or, occas., more) possibilities to show that the speaker thinks that one of them is probably correct, true: **either...or (perhaps)...; whether 〈perhaps〉... or...; (s.o. 〈sth.〉) might have 〈be etc〉...or (perhaps)...;** [in limited contexts] **...or is it...**

«Вон оттуда, — она показала пальцем на балкон третьего этажа, — то ли столкнули голубушку, то ли сама прыгнула...» (Чернёнок 1). "From up there," she said, pointing to a third-floor balcony, "the poor thing was either pushed or she jumped..." (1a). ♦ ...Был он худой, изнурённый, и с утра никогда не понять: не то недоспал, не то переспал... (Ерофеев 2). He was skinny and emaciated, and in the morning it was hard to tell whether he hadn't gotten enough sleep or had overslept (2a). ♦ В воздухе стоял кисловатый дух то ли слегка подгнивающих прошлогодних листьев, устилающих землю, то ли усыхающих ягод черники... то ли древесных соков, бродящих в могучих стволах смешанного леса (Искандер 5). There was a mild tang in the air, perhaps from last year's carpet of leaves gently decaying on the ground, or from drying blueberries...or from tree sap fermenting in the mighty trunks of the mixed forest (5a). ♦ Среди гостей была даже и одна звезда рока, то ли Карл Питерс, то ли Питер Карлтон, долговязый и худой, в золотом пиджаке на голое тело (Аксёнов 7). There was also a bona-fide rock star—Carleton Peters, or was it Peter Carleton?—with stick-figure arms protruding from a gold lamé vest over a bare chest (7a).

Т-115 • ТÓ-ТО ЖЕ; НУ 〈ВОТ〉 ТÓ-ТО ЖЕ all coll [Interj; these forms only] (used to express the speaker's satisfaction with what the interlocutor has just said, often in cases when the interlocutor agrees with the opinion or earlier statement of the speaker) that is correct, now you are talking sensibly, now you understand etc: **there now; that's better 〈right〉; (there now,) what did I tell you?;** [in limited contexts] **I told you so!; aha!**

«Ты умница, — сказал Кязым, разгибаясь, — другого слова не подберёшь». — «То-то же, — сказала Нуца, довольная, — хоть раз в жизни признал меня умной» (Искандер 5). "You're a smart girl," Kyazum said as he straightened up. "No other word for it." "There now," Noutsa said, pleased. "For once in your life you've admitted I'm smart" (5a). ♦ [Кабанова:] ...Только ты смотри, чтобы мне вас не дожидаться! Знаешь, я не люблю этого. [Кабанов:] Нет, маменька, сохрани меня господи! [Кабанова:] То-то же! (Островский 6). [K-ova:] ...But mind I don't have to wait for you too long! You know I don't like it! [K-ov:] Of course not, mother. I'd never dream of being late. [K-ova:] That's better (6c). ♦ «Ты был прав: матч выиграл Каспаров». – «То-то же! В другой раз не будешь со мной спорить!» "You were right, Kasparov won the match." "Aha! Next time you'll know not to argue with me!"

T-116 • ПОКА́ЗЫВАТЬ/ПОКАЗА́ТЬ ТОВА́Р ЛИЦО́М [VP; subj: human; often pfv infin with a finite form of хотеть, уметь etc; fixed WO] to present s.o., sth., or o.s. in such a way as to highlight his, its, or one's most favorable characteristics, aspects etc: X показал товар лицом ≃ X showed s.o. ⟨sth.⟩ off; X showed off; X presented himself ⟨s.o., sth.⟩ to X's ⟨s.o.'s, its⟩ best advantage; X presented sth. in the best possible light; X put his best foot forward.

Потребовалось даже с Запада пускать к себе [в Ибанск] и показывать товар лицом (Зиновьев 1). It even began to be necessary to let foreigners from the West into Ibansk and to show ourselves off to our best advantage (1a).

T-117 • ТОВА́РИЩ ПО НЕСЧА́СТЬЮ [NP; fixed WO] a person who, together with or like another, has fallen into some kind of misfortune or unpleasant situation: **comrade in misfortune ⟨distress⟩; companion in misfortune; fellow sufferer.**

Находясь всё ещё в атмосфере моей трагедии, я считал этих людей с кухни моими товарищами по несчастью (Лимонов 1). Since I was still caught up in the atmosphere of my tragedy, I felt these people from the kitchen were my comrades in misfortune (1a). ♦ Говорили, что Поляшко был когда-то и откуда-то «сослан» в НИИ-9 высоким лицом и одно только имя этого высокого лица внушало Строковскому уважение; говорили, что и сам Строковский должен был идти на серьёзное повышение, да не пошёл, и это тоже было чем-то вроде «ссылки», так вот они с Поляшко – товарищи по несчастью, а это много значит... (Залыгин 1). It was said that Poliashko had once been "banished" to Research Institute No.9 by a highly placed person whose very name filled Strokovsky with awe. It was said that Strokovsky himself was long due for promotion, but it never came, and this was also a sort of "banishment." Thus he and Poliashko were companions in misfortune and this meant a lot (1a). ♦ Находящийся в одном из колымских лагерей мой брат написал мне, что он получил там драгоценный подарок. Товарищ по несчастью, поэт и критик Игорь Поступальский подарил ему в день рождения истрёпанную книжку стихов Пастернака (Гладков 1). [context transl] My brother, who was in one of the Kolyma camps, wrote to me that he had been given a precious gift there. One of his fellow prisoners, the poet and critic Igor Postupalski, had presented him on his birthday with a tattered volume of Pasternak's verse (1a).

T-118 • ТОГДА́ КАК [subord Conj; contrastive, contrastive-temporal, or contrastive-concessive] while at the same time: **while; whereas; when (in fact);** [in limited contexts] **although; even though; by contrast.**

Она сидела неподвижно, опустив голову на грудь; перед нею на столике была раскрыта книга, но глаза её, неподвижные и полные неизъяснимой грусти, казалось, в сотый раз пробегали одну и ту же страницу, тогда как мысли её были далеко... (Лермонтов 1). She sat motionless, her head sunk on her breast, on a table before her lay an open book, but her fixed gaze, full of inexplicable sadness, seemed to be skimming one and the same page for the hundredth time while her thoughts were far away... (1b). ♦ ...Подсудимый, войдя в залу... шагал вперёд как солдат и держал глаза впереди себя, упираясь, тогда как вернее было ему смотреть налево, где в публике сидят дамы, ибо он был большой любитель прекрасного пола... (Достоевский 2). ...The defendant, on entering the courtroom...marched along like a soldier, and kept his eyes fixed straight in front of him, whereas it would have been more correct for him to look to the left where, among the public, the ladies were sitting, since he was a great admirer of the fair

sex... (2a). ♦ Было непонятно, во-первых, как он [котёл] здесь очутился, а во-вторых, как он уцелел, будучи медным, тогда как чугунный не выдержал и лопнул (Искандер 3). They could not understand, in the first place, how it [the kettle] had gotten here, and in the second place, how it had survived, being copper, when the iron one had not withstood the fire and had split (3a). ♦ «Я очень рад буду, – сказал князь. – Скажите, – прибавил он, как будто только что вспомнив что-то и особенно-небрежно, тогда как то, о чём он спрашивал, было главною целью его посещения, – правда, что l'impératrice-mère желает назначения барона Функе первым секретарём в Вену?» (Толстой 4). "Ah! I shall be delighted," said the Prince. "Tell me," he added, with elaborate casualness, as if the question he was about to ask had just occurred to him, when in fact it was the chief purpose of his visit, "is it true that the Dowager Empress wants Baron Funke to be appointed first secretary in Vienna?" (4a). ♦ В простой крестьянской жизни всякий дар человека, если смысл этого дара ясен и нагляден, признаётся окружающими спокойно и безоговорочно. Тогда как в интеллигентной среде... оценки людей гораздо более запутанны и авторитеты гораздо чаще ложны (Искандер 5). In the simple peasant way of life, any gift of a man's, if the significance of the gift be clear and demonstrable, is calmly and unreservedly acknowledged by those around him. In a cultured milieu, by contrast...assessments of men are much more muddled and the experts much more often in error (5a).

T-119 • ВВИДУ́ ТОГО́ ЧТО lit [subord Conj; introduces a clause of reason] taking into account the fact that: **since; as; in view of (the fact that); considering (the fact that).**

Гость ждал и именно сидел как приживальщик, только что сошедший сверху из отведённой ему комнаты вниз к чаю составить хозяину компанию, но смирно молчавший ввиду того, что хозяин занят и об чём-то нахмуренно думает... (Достоевский 2). The visitor sat and waited precisely like a sponger who had just come down from upstairs, from the room assigned to him, to keep his host company at tea, but was humbly silent, since the host was preoccupied and scowling at the thought of something... (2a). ♦ ...Она [труппа] однажды явилась во главе с Шарлем Лагранжем и сообщила Мольеру, что ввиду того, что он соединяет с необыкновенными способностями честность и приятное обращение, труппа просит его не беспокоиться: актёры не уйдут искать счастья на стороне, какие бы выгодные предложения им ни делали (Булгаков 5). ...One day his [Molière's] players came to him, headed by Charles La Grange, and assured him that, in view of his fairness and kindness, as well as his extraordinary talents, he had nothing to worry about—they would not leave to seek their fortunes elsewhere no matter how tempting the offers they received (5a).

T-120 • ВМЕСТО ТОГО́ ЧТОБЫ [subord Conj, contrastive-comparative] in place of (doing something else): **instead of; rather than.**

Он [директор] выпучил глаза и замер, как бы удивляясь, что вместо того, чтобы поскорбеть вместе с ним по поводу нехватки валюты, дядя Сандро ещё требует у него золото (Искандер 3). He [the director] stopped, goggle-eyed, as if amazed that Uncle Sandro was still demanding gold from him instead of grieving with him over the currency shortage (3a).

T-121 • ДЛЯ ⟨РА́ДИ⟩ ТОГО́ ЧТОБЫ [subord Conj; introduces a clause of purpose] for the purpose of: **(in order) to; so as to; with the aim of; in order that; so (that).**

В этот момент, многоуважаемые... читатели, мы вновь применяем технику стоп-кадра и вовсе не для того, чтобы щегольнуть «кинематографическим приёмом»... а по суровой необходимости совершить путешествие в прошлое Фотия Фёкловича (Аксёнов 12). At this moment, my respected readers, we must employ the freeze-frame technique once more, not at all in order to show off the "cinematographic method"...but out of strict necessity to travel into Fotii Feklovich's past... (12a). ♦ [Трофимов:] ...Очевидно, все хорошие разговоры у нас для того только, чтобы отвести глаза себе и другим (Чехов 2). [Т.:] It's obvious that all our fine talk is merely to delude ourselves and others (2a). ♦ «...Провидению угодно было потемнить мой рассудок, вероятно, для того, чтобы не помешать мне испить до дна чашу уготованных мне истязаний...» (Салтыков-Щедрин 2). "...It was the will of Providence to deprive me of my sense with the aim, I suppose, of letting me drain to the dregs the cup of horrors prepared for me..." (2a).

Т-122 • ДО ТОГО [PrepP; Invar; adv or modif] to such a great degree, so intensely (usu. used to show that the high degree of some quality, the intensity of some action etc is the motivation, reason etc for sth. in the surrounding context): **so; so much;** [in limited contexts] **such a** [NP].

«Чтоб вас куриный мор», — отозвался дядя Сандро из-под своей яблони, голосом показывая, что не делает различия между курицей и её хозяйкой, до того обе они ему надоели (Искандер 3). "May you get the chicken plague," Uncle Sandro responded from under the apple tree, his tone indicating that he made no distinction between the hen and her mistress, he was so sick of both of them (3a). ♦ Дома он [Митя] дополнил сумму, взяв взаймы три рубля от хозяев, которые дали ему с удовольствием, несмотря на то, что отдавали последние свои деньги, до того любили его (Достоевский 1). At home he [Mitya] added to the sum, borrowing three roubles from his landlords, who gave it to him gladly, though it was their last money—so much did they love him (1a). ♦ [Наталья Петровна:] Неужели вы можете предполагать... [Ракитин:] Я ничего не предполагаю. [Наталья Петровна:] Неужели ж вы до того меня презираете... [Ракитин:] Перестаньте, ради бога (Тургенев 1). [N.P.:] Surely you aren't suggesting... [R.:] I'm suggesting nothing. [N.:] You can't have such a low opinion of me that... [R.:] Oh stop, for goodness' sake (1d).

Т-123 • ДО ТОГО КАК [subord Conj, temporal] earlier in time than: **before.**

Женя пробиралась на кухню, когда все спали, а утром старалась умываться до того, как проснутся жильцы (Гроссман 2). In the morning Yevgenia would steal into the kitchen when everyone was asleep and try to get washed before they woke up (2a).

Т-124 • ДО ТОГО(...), ЧТО... [subord Conj, correlative] to such a degree that, so intensely that: **so...that; so much that; so much so that; so completely ⟨fully etc⟩ that;** [in limited contexts] **such a** [NP] **that; to the point where.**

Староста, никогда не мечтавший о существовании людей в мундире, которые бы не брали взяток, до того растерялся, что не заперся, не начал клясться и божиться, что никогда денег не давал... (Герцен 1). The head-man, who had never suspected the existence of men in uniform who would not take bribes, lost his head so completely that he did not deny the charge, did not vow and swear that he had never offered money... (1a). ♦ ...[Фёдор Павлович] плакал навзрыд как маленький ребёнок, и до того, что, говорят, жалко даже было смотреть на него... (Достоевский 1). ...He [Fyodor Pavlovich] wept and sobbed like a little child, so much so that they say he was pitiful to see... (1a). ♦ Люди смеялись, смеялись, шутили, шутили и до того дошутились, что сами привыкли и уже всерьёз стали называть море Чёрным (Искандер 3). People laughed and laughed, joked and joked, and joked to the point where they got used to it and started calling the sea Black themselves (3a).

Т-125 • И БЕЗ ТОГО; БЕЗ ТОГО [Particle; these forms only] (some situation, state of affairs etc has been established, some quality or property is present etc) without even adding the factor(s), reason(s) etc (specified or implied by the context): **as it is ⟨was⟩; (even) without that; anyway; anyhow;** [in limited contexts] **already; in any case; enough (already) as it is ⟨without that⟩; already as it is.**

«Вы, конечно, предложите мне дружбу; но ведь она и без того моя» (Гончаров 1). "You will, of course, offer me your friendship, but it is mine as it is" (1a). ♦ «...Человеческие чувства, которые и без того не были в нём глубоки, мелели ежеминутно... (Гоголь 3). The human feelings which had, anyhow, never been very deep in him, grew shallower every minute... (3a). ♦ При слове «пустыня» воображение Феденьки, и без того уже экзальтированное, приобретало такой полёт, что он, не в силах будучи управлять им, начинал очень серьёзно входить в роль погубителя Навозного. Ангел смерти, казалось ему, парит над нечестивым городом... (Салтыков-Щедрин 2). At the word "desert" Fedenka's imagination, already in a state of high exaltation, soared aloft so high that, unable to control it any longer, he began quite seriously to assume the role of Navozny's destroyer. The Angel of Death, it seemed to him, was already spreading his wings over the doomed city (2a). ♦ Он [Пастернак] только попросил и меня обязательно прийти, чтобы на чтении был «кто-то близкий», как он выразился. Разумеется, я и без того собирался быть в этот вечер в театре (Гладков 1). ...He [Pasternak] was very insistent that I should attend, so there would be "someone close to me," as he put it, at the reading. Needless to say, I had fully intended to be there in any case (1a). ♦ «Эх, Пётр Андреич! надлежало бы мне посадить тебя под арест, да ты уж и без того наказан» (Пушкин 2). "Well, I should really put you under arrest, Pyotr Andreitch, but you have been punished enough already without that" (2b). ♦ «Старейшему старейшине нашего села муха влетела в ухо. А он у нас и без того глухой на одно ухо» (Искандер 5). "A fly has flown into the ear of the eldest elder of our village. And he's already deaf in one ear as it is" (5a). ♦ В особенности тяжело было смотреть на город поздним вечером. В это время Глупов, и без того мало оживлённый, окончательно замирал (Салтыков-Щедрин 1). [context transl] The town was especially painful to see in the late evening. None too animated even at best, Foolov at that hour was totally dead (1a). ♦ Наша 54 камера была «спокойной» — старались не отравлять друг другу и без того скверную жизнь (Марченко 1). [context transl] Our cell no. 54 was a peaceful one, we tried not to make life any more miserable for one another than it already was (1a).

Т-126 • И ТОГО [Particle; Invar; foll. by compar form of Adj or Adv] used to emphasize that the comparative form that follows conveys a higher degree of the quality in question than what is stated in the preceding context: **even; still.**

Запретить издание двух лежавших в издательствах рукописей проще простого. Запретить шесть киносценариев, дошедших до режиссёрской разработки, — и того легче (Войнович 1). ...Nothing could have been simpler than stopping the two books in manuscript I had at a publisher's. It was even easier to prohibit the six screenplays of mine that were being worked on by directors (1a).

Т-127 • КРОМЕ ТОГО [Invar; sent adv (parenth); fixed WO] in addition to that (which has been stated, is available etc): **besides (that); furthermore; moreover; what is more.**

Родные Ростовых и Болконских иногда съезжались гостить в Лысые Горы семьями... и жили месяцами. Кроме того, четыре раза в год, в именины и рожденья хозяев, съезжалось до ста человек гостей на один-два дня (Толстой 7). Sometimes whole families of Rostov and Bolkonsky relations came to Bald Hills...and stayed for months. Besides that, four times a year, on the name days and birthdays of the host and hostess, as many as a hundred guests would gather there for a day or two (7a). ♦ Множество мыслей вертелось у меня в голове... Меня должно было радовать то обстоятельство, что редактор появился у меня... Но, с другой стороны, роман ему мог не понравиться... Кроме того, нужно было предложить чаю... Вообще в голове была каша... (Булгаков 12). A host of thoughts whirled in my head....I should have been delighted at his [the editor's] coming to see me....On the other hand he might not like my novel....What is more I should have been offering him some tea....My head was in a thorough muddle... (12a).

T-128 • НЕ БЕЗ ТОГО́ *coll* [PrepP; Invar; usu. indep. remark] (used as a mild affirmative response to a question or to corroborate s.o.'s or one's own statement) there is truth in what has been said: **there's some truth to that; you could say that; there's no denying it; I can't deny it; I guess ⟨suppose⟩ it ⟨he etc⟩ is ⟨does, has etc⟩;** [when confirming that some action or occurrence does take place sometimes] **it happens.**

«Да у тебя, говорю, метка от него [бати] на лбу до сих пор». — «Меня, говорит, и после того много били». — «Ну, и как, говорю, с пользой?» — «Не без того, — говорит, а сам всё отворачивается, отворачивается, — было время подумать» (Максимов 2). "Well, I said, "you've still got a scar on your forehead that my old man gave you." "There were plenty of others beside him who beat me up," he said. "And did it do you any good?" I asked him. "Guess it did," he said, trying all the time to turn away, "I've had plenty of time to think about it since" (2a). ♦ [author's usage] Виктор сел. «Я здорово пьян?» — спросил он. «Не без, — сказал Голем. — Но это неважно...» (Стругацкие 1). Victor sat down. "I'm really plowed, huh?" he asked. "Can't deny it," said Golem. "But never mind..." (1a).

T-129 • НЕ ТОГО́ *highly coll* [Particle; Invar] **1.** [usu. subj-compl with copula (subj: any common noun)] a person (or thing) is not especially good, not as good as he (or it) should be: **X не того ≃ X is not up to scratch ⟨to snuff, to par⟩; X is nothing to brag ⟨to write home⟩ about; X is no great shakes.**

[Ихарев:] Балык, кажется, не того, а икра ещё так и сяк (Гоголь 2). [I.:] The salmon's not up to scratch, but the caviar's satisfactory (2a).

2. ~ *кому* [impers predic with бытьø] s.o. is uncomfortable (physically or emotionally): **X-у не того ≃ X is not quite himself; X doesn't feel like himself;** [in refer. to a physical state only] **X is not feeling quite right ⟨well⟩; X is (a little) under the weather;** [in refer. to an emotional state only] **X is ill at ease;** [in refer. to feeling uncomfortable in one's surroundings] **X doesn't feel at home; X doesn't feel relaxed.**

[Сорин:] Мне, брат, в деревне как-то не того, и, понятная вещь, никогда я тут не привыкну. Вчера лёг в десять и сегодня утром проснулся в девять с таким чувством, как будто от долгого спанья у меня мозг прилип к черепу и всё такое (Чехов 6). [S.:] For some reason, my boy, I'm not quite myself in the country, and, it stands to reason, I'll never get accustomed to it. I went to bed at ten o'clock last night and woke up at nine this morning feeling as though my brain were stuck to my skull from sleeping so long, and all that sort of thing (6a).

T-130 • НЕ́Т ТОГО́ ЧТОБЫ; НЕ́Т ЧТОБЫ ⟨БЫ⟩ *all coll, usu. disapprov* [Particle; these forms only; foll. by infin] used to indicate that s.o. does not do, is not doing, or has not thought to do sth. (usu. an action considered by the speaker to be desirable, beneficial etc): **нет того чтобы сделать Y ≃ s.o. never does ⟨never wants to do etc⟩ Y; it doesn't occur ⟨never occurs⟩ to s.o. to do Y; s.o. doesn't think ⟨never thinks⟩ of doing Y; s.o. doesn't give ⟨never gives⟩ a thought to doing Y.**

«Что ж вы не накрываете на стол? — с удивлением и досадой спросил Обломов. — Нет чтоб подумать о господах?» (Гончаров 1). "Why don't you set the table?" Ilya Ivanovich [Oblomov] asked with vexation and surprise. "Don't you ever think of your masters?" (1b). ♦ «Нет чтобы хорошему примеру подражать, а всё как бы на смех друг друга поднять норовим!» (Салтыков-Щедрин 2). "We never want to imitate a good example. We just try to make fun of one another!" (2a).

T-131 • НИ С ТОГО́ НИ С СЕГО́ [PrepP; Invar; adv; more often used with pfv verbs; fixed WO] unexpectedly and without an

obvious reason: **for no reason (at all ⟨whatsoever⟩); for no good ⟨apparent⟩ reason; without any reason at all; without rhyme or reason;** [in limited contexts] **(suddenly ⟨just⟩) out of the blue;** [in refer. to saying sth. only] **apropos of nothing.**

«Асеев очень сложный человек. Уже здесь в Чистополе он недавно ни с того ни с сего оскорбил меня и даже вынудил жаловаться на него Федину» (Гладков 1). "Aseyev is a very complex man. A little while ago, here in Chistopol, he insulted me for no reason at all, and even forced me to complain to Fedin about him" (1a). ♦ Ни с того ни с сего у поворота перегона Петушки-Роща один за другим стали сходить с полотна паровозы (Максимов 3). For no apparent reason, engines had started leaving the tracks at a bend on the Petushki-Roshcha run (3a). ♦ Николай терпеливо выслушал учительницу, а потом бухнул ни с того ни с сего: «Слышь, Марь Иванна, а Тимофей-то мне проспорил пол-литру [ungrammat = пол-литра]» (Войнович 5). Nikolai patiently heard the teacher out and then blurted out, apropos of nothing: "Listen, Marya Ivanna, I've just won half a liter from Timofei on a bet" (5a). ♦ «Да как же это я вдруг, ни с того ни с сего, [перееду] на Выборгскую сторону...» (Гончаров 1). "But how can I suddenly, without rhyme or reason, move to the Vyborg district?" (1b). ♦ Ольга Петровна собиралась зайти к мадам Кипарисовой и всё не могла собраться. Времени не было, да и неловко как-то. Она не видела Кипарисову года три уже. Как это она ни с того ни с сего вдруг зайдёт? (Чуковская 1). Olga Petrovna intended to call on Mrs. Kiparisova, but couldn't bring herself to. There was no time, and anyway it was a bit awkward. She hadn't seen Mrs. Kiparisova for about three years. She couldn't very well suddenly go and visit her, out of the blue (1a).

T-132 • ПОСЛЕ ТОГО́ КАК [subord Conj, temporal] following or subsequent to the time that: **after;** [in limited contexts] **when.**

После того как был ранен в бою под Глубокой, Григорий провалялся в походном лазарете в Миллерове неделю... (Шолохов 3). After being wounded at Glubokaya, Grigory had spent a week in the field hospital at Millerovo... (3a).

T-133 • СВЕРХ ТОГО́ [PrepP; Invar; sent adv (parenth); fixed WO] in addition to that (which has been stated): **besides (that); what's more; (and) furthermore; moreover; on top of that; ...to boot.**

Некоторое время Байбаков запирался... но когда ему предъявили найденные на столе вещественные доказательства и, сверх того, пообещали полтинник на водку, то вразумился и, будучи грамотным, дал следующее показание... (Салтыков-Щедрин 1). For some time Dormousov refused to speak....But when they confronted him with the evidence that had been found on the desk and promised him fifty kopecks for vodka besides, he saw the light, and, being literate, gave the following deposition (1a). ♦ Слуга старого времени удерживал, бывало, барина от расточительности и невоздержания, а Захар сам любил выпить с приятелями на барский счёт... Сверх того, Захар и сплетник (Гончаров 1). In the old days, servants used to restrain their masters from extravagance and overindulgence; but Zakhar himself liked drinking with his friends at the master's expense....Moreover, Zakhar was a gossip (1b).

T-134 • РЯДИ́ТЬСЯ В ТО́ГУ *кого-чего lit* [VP; subj; human or collect] to try to pass o.s. off as a member of a specific social group, a representative of a specific movement or school of thought, a possessor of specific personality traits etc: **X рядится в тогу Y-a ≃ X dons the garb of Y; X clothes himself in the mantle of Y; X parades (himself) as Y ⟨in Y's garments⟩.**

T-135 • ТО́ЖЕ МНЕ... *coll, derog* [Particle; Invar; fixed WO] used to express one's strong disapproval of s.o. or sth., and one's opinion that he or it is not worthy of his or its name, title etc: **some [NP]!; [NP], indeed!; [NP], my foot!**

«Да врёт она всё, — говорили одни, выслушав гонцов, — тоже мне царица! Мы ещё помним, как она взятки брала помидорами» (Искандер 5). "Oh, she's always telling lies," some said when they heard the heralds. "Some queen! *We* remember how she took bribes of tomatoes" (5a). ♦ Всё это как будто давно готовое бурлило у меня внутри и вдруг вылилось наружу от слов журналиста: «Мы с женой читали вечером [стихи Пастернака] и смеялись»… Тоже мне — ценитель поэзии! (Чуковская 2). All this had long been seething inside me, ready to come out, and had suddenly come pouring out at the journalist's words "my wife and I were reading [Pasternak's poetry] in the evening and it made us laugh"….A connoisseur of poetry, indeed! (2a). ♦ Тоже мне специалист! На простой вопрос не может ответить. Specialist my foot! He can't even answer a simple question.

Т-136 • МА́ЛАЯ ТОЛИ́КА [NP; sing only] **1.** *old-fash ~ чего* [obj or subj] a small amount (of sth.): **a little (bit); a tiny bit; a small quantity; a few;** [in refer. to food only] **a morsel.**

2. usu. получить, дать, отложить и т. п. малую толику *obs* (to get, give, save etc) a small amount of money: **a little something; a small ⟨modest⟩ sum.**

Он [губернатор] как-то втихомолку улучшал своё состояние, как крот где-то под землёю, незаметно, он прибавлял зерно к зерну и отложил-таки малую толику на чёрные дни (Герцен 1). He [the governor] was improving his fortune somehow on the sly, like a mole working unseen underground; he was adding grain to grain and laying by a little something for a rainy day (1a).

3. *obs* [accus only; adv or modif] (to possess some trait, display some characteristic, do sth.) to a small extent: **a little; a (little) bit; somewhat.**

Т-137 • ВЗЯТЬ В ТОЛК *(что)* coll [VP; subj: human; usu. infin with a finite form of не мочь or neg fut; often foll. by a subord clause] to comprehend (sth.): X не мог взять в толк ≃ **X couldn't understand ⟨figure out⟩ (sth.); X couldn't make ⟨could make no⟩ sense of (sth.); X couldn't make head nor ⟨or⟩ tail of (sth.); X couldn't make heads or tails of (sth.);** [in limited contexts] **X couldn't grasp the fact that…**

«Но к чему так громко? Старик услышит, обидится». — «Ничего он не услышит… А и услышит, не возьмёт в толк, — с придурью» (Пастернак 1). "But don't talk so loud. You don't want to hurt the old man's feelings." "He won't hear anything….And if he did, he wouldn't understand—he's not quite right in the head" (1a). ♦ «Что такое? — не могла Романиха в толк взять. — Ведь должно же быть хоть кому-то в этом городе жить хорошо» (Суслов 1). "What is this?" Romanikha could make no sense of it. "There should be someone in the city who's living well" (1a). ♦ …Он никак не мог взять в толк, какого чёрта мельничный жёрнов оказался лежащим на пастухе, а сам пастух при этом оказался лежащим в воде (Искандер 3). …He could not make head nor tail of it—how the devil did the millstone end up lying on the shepherd, and the shepherd lying in the water? (3a). ♦ Тётушка Хрисула не могла взять в толк, что разноязыкой нашей деревенской молодёжи к этому времени проще всего было говорить по-русски (Искандер 5). Auntie Chrysoula could not grasp the fact that by now the young people of our polyglot villages found it easiest to speak Russian (5a).

Т-138 • ЗНАТЬ ⟨ПОНИМА́ТЬ⟩ ТОЛК *в ком-чём* coll; **ЗНАТЬ ПРОК** *obs* [VP; subj: human; if the obj is a count noun, it is usu. pl] to have an understanding of some group of people or type of person; to be extremely knowledgeable in some area, field etc: X знает толк в Y-ах ⟨Y-е⟩ ≃ **X knows what's what in ⟨when it comes to⟩ Y; X knows all there is to know about Y; X knows all about Ys;** [in limited contexts] **X is a connoisseur ⟨a good judge⟩ of thing Y.**

Ты гурман. Ты знаешь толк в еде и в винах… (Аксёнов 2). You're an epicure. You know what's what in food, and in wines… (2a).

…[Арина Власьевна] в хозяйстве, сушенье и варенье знала толк… (Тургенев 2). …[Arina Vlas'evna] knew all there was to know about housekeeping and the drying and preserving of fruit… (2e). ♦ У другого, помоложе, розовое лицо человека, который понимает толк в винах (Булгаков 5). The other man, younger, has the rosy face of a connoisseur of wines (5a). ♦ Эта Муся Борисовна никому ничего не жалела… её считали святой, старухи, знавшие толк в людях, целовали ей платье (Гроссман 2). She [Musya Borisovna] never grudged anyone anything….She had been looked on as a saint; the old women, good judges of character, used to kiss her dress (2a).

Т-139 • С ТО́ЛКОМ coll [PrepP; Invar; adv] (to do sth.) in the way it should be done, using good judgment (usu. producing or attempting to produce a desirable result): **properly; right; the right way; well;** [in limited contexts] **showing ⟨using⟩ good sense; sensibly;** ‖ провести отпуск ⟨неделю в Париже и т. п.⟩ с толком ≃ **make the most of one's vacation ⟨week in Paris etc⟩.**

[Лебедев:] Не велика штука пить, — пить и лошадь умеет. Нет, ты с толком выпей!.. (Чехов 4). [L.:] Drinking's no great trick—even a horse can drink….No, it's knowing how to do it properly! (4a). ♦ «Наказ вам от меня такой: молотите хлеб и день и ночь, до дождей постарайтесь кончить… Зяби вспашите сколько осилите… Смотри, старуха, веди дело с толком!..» (Шолохов 5). "…Let this be my behest to you: thresh that grain day and night, try to finish it before the rains come….Plough up as much land as you can….Run the farm well, woman!.." (5a).

Т-140 • БЕ́З ТОЛКУ ⟨БЕЗ ТО́ЛКУ⟩ coll [PrepP; these forms only; adv] **1.** in an incoherent, senseless, disorderly manner: **haphazardly; carelessly.**

…Много бы можно сделать разных запросов. Зачем, например, глупо и без толку готовится на кухне? (Гоголь 3). …A great number of questions could well be asked. Why, for instance, were the meals in the kitchen prepared so foolishly and haphazardly? (3a).

2. to no purpose, futilely: **uselessly; senselessly; pointlessly; aimlessly; for nothing; in vain; to no avail ⟨purpose⟩.**

[Они] сказали, что такие дураки-одиночки, как я, годятся только чтобы без толку погибнуть. Что моё — впереди. Что я должен расти и учиться. Я учился (Кузнецов 1). They said that fools like myself who did things on their own only got themselves killed uselessly. That my future lay before me. That I had to grow up and learn. And learn I did (1a). ♦ Уже поздно, ночь, но все так боятся проспать, что никто не ложится. Без толку толкаются по избе (Битов 2). It's already late at night, but they are all so afraid of oversleeping that no one goes to bed. Aimlessly they loaf around the cabin (2a). ♦ «Ботинки худые. Чего тут в них без толку лазить по грязи. Он [капитан Миляга], небось, уж давно убёг [*ungrammat* = убежал]» (Войнович 2). "My boots are lousy. No sense in sloshing through the mud in them for nothing. He [Captain Milyaga] must be far away by now" (2a).

Т-141 • НЕ ⟨нельзя, невозможно и т. п.⟩ ДОБИ́ТЬСЯ ТО́ЛКУ *(от кого)* [VP; subj: human] not to receive or be able to get from s.o. a reasonable answer, response, explanation: X не добился толку (от Y-а) ≃ **X didn't ⟨couldn't⟩ get any sense out of Y; X could get no sense out of Y; X didn't ⟨couldn't⟩ get a straight answer (from Y); X got nowhere ⟨couldn't get anywhere⟩ (with Y); X didn't ⟨couldn't⟩ find out (anything) (from Y);** [in limited contexts] **X couldn't get a sensible account (of what had happened ⟨occurred etc⟩).**

…Три инвалида, которым гостиница поручена, так глупы или так пьяны, что от них никакого толку нельзя добиться (Лермонтов 1). …The three invalids to whom the place had been entrusted were either idiots or so drunk that one could not get any sense out of them (1d). ♦ Неподалёку от санатория мы встретили

Людмилу Павловну. Она вернулась утром, и я уже виделась с ней. Про сестру она ничего не узнала. «В прокуратуре народу – труба непротолчёная и никакого толку не добиться» (Чуковская 2). Not far from the rest-home we met Lyudmila Pavlovna. I had already seen her after she had returned that morning. She had not found out anything about her sister. "The Public Prosecutor's office was jammed with people and one could get no sense out of them" (2a). ♦ Не добившись толку в комиссии, добросовестный Василий Степанович решил побывать в филиале её, помещавшемся в Ваганьковском переулке (Булгаков 9). Having gotten nowhere at the Commission, the conscientious Vasily Stepanovich decided to visit its branch on Vagankovsky Lane (9a). ♦ [Наташа:] Вчера в полночь прохожу через столовую, а там свеча горит. Кто зажёг, так и не добилась толку (Чехов 5). [N.:] Last night at midnight I walked through the dining room, and there was a candle burning. Who lighted it? I couldn't find out (5a). ♦ «Они точно дети, от которых не добьёшься толку, как было дело, оттого что все хотят доказать, как они умеют драться» (Толстой 7). "They are like children from whom one can't get a sensible account of what has happened because they all want to show how well they can fight" (7a).

T-142 • СБИВА́ТЬ/СБИТЬ С ТО́ЛКУ *кого coll* [VP; subj: human or abstr] **1.** [more often pfv] to perplex s.o., throw s.o. into a state of (uneasy) confusion, make s.o. unable to see the situation clearly: X сбил Y-а с толку ≃ **X confused ⟨nonplussed, bewildered, muddled, disconcerted, derailed⟩ Y; X got Y confused ⟨flustered⟩; X got Y all mixed up ⟨screwed up, shook up etc⟩; X knocked Y off track ⟨course⟩; X rattled Y; thing X threw Y off.**

Его рассуждения опять сбили Надю с толку (Дудинцев 1). His reasoning had again confused Nadia (1a). ♦ [Говорящий – мул] Молодец мой старик. Что мне в нём нравится, так это то, что никто его не может сбить с толку. Если уж он что-то сам решил, так пусть хоть всем селом навалятся на него, он всё равно будет делать по-своему (Искандер 3). [The speaker is a mule] Good for my old man. What I like is that no one can muddle him. Once he's made up his mind to something, even if the whole village puts pressure on him, he'll still do it his own way (3a). ♦ Гусев мне надоел, и я нарочно болтал разную ерунду, чтобы сбить его с толку (Войнович 5). I was fed up with Gusev and I was purposely babbling all sorts of nonsense to derail him (5a). ♦ «Да у тебя белая горячка, что ль! – заревел взбесившийся наконец Разумихин. – Чего ты комедии-то разыгрываешь! Даже меня сбил с толку...» (Достоевский 3). "Have you got brain fever or what?" Razumikhin bellowed, finally enraged. "What is this farce you're playing? You've even got me all screwed up..." (3c). ♦ «Когда вас спрашивают, вы должны отвечать», – тоном педагога сказал Радов. «Я вам вообще ничего не должен, – сказал я. – Если бы я пришёл вступать в Союз писателей, тогда бы я должен. А я пришёл с вами прощаться». Это их как-то сбило с толку... (Войнович 1). "When you're asked a question, you should answer it," said Radov in a teacherly tone of voice. "I don't have to do anything of the sort," I said. "I would if I were here trying to join the Writers' Union, but I'm here to say good-bye." Somehow that knocked them off course... (1a). ♦ «Вы – не Достоевский», – сказала гражданка, сбиваемая с толку Коровьевым. «Ну, почём знать, почём знать», – ответил тот (Булгаков 9). "You are not Dostoevsky," said the woman, somewhat rattled by Koroviev's logic. "You never can tell, you never can tell," he answered (9a).

2. by serving as a bad example or exerting some influence on s.o., to induce s.o. to change his behavior for the worse, drive s.o. to do sth. wrong: X сбивает Y-а с толку ≃ **X is leading Y astray ⟨into temptation, down the wrong path⟩.**

Чёрт сбил с толку обоих чиновников: чиновники, говоря попросту, перебесились и перессорились ни за что (Гоголь 3). The Devil led the two officials astray: officials, to put it plainly, went crazy and fell out with each other for no reason whatsoever (3c).

T-143 • СБИВА́ТЬСЯ/СБИ́ТЬСЯ С ТО́ЛКУ *coll* [VP; subj: human; more often pfv] finding o.s. in a difficult, confusing situation, to become (anxiously) perplexed, lose one's ability to see the situation clearly, not know what to do: X сбился с толку ≃ **X got ⟨was⟩ confused ⟨nonplussed, bewildered, muddled, disconcerted, derailed, flustered, all mixed up etc⟩; X got ⟨was⟩ knocked off track ⟨course⟩.**

Дед совсем сбился с толку. Места себе не находил. То выйдет, то зайдёт, то присядет, пригорюнившись и тяжко вздыхая, то снова встанет и куда-то уйдёт (Айтматов 1). Grandfather was wholly confused and did not know what to do with himself. He would go outside, come in again, sit down for a minute, sighing heavily and grieving; then stand up and wander out again (1b). ♦ Почему он так сбился с толку, я сказать не могу, скорее всего потому, что разговор сошёл с предусмотренного предварительной разработкой направления (Войнович 1). I can't say why he was knocked off course, most likely because our conversation had departed from the line that had been worked out for it in advance (1a).

T-144 • ...ДА И ТО́ЛЬКО *coll* [used as Particle; Invar; fixed WO] **1.** used when calling or describing some person, thing etc by some name to show that the person, thing etc has all the applicable characteristics of that name: **(a) real ⟨regular, sheer, total⟩ [NP]; (a) [NP], pure and simple; a [NP], a real ⟨regular etc⟩ [NP]; [in limited contexts] really [AdjP].**

Скоро приедет Эдик, и опять разговоры о любви и хватание руками, мученье да и только (Аксёнов 1). Soon Edik would come, and again there'd be talk of love and pawing around, sheer torture... (1a). ♦ «Уж кто-то и пришёл! – сказал Обломов, кутаясь в халат. – А я ещё не вставал – срам да и только!» (Гончаров 1). "Someone has come already!" said Oblomov, wrapping his dressing gown around him. "And I haven't even got up yet – it's really disgraceful!" (1b).

2. used to add emphasis to the named action: **one just ⟨simply⟩ (does sth.).**

Мать его ругает, а он в ответ смеётся, да и только. His mother scolds him and he just laughs in reply. ♦ С этой минуты настойчивый взгляд Ольги не выходил из головы Обломова. Напрасно он во весь рост лёг на спину, напрасно брал самые ленивые и покойные позы – не спится, да и только (Гончаров 1). From that moment Olga's persistent gaze haunted Oblomov. In vain did he stretch out full length on his back, in vain did he assume the laziest and most comfortable positions – he simply could not go to sleep (1a).

T-145 • ТО́ЛЬКО И... [restr Particle; often used in the constructions только и... что ⟨как, как бы⟩] used to single out one action, phenomenon etc in order to emphasize that it is the only one that has a place in the given situation, among the given group of people etc: **only; sole(ly); nothing (else) but; all (one does etc is...).**

...Однажды, одевшись лебедем, он [Грустилов] подплыл к одной купавшейся девице, дочери благородных родителей, у которой только и приданого было что красота... (Салтыков-Щедрин 1). Once, dressed as a swan, he [Melancholov] swam up to a maiden who was bathing – the daughter of noble parents, whose only dowry was her beauty... (1a). ♦ Нынче поутру у колодца только и было толков что об ночном нападении черкесов (Лермонтов 1). This morning, at the well, there was nothing but talk about the night raid of the Circassians (1a). The Cherkess night raid was the sole subject of conversation the spring this morning (1b). ♦ Хотя бы [Аркадий сказал] одно слово в том смысле, что служба в армии – дело серьёзное, но что он постарается держаться. Ничего подобного!.. Отец, мать, бабушка и четыре девочки только и слышали о том, какие мелодии он разучит на саксофоне в ближайшем будущем (Залыгин 1). He [Arkady] might have said something to the effect that army service was no joking matter, but that he would do his best, but he didn't say a word about it.

Far from it. All his father, mother, grandmother, and the four girls heard from him was what tunes he'd soon be learning for the saxophone (1a).

T-146 • ТО́ЛЬКО И ВСЕГО́; И ТО́ЛЬКО *both coll* [indep. sent (usu. the 1st var.), question (both variants), or the concluding clause in a compound or complex sent (both variants); these forms only; fixed WO] (used to emphasize that there are no additional considerations, hidden motives etc beyond what has been stated) only that (which has been stated): **(and ⟨but⟩) that's all ⟨it⟩; it's as simple as that; just…(, that's all); just…, nothing more.**

«Разумеется, если б она мне сама сказала: „Я хочу тебя иметь", то я бы почёл себя в большой удаче, потому что девушка мне очень нравится; но теперь… я жду и надеюсь — и только!» (Достоевский 3). "Naturally, if she herself were to say to me, 'I want to have you,' I'd consider myself highly fortunate, because the girl really appeals to me, but for the moment…I'm waiting and hoping—and that's all!" (3a). ♦ …У меня нет денег, есть только вкус к необычному и странному, и только (Лимонов 1). …I don't have any money, all I have is a taste for the unusual and strange, that's all (1a). ♦ [Репников:] Восстановили против меня дочь и решили, что самое время прийти ко мне с личной просьбой. [Колесов:] Вашу дочь я не восстанавливал. Мы с ней знакомы, и только (Вампилов 3). [R.:] You set my daughter against me and then decided it was the right time to come to me with a personal request. [K.:] I didn't put your daughter up to it. We're just acquaintances (3b).

T-147 • ТО́ЛЬКО ⟨ТО́ЛЬКО-ТО́ЛЬКО, ТО́ЛЬКО ЧТО⟩… КАК… [subord Conj, temporal] used to show that the situation or action presented in the main clause immediately follows the situation or action presented in the subordinate clause: **as soon as; just as; hardly ⟨scarcely, only just⟩…when; no sooner…than; the moment ⟨the minute⟩…**

Только сели в машину, как у неё [девушки] возникла новая идея (Евтушенко 2). As soon as they got back in the car, she [the girl] had another idea (2a). ♦ Только они [друзья] дошли до ручья, как увидели, что навстречу им идёт человек могучего сложения и несёт на плечах дом (Искандер 5). Just as they [the friends] reached the brook they saw a powerfully built man coming toward them, carrying a house on his shoulders (5a). ♦ На другой день поутру я только что стал одеваться, как дверь отворилась, и ко мне вошёл молодой офицер невысокого роста, с лицом смуглым и отменно некрасивым, но чрезвычайно живым (Пушкин 2). The next morning I had only just begun to dress when the door opened and a young officer, not very tall, with a swarthy face that was strikingly unattractive but exceptionally lively, came into the room (2a). ♦ «Только я хочу жениться на полюбившейся мне девушке, вернее, только она захочет меня женить на себе, как мне начинает нравиться другая девушка и я даю стрекача от прежней» (Искандер 5). "The minute I want to marry a girl who's caught my fancy, or rather, the minute she wants me to marry her, I start to like another girl, and I turn tail and run from the first one" (5a).

T-148 • ТО́ЛЬКО ЧТО [Invar; fixed WO] **1.** [AdvP; adv] immediately before (the moment of speech or the moment indicated by the context): **just; just a minute ago.**

Он, конечно, скажет, кого только что встретил на улице… (Федин 1). Of course he would tell whom he had just met on the street… (1a).

2. [subord Conj, temporal] used to show that the situation or action presented in the main clause immediately follows the situation or action presented in the subordinate clause: **as soon as; just as; hardly ⟨scarcely, only just⟩…when; no sooner…than; the moment ⟨the minute⟩…**

Только что смеркло́сь, я велел казаку нагреть чайник по-походному, засветил свечу и сел у стола, покуривая из дорожной трубки (Лермонтов 1). As soon as it was dark, I told my Cossack to heat up the teapot camp-style, then lit a candle and sat down at the table, taking an occasional puff at my travelling pipe (1c). ♦ Оба следили друг за другом, но только что взгляды их встречались, оба, с быстротою молнии, отводили их один от другого (Достоевский 3). Each watched the other, but the moment their eyes met, they both, with lightning speed, averted them again (3a).

T-149 • ТО́ЛЬКО ЧТО НЕ *coll* [Invar; sent adv] **1.** very nearly: **almost; practically; all but; just about;** [in limited contexts] **virtually.**

Три дня терзал её своим великодушием Григорий, а на четвёртый день уехал в район. Да не один, а с Варварой Иняхиной. И Анфиса, когда узнала об этом, только что не перекрестилась от радости. Пускай, пускай будут счастливы! (Абрамов 1). For three days Grigory had tortured her with his magnanimity, and on the fourth day he had left for the district center. Not alone, but with Varvara Inyakhina. When Anfisa had learned about that she had practically crossed herself for joy. Let them be happy! (1a). ♦ Поместив сына по-прежнему в кабинет, он [Василий Иванович] только что не прятался от него и жену свою удерживал от всяких лишних изъявлений нежности (Тургенев 2). Having reinstalled his son in his study he [Vassily Ivanovich] all but hid himself from him and restrained his wife from too exuberant a display of affection (2a).

2. (used to indicate that the attribute, quality etc following the idiom is the only one in a specified or implied series that a person or thing is missing) (a person or thing has all the qualities etc specified or implied) but not…: **except that s.o. is not ⟨sth. does not etc⟩…; the only thing lacking ⟨s.o. lacks⟩ is…; the only thing ⟨problem⟩ is, s.o. ⟨sth.⟩ doesn't ⟨can't etc⟩…; the only thing missing is…; the only thing s.o. ⟨sth.⟩ doesn't have ⟨can't do etc⟩ is…; s.o. ⟨sth.⟩ lacks only…**

Мальчик он неплохой, только что не умеет вести себя. He's basically a good kid, the only thing is he doesn't know how to behave himself.

T-150 • БЛАГОДАРЯ́ ТОМУ́ ЧТО [subord Conj; introduces a clause of reason] by reason of the fact that: **thanks to the fact that; owing ⟨due⟩ to the fact that; because ⟨on account⟩ of the fact that.**

Благодаря тому, что план наступления был разработан очень тщательно, оно с самого начала развивалось успешно. Thanks to the fact that the attack was planned in painstaking detail, it was successful from the very outset.

T-151 • К ТОМУ́ ЖЕ [PrepP; Invar; sent adv] in addition to, along with sth. (mentioned in the preceding context): **moreover; on top of that; …to boot; as well; besides (that);** [in limited contexts] **…into the bargain.**

Кязым по праву считался одним из самых умных людей Чегема. К тому же всем было известно, что он раскрыл несколько преступлений, совершённых в Чегеме и окрестных сёлах… (Искандер 5). Kyazym was rightly considered to be one of the smartest men in Chegem. Moreover, everyone knew that he had solved several crimes committed in Chegem and neighboring villages… (5a). ♦ «…Батя мой мужик был хозяйственный, на все руки мастер: хоть веники, хоть ложки — всё умел и двух лошадей держал к тому же» (Максимов 2). "My father was a good craftsman, he could turn his hand to anything—making brooms, making spoons, he could do it all—and on top of that he kept two horses" (2a). ♦ Из двенадцати [членов правления] сторону Иванько с самого начала активно держали четверо… Пятый член правления был в отъезде, шестой колебался… Седьмой перебегал всё время на ту сторону, которая ему казалась в данный момент сильнее, делая вид, что он тёмный восточный человек, к тому же ещё немножко поэт, не от мира сего и в происходящем не очень-то разбирается (Войнович 3). Of the twelve [members of the board], four actively supported Ivanko's side from the very beginning.…The fifth member of the board was on leave, the sixth was vacillating....The seventh member would always run over to the side that seemed strongest to him at a given moment, pretending that he was an ignorant man of the East, and a bit of a poet to boot, not of this world and not too clear about what was going on (3a). ♦ «Так вот вам бы написать всё это в виде письма в газету...» — «Хорошая идея, но как-то недостойно это делать из тюрьмы, подумают к тому же, что я писал под давлением» (Амальрик 1). "You should put all that in a letter to a newspaper." "That's a good idea; but it doesn't seem quite fitting, somehow, to do it from prison. Besides, people might think I had written the letter under pressure" (1a). ♦ Вот дурак, вот дурак! Да к тому же ещё и нахал, каких мало! (Залыгин 1). The idiot. What an idiot! And what cheek, into the bargain! (1a).

Т-152 • **ТОМУ́ НАЗА́Д** [Invar; adv; used after an NP denoting a span of time; fixed WO] used to denote the amount of time elapsed between a specific point in the past and the moment of speech or the moment indicated: **ago; [in limited contexts] (a week ⟨a few days etc⟩) before ⟨earlier⟩.**

«Несколько дней тому назад вашему сиятельству в одном доме указали на дверь...» (Тургенев 3). "A few days ago your lordship was shown the door in a certain house" (3a). ♦ С неделю тому назад французы получили сапожный товар и полотно и роздали шить сапоги и рубахи пленным солдатам (Толстой 7). The French soldiers had been issued boot leather and linen the week before, and they had given it out to the prisoners to make into boots and shirts (7a).

Т-153 • **В ТОН** [PrepP; Invar] **1.** ~ *(чему)* [the resulting PrepP is adv] in consonance, agreement with: **(be) in tune ⟨harmony, unison⟩ with; go right along with.**

Бабушка напевала какую-то заунывную песню в тон завыванию ветра. Grandma hummed a mournful tune that went right along with the howling of the wind.

2. ~ *(чему)* [usu. subj-compl with copula (subj: concr) or modif] of the same color or a different but compatible shade of the same color: X был в тон Y-у ≃ **X matched Y; X went well with Y ⟨X and Y went well together⟩;** ‖ всё было в тон ≃ **everything matched;** ‖ *Neg* X был не в тон Y-у ≃ **X clashed with Y;** ‖ [when used as a modif] **a matching sth.; sth. to match (sth. else); sth. that matches (sth. else); sth. that goes well with sth. else;** ‖ *Neg* **sth. that clashes with sth. else.**

Он был в синем, достаточно модном, но не вызывающе модном, костюме, в безупречно белой рубашке и галстуке в тон костюму (Аксёнов 2). He had on a smart but not flashy blue suit with a tie to match, and an impeccably white shirt (2a).

3. ~ *чему*. Also: **ПОД ТО́Н** [subj-compl with copula (subj: concr), modif, or adv] in the style, manner, spirit of sth.: **in tune ⟨keeping, harmony⟩ with; in the spirit of.**

На последних трёх страницах склеенного цикла стихов сохранилась карандашная запись, сделанная рукой Б.Л. [Пастернака]. Вот она: «Искренняя, одна из сильнейших (последняя в тот период) попытка жить думами времени и ему в тон» (Ивинская 1). On the last three pages of the typescript [of the cycle of poems], there is the following comment on these poems written in pencil in BL's [Pasternak's] hand: "A sincere and one of the most intense of my endeavors—and the last in that period—to think the thoughts of the era, and to live in tune with it" (1a).

4. ~ *кому* **сказать, ответить** и т. п. [adv] (to say sth., answer etc) in the same spirit, manner (as another, usu. one's interlocutor): **in the same fashion; in the same tone; match(ing) s.o.'s tone.**

«Ты, Самохин, слушать — слушай, да только помалкивай...» — «Наше дело сторона», — в тон ему, чтобы только отвязаться, сказал Фёдор (Максимов 1). "You, Samokhin, listen if you like, but keep it to yourself...." "It's nothing to do with me," Fyodor replied in the same tone, only hoping to be rid of him (1a). ♦ «А ты понял, почему он в последний раз согласился прийти попрощаться с ней?» — «Ясно почему, — ответил Кемал, — он понял, что майор на нас не накапал, и, значит, за нами никто не следит». — «Дурачок, — в тон ему отозвался дядя Сандро, — твой же рассказ я тебе должен объяснять» (Искандер 5). "But did you understand why he consented to come and say good-bye to her the last time?" "It was clear why," Kemal replied. "He realized that the major hadn't squealed, so no one was watching us." "Dumbbell," Uncle Sandro replied, matching his tone, "I have to explain your own story to you" (5a).

Т-154 • **ЗАДАВА́ТЬ/ЗАДА́ТЬ ТОН** [VP] **1.** Also: **ДАВА́ТЬ/ДАТЬ ТОН** *music* [subj: human] to sound the correct pitch (to a choir): X задал тон ≃ **X gave the pitch.**

2. ~ *(кому-чему)*. Also: **ДАВА́ТЬ/ДАТЬ ТОН** *obs* [subj: human or collect; more often impfv] to establish the mood, atmosphere, mode of behavior etc (that is imitated, followed by some person or group of people, or that is accepted, conformed to in some place, organization etc): X задаёт тон ≃ **X sets the tone ⟨the mood⟩.**

...Всё это ленинское нищенствование — игра, партийная линия, чтоб задавать тон, служить примером, «вождь без упрёка» (Солженицын 5). ...This parade of poverty on Lenin's part was a game, the party line, intended to set the tone and provide an example of a "leader beyond reproach" (5a).

3. *obs* [subj: human; impfv only] to act self-importantly, arrogantly: X задаёт тон ≃ **X puts on airs; X walks around with his nose in the air.**

«...[Леницын] заважничал. Тон задаёт» (Гоголь 3). "...[Lenitzin] is making himself important. Putting on airs" (3b).

Т-155 • **НЕ В ТОН** **петь, играть** и т. п. [PrepP; Invar; adv] (to sing, play etc) not in tune (with a given song, piece etc): **out of tune; off-key.**

Т-156 • **ПОПАДА́ТЬ/ПОПА́СТЬ В ТОН** *(кому)* [VP; subj: human] to say or do sth. in keeping with that which is said or done by another or others: X попал Y-у в тон ≃ **X struck the right tone ⟨note⟩.**

«Вы меня понимаете?» — «Отлично понимаю, — серьёзно ответил Стравинский и, коснувшись колена поэта, добавил: — не волнуйтесь и продолжайте». — «Продолжаю», — сказал Иван, стараясь попасть в тон Стравинскому и зная уже по горькому опыту, что лишь спокойствие поможет ему... (Булгаков 9). "Do you understand me?" "I understand very well," Stravinsky answered seriously and, touching the poet's knee, he added: "Don't get upset. Continue please." "I will continue," said Ivan, trying to strike the same tone and knowing from bitter experience that only a calm approach could help him (9a).

Т-157 • **СБАВЛЯ́ТЬ/СБА́ВИТЬ ⟨ПОНИЖА́ТЬ/ПОНИ́ЗИТЬ, СНИЖА́ТЬ/СНИ́ЗИТЬ⟩ ТОН** [VP; subj: human] to begin to speak in a less agitated, irritated way, or in a less aggressive, insolent manner: X сбавил тон ≃ **X softened his tone; X moderated his tone ⟨voice⟩; X toned it down; X toned down ⟨subdued⟩ his voice.**

«Ежели я сегодня не вспашу поле, когда мне лошадь достанется?» — «Лошадь, лошадь...» — Егорша презрительно, не разжимая зубов, цыкнул слюной... Михаил мрачно сдвинул брови, и Егорша сразу же сбавил тон: «Ладно... ладно... Мне-то что» (Абрамов 1). "If I don't plow the plot today when will I get the horse again?" "The horse, the horse...Phthat!" Egorsha scornfully spat without unclenching his teeth....Mikhail frowned grimly and Egorsha toned it down at once. "Okay, okay. What do I care" (1a). ♦ ...Атаман накричал на Мишку... потом сбавил тон, сердито закончил: «Большевикам мы не доверяем защиту Дона!» (Шолохов 4). ...The ataman bawled at him [Mishka], then the ataman lowered his pitch and ended crossly, "We don't trust Bolsheviks with the defense of the Don!" (4a).

T-158 • **ТÓНОМ ВЫ́ШЕ сказать, заговорить** и т. п. [AdvP; Invar; adv; fixed WO] (to say sth., start to speak etc) in a more agitated, irritated tone of voice: X заговорил ~ ≃ **X's voice took on a sharper tone; X raised his voice.**

T-159 • **ТÓНОМ НИ́ЖЕ сказать, заговорить** и т. п. [AdvP; Invar; adv; fixed WO] (to say sth., start to speak etc) more calmly and/or softly (after having raised one's voice in irritation, anger etc): X заговорил ~ ≃ **X softened his tone; X moderated his tone ⟨voice⟩; X toned it down; X lowered his voice ⟨pitch⟩; X toned down ⟨subdued⟩ his voice.**

«Я не позволю вам так со мной разговаривать!» — воскликнула Вера Павловна, и Анна Ивановна сразу же заговорила тоном ниже. "I will not permit you to speak to me this way!" exclaimed Vera Pavlovna, and Anna Ivanovna immediately softened her tone.

T-160 • **(ХОТЬ) ТОПÓР ВЕ́ШАЙ; МÓЖНО ТОПÓР ВЕ́ШАТЬ** *highly coll* [(хоть +) VP$_{imper}$, used as impers predic (1st var.); impers predic with быть$_∅$ (2nd var.); fixed WO (with можно movable)] it is unbearably stuffy, it feels as if there is no air to breathe (in some lodging or room): **you could cut the air with a knife; you can hardly breathe.**

[author's usage] Я люблю набитые ребятами кузова машин, бараки и палатки, хоть там топор можно повесить (Аксёнов 1). What I like is trucks, barracks, tents, so jammed with guys you can hardly breathe (1a).

T-161 • **КАК С ПИ́САНОЙ ТÓРБОЙ носиться** *с кем-чем;* **КАК ДУРÁК ⟨ДУ́РЕНЬ⟩ С (ПИ́САНОЙ) ТÓРБОЙ** *all coll, disapprov* [как + PrepP or NP; these forms only; adv (intensif)] (to relate outwardly to s.o. or sth. undeserving of special attention) with an excessive display of caring, attention etc, exaggerating his or its significance to an extreme degree: X носится с Y-ом как с писаной торбой ≃ **X makes a great ⟨big⟩ fuss over ⟨of⟩ Y; X makes a big to-do over Y; X treats person ⟨animal⟩ Y like someone ⟨something⟩ special; X acts as if person ⟨animal⟩ Y is someone ⟨something⟩ special; [in limited contexts] X is parading Y like a child with a new toy.**

В Краснодаре с ним [Владом] носились как с писаной торбой, наперебой таскали по кабинетам, громогласно рекомендуя: «Поэт-колхозник!» (Максимов 2). The people in Krasnodar made a great fuss of him [Vlad], vying with one another to show him off to a succession of officials, to whom they introduced him loudly and brashly: "This is the peasant poet from a collective farm!" (2a). ♦ [author's usage] «...Крокодил с крыльями — самая простая штука, а возятся с ним, как с писаной торбой» (Стругацкие 3). "A crocodile with wings is a simple enough thing, but he is being treated like something special" (3a). ♦ «Правительство Каледина никто не хочет поддерживать, отчасти даже потому, что он носится со своим паритетом как дурак с писаной торбой» (Шолохов 3). "No one wants to support Kaledin, partly because he's parading his demand for parity like a child with a new toy" (3a).

T-162 • **ВВЕРХ ⟨КВЕ́РХУ⟩ ТОРМÁШКАМИ ⟨ТОР-МÁШКИ** *obs*⟩ *coll* [AdvP] **1.** [adv] with the top downward and the bottom upward: **upside down; topsy-turvy; head over heels; [in limited contexts] turn turtle.**

...Я видел, как кидали мяч в картонную на шарнирах фигуру японского солдата, заставляя её при попадании не то повалиться вверх тормашками, не то... не помню! (Олеша 3). ...I saw balls thrown at the hinged cardboard figure of a Japanese soldier, forcing it either to topple head over heels, or...I don't remember! (3a).

2. ~ **идти, пойти** и т. п. [adv or subj-compl with быть$_∅$ (subj: abstr, often всё)] (of a course of events, s.o.'s everyday life

etc) (to be going or begin to go) not the way it should, in a way contrary to normal: **(be ⟨be going⟩) topsy-turvy; (go) haywire.**

Настёна слушала, как разоряется свёкор, и устало думала: чего уж так убиваться по какой-то железяке, если давно всё идёт вверх тормашками (Распутин 2). Nastyona listened to her father-in-law rant and thought tiredly: why get so excited over a scrap of metal when everything else has been topsy-turvy for so long? (2a).

T-163 • **ЛЕТЕ́ТЬ/ПОЛЕТЕ́ТЬ ВВЕРХ ТОРМÁШ-КАМИ ⟨ТОРМÁШКИ** *obs*⟩ *coll* [VP; subj: usu. abstr, often всё] (of s.o.'s plans, a course of events, s.o.'s life etc) to get completely disrupted, be thrown into disorder: X полетел вверх тормашками ≃ **X was turned upside down; X went topsy-turvy ⟨haywire⟩.**

...Через несколько часов произошло событие, от которого вся её, в общем, налаженная, как она считала, спокойная жизнь полетела вверх тормашками (Некрасов 1). ...Within a few hours what she considered her generally well-ordered and tranquil life was to be turned upside down (1a).

T-164 • **ПЕРЕВЁРТЫВАТЬ ⟨ПЕРЕВОРÁЧИ-ВАТЬ⟩/ПЕРЕВЕРНУ́ТЬ ВВЕРХ ТОРМÁШКАМИ** *что coll* [VP; subj: human or abstr] (in refer. to s.o.'s way of life, a state of affairs etc) to bring abrupt change, disorder, confusion into sth.: X перевернул Y вверх томашками ≃ **X turned Y upside down; X turned Y topsy-turvy.**

T-165 • **СПУСКÁТЬ/СПУСТИ́ТЬ НА ТОРМОЗÁХ** *что coll* [VP; subj: human or collect] to reconcile an unpleasant matter quietly, without creating a stir or punishing those involved: X спустил Y на тормозах ≃ **X settled Y quietly; X soft-pedaled Y.**

T-166 • **ТОСКÁ ЗЕЛЁНАЯ; СКУ́КА ЗЕЛЁНАЯ ⟨СМЕ́РТНАЯ⟩** *all coll* [NP; sing only; usu. VP$_{subj}$ (with быть$_∅$) or obj; usu. this WO] terrible boredom: **intolerable ⟨unbearable, utter⟩ boredom; (s.o. is) bored stiff ⟨to tears, to death⟩; (s.o. is) dying of boredom.**

[Утешительный:] Помнишь, почтеннейший, как я приехал сюды [*ungrammat* = сюда]: один-одинёшенек. Вообразите: знакомых никого. Хозяйка – старуха. На лестнице какая-то поломойка, урод естественнейший... Словом, скука смертная (Гоголь 2). [U.:] Do you recall, dear fellow, my circumstances when I arrived—all alone, not knowing a soul, an old bitch for a landlady, a chambermaid who was an absolute horror....In a word—I was bored stiff (2a). ♦ «...Тоска здесь... зелёная» (Максимов 1). "You could die of boredom here..." (1a).

T-167 • **НАВОДИ́ТЬ/НАВЕСТИ́ ⟨НАГОНЯ́ТЬ/НА-ГНÁТЬ⟩ ТОСКУ́** *на кого* [VP; subj: human or abstr] to evoke despondency in s.o.: X наводит на Y-а тоску ≃ **X depresses Y; X gets Y down; thing X gives Y the blues; [in limited contexts] person X spreads gloom.**

Хозяйственные дрязги наводили на него тоску... (Тургенев 2). The petty troubles of estate management depressed him... (2c). ♦ Вот жёнка! – думал Михаил. Сама держится и на других тоску не нагоняет (Абрамов 1). What a woman! thought Mikhail. She just keeps going and doesn't get other people down (1a). ♦ Ефрем в своей бинтовой, как броневой, обмотке, с некрутящейся головой, не топал по проходу, не нагонял тоски, а, подмостясь двумя подушками повыше, без отрыву читал книгу, навязанную ему вчера Костоглотовым (Солженицын 10). Yefrem, his bandage encasing him like a suit of armor, his head immobilized, was no longer stomping along the corridor spreading gloom. Instead, he had propped himself up with two pillows and was completely absorbed in the book which Kostoglotov had forced upon him the day before (10a).

T-168 • **(И) ТОТ И ДРУГО́Й** [NP (usu. subj or obj) or AdjP (modif)] one and the other: **both**; [in limited contexts, with predic expressing refutation] **neither**.

Ирина Викторовна вышла из троллейбуса, обогнула ограду и тоже подошла к Огню и Могиле. Она видела и то и другое не раз, но теперь всматривалась в прозрачную яркость и в синеву огня с особым вниманием... (Залыгин 1). Irina Viktorovna got out of the bus, stepped round the barrier and approached the flame and the tomb. She had seen both many times before, but now she looked into the bright transparent blue of the flame with special attention... (1a). ♦ Одни скажут: он был добрый малый, другие — мерзавец!.. И то и другое будет ложно (Лермонтов 1). Some will say I was a good fellow, others that I was a swine. Neither will be right (1c).

T-169 • **НЕ ТО́Т** [AdjP; modif or subj-compl with copula (subj: any common noun)] **1.** not identical or similar to the specified or implied person or thing, or to what one or it was like at an earlier time: **(quite) different; not the same;** [in limited contexts] **not the [NP] one ⟨it⟩ once was; not what ⟨like⟩ one ⟨it⟩ used to be;** ‖ не те времена ≃ **times have changed.**

[Маша:] Он [мой муж] казался мне тогда ужасно учёным, умным и важным. А теперь уж не то, к сожалению (Чехов 5). [M.:] In those days he [my husband] seemed to me terribly learned, clever, and important. But now, unfortunately, it is different (5a). ♦ ...Россия уже не та. Выдают чугун Магнитка и Кузнецк... построены первые советские блюминги (Рыбаков 2). ...Russia was not the country she once was. They were already turning out cast-iron at Magnitogorsk and Kuznetsk...and the first Soviet rolling-mills had been built (2a).

2. unsuitable: **not right; (all) wrong; not the right [NP].**

[Таня:] Что ж... Я пойду... [Колесов:] Извините, Таня. Но сами видите — не та обстановка. Возможно, ещё увидимся... (Вампилов 3). [T.:] Oh well... I'd better be off... [K.:] I'm sorry, Tania. But you can see for yourself—the setting is all wrong. Maybe we'll meet again (3a).

T-170 • **НИ ТО́Т НИ ДРУГО́Й** [NP; subj or obj; fixed WO] not one and not the other (of the two named people, things, phenomena etc): **neither; neither [NP]; neither of them ⟨of the two⟩; neither one; neither one nor the other; neither [NP] nor [NP].**

«Водку купить или коньяку?» — «Ни того ни другого» (Семёнов 1). "Shall we get vodka or brandy?" "Neither" (1a). ♦ Под Бородиным происходит столкновение. Ни то ни другое войско не распадаются, но русское войско непосредственно после столкновения отступает так же необходимо, как необходимо откатывается шар, столкнувшись с другим, с большею стремительностью несущимся на него шаром... (Толстой 6). At Borodino the clash occurs. Neither army is destroyed, but immediately after the conflict the Russian army retreats as inevitably as a ball recoils after striking another flying toward it with greater impetus... (6a). ♦ Нет, не высказал Чуйков перед командующим фронтом [Ерёменко] всех своих опасений... Но ни тот ни другой не знали, в чём была причина их неудовлетворённости этой встречей (Гроссман 2). No, he [Chuykov] certainly had not expressed all his fears to Yeremenko....But neither of the two men quite understood why their meeting had been so unsatisfactory... (2a). ♦ И ведь полиция не сама со мной расправлялась, она предпочла делать это руками профессоров и писателей. Однако ни те ни другие доказательств не потребовали и не получили — они поверили на слово полицейским следователям (Эткинд 1). Indeed the police did not deal with me themselves, they preferred to act through the professors and writers. Neither the professors nor the writers, however, either demanded or obtained any proof—they simply took the word of the police investigators (1a).

T-171 • **ОДИ́Н И ТО́Т ЖЕ** [AdjP (modif) or NP (neut only, subj or obj); fixed WO] being exactly the same, not another, or

being exactly identical: **the (very) same [NP]; one and the same [NP]; the selfsame [NP];** ‖ одно и то же ≃ **(one and) the same (thing);** [in limited contexts] **only one thing.**

Так говорил мулла, уважаемый чегемцами человек, потому что он при всех режимах (царском, меньшевистском, большевистском) читал одну и ту же священную книгу Коран... (Искандер 3). So said the mullah, a man respected by the Chegemians because under all regimes (czarist, Menshevik, Bolshevik) he had read one and the same holy book, the Koran... (3a). ♦ В самом деле сходство Пугачёва с моим вожатым было разительно. Я удостоверился, что Пугачёв и он были одно и то же лицо... (Пушкин 2). Indeed, the similarity between Pugachev and my guide was striking. I came to realize that the two were one and the same person (2a). ♦ «Век об одном и том же — какая скука! Педанты, должно быть!» — сказал, зевая, Обломов (Гончаров 1). "Always one and the same thing? What a bore! Pedants, I suppose," said Oblomov, yawning (1b). ♦ Они говорили, что погода стала совершенно другая, что раньше в Москве — так был совершенно другой климат: крепкая зима, жаркое лето, а теперь, что Ленинград, что Москва — одно и то же (Битов 2). They said that the weather had become totally different. Moscow used to have a totally different climate—hard winter, hot summer—but now, Leningrad or Moscow, it's one and the same (2a). ♦ [Таня:] Вечно одно и то же. [Репникова:] Опять ворчишь? Не понимаю, чем ты недовольна. [Таня:] Вечно объедимся, как не знаю кто, а потом весь вечер перевариваем... [Репникова:] Не ешь, никто тебя не заставляет (Вампилов 3). [T.:] It's always the same. [R.:] Are you grumbling again? I don't understand what's bothering you. [T.:] We always overeat like I don't know what and then spend the whole evening digesting.... [R.:] Well don't eat then, no-one's forcing you (3a). ♦ Волей-неволей ему [Кузьме] приходилось... постоянно думать об одном и том же: где достать деньги? (Распутин 1). Like it or not, he [Kuzma] was forced to think of only one thing: where could he get money? (1a).

T-172 • **ТО́Т ЖЕ** [AdjP; modif] **1.** being exactly the same or exactly identical: **the same; the very ⟨exact⟩ same; that very; the ⟨that⟩ selfsame.**

...Подле гордо-стыдливой, покойной подруги спит беззаботно человек. Он засыпает с уверенностью, проснувшись, встретить тот же кроткий, симпатичный взгляд (Гончаров 1). ...With a modest, proud, serene wife at one's side, a man might sleep without a care. He could fall asleep confident that on waking he would meet the same mild, sympathetic gaze (1b). ♦ Народ знал мою девицу Светку, мне тотчас в тот же вечер доносили, если видели её на другой танцплощадке с другим парнем... (Лимонов 1). The people knew my girl Svetka; they would inform me at once, that very night, if they saw her at another dance pavilion with another guy (1a). ♦ Миролюбиво, с видимым дружелюбием пожмут тебе руку, поговорят о скором столетии Ленина... А раздастся в тиши кабинета «звонок», поступят «сигнал», «закрытое письмо», с тем же деловитым дружелюбием выбросят тебя на улицу, оставят без куска хлеба... (Свирский 1). People calmly shake you by the hand with every appearance of friendship, chat about the approaching centenary of Lenin....But if in the silence of their offices the phone rings, or a "signal" comes, or a secret letter, then they'll throw you out on the street with that selfsame businesslike friendliness, leave you to starve... (1a).

2. equivalent in effect, value, status etc to another (or others): **as good ⟨bad etc⟩ as; just ⟨exactly⟩ like; tantamount to.**

[Подколёсин:] ...Надворный советник тот же полковник, только разве что мундир без эполет (Гоголь 1). [P.:] ...A court councilor is as good as a colonel, except perhaps for having no epaulets on his uniform (1c).

T-173 • **ТО́Т ИЛИ ДРУГО́Й ⟨ИНО́Й⟩** [AdjP (modif) or NP (subj or obj)] used when referring to some unspecified member(s) (of a group, category etc): **one...or another; some...or other;** [in limited contexts] **certain.**

…Несмотря на то, что все начальники отделов кадров только тем и занимаются, что вчитываются в анкеты, выискивая несоответствия и изъяны в биографии сотрудников того или иного учреждения, иногда самые невероятные нелепости проходят мимо их бдительного ока (Войнович 1). …Despite the fact that all personnel managers do nothing but pore over questionnaires seeking out inconsistencies and flaws in the biographies of employees of one institution or another, the most incredible absurdities do sometimes slip past their watchful eyes (1a). ♦ Научная ценность её [книги] невелика, так как почти все её идеи в той или иной форме обсуждались в западной литературе такого рода (Зиновьев 2). The scientific value of this book was minimal, as almost all its ideas had already been discussed in some form or other in Western literature of a similar kind (2a). ♦ Молодые наши помпадуры очень часто обращаются ко мне за разъяснениями, как в том или другом случае следует поступить (Салтыков-Щедрин 2). I have often been approached by our young pompadours with requests to advise them what they are to do in certain circumstances (2a).

Т-174 • И ТО́ЧКА *coll* [indep. clause (usu. the concluding clause in a compound or complex sent); Invar; fixed WO] and there is nothing more to be said or done about the matter: **and that's that; and that's final; and that's all there is to it; and that's the end of it; period;** [in limited contexts] **and that settles it; case closed.**

«[Мама] вбила себе в голову, что… мне в институт не поступить — и точка» (Чернёнок 1). "She's [Mother has] gotten it into her head that I won't get into the institute…and that's that" (1a). ♦ (…*За спиной Хороших появляется Еремеев. Он протягивает Хороших деньги.*) [Хороших:] Нет, нет. Сказала, ни грамма [водки] — и точка (Вампилов 2). (*Yeremeyev appears behind Khoroshikh. He holds out some money to her.*) [Kh.:] No, siree. I said no more [vodka], and that's final (2b).

Т-175 • ТО́ЧКА В ТО́ЧКУ; ТОЧЬ-В-ТО́ЧЬ *both coll* [NP or AdvP; these forms only; fixed WO] **1.** [adv] precisely: **exactly; to a T; to the letter; perfectly; letter-perfect;** [in refer. to time] **to the minute; on the button; on the dot.**

[Мурзавецкая:] …Это подлог? за это Сибирь. (*Отдаёт письмо Чугунову.*) …Сам, что ли? [Чугунов:] Где уж самому! Руки трясутся… Племянник. [Мурзавецкая:] Горецкий? [Чугунов:] Он, благодетельница. Думали, ничего из парня не выйдет, не учился нигде и грамоте едва знает, отдали частному землемеру в помощники, так всё одно что бросили… И вдруг какое дарование открылось! Что хотите дайте, точка в точку сделает (Островский 5). [M.:] It's forgery. Siberia for this! (*She hands the letter back to Chugunov*) …Did you do it yourself? [Ch.:] How could I do it? My hands shake. My nephew… [M.:] Goretsky? [Ch.:] It was he, my benefactress. We thought nothing would come of the lad. He never studied; he scarcely knows how to read and write. We apprenticed him to a surveyor; just the same as casting him off. But what a talent he suddenly developed! Give him anything you like, he'll copy it exactly (5a). ♦ Всё вышло так, как думал Михаил. Правда, через милицию Першин его не разыскивал, во всяком случае при нём не заводил речь об этом, а всё остальное — точь-в-точь, тютелька в тютельку (Абрамов 1). It turned out just as Mikhail thought. Granted, Pershin had not gotten the police after him—or at least he made no mention of having done so—but as for the rest: to a T, to a hair (1a). ♦ Опыты эти пока что реальных результатов не давали, хотя некоторые характерные признаки пукса [*nonce word*, гибрид картофеля с помидором] стали уже проявляться: листья и стебли на нём были вроде картофельные, зато корни точь-в-точь помидорные (Войнович 2). So far these experiments had not produced any actual results, although certain characteristics of the PATS [a hybrid of the potato and the tomato] had started to appear: the leaves and stems were potato-like, while the roots were letter-perfect tomato (2a).

2. ~ (похож, походит *на кого-что* и т. п.) [modif or adv] (a person or thing resembles another person or thing) very closely:

X точка в точку похож на Y-a ≃ **X is the spitting image ⟨spit and image⟩ of Y; X is identical in every way (to Y); X looks just like Y; X is an exact copy ⟨replica, duplicate⟩ of Y.**

«Вводят, значит, этого китайца в кремлёвский дом и показывают на какого-то человека, точка в точку похожего на царя Николая» (Искандер 3). "So they bring this Chinaman into a house in the Kremlin and point out a man who's the spitting image of Czar Nicholas" (3a). ♦ Не успели обыватели оглянуться, как из экипажа выскочил Байбаков, а следом за ним в виду всей толпы очутился точь-в-точь такой же градоначальник, как и тот, который, за минуту перед тем, был привезён в телеге исправником! (Салтыков-Щедрин 1). Before the townsfolk could look around, out of the carriage jumped Dormousov, and behind him, in full view of the crowd, appeared a town governor who was the spit and image of the one the commissioner had brought by cart the moment before! (1a). ♦ [Артемий Филиппович (*надевает очки и читает*):] «Почтмейстер точь-в-точь департаментский сторож Михеев…» (Гоголь 4). [A.F.:] (*Puts on his glasses and reads*) "The Postmaster is an exact replica of the department's watchman Mikheyev…" (4a).

Т-176 • ТО́ЧКА ЗРЕ́НИЯ [NP; usu. sing; usu. subj or obj; fixed WO] a way of considering or judging a phenomenon, person, thing etc: **point of view; viewpoint; standpoint; vantage point; perspective;** ‖ с точки зрения *чьей, кого-чего* ≃ **from s.o.'s point of view; from the viewpoint ⟨standpoint, vantage point, perspective⟩ of s.o. ⟨sth.⟩; in the light of sth.; in the eyes of s.o. ⟨sth.⟩;** ‖ стоять на точке зрения *чьей, кого-чего* ⟨стать на точку зрения *чью, кого-чего*⟩ ≃ **side with s.o. ⟨sth.⟩; be on the side of s.o. ⟨sth.⟩;** ‖ отстаивать свою точку зрения ≃ **stick to one's guns; stand firm;** ‖ точка зрения большинства ⟨меньшинства⟩ ≃ **the majority ⟨minority⟩ view.**

Картина слишком пессимистическая, сказал Социолог. Смотря с какой точки зрения, сказал Шизофреник (Зиновьев 1). "That's far too pessimistic a picture," said Sociologist. "From what point of view?" asked Schizophrenic (1a). ♦ Лёва мягко уговаривает Бланка переменить его точку зрения на Есенина (Битов 2). Lyova mildly coaxes Blank to change his viewpoint on Esenin (2a). ♦ Власть, с точки зрения опыта, есть только зависимость, существующая между выражением воли лица и исполнением этой воли другими людьми (Толстой 7). Power, from the standpoint of experience, is merely the relation that exists between the expression of someone's will and the execution of that will by others (7a). ♦ …Закон поэзии — быть выше своего гнева и воспринимать сущее с точки зрения вечности (Солженицын 2). …The laws of poetry command us to rise above our anger and try to see the present in the light of eternity (2a). ♦ Так сочинение давно умершего английского классика стало вдруг злободневным и совершенно непроходимым с точки зрения советской цензуры (Войнович 1). And so, a classic by a long-dead English writer had suddenly become topical and absolutely unpassable in the eyes of Soviet censorship (1a). ♦ …Иногда за ужином разыгрывались схоластические диспуты. Например, так: что более ценно — воля или разум? Рита стояла на точке зрения Фомы Аквинского — за примат разума (Трифонов 5). …Sometimes Scholastic disputes would break out at the supper table. Thus, for example: which was more important—will or reason? Rita was on the side of Thomas Aquinas—for the primacy of reason… (5a). ♦ «Мы добились главного: завтра правление будет докладывать точку зрения большинства» (Войнович 1). "…We got the main thing: tomorrow the board will report the majority view" (1a).

Т-177 • ТО́ЧКА ОТПРАВЛЕ́НИЯ; ОТПРАВНА́Я ТО́ЧКА *both lit* [NP; sing only; fixed WO] the initial, beginning point of a line of reasoning, train of thought, action etc: **point of departure; starting point.**

…Тема слёз непозволительно ширится… вернёмся к отправной её точке (Набоков 1). …The theme of tears is expanding beyond all reason…let us return to its point of departure (1a). ♦

«…Этакое подозрение! Исступлённому-то ипохондрику! При тщеславии бешеном, исключительном! Да тут, может, вся-то точка отправления болезни и сидит!» (Достоевский 3). "…Such a suspicion! For a wild hypochondriac! With such rabid, exceptional vanity! The whole starting point of the illness may well have been sitting right there!" (3c).

Т-178 • НА МЁРТВОЙ ТО́ЧКЕ ⟨НА ТО́ЧКЕ ЗАМЕРЗА́НИЯ *lit*⟩ [PrepP; subj-compl with copula (subj: abstr); fixed WO] some matter (project etc) is in a static state, a state where it shows no advancement, the same state as it was in previously be: X — на мёртвой точке ≃ **X is at ⟨has come to⟩ a complete standstill; X is deadlocked; X has come to a dead stop; X is getting nowhere.**

Т-179 • ДО ТО́ЧКИ¹ дойти, довести *кого coll* [PrepP; Invar; adv] (to reach or drive s.o. to) a hopeless, desperate state, the limits of one's (or his) emotional endurance: X дошёл ⟨довёл себя⟩ ~ ≃ **X reached ⟨was at⟩ the end of his rope ⟨tether⟩; X was at the breaking point;** ‖ Y довёл X-а ~ ≃ **Y pushed X to the limit ⟨to the breaking point⟩;** [in limited contexts] **Y drove X off the deep end.**

«Ничего я не хочу, ничего мне не нужно — пусть только придёт к ней [Марии Михайловне] выздоровление. Мне кажется, что она себя уже довела до точки» (Максимов 2). "Personally I want and need nothing—I only pray that she [Maria Mikhailovna] will recover her health. I actually think she has reached the end of her tether" (2a).

Т-180 • ДО ТО́ЧКИ² знать *кого-что* **изучить, объяснять** *что coll* [PrepP; Invar; adv; often after всё] (to know, learn, explain sth.) fully, completely: **(down) to the last detail; in every ⟨the finest⟩ detail; thoroughly.**

Я хочу объяснить свои поступки до точки… (Марченко 2). I want to explain my actions down to the last detail… (2a).

Т-181 • СДВИ́НУТЬ С МЁРТВОЙ ТО́ЧКИ *что* [VP; subj: human or abstr] to push forward some matter that has long shown no progress: X сдвинул Y с мёртвой точки ≃ **X got Y out of Y's rut; X activated Y; X got Y moving ⟨rolling⟩; X moved Y off dead center.**

[author's usage] По-видимому, прав Виктор Франк; он видит огромную заслугу Пастернака в том, что тот столкнул воз русского романа с мёртвой точки и «повёл его по направлению не беловскому, не прустовскому, не джойсовскому, а по направлению совершенно иному, ещё не нанесённому на карту…» (Ивинская 1). Victor Frank is clearly right when he sees it as Pasternak's great achievement to have gotten the Russian novel out of its rut, taking it "not in the direction mapped out by Bely, Proust, or Joyce, but in a completely new, still uncharted one"… (1a). ♦ …Введение в скульптуру различных материалов уже само собой может сдвинуть её с мёртвой точки, внести в неё известный динамизм (Лившиц 1). …The introduction of diverse materials into sculpture could in itself activate it by giving it a certain dynamism (1a).

Т-182 • СДВИ́НУТЬСЯ ⟨СОЙТИ́⟩ С МЁРТВОЙ ТО́ЧКИ [VP; subj: usu. abstr] (in refer. to a matter that has long shown no progress) to begin moving forward, showing progress: X сдвинулся с мёртвой точки ≃ **X moved off dead center; X got moving ⟨rolling⟩;** [in limited contexts] **person X stopped spinning his wheels.**

[Сахаров] предложил очередной призыв об амнистии, который мы все, конечно, подписали, но прошёл он незамеченным. Мы понимали, однако, что с мёртвой точки сдвинуться надо (Амальрик 1). …He [Sakharov] suggested a routine appeal for amnesty. Naturally, we all signed it, but it went unnoticed. We realized that we had to stop spinning our wheels (1a).

Т-183 • СТА́ВИТЬ/ПОСТА́ВИТЬ ТО́ЧКИ ⟨ВСЕ ТО́ЧКИ, ТО́ЧКУ⟩ НАД ⟨НА *obs*⟩ **И ⟨«И», "I"⟩** [VP; subj: human] to clarify some matter fully and in all its details, leaving no ambiguities: X поставил точки над и ≃ **X dotted the i's and crossed the t's.**

Верно, и чирьи замучили [Михаила], и обещание с его [Першина] стороны насчёт замены было, а всё-таки факт остаётся фактом: самовольно, без разрешения ушёл со сплава, а ежели все ставить точки над «и», то и так сказать можно: дезертировал (Абрамов 1). It was true his [Mikhail's] boils had been plaguing him and that Pershin had made a promise to get him replaced, but facts were facts: absent without leave. He had left the timber floating without permission. To dot the i's and cross the t's, you could indeed say that he had deserted (1a).

< (?) Translation of the French *mettre les points sur les i*. The letter "i" existed in the Russian alphabet prior to the orthography reform of 1917.

Т-184 • БИТЬ В ОДНУ́ ТО́ЧКУ [VP; subj: human or abstr (слова, действия etc)] to direct all one's energies toward a set goal (usu. over a long period of time; often in refer. to arguing the same point persistently): X бьёт в одну точку ≃ **X keeps ⟨has been⟩ hammering away at the same thing ⟨point⟩.**

«Сергей Леонидович, — сказал Ребров, — а как вы полагаете с моим вопросом? Как мне-то быть?» Вновь, как в кабинетике Маревина, возникло грубое вожделение халтурщика: бить в одну точку. А что делать? Явился в таком качестве — и должен вести себя соответственно (Трифонов 1). "But Sergei Leonidovich," said Rebrov, "what's your answer to my question? What am I to do?" As in Marevin's office he felt once again that vulgar compulsion to hammer away at the same point. Well, what else could he do? He had come here as a supplicant, so he might as well behave accordingly (1a).

Т-185 • ПОПАДА́ТЬ/ПОПА́СТЬ В (СА́МУЮ) ТО́ЧКУ *coll* [VP; subj: human; usu. pfv] to say or do exactly the right thing, the precise thing that is fitting at the given moment: X попал в самую точку ≃ **X hit the nail on the head; X hit the bull's-eye ⟨the bull's eye⟩; X hit the mark; X was right on target ⟨on the mark, on the money⟩; X hit it just right; X hit it right on the nose.**

Решения 20-го съезда обнадёжили его [Хикмета] всерьёз, — как многих. Он написал тогда чудесную сатирическую пьесу «А был ли Иван Иванович?», высмеивая советских сателлитов — очевидно, Венгрию и Ракоши. Последовали венгерские события. Хикмет попал в самую точку (Аллилуева 2). The decisions of the Twentieth Congress raised his [Hikmet's] hopes in earnest, as they did those of many others. He wrote a wonderful satirical play called *But Was There an Ivan Ivanovich?* In it he made fun of Soviet satellites—obviously of Hungary and Rakosi. The Hungarian events of 1956 followed. Hikmet had hit the nail on the head (2a). ♦ «Размахались мотыгами! Небось им кажется — они вроде не на поле Сандро, а друг с дружкой усердствуют!» — «В точку попал!» — хором согласились с ним несколько чегемцев, стоящих рядом… (Искандер 5). "They've gone wild with their hoes! I daresay it's not Sandro's field they're doing so zealously—they think they're doing it with each other!" "Bull's eye!" several Chegemians standing nearby chorused in agreement (5a). ♦ «А кто ему доложил о „Канатике"? Не ты?» Варя сказала наугад, но попала в точку (Рыбаков 2). "And I suppose it wasn't you who told him about what happened in the Kanatik!" It was a wild guess, but Varya had hit the mark (2a). ♦ «Это значит опять-таки что: „с умным человеком и поговорить любопытно" — а?» — проскрежетал Иван. «В самую точку изволили-с. Умным и будьте-с» (Достоевский 2). "So once again: 'It's always interesting to talk with an intelligent man'—eh?" Ivan snarled. "Right on the mark, if I may say so, sir. So be intelligent, sir" (2a). ♦ «Если Сын Оленя, — говорили они, — предсказывает, какую подлость учинит подлец, подбавь от себя немного подлости и попадёшь в самую точку» (Искандер 5). "If the Son of the Deer," they said, "predicts the villainy a villain will commit, add a little villainy on your own and you'll hit it just right" (5a).

T-186 • **СТА́ВИТЬ/ПОСТА́ВИТЬ ТО́ЧКУ** [VP; subj: human] **1.** ~ *(на чём)* to cease doing sth. (temporarily or permanently): X поставил точку ≃ **X called it quits; X quit at that; X hung it up; X left it at that;** [in limited contexts] **X called it a day;** ‖ X поставил точку на Y-е ≃ **X closed the book(s) ⟨the door⟩ on Y; X drew the curtain on ⟨over⟩ Y; X laid Y to rest.**

2. ~ *(на ком-чём)* to terminate a relationship with s.o.: X поставил точку на Y-е ≃ **X put an end to thing Y; X was through with person Y; X severed his relationship with person Y; X parted company with person Y.**

[author's usage] Что же касается жены, то его [Вадима] с нею уже ничто не связывало. Отказавшись взять Вадима из больницы, она сама поставила точку в их недолгих и малопонятных и ей и ему взаимоотношениях (Максимов 3). As for his [Vadim's] wife, the last ties between them had been broken long ago. By refusing to take Vadim home from the hospital she had put an end to their brief and—for both of them—incomprehensible liaison (3a).

T-187 • **В ТО́ЧНОСТИ** [PrepP; Invar; adv or modif] (to do sth.) with complete accuracy, (to be like s.o. or sth.) with regard to every detail: **exactly; precisely; to the letter; to a hair; to a T.**

Она [белая олениха] была в точности такая, как Рогатая мать-олениха (Айтматов 1). She [the white doe] was exactly like the Horned Mother Deer (1a). ♦ «Я предложил господину градоначальнику обратиться за помощью в Санкт-Петербург, к часовых и органных дел мастеру Винтергальтеру, что и было ими выполнено в точности» (Салтыков-Щедрин 1). "...[I proposed] to Mr. Town Governor that he turn to St. Petersburg for help, to Winterhalter, master craftsman of clockworks and music boxes; which is precisely what he did" (1a). ♦ «Я счастлив, что имею в настоящий момент возможность сообщить вам, что это поручение я в точности исполнил...» (Федин 1). "I am happy that I am now able to inform you that I carried out your mission to the letter..." (1a). ♦ Десятого октября, в тот самый день, как Дохтуров прошёл половину дороги до Фоминского и остановился в деревне Аристове, приготавливаясь в точности исполнить отданное приказание, всё французское войско... вдруг без причины повернуло влево на новую Калужскую дорогу... (Толстой 7). [context transl] On the tenth of October, the same day on which Dokhturov had covered half the distance to Fominskoe and stopped at the village of Aristovo in preparation for the scrupulous execution of the orders he had been given, the entire French army...for no apparent reason, turned off to the left onto the new Kaluga road... (7a).

T-188 • **ДО ТО́ЧНОСТИ** *obs* [PrepP; Invar; adv] thoroughly, in a very detailed manner: **exactly; precisely; with precision; to the smallest detail; down to the last detail.**

«Мы... всё рассчитали с Дунечкой до точности, и вышло, что дорога возьмёт немного» (Достоевский 3). "...Dunya and I have worked it all out exactly and it comes out that the trip won't cost very much" (3a). ♦ ...Давнишнее ипохондрическое состояние Раскольникова было заявлено до точности многими свидетелями, доктором Зосимовым, прежними его товарищами, хозяйкой, прислугой (Достоевский 3). ...Raskolnikov's long-standing hypochondriac state of mind was attested to with precision by many witnesses, by Dr. Zossimov, former friends, the landlady, the maid (3c).

T-189 • **ТОЧЬ-В-ТО́ЧЬ КАК** [subord Conj, compar] similar or equivalent to: **exactly as ⟨like⟩; just as ⟨like⟩.**

Одет был Митя прилично, в застёгнутом сюртуке, с круглою шляпой в руках и в чёрных перчатках, точь-в-точь как был дня три тому назад в монастыре... (Достоевский 1).

Mitya was respectably dressed in a buttoned frock coat, was holding a round hat, and wearing black leather gloves, exactly as three days before in the monastery... (1a). ♦ Верховые были одеты по-разному — кто в чём, и напоминали сразу и мужиков и солдат, точь-в-точь как красноармейцы сводного полка... (Федин 1). The horsemen were in various dress—in what they had been able to find, and immediately reminded one of both muzhiks and soldiers, exactly like the Red soldiers of the composite regiment... (1a). ♦ «Ах нет, не говорите так!..» — вдруг опять взволновалась и даже раздражилась Соня, точь-в-точь как если бы рассердилась канарейка или какая другая маленькая птичка (Достоевский 3). "Oh, no, don't talk that way!..." Sonya suddenly became ruffled again and was even upset, looking just like a canary or some other little bird that has lost its temper (3a).

T-190 • **ДО ТОШНОТЫ́** *coll* [PrepP; Invar; adv (intensif) or modif] very much, to an extreme degree: **to the point of nausea; ad nauseam;** ‖ X надоел Y-у ~ ≃ **Y is sick to death of X; Y has had it up to here with X;** ‖ X наелся ~ ≃ **X stuffed himself to the gills; X ate himself sick;** ‖ X накормил Y-а ~ ≃ **X stuffed Y to the gills;** ‖ ~ голодный ≃ **sick with hunger;** ‖ ~ однообразный ⟨одинаковый, похожий⟩ ≃ **dreadfully monotonous; disgustingly alike ⟨similar⟩; so alike it's sickening ⟨disgusting etc⟩.**

Пресловутый «Господин из Сан-Франциско» — беспросветен, краски в нём нагромождены до тошноты (Олеша 3). The notorious *Gentleman from San Francisco* is cheerless; the images in it are piled up to the point of nausea (3a).

T-191 • **НИ ТПРУ́ НИ НУ́** *highly coll* [Invar; predic; fixed WO] **1.** [subj: human or collect] one does nothing, takes no action (usu. when some action is expected): X ни тпру ни ну ≃ **X doesn't make a move; X doesn't do a (damn) thing; X won't budge.**

Разве от этих бюрократов чего-нибудь дождёшься? Обещают помочь, а сами — ни тпру ни ну. Do you really expect anything from those bureaucrats? They promise to help, but don't do a damn thing.

2. [subj: abstr or human] some work (a person etc) makes no progress: X ни тпру ни ну ≃ **X isn't getting anywhere; X is going nowhere (fast); thing X isn't moving at all;** [in refer. to beginning an undertaking] **I ⟨he etc⟩ can't get thing X off the ground.**

«...Я уже пятьдесят лет бьюсь над этой проблемой и ни тпру ни ну». (Евтушенко 2). "I've been struggling with the problem for fifty years and still haven't gotten anywhere" (2a).

3. [subj: concr] (of a machine, device, apparatus) sth. is not functioning: X ни тпру ни ну ≃ **X isn't working; X is on the blink ⟨on the fritz⟩.**

T-192 • **КАК ТРАВА́; ТРАВА́ ТРАВО́Й** *both coll* [как + NP (1st var.) or NP; these forms only; subj-compl with быть₀ (subj: a noun denoting food)] sth. is completely tasteless: X как трава ≃ **X tastes like cardboard ⟨wallpaper paste⟩.**

T-193 • **ХОТЬ ТРАВА́ НЕ РАСТИ́** *(кому) coll* [хоть + VP₍imper₎; impers predic; Invar; fixed WO] s.o. is completely indifferent (to sth.), does not care at all (about sth.): (X-у) хоть трава не расти ≃ **X couldn't ⟨could⟩ care less; X doesn't care; X doesn't give a damn ⟨a hoot etc⟩.**

«Любовь? Что это такое, ты хочешь спросить? А это только обозначение обязанностей. Да. Пошлое и... легкомысленное обозначение, которое позволяет человеку в любой момент отказаться от своих самых главных обязанностей: разлюбил, и конец, а там хоть трава не расти...» (Залыгин 1). "Love? You mean, what is it? It's only another name for duty. A tasteless and flippant name...which permits people to abandon their most important obligations whenever they feel like it, so that they can say: 'I don't love her any more, and that's the end of it, and I don't care what happens now...'" (1a).

T-194 • ХУДУ́Ю ⟨ДУРНУ́Ю, СО́РНУЮ⟩ ТРАВУ́ ИЗ ⟨С⟩ ПО́ЛЯ ВО́Н; ХУДА́Я ⟨ДУРНА́Я, СО́РНАЯ⟩ ТРАВА́ ИЗ ПО́ЛЯ ВО́Н [saying] those that are harmful or not needed should be removed (usu. said as an appeal to get rid of a person or people who are considered harmful or useless to society or to some group): ≃ **get rid of the bad apples ⟨the deadwood⟩.**

T-195 • ДЕ́ЛАТЬ/СДЕ́ЛАТЬ ⟨УСТРА́ИВАТЬ/ УСТРО́ИТЬ⟩ ТРАГЕ́ДИЮ (из чего) [VP; subj: human; usu. impfv] to view or present sth. as far more hopeless, problematic etc than it is in reality: X делает из Y-а трагедию ≃ **X makes Y into a tragedy; X makes a tragedy (out) of Y; X acts as if Y were the end of the world.**

Ну, получила ты одну двойку, не надо из этого делать трагедию. So you got one D, don't go making a tragedy out of it.

T-196 • ЧТО И ТРЕ́БОВАЛОСЬ ДОКАЗА́ТЬ *coll* [indep. sent; this form only; fixed WO] used to show that some outcome was expected or predicted earlier by s.o. (when the speaker refers to his own expectation or prediction, the idiom is pronounced with satisfaction often colored by irony): **what did I tell you!; I told you so!; that's just what I ⟨he etc⟩ said ⟨told you etc⟩ before!; just as I ⟨he etc⟩ predicted ⟨expected⟩; just as expected; I knew it all along.**

[Кудимов:] Почему вы молчите? Ведь это вы были на похоронах... [Сарафанов:] Да, я должен признаться... Михаил прав. Я играю на похоронах. На похоронах и на танцах... [Кудимов:] Ну вот! Что и требовалось доказать (Вампилов 4). [K.:] Why don't you say something? I know it was you at the funeral.... [S.:] Yes, I must admit...Mikhail is right. I play at funerals. And at dances.... [K.:] There! What did I tell you? (4a). ♦ Шуз подскочил к своим «Жигулям». Что и требовалось доказать — замок замёрз, ключ не лезет! (Аксёнов 12). Shuz ran over to his Zhiguli. Just as expected, the lock was frozen and his key wouldn't fit! (12a).

< From the Latin *quod erat demonstrandum*, a formula phrase used to conclude the proof of a theorem or the like in mathematics (attributed to the Greek mathematician Euclid, 3rd cent. B.C.).

T-197 • БИТЬ/ЗАБИ́ТЬ ТРЕВО́ГУ [VP; subj: human or collect] to draw attention to impending danger, trouble etc, calling for measures to suppress or fight it: X забил тревогу ≃ **X sounded ⟨raised⟩ the alarm.**

Да, да, именно враги первыми разгадали его замысел и забили тревогу (Искандер 3). Ah, yes—it was the enemy who were the first to guess the meaning of his design and sound the alarm (3a).

T-198 • ЧТО У ТРЕ́ЗВОГО НА УМЕ́, ТО У ПЬЯ́НОГО НА ЯЗЫКЕ́ [saying] when a person is drunk he talks freely, says what he would not say when sober: ≃ **drunkenness reveals what soberness conceals; what soberness conceals, drunkenness reveals; the sober hide what drunks confide; the truth comes out when the spirits go in.**

[author's usage] [Платонов:] Я пьян... пьян... Голова кружится... [Глагольев 1 (в сторону):] Спрошу! Что у трезвого на душе, то у пьяного на языке (Чехов 1). [P.:] I'm drunk—drunk! My head's spinning... [G. Sr. (aside):] I'll ask him. What soberness conceals drunkenness reveals (1a). [P.:] I'm drunk, drunk. My head's spinning. [G. Sr. (aside):] I'll ask my question. The sober hide what drunks confide (1b).

T-199 • ЗАДАВА́ТЬ/ЗАДА́ТЬ ТРЕЗВО́Н(У) *obs, coll* [VP; subj: human; usu. pfv] **1.** ~ *кому* to scold, reprimand s.o.

severely: X задал Y-у трезвону ≃ **X gave it to Y good; X gave Y hell ⟨the business, a good tongue-lashing, a good talking-to⟩; X chewed Y out.**

2. to behave in a loud, unruly, boisterous fashion, often when drinking: X задал трезвону ≃ **X raised hell; X made a ruckus; X had a wild time.**

T-200 • ЗАДАВА́ТЬ/ЗАДА́ТЬ ⟨ДАВА́ТЬ/ДАТЬ⟩ ТРЁПКУ *кому highly coll* [VP] **1.** Also: **ЗАДАВА́ТЬ/ ЗАДА́ТЬ ⟨ДАВА́ТЬ/ДАТЬ⟩ ВЗБУ́ЧКУ ⟨ВЫ́ВО-ЛОЧКУ⟩** *highly coll* [subj: human] to beat s.o. severely: X задал Y-у трёпку ≃ **X gave Y a good beating ⟨thrashing⟩; X knocked ⟨beat⟩ the tar ⟨the crap, the shit etc⟩ out of Y; [in limited contexts] X whipped ⟨flogged⟩ Y.**

[Горецкий:] Глафира Алексеевна, хотите, весь этот забор изломаю?.. [Глафира:] Нет, зачем? [Горецкий:] Как бы я для вас прибил кого-нибудь, вот бы трёпку задал весёлую!.. Глафира Алексеевна, прикажите какую-нибудь подлость сделать! (Островский 5). [Goretsky:] Glafira Alekseyevna, if you want me to, I'll break this fence down. [Glafira:] No. What for? [Goretsky:] If I could thrash someone for your sake, I'd give him a good beating....Glafira Alekseyevna, do command me to do some dirty trick (5a).

2. Also: **ЗАДАВА́ТЬ/ЗАДА́ТЬ ⟨ДАВА́ТЬ/ДАТЬ⟩ ВЗБУ́ЧКУ ⟨ВЫ́ВОЛОЧКУ⟩** *highly coll* [subj: human] to rebuke s.o. severely, reprimand s.o. harshly: X задал Y-у трёпку ≃ **X gave Y a (good) dressing-down ⟨tongue-lashing⟩; X gave Y hell; X bawled ⟨chewed⟩ Y out; X gave it to Y (but good).**

Оставалось и Русанову заснуть. Скоротать ночь, не думать — а уж утром дать взбучку врачам (Солженицын 10). All Rusanov, too, had to do was get to sleep, while away the night, think of nothing, and then tomorrow give the doctors a dressing-down (10a).

3. [subj: human (usu. pl) or collect] to overwhelm and defeat a hostile army, the enemy: X-ы задали трёпку Y-ам ≃ **Xs crushed ⟨routed, clobbered⟩ Ys; Xs ran ⟨drove⟩ Ys into the ground; Xs gave Ys a bashing.**

...Фомин предложил Григорию занять должность начальника штаба. «Надо нам грамотного человека, чтобы ходить... по карте, а то когда-нибудь зажмут нас и опять дадут трёпки» (Шолохов 5). ...Fomin offered Grigory the post of chief of staff. "We need someone who can read, so that we can go by the map, or one day they'll corner us and give us another bashing" (5a).

T-201 • ПОЛУЧА́ТЬ/ПОЛУЧИ́ТЬ ТРЁПКУ ⟨ВЗБУ́ЧКУ, ВЫ́ВОЛОЧКУ⟩ *(от кого) highly coll* [VP; subj: human] **1.** to be severely beaten: X получил трёпку (от Y-а) ≃ **X got a (good) beating ⟨thrashing, whipping, flogging⟩ (from Y); X got the tar ⟨the crap, the shit etc⟩ knocked ⟨beaten⟩ out of him (by Y).**

2. to receive a severe rebuke, harsh reprimand: X получил трёпку (от Y-а) ≃ **X got a (good) dressing-down ⟨tongue-lashing⟩ (from Y); X caught hell (from Y); X got bawled ⟨chewed⟩ out (by Y); X got it in spades (from Y); X got it but good.**

T-202 • ПРОВАЛИ́ТЬСЯ С ТРЕ́СКОМ *coll* [VP; subj: human or a noun denoting some undertaking, venture etc] to fail utterly and completely: X провалился с треском ≃ **X failed shamefully; person X fell flat on his face; thing X fell flat (on its face); X was a complete flop; X bombed (out); person X suffered a complete failure.**

T-203 • ТРЕ́ТИЙ ЛИ́ШНИЙ *coll* [NP; sing only; often used as indep. sent; fixed WO] a third person is not necessary, would cause uncomfortableness or inconvenience in a situation where two people are enough or are happy to be by themselves: (two's company,) three's a crowd; [in limited contexts] fifth wheel; interloper.

T-204 • СООБРАЖА́ТЬ/СООБРАЗИ́ТЬ ⟨СКИ́НУТЬ-СЯ⟩ НА ТРОИ́Х *highly coll* [VP; subj: human, pl; more often pfv; usu. this WO] to share the cost of a bottle of alcohol (usu. vodka) three ways and drink it: Х-ы ⟨X, Y и Z⟩ сообразили на троих ≃ Xs ⟨X, Y, and Z⟩ (chipped in and) split a bottle (of vodka) three ways; Xs ⟨X, Y, and Z⟩ knocked off a bottle between the three of them.

В галичевской песне о том, как «сообразить на троих», рабочий, выпив, уснул (Орлова 1). In Galich's song about how to "split a bottle three ways," a worker, after drinking, falls asleep... (1a). ♦ [author's usage] «Завязали дружбу на троих, потом повторили» (Аксёнов 3). "We laced our ties of friendship by knocking off a bottle between the three of us, and then there was a second" (3a).

T-205 • ИЕРИХО́НСКАЯ ТРУБА́ *lit* [NP; sing only; usu. subj-compl with copula (subj: голос)] a very loud, resounding voice: **stentorian voice.**

< From the name of the city of *Jericho*. According to the Biblical account (Josh. 6), its walls collapsed from the sound of the Israelites' trumpets.

T-206 • НЕТОЛЧЁНАЯ ⟨НЕПРОТОЛЧЁНАЯ⟩ ТРУБА́ (народу, гостей и т. п.) *obs, coll* [NP; these forms only; usu. subj or subj-compl with copula (subj/gen: народу, гостей etc)] there is a huge number of (people, often guests, in some place): **a (whole) slew of people; a huge ⟨whole⟩ crowd of people; scads of people;** [in refer. to many people in a relatively small space] **(some place is) jammed ⟨packed etc⟩ with people.**

Неподалёку от санатория мы встретили Людмилу Павловну. Она вернулась утром, и я уже виделась с ней. Про сестру она ничего не узнала. «В прокуратуре народу – труба непротолчёная и никакого толку не добиться» (Чуковская 2). Not far from the rest-home we met Lyudmila Pavlovna. I had already seen her after she had returned that morning. She had not found out anything about her sister. "The Public Prosecutor's office was jammed with people and one could get no sense out of them" (2a). ♦ ...В предводительском доме... труба нетолчёная. Туда всякий идёт, как в трактир, и всякий не только ест и пьёт, но требует, чтобы его обласкали (Салтыков-Щедрин 2). [context transl] ...The Marshal's house was like a market place. Everybody went there as if it were a public house and everybody not only ate and drank there, but also expected to be well treated (2a).

T-207 • ВЫЛЕТА́ТЬ/ВЫ́ЛЕТЕТЬ В ТРУБУ́ *coll* [VP; usu. pfv] **1.** [subj: human or a noun denoting an enterprise] to become insolvent, financially ruined: X вылетел в трубу ≃ **X went bankrupt ⟨broke, bust, belly up⟩;** [of a person only] **X got wiped out.**

2. [subj: a noun denoting a sum of money, a fortune etc] to be wasted, spent in vain: X вылетел в трубу ≃ **X was squandered ⟨burned, blown⟩; X went ⟨was poured⟩ down the drain; X was frittered ⟨thrown⟩ away.**

3. [subj: abstr] to be lost in vain, to no purpose: X вылетел в трубу ≃ **X went down the tubes ⟨the drain⟩; X went to the dogs; X went ⟨flew⟩ out the window;** [usu. of time] **X was wasted ⟨frittered away, squandered⟩.**

А если меня никто не поддержит? Тогда меня прихлопнут, как муху. Всё моё геройство вылетит в трубу, и никакого толку... (Аксёнов 6). But suppose no one backed me up? In that case, I would be swatted like a fly. All my heroism would go down the tubes, and to no purpose... (6a).

T-208 • ПУСКА́ТЬ/ПУСТИ́ТЬ ⟨ВЫ́ПУСТИТЬ⟩ В ТРУБУ́ *coll* [VP; subj: human; usu. pfv] **1.** ~ *кого* to drive s.o. to bankruptcy, financial ruin: X пустил Y-а в трубу ≃ **X wiped ⟨cleaned⟩ Y out.**

2. ~ *что* [obj: a noun denoting a sum of money, a fortune etc] to waste, spend (money) foolishly, imprudently: X пустил Y в трубу ≃ **X squandered ⟨burned, blew⟩ Y; X poured Y down the drain; X frittered ⟨threw⟩ Y away.**

T-209 • ХОТЬ В ТРУБУ́ ⟨В ТРУ́БЫ⟩ ТРУБИ́ *coll* [хоть + VP_imper; usu. subord clause; these forms only; fixed WO] no matter how much noise you make (you will not wake s.o. up): **(you couldn't wake s.o. up) with a shotgun ⟨a shotgun blast, dynamite⟩.**

T-210 • В ТРУ́БЫ ⟨ВО ВСЕ ТРУ́БЫ, В ТРУБУ́⟩ ТРУБИ́ТЬ (*о ком-чём, про кого-что*) *coll* [VP; subj: human] to tell everyone about s.o. or sth., spread some news or rumors: X во все трубы трубит (об Y-е) ≃ **X spreads the news of ⟨about⟩ Y all over ⟨far and wide⟩; X spreads rumors ⟨gossip⟩ about Y all over ⟨far and wide⟩; X trumpets ⟨broadcasts⟩ the news about ⟨of⟩ Y.**

T-211 • БРАТЬ/ВЗЯТЬ ⟨ПРИНИМА́ТЬ/ПРИНЯ́ТЬ⟩ НА СЕБЯ́ ТРУД [VP; subj: human; foll. by infin; when the verb is negated, the var. труда can also be used; fixed WO] to undertake, pledge, volunteer to do sth.: X взял на себя труд (с)делать Y ≃ **X took it upon ⟨on⟩ himself to do Y; X took upon himself the burden ⟨the labor, the work⟩ of doing Y;** [in limited contexts] **X went to the trouble of doing Y; X made the effort to do Y;** ‖ X любезно взял на себя труд сделать Y ≃ **X was kind ⟨good⟩ enough to do Y;** ‖ [when used as a polite request] вы не возьмёте на себя труд сделать Y? ≃ **would you be so kind ⟨good⟩ as to do Y?**

Но кто же брал на себя труд уведомить отца моего о моём поведении?.. Я терялся в догадках (Пушкин 2). But who then took it on himself to inform my father of my conduct?...I was at a loss (2a). ♦ «Вам всё кажется, что у меня какие-то цели, а потому и глядите на меня подозрительно... Но как я ни желаю сойтись с вами, я всё-таки не возьму на себя труда разуверять вас в противном. Ей-богу, игра не стоит свеч...» (Достоевский 3). "You seem to think the whole time that I have certain ulterior motives and therefore you look upon me with suspicion....But no matter how much I'd like to be friends with you, I'm still not going to take upon myself the labor of convincing you to the contrary. The game's not worth the candle, I swear to God..." (3a). ♦ ...Вы очень талантливы, и я рад, что именно вы взяли на себя труд написать обо мне, о всех нас... (Соколов 1). ...You're very talented, and I'm glad that it was you who took upon yourself the work of writing about me, about all of us... (1a).

T-212 • ДАВА́ТЬ/ДАТЬ СЕБЕ́ ТРУД [VP; subj: human; foll. by infin; usu. neg or condit; fixed WO] to make the effort (to do sth.), considering it necessary, one's responsibility etc; to burden o.s. (with sth.): X не дал себе труда сделать Y ≃ **X did not take the trouble ⟨did not trouble himself, did not take pains⟩ to do Y; X did not bother doing Y.**

«Вот те вопросы, над которыми тебе предстоит задуматься, читатель, и над которыми ты несомненно задумаешься, если дашь себе труд вникнуть в смысл моих слов» (Салтыков-Щедрин 2). "Those are the questions, reader, which you ought to think about and which, we are sure, you will think about, if only you take the trouble to grasp my meaning" (2a). ♦ На следующей станции та же история, и кондуктор уже не давал себе труда объяснить перемену экипажа (Герцен 2). At the next station there was the same business again, and the guard did not even trouble himself to explain the change of carriages (2a). ♦ [Лидия:]

Вся Москва узнает, что мы разорены; к нам будут являться с кислыми лицами, с притворным участием, с глупыми советами... И всё это так искусственно... так оскорбительно! Поверьте, что никто не даст себе труда даже притвориться хорошенько (Островский 4). [L.:] The whole of Moscow will learn that we're bankrupt, they'll come to us with sour faces, feigning sympathy, they'll heap stupid advice on us...and everything they do will be so artificial...so insulting! I tell you, mother, they will not even take pains to disguise their glee (4b). ♦ Без вынутой ленинской главы не было в «Августе» почти ничего, что разумно препятствовало бы нашим вождям напечатать его на родине. Но слишком ненавистен, опасен и подозрителен (не без оснований) был я, чтобы решиться утверждать меня тут печатанием. Я это понимал и не дал себе труда послать рукопись «Августа» советскому издательству... (Солженицын 2). With the Lenin chapter removed, there was hardly anything in the novel [*August 1914*] that could reasonably have prevented our leaders from publishing it in its homeland. But (not without reason) I was an object of such loathing, fear and suspicion that they would never consent to strengthen my position here by publishing me. I understood this, and did not bother sending it [the manuscript] to a Soviet publishing house... (2a).

Т-213 • МАРТЫ́ШКИН ТРУД *coll* [NP; sing only; fixed WO] meaningless, futile work that yields no results: **useless ⟨senseless, pointless⟩ work.**

< From Ivan Krylov's fable "Monkey" («Обезьяна»), 1811.

Т-214 • СИЗИ́ФОВ ТРУД; СИЗИ́ФОВА РАБО́ТА *both lit* [NP; sing only; fixed WO] ceaseless, hard, and futile labor: **labor of Sisyphus; Sisyphean labor.**

Где итог? Или всё это был сизифов труд? (Залыгин 1). Where was the result? Was it all a labour of Sisyphus? (1a).

< From the Greek legend of *Sisyphus*, king of Corinth, who was condemned to roll a heavy stone up a hill in Hades. Each time he neared the top, the stone escaped him and rolled back down to the bottom and he had to start all over again.

Т-215 • БЕЗ ТРУДА́ [PrepP; Invar; adv] (to do sth.) with ease, without having to exert o.s.: **without difficulty; easily; with no trouble at all; without any ⟨a bit of⟩ trouble; not have any trouble ⟨problem⟩ (doing sth.); be easy (for s.o. to do sth.).**

Без труда склонив на свою сторону четырёх солдат местной инвалидной команды и будучи тайно поддерживаема польскою интригою, эта бездельная проходимица овладела умами почти мгновенно (Салтыков-Щедрин 1). Having without difficulty won over four soldiers from the local invalid detachment, and being secretly supported by a Polish intrigue, this scoundrelly ne'er-do-well gained control of people's minds almost instantly (1a). ♦ Матушка не нарадовалась: Лёва — работал, писал, без труда сдал экзамены в аспирантуру... (Битов 2). Mama could not find words for her joy: Lyova worked, wrote, easily passed his examinations for graduate school... (2a). ♦ Мне без труда удаётся располагать к себе людей (Довлатов 1). It has been easy for me to get people to like me (1a).

Т-216 • НЕ СТО́ИТ ТРУДА́ [VP; subj: abstr or infin; 3rd pers only; pres or past] sth. does not deserve the energy that was or will be expended on it: **X не стоит труда ≃ X is not worth the trouble ⟨the effort⟩; [in limited contexts] X is not worth the ⟨s.o.'s⟩ time.**

Т-217 • ПОСЛЕ ТРУДО́В ПРА́ВЕДНЫХ *coll, humor* [PrepP; Invar; adv; fixed WO] after having worked well: **after a job well done; [in limited contexts] after an honest day's work.**

А теперь, после трудов праведных, хорошо бы выпить. Now, after a job well done, I wouldn't mind having a drink.

Т-218 • С ТРУДО́М [PrepP; Invar; adv] having to exert effort and almost not succeeding: **with difficulty; hardly ⟨barely, scarcely⟩ manage (to do sth.); have trouble (doing sth.); find it hard (to do sth.); have difficulty (in) (doing sth.); [in limited contexts] one can ⟨could⟩ hardly ⟨barely, scarcely⟩ (do sth.).**

«А вы читаете по-английски?» — «С трудом, но читаю» (Гончаров 1). "So you read English?" "I do, though with difficulty" (1a). ♦ На седьмой день выступили чуть свет, но так как ночью дорогу размыло, то люди шли с трудом... (Салтыков-Щедрин 1). On the seventh day they got on the march at daybreak, but, since the road had been washed away in the night, the men had trouble walking... (1a). ♦ Очевидно, люди с трудом понимают замаскированные или даже слегка прикрытые высказывания. Им нужно, чтобы всё било прямо в лоб (Мандельштам 1). People evidently find it hard to understand anything that is camouflaged, or even just slightly veiled. They need to have everything said straight out... (1a). ♦ Мысль увидеть императрицу лицом к лицу так устрашала её, что она с трудом могла держаться на ногах (Пушкин 2). The thought of finding herself face to face with the Empress frightened her so much that she could hardly stand on her feet (2a). The thought of coming face to face with the Empress so terrified her that she could scarcely stand up straight (2b).

Т-219 • ПЕРЕСТУПИ́ТЬ ⟨ПЕРЕШАГНУ́ТЬ⟩ ЧЕРЕЗ ТРУП *чей, кого* [VP; subj: human] to ruin s.o.'s life, career etc in order to further one's own aims: **X переступит через Y-ов труп ≃ X will destroy Y; X will crush Y underfoot.**

Т-220 • (только) ЧЕРЕЗ МОЙ ТРУП! *coll* [indep. clause; Invar; fixed WO] used to express a categorical protest against s.o.'s intention to do sth. or to act in a specific way: **over my dead body!**

«[Редактор] Автандил Автандилович хотел с тобой расстаться, но я ему сказал: только через мой труп» (Искандер 6). "Avtandil Avtandilovich [the editor] wanted to bid you farewell, but I told him it would be over my dead body" (6a).

Т-221 • ШАГА́ТЬ ⟨ХОДИ́ТЬ⟩ ПО ТРУ́ПАМ *(чьим, кого)* [VP; subj: human] to destroy others in order to achieve one's own aims: **X шагал по трупам ≃ X made his way over corpses; X crushed others underfoot; X trampled others into the ground.**

Прошло время, когда можно было душить в темноте, убивать безнаказанно, ходить по трупам среди всеобщего безмолвия (Эткинд 1). The time is past when it was possible to stifle people in the dark, to murder with impunity and to make your way over corpses amidst universal silence (1a).

Т-222 • ТРУ́СА ⟨ТРУ́СУ obs⟩ ПРА́ЗДНОВАТЬ; ИГРА́ТЬ/СЫГРА́ТЬ ТРУ́СА *all coll* [VP; subj: human] to experience (and sometimes show) fear, show cowardice, get nervous before undertaking sth. etc: X труса праздновал ≃ **X got scared; X got the jitters; X got (all) weak in the knees; [in refer. to showing fear] X was a chicken ⟨a scaredy-cat⟩; [in refer. to fear before undertaking sth. only] X got cold feet.**

Праздновать труса у всех на виду? Никогда! (Аксёнов 12). "Be cowards in public? Never!" (12a).

Т-223 • ТРЫН-ТРАВА́ *кому, для кого coll* [NP; Invar; subj-compl with бытьø (subj: usu. всё, всё это)] s.o. is not troubled or concerned (about sth. or anything at all): X-у всё трын-трава ≃ [in refer. to a given situation] **it doesn't affect ⟨ruffle⟩ X at all ⟨a bit⟩; it has no effect on X; X doesn't care ⟨couldn't care less, could care less⟩ about it; X doesn't care a straw ⟨a rap etc⟩ for it; it doesn't mean a thing to X; X doesn't take it seriously; [in refer. to s.o.'s general attitude toward things] nothing affects ⟨ruffles⟩ X; X couldn't care less about anything; X doesn't care a fig ⟨a rap⟩ for anything; X doesn't take anything ⟨takes nothing⟩ seriously.**

«Безденежье, бесхлебье, бессапожье!.. Трын-трава бы это было всё, если бы был молод и один» (Гоголь 3). "No money, no bread, no boots! I wouldn't care a straw for all that if only I were young and single" (3b). ♦ «Для Нади всё трын-трава!» — говорила с лёгким осуждением мама. Беспечность тёти Нади вошла в нашей семье в поговорку (Паустовский 1). "Nadya doesn't care a fig for anything!" Mama used to say with a slight reproach in her voice. Aunt Nadya's happy-go-lucky good spirits were proverbial in our family (1b).

Т-224 • МОЛЧА́ТЬ ⟨ПОМА́ЛКИВАТЬ⟩/ПОМОЛ-ЧА́ТЬ В ТРЯ́ПОЧКУ *highly coll* [VP; subj: human; more often impfv; often imper; fixed WO] to keep quiet, not express one's opinions, views, ideas aloud: X молчит в тряпочку ≃ X **keeps his mouth ⟨his trap, his yap⟩ shut; X keeps mum.**

Обыкновенные люди к этому времени уже научились молчать в тряпочку, и шумели только старухи в очередях (Мандельштам 2). By that time ordinary people had learned to keep their mouths shut, and the only ones who still made any fuss were old women standing in queues (2a).

Т-225 • (ЕЩЁ) ТУДА́-СЮДА́ *coll* [AdjP; Invar; subj-compl with copula (subj: any noun) or impers predic] a person (a thing etc) is not bad, is tolerable: X ещё туда-сюда ≃ **X is (more or less) all right; X isn't (so ⟨all that⟩) bad;** [in limited contexts] **X is so-so; X is passable; X will do; thing X is in reasonable shape.**

С непривычки ей было трудно [работать на 12-часовых сменах], особенно ночью. Днём ещё туда-сюда... (Грекова 3). It was hard for her [to work 12-hour shifts] because she wasn't used to such long hours, especially the night shift. But during the day she was more or less all right... (3a). ♦ [Виктория:] Смотреть на него [футбол] — ещё туда-сюда, а так [слушать репортаж по радио] — не понимаю (Вампилов 1). [V.:] It's not so bad if you can watch it [soccer], but listening like this... I don't understand (1a). ♦ Автомобиль почему-то продавался вместе с искусственной пальмой в зелёной кадке. Пришлось купить и пальму. Пальма была ещё туда-сюда, но с машиной пришлось долго возиться... (Ильф и Петров 2). For some reason or other the car was sold together with an artificial palm in a green tub, so he had to take the palm as well. The palm was still in reasonable shape, but the car needed a lot of work (2a).

Т-226 • (И) ТУДА́ И СЮДА́; ТУДА́-СЮДА́; ТУДА́, СЮДА́ *all coll* [AdvP; Invar] **1.** Also: ТУДА́ ДА СЮДА́ *coll;* ТУДЫ́-СЮДЫ́ *substand, regional* [adv] in one direction and then in the other or another: **back and forth; up and down (some place); to and fro; this way and that;** [in limited contexts] **(dash ⟨run etc⟩) around ⟨about⟩.**

Мансуров-Курильский походил по комнате туда-сюда... (Залыгин 1). ...Mansurov-Kurilsky started pacing up and down the room... (1a). ♦ Трещали дрова, таял снег, и чёрные тени солдат туда и сюда сновали по всему занятому, притоптанному в снегу, пространству (Толстой 7). The wood crackled, the snow began to melt, and shadowy figures of soldiers moved to and fro over the occupied space where the snow had been trodden down (7a). ♦ «Ах господи! Да что же это я толкусь туда и сюда, как угорелая...» (Достоевский 3). "Oh, Lord! Why am I dashing around like a madwoman?..." (3b).

2. Also: ТУДЫ́-СЮДЫ́ *substand, regional* [predic (subj: human) or adv] (one looks, searches for s.o. or sth.) in several or many different places: X туда-сюда ≃ [in past contexts] **X looked here and there;** [in limited contexts] **X searched for s.o. ⟨sth.⟩ everywhere.**

«Из крепости убёг зарестованный [*ungrammat* = убежал арестованный] злодей. Туды-сюды искать — нету» (Шолохов 2). "A great villain had escaped from the fortress. The authorities were searching for him everywhere but couldn't find him" (2a).

3. [predic; subj: human] (one attempts to achieve, attain etc sth.) using several or many different approaches: X и туда и сюда ≃ **X (has) tried ⟨acted etc⟩ this way and that ⟨one way and then another⟩; X tried ⟨did⟩ this and that; X tried several different tacks.**

Он наотрез отказался ехать с нами. Я туда, сюда — не смогла уговорить его. He refused outright to go with us. I tried this and that, but I couldn't convince him to change his mind.

Т-227 • НИ ТУДА́ (И) НИ СЮДА́ *coll;* НИ ТУДЫ́ (И) НИ СЮДЫ́ *substand* [AdvP; these forms only; adv or predic; fixed WO] **1.** [subj: human, animal, or concr] some person (animal, or object) cannot move, will not move, cannot be moved etc in any direction from where he (or it) is (standing, sitting, presently located etc): X ни туда и ни сюда ≃ **X won't ⟨can't⟩ move ⟨go⟩ one way or the other; s.o. can't ⟨can't manage to⟩ move X one way or the other; X won't budge; X is stuck.**

Ключ почему-то застрял в скважине и не поворачивался ни туда ни сюда (Гинзбург 2). The key somehow stuck in the lock and I couldn't manage to move it one way or the other (2a).

2. [subj: human or concr] some person (project etc) is not progressing toward the desired goal, some matter (undertaking etc) is not developing: X ни туда и ни сюда ≃ **X is going nowhere (fast); person X isn't getting anywhere; person X is making no headway; X is at a standstill.**

Т-228 • ТО ТУДА́, ТО СЮДА́ [AdvP; Invar; adv; fixed WO] first in one direction, then in another (either back and forth or in random directions): **this way and that; (up and down some place,) now this way, now that; to and fro.**

К Елизавете Павловне присоединилась в первом ряду Чернышевская; и по тому, как мать изредка поворачивала то туда, то сюда голову, поправляя сзади причёску, Фёдор, витавший позади зала, заключил, что ей малоинтересно общество соседки (Набоков 1). Elizaveta Pavlovna was joined in the first row by Mme. Chernyshevski; and from the fact that his mother occasionally turned her head this way and that while adjusting her hairdo from behind, Fyodor, hovering about the hall, concluded that she was little interested in the society of her neighbor (1a). ♦ Там, возле наполовину растасканной на дрова летней читальни, была вытоптанная нашей школой площадка. Старшеклассники, разбившись на две ватаги, проносились по ней то туда, то сюда (Аксёнов 2). There, next to the summer reading room—which had been half torn down for firewood—our school had trampled out a playing field. The upperclassmen, who had split up into two teams, raced up and down it, now this way, now that (2a).

Т-229 • ТУДА́ ЖЕ! *coll* [Particle; Invar] an exclamation directed toward or used in refer. to s.o. who is saying, doing, or trying to do as others do, but who, in the speaker's opinion, cannot, has no right to, or is not in a position to do so: (и ⟨а⟩) X туда же! ≃ **not X, too ⟨as well⟩!; X is no better than the others; so X wants sth. ⟨to do sth.⟩ too!; (so) X is at it, too!;** [in limited contexts] **(and) X too, if you please!**

«Врачи советуют мне бросить курить». — «Хороший совет». — «И ты туда же!» "The doctors tell me to quit smoking." "Good advice." "Not you, too!" ♦ [Шпигельский (*украдкою поглядывая на Ракитина*):] А, видно, не одни нервы страдают, и жёлчь тоже немножко расходилась... [Наталья Петровна:] Ну, и вы туда же! Наблюдайте сколько хотите, доктор, да только не вслух (Тургенев 1). [Sh. (*stealing a look at Rakitin*):] Oh, I see, not just nerves, a little bile, too. [N.:] Not you, as well! Be as observant as you like, but not out loud (1c). ♦ И только усадив патриарха, [Сталин]... с шутливым кряхтением опустился в кресло. «Стареем, владыка, стареем». — «Что вы, что вы, товарищ Сталин!.. Вам ещё жить и жить на благо отечества и народа, русская церковь каждодневно молится за вас!» —

«Эх, поп, поп, и ты туда же», — лениво усмехнулся он про себя... (Максимов 1). And only after he [Stalin] had helped the Patriarch to sit down did he...fall into an armchair with a jocular groan. "We're getting old, Your Eminence, we're getting old." "What are you saying, comrade Stalin, what are you saying?...You must live and prosper a long time yet for the good of the motherland and the people. The Russian church prays for you every day!" "Oh priest, priest, you're no better than the others," he grinned lazily to himself (1a).

Т-230 • ТУДА́ И ОБРА́ТНО ⟨НАЗА́Д⟩ [AdvP; these forms only; adv or postmodif; fixed WO] 1. съездить, сходить, поездка ~ и т. п. (to go, a trip etc) to some place and back again: **there and back;** ‖ поездка ~ ≃ **round trip;** ‖ билет ~ ≃ **round-trip ticket.**

...Там был вопрос, с какой целью еду я в Соединённые Штаты. А я подумал и написал: «Джаст фор фан». То есть, говоря по-нашему, просто для удовольствия... И американские власти этим ответом были, видимо, удовлетворены, потому что через пятнадцать минут мне была выдана виза на четыре года, в течение которых я могу ездить хоть каждый день туда и обратно, если, конечно, хватит денег (Войнович 1). There was a question about my purpose in visiting the United States. I thought for a minute and then I wrote: "Just for fun!" The U.S. authorities apparently found that answer satisfactory, because fifteen minutes later I was granted a visa good for four years, during which time I could go to the United States and back every day of the week — if I had the money, of course (1a).

2. ходить, прогуливаться и т. п. ~ (to walk, pace etc) in one direction and then the other in some place or at some location: **back and forth; over and back.**

Т-231 • В ТУ́ЛУ СО СВОИ́М САМОВА́РОМ НЕ Е́ЗДЯТ [saying] there is no need to bring sth. to a place that already has an abundance of it: ≃ **why ⟨don't⟩ carry water to the river.** Cf. **it's useless to carry ⟨it would be like carrying⟩ coals to Newcastle.**

Т-232 • ТУМА́Н В ГЛАЗА́Х у кого [NP; sing only; VP$_{subj}$ with быть$_∅$] s.o. cannot see clearly, distinctly (because he is exhausted, agitated, not feeling well etc): у Х-а туман в глазах ≃ **everything looks fuzzy to X.**

Т-233 • ТУМА́Н В ГОЛОВЕ́ у кого [NP; sing only; VP$_{subj}$ with быть$_∅$] 1. s.o. has a heavy feeling in his head, is not as alert as usual (from fatigue, illness etc): у Х-а туман в голове ≃ **X's head is in a fog; X's brain is ⟨feels⟩ all fuzzy.**

2. s.o. is confused, is having difficulty understanding sth. etc: у Х-а туман в голове ≃ **X ⟨X's head⟩ is in a fog; X's brain is clouded ⟨fuzzy⟩.**

Т-234 • (КАК) В ТУМА́НЕ [(как +) PrepP; these forms only] 1. видеть, помнить кого-что и т. п. [adv] (to see, remember etc s.o. or sth.) only vaguely, unclearly: **(see s.o. ⟨sth.⟩) as if through a fog ⟨a mist⟩; (have) a cloudy ⟨foggy, hazy⟩ recollection (of s.o. ⟨sth.⟩).**

2. жить, ходить, быть$_∅$ ~ и т. п. [adv or subj-compl with copula (subj: usu. human, occas. abstr, esp. всё)] (of a person) (to live, walk around, be etc) in a state of mental confusion; (of some course of events, everything etc) (to be etc) perceived or remembered by s.o. in an unclear manner: Х был как в тумане ≃ **X was ⟨lived etc⟩ in a fog; X walked around as if in a fog;** [in refer. to a temporary state only] **X was befuddled;** ‖ всё было как в тумане ≃ **everything happened as if in a fog.**

Наташа, по замечанию матери и Сони, казалась по-старому влюблённою в Бориса. Она пела ему его любимые песни... не позволяла поминать ему о старом, давая пони-

мать, как прекрасно было новое; и каждый день он уезжал в тумане, не сказав того, что намерен был сказать, сам не зная, что он делал, и для чего он приезжал, и чем это кончится (Толстой 5). It seemed to her mother and to Sonya that Natasha was in love with Boris as she had been before. She sang his favorite songs to him...and would not allow him to allude to the past, making him feel how delightful the present was; every day he went away in a fog, without having said what he meant to say, not knowing what he was doing, why he continued to go there, or how it would end (5a). ♦ «...Заговелись мы оброк-то получать с Обломовки...» — говорил, опьянев немного, [Иван Матвеевич] Мухояров. «А чёрт с ним, кум!..» — возражал Тарантьев, тоже немного в тумане... (Гончаров 1). "...We've seen the last of the Oblomovka profits," said Ivan Matveyevich, getting a little drunk. "The hell with it brother!..." retorted Tarantyev, also slightly befuddled... (1b). ♦ Соседи вызвали милицию — и дальше пошло всё как в тумане... (Амальрик 1). The neighbors called the police; after that, everything happened as if in a fog... (1a).

Т-235 • НАПУСКА́ТЬ/НАПУСТИ́ТЬ ТУМА́НУ ⟨ТУМА́Н(А)⟩ (В ГЛАЗА́ кому obs); НАВОДИ́ТЬ/НАВЕСТИ́ ТУМА́НУ ⟨ТУМА́Н(А)⟩ all coll, disapprov [VP; subj: human; more often pfv past, infin with a finite form of уметь or любить, or impfv neg imper] to present some matter or issue in an unclear, muddled fashion (usu. in order to hide the actual facts, the true state of affairs): X напустил туману ≃ **X clouded ⟨obscured, fogged⟩ the issue; X confused matters ⟨the issue⟩;** [in limited contexts] **X put up ⟨laid down⟩ a smoke screen ⟨a smokescreen⟩.**

Дамы умели напустить такого тумана в глаза всем, что все, а особенно чиновники, несколько времени оставались ошеломлёнными (Гоголь 3). The ladies succeeded in confusing matters so thoroughly that the population in general and the government employees in particular were momentarily speechless (3e). ♦ [Городничий (в сторону):] О, тонкая штука! Эк куда метнул! Какого туману напустил! разбери, кто хочет (Гоголь 4). [Mayor (aside):] Ah, he's a sly one. So that's his game! He lays down a smokescreen, so you can't tell what's he's after (4f). ♦ «...Опросите тысячу изобретателей... и я уверен, 95 процентов из них скажут, что тов. Шутиков им не помогал, а лишь топил изобретения. Большой мастер напускать тумана, он обманул и вас, тов. редактор!» (Дудинцев 1). "...Ask a thousand inventors...and I am certain that 95 per cent of them would say that Comrade Shutikov had not helped them, but only smothered their inventions. A past master of the smoke screen, he has deceived you, too, comrade editor" (1a).

Т-236 • ЗАВОДИ́ТЬ/ЗАВЕСТИ́ В ТУПИ́К кого [VP; subj: human or abstr; more often pfv] to lead s.o. into a difficult, hopeless situation from which there is no escape: X завёл Y-а в тупик ≃ **X led Y into a dead end ⟨a cul-de-sac⟩; X led Y up ⟨down, into⟩ a blind alley.**

Сумеет ли этот паразит [марксизм] развить в себе творческие потенции или заведёт человечество в тупик типа муравейника или империй древнего (а может быть, и нынешнего) Китая? (Зиновьев 2). Will this parasite [Marxism] be able to develop within itself a creative potential, or will it lead mankind into a cul-de-sac like an anthill or like the empire of ancient (or maybe modern) China? (2a). ♦ ...По характеру вопросов, задаваемых наседкой, очень легко определить, куда следствие клонит и что знает. А дезинформируя их через наседку, можно завести следствие в... тупик... (Буковский 1). ...It was easy to determine in which direction the investigation was headed, and what they knew, from the nature of the questions the snooper asked. And by misinforming them through him, it was possible to lead them into...a blind alley... (1a).

Т-237 • ЗАХОДИ́ТЬ/ЗАЙТИ́ В ТУПИ́К [VP; subj: human, collect, or abstr (дело, дела, спор etc); more often pfv past] (of a

person, a group, a matter, an argument etc) to reach or end up at a point from which further progress cannot be made, the goal in question cannot be attained, the problem in question cannot be solved etc (usu. in cases when all possible means of reaching the desired goal have been exhausted): X зашёл в тупик ≃ **X reached an impasse ⟨a dead end, a deadlock⟩; X ran into a blind alley; thing X was deadlocked; person X came up against a brick wall ⟨a dead end⟩.**

Дела мои зашли в тупик. Долги, семейный разлад, отсутствие перспектив... (Довлатов 1). My life had reached an impasse. Debts, family strife, a lack of perspective... (1a). ♦ Он заявил, что здравоохранение зайдёт в тупик, если изучение вирусов не станет делом государственного значения (Каверин 1). He declared that the health service would inevitably run into a blind alley if the study of viruses was not accorded State importance... (1a). ♦ Примерно с середины лета, окончательно зайдя в тупик, они [следователи] начали следствие по ст[атье] 70 (Буковский 1). Around the middle of the summer they [my investigators] came up against a total dead end and started a new investigation under Article 70 (1a).

Т-238 • СТА́ВИТЬ/ПОСТА́ВИТЬ В ТУПИ́К кого [VP; subj: human or abstr; usu. this WO] (of a person, what a person says, an incomprehensible phenomenon etc) to put s.o. in a difficult position in which he does not know what to do, what to say, how to react etc: X поставил Y-а в тупик ≃ **X baffled ⟨nonplussed, stumped⟩ Y; X put Y in a bad ⟨difficult etc⟩ position; Y was at a loss (for what to say ⟨to do etc⟩); Y didn't know what to say ⟨to do etc⟩; thing X brought Y to ⟨landed Y in⟩ an impasse.**

Администрация их [монахинь-заключённых] ненавидит. Твёрдость духа истязаемых ими женщин их самих ставит в тупик (Ивинская 1). The camp authorities hated them [the imprisoned nuns] and were quite baffled by the firmness of spirit shown by these women they were so cruelly mistreating (1a). ♦ «Почему же письмо необходимо?» – спросил он. «Почему? – повторила она и быстро обернулась к нему с весёлым лицом, наслаждаясь тем, что на каждом шагу умеет ставить его в тупик. – А потому... что вы не спали всю ночь, писали всё для меня; я тоже эгоистка!» (Гончаров 1). "Why was the letter necessary?" he asked. "Why?" she repeated, turning round to him quickly with a gay face, delighted that she could nonplus him at every step. "Because...you did not sleep all night and wrote it all for me. I too am an egoist!" (1a). ♦ [Николай] стал доказывать Пьеру, что никакого переворота не предвидится... Пьер доказывал противное, и так как его умственные способности были сильнее и изворотливее, Николай почувствовал себя поставленным в тупик (Толстой 7). ...Nikolai undertook to demonstrate to Pierre that no revolution was to be expected....Pierre maintained the contrary, and as his intellectual faculties were greater and more resourceful, Nikolai soon felt himself at a loss (7a). ♦ Одно ничтожнейшее обстоятельство поставило его [Раскольникова] в тупик, ещё прежде чем он сошёл с лестницы... Он вдруг увидал, что Настасья не только на этот раз дома, у себя в кухне, но ещё занимается делом... (Достоевский 3). A circumstance of the most trivial kind landed him in an impasse even before he had got to the bottom of the stairs....He suddenly saw that not only was Nastasya at home and in her kitchen, but she was actually doing some work... (3d).

Т-239 • СТАНОВИ́ТЬСЯ/СТАТЬ В ТУПИ́К [VP; subj: human or collect] to end up in a position in which one does not know what to do, what to say, how to react etc, become confused: X стал в тупик ≃ **X was baffled ⟨stumped, nonplussed⟩; X was in a bad ⟨difficult⟩ position; X was at a loss (for what to say ⟨do etc⟩); X didn't know what to say ⟨do etc⟩; X reached ⟨came to, arrived at, was at⟩ an impasse; [in limited contexts] X didn't know what to make of it.**

«Я хочу квартиру хорошую»... – «Гм...» – похоже, она [председатель ревизионной комиссии кооператива] растерялась. Она рассчитывала, что я буду доказывать, что хочу получить именно плохую квартиру... тогда она могла бы мне возражать. А тут стала в тупик (Войнович 3). "I want a good apartment."..."Hmm..." It looked as if she'd [the director of the cooperative's Review Committee had] lost her way. She had counted on my arguing that I wanted to get a really bad apartment...; then she could have objected. But now she was stumped (3a). ♦ Выслушав такой уклончивый ответ, помощник градоначальника стал в тупик (Салтыков-Щедрин 1). When he heard this evasive answer, the assistant town governor was at a loss (1a). ♦ «[Поляк] встретил [меня] так важно, так я и стала в тупик» (Достоевский 1). "He [the Pole] greeted me so pompously I didn't know what to do" (1a). ♦ Может быть, тем бы и кончилось это странное происшествие... если бы дело не усложнилось вмешательством элемента до такой степени фантастического, что сами глуповцы – и те стали в тупик (Салтыков-Щедрин 1). Perhaps this strange episode would have ended like this...if matters had not become complicated by a circumstance so fantastic that even the Glupovites did not know what to make of it (1b).

Т-240 • ТУРУ́СЫ НА КОЛЁСАХ (разводить, подпускать, нести и т. п.)** coll [NP; pl only; fixed WO] foolish, senseless talk, absurdities: **(tell) tall tales ⟨cock-and-bull stories⟩; that's baloney ⟨(a bunch of) twaddle, (a lot of) nonsense etc⟩; (come out with) all kinds of nonsense ⟨cock-and-bull stories etc⟩.**

< The prevailing point of view connects this idiom with «турусы» ⟨or «тарасы»⟩ – the old Russian word for turrets that were moved on wheels and employed when besieging a fortified place. Stories about them were considered unbelievable and grossly exaggerated.

Т-241 • ТО ТУ́Т, ТО ТА́М; ТО ТА́М, ТО ТУ́Т ⟨СЯ́М⟩ all coll [AdvP; these forms only; adv; fixed WO] (some action occurs or similar actions occur, some objects are located etc) in different places, usu. in an alternating fashion (may refer to the way s.o. perceives some objects, people etc as he moves along, as his gaze moves over some area etc): **now here, now there; now here and now there; first here, then there; first in one place and then in another ⟨the other⟩; here and there.**

[Чернышевский] передвигался, как лист, гонимый ветром, нервной, пошатывающейся походкой, и то тут, то там слышался его визгливый голосок (Набоков 1). He [Chernyshevski] moved about like a leaf blown by the wind, with a nervous stumbling gait, and his shrill voice could be heard now here and now there (1a). ♦ Столы были сдвинуты со своих, геометрией подсказанных, правильных мест и стояли то там, то сям, вкривь и вкось... (Битов 2). The tables had been moved from their geometrically suggested correct places to stand here and there, every which way (2a).

Т-242 • ТУ́Т ЖЕ [AdjP; Invar; adv] **1.** in the very place or very close to the place where one is or that is being referred to: **right here ⟨there⟩.**

«...Добрый день, – сказал человек в халате, – мне хотелось бы поговорить...» Тут он положил локти на перила, ладонями подпёр щёки и стал похож на смешную обезьяну в колпаке... Арманда и Барон с изумлением поняли, что он желает разговаривать тут же, на лестнице... (Булгаков 5). "...Good afternoon," said the man in the robe. "We must have a talk...." He rested his elbows on the railing, propped his cheeks with hands, and began to look like a funny monkey in a nightcap. Armande and Baron realized with astonishment that he intended to talk with them right there, on the stairs... (5a).

2. at this or that very moment: **right now ⟨then⟩; (right) there and then ⟨then and there⟩; instantly; on the spot; right away; straight off; immediately; at once.**

…Выходит он на средину, а в руках бумага − форменное донесение по начальству. А так как начальство его было тут же, то тут же и прочёл бумагу вслух всем собравшимся… (Достоевский 1). …He stepped into the middle of the room with a paper in his hand−a formal statement to the authorities. And since the authorities were right there, he read the paper right then to the whole gathering (1a). ♦ Он тут же уснул, а Хикур плакала, плакала, уткнувшись головой в подушку… (Искандер 4). He fell asleep then and there, and Khikur wept, wept with her face buried in the pillow… (4a). ♦ Он ожидал услышать с порога про кольцо, но Фаина была весела, неожиданно ласкова и приветлива, и он удивлялся. Пусть он немного подождёт на лестнице, а она быстренько оденется, и они пойдут гулять. Он ждал. И тут же появилась Фаина, и на ней не было лица. «Что с тобой?!» − воскликнул Лёва… (Битов 2). He had expected to hear about the ring the minute he walked in. But Faina was gay, unexpectedly affectionate, and cordial, and he was amazed. Let him wait a minute on the stairs−she'd get dressed in a jiffy and they'd go for a walk. He waited. Faina reappeared instantly, pale as death. "What's the matter?" Lyova exclaimed… (2a). ♦ [Бабушка:] В нашей молодости мы не знали такого сервиса. Теряешь документы, и тут же их тебе возвращают (Панова 1). [Grandmother:] In our days there was no such service. Now you lose your travel papers, and right away they hand them back to you (1a). ♦ Лёва чуть не расплакался, тут же в коридоре, от радости и от стыда, и взятку принял, тут же поверив, что это именно так, как говорит Бланк (Битов 2). Lyova nearly burst into tears of joy and shame right there in the corridor, and he accepted the bribe, believing immediately that all was just as Blank said (2a). ♦ Требовалось тут же, не сходя с места, изобрести обыкновенные объяснения явлений необыкновенных (Булгаков 9). …He felt obliged to invent at once, right on the spot, some ordinary explanations for extraordinary events (9a). ♦ Другие в его [Юрочки] возрасте и в Берлине побывали, и чёрт знает ещё где («Кое-кто и голову там положил», − перебил его в этом месте Вадим Петрович, но он тут же ответил: «Положили, знаю, но было за что положить») (Некрасов 1). [context transl] Other men of his [Yurochka's] age had been to Berlin and God knows where else ("Some of them gave their lives in Berlin," Vadim Petrovich interrupted him at this point, but Yurochka replied without hesitation: "They gave their lives, I know, but they had something to give them for") (1a).

T-243 • ТУ́Т КАК ТУ́Т *coll* [AdvP; Invar; subj-compl with быть∅ (subj: human, collect, or animal), usu. pres] one appears suddenly and at the precise moment when (he is expected, sth. desirable becomes available, people are talking about him, sth. concerning him happens etc): X тут как тут ≃ **X is there in a flash ⟨like a shot⟩; X is right there; there X is.**

У этого Учреждения создалась такая репутация, что оно всё видит, всё слышит, всё знает, и, если чего не так, оно уже тут как тут (Войнович 2). This Institution acquired the reputation of seeing everything, hearing everything, knowing everything, and, if something was out of line, the Institution would be there in a flash (2a). ♦ …Стоило только потихоньку войти, когда придёт время, в кухню и взять топор, а потом, чрез час (когда всё уже кончится), войти и положить обратно. Но представлялись и сомнения: он [Раскольников], положим, придёт через час, чтобы положить обратно, а Настасья тут как тут, воротилась (Достоевский 3). …He [Raskolnikov] had only to tiptoe into the kitchen when the time came, take the ax, and an hour later (when everything was over) go in again and put it back. But some doubts occurred: suppose he returned an hour later to put it back and Nastasya was right there, having come back herself (3a).

T-244 • ТУ́ЧА ТУ́ЧЕЙ *coll* [NP; Invar; fixed WO] **1.** ~ ходить, прийти и т. п. Also: мрачный **КАК ТУ́ЧА** [subj-compl with copula (subj: human) or modif] morose, sullen, in a bad mood: **(look) gloomy ⟨grim⟩; (walk around) as black as thunder; (look) (as) black as thunder; (look) as black ⟨dark⟩ as a thundercloud.**

«Разумеется, я осёл, − проговорил он, мрачный как туча, − но ведь… и ты тоже» (Достоевский 3). "I know I'm a dope," he said, looking black as thunder, "but then…you're one too." (3a).

2. ~ кого-чего [quantit subj-compl with copula (subj/gen: human or animal)] (in some place there is) a very large or excessive quantity (of animals, insects, or less often, people): **(there's) a multitude ⟨a swarm, a throng, a horde⟩ of** [NPs]; **(there are) droves of** [NPs]; **(some place is) swarming ⟨teeming⟩ with** [NPs].

T-245 • ТУ́ЧИ СГУЩА́ЮТСЯ/СГУСТИ́ЛИСЬ ⟨СОБИРА́ЮТСЯ/СОБРАЛИ́СЬ⟩ *над кем-чем* or **НАД ГОЛОВО́Й** *чьей, кого* [VP_subj] danger is threatening s.o., trouble is coming: над Х-ом ⟨над Х-овой головой⟩ сгущаются тучи ≃ **storm clouds are gathering overhead ⟨over X⟩; there is a dark cloud on the ⟨X's⟩ horizon; trouble is brewing for X; trouble is in the air.**

[author's usage] Предчувствия ожидаемых гонений и бед в это прекрасное воскресное летнее утро в тихом будничном подмосковье представились мне чрезмерностью воображения… По словам Б.Л. [Пастернака], над ним нависла грозовая туча (Гладков 1). On that beautiful summer morning in the peaceful, familiar countryside near Moscow his [Pasternak's] forebodings of troubles and persecutions to come seemed to me the product of excessive imagination….He told me that the storm clouds were gathering over him (1a).

T-246 • ВИ́ШЬ ТЫ *substand* [Interj; Invar] used to express surprise, displeasure etc: **look at that(, will you)!; get a load of this!**

«Вишь ты, − сказал один [мужик] другому, − вон какое колесо!» (Гоголь 3). "Look at that, will you!" said one muzhik to the other. "What a wheel!" (3b).

T-247 • И́ШЬ ТЫ *coll* [Interj; Invar] **1.** used to express surprise, amazement: **would you believe it!; how do you ⟨d'you⟩ like that!; look at that!; (just) look at him ⟨it etc⟩!; how about that!; isn't that something!; well, I'll be!; what do you know!**

«А я, правду сказать… думал, всё, концы. А она [старуха]: кашу, говорит, хочу, варите, говорит, мне кашу. Проголодалась, значит. Ишь ты!» (Распутин 3). "To tell the truth I…thought it was all over. And up she [the old lady] pipes: Make us a bit of *kasha*. She's hungry. Would you believe it!" (3a). ♦ [Гвардеец:] Это даже невероятно… чтобы солдату да вдруг приснился такой волшебный сон… кукла разгуливает по дворцу… Удивительное дело. Ишь ты… Ну, ни дать ни взять − живая девочка (Олеша 7). [G.:] It's incredible that a soldier should have such a magical dream…a doll goes strolling round the palace….Amazing. How d'you like that! A live girl…nothing less (7a). ♦ Иван, хоть и решил с женщиной не разговаривать, не удержался и, видя, как вода хлещет в ванну широкой струёй из сияющего крана, сказал с иронией: «Ишь ты! Как в „Метрополе"!» (Булгаков 9). Although Ivan had made up his mind not to talk to the woman, when he saw a broad stream of water thundering into the bath from a glittering faucet, he could not help saying sarcastically, "Look at that! Just like in the Metropole!" (9b). ♦ Мишка, открыв клавикорды, играл на них одним пальцем. Дворник, подбоченившись и радостно улыбаясь, стоял пред большим зеркалом. «Вот ловко-то! А? Дядюшка Игнат!» − говорил мальчик, вдруг начиная хлопать обеими руками по клавишам. «Ишь ты!» − отвечал Игнат… (Толстой 6). Mishka had opened the clavichord and was strumming on it with one finger. The yard porter, arms akimbo, stood in front of a large mirror smiling with satisfaction. "That's fine! Isn't it? Isn't it, Uncle Ignat?" asked the boy, suddenly beginning to bang on the keyboard with both hands.

"Just look at him!" said Ignat... (6a). ♦ Она смешалась и покраснела. «Ишь ты, ещё краснеет», — про себя удивился Алтынник (Войнович 5). Embarrassed, she blushed. How about that, she still blushes, Altinnik marveled to himself (5a). ♦ Пантелей Прокофьевич деловито оглядел черня́вую головку, торчавшую из вороха тряпья, и не без гордости удостоверил: «Наших кровей... эк-гм... Ишь ты!..» (Шолохов 2). Pantelei briskly surveyed the dark little head poking out of the covers and affirmed with some pride, "Yes, that's our blood all right... Humph!.. Well, I'll be..." (2a). ♦ В долгих застольных беседах Антон удовлетворял детскую любознательность начальника... Разнообразные сведения, получаемые в этих беседах, вызывали у нашего хозяина то радостное изумление: «Ишь ты!», то скептические возгласы: «Скажешь тоже!» (Гинзбург 2). In long conversations around the table, Anton used to try to satisfy the childlike curiosity of the commandant....The varied information acquired in these conversations would elicit from him either a pleasurably astonished "What do you know!" or a skeptical "You don't say!" (2a).

2. used to express disagreement, opposition, refusal, or dissatisfaction: **I like that!; how do you like that!; oh come on!**

[Булычов:] Надобно тебя ругать, а не хочется. [Шура:] Не хочется, значит – не надо. [Булычов:] Ишь ты! Не хочется — не надо. Эдак-то жить легко бы, да нельзя! (Горький 2). [В.:] I ought to be scolding you but I don't feel like it. [Sh.:] If you don't feel like it then you needn't. [B.:] I like that! If you don't want to you needn't! Life would be easy that way, but it can't be done! (2a). ♦ [Сахатов:] ...Мы пришли спрятать предмет. Так куда же спрятать?.. [Василий Леонидыч:] ...Вот что я вам скажу: мужику, одному из этих, в карман. Вот хоть этому. Ты послушай. А, что? Где у тебя карман? [3-ий мужик:] А на что тебе карман! Ишь ты, карман! У меня в кармане деньги (Толстой 3). [S.:] ...We came to hide something. Now where should we hide it?... [V.L.:] ...Here's my idea: Let's put it in the pocket of one of these peasants. How about him? Hey, there! Well? Where's your pocket? [Third Peasant:] What do you want with my pocket? How do you like that? My pocket! I've got money in my pocket (3a).

Т-248 • **НА ТЫ́** *с кем* **быть**₀, **переходить, называть** *кого*, **обращаться** *к кому;* **ГОВОРИ́ТЬ ТЫ** *кому* [PrepP, Invar, subj-compl with copula or adv (1st var.); VP (2nd var.); subj: human] (to address s.o., speak to or with s.o. etc) using the «ты» (informal "you") form of address: X с Y-ом на «ты» ≃ X **is on familiar terms with Y; X addresses Y in the familiar way** ⟨**fashion, manner**⟩; **X uses the familiar form of address with Y;** [in limited contexts] **X is on a first-name basis with Y; X calls Y by Y's first name.** ○ **ОБРАЩЕ́НИЕ НА ТЫ́** [NP; sing only] ≃ **the familiar way one addresses s.o.** ⟨**one is addressed**⟩; **the familiar form (of address).**

Едва поселившись в Павлинове, она уже знала всех соседей, начальника милиции, сторожей на лодочной станции, была на «ты» с молодой директоршей санатория... (Трифонов 4). She'd hardly settled in Pavlinovo when she already knew all the neighbors, the police chief, the watchmen at the wharf, and was on familiar terms with the young directress of the sanatorium... (4a). ♦ «Словом ты вы меня вызываете на тесную дружбу, обязывая и меня говорить вам ты» (Гоголь 3). "By addressing me in so familiar a manner, you show your close friendship for me and oblige me to address you in the familiar fashion" (3a). ♦ ...В кухне он называл меня на «вы», и мне это понравилось, а теперь вдруг на «ты» (Каверин 1). ...In the kitchen, he had spoken to me in the formal way in which grown-ups are addressed and I had liked it, but now he had suddenly changed to the familiar form (1a).

Т-249 • **КРОМЕ́ШНАЯ ТЬМА; КРОМЕ́ШНЫЙ МРАК** [NP; sing only] total darkness: **absolute** ⟨**impenetrable**⟩ **darkness; pitch-darkness.**

Т-250 • **ТЬМА́ ЕГИ́ПЕТСКАЯ** *obs, lit* [NP; sing only] impenetrable darkness: **pitch-darkness; pitch-blackness.**

< From the Biblical account of one of the Egyptian plagues—a supernatural darkness sent by God to punish Egypt (Ex. 10:22).

Т-251 • **ТЬМА-ТЬМУ́ЩАЯ**[1] *coll* [NP; sing only] total darkness: **impenetrable darkness; pitch-darkness.**

Т-252 • **ТЬМА-ТЬМУ́ЩАЯ**[2] *кого-чего coll* [usu. subj or quantit subj-compl with copula (subj/gen: any common noun)] very many, a countless number: **vast numbers; countless multitudes; millions and millions;** [of people and animals only] **hordes and hordes; swarms and swarms.**

...Он получил неслыханный урожай огурцов. Сколько ни шарили в кустах колхозники, проходившие мимо его бахчи, огурцов оставалась тьма-тьмущая (Искандер 3). ...He had an unparalleled crop. No matter how often the cucumber patch was rifled by passing kolkhoz workers, countless multitudes of cucumbers remained (3a). ♦ ...Он [Сталин] уничтожил тьму-тьмущую людей... (Искандер 5). He [Stalin] wiped out millions and millions of people... (5a). ♦ Из-за Дымера кубарем прилетали в сельские полицаи и старосты, рассказывали, что идёт партизан тьма-тьмущая... (Кузнецов 1). Rural *Polizei* [*German* = police] and village elders came pouring in from beyond Dymer, reporting that hordes and hordes of the partisans were advancing... (1a). ♦ «Одно горе — крысы. Тьма тьмущая, отбою нет» (Пастернак 1). "Our only trouble is rats. There are swarms and swarms of them, and you can't get rid of them" (1a).

Т-253 • **ТЮРЬМА́** ⟨**ОСТРО́Г** *obs*⟩ **ПЛА́ЧЕТ** *по ком, по кому, о ком coll* [VP$_{subj}$; usu. pres] s.o. deserves a prison sentence or some other severe form of punishment: по X-у тюрьма плачет ≃ **X should be locked up** ⟨**put in jail**⟩; **X should be (put) behind bars; X should be sent up** ⟨**up the river**⟩.

Т-254 • **ТЮ́ТЕЛЬКА В ТЮ́ТЕЛЬКУ** *coll* [Invar; adv or Particle; fixed WO] precisely (the same as something else, what was expected, conforming to the standard etc): **exactly; to a T; to a hair; to the letter;** [in refer. to time] **to the minute; on the button; on the nose; on the dot.**

«...Их как раз двенадцать, Залогиных-то! Вот тебе и двенадцать кулацких душ! Тютелька в тютельку!» (Евтушенко 2). "...There are exactly twelve Zalogins! There's your twelve kulak souls! Exactly!" (2a). ♦ Всё вышло так, как думал Михаил. Правда, через милицию Першин его не разыскивал, во всяком случае при нём не заводил речь об этом, а всё остальное — точь-в-точь, тютелька в тютельку (Абрамов 1). It turned out just as Mikhail thought. Granted, Pershin had not gotten the police after him—or at least he made no mention of having done so—but as for the rest: to a T, to a hair (1a).

Т-255 • **В ТЯ́ГОСТЬ** *кому* [PrepP; Invar; subj-compl with copula] **1.** [subj: human] one is or becomes an encumbrance to s.o., s.o.'s burdensome responsibility: X стал Y-у в тягость ≃ **X became** ⟨**was**⟩ **a burden to Y.**

«Спасибо за хлеб-соль, за приют. Спасибо за всё. Я сам вижу, что в тягость тебе, но куда же мне деваться? Все ходы у меня закрыты» (Шолохов 5). "Thanks for your hospitality, for sheltering me. Thanks for everything. I can see I'm a burden to you, but where am I to go? All roads are closed to me" (5a).

2. [subj: abstr] sth. is or becomes unpleasant, burdensome for s.o.: X Y-у в тягость ≃ **X is a burden to Y; X is too much (for Y) to bear.**

Т-256 • **ПУСКА́ТЬСЯ/ПУСТИ́ТЬСЯ ВО ВСЕ ТЯ́ЖКИЕ** ⟨**ВО ВСЯ ТЯ́ЖКАЯ** *obs*⟩ *coll, disapprov* [VP; subj: human; more often pfv] **1.** to begin to behave in a morally reprehensible manner (usu. by starting to drink excessively, womanize etc): X пустился во все тяжкие ≃ **X has plunged into dissipation ⟨into a life of moral abandon⟩; X has become a wastrel ⟨a profligate, a rake etc⟩; X has adopted ⟨taken to⟩ a disgraceful ⟨shameful etc⟩ life style; X has abandoned himself to drinking ⟨debauchery etc⟩.**

2. to resort to any means (occas. unlawful) in order to achieve one's aims: X пустился во все тяжкие ≃ **X went to all lengths; X pulled out all the stops; X went all out; X did whatever it took.**

T-257 • ТЯП ДА ЛЯП; ТЯП-ЛЯП *both coll* [Invar; fixed WO] **1.** [adv] (to do sth.) hastily and carelessly: **slapdash; sloppily; in a slipshod way; any old way; bing, bang, boom.**

Книжные полки никуда не годятся, он их сделал тяп-ляп. These bookshelves are good for nothing, he put them together slapdash.

2. [Interj; often used as predic (impers or with subj: всё)] used as an appraisal of how s.o. does sth. quickly but carelessly and crudely: **(slam) bang—and it's done.**

«Вы хотели ведь написать к домовому хозяину?.. Вот бы теперь и написали». — «Теперь, теперь! Ещё у меня поважнее есть дело. Ты думаешь, что это дрова рубить? Тяп да ляп?» (Гончаров 1). "But you were going to write to the landlord, weren't you, sir?...You ought to write him now, sir." "Now, now! I have much more important business to attend to. You think it's just like chopping wood? Bang—and it's done?" (1a).

У-1 • **ХОТЬ УБЕ́Й(ТЕ)** *coll* [хоть + VP$_{imper}$; these forms only; subord clause] **1.** [used with a negated verb as intensif] one absolutely cannot (understand, believe, carry out etc sth.): **I** ⟨**he** etc⟩ **can't for the life of me** ⟨**him** etc⟩ **(do sth.); I** ⟨**he** etc⟩ **couldn't (do sth.) (even) if my** ⟨**his** etc⟩ **life depended on it; I** ⟨**he** etc⟩ **couldn't (do sth.) (even) if you put a gun to my** ⟨**his** etc⟩ **head; I** ⟨**he** etc⟩ **couldn't (do sth.) to save my** ⟨**his** etc⟩ **life; (I'm) hanged if I know** ⟨**understand** etc⟩; **(I'm) damned if I know.**

Это был день решающего боя за Киев, и сейчас, снова переживая его начало, я опять и опять, хоть убейте меня, не могу понять, почему на этой прекрасной, благословенной земле... возможно такое предельное идиотство, как агрессия, война, фашизм (Кузнецов 1). This was the day of the decisive battle for Kiev; and when I relive its beginning I find again and again that I cannot, for the life of me, understand how such a delightful, joyous world...could harbor such boundless idiocies as aggression, war and fascism (1a). ♦ «А я вот, к примеру, считаюсь будто как украинец и жил на Украине, а языка ихнего [*ungrammat* = их], хоть убей, не понимаю» (Войнович 5). "Now take me, for example; I consider myself a Ukrainian, I lived in the Ukraine, but I couldn't speak their language if you put a gun to my head" (5a). ♦ [Городничий:] Ну кто первый выпустил, что он ревизор? Отвечайте. [Артемий Филиппович:] Уж как это случилось, хоть убей, не могу объяснить (Гоголь 4). [Mayor:] Who was it that first spread the rumor that he was the Government Inspector? Answer!... [A.F.:] Damned if I know how it happened (4c).

2. (used to express one's categorical refusal to do sth.) under no circumstances (will one do sth.): **I** ⟨**he** etc⟩ **wouldn't (do sth.) (even) if my** ⟨**his** etc⟩ **life depended on it; I'll be damned if I'll (do sth.);** [in limited contexts] **not on your life!**

Он ни за что не уступит — хоть убей, не уступит. He won't give in for anything; even if his life depended on it he wouldn't give in.

3. used as an emphatic assurance of the truth or correctness of a statement: **strike me dead (on the spot) if (I'm lying** ⟨**it's not true** etc⟩**); I swear to God.**

«В тебе есть что-то несимпатичное, поверь мне! Уж ты мне поверь. Но я тебя люблю. Люблю, хоть тут меня убей!» (Булгаков 12). "There's something nasty about you, you know. There is, believe me. But I like you. I like you, strike me dead on the spot if I'm lying" (12a).

У-2 • **КАК УБИ́ТЫЙ** спит, заснул, уснул *coll* [как + AdjP; nom only; adv (intensif)] (one is sleeping) very soundly, (one fell) quickly into a deep sleep: **(one is sleeping) like a log; (one is) dead to the world; (one was** ⟨**went**⟩**) out like a light; (one fell) dead away** ⟨**asleep**⟩**; (one fell) into a dead sleep.**

«Я намёрзлась дорогой — как убитая спала» (Абрамов 1). "I got so frozen coming here, I slept like a log" (1a). ♦ [Саша:] Принесла я тебе стакан, а ты уж лежишь на диване и спишь как убитый (Чехов 4). [S.:] By the time I brought you a glass, you were lying on a sofa, dead to the world (4b). ♦ ...[Митя] серьёзно уже намеревался не спать всю ночь, но, измучившись, присел как-то на одну минутку, чтобы перевести дух, и мгновенно закрыл глаза, затем тотчас же бессознательно протянулся на лавке и заснул как убитый (Достоевский 1). ...[Mitya] seriously intended not to sleep for the rest of the night, but he became exhausted, sat down for a moment to catch his breath, instantly closed his eyes, then unconsciously stretched out on the bench and fell at once into a dead sleep (1a).

У-3 • **УБИ́ТЬ** ⟨**ПОВЕ́СИТЬ**⟩ **МА́ЛО** *кого за что coll, occas. humor* [VP$_{subj}$ with быть∅, usu. pres; these forms only] not even the most severe punishment could make up for what s.o. has done: убить Х-а мало (за Y) ≃ **hanging** ⟨**death**⟩ **is too good for X;** [humor only] **a pox on X!**

«Мамка нехорошая». — «Твою мамку повесить мало», — отозвался ещё не остывший от злости Михаил (Распутин 3). "Mummy's horrid." "Hanging's too good for that Mummy of yours," replied Mikhail, whose anger still had not cooled (3a). ♦ «...Григорий правильно сказал: об таком подлеце будешь думать — так тебя и убить мало! Нашла присуху!» (Шолохов 5). "...Grigory was right. If you go on thinking about that scoundrel, death will be too good for you! A fine boyfriend you've found!" (5a).

У-4 • **УБИ́ТЬСЯ МО́ЖНО!** *highly coll* [Interj; Invar; fixed WO] used to express great delight, admiration etc: **(s.o.** ⟨**sth.**⟩ **is) a real knockout!; (s.o.** ⟨**sth., it**⟩**) will make you flip!; (s.o.** ⟨**sth.**⟩ **is) breathtaking!; you could lose your head over (s.o.** ⟨**sth.**⟩**)!; I'd sell my soul (for sth.)!**

...Когда Ирина Викторовна вошла в прихожую своей квартиры, Нюрок громко на всю квартиру завопила [, увидев её новую причёску]: «Вот это да — убиться можно! Неотразимо!» (Залыгин 1). When Irina Viktorovna came into the hall of her flat Niurok [, seeing her new hairdo,] let out a whoop for the whole flat to hear: "Isn't that superb! Breathtaking! Irresistible!" (1a). ♦ Нюрок говорит о Никандрове: «Какой мужик — убиться можно!» (Залыгин 1). Niurok says about Nikandrov, "What a man! You could lose your head over him!" (1a).

У-5 • **НА УБО́Й** [PrepP; Invar; adv] **1.** посылать, отправлять, гнать *кого* ~ (to send, drive s.o.) to inevitable death: **(send** ⟨**herd**⟩ **s.o.) to slaughter; (send s.o. off** ⟨**put s.o. somewhere** etc⟩**) to be slaughtered** ⟨**killed, butchered**⟩.

«Ваши генералы в Финляндии и в Польше гнали на убой своих солдат, чтобы убедить нас в своей мнимой слабости» (Копелев 1). "Your generals in Finland and Poland herded your men to slaughter so as to convince us of your false weakness" (1a). ♦ Впереди расположения войск Тучкова находилось возвышение. Это возвышение не было занято войсками. Бенигсен громко критиковал эту ошибку, говоря, что было безумно оставить незанятою командующую местностью высоту и поставить войска под нею. Некоторые генералы выражали то же мнение. Один в особенности с воинскою горячностью говорил о том, что их поставили тут на убой (Толстой 6). In front of Tuchkov's troops was an eminence which was not occupied by troops. Bennigsen loudly criticized this mistake, saying that it was madness to leave an elevation that commanded the surrounding country unoccupied and to place troops below it. Several of the generals expressed the same opinion. One in particular declared with martial vehemence that they were put there to be slaughtered (6a).

2. кормить *кого* ~ *coll.* Also: **КАК НА УБО́Й** *coll* (to feed s.o.) large amounts of food (usu. good, varied food; usu. implies that s.o. ends up eating more than he should or would like to): X кормит Y-а (как) на убой ≃ **X stuffs Y to the gills; X feeds Y until Y is ready to burst; X feeds Y heartily.**

У-6 • **НЕ УБУ́ДЕТ** *кого от чего highly coll* [VP; impers; Invar] sth. (or doing sth.) cannot or will not adversely affect s.o.: X-а (от Y-а) не убудет ≃ **Y** ⟨**it**⟩ **won't** ⟨**can't**⟩ **hurt X; Y** ⟨**it**⟩ **won't kill X; Y** ⟨**it**⟩ **won't do X any harm.**

У-7 • **ИДТИ́/ПОЙТИ́ НА У́БЫЛЬ** [VP] **1.** [subj: usu. abstr or noncount concr] to (begin to) decrease, diminish in quantity, volume, intensity etc: X идёт на убыль ≃ **X is beginning to ebb** ⟨**wane, recede, lessen, die down, subside** etc⟩**; X is on the ebb** ⟨**the wane, the decrease** etc⟩**; X is subsiding** ⟨**ebbing** etc⟩**;** ‖ дни идут на убыль ≃ **the days are getting shorter;** ‖ [in refer. to the diminution of the moon after the full moon] луна идёт на убыль ≃ **the moon is waning ⟨on the wane⟩**; ‖ *Neg* X не идёт на убыль ≃ **X shows no signs of subsiding ⟨weakening etc⟩; X is ⟨has proved (to be)⟩ persistent.**

Жара уже пошла на убыль. The heat has already begun to subside. ♦ Так вот, они утверждают, будто у советского народа вера в коммунизм пошла на убыль (Зиновьев 2). "So, they allege that the faith of the Soviet people in communism is on the ebb" (2a). ♦ Эпидемия поноса упорно не шла на убыль (Гинзбург 2). The diarrhea outbreak proved very persistent (2a).

2. [subj: abstr] to enter its final period, approach its finish: X идёт на убыль ≃ **X is coming to an end ⟨a close⟩; X is winding down;** [of a period of time] **it is late (in the day ⟨the season etc⟩);** ‖ [with subj: годы, дни etc; in refer. to s.o.'s old age, approaching death] X-овы дни идут на убыль ≃ **time is ⟨the sands of time are⟩ running out for X; X is not long for this world.**

Меня накормили сыром и мамалыгой, дед дал мне одну из своих палок, и я пустился в путь, хоть день шёл на убыль и солнце стояло над горизонтом на высоте дерева (Искандер 6). After the women had filled me up on cheese and hominy grits and grandfather had provided me with one of his walking sticks, I finally set off, though by now it was already late in the day and the sun was hanging low in the sky, no higher than the treetops (6a).

У-8 • В УБЫ́ТКЕ ⟨В НАКЛА́ДЕ⟩ быть∅, оставаться и т. п. *coll* [PrepP; these forms only; subj-compl with copula (subj: human or collect); often neg) to suffer material loss: X остался в убытке ≃ **X lost out; X lost (out) by it; X came out a loser;** ‖ *Neg* X в убытке не будет ≃ **X will be no loser (in the transaction ⟨the deal etc⟩); X won't lose anything ⟨will lose nothing⟩;** [in limited contexts] **it will be ⟨person Y will make it⟩ worth X's while.**

[Вася:] Я пятьдесят рубликов накину... В убытке не будем-с... (Островский 11). [V.:] I'll raise the price by fifty roubles.... We shan't lose by it (11a). ♦ «Сколько тебе [за водку]?» – сказал зятёк. «Да что, батюшка, двугривенник всего», – отвечала старуха. «...Дай ей полтину, предовольно с неё». – «Маловато, барин», – сказала старуха, однако ж взяла деньги с благодарностью... Она была не в убытке, потому что запросила вчетверо против того, что стоила водка (Гоголь 3). "How much is it [the vodka]?" the brother-in-law asked the old woman. "It's twenty kopeks altogether, sir." "...Give her ten, that'll be plenty." "It's not quite enough, sir," the woman said, but she looked very pleased as she took the money....She was losing nothing because she had asked four times as much as the drinks were worth in the first place (3e). ♦ Ты бы, начальник, помог устроить парня. В накладе не останешься (Зиновьев 1). "You wouldn't try helping us to get him a place, guv'nor? We'd make it worth your while" (1a).

У-9 • В УБЫ́ТОК кому-чему быть∅, торговать, продать что и т. п.; СЕБЕ́ В УБЫ́ТОК *coll* [PrepP; these forms only; adv, subj-compl with copula (subj: abstr or это etc), or nonagreeing modif] (to operate, trade, sell sth. etc) with material loss to s.o., some enterprise, or o.s.: **(run ⟨function, trade etc⟩) at a loss ⟨a deficit⟩; (run) a loss;** [in limited contexts] **(be) in the red.**

Новому совхозу разрешили в первые годы вести хозяйство... в убыток... (Распутин 4). The new sovkhoz [state-owned farm] was permitted to function at a deficit the first few years... (4a).

У-10 • УВЫ́ И АХ! *coll, humor* [Interj; Invar; fixed WO] used to express regret, lamentation: **alas (and alack)!; woe is me!; dear(ie) me!**

«Знаете, Максим Петрович, я вам устрою индивидуальный билет. Один полетите. Значит, на когда?..» – «...Пожалуй, на послезавтра...» – «Увы и ах, на послезавтра у нас рейса аэрофлотовского нету» (Аксёнов 12). "You know,

Maxim, I'll get you an individual ticket. You'll fly alone. So, what date do you want?"..."I guess the day after tomorrow...." "Oh, dearie me, we don't have an Aeroflot flight the day after tomorrow" (12a).

У-11 • ИЗ УГЛА́ В У́ГОЛ ходить, шагать, слоняться и т. п. [PrepP; Invar; adv; usu. used with impfv verbs; fixed WO] (to walk, pace within a room, office etc) to one end and back or in various directions (usu. when a person is pondering sth., has nothing to do etc): **(pace) from corner to corner; (walk ⟨pace⟩) up and down (the room etc); (walk) to and fro (across the room etc); (pace) back and forth; (walk ⟨pace⟩) all around (the room etc).**

Хозяин, мыча от отчаяния, ходил из угла в угол (Аксёнов 6). The master of the house, groaning with despair, was pacing from corner to corner (6a). ♦ Во время обеденного перерыва Штрум не пошёл в столовую, шагал из угла в угол по своему кабинету (Гроссман 2). Instead of going to the canteen at lunchtime, Viktor paced up and down his office (2a). ♦ Ветер то утихал, то с силой бросал дождь на крышу, и, открывая в полусне глаза, я видела отца, который, опустив голову, ходил из угла в угол, время от времени оглядываясь на меня с робким и беспокойным выражением (Каверин 1). The wind now died down, now flung the [rain]drops violently against the roof, and when I opened my eyes, still half asleep, I saw my father, hanging his head, walking to and fro across the room, glancing at me from time to time with a timid, uneasy expression (1a).

У-12 • ИЗ-ЗА УГЛА́ *coll* [PrepP; Invar; adv or nonagreeing postmodif] **1.** ~ напасть *на кого*, нанести удар *кому*, убить *кого* и т. п. (to attack, kill s.o.) treacherously, without giving him a chance to fight back: **(assault ⟨attack etc⟩ s.o.) from behind ⟨without warning⟩; (stab ⟨shoot⟩ s.o.) in the back;** ‖ нападение из-за угла ≃ **attack from behind; sneak attack; ambush.**

А ведь я нашёл всё, чего искал, даже признание со стороны старого, себядовольного [= самодовольного] мира – да рядом с этим утрату всех верований, всех благ, предательство, коварные удары из-за угла... (Герцен 2). And yet I have found all that I sought, even recognition from this old, complacent world – and along with this I found the loss of all my beliefs, all that was precious to me, have met with betrayal, treacherous blows from behind (2a). ♦ «Если вы меня не убьёте, я вас зарежу ночью из-за угла. Нам на земле вдвоём нет места...» (Лермонтов 1). "If you do not kill me, I shall stab you in the back some night. The world is too small to hold both of us..." (1b).

2. ~ делать *что*, действовать (to do sth.) in a dirty, unfair, deceitful manner: **behind s.o.'s back; underhandedly; in an underhanded manner ⟨fashion⟩.**

У-13 • (КАК ⟨БУ́ДТО, СЛО́ВНО, ТО́ЧНО⟩) ИЗ-ЗА УГЛА́ (ПЫ́ЛЬНЫМ) МЕШКО́М ПРИБИ́Т(ЫЙ) ⟨УДА́РЕН(НЫЙ), ТРА́ХНУТЫЙ⟩ *obsoles* [(как etc +) AdjP; subj-compl with copula, subj: human (all variants) or modif (variants with long-form Part); the Part usu. takes the final position] (of a person) eccentric, quirky, a little crazy: X (как) из-за угла мешком ударен ≃ **(it's as if) X has a few screws loose; X is (a little) flaky ⟨weird, nutty etc⟩.**

У-14 • ПО УГЛА́М шептаться, говорить и т. п. *coll* [PrepP; Invar; adv] (to whisper, talk, gossip about s.o. or sth.) secretively, so that no one can hear: **(talk about sth. etc) behind closed doors; (talk ⟨gossip etc⟩) in whispers ⟨in secret⟩.**

На работе ею недовольны, но открыто пока ничего не говорят, лишь шепчутся по углам. They're not happy with her at work, but so far they just talk about it in whispers rather than say it openly.

У-15 • ПОД УГЛО́М (ЗРЕ́НИЯ) *чего, каким* рассматривать *кого-что* lit [PrepP; these forms only; fixed WO] (to regard s.o. or sth.) in a certain way (as specified): **from the viewpoint ⟨the standpoint, the vantage point, the perspective⟩ of; in the light of; from a ⟨the⟩ [AdjP] point of view.**

Своих знакомых она теперь рассматривала лишь под углом их восприимчивости к её утрате... (Набоков 1). Now she regarded all her friends only in the light of their receptivity toward her loss... (1a).

У-16 • СГЛА́ЖИВАТЬ/СГЛА́ДИТЬ (О́СТРЫЕ) УГЛЫ́ [VP; subj: human; often impfv infin with старается, умеет etc; fixed WO] to (try to) reduce the significance or minimize the intensity of differences, disagreements etc between people: X сглаживает острые углы ≃ **X papers over (the) disagreements ⟨(the) differences etc⟩; X smoothes ⟨papers⟩ things over.**

Конфликтов он не любит, всегда старается сглаживать острые углы. He doesn't like conflicts and always tries to smooth things over.

У-17 • УГОВО́Р ДОРО́ЖЕ ДЕ́НЕГ [saying] if you have agreed to do sth. then you must honestly fulfill your obligation (said as a reminder that sth. agreed upon must be done): ≃ **a promise is a promise; a deal is a deal; a bargain is a bargain.**

У-18 • НА ВСЕХ НЕ УГОДИ́ШЬ [saying] it is impossible to satisfy everyone by your behavior or actions: ≃ **you can't please everyone ⟨everybody⟩; you can't be all things to all people.**

[author's usage] «...Казаки, что же, вообще, довольны жизнью?» — «Кто доволен, а кто и нет. На всякого не угодишь» (Шолохов 2). "Are the Cossacks, in general, satisfied with life?" "Some are, some aren't. You can't please everybody" (2a).

У-19 • ДА́МСКИЙ ⟨ЖЕ́НСКИЙ⟩ УГО́ДНИК *humor or iron* [NP; fixed WO] a man who likes to pursue and romance women: **ladies' man; womanizer; skirt chaser.**

У-20 • ГДЕ ⟨КУДА́⟩ УГО́ДНО [AdvP; these forms only; adv; fixed WO] **1.** ~ *(кому)* at or to any place one desires or chooses: **wherever ⟨anywhere⟩ you ⟨they etc⟩ like ⟨please, want, wish etc⟩.**

Когда сидишь в битком набитом театре в духоте, приятно сознавать, что над одной из дверей... горят буквы: «Запасный выход». В любую минуту можешь встать с кресла и направиться к этим буквам. И выйти на улицу, на воздух, и, пользуясь тем, что вечер лишь начинается, отправиться куда угодно – в ресторан, к приятелю (Трифонов 5). When you sit in a packed, stuffy theater, it is pleasant to see the brightly illuminated emergency exit sign above one of the doorways. At any time, you can get up from your seat and head for this sign. You can step outside into the fresh air and, taking advantage of the fact that the evening is just beginning, you can go wherever you please – to a restaurant or to visit a friend (5a). ♦ Ноздрёв во многих отношениях был многосторонний человек... В ту же минуту он предлагал вам ехать куда угодно, хоть на край света, войти в какое хотите предприятие, менять всё, что ни есть, на всё, что хотите (Гоголь 3). Nozdryov was a man of great versatility in many ways....In the same breath he would offer to go with you anywhere you liked, even to the ends of the earth, to become your partner in any enterprise you might choose, to exchange anything in the world for anything you like (3a).

2. at or to any location (used to emphasize limitless possibilities): **anywhere; anyplace.**

Он перебирал в уме все места, где мог бы быть Трофимович, но тот мог быть где угодно... (Войнович 2). He mentally reviewed all the places Trofimovich could possibly be, but he could be anywhere... (2a).

У-21 • Е́СЛИ ⟨КО́ЛИ obs⟩ УГО́ДНО [these forms only; sent adv (parenth); fixed WO] it could be said: **if you will ⟨wish⟩; perhaps; s.o. ⟨sth.⟩ may (be...).**

«В этом я вижу начало той традиции, которую можно было бы назвать, если угодно, „социалистическим реализмом", если бы в этот термин чаще всего не укутывали нечто противоположное...» (Гладков 1). "I see here the beginning of the tradition which might, if you wish, be called 'Socialist Realism'—if it were not that this phrase now so often masks quite the reverse..." (1a).
♦ Он, если угодно, фат и пустозвон, но умеет произвести впечатление на женщин. He may be a fop and a windbag, but he knows how to impress women.

У-22 • КАК УГО́ДНО [AdvP; Invar; adv; fixed WO] **1.** ~ *(кому)* in whatever manner one desires or chooses: **as ⟨any way, (in) whatever way⟩ you ⟨they etc⟩ like ⟨please, want, wish etc⟩;** [in limited contexts] **as ⟨any way etc⟩ you ⟨they etc⟩ think ⟨see⟩ fit; whatever you ⟨they etc⟩ say; suit yourself ⟨-selves⟩.**

С побочным писателем можно обращаться как угодно. Его можно печатать, можно не печатать, можно хвалить, можно ругать, можно и вовсе не замечать... (Войнович 1). Those in power can deal with these "marginal writers" as they please. They can publish them or not, praise or curse them, pay them no notice... (1a). ♦ [Негина:] Нет, Пётр Егорыч, я поеду. В самом деле, отказываться нехорошо. [Мелузов:] Как вам угодно; это ваше дело (Островский 11). [N.:] No, Pyotr Yegorych, I'm going to go. Indeed, it would be wrong to refuse. [M.:] As you wish; it's your business (11a). ♦ На встревоженные запросы издателя [Фельтринелли] Б.Л. [Пастернак] сначала ответил телеграммой, что тот может поступать, как ему угодно, а потом, после оказанного на него давления, что он просит подождать (Гладков 1). To [the publisher] Feltrinelli's anxious enquiries Pasternak first replied with a telegram telling him to proceed as he thought fit, but later, after pressure had been put on him, he cabled again asking Feltrinelli to wait (1a). ♦ «Фельдмаршал мой, кажется, говорит дело. Как ты думаешь?» Насмешка Пугачёва возвратила мне бодрость. Я спокойно отвечал, что я нахожусь в его власти и что он волен поступать со мною, как ему будет угодно (Пушкин 2). "My field marshal, it seems to me, is talking sense. What do you think?" Pugachev's taunting manner restored my courage. I answered calmly that I was in his power and he was free to deal with me in whatever way he thought fit (2a). ♦ «Я еду в санаторий...» Виктор посмотрел на часы. «Не рано ли?» — сказал он. «Как угодно. Только имейте в виду, с сегодняшнего дня автобус отменили. За нерентабельностью» (Стругацкие 1). "I'm going to the health resort..." Victor looked at his watch. "Isn't it early?" he said. "Suit yourself. Only keep in mind that starting today the bus service has been canceled. It wasn't profitable" (1a). ♦ «Я должен был дать вам совет, а там — как вам угодно» (Шолохов 5). [context transl] "My duty was to advise you, but it's up to you whether you take it" (5a).

2. in any way (used to emphasize that it is inconsequential how): **however; any which way; it doesn't matter how.**

«Книги расставить в определённом порядке?» — «Нет, их можно расставить как угодно». "Should I put these books in any particular order?" "No, you can put them however."

У-23 • КАКО́Й УГО́ДНО [AdjP; modif; fixed WO] **1.** whatever kind one desires or chooses: **any one ⟨whichever⟩ you ⟨they etc⟩ like ⟨please, want etc⟩; any [NP] you ⟨they etc⟩ like ⟨please, want etc⟩; whichever suits your ⟨his etc⟩ fancy.**

2. any thing or kind of thing without specification or identification (used to emphasize the limitless scope covered by the statement in question): **any (one); any [NP] (whatsoever).**

...Виконт готов был стать на сторону какого угодно убеждения или догмата, если имел в виду, что за это ему перепадёт лишний четвертак (Салтыков-Щедрин 1). ...The Vicomte was ready to defend any conviction or dogma whatsoever if he thought it might bring him an extra twenty-five kopecks (1a).

У-24 • **КОГДА́ УГО́ДНО** [AdvP; Invar; adv; fixed WO] **1.** ~ *(кому)* (one can do sth.) at whatever time one likes: **whenever ⟨anytime⟩ you ⟨they etc⟩ like ⟨please, want etc⟩.**

[Негина:] Какие у вас лошади! Вот бы прокатиться как-нибудь. [Великатов:] Когда вам угодно, прикажите только (Островский 11). [N.:] What horses you have! If one could only drive behind them just once! [V.:] Whenever you like. You have only to command (11a). ♦ ...Судебный пристав доложил тогда председателю, что, по внезапному нездоровью или какому-то припадку, свидетель не может явиться сейчас, но только что оправится, то когда угодно готов будет дать своё показание (Достоевский 2). ...The marshal had reported to the presiding judge that, owing to sudden illness or an attack of some kind, the witness could not appear at the moment, but that as soon as he felt better he would be ready to give his testimony whenever they wanted (2a).

2. (sth. could happen) at any given moment: **anytime; at any time.**

Стихийное бедствие может произойти когда угодно. An act of God can happen at any time.

У-25 • **КТО УГО́ДНО** [NP; subj or obj; fixed WO] **1.** any person one desires or chooses: **anyone ⟨whomever⟩ you ⟨they etc⟩ like ⟨please, want, wish etc⟩.**

[Бакин:] По крайней мере, я сделал открытие, которым могу поделиться... [Мелузов:] С кем угодно (Островский 11). [B.:] At least I've made a discovery which I can pass on. [M.:] To who[m]ever you like (11a).

2. any person or people at all (used to emphasize that it is inconsequential who): **anyone ⟨anybody⟩ at all; absolutely anyone ⟨anybody⟩; anyone ⟨anybody⟩ (, it doesn't matter who).**

У-26 • **НЕ УГО́ДНО ЛИ** *кому* [VP; impers predic with бытьₒ; pres or fut; used with infin] **1.** *old-fash* [used as formula phrase] used when making a polite invitation or suggestion to do sth.: **would ⟨wouldn't⟩ you like (to do sth.)?**

Не угодно ли вам пройти в гостиную? Там прохладнее. Wouldn't you like to move into the living room? It's cooler there.

2. used when making an ironically polite request that s.o. do sth.: **would you be so kind ⟨good⟩ as (to do sth.)?; would you be good enough (to do sth.)?**

Не угодно ли вам избавить меня от своего присутствия? Would you be so kind as to relieve me of your presence?

У-27 • **СКО́ЛЬКО УГО́ДНО** [AdvP; Invar; fixed WO] **1.** *(кому)* [adv] as much, as many, or as long as one desires or chooses: **as much ⟨many, long⟩ as you ⟨they etc⟩ like ⟨please, want etc⟩; all you ⟨they etc⟩ like ⟨please, want etc⟩.**

[Негина:] Значит, молодых можно обижать сколько угодно, и они должны молчать (Островский 11). [N.:] But *you* can insult young people as much as you like, and *they* have to keep quiet! (11a). ♦ [Грекова:] Вы можете жить у меня сколько угодно... (Чехов 1). [G.:] You can stay at my house as long as you please (1a). ♦ «Ты, — сказал я себе, — можешь сколько угодно притворяться своим среди этих людей... но если ты не научишься говорить на их языке, они тебе до конца никогда не поверят» (Войнович 4). "You, I said to myself, can pretend to be one of them all you want...but if you don't learn to speak their language, they will never trust you completely" (4a).

2. ~ *(кого-чего)* [adv (quantif) or quantit subj-compl with copula (subj/gen: any common noun)] an unspecified large amount or number: **any number of; countless; [in limited contexts] all you could ever want.**

Сколько угодно можно было слушать об этом рассказы, читать мемуары — и нельзя было себе этого представить... (Солженицын 3). One could listen to any number of tales and read countless memoirs about it, but one could never imagine it... (3a). ♦ Он [Пастернак] жалуется, что последние дни не работается...

«Я знаю, что дело не в помехах, на которые я всё сваливаю, а во мне самом. Помех всегда оказывается в нашем распоряжении сколько угодно, когда работать не хочется» (Гладков 1). He [Pasternak] complained about not having been able to work the last few days....I know...that it's nothing to do with all the hindrances I blame it on, but that it's my own fault. You will always find any number of things to get in the way when you don't *want* to work" (1a).

3. *coll* [indep. remark] (used in response to a request) certainly: **of course; by all means; you bet; sure(ly); I sure will ⟨you sure can etc⟩.**

«Ты можешь мне помочь?» — «Сколько угодно!» "Could you give me a hand?" "You bet!"

У-28 • **ЧТО УГО́ДНО** [NP; subj or obj; fixed WO] **1.** ~ *(кому)* any thing (phenomenon etc) that s.o. desires or chooses: **anything ⟨whatever, any one⟩ you ⟨they etc⟩ like ⟨please, want, wish etc⟩.**

Почему он просил четвёртую комнату? На каком основании? Просить можно что угодно, я тоже могу попросить четыре комнаты, но мне же их никто не даст (Войнович 3). Why did he request a fourth room? On what basis? You can request anything you like. I, too, could request four rooms, but no one would give them to me (3a). ♦ «Государь! — сказал он. — Вы властны требовать от меня что вам угодно...» (Пушкин 2). "Your Majesty," he said, "you're free to demand of me whatever you wish..." (2a).

2. any thing (phenomenon, occurrence etc) whatever (used to emphasize limitless possibilities): **anything at all; anything whatsoever.**

От такого человека, подумали они, можно ожидать что угодно (Лимонов 1). A man like that, they thought, might do anything at all (1a).

У-29 • **В УГО́ДУ** *кому-чему* [PrepP; Invar; the resulting PrepP is adv] (to do sth.) out of a desire to satisfy s.o., gain s.o.'s favor, or in order to further sth.: **(just ⟨in order⟩) to please ⟨oblige⟩ s.o.; for the benefit of sth.; in the interest(s) of sth.**

Может быть, некоторые читатели назовут всё это невероятным, автор тоже в угоду им готов бы назвать всё это невероятным... (Гоголь 3). Perhaps some readers will call this incredible—the author too would be glad to call all this incredible just to please them... (3c). ♦ Он уже готов был нахамить Бланку в угоду Митишатьеву — но что-то не пускало: кровь не давала... (Битов 2). By now he felt ready to be rude to Blank, in order to please Mitishatyev—but something held him back. His blood would not let him... (2a). ♦ Противники коммунизма рассматривают коллективизацию в Советском Союзе просто как насилие и зверство в угоду некоей идеологической или политической идее... (Зиновьев 2). The enemies of communism regard collectivisation in the Soviet Union merely as violence and an atrocity committed for the benefit of some ideological or political idea... (2a).

У-30 • **КРА́СНЫЙ У́ГОЛ** [NP; fixed WO] a place in a peasant hut where icons are hung and a table is placed for honored guests: **icon corner; sacred corner; place of honor.**

«Парамошин, конечно, демагог, крикун... но и ты тоже хорош. К тебе всякий народ ходит, а у тебя в красном углу церковный парад. Так ведь и билет положить недолго!.. По твоей милости и мне... намылят шею...» (Максимов 3). "Paramoshin is a demagogue and a loudmouth, of course. But you're not one to talk—all sorts of people come to your house, and you've got a religious display in the place of honor. That way you'll be handing your party card in before you know where you are....And thanks to you I shall get it in the neck, too" (3a).

У-31 • **МЕДВЕ́ЖИЙ ⟨ГЛУХО́Й⟩ У́ГОЛ** *coll* [NP; fixed WO] a remote, out-of-the-way, and usu. undesirable place: **the boondocks; the sticks; godforsaken place ⟨hole⟩; provincial hole.**

Начальник Ягоднинского райотдела КГБ, пространствовавший всю жизнь по медвежьим углам, сказал мне: «Чем хороша Колыма – в каждом районе есть музыкальные школы!» (Амальрик 1). The chief of the KGB's local department [in Yagodnoye], who had spent his whole life in one godforsaken hole after another, told me: "The great thing about Kolyma is that there are music schools in every [district]" (1a).

У-32 • ЗАГОНЯ́ТЬ/ЗАГНА́ТЬ ⟨ПРИПИРА́ТЬ/ПРИ-ПЕРЕ́ТЬ, ПРИЖИМА́ТЬ/ПРИЖА́ТЬ⟩ В У́ГОЛ *кого coll* [VP; subj: human] by using conclusive arguments or irrefutable facts, to make it impossible for s.o. to deny sth., defend his own position etc: X припёр Y-а в угол ≃ **X drove ⟨forced, backed⟩ Y into a corner.**

…Увольнять Олёну за то, что муж её загнал их в угол, а они ни черта толком не могли возразить ему, – нет, с этим он не согласен (Абрамов 1). …To fire her [Olyona] just because her husband had driven them into a corner and they had not been able to do a damn thing to get back – no, that he could not agree to (1a).

У-33 • СВОЙ ⟨СО́БСТВЕННЫЙ⟩ У́ГОЛ *coll* [NP; sing only; often obj of иметь] one's own living space: **one's own place; a place of one's own; a place one can call one's own.**

«Будем снимать [квартиру]… И запишемся в кооператив». – «Это дорого!» – «Ну и что? Продадим машину… Главное, свой угол… Свой угол», – повторил он упрямо, угрюмо (Ерофеев 3). "We'll rent a place….And sign up for a co-op." "That's expensive!" "So what! We'll sell the car….The main thing is to have our own place…our own place," he repeated stubbornly, morosely (3a). ♦ [Анна Романовна:] Возьмите нас, старых работников культуры, я своего угла не завела за всю жизнь! (Рощин 2). [A.R.:] Take us old members of the Culture Brigade. All my life I never had a place of my own! (2a).

У-34 • У́ГОЛ ЗРЕ́НИЯ *lit* [NP; sing only; fixed WO] a way of regarding a phenomenon, occurrence etc: **point of view; viewpoint; standpoint; vantage point; perspective.**

Ему не приходило в голову, что мой внелитературный жизненный опыт может выдвинуть свежий угол зрения (Солженицын 2). It never occurred to him that my experience of life outside literature might provide a fresh viewpoint (2a). ♦ Время от времени он выискивал новый угол зрения, под которым можно было рассматривать проблему разведения козлотуров… (Искандер 6). …From time to time [he] would discover a new vantage point from which to view the problems of goatibex breeding (6a).

У-35 • КРА́СНЫЙ УГОЛО́К [NP; usu. sing; fixed WO] a room in an institution, dormitory, hotel etc that can be used for various activities – reading, small meetings, instruction etc: **activity room; reading ⟨information, conference, study⟩ room; day room; reading and recreation room.**

Там тебе, на лесопункте, и красный уголок, и столовка, и ларёк – всё, что надо (Абрамов 1). At their logging station they have a recreation and reading room and a canteen and a little store – everything they need (1a).

< The name «красный уголок» is a takeoff on «красный угол» (see У-30), with «красный» in this case meaning "related to a revolution or a socialist regime." Originally used by the Communist Party as a site for Communist agitation, Party functions, and the dispersal of propaganda, the room was later put to more general use, but it long retained certain Party-related features, such as a ready supply of Communist literature.

У-36 • КАК НА (ГОРЯ́ЧИХ) У́ГОЛЬЯХ ⟨У́ГЛЯХ⟩ сидеть, быть∅, чувствовать себя *coll* [как + PrepP; these forms only; adv or subj-compl with copula (subj: human)] (to be) in a state of extreme agitation, uneasiness, or anxiety: X был как

на (горячих) угольях ≃ **X was like a cat on hot bricks; X was on tenterhooks; X was on pins and needles; X was (as) nervous as a cat ⟨a kitten⟩.**

Он в течение всего спора сидел как на угольях и только украдкой болезненно взглядывал на Аркадия (Тургенев 2). He had been sitting on tenterhooks all through the dispute, now and again stealing pained glances at Arkady (2a).

У-37 • КАК УГОРЕ́ЛЫЙ бежать, бегать, метаться, носиться и т. п. *coll* [как + AdjP; nom only; adv (intensif)] (to) run) very fast, not paying attention to anything around one, or (to move about) hurriedly, frantically: **(run ⟨race etc⟩) like one possessed ⟨like a madman, like a madwoman⟩; (run etc) as if one's tail were on fire; (run around ⟨bustle about etc⟩) like mad ⟨like crazy, like a chicken with its head cut off⟩.**

Дуняша бегала взад и вперёд как угорелая и то и дело хлопала дверями… (Тургенев 2). Dunyasha ran hither and thither like one possessed and kept banging the doors… (2e). ♦ [Тишка:] …У нас то туда, то сюда, целый день шаркай по мостовой как угорелый (Островский 10). [T.:] …Around this place, it's go there, come here, and you spend the whole day scraping from street to street, like a madman (10a). ♦ «Ах господи! Да что же это я толькусь туда и сюда, как угорелая…» (Достоевский 3). "Oh, Lord! Why am I dashing around like a madwoman?…" (3b). ♦ «…Я сначала войду, высмотрю обстановку и потом, когда надо будет, свистну: „Иси Перезвон!" – и вы увидите, он тотчас же влетит как угорелый» (Достоевский 1). "I'll go in first, check out the situation, and then at the right moment I'll whistle: *Ici, Perezvon!* And you'll see, he'll come rushing in like mad" (1a). ♦ «Третий день уже носимся по деревням как угорелые» (Ильф и Петров 2). "For three days we've been chasing around the villages like crazy" (2a).

У-38 • УГРЫЗЕ́НИЕ ⟨УКО́Р⟩ СО́ВЕСТИ [NP; more often pl (1st var.); fixed WO] bitter regret for having done wrong, an uneasy feeling of repentance: **pang(s) ⟨twinge(s)⟩ of conscience; (stings of) remorse; (be) conscience-stricken.**

…Сказали: из колхозной бывшей земли бери сколько можешь обработать – обрабатывай. И Спиридон взял, и стал пахать её и засевать без всяких угрызений совести… (Солженицын 3). …He was told to take as much of the former collective farm land as he could work. Spiridon took it and began to plow and sow with not a pang of conscience… (3a). ♦ Он испытывал некоторые угрызения совести за проданного заведующего, но утешал себя тем, что этот заведующий в последнее время так много пил и так неосторожно вёл себя, что рано или поздно сел бы сам и их мог потащить за собой (Искандер 4). He felt some remorse over betraying the manager but consoled himself with the thought that the manager had been drinking so much lately, and behaving so incautiously, that he would have landed in jail anyway sooner or later, and might have taken them all with him (4a).

У-39 • СТА́ВИТЬ/ПОСТА́ВИТЬ ПОД УДА́Р *кого-что* [VP; subj: human or abstr] to put s.o. or sth. in a dangerous position: X поставил Y-а под удар ≃ **X put Y in danger ⟨in jeopardy, at risk⟩; X endangered ⟨jeopardized⟩ Y; [in limited contexts] X left Y open to attack.**

Поняли ли оксфордцы, под какой удар они поставили Зощенко? На него обрушилась вторая волна травли, и он уж больше никогда не поднял головы (Мандельштам 2). Did those Oxford students ever realize what danger they put Zoshchenko in? He was subjected to a second wave of persecution from which he never recovered (2a). ♦ «Сталинская эпоха поставила под удар основы конституции, братство народов, социалистическую законность» (Орлова 1). "The foundations of the Constitution, the fraternity of nations, and socialist legality were put in jeopardy by the Stalinist era" (1a). ♦ Сейчас я легко мог бы найти сто и двести честных писателей и отправить им письма. Но они, как правило, не занимали в СП [Союзе писателей] никаких ведущих постов. Выделив их не по признаку служебному, а душевному, я поставил бы их под удар... (Солженицын 2). It would have been easy for me now to find one hundred or two hundred honest writers and send them letters. But such people did not as a rule occupy the higher posts in the Writers' Union. If I had let myself be guided in my selection by character and not by rank, I would have put them at risk... (2a). ♦ ...Однажды возникла ситуация, когда Лёвина репутация заставляла его поступить... совершенно невыгодным, более того, ставящим всё под удар образом (Битов 2). ...One time a situation arose in which Lyova's reputation forced him to act in a way that was...absolutely disadvantageous, and moreover jeopardized everything (2a). ♦ Громадный воз чепухи въехал во французскую литературу... Кроме того, последовательницы Мадлены Скюдери окончательно засорили язык и даже поставили под удар и самое правописание (Булгаков 5). [context transl] A wagonload of nonsense had invaded French literature.... In addition, the admirers of Madeleine de Scudéry had utterly corrupted the language and even threatened to subvert the orthography (5a).

У-40 • УДА́Р ХВАТИ́Л *кого coll* [VP$_{subj}$] s.o. suddenly became paralyzed or died as the result of an apoplectic stroke: X-а удар хватил ≃ **X had a seizure ⟨a stroke⟩; X dropped dead from a stroke ⟨from apoplexy⟩.**

Я не знаю, жив ли остался священник, по лицу которого катились слёзы. У него был такой вид, что вот-вот его хватит удар (Мандельштам 2). I do not know whether the priest with tears running down his cheeks survived: he looked as though he would have a stroke any moment (2a).

У-41 • В УДА́РЕ [PrepP; Invar] **1.** [subj-compl with copula (subj: human)] one is in an inspired state that makes what he is doing turn out well: X в ударе ≃ **X is in good ⟨top, great, excellent etc⟩ form; X is at his best;** ‖ *Neg* сегодня X не в ударе ≃ **this isn't X's day.**

Четырежды грек менял кости, но ничего не помогало, они ложились так, как хотел скотопромышленник. Он был в ударе и каждый раз из дюжины возможных комбинаций почти безошибочно выбирал наиболее надёжную для продолжения партии (Искандер 3). Four times the Greek changed the dice, but nothing helped; they fell the way the cattle dealer wanted. He was in good form, and every time, from a dozen possible combinations, he almost unerringly chose the one that would keep his game going best (3a).

2. *obs* [subj-compl with быть$_\emptyset$ (subj: human); used with the infin of another verb] one is inclined (to do sth.), is well disposed (toward doing sth.): X в ударе (делать Y) ≃ **X is in the mood (to do Y); X is of a mind (to do Y); X feels like (doing Y).**

У-42 • ПОД УДА́РОМ [PrepP; Invar; subj-compl with copula] **1.** *mil* [subj: collect or a geographical name] some military unit (town etc) is in a vulnerable, undefended position: X оказался под ударом ≃ **X was (left) open to attack; X was exposed to attack ⟨to the enemy⟩.**

2. [subj: human or collect] one is in a precarious, insecure position: X под ударом ≃ **X is in danger ⟨in jeopardy⟩.**

Когда началась реорганизация института, стало ясно, что наш отдел под ударом. When they started reorganizing the institute it became clear that our division was in jeopardy.

У-43 • БЕЗ (ВСЯ́КОГО) У́ДЕРЖУ *coll* [PrepP; these forms only; adv] **1.** (of a person) (to do sth.) immoderately, without restricting o.s.: **uncontrollably; unrestrainedly; with abandon; without (any) restraint; wildly.**

Что касается здешнего председателя, то он, хотя тоже пьёт без всякого удержу, однако, на что-то ещё надеется (Войнович 2). As for their own chairman, well, he too drank uncontrollably but wasn't what you'd call a hopeless case yet (2a). ♦ Главное то, что у меня объявился свой капитал, а потому и пустился я жить в

своё удовольствие, со всем юным стремлением, без удержу, поплыл на всех парусах (Достоевский 1). The chief thing was that I had come into my own money, and with that I threw myself into a life of pleasure, with all the impetuousness of youth, without restraint, under full sail (1a).

2. (of some phenomenon, occurrence etc) (to go on) unceasingly, uninterruptedly, and in such a manner as cannot be contained: **without (a) letup; without stopping; unstoppably.**

Дождь хлещет без удержу уже два дня. It's been pouring without letup for two days already.

У-44 • НЕ ЗНАТЬ (НИКАКО́ГО) У́ДЕРЖУ *(в чём) coll* [VP; subj: human] to show immoderation (in sth.), not control o.s.: X не знает удержу ≃ **X knows no restraint ⟨bounds⟩; X is unrestrained; X goes overboard;** [in limited contexts] **X's desires are ⟨ambition is etc⟩ beyond restraint.**

«Если частное предпринимательство не зажать в железные клещи, то из него вырастают люди-звери, люди биржи, которые знать не хотят удержу в желаниях и в жадности» (Солженицын 10). "If private enterprise isn't held in an iron grip it gives birth to people who are no better than beasts, those stock-exchange people with greedy appetites completely beyond restraint" (10a). ♦ Однажды в Ташкенте она [Ахматова] мне призналась, что в молодости была очень трудной — раздражительной, капризной... не знала удержу, спешила жить и ни с чем не считалась (Мандельштам 2). She [Akhmatova] once confided to me in Tashkent that as a girl she had been quick-tempered, moody, and quite unrestrained, stopping at nothing in her impatience to make the most of life (2a).

У-45 • НЕТ (НИКАКО́ГО) У́ДЕРЖУ *кому, на кого coll* [VP; impers] it is impossible to restrain s.o. in sth.: нет X-у удержу ≃ **there is no holding X back; there is no stopping X; no restraints exist for X;** ‖ [of people fighting] нет (X-у и Y-у) удержу ≃ **there's no pulling X and Y apart.**

Он вдруг ощутил в себе тот восхищающий душу подъём, который всегда предвещал для него риск, дело, власть. В подобные минуты для него не существовало препятствий и не было удержу (Максимов 1). He suddenly sensed within him that elation, that exaltation which always heralded risk, action, power. At such moments no obstacles or restraints existed for him (1a). ♦ «Ну, мыслимое ли это дело: русские, православные люди сцепились между собой, и удержу нету» (Шолохов 5). "Ay, it's beyond me! Russians, true Christians, going for each other like this and there's no pulling you apart" (5a).

У-46 • ЗАКУ́СЫВАТЬ/ЗАКУСИ́ТЬ УДИЛА́ [VP; subj: human] being irritated or agitated, to act rashly, imprudently, without restraint or common sense: X закусил удила ≃ **X took the bit between ⟨in⟩ his teeth.**

«Можно с вами идти?» — спросил он. «Конечно, — не мне с вами опасно, а вам со мной. Но Лондон велик...» — «Я не боюсь, — и тут вдруг, закусивши удила, он быстро проговорил: — Я никогда не возвращусь в Россию...» (Герцен 3). "May I walk with you?" he asked. "Of course; there is no danger for me in being seen with you, though there is for you in being seen with me. But London is a big place." "I am not afraid"—and then all at once, taking the bit between his teeth, he hurriedly burst out: "I shall never go back to Russia..." (3a).

У-47 • В СВОЁ УДОВО́ЛЬСТВИЕ *coll* [PrepP; Invar; adv; fixed WO] **1.** жить ~ (to live) joyfully, lightheartedly, without worries: X живёт ~ ≃ **X lives and enjoys himself; X lives happily; X enjoys (his) life;** [in limited contexts] **X lives a life of pleasure.**

[Костылёв:] Зачем тебя давить? Кому от этого польза? ...Живи знай в своё удовольствие... (Горький 3). [K.:] Why should I hang you? What good would it do anybody?...Live and enjoy yourself!... (3f). ♦ Главное то, что у меня объявился свой капитал, а потому и пустился я жить в своё удовольствие, со всем юным стремлением, без удержу, поплыл на всех парусах (Достоевский 1). The chief thing was that I had come into my own money, and with that I threw myself into a life of pleasure, with all the impetuousness of youth, without restraint, under full sail (1a).

2. (to do sth.) to one's complete satisfaction, to whatever extent one desires: **to one's heart's content; as much ⟨as long⟩ as one pleases ⟨likes, wants etc⟩.**

Меньшевичка Люся Оганджанян уже бывала здесь. И она снова и снова, как Шехерезада, повторяет волшебную сказку о свердловском санпропускнике. Какой он чистый, большой, просторный. Ничем не хуже Сандуновских бань. В раздевалке — огромное зеркало. Мочалки всем выдают. Можно помыться в своё удовольствие (Гинзбург 1). The Menshevik Lucia Oganjanian, who had been there more than once in her time, told us nightly tales, as in the *Arabian Nights*, of the magical delights of the large, clean, spacious disinfection center in Sverdlovsk, just like the famous public baths in Moscow. There was a huge mirror in the changing room, everybody got a wash-cloth, one could wash to one's heart's content... (1b).

У-48 • УДОВО́ЛЬСТВИЕ НИ́ЖЕ СРЕ́ДНЕГО *coll* [NP; sing only; usu. subj-compl with copula (subj: usu. abstr or infin); usu. this WO] an unpleasant experience: **not what I ⟨you⟩ would call fun; no fun; not my ⟨our⟩ idea of a good time; no barrel of laughs.**

Они такие неряхи! Убирать за ними — удовольствие ниже среднего. They're such slobs! Picking up after them is not what you'd call fun.

У-49 • СМА́ТЫВАТЬ/СМОТА́ТЬ У́ДОЧКИ *highly coll* [VP; subj: human] to depart, withdraw, retreat hurriedly (usu. in order to avoid trouble, danger, or when fleeing from an enemy): X сматывает удочки ≃ **X takes off; X takes to his heels; X hightails it (out of here ⟨out of there etc⟩); X beats it; [in limited contexts] X vamooses; ‖ X-у надо сматывать удочки ≃ X has to ⟨should⟩ get out of here ⟨there⟩.**

Уже поздно, мне пора сматывать удочки, а то дома будет скандал. It's already late. I'd better take off or I'll catch hell when I get home.

У-50 • ЗАКИ́ДЫВАТЬ/ЗАКИ́НУТЬ ⟨ЗАБРА́СЫ-ВАТЬ/ЗАБРО́СИТЬ⟩ У́ДОЧКУ *coll* [VP; subj: human] to say or ask sth. indirectly with the purpose of finding out some information: X закинул удочку ≃ **X dropped a hint; X put out a feeler ⟨feelers⟩; X tested the waters.**

...Сейчас не время доказывать свою правоту. Сейчас ей оставалось одно — попытаться извлечь из сложившихся обстоятельств хотя бы маленькую пользу для своих колхозников. И она издалека стала закидывать удочку: «Холод в воде-то бродить. У людей обутки [regional = обуви] нету» (Абрамов 1). [context transl] ...Now was not the time for her to make her point. The only thing she could do now was to try to use the situation to gain some benefit, however small, for her *kolkhozniki*. And she began by casting her line from afar. "Wading around in the water is cold work. My people have no shoes" (1a).

У-51 • ПОЙМА́ТЬ ⟨ПОДДЕ́ТЬ, ПОДЦЕПИ́ТЬ⟩ НА У́ДОЧКУ ⟨УДУ́ *obs*⟩ кого *coll* [VP; subj: human] to outwit, delude s.o. using a cunning ruse: X поймал Y-а на удочку ≃ **X duped ⟨tricked, hoodwinked, conned etc⟩ Y; X got Y on the hook; [in refer. to getting s.o. to marry one] X hooked ⟨snagged, snared⟩ Y.**

[author's usage] [Городничий:] Тридцать лет живу на службе; ни один купец, ни подрядчик не мог провести; мошенников над мошенниками обманывал, пройдох и плутов таких, что весь свет готовы обворовать, поддевал на уду...

(Гоголь 4). [Mayor:] Thirty years I've been in the service; never a merchant, never a contractor that I couldn't get the better of; swindlers upon swindlers and I fooled them, cheats and tricksters out to rob the whole world and I got them on the hook (4b).

У-52 • ПОПАДА́ТЬСЯ/ПОПА́СТЬСЯ ⟨ИДТИ́/ПОЙТИ́, КЛЮ́НУТЬ, ПОЙМА́ТЬСЯ⟩ НА У́ДОЧКУ (кому, к кому) ⟨**НА У́ДОЧКУ** чего, чью⟩ [VP; subj: human] to end up being deceived, duped: X попался на удочку ≃ **X swallowed ⟨took, fell for⟩ the bait; X fell for it; X was hoodwinked ⟨taken in⟩; [in refer. to agreeing to marry s.o.] X got hooked.**

...Он [Липавский] всегда готов был помочь другим — одного подвезти на своей машине, другому достать лекарства... Он был осведомителем того типа, который попадается на удочку по слабости и рад угодить своим жертвам (Амальрик 1). ...He [Lipavsky] was always ready to help others: he would give one person a lift in his car, bring medication to another....He was the kind of informer who takes the bait through weakness and feels guilty toward his victims, so he is glad to do them favors (1a). ♦ «Ну как иной какой-нибудь муж, али юноша вообразит, что он Ликург, али Магомет... — будущий, разумеется, — да и давай устранять к тому все препятствия...» — «Я должен согласиться... что такие случаи действительно должны быть. Глупенькие и тщеславные особенно на эту удочку попадаются; молодёжь в особенности» (Достоевский 3). "Now, what if some man, or youth, imagines himself a Lycurgus or a Muhammad—a future one, to be sure—and goes and starts removing all obstacles to that end...." "I have to agree...that such cases must indeed occur. The vain and silly in particular fall for such bait; young men particularly" (3c). ♦ «А я вам говорю, — кричал старик в ухо великому комбинатору, — что Макдональд на эту удочку не пойдёт! Он не пойдёт на эту удочку!» (Ильф и Петров 2). "But I tell you," the old man shouted into the ear of the great schemer, "MacDonald will not fall for that: He will never fall for that..." (2b).

У-53 • ДАЛЕКО́ НЕ УЕ́ДЕШЬ ⟨НЕ УЙДЁШЬ⟩ на чём, с кем-чем, без кого-чего *coll* [VP; neg pfv fut, gener. 2nd pers sing only; fixed WO] you will not gain, achieve much (from sth., from your dealings with s.o., without s.o., without sth. etc): на X-е ⟨с X-ом, без X-а⟩ далеко не уедешь ≃ **you can't go ⟨get⟩ (very) far with ⟨without⟩ X; thing X doesn't ⟨won't⟩ get you (very) far; X isn't much help; you can't ⟨don't, won't⟩ get very far on thing X.**

В наши дни подружка была сподручнее жены. Подруга разделяет судьбу, а прав у неё нет никаких. Прав мне не нужно было никаких — в любви на «праве» далеко не уедешь (Мандельштам 2). In our times a girl friend was handier than a wife. A girl friend shares a man's life, but has no rights. I did not need any "rights"—in love they are not much help (2a). ♦ [Дорн:] Он мыслит образами, рассказы его красочны, ярки, и я их сильно чувствую. Жаль только, что он не имеет определённых задач. Производит впечатление, и больше ничего, а ведь на одном впечатлении далеко не уедешь (Чехов 6). [D.:] He thinks in images, his stories are vivid, striking, and I am deeply moved by them. It's only a pity that he has no definite purpose. He creates impressions, nothing more, and, of course, you don't get very far on impressions alone (1a).

У-54 • КАК ⟨БУ́ДТО, СЛО́ВНО, ТО́ЧНО⟩ УЖА́ЛЕН-НЫЙ вскочить, броситься, вскрикнуть и т. п. *coll* [как etc + AdjP; nom only; adv] (to jump up, dash out, cry out etc) suddenly, abruptly: **as if ⟨as though⟩ one had been stung ⟨bitten, shot⟩.**

И снова Пата Патарая, вскрикнув, как ужаленный, шмякается на колени, скользит и, раскинув руки, замирает у самых ног товарища Сталина в позе дерзновенной преданности (Искандер 3). Again Pata Pataraya, crying out as if he had been stung, plopped to his knees, slid, and froze with arms outflung in a posture of audacious devotion, at Comrade Stalin's very toes (3a).

У-55 • ДО У́ЖАСА coll [PrepP; Invar; modif or adv (intensif)] very, extremely, to the highest possible degree: **terribly; awfully; dreadfully; frightfully; like you wouldn't believe.**

Я думаю, что Ахматова переоценила его как поэта – ей до ужаса хотелось, чтобы ниточка поэтической традиции не прервалась (Мандельштам 2). I think Akhmatova overestimated him as a poet—she was terribly anxious that the thread of the tradition she represented should not be broken… (2a). ♦ «…Я сам рассеян до ужаса» (Булгаков 9). "I am dreadfully absent-minded myself!" (9a). ♦ «…Действительно, что мне о нём было известно? Да ничего, кроме того, что он был лыс и красноречив до ужаса» (Булгаков 9). "In fact, what did I know about him? Nothing, except that he was bald and frightfully eloquent" (9a).

У-56 • ИЗВИВА́ТЬСЯ УЖО́М coll [VP; subj: human] **1.** ~ *перед кем* to fawn upon s.o., act in a servile manner: X извивается ужом перед Y-ом ≃ **X falls all over Y; X grovels before Y.**

2. Also: **КРУТИ́ТЬСЯ УЖО́М** coll to act in a crafty, sneaky manner, displaying resourcefulness: X извивается ужом ≃ **X weasels around;** ‖ Х-у приходится крутиться ужом ≃ **X has to be cunning ⟨sly, wily⟩; [in limited contexts] X has to live by his wits.**

Когда по радио гремели салюты и голос диктора сообщал о новых победах, лицо Ларичева омрачалось: не его это были победы, не его дело… Его дело – крутиться ужом, исхитряться, добывать, обеспечивать (Грекова 3). When the cannon salutes thundered over the radio and the announcer reported new war victories, Larichev's face darkened: they were not his victories, not his cause. His cause was to weasel around, be cunning, get, obtain (3a).

У-57 • В УЗДЕ́ держать *кого* coll [PrepP; Invar; obj-compl with держать] (to keep s.o.) under strict control: X держит Y-а в узде ≃ **X keeps Y on a tight rein ⟨leash⟩; X keeps a tight rein ⟨leash⟩ on Y; X keeps ⟨holds⟩ Y in check; X keeps Y in line.**

Хитрый и циничный Хрущёв имел… отличный способ держать Королёва «в узде», не применяя к нему грубого насилия, как когда-то сделал Сталин (Владимиров 1). …Khrushchev, crafty and cynical, had an excellent device for keeping Korolyov on a tight rein without having to resort to force as Stalin had done in his day (1a). ♦ Бахметев имел какую-то тень влияния или, по крайней мере, держал моего отца в узде (Герцен 1). Bakhmetev had some shade of influence over my father, or at any rate did keep him in check (1a).

У-58 • ДЕРЖА́ТЬ СЕБЯ́ В УЗДЕ́ coll [VP; subj: human] to refrain from emotional outbursts, control o.s.: X держит себя в узде ≃ **X keeps himself in check; X restrains himself; X keeps a tight rein on himself ⟨his emotions⟩; X keeps a (tight) lid on his emotions.**

Однажды в Ташкенте она [Ахматова] мне призналась, что в молодости была очень трудной – раздражительной, капризной… не знала удержу, спешила жить и ни с чем не считалась. Тогда её слова показались мне неправдоподобными, а она сказала, что просто научилась обуздывать себя. В старости, когда прорвались основные черты характера, я поняла, как трудно было ей держать себя в узде (Мандельштам 2). She [Akhmatova] once confided to me in Tashkent that as a girl she had been quick-tempered, moody, and quite unrestrained, stopping at nothing in her impatience to make the most of life. At the time I found this incredible, even when she explained that she had later learned to control herself. But in her old age, when the basic features of her character broke to the surface again, I could see how hard it was for her to keep herself in check (2a).

У-59 • ГО́РДИЕВ У́ЗЕЛ lit [NP; usu. sing; fixed WO] an extremely complicated problem or great difficulty: **Gordian knot;**

‖ разрубить ⟨рассечь⟩ гордиев узел ≃ **cut (through) the Gordian knot.**

…[Голохвастов] рассказал мне всё дело, прибавив, что именно потому поторопился приехать, чтоб предупредить меня, в чём дело, прежде чем я услышу что-нибудь о размолвке. «Недаром, – сказал я ему шутя, – меня зовут Александром: этот гордиев узел я вам тотчас разрублю» (Герцен 2). …He [Golokhvastov] told me all about it…adding that he had made haste to come to me expressly to warn me what was wrong before I should hear anything of the falling out. "I am not called Alexander for nothing," I said jokingly; "I shall cut this Gordian knot for you at once" (2a).

< From the name of an intricate knot tied by *Gordius*, legendary king of Phrygia, and supposedly cut by Alexander the Great with his sword.

У-60 • ЗАВЯ́ЗЫВАТЬ/ЗАВЯЗА́ТЬ УЗЕЛО́К (НА ПА́МЯТЬ) coll [VP; subj: human] (to try) not to forget sth.: X завяжет (на память) узелок ≃ **X will see that he won't ⟨doesn't⟩ forget it; X will be sure not to forget it; [in limited contexts] X will tie a string around his finger.**

< From the custom of making a knot at the end of a handkerchief so as not to forget something.

У-61 • СВОИ́Х НЕ УЗНА́ЕШЬ coll [VP; subj: human; 2nd and 3rd pers only; fut or subjunctive; fixed WO] you will be punished, beaten (up) severely: **you won't know what hit you; [usu. in refer. to severe beating] your own mother won't recognize you.**

[Трилецкий (в дверях):] Я тебе задам такого доклада, что ты и своих не узнаешь! [Голос Якова:] Барин приказали… [Трилецкий:] Пойди и поцелуйся с своим барином! Он такой же болван, как и ты! (Чехов 1). [T. *in the doorway*:] If you say any more about "announcing" me, you won't know what's hit you. [J. *(off-stage)*:] Master's orders. [T.:] To hell with you and your master, he's as big a fool as you are (1b).

У-62 • У́ЗЫ КРО́ВИ; КРО́ВНЫЕ У́ЗЫ [NP; pl only; fixed WO] a blood relationship: **blood ties ⟨bonds⟩; bonds ⟨the bond⟩ of blood.**

«…Я понял, что дом, где обитаете вы, священ, что ни единое существо, связанное с вами узами крови, не подлежит моему проклятию» (Пушкин 1). "…I understood that the house where you lived was sacred, and that no being related to you by the bond of blood could be subject to my curse" (1a).

У-63 • НЕ УЙДЁТ (*от кого*) coll [VP; subj: any noun (usu. inanim); 3rd pers fut only] there will be time to do sth. later, s.o. will not lose anything by temporarily postponing the action in question: X (от Y-а) не уйдёт ≃ **X isn't going anywhere; X can wait; there will be time enough ⟨plenty of time⟩ for X ⟨for Y to do thing X⟩ (later); X will still be there (later); Y will have a ⟨his⟩ chance (to do thing X) (later).**

«Ученье-то не уйдёт, а здоровья не купишь; здоровье дороже всего в жизни. Вишь, он из ученья как из больницы воротится: жирок весь пропадает, жиденький такой…» (Гончаров 1). "There'll be plenty of time for study, but you can't buy good health. Health is the most precious thing in life. Look, he comes back from school as from a hospital—his fat all gone, looking pale and thin…" (1b). ♦ Это была та блестящая атака кавалергардов, которой удивлялись сами французы… «Что мне завидовать, моё не уйдёт, и я сейчас, может быть, увижу государя!» – подумал Ростов и поскакал дальше (Толстой 4). This was the brilliant charge of the Horse Guards that amazed even the French…. "Why should I envy them? I'll have my chance. I may see the Tsar at any moment now," thought Rostov, and galloped on (4a).

• НЕДАЛЕКО́ ⟨НЕ ТАК УЖ ДАЛЕКО́, НЕ О́ЧЕНЬ ДАЛЕКО́⟩ УЙТИ́ [VP; subj: human; usu. past]

1. *в чём* ~ *(от кого)* not to make significant progress or have much success (in some area, subject matter etc), or not to progress significantly past the level of another (in some area, subject matter etc): в Y-е X недалеко ушёл (от Z-а) ≃ **X didn't get ⟨hasn't got(ten)⟩ very far in ⟨with⟩ Y; X didn't get ⟨hasn't got(ten)⟩ all that far ahead of Z in Y.**

«Ненавижу я этого лекаришку; по-моему, он просто шарлатан; я уверен, что со всеми своими лягушками он и в физике недалеко ушёл» (Тургенев 2). "I detest that wretched little leech; in my opinion he's nothing but a charlatan! I am convinced that for all his frogs he hasn't got very far in physics" (2e). ♦ «И по работе он не так уж далеко ушёл от тебя» (Искандер 5). "He hasn't gotten all that far ahead of you, even in his job" (5a).

2. ~ *от кого* to be very similar to s.o. in some respect: X недалеко ушёл от Y-а ≃ **X is no ⟨not much⟩ better (than Y).**

Он говорил слишком резко, но и ты недалеко от него ушёл. He spoke too harshly, but then you weren't much better.

У-65 • НЕ УКА́З ⟨НЕ УКА́ЗЧИК⟩ *кому coll* [NP; these forms only; subj-compl with быть∅] **1.** [subj: usu. human or collect] one has no right or power to control s.o. or give orders to s.o.: X Y-у не указ ≃ **X is no authority to Y; X can't lay down the law to Y; X can't order ⟨boss⟩ Y around; Y doesn't ⟨won't⟩ take orders from X.**

О Лукашине заговорили в районе. Кто? Откуда такой смельчак взялся, что ему и Подрезов не указ? (Абрамов 1). People in the district office started talking about Lukashin. Who was he? Where did this hothead come from, who doesn't even take orders from Podrezov? (1a).

2. [subj: human, collect, or abstr] there is no reason why some person (organization etc) should be looked upon as a model, standard for s.o. (often because the person or organization in question does not deserve to be so looked upon): X Y-у не указ ≃ **X is not an example for Y to follow; X is no example for Y; Y is not obliged to do what X does.**

«...Нельзя же всякому юноше веровать в такой предрассудок, и ваш юноша не указ остальным» (Достоевский 1). "...Not every young man can believe in such prejudices, and your young man is no example for others" (1a). ♦ «Мы не можем себе этого позволить. Я — солдат. Жизнь кочевая, сегодня здесь, завтра там... Тут не до пелёнок»... — «А как же другие?» — позволила она себе вопрос. «„Другие" мне не указ. Если „другие" глупы, это не значит, что и я должен быть глуп» (Грекова 3). "We can't allow ourselves that. I'm a soldier and lead a wandering life, here today, there tomorrow....We'll have no time for diapers."..."And what about other people?" she permitted herself to ask. "I'm not obliged to do what other people do. If others are stupid it doesn't mean I have to be stupid" (3a).

У-66 • ПО УКА́ЗКЕ *чьей, кого coll* [PrepP; Invar; the resulting PrepP is adv] (to do sth.) because s.o. orders one to: **on orders from s.o.; at s.o.'s command ⟨bidding⟩; (do) what s.o. tells one (to do);** ‖ жить по чужой указке ≃ **let s.o. run one's life.**

«Ты не глупи, Варвара... Тебе не семнадцать лет». — «Да и не сорок. И всю жизнь по твоей указке жить не собираюсь» (Абрамов 1). [context transl] "Don't act silly, Varvara....You're not seventeen years old." "No. And not forty either, and I don't intend to live my whole life under your thumb" (1a).

У-67 • ПОД УКЛО́Н [PrepP; Invar; adv] down the slope of a hill, from a higher to a lower place: **downhill; downward(s).**

Дорога поворачивала направо и шла под уклон. The road turned to the right and dipped downward.

У-68 • БУЛА́ВОЧНЫЙ УКО́Л *obsoles* [NP; fixed WO] **1.** a brief caustic remark: **pinprick ⟨pin-prick⟩; dig; gibe.**

...Она [жена Энгельсона] не могла пропустить ни одного случая, чтоб не кольнуть меня самым злым образом... Наконец булавочные уколы в такое время, когда я весь был задавлен болью и горем, вывели меня из терпенья (Герцен 2). ...She [Engelson's wife] could not let slip any chance for having a spiteful dig at me....Finally these pin-pricks, at a time when I was utterly crushed by grief and distress, drove me out of all patience (2a).

2. a minor trouble: **pinprick; petty annoyance; fleabite.**

У-69 • НЕ В УКО́Р ⟨НЕ В УПРЁК⟩ БУДЬ СКА́ЗАНО *(кому) coll* [these forms only; sent adv (parenth); fixed WO] do not be offended or angered by what I said or am about to say: **no harm meant; no offense meant ⟨intended⟩; don't take it ⟨this⟩ the wrong way, but...; don't take it amiss, but...; if you'll excuse my saying so; (it's) nothing personal.**

«Злодей-то, видно, силён; а у нас всего сто тридцать человек, не считая казаков, на которых плоха надежда, не в укор будь тебе сказано, Максимыч» (Пушкин 2). "The villain is evidently strong, and we have only a hundred and thirty men, not counting the Cossacks, who cannot be relied on, if you'll excuse my saying so, Maksimych" (2a).

У-70 • СТА́ВИТЬ/ПОСТА́ВИТЬ В УКО́Р ⟨В УПРЁК⟩ *кому что obs* [VP; subj: human] to rebuke or blame s.o. for sth.: X поставил Y-у в упрёк Z ≃ **X reproached ⟨reprimanded⟩ Y (for Z); X pinned Z on Y; X put the blame for Z on Y; X considered Z ⟨regarded Z as⟩ blameworthy in Y.**

...Одновременно мы находим в истории совершенно противоположные взгляды на то, что было зло и что было благо: одни данную Польше конституцию и Священный Союз ставят в заслугу, другие в укор Александру (Толстой 7). ...We find at one and the same time quite contradictory views as to what is bad and what is good in history: some people regard giving a constitution to Poland and forming the Holy Alliance as praiseworthy in Alexander, while others regard it as blameworthy (7b).

У-71 • ЗЕЛЁНАЯ У́ЛИЦА [NP; sing only; fixed WO] **1.** a clear path, without obstacles or delays (along which a vehicle can move, a project can develop, a plan can be implemented etc): **a green light all the way; clear passage.**

«Приношу [в издательство] рецензии [на свою брошюру] от светил, — это не проблема. За меня хватаются. Тут же — в план. Зелёная улица» (Зиновьев 2). "I submit [to the publishers] a few testimonials [for my pamphlet] from leading lights—that's no problem. I've got plenty of them. And they immediately include me in their publishing plan. It's a green light all the way" (2a).

2. *obs* a punishment in the Imperial army by which the offending soldier was forced to run between two rows of soldiers who beat him with rods as he ran: **(run ⟨make s.o. run⟩) the gauntlet.**

У-72 • БУ́ДЕТ И НА НА́ШЕЙ ⟨моей, твоей и т. п.⟩ У́ЛИЦЕ ПРА́ЗДНИК [saying] we (I, you etc) too will rejoice, celebrate success etc (said during hard, unsuccessful times in the hope that the person or group in question will eventually be successful, victorious, in a position of power etc): ≃ **our ⟨my, your etc⟩ day ⟨time⟩ will come; we'll ⟨I'll etc⟩ have our ⟨my etc⟩ day, too; every dog has his day.**

«Время работает на нас, — думали они, разноцветно поблёскивая в свете электричества, — наше дело правое, будет и на нашей улице праздник...» (Аржак 1). "Time is on our side," they told themselves, as their many colours gleamed in the electric light. "Our cause is just, our day will come..." (1a).

У-73 • НА У́ЛИЦЕ [PrepP; Invar; usu. subj-compl with быть∅, оказаться etc (subj: human)] **1.** one is (finds o.s. etc) without lodging: **(out) on ⟨in⟩ the street.**

...Соня билась за свою комнату, добилась наконец, дорожит ею, и я не на улице, есть крыша над головой, буду жить у неё и дожидаться, чтобы и мне дали комнату... (Рыбаков 1). Sonya had struggled to get her room and now that she had, it really meant something to her, and, since I wasn't out on the street, but had a roof over my head, I could live with her and wait till they gave me my own place (1a).

2. one is (ends up etc) without work, employment: **(out) on ⟨in⟩ the street;** [in limited contexts] **out the door.**

На фабрике шли массовые увольнения, многие квалифицированные рабочие оказались на улице. There were mass firings at the factory and many skilled laborers ended up on the street.

У-74 • ВЫБРА́СЫВАТЬ/ВЫ́БРОСИТЬ ⟨ВЫКИ́ДЫ-ВАТЬ/ВЫ́КИНУТЬ, ВЫШВЫ́РИВАТЬ/ВЫ́ШВЫР-НУТЬ⟩ НА У́ЛИЦУ *кого* [VP; subj: human or collect] **1.** to evict s.o. from his living quarters, deprive s.o. of lodgings without offering him any other place to stay: X выбросил Y-а на улицу ≃ **X threw ⟨turned, kicked, tossed⟩ Y out on ⟨onto, in, into⟩ the street;** [in limited contexts] **X turned Y out of house and home.**

2. to fire s.o.: X выбросил Y-а на улицу ≃ **X threw ⟨tossed⟩ Y out (on ⟨onto, in, into⟩ the street); X kicked Y out.**

...[Они] расскажут, при случае, что они, Боже упаси, не антисемиты: у них половина друзей — евреи. А раздастся в тиши кабинета «звонок», поступят «сигнал», «закрытое письмо», с тем же деловитым дружелюбием выбросят тебя на улицу, оставят без хлеба... (Свирский 1). ...[They] tell you whenever the opportunity occurs that they aren't anti-Semitic, heaven forbid. Half of their friends are Jews. But if in the silence of their offices the phone rings, or a "signal" comes, or a secret letter, then they'll throw you out on the street with that selfsame businesslike friendliness, leave you to starve... (1a). ♦ [author's usage] «Вы его выкинули из института. Куда ему идти?.. Мы его учили... А вы его на улицу. За что?» (Рыбаков 2). "You've thrown him out of the institute, but where's he supposed to go?...We've taught him and trained him...and you throw him out onto the street! And what for?" (2a).

У-75 • ВЫНОСИ́ТЬ НА У́ЛИЦУ *что* [VP; subj: human; often neg or infin with не надо, не нужно, незачем etc] to divulge a private, intimate matter, make it open to public discussion: X не выносит Y на улицу ≃ **X doesn't make Y public knowledge;** [in limited contexts] **X doesn't tell tales out of school.**

У-76 • С У́ЛИЦЫ *coll, rather derog* [PrepP; Invar; usu. nonagreeing modif or adv] (of a person, people) unfamiliar, altogether unknown: **(a man ⟨people etc⟩) off the street;** ‖ *Neg* человек не с улицы ≃ **not just anybody ⟨anyone⟩.**

Что он [Павел Литвинов] внук Максима Литвинова, бесконечно повторяло и западное радио; тогда всё время подчёркивалось, что такой-то — сын или внук такого-то, диссиденты, дескать, люди не «с улицы»... (Амальрик 1). The fact that he [Pavel Litvinov] was Maxim Litvinov's grandson was endlessly repeated in radio broadcasts from the West. In those days, it was constantly being emphasized that such-and-such a person was the son or grandson of somebody-or-other, as if to say that the dissidents were not just "anybody" (1a). ♦ «Товарищ Сандро — уважаемый человек», — твёрдо сказал чёрный китель. «О чём говорить! — воскликнул сван, сидевший рядом со мной. — Сопровождать генерала Клименко с улицы человека не возьмут» (Искандер 4). "Comrade Sandro is a respected man," Black-Tunic said firmly. "That goes without saying!" exclaimed the Svan sitting next to me. "They don't just pick someone off the street to escort General Klimenko" (4a).

У-77 • БРА́ТЬСЯ/ВЗЯ́ТЬСЯ ЗА УМ *coll* [VP; subj: human; more often pfv; often infin with пора, надо etc] to become more prudent, begin to act judiciously: X взялся за ум ≃ **X came to his senses; X became ⟨grew⟩ sensible ⟨reasonable⟩; X began to act sensibly.**

«...Только напоследок хочу сказать тебе: бросай эту канитель, берись за ум, начинай учиться» (Максимов 2). "...But I want to leave one thought with you before you go: quit fooling around. Act sensibly and start studying" (2a).

У-78 • НАСТАВЛЯ́ТЬ/НАСТА́ВИТЬ НА УМ ⟨НА РА́ЗУМ *obs⟩ кого old-fash, coll* [VP; subj: usu. human] to teach s.o. something good, useful (usu. in the form of sensible advice): X наставил Y-а на ум ≃ **X taught Y some sense; X made Y see sense ⟨the light⟩; X put some sense into Y's head ⟨into Y⟩; X brought Y to Y's senses; X brought Y (back) to reason; X wised Y up.**

[Гордей Карпыч:] Ну, брат, спасибо, что на ум наставил, а то было свихнулся совсем. Не знаю, как и в голову вошла такая гнилая фантазия (Островский 2). [G.K.:] Well, brother, thank you for bringing me back to reason; I almost went out of my mind completely. I don't know how such a rotten notion got into my head (2a).

У-79 • УМ ЗА РА́ЗУМ ЗАХО́ДИТ/ЗАШЁЛ *у кого coll* [VP_subj; fixed WO with the verb movable] s.o. is confused, his thoughts are jumbled, he cannot think coherently (often as a result of pondering some topic for a long time, trying to solve a difficult problem, or being overwhelmed with complex matters): у X-а ум за разум заходит ≃ **X can't think straight ⟨clearly⟩; X's mind is reeling ⟨going (a)round in circles⟩; X doesn't know whether he's coming or going;** [in limited contexts] **(some problem etc) is too much for X's (poor) brain.**

«...Так, например, один горожанин, как мне рассказывали, получив трёхкомнатную квартиру... без всякого пятого измерения и прочих вещей, от которых ум заходит за разум, мгновенно превратил её в четырёхкомнатную, разделив одну из комнат пополам перегородкой» (Булгаков 9). "I heard of one man, for example, who received a three-room apartment and immediately turned the three into four without any fifth dimension or any other things that make your mind reel, simply by dividing one room with a partition" (9a). ♦ ...Часто, начиная думать о самой простой вещи, я впадал в безвыходный круг анализа своих мыслей, я не думал уже о вопросе, занимавшем меня, а думал о том, о чём я думал... Ум за разум заходил... (Толстой 2). ...Frequently, when starting to think of the simplest thing, I entered a vicious circle of mental self-analysis, so that I no longer thought of the original question, but thought only of what I was thinking about....My mind went round in circles (2b). ♦ «...Они [Дмитрий Прокофьич] ещё не знают, кто такая Марфа Петровна». — «Ах, не знаете? А я думала, вам всё уж известно. Вы мне простите, Дмитрий Прокофьич, у меня в эти дни просто ум за разум заходит» (Достоевский 3). "He [Dmitri Prokofich] doesn't know who Marfa Petrovna is yet." "Oh dear, you don't know? And I thought you knew everything already. Please forgive me, Dmitri Prokofich, these days I simply don't know whether I'm coming or going" (3a). ♦ «Фу! перемешал! — хлопнул себя по лбу Порфирий. — Чёрт возьми, у меня с этим делом ум за разум заходит!» (Достоевский 3). "Damn! I've got confused!" Porfiry said, clapping his hand to his forehead. "The devil take it, this case is too much for my poor brain!" (3d).

У-80 • УМ ХОРОШО́, А ДВА ЛУ́ЧШЕ [saying] it is better to confer with s.o. when solving a problem than to try to do it alone (said when asking s.o. for help in solving a problem, offering s.o. one's help in solving a problem etc): ≃ **two heads are better than one.**

«...Русская пословица говорит: „Если есть у кого один ум, то это хорошо, а если придёт в гости ещё умный человек, то будет ещё лучше, ибо тогда будет два ума, а не один только..."» — «Ум хорошо, а два — лучше», — в нетерпении подсказал прокурор... (Достоевский 2). "...The Russian proverb says: 'It is good when someone has one head, but when an intelligent man comes to visit, it is better still, for then there will be two heads and not just one...'" "Two heads are better than one," the prosecutor prompted impatiently... (2a).

У-81 • БЕЗ УМА́ [PrepP; Invar] **1.** ~ *от кого-чего* [the resulting PrepP is subj-compl with быть₀ (subj: human)] one is spellbound, enraptured by s.o. or sth.: X без ума от Y-а ≃ **X is crazy ⟨mad, wild, dotty⟩ about Y; X goes wild ⟨crazy⟩ over Y; X has lost his head over person Y; X is madly ⟨head over heels⟩ in love with person Y; X is head over heels over person Y.**

«...Мы приходим однажды к нашим девушкам. Мою звали Катрин, я её Катей называл, а молоденькую звали Гретой... Мне нравится моя Катя, и я, чувствую, ей нравлюсь, а эти вообще без ума друг от друга» (Искандер 5). "...One time we came to see our girls. Mine was named Katrin—I called her Katya—and the young one was named Greta....I liked my Katya, and she liked me, I could feel it, and the other two were just plain crazy about each other" (5a). ♦ «Откуда вы, Обломов? Не знает Дашеньки! Весь город без ума, как она танцует!» (Гончаров 1). "Where have you been, Oblomov? You don't know Dashenka? Why, the whole town is crazy about her dancing" (1a). ♦ «Великолепный математик был у нас в Юрятине. В двух гимназиях преподавал, в мужской и у нас... Девочки были без ума от него, все в него влюблялись» (Пастернак 1). "We had an excellent [math] teacher in Yuriatin, he taught both in the boys' school and in ours....All the girls were mad about him, they all fell in love with him" (1a). ♦ Ира-Ирунчик оказалась без ума от Аркашки и не могла этого скрыть... (Залыгин 1). Irina/Irunchik turned out to be dotty about Arkady and quite unable to hide it (1a). ♦ Мне была совершенно ясна бессмыслица гартвиговских авантюр, но иные интеллигенты, и в особенности дамы с воспалённым воображением, были от них без ума (Трифонов 5). The absurdity of Gartvig's adventures was perfectly clear to me, but some intellectuals—and especially certain ladies with overly vivid imaginations—went wild over them (5a). ♦ ...Не я один влюбился в неё: все мужчины, посещавшие её дом, были от ней без ума... (Тургенев 3). ...I was not the only one to have fallen in love with her: all the men who visited the house were madly in love with her... (3a).

2. ~ *любить кого, rare что*, **влюбляться *в кого*, быть₀ влюблённым *в кого*** [adv] (to love s.o.) ardently, fervently: **madly; to distraction; beyond all measure.**

Ещё до войны видела однажды Настёна в кино... как городская баба, не зная, чем угодить мужику, которого она без ума любила, кормила его, как маленького, из рук (Распутин 2). Once before the war Nastyona saw a movie...in which a city woman, not knowing how to please the man she loved madly, spoon-fed him like a child (2a). ♦ Гораздо сильнейшее влияние [,чем романы,] имела на меня пьеса, которую я любил без ума. — «Свадьба Фигаро» (Герцен 1). A play which I liked beyond all measure, the *Marriage of Figaro*, had much greater influence on me [than novels] (1a).

У-82 • ВСЯК ⟨ВСЯ́КИЙ, КА́ЖДЫЙ⟩ ПО-СВО́ЕМУ С УМА́ СХО́ДИТ [saying] everyone has his whims, oddities (said condescendingly of s.o. whose behavior, tastes, or actions strike others as unusual): ≃ **everyone is crazy in his own way; we all have our little idiosyncrasies.**

У-83 • ВЫЖИВА́ТЬ/ВЫ́ЖИТЬ ИЗ УМА́ *coll, derog* [VP; subj: human; usu. pfv past] to lose the ability to think, reason sensibly because of old age: X выжил из ума ≃ **X has lost his mind ⟨his senses⟩; X has become ⟨got(ten), grown⟩ senile; X has lost possession of his faculties; X's mind is gone; X has outlived his wits; X is in his dotage.**

...Надо регулярно в Журнале печатать статьи выдающихся (читай: давно выживших из ума) учёных по общим проблемам современной науки (читай: общий банальный трёп по проблемам столетней давности) (Зиновьев 1). ...The Journal was regularly to publish articles by outstanding scientists (i.e. scientists long senile) on the general problems of modern science (i.e. dreary waffle about problems a hundred years old) (1a). ♦ «...[Ста́руха Страусиная Нога] здесь в лесу живёт... местная ведьма. Иногда помогает нам по хозяйству, иногда по ведьминским делам. Но толку от неё мало, совсем из ума выжила» (Искандер 5). "...She [Old Ostrich Leg] lives here in the forest....A local witch. Sometimes she helps us out with the housework, sometimes with witchery. But she's not good for much, her mind's completely gone" (5a). ♦ «Так должно быть! — думал князь Андрей, выезжая из аллеи лысогорского дома. — Она, жалкое невинное существо, остаётся на съедение выжившему из ума старику. Старик чувствует, что виноват, но не может изменить себя» (Толстой 6). "It had to be so!" thought Prince Andrei, as he drove out of the avenue of Bald Hills. "She, poor innocent creature, is left to be victimized by an old man who has outlived his wits. The old man feels he is guilty but cannot change" (6a).

У-84 • ДОВОДИ́ТЬ/ДОВЕСТИ́ ДО УМА́ *coll* [VP; subj: human; often pfv fut or infin with надо, нужно etc] **1.** ~ *кого* to cause s.o. to be sensible, prudent, force s.o. to be reasonable: X доведёт Y-а до ума ≃ **X will bring Y ⟨make Y come⟩ to Y's senses; X will make Y see sense.**

Вернулся драматург, говорил: «Мы их доведём до ума!» (Трифонов 1). The playwright came back into the room and said, "We'll bring them to their senses!" (1a). ♦ «А до ума мы вас, Митёк, доведём, не пойдёте — силой дотащим, для вашей же пользы» (Максимов 2). "We'll make you see sense, though, Mitya—and if you don't, we'll knock it into your head the hard way, for your own good" (2a).

2. ~ *что* to get (a project, work etc) in good condition by making improvements: X доведёт Y до ума ≃ **X will shape Y up; X will get Y in(to) shape; X will whip Y into shape.**

Чтобы довести до ума этот наспех сколоченный дом, нужно вложить в него много денег и труда. It would take a lot of money and work to shape up this hastily thrown-together house.

У-85 • ЛИША́ТЬСЯ/ЛИШИ́ТЬСЯ УМА́ ⟨РАССУ́ДКА⟩; ТЕРЯ́ТЬ/ПОТЕРЯ́ТЬ РАССУ́ДОК [VP; subj: human; usu. pfv past] to become insane: X ума лишился ≃ **X went mad ⟨crazy, out of his mind⟩; X lost his mind.**

Мчал Абдильхан, к седлу пригнувшись чёрной тучей. К аулу, к дому! Сородичи, что волчьей стаей рядом шли, ему кричали на скаку: «Брат твой рассудком тронулся! Ума лишился!» (Айтматов 2). Abdil'khan, crouched low over the saddle, rode on like a black cloud. To the *aul* [the village]! Home! His kinsmen raced beside him like a pack of wolves, shouting, "Your brother is mad! He's gone out of his mind!" (2a).

У-86 • НАБИРА́ТЬСЯ/НАБРА́ТЬСЯ УМА́ ⟨РА́ЗУМА, УМА́-РА́ЗУМА⟩ *coll* [VP; subj: human; usu. pfv (in questions, neg, or infin with хочет, надо бы etc)] to become more serious, sensible, knowledgeable etc: X-у надо (бы) ума набраться ≃ **X should get some sense into his head; X needs to learn some sense ⟨a thing or two⟩; X has much ⟨a lot⟩ to learn;** ‖ *Neg* X ума не набрался ≃ [in limited contexts] **X doesn't know any better.**

«...Дай, говорю, продам [крестьян], да и продал сдуру! — Засим он повесил голову так, как будто сам раскаивался в этом деле, и прибавил: — Вот и седой человек, а до сих пор не набрался ума» (Гоголь 3). "Well, I said to myself, let's sell them [my peasants], and I sold them like a fool!" Then he hung his head as though he were really sorry for what he had done and added: "I may be a grey-haired old man, but I've still got no sense" (3a). ♦ [Зилов:] Думаешь, жена у меня дура. [Вера:] А что, умная?.. Так познакомь меня с ней. [Зилов:] Это зачем? [Вера:] Хочу ума-разума набраться (Вампилов 5). [context transl] [Z.:] Do you think my wife's that stupid? [V.:] You mean she's clever?…Introduce me if she is. [Z.:] Whatever for? [V.:] So I can pick up a few tips (5a).

У-87 • НЕ моего ⟨твоего и т. п.⟩ УМА́ ДЕ́ЛО *coll* [NP$_{gen}$; Invar; subj-compl with быть∅ (subj: это, abstr, or infin), pres only; fixed WO] sth. is beyond s.o.'s ability to understand and/or does not concern s.o.: это не Х-ова ума дело ≃ **X doesn't ⟨wouldn't⟩ understand it and it doesn't have anything to do with him anyway;** [with the focus on s.o.'s inability to understand] **X wouldn't understand (it); it's over X's head; it's out of ⟨beyond⟩ X's depth;** [with the focus on sth.'s not concerning s.o.] **it has nothing to do with X; it's none of X's business ⟨concern⟩; it's not for X to know.**

«А чего же ты слезу сронила?» – допытывалась любознательная старуха. «И чего вам, тётенька, надо? Не вашего ума дело!» (Шолохов 4). "What are you crying about then?" the inquisitive old woman persisted. "Don't bother me, Auntie! You wouldn't understand!" (4a). ♦ «И за это получили из артиллерии?.. С бронепоезда?» – «Разумеется». – «Прискорбно. Достойно сожаления. Впрочем, это не нашего ума дело» (Пастернак 1). "So they were shelled?…From the armored train?" "Of course." "That's bad. All our sympathy. Still, it's none of our business" (1a).

У-88 • ОТ ⟨С⟩ БОЛЬШО́ГО УМА́ *coll, iron* [PrepP; these forms only; adv; usu. used with pfv verbs] (to do sth.) out of stupidity, foolishness: **in one's infinite wisdom; out of sheer brilliance.**

У-89 • С УМА́ СОЙТИ́ ⟨СОЙДЁШЬ⟩! *coll* [Interj; Invar; fixed WO] used to express utter surprise, amazement, delight, a sarcastic reaction to sth. etc: **(truly) unbelievable ⟨amazing, incredible etc⟩!; that's unbelievable ⟨amazing etc⟩!; my goodness!;** [in limited contexts] **you're kidding!; I can't believe it!; it's ⟨she's etc⟩ a knockout!; it'll ⟨she'll etc⟩ make you flip; sth. drives you out of your mind.**

Чуйков вернулся в блиндаж. Гуров, поджидавший его с ужином, сказал: «Николай Иванович, с ума сойти: тихо» (Гроссман 2). He [Chuykov] went back to the bunker. Gurov was waiting for him so they could have supper. "What silence, Nikolay Ivanovich!" said Gurov. "I can't believe it" (2a). ♦ «Я думаю, [он] куда-нибудь в Сибирь подался…» – «А почему в Сибирь?» – «Я там в экспедиции был, с ума сойти как здорово…» (Семёнов 1). "I reckon he's off to Siberia…." "But why Siberia?" "I was out there with an expedition, it's a knockout, great" (1a). ♦ «Вот представьте себе такую историю: старый пёс, – но ещё в соку, с огнём, с жаждой счастья, – знакомится с вдовицей, а у неё дочка, совсем ещё девочка, – знаете, когда ещё ничего не оформилось, а уже ходит так, что с ума сойти» (Набоков 1). "Imagine this kind of thing: an old dog – but still in his prime, fiery, thirsting for happiness – gets to know a widow, and she has a daughter, still quite a little girl – you know what I mean – when nothing is formed yet but already she has a way of walking that drives you out of your mind" (1a).

У-90 • СВОДИ́ТЬ/СВЕСТИ́ С УМА́ *кого coll* [VP] **1.** [subj: human or abstr] to upset, disturb, annoy etc s.o. so greatly that he cannot think coherently: X сводит Y-а с ума ≃ **X drives Y mad ⟨crazy, insane, out of Y's mind etc⟩; X drives Y up the wall.**

«…Он едва самого меня не свёл с ума, доказывая мне, что меня нету!» (Булгаков 9). "He nearly drove *me* mad, trying to prove that I didn't exist" (9b). ♦ «Верите ли, это бредовое сооружение Ирода, – прокуратор махнул рукою вдоль колоннады, так что стало ясно, что он говорит о дворце, – положительно сводит меня с ума» (Булгаков 9). "Would you believe it, this nightmare erected here by Herod," the Procurator waved his hand at the colonnade, and it was clear that he was speaking of the palace, "drives me insane!" (9a). ♦ Отчаяние, бессилье, сознание обмана,

чувство несправедливости, подобное пропасти, уродливые недостатки полярного быта, всё это едва не свело его с ума (Набоков 1). Despair, helplessness, the consciousness of having been deceived, a dizzy feeling of injustice, the ugly shortcomings of arctic life, all this almost drove him out of his mind (1a).

2. [subj: human, abstr, or concr] to enthrall, captivate, charm s.o. overwhelmingly; (of people only) to cause s.o. to fall deeply, passionately in love with one: X сводил Y-а с ума ≃ **X was driving Y out of Y's mind; X was driving Y mad ⟨crazy, wild⟩.**

А что представляла из себя она, если не считать её необъяснимой прелести, сводящей мужчин с ума? (Катаев 2). And what was she, if one didn't count her mysterious charm which drove men out of their minds? (2a).

У-91 • СПЯ́ТИТЬ ⟨СВИХНУ́ТЬ(СЯ), СВОРОТИ́ТЬ, СБРЕ́НДИТЬ⟩ С УМА́ *substand;* **РЕША́ТЬСЯ/РЕШИ́ТЬСЯ УМА́** *obs, substand* [VP; subj: human] **1.** to become insane: X спятил с ума ≃ **X went ⟨was⟩ out of his mind ⟨out of his head, off his rocker, off his nut etc⟩; X lost his marbles.**

Окружат вас мерзкими харями, кикиморами, упырями. Страшно станет. Запьёте пуще прежнего. И чем больше пить будете, тем страшнее будет. Пока не свихнётесь с ума, как бедный Николай Николаевич! (Терц 5). They'll surround you with loathsome snouts, specters, and vampires. You'll be terrified. You'll take to drinking more than ever before. And the more you drink, the more terrified you'll be. Until you go off your rocker like poor Nikolay Nikolayevich! (5a). ♦ «Боже мой! Он что, с ума своротил, этот паршивый Сфинкс?» (Ерофеев 1). My God. What's he up to, has he lost his marbles, this mangy sphinx? (1a).

2. to say or do nonsensical things, act as if one has gone insane: X с ума спятил ≃ **X has gone nuts ⟨crazy, berserk, off his head etc⟩; X must be off his rocker; X has flipped his lid ⟨flipped out⟩.**

«Ты послушал бы, что давеча доктор сказал. „За границу, говорит, ступайте, а то плохо: удар может быть"»… – «Что ж? – хладнокровно сказал Штольц. – В Египте ты будешь через две недели, в Америке через три». – «Ну, брат Андрей, и ты то же! Один толковый человек и был, и тот с ума спятил» (Гончаров 1). "You should have heard what the doctor said this morning. He told me to go abroad or it would be the worse for me: I might have a stroke."…"Well, what about it?" Stolz said coolly. "You can be in Egypt in a fortnight and in America in three weeks." "You, too, old man? You were the only sensible man I knew and you, too, have gone off your head" (1a).

У-92 • СХОДИ́ТЬ/СОЙТИ́ С УМА́ [VP; subj: human] **1.** to become insane: X сошёл с ума ≃ **X went ⟨was⟩ mad ⟨crazy, insane, out of his mind, out of his head⟩; X lost his mind; X went (a)round the bend.**

Чтобы не сойти с ума, надо было действовать решительно и скорее (Пастернак 1). If they were not to go insane they must act quickly and firmly (1a). ♦ «У него всё теперь, всё на земле совокупилось в Илюше, и умри Илюша, он или с ума сойдёт с горя, или лишит себя жизни» (Достоевский 1). "For him, now, everything on earth has come together in Ilyusha, and if Ilyusha dies, he will either go out of his mind from grief or take his own life" (1a).

2. Also: **ПОСХОДИ́ТЬ С УМА́** *coll* [var. with посходить is used with pl subject] to say or do stupid, nonsensical things, act as if one has gone insane: X с ума сошёл ≃ **X has gone (quite) crazy ⟨mad etc⟩; X has gone berserk ⟨nuts etc⟩; X must be crazy ⟨mad, out of his mind etc⟩; X has taken leave of his senses.**

«Они там все вместе с Шутиковым с ума посходили. О трубах только и говорят» (Дудинцев 1). "Shutikov and all the others have gone quite crazy; all they talk about is pipes" (1a). ♦ Что творится во время приёма! Сегодня было 82 звонка. Телефон выключен. Бездетные дамы с ума сошли и идут… (Булгаков 11). The things that go on during visiting hours! The bell rang eighty-two times today. The telephone was disconnected. Childless ladies have gone berserk and are coming in droves... (11a). ♦ [Нина:] Давайте, давайте, оправдывайте его [Васеньку], защищайте. Если хотите, чтобы он совсем рехнулся... [Васенька:] Я с ума хочу сходить, понятно тебе? Сходить с ума и ни о чём не думать! И оставь меня в покое! (*Уходит в другую комнату*) (Вампилов 4). [N.:] Go ahead, go ahead and agree with him [Vasenka], defend him. If you want him to go completely crazy.... [V.:] I want to go nuts, understand? Go nuts and not think about anything! So leave me alone! (*He goes into the other room*) (4b). ♦ «Я вам уже сказал раз! Не приставайте, иначе я прикажу свести вас на берег! Вы с ума сошли!» (Шолохов 5). "I've told you already! Stop accosting me like this, or I'll have you put ashore! You must be mad!" (5a). ♦ «Люди совсем посходили с ума, — покачал головой Соломон Евсеевич. — Мне уже двадцать человек звонили про эти шапки» (Войнович 6). "People have completely taken leave of their senses," said Fishkin, shaking his head. "Twenty phone calls I've had already about these hats" (6a).

3. *coll* [pfv past only; 2nd or 3rd pers only] used to express the speaker's reaction to s.o.'s irrational actions, thoughtless statements etc: ты с ума сошёл! ≃ **you're ⟨you must be⟩ out of your mind ⟨off your head etc⟩!; are you crazy!; you're nuts ⟨crazy etc⟩!**

«Итак, друзья мои, мы, по всей вероятности, будем сматываться отсюда», — сказал Дима... «На родину предков?» — спросил Антон. «Ты с ума сошёл, — возмутился Дима. — В Канаду или США. На худой конец — в Париж» (Зиновьев 2). "Well, then, my friends, we'll probably be pushing off quite soon," said Dima...."To return to the land of your forefathers?" Anton asked. "You must be off your head," said Dima indignantly. "To Canada or to the States. Paris at worst" (2a). ♦ «Он [пассажир] взял её голову в свои руки... и всё сказал. На ухо. Шёпотом. «Ну, вот — слава богу! — ответила она, всё выслушав. — Наконец-то можно пойти и уснуть. Спокойной ночи!» — «Вы с ума сошли?! Как это можно?» (Залыгин 1). ...He [the passenger] took her head in his hands and...told her everything he had to say, whispering in her ear. When he finished she replied, "At last, thank heaven! At last we can go back to bed. Good night!" "Are you crazy! How can you?" (1a). ♦ «Забегает в бар молодой парень и — к бармену: „В двухсотграммовый стакан можете триста граммов коньяка налить?" Бармен с удивлением: „С ума сошли!"» (Чернёнок 2). "A young man runs into a bar and says to the bartender: 'Can you pour three hundred grams of cognac into a two-hundred-gram glass?' The bartender says: 'You're nuts!'" (2a).

4. ~ *(от чего)* [impfv only] to become very agitated, restless, excited etc (in response to worry, alarm, joy etc): X с ума сходит (от Y-a) ≃ [in response to worry, alarm etc] **X is going ⟨is nearly⟩ out of his mind ⟨head⟩ (with Y); X is crazy with Y; Y is driving ⟨is enough to drive⟩ X crazy ⟨mad, insane⟩;** [in response to joy, happiness] **X is (going) wild with Y.**

«Лиза, Лиза! — замахала руками Раечка. — Где ты была? Мы вчера просто с ума сходили...» (Абрамов 1). "Liza! Liza!" shouted Raechka, waving her arms. "Where've you been? We were going out of our minds yesterday" (1a). ♦ «Боже мой, без двадцати двенадцать! Мама, наверное, с ума сошла. Я обещала быть к ужину...» (Ерофеев 3). "Oh my God, it's twenty of twelve! Mama's probably crazy with worry. I promised to be home for supper..." (3a). ♦ «Я с ума сходил от мысли, что скоро опять пойдёт снег. Я не могу видеть, как он падает, падает, падает» (Федин 1). "The thought that snow would soon come again was driving me crazy. I can't bear to see it falling, falling, falling" (1a).

5. ~ *от кого-чего, по кому-чему, по ком coll* [prep obj: more often human; impfv only] to be or become excessively delighted by, excited over s.o. or sth.: X с ума сходит по Y-у ≃ **X is crazy ⟨wild, mad etc⟩ about Y; X goes crazy ⟨wild etc⟩ over Y; X loses his head over Y.**

...Тётушка Хрисула прямо с ума сходила по чёрному инжиру (Искандер 5). ...Auntie Chrysoula was really wild about black

figs (5a). ♦ Женщины от него [Кирсанова] с ума сходили, мужчины называли его фатом и втайне завидовали ему (Тургенев 2). Women lost their heads over him, and men dubbed him a fop but were secretly envious (2c).

У-93 • **УМА́ НЕ ПРИЛОЖУ́; не мочь УМА́ ПРИ-ЛОЖИ́ТЬ** *both coll* [VP; subj: human; usu. main clause in a complex sent; fixed WO] not to know or be able to understand or explain sth.: ума не приложу ≃ **I have (absolutely) no idea; I haven't the faintest ⟨the foggiest⟩ (idea); I can't imagine ⟨figure it out⟩; I can't even begin to guess; I'm at a (complete) loss; it's beyond me.**

«Так что же всё-таки, Альберт Евгеньевич, могло случиться в квартире Деменского?» — возвращая разговор к происшествию, спросил Антон. «Ума не приложу...» (Чернёнок 1). "Well, now what could have happened in Demensky's apartment, Albert Evgenievich?" Anton asked, returning the conversation to the incident. "I have no idea..." (1a). ♦ Жалко шинель, говорит Лопух. Куда она могла деться, ума не приложу (Зиновьев 1). "It's a pity about my greatcoat," said Burdock. "I can't imagine where it could have gone" (1a). ♦ «Нужен он [Костя] м-мне сейчас. Где найти — у-ума не приложу. Если он придёт, то пусть сразу ко мне позвонит» (Семёнов 1). "I n-need him [Kostya] now. Where can I find him—I'm at a complete loss. If he comes, tell him to ring me at once" (1a).

У-94 • **УМА́ ПАЛА́ТА** *(у кого) coll, occas. iron* [NP; Invar; usu. used as VP~subj/gen~ with быть~∅~ (pres or, rare, past) or as subj-compl with быть~∅~ (subj: human); fixed WO] s.o. is very intelligent: у X-a ума палата ≃ **X has a lot of brains; X is (as) smart as they come; X is (as) smart as a whip; X is (as) sharp as a tack; X is big ⟨long⟩ on brains.**

У-95 • **В ЗДРА́ВОМ УМЕ́ (И ТВЁРДОЙ ПА́МЯТИ); В ПО́ЛНОМ УМЕ́; В ПО́ЛНОМ ⟨ЗДРА́ВОМ, ТВЁР-ДОМ⟩ РАССУ́ДКЕ; В ПО́ЛНОЙ ⟨ТВЁРДОЙ⟩ ПА́МЯТИ** [PrepP; these forms only; subj-compl with copula (subj: human), nonagreeing modif, or adv; fixed WO] one is psychologically normal, sane: **in one's right mind; of sound mind; in full possession ⟨command⟩ of one's faculties; in full possession of one's senses.**

[Кири:] Необходимо сейчас же избрать нового правителя. [Лики:] Ага! Понял! Но кого? [Кири:] Меня. [Лики:] Ты — как, в здравом уме? (Булгаков 1). [K.:] We must choose a new leader immediately. [L.:] Aha! I see! But who? [K.:] Me. [L.:] You?! Are you in your right mind? (1a). ♦ «Нервная система истощена, — заключил доктор, — покой нужен». И другие с ним согласились. «Но человек перед нами в здравом уме и памяти» (Суслов 1). "Nervous exhaustion," the doctor concluded. "Needs rest." And the others agreed with him. "But the patient in question is of sound mind" (1a). ♦ ...[Я] даже смог убедиться в том, что геройский мэр Дижона, несмотря на свои 94 года, абсолютно в здравом уме (Свирский 1). I was able to prove to my own satisfaction that the heroic mayor of Dijon, despite his ninety-four years, was absolutely in full command of his faculties (1a). ♦ «...[Свидригайлов] оставил в своей записной книжке несколько слов, что он умирает в здравом рассудке и просит никого не винить в его смерти» (Достоевский 3). "He [Svidrigailov] left a few words in his notebook to the effect that he was dying in full possession of his faculties and requested that no one be blamed for his death" (3d). ♦ «Я не думаю, что умру... Но на всякий случай... Находясь в твёрдом уме и так далее... Евгений, не оставь Лёлю... Женись на ней... Не хочешь?» (Шолохов 4). "I don't think I'll die... But just in case... I hereby, while in full possession of my senses, and so on... Yevgeny, don't leave Olga... Marry her... Don't you want to?" (4a).

У-96 • **В СВОЁМ УМЕ́** *coll* [PrepP; Invar; usu. subj-compl with copula (subj: human); often neg; fixed WO] one is in a healthy mental state, sane: X в своём уме ≃ **X is in his right mind; X is of sound mind;** ‖ *Neg* X не в своём уме ≃ **X is out of his mind; X is off his head ⟨off his rocker etc⟩.**

«Экспертиза медиков стремилась доказать нам, что подсудимый не в своём уме и маньяк. Я утверждаю, что он именно в своём уме, но что это-то и всего хуже...» (Достоевский 2). "The medical experts strove to prove to us that the defendant is out of his mind and a maniac. I insist that he is precisely in his right mind, and so much the worse for him..." (2a). ♦ [Мелания:] Докажем, что завещатель не в своём уме был... (Горький 2). [M.:] We can prove that the man was not in his right mind when he made the will (2b). ♦ «Они, наверное, не в своём уме... До чего доводит слепая ненависть...» (Свирский 1). "They're obviously out of their minds....That's where blind hatred leads you" (1a).

У-97 • В УМЕ́ [PrepP; Invar] **1.** считать, решать ~ и т. п. [adv] (to count, solve a problem etc) mentally, without writing anything down (may refer to the unwritten transfer of a number from one column to another when doing an arithmetical calculation; the whole problem may or may not be written down): **(count ⟨add etc⟩) in one's head ⟨mind⟩;** [in refer. to the unwritten transfer of a number] **carry (in one's head).**

Была у Александра Ивановича удивительная способность. Он мгновенно умножал и делил в уме большие трёхзначные и четырёхзначные числа (Ильф и Петров 2). Alexander Ivanovich had a remarkable gift. With lightning speed he could multiply and divide in his mind large three-digit and four-digit figures (2b). ♦ Ничего, кое-как [Маргарита Антоновна] пересчитывала, делила на бумажке уголком, вспоминая школьные правила: «пять пишем, два в уме...» (Грекова 3). Never mind, somehow she recalculated, divided on the corner of the page, recalling the school rules: write five, carry the two (3a).

2. прикидывать, взвешивать ~ и т. п. [adv] (to consider, contemplate, weigh etc sth.) mentally, without saying anything aloud: **inwardly; in one's mind; to oneself.**

Пантелей никогда не ругал бывшего друга ни вслух, ни в уме (Аксёнов 6). Pantelei never swore at his former friend, neither inwardly or aloud (6a).

3. *coll* [subj-compl with быть∅ (subj: human, usu. 2nd pers), pres only; used (usu. in questions) as Interj] (used to express amazement, indignation, resentment etc in refer. to sth. said or done by the interlocutor) do you know what you are saying (or doing)?: да ты в уме? ≃ **are you in your right mind?; are you out of your mind?; are you off your head ⟨rocker etc⟩?; what are you saying ⟨doing⟩?**

«Убил отца он [Смердяков], а не брат. Он убил, а я его научил убить... Кто не желает смерти отца?..» — «Вы в уме или нет?» — вырвалось невольно у председателя (Достоевский 2). "It was he [Smerdyakov] who killed father, not my brother. He killed him, and killed him on my instructions....Who doesn't wish for his father's death?..." "Are you in your right mind?" inadvertently escaped from the judge (2a).

У-98 • ДЕРЖА́ТЬ В УМЕ́ ⟨В ГОЛОВЕ́⟩ *coll* [VP; subj: human] **1.** ~ *кого-что* to think about s.o. or sth. constantly: X держит Y-а в уме ≃ **X keeps thinking about Y; X dwells on thing Y.**

2. ~ *что* to retain sth. in one's memory: X держит в уме Y ≃ **X keeps ⟨stores⟩ Y in X's head; X's mind holds Y.**

В секретариате [Ежов] проявил себя хорошо, помнил, кто, где, когда, на каком месте работал, держал в голове сотни фамилий (Рыбаков 2). He [Yezhov] had proved himself at the secretariat. He had remembered who had worked where, when, and on what, and he kept hundreds of names in his head (2a). ♦ Как-то он [Иван] сказал писателю, чтобы тот перестал записывать и держал бы в уме свои жизненные наблюдения (Аксёнов 1). Once he [Ivan] told the writer to stop writing things down and to store his observations in his head (1a). ♦ Занимая неприметную и

низкооплачиваемую должность колхозного кладовщика, Гладышев зато имел много свободного времени для пополнения знаний и держал в своей маленькой головке столько различных сведений из различных областей, что люди, знакомые с ним, только вздыхали завистливо и уважительно — вот это, мол, да! (Войнович 2). Though he held the undistinguished and low-paying position of kolkhoz warehouseman, Gladishev did have a lot of free time for supplementing his knowledge, and his mind held such diverse information from such diverse fields that people who knew him could only sigh with envy and respect. He's really something! they'd say (2a).

3. ~ *что* [often neg; often foll. by a что-clause] to think or think up sth. and retain it in one's head: X держит Y в уме ≃ **X has Y in mind; X has Y in his head;** ‖ *Neg* X и в уме не держал Y-а ≃ **X never even imagined ⟨dreamed of⟩ Y; X never even thought (of) Y; Y never (even) occurred to X.**

«...Ресслих эта шельма, я вам скажу, она ведь что в уме держит: я наскучу, жену-то брошу и уеду, а жена ей достанется, она её и пустит в оборот...» (Достоевский 3). "...This Resslich woman's a sly old devil, let me tell you, and look what she has in mind: I'll get fed up, abandon my wife and go away, and then she'll get the wife and put her into circulation..." (3a).

У-99 • МЕША́ТЬСЯ/ПОМЕША́ТЬСЯ ⟨ТРО́НУТЬСЯ, ПОВРЕДИ́ТЬСЯ⟩ В УМЕ́ ⟨В РАССУ́ДКЕ, УМО́М, РАССУ́ДКОМ⟩ *substand* [VP; subj: human] to be or become insane: X помешался в уме ≃ **X went ⟨was⟩ mad ⟨out of his mind, off his nut, off his rocker etc⟩; X lost his mind; X was touched (in the head).**

Мчал Абдильхан, к седлу пригнувшись чёрной тучей. К аулу, к дому! Сородичи, что волчьей стаей рядом шли, ему кричали...: «Брат твой рассудком тронулся! Ума лишился!» (Айтматов 2). Abdil'khan, crouched low over the saddle, rode on like a black cloud. To the *aul* [the village]! Home! His kinsmen raced beside him like a pack of wolves, shouting, "Your brother is mad! He's gone out of his mind!" (2a). ♦ Сергея и его разоблачителя судило заочно ОСО, каждый получил по четвертной — 25 лет — по трём пунктам 58-ой статьи: 8-ой — террор, 10-ый — антисоветская пропаганда, 11-ый, — контрреволюционная организация. «Тот болван потом узнал, что за платину ему больше десятки и не карячилось. И считался бы хозяйственником, указником, а не врагом народа. Он чуть умом не тронулся» (Копелев 1). Sergei and his exposer were tried *in absentia* by the Special Commission, each got a quarter—twenty-five years—on three paragraphs of Article 58: 8 (terrorism), 10 (anti-Soviet propaganda), and 11 (counterrevolutionary organization). "That idiot later learned that he wouldn't have gotten more than ten years for the platinum. And he would have been considered an economic criminal, and not an enemy of the state. He almost went off his nut" (1a). ♦ «В последние дни он, сидя у меня, бредил. Я видела, что он мешается в уме» (Достоевский 2). "In the past few days, sitting with me, he was raving. I saw that he was losing his mind" (2a).

У-100 • НА УМЕ́ *у кого* [PrepP; Invar; the resulting PrepP is usu. subj-compl with быть∅ (subj: abstr or, less often, human)] some thing (or, occas., person) occupies s.o.'s thoughts: у Y-а на уме X ≃ **X is on Y's mind; Y has X on Y's mind; Y has X on the brain;** [of some trick, mischief etc] **Y is up to something; Y has something up his sleeve;** ‖ у Y-а одно ⟨один X, только X⟩ на уме ≃ **X is all Y thinks of; all Y thinks of is X; Y has only one thing on his mind—X; Y thinks of nothing but X; Y is obsessed ⟨has an obsession⟩ with X;** [in limited contexts] **Y has a one-track mind.**

Нет, надо скорей повидать Андрея, узнать, что у него на уме (Распутин 2). No, she had to see Andrei soon, to find out what was on his mind (2a). ♦ Величавая дикость прежнего времени исчезла без следа; вместо гигантов, сгибавших подковы и ломавших целковые, явились люди женоподобные, у которых были на уме только милые непристойности (Салтыков-Щедрин 1). The majestic savagery of former times disappeared without a trace; instead of giants bending horseshoes and breaking silver rubles, there were effeminate men who had only sweet indecencies on their minds (1a). ♦ «На уме мальчики, лак для ногтей, губная помада морковного цвета, разбирается» (Рыбаков 2). "Boys on the brain, painted fingernails, lipstick the color of carrots, she knows it all" (2a). ♦ «Ну, Егор, с тобой не соскучишься. Что же у тебя на уме, парень?» (Шукшин 1). "Well, Egor, with you it's never boring. What are you up to now, I wonder?" (1a). ♦ Степан Андреянович, сливая в чугун воду, покачал головой: «У нашего Егора одно на уме — клуб» (Абрамов 1). Stepan Andreyanovich shook his head as he poured water into the kettle, and he said, "Our Egor has only one thing on his mind: the club" (1a). ♦ «У тебя одно на уме — войти в историю» (Терц 4). "You've got this obsession with becoming a historical figure" (4a).

У-101 • ПЕРЕБИРА́ТЬ/ПЕРЕБРА́ТЬ В УМЕ́ ⟨В ПА́МЯТИ, В МЫ́СЛЯХ, В ГОЛОВЕ́⟩ *кого-что* [VP; subj: human; obj: if a count noun, usu. pl] to examine and re-examine sth. mentally, considering various possibilities (circumstances, people etc) in turn: X перебрал в уме Y-ов ≃ **X turned Ys over in X's mind; X went over Ys in X's mind; X sorted through Ys; X thought back over Ys; X mentally reviewed Ys.**

Я одолеваю этот путь как на крыльях, не замечая ни мороза, ни обледенелых колдобин под ногами... Снова и снова перебираю в памяти то, что сказал Б.Л. [Пастернак] (Гладков 1). The whole way I felt as if borne up on wings, oblivious of the frost and the icy potholes underfoot....Again and again I went over in my mind what Pasternak had said (1a). ♦ ...Чонкин задумался, стал перебирать в уме возможные варианты. И придумал (Войнович 2). Deep in thought, Chonkin began sorting through all the possible alternatives. Finally he came up with the solution (2a). ♦ Он перебрал в уме все места, где мог бы быть Трофимович, но тот мог быть где угодно... (Войнович 2). He mentally reviewed all the places Trofimovich could possibly be, but he could be anywhere... (2a).

У-102 • СВОЁ НА УМЕ́ *у кого coll* [Invar; used as VP_subj with быть∅; fixed WO] s.o. has a plan (intention etc) that he is not revealing: у X-а своё на уме ≃ **X has something up his sleeve.**

В ауле множество собак встретило нас громким лаем. Женщины, увидя нас, прятались; те, которых мы могли рассмотреть в лицо, были далеко не красавицы. «Я имел гораздо лучшее мнение о черкешенках», — сказал мне Григорий Александрович. «Погодите», — отвечал я усмехаясь. У меня было своё на уме (Лермонтов 1). At his village, a lot of dogs met us with loud barking. The women hid at the sight of us. Those whose faces we were able to make out were far from being beauties. "I had a far better opinion of Circassian women," said Pechorin to me. "Just wait!" I replied with a smile. I had something up my sleeve (1a).

У-103 • СЕБЕ́ НА УМЕ́ *coll* [Invar; usu. subj-compl with быть∅ (subj: human), pres or past; fixed WO] one is guarded, tight-lipped (with regard to his plans, intentions etc), guileful, protective of his own interests etc (the focus may be on any combination of the above elements; may imply that one's plans etc are not aboveboard): X себе на уме ≃ **X is secretive ⟨close-mouthed, sly etc⟩; X is secretive and wily ⟨sly, mindful of his own interests etc⟩; X plays a deep game.**

...Свидригайлов вдруг опять рассмеялся. Раскольникову явно было, что это на что-то твёрдо решившийся человек и себе на уме (Достоевский 3). ...Svidrigailov suddenly laughed again. It was obvious to Raskolnikov that this was a man with his mind firmly set on something and one who was also secretive (3a). ♦ Вообще Куник Глебову не нравился. Он был какой-то очень молчаливый, неприветливый... и себе на уме (Трифонов 2). Glebov disliked Kunik. He was so very taciturn, unfriendly, secretive

and wily (2a). ♦ Тут же кстати он [градоначальник] доведался, что глуповцы, по упущению, совсем отстали от употребления горчицы, а потому на первый раз ограничился тем, что объявил это употребление обязательным; в наказание же за ослушание прибавил ещё прованское масло... Но глуповцы тоже были себе на уме. Энергии действия они с большою находчивостью противопоставили энергию бездействия. «Что хошь [ungrammat = хочешь] с нами делай! — говорили одни, — хошь — на куски режь; хошь — с кашей ешь, а мы не согласны!» (Салтыков-Щедрин 1). At this point he [the governor] received the timely information that the Foolovites, out of negligence, had completely given up the use of mustard, and for that reason he confined himself at first to declaring its use obligatory; as punishment for disobedience he added olive oil besides....But the Foolovites, too, could play a deep game. To the energy of action they very resourcefully opposed the energy of inaction. "Do with us what you will!" said some. "Cut us into pieces, eat us with kasha, but we're not agreed!" (1a).

У-104 • БЕЗ У́МОЛКУ *говорить, болтать, трещать* и т. п. [PrepP; Invar; adv] (to talk, chatter, chirp etc) without stopping or growing quiet: **nonstop; without pause ⟨letup, a break⟩; incessantly; continuously; unceasingly.**

Завтрак продолжался долго. За первою бутылкой шампанского последовала другая, третья и четвёртая... Евдоксия болтала без умолку... (Тургенев 2). The lunch dragged on a long while. The first bottle of champagne was followed by another, a third, and even a forth....Evdoksya chattered without pause... (2b). ♦ «Государь, предупреждаю вас, что она в белой горячке и третий день как бредит без умолку» (Пушкин 2). "Your Majesty, I must warn you that she's in a delirium and has been raving incessantly for the last three days" (2a). ♦ Тогда заговорили все казачьи пулемёты, на опушинах леса жарко, без умолку зачастили винтовочные выстрелы... (Шолохов 5). Then all the Cossack machine-guns spoke at once, rifle shots cracked feverishly and continuously on the forest edge... (5a). ♦ Пока ехали, Антон без умолку болтал о своей новой идеологии, может быть, он решил за дорогу до аэропорта обратить и дедушку в свою веру (Аксёнов 7). [context transl] All the way to the airport Anton babbled on about his new ideology, as if trying to convert his grandfather in the time allotted (7a).

У-105 • ДОХОДИ́ТЬ/ДОЙТИ́ СВОИ́М ⟨(СВОИ́М) СО́БСТВЕННЫМ⟩ УМО́М *до чего;* **СВОИ́М УМО́М** *додуматься, догадаться* и т. п. *all coll* [VP (subj: human, more often pfv) or NP_instrum (Invar, adv)] to understand (figure out, guess etc) the sense or meaning of sth. independently, without assistance or guidance from anyone: X дошёл до Y-а своим умом ≃ **X worked ⟨figured⟩ it ⟨Y⟩ out himself ⟨by himself, for himself, on his own⟩; X came to it ⟨the conclusion, the solution etc⟩ by himself ⟨on his own⟩.**

«А в книжках этих каждый про своё брешет, поди разберись, где правда? Без книжек, своим умом дойти — самое дело...» (Максимов 2). "All those people who write books keep telling us different things — so how are *we* to know what's right and what to believe? Best thing to do is to work things out for yourself without any of them books..." (2a). ♦ «Да где же это видано, чтобы народ сам по себе собирался без всякого контроля со стороны руководства?» У Килина внутри всё остыло. «Так ведь, Сергей Никанорыч, ты же сам... вы ж сами говорили: стихийный митинг...» — «Стихией, товарищ Килин, нужно управлять!» — отчеканил Борисов. В трубке что-то щёлкнуло... [Килин] перевёл дыхание... Ведь всё так просто и понятно. Мог и сам своим умом догадаться: стихией нужно управлять (Войнович 2). "Who ever heard of people assembling all by themselves, without any control on the part of the leadership?" Kilin went cold inside. "But listen, Sergei Nikanorich, I mean, you said so yourself — a spontaneous meeting..." "Spontaneity, Comrade Kilin, must be controlled!" rapped out Borisov. Something clicked in the receiver....[Kilin] took a deep breath....Of course, it's all so simple, so easy to understand. I could have figured it out myself. Spontaneity must be controlled (2a). ♦ «...Коли бога бесконечного нет, то и нет никакой добродетели, да и не надобно её тогда вовсе...» — «Своим умом дошёл-с?» — криво усмехнулся Иван. — «Вашим руководством-с» (Достоевский 2). "...If there's no infinite God, then there's no virtue either, and no need of it at all...." "Did you figure it out for yourself?" Ivan grinned crookedly. "With your guidance, sir" (2a). ♦ «В какой-нибудь из греческих книг ты прочёл об этом?» — «Нет, я своим умом дошёл до этого» (Булгаков 9). "Did you read this in some Greek book?" "No, I came to it by myself" (9a).

У-106 • ЖИТЬ СВОИ́М ⟨СО́БСТВЕННЫМ⟩ УМО́М *coll* [VP; subj: human] to be independent in one's actions, hold to one's views, act in accordance with one's convictions: X живёт своим умом ≃ **X thinks for himself; X has a mind of his own; X lives his own way ⟨life⟩.**

[Кулигин:] Пора бы уж вам, сударь, своим умом жить (Островский 6). [K.:] It's high time, sir, you started to think for yourself (6a). ♦ «Что ж, Иван, живи своим умом, я тебе больше не советчик...» (Максимов 1). "All right, Ivan, live your own way. I shan't give you any more advice" (1a).

У-107 • ЖИТЬ ЧУЖИ́М УМО́М *coll* [VP; subj: human] not to be independent in one's actions, to adhere to and act in accordance with another's or others' views, convictions: X живёт чужим умом ≃ **X lives as others tell him to; X lets other people ⟨someone else⟩ think for him.**

У-108 • ЗА́ДНИМ УМО́М КРЕ́ПОК *coll* [AdjP; subj-compl with быть∅ (subj: human), pres only] one comprehends a situation, understands what must be done, which decision is the best etc only when it is too late, after the fact, when the time for taking proper action has passed: X задним умом крепок ≃ **X is wise after the event; X possesses the wisdom of hindsight.** Cf. **be a good Monday morning quarterback.**

[Женя:] Ох! Если бы ты могла забежать на десять лет вперёд. [Валя:] Все крепки задним умом (Рощин 1). [Zh.:] Oh, if only you could jump ten years ahead! [V.:] We're all wise after the event (1a).

< From the saying «Русский человек задним умом крепок» ("A Russian is wise after the event").

У-109 • РАСКИ́ДЫВАТЬ/РАСКИ́НУТЬ ⟨ПОРАСКИ́НУТЬ⟩ УМО́М ⟨МОЗГА́МИ⟩ *coll* [VP; subj: human] to deliberate, ponder sth.: X пораскинул умом ≃ **X thought ⟨mulled⟩ it over; X thought about it;** ‖ *Imper* пораскинь умом! ≃ **(just) think it over; (just) think about it; put your brain to work!; use your brain(s) ⟨head⟩!; put on your thinking cap!**

«Заберу детей и уйду к своим. Больше жить с ним не буду...» — «Только уйтить [*ungrammat* = уйти] от родного мужа нелегко... Пораскинь умом — сама увидишь» (Шолохов 5). "I'll take the children and go back to my own folk. I won't live with him any more...." "But it's not easy to leave your own husband....Just think it over and you'll see" (5a). ♦ ...Он вдруг спросил с хитроватой улыбкой, не попахивает ли корень шелковицей. «Вроде, — сказал я, — а что?» — «А ты пораскинь умом», — сказал он... (Искандер 3). ...He suddenly asked with a crafty smile whether the root didn't smell like mulberry. "Sort of," I said. "Why?" "Think about it," he said... (3a).

У-110 • С УМО́М; С СООБРАЖЕ́НИЕМ *both coll* [PrepP; these forms only; adv] (to do sth.) judiciously, in a sensible manner: **sensibly; levelheadedly; using one's head; using common sense ⟨one's wits⟩; intelligently; (having) one's wits about one.**

Прежде всего надо сделать более свободными поездки за границу. Любого выпускать, конечно, нельзя. Нужен отбор... Надо надёжных выпускать. Но с умом (Зиновьев 2). The first thing would be to make foreign travel easier. Of course, you can't just let anyone go. You have to be selective....You can let out only reliable people. But it must be done intelligently (2a). ♦ «Ты ему [бедуину] на верёвке свой товар опускаешь, он тебе на палке свой поднимает... Если ты ему раньше свой товар опустил, он его схватил и бежать... Тут надо всё с умом делать» (Войнович 1). "You lower your stuff down to him [the Bedouin] on a rope, and he lifts his up to you on a stick....If you lower your stuff down to him first, he'll grab it and run....You need your wits about you the whole time" (1a).

У-111 • ДО УМОПОМРАЧЕ́НИЯ *coll, often humor* [PrepP; Invar; adv (intensif) or modif] to the highest, most extreme degree possible: **terribly; tremendously; awfully; dreadfully; desperately;** [in limited contexts] **(be) crazy about.**

Она любит балет до умопомрачения. She's crazy about ballet. ♦ Я до умопомрачения был возмущён (Зиновьев 2). [context transl] I was practically beside myself with fury (2a).

У-112 • ХОТЬ УМРИ́ ⟨УМИРА́Й⟩ *coll* [хоть + VP$_{imper}$; subord clause; these forms only] (s.o. will or must accomplish sth.) without fail, whatever the cost: **even if it kills me ⟨you, him etc⟩; no matter what; come hell or high water.**

У-113 • НИ УМУ́ НИ СЕ́РДЦУ (ничего) не говорить, не давать *coll* [NP$_{dat}$; Invar; indir obj; fixed WO] neither (to stir) s.o.'s intellect nor (to touch) s.o.'s emotions to any degree: **(speak) neither to the mind nor (to) the heart; (offer) nothing for either the intellect or the emotions ⟨the heart⟩; (have) neither appeal nor substance.**

Беневоленский же возражал, что... такое выражение, как «мера возможности», ничего не говорит ни уму, ни сердцу... (Салтыков-Щедрин 1). ...Benevolensky objected that...an expression like "insofar as possible" spoke neither to the mind nor the heart... (1a). ♦ «Неужели же вам понравились эти зайцы?» — «Зайцы! — Он презрительно махнул рукой. — Кто говорит о зайцах? Глупая игра, не дающая ни уму ни сердцу» (Грекова 1). "Did you really like those rabbits?" "Rabbits"—he waved his hand contemptuously—"who's talking about rabbits? A stupid game holding nothing for either the intellect or the emotions" (1b).

У-114 • УМУ́ НЕПОСТИЖИ́МО [Invar; subj-compl with быть∅ (subj: a clause) or impers predic; fixed WO] sth. is absolutely unfathomable, impossible to comprehend or explain: **it's beyond (all) understanding ⟨belief⟩; it's inconceivable; it boggles the mind; the mind cannot grasp it; it defies understanding; it's beyond me.**

Толпа окружала лежавший на земле окровавленный человеческий обрубок. Изувеченный ещё дышал. У него были отрублены правая рука и левая нога. Было уму непостижимо, как на оставшейся другой руке и ноге несчастный дополз до лагеря (Пастернак 1). They [the crowd] stood around a bleeding stump of a man lying on the ground. His right arm and left leg had been chopped off. It was inconceivable how, with his remaining arm and leg, he had crawled to the camp (1a). ♦ «Нет, это просто удивительно, что мне удалось от неё удрать. Уму непостижимо, и как это она меня выпустила?» (Стругацкие 1). "No, it's just amazing that I managed to get away from her. It boggles the mind—how did she let me?" (1a). ♦ И что он рассказывал о немцах, о том, что они вытворяют, уму непостижимо, поверить невозможно (Рыбаков 1). As for what he told us about the Germans, what they were up to, the mind just couldn't grasp it, it was impossible to believe (1a).

У-115 • УЧИ́ТЬ/НАУЧИ́ТЬ УМУ́-РА́ЗУМУ *кого coll* [VP; subj: human or, less often, abstr; more often impfv; if pfv, usu. fut or subjunctive; more often this WO] to teach s.o. something good, helpful, admonish s.o., give s.o. advice on how to act or live: X научит Y-а уму-разуму ≃ **X will teach Y some**

(good) sense; **X will make Y see sense**; [when punishment is implied] **X will knock some sense into Y.**

...Надо сшибать с него спесь, учить его уму-разуму, этакого дурачка долговязого! (Трифонов 3). This lanky upstart should be taken down a peg or two and taught some sense (3a). ♦ «А этот, — она снисходительно кивнула в сторону мальчишки... — совсем от рук отбился, никакого сладу с ним нет. Был бы отец, научил к уму-разуму...» (Максимов 1). "But as for him," she gave a contemptuous nod in the direction of the boy... "he's got completely out of hand, I can't do anything with him. If his father was here he'd knock some sense into him..." (1a).

У-116 • В УНИСÓН [PrepP; Invar; adv] **1. петь, звучать ~** *(с чем) music* (to sing, sound notes etc) at the same pitch or in octaves: **in unison.**

2. ~ с чем, чему corresponding exactly to the mood, emotional spirit (of some person, group, happening etc): **in unison with; in harmony ⟨tune, keeping⟩ with; harmonize with.**

Музыка звучала в унисон моему меланхоличному настроению. The music was in keeping with my melancholy mood. ♦ «В воздухе чувствовалось дыхание приближающейся грозы». Этой фразой я завершу роман «В поисках радости»... Приближающаяся гроза оживляет пейзаж и звучит в унисон событиям: лёгкий намёк на революцию, на любовь моего Вадима к Татьяне Кречет... (Терц 4). "The breath of an approaching thunderstorm could be sensed in the air." With this phrase I would end my novel *In Search of Joy*....An approaching storm would enliven the landscape and harmonize with the novel's events, introducing a faint hint of revolution and of the love of my hero Vadim for Tatyana Krechet (4a).

3. ~ с кем-чем (to do sth.) in coordination, together (with s.o. or sth.): **as one; in unison.**

4. ~ отвечать (to answer) with the same inflection, intonation, expressing the same emotion (as one's interlocutor): **in the same fashion ⟨spirit, tone⟩; match(ing) s.o.'s tone.**

У-117 • ДО УПÁДУ ⟨-а⟩ *coll* [PrepP; these forms only; adv; usu. used with impfv verbs] (to do sth.) until one is completely exhausted, drained: **till ⟨until⟩ one drops; to the point of collapse ⟨exhaustion⟩; wear o.s. out (doing sth.);** ‖ смеяться ⟨хохотать⟩ ~ ≃ **laugh till one splits his sides; laugh o.s. silly; laugh one's head off;** ‖ веселиться ~ ≃ **have a ball; thoroughly enjoy o.s.**

«А я всё больше нажимал на производство. Вкалывал до упаду» (Копелев 1). "And I kept pushing the production part. I worked till I dropped" (1a). ♦ [Иванов:] Надо бы хохотать до упаду над моим кривляньем, а ты — караул! (Чехов 4). [I.:] You should laugh yourself silly at my antics, not sound the alarm-bell! (4b). ♦ Грузовики Старкомхоза и Мельстроя развозили детей... Несовершеннолетнее воинство потряхивало бумажными флажками и веселилось до упаду (Ильф и Петров 1). The children were riding in trucks belonging to the Stargorod communal services and the grain-mill-and-elevator-construction administration....The junior army waved paper flags and thoroughly enjoyed themselves (1a).

У-118 • В УПÓР [PrepP; Invar; adv] **1. подойти, подступить к кому, столкнуться ~ и т. п.** (to approach, come up to etc s.o.) very closely, so that hardly any distance separates one from s.o., (to run) directly, right (into s.o.): **face to face; eyeball-to-eyeball; right up to;** [in limited contexts] **(be) close up to.**

[extended usage] Человек взмахнул руками, вцепился в мою шубу, потряс меня, прильнул и стал тихонько выкрикивать: «Голубчик мой... доктор... скорее... умирает она»... Я взял безжизненную руку... Под пальцами задрожало мелко, часто, потом стало срываться, тянуться в нитку. У меня похолодело привычно под ложечкой, как всегда, когда я в упор видел смерть (Булгаков 6). The man waved his arms, clutched my fur coat and shook me as he pressed against me, moaning softly: "Oh, doctor...my dear fellow...quickly...she's dying."...I took the lifeless arm....I could feel a thin, rapid flutter which broke off and picked up again as a mere faint thread. I felt the customary stab of cold in the pit of my stomach as I always do when I see death face to face (6a). ♦ ...Штабс-капитан быстрым жестом схватил порожний стул... и поставил его чуть не посредине комнаты; затем, схватив другой такой же стул для себя, сел напротив Алёши, по-прежнему к нему в упор и так, что колени их почти соприкасались вместе (Достоевский 1). ...The captain seized an empty chair...and placed it almost in the middle of the room; then, seizing another chair, just like the first, for himself, he sat facing Alyosha, as close up to him as before, so that their knees almost touched (1a).

2. стрелять, целиться в кого-что, убить кого ~ и т. п. (to shoot, aim at s.o. or sth., kill s.o. etc) from a very short distance away, having moved right up to him or it: **point-blank; at point-blank ⟨close⟩ range.**

Высокий белобровый австриец... почти в упор выстрелил в Григория с колена. Огонь свинца опалил щёку. Григорий повёл пикой, натягивая изо всей силы поводья (Шолохов 2). A tall fair-browed Austrian...fired almost point-blank at Grigory from a kneeling position. The heat of the molten lead scorched Grigory's cheek. He aimed his lance and reined in with all his strength (2a). ♦ Вдруг слева ослепительно вспыхнуло — Борька подскочил и щёлкнул почти в упор (Трифонов 1). Suddenly there was a blinding flash from the left — it was Borka who had jumped forward and clicked his camera at almost point-blank range (1a). ♦ Долохов, бежавший рядом с Тимохиным, в упор убил одного француза... (Толстой 4). Dolokhov, running beside Timokhin, killed a Frenchman at close range... (4a).

3. смотреть на кого, рассматривать, разглядывать кого-что ~ и т. п. (to look at, examine etc s.o. or sth.) directly and intently: **look point-blank at; stare ⟨look⟩ straight ⟨right⟩ at ⟨into⟩; stare hard ⟨fixedly⟩ at.**

«А что он сделал?» — спросил Сталин и в упор посмотрел на Берию. «Болтает лишнее, выжил из ума», — сказал Берия (Искандер 3). "What has he done?" Stalin asked. He looked point-blank at Beria. "He blabs too much, he's gotten senile," Beria said (3a). ♦ Сталин медленно поднялся, не протянул руки, продолжал в упор смотреть на Будягина (Рыбаков 2). Without extending his hand, Stalin got up slowly and continued to look straight at Budyagin (2a). ♦ «Это что ещё такое?» — вскричал [Иван Фёдорович], вглядываясь в упор в лицо пристава, и вдруг, схватив его за плечи, яростно ударил об пол (Достоевский 2). "What is the meaning of this?" Ivan Fyodorovich exclaimed, staring straight into the marshal's face, and suddenly, seizing him by the shoulders, he flung him violently to the floor (2a). ♦ «Ухожу в армию, сын. К матери поедешь». — «Не хочу туда, — нахлынился Влад... — У деда Савелия останусь». Влад сказал и тут же осёкся. Отец смотрел в упор, излучая на него столько горечи и снисходительного презрения, что он не выдержал, сдался... (Максимов 2). "I'm going away to join the army, son. You must go back to your mother." "I don't want to," Vlad objected.... "I'll stay with grandfather." As Vlad said this he stopped short. His father stared hard at him, radiating such bitterness and condescending scorn that his resistance faltered and he capitulated (2a). ♦ «Трою основали Тевкр, Дардан, Иллюс и Трос», — разом отчеканил мальчик и в один миг весь покраснел, так покраснел, что на него жалко стало смотреть. Но мальчики все на него глядели в упор... (Достоевский 1). "Troy was founded by Teucer, Dardanus, Ilius, and Tros," the boy rapped out at once, and instantly blushed all over, blushed so much that it was pitiful to see. But all the boys stared fixedly at him... (1a).

4. сказать, спросить ~ (to say, ask) directly and in plain terms: **point-blank; flat out; bluntly.**

«Где брала?» — в упор спросил Николай. «Чего?» — испугалась учительница. «Да танкетки ж», — нетерпеливо сказал Николай (Войнович 5). "Where'd you get them?" Nikolai asked point-blank. "Get what?" said the teacher, quite startled. "The shoes, the shoes," said Nikolai impatiently (5a). ♦ «Осмелюсь узнать, служить изволили?» — «Нет, учусь...» — ответил молодой человек, отчасти удивлённый и особенным витиеватым тоном речи, и тем, что так прямо, в упор, обратились к нему (Достоевский 3). "May I venture to inquire, pray: have you been in the service?" "No, I study..." replied the young man, taken aback partly by the peculiar, orotund manner of the other's speech and partly by the fact that he had been so directly and bluntly addressed (3a).

У-119 • **В УПО́Р НЕ ВИ́ДЕТЬ** *кого highly coll* [VP; subj: human; pres or past; fixed WO] to ignore s.o. completely, usu. in a demonstrative fashion: X Y-а в упор не видит ≃ **X looks right through ⟨past⟩ Y; X pretends not to see Y; X snubs Y.**

Он зазнался, старых друзей в упор не видит. He's gotten a swelled head, and he snubs his old friends.

У-120 • **ДЕ́ЛАТЬ/СДЕ́ЛАТЬ УПО́Р** *на что, на чём* [VP; subj: human] to underscore sth., pay or call special attention to sth.: X делает упор на Y ≃ **X emphasizes ⟨stresses, underlines⟩ Y; X places ⟨lays⟩ (the) emphasis on Y; X lays special stress on Y.**

Хардин, адвокат Убожко, делал упор на то, что Убожко — психопат... (Амальрик 1). Khardin, defense counsel for Ubozhko, emphasized his client's psychopathic personality (1a). ♦ «И христиане, не выдумав ничего нового, точно так же создали своего Иисуса, которого на самом деле никогда не было в живых. Вот на это-то и нужно сделать главный упор...» (Булгаков 9). "And the Christians, lacking any originality, invented their Jesus in exactly the same way. In fact, he never lived at all. That's where the emphasis has got to be placed" (9b).

У-121 • **ДО УПО́РА** *напиться, пьян* и т. п. *slang* [PrepP; Invar; modif or adv (intensif)] (to get or be) extremely (drunk): X был пьян ⟨напился⟩ ~ ≃ **X was ⟨got⟩ blind drunk; X was ⟨got⟩ smashed ⟨plastered, pickled, stewed etc⟩; X was loaded ⟨stewed⟩ to the gills.**

У-122 • **НАЙТИ́ УПРА́ВУ** *на кого coll* [VP; subj: human] to curtail s.o.'s arbitrary or lawless actions, often punishing him as well: X найдёт на Y-а управу ≃ **X will find a way to stop Y;** [in limited contexts] **X will not let Y get away with it;** [in refer. to illegal or criminal actions only] **X will get the law after Y.**

У-123 • **УПРА́ВЫ НЕТ** *на кого coll* [VP; impers] it is impossible to control s.o., keep s.o. from acting reprehensibly etc: на X-а управы нет ≃ **there is no way to stop ⟨restrain etc⟩ X; there is no (way of) stopping ⟨restraining etc⟩ X; there is no way ⟨it is impossible⟩ to keep X in check ⟨in line, under control etc⟩.**

«...Управы на них нет. Хорошенький пример контингенту показывают! Не хозяйство, а кабак круглосуточный!» (Максимов 1). "There's no way of stopping them. A very good example they give to the men! They never do a stroke of work—it's round-the-clock drinking" (1a).

У-124 • **НА УРА́** [PrepP; Invar; adv] **1.** взять, захватить *что* (крепость, город и т. п.) ~ (to take, seize sth.—a fortress, town etc) by a swift assault, attack: **by storm.**

2. *coll* (to venture sth.) without adequate preparation, hoping to be aided by luck, or (to succeed in accomplishing sth.) even though one did not prepare adequately, aided by luck: **on luck alone.**

«Ты что, надеешься сдать экзамен на ура?» — спросила мать, видя, что Сергей даже не притронулся к учебникам. "What, do you expect to pass your exam on luck alone?" asked Sergei's mother, seeing that he hadn't even touched his books.

3. прошёл, приняли *кого-что* и т. п. ~ *coll* sth. went excellently, s.o. or sth. was received with enthusiasm: (s.o.

⟨sth.⟩ was) a hit ⟨a smash, a smash hit⟩; (s.o. ⟨sth.⟩ was) a tremendous ⟨smashing, great etc⟩ success; (sth.) went off tremendously ⟨wonderfully etc⟩; (s.o. ⟨sth.⟩ was received) enthusiastically; (s.o. ⟨sth.⟩ was received) with hurrahs; [in limited contexts] (pass an exam ⟨a test etc⟩) with flying colors.

...Читка прошла «на ура», и по дороге домой Маяковский был в прекрасном настроении... (Катаев 3). ...The reading was a tremendous success and on the way home Mayakovsky was jubilant... (3a). ♦ С того письма, нет, уже с «Августа» начинается процесс раскола моих читателей, потери сторонников, и со мной остаётся меньше, чем уходит. «На ура» принимали меня пока я был, по видимости, только против сталинских злоупотреблений... (Солженицын 2). It is not from this letter, but earlier, from the appearance of *August 1914*, that we must date the schism among my readers, the steady loss of supporters, with more leaving me than remained behind. I was received with "hurrahs" as long as I appeared to be against Stalinist abuses only... (2a). ♦ Так или иначе, а Ирина Викторовна прошла в НИИ-9 «на ура»... (Залыгин 1). All in all Irina Viktorovna passed the test with flying colours... (1a).

У-125 • **В У́РОВЕНЬ** [PrepP; Invar; adv] **1.** становиться, ставить *кого* ~ *с кем obs.* Also: **НА (ОДИ́Н) У́РОВЕНЬ** (to end up or put s.o.) in(to) the same category as another (with regard to morals, conduct etc): **on the same level as; on a par ⟨a level⟩ with; in a class with.**

Вероятно, по её замыслу, я должна была осознать, что своим неслыханным поступком я поставила себя на один уровень с уголовниками (Гинзбург 2). Presumably her idea was that I should be made to realize that my unprecedented action had put me on a level with common criminals (2a).

2. идти, развиваться, стоять и т. п. ~ *с чем* (to move, develop etc) at a pace equal to that of (some branch of science, technology etc, or the times in general), (to be) in full conformity with (some requirements): **keep ⟨stay⟩ abreast of ⟨with⟩; keep up with; keep pace (with);** ‖ X идёт в уровень с веком ≃ **X keeps ⟨stays⟩ abreast of the times; X keeps up with the times; X keeps ⟨is⟩ in step with the times; X keeps up-to-date.**

«Кажется, я всё делаю, чтобы не отстать от века: ...читаю, учусь, вообще стараюсь стать в уровень с современными требованиями...» (Тургенев 2). "I thought I was doing everything to keep up with the times:...I read, I study, I try in every way to keep abreast with the requirements of the age..." (2c).

У-126 • **НА У́РОВНЕ** [PrepP; Invar] **1.** ~ *чего* [the resulting PrepP is subj-compl with copula (subj: human or concr)] at or on the same horizontal plane as s.o. or sth.: **at the level of; at ⟨on⟩ a level with; level with.**

Когда она присела на корточки, её глаза оказались на уровне глаз ребёнка. When she squatted down her eyes were on a level with the child's.

2. ~ *кого, каком* [the resulting PrepP is adv or nonagreeing postmodif] at the specified level, involving people of the specified rank, status etc: **at the level of; at (the) [AdjP] level;** ‖ на высоком ⟨высшем⟩ уровне ≃ **at the highest level;** ‖ встреча ⟨совещание⟩ на высшем уровне ≃ **summit (meeting ⟨conference⟩).**

Такие «проблемы» приходилось ежедневно решать на самом высшем уровне с огромными потерями времени, с невероятными расходами, при сильнейшем нервном напряжении (Владимиров 1). Such problems had to be resolved every day at the highest level with tremendous loss of time, unbelievable expense and extreme nervous strain (1a). ♦ Забавное зрелище представляют... встречи на высшем уровне, когда встречаются главы политической власти Запада и неполитической власти Ибанска (Зиновьев 1). ...Summit meetings between the leaders of the political powers of the West and the leaders of the non-political power of Ibansk present an amusing spectacle (1a).

3. *coll* [subj-compl with copula (subj: any noun)] a person (thing, organization etc) meets the strictest standards: **X на уровне** ≃ **X is up to the mark; X is up to par ⟨snuff, scratch⟩; X can pass muster.**

У-127 • ДАТЬ УРÓК *кому* [VP; subj: human] to reprimand or punish s.o. in such a way as to ensure that he will improve his behavior and not act similarly again: **X дал Y-у урок** ≃ **X taught ⟨gave⟩ Y a (good ⟨painful etc⟩) lesson; X taught Y a thing or two.**

«О, ему надо дать урок, чтоб этого вперёд не было! Попрошу *ma tante* отказать ему от дома: он не должен забываться...» (Гончаров 1). "He must be taught a lesson, so it doesn't happen again! I'll tell *ma tante* not to permit him to come to the house: he must not again forget himself" (1b). ♦ «Что же вы намерены делать?» — «Дать ему такой урок, которого он долго не забудет» (Герцен 3). "What do you intend to do?" "Give him such a lesson as he will not forget for some time" (3a).

У-128 • (И) В УС (СЕБÉ) НЕ ДУТЬ *coll* [VP; subj: human; usu. pres or past; fixed WO] not to care (about sth. one should care about, or about anything at all): **X и в ус не дует** ≃ **X doesn't give a damn; X couldn't ⟨could⟩ care less.**

Есть такие молодцы, что весь век живут на чужой счёт, наберут, нахватают справа, слева, да и в ус не дуют! Как они могут покойно уснуть, как обедают — непонятно! (Гончаров 1). There were, of course, those clever fellows who lived their entire lives at other people's expense, grabbing right and left, never giving a damn! How could they sleep in peace? How could they enjoy their dinner? Incomprehensible! (1b).

У-129 • МОТÁТЬ ⟨НАМÁТЫВАТЬ⟩/НАМОТÁТЬ (СЕБÉ) НА УС *coll* [VP; subj: human; often imper] to pay special attention to and remember sth. (sometimes so that it can be taken into consideration when making future plans, decisions etc): **X намотал себе на ус** ≃ **X took note (of sth.); X made a mental note (of sth.); X stored (sth.) away in his mind; X kept in mind (that...);** ‖ *Imper* **намотай (себе) на ус** ≃ **(and) don't (you) forget it.**

Передонов был ошеломлён. Наскажет чего и не было, а жандармский на ус намотает и, пожалуй, напишет в министерство. Это скверно (Сологуб 1). Peredonov was stunned. She might say a lot of things, true and untrue, which the police lieutenant might take note of and, perhaps, report to the ministry. It promised to be a nasty business (1a). ♦ Бунин в прекрасном, несколько саркастическом настроении. Он искоса смотрит на могучую даму... «Вам, Елена Васильевна, не хватает маленьких чёрных усиков, и вы — вылитый... Пётр Великий»... Мотаю себе на ус, обобщая бунинскую находку: «дамское лицо Петра» (Катаев 3). Bunin is in a splendid, rather sarcastic mood. He glances sideways at the forceful corpulent lady...."All you need, Elena Vasilyevna, is a little black moustache and you would be the image of—Peter the Great."...I stored the incident away in my mind, generalizing Bunin's discovery as "the feminine face of Peter" (3a). ♦ ...[Смерды] мотали себе на ус, что если долгое время не будет у них дождя или будут дожди слишком продолжительные, то они могут своих излюбленных богов высечь... (Салтыков-Щедрин 1). ...They [the peasants] kept in mind that if they had no rain for a long time or if the rains lasted too long, they could flog their chosen gods... (1a). ♦ «Слушайте, что брат-то говорит, — наставительно сказала Лизка. — Наматывайте себе на ус» (Абрамов 1). "Listen to what your brother's saying," said Lizka didactically, "and don't forget it" (1a).

У-130 • СÁМИ С УСÁМИ *coll;* **САМ С УСÁМ** *substand* [AdjP; these forms only; subj-compl with быть∅ (subj: human),

usu. 1st pers; fixed WO] we are (or I am) not stupid, we (or I) understand things (or the matter in question) perfectly well (no worse than others): мы сами с усами ≃ **we weren't ⟨I wasn't⟩ born yesterday (either); we ⟨I⟩ know what's what (too); we ⟨I⟩ know a thing or two about (sth.) ourselves ⟨myself⟩.**

Это она и есть, она самая – Кроваткина. Сущая ведьма. Ухо к дверям приложит и контролирует, о чём мы с вами беседуем. Уж я её чувствую, знаю. Раз говорю – значит знаю! У меня на это дело такое осязание есть. Сами с усами (Терц 5). That's who it is, Krovatkina in person. A real witch. Glues her ear to the door and keeps a check on our conversation. Oh, I can sense her all right; I know. If I say so, that means I know! I've got a feeling for those things, wasn't born yesterday (5a). ♦ Больной завозился... Кое-кто из солдат засмеялся. «Жалеете вы его, ребятки, напрасно. Жалостью вы не поможешь, не такое теперь время. Вас тоже пожалеть надо...» Семидолец перебил его: «Ты зубы-то не заговаривай, мил-человек, мы сами с усами. Ты... скажи, что тебе про Расею [*ungrammat* = Россию] известно?» (Федин 1). The sick man began to toss about....One or two of the soldiers laughed. "Your pity for him is a waste of time, boys. Pity won't help him, it's not the time for it now. You are also to be pitied...." The man from Semidol cut him short: "Don't you spin us no fine yarns, kind sir, we know what's what. You tell us...what you know about Russia" (1a).

У-131 • МЕДВÉЖЬЯ УСЛÚГА *coll* [NP; sing only; usu. obj of оказать; fixed WO] an action or gesture intended to help s.o. that unwittingly turns out to cause him trouble, discomfort etc: **a good deed that backfired; misdirected good intentions; (unintentional) disservice; (do) more harm than good;** [in limited contexts] **a lot of help *that* was!**

Соколов помялся: «Такое чувство, Виктор Павлович, что ваши хвалители и поклонники оказывают вам медвежью услугу, — начальство раздражается» (Гроссман 2). Sokolov hesitated for a moment. "I get the feeling, Viktor Pavlovich, that the people who sing your praises so unreservedly are doing you a disservice. It upsets the authorities" (2a).

< From Ivan Krylov's fable "Hermit and Bear" («Пустынник и Медведь»), 1808.

У-132 • УСЛÚГА ЗА УСЛÚГУ [saying] sth. nice done for s.o. is or will be reciprocated: ≃ **one good turn deserves another;** [in limited contexts] **(you) scratch my back and I'll scratch yours; one hand washes the other.**

Мандельштам решил пристроить урбаниста комсомольскому Авербаху. Мальчишку Авербах взял рассыльным, а Мандельштама попросил перевести — услуга за услугу — стишок какого-то революционного венгра (Мандельштам 2). M[andelstam] sent the young urbanist to Averbakh, who took him on as an errand boy. On the principle that one good turn deserves another, Averbakh commissioned M[andelstam] to translate a poem by some Hungarian revolutionary (2a).

У-133 • ГОТÓВЫЙ К УСЛÚГУ *obs* [formula phrase; fixed WO] a polite closing phrase before the signature in a letter: **(I remain) your (most) humble servant; I am, (dear) Sir ⟨Madam⟩, your (most) humble servant; (I remain) at your service.**

«В любом случае вы дискредитируете советскую власть, которую на вашей должности вы собой представляете. Засим остаюсь готовый к услугам гр. В. Войнович» (Войнович 3). "In any case, you discredit the Soviet regime, which through your office you represent. I remain, ever, at your service, Ct. V. Voinovich" (3a).

У-134 • К ВÁШИМ ⟨ТВОЙМ⟩ УСЛÚГАМ *obs* [PrepP; these forms only; used as formula phrase or as subj-compl with быть∅ (subj: я or мы); fixed WO] used to express one's readiness to be of service: **(I am ⟨we are⟩) at your service ⟨disposal⟩.**

«...Но, серьёзно, у меня есть много кой о чём переговорить с вами, барон!» — «К вашим услугам...» (Салтыков-Щедрин 2). "But, seriously, I've lots of things to discuss with you, baron." "At your service..." (2a). ♦ «Вы можете мне помочь в моих агрономических работах; вы можете дать мне какой-нибудь полезный совет». — «Я к вашим услугам, Николай Петрович» (Тургенев 2). "You can be of assistance to me in my agricultural work; you can give me some useful advice." "I am at your service, Nikolai Petrovich..." (2b).

У-135 • К УСЛУ́ГАМ чьим, кого obs [PrepP; Invar; the resulting PrepP is subj-compl with copula (subj: human or concr)] s.o. or sth. is offered to some person for his use: X к Y-овым услугам ≃ **X is at Y's service ⟨disposal⟩.**

«Хотите пороху понюхать? — сказал он Пьеру. — Да, приятный запах. Имею честь быть обожателем супруги вашей, здорова она? Мой привал к вашим услугам» (Толстой 6). "So you want to smell gunpowder?" he said to Pierre. "Yes, it's a pleasant smell. I have the honor to be one of your wife's adorers. Is she well? My quarters are at your disposal" (6a).

У-136 • НЕ УСПЕ́Л ⟨НЕ УСПЕ́ЕШЬ и т. п.⟩... КАК... [used as temporal correlative Conj; не успел etc is foll. by pfv infin; fixed order of clauses] (of two actions, one of which immediately follows the other) the moment one does one thing (or sth. happens) something else happens: **hardly ⟨barely⟩...when ⟨and⟩; no sooner...than.**

[Артемий Филиппович:] Больной не успеет войти в лазарет, как уже здоров... (Гоголь 4). [A.F.:] A sick man hardly gets into the infirmary and he's already well... (4a). [A.F.:] A patient no sooner sets foot in the hospital than he's cured (4f).

У-137 • С ТЕМ ЖЕ ⟨ТАКИ́М ЖЕ, ОДИНА́КОВЫМ⟩ УСПЕ́ХОМ coll, often iron [PrepP; these forms only; adv; fixed WO] with a similar lack of success (used when comparing the results of a real action, approach etc with those of an exaggerated one invented by the speaker): **might ⟨could⟩) just as well ⟨easily⟩; (might) equally well; with equal ⟨exactly the same⟩ success.**

...Я начала вдруг настойчиво писать на материк, чтобы выслали... копии моих документов об образовании. Ну пусть только университетский диплом. Юля уверяла меня, что я с таким же успехом могла бы попросить, чтобы мне выслали звезду с неба (Гинзбург 2). ...I dashed off various letters to the mainland requesting copies...of my academic documents. At the very least, a copy of my university diploma. Julia assured me that I might equally well ask them to send me a star from the sky (2a). ♦ После первого же урока я убедился, что объяснять Марусе что бы то ни было совершенно бессмысленно. Она ничего не могла понять... С таким же успехом, как Марусю, я мог бы обучать истории, географии и русскому языку попугая (Паустовский 1). I was convinced after the first lesson that it would make no sense at all to try to explain anything to Marusa. She could not understand a thing....I could have taught history, geography, and Russian grammar to a parrot with exactly the same success (1b).

У-138 • ИЗ ПЕ́РВЫХ УСТ узнать, услышать что [PrepP; Invar; adv; fixed WO] (to find out, hear sth.) from an eyewitness (eyewitnesses), or a participant (participants): **(straight) from the horse's mouth; from s.o.'s own lips; firsthand; from the source.**

У-139 • ИЗ ТРЕ́ТЬИХ ⟨ВТОРЫ́Х⟩ УСТ узнать, услышать что [PrepP; these forms only; adv; fixed WO] (to find out, hear sth.) not from eyewitnesses or direct participants, but through an intermediary (intermediaries): **at second hand; secondhand; thirdhand; through the grapevine.**

У-140 • ИЗ УСТ чьих, кого узнать, услышать что [PrepP; Invar; the resulting PrepP is adv] (to find out, hear sth.) from the named person: **from s.o.'s lips; from (the mouth of); coming from.**

Он надеялся увидеть графиню Румянцеву и, может быть, даже из её уст услышать подтверждение случившемуся (Окуджава 2). He hoped to find Countess Rumyantseva there, and perhaps obtain a confirmation of the incident from her (2a). ♦ Такие слова — из уст профессора? Трудно поверить! Such words coming from a professor? Hard to believe!

У-141 • ИЗ УСТ В УСТА́ переходить, передавать(ся) [PrepP; Invar; adv; usu. used with impfv verbs; fixed WO] (of rumors, stories, news, jokes etc) (to be passed, conveyed) orally from one person to another: **be spread ⟨pass around etc⟩) by word of mouth; be going (a)round; go ⟨make⟩ the rounds.**

В ту пору Самиздата почти не было. Стихи из уст в уста... передавались, но только политические (Эткинд 1). In those days there was virtually no Samizdat. There were poems passed around by word of mouth...but they were always political (1a). ♦ ...Боевые орлы отливались из чистого золота и серебра — передавалось из уст в уста какое-то замечание профессора (Домбровский 1). ...The rumour was going round, based on one of the professor's remarks, that Roman eagles had been made of pure gold and silver (1a). ♦ Об её поступке уже несколько лет передавали из уст в уста (Гинзбург 2). The tale of her exploit had made the rounds for many years now (2a).

У-142 • ВКЛА́ДЫВАТЬ/ВЛОЖИ́ТЬ что **В УСТА́** чьи, кого, кому lit [VP; subj: human; direct obj: usu. слова, мысли etc] (usu. in refer. to the words that an author has his characters say) to get s.o. to say certain words, voice certain thoughts: X вложил Y-и в Z-овы уста ≃ **X put ⟨placed⟩ Ys into Z's mouth ⟨into the mouth of Z⟩.**

«Автор пишет на языке, имеющем мало общего с русским. Он любит выдумывать слова. Он... вкладывает в уста действующих лиц торжественные, но не совсем грамотные сентенции...» (Набоков 1). "The author writes in a language having little in common with Russian. He loves to invent words. He...places solemn but not quite grammatical maxims in the mouths of his characters..." (1a).

У-143 • БЕЗ У́СТАЛИ [PrepP; Invar; adv; used with impfv verbs] (to do sth.) continuously, (of animates only) without experiencing a desire or need to stop and rest: **incessantly; unceasingly; tirelessly; indefatigably; without stopping ⟨getting tired⟩.**

Он веселился без устали, почти ежедневно устраивал маскарады... (Салтыков-Щедрин 1). He made merry tirelessly, arranged masquerades almost every day... (1a). ♦ Без устали звонил телефон — звали Веру Платоновну (Грекова 3). The telephone rang unceasingly for Vera Platonovna (3a). ♦ Фомин и его соратники каждый по-своему убивали время: ...Фомин и Чумаков без устали играли в самодельные, вырезанные из бумаги карты; Григорий бродил по острову, подолгу просиживал возле воды (Шолохов 5). Fomin and his men each found their own ways of passing the time....Fomin and Chumakov played indefatigably with makeshift cards; Grigory roamed about the island and sat for long hours by the water (5a). ♦ Откуда мне знать, нужен ли парню отец, когда у парня рост метр восемьдесят, канадская стрижка, бас, когда он может три часа танцевать без устали... (Трифонов 5). How am I to judge whether a boy needs a father when the boy in question is taller than I am, has a bass voice and a mod haircut; when he can dance for three hours without getting tired... (5a). ♦ Он оказался болтливым, надоедливым собеседником. Чай поглощал без устали (Шолохов 4). [context transl] He turned out to be a garrulous companion, and his thirst for tea was insatiable (4a).

У-144 • НЕ ЗНАТЬ У́СТАЛИ [VP; subj: human] to be hardy, strong, in a condition to work for long stretches of time without getting tired: X не знает устали ≃ **X is indefatigable** ⟨**tireless**⟩; **X's energy never runs out.**

У-145 • ВА́ШИМИ ⟨ТВОИ́МИ⟩ БЫ УСТА́МИ (ДА) МЁД ПИТЬ [saying] it would be good if everything would turn out as you say (said in response to favorable predictions, assumptions, comforting words etc): ≃ **may your words come true; from your mouth ⟨lips⟩ to God's ear(s).**

«Франция спит, мы её разбудим». Мне оставалось сказать: «Дай бог вашими устами мёд пить!» (Герцен 3). "France is asleep, but we shall wake her up." There was nothing left for me to say but, "God grant that your words may come true!" (3a).

У-146 • В УСТА́Х чьих, кого [PrepP; Invar; the resulting PrepP is adv] when spoken, verbalized by s.o.: **coming from s.o. ⟨from s.o.'s lips⟩; on s.o.'s lips.**

«Комаровский был там». — «Разве? Вполне возможно...» — «Отчего ты покраснела?» — «От звука „Комаровский" в твоих устах» (Пастернак 1). "Komarovsky was there." "Was he? Quite possible...." "Why are you blushing?" "At the sound of Komarovsky's name coming from you" (1a). ♦ Француз, к сожалению, очень скоро ушёл, на прощанье... сказал: «Я думаю, это лучше для вас — что вас бросила жена». В его устах это звучало убедительно... (Лимонов 1). The Frenchman very soon left, unfortunately. In parting he...said, "I think you're better off that your wife deserted you." On his lips this sounded convincing (1a).

У-147 • НА УСТА́Х [PrepP; Invar] **1.** *(у кого)* ~ *obs* [subj-compl with быть₀ (subj: usu. abstr) or adv] sth. is about to be said, mentioned, s.o. is ready to say, mention sth.: X был у Y-а на устах ≃ **X was on ⟨rose to⟩ Y's lips; Y was ready ⟨about⟩ to say ⟨ask, mention etc⟩ X.**

«Эпоха умрёт с моим именем на устах» (Олеша 2). "Our epoch will die with my name on its lips" (2a). ♦ По связи воспоминаний, Пьер мгновенно перенёсся воображением к тому времени, когда он, утешая её, сказал ей, что ежели бы он был не он, а лучший человек в мире и свободен, то он на коленях просил бы её руки, и то же чувство жалости, нежности, любви охватило его, и те же слова были у него на устах. Но она не дала ему времени сказать их (Толстой 6). By an association of ideas Pierre was instantly carried back to the time when, trying to comfort her, he had said that if he were not himself but the best man in the world and free, he would be on his knees begging for her hand, and the same feeling of pity, tenderness, and love took posession of him and the same words rose to his lips. But she did not give him time to utter them (6a).

2. *у кого* ~ [subj-compl with быть₀ (subj: usu. abstr)] sth. is continually mentioned, discussed, repeated: X у Y-ов на устах ≃ **X is on Ys' lips; X keeps popping ⟨cropping⟩ up (in conversation);** ‖ X у всех на устах ≃ **X is on everybody's lips ⟨on every lip, on every tongue⟩; everyone is talking about X.**

...Широкому кругу читателей он [Бунин] был мало заметен среди шумной толпы — как он с горечью выразился — «литературного базара». Его затмевали звёзды первой величины, чьи имена были на устах у всех: Короленко, Куприн, Горький, Леонид Андреев, Мережковский, Фёдор Сологуб... (Катаев 3). ...For the wider public he [Bunin] did not stand out from among the noisy crowd of what he bitterly called the "literary bazaar." He was overshadowed by stars of the first magnitude, whose names were on every lip: Korolenko, Kuprin, Gorky, Leonid Andreyev, Merezhkovsky, Fyodor Sologub... (3a).

У-148 • ГА́ДКИЙ УТЁНОК *coll* [NP; sing only; fixed WO] an unattractive, plain child who grows up to become a very attractive, accomplished adult: **ugly duckling.**

< From the Russian translation of Hans Christian Andersen's story of that title.

У-149 • УТОПА́ЮЩИЙ ХВАТА́ЕТСЯ (И) ЗА СОЛО́МИНКУ [saying] a person in a hopeless situation will do anything to try to extricate himself from it, including taking measures that obviously will not help: ≃ **a drowning man will grasp ⟨clutch, catch⟩ at a straw ⟨at straws⟩.**

[Лидия:] Ради бога, maman! подите к моему мужу, позовите его сюда, скажите, что я умираю... [Надежда Антоновна:] Я сейчас еду. *(Уходит.) (Входит Андрей.)* [Андрей:] Господин Глумов. [Лидия *(привстав):*] Принимать его или нет? Ещё муж придёт или нет, неизвестно. Утопающий хватается за соломинку. *(Андрею.)* Проси! (Островский 4). [L.:] For heaven's sake, mamma, go to my husband and call him here. Tell him I'm dying.... [N.A.:] I'll go this minute. *(She goes out.) (Andrey comes in.)* [A.:] Mr. Glumov. [L. *(who has risen):*] Shall I receive him or not? I still don't know whether my husband will come. A drowning man catches at a straw. *(To Andrey.)* Show him in! (4a).

У-150 • ВЕЗЁТ КАК УТО́ПЛЕННИКУ *кому coll, humor* [VP; impers; usu. pres or past] s.o. is very unlucky: X-у везёт как утопленнику ≃ **X has rotten ⟨the worst etc⟩ luck; X has no luck at all; talk about bad ⟨rotten etc⟩ luck!; just X's luck!**

У-151 • ДО́БРОЕ У́ТРО; С ДО́БРЫМ У́ТРОМ [formula phrase; these forms only; fixed WO] a morning greeting (said upon meeting s.o.): **good morning.**

...Музыка неожиданно глохнет, и Тишка появляется на кухне умытый, причёсанный, аккуратно одетый... «Здорово, папан!» — «Доброе утро!» Тишка садится завтракать (Войнович 6). Suddenly the music stops, and Tishka appears in the kitchen, washed, combed, and neatly dressed...."Morning, Papa!" "Good morning!" Tishka sits down to breakfast (6a).

У-152 • У́ТРО ВЕ́ЧЕРА МУДРЕНЕ́Е [saying] (when faced with a decision in the evening,) it is better to put it off until the next morning (since the situation may change, things will appear different to one in the morning, and one generally makes better decisions when his mind is fresh): ≃ **night brings ⟨is the mother of⟩ counsel; things will ⟨always⟩ look better ⟨brighter⟩ in the morning; one's mind is always sharper in the morning; (let's) sleep on it.**

«Ладно, ложись, утро вечера мудренее, хотя здесь и не разберёшь, когда утро, а когда вечер» (Максимов 2). "OK, you'd better get some sleep. Things always look brighter in the morning — although I must say it's hard to tell morning from evening in this part of the world" (2a). ♦ Зеф был голоден и зол, он наладился было поспать, но Максим ему не дал. «Спать будешь потом... Завтра, может быть, будем на фронте, а до сих пор ни о чём толком не договорились...» Зеф проворчал, что договариваться не о чем, что утро вечера мудренее, что Максим сам не слепой и должен видеть, в какой они оказались трясине... (Стругацкие 2). Zef, hungry and irritated, was about to fall asleep, but Maxim wouldn't let him. "You'll sleep later. We'll probably be at the front tomorrow and we haven't come to agreement about anything yet." Zef muttered that there was nothing to agree about; that one's mind was always sharper in the morning; that Maxim was not blind and must see what a quagmire they were in... (2a). ♦ ...Слова-то телеграммы никак не складываются. Что-то наскрёб, но совсем без ругани, понёс показывать — А.Т. [Твардовский] разгневался: слабо, не то! Я его мягко похлопал по спине, он пуще вскипел: «Я — не нервный! Это — вы нервный!» Ну, ин так. Не пишется. Утро вечера мудреней, дайте подумать, завтра утром пошлю, обещаю (Солженицын 2). ...The words wouldn't fit together in my telegram. I scrawled something, without a word of abuse in it, and took it to show A.T. [Tvardovsky] — who got angry: too feeble, no good at all! I patted him gently on the back, and he was even more furious: "I'm not the nervous one! You are!" Well, maybe so. Anyway, I can't write it. Let's sleep on it. Give me time to think. I'll send it in tomorrow morning, I promise (2a).

У-153 • **НЕНАСЫ́ТНАЯ УТРО́БА** *highly coll* [NP; usu. sing] **1.** a voracious person or animal, one with an insatiable appetite: **glutton; chowhound.**

2. *derog* a grasping, avaricious person: **greedy bastard ⟨bitch, old bag etc⟩.**

У-154 • **ДЕМЬЯ́НОВА УХА́** [NP; sing only; fixed WO] sth. that is importunately offered, thrust upon s.o. in excessive quantity (and is therefore irritating): **too much of a good thing.**

< The title of Ivan Krylov's fable "Demyan's Fish Soup" («Демьянова уха»), 1813.

У-155 • **НИ У́ХА НИ РЫ́ЛА** не смыслить, не понимать *(в чём),* не знать *substand* [NP_gen; Invar; obj; fixed WO] (to understand, know) absolutely nothing (about sth.): X ~ не смыслит (в Y-e) ≃ **X doesn't know ⟨understand⟩ a (damn) thing (about Y); X doesn't know his ass from his elbow ⟨from a hole in the ground⟩.**

В юртах, в столовой, везде разговаривали и спорили уже только о новых «парашах»... «Хорошо, если сразу не прикончат...» — «Отправят большинство, но полсотни самых незаменимых оставят здесь...» — «А кто будет решать, кого считать незаменимыми? Антону, например, нужен ты со своими артикуляциями и прочими хренациями. А Недоумову [nickname of Naumov] на всё начхать. Он же ни уха ни рыла не петрит [*substand* = не понимает]» (Копелев 1). In the yurts, in the dining room, the only talk and arguments were about the new rumors.... "We'll be lucky if they don't finish us off right away"; "They'll send most of us away, but about fifty of the most indispensable ones will stay here."..."Who gets to determine who's indispensable? Anton, for instance, needs you with your articulations and other shit. But stupid Naumov doesn't give a damn about anyone. He doesn't understand a thing about anything" (1a). ♦ ...Если случайно оказывалось, что в какой-то области человеческих знаний проявлял он [номенклатурный работник] некоторые способности или познания, то его тут же перекидывали в другую область, постепенно доводя до той, в которой он не смыслил ни уха ни рыла... (Войнович 4). And if by chance it so happened that [a member of the nomenclature] displayed skill or knowledge in some area of human endeavor, he would immediately be booted to another field until, by degrees, he was brought to that field where he did not know his ass from his elbow... (4a).

У-156 • **В ОДНО́ У́ХО ВХО́ДИТ/ВОШЛО́, (А) В ДРУГО́Е ВЫХО́ДИТ/ВЫ́ШЛО** *coll* [VP; subj: всё, слова etc, usu. omitted; fixed WO] sth. said passes s.o. by without that person's really hearing or assimilating it (because he is not listening attentively): **it goes ⟨s.o.'s words etc go⟩ in one ear and out the other.**

У-157 • **В У́ХО ⟨ПО́ УХУ⟩** дать, заехать, съездить *кому,* получить и т. п. *highly coll* [PrepP; these forms only; adv] (to deliver or receive) a powerful blow to the side of the head: X дал Y-у по уху ≃ **X boxed Y's ear(s); X boxed ⟨clouted, bashed⟩ Y on the ear;** ‖ Y получил в ухо ≃ **Y got a box ⟨a clout⟩ on the ear.**

«Он [твой муж] заслуженный ангел республики, он ни разу не заехал тебе в ухо, не вынудил тебя выцарапать ему ни одного глаза...» (Залыгин 1). "...He [your husband] deserves the order of Angel of the Soviet Union! He's never once boxed your ears, never forced you to scratch his eyes out, not even one eye" (1a). ♦ «Он вас побранил, а вы его выругайте; он вас в рыло, а вы его в ухо, в другое, в третье — и разойдитесь; а мы вас уж помирим» (Пушкин 2). "If he swore at you, you curse him back; if he hit you in the mug, you bash him on the ear; and once more, and again; and then go your separate ways; we'll see to it that you make up" (2a).

У-158 • **ДЕРЖА́ТЬ У́ХО ВОСТРО́** *coll;* **ДЕРЖА́ТЬ У́ШКИ НА МАКУ́ШКЕ** *coll, usu. humor* [VP; subj: human; often imper or infin with надо, нужно, следует etc; usu. this WO] **1.** ~ *с кем* not to trust s.o., to be very cautious with s.o.: с Y-ом держи ухо востро ≃ **be on your guard with Y; be very careful with Y; watch Y carefully;** [in refer. to caution when speaking with s.o. or in s.o.'s presence] **watch what you say when Y is around ⟨when you talk to Y etc⟩.**

[Хлестаков:] Я еду в Саратовскую губернию, в собственную деревню. [Городничий (*в сторону, с лицом, принимающим ироническое выражение):*] В Саратовскую губернию! А? И не покраснеет! О, да с ним нужно ухо востро (Гоголь 4). [Kh.:] I'm on my way to my own estate in the province of Saratov. [Mayor (*aside with an ironical expression*):] In the province of Saratov! And not a blush! Oh, you have to be on your guard with him (4c). ♦ «...С Юркой со своим ухо держи востро». — «Как это „востро"? Почему?» — «...Думаю я, что нет для него ничего святого». — «Конечно, в бога он верит». — «Я не про бога говорю... Я к тому, что нету в нём доброты, души нет. А раз нет души, так и святого ничего нету» (Михайловская 1). "...Be very careful with your Yuri." "What do you mean by 'careful'? Why?" "...I think that nothing is sacred to him." "Of course, he doesn't believe in God." "I am not speaking of God. What I mean is, there is no kindness in him, no soul. And if there is no soul, there is nothing sacred" (1a).

2. to be cautious, attentive, vigilant (in order to avoid danger or trouble, protect one's interests etc): X-у надо держать ухо востро ≃ **X must ⟨has to⟩ be on his guard ⟨on the alert⟩; X must keep his eyes and ears open; X must ⟨has got to etc⟩ keep his ear to the ground ⟨keep his ears pricked⟩; X must keep a sharp lookout;** [in limited contexts] **you can't be too careful.**

Она знала, её научили, что здесь [на Западе] ухо надо держать востро (Войнович 1). She knew, for she had been taught well, that in the West you have to be on your guard (1a). ♦ Сердце неугомонного старичка билось тревожно, он ходил по пустым своим комнатам и прислушивался. Надо было держать ухо востро: мог где-нибудь сторожить её [Грушеньку] Дмитрий Фёдорович, а как она постучится в окно... то надо было отпереть двери как можно скорее... (Достоевский 1). The irrepressible old man's heart was beating anxiously; he paced his empty rooms and listened. He had to be on the alert: Dmitri Fyodorovich could be watching out for her [Grushenka] somewhere, and when she knocked at the window...he would have to open the door as quickly as possible... (1a). ♦ ...Ребров знал, что при Лялином мягкосердечии самая страстная ненависть может легко перекинуться в страстное сожаление, даже в сочувствие, тут надо держать ухо востро (Трифонов 1). ...With Lyalya's softheartedness Rebrov knew that the strongest hatred could easily transform itself into feelings of pity or even sympathy, so here he would have to keep his eyes and ears open (1a). ♦ «Ребята мои умничают. Они воры. Мне должно держать ухо востро; при первой неудаче они свою шею выкупят моею головою» (Пушкин 2). "My fellows are always trying to be clever. They're crooks. I've got to keep my ears pricked: at the first sign of failure they'll try to save their necks in exchange for my head" (2a). ♦ «Я бы тебя... не поставил на этот пост, не положено кандидату, но господин ротмистр приказал... Ты держи ухо востро, Мак» (Стругацкие 2). "If it were up to me, I wouldn't have assigned you to this post. It's never given to candidates, but the captain ordered it. Keep a sharp lookout, Mac" (2a).

У-159 • **НА́ УХО** говорить, сказать, шептать [PrepP; Invar; adv] (to say, whisper sth.) quietly, in secret, with one's lips close to the ear of the hearer: **in(to) s.o.'s ear.**

Присутствие Бланка и Готтиха раскаляло беседу... То, что ни в коем случае не предназначалось для ушей Готтиха, кричалось на ухо Бланку, а то, что не годилось для ушей Бланка, хором вшёптывалось Готтиху (Битов 2). The presence of Blank and Gottich raised the conversation to fever pitch. Anything not meant under any circumstances for Gottich's ears was shouted in Blank's ear, and anything not fit for Blank's ears was whispered in unison in Gottich's (2a). ♦ «А за деньгами он не постоит, — Коровьев оглянулся, а затем шепнул на ухо председателю: — миллионер!» (Булгаков 9). "Money's no object with him." Koroviev looked around, then whispered into the chairman's ear, "A millionaire!" (9a).

У-160 • **РЕ́ЗАТЬ У́ХО ⟨У́ШИ, СЛУХ⟩** *(кому чем) coll* [VP; subj: abstr (usu. слова, пение, брань etc); usu. pres or past] to make an unpleasant impression on the ear (because of its sound quality, style, content etc): X режет ухо ≃ **X grates on ⟨upon⟩ the ⟨person Y's⟩ ear(s); X offends the ⟨person Y's⟩ ear(s); X is jarring to the ear(s); X pains the ear(s).**

У-161 • **ТУГ ⟨ТУГОВА́Т, КРЕПЮ́К, ТУГО́Й, ТУГО-ВА́ТЫЙ, КРЕ́ПКИЙ⟩ НА́ УХО** *coll* [AdjP; subj-compl with copula, subj: human (all variants) or modif (variants with long-form Adj)] lacking the ability to hear or hear well: X туг на ухо ≃ **X is hard of hearing; X is (almost) deaf;** ‖ X туговат на ухо ≃ **X is a bit ⟨a little⟩ hard of hearing; X is a little on the deaf side.**

«...К чему так громко? Старик услышит, обидится». — «Ничего он не услышит, туг на ухо. А и услышит, не возьмёт в толк, — с придурью» (Пастернак 1). "...Don't talk so loud. You don't want to hurt the old man's feelings." "He won't hear anything, he's deaf. And if he did, he wouldn't understand—he's not quite right in the head" (1a). ♦ [Жевакин:] Позвольте... спросить: с кем-с имею счастье изъясняться? [Иван Павлович:] В должности экзекутора, Иван Павлович Яичница. [Жевакин *(не дослышав)*:] Да, я тоже перекусил... [Иван Павлович:] Нет, кажется, вы не так поняли: это фамилия моя — Яичница. [Жевакин *(кланяясь)*:] Ах, извините. Я немножко туговат на ухо (Гоголь 1). [Zh.:] ...Allow me to ask, With whom do I have the pleasure of conversing? [I.P.:] Omelet, managing clerk. [Zh. *(not catching the last words)*:] Yes, I also had a bite... [I.P.:] No, it seems you didn't understand me correctly. That's my name—Omelet. [Zh. *(bowing)*:] Oh, I beg your pardon. I'm a bit hard of hearing (1b).

У-162 • **У́ХО В У́ХО ⟨К У́ХУ⟩** *с кем идти, бежать* и т. п.; **НОЗДРЯ́ В НОЗДРЮ́** *all coll* [NP; these forms only; adv] (usu. of animals) (to go, run) next to, parallel with another or each other: **side by side; neck and neck.**

У-163 • **УХОДИ́ТЬ/УЙТИ́ В СЕБЯ́** [VP; subj: human; fixed WO] **1.** to become unsociable, avoid people: X ушёл в себя ≃ **X withdrew into himself; X retreated into his shell.**

Иногда, отдаляясь и уходя в себя или в дружбу с кем-нибудь, он [Мандельштам] выпускал меня на свободу (Мандельштам 2). Occasionally, withdrawing into himself, or into his friendship with someone, he [Mandelstam] would let me be for a while (2a).

2. Also: **УГЛУБЛЯ́ТЬСЯ/УГЛУБИ́ТЬСЯ В СЕБЯ́** to become temporarily self-absorbed, concentrating on one's own thoughts and/or feelings: X ушёл в себя ≃ **X withdrew ⟨retreated⟩ into himself; X became ⟨was⟩ engrossed ⟨submerged⟩ in his own thoughts.**

Зарипа... горько зарыдала, уйдя вся в себя, в свою боль и утрату (Айтматов 2). She [Zaripa] wept bitterly, completely retreating into herself, into her pain and her loss (2a). ♦ ...[Маяковский] надолго замолчал, ушёл глубоко в себя (Катаев 3). ...He [Mayakovsky] plunged into a long silence, deeply submerged in his own thoughts (3a).

У-164 • **ПРИНИМА́ТЬ/ПРИНЯ́ТЬ УЧА́СТИЕ** *в ком* [VP; subj: human; fixed WO] to show s.o. kindness, attention, usu. by aiding him: X принимает участие в Y-е ≃ **X shows**

concern for Y; X takes an interest in Y; X helps ⟨tries to help⟩ Y; X gives ⟨shows⟩ Y (some) support.

В тот период не только на каторге, но и в дальних ссылках сохранились товарищество и взаимопомощь. На воле с этим давно покончили, но Чердынь жила традициями, и кастелянша приняла в нас горячее участие (Мандельштам 1). At that time the tradition of comradeship and mutual help still lingered on both in the forced-labor camps and in remote places of exile such as ours. In the world beyond, all this was a thing of the past, but Cherdyn was faithful to the old ways, and the housekeeper showed warm concern for us (1a). ♦ ...Он принял в сиротах участие лично и особенно полюбил младшего из них, Алексея, так что тот долгое время даже и рос в его семействе (Достоевский 1). He took a personal interest in the orphans, and came especially to love the younger one, Alexei, who for a long time even grew up in his family (1a). ♦ «Это он мне вместо спасибо! — горько подумал он. — За то, что я принял в нём участие! Вот уж, действительно, дрянь!» (Булгаков 9). "That's what I get instead of thanks," he thought bitterly, "for trying to help him! What a louse!" (9a).

У-165 • **НЕ УЧИ́ УЧЁНОГО** *coll* [imper sent; occas. used without negation to convey the same meaning; fixed WO] do not give advice to those who are more experienced at sth. than you are: **an old fox needs not ⟨doesn't need⟩ to be taught tricks; don't (try to) teach your grandmother to suck eggs.**

«Неплохо, — сказал Антон, прочитав моё сочинение. — Только вот тебе мой совет: ...в Главлит дай липу, а не подлинник... Иначе не пропустят. И на конгресс не поедешь». — «Само собой разумеется, — сказал я, возбуждённый удачей. — Не учи учёного» (Зиновьев 2). "That's not bad," said Anton when he'd read the work. "But here's my advice: don't give the real thing to the censorship; give them a bit of window-dressing....Otherwise they'll never pass it, and you'll never make it to the Congress." "But of course!" I said elated by my success. "Don't teach your grandmother to suck eggs!" (2a).

У-166 • **УЧЕ́НЬЕ СВЕТ, (А) НЕУЧЕ́НЬЕ ТЬМА** [saying] said, often jokingly, to emphasize the importance of knowledge, education (usu. when advising s.o. to study): ≃ **knowledge is power; knowledge is light, and ignorance is darkness.**

Пословица «ученье свет, а неученье тьма» бродила уже по сёлам и деревням вместе с книгами, развозимыми букинистами (Гончаров 1). The proverb "Knowledge is light, and ignorance is darkness" was slowly finding its way into villages and hamlets, along with the books sold by book peddlers (1b).

У-167 • **БРАТЬ/ВЗЯТЬ ⟨СТА́ВИТЬ/ПОСТА́ВИТЬ⟩ НА УЧЁТ** *кого-что* [VP; subj: human or collect] to put s.o. or sth. on a list: X взял Y-а на учёт ≃ **X registered Y.**

У-168 • **СТАНОВИ́ТЬСЯ/СТАТЬ ⟨ВСТАВА́ТЬ/ВСТАТЬ, БРА́ТЬСЯ/ВЗЯ́ТЬСЯ⟩ НА УЧЁТ** *где* [VP; subj: human] to place one's name or have one's name placed on a list (at some organization, office etc): X стал на учёт ≃ **X got ⟨was⟩ registered; X registered; X got ⟨was⟩ listed (with s.o.).**

«Вы, гражданин Шариков, говорите... несознательно. На воинский учёт необходимо взяться». — «На учёт возьмусь, а воевать — шиш с маслом», — неприязненно ответил Шариков... (Булгаков 11). "Citizen Sharikov, your words are...lacking in social consciousness. It is most essential to be registered in the military rolls." "I'll register, but if it comes to fighting, they can kiss..." Sharikov answered coldly... (11a). ♦ Его задержали на регистрации недолго. Поспешно отметив удостоверение, секретарь военкома сказал: «Зайдите в политбюро при Дончека. Вам, как бывшему офицеру, надлежит взяться у них на учёт» (Шолохов 5). His registration did not take long. After hurriedly marking his papers, the secretary said, "Go and see the Political

Bureau of the Don Emergency Commission. As a former officer, you've got to be listed with them" (5a).

У-169 • **БЕЗ УЧЁТА** *чего* [PrepP; Invar; the resulting PrepP is adv] without allowing for sth.: **without taking sth. into account ⟨into consideration⟩; without considering sth.;** [in limited contexts] **if you ignore sth.**

До Коряжска было шестьдесят пять километров, то есть часа два езды с учётом местных дорог и без учёта странностей Володиного характера (Аксёнов 3). It was about 65 kilometers to Koryazhsk, or a two hour drive if you take into consideration the condition of local roads and ignore the peculiarities of Volodya's personality (3a).

У-170 • **СНИМА́ТЬ/СНЯТЬ С УЧЁТА** *кого* [VP; subj: human or collect] to take s.o.'s name off a list (of members or those registered for sth.): X снял Y-а с учёта ≃ **X removed ⟨struck⟩ Y ⟨Y's name⟩ from the books ⟨the roster, the rolls, the register⟩; X took Y off the register ⟨the books etc⟩.**

Я положил на подоконничек, обращённый в его сторону, повестку и воинский билет. Раскрыв эту мою книжечку и полистав... он вскинул на меня очень учтивый взгляд и сказал, что просит меня подождать, пока он снимет меня с учёта (Олеша 3). I put my notification and my service card down on the windowsill, facing in his direction. Having opened my booklet and thumbed through it...he glanced at me with a very courteous look and said he would ask me to wait while he removed me from the rolls (3a).

У-171 • **СНИМА́ТЬСЯ/СНЯ́ТЬСЯ С УЧЁТА** [VP; subj: human] to have one's name taken off a list (of members or those registered for sth.): X снялся с учёта ≃ **X had his name removed ⟨stricken⟩ from the books ⟨the roster, the rolls etc⟩; X had his name stricken from ⟨taken off⟩ the register ⟨the books etc⟩.**

У-172 • **НА УЧЁТЕ** [PrepP; Invar; subj-compl with быть₀] **1.** ~ *где.* Also: **СОСТОЯ́ТЬ ⟨СТОЯ́ТЬ⟩ НА УЧЁТЕ** [VP; subj: human] one is placed on a list (at some organization, office etc): X на учёте ≃ **X is registered; X is on the books; X is numbered** (in some records etc); ‖ X на учёте в милиции ≃ **X has a (police) record;** ‖ X на учёте в психиатрической больнице ⟨туберкулёзном диспансере и т. п.⟩ ≃ **X is under psychiatric observation; X is registered as a mental ⟨TB etc⟩ patient ⟨case⟩.**

«Хочешь подробности о ней узнать, зайди в детскую комнату шестого отделения милиции. Она там на учёте стояла» (Чернёнок 1). "If you want to know more about her, drop by the juveniles' room of the Sixth Precinct. She has a record there" (1a). ♦ ...Потом женщина вышла к Рите и сказала, что забирает Нюру на месяц в больницу, в психиатрическую. Ничего страшного, особый вид шизофрении. Оказывается, Нюра давно уже на учёте, а мы не знали (Трифонов 5). Then the woman came out and told Rita that she was taking Nyura to the hospital for a month, to the psychiatric hospital. Nothing frightening, just a particular form of schizophrenia. It turned out that Nyura had been under observation for a long time, and we hadn't known anything about it (5a).

2. [subj: human, concr, or count abstr, often preceded by каждый] the person or thing named is important, has significance: каждый X на учёте ≃ **every X counts ⟨matters⟩; every X is significant ⟨precious⟩.**

Людей у нас не хватает, каждый человек на учёте. We're short of people, every man counts.

У-173 • **С УЧЁТОМ** *чего* [PrepP; Invar; the resulting PrepP is adv] allowing for: **taking ⟨if you take⟩ into account ⟨into consideration⟩.**

...Она хотела бы знать, как лучше написать место о моём выступлении [на симпозиуме] с учётом требований Барского (Зиновьев 2). ...She wanted to know how best to write the passage about my [presentation at the symposium] while taking Barskiy's demands into account (2a). ♦ До Коряжска было шестьдесят пять километров, то есть часа два езды с учётом местных дорог и без учёта странностей Володиного характера (Аксёнов 3). It was about 65 kilometers to Koryazhsk, or a two hour drive if you take into consideration the condition of local roads and ignore the peculiarities of Volodya's personality (3a).

У-174 • **НЕ ВЕ́РИТЬ/НЕ ПОВЕ́РИТЬ (СВОИ́М) УША́М** *coll* [VP; subj: human] to be extremely surprised by sth. one has heard and wonder if it really could be so: X ушам своим не верит ≃ **X can't ⟨didn't, can hardly, is unable to, is hardly able to⟩ believe his ears.**

«Вы, кажется, не расположены сегодня петь? Я и просить боюсь», — спросил Обломов... «Жарко!» — заметила тётка. «Ничего, я попробую», — сказала Ольга и спела романс. Он слушал и не верил ушам. Это не она: где прежний, страстный звук? (Гончаров 1). "I don't suppose you feel like singing today, do you? I'm afraid to ask you," Oblomov said....."It's too hot!" her aunt remarked. "Never mind, I'll try," said Olga, and she sang one song. He listened and could not believe his ears. It was not she: where was the former note of passion? (1b). ♦ Я просто ушам не поверила, когда уже на исходе развода утомлённая Верка небрежно бросила мне: «В гостиницу пойдёшь... Бригадир — Анька Полозова» (Гинзбург 1). I could hardly believe my ears when, after the rest of the team had passed through the gate, she said to me casually: "You're to work in the guesthouse. Report to Anka Polozova" (1b). ♦ «Так... кто же... убил?..» — «Как кто убил?.. — переговорил он, точно не веря ушам своим, — да *вы* убили, Родион Романыч!» (Достоевский 3). "So then...who...did the murder?"..."What? Who did the murder?" he echoed, as though unable to believe his ears. "Why *you* did, Rodion Romanich!" (3a). ♦ Пьер, приподняв плечи и разинув рот, слушал то, что говорила ему Марья Дмитриевна, не веря своим ушам (Толстой 5). Pierre hunched his shoulders and listened open-mouthed to what Marya Dmitrievna was saying, hardly able to believe his ears (5a).

У-175 • **ест, уписывает** и т. п. **так, что ЗА УША́МИ ТРЕЩИ́Т** *coll, humor* [VP; impers; used with verbs of eating as intensif; fixed WO] (one eats) with a great appetite, voraciously: X ест так, что за ушами трещит ≃ **X wolfs down thing Y; X gobbles up thing Y; X shovels it in; X eats ravenously ⟨greedily⟩.**

...[Юра] даже не смотрел в сторону мясного... а только рубал [*slang* = ел] свои апельсинчики так, что за ушами трещало (Аксёнов 1). Yura...hadn't even looked at the meat dish...but was only digging into his oranges, wolfing them down (1a).

У-176 • **СВОИ́МИ ⟨(СВОИ́МИ) СО́БСТВЕННЫМИ⟩ УША́МИ слышать** *что coll* [NP_instrum; these forms only; adv; fixed WO] (to hear sth.) oneself: **(hear sth.) with one's own (two) ears; (hear sth.) for o.s.**

Комендант немедленно посадил урядника под караул, а Юлая назначил на его место. Эта новость принята была казаками с явным неудовольствием. Они громко роптали, и Иван Игнатьич, исполнитель комендантского распоряжения, слышал своими ушами, как они говорили: «Вот уж тебе будет, гарнизонная крыса!» (Пушкин 2). The commandant immediately took the sergeant into custody and appointed Iulai in his place. The Cossacks took this new development with manifest displeasure. They grumbled loudly, so much so that Ivan Ignatich, who executed the commandant's order, heard with his own ears, "You'll live to regret that, garrison rat!" (2a).

У-177 • ХЛО́ПАТЬ УША́МИ *coll, disapprov* [VP; subj: human] **1.** while listening to sth., not to understand or grasp what is being said: X ушами хлопает ≃ **X looks blank.**

…Сослужил Лебедев ещё одну службу: подстроил чтение вслух «Тёркина на том свете». Иностранцы ушами хлопали, Хрущёв смеялся… (Солженицын 2). …Lebedev performed another public service. He arranged a reading of "Tyorkin in the Next World." The foreigners looked blank, but Khrushchev laughed… (2a).

2. to be idle, inactive (when the situation requires decisive, energetic action, often under circumstances when taking concrete action would keep sth. harmful from happening or would allow one to obtain sth. valuable, advance one's career etc): X хлопает ушами ≃ **X sits on his hands; X sits around ⟨here, there** etc⟩ **doing nothing; X does nothing.**

«Вот, — сказал Трёшкин, проводив Ефима долгим тяжёлым взглядом. — У меня кот пропал, а ему шапку дают из кота. Как же это понять?» — «Если мы будем ушами хлопать, они и из нас шапки наделают», — сказал Черпаков (Войнович 6). "There," Tryoshkin said, following Yefim with a long heavy stare. "My tomcat disappears, and they give him a hat made of tomcat fur. How am I to interpret that?" "If we sit here long enough, doing nothing, they'll make hats out of us, too," Cherpakov said (6a).

У-178 • ВЫ́ЛИТЬ УША́Т ПОМО́ЕВ *на кого;* ОКАТИ́ТЬ УША́ТОМ ПОМО́ЕВ *кого coll, disapprov* [VP; subj: human] to disgrace, defame s.o. unjustly: X вылил на Y-а ушат помоев ≃ **X dragged Y through the mud ⟨the mire, the muck⟩; X threw ⟨slung, flung⟩ mud ⟨dirt⟩ at Y; X smeared Y ⟨Y's name⟩.**

У-179 • ДО УШЕ́Й [PrepP; Invar; adv (intensif)] **1.** покраснеть, вспыхнуть и т. п. ~ (to blush) very intensely: **to (the tips of) one's ears.**

Он, казалось, был очень стыдлив, потому что каждая малость заставляла его краснеть до самых ушей… (Толстой 2). He was apparently very bashful, for every trifle made him blush to the tips of his ears… (2c). ♦ Катя… с недоумением подняла глаза на Базарова — и, встретив его быстрый и небрежный взгляд, вспыхнула вся до ушей (Тургенев 2). Katya…lifted her eyes to Bazarov with a puzzled look, and meeting his quick casual glance she blushed to her ears (2c).

2. улыбаться и т. п. ~ (to smile) very broadly: **(grin) from ear to ear.**

У-180 • ДОХОДИ́ТЬ/ДОЙТИ́ ДО УШЕ́Й *чьих, кого* [VP; subj: abstr] to become known to s.o.: X дошёл до ушей Y-а ≃ **X reached Y's ears ⟨the ears of Y⟩.**

К счастью, вся эта история не дошла до ушей Нестора Аполлоновича… (Искандер 3). Fortunately, none of this story reached the ears of Nestor Apollonovich… (3a).

У-181 • НЕ ВИДА́ТЬ КАК СВОИ́Х УШЕ́Й *кому кого-чего coll* [VP; impers; usu. infin; usu. this WO] (in refer. to a desirable person, thing etc) s.o. will never win over, attract to o.s. etc (the person in question); s.o. will never obtain (the thing in question), achieve (the end in question) etc: не видать X-у Y-а как своих ушей ≃ **X will never get ⟨get hold of, get his hands on, get near, get to see** etc⟩ **Y; there's no way X will ever get ⟨get hold of** etc⟩ **Y; X can forget about (getting) Y; Y is out of X's reach;** [in limited contexts] **like hell X will get ⟨get to see, be able to go to see⟩ Y; X can kiss thing Y good-bye.**

«Меня же за одно намерение сочинить подпольную книжку выгонят из партии и с работы. А с вами что будет? Сашку укатают в Сибирь, а тебе института не видать тогда как своих ушей» (Зиновьев 2). "If I so much as had a thought of writing an underground book I'd be expelled from the party and sacked. And what'd happen to you? Sashka'd have to go off to Siberia, and you'd

never get to see the inside of any institute" (2a). ♦ «Здравия желаю, товарищ майор! Говорит Паськов. У меня в кабинете… один из ваших… Просится на передовую. Хорошо. Передаю трубку». — «Привет, — говорю, — товарищ Кидалла». — «Здравствуй, мерзавец. Фронта тебе не видать как своих ушей. Ты числишься за органами» (Алешковский 1). "Good morning, Comrade Major. Paskov here. I have one of yours in my office… Wants to go to the front. Okay. I'll put him on." "Hi, Comrade Kidalla," I said. "Hello, scumbag. Like hell you're going to the front. You're working for the agency" (1a).

У-182 • ПРОПУСКА́ТЬ/ПРОПУСТИ́ТЬ МИМО УШЕ́Й *что coll* [VP; subj: human; obj: слова, замечание, вопрос etc; more often this WO] intentionally not to take notice of or react to what is being said or has been said: X пропустил Y мимо ушей ≃ **X turned a deaf ear to Y; X took no notice of Y; X paid no attention ⟨heed⟩ to Y; X let Y pass (unnoticed); X ignored Y; Y went ⟨X let Y go⟩ in one ear and out the other.**

Надо сказать, что обычно слушатель пропускал мимо ушей замечание относительно крутизны берега [, куда мельник должен был подняться со своим десятипудовым грузом]… (Искандер 3). Admittedly, the listener usually turned a deaf ear to the remark about the steepness of the bank [that the miller had to climb up with his four-hundred-pound load] (3a). ♦ «Ты же знаешь, твой Гриша никогда ничего нам не рассказывает о своих делах!» В другой раз Ляля пропустила бы фразу мимо ушей, сочла бы её нормальной, но теперь, когда она едва сдерживалась от того, чтобы не накричать на мать, она не могла смолчать и ответила тоже с нажимом: «Но можно и самой поинтересоваться, правда же?» (Трифонов 1). "You ought to know by now that your Grisha never tells us anything about his work!" Normally Lyalya wouldn't have paid any attention to such a remark, considering it merely normal. But on this occasion, when she could barely keep from screaming at her mother, she simply could not keep quiet and replied in an equally aggressive tone, "But you could at least express an interest, couldn't you?" (1a). ♦ Он [Ефим] бросил трубку, но через минуту поднял её снова. «Извини, я погорячился», — сказал он Баранову. «Бывает, — сказал тот великодушно. — Кстати, в поликлинике работает новый психиатр…» Ефим пропустил подковырку мимо ушей и спросил, что именно Баранову известно о шапках (Войнович 6). He [Yefim] slammed down the receiver, but a minute later picked it up again and dialed Kostya [Baranov]. "Sorry I blew up." "Nerves. I understand," Kostya said magnanimously. "Incidentally, the clinic has a new psychiatrist…." Yefim let the dig pass and asked what, exactly, Kostya knew about the hats (6a). ♦ Я усомнился в его компетенции, когда он [философ] сказал мне, что во всяком случае советские люди никогда не знали голода. Я спросил его, слышал ли он что-нибудь о голоде на Украине, стоившем жизни нескольким миллионам людей, или в блокаде Ленинграде… Он пропустил сказанное мною мимо ушей и продолжал спорить (Войнович 1). …I doubted his [the philosopher's] competence when he told me that in any case Soviet people had never known hunger. I asked him if he had ever heard of the famine in the Ukraine which cost several million people their lives or of the siege of Leningrad….What I said went in one ear and out the other, and he continued to argue (1a).

У-183 • ВО ВСЕ У́ШИ *слушать coll* [PrepP; Invar; adv (intensif); fixed WO] (to listen) very attentively, missing nothing: X слушал ~ ≃ **X was all ears; X hung on every word (person Y said); X hung on Y's every word.**

У-184 • ЗА́ УШИ НЕ ОТТЯ́НЕШЬ ⟨НЕ ОТТА́ЩИШЬ⟩ *(кого от кого-чего) coll* [VP; neg pfv fut, gener. 2nd pers sing only] (some food is so tasty, or some person, event etc is so interesting, appealing that) it is impossible to tear s.o. away from it or him: X-а (от Y-а) за уши не оттянешь ≃ **wild horses couldn't drag X away (from Y).**

У-185 • **НАВОСТРИ́ТЬ** ⟨**НАСТОРОЖИ́ТЬ**⟩ **У́ШИ** ⟨**СЛУХ**⟩ *coll* [VP; usu. this WO] **1.** [subj: animal; usu. past or Verbal Adv] (usu. of a dog or horse) to become very alert, raise the ears so as to listen intently (upon hearing some sound): X навострил уши ≃ X pricked up his ears; X cocked his ears.

2. [subj: human; usu. past] to prepare to listen or to begin listening with intense attention and interest: X навострил уши ≃ X pricked up his ears; X cocked his ears; [in limited contexts] X was all ears.

Всё время обеда Анна Михайловна говорила о слухах войны, о Николушке… Наташа, из всего семейства более всех одарённая способностью чувствовать оттенки интонаций, взглядов и выражений лиц, с начала обеда насторожила уши и знала, что что-нибудь есть между её отцом и Анной Михайловной и что-нибудь касающееся брата и что Анна Михайловна приготавливает (Толстой 4). All during dinner Anna Mikhailovna talked of rumors concerning the war and of Nikolushka….Natasha, who of all the family was the most gifted with the faculty of catching the subtleties of an intonation, a glance, or the expression of a face, pricked up her ears at the beginning of dinner and felt that there was some secret between her father and Anna Mikhailovna, that it had something to do with her brother, and that Anna Mikhailovna was preparing them for it (4a). ♦ Ребёнок, навострив уши и глаза, страстно впивался в рассказ (Гончаров 1). The child, all eyes and ears, listened to the story with passionate absorption (1b).

У-186 • **НАДУВА́ТЬ** ⟨**ДУТЬ**⟩/**НАДУ́ТЬ** ⟨**ПЕТЬ/ НАПЕ́ТЬ, НАЖУЖЖА́ТЬ, НАТРУБИ́ТЬ**⟩ **В У́ШИ** *кому (что) substand* [VP; subj: human] to tell s.o. gossip, incorrect, superfluous, absurd things: X надул Y-у в уши ≃ X poured twaddle into Y's ear; X filled Y's head with stories; X gave Y a lot of bull ⟨crap etc⟩.

[Сатин:] Чепуха! Никуда ты не пойдёшь… Старик! Чего ты надул в уши этому огарку? [Актёр:] Врёшь! Дед! Скажи ему, что он — врёт! Я — иду! [S.:] Nonsense! You won't go, you know you won't….Old man! What twaddle have you been pouring into this fellow's ear? [A.:] That's a lie! Grandad, tell him he's lying. I *will* go (3d). ♦ С отцом они встретились как-то отчуждённо. Пантелей Прокофьевич (нажужжал ему в уши Петро) хмуро присматривался к Григорию… (Шолохов 3). There was a touch of estrangement in his [Grigory's] meeting with his father. Petro had filled the old man's head with stories and he now kept a surly watchful eye on Grigory… (3a).

У-187 • **ПО́ УШИ; ПО СА́МЫЕ У́ШИ** *both coll* [PrepP; these forms only; adv (intensif)] **1.** влюбиться, влюблён и т. п. *в кого* ~ (to be or fall) deeply (in love): (be ⟨fall⟩) head over heels (in love with s.o.); (be ⟨fall⟩) madly (in love with s.o.).

«Ясное дело, девушка втрескалась в него по уши» (Искандер 5). "No question, the girl was head over heels in love with him" (5a). ♦ [Войницкий:] Дайте себе волю хоть раз в жизни, влюбитесь поскорее в какого-нибудь водяного по самые уши… (Чехов 3). [V.:] Let yourself go for once in your life and fall madly in love with a river-god… (3c).

2. ~ уйти, погрузиться *во что*, увязнуть, быть₀ *в чём*, often **в работе, в хлопотах** и т. п. (to have become) fully overwhelmed by and deeply involved in (some work, concerns etc): (be ⟨sink⟩) up to one's ears ⟨neck⟩ (in sth.); [usu. in refer. to work] (be) awash (in sth.).

[Иванов:] …Я поддался слабодушию и по уши увяз в этой гнусной меланхолии… (Чехов 4). [I.:] …I've given way to cowardice and am sunk up to my ears in this loathsome melancholy… (4a). ♦ Когда день полон грохота и человек по уши погружён в котёл войны, он не в силах понять, увидеть свою жизнь… (Гроссман 2). When a man is plunged up to his neck into the cauldron of war, he is quite unable to look at his life and understand anything… (2a).

3. быть₀, сидеть, увязнуть в долгах ~; влезть, залезть в долги ~ (to be or get) very deeply (in debt): (be ⟨sink⟩) up to one's ears ⟨neck⟩ in debt; (be) mired ⟨buried⟩ in debts; (be) deep in the hole.

У-188 • **ПРОЖУЖЖА́ТЬ** ⟨**ПРОТРУБИ́ТЬ, ПРО- ГУДЕ́ТЬ**⟩ **(ВСЕ) У́ШИ** *кому (о ком-чём, про кого-что)* и т. п. *coll* [VP; subj: human or радио, телевидение etc] to annoy, tire s.o. with constant talk about one and the same thing: X прожужжал Y-у все уши (о Z-е) ≃ X dinned Z into Y's ears; person X talked Y's ear(s) off (about Z).

Её [Ахматову] запугивали, ей грозили, за ней посылали топтунов, откормленных бездельников… а свои стихи она всё же написала. Все расходы пошли в прорву… Другой вопрос, кому это нужно и как согласуется с «режимом экономии», о котором нам прожужжали уши? (Мандельштам 2). Despite all intimidation and threats, despite surveillance by the well-fed oafs ordered to follow her…she [Akhmatova] still managed to write her poems. All the expense involved was thrown down the drain…. One might well ask who needs it, and how it jibes with all the frantic appeals for economy which are constantly being dinned into our ears (2a).

У-189 • **ПРОСЛУ́ШАТЬ (ВСЕ) У́ШИ** *coll* [VP; subj: human] to listen attentively and closely for a long time, hoping to hear sth.: X прослушал все уши ≃ X had ⟨kept⟩ his ears open.

У-190 • **РАЗВЕ́ШИВАТЬ/РАЗВЕ́СИТЬ У́ШИ** *coll* [VP; subj: human] to listen intently and enthusiastically to s.o., trusting that what he says is true: X развесил уши ≃ X listened open-mouthed; X hung on person Y's every word; X hung on the words ⟨the lips⟩ of person Y; X drank it all in; [in refer. to lies, fabrications etc] X swallowed it whole; X lapped it (all) up.

Эта весёлая чушь преподносилась таким обворожительным басом, что публика слушала, развесив уши (Лившиц 1). Maiakovsky delivered this cheerful nonsense in such a charming bass voice that the audience listened open-mouthed (1a). ♦ «И говорить [Хохлушкин] большой мастер… только уши развешивай» (Максимов 1). "And he's a real talker….You just sit there and drink it all in" (1a). ♦ [Подколёсин:] …Невеста должна знать по-французски. [Кочкарёв:] Почему же? [Подколёсин:] Да потому, что… уж я не знаю почему, а всё уж будет у ней не то. [Кочкарёв:] Ну, вот. Дурак сейчас один сказал, а он и уши развесил (Гоголь 1). [P.:] A young lady should speak French. [K.:] What for? [P.:] Why? Because… I really don't know why. But without French she won't be quite it. [K.:] There he goes again! Some fool said it, and he lapped it up (1b).

У-191 • **ТАЩИ́ТЬ** ⟨**ТЯНУ́ТЬ**⟩ **ЗА́ УШИ** *кого coll* [VP; subj: human] **1.** to help an incapable, unenterprising, or inactive person in every possible way (usu. in his studies, work, career advancement etc): X тащил Y-а за уши ≃ X dragged ⟨yanked⟩ Y up the ladder ⟨up through the ranks etc⟩; [in limited contexts] X dragged Y out of Y's rut.

Про Алферова говорили, что он из захудалых казачьих офицеришек выбился в люди лишь благодаря своей жене — бабе энергичной и умной; говорили, что она тянула бездарного супруга за уши и до тех пор не давала ему дыхнуть, пока он, три раза срезавшись, на четвёртый всё же выдержал экзамен в академию (Шолохов 3). Alferov was said to have made his way up from being a lowly Cossack officer only thanks to his energetic and intelligent wife; she had dragged her dull-witted spouse out of his rut and never let him rest until, after three failures, he had passed the Academy entrance examination (3a).

2. to pressure or force s.o. to perform some action, participate in sth., adopt some doctrine etc: X тащил Y-а за уши ≃ X dragged Y (into ⟨to⟩ sth.) by the ears ⟨by the scruff of the neck⟩; X dragged Y (into ⟨to⟩ sth.) kicking and screaming.

«Надо активнее разоблачать ловкачей», — сказал Дмитрий Алексеевич шутливым тоном, всё ещё с удивлением посматривая по сторонам. «Активнее! Учёный не всегда приспособлен к такой борьбе. Иного за уши тащи бороться, а он не может...» (Дудинцев 1). "One must expose these dodgers more actively!" Dmitri said in a jocular tone, still looking about him in wonder. "More actively! Scientists are not always adapted to fighting such battles. You can drag some of them to the fight by the ears and they are still incapable of it!" (1a).

У-192 • У́ШИ ВЯ́НУТ *(у кого слушать кого-что) coll* [VP$_{subj}$; pres or, rare, past; fixed WO] it is unpleasant or repulsive for s.o. to listen to some person, story etc (because what is being said is ridiculous, offensive etc): (у X-а) уши вянут ≃ **it makes X sick (to listen to s.o. ⟨hear sth. etc⟩); it turns X's stomach (to listen to sth.** etc); **X can't stand listening to s.o. ⟨sth.⟩.**

«Ты опять говоришь вздор! Уши вянут тебя слушать» (Трифонов 3). "You're talking nonsense again. It makes me sick to listen to you" (3a).

У-193 • У́ШКИ НА МАКУ́ШКЕ *у кого coll, usu. humor* [Invar; VP$_{subj}$ with быть$_∅$; fixed WO] s.o. is alert and prepared to listen very closely to sth. that has attracted his attention: у X-а ушки на макушке ≃ **X has ⟨keeps⟩ his ears open; X has pricked up his ears; X is all ears.**

«Ишь ведь сколько нумеров велел натащить! Подозрительно, а?» – «Ну, скажите». – «Ушки на макушке?» (Достоевский 3). "Look how many newspapers I told them to bring me! Suspicious, eh?" "Well, you tell me." "Are your ears pricked up?" (3a).

У-194 • ЗА УШКО́ ДА НА СО́ЛНЫШКО (вывести, вытащить *кого и т. п.) coll* [PrepP; Invar; predic with subj: human (or adv when used with a verb); can be used in past, pres, and fut contexts; fixed WO] to expose s.o. who is doing sth. reprehensible or illegal, make s.o. answer for his actions, see to it that s.o. gets punished: X Y-а за ушко да на солнышко ≃ [in past contexts] **X dragged Y out into the open ⟨the sunshine⟩; X pulled the plug ⟨blew the whistle⟩ on Y.**

У-195 • В УЩЕ́РБ *кому-чему* [PrepP; Invar; the resulting PrepP is adv or subj-compl with copula (subj: abstr)] causing harm, losses to s.o. or sth.: **to s.o.'s ⟨one's (own)⟩ detriment ⟨disadvantage⟩; to the detriment of s.o. ⟨sth.⟩; at the expense of sth.;** [in limited contexts] **one ⟨s.o.⟩ is only harming ⟨hurting⟩ himself (by doing sth.).**

«Мы пошли ему навстречу!.. Мы в ущерб себе согласились с его просьбой!» (Трифонов 3). "We met him halfway....We agreed to his request to our own detriment" (3a). ♦ ...Фёдор Павлович всю жизнь свою любил представляться, вдруг проиграть пред вами какую-нибудь неожиданную роль, и, главное, безо всякой иногда надобности, даже в прямой ущерб себе, как в настоящем, например, случае (Достоевский 1). ...All his life...Fyodor Pavlovich was fond of play-acting, of suddenly taking up some unexpected role right in front of you, often when there was no need for it, and even to his own real disadvantage, as, for instance, in the present case (1a). ♦ ...В Москву сообщили, будто Рязанов затеял внеплановое строительство в ущерб заводу, заставляет людей работать без оплаты (Рыбаков 2). ...Moscow had received a report that Ryazanov had started non-plan construction to the detriment of the plant and that he was forcing people to work without pay (2a). ♦ [Кручинина:] У меня уж слишком сильно воображение и, кажется, в ущерб рассудку (Островский 3). [K.:] I have too lively an imagination—at the expense of good sense, I fear (3a). ♦ «[Вы] просто не имеете здравого рассудка! Вы запираетесь в ущерб самому себе...» (Шолохов 2). "You simply have no common sense! You are only harming yourself by your denials..." (2a).

У-196 • НА УЩЕ́РБЕ [PrepP; Invar; usu. subj-compl with быть$_∅$] **1.** [subj: луна, месяц] (of the crescent moon) the moon is beginning to decrease gradually in size: луна на ущербе ≃ **the moon is waning ⟨on the wane⟩.**

«Не будет, батя, дела... Месяц на ущербе»... Старик закурил, поглядел на солнце, застрявшее по ту сторону коряги. «Сазан, он разно берёт. И на ущербе иной раз возьмётся» (Шолохов 2). "We won't get anything today, Dad... Moon's on the wane."...The old man lighted up [his cigarette] and glanced at the sun, now snagged behind the sunken tree. "Carp bite at different times. Even with a waning moon" (2a).

2. [subj: abstr] sth. is receding, nearing the end: X на ущербе ≃ **X is nearly ⟨almost⟩ over; X is on the decline ⟨on the wane⟩; X is waning ⟨fading, dying out⟩; X is almost gone; X is almost at an end; X is drawing to a close ⟨to an end⟩.**

«Вроде, на ущербе жизнь твоя холостяцкая, Вася?» (Максимов 3). "Vasilii, my boy...it looks as though your bachelor days are nearly over" (3a).

Ф

Ф-1 • **В ФАВО́РЕ** *у кого* **быть₀, оказаться; В ФАВО́Р к кому попасть** [PrepP; these forms only; usu. subj-compl with copula (subj: human or collect)] one is well-liked by and receives patronage from s.o.: X в фаворе у Y-а ≃ **X is in favor with Y; X is in Y's favor ⟨good graces, good books⟩;** [in limited contexts] **X is a favorite of Y ⟨Y's⟩;** ‖ *Neg* X не в фаворе у Y-а ≃ **X is in disfavor with Y; X is out of favor with Y; X is in Y's bad books;** [in limited contexts] **X has fallen from grace with Y.**

«Мне думалось, что его цель вступления в братство состояла только в желании сблизиться с людьми, быть в фаворе у находящихся в нашей ложе» (Толстой 5). "It seemed to me that his object in entering the Brotherhood was merely to be intimate and in favor with the members of our Lodge" (5a).

Ф-2 • **СТА́ВИТЬ/ПОСТА́ВИТЬ ПЕРЕД (СВЕРШИ́В-ШИМСЯ ⟨СОВЕРШИ́ВШИМСЯ⟩) ФА́КТОМ** *кого-что* [VP; subj: human or collect] to inform s.o. of sth. that is already done or accomplished (and usu. irreversible): X поставил Y-а перед (свершившимся) фактом ≃ **X presented ⟨confronted⟩ Y with a *fait accompli*; Y was faced with a *fait accompli.***

[Он:] Я тебе говорю, нам надо расписаться. Поставить всех перед фактом (Рощин 1). [He:] I tell you, we must register at the [marriage] registry office. We'll present everybody with a *fait accompli* (1a).

Ф-3 • **ДЕРЖА́ТЬ ФАСО́Н** *highly coll*; **ДАВИ́ТЬ ФАСО́Н** *slang* [VP; subj: human] to behave in an ostentatious manner in an attempt to impress others (often in refer. to how one dresses or one's general appearance): X держит фасон ≃ **X shows off; X tries to make an impression; X puts on the dog.**

Панин уважал нашу слабость к «отвлечённой» музыке, не мешал нам и отгонял других. Но некоторые полагали, что мы просто «давим фасон», притворяемся, будто бренчанье и пиликанье предпочитаем частушкам, хорам, опереттам (Копелев 1). Panin respected our weakness for "abstract" music; he did not disturb us and chased away others who might. But some thought that we were "just showing off," pretending that we preferred the plunking and plinking to *chastushka* ditties, choruses, and operettas (1a).

Ф-4 • **НЕ ФАСО́Н ⟨НЕ МОДЕ́ЛЬ⟩** *(кому)* *obs, substand* [NP; these forms only; subj-compl with быть₀ (subj: usu. infin, a clause, or это)] sth. (or doing sth.) is not suitable, proper, good: (X-у) делать Y не фасон ≃ **X shouldn't do Y; Y is not the thing to do; it's not ⟨it wouldn't be⟩ right (for X) to do Y.**

Ф-5 • **ФЕДО́Т, ДА НЕ ТОТ** [saying] the person or thing in question looks like or has some of the characteristics of the named category of people or things, but is not entirely authentic or deserving of being called a member of that category: ≃ **he's ⟨it's etc⟩ not the real thing; he ⟨it etc⟩ seems to..., but not really; he ⟨it etc⟩ is kind of..., but not really; he ⟨it etc⟩ is sort of..., but not quite; there's...and there's... ⟨there are..., and there are...⟩, you mustn't go by the label.**

«А здесь разве не тайга?» — «Тайга-то тайга... Только Федот, да не тот... Наше Беличье — оазис в пустыне» (Гинзбург 2). "Isn't this taiga, then?" "I suppose it is. But there's taiga and there's taiga. You mustn't go by the label. Our Belichye is an oasis in the desert" (2a).

Ф-6 • **К ЯДРЁНОЙ ⟨ЕДРЁНОЙ, ЕДРЕ́НЕ⟩ ФЕ́НЕ (послать** *кого-что)* *vulg* [PrepP; these forms only; usu. used as

---

Interj or adv; fixed WO] used to express anger, irritation, scorn directed toward s.o. or sth., or a desire to get rid of s.o. or sth.: **damn it!; shove it!; to ⟨the⟩ hell with you ⟨him etc⟩!;** ‖ выгнать ⟨вышвырнуть и т. п.⟩ *кого* к ядрёной фене ≃ **throw s.o. the hell out of here ⟨there etc⟩; kick ⟨throw⟩ s.o.'s (goddamned ⟨fucking, bloody etc⟩ ass out of here ⟨there etc⟩;** ‖ расстрелять *кого* к ядрёной фене ≃ **blast s.o.'s goddamned ⟨bloody etc⟩ brains out; blow s.o. to (goddamned ⟨bloody etc⟩) hell.**

...К ядрёной фене, завтра же с утра в ОВИР за формулярами, линять отсюда, линять, линять... (Аксёнов 7). ...This is it, damn it. Tomorrow morning I'm going to see about emigration forms. I've got to get out of here, I've got to get out... (7a). ♦ «Я просто так рассуждал: если равенство — так всем равенство, а если нет — так к ядрёной фене...» (Солженицын 3). "I've simply come to the conclusion that if it's to be equality, then it must be equality for everyone, and if it isn't, then shove it" (3a).

Ф-7 • **ДО ФЕ́НИ ⟨ФОНАРЯ́⟩** *highly coll* [PrepP; these forms only; subj-compl with быть₀ (subj: any noun, often это, всё, всё это)] some person or thing does not matter to s.o. or interest s.o. at all: X Y-у до феньки ≃ **Y doesn't give a damn about ⟨for⟩ X; Y doesn't give a crap ⟨a hoot etc⟩ about X; Y couldn't give a good goddamn about X.**

[author's usage] ...Мсти им всем за их нектар, за их амброзию, хоть она нам и до феньки... (Аксёнов 6). Vengeance on them all for their nectar, their ambrosia, even though we don't give a damn for the stuff (6a). ♦ «...До сегодняшнего дня мне было, как говорится, до фени, живёт ли где-то подобный Шевчук или нет» (Войнович 4). "...Up until today, I couldn't have, as they say, given a good goddamn whether there was any such Shevchuk alive anywhere" (4a).

Ф-8 • **ХОДИ́ТЬ ФЕ́РТОМ** *highly coll* [VP; subj: human] **1.** *obsoles*. Also: **СТОЯ́ТЬ ФЕ́РТОМ** *obsoles, highly coll* to walk or stand with one's hands on one's hips (i.e., in a position resembling the Russian letter «Ф»): X ходил ⟨стоял⟩ фертом ≃ **X walked ⟨stood⟩ with ⟨his⟩ arms akimbo.**

2. Also: **ГЛЯДЕ́ТЬ ⟨СМОТРЕ́ТЬ и т. п.⟩ ФЕ́РТОМ** *highly coll* to carry o.s. in an overconfident, conceited manner, look self-satisfied: X ходит ⟨глядит⟩ фертом ≃ **X struts about; X swaggers; X looks smug ⟨cocky, snooty⟩.**

< «Ферт» is the antiquated name of the letter «Ф».

Ф-9 • **ВСЕ́МИ ФИ́БРАМИ ⟨СИ́ЛАМИ⟩ ДУШИ́ ненавидеть, презирать** *кого-что,* **стремиться** *к чему* и т. п. *rather lit* [NP_instrum; these forms only; adv (intensif); fixed WO] (to hate, despise s.o. or sth., want sth. etc) very intensely: **(hate ⟨detest etc⟩ s.o. ⟨sth.⟩) with every fiber of one's being; (hate etc s.o. ⟨sth.⟩) with a passion; (want sth.) with all one's being ⟨heart, soul, heart and soul⟩.**

...Павел Петрович всеми силами души своей возненавидел Базарова: он считал его гордецом, нахалом, циником, плебеем (Тургенев 2). ...Pavel Petrovich detested Bazarov with every fibre of his being: he regarded him as an arrogant, impudent fellow, a cynic and a vulgarian (2c).

Ф-10 • **НА́ ФИГ** *highly coll, rude* [PrepP; Invar] **1. (послать)** *кого-что* ~ [usu. Interj or adv] used to express anger, a desire to get rid (or rid o.s.) of s.o. or sth.: **to ⟨the⟩ hell with you ⟨him etc⟩; (tell s.o. to) go to hell.**

«...Город тоже мне... Не Москва. Может, кому он и нравится, мне лично не то чтобы очень. Ну его на фиг!»

(Аксёнов 5). "...Some town, I must say....It's no Moscow. There may be those who like it, but they can have it as far as I'm concerned. To hell with it!" (5a).

2. ~ (нужно, сдалось *кому* **и т. п.)** [adv (neg intensif)] used (often in a rhetorical question) to express one's contempt for sth. and one's opinion that it is absolutely useless, not needed by one or s.o. etc: **what the hell do I ⟨does he etc⟩ want ⟨need⟩ with it ⟨that etc⟩?; what the hell do I ⟨does he etc⟩ need it ⟨*that* etc⟩ for!; who (the hell) needs it ⟨them etc⟩!;** [in limited contexts] **s.o. can take his [NP] and go to hell.**

«Я принёс тебе ежа». — «На фиг мне ёж?» "I've brought you a hedgehog." "What the hell do I want with a hedgehog?" ♦ Обманула, а теперь сочувствует? На фиг мне нужно её сочувствие! First she deceives me and now she says she feels for me! She can take her sympathy and go to hell!

Ф-11 • КУРИ́ТЬ ⟨ВОСКУРЯ́ТЬ, ЖЕЧЬ⟩ ФИМИА́М *кому* *lit, often iron* [VP; subj: human] to extol, acclaim s.o. in an excessive, overly flattering way: X курит Y-у фимиам ≃ **X sings Y's praises ⟨the praises of Y⟩; X praises Y to the skies.**

Да, подхалимы и угодники курят Сталину фимиам, но он [Саша] никогда никому об этом не говорил... (Рыбаков 2). Sure...toadies and time-servers sang Stalin's praises, but he'd [Sasha had] never spoken to anyone about this... (2a).

< From the custom of burning incense («фимиам», borrowed from Greek) in temples while extolling a deity.

Ф-12 • ПОД ФЛА́ГОМ *чего, каким usu. media* [PrepP; Invar; the resulting PrepP is adv] **1.** in the name of sth., using sth. as a slogan: **under the banner of.**

2. concealing one's true intentions, purposes under the appearance of something else: **under the guise ⟨the pretext⟩ of.**

Под флагом укрепления дисциплины труда служащим запретили пользоваться служебным телефоном в личных целях. Under the pretext of maintaining discipline in the workplace, workers were forbidden to use office telephones for personal matters.

Ф-13 • ВЫКИ́ДЫВАТЬ/ВЫ́КИНУТЬ ФО́КУС ⟨ФО́КУСЫ, ФО́РТЕЛЬ, ФО́РТЕЛИ⟩ *coll* [VP; subj: human; variants with фокусы, фортели are usu. impfv; variants with фокус, фортель are usu. pfv] to do sth. unexpected, unusual, often absurd: X выкинул фокус ≃ **X played a trick; X pulled a stunt ⟨a trick⟩.**

Наконец кассу открывают... «Граждане, в общие и плацкартные вагоны билетов нет!» — кричит кассирша... «Не знают, как деньги выманить, — возмущается толстая... тётка. — Понаделали мягких вагонов — кому они нужны?.. Вот ещё раз, два такие фокусы выкинете, и ни один человек к вам не пойдёт» (Распутин 1). At last the ticket office opened...."No second- or third-class tickets, citizens," shouted the cashier...."Anything to get money out of us," blustered a fat woman...."Who wants their first-class carriages?...Play this trick once too often and you'll not have anybody using the railways" (1a).

Ф-14 • ФОМА́ НЕВЕ́РНЫЙ ⟨НЕВЕ́РУЮЩИЙ⟩ [NP; sing only; fixed WO] a skeptical person who is hard to convince of something: **a doubting Thomas.**

< From the Biblical account of the apostle Thomas, who did not believe that Christ had risen from the dead until he saw and touched the wounds (John 20:24–29).

Ф-15 • КРА́СНЫЙ ФОНА́РЬ *obs* [NP; sing only] an establishment where prostitutes live and entertain their clients: **brothel; whorehouse; house of ill repute ⟨ill fame⟩;** [in limited contexts] **call house.** Cf. red-light district.

Ф-16 • СТА́ВИТЬ/ПОСТА́ВИТЬ ФОНА́РЬ *кому;* **НАСТА́ВИТЬ ФОНАРЕ́Й** *all coll* [VP; subj: human] to hit s.o.

in such a way that he ends up with a bruise near or around the eye: X поставил Y-у фонарь ≃ **X gave Y a black eye ⟨a shiner⟩; X blackened Y's eye.**

[Городничий:] Да сказать Держиморде, чтобы не слишком давал воли кулакам своим: он... всем ставит фонари под глазами: и правому и виноватому (Гоголь 4). [Mayor:] And tell Derzhimorda not to be too free with his fists. He gives black eyes both to the guilty and the innocent... (4c).

Ф-17 • ЗОЛОТО́Й ФОНД *кого-чего rhet, lit* [NP; sing only; fixed WO] the best, most valuable, most important people (achievements, works of art or literature etc): **the gold reserve (of s.o. ⟨sth.⟩).**

Все переводчики разбиты на группы: английская, французская, скандинавская... В каждой группе есть свои корифеи... Корифеи давно работают в «Интуристе», прекрасно знают язык. Их берегут, ими дорожат. Это «золотой фонд» «Интуриста» (Михайловская 1). All interpreters are broken up into groups: English, French, Scandinavian. Each group has its star[s]....The stars have worked for Intourist for a long time, they know their languages perfectly. They are protected, they are treasured. They are the "gold reserve" of Intourist (1a).

Ф-18 • ЗАТКНУ́ТЬ ФОНТА́Н *highly coll, rude* [VP; subj: human; usu. imper; fixed WO] to stop talking: заткни фонтан ≃ **put a lid on it!; cork it!; dry up!; give it a rest!; turn it off!**

[Телегин *(плачущим голосом)*:] Ваня, я не люблю, когда ты это говоришь. Ну, вот, право... Кто изменяет жене или мужу, тот, значит, неверный человек, тот может изменить и отечеству! [Войницкий *(с досадой)*:] Заткни фонтан, Вафля! (Чехов 3). [T. *(in a tearful voice)*:] Vanya, I don't like to hear you talk like that. Really, you know, anyone who betrays a wife or husband is a person you cannot trust, a person who might betray his country, too. [V. *(with vexation)*:] Dry up, Waffles! (3e).

< From the aphorism «Если у тебя есть фонтан, заткни его: дай отдохнуть и фонтану» ("If you have a fountain, turn it off: give the fountain a rest, too"), by Kozma Prutkov (published in «Плоды раздумья», 1854). Kozma Prutkov, a fictitious writer, was the creation of Count Aleksei Tolstoi and the brothers Zhemchuzhnikov—Aleksei and Vladimir, with occasional contributions from a third brother, Aleksandr.

Ф-19 • НЕ ФОНТА́Н *coll, often humor* [NP; Invar; subj-compl with быть₀ (subj: abstr or concr)] sth. is mediocre, not very good: X не фонтан ≃ **X is nothing special; X is no great shakes ⟨no prize, no gem⟩; X is nothing to brag ⟨to write home⟩ about.**

«Вот, — схватил он со стола газету и сунул Ефиму. — „Всегда с партией, всегда с народом". Хорош заголовок?» — «Мм-м», — замялся Ефим. — «Мму! — передразнил Каретников, замычав по-коровьи. — Не мучайся и не мычи, я и так вижу, что морду воротишь. Название не фонтан, но зато просто и без прикрас» (Войнович 6). "Here." He grabbed the newspaper from his desk and thrust it at Yefim. "'Always with the Party, Always with the People.' Nice headline, eh?" "Mmm..." Yefim began hesitantly. "Mmooo!" Karetnikov lowed, mimicking. "Don't squirm, don't mumble. I can see you're turning up your nose. The title's no gem. It's simple, though, straightforward" (6a).

Ф-20 • В ФО́РМЕ *(какой)* **быть₀, оказаться, чувствовать себя; В ФО́РМУ входить, приходить** [PrepP; these forms only; subj-compl with copula; subj: human, collect (команда, класс etc), or, occas., animal] (often of a performer, public speaker, athlete, or animal in competition) (to be in or get into) the physical or mental condition in which one's strengths, abilities, skills etc are or can be displayed to their fullest: X в (хорошей) форме ≃ **X is in good ⟨fine⟩ form; X is at his best; X is in top ⟨great etc⟩ shape;** [usu. in sporting contexts] **X is at the top of**

his game; ‖ *Neg* X не в форме ≃ **X is not up to par**; [usu. in refer. to one's level of fitness] **X is out of shape.**

Рейно говорил в палате о выдержке, мужестве. Когда он кончил, Тесса его поздравил: «Ты сегодня в форме…» (Эренбург 4). Reynaud spoke in the Chamber about firmness and courage. When he finished his speech, Tessa congratulated him. "You were in good form today" (4a). ♦ Так уж получалось, что, когда Фаина жаловалась на то, что плохо выглядит, то казалась Лёве наиболее красивой, любимой и близкой… Его радовало, когда она бывала измученной, слабой и несчастной… и наоборот, пугало, когда она была «в форме»: красивой, уверенной, бодрой (Битов 2). Thus it was that when Faina complained of looking bad she seemed to Lyova most beautiful, beloved, and close.…It gladdened him when she was exhausted, weak, and unhappy…and vice versa, it frightened him when she was "at her best": beautiful, confident, cheerful (2a).

Ф-21 • ПО ВСЕЙ ФÓРМЕ [PrepP; Invar; fixed WO] **1.** Also: **ПО ФÓРМЕ** [adv or nonagreeing modif] according to protocol, according to a prescribed set of standards: **according to (all) the rules ⟨regulations⟩; as (is) required; proper(ly); in the proper way.**

«Да подозревай я вас хоть немножко, так ли следовало мне поступить? Мне, напротив, следовало бы сначала усыпить подозрения ваши, и виду не подать, что я об этом факте уже известен… Следовало бы по всей форме от вас показание-то отобрать, обыск сделать, да, пожалуй, ещё вас и заарестовать…» (Достоевский 3). "If I had suspected you even a tiny bit, is that the way I should have acted? On the contrary, I should have begun by lulling your suspicions and not giving a sign that I was already in possession of that fact.…I should have taken evidence from you according to all the regulations, I should have made a search and probably even have arrested you…" (3a). ♦ [Саша] мог бы спросить [Алферова]: для чего вы меня вызвали? Для допроса? Тогда ведите его по всей форме… (Рыбаков 2). He [Sasha] could have asked why he had been summoned. For an interrogation? If so, then he [Alferov] ought to get on with it in the proper way… (2a).

2. *coll.* Also: **ПО ФÓРМЕ; ВО ВСЕЙ ФÓРМЕ** *obs* [adv] in keeping with high standards: **in fine style.**

[Гордей Карпыч:] Сколько раз говорил я тебе: хочешь сделать у себя вечер, позови музыкантов, чтобы это было во всей форме… [Пелагея Егоровна:] Ну уж, куда нам музыкантов… старухам (Островский 2). [G.K.:] How many times have I said: if you want to have some amusement, hire musicians and do it in fine style.… [P.E.:] What does us old ladies want with musicians? (2b).

3. *obs.* Also: **ВО ВСЕЙ ФÓРМЕ** *obs* [nonagreeing modif] (one is a certain type of person) entirely: **a real ⟨regular⟩ [NP]; a full-fledged ⟨full-blown⟩ [NP]; an honest-to-goodness ⟨-God⟩ [NP].**

«…В трёх верстах от города стоял драгунский полк… Офицеры, сколько их ни было, сорок человек одних офицеров было в городе; как начали мы, братец, пить… Штабс-ротмистр Поцелуев… такой славный! усы, братец, такие!.. Поручик Кувшинников… Ах, братец, какой премилый человек! вот, уж можно сказать, во всей форме кутила» (Гоголь 3). "…There was a regiment of dragoons stationed three versts from town.…All the officers—there must have been at least forty of them—were in town to a man; and we started drinking, brother.…Captain Potseluev—such a nice fellow! You should have seen his mustache, brother; that long!…Lieutenant Kuvshinnikov, too—such a charming fellow, brother, a full-blown rake, I'd say" (3c).

Ф-22 • ДЛЯ ФÓРМЫ [PrepP; Invar] **1.** [adv] in order to adhere to established procedure, rules: **for the sake of form ⟨protocol⟩; for good form; as a matter of procedure ⟨protocol⟩; as a formality.**

…К вечеру она [Амалия], для формы, созвала опытнейших городских будочников и открыла совещание (Салтыков-Щедрин 1). …That evening, for the sake of form, [Amalia] called all the most experienced constables together and held a conference (1b). Toward evening…, for good form, [Amalia] summoned the most experienced municipal patrolmen and opened a conference (1a).

2. Also: **ДЛЯ ПРОФÓРМЫ** [adv or subj-compl with быть⌀ (subj: human, abstr, or concr)] in order to create the impression that all is as it should be: **for the sake of appearances; for appearance' sake; as a matter of form; (just) for show; pro forma.**

Секретарь тут лишь для проформы, его можно в расчёт не принимать (Зиновьев 1). "Secretary's only there for the sake of appearances; you can ignore him" (1a). ♦ Во всю дорогу был он [Селифан] молчалив, только похлёстывал кнутом и не обращал никакой поучительной речи к лошадям, хотя чубарому коню, конечно, хотелось бы выслушать что-нибудь наставительное, ибо в это время вожжи всегда как-то лениво держались в руках словоохотного возницы и кнут только для формы гулял поверх спин (Гоголь 3). During the whole trip he [Selifan] was silent, merely flicking his whip from time to time, without addressing any diatribes to the horses, although the dappled horse, of course, would have liked to hear something instructive, for during those speeches the reins always slackened somehow in the hands of the garrulous driver and the whip strayed only *pro forma* over their backs (3c).

Ф-23 • ДЕРЖÁТЬ ФОРС *highly coll* [VP; subj: human] to appear calm, poised, brave etc in an embarrassing situation, troublesome circumstances etc: X держит форс ≃ **X keeps ⟨puts⟩ up a (brave) front; X puts on a brave face; X keeps a stiff upper lip.**

«Товарищ майор, — говорю стальным голосом, — прошу вас немедленно покинуть помещение!» Вижу, растерялся, но форс держит (Искандер 5). "Comrade Major," I said in a steely voice, "please leave the premises immediately!" He was flustered, I saw, but still keeping up a front (5a).

Ф-24 • ДЛЯ ФÓРСУ ⟨-а⟩ *highly coll* [PrepP; these forms only; usu. adv] simply in order to impress others: **for show; (just) to show off; to cut a dash.**

Он в теннис не играет — носит с собой ракетку только для форса. He doesn't play tennis—he carries a racket with him just for show.

Ф-25 • ДАВÁТЬ/ДАТЬ ФÓРУ *кому coll* [VP; subj: human; more often pfv] **1.** to give s.o. an advantage over o.s. (often in a game, competition etc): X дал Y-у фору ≃ **X gave Y a handicap ⟨a head start⟩; X let Y get a jump on X.**

Когда чемпион школы по шахматам играл с кем-либо из школьников, он обычно снимал с доски одну из своих пешек до начала партии — давал фору более слабому противнику. When the school chess champion played another student, he would usually take one of his pawns off the board before starting the game, thus giving his weaker opponent a handicap. ♦ [author's usage] …В самой глубине души мне хотелось, чтобы восторжествовала не убогая реальность действительности, а фантастическая реальность; хотелось, чтобы жизнь была глубже, таинственней. Поэтому, признав первого владельца кабинета эндурцем, я как бы дал фору маловероятной мистике… (Искандер 5). …At the bottom of my heart I wanted a fantastical reality to triumph, not the squalid reality of daily life; I wanted life to be deeper, more mysterious. That was why I had given the improbable mystique a head start, as it were, by identifying the owner of the first office as an Endursky (5a).

2. [usu. pfv] to be substantially superior to s.o. in some area: X даст Y-у фору ≃ **X will ⟨can⟩ run circles ⟨rings⟩ around Y; X will leave Y in the dust; X will outclass ⟨outshine etc⟩ Y.**

По скорости чтения Петя давал фору всем своим одноклассникам. When it came to reading speed, Petya ran circles around all his classmates.

Ф-26 • ВО ФРОНТ ⟨**ФРУНТ** *obs*⟩ **вытянуться, стать, стоять** и т. п. [PrepP; these forms only; adv] (to come) to or (to be) in a position with one's arms at one's sides and one's heels together: **(come) to attention; (stand) at attention.**

Подходя к комендантскому дому, мы увидели на площадке человек двадцать стареньких инвалидов с длинными косами и в треугольных шляпах. Они выстроены были во фрунт (Пушкин 2). As we approached the commandant's house, we saw in a small square some twenty doddering veterans wearing three-cornered hats over their long hair. They were lined up, standing at attention (2a).

Ф-27 • НА ДВА ФРО́НТА бороться, вести борьбу, работать, успевать и т. п. *coll* [PrepP; Invar; adv; fixed WO] (to fight, struggle) against two sides simultaneously, (to work, succeed) in two areas simultaneously etc: **on two fronts.**

«Осуществляя этот план, мы должны бороться на два фронта: против того, чтобы Москва осталась "большой деревней", и против излишеств урбанизации» (Рыбаков 2). "In carrying out this plan, we will be fighting on two fronts: first, against the idea that Moscow should remain a 'big village,' and second, against excesses in urban development" (2a).

Ф-28 • ЕДИ́НЫМ ФРО́НТОМ действовать, выступать и т. п. [NP$_{instrum}$; Invar; adv; fixed WO] (to act) as one, showing solidarity: **(present ⟨put up⟩) a united front; (make) common cause.**

[Мать:] Я только хочу сказать, чтобы вы... понимаете, если у них не будет никакой поддержки, если мы будем выступать, так сказать, единым фронтом... Он ведь тоже совсем мальчик, зачем ему это? Искалечат себе жизнь! Никакой любви здесь нет, поймите! Туман, больше ничего (Рощин 1). [Mother:] I just want to say that you and I...you understand, don't you, that if they have no support, if we present a united front, so to speak....He's only a boy after all, so why let him do this to himself? They'll ruin their lives. There's no love here, you realize! It's a romantic mist, that's all it is (1b).

Ф-29 • ФУ́-ТЫ; ФУ́-ТЫ, НУ́-ТЫ! *both coll* [Interj; these forms only; fixed WO] used to express surprise, irritation etc (usu. colored by irony): **la-di-da!; my, my!; well, well!; isn't that ⟨he etc⟩ something!; ooh!;** [when said without irony] **good grief!; my goodness!;** ‖ **фу-ты ну-ты, какой важный!** ≃ **isn't** *he* **hoity-toity ⟨snooty etc⟩!**

«Что же ты проходишь мимо не здороваясь?» — «Фу-ты, ну-ты, какой ты обидчивый!» "What's this, you walk by and don't even say hello?" "My, my, awfully touchy, aren't we!" ♦ [Городничий:] Фу-ты, какая невидаль! Оттого, что ты шестнадцать самоваров выдуешь в день, так оттого и важничаешь? (Гоголь 4). [Mayor:] Ooh, aren't you a wonder! Swill down sixteen pots of tea a day — is that anything to put on airs about? (4b). ♦ Вхожу я в кабинет, за столом директор — фу-ты, ну-ты, какой важный! I go into the office, the director is sitting at his desk, and isn't *he* hoity-toity!

Ф-30 • ПРОЙТИ́ ⟨ВЫ́ЙТИ, ПРОСКОЧИ́ТЬ⟩ ФУ́КСОМ *obs, coll* [VP; subj: usu. human or concr] to make it through (some test, bureaucratic process etc) by chance: **by some (lucky) fluke.**

Хоть десяток отказов! Пиши дальше! И в конце концов, по закону больших чисел, пропуск твой проскочит фуксом через бюрократическую машину (Гинзбург 2). You might have had ten refusals. But never mind, slap in another application! Finally, according to the law of averages, your pass would emerge by some lucky fluke from the bureaucratic machine (2a).

Ф-31 • ВОТ ТАК ФУНТ! ВОТ ТЕ ФУНТ! *both highly coll* [Interj; these forms only; fixed WO] used to express surprise, perplexity, disappointment (usu. in reaction to sth. unexpected):

you don't say!; (well,) how do you like that!; (well,) I like that!; well, I'll be (darned ⟨damned⟩)!; (well,) how about that!; [in limited contexts] bless me if...

«А в тоне вашем, простите, содержится некий елей, нечто этакое, не то поповское, не то толстовское». — «Иначе не может быть, — сказал Иконников, — ведь я был толстовцем». — «Вот так фунт», — сказал Михаил Сидорович [Мостовской] (Гроссман 2). "But there's something rather unctuous, if I may say so, in your tone of voice. You sound like a priest or a Tolstoyan." "That's hardly surprising," said Ikonnikov. "I used to be a Tolstoyan." "You don't say!" exclaimed Mostovskoy (2a). ♦ «Вы обратили внимание, на юрятинских путях стрелочница нам кулаком грозила? Вот те фунт, думаю, в сторожихи на дорогу Глафира определилась. Но, кажется, не она. Слишком стара» (Пастернак 1). "You saw the woman at the switch, who shook her fist at us? Bless me, I thought, if it isn't Glafira gone to work on the railway. But I don't think it was Glafira, she looked too old" (1a).

Ф-32 • НЕ ФУНТ ИЗЮ́МУ ⟨-а⟩ *coll, often humor* [NP; these forms only; subj-compl with быть$_\varnothing$ (subj: usu. abstr), usu. pres; fixed WO] sth. is no trifle, is a serious matter, is not to be taken lightly: **X не фунт изюму** ≃ **X is nothing to sneeze ⟨laugh⟩ at; X is no joke.**

Сколько видел Фёдор за свою короткую жизнь, сколько слышал, войны хлебнул четыре ровных годика, тоже не фунт изюма... (Максимов 1). Fyodor had seen and heard a good deal in his short life. He'd supped four full years of war, which is also no joke (1a).

Ф-33 • ПОЧЁМ ФУНТ ЛИ́ХА узнать, знать, понять и т. п. *coll* [subord clause; Invar; fixed WO] (to know, learn) what severe hardship is (by personally experiencing an ordeal, hard time etc): **what real trouble ⟨misfortune, suffering, misery etc⟩ is; what hard times are (really like ⟨all about⟩).**

«Жена воспитывалась в детском доме. Сирота... Она с детства узнала, почём фунт лиха стоит...» (Шолохов 1). "My wife had been brought up in a children's home. She was an orphan....She had known what real trouble was since she was a kid" (1c).

Ф-34 • НА ФУФУ́ *obsoles, highly coll* [PrepP; Invar; adv] (to do sth.) haphazardly, without proper care, thought, attention etc: **carelessly; slapdash; in a slipshod ⟨slapdash⟩ manner.**

Ему ничего важного нельзя поручать: всё делает на фуфу. You can't trust anything important to him, he does everything slapdash.

Ф-35 • ПОДНИМА́ТЬ ⟨ПОДЫМА́ТЬ⟩/ПОДНЯ́ТЬ ⟨ПОДДЕВА́ТЬ/ПОДДЕ́ТЬ⟩ НА ФУФУ́ кого *obs, coll* [VP; subj: human] to delude, deceive s.o.: **X поднял Y-а на фуфу** ≃ **X pulled the wool over Y's eyes; X took Y in ⟨for a ride⟩; X hoodwinked Y.**

[Нелькин:] Осмотритесь: вас подымают на фуфу! У вас крадут дочь!.. (Сухово-Кобылин 2). [N.:] Look around you: you're being taken in. They are stealing your daughter!... (2a).

Ф-36 • ПОЙТИ́ ⟨СОЙТИ́⟩ НА ФУФУ́ *obs, coll* [VP; subj: usu. abstr] to fail to succeed, end in failure: **X пошёл на фуфу** ≃ **X fell through; X fizzled (out); X came to nothing ⟨to naught⟩.**

[Кречинский:] ...[Он] влепит своим хамским почерком имя моё в книгу, и как гром какой разразится по Москве весть! И кончено, и всё кончено. Свадьба пошла на фуфу; от этого проклятого миллиона остаётся дым какой-то, чад, похмелье и злость... да, злость!.. (Сухово-Кобылин 2). [K.:] He'll scrawl my name in the book with that boorish handwriting of his, and the news is bound to reverberate throughout Moscow like a clap of thunder! And that'll be the end of it, the end of everything! The marriage'll fizzle out, and all that'll be left of that damn million'll be nothing but a puff of smoke, fumes, a hangover, and malice...yes, malice (2b).

X

X-1 • ИЗ ХА́МА НЕ СДЕ́ЛАЕШЬ ⟨НЕ БУ́ДЕТ⟩ ПА́НА [saying] a rude, uncouth person cannot become refined and well-mannered: ≃ **you can't make a silk purse out of a sow's ear.**

X-2 • ВЫДЕ́РЖИВАТЬ/ВЫ́ДЕРЖАТЬ ХАРА́КТЕР *coll* [VP; subj: human] to adhere firmly and resolutely to a decision, displaying strength of character (or, occas., stubbornness): X выдержал характер ≃ **X stood ⟨held⟩ firm; X hung tough; X didn't ⟨wouldn't⟩ give in ⟨budge, back down⟩; X maintained his stand; X held out; X stuck it out;** ‖ *Neg* X не выдержал характера ≃ **X gave ⟨caved⟩ in; X gave way ⟨folded, buckled⟩.**

Как он ни горячился, называл их мошенниками, разбойниками, грабителями проезжающих, намекнул даже на страшный суд, но кузнецов ничем не пронял; они совершенно выдержали характер: не только не отступились от цены, но даже провозились за работой вместо двух часов целых пять с половиною (Гоголь 3). However much he fumed, calling them scoundrels, brigands, robbers who fleeced travellers, and even hinting at the Day of Judgement, he made no impression whatever on the blacksmiths: they stood firm and not only stuck to their original price, but took five and a half hours over their work instead of two (3a). ♦ После часто мне надо было выдерживать увещания отца, который говорил, что необходимо *кюльтивировать* это знакомство и что я не могу требовать, чтоб человек в таком положении, как Ивин, занимался мальчишкой, как я; но я выдержал характер довольно долго (Толстой 2). Afterwards I frequently had to endure the exhortations of my father, who said that it was essential to *cultiver* this acquaintance and that I could not demand of a man in Ivin's position that he bother himself about a mere boy like myself; but I maintained my stand for quite a long time (2b).

X-3 • ПОКА́ЗЫВАТЬ/ПОКАЗА́ТЬ ХАРА́КТЕР *(кому)*; ПРОЯВЛЯ́ТЬ/ПРОЯВИ́ТЬ ХАРА́КТЕР *both coll* [VP; subj: human] to demonstrate forcefulness, will, strong-mindedness etc: X показал характер ≃ **X showed some muscle (to Y); X showed his mettle; X showed what he was made (out) of.**

Ревкин понял, что Ермолкину и тем, кто стоит за его спиной, пора показать характер (Войнович 4). Revkin realized that it was time to show some muscle to Ermolkin and those behind him (4a). ♦ Конечно, последовательнее было бы стоять на своём. Но тогда и ему придётся проявлять характер. И чем дело кончится, неизвестно (Войнович 5). Of course it would have been more consistent of me to stand my ground. But then he would have had to show what he was made out of, too. There'd have been no telling where it all would end (5a).

X-4 • НЕ СОЙТИ́СЬ ХАРА́КТЕРАМИ ⟨ХАРА́КТЕ-РОМ⟩ *(с кем) coll* [VP; subj: human; if there is no prep obj, subj: pl] to be ill-matched with regard to disposition, not to have a congenial relationship with s.o.: X и Y ⟨X с Y-ом⟩ не сошлись характерами ≃ **X and Y are ⟨were⟩ incompatible; X doesn't ⟨didn't⟩ get along with Y; X and Y didn't hit it off.**

[Репников:] На свадьбе стало ясно, что [жених и невеста] не сошлись характерами... Любопытно... (Вампилов 3). [R.:] At the wedding it became clear they [the bride and groom] were incompatible...that's odd... (3b). ♦ «Характером, значит, с Дёминой не сошёлся? Кто ж с ней, с язвой, сойдётся, покойник разве?» (Максимов 2). "So you didn't exactly hit it off with Dyomina, eh? I don't know who can get on with that old witch, except a corpse maybe" (2a).

X-5 • В ХАРА́КТЕРЕ *чьём, кого* [PrepP; Invar; the resulting PrepP is subj-compl with быть∅ (subj: abstr or infin); often neg] it is characteristic of or natural for s.o. (to do sth.): X ⟨делать X⟩ в Y-овом характере ≃ **X ⟨doing X⟩ is in (keeping with) Y's character; X ⟨doing X⟩ is in character for Y; it's (just) like Y (to do X); X ⟨doing X⟩ is typical of Y;** ‖ *Neg* X ⟨делать X⟩ не в Y-овом характере ≃ **it's out of character for Y (to do X); it's not in Y (to do X); it's not (in) Y's nature (to do X); it's unlike Y (to do X).**

Приглашение доброе и деловое, вполне в его характере... (Орлова 1). The invitation was kind and businesslike, completely in keeping with his character... (1a). ♦ [Пепел:] Ну... говори... [Василиса:] Что же говорить? Насильно мил не будешь... и не в моём это характере милости просить... (Горький 3). [P.:] Well, if you have anything to say—[V.:] What is there to say? You can't force one to like you—and it's not in my character to beg for alms (3b). ♦ «...Вы связали меня данным словом, от которого теперь отрекаетесь... и наконец... наконец, я вовлечён был, так сказать, через то в издержки...» Эта последняя претензия до того была в характере Петра Петровича, что Раскольников... вдруг не выдержал и—расхохотался (Достоевский 3). "...You bound me with your promise and now you're going back on it...and anyway...anyway, I was led, so to speak, into expense because of that..." This last complaint was so in character for Mr. Luzhin that Raskolnikov...suddenly gave way and—burst out laughing (3a). ♦ ...Я думаю, отец знал о гибели своих детей. Дядя Гриша вряд ли скрыл бы от него этот факт, это было не в его характере (Рыбаков 1). ...I think father knew about the death of his children. Uncle Grisha wouldn't have kept it from him, it wasn't his nature (1a). ♦ [Линевский:] Если только он меня не уволил. Скорей всего уволил. Скорей всего. Не в его характере не уволить (Панова 1). [L.:] If only he hasn't fired me. Probably has, though. Probably has. It would be unlike him not to (1a).

X-6 • МОЯ́ ⟨твоя́ и т. п.⟩ ХА́ТА С КРА́Ю *coll, usu. disapprov* [sent; these forms only; rarely used in refer. to the 1st person—variants with моя and наша usu. refer. to the interlocutor(s) or a third party; fixed WO] (said, usu. disapprovingly, to or about s.o. who refuses to be involved in some matter that requires courage, determination, selflessness) it does not concern me (you etc): X-ова хата с краю ≃ **it's no concern ⟨business⟩ of X's; it has nothing to do with X; it's not X's affair; it's none of X's business ⟨concern⟩.**

«Меня в деревне Иван Акимычем кликали. Калачёв фамилиё [*ungrammat* = фамилия]...» Пожалуй, Влад и до этого знал: такими калачёвыми земля держится, но только теперь... при всем уважении к ним—этим калачёвым,—с горечью усвоил, что ими же держится и всякая на земле неправда. Мы люди маленькие. Наша хата с краю. До Бога высоко, до царя далеко... Вот набор их нехитрых истин, под которые они тянут своё ярмо через всю жизнь... (Максимов 2). "Back home they call me Ivan Akimych. Kalachev's my last name...." Vlad already knew that it was Kalachev and his kind who keep the globe turning, but only now, with all due respect to the Kalachevs of this world, has he come to the sad realization that it is they who also enable all forms of injustice to flourish. We're only small folk. It's no concern of ours. God's too high to help us, the tsar's too far away....This is the sum total of the simple-minded truths with the aid of which they drag their yoke through life... (2a). ♦ ...Скорее всего, это было проявлением особого советского этикета, который твёрдо соблюдался нашим народом в течение многих десятилетий: раз начальство ссылает, значит—так и надо, а моя хата с краю... (Мандельштам 1). Most probably it was a case of the peculiar Soviet etiquette that has been carefully observed for several decades now: if the authorities are sending someone into exile, all well and good, it's none of our business (1a).

< Abbreviated version of the saying «Моя хата с краю, (я) ничего не знаю» ("My hut is set apart, and I don't know anything").

Х-7 • Э́ТОГО ЕЩЁ (ТО́ЛЬКО) НЕ ХВАТА́ЛО 〈НЕДОСТАВА́ЛО〉!; ТО́ЛЬКО Э́ТОГО (И) НЕ ХВАТА́ЛО 〈НЕДОСТАВА́ЛО〉!; ЕЩЁ ЧЕГО́ НЕ ХВАТА́ЛО! *all coll* [Interj; these forms only; the verb is usu. in the final position] (used to express one's dissatisfaction with, indignation at, disapproval of etc some action, event, or circumstance; also used to express one's sharp and rather rude refusal to do what another has suggested) this is intolerable, unacceptable: **that's all I 〈we〉 need!; this is 〈that's〉 the limit!; that is 〈that's〉 going too far!; this is (really) too much!; that's the last straw!**

«Слов, конечно, они [немки] не понимали, но всё ясно было и без слов: я выгнал майора... „Майор гестапо?" – спрашивает у меня Катя. „Найн, найн," – говорю. Этого ещё не хватало» (Искандер 5). "They [the German girls] hadn't understood the words, of course, but all was clear even without words: I'd thrown out the major....'Major – Gestapo?' Katya asked me. 'Nein, nein,' I said. That's all we needed!" (5a). ♦ «Господин сотник, что это за чёрт? Приведите свой взвод в порядок, этого ещё недоставало!» (Шолохов 2). "What the devil are you doing, Lieutenant! Put your troop in order! This is the limit..." (2a). ♦ Гладышев вдруг заметил, что на переднем копыте мерина нет подковы. «Этого ещё не хватало», – пробормотал он... (Войнович 2). Suddenly Gladishev noticed that there was no shoe on the gelding's front hoof. "That's the limit," he muttered (2a). ♦ «Ты должна знать, моя милая, были ли написаны завещание и письмо и уничтожены ли они. И ежели почему-нибудь они забыты, то ты должна знать, где они, и найти их, потому что...» – «Этого только недоставало!» – перебила его княжна... (Толстой 4). "You, my dear, ought to know whether the will and letter were written, and whether or not they have been destroyed. And if they have somehow been overlooked, then you must know where they are and must find them, because –" "That is going too far!" the Princess interrupted... (4a).

Х-8 • (ВОН 〈ВОТ〉) КУДА́ ХВАТИ́Л 〈МАХНУ́Л〉! *highly coll;* ЭК(А) (КУДА́) ХВАТИ́Л! *substand* [sent; pfv past only; fixed WO] what you (he etc) said is grossly exaggerated, foolish etc: **(now) that is 〈that's〉 going too far!; where'd you 〈he etc〉 get that from?; what will you 〈he etc〉 say next?; what put that idea into your 〈his etc〉 head?; [in limited contexts] you have really surpassed yourself 〈he has really surpassed himself etc〉!**

«...Не видать книг у вас! – сказал Пенкин. – Но умоляю вас, прочтите одну вещь; готовится великолепная... поэма: „Любовь взяточника к падшей женщине"... Я слышал отрывки – автор велик! В нём слышится то Дант, то Шекспир...» – «Вон куда хватили!» (Гончаров 1). "...I don't see any books in your room!" said Pyenkin. "But one thing I urge you to read: a magnificent...poem: 'The Love of an Extortionist for a Fallen Woman'....I have heard extracts from it – the author is great! It has the ring of Dante...Shakespeare..." "Now that is going too far!" (1b). ♦ [Аммос Фёдорович:] Это значит вот что: Россия... да... хочет вести войну, и министерия-то, вот видите, и подослала чиновника, чтобы узнать, нет ли где измены. [Городничий:] Эк куда хватили! (Гоголь 4). [A.F.:] Here's what I mean now: Russia...um, yes...wants to start war, and the ministry now, you see, has sent out a man to find out if there isn't treason somewhere. [Mayor:] Where'd you get that from! (4a). ♦ «Кто ж станет покупать их [мёртвые души]? Ну, какое употребление он может из них сделать?» – «А может, в хозяйстве-то как-нибудь под случай понадобятся...» – возразила старуха... «Мёртвые в хозяйстве! Эк куда хватили! Воробьёв разве пугать по ночам в

вашем огороде, что ли?» (Гоголь 3). "Who will want to buy them [dead souls]? To what use can one put them?" "But perhaps they can be put to some use in the household on an occasion..." retorted the old woman....."Dead men to be put to use in the household! You have really surpassed yourself! What for, pray? To set them up on poles to scare off sparrows in your vegetable garden at night, or what?" (3c).

Х-9 • МЁРТВАЯ ХВА́ТКА, usu. вцепиться *в кого-что*, держать *кого-что* и т. п. мёртвой хваткой [NP; sing only] a very tight hold on s.o. or sth.: **(seize 〈hold〉 s.o. 〈sth.〉 in) a death 〈iron, mortal〉 grip; (seize 〈hold, grip etc〉 s.o. 〈sth.〉 in) a stranglehold.**

К их удивлению, у двери, ведущей со сцены в переулок, лежал на спине целый и невредимый гамбсовский стул. Издав собачий визг, Ипполит Матвеевич вцепился в него мёртвой хваткой (Ильф и Петров 1). To their surprise, the Hambs chair was lying on its back, undamaged, at the exit from the stage to the street. Growling like a dog, Ippolit Matveyevich seized it in a death grip (1a). ♦ ...Рука Николая мёртвой хваткой вцепилась в расстёгнутый ворот гостя... (Максимов 3). ...Nikolai's hand seized his guest's open collar in an iron grip (3a). ♦ Он сейчас мечтал о том, чтобы встретить Читу и того, второго. О, сейчас бы он знал, что надо сделать! Сейчас бы он бросился на них и вцепился мёртвой хваткой (Семёнов 1). He was dreaming now that he would meet Cheetah and that other one. Oh, now he would know what to do! Now he would hurl himself upon them and seize them in a mortal grip (1a). ♦ Он... сделал хищные глаза, высоко подпрыгнул и стремительно схватил в воздухе за горло воображаемую Россию. Он вцепился в неё мёртвой хваткой, зашипел, швырнул её под ноги и начал остервенело топтать лакированными ботинками. При этом он испускал воинственные крики и рычал, как бешеный тигр (Паустовский 1). ...He glared savagely, leapt high into the air and seized an imaginary Russia by the throat. He gripped her in a stranglehold, spat, hurled her to the ground, kicked and trampled her with his polished boots, uttering war whoops and snarling like an enraged tiger (1a).

< Originally referred to the way dogs and certain other animals tightly lock their jaws on a foe or prey through spasmodic muscular contraction.

Х-10 • ДЕРЖА́ТЬ ХВОСТ ТРУБО́Й 〈МОРКО́ВКОЙ, ПИСТОЛЕ́ТОМ〉 *highly coll, humor* [VP; subj: human; usu. imper; fixed WO] to remain hopeful, cheerful, and brave (usu. in refer. to coping with difficult circumstances or some challenge): держи хвост трубой ≃ **keep your chin 〈spirits〉 up; hang in there; cheer up.**

Х-11 • ЗАДИРА́ТЬ/ЗАДРА́ТЬ ХВОСТ *highly coll, rude* [VP; subj: human] to behave arrogantly, show no regard for anyone or anything: X задирает хвост ≃ **X is 〈acts〉 stuck-up 〈snotty, uppity etc〉; X has 〈sticks〉 his nose in the air; X acts high-and-mighty.**

Х-12 • (И) В ХВОСТ И В ГРИ́ВУ *highly coll* [PrepP; these forms only; adv (intensif); fixed WO] to an extreme degree, as intensely as possible: **with all one's might; with might and main; with all 〈everything〉 one's got 〈one has〉; like nobody's business;** ∥ гнать 〈погонять〉 (лошадей) ~ ≃ **drive the 〈one's etc〉 horses for all they are worth; drive not sparing the 〈one's etc〉 horses;** ∥ бить 〈лупить〉 *кого* ~ ≃ **beat s.o. good and hard; beat the tar 〈the (living) daylights etc〉 out of s.o.;** ∥ [in refer. to a hostile army, the enemy] лупить *кого* ~ ≃ **give s.o. a good thrashing.**

«...Он тебя эксплуатирует в хвост и в гриву» (Трифонов 1). "...He exploits you like nobody's business" (1a).

Х-13 • НАКРУТИ́ТЬ ХВОСТ *кому highly coll;* НАКРУТИ́ТЬ ХВОСТА́ *substand* [VP; subj: human] to reprimand

[753]

s.o. sharply or harshly: X накрутил Y-у хвост ≃ **X gave Y hell; X let Y have it (with both barrels); X chewed ⟨bawled⟩ Y out.**

X-14 • НАСТУПА́ТЬ/НАСТУПИ́ТЬ НА ХВОСТ *кому highly coll* [VP] **1.** [subj: human or collect] to be following s.o. very closely and be about to catch up to him: X наступает Y-у на хвост ≃ **X is (right) on Y's tail; X is in hot pursuit of Y; X is breathing down Y's neck.**

Они поспешно отходили – противник наступал им на хвост. They were beating a fast retreat because the enemy was right on their tail.

2. [subj: human] to offend s.o., encroach upon his sphere of interests: X наступил Y-у на хвост ≃ **X stepped on Y's toes.**

«Не злись... ты злишься, как будто я тебя девочку увёл. Ведь она же ничья была, совершенно одна и ничья, я никому не наступил на хвост...» (Аксёнов 7). "Pipe down...pipe down! You'd think she was yours the way you're reacting. She's a free agent, her own woman. I haven't stepped on anybody's toes" (7a).

X-15 • ПОДЖИМА́ТЬ/ПОДЖА́ТЬ ⟨ПРИЖИМА́ТЬ/ ПРИЖА́ТЬ, ПОДВЁРТЫВАТЬ/ПОДВЕРНУ́ТЬ, ОПУСКА́ТЬ/ОПУСТИ́ТЬ⟩ ХВОСТ ⟨ХВОСТЫ́⟩ *all highly coll* [VP; subj: human] to retreat, surrender, give up one's course of action because one experiences a loss of self-confidence, apprehension, humiliation etc (often in circumstances when one encounters strong, unexpected opposition, when one suddenly becomes afraid of the possible consequences of one's actions etc): X поджал хвост ≃ **X tucked ⟨stuck, went away with etc⟩ his tail between his legs.**

«Больно спесив Кирила Петрович! а небось поджал хвост, когда Гришка мой закричал ему: „Вон, старый пёс! долой со двора!"» (Пушкин 1). "Kirila Petrovich is proud all right, but he certainly went away with his tail between his legs when Grisha shouted to him: 'Go on, you old cur! Get out of here!'" (1b). ♦ «...Сегодня он действительно его выгнал. Это так и было. Ну, а тот рассердился... Ораторствовал здесь, знания свои выставлял, да и ушёл, хвост поджав...» (Достоевский 3). "...Today he really did send him packing. That's exactly what happened. And then the other character lost his temper....Made a speech or two, showed off his knowledge and then left with his tail between his legs" (3a).

X-16 • ПРИЩЕМЛЯ́ТЬ/ПРИЩЕМИ́ТЬ ⟨ПРИЖИМА́ТЬ/ПРИЖА́ТЬ *obs*⟩ **ХВОСТ ⟨ХВОСТЫ́⟩** *кому highly coll* [VP; subj: human; more often pfv] to humble s.o. and/ or force him to act in accordance with one's wishes: X прищемит Y-у хвост ≃ **X will take ⟨bring⟩ Y down a peg ⟨a notch⟩ (or two); X will bring Y in line ⟨to heel⟩.**

[author's usage] Я не сомневаюсь, что [директор издательства] Котов, торгуясь, не сомневался в том, что Мариетта [Шагинян] добьётся своего. Он просто хотел... ущемить ей хвост (Мандельштам 2). I have no doubt that all the time he was haggling with her [Marietta Shaginian], Kotov [the director of the publishing house] knew perfectly well that she would get her way in the end. He simply wanted to take her down a peg or two... (2a).

X-17 • РАСПУСКА́ТЬ/РАСПУСТИ́ТЬ (ПАВЛИ́НИЙ ⟨ПЫ́ШНЫЙ⟩) ХВОСТ *(перед кем) coll* [VP; subj: human] to flaunt, talk or behave in a pretentious way, trying to impress s.o. (with one's erudition, skills etc): X распускает хвост (перед Y-ом) ≃ **X struts like a peacock; X struts his stuff; X puts on ⟨gives himself⟩ airs; X shows off (in front of Y).**

Мандельштам... очень следил, чтобы и я не распускала хвост (Мандельштам 2). M[andelstam]...always watched me very carefully in case I tried to put on airs... (2a). ♦ Это был мрачный, возбудимый старик, непризнанный гений, жертва бутылки. Людей вообще он терпеть не мог, но для Верочки делал исключение. Куражился перед ней, распускал хвост, поражая

обилием знаний (Грекова 3). He was a gloomy, nervous old man, an unrecognized genius who drank too much. He could not stand people in general, but made an exception for Verochka. He showed off in front of her, amazing her with his fantastic knowledge (3a).

X-18 • УКОРОТИ́ТЬ ХВОСТ *кому highly coll* [VP; subj: human] to deflate s.o.'s ego, humble s.o. and often make him more obedient: X укоротил Y-у хвост ≃ **X took Y down a peg (or two); X cut Y down to size; X got Y (back) in line.**

X-19 • ХВАТА́ТЬ/СХВАТИ́ТЬ ⟨УХВАТИ́ТЬ, ЛОВИ́ТЬ/ПОЙМА́ТЬ⟩ ЗА ХВОСТ *что coll* [VP; subj: human] **1.** ~ **славу, счастье, фортуну** и т. п. (in refer. to fame, happiness, fortune etc) to (strive to) attain something that is difficult to attain: X схватил Y за хвост ≃ **X grabbed ⟨seized⟩ Y by the tail.**

Меня он тогда считал счастливцем, схватившим за хвост жар-птицу (Гладков 1). At this time he looked on me as someone favoured by fortune who had seized the fire-bird by the tail (1a).

2. ~ **идею, тему** и т. п. suddenly to think up (a good idea), find (a successful solution): X ухватил за хвост Y ≃ **X hit ⟨lighted⟩ (up)on Y.**

X-20 • В ХВОСТЕ́ *(чего, occas. кого)* **идти, плестись, оказаться, оставить** *кого* и т. п. [PrepP; Invar; adv, subj-compl with copula (subj: human or collect), or obj-compl with оставить etc (obj: human or collect)] (to be) unable to keep up with some person or group, or (to leave some person or group) behind one and unable to keep up as one progresses ahead: **(lag ⟨trail, fall, leave s.o. lagging, leave s.o. trailing** etc⟩) **behind; (be) at the tail ⟨tag⟩ end (of sth.); [in refer. to studies only] (be) at the bottom of the class.**

[Генерал:] ...По *чьей* вине следователи всё ещё плетутся в хвосте? По вине руководителей отделов, да! (Солженицын 9). [General:] ...Whose fault is it that the investigators are trailing behind? It's the fault of the heads of departments, yes! (9a). ♦ R – всё тот же, всё тот же. По Тэйлору и математике — он всегда шёл в хвосте (Замятин 1). R. is the same as ever. In Taylor and in mathematics he was always at the bottom of the class (1a).

X-21 • ВИСЕ́ТЬ ⟨ПОВИ́СНУТЬ⟩ НА ХВОСТЕ́ *(кого, у кого);* **НА ХВОСТЕ́** *all coll* [VP or PrepP (Invar, subj-compl with copula); subj: human or collect] (of a pursuer, an athlete in competition, or enemy troops) to be following s.o. very closely and be about to catch up to him: X висел на хвосте у Y-а ≃ **X was (right) on Y's tail; X was right behind Y; X was closing in on Y.**

«Зараз [*regional* = сейчас, только что] разведка вернулась, говорят, что бугор пустой. Стало быть, Журавлёв потерял нас, а то бы он теперь на хвосте висел» (Шолохов 5). "Our patrol has just come in, they say there's no one on the hill. Zhuravlyov must have lost us or he'd be on our tail right now" (5a).

X-22 • МЫШИ́НЫЙ ⟨КРЫСИ́НЫЙ⟩ ХВО́СТИК ⟨ХВОСТ⟩ *coll, derog* [NP; fixed WO] a very thin plait or lock of hair: **ratty little braid ⟨hank⟩.**

X-23 • С ХВО́СТИКОМ; С ХВОСТО́М *both coll* [PrepP; these forms only; usu. used with a Num or quantit NP as nonagreeing postmodif] (used when expressing s.o.'s age or, less often, the time, size, or quantity of sth. as an approximation rounded down to the nearest convenient figure) (the figure named) with a small excess: **a little over...; a little more than...; ...and then some; ...plus; [Num]-odd...; [in limited contexts] not much over...; not much more than...; [in refer. to clock time only] a little past...**

На вид Борису Ивановичу было лет пятьдесят с хвостиком. Boris Ivanovich looked to be a little over fifty. ♦ «Я вам, кажется, надоел?» — «Совсем нет, только я немного устал, хочу спать, я встал в шесть часов, а теперь два с хвостиком» (Герцен 3). "I am afraid I am boring you?" "Not at all, only I am a little tired and sleepy. I got up at six and now it is a little past two" (3a).

X-24 • ВЕРТЕ́ТЬ/ЗАВЕРТЕ́ТЬ 〈КРУТИ́ТЬ/ЗАКРУ-ТИ́ТЬ〉 ХВОСТО́М *highly coll, disapprov* [VP; subj: human] (often in refer. to answering a question directly, answering for sth. etc) to (try to) evade sth.: X вертит хвостом ≃ **X is trying to weasel his way out of it; X is hedging 〈beating around the bush〉;** [in limited contexts] **X is trying to confuse the issue.**

«Долго ли нам [= нашему городу] гореть будет?» — спросили они… Но лукавый бригадир только вертел хвостом и говорил, что ему с богом спорить не приходится (Салтыков-Щедрин 1). "Is it long we [our town] must burn?" they asked.…But the sly brigadier only tried to confuse the issue by saying that it was not for him to quarrel with God (1a).

X-25 • ВИЛЬНУ́ТЬ ХВОСТО́М *highly coll, usu. disapprov* [VP; subj: human] to leave s.o. or some place suddenly and quickly (often in order to avoid s.o.'s company, doing an unpleasant chore etc): X вильнул хвостом ≃ **X cut 〈skipped〉 out (on s.o.); X up and left; X turned round and left 〈disappeared〉; X did a disappearing act.**

Я её попросила вывести собаку, а она вместо этого вильнула хвостом и исчезла на весь день. I asked her to walk the dog, but instead she cut out and disappeared for the entire day.

X-26 • ВИЛЯ́ТЬ/ЗАВИЛЯ́ТЬ ХВОСТО́М *highly coll* [VP; subj: human; usu. impfv] **1.** (often in refer. to answering a question directly, answering for sth. etc) to (try to) evade sth.: X виляет хвостом ≃ **X is trying to weasel his way out of it; X is hedging 〈beating around the bush〉;** [in limited contexts] **X is trying to confuse the issue.**

2. ~ *перед кем* to ingratiate o.s. before s.o., be subservient, try desperately to please s.o.: X виляет хвостом перед Y-ом ≃ **X falls all over Y; X kowtows before 〈to〉 Y; X kisses up to Y.**

Грубый и хамоватый с подчинёнными, он хорошо умел вилять хвостом перед начальством. Rude and boorish to his subordinates, he really knew how to kiss up to the bosses.

X-27 • НЕ ВЕЛИКА́ 〈НЕ БОЛЬША́Я〉 ХИ́ТРОСТЬ *coll* [NP; these forms only; subj-compl with быть∅ (subj: infin), pres only; more often this WO] doing sth. is not complicated, does not require any special talent or effort: сделать X не велика хитрость ≃ **it's 〈doing X is〉 no big deal 〈thing〉; it doesn't take 〈require〉 any great skill to do X; it doesn't take a genius to do X.**

Посадить рассаду — не велика хитрость, а попробуй цветы из семян вырастить! It doesn't take any great skill to plant seedlings, but just try to grow flowers from seeds!

X-28 • (ВСЁ) ХИ́ХАНЬКИ ДА ХА́ХАНЬКИ 〈ХА́-ХАНЬКИ ДА ХИ́ХАНЬКИ〉 *coll, disapprov* [NP; pl only] (in refer. to s.o.'s frivolous attitude toward everything, unserious approach to his duties, lack of due concern in handling serious problems etc) (everything is) jokes and laughter (for s.o.): всё у X-а ~ ≃ **everything is a big joke to X; X doesn't take things 〈anything etc〉 seriously.**

X-29 • ВОДИ́ТЬ ХЛЕ́Б-СО́ЛЬ *с кем obs* [VP; subj: human] to maintain friendly relations with s.o. and visit with him often: X водит хлеб-соль с Y-ом ≃ **X exchanges frequent visits with Y; X is entertained by Y in Y's house and entertains Y (in X's house); X and Y are frequent guests in each other's homes 〈at each other's tables〉.**

…Тот же читатель, который на жизненной своей дороге будет дружен с таким человеком, будет водить с ним хлеб-соль и проводить приятно время, станет глядеть на него косо, если он очутится героем драмы или поэмы (Гоголь 3). …The very reader who will make friends with such a person in life, exchange frequent visits with him, and enjoy spending time together, will look askance at him if he is made the hero of a drama or a poem (3c). …The very same reader who would make friends with such a man in the course of his life, would entertain him in his house and be entertained by him and spend a pleasant time with him, will be sure to look askance at him if he is made the hero of a drama or an epic poem (3a).

X-30 • ДА́РОМ 〈ЗРЯ〉 ХЛЕБ ЕСТЬ *coll, disapprov* [VP; subj: human] to live or work unproductively: X даром хлеб ест ≃ **X doesn't earn his keep 〈his daily bread〉;** [in refer. to one's life style] **X idles away his time;** [in refer. to working] **X isn't worth his salt.**

[author's usage] Глядя на быстрые руки невестки, бесшумно скользящие над столом, Василий, по их натруженной огрубелости, безошибочно определил, во сколько обходится ей благополучие и гостеприимство мужниного дома: «Не задаром ты, Мария Ильинична, здесь свой хлеб ешь, ой не задаром!» (Максимов 3). Watching his sister-in-law's quick hands darting silently about the table, Vasilii Vasilievich could tell from their work-worn roughness what a price she had had to pay for the prosperity and hospitality of her husband's home. "You earn your keep all right, Maria Ilyinichna," he thought (3a). ♦ [Соня:] Я и дядя Ваня работали без отдыха, боялись потратить на себя копейку и всё посылали тебе… Мы не ели даром хлеба! (Чехов 3). [S.:] Uncle Vanya and I have worked without rest, afraid to spend a kopeck on ourselves, we sent everything to you.…We earned our daily bread (3a). ♦ «Сидим тут, бюрократы проклятые, бумажки перекладываем, ничего не смотрим, хлеб зря едим!» (Солженицын 12). "We sit here like a damned lot of bureaucrats trading papers, not seeing past the ends of our noses—we're not worth our salt" (12a).

X-31 • ЕСТЬ СВОЙ ХЛЕБ *coll* [VP; subj: human] to earn one's own living: X ест свой хлеб ≃ **X eats his own bread; X supports himself;** [in limited contexts] **X makes it on his own.**

[Софья Егоровна:] Мы будем людьми, Мишель! Мы будем есть свой хлеб, мы будем проливать пот, натирать мозоли… (Чехов 1). [S.E.:] We'll be decent people, Michael. We shall eat our own bread. We shall live by the sweat of our own brows. We shall have calloused hands (1a).

X-32 • ЕСТЬ ХЛЕБ *чей, кого;* **ЕСТЬ ЧУЖО́Й ХЛЕБ** *both coll* [VP; subj: human] to live at the expense of another or others: X ест Y-ов 〈чужой〉 хлеб ≃ **X eats Y's 〈another's〉 bread 〈food〉; X lives off (of) Y 〈off (of) others〉.**

Ну, вот хотя бы мои родители — скромные, тихие, честные люди. Но они журналисты, они создают ту самую пропаганду, которая так подло обманула меня… А я сам, разве я был лучше? Мало того, что я ел их хлеб, — я ещё был пионером, я участвовал в работе этой страшной машины, продукцией которой были либо трупы, либо палачи (Буковский 1). Take my own parents, for example—modest, quiet, honorable people. But they were journalists, writing the very propaganda that had so vilely deceived me.…And was I any better myself? It wasn't just that I ate their bread. I had been a Pioneer, I had participated in the work of this terrible machine whose end product was either hangmen or corpses (1a). ♦ «Есть наш хлеб тебе не стыдно, а мне ты смеешь колоть глаза какой-то шлюхой, учить нас приехал, убирайся в свою Швейцарию, швабский ублюдок!» (Рыбаков 1). "You're not ashamed to eat our food, yet you've got the nerve to throw some cheap whore in my face, you came here to teach us, well, now you can clear off back to Switzerland, you mongrel kraut!" (1a).

X-33 • ЗАБЫВА́ТЬ/ЗАБЫ́ТЬ ХЛЕБ-СО́ЛЬ *чью, какую obs, disapprov* [VP; subj: human; usu. this WO] to show a complete lack of appreciation for s.o.'s hospitality and an unwillingness to reciprocate his kindness: X забыл Y-ову хлеб-соль ≃ **X repaid Y's kindness ⟨hospitality⟩ with ingratitude.**

X-34 • И ТО́ ХЛЕБ *coll* [usu. indep. sent or clause; Invar; fixed WO] it is good that at least I (we, you etc) have this (used to express one's satisfaction with, or opinion that another should be satisfied with, sth. meager when getting more is impossible): **(at least) it's ⟨that's⟩ something; something is better than nothing; I'll ⟨we'll⟩ settle for that; I'll take what I can get ⟨you've got to take what you can get⟩ etc.**

«Поздравляю, старик! Только сейчас твою рожу по телевизору показали. Правда, в толпе и на сотую долю секунды, но для начала и то хлеб» (Зиновьев 2). "Congratulations, old man! I have just seen your mug on television. It's true you were only one of a crowd, and you were only there for about a hundredth of a second, but it's something for a start" (2a). ♦ «Между прочим, мой Тенго помог мне с оползнем»... — «Значит, выплатили?» — «Нет, бетонную канаву провели за счёт горсовета, и то хлеб...» (Искандер 3). "By the way, my Tengo helped me with the landslide."..."They paid you, then?" "No, they ran a concrete conduit at the city soviet's expense—I'll settle for that" (3a).

X-35 • ОТБИВА́ТЬ/ОТБИ́ТЬ ⟨ПЕРЕБИВА́ТЬ/ПЕРЕБИ́ТЬ *obs*⟩ **ХЛЕБ** *у кого coll* [VP; subj: human] to deprive another person of earnings or an opportunity to earn money by taking up his work; *by extension* to (try to) take attention, praise etc away from s.o. by infringing on his area of activity: X отбивает хлеб у Y-а ≃ **X is taking ⟨is trying to take, is stealing etc⟩ (the) bread out of Y's mouth; X is doing ⟨is trying to do⟩ Y out of a ⟨Y's⟩ job;** [extended usage] **X is stealing the spotlight from Y.**

[Фёкла:] Знаешь ли ты, мать моя, ведь меня чуть было не прибили, ей-богу! Старуха-то, что женила Афёровых, так было приступила ко мне: «Ты такая и этакая, только хлеб перебиваешь, знай свой квартал», — говорит (Гоголь 1). [F.:] Do you know, my dear, I was almost beaten up—yes, by God! The old woman that married the Afyorovs, she comes up to me. "You're a so and so," she says, "taking the bread out of the mouths of honest people. Stick to your own district" (1b). ♦ [Коринкина:] А коли у ней деньги, так зачем она в актрисы пошла, зачем рыщет по России, у нас хлеб отбивает? (Островский 3). [K.:] And if she has so much money, why should she be an actress? Why should she go travelling about Russia, stealing the bread out of our mouths? (3a). ♦ «Дмитрий Алексеевич, — начал Урюпин... — Вот тут мы... вот, так сказать, наша с Валерием Осиповичем попытка отбить у вас хлеб...» (Дудинцев 1). "Comrade Lopatkin," Uriupin began.... "We have here...well—that is Comrade Maxiutenko's and my attempt to do you out of your job!" (1a). ♦ «Кто чем угощает, а Кемал рассказом, — уточнил дядя Сандро, насмешливо поглядывая на Кемала, — отбивает хлеб у своего дяди» (Искандер 5). [context transl] "Some people treat you to one thing, Kemal to a story," Uncle Sandro said, making it more precise, with a mocking glance at Kemal. "He takes the story right out of his uncle's mouth" (5a).

X-36 • САДИ́ТЬСЯ/СЕСТЬ НА ХЛЕБ И (НА) ВО́ДУ *coll* [VP; subj: human; the verb may take the final position, otherwise fixed WO] to limit one's food intake to the minimum of staple food: X сел на хлеб и воду ≃ **X limited himself to bread and water.**

X-37 • САЖА́ТЬ/ПОСАДИ́ТЬ НА ХЛЕБ И (НА) ВО́ДУ *кого coll* [VP; subj: human; the verb may take the final position, otherwise fixed WO] to punish s.o. with hunger by

limiting his food intake to the minimum of staple food: X посадит Y-а на хлеб и воду ≃ **X will keep ⟨put⟩ Y on bread and water.**

Я старался вообразить себе капитана Миронова, моего будущего начальника, и представлял его строгим, сердитым стариком, не знающим ничего, кроме своей службы, и готовым за всякую безделицу сажать меня под арест на хлеб и на воду (Пушкин 2). I tried to picture Captain Mironov, my future commanding officer, and the picture that came to my mind was that of a strict, bad-tempered old man, knowing nothing outside the Service, and ready to put me under arrest on bread and water for the merest trifle (2b).

X-38 • ХЛЕБ ДА ⟨И⟩ СОЛЬ!; ХЛЕ́Б-СО́ЛЬ! *all obs, now used as an imitation of peasants' old-fashioned speech* [formula phrase; these forms only; fixed WO] **1.** a greeting, salutation to those who are seated around the table at a meal: **good appetite!; enjoy your meal!**

В дворницкую вошёл Юрий Андреевич с двумя вёдрами. «Хлеб да соль». — «Просим вашей милости. Садись, гостем будешь» (Пастернак 1). Yurii Andreievich came in with two buckets. "Good appetite." "Make yourself at home. Sit down and have dinner with us" (1a).

2. an invitation to a person or persons who arrive at mealtime and find another or others at the table, eating: **you're welcome to join me ⟨us⟩; please join me ⟨us⟩.**

< See X-40.

X-39 • ХЛЕБ НАСУ́ЩНЫЙ [NP; sing only] **1.** the food or money a person needs in order to live; a person's means of subsistence: **one's ⟨s.o.'s⟩ daily bread.**

Мой отец тоже остался без работы. И встала проблема — чем заняться? Как заработать на хлеб насущный? (Рыбаков 1). My father was also out of work. The question was, what could he do for a living? How could he earn his daily bread? (1a).

2. that which is most important, essential, that which some person (group etc) cannot do without: **lifeblood.**

< From the Bible (Matt. 6:11).

X-40 • ХЛЕ́Б-СО́ЛЬ *coll* [NP; sing only; usu. obj or subj] food cordially and generously given to a guest; *by extension* warm and generous treatment of a guest: **bread and salt; (share ⟨offer⟩) one's bread; hospitality.**

«Вот почему я особенно вам благодарна, Родион Романыч, что вы не погнушались моим хлебом-солью, даже и при такой обстановке...» (Достоевский 3). "That is why I am so especially grateful to you, Rodion Romanych, for not scorning my bread and salt, even in such circumstances..." (3c). ♦ ...Вообще они были народ добрый, полны гостеприимства, и человек, вкусивший с ними хлеба-соли или просидевший вечер за вистом, уже становился чем-то близким... (Гоголь 3). In general, they were kindly and very hospitable, and anyone who had partaken of their hospitality or spent an evening playing whist with them became one of them... (3d).

< From an old Slavic custom (still occasionally observed, especially in the countryside) of presenting a round loaf of bread and some salt to a guest of honor as a sign of respect and welcome.

X-41 • ПЕРЕБИВА́ТЬСЯ С ХЛЕ́БА НА КВАС ⟨С ХЛЕ́БА НА́ ВОДУ or НА ВО́ДУ, С КУСКА́ НА КУСО́К, С КО́РОЧКИ НА КО́РОЧКУ, С ГРОША́ НА КОПЕ́ЙКУ⟩ *coll* [VP; subj: human; the verb may take the final position, otherwise fixed WO] to be very poor, endure financial hardship: X перебивается с хлеба на квас ≃ **X lives from hand to mouth; X barely ⟨hardly, scarcely⟩ manages to keep body and soul together ⟨to scrape by⟩.**

А Афродита вела причитания дальше, рисуя перед своим слушателем картину безрадостного будущего своего и ребёнка: «...Будем перебиваться с хлеба на воду, будем с голоду помирать…» (Войнович 4). But Aphrodite took her lamentations further, conjuring up for her listener her own and her child's joyless future: "…We'll live from hand to mouth, we'll die of hunger…" (4a).

X-42 • **НЕСО́ЛОНО ХЛЕБА́ВШИ** уходить, уезжать, возвращаться и т. п. *coll* [Verbal Adv; Invar; adv; fixed WO] (to leave, return home etc) not having gotten what one came for, disappointed: **empty-handed; having gotten nothing ⟨with nothing to show⟩ for one's pains ⟨efforts⟩; without having accomplished anything ⟨a thing⟩; having accomplished nothing.**

Чаще всего такие купцы уходили несолоно хлебавши. Ну, а иногда и слаживалось дельце (Гинзбург 2). More often than not merchants such as these went away empty-handed. But occasionally they did get themselves a deal (2a). ♦ Молчание становилось тягостным. Такое молчание бывает… у пассажиров машины, которые легко мчались несколько часов к цели – и вдруг у самой цели оказалось, что нет моста. Паводок снёс. Надо возвращаться обратно несолоно хлебавши. Или искать новый объезд. По дальней кривой (Свирский 1). The silence grew heavier. Such a silence is found…among passengers who have been traveling several hours toward their destination, only to arrive and find that the bridge has been swept away by the flood. They know they must set off back the way they have come with nothing to show for their pains. Or find a new way around—a very long detour (1a).

X-43 • **НА ХЛЕБА́Х; НА ХЛЕБА́** [PrepP; these forms only; the resulting PrepP is usu. adv] **1.** **на хлебах** *у кого* **жить, на хлеба** *к кому* **идти** *both obs* (to live or begin to live) in s.o.'s home, paying money in exchange for lodging and meals: **(get) room and board (in s.o.'s home); be ⟨become⟩ a boarder (in s.o.'s home).**

«…Жили мы тогда в приходе Пантелеймона, близ Соляного Городка, на хлебах у одной почтенной немки, платя за всё по пятьдесят рублей на ассигнации в месяц…» (Салтыков-Щедрин 2). "…We lived at the time in the Panteleymon parish near the Salt Township, as boarders of a worthy German lady, paying her altogether fifty roubles in notes a month…" (2a).

2. **на хлебах** *чьих* **жить, на хлеба** *чьи* **идти, держать** *кого* **на своих хлебах** и т. п. *all old-fash, coll* to be or become s.o.'s dependent or have s.o. as one's dependent: X живёт на Y-овых хлебах ≃ **X is supported by Y; X lives at Y's expense; X lives off (of) Y;** ‖ Y держит X-а на своих хлебах ≃ **Y keeps X (in Y's home ⟨here etc⟩) at Y's expense.**

«Вот о чём я раздумывал. Нельзя ли было бы сговориться с Самдевятовым, на выгодных для него условиях, чтобы он полгода продержал нас на своих хлебах…» (Пастернак 1). "This is what I was thinking. Couldn't we come to an agreement with Samdeviatov—we'd have to give him profitable terms, of course—so that he should keep us here for six months at his expense…" (1a).

X-44 • **СИДЕ́ТЬ НА ХЛЕ́БЕ И (НА) ВОДЕ́** *coll* [VP; subj: human; the verb may take the final position, otherwise fixed WO] to live in poverty, experience hunger: X сидит на хлебе и воде ≃ **X lives on bread and water; X goes hungry.**

X-45 • **ХЛЕ́БОМ НЕ КОРМИ́** *кого coll* [VP$_{imper}$; Invar; fixed WO] s.o. absolutely loves doing sth., it is his favorite thing to do: X-а хлебом не корми (, только дай делать Y) ≃ **nothing pleases X so much (as doing Y); there's nothing X likes better (than doing Y).**

[Курчаев:] Его хлебом не корми, только приди совета попроси (Островский 9). [K.:] Nothing pleases him so much as having his advice sought (9b).

X-46 • **РАЗВЕ́РЗЛИСЬ ⟨ОТВЕ́РЗЛИСЬ⟩ ХЛЯ́БИ НЕБЕ́СНЫЕ** *obs, lit, humor* [VP$_{subj}$; usu. past; usu. this WO] heavy rains began to fall: **the heavens opened; the skies opened up.**

< From the Biblical account of the Flood (Gen. 7:11, Old Church Slavonic text).

X-47 • **ХМЕЛЬ ВЫ́ЛЕТЕЛ ⟨ВЫ́СКОЧИЛ, ВЫ́ШЕЛ⟩ ИЗ ГОЛОВЫ́** *у кого coll* [VP$_{subj}$] s.o. under the influence of alcohol suddenly became (more) quick and alert (usu. out of fear, strong emotion etc): хмель вылетел у X-а из головы ≃ **X sobered up ⟨thing Y sobered up X⟩ in a flash ⟨in a hurry⟩; X's head cleared up fast.**

Когда он увидел, что парни достают ножи, хмель сразу вылетел у него из головы. When he saw that the guys were taking out knives, he sobered up in a flash.

X-48 • **ПОД ХМЕЛЬКО́М** *coll;* **ПОД ХМЕ́ЛЕМ** *obsoles* [PrepP; these forms only; subj-compl with copula (subj: human) or adv] in a slightly intoxicated state: **tipsy; a little tight; slightly ⟨a little⟩ drunk.**

Начальник тюрьмы полковник Петренко приходил ко мне по вечерам под хмельком, как старый приятель (Буковский 1). The prison governor, Colonel Petrenko, would come and visit me in the evening, when he was tipsy, like an old friend (1a). ♦ Брюнетка, склонясь над тазом, готовилась к встрече с Николаем Васильевичем, который, как бывало, бежал под хмельком по морозцу (Терц 8). The brunette, bent over a basin, was preparing for her meeting with Nikolay Vasilyevich, who, as had happened before, was running, slightly drunk, through the cold (8a).

X-49 • **ВО ХМЕЛЮ́** [PrepP; Invar; adv or subj-compl with быть$_\theta$ (subj: human)] when (one is) in an intoxicated state: **when (one is) loaded; (when one is) under the influence; (when one is) in one's cups.**

Тихий и уступчивый по натуре, отец во хмелю терял рассудок… (Максимов 1). Quiet and amenable by nature, he became irrational in his cups… (1a). ♦ «Как вы изволили тогда приходить, может во хмелю, и дворников в квартал звали и про кровь спрашивали, обидно мне стало, что втуне оставили и за пьяного вас почли» (Достоевский 3). "When you came that time, maybe under the influence, and told the caretakers to go to the precinct, and asked about blood, I felt bad because it all came to nothing, and you were taken for drunk" (3c).

X-50 • **ХОТЬ БЫ ХНЫ** *highly coll* [Invar; predic] **1.** ~ *(кому) disapprov* [impers or with subj: human] one or s.o. is completely indifferent to, unconcerned about etc sth.: X-у ⟨X⟩ хоть бы хны ≃ **X couldn't ⟨could⟩ care less; X doesn't care (at all ⟨in the least etc⟩); X doesn't give a damn ⟨a hoot, a darn etc⟩; it doesn't mean a thing to X.**

«[Ты] мог бы встретить, – капризно и запальчиво выкрикивала она сквозь слёзы. – Думала, не дойду, думала, упаду, а… ему хоть бы хны» (Распутин 2). "You could have met me," she cried through her tears crankily. "I thought I wouldn't make it, I thought I would fall, and…you don't care!" (2a).

2. ~ *кому* [impers] sth. does not affect or cause any reaction in s.o.: X-у хоть бы хны ≃ **it doesn't bother ⟨ruffle⟩ X a bit ⟨at all⟩; it has little ⟨no⟩ effect on X; X doesn't turn a hair;** [in refer. to physical sensations, usu. pain] **X doesn't even feel it.**

Один человек, допустим, такой это весёлый-весёлый, что с ним хоть что ни случись — ему хоть бы хны, плюнет и дальше жить пойдёт (Попов 1). One person, let's say, is so cheerful and jolly that no matter what happens to him, it doesn't bother him a bit; he just shrugs it off and goes on living (1a). ♦ «Ты её [тётушку Хрисулу] трахнул фасолевой подпоркой, а ей хоть бы хны?!» — сказал Чунка, не глядя вниз (Искандер 5). "You bonked her [Auntie Chrysoula] with a beanpole, and she didn't even feel it?" Chunka said without looking down (5a).

X-51 • ДАВА́ТЬ/ДАТЬ ЗА́ДНИЙ ХОД *coll* [VP; subj: human] to retract or reverse a decision, a promise, one's consent, one's support for s.o. or sth. etc: X дал задний ход ≃ **X backed down ⟨off, out⟩; X back-pedaled ⟨retreated⟩; X went back (on his word ⟨promise⟩); X changed his tune; X did a flip-flop.**

«...Сто́ило этому Тетерину объяснить, что его поведение преступно, как сразу же дал задний ход» (Тендряков 1). "...As soon as I pointed out to him [Teterin] that he was committing a criminal offence, he backed down straight away" (1a). ♦ ...Блатные действовали группками, а остальные каждый за себя — если удавалось объединиться, блатные давали задний ход (Амальрик 1). The thugs...operated in groups, whereas the other prisoners acted individually. But sometimes the latter managed to join forces, and then the thugs would retreat (1a).

X-52 • ДАВА́ТЬ/ДАТЬ ХОД *чему*, usu. **заявлению, жалобе, делу** и т. п. [VP; subj: human or collect] (in refer. to an application, complaint, case etc) to direct sth. to the appropriate authorities for review, processing, and proper action or advance sth. along the course of proper action: X дал ход Y-у ≃ **X took action on Y; X acted ⟨moved⟩ on Y; X moved Y along; X followed up on Y; [in legal contexts] X started proceedings;** ‖ *Neg* X не дал хода Y-у ≃ **X tabled ⟨shelved, held up⟩ Y.**

Строго говоря, совсем не была исключена возможность того, что Белый дом даст ход доносу Кривошея (Гинзбург 2). Strictly speaking, the possibility that the White House would take action on Krivoshei's denunciation was in no way excluded (2a). ♦ Кунта знал, что таких людей в сельсовете не любят и жалобе, если только он пожалуется, дадут ход (Искандер 4). Kunta knew that the village soviet had no love for such men; he had only to file a complaint and they would act on it (4a). ♦ [Брат Сила:] Врать вредно, дорогой актёр. Придётся тебе сесть в тюрьму, красавчик, где ты долго будешь кормить клопов. А делу мы всё равно ход дадим (Булгаков 8). [Brother Force:] Lying is harmful, dear actor. It will be necessary to put you in the dungeon, pretty boy, where you will feed the bedbugs for a long time to come. And we are going to move this case along anyway (8a). ♦ Начальство и суд не могли не дать хода делу... (Достоевский 1). The authorities and the court could not avoid starting proceedings... (1a).

X-53 • ИДТИ́/ПОЙТИ́ В ХОД ⟨В ДЕ́ЛО *coll*⟩ [VP; subj: concr, abstr, or animal (if count noun, usu. pl)] to be or start to be used: X-ы пошли в ход ≃ **Xs were put to use; Xs were used ⟨utilized⟩; (we ⟨they etc⟩) used ⟨utilized⟩ Xs; (I ⟨he etc⟩) made use of Xs.**

«Чем только они кормятся?» — проговорил мой старик. «А у них всё в ход идёт, — сказал Колчерукий, — жучки, паучки, червячки» (Искандер 3). "But what do they live on?" my old man said. "They use everything," Bad Hand said. "Beetles, spiders, worms" (3a).

X-54 • НА ПО́ЛНЫЙ ХОД [PrepP; Invar; fixed WO] **1.** ~ **работать, пускать** *что* и т. п. [adv] (usu. of a factory, plant etc) (to operate, set sth. operating etc) at maximum potential, maximum output: **(operate) at full capacity; (go) (at) full blast.**

Завод работает на полный ход. The factory is operating at full capacity.

2. [usu. adv or subj-compl with бытьø (subj: usu. abstr)] (to be) in the highest state of growth, development: **at its height ⟨peak⟩; going strong; in full swing; booming.**

Там торговля идёт на полный ход. Trade there is going strong.

X-55 • ПО́ЛНЫЙ ХОД ⟨ВПЕРЁД⟩! [sent; these forms only; fixed WO] (a command that a ship, train etc) go at top speed: **full speed ahead!; at full throttle!**

X-56 • ПУСКА́ТЬ/ПУСТИ́ТЬ В ХОД *что* [VP; subj: human; usu. this WO] **1.** [usu. pfv] to set sth. (usu. a factory,

plant etc) operating: X пустил Y в ход ≃ **X got ⟨set⟩ Y going ⟨running⟩.**

«Он временно принял директорство над филиалом. На весь наладочный период. Пустит машину в ход, подготовит директора из местных и только тогда вернётся» (Залыгин 1). "He's taken on temporary directorship of the branch till it gets started properly. He'll set things running, train a local man as director, and won't come back till he's done it" (1a).

2. Also: ПУСКА́ТЬ/ПУСТИ́ТЬ В ДЕ́ЛО [var. with дело is used in refer. to a tool, weapon etc] to employ or start to employ (some means, device, instrument etc) in order to achieve one's goal: X пустил в ход Y ≃ **X put Y to use; X used ⟨utilized⟩ Y; X made use of Y; X brought Y into play ⟨into service, into action⟩; [in limited contexts] X set Y in motion; X resorted to Y;** ‖ X пустил в ход своё обаяние ⟨все свои чары и т. п.⟩ ≃ **X turned on the ⟨all his⟩ charm;** ‖ X пустил в ход всё ⟨все средства⟩ ≃ **X used all possible ⟨available⟩ means; X did everything in his power.**

У них есть оружие. Они пустят его в ход (Аксёнов 6). They have weapons. They are going to put them to use (6a). ♦ «Эндурцы испокон веков ядами промышляют. Они с такой хитростью яды пускают в ход — ни один прокурор не подкопается» (Искандер 5). "The Endurskies have dealt in poisons since time immemorial. They're so sly about using poisons that no prosecutor has ever trapped them" (5a). ♦ «Я... пустил в ход величайшее и незыблемое средство к покорению женского сердца, средство, которое никогда и никого не обманет и которое действует решительно на всех до единой, без всякого исключения. Это средство известное — лесть» (Достоевский 3). "I...brought into play the greatest and most reliable of all instruments for the subjugation of the female heart, the instrument that never fails, that works on absolutely every single woman without exception. This instrument is well-known: flattery" (3a). ♦ Испуганные буржуа травили революцию, как дикого зверя; всё было пущено в ход: клевета и слезоточивые газы, демагогия и тюрьмы (Эренбург 4). The terrified bourgeois hunted down the revolution like a wild animal. Every weapon was brought into service: slander and tear-gas, demagogy and imprisonment (4a). ♦ ...Пуская в ход весь аппарат своей поржавелой, скрипучей, но всё такой же извилистой логики, [Чернышевский] сначала мотивировал свою досаду тем, что его считают за вором, желавшим наживать капитал, а затем объяснял, что гнев его был, собственно, напоказ, ради Ольги Сократовны... (Набоков 1). ...Setting in motion the whole apparatus of his logic—rusty, creaky but still as wriggly as ever, he [Chernyshevski] at first justified his ire by the fact that he was being taken for a thief who wished to acquire capital, and then explained that his anger was actually only a sham for Olga Sokratovna's sake... (1a). ♦ [Юлия:] Сейчас сюда приедет министр финансов, и я пущу в ход все свои чары и узнаю, что они затевают (Шварц 3). [J.:] The Minister of Finance will be here any minute, and I'll turn on all my charm and find out what they're cooking up (3a).

3. to introduce sth. into general, common usage, promote the dissemination of sth.: X пустил в ход Y ≃ **X put Y in(to) circulation; X brought Y into widespread use; X started Y.**

«Ты представляешь, какие откроются перспективы, если пустить твоё открытие в ход!» (Аксёнов 6). "Just imagine what prospects could open up if your discovery were to be put into circulation!" (6a). ♦ Кто пустил его [Самиздат] в ход, неизвестно, как он работает, понять нельзя... (Мандельштам 2). Who started it [samizdat], nobody knows, and the way it works is beyond our comprehension... (2a).

X-57 • В ХО́ДЕ *чего* [PrepP; Invar; Prep; the resulting PrepP is adv] while some action is being carried out or process is going on: **during; in ⟨during, over⟩ the course of.**

Сперва очень настороженный и недоверчивый, Демичев в ходе двухчасовой беседы потеплел ко мне и во всё поверил

(Солженицын 2). Demichev was very much on his guard, very suspicious to begin with, but in the course of our two-hour conversation he warmed to me, and ended by believing everything I said (2a). ♦ [Болоснин:] Вот в чём ужас — что в ходе этой войны в глазах простого народа право называться русскими захватили большевики (Солженицын 9). [B.:] That's the horror of it—during the course of this war, in the eyes of ordinary people, it is the Bolsheviks who have usurped the right to be called Russian (9a).

X-58 • **НЕДАЛЕКО́ ХОДИ́ТЬ (ЗА ПРИМЕ́РОМ ⟨ПРИМЕ́РАМИ⟩); НЕДАЛЕКО́ ИСКА́ТЬ; (ЗА ПРИМЕ́РОМ ⟨ПРИМЕ́РАМИ⟩) ДАЛЕКО́ ХОДИ́ТЬ НЕ НУ́ЖНО ⟨НЕ НА́ДО, НЕ ПРИХО́ДИТСЯ⟩** all coll [VP; impers predic; these forms only; usu. this WO] it is easy to cite an example (examples) or find proof of (sth. stated in general terms in the immediately preceding context): **you don't have ⟨need⟩ to go far ⟨to look hard⟩ (to find examples ⟨evidence⟩); you needn't go far ⟨look hard⟩ (to find examples ⟨evidence⟩).**

«Растут подозрительность, доносы, интриги, ненавистничество... За примером далеко ходить не приходится» (Пастернак 1). "There is more and more suspicion—informers, intrigues, hatreds....We don't have to go far to find evidence of it" (1a). ♦ [Вера] каялась, что не взяла [Виталия] в руки, не перевоспитала... Другие же перевоспитывают!.. И за примерами ходить недалеко (Грекова 3). She [Vera] was sorry, and wished that she had taken him [Vitaly] in hand, reformed him. After all, others do reform people! You didn't need to look hard to find examples (3a). ♦ [Беркутов:] ...В последнее время много стало открываться растрат, фальшивых векселей и других бумаг, подлогов и вообще всякого рода хищничества. Ну, а по всем этим операциям находятся и виновные... [Чугунов:] Шутить изволите. [Беркутов:] Какие шутки! Да вот, недалеко ходить, сейчас один молодой человек сам сознался, что наделал фальшивых векселей (Островский 5). [B.:] ...Recently there have come to light many embezzlements, bogus promissory notes, forgeries of other sorts, and in general all sorts of knavery. Well, the guilty persons in all these operations are being discovered.... [Ch.:] You're joking. [B.:] Not much! Why, you needn't go far,—a certain young man has just confessed that he's been forging notes (5a).

X-59 • **ХОДИ́ТЬ ⟨КРУЖИ́ТЬ, ПЕТЛЯ́ТЬ и т. п.⟩ ВОКРУ́Г ⟨КРУГО́М⟩ ДА О́КОЛО** coll [VP; subj: human] to speak in a roundabout way, avoid expressing sth. directly or answering some question: X ходит вокруг да около ≃ **X beats around ⟨about⟩ the bush.**

[author's usage] «Всё вокруг да около...» — отметил про себя председатель [Голубев] и решил пощупать собеседника с другого конца, затронуть вопросы внешней политики (Войнович 2). He beats around the bush...the chairman [Golubev] observed to himself. Golubev decided to take a different tack—foreign affairs (2a).

X-60 • **ХОДИ́ТЬ НА ПОЛУСО́ГНУТЫХ** (перед кем) coll [VP; subj: human] to behave (toward s.o.) in a fawning, obsequious manner: X ходит перед Y-ом на полусогнутых ≃ **X bows and scrapes before ⟨to⟩ Y.**

Из института Павлу пришлось уйти: ходить на полусогнутых перед начальством он не умел, а без этого там нельзя было пробиться. Pavel had to leave the institute because he was not one to bow and scrape to the bosses, and without doing that it was impossible to make your way up the ladder.

X-61 • **НЕ ХОДО́К ⟨НЕ ЕЗДО́К⟩** [NP; these forms only; subj-compl with copula (subj: human)] one will not or will never again go to a specified place, type of event etc: в место Y X (больше) не ходок ≃ **X won't ⟨will never⟩ set foot in place Y (again); X won't ⟨will never⟩ be seen in place Y ⟨at a party etc⟩** (again); X won't ⟨will never⟩ show his face in place Y ⟨at a party etc⟩ (again); no more going to place Y ⟨to parties etc⟩ for X.

На этой невесёлой свадьбе не пили самогонки, не орали песен. Прохор Зыков, бывший на свадьбе за дружка, на другой день долго отплёвывался и жаловался Аксинье: «...Я теперича [substand = теперь] на эти новые свадьбы не ходок. На собачьей свадьбе и то веселей...» (Шолохов 5). At this dreary wedding no one drank home-brewed vodka and no songs were bawled in tipsy voices. Prokhor Zykov, who had been best man, spent most of the next day complaining to Aksinya and spitting in disgust. "...No more of these new-fangled weddings for me! It's more fun at a dog's wedding" (5a).

X-62 • **ПО́ЛНЫМ ХО́ДОМ** [NP_instrum; Invar; adv; fixed WO]
1. идти, нестись и т. п. ~ (of the movement of a train, ship etc) (to go, race etc) at maximum speed: **at full ⟨top⟩ speed; full speed (ahead).**

Мы увидели вдалеке поезд, который шёл полным ходом. We saw in the distance a train going full speed ahead.

2. идти, двигаться, протекать и т. п. ~ (of some work, preparations for sth. etc) (to go, proceed etc) at full capacity, maximum intensity: **(go) at full speed; (go) full speed (ahead); (go) (at) full blast; (be) in full swing.**

Подготовка к программе «Аполлон» шла в США полным ходом (Владимиров 1). Preparations for the Apollo programme were going at full speed in America (1a). ♦ «Экспертиза по обуви движется?» — спросила Маковкина. «Полным ходом...» (Чернёнок 2). "How's the shoe analysis?" Makovkina asked. "Going full blast..." (2a). ♦ Цивилизация края шла полным ходом, хотя иногда натыкалась на неожиданные препятствия (Искандер 3). The process of civilizing the area was in full swing, although it sometimes stumbled against unexpected obstacles (3a).

X-63 • **СВОИ́М ХО́ДОМ** [NP_instrum; Invar; adv; fixed WO]
1. идти, прийти, дойти и т. п. ~ (of a person, animal, or vehicle) (to go, move along etc) independently, without assistance: **under one's ⟨its⟩ own steam ⟨power⟩; on one's ⟨its⟩ own; by oneself ⟨itself⟩;** [of a person only] **on one's own two feet.**

Под утро все новоиспечённые офицеры... частично своим собственным ходом, частично с помощью товарищей и аборигенов вернулись в казарму в целости и сохранности... (Зиновьев 1). By morning all the newly fledged officers had returned to barracks safe and sound, partly under their own steam and partly with the help of their comrades and the aboriginal population (1a). ♦ Увезли деда Максима: на берег его вели под руки, своим ходом дед идти не мог (Распутин 4). They took away Grandpa Maxim: they held him up and walked him to the shore, he couldn't get there on his own (4a).

2. идти, развиваться ~ (of a process, matter etc) (to proceed, develop) normally, the usual way and at the usual pace, unaffected by circumstances: **(proceed) at its own pace; (take) its course; (be going) as it should.**

«Как твой бизнес? Не развалился, пока тебя не было?» — «Да нет, всё в порядке, всё идёт своим ходом». "How's your business? It didn't fall apart while you were away, did it?" "No, everything's fine, everything's going as it should."

X-64 • **ЧЕРЕПА́ШЬИМ ХО́ДОМ идти, двигаться** и т. п. coll [NP_instrum; Invar; adv; fixed WO] (to go, move etc) very slowly: **at a snail's pace.**

X-65 • **В ХОДУ́; В БОЛЬШО́М ХОДУ́** both coll [PrepP; these forms only; subj-compl with быть∅ (subj: usu. abstr)] sth. occurs widely, enjoys popularity, is in general use: X в (большом) ходу ≃ **X is widespread ⟨current, (very) popular, fashionable⟩; X is in (great) demand ⟨in style, in vogue⟩;** || Neg X не в ходу ≃ **X is outmoded ⟨passé, out of style etc⟩.**

...Вообще пользование канвой лермонтовских стихов для шуток было так в ходу, что, в конце концов, становилось карикатурой на самое искусство пародии.. (Набоков 1). ...The use of some of Lermontov's lyrical poems as a canvas for journalistic jokes about people and events was in general so widespread that in the long run it turned into a caricature of the very art of parody... (1a). ♦ Прочитав фразу про плен, я опять умилился и подумал, что, видимо, именно тогда учёные и другие общественные деятели стали попадать в плен. Помнится, в самые ранние школьные годы это выражение было в ходу, и я довольно картинно представлял себе этих самых учёных, попавших в плен к буржуям (Искандер 3). Reading the phrase about imprisonment, I was again filled with emotion. It struck me that this was just about the time when scholars and other public figures began to be taken prisoner. As I recall, this expression was current when I first started school, and I had a rather picturesque image of these scholars who had been taken prisoner by the bourgeoisie (3a). ♦ «Но я просто не могу себе представить его в роли грабителя». – «Почему?» – «Ну, теория квадратного подбородка, дегенеративного черепа и низкого лба, я это имею в виду. Ламброзо и его школа.» – «...Ламброзо у нас не в ходу» (Семёнов 1). "But I simply can't see him as a robber." "Why?" "You know, the theory of the square chin, degenerate skull and low forehead, that's what I have in mind; Lombroso and his school." "...Lombroso's not popular with us in this country" (1a). ♦ [Варравин:] Сделаем христианское дело; поможем товарищу – а?.. Нынче всё общинное в ходу, а с философской точки зрения, что же такое община, как не складчина? (Сухово-Кобылин 3). [V.:] Let's do the Christian thing; let's help a comrade, shall we?...Nowadays everything communal is fashionable, and from a philosophical standpoint, what is a community if not a pooling of resources? (3a). ♦ Вообще, политическая мечтательность была в то время в большом ходу... (Салтыков-Щедрин 1). Political dreaminess was generally in vogue then... (1a).

Х-66 • ДАТЬ ХО́ДУ *highly coll* [VP; subj: human, collect, or animal] to flee, run away (from s.o. or sth.): X дал ходу ≃ **X took ⟨ran⟩ off; X took to his heels; X turned tail (and ran); X beat it.**

[Мышлаевский:] ...Он, значит, при тебе ходу дал? [Шервинский:] При мне: я был до последней минуты (Булгаков 4). [M.:] ...Does this mean he took off while you were there? [Sh.:] While I was there: I was there until the very last minute (4a). ♦ [Первый офицер:] У меня, господин капитан, пятерых во взводе не хватает. По-видимому, ходу дали (Булгаков 4). [First Officer:] Captain, five of my platoon are missing. Apparently they've run off (4a).

Х-67 • НА ХОДУ́ [PrepP; Invar] **1.** *coll* [subj-compl with бытьø (subj: a noun denoting a vehicle, factory etc)] sth. is in working condition, working as it should: X на ходу ≃ [of a vehicle] **X is in running ⟨working⟩ order;** [of a factory, plant etc] **X is operational.**

2. ~ **вскочить, соскочить** и т. п. [adv] (to jump into, jump off etc a vehicle, horse etc) while it is in motion: **while (the car ⟨the horse etc⟩) is moving; (jump into ⟨onto, from⟩) a ⟨the⟩ moving (car ⟨train etc⟩); (jump into a car ⟨jump out of a boat etc⟩) as it is pulling out ⟨pulling in, floating out etc⟩.**

Трамвай начал делать круг... Зоя ловко соскочила на ходу, потому что отсюда было короче (Солженицын 10). The [trolley] car had already begun its turn around the circle....[Zoya] jumped off deftly while the car was moving, so as to cut down the distance she would have to walk (10b). ♦ Отомкнув баркас, он [Митька] с силой толкнул его от коряги, вскочил на ходу (Шолохов 2). He [Mitka] unhitched the boat, pushed it hard and jumped in as it floated out (2a).

3. [adv] (of a person) (to do sth.) while continuing to move: **as one walks ⟨goes⟩ (along); on the move ⟨the go⟩; without stopping.**

Перед собой он держал половинку арбуза и ел из неё на ходу столовой ложкой (Аксёнов 6). In one hand he held half a watermelon, which he was eating with a tablespoon as he walked along (6a). ♦ ...Буш, как фокусник, извлёк из воздуха тетрадь и стал на ходу читать... (Набоков 1). ...Busch, like a conjurer, plucked a notebook out of the air and began to read on the move... (1a). ♦ Статный австрийский офицер со спортсменской выправкой шёл под конвоем на вокзал. Ему улыбнулись две барышни, гулявшие по перрону. Он на ходу очень ловко раскланялся и послал им воздушный поцелуй (Шолохов 2). A fine-looking Austrian officer with the bearing of an athlete was being taken under guard to the station building. Two young ladies strolling along the platform smiled at him. He managed a very neat bow without stopping and blew them a kiss (2a).

4. *coll* [adv] (to do sth.) hastily, without giving it one's full attention, or while in the process of doing something else: **on the go; on the move.**

Не стал читать страницу из «Дневника» Делакруа... чтобы не прочесть её кое-как, на ходу... (Олеша 3). I didn't begin reading a page in Delacroix's *Diary*...in order not to read it haphazardly, on the go... (3a).

5. *coll* [adv] quickly, without thinking or preparation: **on the spur of the moment;** [in refer. to saying sth., answering etc] **off the top of one's head.**

...Нужно было разобраться в речевом коде землян. Без помощи специального устройства, на ходу, это не просто (Обухова 1). He had to decipher the speech code of the Earthmen. This was not easy on the spur of the moment, without special instruments (1a).

Х-68 • НА ХОДУ́ ПОДМЁТКИ РВЁТ ⟨РЕ́ЖЕТ⟩ *highly coll, occas. disapprov* [VP; subj: human; 3rd pers only; fixed WO] one is extremely resourceful and aggressive (in attaining sth.): X на ходу подмётки рвёт ≃ **X (certainly) doesn't waste any time; X is a (real) go-getter;** [in limited contexts] **X is slick ⟨a slick customer⟩; X is pretty brazen; X is (a young man ⟨woman⟩) on the make; X is a ⟨one⟩ fast climber; X is pushing his way to the top.**

Ну и парень – на ходу подмётки рвёт: только две недели, как поступил на работу, а уже без него начальник и часу прожить не может. What a shrewd guy, he certainly doesn't waste any time: he's been on the job for all of two weeks and already the boss can't get by for a single hour without him. ♦ Из-за поворота выкатил встречный «ЗИЛ» Жорки Борбаряна... «Э-и-ей, дядя Митя!» – крикнул Жорка, высовывая голову из окна, и в голосе его, конечно, было восхищение сноровкой старшего товарища. Дядя Митя только успел ему сделать ручкой. Жорку он уважал. Подпирает молодёжь, на ходу подмётки рвёт (Аксёнов 10). From round a bend Zhorka Borbaryan's Zil came at them....«Heh-e-eh, Old Mitya!» Zhorka shouted, sticking his head out of the window, his voice, of course, full of delight at his old mate's technique. Mitya had time only to wave. He had a great respect for Zhorka. These youngsters were pushing their way in—brazen they were (10a).

Х-69 • НЕ ДАВА́ТЬ/НЕ ДАТЬ ХО́ДУ ⟨-а⟩ *кому* [VP; subj: human or collect; often 3rd pers pl with indef. refer.] to deprive s.o. of the opportunity to make full use of his abilities, obstruct s.o.'s advancement at work etc: X не даёт Y-у ходу ≃ **X holds Y back; X doesn't give Y a chance; X doesn't let Y get ahead; X blocks Y's advancement ⟨promotion⟩; X stands in Y's way.**

Ему надо искать другую работу, в институте ему не дадут хода. He should look for another job, they won't let him get ahead at the institute.

Х-70 • НЕТ ХО́ДУ ⟨-а⟩ *кому coll* [VP; impers] all opportunities are denied s.o. (usu. in refer. to s.o.'s career opportunities, promotion at the workplace etc): Х-у нет ходу ≃ **every path ⟨way⟩ is barred to X; all roads ⟨routes⟩ are barred to X; all doors are closed to X; there's ⟨X has⟩ no hope of getting ahead.**

[Сатин:] Тюрьма, дед! Я четыре года семь месяцев в тюрьме отсидел... а после тюрьмы — нет ходу! (Горький 3). [S.:] Prison, Grandpa. I spent four years and seven months in prison, and after that I found every way barred to me (3e).

Х-71 • ПРИБАВЛЯ́ТЬ/ПРИБА́ВИТЬ ⟨ПОДДАВА́ТЬ/ ПОДДА́ТЬ, НАДДАВА́ТЬ/НАДДА́ТЬ⟩ ХО́ДУ *coll* [VP; subj: human, collect, or a noun denoting a vehicle] to begin to move more quickly: X прибавил ходу ≃ **X picked up speed; X sped up; X started going faster; X increased his ⟨its⟩ speed;** [of a driver] **X stepped on it ⟨the gas⟩;** [of a person walking] **X quickened his pace ⟨his step⟩; X picked up the pace.**

Заслышав конский топот, Христоня оглянулся и заметно наддал ходу (Шолохов 5). At the sound of hooves behind him, Khristonya glanced back and increased his speed perceptibly (5a).

Х-72 • С ХО́ДУ [PrepP; Invar; adv] **1.** (of people, esp. attacking troops in cavalry or armored vehicle units, or of animals, esp. horses) (to do sth.) while continuing to move: **as one ⟨it⟩ goes; while in motion; without stopping;** [of a horse and rider only] **without breaking stride.**

С ходу отстреливаясь, они скакали в сторону леса. They galloped toward the woods, returning fire as they went.

2. *coll* instantly and without preparation or contemplation: **right away; straight off; immediately; right off the bat; just like that; on the spur of the moment; (right) then and there ⟨there and then⟩;** ‖ сказать *что* ⟨ответить⟩ ~ ≃ **say sth. ⟨answer⟩ off the top of one's head;** ‖ отвергнуть *кого-что* ~ ≃ **reject s.o. ⟨sth.⟩ out of hand.**

И вот Б.Л. [Пастернак] явился на Лубянку и с ходу начал препираться со следователем Семёновым, требуя от него выдачи «моего ребёнка» (Ивинская 1). And so BL [Pasternak] went to the Lubianka, where he immediately began to remonstrate with [the interrogator] Semionov, demanding that "my child" be handed over to him (1a). ♦ [Ольга Николаевна:] А почему Надя тебя не выставила? [Лукашин:] Наверно, ей этого не хотелось... [Ольга Николаевна:] Думаешь, понравился ей? [Лукашин:] Этого я не знаю... Но она мне понравилась! [Ольга Николаевна:] Прямо вот так, с ходу? (Брагинский и Рязанов 1). [O.N.:] Why didn't Nadya turn you out? [L.:] I suppose she didn't. [O.N.:] You think she likes you? [L.:] That I don't know....I know I like her! [O.N.:] Straightaway? Right off the bat? (1a). ♦ «Но я так с ходу не могу определить достоинства и недостатки такой большой рукописи. Позвольте мне хотя бы один вечер...» (Зиновьев 2). "But I can't determine the qualities and demerits of a manuscript this size just like that. Can you give me an evening at least..." (2a).

Х-73 • ХОДИ́ТЬ ⟨ЗАХОДИ́ТЬ⟩ ХОДУНО́М ⟨ХО́ДО-РОМ *obs*⟩ *coll;* **ХОДИ́ТЬ ⟨ЗАХОДИ́ТЬ⟩ ХО́ДНЕМ ⟨ХОДЕНЁМ⟩** *obs, substand* [VP; usu. impfv] **1.** [subj: usu. concr] to move from side to side or up and down with quick, jerky movements: X ходил ходуном ≃ **X shook (violently ⟨furiously⟩); X trembled ⟨vibrated⟩;** [of the human body or a part of the body] **X bobbed up and down; X quaked.**

Векслер видел, что рассказ его тронул меня, и наверное потому ходуном ходила его рука, когда он закуривал, отвернувшись от ветра (Чуковская 2). Veksler saw that the story had touched me and it was probably this that made his hand shake as he lit a cigarette, turning away against the wind (2a). ♦ Это бомбили уже советские самолёты, и в кромешной тьме взрывы бомб казались особенно близкими и мощными. Кровать так и ходила ходуном, и весь домик пошатывало, как при землетрясении (Кузнецов 1). It was Soviet planes that were doing the bombing, and in the pitch darkness the bomb explosions seemed to be particularly

near and heavy. The bed trembled and the whole house shook as if it was an earthquake (1b). ♦ Огромная туша капитана колышется от смеха, брюхо трясётся и ходит ходуном (Марченко 2). The captain's huge frame shook with laughter, his belly bobbing up and down (2a).

2. [subj: usu. всё or a noun denoting a place and referring to the people in that place] to be very agitated, in a state of unrest, agitation, turmoil: место X ⟨всё в месте X⟩ ходило ходуном ≃ **there was a great commotion in place X; all hell broke loose in place X; place X was in a frenzy ⟨an uproar⟩; everyone in place X was frantic.**

Семья готовилась к приезду гостей, и в доме всё ходило ходуном. The family was preparing for the arrival of their guests, and the house was in a frenzy.

Х-74 • ЗНАТЬ ВСЕ ХОДЫ́ И ВЫ́ХОДЫ ⟨ХОДЫ́-ВЫ́ХОДЫ⟩ *(чего, где) coll* [VP; subj: human; the verb may take the final position, otherwise fixed WO] to be very experienced in all the details, intricacies etc (of a profession, job etc): X знает все ходы и выходы ≃ **X knows all the ins and outs; X knows the ropes ⟨(all) the tricks of the trade⟩; X knows what's what.**

«Ты вот лучше скажи — у начальства близко, все ходы-выходы знаешь: хлопотать мне насчёт пенсии?» (Абрамов 1). "...You can tell me this: Should I go and see about getting a pension? You're close to the bosses; you know all the ins and outs" (1b). ♦ Он понял так, что теперь самое верное средство — это начать во все места просьбы писать. «Знаю я одного человека, — обратился он к глуповцам, — не к нему ли нам наперёд поклониться сходить?.. Таков этот человек, что все ходы и выходы знает!» (Салтыков-Щедрин 1). As he conceived it, the most reliable expedient now was to begin writing petitions to all government offices. "I know a little man," he said to the Foolovites. "Oughtn't we go and pay our respects to him first?...He's the sort of man as knows the ropes!" (1a).

Х-75 • ХОЖДЕ́НИЕ ПО МУ́КАМ *lit* [NP; fixed WO] a series of trying experiences in life, one following another: **a ⟨one⟩ long ordeal; (going through) purgatory.**

< From the ancient Christian belief reflected in the Old Russian apocryphal text *Descent of the Virgin into Hell* («Хождение Богородицы по мукам», 12th cent.), that the souls of the deceased endure forty days of torment immediately after death. The phrase came into widespread use after the publication of a trilogy under the same title by Aleksei Tolstoi (1921–41, translated into English as *Road to Calvary*).

Х-76 • САМ СЕБЕ́ ХОЗЯ́ИН ⟨ГОСПОДИ́Н, ГО-ЛОВА́⟩; САМА́ СЕБЕ́ ХОЗЯ́ЙКА ⟨ГОСПОЖА́, ГО-ЛОВА́⟩ *all coll* [NP; subj-compl with быть∅ (subj: human); fixed WO] a person who is completely independent in his or her actions and judgment, who acts as he or she chooses: X сам себе хозяин ≃ **X is his own man ⟨master, boss, person⟩;** ‖ X сама себе хозяйка ≃ **X is her own woman ⟨master, mistress, boss, person⟩.**

«...Заходил тут ко мне один, интересовался: кто, мол, да что, мол, ты такое...» — «Я сам себе хозяин... Я из-под Чарджоу две огнестрельных вывез. Тебе ли меня не знать, Александр Петрович!» (Максимов 3). "...A man called on me, wanted to know about you, who you were, what you were like...." "I'm my own man. I brought two bullet wounds back from Chardzhou. Surely you know me well enough, Alexandr Petrovich!" (3a). ♦ [Тарелкин:] Родни нет, детей нет; семейства не имею; никому не должен... сам себе господин! (Сухово-Кобылин 3). [T.:] No relatives, no children; I have no family: I don't owe anybody a thing....I'm my own master! (3a). ♦ [Квашня:] Чтобы я, — говорю, — свободная женщина, сама себе хозяйка, да кому-нибудь в паспорт вписалась, чтобы я мужчине в крепость себя отдала — нет! (Горький 3). [К.:] That I, a free woman and my own mistress, says I — that I should enter myself in somebody else's passport and make myself a man's slave — never! (3b). ♦ ...Потом [Соня] говорит: «И у меня хорошая новость». И показывает ордер на комнату в новом доме горсовета. Действительно — удача!.. «Теперь, — говорит Соня, — я ни от кого не завишу, плюю на них, захочу — обменяю на Москву или Ленинград, теперь я сама себе хозяйка...» (Рыбаков 1). Then she [Sonya] said, "I've got some good news, too." She showed me an order giving her a room in a new municipal block. It really was good luck...."Now I'm not dependent on anyone," she said. "To hell with the lot of them. If I feel like it, I can swap it for a room in Moscow or Leningrad, now I'm my own boss" (1a).

X-77 • ХОЗЯ́ИН 〈ХОЗЯ́ЙКА〉 ПОЛОЖЕ́НИЯ [NP; usu. subj-compl with copula, nom or instrum (subj: human); fixed WO] the person who is in control of the situation in question, in a position to direct the development of events: X — хозяин 〈хозяйка〉 положения ≃ X is (the) master 〈(the) mistress〉 of the situation; [in limited contexts] X is in the driver's seat.

«И вот... я решу — в чём будет состоять моё дело, как поступлю я — хозяин положения!» (Залыгин 1). "And I'll decide...where my duty lies and what I, as master of the situation, shall do about it" (1a).

X-78 • ХОЗЯ́ИН 〈ГОСПОДИ́Н〉 СВОЕГО́ СЛО́ВА 〈СВОЕМУ́ СЛО́ВУ〉 coll [NP; subj-compl with copula, nom or instrum (subj: human)] a person who fulfills his promises, does what he pledges to do: X хозяин своего слова ≃ X is as good as his word; X is a man of his word; X keeps his word.

[Нина:] [Мой жених] волевой, целеустремлённый... Много он на себя не берёт, но он хозяин своему слову. Не то что некоторые (Вампилов 4). [N.:] He's [my fiancé is] headstrong and purposeful....He won't take on more than he can handle, but he's as good as his word. Not like some... (4a).

X-79 • ОБДАВА́ТЬ/ОБДА́ТЬ ХО́ЛОДОМ кого [VP; subj: human] to receive s.o. in a cold, unfriendly manner, making it clear that he is not wanted (in some place): X обдал Y-а холодом ≃ X gave Y the cold shoulder; X turned a cold shoulder to Y; X cold-shouldered Y.

X-80 • НАДЕВА́ТЬ/НАДЕ́ТЬ 〈ВЕ́ШАТЬ/ПОВЕ́СИТЬ〉 (СЕБЕ́) ХОМУ́Т НА ШЕ́Ю; НАДЕВА́ТЬ/ НАДЕ́ТЬ НА СЕБЯ́ ХОМУ́Т 〈ЯРМО́〉 all coll [VP; subj: human] to inconvenience o.s. excessively, cause o.s. needless worry, limit one's freedom of action (occas. in refer. to getting married, more often with male subjects): X надел себе хомут на шею ≃ X took a burden on himself; X hung 〈took〉 a yoke on his neck.

Работа авторского коллектива над книгой, подобной нашей, это месяцы и годы напряжённой жизни, о которой можно написать романы действительно пострашнее романов Достоевского и Бальзака... За каким же чёртом, спрашивается, я надел этот хомут на свою шею? (Зиновьев 2). The work of a collective on a book like ours means months and years of tension which could be the subject of novels truly more terrifying than those of Dostoievsky and Balzac....You might well ask why the hell I took this burden on myself? (2a).

X-81 • ЗА́ЖИВО ХОРОНИ́ТЬ/ПОХОРОНИ́ТЬ кого coll [VP; subj: human] to consider s.o. useless, not suitable for anything, dismiss s.o. as worthless: X Y-а заживо хоронит ≃ X writes Y off; X gives Y up as hopeless; [in limited contexts] X sends 〈puts〉 Y out to pasture.

X-82 • ЗА́ЖИВО ХОРОНИ́ТЬ/ПОХОРОНИ́ТЬ СЕБЯ́ obs, lit [VP; subj: human] to refuse o.s. contact with society and the outside world, live in seclusion (often when one is still young and in his prime): X заживо похоронил себя ≃ X lived like a hermit; X holed himself up; X buried himself alive.

[Глафира:] Я должна прятаться от всех, заживо похоронить себя, а я ещё молода, мне жить хочется... (Островский 5). [G.:] I have to hide away from everyone; I have to bury myself alive. But I'm young yet; I want to live (5a).

X-83 • ВСЕГО́ ХОРО́ШЕГО 〈ДО́БРОГО〉!; ВСЕГО́ (НАИ)ЛУ́ЧШЕГО! [formula phrase; these forms only; also used as obj of желать/пожелать] (used when parting with s.o. or in concluding a nonofficial letter) may everything go well for you: all the best!; best of luck!; the best of luck to you!; best regards!; take care (of yourself).

[Маша:] Ну-с, позвольте пожелать вам всего хорошего. Не поминайте лихом (Чехов 6). [M.:] Well, I wish you all the best. Don't think badly of me (6a). ♦ «До свиданья», — сказал он полицмейстеру. «Всего хорошего», — ответствовал тот (Стругацкие 1). "Good-bye," he said to the police chief. "Best regards," said the chief (1a).

X-84 • ХОРО́ШЕНЬКОГО 〈ХОРО́ШЕГО〉 ПОНЕМНО́ЖКУ coll, often iron or humor [sent; these forms only; fixed WO] sth. pleasant or good should be enjoyed in small quantities (used to convey the speaker's belief that he or another has had enough of sth. pleasurable or, when used ironically, sth. unpleasant): don't 〈you mustn't etc〉 overdo a good thing; enough is enough.

Аванесян решительно поднялся и, старательно избегая её взгляда, сделал шаг к выходу. В его поспешности было что-то суетливо-жалкое. «Хорошенького понемножку, погрелся, пора и честь знать» (Максимов 3). Avanesyan rose resolutely, and moved toward the door, carefully avoiding her eyes. There was something pathetic in his haste. "Mustn't overdo a good thing. I've warmed up, and I mustn't disturb you anymore" (3a).

X-85 • НЕ ПО́ ХОРОШУ МИЛ, А ПО́ МИЛУ ХОРО́Ш [saying] there are no absolute standards for beauty, goodness etc, and people tend to consider those they like to be more beautiful, good etc than others might consider them to be: ≃ beauty is in the eye of the beholder; it's not those who are fair we love, but those we love who are fair.

«Мне кажется, что ты не можешь любить меня, что я так дурна... и всегда... а теперь... в этом по...» — «Ах, какая ты смешная! Не по хорошу мил, а по милу хорош» (Толстой 7). "It seems to me that you can't love me, that I am so ugly...always...and now...in this condi—" "Oh, how absurd you are! It's not those who are fair we love, but those we love who are fair" (7a).

X-86 • ГДЕ ХОТЕ́НЬЕ, ТАМ И УМЕ́НЬЕ [saying] if a person wants sth. very much or is determined to do sth., he will find a way to obtain or do it no matter how difficult it is: ≃ where there's a will there's a way.

X-87 • НА ВСЯ́КОЕ ХОТЕ́НЬЕ ЕСТЬ ТЕРПЕ́НЬЕ [saying] you must learn how to wait patiently because not everything that you want can be gotten immediately (usu. said jokingly, often to children, when s.o. exhibits impatience and wants his wish fulfilled immediately): ≃ everything comes to him who waits.

X-88 • ÉСЛИ ХОТИ́ТЕ 〈ХО́ЧЕШЬ〉 [these forms only; sent adv (parenth); fixed WO] it is acceptable, possible, reasonable to present (phrase or rephrase) sth. the way the speaker is about to

present (phrase or rephrase) it: **if you will; if you prefer; one could even say…**; [in limited contexts] **perhaps.**

Он человек малообразованный, если хотите, попросту невежественный. He's a poorly educated man, simply ignorant, if you will. ♦ …[Секретари Московского отделения Союза писателей РСФСР] составили сугубо секретный протокол, окончательно лишивший меня высокого звания советского писателя. Но этому последнему акту драмы или, если хотите, комедии, которую Лидия Чуковская назвала «процессом исключения», предшествовали три предварительных акта… (Войнович 1). …[The secretaries of the Moscow branch of the Russian Writers' Union] drew up a top-secret document depriving me once and for all of the high calling of Soviet writer. This last act in the drama, or, if you prefer, the comedy, which Lydia Chukovsky has called the expulsion process, had been preceded by three acts… (1a). ♦ «Хоть мы идём и разными путями, но я глубокий поклонник вашего таланта. Даже если хотите — ученик. Ваш и Хлебникова» (Катаев 3). "Though we are following different paths, I am a profound admirer of your talent. Perhaps even a pupil. Yours and Khlebnikov's" (3a).

X-89 • КАК ХОТИ́ТЕ ⟨ХО́ЧЕШЬ⟩ [these forms only; fixed WO] **1.** [subord clause] (you can do sth.) any way you want, (you can do) whatever you choose: **(do) as you please ⟨will, wish, like⟩;** [in limited contexts] **(do) whatever you want.**

[Митя:] …Судите, как хотите, я весь тут-с: я вашу дочку полюбил душою-с (Островский 2). [M.:] You must judge me as you will; here I stand, just as I am. But I love your daughter with all my heart (2b). ♦ «Так пойдёшь ужинать?» — «Не хочется». — «Дело хозяйское. Как хочешь» (Залыгин 1). "Are you going to get supper?" "I don't feel like it." "Suit yourself. Do as you like" (1a). ♦ «Ирма, иди в машину, на твоём месте я бы тоже пошёл в машину»… Бол-Кунац сказал вежливо: «Благодарю вас, господин Банев, но, право, я лучше останусь». — «Как хочешь» (Стругацкие 1). "Irma…go to the car, you're soaking wet. Bol-Kunats, if I were you I'd also get into the car."…Bol-Kunats looked at him politely. "Thank you, Mr. Banev, but I think I'd better stay." "Whatever you want" (1a).

2. [sent adv (parenth); usu. foll. by a clause introduced by Conj «а» or «но»] (usu. used when objecting to s.o.'s statement or when anticipating an objection to one's own statement) whether you agree with me or not, regardless of whether you think the way I do: **say what you like ⟨will⟩, but…; that's all very well, but…;** [in limited contexts] **all the same.**

«Нет, господа, как хотите, а Коршунова превзойти невозможно! Дракон, а не человек!» (Шолохов 5). "No, gentlemen, say what you like, but Korshunov is unbeatable! He's not a man but a dragon!" (5a).

X-90 • ХОТЬ ⟨ХОТЯ́⟩ БЫ… [these forms only] **1.** [subord Conj, concessive] used to express hypothetical concession: **even if.**

«Я хотела уж зайти к Катерине Ивановне…»… — «Катерина Ивановна ведь вас чуть не била, у отца-то?» — «Ах нет, что вы, что вы это, нет!.. Господи, била! А хоть бы и била, так что ж! Ну так что ж? Вы ничего, ничего не знаете…» (Достоевский 3). "I was even going to go to Katerina Ivanovna…"…"But Katerina Ivanovna all but beat you when you lived at your father's?" "Ah, no, what are you saying, no!…Beat me—Lord! And even if she did beat me, what of it! Well, what of it! You know nothing, nothing…" (3c).

2. [Particle] (used to show that the person, thing, phenomenon etc named is less than optimal) if nothing better, more substantial, more important etc: **at least; if nothing else;** [in limited contexts] **if only.**

…Видно, его могучая, замкнутая в своей безысходности страсть нуждалась в поддержке доброжелателей или хотя бы зрителей (Искандер 5). …His mighty passion, locked in hopeless-

ness, must have needed the support of well-wishers, or at least spectators (5a). ♦ Затянувшись дымом и глядя на меня с необычной внимательностью, она сказала: «Чем обогатилась? Хотя бы тем, что лучше узнала твой характер» (Трифонов 5). Inhaling on her cigarette and gazing at me with unusual attentiveness, she said, "In what way was I enriched by it? Well, if nothing else, I gained a better understanding of your character" (5a).

3. [intensif Particle; used with a verb in the affirmative] used to indicate that sth. that was to be expected did not take place: **not even.**

[Телятев:] Выпили по бутылке, и хоть бы краска в лице прибавилась… (Островский 4). [T.:] We had a bottle each and his face didn't even colour… (4b).

4. [exemplifying Particle] as an example: **for example; for instance.**

Сколько всего напридумано ими, безвестными следователями соответствующих органов. Возьмите хотя бы знаменитую теперь стенограмму процесса Бухарина и других (Войнович 3). How much of all this did they make up themselves, the unsung investigators of the appropriate organs! Take for example the now famous shorthand report of the trial of Bukharin et al. (3a). ♦ «Ещё между собой придётся воевать. Ты как думаешь?»… — «С кем воевать-то?» — «Мало ли с кем… Хотя бы с большевиками»… — «Нам с ними нечего делить» (Шолохов 3). "There's still some fighting to be done among ourselves, don't you think?"…"Who have we got to fight?" "Plenty of people….The Bolsheviks, for instance."…"We've got no quarrel with them" (3a).

5. [Particle] (used to express a wish or desire) it would be good if: **if only; would that; I wish…;** [in limited contexts] **oh, that…**

[Нина:] У меня в руке только одна горошина. Я загадала: идти мне в актрисы или нет? Хоть бы посоветовал кто. [Тригорин:] Тут советовать нельзя (Чехов 6). [N.:] There's just one pea in my hand. I was trying to tell my fortune: should I become an actress or not? If only someone would advise me. [T.:] No one can about that (6c). ♦ «Хоть бы Штольц скорей приехал!» — сказал он (Гончаров 1). "I wish Stolz would hurry up and come," he said (1a).

X-91 • ХОХОТУ́Н НАПА́Л *на кого* coll [VP$_{subj}$; fixed WO] s.o. has been overcome by a desire to laugh and cannot contain his laughter: на X-а хохотун напал ≃ **X had a fit of laughter.**

X-92 • МНО́ГОГО ⟨ИШЬ ЧЕГО́⟩ ХО́ЧЕТ/ЗАХОТЕ́Л coll [sent; 3rd or 2nd pers (var. with многого); 3rd pers only, but may refer to the interlocutor (var. with ишь чего); pres or pfv past only; fixed WO] your (his etc) requests, expectations, demands etc are extreme and unreasonable (and if their fulfillment depends on me, I will not fulfill them): **that's too much!; that's a tall order!; you must be kidding!; you have to be joking!;** [in limited contexts] **(now) that's going (a bit) too far!**

«Ты, как я, пиши смело, морду не вороти: „Всегда с партией, всегда с народом". Да посиди лет десять-двадцать-тридцать с важной и кислой рожей в президиумах, да произнеси сотню-другую казённых речей, вот после этого и приходи за шапкой. А то ишь чего захотел!» (Войнович 6). "You must write boldly, as I do, without turning up your nose: 'Always with the Party, Always with the People.' And sit in presidiums for ten, twenty, thirty years wearing a solemn sourpuss face. And deliver a few hundred bureaucratic speeches. *Then* come for your hat. Otherwise—you have to be joking" (6a).

X-93 • (И) ХО́ЧЕТСЯ И КО́ЛЕТСЯ coll, humor [VP; impers; these forms only; fixed WO] s.o. is torn between the desire to do sth. and the fear of doing it because of the risk, danger, or loss that might be involved: **I want ⟨he wants etc⟩ to, but I'm ⟨he's etc⟩ scared ⟨wavering, hanging back⟩; I ⟨you etc⟩ want to,**

but…; the cat loves fish but hates water; honey is sweet, but the bee stings.

X-94 • **ХО́ЧЕШЬ НЕ ХО́ЧЕШЬ** *coll;* **РАД (И́ЛИ) НЕ РАД** *coll;* **ХОШЬ НЕ ХОШЬ** *substand* [these forms only; sent adv (parenth)] regardless of whether desired, liked etc or not: **(whether you) like it or not ⟨no⟩; (whether you) want to or not; whether he ⟨she etc⟩ likes it or not ⟨wants to or not⟩; willy-nilly; [in limited contexts] one can't help (doing sth.).**

«Расставаться нам с тобой пора, хочешь не хочешь» (Владимов 1). "Like it or not, it's time for you and me to say goodbye" (1a). ♦ Им с Казангапом времени не хватало передохнуть, потому что, хочешь не хочешь, приходилось… делать по разъезду всю работу, в какой только возникала необходимость (Айтматов 2). Kazangap and he had no time to rest properly because, want to or not, they…had to do all the jobs which needed to be done [at the junction] (2a). ♦ Хочешь не хочешь, а надо идти к следователю. Дудыреву придётся самому за себя постоять (Тендряков 1). Whether he liked it or not he had to go to the Assistant Prosecutor: Dudyrev would have to take care of himself (1a). ♦ «Что всё это значит?» — спросил Лучников. Он злился. Двое уже знают некий секрет, который собираются преподнести третьему, несведущему. Хочешь не хочешь, но в эти минуты чувствуешь себя одураченным (Аксёнов 7). "What's going on here?" asked Luchnikov. He was beginning to lose his temper. When two people are in possession of a secret and haven't quite come round to letting a third person in on it, the third person can't help feeling exasperated (7a).

X-95 • **ЕШЬ ⟨ПЕЙ, БЕРИ́ и т. п.⟩ — НЕ ХОЧУ́** *coll* [sent; these forms only; fixed WO] in some place there is a great quantity of food, drink, some item etc and one is free to eat, drink, or avail o.s. of it without limit or restriction: **there is more than one could ever want ⟨one could possibly eat, one could take etc⟩; one can eat ⟨drink etc⟩ to one's heart's content; one can eat ⟨drink, take etc⟩ as much as one likes ⟨wants⟩.**

«Они оказались действительно среди развалов богатств — бери не хочу!» (Битов 2). "They found themselves really among mountains of riches—more than they could take!" (2a). ♦ «Я уж как-нибудь сам с собой управлюсь… Теперь, вон, в столовой любо-дорого… На четыре гривенника ешь — не хочу…» (Максимов 3). "I can get by somehow on my own….It's a real treat over there in the canteen nowadays….Eat as much as you like for a few coppers…" (3a).

X-96 • **ЗАДАВА́ТЬ/ЗАДА́ТЬ ХРАПОВИ́ЦКОГО** *coll, humor;* **ЗАДАВА́ТЬ/ЗАДА́ТЬ ХРАПАКА́** *substand* [VP; subj: human] to sleep soundly, usu. snoring: X задаёт храповицкого ≃ **X is having himself a good (sound) sleep ⟨a good snore⟩; X is sawing wood.**

[Расплюев:] …И вот — невредим, жив и скажу: ну, дайте только пообедать да задать… храповицкого… (Сухово-Кобылин 2). [R.:] …Here I am—alive and in one piece and I'll say this: all I need is a little food in my belly and a place I can have me a good snore… (2b).

X-97 • **ЛОМА́ТЬ ХРЕБЕ́Т** [VP] **1.** *substand* [subj: human] to work, labor to the point of exhaustion, wear o.s. out with hard (usu. menial) work (usu. in an attempt to earn enough money to live on, often with the implication that one is being exploited by s.o.): X ломает хребет ≃ **X is breaking his back; X is working his fingers to the bone; X is working his tail ⟨butt etc⟩ off.**

2. ~ *кому-чему usu. media.* Also: **СЛОМА́ТЬ ХРЕБЕ́Т** *usu. media* [subj and indir obj: human or collect] to destroy or severely damage (some person, group, movement etc): X ломает Y-у хребет ≃ **X breaks ⟨destroys⟩ Y; X breaks Y's back.**

«А с Першиным, между прочим, советую не ссориться. Не забывай, кто его поставил». — «Ну и что?» — «А то. Подрезов не таким, как ты, хребет ломает» (Абрамов 1). "By the way, I advise you not to fall out with Pershin. Don't forget who put him there." "What about it?" "Just this: Podrezov can break bigger people than you" (1a).

X-98 • **СТАНОВО́Й ХРЕБЕ́Т** *чего;* **СТАНОВА́Я ЖИ́ЛА** *both media* [NP; sing only; usu. subj-compl with copula (subj: abstr or concr); fixed WO] the most important, sustaining part (of sth.): **backbone; mainstay; foundation.**

< Formerly used in substandard speech in reference to the spinal column.

X-99 • **СТА́РЫЙ ХРЕН** *highly coll, rude* [NP; usu. sing] a reference to or way of addressing an old man: **old fogy ⟨geezer, devil, coot, grumbler, fart⟩.**

«Съезди завтра к старому хрену. Скажи, чтоб на бюро ехал» (Абрамов 1). "Go over and see the old fogy tomorrow and tell him to come in to the office" (1a). ♦ [Шеметова:] Здравствуйте, Сергей Георгиевич. [Бакченин:] Боже мой, Оля! Сколько лет, сколько зим! Смотришь… Старый хрен, да? [Шеметова:] Это сильно сказано. Разумеется, постарели оба (Панова 1). [Sh.:] Hello, Sergei Georgievich. [B.:] My god! Olya! It's been ages! I guess I'm…an old geezer. [Sh.:] That's putting it rather strongly. We've both gotten older (1a).

X-100 • **ХРЕН В ПЯ́ТКУ ⟨В ГО́ЛОВУ⟩** *кому substand, rather vulg* [Interj; these forms only; fixed WO] used to express surprise, admiration, delight, or resentment, indignation etc: **that ⟨you etc⟩ son of a gun ⟨a bitch⟩!; damn you ⟨him etc⟩!; I'll be damned ⟨darned⟩!**

X-101 • **ХРЕН РЕ́ДЬКИ НЕ СЛА́ЩЕ** [saying] one person (thing, option etc) is as bad as the other, neither is any better than the other (usu. said when making a comparison or considering a replacement): ≃ **it's six of one and half a dozen of the other; it's a choice between the devil and the deep blue sea.**

X-102 • **НА ХРЕНА́; НА́ ХРЕН; НА КОЙ ХРЕН** *all highly coll, rude* [PrepP; these forms only; adv] used in questions, rhetorical questions, and exclamations to express annoyance, irritation, and/or a complete lack of interest in s.o. or sth.: **why the hell ⟨the devil, the frig⟩; what the hell ⟨the devil, the frig⟩ (for); why in ⟨the⟩ blazes; the hell with (s.o. ⟨sth.⟩).**

Я сейчас сидел и думал, — продолжал отец, — на кой хрен нам нужна халупа, там же нет ничего хорошего… (Соколов 1). I was just sitting and thinking—continued father,—why the hell do we need that hovel, there's nothing good out there… (1a). ♦ «Путается, хочет всё объяснить, а на хрена нам его объяснения?» (Искандер 5). "He kept getting tangled up, wanting to explain everything. What the frig did we want with his explanations?" (5a). ♦ «Какая баба!.. Ей бы и быть председателем. И на хрена нам кого-то со стороны искать» (Абрамов 1). "…What a woman!…If only she could be Chairwoman. And the hell with searching for one on the outside" (1a).

X-103 • **НИ ХРЕНА́ СЕБЕ́!** *highly coll, rather vulg* [Interj; fixed WO] used to express surprise coupled with admiration: **ain't that something!; no shit!; no kidding!**

«Представляешь, их сын попал в олимпийскую сборную». — «Ни хрена себе!» "Would you believe it, their son made the Olympic team!" "No shit!"

X-104 • **КАК У ХРИСТА́ ЗА ПА́ЗУХОЙ** жить, быть₀ и т. п. *coll* [как + PrepP; Invar; adv or subj-compl with copula (subj: human); fixed WO] (to live, be etc) in complete comfort, free from worry, hardship, danger etc: **(live) in clover; (be) without a care in the world; (be able to) rest easy; (feel) as safe as could be; (be) as safe as in God's pocket; (one) couldn't be cozier in the good Lord's pocket.**

Целый год мы жили как у Христа за пазухой (Мандельштам 2). For a year we lived in clover (2a). ♦ На его глазах она из девочки-ординатора стала таким схватчивым диагностом, что он верил ей не меньше, чем самой Донцовой. За такими диагностами хирург, даже скептик, живёт как у Христа за пазухой (Солженицын 10). Before his eyes she had turned from a girl intern into such a perceptive diagnostician that he trusted her no less than he trusted Dontsova herself. With a diagnostician like that, even a skeptical surgeon could rest easy (10b). ♦ «Здесь тебе возле печки теплей будет... Здесь ты как у Христа за пазухой...» (Распутин 3). "You'll be nice and warm here by the stove....You couldn't be cosier in the good Lord's pocket" (3a).

X-105 • ХРИСТА́ РА́ДИ [PrepP; Invar; usu. this WO] **1.** *obsoles* [Interj] an exclamation used by beggars asking for alms: **for Christ's ⟨God's⟩ sake; for the love of Christ ⟨God⟩; in Christ's ⟨God's⟩ name.**

2. ~ просить, побираться *obs* [adv] to lead the life of a beggar, ask for charity: X просит ~ ≃ **X begs his bread; X lives on alms.**

3. жить, делать *что* ~ *obs* [adv] (to live) at s.o.'s expense, benefiting from his generosity or (to do sth.—feed s.o., give s.o. shelter etc) as an act of generosity: **(live ⟨get sth. etc⟩) free of charge thanks to s.o.'s kindness; (do sth.) out of kindness ⟨out of the goodness of one's heart, out of pity** etc⟩.

4. *coll* [sent adv (parenth)] please, I beseech you (used to make a request emphatic): **for Christ's ⟨God's, heaven's⟩ sake; for the love of Christ ⟨God, Jesus⟩; in Christ's ⟨God's, Jesus'⟩ name.**

«Э, да у вас, гражданин, червонцев-то куры не клюют. Ты бы со мной поделился! А?» — «Оставь ты меня, Христа ради», — испугался буфетчик и проворно спрятал деньги (Булгаков 9). "Hey, citizen, you're rolling in chervontsy!...Why not share them with me, eh?" "Let me be, for Christ's sake!" the bartender was frightened and quickly hid the money (9a). ♦ «...Скажи честно, ради Христа, без заученных фраз, это ли нужно России?» (Пастернак 1). "Tell me honestly, for the love of Christ, without any fine phrases, is this really what Russia needs?" (1a). ♦ «Идёт странница, стонет, за живот хватается... И просит: отвезите меня Христа ради в больницу, заплачу я, не пожалею денег» (Пастернак 1). "She [the beggar woman] was walking along and moaning and clutching her belly....In Christ's name, she begged, take me to the hospital, I'll pay you whatever you like" (1a).

X-106 • ХРИСТО́М-БО́ГОМ просить, умолять *obs* [NP_instrum; Invar; adv (intensif)] (to implore, beg s.o.) earnestly, beseechingly: **in Christ's ⟨God's⟩ name; for the love of Christ ⟨God, Jesus⟩; for Christ's ⟨God's⟩ sake.**

Он тридцатилетним опытом знал, что... ещё два раза остановят его и пошлют за забытыми вещами, и уже после этого ещё раз остановят, и графиня сама высунется к нему в окно и попросит его Христом-богом ехать осторожнее на спусках (Толстой 6). His thirty years' experience had taught him that...he would be stopped at least twice for some forgotten article that would have to be sent for, and then again for the Countess to lean out the window and beg him in God's name to drive carefully down the hill (6a). ♦ «Егор, — взмолилась Люба. — Христом-богом прошу, скажи, они ничего с тобой не сделают?» (Шукшин 1). "Egor!" beseeched Lyuba. "Please, for the love of Christ, tell me they're not going to do anything to you" (1a).

X-107 • НЕТ ХУ́ДА БЕЗ ДОБРА́ [saying] every difficult or unpleasant situation brings something good along with it (usu. said when something good or useful arises out of a misfortune or trouble that has already passed): ≃ **every cloud has a silver lining; there is no great loss without some small gain.**

...[Ирине Викторовне] пока что никакой диеты не требуется... Нет худа без добра: в молодости она часто прихварывала, а должно быть, тогда-то и были заложены её формы. Хворь прошла, формы – остались! (Залыгин 1). ...She [Irina Viktorovna] didn't need to watch her diet yet....Every cloud has a silver lining: as a girl she'd been sickly, just at the time when her figure was taking shape. The sickness had passed, but the slim figure had remained (1a). ♦ ...Среди мирных подпольных фабрик Эндурска появилась сверхподпольная трикотажная фабрика, выпускающая изделия из «джерси» и работающая на японских станках... В один прекрасный день в Эндурске сгорел подпольный склад [, принадлежавший конкурентам этой трикотажной фабрики,] с огромным запасом временно законсервированных нейлоновых кофточек... Но, как говорится, нет худа без добра. С этих пор лекторы Эндурска и Мухуса с немалым успехом используют эту историю как наглядный пример, подтверждающий тезис о хищническом характере частнособственнического развития... (Искандер 3). ...Among the peaceful underground factories of Endursk, there had appeared a supersecret knitting mill which turned out articles made of jersey and used Japanese machines....One fine day the underground warehouse in Endursk [owned by the competitors of that knitting mill] burned down, and with it a huge stock of nylon blouses....But, as they say, there is no great loss without some small gain. Ever since, the lecturers of Endursk and Mukhus have used this story with considerable success as a graphic example supporting the proposition that the development of private ownership is rapacious in character... (3a).

X-108 • НЕ ХУ́ДО ⟨НЕ ДУ́РНО, НЕ ПЛО́ХО⟩ (БЫ) *coll* [these forms only; impers predic with быть_∅; usu. foll. by infin; fixed WO] it would not be bad, it is desirable, advisable (to do sth.): **it's not ⟨it wouldn't be⟩ a bad idea (for s.o. to do sth.); it wouldn't be a bad thing (if s.o. did sth. ⟨for s.o. to do sth.⟩); it would be a good idea (for s.o. to do sth.); it won't ⟨wouldn't, couldn't⟩ hurt (s.o. to do sth.); s.o. wouldn't do badly (by doing sth.).**

[Кочкарёв:] Да ведь ты сейчас объявил, что хочешь [жениться]. [Подколёсин:] Я говорил только, что не худо бы (Гоголь 1). [K.:] But you just now said that you wanted to [get married]. [P.:] I only said that it wouldn't be a bad idea (1a). ♦ «...Псарня чудная, вряд людям вашим житьё такое ж, как вашим собакам». Один из псарей обиделся. «Мы на своё житьё, — сказал он, — благодаря бога и барина не жалуемся, а что правда, то правда, иному и дворянину не худо бы променять усадьбу на любую здешнюю конурку» (Пушкин 1). "...The kennels are marvellous...but I don't imagine your servants live as well as your dogs." One of the grooms took offence at this remark. "Thanks to God and our master, we have no complaints about how we live," he said, "but it's only true to say that some noblemen wouldn't do badly by exchanging their estate for any one of our kennels here" (1b).

X-109 • ХУ́ДО-БЕ́ДНО *coll* [AdvP; Invar; adv] **1.** used to show that sth. is done less smoothly, completely etc than desired: **somehow (manage to...); somehow or other.**

Друзей и знакомых у Александра Николаевича было множество, один помог ему достать кирпич, другой — доски, третий — цемент, и так, худо-бедно, за два года дом был построен. Aleksandr Nikolaevich had many friends and acquaintances; one helped him to get bricks, another—lumber, a third—cement, and in that way, over the course of two years, his house somehow or other got built. ♦ «Я сюда [в лагерь] на дармовые харчи не просился, — ответил зэк. — Я на заводе работал. Худо-бедно, а себя и свою семью сам кормил. Какой же я тунеядец?» (Марченко 1). [context transl] "I didn't ask to come here and get my grub free," replied the con. "I used to work in a factory—the pay was rotten but still I used to keep myself and my family, so how does that make me a parasite?" (1a).

2. [usu. foll. by a quantit NP] not less than: **at (the very) least; as a bare minimum.**

Ремонт обойдётся нам, худо-бедно, в пятнадцать тысяч рублей. The repairs will cost us about fifteen thousand rubles at the very least.

X-110 • **ХУДО́ЖНИК ОТ СЛО́ВА «ХУ́ДО»** *coll* [NP; fixed WO] a very unskilled, worthless painter: **painter with the stress on "pain."**

Зашёл Начальник Караула и сказал, что Мазила — художник от слова «худо»... (Зиновьев 1). The guard commander came in and said that Dauber was a painter with the stress on "pain"... (1a).

Ц-1 • ПРИ ЦАРЕ́ ГОРО́ХЕ *coll, humor* [PrepP; Invar; adv; fixed WO] long ago: **in the olden days; in days of yore; ages ago; in the year one.**

«Казалось бы, чего тут хитрого, ещё при царе Горохе телефоны умели проверять на слух, но ваши работники, Абрам Менделевич, оказывается, не умеют...» (Копелев 1). "You would think there was nothing so complicated about it, even in the olden days they knew how to test telephones by ear, but your workers, Abram Mendelevich, it turns out, don't know how" (1a). ♦ А отец его, рыбопромышленник, владевший когда-то, при царе Горохе, двумя баркасами «астраханками», рассказывал, что в его времена и по пять пудов ловились (Трифонов 1). His father, who way back when, in the year one, had been a fish merchant and had owned two Astrakhan longboats, used to tell how in his day they would catch sturgeon weighing close to 200 pounds (1a).

Ц-2 • С ЦАРЁМ В ГОЛОВЕ́ *obs* [PrepP; Invar; subj-compl with быть∅ (subj: human), pres or past; fixed WO] one is clever, practical, one knows how to get things done etc: X с царём в голове ≃ **X has a good head on his shoulders; X is smart;** [in limited contexts] **X is shrewd.**

Ц-3 • ЦАРИ́ЦА НЕБЕ́СНАЯ *obs* [NP; sing only; fixed WO] Mary, the mother of Jesus: **Our Lady (in Heaven); Holy Queen of Heaven; Holy Mother.**

[1-й мужик:] Только бы свершилось дело. [3-й мужик:] Царицу небесную просить надо. Авось смилосердуется (Толстой 3). [1st Peasant:] ...If only we can get our business done. [3rd Peasant:] We must pray to Our Lady in Heaven. Maybe she'll take pity (3b). ♦ «...Мы никуда не поедем! Ехать — так всем, а не ехать — так никому!»... — «Ну, коли так — остаёмся! Укрой и оборони нас, царица небесная!» (Шолохов 4). "We're not going anywhere! If one goes, we all go, or not at all!"..."Well, if that's how things are, we'll stay. Shield and protect us, Holy Queen of Heaven!" (4a).

Ц-4 • В НЕ́КОТОРОМ ЦА́РСТВЕ, В НЕ́КОТОРОМ ГОСУДА́РСТВЕ *folk poet* [PrepP; Invar; adv; fixed WO] the formulaic beginning of many Russian folk tales: **once upon a time (in a faraway kingdom); a long time ago in a land far away; long ago and far away.**

[Марат:] В некотором царстве, в некотором государстве жил старик со своей старухой... (Арбузов 4). [M.:] Once upon a time there lived an old man with his old woman... (4a).

Ц-5 • СО́ННОЕ ЦА́РСТВО *coll* [NP; sing only; fixed WO] (in some place there is) peace and silence because everyone is fast asleep; *by extension* inactivity in the workplace: **the land of Nod; dreamland;** [extended usage] у нас в отделе — сонное царство ≃ **everyone in our department is just whiling away the time; our department is totally dead.**

У вас тут, я вижу, сонное царство: и отец спит, и дети. I see everyone here is in the land of Nod: Dad's asleep and the kids are, too. ♦ В нашем отделе работы по горло — еле справляемся, а у них в отделе — сонное царство: клиентов нет, никто ничего не делает. In our department we're up to our necks in work and can hardly manage, whereas their department is totally dead: they have no clients and nobody does anything.

Ц-6 • ТРИДЕВЯ́ТОЕ ⟨ТРИДЕСЯ́ТОЕ⟩ ЦА́РСТВО ⟨ГОСУДА́РСТВО⟩ *folk poet* [NP; sing only; fixed WO] in Russian fairy tales, a very distant land; *by extension* any very distant place: **faraway land ⟨place⟩; faraway kingdom; kingdom beyond the sea(s); never-never land.**

Я выключила радио... и начала читать ей [Лёльке] сказку... «Прощай, красна девица, — печально сказал он. — Лечу я за тридевять земель, в тридевятое царство, в тридесятое государство. Если любишь, ищи меня там» (Чуковская 2). I turned the radio off...and started to read her [Lyolka] a fairy-story...."Farewell, lovely maiden," he said sadly, "I am flying off to the other end of the world, to a kingdom beyond the seas. If you love me look for me there" (2a). ♦ Положим, например, существует канцелярия, не здесь, а в тридевятом государстве... (Гоголь 3). Let us suppose, for instance, that there is a government office, not here but in some never-never land... (3c).

Ц-7 • ЦА́РСТВО ⟨ЦА́РСТВИЕ⟩ НЕБЕ́СНОЕ *obs* [NP; sing only; fixed WO] **1.** paradise, heaven: **the kingdom of heaven; the heavenly kingdom; the kingdom of God.**

При его слабости к съедобному, Гена, разумеется, даже в обмен на Царствие Небесное не согласился бы умереть до обеда (Максимов 2). With his weakness for food, Gena would never, of course, have agreed to die before lunch, even in exchange for the Kingdom of Heaven (2a).

2. ~ *кому* [usu. indep. sent] a wish that the deceased spend the afterlife in paradise: царство Х-у небесное ≃ **God rest X's soul; may X rest in peace; may the kingdom of heaven be X's; may X's soul rest in the kingdom of heaven.**

«Батюшка Сергея Сергеевича умер», — сообщил Иван Васильевич. «Царство небесное», — сказала старушка вежливо... (Булгаков 12). "Sergei Sergeyevich's father is dead," put in Ivan Vasilievich. "God rest his soul," said the old lady politely (12a). ♦ «Ну, что отец?» — «Вчера получил известие о его кончине», — коротко сказал князь Андрей. Кутузов испуганно-открытыми глазами посмотрел на князя Андрея, потом снял фуражку и перекрестился: «Царство ему небесное!» (Толстой 6). "And how's your father?" "I received news of his death yesterday," replied Prince Andrew abruptly. Kutuzov looked at him with eyes wide open with dismay, and then took off his cap and crossed himself: "May the kingdom of Heaven be his!" (6b). ♦ «Ну, давай, кум, помянем Каледина, покойного атамана. Царство ему небесное!» (Шолохов 3). "Well, kinsman, let's drink to Kaledin, our late ataman. May his soul rest in the kingdom of heaven!" (3a).

Ц-8 • ЦАРЬ И БОГ [NP; nom only; subj-compl with copula (subj: human)] **1.** a person who possesses unlimited authority, power: **lord and master; (be) like God Almighty.**

Кругом на сотни километров была одна тайга, и жаловаться на произвол начальника экспедиции было некому: он был здесь царь и бог. For hundreds of kilometers around there was nothing but taiga, and there was no one to complain to about the tyranny of the expedition leader: here, he was lord and master.

2. an excellent specialist, a person who is very knowledgeable in some field or about some matter: **topnotch expert; master hand; whiz; (one knows sth.) inside out.**

Давай попросим Роберта помочь тебе с компьютером, он в этом деле царь и бог. Let's ask Robert to help you with the computer, he's a whiz at computers.

Ц-9 • ЦАРЬ ⟨ОТЕ́Ц⟩ НЕБЕ́СНЫЙ *obs* [NP; sing only; fixed WO] **1.** God: **Heavenly ⟨Divine⟩ Father.**

2. [used as Interj] used to express fright, offense, astonishment etc: **God Almighty!; good God (in heaven)!**

«Кто просил тебя писать на меня доносы? разве ты приставлен ко мне в шпионы?» — «Я? писал на тебя доносы? — отвечал Савельич со слезами. — Господи царю небесный! Так изволь-ка прочитать, что пишет ко мне барин: увидишь, как я доносил на тебя» (Пушкин 2). "Who told you to write and inform on me? Or were you assigned to spy on me?" "Me write and inform on you?" Savelich replied in tears. "God Almighty! Just read, if you please, what the master writes to me: you'll see if I've been informing on you" (2a).

Ц-10 • **БЕЗ ЦАРЯ́ В ГОЛОВЕ́** *coll* [PrepP; Invar; usu. subj-compl with быть∅ (subj: human), pres or past, or nonagreeing postmodif; fixed WO] one is very dull-witted, foolish: X без царя в голове ≃ **X has no brains; X has nothing upstairs; X doesn't have a brain in his head;** ‖ [when used as nonagreeing postmodif] **a person ⟨a man, a woman⟩ with nothing upstairs.**

«Ты, Митёк, известно, без царя в голове, молотишь, что ни попадя...» (Максимов 2a). "Mitya, we know you haven't any brains and you don't often hit the nail on the head..." (2a). ♦ Хлестаков, молодой человек лет 23-х, тоненький, худенький; несколько приглуповат и, как говорят, без царя в голове (Гоголь 4). Khlestakov, a young man, about twenty-three, slim, slender; a bit silly, and, as they say, with nothing upstairs (4a).

Ц-11 • **времена, времён ЦАРЯ́ ГОРО́ХА** *coll, humor* [NP_{gen}; Invar; nonagreeing postmodif; fixed WO] (in or from) very remote times: **(in ⟨from⟩) the olden days; (in ⟨from⟩) the days of yore; ages ago; (in ⟨from⟩) the year one.**

Ц-12 • **КАК ⟨ЧТО⟩ МА́КОВ ЦВЕТ** *folk poet* [как or что + NP; these forms only; fixed WO] **1.** ~ **румян(ый), зардеться** и т. п. [modif or adv (intensif)] (of s.o.'s face) (to be, turn etc) very red, resembling the color of a poppy: **beet ⟨bright, poppy⟩ red.**

Дуняшка вспыхнула, как маков цвет, – сквозь слёзы посмотрела на Григория. Он не сводил с неё злого взгляда... (Шолохов 5). Dunyashka blazed poppy red and stared at Grigory through tears. He kept his angry gaze upon her... (5a).

2. расцвести ~ [adv] (of a young woman) to develop, mature into a beautiful woman: X расцвела как маков цвет ≃ **X blossomed into a real beauty.**

Ц-13 • **В ЧЁРНОМ ЦВЕ́ТЕ видеть, представлять** *кого-что* [PrepP; Invar; adv; usu. used with impfv verbs; fixed WO] (to see, perceive, portray etc s.o. or sth. as) exaggeratedly gloomy, unattractive, worse than he or it actually is: **(see ⟨view⟩ s.o. ⟨sth.⟩) in a bad ⟨negative⟩ light; (paint ⟨see⟩ s.o. ⟨sth.⟩) in somber colors; (look) on the dark side (of things).**

Он пессимист, всегда видит всё в чёрном цвете. He's a pessimist—he always looks on the dark side of things.

Ц-14 • **ВО ⟨В⟩ ЦВЕ́ТЕ ЛЕТ ⟨СИЛ⟩** [PrepP; these forms only; subj-compl with быть∅ (subj: human), obj-compl with знать, оставить etc (obj: human), or adv; fixed WO] the years when one's or s.o.'s mental and physical abilities are at their peak: **in one's prime; in the prime of life; at the height of one's powers.**

Он погиб во цвете лет, оставив молодую жену с ребёнком. He was killed in his prime, leaving behind a young wife and child.

Ц-15 • **ПЫ́ШНЫМ ЦВЕ́ТОМ расцвести, распуститься** и т. п. [NP_{instrum}; Invar; adv; usu. used with pfv verbs; fixed WO] (to develop) extensively, in full measure (in contemp. usage, usu. used ironically of negative qualities and phenomena): **blossom; flourish; thrive; reach full flower;** [of negative phenomena only] **run rampant.**

Талант его расцвёл пышным цветом лишь в последний период его жизни. It was only in the last period of his life that his talent blossomed. ♦ В труппе театра пышным цветом расцвели зависть и взаимная злоба. Jealousy and mutual loathing ran rampant in the theater company.

Ц-16 • **ЭТО ЕЩЁ ⟨ТО́ЛЬКО⟩ ЦВЕТО́ЧКИ ⟨ЦВЕ́-ТИКИ, ЦВЕТКИ́⟩, А Я́ГОДКИ (БУ́ДУТ) ВПЕ-**

РЕДИ́ [saying; often only the first half of the saying is used] this first thing, beginning stage etc is bad, but what is to come will be many times worse: ≃ **this is only the half of it (, there are more "treats" in store); this is just a taste of what's to come; this is only ⟨just⟩ the beginning (, there's much more to come ⟨the real stuff comes later⟩); the worst is yet to come; you ain't seen nothin' yet;** [said ironically] **the best is yet to come.**

[Лебедев:] Тебе в приданое назначается пятнадцать тысяч рублей серебром... Вот... Смотри, чтоб потом разговоров не было! Постой, молчи! Это только цветки, а будут ещё ягодки. Приданого тебе назначено пятнадцать тысяч, но, принимая во внимание, что Николай Алексеевич должен твоей матери девять тысяч, из твоего приданого делается вычитание... (Чехов 4). [L.:] Your dowry's to be fifteen thousand rubles. Now look, we don't want arguments afterwards. No, don't speak, this is only the half of it, there are more treats in store. Your dowry's to be fifteen thousand, but as Nicholas owes your mother nine thousand, that's being deducted from the dowry (4b). ♦ «[Сталин] кровь из мужика пьёт... Но это ещё цветочки. Ягодки у вас обоих впереди» (Алешковский 1). "[Stalin] sucks the peasants' blood....But that's just the beginning. The real stuff comes later" (1a).

Ц-17 • **СРЫВА́ТЬ ЦВЕТЫ́ УДОВО́ЛЬСТВИЯ** *obsoles, lit* [VP; subj: human; fixed WO] to give o.s. in a carefree manner to the joys of life: X срывал цветы удовольствия ≃ **X enjoyed the finer things in life; X indulged in life's little pleasures; X picked the flowers ⟨gathered the blossoms⟩ of pleasure.**

[source] [Хлестаков:] Я люблю поесть. Ведь на то живёшь, чтобы срывать цветы удовольствия (Гоголь 4). [Kh.:] I like a good meal. But, then, what is life for if not to pick the flowers of pleasure? (4c).

< From Nikolai Gogol's *The Inspector General* («Ревизор»), 1836.

Ц-18 • **уходи, убирайся, пусть убирается** и т. п. **ПОКА́ ЦЕЛ** *coll;* **ПОКУ́ДА ЦЕЛ** *substand* [subord clause; fixed WO] (go, get out, s.o. should get out etc) before you are (he is etc) harmed, while there is still time: **while you're ⟨he's etc⟩ still in one piece; before you get ⟨he gets etc⟩ hurt.**

«Марш!» — крикнул он на офицеров. «Хорошо же! — не робея и не отъезжая, кричал маленький офицер. — Разбойничать, так я вам...» — «К чёрту марш скорым шагом, пока цел». И Денисов повернул лошадь к офицеру (Толстой 5). "Now, march!" he shouted at the officers. "Very well then!" cried the little officer, not in the least intimidated and not moving. "If you're determined to go through with this raid, then I'll—" "Go to hell! Quick march, while you're still in one piece!" And Denisov turned his horse and made for the officer (5a). ♦ [Бусыгин:] Слушай. Беги отсюда, пока цел (Вампилов 4). [B.:] Look, get out of here before you get hurt (4a).

Ц-19 • **БИТЬ МИМО ЦЕ́ЛИ** [VP; subj: abstr or, occas., human] (usu. of an argument, criticism etc) to be ineffective, fail to attain the desired result: X бил мимо цели ≃ **X didn't have any ⟨had no⟩ effect ⟨impact⟩; X didn't make any impact.**

Нина приводила десятки аргументов, пытаясь отговорить мужа от сомнительной сделки, но все они били мимо цели. Nina tried dozens of different arguments in an attempt to talk her husband out of getting involved in a shady deal, but they had no effect.

Ц-20 • **ЦЕЛИКО́М И ПО́ЛНОСТЬЮ** *coll* [AdvP; Invar; adv; fixed WO] wholly, totally: **(utterly and) completely; fully; entirely;** [in limited contexts] **lock, stock, and barrel.**

Наша работа целиком и полностью зависит от качества сырья. Our work is entirely dependent on the quality of the raw materials.

Ц-21 • **В ЦÉЛОСТИ И СОХРÁННОСТИ ⟨НЕВРЕДИ́-МОСТИ⟩ бытьₒ, доставить** *кого-что,* **вернуть** *что* и т. п.; **В ЦÉЛОСТИ-СОХРÁННОСТИ** *all coll* [PrepP; these forms only; usu. subj-compl with copula: human or concr) or obj-compl with доставить etc (obj: human or concr); fixed WO] (a person or thing is, to deliver a person or thing, return a thing etc) unhurt, undamaged: **safe and sound; unharmed; (all) in one piece;** [of a person only] **alive and well;** [of a thing only] **intact; in (good) working order.**

Под утро все новоиспечённые офицеры... частично своим собственным ходом, частично с помощью товарищей и аборигенов вернулись в казарму в целости и сохранности... (Зиновьев 1). By morning all the newly fledged officers had returned to barracks safe and sound, partly under their own steam and partly with the help of their comrades and the aboriginal population (1a). ♦ Мансурову даже казалось, что если он перестанет запрещать — завтра же всё рухнет, полетит в тартарары, вся семья погибнет, разве только он один и останется в целости и сохранности, так что он вовсе и не о себе заботился, запрещая, а о других (Залыгин 1). It actually seemed to him that if he once stopped forbidding things everything would crumble into ruins the next day, everything would fall to pieces, the family would perish. He himself would remain unharmed, which proved that it wasn't himself he was concerned about when he exercised his right of veto. It was others (1a). ♦ Вот твой велосипед, возвращаю его в целости и сохранности. Here's your bike—I'm returning it all in one piece.

Ц-22 • **ЦÉЛЫЙ И НЕВРЕДИ́МЫЙ ⟨ЦЕЛ И НЕВРЕДИ́М⟩** [AdjP; usu. subj-compl with copula (subj: human or concr), occas. detached modif (var. with long-form Adj only); fixed WO] unhurt, in fine condition: **safe and sound; unharmed; (all) in one piece;** [of a person only] **alive and well; alive and in one piece;** [of a thing only] **undamaged; intact.**

Ему бы этот год перетерпеть в горах, и он целым и невредимым вернулся бы в свою семью (Искандер 4). He should have waited out the year in the mountains, and he would have come back to his family safe and sound (4a). ♦ [Вершинин:] Когда начался пожар, я побежал скорей домой; подхожу, смотрю — дом наш цел и невредим и вне опасности... (Чехов 5). [V.:] When the fire began, I ran home fast; got there, looked...our house was unharmed and out of danger... (5c). ♦ К их удивлению, у двери, ведущей со сцены в переулок, лежал на спине целый и невредимый гамбсовский стул. Издав собачий визг, Ипполит Матвеевич вцепился в него мёртвой хваткой (Ильф и Петров 1). To their surprise, the Hambs chair was lying on its back, undamaged, at the exit from the stage to the street. Growling like a dog, Ippolit Matveyevich seized it in a death-grip (1a).

Ц-23 • **БИТЬ (ПРЯ́МО) В ЦЕЛЬ** [VP; subj: abstr or, occas., human] (usu. of arguments, criticism, advice etc) to be effective, attain the desired result: X бил в цель ≃ **X achieved its ⟨his⟩ aim ⟨goal⟩; X was (right) on target ⟨on the mark⟩; X hit the mark.**

Точно и чётко поставленные вопросы следователя били прямо в цель, и на следующий день преступник сознался во всём. The precise and meticulously phrased questions of the investigator were right on target, and the following day the criminal made a full confession. ♦ ...Его [Миляги] советы всегда оказывались точными, немногословными, но всегда били в цель (Войнович 4). [Milyaga's] advice was precise and terse but always on the mark (4a).

Ц-24 • **ЦЕЛЬ ОПРÁВДЫВАЕТ СРÉДСТВА** [saying] if a goal is good, then any method of achieving it, however unfair, violent etc, is justified: ≃ **the end justifies the means.**

Цель оправдывает средства, говорила она Участковому, обещавшему за флакон парижских духов скомпрометировать Сожительницу... (Зиновьев 1). "The end justifies the means," she said to the Fuzz, who had promised, at the price of a phial of Parisian perfume, to compromise Mistress... (1a).

Ц-25 • **С ЦÉЛЬЮ** [PrepP; Invar] **1.** ~ *чего.* Also: **В ЦÉЛЯХ** [Prep; the resulting PrepP is adv] having (sth.) as one's goal: **with the purpose ⟨the aim, the object, the motive⟩ of; for** [AdjP] **⟨[NP]⟩ purposes.**

...Он с негодованием отверг даже предположение о том, что брат мог убить с целью грабежа... (Достоевский 2). ...He indignantly rejected even the suggestion that his brother could have killed with the purpose of robbery... (2a). ♦ Версия у него была такая: Сандро убил бухгалтера с целью грабежа... (Искандер 3). This was his version of the story: Sandro had killed the bookkeeper with the motive of robbery... (3a). ♦ ...Гитлеровцы широко использовали его имя в целях своей пропаганды (Рыбаков 1). The Nazis did use his name widely for propaganda purposes (1a).

2. [used with infin; the resulting PrepP is adv] as a means to (achieving sth.): **with the aim ⟨the purpose, the intention, the object, the motive⟩ of (doing sth.); for the purpose of (doing sth.); (in order) to; with a view to (doing sth.).**

Колония была заключена в сравнительно изолированное помещение с целью наблюдать законы крысиной жизни в чистом виде (Зиновьев 1). The colony was housed in a fairly isolated environment with the aim of observing the laws of rodent life in their pure form (1a). ♦ «...Вы напросились ко мне в гости именно с целью подсмотреть и подслушать всё, что можно» (Булгаков 9). "...You invited yourself to see me with the intention of spying and eavesdropping as much as you could" (9b). ♦ Видно было, что этот план давно был составлен Армфельдом и что он теперь изложил его не столько с целью отвечать на предлагаемые вопросы, на которые план этот не отвечал, сколько с целью воспользоваться случаем высказать его (Толстой 6). It was obvious that this plan had been formulated by Armfeldt long ago, and put forward now not so much with the object of meeting the present problem, to which it offered no solution, as to avail himself of the opportunity of airing it (6a).

Ц-26 • **КРÁСНАЯ ЦЕНÁ** *чему coll* [NP; sing only; usu. subj or subj-compl with бытьₒ (subj: a noun denoting a specified amount of money); fixed WO] the most s.o. thinks that sth. is worth, the highest price that s.o. would be willing to pay for sth.: X-у красная цена — десять рублей ≃ **X isn't worth more than ten rubles; ten rubles is the top ⟨the best⟩ price (that s.o. would offer) for X; s.o. would pay ten rubles tops for X; the most s.o. would pay for X is ten rubles.**

«Я полагаю с своей стороны...: по восьми гривен за душу, это самая красная цена!» (Гоголь 3). "I, for my part, would offer eighty kopecks per soul....This is the top price" (3c).

Ц-27 • **В ЦЕНÉ** [PrepP; Invar; subj-compl with бытьₒ] **1.** [subj: concr (count pl or mass)] (some category of items) is highly valued and therefore has a high market price: X-ы в цене ≃ **Xs are (very ⟨quite, rather⟩) costly; Xs are highly priced ⟨high-priced⟩; the price of Xs is high; Xs are worth (quite) a bit; Xs are worth a pretty penny; Xs bring ⟨fetch⟩ a good price; Xs are in demand;** ‖ *Neg* X-ы не в цене ≃ **Xs don't fetch ⟨bring⟩ much.**

«Хлеб был хорош и в цене, и в марте или апреле вы получите деньги...» (Гончаров 1). "The harvest was good, the price high, and you can get the money in March or April..." (1b). ♦ Батько ещё в начале весны повёз в Крым на продажу табак... Табак был тогда в цене (Гоголь 5). Just at the beginning of spring Father went with the wagons to the Crimea to sell tobacco;...tobacco brought a good price in those days (5a). ♦ Нашатырь... был в цене. Он заменял дрожжи (Паустовский 1). Ammonia was in demand. It was a substitute for yeast (1a). ♦ [Анчугин:] Часы теперь не в цене (Вампилов 1). [A.:] Watches don't fetch much these days (1a).

2. [subj: human (usu. pl) or abstr] (people of some category, items of some type etc) are considered to be of great value (among some group, in some place etc): X-ы в цене ≃ **Xs are highly valued.**

Опытный и честный работник всегда в цене. An experienced and honest worker is always highly valued.

Ц-28 • ДОРОГО́Й ЦЕНО́Й достаться *кому,* добиться, достигнуть *чего,* заплатить *за что* и т. п. [NP$_{instrum}$; Invar; adv; fixed WO] (to attain, get, accomplish etc sth.) at the cost of great effort, sacrifice etc: X достался Y-у ⟨Y добился X-а и т. п.⟩ дорогой ценой ≃ **Y paid dearly ⟨a high price, a heavy price⟩ for X; X came to Y at a great price ⟨at great cost⟩.**

Мы действительно многого не знали и не понимали, и знание далось нам дорогой ценой (Мандельштам 1). We really didn't know and understand many things—and we paid a heavy price for our ignorance (1a). ♦ …Никто не отнимет у меня права иметь своё собственное мнение о так называемой «эпохе сталинизма». Слишком дорогой ценой оно мне досталось, с трудом и с болью приобреталось… (Аллилуева 2). …No one can take away from me the right to have my own opinion of the so-called "Epoch of Stalinism." It had come to me at too great a price, had been reached through hardship and pain… (2a).

Ц-29 • ЛЮБО́Й ЦЕНО́Й [NP$_{instrum}$; Invar; adv; fixed WO] by any means available, regardless of the time, effort, risk etc involved: **at any cost ⟨price⟩; at all costs; at whatever (the) cost; no matter (what) the cost; no matter what the sacrifice.**

«Надо открыть любой ценой замок», – говорил Ершов (Кузнецов 1). "We have to get that lock open at any cost," said Yershov (1a). ♦ «Задержите противника сами любой ценой. Резервов у меня нет», – сказал Родимцев (Гроссман 2). "You must stop the enemy yourselves, at whatever the cost," said Rodimtsev. "There are no reserves" (2a). ♦ «Я ничего не ищу. Спасти Россию… спасти во что бы то ни стало, любой ценой!» (Шолохов 3). "I seek nothing for myself. We must save Russia—at all costs, no matter what the sacrifice!" (3a).

Ц-30 • ЦЕНТР ТЯ́ЖЕСТИ *(чего)* [NP; sing only; fixed WO] the most essential, important part (of sth.): **the main ⟨chief, focal⟩ point; the focus; the essence; the sum and substance.**

Ц-31 • ЗНАТЬ СЕБЕ́ ЦЕ́НУ *coll* [VP; subj: human; pres or past] to evaluate accurately and appreciate fully one's own abilities, merits etc: **X знает себе цену ≃ X knows his own worth.**

«Баб-то, конечно, по военному времю [*ungrammat* = времени] много свободных, – размышлял счетовод, – да такую, как Зинаида, днём с огнём не найдёшь. А ежели и найдёшь, так та, которая себе цену знает, нешто пойдёт за мужика, у которого пять детей и одна рука» (Войнович 4). Of course, there's lots of women around during wartime, reflected the bookkeeper, but ones like Zinaida are scarce as hen's teeth. And if you do find one like her, she'll know her own worth and wouldn't be likely to marry a man with five children and one arm (4a).

Ц-32 • ЗНАТЬ ⟨less often **УЗНАВА́ТЬ/УЗНА́ТЬ**⟩ **ЦЕ́НУ** *кому-чему* [VP; subj: usu. human] to assess correctly the value of s.o. or sth. (occas. refers to a negative evaluation): X знает цену Y-у ≃ **X knows Y's worth ⟨the worth of Y⟩; X knows what Y is (really) worth; X knows the (true) value of Y;** [in refer. to a negative evaluation only] **X knows Y for what Y is.**

Чем вызван был такой успех? Ведь цену своим рассказам я знаю. Не такие уж они замечательные (Довлатов 1). What was the reason for my success? After all, I knew the true value of my stories. They weren't all *that* remarkable (1a). ♦ И хотя мать не верила Иосифу, знала ему цену, но доверилась дедушке: другого выхода не было (Рыбаков 1). Mother didn't trust Yosif, she knew him for what he was, but she did trust grandfather, and there was no other way out (1a).

Ц-33 • ЗНАТЬ ЦЕ́НУ ДЕНЬГА́М ⟨КОПЕ́ЙКЕ *coll*⟩ [VP; subj: human] to be thrifty, economical (usu. after having experienced need): X знает цену деньгам ≃ **X knows the value of money ⟨of a ruble, of a dollar⟩.**

Рано лишившись родителей, Антон работал по двенадцать часов в сутки, чтобы прокормить себя и сестрёнку, и хорошо знал цену деньгам. Anton lost his parents at a young age and worked twelve hours a day to feed himself and his little sister. He really knew the value of money.

Ц-34 • НАБИВА́ТЬ/НАБИ́ТЬ СЕБЕ́ ЦЕ́НУ *coll* [VP; subj: human; usu. pres or past] to (try to) better s.o.'s opinion of o.s., make o.s. look more important to others (usu. in order to achieve a certain status, obtain sth. etc): X набивает себе цену ≃ **X is building himself up (in s.o.'s eyes); X is trying to enhance his own value ⟨image⟩; X is trying to convince s.o. of how invaluable ⟨indispensable etc⟩ X is; X is trying to make s.o. appreciate X (more).**

Рассказывая новому начальнику, как неохотно её отпускали с предыдущего места работы, она надеялась набить себе цену. By telling her new boss stories about how they hated to see her leave her old job, she hoped to build herself up in his eyes.

Ц-35 • НАБИВА́ТЬ/НАБИ́ТЬ ЦЕ́НУ *на что coll* [VP; subj: usu. human] to raise the price of some merchandise: X набивает цену на Y ≃ **X jacks ⟨hikes⟩ up the price of Y.**

«Легко жить Ракитину: „Ты, – говорит он мне сегодня, – о расширении гражданских прав человека хлопочи лучше али хоть о том, чтобы цена на говядину не возвысилась…" Я ему на это и отмочил: „А ты, говорю, без бога-то, сам ещё на говядину цену набьёшь… и накопотишь рубль на копейку"» (Достоевский 2). "Life is simple for Rakitin: 'You'd do better to worry about extending man's civil rights,' he told me today, 'or at least about not letting the price of beef go up….' But I came back at him: 'And without God,' I said, 'you'll hike up the price of beef yourself…and make a rouble on every kopeck'" (2a).

Ц-36 • ЦЕНЫ́ НЕТ *кому-чему* [VP; impers] s.o. or sth. possesses such admirable or remarkable qualities that his or its worth cannot be overestimated: X-у цены нет ≃ **X is invaluable ⟨priceless⟩; X is worth his ⟨its etc⟩ weight in gold; X is beyond price.**

«…Последняя возможность мне бросить [агрономические] курсы – сейчас, в августе, пока год только один потерян… На что мне эта агрономия?..» – «…[Отец] никогда не простит. И вообще – говоришь вздор. Тебе полный расчёт, единственный резон кончать именно агрономические курсы. Тебе цены не будет здесь» (Солженицын 1). "This is my last chance to give up my studies…right now, this August, while I've only wasted one year…. What do I want with agricultural science?…"…"He [Father] would never forgive you. Anyway, you're talking nonsense. There's every reason for you to finish your agronomy course, it's the only sensible thing you can do. You'd be invaluable around here" (1a). ♦ Буффоны в масках охрипшими в гвалте голосами клялись, что нет на свете такой болезни, при которой не помог бы волшебный орвьетан… «Позвольте мне коробочку орвьетана, – говорит некий соблазнившийся Сганарель, – сколько она стоит?» – «Сударь, – отвечает шарлатан, – орвьетан – такая вещь, что ей цены нету!» (Булгаков 5). Masked buffoons swear in voices gone hoarse with shouting that there is no sickness in the world that cannot be cured by magical orviétan [a nostrum]…."Let me have some orviétan," says a certain Sganarelle, tempted by the extravagant promises. "How much is it?" "Sir," replies the charlatan, "orviétan is priceless!" (5a). ♦ «…Ей [газете] бы цены не было, если б её без закорючек выпускали» (Искандер 5). "It'd [the newspaper would] be worth its weight in gold if they'd issue it without all these crooked little lines" (5a).

Ц-37 • **КАК ⟨БУ́ДТО, СЛО́ВНО, ТО́ЧНО⟩ С ЦЕПИ́ ⟨С ПРИ́ВЯЗИ⟩ СОРВА́ТЬСЯ** *coll, often disapprov* [VP; subj: human; past or Verbal Adv; fixed WO] **1.** [usu. after вбежал, помчался etc] one ran in, raced, took off etc headlong: X вбежал ⟨помчался и т. п.⟩ как с цепи сорвался ≃ **X ran in ⟨took off etc⟩ like one possessed; X took off** etc **like a wild animal ⟨like a bat out of hell⟩.**

2. one acts, behaves etc irrationally, in an extreme, uncontrolled, wild manner: X как с цепи сорвался ≃ **X acted ⟨was⟩ like a mad dog on the loose ⟨a mad dog broke loose⟩; X acted like one possessed; X acted like a wild man ⟨woman⟩.**

[Кудряш:] Ну, да та [Кабаниха] хоть, по крайности, всё под видом благочестия, а этот [Дикой] как с цепи сорвался! (Островский 6). [K.:] At least she [Kabanova] serves her words up with a sauce of piety, but Dikoy—he's like a mad dog broke loose (6b). ♦ Словно сорвавшись с цепи, КГБ больше ни перед чем не останавливался (Буковский 1). [context transl] Now, as if let off the leash, the KGB stopped at nothing (1a).

Ц-38 • **КИТА́ЙСКИЕ ЦЕРЕМО́НИИ** *usu. humor or iron* [NP; pl only; fixed WO] an excessive display of politeness or formality: **standing on ceremony.**

Тебе понравятся Мария Семёновна и её муж: они люди простые и китайских церемоний не любят. You'll like Marya Semyonovna and her husband: they're regular people who don't like standing on ceremony.

Ц-39 • **НА ЦУГУ́НДЕР брать, тянуть** *кого obs, now humor* [PrepP; Invar; adv] (to take s.o. away) for severe punishment (often putting him in jail): X-а тянут на цугундер ≃ **X is being hauled off ⟨taken away⟩; they're hauling X off ⟨taking X away⟩; X is being tossed in the clink ⟨the slammer, the hoosegow etc⟩.**

«Пролетарский поэт — и восхищался стихами контрика? И никто не донёс? И никого из вас не взяли, как говорится, „на цугундер"?» (Копелев 1). "A proletarian poet enjoying the poetry of a 'contra'? And no one denounced him? And none of you was taken away?" (1a). ♦ «Если у тебя ещё хоть один только раз в твоём благородном доме произойдёт скандал, так я тебя самоё на цугундер, как в высоком слоге говорится» (Достоевский 3). "If a scandal takes place in your respectable house just once more, then I will personally, as they say in high society, toss you in the clink" (3b).

< From the German *zu Hundert* (?), of uncertain derivation. It may mean "to arrest."

Ц-40 • **ЦЫПЛЯ́Т ПО О́СЕНИ СЧИТА́ЮТ** [saying] one should not rejoice until the outcome of sth. is clear (said when s.o. is confident that an endeavor will turn out successfully when it is still too early to be sure): ≃ **don't count your chickens before they're hatched.**

Ц-41 • **НА ЦЫ́ПОЧКАХ ходить, стоять; НА ЦЫ́ПОЧКИ стать, подняться и т. п.** [PrepP; these forms only; adv] (to walk, stand etc) on one's toes: **(walk ⟨stand, get etc⟩) on tiptoe; (stand etc) on one's tiptoes; tiptoe.**

Взобравшись на третий этаж, Княжицкий отпер своим ключом дверь, бесшумно притворил её и на цыпочках двинулся по коридорчику (Аржак 3). Knyazhitsky got up to the third floor, unlocked the door, closed it silently and crept along the passage on tiptoe (3a). ♦ В начале пятого часа Захар осторожно, без шума, отпер переднюю и на цыпочках пробрался в свою комнату... (Гончаров 1). Shortly after four o'clock Zakhar cautiously and noiselessly opened the front door and tiptoed to his room (1b).

Ц-42 • **ХОДИ́ТЬ НА ЦЫ́ПОЧКАХ** *перед кем coll* [VP; subj: human] to behave cautiously, deferentially, obediently in dealing with s.o. so as not to anger, displease, or fall out of favor with him: X ходит на цыпочках перед Y-ом ≃ **X walks on tiptoe ⟨tippytoe⟩ in Y's presence ⟨before Y, in front of Y⟩.**

«Неужто наши старцы так и не велят Хабугу изгнать его?» — «Наши старцы перед Хабугом на цыпочках ходят!» (Искандер 5). "I can't believe our elders won't order old Khabug to banish him!" "Our elders walk on tippytoe in front of old Khabug" (5a).

Ч

Ч-1 • В ЧАДУ́ [PrepP; Invar] **1.** Also: **КАК ⟨КАК БУ́ДТО⟩ В ЧАДУ́** [adv or subj-compl with быть∅ (subj: human)] (to do sth., be) in a state of mental confusion or emotional turmoil: **(as if) in a fog ⟨a trance⟩; dazed; in a daze.**

Теперь-то мне понятны мои дружбы, это только две, наиболее запомнившиеся, были и другие, но много лет я жил как в чаду, и только моя трагедия вдруг открыла мне глаза, я смог посмотреть на свою жизнь с неожиданной точки зрения (Лимонов 1). My friendships are intelligible to me now. Those were but two, the most memorable; there were others, but for many years I lived as if in a fog, and only when my tragedy opened my eyes did I suddenly see my life from a new perspective (1a). ♦ «Говорю тебе, [Григорий] живой и здоровый, морду наел во какую!»… Аксинья слушала, как в чаду… Она опомнилась только у мелеховской калитки (Шолохов 5). "I tell you he's [Grigory is] safe and sound, and real fat in the face!"…Aksinya listened as if in a trance. She came to herself only at the Melekhovs' gate (5a). ♦ Я был в чаду… Я плохо соображал, что же будет дальше. Я рвался в Москву, но поезда ещё не ходили (Паустовский 1). I was dazed….I could not imagine what would happen next. I longed to be in Moscow. But no trains were running (1a).

2. ~ *чего*, often **увлечений, удовольствий, романов** и т. п. [the resulting PrepP is adv] being completely absorbed by sth. (often passions, pleasures, love affairs etc): **in the whirl ⟨swirl⟩ of sth.; being caught up in sth.;** [in limited contexts] **amid the hurly-burly of sth.; in the hustle and bustle of sth.**

Жизнь его [Пьера] между тем шла по-прежнему, с теми же увлечениями и распущенностью… В чаду своих занятий Пьер, однако, по прошествии года начал чувствовать, как та почва масонства, на которой он стоял, тем более уходила из-под его ног, чем твёрже он старался стать на ней (Толстой 5). Meanwhile his [Pierre's] life continued as before, with the same passions and dissipations….Amid the hurly-burly of his activities, however, before the year was out Pierre began to feel as though the more firmly he tried to rest upon the ground of Freemasonry on which he had taken his stand, the more it was giving way under him (5a).

Ч-2 • ГОНЯ́ТЬ ЧАЙ *(с кем) highly coll, often humor* [VP; subj: human, often pl] to drink tea in an unhurried manner and with great enjoyment, pleasurably occupy o.s. with drinking tea (usu. for an extended period of time and consuming great quantities): Х-ы чаи гоняют ≃ **Xs sit (around) drinking tea; Xs spend their time drinking tea.**

Ч-3 • НА ЧАЙ¹ давать *кому*, **брать, получать, просить** и т. п. *coll;* **НА ЧАЁК** *obs, coll, humor* [PrepP; these forms only; obj] (to give s.o., take, receive, ask for etc) a small monetary reward for a minor service: X дал Y-у ⟨Y получил⟩ ~ ≃ **X gave Y ⟨Y received⟩ a tip ⟨tips⟩; X gave Y ⟨Y received⟩ a ruble ⟨two rubles etc⟩ as ⟨for⟩ a tip; X tipped Y.**

Носильщики, но не те, которых мы сначала подрядили, а какие-то новые, подхватили багаж. Мне… сказали, что я могу ни о чём не беспокоиться: всё будет доставлено прямо в вагон. И я заметила, что первые носильщики даже не подошли ко мне поклянчить на чай, а просто испарились… (Мандельштам 1). Some porters—not the ones we had hired, but some new ones—picked up my luggage. They told me I needn't worry and that everything would be taken right through to the train. I noticed that the first ones didn't come up to beg for tips, but just vanished (1a). ♦ Ящик был такой тяжёлый, что почтальон с трудом внёс его в комнату и потребовал рубль «на чай» (Чуковская 1). The crate was so heavy that the mailman had a hard time bringing it into the room, and demanded a ruble as a tip (1a). ♦ «Расчёт, Андрей, принимай! Вот тебе пятнадцать рублей за тройку, а вот пятьдесят на водку…

за готовность, за любовь твою…» – «Боюсь я, барин… – заколебался Андрей, – пять рублей на чай пожалуйте, а больше не приму» (Достоевский 1). "Your pay, Andrei, take it! Fifteen roubles for the troika, and fifty for vodka…for your willingness, your love…" "I'm afraid, your honor…," Andrei hesitated. "Give me five roubles for a tip, if you like, but I won't take more" (1a). ♦ Когда почтальонша приносит мне денежный перевод и мне приходится заполнять бланк, я всегда вынужден у неё спрашивать, какое у нас число и какой год. Иногда бывает неудобно. Правда, я всегда даю им на чай, и почтальонши обычно радостно отвечают на мой вопрос (Искандер 4). When the postwoman brings me a money order and I have to fill out the form, I'm always forced to ask her what day of the month it is and what year. Sometimes it's awkward. Granted, I always tip them, and they're usually glad to answer my question (4a).

Ч-4 • НА ЧАЙ² приглашать, звать *кого (к кому)* и т. п.; **НА ЧА́ШКУ ЧА́Я ⟨-ю⟩** [PrepP; these forms only; adv] (to invite s.o. over) to partake of tea (and refreshments): **(invite s.o.) to tea; (invite s.o. over ⟨(a)round etc⟩) for (a cup of) tea.**

…Губернатор сделал ему приглашение пожаловать к нему того же дня на домашнюю вечеринку, прочие чиновники тоже, с своей стороны, кто на обед, кто на бостончик, кто на чашку чаю (Гоголь 3). …The governor invited him that same evening to a party and the other civil servants, for their part, also invited him, one to dinner, another to a game of boston, and a third to tea (3a). ♦ В этот день он пригласил к себе своего фельдфебеля на чашку чая (Федин 1). That day he had invited his sergeant-major round for a cup of tea (1a).

Ч-5 • ЧАЙ ДА ⟨И⟩ СА́ХАР!; ЧАЙ С СА́ХАРОМ! *all obs, substand* [formula phrase; these forms only; fixed WO] a greeting expressing kind wishes to s.o. found drinking tea: **enjoying your tea, I hope!**

Ч-6 • АДМИРА́ЛЬСКИЙ ЧАС *obs, humor* [NP; sing only] noon, the time for a lunch break: **lunchtime.**

< Starting in 1865, the beginning of the lunch break in St. Petersburg was signaled at 12 noon by a shot fired from one of the admiralty cannons.

Ч-7 • БИ́ТЫЙ ЧАС *coll, disapprov* [NP; Invar; adv; usu. this WO] (for) a very long time, an hour or more (usu. said with frustration, vexation to express the opinion that an hour is a very long time to spend or waste on the matter in question): **(for) the longest time; (for) a whole ⟨good, solid⟩ hour.**

Знаешь, я битый час не мог взять в толк, что он мне говорит (Зиновьев 1). You know, for a whole hour I couldn't understand what he was getting at (1a). ♦ Рита сидела в своём любимом кресле под торшером, курила сигарету и только что отговорила с кем-то битый час по телефону (Трифонов 5). Rita was sitting smoking in her favorite armchair by the standing lamp after having just talked to someone on the phone for a solid hour (5a).

Ч-8 • В ДО́БРЫЙ ЧАС!; ЧАС ДО́БРЫЙ! *coll* [formula phrase; these forms only; usu. this WO (1st var.), fixed WO (2nd var.)] used to wish s.o. success, prosperity etc, usu. when he is about to begin some important undertaking or set out on a trip: **good luck (to you)!; the best of luck!; all the best (to you)!; I wish you luck!;** [as a wish for a successful trip only] **have a good ⟨safe, nice⟩ trip; have a safe ⟨good⟩ journey.**

«Ну, с богом. Час добрый», – проговорил старик, крестясь. Петро привычным движением вскинул в седло своё сбитое тело, поправил позади складки рубахи, стянутые пояском. Конь пошёл к воротам (Шолохов 2). "Well, God be with ye! Good luck," the old man said, making the sign of the cross. With habitual ease Petro swung his well-knit body into the saddle and straightened the back folds of his belted shirt. The horse walked to the gate (2a). ♦ «Венчайся себе, пожалуй, противузаконного ничего нет; но лучше бы было семейно да кротко... Ну, господь с вами, в добрый час...» (Герцен 1). "Get married if you like, there is nothing unlawful here; but it would be better to do it peacefully, with the consent of the family....Well, the Lord be with you! Good luck to you..." (1a). ♦ После завтрака Пантелей Прокофьевич собрался ехать, но тут пришёл хуторской атаман. «Сказал бы — в час добрый, да погоди, Пантелей Прокофич, не выезжай» (Шолохов 5). After breakfast Pantelei was about to set off for the fields again, but the village ataman appeared. "I was going to wish you a good journey, Pantelei Prokofievich, but wait a bit, don't go yet" (5a).

Ч-9 • В НЕДО́БРЫЙ ⟨НЕ В ДО́БРЫЙ⟩ ЧАС coll
[PrepP; these forms only; adv] (s.o. did sth., sth. happened) at an unfortunate time, a time foreboding trouble: **in an evil hour; on a black day; (it was) a black day.**

Право, плохой знак, если Мари забежит на чужой двор. Непременно после её появления в хозяйстве случится какая-нибудь беда: захворает лошадь, или сломается жнейка, или — по меньшей мере — прокиснет молоко... Не иначе как сидел в девчонке какой-то бес, и родилась она не в добрый час (Федин 1). It was truly a bad sign if Marie ever ran into someone else's yard. After her appearance some kind of trouble was sure to happen on that farm: a horse would fall sick, or a reaper would break, or—at the very least—the milk would go sour....It was as if nothing less than a demon had settled in the wench, and she had been born in an evil hour... (1a). ♦ [Калошин:] ...Не в добрый час я связался с гостиницей, не в добрый час (Вампилов 1). [K.:] ...It was a black day when I took on this hotel job, a black day (1a).

Ч-10 • В СВОЙ ЧАС
[PrepP; Invar; adv; fixed WO] at a suitable moment, at the appropriate time: **at the proper ⟨right⟩ moment; at the ⟨in its⟩ proper time; when the time is right; in due time;** [in refer. to death only] **(die) at the appointed hour; (die) a timely death;** [in limited contexts] **(die) when one's time comes;** ‖ Neg (умереть) не в свой час ≃ **(die) before one's time; (die) an untimely death.**

Всё ещё ночь... с трудом верится, что ничего не случится и в свой час придёт рассвет и наступит утро (Распутин 1). It was still night...it was hard to believe that dawn would come in its proper time and day would follow (1a). ♦ «Понимаешь, черви, вам всем полагаются, ты тоже с ними в свой час увидишься, но чтоб меня волки выкопали себе на харч, этого ж я не заслужил» (Владимов 1). "I don't mind about the worms, because worms get everybody in the end—they'll get you when your time comes—but I didn't deserve to be dug up and eaten by the wolves" (1a).

Ч-11 • ЗВЁЗДНЫЙ ЧАС (чей, кого) lit, occas. iron
[NP; sing only; fixed WO] the moment or period (in s.o.'s life, some field etc) when the greatest success or triumph is achieved, the greatest accomplishments are made etc: **shining ⟨finest, brightest⟩ hour; s.o.'s ⟨one's⟩ moment of glory.**

Никто, как я понял, не желает колоться [slang = признаваться] и брать дело на себя. Молчат, как вполне нормальные люди с развитым инстинктом самосохранения. Наконец кто-то, почуявший свой звёздный час, сказал: «Разрешите доложить?» (Алешковский 1). Nobody wanted to open his mouth and take the rap. They all keep their traps shut, like any normal guy with a well-developed instinct for self-preservation. Finally someone who felt his moment of glory had come said, "Permission to report" (1a).

Ч-12 • КОТО́РЫЙ ЧАС
[Invar; used as a question or subord clause; fixed WO] what the time of day is (usu. used when asking the time): который час? ≃ **what time is it?; what's the time?;** [in limited contexts] **do you have the time?**

[Лопахин:] Пришёл поезд, слава богу. Который час? [Дуняша:] Скоро два (Чехов 2). [L.:] The train is in, thank God. What time is it? [D.:] Nearly two (2a). ♦ Дважды уже мимо Пантелея прошли дружинники... Они беседовали увлечённо, но всякий раз, проходя мимо Пантелея, внимательно его оглядывали... «Который час, не скажете?» — спросил дружинник (Аксёнов 6). Twice already a group of vigilantes had walked past Pantelei....Although they were absorbed in their conversation, every time they passed Pantelei, they looked him over intently...."What's the time, please?" asked one of the vigilantes (6a).

Ч-13 • МЁРТВЫЙ ⟨ТИ́ХИЙ⟩ ЧАС
[NP; sing only] the time of rest, sleep after lunch in hospitals, sanatoriums, kindergartens etc: **rest ⟨nap⟩ time; quiet ⟨rest⟩ hour.**

Мандельштам откармливал меня молоком и виноградом и требовал, чтобы я лежала в мёртвый час, как велели врачи (Мандельштам 2). M[andelstam] made me drink milk and eat grapes, and insisted that I lie down during the rest hour prescribed by the doctors (2a).

Ч-14 • НЕ РОВЁН ЧАС old-fash, coll
[sent; Invar; often used as sent adv; fixed WO] **1.** (in refer. to an action, event etc specified or implied by the context) used to express fear that sth. unpleasant or dangerous may happen: **who knows; you never know; one never knows.**

«Пожалуйте только расписочку». — «Да на что ж вам расписка?» — «Всё, знаете, лучше расписочку. Не ровён час, всё может случиться» (Гоголь 3). "Please let me have a receipt." "What do you want a receipt for?" "It's always better to have a receipt. Who knows, anything might happen" (3a). ♦ ...Не ровён час — какой-нибудь офицер Петровского полка, находясь в столице, мог заглянуть на один из наших вечеров и, увидев меня на эстраде, сделать соответствующие «организационные» выводы, угрожавшие мне по меньшей мере годичным заключением в дисциплинарном батальоне (Лившиц 1). One never knows—some officer from the Petrovsky regiment who happened to be in the capital might drop in on one of our meetings; he would see me on the rostrum, make the appropriate "disciplinary" inferences and threaten me with at least a year's detention in the penal battalion (1a).

2. used to indicate that some unspecified dangerous, unpleasant etc thing may happen (often used as a conclusion after a warning): **you never know what might happen; all kinds of things could happen; something might ⟨could⟩ go wrong.**

Деньги надо хранить в банке: не ровён час. You should keep your money in the bank—you never know what might happen.

Ч-15 • СМЕ́РТНЫЙ ⟨ПОСЛЕ́ДНИЙ⟩ ЧАС (чей, кого)
[NP; sing only] **1.** the moment a person dies or the actual occurrence of a person's death: **the time ⟨the moment⟩ of one's ⟨s.o.'s⟩ death; one's ⟨s.o.'s⟩ time to die; the hour of death;** [in limited contexts] **death.**

«Наш бог... послал мне этого мальчика в утешение, чтобы было кому радовать меня на старости лет и было кому закрыть мне глаза в смертный час» (Искандер 5). "Our God...has sent me this little boy for consolation, so that I will have someone to gladden my old age and someone to close my eyes in the hour of death" (5a). ♦ Всего только один день остаётся жить ему [колдуну]... Может быть, он уже и кается перед смертным часом, только не такие грехи его, чтобы бог простил ему (Гоголь 5). He [the sorcerer] had but one day left to live....Perhaps he was already repenting on the eve of death; but his sins were not such as God would forgive (5a).

2. the relatively brief time preceding the actual point of a person's death: **(one's ⟨s.o.'s⟩) last hours (of life); (one's ⟨s.o.'s⟩) final ⟨dying⟩ hour(s).**

Бог мой, какую горькую чашу надо испить, чтобы и в свой последний час [говорить] об этом! Только об этом... (Свирский 1). My God, what a bitter cup it must be, to have to talk about that in one's last hours of life! Only of that... (1a).

Ч-16 • ЧАС В ЧАС *coll* [NP; Invar; adv] at the precise hour (expected, predicted, anticipated etc): **right ⟨precisely⟩ at the appointed ⟨expected etc⟩ time ⟨hour⟩; (predict ⟨prophesy etc⟩ sth.) (right) to the very hour;** [in limited contexts] **right on time.**

«...Я тебе рассказывала, кажется, как Кирюша день в день, час в час предсказал покойнику папеньке его кончину» (Толстой 2). "I believe I told you how Kiryusha prophesied the end of poor Papa, right to the very day and hour" (2b).

Ч-17 • ЧАС ОТ ЧАСУ ⟨ОТ ЧАСУ⟩ [NP; Invar; adv; used with impfv verbs] (in refer. to the gradual intensification or diminishing of sth.) continuously over the course of time: **by the hour ⟨the minute⟩; every hour ⟨minute⟩; with every ⟨each⟩ passing hour ⟨minute⟩; hour by hour.**

Между тем здоровье Андрея Гавриловича час от часу становилось хуже (Пушкин 1). In the meantime, Andrei Gavrilovich's condition worsened by the hour (1a). ♦ Ветер... час от часу становился сильнее (Пушкин 2). The wind...was becoming stronger by the minute (2a). The wind...was growing stronger every minute (2b). ♦ В этом беспорядочном переплетении трав и деревьев без оттенка и запаха таилась какая-то едва ощутимая угроза, от которой на душе час от часу становилось всё сиротливей и неуютнее (Максимов 1). In this disordered tangle of trees and grasses without odour or nuance there was some scarcely perceptible menace, which made his soul feel more orphaned and ill at ease with every passing minute (1a).

Ч-18 • ЧАС ОТ ЧАСУ НЕ ЛЕГЧЕ *coll* [sent with бытьø (usu. pres); fixed WO] the situation becomes worse with each new piece of information or each new development (used, usu. in a dialogue, to express annoyance when news is received of new trouble or new difficulties): **it gets ⟨is getting⟩ worse all the time; it gets ⟨is getting⟩ worse by the minute ⟨every minute⟩; it gets ⟨is getting⟩ worse and worse; things are going from bad to worse; it's one thing on top of another.**

Нюрок и тут взбеленилась: «...Неужели ты не видишь, что он давно умеет делать, чтобы за него всё делали?.. Он всегда кого-нибудь эксплуатирует — мать, отца, каких-то там приятелей, а прежде всего приятельниц!» Час от часу было не легче. Ирина Викторовна спросила: «Значит, ты меня окунаешь, милая? В действительность?» (Залыгин 1). Niurok lost her temper completely: "...Can't you see he knows how to arrange things so that other people do everything for him?...He's forever exploiting somebody—his mother, his father, his friends, but most of all his girlfriends." It was getting worse all the time. Irina Viktorovna asked, "Giving me a crash course in reality, are you, my dear?" (1a). ♦ [Маша:] Тебя исключают из университета... [Колесов:] Да он [ректор] что, озверел, что ли? [Маша:] Полегче. Эта девочка, между прочим, дочь [ректора] Владимира Алексеевича. [Колесов:] Вы — дочь? [Таня:] Что поделаешь. [Колесов:] Час от часу не легче... (Вампилов 3). [M.:] You're being expelled from the university.... [K.:] What happened, did he [the Provost] go wild, is that it? [M.:] Take it easy. This girl, by the way, is [the Provost] Vladimir Alekseyevich's daughter. [K.:] You're—his daughter? [T.:] What can I do... [K.:] It's getting worse every minute (3b). ♦ «Да как обвенчаться! — проговорил Пьер на слова Марьи Дмитриевны. — Он не мог обвенчаться: он женат». — «Час от часу не легче, —проговорила Марья Дмитриевна. — Хорош мальчик! То-то мерзавец! А она ждёт, второй день ждёт» (Толстой 5). "But how could there be a marriage?" exclaimed Pierre at Marya Dmitrievna's last words. "He couldn't marry her—he's already married!" "It gets worse and worse!" cried Marya Dmitrievna. "A fine fellow! He's certainly a scoundrel! And there she sits waiting—she's

been expecting him for two days" (5a). ♦ «Зачем же им этот ядовитый сок, — встревожился мой старик, — кого они собираются травить?» — «Нет, — успокоил его старый арап, — травить они никого не собираются — ни людей, ни скотину. Этот сок им нужен для аэропланов. Аэропланы без этого сока взлететь не могут, могут только ехать по земле, как машины» — «Час от часу не легче», — сказал мой старик (Искандер 3). "What do they want with this poisonous juice?" my old man asked anxiously. "Whom are they planning to poison?" "No," the old black soothed him, "they're not planning to poison anyone, neither men nor beasts. They need the juice for airplanes. Airplanes can't fly without it, they can only run along the ground like trucks." "Things are going from bad to worse," my old man said (3a).

Ч-19 • ЧАС ПРОБИЛ ⟨НАСТАЛ, ПРИШЁЛ⟩ *(чей, кого);* **УДАРИЛ ЧАС** [VP$_{subj}$] the time has arrived (for s.o. to do sth., for sth. important to happen etc): **(X-ов) час пробил ≃ X's hour ⟨turn, time⟩ has come; X's ⟨the⟩ hour has struck.**

«Дело вот в чём, — начал Иван, чувствуя, что настал его час, — меня в сумасшедшие вырядили, никто не желает меня слушать!..» (Булгаков 9). "The point is this," began Ivan, feeling that his hour had come. "They've rigged me out here as a madman, and no one wants to listen to me!..." (9a). ♦ «Вы обещали встать вместе со мной на спасение родины, когда я найду это нужным. Час пробил — родина накануне смерти!» (Шолохов 3). "You promised to join with me in saving the Motherland when I should find it necessary. That hour has struck—the Motherland is in peril!" (3a).

Ч-20 • ЧЕРЕЗ ⟨В⟩ ЧАС ПО ЧАЙНОЙ ЛОЖКЕ; ЧЕРЕЗ ⟨В⟩ ЧАС ПО (СТОЛОВОЙ) ЛОЖКЕ *all coll* [PrepP; these forms only; adv; used with impfv verbs; fixed WO] (to do sth.) very slowly or taking an excessively long time (usu. in refer. to an activity that can and should be done more quickly): **at a snail's pace; drag sth. out; in dribs and drabs.**

Он мог бы проверить библиографию за день, а он всё делает медленно — через час по чайной ложке, и кто его знает, когда закончит. He could have checked the bibliography in a day, but he is doing it slowly, in dribs and drabs, and who knows when it will be done.

Ч-21 • ЖДАТЬ ⟨ОЖИДАТЬ, ДОЖИДАТЬСЯ/ДОЖДАТЬСЯ⟩ СВОЕГО ЧАСА [VP; subj: human or, less common, abstr or concr] (of a person) to await the most suitable, opportune time to do sth.; (of a thing—an invention, idea etc) to be held in a state of readiness until a suitable, opportune moment comes: **X ждёт своего часа ≃ X is awaiting ⟨waiting for⟩ the proper ⟨right⟩ moment; X is waiting for the time to be right; person X is biding his time; ‖ X дождался своего часа ≃ this is what X has been waiting for.**

Всё это, незаконченное, сумбурное, грудами черновиков лежало в бесчисленных папках, ожидая своего часа (Трифонов 1). All of this unfinished muddle lay heaped in draft notebooks inside innumerable folders, awaiting the right moment for completion (1a). ♦ Они [работавшие в лагерях разжалованные работники МВД] пристроились... и ждали своего часа. Верили, что они с их опытом ещё пригодятся, что их ещё позовут. И дождались (Марченко 1). They [demoted MVD men working in the camps] settled in there and bided their time. They were confident that their experience would be needed again, that they would be recalled. And they were right (1a). ♦ «Дождались станишники [*phonetic spelling* = станичники] своего часа. И уж они, будьте покойны, они своё возьмут» (Максимов 3). "This is just what the Cossacks have been waiting for. They'll take their revenge, don't you worry" (3a).

Ч-22 • ПО ЧАСАМ [PrepP; Invar; adv]   **1.** in correspondence with a fixed time schedule: **according to schedule; according to a strict timetable; (right) on schedule ⟨on time⟩; by the clock.**

Она кормит ребёнка точно по часам. She feeds her baby according to a strict timetable. ♦ Что же бы делали Соня, граф и графиня… ежели бы не было этих пилюль по часам, питья тёпленького, куриной котлетки и всех подробностей жизни, предписанных доктором, соблюдать которые составляло занятие и утешение для окружающих? (Толстой 6). What would Sonya and the Count and Countess have done…had there not been those pills to administer by the clock, the warm drinks, the chicken patties, and all the rest of the regimen prescribed by the doctors, the carrying out of which kept them occupied and provided consolation? (6a).

2. obs [used with impfv verbs] (in refer. to a gradual intensification or diminishing of sth.) constantly over the course of time: **with every ⟨each⟩ passing hour; every hour; by the hour; hour by hour.**

Ч-23 • **НА ЧАСА́Х стоять, быть**∅ [PrepP; Invar; subj-compl with copula (subj: human)] to perform the duty of a guard, watch over sth.: X стоит на часах ≃ **X stands (on) guard; X keeps ⟨stands⟩ watch.**

…Один из юнкеров стоял на часах у двери, не спуская глаз с мотоциклетки у подъезда… (Булгаков 3). A cadet stood on guard at the door keeping constant watch on the motor-cycle and sidecar parked outside… (3a).

Ч-24 • **ПО МОЕ́Й ⟨твоей и т. п.⟩ ЧА́СТИ** coll [PrepP; these forms only; subj-compl with быть∅ (subj: usu. abstr or infin)] sth. pertains to my (your etc) area of expertise, interest, jurisdiction, involvement etc: X по Y-овой части ≃ **X is (in) Y's department; X is (right) in Y's line ⟨up Y's alley⟩; X is Y's specialty; ‖ Neg** X не по Y-овой части ≃ **X is outside Y's province; X is out of Y's line ⟨province⟩; X is off Y's beat.**

«Виктор, откупорьте бутылку; это по вашей части» (Тургенев 2). "Victor, uncork a bottle; that's your department" (2f). ♦ [Нелькин:] Как тебе колоколов не знать: это по твоей части (Сухово-Кобылин 2). [N.:] Who but you should know about bells? That's right in your line (2a). ♦ «Нигилист — это человек, который не склоняется ни перед какими авторитетами, который не принимает ни одного принципа на веру…» — «Ну, это, я вижу, не по нашей части» (Тургенев 2). "A nihilist is a man who does not bow to any authorities, who does not take any principle on trust…" "Well, I can see that this is outside our province" (2f).

Ч-25 • **ПО ЧА́СТИ** coll [PrepP; Invar] **1.** ~ чего, less often кого. Also: **В ЧА́СТИ** [Prep; the resulting PrepP is adv] concerning (sth.): **as regards; in ⟨with⟩ regard to; with respect to; as far as…goes; in the field ⟨area, realm⟩ of; when it comes to; apropos of; about.**

…По части музыкальных инструментов, надо прямо сказать, в Чегеме не густо… (Искандер 3). …As regards musical instruments, it must be plainly stated that Chegem did not have a great variety… (3a). ♦ «Все-то мы, все без исключения, по части науки, развития, мышления, изобретения, идеалов, желаний, либерализма, рассудка, опыта и всего, всего, всего, всего ещё в первом предуготовительном классе гимназии сидим!» (Достоевский 3). "With regard to science, development, thought, invention, ideals, aspirations, liberalism, reason, experience, and everything, everything, everything, we're all, without exception, still sitting in the first grade!" (3c). ♦ За такой стиль, конечно, надо убивать, но… я промямлил, что по части стиля у него всё в порядке, хотя есть некоторые шероховатости… (Войнович 6). For such writing a man should be shot. But…I mumbled that as far as style went, he was in good shape, though there were a few rough spots… (6a). ♦ [Суходолов:] Ты чистый жрец искусства. Виртуоз на скрипке, а также виртуоз по части женских сердец… (Погодин 1). [S.:] You're a pure priest of art. A virtuoso on the violin, and a virtuoso in the field of ladies' hearts… (1a). ♦ …Он [Турганов] проявил немалую изобретательность по части мелких махинаций (Войнович 3). …Turganov demonstrated no little inventiveness in the area of petty intrigues (3a). ♦ «Конечно, я не буду

врать, что у ней [жены] ко мне возражений совсем не имеется. Имеются, особенно вот… по части выпивки» (Распутин 3). "Of course I can't say she [my wife] hasn't no grounds for complaint. She has, specially when it comes to the booze…" (3a). ♦ Кемала лишили водительских прав чуть ли не на полгода… Однако он, будучи человеком крайне ленивым по части ходьбы, с таким наказанием никак не мог смириться (Искандер 5). They took Kemal's license away for nearly six months.…Being a man extremely lazy about walking, however, he couldn't possibly resign himself to such a punishment (5a). ♦ [Глаголев 1:] Мы, сказал он, поумнели по части женщин… (Чехов 1). [G. Sr.:] We've grown more intelligent about women, he said… (1a).

2. ~ какой (работать, служить, пойти и т. п.) [the resulting PrepP is adv] in some field of knowledge, interest, or in some sphere of activity: **in the area ⟨realm, sphere⟩ of; ‖** по торговой ⟨медицинской и т. п.⟩ части ≃ **in trade ⟨medicine etc⟩; ‖** по этой части ≃ **in these ⟨such⟩ matters; in this regard; in that department.**

…Дедушка Рахленко решил пустить его [Якоба] по торговой части (Рыбаков 1). …Grandfather Rakhlenko decided to get him [Jakob] going in trade (1a). ♦ «…Ваське быть бы по торговой части, как дедушка Тихон» (Войнович 6). "…Vaska Karetnikov should have been in business, like his Grandpa Tikhon" (6a). ♦ Избран был комитет из самых опытных по этой части обывателей… (Салтыков-Щедрин 2). A committee of citizens who were most expert in such matters was chosen… (2a). ♦ [Мелузов:] Не о платье же мы будем говорить, это не мой предмет; по этой части я в преподаватели не гожусь (Островский 11). [M.:] We're not going to talk about clothes, that's not my subject: I'm not suited to instruct in that department (11a).

Ч-26 • **РАЗРЫВА́ТЬСЯ ⟨РВА́ТЬСЯ⟩ НА ЧА́СТИ** coll [VP; subj: human] to try frantically to do many things at the same time: X разрывается на части ≃ **X is going in ten different directions ⟨trying to do ten (different) things etc⟩ at the same time; X is running around like a madman ⟨a madwoman⟩.**

У меня столько дел, что я просто разрываюсь на части. I've got so much to do that I'm running around like a madwoman.

Ч-27 • **РВАТЬ ⟨РАЗРЫВА́ТЬ⟩ НА ЧА́СТИ** кого coll [VP; subj: human, pl, usu. omitted; usu. 3rd pers pl with indef. refer.] (in refer. to many people's simultaneous demands of s.o., invitations to s.o. etc) to besiege s.o. with requests, invitations etc, ask that s.o. provide services to many people at the same time etc: X-а рвут на части ≃ **X is being pulled in a thousand ⟨a dozen etc⟩ different directions; they want X to be in five ⟨ten etc⟩ places at the same time; everyone and his brother is making demands on X's time; X is overwhelmed by requests for his services ⟨demands for his services, invitations etc⟩.**

Когда он изредка приезжал в родной город, друзья разрывали его на части, наперебой приглашая в гости. When he would return to his hometown for an occasional visit, his friends would pull him in a dozen different directions, all vying for the opportunity to entertain him in their homes. ♦ В нашем городке всего два зубных врача, их просто рвут на части. There are only two dentists in our town, and they're overwhelmed by demands for their services.

Ч-28 • **В ЧА́СТНОСТИ** [PrepP; Invar; sent adv (often parenth)] used to single out and emphasize a specific case, example etc: **in particular; particularly; specifically; especially.**

«Как только полк отзовут, мы строго покараем всех нарушителей дисциплины, и в частности тех красноармейцев, которые говорили сообщённое вами сейчас… Надо принять срочные меры по локализации этой опасности. Прошу вас держать в секрете наш разговор» (Шолохов 4). "As soon as the regiment is taken out of line we'll crack down on all infringers of discipline and particularly those who said what you've just reported....Urgent measures must be taken to localise this danger. Please keep our conversation secret" (4a).

Ч-29 • ИЗБИРА́ТЬ/ИЗБРА́ТЬ БЛАГУ́Ю ЧАСТЬ *obs, lit*
[VP; subj: human] (usu. said sarcastically of a person who chooses the safest, most convenient etc option) to choose the best alternative: X избрал благую часть ≃ **X chose the better part.**

...Я сказал ему, что мне ужасно нравится его морская жизнь, что он из всех эмигрантов избрал благую часть (Герцен 2). ...I told him how immensely I liked his seafaring life, and that of all the exiles he was the one who had chosen the better part (2a).

< From the Biblical account of Christ's visit to Mary and Martha's home. While Martha was busy serving, Mary chose "that good part" and listened to Christ's words (Luke 10:38–42).

Ч-30 • БО́ЛЬШЕЙ ЧА́СТЬЮ; ПО БО́ЛЬШЕЙ ЧА́СТИ
[NP$_{instrum}$ or PrepP; these forms only; adv or sent adv (often parenth)] **1.** (for) the greatest part, predominantly: **for the most part; mostly; [in limited contexts] in most respects; the majority (of); the greater part of.**

Внуку гораздо больше тех трагедий, в которых выступал Бельроз, нравились бургонские фарсы, грубые и лёгкие фарсы, заимствованные большею частью у итальянцев и нашедшие в Париже прекрасных исполнителей... (Булгаков 5). The grandson...preferred the farces to the tragedies enacted by Bellerose. These crude and light farces, borrowed for the most part from the Italians, had found in Paris most excellent performers... (5a). ♦ Крепости выстроены были в местах, признанных удобными, заселены по большей части казаками... (Пушкин 2). Forts were built in convenient locations and settled mostly by Cossacks... (2a). ♦ ...История показывает нам, что ни Людовики XI-е, ни Меттернихи, управлявшие миллионами людей, не имели никаких особенных свойств силы душевной, а, напротив, были по большей части нравственно слабее каждого из миллионов людей, которыми они управляли (Толстой 7). ...History shows us that neither a Louis XI nor a Metternich, who ruled over millions of men, had any particular moral qualities, but on the contrary, that they were in most respects morally weaker than any of the millions they governed (7a). ♦ Солдаты с винтовками, в грязных обмотках и разбухших бутсах сидели... на мокром полу. Большей частью это были солдаты-фронтовики, застрявшие в Москве после Брестского мира (Паустовский 1). The soldiers, in dirty foot rags and sodden boots, their rifles beside them, sat on the muddy floor. The majority were men from the front, stranded in Moscow since the conclusion of the Treaty of Brest-Litovsk (1a).

2. most often, usually: **more often than not; most of the time; as a rule; generally; by and large; [in limited contexts] (spend) most of one's time.**

...Он по большей части к обеду был несколько навеселе (Герцен 1). ...More often than not he was somewhat tipsy by dinnertime (1a). ♦ ...Все две недели, как жил болезненный мальчик, [Григорий] почти не глядел на него, даже замечать не хотел и большей частью уходил из избы (Достоевский 1). ...For the two weeks that the sickly boy lived, he [Grigory] scarcely ever looked at him, did not even want to notice him, and kept away from the house most of the time (1a). ♦ Между собеседниками по большей части царствует глубокое молчание: все видятся ежедневно друг с другом; умственные сокровища взаимно исчерпаны и изведаны, а новостей извне получается мало (Гончаров 1). As a rule, deep silence reigned among them: they saw each other every day, and had long ago explored and exhausted all their intellectual treasures, and there was little news from the outside world (1a). ♦ Он [Кутузов] днём часто неожиданно задрёмывал; но ночью он, лёжа нераздетый на своей постели, большею частью не спал и думал (Толстой 7). He [Kutuzov] often fell asleep unexpectedly in the day-time, but at night, lying on his bed without undressing, he generally remained awake thinking (7b). ♦ Пастернак большей частью жил в Переделкине, где я бывал редко (Гладков 1).

...Pasternak spent most of his time in Peredelkino, which I visited only rarely (1a).

Ч-31 • С ЧА́СУ НА ЧАС
[PrepP; Invar; adv] **1.** (of sth. that is expected, awaited) (sth. will happen) very soon: **any time now; any moment ⟨minute⟩ (now); at any moment (now).**

«С часу на час жду, что [Миколка] придёт от показания отказываться» (Достоевский 3). "I'm expecting him [Mikolka] to come any time now and deny his evidence" (3c). ♦ Он был в отлучке, но Обломов ждал его с часу на час (Гончаров 1). He was away, but Oblomov was expecting him back any moment (1a). ♦ Семён ждал, что с часу на час приедет отец парня – Михайло (Тендряков 1). Simon expected the boy's father, Mikhailo Lyskov, to arrive any minute (1a). ♦ С часу на час должно было и нам ожидать нападения Пугачёва (Пушкин 2). We could expect Pugachev's attack at any moment (2a). ♦ «Ваших, то есть мамашу и сестрицу, жду с часу на час... Приискал им на первый случай квартиру...» (Достоевский 3). "I'm expecting your people, that is your mama and sister, at any moment now... I've found them rooms for the time being—" (3a).

2. continuously over the course of time: **with each ⟨every⟩ passing hour; by the hour; hour by hour.**

Вода продолжала подниматься, и ситуация с часу на час становилась всё более угрожающей. The water continued to rise, and the situation became more and more threatening with each passing hour.

Ч-32 • КАК ЧАСЫ́ работать, действовать *coll* [как + NP; Invar; adv; more often used with impfv verbs] (to work, run, go) smoothly, with precision: **like clockwork; [of a motor, a car etc] (sth.) purrs like a kitten.**

Мотор работает как часы. The engine is purring like a kitten.

Ч-33 • ЧАСЫ́ ⟨ЧАС⟩ ПИК [NP; fixed WO] the busiest time(s) of day (for transport, when traffic is heaviest or the crowds are the greatest, or at the workplace, when the workload is heaviest or the level of activity is the greatest): **busiest time(s) of (the) day; peak (hour ⟨hours⟩); [in refer. to transport only] rush hour; [in refer. to the workplace only] most hectic ⟨most frantic, craziest etc⟩ time(s) of (the) day.**

Ч-34 • МИНОВА́ЛА (Э́ТА ⟨СИЯ́⟩) ЧА́ША кого *lit*
[VP$_{subj}$] s.o. has been spared some ordeal, misfortune: X-а миновала эта чаша ≃ **this cup has passed from X.**

Уже собравшись и купив билет, она [Ахматова] задумалась, стоя у окна. «Молитесь, чтобы вас миновала эта чаша?» – спросил Пунин, умный, жёлчный и блестящий человек (Мандельштам 1). When she [Akhmatova] had packed and bought her ticket, her brilliant, irritable husband Punin asked her, as she stood in thought by a window: "Are you praying that this cup should pass from you?" (1a).

< From the Bible (Matt. 26:39).

Ч-35 • ПО́ЛНАЯ ЧА́ША [NP; sing only; subj-compl with бытьø (subj: usu. дом); fixed WO] s.o. has (in s.o.'s house there is) an abundance of everything: **(a house) of plenty; (live) in plenty; (have) plenty of everything (in the house).**

И дом его полная чаша, и гостей, бывало, полон двор, так что жена его и пять дочерей едва успевали их обслуживать (Искандер 3). His was a house of plenty, and guests used to fill the yard, so that his wife and five daughters could hardly take care of them (3a). ♦ [Матрёна:] Дом, слава богу, полная чаша (Толстой 1). [M.:] They live in plenty, thank God (1a). ♦ «Пока она у нас жила, дом был полная чаша» (Пастернак 1). "We had plenty of everything in the house as long as she was living with us" (1a).

Ч-36 • ЧА́ША чья ПЕРЕПО́ЛНИЛАСЬ; ЧА́ША ⟨МЕ́РА⟩ чьего ТЕРПЕ́НИЯ ПЕРЕПО́ЛНИЛАСЬ *all*

lit [VP$_{subj}$; the verb may take the initial position, otherwise fixed WO] s.o. cannot tolerate sth. any longer: X-ова чаша переполнилась ≃ **X's patience ran out ⟨was exhausted, reached its limit⟩; thing Y brought X to the limit of X's endurance; thing Y was more than X could bear.**

Когда доставку мебели отложили в третий раз, чаша моего терпения переполнилась и я отказалась от покупки. When they put off delivering the furniture for the third time, my patience ran out and I canceled my order. ♦ [author's usage] И даже если Лёвина чаша переполнялась от такого глумления, он лишь срывался, как правило, на глупую и позорную грубость... (Битов 2). Even if such desecration brought Lyova to the limit of his endurance, as a rule he merely descended to foolish and ignominious rudeness... (2a).

Ч-37 • БРОСА́ТЬ/БРО́СИТЬ ⟨КЛАСТЬ/ПОЛОЖИ́ТЬ⟩ НА ЧА́ШУ ⟨ЧА́ШКУ⟩ ВЕСО́В *что lit* [VP; subj: human] (often in refer. to one's professional reputation, authority, the prestige of one's firm etc) to use sth. in the hope of gaining the advantage or a victory in some matter or area: X бросил на чашу весов Y ≃ **X used Y in an attempt to tip ⟨tilt⟩ the scale(s) in his favor; X used Y in an attempt to turn the tide in his favor.**

Ч-38 • ПЕРЕПОЛНЯ́ТЬ/ПЕРЕПО́ЛНИТЬ ЧА́ШУ (*чьего* ТЕРПЕ́НИЯ) *lit* [VP; subj: abstr; usu. pfv; fixed WO] to drive s.o. to the limit of his patience, forbearance: X переполнил чашу Y-ва терпения ≃ **X brought Y to the limit of Y's endurance; X was more than Y could bear; X exhausted Y's patience;** [in limited contexts] **X was the last straw ⟨the straw that broke the camel's back⟩.**

Больше я выручать тебя не буду. Твоя последняя выходка переполнила чашу моего терпения. I'm not going to bail you out anymore. Your last stunt was the straw that broke the camel's back.

Ч-39 • ПИТЬ/ИСПИ́ТЬ ⟨ВЫ́ПИТЬ, ДОПИ́ТЬ⟩ (ГО́РЬКУЮ) ЧА́ШУ (ДО ДНА); ПИТЬ/ИСПИ́ТЬ ⟨ВЫ́ПИТЬ⟩ (ДО ДНА) ГО́РЬКУЮ ⟨ПО́ЛНУЮ⟩ ЧА́ШУ *чего all elev* [VP; subj: human; usu. pfv] to endure the full pain and suffering associated with some adverse situation, misfortune etc, suffer a great deal: X испил горькую чашу до дна ≃ **X drained ⟨drank⟩ the cup (of misery ⟨grief etc⟩) to the dregs; X drained ⟨drank⟩ the bitter cup; X drank this ⟨that⟩ cup (to the dregs).**

«Ты уезжаешь?» Виар смутился: «Да. То есть лично я остаюсь. Я выпью чашу до дна. Но я отправляю картины. Я не вправе рисковать моей коллекцией!» (Эренбург 4). "Are you going away?" he asked. Villard looked embarrassed. "Yes," he said. "That is, personally I'm remaining. I'm going to drain the cup to the dregs. But I'm sending my pictures away. I've got no right to risk my collection" (4a). ♦ «...Провидению угодно было потемнить мой рассудок, вероятно, для того, чтобы не помешать мне испить до дна чашу уготованных мне истязаний...» (Салтыков-Щедрин 2). "...It was the will of Providence to deprive me of my sense with the aim, I suppose, of letting me drain to the dregs the cup of horrors prepared for me..." (2a). ♦ ...Куда идти, какой стороны держаться, ей [Настёне] открылось. Для Настёны это значило не трепыхаться, смириться с тем, что есть, и не перечить судьбе. Что будет, то пускай и будет. Она ещё не прибилась окончательно к этому решению, но уже понимала, что никуда ей от него не деться. Видно, придётся испить свою горькую чашу до дна. Отступать поздно (Распутин 2). ...At least she [Nastyona] knew where to go and which side to stay on. For Nastyona this meant not fretting, resigning herself to what was, and not arguing with her fate. What would be, well, let it be. She wasn't yet cornered into her decision, but she understood that there was no avoiding it. It looked as if she'd have to drain the bitter cup. It was too late to retreat (2a). ♦ Он остановился на мгновение, чтобы пере-

вести дух, чтоб оправиться, чтобы войти *человеком*. «А для чего? зачем? — подумал он вдруг, осмыслив своё движение. — Если уж надо выпить эту чашу, то не всё ли уж равно? Чем гаже, тем лучше» (Достоевский 3). He stopped for a moment to catch his breath, to straighten up and go in *like a man*. But he thought suddenly, reflecting on this impulse of his: "What for? Why? If I must drink this cup, does it make any difference? The fouler the better!" (3a).

< From the Bible (Isa. 51:17).

Ч-40 • ПА́ЧЕ ЧА́ЯНИЯ *lit;* СВЕРХ ⟨ПРОТИВ⟩ ВСЯ́КОГО ЧА́ЯНИЯ *obs, lit* [AdvP or PrepP; these forms only; sent adv (parenth); fixed WO] in opposition to or exceeding what is or would be expected: **contrary to (all) expectation(s); against all (one's) expectations;** [in limited contexts] **by any chance.**

Секретарь [суда] повторил ему своё приглашение подписать своё полное и совершенное удовольствие или явное неудовольствие, если паче чаяния чувствует по совести, что дело его есть правое... (Пушкин 1). The [court] secretary repeated his invitation: to subscribe his full and complete satisfaction or his manifest dissatisfaction, if, contrary to expectations, he truly felt his own case was just... (1b). ♦ Матушка была ещё мною брюхата, как уже я был записан в Семёновский полк сержантом... Если бы паче всякого чаяния матушка родила дочь, то батюшка объявил бы куда следовало о смерти неявившегося сержанта, и дело тем бы и кончилось (Пушкин 2). I was still in my dear mother's womb when they registered me as a sergeant in the Semenovskii Regiment....If against all expectations my mother had delivered a baby girl, my father would have simply informed the appropriate authorities that the sergeant could not report for duty because he had died, and that would have been the end of that (2a). ♦ «Спасти вас не в моей власти, вы сами видите. Но приложу старанье, какое могу, чтобы облегчить вашу участь и освободить. Не знаю, удастся ли это сделать, но буду стараться. Если же, паче чаяния, удастся, Павел Иванович, я попрошу у вас награды за труды: бросьте все эти поползновенья на эти приобретенья» (Гоголь 3). "It is not in my power to save you; you see it yourself. But I shall try to do what I can to alleviate your lot and set you free. I don't know whether I shall succeed but I shall try. But if, against all my expectations, I do succeed, Pavel Ivanovich, I shall ask a reward from you for my troubles: give up all your attempts to acquire property" (3c). ♦ «Я себя не боюсь, я двужильный, но если бы, паче чаяния, я свалился, не глупи, пожалуйста, и дома [меня] не оставляй. Моментально в больницу» (Пастернак 1). "I'm not worried about myself, I've got nine lives, but if by any chance I should get ill, you will be sensible, won't you, you mustn't keep me at home. Get me into the hospital at once" (1a).

Ч-41 • ДО ЧЕГО́... [Particle; Invar; often used in exclamations] **1.** very, extremely: [when foll. by AdjP or AdvP] **how...; so...;** [when foll. by NP containing a modif] **what (a)...**

[Ирина:] Милая наша московская квартира, до чего же ты облезлая! (Розов 3). [I.:] Our darling Moscow apartment, how shabby you are! (3a). ♦ «А яблок этих самых — всю зиму лопаем; и мочим, и сушим — никак не справиться, до чего много!» (Федин 1). "And as for those apples, we gorge 'em all winter; and soak 'em, and dry 'em—can't get rid of 'em nohow, there's so many!" (1a). ♦ До чего умная корова! — и здесь, где скот одичал без выпасов и присмотра... она сама каждый день приходит домой (Распутин 4). What a smart cow!—even here, where the cattle had run wild without pastures or attention...she came home every day on her own (4a).

2. [used with a verb] to a very high degree: **so (very) much; how much...; so; so incredibly ⟨very⟩;** [when the verb is translated by AdjP or Part] **how (very);** ‖ до чего ты меня напугал ≃ **you scared me so badly; you got me so scared; you gave me such a scare.**

«Я тебя искал, кулацкое отродье… чтобы сказать, до чего я жалею, что не упёк вас в тридцатом в Сибирь!» (Искандер 5). "I was looking for you, you spawn of a kulak…to say how very sorry I am that I didn't pack you off to Siberia in 1930!" (5a).

3. [used with a verb] (to drive s.o.) to an extreme condition, or (to arrive) at an extreme condition (usu. with the implication that the condition in question is undesirable): до чего X довёл Y-a ≃ **what a (sorry) state X has driven Y to; what X has driven Y to; the state X has driven Y to;** ‖ до чего X дошёл ≃ **what a (sorry) state X ended up in; the state X ended up in; [in limited contexts]** **to what extent X has gone downhill; how far downhill X has gone; X deteriorated to such an extent that…**

Посмотри, до чего ты довёл мать: она из-за тебя сон потеряла. Look what you've driven your mother to, she's lost sleep over you.

Ч-42 • ЕЩЁ ЧЕГО! *coll* [Interj; Invar; fixed WO] used to express one's rejection of some suggestion or offer, one's refusal to comply with some request, one's total disagreement with sth. etc: **what next!; no way!; not on your life!; you've got to be kidding!; that's (asking) too much!; that's all I ⟨we etc⟩ need!**

[Таня *(вдруг подняв голову)*:] Перестань глаза таращить, я тебе сказала. [Геннадий:] Пойдём посидим во дворе на лавочке. [Таня:] Ещё чего! (Розов 2). [T. *(raising her head suddenly)*:] Stop staring at me like that, I've told you already. [G.:] Let's go out and sit on the bench in the yard. [T.:] What next! (2a). ♦ «Ма-маша, — спросил Садчиков лифтёршу, — а у вас к-кабина вниз ходит?» — «Ещё чего! — ответила лифтёрша. — …Только вверх, а оттеда [*ungrammat* = оттуда] — одиннадцатым номером…» (Семёнов 1). "Dearie," said Sadchikov to the lift woman, "does your lift go down?…" "Not on yer life!" replied the lift woman. "…Only up. Yer comes down on yer feet" (1a). ♦ Егорша… хлопнул Михаила по плечу: «Давай! Цепляй какие в колхозе найдутся телеги да сани. За один раз привезу весь ваш урожай»… — «А что, Михаил, — заговорили бабы, — чем лошадей маять, пущай прокатится» — «Ещё чего! Играть будем или хлеб молотить?» (Абрамов 1). Egorsha…slapped Mikhail on the shoulder. "Come on then! Get hold of all the carts and sledges you can find on the farm and I'll bring your whole harvest in for you in one fell swoop."…"Why not, Mikhail? Why wear the horses out? Let him have his little drive." "That's all we need! Are we gonna play games or thresh grain?" (1a).

Ч-43 • НÉ ДЛЯ ЧЕГО *(кому) что делать coll* [PrepP; Invar; subj-compl with бытьₒ (subj: infin)] it would be pointless for s.o. to do (or attempt to do) sth., doing sth. is illogical, unnecessary etc: X-у не для чего делать Y ≃ **there's no reason for X to do Y; there's no reason for doing Y; it would make no sense for X to do Y.**

«…Если общество устроить нормально, то разом и все преступления исчезнут, так как не для чего будет протестовать, и все в один миг станут праведными» (Достоевский 3). "…If society itself is normally set up, all crimes will at once disappear, because there will be no reason for protesting and everyone will instantly become righteous" (3c).

Ч-44 • НÉ С ЧЕГО *жить (кому) substand* [PrepP; Invar; subj-compl with бытьₒ (subj: жить)] (to be) without money or any means to feed and support o.s., one's family etc: X-у было не с чего жить ≃ **X had nothing to live on; X had no money to put food on the table.**

Ч-45 • С ЧЕГО *coll* [PrepP; Invar; adv; used in questions and subord clauses] for what reason, on what grounds: **why; what for; what makes him ⟨her etc⟩ (do sth.); what makes that happen; how come; what could have caused that.**

[Соня:] А ты, дядя Ваня, опять напился с доктором. Подружились ясные соколы. Ну, тот уж всегда такой, а ты-то с

чего? (Чехов 3). [S.:] Uncle Vanya, you've been drinking with the doctor again. You're a fine pair! He's always been like that, but why do you have to do it? (3a). ♦ «А что с Лобановым?» — «Всё то же. А теперь ещё новую песню завёл: дай ему направление в район». — «Дала?» — «С чего? Температура нормальная, стул нормальный» (Абрамов 1). "What's with Lobanov?" "Same as before, except now he's started on a new song and dance: I should give him a referral certificate to the district hospital." "Did you?" "What for? His temperature's normal; his stools are normal" (1a). ♦ «С чего у тебя припадки-то чаще?» (Достоевский 1). "How come you're having more attacks now?" (1a). ♦ «Вот новость! Обморок! С чего бы!» — невольно воскликнул Базаров, опуская Павла Петровича на траву (Тургенев 2). "Here's something new! A swoon! What could have caused that!" Bazarov exclaimed involuntarily, lowering Pavel Petrovich on to the grass (2e). ♦ «Здравствуй, внучек. Что невесел?» — «…С чего тут веселиться, бабусь, с работы выперли, жить негде…» (Суслов 1). [context transl] "Hello, sonny. Why so sad?" "What's to be happy about, granny? They kicked me out of my job, and I've got nowhere to live…" (1a). ♦ «Она сделает мир шахматной доской, эта проклятая кибернетика! Она превратит людей в роботов!» — «Ты с чего это?» — поинтересовался Костенко (Семёнов 1). [context transl] "That damned cybernetics is turning the world into a chess board! It's turning people into robots!" "Who started you off on that?" inquired Kostyenko (1a).

Ч-46 • ЧЕГÓ РÁДИ *coll* [PrepP; Invar; adv; fixed WO] for what reason (often used in questions to express the speaker's bewilderment, annoyance etc): **what for?; why (on earth)?; why should…?; what's the point of…?**

[Тригорин:] Сын [Аркадиной] ведёт себя крайне бестактно. То стрелялся, а теперь, говорят, собирается меня на дуэль вызвать… А чего ради? (Чехов 6). [T.:] Her [Arkadina's] son is behaving most tactlessly. First he shoots himself, and now they say he's going to challenge me to a duel. And what for? (6a).

Ч-47 • ЧЕГÓ ТÓЛЬКО НЕТ *у кого, где;* **ЧЕГÓ-ЧЕГÓ (ТÓЛЬКО) НЕТ** *all coll* [VP~subj/gen~; pres or past; fixed WO] s.o. has (or in some place there is) a great variety and/or a great abundance of things: у X-a ⟨в месте Y⟩ чего только нет ≃ **X ⟨place Y⟩ has (just about) everything under the sun; you name it, X ⟨place Y⟩ has (got) it; you name it, it's there ⟨here⟩; X wants for ⟨lacks⟩ nothing.**

…Автолавка — это тебе не камни и не травы какие-то. Чего там только нет, в автолавке! (Айтматов 1). …The mobile shop wasn't a collection of stones or some species of grass. It had just about everything under the sun, that mobile shop! (1b). ♦ …Пока находился он [Кириленко] на своём высоком посту, пока ездил на нескольких машинах, чего у него только не было (Войнович 1). …As long as he held his high position and traveled in motorcades, Kirilenko wanted for nothing (1a).

Ч-48 • ЛИ́ШНИЙ ЧЕЛОВÉК [NP; fixed WO] in 19th-cent. Russian literature, a character who is unable to apply his talents, who finds himself in a state of discord with the surrounding world etc: **superfluous man.**

< The phrase became current after the publication of Ivan Turgenev's *Diary of a Superfluous Man* («Дневник лишнего человека»), 1850.

Ч-49 • ПОСЛÉДНИЙ ЧЕЛОВÉК *coll* [NP; subj-compl with бытьₒ, nom or instrum (subj: human), or obj-compl with считать (obj: human); fixed WO] an inferior, insignificant person who has no status or power in society or the workplace: **the lowest of the low; a (real) nothing; [in limited contexts] low man on the totem pole.**

Я ни во что не ставлю русскую эмиграцию, считаю их последними людьми, жалкими, нелепыми… (Лимонов 1). I think very little of the Russian emigration, I consider them the lowest of the low, pathetic, absurd… (1a).

Ч-50 • **ЧЕЛОВÉК В ФУТЛЯ́РЕ** [NP; sing only; fixed WO] a person who immerses himself in narrow-minded interests, who is afraid of anything new, who isolates himself from the outside world: **man (who lives) in a cocoon ⟨a shell⟩.**

< Title of a short story by Anton Chekhov, 1898, commonly translated as "The Man in a Case."

Ч-51 • **ЧЕЛОВÉК НАСТРОÉНИЯ** [NP; usu. subj-compl with быть∅ (subj: human); fixed WO] a person whose actions are determined by his moods: **man ⟨woman, person⟩ of many moods.**

Ч-52 • **ЧЕЛОВÉК ПРЕДПОЛАГÁЕТ, А БОГ РАСПОЛАГÁЕТ** [saying] people may make plans, but it is God or fate that determines whether those plans will be realized (usu. said when a person's life does not turn out the way he had hoped or expected): ≃ **man proposes, (but) God disposes.**

«Шесть лет и семь месяцев я жил в городе у сапожного мастера, и хозяин любил меня. Он сказал: „Карл хороший работник, и скоро он будет моим Geselle [подмастерьем]!", но... человек предполагает, а бог располагает... в 1796 году была назначена Conscription [рекрутский набор], и все, кто мог служить, от восемнадцати до двадцати первого года должны были собраться в город» (Толстой 2). "For six years and seven months I lived in town at the cobbler's and my master liked me. He said: 'Karl is a good workman and soon he will be my *Geselle*!' but...man proposes, God disposes...in seventeen ninety-six conscription was introduced and all who could serve and were between the ages of eighteen and twenty-one had to gather in the town" (2b).

Ч-53 • **НЕ СЧИТÁТЬ ЗА ЧЕЛОВÉКА** *кого* coll [VP; subj: human] to have an extremely low opinion of s.o. and consider him unworthy of being called a human being: **X Y-a за человека не считает ≃ X doesn't consider Y a person.**

«Ты думаешь, ты любишь?! Как же! Да ты за человека никого не считаешь» (Битов 2). "You think you love? Sure! But you don't consider anyone a person" (2a).

Ч-54 • **ЧТÓБЫ УЗНÁТЬ ЧЕЛОВÉКА, НÁДО С НИМ ПУД СÓЛИ СЪÉСТЬ** [saying] in order to know a person well, you must spend a great deal of time with him: ≃ **you must eat a peck of salt with someone before you know him; you have to winter and summer with people to know them;** [in limited contexts] **before you choose a friend eat a bushel of salt with him; eat a peck of salt with a man before you trust him.**

Ч-55 • **БИТЬ ⟨УДАРЯ́ТЬ/УДÁРИТЬ⟩ ЧЕЛÓМ** *obs, now used in stylized speech* [VP; subj: human] **1.** ~ *(кому)* to bow respectfully when greeting s.o. (often as a sign of deference, subordination): **X бил челом Y-у ≃ X bowed low to Y; X bowed humbly before Y.**

2. ~ *кому* to request (sth.) respectfully and deferentially: **X бил челом Y-у ≃ X humbly implored ⟨begged⟩ Y; X asked Y most humbly; X made (a) humble petition to Y.**

[Хлестаков:] А что вы, любезные? [Купцы:] Челом бьём вашей милости. [Хлестаков:] А что вам угодно? (Гоголь 4). [Kh.:] What is it, my good fellows? [Merchants:] We make humble petition to Your Grace. [Kh.:] Well, and what do you want? (4b).

3. ~ *(кому) на кого* to complain to s.o. (in a position of authority) about another person's wrongdoings: **X челом бил Y-у на Z-a ≃ X made humble petition to Y against Z; X lodged a complaint (to Y) against Z.**

[Хлестаков:] Что тебе нужно? [Слесарша:] ...На городничего челом бью! (Гоголь 4). [Kh.:] What do you want? [Locksmith's wife:] ...I make humble petition to you against the Prefect! (4b). ♦ [Скотинин:] Сколько меня соседи ни обижали, сколько

убытку ни делали, я ни на кого не бил челом... (Фонвизин 1). [S.:] No matter how much my neighbors have offended me, no matter how many losses they've caused me, I've not lodged a complaint against anyone... (1a).

4. ~ *кому за что* to express profound gratitude: **X бил челом Y-у ≃ X bowed low ⟨bowed down⟩ to Y in gratitude; X offered Y humble thanks.**

Ч-56 • **ЧÉЛЮСТЬ ОТВИ́СЛА ⟨ОТВАЛИ́ЛАСЬ⟩** *у кого highly coll* [VP_subj] s.o.'s face shows astonishment, s.o. gapes in amazement: **у X-a отвисла челюсть ≃ X's jaw dropped; X's mouth fell ⟨dropped, hung⟩ open.**

...Мерзавцы не давали Тане и рта раскрыть. Наконец она стряхнула руку «Ходока» со своего бедра и небрежно щёлкнула его по носу. У обоих... челюсти отвисли (Аксёнов 7). ...Tanya had still not been able to get a word in edgewise. At last she brushed Stud's hand off her thigh and gave him a punch in the nose. Both men's jaws dropped (7a).

Ч-57 • **НИ ПРИ ЧЁМ¹ (тут, здесь)** coll [PrepP; Invar; subj-compl with быть∅] **1.** [subj: human or collect] a person or group is not involved in the matter at hand (often implies that the person or group in question is not guilty in the given matter): **X (тут) ни при чём ≃ X has nothing to do with it (at all); X doesn't come into it at all; X plays no part in it;** [in limited contexts] **it's not X's fault ⟨doing etc⟩; X is not responsible ⟨at fault etc⟩.**

«Ах, вы считаете, что во всём виновата я? А ваш Виктор был ни при чём?» (Трифонов 4). "Ah, you consider me guilty for everything? And your Viktor had nothing to do with it?" (4a). ♦ «Что ты всё валишь на Андропова? Он вообще ни при чём» (Солженицын 2). "Why do you keep blaming Andropov for everything? He doesn't come into it at all" (2a). ♦ Софья Александровна... не может простить Советской власти высылки Саши. Но если даже это ошибка, то Советская власть здесь ни при чём, от ошибок не избавлена никакая власть (Рыбаков 2). Sofya Alexandrovna was...unable to forgive the Soviet regime for Sasha's exile. But even if that had been a mistake, the Soviet regime as such was not at fault, there wasn't a government in the world that did not make mistakes (2a).

2. [subj: concr or abstr] sth. has no relevance to the matter or topic at hand: **X (тут) ни при чём ≃ X has nothing to do with it ⟨sth.⟩ (at all); X is irrelevant ⟨unrelated, beside the point⟩.**

...[Мадлена] сочинила роман под названием «Клелия (Римская история)». Римская история была в нём, собственно, ни при чём. Изображены были под видом римлян видные парижане (Булгаков 5). ...[Madeleine] composed a novel she titled *Clélie, A Roman Story*. Properly speaking, Rome had nothing to do with the story at all. Under the guise of Romans, the novel depicted eminent Parisians (5a). ♦ [context transl] «Ты чего же — большевик?» — «Прозвище тут ни при чём... Дело не в прозвище, а в правде» (Шолохов 3). "What are you then—a Bolshevik?" "The name makes no difference....It's not the name that matters, but the truth" (3a).

Ч-58 • **НИ ПРИ ЧЁМ² остаться** coll [PrepP; Invar; subj-compl with остаться (subj: human)] one is left without anything at all, usu. without having attained sth. desired or expected: **X остался ни при чём ≃ X was left with nothing; X was left out in the cold.**

Всем дали премии, а я снова остался ни при чём. Everybody else got a bonus, but again I was left with nothing.

Ч-59 • **НИ С ЧЕМ** coll [PrepP; Invar] **1. остаться, оставить** *кого* ~ [subj-compl with остаться (subj: human) or obj-compl with оставить (obj: human)] (to end up or leave s.o.) without any money or means of subsistence: **(be left ⟨leave s.o.⟩) with nothing; (leave s.o.) nothing; (be left ⟨leave s.o.⟩) penniless.**

[Анна Петровна:] Как бы папенька-то твой не мотал без памяти, так бы другое дело было, а то оставил нас почти ни с чем (Островский 1). [A.P.:] If only your papa hadn't spent his money like water, then everything'd be different. As it is, he left us almost nothing at all (1a).

2. остаться, уйти, уехать, вернуться и т. п. ~ [subj-compl with остаться etc (subj: human); more often used with pfv verbs] (to end up, go away, come back etc) without what one had hoped to attain, not having achieved the desired results: **with nothing; empty-handed; (be left) high and dry; without having achieved ⟨accomplished⟩ anything;** [in limited contexts] **nothing comes out of it.**

Приходил, чтобы поговорить о хозяйстве, потолковать. Ушёл ни с чем (Пильняк 1). He came to have a word about the housekeeping, to have a chat. He went away with nothing (1a). ♦ Были скромно, даже бедно одетые люди, которые внезапно для меня получали два бесплатных места в четвёртом ряду, и были какие-то хорошо одетые, которые уходили ни с чем (Булгаков 12). There were people who were modestly, even poorly dressed who to my amazement were suddenly given two free tickets in the fourth row and there were some well-dressed ones who went out empty-handed (12a). ♦ ...Барышников забрала милиция, и Сударь, приехав в субботу к условленному месту, остался ни с чем (Семёнов 1). ...The police rounded up the middlemen and Squire, arriving at his customary spot, was left high and dry (1a). ♦ ...[Майор Бадьин] стал задавать профессору вопросы о Лопаткине и Наде. Он получил жёсткий ответ: «...Позвольте мне не сообщать вам ничего»... Так Бадьин и ушёл ни с чем (Дудинцев 1). ...[Major Badyin] began asking the professor questions about Lopatkin and Nadia. He received a fierce reply: "...Permit me not to answer you."...And Badyin left without having achieved anything (1a).

Ч-60 • ПРЕ́ЖДЕ ⟨РА́НЬШЕ⟩ ЧЕМ; ПРЕ́ЖДЕ НЕ́-ЖЕЛИ *lit* [subord Conj, temporal] used to show that what is stated in the main clause precedes what is stated in the subordinate clause: **before.**

Но прежде чем приступим к описанию сего торжества и дальнейших происшествий, мы должны познакомить читателя с лицами для него новыми... (Пушкин 1). But before we embark on a description of this celebration or relate the ensuing events, we must acquaint the reader with certain personages who are...new to him... (1a).

Ч-61 • ПРИ ЧЁМ (тут ⟨здесь⟩) *coll* [PrepP; Invar; subj-compl with быть₀ (subj: any noun); used in questions, exclamations, and subord clauses] what relationship the person, thing etc in question has to the matter at hand: при чём (тут) X? ≃ **what does X have ⟨what has X got⟩ to do with it?; what's all this about X?**

[Бусыгин:] Ты что, не видишь, что с пацаном делается из-за этой женщины? [Сильва:] А я-то тут при чём? (Вампилов 4). [B.:] Can't you see what's happening to the kid because of that woman? [S.:] But what have I got to do with it? (4b). ♦ «Господи! При чём тут доброта! Никакой тут доброты нет...» (Гинзбург 2). "Heavens above! What's all this about kindness? It's not a question of kindness..." (2a). ♦ «Кто это?» – на чистом русском языке спросил высокий. «Пленный, товарищ генерал... Капитан гестапо»... – «При чём здесь гестапо?» – заспорил Ревкин и дал краткие разъяснения по поводу личности капитана (Войнович 2). [context transl] "Who is this," asked the tall one in perfect Russian. "The prisoner, Comrade General....A captain in the Gestapo."..."What are you talking about, Gestapo?" objected Revkin and offered a brief explanation concerning the person of Captain Milyaga (2a).

Ч-62 • ЧЕМ НЕ... *coll* [Invar; used (with NP that follows it) as indep. sent, usu. as a rhet question or exclamation] the person (thing etc) named has all or most of the qualities, characteristics to qualify him (it etc) as a member of the category to which he (it etc) is said to belong: **(s.o. ⟨sth.⟩) is nothing short of a [NP]; (s.o. ⟨sth.⟩) is a perfectly good [NP]; (s.o. ⟨sth.⟩) is a regular [NP]; how's that for a [NP]?**

Приезжай отдыхать к нам. У нас тут и речка, и песчаный пляж — чем не курорт! Come vacation at our place. We've got a stream and a sandy beach—it's nothing short of a resort! ♦ На маленьком клочке земли за домом посадили два куста помидоров, укроп и петрушку. Чем не огород! On the little patch of land behind the house they planted two tomato plants, dill, and parsley. A regular garden! ♦ Слушали: «О неправильном поведении председателя правления Б.А. Турганова». Постановили: «Предложить тов. Турганову письменно до 22 мая объяснить свои действия. До представления письменных объяснений и их рассмотрения отстранить Б.А. Турганова от обязанностей председателя правления»... Чем вам не процесс импичмента? (Войнович 3). Discussed: Board Chairman B. A. Turganov's irregular conduct. Resolved: Comrade Turganov required to explain his actions in writing by May 22. Until presentation of the written explanations and their examination, B. A. Turganov to be relieved of his duties as board chairman....How's that for an impeachment process? (3a).

Ч-63 • ЧЕМ... ТЕМ... [subord Conj, correlative; used with compar forms of Adj or Adv] used to show that the action in the second clause develops proportionally to the action in the first clause in terms of intensity: **the...the...**

Чем больше он думал обо всём этом, тем меньше он во всём этом разбирался (Гроссман 2). The more he thought about it all, the less he understood (2a).

Ч-64 • СИДЕ́ТЬ НА ЧЕМОДА́НАХ ⟨НА УЗЛА́Х⟩ *coll* [VP; subj: human] to be waiting to leave, having already packed one's luggage: X сидит на чемоданах ≃ **X has his bags packed and ready to go; X is packed and ready to go; X is waiting with his bags packed;** [in limited contexts] **X is sitting on his suitcase(s).**

Мы уже сидели на чемоданах, но заболела мама и поездку к морю пришлось отложить. We were all packed and ready to go, but Mom got sick and our trip to the sea had to be postponed.

Ч-65 • К ЧЕМУ́ *coll* [PrepP; Invar; adv; used in questions and subord clauses (often without a verb)] **1.** for what purpose: **what for?; whatever for?; what's the use ⟨the point⟩ (of...)?;** [in limited contexts] **why (on earth)?;** ‖ к чему этот разговор ⟨к чему вы мне это говорите и т. п.⟩? ≃ **what are you driving at?; what is (all) this leading to?**

[Беляев:] Отдайте ей эту записку и скажите... Нет, не говорите ей ничего. К чему? (Тургенев 1). [B.:] Give her this note and tell her— No, don't tell her anything. What's the use? (1b). ♦ ...Я отмахивалась почти с досадой, когда Антон уже несколько раз повторял мне, что у него появилась надежда на досрочное освобождение. К чему такие детские разговоры! (Гинзбург 2). I was incredulous and almost annoyed when Anton kept telling me that he now had hopes of early release. What was the point of such childish talk? (2a). ♦ «...К чему же эта дуэль, это убийство? Или я убью его, или он попадёт мне в голову, в локоть, в коленку. Уйти отсюда, бежать, зарыться куда-нибудь» (Толстой 5). "...Why this duel, this murder? Either I shall kill him, or he will put a bullet into my head, my elbow or my knee. Can't I get away from here, run away, bury myself somewhere?" (5a). ♦ «Но к чему я говорю вам это всё? Для вас ведь это кимвал бряцающий, пустые звуки» (Пастернак 1). "But why on earth am I telling you all this? To you it must be the tinkling of a cymbal—just words" (1a). ♦ [Репников:] Послушайте, Колесов, я признаю ваши способности. Но учтите, способных людей много. Очень много. Гораздо больше, чем учёных. Не правда ли? [Колесов:] Владимир Алексеевич, к чему этот разговор? (Вампилов 3). [R.:] Listen, Kolesov, I recognize your abilities. But remember, there are a lot of capable people. A great many. Far more than there are scientists. Isn't that true? [K.:] Vladimir Alekseyevich, what are you driving at? (3b).

[R.:] Listen, Koliosov, I admit you have ability. But bear in mind that there are many able people. A great many. A lot more than there are scientists. Isn't that so? [K.:] Vladimir Alekseevich, what's all this leading to? (3a).

2. what the significance or possible consequences of sth. are: **к чему (бы) это?** ≃ **what could that mean?; why should this ⟨that⟩ be?**

«У нас мулица ожеребилась... К чему бы это?»... – «Не положено по природе. Хотим узнать, что предзнаменует» (Искандер 5). "Our mule has foaled....Why should this be?"..."It's not supposed to happen in nature. We want to find out what it portends" (5a).

Ч-66 • НЕ́ К ЧЕМУ *(кому)* coll [PrepP; Invar; subj-compl with быть∅ (subj: infin)] it would be pointless for s.o. to do sth. because no advantage would come of it, nothing would be achieved by it etc: делать X (Y-у) не к чему ≃ **there is no point ⟨sense⟩ in (Y's) doing X; it makes no sense (for Y) to do X; there is no need ⟨reason⟩ (for Y) to do X; it's useless (for Y) (to do X); [when used as indep. remark only] (there's) no need for that.**

[Терентий:] Не станем мы вместе с тобой в кино ходить, батя. *(Отдаёт ему билеты.)* Не к чему (Арбузов 2). [T.:] Dad, we are not going to the cinema together. *(Returns the tickets to him.)* There is no point... (2a).

Ч-67 • НИ К ЧЕМУ́ coll [Invar] **1.** *(кому)* [subj-compl with copula (subj: any noun, most often concr)] a thing (or, less often, a person or group) is not needed by s.o., cannot be used by s.o. (and, therefore, s.o. does not want to deal with it or him): X Y-у ни к чему ≃ **X is of no ⟨isn't of any⟩ use to Y; X isn't (of) much use to Y; Y has no use for X; Y has no need of ⟨for⟩ X; [in limited contexts] X won't help; thing X won't do any good.**

Она [медсестра] совсем была девочка, но роста высокого, тёмненькая и с японским разрезом глаз. На голове у неё так сложно было настроено, что ни шапочка, ни даже косынка никак не могли бы этого покрыть... Всё это было Олегу совсем ни к чему, но он с интересом рассматривал её белую корону... (Солженицын 10). She [the nurse] was no more than a girl, but quite tall, with a dark complexion and a Japanese slant to her eyes. Her hair was piled on top of her head in such a complicated way that no cap or scarf would ever have been able to cover it....None of this was much use to Oleg, but still he studied her white tiara with interest... (10a). ♦ «Ведь ему безразлично, покойнику, – шёпотом сипел Коровьев, – ему теперь, сами согласитесь, Никанор Иванович, квартира эта ни к чему» (Булгаков 9). "After all, it is all the same to him—to the dead man," Koroviev hissed in a loud whisper. "You will agree yourself, Nikanor Ivanovich, that he has no use for the apartment now?" (9a). ♦ «Вот вы пренебрежительно отозвались о космосе, а ведь спутник, ракеты — это великий шаг, это восхищает, и согласитесь, что ни одно членистоногое не способно к таким свершениям»... — «Я мог бы возразить, что космос членистоногим ни к чему» (Стругацкие 3). "You scoffed at the cosmos, yet the sputniks and rockets are a great step forward—they're amazing, and you must agree that not a single arthropod is capable of doing it."..."I could argue by saying that arthropods have no need for the cosmos" (3a). ♦ [Кай:] А слёзы нам ни к чему. Без них, будьте любезны (Арбузов 2). [K.:] Tears won't help. No tears, if you please (2a).

2. [subj-compl with copula (subj: infin, deverbal noun, or это)] some action is unnecessary, useless, futile: делать X ни к чему ≃ **there's no point ⟨sense⟩ in doing X; (there's) no need to do X; it's pointless to do X; there's little use doing X; [in limited contexts] doing X isn't doing ⟨won't do⟩ (person Y) any good.**

Продолжать этот разговор было ни к чему (Распутин 2). There was no point in continuing the conversation (2a). ♦ ...[Настёна] опустила вёсла... Она и без того отплыла достаточно, дальше грести ни к чему (Распутин 2). ...[Nastyona] dropped the oars....She was far enough away as it was, there was no need to row any further (2a). ♦ «Володя, чтобы не было недоразумений. Я разделяю линию партии. Будем держать свои взгляды при себе. Ни к чему бесполезные споры» (Рыбаков 2). "Volodya, just so there won't be any misunderstandings, I want you to know that I accept the Party line. Let's keep our views to ourselves. No need to have pointless arguments" (2a). ♦ Всё это описывать ни к чему. Просто надо проклясть негодяев, чьей волей творилось подобное! (Ивинская 1). It is pointless to try and describe such things. All one can do is curse the evil men by whose orders they were perpetrated (1a). ♦ «Слушайте, Виктор, – сказал Голем. – Я позволил вам болтать на эту тему только для того, чтобы вы испугались, и не лезли в чужую кашу. Вам это совершенно ни к чему. Вы и так уже на заметке...» (Стругацкие 1). "Listen, Victor," said Golem. "I've allowed you to shoot your mouth off on this topic only to get you scared, to stop you from sticking your nose into other people's business. This isn't doing you any good. They've got an eye on you as it is" (1a).

3. [adv] without reason or cause: **for no (good) reason; for no apparent reason; to no purpose.**

И ни к чему, некстати — у меня вырвалось (если бы я удержался): «А скажите: вам когда-нибудь случалось пробовать никотин или алкоголь?» (Замятин 1). And inappropriately, to no purpose, the words broke out (if I had only restrained myself!): "Tell me, have you ever tasted nicotine or alcohol?" (1a).

Ч-68 • ЗАМОРИ́ТЬ ЧЕРВЯЧКА́ ⟨ЧЕРВЯКА́ *obs⟩* coll [VP; subj: human] to alleviate one's hunger by having a little something to eat: X заморил червячка ≃ **X took the edge off his hunger; X had a snack ⟨a bite to eat⟩.**

Заморив червячка, мы опять разговорились о разных вещах (Кожевников 1). After we'd had a snack, we talked about different things (1a).

Ч-69 • СВОИ́М ЧЕРЕДО́М идти, пойти, течь и т. п. coll; **СВОЕ́Й ЧЕРЕДО́Й** obs [NP$_{instrum}$; these forms only; adv; fixed WO] (usu. of life, a course of events etc) (to go etc) the same way as previously, following the normal routine: **take ⟨resume⟩ its normal ⟨usual⟩ course; go ⟨go on⟩ as usual ⟨as always, the same as usual, the same as always, just as before⟩; [in limited contexts] (run) its course; (be) business as usual.**

...У нас в школе всё идёт своим чередом. И вдруг на уроке по политической подготовке встаёт курсант Васильев и, покраснев от напряжения... спрашивает: «Товарищ старший лейтенант, а почему у нас, в Советском Союзе, евреев не расстреливают?» (Войнович 1). ...In our school things continued to take their normal course. Then suddenly, one day during a political-education class, cadet Vasilev rose, red-faced with tension, and asked: "Comrade First Lieutenant, why don't we shoot the Jews in the Soviet Union?" (1a). ♦ И день пошёл своим чередом (Каверин 1). And the day took its usual course (1a). ♦ Жизнь Василия Васильевича текла своим чередом (Максимов 3). Life for Vasilii Vasilievich went on as usual (3a). ♦ «Антон, – сказал дон Кондор. – Во вселенной тысячи планет, куда мы ещё не пришли и где история идёт своим чередом» (Стругацкие 4). "Anton," said Don Kondor, "there are thousands of other planets in the universe which we have not yet visited and where history runs its course" (4a).

Ч-70 • КАК ЧЕРЕПА́ХА идти, ехать, плестись, тащиться coll [как + NP; adv] (usu. of a person or vehicle) (to go, trudge along etc) very slowly: **(creep along) at a snail's pace; [in limited contexts] drag one's feet.**

Ч-71 • НАЗЫВА́ТЬ/НАЗВА́ТЬ ЧЁРНОЕ БЕ́ЛЫМ (И БЕ́ЛОЕ ЧЁРНЫМ) ⟨БЕ́ЛОЕ ЧЁРНЫМ (И ЧЁРНОЕ БЕ́ЛЫМ)⟩; ВЫДАВА́ТЬ/ВЫ́ДАТЬ ⟨ПРИНИМА́ТЬ/ПРИНЯ́ТЬ⟩ ЧЁРНОЕ ЗА БЕ́ЛОЕ (И БЕ́ЛОЕ ЗА ЧЁРНОЕ) ⟨БЕ́ЛОЕ ЗА ЧЁРНОЕ (И ЧЁРНОЕ ЗА БЕ́ЛОЕ)⟩ [VP; subj: human] to interpret, represent, or perceive sth. as the opposite of what it really is: X называет чёрное белым ⟨принимает чёрное за белое (и белое за чёрное) и т. п.⟩ ≃ **X calls black white (and white black); X says ⟨swears⟩ that black is white (and white is black); X sees ⟨presents⟩ black as white (and white as black); X sees a negative as a positive (and a positive as a negative).**

Ч-72 • **ЧЁРНЫМ ПО БЕ́ЛОМУ** написано, напечатано и т. п. [Invar; adv; more often used with pfv verbs; fixed WO] (written, printed etc) very clearly and unambiguously: **stated ⟨laid out etc⟩) in the clearest possible terms; (stated etc) in no uncertain terms.**

Ч-73 • **КАК ЧЁРТ ⟨ЧЕ́РТИ⟩** злой, усталый и т. п. *coll* [как + NP; nom only; modif or adv (intensif)] (of a person) extremely (angry, tired etc): **as hell;** ‖ X злой как чёрт ≃ **X is fuming ⟨mad⟩; X is mad as a hornet; X is in a filthy temper;** ‖ X устал как чёрт ≃ **X is dead on his feet; X is dead beat.**

Ещё за дверью я услышал, что они о чём-то спорят, а когда вошёл, увидел, что Мишка зол как чёрт и у Нины красные пятна на лице (Аржак 2). I had heard them arguing about something while I was still outside and when I went in I saw that Mishka looked as angry as hell and that Nina had red blotches on her cheeks (2a). ♦ Ждёшь, злой как чёрт, — когда же пустят в моечную... (Марченко 1). Then you wait there, in a filthy temper, for them to let you into the washroom (1a). ♦ «Сразу будете отдыхать или сначала поужинаете?» — «Нет, нет, спать, сразу спать, устал как чёрт» (Максимов 1). "D'you want to rest straight away, or will you have supper first?" "No, no. I want to sleep, I want to sleep now, I'm dead beat" (1a).

Ч-74 • **КАК ЧЁРТ ЛА́ДАНА** бояться *кого-чего coll* [как + NP; Invar; adv (intensif); fixed WO] (to fear s.o. or sth.) very intensely: **like the devil fears holy water.**

Хорошего администратора из меня не выйдет: боюсь ответственности как чёрт ладана. I would never make a good administrator: I fear responsibility like the devil fears holy water.

Ч-75 • **КАК ЧЁРТ ОТ ЛА́ДАНА** бежать, бегать, убегать *от кого-чего* и т. п. *coll* [как + NP; Invar; adv; fixed WO] (to run or keep away from s.o. or sth.) trying to avoid him or it by all possible means: **(flee sth.) like the devil flees incense; run from sth. like the devil (away) from holy water; (avoid s.o. ⟨sth.⟩) like the plague.**

Ч-76 • **КОЙ ⟨КАКО́Й⟩ ЧЁРТ** *highly coll, rude* [NP; these forms only] **1.** [usu. used as subj] used to express irritation, annoyance: **why ⟨what, who⟩ the devil ⟨the hell⟩; what in hell.**

...То, что он участок свой загубил, это пострашнее всего. Да, загубил. Кой чёрт уродится, ежели уже трава выросла, а поле ещё не пахано (Абрамов 1). ...That he had ruined his own plot—that was the most terrible thing. Yes, ruined it. What the hell was going to grow if the grass was up already and the field hadn't even been plowed yet? (1a).

2. [Interj] said with aggravation to express disagreement with or a denial of sth. stated previously (the word or phrase disagreed with or denied is usu. repeated after the idiom): **like hell; what the hell are you talking about,...; what the hell do you mean by...**

«Ты что здесь делаешь?» — спросил дядя Кязым у Кунты. «А ты что, тоже заблудился?» — ответил Кунта вопросом на вопрос. «Кой чёрт я заблудился, — ответил ему дядя Кязым, — я в собственном сарае...» (Искандер 4). "What are you doing here?" Uncle Kyazym asked Kunta. "Why, are you lost too?" Kunta said, answering a question with a question. "Like hell I'm lost," Uncle Kyazym replied. "I'm in my own barn..." (4a). ♦ «У тебя, кум, славный табак! Где ты берёшь его?» — «Кой чёрт, славный! — отвечал кум. — Старая курица не чихнёт!» (Гоголь 5).

"You have splendid snuff, friend! Where do you get it?" "Splendid! What the hell do you mean by splendid?" answered the friend...."It wouldn't make an old hen sneeze!" (5a).

Ч-77 • **НА КОЙ ЧЁРТ ⟨ДЬЯ́ВОЛ, ЛЕ́ШИЙ, БЕС⟩; НА ЧЁРТА; НА ⟨ДЛЯ⟩ КАКО́ГО ЧЁРТА ⟨ДЬЯ́-ВОЛА⟩; НА (КАКО́ГО) ШУ́ТА; ЗА КАКИ́М ЧЁР-ТОМ ⟨ДЬЯ́ВОЛОМ, ЛЕ́ШИМ, БЕ́СОМ⟩** *all highly coll, often rude;* **НА КОЙ ПЁС ⟨ЛЯД, ПРАХ⟩** *substand* [PrepP; these forms only; adv] why, for what reason (usu. used to express annoyance or irritation; occas. used to express indifference): **why ⟨how etc⟩ the hell ⟨the devil, the heck, the dickens⟩; what the hell ⟨the devil⟩ (for); why in blazes; the devil (only) knows why ⟨what for⟩; why ⟨how etc⟩ the hell ⟨the heck, on earth, in the world⟩.**

«И на кой чёрт я не пошёл прямо на стрельцов!» — с горечью восклицал Бородавкин... (Салтыков-Щедрин 1). "Why the Devil didn't I go straight for the Musketeers!" exclaimed Borodavkin with bitterness... (1b). ♦ «Лев Григорьич!.. Зачем вы ходите по вечерам? Что вам тут делать?.. Да на кой чёрт нам тут ещё филологи! Ха-ха-ха!.. Ведь вы же не инженер!» (Солженицын 3). "Lev Grigorich!...Why come here nights? What is there for you to do here?...What the hell do we need philologists for! Ha, ha, ha!...After all, you're no engineer!" (3a). ♦ «А может, это „товарищи" за мной приехали?» Игорь решительно возразил: «Они в „Чайках" не ездят, да потом на кой ты им чёрт сдался?..» (Аксёнов 6). "Or perhaps the 'comrades' have come to get me?" Igor objected vigorously. "They don't drive Chaikas, and in any case, why on earth should they bother about you?..." (6a).

Ч-78 • **НЕ ТАК СТРА́ШЕН ЧЁРТ, КАК ЕГО́ МА-ЛЮ́ЮТ** [saying] although the person, place, phenomenon etc in question is bad, he or it is not so terrible as he or it seems to be or is said to be (usu. said to hearten s.o. who fears some new place, some unfamiliar circumstances, some person in a position of power etc; also used to describe one's experiences at such a place, in such a circumstance, or with such a person; occas. used in response to another's attempt to intimidate one): ≃ **the devil is not so ⟨as⟩ black as he is painted.**

Густой... туман стоял над Эльгеном, когда наши машины въехали на его главную магистраль... Мимо нас, по направлению к лагерю, шли длинные вереницы «работяг», окружённых конвоирами... «Да не сокрушайтесь сильно-то... Эльген да Эльген... Не так страшен чёрт, как его малюют» (Гинзбург 1). Elgen was covered with thick mist as we drove along its main thoroughfare....Long lines of workers, surrounded by guards, filed past us on their way to camp...."Don't get too down-hearted. We're at Elgen all right but the devil isn't always as black as he's painted" (1a).

Ч-79 • **НИ ОДИ́Н ЧЁРТ** *highly coll* [NP; nom sing only; subj; used with negated verbs] absolutely no one: **not a (living) soul; not one person ⟨one of them etc⟩.**

Гнали письма в единственную отдушину, через смутную Польшу (ни один чёрт не знал, кстати говоря, что в ней творится и что это за такая новая страна — Польша) в Германию... (Булгаков 3). They sent off letters through the only escape-hole across turbulent, insecure Poland (not one of them, incidentally, had the slightest idea what was going on there or even what sort of place this new country—Poland—was) to Germany... (3a).

Ч-80 • **ОДИ́Н ЧЁРТ** *highly coll* [NP; Invar] **1.** [usu. subj-compl with быть∅ (subj: usu. two or more clauses or abstr NPs)] two or more phenomena (notions etc) are exactly identical: X и Y — один чёрт ≃ **X and Y are the same damned thing.**

«...Которые в бога не веруют, ну те о социализме и об анархизме заговорят, о переделке всего человечества по новому штату, так ведь это один же чёрт выйдет, всё те же вопросы, только с другого конца» (Достоевский 1). "...Those who do not believe in God, well, they will talk about socialism and anarchism, about transforming the whole of mankind according to a new order, but it's the same damned thing, the questions are all the same, only from the other end" (1a).

2. *(кому)* [subj-compl with быть₀ (subj: usu. это or a clause) or impers predic with быть₀] (the difference, if any, between two or more expressed or implied options is) unimportant or of little or no significance (to s.o.): (Х-у) один чёрт ≃ **it doesn't make a damn bit of difference (to X); it doesn't matter one damn bit (to X); it doesn't damn well make any difference (to X); X doesn't give a damn; it comes to the same damn thing.**

...Первый выстрел дают по живой мишени, а потом два в воздух. Не один ли чёрт, зэку всё равно погибать... (Марченко 1). ...The first shot is fired at the living target and then two shots into the air. Well, what difference does it damn well make—the con's bound to die... (1a). ♦ Он быстро брился, включив газовую колонку и полоская кисточку под горячей струёй, потом мыл лицо над старым, пожелтевшим, с отбитым краем умывальником — его давно полагалось сменить, но Фандеевым один чёрт, над каким умывальником мыться, а Ираида Васильевна жалела деньги... (Трифонов 4). He shaved quickly, turning on the water heater and rinsing the brush under the hot stream, then washed his face over the old yellowed washstand with the broken corner—it was supposed to have been replaced a long time ago, but the Fandeevs didn't give a damn what kind of washstand they washed up over, and Iraida Vasilievna begrudged the money... (4a).

Ч-81 • (САМ) ЧЁРТ НЕ БРА́Т *кому coll* [VP_subj with быть₀; usu. pres] (in refer. to s.o. who acts with extreme independence, daring, audacity etc) nothing frightens s.o., s.o. boldly takes on any task, challenge, opponent etc, no one can compete with or intimidate s.o. (in the named area): сам чёрт X-у не брат ≃ **the devil himself is ⟨would be⟩ no match for X; X would take on the devil himself.**

...В центре круга Диана отплясывала с тем самым желтолицым пижоном, обладателем орлиного профиля. У неё горели глаза, горели щёки, волосы летали над плечами, и чёрт был ей не брат (Стругацкие 1). In the center of the circle Diana was engaged in a wild dance with the sallow-faced fop, the owner of the eagle's profile. Her eyes burned, her cheeks burned, her hair flew above her shoulders, the devil himself was no match for her (1a). ♦ Феоктистов долго соображал, кто же из белоцерковских извозчиков самый отчаянный... «Ну что ж, позовём Брегмана, отпетого старика, — решил, наконец, Феоктистов. — Ему сам чёрт не брат» (Паустовский 1). Feoktistov sat for a long time pondering as to which of the drivers in Belaya Tserkov was indeed the most reckless...."Well, why not—let's call Bregman, the old rascal," Feoktistov decided at last. "He'd take on the devil himself" (1a).

Ч-82 • САМ ЧЁРТ ⟨НИ ОДИ́Н ЧЁРТ, И ЧЁРТ⟩ не разберёт, не поймёт *coll* [NP; nom sing only; subj] no one (will understand sth.), it is absolutely impossible (to make sth. out): **the devil himself (couldn't figure sth. out ⟨would be hard put to know sth.** etc⟩).

«Сам чёрт не разберёт, кто тут плохой, кто хороший...» (Гинзбург 2). "The devil himself would be hard put to know who's good and who's bad around here" (2a).

Ч-83 • (САМ) ЧЁРТ НО́ГУ ⟨ГО́ЛОВУ⟩ СЛО́МИТ *(в чём, где) coll* [VP_subj; these forms only; fixed WO] some matter is so convoluted, intricate, or confused that it is impossible to understand, make sense of, or clarify it: сам чёрт ногу сломит (в Х-е) ≃ **it ⟨X⟩ could trip up the devil himself; the devil himself would be stumped ⟨at a loss⟩; s.o. would have the devil's own time with X ⟨trying to make sense of X⟩.**

Анкеты бывают разные. Бывают попроще, бывают потруднее, а бывают такие, что чёрт ногу сломит (Войнович 1). There are various types of questionnaires. Some are a bit easier than others, some a bit more difficult; then there are those that could trip up the devil himself (1a).

Ч-84 • ТЬФУ ⟨ФУ⟩ ТЫ ЧЁРТ ⟨ПРО́ПАСТЬ⟩!; ТЬФУ ЧЁРТ ⟨ПРО́ПАСТЬ⟩! *all highly coll* [Interj; these forms only; fixed WO] used to express vexation, annoyance: **what the hell ⟨the devil⟩!; to ⟨the⟩ hell with it!; damn it!**

«Фу ты чёрт! — неожиданно воскликнул мастер, — ...нет, послушай, ты же умный человек и сумасшедшей не была. Ты серьёзно уверена в том, что мы вчера были у сатаны?» (Булгаков 9). "What the devil!" the Master exclaimed suddenly. "...No, listen, you are an intelligent woman, and you were not mad....Are you quite certain that we visited Satan the other night?" (9a). ♦ Куницер вздрогнул. Горячие эти глазки и даже не столько глазки, сколько презрение в них, что-то ему напомнили. Что? Воспоминание уже улетело, едва коснувшись лба совиным крылышком. Тьфу ты пропасть! (Аксёнов 6). Kunitser gave a start. Those hot eyes, and not so much the eyes as the contempt in them, reminded him of something. What? The memory had already flown, having barely touched his brow like an owl's wing. To hell with it! (6a). ♦ [Нелькин:] Я спрашиваю, где вы? [Муромский:] Как где? Здесь, ну вот здесь. [Нелькин:] Где здесь? [Муромский *(рассердившись)*:] Фу ты пропасть! Ну, здесь! (Сухово-Кобылин 2). [N.:] I'm asking you, where are you? [M.:] What do you mean, where am I? I'm here, right here. [N.:] Where is here? [M. *(losing his temper)*:] Damn it, here! Here, I say! (2a).

Ч-85 • ЧЕМ ЧЁРТ НЕ ШУ́ТИТ [saying] all kinds of things could happen, anything can happen (used to express the fear that sth. bad might happen, or the hope that sth. desirable but unlikely will happen): ≃ **(there's) no telling what could ⟨might⟩ happen; you can never tell what might happen; you never can tell; you never know; stranger things have happened; anything's possible.**

К Анфисе Петровне он не собирался заходить. Откуда у неё деньги? На тех же трудоднях сидит. Но у неё был свет, и он свернул в заулок. Чем чёрт не шутит! А вдруг да выгорит (Абрамов 1). He had not intended to visit Anfisa Petrovna. How could she have any money? She had the same workdays under her belt as everybody else. But there was a light on, so he turned into her yard. No telling what could happen. He might just strike it lucky! (1a). ♦ Теперь мне светила вполне определённая цель — предложить эту рукопись толстым журналам. Может быть, «Юности», где я уже печатала свои очерки? Или — чем чёрт не шутит! — даже «Новому миру», где уже появился к тому времени «Иван Денисович»? (Гинзбург 2). I had assigned myself a specific aim: to offer the manuscript to the major journals. Perhaps to *Yunost,* where I had already published some of my pieces. Or—you never know your luck—even to *Novy Mir,* which by that time had already published *Ivan Denisovich* (2a). ♦ «Вы напишете пьесу, а мы её и поставим. Вот будет замечательно! А?.. И знаете ли, чем чёрт не шутит, вдруг старика удастся обломать...» (Булгаков 12). "You write your play and we'll put it on. Won't that be marvelous, eh?...And who knows, stranger things have happened—perhaps the old man himself may decide to produce it!" (12a).

< Abbreviated form of the saying «Чем чёрт не шутит, пока ⟨когда⟩ Бог спит» ("The devil plays all kinds of tricks while God is asleep").

Ч-86 • ЧЁРТ В СТУ́ПЕ *obs, coll* [NP; sing only; subj-compl with быть₀ (subj: usu. это) or obj of наговорить, наобещать etc] words (statements etc) devoid of logic, meaning, common sense etc: **balderdash; poppycock; tommyrot; nonsense.**

[Кречинский *(Сочиняет письмо, перечитывает, марает, опять пишет)*:] Вот работа: даже пот прошиб. *(Отирает лицо и пробегает письмо.)* Гм... м... м... м... Мой тихий ангел… милый… милый сердцу уголок семьи… м… м… м… нежное созвездие… чёрт знает, какого вздору!.. чёрт в ступе… сапоги всмятку и так далее (Сухово-Кобылин 2). [K. (*Composes the letter, reads it over, crosses out, writes again.*):] This is what I call real work; why I've even started sweating. (*Wipes his face and quickly peruses the letter.*) Hm-m-m-m…My gentle angel… family haven so dear to the heart…hm…mm…hm…tender constellation…devil knows what nonsense!…Balderdash, tommyrot, and the like (2b).

Ч-87 • ЧЁРТ ВОЗЬМИ ⟨ПОБЕРИ, ПОДЕРИ, ДЕРИ⟩!

highly coll [Interj; these forms only; often used as sent adv (parenth); fixed WO] used to express indignation, vexation, astonishment, or, occas., admiration, joy etc: **(well,) I'll be damned!; what the hell ⟨the devil⟩!; (God) damn it (all)!; (god)dammit ⟨(god) damn it⟩; the devil take it!; oh hell!; good God!**

[Городничий:] Да, признаюсь, господа, я, чёрт возьми, очень хочу быть генералом (Гоголь 4). [Mayor:] Yes, I must admit, ladies and gentlemen, God damn it, I very much want to be a general (4a). ♦ Я сам был мальчик, и существование какого-то чудо-мальчика вывело меня из равновесия. Я сам был, чёрт возьми, чудо-мальчик (Олеша 3). I myself was a boy, and the existence of some boy-wonder rather upset my sense of equilibrium. Why, damn it, I was a boy-wonder myself (3a). ♦ «Господи, — сказал Голем. — Как будто мне не хочется остаться! Но нужно же немножко думать головой! Нужно же разбираться, чёрт побери, что хочется и что должно…» (Стругацкие 1). "Christ," said Golem. "As if I didn't want to stay. But you have to use your head a little. There's a difference, goddamnit, between what you feel like doing and what you have to do" (1a). ♦ Я перечитал письмо два раза. Приятно, чёрт побери, получить неожиданное письмо от старых друзей (Войнович 5). I read the letter twice. Dammit but it's good to get a letter you didn't expect from an old friend (5a). ♦ Чёрт возьми, подумал Крикун, когда эту характеристику прочитал ему из своей записной книжечки Брат (Зиновьев 1). Good God, thought Bawler, when Brother read this character assessment to him from his notebook (1a).

Ч-88 • ЧЁРТ ⟨less often БЕС, ЛЕШИЙ⟩ ДЁРНУЛ кого; НЕЛЁГКАЯ ДЁРНУЛА

all highly coll [VP$_{subj}$; usu. foll. by pfv infin] (used to express displeasure or regret over an imprudent, inappropriate etc action, behavior, or statement) for some incomprehensible reason s.o. (often the speaker) said or did sth. that he should not have: **чёрт дёрнул X-a (сделать Y) ≃ what the hell ⟨in the world⟩ possessed X (to do Y)?; it must have been the devil's prompting (that made X do Y); it must have been the devil who prompted X (to do Y); the devil got ⟨must have got(ten)⟩ into X; I don't know what got into X.**

И дёрнула же меня нелёгкая связаться с этим анализом понятий! (Зиновьев 2). And what in the world had possessed me to get myself mixed up in this analysis of concepts? (2a). ♦ В одном из больших окон каменного дома — квартиры начальства — я вдруг вижу своё отражение. Ну и вид! Дёрнула же меня нелёгкая ещё обшить телогрейку у ворота этой драной кошкой! (Гинзбург 2). In one of the large windows of a brick building, an apartment house where the bosses lived, I suddenly saw my reflection. What a sight I was! It must have been the devil's prompting that caused me to sew that strip of moulting cat fur onto the collar of my jacket! (2a). ♦ «Тебе не легко будет сообщить им [родителям] это известие [об отъезде]. Они всё рассуждают о том, что мы через две недели делать будем». — «Не легко. Чёрт меня дёрнул сегодня подразнить отца… Он очень сконфузился, а теперь мне придётся вдобавок его огорчить…» (Тургенев 2). "You're not going to find it easy to break it [the news of your leaving] to them [your parents]. They are always discussing what we are going to do in two weeks' time." "No, it won't be easy. The Devil got into me today to annoy Father.…He was quite overcome, and now I shall have to disappoint him into the bargain" (2e). ♦ «Сука! Стерва!.. Я спрашиваю, что у тебя с ним было? Ну?» — «Целовались…» —

захлёбываясь слезами, сказала Лизка… «И всё?» — «А чего ещё…» Михаил схватился руками за голову… Да как он мог подумать такое о сестре! О Лизке… О своей Лизке… «Ну, ну, сестра… Наплевать. Выкинь ты эту всю чепуху из головы. Ну, наорал… Дёрнул меня чёрт…» (Абрамов 1). "Bitch! Lousy bitch!…I'm asking you: What happened between you? Well?" "We kissed," said Lizka, choking with tears.…"Was that all?" "What else…?" Mikhail clasped his head in his hands.…How could he think that his sister…Lizka…his Lizka.…"It's all right, sister. To hell with him. Toss all that nonsense out of your head. The way I barked at you…I don't know what got into me" (1a).

Ч-89 • ЧЁРТ ⟨БЕС, ЛЕШИЙ, ШУТ⟩ ЕГО ⟨её и т. п.⟩ ЗНАЕТ *highly coll*; ПЁС ЕГО ⟨её и т. п.⟩ ЗНАЕТ *substand*; ХРЕН ЕГО ⟨её и т. п.⟩ ЗНАЕТ *vulg* [VP$_{subj}$; these forms only; usu. used as indep. sent in response to the interlocutor's question or statement, or as the main clause in a complex sent; fixed WO] **1.** Also: ЧЁРТ ⟨ШУТ⟩ ЕГО ⟨её и т. п.⟩ РАЗБЕРЁТ; ЧЁРТ ЕГО ⟨её и т. п.⟩ ДУШУ ЗНАЕТ *all highly coll* no one knows or it is impossible for s.o. to know: **the devil (only) knows; God ⟨goodness⟩ (only) knows; who the hell can tell?; (I'll be) damned if I know ⟨can figure it out etc⟩; you can't tell what the hell ⟨the devil⟩ (s.o. is saying ⟨s.o. means etc⟩).**

«А кто же эта Аннушка?» Этот вопрос немного расстроил Ивана, лицо его передёрнуло. «Аннушка здесь совершенно не важна, — проговорил он, нервничая, — чёрт её знает, кто она такая. Просто дура какая-то с Садовой» (Булгаков 9). "And who is this Annushka?" This question somewhat unsettled Ivan, and his face twitched. "Annushka is absolutely irrelevant here," he said, becoming nervous. "The devil knows who she is. Some fool from Sadovaya" (9a). ♦ Чёрт его знает, какой реакции он ожидал на свою благодушную отповедь (Стругацкие 1). God only knows what kind of reaction he expected from his well-intended lecture (1a). ♦ Председатели колхозов на задних лапах перед ним [Егоршей], потому что пёс его знает, что он напоёт хозяину, когда останется с ним с глазу на глаз (Абрамов 1). Kolkhoz chairmen danced attendance upon him [Egorsha] since God knew what he would pass on to the Boss when he was with him eyeball to eyeball (1a). ♦ «Ужасные бестии эти азиаты! Вы думаете, они помогают, что кричат? А чёрт их разберёт, что они кричат? Быки-то их понимают; запрягите хоть двадцать, так коли они крикнут по-своему, быки всё ни с места…» (Лермонтов 1). "They're terrific rogues, these Asiatics! You don't think their yelling helps much, do you? You can't tell what the devil they're saying. But the oxen understand them all right; hitch up twenty of the beasts if you wish and they won't budge once those fellows begin yelling in their tongue…" (1b).

2. used to express annoyance, indignation, surprise, perplexity etc: **what ⟨why, how etc⟩ the hell; damn it (all); (god)dammit; I'll be damned.**

Я несу командиру полка очень ответственный пакет. Чёрт его знает, где он, этот командир полка! (Окуджава 1). I'm taking a very important package to the regimental commander. Where the hell can the man be? (1a).

Ч-90 • ЧЁРТ ЗНАЕТ кто, что, как, какой, где, куда, откуда, почему, сколько *highly coll* [VP$_{subj}$; Invar; fixed WO] **1.** no one knows or it is impossible to know (who, what, how etc): **the devil (only) knows (who ⟨what, how etc⟩); goodness ⟨God, heaven⟩ (only) knows (who etc); (I'll be) damned if I know (who etc).**

[Почтмейстер:] В том-то и штука, что он и не уполномоченный и не особа! [Городничий:] Что ж он, по-вашему, такое? [Почтмейстер:] …Чёрт знает что такое (Гоголь 4). [P.:] Well, you see, that's just the point: he's not a personage and not in a position of authority. [Mayor:] What is he then in your opinion? [P.:] …Goodness only knows what he really is (4c). ♦ «Эта девушка мне нравится. Чёрт знает почему, но нравится» (Евтушенко 1). "I like this girl. God knows why, but I do…" (1a). ♦ Да, вот так быть за председателя колхоза, когда ты в то же время и главный подвозчик дров, и сена, и чёрт знает ещё чего. Каждый, кому не лень, глотку на тебя дерёт (Абрамов 1). Yes, that's what it was like to be acting *kolkhoz* Chairman when you were also the chief source of firewood and hay and heaven knows what else. Anyone who felt like it would give you a bawling out (1a).

2. [Interj] used to express anger, indignation, a negative attitude toward sth., or admiration, reaction to an unexpected development etc: **the devil (only) knows (who ⟨what etc⟩)!; dammit!; good Lord!**

[Кочкарёв:] Будто у них [женщин] только что ручки!.. У них, брат… У них, брат, просто чёрт знает чего нет (Гоголь 1). [K.:] As though they [women] only had nice little hands.…They've got.…The Devil only knows what they haven't got (1a). ♦ [Кочкарёв:] Ты рассмотри только глаза её: ведь это чёрт знает, что за глаза: говорят, дышат (Гоголь 1). [K.:] Look at her eyes. Dammit, what eyes! They speak, they breathe (1b).

Ч-91 • **ЧЁРТ ЗНА́ЕТ ⟨ЧЁРТ-ТЕ⟩ ГДЕ** быть∅, оказа́ться, находи́ться и т. п. *coll, disapprov* [AdvP; these forms only; subj-compl with copula (subj: human, collect, or concr) or adv] (to be, find o.s., be located etc) very far away and/or in a very undesirable place: **the devil knows where; God ⟨Lord, the Lord⟩ knows where.**

…Вдруг — трах-бах — [Чонкина] вызвали в казарму, выдали винтовку, скатку, вещмешок, усадили в самолёт, и через каких-нибудь полтора часа Чонкин был уже чёрт-те где, в какой-то деревне, о которой он до этого никогда не слыхал… (Войнович 2). …Suddenly—bango—he [Chonkin] was summoned to barracks, issued a rifle, a greatcoat roll, and a knapsack, put in an airplane, and an hour and a half later he was already the devil knows where, in some village he had never heard of before… (2a).

Ч-92 • **ЧЁРТ ЗНА́ЕТ ⟨ЧЁРТ-ТЕ⟩ СКО́ЛЬКО** *(кого-чего)* *coll* [AdvP; these forms only; usu. quantit compl with copula (subj/gen: any common noun); fixed WO] (s.o. has or in some place there is) a very great number or amount of (people, things, some type of person or thing etc): **a hell of a lot.**

«Припасов много у вас?» — «Чёрт-те сколько!» — «Орудий?» — «Восемь…» (Шолохов 4). "How're you off for supplies? Plenty?" "A hell of a lot!" "What about guns?" "Eight…" (4a).

Ч-93 • **ЧЁРТ ЗНА́ЕТ ⟨ЧЁРТ-ТЕ⟩ ЧТО** *coll, disapprov* [NP] **1.** ~ твори́тся, начина́ется и т. п.; говори́ть, городи́ть и т. п. ~ [usu. subj or obj] something incredible, outrageous that evokes surprise or indignation, exceeds the speaker's expectations, or is hard to believe (is going on, is beginning etc); (to say, prattle etc) something incredible, outrageous etc: **the devil ⟨God⟩ knows what; the oddest ⟨damnedest⟩ thing(s); something unimaginable;** [in refer. to sth. spoken, written etc only] **some damned nonsense; all sorts of rubbish.**

[Маша:] Вам шестьдесят лет, а вы, как мальчишка, всегда городите чёрт знает что (Чехов 5). [M.:] You are sixty years old, and you are like a little boy, always prattling the devil knows what (5c). [M.:] You are sixty years old, but you're like a little boy, always prattling some damned nonsense (5a). ♦ «Это, наверное, ужасно глупо, что я вас пригласила, да? Вы думаете обо мне чёрт знает что». — «Точно». — «А какая разница, в конце концов?» (Семёнов 1). "It's stupid of me, I suppose, to invite you round, eh? You must be thinking God knows what about me." "That's right." "But what's the difference, when all's said and done?" (1a). ♦ Об исчезнувших [жильцах] и о проклятой квартире долго в доме рассказывали всякие легенды… Квартира простояла пустой… только неделю, а затем в неё вселились — покойный Берлиоз с супругой и этот самый Стёпа тоже с супругой. Совершенно естественно, что, как только они попали в окаянную квартиру, и у них началось чёрт знает что (Булгаков 9).

Legends of all kinds about the mysterious apartment and its vanishing lodgers circulated in the building for some time.…The flat only remained empty for a week before Berlioz and his wife and Stepa and his wife moved into it. Naturally as soon as they took possession of the haunted apartment the oddest things started happening to them too (9b). ♦ В кабинете учёного началось чёрт знает что: головастики расползлись из кабинета по всему институту, в террариях и просто на полу, во всех закоулках завывали зычные хоры, как на болоте (Булгаков 10). The scientist's office became the scene of something unimaginable: the tadpoles crawled off everywhere throughout the Institute. From the terraria, from the floor, from every nook and cranny came loud choruses as from a bog (10a). ♦ …[Местная газета «Большевистские темпы»] печатала чёрт-те чего, а о пропавшем Учреждении — ни гугу (Войнович 2). …[The local newspaper *Bolshevik Tempos*] was printing all sorts of rubbish, but that the Institution had vanished, not one peep (2a).

2. (это) ~ ! Also: **(ЭТО) ЧЁРТ ЗНА́ЕТ ЧТО ТАКО́Е!** [Interj] used to express aggravation, indignation, perplexity etc with regard to sth.: **the devil (only) knows what's going on ⟨what it means etc⟩!; it's the devil knows what!; what the devil ⟨the hell⟩!; what in hell ⟨in blazes⟩!**

Персиков бушевал. «Это чёрт знает что такое, — скулил он, разгуливая по кабинету и потирая руки в перчатках, — это неслыханное издевательство надо мной и над зоологией» (Булгаков 10). Persikov was raging. "The devil only knows what's going on," he whimpered, pacing the office and rubbing his gloved hands. "It's unprecedented mockery of me and of zoology" (10b). ♦ «Они не верят. Сидят в Париже и думают, что здесь самая обыкновенная, мирная война! Здесь не война, здесь чёрт знает что такое!» (Эренбург 2). "They won't believe me. They sit in Paris and think that this is an ordinary war. It isn't a war, it's the devil knows what" (2a).

Ч-94 • **ЧЁРТ НЕСЁТ[1]/ПРИНЁС** *кого;* **ЧЁРТИ НЕСУ́Т/ПРИНЕСЛИ́; НЕЛЁГКАЯ НЕСЁТ/ПРИНЕСЛА́** *all highly coll, disapprov* [VP$_{subj}$] **1.** [if impfv, pres only] used to express displeasure, annoyance when an unwelcome visitor arrives at the wrong or an inopportune time: чёрт несёт ⟨принёс⟩ X-a ≃ **the devil must have brought X; the devil must have made X come; damn X coming here; why the devil did X have to come (here)?** ‖ кого чёрт несёт? ≃ **who the devil ⟨the hell, in blazes⟩ can ⟨could⟩ that ⟨it⟩ be?**

«Что, кум, ведь плохо!»… — «Да, чёрт его [Штольца] принёс! — яростно возразил Тарантьев. — Каков шельма, этот немец! Уничтожил доверенность да на аренду имение взял!» (Гончаров 1). "Well, old man.…Things don't look very bright, do they?" "No," Tarantyev replied furiously; "the devil must have brought him [Stolz]! What a rogue that German is! Destroyed the deed of trust and got the estate on a lease!" (1a). ♦ «По разговору видно, что он женится на его [Роди] сестре и что Родя об этом, перед самой болезнью, письмо получил…» — «Да; чёрт его принёс теперь; может быть, расстроил всё дело» (Достоевский 3). "From what he says it seems he's supposed to be marrying his [Rodya's] sister and Rodya received a letter about it just before his illness—" "Yes. Damn him coming here now. He might have upset the whole applecart" (3a). "You could see from what they said that he's marrying his [Rodya's] sister, and that Rodya got a letter about it just before his illness…" "Yes; why the devil did he have to come now; he may have spoiled the whole thing" (3c). ♦ «Кого… принесла нелёгкая? Отстали бы уж, наконец, совсем!» (Максимов 3). "Who the devil can it be? Why can't they leave me alone once and for all?" (3a). ♦ …Вдруг звонок в дверь. Иду открывать, мысленно по дороге чертыхаясь: кого ещё там нелёгкая на ночь глядя принесла? (Войнович 1). …All of a sudden the doorbell rang. I went to the door, cursing on the way: Who the hell could it be at this time of night? (1a).

2. Also: **ЧЁРТ ЗАНЁС ⟨ПОНЁС⟩; ЧЁРТИ ЗАНЕСЛИ́/ПОНЕСЛИ́; НЕЛЁГКАЯ ЗАНЕСЛА́**

⟨ПОНЕСЛА́⟩; НЕЧИ́СТАЯ СИ́ЛА НЕСЁТ/ПРИ-НЕСЛА́ ⟨ЗАНЕСЛА́, ПОНЕСЛА́⟩ all highly coll, disapprov [usu. pfv] (used to express displeasure or regret caused by s.o.'s or one's decision to go somewhere) it is unclear why or the speaker has no idea why he or s.o. is going to, is headed for, or has arrived at some place: чёрт занёс X-а в место Y ≃ **the devil knows what brought X ⟨what made X come⟩ to place Y; what the devil ⟨the hell, the dickens, in blazes⟩ did X (have to) come ⟨go⟩ to place Y for?**

«Тише ори... всех погубишь, чёрт сопливый. Слышишь, Штрезенака рыщут — шастают... Вот они. Замри... Ну, твоё счастье, — далеко. Прошли мимо. Кой чёрт тебя сюда понёс?» (Пастернак 1). "Not so loud. You'll give us all away, you devil. Can't you hear—Strese's crowd are prowling up and down....There they are. Don't breathe....Lucky for you they've gone by....What the devil did you have to come here for?" (1a).

Ч-95 • ЧЁРТ НЕСЁТ²/ПОНЁС кого; НЕЛЁГКАЯ НЕСЁТ/ПОНЕСЛА́ all highly coll [VP_subj; these forms only; foll. by infin] (in refer. to a reckless, foolhardy action) s.o. is going to do or has done sth. foolish: чёрт понёс X-а сделать Y ≃ **the devil must have prompted X to do Y; for some damn reason X did Y;** ‖ зачем чёрт несёт ⟨понёс⟩ X-а делать Y? ≃ **what the devil ⟨the hell, the dickens, in blazes⟩ would X do Y for?; why the devil ⟨the hell, the dickens, in blazes⟩ is X going to do Y?; why the devil ⟨the hell, the dickens, in blazes⟩ does X want to do Y?;** [past only] **what the devil ⟨the hell, the dickens, in blazes⟩ made X do Y?**

«И зачем нас нелёгкая несёт воевать с Бонапартом?» — сказал Шиншин (Толстой 4). "And why the devil are we going to fight Bonaparte?" asked Shinshin (4a). ♦ «Всё это, брат, хорошо; одно нехорошо: зачем тебя чёрт несёт жениться?» (Пушкин 2). "That's all very well, brother; one thing is not, however: why the devil do you want to get married?" (2b).

Ч-96 • ЧЁРТ ⟨НЕЛЁГКАЯ⟩ НО́СИТ кого; ЧЁРТИ НО́СЯТ all highly coll, rude [VP_subj; often used in questions] **1.** Also: **ЧЁРТИ ТАСКА́ЮТ; ЧЁРТ ТАСКА́ЕТ** both highly coll, rude s.o. is not where he is needed or supposed to be, s.o. is wandering about somewhere and cannot be found: где X-а чёрт носит? ≃ **where the hell ⟨the devil, the dickens, in blazes⟩ is X?;** ‖ X-а где-то чёрт носит ≃ **the devil knows where X is; X is off hell ⟨the devil⟩ knows where.**

[Городничий:] Где вас чёрт таскает? [Держиморда:] Был по приказанию... (Гоголь 4). [Mayor:] Where the devil have you been? [D.:] I was acting on your orders... (4d).

2. Also: **ЛЕ́ШИЙ ⟨БЕС⟩ НО́СИТ** highly coll, rude [obj: often кого-то, кого] s.o. is outside and in the vicinity of the speaker(s) at an unusual and/or inappropriate time (used to express annoyance, displeasure etc): X-а ⟨кого-то⟩ чёрт носит ≃ **for some damn reason X ⟨somebody⟩ is hanging around here ⟨there etc⟩; why the hell ⟨the devil, the dickens, in blazes⟩ would X ⟨anybody⟩ want to be out at this hour ⟨outside at this hour, out there at this time of night⟩ etc?;** ‖ кого чёрт носит? ≃ **who the hell ⟨the devil etc⟩ could that be (at that hour)?; who the hell ⟨the devil etc⟩ is that?**

Ч-97 • ЧЁРТ ⟨БЕС, ЛУКА́ВЫЙ, НЕЧИ́СТЫЙ (ДУХ), ГРЕХ obs⟩ **ПОПУ́ТАЛ (кого); НЕЛЁГКАЯ ⟨НЕЧИ́-СТАЯ СИ́ЛА⟩ ПОПУ́ТАЛА; ЧЁРТ ДОГАДА́Л** all highly coll [VP_subj; usu. past; fixed WO] s.o. yielded to temptation (and did sth., usu. sth. reprehensible): (X-а) чёрт попутал ≃ **the devil tripped X up ⟨led X astray⟩; the devil must have been at X's elbow; the devil made X do it; the devil misled X; it was the devil's work; the devil had a hand in this;** [in limited contexts] **the devil got there first.**

«Я не верю, чтобы из нас был кто-нибудь благоразумным. Если я вижу, что иной даже и порядочно живёт, собирает и копит деньги, не верю я и тому. На старости и его чёрт попутает: спустит потом всё вдруг» (Гоголь 3). "I don't believe that any of us has any sense. If I see any of us leading a decent life, making and saving money—I don't trust even him. When he grows older, the devil will be sure to lead him astray: he will squander it all later on" (3a). ♦ «Сам не знаю, как я убёг [ungrammat = убежал]: должно, нечистый попутал...» (Шолохов 5). "I don't know what made me desert. The devil must have been at my elbow..." (5a). ♦ [Один из купцов:] Лукавый попутал. И закаемся вперёд жаловаться (Гоголь 4). [One of the Merchants:] The devil misled us. We swear never to complain again (4d). ♦ «Приказчик мой задрожал и повалился генералу в ноги. „Батюшка, виноват — грех попутал — солгал"» (Пушкин 1). "My steward went all a-tremble and threw himself at the general's feet. 'Gracious sir, I am guilty: it was the devil's work—I lied'" (1a). ♦ Не подлежит сомнению, что ещё год-другой и молодой фон Витте стал бы командующим ВСЮРа [Вооружённых Сил Юга России], но тут его бес попутал, тот же самый бес, что и нас всех уловил, Андрюша, — любовь к ЕДИНОЙ-НЕДЕЛИМОЙ-УБОГОЙ и ОБИЛЬНОЙ-МОГУЧЕЙ и БЕССИЛЬНОЙ... (Аксёнов 7). Another year or two and young General von Witte would doubtless have been named commander in chief of the armed forces of South Russia, but the devil got there first, the same devil that tempts us all, Andrei: love, love for the glorious, the pitiful, the powerful, the vulnerable, the one-and-only motherland... (7a).

Ч-98 • ЧЁРТ ⟨ШУТ⟩ С ТОБО́Й ⟨с ним и т. п.⟩ highly coll; **ПЁС ⟨ПРАХ⟩ С ТОБО́Й ⟨с ним и т. п.⟩** substand; **ХРЕН С ТОБО́Й ⟨с ним и т. п.⟩** vulg [Interj; these forms only; fixed WO] used to express reluctant agreement, concession, or complete indifference: чёрт с X-ом ≃ **to ⟨the⟩ hell ⟨heck⟩ with X; who (the hell ⟨the heck⟩) cares; damn ⟨screw, bugger etc⟩ X.**

[Марат:] Я бы тебе сказал, кто ты. Но я не скажу. [Лика:] Ну и чёрт с тобой (Арбузов 4). [M.:] I could tell you what you are. But I shan't. [L.:] Then to hell with you (4a). ♦ «Сердце бьётся или не бьётся?» — «А кто его знает... Я же не врач и в этом деле без особого понимания...» — «Ладно, хрен с ним, пусть лежит» (Войнович 2). "Is his heart beating or isn't it?" "Who knows....I'm no doctor. I don't know much about this kind of stuff."... "All right, the hell with him, let him lie there" (2a). ♦ Лицо Бунина искривилось, как будто его внезапно ударили под вздох, и он даже вскрикнул «ой!», но сейчас же взял себя в руки и устало махнул рукой: «А, чёрт с ним!» (Катаев 3). Bunin's face twisted, as though from a sudden blow in the solar plexus. He even gasped, but at once took a grip on himself and waved the matter aside. "Oh, who cares!" (3a). ♦ «Достань мне вина [here = водки] и закуски». — «Курева я достать не могу». — «Хрен с ним, вина достань». — «За спасибо водку не дают» (Рыбаков 1). "Get me vodka and something to smoke." "A smoke I can't get." "Bugger the tobacco, get me the vodka." "They don't give it away, you know" (1a).

Ч-99 • ЧЁРТ ⟨ЛЕ́ШИЙ, ШУТ⟩ ТЕБЯ́ ⟨его и т. п.⟩ ВОЗЬМИ́ ⟨ПОБЕРИ́, (ПО)ДЕРИ́⟩! highly coll, usu. rude; **ПЁС ТЕБЯ́ ⟨его и т. п.⟩ ВОЗЬМИ́!** substand, rude; **ПРАХ ТЕБЯ́ ⟨его и т. п.⟩ ВОЗЬМИ́ ⟨ПОБЕРИ́⟩!** substand, rude; **ЛЯД ТЕБЯ́ ⟨его и т. п.⟩ ПОБЕРИ́!** substand, rude; **ЧЁРТ БЫ ТЕБЯ́ ⟨его и т. п.⟩ ВЗЯЛ ⟨(ПО)БРА́Л, (ПО)ДРА́Л⟩!** highly coll, rude [Interj; these forms only; fixed WO] used to express indignation, irritation, resentment or, less often, surprise, admiration etc (caused by s.o.'s words, s.o.'s deeds, some happening etc): [in refer. to indignation, irritation etc] **(God) damn you ⟨him etc⟩!; to ⟨the⟩ hell with you ⟨him etc⟩!; the devil take you ⟨him etc⟩!; blast you ⟨him etc⟩!; what ⟨where etc⟩ the devil!;** [in limited contexts] **you ⟨the⟩ little**

devil; [in refer. to surprise, admiration etc] **(well,) I'll be damned!; what the hell!**

[Михаил:] ...Эти подлецы требуют, чтобы я прогнал мастера Дичкова... да! Грозят бросить работу... чёрт бы их... (Горький 1). [M.:] Those wretches are demanding that I sack Dichkov, the foreman...*demanding!* They threaten to stop work if I don't, damn them! (1b). ♦ «Бонапарте...» – начал было Долохов, но француз перебил его. «Нет Бонапарте. Есть император! Sacré nom...» – сердито крикнул он. «Чёрт его дери, вашего императора!» (Толстой 4). "Bonaparte—" began Dolokhov, but the Frenchman interrupted him. "Not Bonaparte—he's the Emperor, *sacré nom!*" he shouted angrily. "To hell with your Emperor!" (4a). ♦ Узнав о предстоящем визите [Виара], Андре вспомнил рассказ Пьера и поморщился: «Чёрт бы его побрал!..» (Эренбург 4). André, hearing of Villard's intended visit, remembered what Pierre had told him and frowned. The devil take him! (4a). ♦ [Базильский:] И не мешайте мне работать, чёрт вас возьми! (Вампилов 1). [B.:] And stop preventing me working, blast you! (1a). ♦ Остановившись у крайней избы, капитан услышал за калиткой строгий женский голос: «Борька, шут тебя подери, ты пойдёшь домой или нет, или хочешь, чтобы я тебя хворостиной огрела» (Войнович 2). Stopping at the first hut, the captain heard a woman scolding somebody behind the gate. "Borka, you little devil, are you coming home or do you want me to warm your butt with my switch?" (2a). ♦ Воздушные акробаты выделывали такие удивительные трюки, что у Геши время от времени вырывалось: «Чёрт тебя возьми!» The aerial acrobats were performing such amazing tricks that from time to time Gesha would exclaim: "Well, I'll be damned!"

Ч-100 • **ЧЁРТ УНЁС** *кого;* **НЕЛЁГКАЯ УНЕСЛА́** *both highly coll* [VP~subj~] **1.** *disapprov* [often used in questions] s.o. has disappeared, is not where he is needed or is supposed to be; s.o. is wandering about somewhere and cannot be found: Х-а куда-то чёрт унёс ≃ **the devil ⟨God⟩ (only) knows where X is ⟨went⟩**; ‖ куда Х-а чёрт унёс? ≃ **where the devil ⟨the hell, in blazes⟩ did X go ⟨could X have gone⟩?**

2. [more often past] s.o. finally left (used to express relief, satisfaction that an unwanted visitor or guest has departed): (наконец-то) Х-а унёс чёрт ≃ **at long last (X is gone)!**

Ч-101 • **ЧТО ЗА ЧЁРТ ⟨ДЬЯ́ВОЛ** *obsoles,* **ПРО́ПАСТЬ** *obs⟩!* *highly coll* [Interj; these forms only] used to express perplexity or displeasure on account of sth. completely incomprehensible or unexpected: **what the hell ⟨the devil⟩!; what the hell ⟨the devil⟩ is going on here ⟨are you doing etc⟩?; what on earth!**

Сколько я ни листал подшивки за три года, ни одного материала по козлотуру в них не оказалось. Что за чёрт, подумал я, ведь первый большой материал о козлотуре был напечатан примерно через неделю после первой информации (Искандер 4). As carefully as I went through the files for the three years, I couldn't turn up one piece on the goatibex. What the hell, I thought—after all, the first big piece on the goatibex was carried about a week after the first report (4a). ♦ «...Кто это, по-вашему, Владимир Ипатьич?» Персиков сдвинул очки на лоб, потом передвинул их на глаза, всмотрелся в рисунок и сказал в крайнем удивлении: «Что за чёрт. Это... да это анаконда, водяной удав...» (Булгаков 10). "What would you say it is, Vladimir Ipatyich?" Persikov pushed his glasses up on his forehead, then slipped them down again, peered at the picture, and said with extreme astonishment, "What the devil! It's...why, it's an anaconda, a river boa!" (10a). ♦ «Господин сотник, что это за чёрт? Приведите свой взвод в порядок» (Шолохов 2). "What the devil are you doing, Lieutenant! Put your troop in order!" (2a).

Ч-102 • **ДО ЧЁРТА** *highly coll* [PrepP; Invar] **1.** ~ **устать, надоесть, злой** и т. п. [adv (intensif)] (to be tired, fed up, angry etc) to the utmost degree, extremely: **as hell; awfully; terribly;** ‖

Х-у до чёрта надоело (делать Y) ≃ **X is sick to death (of doing Y); X has had it up to here (with doing Y).**

Мне позвонил пьяный Олеша и долго плакался по телефону, что всё до чёрта надоело (Мандельштам 2). The drunken Olesha telephoned me and bewailed the whole business at great length, saying he was sick to death of everything (2a).

2. ~ *кого-чего (где, у кого).* Also: **ДО ФИГА́** *highly coll* [usu. quantit compl with copula (subj/gen: any common noun)] (s.o. has or in some place there is) a very large or excessive quantity (of people, some category of people, things etc) or a very large or excessive amount (of some substance, some quality etc): Х-ов (у Y-а ⟨в месте Z⟩) было до чёрта ≃ **there are ⟨Y has⟩ a hell of a lot ⟨tons etc⟩ of Xs; there are Xs galore (in place Z); (place Z is) packed ⟨crammed⟩ with Xs.**

Смешных странностей и у моего старика до чёрта (Искандер 3). My old man has a hell of a lot of funny quirks (3a). ♦ ...Народу на земле до чёрта, и каждому хочется куда-то подвинуться (Войнович 4). The world is packed with people and every one wants to get ahead (4a).

Ч-103 • **КАКО́ГО ЧЁРТА ⟨ДЬЯ́ВОЛА, БЕ́СА, ЛЕ́ШЕГО, ШУ́ТА⟩** *all highly coll* [NP~gen~; these forms only; used in questions and subord clauses; fixed WO] **1.** [adv] why, what for: **why the devil ⟨the hell, in hell, in blazes⟩; what the hell ⟨the devil⟩ for.**

«Зачем вы вернулись? – спросил я. – Какого чёрта вы вернулись?» (Олеша 2). "Why did you come back?" I asked. "Why the hell did you come back?" (2a). ♦ ...Вечно я им поперёк горла, а они мне. Так какого же чёрта мне вдруг стать послушным и шёлковым теперь, за решёткой? (Марченко 2). ...I'm a thorn in their flesh and they in mine. So why in blazes should I suddenly be meek as a lamb behind bars? (2a). ♦ Всё начинало злить меня. Какого чёрта я здесь сижу (Лимонов 1). It all began to irritate me. What the hell was I sitting here for? (1a).

2. ~ **надо, нужно, не хватает** *кому* [obj] what is it (that s.o. needs, that is lacking for s.o. etc)?: какого чёрта Х-у надо? ≃ **what the devil ⟨the hell, in hell, in blazes⟩ (does X want ⟨need⟩)?; what does X want ⟨need⟩, damn it?**

«А какого чёрта ему надо?» – подумал Бездомный и нахмурился (Булгаков 9). "What the devil does he want?" Homeless thought, frowning (9a). ♦ «Не надо... переводов...» – пробормотал Раскольников, уже спускаясь с лестницы. «Так какого же тебе чёрта надо?» – закричал сверху Разумихин (Достоевский 3). "I don't need...translations..." muttered Raskolnikov, who was already descending the stairs. "What the hell do you need, then?" Razumikhin shouted from above (3b). "I don't need any...translations..." Raskolnikov muttered, already on his way downstairs. "Well, what *do* you need then, damn it?" Razumikhin shouted from above (3d).

Ч-104 • **НИ ЧЕРТА́; НИ ХРЕНА́; НИ ФИГА́** *all highly coll* [NP~gen~; these forms only] **1.** ~ **не знать, не понимать, не получать, не получаться, не делать, не делаться** и т. п. Also: **НИ ШУТА́; НИ ЛЕ́ШЕГО** *both highly coll* [obj or subj/gen] (to know, understand, receive, do etc) absolutely nothing; not (to be done, work out, be understood etc) at all: **not (know ⟨understand, do etc⟩) a damn ⟨damned, goddamn, frigging⟩ thing; not (understand sth. etc) one damned bit; [in limited contexts] not be able to make any goddamn sense of sth.**

«Не нужно нам никакой квартиры, – сказал Дмитриев задыхающимся голосом. – Не нужно, понятно тебе? Во всяком случае, *мне* не нужно. Мне, мне! Ни чёрта мне не нужно, абсолютно ни чёрта» (Трифонов 4). "We don't need any apartment at all," said Dmitriev in a choked voice. "We don't need it, you understand? In any case *I* don't need it. I, me! I don't need a damn thing, absolutely not a damn thing" (4a). ♦ «...Лётчик [он] был первоклассный, в воздухе ни хрена не боялся!» (Искандер 5).

"...He was a first class pilot. In the air, he wasn't afraid of a frigging thing" (5a). ♦ Владимир Семёнович, а как всё это с вашим писательством согласуется?» — «Как согласуется? Никак не согласуется! Ни хрена не согласуется...» (Аржак 1). "But Vladimir Semyonovich, how does all this fit in with your job as a writer?" "How does it fit in? It doesn't. Not one damned bit" (1a). ♦ «Кто это?» — на чистом русском языке спросил высокий. «Пленный, товарищ генерал... Капитан гестапо»... — «При чём здесь гестапо?» — заспорил Ревкин и дал краткие разъяснения по поводу личности капитана. «Но я же его допрашивал... Он сказал, что расстреливал коммунистов и беспартийных». — «Ни хрена не могу...» — запутался вконец [генерал] Дрынов (Войнович 2). "Who is this," asked the tall one in perfect Russian. "The prisoner, Comrade General....A captain in the Gestapo."..."What are you talking about, Gestapo?" objected Revkin and offered a brief explanation concerning the person of Captain Milyaga. "But it was me who questioned him....He told me he had shot Communists and non-Party members." "I can't make any goddamn sense of it," said [General] Drinov, thoroughly confused (2a).

2. [impers predic; often used as indep. clause] sth. does not have any (negative) effect on s.o. at all, in no way reflects on s.o.: **it doesn't harm ⟨affect etc⟩ s.o. one damn bit; it's nothing for s.o.**

Ты посмотри на него! Пять километров пробежал и — ни черта, даже не устал. Just look at him! He ran five kilometers and it didn't affect him one damn bit, he isn't even tired.

Ч-105 • **У ЧЁРТА НА КУЛИ́ЧКАХ ⟨НА РОГА́Х⟩** жить, быть∅, находиться и т. п. *coll;* **У ДЬЯ́ВОЛА НА РОГА́Х** *coll;* **К ЧЁРТУ ⟨К ЧЕРТЯ́М⟩ НА КУ-ЛИ́ЧКИ ⟨НА РОГА́⟩** уехать, забраться и т. п. *coll;* **К ДЬЯ́ВОЛУ НА РОГА́** *coll* [PrepP; these forms only; adv or subj-compl with copula (subj: usu. human, collect, or a geographical name); fixed WO] (to live, be etc or go, go away etc) in or to a remote and sometimes desolate, undesirable place: **at ⟨to⟩ the ends of the earth; in ⟨to⟩ the middle of nowhere; at ⟨to⟩ the back of beyond; in ⟨to⟩ some godforsaken place ⟨hole⟩; in ⟨to⟩ the sticks;** ‖ у чёрта на кули́чках, в месте Z ⟨к чёрту на кулички в место Z⟩ ≃ **in ⟨to, for⟩ the distant sticks of place Z.**

«...Согласна на всё, согласна проделать эту комедию с натиранием мазью, согласна идти к чёрту на кулички» (Булгаков 9). "I agree to everything, I'll go through the whole routine of smearing on the ointment, I'll go to the ends of the earth!" (9b). ♦ И теперь, подаваясь в дальние края, к чёрту на кулички, на Курилы... Фёдор уверен был, что пройдёт не так много времени и его опять потянет сюда... (Максимов 1). And now, on his way to distant parts, to the back of beyond, to the Kurile Islands,... Fyodor was convinced that it would not be that long before he would be drawn to come back here... (1a). ♦ [author's usage] Заём, налоги, хлебозаготовки, лес — всё уполномоченный [райкома Ганичев]! Тащись к дьяволу на кулички (Абрамов 1). [The District Committee representative] Ganichev had to do it all: the Loan, the taxes, the grain procurements, the timber. He had to go to all sorts of godforsaken places (1a). ♦ Его не повысят ни в должности, ни в звании. Каждый начальник постарается от него избавиться... Его в конце концов загонят к чёрту на кулички... (Войнович 5). Neither his duties nor his rank would ever be increased. Every higher officer would try to get rid of him....In the end, he'd be sent to some God-forsaken hole... (5a). ♦ ...[Ефим] немедленно выскочил из дому, схватил такси и попёрся к Баранову к чёрту на кулички в Беляево-Богородское... (Войнович 6). ...Yefim immediately ran out, grabbed a taxi, and set off for the distant sticks of Belyaevo-Bogorodskoe... (6a).

Ч-106 • **ЧЁРТА ⟨БЕ́СА⟩ ЛЫ́СОГО** *highly coll* [NP_accus; these forms only; fixed WO] **1.** [Interj] nothing of the kind, absolutely not (used to express vehement disagreement, rejection,

usu. when sharply objecting to sth.): **like ⟨the⟩ hell (one does ⟨will etc⟩)!; no way ⟨not a chance⟩ in hell!; hell, no!**

«Мы проворно поворачивались, мы думали: достаточно изменить способ производства — и сразу изменятся люди. А — чёрта лысого! А — нисколько не изменились. Человек есть биологический тип! Его меняют тысячелетия!» (Солженицын 10). "We made a very quick turnaround, we thought it was enough to change the mode of production and people would immediately change with it. But did they? The hell they did! They didn't change a bit. Man is a biological type. It takes thousands of years to change him" (10a).

2. ~ получить, дать, понять и т. п. [obj] (to receive, give, understand etc) absolutely nothing: **not a damn thing.**

«Продай мне душ одних, если уж ты такой человек, что дрожишь из-за этого вздору». — «Чёрта лысого не получишь! Хотел было, даром хотел отдать, но теперь вот не получишь же!» (Гоголь 3). "Sell me your souls by themselves, if you're the sort of man who gets worked up over such nonsense." "You won't get a damn thing from me. I was going to let you have them for nothing, but now you shan't have them" (3a).

Ч-107 • **ЧЁРТА С ДВА!** *highly coll* [Invar; fixed WO] **1.** [Interj] absolutely not (used to express vehement disagreement, energetic refusal): **like ⟨the⟩ hell (one does ⟨will etc⟩)!; hell, no!; no way ⟨not a chance⟩ in hell!**

Правда, уже в наше время, когда начальство на поминальные и праздничные пиршества запросто приезжает на служебных машинах, эти проклятые подражатели опять-таки приспособились к обстоятельствам. Например, какой-нибудь лавочник, имеющий свою «Волгу», будучи приглашённым на такое пиршество, думаете, просто садится в свою машину и приезжает? Чёрта с два! Нет, он... нанимает шофёра... Поди пойми, лавочник он или начальник... (Искандер 3). Admittedly, in our own day, when the authorities arrive at funeral and holiday feasts without fanfare, in official cars, these damned imitators have again adapted to circumstances. For example, some store manager who has his own Volga: if he's invited to such a feast, do you think he just gets in his car and comes? Hell, no! He hires a chauffeur....Just try and figure out whether he's a store manager or an official... (3a). ♦ Вы думаете, он, манекен, демонстрирует вам костюм новейшего покроя? Чёрта с два! Он хочет доказать, что можно быть человеком и без души (Искандер 6). [context transl] Do you really believe that the mannequin's only function is to model a suit of clothes? Don't be naive! The mannequin wants to prove to us that it is possible to be a human being even when lacking a soul (6a).

2. [adv (neg intensif); used with pfv verbs] in no case, not under any circumstances: **like hell (one will do sth.); (one) sure as hell (won't do sth.); one damn well (won't do sth.); there's no way in hell (one will do sth.); no way (will one do sth.).**

«Да так поломаешь рога. Дай мне», — подошёл Сейдахмат. «Прочь! Я сам! Чёрта с два — поломаешь!» — прохрипел Орозкул, взмахивая топором (Айтматов 1). "Wait, you'll smash the horns like that," said Seidakhmat, approaching. "Give it to me." "Keep off. I'll do it myself," said Orozkul hoarsely, waving the axe. "Like hell I'll smash them up" (1b). ♦ «А когда вы пришли в виде киевского надзирателя, я сразу понял, что вы мелкий жулик. К сожалению, я ошибся. Иначе чёрта с два вы бы меня нашли» (Ильф и Петров 2). "...And when you came here as a Kiev militiaman, I knew at once that you were a petty blackmailer. Unfortunately, I was wrong. Otherwise you damn well wouldn't have found me" (2a). ♦ «Чёрта с два в их возрасте я стал бы читать мои книги» (Стругацкие 1). "No way you would have caught me reading my books when I was their age" (1a).

Ч-108 • **В О́БЩИХ ⟨ГЛА́ВНЫХ, ОСНОВНЫ́Х⟩ ЧЕР-ТА́Х** *lit* [PrepP; these forms only; adv] (usu. in refer. to the way some information is conveyed, presented, remembered etc) without details, in general: **in rough ⟨broad⟩ outline; in general**

⟨broad⟩ terms; [in limited contexts] along general lines; (give s.o. ⟨have⟩) a general idea (of sth.); (give s.o. etc) a general account ⟨description etc⟩; (tell s.o. ⟨understand, grasp etc⟩) roughly (what is going on ⟨has happened etc⟩).

[Серебряков:] Нужно изыскать такие меры, которые гарантировали бы нам постоянную, более или менее определённую цифру дохода. Я придумал одну такую меру… Минуя детали, изложу её в общих чертах (Чехов 3). [S.:] We must seek some means which would guarantee us a permanent, and more or less definite income. I have thought of one such measure.…Omitting details, I shall put it before you in rough outline (3a). ♦ Конечно, Нюрок ждала хотя бы краткой, в общих чертах, информации о том, как прошёл новогодний вечер у Канунниковых: кто в чём был, как выглядела Леночка, вообще кто как выглядел, какие там были сказаны интересные слова… (Залыгин 1). Niurok naturally expected at least a short, general account of the Kannunnikovs' New Year party: who was wearing what, how Lena looked, how everybody else looked, what gossip she'd heard… (1a). ♦ [Отец] заперся в кабинете. Потом впустил мать. Они долго шептались о чём-то… Лёва и без них уловил в общих чертах, что произошло (Битов 2). He [Father] locked himself in the study. Then he let Mother in. They whispered about something for a long time.…Even without them, Lyova grasped roughly what had happened (2a).

Ч-109 • **ДО ЧЁРТИКОВ** *coll* [PrepP; Invar; adv (intensif)] **1.** ~ **надоело, наскучило, жаль** и т. п. (s.o. is bored, is aggravated, feels sorry for another etc) to an extreme degree: **extremely; awfully; terribly; dreadfully;** ‖ X-у до чёртиков надоел Y ⟨надоело делать Y⟩ ≃ **X is utterly fed up with Y ⟨with doing Y⟩; X is sick and tired of Y ⟨of doing Y⟩; X has had it up to here with Y ⟨with doing Y⟩.**

Василий всё время дремал, иногда засыпал, и тогда хромой вороной, которому явно до чёртиков надоело хромать неизвестно куда, сбавлял шаг, переступал всё тише и тише, пока совсем не останавливался (Кузнецов 1). Vasili was dozing the whole time and sometimes fell right off to sleep, and then our poor lame nag, obviously utterly fed up with limping along not knowing where he was going, would gradually reduce his pace until he stopped altogether (1b). ♦ Мансурову-Курильскому, Аркашке и свекрови она объяснила, что ей до чёртиков надоел весь тот вид, в котором она неизвестно почему существует едва ли не четверть века… (Залыгин 1). She explained to Mansurov-Kurilsky, Arkady, and her mother-in-law that she was sick and tired of the form in which she had existed, without knowing why, for nearly a quarter of a century (1a).

2. ~ **допиться, напиться** и т. п. (to get or be drunk) to an extreme degree: X допился ~ ≃ **X was ⟨got⟩ blind ⟨stone⟩ drunk; X got drunk out of his mind ⟨gourd⟩; X drank himself silly ⟨cockeyed etc⟩; X got drunk as hell.**

«Ну, пьян человек, до чёртиков и будет пить запоем ещё неделю…» (Достоевский 1). "Well, the man is drunk, drunk out of his mind, and he'll go on drinking for another week…" (1a). ♦ «Мне кажется, здесь убийство. С симуляцией несчастного случая». — «Почему вы так думаете? – спросил Костенко. – Напился до чёртиков и сгорел» (Семёнов 1). "It looks like murder to me. Disguised as an accident." "What makes you think that?" asked Kostyenko. "He drank himself silly and set fire to himself" (1a).

Ч-110 • **К ЧЁРТУ¹ ⟨К ЧЕРТЯ́М, КО ВСЕМ ЧЕРТЯ́М, К ЧЕРТЯ́М СОБА́ЧЬИМ⟩** *highly coll;* **К ЧЁРТОВОЙ МА́ТЕРИ ⟨БА́БУШКЕ⟩** *highly coll, rude* [PrepP; these forms only] **1. послать, выгнать, вышвырнуть** и т. п. *кого* ~. Also: **К ЛЁШЕМУ** *highly coll;* **К ⟨КО ВСЕМ⟩ СВИНЬЯ́М** *substand, rude* [adv] to send s.o. away or drive s.o. out rudely (often when rejecting s.o.'s requests, claims, demands etc): **tell s.o. to go to the devil ⟨to hell⟩; throw ⟨kick⟩ s.o. the hell out (of some place).**

Панкрат… явился в кабинет и вручил Персикову великолепнейшую атласную визитную карточку. «Он тамотко [*regional* = там]», — робко прибавил Панкрат… «Гони его к чёртовой матери», — монотонно сказал Персиков и смахнул карточку под стол (Булгаков 10). …Pankrat entered the office and handed Persikov a magnificent satiny calling card. "He's out there," Pankrat added timidly.…"Tell him to go to hell," Persikov said in a monotone, and he threw the card under the table (10b). ♦ «Разрешите, мессир, его [Стёпу] выкинуть ко всем чертям из Москвы?» (Булгаков 9). "Permit me, Messire, to throw him [Styopa] the hell out of Moscow?" (9a).

2. ну тебя ⟨его и т. п.⟩ ~ !; **иди ⟨пошёл, убирайся и т. п.⟩** ~ ! Also: **К ЛЁШЕМУ** *highly coll;* **К ⟨КО ВСЕМ⟩ СВИНЬЯ́М** *substand, rude;* **К ЛЯ́ДУ** *substand, rude* [adv] used to express irritation, anger, contempt directed at s.o. or sth., a desire to be rid of s.o. or sth.: **to ⟨the⟩ hell with you ⟨him etc⟩!; go ⟨let him etc go⟩ to (bloody) hell ⟨to the devil⟩!; get ⟨let him etc get⟩ the hell out of here!**

Разговоры на тему о психике таких индивидов, как Хозяин и Хряк, беспредметны… Да ну их к чёртовой матери! Кто они такие, чтобы забивать свою голову их жалкими персонами? (Зиновьев 1). Conversations about the psyche of such individuals as the Boss and Hog are conversations without a subject.…The hell with them all! Who are they anyway, that we should be bothering our heads with their miserable personas! (1a). ♦ Женщина рассмеялась: «Да ну тебя к лешему, скаред! Я пошутила…», — и пошла вниз (Булгаков 9). The woman laughed. "Oh, go to hell, you old miser! I was only joking." And she went on downstairs (9b). ♦ «Слушай, дед… иди-ка ты отсюдова [*ungrammat* = отсюда] к чёртовой матери. Я этими байками сыт по горло» (Максимов 3). "Listen, Grandpa, why don't you go to bloody hell. I'm fed up to the teeth with your bedtime stories" (3a). ♦ «Бери три тысячи и убирайся ко всем чертям, да и Врублевского с собой захвати — слышишь это? Но сейчас же, сию же минуту, и это навеки, понимаешь, пане, навеки вот в эту самую дверь и выйдешь» (Достоевский 1). "Take three thousand and go to the devil, and don't forget Vrublevsky—do you hear? But now, this minute, and forever, do you understand, *panie*, you'll walk out this door forever" (1a).

3. ~ **(кого-что)!** Also: **К ЛЁШЕМУ** *highly coll* [Interj] used to express protest, a complete rejection of s.o. or sth.: **damn it ⟨him⟩!; the ⟨to⟩ hell with this ⟨him etc⟩!; to the devil with this ⟨him etc⟩!**

К чёрту! К чёртовой матери! Я не могу позволить им убить себя. Я должен жить (Аржак 1). Damn it! To hell with it! I couldn't let them kill me! I must live (1a). ♦ «К чёрту музей, к чёрту Карла Эберсокса, я хочу на воздух, на солнце!» (Федин 1). "To the devil with the museum, to the devil with Karl Ebersocks, I want air, sunshine!" (1a).

4. взорвать *что,* **взорваться, разлететься, развалиться** и т. п. — [adv] (to blow up, collapse, be ruined etc) completely, irretrievably: **dammit, the damn…; ⟨blow ⟨smash⟩ sth.⟩ to bits ⟨to smithereens⟩; (burst) into bits ⟨into smithereens⟩;** [in limited contexts] **shot to hell; to hell and gone.**

5. [formula phrase] used in response to «ни пуха ни пера», which is a wish for success or luck in sth.: **I'll do my best!; thanks!** (See П-665.)

Ч-111 • **К ЧЁРТУ² ⟨К ЧЕРТЯ́М, К БЕ́СУ, К ДЬЯ́ВОЛУ, К ЛЁШЕМУ, К НЕЧИ́СТОМУ, К ШУ́ТУ⟩** *coll;* **К ЧЁРТОВОЙ МА́ТЕРИ ⟨БА́БУШКЕ⟩** *highly coll* [PrepP; these forms only; sent adv (parenth); used after interrog pronouns and adverbs (usu. какой, куда)] used to indicate or emphasize the rhetorical and/or ironic nature of a statement: **what the hell kind of** [NP] **is this ⟨is he etc⟩; some bloody** [NP] **he is ⟨you are etc⟩.**

«Какая, к чёрту, в Семидоле революция? Четыре маслобойки и одна мельница… Весь город пополз ко всенощной, к

Покрову пресвятой богородицы» (Федин 1). "What the hell kind of revolution is there in Semidol? Four creameries and one windmill....The whole town's crept off to vespers, to the Feast of the Intercession of the Holy Virgin" (1a). ♦ [Зилов:] *(Тычет пальцем в открытую дверь, через которую видна освещённая улица.)* Что это?.. Разве это ночь? Ну? Светло как днём! Какая это к чёрту ночь! (Вампилов 5). [Z.:] *(Points at open door, through which the brightly lit street can be seen.)* What's that?...Call that night, do you? It's as bright as day! Some bloody night that! (5a). ♦ [1-й гость:] Какая тут, к нечистому, любовь, ежели с самого обеда ни рюмки? (Чехов 4). [context transl] [First Guest:] How the devil can I think of love when I haven't had a single glass of anything since dinner? (4a).

Ч-112 • ЛЕЗТЬ/ПОЛЕ́ЗТЬ К ЧЁРТУ В ЗУ́БЫ *highly coll* [VP; subj: human] to do sth. risky, dangerous, not thinking about the consequences: X лезет к чёрту в зубы ≃ **X sticks his neck out; X puts ⟨sticks⟩ his head in the lion's mouth.**

Ч-113 • ЛЕТЕ́ТЬ/ПОЛЕТЕ́ТЬ ⟨ИДТИ́/ПОЙТИ́⟩ К ЧЁРТУ *coll;* **ЛЕТЕ́ТЬ/ПОЛЕТЕ́ТЬ ⟨ИДТИ́/ ПОЙТИ́⟩ К ЧЕРТЯ́М ⟨КО ВСЕМ ЧЕРТЯ́М, К ЧЕРТЯ́М СОБА́ЧЬИМ, К ЧЁРТОВОЙ МА́ТЕРИ⟩** *highly coll* [VP; subj: abstr or, rare, concr] (usu. of some plans, matters, s.o.'s life etc) to move toward a state of collapse or be totally ruined: X полетел к чёрту ≃ **X went to hell; X went (all) to pieces; X went to the devil ⟨to the dogs⟩; X went down the drain ⟨the tube(s)⟩.**

«Недостоин, негодяй, упоминания, не то что слёз. Вот почему говорю я, что всё теперь полетело к чёрту. Дети стали предателями, и отцы почерствели» (Федин 1). "He's not worth remembering, the good for nothing, let alone tears. That's why I say that everything's gone to the devil now. Children have become traitors and fathers have become hardened" (1a). ♦ Надо сказать, что мне тридцать один год. Со спортом всё покончено, однако я стараюсь не опускаться. Утренняя гимнастика, абонемент в плавательный бассейн — без этого не обходится. Правда, все эти гигиенические процедуры — а иначе их не назовёшь — летят к чертям, когда я завожусь (Аксёнов 8). I should mention that I am thirty one, past sport, but trying not to let myself go. Morning gymnastics, season's tickets at a swimming pool—those are a must. It's true all this health habit—there is no other word for it—goes down the drain when I get wound up (8a). ♦ Я старался по почерку угадать расположение духа, в котором писано было письмо; наконец решился его распечатать и с первых строк увидел, что всё дело пошло к чёрту (Пушкин 2). [context transl] I attempted to divine from the handwriting the mood in which the letter had been written. At last I resolved to open it and saw from the first few lines that all my hopes were lost (2b).

Ч-114 • НИ К ЧЁРТУ (не годится, не годный, не годен) *all coll* [PrepP; Invar; subj-compl with copula (subj: human, abstr, or concr) or, when used with не годится etc, adv or modif (intensif)] some person is without merit, not suited for anything, sth. is worthless, of bad quality, in a bad state, or unsuitable for the matter in question: X ни к чёрту (не годится) ≃ **X isn't worth a damn; X isn't good for anything; X is good for nothing; [in limited contexts] X is hopeless; thing X is shot to pieces.**

Да, Кязым знал, что всё ещё силён, но сердце у него ни к чёрту не годилось (Искандер 5). Yes, Kyazym knew he was still strong, but his heart wasn't worth a damn (5a). ♦ «Очень возможно, что куры у него вылупятся. Но ведь ни вы, ни я не можем сказать, какие это куры будут... может быть, они ни к чёрту не годные куры» (Булгаков 10). "It is very possible that the hens will hatch. But neither you nor I can say what kind of hens they will be. Perhaps they won't be good for anything" (10a). ♦ Я прочитал [гостям] вторую порцию [своего романа]... «Язык ни к чёрту! Но занятно...» (Булгаков 12). I read the second part [of my novel to my guests].... "The language is hopeless! But it's intriguing..." (12a). ♦

Оказывается, нервная система у неё ни к чёрту, и обезболивание плохо подействовало (Свирский 1). It turned out that her nervous system was all shot to pieces, and the anesthetic wasn't working properly (1a).

Ч-115 • ОДНОМУ́ ЧЕРТУ ИЗВЕ́СТНО *highly coll* [AdjP; Invar; subj-compl with бытьø (subj: usu. a clause); usu. pres; fixed WO] it is unknown to anyone: **the devil ⟨God⟩ (only) knows; only the devil ⟨God⟩ knows; (I'll be) damned if I know.**

Уже целую неделю льёт дождь, и одному чёрту известно, когда это кончится. It's been raining a whole week already, and the devil only knows when it's going to let up.

Ч-116 • ПОДВОДИ́ТЬ/ПОДВЕСТИ́ ЧЕРТУ́ [VP; subj: human] **1.** ~ *(под чем) coll* to stop, conclude, sum up sth.: X подвёл черту ≃ **X closed the books (on sth.); X put an end (to sth.); X brought sth. to an end ⟨a close⟩; X tallied up the score.**

2. to suspend the acceptance of nominations, speeches etc at a meeting: X подвёл черту ≃ **X closed the nominations ⟨the discussion⟩; [in limited contexts] X concluded the session;** ‖ X предложил подвести черту ≃ **X moved that the nominations ⟨the discussion⟩ be closed.**

«Есть предложение прекратить прения и подвести черту» (Стругацкие 3). "There is a motion to end the debate and to conclude the session" (3a).

Ч-117 • ПРОВАЛИ́СЬ (ТЫ ⟨вы, он, она, они⟩) К ЧЁРТУ *highly coll, rude* [Interj; these forms only; fixed WO] used to express anger, strong dissatisfaction, a desire to rid o.s. of s.o. or sth. etc: провались X к чёрту ≃ **to hell ⟨to the devil⟩ with X; let X go to hell ⟨to the devil⟩; X can go to hell ⟨to the devil⟩.**

Проезжий... поглядывал в окно и посвистывал к великому неудовольствию смотрительши, сидевшей за перегородкой. «...Эк посвистывает, — чтоб он лопнул, окаянный басурман... Дай ему лошадей, да провались он к чёрту» (Пушкин 1). The traveler...looked through the window and whistled—an action that greatly annoyed the stationmaster's wife, who was sitting behind the partition. "...Ugh, he does whistle, may he be struck dumb, the damned infidel....Give him some horses and let him go to the devil!" (1a).

Ч-118 • ХОТЬ К ЧЁРТУ (НА РОГА́ ⟨В ЗУ́БЫ, В ПЕ́КЛО⟩) бежать, отправить *кого* и т. п.; **ХОТЬ К ЧЕРТЯ́М ⟨КО ВСЕ́М ЧЕРТЯ́М⟩** *all highly coll* [хоть + PrepP; these forms only; adv; fixed WO] to any place at all, even a dangerous or highly undesirable one: **(even) to the devil himself; (even) to hell itself.**

...Я три ночи не спал, измучился и начинал сердиться. «Веди меня куда-нибудь, разбойник! хоть к чёрту, только к месту!» — закричал я (Лермонтов 1). I'd had no sleep for three nights and was tired....I began to lose my temper. "Take me anywhere, damn you!" I shouted. "To the devil himself, as long as it's a place to sleep" (1c).

Ч-119 • В ЧЕСТИ́ *у кого, где obsoles, coll* [PrepP; Invar; subj-compl with бытьø; often neg] **1.** [subj: usu. human, collect, or abstr] a person (group, idea etc) enjoys the respect of s.o., recognition in some place etc: X в чести у Y-ов ≃ **X is highly regarded by Ys; Ys hold person X in high regard ⟨esteem⟩;** ‖ *Neg* X у Y-ов не в чести ≃ **X is viewed with disfavor by Ys; Ys don't think much of X.**

2. [subj: usu. human] one enjoys popularity with s.o. (usu. with some group of people): X у Y-ов в чести ≃ **X is popular with Ys; X is a (great) favorite of Ys; [in limited contexts] Ys are keen on X.**

«Я еврейка, ты разве не замечал? Еврейки теперь у вас не в чести» (Максимов 1). "I'm a Jew, hadn't you noticed? You Russians aren't very keen on Jewish women at the moment" (1a).

Ч-120 • ИЗ ЧЕСТИ *obs* [PrepP; Invar; adv] (to do sth.) out of respect for s.o., as a sign of respect: **do s.o. the honor (of doing sth.).**

[Кречинский:] Разве я вам в платеже отказываю? Я прошу вас из чести подождать два-три дня (Сухово-Кобылин 2). [K.:] Am I refusing to pay? All I am asking is that you do me the honor of waiting two or three days (2a).

Ч-121 • К ЧЕСТИ *чьей, кого* (надо сказать, нужно заметить и т. п.) [PrepP; Invar; the resulting PrepP is usu. sent adv] (to say or mention sth. with regard to some person or group) acknowledging a good point, merit etc of that person or group: **to s.o.'s credit; in s.o.'s favor.**

Неловко ездить в автобусе и громко разговаривать «об умном». А Лёва как раз способен увлечься и что-нибудь такое брякнуть не к месту. Хотя к чести его могу добавить, что он легко краснеет (Битов 2). It's awkward having a loud "intelligent" conversation on the bus. And Lyova is just the kind to get carried away and blurt out something inappropriate. Although, to his credit, I can add that he blushes easily (2a). ♦ …Если бы Чичиков встретил его [Плюшкина]… где-нибудь у церковных дверей, то, вероятно, дал бы ему медный грош. Ибо к чести героя нашего нужно сказать, что сердце у него было сострадательно… (Гоголь 3). …If Chichikov had met him [Plyushkin]…at the entrance of a church, he would in all likelihood have given him a copper coin. For be it said in our hero's favour that his heart was compassionate… (3d).

Ч-122 • МНОГО ЧЕСТИ *(кому, для кого)* coll, disapprov [usu. indep. sent (with быть∅, pres or fut)] s.o. does not merit sth., is not worthy of sth.: много чести X-у ≃ **X doesn't deserve the honor; that's too good for X.**

«Мамка нехорошая». — «Твою мамку повесить мало», — отозвался ещё не остывший от злости Михаил. «Давай, папка, повесим её и поглядим». — «…Сильно много чести ей будет» (Распутин 3). "Mummy's horrid." "Hanging's too good for that Mummy of yours," replied Mikhail, whose anger still had not cooled. "Ooh, let's hang her, Daddy, and see what happens." "…She doesn't deserve the honour" (3a).

Ч-123 • НЕ ДЕЛАТЬ ЧЕСТИ *кому* [VP; subj: abstr] (of some action, mode of behavior etc) to characterize s.o. negatively: X не делает чести Y-у ≃ **X does Y no honor; X doesn't do Y any credit.**

[Гурмыжская:] …Светские дамы им [Булановым] увлекались. [Аксюша:] Чести им не делает (Островский 7). [G.:] …Fashionable ladies have been in love with him [Bulanov]. [A.:] That does them no honor (7a). ♦ «Почему вы его [Анатолия] не арестовали?..» — «За что?»… — «Представьте себе… Анатолий бабник и… водку пьёт»… — «Это не делает ему чести — и только». — «Значит, вы его ни в чём не обвиняете?» — «А в чём мне его обвинять?» (Чернёнок 2). "Why haven't you arrested him [Anatoly]?" "For what?"…"Well, you know…Anatoly is a womanizer and…drinks vodka."…"That doesn't do him any credit, but that's all." "That means you're not charging him with anything?" "What should I charge him with?" (2a).

Ч-124 • НЕ ОТКАЗАТЬ В ЧЕСТИ *кому* old-fash [VP; subj: human; foll. by pfv infin; often imper] (usu. used to extend a courteous invitation or convey a polite request) to favor s.o. by doing sth., deem s.o. worthy (of one's presence etc): X не откажет (Y-у) в чести сделать Z ≃ **X will do Y the honor (of doing Z); X will not deny ⟨refuse⟩ Y the honor (of X's doing Z).**

Ч-125 • ПО ЧЕСТИ¹ [PrepP; Invar; adv] **1.** (to do sth.) properly, as it should be done, in good faith: **honestly; the right way.**

Конечно, и Олег мог бы так же полезть, и была б его верная полка, но насточертело это за прошлые годы, хотелось по чести… (Солженицын 10). Of course it was a ruse Oleg could have tried, and he'd have had a proper bunk to himself. But the past years had made him tired of such tricks. He wanted things done honestly… (10a).

2. ~ сказать, говорить (to say sth., speak) frankly, truthfully: **on one's honor; candidly; sincerely; (be) honest (with s.o.).**

«Говорю вам по чести, что если бы я и всего лишился моего имущества… я бы не заплакал» (Гоголь 3). "I tell you on my honor that if I had lost all my property…I wouldn't have shed a tear" (3c). ♦ «Каждый ваш шаг вызывает против вас огонь. Даже я, скажу вам по чести, даже я был вынужден иногда преграждать вам путь» (Дудинцев 1). "Every step you take draws the fire toward yourself! Even I, I tell you candidly, even I was forced at times to bar your way!" (1a). ♦ «По чести скажу вам: я до сих пор без памяти от вашего „Бригадира"» (Гоголь 5). "I tell you sincerely, I have not yet got over my delight at your *Brigadier*" (5a).

Ч-126 • ПО ЧЕСТИ²; ПО ЧЕСТИ СКАЗАТЬ ⟨ГОВОРЯ⟩ [these forms only; sent adv (parenth)] (used to introduce a personal opinion or to admit sth.) speaking totally honestly, openly: **to tell (you) the truth; in all honesty; to tell the honest truth; truth to tell; if the truth be told; (quite) frankly.**

Он хотел бы именно так истолковать своё равнодушие, чтобы стать как все, не быть уродом, но, по чести, он не мог так себя в этот миг истолковать (Битов 2). He would have liked to explain his apathy in just this way, so as to become like everyone else and not be a freak, but in all honesty he could not so explain himself at this instant (2a). ♦ [Тятин:] По чести говоря, Андрей, не нравится мне это… (Горький 2). [T.:] Frankly, Andrei, I don't like it… (2a).

Ч-127 • УДОСТАИВАТЬ/УДОСТОИТЬ *кого* **ЧЕСТИ** *(какой)* often iron [VP; subj: human; often foll. by infin] to show one's respect for s.o., confer a distinction upon s.o. by doing sth.: X удостоил Y-а чести (сделать Z) ≃ **X did Y the honor (of doing Z); X bestowed an honor on ⟨upon⟩ Y by doing Z; X conferred an honor on Y by doing Z; X honored Y (by doing Z); X showed his respect for Y by doing Z; ‖ не каждого ⟨не всех⟩ удостаивают такой чести ≃ not everyone is given ⟨afforded etc⟩ such an honor.**

«…Дворянство здешнее удостоило меня чести избрания в предводители…» (Толстой 5). "…The local nobility have done me the honor of electing me their marshal…" (5a). ♦ Здесь меня допрашивали и сам хозяин кабинета, и комиссия, созданная для расследования моей деятельности (можно гордиться — такой чести не каждого удостаивали)… (Войнович 3). Here I was interrogated by the owner of the office himself, by the commission set up to investigate my activities (I should be proud, not everyone is given such an honor)… (3a).

Ч-128 • УДОСТАИВАТЬСЯ/УДОСТОИТЬСЯ ЧЕСТИ *(какой)* often iron [VP; subj: human; often foll. by infin] to be distinguished by being allowed or being able to do sth.: X удостоился чести (делать Y) ≃ **X had ⟨was given, was afforded⟩ the honor (of doing Y); X was chosen for this honor ⟨for the honor of doing Y⟩.**

У одного подъезда мы удостоились чести лицезреть нашего лилипута-мэра… (Лимонов 1). In front of one building we had the honor of beholding with our own eyes our Lilliputian mayor (1a). ♦ «Почему этой чести удостоились именно мы, а не кто-нибудь другой?» (Пастернак 1). "Why should we be chosen for this honor, rather than anyone else?" (1a).

Ч-129 • БЫЛА БЫ ЧЕСТЬ ПРЕДЛОЖЕНА ⟨ПРИЛОЖЕНА *obs*⟩ coll [sent; these forms only; fixed WO] used to express indifference toward another's refusal to accept an invitation or offer, or his refusal to agree to sth.: **at least I offered 〈tried, asked** etc〉; **it's your loss; you had your chance.**

Не хочешь ехать с нами — не надо, была бы честь предложена. If you don't want to come with us, don't come—at least I offered.

Ч-130 • В ЧЕСТЬ *кого-чего* [PrepP; Invar; the resulting PrepP is adv] out of respect or appreciation for s.o. or s.o.'s accomplishments, and/or in memory of s.o. or sth.: **in s.o.'s honor; in honor of s.o. 〈sth.〉.**

Граф Илья Андреич... через минуту явился, неся большое серебряное блюдо, которое он поднёс князю Багратиону. На блюде лежали сочинённые и напечатанные в честь героя стихи (Толстой 5). Count Ilya Andreyevich...reappeared a minute later...carrying a large silver salver, which he presented to Prince Bagration. On it lay some verses composed and printed in the hero's honor (5a). ♦ Через три года у Харлампо было трое детей. Первую, девочку, в честь тётушки назвали Сулой (Искандер 5). Inside of three years Harlampo had three children. The first, a girl, was named Soula in honor of her auntie (5a).

Ч-131 • ДЕ́ЛАТЬ/СДЕ́ЛАТЬ ЧЕСТЬ [VP] **1.** ~ *кому* [subj: human] to show respect to s.o., confer a distinction upon s.o. by doing sth.: X сделал Y-у честь ≃ **X did Y the honor of doing Z; X honored Y (by doing Z); X bestowed an honor on 〈upon〉 Y (by doing Z); X extended an honor to Y (by doing Z); X did Y an honor by doing Z.**

В немного времени он [Чичиков] совершенно успел очаровать их. Помещик Манилов... был от него без памяти. Он очень долго жал ему [Чичикову] руку и просил убедительно сделать ему честь своим приездом в деревню... (Гоголь 3). It did not take him [Chichikov] long to charm both of them completely. Landowner Manilov...simply lost his head over Chichikov. He kept shaking his hand for quite some time and besought him most convincingly to do him, Manilov, the honor of visiting him on his estate... (3c). ♦ Тарантьев вообще постоянно был груб в обращении со всеми, не исключая и приятелей, как будто давал чувствовать, что, заговаривая с человеком, даже обедая или ужиная у него, он делает ему большую честь (Гончаров 1). ...[Tarantyev] was generally rude to everyone, including his friends, as though making it clear that he bestowed a great honour on a person by talking to him or having dinner or supper at his place (1a). ♦ Эти господа, по-видимому, охотно, как *своего* (честь, которую они делали немногим), приняли в свой кружок князя Андрея (Толстой 4). These gentlemen received Prince Andrew as one of themselves, an honour they did not extend to many (4b).

2. *coll* [subj: human; pfv only; usu. imper] used to express encouragement, prompting (when inviting s.o. to do sth.): сделай честь ≃ **do us the honor.**

«Ты, Авдеич, лучше рассказал бы молодым, как ты в Санкт-Петербурге разбойника споймал [*ungrammat* = поймал]», — предложил Мирон Григорьевич... «Что там рассказывать-то», — заскромничал Авдеич. «Расскажи!» — «Просим!» — «Сделай честь, Авдеич!» (Шолохов 2). "Come on, Avdeich, you'd do better to tell us the story of how you caught a brigand in St. Petersburg when you were young," Miron suggested...."What is there to tell," Avdeich became suddenly modest. "Tell us!" "Yes, go on!" "Do us the honor, Avdeich!" (2a).

3. ~ *кому-чему* [subj: abstr or (less common) human; if subj: human, indir obj is usu. collect; impfv only] (of some action, quality etc) to improve s.o.'s reputation, (of some person) to add to the honor of some group or organization etc: X делает Y-у честь ≃ **X does Y credit 〈honor〉; thing X is to Y's credit; X is a credit 〈an honor〉 to Y; X brings honor to Y.**

«...У этого идиота промелькнуло одно весьма и весьма любопытное замечание, сделавшее бы честь и поумнее его наблюдателю...» (Достоевский 2). "...This idiot let drop one very, very curious remark, which would do honor even to a more intelligent observer..." (2a).

Ч-132 • ЗАЩИЩА́ТЬ ЧЕСТЬ МУНДИ́РА *usu. disapprov* [VP; subj: human] to uphold (sometimes through unscrupulous means) the reputation of some organization, one's departmental interests etc: X будет защищать честь мундира ≃ **X will defend 〈uphold〉 the honor of the company; X will protect the good name of his company 〈organization** etc〉.

Ч-133 • ИМЕ́ТЬ ЧЕСТЬ *obs, now used in stylized speech* [VP; subj: human; foll. by infin] (usu. used in direct address to show one's respect for a person of higher standing) to have the opportunity and/or distinction (of doing sth.): **have the honor (of doing 〈to do〉 sth.); have the privilege 〈the pleasure〉 (of doing sth.); be honored 〈privileged〉 (to do sth.); [in limited contexts] it's an honor 〈a privilege, a pleasure〉 (to do sth.).**

«Что вы мне предъявляете? И с кем я вообще имею честь беседовать?» (Семёнов 1). "What are you charging me with? And anyway, to whom have I the honour of speaking?" (1a). ♦ «Прежде так купцы писали: честь имеем сообщить, что в наш торговый дом на равных правах вошёл Иван Иваныч Сидоров» (Федин 1). "Once merchants used to write: We have the honor to inform you that Ivan Ivanich Sidorov has entered our firm on an equal footing" (1a). ♦ [Коробкин:] Имею честь поздравить Антона Антоновича! (Гоголь 4). [K.:] It's a privilege to congratulate you, Anton Antonovich (4f).

Ч-134 • ИМЕ́Ю ЧЕСТЬ БЫТЬ 〈ПРЕБЫВА́ТЬ, ОСТАВА́ТЬСЯ〉... *obs* [formula phrase; these forms only; fixed WO] a courteous closing to a letter: **I have the honor to remain...**

Ч-135 • ОКА́ЗЫВАТЬ/ОКАЗА́ТЬ ЧЕСТЬ *кому-чему* [VP; subj: human] to show one's respect for s.o. (or some group), confer a distinction on s.o. by doing sth.: X оказал Y-у честь ≃ **X did Y an honor (by doing Z); X did Y the honor of doing Z; X honored Y (by doing Z).**

«Приехал в СССР! Думал, оказал большую честь Советскому Союзу, а здесь, как выяснилось, надо работать» (Рыбаков 2). "He came to the U.S.S.R.! Thought he was doing the Soviet Union a great honor, but then he discovered that in the Soviet Union you have to work" (2a). ♦ [Мольер:] Актёры группы Господина, всевернейшие и всеподданейшие слуги ваши, поручили мне благодарить вас за ту неслыханную честь, которую вы оказали нам, посетив наш театр... (Булгаков 8). [M.:] The actors of the Troupe de Monsieur, your most faithful and submissive servants, have asked me to thank you for the unparalleled honor which you have done us by visiting our theater... (8a).

Ч-136 • ОТДАВА́ТЬ/ОТДА́ТЬ ЧЕСТЬ [VP; subj: human] **1.** ~ *кому* to greet s.o. in a military fashion by raising one's right hand to the side of one's forehead or cap: X отдал честь Y-у ≃ **X saluted Y; X raised his hand in (a) salute.**

Они прошли мимо поста. Люсьен отдал честь (Эренбург 4). They passed a military post. Lucien saluted (4a).

2. ~ *кому* to show s.o. one's full appreciation of his qualities, achievements etc: X отдал Y-у честь ≃ **X paid 〈showed〉 honor to Y; X honored Y; [in limited contexts] X gave Y credit.**

Тому, что Багратион выбран был героем в Москве, содействовало и то, что он не имел связей в Москве и был чужой. В лице его отдавалась честь боевому, простому, без связей и интриг, русскому солдату... (Толстой 5). And what was also conducive to his [Bagration's] being chosen as Moscow's hero was the fact that he had no connections in the city and was virtually a stranger there. In his person honor was paid to the simple combat soldier, unsupported by connections or intrigue... (5a).

3. ~ *чему humor* to accept (and fully enjoy) some food or drink that is offered to one: X отдал честь Y-у ≃ **X did Y the honor of having some; X did Y justice.**

Вообще-то я не пью, но не могу не отдать честь вашему коньяку. Generally I don't drink, but I certainly won't deny your brandy the honor of having some.

Ч-137 • ПОРА́ ⟨НА́ДО⟩ (И) ЧЕСТЬ ЗНАТЬ *coll* [sent; these forms only; usu. this WO] **1.** the time has come to cease, stop sth.: **it's (high) time to stop ⟨to quit⟩; you ⟨he etc⟩ ought to know when to stop ⟨to quit⟩; you've ⟨he's etc⟩ got to know when to call it quits; enough is enough; there's a limit to everything;** [in limited contexts] **your ⟨his etc⟩ time is up; you ⟨he etc⟩ shouldn't overdo it; let's not overdo it.**

«Слушайте, оставьте споры, пора и честь знать, ведь остальные спать хотят» (Шолохов 2). "Enough argument, you fellows. There's a limit to everything. Other people want some sleep" (2a). ♦ «...А старухе скажи, что, дескать, пора умирать, зажилась, надо знать и честь» (Лермонтов 1). "And tell the old woman it's time she died; she's lived long enough and ought to know when her time's up" (1b).

2. the time has come for s.o. to leave, go away: **it's (high) time for me ⟨you etc⟩ to leave ⟨to go⟩; it's (high) time I was on my way ⟨you were going⟩ etc; I ⟨you etc⟩ mustn't outstay my ⟨your etc⟩ welcome;** [in limited contexts] **I ⟨you etc⟩ have outstayed my ⟨your etc⟩ welcome; I ⟨you etc⟩ mustn't disturb s.o. anymore.**

[Бусыгин:] Хорошо мы погостили, весело, но пора и честь знать (Вампилов 4). [V.:] We've had a good time, enjoyed our stay, and now it's time we were on our way (4a). ♦ [Варя:] Что ж, господа? Третий час, пора и честь знать (Чехов 2). [V.:] Well, gentlemen? It's after two, high time you were going (2a). ♦ Аванесян решительно поднялся и, старательно избегая её взгляда, сделал шаг к выходу. В его поспешности было что-то суетливо-жалкое. «Хорошенького понемножку, погрелся, пора и честь знать» (Максимов 3). Avanesyan rose resolutely, and moved toward the door, carefully avoiding her eyes. There was something pathetic in his haste. "Mustn't overdo a good thing. I've warmed up, and I mustn't disturb you anymore" (3a).

Ч-138 • СЧИТА́ТЬ/ПОСЧИТА́ТЬ ⟨СЧЕСТЬ, ПОЧЕСТЬ *obs*, **СТА́ВИТЬ/ПОСТА́ВИТЬ** *obs*⟩ **ЗА ЧЕСТЬ** *что* [VP; subj: human] to deem sth. an honor for o.s.: X считает за честь Y ⟨сделать Y⟩ ≃ **X is honored by Y; X considers it an honor to do Y.**

Я считаю за честь ваше предложение работать вместе. I am honored by your suggestion that we work together. ♦ «...[Авдотья Романовна] потребовала от меня, чтоб я оставил бедную Парашу в покое... Я, разумеется, почёл за честь удовлетворить её желанию...» (Достоевский 3). "...[Avdotya Romanovna] demanded that I leave poor Parasha alone....I naturally considered it an honor to satisfy her wish..." (3c).

Ч-139 • ЧЕСТЬ И МЕ́СТО *obs, coll, now humor* [NP; Invar; fixed WO] **1.** *(кому)* ~ [formula phrase] (a polite invitation to a person who has just arrived) please sit down and join the company: **please take ⟨have⟩ a seat; please be seated; please join us.**

«А, ваше благородие! — сказал Пугачёв, увидя меня. — Добро пожаловать; честь и место, милости просим» (Пушкин 2). "Ah, Your Honor!" said Pugachev on seeing me. "Welcome. Please be seated" (2a).

2. *кому где* ~ [impers predic] s.o. is accepted gladly, willingly: X-у в месте Y честь и место ≃ **X is welcomed in place Y with open arms; X is most welcome in place Y.**

Хорошему специалисту у нас в институте всегда честь и место. In our institute a good specialist is always welcomed with open arms.

Ч-140 • ЧЕСТЬ ИМЕ́Ю *obs* [formula phrase; Invar] **1.** a greeting said upon meeting s.o.: **what an honor; an honor, to be sure; (this is) quite an honor.**

2. Also: **ЧЕСТЬ ИМЕ́Ю КЛА́НЯТЬСЯ** *obs* [the var. with кланяться has fixed WO] said when parting with s.o.: **allow me to bid you farewell; I shall take my leave of you (, sir ⟨madam⟩); I (have the honor to) bid you good-bye ⟨good-by, good day⟩; good day to you.**

[Глумов:] Я не нужен вашему превосходительству? [Крутицкий:] Нет. [Глумов:] Честь имею кланяться (Островский 9). [G.:] You don't need me any more, sir? [K.:] No. [G.:] I shall then take my leave of you, sir (9a). ♦ [Астров:] Ну, честь имею, господа... *(Елене Андреевне.)* Если когда-нибудь заглянете ко мне, вот вместе с Софьей Александровной, то буду искренно рад (Чехов 3). [A.:] Well, I have the honor to bid you good-by, ladies and gentlemen. *(To Elena)* If you would look in on me some time, you and Sonia here, I'd be very glad—truly (3d).

Ч-141 • ЧЕСТЬ ЧЕ́СТЬЮ; ЧЕСТЬ ПО ЧЕ́СТИ *both coll* [NP; these forms only; adv (more often used with pfv verbs) or subj-compl with бытьø (subj: всё); fixed WO] in a suitable, appropriate manner, in the correct manner: **properly; the right way; (sth. is done ⟨handled etc⟩) just ⟨exactly⟩ like ⟨as⟩ it should be (done ⟨handled etc⟩); (do sth.) just ⟨exactly⟩ like one should (do it);** [in limited contexts] **as is right and proper; fair and square; by ⟨according to⟩ the rules ⟨the book⟩; (open and) aboveboard.**

Отец сделал всё честь честью и распрощался со своими родителями теперь уже навсегда (Рыбаков 1). Father did everything properly and said good-bye to his parents, this time for good (1a). ♦ [Матрёна:] Иди, родной, честь честью благословенье сделай... (Толстой 1). [M.:] Come, give them your blessing, as is right and proper... (1c). ♦ Дедушка кивает в сторону нахала приказчика: «А кто этот человек?» — «Это мой бывший приказчик», — заикаясь, отвечает Кусиел. «Ты с ним рассчитался?» — «Рассчитался». — «Полностью и честь честью?» — «Полностью и честь честью» (Рыбаков 1). Grandfather nodded in the direction of the loutish assistant, "Then who is that man?" "That's my ex-assistant," replied Kusiel with a stammer. "Have you settled up with him?" "Yes." "In full, everything fair and square?" "Everything fair and square" (1a). ♦ «Короче, женился я на ней. Все честь по чести, зарегистрировались...» (Максимов 3). "To cut a long story short, I married her. All open and aboveboard. We even went to the registry office" (3a).

Ч-142 • ПРОСИ́ТЬ ЧЕ́СТЬЮ *(кого) obsoles, highly coll* [VP; subj: human; often 1st pers] to request that s.o. comply so that there will be no need to resort to force or threats: я тебя честью прошу ≃ **I am asking you nicely ⟨politely⟩.**

Ч-143 • С ЧЕ́СТЬЮ [PrepP; Invar; adv] in a manner deserving honor and respect: **with honor; honorably; with distinction.**

Индустрия смерти набирала силу, и надо было готовиться к обороне, обороне с пустыми руками, в которой они погибнут, но погибнут с честью (Рыбаков 1). The death industry was gathering force and the people had to prepare to defend themselves, to defend themselves with their bare hands, to die in the act, but to die with honor (1a). ♦ Она имела в виду, что даже поймав осквернённый инжир, Деспина могла с честью выйти из этого положения, просто перебросив этот инжир ей, тётушке Хрисуле (Искандер 5). She meant that even after catching the defiled fig, Despina could have remedied the situation honorably, simply by throwing the fig to her, Auntie Chrysoula (5a).

Ч-144 • ЗАДАВА́ТЬ/ЗАДА́ТЬ ⟨ДАВА́ТЬ/ДАТЬ⟩ ЧЁСУ *substand* [VP; subj: human; more often pfv] **1.** ~ *кому.* Also: **ЗАДАВА́ТЬ/ЗАДА́ТЬ ЧЁСКУ** *substand* to reprimand s.o. harshly, take severe disciplinary measures: X задаст Y-у чёсу ≃ **X will make it hot for Y; X will show ⟨fix⟩ Y; X will give it to Y good; X will let Y have it; X will give Y hell.**

2. ~ *кому* [subj: usu. pl] to fight s.o. (usu. a hostile army, the enemy) vehemently, overwhelming or defeating him: Х-ы дали Y-ам чёсу ≃ **Xs clobbered ⟨routed, crushed⟩ Ys.**

3. to run away swiftly: Х задал чёсу ≃ **X hightailed it (out of here ⟨up the road, down the street etc⟩); X beat it; X split; X ran ⟨made a run⟩ for it.**

Ч-145 • **НЕ ЧЕТА́** *кому-чему* [NP; Invar; subj-compl with быть∅ (subj: usu. human, occas. any common noun); if subj: human, indir obj is also human etc] a person, thing etc is significantly better (with regard to some quality, some characteristic, social status, educational background etc) than another person, thing etc (may refer to a potential spouse): Х Y-у не чета ≃ **X is a cut above Y; X (completely) outclasses Y; Y is no match for X; there's no comparing Y to X; Y is not X's equal; X is not like Y.**

Боже мой, думал Михаил, сколько у них было надежд, когда Лукашина председателем назначили! Вот, думали, дождались хозяина. Этот не чета Першину. Этот колхоз поведёт (Абрамов 1). My God, thought Mikhail, what hopes they'd had when they appointed Lukashin as Chairman! Now we've got a real boss, they had thought. This one's a good cut above Pershin. This one'll steer the *kolkhoz* (1a). ♦ Вот настоящий мужчина, подумал я, настоящий герой, не чета... этому дешёвому московскому сброду (Аксёнов 6). Now there's a real man, I thought, a real hero who completely outclasses...all that cheap Moscow riffraff (6a). ♦ [Барон *(Насте)*:] Ты должна понимать, что я — не чета тебе! Ты... мразь! (Горький 3). [B. *(to Nastya)*:] You have to understand...you're not my equal. You're—dirt under my feet! (3b). ♦ Короче говоря, важный был человек Кириленко, не нам с вами чета (Войнович 1). In short, Kirilenko was an important man, not like you and me (1a).

Ч-146 • **НА ЧЕТВЕРЕ́НЬКАХ** *стоять, ползти и т. п. coll;* **НА КАРА́ЧКАХ** *substand;* **НА ЧЕТВЕРЕ́НЬКИ** *становиться,* (в)*стать coll;* **НА КАРА́ЧКИ** *substand* [PrepP; these forms only; adv] (to be, crawl, get down, get up etc) on one's hands and knees: **on all fours.**

Людмила вернулась как раз в тот момент, когда Алтынник, ползая по полу на карачках, показывал, как именно старшина де Голль учит молодых солдат мыть полы (Войнович 5). Ludmilla returned just as Altinnik was crawling on all fours across the floor to demonstrate de Gaulle's method of teaching a raw recruit the proper way to wash floors (5a).

Ч-147 • **ЧИН ЧИ́НОМ; ЧИН ПО ЧИ́НУ** *both coll;* **ЧИН ЧИНАРЁМ** *substand, humor* [NP; these forms only; adv or subj-compl with быть∅ (subj: всё); fixed WO] in a suitable, appropriate manner, in the correct manner: **the right way; just right; properly; (sth. is done ⟨handled etc⟩) just ⟨exactly⟩ like it should be (done ⟨handled etc⟩); (do sth.) just ⟨exactly⟩ like ⟨as⟩ one should (do it);** [in limited contexts] **all neat and proper.**

«Помню, когда пацаном был, мы все в «начинку» играли. Завернёшь, бывало, мусору какого в белый листок, ленточкой броской чин чинарём перевяжешь и бросишь на тротуар, а сам сидишь за забором и смотришь в щёлку: кто подберёт?» (Максимов 3). "I remember when I was a kid we were always playing 'parcels.' You wrapped up some rubbish in a sheet of white paper, tied it up all neat and proper with a bright ribbon, dropped it on the pavement, sat yourself down behind a fence, and looked through the crack to see who'd pick it up" (3a).

Ч-148 • **В (БОЛЬШИ́Х ⟨КРУ́ПНЫХ и т. п.⟩) ЧИНА́Х** *obs* [PrepP; these forms only; subj-compl with быть∅ (subj: human)] one has a high civilian or military position: Х в (больших) чинах ≃ **X holds a high rank; X is of high rank; X is a man of high position; X is a high-ranking (officer ⟨official etc⟩).**

[Отрадина:] Так [он] хорошей фамилии, в больших чинах? (Островский 3). [O.:] Does he come from an influential family? Is he a man of high position? (3a). ♦ [Болоснин:] Отец мой... в больших чинах, генерал (Солженицын 9). [B.:] My father is...a high-ranking officer—a General (9a).

Ч-149 • **БЕЗ ЧИНО́В** *obs, now humor* [PrepP; Invar; adv (occas. used as indep. remark)] without observing accepted conventions regarding rules of behavior between people of different rank, position, title etc: **without ceremony ⟨formalities⟩; without ⟨not⟩ standing on ceremony;** [as a suggestion, invitation] **don't ⟨let's not⟩ stand on ceremony; let's forget about rank; let's forgo ⟨dispense with⟩ the formalities.**

[Стародум:] Я говорю без чинов. Начинаются чины — перестаёт искренность (Фонвизин 1). [S.:] I speak without formalities. Where formalities begin, sincerity ends (1a). ♦ [Хлестаков:] Что вы, господа, стоите? Пожалуйста, садитесь! [Городничий:] Чин такой, что ещё можно постоять. [Артемий Филиппович:] Мы постоим. [Лука Лукич:] Не извольте беспокоиться. [Хлестаков:] Без чинов, прошу садиться (Гоголь 4). [Kh.:] Why are you standing, gentlemen? Please sit down. [Mayor:] A person of my rank, sir, can stand. [A.F.:] We don't mind standing, sir. [L.L.:] Don't worry sir. [Kh.:] Don't stand on ceremony, gentlemen. Do sit down (4c).

Ч-150 • **НЕ ПО ЧИ́НУ БЕРЁШЬ!** *obs, coll* [sent; Invar; fixed WO] you are allowing yourself more than is customary for s.o. in your position, you are going too far: **you are overstepping your rank; that's not a thing for someone in your position ⟨of your rank etc⟩ to do; you are (stepping) out of line; you mustn't ⟨can't⟩ behave like that in your position.**

«...Говорит Настасья Ивановна, что ты... надерзил Ивану Васильевичу? Расстроил его? Он тебе стал советы подавать, а ты в ответ Настасья Иванна, — фырк! Фырк! Ты меня прости, но это слишком! Не по чину берёшь!» (Булгаков 12). "...Nastasya Ivanovna said...that you'd annoyed Ivan Vasilievich somehow, upset him? He started to give you some advice and you just sniffed at him! Sniffed! I'm sorry, old man, but really that's going a bit far! You can't behave like that in your position!" (12a).

< From Nikolai Gogol's *The Inspector General* («Ревизор»), 1836. Originally the expression meant "You are taking bigger bribes than someone of your rank is entitled to."

Ч-151 • **ПО ЧИ́НУ** *(кому)* [PrepP; Invar; subj-compl with быть∅ (subj: abstr or infin) or adv] in accordance with one's or s.o.'s position, title, status: **according to ⟨in keeping with, as befits etc⟩ one's ⟨s.o.'s⟩ rank;** [in limited contexts] **(s.o. is obliged ⟨permitted etc⟩) by his rank ⟨office etc⟩ (to do sth.); s.o.'s rank ⟨office, status etc⟩ gives s.o. (some privilege ⟨responsibility etc⟩);** || *Neg* [in limited contexts] **who is s.o. (to do sth.)?**

Им положено по чину интересоваться всем тем, к чему они сами не испытывают никакого интереса и в чём ничего не смыслят (Зиновьев 1). "They're obliged by their office to take an interest in everything they haven't the slightest interest in and which means nothing at all to them" (1a). ♦ В это время генерал Дрынов сидел в блиндаже под тремя накатами и следил за происходящим сквозь перископ. Не то чтобы он был так труслив (храбрость свою он неоднократно уже показывал), просто он считал, что генералу по чину положено сидеть в блиндаже и передвигаться исключительно на бронетранспортёре (Войнович 2). General Drinov was sitting in his dugout, three floors down, following the action through a periscope. It was not that he was cowardly (he had already proven his courage many times over), he simply considered that a general's rank gave him the privilege of sitting in dugouts and traveling exclusively in armored carriers (2a). ♦ Господин Меркатор не раз намекал Кузенкову, что был бы счастлив принять его у себя дома, в городской квартире или на «ля «даче» в Карачели… однако Марлен Михайлович всякий раз мягко отклонял эти намёки, и Меркатор сразу показывал, что понимает отказ и даже как бы извиняется за своё нахальство: залетел, мол, высоко, не по чину (Аксёнов 7). More than once Mr. Mercator had hinted that he would be happy to invite Marlen Mikhailovich to his flat in town or his dacha in Karachel….But each time the subject came up, Marlen Mikhailovich gently changed it, and Mr. Mercator would make it clear he understood and all but apologize for having been so forward: who was he to invite so high an official to his house? (7a).

Ч-152 • В ТОМ ЧИСЛÉ (И…) [PrepP; Invar; used as coord Conj; indicator of appos] used after naming a group or category to specify one or more members, objects, facts etc included in that group or category: **including; and that includes;** [in limited contexts] **…among them; …included;** [in refer. to an extreme, striking etc case] **even.**

Опять все, в том числе хозяйка и её сын, хлебали из общей миски (Рыбаков 2). Again everyone, including the old woman and her son, ate from the same pot (2a). ♦ Он говорил: «Зря не сажают», считал, что посажена по ошибке маленькая кучка людей, в том числе и он, остальные репрессированы за дело… (Гроссман 2). He had repeated, "You don't get arrested for nothing," believing that only a tiny minority, himself among them, had been arrested by mistake. As for everyone else—they had deserved their sentences (2a). ♦ В моё время… люди изданные на Западе книги не только у себя дома, на семь замков заперишись, читали, а где попало, в том числе и в общественном транспорте (Войнович 1). In my time…people did not read books published in the West only at home with every lock on every door locked, but indulged wherever they happened to be, even on public transportation (1a).

Ч-153 • ПО ПÉРВОЕ ЧИСЛÓ всыпать, задать, влететь *кому*, получить и т. п. coll [PrepP; Invar; adv (intensif); fixed WO] (to reprimand, punish, beat, defeat etc s.o.) severely, harshly: X всыпал Y-у по первое число ≃ **X gave it to Y good; X let Y have it;** [in refer. to reprimands only] **X gave Y what for; X gave Y hell; X raked Y over the coals;** [in military and sporting contexts] X-ы всыпали Y-ам по первое число ≃ **Xs clobbered ⟨routed⟩ Ys; Xs ran ⟨drove⟩ Ys into the ground;** ‖ X получил по первое число ≃ **X got it good;** [in refer. to reprimands or punishment only] **X got ⟨caught⟩ it in the neck;** [in refer. to reprimands only] **X caught hell.**

«Смотри, Пашка, узнает мать, что ты куришь, — всыплет тебе по первое число». — «Не узнает». "Watch out, Pashka, if mom finds out you smoke she'll give it to you good." "She won't find out." ♦ «И вдруг встаёт Ирина и говорит… В общем, неважно, что именно она говорила. Вложила им по первое число. И я немного добавил» (Аржак 2). "Then suddenly Irina gets up and says—as a matter of fact, it doesn't matter what she said. She really gave them what for. And I added a thing or two" (2a).

Ч-154 • ЗÁДНИМ ЧИСЛÓМ coll [NP_{instrum}; Invar; adv; fixed WO] **1.** помечать *что*, оформлять *кого-что* to mark some document with a date that is earlier than the date on which the mark is made: **predate; backdate; antedate.**

2. ~ понять *что*, сообразить, оценить *кого-что*, жалеть, испугаться и т. п. (to understand sth., figure sth. out, appreciate s.o. or sth., regret having done sth., get scared etc) at some point after the event, action etc in question has already taken place or been carried out: **in ⟨with⟩ hindsight; after the event ⟨the fact⟩; in retrospect; later (on);** [in limited contexts] **looking back on it.**

Настёна и не подозревала в себе этой порчи и пошла замуж легко, заранее зная бабью судьбу, радуясь самой большой перемене в своей жизни и немножко, задним числом, как это обычно бывает, жалея, что походила в девках мало (Распутин 2). Nastyona had not even suspected that there was something wrong with her and she entered marriage easily, knowing a woman's fate, happy about the greatest change in her life and only being sorry a little, in hindsight, as usually happens, about not having remained unmarried longer (2a). ♦ Сейчас, задним числом, я думаю, что у кагебешников даже и шанса не было не сдаться. Вопрос о моём отъезде был решён на каких-то верхах, им недоступных. И нарушать решение верхов им было не под силу (Войнович 1). Now, with hindsight, I think the KGB had no choice but to give in. The question of my leaving the country had been decided high up, on levels to which these men had no access. It was not in their power to violate such a decision (1a). ♦ Перед отправкой в Саматиху Ставский впервые принял О. М[андельштама]. Мы тоже сочли это добрым знаком. На самом же деле, ему, наверное, понадобился добавочный материал для «рецензии» на Мандельштама, то есть для характеристики, предваряющей его арест. Иногда такие характеристики писались задним числом, когда человек уже находился в тюрьме, иногда перед арестом (Мандельштам 1). Before sending us to Samatikha, Stavski had received M[andelstam] for the first time. This also we had taken as a good sign. But in fact Stavski probably wanted to see M[andelstam] only to make it easier for him to write his report—the sort of report always written on a man about to be arrested. Such reports were sometimes written after the event, when the person in question had already been arrested, and sometimes beforehand (1a).

Ч-155 • ПО ЧИ́СТОЙ демобилизовать *кого*, демобилизоваться, списать *кого* coll [PrepP; Invar; adv] (to dismiss s.o. or be dismissed from military service) entirely and forever: **(be) completely discharged; (give s.o. ⟨get⟩) a complete ⟨full⟩ discharge.**

Глубокий осенью 1917 года стали возвращаться с фронта казаки. Пришёл постаревший Христоня с тремя казаками, служившими с ним в 52-м полку. Вернулись уволенные по чистой, по-прежнему голощёкий Аникушка, батарейцы Томилин Иван и Яков Подкова, за ними — Мартин Шамиль, Иван Алексеевич, Захар Королёв, нескладно длинный Борщёв… (Шолохов 3). Late in the autumn of 1917 the Cossacks started coming home from the front. Khristonya, looking much older, returned with three other Cossacks who had served with him in the 52nd Regiment. Anikei, as hairless as ever, and gunners Ivan Tomilin and Horseshoe Yakov with a complete discharge were followed by Martin Shamil, Ivan Alexeyevich Kotlyarov, Zakhar Korolyov, and the tall ungainly Borshchev… (3a).

Ч-156 • НА ВСЯ́КИЙ ЧИХ ⟨НА ВСЯ́КОЕ ЧИХА́НЬЕ⟩ НЕ НАЗДРА́ВСТВУЕШЬСЯ coll [saying] (used to indicate that some comment, rumor, gossip etc does not deserve attention) you should not let what others say bother you, since it is impossible to satisfy everyone by your behavior or actions: ≃ **let it go; don't pay any attention; don't pay it any mind; it's not worth your time;** [in limited contexts] **there's no pleasing everybody.**

[Анна Петровна:] …Ещё тут сплетни какие-то распустили про Машеньку! На что это похоже! [Добротворский:] На всякое чиханье, сударыня, не наздравствуешься (Островский 1). [A.P.:] …They've even spread abroad some scandal about Mashenka! How outrageous! [D.:] There's no pleasing everybody, madam (1b).

Ч-157 • НЕ ВÉРИТЬ НИ В ЧОХ, НИ В СОН (, НИ В ПТИ́ЧИЙ ГРАЙ) coll [VP; subj: human] not to believe in the existence of or fear any supernatural forces, not to be superstitious: X не верил ни в чох ни в сон ≃ **X feared ⟨believed in⟩ neither God nor the devil; X believed in neither heaven nor hell.**

Ч-158 • ДО ЧРЕЗВЫЧА́ЙНОСТИ [PrepP; Invar; modif] to a very high degree: **extremely; exceptionally; incredibly;** [in limited contexts] **unbearably.**

До чрезвычайности приятный негр… почитывал какой-то журнальчик… (Аксёнов 12). An extremely pleasant black man…sat reading a magazine… (12a). ♦ Дни стояли жаркие до чрезвычайности. Над полями видно было ясно, как переливался прозрачный, жирный зной (Булгаков 10). The days were unbearably hot. You could see the dense, transparent heat wavering over the fields (10a).

Ч-159 • (А) МНЕ́-ТО ⟨тебе́-то и т. п.⟩ ЧТО? *coll* [sent; these forms only; fixed WO] that does not have any relation to me (you etc), that does not interest or concern me (him etc): (a) мне-то ⟨тебе-то, ему-то и т. п.⟩ что? ≃ **what's it to me ⟨you, him etc⟩?; what do I ⟨do you, does he etc⟩ care?; I ⟨he etc⟩ couldn't care less; it's no skin off my ⟨your, his etc⟩ nose.**

«Говорят, будут сливать несколько отделов». — «Тебе-то что! Твоего отдела это не коснётся». "I hear they're going to merge several departments." "What do you care, your department won't be affected."

Ч-160 • А ЧТО? *coll* [Invar] **1.** [indep. remark] what is your reason for asking or saying this (used in response to a question or as a remark intended to induce the interlocutor to continue speaking, to give an explanation): **why (do you ask ⟨say that⟩)?; what about it ⟨him etc⟩?; what of it?; [in limited contexts] why not?; what's wrong with it ⟨that⟩?**

[Клавдия Васильевна:] Где Олег? [Геннадий:] А что?.. Зачем он вам? (Розов 2). [K.V.:] Where's Oleg? [G.:] What about it?…What do you need him for? (2a). ♦ «У мамы отпуск, у папы отпуск, у меня каникулы, вот мы сюда и приехали на пять дней покататься на лыжах». — «Прямо так вот взяли и приехали?» — «Ну да. А что?» (Войнович 1). "Mama's on vacation, Papa's on vacation, and it's school break, so we came to ski for five days." "You just up and came?" "That's right. Why not?" (1a).

2. [Particle] used in the beginning of a question or exclamation to add emphasis to it or to draw the interlocutor's attention to it: **listen; look; say; hey; [in limited contexts] what.**

[Гомыра:] Не поверите, не принимал сегодня ни грамма и сейчас не хочу. А что, ребята, может, я желаю воспоминания сохранить об этом вечере? (Вампилов 3). [G.:] You won't believe it, but I haven't had a drop today, and now I don't want any. Look fellows, maybe I want to cherish some memories of this evening? (3b). ♦ «А что, коньячку не выпьешь?..» — «Нет, не надо, благодарю. Вот этот хлебец возьму с собой, коли дадите…» (Достоевский 1). "Say, how about a little cognac?…" "No, no, thank you. But I'll take this bread with me, if I may…" (1a). ♦ «Давай пойдём в кино». — «А что, совсем неплохая идея». "Let's go to the movies." "Hey, that's not a bad idea." ♦ Я долго вертел в руках этот бесценный документ [ордер на квартиру] и увидел запись, сделанную на обратной стороне, что моя семья состоит «из одного чел». «Как же это из одного?» — спросил я управдома. «А что, жена уже родила?» — спросил он (Войнович 3). I turned this priceless document [assigning us an apartment] around in my hands for a long time and saw the entry, made on the reverse side, that my family consisted of one person. "What do you mean, of one person?" I asked the building manager. "What, did your wife give birth already?" he asked (3a).

Ч-161 • ВО́Т ⟨ВО́Н⟩ ОНО́ ЧТО! *coll* [Interj; these forms only; fixed WO] used to express surprise, amazement, sudden understanding etc: **so that's it!; so that's what ⟨how⟩ it is!; so that's ⟨this is⟩ what it's all about!; so that's what happened!; (now) I see ⟨understand, get it⟩!; [in limited contexts] how about that!; really!; so that's why…; so that's where s.o. got sth. ⟨why s.o. did sth. etc⟩.**

…[Я] сказал, что ни с кем не общаюсь и нигде не бываю. «…Но вы же были на художественной выставке и там смотрели абстрактные картины». Ах, вот оно что! Хотя это была выставка совершенно официальная и никто не преду-

преждал, что ходить на неё не надо, но как советский человек я должен был понимать, что на абстрактные картины лучше всё-таки не смотреть (Войнович 1). I said that I didn't associate with anyone and didn't go anywhere. "…You've been to an art exhibit, and you looked at abstract paintings." Oh, so that was it! Even though that exhibit had been entirely official, and no one had warned me not to go there, as a good Soviet I should have known that, no matter what, it's best to avoid looking at abstract paintings (1a). ♦ Вот оно что! Письмо не дошло до адресата, потому что в адресе ошибка! So that's what happened! The letter didn't get to the addressee because there was a mistake in the address! ♦ Конференция, старая лошадь, новые сады, бюллетени и лаванда, овечки с паспортами. Ах, вот оно что! Какой-то французский реакционный префект выслал этих колхозников из Франции, не постеснявшись заявить публично, что они поселились в районе, где интересы национальной обороны требуют повышенной бдительности (Войнович 1). A conference, an old horse, new orchards, bulletins and lavender, sheep with passports. Ah, now I see! Some reactionary French prefect deported those kolkhozniks from France and was not ashamed to state publicly that they had settled in an area where national defense interests required increased vigilance (1a). ♦ «Оказывается, когда пьёшь вниз головой, быстро хмелеешь. Хмель сразу же стекает в голову» — «Ах, вот оно что», — сказал Объедало и успокоился (Искандер 5). "When you drink head down, it turns out, you get tipsy fast. The tipsiness runs straight to your head." "Really?" Trencherman said, mollified (5a). ♦ [Саяпин:] …Без жены он, сам знаешь, ни шагу. [Зилов:] А он жену вчера на юг отправил. [Саяпин:] Вот оно что. То-то загулял мужик… (Вампилов 5). [S.:] …You know he doesn't make a move without his wife. [Z.:] But he sent her off to the south yesterday. [S.:] So that's why the guy is cutting loose… (5b).

Ч-162 • ВО́Т ЧТО *coll* [Interj or Particle; Invar; fixed WO] used to introduce and draw the interlocutor's attention to a statement, or, when used at the end of a statement, to conclude and add emphasis to that statement: [when introducing a statement] **now, listen to me; look here; here's the thing ⟨the story, the deal⟩; [when recalling sth. one had not been able to recall earlier in the conversation] oh yes (, that's it); [when concluding a statement] that's what it is; that's the thing; that's what; [in limited contexts] that's the trouble.**

«Вот что, станишники [phonetic spelling = станичники]! Нам тут делать нечего. Надо уходить…» (Шолохов 3). "Now, listen to me, Cossacks! There's no point in our staying here. We've got to get away…" (3a). ♦ [Полуорлов:] Вот что! Не надо извращать моих слов (Рощин 2). [P.:] Look here! You don't need to twist my words (2a). ♦ «Да, вот что, — вспомнил он. — Тётка твоя чулки просила купить…» (Абрамов 1). "Oh yes," he remembered. "Your aunt asked me to buy her some stockings…" (1a). ♦ «Вы не хотите, чтоб я любил вас, вот что!» — воскликнул я мрачно… (Тургенев 3). "You don't want me to love you—that's what it is," I burst out gloomily… (3b). ♦ «Худо у меня, Михаил, дома, худо». — «А чего? С Марьей поцапались?» — «Ах, кабы только с Марьей! Валентина у меня больна — вот что» (Абрамов 1). "It's bad at my place, Mikhail, bad." "Why? Have you been quarreling with Marya?" "Oh, if it were only Marya. My Valentina is sick, that's the trouble" (1b).

Ч-163 • ДА ЧТО́…! *coll* [Particle; Invar; foll. by NP] used in exclamations to show that the commentary in the preceding context, which refers to the person(s), thing(s) etc reintroduced by the idiom, is in some way an understatement or does not reflect the entirety of the situation, and that what is to follow is both more extreme and closer to the truth: **what am I saying, [+ the word or phrase in question from the preceding context]; s.o. ⟨sth.⟩ isn't the half of it!; and not just ⟨only⟩…!**

«Вы, может быть, думаете, что наука — это лёгкое дело? Это, сударыня, годы труда, самоотверженного и незаметного! Да что там годы — вся жизнь!» (Каверин 1). "Perhaps you think that scientific research is an easy thing? Madam, it means years of labour, selfless and unregarded! What am I saying: years—one's whole life!" (1a). ♦ И тут не только дети, но и все друзья Джамхуха завизжали от восторга! Да что друзья Джамхуха, даже куры радостно закудахтали... (Искандер 5). Not just the children but all Jamkhoukh's friends, too, now squealed with delight! And not just Jamkhoukh's friends, even the chickens set up a glad cackle... (5a).

Ч-164 • **ÉСЛИ ЧТО** coll; **ÉЖЕЛИ ЧТО** highly coll [subord clause; Invar; fixed WO] if some trouble should occur or need should arise: **if something ⟨anything⟩ happens ⟨should happen⟩; if anything happens ⟨should happen⟩ to me ⟨it etc⟩; in case something ⟨anything⟩ happens; if anything comes ⟨crops⟩ up; if need be; if something ⟨anything⟩ goes wrong; if things go wrong ⟨take a wrong turn⟩; in the event of trouble; if there's any trouble;** [in limited contexts] **any tricks (and...).**

[Гомыра:] Я это к тому говорю, что раз уж он попал в такую историю, то пусть он знает... *(Обращаясь к Букину.)* Короче, если что, то знай, Вася, у тебя есть друзья, которые не бросят тебя на произвол судьбы (Вампилов 3). [G.:] I'm saying this so that, since he's got himself into a situation like this, he'll know... *(Turns to Bukin.)* In other words, if anything happens, Vasia, you know you've got friends who won't just leave you to your fate (3a). ♦ «...У меня здесь секретная документация, если что, голову с меня сымут [*substand* — снимут]...» (Максимов 2). "...I'm carrying secret documents, and if anything happens to them my head will roll..." (2a). ♦ «До свиданья, Сын Оленя!.. Если что — дай знать! Чем можем — поможем!» (Искандер 5). "Good-bye, Son of the Deer....If anything comes up, let us know! We'll help any way we can!" (5a). ♦ Новый тихий и глупый Заибан тут же приказал подготовить ему речь для празднования юбилея Ларька... И намекнул, что ежели что, так он посадит. Не остановится! (Зиновьев 1). This new insipid and stupid Leadiban immediately had a speech prepared for him to deliver on the anniversary of the Shop...and he made it very plain that if things went wrong he wouldn't hesitate to make an arrest or two (1a). ♦ «Ну гляди, — ...пригрозил Алтынник, — если что, всех вас перережу, под расстрел пойду, а жить с Людкой не буду» (Войнович 5). "But now listen"—Altinnik decided to throw in a threat...—"any tricks and I'll cut all of you to ribbons. I'll take a firing squad over living with Ludmilla" (5a). ♦ Они посоветовали мне проситься в санитары: всё-таки, если что, так врачи близко, будут подлечивать помаленьку (Марченко 1). [context transl] They advised me to apply for work as an orderly: it was close to the doctors, just in case, and they would treat me a bit on the side (1a).

Ч-165 • **ЗА ЧТÓ; ЗА ЧТÓ ПРО ЧТÓ** coll [PrepP; these forms only; adv; used in questions and subord clauses] for what reason or cause: **what for; why; whatever for.**

«Я решился драться с вами». — «Со мной?» — «Непременно с вами». — «Да за что? помилуйте». — «Я бы мог объяснить вам причину, — начал Павел Петрович. — Но я предпочитаю умолчать о ней» (Тургенев 2). "I have decided to fight you." Bazarov opened his eyes wide. "Me?" "Precisely." "But what for, pray?" "I could explain the reason to you," began Pavel Petrovich, "but I prefer to keep silent about it" (2c). ♦ «Тебе бы следовало уважать в нём моего приятеля...» — «Уважать немца? — с величайшим презрением сказал Тарантьев. — За что это?» — «Я уж тебе сказал, хоть бы за то, что он вместе со мной рос и учился» (Гончаров 1). "You ought to respect him as my friend..." "To respect a German?" Tarantyev said with the utmost contempt. "Why should I?" "But I've just told you—if for nothing else then because we grew up and went to the same school together" (1a).

Ч-166 • **НА ЧТÓ¹** *кому кто-что* coll [PrepP; Invar; adv; used in questions without a verb and in subord clauses] for what purpose (does s.o. need some person or thing): на что Y-у X? ≃ **why does Y need X?; what does Y need X for?; what does Y want**

with X?; [when said ironically, mockingly etc] **what good ⟨use⟩ is X to Y?; what is X to Y?; what does Y care about X?**

...Помнили, что так же, как и теперь, в руках его торчала целая пачка радужных и он разбрасывал их зря, не торгуясь, не соображая и не желая соображать, на что ему столько товару, вина и проч.? (Достоевский 1). ...They remembered that he had a whole wad of money sticking out of his hand, just as now, and was throwing it around for nothing, without bargaining, without thinking and without wishing to think why he needed such a quantity of goods, wines, and so forth (1a). ♦ Большую часть наук читал он сам. Без педантских терминов, напыщенных воззрений и взглядов, умел он передать самую душу науки, так что и малолетнему было видно, на что она ему нужна (Гоголь 3). He taught most of the subjects himself, he knew how to convey the very essence of a subject without using any pedantic terms or pompous theories and opinions, so that even a small boy could grasp immediately what he needed it for (3a). ♦ [Лука:] Стихи-и! А на что они мне, стихи-то? (Горький 3). [L.:] Poetry? What do I want with poetry? (3d). ♦ «Да... я... я... я желала его смерти! Да, я желала, чтобы скорее кончилось... Я хотела успокоиться... А что ж будет со мной? На что моё спокойствие, когда его не будет!» — бормотала княжна Марья... (Толстой 6). "Yes...I—I wished for his death! Yes...I wanted it to end sooner... so that *I* could be at peace. But what will become of me? What good will peace be to me when he is gone?" Princess Marya murmured... (6a). ♦ [Аннушка:] Ты меня, братец, отпусти домой! На что я тебе? (Островский 8). [A.:] Brother, let me go home! What use am I to you? (8a). ♦ [Хомич:] Я инженер, я талантливый человек. [Граня:] На что мне твой ум? На что мне твой ум? (Солженицын 8). [Kh.:] I'm an engineer, I've got talent.... [G.:] What do I care about your brains? What do I care? (8a).

Ч-167 • **НА ЧТÓ²** (..., а ⟨но⟩); **УЖ НА ЧТÓ** (..., а ⟨но⟩) *both* coll [Particle; these forms only] **1.** despite the fact that the person or thing in question possesses the named quality to a high degree, displays the named characteristics to a great extent etc: (уж) на что X..., а ⟨но⟩ и он... ≃ **(as)...as X is, even he ⟨it etc⟩...; even X, as...as he ⟨it etc⟩ is,...; heaven knows X is..., but ⟨yet, and⟩ he ⟨it etc⟩...**

Уж на что Пётр дурак, но даже он сообразил, в чём дело. Stupid as Pyotr is, even he figured out what this was all about. ♦ Даже Самсик — уж на что не Брежнев, но и о нём поползли слухи от котельной «Советского пайщика»... (Аксёнов 6). Even Samsik—heaven knows, no Brezhnev he!—caused rumors to start emanating from the boiler room of the Soviet Shareholder... (6a).

2. [foll. by AdjP; used in exclamations] extremely, to a high degree: **how [AdjP]!; what (a) [NP]!; (s.o. ⟨sth.⟩) is so [AdjP]!**

Таких роз, как у нас, ни у кого нет. Уж на что хороши! No one has roses like ours. What beauties!

Ч-168 • **НÉ ЗА ЧТО** coll [formula phrase; Invar] used in response to an expression of thanks: **don't mention it; it was nothing ⟨no trouble⟩ (at all); no problem;** [in limited contexts] **my pleasure.**

«Спасибо, Нина Евгеньевна». — «Не за что. Я на работе» (Грекова 3). "Thank you, Nina Evgenievna." "Don't mention it. This is my job" (3a).

Ч-169 • **НÉ НА ЧТО** жить, купить *что* и т. п. coll [PrepP; Invar; subj-compl with быть∅ (subj: infin)] s.o. has no money at all or not enough money to buy sth.: **(s.o.) has nothing (to buy sth. with ⟨to live on⟩).**

Не только драгоценных металлов и мехов не получали обыватели в обмен за свои продукты, но и не на что было купить даже хлеба (Салтыков-Щедрин 1). Not only did the townsfolk receive no precious metals or furs in exchange for their products, they had nothing even to buy bread with (1a).

Ч-170 • НЕ ЧТО́ ИНО́Е, КАК... [NP; used as intensif Particle; foll. by NP (inanim or, rare, human); fixed WO] the named thing itself: не что иное, как X ≃ **nothing but X; nothing less ⟨else, other, more⟩ than X.**

...Честолюбие есть не что иное, как жажда власти... (Лермонтов 1). ...Ambition is nothing but greed for power... (1b). ...Ambition is nothing else than thirst for power... (1a). ♦ Публика начала даже склоняться в пользу того мнения, что вся эта история есть не что иное, как выдумка праздных людей... (Салтыков-Щедрин 1). The assemblage even began to incline toward the opinion that this whole incident was no more than the fabrication of idle people... (1a).

Ч-171 • НИ ЗА ЧТО́[1]; НИ ЗА ЧТО НА СВЕ́ТЕ *both coll* [PrepP; these forms only; adv; used with negated verbs (more often pfv fut or subjunctive); fixed WO] under no conditions or circumstances: **not for anything (in the world ⟨on earth⟩); not for (all) the world; on no ⟨not on any⟩ account; not at any price; nothing on earth (would ⟨could⟩ make one do sth.);** [in limited contexts] **not on your life!; no way! no dice!; nothing doing; no matter what; never.** Cf. **not for all the tea in China.**

«...Мне ни за что не хотелось бы расстаться с вами» (Булгаков 9). "I would not like to part with you for anything" (9a). ♦ Понять его [приказ] Руслан не мог, но не согласился бы ни за что на свете (Владимов 1). It was not that Ruslan could not understand the order; he would not have accepted it for anything in the world (1a). ♦ «...Вот какие у меня подозрения: они, то есть секунданты, должно быть, несколько переменили свой прежний план и хотят зарядить пулею один пистолет Грушницкого... Как вы думаете? Должны ли мы показать им, что догадались?» — «Ни за что на свете, доктор!» (Лермонтов 1). "...Here are my suspicions: they, that is to say the seconds, have apparently altered somewhat their former plan and want to load, with a bullet, only Grushnitski's pistol....What do you think, should we show them that we have found them out?" "Not for anything on earth, doctor!" (1a). ♦ ...Кузнец, который был издавна не в ладах с ним, при нём ни за что не отважится идти к дочке, несмотря на свою силу (Гоголь 5). ...The blacksmith, who had for a long time been on bad terms with him, would on no account have ventured, strong as he was, to visit the daughter when the father was at home (5a). ♦ Он договорить ещё не успел, я уже понял: ни за что не поеду! (Солженицын 2). Before he had finished speaking, my mind was made up. Nothing on earth would make me go! (2a). ♦ [Бусыгин:] Мы едем домой. [Сильва:] Ни за что (Вампилов 4). [B.:] We're going home. [S.:] Not on your life! (4a). [B.:] We're going home. [S.:] No dice (4b).

Ч-172 • НИ ЗА ЧТО́[2]; НИ ЗА ЧТО́ НИ ПРО ЧТО́; НИ ЗА́ ЧТО НИ ПРО́ ЧТО *all coll* [PrepP; these forms only; adv; more often used with pfv verbs; fixed WO] **1. погибнуть, пропасть** и т. п. ~ (of a person) (to perish, be destroyed etc) to no purpose, futilely: **(all) for nothing ⟨naught⟩; (all) in vain.**

Здесь ни за что погиб мой отец... Ни за грош пропала моя собственная жизнь (Зиновьев 1). "My Father died here for nothing....My own life has been ruined for nothing" (1a).

2. обидеть, оскорбить, ударить, ругать, арестовать *кого* и т. п. ~ (to offend, insult, hit, berate, arrest etc s.o.) without any reason or grounds for doing so: **for no reason (at all); for no reason whatever ⟨whatsoever⟩; for no good ⟨particular⟩ reason; for nothing (at all); for nothing, for no reason; just for the hell of it; (quarrel) over nothing.**

Настёна обычно отмалчивалась, она научилась этому ещё в то... лето, когда обходила с Катькой ангарские деревни и когда каждый, кому не лень, мог ни за что ни про что её облаять (Распутин 2). Nastyona usually held her peace. She had learned how that summer when she and Katya made the rounds of the Angara villages and anyone who felt like it could shower her with curses for no reason at all (2a). ♦ Чёрт сбил с толку обоих чинов-

ников: чиновники, говоря попросту, перебесились и пересорились ни за что (Гоголь 3). The Devil led the two officials astray: the officials, to put it plainly, went crazy and fell out with each other for no reason whatsoever (3c). ♦ ...Я защищал людей, которых сажали, как принято выражаться, за убеждения, или, иначе говоря, ни за что (Войнович 1). ...I spoke out in defense of people who, as we usually say, were imprisoned for their convictions, or, to put it another way, for nothing at all (1a). ♦ «Значит, вас арестовали ни за что ни про что? Мы сажаем невинных людей?» (Рыбаков 2). "So, you were arrested for nothing, for no reason? We put innocent people in prison, do we?" (2a). ♦ ...Эти умники из Кенгура... вполне могут засадить человека ни за что ни про что (Искандер 4). ...Those wiseacres from Kengur...were quite capable of putting a man in prison just for the hell of it (4a).

Ч-173 • НУ И ЧТО́ (ЖЕ)? *coll* [sent; Invar; fixed WO] used in response to s.o.'s statement to ask for an explanation of its significance (often said pointedly to express disagreement with the implications of what was said, one's opinion that the statement is irrelevant etc): **so what?; (and ⟨so, well,⟩) what of it?; so?; (well,) what about it?**

[Мечеткин:] Между прочим, уже десять девятого. [Хороших:] Ну и что? [Мечеткин:] Опаздываете, Анна Васильевна (Вампилов 2). [M.:] By the way, it is now ten minutes past eight. [A.:] So what? [M.:] You're late, Anna Vassilievna (2a). ♦ Да, да держал пастухов! Ну и что?! За три года работы пастух получал тридцать коз, после чего мог уйти и заводить собственное хозяйство (Искандер 3). Yes, he did keep shepherds! And what of it? For three years' work a shepherd received thirty goats, after which he could leave and start his own farm (3a). ♦ «Тётя Муза, — говорю я, — вы помните, как мне всегда хотелось поехать на юг? Так вот! Я до сих пор хочу на юг». — «Ну и что?» — говорит тётя Муза... (Михайловская 1). "Aunt Musa," I say, "do you remember how I have always wanted to go to the South? So, I still want to go to the South." "Well, what about it?" says Aunt Musa... (1a).

Ч-174 • НУ ЧТО́ *coll* [Particle; Invar] used to induce one's interlocutor to answer a question: **well; so.**

«Здравствуй, Илья. Как я рад тебя видеть! Ну что, как ты поживаешь? Здоров ли?» — спросил Штольц (Гончаров 1). "Good morning, Ilya, I'm so glad to see you! Well, how are you? All right?" asked Stolz (1a).

Ч-175 • ХОТЬ БЫ ЧТО́ *coll* [Invar; predic] **1. ~** *(кому) disapprov* [impers] s.o. is totally indifferent to sth.: X-у хоть бы что ≃ **X couldn't ⟨could⟩ care less; X doesn't give a hoot ⟨a damn, a darn⟩; X doesn't care a hang; X doesn't care; it means nothing ⟨it doesn't mean a thing⟩ to X.**

«Смотрю, у обочины под кустом сидит на мотоцикле товарищ Красивый Фуражкин, автоинспектор, газету читает, а мимо грузовики идут, хоть бы что» (Аксёнов 10). "I see at the side of the road, under a bush, sitting on his motor-bike—Comrade Smart-Hat, traffic-cop. He's reading a newspaper while lorries go by, he couldn't care less" (10a). ♦ [Ксения:] Отец-то крёстный — болеет, а тебе хоть бы что... (Горький 2). [K.:] Here's your godfather lying sick, and you don't care a hang (2a).

2. ~ *кому* or *кто* [impers or, less often, with subj: human] sth. (fatigue, physical or emotional stress, alcohol etc) has no impact on s.o., in no way reflects on s.o.: X-у хоть бы что ≃ **it doesn't affect ⟨tell on⟩ X at all ⟨a bit⟩; it has no effect on X; it's nothing for X;** [in refer. to emotional stress] **it doesn't ruffle X at all ⟨a bit⟩;** [in refer. to doing sth. dangerous, difficult etc] **(X does sth.) without turning a hair.**

Он может один выпить бутылку водки — и хоть бы что! He can drink a whole bottle of vodka all by himself—and it doesn't affect him a bit. ♦ [Миронов:] Отчаянный, однако, у вас водитель, товарищ председатель. Гонит в самую пургу, хоть бы что! (Салынский 1). [M.:] You've got a fearless chauffeur, Comrade Chairman. She drives through a blizzard without turning a hair! (1a).

Ч-176 • **ХОТЬ ТЫ ЧТО** *highly coll* [subord clause; Invar] regardless of what one does (the desired outcome is unattainable): **try as you ⟨he etc⟩ may ⟨might⟩; no matter what you do ⟨try⟩; it's a lost cause; it's hopeless.**

«Рафаэля считают чуть не дураком, потому что это, мол, авторитет; а сами бессильны и бесплодны до гадости, у самих фантазия дальше „Девушки у фонтана" не хватает, хоть ты что! И написана-то девушка прескверно» (Тургенев 2). "Raphael they practically regard as a fool because, if you please, he is an authority. Yet they themselves are so impotent and sterile that their imagination cannot rise above *Girl at the Fountain*, try as they may. And the girl is abominably drawn" (2c). ♦ Никакими доводами нельзя убедить его бросить курить, хоть ты что! There's no argument in the world that will make him quit smoking. It's a lost cause.

Ч-177 • **ЧТО БЫ ⟨Б⟩...** *coll* [modal Particle; Invar] (used in exclamations to express the wish that s.o. do sth. or that sth. happen, express frustration that s.o. did not do sth. or that sth. did not happen etc) it would be (or would have been) good if: **why don't...; why not...; it would be ⟨might be, would have been etc⟩ nice if...;** [in limited contexts] **if only...**

Что бы тебе помолчать. Why don't you keep quiet. ♦ Вот так же и в случае с корейским самолётом. Что бы сказать попросту: самолёт был сбит. Так нет, ушёл в сторону Японского моря (Войнович 1). The same was true in the case of the Korean airliner. Why not say simply that the plane was shot down? No, the plane went off in the direction of the Sea of Japan (1a).

Ч-178 • **ЧТО ДО... (ТО ⟨ТАК⟩...)** [subord Conj] as concerns (s.o. or sth.): что до X-а (, то...) ≃ **as ⟨so⟩ far as X is concerned; as for ⟨to⟩ X; when it comes to X; for person X's part.**

«Что же до меня, то я давно уже положил не думать о том: человек ли создал бога или бог человека?» (Достоевский 1). "As for me, I long ago decided not to think about whether man created God or God created man" (1a). ♦ Что до того, как вести себя... поддержать этикет, множество приличий самых тонких, а особенно наблюсти моду в самых последних мелочах, то в этом они [дамы города N.] опередили даже дам петербургских и московских (Гоголь 3). As to the ways in which they [the ladies of the town of N—] conducted themselves...observed the etiquette with its multitude of the subtlest proprieties, and responded to the minutest dictates of fashion—in these things they surpassed even the ladies of Petersburg and Moscow (3c). ♦ «Впрочем, что до меня, — сказал он, — мне, признаюсь, более всех нравится полицеймейстер» (Гоголь 3). "For my part," he said, "I must confess that I liked the chief of police best of all" (3a).

Ч-179 • **ЧТО, ÉСЛИ ⟨ÉСЛИ Б(Ы)⟩; ЧТО, ÉЖЕЛИ ⟨ÉЖЕЛИ Б(Ы)⟩** *highly coll* [these forms only; fixed WO] **1.** used to introduce a question expressing inquiry, apprehension etc: **what if...; suppose...**

Он пошёл тише, тише, тише, одолеваемый сомнениями. «А что, если она кокетничает со мной?.. Если только...» Он остановился совсем, оцепенел на минуту. «Что, если тут коварство, заговор...» (Гончаров 1). He walked slower and slower, overcome with doubts. "And what if she is just flirting with me? If only—" He stopped altogether, rooted to the spot for a moment. "What if it is treachery, a plot?..." (1a). ♦ [Хлестаков:] Что, если в самом деле он [городничий] потащит меня в тюрьму? (Гоголь 4). [Kh.:] Suppose he [the Mayor] really does haul me off to jail? (4b).

2. used to introduce a question expressing a suggestion, invitation, request: **why not...; why don't...; how about...; what if...; what about...**

Что, если пойти вечером в кино? How about going to the movies tonight? ♦ Некоторые довольно интеллигентные люди, замечая отдельные недостатки, которые всё ещё имеют место в нашей стране, думают: а что, если слегка потеснить большевиков, чтобы в дальнейшем, устранив эти недостатки, перестать их теснить? (Искандер 4). There are certain rather well-informed people who notice the isolated shortcomings that still exist in our country and think: What if we crowd the Bolsheviks a little, with the idea that we'll stop crowding them in the future, when we've eliminated these deficiencies? (4a).

Ч-180 • **ЧТО Ж(Е)** *coll* [Particle; Invar] **1.** Also: **ЧЕГО Ж(Е)** *highly coll;* **ЧТО (ЖЕ) ЭТО** *coll* [used in questions and subord clauses] for what reason?: **why?; what for?; how come?**

«Эхе, хе! двенадцать часов! — сказал... Чичиков, взглянув на часы. — Что ж я так закопался?» (Гоголь 3). "Oh, my, it's twelve o'clock already," said Chichikov, glancing at his watch. "Why have I been lingering over the stuff so long?" (3c). ♦ ...[Я] сказал: «Я твой господин, а ты мой слуга. Деньги мои. Я их проиграл, потому что так мне вздумалось. А тебе советую не умничать и делать то, что тебе приказывают». Савельич так был поражён моими словами, что всплеснул руками и остолбенел. «Что же ты стоишь! — закричал я сердито (Пушкин 2). ...[I said,] "I am your master, you are my servant. The money is mine. I lost it at billiards because that was my pleasure. As for you, I advise you not to try to be clever, but to do what you're told." Savelich was so struck by my words that he just threw up his hands and stood rooted to the ground. "What are you waiting for?" I bawled at him angrily (2a).

2. used to introduce questions, often rhetorical ones, or exclamations (when the question or exclamation is positively phrased, a negative response is expected; when the question or exclamation is negatively phrased, a confirmation or expression of agreement is expected): **what; (and) so;** [in limited contexts] **you don't expect ⟨think⟩?**

«Мы к товарищу председателю [Голосову]...» — «Голосова сейчас здесь нет, он ушёл». По кустам прокатился глухой смех. «Это вы, товарищ, изволили сказать несправедливо...» — «Вот чудаки! — воскликнул Покисен. — Что же, я вам врать, что ли, буду? Голосов вышел в сад» (Федин 1). "We want the comrade chairman [Golosov]...." "Golosov isn't here at the moment, he went out." A hollow laugh rolled through the bushes. "Now you're speaking falsely, Comrade." "What fools!" exclaimed Pokisen. "What, d'you think I'm going to lie to you? Golosov's gone out to the orchard" (1a). ♦ Соколов рассказал, что Гавронов заговорил о том, что работа Штрума противоречит ленинским взглядам на природу материи... «Что же, так никто и не возражал?» — «Пожалуй, нет» (Гроссман 2). Sokolov said that Gavronov had asserted that Viktor's work contradicted the Leninist view of the nature of matter.... "And no one stood up for me?" "I don't think so" (2a). ♦ «Что ж мне, лгать, что ли, на старости лет?» — оправдывался Захар (Гончаров 1). "You don't expect me to go around telling lies at my age, do you?" Zakhar protested (1b).

3. used in a dialogue to induce one's interlocutor to answer a question or give an explanation: **well; now; (and) what about it?; (and) what of it?;** [in limited contexts] **...I suppose.**

«...Как проехать отсюда к Плюшкину, так, чтобы не мимо господского дома?» Мужик, казалось, затруднился таким вопросом. «Что ж, ты не знаешь?» — «Нет, барин, не знаю» (Гоголь 3). "How can we drive to Pliushkin's place from here without passing by the manor house?" The peasant seemed puzzled by the question. "Well, don't you know?" "No, sir, I don't" (3c). ♦ «Что ж, тебе не хотелось бы так пожить?»... — «И весь век так?» — спросил Штольц. «До седых волос, до гробовой доски. Это жизнь!» (Гончаров 1). "Now, wouldn't you like to live like that?"... "To live like that all the time?" "Till you grow gray—till you are laid in the grave! That is life!" (1b). ♦ «Я офицер и дворянин; вчера ещё дрался против тебя, а сегодня еду с тобой в одной кибитке, и счастие всей моей жизни зависит от тебя». — «Что ж? — спросил Пугачёв. — Страшно тебе?» (Пушкин 2). "I am an officer and a nobleman; only yesterday I was fighting against you; yet today I'm riding in the same wagon with you, and the happiness of my whole life depends on you." "And what about it?" asked Pugachev.

"Are you scared?" (2a). ♦ «Он, что же, по-советски женился?» — «Не знаю. Думаю – да», – ответил Старцов (Федин 1). "He had a Soviet wedding, I suppose?" "I don't know. I think so—yes," replied Startsov (1a).

4. Also: **НУ ЧТО Ж(Е)** *coll* used to introduce a remark expressing concession, agreement: **well (then); all right then.**

…В тени яблони дожидается его какой-то крестьянин, ви-димо, приехавший к нему за советом. Крестьянин встаёт и почтительно кланяется ему. Что ж, придётся побеседовать с ним, дать ему дельный совет (Искандер 3). …A peasant has been waiting for him in the shade of an apple tree. The peasant, who has evidently come to him for advice, stands up and bows to him respectfully. Well, he'll have to take the time to chat with him, give him some sensible advice (3a). ♦ «Со мной в дороге легко». – «Ну что ж, идём», – сказал Джамхух, и они пошли (Искандер 5). "Traveling with me is no trouble." "Well then, let's go," Jamkhoukh said, and they started out (5a). ♦ «Позвонил я первому секретарю обкома, хотел проститься… а помощник его… сказал: „Товарищ Пряхин с вами говорить не может. Занят". … Я ему говорю, уезжаю сегодня, сам знаешь. А он мне: что ж, тогда напишите, обратитесь в письменной форме» (Гроссман 2). "I phoned the first secretary of the *obkom* [Oblast Party Committee] to say goodbye.…But his assistant…said: 'Comrade Pryakhin's unable to speak to you. He's engaged.' So I said to him: 'I'm leaving today. You know that very well.' 'All right then,' he said, 'you can address him in writing'" (2a).

Ч-181 • ЧТО Ж(Е) ТАКОГО ⟨ТАКОЕ⟩?; ЧТО (Ж ⟨ЖЕ⟩) (ТУТ) ТАКОГО? *all coll* [indep. clause; these forms only] what is unusual (whether good or bad) about that?: **so what (if…)?; what of it (if…)?; what's wrong with that?; what's the big deal?; what's so special ⟨terrible, wonderful etc⟩ about that?**

[Фёкла:] Впрочем, что ж такого, что иной раз выпьет лишнее – ведь не всю же неделю бывает пьян; иной день выберется и трезвый (Гоголь 1). [F.:] But what of it if he has a drop too much now and then? He's not drunk all week. Some days he turns up sober (1b). ♦ [Колесов:] …Зря вы от свадьбы отказываетесь. Пожалеете, Таня. [Таня:] Ничего, переживу как-нибудь. [Колесов:] Ну, смотрите. А то приходите, если вздумаете. Комната сорок два – запомнили? [Таня:] Как? Вы опять меня приглашаете? А с Голошубовой как же? [Колесов:] Приглашаю и вас и Голошубову. Что тут такого? Места всем хватит – свадьба (Вампилов 3). [K.:] …You shouldn't turn down the wedding. You'll be sorry, Tanya. [T.:] Never mind. I'll survive, somehow. [K.:] Well, it's up to you. But if you change your mind, come anyway. Room forty-two—got it? [T.:] What? You're inviting me again? What about Goloshubova? [K.:] I'm inviting you and Goloshubova. What's wrong with that? There's room for everybody—it's a wedding! (3b).

Ч-182 • ЧТО ЗА… *coll* [Particle; Invar] **1.** [used in questions and obj or subj clauses] used when asking the interlocutor to describe the character, personality etc of the named person(s), or the nature, characteristics etc of the named thing: **what kind ⟨sort⟩ of (a) [NP] is (s.o. ⟨sth.⟩)?; what is s.o. ⟨sth.⟩ like?; what is (s.o. ⟨sth.⟩)?**

«А насчёт квартиры я вам вот что скажу: соглашайтесь. Нет, не кидайтесь так сразу. Скажите, что вам надо по-думать, посмотреть, что за квартира…» (Войнович 3). "But here's what I have to say to you about the apartment: agree. No, don't just give in right away. Say that you have to think it over, see what kind of apartment it is…" (3a). ♦ «А что за человек этот Пугачёв?» – спросила комендантша (Пушкин 2). "And what sort of a man is this Pugachev?" asked the commandant's wife (2b). ♦ «…Вы мне должны описать маменьку с дочкой. Что они за люди?» (Лермонтов 1). "…You must give me a description of the mother and daughter. What are they like?" (1c). ♦ «Максим Максимыч, – сказал я, подошедши к нему, – а что за бумаги вам оставил

Печорин?» (Лермонтов 1). "Maxim Maximych," said I, walking up to him. "What were the papers Pechorin left you?" (1b).

2. (used in exclamations expressing the speaker's feeling about or emotional reaction to some person, thing, or phenomenon) (s.o. or sth. is) very (pretty, nice, revolting etc): **what a [NP]!; what a beautiful ⟨terrible etc⟩ [NP]!; (he ⟨it etc⟩) is such a [NP]; (he ⟨she etc⟩) is such an exquisite ⟨beautiful etc⟩ [NP]; [when the Russian NP is translated by an AdjP] how [AdjP].**

[Альда:] Что за славный лесочек! (Солженицын 11). What a gorgeous little wood! (11a). ♦ [Гаврюшка:] Как подумаешь, что за житьё господам на свете! Куда хошь [*substand* = хочешь] катай! (Гоголь 2). [G.:] What a fine life the gentry lead, when you think of it! Drive about wherever you like! (2b). ♦ «Ты любишь эту арию? Я очень рад: её прекрасно поёт Ольга Ильинская. Я познакомлю тебя – вот голос, вот пение! И сама она что за очаровательное дитя!» (Гончаров 1). "You are fond of that aria? That's fine! Olga Ilyinsky sings it beautifully. I'll introduce you to her. She has a lovely voice and she sings wonderfully. And she herself is such a charming child!" (1a). ♦ «Что за страсть убивать время с этим болваном!» (Гончаров 1). "How awful to waste your time with a blockhead like that!" (1b).

Ч-183 • ЧТО К ЧЕМУ знать, понимать, соображать, разобраться, объяснить и т. п. *coll* [Invar; usu. used as an obj clause; fixed WO] (to know, understand, grasp, explain etc) how a business, process etc operates, or what the situation is or demands: **what's what; what it's all about; (know) the score; what is afoot; what's happening ⟨going on⟩; [in limited contexts] size up (sth.); (get) the point; understand things.**

«В конторе телефон есть? Мне позвонить надо». – «Чего ж сразу звонить? – обиделся Голубев. – Вы бы сперва посмот-рели, что к чему, с народом бы поговорили». – «…Зачем мне говорить с народом? Мне с начальством поговорить надо» (Войнович 2). "Is there a telephone in your office? I need to make a call." "Why call right away?" said Golubev, taking offense. "First you should see what's what, have a little talk with the people." "…Why should I talk with the people? I need to talk with my superiors" (2a). ♦ Почему лошадь можно бить, а меня нельзя? Наоборот, при-сутствие во мне «развитого сознания» это более допускает, поскольку я понимаю что к чему и, значит, мне легче (Терц 3). Why should it be so wrong to beat my dog, but all right to beat a horse, rather than the other way round? My possession of a "developed consciousness" means that I can at least understand what it's all about and hence more easily bear it (3a). ♦ Она, видно, догадалась, что здесь к чему, но виду не подала… (Максимов 2). She had obvi-ously guessed what was afoot but gave no sign of it (2a). ♦ «Недотёпа, правда, но дело знает… Пускай осмотрится, прикинет, что к чему. А мы пока покурим» (Максимов 3). "He's obviously half-baked, but he knows his job.…Let him take a look around and size up the job. We'll have a smoke while we wait" (3a). ♦ Тут некоторые из слушателей, поняв что к чему, вспомнили свою давнюю обиду на товарища Сталина… (Искандер 3). Some of the lis-teners, once they got the point, recalled their own long-ago resentment at Comrade Stalin… (3a).

Ч-184 • ЧТО ЛИ *coll* [Particle; Invar] **1.** used to express uncertainty, indecisiveness, hesitation, assumption: **perhaps; maybe; or something; or whatever; I suppose.**

…На Западе [мор] удивительным образом задержался как раз на польской и румынской границах. Климат, что ли, там был иной или сыграли роль заградительные кордонные меры, принятые соседними правительствами, но факт тот, что мор дальше не пошёл (Булгаков 10). In the west, it [the plague] halted miraculously exactly on the Polish and Rumanian borders. Perhaps the climate in these countries was different, or perhaps the quarantine established by the neighboring governments had done its job, but the fact remains that the plague had gone no further (10a). ♦ [Спиридоньевна:] Да где сам-то: дома, видно, нет? [Мат-рёна:] К священнику, что ли, пошёл – не знаю… (Писемский 1). [S.:] And where is he? I see he's not home. [M.:] I don't know....Maybe he's gone to the priest (1a). ♦ Что она там делает? Гладит, что ли? (Трифонов 4). What was she doing there? Ironing or something? (4a). ♦ Рассказ, следовательно, о разладе между чистыми устремлениями юности и последующим попаданием, что ли, в плен житейской суете, заставляющей терять эту чистоту... (Олеша 3). The story, it follows, is about the conflict between the pure strivings of youth and the subsequent fall, or whatever, into bondage to a daily routine which forces one to lose that purity... (3a). ♦ [Атуева:] ...А вы, говорит, заодно с Кречинским-то, что ли? (Сухово-Кобылин 1). [А.:] ...He says to me, Well, I suppose you and Krechinsky see eye to eye, eh? (1a).

2. [used in questions, rhet questions, exclamations] used to express doubt, bewilderment, incredulity etc: **or what?; what?;** [in limited contexts] **what am I ⟨are you** etc⟩...?; **is that it?;** [may be translated as part of general context].

«Откуда угрозыску стало известно, что я в „Орбите" гулял? Следили за мной, что ли?» (Чернёнок 1). "How did CID find out that I was partying at the Orbit? Were you watching me, or what?" (1a). ♦ «Вот чудаки! — воскликнул Покисен. — Что же, я вам врать, что ли, буду?» (Федин 1). "What fools!" exclaimed Pokisen. "What, d'you think I'm going to lie to you?" (1a). ♦ [Маша:] Тебя исключают из университета... [Колесов:] Да он [ректор] что, озверел, что ли? (Вампилов 3). [М.:] You're being expelled from the university.... [К.:] What happened, did he [the Provost] go wild, is that it? (3b). ♦ Но, спрашивается, зачем нам этот мракобес, что, у нас нет своих забот, что ли? (Искандер 4). But, I ask you, what do we want with this obscurantist, don't we have enough troubles of our own? (4a).

3. [usu. used with imper] used to express exhortation: **do** [foll. by imper]; **why don't you...?; ..., will you?;** [in limited contexts] **shall we...?**

«Отсаживай, что ли, нижегородская ворона!» — кричал чужой кучер (Гоголь 3). "Back up, why don't you, you Nizhni Novgorod crow!" shouted the strange coachman (3c). ♦ [Пепел:] Барон! Идём в трактир... [Барон:] Готов! Ну, прощай, старик... Шельма ты! [Лука:] Всяко бывает, милый... [Пепел (у двери в сени):] Ну, идём, что ли! (Горький 3). [Р.:] Baron, come on to the tavern! [В.:] I'm ready! Well, good-by, old man!...You're a rascal! [L.:] There are all sorts of folks, my friend. [P. (at the door of the hall):] Well, come on, will you! (3f). ♦ «Так что ж, матушка, по рукам, что ли?» — говорил Чичиков (Гоголь 3). "Well, my dear lady, shall we call it a deal?" Chichikov was saying (3c).

Ч-185 • ЧТО НИ... (ТО...) [subord Conj, correlative] (used to show that the stated phenomenon, situation etc repeats regularly with respect to time or space; also used to show that each member of the stated group falls into the stated category) **each or almost each: each; every; each and every; there isn't ⟨there's hardly⟩ a day ⟨a year** etc⟩ **without a** [NP].

Мне казалось, что я здорово поднаторела в лагерной медицине, а тут что ни слово — то загадка... (Гинзбург 2). I thought I had acquired a pretty good working knowledge of camp medicine, but here each word was a riddle... (2a). ♦ Гнусный шантаж, обман. У них — что ни слово, то ложь (Иоффе 1). Despicable blackmail and deceit. Every word these people utter is a lie (1a). ♦ [Треплев:] Потом я, когда уже вернулся домой, получал от неё письма. Письма умные, тёплые, интересные; она не жаловалась, но я чувствовал, что она глубоко несчастна; что ни строчка, то больной, натянутый нерв (Чехов 6). [context transl] [Т.:] Afterward, when I had come back home, I received letters from her—clever, warm, interesting letters; she didn't complain, but I felt that she was profoundly unhappy; there was not a line that didn't betray her sick, strained nerves (6a).

Ч-186 • ЧТО (...) НИ...; ЧТО БЫ (...) НИ... [NP; used as subord Conj, concessive] regardless of what: **whatever; no matter what;** [in limited contexts] **everything.**

О чём бы разговор ни был, он всегда умел поддержать его... (Гоголь 3). Whatever topic the conversation turned upon, he could always keep it up (3c). ♦ ...Она ему в рот смотрела, что бы он ни говорил (Битов 2). She listened spellbound no matter what he said (2a). ♦ Лишь только они с Анисьей принялись хозяйничать в барских комнатах вместе, Захар что ни сделает, окажется глупостью (Гончаров 1). As soon as he and Anisya began to look after Oblomov's rooms together, everything Zakhar did turned out to be stupid (1a).

Ч-187 • ЧТО ТА́К? coll [sent; Invar; fixed WO] for what reason?: **how's ⟨how is⟩ that?; why's ⟨why is⟩ that?; how come?; why so?; why?; what makes you ⟨why do you⟩ say that?;** [in response to a negative statement] **why not?**

«Не хотите ли подбавить рома? — сказал я моему собеседнику: — у меня есть белый из Тифлиса; теперь холодно». — «Нет-с, благодарствуйте, не пью». — «Что так?» (Лермонтов 1). "Have some rum in it?" I asked my companion. "I've got some white rum from Tiflis. It's turned cold now." "Thanks all the same, I don't drink." "How is that?" (1c). ♦ «Мне твою мать особенно жалко». — «Что так?» (Тургенев 2). "I feel particularly sorry for your mother." "Why's that?" (2b). "I'm especially sorry for your mother." "Why so?" (2e).

Ч-188 • ЧТО ТАКО́Е [NP; Invar; fixed WO] **1.** [predic; subj: human, abstr, or concr; used in questions and subord clauses] what (the person or thing in question) is or represents: **что такое X?** ≃ **what is X (exactly ⟨really⟩)?; what is X like?; what sort of (a)** [NP] **is X?; what is the nature of thing X?;** ‖ ...вот что такое X! ≃ **that's what X is!; that's the kind of** [NP] **X is.**

«Что такое общество?» — задал он себе вопрос... (Салтыков-Щедрин 2). "What is society?" he asked himself... (2a). ♦ «Ma tante, вы читали эту книгу — что это такое?»... — «Ах, какая гадость!» (Гончаров 1). "You've read this book, Auntie....What is it like?" "Oh, it's horrible!" (1a). ♦ [Городничий:] Только бы мне узнать, что он такое и в какой мере нужно его опасаться (Гоголь 4). [Mayor:] All I want is to find out what sort of person he is and how much I have to be afraid of him (4c). ♦ «Когда раньше, на воле, я читал в книгах, что мудрецы думали о смысле жизни, или о том, что такое счастье, — я мало понимал эти места» (Солженицын 3). "When I was free and used to read books in which wise men pondered the meaning of life or the nature of happiness, I understood very little of those passages" (3a). ♦ «Замётов, он соскандалит что-нибудь на французский манер в неприличном заведении, за стаканом шампанского или донского — вот что такое ваш Замётов!» (Достоевский 3). "He'd [Zamyotov would] go and cause a French-style scandal in some disreputable establishment, over a glass of champagne or Don wine — that's what your Zamyotov is!" (3c).

2. coll [foll. by infin; usu. used in subord clauses] what the significance, possible repercussions etc of some action are: **what it means (to do sth.).**

«Влепят вам десять лет, вот тогда колхозники будут знать, что такое оскорблять председателя колхоза...» (Рыбаков 2). "You'll get ten years for that, and then the kolkhozniks will know what it means to insult the kolkhoz chairman" (2a).

3. coll [indep. sent] what is taking place? what is wrong?: **what's the matter?; what is it ⟨this⟩?; what's going on?**

«Приходит раз Герасим Николаевич [Горностаев] к Августе Авдеевне в кабинет... Подошёл к окну, побарабанил пальцами по стеклу, стал насвистывать что-то очень печальное и знакомое до ужаса. Вслушалась, оказалось — траурный марш Шопена. Не выдержала, сердце у неё по человечеству заныло, пристала: „Что такое? В чём дело?"» (Булгаков 12). "One day Gornostayev came into Augusta Avdeyevna's office....He went over to the window, drummed his fingers on the glass and began to whistle a sad, terribly familiar snatch of music. She listened for a moment and recognized Chopin's *Funeral March*. Unable to contain herself, filled with human kindness, she asked, 'What's the matter? What is it?'" (12a). ♦ «Вот, возьмите [розу]», — сказала она, но тотчас же отдёрнула протянутую руку и, закусив губы, глянула на вход беседки, потом приникла ухом. «Что такое? – спросил Базаров. – Николай Петрович?» (Тургенев 2). "Here, take it [the rose]," she said, but at once drew back her outstretched hand, and, biting her lips looked towards the entrance of the arbor, then listened. "What is it?" asked Bazarov. "Nikolai Petrovich?" (2b).

Ч-189 • ЧТО ⟨ЧЕГО⟩ (УЖ) ТАМ; ЧТО ⟨ЧЕГО⟩ (УЖ) ТУТ *all coll* [Invar] **1.** [Particle] used to express unenthusiastic agreement: **well, all right ⟨OK⟩; why not.**

«Дамы, можно рассказать грубоватый анекдот?» — «Рассказывай, чего уж там». "May I tell an off-color joke, ladies?" "Well, OK, go ahead."

2. [Particle] used to emphasize that sth. is insignificant, not worth worrying about etc: **never mind; (it's) no big deal; it's nothing.**

…Он всё нёс банальщину и тривиальщину, всё воображал… что, чего там, и так сойдёт… (Стругацкие 1). …He kept on going with his banalities and trivialities, imagining…that never mind, he'd make it (1a).

3. [adv] for what reason (implying that there is no reason for doing sth.): **why; why should one…; (there's) no point in (doing sth.).**

[Сильва:] Я считаю, лучше сказать сразу! Честно и откровенно!.. Чего тут темнить, когда всё уже ясно? (Вампилов 4). [S.:] I think it's better to say it right out! Honestly and openly!…Why hide anything when it's already clear? (4b). ♦ [Лизавета Ивановна:] А вы про это тише говорите. [Второй жилец:] Чего там тише. Это не политика (Олеша 6). [L.I.:] You better speak more quietly about it. [Second Tenant:] Why should I, I'm not speaking about politics (6a).

Ч-190 • ЧТО-ТО НЕ ТАК ⟨НЕ ТО⟩ *coll* [these forms only; usu. indep. sent or obj clause with быть∅; fixed WO] sth. about the situation is suspicious, not quite as it should be: что-то не так ≈ **something is wrong ⟨amiss, out of line, just not right, not quite right** etc⟩; **there is something wrong ⟨amiss** etc⟩; [in limited contexts] **something smells fishy ⟨funny⟩.**

«Хороший дом, — сказал мой старик, кивнув головой, — вызывай хозяина, поговорим, поторгуемся…» — «Хозяина нет, — сказал Сандро, — дом продаёт горсовет». — «А хозяин что, умер?»… — «Не то чтобы умер… здесь жил один грек. Так его вместе с женой арестовали и в Сибирь отправили…» — «Вот оно как», — сказал мой старик и замолчал. Сандро тоже молчал. Я же сразу почувствовал, что здесь что-то не то! (Искандер 3). "It's a good house," my old man said with a nod. "Call out the owner, let's talk, let's drive a bargain." "There isn't any owner," Sandro said. "The city soviet is selling the house." "What, did the owner die?"…"It's not that he died….A Greek lived here. He and his wife were arrested and sent to Siberia." "So that's it," my old man said, and fell silent. Sandro was also silent. I knew there was something wrong here! (3a). ♦ Так бы он и меня заподозрил в связи с Фаиной, как на меня взглянул… Да, он безукоризненно почувствовал и заподозрил что-то не то (Битов 2). The way he looked at me, he may even have suspected me of a liaison with Faina. Yes, he unerringly sensed and suspected something amiss (2a). ♦ «Странно, — подумал Виктор. — В чём дело?..» Что-то здесь было не так (Стругацкие 1). "Funny," thought Victor. "What's going on?" Something was not quite right (1a). ♦ «Послушай, — сказала она, — тут есть какая-то ложь, что-то не то…» (Гончаров 1). "Listen," she said, "there is something wrong, some sort of lie in all this…" (1b).

Ч-191 • ЧТО ТЫ ⟨ВЫ⟩!; ДА ЧТО ТЫ ⟨ВЫ⟩! *all coll* [Interj; these forms only] **1.** used to express surprise, bewilderment, fright etc: **you don't say (so)!; what do you mean!; good Lord!; how can that be!; really!; is that so!**

«Какое следствие? Никакого следствия не будет!..» — «Что ты, кум! Как гора с плеч! Выпьем!» — сказал Тарантьев (Гончаров 1). "Who's going to prosecute you? There won't be any prosecution…." "You don't say so, old man! Ugh, what a weight off my mind! Let's have a drink!" said Tarantyev (1a). ♦ «Я устроюсь скоро, очень скоро, Мари». — «Ну, как ты думаешь, с полгода, или…» — «Что ты, Мари! Месяца два, самое большее…» (Федин 1). "I'll get settled quickly, very quickly, Marie." "Well what do you think, in six months, or…?" "What do you mean, Marie! Two months at the very most…" (1a). ♦ «Деньги нужны: осенью женюсь», — прибавил Судьбинский. «Что ты! В самом деле? На ком?» (Гончаров 1). "I need money," added Sudbinsky. "I'm getting married in the autumn." "Good Lord! Really? To whom?" (1a). ♦ «Аня, с сегодняшнего дня я не работаю в трибунале». — «Да что ты? Куда же тебя?» (Шолохов 3). "Anna, from today I shan't be working for the tribunal any more." "Really? Where are they sending you?" (3a).

2. Also: **НУ ЧТО ТЫ ⟨ВЫ⟩!** *coll* used to express a skeptical or sarcastic reaction to the interlocutor's statement: **come ⟨go⟩ on!; oh come!; good Lord (,…indeed)!; what are you talking about!; the things you say!; [in limited contexts] oh, get away with you!**

[Себейкин:] Есть [водка]? [Вася:] Да что ты, полно! [Себейкин:] Надо же! Водка осталась! Когда это такое было-то! (Рощин 2). [S.:] Is there any [vodka] left? [V.:] Com'on, there's plenty! [S.:] What do you know! There's vodka left! When has that ever happened before? (2a). ♦ «Очень весело будет за вас под расстрел идти». — «Да что вы! Опомнитесь!» (Пастернак 1). "A nice thought, to have to face a firing squad on your account!" "Oh, come! Be sensible" (1a). ♦ [Артемий Филиппович:] У вас что ни слово, то Цицерон с языка слетел. [Аммос Фёдорович:] Что вы! Что вы: Цицерон! Смотрите, что выдумали (Гоголь 4). [Art.F.:] As soon as you open your mouth, it might be Cicero himself making a speech. [Am.F.:] Good Lord, Cicero indeed! The things you think of! (4c). ♦ [Смельская:] …Едем скорей! [Негина:] Куда? [Смельская:] Кататься, я на лошадях Ивана Семёныча… [Негина:] Право, не знаю. [Смельская:] Да что ты, помилуй! Об чём тут думать! Разве отказаться можно? (Островский 11). [S.:] …We must be off at once! [N.:] Where? [S.:] For a drive—I've got Ivan Semyonych's horses…. [N.:] I really don't know… [S.:] Oh, get away with you! What is there to think about, for heaven's sake! How can you possibly refuse? (11a).

3. Also: **НУ ⟨НЕТ,⟩ ЧТО ТЫ ⟨ВЫ⟩!** *coll* used to express one's disagreement with or a denial of some statement, or as a negative answer to a question: **what do you mean!; what are you saying!; what are you talking about!; (no,) not at all; (no,) it's out of the question; good heavens, no!; certainly not; of course not.**

[Макарская:] Вы в каком суде разводились? [Сильва:] Ну что вы! Никогда этого не было (Вампилов 4). [M.:] In what court did you get your divorce? [S.:] What do you mean! I never had one (4b). ♦ «Позволь и тебя спросить…: считаешь ты и меня, как Дмитрия, способным пролить кровь Езопа, ну, убить его, а?» — «Что ты, Иван! Никогда и в мыслях этого у меня не было!» (Достоевский 1). "…Let me ask you: do you consider me capable, like Dmitri, of shedding Aesop's blood, well, of killing him? Eh?" "What are you saying, Ivan! The thought never entered my mind!" (1a). ♦ «Виктор Павлович, мы не мешаем вам своими разговорами?» — «Нет, нет, что вы», — сказал Штрум… (Гроссман 2). "Viktor Pavlovich, will it disturb you if we go on talking?" "No, no. Not at all," said Viktor (2a). ♦ «Может, всё-таки останешься?» — «Нет, что ты! Она подымет на ноги всю московскую милицию!» (Ерофеев 3). "You don't think you could stay?" "No, it's out of the question! She'd have the whole Moscow police force out looking for me!" (3a). ♦ [Анастасия Ефремовна:] Вы тоже к нам? [Катя:] Что вы! У меня родная сестра в Москве (Розов 1). [A.E.:] Are you going to stay with us? [K.:] Of course not! I have a sister in Moscow… (1a).

Ч-192 • ЧТÓ-ЧТÓ ⟨чего-чего и т. п.⟩, А... coll [NP + Conj; used as a restr. marker] used to single out one thing, phenomenon etc (or group of things, phenomena etc) among others: что-что, а X ⟨делать X⟩... ≃ perhaps not something else, but (s.o. will do ⟨give etc⟩) X; if anything, X is...; whatever else..., but...; say what you like, but...; [when foll. by a clause with negated predic] that's the last thing (s.o. will do etc); ‖ чего-чего, а X-а... ⟨чему-чему, а X-у... и т. п.⟩ ≃ if there's anything..., it's X; there's one thing...and that's X.

[Аркадина:] На мне был удивительный туалет... Что-что, а уж одеться я не дура (Чехов 6). [A.:] I wore a lovely dress. Say what you like, but I do know how to dress (6b). ♦ Лукерья опять усмехнулась и сказала: «Да уж чего-чего, а красоты твоей невестушке не занимать» (Абрамов 1). Lukerya grinned again and said, "Yes, there's one thing you can't deny your daughter-in-law, and that's beauty" (1a).

Ч-193 • ЧУТЬ ЧТÓ coll [subord clause; Invar; fixed WO] **1.** in case some new development (usu. trouble) should occur: if something ⟨anything⟩ happens ⟨should happen⟩; in case something ⟨anything⟩ happens; if anything crops up; if something ⟨anything⟩ goes ⟨should go⟩ wrong; in the event of trouble; if there's any trouble.

[Кудряш:] А мать-то не хватится?.. [Варвара:] У неё первый сон крепок... Да и Глаша стережёт; чуть что, она сейчас голос подаст (Островский 6). [K.:] But that ma of yours—no danger of her catching on?... [V.:] She sleeps like a log the first half of the night....Besides, Glasha is keeping watch; she'll let us know directly if anything goes wrong (6b).

2. when even the most minor problem, unpleasantness, complication etc arises, or even without any cause at all (one acts as stated): at the slightest excuse ⟨provocation⟩; at the least little thing; at the drop of a hat.

В баню нас водили обычно два надзирателя, Ваня и Саня. Ваня маленький, чёрный, злой; у него была кличка «Цыган». Чуть что — орёт, кроет матом, грозит, дерётся (Марченко 1). We were usually taken to the bath house by two warders, Vanya and Sanya. Vanya was short, dark and bad-tempered. His nickname was "Gipsy." At the slightest excuse he started bellowing, cursing, threatening and pummeling you (1a). ♦ [Аннунциата:] Он очень вспыльчив, и чуть что — стреляет из пистолета (Шварц 3). [A.:] He's very quick-tempered and, at the least little thing, shoots his pistol (3a).

Ч-194 • ЛИШÁТЬСЯ/ЛИШÍТЬСЯ ЧУВСТВ; ПÁ-ДАТЬ/УПÁСТЬ БЕЗ ЧУВСТВ ⟨БЕЗ СОЗНÁНИЯ, БЕЗ ПÁМЯТИ⟩; ТЕРЯ́ТЬ/ПОТЕРЯ́ТЬ СОЗНÁНИЕ [VP; subj: human] to become unconscious: X лишился чувств ≃ X lost consciousness; X passed out; X fainted; X fell down unconscious.

В это самое время меня сильно кольнуло в грудь пониже правого плеча; я упал и лишился чувств (Пушкин 2). At that moment I felt a sharp stab in my chest just under the right shoulder; I fell down and lost consciousness (2a). ♦ Он такой дубина колошматил нас, что я чуть сознание не потерял (Искандер 3). He thrashed us with such a big staff that I almost passed out (3a). ♦ ...Он объявил, что нарочно лежал как без чувств, чтоб их испугать, но правда была в том, что он и в самом деле лишился чувств, как и признался потом сам, уже долго спустя, своей маме (Достоевский 1). ...He announced that he had pretended to be unconscious on purpose to frighten them, but the truth was that he had indeed fainted, as he himself later confessed long afterwards to his mama (1a). ♦ Однажды, среди студенческого сбора, он вдруг встал, поднял, изящно изогнувшись, руку, как будто просил слова, и в этой скульптурной позе упал без чувств (Набоков 1). Once at a student gathering he suddenly stood up, gracefully raised his curved arm, as if requesting permission to speak, and in this sculpturesque pose fell down unconscious (1a).

Ч-195 • В РАСТРЁПАННЫХ ЧУ́ВСТВАХ coll, usu. humor [PrepP; Invar; subj-compl with бытьø (subj: human) or adv] in a state of great agitation, emotional disturbance, confusion: (one is ⟨one does sth., one does sth. when he is⟩) in an emotional turmoil; (one is ⟨one does sth. etc⟩) in a state of emotional turmoil; (one is) all shook up; (one is) thrown off balance; (one is) shaken.

Так, теперь всё ясно. В растрёпанных чувствах [Нина] забыла «заказец», а ведь именно за заказчиком приезжала контра на «Жигулях» (Аксёнов 6). So everything was now clear. In the emotional turmoil Nina had forgotten her little "job," and obviously that counterrevolutionary in the Zhiguli had come with the intention of collecting it (6a).

Ч-196 • ПРИВОДИ́ТЬ/ПРИВЕСТИ́ В ЧУ́ВСТВО кого [VP] **1.** Also: ПРИВОДИ́ТЬ/ПРИВЕСТИ́ В СОЗНÁ-НИЕ ⟨В ПÁМЯТЬ obs⟩ [subj: human or abstr] to cause s.o. to regain consciousness, come out of a stupor etc: X привёл Y-а в чувство ≃ X brought Y to Y's senses; X brought Y (a)round.

...Он привёл [мертвецки пьяного] музыканта в чувство, а через час тот уже настраивал непослушными пальцами свой инструмент у него за сценой (Максимов 2). ...He brought the [dead-drunk] musician to his senses, and an hour later Govorukhin's somewhat wooden fingers were tuning his instrument backstage at the club (2a).

2. [subj: human] to take decisive measures and cause s.o. to stop doing sth. offensive, reprehensible, undesirable etc, make s.o. act sensibly: X привёл Y-а в чувство ≃ X brought Y (back) to Y's senses.

[Репников:] ...Что он [Колесов] натворил? [Милиционер:] ...[Ваш студент] нанёс телесные повреждения музыканту Шафранскому. [Колесов:] Этот тип ворвался в номер, стал кричать, оскорбил женщину, и меня он оскорбил. Я привёл его в чувство... (Вампилов 3). [R.:] ...What do you want him [Kolesov] for? [Policeman:] ...[Your student] inflicted bodily harm on the musician, Shafransky. [K.:] That character forced his way into the room and started yelling. He insulted the woman, and he insulted me too, I brought him to his senses... (3b).

Ч-197 • ПРИХОДИ́ТЬ/ПРИЙТИ́ В ЧУ́ВСТВО ⟨В СОЗНÁНИЕ, В ПÁМЯТЬ obs⟩ [VP; subj: human] to come out of a state of unconsciousness, semiconsciousness, drowsiness etc: X пришёл в чувство ≃ X regained consciousness; X came to; X came (a)round.

К вечеру ему стало легче, больной пришёл в память (Пушкин 1). By the evening the patient's condition improved, and he regained consciousness (1a).

Ч-198 • СТÁДНОЕ ЧУ́ВСТВО usu. disapprov [NP; sing only] the inclination to conform to the behavior of the crowd: herd instinct.

«Зачем ты накупил столько лотерейных билетов? Ведь всё равно не выиграешь» — «Стадное чувство: все покупали помногу — и я купил». "Why did you buy so many lottery tickets? You won't win anything anyway." "It was the herd instinct. Everyone was buying a lot so I bought a lot too."

Ч-199 • ЧУ́ВСТВО ЛÓКТЯ [NP; sing only; fixed WO] mutual support and loyalty between friends: (feeling of) camaraderie; (sense of) fellowship.

Я не отворачиваюсь от своей юности. Тогда возникло доверие к миру, ощущение добрых и ясных человеческих связей, то чувство локтя, без которого мне невозможно существовать (Орлова 1). I am not turning my back on my youth. A belief in the world emerged in those days, a feeling for clear-cut and good human relations, that sense of fellowship without which it is impossible for me to exist (1a).

Ч-200 • ЧУДЕСА́ В РЕШЕТЕ́ *coll* [NP; pl only; often used as exclamation; fixed WO] an astonishing, highly unusual thing, occurrence, phenomenon etc: **no less than a miracle; a real wonder; (will) wonders never cease; truly amazing.**

Несколько зная язык, он писал статью начерно, оставляя пробелы, вкрапливая русские фразы и требуя от Фёдора Константиновича дословного перевода своих передовичных словец: ...чудеса в решете... пришла беда – растворяй ворота... (Набоков 1). Having a smattering of the language, he wrote his article out in rough, with gaps and Russian phrases interspersed, and demanded from Fyodor a literal translation of the usual phrases found in leaders:...wonders never cease...troubles never come singly... (1a).

Ч-201 • ЧУ́ДО КАК... *obs, coll* [Invar; modif] (usu. refers to a high degree of some positive quality) very, extremely: **amazingly; wonderfully; incredibly.**

[Кречинский:] ...Как вы отдохнули после вчерашнего бала? [Лидочка:] У меня голова что-то болит. [Кречинский:] А ведь чудо как было весело! [Лидочка:] Ах, чудо как весело! (Сухово-Кобылин 2). [K.:] Have you rested well after the ball?... [L.:] I have a slight headache. [K.:] What a wonderfully gay time we had! [L.:] Oh, yes, wonderfully gay (2a).

Ч-202 • СИ́НИЙ ЧУЛО́К *disapprov or derog* [NP; fixed WO] a woman who is absorbed exclusively in scholarly interests (and usu. devoid of femininity): **bluestocking.**

«...Она презирает меня, я знаю. Нина – синий чулок. Я не ставлю ей это в вину, уважаю её стремления, она общественница, это хорошо, прекрасно! Но не все созданы такими» (Рыбаков 2). "She despises me, I know, because she's a bluestocking, but I don't mind. I admire her ambition. She's socially minded and that's good, that's wonderful. But we're not all made the same way" (2a).

< Loan translation of the English "bluestocking."

Ч-203 • КАК ЧУМЫ́ бояться, избегать *кого-чего coll* [как + NP; Invar; adv (intensif)] (to fear sth.) intensely, (to avoid sth.) in every possible way: **like the plague.**

Зелёного автомобиля стали бояться, как чумы (Ильф и Петров 2). People began to fear the green automobile like the plague (2b).

Ч-204 • НИ ЧУ́ТОЧКИ *coll* [NP$_{gen}$; Invar; adv (intensif); used with a negated predic] not even in the smallest degree: **not a ⟨one, the slightest⟩ bit; not in the least ⟨the slightest⟩.**

Почему ты думаешь, что я эту собаку боюсь? Мне ни чуточки не страшно. Я её даже погладить могу. Why do you think I'm afraid of that dog? I'm not one bit afraid. Look, I can even pet it!

Ч-205 • ЧУ́ТЬ БЫЛО НЕ...; ЧУ́ТЬ-ЧУ́ТЬ БЫЛО НЕ... [Particle; these forms only; usu. foll. by a pfv past verb, Part, or Verbal Adv] s.o. was about to do sth. but did not, or began doing sth. but quickly stopped; sth. was about to happen but did not, or began happening but was quickly interrupted: **(very) nearly; almost; all but; (be) on the verge of (doing sth. ⟨happening⟩).**

«Дура – чуть было не вышла замуж» (Грекова 3). "Fool...you nearly got married" (3a). ♦ «[Я] чуть было не прошёл мимо великого начинания». – «А что, если бы прошли?» – говорил я. «Не говори», – отвечал Платон Самсонович и снова вздрагивал (Искандер 6). "To think that I almost let this great undertaking slip through my fingers!" "Well, and what if you had?" I would ask. "Don't even suggest such a thing," he [Platon Samsonovich] would answer, wincing once again (6a). ♦ После чаю он уже приподнялся с своего ложа и чуть было не встал; поглядывая на туфли, он даже начал спускать к ним одну ногу с постели, но тотчас же опять подобрал её (Гончаров 1). When he had drunk his tea, he sat up and all but got out of bed; glancing at his slippers, he even commenced lowering one foot toward them, but immediately drew it back again (1b). ♦ «...Два-три раза он чуть-чуть было не сознался вполне, почти намекал и только разве не договаривал...» (Достоевский 2). "Two or three times he was on the verge of confessing outright, almost hinted at it, and stopped just short of telling all" (2a).

Ч-206 • ЧУ́ТЬ ЛИ НЕ...; ЕДВА́ ЛИ НЕ... [Particle; these forms only; foll. by NP, AdjP, or AdvP] **1.** Also: **ЧУ́ТЬ ЧТО НЕ...** *obs* almost but not quite or entirely: **almost; nearly; practically; virtually;** [in limited contexts] **barely; just about.**

Их первую встречу (летом 56 года) Чернышевский спустя чуть ли не тридцать лет (когда писал и о Некрасове) вспоминал со знакомой нам уже детальностью... (Набоков 1). Their first meeting (summer 1856) was recalled almost thirty years later by Chernyshevski (when he also wrote about Nekrasov) with his familiar wealth of detail... (1a). ♦ ...В те далёкие, незлопамятные времена чудеса происходили чуть ли не каждый день (Искандер 5). ...In those far-off, forgiving times miracles took place nearly every day (5a). ♦ Слава Голубев соскочил на перрон чуть ли не первым... (Чернёнок 2). Slava Golubyov was practically the first to jump down to the platform... (2a). ♦ Он [Сталин] и теперь... представляет себя чуть ли не инициатором и вдохновителем ленинских решений (Рыбаков 2). Even now...he [Stalin] presented himself virtually as the initiator and inspirer of Lenin's decisions (2a). ♦ ...Как-то так случилось, что с семьёй Ефима Петровича он расстался чуть ли не тринадцати лет, перейдя в одну из московских гимназий и на пансион к какому-то опытному и знаменитому тогда педагогу... (Достоевский 1). ...It somehow happened that he parted from Yefim Petrovich's family when he was barely thirteen, passing on to one of the Moscow secondary schools and boarding with a certain experienced and then-famous pedagogue... (1a). ♦ Собрание ленинградских писателей вёл приехавший из Москвы Константин Симонов... Был он в зените славы... Любимец публики и сталинский любимец, многократно осыпанный Сталинскими премиями и орденами. Да к тому же ещё чуть ли не герой войны (Войнович 1). [context transl] The meeting of the Leningrad writers was run by Konstantin Simonov, who had come from Moscow....He was at the height of his fame....The darling of the public as well as of Stalin, he had been heaped with prizes and decorations. And, on top of that, he was something of a war hero (1a).

2. apparently, it seems: **possibly; perhaps; must** [+ infin]; **most likely.**

...Они возмечтали, что счастье принадлежит им по праву и что никто не в силах отнять его у них. Победа над Наполеоном ещё более утвердила их в этом мнении, и едва ли не в эту самую эпоху сложилась знаменитая пословица: шапками закидаем! – которая впоследствии долгое время служила девизом глуповских подвигов на поле брани (Салтыков-Щедрин 1). ...They started dreaming that happiness belonged to them by right and that no one had the power to take it away from them. The victory over Napoleon convinced them of this opinion still more firmly. The famous saying "It's in the bag!"—which afterwards served for a long time as the motto for Foolovian exploits on the field of battle—must have arisen in this period (1a). ♦ ...Действительная причина его увольнения заключалась едва ли не в том, что он был когда-то в Гатчине истопником... (Салтыков-Щедрин 1). ...The real reason for his dismissal most likely lay in the fact that he had at one time been a stoker in Gatchina... (1b).

Ч-207 • ЧУ́ТЬ НЕ [Particle; Invar] **1.** Also: **ЕДВА́ НЕ; ЧУ́ТЬ-ЧУ́ТЬ НЕ** [usu. foll. by a pfv past verb, Part, or Verbal Adv] s.o. was about to do sth. but did not, or began doing sth. but quickly stopped; sth. was about to happen but did not, or began happening but was quickly interrupted: **almost; (very) nearly; all**

but; (be) on the verge of (doing sth. ⟨happening⟩); [of a person only] (come) near to (doing sth.).

В войну сад едва не погиб (Трифонов 1). During the war the garden had almost perished (1a). ♦ «...Не дай господи, как он рассердился! чуть-чуть не отдал под суд» (Лермонтов 1). "...Goodness, how furious he was! He very nearly had us court-martialed" (1a). ♦ ...В движениях девушки...было что-то такое очаровательное, повелительное, ласкающее, насмешливое и милое, что я чуть не вскрикнул от удивления и удовольствия... (Тургенев 3). ...There was in the movements of the young girl...something so fascinating, imperious, caressing, mocking, and charming, that I nearly cried out with wonder and delight... (3a). ...There was something so charming, so imperative, so gracious, amusing, and pleasant in the girl's movements, that I all but cried out with amazement and delight... (3c).

2. [usu. foll. by NP, AdjP, or AdvP] almost but not quite or entirely: **almost; nearly; practically; virtually;** [in limited contexts] **barely; just about.**

«Ну, веришь, Порфирий, [Раскольников] сам едва на ногах, а чуть только мы, я да Зосимов, вчера отвернулись — оделся и удрал потихоньку и куролесил где-то чуть не до полночи...» (Достоевский 3). "Now, would you believe it, Porfiry, he [Raskolnikov] could hardly stand, and yet the minute we, that is Zosimov and I, turned our backs on him yesterday, he got dressed and sneaked out on the sly and was whooping it up somewhere till almost midnight..." (3a). ♦ «Мне сказывали, что в Риме наши художники в Ватикан ни ногой. Рафаэля считают чуть ли не дураком, потому что это, мол, авторитет; а сами бессильны и бесплодны до гадости...» (Тургенев 2). "I am told that in Rome our artists never set foot in the Vatican. Raphael they practically regard as a fool because, if you pleaese, he is an authority. Yet they themselves are so impotent and sterile..." (2c).

Ш-1 • ДЕ́ЛАТЬ/СДЕ́ЛАТЬ ШАГ НАВСТРЕ́ЧУ *(кому-чему)* [VP; subj and obj: human or collect; the verb may take the final position, otherwise fixed WO] to show the initiative in establishing or improving relations with s.o. (may refer to making an effort to meet s.o., reconcile a conflict with s.o. etc): X сделал шаг навстречу (Y-у) ≃ **X took the first step (to meet Y 〈make up with Y etc〉);** [in limited contexts] **X made a conciliatory gesture (toward Y).**

Любой интеллигентный человек тут понял бы, что надо же сделать шаг навстречу. Но Оглоед ничего этого понять не мог. Он не оценил тактичности Павла Николаевича (Солженицын 10). Any educated man would have seen at this point that it was time to make a conciliatory gesture, but Bone-chewer couldn't understand this. He couldn't appreciate Pavel Nikolayevich's tact (10a).

Ш-2 • ДЕРЖА́ТЬ ШАГ 〈НО́ГУ〉 [VP; subj: human or collect] to march in time with others: X-ы держали шаг ≃ **Xs kept 〈marched〉 in step.**

Ш-3 • ЛО́ЖНЫЙ 〈НЕВЕ́РНЫЙ〉 ШАГ [NP; sing only; fixed WO] an erroneous action, mistake: **false move 〈step〉; wrong move 〈step〉; misstep.**

Колебания матери можно понять: один неверный шаг — и конец! (Рыбаков 1). It's easy to understand mother's hesitation, one false step and it would be the end! (1a).

Ш-4 • НА ШАГ *от чего* [PrepP; Invar; the resulting PrepP is usu. subj-compl with copula (subj: human)] (often in refer. to death, committing a sin, being in an accident etc) one is very close to (doing) sth.: X был на шаг от Y-а ≃ **X was one step away from (doing) Y; X was on the verge 〈the brink〉 of (doing) Y.**

Михаил так переживал смерть жены, что был на шаг от самоубийства. Mikhail took his wife's death so hard that he was on the verge of committing suicide.

Ш-5 • НИ НА ШАГ [PrepP; Invar] **1.** ~ *(не отставать, не отходить и т. п.) от кого-чего.* Also: **НИ НА ПЯДЬ** *coll* [adv or predic (with subj: usu. human or animal)] not (to fall behind s.o. or sth.) even the slightest distance (when walking, running etc): X не отходил 〈не отставал〉 от Y-а ~ ≃ **X stayed right on person Y's heels 〈tail〉.**

Мы бежали по улице, и собака не отставала ни на шаг. We ran down the street, and the dog stayed right on our heels.

2. ~ *(не отходить, не отставать и т. п.) от кого-чего,* не *отпускать кого.* Also: **НИ НА ПЯДЬ** *coll* [adv or predic (with subj: human or animal)] not (to be far from s.o.) for even the slightest amount of time: X не отходит от Y-а ~ ≃ **X is never more than a few steps 〈feet〉 away from Y; X doesn't leave Y 〈Y's side〉 for an instant 〈a moment, a second, a minute〉; X sticks 〈stays〉 close to Y all the time 〈at all times etc〉; X stays glued to Y's side;** ‖ Y не отпускает X-а (от себя) ~ ≃ **Y doesn't let 〈never lets〉 X out of Y's sight.**

«...Здесь отец мне твердит: „Мой кабинет к твоим услугам — никто тебе мешать не будет"; а сам от меня ни на шаг» (Тургенев 2). "Here father keeps on repeating: 'My study's at your disposal—nobody will be in your way,' but he doesn't leave my side for a minute" (2a). ♦ «Сань, а ты меня бы туда не взял как-нибудь?» — «Да пошли хоть сейчас... Только от меня ни на шаг!» (Аксёнов 6). "Sanya, I suppose you couldn't take me down there, could you?" "Sure, let's go now if you like....Only stick close to me at all times" (6a). ♦ В первые дни после его возвращения из лесу или со сплава двойнята ни на шаг от него... (Абрамов 1). For the

first few days after he came back from the forest or the river, the twins would never let him out of their sight... (1a).

3. ~ *без кого* [predic; subj: human] not to do or undertake anything (without s.o.'s consent or permission): X без Y-а ~ ≃ **X doesn't (dare to) take a step 〈make a move〉 without Y 〈Y's permission, Y's go-ahead, Y's OK〉.**

4. ~ *без кого-чего* [predic; impers or with subj: human] to be unable to function, act etc without s.o. or sth.: X без Y-а ~ ≃ **X won't 〈can't, doesn't etc〉 do anything 〈go anywhere etc〉 without Y; X is lost 〈helpless〉 without Y;** [in limited contexts] **X can't get along without Y.**

Наша Лена без своей любимой куклы ни на шаг. Our Lena's lost without her favorite doll.

5. ~ *не продвинуть что,* не продвинуться, не отступать *от чего* и т. п. [adv] not (to move some matter ahead, advance, deviate from some regulations etc) to any extent or in any way: **not (by) one 〈a, a single〉 step; not in the least; not at all; not one bit.**

«Я — по закону-с! Не отступая-с... ни на шаг-с... ни на волос-с!» (Салтыков-Щедрин 2). "I'm acting according to law! Without deviating by a single step...not by a hair's breadth, sir!" (2a). ♦ Пьер с главноуправляющим каждый день *занимался.* Но он чувствовал, что занятия его ни на шаг не подвигали дела (Толстой 5). Every day Pierre *went into things* with his head steward. But he felt that this did not forward matters in the least (5a). ♦ ...Внутри, кажется, что-то точило его [Гришу] непобедимо. Ведь его собственные дела не продвинулись ни на шаг... (Трифонов 1). ...Inside something seemed to be eating away at Grisha, something which he could not control. After all, his own career hadn't moved forward at all... (1a).

Ш-6 • ОДИ́Н ШАГ *от чего до чего coll* [NP; sing only; usu. impers predic with copula; fixed WO] it does not take much for one phenomenon, condition, emotion etc to develop into another more serious, significant etc one or to turn into an opposite or contrasting one: от X-а до Y-а один шаг ≃ **it's only one 〈a short, a single〉 step from X to Y; it's but a short 〈a single〉 step from X to Y; Y is only one 〈just a〉 step away from X; from X to Y is but a single step.**

Если для охранника охрана — задача политическая, то такой охранник ненадёжен: политические взгляды могут меняться. Даже личная симпатия ненадёжна: от симпатии до антипатии один шаг (Рыбаков 2). If security officials regarded their work as political, then they were unreliable, as political views were changeable. Even personal sympathy was unreliable, for it was only one step from sympathy to antipathy (2a). ♦ ...Издали казалось, что солдатики иронически улыбаются. А от иронии до крамолы — один шаг (Салтыков-Щедрин 1). ...From a distance it looked as though they [the soldiers] were smiling ironically. And from irony to sedition is but a single step! (1b).

Ш-7 • СДЕ́ЛАТЬ ПЕ́РВЫЙ ШАГ *(к чему)* [VP; subj: human; the verb may take the final position, otherwise fixed WO] **1.** to undertake an initial action toward some goal: X сделал первый шаг ≃ **X took the first step.**

«Я сам хотел добра людям и сделал бы сотни, тысячи добрых дел вместо одной этой глупости... Этою глупостью я хотел только поставить себя в независимое положение, первый шаг сделать... Но я, я и первого шага не выдержал, потому что я — подлец!» (Достоевский 3). "I myself wanted to do good to people and I'd have done hundreds and thousands of good deeds to make up for that one stupidity....By that stupidity I merely wanted to place myself in an independent position, to take the first step....But I— I couldn't even endure the first step, because I'm vile!" (3a).

2. to be the first to act in establishing or improving relations with another (may refer to making an effort to meet s.o., reconcile a conflict with s.o. etc): X сделал первый шаг ≃ **X took the first step; X made the first move.**

«Я очень хорошо понял, с первого взгляда, что тут дело плохо, и – что вы думаете? – решился было и глаз не подымать на неё. Но Авдотья Романовна сама сделала первый шаг...» (Достоевский 3). "I understood very well, at first glance, that things were bad here, and—what do you think?—I decided not even to raise my eyes to her. But Avdotya Romanovna herself took the first step..." (3c).

Ш-8 • ЧТО НИ ШАГ (, то...) *coll* [subord clause; Invar; used as adv; fixed WO] everywhere: **at every step ⟨turn⟩; everywhere you look (you see ⟨there is etc⟩...).**

В этом городе что ни шаг, то ресторан. In that town, everywhere you look you see a restaurant.

Ш-9 • ШАГ ВПЕРЁД [NP; sing only; often subj-compl with copula (subj: abstr); fixed WO] movement toward improvement, progress etc: **(sth. is ⟨one takes etc⟩) a step forward; (sth. is ⟨one takes etc⟩) a step in the right direction;** ‖ (сделать) большой ⟨огромный⟩ шаг вперёд ≃ **(make) a quantum leap;** ‖ *Neg* ни шагу вперёд (не сделать) ≃ **(make) no headway ⟨progress⟩.**

«Я считаю Вана большим талантом. Он настойчив, упрям и беспощаден к себе. Каждая новая картина его – шаг вперёд» (Федин 1). "I consider Wahn a major talent. He is persistent, stubborn and merciless with himself. Every new picture of his is a step forward" (1a).

Ш-10 • ШАГ ЗА ШАГОМ ⟨ШАГ ЗА ШАГ *obs*⟩ [these forms only; adv; usu. used with impfv verbs; fixed WO] **1.** (to do sth. or sth. happens) steadily: **step by step; little by little; one step at a time.**

«Ты говоришь Бонапарте; но Бонапарте, когда он работал, шаг за шагом шёл к своей цели, он был свободен, у него ничего не было, кроме его цели, – и он достиг её» (Толстой 4). "...You talk of Bonaparte—why, when he was working toward his goal, he went forward step by step; he was free; he had nothing except his goal to consider, and he attained it" (4a).

2. consecutively, doing each action in its proper order: **step by step.**

«Учёные различных стран напишут подробные исследования его произведений и шаг за шагом постараются проследить его таинственную жизнь» (Булгаков 5). "Scholars in diverse lands will write detailed analyses of his works, seeking step by step to reconstruct the mysterious thread of his life" (5a).

Ш-11 • СЕМИМИ́ЛЬНЫМИ ⟨ГИГА́НТСКИМИ⟩ ШАГА́МИ идти, двигаться вперёд и т. п. *media or lit* [NP_instrum; these forms only; adv; used with impfv verbs; fixed WO] (to proceed, develop) quickly and efficiently: **(make) rapid ⟨giant, great⟩ strides; (take) giant steps; (make) amazing progress.**

Ш-12 • В ДВУХ ⟨В ТРЁХ, В НЕ́СКОЛЬКИХ⟩ ШАГА́Х *(от кого-чего) coll* [PrepP; these forms only; adv or subj-compl with copula (subj: concr); fixed WO] very close (to s.o. or sth.), very near: **within a stone's throw of; a stone's throw away ⟨away from, from⟩; two ⟨a few⟩ steps away ⟨away from, from⟩; within a few steps; no distance at all; right ⟨just⟩ near here ⟨there etc⟩; right ⟨just⟩ around the corner.**

Я... даже в Историческом музее, в двух шагах от Кремля работал... (Солженицын 2). I was able...even to work in the Historical Museum, a stone's throw from the Kremlin (2a). ♦ «Там Безбородкин сад... Нева в двух шагах, свой огород – ни пыли, ни духоты!» (Гончаров 1). "There you would have the Bezborodkin Park; you'd be...two steps from the Neva, have your own kitchen garden—and no dust, none of that oppressive heat!" (1b). ♦ «Знаете ли что? Пойдёмте теперь к ней все вместе. Она живёт отсюда в двух шагах» (Тургенев 2). "Do you know what? Let's all go to call on her now, together. She lives just near here" (2e).

Ш-13 • ПЕ́РВЫЕ ШАГИ́ *(кого, чьи, в чём, на чём);* **ПЕ́РВЫЙ ШАГ** *(кого, чей, в чём, на чём)* [NP; fixed WO] (often in refer. to s.o.'s actions in the initial stage of his career) the first action(s), measure(s) etc taken in some area and/or toward the realization of some goal, plan etc: **first step(s); first move(s).**

Она напомнила ему правду: первыми шагами своими в службе он был обязан её отцу (Толстой 4). She had only reminded him of what was true: he was indebted to her father for his first steps in the service (4a). ♦ ...Несмотря на то что первые шаги Прыща были встречены глуповцами с недоверием, они не успели и оглянуться, как всего у них очутилось против прежнего вдвое и втрое (Салтыков-Щедрин 1). ...Despite the mistrust with which the Foolovites greeted Pimple's first moves, before they knew it they had two or three times as much of everything as before (1a).

Ш-14 • С ПЕ́РВЫХ ШАГО́В *(чего)* [PrepP; Invar; adv; fixed WO] from the start of some activity, process, endeavor: **from its first ⟨earliest⟩ steps ⟨stages⟩; from the outset; from the very beginning;** [in limited contexts] **from the infancy (of sth.).**

Всем, может быть, стало понятно ещё с самых первых шагов, что это совсем даже и не спорное дело, что тут нет сомнений, что, в сущности, никаких бы и прений не надо... (Достоевский 2). It perhaps became clear to everyone from the very outset that this was not a controversial case at all, that there were no doubts here, that essentially there was no need for any debate... (2a).

Ш-15 • ЧЕРЕПА́ШЬИМ ША́ГОМ идти, двигаться и т. п. *coll* [NP_instrum; Invar; adv; fixed WO] (to proceed, move) very slowly (often in refer. to the development of an undertaking, project etc): **at a snail's pace.**

Ш-16 • ША́ГОМ МАРШ! [Invar; usu. indep. sent; fixed WO] a command to begin marching: **forward, march!**

«Полк, равняйсь!.. Смирно! С места с песней шагом... – полковник выдержал паузу – ...марш!» (Войнович 2). "Regiment, dress!...Attention! Now, singing, forward..." the colonel prolonged the pause "...march!" (2a).

Ш-17 • В ШАГУ́ узки, тесны и т. п. [PrepP; Invar; adv] (some pants, trousers etc are tight, too small) in the area where the tops of the trouser legs come together (such that the wearer cannot take long steps because of the risk of ripping the fabric): **(tight) in the crotch ⟨the seat⟩.**

Ш-18 • НА КА́ЖДОМ ШАГУ́ [PrepP; Invar; adv; used with impfv verbs; fixed WO] constantly and/or everywhere: **at every step ⟨turn⟩;** [in limited contexts] **all around (s.o.); all over the place.**

На каждом шагу встречаю доброжелателей, которые предупреждают. Вам надо смотреть в оба, вы должны бороться (Войнович 1). At every step I was meeting well-wishers who forewarned me. "You have to keep your eyes open, you should put up a fight" (1a). ♦ Они тебе лгут на каждом шагу, а от тебя требуют безусловной правдивости (Зиновьев 1). They lie to you at every turn, but from you They demand unconditional truth (1a). ♦ Удивительно, как это так наука до сих пор не открыла и не доказала вполне научно и логично – переселение душ. А примеры – на каждом шагу (Терц 2). It is amazing that science has not yet discovered and given a complete logical proof of the transmigration of souls. Yet there are examples all around us (2a).

♦ Мы проедали деньги [, полученные за плакаты,] в кофейнях и кондитерских. Они открывались на каждом шагу... (Мандельштам 2). We spent it [the money we got for our posters] in the coffeehouses and pastry shops which were being opened all over the place... (2a). ♦ [context translation] Я был избавлен от необходимости собирать справки о личности Иванько, сведения о нём сыпались на меня на каждом шагу (Войнович 1). I was spared the necessity of gathering information on Ivanko—reports on him rained down on me (1a).

Ш-19 • НЕ ДАВА́ТЬ/НЕ ДАТЬ ША́ГУ СТУПИ́ТЬ ⟨СДЕ́ЛАТЬ⟩ (кому) coll [VP; subj: human; more often impfv; often 3rd pers pl with indef. refer.] to constrain, limit s.o.'s actions, activities etc severely, not letting s.o. do anything independently, without one's permission: X Y-у шагу не даёт ступить ≃ **X doesn't let Y take a (single) step ⟨make a (single) move⟩ on Y's own; Y can't take a single step ⟨make a single move⟩ without X's go-ahead ⟨approval, say-so etc⟩.**

Сына они всё ещё считают ребёнком, шагу ему не дают ступить. They still consider their son a child and don't let him make a move without their go-ahead.

Ш-20 • НИ ША́ГУ [NP_gen; Invar] **1.** ~ (дальше, вперёд, назад и т. п.) [indep. sent used as imper] do not move (used as a command forbidding s.o. to move from the precise spot where he is standing): **not a ⟨one⟩ step farther!; freeze!; stay where you are!; stay put!; don't move ⟨budge⟩ (an inch)!**

2. ~ к кому, куда coll [predic; subj: human; usu. used as imper] not to visit s.o. or go to some place at all (usu. used as an order or warning): Imper к Y-у ⟨в место Z⟩ – ни шагу ≃ **don't ⟨don't you dare etc⟩ set foot in Y's house ⟨at Y's apartment, in place Z etc⟩; don't even think about going to Y's house ⟨Y's apartment, place Z etc⟩; don't even think about going to see Y.**

3. ~ откуда coll [predic; subj: human (often omitted)] not to leave some place (for a certain period of time or ever) (often used as a command): Imper из места Z ни шагу ≃ **don't set foot outside ⟨out of⟩ place Z.**

[Мурзавецкая:] Смотреть за Аполлоном Викторычем, чтоб ни шагу из дому! (Островский 5). [M.:] Watch out for Apollon Viktorovich. Don't let him set foot out of the house! (5a).

4. ~ не сделать, не предпринять [obj] not (to do or make any attempt to do) anything (in a situation where some action is expected, required etc): **not make a (single) move; not take any steps; [in limited contexts] make no effort (to do sth.).**

5. ~ (не отставать, не отходить и т. п.) от кого-чего [adv or predic (subj: usu. human or animal)] not (to fall behind s.o. or sth.) even the slightest distance (when walking, running etc): X не отставал ⟨не отходил⟩ от Y-а ≃ **X stayed right on person Y's heels ⟨tail⟩.**

6. ~ от кого-чего (не отходить и т. п.) [adv or predic (with subj: human or animal)] not (to be far from s.o.) for even the slightest amount of time: X не отходит от Y-а ≃ **X is never more than a few steps ⟨feet⟩ away from Y; X doesn't leave Y ⟨Y's side⟩ for an instant ⟨a second, a minute⟩; X sticks ⟨stays⟩ close to Y all the time ⟨at all times etc⟩; X stays glued to Y's side.**

7. ~ без кого [predic; subj: human] not to do or undertake anything (without s.o.'s consent, permission): X без Y-а ~ ≃ **X doesn't (dare ⟨dare to⟩) take a step ⟨make a move⟩ without Y ⟨Y's permission, Y's go-ahead, Y's OK etc⟩.**

[Саяпин:] ...Без жены он, сам знаешь, ни шагу. [Зилов:] А он жену вчера на юг отправил. [Саяпин:] Вот оно что. То-то загулял мужик... (Вампилов 5). [S.:] ...You know he doesn't make a move without his wife. [Z.:] But he sent her off to the south yesterday. [S.:] So that's why the guy is cutting loose... (5b).

8. ~ без кого-чего [predic; impers or with subj: human] to be unable to function, act etc without s.o. or sth.: X без Y-а ~ ≃ **X won't ⟨can't, doesn't etc⟩ do anything ⟨do a thing, go anywhere etc⟩ without Y; X is lost ⟨helpless⟩ without Y; [in limited contexts] X can't get along ⟨make it⟩ without Y.**

«Ведь не обходится же военная музыка без специалистов с высшим образованием?» – «Но без тебя-то, Аркадий, любая музыка обойдётся! Я в этом нисколько не сомневаюсь!» – «Ещё бы, конечно! Но ведь мне-то без неё – куда? Я без неё – ни шагу...» (Залыгин 1). "How can martial music get along without specialists with higher education?" "Any music can get along without you, Arkady! I've no doubt about that." "Of course it can! But how can I get along without it? Without it I can't do a thing..." (1a).

Ш-21 • ПРИБАВЛЯ́ТЬ/ПРИБА́ВИТЬ ША́ГУ [VP; subj: human or collect] to begin to walk faster: X прибавил шагу ≃ **X quickened his pace ⟨step(s)⟩; X picked up the pace.**

Она было прибавила шагу, но, увидя лицо его, подавила улыбку и пошла покойнее... (Гончаров 1). She had quickened her pace, but seeing his face, suppressed a smile, and walked on more calmly... (1a). ♦ Мари прибавила шагу. Несколько минут они молчали (Федин 1). Marie quickened her step. For a few minutes they were silent (1a).

Ш-22 • ША́ГУ (ЛИ́ШНЕГО) НЕ СДЕ́ЛАТЬ (для кого-чего); **НИ ША́ГУ НЕ СДЕ́ЛАТЬ** [VP; subj: human] not to expend any effort in order to help s.o. or attain sth.: X шагу (лишнего) не сделает для Y-а ≃ **X won't go a step out of his way for (the sake of) Y; X won't lift a finger to help person Y ⟨attain thing Y etc⟩.**

Он был беден, мечтал о миллионах, а для денег не сделал бы лишнего шагу... (Лермонтов 1). He was poor and dreamed of possessing millions, but he would not have gone a step out of his way for the sake of money (1b).

Ш-23 • ША́ГУ НЕ́ГДЕ ⟨НЕ́КУДА⟩ СТУПИ́ТЬ (где) coll [these forms only; impers predic with быть₀] some place is very crowded (usu. with people): (в месте X) шагу негде ступить ≃ **there's no room to move ⟨to breathe, to swing a cat etc⟩ (in place X).**

Ш-24 • ША́ГУ НЕЛЬЗЯ́ ⟨НЕВОЗМО́ЖНО, НЕ МОЧЬ, НЕ СМЕТЬ⟩ СТУПИ́ТЬ ⟨СДЕ́ЛАТЬ⟩ coll [impers predic with быть₀ (variants with нельзя, невозможно) or VP (subj: human)] **1.** ~ (без кого-чего) s.o. is unable to act independently (because he is insecure, because another prohibits it etc): X шагу ступить не может ≃ **X can't ⟨doesn't dare (to)⟩ take a step ⟨make a move⟩ on his own ⟨without person Y's permission, without person Y's go-ahead etc⟩.**

[Муров:] Я совершеннолетний, а не смею ступить шагу без позволения... (Островский 3). [M.:] ...Here I am, a grown man, and I cannot take a step without her permission... (3a).

2. ~ без кого-чего s.o. cannot function, act etc without another person or some thing: X шагу ступить не может без Y-а ≃ **X is lost ⟨helpless⟩ without Y; X can't get along ⟨manage, do anything etc⟩ without Y; X can't ⟨can barely etc⟩ take a (single) step without Y.**

Прошло несколько дней с тех пор, как исчезло ведомство капитана Миляги, но в районе никто этого не заметил. И ведь пропала не иголка в сене, а солидное Учреждение, занимавшее в ряду других учреждений весьма заметное место. Такое учреждение, что без него вроде и шагу ступить нельзя (Войнович 2). Several days had passed since Captain Milyaga's department had vanished, but nobody in the district seemed to notice. And after all it wasn't a needle that had vanished in a haystack but a reputable Institution which occupied a prominent place among other institutions. An Institution without which you could barely take a single step (2a).

Ш-25 • **ОДНА́ ША́ЙКА** ⟨**ША́ЙКА-ЛЕ́ЙКА, ЛА́-ВОЧКА**⟩ *highly coll, usu. disapprov* [NP; these forms only; subj-compl with быть∅ (subj: human, pl)] (the people in question) are similar to each other, have the same characteristics—usu. the same faults: все они ⟨вы⟩ одна шайка-лейка ≃ **they're ⟨you're⟩ all birds of a feather; they're ⟨you're⟩ all of the same ilk ⟨stripe, sort etc⟩; they're ⟨you're⟩ all one gang;** [in refer. to scheming, plotting etc] **they're ⟨you're⟩ in cahoots.**

Ш-26 • **ША́ПКАМИ ЗАКИДА́ТЬ** *кого coll* [VP; subj: human; usu. fut (1st pers pl закидаем or neg pfv fut, gener. 2nd pers sing не закидаешь); fixed WO] to defeat s.o. quickly and easily (usu. used when brazenly predicting a quick victory over s.o.): (мы Y-ов) шапками закидаем ≃ **we'll bag an easy win over Ys; it's in the bag; we'll beat Ys all hollow; it's going to be a walkover; we'll win an easy victory over Ys;** ‖ *Neg* шапками Y-ов не закидаешь ≃ **you won't get Ys that easily.**

«Мы головотяпы! Нет нас в свете народа мудрее и храбрее! Мы даже кособрюхих... шапками закидали!» — хвастали головотяпы (Салтыков-Щедрин 1). "We are the Knockheads! There is no race in the world wiser or braver than we! We even bagged an easy win over the Skewbellies...!" boasted the Knockheads (1a). ♦ ...Они возмечтали, что счастье принадлежит им по праву и что никто не в силах отнять его у них. Победа над Наполеоном ещё более утвердила их в этом мнении, и едва ли не в эту самую эпоху сложилась знаменитая пословица: шапками закидаем! — которая впоследствии долгое время служила девизом глуповских подвигов на поле брани (Салтыков-Щедрин 1). ...They started dreaming that happiness belonged to them by right and that no one had the power to take it away from them. The victory over Napoleon convinced them of this opinion still more firmly. The famous saying "It's in the bag!"—which afterwards served for a long time as the motto for Foolovian exploits on the field of battle—must have arisen in this period (1a). ♦ Тут, наконец, до Марлена Михайловича дошло: вот она — главная причина сегодняшнего высокого совещания. Обеспокоены «поворотом на 180 градусов», перепугались, как бы не отплыл от них в недосягаемые дали Остров Крым, как бы не отняли того, что давно уже считалось личной собственностью. Ага, сказал он себе не без торжества, шапками тут нас не закидаешь (Аксёнов 7). In a flash Marlen Mikhailovich realized what the meeting was for. They were upset by the about face, concerned that the Island of Crimea would float out of their reach, that they would be robbed of what they had long considered their due. Sorry, gentlemen, he said to himself triumphantly, you won't get us that easily! (7a).

Ш-27 • **ДАВА́ТЬ/ДАТЬ ПО ША́ПКЕ** *кому highly coll* [VP; subj: human; usu. pfv; often 3rd pers pl with indef. refer.] to drive away, dismiss, punish, or reprimand s.o. (as implied by the context): Y-у дадут по шапке ≃ **they'll give it to Y in the neck; they'll really give it to Y; they'll give it to Y good; Y will get it good ⟨get it in the neck, catch it in the neck, really get it⟩;** [in limited contexts] **they'll boot ⟨throw⟩ Y out; they'll send Y packing; they'll give Y the boot;** [in refer. to firing only] **Y will get ⟨they'll give Y⟩ the sack ⟨the ax⟩; Y will get ⟨be⟩ canned.**

Ш-28 • **ПО ША́ПКЕ** *кого-что highly coll* [PrepP; Invar; predic; usu. impers or with subj: human] to free o.s. of a person, thing etc one considers undesirable or abandon sth. tedious, unproductive etc: X-а по шапке ≃ [past context] **he ⟨I etc⟩ got rid of X; he ⟨I etc⟩ sent X packing; he ⟨I etc⟩ threw X out; he ⟨I etc⟩ gave X the boot; he ⟨they etc⟩ ousted X;** [in refer. to an undertaking] **he ⟨I etc⟩ bagged X;** [in refer. to firing only] **he ⟨I etc⟩ gave X the ax ⟨the sack⟩.**

[Войницев:] И откуда у вас, у женщин, берётся столько тоски? Ну чего тосковать? Полно! Будь весела!.. Нельзя ли эту тоску, как говорит Платонов, по шапке? (Чехов 1). [V.:] Why are you women always so terribly depressed? Why on earth should you feel depressed? Come, cheer up, darling!...Can't you send this depression packing, as Platonov says? (1a). ♦ Ты говоришь, нет больше сил с твоим пьяницей жить? А ты его по шапке! So you say you can't stand to live with your drunken husband anymore? Then throw the bum out!

Ш-29 • **ПОЛУЧА́ТЬ/ПОЛУЧИ́ТЬ ПО ША́ПКЕ** *highly coll* [VP; subj: human] to be driven away, dismissed, punished, or reprimanded (as implied by the context): X получил по шапке ≃ **X got ⟨caught⟩ it in the neck; X really got it; X got it good;** [in limited contexts] **X got ⟨was⟩ thrown out; X was sent packing; X got the boot;** [in refer. to firing only] **X got the sack ⟨the ax⟩; X got sacked ⟨canned, axed⟩.**

Ш-30 • **ЛОМА́ТЬ ⟨ЛОМИ́ТЬ** *obs*⟩ **ША́ПКУ** *перед кем coll* [VP; subj: human] **1.** *obs* to remove one's cap (and bow) in greeting as a sign of respect: X ломал шапку перед Y-ом ≃ **X doffed his cap to Y;** [in limited contexts] **X bowed to Y, cap in hand.**

Раздался топот конских ног по дороге... Мужик показался из-за деревьев. Он гнал двух спутанных лошадей перед собою и, проходя мимо Базарова, посмотрел на него как-то странно, не ломая шапки, что, видимо, смутило Петра, как недоброе предзнаменование (Тургенев 2). The tramp of horses' hoofs was heard along the road....A peasant came into sight from behind the trees. He was driving before him two horses hobbled together, and as he passed Bazarov he looked at him rather strangely, without doffing his cap, which it was easy to see disturbed [the valet] Peter, as an unlucky omen (2b).

2. to humble o.s. before s.o., behave in a servile manner: X ломает шапку перед Y-ом ≃ **X bows and scrapes before ⟨to⟩ Y; X grovels before Y.**

[Платонов:] Он благодеяния делает, обеды даёт, всеми уважаем, все перед ним шапку ломают... (Чехов 1). [P.:] He contributes to public charities, he gives public dinners, he is a respected member of society, everyone bows and scrapes to him (1a).

Ш-31 • **ПОД КРА́СНУЮ ША́ПКУ** *попасть, отдать кого;* **ПОД КРА́СНОЙ ША́ПКОЙ** *ходить и т. п. both obs, substand* [PrepP; these forms only; adv or subj-compl with copula (subj: human); fixed WO] (to become, give s.o. over to be, serve as etc) a soldier: **(be ⟨send s.o. etc⟩) under a red cap.**

«Этому охотнику ещё года три надо под красную шапку походить». – «Это ты об армии, Миша?» (Абрамов 1). "Your hunter has a three-year stretch under a red cap to go yet." "You mean the army, Misha?" (1a).

Ш-32 • **БЕ́ЛЫЙ ШАР** *old-fash* [NP] a vote for: **yes-vote.**

< Formerly, «белый шар» ("a white ball") was placed in a ballot box to cast a positive vote.

Ш-33 • **ПРО́БНЫЙ ШАР** *lit* [NP; sing only; fixed WO] an action or method that serves as a means of finding out sth.: **trial balloon ⟨run⟩; test run.**

Ш-34 • **ЧЁРНЫЙ ШАР** *old-fash* [NP] a vote against: **blackball; no-vote;** ‖ положить *(кому)* чёрный шар ≃ **blackball (s.o.).**

«Я сам позавидовал ему на защите [диссертации]. Молодость, чистота и вместе с тем какая зрелая, глубокая любовь к своему делу? Разумеется, это чувство не могло заставить меня положить чёрный шар» (Каверин 1). "I myself envied him for his defence [of his dissertation]. Youth, single-mindedness, and along with it such a deep, mature love for his work. Of course, that feeling wasn't strong enough to make me blackball him" (1a).

< Formerly, «чёрный шар» ("a black ball") was placed in a ballot box to cast a negative vote.

Ш-35 • **НА ШАРА́П** *obs, substand* [PrepP; Invar; usu. indep. sent] a call to snatch whatever one can when something is tossed into a crowd: **grab it ⟨what you can⟩.**

Ш-36 • **КРУТИ́ТЬ ⟨ВЕРТЕ́ТЬ, ЗАВОДИ́ТЬ/ЗА-ВЕСТИ́⟩ ШАРМА́НКУ** *highly coll, disapprov* [VP; subj: human] to repeat sth. incessantly or bring up the same subject repeatedly: X крутит шарманку ≃ **X keeps harping on the same string ⟨thing, subject etc⟩; X keeps repeating the same thing over and over; X goes on like a broken ⟨a phonograph⟩ record.**

Юрий Андреевич лёг ничком на койку, лицом в подушку. Он всеми силами старался не слушать оправдывавшегося Ливерия... «Завёл шарманку, дьявол! Заработал языком!..» – вздыхал про себя и негодовал Юрий Андреевич (Пастернак 1). Yurii Andreievich lay down flat on his bunk, his face on his pillow, doing his utmost not to listen to Liberius justifying himself.... "Just like a phonograph record, the devil!" Yurii Andreievich raged in silent indignation. "He can't stop"(1a).

Ш-37 • **ХОТЬ ШАРО́М ПОКАТИ́** *где coll* [хоть + VP$_{imper}$; Invar; impers predic with быть∅; fixed WO] there is no one, nothing, or none of some type of person or thing present or available in some place (often in refer. to a complete lack of food or belongings in s.o.'s home): в месте X хоть шаром покати ≃ **there is no [NP] ⟨not a single [NP], not a bite to eat etc⟩ in place X; you can search place X and not find one [NP] ⟨a single [NP]⟩; place X is (as) bare as a bone.**

«А что, бабоньки, нету ведь у нас в институте мужчин, хоть шаром покати! Одни только и. о. [исполняющие обязанности]?»... – «Чёрт с ними, с мужиками, но ведь и женщины из-за этого лишены своего самого сильного оружия – любовных чар! Кого очаровывать-то: исполняющих обязанности, да?» (Залыгин 1). "Too bad, eh, girls! Not a single real man in the whole institute, not one! Nothing but understudies."... "To hell with them! Men! Trouble is there's no one for us women to use our strongest weapon on—charm! No point trying to charm understudies, is there?"(1a). ♦ В доме хоть шаром покати – никакой еды. О. М[андельштам] отправился к соседям раздобыть что-нибудь на ужин Анне Андреевне... (Мандельштам 2). There wasn't a bite to eat in the house and M[andelstam] went around to the neighbors to try and get something for Akhmatova's supper (2a). ♦ «Остался [я] один. Родни – нигде, никого, ни одной души» (Шолохов 1). "I was left entirely alone. You could search the whole world and not find one relation of mine, not a single soul" (1a). ♦ «По базу хоть шаром покати, хворостины на растопку – и то не найдёшь. Вот до чего дожили!» (Шолохов 5). "The yard's as bare as a bone, there's not even a twig to light a fire with. That's what we've come to!" (5a).

Ш-38 • **И ША́ТКО И ВА́ЛКО (И НА́ СТОРОНУ)** *жить, делать что* и т. п. *obs, coll* [AdvP; these forms only; adv; usu. used with impfv verbs; fixed WO] (to live, do sth. etc) very badly: **I couldn't be worse ⟨it couldn't be worse, he couldn't have done it worse etc⟩; as bad as can be.**

Ш-39 • **НИ ША́ТКО НИ ВА́ЛКО** *жить, работать* и т. п. *coll;* **НИ ША́ТКО НИ ВА́ЛКО НИ НА́ СТОРОНУ** *obs, coll* [AdvP; these forms only; adv; usu. used with impfv verbs; fixed WO] (to do sth., live) neither well nor poorly, in a mediocre way: **so-so; fair to middling; (be) not good, not bad.**

Два дня прошли ни шатко ни валко: трезво, угрюмо. На третий день [Таля] опять стал просить водки, да как-то нахально, злобно... (Грекова 3). Two sober, glum days passed—not good, not bad. On the third day he [Talya] again began to get angry, rudely asking for vodka (3a).

Ш-40 • **ТРЕЩА́ТЬ ПО (ВСЕМ) ШВАМ** *coll* [VP; subj: usu. abstr, often всё; usu. this WO] to be collapsing, heading for ruin: X трещит по всем швам ≃ **X is coming ⟨falling⟩ apart at the seams; X is falling apart; X is falling ⟨going⟩ to pieces; X is coming unglued.**

...Два-три крохотных события, две-три случайные встречи, и мир, взлелеянный [Петром Васильевичем] с такой любовью, с таким тщанием, начинал терять свою устойчивость, трещать по швам, разваливаться на глазах (Максимов 3). Two or three trivial events, two or three chance meetings, and the world he [Pyotr Vasilievich] had cherished with such loving care began to crumble, fall apart, disintegrate before his very eyes (3a).

Ш-41 • **КАК ШВЕД (ПОД ПОЛТА́ВОЙ)** *пропал, погиб, горит* и т. п. *coll, often humor* [как + NP; nom only; adv; fixed WO] (one was or is about to be) destroyed, ruined; (one finds o.s.) in a hopeless, disastrous situation: **(perish ⟨be destroyed etc⟩) like a Swede at Poltava; go up in smoke;** [when the verb is in fut or subjunctive] **(perish ⟨be destroyed etc⟩) as surely as a Swede at Poltava.**

«С хорошею, может быть, душой был человек, а вот пропал, как швед, от пьянства и беспорядка!» (Достоевский 2). "He was probably a man of good soul, and then came to grief like a Swede at Poltava, from drinking and disorder!" (2a). ♦ «Воровал мой оголец, как ни попадя [*ungrammat* = всё, что попадётся]. Я тряпьё на базар таскала. Сколько верёвочке ни виться... Сгорели мы, как шведы. Он подельников выгораживал, всё на себя взял, ему на всю катушку, а мне, по моей глупости, – пять без поражения» (Максимов 3). "He stole everything he could lay his hands on, this man of mine. I used to take it all down to the market to sell. It caught up with us in the end. We went up in smoke. He wouldn't squeal on his mates, he took all the blame, so they gave him the full treatment and I got five years without deprivation of rights for being stupid" (3a).

< Refers to the 1709 battle at *Poltava*, in which Russian troops won a decisive victory over the Swedes.

Ш-42 • **И ШВЕЦ, И ЖНЕЦ, И НА ДУДЕ́ ⟨И В ДУДУ́⟩ ИГРЕ́Ц** *coll, usu. humor* [NP; sing only; subj-compl with быть∅, nom only (subj: human); fixed WO] a person who is skillful at many different kinds of work: **jack-of-all-trades.**

«[Сутырин] задавала, конечно... зато, как говорят, на все руки: и швец, и жнец, и на дуде игрец, обломается» (Максимов 3). "He's [Sutyrin is] a show-off, of course, but he can turn his hand to anything. Jack-of-all-trades. He'll shape up" (3a).

Ш-43 • **ВИСЕ́ТЬ ⟨ПОВИ́СНУТЬ⟩ НА ШЕ́Е** *у кого coll* [VP; subj: human] **1.** (usu. in refer. to a smaller person embracing a taller, stronger etc one) to wrap one's arms around s.o.'s neck in an embrace and continue to embrace him for some time (expressing affection, joy etc): X висит у Y-а на шее ≃ **X hangs (up)on Y's neck;** ∥ X повис на шее у Y-а ≃ **X threw his arms around Y ⟨around Y's neck⟩; X threw himself on Y's neck.**

2. *disapprov* to burden s.o. by being dependent on him for care, monetary support etc: X висит у Y-а на шее ≃ **X is a (heavy) burden to ⟨on⟩ Y; X is a millstone around Y's neck.**

Прожить на свою пенсию Иван Петрович не мог, и он устроился на работу, чтобы не висеть на шее у детей. Ivan Petrovich's pension wasn't enough to live on, and he got himself a job so that he wouldn't be a burden on his children.

Ш-44 • **ДАВА́ТЬ/ДАТЬ ПО ШЕ́Е** *кому coll;* **ДАВА́ТЬ/ ДАТЬ ПО ШЕ́ЯМ** *substand* [VP; subj: human] **1.** Also: **ДАВА́ТЬ/ДАТЬ В ШЕ́Ю** *coll;* **НАДАВА́ТЬ ПО ШЕ́Е ⟨В ШЕ́Ю⟩** *coll;* **НАДАВА́ТЬ ПО ШЕ́ЯМ** *substand* to hit or beat s.o.: X дал Y-у по шее ≃ **X gave Y a thrashing ⟨a**

beating⟩; X walloped Y; X beat Y up; X clouted Y (over the head).

Не может быть, не может быть, думал Шалико, вот сейчас даст мне по шее и отпустит (Искандер 4). It can't be, it can't be, Shaliko thought, he's going to give me a thrashing and let me go (4a). ♦ На тёмной и пустой улице шофёр надавал Лёве по шее и, резко, с матом, газанув, уехал (Битов 2). On the dark and empty street, the driver walloped Lyova, then stepped hard on the gas and drove away, swearing (2a). ♦ Огороды были бесконечные, солнце пекло. Я халтурил: присыпал землёй сорняки, — хотя Садовник иногда шёл по нашим следам, разгребал землю, тогда давал по шее (Кузнецов 1). There was no end to the gardens and the sun was scorching hot. I used to cheat: I just covered the weeds with earth, although the Gardener would sometimes check up on us and uncover the weeds, and then clout us over the head (1b).

2. [often 3rd pers pl with indef. refer.] to punish s.o. severely; (in job-related contexts) to fire s.o.: X даст Y-у ⟨Y-у дадут⟩ по шее ≃ X will give it to Y ⟨Y will get it⟩ in the neck; X will give Y ⟨Y will get⟩ hell; [in refer. to firing] X will give Y ⟨Y will get⟩ the sack ⟨the ax, the boot⟩; X will can Y; Y will get booted ⟨canned⟩; Y will get kicked out; X will kick Y out.

Я создатель новой науки. Но, увы, пользы для себя из этого не извлеку. А если Вы выдадите меня, мне ещё за это по шее дадут (Зиновьев 1). "I am the founder of a new science. But unfortunately I won't be able to get any personal benefit from it. And if you betray me I'll get it in the neck" (1a).

Ш-45 • СИДЕ́ТЬ НА ШЕ́Е чьей ⟨НА ГОРБУ́ чьём⟩, у кого; ЖИТЬ НА ШЕ́Е all coll, disapprov [VP; subj: human] to burden s.o. by being dependent on him for care, monetary support etc: X сидит у Y-а на шее ≃ X is a (heavy) burden to ⟨on⟩ Y; X is a millstone around Y's neck; X hangs (a)round Y's neck; [in limited contexts] X lives off Y.

…Работать [отцу] надо, содержать семью надо, нельзя с женой и детьми сидеть на шее у дедушки Рахленко (Рыбаков 1). …He [father] had to work, he had his family to support and he couldn't let himself and his wife and children hang round grandfather Rakhlenko's neck (1a). ♦ Сами не вырабатывая ничего, кроме ненужных бумаг, они [важные лица] попрекали каждого входящего, будто именно он и живёт на шее у государства… (Войнович 4). Themselves producing nothing but useless paper, they [important people] reproached each caller as if it were he precisely who was living off the state… (4a).

Ш-46 • КАК ШЁЛКОВЫЙ coll [как + AdjP; nom only; subj-compl with copula (subj: human) or adv] one is well-behaved, one acts obediently (occas. out of fear): (as) good as gold; [in limited contexts] (as) meek as a lamb.

Шунечка, пока шёл скандал, ни во что не вмешивался, а когда всё кончилось, вызвал к себе мальчиков и что-то им внушал наедине… после чего они два дня были как шёлковые (Грекова 3). While the row was going on Shunechka did not interfere, but when it was all over he called in the boys and drummed something into them. For two days after that they were good as gold (3a).

Ш-47 • ШЕ́РОЧКА ⟨МАШЕ́РОЧКА⟩ С МАШЕ́РОЧ-КОЙ obs, humor [NP; these forms only; fixed WO] girls or women dancing together in pairs (usu. because of a shortage of men): one girl ⟨gal⟩ (dances) with another.

< From the French ma chère, the form of address formerly used by finishing-school girls in Russia.

Ш-48 • ГЛА́ДИТЬ/ПОГЛА́ДИТЬ ПО ШЕ́РСТИ ⟨ПО ШЕ́РСТКЕ⟩ кого coll [VP; subj: human] to do or say sth. that is pleasing to s.o., makes s.o. feel good: X погладил Y-а по шерсти ≃ X complimented ⟨praised, flattered etc⟩ Y; [in limited contexts] X stroked Y's ego; X smoothed Y's rumpled feathers.

Ш-49 • ГЛА́ДИТЬ/ПОГЛА́ДИТЬ ПРОТИВ ШЕ́РСТИ ⟨ПРОТИВ ШЁРСТКИ, НЕ ПО ШЕ́РСТИ, НЕ ПО ШЁРСТКЕ⟩ кого coll [VP; subj: human] to annoy or displease a person by saying or doing sth. that he does not like: X погладил Y-а против шёрстки ≃ X ruffled Y's feathers; X pushed ⟨pressed⟩ Y's buttons; [in limited contexts] X rubbed Y the wrong way.

Тут Лизка немного покривила душой. На самом-то деле она знала, из-за чего взъелся на них председатель [Першин]. Из-за критики. Из-за того, что он, Михаил, против шерсти погладил Першина (Абрамов 1). Lizka was playing somewhat false here. She did in fact know why the Chairman [Pershin] was out to get them: because of the criticism, because Mikhail had rubbed Pershin the wrong way (1a).

Ш-50 • ПРОТИВ ШЕ́РСТИ ⟨ПРОТИВ ШЁРСТКИ, НЕ ПО ШЕ́РСТИ, НЕ ПО ШЁРСТКЕ⟩ кому, для кого highly coll [PrepP; these forms only; subj-compl with copula (subj: abstr)] sth. is displeasing, irritating to s.o.: X Y-у не по шерсти ≃ X goes against the grain; X rubs Y the wrong way; X ticks Y off.

Ш-51 • БРОСА́ТЬСЯ/БРО́СИТЬСЯ ⟨КИДА́ТЬСЯ/КИ́НУТЬСЯ⟩ НА ШЕ́Ю (к) кому coll [VP; subj: human] 1. to rush to embrace s.o., throwing one's arms around his neck: X бросился Y-у на шею ≃ X threw ⟨flung⟩ himself on Y's neck; X threw his arms (a)round Y's neck; X fell on Y's neck.

«Только едва он коснулся двери, как она вскочила, зарыдала и бросилась ему на шею. — Поверите ли? я, стоя за дверью, также заплакал, то есть, знаете, не то чтоб заплакал, а так — глупость!» (Лермонтов 1). "But barely had he touched the door, than she jumped up, burst into sobs and threw herself on his neck. Would you believe it? As I stood behind the door, I, too, began to cry; I mean, you know, it was not really crying, it was just — oh, silliness!" (1a). ♦ Он хотел кинуться на шею Печорину, но тот довольно холодно, хотя с приветливой улыбкой, протянул ему руку (Лермонтов 1). …He was about to fall on Pechorin's neck, but the latter, rather coolly, though with a friendly smile, stretched out his hand (1a).

2. [subj: female] to make persistent attempts to win a man's love by forcing one's attentions upon him: X бросается Y-у на шею ≃ X throws herself at Y; X runs ⟨chases⟩ after Y; X chases Y.

[Платонов:] Я сделаю из тебя то, что делал я из всех женщин, бросавшихся мне на шею… Я сделаю тебя несчастной! (Чехов 1). I'll make you what I've made all the women who've thrown themselves at me — miserable (1b).

Ш-52 • В ШЕ́Ю ⟨В ТРИ ШЕ́И⟩ гнать, выгнать, вытолк-нуть и т. п. highly coll, rude [PrepP; these forms only; adv] (to turn, drive, push etc s.o. out) rudely, with verbal abuse or blows: X выгнал Y-а в шею ≃ X kicked Y out; X threw Y out (on Y's ear ⟨ass⟩); X sent Y packing.

«Должность хорошая, старинная: сиди только важнее на стуле… да не отвечай сразу, когда кто придёт, а сперва зарычи, а потом уж пропусти или в шею вытолкай, как понадобится» (Гончаров 1). "It's a good, old-fashioned job: all you have to do is sit on a chair and look important…and not answer at once when some one comes, but first give a growl, and then let them in or kick them out, as the case may be" (1b). ♦ «Непостоянны сильные мира сего, — говорил Мольер Мадлене, — и дал бы я совет всем комедиантам. Если ты попал в милость, сразу хватай всё, что тебе полагается. Не теряй времени, куй железо, пока горячо. И уходи сам, не дожидайся, пока тебя выгонят в шею!..» (Булгаков 5). "How inconstant are the mighty of this world," Molière said to Madeleine. "And I would give this advice to all players: if you happen to win favor, seize everything you can at once. Lose no time, strike while the iron is hot. And leave of your own choice, don't wait till you are thrown out!…" (5a).

Ш-53 • **ВЕ́ШАТЬСЯ НА ШЕ́Ю** *кому;* **ВИ́СНУТЬ НА ШЕ́Е** *у кого both coll* [VP; subj: human] **1.** to embrace s.o., hug s.o. with one's arms around his neck (expressing affection, joy etc): X виснет у Y-а на шее ≃ **X hangs (up)on Y's neck.**

2. *disapprov* [subj: female] to make persistent attempts to win a man's love by forcing one's attentions upon him: X вешается Y-у на шею ≃ **X throws herself at Y; X runs ⟨chases⟩ after Y; X chases Y.**

Ш-54 • **НАМЫ́ЛИТЬ ⟨НАМЯ́ТЬ⟩ ШЕ́Ю** *кому substand* [VP; subj: human] **1.** Also: **НАЛОМА́ТЬ ШЕ́Ю; НА-КОСТЫЛЯ́ТЬ ШЕ́Ю ⟨В ШЕ́Ю, ПО ШЕ́Е⟩** *all substand* to beat s.o. severely: X намылит Y-у шею ≃ **X will give Y a good beating ⟨thrashing etc⟩; X will beat Y up.**

2. Also: **МЫ́ЛИТЬ ШЕ́Ю; МЫ́ЛИТЬ/НАМЫ́ЛИТЬ ХО́ЛКУ** *both substand* to reproach s.o. severely, upbraid s.o.: X намылил Y-у шею ≃ **X gave Y hell ⟨the business, a tongue-lashing⟩; X bawled ⟨chewed⟩ Y out; Y got it in the neck; Y got a good talking-to;** [in limited contexts] **X settled Y's hash.**

«Садчиков, я повторил тебе уже три раза — выполняй то, что предписано. Холку потом мне будут мылить, а не тебе» (Семёнов 1). "Sadchikov, I've told you three times already—carry out your instructions. It's me that'll get it in the neck afterwards, not you" (1a). ♦ Зимнюю сессию он одолел «еле можахом», с хвостами, затевал разговор об академическом отпуске, даже пошёл без моего ведома в поликлинику, надеясь получить у врачей справку для отпуска, но там ему намылили шею (Трифонов 5). He had barely made it through the fall semester (as it was, he had a couple of incompletes) and was starting to talk about taking a leave of absence. Without my knowledge he had even gone to the polyclinic, hoping to get a leave of absence on medical grounds; instead he had gotten a good scolding (5a). ♦ «А откуда вам известно про его штуки?» — «Говорили в институте...» — «Чего ж вы ему тогда холку не намылили?» — «Не пойман — не вор» (Семёнов 1). "How do you come to know so much about his tricks?" "They were talked about at the Institute...." "Why didn't you settle his hash at that time?" "You're not a thief till you're caught" (1a).

Ш-55 • **САДИ́ТЬСЯ/СЕСТЬ НА ШЕ́Ю** *coll, disapprov* [VP; subj: human] **1.** ~ *чью, кого, кому* to (begin to) burden s.o. by becoming dependent on him for care, financial support etc: X сядет Y-у на шею ≃ **X will become a (heavy) burden to ⟨on⟩ Y;** [in limited contexts] **X will live ⟨sponge⟩ off Y.**

В Игарке Влада ожидало разочарование: начальство переехало в Ермаково, жаловаться было некому, расчёт получить негде. Снова садиться на шею Мухаммеду в ожидании лучших времён он не решился. Оставалось тем же манером пуститься дальше — на Ермаковский маяк (Максимов 2). [context transl] Disappointment awaited Vlad in Igarka: the expedition's headquarters had moved to Yermakovo, so there was no one to whom he could complain and no one to pay him off. He decided against imposing himself again on Mukhammed while waiting for better times. The only thing to do was to press on to Yermakovo on foot (2a).

2. to make persistent demands of s.o., force s.o. to satisfy one's will, assert one's control over s.o. etc: X сядет Y-у на шею ≃ **X will walk all over Y; X will be on Y's back; X will take advantage of Y; X will push Y around.**

«Погрубее надо с ними [женщинами], пожёстче. Главное — ни намёка на перспективы. А то на шею сядут» (Евтушенко 2). *You have to be tougher with them* [women], *harder*, he thought. *Most important, not a hint of marriage. Otherwise, they'll be on your back forever* (2a).

Ш-56 • **САЖА́ТЬ/ПОСАДИ́ТЬ** *кого* **НА ШЕ́Ю** *чью, кому coll* [VP; subj: human] **1.** to thrust responsibility for some

person, some person's cares etc on s.o. who does not want it: X посадил Y-а на шею Z-у ≃ **X burdened ⟨saddled⟩ Z with Y.**

[Ксения:] Чего я от него [Егора] не терпела! Дочь прижил на стороне да посадил на мою шею (Горький 2). [K.:] The things I've had to stand from him [Yegor]! Brought in a bastard daughter from somewhere and burdened me with her (2b).

2. to force s.o. to take on some unwanted person (as an employee, team member etc): X посадил Y-а Z-у на шею ≃ **X burdened ⟨saddled, stuck⟩ Z with Y.**

Никто из заведующих лабораториями не хотел посадить на шею своим сотрудникам студентов-стажёров, которые только мешали бы им работать. None of the laboratory supervisors wanted to saddle their staff members with student trainees who would only get in the way.

Ш-57 • **СВЕРНУ́ТЬ ШЕ́Ю ⟨ГО́ЛОВУ⟩** *кому coll* [VP; subj: human] **1.** to kill (a bird or animal) by breaking its neck or decapitating it: X свернул шею Y-у ≃ **X chopped ⟨yanked⟩ off Y's head; X snapped Y's neck.**

[Гаттерас:] Я вас уверяю, лорд, этой проклятой птице необходимо свернуть голову. От неё житья нет (Булгаков 1). [G.:] My lord, I tell you that damned bird must have its head yanked off. He makes life impossible (1a).

2. Also: **СЛОМИ́ТЬ ШЕ́Ю ⟨ГО́ЛОВУ⟩** *obs;* **СВЕРНУ́ТЬ БАШКУ́** *substand* (usu. used as a threat) to do s.o. great physical harm, even kill him: X свернёт Y-у шею ≃ **X will wring ⟨break⟩ Y's neck; X will kill ⟨murder⟩ Y.**

[Бубнов:] Дуришь ты, Василий. Чего-то храбрости у тебя много завелось... гляди, храбрость у места, когда в лес по грибы идёшь... а здесь она — ни к чему... Они тебе живо голову свернут... (Горький 3). [B.:] You're playing the fool, Vassily. What's all this showing off how brave you are? Bravery is all right when you go picking mushrooms in the woods. It's not much use in these parts. They'll wring your neck in no time here (3b). ♦ [Бубнов:] Ваську ждёшь? Гляди — сломит тебе голову Васька... (Горький 3). [B.:] Waiting for Vaska? You watch out, Vaska'll break your neck... (3a).

Ш-58 • **СЛОМА́ТЬ ⟨СЛОМИ́ТЬ** *obs⟩* **(СЕБЕ́) ШЕ́Ю ⟨ГО́ЛОВУ⟩** *coll;* **СВИХНУ́ТЬ (СЕБЕ́) ШЕ́Ю** *coll* [VP; subj: human] **1.** Also: **СВЕРНУ́ТЬ (СЕБЕ́) ШЕ́Ю ⟨ГО́ЛОВУ⟩** *coll;* **СВЕРНУ́ТЬ (СЕБЕ́) БАШКУ́** *substand* [usu. fut or infin with мочь, бояться, рисковать etc] to get seriously injured or killed: X свернёт себе шею ≃ **X will break his neck; X will get himself killed;** ‖ X рискует свернуть себе шею ≃ **X is risking his neck.**

[Тишка:] ...Ууух!!! *(Свёртывается с лестницы; она падает. Шум. Вбегают слуги.)* [Атуева *(кричит)*:] Боже мой!.. Батюшки!.. Он себе шею сломит (Сухово-Кобылин 2). [T.:] Ouch!!! *(Tumbles from the ladder; it falls after him. Noise. Servants run in.)* [A. *(shouting)*:] My God!... Help!... He'll break his neck (2b).

2. ~ *(на чём)* to suffer complete failure, defeat in sth. (often damaging one's career or losing one's social status as a result): X свернёт себе шею (на Y-е) ≃ **X will come a cropper; X will fall flat on his face (in Y);** [in limited contexts] **X will cut his own throat;** ‖ X рискует свернуть себе шею ≃ **X is risking his neck.**

Высокий тенор Берлиоза разносился в пустынной аллее, и по мере того, как Михаил Александрович забирался в дебри, в которые может забираться, не рискуя свернуть себе шею, лишь очень образованный человек, — поэт узнавал всё больше и больше интересного и полезного... (Булгаков 9). The editor's high tenor resounded in the deserted avenue. And, as he delved deeper and deeper into jungles where only a highly educated man could venture without risking his neck, the poet learned more and more fascinating and useful facts... (9a).

Ш-59 • ЗА ШИ́ВОРОТ *coll* [PrepP; Invar; adv] **1.** ~ *(кому)* попасть и т. п. (to fall, land etc) on the skin of the dorsal side of s.o.'s neck, inside the collar: **on the nape ⟨back⟩ of s.o.'s ⟨the⟩ neck.**

2. взять, схватить, держать и т. п. *кого* (in refer. to a person) (to seize, grab, hold etc s.o.) by the part of his clothing that encircles the neck or, possibly, by the back of the neck itself; (in refer. to an animal) (to seize, take hold of an animal) by the back of the neck: **by the scruff of the neck;** [in refer. to a person only] **by the collar.**

Основное обвинение отец решительно отверг, но то, что он не сгрёб Лёву за шиворот и не вышвырнул тут же из кабинета, само по себе было очень примечательно (Битов 2). Father emphatically rejected the main accusation, but the mere fact that he didn't scoop Lyova up by the scruff of the neck and fling him right out of the study was very noteworthy (2a). ♦ ...Он [R-13] огромными скачками — со скамьи на скамью — отвратительный и ловкий, как горилла — уносил её вверх... Я, как таран, пропорол толпу — на чьи-то плечи — на скамьи — и вот уже близко, вот схватил за шиворот R: «Не сметь! Не сметь, говорю. Сейчас же...» (Замятин 1). ...He [R-13], repulsive and agile as a gorilla, was carrying her up, away, bounding in huge leaps from bench to bench....Like a battering ram, I tore through the crowd, stepping on shoulders, benches—and now I was upon them; I seized R by the collar: "Don't you dare! Don't you dare, I say. Let her go. This very moment!" (1a).

Ш-60 • ШИ́ВОРОТ-НАВЫ́ВОРОТ *coll* [AdvP; Invar; adv or subj-compl with copula (subj: usu. всё)] **1.** in refer. to the physical placement of some object or objects, the way a piece of clothing is worn etc) in a direction, order, position etc opposite to the customary one: **backward(s); inside ⟨wrong side⟩ out; upside down.**

...Во дворике, впритык к стене, огородик на полторы сотки, на который требуется возить землю, чтобы выросло что-то, потому что отмерен он на камнях и глине, — и это было тоже диковинно: отчего так шиворот-навыворот — не огород на земле, а землю на огород (Распутин 4). ...In the yard, up against the wall, there was a tiny garden, for which you had to haul in soil to grow anything because it was set up in stones and clay—and that was very strange too: why was it so backwards—you didn't have a garden on the soil, you had to have soil on top of the garden (4a).

2. идти, получаться, быть₀ и т. п. ~ (often in refer. to some matter, s.o.'s life etc) (to go, come out, be etc) opposite to the way it should be, not as it is supposed to be: **topsy-turvy; backward(s); upside down;** ‖ сделать *что* ~ ≃ **put the cart before the horse.**

...Тут брехня на брехне, всё шиворот-навыворот. Егорша передовой... Егорша новый... С Егорши пример надо брать... (Абрамов 1). ...This was one piece of garbage after another, everything turned topsy-turvy. Egorsha the progressive...Egorsha the New Man...One should take Egorsha as an example... (1a). ♦ «У нас всё шиворот-навыворот... Что за народ! На войну мужиков провожали — пели, а встречают — как на похоронах» (Распутин 2). "Everything is backwards here....What a group! They sang when they sent off their men to war and they welcome them like it's a funeral" (2a).

Ш-61 • ЗАДАВА́ТЬ/ЗАДА́ТЬ ШИК ⟨ШИ́КУ⟩ *highly coll* [VP; subj: human] to live or do sth. lavishly, striving to make an impression on others and being aware that one is succeeding: X задаст шику ≃ **X will live ⟨do sth.⟩ in ⟨high ⟨grand⟩) style; X will put on the dog ⟨the ritz⟩.**

Вернувшись в Москву из провинции с большими деньгами, Свиридов стал задавать шик: отделал новый дом по последней моде и щедро поил и кормил в нём гостей. When Sviridov returned to Moscow from the provinces with a great deal of money, he began to live in high style: he remodeled his new home according to the latest fashion, and lavishly wined and dined guests there. ♦ [Аннушка:] Там старик-то и помер, да и отказал все свои деньги и все пески золотые Таисе Ильинишне, вот она и разбогатела. Приехала сюда, да теперь шику и задаёт (Островский 3). [A.:] There the old fellow dies and leaves all his money and his gold-fields to Taisa. That's how she got her money. She came back after he died and she's been living in style ever since (3a).

Ш-62 • ШИ́ЛА В МЕШКЕ́ НЕ УТАИ́ШЬ [saying] you cannot hide something that reveals itself on its own or gives itself away (said when a person tries to conceal an act, deed, emotion etc that makes itself apparent): ≃ **murder will out; (the) truth will out ⟨will come to light⟩;** [in limited contexts] **love (and a cough) cannot be hidden.**

Ш-63 • МЕНЯ́ТЬ/СМЕНЯ́ТЬ ШИ́ЛО НА МЫ́ЛО *coll* [VP; subj: human; the verb may take the final position, otherwise fixed WO] to rid o.s. of an undesirable person or thing only to find o.s. with a worse person or thing, extricate o.s. from a bad situation only to find o.s. in a worse situation etc: X сменял шило на мыло ≃ **X jumped out of the frying pan into the fire; X traded bad for worse; X traded something bad for something (even) worse.**

[author's usage] «Он за что сидел-то?» — «За кражу...» — и Люба беспомощно посмотрела на подругу. «Шило на мыло, — сказала та. — Пьяницу на вора... Ну и судьбина тебе выпала! Живи одна, Любка» (Шукшин 1). "What was he in prison for?" "Burglary..." And Lyuba looked at her friend helplessly. "Out of the frying pan into the fire," said the latter. "A drunkard for a thief. What a terrible fate, poor thing. Live alone, Lyuba" (1a).

Ш-64 • ПОПЕРЁК СЕБЯ́ ШИ́РЕ ⟨ТО́ЛЩЕ⟩ *highly coll* [AdjP; these forms only; subj-compl with copula (subj: human); fixed WO] (to be or have become) very fat: X (стал) поперёк себя шире ≃ **X is ⟨has grown, has become⟩ wider than he is tall; X is ⟨has become⟩ a butterball; X is ⟨has gotten to be⟩ like the side of ⟨as big as⟩ a house.**

[author's usage] [Гусев:] ...У всех наших девочек вот такие дети, и все они стали шире себя... (Рощин 1). [G.:] ...All the girls I went to school with have children so high, and they've all grown wider than they're tall... (1b).

Ш-65 • ВО ВСЮ ШИРЬ [PrepP; Invar; adv; fixed WO] **1.** very broadly, without bounds: **to its full width; in all its vastness.**

Во всю ширь раскинулась приволжская степь. The steppes of the Volga stretched out in all their vastness.

2. развернуться, развернуть *что* ~ и т. п. (in refer. to the development of some matter, s.o.'s displaying his qualities etc) as fully as possible: **to the fullest; in full measure; to the full(est) extent.**

Ш-66 • ШИ́ТО-КРЫ́ТО ⟨ШИ́ТО И КРЫ́ТО, ШИ́ТО ДА КРЫ́ТО⟩ делается, остаётся и т. п. *coll* [AdvP; these forms only; subj-compl with copula (subj: всё) or adv] sth. is or remains secret, concealed from others, sth. is done in complete secrecy: всё было шито-крыто ≃ **everything was kept hush-hush ⟨dark, under wraps, under cover⟩; it was all hushed up;** [in limited contexts] **everything was swept under the rug ⟨the carpet⟩;** ‖ сделай так, чтобы всё было шито-крыто ≃ **make ⟨be⟩ sure nobody gets wind of it.**

Иосиф ездил за золотом в Харьков, Киев, Москву, даже в среднюю Азию, но никогда не попадался, всё было шито-крыто... (Рыбаков 1). Yosif used to travel to Kharkov, Kiev, and Moscow to get the gold, even to Central Asia; he was never caught, everything was kept hush-hush (1a). ♦ Неужели она забеременела и, как сестра её, ничего не сказав ему, уехала в деревню?!

Проклятые дикарки! Ведь здесь в городе всё это можно обделать так, что всё будет шито-крыто (Искандер 4). Could she really have gotten pregnant and gone off to the country without saying anything to him, just like her sister? Damned savages! Here in the city it could all have been arranged so that everything would be kept dark (4a). ♦ «...И вы заметьте, они его поместили на квартире, где других гимназистов нет, он там один, так что всё шито-крыто, думали, останется» (Сологуб 1). "...And observe that they have placed him in a house where there are no other students. He is there alone where they thought everything could be kept under cover" (1a). ♦ [Варвара:] А по-моему: делай, что хочешь, только бы шито да крыто было (Островский 6). [V.:] As I see it, do what you like so long as nobody gets wind of it (6b).

Ш-67 • ШИШ В КАРМА́НЕ *у кого highly coll* [NP; sing only; often VP$_{subj}$ with быть$_{\varnothing}$] s.o. has no money: **у Х-а шиш в кармане** ≃ **X is (flat) broke; X doesn't have a kopeck ⟨a penny, a dime etc⟩ to his name ⟨in his pocket⟩; X doesn't have two nickels to rub together.**

«Видишь, что человеку [пассажиру] надо ехать, а он от тебя по вагону прячется, — значит, у него в кармане шиш» (Паустовский 1). "You can see the man [the passenger] has to go somewhere, but he's trying to hide from you—it means he hasn't a kopeck in his pocket" (1b).

Ш-68 • НИ ШИША́ *highly coll* [NP$_{gen}$; Invar; obj or subj/gen] **1.** ~ **нет** *у кого*, **не дать, не получить** и т. п. (to have, give, receive etc) no money, nothing at all: **not (so much as) a kopeck ⟨a penny, a dime etc⟩; (be) without a kopeck ⟨a penny, a dime etc⟩; not a bean; zero; not a fig.**

«...Имеешь ты какое-нибудь влияние на тех-то, на мать да сестру? Осторожнее бы с ним [Раскольниковым] сегодня...» — «Сговорятся!» — неохотно ответил Разумихин. «И чего он так на этого Лужина? Человек с деньгами, ей, кажется, не противен... а ведь у них ни шиша?» (Достоевский 3). "Incidentally, do you have any influence over those two, the mother and the sister? They should be more careful with him today...." "They'll manage!" Razumikhin answered reluctantly. "And why is he so much against this Luzhin? The man has money, she doesn't seem averse to him...and they don't have a bean, do they?" (3c). ♦ Оказывается, на днях тем, кто едет на дальний сенокос, правление выписало по три килограмма ячменной муки, а им [Пряслиным] ни шиша (Абрамов 1). It turned out that the people who had been sent out to the remote hayfields had recently been issued three kilos of barley flour, while they [the Pryaslins] had been given zero (1a). ♦ «Денег он не просит, правда, а всё же от меня ни шиша не получит» (Достоевский 1). "It's true he's never asked for money, and he won't get a fig out of me anyway" (1a).

2. ~ **не знать, не смыслить** и т. п.; ~ **не светит** и т. п. (to know, understand etc) absolutely nothing; (there is) absolutely no chance (of obtaining, achieving, realizing etc sth.): [in refer. to knowing, understanding etc] **not a damn(ed) ⟨goddamn(ed), frigging⟩ thing; not one damn(ed) bit;** [in limited contexts] **not be able to make any goddamn(ed) sense of sth.;** [in refer. to being unable to obtain, achieve etc sth.] **there's no chance in hell...; (s.o.) hasn't a snowball's chance in hell...; there's absolutely no way in the world...**

Ш-69 • НА КАКИ́Е ШИШИ́ *highly coll* [PrepP; Invar; adv; usu. used in questions] what money will or did s.o. use (to do sth.) (usu. implying a lack of money or an assumed lack of money): **on ⟨with⟩ what money; what is one going to use ⟨did one use, does one plan on using etc⟩ for money?; where's the money ⟨the cash, the dough⟩ coming from ⟨where did the money etc come from⟩?**

[Галька:] ...Мы свою [машину] купим, «Волгу»! [Петюня:] Ха! «Волгу»! На какие шиши?! Сколько твой батя зарабатывает, знаешь? (Салынский 1). [G.:] We'll be buying a Volga! [P.:] Huh! A Volga! Where's the cash coming from? How much does your dad earn, do you know? (1a).

Ш-70 • БОЛЬША́Я ⟨ВА́ЖНАЯ, КРУ́ПНАЯ⟩ ШИ́ШКА *coll, iron or humor* [NP; usu. subj-compl with copula, nom or instrum (subj: human); fixed WO] an important, influential person: **big wheel ⟨cheese, shot⟩; bigwig;** [esp. of a military person] **brass hat.**

...И Вадька Батон стал в своей области важной шишкой. Не знаю точно, какой, меня это не интересует (Трифонов 2). ...In his particular sphere even Vadim French Loaf became a big wheel, although I don't know exactly what it was, because it was of no interest to me... (2a). ♦ Вот, брат, как надо устраиваться! Квартирка из трёх комнат, свёкор — большая шишка... (Абрамов 1). That's the way to live, brother! Three-room apartment—her father-in-law's a big cheese... (1a). ♦ В конце концов я узнал, что Иванько Сергей Сергеевич, 1925 года рождения: а) родственник бывшего председателя КГБ Семичастного; б) ближайший друг бывшего представителя СССР в Организации Объединённых Наций... Николая Т. Федоренко; в) сам по себе тоже большая шишка (Войнович 3). In the end, I learned that Ivanko, Sergei Sergeevich, born 1925, was: a. A relative of the former director of the KGB, Semichastny. b. A close friend of Nikolai T. Fedorenko, the former Soviet representative to the United Nations.... c. A big shot in his own right (3a).

Ш-71 • ШИ́ШКА НА РО́ВНОМ МЕ́СТЕ *coll, derog* [NP; usu. subj-compl with copula, nom or instrum (subj: human); fixed WO] a person who exaggerates his own importance (usu. said in refer. to s.o.'s position, office): **a small fry who thinks he's a big fish;** [said ironically] **big cheese; big shot.**

Ш-72 • ВСЕ ШИ́ШКИ ВА́ЛЯТСЯ *на кого* or **НА ГО́ЛОВУ** *чью, кому coll* [VP$_{subj}$; usu. pres; fixed WO] a lot of troubles (or all the troubles that arise in a given situation) befall or are befalling s.o.: **на Х-а все шишки валятся** ≃ **X is ⟨has been⟩ up to his neck in troubles; X has had trouble after trouble; it's as if trouble seeks X out; X has ⟨has had⟩ more than his share of troubles; X is ⟨has been⟩ inundated with troubles; X can't win for losing;** [in limited contexts, usu. when a contrast with another or others is drawn or implied] **X gets ⟨takes⟩ all the lumps; X is the one getting ⟨taking⟩ all the lumps; X gets ⟨is the one getting⟩ all the blame.**

< From the saying «На бедного Макара все шишки валятся». See M-4.

Ш-73 • БРАТЬ/ВЗЯТЬ ЗА ШКИ́РКУ *кого highly coll* [VP; subj: human] to force s.o. into a position in which he must obey one: **X возьмёт Y-а за шкирку** ≃ **X will put the screws ⟨the squeeze⟩ on Y; X will have Y over a barrel; X will get Y where X wants him.**

Ш-74 • СВОЯ́ ШКУ́РА *coll* [NP; sing only; obj or subj; usu. this WO] one's own life, well-being, career etc: **one's own skin ⟨hide⟩;** ∥ спасать свою шкуру *usu. derog* ≃ **save one's own skin ⟨hide⟩;** ∥ думать о своей шкуре ⟨дорожить своей шкурой, дрожать за свою шкуру и т. п.⟩ *derog* ≃ **think of saving ⟨want to save, look out for, worry about (saving), be afraid for etc⟩ one's own skin ⟨hide⟩;** ∥ *Neg* не жалеть своей шкуры ⟨не дрожать за свою шкуру и т. п.⟩ ≃ **not mind risking one's (own) skin ⟨hide⟩.**

Он [дедушка] видел его [Иосифа] насквозь: врёт, будто детей увезли в Польшу, — детей расстреляли; врёт, будто где-то ещё сохранились гетто, —они уничтожены вместе с их обитателями... Всё врёт... думает только о своей шкуре... (Рыбаков 1). He [grandfather] saw right through Yosif. Yosif was lying when he said they might have transported the children to Poland, they had shot them. He'd lied when he said some ghettoes still survived, they'd been liquidated together with their inhabitants....It was all lies...he was only thinking of saving his own skin (1a). ♦ «Люди трусы. Видят, как жулик в карман лезет, — отвернутся, потому что за свою шкуру дрожат» (Семёнов 1). "People are cowards. When they see a thief's hand in somebody's pocket they turn away, because they're afraid for their own skins" (1a). ♦ «Так, Лашков, так, Вася, — отчеканила она. — Так. Выходит, о шкуре своей печёшься? А я как? — она невольно повторила вопрос, заданный им Калинину. — Как я?» (Максимов 3). "All right, Lashkov, all right, Vasilii," she said slowly and distinctly. "Right. So you're worried about your own skin, are you? And what about me?" Without realizing it she was repeating his question to Kalinin. "What about me?" (3a). ♦ «...Ежели вашей светлости понадобится человек, который бы не жалел своей шкуры, то извольте вспомнить обо мне...» (Толстой 6). "...If Your Serene Highness has need of a man who doesn't mind risking his skin, please think of me" (6a).

Ш-75 • В ШКУ́РЕ *чьей, кого coll* [PrepP; Invar; the resulting PrepP is subj-compl with copula (subj: human); often used in condit clauses] one is, finds o.s. in another's (usu. unenviable) position (implying that only a person who has been in that position can understand how bad, difficult etc it is): **in s.o.'s skin ⟨shoes, place⟩.**

«Ты, Лиза, не была в нашей шкуре и не говори» (Распутин 2). "You haven't been in our skins, Liza, so don't you talk about it" (2a).

Ш-76 • НА СВОЕ́Й ШКУ́РЕ *испытать что*; **НА (СВОЕ́Й) СО́БСТВЕННОЙ ШКУ́РЕ** *both coll* [PrepP; these forms only; adv; fixed WO] (to experience, live through sth.) personally, so that one understands it intimately: X на своей шкуре испытал Y ≃ **X (has) experienced Y firsthand ⟨at first hand⟩; X went ⟨has gone⟩ through Y himself; X knows ⟨learned etc⟩ what Y feels ⟨is⟩ like.**

В этот... период жизни с Альбиной дано было Лёве на своей шкуре испытать всю силу и ужас собственной НЕ любви (именно отдельно НЕ, а не вместе: просто нелюбовь — просто эмоция)... (Битов 2). In this period of his life with Albina...Lyova was allowed to experience firsthand the full force and horror of his own *not*-love (precisely, *not*-love: mere unlove is mere emotion)... (2a). ♦ Даже чечено-ингуши и калмыки... на своей шкуре испытавшие мудрость сталинской национальной политики (они все были высланы Сталиным в места не столь отдалённые), — и те тоже очень возмущаются... (Ивинская 1). Even the Chechens, Ingush, and Kalmyks, who had experienced at first hand the wisdom of Stalin's policies toward the minorites (they were deported, men, women, and children, to remote areas of the country), joined in the chorus of indignation... (1a). ♦ Снова долг заставляет меня свидетельствовать о том, что пока ещё, по-моему, никто не рассказал, а мне довелось испытать на собственной шкуре (Марченко 2). Duty once more compels me to tell what I think has not yet been told by anyone and what I went through myself (2a). ♦ «Я ведь тоже за Сталина. Но хотелось бы поменьше славословий — режут ухо». — «Непонятное ещё не есть неправильное, — ответил Марк, — верь в партию, в её мудрость. Начинается строгое время». Саша усмехнулся. «Сегодня на своей шкуре испытал» (Рыбаков 2). "I mean, I'm for Stalin, but I just wish there was a bit less glorification. It grates on me." "Something not understood is not the same as something wrong," Mark replied. "You must believe in the Party and its wisdom. Things are going to get tough." Sasha laughed. "Yes...I learned what that's like today" (2a).

Ш-77 • ВЛЕЗА́ТЬ/ВЛЕЗТЬ В ШКУ́РУ ⟨В КО́ЖУ⟩ *чью, кого coll* [VP; subj: human; often pfv imper or infin used with a finite form of another verb] to imagine, picture, put etc o.s. in another's (usu. unenviable) position: влезь в Y-ову шкуру ≃ **crawl inside Y's skin; put yourself in ⟨step into⟩ Y's shoes.**

«Казалось бы, чего легче понять ближнего! Надо только хоть на мгновение влезть в его шкуру, поставить себя на его место, и ты всегда будешь поступать правильно» (Максимов 2). "You'd think there was nothing easier than to understand your fellow-man. You only have to crawl inside his skin for a moment, to put yourself in his place—and you'll always act decently" (2a). ♦ «Вот попал [в тюрьму], чёрт шелудивый, а я с тремя [детьми] живи, — и все колготят: хлеба! И иде [*ungrammat* = где] я его возьму, хлеба-то? Жилы они из меня все вытянули»... Женщина в берете сказала вполголоса: «Зачем вы? Не надо»... — «Вам оно, конечно, что!.. А вы в мою шкуру влезьте, не таким голосом запоёте» (Максимов 3). "Got caught, the miserable devil, and left me with three [children] on my hands, and all they can yell about is food. Where'm I supposed to get it from? They've tortured the life out of me...."...The woman in the beret spoke in a low voice. "Why do you talk like that? You mustn't...." "Oh, it doesn't mean much to you, of course....You put yourself in my shoes and you'd sing a different tune" (3a).

Ш-78 • ДЕЛИ́ТЬ ШКУ́РУ НЕУБИ́ТОГО МЕДВЕ́ДЯ *coll* [VP; subj: human; the verb may take the final position, otherwise fixed WO] to count on future benefits that may never materialize, divide expected profits etc from a job not yet accomplished: X-ы делят шкуру неубитого медведя ≃ **Xs should catch the bear before they sell his skin; Xs are dividing up the bearskin before the bear is shot; Xs are counting their chickens (before they hatch ⟨are hatched⟩); Xs should first catch their hare ⟨rabbit⟩, then go about skinning it.**

В вопросе о предоставлении независимости Украине я... выразил сомнение в целесообразности делить шкуру неубитого медведя сейчас, именно сейчас, когда Советское государство столь сильно, как никогда (Лимонов 1). On the question of granting independence to the Ukraine, I...expressed doubt as to the expediency of dividing up the bearskin before the bear was shot, especially right now, when the Soviet government was stronger than ever (1a). ♦ «Я жду с нетерпением, когда мы получим четвёртую комнату, чтобы оборудовать тебе кабинет». — «Нет, — возразил он. — ...Я хочу, чтобы в этой комнате был твой будуар». — ...«А тебе не кажется, — спросила жена, — что мы делим шкуру неубитого медведя, что этот негодяй с беременной женой настроит против нас весь кооператив и они опять проголосуют против?» (Войнович 3). "I can't wait until we get that fourth room so we can set up a study for you." "No," he objects. "...I want that room to be your boudoir."..."But don't you think," his wife asks, "that we're counting our chickens, that the scoundrel with the pregnant wife will get the whole cooperative against us and that they'll vote 'no' again?" (3a).

Ш-79 • ДРАТЬ/СОДРА́ТЬ ШКУ́РУ *с кого highly coll* [VP; subj: human] **1.** [usu. fut or subjunctive] (usu. used as a threat) to whip or beat s.o. severely; *by extension* to deal cruelly with s.o. in a more general sense: X сдерёт шкуру с Y-а ≃ **X will have Y's hide; X will skin ⟨flay⟩ Y alive; X will beat the hide off Y.**

«Признавайся, — помилуем, не признаешься — шкуру с тебя сдерём, кости переломаем и повесим как шпиона...» (Копелев 1). "Confess, and we'll pardon you; don't confess, we'll skin you alive, break all your bones, and hang you as a spy" (1a). ♦ «Вывезут сенаторы. Кайо поклялся содрать шкуру с Блюма» (Эренбург 4). "The senators will come to the rescue. Caillaux has sworn to flay Blum alive" (4a). ♦ «...Коли шкуру драть с человека станут, так он во всём признается, чего и не было» (Сологуб 1). "...If you beat the hide off a man, he will confess to anything — even things that never happened" (1a).

2. Also: **ДРАТЬ ⟨СДИРА́ТЬ⟩/СОДРА́ТЬ СЕМЬ ШКУР ⟨(ПО) ДВЕ ШКУ́РЫ, (ПО) ТРИ ШКУ́РЫ⟩** *highly coll* being in a position of power, to exploit s.o. pitilessly by making him pay large taxes, very high interest, exorbitant prices etc: X драл шкуру с Y-a ≃ **X exploited Y mercilessly; X skinned Y; X squeezed Y dry; X took the food out of Y's mouth ⟨the bread off Y's table⟩**.

«Мы с голоду на улицах подыхаем, а вы с нас последнюю шкуру содрать хотите!..» (Пильняк 1). "We're croaking on the streets from hunger, and you want to skin us even more!" (1a).

Ш-80 • СПУСКА́ТЬ/СПУСТИ́ТЬ ⟨СНЯТЬ⟩ ШКУ́РУ ⟨ТРИ ШКУ́РЫ, СЕМЬ ШКУР⟩ с кого *highly coll* [VP; subj: human; usu. fut or subjunctive] to subject s.o. to extremely cruel physical punishment (usu. a beating); *by extension* to deal cruelly with s.o. in a more general sense (often used as a threat): X с Y-a шкуру спустит ≃ **X will skin ⟨flay⟩ Y alive; X will flay the hide off Y; X will beat the hide off Y; X will knock ⟨beat⟩ the hell out of Y; X will have Y's hide.**

«Выслушал он всё разъяснение Апокалипсиса — и про зверя, и про дракона, и что значит число шестьсот шестьдесят шесть... Потом встал, потянулся, обошёл вокруг моего стула и с тоской говорит: „Ох, попался бы ты мне два года назад, ведь я бы с тебя всю шкуру спустил!.."» (Терц 3). "He listened to my explanation of the Revelation, about the beast and the dragon, and about the meaning of the number six hundred three score and six....Then he got up, stretched himself, went round and stood at the back of my chair and said: 'Oh, if you had only come into my hands two years ago I would have skinned you alive!'" (3a). ♦ «Если ты мне во всём признаешься, так я тебя не высеку, дам ещё пятак на орехи. Не то я с тобою сделаю то, чего ты не ожидаешь. Ну!» Мальчик не отвечал ни слова и стоял, потупя голову и приняв на себя вид настоящего дурачка. «Добро, — сказал Кирила Петрович, — запереть его куда-нибудь да смотреть, чтоб он не убежал, или со всего дома шкуру спущу» (Пушкин 1). "If you tell me everything, I won't flog you, and will even give you five copecks for nuts. If you don't, I'll do something to you that you little expect. Well?" The boy still made no reply, but stood with his head bent, assuming an expression of veritable idiocy. "Right!" said Kirila Petrovich. "Lock him up somewhere, and see that he doesn't run away, or I'll have the whole household flayed alive" (1b). ♦ «Он... от власти пьяный и готов шкуру с другого спустить, лишь бы усидеть на этой полочке» (Шолохов 4). "He was...drunk with power, and ready to flay the hide off anyone else to stay that way" (4a). ♦ «Так что вы аккуратней, чтоб никакого шума. Если наружу слыхать будет, или кто пожалится [dial = пожалуется], и с меня шкуру снимут, и вас накажут» (Копелев 1). "So you be careful not to make any noise. If I hear it outside, or if anyone complains, they'll have my hide, and you'll be punished" (1a).

Ш-81 • КУДА́ НИ ШЛО *coll* [Invar; fixed WO] **1.** [usu. used as Particle] let it be so, agreed (used to express hesitant agreement): **very well; all right (then); so be it.**

[Астров:] Пока здесь никого нет, пока дядя Ваня не вошёл с букетом, позвольте мне... поцеловать вас... На прощанье... Да? (*Целует её в щёку*)... [Елена Андреевна:] Желаю вам всего хорошего. (*Оглянувшись*) Куда ни шло, раз в жизни! (*Обнимает его порывисто...*) (Чехов 3). [A.:] Before anyone comes in, before Uncle Vanya turns up with his bunch of flowers, allow me — to kiss you good-bye. May I? (*Kisses her cheek*.)... [E.A.:] I wish you every happiness. (*Looks round.*) Oh, all right then, just for once in a lifetime. (*Embraces him impulsively...*) (3c). ♦ «Вам пришла фантазия испытать на мне свой рыцарский дух. Я бы мог отказать вам в этом удовольствии, да уж куда ни шло!» (Тургенев 2). "You have taken it into your head to test your chivalrous spirit on me. I could refuse you this satisfaction but — so be it!" (2c).

2. [predic; subj: infin, это, or any noun] acceptable, adequate to some degree (used to express mild approval): X — (ещё) куда ни шло ≃ **X is not so ⟨that⟩ bad; X is more or less all right; X is okay; X can be tolerated; doing X makes sense.**

Родители Марка не одобряли его расточительства. «Снять дорогую, но удобную квартиру, — говорили они, — это куда ни шло, но купить ещё и новую машину — это уж слишком». Mark's parents did not approve of his extravagance. "Renting an expensive yet comfortable apartment is more or less all right," they would say, "but buying a new car on top of it is going too far." ♦ Обстановка на работе становилась для Тани всё труднее: терпеть придирки начальника — это ещё куда ни шло, но чувствовать враждебность сотрудников было выше её сил. The situation at work became more and more difficult for Tanya: as for her boss's constant faultfinding, that could be tolerated, but the animosity of her coworkers was more than she could take.

Ш-82 • СНИМА́ТЬ/СНЯТЬ ШЛЯ́ПУ перед кем-чем *lit* [VP; subj: human] to exhibit great respect toward s.o., s.o.'s achievements, s.o.'s deeds etc: X снимает шляпу перед Y-ом ≃ **X takes off his hat to Y.**

Ш-83 • БРАТЬ/ВЗЯТЬ В ШО́РЫ кого; ДЕРЖА́ТЬ В ШО́РАХ [VP; subj: human] to repress s.o., limit his freedom of action: X взял Y-a в шоры ⟨держал Y-a в шорах⟩ ≃ **X clamped down on Y; X tightened the reins ⟨kept a tight rein⟩ on Y.**

Мать никогда не держала Веру в шорах — отношения между ними были дружескими, доверительными. Vera's mother never kept a tight rein on her — their relationship was friendly and trusting.

Ш-84 • СКРЕ́ЩИВАТЬ/СКРЕСТИ́ТЬ ШПА́ГИ ⟨МЕЧИ́, ОРУ́ЖИЕ⟩ (с кем) *lit* [VP; subj: human] **1.** *obs* to fight with s.o. one on one in battle or a duel: X скрестил шпаги с Y-ом ⟨X и Y скрестили шпаги⟩ ≃ **X crossed swords with Y ⟨X and Y crossed swords⟩.**

2. to enter into an ideological, political etc argument with s.o., defending one's position, interests etc: X скрестит шпаги с Y-ом ≃ **X will cross swords ⟨lock horns⟩ with Y.**

«Прежде чем скрещивать оружие с инженером Лопаткиным, — пробасил он, — я хочу сказать несколько слов критики в адрес почтенных представителей НИИ-Центролита» (Дудинцев 1). "Before I cross swords with Engineer Lopatkin," he growled, "I would like to address a few words of criticism to the respected representatives of C.S.I.F.R. [the Central Scientific Institute of Foundry Research]" (1a).

Ш-85 • ПОДПУСКА́ТЬ/ПОДПУСТИ́ТЬ ШПИ́ЛЬКИ ⟨ШПИ́ЛЬКУ⟩ (кому, по поводу чего и т. п.); ПУ-СКА́ТЬ/ПУСТИ́ТЬ ШПИ́ЛЬКИ ⟨ШПИ́ЛЬКУ⟩ *all coll* [VP; subj: human; var. with шпильки is usu. impfv; var. with шпильку is usu. pfv] to make caustic remarks or a caustic remark (to s.o.): X подпускал шпильки ⟨подпустил шпильку⟩ (Y-у ⟨по поводу Z-а⟩) ≃ **X made digs ⟨a dig⟩ (at Y ⟨about Z⟩);** [usu. in refer. to lighthearted teasing] **X needled Y.**

[Андрей:] Господин Харман знает русский язык, так что если вы начнёте пускать шпильки по поводу принадлежности его к капиталистическому обществу — то получится неловкость (Олеша 6). [A.:] Mr. Harman knows Russian, so if you start making digs about his being a capitalist — well, it would be awkward (6a). ♦ Жить с ним в одной комнате я не хотел бы — все говорят, что он любит подпускать шпильки (Эренбург 3). "Not that I would like to live in the same room with him, everybody says he likes to needle people" (3a).

Ш-86 • ОСТАВА́ТЬСЯ/ОСТА́ТЬСЯ БЕЗ ШТАНО́В *highly coll, often humor* [VP; subj: human; more often pfv] to be left without any means, be ruined financially: X останется без штанов ≃ **X will end up flat broke; X will end up losing his shirt; X will be left penniless ⟨without his shirt, without a pot to piss in⟩; X won't have two nickels to rub together.**

Будешь играть в рулетку — без штанов останешься. If you play roulette you'll end up losing your shirt.

Ш-87 • ПРОТИРА́ТЬ ⟨ПРОСИ́ЖИВАТЬ⟩ ШТАНЫ́
highly coll, humor or iron [VP; subj: human] to work or study long hours, usu. very diligently (in refer. to a job – often a clerical one – or other occupation that the speaker considers unworthy of such diligence): X протирает штаны ≃ **X wears out the seat of his pants.**

«Сажа валит из труб — это убыток и одновременно напоминание: есть приказ... о ликвидации убытков, над чем мы ежедневно просиживаем штаны» (Дудинцев 1). "If soot pours from a chimney, that is a loss and at the same time a reminder: there is an order...about the reduction of losses and we wear out the seats of our pants day after day trying to achieve this" (1a).

Ш-88 • ПО ШТА́ТУ ПОЛАГА́ЕТСЯ ⟨ПОЛО́ЖЕНО⟩
кому occas. humor [VP or subj-compl with быть₀ (var. with положено); subj: это, такое etc or infin] (some action, manner of behavior etc) corresponds to s.o.'s position, social status, merits etc: X-у по штату положено делать Y ≃ **it befits ⟨is appropriate to⟩ X's station ⟨rank etc⟩ to do Y; it ⟨doing Y⟩ is in keeping with X's position ⟨station, status etc⟩; it's X's job ⟨duty etc⟩ to do Y; X is supposed to ⟨has to etc⟩ do Y, it's his job ⟨duty etc⟩.**

Никто не знает, сколько у нас классов чиновников, кроме самих чиновников, но они-то отлично разбираются в тонкой структуре и не возьмутся за лом, если такое им по штату не положено (Мандельштам 2). Nobody knows how many different grades of officials we have, but they themselves have a very keen sense of all the nuances, and none of them would dream of wielding a crowbar if it were not appropriate to his station (2a). ♦ «А я — инженер человеческих душ, мне по штату положено душу уловить, изучить и затем, используя накопленный материал, глаголом жечь сердца людей» (Аржак 2). "But I'm an engineer of human souls. It's my job to capture the soul, study it and then, with the knowledge I've accumulated, to set the hearts of men on fire with my words" (2a). ♦ «Когда раньше, на воле, я читал в книгах, что мудрецы думали о смысле жизни, или о том, что такое счастье, — я мало понимал эти места. Я отдавал им должное: мудрецам и по штату положено думать» (Солженицын 3). "When I was free and used to read books in which wise men pondered the meaning of life or the nature of happiness, I understood very little of those passages. I gave them their due: wise men are supposed to think. It's their profession" (3a).

Ш-89 • ВОТ ТАК ШТУ́КА!; ВОТ ТАК ⟨ЭТО⟩ НО́МЕР! *all coll* [Interj; these forms only; fixed WO] used to express surprise, disappointment, perplexity etc (usu. in reaction to sth. unexpected): **(well,) how do you like that!; (well,) I like that!; well, I'll be darned ⟨damned⟩!; what a mess ⟨a business⟩!; well, what do you know!; [in limited contexts] that's a new ⟨good⟩ one!**

«Вот так штука, вот так штука», — шептал он, отходя и чувствуя, как сзади, от затылка до пят, наваливается на него бремя бессонной ночи... (Набоков 1). "What a mess, what a mess," he whispered, stepping away and feeling, from behind, the weight of a sleepless night settling on him from head to heels... (1a). ♦ «Понимаю, понимаю. У него буква „В" была на визитной карточке. Ай-яй-яй, вот так штука!.. Так он, стало быть, действительно мог там быть с Понтия Пилата? Ведь он уже тогда родился? А меня сумасшедшим называют!» — прибавил Иван, в возмущении указывая на дверь (Булгаков 9). "I see, I see it now! That letter 'W' on his card. Oh, oh, what a business!...So he really could have been there with Pontius Pilate? He had already been born at the time, hadn't he? And they call me mad!" he [Ivan] added, indignantly pointing at the door (9a). ♦ «Что нибудь случилось?» Лена сказала, что у Саши неприятности и её отец звонил

[директору института] Глинской. Несгибаемый Сашка! Вот это номер! (Рыбаков 2). "Has anything happened?" Lena replied that Sasha was having some problems and her father had telephoned [the director of the institute] Glinskaya. So, the unbending Sasha! Well, what do you know? (2a).

Ш-90 • НЕ ШТУ́КА; НЕ ВЕЛИКА́ ШТУ́КА *both obsoles, coll* [NP; these forms only; subj-compl with быть₀ (subj: usu. infin or abstr), pres only] doing sth. does not require much work or great effort, sth. or dealing with sth. is not difficult: сделать X не штука ≃ **X ⟨doing X⟩ is nothing ⟨no great trick⟩; there's nothing to it; it's not hard at all (to do X).**

«Придёт муж [Степан] — небось, бросишь меня? Побоишься?» — «Мне что его бояться... Степан придёт — это не штука. Батя вон меня женить собирается» (Шолохов 2). "You'll give me up when my husband [Stepan] comes back, won't you? You'll be afraid?" "Why should I be afraid of him?...Stepan coming back—that's nothing. It's my Dad; he wants to marry me off" (2a). ♦ [Лебедев:] Не велика штука пить, — пить и лошадь умеет. Нет, ты с толком выпей!.. (Чехов 4). [L.:] Drinking's no great trick—even a horse can drink....No, it's knowing how to do it properly! (4a). [L.:] Drinking? There's nothing to it, even a horse can drink. No, the thing is to drink properly (4b).

Ш-91 • ОТМА́ЧИВАТЬ/ОТМОЧИ́ТЬ ⟨ОТКА́ЛЫВАТЬ/ОТКОЛО́ТЬ, ВЫКИ́ДЫВАТЬ/ВЫКИНУТЬ, УДРА́ТЬ *obs*⟩ ШТУ́КУ ⟨ШТУ́КИ⟩ *highly coll* [VP; subj: human; variants with штуки are usu. impfv; variants with штуку are usu. pfv] to do sth. unexpected, unusual, absurd: X отмочил штуку ≃ **X pulled a stunt ⟨a trick, a number⟩; X played a trick.**

Тогда Стёпа отколол такую штуку: стал на колени перед неизвестным курильщиком и произнёс: «Умоляю, скажите, какой это город?» (Булгаков 9). Then Styopa pulled a crazy stunt; he dropped on his knees before the unknown smoker and asked: "I implore you, tell me what city is this?" (9a). ♦ ...Кот отмочил штуку почище номера с чужими часами. Неожиданно поднявшись с дивана, он на задних лапах подошёл к подзеркальному столику, передней лапой вытащил пробку из графина, налил воды в стакан, выпил её, водрузил пробку на место и гримировальной тряпкой вытер усы (Булгаков 9). ...The tom pulled an even neater trick [than the watch trick]. Suddenly getting up from the sofa, he walked up to the dressing table under the mirror, drew the cork out of the carafe with his front paw, poured some water into a glass, drank it, restored the cork to its proper place and wiped his whiskers with the make-up cloth (9a).

Ш-92 • КАК ШТЫК прийти, явиться, быть₀ и т. п. *coll* [как + NP; nom only; subj-compl with copula (subj: human) or adv] (to come to, appear at some place) unfailingly and at the appointed time (if the time is indicated or implied): **(on time and) without fail;** [with the focus on the exact time] **on the dot ⟨on the nose, on the button⟩.**

«Зачем тебе отпуск?» — спросил Андриолли. «К матери надо съездить, крышу покрыть. Пишет: текёт [*ungrammat =* течёт] крыша-то. На недельку, Матвей Матвеич. В тот понедельник как штык на работе буду», — заверил он в слабой надежде (Войнович 5). "What do you need leave for?" asked Andriolli. "I've got to go to my mother's and mend the roof. She wrote and told me it's leaking. Just for a week, Matvei Matveevich. I'll be back on the job next Monday. On the dot," he assured the director without much hope (5a).

Ш-93 • В ШТЫКИ́ встретить, принять *кого-что coll* [PrepP; Invar; adv] (to react to s.o. or sth.) with hostility, (to be) violently opposed to sth., ready to argue or fight with s.o. about sth.: **react to s.o. ⟨sth.⟩ with open ⟨extreme⟩ hostility; (give s.o. ⟨sth.⟩) a hostile reception; (be) up in arms over ⟨about, at⟩ sth.**

Все мои домашние встретили в штыки моё предложение официально удочерить Тоню (Гинзбург 2). All the members of my household were up in arms at my proposal to adopt Tonya (2a).

Ш-94 • ШУ́БЫ НЕ СОШЬЁШЬ *из чего coll, usu. humor;* **НЕ ШУ́БУ ШИТЬ** *obs, coll* [VP; these forms only; neg pfv fut, gener. 2nd pers sing (1st var.); impers predic (2nd var.); fixed WO] sth. is or will be of no practical use whatsoever: **it ⟨that⟩ won't ⟨doesn't⟩ do you ⟨me etc⟩ any good; it won't put clothes on your ⟨his etc⟩ back;** [in limited contexts] **it won't fill your ⟨his etc⟩ belly.**

Ш-95 • ПОД ШУМО́К *coll* [PrepP; Invar; adv] (to do sth., usu. sth. that would be disapproved of by those present) secretly, unobserved by others, making use of general noise and/or confusion to cover o.s.: **in (the midst of) all the confusion ⟨the commotion, the bustle etc⟩; taking advantage of the commotion ⟨the confusion, the bustle etc⟩; using the commotion ⟨the confusion etc⟩ to one's advantage; while the racket ⟨all this etc⟩ is going on;** [in limited contexts] **quietly; on the quiet.**

И тут только я, зачарованный его таинственным рассказом, догадался, что он под шумок выпил всю нашу оставшуюся водку (Попов 1). And only then did I, entranced by his mysterious tale, guess the truth—that in all the commotion he had drunk up what vodka we had left (1a). ♦ Все засуетились. Комендант бросился вызывать машину, Хлебовводов отпаивал Лавра Федотовича боржомом, а Фарфуркис забрался в сейф и принялся искать соответствующие дела. Я под шумок схватил Говоруна за ногу и выбросил его вон (Стругацкие 3). Everyone started bustling. The commandant ordered the car, Khlebovvodov plied Lavr Fedotovich with mineral water, and Farfurkis dug around for the necessary documents. I took advantage of the bustle, grabbed Gabby by the leg, and threw him out (3a). ♦ «А кто бомбу бросил? Ну, не бомбу, — гранату?» — «Господи, да разве это мы?» — «А кто же?» — «А почём я знаю. Кто-то другой. Видит, суматоха, дай, думает, под шумок волость взорву» (Пастернак 1). "Well, who threw it? The bomb or the grenade or whatever it was." "My God! You don't think we did?" "Who did, then?" "How should I know? It must have been someone else. Somebody sees all this hullabaloo going on and says to himself: 'Why shouldn't I blow the place up while the racket is going on...'" (1a). ♦ Среди этой общей тревоги об шельме Анельке совсем позабыли. Видя, что дело её не выгорело, она под шумок снова переехала в свой заезжий дом, как будто за ней никаких пакостей и не водилось... (Салтыков-Щедрин 1). In the general commotion, the rascal Anelka was completely forgotten. Seeing that the deal had not come off, she moved back to her inn on the quiet, just as if she hadn't been playing dirty tricks... (1a).

Ш-96 • НАДЕ́ЛАТЬ (много) ШУ́МУ ⟨-а⟩ *coll* [VP; subj: abstr or concr] to give rise to much talk, attract general attention: X наделал шуму ≃ **X caused ⟨created⟩ a sensation ⟨a stir⟩;** [in limited contexts] **X made a splash.**

Картина наделала много шуму, и, в конце концов, её сняли до закрытия выставки (Искандер 4). The painting caused quite a sensation, and they finally took it down before the exhibition closed (4a). ♦ «...Я сказал ваше имя... Оно было ей известно. Кажется, ваша история там наделала много шума!» (Лермонтов 1). "She knew your name when I mentioned it. Your affair seems to have caused quite a stir" (1c).

Ш-97 • ШУТ ГОРО́ХОВЫЙ; ЧУ́ЧЕЛО ⟨ПУ́ГАЛО⟩ ГОРО́ХОВОЕ *all coll* [NP; sing only (variants with чучело and пугало); fixed WO] **1.** *disapprov* [often subj-compl with copula (subj: human)] a person dressed funnily, unbecomingly, or out of fashion: **(look ⟨be dressed⟩ like) a scarecrow ⟨a clown⟩.**

Посмотри на себя в зеркало. Ты выглядишь как чучело гороховое! Где ты взяла эти лохмотья? Just look at yourself in the mirror. You look like a clown! Where did you get those rags from anyway?

2. *disapprov* [often subj-compl with copula (subj: human)] a person whose jokes or behavior seem bizarre to others and make him an object of ridicule: **buffoon; clown; laughingstock.**

...Этот самоуверенный Базаров и не подозревал, что он в их [мужиков] глазах был всё-таки чем-то вроде шута горохового... (Тургенев 2). ...Bazarov the self-confident did not for a moment suspect that in their [the peasants'] eyes he was after all nothing but a sort of buffoon (2c). ♦ [Войницкий:] Что ж, я — сумасшедший, невменяем, я имею право говорить глупости. [Астров:] Стара штука. Ты не сумасшедший, а просто чудак. Шут гороховый (Чехов 3). [V.:] Well, I'm not responsible, I have a right to say silly things. [A.:] That's a stale trick. You're not insane, you're just a crackpot. A clown (3a).

3. *derog* [usu. used as Interj when addressing s.o.] an abusive expression used to show the speaker's strong negative feelings toward s.o. or to humiliate s.o.: **idiot; fool; jerk; shithead.**

Ш-98 • РАЗЫ́ГРЫВАТЬ (ИЗ СЕБЯ́) ШУТА́ ⟨ГОРО́ХОВОГО⟩; СТРО́ИТЬ ⟨ДЕ́ЛАТЬ, КО́РЧИТЬ⟩ ИЗ СЕБЯ́ ШУТА́ *coll, disapprov* [VP; subj: human] to behave in an absurd, ridiculous, outlandish way: X разыгрывает из себя шута ≃ **X plays the clown ⟨the fool, the buffoon⟩; X acts like a clown ⟨a fool, a buffoon⟩.**

[Митя] заметил только, надевая платье, что оно богаче его старого платья и что он бы не хотел «пользоваться». Кроме того, «унизительно узко. Шута, что ли, я горохового должен в нём разыгрывать... к вашему наслаждению!» (Достоевский 1). He [Mitya] merely observed, as he was putting the clothes on, that they were more costly than his old ones, and that he did not want "to gain by it." And besides, "they're embarrassingly tight. Shall I play the buffoon in them...for your pleasure?" (1a).

Ш-99 • ШУТИ́ТЬ НЕ ЛЮ́БИТ; НЕ ШУ́ТИТ; ШУТИ́ТЬ НЕЛЬЗЯ́ *с кем-чем all coll* [VP; subj: human, collect, or a noun denoting a natural phenomenon (1st and 2nd variants); impers predic with быть∅, pres only (3rd var.); fixed WO (1st var.)] a person (group, or force of nature) should be taken seriously, paid serious attention to, obeyed etc because he (or it) may cause trouble (if s.o. is careless, disobedient etc): X шутить не любит ≃ **X is not to be taken lightly; X is not something ⟨someone⟩ to mess with; there's no fooling around with X;** [of a person only] **X doesn't ⟨won't⟩ stand for any nonsense; X dislikes being trifled with;** ‖ X шутить этим ⟨такими вещами и т. п.⟩ не любит ≃ **X doesn't treat such things ⟨things like this etc⟩ lightly.**

«А ты вот лучше деньги-то за полгода вперёд отдай». — «У меня нет денег». — «Где хочешь достань; брат кумы, Иван Матвеич, шутить не любит» (Гончаров 1). "You'd better let me have the rent for six months in advance." "I haven't any money." "Well, you can get it. My friend's brother [Ivan Matveyevich] won't stand for any nonsense" (1b). ♦ Прачка Палашка, толстая и рябая девка, и кривая коровница Акулька как-то согласились в одно время кинуться матушке в ноги, винясь в преступной слабости и с плачем жалуясь на мусье, обольстившего их неопытность. Матушка шутить этим не любила и пожаловалась батюшке (Пушкин 2). The washerwoman Palashka, a fat and pockmarked wench, and the one-eyed dairymaid Akulka somehow decided to throw themselves at my mother's feet at the same time, confessing to a reprehensible weakness and complaining in tears against the *mounseer*, who had seduced their innocence. My mother did not treat such things lightly, and complained to my father (2a).

Ш-100 • НЕ ШУ́ТКА *coll* [NP; Invar; subj-compl with быть∅, pres only] **1.** [subj: a quantit NP] the amount or quantity of people (things etc) in question is considerable, is relatively large: **no small number ⟨amount, sum etc⟩; no piddling amount; a**

hefty number ⟨amount⟩; **nothing to sneeze at**; [in limited contexts] **it counts for something.**

Мелодия уплывала за кладбищенские кроны, а Пётр Васильевич, поворачивая к дому, озаботился про себя: «Надо бы как-нибудь днями зайти, посочувствовать. Сколько вёрст вместе намотали, не шутка. Да, надо...» (Максимов 3). The melody floated away over in the cemetery treetops, and Pyotr Vasilievich made an anxious mental note, as he turned for home. "Ought to drop in someday soon, offer my sympathy. Chalked up a few miles together, we did...Counts for something. Yes, I ought to..." (3a).

2. [subj: usu. abstr or a clause, occas. concr] some action (phenomenon etc) should be taken seriously, considered significant (because it may have serious consequences, is a significant accomplishment etc): **no joke; no laughing matter; nothing to sneeze at; not to be sneezed at.**

«И опять я возгордился им ужасно! Как ни крути, а мой родной сын — капитан и командир батареи, это не шутка!» (Шолохов 1). "And again I was terribly proud of him. Say what you like: my own son was a captain and a battery commander; that's not to be sneezed at!" (1a).

3. [subj: infin] doing sth. is not easy, requires resolve, effort, courage etc: **no easy task; quite a feat.**

Закончить аспирантуру за два года — это не шутка. Обычно на это уходит пять-шесть лет. Getting a doctorate in two years is quite a feat. It usually takes five or six years.

Ш-101 • ШУ́ТКА ЛИ; ШУ́ТКА (ЛИ) СКАЗА́ТЬ *all coll* [these forms only; sent adv, parenth (all variants); indep. clause or predic with subj: infin (1st var.); fixed WO] it is very important, serious, not a trifle (because it may have serious consequences, is a significant accomplishment etc; sometimes used to express surprise at or admiration of the importance of sth.): **it's no joke; it's no laughing ⟨small⟩ matter;** [in limited contexts] **seriously.**

Как только разносится слух, что в лагерь едет Громов, поднимается страшный переполох. Шутка ли, сам Громов! (Марченко 1). As soon as word goes round that Gromov is on his way to the camp there's a terrible hustle and bustle. It's no joke — Gromov in person! (1a). ♦ «Шутка ли, целая жизнь дана нам для собственного испытания, и даже если мы её плохо начали, есть время всё исправить!» (Искандер 5). "Seriously, a whole life is given us for self-examination, and even if we have begun badly, there is time to rectify all!" (5a).

Ш-102 • В КА́ЖДОЙ ШУ́ТКЕ ЕСТЬ ДО́ЛЯ ПРА́ВДЫ [saying] every joke contains or is somehow based upon sth. serious or truthful: ≃ **in every joke there's a grain of truth; there is many a true word spoken in jest; many a true word is spoken in jest.**

[author's usage] Всё это говорится в подчёркнуто шутливом тоне, но при этом она бросает на меня быстрый и тревожный взгляд. Она боится, что в шутке есть доля истины (Войнович 5). [context transl] She made a point of saying all this jokingly, yet at the same time she kept casting quick, worried looks at me. She was afraid there might be some truth in her jest (5a). ♦ [author's usage] Как-то Бунин сказал мне, что если бы он был очень богат, то не стал бы жить на одном месте, заводить хозяйство, квартиру, библиотеку, гардероб, а путешествовал бы по всему земному шару, останавливаясь в хороших, комфортабельных гостиницах и живя там столько, сколько живётся... Он говорил в шутливом тоне, но, я думаю, в этом заключалась большая доля правды (Катаев 3). [context transl] One day Bunin told me that if he were very rich he would never live in one place, building up a home, a flat, a library, a wardrobe. He would rather travel all over the world, staying at good, comfortable hotels and living there as long as he wished....He spoke in a joking way, but I believe there was a great deal of truth in what he said (3a).

Ш-103 • ШУ́ТКИ В СТО́РОНУ; ШУ́ТКИ ПРОЧЬ [usu. indep. clause; these forms only; fixed WO] speaking seriously; it is time to become serious (used as an appeal or proposal to begin to discuss sth. in a serious manner, get to the matter at hand): **(all) joking ⟨kidding⟩ aside; let's get serious; this is no time for joking.**

«Молчи, я тебе пинков надаю!» — «...Коли пинки, значит, веришь в мой реализм, потому что призраку не дают пинков. Шутки в сторону: мне ведь всё равно, бранись, коли хочешь, но всё же лучше быть хоть каплю повежливее...» (Достоевский 2). "Shut up or I'll kick you!" "...If it comes to kicks, that means you must believe in my realism, because one doesn't kick a ghost. Joking aside: it's all the same to me, abuse me if you like, but still it would be better to be a bit more polite..." (2a). ♦ [Серебряков:] Я пригласил вас, господа, чтобы объявить вам, что к нам едет ревизор. Впрочем, шутки в сторону. Дело серьёзное (Чехов 3). [S.:] I have invited you here, ladies and gentlemen, to announce that the Government Inspector is about to pay us a visit. However, this is no time for joking. This is a serious matter (3b).

Ш-104 • ШУ́ТКИ ПЛО́ХИ *с кем-чем coll* [VP$_{subj}$ with быть$_\emptyset$; usu. pres; fixed WO] some person (group, or force of nature) should be dealt with seriously, with caution, otherwise unpleasant consequences or troubles may follow: **с Х-ом шутки плохи ≃ X is not to be trifled with; don't ⟨you shouldn't⟩ fool ⟨mess⟩ around with X; person X is not a person to play ⟨toy etc⟩ with;** [in limited contexts] **person X is a tough customer.**

Бедняга Маяна не знала, что с природою шутки плохи... (Искандер 4). Poor Mayana did not know that nature is not to be trifled with (4a). ♦ [Шелавина:] ...Если он обманет меня, так ему же хуже. Со мной шутки плохи (Островский 3). [Sh.:] ...If he deceives me it will be the worse for him. I'm not a person to play with (3a). ♦ Гено снизу вверх оглядел маленькую гневную фигуру помощника лесничего и что-то сказал в том духе, что шутки с ним плохи (Искандер 4). From the ground, Geno looked up at the small angry figure of the assistant forest warden and said something to the effect that he was a tough customer (4a).

Ш-105 • ШУ́ТКИ ⟨ШУ́ТКУ *rare*⟩ ШУТИ́ТЬ *coll* [VP; subj: human; usu. this WO] **1.** [often infin with нечего, не собираюсь etc or neg infin with пришёл, приехал etc] to say or do sth. to amuse o.s. and/or others: **X шутки шутит ≃ X is making jokes; X is kidding ⟨fooling⟩ around;** ‖ X и Y шутки шутят ≃ **X and Y are exchanging jokes;** ‖ *Neg* X не шутки шутить пришёл ≃ **X is in no mood to joke (around) ⟨to play games⟩;** ‖ *Neg Imper* ты шутки ⟨шуток⟩ не шути ≃ **keep your jokes to yourself.**

[Любим Карпыч:] Брат, погоди, не гони! Ты думаешь, Любим Торцов пришёл шутки шутить, паясничать, ты думаешь, пьян Любим Торцов? (Островский 2). [L.K.:] Wait, brother, don't turn me out! Do you think Lyubim Tortsov has come to make jokes? Do you think Lyubim Tortsov is drunk? (2a). ♦ «Скворцы» встрепенулись и, считая предмет исчерпанным, вознамерились было, по обыкновению, шутки шутить, но Собачкин призвал их к порядку... (Салтыков-Щедрин 2). The "starlings" stirred in their seats and, thinking the subject exhausted, were about to resume their usual occupation of exchanging jokes, but Sobachkin called them to order (2a). ♦ Он зарычал — грозно, яростно, исступлённо, показывая, что не шутки он будет шутить, но убивать, и сам готов умереть... (Владимов 1). He growled — angrily, menacingly, savagely, to show that he was in no mood to joke but ready to kill or to die himself... (1a). ♦ ...Дошла очередь записываться в охотники, а охотников-то и не оказалось... «Ты чего ж, Аникей, не пишешься?» И Аникушка бормотал: «Молодой я ишо [*ungrammat* = ещё]... Вусов [*influenced by Ukrainian* вуса = усы] нету...» — «Ты шутки не шути! Ты что, на смех нас подымаешь?» — вопил у него под ухом старик Кашулин (Шолохов 3). The time came for the volunteers to sign up, but there were no volunteers....“Why don't you put your name down, Anikei?” To which Anikei muttered, “I'm a bit too young. Haven't grown any whiskers yet.” “Keep your jokes to yourself! Are you trying to make fun of us?” old Kashulin howled into his ear (3a).

2. ~ *над кем, с кем* to mock s.o., jeer at s.o.: X шутки шутит над Y-ом ≃ **X is making fun of Y; X is making ⟨trying to make⟩ a fool of Y.**

[Атуева *(начинает сердиться)*:] Теперь выше! Ниже!! Выше!!! Ниже!! Ах ты, боже мой! А, да что ты, дурак, русского языка не понимаешь?.. [Тишка:] Помилуйте, как не понимать!.. Я понимаю-с, я оченю [*substand* = очень], сударыня, понимаю. [Атуева *(нетерпеливо)*:] Что ты там болтаешь?.. А! Ты, разбойник, со мною шутку шутишь, что ли?.. (Сухово-Кобылин 2). [A. *(starting to get angry)*:] Now higher a little! Lower!! Higher!!! Lower!! Oh, my God, Tishka! What are you, a fool, don't you understand Russian at all? [T.:] By your leave, Ma'am, of course I do! I understand, Your Ladyship, I most certainly understand. [A. *(impatiently)*:] What are you yapping about?.. Oh! Are you trying to make a fool of me, you scoundrel you?! (2b).

Ш-106 • ШУ́ТКИ ШУ́ТКАМИ ⟨ШУ́ТКА ШУ́ТКОЙ⟩, а ⟨но⟩… *coll* [these forms only; usu. a clause in a compound sent; fixed WO] (used to introduce a response to, or as a rejoinder for, an exaggerated, humorous, or nonserious statement) speaking seriously, without exaggeration: **joking aside ⟨apart⟩; kidding aside; it's all very well to joke, but…**

«Канцлер на меня сердится, — сказал прокурор. — Мне это чертовски неприятно». — «Хорошо, — сказал Странник. — Я ему то передам». — «Шутки шутками, — сказал прокурор, — а если бы ты замолвил словечко…» (Стругацкие 2). “Chancellor is angry with me,” said the prosecutor. “It's damned unpleasant for me.” “All right, I'll tell him that.” “Joking aside, if you could put in a word for me…” (2a). ♦ [Чебутыкин:] Солёный воображает, что он Лермонтов, и даже стихи пишет. Вот шутки шутками, а уж у него третья дуэль (Чехов 5). [Ch.:] Solyony imagines he's a second Lermontov. He even writes poetry. Joking apart, though, it's his third duel (5b).

Ш-107 • В ШУ́ТКУ; РА́ДИ ⟨ДЛЯ⟩ ШУ́ТКИ [PrepP; these forms only; usu. adv] (to do sth.) in order to provoke amusement, laughter, not seriously: **as ⟨for, by way of⟩ a joke; in jest; (say sth.) jokingly ⟨jestingly⟩; (say sth.) (with) tongue in cheek; [in limited contexts] be (just) a joke.**

[Аркадина:] Ради шутки я готова слушать и бред, но ведь тут претензии на новые формы, на новую эру в искусстве (Чехов 6). [A.:] As a joke, I'm willing to listen even to madness, but, you know, this had pretensions to new forms, to a new era in art (6c). ♦ «Можно ли писать по-русски без глаголов? Можно – для шутки» (Набоков 1). “Is it possible to write Russian without verbs? Yes, it is – for a joke” (1a). ♦ Таким образом чегемцы, якобы в шутку, пытались узнать у Баграта, чего он добивается у тёти Маши… (Искандер 3). Thus the Chegemians, as if in jest, tried to find out from Bagrat what he was after at Aunt Masha's… (3a). ♦ Господа, и старый князь, и молодой, и управляющий, уважали его и в шутку называли министром (Толстой 6). Both the young and the old Prince, and the steward, respected him and jestingly called him the “Minister” (6a). ♦ «Подойдите сюда, Алексей Фёдорович, — продолжала Lise, краснея всё более и более, — дайте вашу руку, вот так. Слушайте, я вам должна большое признание сделать: вчерашнее письмо я вам не в шутку написала, а серьёзно…» (Достоевский 1). “Come here, Alexei Fyodorovich,” Lise went on, blushing more and more, “give me your hand, so. Listen, I must make you a great confession: yesterday's letter was not a joke, it was serious…” (1a).

Ш-108 • НЕ НА ШУ́ТКУ рассердиться, испугать(ся), встревожить(ся), увлечься и т. п. [PrepP; Invar; adv (inten-

sif)] (to become) extremely (angry, frightened, upset, enamored etc): **really; genuinely; seriously; (quite) in earnest.**

На этот раз дед рассердился совсем не на шутку (Распутин 1). This time the old man really did take offence (1a). ♦ …В последнее время хоть мальчик и не любил переходить в своих шалостях известной черты, но начались шалости, испугавшие мать не на шутку… (Достоевский 1). Of late…though the boy did not like to overstep a certain line in his pranks, there began to be some pranks that genuinely frightened his mother… (1a). ♦ После краха с нашим последним обменом дед перепугался не на шутку (Кузнецов 1). After the failure of our last attempt at bartering things my grandfather got seriously scared (1b). ♦ Проснулся он [Лёва] резко, и в нём сразу возникло подозрение, что он проспал… Лёва выбежал из избы, чтобы увидеть, как стало светло, что напротив выгоняют корову, и не на шутку встревожился… (Битов 2). He [Lyova] woke abruptly, and immediately had a suspicion that he had overslept….Lyova ran out of the cabin to see how light it had grown. Someone across the way was driving a cow out, and he became alarmed in earnest (2a). ♦ Вернер человек замечательный по многим причинам. Он скептик и матерьялист, как все почти медики, а вместе с этим поэт, и не на шутку, — поэт на деле всегда и часто на словах… (Лермонтов 1). Werner is in many respects a remarkable man. He is a sceptic and a materialist like most medical men, but he is also a poet, and that quite in earnest – a poet in all his deeds and frequently in words… (1b).

Ш-109 • СЫГРА́ТЬ ШУ́ТКУ *с кем coll;* **СЫГРА́ТЬ ШТУ́КУ** *obsoles, coll* [VP; subj: human or abstr] to do sth. mischievous, unkind to s.o., causing him grief, embarrassment etc: X сыграл штуку с Y-ом ≃ **X played a trick on Y;** [in limited contexts] **X played a practical joke on Y;** ‖ X сыграл с Y-ом злую ⟨скверную и т. п.⟩ шутку ≃ **X played a nasty ⟨mean etc⟩ trick on Y.**

«Слышал ты, какую без тебя сыграл с нами штуку Леницын? Захватил пустошь» (Гоголь 3). “Have you heard what trick Lenitsyn played on us while you were away? He has grabbed our wasteland” (3c).

Ш-110 • БЕЗ ШУ́ТОК [PrepP; Invar] **1.** [sent adv (usu. parenth)] speaking in earnest: **(all) joking ⟨kidding⟩ aside; joking apart; (speaking) seriously.**

Но без шуток: было очень красиво, очень тихо (Набоков 1). But joking aside, it really was all very beautiful, very quiet (1a). ♦ «Нет, без шуток, батюшка, она [княжна Марья] очень уродлива? А?» — …спросил он [Анатоль], как бы продолжая разговор, не раз ведённый во время путешествия (Толстой 4). “Joking apart, father, is she [Princess Marya] very hideous? Eh?” Anatol asked his father, as if continuing a subject that had been discussed more than once during the journey (4a).

2. [adv] (to say or do sth.) in earnest, without joking: **in all seriousness; seriously; earnestly.**

Ш-111 • КРОМЕ ШУ́ТОК [PrepP; Invar; sent adv (parenth) or indep. remark] speaking in earnest: **(all) joking ⟨kidding⟩ aside; joking apart; (speaking) seriously;** [when questioning or confirming sth. stated previously] **no kidding? ⟨!⟩; you're kidding! ⟨are you kidding? etc⟩; really? ⟨!⟩**

«Но кроме шуток, ведь протоплазма эта состоит из людей, из отдельных личностей…» (Аксёнов 6). “But all joking aside, this protoplasm of yours consists of human beings, of individual personalities…” (6a). ♦ «Вчера моя сестра родила тройню». — «Кроме шуток?» — «Кроме шуток». “Yesterday my sister had triplets.” “No kidding?” “No kidding.”

Ш-112 • НЕ ДО ШУ́ТОК ⟨НЕ ДО СМЕ́ХУ⟩ [PrepP; these forms only; impers predic with быть∅] **1.** ~ *(кому)* sth. is a serious matter, not to be laughed about or taken lightly: **it's no laughing ⟨joking⟩ matter; it's not something to laugh at ⟨joke about⟩; it's no joke; this is no time for joking.**

...Потом всё поворачивается такой стороной, что не до шуток. Правда, происходит не сразу. Года через полтора (Трифонов 6). Later…things take a turn that is no joking matter. True, this does not happen immediately, but about a year and a half later (6a). ♦ «...Потрудитесь снять и носки». — «Вы не шутите? Это действительно так необходимо?» — сверкнул глазами Митя. «Нам не до шуток», — строго отпарировал Николай Парфёнович (Достоевский 1). "...May I also trouble you to take off your socks?" "You must be joking! Is it really so necessary?" Mitya flashed his eyes. "This is no time for joking," Nikolai Parfenovich parried sternly (1a).

2. ~ *кому* s.o. is not in a lighthearted mood, not inclined to look at the given situation in a humorous way: X-у не до шуток ≃ **X is in no mood for jokes ⟨joking⟩; X is in no mood to fool ⟨joke⟩ around.**

...В тот день Владу было не до шуток. Голодный, без копейки денег... он сразу сделался игрушкой в руках судеб, от которых, как известно, спасенья нет (Максимов 2). At the time…Vlad was in no mood for jokes. Hungry, without a kopeck to his name…he became a plaything in the hands of fate—from which, as we know, there is no salvation (2a).

Ш-113 • **НЕ ШУТЯ́** [Verbal Adv; Invar] **1.** [adv] in a serious way, genuinely: **seriously; in all seriousness; (quite) in earnest; earnestly; (one is) serious.**

«Как? Вы не шутя думаете сладить с целым народом?» (Тургенев 2). "What? Do you seriously think you can take on the whole nation?" (2c). ♦ «Ваше имя в списке. Говорю это не шутя, я сам видел...» (Пастернак 1). "Your name is on the list—I am telling you this in all seriousness, I've seen it myself" (1a). ♦ Иные ужасно обиделись, и не шутя, что им ставят в пример такого безнравственного человека, как Герой Нашего Времени (Лермонтов 1). Some were dreadfully offended, quite in earnest, that such an immoral person as the Hero of Our Time should be set as a model to them (1a). ♦ От отца своего он перенял смотреть на всё в жизни, даже на мелочи, не шутя... (Гончаров 1). He had his father's way of looking earnestly at everything—even the trivia of life... (1b).

2. [sent adv (parent)] speaking in earnest: **(all) joking ⟨kidding⟩ aside; joking apart; (speaking) seriously.**

[Анна Петровна *(смеётся)*:] Вы даже простого каламбура не можете сказать без злости. Злой вы человек. *(Серьёзно.)* Не шутя, граф, вы очень злы (Чехов 4). [А.Р. *(laughs)*:] You can't even make a simple joke without malice. You're a malicious person. *(Seriously.)* Joking aside, Count, you are exceedingly malicious (4a).

Ш-114 • **НИ ШЬЁТ НИ ПÓРЕТ** *coll, often disapprov* [VP; subj: human; 3rd or 2nd pers, pres only; fixed WO] one takes no definite action on sth., refrains from a definite decision etc: X ни шьёт ни порет ≃ **X is sitting on it; X is dragging his feet; X (still) hasn't moved on it; [in limited contexts] X is just sitting there twiddling his thumbs.**

Мы ему много раз говорили, что пора подавать документы в университет, а он ни шьёт ни порет. We've told him over and over again that it's time to send in his college application, but he's dragging his feet. ♦ «Мама, ты чего ни шьёшь ни порешь? — начала, не мешкая, распоряжаться Лизка. — Самовар будем греть или баню затоплять?» (Абрамов 1). "Mama, why are you just sitting there twiddling your thumbs?" asked Lizka, promptly taking control. "Aren't we going to heat up the samovar or get the bathhouse going?" (1a).

Щ-1 • ОТ СВОИ́Х ЩЕДРО́Т дарить, давать *кому что* и т. п.; **ОТ ЩЕДРО́Т** *кого both obs, now humor or iron* [PrepP; these forms only; adv] (to give, donate etc sth. to s.o.) as an act of kindness, showing generosity: **out of largesse ⟨kindness⟩; out of the kindness of one's heart.**

Щ-2 • ЗА О́БЕ ЩЁКИ ⟨ЩЕКИ́⟩ уплетать, уписывать, уминать *что coll* [PrepP; Invar; adv; used with impfv verbs; fixed WO] (of a person) (to eat) greedily and with a great appetite: X уплетает (Y) ~ ≃ **X is stuffing himself with Y; X is wolfing down Y; X is gobbling up Y.**

[author's usage] [Шпигельский:] Вхожу я в людскую, спрашиваю больного кучера, глядь! а мой больной сидит за столом и в обе щёки уписывает блин с луком (Тургенев 1). [Sh.:] I went into the servants' hall and asked for the sick driver. Lo and behold! My patient sitting at table, stuffing himself with onion pancakes (1c). ♦ Если Вадима ещё не было, [Кира] пыталась работать, поминутно глядя на часы, если же он был, готовила на плитке яичницу или сосиски, которые он уплетал за обе щёки, утверждая, что ничего вкуснее во всю жизнь не ел (Некрасов 1). If Vadim had not yet arrived she [Kira] would try to work, but her eyes constantly strayed to her watch. If he was there she would cook sausages and eggs on the hot plate and he would wolf them down, declaring that he had never eaten anything tastier in his whole life (1a).

Щ-3 • ЗА ЧУЖО́Й ЩЕКО́Й ЗУБ НЕ БОЛИ́Т [saying] one does not or cannot feel the pain of another or truly empathize with his grief, misfortune etc: ≃ **your neighbor's toothache can't ⟨won't⟩ hurt you; when your tooth doesn't ache, you can't sympathize with another's aching tooth; we can always bear our neighbors' misfortunes; your neighbor's burden is always light.**

Да если б на Западе хоть расшумели о моём романе, если б арест его стал всемирно-известен — я, пожалуй, мог бы и не беспокоиться, я как у Христа за пазухой мог бы продолжать свою работу. Но они молчали!.. За чужой щекою зуб не болит (Солженицын 2). If only someone in the West had raised an outcry, if the whole world had been told that my novel had been impounded, I should have been in clover, I could have gone on working without a care in the world. But they were silent!...Your neighbor's toothache won't hurt you (2a).

Щ-4 • БОРЗЫ́МИ ЩЕНКА́МИ брать, давать *кому iron or humor* [NP$_{instrum}$; Invar; adv; fixed WO] (to take or give as a bribe) something other than money: **token(s) (of gratitude).**

< From Nikolai Gogol's *The Inspector General* («Ревизор»), 1836. Borzoi puppies («борзые щенки») were what Judge Lyapkin-Tyapkin, a character in the play, admitted to accepting as bribes.

Щ-5 • КАК ЩЕ́ПКА худой, тощий *coll* [как + NP; Invar; modif; fixed WO] (of a person) extremely thin: **(as) thin as a rail ⟨a rake, a reed⟩; (as) skinny as a toothpick.**

Щ-6 • ПОДНИМА́ТЬ ⟨ПОДЫМА́ТЬ⟩/ПОДНЯ́ТЬ НА ЩИТ *кого-что lit* [VP; subj: human] to praise, extol s.o. or sth. excessively: X поднимает на щит Y-а ≃ **X turns person Y into a hero; X makes a hero out of person Y; X hero-worships person Y; X praises Y to the skies; X extols the virtues of Y; X puts person Y on a pedestal.**

Работая над своей книгой, он ничего не заимствовал у «родоначальника» советской космонавтики Циолковского, ибо никакого Циолковского не знал (и никто не знал, пока в начале тридцатых годов Циолковский не был поднят на щит советской пропагандой) (Владимиров 1). In writing his book he borrowed nothing from the "founder" of Soviet astronautics, Tsiolkovsky, because he knew nothing about Tsiolkovsky. (Nor did anybody else, until, at the beginning of the thirties, Tsiolkovsky was turned into a hero by Soviet propaganda) (1a).

Щ-7 • НА ЩИТЕ́ вернуться, прийти и т. п. *lit* [PrepP; Invar; usu. adv] (to return etc) vanquished, a loser: **(return) (up)on one's shield; (return ⟨come back⟩) defeated.**

< According to Plutarch and other sources, a Spartan woman seeing her son off to battle handed him his shield («щит») and said, "Either this or upon this" (Plutarch, *Moralia*, "Sayings of Spartan Women," 16). These words are traditionally interpreted as meaning "Return victorious or be brought home dead upon your shield."

Щ-8 • СО ЩИТО́М вернуться, прийти и т. п. *lit* [PrepP; Invar; usu. adv] (to return etc) having gained victory: **(return) with one's shield; (return) victorious ⟨a winner, triumphant⟩; [in limited contexts] (return etc) with a success story.**

О том, чтобы заявиться к своим, не могло быть и речи: он посмел бы это сделать только «со щитом» (Максимов 2). There was no question of turning up on his family's doorstep: he would only have dared to do that if he could arrive with a success story (2a).

< See Щ-7.

Э

Э-1 • ХОДЯ́ЧАЯ ⟨ЖИВА́Я⟩ ЭНЦИКЛОПЕ́ДИЯ; ХОДЯ́ЧИЙ УНИВЕРСИТЕ́Т; ЖИВО́Й СПРА́ВОЧ-НИК *all humor* [NP; sing only] a person possessing extensive knowledge in various fields, capable of providing an answer to any question: **walking encyclopedia ⟨dictionary⟩; mine of information.**

Говорили, что он не только помнит наизусть «Капитал» и «Анти-Дюринг», но и, хорошо разбираясь в местных проблемах, держит в голове все цифры показателей промышленного и сельскохозяйственного производства... Его называли ходячей энциклопедией... (Войнович 4). It was...said that he not only knew *Das Kapital* and *Anti-Dühring* but also had a good grasp of local problems, knew by heart all the figures for the indices concerning industrial and agricultural production....People called him a walking encyclopedia... (4a).

Э-2 • ПЕРЕДАВА́ТЬ/ПЕРЕДА́ТЬ ЭСТАФЕ́ТУ *кому usu. media* [VP; subj: human] to entrust s.o. (usu. one's follower or followers) with, and encourage s.o. to continue developing, one's ideas, traditions, undertakings: X передал эстафету Y-у ≃ **X passed Y the baton ⟨the torch⟩; X handed (on) the torch to Y.**

Э-3 • ПРИНИМА́ТЬ/ПРИНЯ́ТЬ ЭСТАФЕ́ТУ *от кого, у кого usu. media* [VP; subj: human] to continue developing s.o.'s ideas, carrying on s.o.'s traditions, furthering s.o.'s undertakings etc: X принял эстафету от Y-a ≃ **X took the torch ⟨the baton⟩ from Y; X carried on Y's work ⟨the tradition⟩.**

«Как ты наивен, — прошептала Нина. — Бедный, бедный, бедный мой мальчик...»... Приняла эстафету от мамочки! Сучья сердобольность, видно, у них в крови! (Аксёнов 6). "How naïve you are," whispered Nina. "My poor, poor, poor boy."...She has picked up the baton from her mother! Obviously all that big-deal compassion is in their blood (6a).

Э-4 • В ТРИ ЭТАЖА́ загнуть, крыть *кого и т. п. highly coll* [PrepP; Invar; adv (intensif); fixed WO] (to swear, curse etc) fiercely, using expletives: X загнул ⟨крыл Y-a⟩ ~ ≃ **X cursed a blue streak; X cursed Y up and down; X turned the air blue; X let loose a (terrific ⟨incredible etc⟩) hail of curses (at Y).**

Воркута стоял в очереди за бандеролью и вот как загнёт в три этажа! Цензор, видно, решил показать, что тоже не лаптем щи хлебает, тоже кое-что умеет — и отозвался ещё похлеще (Марченко 1). He [Vorkuta] was lining up for printed packets when, all of a sudden he let loose a terrific hail of curses. The censor evidently decided to show that he wasn't born yesterday either and also knew a thing or two—and sent back an even bluer reply (1a).

Э-5 • ПО ЭТА́ПУ отправлять, гнать *кого и т. п.*; ЭТА́П-НЫМ ПОРЯ́ДКОМ [PrepP (1st var.); NP$_{instrum}$ (2nd var.); these forms only; adv] (in refer. to the transfer of prisoners who are) watched over by a special police unit: **(send ⟨transport etc⟩ s.o.) under guard ⟨under (police) escort⟩.**

[Несчастливцев:] Мне, братец, только мигнуть, и пойдёшь ты по этапу на место жительства, как бродяга (Островский 7). [N.:] I've only to beckon, my boy, and you'll go to your home city under guard, as a vagabond (7a). ♦ [Дудукин:] ...В одно прекрасное утро его из дому совсем выгнали; тогда он пристал к какой-то бродячей труппе и переехал с ней в другой город. Оттуда его, за неимением законного вида, отправили по этапу на место жительства (Островский 3). [D.:] One fine morning he was thrown out of the house altogether. He joined a troupe of strolling players and went with them to another town, but when it was discovered he had no passport he was sent home under police escort (3a).

Э-6 • ВОТ Э́ТО ДА́! *coll* [Interj; Invar; fixed WO] used to express delight, admiration, amazement etc: **how about that!; (well,) how do you like that!; that beats all!; that's a new ⟨a good⟩ one!; that's the way!; that's it!; he ⟨she etc⟩ is really something!; isn't that superb ⟨fabulous etc⟩!**

На удивление всем, он ахнул до дна почти полный стакан водки и, оглушённый, замотал старой головой. «Вот это да!» (Айтматов 1). ...To everyone's surprise, he gulped down almost a full glass in a single breath. Then, stunned, he shook his old head. "That's the way!" (1a). ♦ ...Когда Ирина Викторовна вошла в прихожую своей квартиры, Нюрок громко на всю квартиру завопила [, увидев её новую причёску]: «Вот это да — убиться можно! Неотразимо!» (Залыгин 1). When Irina Viktorovna came into the hall of her flat Niurok [seeing her new hairdo] let out a whoop for the whole flat to hear: "Isn't that superb? Breathtaking! Irresistible!" (1a).

Э-7 • Э́ТО СА́МОЕ *substand* [NP; Invar; parenth; fixed WO] used as a filler when the speaker cannot immediately recall a word, formulate his thoughts etc: **er; um; you know; like.**

Э-8 • Э́ТО (УЖ ⟨УЖЕ́⟩) СЛИ́ШКОМ *coll* [sent with быть$_\emptyset$; fixed WO] this exceeds the limits of the acceptable, permissible etc: **that ⟨this⟩ is ⟨would be⟩ going too far;** [in refer. to exaggeration] **s.o. is ⟨that would be⟩ spreading it (on) too thick(ly).**

Он уже хотел было выразиться в таком духе, что, наслышась о добродетелях [Плюшкина]... почёл долгом принести лично дань уважения, но спохватился и почувствовал, что это слишком (Гоголь 3). He was about to venture an explanation in the vein that having heard of Pliushkin's virtues...he had deemed it his duty to pay him his due tribute of respect in person, but he reined up in time, realizing that it would be spreading it too thickly (3c).

Э-9 • ПРИ Э́ТОМ [PrepP; Invar; sent adv; often preceded by Conj «и» or «но»] in addition to, along with (some previously mentioned action, characteristic etc; a contrast may be implied): **(and ⟨but, yet⟩) at the same time;** [in limited contexts] **while ⟨as one is⟩ doing sth.; in the process; thus; as well; on top of this ⟨that⟩; ...to boot; in so doing;** ‖ при всём этом ≃ **with all this ⟨while all this is⟩ going on; on top of all that ⟨of everything else⟩;** ‖ но при (всём) этом ≃ **but for all that.**

Удивительное было лицо у Чепыжина — простое, даже грубое, скуластое, курносое, мужицкое и при этом уж до того... тонкое, куда там лондонцам, куда там лорду Кельвину (Гроссман 2). Chepyzhin had an extraordinary face. It was simple, coarse, with high cheekbones and a snub nose, the face of a peasant—yet at the same time it was...as to be the envy of any Englishman, even Lord Kelvin (2a). ♦ Персиков забыл о своих амёбах и в течение полутора часа по очереди с Ивановым припадал к стеклу микроскопа. При этом оба учёные перебрасывались оживлёнными, но непонятными простым смертным словами (Булгаков 10). Persikov forgot his amoebas and for the next hour and a half took turns with Ivanov at the microscope lens. As they were doing this both scientists kept exchanging animated comments incomprehensible to ordinary mortals (10b). ♦ На стене [летней уборной] справа, наколотые на гвоздик, висели квадратные куски газет. Чонкин срывал их по очереди и прочитывал, получая при этом немало отрывочных сведений по самым разнообразным вопросам (Войнович 2). Squares of newspaper had been nailed to the wall [of the summer outhouse] on Chonkin's right. He tore them off one after the other and read them through, thus acquiring no little fragmentary information on the most diverse matters (2a).

Ю

Ю-1 • В Ю́БКЕ *iron or humor* [PrepP; Invar; usu. nonagreeing postmodif] used to liken a woman to a well-known fictitious male character (or, less often, a real male figure) who embodies some trait to an extreme extent (e.g., greed, envy, gluttony); occas. used when describing a woman who works, has dealings etc in a traditionally male profession, sphere of interest etc: **a female (version of)...; ...in a skirt; ...in female form; (s.o.'s) female counterpart.**

Наша бабушка — настоящий детектив, Шерлок Холмс в юбке. Our grandmother's a real detective — Sherlock Holmes in a skirt.

Ю-2 • ДЕРЖА́ТЬСЯ ЗА Ю́БКУ *чью* ⟨ЗА БА́БЬЮ Ю́БКУ⟩ *coll, disapprov* [VP; subj: human, male] to be completely under the control of, and fully dependent on, some woman (one's wife, mother etc): X держится за Y-ову ⟨за бабью⟩ юбку ≃ **X clings ⟨is tied⟩ to Y's ⟨to a woman's⟩ apron strings.**

Когда князь Андрей вошёл в кабинет, старый князь... сидел за столом и писал. Он оглянулся. «Едешь?» И он опять стал писать. «Пришёл проститься». — «Целуй сюда, — он показал щёку, — спасибо, спасибо!» — «За что вы меня благодарите?» — «За то, что не просрочиваешь, за бабью юбку не держишься. Служба прежде всего» (Толстой 4). When Prince Andrei entered the study, his father...sat at the table writing. He looked up. "Going?" And he went on writing. "I have come to say good-bye." "Kiss me here," he indicated his cheek. "Thanks, thanks." "What are you thanking me for?" "For not dilly-dallying, for not being tied to a woman's apron strings. Duty before everything" (4a).

Ю-3 • Ю́МОР ВИ́СЕЛЬНИКА *iron* [NP; fixed WO] gloomy humor, jokes, witticisms of a person in a difficult and inescapable situation: **gallows humor.**

< Loan translation of the German *Galgenhumor*.

Я

Я-1 • (ВОТ) Я ТЕБЯ ⟨его, её, вас, их⟩ *highly coll* [Interj; these forms only; fixed WO] used (sometimes after a command) as a threat to the person addressed or to another person: **I'll show you** ⟨**him** etc⟩ **(what's what)!; I'll get** ⟨**fix**⟩ **you** ⟨**him** etc⟩!; **I'll give it to you** ⟨**him** etc⟩ **(good)!; I'll make it hot for you** ⟨**him** etc⟩!; **I'll give you** ⟨**him** etc⟩ **what for!**

«Ах, Рабинович! – говорит начальник... – Да ты что, – говорит, – Рабинович! Да кто тебе разрешил, Рабинович? Да я тебя, Рабинович!» (Войнович 1). "Ah, Rabinovich!" said the chief...."What do you think you're doing, Rabinovich? Who gave you permission? I'll show you, Rabinovich!" (1a). ♦ ...[Они] решили: сечь аманатов до тех пор, пока не укажут, где слобода. Но странное дело! чем больше секли, тем слабее становилась уверенность отыскать желанную слободу! Это было до того неожиданно, что Бородавкин растерзал на себе мундир и, подняв правую руку к небесам, погрозил пальцем и сказал: «Я вас!» (Салтыков-Щедрин 1). ...[They] decided to flog the hostages until they pointed out where the settlement was. But it was a strange thing: the more they flogged, the weaker became the certitude of their finding the desired settlement! This was so unexpected that Wartkin rent his uniform, and raising his right hand to the heavens he shook his finger threateningly and said, "I'll get you!" (1a). ♦ ...Четыре человека отделились и во весь опор подскакали под самую крепость. Мы в них узнали своих изменников. Изменники кричали: «Не стреляйте; выходите вон к государю. Государь здесь!» – «Вот я вас! – закричал Иван Кузьмич. – Ребята! стреляй!» (Пушкин 1). ..Four men broke away from the main body of people and galloped at full speed right up to the fortress. We recognised them as our Cossack traitors....The traitors cried: "Don't fire. Come out to the Tsar. The Tsar is here!" "I'll give it to you!" shouted Ivan Kuzmitch. "Right, lads—fire!" (1b).

Я-2 • Я НЕ Я *coll* [usu. indep. clause; Invar; fixed WO] I do not know anything because I am not involved: **it has nothing to do with me; search** ⟨**beats**⟩ **me; I haven't the foggiest.**

Я и виду не покажу, что знаю об этом деле. А если спросят, то скажу: «Я не я, в первый раз об этом слышу». I won't let on that I know anything about it. And if they ask me I'll say, "Search me, this is the first I've heard of it."

< From the saying «Я не я, и лошадь не моя (, и я не извозчик)» – "I am not I, and the horse is not mine (and I am not a coachman)."

Я-3 • В Я́БЛОКАХ [PrepP; Invar; postmodif] (of a horse's coat) marked with dark, roundish spots: **dappled;** ‖ серый в яблоках ≃ **dapple-gray.**

Посмотри, какой красивый конь, серый в яблоках. Look, what a beautiful dapple-gray horse.

Я-4 • Я́БЛОКО ⟨Я́БЛОЧКО⟩ **ОТ Я́БЛОНИ** ⟨Я́Б-ЛОНЬКИ⟩ **НЕДАЛЕКО́ ПА́ДАЕТ** [saying] children usually resemble their parents in character, habits etc (usu. said disapprovingly when children have the same faults as their parents): ≃ **the apple never falls far from the tree; it runs in the family; like father, like son** ⟨**daughter, child**⟩**; like mother like daughter** ⟨**son, child**⟩**; as the baker so the buns, as the father so the sons.**

Я-5 • Я́БЛОКО РАЗДО́РА *между кем-чем lit* [NP; sing only; fixed WO] the cause of a quarrel, argument, serious disagreement: **apple of discord; bone of contention.**

Маленький островок, лежавший посредине пограничной реки, долгие годы был яблоком раздора между двумя государствами. A small island in the middle of a river that divided two countries was a bone of contention between those governments for many years.

< From the Greek myth of a golden apple inscribed "for the most beautiful," which caused a dispute among Aphrodite, Athena, and Hera, each of whom claimed the apple for herself.

Я-6 • Я́БЛОКУ НЕ́ГДЕ ⟨НЕ́КУДА⟩ **УПА́СТЬ** [these forms only; impers predic with быть∅] some place is so full of people or things that there is no free space: **there's no room to sneeze** ⟨**to turn around**⟩**; there's hardly** ⟨**barely, scarcely**⟩ **room to breathe** ⟨**to move an elbow** etc⟩**; there isn't room to swing a cat.**

«А была такая давка, что и яблоку негде было упасть» (Гоголь 3). "The crush had been such that there wasn't room to sneeze" (3b). ♦ ...Комната наполнилась так, что яблоку упасть было негде (Достоевский 3). ...The room had become so full of people that there was hardly room to move an elbow (3d). ♦ В громадном зале яблоку негде было упасть (Лившиц 1). In the huge hall there wasn't room to swing a cat (1a).

Я-7 • БО́ЕК ⟨БО́ЙКИЙ⟩ **НА ЯЗЫ́К** ⟨НА СЛОВА́⟩ [AdjP; subj-compl with copula, subj: human (all variants) or modif (variants with long-form Adj); usu. this WO] a person who is quick in conversation, eloquent: X боек на язык ≃ **X has a quick** ⟨**ready**⟩ **tongue; X is quick-tongued; X has a ready** ⟨**quick**⟩ **wit.**

...Наш парень, наглый и очень бойкий на язык дома, совершенно меняется с чужими людьми (Трифонов 5). ...However bold and quick-tongued our son might be at home, he changed completely in the presence of strangers (5a).

Я-8 • ВЫ́СУНУВ ⟨ВЫ́СУНУВШИ, ВЫ́СУНЯ *obs*⟩ **ЯЗЫ́К** ⟨ЯЗЫКИ́ *rare*⟩ *coll* [Verbal Adv; these forms only; usu. used with impfv verbs; var. with язык may be used with pl subj; fixed WO] **1.** бежать, удирать и т. п. ~ (to run, run away) very quickly: **like the dickens; like mad; like a bat out of hell.**

Мальчишки залезли в колхозный сад, но сторож их заметил, и им пришлось удирать, высунув язык. The boys got into the kolkhoz garden, but the guard saw them and they had to run like the dickens.

2. бегать, мотаться и т. п. ~ (to run, be on the go etc) nonstop, without taking a breather (because one is overwhelmed by the number of things he has to do): **with one's tongue hanging out; like mad; till one is dropping in his tracks.**

Я такой же кинозритель, какой в своё время был театрал. Но сыновья мои большие любители, и когда кинофестиваль, бегают по Москве высунув язык и меня тащат... (Рыбаков 1). I'm about as much of a film-goer as I used to be a theatre-goer in the old days, but my sons are great film-fans and during the festival they rush all over Moscow with their tongues hanging out, and dragging me along with them (1a).

Я-9 • ДЕРЖА́ТЬ ЯЗЫ́К ЗА ЗУБА́МИ ⟨НА ПРИ́ВЯЗИ *obs*⟩ *coll* [VP; subj: human; often imper or infin with надо, должен, советовать, просить etc] to remain silent, not revealing some information, expressing some opinion etc: X держал язык за зубами ≃ **X kept his mouth shut; X held his tongue; X kept his tongue in check;** [in limited contexts] **X didn't breathe a word about sth. (to s.o.).**

«...Я тебе советую держать язык за зубами» (Каверин 1). "...My advice to you is to keep your mouth shut" (1a). ♦ Ика насмешливо заметил, что миллионерами в Америке становятся не только чистильщики ботинок, но и мафиози. Варя вспыхнула, посоветовала Ике держать язык за зубами (Рыбаков 2). Ika had joked that it wasn't only shoeshine boys who became millionaires in America, it was also the Mafiosi. Varya had flared up and told Ika to hold his tongue (2a).

Я-10 • ДЁРНУЛО ЗА ЯЗЫ́К *кого coll;* **ЧЁРТ** ⟨less often **БЕС, ЛЕ́ШИЙ⟩ ДЁРНУЛ ЗА ЯЗЫ́К** *highly coll;* **НЕЛЁГКАЯ ДЁРНУЛА ЗА ЯЗЫ́К** *highly coll* [VP, impers (1st var.); VP$_{subj}$ (other variants)] used to express the speaker's extreme regret, anger, or annoyance over the fact that he or another person said sth. inappropriate, offensive, out of place etc: дёрнуло ⟨чёрт дёрнул⟩ Х-а за язык ≃ **what ⟨something must have⟩ possessed X to say that!; why the hell ⟨in blazes, on earth⟩ did X (have to) say that?; what the hell ⟨in blazes, on earth⟩ did X say that for?; X and his big mouth!; there goes X with his big mouth!**

И дёрнуло ж меня за язык! Промолчи я насчёт его топорика, ничего бы не было (Искандер 4). What had possessed me to say that! If I'd kept quiet about his ax, nothing would have happened (4a). ♦ «Ты-то выпьешь со мной на радостях?» — спросил он. И тотчас же с тревогой подумал: «Ну, вот и опять дёрнул меня чёрт за язык!» (Шолохов 5). "You'll have one [a drink] with me to celebrate, won't you?" he asked. And at once the alarming thought crossed his mind, "There I go again with my big mouth!" (5a).

Я-11 • ДЛИ́ННЫЙ ЯЗЫ́К *coll, disapprov* [NP] **1.** ~ *чей, кого* [fixed WO] excessive talkativeness, the inability to keep a secret or restrain o.s. in conversation: **big mouth; loose tongue.**

2. *у кого* ~ [VP$_{subj}$ with copula] s.o. is excessively talkative, says too much, is unable to keep a secret: у Х-а длинный язык ≃ **X talks too much; X has a big mouth; X has a loose tongue; X is loose-lipped ⟨loose-tongued⟩.**

Нашему Андрюше доверять тайны нельзя — слишком уж длинный у него язык. You can't confide secrets to our Andryusha—he's too loose-tongued.

Я-12 • ЗЛОЙ НА ЯЗЫ́К [AdjP; modif or subj-compl with copula (subj: human); fixed WO] a person who speaks in a malicious, mocking, sarcastic manner: **evil-tongued; mean-tongued.**

Злые на язык чегемцы говорили, что она [тётя Катя] выслеживает больных собак и, высмотрев, какие они травы кусают, разводит их у себя в огороде (Искандер 3). Evil-tongued Chegemians said that she [Aunt Katya] followed sick dogs to see what kinds of herbs they ate, and then raised them in her garden (3a).

Я-13 • ЗЛОЙ ЯЗЫ́К [NP; sing only] **1.** ~ *чей, кого* [NP; sing only] a person's habit of saying unkind, mocking etc things at the expense of s.o. or sth.: **malicious ⟨spiteful, vicious, evil, sharp etc⟩ tongue.**

Так как никому не было пощады, то никто особенно не сердился на злой язык доктора (Герцен 1). Since no one was spared, no one particularly resented the doctor's spiteful tongue (1a). ♦ …Его обыкновенная угрюмость, крутой нрав и злой язык имели сильное влияние на молодые наши умы (Пушкин 3). …His habitual sullenness, acrimonious temper, and sharp tongue made a strong impression on our young minds (3a).

2. ~ *у кого* [VP$_{subj}$ with copula] s.o. speaks in an unkind, mocking, sarcastic manner: у Х-а злой язык ≃ **X has a malicious ⟨spiteful, vicious, evil etc⟩ tongue; X is evil-tongued.**

У него был злой язык: под вывескою его эпиграммы не один добряк прослыл пошлым дураком (Лермонтов 1). He had a malicious tongue, and, branded by his epigrams, more than one good soul came to be regarded as a vulgar fool (1b).

Я-14 • НАХОДИ́ТЬ/НАЙТИ́ О́БЩИЙ ЯЗЫ́К *(с кем)* [VP; subj: human; if there is no obj, subj: pl; usu. this WO] to

discover a basis for mutual understanding, such as common interests, values, views etc: X и Y нашли общий язык ≃ **X and Y found a common language; X and Y found (some) common ground; X and Y found (they had) much in common; X and Y came to speak the same language.**

«…Если мы не найдём общего языка, если вы меня пошлёте сейчас подальше, я и это пойму, поверьте…» (Аксёнов 7). "…If we, shall we say, fail to find a common language, if you tell me to go to blazes, I'll understand, believe me" (7a). ♦ …Я работал в «Русском деле» корректором, как и Алька. Мы сидели тогда друг против друга и быстро нашли общий язык (Лимонов 1). …I was a proofreader in *Russkoe Delo*, as was Alexander—we had sat across from each other there and quickly found much in common (1a).

Я-15 • О́БЩИЙ ЯЗЫ́К *(у кого с кем)* [NP; sing only; fixed WO] common interests, values, views etc that allow two or more people to find mutual understanding: **(have ⟨share etc⟩) a common language; (speak) the same language; (share) common ground; [in limited contexts] (be) on the same wavelength.**

Я-16 • ОСТЁР ⟨О́СТРЫЙ⟩ НА ЯЗЫ́К *coll* [AdjP; subj-compl with copula, subj: human (all variants) or modif (var. with long-form Adj); fixed WO] a person who is sarcastic and biting in conversation: X остёр на язык ≃ **X has a sharp tongue; X is sharp-tongued.**

Я-17 • О́СТРЫЙ ЯЗЫ́К [NP; sing only] **1.** ~ *чей, кого.* Also: **О́СТРЫЙ ЯЗЫЧО́К** *coll* s.o.'s ability to say and habit of saying sarcastic, cutting things in conversation: **sharp ⟨biting, barbed, quick etc⟩ tongue.**

Мужчины побаивались Машенькиного острого язычка: она могла такое сказать, что потом над неудачником долго потешался весь отдел. The men feared Masha's sharp tongue: she could say things that would have the entire department laughing at you for a long time to come.

2. *у кого* ~ [VP$_{subj}$ with copula] s.o. is witty, sarcastic in conversation: у Х-а острый язык ≃ **X is sharp-tongued ⟨tart-tongued⟩; X has a sharp ⟨biting, quick etc⟩ tongue.**

«Был сегодня у неё [Елизаветы], угощала чаем с халвой… Острый язык, в меру умна…» (Шолохов 2). "Called on her [Yelizaveta] today, she gave me tea and halvah….Sharp tongue, moderately clever…" (2a).

Я-18 • ОТСО́ХНИ (у меня) ЯЗЫ́К *substand* [Interj; Invar; often foll. by a clause introduced by если, коли; fixed WO] used to emphasize the truth of a statement or the sincerity of a promise: **may my tongue dry up and fall off; may my tongue wither ⟨fall out⟩.**

Я-19 • ПОКА́ЗЫВАТЬ/ПОКАЗА́ТЬ ЯЗЫ́К *кому* [VP; subj: human] to poke one's tongue out of one's mouth in s.o.'s direction in order to tease, mock, provoke etc him: X показал язык Y-у ≃ **X stuck his tongue out ⟨stuck out his tongue⟩ (at Y).**

Глохнут внешние звуки под водой, и в ушах остаётся лишь журчанье. И он, таращя глаза, старательно смотрит на всё то, что можно увидеть под водой. Глаза щиплет, глазам больно, но он горделиво улыбается себе и даже язык показывает в воде. Это он бабке. Пусть знает, вовсе и не утонет он, и вовсе ничего не боится (Айтматов 1). Under the water all outside sounds vanish—you hear only the rushing of the stream. Keeping his eyes wide open, he stared hard to see everything that could be seen. His eyes prickled and hurt, but he smiled proudly to himself and even stuck his tongue out. That was for grandma. Let her know. He wouldn't drown. And he wasn't afraid of anything (1a).

Я-20 • **ПОПАДА́ТЬ/ПОПА́СТЬ ⟨ПОПАДА́ТЬСЯ/ ПОПА́СТЬСЯ⟩ НА ЯЗЫ́К ⟨НА ЯЗЫЧО́К⟩** (к) *кому coll* [VP; subj: human] to become the subject of gossip or (usu. unkind) conversation: X попал(ся) Y-у на язык ≃ **X fell victim to Y's tongue; X is the victim of Y's tongue; Y's tongue is wagging about X.**

…Я стал перебирать присутствующих и отсутствующих наших знакомых, сначала выказывал смешные, а после дурные их стороны. Жёлчь моя взволновалась; я начал шутя — и кончил искренней злостью… «Вы опасный человек, — сказала она мне: — я бы лучше желала попасться в лесу под нож убийцы, чем вам на язычок…» (Лермонтов 1). …I went through all our acquaintances, present and absent, pointing out their comic features, then their bad ones. I was in a jaundiced mood, and though I began in jest, I was being really spiteful at the end.… "You're a dangerous man," she said. "I'd rather fall victim to a cut-throat's knife in the forest than to your tongue" (1c). ♦ «Нашим бабам только попади на язык, такого наговорят!» (Максимов 3). "Once our women's tongues start wagging about you, there's no knowing what they'll say" (3a).

Я-21 • **ПРИДЕ́РЖИВАТЬ/ПРИДЕРЖА́ТЬ ⟨ПОПРИ-ДЕРЖА́ТЬ⟩ ЯЗЫ́К ⟨ЯЗЫЧО́К⟩** *coll* [VP; subj: human; usu. imper or infin with надо] to refrain from talking or arguing, keep silent: (по)придержи язык ≃ **hold your tongue; keep your mouth shut; control ⟨curb, restrain⟩ your tongue.**

«Даю тебе два дня, — объявил последнее решение уполномоченный. — Не уплатишь — пеняй на себя. Опишем имущество». — «А есть такой закон?»… — «Есть». — «Ну нет, товарищ Черёмный, это ты малость призагнул…» — «Не призагнул. А язык советую попридержать» (Абрамов 1). "I'm giving you two days," was the official's final decision. "If you don't pay up you have only yourself to blame. We'll seize your property." "Is that legal?" "Yes." "But Comrade Cheryomny, that's a bit rough…" "It's not a bit rough. And I would advise you to hold your tongue" (1a). ♦ [Лука:] Приятного вам аппетиту!.. [Василиса *(оборачиваясь):*] По-придержи язык…гриб поганый! *(Уходит с мужем за угол.)* (Горький 3). [L.:] Have a good meal!… [V. *(turning around):*] Keep your mouth shut…you stinking toadstool!… *(Goes around the corner with her husband.)* (3a). ♦ Тут он и спохватился было, видя, что солгал вовсе напрасно и мог таким образом накликать на себя беду, но языка никак уже не мог придержать (Гоголь 3). Here he realized that he had told quite an unnecessary lie which might get him into trouble but he was simply unable to restrain his tongue (3c).

Я-22 • **ПРИКУ́СЫВАТЬ/ПРИКУСИ́ТЬ ⟨ЗАКУ-СИ́ТЬ⟩ ЯЗЫ́К ⟨ЯЗЫЧО́К⟩** *coll* [VP; subj: human; usu. pfv past or imper] to fall silent suddenly or refrain from saying sth.: X прикусил язык ≃ **X bit ⟨held, bridled etc⟩ his tongue; X kept his mouth shut ⟨closed⟩; X bit back a remark.**

«Бог милостив: солдат у нас довольно, пороху много, пушку я вычистил. Авось дадим отпор Пугачёву…» — «А что за человек этот Пугачёв?» — спросила комендантша. Тут Иван Игнатьич заметил, что проговорился, и закусил язык. Но уже было поздно. Василиса Егоровна принудила его во всём признаться, дав ему слово не рассказывать о том никому (Пушкин 2). "The Lord is merciful: we have enough soldiers and plenty of powder, and I've cleaned out the cannon. With a little luck we'll drive back Pugachev.…" "And what sort of a man is Pugachev?" asked the captain's wife. Ivan Ignatich now realized that he had let the cat out of the bag, and he bit his tongue. But it was too late. Vasilisa Egorovna, giving her word not to pass the secret to anyone, made him reveal the whole thing (2a). ♦ «Ты не у себя в Чегеме», — огрызнулся писарь, видимо, осмелев от выпитого. «Чтоб раздавить жабу, не обязательно ехать в Чегем», — сказал дядя Сандро и так посмотрел на писаря, что тот сразу же отрезвел и прикусил язык (Искандер 3). "You're not at home in Chegem," the clerk snarled, evidently made bold by drink. "I don't have to go to Chegem to squash a toad," Uncle Sandro said, with a look that

instantly made the clerk sober up and hold his tongue (3a). ♦ Ребров видел, что Ляля накалена, изнемогает от материнской враж-дебности — тёща мучила её молчанием четвёртые сутки, чем-то это должно было разрешиться, надо было прикусить язык, но Ребров потерял равновесие (Трифонов 1). Rebrov could see that Lyalya was tense and worn out from her mother's hostility—this being the fourth day that her mother had given her the silent treatment. The situation would have resolved itself somehow, so he should have kept his mouth shut—but he lost his self-control (1a).

Я-23 • **ПРОГЛОТИ́ТЬ ЯЗЫ́К;** often **БУ́ДТО ⟨КАК БУ́ДТО, СЛО́ВНО, ТО́ЧНО⟩ ЯЗЫ́К ПРОГЛОТИ́Л** *coll* [VP; subj: human; usu. past; often used in questions] to keep or fall silent, refrain from saying anything (out of fear, embarrass-ment, a lack of confidence etc, or in an attempt not to reveal sth.): X как будто язык проглотил ≃ **it was as if ⟨as though⟩ X had swallowed ⟨lost⟩ his tongue;** ‖ ты что, язык проглотил? ≃ **(what,) has the cat got your tongue?**

Бабушка пыталась выяснить у Алёши, кто разбил салат-ницу, но тот молчал, словно язык проглотил. Grandma tried to find out from Alyosha who had broken the salad bowl, but he kept silent, as if he had swallowed his tongue.

Я-24 • **ПРО́СИТСЯ НА ЯЗЫ́К** [VP; subj: слово, имя etc] (of a word, phrase etc that s.o. is eager to say) sth. is about to be said: X просится на язык ≃ **X is on the tip of person Y's tongue; person Y is dying ⟨itching⟩ to say X.**

Я-25 • **РАЗВЯ́ЗЫВАТЬ/РАЗВЯЗА́ТЬ ЯЗЫ́К** *coll* [VP]
1. ~ *кому* [subj: abstr or a noun denoting an alcoholic beverage] to encourage, induce a person to begin talking, speak freely, without reservation: X развязал язык Y-у ≃ **X loosened Y's tongue.**

Выпитое ли вино, или потребность откровенности, или мысль, что этот человек не знает и не узнает никого из дей-ствующих лиц его истории, или всё вместе развязало язык Пьеру. И он… рассказал всю свою историю: и своё же-нитьбу, и историю любви Наташи к его лучшему другу, и её измену, и все свои несложные отношения к ней (Толстой 6). Whether it was the wine he had drunk or an impulse of frankness or the thought that this man did not, and never would, know any of those who played a part in his story, or whether it was all these things together, something loosened Pierre's tongue.…He told the whole story of his life: his marriage, Natasha's love for his best friend, her betrayal of him, and all his own simple relations with her (6a).

2. ~ *кому* [subj: human] to force, impel a person to speak, divulge a secret: X развяжет Y-у язык ≃ **X will loosen Y's tongue; X will make Y talk.**

3. [subj: human] fearing punishment, reprisal, to speak after a silence and divulge some secret: X развязал язык ≃ **X started talking;** [in limited contexts] **X came clean.**

«Ещё раз повторяю вам, что на подобные вопросы отве-чать не стану». — «На выбор: или ты, собака, сейчас же развяжешь язык, или через десять минут будешь поставлен к стенке! Ну?!» (Шолохов 5). "I repeat, I refuse to answer such questions." "You have the choice. Either you come clean, you dog, or in ten minutes from now we'll have you up against a wall! Now then?" (5a).

4. *often disapprov* [subj: human] to become talkative (usu. after a silence), talk a great deal: X развязал язык ≃ **X began to talk ⟨a lot⟩; X began to wag his tongue; X began to jabber ⟨chatter⟩ away.**

Я-26 • **РАСПУСКА́ТЬ/РАСПУСТИ́ТЬ ЯЗЫ́К** *coll, dis-approv* [VP; subj: human] to become too talkative, speak exces-sively, without restraint: X распустил язык ≃ **X talked too much ⟨too freely⟩; X wagged ⟨began to wag⟩ his tongue;** ‖ *Neg*

Imper не распускай язык ≃ **shut your mouth; quit wagging ⟨don't wag⟩ your tongue; put a sock in it; put a lid on it.**

В это мгновение чёрный китель поднял голову и начал что-то выговаривать своему земляку. Сван, что сидел на корточках, добродушно оправдывался, поглядывая в нашу сторону, как на союзников. Чёрный китель постепенно успокоился и на интонации мелкого административного раздражения замолк. «Язык не распускай», – сказал он ему в конце по-русски... (Искандер 4). At that instant, Black-Tunic raised his head and began saying something to his countryman. The Svan who was sitting on his haunches defended himself good-naturedly, glancing in our direction as if we were allies. Black-Tunic gradually wound down and concluded in a tone of petty administrative irritation. "Don't wag your tongue," he said finally, in Russian... (4a).

Я-27 • СЛАБ ⟨СЛА́БЫЙ⟩ НА ЯЗЫ́К *obsoles, substand* [AdjP; subj-compl with copula (subj: human, both variants) or modif (var. with long-form Adj); fixed WO] a person who is too talkative, has a tendency to talk unrestrainedly: X слаб на язык ≃ **X has a loose tongue; X talks nonstop; X has trouble keeping his mouth shut; X can't keep his tongue still; X is a blabbermouth.**

Я-28 • СУКО́ННЫЙ ЯЗЫ́К; СУКО́ННАЯ РЕЧЬ [NP] inexpressive, colorless, unimaginative language: **dull ⟨vapid, uninspired, insipid⟩ language.**

Он и личные письма пишет таким же суконным языком, как и деловые бумаги. He writes personal letters in the same vapid language that he uses for business documents.

Я-29 • ТОЧИ́ТЬ/ПОТОЧИ́ТЬ ЯЗЫ́К *highly coll* [VP; subj: human] **1.** to engage in idle chatter: X точит язык ≃ **X wags his tongue; X shoots the breeze ⟨the bull⟩; X flaps his jaws ⟨gums⟩; X gabs ⟨jabbers, chatters⟩ away.**

По субботам у Марьи Семёновны собиралось небольшое дамское общество. За чашкой чая дамы точили языки, обсуждая последние городские новости. On Saturdays a small group of ladies would gather at Marya Semyonovna's home. Over tea they would wag their tongues, discussing the latest news of the city.

2. ~ на ком [impfv only] to gossip maliciously, make snide or mocking remarks about s.o.: X точит язык на Y-е ≃ **X picks Y apart; X makes sport ⟨fun⟩ of Y; X makes Y the butt of X's ridicule ⟨jokes⟩.**

Я-30 • ТЯНУ́ТЬ ЗА ЯЗЫ́К *кого coll* [VP; subj: human (often никто or, in rhet questions, кто, кто-нибудь etc); often 3rd pers pl with indef. refer.; often neg) to compel s.o. to speak, answer, or say sth.: X Y-а за язык не тянул ≃ **X didn't force Y to talk ⟨say it⟩; X didn't drag ⟨force⟩ it out of Y; [in limited contexts] X didn't try to pump Y for information.**

«Да, Фома Гурьянович. Я, собственно... Мы, собственно... Мы уверены, что [преступник] – среди этих пяти». (А что он мог ещё сказать?..) Фома слегка прищурил глаз. «Вы *отвечаете* за свои слова?» – «Да, мы... Да... отвечаем...»... – «Смотрите, я за язык не тянул» (Солженицын 3). "Yes, Foma Guryanovich. I, to be sure...we certainly...we are convinced that he [the criminal] is among these five." What else could he say? [Foma] Oskolupov squinted one eye. "Will you *answer* for what you say?" "Yes, we...yes...we will answer."..."Listen here, I didn't force you to talk" (3a). ♦ «Всё случившееся я считаю большой ошибкой», – начала Роза. «Ошибки бывают разные!» – «Я считаю это политической ошибкой». – «Так и надо говорить сразу, не когда тянут за язык» (Рыбаков 2). "I regard the whole affair as a big mistake," Rosa Poluzhan began. "Mistakes can be of all sorts..." "I regard this one as a political mistake." "You should have said so straightaway; we shouldn't have to drag it out of you" (2a). ♦ «Да вы не подумайте, что вас за язык тянут. Виталий меня знает, я не из тех...» (Аксёнов 7). "Please

don't think I'm trying to pump you for information. Vitaly will tell you. That's not my style..." (7a).

Я-31 • УКОРОТИ́ТЬ ЯЗЫ́К *highly coll* [VP] **1.** ~ *кому* [subj: human or abstr; often infin with надо, нужно etc] to force s.o. to stop saying rude or inappropriate things or sth. he should not say: X укоротит Y-у язык ≃ **X will shut Y up; X will shut Y's mouth ⟨trap⟩ for him; X will silence Y.**

У властей было достаточно способов укоротить язык недовольным, самых активных могли в двадцать четыре часа вышвырнуть из города. The authorities had plenty of ways to silence dissenters, and they could throw the most vocal ones out of the city within twenty-four hours.

2. [imper only] stop talking: укороти язык ≃ **shut up!; shut your mouth ⟨trap, face⟩!; hold your tongue!**

Я-32 • ЧЕСА́ТЬ/ПОЧЕСА́ТЬ ⟨ТРЕПА́ТЬ/ПОТРЕ-ПА́ТЬ⟩ ЯЗЫ́К ⟨ЯЗЫКО́М⟩; МОЗО́ЛИТЬ/ПОМО-ЗО́ЛИТЬ ЯЗЫ́К; МОЛО́ТЬ/ПОМОЛО́ТЬ ⟨ТРЕ-ЩА́ТЬ/ПОТРЕЩА́ТЬ⟩ ЯЗЫКО́М *all coll* [VP; subj: human; often infin with любит, хочется etc or impfv infin with хватит, нечего etc] to talk to no purpose, saying nothing important, occupy o.s. with empty chatter: X чешет язык ≃ **X is wagging his tongue ⟨chin⟩; X is flapping his jaw ⟨gums⟩; X is gabbing ⟨jabbering, prattling etc⟩ (on);** ∥ X-ы чешут языки ≃ **Xs are chewing the fat ⟨the rag⟩; Xs are shooting the breeze ⟨the bull⟩.**

«Довольно чесать языком! Ещё писатель называется!» – не раз возмущался я его способностью вечно плести всякую чушь (Терц 4). "Stop wagging your tongue! Call yourself a writer?" I often said in indignation at his capacity for perpetually concocting every possible kind of nonsense (4a). ♦ «Валяй, Пряслин! – Першин взмахнул кулаком. – Покажем, на что способна советская молодёжь... Партия тебе доверяет». И пошёл чесать языком – про эпоху, про восстановительный период, про кадры. Как будто с трибуны высказывается (Абрамов 1). "Go to it, Pryaslin," said Pershin with a swing of his fist. "Let's show 'em what Soviet youth can do....The Party is placing its trust in you." He went jabbering on about the era, the period of reconstruction, cadres, as if he were on a rostrum making a speech (1a). ♦ «С этими интеллигентами только и знай чай пить интересно. Больно складно языками чешут» (Максимов 3). "Those intellectuals are only interesting at tea-time. They're mighty good at chewing the rag" (3a).

Я-33 • ЧТОБ У ТЕБЯ́ ⟨у него, твой, его и т. п.⟩ ЯЗЫ́К ОТСО́Х *highly coll, rude* [Interj; these forms only; fixed WO] an evil wish directed at a person who brings bad news or speaks inappropriately or too much: **may your ⟨his etc⟩ tongue wither ⟨dry up⟩ (and fall off).**

«Кязым, – несколько раз, склоняясь к нему, говорил на пиру Даур, – помни, что ты утолил мою жизнь, а мне недолго осталось! Но я теперь ни о чём не жалею!» – «Чтоб твой язык отсох, Даур» – дважды вскричала его бедная мать, уловив его слова. – Зачем ты убиваешь меня!» (Искандер 5). "Kyazym," Daur told him several times at the feast, leaning over to him, "remember that you've comforted my life, and I don't have long to live! But now I have no regrets!" "May your tongue wither, Daur!" his poor mother cried, the two times that she caught his words. "Why are you killing me!" (5a). ♦ «Верни моего сына!» – крикнула ему вслед старуха. «Чтоб язык твой отсох» – бормотнул мой старик... (Искандер 3). "Bring back my son!" the old woman shouted after him. "May your tongue dry up," my old man muttered (3a).

Я-34 • ЭЗО́ПОВ ⟨ЭЗО́ПОВСКИЙ⟩ ЯЗЫ́К; ЭЗО́ПОВ-СКАЯ РЕЧЬ *all lit* [NP; sing only; fixed WO] an allegorical expression of thoughts: **Aesopian language.**

Работая с Усовой в Ташкенте в университете, мы не искали стукачей, потому что «писали» все. И мы упражнялись в эзоповом языке (Мандельштам 1). When Alisa Usov and I later taught at Tashkent University, there was no point in trying to pick up informers, because we knew everybody "wrote." And we tried to become adept in Aesopian language (1a).

< From *Aesop*, the name of the Greek fabulist.

Я-35 • ЯЗЫ́К БЕЗ КОСТЕ́Й *у кого coll, disapprov* [VP~subj~ with быть~ø~, pres only; fixed WO] s.o. is very talkative, says things he should not, is not careful about what he says: у X-а язык без костей ≃ **X has a loose tongue; X's tongue runs away with him; X runs off at the mouth; X's tongue is out of control; X's tongue is always wagging.**

«Ишь, сопит! Обиделся, видно, малолетка... Я ведь так, не со зла... Язык без костей, вот и мелю...» (Максимов 2). "Hell, he's snivelling! Must have offended him....Don't mind me, kid, I don't mean any harm. My tongue runs away with me and I say all kinds of junk..." (2a). ♦ «Молотишь, папаня, что ни попадя, язык без костей» (Максимов 1). "You're talking a lot of rubbish, Dad, your tongue's out of control" (1a). ♦ «У нас, знаешь, в деревне языки без костей — кому чего на ум взбредёт, то и болтают». — «А чего болтают, — возразила Ксения. — Хоть и деревня, а тоже народ живёт не дурее других. Болтать зря не будут» (Войнович 4). "You know, tongues are always wagging in this village; someone gets an idea, they've got to blab about it." "What do you mean blab," objected Ksenia. "It might be a village but people here don't live any worse than other people. We don't go in for idle talk" (4a).

Я-36 • ЯЗЫ́К ДО КИ́ЕВА ДОВЕДЁТ [saying] inquiries can always help one to find what one needs (said when a person does not know how to get somewhere): ≃ **he who uses his tongue will reach his destination; he who has a tongue can find his way; you can always find the way by asking. Cf. he who has a tongue goes to Rome.**

Я-37 • ЯЗЫ́К ЗАПЛЕТА́ЕТСЯ *у кого coll* [VP~subj~; pres or past] s.o. is unable to speak articulately, distinctly (from drunkenness, fatigue, embarrassment etc): у X-а язык заплетается ≃ **X is stammering; X is tripping (all) over his tongue; X's speech is thick; X can hardly get his tongue (a)round the words;** [in limited contexts] **X's speech is slurred.**

[Лебедев:] Николаша, совестно мне, краснею, язык заплетается, но, голубчик, войди в моё положение, пойми, что я человек подневольный, негр, тряпка... (Чехов 4). [L.:] Nikolasha, I feel ashamed, I'm blushing and stammering, but, my dear boy, put yourself in my place, try to understand that I am helpless, a slave, a milksop... (4a). ♦ «Только винцо-то [*here* = водка] у нас, сам знаешь, — поддельное...» — «Это почему же поддельное?» — изумился Лёня столь откровенной наглости. Приняв двойную порцию, мерзавец раскраснелся, распарился, глаза у него тоже достаточно посоловели, язык заплетался... Но, заплетаясь, настаивал, что винцо, — поддельное, получаемое из обыкновенной воды — путём гипноза... (Терц 6). "Our only trouble is this substitute vodka they give us as you know." "What d'you mean — substitute?" Lenny was staggered by the brazen insolence of the man. After his double portion he was red in the face and sweating like a pig, his eyes glazed and his speech slurred....But although he could hardly get his tongue round the words, he went on insisting that the vodka was a substitute, produced out of plain water by hypnosis (6a).

Я-38 • ЯЗЫ́К МОЙ – ВРАГ МОЙ [saying] an unnecessarily loquacious, unrestrained person only harms himself: ≃ **my tongue is my (worst) enemy; I am my own worst enemy; me and my big mouth.**

«Пришёл брат Урусов, беседовали о суетах мира. Рассказывал о новых предначертаниях государя. Я начал было осуждать, но вспомнил о своих правилах и слова благодетеля нашего о том, что истинный масон должен быть усердным деятелем в государстве, когда требуется его участие, и спокойным созерцателем того, к чему он не призван. Язык мой – враг мой» (Толстой 5). "Brother Urusov came and we talked about the vanities of the world. He told me of the Tsar's new projects. I was on the point of criticizing them when I remembered my rules and my benefactor's words – that a true Freemason should be a zealous worker for the State when his services are required, and a reflective observer when not called upon to assist. My tongue is my enemy" (5a).

Я-39 • ЯЗЫ́К НА ПЛЕЧЕ́ ⟨НА ПЛЕЧО́⟩ *(у кого) coll* [VP~subj~ with быть~ø~; pres only; fixed WO] s.o. is very tired, exhausted (from physical exertion, work etc): (у X-а) язык на плече ≃ **X is ready to drop (from exhaustion); X is dead on his feet; X is dead beat.**

«На самом верху холодно, дуют очень вредные для здоровья сквозняки, падать оттуда смертельно, ступеньки скользкие, опасные, и ты отлично знаешь это, и всё равно лезешь, карабкаешься — язык на плечо» (Стругацкие 2). "It's cold and drafty up there — bad for the health — and a fall can be fatal. The rungs are slippery. It's a funny thing: you're aware of the dangers, and you're practically ready to drop from exhaustion, yet you keep fighting your way up" (2a). ♦ «Я ещё в детстве пускал змеев, отец драл меня! А на заводе был, семь километров в аэроклуб ходил после работы, язык на плече, а ни одного занятия не пропустил» (Гроссман 2). "As a kid, I was always flying kites. My father used to thrash me for it. And when I was at the factory, I used to walk seven kilometres to the flying club after work. I was dead beat. But I didn't miss a single lesson" (2a).

Я-40 • ЯЗЫ́К НЕ ПОВОРА́ЧИВАЕТСЯ ⟨НЕ ПОВЁРТЫВАЕТСЯ, НЕ ВОРО́ЧАЕТСЯ *obs*⟩**/НЕ ПОВЕРНУ́ЛСЯ ⟨НЕ ПОВОРОТИ́ЛСЯ** *obs*⟩ *(у кого)* сказать, спросить и т. п. *coll* [VP~subj~; used without negation to convey the opposite meaning, usu. in the constructions как язык поворачивается, если повернётся язык etc] s.o. does not have the courage, resolve etc to say or ask sth. (usu. when having to break bad news to s.o., when saying sth. that may embarrass the hearer, or when lying): у X-а язык не поворачивается сказать Y ≃ **X can't bring ⟨get⟩ himself to say Y; X's tongue refuses to ⟨won't⟩ say ⟨repeat⟩ Y; X's tongue refuses to obey him; X doesn't have the nerve ⟨the heart, the gall⟩ to say Y; X can't work up the nerve to say Y;** ‖ как у тебя язык поворачивается? ≃ **how can ⟨could⟩ you say such things ⟨such a thing⟩?; the things you say!**

Как же можно обмануть его, нарушить слово? Зря обещала, но *обещала*! У неё не повернётся язык сказать «нет» (Рыбаков 2). How could she possibly deceive him by breaking her word? She may have made an idle promise, but it was a promise just the same. She simply couldn't bring herself to say "No" (2a). ♦ «...Он эту фразу, которую у меня даже язык не поворачивается повторить, сказал не когда-нибудь, не двадцать первого июня и не двадцать третьего, а именно двадцать второго...» (Войнович 4). "...His words, which my tongue refuses to repeat, were not just spoken at any old time, not on the twenty-first of June and not on the twenty-third but, precisely, on the twenty-second..." (4a). ♦ ...Она мысленно представляла себе, как бы она вошла в клуб с Егоршей... Но она не посмела отпроситься у брата. В другое бы время проще простого: сбегаю на часик в клуб, ладно? А сегодня язык не поворачивается (Абрамов 1). ...She imagined to herself what it would be like going into the club with Egorsha....But she could not get up the courage to ask her brother's permission. At any other time it would be the simplest thing in the world: I'm going over to the club for an hour, okay? But today she could not work up the nerve (1a). ♦ «Товарищи! Товарищи! Что я слышу? Да как у вас поворачивается язык?» (Солженицын 3). "Comrades! Comrades! What do I hear? How can you say such things?" (3a).

Я-41 • ЯЗЫ́К ОТНЯ́ЛСЯ (у кого) coll [VP$_{subj}$; Invar] s.o. suddenly lost the ability to speak (usu. from surprise, fear, fright etc): у X-а язык отнялся ≃ X lost his tongue; X's tongue froze; X was speechless (with terror ⟨fear etc⟩); X was (struck) dumb (with fear ⟨astonishment etc⟩).

«Ты кто такой? – властно спросил он. – ...Чего же молчишь? Язык отнялся? Кто такой, спрашиваю». – «Красноармеец» (Шолохов 5). "Who are you?" he asked sternly.... "Why don't you speak? Lost your tongue? Who are you, I said." "I'm in the Red Army" (5a). ♦ «Ой, батюшки светы, дорогие товарищи, что с нами сделалось... Дрожим, ни живы ни мёртвы, язык отнялся от ужаса!..» (Пастернак 1). "Oh, God in heaven, need I tell you the state we were in....We were shaking all over, half dead with fright and speechless with terror!" (1a).

Я-42 • ЯЗЫ́К ПЛО́ХО ПОДВЕ́ШЕН ⟨ПРИВЕ́ШЕН⟩ у кого coll [VP$_{subj}$ with быть$_\emptyset$; pres or past] s.o. is inarticulate, cannot speak smoothly: у X-а язык плохо подвешен ≃ X doesn't speak well; X is not good with words; X isn't a good speaker.

Зря вы поручили докладывать о проекте Бочкарёву. Язык у него подвешен плохо, ни на один вопрос вразумительно ответить не сможет. It's too bad you assigned the presentation of the project to Bochkaryov. He's not good with words and won't be able to answer a single question clearly.

Я-43 • ЯЗЫ́К чей, (у) кого ПРИЛИ́П ⟨ПРИСО́Х⟩ К ГОРТА́НИ coll [VP$_{subj}$] s.o. suddenly lost the ability to speak (from surprise, amazement, fright etc): у X-а язык прилип к гортани ≃ X's tongue froze; X lost his tongue; X was speechless ⟨tongue-tied, dumbstruck⟩; X was struck dumb.

...В это самое время увидел [бригадир] Алёнку и почувствовал, что язык у него прилип к гортани (Салтыков-Щедрин 1). ...Just then he [the brigadier] caught sight of Alyonka and felt himself tongue-tied (1a).

Я-44 • ЯЗЫ́К ПРОГЛО́ТИШЬ coll, approv [VP; pfv fut, gener. 2nd pers sing only] (of food) very tasty: it makes your mouth water; it's mouth-watering; it melts in your mouth.

Обед был – язык проглотишь. Dinner was mouth-watering.

Я-45 • ЯЗЫ́К РАЗВЯ́ЗЫВАЕТСЯ/РАЗВЯЗА́ЛСЯ у кого coll [VP$_{subj}$] s.o. begins to talk a lot, becomes talkative (often as a consequence of drinking alcoholic beverages): у X-а развязался язык ≃ X's tongue loosened (up); X became chatty; X's tongue began to wag.

Володя фуганул полный стакан [«Столичной»], и язык у него тогда развязался (Аксёнов 12). He [Volodya] slugged down a full glass [of Stolichnaya], and his tongue loosened (12a). ♦ С годами у неё стал слишком развязываться язык, сказывался, видно, возраст... (Максимов 1). With the passing years her tongue had begun to wag too freely—evidently the effect of age... (1a).

Я-46 • ЯЗЫ́К СЛОМА́ЕШЬ; ЯЗЫ́К СЛОМА́ТЬ МО́ЖНО coll [VP; pfv fut, gener. 2nd pers sing (1st var.); Invar, impers predic with быть$_\emptyset$ (2nd var.); fixed WO (1st var.)] some word (combination of words, phrase etc) is very difficult to pronounce: it's a (real) jawbreaker ⟨tongue twister⟩; you can't ⟨it's impossible to⟩ get your tongue around it; you'd tie your tongue in knots trying to say it ⟨to talk like that etc⟩.

Ну и имя! Язык сломаешь! What a name! A real jawbreaker! ♦ До прошлого года у старухи на тумбочке стояло радио, и она сама крутила на нём чёрное, как пуговка, колёсико: в одном месте поют, в другом плачут, в третьем горгочут [dial = говорят] не по-нашему, в четвёртом не по-ихнему и не по-нашему – язык сломать можно, а они всё горгочут и горгочут (Распутин 3). Up till last year the old lady had had a radio on her bedside table, and she used to twiddle the black knob herself: here she'd find singing, there—weeping, further on—somebody gabbling away in some foreign language, further still—something that wasn't Russian and wasn't foreign either. You'd tie your tongue in knots trying to talk like that (3a).

Я-47 • ЯЗЫ́К ХОРОШО́ ⟨НЕПЛО́ХО, ЗДО́РОВО и т. п.⟩ ПОДВЕ́ШЕН ⟨ПРИВЕ́ШЕН⟩ у кого; ХОРОШО́ ⟨НЕПЛО́ХО и т. п.⟩ ПОДВЕ́ШЕННЫЙ ЯЗЫ́К all coll [VP$_{subj}$ with быть$_\emptyset$ (variants with short-form Part); pres or past; NP (variants with long-form Part)] s.o. is articulate, eloquent: у X-а язык хорошо подвешен ≃ X has the gift of gab; X has a way with words; X is smooth-tongued; X has a glib tongue; X is a good speaker; X speaks well.

Старуху использовали для всех приезжающих журналистов – у неё был ловко подвешенный язык. Активная колхозница, она работала безотказно, куда бы её ни послали (Мандельштам 2). The old woman was...always produced for the benefit of visiting journalists because she was a model member of her kolkhoz who always did everything asked of her and also had the gift of gab (2a).

Я-48 • ЯЗЫ́К ЧЕ́ШЕТСЯ/ЗАЧЕСА́ЛСЯ у кого coll [VP$_{subj}$; usu. impfv] s.o. feels an uncontrollable urge to say sth., to speak: у X-а язык чешется ≃ X ⟨X's tongue⟩ is itching (to say sth.); X is itching to speak; X is bursting (to say sth.); X just can't wait (to say sth.).

...Хотя язык у неё и чесался, рассказывать побоялась, памятуя Прохорово наставление: «Так и знай: скажешь об этом кому хоть слово – положу тебя головой на дровосеку, язык твой поганый на аршин вытяну и отрублю» (Шолохов 5). ...Although she was itching to speak, she was afraid, remembering Prokhor's warning, "Mark my words. If you so much as breathe a word to anyone about it, I'll put your head on the chopping block, pull your tongue out till it's a yard long, and cut it off" (5a).

Я-49 • БЕЗ ЯЗЫКА́ быть$_\emptyset$, остаться obsoles [PrepP; Invar; subj-compl with copula (subj: human)] to have lost permanently or temporarily the ability to speak: X остался без языка ≃ X was unable to speak; X was incapable of speaking ⟨speech⟩; [of a temporary inability to speak] X was tongue-tied.

Прошло несколько дней, и я узнала, что у Кривицкого – второй удар. Теперь он опять без языка и почти неподвижен (Гинзбург 2). A few days went by and I learned that Krivitsky had had a second stroke. He was once more unable to speak and almost unable to move (2a). ♦ Дело касалось его старинного друга... положение было отвратительное, разбирательство очень тяжёлое и чреватое (друг этот не то что-то написал, не то что-то подписал, не то напечатал, не то вслух сказал...), Лёва не то был замешан, не то касался боком... От него – требовалось. Он совсем потерял себя и ходил вовсе без лица и без языка... (Битов 2). The affair concerned an old friend...the situation was wretched, the investigation very painful and highly charged (the friend had maybe written something, or signed something, or printed it, or said it aloud...), Lyova was either implicated or indirectly involved... Something was required of him. He utterly lost his composure and went around totally blank-faced and tongue-tied... (2a).

Я-50 • НЕ СХОДИ́ТЬ С ЯЗЫКА́ ⟨С УСТ⟩ (у) кого [VP; subj: слово, имя etc] (of a word, name etc that is key to some topic of conversation) to be continually said, mentioned in conversation: X не сходит у Y-а с языка ≃ X is constantly on Y's tongue; X is always on Y's lips; X keeps coming up (in conversation); Y never stops talking about X; ‖ X не сходит с языков в месте Z ≃ X is on all tongues in place Z.

Эти имена наших «национальных героев» не сходили у нас с языка (Лимонов 1). The names of these "national heroes" of ours were always on our lips (1a). ♦ ...Господин Мольер и его комедианты... репетировали «Тартюфа» под новым названием «Обманщик»... Успех был огромный. Но на другой же день в Пале-Рояль явился пристав парижского парламента и вручил господину Мольеру официальное предписание немедленно прекратить представления «Обманщика»... Слова «Тартюф» и «Обманщик» не сходили с языков в Париже... (Булгаков 5). ...Monsieur de Molière and his players...rehearsed *Tartuffe* under a new title, *The Impostor*....The play's success was enormous. On the very next day, however, a bailiff of the parliament of Paris appeared at the Palais Royal and handed Monsieur de Molière an official order...to halt performances of *The Impostor* at once....*Tartuffe* and *The Impostor* were on all tongues in Paris... (5a).

Я-51 • СРЫВА́ТЬСЯ/СОРВА́ТЬСЯ ⟨СЛЕТА́ТЬ/СЛЕТЕ́ТЬ⟩ С ЯЗЫКА́ ⟨С УСТ, С ГУБ⟩ (у кого) [VP; subj: слово, имя etc; usu. pfv] to be uttered involuntarily and unexpectedly: X сорвался у Y-а с языка ≃ **X escaped ⟨burst from⟩ Y's lips; Y let X slip; X was ⟨Y made⟩ a slip of the tongue; X (just) slipped ⟨popped, flew⟩ out (of Y's mouth); Y said something he shouldn't have ⟨didn't want to say⟩.**

Он встал и быстро удалился, как бы испугавшись слов, сорвавшихся у него с языка (Тургенев 2). He got up and walked quickly away, as though frightened by the words which had burst from his lips (2e). ♦ «Зачем же ты предлагал мне переехать?..» – «Я думал, что другие, мол, не хуже вас, да переезжают, так и нам можно...» – сказал Захар... Он [Обломов] вникал в глубину этого сравнения и разбирал... сознательно ли оскорбил его Захар, то есть убеждён ли он был, что Илья Ильич всё равно, что «другой», или так это сорвалось у него с языка... (Гончаров 1). "...Why do you suggest moving?..." "I was just thinking, well, other people, they're no worse than us, and if they can move, we can—"....He [Oblomov] tried to get to the bottom of this comparison by analyzing...whether Zakhar had insulted him consciously; in other words, whether he was convinced that his master was the same as "other people," or whether the words had slipped out... (1b). ♦ «Пьяная женщина, – говорит дамочка, что роман про... нашего Сакуненко собирается писать, – отвратительное зрелище». – «Помолчала бы, дама! – крикнул я. – Чего вы знаете про неё? Простите, – сказал я, подумав, – с языка сорвалось» (Аксёнов 1). "A drunken woman," says the dame that's planning to write the novel about...our Sakunenko, "is a disgusting sight." "You should keep quiet lady!" I shouted. "What do you know about her?—I'm sorry," I said, catching myself, "it just popped out" (1a). ♦ Все эти отклики и разговоры сдержали Раскольникова, и слова «я убил», может быть, готовившиеся слететь у него с языка, замерли в нём (Достоевский 3). All these comments and remarks checked Raskolnikov and the words, "I killed," which were perhaps about to come flying out, died away on his lips (3a). ♦ Энгельсон уверял его... что у него сорвалась эта глупость нечаянно с языка (Герцен 2). Engelson assured him...that the stupid phrase had been a slip of the tongue (2a). ♦ [Иванов:] Сарра, замолчи, уйди, а то у меня с языка сорвётся слово! (Чехов 4). [I.:] Sarah, stop this and go away or I'll say something I shouldn't (4b). ♦ «Почему вы не хотите взять на себя командование? Казаки вас уважают. За вами они охотно пошли бы». – «Мне это не надо, я у вас короткий гость», – сухо ответил Григорий и отошёл к коню, сожалея о нечаянно сорвавшемся с языка неосторожном признании (Шолохов 5). [context transl] "Why don't you take over command? The Cossacks respect you. They'd gladly follow you." "That's not for me, I won't be staying with you much longer," Grigory replied drily and returned to his horse, regretting the careless admission he had made (5a).

Я-52 • ГОВОРИ́ТЬ НА РА́ЗНЫХ ЯЗЫКА́Х [VP; subj: human (pl) or, occas., collect] (of two or more people or groups) not to understand one another, not to have any basis for mutual understanding (as a result of having markedly different opinions, perspectives, tastes etc): X и Y говорят на разных языках ≃ **X and Y speak ⟨are speaking⟩ different languages; X and Y do not speak a common ⟨the same⟩ language; X and Y are on different wavelengths; X and Y talk ⟨are talking⟩ at cross-purposes.**

[Кавалеров:] Вы ничего не хотите говорить? Вы притворяетесь, что не понимаете меня? Или мы на разных языках говорим? Ну да, конечно, на разных... Вы коммунист, строитель, а я жалкий интеллигент (Олеша 6). [K.:] Don't you want to say something? Are you pretending not to understand me? Or are we speaking different languages? Yes, that's it, different languages. You're a communist, a builder, and I'm just a pathetic intellectual (6a). ♦ Открывается заседание. Весь смысл происходящего в том, что героиня не понимает, в чём её обвиняют. Судьи и писатели возмущены, почему она отвечает невпопад. На суде встретились два мира, говорящие... на разных языках (Мандельштам 2). The trial begins, and the main point to emerge from the proceedings is that the heroine has not the faintest idea what she is being accused of. Her judges and fellow writers are indignant because her answers bear no relation to the questions she is asked. The trial is an encounter between two different worlds in which the two sides are talking at cross purposes... (2a).

Я-53 • ВЕРТЕ́ТЬСЯ НА ЯЗЫКЕ́ у кого coll [VP] **1.** [subj: слово, вопрос etc or infin] (of sth. that the speaker is eager to say) to be about to be said, asked etc: X вертится у Y-а на языке ≃ **X is on the tip of Y's tongue; Y is itching ⟨dying⟩ to say X; [in limited contexts] X keeps coming to the tip of Y's tongue.**

День был жаркий, и человек в плаще выглядел странно. Когда он подошёл ближе, я узнал Б.Л. [Пастернака] и окликнул его. Он улыбнулся, подошёл и сел рядом. У меня вертелось на языке посоветовать ему снять плащ, но я не решался (Гладков 1). ...It was a hot day for anyone to be wearing a coat. When this strange figure got closer I recognized Pasternak and called out to him. He smiled, came over and sat down close to me. It was on the tip of my tongue to suggest he might feel better without his coat on, but I refrained (1a). ♦ ...Долго ещё у него вертелся на языке всякий вздор... (Гоголь 3). ...For a long while yet all sorts of nonsense kept coming to the tip of his tongue... (3b).

2. [subj: usu. имя, фамилия, название etc] (of sth. that the speaker knows well and is trying to recall) to be momentarily forgotten by s.o.: X вертится у Y-а на языке ≃ **X is (right) on the tip of Y's tongue; [in limited contexts] X will not come to Y.**

Потом я ещё раз увидел растение, осыпанное ярко-красными, как бы светящимися цветами – сигналами калифорнийской зимы, – но я уже забыл, как оно называется. Его название вертелось на языке, я мучительно напрягал память, но не мог вспомнить... (Катаев 2). Later I again saw that plant, sprinkled with the bright red glowing flowers that herald the Californian winter, but I had forgotten its name. Its name was on the tip of my tongue, I strained my memory to the utmost, but I couldn't recall it... (2a).

Я-54 • НА ЯЗЫКЕ́ у кого [PrepP; Invar; the resulting phrase is usu. subj-compl with быть₀] **1.** [subj: вопрос, слово etc] some question (word etc) is about to be asked, said by s.o. (who is eager to ask or say it): X у Y-а на языке ≃ **X is on the tip of Y's tongue; Y has X on the tip of his tongue.**

На языке у него было множество вопросов, но задать их так и не удалось. He had many questions on the tip of his tongue, but didn't get to ask them.

2. [subj: abstr] sth. is continually mentioned, discussed, repeated: X у Y-ов на языке ≃ **X keeps popping ⟨cropping⟩ up (in conversation); Ys keep ⟨are always, are constantly⟩ talking about X; Ys talk about X all the time;** ‖ X у всех на языке ≃ **X is on everyone's lips; X is the talk of the town.**

Его злоключения у всех на языке – мне уже трое сегодня говорили об этом. His misadventures are the talk of the town—I've heard about them from three people already today.

Я-55 • ЗЛЬІЕ ЯЗЫКИ́ [NP; usu. subj (pl only); sing can be used as appos; fixed WO] people who engage in base gossip, slanderers: **evil ⟨malicious, venomous⟩ tongues; malicious gossips ⟨gossipers, gossipmongers⟩; people ⟨men, women⟩ with evil ⟨malicious, venomous⟩ tongues.**

Ходил слушок, что Жан-Батист, отец, помимо торговли креслами и обоями, занимался и отдачею денег взаймы за приличные проценты. Не вижу в этом ничего предосудительного для коммерческого человека. Но злые языки утверждали, что Поклен-отец несколько пересаливал в смысле процентов и что будто бы драматург Мольер, когда описывал противного скрягу Гарпагона, вывел в нём своего родного отца (Булгаков 5). It was rumored on the quiet that Jean-Baptiste the father, in addition to selling armchairs and wallpaper, engaged in lending money at handsome interest. I see nothing prejudicial in that for a merchant. But evil tongues asserted that Poquelin the elder somewhat overdid it in regard to interest extracted, and that the playwright Molière depicted his own father in the image of the revolting miser Harpagon (5a). ♦ Злые языки утверждают, что Коля Зархиди вознаградил дядю Сандро через Дашу... (Искандер 3). Malicious tongues assert that Kolya Zarhidis rewarded Uncle Sandro by way of Dasha... (3a). ♦ Это был старый холостяк Шиншин, двоюродный брат графини, злой язык, как про него говорили в московских гостиных (Толстой 4). This was Shinshin, an old bachelor and cousin of the Countess, a man with a venomous tongue, according to the talk in the drawing rooms of Moscow (4a).

Я-56 • ЧЕСА́ТЬ/ПОЧЕСА́ТЬ ЯЗЫКИ́ ⟨ЯЗЫЧКИ́, ЯЗЫКА́МИ⟩ (*о ком, про кого,* **на чей** *счёт*) *coll* [VP; subj: human pl] to engage in empty conversation, usu. gossip: Х-ы ⟨Х и Y⟩ чешут языки (про Z-а) ≃ **Xs ⟨X and Y⟩ wag their tongues (about Z); Xs ⟨X and Y⟩ beat their gums (about Z); Xs ⟨X and Y⟩ gab (about Z);** [not in refer. to gossip] **Xs ⟨X and Y⟩ shoot the breeze ⟨the bull⟩.**

«На чужой роток не накинешь платок, — сказал хозяин, — а впрочем, в наших палестинах, известно, кумушкам что и делать, как не язычки чесать» (Сологуб 1). "You can't stop people from talking," said the host, "and besides, it is well known that the scandalmongers in our provincial Palestines have nothing to do but wag their tongues" (1a). ♦ ...На четвёртый день [Григорий] уехал в район. Да не один, а с Варварой Иняхиной... Сколько она [Анфиса] слёз тогда пролила! И из-за чего? Из-за того, что бабы на каждом перекрёстке судачат да языком чешут (Абрамов 1). ...On the fourth day he [Grigory] had left for the district center. Not alone but with Varvara Inyakhina....Then the floodgates had opened! But why?...It was because of those women tittle-tattling and gabbing on every corner (1a). ♦ Ну, посидели они, как водится, выпили джин или виски, само собой, без закуски, почесали языками, да и пора расходиться (Войнович 1). They sat together for a while, drinking whiskey or gin, but not chasing them with appetizers the way Russians do, shooting the breeze until it was time for Rabinovich to go (1a).

Я-57 • БОЛТА́ТЬ ЯЗЫКО́М *coll* [VP; subj: human] **1.** to talk far too much and about nonsense, rubbish: Х болтает языком ≃ **X babbles ⟨prattles, jabbers⟩ away ⟨on (and on)⟩; X blathers; X runs off at the mouth; X beats his gums; X flaps his jaw ⟨gums⟩.**

Прогоревший начисто глава Блестящего Театра подошёл к окну и в виртуозных выражениях проклял Париж... Потом он обругал парижскую публику, которая ничего не понимает в искусстве, и к этому добавил, что в Париже есть только один порядочный человек, и этот человек — королевский мостовщик Леонар Обри. Он долго ещё болтал языком, не получая ответа... (Булгаков 5). The head of the Illustrious Theater, flat broke, went over to the window and heaped curses of consummate eloquence on Paris....Then he proceeded to pile abuse upon the Paris public, which had no inkling of what art was, and added that there was

only one decent man in Paris, and that was the Royal paver, Léonard Aubry. He babbled on for a long time, receiving no answer... (5a).

2. to talk to no purpose (promising sth. one cannot or will not deliver, expressing an unfounded opinion etc): Х болтает языком ≃ **X throws words around; X is spouting (a lot of) hot air; X is all talk.**

Он только зря языком болтает, а как до дела дойдёт — ничего не сделает. He's just throwing words around—when it comes right down to it, he won't do anything.

3. to talk freely and indiscreetly: Х болтает языком ≃ **X talks too much; X says whatever comes ⟨pops⟩ into his head.**

Голем сказал: «Вы намёки понимаете?» — «Иногда, — ответил Виктор. — Когда знаю, что это намёки. А что?» — «Так вот обратите внимание: намёк. Перестаньте трепаться». «Гм, — пробормотал Виктор. — И как прикажете это понимать?» — «Как намёк. Перестаньте болтать языком» (Стругацкие 1). "Can you take a hint?" asked Golem. "Sometimes," said Victor. "When I know it's a hint. What of it?" "Here's a hint. Stop shooting your mouth off." "Hm," mumbled Victor. "And how would you like me to understand that?" "As a hint. Stop talking so much" (1a).

Я-58 • РУ́ССКИМ ЯЗЫКО́М говорить, спрашивать и т. п. *coll* [NP_{instrum}; Invar; adv; fixed WO] (usu. said with irritation when the speaker must repeat sth. because of the interlocutor's failure to understand, unwillingness to comply etc) (to say, ask etc sth.) perfectly clearly: **in plain Russian; in plain language ⟨words⟩; in no uncertain terms.**

«Алтынник! — распалялся майор. — Я вас русским языком спрашиваю, где вы нашли эту Людмилу Сырову? Кто вам давал право жениться без разрешения командира полка?» (Войнович 5). "Altinnik!" The major was growing incensed, "I'm asking you in plain Russian who this Ludmilla Sirova is? Who gave you the right to get married without the permission of the regimental commander?" (5a). ♦ [Лопахин:] Вам говорят русским языком, имение ваше продаётся, а вы точно не понимаете (Чехов 2). [L.:] You're told in plain language that your estate's going to be sold, and you don't seem to understand (2b).

Я-59 • ВЫ́ЕДЕННОГО ЯЙЦА́ НЕ СТО́ИТ *coll* [VP; subj: usu. abstr; usu. 3rd pers, pres or past] not to be worth anything, not warrant attention: Х выеденного яйца не стоит ≃ **X isn't worth a (tinker's) damn; X isn't worth wasting your ⟨his etc⟩ breath on; X isn't worth a plugged nickel ⟨a brass farthing, a straw⟩; X isn't worth beans.**

[Муромский:] ...Эти два свидетеля выеденного яйца не стоят (Сухово-Кобылин 1). [M.:] ...These two witnesses aren't worth a damn (1a). ♦ ...Состряпали дело, написали фельетон, ошельмовали порядочных людей, десять человек, в том числе и моего отца. Отец сказал, что всё это чепуха, неправда, яйца выеденного не стоит. Но он был наивный человек, мой отец (Рыбаков 1). ...The case was cooked up, and the article written to defame decent people, ten in all, including my father. Father said the whole thing was rubbish, untrue, and not worth wasting one's breath on. But father was naïve (1a). ♦ [Павлу Евграфовичу] не хотелось показывать своего полнейшего равнодушия при виде её слёз, но [он] не мог себя пересилить. Чепуха всё это. Яйца выеденного не стоит (Трифонов 6). He [Pavel Evgrafovich] was reluctant to show his utter indifference at the sight of her tears, but was unable to control himself. The whole thing was nonsense. Not worth a brass farthing (6a). ♦ «...Эти господа немцы завтра не выиграют сражение, а только нагадят, сколько их сил будет, потому что в его немецкой голове только рассуждения, не стоящие выеденного яйца, а в сердце нет того, что одно только и нужно на завтра, — то, что есть в Тимохине» (Толстой 6). "...Those German gentlemen won't win the battle tomorrow but will only make a filthy mess of it, insofar as they can, because they have nothing in their German heads but theories, which are not worth a straw, and their hearts lack the one thing needed for tomorrow – what Timokhin has" (6a).

Я-60 • ЯЙЦА КУ́РИЦУ НЕ У́ЧАТ [saying] s.o. young and inexperienced should not try to educate s.o. older and more experienced (said in scorn when a young person gives advice to an older person): ≃ **don't teach your grandmother to suck eggs.**

Я-61 • ВЫ́ЕДЕННОЕ ЯЙЦО́ *obs, coll* [NP; sing only; fixed WO] a trifle, an insignificant matter: **trifling 〈piddling〉 matter; matter of trivial importance 〈of no concern〉; nothing at all; small potatoes.**

...[Бородавкин] поражал расторопностью и какою-то неслыханной административной въедчивостью, которая с особенной энергией проявлялась в вопросах, касавшихся выеденного яйца (Салтыков-Щедрин 1). ...Wartkin was striking for his snappy efficiency and an unprecedented administrative voracity, which manifested itself with especial energy in matters that were small potatoes (1a).

Я-62 • БРО́СИТЬ 〈КИ́НУТЬ〉 Я́КОРЬ *где, куда* [VP; subj: human; usu. this WO] to stop moving from place to place and settle somewhere permanently or for a long period of time: X бросил якорь в месте Y ≃ **X cast anchor 〈settled down, put down roots〉 in place Y.**

Я устал переезжать с места на место, хочу бросить якорь где-нибудь на юге. I'm tired of moving from place to place, I want to cast anchor somewhere in the South.

Я-63 • Я́КОРЬ СПАСЕ́НИЯ *lit* [NP; sing only; fixed WO] a last means or prospect (of saving a hopeless or embarrassing situation): **last hope 〈resort〉; last means of salvation.**

Я-64 • НЕ РОЙ ДРУГО́МУ Я́МУ (-ы), САМ В НЕЁ ПОПАДЁШЬ [saying] s.o. who wishes trouble on, or makes trouble for, others can find himself in trouble: ≃ **he who digs a pit for others may fall himself therein; curses like chickens come home to roost; he who mischief hatches mischief catches; when you plot mischief for others, you're preparing trouble for yourself.**

Я-65 • РЫТЬ/ВЫ́РЫТЬ 〈КОПА́ТЬ/ВЫ́КОПАТЬ〉 Я́МУ *кому, под кого coll, disapprov* [VP; subj: human; usu. impfv] to prepare serious trouble for s.o., scheme against s.o.: X роет яму под Y-a ≃ **X is plotting Y's downfall; X is plotting 〈cooking up〉 trouble for Y; X is digging a hole 〈a pit〉 for Y.**

Я-66 • ДВУЛИ́КИЙ Я́НУС *lit, disapprov* [NP; sing only; fixed WO] a deceitful, hypocritical person: **double-faced Janus; two-faced Janus; (s.o. is) Janus-faced.**

«Этот случай должен показать, что нельзя быть двуликим Янусом и сидеть между двух стульев» (Эткинд 1). "This case should be a lesson to us that one must not act like a two-faced Janus, sitting on the fence..." (1a).

< From *Janus*, the ancient Roman god of doorways and gates. Janus was represented with one head and two faces that looked in opposite directions.

Я-67 • НАКЛЕ́ИВАТЬ/НАКЛЕ́ИТЬ 〈ПРИКЛЕ́И-ВАТЬ/ПРИКЛЕ́ИТЬ, ЛЕПИ́ТЬ/ПРИЛЕПИ́ТЬ〉 ЯРЛЫКИ́ 〈ЯРЛЫ́К〉 *(кому, на кого-что) disapprov* [VP; subj: human] to call some person, phenomenon etc by a name that places him or it into a ready-made category (upon having evaluated him or it superficially or one-sidedly; may be used to categorize s.o. in the context of a political or ideological struggle): X наклеил ярлык Y-у ≃ **X stuck 〈pinned〉 a label on Y; X**

stuck the label of [NP] on Y; X tagged Y with a label; X labeled Y.

«Ах, какой вздор все эти направления! Кем меня только не объявляли критики: и декадентом, и символистом, и мистиком, и реалистом, и неореалистом, и богоискателем, и натуралистом, да мало ли ещё каких ярлыков на меня не наклеивали, так что в конце концов я стал похож на сундук, совершивший кругосветное путешествие...» (Катаев 3). "Oh, what a lot of nonsense all these trends are! According to the critics I am a decadent, a symbolist, a mystic, a realist, a neorealist, a god-seeker, a naturalist and God knows what else. They have stuck so many labels on me that I feel like a suitase that has travelled all round the world..." (3a). ♦ Саше нравилось, что Столпер гоняет этих чиновников. Так он будет гонять и Баулина, и всех, кто приклеил ему, Саше, ярлык врага (Рыбаков 2). It pleased Sasha to hear Stolper getting on these officials, just as he would get on Baulin and all the others who had stuck the label of enemy on him (2a). ♦ Все они [те, кто некогда был в оппозиции или был несогласен со Сталиным,] были названы агентами иностранного империализма. Такой же ярлык был приклеен тем, кто даже не участвовал в оппозиции, но попал в «чистки» 1937–38 годов, – так как это самый простой и верный способ дискредитировать политических деятелей в глазах народа (Аллилуева 2). They [those who had been in the opposition or who had disagreed with Stalin] were called "agents of foreign imperialism." And those who had not taken part in any opposition but had simply been victims of the 1937–38 "purges" were also tagged with the same label. It was the surest and simplest way of discrediting politicians in the eyes of the people (2a).

Я-68 • ЗАМНЁМ ДЛЯ Я́СНОСТИ *coll* [usu. indep. sent; Invar] let us not speak of this (anymore) in order to avoid embarrassment, hard feelings, offense etc: **let's give it 〈this topic etc〉 a rest; let's not talk about that; [in limited contexts] you know what I mean.**

«Федька, Федька Косой меня упёк. Ох, зверь-человек... И заданьем твёрдым обкладывал, и из лесу по месяцам не выпускал... А и зазря, как потом выяснилось. Тамошние власти поумнее – с меня и вину всю сняли»... – «Ну ладно, – важно, как если бы он вёл собрание, сказал Егорша. – Этот вопрос для ясности замнём» (Абрамов 1). "Fedka, Fedka Kosoi did me in. Oh, what a monster of a man....He made me pay more taxes...and wouldn't let me leave the forest for months on end. All to no avail, as it turned out later: the authorities out there were smarter than him; they said I was completely innocent."..."All right then," said Egorsha in a pompous voice, as if he was conducting a meeting. "Let's give that topic a rest" (1a). ♦ ...Временами приходилось ему и показать товарищам кое-какими внешними признаками, что он «свой» – ну, там, матюкаться в тесном кругу, ну, демонстрировать страсть к рыбалке, сдержанное почтение к генералиссимусу... интерес к «деревенской литературе»... и, конечно же, посещать... хм... гм... замнём для ясности, товарищи,... ну, в общем, финскую баню (Аксёнов 7). ...Every once in a while he would throw the comrades an external sop to remind them that he was really one of the gang—say, use a dirty word or two in private, make a big thing out of going fishing, show a certain muted respect for Generalissimo Iosif S....comment favorably on recent village prose...and naturally take part in the...um...you know what I mean, Comrades...the...the Finnish bath ritual (7a).

Я-69 • НА ЯТЬ *old-fash, coll* [PrepP; Invar] **1.** [subj-compl with copula (subj: any common noun) or nonagreeing postmodif] very good, excellent in quality, form etc: **with a capital A 〈B etc〉; one in a million; a [NP] in the finest sense of the word.**

[Шервинский:] Вы красивая, умная, как говорится, интеллектуально развитая. Вообще женщина на ять. Аккомпанируете прекрасно на рояле. А он рядом с вами – вешалка, карьерист, штабной момент (Булгаков 4). [Sh.:] You are beautiful, intelligent, intellectually developed, as they say. In general a woman with a capital "W." You are a fine accompanist on the piano. And compared to you he's a coat rack, a careerist, a headquarters nothing (4a). ♦ Вы сами видите, что это рояль, как говорится, **на ять**: и звук прекрасный, и отделка великолепная. You can see for yourself, this piano is, as they say, one in a million: the tone is excellent and the ornamentation extraordinary.

2. сделать *что* ~ [adv] (to do sth.) excellently: **to a T; to perfection; perfectly; splendidly;** ‖ **знать** *что* ~ **know sth. inside out; know sth. backward and forward.**

«По сравнению с нынешней мебелью, которая разваливается через год, старая мебель была сработана на ять, — сказал дед. — Этот стул, к примеру, служит уже третьему поколению семьи Афанасьевых». "As compared with furniture of today, which falls apart in a year, old furniture was splendidly crafted," said Grandfather. "This chair, for example, is already serving the third generation of Afanasyevs."

Я-70 • В ДÓЛГИЙ Я́ЩИК **откладывать** *(что)* coll [PrepP; Invar; adv; the verb is usu. negated or used with нельзя, не надо, незачем etc; often Verbal Adv не откладывая; fixed WO] (of a person or group) (to postpone some matter) for an indefinite period: X не откладывает дел в долгий ящик ≃ **X doesn't put things off (indefinitely);** ‖ не откладывая в долгий ящик ≃ **right away; without delay; losing no time.**

Чтобы уменьшить круг подозреваемых, Антон решил, не откладывая в долгий ящик, точно установить, когда Овчинников уехал в Раздумье (Чернёнок 1). In order to cut down the list of suspects, Anton decided to determine right away when Ovchinnikov had set off for Razdumie (1a). ♦ Два-три развратных губернатора воспитали вятских дам, и Тюфяев, привыкнувший к ним, не откладывая в долгий ящик, прямо стал говорить ей [Р.] о своей любви (Герцен 1). Two or three dissolute governors before him had kept Vyatka ladies as mistresses, and Tyufyayev, being used to such women, lost no time but at once began making declarations of love to her [Madame R.] (1a).

Я-71 • СЫ́ГРАТЬ В Я́ЩИК *substand* [VP; subj: human] to die: X сыграл в ящик ≃ **X kicked the bucket; X popped off.**

«Вот вы, например, мужчина видный, возвышенного роста, хотя и худой. Вы, считается, ежели, не дай бог, помрёте, что в ящик сыграли. А который человек торговый, бывшей купеческой гильдии, тот, значит, приказал долго жить» (Ильф и Петров 1). "Now you, for instance. You're distinguished-looking and tall, though a bit on the thin side. If you should die, God forbid, they'll say you popped off. But a tradesman, who belonged to the former merchants' guild, would breathe his last" (1a).

Я-72 • Я́ЩИК ПАНДÓРЫ *lit* [NP; sing only; fixed WO] a source of misfortune or disaster: **Pandora's box.**

< In Greek mythology the gods used a beautiful woman, Pandora, to punish mankind for Prometheus's theft of fire. They sent her to earth with a box full of all the evils that could befall mankind, certain that she would give in to her curiosity and open the box, thus releasing those evils into the world.

BIBLIOGRAPHY

The Bibliography identifies the literary and reference works cited and used in the preparation of this dictionary. The names of literary authors are presented alphabetically in Russian (surname, given name, and patronymic) followed by the English transliteration (surname and given name only). The English transliterations of authors' names do not adhere to a single transliteration system but, rather, follow the spelling currently used by the Library of Congress (with diacritics omitted). Literary authors' birth dates and, when applicable, death dates are provided because idiom usage can change over time, and an author's choice and use of idioms are best understood in relation to the time frame within which the author wrote. In addition, the Bibliography includes the real names of authors who wrote under pseudonyms; the real names appear only within the pseudonym entry and are transliterated.

When multiple works from a collection by a single author (or team of authors) are used in the dictionary, the full citation is given only at the first occurrence of the collection in the Bibliography, with all subsequent occurrences being cross-referred back to that initial citation. All works and translations from anthologies are cross-referred to subsection B of the Bibliography, "Anthologies," where a full bibliographic citation is presented. When a collection or anthology is translated by a single translator (or team of translators), the translator's name is indicated only in the full bibliographic citation for the volume. Cross references to that bibliographic citation do not repeat the translator's name. However, when the works included in a collection or anthology are translated by different translators, all references to that edition include the name of the translator who translated the work in question.

Because in this dictionary the source of each citation has been identified with only its author's surname (in Russian) followed by the number assigned to the relevant work, a special numbering convention has been employed to distinguish works by two authors with the same name and first initial, Venedikt Erofeev and Viktor Erofeev. The cited work by Venedikt Erofeev has been identified as Ерофеев 1, while works by Viktor Erofeev have been numbered starting with Ерофеев 2.

In some instances two editions of a work have been consulted as sources for citations: an earlier, less carefully edited version (usually published in the West), and a later, more carefully edited version (published in the former Soviet Union). Where applicable, both editions have been listed in the Bibiliography.

I. DICTIONARIES AND REFERENCE SOURCES (Selected Bibliography)

A. *Russian*

Ашукин, Н.С., М.Г. Ашукина. *Крылатые слова: Литературные цитаты, образные выражения.* Изд. 2-е, доп. Москва: Гос. изд-во художественной лит-ры, 1960; Изд. 3-е, Москва: Изд-во «Правда», 1986.

Быстрова, Е.А., А.П. Окунева, Н.М. Шанский. *Учебный фразеологический словарь русского языка: Пособие для учащихся национальных школ.* Ленинград: «Просвещение», 1984.

Даль, В.И. *Толковый словарь живого великорусского языка.* Тт. 1–4. Москва: Гос. изд-во иностранных и национальных словарей, 1955. (Набрано и напечатано со второго издания 1880–1882 гг.)

Жуков, В.П. *Школьный фразеологический словарь русского языка: Пособие для учащихся.* Москва: «Просвещение», 1980.

Жуков, В.П., М.И. Сидоренко, В.Т. Шкляров. *Словарь фразеологических синонимов русского языка.* Москва: «Русский язык», 1987.

Кохтев, Н.Н., Д.Э. Розенталь. *Русская фразеология.* Москва: «Русский язык», 1986.

Мельчук, И.А., А.К. Жолковский. *Толково-комбинаторный словарь современного русского языка: Опыты семантико-синтаксического описания русской лексики = Explanatory Combinatorial Dictionary of Modern Russian.* Вена: 1984. (*Wiener Slawistischer Almanach. Sonderband;* 14.)

Михельсон, М.И. *Русская мысль и рѣчь: Свое и чужое: Опыт русской фразеологии.* The Hague: Mouton, 1969. (Reprint. С.-Петербургъ, 1912.)

Ожегов, С.И., Н.Ю. Шведова. *Толковый словарь русского языка.* Москва: «Азъ» Ltd., 1992.

Орфоэпический словарь русского языка: Произношение, ударение, грамматические формы. Под ред. Р.И. Аванесова. Изд. 2-е, стереотипное. Москва: «Русский язык», 1985, c1983.

Словарь русского языка в четырех томах. Главный редактор А.П. Евгеньева. Изд. 2-е, испр. и доп. Москва: «Русский язык», 1981–1984.

Словарь современного русского литературного языка. Тт. 1–17. Москва-Ленинград: Изд-во Академии наук СССР; Изд-во «Наука», 1950–1965.

Словарь современного русского литературного языка в 20 томах. Тт. 1-⟨4⟩. Главный редактор К.С. Горбачевич. Изд. 2-е, перер. и доп. Москва: «Русский язык», 1991-⟨1993⟩.

Толковый словарь русского языка. Под ред. Д.Н. Ушакова. Cambridge, Mass.: Slavica Publishers, 1974. 4 v. in 3. (Reprint. Москва: «Советская энциклопедия», 1934–1940. Тт. 1–4.)

Фелицына, Н.М., В.М. Мокиенко *Русские фразеологизмы: Лингвострановедческий словарь.* Москва: «Русский язык», 1990.

Фелицына, В.П., Ю.Е. Прохоров. *Русские пословицы, поговорки и крылатые выражения: Лингвострановедческий словарь.* Москва: Изд-во «Русский язык», 1979.

Фразеологический словарь русского литературного языка конца XVIII-XX в. в двух томах. Под ред. А.И. Федорова. Новосибирск: «Наука», 1991.

Фразеологический словарь русского языка. Под ред. А.И. Молоткова. Москва: Изд-во «Советская энциклопедия», 1967; Изд. 3-е, стереотипное, Москва: Изд-во «Русский язык», 1978.

Шанский, Н.М., В.И. Зимин, А.В. Филиппов. *Опыт этимологического словаря русской фразеологии.* Москва: «Русский язык», 1987.

Яранцев, Р.И. *Словарь-справочник по русской фразеологии.* Москва: «Русский язык», 1981.

B. *Bilingual*

Андрейчина, К., С. Влахов, С. Димитрова, К. Запрянова. *Русско-болгарский фразеологический словарь.* Москва: Изд-во «Русский язык»; София: Гос. изд-во «Наука и искусство», 1980.

Апресян, Ю.Д., Эрна Палл. *Русский глагол – венгерский глагол: Управление и сочетаемость = Orosz ige – magyar ige: Vonzatok és kapcsolódások.* Тт. 1–2. Будапешт: Танкёньвкиадо, 1982.

Буковская, М.В., С.И. Вяльцева и др. *Словарь употребительных английских пословиц.* Изд. 3-е, стереотипное. Москва: «Русский язык», 1990, c1985.

Гуревич, В.В., Ж.А. Дозорец. *Краткий русско-английский фразеологический словарь.* Москва: «Русский язык», 1988.

Квеселевич, Д.И., В.П. Сасина. *Русско-английский словарь междометий и релятивов.* Москва: «Русский язык», 1990.

Кузьмин, С.С., Н.Л. Шадрин. *Русско-английский словарь пословиц и поговорок.* Москва: «Русский язык», 1989.

Кунин, А.В. *Англо-русский фразеологический словарь = English-Russian Phraseological Dictionary.* Изд. 4-е, перер. и доп. Москва: «Русский язык», 1984.

Русско-английский словарь. Под общим руководством А.И. Смирницкого; авторы О.С. Ахманова и др. Изд. 13-е, испр. и доп. Москва: «Русский язык», 1985.

Русско-армянский фразеологический словарь. Под ред. Р.Л. Мелкумяна и П.М. Погосяна. Ереван: Изд-во Ереванского университета, 1975.

Сташайтене, В., Й. Паулаускас. *Русско-литовский фразеологический словарь.* Вильнюс: «Мокслас», 1985.

Уолш, И.А., В.П. Берков. *Русско-английский словарь крылатых слов.* Москва: «Русский язык», 1984.

Шкляров, В.Т., Р. Эккерт, Х. Энгельке. *Краткий русско-немецкий фразеологический словарь.* Москва: Изд-во «Русский язык», 1977.

Katzner, Kenneth. *English-Russian, Russian-English Dictionary.* New York: Wiley, 1984.

Wheeler, Marcus. *The Oxford Russian-English Dictionary.* Oxford: Clarendon, 1972; 2nd ed., 1992, c1984.

C. *English*

American Expressions: A Thesaurus of Effective and Colorful Speech. Edited by Robert B. Costello, consulting editor Jess Stein. New York: McGraw-Hill, 1981.

The American Heritage Dictionary of the English Language. Anne H. Soukhanov, executive editor. 3rd ed. Boston: Houghton Mifflin, 1992.

The BBI Combinatory Dictionary of English. Compiled by Morton Benson, Evelyn Benson and Robert Ilson. Amsterdam; Philadelphia: John Benjamins, 1986.

A Dictionary of American Idioms. Based on the earlier edition edited by M.T. Boatner, J.E. Gates, and Adam Makkai. 2nd ed. rev. and thoroughly updated by Adam Makkai. New York: Barron's, c1987.

A Dictionary of American Proverbs. Wolfgang Mieder, editor in chief; Stewart A. Kingsbury, Kelsie B. Harder, editors. New York: Oxford Univ. Press, 1992.

Lewin, Esther and Albert E. Lewin. *The Random House Thesaurus of Slang.* New York: Random House, 1988.

Longman Dictionary of English Idioms. Thomas Hill Long, editorial director. Harlow [England]: Longman, 1979.

Oxford Dictionary of Current Idiomatic English. V. 1. *Verbs with Prepositions & Particles* / A.P. Cowie, R. Mackin. V. 2. *Phrase, Clause & Sentence Idioms* / A.P. Cowie, R. Mackin, I.R. McCaig. Oxford: Oxford Univ. Press, 1975–1983.

Partridge, Eric. *A Dictionary of Clichés.* 5th ed. London; Boston: Routledge & Kegan Paul, 1985, c1978.

The Random House Dictionary of the English Language. Stuart Berg Flexner, editor in chief; Leonore Crary Hauck, managing editor. 2nd ed., unabridged. New York: Random House, 1987.

Rogers, James. *The Dictionary of Cliches*. New York: Ballantine Books, 1985.

Spears, Richard A. *NTC's American Idioms Dictionary*. Associate editor, Linda Schinke-Llano. Lincolnwood, Ill.: National Textbook Company, 1989, c1987.

Whiting, Bartlett Jere. *Modern Proverbs and Proverbial Sayings*. Cambridge, Mass.: Harvard Univ. Press, 1989.

II. LITERARY SOURCES

A. *Authors*

АБРАМОВ, ФЕДОР АЛЕКСАНДРОВИЧ/ABRAMOV, FEDOR (1920–1983)

1. *Две зимы и три лета*. Ижевск: Удмуртия, 1982.
   1a. *Two Winters and Three Summers*. Transl. Jacqueline Edwards and Mitchell Schneider. San Diego: Harcourt Brace Jovanovich, 1984.
   1b. *Two Winters and Three Summers*. Transl. D.B. Powers and Doris C. Powers. Ann Arbor: Ardis, 1984.

АЙТМАТОВ, ЧИНГИЗ/AITMATOV, CHINGIZ (b. 1928)

1. «Белый пароход». *Новый мир*, 1970, 1, 31–100.
   1a. *The White Ship*. Transl. Mirra Ginsburg. New York: Crown Publishers, 1972.
   1b. *The White Steamship*. Transl. Tatyana and George Feifer. London: Hodder and Stoughton, 1972.

2. «И дольше века длится день». *Новый мир*, 1980, 11, 3–185.
   2a. *The Day Lasts More Than a Hundred Years*. Transl. John French. Bloomington: Indiana Univ. Press, 1983.

АКСЕНОВ, ВАСИЛИЙ ПАВЛОВИЧ/AKSENOV, VASILII (b. 1932)

1. «Апельсины из Марокко». См. (его) *Катапульта*. Москва: Советский писатель, 1964, 117–261.
   1a. "Oranges from Morocco." Transl. Susan Brownsberger. In (his) *The Steel Bird and Other Stories*. Ann Arbor: Ardis, 1979, 163–263.

2. «Завтраки сорок третьего года». См. Аксенов-1, 89–99.
   2a. "The Lunches of '43." Transl. Susan Brownsberger. See Aksenov-1a, 89–96.

3. «Затоваренная бочкотара». См. (его) *Затоваренная бочкотара. Рандеву: Повести*. Нью-Йорк: Серебряный век, 1980, 9–102.
   3a. "Surplussed Barrelware." In (his) *Surplussed Barrelware*. Ed. and transl. Joel Wilkinson and Slava Yastremski. Ann Arbor: Ardis, 1985, 23–102.

4. «Маленький Кит, лакировщик действительности». См. (его) *Право на остров*. Ann Arbor: Эрмитаж, 1983, 78–90.
   4a. "Little Whale, Varnisher of Reality." Transl. Susan Brownsberger. See Aksenov-1a, 78–88.

5. «На полпути к луне». См. (его) *На полпути к луне: Книга рассказов*. Москва: Советская Россия, 1966, 150–169.
   5a. "Half-way to the Moon." Transl. R. Hingley. See ANTHOL-13, 121–144.

6. *Ожог: Поздние шестидесятые, ранние семидесятые (роман в трех книгах)*. Ann Arbor: Ardis, 1980.
   6a. *The Burn: Late Sixties-Early Seventies: A Novel in Three Books*. Transl. Michael Glenny. New York: Random House, 1984.

7. *Остров Крым*. Ann Arbor: Ardis, 1981.
   7a. *The Island of Crimea*. Transl. Michael Henry Heim. New York: Random House, 1983.

8. «Перемена образа жизни». См. Аксенов-1, 75–88.
   8a. "Changing a Way of Life." Transl. Rae Slonek. See Aksenov-1a, 138–148.

9. «Победа – рассказ с преувеличениями». См. Аксенов-4, 91–97.
   9a. "Victory—a Story with Exaggerations." Transl. Greta Slobin. See Aksenov-1a, 55–59.

10. «Товарищ Красивый Фуражкин». См. ANTHOL-19, 161–211.
    10a. "Comrade Smart-Hat." Transl. A. Wood. See ANTHOL-19, 161–211.

11. «Четыре темперамента (комедия)». См. ANTHOL-4, 636–696.
    11a. "The Four Temperaments: A Comedy in Ten Tableaux." Transl. B. Jakim. See ANTHOL-16, 532–586.

12. *Скажи изюм*. Ann Arbor: Ardis, 1985.
    12a. *Say Cheese*. Transl. Antonina W. Bouis. New York: Random House, 1989.

АЛЕШКОВСКИЙ, ЮЗ (ИОСИФ) ЕФИМОВИЧ/ALESHKOVSKII, IUZ (b. 1929)

1. *Кенгуру*. Ann Arbor: Ardis, 1981.
   1a. *Kangaroo*. Transl. Tamara Glenny. New York: Farrar, Straus & Giroux, 1986.

АЛЛИЛУЕВА, СВЕТЛАНА ИОСИФОВНА/ALLILUEVA, SVETLANA (b. 1925)

1. *Двадцать писем к другу*. Нью-Йорк: Русская книга, 1981.
   1a. *Twenty Letters to a Friend*. Transl. Priscilla Johnson McMillan. New York: Harper & Row, 1967.

2. *Только один год*. New York: Harper & Row, 1969.
   2a. *Only One Year*. Transl. Paul Chavchavadze. New York: Harper & Row, 1969.

АМАЛЬРИК, АНДРЕЙ АЛЕКСЕЕВИЧ/AMALRIK, ANDREI (1938–1981)

1. *Записки диссидента*. Ann Arbor: Ardis, 1982.
   1a. *Notes of a Revolutionary*. Transl. Guy Daniels. New York: Knopf, 1982.

АРБУЗОВ, АЛЕКСЕЙ НИКОЛАЕВИЧ/ARBUZOV, ALEKSEI (1908–1986)

1. «Двенадцатый час». См. (его) *Драмы*. Москва: Искусство, 1969, 195–270.
   1a. "The Twelfth Hour." In (his) *Selected Plays of Aleksei Arbuzov*. Transl. Ariadne Nicolaeff. Oxford; New York: Pergamon Press, 1982, 149–212.

2. «Жестокие игры». *Театр*, 1978, 4, 140–167.
   2a. "Cruel Games." See Arbuzov-1a, 77–148.

3. «Мое загляденье». См. (его) *Выбор: Сборник пьес*. Москва: Советский писатель, 1976, 197–256.
   3a. "Lovely to Look At!" See Arbuzov-1a, 215–266.

4. «Мой бедный Марат». См. Арбузов-1, 435–512.
   4a. "The Promise." See Arbuzov-1a, 5–73.

5. «Сказки старого Арбата». См. Арбузов-3, 5–64.
   5a. "Once Upon a Time (Tales of the Old Arbat)." See Arbuzov-1a, 269–322.

АРЖАК, НИКОЛАЙ/ARZHAK, NIKOLAI [Pseud. of DANIEL, IULII MARKOVICH (1925–1988)]

1. «Говорит Москва». См. (его) *Говорит Москва: Повести и рассказы*. Нью-Йорк: Международное литературное содружество, 1966, 11–63.
   1a. *This is Moscow Speaking*. In (his) *This is Moscow Speaking, and Other Stories*. Transl. Stuart Hood, Harold Shukman and John Richardson. London: Collins & Harvill, 1968, 19–66.

2. «Искупление». См. Аржак-1, 97–159.
   2a. "Atonement." See Arzhak-1a, 75–134.

3. «Человек из МИНАП'а». См. Аржак-1, 71–96.
   3a. "The Man from Minap." See Arzhak-1a, 135–159.

АРКАНОВ, АРКАДИЙ МИХАЙЛОВИЧ/ARKANOV, ARKADII (b. 1933)

1. «И все раньше и раньше опускаются синие сумерки». См. ANTHOL-4, 500–508.
   1a. "And Ever More Early the Dark Blue of Twilight Descends." Transl. George Saunders. See ANTHOL-16, 425–432.

2. «И снится мне карнавал». См. ANTHOL-4, 509–518.
   2a. "I Dream of a Carnival." Transl. George Saunders. See ANTHOL-16, 432–440.

АХМАДУЛИНА, БЕЛЛА АХАТОВНА/AKHMADULINA, BELLA (b. 1937)

1. «Много собак и собака». См. ANTHOL-4, 21–47.
   1a. "The Many Dogs and the Dog." Transl. H. William Tjalsma. See ANTHOL-16, 6–29.

БИТОВ, АНДРЕЙ ГЕОРГИЕВИЧ/BITOV, ANDREI (b. 1937)

1. «Прощальные деньки». См. ANTHOL-4, 326–371.
   1a. "Days of Leavetaking." Transl. George Saunders. See ANTHOL-16, 273–315.

2. *Пушкинский дом*. Ann Arbor: Ardis, 1978.
   Пушкинский дом. Москва: Современник, 1989. [consulted for punctuation]
   2a. *Pushkin House*. Transl. Susan Brownsberger. New York: Farrar, Straus & Giroux, 1987.

БОГДАНОВ, АЛЕКСАНДР АЛЕКСАНДРОВИЧ/BOGDANOV, ALEKSANDR (1873–1928)

1. *Красная звезда: Роман-утопия*. Hamburg: Helmut Buske Verlag, 1979. Reprint. Ленинград: Изд-во «Красная газета», 1929.
   Красная звѣзда: утопія. С.-Петербургъ: «Т-во Художественной печати», 1908.
   1a. *Red Star. The First Bolshevik Utopia*. Transl. Charles Rougle. Bloomington: Indiana Univ. Press, 1984.

БРАГИНСКИЙ, ЭМИЛЬ (ЭММАНУЭЛЬ) ВЕНИАМИНОВИЧ/BRAGINSKII, EMIL (b. 1921) and РЯЗАНОВ, ЭЛЬДАР АЛЕКСАНДРОВИЧ/RIAZANOV, ELDAR (b. 1927)

1. «Ирония судьбы, или С легким паром». См. (их) *Ирония судьбы, или С легким паром: Комедии для театра*. Москва: Советский писатель, 1983, 5–64.
   1a. "The Irony of Fate, or I Hope You Enjoyed Your Bath." Transl. Robert Daglish. *Soviet Literature*, 1978, 12, 36–83.

БУКОВСКИЙ, ВЛАДИМИР КОНСТАНТИНОВИЧ/BUKOVSKII, VLADIMIR (b. 1942)

1. «И возвращается ветер...» Нью-Йорк: Хроника, 1978.
   1a. *To Build a Castle: My Life as a Dissenter*. Transl. Michael Scammell. New York: Viking Press, 1978.

БУЛГАКОВ, МИХАИЛ АФАНАСЬЕВИЧ/BULGAKOV, MIKHAIL (1891–1949)

1. «Багровый остров». См. (его) *Адам и Ева. Багровый остров. Зойкина квартира: Пьесы*. 2-е изд. Paris: YMCA-Press, 1974, 79–192.
   1a. "The Crimson Island." In (his) *The Early Plays of Mikhail Bulgakov*. Transl. Carl and Ellendea Proffer. Bloomington: Indiana Univ. Press, 1972, 241–347.

2. *Бег*. См. (его) *Пьесы*. Москва: Советский писатель, 1986, 123–186.
   2a. *Flight*. Transl. Mirra Ginsburg. New York: Grove Press, 1969.

3. «Белая гвардия». См. (его) *Белая гвардия. Театральный роман. Мастер и Маргарита: Романы*. Ленинград: Художественная литература, 1978, 11–270.
   3a. *The White Guard*. Transl. Michael Glenny. New York: McGraw-Hill, 1971.

4. «Дни Турбиных». См. (его) *Пьесы*. Москва: Советский писатель, 1986, 47–122.
   4a. "The Days of the Turbins." See Bulgakov-1a, 1–93.
   4b. "The Days of the Turbins." See ANTHOL-23, 255–334.
   4c. "The Days of the Turbins." Transl. R. Daglish. See ANTHOL-7, 265–350.

5. «Жизнь господина де Мольера». См. (его) *Избранная проза*. Москва: Художественная литература, 1966, 351–504.
   5a. *The Life of Monsieur de Molière*. Transl. Mirra Ginsburg. New York: Funk & Wagnalls, 1970.

6. «Записки юного врача». См. Булгаков-5, 45–108.
   6a. *A Country Doctor's Notebook*. Transl. Michael Glenny. London: Collins & Harvill, 1975.

7. «Зойкина квартира». См. Булгаков-1, 193–252.
   7a. "Zoya's Apartment." See Bulgakov-1a, 95–108.

8. «Кабала святош». См. (его) *Пьесы*. Москва: Советский писатель, 1986, 187–236.
   8a. "A Cabal of Hypocrites." See Bulgakov-1a, 349–418.

9. «Мастер и Маргарита». См. Булгаков-3, 421–812.
   «Мастер и Маргарита». См. (его) *Собрание сочинений в пяти томах*, т. 5. Москва: «Художественная литература», 1989, 7–384. [consulted for punctuation]
   9a. *The Master and Margarita*. Transl. Mirra Ginsburg. New York: Grove Press, 1967.
   9b. *The Master and Margarita*. Transl. Michael Glenny. New York: Harper & Row, 1967.

10. «Роковые яйца». См. (его) *Дьяволиада: Рассказы*. Москва: Недра, 1925, 44–124.
   «Роковые яйца». См. (его) *Собрание сочинений в пяти томах*. Москва: «Художественная литература», 1989–1990, т. 2, 45–116. [consulted for punctuation]
   10a. "The Fatal Eggs." See ANTHOL-20, 53–133.
   10b. "The Fatal Eggs." Transl. Carl R. Proffer. In (his) *Diaboliad and Other Stories*. Bloomington: Indiana Univ. Press, 1972, 48–134.

11. *Собачье сердце*. Paris: YMCA-Press, 1969.
   «Собачье сердце». См. (его) *Собрание сочинений в пяти томах*. Москва: «Художественная литература», 1989–1990, т. 2, 119–208. [consulted for punctuation]
   11a. *Heart of a Dog*. Transl. Mirra Ginsburg. New York: Grove Press, 1968.
   11b. *The Heart of a Dog*. Transl. Michael Glenny. New York: Harcourt, Brace & World, 1968.

12. «Театральный роман». См. Булгаков-3, 271–420.
   «Записки покойника (театральный роман)». См. (его) *Собрание сочинений в пяти томах*. Москва: «Художе-

ственная литература», 1989–1990, т. 4, 401–542. [consulted for punctuation]

   12a. *Black Snow: A Theatrical Novel*. Transl. Michael Glenny. New York: Simon & Schuster, 1967.

БУНИН, ИВАН АЛЕКСЕЕВИЧ/BUNIN, IVAN (1870–1953)

1. *Темные аллеи*. Paris: La Presse Française et Étrangère, 1946.
   1a. *Dark Avenues, and Other Stories*. Transl. Richard Hare. Westport, Conn.: Hyperion Press, 1977 (Reprint. London: John Lehmann, 1949.)

ВАМПИЛОВ, АЛЕКСАНДР ВАЛЕНТИНОВИЧ/ VAMPILOV, ALEKSANDR (1937–1972)

1. «Провинциальные анекдоты». См. (его) *Прощание в июне: Пьесы*. Москва: Советский писатель, 1977, 225–282.
   1a. "Provincial Anecdotes." Transl. Kevin Windle. In (his) *Farewell in June: Four Russian Plays*. St. Lucia, Queensland: Univ. of Queensland Press, 1983, 219–273.
2. «Прошлым летом в Чулимске». См. Вампилов-1, 283–351.
   2a. "Last Summer in Chulimsk." Transl. Margaret Wettlin. See ANTHOL-17, 467–542.
   2b. *Last Summer in Chulimsk*. Transl. Alma H. Law. Arlington, Va.: Theatre Research Associates, 1979.
3. «Прощание в июне». См. Вампилов-1, 5–66.
   3a. "Farewell in June." Transl. Amanda Metcalf. See Vampilov-1a, 1–62.
   3b. *Farewell in June*. Transl. Alma H. Law. Arlington, Va.: Theatre Research Associates, 1980.
4. «Старший сын». См. Вампилов-1, 67–138.
   4a. "The Elder Son." Transl. Kevin Windle. See Vampilov-1a, 63–133.
   4b. *The Elder Son*. Transl. Alma H. Law. Arlington, Va.: Theatre Research Associates, 1980.
   4c. "The Elder Son." See ANTHOL-10, 282–355.
5. «Утиная охота». См. Вампилов-1, 139–224.
   5a. "Duck-Shooting." Transl. Kevin Windle. See Vampilov-1a, 135–217.
   5b. *Duck Hunting*. Transl. Alma H. Law. New York: Dramatists Play Service, 1980.

ВАХТИН, БОРИС БОРИСОВИЧ/VAKHTIN, BORIS (1930–1981)

1. «Дубленка». См. ANTHOL-4, 444–490.
   1a. "The Sheepskin Coat." Transl. George Saunders. See ANTHOL-16, 373–416.

ВЛАДИМИРОВ, ЛЕОНИД ВЛАДИМИРОВИЧ/ VLADIMIROV, LEONID (b. 1924)

1. *Советский космический блеф*. Frankfurt/Main: Posev, 1973.
   1a. *The Russian Space Bluff*. Transl. David Floyd. New York: Dial Press, 1973.

ВЛАДИМОВ, ГЕОРГИЙ НИКОЛАЕВИЧ/VLADI-MOV, GEORGII (b. 1931)

1. *Верный Руслан: История караульной собаки*. Frankfurt/Main: Posev, 1975.
   1a. *Faithful Ruslan: The Story of a Guard Dog*. Transl. Richard Adams. New York: Simon & Schuster, 1979.

ВОЙНОВИЧ, ВЛАДИМИР НИКОЛАЕВИЧ/VOINO-VICH, VLADIMIR (b. 1932)

1. *Антисоветский Советский Союз*. Ann Arbor: Ardis, 1985.
   1a. *The Anti-Soviet Soviet Union*. Transl. Richard Lourie. San Diego: Harcourt Brace Jovanovich, 1986.
2. *Жизнь и необычайные приключения солдата Ивана Чонкина*. Paris: YMCA-Press, 1976.

   2a. *The Life and Extraordinary Adventures of Private Ivan Chonkin*. Transl. Richard Lourie. New York: Bantam Books, 1979.
3. *Иванькиада*. Ann Arbor: Ardis, 1976.
   3a. *The Ivankiad*. Transl. David Lapeza. New York: Farrar, Straus & Giroux, 1977.
4. *Претендент на престол: Новые приключения солдата Ивана Чонкина*. Paris: YMCA-Press, 1979.
   4a. *Pretender to the Throne: The Further Adventures of Private Ivan Chonkin*. Transl. Richard Lourie. New York: Farrar, Straus & Giroux, 1979.
5. *Путем взаимной переписки*. Paris: YMCA-Press, 1979.
   5a. *In Plain Russian: Stories*. Transl. Richard Lourie. New York: Farrar, Straus & Giroux, 1979.
6. *Шапка*. London: Overseas Publications Interchange, 1988.
   6a. *The Fur Hat*. Transl. Susan Brownsberger. San Diego: Harcourt Brace Jovanovich, 1989.

ГЕРЦЕН, АЛЕКСАНДР ИВАНОВИЧ/HERZEN, ALEKSANDR (1812–1870)

1. *Былое и думы*, части 1–3. См. (его) *Былое и думы* [в двух томах]. Москва: Художественная литература, 1969, т. 1, 21–333.
   1a. *My Past and Thoughts*, parts 1–3. In (his) *My Past and Thoughts* [in four volumes]. Transl. Constance Garnett. Rev. by Humphrey Higgens. New York: Knopf, 1968, v. 1.
2. *Былое и думы*, части 4–5. См. Герцен-1, т. 1, 334–838.
   2a. *My Past and Thoughts*, parts 4–5. See Herzen-1a, v. 2.
3. *Былое и думы*, части 6–8. См. Герцен-1, т. 2, 7–414.
   3a. *My Past and Thoughts*, parts 6–8. See Herzen-1a, v. 3.

ГИНЗБУРГ, ЕВГЕНИЯ СЕМЕНОВНА/GINZBURG, EVGENIIA (1906–1977)

1. *Крутой маршрут*. Frankfurt/Main: Posev, 1967.
   1a. *Into the Whirlwind*. Transl. Paul Stevenson and Manya Harari. London: Collins & Harvill, 1967.
   1b. *Journey into the Whirlwind*. Transl. Paul Stevenson and Max Hayward. New York: Harcourt Brace Jovanovich, 1967.
2. *Крутой маршрут: Том второй*. Milano: Arnoldo Mondadori, 1979.
   2a. *Within the Whirlwind*. Transl. Ian Boland. London: Collins & Harvill, 1981.

ГЛАДКОВ, АЛЕКСАНДР КОНСТАНТИНОВИЧ/ GLADKOV, ALEKSANDR (1912–1976)

1. *Встречи с Пастернаком*. Paris: YMCA-Press, 1973.
   1a. *Meetings with Pasternak*. Transl. Max Hayward. London: Collins & Harvill, 1977.

ГОГОЛЬ, НИКОЛАЙ ВАСИЛЬЕВИЧ/GOGOL, NIKO-LAI (1809–1852)

1. «Женитьба». См. (его) *Собрание художественных произведений в пяти томах*. Изд. 2. Москва: Изд-во Академии наук СССР, 1960–1961, т. 4, 213–287.
   1a. *Marriage*. Transl. Bella Costello. Manchester: Manchester Univ. Press; New York: Barnes & Noble, 1969.
   1b. "Marriage." In (his) *The Theater of Nikolay Gogol: Plays and Selected Writings*. Transl. Milton Ehre and Fruma Gottschalk. Chicago: Univ. of Chicago Press, 1980, 1–50.
   1c. "Marriage." In (his) *The Collected Tales and Plays of Nikolai Gogol*. Transl. Constance Garnett. Rev. by Leonard J. Kent. New York: Pantheon Books, 1964, 676–724.
2. «Игроки» См. Гоголь-1, т. 4, 291–339.
   2a. "The Gamblers." See Gogol-1b, 131–164.
   2b. "The Gamblers." See Gogol-1c, 726–759.
3. *Мертвые души*. См. Гоголь-1, т. 5.
   3a. *Dead Souls*. Transl. David Magarshack. Baltimore: Penguin Books, 1969.

3b. *Dead Souls*. Transl. Bernard Guilbert Guerney. New York: Modern Library, 1965.

3c. *Dead Souls*. Transl. Helen Michailoff. New York: Washington Square Press, 1964.

3d. *Dead Souls*. Transl. George Reavey. New York: W.W. Norton, 1971.

3e. *Dead Souls*. Transl. Andrew R. MacAndrew. New York: New American Library, 1961.

4. «Ревизор» См. Гоголь-1, т. 4, 5–122.

4a. "The Inspector General." See ANTHOL-6, 231–314.

4b. "The Inspector." See ANTHOL-11, 215–318.

4c. "The Government Inspector." See ANTHOL-21, 1–84.

4d. "The Inspector." Transl. John Laurence Seymour and George Rapall Noyes. See ANTHOL-14, 157–232.

4e. *The Government Inspector*. Transl. Edward O. Marsh and Jeremy Brooks. London: Methuen, 1968.

4f. "The Government Inspector." See Gogol-1b, 51–130.

5. «Вечера на хуторе близ Диканьки». См. Гоголь-1, т. 1, 9–303.

5a. "Evenings on a Farm near Dikanka." See Gogol-1c, 3–206.

ГОНЧАРОВ, ИВАН АЛЕКСАНДРОВИЧ/GONCHAROV, IVAN (1812–1891)

1. *Обломов*. См. (его) *Собрание сочинений в восьми томах*. Москва: Гос. изд-во художественной литературы, 1953–1955, т. 4.

1a. *Oblomov*. Transl. David Magarshack. Baltimore: Penguin Books, 1978, c1954.

1b. *Oblomov*. Transl. Ann Dunnigan. New York: New American Library, 1963.

ГОРЕНШТЕЙН, ФРИДРИХ НАУМОВИЧ/GORENSHTEIN, FRIDRIKH (b. 1932)

1. «Ступени». См. ANTHOL-4, 215–313.

1a. "Steps." Transl. Barry Rubin and Vladimir Lunis. See ANTHOL-16, 176–261.

ГОРЬКИЙ, МАКСИМ/GORKY, MAKSIM [Pseud. of PESHKOV, ALEKSEI MAKSIMOVICH (1868–1936)]

1. «Враги». См. (его) *Полное собрание сочинений: Художественные произведения в двадцати пяти томах*. Москва: Наука, 1968–1976, т. 7, 485–562.

1a. "Enemies." In (his) *The Lower Depths and Other Plays*. Transl. Alexander Bakshy in collab. with Paul S. Nathan. New Haven: Yale Univ. Press, 1945, 75–150.

1b. *Enemies*. Transl. by Kitty Hunter-Blair and Jeremy Brooks. London: Eyre Methuen, 1972.

1c. "Enemies." In (his) *Five Plays*. Transl. Margaret Wettlin. Moscow: Progress Publishers, [1957?], 301–381.

2. «Егор Булычов и другие». См. Горький-1, т. 19, 5–60.

2a. "Yegor Bulichov and Others." Transl. Margaret Wettlin. See ANTHOL-7, 27–86.

2b. "Yegor Bulychov and Others." Transl. Anthony Wixley. See ANTHOL-12, 1–79.

3. «На дне». См. Горький-1, 107–182.

3a. "The Lower Depths." See ANTHOL-23, 83–162.

3b. "The Lower Depths." See Gorky-1a, 1–74.

3c. *The Lower Depths*. Transl. Kitty Hunter-Blair and Jeremy Brooks. London: Eyre Methuen, 1973.

3d. "The Lower Depths." See Gorky-1c, 107–185.

3e. "The Lower Depths." See ANTHOL-21, 283–362.

3f. "Down and Out." Transl. George Rapall Noyes and Alexander Kaun. See ANTHOL-15, 625–689.

ГРЕКОВА, И./GREKOVA, I. [Pseud. of VENTTSEL, ELENA SERGEEVNA (b. 1907)]

1. «Дамский мастер». См. (ее) *Под фонарем*. Москва: Советская Россия, 1966, 65–117.

1a. "The Lady's Hairdresser." Transl. Larry Gregg. *Russian Literature Triquarterly*, No. 5 (Winter 1973), 223–264.

1b. "Ladies' Hairdresser." Transl. Michel Petrov. In (her) *Russian Women: Two Stories*. San Diego: Harcourt Brace Jovanovich, 1983, 1–61.

2. «За проходной». *Новый мир*, 1962, 7, 110–131.

2a. "Beyond the Gates." Transl. Eve Manning. See ANTHOL-22, 61–104.

3. «Хозяйка гостиницы». См. (ее) *Кафедра: Повести*. Москва: Советский писатель, 1983, 237–413.

3a. "The Hotel Manager." Transl. Michel Petrov. See Grekova-1b, 63–304.

ГРОССМАН, ВАСИЛИЙ СЕМЕНОВИЧ/GROSSMAN, VASILII (1905–1964)

1. *Все течет...* Frankfurt/Main: Posev, 1970.

1a. *Forever Flowing*. Transl. Thomas P. Whitney. New York: Harper & Row, 1972.

2. *Жизнь и судьба: Роман*. Lausanne: L'Age d'Homme, 1980.

2a. *Life and Fate: A Novel*. Transl. Robert Chandler. London: Collins & Harvill, 1985.

ДОВЛАТОВ, СЕРГЕЙ ДОНАТОВИЧ/DOVLATOV, SERGEI (1941–1990)

1. *Невидимая книга*. Ann Arbor: Ardis, 1977.

1a. *The Invisible Book*. Transl. Katherine O'Connor and Diana L. Burgin. Ann Arbor: Ardis, 1979.

ДОМБРОВСКИЙ, ЮРИЙ ОСИПОВИЧ/DOMBROVSKII, IURII (1909–1978)

1. *Хранитель древностей*. Москва: Советская Россия, 1966.

1a. *The Keeper of Antiquities*. Transl. M. Glenny. New York: McGraw-Hill, 1969.

ДОСТОЕВСКИЙ, ФЕДОР МИХАЙЛОВИЧ/DOSTOYEVSKY, FYODOR (1821–1881)

1. *Братья Карамазовы*, кн. 1–10. См. (его) *Полное собрание сочинений в тридцати томах*. Ленинград: Изд-во «Наука», 1972–1990, т. 14.

1a. *The Brothers Karamazov: A Novel in Four Parts with Epilogue*. Transl. Richard Pevear and Larissa Volokhonsky. San Francisco: North Point Press, 1990, bks. 1–10, 7–562.

2. *Братья Карамазовы*, кн. 11–12, эпилог. См. Достоевский-1, т. 15.

2a. *The Brothers Karamazov*, bks. 11–12, Epilogue. See Dostoyevsky-1a, 563–776.

3. *Преступление и наказание*. См. Достоевский-1, т. 6.

3a. *Crime and Punishment*. Transl. Michael Scammell. New York: Washington Square Press, 1976, c1972.

3b. *Crime and Punishment*. Transl. Sidney Monas. New York: New American Library, 1968.

3c. *Crime and Punishment*. Transl. Richard Pevear and Larissa Volokhonsky. New York: Knopf, 1992.

3d. *Crime and Punishment*. Transl. David McDuff. Harmondsworth, Middlesex [England]: Penguin Books, 1991.

ДУДИНЦЕВ, ВЛАДИМИР ДМИТРИЕВИЧ/DUDINTSEV, VLADIMIR (b. 1918)

1. *Не хлебом единым*. Москва: Художественная литература, 1968.

1a. *Not by Bread Alone*. Transl. Edith Bone. New York: Dutton, 1957.

ЕВТУШЕНКО, ЕВГЕНИЙ АЛЕКСАНДРОВИЧ/YEVTUSHENKO, YEVGENY (b. 1933)

1. «Ардабиола». *Юность*, 1981, 3, 11–37.

1a. *Ardabiola*. Transl. Armorer Wason. New York: St. Martin's Press, 1984.

2. *Ягодные места*. Москва: Советский писатель, 1982.
   2a. *Wild Berries*. Transl. Antonina W. Bouis. New York: William Morrow, 1984.

ЕРОФЕЕВ, ВЕНЕДИКТ ВАСИЛЬЕВИЧ/EROFEEV, VENEDIKT (b. 1933)

1. *Москва-Петушки*. 2e éd. Paris: YMCA-Press, 1981.
   1a. *Moscow to the End of the Line*. Transl. H. W. Tjalsma. New York: Taplinger, 1980.

ЕРОФЕЕВ, ВИКТОР ВЛАДИМИРОВИЧ/EROFEEV, VIKTOR (b. 1947)

2. «Приспущенный оргазм столетья». См. ANTHOL-4, 543–552.
   2a. "A Fin de Siecle Orgasm." Transl. Martin Horwitz. See ANTHOL-16, 457–465.
3. «Трехглавое детище». См. ANTHOL-4, 552–614.
   3a. "A Creation in Three Chapters." Transl. Martin Horwitz. See ANTHOL-16, 471–526.
4. «Ядрена Феня». См. ANTHOL-4, 537–543.
   4a. "Humping Hannah." Transl. Martin Horwitz. See ANTHOL-16, 465–471.

ЗАЛЫГИН, СЕРГЕЙ ПАВЛОВИЧ/ZALYGIN, SERGEI (b. 1913)

1. «Южноамериканский вариант». См. (его) *Собрание сочинений в четырех томах*. Москва: Молодая гвардия, 1979–1980, т. 3, 5–220.
   1a. *The South American Variant*. Transl. Kevin Windle. St. Lucia, Queensland: Univ. of Queensland Press, 1979.

ЗАМЯТИН, ЕВГЕНИЙ ИВАНОВИЧ/ZAMIATIN, EVGENII (1884–1937)

1. *Мы*. New York: Inter-Language Literary Associates, 1973.
   1a. *We*. Transl. Mirra Ginsburg. New York: Viking Press, 1972.
   1b. *We*. Transl. Gregory Zilboorg. New York: Dutton, 1952.

ЗИНОВЬЕВ, АЛЕКСАНДР АЛЕКСАНДРОВИЧ/ ZINOVIEV, ALEKSANDR (b. 1922)

1. *Зияющие высоты*. Lausanne: L'Age d'Homme, 1976.
   1a. *The Yawning Heights*. Transl. Gordon Clough. New York: Random House, 1978.
2. *Светлое будущее*. Lausanne: L'Age d'Homme, 1978.
   2a. *The Radiant Future*. Transl. Gordon Clough. New York: Random House, 1980.

ИВИНСКАЯ, ОЛЬГА ВСЕВОЛОДОВНА/IVINSKAIA, OLGA (b. 1913)

1. *В плену времени: Годы с Борисом Пастернаком*. Paris: Fayard, 1978.
   1a. *A Captive of Time*. Transl. Max Hayward. Garden City, N.Y.: Doubleday, 1978.

ИЛЬФ, ИЛЬЯ/ILF, ILIA [Pseud. of FAINZILBERG, ILIA ARNOLDOVICH (1897–1937)] и ПЕТРОВ, ЕВГЕНИЙ/ PETROV, EVGENII [Pseud. of KATAEV, EVGENII PETROVICH (1903–1942)]

1. «Двенадцать стульев». См. (их) *Собрание сочинений в пяти томах*. Москва: Гос. изд-во художественной литературы, 1961, т. 1, 5–382.
   1a. "The Twelve Chairs." In (their) *The Complete Adventures of Ostap Bender*. Transl. John H.C. Richardson. New York: Random House, 1962.
2. «Золотой теленок». См. Ильф и Петров-1, т. 2, 5–386.
   2a. "The Golden Calf." See Ilf and Petrov-1a.
   2b. *The Little Golden Calf*. Transl. Charles Malamuth. New York: Holt Rinehart & Winston, 1961.

ИОФФЕ, МАРИЯ МИХАЙЛОВНА/JOFFE, MARIA (b. 1900)

1. *Одна ночь: Повесть о правде*. Нью-Йорк: Хроника, 1978.
   1a. *One Long Night: A Tale of Truth*. Transl. Vera Dixon. Clapham [England]: New Park Publications, 1978.

ИСКАНДЕР, ФАЗИЛЬ АБДУЛОВИЧ/ISKANDER, FAZIL (b. 1929)

1. «Возмездие». См. ANTHOL-4, 425–443.
   1a. "Vengeance." Transl. Carl R. Proffer. See ANTHOL-16, 358–373.
2. ffiMalenhkij gigant bolhßogo seksaffl. Sm. ANTHOL-4, 381–425.
   2a. "A Sexy Little Giant." Transl. Carl R. Proffer. See ANTHOL-16, 322–358.
3. *Сандро из Чегема*. Ann Arbor: Ardis, 1979, chapters 1–11. *Сандро из Чегема: Роман*, кн. 1–3. Москва: Московский рабочий, 1989. [consulted for punctuation]
   3a. *Sandro of Chegem*. Transl. Susan Brownsberger. New York: Vintage, 1983.
4. *Сандро из Чегема*. Ann Arbor: Ardis, 1979, chapters 12–16.
   4a. *The Gospel According to Chegem: Being the Further Adventures of Sandro of Chegem*. Transl. Susan Brownsberger. New York: Vintage, 1984, 3–66, 179–224, 262–300, 364–398.
5. *Сандро из Чегема: Новые главы*. Ann Arbor: Ardis, 1981. «Джамхух-Сын Оленя». *Юность*, 1982, 3, 36–51; 4, 41–57.
   5a. *The Gospel According to Chegem: Being the Further Adventures of Sandro of Chegem*. See Iskander-4a, 67–178, 225–261, 301–363.
6. «Созвездие Козлотура». См. (его) *Время счастливых находок*. Москва: Молодая гвардия, 1973, 308–430.
   6a. *The Goatibex Constellation*. Transl. Helen Burlingame. Ann Arbor: Ardis, 1982.

КАВЕРИН, ВЕНИАМИН АЛЕКСАНДРОВИЧ/ KAVERIN, VENIAMIN (1902–1989)

1. *Открытая книга*. Москва: Молодая гвардия, 1953.
   1a. *Open Book*. Transl. Brian Pearce. London: Lawrence & Wishart, 1955.
2. *Художник неизвестен*. Ленинград: Изд-во писателей в Ленинграде, 1931.
   2a. *The Unknown Artist*. Transl. P. Ross. Westport, Conn.: Hyperion Press, 1973. (Reprint. London: John Westhouse, 1947.)

КАЗАКОВ, ЮРИЙ ПАВЛОВИЧ/KAZAKOV, IURII (1927–1982)

1. «Адам и Ева». См. (его) *Двое в декабре*. Москва: Молодая гвардия, 1966, 62–86.
   1a. "Adam and Eve." Transl. Manya Harari. See ANTHOL-13, 92–120.
2. «Голубое и зеленое». См. Казаков-1, 163–189.
   2a. "The Blue and the Green." Transl. Gabriella Azrael. See ANTHOL-22, 170–204.

КАТАЕВ, ВАЛЕНТИН ПЕТРОВИЧ/KATAEV, VALENTIN (1897–1986)

1. «Время, вперед!» См. (его) *Собрание сочинений в пяти томах*. Москва: Гос. изд-во художественной литературы, 1956–1957, т. 1, 197–520.
   1a. *Time, Forward!* Transl. Charles Malamuth. Bloomington: Indiana Univ. Press, 1976.
2. «Святой колодец». См. (его) *Святой колодец. Трава забвенья*. Москва: Советский писатель, 1969, 5–120.

2a. *The Holy Well*. Transl. Max Hayward and Harold Shukman. New York: Walker, 1967.

3. «Трава забвенья». См. Катаев-2, 121–343.
    3a. *The Grass of Oblivion*. Transl. Robert Daglish. London: Macmillan, 1969.

КОЖЕВНИКОВ, ПЕТР АЛЕКСЕЕВИЧ/KOZHEVNIKOV, PYOTR (b. 1953)

1. «Две тетради». См. ANTHOL-4, 49–88.
    1a. "Two Diaries." Transl. Ellendea Proffer. See ANTHOL-16, 30–63.

КОПЕЛЕВ, ЛЕВ ЗИНОВЬЕВИЧ/KOPELEV, LEV (b. 1912)

1. *Утоли мои печали*. Ann Arbor: Ardis, 1981.
    1a. *Ease My Sorrows: A Memoir*. Transl. Antonina W. Bouis. New York: Random House, 1983.

КОРОТЮКОВ, АЛЕКСЕЙ КОНСТАНТИНОВИЧ/KOROTIUKOV, ALEKSEI (b. 1932)

1. *Нелегко быть русским шпионом*. Ann Arbor: Эрмитаж, 1982.
    1a. *It's Hard to Be a Russian Spy*. Transl. Joseph Kiegel. New York: Pocket Books, 1985.

КУЗНЕЦОВ, АНАТОЛИЙ ВАСИЛЬЕВИЧ/KUZNETSOV, ANATOLII (1929–1979)

1. *Бабий Яр: Роман-документ*. Москва: Молодая гвардия, 1967.
    1a. *Babi Yar: A Documentary Novel*. Transl. Jacob Guralsky. New York: Dial Press, 1967.
    1b. *Babi Yar: A Document in the Form of a Novel*. Transl. David Floyd. New York: Farrar, Straus & Giroux, 1970.

ЛЕРМОНТОВ, МИХАИЛ ЮРЬЕВИЧ/LERMONTOV, MIKHAIL (1814–1841)

1. «Герой нашего времени». См. (его) *Собрание сочинений в четырех томах*. Ленинград: Изд-во Академии наук СССР, 1958–1959, т. 4, 275–474.
    1a. *A Hero of Our Time*. Transl. Vladimir Nabokov in collab. with Dmitri Nabokov. Garden City, N.Y.: Doubleday, 1958.
    1b. *A Hero of Our Time*. Transl. Martin Parker. Moscow: Raduga Publishers, 1985.
    1c. *A Hero of Our Time*. Transl. Paul Foote. Baltimore: Penguin Books, 1966.
    1d. *A Hero of Our Time*. Transl. Philip Longworth. New York: New American Library, 1964.
    1e. *A Hero of Our Time*. Transl. Reginald Merton. London: Folio Society, 1980.

ЛИВШИЦ, БЕНЕДИКТ КОНСТАНТИНОВИЧ/LIVSHITS, BENEDIKT (1886–1939)

1. *Полутораглазый стрелец*. Нью-Йорк: Изд-во им. Чехова, 1978.
    1a. *The One and a Half-Eyed Archer*. Transl. John E. Bowlt. Newtonville, Mass.: Oriental Research Partners, 1977.

ЛИМОНОВ, ЭДУАРД/LIMONOV, EDUARD [Pseud. of SAVENKO, EDUARD VENIAMINOVICH (b. 1941)]

1. *Это я – Эдичка*. 2-е изд. New York: Index Publishers, 1982.
    1a. *It's Me, Eddie: A Fictional Memoir*. Transl. S.L. Campbell. New York: Random House, 1983.

МАКСИМОВ, ВЛАДИМИР ЕМЕЛЬЯНОВИЧ/MAKSIMOV, VLADIMIR (b. 1932)

1. *Ковчег для незваных*. Frankfurt/Main: Posev, 1979.
    1a. *Ark for the Uncalled*. Transl. Julian Graffy. London: Quartet Books, 1984.

2. *Прощание из ниоткуда*. См. (его) *Собрание сочинений*. Frankfurt/Main: Posev, 1973–1979, т. 4.

2a. *Farewell from Nowhere*. Transl. Michael Glenny. London: Collins & Harvill, 1978.

3. *Семь дней творения*. См. Максимов-2, т. 2.
    3a. *The Seven Days of Creation*. [Transl. not indicated] New York: Knopf, 1975.

МАНДЕЛЬШТАМ, НАДЕЖДА ЯКОВЛЕВНА/MANDELSHTAM, NADEZHDA (1899–1980)

1. *Воспоминания*. Нью-Йорк: Изд-во им. Чехова, 1970.
    1a. *Hope Against Hope: A Memoir*. Transl. Max Hayward. New York: Atheneum, 1970.

2. *Вторая книга*. Paris: YMCA-Press, 1972.
    2a. *Hope Abandoned*. Transl. Max Hayward. New York: Atheneum, 1974.

МАРЧЕНКО, АНАТОЛИЙ ТИХОНОВИЧ/MARCHENKO, ANATOLII (1938–1986)

1. *Мои показания*. Frankfurt/Main: Posev, 1973.
    1a. *My Testimony*. Transl. Michael Scammell. New York: Dutton, 1969.

2. *От Тарусы до Чуны*. Нью-Йорк: Хроника, 1976.
    2a. *From Tarusa to Siberia*. Ed. and Introd. Joshua Rubinstein. Royal Oak, Mich.: Strathcona, 1980.

МАЯКОВСКИЙ, ВЛАДИМИР ВЛАДИМИРОВИЧ/MAYAKOVSKY, VLADIMIR (1893–1930)

1. «Клоп». См. (его) *Полное собрание сочинений в тринадцати томах*. Москва: Гос. изд-во художественной литературы, 1955–1961, т. 11, 215–274.
    1a. "The Bedbug." Transl. Max Hayward. In (his) *The Bedbug and Selected Poetry*. New York: Meridian Books, 1960, 239–303.
    1b. "The Bedbug." See ANTHOL-23, 335–379.
    1c. "The Bedbug." In (his) *The Complete Plays of Vladimir Mayakovsky*. Transl. Guy Daniels. New York: Washington Square Press, 1968, 141–196.

МИХАЙЛОВСКАЯ, КИРА НИКОЛАЕВНА/MIKHAILOVSKAIA, KIRA (b. 1935)

1. *Переводчица из «Интуриста»*. Москва: Советский писатель, 1964.
    1a. *My Name is Asya*. Transl. Catherine A. Burland. New York: McGraw-Hill, 1966.

НАБОКОВ, ВЛАДИМИР ВЛАДИМИРОВИЧ/NABOKOV, VLADIMIR (1899–1977)

1. *Дар*. Нью-Йорк: Изд-во им. Чехова, 1952.
    1a. *The Gift*. Transl. Michael Scammell with the collaboration of the author. New York: Putnam, 1963.

НЕКРАСОВ, ВИКТОР ПЛАТОНОВИЧ/NEKRASOV, VIKTOR (1911–1987)

1. *Кира Георгиевна*. Cambridge: Cambridge Univ. Press, 1967.
    1a. *Kira Georgievna*. Transl. Walter N. Vickery. New York: Pantheon Books, 1962.

ОБУХОВА, ЛИДИЯ АЛЕКСЕЕВНА/OBUKHOVA, LIDIIA (b. 1924)

1. *Лилит: Фантастические повести*. Москва: Знание, 1966.
    1a. *Daughter of the Night: A Tale of Three Worlds*. Transl. Mirra Ginsburg. New York: Macmillan, 1974.

ОКУДЖАВА, БУЛАТ ШАЛВОВИЧ/OKUDZHAVA, BULAT (b. 1924)

1. «Будь здоров, школяр». См. ANTHOL-5, 50–75.
    1a. "Goodluck, Schoolboy!" Transl. John Richardson. See ANTHOL-13, 149–181.

2. *Путешествие дилетантов: Из записок отставного поручика Амирана Амилахвари*. Москва: Советский писатель, 1980.
   2a. *Nocturne: From the Notes of Lieutenant Amiran Amilakhvari, Retired*. Transl. Antonina W. Bouis. New York: Harper & Row, 1978.

ОЛЕША, ЮРИЙ КАРЛОВИЧ/OLESHA, IURII (1899–1960)

1. «Вишневая косточка». См. (его) *Рассказы. Избранные сочинения*. Москва: Гос. изд-во художественной литературы, 1956, 261–269.
   1a. "The Cherry Stone." In (his) *Envy and Other Works*. Transl. A.R. MacAndrew. Garden City, N.Y.: Doubleday, 1967, 147–157.
2. «Зависть». См. Олеша-1, 23–128.
   2a. "Envy." See Olesha-1a, 1–121.
3. *Ни дня без строчки*. Москва: Советская Россия, 1965.
   3a. *No Day Without a Line*. Transl. Judson Rosengrant. Ann Arbor: Ardis, 1979.
4. «Цепь». См. Олеша-1, 254–260.
   4a. "The Chain." See Olesha-1a, 123–130.
5. «Человеческий материал». См. Олеша-1, 249–253.
   5a. "Human Material." See Olesha-1a, 195–200.
6. «Заговор чувств». См. (его) *Пьесы. Статьи о театре и драматургии*. Москва: Искусство, 1968, 13–89.
   6a. "The Conspiracy of Feelings." In (his) *The Complete Plays*. Ed. and transl. Michael Green and Gerome Katsell. Ann Arbor: Ardis, 1983, 13–66.
7. «Три толстяка: Пьеса в четырех действиях». См. Олеша-6, 171–253.
   7a. "The Three Fat Men: A Play in Four Acts." See Olesha-6a, 127–183.

ОРЛОВА, РАИСА ДАВЫДОВНА/ORLOVA, RAISA (1918–1989)

1. *Воспоминания о непрошедшем времени: Москва, 1961–1981 гг*. Ann Arbor: Ardis, 1983.
   1a. *Memoirs*. Transl. Samuel Cioran. New York: Random House, 1983.

ОСТРОВСКИЙ, АЛЕКСАНДР НИКОЛАЕВИЧ/ OSTROVSKY, ALEKSANDR (1823–1886)

1. «Бедная невеста». См. (его) *Полное собрание сочинений в двенадцати томах*. Москва: Искусство, 1973–1980, т. 1, 192–279.
   1a. "The Poor Bride." In (his) *Five Plays of Alexander Ostrovsky*. Transl. Eugene K. Bristow. New York: Pegasus, 1969, 109–202.
   1b. "The Poor Bride." Transl. John Laurence Seymour and George Rapall Noyes. See ANTHOL-14, 329–406.
2. «Бедность не порок». См. Островский-1, т. 1, 328–378.
   2a. "Poverty is No Crime." In (his) *Plays by Alexander Ostrovsky*. Transl. George Rapall Noyes. New York: Scribner, 1917, 65–133.
   2b. "Poverty is No Crime." In (his) *Plays*. Transl. Margaret Wettlin. Moscow: Progress, 1974, 80–157.
3. «Без вины виноватые». См. Островский-1, т. 5, 353–424.
   3a. "More Sinned Against Than Sinning." See Ostrovsky-2b, 369–473.
4. «Бешеные деньги». См. Островский-1, т. 3, 165–248.
   4a. "Fairy Gold." Transl. Camilla Chaplin Daniels and George Rapall Noyes. *Poet Lore*, v. 40, no. 1, 1929, 1–80.
   4b. "Easy Money." In (his) *Easy Money and Two Other Plays*. Transl. David Magarshack. Westport, Conn.: Greenwood Press, 1970, 95–186. (Reprint. London: Allen & Unwin, 1944.)
5. «Волки и овцы». См. Островский-1, т. 4, 113–207.
   5a. "Wolves and Sheep". Transl. Inez Sachs Colby and George Rapall Noyes. *Poet Lore*, v. 37, no. 2, 1926, 159–253.
   5b. "Wolves and Sheep." See Ostrovsky-4b, 187–289.
6. «Гроза». См. Островский-1, т. 2, 209–266.
   6a. "The Storm." See ANTHOL-6, 315–374.
   6b. "The Storm." See Ostrovsky-2b, 158–251.
   6c. "The Storm." See ANTHOL-21, 85–153.
   6d. "Thunder." See ANTHOL-11, 319–394.
   6e. "The Thunderstorm." Transl. F. White and George Rapall Noyes. See ANTHOL-24, 608–641.
   6f. "The Storm." See Ostrovsky-1a, 203–276.
   6g. *The Storm*. Transl. Constance Garnett. Boston: J.W. Luce, 1907.
7. «Лес». См. Островский-1, т. 3, 249–338.
   7a. *The Forest: Comedy in Five Acts*. Transl. Clara Vostrovsky Winlow and George Rapall Noyes. New York: French, 1926.
   7b. "The Forest." See Ostrovsky-1a, 357–459.
   7c. *The Forest*. Transl. Tom Cole (for Milwaukee Repertory Theater) Pre-rehearsal text. [s.l.: s.n.] 1983.
8. «На бойком месте». См. Островский-1, т. 2, 543–588.
   8a. "At the Jolly Spot." Transl. Jane Paxton Campbell and George Rapall Noyes. *Poet Lore*, v. 36, no. 1, 1925, 1–44.
9. «На всякого мудреца довольно простоты». См. Островский-1, т. 3, 7–79.
   9a. "Even a Wise Man Stumbles." See Ostrovsky-4b, 13–93.
   9b. "Even the Wise Can Err." See Ostrovsky-2b, 252–367.
   9c. "The Scoundrel." See Ostrovsky-1a, 277–356.
10. «Свои люди – сочтемся». См. Островский-1, т. 1, 85–152.
   10a. "It's a Family Affair–We'll Settle It Ourselves." Transl. Eugene K. Bristow. See Ostrovsky-1a, 29–108.
   10b. "It's a Family Affair–We'll Settle It Ourselves." See Ostrovsky-2a, 213–305.
11. «Таланты и поклонники». См. Островский-1, т. 5, 210–280.
   11a. *Artistes and Admirers*. Transl. Elisabeth Hanson. Manchester: Manchester Univ. Press; New York: Barnes & Noble, 1970.

ПАНОВА, ВЕРА ФЕДОРОВНА/PANOVA, VERA (1905–1973)

1. «Сколько лет, сколько зим!» *Новый мир*, 1966, 7, 3–38.
   1a. "It's Been Ages!" See ANTHOL-8, 207–259.

ПАСТЕРНАК, БОРИС ЛЕОНИДОВИЧ/PASTERNAK, BORIS (1890–1960)

1. *Доктор Живаго*. Ann Arbor: Univ. of Michigan Press, 1959.
   1a. *Doctor Zhivago*. Transl. Max Hayward and Manya Harari. New York: Pantheon, 1958.

ПАУСТОВСКИЙ, КОНСТАНТИН ГЕОРГИЕВИЧ/ PAUSTOVSKY, KONSTANTIN (1892–1968)

1. *Повесть о жизни*. См. (его) *Собрание сочинений в шести томах*. Москва: Гос. изд-во художественной литературы, 1957–1958, т. 3.
   1a. *Story of a Life*. Transl. Manya Harari and Michael Duncan. London: Harvill Press, 1964.
   1b. *The Story of a Life*. Transl. Joseph Barnes. New York: Pantheon Books, 1964.

ПИЛЬНЯК, БОРИС/PILNIAK, BORIS [Pseud. of VOGAU, BORIS ANDREEVICH (1894–1937?)]

1. «Голый год». См. (его) *Избранные произведения*. Москва: Художественная литература, 1976, 29–184.
   1a. *The Naked Year*. Transl. Alexander R. Tulloch. Ann Arbor: Ardis, 1975.

ПИСЕМСКИЙ, АЛЕКСЕЙ ФЕОФИЛАКТОВИЧ/PISEMSKII, ALEKSEI (1820–1881)

1. «Горькая судьбина». См. (его) *Собрание сочинений в девяти томах*. Москва: Изд-во «Правда», 1959, т. 9, 179–233.
   1a. "A Bitter Fate." Transl. Alice Kagan and George Rapall Noyes. See ANTHOL-14, 407–456.

ПЛАТОНОВ, АНДРЕЙ ПЛАТОНОВИЧ/PLATONOV, ANDREI (1899–1951)

1. *Котлован*. Ann Arbor: Ardis, 1973.
   1a. *The Foundation Pit*. Transl. Mirra Ginsburg. New York: Dutton, 1975.
   1b. *The Foundation Pit*. Transl. Thomas P. Whitney. Bilingual ed. Ann Arbor: Ardis, 1973.

ПОГОДИН, НИКОЛАЙ ФЕДОРОВИЧ/POGODIN, NIKOLAI (1900–1962)

1. «Сонет Петрарки». См. ANTHOL-3, 300–351.
   1a. "A Petrarchan Sonnet." See ANTHOL-8, 81–138.

ПОПОВ, ЕВГЕНИЙ АНАТОЛЬЕВИЧ/POPOV, EVGENII (b. 1946)

1. «Чертова дюжина рассказов». См. ANTHOL-4, 113–188.
   1a. "A Baker's Dozen of Stories." Transl. George Saunders. See ANTHOL-16, 85–153.

ПУШКИН, АЛЕКСАНДР СЕРГЕЕВИЧ/PUSHKIN, ALEKSANDR (1799–1837)

1. «Дубровский». См. (его) *Собрание сочинений в десяти томах*. Москва: Гос. изд-во художественной литературы, 1959–1962, т. 5, 148–232.
   1a. "Dubrovskii." In (his) *Alexander Pushkin: Complete Prose Fiction*. Transl. Paul Debreczeny. Stanford, Calif.: Stanford Univ. Press, 1983, 145–210.
   1b. "Dubrovsky." In (his) *The Complete Prose Tales of Alexander Sergeyevich Pushkin*. Transl. Gillon R. Aitken. New York: Norton, 1966, 179–271.
2. «Капитанская дочка». См. Пушкин-1, т. 5, 555–563.
   2a. "The Captain's Daughter." See Pushkin-1a, 266–357.
   2b. "The Captain's Daughter." See Pushkin-1b, 335–475.
3. «Повести покойного Ивана Петровича Белкина». См. Пушкин-1, т. 5, 45–118.
   3a. "The Tales of the Late Ivan Petrovich Belkin." See Pushkin-1a, 62–119.
   3b. "The Tales of the Late Ivan Petrovitch Belkin." See Pushkin-1b, 61–140.

РАСПУТИН, ВАЛЕНТИН ГРИГОРЬЕВИЧ/RASPUTIN, VALENTIN (b. 1937)

1. «Деньги для Марии». См. (его) *Повести*. Изд. 2-е. Москва: Молодая гвардия, 1978, 557–653.
   1a. "Money for Maria." Transl. Margaret Wettlin. See (his) *Money for Maria and Borrowed Time*. London: Quartet Books, 1981, 1–142.
2. «Живи и помни». См. Распутин-1, 197–393.
   2a. *Live and Remember*. Transl. Antonina W. Bouis. New York: Macmillan, 1978.
3. «Последний срок». См. Распутин-1, 395–555.
   3a. "Borrowed Time." Transl. Kevin Windle. See Rasputin-1a, 143–374.
4. «Прощание с Матерой». См. Распутин-1, 13–195.
   4a. *Farewell to Matyora*. Transl. Antonina W. Bouis. New York: Macmillan, 1979.

РОЗОВ, ВИКТОР СЕРГЕЕВИЧ/ROZOV, VIKTOR (b. 1913)

1. «В добрый час!» См. ANTHOL-1, 267–346.
   1a. "The Young Graduates." See ANTHOL-18, 203–313.
2. «В поисках радости». См. (его) *В добрый час: Пьесы*. Москва: Советский писатель, 1973, 137–208.
   2a. "In Search of Happiness." Transl. Robert Daglish. See ANTHOL-7, 705–788.
3. «Вечно живые». См. ANTHOL-2, 626–680.
   3a. "Alive Forever." See ANTHOL-8, 19–80.
4. «С вечера до полудня». См. Розов-2, 401–458.
   4a. "From Night Till Noon." Transl. Robert Daglish. See ANTHOL-17, 305–376.

РОЩИН, МИХАИЛ МИХАЙЛОВИЧ/ROSHCHIN, MIKHAIL (b. 1933)

1. «Валентин и Валентина». См. (его) *Пьесы*. Москва: Искусство, 1980, 203–280.
   1a. *Valentin and Valentina*. Transl. Irene Arn Vacchina and Edward Hastings. Chicago: Dramatic Publishing Company, 1978.
   1b. "Valentin and Valentina." Transl. Alex Miller. See ANTHOL-17, 377–466.
2. «Старый новый год». См. Рощин-1, 63–140.
   2a. *The Old New Year*. Transl. Alma H. Law. Arlington, Va.: Theatre Research Associates, 1979.

РЫБАКОВ, АНАТОЛИЙ НАУМОВИЧ/RYBAKOV, ANATOLII (b. 1911)

1. *Тяжелый песок*. Москва: Советский писатель, 1979.
   1a. *Heavy Sand*. Transl. Harold Shukman. New York: Viking Press, 1981.
2. *Дети Арбата*. Москва: Советский писатель, 1987.
   2a. *Children of the Arbat*. Transl. Harold Shukman. Boston: Little, Brown, 1988.

САЛТЫКОВ-ЩЕДРИН, МИХАИЛ ЕВГРАФОВИЧ/SALTYKOV, MIKHAIL (1826–1889)

1. «История одного города». См. (его) *Собрание сочинений в двадцати томах*. Москва: Художественная литература, 1965–1977, т. 8, 263–433.
   1a. *The History of a Town: or, The Chronicle of Foolov*. Transl. Susan Brownsberger. Ann Arbor: Ardis, 1982.
   1b. *The History of a Town*. Transl. I. P. Foote. Oxford: Willem A. Meeuws, 1980.
2. «Помпадуры и помпадурши». См. Салтыков-Щедрин-1, т. 8, 5–261.
   2a. *The Pompadours: A Satire on the Art of Government*. Transl. David Magarshack. Ann Arbor: Ardis, 1985.

САЛЫНСКИЙ, АФАНАСИЙ ДМИТРИЕВИЧ/SALYNSKII, AFANASII (b. 1920)

1. «Мария». См. (его) *Драмы и комедии*. Москва: Искусство, 1977, 399–466.
   1a. "Maria." Transl. Robert Daglish. See ANTHOL-17, 229–304.

СВИРСКИЙ, ГРИГОРИЙ ЦЕЗАРЕВИЧ/SVIRSKII, GRIGORII (b. 1921)

1. *Заложники: Роман-документ*. Paris: Les Éditeurs Réunis, 1974.
   1a. *Hostages: The Personal Testimony of a Soviet Jew*. Transl. Gordon Clough. New York: Knopf, 1976.

СЕМЕНОВ, ЮЛИАН СЕМЕНОВИЧ/SEMENOV, IULIAN (b. 1931)

1. *Петровка, 38*. Москва: Молодая гвардия, 1964.
   1a. *Petrovka 38*. Transl. Michael Scammell. New York: Stein and Day, 1965.

СОКОЛОВ, САША (АЛЕКСАНДР ВСЕВОЛОДОВИЧ)/SOKOLOV, SASHA (b. 1943)

1. *Школа для дураков*. Ann Arbor: Ardis, 1976.
   1a. *A School for Fools*. Transl. Carl R. Proffer. Ann Arbor: Ardis, 1977.

СОЛЖЕНИЦЫН, АЛЕКСАНДР ИСАЕВИЧ/SOLZHENITSYN, ALEKSANDR (b. 1918)

1. *Красное колесо. Узел 1: Август четырнадцатого*. Вермонт; Париж: YMCA-Press, 1983. (His *Собрание сочинений*, т. 11)
   1a. *August 1914: The Red Wheel/Knot 1*. Transl. H.T. Willetts. New York: Farrar, Straus & Giroux, 1989.

2. *Бодался теленок с дубом: Очерки литературной жизни*. Paris: YMCA-Press, 1975.
   2a. *The Oak and the Calf: Sketches of Literary Life in the Soviet Union*. Transl. Harry Willetts. New York: Harper & Row, 1979.

3. *В круге первом*. New York: Harper & Row, 1968.
   3a. *The First Circle*. Transl. Thomas P. Whitney. New York: Harper & Row, 1968.

4. «Для пользы дела». См. (его) *Рассказы*. Frankfurt/Main: Posev, 1976, 261–319.
   4a. "For the Good of the Cause." See (his) *Stories and Prose Poems*. Transl. Michael Glenny. New York: Farrar, Straus & Giroux, 1970, 53–123.
   4b. "For the Good of the Cause." Transl. Max Hayward and David Floyd. See ANTHOL-9, 125–170.

5. *Ленин в Цюрихе: Главы*. Paris: YMCA-Press, 1975.
   5a. *Lenin in Zurich: Chapters*. Transl. H.T. Willetts. New York: Farrar, Straus & Giroux, 1976.

6. «Матренин двор». См. Солженицын-4, 215–259.
   6a. "Matryona's Home." Transl. H.T. Willets. See ANTHOL-13, 51–91.
   6b. "Matryona's House." See Solzhenitsyn-4a, 3–52.

7. «Один день Ивана Денисовича». См. Солженицын-4, 5–143.
   7a. *One Day in the Life of Ivan Denisovich*. Transl. Max Hayward and Ronald Hingley. New York: Bantam, 1970, 1963.
   7b. *One Day in the Life of Ivan Denisovich*. Transl. Ralph Parker. New York: Dutton, 1963.
   7c. *One Day in the Life of Ivan Denisovich*. Transl. H.T. Willetts. New York: The Noonday Press; Farrar, Straus & Giroux, 1991.

8. «Олень и шалашовка». См. (его) *Собрание сочинений в шести томах*. Frankfurt/Main: Posev, 1969–1970, т. 5, 7–124.
   8a. *The Love-Girl and the Innocent*. Transl. Nicholas Bethell and David Burg. New York: Farrar, Straus & Giroux, 1969.

9. «Пленники». См. (его) *Пьесы и киносценарии*. Paris: YMCA-Press, 1981, 125–250.
   9a. *Prisoners: A Tragedy*. Transl. Helen Rapp and Nancy Thomas. London: Bodley Head, 1981.

10. *Раковый корпус*. См. Солженицын-8, т. 2.
    10a. *Cancer Ward*. Transl. Nicholas Bethell and David Burg. New York: Bantam Books, 1969.
    10b. *The Cancer Ward*. Transl. Rebecca Frank. New York: Dell, 1968.

11. «Свеча на ветру: свет, который в тебе». См. Солженицын-8, т. 5, 125–205.
    11a. *Candle in the Wind*. Transl. Keith Armes with Arthur Hudgins. Minneapolis: Univ. of Minnesota Press, 1973.

12. «Случай на станции Кречетовка». См. Солженицын-4, 145–213.
    12a. "An Incident at Krechetovka Station." See Solzhenitsyn-4a, 167–240.
    12b. "An Incident at Krechetovka Station." Transl. Helen Colaclides. See ANTHOL-9, 42–91.

СОЛОГУБ, ФЕДОР КУЗЬМИЧ/SOLOGUB, FYODOR [Pseud. of TETERNIKOV, FEDOR KUZMICH (1863–1927)]

1. *Мелкий бес*. Chicago: Russian Language Specialties, 1966.
   1a. *The Petty Demon*. Transl. Andrew Field. New York: Random House, 1962.

СТРУГАЦКИЙ, АРКАДИЙ НАТАНОВИЧ/STRUGATSKII, ARKADII (1925–1991) и СТРУГАЦКИЙ, БОРИС НАТАНОВИЧ/STRUGATSKII, BORIS (b. 1933)

1. *Гадкие лебеди*. Frankfurt/Main: Posev, 1972.
   1a. *The Ugly Swans*. Transl. Alice Stone Nakhimovsky and Alexander Nakhimovsky. New York: Macmillan, 1979.

2. *Обитаемый остров*. Москва: Детская литература, 1971.
   2a. *Prisoners of Power*. Transl. Helen Saltz Jacobson. New York: Macmillan, 1977.

3. «Сказка о тройке». См. (их) *Улитка на склоне. Сказка о тройке*. Frankfurt/Main: Posev, 1972.
   3a. "Tale of the Troika." Transl. Antonina W. Bouis. In (their) *Roadside Picnic. Tale of the Troika*. New York: Macmillan, 1977.

4. «Трудно быть богом». См. (их) *Трудно быть богом. Понедельник начинается в субботу*. Москва: Молодая гвардия, 1966.
   4a. *Hard to Be a God*. Transl. Wendayne Ackerman with Forrest J. Ackerman. New York: Seabury Press, 1973.

СУСЛОВ, АЛЕКСАНДР ВАСИЛЬЕВИЧ/SUSLOV, ALEKSANDR (b. 1950)

1. «Плакун-Город». *Грани*, 103, 1977, 3–95.
   1a. *Loosestrife City*. Transl. David Lapeza. Ann Arbor: Ardis, 1980.

СУХОВО-КОБЫЛИН, АЛЕКСАНДР ВАСИЛЬЕВИЧ/SUKHOVO-KOBYLIN, ALEKSANDR (1817–1903)

1. «Дело». См. (его) *Трилогия*. Москва-Ленинград: Гос. изд-во художественной литературы, 1959, 121–220.
   1a. "The Case." In (his) *The Trilogy of Alexander Sukhovo-Kobylin*. Transl. Harold B. Segel. New York: Dutton, 1969, 87–194.

2. «Свадьба Кречинского». См. Сухово-Кобылин-1, 43–120.
   2a. *Krechinsky's Wedding*. Transl. Robert Magidoff. Ann Arbor: Univ. of Michigan Press, 1961.
   2b. "Krechinsky's Wedding." See Sukhovo-Kobylin-1a, 1–86.

3. «Смерть Тарелкина». См. Сухово-Кобылин-1, 221–290.
   3a. "The Death of Tarelkin." See Sukhovo-Kobylin-1a, 195–264.

ТЕНДРЯКОВ, ВЛАДИМИР ФЕДОРОВИЧ/TENDRIAKOV, VLADIMIR (1923–1984)

1. «Суд». См. (его) *Three Novellas*. Oxford: Pergamon Press, 1967, 103–178.
   1a. "Justice." Transl. Olive Stevens. In (his) *Three, Seven, Ace & Other Stories*. New York: Harper & Row, 1973, 71–159.

ТЕРЦ, АБРАМ/TERTS, ABRAM [Pseud. of SINIAVSKII, ANDREI DONATOVICH (b. 1925)]

1. «В цирке». См. (его) *Фантастический мир Абрама Терца*. Нью-Йорк: Международное литературное содружество, 1967, 42–63.
   «В цирке». См. (его) *Собрание сочинений в двух томах*. Москва: СП «Старт», 1992, т. 1. [consulted for punctuation]
   1a. "At the Circus." Transl. Ronald Hingley. In (his) *Fantastic Stories by Abram Tertz*. New York: Grosset & Dunlap, 1967, 145–168.

2. «Гололедица». См. Терц-1, 108–174.
   2a. "The Icicle." Transl. Max Hayward. See Terts-1a, 33–121.

3. *Голос из хора*. London: Stenvalley Press, 1973.
   «Голос из хора». См. (его) *Собрание сочинений в двух*

томах. Москва: СП «Старт», 1992, т. 1, 437–669. [consulted for punctuation]

   3a. *A Voice from the Chorus.* Transl. Kyrill FitzLyon and Max Hayward. New York: Farrar, Straus & Giroux, 1976.

  4. «Графоманы». См. Терц-1, 77–107.

   4a. "Graphomaniacs." Transl. Ronald Hingley. See Terts-1a, 169–214.

  5. «Квартиранты». См. Терц-1, 64–76.

   5a. "Tenants." Transl. Ronald Hingley. See Terts-1a, 123–144.

  6. «Любимов». См. Терц-1, 277–397.

   6a. *The Makepeace Experiment.* Transl. Manya Harari. New York: Pantheon Books, 1965.

  7. «Суд идет». См. Терц-1, 197–276.

   7a. *The Trial Begins.* Transl. Max Hayward. New York: Pantheon Books, 1960.

  8. «Ты и я». См. Терц-1, 42–63.

   8a. "You and I." Transl. Max Hayward. See Terts-1a, 1–32.

ТОЛСТОЙ, ЛЕВ НИКОЛАЕВИЧ/TOLSTOY, LEO (1828–1910)

  1. «Власть тьмы». См. (его) *Собрание сочинений в двенадцати томах.* Москва: Гос. изд-во художественной литературы, 1958–1959, т. 10, 187–266.

   1a. "The Power of Darkness." See ANTHOL-6, 375–454.

   1b. "The Power of Darkness." Transl. George Rapall Noyes and George Z. Patrick. See ANTHOL-15, 547–623.

   1c. "The Power of Darkness." See ANTHOL-21, 155–230.

  2. *Детство, отрочество, юность.* См. Толстой-1, т. 1.

   2a. *Childhood, Boyhood and Youth.* Transl. Louise and Aylmer Maude. London: Oxford Univ. Press, 1961 (c1947).

   2b. *Childhood, Boyhood & Youth.* Transl. Michael Scammell. New York: McGraw-Hill, 1965.

   2c. *Childhood, Boyhood, Youth.* Transl. Rosemary Edmonds. Harmondsworth, Middlesex [England]: Penguin Books, 1973, c1964.

   2d. *Childhood, Boyhood, & Youth.* Transl. Alexandra and Sverre Lyngstad. New York: Washington Square Press, 1968, c1967.

  3. «Плоды просвещения». См. Толстой-1, т. 10, 387–484.

   3a. "The Fruits of Enlightenment." In (his) *Darkness and Light: Three Short Works by Tolstoy.* Ed. Peter Rudy. New York: Holt Rinehart & Winston, 1965, 163–266.

   3b. *The Fruits of Enlightenment.* Transl. Michael Frayn. London: Eyre Methuen, 1979.

  4. *Война и мир, том первый.* См. Толстой-1, т. 4.

   4a. *War and Peace* (volume 1). Transl. Ann Dunnigan. New York: Signet, 1968, 27–360.

   4b. *War and Peace* (volume 1). Transl. Louise and Aylmer Maude. Oxford; New York: Oxford Univ. Press, 1991, 3–308.

  5. *Война и мир, том второй.* См. Толстой-1, т. 5.

   5a. *War and Peace* (volume 2). See Tolstoy-4a, 361–726.

   5b. *War and Peace* (volume 2). See Tolstoy-4b, 309–641.

  6. *Война и мир, том третий.* См. Толстой-1, т. 6.

   6a. *War and Peace* (volume 3). See Tolstoy-4a, 727–1114.

   6b. *War and Peace* (volume 3). See Tolstoy-4b, 645–996.

  7. *Война и мир, том четвертый.* См. Толстой-1, т. 7.

   7a. *War and Peace* (volume 4). See Tolstoy-4a, 1115–1455.

   7b. *War and Peace* (volume 4). See Tolstoy-4b, 999–1315.

ТРИФОНОВ, ЮРИЙ ВАЛЕНТИНОВИЧ/TRIFONOV, YURII (1925–1981)

  1. «Долгое прощание». См. (его) *Избранные произведения в двух томах.* Москва: Художественная литература, 1978, т. 2, 126–212.

   1a. "The Long Goodbye." Transl. Helen P. Burlingame. In (his) *The Long Goodbye.* Ann Arbor: Ardis, 1978, 201–353.

  2. «Дом на набережной». См. (его) *Повести.* Москва: Советская Россия, 1978, 371–506.

   2a. "The House on the Embankment." In (his) *Another Life and The House on the Embankment.* Transl. Michael Glenny. New York: Simon & Schuster, 1983, 187–350.

  3. «Другая жизнь». См. Трифонов-2, 223–370.

   3a. "Another Life." See Trifonov-2a, 9–186.

  4. «Обмен». См. Трифонов-1, т. 2, 7–62.

   4a. "The Exchange." Transl. Ellendea Proffer. See Trifonov-1a, 17–97.

  5. «Предварительные итоги». См. Трифонов-1, т. 2, 63–125.

   5a. "Taking Stock." Transl. Helen P. Burlingame. See Trifonov-1a, 99–200.

  6. «Старик». См. (его) *Вечные темы.* Москва: Советский писатель, 1984, 5–196.

   6a. *The Old Man.* Transl. Jacqueline Edwards and Mitchell Schneider. New York: Simon & Schuster, 1984.

ТУРГЕНЕВ, ИВАН СЕРГЕЕВИЧ/TURGENEV, IVAN (1818–1883)

  1. «Месяц в деревне». См. (его) *Сочинения в двенадцати томах.* Изд. 2-е, испр. и доп. Москва: Наука, 1978–1986, т. 4, 285–397. (Part of his *Полное собрание сочинений и писем в тридцати томах*)

   1a. "A Month in the Country." In (his) *Three Famous Plays.* Transl. Constance Garnett. New York: Hill & Wang, 1959, 1–127.

   1b. "A Month in the Country." Transl. George Rapall Noyes. See ANTHOL-14, 233–327.

   1c. *A Month in the Country.* Transl. Ariadne Nicolaeff. New York: Dramatists Play Service, 1980.

   1d. *A Month in the Country.* Transl. Richard Newnham. San Francisco: Chandler, 1962.

   1e. "A Month in the Country." Transl. Max S. Mandell. In (his) *The Plays of Ivan S. Turgenev.* V. 2. New York: Macmillan, 1924, 345–488.

  2. «Отцы и дети». См. (его) *Сочинения в пятнадцати томах.* Москва-Ленинград: Наука, 1960–1968, т. 8, 193–402. (Part of his *Полное собрание сочинений и писем в двадцати восьми томах*)

   2a. *Fathers and Sons.* Transl. Bernard Isaacs. Moscow: Foreign Languages Publishing House, [1947?].

   2b. *Fathers and Sons.* Transl. Ralph E. Matlaw. (Substantially new transl. based on Constance Garnett's transl.) New York: Norton, 1966.

   2c. *Fathers and Sons.* Transl. Rosemary Edmonds. Harmondsworth, Middlesex [England]: Penguin Books, 1981, c1965.

   2d. *Fathers and Sons.* Transl. Bernard Guilbert Guerney. New York: The Modern Library, 1961.

   2e. *Fathers and Sons.* Transl. Avril Pyman. London: J.M. Dent; New York: Dutton, 1962.

   2f. "Fathers and Sons." Transl. Harry Stevens. In (his) *The Borzoi Turgenev.* New York: Knopf, 1950, 165–352.

  3. «Первая любовь». См. Тургенев-2, т. 9, 7–76.

   3a. "First Love." Transl. David Magarshack. In (his) *First Love and Other Tales.* New York: W.W. Norton, 1968, 142–218.

   3b. *First Love.* Transl. Isaiah Berlin. With an introduction by V.S. Pritchett. Harmondsworth, Middlesex [England]: Penguin Books, 1978.

   3c. "First Love." See Turgenev-2f, 353–412.

ФЕДИН, КОНСТАНТИН АЛЕКСАНДРОВИЧ/FEDIN, KONSTANTIN (1892–1977)

  1. *Города и годы.* Москва: Гос. изд-во художественной литературы, 1957.

   1a. *Cities and Years.* Transl. Michael Scammell. Westport, Conn.: Greenwood Press, 1975. (Reprint. New York: Dell Pub. Co., 1962.)

ФОНВИЗИН, ДЕНИС ИВАНОВИЧ/FONVIZIN, DENIS (1745–1792)

1. «Недоросль». См. (его) *Собрание сочинений в двух томах*. Москва: Гос. изд-во художественной литературы, 1959, т. 1, 105–177.
   - 1a. "The Minor." Transl. Marvin Kantor. In (his) *Dramatic Works of D.I. Fonvizin*. Bern: Herbert Lang; Frankfurt/Main: Peter Lang, 1974, 87–134.
   - 1b. "The Minor." See ANTHOL-6, 21–83.
   - 1c. "The Infant." See ANTHOL-11, 47–124.
   - 1d. "The Young Hopeful." Transl. George Z. Patrick and George Rapall Noyes. See ANTHOL-14, 27–84.

ЧЕРНЕНОК, МИХАИЛ ЯКОВЛЕВИЧ/CHERNYO-NOK, MIKHAIL (b. 1931)

1. «Ставка на проигрыш». *Сибирские огни*, 1979, 2, 74–125.
   - 1a. *Losing Bet*. Transl. Antonina W. Bouis. Garden City, N.Y.: Dial Press, 1984.

2. «Ставка на проигрыш». *Сибирские огни*, 1979, 3, 41–102.
   - 2a. *Losing Bet*. Transl. Antonina W. Bouis. Garden City, N.Y.: Dial Press, 1984.

ЧЕХОВ, АНТОН ПАВЛОВИЧ/CHEKHOV, ANTON (1860–1904)

1. «Пьеса без названия (Платонов)». См. (его) *Собрание сочинений в двенадцати томах*. Москва: Гос. изд-во художественной литературы, 1960–1964, т. 9, 5–178.
   - 1a. *Platonov*. Transl. David Magarshack. New York: Hill & Wang, 1964.
   - 1b. "Platonov." In (his) *The Oxford Chekhov*. V. 2. Transl. Ronald Hingley. London: Oxford Univ. Press, 1967, 9–162.

2. «Вишневый сад». См. Чехов-1, т. 9, 607–662.
   - 2a. "The Cherry Orchard." In (his) *Chekhov: The Major Plays*. Transl. Ann Dunnigan. New York: New American Library, 1964, 313–380.
   - 2b. "The Cherry Orchard." In (his) *Four Plays*. Transl. David Magarshack. New York: Hill & Wang, 1969, 187–244.
   - 2c. "The Cherry Orchard." In (his) *Chekhov: Five Major Plays*. Transl. Ronald Hingley. New York: Oxford Univ. Press, 1977, 267–310.
   - 2d. "The Cherry Orchard." In (his) *Best Plays by Chekhov*. Transl. Stark Young. New York: Random House, 1956, 225–296.

3. «Дядя Ваня». См. Чехов-1, т. 9, 482–532.
   - 3a. "Uncle Vanya." See Chekhov-2a, 171–231.
   - 3b. "Uncle Vanya." See Chekhov-2b, 63–114.
   - 3c. "Uncle Vanya." See Chekhov-2c, 145–195.
   - 3d. "Uncle Vanya." See Chekhov-2d, 71–135.
   - 3e. *Uncle Vanya*. Transl. Tyrone Guthrie and Leonid Kipnis. Minneapolis: Univ. of Minnesota Press, 1969.

4. «Иванов». См. Чехов-1, т. 9, 216–283.
   - 4a. "Ivanov." See Chekhov-2a, 23–101.
   - 4b. "Ivanov." See Chekhov-1b, 163–227.

5. «Три сестры». См. Чехов-1, т. 9, 533–601.
   - 5a. "The Three Sisters." See Chekhov-2a, 233–312.
   - 5b. "The Three Sisters." See Chekhov-2b, 115–185.
   - 5c. "The Three Sisters." See Chekhov-2d, 137–223.
   - 5d. *The Three Sisters*. Transl. Randall Jarrell. London: Macmillan, 1969.

6. «Чайка». См. Чехов-1, т. 9, 426–481.
   - 6a. "The Sea Gull." See Chekhov-2a, 103–170.
   - 6b. "The Sea Gull." See Chekhov-2b, 1–61.
   - 6c. "The Sea Gull." See ANTHOL-23, 23–82.
   - 6d. "The Sea Gull." See Chekhov-2d, 1–70.

ЧУКОВСКАЯ, ЛИДИЯ КОРНЕЕВНА/CHUKOV-SKAIA, LIDIIA (b. 1907)

1. *Опустелый дом*. Париж: Пять континентов, 1965.
   - 1a. *The Deserted House*. Transl. Aline B. Werth. New York: Dutton, 1967.

2. *Спуск под воду*. Нью-Йорк: Изд-во им. Чехова, 1972.
   - 2a. *Going Under*. Transl. Peter M. Weston. New York: Quadrangle/The New York Times Book Co., 1972.

ШВАРЦ, ЕВГЕНИЙ ЛЬВОВИЧ/SHVARTS, EVGENII (1896–1958)

1. «Голый король». См. (его) *Пьесы*. Ленинград: Советский писатель, 1962, 89–166.
   - 1a. "The Naked King." In (his) *The Naked King; The Shadow; &, The Dragon*. Transl. Elisaveta Fen. London: Marion Boyars, 1976, 13–166.

2. «Дракон». См. Шварц-1, 311–384.
   - 2a. "The Dragon." See Shvarts-1a, 189–277.
   - 2b. "The Dragon." Transl. Robert Daglish. See ANTHOL-7, 619–696.

3. «Тень». См. Шварц-1, 233–309.
   - 3a. "The Shadow." See ANTHOL-23, 381–458.

ШОЛОХОВ, МИХАИЛ АЛЕКСАНДРОВИЧ/SHOLO-KHOV, MIKHAIL (1905–1984)

1. «Судьба человека». См. (его) *Собрание сочинений в восьми томах*. Москва: «Правда», 1962, т. 8, 22–54.
   - 1a. "One Man's Destiny." Transl. H.C. Stevens. In (his) *One Man's Destiny: and Other Stories, Articles and Sketches, 1923–1963*. New York: Knopf, 1967, 9–45.
   - 1b. "The Fate of a Man." Transl. Miriam Morton. In (his) *Fierce and Gentle Warriors*. Garden City, N.Y.: Doubleday, 1967, 65–109.
   - 1c. "The Fate of a Man." Transl. Robert Daglish. In (his) *Collected Works in Eight Volumes*. Moscow: Raduga, 1984, v. 8, 243–283.

2. *Тихий Дон, книга первая*. См. Шолохов-1, т. 2.
   - 2a. *Quiet Flows the Don, Book One*. (His *Collected Works in Eight Volumes*, v. 2.) Transl. Robert Daglish. Moscow: Raduga, 1984.
   - 2b. *And Quiet Flows the Don, Book One*. Transl. Stephen Garry (rev. and completed by Robert Daglish). Moscow: Foreign Languages Publishing House, n.d.

3. *Тихий Дон, книга вторая*. См. Шолохов-1, т. 3.
   - 3a. *Quiet Flows the Don, Book Two*. See Sholokhov-2a, v. 3.
   - 3b. *And Quiet Flows the Don, Book Two*. See Sholokhov-2b.

4. *Тихий Дон, книга третья*. См. Шолохов-1, т. 4.
   - 4a. *Quiet Flows the Don, Book Three*. See Sholokhov-2a, v. 4.

5. *Тихий Дон, книга четвертая*. См. Шолохов-1, т. 5.
   - 5a. *Quiet Flows the Don, Book Four*. See Sholokhov-2a, v. 5.

ШУКШИН, ВАСИЛИЙ МАКАРОВИЧ/SHUKSHIN, VASILII (1929–1974)

1. «Калина красная». См. (его) *Избранные произведений в двух томах*. Москва: Молодая гвардия, 1975, т. 1, 417–492.
   - 1a. *Snowball Berry Red & Other Stories*. Transl. Donald M. Fiene. Ann Arbor: Ardis, 1979, 125–199.

ЭРДМАН, НИКОЛАЙ РОБЕРТОВИЧ/ERDMAN, NIKOLAI (1902–1970)

1. *Самоубийца*. Ann Arbor: Ardis, 1980.
   - 1a. "The Suicide." In (his) *The Mandate. The Suicide*. Transl. George Genereux, Jr., and Jacob Volkov. Ann Arbor: Ardis, 1975.

ЭРЕНБУРГ, ИЛЬЯ ГРИГОРЬЕВИЧ/ERENBURG, ILIA (1891–1967)

1. *Буря*. См. (его) *Собрание сочинений в девяти томах*. Москва: Гос. изд-во художественной литературы, 1962–1967, т. 5.

1a. *The Storm.* Transl. J. Fineberg. New York: Gaer Associates, 1949.

2. *Любовь Жанны Ней.* Рига: Изд-во О.Д. Строк, 1925/26.
   2a. *The Love of Jeanne Ney.* Transl. Helen Chrouschoff Matheson. Garden City, N.Y.: Doubleday, Doran, 1930.

3. *Оттепель.* Москва: Советский писатель, 1954.
   3a. *The Thaw.* Transl. Manya Harari. Chicago: H. Regnery, 1955.

4. *Падение Парижа.* См. Эренбург-1, т. 4, 67–540.
   4a. *The Fall of Paris.* Transl. Gerard Shelley. New York: Knopf, 1943.

ЭТКИНД, ЕФИМ ГРИГОРЬЕВИЧ/ETKIND, EFIM (b. 1918)

1. *Записки незаговорщика.* London: Overseas Publication Interchange, 1977.
   1a. *Notes of a Non-Conspirator.* Transl. Peter France. Oxford: Oxford Univ. Press, 1978.

B. *Anthologies*

1. *Антология советской драматургии.* Магадан: Магаданское книжное изд-во, 1972.

2. *Литературная Москва.* [Сборник первый.] Москва: Гос. изд-во художественной литературы, 1956.

3. *Литературная Москва.* Сборник второй. Москва: Гос. изд-во художественной литературы, 1956.

4. *Метрополь: Литературный альманах.* Составили: В. Аксенов, А. Битов, Вик. Ерофеев, Ф. Искандер, Евг. Попов. Анн Арбор: Ардис, 1979.

5. *Тарусские страницы.* Калуга: Калужское книжное изд-во, 1961.

6. *An Anthology of Russian Plays.* V. 1, 1790–1890. Ed., transl., and introduced by F.D. Reeve. New York: Vintage, 1961.

7. *Classic Soviet Plays.* Compiled by Alla Mikhailova. Moscow: Progress, 1979.

8. *Contemporary Russian Drama.* Selected and transl. by Franklin D. Reeve. With a preface by Victor Rozov. New York: Pegasus, 1968.

9. *Fifty Years of Russian Prose.* V. 2. Ed. by Krystyna Pomorska. Cambridge, Mass.: The MIT Press, 1971.

10. *Five of the Best Soviet Plays of the 1970s.* Transl. by Maya Gordeyeva and Mike Davidow. Moscow: Raduga, 1983.

11. *Four Russian Plays.* Transl. with an introduction and notes by Joshua Cooper. Harmondsworth, Middlesex [England]: Penguin Books, 1972.

12. *Four Soviet Plays.* Moscow: Co-operative Publishing Society of Foreign Workers in the USSR, 1937.

13. *Half-Way to the Moon.* Ed. by P. Blake and M. Hayward. New York: Holt Rinehart & Winston, 1964.

14. *Masterpieces of the Russian Drama.* V. 1. Selected and ed. with an introduction by George Rapall Noyes. New York: Dover Publications, c1961 [originally c1933].

15. *Masterpieces of the Russian Drama.* V. 2. Selected and edited by George Rapall Noyes. New York: Dover Publications, c1961 [originally c1933].

16. *Metropol: Literary Almanac.* Ed. by Vasily Aksyonov, Viktor Yerofeyev, Fazil Iskander, Andrei Bitov, and Yevgeny Popov. New York: Norton, 1982.

17. *Nine Modern Soviet Plays.* Compiled and prefaced by Victor Komissarzhevsky. Moscow: Progress, 1977.

18. *Russian Plays for Young Audiences.* Transl. and ed. with an introduction by Miriam Morton. Rowayton, Conn.: New Plays Books, 1977.

19. *Soviet Short Stories.* V. 2. Ed. by Peter Reddaway. Baltimore: Penguin Books, 1968. ⟨Parallel texts in Russian and English.⟩

20. *The Fatal Eggs and Other Soviet Satire.* Ed. and transl. by Mirra Ginsburg. New York: Grove Press, 1968.

21. *The Storm and Other Russian Plays.* Transl. and introduced by David Magarshack. New York: Hill & Wang, 1960.

22. *The Young Russians: A Collection of Stories About Them.* Ed. by Thomas P. Whitney. New York: Macmillan, 1972.

23. *Twentieth-Century Russian Plays: An Anthology.* Transl. by F.D. Reeve. New York: W.W. Norton, 1963.

24. *World Drama. An Anthology.* Ed. by Barrett H. Clark. New York: Dover Publications, 1933.

INDEX

The Index consists of main entries, or headwords, each with one or more subentries. The headwords represent the significant words of the idioms in the dictionary. Significant words are usually content words. The headwords appear in boldface capital letters, are presented in the precise form (with respect to case, number, etc.) in which they occur in an idiom or idioms, and are ordered alphabetically.

Subentries appear in lightface lower case letters and are in alphabetical (word-by-word) order under the headword. Each subentry to a headword is an idiom in which that headword occurs. This subentry idiom is followed by the letter-number indicator of its location in the dictionary. For example, the idiom В САМЫЙ РАЗ, which appears as Р-19 in the dictionary, is entered under the content words САМЫЙ and РАЗ:

САМЫЙ
  в самый раз, Р-19

РАЗ
  в самый раз, Р-19

Proverbs and sayings are entered under their first three content words and under other especially significant words.

Many idioms in the dictionary have morphological, lexical, and/or aspectual variants. To avoid cluttering the Index, such variants have been presented together when feasible (that is, when no other idioms intervene alphabetically and no difficulties in finding a variant are foreseen). The ordering of variants in the Index does not always correspond to the ordering of variants in the dictionary proper because the Index observes strict alphabetical order. For example, the idiom НАДУВАТЬ/НАДУТЬ ГУБЫ 〈ГУБКИ〉 (Г-440) is listed under each of its four content words (НАДУВАТЬ, НАДУТЬ, ГУБЫ, and ГУБКИ). Under НАДУВАТЬ and НАДУТЬ the variants губы and губки are listed together, since combining them causes no problems in locating any variant of the idiom.

НАДУВАТЬ
  надувать губки 〈губы〉, Г-440

НАДУТЬ
  надуть губки 〈губы〉, Г-440

For idioms like КАЖДАЯ 〈ВСЯКАЯ, ЛЮБАЯ〉 СОБАКА (С-441), variants have been presented separately in the Index for two reasons: first, several other idioms come between the variants alphabetically; and second, it is easier to scan this column of idioms when each variant is presented independently.

СОБАКА
  всякая собака, С-441
  каждая собака, С-441
  как собака, С-442
  как собака на сене, С-443
  как собака палку, С-444
  любая собака, С-441

Many idioms contain the variants КАК 〈БУДТО, СЛОВНО, ТОЧНО〉. To avoid redundancy, such idioms are entered as follows:

1) under КАК, БУДТО, СЛОВНО, and ТОЧНО (that is, four Index occurrences)

2) under each other content word as the basic variant как*…, with the asterisk indicating that the variants будто, словно, and точно (or some combination of them) are also found in the indicated entry. Idioms containing the variants КАК БУДТО 〈СЛОВНО, ТОЧНО〉 are treated similarly, with как будто* indicating the existence of other variants. For example, the idiom КАК 〈БУДТО, СЛОВНО, ТОЧНО〉 НА СМЕХ (С-402) is entered in the Index as follows:

БУДТО
  будто на смех, С-402

КАК
  как на смех, С-402

СЛОВНО
  словно на смех, С-402

СМЕХ
  как* на смех, С-402

ТОЧНО
  точно на смех, С-402

When aspectual variants are combined and the imperfective aspect precedes the perfective alphabetically, the variants are separated by a slash, as in the dictionary proper. For example, the idiom СБИВАТЬ/СБИТЬ С ТОЛКУ (Т-142) is entered under ТОЛКУ as follows:

ТОЛКУ
  сбивать/сбить с толку, Т-142

(The idiom is, of course, entered under each verb as well.)

When the perfective aspect precedes the imperfective alphabetically, the imperfective is presented in angle brackets following the perfective. For example, the idiom ДОВОДИТЬ/ДОВЕСТИ ДО СОЗНАНИЯ (С-465) is entered under СОЗНАНИЯ as follows:

СОЗНАНИЯ
  довести 〈доводить〉 до сознания, С-465

In compliance with the rule of alphabetization, the perfective and the imperfective may be presented as separate Index entries.

Hyphenated idioms are generally presented under the first word. For example, ТАК-СЯК (Т-6) is entered only under ТАК. In those cases where the first word is not perceived as a content word, the hyphenated idiom itself is used as an Index heading:

БОЙ-БАБА
  бой-баба, Б-146

Homographic forms are combined under one Index headword. For example, in some idioms listed under the headword ДОРОГОЙ, дорогой is an instrumental singular adjective (Ц-28, Д-402), whereas in others it is an instrumental singular noun (Д-272, Д-273, Д-274):

ДОРОГОЙ
  дорогой ценой, Ц-28
  идти прямой дорогой, Д-272
  идти своей дорогой, Д-273
  обойти 〈обходить〉 десятой дорогой, Д-274
  пойти своей дорогой, Д-273
  с дорогой душой, Д-402

А

А
от а до зет, А-1
от а до я, А-1

АБОРДАЖ
брать/взять на абордаж, А-2

АБСОЛЮТНЫЙ
абсолютный слух, С-352

АБЦУГА
с первого абцуга, А-3

АБЦУГУ
по первому абцугу, А-3

АВАНСЫ
делать авансы, А-4

АВГИЕВЫ
авгиевы конюшни, К-273

АВОСЬ
авось да небось, А-5
авось, небось да как-нибудь, А-5
на авось, А-6

АД
ад кромешный, А-7

АДАМА
в костюме Адама, К-331
от ⟨с⟩ Адама, А-8

АДАМОВА
адамова голова, Г-193

АДАМОВЫ
адамовы веки, В-24
адамовы времена, В-24

АДМИНИСТРАТИВНЫЙ
административный восторг, В-280

АДМИРАЛЬСКИЙ
адмиральский час, Ч-6

АДРЕС
в адрес, А-9

АДРЕСУ
не по адресу, А-10
по адресу, А-11
проезжаться/проехаться по адресу, С-712
пройтись ⟨прохаживаться⟩ по адресу, С-712

АЖУРЕ
в (полном) ажуре, А-12

АЗА
аза в глаза, А-13
ни аза, А-13
ни аза в глаза, А-13
от аза до ижицы, А-1

АЗАРТ
войти в азарт, А-14
впадать/впасть в азарт, А-14
входить в азарт, А-14
прийти ⟨приходить⟩ в азарт, А-14

АЗБУЧНАЯ
азбучная истина, И-82

АЗОВ
с азов, А-15

АЙ
ай да...!, А-16

ай да ну!, Н-252

АККОРД
заключительный аккорд, А-17

АККУРАТ
в аккурат, А-18

АККУРАТЕ
в аккурате, А-19

АКРИДАМИ
питаться акридами (и диким мёдом), А-20
питаться акридами и мёдом, А-20

АКЦЕНТ
делать/сделать акцент, А-21

АКЦЕНТЫ
расставлять/расставить акценты, А-22

АКЦИИ
акции падают, А-23
акции повысились ⟨повышаются⟩, А-24
акции поднимаются/поднялись, А-24
акции упали, А-23

АЛЛАХ
аллах (его) ведает ⟨знает⟩, Б-93

АЛЛАХУ
одному аллаху ведомо ⟨известно⟩, Б-138

АЛМАЗ
свой глаз — алмаз (, а чужой — стекло), Г-41

АЛМАЗНАЯ
алмазная свадьба, С-25

АЛТЫН
не было ни гроша, да (и) вдруг алтын, Г-417

АЛТЫНА
ни алтына, Г-418

АЛЬФА
альфа и омега, А-25

АЛЬФЫ
от альфы до омеги, А-1

АМБИЦИЮ
вламываться/вломиться в амбицию, А-26
войти в амбицию, А-26
впадать/впасть в амбицию, А-26
входить в амбицию, А-26
удариться ⟨ударяться⟩ в амбицию, А-26

АМЕРИКИ
открытие Америки, А-27

АМЕРИКУ
открывать/открыть Америку, А-27

АНАФЕМЕ
предавать/предать анафеме, А-28

АНГЕЛА
день ангела, Д-152

АНДРОНЫ
андроны едут, А-29

АННИБАЛОВА
аннибалова клятва, К-146

АННИБАЛОВСКАЯ
аннибаловская клятва, К-146

АНТИК
антик с гвоздикой ⟨с мармеладом⟩, А-30

АНТИМОНИИ
разводить антимонии, А-31

АНТОНИЯ
вкушать от пищи святого Антония, П-160
сидеть на пище святого Антония, П-160

АПЕЛЬСИНАХ
как свинья в апельсинах, С-82

АППЕТИТ
аппетит приходит во время еды, А-32
волчий аппетит, А-33

АППЕТИТА
приятного аппетита!, А-34

АПТЕКЕ
как в аптеке, А-35

АРАПА
брать/взять на арапа, А-36
заправлять арапа, А-37
на арапа, А-38

АРЕДОВЫ
аредовы веки, В-25

АРЕСТАНТОВ
сорок бочек арестантов, Б-186

АРИАДНИНА
Ариаднина нить, Н-103

АРИАДНЫ
нить Ариадны, Н-103

АРИДОВЫ
аридовы веки, В-25

АРКАДСКАЯ
аркадская идиллия, И-24

АРКАНЕ
затащить ⟨затянуть⟩ на аркане, А-39
потащить ⟨потянуть⟩ на аркане, А-39
тащить ⟨тянуть⟩ на аркане, А-39

АРТИЛЛЕРИЯ
тяжёлая артиллерия, А-40

АРХИВ
сдавать/сдать в архив, А-41

АРШИН
как* аршин проглотил, А-42
видеть на аршин в землю ⟨под землёй, под землю⟩, А-46
мерить ⟨мерять⟩ на... аршин, А-43
мерить ⟨мерять⟩ на один аршин, А-44
мерить ⟨мерять⟩ на свой аршин, А-45

АРШИНА
видеть на два аршина в

землю ⟨под землёй, под землю⟩, А-46
видеть на три аршина в землю ⟨под землёй, под землю⟩, А-46

АРШИНОМ
мерить ⟨мерять⟩... аршином, А-43
мерить ⟨мерять⟩ одним аршином, А-44
мерить ⟨мерять⟩ своим аршином, А-45

АТМОСФЕРУ
накалить ⟨накалять⟩ атмосферу, А-47
разрядить атмосферу, А-48

АТТИЧЕСКАЯ
аттическая соль, С-475

АУКНЕТСЯ
как аукнется, так и откликнется, А-49

АХ
увы и ах!, У-10

АХИ
ахи да ⟨и⟩ охи, А-50
охи да ⟨и⟩ ахи, А-50

АХИЛЛЕСОВА
ахиллесова пята ⟨пятка⟩, П-677

АХИНЕЮ
нести ахинею, В-99
плести ахинею, В-99
понести ахинею, В-99
пороть ахинею, В-99

АХТИ
не ахти, А-51, А-52
не ахти как, А-51
не ахти какой, А-52
не ахти сколько, А-53

Б

БАБА
базарная баба, Б-1
не было у бабы хлопот ⟨забот⟩, (так) купила баба порося, Б-2
не знала баба горя, (так) купила (баба) порося, Б-2

БАБКИ
подбивать/подбить бабки, Б-3
подсчитать ⟨подсчитывать⟩ бабки, Б-3

БАБУШКА
бабушка ворожит, Б-4
бабушка (ещё) надвое гадала ⟨сказала⟩, Б-5
вот тебе, бабушка, и Юрьев день!, Б-6

БАБУШКЕ
к ёбаной ⟨ебене⟩ бабушке, М-50
к едрёной бабушке, М-45
к чёртовой бабушке, Ч-110, Ч-111

расскажи ⟨рассказывай⟩ это своей бабушке, Б-7

БАБУШКИНЫ
бабушкины сказки, С-217

БАБЫ
не было у бабы хлопот ⟨забот⟩, (так) купила (баба) порося, Б-2
у бабы волос долог, а ⟨да⟩ ум короток, Б-8

БАБЬЕ
бабье лето, Л-66

БАБЬИ
бабьи сказки, С-217

БАБЬЮ
держаться за бабью юбку, Ю-2

БАЗАРНАЯ
базарная баба, Б-1

БАЗАРНЫЙ
грош цена в базарный день, Г-410

БАЗУ
подвести ⟨подводить⟩ базу, Б-9

БАКИ
вкрутить ⟨вкручивать⟩ баки, Б-10
забивать/забить баки, Б-10

БАКЛУШИ
бить баклуши, Б-11

БАЛ
(и) кончен бал, Б-12
с корабля на бал, К-291

БАЛАЛАЙКА
бесструнная балалайка, Б-13

БАЛАНДУ
травить баланду, Б-14

БАЛДОЙ
под балдой, Б-15

БАЛОВЕНЬ
баловень судьбы ⟨счастья⟩, Б-16
баловень фортуны, Б-16

БАЛЬЗАМ
проливать/пролить бальзам на раны, Б-17

БАЛЯСЫ
поточить балясы, Л-177
точить балясы, Л-177

БАННЫЙ
как* банный лист, Л-78

БАНЮ
задавать/задать баню, Б-18

БАРАБАНЩИК
отставной козы барабанщик, К-172

БАРАН
как баран, Б-19
как баран на новые ворота, Б-20
не баран начихал, Б-21

БАРАНАМ
вернёмся к нашим баранам, Б-22

БАРАНИЙ
гнуть в бараний рог, Р-120

свернуть в бараний рог, Р-120
скрутить в бараний рог, Р-120
согнуть в бараний рог, Р-120

БАРАНОВ
как стадо баранов, С-539

БАРАНЬЯ
баранья голова, Г-194

БАРАШЕК
барашек в бумажке, Б-23

БАРИН
сидеть как барин, Б-24

БАРИНОМ
сидеть барином, Б-24

БАРСКОГО
крохи ⟨крошки⟩ с барского стола, К-418

БАРСКУЮ
на барскую ногу, Н-177

БАРХАТНЫЙ
бархатный сезон, С-108

БАРЫШНЯ
кисейная барышня, Б-25

БАРЬЕР
брать/взять барьер, Б-26

БАРЬЕРЫ
брать/взять барьеры, Б-26

БАСНЯМИ
соловья баснями не кормят, С-473

БАТЬКИ
не лезь поперёд батьки в пекло, Б-27
прежде батьки в петлю не лезь ⟨не суйся⟩, Б-27

БАТЮШКЕ
по батюшке, Б-28

БАТЮШКИ
батюшки мои!, Б-29
батюшки светы ⟨святы⟩!, Б-29

БАШ
баш на баш, Б-30

БАШКА
башка разламывается ⟨раскалывается⟩, Г-209
башка трещит, Г-209
дубовая башка, Г-211
дурья башка, Г-212
мякинная башка, Г-212
отчаянная башка, Г-216
пустая башка, Г-217

БАШКУ
брать себе в башку, Г-246
вбивать в башку, Г-245
вбивать себе в башку, Г-246
вбить в башку, Г-245
вбить себе в башку, Г-246
вдалбливать/вдолбить в башку, Г-245
взять себе в башку, Г-246
вколачивать/вколотить в башку, Г-245
втемяшивать в башку, Г-245
втемяшивать себе в башку, Г-246

втемяшить в башку, Г-245
втемяшить себе в башку, Г-246
забивать себе в башку, Г-246
забирать себе в башку, Г-246
забить себе в башку, Г-246
забрать себе в башку, Г-246
свернуть башку, Ш-57, Ш-58
свернуть себе башку, Ш-58

БАШМАК
под башмак, Б-31

БАШМАКОМ
под башмаком, Б-31

БАШМАЧКОМ
под башмачком, Б-31

БАШНЯ
башня из слоновой кости, Б-32

БЕ
ни бе ни ме (ни кукареку), Б-33

БЕГАТЬ
бегать глазами, Г-50

БЕГАХ
в бегах, Б-34

БЕГАЮТ
глаза бегают, Г-50
мурашки бегают по коже ⟨по спине, по телу⟩, М-291

БЕГИ
дают — бери, бьют — беги, Д-29

БЕГОТНЯ
мышиная беготня, В-209

БЕГУ
на бегу, Б-35

БЕГУТ
крысы бегут с тонущего корабля, К-435
мурашки бегут по коже ⟨по спине, по телу⟩, М-291

БЕД
семь бед — один ответ, Б-36

БЕДА
беда в одиночку не ходит, Б-37
беда не приходит ⟨не ходит⟩ одна, Б-37
беда никогда не приходит ⟨не ходит⟩ одна, Б-37
велика беда, Б-41
лиха беда, Б-38
лиха беда начало ⟨начать⟩, Б-39
не беда, Б-40
не велика беда, Б-41
попытка не пытка, а спрос не беда, П-356
пришла беда — отворяй ⟨открывай, растворяй⟩ ворота, Б-42
что за беда, Б-43

БЕДЕ
друзья познаются

⟨узнаются⟩ в беде, Д-315

БЕДНОГО
на бедного Макара все шишки валятся, М-4

БЕДНОСТЬ
бедность не порок, Б-44

БЕДНЫХ
в пользу бедных, П-323

БЕДОВАЯ
бедовая голова ⟨головушка⟩, Г-195

БЕДУ
на беду, Б-45

БЕДЫ
долго ли до беды, Г-390
недолго (и) до беды, Г-390

БЕЖИТ
на ловца и зверь бежит, Л-121

БЕЗДНА
бездна премудрости, Б-47

БЕЗДОННАЯ
бездонная бочка, Б-187

БЕЗРЫБЬЕ
на безрыбье и рак рыба, Б-48

БЕЗУМИЯ
до безумия, Б-49

БЕЗУМНЫХ
с безумных глаз, Г-37

БЕЙ
не бей лежачего, Л-46

БЕЙСЯ
хоть головой об стенку ⟨стену⟩ бейся, Г-242

БЕЛА
дела как сажа бела, Д-56
среди ⟨средь⟩ бела дня, Д-213

БЕЛАЯ
белая ворона, В-273
белая кость, К-328

БЕЛЕНЫ
белены объелся, Б-50

БЕЛЕНЬКИМИ
полюбите нас чёрненькими, а беленькими всякий полюбит, П-326

БЕЛИБЕРДУ
нести/понести белиберду, В-99

БЕЛКА
(вертеться) как* белка в колесе, Б-51
кружиться ⟨крутиться⟩ как* белка в колесе, Б-51

БЕЛОГО
довести ⟨доводить⟩ до белого каления, К-34
дойти ⟨доходить⟩ до белого каления, К-35
света белого не видеть, С-66
сказка про белого бычка, С-214
среди ⟨средь⟩ белого дня, Д-213

БЕЛОЕ
белое пятно, П-685
выдавать белое за чёрное (и чёрное за белое), Ч-71
выдавать чёрное за белое (и белое за чёрное), Ч-71
выдать белое за чёрное (и чёрное за белое), Ч-71
выдать чёрное за белое (и белое за чёрное), Ч-71
назвать белое чёрным (и чёрное белым), Ч-71
назвать чёрное белым и белое чёрным, Ч-71
называть белое чёрным (и чёрное белым), Ч-71
называть чёрное белым и белое чёрным, Ч-71
принимать белое за чёрное (и чёрное за белое), Ч-71
принимать чёрное за белое (и белое за чёрное), Ч-71
принять белое за чёрное (и чёрное за белое), Ч-71
принять чёрное за белое (и белое за чёрное), Ч-71

БЕЛОМ
во всём белом свете, С-39
на (всём) белом свете, С-39
не жилец на белом свете, Ж-72

БЕЛОМУ
по белому свету, С-39
чёрным по белому, Ч-72

БЕЛУ
по белу свету, С-39

БЕЛУГОЙ
зареветь (реветь) белугой, Б-52

БЕЛЫЕ
белые мухи, М-298

БЕЛЫЙ
белый билет, Б-62
белый свет, С-39
белый шар, Ш-32
в белый свет как в копеечку, С-40

БЕЛЫМ
назвать (называть) белое чёрным и чёрное белым, Ч-71
назвать (называть) чёрное белым (и белое чёрным), Ч-71

БЕЛЫМИ
шито белыми нитками, Н-98

БЕЛЫХ
в белых перчатках, П-111
до белых мух, М-293

БЕЛЬЕ
копаться в (чужом) грязном белье, Б-53
рыться в (чужом) грязном белье, Б-53

БЕЛЬМА
вылупить (выпучить, выпялить) бельма, Г-100

лупить бельма, Г-100
пучить бельма, Г-100
пялить бельма, Г-100
разуй бельма, Г-94

БЕЛЬМЕСА
ни бельмеса, Б-54

БЕЛЬМО
бельмо в (на) глазу, Б-55
как* бельмо в (на) глазу, Б-55

БЕНЕФИС
устроить бенефис, Б-56

БЕРЕГА
молочные реки и кисельные берега, Р-107
молочные реки, кисельные берега, Р-107

БЕРЕГИ
береги (платье снову, а) честь смолоду, П-167

БЕРЕДИТЬ
бередить душу, Д-406
бередить рану (раны), Р-78
бередить сердце, Д-406

БЕРЕЖЁНОГО
бережёного (и) бог бережёт, Б-57

БЕРЕЖЁТ
бережёного (и) бог бережёт, Б-57
копейка рубль бережёт, К-279

БЕРЁЗОВАЯ
берёзовая каша, К-106

БЕРЁЗОВЫЙ
пень берёзовый, П-83

БЕРЁТ
ваша берёт, Б-58
зло берёт, З-132
злость берёт, З-132
наша берёт, Б-58
смелость города берёт, С-390
твоя берёт, Б-58

БЕРЁШЬ
не по чину берёшь!, Ч-150

БЕРИ
бери — не хочу, Х-95
дают — бери, бьют — беги, Д-29

БЕРУТ
завидки берут, З-19

БЕС
бес дёрнул, Ч-88
бес дёрнул за язык, Я-10
бес его знает, Ч-89
бес носит, Ч-96
бес попутал, Ч-97
на кой бес, Ч-77

БЕСА
беса лысого, Ч-106
какого беса?, Ч-103

БЕСИТЬСЯ
с жиру беситься, Ж-78

БЕСКОНЕЧНОСТИ
до бесконечности, Б-59

БЕСОМ
за каким бесом, Ч-77

рассыпаться мелким бесом, Б-60

БЕСПЛАТНОЕ
бесплатное приложение, П-529

БЕСПЛОДНАЯ
бесплодная смоковница, С-412

БЕССТРУННАЯ
бесструнная балалайка, Б-13

БЕСТИЯ
продувная бестия, Б-61

БЕСУ
к бесу, Ч-111

БЕШЕНЫЕ
бешеные деньги, Д-168

БИЛЕТ
белый билет, Б-62
волчий билет, Б-63
выложить билет (на стол), Б-65
жёлтый билет, Б-64
положить билет (на стол), Б-65

БИРЮКОМ
глядеть бирюком, Б-67
жить бирюком, Б-66
сидеть бирюком, Б-67
смотреть бирюком, Б-67

БИРЮЛЬКИ
игра в бирюльки, Б-68
играть в бирюльки, Б-68

БИСЕР
метать (рассыпать) бисер перед свиньями, Б-69

БИТА
карта бита, К-87

БИТВЫ
поле битвы, П-296

БИТКОМ
битком набить, Н-2
битком набиться, Н-2

БИТЫЙ
битый час, Ч-7

БИТЬ
бить баклуши, Б-11
бить в глаза, Г-44
бить в набат, Н-1
бить в нос, Н-206
бить в одну точку, Т-184
бить в цель, Ц-23
бить во все колокола, К-201
бить его же (собственным) оружием, О-105
бить как* обухом по голове, О-31
бить ключом, К-145
бить мимо цели, Ц-19
бить набат, Н-1
бить наверняка, Б-70
бить некому, Б-71
бить отбой, О-129
бить по карману, К-85
бить по рукам, Р-243
бить прямо в цель, Ц-23
бить рублём, Р-200

бить себя в грудь, Г-421
бить тревогу, Т-197
бить челом, Ч-55
бить через край, К-352
из пушек (пушки) по воробьям бить, П-666

БИТЬСЯ
биться как рыба об лёд, Р-378
биться об заклад, З-45

БИТЬЯ
мальчик для битья, М-20

БИШЬ
то бишь, Т-111

БЛАГ
всех благ, Б-72

БЛАГА
ни за какие блага (в мире), Б-73

БЛАГИМ
благим матом, М-47

БЛАГО
почесть (рассудить) за благо, Б-74
счесть за благо, Б-74

БЛАГОДАРЮ
покорнейше (покорно) благодарю, Б-75

БЛАГОДАРЯ
благодаря тому что, Т-150

БЛАГОДАТЬ
тишь да (и) гладь да (и) божья благодать, Т-102

БЛАГОНАДЁЖЕН
будь благонадёжен, Б-226

БЛАГОНАДЁЖНЫ
будьте благонадёжны, Б-226

БЛАГОРОДНОЕ
риск — благородное дело, Р-119

БЛАГОРОДНЫЙ
благородный жест, Ж-23

БЛАГУЮ
избирать/избрать благую часть, Ч-29

БЛАЖЕННОЙ
блаженной памяти, П-30

БЛАЖЕННОМ
в блаженном неведении, Н-58

БЛАЖЕНСТВА
на верху блаженства, В-57

БЛАТУ
по блату, Б-76

БЛЕЗИРУ
для блезиру, Б-77

БЛЕСКЕ
во всём блеске, Б-78

БЛЕСКОМ
с блеском, Б-79

БЛЕСТИТ
не всё то золото, что блестит, З-183

БЛИЖЕ
ближе к делу, Д-142
своя рубаха (рубашка) ближе к телу, Р-190

БЛИЖНИЙ
не ближний свет, С-50

БЛИЗКИЙ
не близкий свет, С-50

БЛИЗКО
близко локоть, да не
укусишь, Л-130
принимать/принять
близко к сердцу, С-149

БЛИЗОК
близок локоть, да не
укусишь, Л-130
не близок свет, С-50

БЛИН
первый блин (всегда)
комом, Б-80

БЛИНЫ
печь как блины, Б-81

БЛИСТАТЬ
блистать (своим)
отсутствием, О-170

БЛОХ
выискивать блох, Б-82
ловить блох, Б-82

БЛУДНЫЙ
блудный сын, С-732

БЛУЖДАТЬ
блуждать в потёмках,
П-423

БЛЮДЕ
как на блюде, Б-83
на блюде, Б-84

БЛЮДЕЧКЕ
как на блюдечке, Б-83
на блюдечке, Б-84
на блюдечке с голубой
〈золотой〉 каёмочкой,
Б-84

БОБАХ
гадание на бобах, Г-450
гадать на бобах, Г-450
на бобах, Б-85

БОБРА
убить бобра, Б-86

БОБЫ
бобы разводить, Б-87

БОГ
бережёного (и) бог
бережёт, Б-57
бог в помочь 〈помощь〉,
Б-99
бог ведает, Б-93
бог велел 〈велит〉, Б-122
бог весть, Б-93
бог даёт, Б-88
бог дал, Б-88, Б-89
бог дал, бог и взял, Б-90
бог даст, Б-91
бог даст день, бог даст
пищу, Б-92
бог даст день, даст и
пищу, Б-92
бог его ведает, Б-93
бог его знает, Б-93
бог знает, Б-93, Б-94
бог знает как, Б-95
бог знает сколько, Б-96
бог знает что, Б-97
бог миловал, Б-98

бог мой!, Б-142
бог на помочь 〈помощь〉,
Б-99
бог не выдаст, свинья не
съест, Б-100
бог не обидел, Б-101
бог несёт, Б-102
бог помочь, Б-99
бог прибрал, Б-103
бог привёл, Б-89
бог принёс, Б-102
бог с тобой, Б-104
бог троицу любит, Б-105
бог ты мой!, Б-142
видит бог, Б-106
вот (тебе) бог, а вот порог,
Б-107
да разразит меня бог,
Б-125
да разразит тебя бог,
Г-407
давай бог ноги, Б-108
дай бог, Б-109
дай бог всем..., Б-110
дай бог всякому, Б-110
дай бог здоровья, Б-111
дай бог каждому..., Б-110
дай бог любому..., Б-110
дай бог ноги, Б-108
дай бог памяти 〈память〉,
Б-112
и бог велел 〈велит〉, Б-122
избави бог, Б-143
как бог на душу положит,
Б-113
как бог свят, Б-114
кто рано встаёт, тому бог
(по)даёт, В-346
не бог весть как, Б-115
не бог весть какой, Б-116
не бог весть сколько, Б-117
не бог весть что, Б-118
не бог знает как, Б-115
не бог знает какой, Б-116
не бог знает сколько, Б-117
не дай бог, Б-119
не приведи бог, Б-119
не приведи бог сколько,
Б-120
оборони бог, Б-143
один бог ведает, Б-138
один бог знает, Б-138
побей меня бог, Б-125
покарай меня бог, Б-125
помилуй бог, Б-121
помогай бог, Б-99
пусть разразит тебя бог,
Г-407
разрази меня бог, Б-125
сам бог велел 〈велит〉,
Б-122
сколько бог на душу
положит, Б-123
сохрани бог, Б-143
счастлив твой бог, Б-124
убей (меня) бог, Б-125
упаси бог, Б-143
царь и бог, Ц-8
человек предполагает, а
бог располагает, Ч-52
чем бог послал, Б-126

что бог даст, Б-127
что бог на душу положит,
Б-128
что бог послал, Б-126

БОГА
бога бы побоялся, Б-130
бога ради, Б-131
брать на бога, П-669
в бога (душу) мать, М-55
взять на бога, П-669
на бога надейся, а сам не
плошай, Б-129
от бога, М-162
побойся бога, Б-130
ради бога, Б-131
ради (самого) господа
бога, Б-131

БОГАТЫ
чем богаты, тем и рады,
Б-132

БОГИ
не боги горшки обжигают,
Б-133

БОГОМ
богом обижен(ный), Б-134
все (мы) под богом ходим,
Б-135
с богом, Б-136

БОГУ
ни богу свечка 〈свеча〉 ни
чёрту кочерга, Б-137
одному богу ведомо, Б-138
одному богу известно,
Б-138
отдавать/отдать богу
душу, Б-139
слава богу, С-244

БОДЯГУ
разводить бодягу, Б-140

БОЕВОЕ
боевое крещение, К-384

БОЕК
боек на слова, Я-7
боек на язык, Я-7

БОЕМ
смертным боем, Б-141

БОЖЕ
боже мой!, Б-142
боже оборони, Б-143
боже сохрани, Б-143
боже ты мой!, Б-142
боже упаси, Б-143
избави боже, Б-143
не дай боже, Б-119
не приведи боже, Б-119
ни боже мой, Б-144

БОЖЕСКИЙ
привести 〈приводить〉 в
божеский вид, В-113
придавать/придать
божеский вид, В-113

БОЖЕСКОЕ
наказание божеское, Н-21

БОЖЕСКУЮ
сделай(те) божескую
милость, М-161
яви(те) божескую
милость, М-161

БОЖИЕМ
в страхе божием, С-631

БОЖИЙ
божий одуванчик, О-84
божий свет, С-39
вывести 〈выводить〉 на
свет божий, С-41
всплывать/всплыть на
свет божий, С-44
выплывать/выплыть на
свет божий, С-44
выступать/выступить на
свет божий, С-44
извлекать/извлечь на свет
божий, С-47
каждый божий день, Д-161
как божий день, Д-162
на свет божий не глядел
〈не смотрел〉 бы, С-48
перст божий, П-108
раб божий, Р-1

БОЖЬЕГО
света божьего не видеть,
С-66
света 〈свету〉 божьего
невзвидеть, С-67

БОЖЬЕЙ
божьей милостью, М-162

БОЖЬЕМ
в страхе божьем, С-631

БОЖЬЯ
божья коровка, К-314
искра божья, И-75
тишь да 〈и〉 гладь да 〈и〉
божья благодать, Т-102

БОЗЕ
почить в бозе, Б-145

БОИТСЯ
дело мастера боится, Д-85
пуганая ворона (и) куста
боится, В-275

БОЙ
давать/дать бой, Б-147
объявить 〈объявлять〉
бой, Б-148
рваться в бой, Б-149

БОЙ-БАБА
бой-баба, Б-146

БОЙ-ДЕВКА
бой-девка, Б-146

БОЙКИЙ
бойкий на слова, Я-7
бойкий на язык, Я-7

БОЙКОЕ
бойкое перо, П-99

БОК
бок о бок, Б-150
о бок, Б-150
с боку на бок, Б-161

БОКА
брать/взять за бока, Б-151
держаться за бока, Ж-35
за бока, Б-151
нагреть бока, Б-152
наломать бока, Б-152
намять бока, Б-152
обломать бока, Б-152
помять бока, Б-152
хвататься за бока, Ж-35

БОКАЛ(Ы)
поднимать/поднять
бокал(ы), Б-153

БОКАМИ
 отдуваться своими
  〈собственными〉
  боками, Б-154
БОКОВУЮ
 на боковую, Б-155
БОКОМ
 выйти 〈выходить〉 боком,
  Б-156
 под боком, Б-157
БОКУ
 лежать на боку, Б-158
 по боку, Б-159
 подойти 〈подходить〉 с
  другого боку, Б-160
 с боку на бок, Б-161
 с какого боку, Б-162
 с какого боку подойти
  〈подступиться〉, Б-163
БОЛВАН
 болван стоеросовый, Д-317
БОЛЕЕ
 более или менее, Б-164
 более того, Б-165
 более чем..., Б-166
 всё более и более, Б-167
 далее – более, Д-18
 не более, Б-168
 не более 〈и〉 не менее,
  М-197
 не более того, Б-168
 ни более 〈и〉 ни менее,
  М-197
 тем более, Т-64
 тем более что, Т-65
БОЛЕЗНИ
 болезни роста, Б-169
БОЛЕТЬ
 болеть душой, Д-395
 болеть сердцем, Д-395
БОЛИТ
 голова болит, Г-197
 душа болит, Д-364
 за чужой щекой зуб не
  болит, Щ-3
 сердце болит, Д-364
 у кого что болит, тот о
  том и говорит, Б-170
 что у кого болит, тот о
  том и говорит, Б-170
БОЛОТО
 всяк кулик своё болото
  хвалит, К-467
 ну тебя в болото!, Б-171
БОЛТАТЬ
 болтать ерунду, В-99
 болтать на ветер, В-68
 болтать чепуху, В-99
 болтать языком, Я-57
БОЛЬНО
 больно жирно (будет),
  Б-217
БОЛЬНОЕ
 больное место, М-110
БОЛЬНОЙ
 больной вопрос, В-258
 валить с больной головы
  на здоровую, Г-284
 перекладывать с больной
  головы на здоровую,
  Г-284

сваливать/свалить с
  больной головы на
  здоровую, Г-284
БОЛЬНУЮ
 задевать/задеть (за)
  больную струну, С-649
 затронуть (за) больную
  струну, С-649
 наступать/наступить на
  больную мозоль, М-230
 тронуть (за) больную
  струну, С-649
БОЛЬШАЯ
 большая дорога, Д-263
 большая нужда, Н-253
 большая разница, Р-58
 большая рука, Р-225
 большая шишка, Ш-70
 не большая хитрость, Х-27
БОЛЬШЕ
 больше жизни!, Ж-37
 больше того, Б-165
 больше чем..., Б-166
 всё больше, Б-172
 всё больше и больше,
  Б-167
 дальше – больше, Д-18
 не больше, Б-168
 не больше 〈и〉 не меньше,
  М-197
 не больше того, Б-168
 ни больше 〈и〉 ни меньше,
  М-197
 чем дальше в лес, тем
  больше дров, Л-59
БОЛЬШЕЕ
 самое большее, Б-173
БОЛЬШЕЙ
 большей частью, Ч-30
 для большей важности,
  В-2
 по большей части, Ч-30
БОЛЬШИЕ
 большие дела, Д-68
 две большие разницы,
  Р-60
 делать большие глаза,
  Г-66
 подавать большие
  надежды, Н-9
 сделать большие глаза,
  Г-66
БОЛЬШИМ
 под большим вопросом,
  В-263
БОЛЬШИМИ
 смотреть большими
  глазами, Г-66
БОЛЬШИНСТВЕ
 в большинстве 〈своём〉,
  Б-174
БОЛЬШИХ
 в больших чинах, Ч-148
БОЛЬШОГО
 большого сердца, С-121
 от 〈с〉 большого ума, У-88
БОЛЬШОЕ
 большое дело, Д-68
 большое сердце, С-129
 большому кораблю –
  большое плавание,
  К-290

самое большое, Б-173
БОЛЬШОЙ
 большой души, С-121
 большой руки, Р-276
 на большой, П-4
 на большой палец, П-4
 по большой, Б-175
 разбойник с большой
  дороги, Р-41
 с большой буквы, Б-239
 сам большой, Б-176
БОЛЬШОМ
 в большом ходу, Х-65
БОЛЬШОМУ
 большому кораблю –
  большое плавание,
  К-290
 к большому сожалению,
  С-464
 по большому, Б-177
 по большому счёту, С-725
БОЛЬШУЮ
 на большую ногу, Н-177
БОМБА
 влетать/влететь как
  бомба, Б-178
БОМБОЙ
 влетать/влететь бомбой,
  Б-178
БОРЗЫМИ
 борзыми щенками, Щ-4
БОРОДОЙ
 с бородой, Б-179
БОРОДУ
 в бороду, Б-180
БОРОЛИСЬ
 за что боролись, на то и
  напоролись, Б-181
БОРОТЬСЯ
 бороться его же
  〈собственным〉
  оружием, О-105
 бороться с (самим) собой,
  Б-182
БОРТ
 бросать/бросить за борт,
  Б-183
 выбрасывать/выбросить
  за борт, Б-183
 выкидывать/выкинуть за
  борт, Б-183
 вышвыривать/
  вышвырнуть за борт,
  Б-183
БОРТОМ
 за бортом, Б-184
БОРУ
 и с бору и с сосенки, Б-185
 с бору да с сосенки, Б-185
 с бору по сосенке, Б-185
БОСУ
 на босу ногу, Н-172
БОСУЮ
 на босую ногу, Н-172
БОЧЕК
 сорок бочек арестантов,
  Б-186
БОЧКА
 бездонная бочка, Б-187

бочка Данаид, Б-188
 как бочка, Б-189
 пороховая бочка, Б-190
БОЧКЕ
 к каждой бочке затычка,
  Б-191
 как сельдей 〈сельди〉 в
  бочке, С-115
 ко всякой бочке затычка,
  Б-191
 ложка дёгтю в бочке мёда
  〈мёду〉, Л-128
БОЧКУ
 деньги на бочку, Д-169
 катить/покатить бочку,
  Б-192
БОЮ
 брать/взять с бою, Б-193
БОЮСЬ
 боюсь назвать, Б-194
 боюсь сказать, Б-194
БОЯ
 поле боя, П-296
БОЯТЬСЯ
 волков бояться – в лес не
  ходить, В-231
БРАЗДЫ
 бразды правления, Б-195
БРАЛ
 чёрт бы тебя брал!, Ч-99
БРАНИ
 поле брани, П-296
БРАНЬ
 брань на вороту не виснет,
  Б-196
БРАНЯТСЯ
 милые бранятся – только
  тешатся, М-163
БРАТ
 ваш брат, Б-197
 наш брат, Б-198
 ни сват ни брат, С-31
 сам чёрт не брат, Ч-81
 свой брат, Б-199
 свой своему поневоле брат
  〈друг〉, Б-200
 чёрт не брат, Ч-81
БРАТА
 на брата, Б-201
 с брата, Б-202
БРАТСКАЯ
 братская могила, М-200
БРАТЬ
 брать барьер(ы), Б-26
 брать быка за рога, Б-256
 брать в ежовые рукавицы,
  Р-241
 брать в оборот, О-16
 брать в переплёт, П-94
 брать в работу, О-16
 брать в расчёт, Р-91
 брать в руки, Р-277, Р-278
 брать в свои руки, Р-278
 брать в соображение,
  С-487
 брать в шоры, Ш-83
 брать верх, В-53
 брать волю, В-247
 брать голыми руками,
  Р-253

брать горлом, Г-346
брать грех на душу, Г-382
брать за бока, Б-151
брать за глотку, Г-335
брать за горло, Г-335
брать за грудки, Г-420
брать за душу, Д-407
брать за жабры, Ж-1
брать за живое, Ж-30
брать за сердце, Д-407
брать за шкирку, Ш-73
брать измором, И-51
брать моду, М-210
брать на абордаж, А-2
брать на арапа, А-36
брать на бога, П-669
брать на буксир, Б-241
брать на вооружение,
    В-257
брать на глотку, Г-336
брать на горло, Г-336
брать на заметку, З-54
брать на замечание, З-54
брать на измор, И-51
брать на испуг, И-80
брать на карандаш, К-69
брать на караул, К-71
брать на мушку, П-555
брать на откуп, О-152
брать на примету, П-538
брать на прицел, П-555
брать на пушку, П-669
брать на себя, Б-203
брать на себя смелость,
    С-389
брать на себя труд, Т-211
брать на учёт, У-167
брать начало, Н-36
брать ноги в руки, Н-140
брать под караул, С-624
брать под козырёк, К-173
брать под обстрел, О-29
брать под своё крылышко,
    К-429
брать под сомнение, С-478
брать под стражу, С-624
брать пример, П-530
брать расчёт, Р-90
брать с бою, Б-193
брать своё, С-84
брать своё начало, Н-36
брать своё слово назад
    ⟨обратно⟩, С-280
брать свои слова назад
    ⟨обратно⟩, С-280
брать себе в башку, Г-246
брать себе в голову, Г-246
брать себя в руки, Р-279
брать силу, С-188
брать слова назад
    ⟨обратно⟩, С-280
брать слово, С-306, С-307
брать слово назад
    ⟨обратно⟩, С-280
брать сторону, С-609
в рот не брать, Р-171
капли в рот не брать, К-60
маковой росинки в рот не
    брать, К-60
много на себя брать, Б-204
не брать в руки, Р-297

ни капли в рот не брать,
    К-60
БРАТЬСЯ
    браться за оружие, О-102
    браться за перо, П-100
    браться за ум, У-77
    браться на учёт, У-168
    браться не за своё дело,
        Д-69
БРЕВНА
    в чужом глазу сучок
        видим, а в своём ⟨и⟩
        бревна не замечаем,
        Г-140
БРЕД
    бред сивой кобылы, Б-205
БРЕМЕНИ
    разрешаться/разрешиться
        от бремени, Б-206
БРЕШЬ
    пробить брешь, Б-207
БРИЛЛИАНТОВАЯ
    бриллиантовая свадьба,
        С-25
БРИТЬ
    брить лбы ⟨лоб⟩, Л-115
БРОВЬ
    не в бровь, а ⟨прямо⟩ в
        глаз, Б-208
БРОВЬЮ
    бровью не ведёт/не повёл,
        Б-209
    бровью не шевельнул,
        Б-209
    и бровью не ведёт/не
        повёл, Б-209
    и бровью не шевельнул,
        Б-209
    стоит только бровью
        повести ⟨шевельнуть⟩,
        Б-210
    только бровью повести
        ⟨шевельнуть⟩, Б-210
БРОДИТ
    кровь бродит, К-403
БРОДИТЬ
    бродить в потёмках, П-423
БРОДУ
    не зная ⟨не спросясь⟩
        броду, не суйся в воду,
        Б-211
БРОСАЕТ
    бросает в краску, К-366
БРОСАТЬ
    бросать в глаза, Л-93
    бросать в жар ⟨и в холод⟩,
        Ж-2
    бросать в лицо, Л-93
    бросать взгляд, В-95
    бросать грязью, Г-434
    бросать деньгами, Д-165
    бросать жребий, Ж-83
    бросать за борт, Б-183
    бросать камень, К-37
    бросать камень в огород,
        К-47
    бросать каменья(ми), К-37
    бросать камешек
        ⟨камешки⟩ в огород,
        К-47

бросать камнем, К-37
бросать камни в огород,
    К-47
бросать на ветер, В-67,
    В-68
бросать на чашку ⟨чашу⟩
    весов, Ч-37
бросать оружие, О-104
бросать перчатку, П-112
бросать свет, С-56
бросать тень, Т-73
бросать в жар, то в
    холод, Ж-2
БРОСАТЬСЯ
    бросаться в глаза, Г-45
    бросаться в голову, Г-280
    бросаться в нос, Н-206
    бросаться деньгами, Д-165
    бросаться на шею, Ш-51
    бросаться наутёк, П-637
    бросаться обещаниями,
        С-295
    бросаться словами, С-295
БРОСИЛ
    поматросил и бросил,
        П-328
БРОСИЛАСЬ
    краска бросилась в лицо,
        К-400
    кровь бросилась в голову,
        К-399
    кровь бросилась в лицо,
        К-400
БРОСИЛО
    бросило в краску, К-366
БРОСИТЬ
    бросить в глаза, Л-93
    бросить в жар ⟨и в холод⟩,
        Ж-2
    бросить в лицо, Л-93
    бросить взгляд, В-95
    бросить грязью, Г-434
    бросить жребий, Ж-83
    бросить за борт, Б-183
    бросить камень, К-37
    бросить камнем, К-37
    бросить на ветер, В-67,
        В-68
    бросить на чашку ⟨чашу⟩
        весов, Ч-37
    бросить оружие, О-104
    бросить палку, П-11
    бросить перчатку, П-112
    бросить свет, С-56
    бросить тень, Т-73
    бросить якорь, Я-62
БРОСИТЬСЯ
    броситься в глаза, Г-45
    броситься в голову, Г-280
    броситься в ноги, Н-141
    броситься в нос, Н-206
    броситься на шею, Ш-51
    броситься наутёк, П-637
БРОСЬ
    оторви да ⟨и⟩ брось, О-161
    хоть брось, Б-212
БРОШЕН
    жребий брошен, Ж-84
БРУДЕРШАФТ
    пить/выпить ⟨на⟩
        брудершафт, Б-213

БРЮКИ
    руки в брюки, Р-313
БРЮХЕ
    ползать на брюхе, Б-214
БРЮХО
    на голодное брюхо, Ж-14
    на сытое брюхо, Ж-15
БРЯЦАНИЕ
    бряцание оружием, О-106
БРЯЦАТЬ
    бряцать оружием, О-106
БУБЛИКА
    дырка от бублика, Д-439
БУДЕМ
    будем здоровы, Б-228
    все там будем, Б-215
    на том стояли, стоим и
        стоять будем, С-577
БУДЕТ
    больно жирно будет, Б-217
    будет день, будет пища,
        Б-92
    будет и на нашей улице
        праздник, У-72
    будь что будет, Б-232
    видно будет, Б-216
    да будет земля пухом,
        З-128
    жирно будет, Б-217
    из хама не будет пана, Х-1
    нога ⟨ноги⟩ не будет,
        Н-148
    перемелется — мука будет,
        М-287
    плохо будет, Б-219
    пусть будет земля пухом,
        З-128
    слишком жирно будет,
        Б-217
    то ли ⟨ещё⟩ будет, Б-218
    худо будет, Б-219
    что будет, то будет, Б-220
БУДЕШЬ
    много будешь знать —
        скоро состаришься,
        З-173
    насильно мил не будешь,
        Б-221
    тише едешь — дальше
        будешь, Е-3
БУДИТЬ
    будить зверя, З-98
БУДТО
    бить будто обухом по
        голове, О-31
    будто аршин проглотил,
        А-42
    будто банный лист, Л-78
    будто белка в колесе, Б-51
    будто бельмо в ⟨на⟩ глазу,
        Б-55
    будто бы, Б-222
    будто в воду глядел, В-184
    будто в воду канул, В-185
    будто в воду опущенный,
        В-186
    будто в воду смотрел,
        В-184
    будто варом обдало, В-8
    будто ветром сдувало
        ⟨сдуло, сдунуло⟩, В-78

будто водой смыло, В-180
будто гора с плеч (свалилась), Г-316
будто гром среди ясного неба, Г-405
будто иголка в стоге ⟨в стогу⟩ сена, И-2
будто из-за угла (пыльным) мешком прибит(ый) ⟨трахнутый, ударен(ный)⟩, У-13
будто из земли, З-115
будто из-под земли, З-115
будто корова языком слизала ⟨слизнула⟩, К-310
будто курица лапой, К-479
будто Мамай прошёл, М-22
будто маслом по сердцу, М-38
будто на иголках, И-5
будто на ладони ⟨на ладонке, на ладошке⟩, Л-13
будто на подбор, П-238
будто на пожар, П-265
будто на смех, С-402
будто нарочно, Н-31
будто ножом отрезало, Н-189
будто обухом по голове, О-31
будто по волшебству, В-245
будто по команде, К-211
будто по манию волшебного жезла, М-27
будто по мановению волшебного жезла, М-27
будто по мановению волшебной палочки, М-27
будто по писаному, П-157
будто подменили, П-246
будто потерянный, П-427
будто рукой сняло, Р-332
будто с неба свалиться ⟨упасть⟩, Н-46
будто с привязи сорваться, Ц-37
будто с цепи сорваться, Ц-37
будто свинцом налита, С-78
будто сквозь землю провалился, З-120
будто сквозь сон, С-481
будто снег на голову, С-430
будто ужаленный, У-54
будто холодной водой облить ⟨окатить⟩, В-181
будто язык проглотил, Я-23
вертеться будто белка в колесе, Б-51
как будто (бы), К-11
как будто в чаду, Ч-1
как будто пелена падает (с глаз), П-76

как будто пелена спадает/ спала (с глаз), П-76
как будто пелена упала (с глаз), П-76
как будто подменили, П-246
как будто покров падает (с глаз), П-76
как будто покров спадает/ спал (с глаз), П-76
как будто покров упал (с глаз), П-76
как будто с неба свалиться ⟨упасть⟩, Н-46
как будто язык проглотил, Я-23
кружиться ⟨крутиться⟩) будто белка в колесе, Б-51
ударить ⟨ударять⟩ будто обухом по голове, О-31
БУДУ
землю есть буду, З-118
(я) не я буду, Б-223
БУДУТ
это ещё ⟨только⟩ цветики ⟨цветки, цветочки⟩, а ягодки будут впереди, Ц-16
БУДУЩЕЕ
заглядывать/заглянуть в будущее, Б-224
БУДУЩЕМ
в будущем, Б-225
БУДЬ
будь благонадёжен, Б-226
будь добр, Б-227
будь друг ⟨другом⟩, Д-313
будь здоров, Б-228, Б-229
будь любезен, Б-227
будь моя воля, В-252
будь покоен, Б-235
будь ты неладен, Б-230
будь ты (трижды) проклят, Б-231
будь что будет, Б-232
будь я (трижды) проклят, Б-233
не будь дура ⟨дурак⟩, Д-331
не будь дурён ⟨дурна⟩, Д-331
не в обиду будь сказано, О-4
не в укор будь сказано, У-69
не в упрёк будь сказано, У-69
не во гнев будь сказано, О-4
не к ночи будь помянут, Н-243
не к ночи будь сказано, Н-243
не тем будь помянут, Б-234
БУДЬТЕ
будьте благонадёжны, Б-226
будьте добры, Б-227

будьте здоровы, Б-228
будьте любезны, Б-227
будьте покойны, Б-235
БУЗИНА
в огороде бузина, а в Киеве дядька, О-68
БУЙНАЯ
буйная голова ⟨головушка⟩, Г-195
БУКВА
буква в букву, Б-236
буква закона, Б-237
БУКВОЙ
мёртвой буквой, Б-238
БУКВУ
буква в букву, Б-236
БУКВЫ
с большой буквы, Б-239
БУКОЙ
глядеть букой, Б-240
смотреть букой, Б-240
БУКСИР
брать/взять на буксир, Б-241
БУЛАВКИ
на булавки, Б-242
БУЛАВОЧНУЮ
в ⟨с⟩ булавочную головку, Г-233
БУЛАВОЧНЫЙ
булавочный укол, У-68
БУМ-БУМ
ни бум-бум, Б-54
БУМАГА
бумага всё стерпит, Б-243
бумага не краснеет, Б-243
БУМАГЕ
на бумаге, Б-244
БУМАГУ
лечь на бумагу, Б-245
ложиться на бумагу, Б-245
марать бумагу, Б-246
БУМАЖКЕ
барашек в бумажке, Б-23
БУМАЖНАЯ
бумажная душа, Д-378
бумажная крыса, К-434
БУРИДАНОВ
буриданов осёл, О-108
БУРКУ
укатали ⟨умыкали, уходили⟩ бурку крутые горки, С-160
БУРЯ
буря в стакане воды, Б-247
БУТЫЛКЕ
прикладываться к бутылке, Б-248
БУТЫЛКУ
заглядывать в бутылку, Б-248
лезть/полезть в бутылку, Б-249
раздавить бутылку, Б-250
БУХТА-БАРАХТА
с бухта-барахта, Б-251
БУХТЫ-БАРАХТЫ
с бухты-барахты, Б-251

БЫВАЕТ
дыма без огня не бывает, Д-437
и на старуху бывает проруха, С-549
свято место пусто не бывает, М-121
БЫВАЛО
как не бывало, Б-252
как ни в чём не бывало, Б-253
ничего не бывало, Б-254
ничуть не бывало, Б-254
БЫВАТЬ
бывать в переделках ⟨в переделке⟩, П-95
бывать в передрягах ⟨в передряге⟩, П-95
бывать в переплётах ⟨в переплёте⟩, П-95
двум смертям ⟨двух смертей⟩ не бывать, а одной не миновать, С-399
БЫВАЮТ
и у стен бывают уши, С-559
БЫК
как бык, Б-255
БЫКА
брать/взять быка за рога, Б-256
схватить быка за рога, Б-256
хватать быка за рога, Б-256
БЫЛ
был да сплыл, Б-257
в чём был, Б-259
и был таков, Б-258
как был, Б-259
кто бы (то) ни был, Б-260
БЫЛА
была бы моя воля, В-252
была бы честь предложена ⟨приложена⟩, Ч-129
была не была, Б-261
чтоб нога не была, Н-148
БЫЛИ
были когда-то и мы рысаками, Р-393
БЫЛО
где бы то ни было, Б-262
как бы там ни было, Б-263
как бы то ни было, Б-263
какой бы то ни было, Б-264
когда бы то ни было, Б-265
кто бы то ни было, Б-266
куда бы то ни было, Б-262
маковой росинки во рту не было, Р-161
не было бы счастья, да несчастье помогло, С-693
не было заботы!, З-7
не было ни гроша, да (и) вдруг алтын, Г-417
не было печали, (так) черти накачали, П-137

не было у бабы хлопот
⟨забот⟩, (так) купила
(баба) порося, Б-2
не тут-то было, Б-267
ни (маковой) росинки во
рту не было, Р-161
ничего во рту не было,
Р-161
почему бы то ни было,
Б-268
сколько бы то ни было,
Б-269
чей бы то ни было, Б-270
что бы то ни было, Б-271
что было духу, Д-361
что было мочи, М-271
что было сил(ы), М-271
что было, то прошло (и
быльём поросло), Б-275
чтоб ноги не было, Н-148
чтоб пусто было, Б-273
чтобы духу не было, Д-362
чтобы не было повадно,
Б-272
чтобы неповадно было,
Б-272
чуть было не..., Ч-205
чуть-чуть было не...,
Ч-205

БЫЛЬЁМ
быльём поросло, Б-274
что было, то прошло (и
быльём поросло), Б-275

БЫЛЬЮ
былью поросло, Б-274

БЫСТРОТОЮ
с быстротою молнии,
Б-276

БЫТ
войти ⟨входить⟩ в быт,
Ж-50

БЫТЬ
быть бычку на верёвочке,
Б-283
быть не может!, М-214
быть по сему, Б-277
должно быть, Б-278
и разговора ⟨разговору⟩
быть не может, Р-51
и речи быть не может,
Р-112
имею честь быть, Ч-134
какой может быть
разговор!, Р-50
может быть, М-213
надо быть, Б-279
не до жиру, быть бы живу,
Ж-77
не может быть!, М-214
не может быть и речи,
Р-112
речи быть не может, Р-112
стало быть, С-541
так и быть, Б-280
так тому и быть, Б-281
чему быть, того ⟨тому⟩ не
миновать, Б-282

БЫЧКА
сказка про белого бычка,
С-214

БЫЧКУ
быть бычку на верёвочке,
Б-283

БЬЮТ
дают — бери, бьют —
беги, Д-29
лежачего не бьют, Л-45

БЮДЖЕТА
выйти ⟨выходить⟩ из
бюджета, Б-284

В

ВА-БАНК
играть ва-банк, И-25
идти/пойти ва-банк, И-25
сыграть ва-банк, И-25

ВАВИЛОНСКОЕ
вавилонское
столпотворение, С-596

ВАВИЛОНЫ
выводить вавилоны, В-33
писать вавилоны, В-33

ВАГОН
вагон и маленькая
тележка, В-1

ВАЖНАЯ
важная птица, П-615
важная шишка, Ш-70

ВАЖНОСТИ
для (большей) важности,
В-2
для пущей важности, В-2

ВАЖНОСТЬ
велика важность!, В-3
не велика важность, В-4
что за важность!, В-3
эка важность!, В-3

ВАЛ
девятый вал, В-5

ВАЛААМОВА
валаамова ослица
(заговорила), О-112

ВАЛИТСЯ
валится из рук, Р-207

ВАЛИТЬ
валить в (одну) кучу, К-498
валить с больной головы
на здоровую, Г-284
валить с ног, Н-112
валом валить, В-6

ВАЛИТЬСЯ
валиться с ног, Н-113

ВАЛКО
и шатко и валко (и на
сторону), Ш-38
ни шатко ни валко (ни на
сторону), Ш-39

ВАЛОМ
валом валить/повалить,
В-6

ВАЛТАСАРОВ
валтасаров пир, П-151

ВАЛТАСАРОВО
валтасарово пиршество,
П-151

ВАЛЯЕТСЯ
на дороге не валяется,
Д-268

на земле не валяется,
Д-268
на полу не валяется, Д-268
на улице не валяется,
Д-268

ВАЛЯЛСЯ
конь (ещё) не валялся,
К-267

ВАЛЯТСЯ
все шишки валятся на
голову, Ш-72
на бедного Макара все
шишки валятся, М-4

ВАЛЯТЬ
валять ваньку, Д-333
валять дурака, Д-333
валять дурочку, Д-333

ВАЛЯТЬСЯ
валяться в ногах ⟨в
ножках⟩, Н-130
валяться от смеха ⟨от
хохота⟩, С-406
валяться с хохоту, С-406
валяться со смеху, С-406

ВАМ
вот вам!, Т-48
вот вам и весь разговор
⟨сказ⟩, Р-46
вот вам крест!, К-380
говорю ⟨говорят⟩ вам,
Г-177
доложу (я) вам, Д-247
как вам сказать, С-205
наше вам (с кисточкой),
К-124

ВАНЬКУ
валять ваньку, Д-333
корчить ваньку, Д-333
ломать ваньку, Д-333
свалять ваньку, Д-333

ВАРВАРЕ
любопытной Варваре нос
оторвали, В-7

ВАРИТ
голова варит, Г-199
котелок варит, Г-199

ВАРИТЬСЯ
в котле вариться, К-340
вариться в котле, К-339,
К-340
вариться в собственном
соку, С-470
как* в котле вариться,
К-340

ВАРОМ
как* варом обдало, В-8

ВАРФОЛОМЕЕВСКАЯ
варфоломеевская ночь,
Н-244

ВАРЯТ
мозги варят, Г-199

ВАС
знаем мы вас!, З-142
ну я вас спрашиваю!,
С-525
с чем вас и поздравляем
⟨поздравляю⟩, П-272
я вас спрашиваю!, С-525

ВАШ
ваш брат, Б-197

ваш покорнейший слуга,
С-346
ваш покорный слуга, С-346

ВАША
ваша берёт, Б-58
ваша взяла, Б-58
ваша власть, В-164
ваша правда, П-478
ваша сестра, С-154
воля ваша, В-254

ВАШЕ
ваше здоровье!, З-105
за ваше здоровье!, З-105
с ваше, М-211

ВАШЕГО
с вашего позволения
⟨разрешения⟩, П-268

ВАШЕМУ
к вашему сведению, С-33

ВАШИ
в ваши края, К-376

ВАШИМ
и нашим и вашим, Н-45
к вашим услугам, У-134

ВАШИМИ
вашими бы устами (да)
мёд пить, У-145
вашими молитвами, М-231

ВАШИХ
в ваших краях, К-376
и ваших нет, В-9

ВАШУ
вашу мать, М-55
ёб вашу мать, М-50
так вашу мать, М-55

ВБИВАТЬ
вбивать в башку, Г-245
вбивать в голову, Г-245
вбивать клин, К-134
вбивать себе в башку,
Г-246
вбивать себе в голову,
Г-246

ВБИТЬ
вбить в башку, Г-245
вбить в голову, Г-245
вбить клин, К-134
вбить осиновый кол (в
могилу), К-177
вбить себе в башку, Г-246
вбить себе в голову, Г-246

ВВЕРХ
вверх дном, Д-208
вверх ногами, Н-125
вверх тормашками
⟨тормашки⟩, Т-162
глядеть снизу вверх, С-419
лететь вверх тормашками
⟨тормашки⟩, Т-163
перевернуть
⟨перевёртывать⟩ вверх
тормашками, Т-164
переворачивать вверх
тормашками, Т-164
полететь вверх
тормашками
⟨тормашки⟩, Т-163
руки вверх!, Р-314
смотреть снизу вверх,
С-419

[858]

ВЕРОЙ-ПРАВДОЙ, В-41

ВЕРОЯТНОСТИ
по всей вероятности, В-42

ВЁРСТ
для друга ⟨для милого дружка⟩ ⟨и⟩ семь вёрст не околица, Д-312
за семь вёрст киселя есть ⟨хлебать⟩, В-43
семь вёрст до небес (и всё лесом), В-44

ВЕРСТА
коломенская верста, В-45

ВЕРСТУ
в коломенскую версту, В-45
за версту, В-46
обойти ⟨обходить⟩ за версту, В-48
с коломенскую версту, В-45

ВЕРСТЫ/ВЁРСТЫ
мерить ⟨мерять⟩ вёрсты, В-47
обойти ⟨обходить⟩ за три версты, В-48

ВЕРТЕТЬ
вертеть хвостом, Х-24
вертеть шарманку, Ш-36
вола вертеть, В-220

ВЕРТЕТЬСЯ
вертеться в голове, Г-226
вертеться волчком, В-244
вертеться вьюном, В-393
вертеться как* белка в колесе, Б-51
вертеться на глазах, Г-104
вертеться на языке, Я-53
вертеться перед глазами, Г-104
вертеться под ногами, Н-126

ВЕРТИ
как ни верти, К-427
как там ⟨тут⟩ ни верти, К-427

ВЕРТИСЬ
как ⟨там⟩ ни вертись, К-428

ВЕРУ
давать/дать веру, В-49
на веру, В-50
обратить ⟨обращать⟩ в свою веру, В-51
принимать/принять на веру, В-52

ВЕРХ
брать/взять верх, В-53
держать верх, В-54
забирать/забрать верх, В-53
одержать ⟨одерживать⟩ верх, В-53

ВЕРХАМ
скользить по верхам, В-55

ВЕРХИ
хватать верхи, В-55

ВЕРХОВ
нахвататься верхов, В-55

ВЕРХОМ
ездить верхом, Е-7

с верхом, В-56
садиться/сесть верхом, С-1

ВЕРХУ
на верху блаженства, В-57

ВЕРХУШЕК
нахвататься верхушек, В-55

ВЕРХУШКИ
хватать верхушки, В-55

ВЕРШИТЕЛЬ
вершитель судеб, В-58

ВЕРШКА
от горшка два ⟨три⟩ вершка, Г-355

ВЕРШКИ
хватать вершки, В-55

ВЕРШКОВ
нахвататься вершков, В-55

ВЕС
иметь вес, В-59
на вес золота, В-60
удельный вес, В-61

ВЕСЁЛУЮ
делать весёлую мину при плохой игре, М-167
под весёлую руку, Р-354
сделать весёлую мину при плохой игре, М-167
устраивать/устроить весёлую жизнь, Ж-65

ВЕСНЫ
одна ласточка весны не делает, Л-33

ВЕСОВ
бросать на чашку ⟨чашу⟩ весов, Ч-37
бросить на чашку ⟨чашу⟩ весов, Ч-37
класть на чашку ⟨чашу⟩ весов, Ч-37
положить на чашку ⟨чашу⟩ весов, Ч-37

ВЕСТИ
вести начало, Н-37
вести речь, Р-113
вести своё начало, Н-37
вести свою линию, Л-75
вести себя, В-62
пропасть без вести, В-63
худые вести не лежат на месте, В-64
худые вести не сидят на насесте, В-64

ВЕСТЬ
бог весть, Б-93, Б-94
не бог весть как, Б-115
не бог весть какой, Б-116
не бог весть сколько, Б-117
не бог весть что, Б-118

ВЕСУ
на весу, В-65

ВЕСЬ
весь вышел, В-390
весь наружу, В-66
весь свет в окошке, С-74
весь сыр-бор ⟨загорелся⟩, С-737
во весь голос, Г-299

во весь дух, Д-342
во весь мах, Д-342
во весь народ, Н-29
во все опор, Д-342
во весь рост, Р-167
во весь рот, Р-173
во весь скок, С-227
вот (вам) и весь разговор ⟨сказ⟩, Р-46
вот тебе и весь разговор ⟨сказ⟩, Р-46
и весь разговор ⟨сказ⟩, Р-46
на весь народ, Н-29
обивать/обить весь порог, П-377
перевернуть весь мир ⟨свет⟩, М-183
пир на весь мир, П-153
пообивать/пообить весь порог, П-377

ВЕТЕР
болтать на ветер, В-68
бросать/бросить на ветер, В-67, В-68
ветер в голове, В-69
ветер в карманах ⟨в кармане⟩, В-70
ветер свистит в карманах ⟨в кармане⟩, В-70
выбрасывать/выбросить на ветер, В-67
говорить на ветер, В-68
какой ветер занёс?, В-79
кидать/кинуть на ветер, В-67
куда ветер дует, В-71
откуда ветер дует, В-71
пускать/пустить на ветер, В-67
швырнуть ⟨швырять⟩ на ветер, В-67

ВЕТЕРКОМ
подбит(ый) ветерком, В-80
с ветерком, В-72
с ветерком в голове, В-73

ВЕТРА
догоняй ветра в поле, В-74
ищи ветра в поле, В-74
ищи-свищи ветра в поле, В-74
мочиться против ветра, В-75
попутного ветра, В-76

ВЕТРАМИ
какими ветрами (занесло)?, В-79

ВЕТРЕНАЯ
ветреная голова ⟨головушка⟩, Г-196

ВЕТРИЛ
без руля и без ветрил, Р-372

ВЕТРОМ
ветром шатает, В-77
как* ветром сдувало, В-78
как* ветром сдуло ⟨сдунуло⟩, В-78
каким ветром (занесло)?, В-79

подбит(ый) ветром, В-80

ВЕТРУ
держать нос по ветру, Н-212
до ветру, В-81
пускать/пустить по ветру, В-82

ВЕТРЫ
какие ветры занесли?, В-79

ВЕТРЯНАЯ
ветряная мельница, М-69

ВЕТРЯНЫМИ
воевать с ветряными мельницами, М-70
сражаться с ветряными мельницами, М-70

ВЕЧЕР
добрый вечер, В-83
ещё не вечер, В-84

ВЕЧЕРА
утро вечера мудренее, У-152

ВЕЧНАЯ
вечная история, И-86
вечная память, П-41

ВЕЧНОСТЬ
кануть в вечность, В-85
отойти в вечность, В-86

ВЕЧНЫЕ
на веки вечные, В-28

ВЕЧНЫЙ
вечный покой, П-283

ВЕЧНЫМ
заснуть вечным сном, С-432
почивать вечным сном, С-436
почить вечным сном, С-432
спать вечным сном, С-436
уснуть вечным сном, С-432

ВЕШАЙ
(хоть) топор вешай, Т-160

ВЕШАЛКЕ
как на вешалке, В-87

ВЕШАТЬ
вешать голову, Г-247
вешать камень на шею, К-38
вешать лапшу на уши, Л-31
вешать нос (на квинту), Н-208
вешать себе камень на шею, К-38
вешать себе хомут на шею, Х-80
вешать хомут на шею, Х-80
можно топор вешать, Т-160
собак вешать, С-439

ВЕШАТЬСЯ
вешаться на шею, Ш-53

ВЕЩЕЙ
в натуре вещей, П-543
в порядке вещей, П-398
в природе вещей, П-543
положение вещей, П-307

ВЕЩИ
глядеть на вещи, В-89
назвать вещи настоящими
⟨своими,
собственными⟩
именами, В-88
называть вещи
настоящими ⟨своими,
собственными⟩
именами, В-88
смотреть на вещи, В-89

ВЕЩЬ
вещь в себе, В-90
понятная вещь, Д-124
странная вещь, Д-131

ВЗАД
взад-вперёд ⟨взад и
вперёд⟩, В-91
ни взад (и) ни вперёд, В-92

ВЗБРЕДАТЬ
взбредать в голову ⟨на
мысль, на ум⟩, Г-248

ВЗБРЕСТИ
взбрести в голову ⟨на
мысль, на ум⟩, Г-248

ВЗБУЧКУ
давать/дать взбучку, Т-200
задавать/задать взбучку,
Т-200
получать/получить
взбучку, Т-201

ВЗВАЛИВАТЬ
взваливать на плечи, П-189

ВЗВАЛИТЬ
взвалить на плечи, П-189

ВЗВЕСИТЬ
взвесить каждое слово,
С-281
взвесить свои слова, С-281

ВЗВЕШИВАТЬ
взвешивать каждое слово,
С-281
взвешивать свои слова,
С-281

ВЗВОДЕ
на взводе, В-93
на втором взводе, В-93
на первом взводе, В-93
на седьмом взводе, В-94
на третьем взводе, В-94

ВЗВЫТЬ
волком взвыть, В-232

ВЗГЛЯД
бросать/бросить взгляд,
В-95
взгляд не отрывается,
Г-58
кидать/кинуть взгляд,
В-95
куда ни кинешь ⟨ни кинь⟩
взгляд, Г-137
на взгляд, В-96
на первый взгляд, В-97
прятать взгляд, Г-91

ВЗГЛЯДА
не спускать взгляда, Г-31
с первого взгляда, В-98

ВЗГЛЯДЕ
при первом взгляде, В-98

ВЗГЛЯДОМ
впиваться/впиться
взглядом, Г-105

куда ни кинешь ⟨ни кинь⟩
взглядом, Г-137
мерить взглядом, Г-109
проводить ⟨провожать⟩
взглядом, Г-112
пронзать/пронзить
взглядом, Г-113
смерить взглядом, Г-109
шарить взглядом, Г-124

ВЗГЛЯДУ
по первому взгляду, В-98
с первого взгляду, В-98

ВЗГЛЯНУТЬ
взглянуть другими
⟨иными⟩ глазами, Г-120
взглянуть правде в глаза
⟨в лицо⟩, П-483

ВЗДОР
городить вздор, В-99
молоть вздор, В-99
нагородить вздор, В-99
нести/понести вздор, В-99
пороть вздор, В-99

ВЗДОХ
испускать/испустить
последний вздох, Д-346
под вздох, Л-125

ВЗДОХА
до последнего вздоха,
Д-443

ВЗДОХИ
охи да ⟨и⟩ вздохи, О-175

ВЗДОХНУТЬ
вздохнуть некогда, В-100
свободно вздохнуть, В-101

ВЗДУМАЙ(ТЕ)
не вздумай(те), В-102

ВЗЛЕТАТЬ
взлетать в ⟨на⟩ воздух,
В-203

ВЗЛЕТЕТЬ
взлететь в ⟨на⟩ воздух,
В-203
взлететь на Геликон, Г-14

ВЗОР
ласкать взор, Г-25
прятать взор, Г-91
радовать взор, Г-36

ВЗОРА
не спускать взора, Г-31

ВЗОРОМ
проводить ⟨провожать⟩
взором, Г-112

ВЗЫЩИ(ТЕ)
не взыщи(те), В-103

ВЗЯЛ
бог дал, бог и взял, Б-90
всем взял, В-104
господь дал, господь и
взял, Б-90
откуда ты взял?, В-105
с чего ты взял?, В-105
чёрт бы тебя взял!, Ч-99

ВЗЯЛА
ваша взяла, Б-58
злость взяла, З-132
наша взяла, Б-58
твоя взяла, Б-58

ВЗЯЛАСЬ
откуда прыть взялась,
П-609

ВЗЯЛО
зло взяло, З-132

ВЗЯЛОСЬ
откуда что взялось!, В-106

ВЗЯЛСЯ
взялся за гуж, не говори,
что не дюж, Г-443

ВЗЯТКИ
взятки гладки, В-107

ВЗЯТЬ
в рот нельзя взять, Р-172
взять барьер(ы), Б-26
взять б*ы*ка за рога, Б-256
взять в ежовые рукавицы,
Р-241
взять в оборот, О-16
взять в переплёт, П-94
взять в работу, О-16
взять в расчёт, Р-91
взять в руки, Р-277, Р-278
взять в свои руки, Р-278
взять в соображение,
С-487
взять в толк, Т-137
взять в шоры, Ш-83
взять верх, В-53
взять волю, В-247
взять голыми руками,
Р-253
взять горлом, Г-346
взять грех на душу, Г-382
взять да (и), В-108
взять за бока, Б-151
взять за глотку, Г-335
взять за горло, Г-335
взять за грудки, Г-420
взять за душу, Д-407
взять за жабры, Ж-1
взять за живое, Ж-30
взять за правило, П-489
взять за сердце, Д-407
взять за шкирку, Ш-73
взять и, В-108
взять измором, И-51
взять моду, М-210
взять на абордаж, А-2
взять на арапа, А-36
взять на бога, П-669
взять на буксир, Б-241
взять на вооружение,
В-257
взять на глотку, Г-336
взять на горло, Г-336
взять на заметку, З-54
взять на замечание, З-54
взять на измор, И-51
взять на испуг, И-80
взять на карандаш, К-69
взять на караул, К-71
взять на мушку, П-555
взять на откуп, О-152
взять на примету, П-538
взять на прицел, П-555
взять на пушку, П-669
взять на себя, Б-203
взять на себя смелость,
С-389
взять на себя труд, Т-211
взять на учёт, У-167
взять ноги в руки, Н-140
взять ногу, Н-169

взять под караул, С-624
взять под козырёк, К-173
взять под обстрел, О-29
взять под своё крылышко,
К-429
взять под сомнение, С-478
взять под стражу, С-624
взять правилом, П-489
взять пример, П-530
взять расчёт, Р-90
взять с бою, Б-193
взять с места, М-88
взять своё, С-84
взять своё слово назад
⟨обратно⟩, С-280
взять свои слова назад
⟨обратно⟩, С-280
взять себе в башку, Г-246
взять себе в голову, Г-246
взять себе за правило,
П-489
взять себе правилом,
П-489
взять себя в руки, Р-279
взять силу, С-188
взять слова назад
⟨обратно⟩, С-280
взять слово, С-306, С-307
взять слово назад
⟨обратно⟩, С-280
взять сторону, С-609
капли в рот не взять, К-60
маковой росинки в рот не
взять, К-60
много на себя взять, Б-204
ни дать ни взять, Д-28
ни капли в рот не взять,
К-60
что взять, В-216

ВЗЯТЬСЯ
взяться за оружие, О-102
взяться за перо, П-100
взяться за ум, У-77
взяться на учёт, У-168
взяться не за своё дело,
Д-69

ВИД
выставить ⟨выставлять⟩
на вид, В-109
делать вид, В-110
на вид, В-111
напускать/напустить на
себя вид, В-112
поставить на вид, В-114
привести ⟨приводить⟩ в
божеский
⟨христианский⟩ вид,
В-113
придавать/придать
божеский
⟨христианский⟩ вид,
В-113
сделать вид, В-110
ставить на вид, В-114

ВИДА
выпускать/выпустить из
вида, В-141
для вида, В-115
исчезать/исчезнуть из
вида, Г-42
не подавать/не подать
вида, В-116

не показать ⟨не
показывать⟩ вида, В-116
потерять из вида, В-140
скрываться/скрыться из
вида, Г-42
терять из вида, В-140
упускать/упустить из
вида, В-141

ВИДАЛ
в гробу видал, Г-402
не видал, В-117
свет не видал, С-59
чего я здесь не видал?,
В-118
чего я там ⟨тут⟩ не
видал?, В-118

ВИДАЛИ
глаза бы (мои) не видали,
Г-51

ВИДАННОЕ
виданное ли (это) дело,
Д-72

ВИДАНО
где видано?, В-119
где ж(е) это видано?, В-119
где это видано?, В-119

ВИДАТЬ
видать (всякие) виды,
В-142
видать птицу ⟨сокола⟩ по
полёту, П-616
зги не видать, З-104
конца не видать, К-251
конца и краю ⟨конца-
краю⟩ не видать, К-251
не видать как своих ушей,
У-181
ни зги не видать, З-104
ни конца ни краю не
видать, К-251
от земли не видать, З-116

ВИДАХ
в видах, В-120

ВИДЕ
в виде, В-121
в лучшем виде, В-122
в чистом виде, В-123
при виде, В-124

ВИДЕЛ
в гробу видел, Г-402
свет не видел, С-59
только и видел, В-125
чего я здесь не видел?,
В-118
чего я там ⟨тут⟩ не
видел?, В-118

ВИДЕЛИ
глаза бы (мои) не видели,
Г-51
только и видели, В-125

ВИДЕТЬ
в упор не видеть, У-119
видеть на аршин в землю
⟨под землёй, под
землю⟩, А-46
видеть на два ⟨три⟩
аршина в землю ⟨под
землёй, под землю⟩,
А-46
видеть насквозь, В-126

видеть не может, В-127
глядеть в книгу и видеть
фигу, К-148
десятый сон видеть, С-483
за деревьями леса не
видеть, Д-178
зги не видеть, З-104
из-за деревьев леса не
видеть, Д-178
изволите ⟨изволишь⟩
видеть, И-45
не видеть дальше своего
носа, Н-225
не видеть дальше (своего)
собственного носа,
Н-225
не видеть покою ⟨покоя⟩,
П-288
ни зги не видеть, З-104
по глазам видеть, Г-103
света белого ⟨божьего⟩ не
видеть, С-66
света не видеть, С-66
седьмой сон видеть, С-483
смотреть в книгу и видеть
фигу, К-148

ВИДИМ
в чужом глазу сучок
видим, а в своём (и)
бревна не замечаем,
Г-140

ВИДИМО
видимо-невидимо, В-128
и видимо и невидимо,
В-128

ВИДИМОЕ
видимое дело, Д-73

ВИДИМОСТИ
для видимости, В-115
по (всей) видимости, В-129

ВИДИТ
видит бог, Б-106
видит око, да зуб неймёт,
О-89
рыбак рыбака видит
издалека, Р-383
спит и видит, С-519
спит и во сне видит, С-519
хоть видит око, да зуб
неймёт, О-89

ВИДИТЕ
видите ли, В-130
вот видите!, В-131
как видите, В-132

ВИДИШЬ
видишь ли, В-130
вот видишь!, В-131
как видишь, В-132

ВИДНА
видна птица по полёту,
П-616

ВИДНО
видно будет, Б-216
видно птицу ⟨сокола⟩ по
полёту, П-616
зги не видно, З-104
как видно, В-133
конца и краю ⟨конца-
краю⟩ не видно, К-251
конца не видно, К-251

ни зги не видно, З-104
ни конца ни краю не
видно, К-251
от земли не видно, З-116
по глазам видно, Г-103

ВИДОМ
ни под каким видом, В-134
под видом, В-135
с убитым видом, В-136

ВИДУ
в виду, В-137
выпускать/выпустить из
виду, В-141
для виду, В-115
иметь в виду, В-138
исчезать/исчезнуть из
виду, Г-42
на виду, В-139
не подавать/не подать
виду, В-116
не показать ⟨не
показывать⟩ виду, В-116
по виду, В-111
поиметь в виду, В-138
потерять из виду, В-140
с виду, В-111
скрываться/скрыться из
виду, Г-42
терять из виду, В-140
упускать/упустить из виду,
В-141

ВИДЫ
видать (всякие) виды,
В-142
видывать (всякие) виды,
В-142
иметь виды, В-143

ВИДЫВАЛ
свет не видывал, С-59

ВИДЫВАТЬ
видывать (всякие) виды,
В-142

ВИЛАМИ
(ещё) вилами на ⟨по⟩ воде
писано, В-144

ВИЛЬНУТЬ
вильнуть хвостом, Х-25

ВИЛЯТЬ
вилять хвостом, Х-26

ВИНЕ
по вине, В-145

ВИНОВАТ
всегда виноват
стрелочник, С-634
стрелочник виноват, С-634

ВИНОГРАД
зелен виноград, В-146

ВИНТИКА
винтика (в голове) не
хватает ⟨недостаёт⟩,
В-147

ВИНТИКОВ
винтиков (в голове) не
хватает ⟨недостаёт⟩,
В-147

ВИНУ
вменить ⟨вменять⟩ в вину,
В-148
поставить в вину, В-148
ставить в вину, В-148

ВИСЕЛЬНИКА
юмор висельника, Ю-3

ВИСЕТЬ
висеть в воздухе, В-208
висеть на волоске, В-239
висеть на нитке ⟨на
ниточке⟩, В-239
висеть на носу, Г-234
висеть на плечах, П-185
висеть на телефоне, Т-55
висеть на хвосте, Х-21
висеть на шее, Ш-43
висеть над головой, Г-234

ВИСНЕТ
брань на вороту не виснет,
Б-196

ВИСНУТЬ
виснуть на шее, Ш-53

ВИТАТЬ
витать в облаках ⟨в
эмпиреях⟩, О-8
витать между небом и
землёй, О-8

ВИТЬ
вить верёвки, В-37
вить (себе) гнездо, Г-156
сколько верёвку
⟨верёвочку⟩ ни вить, а
концу быть, В-38

ВИТЬСЯ
виться вьюном, В-393
как верёвочке ни виться, а
конец будет, В-38
сколько верёвочке ни
виться, а конец будет,
В-38

ВИШЬ
вишь ты, Т-246

ВКЛАД
внести ⟨вносить⟩ свой
вклад, В-149

ВКЛАДЫВАТЬ
вкладывать в уста, У-142
вкладывать душу, Д-409
вкладывать сердце, Д-409

ВКОЛАЧИВАТЬ
вколачивать в башку,
Г-245
вколачивать в голову,
Г-245

ВКОЛОТИТЬ
вколотить в башку, Г-245
вколотить в голову, Г-245

ВКОПАННЫЙ
как* вкопанный, В-150

ВКОСЬ
вкось и вкривь, В-151
вкось и впрямь, В-151
вкривь и вкось, В-151
и вкривь и вкось, В-151

ВКРАДЫВАТЬСЯ
вкрадываться в доверие,
Д-225
вкрадываться в милость,
М-156

ВКРАСТЬСЯ
вкрасться в доверие, Д-225
вкрасться в милость,
М-156

ВКРИВЬ
вкось и вкривь, В-151
вкривь и вкось, В-151
вкривь и впрямь, В-151
и вкривь и вкось, В-151

ВКРУТИТЬ
вкрутить баки, Б-10

ВКРУЧИВАТЬ
вкручивать баки, Б-10

ВКУС
войти ⟨входить⟩ во вкус,
В-152
на вкус, В-153
на вкус (и) на цвет
товарища ⟨товарищей⟩
нет, В-154

ВКУСАХ
о вкусах не спорят, В-155

ВКУСЕ
во вкусе, В-156

ВКУСИТЬ
вкусить плоды, П-196

ВКУСОМ
со вкусом, В-157

ВКУСУ
по вкусу, В-158

ВКУШАТЬ
вкушать плоды, П-196
вкушать от пищи святого
Антония, П-160

ВЛАГАТЬ
влагать душу, Д-409
влагать сердце, Д-409

ВЛАДЕТЬ
владеть даром слова,
С-331
владеть кистью, К-125
владеть пером, П-101
владеть словом, С-331
владеть собой, В-159

ВЛАДЫКА
своя рука владыка, Р-234

ВЛАМЫВАТЬСЯ
вламываться в амбицию,
А-26

ВЛАСТИ
в моей власти, В-160
во власти, В-160, В-161
отдаваться/отдаться
власти, В-165
предаваться/предаться
власти, В-165
у власти, В-162

ВЛАСТИТЕЛЬ
властитель дум, В-163

ВЛАСТЬ
ваша власть, В-164
забирать/забрать власть,
С-188
отдаваться/отдаться во
власть, В-165
потерять ⟨терять⟩ власть
над собой, В-166

ВЛАСТЬЮ
под властью, В-161

ВЛЕЗАТЬ
влезать в доверие, Д-225
влезать в долг(и), Д-237
влезать в душу, Д-410

влезать в кожу, Ш-77
влезать в шкуру, Ш-77

ВЛЕЗЕТ
сколько влезет, В-167

ВЛЕЗЕШЬ
не влезешь, В-168

ВЛЕЗТЬ
без мыла в душу влезть,
М-307
влезть в доверие, Д-225
влезть в долг(и), Д-237
влезть в душу, Д-410
влезть в кожу, Ш-77
влезть в шкуру, Ш-77

ВЛЕПИТЬ
влепить горячих, Г-364

ВЛЕТАТЬ
влетать бомбой, Б-178
влетать в копеечку ⟨в
копейку⟩, К-276
влетать как бомба, Б-178

ВЛЕТЕТЬ
влететь бомбой, Б-178
влететь в копеечку ⟨в
копейку⟩, К-276
влететь как бомба, Б-178

ВЛЕЧЬ
влечь за собой, В-169

ВЛИВАТЬ
вливать живую ⟨свежую⟩
струю, С-650

ВЛИПАТЬ
влипать в историю, И-85

ВЛИПНУТЬ
влипнуть в историю, И-85

ВЛИТЬ
влить живую ⟨свежую⟩
струю, С-650

ВЛОЖИТЬ
вложить в уста, У-142
вложить душу, Д-409
вложить меч в ножны,
М-137
вложить сердце, Д-409

ВЛОМИТЬСЯ
вломиться в амбицию,
А-26

ВМЕНИТЬ
вменить в вину, В-148
вменить в обязанность,
О-41

ВМЕНЯТЬ
вменять в вину, В-148
вменять в обязанность,
О-41

ВМЕСТЕ
вместе с тем, Т-59
вместе тесно, а врозь
скучно, В-170

ВМЕСТО
вместо того чтобы, Т-120

ВМЕШИВАТЬСЯ
вмешиваться не в своё
дело, Д-111

ВНЕСТИ
внести живую ⟨свежую⟩
струю, С-650
внести свой вклад, В-149
внести свою лепту, Л-54

ВНЕШНОСТЬ
внешность обманчива,
В-171

ВНИЗ
глядеть сверху вниз, С-418
идти вниз, Г-352
катиться вниз, Г-352
пойти вниз, Г-352
покатиться вниз, Г-352
смотреть сверху вниз,
С-418

ВНИМАНИЕ
принимать/принять во
внимание, В-172

ВНИМАНИЯ
ноль внимания (, фунт
презрения), Н-196
оставить ⟨оставлять⟩ без
внимания, В-173

ВНОВЬ
вновь испечённый, И-79

ВНОСИТЬ
вносить живую ⟨свежую⟩
струю, С-650
вносить свой вклад, В-149
вносить свою лепту, Л-54

ВНУТРИ
снаружи мило, а внутри
гнило, С-427

ВОГНАТЬ
вогнать в гроб, Г-396
вогнать в краску, К-367
вогнать в пот, П-418
вогнать в убыток, Р-89

ВОДА
десятая вода на киселе,
В-175
живая вода, В-174
как с гуся вода, Г-449
под лежач(ий) камень (и)
вода не течёт, К-45
седьмая вода на киселе,
В-175
темна вода во облацех,
В-176

ВОДЕ
в мутной воде рыбу
ловить, В-177
вилами на ⟨по⟩ воде
писано, В-144
ещё вилами на ⟨по⟩ воде
писано, В-144
как рыба в воде, Р-380
сидеть на хлебе и (на)
воде, Х-44

ВОДИТСЯ
как водится, В-178

ВОДИТЬ
водить за нос, Н-209
водить компанию, К-218
водить на помочах, П-335
водить хлеб-соль, Х-29

ВОДОЙ
водой не замутит, В-193
водой не разлить ⟨не
разольёшь⟩, В-179
как* водой смыло, В-180
как* холодной водой
облить ⟨окатить⟩, В-181
облить холодной водой,
В-181

окатить холодной водой,
В-181

ВОДУ
возить воду, В-182
вывести ⟨выводить⟩ на
свежую ⟨чистую⟩ воду,
В-183
и концы в воду, К-258
идти в огонь и в воду, О-64
как* в воду глядел, В-184
как* в воду канул, В-185
как* в воду опущенный,
В-186
как* в воду смотрел, В-184
концы в воду, К-258
лить воду на мельницу,
В-187
мутить воду, В-188
не зная ⟨не спросясь⟩
броду, не суйся в воду,
Б-211
носить воду в решете
⟨решетом⟩, В-189
обжёгся ⟨обжёгшись⟩ на
молоке, дуешь ⟨будешь
дуть⟩ и на воду, М-239
перебиваться с хлеба на
воду, Х-41
пойти в огонь и в воду,
О-64
посадить на хлеб и (на)
воду, Х-37
пройти (и) огонь и воду (и
медные трубы), О-65
пройти сквозь ⟨через⟩
огонь и воду (и медные
трубы), О-65
прятать концы в воду,
К-262
с лица не воду пить, Л-86
садиться на хлеб и (на)
воду, Х-36
сажать на хлеб и (на) воду,
Х-37
сесть на хлеб и (на) воду,
Х-36
спрятать концы в воду,
К-262
схоронить концы в воду,
К-262
таскать воду в решете
⟨решетом⟩, В-189
толочь воду (в ступе),
В-190
хоронить концы в воду,
К-262
хоть в воду, В-191
черпать воду решетом,
В-189

ВОДЫ
буря в стакане воды, Б-247
в ложке воды утопить,
Л-129
воды в рот набрать, В-192
воды не замутит, В-193
воды утекло, В-194
выйти сухим из воды,
В-195
вылить ушат холодной
воды, В-181
выходить сухим из воды,
В-195

ни на волосок, В-237
ВОЛОСЫ
  волосы встали ⟨встают⟩
    дыбом, В-241
  волосы поднимаются/
    поднялись дыбом, В-241
  волосы стали
    ⟨становятся⟩ дыбом,
    В-241
  драть на себе волосы,
    В-243
  притягивать/притянуть за
    волосы, В-242
  рвать на себе волосы,
    В-243
ВОЛОЧИТЬ
  едва ⟨еле⟩ ноги волочить,
    Н-144
  насилу ноги волочить,
    Н-144
  с трудом ноги волочить,
    Н-144
  чуть ноги волочить, Н-144
ВОЛЧИЙ
  волчий аппетит, А-33
  волчий билет, Б-63
  волчий паспорт, Б-63
ВОЛЧКОМ
  вертеться волчком, В-244
ВОЛШЕБНИК
  маг и волшебник, М-1
ВОЛШЕБНОГО
  как* по манию волшебного
    жезла, М-27
  как* по мановению
    волшебного жезла, М-27
ВОЛШЕБНОЙ
  как* по мановению
    волшебной палочки,
    М-27
ВОЛШЕБСТВУ
  как* по волшебству, В-245
ВОЛЫНКУ
  разводить волынку, В-246
  тянуть волынку, В-246
ВОЛЬНАЯ
  вольная пташка, П-617
  вольная птица, П-617
ВОЛЬНОМ
  на вольном воздухе, В-206
ВОЛЬНОМУ
  вольному воля, В-253
ВОЛЬНЫЙ
  вольный казак, К-5
  на вольный воздух, В-206
ВОЛЮ
  брать/взять волю, В-247
  давать волю, В-248
  давать волю кулакам,
    В-249
  давать волю рукам, В-250
  давать волю языку, В-251
  дать волю, В-248
  дать волю кулакам, В-249
  дать волю рукам, В-250
  дать волю языку, В-251
ВОЛЯ
  будь моя воля, В-252
  была бы моя воля, В-252

вольному воля, В-253
  воля ваша ⟨твоя⟩, В-254
  моя бы воля, В-252
  последняя воля, В-255
ВОН
  вон куда махнул!, Х-8
  вон куда хватил!, Х-8
  вон оно что!, Ч-161
  глядеть вон, С-415
  дурная трава из поля вон,
    Т-194
  дурную траву из ⟨с⟩ поля
    вон, Т-194
  дух вон, Д-344
  душа вон, Д-344
  из головы вон, Г-287
  из кожи вон вылезать
    ⟨лезть⟩, К-162
  из памяти вон, Г-287
  из рук вон, Р-212
  из ряда вон, Р-399
  из ряда вон выходящий,
    Р-400
  из ряду вон, Р-399
  из ума вон, Г-287
  из шкуры вон вылезать
    ⟨лезть⟩, К-162
  кто старое вспомянет
    ⟨помянет⟩, тому глаз
    вон, С-546
  с глаз долой – из сердца
    вон, Г-39
  смотреть вон, С-415
  сорная трава из поля вон,
    Т-194
  сорную траву из ⟨с⟩ поля
    вон, Т-194
  хоть святых вон выноси
    ⟨неси, уноси⟩, С-90
  худая трава из поля вон,
    Т-194
  худую траву из ⟨с⟩ поля
    вон, Т-194
ВОНЯЕТ
  рыба с головы воняет,
    Р-382
ВООБРАЖАТЬ
  (много) воображать о
    себе, В-256
ВООБРАЖЕНИЯ
  игра воображения, И-10
ВООБЩЕ
  вообще говоря, Г-169
ВООРУЖАТЬСЯ
  вооружаться терпением,
    Т-83
ВООРУЖЕНИЕ
  брать/взять на
    вооружение, В-257
  принимать/принять на
    вооружение, В-257
ВООРУЖИТЬСЯ
  вооружиться терпением,
    Т-83
ВОПИЮТ
  камни вопиют, К-48
ВОПИЮЩЕГО
  глас вопиющего в
    пустыне, Г-143
ВОПИЮЩИЙ
  глас ⟨голос⟩, вопиющий в
    пустыне, Г-143

ВОПЛОТИТЬ
  воплотить в жизнь, Ж-49
ВОПЛОЩАТЬ
  воплощать в жизнь, Ж-49
ВОПРОС
  больной вопрос, В-258
  вопрос жизни и ⟨или⟩
    смерти, В-259
  поставить вопрос ребром,
    В-260
  поставить под вопрос,
    В-261
  ставить вопрос ребром,
    В-260
  ставить под вопрос, В-261
  что за вопрос!, В-262
ВОПРОСОМ
  под (большим) вопросом,
    В-263
ВОР
  вор у вора дубинку украл,
    В-264
  не пойман – не вор, В-265
ВОРА
  вор у вора дубинку украл,
    В-264
ВОРЕ
  на воре шапка горит, В-266
ВОРОБЕЙ
  слово не воробей, вылетит
    – не поймаешь, С-328
  старый воробей, В-267
  стреляный воробей, В-267
ВОРОБЬИНОГО
  короче воробьиного носа,
    Н-224
ВОРОБЬИНЫЙ
  с воробьиный нос, Н-218
ВОРОБЬЯ
  старого воробья на мякине
    не проведёшь, В-268
ВОРОБЬЯМ
  из пушек ⟨пушки⟩ по
    воробьям бить ⟨палить,
    стрелять⟩, П-666
ВОРОВСТВА
  простота хуже воровства,
    П-586
ВОРОЖИТ
  бабушка ворожит, Б-4
ВОРОН
  ворон ворону глаз не
    выклюет, В-269
  ворон ловить, В-270
  ворон считать, В-270
  куда ворон костей не
    заносил, В-271
  чёрный ворон, В-272
ВОРОНА
  белая ворона, В-273
  ворона в павлиньих
    перьях, В-274
  ни пава ни ворона, П-1
  пуганая ворона (и) куста
    боится, В-275
ВОРОНОК
  чёрный воронок, В-272
ВОРОНУ
  ворон ворону глаз не
    выклюет, В-269

ВОРОНЫХ
  на вороных не объедешь,
    К-387
  прокатить на вороных,
    В-276
ВОРОТ
  от ворот поворот, В-277
  у ворот, В-278
ВОРОТА
  как баран на новые
    ворота, Б-20
  ни в какие ворота (не
    лезет), В-279
  пришла беда – отворяй
    ⟨открывай, растворяй⟩
    ворота, Б-42
ВОРОТИТ
  с души воротит, Д-393
ВОРОТИТЬ
  воротить гору ⟨горы⟩,
    Г-358
  воротить морду, Н-210
  воротить нос, Н-210
  воротить рожу ⟨рыло⟩,
    Н-210
ВОРОТУ
  брань на вороту не виснет,
    Б-196
ВОРОЧАЕТСЯ
  язык не ворочается, Я-40
ВОРОЧАТЬ
  ворочать горами ⟨горы⟩,
    Г-358
  ворочать мозгами, М-221
ВОСЕМЬДЕСЯТ
  поворот на сто
    восемьдесят градусов,
    П-225
ВОСКЛИЦАТЬ
  восклицать осанну, О-107
ВОСКУРЯТЬ
  воскурять фимиам, Ф-11
ВОСПОМИНАНИЙ
  отойти ⟨отходить⟩ в
    область воспоминаний,
    О-11
  уйти ⟨уходить⟩ в область
    воспоминаний, О-11
ВОСПРЯНУТЬ
  воспрянуть духом, Д-352
ВОСТОРГ
  административный
    восторг, В-280
  телячий восторг, В-281
ВОСТРИТЬ
  вострить зуб(ы), З-204
ВОСТРО
  держать ухо востро, У-158
ВОСТРЫЙ
  нож вострый, Н-182
ВОСХОДЯЩАЯ
  восходящая звезда, З-90
ВОСХОДЯЩЕЕ
  восходящее светило, З-90
ВОТ
  а вот поди (ж) ты!, П-243
  вот бог, а вот порог, Б-107
  вот в чём собака зарыта,
    С-440

вот в этом и зарыта собака, С-440
вот вам!, Т-48
вот вам и весь разговор ⟨сказ⟩, Р-46
вот вам крест!, К-380
вот видите ⟨видишь⟩!, В-131
вот-вот, В-282
вот, вот, В-283
вот где сидит, С-161
вот где собака зарыта, С-440
вот ещё!, Е-28
вот ещё новости ⟨новость⟩!, Н-110
вот здесь и зарыта собака, С-440
вот и весь разговор ⟨сказ⟩, Р-46
вот и всё, В-324
вот и вся недолга, В-349
вот как, К-10
вот какие пироги, П-154
вот какой…, К-22
вот куда махнул!, Х-8
вот куда хватил!, Х-8
вот мило!, М-152
вот наказание, Н-21
вот невидаль ⟨невидальщина⟩!, Н-65
вот новости ⟨новость⟩!, Н-110
вот оно что!, Ч-161
вот поди ж!, П-243
вот поди (ж) ты!, П-243
вот так…!, Т-2
вот так клюква!, К-143
вот так номер!, Ш-89
вот так так!, Р-20
вот так фунт!, Ф-31
вот так штука!, Ш-89
вот те (и) здравствуй(те)!, З-109
вот те и на!, Р-20
вот те и раз!, Р-20
вот те крест!, К-380
вот те на!, Р-20
вот те раз!, Р-20
вот те фунт!, Ф-31
вот тебе!, Т-48
вот тебе, бабушка, и Юрьев день!, Б-6
вот тебе бог, а вот порог, Б-107
вот тебе и…, Т-49
вот тебе и весь разговор ⟨сказ⟩, Р-46
вот тебе и вся недолга, В-349
вот тебе и здравствуй(те)!, З-109
вот тебе и на!, Р-20
вот тебе и раз!, Р-20
вот тебе крест!, К-380
вот тебе на!, Р-20
вот тебе раз!, Р-20
вот то-то же, Т-115
вот то-то и есть, Т-105
вот то-то и оно ⟨оно-то⟩, Т-105

вот то-то оно и есть, Т-105
вот тут ⟨тут-то⟩ и зарыта собака, С-440
вот что, Ч-162
вот это да!, Э-6
вот это мило!, М-152
вот это номер!, Ш-89
вот это я понимаю!, П-338
вот я тебя, Я-1
да вот поди (ж) ты!, П-243
и вот на столечко ⟨столько⟩, С-598
и вот столько, С-598
ни вот на столечко ⟨столько⟩, С-598
ну вот ещё!, Е-28
разве вот, Р-45
так вот, Т-13
ВОТКНУТЬ
иголки негде ⟨некуда⟩ воткнуть, И-8
иголку негде ⟨некуда⟩ воткнуть, И-8
ВОШЛО
в одно ухо вошло, (а) в другое вышло, У-156
ВОШЬ
ядрёна вошь!, В-284
ВПАДАТЬ
впадать в азарт, А-14
впадать в амбицию, А-26
впадать в детство, Д-190
впадать в крайности, К-358
впадать в крайность, К-361
впадать в младенчество, Д-190
впадать в немилость, Н-78
впадать в раж, Р-17
впадать в ребячество, Д-190
ВПАСТЬ
впасть в азарт, А-14
впасть в амбицию, А-26
впасть в детство, Д-190
впасть в крайность, К-361
впасть в младенчество, Д-190
впасть в немилость, Н-78
впасть в раж, Р-17
впасть в ребячество, Д-190
ВПЕРЁД
взад-вперёд ⟨взад и вперёд⟩, В-91
давать/дать двадцать ⟨десять, сто⟩ очков вперёд, О-191
забегать/забежать вперёд, З-3
заглядывать/заглянуть вперёд, Б-224
ни взад (и) ни вперёд, В-92
ногами вперёд, Н-127
полный вперёд!, Х-55
шаг вперёд, Ш-9
ВПЕРЕДИ
это ещё ⟨только⟩ цветики ⟨цветки, цветочки⟩, а ягодки (будут) впереди, Ц-16

ВПИВАТЬСЯ
впиваться взглядом, Г-105
впиваться глазами, Г-105
ВПИСАТЬ
вписать новую страницу, С-625
ВПИТАТЬ
впитать с молоком матери, М-241
ВПИТЫВАТЬ
впитывать с молоком матери, М-241
ВПИТЬСЯ
впиться взглядом, Г-105
впиться глазами, Г-105
ВПЛОТЬ
вплоть до, В-285
ВПРАВИТЬ
вправить мозги, М-222
ВПРАВЛЯТЬ
вправлять мозги, М-222
ВПРЕДЬ
впредь до, В-286
ВПРОК
идти/пойти впрок, И-26
ВПРОСАК
попадать(ся) впросак, П-347
попасть(ся) впросак, П-347
ВПРЯМЬ
вкось и впрямь, В-151
вкривь и впрямь, В-151
ВРАГ
язык мой – враг мой, Я-38
ВРАЖИЙ
вражий сын, С-734
ВРАЗРЕЗ
идти/пойти вразрез, И-27
ВРАСПЛОХ
застать врасплох, З-79
застигнуть врасплох, З-79
ВРАСТАТЬ
врастать корнями, К-305
ВРАСТИ
врасти корнями, К-305
ВРЕД
во вред, В-287
ВРЕЗАТЬ
врезать дуба ⟨дубаря⟩, Д-316
ВРЕЗАТЬСЯ
врезаться в памяти ⟨в память⟩, П-42
ВРЕМЁН
с незапамятных времён, В-288
ВРЕМЕНА
адамовы времена, В-24
во времена оны, В-305
во все времена, В-289
ВРЕМЕНАМ
по временам, В-290
по тем временам, В-291
ВРЕМЕНЕМ
со временем, В-292
тем временем, В-293
ВРЕМЕНИ
в скором времени, В-294

время от времени, В-308
до времени, В-295
до настоящего времени, Д-163
до поры до времени, П-393
до сего времени, Д-163
до этого времени, Д-163
за давностью времени, Д-10
знамение времени, З-164
ко времени, В-296
не ко времени, В-296
от времени до времени, В-308
отставать/отстать от времени, В-297
прежде времени, В-298
раньше времени, В-298
с течением времени, Т-95
ВРЕМЯ
аппетит приходит во время еды, А-32
в одно прекрасное время, Д-150
в первое время, В-299
в последнее время, В-300
в своё время, В-301
в то время как, В-302
в то же время, В-303
во время, В-304
во время оно, В-305
время – деньги, В-306
время не ждёт, В-307
время не терпит, В-307
время от времени, В-308
время работает, В-309
время терпит, В-310
всё в своё время, В-312
всё время, В-311
всему своё время, В-312
всякому овощу своё время, О-44
выиграть ⟨выигрывать⟩ время, В-313
делу время, (а) потехе час, Д-144
детское время, В-314
каждому овощу своё время, О-44
на время, В-315
на первое время, В-316
одно время, В-317
отживать/отжить своё время, В-21
первое время, В-299
последнее время, В-300
самое время, В-318
тянуть время, В-319
убивать/убить время, В-320
ВРИ
ври, да не завирайся, В-321
ВРОДЕ
вроде бы, В-322
вроде как, В-322
ВРОЗЬ
вместе тесно, а врозь скучно, В-170
ВРЯД
вряд ли, В-323
ВСАСЫВАТЬ
всасывать с молоком матери, М-241

ВСЕ/ВСЁ

бить во все колокола, К-201

бумага всё стерпит, Б-243

в темноте все кошки серы, К-349

во все времена, В-289

во все глаза, Г-47

во всё горло, Г-337

во все концы, К-257

во все лопатки, Л-134

во все носовые завёртки, З-14

во все трубы трубить, Т-210

во все уши, У-183

вот и всё, В-324

всё более и более, Б-167

всё больше, Б-172

всё больше и больше, Б-167

всё в своё время, В-312

всё время, В-311

все глаза высмотреть, Г-48

все глаза проглядеть ⟨просмотреть⟩, Г-48

всё едино, В-327

всё ещё, Е-24

всё же, В-325

все за одного, один за всех, О-73

все ⟨всё⟩ и вся, В-326

все мы люди, все (мы) человеки, Л-166

все мы под богом ходим, Б-135

всё на месте, М-101

всё на своём месте, М-101

всё наружу, В-66

всё одно, В-327

всё одно как ⟨что⟩, В-328

все под богом ходим, Б-135

всё равно, В-327

всё равно как ⟨что⟩, В-328

всё та же песня, П-121

все там будем, Б-215

всё хаханьки да хиханьки, Х-28

всё хиханьки да хаханьки, Х-28

всё хорошо, что хорошо кончается, К-264

все шишки валятся на голову, Ш-72

выжать ⟨выжимать⟩ все соки, С-467

выматывать все жилы, Ж-74

выматывать все кишки, К-129

вымотать все жилы, Ж-74

вымотать все кишки, К-129

выплакать все глаза, Г-49

высасывать/высосать все соки, С-467

вытягивать все жилы, Ж-74

вытягивать все кишки, К-129

вытянуть все жилы, Ж-74

вытянуть все кишки, К-129

гори всё прахом, О-55

жечь все мосты, К-289

за всё про всё, В-329

зазвонить во все колокола, К-202

заказать ⟨заказывать⟩ все пути, П-656

застёгнут(ый) на все пуговицы, П-624

звонить во все колокола, К-202

знать все ходы-выходы ⟨ходы и выходы⟩, Х-74

и всё, В-324

и всё такое (прочее), В-330

и всё тут, В-331

кончить все счёты, С-727

куда ни кинь, всё клин, К-136

лезть во все дырки, Д-440

мастер ⟨мастерица⟩ на все руки, М-42

мешать все карты, К-98

на бедного Макара все шишки валятся, М-4

на все корки, К-296

на все лады, Л-16

на всё про всё, В-332

на все руки, Р-294

на все сто, С-576

на все сто процентов, С-576

на все четыре стороны, С-615

нажать все пружины, П-75

нажать на все кнопки, К-149

нажать на все педали, П-75

нажать на все пружины, П-75

нажимать все пружины, П-75

нажимать на все кнопки, К-149

нажимать на все педали, П-75

нажимать на все пружины, П-75

не все дома, Д-255

не всё же, В-333

не всё коту масленица (,бывает и великий пост), К-341

не всё то золото, что блестит, З-183

ночью все кошки серы, К-349

обивать/обить все пороги, П-377

один за всех, все за одного, О-73

паршивая овца всё стадо портит, О-46

переломать все кости, К-321

покончить все счёты, С-727

пообивать/пообить все пороги, П-377

попутать все карты, К-98

поставить всё на место, М-98

поставить всё на одну карту, К-93

поставить всё на своё место, М-98

поставить всё на свои места, М-98

поставить все точки на ⟨над⟩ и, Т-183

прогудеть все уши, У-188

прожужжать все уши, У-188

проплакать все глаза, Г-49

прослушать все уши, У-189

протрубить все уши, У-188

пускаться/пуститься во все тяжкие, Т-256

путать все карты, К-98

раззвонить во все колокола, К-202

растрезвонить во все колокола, К-202

семь вёрст до небес и всё лесом, В-44

сжечь ⟨сжигать⟩ все мосты, К-289

склонять на все лады, Л-17

смешать все карты, К-98

спутать все карты, К-98

ставить всё на место, М-98

ставить всё на одну карту, К-93

ставить всё на своё место, М-98

ставить всё на свои места, М-98

ставить все точки на ⟨над⟩ и, Т-183

терпение и труд всё перетрут, Т-80

трезвонить во все колокола, К-202

ударить/ударять во все колокола, К-201

ВСЕГДА

всегда виноват стрелочник, С-634

первый блин всегда комом, Б-80

сапожник всегда без сапог, С-19

ВСЕГО

всего доброго!, Х-83

всего лучшего!, Х-83

всего-навсе, В-334

всего-навсего, В-334

всего наилучшего!, Х-83

всего ничего, В-335

всего хорошего!, Х-83

от всего сердца, С-123

превыше всего, П-501

прежде всего, В-336

ради всего святого, Б-131

сверх всего, В-337

скорее всего, С-232

со всего маха ⟨маху⟩, М-58

со всего плеча, П-182

со всего размаха ⟨размаху⟩, Р-56

только и всего, Т-146

ВСЕЙ

во всей красе, К-363

во всей наготе, Н-4

во всей поре, П-369

во всей своей красе, К-363

во всей своей наготе, Н-4

во всей форме, Ф-21

всей душой, Д-396

изо всей мочи, М-271

изо всей силы, С-167

от всей души, Д-392

по всей вероятности, В-42

по всей видимости, В-129

по всей форме, Ф-21

при всей честной компании, Н-30

ВСЕМ/ВСЁМ

во всём блеске, Б-78

во всём параде, П-57

всем взял, В-104

всем и каждому, В-343

всем сердцем, Д-396

всем сестрам по серьгам, С-156

всем скопом, С-230

дай бог всем, Б-110

за всем тем, В-338

идти ко всем чертям, Ч-113

ко всем свиньям, Ч-110

ко всем чертям, Ч-110

лететь ко всем чертям, Ч-113

на всём готовом, Г-369

на всём скаку, С-219

по всем правилам, П-485

по всем правилам искусства, П-486

по всем статьям, С-555

пойти ко всем чертям, Ч-113

полететь ко всем чертям, Ч-113

при всём народе, Н-30

при всём параде, П-57

при всём (при) том, В-338

при всём честном народе, Н-30

просклонять по всем падежам, П-2

склонять по всем падежам, П-2

со всем тем, В-338

трещать по всем швам, Ш-40

хоть ко всем чертям, Ч-118

ВСЕМИ

всеми печёнками, П-141

всеми силами, С-175

всеми силами души, Ф-9

всеми фибрами души, Ф-9

со всеми онёрами, О-93

со всеми потрохами, П-437

ВСЕМУ

всему своё время, В-312

конец — всему делу венец, К-233

по всему, В-339

ВСЕОРУЖИИ

во всеоружии, В-340

ВСЕРЬЁЗ
всерьёз и надолго, В-341
ВСЕУСЛЫШАНИЕ
во всеуслышание, В-342
ВСЕХ
во всех отношениях, О-160
все за одного, один за всех,
О-73
всех благ, Б-72
всех и каждого, В-343
всех мастей, М-41
изо всех сил, С-167
кричать на всех
перекрёстках, П-92
на всех не угодишь, У-18
на всех парах, П-60
на всех парусах, П-60
на всех рысях, Р-394
один за всех, все за одного,
О-73
просклонять во всех
падежах, П-2
склонять во всех падежах,
П-2
со всех концов, К-256
со всех ног, Н-117
ВСКОЧИТЬ
вскочить в копеечку ⟨в
копейку⟩, К-276
ВСКРУЖИЛАСЬ
голова вскружилась, Г-200
ВСКРУЖИТЬ
вскружить голову, Г-253
ВСЛЕД
вслед за, В-344
вслед за тем, В-345
ВСМЯТКУ
сапоги всмятку, С-15
ВСОСАТЬ
всосать с молоком матери,
М-241
ВСПАДАТЬ
вспадать на мысль, Г-271
вспадать на ум, Г-271
ВСПАСТЬ
вспасть на мысль, Г-271
вспасть на ум, Г-271
ВСПЛЫВАТЬ
всплывать в памяти, П-31
всплывать на поверхность,
П-217
всплывать на свет божий,
С-44
всплывать наружу, П-217
ВСПЛЫТЬ
всплыть в памяти, П-31
всплыть на поверхность,
П-217
всплыть на свет божий,
С-44
всплыть наружу, П-217
ВСПОМИНАТЬ
вспоминать добром
⟨добрым словом⟩,
Д-222
ВСПОМНИТЬ
вспомнить добром
⟨добрым словом⟩,
Д-222
ВСПОМЯНЕТ
кто старое вспомянет,
тому глаз вон, С-546

ВСПЯТЬ
повернуть колесо истории
вспять, К-196
ВСТАВАТЬ
вставать левой ногой,
Н-142
вставать на дыбы, Д-434
вставать на ноги, Н-157
вставать на очередь, О-186
вставать на путь, П-662
вставать на сторону, С-609
вставать на учёт, У-168
вставать не с той ноги,
Н-142
вставать перед глазами,
Г-106
вставать с левой ноги,
Н-142
вставать стеной, С-566
ВСТАВЛЯТЬ
вставлять палки в колёса,
П-9
ВСТАЁТ
кто рано встаёт, тому бог
(по)даёт, В-346
ВСТАЛИ
волосы встали дыбом,
В-241
ВСТАЛО
встало на свои места ⟨на
(своё) место⟩, М-99
ВСТАТЬ
встать в позу, П-273
встать горой, Г-350
встать грудью, Г-427
встать колом в горле,
К-206
встать костью в глотке,
К-206
встать костью в горле,
К-206
встать левой ногой, Н-142
встать на дороге, П-652
встать на дыбы, Д-434
встать на место, М-124
встать на ноги, Н-157
встать на одну доску,
Д-296
встать на очередь, О-186
встать на пути, П-652
встать на путь, П-662
встать на сторону, С-609
встать на учёт, У-168
встать не с той ноги, Н-142
встать перед глазами,
Г-106
встать под знамёна ⟨под
знамя⟩, З-167
встать поперёк горла,
Г-332
встать поперёк дороги,
П-652
встать поперёк пути,
П-652
встать с левой ноги, Н-142
встать стеной, С-566
не встать мне ⟨нам⟩ с
(этого) места!, М-92
(чтоб) не встать мне
⟨нам⟩ с (этого) места!,
М-92

ВСТАЮТ
волосы встают дыбом,
В-241
ВСТРЕТИТЬСЯ
встретиться на узкой
дороге ⟨дорожке⟩, Д-289
ВСТРЕЧАТЬСЯ
встречаться на узкой
дороге ⟨дорожке⟩, Д-289
ВСТРЕЧАЮТ
по одёжке встречают, по
уму провожают, О-70
по платью встречают, по
уму провожают, О-70
ВСТРЕЧНЫЙ
встречный и поперечный
⟨встречный-
поперечный⟩, В-347
всякий встречный, В-347
всякий встречный и
поперечный ⟨встречный-
поперечный⟩, В-347
каждый встречный, В-347
каждый встречный и
поперечный ⟨встречный-
поперечный⟩, В-347
первый встречный, В-348
ВСТУПАТЬ
вступать в возраст, В-210
вступать в года, В-210
вступать в дело, Д-74
вступать в жизнь, Ж-50
вступать в законную силу,
С-187
вступать в лета, В-210
вступать в свои права,
П-469
вступать в силу, С-187
вступать в строй, С-637
вступать на путь, П-662
ВСТУПИТЬ
вступить в возраст, В-210
вступить в года, В-210
вступить в дело, Д-74
вступить в жизнь, Ж-50
вступить в закон, З-47
вступить в законную силу,
С-187
вступить в лета, В-210
вступить в свои права,
П-469
вступить в силу, С-187
вступить в строй, С-637
вступить на путь, П-662
ВСЫПАТЬ
всыпать горячих, Г-364
ВСЮ
во всю глотку, Г-337
во всю ивановскую, И-1
во всю мочь, М-271
во всю носовую завёртку,
З-14
во всю прыть, П-608
во всю рысь, Р-394
во всю силу, С-186
во всю ширь, Ш-65
выматывать/вымотать
всю душу, Д-415
вытягивать/вытянуть всю
душу, Д-415

на всю железку, Ж-11
на всю катушку, К-103
перевернуть
⟨перевёртывать⟩ всю
душу, Д-429
переворачивать
⟨переворотить⟩ всю
душу, Д-429
ВСЮДУ
куда ни кинь, всюду клин,
К-136
ВСЯ
вот (тебе) и вся недолга,
В-349
все ⟨всё⟩ и вся, В-326
и вся недолга, В-349
пускаться/пуститься во
вся тяжкая, Т-256
ВСЯК
всяк кулик своё болото
хвалит, К-467
всяк по-своему с ума
сходит, У-82
всяк сверчок знай свой
шесток, С-38
ВСЯКАЯ
всякая всячина, В-351
всякая собака, С-441
ВСЯКИЕ
видать всякие виды, В-142
видывать всякие виды,
В-142
ВСЯКИЙ
всякий встречный, В-347
всякий встречный и
поперечный ⟨встречный-
поперечный⟩, В-347
всякий дурак может/
сможет, Д-328
всякий по-своему с ума
сходит, У-82
на всякий пожарный
случай, С-372
на всякий роток не
накинешь платок, Р-186
на всякий случай, С-373
на всякий чих не
наздравствуешься, Ч-156
ВСЯКИМ
вопреки всяким
ожиданиям, О-85
ВСЯКИХ
без всяких, В-350
без всяких задних мыслей,
М-311
без всяких околичностей,
О-7
без всяких разговоров,
Р-52
безо всяких, В-350
против всяких ожиданий,
О-85
сверх всяких ожиданий,
О-85
ВСЯКО
не всяко лыко в строку,
Л-155
ВСЯКОГО
без всякого разговора, Р-52
без всякого сомнения,
С-480

без всякого удержу, У-43
вне всякого сомнения,
   С-480
всякого рода, Р-126
на всякого мудреца
   довольно простоты,
   М-279
против всякого ожидания,
   О-85
против всякого чаяния,
   Ч-40
сверх всякого ожидания,
   О-85
сверх всякого чаяния, Ч-40

ВСЯКОЕ
на всякое хотенье есть
   терпенье, Х-87
на всякое чиханье не
   наздравствуешься, Ч-156
не всякое лыко в строку,
   Л-155
поставить всякое лыко в
   строку, Л-156
ставить всякое лыко в
   строку, Л-156

ВСЯКОЙ
без всякой задней мысли,
   М-311
всякой твари по паре, Т-46
ко всякой бочке затычка,
   Б-191
ниже всякой критики,
   К-390
сверх всякой меры, М-87
свыше всякой меры, М-87

ВСЯКОМ
во всяком случае, С-369

ВСЯКОМУ
вопреки всякому
   ожиданию, О-85
всякому овощу своё время,
   О-44
дай бог всякому, Б-110

ВСЯКУЮ
потерять всякую совесть,
   С-457
разменивать на всякую
   мелочь, М-65
размениваться на всякую
   мелочь, М-66
разменять на всякую
   мелочь, М-65
разменяться на всякую
   мелочь, М-66

ВСЯЧЕСКАЯ
суета сует и всяческая
   суета, С-669

ВСЯЧИНА
всякая всячина, В-351

ВТАПТЫВАТЬ
втаптывать в грязь, Г-432

ВТЕМЯШИВАТЬ
втемяшивать в башку,
   Г-245
втемяшивать в голову,
   Г-245
втемяшивать себе в башку,
   Г-246
втемяшивать себе в
   голову, Г-246

ВТЕМЯШИТЬ
втемяшить в башку, Г-245
втемяшить в голову, Г-245
втемяшить себе в башку,
   Г-246
втемяшить себе в голову,
   Г-246

ВТЕРЕТЬ
втереть очки, О-189

ВТЕРЕТЬСЯ
втереться в доверие, Д-225
втереться в милость,
   М-156

ВТИРАТЬ
втирать очки, О-189

ВТИРАТЬСЯ
втираться в доверие, Д-225
втираться в милость,
   М-156

ВТОПТАТЬ
втоптать в грязь, Г-432

ВТОРАЯ
вторая молодость, М-236
вторая натура, Н-33
вторая скрипка, С-237
привычка – вторая
   натура, П-518

ВТОРОГО
до второго пришествия,
   П-558

ВТОРОМ
на втором взводе, В-93

ВТОРОМУ
по второму кругу, К-424

ВТОРУЮ
играть вторую скрипку,
   С-239

ВТОРЫХ
до вторых петухов, П-135
из вторых рук, Р-209
из вторых уст, У-139
на вторых ролях, Р-158
после вторых петухов,
   П-136

ВУЛКАНЕ
как на вулкане, В-352

ВХОДИТ
в одно ухо входит, (а в
   другое выходит, У-156

ВХОДИТЬ
входить в азарт, А-14
входить в амбицию, А-26
входить в быт, Ж-50
входить в возраст, В-210
входить в года, В-210
входить в голову, Г-271
входить в доверие, Д-226
входить в долг(и), Д-237
входить в душу, Д-411
входить в жизнь, Ж-50
входить в колею, К-198
входить в курс, К-484
входить в лета, В-210
входить в милость, М-157
входить в мысль, Г-271
входить в норму, Н-204
входить в обычное русло,
   К-198
входить в обычную колею,
   К-198

входить в привычное
   русло, К-198
входить в привычную
   колею, К-198
входить в плоть и кровь,
   П-199
входить в поговорку, П-411
входить в положение,
   П-304
входить в пословицу, П-411
входить в привычку, П-519
входить в раж, Р-17
входить в роль, Р-153
входить в русло, К-198
входить в своё русло,
   К-198
входить в свои права,
   П-469
входить в свою колею,
   К-198
входить в сердце, Д-411
входить в силу, С-187
входить в строй, С-637
входить в тело, Т-57
входить в ум, Г-271
входить во вкус, В-152

ВЧЕРАШНЕГО
искать вчерашнего дня,
   Д-160

ВЧЕРАШНИЙ
вчерашний день, Д-151
искать вчерашний день,
   Д-160

ВЪЕХАТЬ
на чужой спине в рай
   въехать, Г-323
на чужом горбу в рай
   въехать, Г-323

ВЫ
вы только подумайте!,
   П-259
говорить вы, В-354
да что вы!, Ч-191
идите вы (куда
   подальше!, И-23
иду на вы, В-353
на вы, В-354
нет, вы только
   подумайте!, П-259
нет, что вы!, Ч-191
ну что вы!, Ч-191
что вы!, Ч-191
что вы говорите!, Г-168

ВЫБИВАЕТСЯ
клин клином выбивается,
   К-135

ВЫБИВАТЬ
выбивать дурь (из
   головы), Д-340
выбивать из головы, Г-285
выбивать из колеи, К-181
выбивать из седла, С-107
выбивать почву из-под
   ног, П-451

ВЫБИВАТЬСЯ
выбиваться в люди, Л-168
выбиваться из колеи,
   К-182
выбиваться из сил, С-164
выбиваться на (широкую)
   дорогу, Д-277

ВЫБИВАЮТ
клин клином выбивают,
   К-135

ВЫБИРАТЬ
выбирать выражения,
   В-375
выбирать слова, В-375

ВЫБИТЬ
выбить дурь (из головы),
   Д-340
выбить из головы, Г-285
выбить из колеи, К-181
выбить из седла, С-107
выбить почву из-под ног,
   П-451

ВЫБИТЬСЯ
выбиться в люди, Л-168
выбиться из колеи, К-182
выбиться из сил, С-164
выбиться на (широкую)
   дорогу, Д-277

ВЫБОР
на выбор, В-355

ВЫБРАСЫВАТЬ
выбрасывать дурь из
   головы, Д-341
выбрасывать за борт,
   Б-183
выбрасывать на ветер,
   В-67
выбрасывать на помойку,
   П-334
выбрасывать на улицу,
   У-74
выбрасывать номер
   ⟨номера⟩, Н-198

ВЫБРОСИТЬ
выбросить дурь из
   головы, Д-341
выбросить за борт, Б-183
выбросить из головы,
   Г-286
выбросить из памяти,
   Г-286
выбросить на ветер, В-67
выбросить на помойку,
   П-334
выбросить на улицу, У-74
выбросить номер
   ⟨номера⟩, Н-198
выкрасить да ⟨и⟩
   выбросить, В-368

ВЫБРОСЬ
оторви да ⟨и⟩ выбрось,
   О-161

ВЫБЫВАТЬ
выбывать из строя, С-643

ВЫБЫТЬ
выбыть из строя, С-643

ВЫВЕДЕТ
куда кривая выведет,
   К-386

ВЫВЕЗЕТ
кривая вывезет, К-385
куда кривая вывезет, К-386
куда кривая ни вывезет,
   К-386

ВЫВЕЗТИ
вывезти в свет, С-42
вывезти на плечах, П-186

вывезти на своём горбу,
П-186
вывезти на своих плечах,
П-186
вывезти на себе, П-186
вывезти на собственном
горбу, П-186
вывезти на собственных
плечах, П-186

ВЫВЕРНУЛО
вывернуло наизнанку,
В-358

ВЫВЕРНУТЬ
вывернуть душу, Д-412,
Д-413
вывернуть душу
наизнанку, Д-413
вывернуть карманы, К-77
вывернуть наизнанку,
В-359
вывернуть свои карманы,
К-77

ВЫВЕРНУТЬСЯ
вывернуться наизнанку,
В-360

ВЫВЕСТИ
вывести в люди, Л-167
вывести в расход, Р-88
вывести из заблуждения,
З-5
вывести из себя, В-356
вывести из строя, С-642
вывести из терпения, Т-84
вывести на дорогу, Д-276
вывести на путь, Д-276
вывести на свежую воду,
В-183
вывести на свет божий,
С-41
вывести на чистую воду,
В-183
вывести наружу, В-357

ВЫВОДИТЬ
выводить в люди, Л-167
выводить в расход, Р-88
выводить вавилоны, В-33
выводить вензеля, К-379
выводить из заблуждения,
З-5
выводить из себя, В-356
выводить из строя, С-642
выводить из терпения,
Т-84
выводить на дорогу, Д-276
выводить на путь, Д-276
выводить на свежую воду,
В-183
выводить на свет божий,
С-41
выводить на чистую воду,
В-183
выводить наружу, В-357

ВЫВОЗИТ
кривая вывозит, К-385

ВЫВОЗИТЬ
вывозить в свет, С-42
вывозить на плечах, П-186
вывозить на своём горбу,
П-186
вывозить на своих плечах,
П-186

вывозить на себе, П-186
вывозить на собственном
горбу, П-186
вывозить на собственных
плечах, П-186

ВЫВОЛОЧКУ
давать/дать выволочку,
Т-200
задавать/задать
выволочку, Т-200
получать/получить
выволочку, Т-201

ВЫВОРАЧИВАЕТ
выворачивает наизнанку,
В-358
душу выворачивает, Д-412

ВЫВОРАЧИВАТЬ
выворачивать душу, Д-412,
Д-413
выворачивать душу
наизнанку, Д-413
выворачивать карманы,
К-77
выворачивать наизнанку,
В-359
выворачивать свои
карманы, К-77

ВЫВОРАЧИВАТЬСЯ
выворачиваться
наизнанку, В-360

ВЫВОРОТИЛО
выворотило наизнанку,
В-358

ВЫВОРОТИТЬ
выворотить наизнанку,
В-359

ВЫДАВАТЬ
выдавать белое за чёрное
(и чёрное за белое), Ч-71
выдавать головой, Г-235
выдавать замуж, В-361
выдавать себя, В-362
выдавать чёрное за белое
(и белое за чёрное), Ч-71

ВЫДАЙ(ТЕ)
не выдай(те), В-363

ВЫДАНЬЕ
на выданье, В-364

ВЫДАСТ
бог не выдаст, свинья не
съест, Б-100
господь не выдаст, свинья
не съест, Б-100

ВЫДАТЬ
выдать белое за чёрное (и
чёрное за белое), Ч-71
выдать головой, Г-235
выдать замуж, В-361
выдать себя, В-362
выдать чёрное за белое (и
белое за чёрное), Ч-71

ВЫДЕЛКИ
овчинка выделки не стоит,
О-48

ВЫДЕЛЫВАТЬ
выделывать вензеля, В-33
выделывать коленца
⟨коленце⟩, К-191
выделывать крендели,
В-33

выделывать кренделя,
В-33, К-379
выделывать курбеты,
К-379
выделывать мыслете, В-33
выделывать ногами
вензеля ⟨кренделя,
крендели, мыслете⟩,
В-33

ВЫДЕРЖАТЬ
выдержать роль, Р-154
выдержать характер, Х-2

ВЫДЕРЖИВАТЬ
выдерживать марку, М-31
выдерживать роль, Р-154
выдерживать характер,
Х-2
не выдерживать критики,
К-390
не выдерживать никакого
сравнения, С-531
не выдерживать никакой
критики, К-390
не выдерживать
сравнения, С-531

ВЫДУМАЕТ
пороха ⟨пороху⟩ не
выдумает, П-382

ВЫДУМКИ
голь на выдумки хитра,
Г-311

ВЫЕДЕННОГО
выеденного яйца не
стоит, Я-59

ВЫЕДЕННОЕ
выеденное яйцо, Я-61

ВЫЕЗЖАТЬ
выезжать в свет, С-43

ВЫЕСТ
стыд не дым, глаза не
выест, С-652

ВЫЕХАТЬ
выехать в свет, С-43

ВЫЖАТЫЙ
выжатый лимон, Л-72

ВЫЖАТЬ
выжать сок, С-467
выжать все соки, С-467
выжать (последние) соки,
С-467

ВЫЖЕЧЬ
выжечь калёным железом,
Ж-13

ВЫЖИВАТЬ
выживать из памяти, П-32
выживать из ума, У-83

ВЫЖИГАТЬ
выжигать калёным
железом, Ж-13

ВЫЖИМАТЬ
выжимать сок, С-467
выжимать все соки, С-467
выжимать (последние)
соки, С-467

ВЫЖИТЬ
выжить из памяти, П-32
выжить из ума, У-83

ВЫЖМИ
хоть выжми, В-365

ВЫЗВАТЬ
вызвать к жизни, Ж-40
вызвать на ковёр, К-152

ВЫЗОВОМ
с вызовом, В-366

ВЫЗЫВАТЬ
вызывать к жизни, Ж-40
вызывать на ковёр, К-152

ВЫИГРАТЬ
выиграть время, В-313

ВЫИГРЫВАТЬ
выигрывать время, В-313

ВЫИГРЫШЕ
в выигрыше, В-367

ВЫИСКИВАТЬ
выискивать блох, Б-82

ВЫЙДЕТ
(этот) номер не выйдет,
Н-201

ВЫЙТИ
выйти боком, Б-156
выйти в люди, Л-168
выйти в свет, С-46
выйти в тираж, Т-99
выйти замуж, В-387
выйти из бюджета, Б-284
выйти из возраста, В-211
выйти из доверия, Д-227
выйти из игры, И-19
выйти из колеи, К-182
выйти из лет, В-211
выйти из пелёнок, П-78
выйти из-под кисти, К-123
выйти из-под пера, П-87
выйти из-под резца, Р-106
выйти из положения,
П-311
выйти из роли, Р-151
выйти из своей скорлупы,
С-234
выйти из себя, В-388
выйти из строя, С-643
выйти из терпения, Т-82
выйти на дорогу, Д-277
выйти на панель, П-51
выйти на широкую дорогу,
Д-277
выйти сухим из воды,
В-195
выйти фуксом, Ф-30

ВЫКАТИТЬ
выкатить глаза, Г-100

ВЫКАТЫВАТЬ
выкатывать глаза, Г-100

ВЫКИДЫВАТЬ
выкидывать дурь из
головы, Д-341
выкидывать за борт, Б-183
выкидывать коленца
⟨коленце⟩, К-191
выкидывать кренделя,
К-379
выкидывать на улицу,
У-74
выкидывать номер
⟨номера⟩, Н-198
выкидывать фокус
⟨фокусы⟩, Ф-13
выкидывать фортели
⟨фортель⟩, Ф-13

ВЫКИДЫВАТЬ ШТУКИ
выкидывать штуки
⟨штуку⟩, Ш-91

ВЫКИНЕШЬ
из песни слова не
выкинешь, П-117

ВЫКИНУТЬ
выкинуть дурь из головы,
Д-341
выкинуть за борт, Б-183
выкинуть из головы, Г-286
выкинуть из памяти, Г-286
выкинуть коленца
⟨коленце⟩, К-191
выкинуть на улицу, У-74
выкинуть номер ⟨номера⟩,
Н-198
выкинуть фокус ⟨фокусы⟩,
Ф-13
выкинуть фортели
⟨фортель⟩, Ф-13
выкинуть штуки ⟨штуку⟩,
Ш-91

ВЫКЛАДЫВАТЬ
выкладывать душу, Д-414

ВЫКЛЮЕТ
ворон ворону глаз не
выклюет, В-269

ВЫКОЛАЧИВАТЬ
выколачивать дурь (из
головы), Д-340

ВЫКОЛИ
хоть глаз ⟨глаза⟩ выколи,
Г-43

ВЫКОЛОТИТЬ
выколотить дурь (из
головы), Д-340

ВЫКОЛОТИШЬ
гвоздём не выколотишь,
К-137
дубиной не выколотишь,
К-137
клином не выколотишь,
К-137

ВЫКОПАТЬ
выкопать яму, Я-65

ВЫКРАСИТЬ
выкрасить да ⟨и⟩
выбросить, В-368

ВЫКУСИ
на ⟨на-ка, на-кась, на-
кася⟩, выкуси!, В-369

ВЫЛЕЗАТЬ
из кожи (вон) вылезать,
К-162
из шкуры (вон) вылезать,
К-162

ВЫЛЕТАТЬ
вылетать в трубу, Т-207
вылетать из головы, Г-287
вылетать из памяти, Г-287
пулей вылетать, П-630
стрелой вылетать, П-630

ВЫЛЕТЕЛ
хмель вылетел из головы,
Х-47

ВЫЛЕТЕТЬ
вылететь в трубу, Т-207
вылететь из головы, Г-287
вылететь из памяти, Г-287

как пробка вылететь,
П-561
пробкой вылететь, П-561
пулей вылететь, П-630
стрелой вылететь, П-630

ВЫЛЕТИТ
слово не воробей, вылетит
— не поймаешь, С-328

ВЫЛИТЬ
вылить ушат помоев,
У-178
вылить ушат холодной
воды, В-180

ВЫЛОЖИТЬ
выложить билет (на стол),
Б-65
выложить душу, Д-414
выложить партбилет (на
стол), Б-65

ВЫЛУПИТЬ
вылупить бельма, Г-100
вылупить глаза, Г-100
вылупить зенки, Г-100

ВЫМАНИТЬ
калачом не выманить,
К-31

ВЫМАТЫВАТЬ
выматывать все жилы,
Ж-74
выматывать все кишки,
К-129
выматывать (всю) душу,
Д-415
выматывать жилы, Ж-74
выматывать кишки, К-129
выматывать нервы, Н-83

ВЫМЕСТИ
вымести железной метлой,
М-135

ВЫМЕСТИТЬ
выместить сердце, С-130

ВЫМЕТАТЬ
выметать железной
метлой, М-135

ВЫМЕЩАТЬ
вымещать сердце, С-130

ВЫМОТАТЬ
вымотать все жилы, Ж-74
вымотать все кишки,
К-129
вымотать (всю) душу,
Д-415
вымотать жилы, Ж-74
вымотать кишки, К-129
вымотать нервы, Н-83

ВЫМЫТЬ
вымыть голову, Г-258

ВЫНЕСЕТ
кривая вынесет, К-385
куда кривая вынесет,
К-386
куда кривая ни вынесет,
К-386

ВЫНЕСТИ
вынести за скобки, С-226
вынести на плечах, П-186
вынести на своём горбу,
П-186
вынести на своих плечах,
П-186

вынести на себе, П-186
вынести на собственном
горбу, П-186
вынести на собственных
плечах, П-186
вынести сор из избы,
С-494

ВЫНИМАТЬ
вынимать душу, Д-416

ВЫНОСИ
хоть святых (вон) выноси,
С-90

ВЫНОСИТ
кривая выносит, К-385

ВЫНОСИТЬ
выносить за скобки, С-226
выносить на плечах, П-186
выносить на своём горбу,
П-186
выносить на своих плечах,
П-186
выносить на себе, П-186
выносить на собственном
горбу, П-186
выносить на собственных
плечах, П-186
выносить на улицу, У-75
выносить сор из избы,
С-494

ВЫНУТЬ
вынуть душу, Д-416

ВЫНЬ
вынь да положь, В-370

ВЫПАДАТЬ
выпадать из памяти, Г-287

ВЫПАСТЬ
выпасть из памяти, Г-287

ВЫПИСЫВАТЬ
выписывать вензеля, В-33
выписывать крендели,
В-33
выписывать кренделя,
В-33, К-379
выписывать курбеты,
К-379
выписывать мыслете, В-33
выписывать ногами
вензеля ⟨кренделя,
крендели, мыслете⟩,
В-33

ВЫПИТЬ
выпить брудершафт, Б-213
выпить горькую чашу (до
дна), Ч-39
выпить до дна горькую
⟨полную⟩ чашу, Ч-39
выпить кровь, К-407
выпить на брудершафт,
Б-213
выпить на ты, Б-213
выпить полную чашу, Ч-39
выпить чашу (до дна),
Ч-39

ВЫПЛАКАТЬ
выплакать (все) глаза,
Г-49

ВЫПЛЫВАТЬ
выплывать на свет божий,
С-44
выплывать наружу, П-217

ВЫПЛЫТЬ
выплыть на свет божий,
С-44
выплыть наружу, П-217

ВЫПРОСИШЬ
зимой снега ⟨снегу⟩ не
выпросишь, С-431

ВЫПУСКАТЬ
выпускать в свет, С-45
выпускать вожжи, В-199
выпускать из вида ⟨виду⟩,
В-141
выпускать из глаз, В-141
выпускать из рук, Р-208
выпускать когти, К-158
выпускать с глаз, В-141
не выпускать из рук, Р-214
не выпускать из рук меча,
Р-215
не выпускать из рук
оружия, Р-215

ВЫПУСТИТЬ
выпустить в свет, С-45
выпустить в трубу, Т-208
выпустить вожжи, В-199
выпустить из вида ⟨виду⟩,
В-141
выпустить из глаз, В-141
выпустить из рук, Р-208
выпустить кишки, К-130
выпустить когти, К-158
выпустить с глаз, В-141

ВЫПУЧИТЬ
выпучить бельма, Г-100
выпучить глаза, Г-100
выпучить зенки, Г-100

ВЫПЯЛИТЬ
выпялить бельма, Г-100
выпялить глаза, Г-100
выпялить зенки, Г-100

ВЫРАЖАЯСЬ
мягко выражаясь, В-371

ВЫРАЖЕНИЕ
извини(те) за выражение,
В-372
прости(те) за выражение,
В-372

ВЫРАЖЕНИЕМ
с выражением, В-373

ВЫРАЖЕНИЯ
без выражения, В-374
выбирать выражения,
В-375

ВЫРВАТЬ
вырвать из души, С-122
вырвать из сердца, С-122
вырвать с корнем, К-302

ВЫРОСТ
на вырост, В-376

ВЫРУБИШЬ
что написано пером, того
не вырубишь топором,
П-103

ВЫРЫВАТЬ
вырывать из души, С-122
вырывать из сердца, С-122
вырывать с корнем, К-302

ВЫРЫТЬ
вырыть яму, Я-65

ВЫСАСЫВАТЬ
высасывать все соки,
С-467

высасывать из пальца, П-14
высасывать кровь, К-407
высасывать последние соки, С-467
высасывать сок(и), С-467

ВЫСКАКИВАТЬ
выскакивать из головы, Г-287
выскакивать из памяти, Г-287

ВЫСКОЧИЛ
хмель выскочил из головы, Х-47

ВЫСКОЧИТЬ
выскочить из головы, Г-287
выскочить из памяти, Г-287
как пробка выскочить, П-561
пробкой выскочить, П-561

ВЫСЛУГА
выслуга лет, В-377

ВЫСМОТРЕТЬ
(все) глаза высмотреть, Г-48

ВЫСОВЫВАТЬ
высовывать нос, Н-211

ВЫСОКИЕ
высокие материи, М-46

ВЫСОКО
высоко держать знамя, З-165
высоко думать о себе, В-256
высоко летать, Л-65
высоко мнить о себе, В-256

ВЫСОКОГО
наплевать с высокого дерева, Д-176
плевать с высокого дерева, Д-176
птица высокого полёта, П-619

ВЫСОКОЙ
высокой пробы, П-564

ВЫСОСАТЬ
высосать все соки, С-467
высосать из пальца, П-14
высосать кровь, К-407
высосать последние соки, С-467
высосать сок(и), С-467

ВЫСОТЕ
на высоте, В-378
на высоте положения, В-378
на должной высоте, В-378

ВЫСОТЫ
с высоты птичьего полёта, В-379
с высоты своего величия, В-380

ВЫСТАВИТЬ
выставить за дверь, Д-34
выставить на вид, В-109
выставить напоказ ⟨наружу⟩, В-109

ВЫСТАВКУ
хоть на выставку, В-381

ВЫСТАВЛЯТЬ
выставлять за дверь, Д-34
выставлять на вид, В-109
выставлять напоказ ⟨наружу⟩, В-109

ВЫСТРЕЛ
на выстрел, В-382
на пушечный выстрел, В-383
холостой выстрел, В-384

ВЫСТУПАТЬ
выступать гоголем, Г-178
выступать на свет божий, С-44
выступать на сцену, С-686

ВЫСТУПИТЬ
выступить на свет божий, С-44
выступить на сцену, С-686

ВЫСУНУВ
высунув язык ⟨языки⟩, Я-8

ВЫСУНУВШИ
высунувши язык ⟨языки⟩, Я-8

ВЫСУНУТЬ
высунуть нос, Н-211

ВЫСУНЯ
высуня язык ⟨языки⟩, Я-8

ВЫСШЕЙ
в высшей степени, С-571
высшей марки, М-29
высшей пробы, П-564

ВЫТАРАЩИТЬ
вытаращить глаза, Г-100

ВЫТАСКИВАТЬ
вытаскивать из грязи, Г-430

ВЫТАЩИТЬ
вытащить из грязи, Г-430

ВЫТАЩИШЬ
клещами не вытащишь, К-132

ВЫТРЯСТИ
вытрясти душу, Д-417
вытрясти карман, К-77

ВЫТЬ
волком выть, В-232
с волками жить — по-волчьи выть, В-229

ВЫТЯГИВАТЬ
вытягивать все жилы, Ж-74
вытягивать все кишки, К-129
вытягивать (всю) душу, Д-415
вытягивать жилы, Ж-74
вытягивать кишки, К-129
вытягивать руки по швам, Р-285
клещами вытягивать, К-133

ВЫТЯНЕШЬ
клещами не вытянешь, К-132

ВЫТЯНУЛАСЬ
физиономия вытянулась, Л-96

ВЫТЯНУЛОСЬ
лицо вытянулось, Л-96

ВЫТЯНУТЬ
вытянуть все жилы, Ж-74
вытянуть все кишки, К-129
вытянуть (всю) душу, Д-415
вытянуть жилы, Ж-74
вытянуть кишки, К-129
вытянуть ноги, Н-155
вытянуть руки по швам, Р-285

ВЫХОД
выход из положения, П-311
давать/дать выход, В-385

ВЫХОДЕЦ
выходец с того света, В-386

ВЫХОДИТ
в одно ухо входит, (а) в другое выходит, У-156
не выходит из головы, Г-291
не выходит из памяти, Г-291
не выходит из ума, Г-291

ВЫХОДИТЬ
выходить боком, Б-156
выходить в люди, Л-168
выходить в свет, С-46
выходить в тираж, Т-99
выходить замуж, В-387
выходить из бюджета, Б-284
выходить из возраста, В-211
выходить из доверия, Д-227
выходить из игры, И-19
выходить из колеи, К-182
выходить из лет, В-211
выходить из пелёнок, П-78
выходить из-под кисти, К-123
выходить из-под пера, П-87
выходить из-под резца, Р-106
выходить из положения, П-311
выходить из роли, Р-151
выходить из своей скорлупы, С-234
выходить из себя, В-388
выходить из строя, С-643
выходить из терпения, Т-82
выходить на дорогу, Д-277
выходить на панель, П-51
выходить на широкую дорогу, Д-277
выходить сухим из воды, В-195

ВЫХОДЫ
знать все ходы-выходы ⟨ходы и выходы⟩, Х-74

ВЫХОДЯЩИЙ
из ряда вон выходящий, Р-400

ВЫЧЁРКИВАТЬ
вычёркивать из памяти, П-33

вычёркивать из своей жизни, Ж-41

ВЫЧЕРКНУТЬ
вычеркнуть из памяти, П-33
вычеркнуть из своей жизни, Ж-41

ВЫЧЕТОМ
за вычетом, В-389

ВЫШВЫРИВАТЬ
вышвыривать за борт, Б-183
вышвыривать на улицу, У-74

ВЫШВЫРНУТЬ
вышвырнуть за борт, Б-183
вышвырнуть на улицу, У-74

ВЫШЕ
выше головы, Г-288
выше головы не прыгнешь, Г-289
выше сил, С-165
головой выше, Г-260
на голову выше, Г-260
поднимай ⟨подымай⟩ выше!, П-248
стать выше, С-620
стоять выше, С-620
тоном выше, Т-158

ВЫШЕЛ
весь вышел, В-390
мордой не вышел, Р-390
не вышел, В-391
рожей не вышел, Р-390
рылом не вышел, Р-390
хмель вышел из головы, Х-47

ВЫШИБАЕТСЯ
клин клином вышибается, К-135

ВЫШИБАТЬ
вышибать дурь (из головы), Д-340
вышибать дух, Д-343
вышибать душу, Д-343
вышибать из колеи, К-181
вышибать из седла, С-107
вышибать почву из-под ног, П-451

ВЫШИБАЮТ
клин клином вышибают, К-135

ВЫШИБЕШЬ
гвоздём не вышибешь, К-137
дубиной не вышибешь, К-137
клином не вышибешь, К-137
плетью не вышибешь, П-173

ВЫШИБИТЬ
вышибить дурь (из головы), Д-340
вышибить дух, Д-343
вышибить душу, Д-343
вышибить из колеи, К-181
вышибить из седла, С-107

в глазах мутится
⟨позеленело,
помутилось,
потемнело⟩, Г-127
в глазах темнеет, Г-127
в глазах чертенята
⟨чёртики⟩ (прыгают),
Г-128
вертеться на глазах, Г-104
двоится в глазах, Г-129
зарябило в глазах, Г-131
на глазах, Г-130
нет стыда в глазах, С-653
рябит в глазах, Г-131
свет померк в глазах, С-61
стоять в глазах, Г-121
троится в глазах, Г-129
туман в глазах, Т-232

ГЛАЗЕ
ни в одном глазе, Г-141
хоть бы в одном глазе,
Г-141

ГЛАЗЕНАПА
запускать/запустить
глазенапа, Г-75
продирать/продрать
глазенапа, Г-89

ГЛАЗКАМИ
постреливать глазками,
Г-122
стрельнуть ⟨стрелять⟩
глазками, Г-122

ГЛАЗКИ
делать глазки, Г-132
протереть глазки, Г-90
строить глазки, Г-132

ГЛАЗКОМ
одним глазком, Г-133

ГЛАЗОК
на глазок, Г-26
свой глазок — смотрок,
Г-41

ГЛАЗОМ
глазом мигнуть
⟨моргнуть⟩, Г-135
глазом не ведёт, Б-209
глазом не моргнуть, Г-134
глазом не повёл, Б-209
и глазом мигнуть
⟨моргнуть⟩, Г-135
и глазом не ведёт/не
повёл, Б-209
каким глазом, Г-136
куда ни кинешь ⟨ни кинь⟩
глазом, Г-137
невооружённым глазом,
Г-138
одним глазом, Г-133, Г-139
простым глазом, Г-138

ГЛАЗУ
бельмо в ⟨на⟩ глазу, Б-55
в чужом глазу сучок
видим, а в своём (и)
бревна не замечаем,
Г-140
как* бельмо в ⟨на⟩ глазу,
Б-55
куда хватало глазу, Г-27
насколько хватало глазу,
Г-27

ни в одном глазу, Г-141
одна радость в глазу, Р-14
с глазу на глаз, Г-142
сколько хватало глазу,
Г-27
у семи нянек дитя без
глазу, Н-268
хоть бы в одном глазу,
Г-141

ГЛАС
глас вопиющего в
пустыне, Г-143
глас, вопиющий в
пустыне, Г-143

ГЛАСА
ни гласа ни воздыхания,
Г-144

ГЛАСНОСТИ
предавать/предать
гласности, Г-145

ГЛИНЯНЫХ
колосс на глиняных ногах,
К-208

ГЛОТАТЬ
глотать слёзы, С-267
глотать слова, С-282
глотать слюнки, С-386

ГЛОТКА
лужёная глотка, Г-146
медная глотка, Г-146

ГЛОТКЕ
встать ⟨стать, стоять⟩
костью в глотке, К-206

ГЛОТКУ
брать за глотку, Г-335
брать на глотку, Г-336
в глотку не идёт ⟨не лезет,
не пойдёт, не полезет⟩,
К-491
взять за глотку, Г-335
взять на глотку, Г-336
во всю глотку, Г-337
драть глотку, Г-339
заткнуть ⟨затыкать⟩
глотку, Г-147
кусок в глотку не идёт ⟨не
лезет, не пойдёт, не
полезет⟩, К-491
надрывать ⟨надсаживать⟩
глотку, Г-339
наступать/наступить на
глотку, Г-335
промочить глотку, Г-343
распускать/распустить
глотку, Г-344
расстегнуть глотку, Р-182
рвать глотку, Р-339
схватить ⟨хватать⟩ за
глотку, Г-335

ГЛУБИНЕ
в глубине веков, Г-148
в глубине души, Г-149
в глубине сердца, Г-149

ГЛУБИНЫ
до глубины души, Г-150
до глубины сердца, Г-150
из глубины веков, Г-151
из глубины прошлого,
Г-151
от глубины души, Г-152

ГЛУБОКИМ
с глубоким почтением,
П-463

ГЛУБОКОМУ
к глубокому сожалению,
С-464

ГЛУХАЯ
глухая тетеря, Т-91

ГЛУХОЙ
глухой тетерев, Т-91
глухой угол, У-31

ГЛЯДЕЛ
как* в воду глядел, В-184
на свет (божий) не глядел
бы, С-48

ГЛЯДЕЛИ
глаза бы (мои) не глядели,
Г-51

ГЛЯДЕТЬ
глядеть бирюком, Б-67
глядеть букой, Б-240
глядеть в глаза, Г-96, Г-97
глядеть в гроб, М-205
глядеть в книгу и видеть
фигу, К-148
глядеть в корень, К-295
глядеть в кусты, К-497
глядеть в лес, Л-57
глядеть в лицо, Г-97
глядеть в могилу, М-205
глядеть в оба, С-414
глядеть в оба глаза, С-414
глядеть в рот, Р-184
глядеть волком, В-233
глядеть вон, С-415
глядеть глазами, Г-119
глядеть другими ⟨иными⟩
глазами, Г-120
глядеть из рук, Р-221
глядеть косо, С-416
глядеть на вещи, В-89
глядеть не на что, С-417
глядеть по сторонам,
С-604
глядеть правде в глаза ⟨в
лицо⟩, П-483
глядеть прямо в глаза,
Г-98
глядеть сверху вниз, С-418
глядеть свысока, С-418
глядеть сквозь пальцы,
П-27
глядеть смело в глаза,
Г-98
глядеть смерти в глаза ⟨в
лицо⟩, С-394
глядеть снизу вверх, С-419
глядеть со своей
колокольни, К-204
глядеть фертом, Ф-8
как сыч глядеть, С-740
сычом глядеть, С-740

ГЛЯДИ
того (и) гляди, Г-153

ГЛЯДИТ
как ⟨сколько⟩ волка ни
корми, (а) он ⟨всё⟩ в лес
глядит, В-228

ГЛЯДЯ
на ночь глядя, Н-246

ГЛЯДЯТ
куда глаза глядят, Г-78

ГЛЯНЕЦ
навести ⟨наводить⟩
глянец, Г-154

ГНАТЬСЯ
гнаться за двумя зайцами,
3-36

ГНЕВ
менять гнев на милость,
Г-155
не во гнев будь сказано,
О-4
переменить ⟨положить,
преложить⟩ гнев на
милость, Г-155
сменить ⟨сменять⟩ гнев на
милость, Г-155

ГНЕЗДО
вить (себе) гнездо, Г-156
осиное гнездо, Г-157
свить (себе) гнездо, Г-156

ГНИЁТ
рыба с головы гниёт, Р-382

ГНИЛО
снаружи мило, а внутри
гнило, С-427

ГНУТЬ
гнуть в бараний рог, Р-120
гнуть в дугу, Р-120
гнуть в три дуги ⟨в три
погибели⟩, Р-120
гнуть горб, С-513
гнуть своё, Л-75
гнуть свою линию, Л-75
гнуть спину, С-513, С-514
гнуть хребет, С-513, С-514

ГОВОРИ
взялся за гуж, не говори,
что не дюж, Г-443
и не говори, Г-162
как ни говори, Г-163
не говори, Г-162
не говори гоп, пока не
перепрыгнешь ⟨не
перескочишь⟩, Г-158
что ни говори, Г-163

ГОВОРИЛ
а ⟨ну⟩ что я говорил!,
Г-159
что я говорил!, Г-159

ГОВОРИТ
говорит как пишет, Г-160
кровь говорит, К-401
сам за себя говорит, Г-161
у кого что болит, тот о
том и говорит, Б-170
что у кого болит, тот о
том и говорит, Б-170

ГОВОРИТЕ
и не говорите, Г-162
как ни говорите, Г-163
не говорите, Г-162
что вы говорите!, Г-168
что ни говорите, Г-163

ГОВОРИТСЯ
как говорится, Г-164

ГОВОРИТЬ
говорить в пользу, П-324
говорить вы, В-354

говорить дело, Д-76
говорить загадками, З-27
говорить на ветер, В-68
говорить на разных
  языках, Я-52
говорить по делу, Д-143
говорить правду-матку (в
  глаза), П-484
говорить с твоего
  ⟨чужого⟩ голоса, Г-306
говорить ты, Т-248
да что (и) говорить, Г-167
да что там ⟨тут⟩
  говорить, Г-167
ещё ни о чём не говорить,
  Г-165
нечего и говорить, Г-166
ни о чём не говорить,
  Г-165
что (и) говорить, Г-167
что там ⟨тут⟩ говорить,
  Г-167

ГОВОРИШЬ
что ты говоришь!, Г-168

ГОВОРЮ
говорю вам ⟨тебе⟩, Г-177
я уж(е) не говорю, Г-173

ГОВОРЯ
в сущности говоря, С-684
вообще говоря, Г-169
иначе говоря, Г-170
к примеру говоря, П-534
к слову говоря, С-338
коротко ⟨короче⟩ говоря,
  Г-171
кстати говоря, С-206
между нами говоря, Г-172
мягко говоря, В-371
не говоря, Г-173
не говоря дурного слова,
  С-284
не говоря уж(е), Г-173
не говоря худого слова,
  С-284
откровенно говоря, Г-174
по правде говоря, П-482
по совести говоря, С-452
по существу говоря, С-684
по чести говоря, Ч-126
попросту говоря, Г-175
правду говоря, П-482
собственно говоря, Г-176
честно говоря, Г-174

ГОВОРЯТ
в доме повешенного не
  говорят о верёвке, Д-259
говорят вам ⟨тебе⟩, Г-177

ГОГОЛЕМ
выступать гоголем, Г-178
ходить гоголем, Г-178

ГОД
год от года ⟨году⟩, Г-179
из года ⟨году⟩ в год, Г-181
раз в год по обещанию,
  Р-27
с года ⟨году⟩ на год, Г-179

ГОДА
входить/войти ⟨вступать/
  вступить⟩ в года, В-210
год от года, Г-179

года вышли, Г-180
года подошли ⟨подходят⟩,
  Г-191
из года в год, Г-181
мафусаиловы года, В-19
обещанного три года
  ждут, Г-182
с года на год, Г-179

ГОДАМ
не по годам, Г-183

ГОДАМИ
с годами, Г-184

ГОДАХ
в годах, Г-185

ГОДИТСЯ
в подмётки не годится,
  П-247
куда это годится!, Г-186
никуда не годится, Г-187

ГОДИТЬСЯ
годиться в матери, Г-188
годиться в отцы, Г-188
годиться в сыновья, Г-188

ГОДНЫЙ
никуда не годный, Г-189

ГОДУ
без году неделю ⟨неделя⟩,
  Г-190
год от году, Г-179
из году в год, Г-181
с году на год, Г-179

ГОДЫ
годы вышли, Г-180
годы подошли
  ⟨подходят⟩, Г-191

ГОЛ
гол как сокол, С-468

ГОЛОВ
сколько голов, столько (и)
  умов, Г-192

ГОЛОВА
адамова голова, Г-193
баранья голова, Г-194
бедовая голова, Г-195
буйная голова, Г-195
ветреная голова, Г-196
голова болит, Г-197
голова в голову, Г-198
голова варит, Г-199
голова вскружилась, Г-200
голова два уха, Г-203
голова еловая, Г-201
голова забита, Г-202
голова и два уха, Г-203
голова идёт кругом, Г-204
голова мякиной набита,
  Г-208
голова на плечах, Г-205
голова пошла кругом,
  Г-204
голова пухнет, Г-206
голова разламывается
  ⟨раскалывается⟩, Г-209
голова распухла, Г-206
голова садовая, Г-207
голова соломой набита,
  Г-208
голова трещит, Г-209
голова трухой набита,
  Г-208

горячая голова, Г-210
дубовая голова, Г-211
дурья голова, Г-212
дырявая голова, Г-213
забубённая голова, Г-214
закружилась голова, Г-215
или грудь в крестах, или
  голова в кустах, Г-425
кружится голова, Г-215
либо грудь в крестах, либо
  голова в кустах, Г-425
мякинная голова, Г-212
отчаянная голова, Г-216
пустая голова, Г-217
сам ⟨сама⟩ себе голова,
  Х-76
светлая голова, Г-218
своя голова на плечах,
  Г-219
тяжёлая голова, Г-220
умная голова, Г-221
чугунная голова, Г-222
шальная голова, Г-223

ГОЛОВАХ
в головах, Г-224
о двух головах, Г-225
ходить на головах, Г-230

ГОЛОВЕ
без царя в голове, Ц-10
бить как* обухом по
  голове, О-31
вертеться в голове, Г-226
ветер в голове, В-69
винтика ⟨винтиков⟩ в
  голове не хватает
  ⟨недостаёт⟩, В-147
гвоздём засесть ⟨сидеть⟩ в
  голове, Г-12
гладить по голове, Г-232
держать в голове, У-98
заклёпки ⟨заклёпок⟩ в
  голове не хватает
  ⟨недостаёт⟩, В-147
закружилось в голове,
  Г-215
засесть в голове, Г-12
зашумело в голове, Г-231
как* обухом по голове,
  О-31
каша в голове, К-109
клёпки ⟨клёпок⟩ в голове
  не хватает ⟨недостаёт⟩,
  В-147
мутится в голове, Г-227
не укладывается в голове,
  Г-228
не умещается в голове,
  Г-228
перебирать/перебрать в
  голове, У-101
погладить по голове, Г-232
помутилось в голове, Г-227
с ветерком в голове, В-73
с царём в голове, Ц-2
сидеть в голове, Г-12
туман в голове, Т-233
ударить ⟨ударять⟩ как*
  обухом по голове, О-31
уложить в голове, Г-229
ходить на голове, Г-230
хоть кол на голове теши,
  К-178

шариков в голове не
  хватает ⟨недостаёт⟩,
  В-147
шумит в голове, Г-231

ГОЛОВКЕ
гладить/погладить по
  головке, Г-232

ГОЛОВКУ
в ⟨с⟩ булавочную головку,
  Г-233

ГОЛОВОЙ
висеть над головой, Г-234
выдавать/выдать головой,
  Г-235
головой выше, Г-260
заплатить головой, Г-236
ответить ⟨отвечать⟩
  головой, Г-237
поплатиться головой,
  Г-236
поручиться головой, Г-238
ручаться головой, Г-238
с головой, Г-239, Г-240
с непокрытой головой,
  Г-241
с повинной головой, П-219
тучи сгустились
  ⟨сгущаются⟩ над
  головой, Т-245
тучи собираются/
  собрались над головой,
  Т-245
хоть в омут ⟨в прорубь⟩
  головой, В-191
хоть головой об стенку
  ⟨стену⟩ бейся, Г-242

ГОЛОВОМОЙКУ
давать/дать головомойку,
  Г-243
задавать/задать
  головомойку, Г-243
получать/получить
  головомойку, Г-244
устраивать/устроить
  головомойку, Г-243

ГОЛОВУ
брать себе в голову, Г-246
бросаться/броситься в
  голову, Г-280
в голову, Г-224
в первую голову, О-183
вбивать в голову, Г-245
вбивать себе в голову,
  Г-246
вбить в голову, Г-245
вбить себе в голову, Г-246
вдалбливать/вдолбить в
  голову, Г-245
вешать голову, Г-247
взбредать/взбрести в
  голову, Г-248
взять себе в голову, Г-246
вколачивать/вколотить в
  голову, Г-245
войти в голову, Г-271
все шишки валятся на
  голову, Ш-72
вскружить голову, Г-253
втемяшивать в голову,
  Г-245
втемяшивать себе в
  голову, Г-246

втемяшить в голову, Г-245
втемяшить себе в голову,
  Г-246
входить в голову, Г-271
вымыть голову, Г-258
голова в голову, Г-198
голову прозакладывать
  ⟨прозакладываю⟩,
  Г-249
давать/дать голову на
  отсечение, Г-250
дурить голову, Г-257
забивать голову, Г-251
забивать себе в голову,
  Г-246
забить голову, Г-251
забить себе в голову, Г-246
забирать/забрать себе в
  голову, Г-246
задурить голову, Г-257
закружить голову, Г-253
закрутить голову, Г-254
заморочить голову, Г-257
западать/запасть в голову,
  Д-421
иметь голову на плечах,
  Г-205
как* снег на голову, С-430
кидаться/кинуться в
  голову, Г-280
кровь бросилась
  ⟨кинулась, ударила⟩ в
  голову, К-399
кружить голову, Г-253
крутить голову, Г-254
лезть в голову, Г-255
ломать (себе) голову,
  Г-256
морочить голову, Г-257
моча в голову ударила,
  М-268
мылить голову, Г-258
мыть голову, Г-258
на голову, Г-259
на голову выше, Г-260
на мою голову, Г-261
на свежую голову, Г-262
на свою голову, Г-263
навязаться
  ⟨навязываться⟩ на
  голову, Г-264
намылить голову, Г-258
напудрить голову, Г-258
не идёт/не пойдёт в
  голову, Г-265
нейдёт в голову, Г-265
опускать/опустить голову,
  Г-247
очертя голову, Г-266
повесить голову, Г-247
повинную голову (и) меч не
  сечёт, Г-267
поднимать/поднять
  голову, Г-268
полезть в голову, Г-255
положить (свою) голову,
  Г-252
поломать (себе) голову,
  Г-256
посыпать (себе) голову
  пеплом, Г-269

потерять голову, Г-279
прийти в голову, Г-271
приклонить голову, Г-270
принести ⟨приносить⟩
  повинную голову, П-220
приходить в голову, Г-271
прятать голову под крыло,
  Г-272
пудрить голову, Г-258
с ног на голову, Н-115
садиться на голову, Г-273
сам чёрт голову сломит,
  Ч-83
свернуть голову, Ш-57
свернуть себе голову, Ш-58
себе на голову, Г-263
сесть на голову, Г-273
склонить ⟨склонять⟩
  голову, Г-274
сложить (свою) голову,
  Г-252
сломать голову, Ш-58
сломать себе голову, Ш-58
сломить голову, Ш-57,
  Ш-58
сломить себе голову, Ш-58
сломя голову, Г-275
снявши голову, по волосам
  не плачут, Г-276
снять голову, Г-277
совать голову в петлю,
  Г-278
сорвать голову, Г-277
спрятать голову под
  крыло, Г-272
сунуть голову в петлю,
  Г-278
схватиться за голову, Г-281
терять голову, Г-279
ударить ⟨ударять⟩ в
  голову, Г-280
хвататься за голову, Г-281
хрен в голову, Х-100
через голову, Г-282
чёрт голову сломит, Ч-83

ГОЛОВУШКА
бедовая головушка, Г-195
буйная головушка, Г-195
ветреная головушка, Г-196
забубённая головушка,
  Г-214
отчаянная головушка,
  Г-216
умная головушка, Г-221

ГОЛОВЫ
без головы, Г-283
в головы, Г-224
валить с больной головы
  на здоровую, Г-284
выбивать дурь из головы,
  Д-340
выбивать из головы, Г-285
выбить дурь из головы,
  Д-340
выбить из головы, Г-285
выбрасывать/выбросить
  дурь из головы, Д-341
выбросить из головы,
  Г-286
выкидывать/выкинуть
  дурь из головы, Д-341

выкинуть из головы, Г-286
выколачивать/выколотить
  дурь из головы, Д-340
вылетать/вылететь из
  головы, Г-287
выскакивать/выскочить из
  головы, Г-287
выше головы, Г-288
выше головы не
  прыгнешь, Г-289
вышибать/вышибить дурь
  из головы, Д-340
головы летят/полетели,
  Г-290
из головы вон, Г-287
не выходит из головы,
  Г-291
не идёт из головы, Г-291
не снести ⟨не сносить⟩
  головы, Г-292
нейдёт из головы, Г-291
от головы до ног ⟨до пят,
  до пяток⟩, Г-293
перекладывать с больной
  головы на здоровую,
  Г-284
поднимать/поднять
  головы, Г-268
положить (свои) головы,
  Г-252
рыба с головы воняет
  ⟨гниёт, тухнет⟩, Р-382
с головы, Б-202
с головы до ног ⟨до пят,
  до пяток⟩, Г-293
с головы на ноги, Г-294
с ног до головы, Г-293
сваливать/свалить с
  больной головы на
  здоровую, Г-284
сложить (свои) головы,
  Г-252
улетучиваться/
  улетучиться из головы,
  Г-287
хмель вылетел ⟨выскочил,
  вышел⟩ из головы, Х-47

ГОЛОД
голод не тётка, Г-295
ГОЛОДНОГО
как из голодного края,
  К-374
сытый голодного не
  разумеет, С-739
ГОЛОДНОЕ
на голодное брюхо, Ж-14
ГОЛОДНЫЙ
на голодный желудок,
  Ж-14
ГОЛОДОМ
морить голодом, Г-296
ГОЛОЙ
голой рукой, Р-254
ГОЛОМ
на голом месте, М-105
ГОЛОМУ
с миру по нитке — голому
  рубаха ⟨рубашка⟩,
  М-194
ГОЛОС
в голос, Г-297

в один голос, Г-298
в полный голос, Г-299
во весь голос, Г-299
голос, вопиющий в
  пустыне, Г-143
голос сорвался
  ⟨срывается⟩, Г-300
повысить ⟨повышать⟩
  голос, Г-301
подавать/подать голос,
  Г-302
поднимать/поднять голос,
  Г-303
подымать голос, Г-303
понижать/понизить голос,
  Г-304
сорвать ⟨срывать⟩ голос,
  Г-305
ГОЛОСА
говорить с твоего
  ⟨чужого⟩ голоса, Г-306
петь с твоего ⟨чужого⟩
  голоса, Г-306
с голоса, Г-307
ГОЛОСЕ
в голосе, Г-308
ГОЛОСОМ
дурным голосом, Г-309
не своим голосом, Г-310
полным голосом, Г-299
ГОЛУБАЯ
в жилах течёт голубая
  кровь, К-398
голубая кровь, К-398
ГОЛУБОЙ
голубой крови, К-398
на блюдечке с голубой
  каёмочкой, Б-84
ГОЛЫЙ
голый король, К-315
король-то голый, К-315
ГОЛЫМИ
брать/взять голыми
  руками, Р-253
забрать голыми руками,
  Р-253
голыми руками, Р-254
ГОЛЬ
голь кабацкая, Г-312
голь на выдумки хитра,
  Г-311
голь перекатная, Г-312
ГОМОРР
Содом и Гоморр, С-463
ГОМОРРА
Содом и Гоморра, С-463
ГОНОР
сбивать/сбить гонор,
  С-508
сшибать/сшибить гонор,
  С-508
ГОНЯЛ
куда Макар телят не
  гонял, М-3
ГОНЯТЬ
гонять чаи, Ч-2
лодыря гонять, Л-122
ГОНЯТЬСЯ
гоняться за двумя
  зайцами, З-36

ГОП

не говори гоп, пока не перепрыгнешь ⟨не перескочишь⟩, Г-158

ГОРА

гора родила мышь, Г-313

гора с горой не сходится, а человек с человеком (всегда) сойдётся, Г-314

гора с плеч (свалилась), Г-316

если гора не идёт к Магомету, то Магомет идёт к горе, Г-315

как* гора с плеч (свалилась), Г-316

ГОРАЗД

кто во что горазд, Г-317

ГОРАМИ

ворочать горами, Г-358

двигать горами, Г-358

не за горами, Г-318

ГОРБ

гнуть горб, С-513

ломать горб, С-513

ГОРБАТОГО

горбатого могила исправит, Г-319

ГОРБОМ

своим горбом, Г-320

собственным горбом, Г-320

чужим горбом, Г-321

ГОРБУ

вывезти ⟨вывозить⟩ на своём ⟨на собственном⟩ горбу, П-186

вынести ⟨выносить⟩ на своём ⟨на собственном⟩ горбу, П-186

на своём ⟨на собственном⟩ горбу, Г-322

на чужом горбу в рай въехать, Г-323

сидеть на горбу, Ш-45

ГОРДИЕВ

гордиев узел, У-59

ГОРЕ

горе луковое, Г-324

горе мыкать, Г-325

завивать/завить горе верёвочкой, Г-326

заливать/залить горе, Г-327

и смех и горе, С-401

когда рак (на горе) свистнет, Р-71

на горе, Г-328

пока рак (на горе) свистнет, Р-71

смех и горе, С-401

ГОРЕМ

с горем пополам, Г-393

ГОРЕТЬ

гореть на работе, Р-5

ГОРИ

гори всё прахом, О-55

гори огнём, О-55

гори (оно) прахом, О-55

гори (оно) синим огнём ⟨пламенем⟩, О-55

гори (оно) ясным огнём ⟨пламенем⟩, О-55

ГОРИЗОНТА

с горизонта, Г-329

ГОРИЗОНТЕ

на горизонте, Г-330

ГОРИТ

горит в руках, Р-270

земля горит под ногами, З-123

кровь горит, К-403

на воре шапка горит, В-266

не горит, Г-331

сыр-бор горит, С-737

ГОРКИ

укатали ⟨умыкали, уходили⟩ бурку ⟨сивку⟩ крутые горки, С-160

ГОРКУ

идти под горку, Г-352

катиться под горку, Г-352

пойти под горку, Г-352

покатиться под горку, Г-352

ГОРЛА

встать поперёк горла, Г-332

становиться/стать поперёк горла, Г-332

стоять поперёк горла, Г-333

ГОРЛЕ

встать колом в горле, К-206

встать костью в горле, К-206

застревать/застрять в горле, Г-334

клубок в горле (стоит ⟨застрял⟩), К-142

ком(ок) в горле (стоит ⟨застрял⟩), К-142

стать колом в горле, К-206

стать костью в горле, К-206

стоять колом в горле, К-206

стоять костью в горле, К-206

ГОРЛО

брать за горло, Г-335

брать на горло, Г-336

в горло не идёт ⟨не лезет, не пойдёт, не полезет⟩, К-491

взять за горло, Г-335

взять на горло, Г-336

во всё горло, Г-337

держать за горло, Г-338

драть горло, Г-339

заткнуть ⟨затыкать⟩ горло, Г-147

кусок в горло не идёт ⟨не лезет, не пойдёт, не полезет⟩, К-491

надрывать горло, Г-339

надсаживать горло, Г-339

наступать/наступить на горло, Г-335

перегрызть горло, Г-340

перехватить ⟨перехватывать⟩ горло, Г-341

по горло, Г-342

промочить горло, Г-343

распускать/распустить горло, Г-344

рвать горло, Г-339

схватить за горло, Г-335

сыт по горло, Г-345

хватать за горло, Г-335

ГОРЛОМ

брать/взять горлом, Г-346

ГОРЛУ

клубок к горлу подкатил(ся) ⟨подступил⟩, К-142

ком(ок) к горлу подкатил(ся) ⟨подступил⟩, К-142

подкатить(ся) к горлу, Г-347

подкатывать(ся) к горлу, Г-347

подступать/подступить к горлу, Г-347

с ножом к горлу, Н-193

ГОРОД

за город, Г-348

ГОРОДА

смелость города берёт, С-390

ГОРОДИТЬ

городить вздор ⟨ерунду, околёсицу⟩, В-99

городить чепуху ⟨чушь⟩, В-99

огород городить, О-67

ГОРОДОМ

за городом, Г-348

ГОРОДУ

ни к селу ни к городу, С-114

ГОРОЙ

встать горой, Г-350

гора с горой не сходится, а человек с человеком (всегда) сойдётся, Г-314

дуй тебя горой!, Г-349

пир горой, П-153

раздуй тебя горой!, Г-349

стать горой, Г-350

стоять горой, Г-350

ГОРОХ

как в стенку ⟨стену⟩ горох, С-565

как об стенку ⟨стену⟩ горох, С-565

как от стенки ⟨стены⟩ горох, С-565

что стене ⟨стенке⟩ горох, С-565

ГОРОХА

царя Гороха, Ц-11

ГОРОХЕ

при царе Горохе, Ц-1

ГОРОХОВОГО

разыгрывать (из себя) шута горохового, Ш-98

ГОРОХОВОЕ

пугало гороховое, Ш-97

чучело гороховое, Ш-97

ГОРОХОВЫЙ

шут гороховый, Ш-97

ГОРОХОМ

как в стенку ⟨стену⟩ горохом, С-565

как об стенку ⟨стену⟩ горохом, С-565

ГОРТАНИ

язык прилип ⟨присох⟩ к гортани, Я-43

ГОРУ

воротить гору, Г-358

идти в гору, Г-351

идти под гору, Г-352

как на каменную гору, Г-353

катиться под гору, Г-352

лезть в гору, Г-351

на кудыкину гору, Г-354

переть в гору, Г-351

пойти под гору, Г-352

покатиться под гору, Г-352

полезть в гору, Г-351

свернуть гору, Г-358

своротить гору, Г-358

ГОРШКА

от горшка два ⟨три⟩ вершка, Г-355

ГОРШКИ

не боги горшки обжигают, Б-133

ГОРШКОМ

хоть горшком назови, только в печку не ставь, Г-356

ГОРШОК

под горшок, Г-357

ГОРЫ

воротить ⟨ворочать⟩ горы, Г-358

двигать горы, Г-358

златые ⟨золотые⟩ горы, Г-359

свернуть горы, Г-358

своротить горы, Г-358

ГОРЬКА

пилюля горька, П-150

ГОРЬКАЯ

горькая пилюля, П-150

как горькая редька, Р-102

ГОРЬКИЙ

горький опыт, О-96

ГОРЬКИМ

горьким опытом, О-96

ГОРЬКОЙ

пуще горькой редьки, Р-102

хуже горькой редьки, Р-102

ГОРЬКОМ

на (своём) горьком опыте, О-96

ГОРЬКУЮ

выпить горькую чашу (до дна), Ч-39

допить горькую чашу (до дна), Ч-39

испить горькую чашу (до дна), Ч-39

запить горькую, Г-360

ГОРЮ
пить горькую, Г-360
пить горькую чашу (до дна), Ч-39

ГОРЮ
слезами горю не поможешь, С-261

ГОРЮШКА
и горюшка мало, Г-361
хватить горюшка, Г-363
хлебнуть горюшка, Г-363

ГОРЯ
и горя мало, Г-361
намыкаться горя, Г-325
не знала баба горя, (так) купила (баба) порося, Б-2
с горя, Г-362
хватить горя, Г-363
хлебнуть горя, Г-363

ГОРЯТ
рукописи не горят, Р-342

ГОРЯЧАЯ
горячая голова, Г-210

ГОРЯЧЕМУ
по горячему следу, С-255

ГОРЯЧИМ
по горячим следам, С-255

ГОРЯЧИХ
влепить горячих, Г-364
всыпать горячих, Г-364
как на горячих углях ⟨угольях⟩, У-36

ГОРЯЧКУ
пороть горячку, Г-365

ГОРЯЧО
куй железо, пока горячо, Ж-12

ГОРЯЧУЮ
под горячую руку, Р-355

ГОСПОД
слуга двух господ, С-347

ГОСПОДА
ради (самого) господа (бога), Б-131

ГОСПОДИ
избави господи, Б-143
не дай господи, Б-119
не приведи господи, Б-119
не приведи господи сколько, Б-120
прости господи, Г-366, Г-367
слава те ⟨тебе⟩ господи, С-244

ГОСПОДИН
господин своего слова ⟨своему слову⟩, Х-78
сам себе господин, Х-76

ГОСПОДНЕ(Е)
наказание господне(е), Н-21

ГОСПОДНИ
неисповедимы пути господни, П-648

ГОСПОДСКОГО
крохи ⟨крошки⟩ с господского стола, К-418

ГОСПОДУ
одному господу ведомо ⟨известно⟩, Б-138

ГОСПОДЬ
господь ведает, Б-93
господь дал, господь и взял, Б-90
господь его ведает, Б-93
господь (его) знает, Б-93
господь не выдаст, свинья не съест, Б-100
господь прибрал, Б-103
господь с тобой, Б-104
да разразит меня господь, Б-125
да разразит тебя господь, Г-407
не приведи господь, Б-119
оборони господь, Б-143
один господь-бог ведает, Б-138
один господь-бог знает, Б-138
побей меня господь, Б-125
покарай меня господь, Б-125
пусть разразит тебя господь, Г-407
разрази меня господь, Б-125
сохрани господь, Б-143
убей меня господь, Б-125
упаси господь, Б-143
чем господь послал, Б-126

ГОСПОЖА
сама себе госпожа, Х-76

ГОСТЯХ
в гостях хорошо, а дома лучше, Г-368

ГОСУДАРСТВЕ
в некотором царстве, в некотором государстве, Ц-4

ГОСУДАРСТВО
тридевятое ⟨тридесятое⟩ государство, Ц-6

ГОТОВ
готов сквозь землю провалиться, З-117

ГОТОВО
раз-два ⟨раз-раз⟩ и готово, Р-30

ГОТОВОМ
на всём готовом, Г-369

ГОТОВЫЙ
готовый к услугам, У-133

ГРАДУСЕ
в градусе, Г-370

ГРАДУСОВ
поворот на сто восемьдесят градусов, П-225

ГРАДУСОМ
под градусом, Г-370

ГРАЙ
не верить ни в чох, ни в сон, ни в птичий грай, Ч-157

ГРАММ
девять грамм, Г-371

ГРАМОТА
китайская грамота, Г-372
тарабарская грамота, Г-372
филькина грамота, Г-373

ГРАНА
ни грана, Г-374

ГРАНИ
на грани, Г-375
стереть грани, Г-376
стёрлись грани, Г-377
стирать грани, Г-376
стираются грани, Г-377

ГРАНИТЬ
гранить мостовую, М-265

ГРАНИЦАХ
держать себя в границах (приличия), Р-75

ГРАНИЦЕЙ
за границей, Г-378

ГРАНИЦУ
за границу, Г-378

ГРАНИЦЫ
из-за границы, Г-378

ГРАНЬ
провести ⟨проводить⟩ грань, Г-379
стереть ⟨стирать⟩ грани, Г-376

ГРАТА
персона грата, П-104
персона нон грата, П-105

ГРЕБЁНКУ
остричь под одну гребёнку, Г-381
под гребёнку, Г-380
подстригать/подстричь под одну гребёнку, Г-381
стричь под одну гребёнку, Г-381

ГРЕСТИ
грести лопатой, Л-136

ГРЕТЬ
греть руки, Р-284

ГРЕХ
брать грех на душу, Г-382
ввести ⟨вводить⟩ в грех, Г-383
взять грех на душу, Г-382
грех один, Г-384
грех попутал, Ч-97
есть грех, Г-385
есть такой ⟨тот⟩ грех, Г-385
и смех и грех, С-401
как на грех, Г-386
как смертный грех, Г-387
на грех, Г-386
не грех, Г-388
принимать/принять грех на душу, Г-382
смертный грех, Г-389
смех и грех, С-401

ГРЕХА
долго ли до греха, Г-390
недолго (и) до греха, Г-390
нечего (и) греха таить, Г-392
от греха подальше, Г-391
хватить греха на душу, Г-382
чего (и) греха таить, Г-392
что (и) греха таить, Г-392

ГРЕХИ
(и) рад бы в рай, да грехи не пускают, Р-67

ГРЕХОМ
с грехом пополам, Г-393

ГРЕЧЕСКИХ
до греческих календ, К-33

ГРЕЧНЕВАЯ
гречневая каша сама себя хвалит, К-107

ГРЕШНЫМ
грешным делом, Д-138

ГРИБ
съесть гриб, Г-394

ГРИБОВ
дешевле грибов, Р-110

ГРИБЫ
как грибы (после дождя), Г-395

ГРИВУ
(и) в хвост и в гриву, Х-12

ГРОБ
вгонять/вогнать в гроб, Г-396
глядеть в гроб, М-205
гроб повапленный, Г-397
загнать в гроб, Г-396
краше в гроб кладут, Г-398
лечь в гроб, М-206
по гроб дней, Г-399
по гроб жизни, Г-399
свести ⟨сводить⟩ в гроб, Г-396
смотреть в гроб, М-205
сойти в гроб, М-206
сходить в гроб, М-206
уложить в гроб, Г-396
хоть в гроб ложись, Г-400

ГРОБА
до гроба, Г-401
на краю гроба, К-371
у края гроба, К-371

ГРОБОВОЙ
до гробовой доски, Д-292

ГРОБУ
в гробу видал ⟨видел⟩, Г-402
одной ногой в гробу, Н-162
перевернуться ⟨перевёртываться⟩ в гробу, Г-403
переворачиваться в гробу, Г-403
стоять одной ногой в гробу, Н-162

ГРОМ
гром не грянет, мужик не перекрестится, Г-404
да поразит меня гром, Г-406
да разразит меня гром, Г-406
как* гром среди ясного неба, Г-405
метать гром и молнию, Г-409
порази меня гром (на этом месте), Г-406
порази тебя гром, Г-407
пускай поразит ⟨разразит⟩ меня гром, Г-406
пусть поразит ⟨разразит⟩ меня гром, Г-406

разрази меня гром (на этом месте), Г-406
разрази тебя гром, Г-407
убей меня гром (на этом месте), Г-406

ГРОМОМ
как громом оглушить, Г-408
как громом поразить, Г-408
порази тебя громом, Г-407
разрази тебя громом, Г-407

ГРОМЫ
метать громы, Г-409
метать громы и молнии ⟨громы-молнии⟩, Г-409

ГРОШ
в (медный) грош не ставить, Г-412
грош цена (в базарный день), Г-410
за грош, Г-419
за грош удавится, К-282
и в (медный) грош не ставить, Г-412
и на грош, Г-414
ломаный грош цена, Г-410
медный грош цена, Г-410
на грош, Г-411, Г-414
ни в грош не ставить, Г-412
ни за грош, Г-413
ни на грош, Г-414
последний грош ребром поставить ⟨ставить⟩, К-284

ГРОША
без гроша (в кармане), Г-415
без гроша денег, Г-415
гроша ломаного не стоит, Г-416
гроша медного не стоит, Г-416
и гроша не стоит, Г-416
не было ни гроша, да (и) вдруг алтын, Г-417
ни гроша, Г-418
ни гроша не стоит, Г-416
перебиваться с гроша на копейку, Х-41

ГРОШИ
за гроши, Г-419
на медные гроши, Д-172

ГРУДИ
оборвалось в груди, С-141
отогревать/отогреть змею на груди, З-139
оторвалось в груди, С-141
пригревать/пригреть змею на груди, З-139
согревать/согреть змею на груди, З-139

ГРУДКИ
брать/взять за грудки, Г-420
схватить за грудки, Г-420
хватать за грудки, Г-420

ГРУДЬ
бить себя в грудь, Г-421

грудь в грудь, Г-422
грудь на грудь, Г-423
грудь с грудью, Г-424
или грудь в крестах, или голова в кустах, Г-425
либо грудь в крестах, либо голова в кустах, Г-425
надрывать грудь, Г-426
надсаживать грудь, Г-426

ГРУДЬЮ
встать грудью, Г-427
грудь с грудью, Г-424
стать грудью, Г-427
стоять грудью, Г-427

ГРУЗДЕМ
назвался груздем, полезай в кузов, Г-428

ГРУЗОМ
лежать мёртвым грузом, Г-429

ГРУППЫ
инвалид пятой группы, И-67

ГРЫЗУТСЯ
свои собаки грызутся, чужая не подходи ⟨не приставай⟩, С-447

ГРЯДУЩИЙ
на сон грядущий, С-482

ГРЯЗИ
вытаскивать/вытащить из грязи, Г-430
из грязи (да) в князи, Г-431

ГРЯЗНОМ
копаться в (чужом) грязном белье, Б-53
рыться в (чужом) грязном белье, Б-53

ГРЯЗЬ
втаптывать/втоптать в грязь, Г-432
затаптывать/затоптать в грязь, Г-432
лить грязь, Г-436
месить грязь, Г-433
не ударить лицом в грязь, Л-102

ГРЯЗЬЮ
бросать/бросить грязью, Г-434
забрасывать/забросать грязью, Г-434
закидывать/закидать грязью, Г-434
зарастать/зарасти грязью, Г-435
кидать/кинуть грязью, Г-434
обливать/облить грязью, Г-436
поливать/полить грязью, Г-436
смешать ⟨смешивать⟩ с грязью, Г-437

ГРЯНЕТ
гром не грянет, мужик не перекрестится, Г-404

ГУБ
слетать/слететь с губ, Я-51

сорваться ⟨срываться⟩ с губ, Я-51

ГУБА
губа не дура, Г-438

ГУБАХ
материно ⟨материнское⟩ молоко на губах не обсохло, М-240
молоко на губах не обсохло, М-240

ГУБЕРНАТОРСКОГО
положение хуже губернаторского, П-308

ГУБЕРНИЯ
пошла писать губерния, Г-439

ГУБКИ
надувать/надуть губки, Г-440

ГУБЫ
надувать/надуть губы, Г-440
разжать ⟨разжимать⟩ губы, Г-441

ГУГУ
ни гугу, Г-442

ГУЖ
взялся за гуж, не говори, что не дюж, Г-443

ГУЛЬКИН
с гулькин нос, Н-218

ГУЛЯЙ
кончил дело — гуляй смело, Д-110

ГУЛЯТЬ
гулять по рукам, Р-244

ГУСЕЙ
дразнить/раздразнить гусей, Г-444

ГУСИНАЯ
гусиная кожа, К-160

ГУСИНЫЕ
гусиные лапки, Л-23

ГУСТО
не густо, Г-445
разом густо, разом пусто, Р-62

ГУСЬ
гусь лапчатый, Г-446
гусь свинье не товарищ, Г-447
каков гусь!, Г-448
ну и гусь!, Г-448
хорош гусь!, Г-448
что за гусь!, Г-448

ГУСЯ
как с гуся вода, Г-449

ГУЩЕ
гадание на кофейной гуще, Г-450
гадать на кофейной гуще, Г-450

Д

ДА
да будет земля пухом, З-128

да и, Д-1
да ну?, Д-2
да ну тебя!, Т-51

ДАВАЙ
давай бог ноги, Б-108
живи и жить давай другим, Ж-29

ДАВАТЬ
давать бой, Б-147
давать в шею, Ш-44
давать веру, В-49
давать взбучку, Т-200
давать волю, В-248
давать волю кулакам, В-249
давать волю рукам, В-250
давать волю языку, В-251
давать выволочку, Т-200
давать выход, В-385
давать головомойку, Г-243
давать голову на отсечение, Г-250
давать двадцать очков вперёд, О-191
давать дёру, Д-183, Д-184
давать десять очков вперёд, О-191
давать дорогу, Д-278
давать драла, Д-304
давать драпа ⟨драпака, драпу⟩, Д-304
давать дуба ⟨дубаря⟩, Д-316
давать жару, Ж-6
давать жизни, Ж-42
давать задний ход, Х-51
давать знак, З-155
давать знать, Д-3
давать исход, В-385
давать коленкой ⟨коленом⟩ под зад, К-189
давать круг, К-420
давать лататы, Д-304
давать маху, М-57
давать начало, Н-38
давать о себе знать, Д-4
давать осечку, О-110
давать острастку, О-125
давать отбой, О-130
давать ответ, О-134
давать отпор, О-163
давать отставку, О-167
давать петуха, П-133
давать пить, Д-6
давать пищу, П-161
давать по мозгам, М-219
давать по носу, Н-238
давать по рукам, Р-245
давать по шапке, Ш-27
давать по шее ⟨по шеям⟩, Ш-44
давать поблажки ⟨поблажку⟩, П-209
давать повадку, П-209
давать повод, П-221
давать подножку, Н-188
давать подписку, П-253
давать понять, Д-5
давать потачку, П-209
давать почувствовать, Д-5

давать прикурить, Д-6
давать промах
⟨промашку⟩, П-571
давать руку на отсечение,
Г-250
давать сдачи ⟨сдачу⟩, С-92
давать себе отчёт, О-172
давать себе слово, С-310
давать себе труд, Т-212
давать себя знать, Д-7
давать себя чувствовать,
Д-7
давать слабину, С-243
давать слово, С-311, С-312
давать сто очков вперёд,
О-191
давать стрекача
⟨стречка⟩, С-633
давать таску, Т-45
давать тёку, Д-304
давать тон, Т-154
давать трёпку, Т-200
давать тягу, Д-304
давать фору, Ф-25
давать ход, Х-52
давать чёсу, Ч-144
давать чувствовать, Д-5
не давать в обиду, О-5
не давать житья, Ж-82
не давать ни отдыха ни
срока, О-141
не давать покою ⟨покоя⟩,
П-287
не давать прохода
⟨проходу⟩, П-594
не давать себя в обиду, О-6
не давать спуска ⟨спуску⟩,
С-529
не давать хода ⟨ходу⟩,
Х-69
не давать шагу сделать
⟨ступить⟩, Ш-19

ДАВАТЬСЯ
диву даваться, Д-193
не даваться в обиду, О-6

ДАВИТЬ
давить на мозги, М-223
давить фасон, Ф-3

ДАВЛЕНИЕМ
под давлением, Д-8

ДАВНО
давно бы так!, Д-9

ДАВНОСТЬЮ
за давностью времени,
Д-10
за давностью лет, Д-10

ДАВШИ
давши слово, держись, а не
давши, крепись, С-285
не давши слова, крепись, а
давши, держись, С-285

ДАДУТ
как пить дадут, П-158

ДАЁТ
бог даёт, Б-88
кто рано встаёт, тому бог
даёт, В-346

ДАЙ
дай бог, Б-109
дай бог всем, Б-110

дай бог всякому, Б-110
дай бог здоровья, Б-111
дай бог каждому
⟨любому⟩…, Б-110
дай бог ноги, Б-108
дай бог памяти ⟨память⟩,
Б-112
дай ему палец, он и всю
руку откусит, П-3
дай срок, С-537
не дай бог ⟨боже,
господи⟩ Б-119
не сули журавля в небе, а
дай синицу в руки, С-195

ДАЙТЕ
дайте срок, С-537

ДАЛ
бог дал, Б-88, Б-89
бог дал, бог и взял, Б-90
господь дал, господь и
взял, Б-90
дорого бы дал, Д-11
много бы дал, Д-11
чего бы не дал, Д-11

ДАЛЕЕ
далее — более, Д-18
и так далее, Т-5
не далее, Д-12
не далее как, Д-13
не далее чем, Д-13

ДАЛЁКИЙ
далёкий прицел, П-556

ДАЛЕКО
далеко до, Д-14
далеко за, Д-15
далеко не, Д-16
далеко не уедешь ⟨не
уйдёшь⟩, У-53
далеко уйти ⟨пойти⟩,
П-275
далеко хватить, З-85
далеко ходить не надо ⟨не
нужно, не приходится⟩,
Х-58
за примерами ⟨примером⟩
далеко ходить не надо
⟨не нужно, не
приходится⟩, Х-58
зайти ⟨заходить⟩
(слишком) далеко, З-85
не очень далеко уйти, У-64
не так уж далеко уйти,
У-64
слишком далеко хватить,
З-85

ДАЛЬНЕЙШЕМ
в дальнейшем, Д-17

ДАЛЬНИЕ
дальние проводы —
лишние слёзы, П-566

ДАЛЬНИЙ
дальний прицел, П-556

ДАЛЬНИХ
без дальних разговоров,
С-274
без дальних слов, С-274

ДАЛЬШЕ
дальше — больше, Д-18
дальше ехать некуда, Н-74
дальше (идти) некуда,
Н-74

не видеть дальше своего
носа, Н-225
не видеть дальше (своего)
собственного носа,
Н-225
не дальше, Д-12
не дальше как, Д-13
не дальше чем, Д-13
не идти дальше, И-31
тише едешь — дальше
будешь, Е-3
чем дальше в лес, тем
больше дров, Л-59

ДАМ
я тебе дам!, Д-19

ДАМА
дама сердца, Д-20

ДАМКАХ
в дамках, Д-21

ДАМОКЛОВ
дамоклов меч, М-138

ДАМОКЛОВЫМ
под дамокловым мечом,
М-138

ДАМСКИЙ
дамский угодник, У-19

ДАНАИД
бочка Данаид, Б-188

ДАНАЙЦЕВ
дары данайцев, Д-26

ДАННОМ
в данном случае, С-358

ДАНЬ
заплатить дань, Д-22
отдавать/отдать дань,
Д-22
платить дань, Д-22

ДАР
дар речи, Д-23
дар слова, Д-23

ДАРЁНОМУ
дарёному коню в зубы не
смотрят, К-272

ДАРМОВЩИНКУ
на дармовщинку, Д-24

ДАРМОВЩИНУ
на дармовщину, Д-24

ДАРОВАТЬ
даровать жизнь, Ж-51

ДАРОВОМУ
даровому коню в зубы не
смотрят, К-272

ДАРОВЩИНКУ
на даровщинку, Д-24

ДАРОВЩИНУ
на даровщину, Д-24

ДАРОМ
владеть даром слова,
С-331
даром не возьму, В-218
даром не надо ⟨не нужно⟩,
В-218
даром хлеб есть, Х-30
даром что, Д-25
не проходит/не прошёл
даром, П-596

ДАРЫ
дары данайцев, Д-26

ДАСТ
бог даст, Б-91

бог даст день, бог даст
пищу, Б-92
бог даст день, даст и
пищу, Б-92
как пить даст, П-158
что бог даст, Б-127

ДАТА
круглая дата, Д-27

ДАТЬ
дать бой, Б-147
дать в шею, Ш-44
дать веру, В-49
дать взбучку, Т-200
дать волю, В-248
дать волю кулакам, В-249
дать волю рукам, В-250
дать волю языку, В-251
дать выволочку, Т-200
дать выход, В-385
дать газ, Г-2
дать головомойку, Г-243
дать голову на отсечение,
Г-250
дать двадцать очков
вперёд, О-191
дать дёру, Д-183, Д-184
дать десять очков вперёд,
О-191
дать дорогу, Д-278
дать драла, Д-304
дать драпа ⟨драпака,
драпу⟩, Д-304
дать дуба ⟨дубаря⟩, Д-316
дать исход, В-385
дать жару, Ж-6
дать жизни, Ж-42
дать жизнь, Ж-52
дать задний ход, Х-51
дать знак, З-155
дать знать, Д-3
дать коленкой ⟨коленом⟩
под зад, К-189
дать круг, К-420
дать крюк(у), К-438
дать лататы, Д-304
дать леща, Л-71
дать маху, М-57
дать начало, Н-38
дать ногу, Н-169
дать о себе знать, Д-4
дать осечку, О-110
дать острастку, О-125
дать отбой, О-130
дать отпор, О-163
дать отставку, О-167
дать петуха, П-133
дать пить, Д-6
дать пищу, П-161
дать по мозгам, М-219
дать по носу, Н-238
дать по рукам, Р-245
дать по шапке, Ш-27
дать по шее ⟨по шеям⟩,
Ш-44
дать поблажки
⟨поблажку⟩, П-209
дать повадку, П-209
дать повод, П-221
дать подножку, Н-188
дать подписку, П-253
дать понять, Д-5

дать потачку, П-209
дать почувствовать, Д-5
дать прикурить, Д-6
дать промах ⟨промашку⟩,
П-571
дать руку на отсечение,
Г-250
дать сдачи ⟨сдачу⟩, С-92
дать себе отчёт, О-172
дать себе слово, С-310
дать себе труд, Т-212
дать себя знать, Д-7
дать себя почувствовать,
Д-7
дать себя чувствовать, Д-7
дать слабину, С-243
дать слово, С-311, С-312
дать сто очков вперёд,
О-191
дать стрекача ⟨стречка⟩,
С-633
дать таску, Т-45
дать тёку, Д-304
дать тон, Т-154
дать трёпку, Т-200
дать тягу, Д-304
дать урок, У-127
дать фору, Ф-25
дать ход, Х-52
дать ходу, Х-66
дать чёсу, Ч-144
как пить дать, П-158
не дать в обиду, О-5
не дать житья, Ж-82
не дать прохода
⟨проходу⟩, П-594
не дать себя в обиду, О-6
не дать спуска ⟨спуску⟩,
С-529
не дать хода ⟨ходу⟩, Х-69
не дать шагу сделать
⟨ступить⟩, Ш-19
ни дать ни взять, Д-28

ДАТЬСЯ
диву даться, Д-193
не даться в обиду, О-6

ДАЮТ
дают – бери, бьют –
беги, Д-29
лавры не дают покоя, Л-5
лавры не дают спать, Л-5

ДВА
в два счёта, С-715
видеть на два аршина в
землю ⟨под землёй, под
землю⟩, А-46
голова (и) два уха, Г-203
два сапога пара, С-14
двадцать два несчастья,
Н-88
действовать на два лагеря,
Л-7
как дважды два ⟨четыре⟩,
Д-31
на два слова, П-67
на два фронта, Ф-27
ни два ни полтора, Д-30
от горшка два вершка,
Г-355
ум хорошо, а два лучше,
У-80

чёрта с два!, Ч-107
ДВАДЦАТОЕ
дело двадцатое, Д-81
ДВАДЦАТЬ
давать/дать двадцать
очков вперёд, О-191
двадцать два несчастья,
Н-88
опять двадцать пять!,
О-97
ДВАЖДЫ
как дважды два ⟨четыре⟩,
Д-31
ДВЕ
две большие разницы,
Р-60
две капли воды, К-59
драть (по) две шкуры,
Ш-79
как две капли воды, К-59
сдирать/содрать (по) две
шкуры, Ш-79
ДВЕРЕЙ
день открытых дверей,
Д-156
у дверей, В-278
ДВЕРИ
двери закрыты, Д-32
закрывать/закрыть двери
дома, Д-32
ломиться в открытые
двери, Д-36
открывать/открыть
двери, Д-33
стучаться в двери, Д-37
ДВЕРЬ
выставить ⟨выставлять⟩
за дверь, Д-34
дверь в дверь, Д-35
дверь дома закрыта, Д-32
ломиться в открытую
дверь, Д-36
открывать/открыть
дверь, Д-33
показать ⟨показывать⟩
(на) дверь, Д-38
стучаться в дверь, Д-37
указать ⟨указывать⟩ (на)
дверь, Д-38
ДВЕРЬЮ
хлопнуть дверью, Д-39
ДВЕРЯХ
при закрытых дверях,
Д-40
ДВИГАТЬ
двигать горами ⟨горы⟩,
Г-358
ДВИНУТЬ
пальцем не двинуть, П-22
ДВОИТСЯ
двоится в глазах, Г-129
ДВОИХ
на своих (на) двоих, Д-41
ДВОР
идти на попятный двор,
П-357
на двор, Д-42
на попятный двор, П-357
пойти на попятный двор,
П-357

проходной двор, Д-43
ДВОРА
ни кола ни двора, К-179
ДВОРЕ
на дворе, Д-44
ДВОРУ
ко двору, Д-45
ДВОРЯНСТВЕ
мещанин во дворянстве,
М-146
ДВУЛИКИЙ
двуликий Янус, Я-66
ДВУМ
двум смертям не бывать,
а одной не миновать,
С-399
ДВУМЯ
гнаться ⟨гоняться⟩ за
двумя зайцами, З-36
переброситься двумя
словами, С-335
перекинуться двумя
словами, С-335
перемолвиться двумя
словами, С-335
погнаться за двумя
зайцами, З-36
сидеть между двумя
стульями, С-651
ДВУХ
в двух словах, С-300
в двух шагах, Ш-12
двух слов связать не мочь,
С-275
двух смертей не бывать, а
одной не миновать,
С-399
из двух зол меньшее, З-180
меж ⟨между⟩ двух огней,
О-54
о двух головах, Г-225
палка о двух концах, П-7
сидеть между двух
стульев, С-651
слуга двух господ, С-347
старый друг лучше новых
двух, Д-311
убивать/убить двух
зайцев, З-38
ДЕВА
старая дева, Д-46
ДЕВАТЬ
девать некуда, Д-47
не знать, куда глаза
девать, Г-83
не знать, куда себя девать,
З-175
ДЕВАТЬСЯ
деваться некуда, Д-48
не знать, куда деваться,
З-174
ДЕВИЦА
красная девица, Д-49
ДЕВИЧЬЯ
девичья память, П-44
ДЕВКА
бой-девка, Б-146
красная девка, Д-49
ДЕВКАХ
в девках, Д-50

ДЕВУШКА
красная девушка, Д-49
ДЕВЯТОЕ
дело девятое, Д-81
ДЕВЯТЫЙ
девятый вал, В-5
ДЕВЯТЬ
девять грамм, Г-371
ДЁГТЮ
ложка дёгтю в бочке мёда
⟨мёду⟩, Л-128
ДЕЙСТВОВАТЬ
действовать на два лагеря,
Л-7
действовать на нервы,
Н-81
ДЕКОРАЦИИ
менять декорации, Д-51
переменить декорации,
Д-51
сменить декорации, Д-51
ДЕКОРАЦИЙ
перемена декораций, Д-51
ДЕЛ
заплечных дел мастер,
Д-52
между дел, Д-140
наделать дел, Д-53
не у дел, Д-54
ДЕЛА
большие дела, Д-68
дела идут, контора пишет,
Д-55
дела как сажа бела, Д-56
дела табак, Д-95
дела труба, Д-95
нет дела, Д-57
ну и дела!, Д-58
по сути дела, С-680
суть дела, С-681
ДЕЛАЕТ
одна ласточка весны не
делает, Л-33
только и делает, З-144
ДЕЛАЕТСЯ
скоро сказка сказывается,
а ⟨да⟩ не скоро дело
делается, С-215
что делается!, Д-59
ДЕЛАТЬ
делать авансы, А-4
делать акцент, А-21
делать большие глаза,
Г-66
делать весёлую мину при
плохой игре, М-167
делать вид, В-110
делать глазки, Г-132
делать из мухи слона,
М-299
делать из себя шута, Ш-98
делать карьеру, К-100
делать круг, К-420
делать круглые глаза, Г-66
делать на караул, К-71
делать нечего, Д-60
делать поблажки
⟨поблажку⟩, П-209
делать погоду, П-231
делать под козырёк, К-173

ДЕРЁТ

мороз по коже ⟨по спине⟩ дерёт, М-258

ДЕРЖАТ

едва ⟨еле⟩ ноги держат, Н-143

ноги не держат, Н-149

ДЕРЖАТЬ

высоко держать знамя, З-165

держать в голове, У-98

держать в ежовых рукавицах, Р-241

держать в известном отдалении, Р-84

держать в мыслях, М-316

держать в памяти, П-34

держать в почтительном отдалении, Р-84

держать в руках, Р-271

держать в уме, У-98

держать в чёрном теле, Т-54

держать в шорах, Ш-83

держать верх, В-54

держать вожжи в руках, В-200

держать за горло, Г-338

держать камень за пазухой, К-39

держать карты к орденам, К-96

держать курс, К-485

держать линию, К-485

держать марку, М-31

держать на известном расстоянии, Р-84

держать на коротком поводке, П-222

держать на помочах, П-335

держать на почтительном расстоянии, Р-84

держать на привязи, П-520

держать на примете, П-536

держать на расстоянии, Р-84

держать ногу, Ш-2

держать нос по ветру, Н-212

держать ответ, О-134

держать пари, П-63

держать под сукном, С-672

держать при себе, Д-179

держать путь, П-655

держать рот на замке, Р-174

держать руки по швам, Р-285

держать руку, С-611

держать своё слово, С-313

держать себя, Д-180

держать себя в границах ⟨приличия⟩, Р-75

держать себя в рамках ⟨приличия⟩, Р-75

держать себя в руках, Р-272

держать себя в узде, У-58

держать сердце, С-131

держать слово, С-313

держать сторону, С-611

держать ухо востро, У-158

держать ушки на макушке, У-158

держать фасон, Ф-3

держать форс, Ф-23

держать хвост морковкой, Х-10

держать хвост пистолетом, Х-10

держать хвост трубой, Х-10

держать шаг, Ш-2

держать язык за зубами, Я-9

держать язык на привязи, Я-9

зла не держать, З-131

так держать!, Д-181

ДЕРЖАТЬСЯ

держаться в известном отдалении, Р-85

держаться в почтительном отдалении, Р-85

держаться за бабью юбку, Ю-2

держаться за бока, Ж-35

держаться за живот ⟨за животики, за животы⟩, Ж-35

держаться за юбку, Ю-2

держаться на волоске, В-239

держаться на известном расстоянии, Р-85

держаться на нитке ⟨на ниточке⟩, В-239

держаться на почтительном расстоянии, Р-85

держаться на расстоянии, Р-85

едва ⟨еле⟩ держаться на ногах, Н-131

зубами держаться, З-189

на ногах не держаться, Н-131

с трудом держаться на ногах, Н-131

чуть держаться на ногах, Н-131

ДЕРЖИ

держи карман ⟨шире⟩, К-78

ДЕРЖИСЬ

давши слово, держись, а не давши, крепись, С-285

не давши слова, крепись, а давши, держись, С-285

только держись!, Д-182

ДЕРЖИТ

(и) как ⟨ещё⟩ земля держит, З-126

(и) как только земля держит, З-126

ДЕРЖИТСЯ

в чём ⟨только⟩ душа держится, Д-363

земля держится, З-124

пока душа держится в теле, Д-377

ДЕРИ

чёрт дери!, Ч-87

леший тебя дери!, Ч-99

чёрт тебя дери!, Ч-99

шут тебя дери!, Ч-99

ДЁРНУЛ

бес дёрнул, Ч-88

бес дёрнул за язык, Я-10

леший дёрнул, Ч-88

леший дёрнул за язык, Я-10

чёрт дёрнул, Ч-88

чёрт дёрнул за язык, Я-10

ДЁРНУЛА

нелёгкая дёрнула, Ч-88

нелёгкая дёрнула за язык, Я-10

ДЁРНУЛО

дёрнуло за язык, Я-10

ДЁРУ

давать/дать дёру, Д-184

задавать/задать дёру, Д-184

ДЕРУТСЯ

паны дерутся, а у хлопцев ⟨холопов⟩ чубы болят ⟨трещат⟩, П-54

свои собаки дерутся, чужая не подходи ⟨не приставай⟩, С-447

ДЕРЬМО

дерьмо на палочке, Д-185

ДЕРЬМОМ

смешать ⟨смешивать⟩ с дерьмом, Г-437

ДЕСКАТЬ

так и так дескать, Т-18

ДЕСЯТАЯ

десятая вода на киселе, В-175

десятая спица в колеснице, С-520

ДЕСЯТКА

не из робкого ⟨трусливого⟩ десятка, Д-186

не из храброго десятка, Д-187

не робкого ⟨трусливого⟩ десятка, Д-186

не храброго десятка, Д-187

ДЕСЯТОГО

до десятого пота, П-421

ДЕСЯТОЕ

дело десятое, Д-81

из пятого в десятое, П-688

пятое через десятое, П-688

с пятого на десятое, П-688

через пятое на десятое, П-688

ДЕСЯТОЙ

обойти ⟨обходить⟩ десятой дорогой, Д-274

ДЕСЯТЫЙ

десятый сон видеть, С-483

десятый сон снится, С-483

ДЕСЯТЬ

давать/дать десять очков вперёд, О-191

десять потов сгонять/ согнать, П-429

десять потов сошло, П-430

десять потов спускать/ спустить, П-429

ДЕТЕЙ

не детей крестить, Д-188

ДЕТИШКАМ

детишкам на молочишко, Д-189

ДЕТСКАЯ

детская забава, И-18

детская игрушка, И-18

ДЕТСКИЕ

детские игрушки, И-18

ДЕТСКИЙ

детский лепет, Л-52

ДЕТСКОЕ

детское время, В-314

ДЕТСТВО

впадать/впасть в детство, Д-190

ДЕТЬ

деть некуда, Д-47

не знать, куда глаза деть, Г-83

не знать, куда деть себя, З-174

не знать, куда себя деть, З-175

ДЕТЬСЯ

деться некуда, Д-48

не знать, куда деться, З-174

никуда не деться, Д-149

ДЕШЕВЛЕ

дешевле грибов, Р-110

дешевле пареной репы, Р-110

ДЁШЕВО

дёшево и сердито, Д-191

дёшево отделаться, О-139

и дёшево и сердито, Д-191

ДИВО

на диво, Д-192

ДИВУ

диву даваться/даться, Д-193

ДИКИМ

питаться акридами (и диким мёдом), А-20

ДИКОВИНКУ

в диковинку, Д-194

ДИКОВИНУ

в диковину, Д-194

ДИКТОВКУ

под диктовку, Д-195

ДИНАМО

крутить динамо, Д-196

провернуть ⟨прокрутить⟩ динамо, Д-196

ДИТЯ

у семи нянек дитя без глазу, Н-268

чем бы дитя ни тешилось, лишь бы не плакало, Д-197

ДИФИРАМБЫ

петь/пропеть дифирамбы, Д-198

[884]

как долго, Д-240
не долго думаючи, Д-327
не долго думая, Д-327
не заставить себя долго
    ждать, З-78
не заставить себя долго
    просить, З-76
не заставить себя долго
    упрашивать, З-76
не заставлять себя долго
    ждать, З-78
приказать долго жить,
    П-526
ДОЛГОМ
первым долгом, Д-141
ДОЛГУ
в долгу, Д-241
в долгу как в шелку, Д-242
не оставаться/не остаться
    в долгу, Д-243
по долгу, Д-244
ДОЛЕ
в доле, Д-245
ДОЛЖНО
должно быть, Б-278
ДОЛЖНОЕ
отдавать/отдать должное,
    Д-246
ДОЛЖНОЙ
на должной высоте, В-378
ДОЛЖНУЮ
отдавать/отдать должную
    справедливость, Д-246
ДОЛОГ
у бабы волос долог, а ⟨да⟩
    ум короток, Б-8
ДОЛОЖУ
доложу (я) вам ⟨тебе⟩,
    Д-247
ДОЛОЙ
с глаз долой, Г-38
с глаз долой — из сердца
    вон, Г-39
с копыт долой, К-286
с плеч долой, П-175
с рук долой, П-175
ДОЛЮ
в долю, Д-245
на долю, Д-248
ДОЛЯ
в каждой шутке есть доля
    правды, Ш-102
доля истины, Д-249
доля правды, Д-249
львиная доля, Д-250
ДОМ
ввести ⟨вводить⟩ в дом,
    Д-251
дом терпимости, Д-252
жёлтый дом, Д-253
публичный дом, Д-252
сумасшедший дом, Д-253
ДОМА
в гостях хорошо, а дома
    лучше, Г-368
дверь дома закрыта, Д-32
дома (и) стены помогают,
    С-570
друг дома, Д-308
закрывать/закрыть двери
    дома, Д-32

как (у себя) дома, Д-254
не все дома, Д-255
отбиваться/отбиться от
    дома, Д-256
отказать ⟨отказывать⟩ от
    дома, Д-257
ДОМАХ
в лучших домах
    Филадельфии, Д-258
ДОМЕ
в доме повешенного не
    говорят о верёвке, Д-259
ДОМИК
карточный домик, Д-260
ДОМОМ
жить одним домом, Д-261
ДОНА
нести (и) с Дона и с моря,
    Д-262
ДОНИЗУ
сверху донизу, С-37
ДОПИТЬ
допить (горькую) чашу (до
    дна), Ч-39
ДОРОГ
мал золотник, да дорог,
    З-182
ДОРОГА
большая дорога, Д-263
дорога ложка к обеду,
    Л-127
избитая дорога, Д-288
прямая дорога, Д-264
скатертью дорога, С-221
столбовая дорога, Д-265
торная дорога, Д-266
туда и дорога, Д-267
ДОРОГЕ
встать на дороге, П-652
встретиться ⟨встречаться⟩
    на узкой дороге, Д-289
на дороге не валяется,
    Д-268
на дурной дороге, П-644
на ложной дороге, П-643
на плохой дороге, П-644
на правильной дороге,
    П-645
на хорошей дороге, П-647
по дороге, Д-269
по ложной дороге, П-643
по правильной дороге,
    П-645
по хорошей дороге, П-647
пойти по дурной ⟨плохой,
    худой⟩ дороге, Д-270
сталкиваться/столкнуться
    на узкой дороге, Д-289
становиться/стать на
    дороге, П-652
стоять на дороге, П-652
ДОРОГИ
встать поперёк дороги,
    П-652
дороги разошлись
    ⟨расходятся⟩, П-649
разбойник с большой
    дороги, Р-41
с дороги, Д-271
сбивать с дороги, П-650

сбиваться с дороги, П-651
сбить с дороги, П-650
сбиться с дороги, П-651
становиться/стать поперёк
    дороги, П-652
стоять поперёк дороги,
    П-652
ДОРОГО
дорого бы дал, Д-11
дорого заплатить, З-68
дорого отдавать/отдать
    свою жизнь, Ж-53
дорого продавать/продать
    свою жизнь, Ж-53
ДОРОГОЙ
дорогой ценой, Ц-28
идти прямой дорогой,
    Д-272
идти своей дорогой, Д-273
обойти ⟨обходить⟩
    десятой дорогой, Д-274
пойти своей дорогой,
    Д-273
с дорогой душой, Д-402
ДОРОГУ
в дорогу, Д-275
выбиваться/выбиться на
    (широкую) дорогу, Д-277
вывести ⟨выводить⟩ на
    дорогу, Д-276
выйти на (широкую)
    дорогу, Д-277
выходить на (широкую)
    дорогу, Д-277
давать/дать дорогу, Д-278
забывать/забыть дорогу,
    Д-279
заказать ⟨заказывать⟩
    дорогу, Д-656
заступать/заступить
    дорогу, Д-280
на дорогу, Д-281
на дурную дорогу, П-644
на ложную дорогу, П-643
на плохую дорогу, П-644
на правильную дорогу,
    П-645
на хорошую дорогу, П-647
найти ⟨находить⟩ дорогу
    к сердцу, Д-282
перебегать/перебежать
    дорогу, Д-283
перейти дорогу, Д-283
перебивать/перебить
    дорогу, Д-283
перейти ⟨переходить⟩
    дорогу, Д-283
пробивать дорогу, Д-285
пробивать себе дорогу,
    Д-284
пробить дорогу, Д-285
пробить себе дорогу,
    Д-284
прокладывать дорогу,
    Д-285
прокладывать себе дорогу,
    Д-286
пролагать/проложить
    дорогу, Д-285
проложить себе дорогу,
    Д-286

уступать/уступить дорогу,
    Д-278
ДОРОЖЕ
себе дороже (стоит), Д-287
уговор дороже денег, У-17
ДОРОЖКА
избитая дорожка, Д-288
проторённая дорожка,
    Д-288
скатертью дорожка, С-221
ДОРОЖКЕ
встретиться ⟨встречаться⟩
    на узкой дорожке, Д-289
катиться по скользкой
    дорожке, П-197
на дурной дорожке, П-644
на плохой дорожке, П-644
пойти по дурной ⟨плохой,
    худой⟩ дорожке, Д-270
покатиться по скользкой
    дорожке, П-197
сталкиваться/столкнуться
    на узкой дорожке, Д-289
ДОРОЖКУ
на дурную дорожку, П-644
на плохую дорожку, П-644
перебегать/перебежать
    дорожку, Д-283
перебивать/перебить
    дорожку, Д-283
перейти ⟨переходить⟩
    дорожку, Д-283
ДОРОС
нос не дорос, Н-215
ДОСКА
как доска, Д-290
ДОСКЕ
стоять на одной доске,
    Д-291
ДОСКИ
до гробовой доски, Д-292
ДОСКУ
в доску, Д-293
встать на одну доску,
    Д-296
поставить на одну доску,
    Д-295
свой в доску, Д-294
свой парень в доску, Д-294
ставить на одну доску,
    Д-295
становиться/стать на одну
    доску, Д-296
ДОСТАЁТ
достаёт духу, Д-360
ДОСТАЛО
достало духу, Д-360
ДОСТАЛОСЬ
солоно досталось, П-551
ДОСТАНЕШЬ
рукой не достанешь, Р-338
ДОСТАТЬ
рукой не достать, Р-338
ДОСТОИНСТВА
ниже (своего) достоинства,
    Д-297
ДОСТОИНСТВУ
оценивать/оценить по
    достоинству, Д-298

[885]

ДОСТУП
найти ⟨находить⟩ доступ к сердцу, Д-282

ДОХЛОЕ
дохлое дело, Д-97

ДОХЛЫЙ
дохлый номер, Д-97

ДОХНУТ
мухи дохнут, М-302

ДОХНУТЬ
дохнуть негде, Д-299
дохнуть некогда, Д-300
дохнуть нельзя, Д-299
дохнуть нечем, Д-299
не сметь дохнуть, С-400

ДОХОДИТ
дело доходит до, Д-82

ДОХОДИТЬ
доходить до белого каления, К-35
доходить до сознания, С-466
доходить до сумы, М-190
доходить до ушей, У-180
доходить своим умом, У-105
доходить ⟨своим⟩ собственным умом, У-105

ДОХОДЯТ
руки не доходят, Р-318

ДОЧКА
маменькина дочка, Д-301

ДОЧЬ
собачья дочь, Д-302
сучья дочь, Д-302

ДОШЛИ
руки не дошли, Р-318

ДОШЛО
дело дошло до, Д-82

ДРАБАДАН
в драбадан, Д-435

ДРАЖАЙШАЯ
дражайшая половина, П-303

ДРАЗНИТЬ
дразнить гусей, Г-444

ДРАКИ
после драки кулаками не машут, Д-303

ДРАЛ
чёрт бы тебя драл!, Ч-99

ДРАЛА
давать/дать драла, Д-304
задавать/задать драла, Д-304

ДРАНАЯ
драная кошка, К-342

ДРАПА
давать/дать драпа, Д-304
задавать/задать драпа, Д-304

ДРАПАКА
давать/дать драпака, Д-304
задавать/задать драпака, Д-304

ДРАПУ
давать/дать драпу, Д-304

задавать/задать драпу, Д-304

ДРАТЬ
драть глотку, Г-339
драть горло, Г-339
драть две шкуры, Ш-79
драть козла, К-166
драть на себе волосы, В-243
драть нос, Н-213
драть по две ⟨три⟩ шкуры, Ш-79
драть семь шкур, Ш-79
драть три шкуры, Ш-79
драть шкуру, Ш-79

ДРЕВУ
растекаться мыслью по древу, М-313

ДРЕЗИНУ
в дрезину, Д-435

ДРЕМАТЬ
не дремать, Д-305

ДРЕМУЧИЙ
дремучий лес, Л-58

ДРОБИНА
как слону дробина, С-344
что слону дробина, С-344

ДРОБИНКА
как слону дробинка, С-344
что слону дробинка, С-344

ДРОВ
наломать дров, Д-306
чем дальше в лес, тем больше дров, Л-59

ДРОВА
кто в лес, кто по дрова, Л-55
дрова рубят — щепки летят, Л-56

ДРОГНЕТ
рука не дрогнет, Р-230

ДРОЖАТ
коленки дрожат, К-188

ДРОЖАТЬ
дрожать за каждую копейку, К-281
дрожать над ⟨каждой⟩ копейкой, К-281

ДРОЖЖАХ
как на дрожжах, Д-307

ДРУГ
будь друг, Д-313
друг дома, Д-308
друг друга, Д-309
друг другу ⟨дружке⟩, Д-309
друг дружку, Д-309
друг на друга ⟨на дружку⟩, Д-309
друг о друге ⟨о дружке⟩, Д-309
свой своему поневоле друг, Б-200
скажи мне, кто твой друг, и я скажу ⟨тебе⟩, кто ты, Д-310
старый друг лучше новых двух, Д-311

ДРУГА
для друга ⟨и⟩ семь вёрст не околица, Д-312

друг друга, Д-309
друг на друга, Д-309

ДРУГАЯ
другая музыка, М-283
другая сторона медали, С-602
одна нога здесь, ⟨а⟩ другая там, Н-123
совсем другая история, И-89

ДРУГЕ
друг о друге, Д-309

ДРУГИМ
живи и жить давай другим, Ж-29
один за другим, О-74

ДРУГИМИ
взглянуть другими глазами, Г-120
глядеть другими глазами, Г-120
другими словами, С-296
поглядеть другими глазами, Г-120
посмотреть другими глазами, Г-120
смотреть другими глазами, Г-120

ДРУГИХ
прятаться/спрятаться за других, С-516

ДРУГОГО
из другого теста, Т-89
испечён из другого теста, Т-89
ничего другого не остаётся/не останется, О-122
подойти ⟨подходить⟩ с другого боку, Б-160
сделан из другого теста, Т-89

ДРУГОЕ
в одно ухо вошло, ⟨а⟩ в другое вышло, У-156
в одно ухо входит, ⟨а⟩ в другое выходит, У-156
другое дело, Д-98
перевести ⟨переводить⟩ разговор на другое, Р-48

ДРУГОЙ
другой коленкор, К-190
другой раз, Р-21
другой разговор, Р-47
другой табак, К-190
и тот и другой, Т-168
из другой оперы, О-94
ни тот ни другой, Т-170
отбывать/отбыть в другой мир, М-184
переселиться ⟨переселяться⟩ в другой мир, М-184
с одной стороны... с другой ⟨стороны⟩, С-616
тот и другой, Т-168
тот или другой, Т-173
уйти ⟨уходить⟩ в другой мир, М-184

ДРУГОМ
будь другом, Д-313

ДРУГОМУ
не рой другому яму ⟨ямы⟩, сам в неё попадёшь, Я-64
расскажи ⟨рассказывай⟩ это кому-нибудь другому, Б-7

ДРУГУ
друг другу, Д-309

ДРУГУЮ
перевести ⟨переводить⟩ разговор на другую тему, Р-48

ДРУЖБА
дружба дружбой, а служба службой, Д-314

ДРУЖБОЙ
дружба дружбой, а служба службой, Д-314

ДРУЖБУ
не в службу, а в дружбу, С-349

ДРУЖЕСКОЙ
на дружеской ноге, Н-135

ДРУЖЕСКУЮ
на дружескую ногу, Н-135

ДРУЖКА
для милого дружка ⟨и⟩ семь вёрст не околица, Д-312

ДРУЖКЕ
друг дружке, Д-309
друг о дружке, Д-309

ДРУЖКУ
друг дружку, Д-309
друг на дружку, Д-309

ДРУЗЕЙ
не имей сто рублей, ⟨а⟩ имей сто друзей, Р-199

ДРУЗЬЯ
друзья познаются ⟨узнаются⟩ в беде, Д-315

ДРЯНЬ
дело дрянь, Д-91

ДУБА
врезать дуба, Д-316
давать/дать дуба, Д-316

ДУБАРЯ
врезать дубаря, Д-316
давать/дать дубаря, Д-316

ДУБИНА
дубина стоеросовая, Д-317

ДУБИНКУ
вор у вора дубинку украл, В-264

ДУБИНОЙ
дубиной не выколотишь ⟨не вышибешь⟩, К-137

ДУБОВАЯ
дубовая башка, Г-211
дубовая голова, Г-211

ДУГИ
в три дуги, П-228
гнуть/согнуть в три дуги, Р-120

ДУГУ
в дугу, П-228
гнуть/согнуть в дугу, Р-120

ДУДЕ
и швец, и жнец, и на дуде игрец, Ш-42

ДУДЕТЬ
в одну дудку ⟨дуду⟩ дудеть, Д-320
в ту же дудку ⟨дуду⟩ дудеть, Д-320

ДУДКЕ
плясать/поплясать по дудке, Д-319

ДУДКУ
в одну дудку дудеть, Д-320
в ту же дудку дудеть, Д-320
дуть в дудку, Д-318
плясать/поплясать под дудку, Д-319

ДУДОЧКЕ
плясать/поплясать по дудочке, Д-319

ДУДОЧКУ
плясать/поплясать под дудочку, Д-319

ДУДУ
в одну дуду дудеть, Д-320
в ту же дуду дудеть, Д-320
и швец, и жнец, и в дуду игрец, Ш-42

ДУЕТ
куда ветер дует, В-71
откуда ветер дует, В-71

ДУЕШЬ
обжёгся ⟨обжёшись⟩ на молоке, дуешь и на воду, М-239

ДУЙ
дуй тебя горой!, Г-349

ДУЛЯ
дуля в кармане, К-458

ДУМ
властитель дум, В-163

ДУМАТЬ
высоко думать о себе, В-256
думать-гадать, Д-321
думать да ⟨и⟩ гадать, Д-321
и думать забыть, Д-322
много думать о себе, В-256
надо думать, Д-323
не думать и не гадать, Д-324
не думать, не гадать, Д-324
нечего и думать, Д-325

ДУМАЮ
я думаю!, Д-326

ДУМАЮЧИ
не долго думаючи, Д-327

ДУМАЯ
не долго думая, Д-327

ДУРА
губа не дура, Г-438
дура дурой, Д-329
не будь дура, Д-331
не дура, Д-332

ДУРАК
всякий дурак может/ сможет, Д-328

ДУРАК
дурак дураком, Д-329
дурак стоеросовый, Д-317
каждый дурак может/ сможет, Д-328
как дурак с ⟨писаной⟩ торбой, Т-161
круглый дурак, Д-330
набитый дурак, Д-330
не будь дурак, Д-331
не дурак, Д-332
петый дурак, Д-330

ДУРАКА
валять дурака, Д-333
ищи дурака!, Д-334
корчить дурака, Д-333
ломать дурака, Д-333
нашёл дурака!, Д-334
не на дурака напал, Д-335
разыграть ⟨разыгрывать⟩ дурака, Д-336
свалять дурака, Д-333

ДУРАКАМ
дуракам закон не писан, Д-337

ДУРАКАХ
в дураках, Д-338

ДУРАКОВ
без дураков, Д-339
ищи дураков!, Д-334
нашёл дураков!, Д-334
нет дураков!, Д-334

ДУРАКОМ
дурак дураком, Д-329

ДУРАКУ
дураку закон не писан, Д-337

ДУРАХ
в дурах, Д-338

ДУРЁН
не будь дурён, Д-331

ДУРЕНЬ
как дурень с ⟨писаной⟩ торбой, Т-161

ДУРИТЬ
дурить голову, Г-257

ДУРНА
не будь дурна, Д-331

ДУРНАЯ
дурная трава из поля вон, Т-194

ДУРНО
не дурно (бы), Х-108
дурно кончить, К-266

ДУРНОГО
не говоря дурного слова, С-284

ДУРНОЙ
дурной глаз, Г-24
дурной пример заразителен, П-535
на дурной дороге ⟨дорожке⟩, П-644
на дурной путь, П-644
пойти по дурной дороге ⟨дорожке⟩, Д-270

ДУРНОМ
на дурном пути, П-644

ДУРНУЮ
дурную траву из ⟨с⟩ поля вон, Т-194

на дурную дорогу ⟨дорожку⟩, П-644

ДУРНЫЕ
дурные примеры заразительны, П-535

ДУРНЫМ
дурным голосом, Г-309

ДУРОЙ
дура дурой, Д-329

ДУРОЧКУ
валять дурочку, Д-333
ищи дурочку, Д-334
корчить дурочку, Д-333
ломать дурочку, Д-333
нашёл дурочку, Д-334
свалять дурочку, Д-333
строить дурочку, Д-333

ДУРУ
ищи дуру, Д-334
нашёл дуру, Д-334
не на дуру напал, Д-335
разыграть ⟨разыгрывать⟩ дуру, Д-336

ДУРЬ
выбивать/выбить дурь (из головы), Д-340
выбрасывать/выбросить дурь из головы, Д-341
выкидывать/выкинуть дурь из головы, Д-341
выколачивать/выколотить дурь (из головы), Д-340
вышибать/вышибить дурь (из головы), Д-340

ДУРЬЮ
с дурью, П-522

ДУРЬЯ
дурья башка, Г-212
дурья голова, Г-212

ДУТАЯ
дутая величина, В-30

ДУТЫЙ
дутый пузырь, П-627

ДУТЬ
в ус (себе) не дуть, У-128
дуть в дудку, Д-318
дуть в уши, У-186
и в ус (себе) не дуть, У-128
обжёгся ⟨обжёгшись⟩ на молоке, будешь дуть и на воду, М-239

ДУХ
во весь дух, Д-342
вышибать/вышибить дух, Д-343
дух вон, Д-344
дух замер ⟨замирает⟩, С-136
дух занимает(ся), Д-345
дух заняло ⟨занялся⟩, Д-345
дух захватило ⟨захватывает⟩, Д-345
дух спёрло, Д-345
испустить дух, Д-346
на дух, Д-347
нечистый дух, С-171
нечистый дух попутал, Ч-97
перевести ⟨переводить⟩ дух, Д-348

перехватило ⟨перехватывает⟩ дух, Д-345

ДУХА
набираться/набраться духа, Д-358
не переводя духа, Д-444
присутствие духа, П-549
расположение духа, Р-79
состояние духа, Р-79

ДУХАХ
не в духах, Д-351

ДУХЕ
в духе, Д-349, Д-350
в таком (же) духе, Д-350
в том (же) духе, Д-350
в этом (же) духе, Д-350
не в духе, Д-351

ДУХОМ
воспрянуть духом, Д-352
единым духом, Д-354
ни сном ни духом, С-434
нищие духом, Д-353
одним духом, Д-354
падать/пасть духом, Д-355
питаться святым духом, Д-356
святым духом, Д-357
собираться/собраться с духом, Д-358
упасть духом, Д-355
чтобы духом не пахло, Д-362

ДУХУ
достаёт/достало духу, Д-360
как на духу, Д-359
набираться/набраться духу, Д-358
не переводя духу, Д-444
ни слуху ни духу, С-357
хватает/хватило духу, Д-360
что было духу, Д-361
что есть духу, Д-361
чтобы духу не было, Д-362

ДУША
бумажная душа, Д-378
в чём (только) душа держится, Д-363
душа болит, Д-364
душа в душу, Д-365
душа в пятках, Д-374
душа вон, Д-344
душа замерла ⟨замирает⟩, С-136
душа моя, Д-366
душа надрывается, Д-367
душа нараспашку, Д-368
душа не лежит, Д-368
душа не на месте, Д-370
душа не принимает, Д-371
душа общества, Д-372
душа переболела, Д-364
душа перевернулась ⟨переворачивается⟩, Д-373
душа разрывается (на части), С-142

душа рвётся на части, С-142
душа уходит/ушла в пятки, Д-374
еле-еле душа в теле, Д-363
заячья душа, Д-375
ни одна (живая) душа, Д-376
пока душа держится в теле, Д-377
чернильная душа, Д-378
чужая душа – потёмки, Д-379
широкая душа, Н-34

ДУШАМ
по душам, Д-380

ДУШЕ
в душе, Д-381
как душе угодно, Д-382
камень на душе, К-40
кошки скребут на душе, К-348
на душе, Д-383
отлегло на душе, С-126
по душе, Д-380, Д-384
свинец на душе, С-77
сколько душе угодно, Д-385
скребёт на душе, К-348
читать в душе, Д-386
что душе угодно, Д-387

ДУШЕВНОЙ
в ⟨по⟩ простоте душевной, П-587

ДУШИ
большой души, С-121
в глубине души, Г-149
в простоте души, П-587
всеми силами души, Ф-9
всеми фибрами души, Ф-9
вырвать ⟨вырывать⟩ из души, С-122
для души, Д-388
до глубины души, Г-150
души не чаять, Д-389
камень с души свалился, К-43
мёртвые души, Д-390
на пропой души, П-577
ни души, Д-391
ни единой (живой) души, Д-391
ни живой души, Д-391
ни одной (живой) души, Д-391
от всей души, Д-392
от глубины души, Г-152
от души, Д-392
от полноты души, П-302
отлегло от души, С-126
по простоте души, П-587
с души воротит ⟨рвёт, тянет⟩, Д-393

ДУШИТЬ
душить в объятиях, О-38

ДУШКОМ
с душком, Д-394

ДУШОЙ
болеть душой, Д-395
всей душой, Д-396

душой и телом, Д-397
за душой, Д-398
кривить душой, Д-399
ни душой ни телом, Д-400
отдохнуть ⟨отдыхать⟩ душой, Д-401
покривить душой, Д-399
с дорогой душой, Д-402
с душой, Д-403
с лёгкой душой, С-145
с открытой душой, Д-404
сидеть над душой, Д-405
стоять над душой, Д-405
торчать над душой, Д-405

ДУШУ
без мыла в душу влезть ⟨лезть⟩, М-307
бередить душу, Д-406
брать грех на душу, Г-382
брать за душу, Д-407
в бога душу мать, М-55
в одну душу, Д-408
взять грех на душу, Г-382
взять за душу, Д-407
вкладывать душу, Д-409
влагать душу, Д-409
влезать/влезть в душу, Д-410
вложить душу, Д-409
войти ⟨входить⟩ в душу, Д-411
вывернуть душу, Д-412, Д-413
вывернуть душу наизнанку, Д-413
выворачивать душу, Д-412, Д-413
выворачивать душу наизнанку, Д-413
выкладывать/выложить душу, Д-414
выматывать/вымотать (всю) душу, Д-415
вынимать/вынуть душу, Д-416
вытрясти душу, Д-417
вытягивать/вытянуть (всю) душу, Д-415
вышибать/вышибить душу, Д-343
душа в душу, Д-365
душу выворачивает, Д-412
за милую душу, Д-418
забирать/забрать за душу, Д-407
заглядывать/заглянуть в душу, Д-419
закрадываться/закрасться в душу, Д-420
залезать/залезть в душу, Д-410
западать/запасть в душу, Д-421
изливать/излить душу, Д-422
как бог на душу положит, Б-113
класть душу, Д-423
леденить душу, К-406
лезть в душу, Д-410
лечь свинцом на душу, С-79

надорвать ⟨надрывать⟩ душу, Д-424
наплевать в душу, Д-430
облегчать/облегчить душу, Д-425
отвести ⟨отводить⟩ душу, Д-426
отдавать/отдать богу душу, Б-139
открывать/открыть душу, Д-427
отпустить душу на покаяние, Д-428
перевернуть (всю) душу, Д-429
перевёртывать (всю) душу, Д-429
переворачивать ⟨переворотить⟩ (всю) душу, Д-429
плевать ⟨плюнуть⟩ в душу, Д-430
по душу, Д-431
положить душу, Д-423
принимать/принять грех на душу, Г-382
разбередить душу, Д-406
раскрывать/раскрыть душу, Д-427
распахивать/распахнуть душу, Д-427
сколько бог на душу положит, Б-123
травить душу, Д-432
тянуть душу, Д-433
тянуть за душу, Д-433
хватать за душу, Д-407
хватить греха на душу, Г-382
чёрт его душу знает, Ч-89
что бог на душу положит, Б-128

ДЫБОМ
волосы встали ⟨встают⟩ дыбом, В-241
волосы поднимаются/поднялись дыбом, В-241
волосы стали ⟨становятся⟩ дыбом, В-241

ДЫБЫ
вставать/встать на дыбы, Д-434
на дыбы, Д-434
становиться/стать на дыбы, Д-434

ДЫМ
в дым, Д-435
дым идёт коромыслом ⟨столбом⟩, Д-436
дым коромыслом, Д-436
дым пошёл коромыслом ⟨столбом⟩, Д-436
дым стоит коромыслом ⟨столбом⟩, Д-436
дым столбом, Д-436
стыд не дым, глаза не выест, С-652

ДЫМА
дыма без огня не бывает, Д-437

нет дыма без огня, Д-437

ДЫМИНУ
в дымину, Д-435

ДЫМОВАЯ
дымовая завеса, З-15

ДЫР
до дыр, Д-438

ДЫРКА
дырка от бублика, Д-439

ДЫРКИ
лезть во все дырки, Д-440

ДЫРУ
заткнуть ⟨затыкать⟩ дыру, Д-441

ДЫРЫ
заткнуть ⟨затыкать⟩ дыры, Д-441

ДЫРЯВАЯ
дырявая голова, Г-213
дырявая память, П-44

ДЫРЯВЫЕ
дырявые руки, Р-287

ДЫХ
под дых, Л-125

ДЫХАНИЕ
дыхание занимает(ся), Д-345
дыхание заняло ⟨занялось⟩, Д-345
дыхание захватило ⟨захватывает⟩, Д-345
дыхание спёрло, Д-345
затаив дыхание, Д-442
перевести ⟨переводить⟩ дыхание, Д-348
перехватило ⟨перехватывает⟩ дыхание, Д-345

ДЫХАНИЯ
до последнего дыхания, Д-443
не переводя дыхания, Д-444

ДЫХНУТЬ
дыхнуть негде, Д-299
дыхнуть некогда, Д-300
дыхнуть нельзя, Д-299
дыхнуть нечем, Д-299
не сметь дыхнуть, С-400

ДЫШАТЬ
дышать на ладан, Л-12
еле ⟨едва⟩ дышать, Д-445
чуть дышать, Д-445

ДЫШИТ
чем дышит, Д-446

ДЫШЛО
закон что дышло: куда повернёшь ⟨повернул⟩, туда и вышло, З-49

ДЬЯВОЛ
на кой дьявол, Ч-77
что за дьявол!, Ч-101

ДЬЯВОЛА
для какого дьявола, Ч-77
какого дьявола?, Ч-103
на какого дьявола, Ч-77
у дьявола на рогах, Ч-105

ДЬЯВОЛОМ
за каким дьяволом, Ч-77

ДЬЯВОЛУ
к дьяволу, Ч-111
к дьяволу на рога, Ч-105

ДЮЖ
взялся за гуж, не говори, что не дюж, Г-443

ДЮЖИНА
чёртова дюжина, Д-447

ДЯДЬКА
в огороде бузина, а в Киеве дядька, О-68

Е/Ё

ЁБ
ёб вашу мать, М-50
ёб твою мать, М-50

ЁБАНОЙ
к ёбаной бабушке, М-50
к ёбаной матери, М-50

ЕБЕНЕ
к ебене бабушке, М-50
к ебене матери, М-50

ЕВРОПАМ
галопом по европам, Е-1

ЕВЫ
в костюме Евы, К-331

ЕГИПЕТСКАЯ
египетская казнь, К-8
египетская работа, Р-2
тьма египетская, Т-250

ЕГИПЕТСКИЙ
египетский труд, Р-2

ЕГО
аллах его ведает ⟨знает⟩, Б-93
бес его знает, Ч-89
бить его же ⟨собственным⟩ оружием, О-105
бог его ведает ⟨знает⟩, Б-93
бороться его же ⟨собственным⟩ оружием, О-105
господь его ведает ⟨знает⟩, Б-93
едят его мухи!, М-300
кто его знает, З-143
леший его знает, Ч-89
пёс его знает, Ч-89
пускай его, П-639
пусть его, П-639
с чем его едят, Е-5
так его!, Т-14
указать ⟨указывать⟩ его место, М-123
хрен его знает, Ч-89
чёрт его душу знает, Ч-89
чёрт его знает, Ч-89
чёрт его разберёт, Ч-89
чтоб его!, Р-63
чтоб его разорвало!, Р-63
шут его знает, Ч-89
шут его разберёт, Ч-89

ЕДВА
едва держаться на ногах, Н-131
едва дышать, Д-445

едва... как, Е-2
едва ли, В-323
едва ли не..., Ч-206
едва лишь, Е-2
едва не, Ч-207
едва ноги волочить, Н-144
едва ноги держат ⟨носят⟩, Н-143
едва ноги передвигать, Н-144
едва ноги таскать ⟨тащить, тянуть⟩, Н-144
едва стоять на ногах, Н-131
едва только, Е-2
едва только... как, Е-2

ЕДЕШЬ
тише едешь – дальше будешь, Е-3

ЕДИНО
всё едино, В-327

ЕДИНОГО
до единого, О-81
с единого маху, М-56

ЕДИНОЙ
до единой, О-81
ни единой ⟨живой⟩ души, Д-391
ни единой йоты, Й-2

ЕДИНОМУ
по единому росчерку пера, Р-170
привести ⟨приводить⟩ к единому знаменателю, З-162

ЕДИНСТВЕННЫЙ
единственный в своём роде, Р-134

ЕДИНУЮ
ни на единую йоту, Й-1

ЕДИНЫЙ
в единый миг, М-147

ЕДИНЫМ
единым духом, Д-354
единым махом, М-56
единым росчерком пера, Р-170
единым фронтом, Ф-28
не обмолвиться ни единым словом, С-333

ЕДРЕНЕ
к едрене фене, Ф-6

ЕДРЁНОЙ
к едрёной бабушке, М-45
к едрёной матери, М-45
к едрёной фене, Ф-6

ЕДУН
едун напал, Е-4

ЕДУТ
андроны едут, А-29

ЕДЫ
аппетит приходит во время еды, А-32

ЕДЯТ
едят его мухи!, М-300
с чем его едят, Е-5

ЕЁ
пускай её, П-639

пусть её, П-639
указать ⟨указывать⟩ её место, М-123

ЕЖЕЛИ
в (том) случае, ежели, С-367
ежели (уж) на то пошло, П-465
ежели что, Ч-164
что, ежели, Ч-179
что, ежели б(ы), Ч-179

ЕЖОВЫЕ
брать/взять в ежовые рукавицы, Р-241
ежовые рукавицы, Р-242

ЕЖОВЫХ
держать в ежовых рукавицах, Р-241

ЕЖУ
(и) ежу понятно, Е-6

ЕЗДИТЬ
ездить верхом, Е-7

ЕЗДОК
не ездок, Х-61

ЕЗДЯТ
в Тулу со своим самоваром не ездят, Т-231

ЕЙ-БОГУ
ей-богу, Е-8

ЁКАЕТ
сердце ёкает, С-136

ЁКНУЛО
сердце ёкнуло, С-136

ЕЛ
мало каши ел, К-113

ЕЛЕ
еле держаться на ногах, Н-131
еле дышать, Д-445
еле-еле душа в теле, Д-363
еле можахом ⟨можаху⟩, М-212
еле ноги волочить, Н-144
еле ноги держат ⟨носят⟩, Н-143
еле ноги передвигать, Н-144
еле ноги таскать ⟨тащить, тянуть⟩, Н-144
еле стоять на ногах, Н-131

ЁЛКИ
ёлки зелёные!, Е-9
ёлки-моталки!, Е-9
ёлки-палки!, Е-9

ЕЛОВАЯ
голова еловая, Г-201

ЕМЕЛЯ
мели, Емеля, твоя неделя, Е-10

ЕРЕСЬ
нести ересь, В-99
плести ересь, В-99
понести ересь, В-99

ЕРУНДА
ерунда на постном масле, Е-11

ЕРУНДУ
болтать ерунду, В-99
городить ерунду, В-99

молоть ерунду, В-99
нагородить ерунду, В-99
нести/понести ерунду, В-99
пороть ерунду, В-99

ЕСЛИ
в (том) случае если, С-367
если бы да кабы, Е-12
если гора не идёт к Магомету, то Магомет идёт к горе, Г-315
если на то пошло, П-465
если память не изменяет, П-43
если позволите, П-270
если угодно, У-21
если уж на то пошло, П-465
если хотите ⟨хочешь⟩, Х-88
если что, Ч-164
как если бы, К-11
на (тот) случай если, С-377
что, если, Ч-179
что, если б(ы), Ч-179

ЕСТЬ
в каждой шутке есть доля правды, Ш-102
вот то-то (оно) и есть, Т-105
даром хлеб есть, Х-30
зря хлеб есть, Х-30
есть глазами, Г-107
есть грех, Г-385
есть ещё порох в пороховницах, П-379
есть маленько, Е-13
есть немного, Е-13
есть просит, Е-14
есть свой хлеб, Х-31
есть такое дело, Д-99
есть такой ⟨тот⟩ грех, Г-385
есть хлеб, Х-32
есть чужой хлеб, Х-32
за семь вёрст киселя есть, В-43
землю есть буду, З-118
и есть, Е-15
и у стен есть уши, С-559
как есть, Е-16
какой ни (на) есть, Е-17
кто ни (на) есть, Е-18
на всякое хотенье есть терпенье, Х-87
поедом есть, Е-19
(своя) рука есть, Р-345
сколько ни на есть, Е-20
так (оно) и есть, Е-21
то есть, Т-113
то-то (оно) и есть, Т-105
что есть духу, Д-361
что есть мочи, М-271
что есть сил(ы), М-271
что ни (на) есть, Е-22, Е-23

ЕХАТЬ
дальше ехать некуда, Н-74

ЕШЬ
ешь – не хочу, Х-95

ЕЩЁ
бабушка ещё надвое гадала ⟨сказала⟩, Б-5

вот ещё!, Е-28
вот ещё новости
⟨новость⟩!, Н-110
всё ещё, Е-24
да ещё как, Е-27
есть ещё порох в
пороховницах, П-379
ещё бы!, Е-25
ещё вилами на ⟨по⟩ воде
писано, В-144
ещё и ещё, Е-26
ещё как, Е-27
ещё не вечер, В-84
ещё ни о чём не говорить,
Г-165
ещё туда-сюда, Т-225
ещё чего!, Ч-42
ещё чего не хватало!, Х-7
и ещё как, Е-27
(и) как ещё земля держит
⟨носит, терпит⟩, З-126
конь ещё не валялся, К-267
мало того что... ещё и...,
М-14
ну вот ещё!, Е-28
то ли ещё будет, Б-218
это ещё цветики ⟨цветки,
цветочки⟩, а ягодки
(будут) впереди, Ц-16
это ещё что за новости
⟨новость⟩!, Н-110
этого ещё (только) не
хватало ⟨недоставало⟩!,
Х-7

Ж

ЖАБРЫ
брать/взять за жабры,
Ж-1
ЖАЖДАТЬ
жаждать крови, К-392
ЖАЛЕТЬ
живота (своего) не жалеть,
Ж-43
жизни (своей) не жалеть,
Ж-43
не жалеть красок, К-368
ЖАЛОВАТЬ
просим ⟨прошу⟩ любить
да ⟨и⟩ жаловать, П-602
ЖАР
бросать в жар (и в холод),
Ж-2
бросать то в жар, то в
холод, Ж-2
бросить в жар (и в холод),
Ж-2
кидать в жар (и в холод),
Ж-2
кидать то в жар, то в
холод, Ж-2
кинуть в жар (и в холод),
Ж-2
чужими руками жар
загребать, Р-266
ЖАРЕНЫЙ
жареный петух не клевал/
не клюнул, П-130

ЖАРЕНЫМ
запахло жареным, Ж-3
пахнет жареным, Ж-3
ЖАРКО
небу жарко, Н-57
ни жарко ни холодно, Ж-4
ни холодно ни жарко, Ж-4
ЖАРОМ
с жаром, Ж-5
ЖАРУ
давать/дать жару, Ж-6
задавать/задать жару,
Ж-6
подбавить ⟨подбавлять⟩
жару, Ж-7
поддавать/поддать жару,
Ж-7
с пылу, с жару, П-671
ЖАТЬ
жать сок(и), С-467
ЖВАЧКУ
жевать ⟨пережёвывать⟩
жвачку, Ж-8
ЖДАТЬ
ждать не дождаться, Ж-9
ждать своего часа, Ч-21
ждать у моря погоды,
М-259
заставить ⟨заставлять⟩
себя ждать, З-77
не ждать, не гадать, Д-324
не заставить ⟨не
заставлять⟩ себя (долго)
ждать, З-78
сидеть у моря да ⟨и⟩
ждать погоды, М-259
ЖДЁТ
время не ждёт, В-307
дело не ждёт, В-307
ЖДИ
того и жди, Г-153
ЖДУТ
обещанного три года
ждут, Г-182
семеро одного не ждут,
Ж-10
ЖЕВАТЬ
жевать жвачку, Ж-8
жевать мочалку ⟨мочало⟩,
М-269
ЖЕЗЛА
как* по манию волшебного
жезла, М-27
как* по мановению
волшебного жезла, М-27
ЖЕЛАЕМ
здравия желаем!, З-108
ЖЕЛАТЬ
оставляет желать лучшего
⟨многого⟩, Л-151
ЖЕЛАЮ
здравия желаю!, З-108
ЖЕЛЕЗКУ
на всю железку, Ж-11
на полную железку, Ж-11
ЖЕЛЕЗНОЙ
вымести ⟨выметать⟩
железной метлой, М-135
ЖЕЛЕЗО
куй железо, пока горячо,
Ж-12

ЖЕЛЕЗОМ
выжечь ⟨выжигать⟩
калёным железом, Ж-13
ЖЕЛТОРОТЫЙ
желторотый птенец, П-614
ЖЁЛТЫЙ
жёлтый билет, Б-64
жёлтый дом, Д-253
ЖЕЛУДОК
на голодный желудок,
Ж-14
на пустой желудок, Ж-14
на сытый желудок, Ж-15
на тощий желудок, Ж-14
ЖЕНА
муж да ⟨и⟩ жена – одна
сатана, М-282
ЖЕНИЛИ
без меня меня женили,
Ж-16
ЖЕНИХОМ
смотреть женихом, Ж-17
ЖЕНСКИЙ
женский угодник, У-19
ЖЕНЩИН
не знать женщин, Ж-18
ЖЕНЩИНЫ
не знать ни одной
женщины, Ж-18
ЖЕРЕБЧИК
мышиный жеребчик, Ж-19
ЖЕРТВОЙ
пасть жертвой, Ж-20
ЖЕРТВУ
принести в жертву, Ж-21
принести жертву, Ж-22
приносить в жертву, Ж-21
приносить жертву, Ж-22
ЖЕРТВЫ
принести ⟨приносить⟩
жертвы, Ж-22
ЖЕСТ
благородный жест, Ж-23
красивый жест, Ж-23
широкий жест, Ж-23
ЖЁСТКО
мягко стелет, да жёстко
спать, С-557
ЖЕЧЬ
жечь все мосты, К-289
жечь за собой мосты,
К-289
жечь корабли ⟨мосты⟩,
К-289
жечь свои корабли
⟨мосты⟩, К-289
жечь фимиам, Ф-11
ЖИВ
жив-здоров, Ж-24
жив и здоров, Ж-24
жив курилка!, К-478
ни жив ни мёртв, Ж-25
ЖИВАЯ
живая вода, В-174
живая летопись, Л-67
живая энциклопедия, Э-1
ни одна живая душа,
Д-376
ЖИВЁТЕ
как живёте-можете?, Ж-28

ЖИВЁШЬ
за здорово живёшь, Ж-26
здорово живёшь, Ж-26,
Ж-27
как живёшь-можешь?,
Ж-28
ЖИВИ
век живи, век учись, В-16
живи и жить давай
другим, Ж-29
ЖИВОГО
живого места не осталось
⟨нет⟩, М-89
ЖИВОЕ
брать/взять за живое,
Ж-30
живое слово, С-314
забирать/забрать за
живое, Ж-30
задевать/задеть за живое,
Ж-30
затрагивать/затронуть за
живое, Ж-30
ЖИВОЙ
в порядке живой очереди,
П-399
живой-здоровый, Ж-24
живой и здоровый, Ж-24
живой нитки нет ⟨не
осталось⟩, Н-101
живой портрет, П-387
живой рукой, Р-331
живой справочник, Э-1
ни (единой) живой души,
Д-391
ни живой ни мёртвый,
Ж-25
ни одной живой души,
Д-391
ни одной живой нитки не
осталось ⟨нет⟩, Н-101
ЖИВОМУ
по живому резать, Ж-31
ЖИВОТ
держаться за живот, Ж-35
живот подвело ⟨подводит,
подтянуло⟩, Ж-32
класть живот (свой), Ж-55
надорвать ⟨надрывать⟩
живот, Ж-33
не на живот, а на смерть,
Ж-58
подтягивать/подтянуть
живот, Ж-34
положить живот (свой),
Ж-55
хвататься за живот, Ж-35
ЖИВОТА
живота (своего) не жалеть,
Ж-43
ЖИВОТИКИ
держаться за животики,
Ж-35
животики подвело
⟨подводит, подтянуло⟩,
Ж-32
надорвать ⟨надрывать⟩
животики, Ж-33
хвататься за животики,
Ж-35

ЖИВОТЫ
держаться за животы,
Ж-35
животы подвело
⟨подводит, подтянуло⟩,
Ж-32
надорвать ⟨надрывать⟩
животы, Ж-33
подтягивать/подтянуть
животы, Ж-34
хвататься за животы,
Ж-35

ЖИВУ
не до жиру, быть бы живу,
Ж-77

ЖИВУТ
живут (же) люди!, Л-169

ЖИВУЮ
вливать/влить живую
струю, С-650
внести ⟨вносить⟩ живую
струю, С-650
на живую нитку, Н-102
на живую руку, Р-346

ЖИВЫЕ
живые мощи, М-274

ЖИВЫМ
живым манером, Р-331

ЖИВЫХ
в живых, Ж-36

ЖИВЬЁМ
съесть живьём, С-731

ЖИЗНИ
больше жизни!, Ж-37
в жизни, Ж-38
вернуть к жизни, Ж-39
возвратить ⟨возвращать⟩
к жизни, Ж-39
вопрос жизни и ⟨или⟩
смерти, В-259
вызвать ⟨вызывать⟩ к
жизни, Ж-40
вычёркивать/вычеркнуть
из своей жизни, Ж-41
давать/дать жизни, Ж-42
жизни (своей) не жалеть,
Ж-43
лишать жизни, Ж-44
лишаться жизни, Ж-45
лишить жизни, Ж-44
лишиться жизни, Ж-45
на закате жизни, З-44
на склоне жизни, С-224
отставать/отстать от
жизни, Ж-46
по гроб жизни, Г-399
подавать/подать признаки
жизни, П-524
подруга жизни, П-255
прожигатель
⟨прожигательница⟩
жизни, Ж-63
решать жизни, Ж-44
решаться жизни, Ж-45
решить жизни, Ж-44
решиться жизни, Ж-45
свет жизни, С-60
спутник ⟨спутница⟩
жизни, С-530
уйти ⟨уходить⟩ из жизни,
Ж-47

ЖИЗНЬ
в жизнь, Ж-38
вдохнуть жизнь, Ж-48
войти в жизнь, Ж-50
воплотить ⟨воплощать⟩ в
жизнь, Ж-49
вступать/вступить в
жизнь, Ж-50
входить в жизнь, Ж-50
даровать жизнь, Ж-51
дать жизнь, Ж-52
дорого отдавать/отдать
свою жизнь, Ж-53
дорого продавать/продать
свою жизнь, Ж-53
жизнь прожить — не поле
перейти, Ж-54
заедать/заесть (чужую)
жизнь, В-18
класть жизнь, Ж-55
кончать/кончить жизнь,
Ж-56
мыкать жизнь, В-20
не жизнь, а масленица
⟨малина⟩, Ж-57
не на жизнь, а на смерть,
Ж-58
ни в жизнь, Ж-59
отдавать/отдать жизнь,
Ж-60
отравлять жизнь, Ж-61
подарить жизнь, Ж-51
покончить жизнь
самоубийством, П-285
положить жизнь, Ж-55
претворить ⟨претворять⟩
в жизнь, Ж-49
провести ⟨проводить⟩ в
жизнь, Ж-62
прожигать жизнь, Ж-63
путёвка в жизнь, П-641
собачья жизнь, Ж-64
устраивать/устроить
весёлую жизнь, Ж-65

ЖИЗНЬЮ
играть жизнью (и
смертью), Ж-66
играть своей жизнью,
Ж-66
между жизнью и смертью,
Ж-67
покончить с жизнью,
П-285
покончить счёты с
жизнью, П-285
поплатиться жизнью,
Г-236

ЖИЛ
жил-был, Ж-68
чтоб я так жил!, Ж-69

ЖИЛА
становая жила, Х-98

ЖИЛАХ
в жилах течёт голубая
кровь, К-398
кровь заиграла в жилах,
К-403
кровь застывает/застыла
в жилах, К-405
кровь играет в жилах,
К-403

кровь леденеет в жилах,
К-405
кровь стынет в жилах,
К-405
кровь холодеет в жилах,
К-405

ЖИЛЕТКИ
от жилетки рукава, Ж-70

ЖИЛЕТКУ
плакать(ся) в жилетку,
Ж-71
поплакать(ся) в жилетку,
Ж-71

ЖИЛЕЦ
не жилец (на белом свете),
Ж-72
не жилец на (этом) свете,
Ж-72

ЖИЛКУ
попадать/попасть в
(самую) жилку, Ж-73

ЖИЛУ
попадать/попасть в
(самую) жилу, Ж-73

ЖИЛЫ
выматывать/вымотать
(все) жилы, Ж-74
вытягивать/вытянуть
(все) жилы, Ж-74
тянуть жилы, Ж-74

ЖИР
растрясать/растрясти
жир, Ж-75
сбрасывать/сбросить жир,
Ж-75
сгонять/согнать жир,
Ж-75
спускать/спустить жир,
Ж-75

ЖИРКОМ
заплывать/заплыть
жирком, Ж-76

ЖИРНО
больно ⟨слишком⟩ жирно
(будет), Б-217
жирно будет, Б-217

ЖИРОК
растрясать/растрясти
жирок, Ж-75
спускать/спустить жирок,
Ж-75

ЖИРОМ
заплывать/заплыть
жиром, Ж-76

ЖИРУ
не до жиру, быть бы живу,
Ж-77
от жиру лопаться/
лопнуть, Ж-79
с жиру беситься, Ж-78
с жиру лопаться/лопнуть,
Ж-79

ЖИСТЬ
ни в жисть, Ж-59

ЖИТЕЙСКОЕ
дело житейское, Д-83

ЖИТЬ
велеть долго жить, П-526
живи и жить давай
другим, Ж-29

жить бирюком, Б-66
жить в веках, В-23
жить в людях, Л-174
жить на шее, Ш-45
жить одним домом, Д-261
жить припеваючи, Ж-80
жить своим умом, У-106
жить сегодняшним днём,
Д-204
жить собственным умом,
У-106
жить чужим умом, У-107
как сыч жить, С-741
приказать долго жить,
П-526
с волками жить — по-
волчьи выть, В-229
сычом жить, С-741

ЖИТЬЁ
не житьё, а малина
⟨масленица⟩, Ж-57

ЖИТЬЯ
житья не стало, Ж-81
житья нет, Ж-81
не давать/не дать житья,
Ж-82

ЖМУРКИ
игра в жмурки, П-610
играть в жмурки, П-610

ЖНЕЦ
и швец, и жнец, и в дуду
⟨и на дуде⟩ игрец, Ш-42

ЖРЕБИЙ
бросать/бросить жребий,
Ж-83
жребий брошен, Ж-84
кидать/кинуть жребий,
Ж-83
метать/метнуть жребий,
Ж-83

ЖУРАВЛЬ
журавль в небе, Ж-85
лучше синица в руках ⟨в
руки⟩, чем журавль в
небе, С-195

ЖУРАВЛЯ
не сули журавля в небе, а
дай синицу в руки, С-195

ЖУТИ
до жути, Ж-86

З

ЗА
за и против, З-1

ЗАБАВА
детская забава, И-18

ЗАБВЕНИЮ
предавать/предать
забвению, З-2

ЗАБВЕНИЯ
кануть в реку забвения,
Л-68

ЗАБЕГАЛИ
мурашки забегали по
коже, М-291
мурашки забегали по
спине ⟨по телу⟩, М-291

ЗАБЕГАТЬ
забегать вперёд, З-3

ЗАБЕЖАТЬ
забежать вперёд, З-3
ЗАБИВАТЬ
забивать баки, Б-10
забивать голову, Г-251
забивать козла, К-167
забивать мозги, Г-251
забивать себе в башку,
 Г-246
забивать себе в голову,
 Г-246
ЗАБИРАТЬ
забирать в руки, Р-288
забирать верх, В-53
забирать власть, С-188
забирать за душу, Д-407
забирать за живое, Ж-30
забирать за сердце, Д-407
забирать себе в башку,
 Г-246
забирать себе в голову,
 Г-246
забирать силу, С-188
ЗАБИТА
голова забита, Г-202
ЗАБИТЬ
забить баки, Б-10
забить в набат, Н-1
забить голову, Г-251
забить ключом, К-145
забить козла, К-167
забить мозги, Г-251
забить осиновый кол (в
 могилу), К-177
забить отбой, О-129
забить себе в башку, Г-246
забить себе в голову, Г-246
забить тревогу, Т-197
ЗАБЛУДИТЬСЯ
заблудиться в трёх соснах,
 С-500
ЗАБЛУДШАЯ
заблудшая овечка (овца),
 О-45
ЗАБЛУЖДЕНИЕ
ввести (вводить) в
 заблуждение, З-4
ЗАБЛУЖДЕНИЯ
вывести (выводить) из
 заблуждения, З-5
ЗАБОТ
не было у бабы забот,
 (так) купила (баба)
 порося, Б-2
ЗАБОТА
не моя забота, З-6
ЗАБОТЫ
не было заботы!, З-7
ЗАБРАЛОМ
с открытым забралом, З-8
с поднятым забралом, З-8
ЗАБРАСЫВАТЬ
забрасывать грязью, Г-434
забрасывать камнями,
 Г-434
забрасывать удочку, У-50
ЗАБРАТЬ
забрать в руки, Р-288
забрать верх, В-53
забрать власть, С-188

забрать голыми руками,
 Р-253
забрать за душу, Д-407
забрать за живое, Ж-30
забрать за сердце, Д-407
забрать себе в башку,
 Г-246
забрать себе в голову,
 Г-246
забрать силу, С-188
ЗАБРИВАТЬ
забривать лбы (лоб),
 Л-115
ЗАБРИТЬ
забрить в рекруты (в
 солдаты), Л-115
забрить лоб (лбы), Л-115
забрить лоб в рекруты (в
 солдаты), Л-115
ЗАБРОСАТЬ
забросать грязью, Г-434
забросать камнями, Г-434
ЗАБРОСИТЬ
забросить удочку, У-50
ЗАБУБЁННАЯ
забубённая голова
 (головушка), Г-214
ЗАБЫВАТЬ
забывать дорогу, Д-279
забывать себя, З-9
забывать хлеб-соль, Х-33
себя не забывать, З-10
ЗАБЫЛ
что я там (тут) забыл?,
 З-11
ЗАБЫТЬ
забыть дорогу, Д-279
забыть себя, З-9
забыть хлеб-соль, Х-33
и думать забыть, Д-322
не забыть, З-12
себя не забыть, З-10
ЗАВАЛИСЬ
хоть завались, З-13
ЗАВАРИВАЕТСЯ
заваривается каша, К-108
ЗАВАРИВАТЬ
заваривать кашу, К-115
ЗАВАРИЛ
сам кашу заварил, сам и
 расхлёбывай, К-118
ЗАВАРИЛАСЬ
заварилась каша, К-108
ЗАВАРИТЬ
заварить кашу, К-115
ЗАВЕДЁННАЯ
как заведённая машина,
 М-59
ЗАВЕДЁННЫЙ
как заведённый, М-59
ЗАВЕРТЕТЬ
завертеть хвостом, Х-24
ЗАВЁРТКИ
во все носовые завёртки,
 З-14
ЗАВЁРТКУ
во всю носовую завёртку,
 З-14
ЗАВЕСА
дымовая завеса, З-15

завеса падает (с глаз), З-16
завеса спадает/спала (с
 глаз), З-16
завеса упала (с глаз), З-16
ЗАВЕСТИ
завести в тупик, Т-236
завести глаза, Г-70
завести шарманку, Ш-36
ЗАВЕСТИСЬ
завестись с одного
 оборота, П-316
завестись с пол-оборота,
 П-316
завестись с полуоборота,
 П-316
ЗАВЕСУ
приоткрывать/
 приоткрыть завесу, З-17
приподнимать/
 приподнять завесу, З-17
снимать/снять завесу, З-18
сорвать (срывать) завесу,
 З-18
ЗАВИВАТЬ
завивать горе верёвочкой,
 Г-326
ЗАВИДКИ
завидки берут, З-19
ЗАВИДУЩИЕ
руки загребущие, глаза
 завидущие, Р-315
ЗАВИЛЯТЬ
завилять хвостом, Х-26
ЗАВИНТИТЬ
завинтить гайки, Г-8
ЗАВИНЧИВАНИЕ
завинчивание гаек, Г-8
ЗАВИНЧИВАТЬ
завинчивать гайки, Г-8
ЗАВИРАЙСЯ
ври, да не завирайся, В-321
ЗАВИСИМОСТИ
в зависимости, З-20
ЗАВИСТЬ
на зависть, З-21
ЗАВИТЬ
завить горе верёвочкой,
 Г-326
ЗАВОДЕ
(и) в заводе нет, З-22
ЗАВОДИТЬ
заводить в тупик, Т-236
заводить глаза, Г-70
заводить шарманку, Ш-36
ЗАВОДИТЬСЯ
заводиться с одного
 оборота, П-316
заводиться с пол-оборота,
 П-316
заводиться с полуоборота,
 П-316
ЗАВОДЬ
тихая заводь, З-23
ЗАВТРА
до завтра, З-24
заглядывать/заглянуть в
 завтра, Б-224
не откладывай на завтра
 то, что можешь

(можно) сделать
 сегодня, О-149
ЗАВТРАКАМИ
кормить завтраками, З-25
ЗАВТРАШНИЙ
завтрашний день, Д-159
ЗАВЯЗАТЬ
завязать узелок (на
 память), У-60
ЗАВЯЗКУ
по (самую) завязку, З-26
под (самую) завязку, З-26
ЗАВЯЗЫВАТЬ
завязывать узелок (на
 память), У-60
ЗАГАДКАМИ
говорить загадками, З-27
ЗАГАДКИ
играть в загадки, З-27
ЗАГИБАТЬ
загибать/загнуть салазки,
 С-4
ЗАГЛЯДЕНЬЕ
на загляденье, З-28
ЗАГЛЯДЫВАТЬ
заглядывать в будущее,
 Б-224
заглядывать в бутылку,
 Б-248
заглядывать в душу, Д-419
заглядывать в завтра,
 Б-224
заглядывать в рюмку
 (рюмочку), Б-248
заглядывать в сердце,
 Д-419
заглядывать вперёд, Б-224
ЗАГЛЯНУТЬ
заглянуть в будущее, Б-224
заглянуть в душу, Д-419
заглянуть в завтра, Б-224
заглянуть в сердце, Д-419
заглянуть вперёд, Б-224
ЗАГНАТЬ
загнать в гроб, Г-396
загнать в могилу, М-204
загнать в угол, У-32
ЗАГНУТЬ
загнуть салазки, С-4
ЗАГОВАРИВАТЬ
заговаривать зубы, З-196
ЗАГОВЕНЬЯ
до морковкина заговенья,
 З-29
ЗАГОВОР
заговор молчания, З-30
ЗАГОВОРИЛА
валаамова ослица
 заговорила, О-112
кровь заговорила, К-401
ЗАГОВОРИТЬ
заговорить зубы, З-196
ЗАГОНЕ
в загоне, З-31
ЗАГОНЯТЬ
загонять в угол, У-32
ЗАГОРЕЛАСЬ
Москва от копеечной
 свечки загорелась, М-261

ЗАГОРЕЛСЯ
(весь) сыр-бор загорелся, С-737

ЗАГРЕБАТЬ
загребать лопатой, Л-136
чужими руками жар загребать, Р-266

ЗАГРЕБУЩИЕ
руки загребущие (, глаза завидущие), Р-315

ЗАД
давать/дать коленкой ⟨коленом⟩ под зад, К-189
коленкой ⟨коленом⟩ под зад, К-189

ЗАДАВАТЬ
задавать баню, Б-18
задавать взбучку ⟨выволочку⟩, Т-200
задавать головомойку, Г-243
задавать дёру, Д-183, Д-184
задавать драла, Д-304
задавать драпа ⟨драпака, драпу⟩, Д-304
задавать жару, Ж-6
задавать звону, З-101
задавать лататы, Д-304
задавать острастку, О-125
задавать пару, П-65
задавать перцу, П-110
задавать пфеферу, П-110
задавать стрекача ⟨стречка⟩, С-633
задавать таску, Т-45
задавать тёку, Д-304
задавать тон, Т-154
задавать трезвон(у), Т-199
задавать трёпку, Т-200
задавать тягу, Д-304
задавать фееру, П-110
задавать храпака ⟨храповицкого⟩, Х-96
задавать чёску ⟨чёсу⟩, Ч-144
задавать шик(у), Ш-61

ЗАДАВИТЬ
муху задавить, М-306

ЗАДАМ
я тебе задам!, Д-19

ЗАДАТЬ
задать баню, Б-18
задать взбучку ⟨выволочку⟩, Т-200
задать головомойку, Г-243
задать дёру, Д-183, Д-184
задать драла, Д-304
задать драпа ⟨драпака, драпу⟩, Д-304
задать жару, Ж-6
задать звону, З-101
задать лататы, Д-304
задать острастку, О-125
задать пару, П-65
задать перцу, П-110
задать пфеферу, П-110
задать стрекача ⟨стречка⟩, С-633
задать таску, Т-45

задать тёку, Д-304
задать тон, Т-154
задать трезвон(у), Т-199
задать трёпку, Т-200
задать тягу, Д-304
задать фееру, П-110
задать храпака ⟨храповицкого⟩, Х-96
задать чёску ⟨чёсу⟩, Ч-144
задать шик(у), Ш-61

ЗАДВОРКАХ
на задворках, З-32

ЗАДЕВАТЬ
задевать больную струну, С-649
задевать за больную струну, С-649
задевать за живое, Ж-30
задевать (за) чувствительную струну, С-649

ЗАДЕТЬ
задеть больную струну, С-649
задеть за больную струну, С-649
задеть за живое, Ж-30
задеть (за) чувствительную струну, С-649

ЗАДИРАТЬ
задирать нос, Н-213
задирать хвост, Х-11

ЗАДНЕЙ
без (всякой) задней мысли, М-311

ЗАДНЕМ
на заднем плане, П-163

ЗАДНИЕ
становиться/стать на задние лапки, Л-25

ЗАДНИЙ
давать/дать задний ход, Х-51
на задний план, П-163

ЗАДНИМ
задним умом крепок, У-108
задним числом, Ч-154

ЗАДНИХ
без (всяких) задних мыслей, М-311
без задних ног, Н-111
на задних лапах ⟨лапках⟩, Л-22
стоять на задних лапах ⟨лапках⟩, Л-22
ходить на задних лапах ⟨лапках⟩, Л-22

ЗАДНЯЯ
задняя мысль, М-311

ЗАДОМ
задом наперёд, З-33

ЗАДОРИНКИ
без задоринки, С-682
без сучка без ⟨и⟩ задоринки, С-682
ни сучка ни задоринки, С-683

ЗАДРАТЬ
задрать нос, Н-213

задрать хвост, Х-11

ЗАДУРИТЬ
задурить голову, Г-257

ЗАДУШИТЬ
задушить в объятиях, О-38

ЗАЕДАТЬ
заедать век ⟨жизнь⟩, В-18
заедать чужой век ⟨чужую жизнь⟩, В-18

ЗАЕСТЬ
заесть век ⟨жизнь⟩, В-18
заесть чужой век ⟨чужую жизнь⟩, В-18

ЗАЕХАТЬ
не туда заехать, З-34

ЗАЖАТЬ
зажать в кулак ⟨в кулаке⟩, К-463
зажать рот, Р-176

ЗАЖИВЁТ
до свадьбы заживёт, С-29

ЗАЖИВО
заживо похоронить, Х-81
заживо похоронить себя, Х-82
заживо хоронить, Х-81
заживо хоронить себя, Х-82
погребать/погрести себя заживо, П-233

ЗАЖИМАТЬ
зажимать в кулак ⟨в кулаке⟩, К-463
зажимать рот, Р-176

ЗАЗВОНИТЬ
зазвонить в ⟨во все⟩ колокола, К-202

ЗАЗРЕНИЯ
без зазрения совести, З-35

ЗАЗРИЛА
совесть зазрила, С-458

ЗАИГРАЛА
кровь заиграла (в жилах), К-403

ЗАЙТИ
зайти в тупик, Т-237
зайти (слишком) далеко, З-85

ЗАЙЦАМИ
гнаться за двумя зайцами, З-36
гоняться за двумя зайцами, З-36
за двумя зайцами погонишься, ни одного не поймаешь, З-37
погнаться за двумя зайцами, З-36

ЗАЙЦЕВ
убивать/убить двух зайцев, З-36

ЗАКАЖЕШЬ
не закажешь, З-39

ЗАКАЗ
как на заказ, З-41
на заказ, З-40

ЗАКАЗАТЬ
заказать все пути, П-656
заказать дорогу, П-656

заказать путь, П-656

ЗАКАЗУ
как по заказу, З-41
по заказу, З-42

ЗАКАЗЫВАТЬ
заказывать все пути, П-656
заказывать дорогу, П-656
заказывать путь, П-656

ЗАКАЛА
старого закала, З-43

ЗАКАНЧИВАТЬСЯ
заканчиваться ничем, К-265

ЗАКАТЕ
на закате дней, З-44
на закате жизни, З-44

ЗАКАТИЛОСЬ
сердце закатилось, С-135

ЗАКАТИТЬ
закатить глаза, Г-70

ЗАКАТЫВАЕТСЯ
сердце закатывается, С-135

ЗАКАТЫВАТЬ
закатывать глаза, Г-70

ЗАКВАСКИ
старой закваски, З-43

ЗАКИДАТЬ
закидать грязью, Г-434
закидать камнями, Г-434
шапками закидать, Ш-26

ЗАКИДЫВАТЬ
закидывать грязью, Г-434
закидывать камнями, Г-434
закидывать словечко, С-315
закидывать слово ⟨словцо⟩, С-315
закидывать удочку, У-50

ЗАКИНУТЬ
закинуть словечко, С-315
закинуть слово ⟨словцо⟩, С-315
закинуть удочку, У-50

ЗАКИПЕЛА
кровь закипела, К-403

ЗАКИПЕТЬ
закипеть ключом, К-145

ЗАКЛАД
биться об заклад, З-45
побиться об заклад, З-45
удариться об заклад, З-45

ЗАКЛАДЫВАТЬ
закладывать за галстук, Г-10
закладывать основу ⟨основы⟩, О-118
закладывать фундамент, О-118

ЗАКЛЁПКИ
заклёпки (в голове) не хватает ⟨недостаёт⟩, В-147

ЗАКЛЁПОК
заклёпок (в голове) не хватает ⟨недостаёт⟩, В-147

ЗАКЛЮЧЕНИЕ
в заключение, З-46

ЗАПАХЛО
запахло жареным, Ж-3
запахло палёным, Ж-3
запахло порохом, П-383

ЗАПЕЛА
рано пташечка запела, как бы кошечка не съела, П-612

ЗАПЕТЬ
запеть соловьём, С-472
лазаря запеть, Л-18

ЗАПИНКИ
без запинки, З-67

ЗАПИТЬ
запить горькую, Г-360
запить мёртвую, Г-360

ЗАПЛАТИТЬ
дорого заплатить, З-68
заплатить головой, Г-236
заплатить дань, Д-22

ЗАПЛЕТАЕТСЯ
язык заплетается, Я-37

ЗАПЛЕТАЮТСЯ
ноги заплетаются, Н-147

ЗАПЛЕЧНЫЙ
заплечный мастер, Д-52

ЗАПЛЕЧНЫХ
заплечных дел мастер, Д-52

ЗАПЛЫВАТЬ
заплывать жирком ⟨жиром⟩, Ж-76

ЗАПЛЫТЬ
заплыть жирком ⟨жиром⟩, Ж-76

ЗАПОЛЗАЛИ
мурашки заползали по коже, М-291
мурашки заползали по спине ⟨по телу⟩, М-291

ЗАПРАВЛЯТЬ
заправлять арапа, А-37

ЗАПРЕТНЫЙ
запретный плод, П-195

ЗАПРЕТОМ
под запретом, З-69

ЗАПУДРИТЬ
запудрить мозги, М-229

ЗАПУСКАТЬ
запускать глаза ⟨глазенапа⟩, Г-75
запускать лапу, Р-343
запускать руку, Р-343
запускать словечко, С-315

ЗАПУСТЕНИЯ
мерзость запустения, М-79

ЗАПУСТИТЬ
запустить глаза ⟨глазенапа⟩, Г-75
запустить лапу, Р-343
запустить руку, Р-343
запустить словечко, С-315

ЗАПЯТОЙ
до последней запятой, З-70

ЗАРАЗИТЕЛЕН
дурной пример заразителен, П-535

ЗАРАЗИТЕЛЬНЫ
дурные примеры заразительны, П-535

ЗАРАСТАТЬ
зарастать грязью, Г-435
зарастать мохом, М-267

ЗАРАСТИ
зарасти грязью, Г-435
зарасти мохом, М-267

ЗАРЕВЕТЬ
зареветь белугой, Б-52

ЗАРЕЖЬ
хоть зарежь, З-71

ЗАРЕЖЬТЕ
хоть зарежьте, З-71

ЗАРЕЗАТЬ
без ножа зарезать, Н-185

ЗАРЕЗУ
до зарезу, З-72

ЗАРЖАВЕЕТ
не заржавеет, П-574

ЗАРИ
от зари до зари, З-73

ЗАРОДЫШЕ
в зародыше, З-74

ЗАРОНИТЬ
заронить зерно, И-76
заронить искру, И-76
заронить семя, И-76

ЗАРУБИТЬ
зарубить (себе) на лбу ⟨на носу⟩, Н-235

ЗАРЫВАТЬ
зарывать талант (в землю), Т-37

ЗАРЫТА
вот в чём собака зарыта, С-440
вот в этом и зарыта собака, С-440
вот где собака зарыта, С-440
вот здесь и зарыта собака, С-440
вот тут ⟨тут-то⟩ и зарыта собака, С-440

ЗАРЫТЬ
зарыть талант (в землю), Т-37

ЗАРЯ
ни свет ни заря, С-51

ЗАРЯБИЛО
зарябило в глазах, Г-131

ЗАСВЕРКАЛИ
только пятки засверкали, П-683

ЗАСЕСТЬ
гвоздём засесть в голове ⟨в мозгу⟩, Г-12
засесть в голове ⟨в мозгу⟩, Г-12

ЗАСЛАБИЛА
гайка заслабила, Г-6

ЗАСЛУГАМ
по заслугам, З-75

ЗАСНУТЬ
заснуть вечным ⟨могильным, последним⟩ сном, С-432

ЗАСТАВИТЬ
заставить себя ждать, З-77
не заставить себя долго ждать, З-78

не заставить себя долго просить ⟨упрашивать⟩, З-76
не заставить себя ждать, З-78

ЗАСТАВЛЯТЬ
заставлять себя ждать, З-77
не заставлять себя (долго) ждать, З-78

ЗАСТАТЬ
застать врасплох, З-79

ЗАСТЁГНУТ(ЫЙ)
застёгнут(ый) на все пуговицы, П-624

ЗАСТИГНУТЬ
застигнуть врасплох, З-79

ЗАСТРЕВАТЬ
застревать в горле, Г-334

ЗАСТРЯЛ
клубок в горле застрял, К-142
ком(ок) в горле застрял, К-142

ЗАСТРЯТЬ
застрять в горле, Г-334

ЗАСТУПАТЬ
заступать дорогу, Д-280

ЗАСТУПИТЬ
заступить дорогу, Д-280

ЗАСТЫВАЕТ
кровь застывает в жилах, К-405

ЗАСТЫЛА
кровь застыла (в жилах), К-405

ЗАСУЧИВ
засучив рукава, Р-239

ЗАСЫПКУ
на засыпку, З-80

ЗАТАИВ
затаив дыхание, Д-442

ЗАТАПТЫВАТЬ
затаптывать в грязь, Г-432

ЗАТАЩИТЬ
затащить на аркане, А-39

ЗАТЕЙ
без затей, З-81

ЗАТЕМ
затем что, З-82

ЗАТКНУТЬ
заткнуть глотку, Г-147
заткнуть горло, Г-147
заткнуть дыру ⟨дыры⟩, Д-441
заткнуть за пояс, П-466
заткнуть прорехи ⟨прореху⟩, Д-441
заткнуть рот, Р-176
заткнуть фонтан, Ф-18

ЗАТОПТАТЬ
затоптать в грязь, Г-432

ЗАТРАГИВАТЬ
затрагивать за живое, Ж-30

ЗАТРОНУТЬ
затронуть (за) больную струну, С-649

затронуть за живое, Ж-30
затронуть (за) чувствительную струну, С-649

ЗАТРЯСЛИСЬ
поджилки затряслись, П-242

ЗАТЫКАТЬ
затыкать глотку, Г-147
затыкать горло, Г-147
затыкать дыру ⟨дыры⟩, Д-441
затыкать прорехи ⟨прореху⟩, Д-441
затыкать рот, Р-176

ЗАТЫЛКАХ
чесать в затылках, З-84

ЗАТЫЛКЕ
глаза на затылке, Г-53
чесать в затылке, З-84

ЗАТЫЛКИ
чесать затылки, З-84

ЗАТЫЛОК
в затылок, З-83
чесать затылок, З-84

ЗАТЫЧКА
к каждой бочке затычка, Б-191
ко всякой бочке затычка, Б-191

ЗАТЯНУТЬ
затянуть на аркане, А-39

ЗАХВАТИЛО
дух захватило, Д-345
дыхание захватило, Д-345

ЗАХВАТЫВАЕТ
дух захватывает, Д-345
дыхание захватывает, Д-345

ЗАХОДИТ
мозга за мозгу заходит, М-218
ум за разум заходит, У-79

ЗАХОДИТСЯ
сердце заходится, С-137

ЗАХОДИТЬ
заходить в тупик, Т-237
заходить (слишком) далеко, З-85
заходить ходенём ⟨ходнем, ходором⟩, Х-73
заходить ходуном, Х-73

ЗАХОТЕЛ
ишь чего захотел, Х-92
многого захотел, Х-92

ЗАХОЧЕТ
левая нога захочет, Н-119

ЗАЧЕСАЛИСЬ
руки зачесались, Р-324

ЗАЧЕСАЛСЯ
язык зачесался, Я-48

ЗАШЁЛ
ум за разум зашёл, У-79

ЗАШИБАТЬ
зашибать деньгу, Д-175
зашибать монету, Д-175

ЗАШИБИТЬ
зашибить деньгу, Д-175

продирать/продрать
зенки, Г-89
пучить ⟨пялить⟩ зенки,
Г-100
ЗЕРНО
заронить зерно, И-76
ЗЕТ
от а до зет, А-1
ЗИМ
сколько лет, сколько зим!,
Л-62
ЗИМОЙ
зимой снега ⟨снегу⟩ не
выпросишь, С-431
ЗИМУЮТ
знать, где раки зимуют,
Р-72
показать, где раки
зимуют, Р-73
узнать, где раки зимуют,
Р-74
ЗЛА
зла не держать, З-131
зла не помнить, З-131
любовь зла — полюбишь и
козла, Л-162
ЗЛАТОЙ
златой телец, Т-56
ЗЛАТЫЕ
златые горы, Г-359
ЗЛАЧНОЕ
злачное место, М-111
ЗЛО
зло берёт/взяло, З-132
зло разбирает/разобрало,
З-132
сорвать ⟨срывать⟩ зло,
З-133
употребить во зло, З-134
ЗЛОБА
злоба дня, З-135
ЗЛОБУ
на злобу дня, З-136
ЗЛОЙ
злой гений, Г-17
злой на язык, Я-12
злой язык, Я-13
ЗЛОСТИ
лопаться от злости, З-137
лопнуть от ⟨со⟩ злости,
З-138
ЗЛОСТЬ
злость берёт/взяла, З-132
злость разбирает/
разобрала, З-132
ЗЛЫЕ
злые языки, Я-55
ЗМЕЮ
отогревать/отогреть змею
за пазухой ⟨на груди⟩,
З-139
пригревать/пригреть
змею за пазухой ⟨на
груди⟩, З-139
согревать/согреть змею за
пазухой ⟨на груди⟩,
З-139
ЗМЕЯ
змея подколодная, З-140

ЗМИЯ
до зелёного змия, З-141
ЗНАЕМ
знаем мы вас!, З-142
ЗНАЕТ
аллах (его) знает, Б-93
бес его знает, Ч-89
бог его знает, Б-93
бог знает, Б-93, Б-94
бог знает как, Б-95
бог знает сколько, Б-96
бог знает что, Б-97
господь (его) знает, Б-93
знает кошка, чьё мясо
съела, К-343
кто (его) знает, З-143
леший его знает, Ч-89
не бог знает как, Б-115
не бог знает какой, Б-116
не бог знает сколько, Б-117
один бог ⟨господь-бог⟩
знает, Б-138
пёс его знает, Ч-89
слышал звон, да не знает,
где он, З-99
только и знает, З-144
хрен его знает, Ч-89
чёрт его душу знает, Ч-89
чёрт его знает, Ч-89
чёрт знает, Ч-90
чёрт знает где, Ч-91
чёрт знает сколько, Ч-92
чёрт знает что, Ч-93
чёрт знает что такое!,
Ч-93
шут его знает, Ч-89
это чёрт знает что такое!,
Ч-93
ЗНАЕТЕ
знаете ли, З-145
ну знаете ли, З-148
ЗНАЕШЬ
знаешь ли, З-145
как знаешь, З-146
не знаешь, где найдёшь,
где потеряешь, З-147
ну знаешь ли!, З-148
слышал звон, да не
знаешь, где он, З-99
ЗНАЙ
всяк сверчок знай свой
шесток, С-38
знай наших!, З-149
знай сверчок свой шесток,
С-38
знай себе, З-150
так и знай, З-151
то и знай, З-152
ЗНАЙТЕ
так и знайте, З-151
ЗНАК
в знак, З-153
в знак памяти, З-154
давать/дать знак, З-155
молчание — знак согласия,
М-244
подавать/подать знак,
З-155
поставить знак равенства,
З-156

ставить знак равенства,
З-156
ЗНАКОМ
под знаком, З-157
ЗНАКОМСТВА
с первого знакомства,
З-158
ЗНАКОМСТВО
шапочное ⟨шляпочное⟩
знакомство, З-159
ЗНАКОМСТВУ
по знакомству, З-160
ЗНАКОМЫЙ
шапочный знакомый, З-161
ЗНАЛА
не знала баба горя, (так)
купила (баба) порося,
Б-2
ЗНАМЁНА
встать под знамёна, З-167
становиться/стать под
знамёна, З-167
ЗНАМЕНАТЕЛЮ
привести ⟨приводить⟩ к
единому ⟨к общему, к
одному⟩ знаменателю,
З-162
ЗНАМЕНЕМ
под знаменем, З-163
ЗНАМЕНИЕ
знамение времени, З-164
ЗНАМЯ
встать под знамя, З-167
высоко держать знамя,
З-165
поднимать/поднять
знамя, З-166
становиться/стать под
знамя, З-167
ЗНАТЬ
давать знать, Д-3
давать о себе знать, Д-4
давать себя знать, Д-7
дать знать, Д-3
дать о себе знать, Д-4
дать себя знать, Д-7
знать все ходы-выходы
⟨ходы и выходы⟩, Х-74
знать, где раки зимуют,
Р-72
знать меру, М-83
знать не знаю (, ведать не
ведаю), З-168
знать не хочу, З-169
знать про себя, З-170
знать прок, Т-138
знать своё место, М-112
знать себе цену, Ц-31
знать счёт деньгам, С-702
знать толк, Т-138
знать цену, Ц-32
знать цену деньгам
⟨копейке⟩, Ц-33
износу не знать, И-53
интересно знать, З-171
как знать, З-172
много будешь знать —
скоро состаришься,
З-173
надо (и) совесть знать,
С-456

надо (и) честь знать, Ч-137
не знать женщин ⟨ни
одной женщины⟩, Ж-18
не знать, куда глаза
девать/деть, Г-83
не знать, куда деваться/
деть себя ⟨деться⟩, З-174
не знать, куда себя девать/
деть, З-175
не знать, на каком свете,
С-72
не знать никакого удержу,
У-44
не знать покою ⟨покоя⟩,
П-288
не знать счёта деньгам,
С-717
не знать удержу, У-44
не знать устали, У-144
не могу знать, М-209
пора (и) совесть знать,
С-456
пора (и) честь знать, Ч-137
почём знать, З-172
почём мне знать, З-176
сносу не знать, И-53
совесть знать надо, С-454
ЗНАЧИТ
что значит, З-177
что сей сон значит?, С-486
ЗНАЧИТЬ
ничего не значить, З-178
ЗНАЮ
знать не знаю (, ведать не
ведаю), З-168
как не знаю кто, З-179
почём я знаю, З-176
ЗНАЯ
не зная броду, не суйся в
воду, Б-211
ЗОЛ
из двух зол меньшее, З-180
ЗОЛОТА
на вес золота, В-60
ЗОЛОТАЯ
золотая рота, Р-185
золотая свадьба, С-26
золотая середина, С-151
ЗОЛОТЕ
купаться в золоте, З-181
ЗОЛОТИТЬ
золотить пилюлю, П-147
ЗОЛОТНИК
мал золотник, да дорог,
З-182
ЗОЛОТО
не всё то золото, что
блестит, З-183
слово — серебро, молчание
– золото, С-329
ЗОЛОТОЕ
золотое дно, Д-207
ЗОЛОТОЙ
золотой дождь, Д-231
золотой мешок, М-143
золотой телец, Т-56
золотой фонд, Ф-17
на блюдечке с золотой
каёмочкой, Б-84
ЗОЛОТЫЕ
золотые горы, Г-359

золотые руки, Р-289

ЗОНДИРОВАТЬ
зондировать почву, П-452

ЗОНТИК
как рыбе ⟨рыбке⟩ зонтик,
Р-384

ЗРЕНИЯ
под углом зрения, У-15
поле зрения, П-297
точка зрения, Т-176
угол зрения, У-34

ЗРЯ
зря хлеб есть, Х-30
почём зря, П-457

ЗУБ
видит око, да зуб неймёт,
О-89
вострить зуб, З-204
за чужой щекой зуб не
болит, Щ-3
зуб на зуб не попадает,
З-184
иметь зуб, З-185
на один зуб, З-186
ни на зуб ⟨ногой⟩, З-187
ни в зуб толкнуть, З-187
око за око зуб за зуб, О-88
острить зуб, З-204
попадать(ся) на зуб, З-194
попасть(ся) на зуб, З-194
точить зуб, З-204
хоть видит око, да зуб
неймёт, О-89

ЗУБАМ
не по зубам, З-188

ЗУБАМИ
держать язык за зубами,
Я-9
зубами держаться, З-189
щёлкать зубами, З-190

ЗУБАХ
навязнуть в зубах, З-191

ЗУБКИ
почесать ⟨чесать⟩ зубки,
З-205

ЗУБОВ
до зубов, З-192

ЗУБОВНЫЙ
скрежет зубовный, С-236

ЗУБОВНЫМ
со скрежетом зубовным,
С-236

ЗУБОК
на зубок, З-193
попадать(ся) на зубок,
З-194
попасть(ся) на зубок, З-194

ЗУБЫ
в зубы, З-195
вострить зубы, З-204
глаза и зубы разгорелись,
Г-63
дарёному ⟨даровому⟩
коню в зубы не смотрят,
К-272
заговаривать/заговорить
зубы, З-196
зубы на полку, З-198
зубы проесть, З-197
зубы разгорелись, Г-63

зубы съесть, З-197
класть зубы на полку,
З-198
лезть к чёрту в зубы, Ч-112
ломать зубы, З-199
обломать зубы, З-199
острить зубы, З-204
показать ⟨показывать⟩
зубы, З-200
полезть к чёрту в зубы,
Ч-112
положить зубы на полку,
З-198
почесать зубы, З-205
разжать ⟨разжимать⟩
зубы, Г-441
скалить зубы, З-201
сквозь зубы, З-202
сломать зубы, З-199
стиснуть зубы, З-203
точить зубы, З-204
хоть к чёрту в зубы, Ч-118
чесать зубы, З-205

ЗУДЯТ
руки зудят, Р-324

ЗЮЗЯ
как зюзя, З-206

И

ИВАН
Иван, не помнящий
родства, Р-136

ИВАНОВСКУЮ
во всю ивановскую, И-1

ИГОЛКА
иголка в сене, И-2
иголка в стогу сена, И-2
как* иголка в стоге ⟨в
стогу⟩ сена, И-2
куда иголка, туда и нитка,
И-3
не иголка, И-4

ИГОЛКАХ
как* на иголках, И-5

ИГОЛКИ
до иголки, И-6
иголки не подпустишь ⟨не
подточишь⟩, И-7
иголки негде воткнуть, И-8
иголки некуда воткнуть,
И-8
на иголки, Б-242
нельзя иголки подпустить
⟨подточить⟩, И-7
с иголки, И-9

ИГОЛКОЙ
как нитка с иголкой, Н-97

ИГОЛКУ
иголку негде воткнуть, И-8
иголку некуда воткнуть,
И-8

ИГОЛОЧКИ
с иголочки, И-9

ИГОЛЬНОЕ
легче верблюду пройти в
⟨сквозь⟩ игольное ушко,
В-35

ИГРА
игра в бирюльки, Б-68

игра в жмурки, П-610
игра в кошки-мышки,
К-347
игра в молчанку, М-247
игра в прятки, П-610
игра в слова, С-297
игра воображения, И-10
игра не стоит свеч, И-11
игра природы, И-12
игра слов, И-13
игра словами, С-297
игра случая, И-14
игра судьбы, И-14

ИГРАЕТ
кровь играет (в жилах),
К-403

ИГРАТЬ
играть в бирюльки, Б-68
играть в жмурки, П-610
играть в загадки, З-27
играть в кошки-мышки,
К-347
играть в молчанки ⟨в
молчанку⟩, М-247
играть в опасную игру,
И-15
играть в прятки, П-610
играть в слова, С-297
играть в четыре руки,
Р-290
играть ва-банк, И-25
играть вторую скрипку,
С-239
играть глазами, Г-108
играть жизнью (и
смертью), Ж-66
играть на нервах, Н-80
играть на публику, П-623
играть на руку, Р-344
играть первую роль, Р-155
играть первую скрипку,
С-240
играть роль, Р-156
играть с огнём, О-57
играть своей жизнью,
Ж-66
играть словами, С-297
играть со смертью, Ж-66
играть труса, Т-222
играть комедию, К-215
не играть (никакой) роли,
Р-152

ИГРЕ
делать/сделать весёлую
⟨хорошую⟩ мину при
плохой игре, М-167

ИГРЕЦ
и швец, и жнец, и в дуду
⟨и на дуде⟩ игрец, Ш-42

ИГРУ
играть в опасную игру,
И-15
раскрывать/раскрыть
игру, И-16

ИГРУШКА
детская игрушка, И-18
как ⟨словно⟩ игрушка,
И-17

ИГРУШКИ
детские игрушки, И-18

ИГРЫ
выйти ⟨выходить⟩ из
игры, И-19

ИДЕЕ
по идее, И-20

ИДЁТ
в глотку не идёт, К-491
в горло не идёт, К-491
голова идёт кругом, Г-204
дело идёт, Д-84, Р-114
дым идёт коромыслом,
Д-436
дым идёт столбом, Д-436
если гора не идёт к
Магомету, то Магомет
идёт к горе, Г-315
идёт на лад, Л-9
кусок в глотку не идёт,
К-491
кусок в горло не идёт,
К-491
мороз по коже ⟨по спине⟩
идёт, М-258
не идёт в голову, Г-265
не идёт из головы, Г-291
не идёт из памяти ⟨из
ума⟩, Г-291
не идёт на ум, Г-265
речь идёт, Р-114

ИДЕЯ
идея фикс, И-21

ИДИ
иди (куда) подальше!,
И-23
иди ты (куда) подальше!,
И-23
иди ты!, И-22

ИДИЛЛИЯ
аркадская идиллия, И-24

ИДИТЕ
идите вы (куда)
подальше!, И-23
идите (куда) подальше!,
И-23

ИДТИ
дальше идти некуда, Н-74
идти в гору, Г-351
идти в дело, Х-53
идти в Каноссу, К-53
идти в люди, Л-170
идти в ногу, Н-170
идти в огонь и в воду, О-64
идти в руки, Р-303
идти в ход, Х-53
идти ва-банк, И-25
идти вниз, Г-352
идти впрок, И-26
идти вразрез, И-27
идти к венцу, В-31
идти к делу, Д-145
идти к чёртовой матери,
Ч-113
идти к чёрту, Ч-113
идти к чертям (собачьим),
Ч-113
идти ко всем чертям, Ч-113
идти ко дну, Д-209
идти на дно, Д-209
идти на крайность, К-362
идти на мировую, М-187

идти на панель, П-51
идти на поводу, П-223
идти на попятную, П-357
идти на попятный (двор),
  П-357
идти на рожон, Р-145
идти на убыль, У-7
идти на удочку, У-52
идти навстречу, И-28
идти напролом, И-29
идти насмарку, И-30
идти по линии
  наименьшего
  сопротивления, Л-73
идти по миру, М-190
идти по наклонной
  плоскости, П-197
идти по пути наименьшего
  сопротивления, Л-73
идти по следам, С-599
идти по стопам, С-599
идти под венец, В-31
идти под горку ⟨гору⟩,
  Г-352
идти под откос, О-150
идти под уклон, Г-352
идти прахом, П-498
идти против совести,
  С-449
идти против течения, Т-97
идти прямой дорогой,
  Д-272
идти прямым путём,
  Д-272
идти с сумой, М-190
идти своей дорогой, Д-273
идти своим путём, Д-273
идти шаг в шаг, Н-170
не идти в сравнение, С-531
не идти в счёт, С-707
не идти дальше, И-31
не идти ни в какое
  сравнение, С-531
ИДУ
  иду на вы, В-353
ИДУТ
  дела идут, контора пишет,
    Д-55
  слова не идут с языка,
    С-292
ИЕРИХОНСКАЯ
  иерихонская труба, Т-205
ИЖЕ
  и иже с ним ⟨с ними⟩,
    И-32
ИЖИЦУ
  прописать ижицу, И-33
ИЖИЦЫ
  от аза до ижицы, А-1
ИЗБА
  не красна изба углами, а
    красна пирогами, И-34
ИЗБАВИ
  избави бог ⟨боже,
    господи⟩, Б-143
ИЗБЕЖАНИЕ
  во избежание, И-35
ИЗБИЕНИЕ
  избиение младенцев, И-36
ИЗБИРАТЬ
  избирать благую часть,
    Ч-29

ИЗБИТАЯ
  избитая дорога
    ⟨дорожка⟩, Д-288
ИЗБРАННЫХ
  много званых, но мало
    избранных, З-88
ИЗБРАТЬ
  избрать благую часть,
    Ч-29
ИЗБУШКА
  избушка на курьих
    ножках, И-37
ИЗБЫ
  вынести ⟨выносить⟩ сор
    из избы, С-494
ИЗБЫТКЕ
  в избытке, И-38
ИЗБЫТКОМ
  с избытком, И-38
ИЗВЕСТНО
  как известно, И-39
  одному аллаху известно,
    Б-138
  одному богу известно,
    Б-138
  одному господу известно,
    Б-138
  одному чёрту известно,
    Ч-115
ИЗВЕСТНОЕ
  известное дело, Д-106
ИЗВЕСТНОМ
  держать в известном
    отдалении, Р-84
  держать на известном
    расстоянии, Р-84
  держаться в известном
    отдалении, Р-85
  держаться на известном
    расстоянии, Р-85
ИЗВЕСТНОСТЬ
  поставить ⟨ставить⟩ в
    известность, И-40
ИЗВИВАТЬСЯ
  извиваться ужом, У-56
ИЗВИНИ
  извини за выражение,
    В-372
  извини подвинься, И-41
  нет, извини, И-42
  нет, уж ⟨это⟩ извини, И-42
ИЗВИНИТЕ
  извините за выражение,
    В-372
  извините подвиньтесь,
    И-41
  нет, извините, И-42
  нет, уж ⟨это⟩ извините,
    И-42
ИЗВЛЕКАТЬ
  извлекать на свет (божий),
    С-47
ИЗВЛЕЧЬ
  извлечь на свет (божий),
    С-47
ИЗВОДИТЬ
  изводить порох, П-380
ИЗВОЗЧИК
  как извозчик, И-43

ИЗВОЛИТЕ
  изволите видеть, И-45
  чего изволите, И-44
ИЗВОЛИШЬ
  изволишь видеть, И-45
ИЗВОЛЬТЕ
  извольте радоваться, И-46
ИЗДАЛЕКА
  начать ⟨начинать⟩
    издалека, Н-42
  рыбак рыбака видит
    издалека, Р-383
ИЗДЕРЖКИ
  ввести ⟨вводить⟩ в
    издержки, Р-89
ИЗДЫХАНИИ
  при последнем издыхании,
    И-47
ИЗДЫХАНИЯ
  до последнего издыхания,
    Д-443
ИЗЖИВАТЬ
  изживать себя, И-48
ИЗЖИТЬ
  изжить себя, И-48
ИЗЛИВАТЬ
  изливать душу, Д-422
ИЗЛИТЬ
  излить душу, Д-422
ИЗЛИШКОМ
  с излишком, И-49
ИЗЛИШНИ
  комментарии излишни,
    К-217
ИЗМЕНИТЬ
  изменить (самому) себе,
    И-50
ИЗМЕНИТЬСЯ
  измениться в лице, Л-91
ИЗМЕНЯЕТ
  если память не изменяет,
    П-43
ИЗМЕНЯТЬ
  изменять (самому) себе,
    И-50
ИЗМОР
  брать/взять на измор,
    И-51
ИЗМОРОМ
  брать/взять измором,
    И-51
ИЗМОТАТЬ
  измотать нервы, Н-83
ИЗНОС
  на износ, И-52
ИЗНОСА
  износа нет, И-53
ИЗНОСУ
  износу не знать, И-53
  износу нет, И-53
ИЗОБИЛИЯ
  рог изобилия, Р-121
ИЗРУБИТЬ
  изрубить в капусту, К-68
  изрубить в лапшу, К-68
ИЗЮМА
  не фунт изюма, Ф-32
ИЗЮМУ
  не фунт изюму, Ф-32

ИКРУ
  метать икру, И-54
ИМ
  имя (же) им легион, И-63
ИМЕЕМ
  что имеем, не храним,
    потерявши, плачем,
    И-55
ИМЕЕТСЯ
  (своя) рука имеется, Р-345
ИМЕЙ
  имей совесть, С-454
  не имей сто рублей, (а)
    имей сто друзей, Р-199
ИМЕЙТЕ
  имейте совесть, С-454
ИМЕНА
  склонять имена, П-2
ИМЕНАМИ
  назвать ⟨называть⟩ вещи
    настоящими ⟨своими,
    собственными⟩
    именами, В-88
ИМЕНЕМ
  с именем, И-56
ИМЕНИ
  от имени, И-57
ИМЕНИННИК
  сидеть как именинник,
    И-58
ИМЕНИННИКОМ
  смотреть именинником,
    И-59
ИМЕНИННИЦА
  сидеть как именинница,
    И-58
ИМЕНИННИЦЕЙ
  смотреть именинницей,
    И-59
ИМЕНИНЫ
  чёрствые именины, И-60
ИМЕТЬ
  в мыслях не иметь, М-317
  иметь в виду, В-138
  иметь вес, В-59
  иметь виды, В-143
  иметь голову на плечах,
    Г-205
  иметь дело, Д-107
  иметь зуб, З-185
  иметь место, М-113
  иметь на примете, П-536
  иметь под собой почву,
    П-453
  иметь почву под ногами,
    П-450
  иметь руку, Р-345
  иметь сердце, С-131
  иметь твёрдую почву под
    ногами, П-450
  иметь честь, Ч-133
  не иметь ничего общего,
    О-33
  не иметь понятия, П-342
  ничего не иметь против,
    И-61
  совесть иметь надо, С-454
ИМЕЮ
  имею честь быть

〈пребывать,
    оставаться〉, Ч-134
честь имею, Ч-140
честь имею кланяться,
    Ч-140

ИМЕЮТ
(и) стены имеют уши,
    С-559

ИМЯ
во имя, И-62
имя (же) им легион, И-63
на имя, И-64
сделать себе имя, И-65
склонять имя, П-2
составить себе имя, И-65

ИНАЧЕ
иначе говоря, Г-170
не иначе (как), И-66
так или иначе, Т-19

ИНАЯ
иная музыка, М-283

ИНВАЛИД
инвалид пятого пункта,
    И-67
инвалид пятой группы,
    И-67

ИНОЕ
иное дело, Д-98
не что иное, как…, Ч-170

ИНОЙ
иной коленкор, К-190
иной табак, К-190
иной раз, Р-21
не кто иной, как…, К-450
тот или иной, Т-173
отбывать/отбыть в иной
    мир, М-184
переселиться
    〈переселяться〉 в иной
    мир, М-184
уйти 〈уходить〉 в иной
    мир, М-184

ИНТЕРЕСА
из спортивного интереса,
    И-68

ИНТЕРЕСАХ
в интересах, И-69

ИНТЕРЕСЕ
при пиковом интересе,
    И-70

ИНТЕРЕСНО
интересно знать, З-171

ИНТЕРЕСНОМ
в интересном положении,
    П-310

ИНЫМИ
взглянуть иными глазами,
    Г-120
глядеть иными глазами,
    Г-120
иными словами, С-296
поглядеть иными глазами,
    Г-120
посмотреть 〈смотреть〉
    иными глазами, Г-120

ИОВ
Иов многострадальный,
    И-71

ИРОНИИ
по иронии судьбы, И-72

ИРОНИЯ
ирония судьбы, И-72

ИСКАТЕЛЬ
искатель приключений,
    И-73

ИСКАТЕЛЬНИЦА
искательница
    приключений, И-73

ИСКАТЬ
искать вчерашнего дня
    〈вчерашний день〉,
    Д-160
недалеко искать, Х-58
искать руки, Р-307

ИСКЛЮЧЕНИЕМ
за исключением, И-74

ИСКРА
искра божья, И-75

ИСКРОШИТЬ
искрошить в лапшу, К-68

ИСКРУ
заронить искру, И-76

ИСКРЫ
искры из глаз посыпались,
    И-77

ИСКУССТВА
по всем правилам
    искусства, П-486

ИСКУССТВОВЕД
искусствовед в штатском,
    И-78

ИСКУССТВУ
из любви к искусству,
    Л-159

ИСКУШАТЬ
искушать провидение,
    С-665
искушать судьбу, С-665

ИСПЕЧЁН
испечён из другого 〈не из
    того〉 теста, Т-89

ИСПЕЧЁННЫЙ
вновь испечённый, И-79

ИСПЕЧЕНЫ
испечены из одного (и того
    же) теста, Т-90
испечены из разного теста,
    Т-89
испечены из того же теста,
    Т-90

ИСПИТЬ
испить горькую чашу (до
    дна), Ч-39
испить (до дна) горькую
    〈полную〉 чашу, Ч-39
испить чашу (до дна), Ч-39

ИСПОКОН
испокон века, В-22

ИСПОРТИТЬ
испортить воздух, В-205
испортить крови, К-408
испортить музыку, О-1
испортить нервы, Н-83
испортить обедню, О-1
испортить себе крови,
    К-409

ИСПОРТИШЬ
каши 〈кашу〉 маслом не
    испортишь, К-116

ИСПРАВИТ
горбатого могила
    исправит, Г-319

ИСПУГ
брать/взять на испуг, И-80

ИСПУГОМ
отделаться
    〈отделываться〉 лёгким
    испугом, И-81

ИСПУСКАТЬ
испускать последний
    вздох, Д-346

ИСПУСТИТЬ
испустить дух, Д-346
испустить последний
    вздох, Д-346

ИСПЫТЫВАТЬ
испытывать провидение,
    С-665
испытывать судьбу, С-665
испытывать терпение,
    Т-79

ИСТЕРЕТЬ
истереть в (мелкий)
    порошок, П-386

ИСТИНА
азбучная истина, И-82
прописная истина, И-83

ИСТИННОГО
сбивать с пути истинного,
    П-650
сбиваться с пути
    истинного, П-651
сбить с пути истинного,
    П-650
сбиться с пути истинного,
    П-651

ИСТИННОЕ
показать своё истинное
    лицо, Л-98

ИСТИННЫЙ
направить 〈направлять〉
    на путь истинный,
    П-658
наставить 〈наставлять〉
    на путь истинный,
    П-658
обратиться на путь
    истинный, П-659
обратить 〈обращать〉 на
    путь истинный, П-658

ИСТИНЫ
доля истины, Д-249
направить 〈направлять〉
    на путь истины, П-658
наставить 〈наставлять〉
    на путь истины, П-658
обратиться на путь
    истины, П-659
обратить 〈обращать〉 на
    путь истины, П-658
сбивать с пути истины,
    П-650
сбиваться с пути истины,
    П-651
сбить с пути истины,
    П-650
сбиться с пути истины,
    П-651

ИСТОРИИ
на свалке истории, С-30

на свалку истории, С-30
повернуть колесо истории
    вспять 〈назад〉, К-196

ИСТОРИЮ
влипать/влипнуть в
    историю, И-85
войти в историю, И-84
попадать/попасть в
    историю, И-85

ИСТОРИЯ
вечная история, И-86
история с географией, И-87
история умалчивает, И-88
обычная история, И-86
совсем другая история,
    И-89

ИСТРАТИТЬ
истратить по мелочам 〈по
    мелочи〉, М-65

ИСТРЕПАТЬ
истрепать нервы, Н-83

ИСТУКАН
как истукан, И-90

ИСХОД
давать/дать исход, В-385

ИСХОДЕ
в исходе, И-91
на исходе, И-91

ИСХОДУ
к исходу, И-91

ИСЧЕЗАТЬ
исчезать из вида 〈виду〉,
    Г-42
исчезать из глаз, Г-42

ИСЧЕЗНУТЬ
исчезнуть из вида 〈виду〉,
    Г-42
исчезнуть из глаз, Г-42

ИТОГ
подвести 〈подводить〉
    итог, И-92

ИТОГЕ
в (конечном) итоге, И-93

ИТОГИ
подвести 〈подводить〉
    итоги, И-92

ИУДЕЙСКА
страха ради иудейска,
    С-629

ИУДИН
иудин поцелуй, П-447

ИУДИНО
иудино лобзание, П-447

ИУДЫ
поцелуй Иуды, П-447

ИХ
пускай их, П-639
пусть их, П-639

ИШЬ
ишь ты, Т-247
ишь чего захотел 〈хочет〉,
    Х-92

ИЩИ
ищи ветра в поле, В-74
ищи да свищи, В-74
ищи дурака 〈дураков〉!,
    Д-334
ищи дурочку 〈дуру〉!,
    Д-334

ищи-свищи (ветра в поле),
В-74
ИЩУТ
от добра добра не ищут,
Д-219

Й

ЙОТУ
и на йоту, Й-1
ни на (единую) йоту, Й-1
ни на одну йоту, Й-1
ЙОТЫ
ни (единой) йоты, Й-2
ни одной йоты, Й-2

К

КАБАЦКАЯ
голь кабацкая, Г-312
КАБЛУКОМ
под каблуком, К-1
КАБЛУЧКОМ
под каблучком, К-1
КАБЫ
если бы да кабы, Е-12
КАВЫЧКАХ
в кавычках, К-2
КАДИЛО
раздувать/раздуть кадило,
К-3
КАЁМОЧКОЙ
на блюдечке с голубой
〈золотой〉 каёмочкой,
Б-84
КАЖДАЯ
каждая собака, С-441
КАЖДОГО
всех и каждого, В-343
на каждого мудреца
довольно простоты,
М-279
КАЖДОЕ
взвесить 〈взвешивать〉
каждое слово, С-281
ловить каждое слово,
С-317
КАЖДОЙ
в каждой шутке есть доля
правды, Ш-102
дрожать над каждой
копейкой, К-281
к каждой бочке затычка,
Б-191
каждой твари по паре,
Т-46
трястись над каждой
копейкой, К-281
КАЖДОМ
на каждом шагу, Ш-18
КАЖДОМУ
всем и каждому, В-343
дай бог каждому, Б-110
каждому овощу своё
время, О-44
каждому своё, К-4
КАЖДУЮ
дрожать за каждую
копейку, К-281

считать каждую копейку,
К-285
трястись за каждую
копейку, К-281
КАЖДЫЙ
каждый божий день, Д-161
каждый встречный, В-347
каждый встречный и
поперечный 〈встречный-
поперечный〉, В-347
каждый дурак может/
сможет, Д-328
каждый по-своему с ума
сходит, У-82
КАЖЕТСЯ
небо в 〈с〉 овчинку
кажется, Н-53
КАЖИННЫЙ
кажинный раз на этом
(самом) месте, Р-22
КАЗАК
вольный казак, К-5
КАЗАЛОСЬ
казалось бы, К-6
как казалось, К-7
КАЗАНСКАЯ
казанская сирота, С-197
КАЗАНСКИЙ
казанский сирота, С-197
КАЗАТЬ
не казать глаз, Г-28
не казать носа 〈носу〉,
Н-226
КАЗАТЬСЯ
казаться на глаза, Г-87
КАЗЁННОЙ
по казённой надобности,
Н-13
КАЗНОЙ
тряхнуть казной, М-272
КАЗНЬ
египетская казнь, К-8
КАИНА
печать Каина, П-139
КАИНОВА
каинова печать, П-139
КАИНОВО
каиново клеймо, П-139
КАК
а как же!, К-9
а то как же!, К-9
бить как обухом по голове,
О-31
биться как рыба об лёд,
Р-378
бог знает как, Б-95
в белый свет как в
копеечку, С-40
в долгу как в шелку, Д-242
в то время как, В-302
везёт как утопленнику,
У-150
вертеться как белка в
колесе, Б-51
влетать/влететь как
бомба, Б-178
во как, К-10
вот как, К-10
вроде как, В-322

всё одно как, В-328
всё равно как, В-328
говорит как пишет, Г-160
гол как сокол, С-468
да ещё как, Е-27
дела как сажа бела, Д-56
до того как, Т-123
едва... как, Е-2
едва только... как, Е-2
ещё как, Е-27
и ещё как, Е-27
и как (ещё) земля держит
〈носит, терпит〉, З-126
и как только земля держит
〈носит, терпит〉, З-126
как аршин проглотил,
А-42
как аукнется, так и
откликнется, А-49
как банный лист, Л-78
как баран, Б-19
как баран на новые
ворота, Б-20
как без рук, Р-213
как белка в колесе, Б-51
как бельмо в 〈на〉 глазу,
Б-55
как бог на душу положит,
Б-113
как бог свят, Б-114
как божий день, Д-162
как бочка, Б-189
как будто (бы), К-11
как будто в чаду, Ч-1
как будто пелена падает (с
глаз), П-76
как будто пелена спадает/
спала (с глаз), П-76
как будто пелена упала (с
глаз), П-76
как будто подменили,
П-246
как будто покров падает (с
глаз), П-76
как будто покров спадает/
спал (с глаз), П-76
как будто покров упал (с
глаз), П-76
как будто с неба свалиться
〈упасть〉, Н-46
как будто язык проглотил,
Я-23
как бы..., К-12
как бы не..., К-13
как бы не так!, К-14
как бы ни..., К-16
как бы там 〈то〉 ни было,
Б-263
как бы чего не вышло,
В-392
как бык, Б-255
как был, Б-259
как в аптеке, А-35
как в воду глядел, В-184
как в воду канул, В-185
как в воду опущенный,
В-186
как в воду смотрел, В-184
как в котле вариться
〈кипеть〉, К-340
как в лесу, Л-61

как в прорву, П-579
как в стенку 〈в стену〉
горох 〈горохом〉, С-565
как в тёмном лесу, Л-61
как в тумане, Т-234
как в чаду, Ч-1
как вам сказать, С-205
как варом обдало, В-8
как верёвочке ни виться, а
конец будет, В-38
как ветром сдувало
〈сдуло, сдунуло〉, В-78
как видишь, В-132
как видно, В-133
как вкопанный, В-150
как водится, В-178
как водой смыло, В-180
как воздух, В-204
как вол, В-219
как волк, В-225
как волка ни корми, (а) он
(всё) в лес глядит
〈смотрит〉, В-228
как говорится, Г-164
как гора с плеч
(свалилась), Г-316
как горькая редька, Р-102
как грибы (после дождя),
Г-395
как гром среди ясного
неба, Г-405
как громом поразить
〈оглушить〉, Г-408
как дважды два (четыре),
Д-31
как две капли воды, К-59
как день, Д-162
как долго, Д-240
как дома, Д-254
как доска, Д-290
как дурак 〈дурень〉 с
(писаной) торбой, Т-161
как душе угодно, Д-382
как если бы, К-11
как есть, Е-16
как ещё земля держит
〈носит, терпит〉, З-126
как же, К-15
как же, как же, К-15
как живёте-можете
〈живёшь-можешь〉?,
Ж-28
как за каменной стеной,
С-567
как заведённая машина,
М-59
как заведённый, М-59
как земля держит 〈носит,
терпит〉, З-126
как зеницу ока, З-130
как знаешь, З-146
как знать, З-172
как зюзя, З-206
как иголка в стоге 〈в
стогу〉 сена, И-2
как игрушка, И-17
как из ведра, В-14
как из голодного края,
К-374
как из-за угла (пыльным)
мешком прибит(ый)

не видать как своих ушей,
У-181
не далее как ⟨чем⟩..., Д-13
не дальше как ⟨чем⟩...,
Д-13
не иначе как, И-66
не кто иной, как..., К-450
не успеешь ⟨не успел⟩...
как..., У-136
не что иное, как..., Ч-170
нет как нет, Н-91
обдирать/ободрать как
липку, Л-76
обирать/обобрать как
липку, Л-76
облупить как липку, Л-76
обчистить как липку, Л-76
перед тем как, Т-62
печь как блины, Б-81
по мере того как..., М-78
подобно тому как, П-249
поминай как звали, П-330
после того как, Т-132
потому как, П-435
равно как (и), Р-6
раз как-то, Р-24
рано пташечка запела, как
бы кошечка не съела,
П-612
руки как крюки, Р-317
с тех пор как, П-366
сидеть как барин, Б-24
сидеть как именинник
⟨именинница⟩, И-58
сил нет, как, С-170
слышно, как муха
пролетит, М-297
смотря как, С-422
стоять как столб, С-592
так же как (и), Т-15
так как, Т-20
тогда как, Т-118
только... как..., Т-147
только-только... как...,
Т-147
только что... как..., Т-147
точь-в-точь как, Т-189
тут как тут, Т-243
ударить ⟨ударять⟩ как
обухом по голове, О-31
чудо как..., Ч-201
щёлкать как орехи
⟨орешки⟩, О-100

КАКАЯ
какая компания, К-223
какая муха укусила, М-295
какая невидаль
⟨невидальщина⟩!, Н-65
какая печаль, П-138
какая разница?, Р-59

КАКИЕ
вот какие пироги, П-154
какие ветры занесли?, В-79
на какие шиши, Ш-69
ни в какие ворота (не
лезет), В-279
ни за какие блага (в мире),
Б-73
ни за какие деньги, Д-173
ни за какие коврижки,
К-153

ни за какие пряники, К-153
ни за какие сокровища (в
мире), Б-73

КАКИМ
за каким бесом, Ч-77
за каким дьяволом, Ч-77
за каким лешим, Ч-77
за каким чёртом, Ч-77
каким ветром (занесло)?,
В-79
каким глазом, Г-136
каким образом, О-20
ни под каким видом, В-134
ни под каким соусом,
С-502

КАКИМИ
какими ветрами
(занесло)?, В-79
какими глазами, Г-115,
Г-136
какими судьбами?, С-663
с какими глазами, Г-115

КАКИХ
до каких пор, П-358
с каких пор, П-363

КАКОВ
каков поп, таков и приход,
П-343
каков гусь!, Г-448

КАКОГО
какого беса?, Ч-103
какого дьявола?, Ч-103
какого лешего?, Ч-103
какого рожна, Р-143
какого чёрта?, Ч-103
какого шута?, Ч-103
для какого дьявола, Ч-77
для какого чёрта, Ч-77
на какого дьявола, Ч-77
на какого чёрта, Ч-77
на какого шута, Ч-77
с какого боку, Б-162
с какого боку подойти
⟨подступиться⟩, Б-163

КАКОЕ
какое дело, Д-108
какое там ⟨тут⟩!, К-21
кому какое дело, что кума
с кумом сидела, Д-109
наказание какое-то, Н-21
не идти ни в какое
сравнение, С-531

КАКОЙ
во какой, К-22
вот какой..., К-22
какой бы ни..., К-23
какой бы то ни было,
Б-264
какой ветер занёс?, В-79
какой может быть
разговор!, Р-50
какой ни..., К-23
какой ни (на) есть, Е-17
какой ни попало, П-350
какой-никакой, К-24
какой попало, П-350
какой придётся, П-350
какой разговор!, Р-50
какой такой..., К-25
какой там ⟨тут⟩...!, К-26

какой угодно, У-23
какой хотите, К-27
какой хочешь, К-27
какой чёрт, Ч-76
на какой конец?, К-234
на какой предмет?,
П-506
не ахти какой, А-52
не бог весть ⟨знает⟩
какой, Б-116
ни в какой мере, М-73
с какой радости?, Р-11
с какой стати?, С-550
с какой стороны подойти
⟨подступиться⟩, Б-163
смотря какой, С-422
хоть какой, К-27

КАКОМ
на каком основании?, О-113
не знать, на каком свете,
С-72
ни в каком разе, С-370
ни в каком случае, С-370

КАКУЮ
ни в какую, К-28

КАЛАНЧА
каланча пожарная, К-29

КАЛАЧ
тёртый калач, К-30

КАЛАЧИ
на калачи, О-99

КАЛАЧОМ
калачом не выманить,
К-31
калачом не заманить, К-32

КАЛЕНД
до греческих календ, К-33

КАЛЕНИЯ
довести ⟨доводить⟩ до
белого каления, К-34
дойти ⟨доходить⟩ до
белого каления, К-35

КАЛЁНЫМ
выжечь ⟨выжигать⟩
калёным железом, Ж-13

КАЛИФ
калиф на час, К-36

КАЛОШУ
посадить в калошу, Л-143
садиться в калошу, Л-142
сажать в калошу, Л-143
сесть в калошу, Л-142

КАМЕННОЙ
как за каменной стеной,
С-567

КАМЕННУЮ
как на каменную гору
⟨стену⟩, Г-353

КАМЕНЬ
бросать камень, К-37
бросать камень в огород,
К-47
бросить камень, К-37
вешать (себе) камень на
шею, К-38
держать камень за
пазухой, К-39
камень на душе, К-40
камень на сердце, К-40
камень на шее, К-41

камень преткновения, К-42
камень с души свалился,
К-43
камень с сердца свалился,
К-43
кидать камень, К-37
кидать камень в огород,
К-47
кинуть камень, К-37
краеугольный камень,
К-44
нашла коса на камень,
К-318
носить камень за пазухой,
К-39
повесить (себе) камень на
шею, К-38
под лежач(ий) камень (и)
вода не течёт, К-45
пробный камень, К-46
пускать/пустить камень,
К-37
сердце не камень, С-139

КАМЕНЬЯ
бросать каменья, К-37

КАМЕНЬЯМИ
бросать каменьями, К-37

КАМЕШЕК
бросать камешек в огород,
К-47
кидать камешек в огород,
К-47
камешек в огород, К-47

КАМЕШКИ
бросать камешки в огород,
К-47
кидать камешки в огород,
К-47
камешки в огород, К-47
подводные камешки, К-49

КАМНЕ
камня на камне не
оставить ⟨не
оставлять⟩, К-50
камня на камне не
осталось, К-50

КАМНЕМ
бросать/бросить камнем,
К-37
кидать/кинуть камнем,
К-37
пускать/пустить камнем,
К-37

КАМНИ
бросать камни в огород,
К-47
камни вопиют/возопили,
К-48
кидать камни в огород,
К-47
подводные камни, К-49

КАМНЯ
камня на камне не
оставить ⟨не
оставлять⟩, К-50
камня на камне не
осталось, К-50

КАМНЯМИ
забрасывать/забросать
камнями, Г-434

[903]

закидать ⟨закидывать⟩
камнями, Г-434

КАНВА
хронологическая канва,
К-51

КАНИТЕЛЬ
развести ⟨разводить⟩
канитель, К-52
тянуть канитель, К-52

КАНОССУ
идти/пойти в Каноссу,
К-53

КАНУЛ
как* в воду канул, В-185

КАНУТЬ
кануть в вечность, В-85
кануть в Лету, Л-68
кануть в прошлое, П-601
кануть в реку забвения,
Л-68

КАНЦЕЛЯРИЯ
небесная канцелярия, К-54

КАНЦЕЛЯРСКАЯ
канцелярская крыса, К-434

КАПАТЬ
капать на мозги, М-224

КАПЕЛЬКИ
до (последней) капельки,
К-57
ни капельки, К-61

КАПЕЛЬКУ
на капельку, К-62
ни на капельку, К-61

КАПИТАЛ
капитал приобрести и
невинность соблюсти,
К-55

КАПЛЕ
капля по капле, К-65
по капле, К-65

КАПЛЕЙ
капля за каплей, К-65

КАПЛЕТ
не каплет, К-56

КАПЛИ
две капли воды, К-59
до капли, К-57
до последней капли, К-57
до последней капли крови,
К-58
как две капли воды, К-59
капли в рот не брать/не
взять, К-60
ни капли, К-61
ни капли в рот не брать/не
взять, К-60

КАПЛЮ
капля в каплю, К-63
на каплю, К-62
ни на каплю, К-61

КАПЛЯ
капля в каплю, К-63
капля в море, К-64
капля за каплей, К-65
капля моего мёду, К-66
капля, переполнившая
чашу, К-67
капля по капле, К-65
последняя капля, К-67

КАПЛЯМ
по каплям, К-65

КАПУСТУ
изрубить ⟨рубить⟩ в
капусту, К-68

КАРАНДАШ
брать/взять на карандаш,
К-69

КАРАНДАШЕ
в карандаше, К-70

КАРАУЛ
брать на караул, К-71
брать под караул, С-624
взять на караул, К-71
взять под караул, С-624
делать на караул, К-71
закричать караул, К-72
крикнуть караул, К-72
кричать караул, К-72
почётный караул, К-73
сделать на караул, К-71
хоть караул кричи, К-74

КАРАУЛОМ
под караулом, С-623

КАРАЧКАХ
на карачках, Ч-146

КАРАЧКИ
на карачки, Ч-146

КАРАЧУН
карачун пришёл, К-75

КАРГА
старая карга, К-76

КАРМАН
вытрясти карман, К-77
держи карман (шире),
К-78
за словом в карман не
лазит ⟨не лезет, не
полезет⟩, С-332
за словом в карман не
ходит, С-332
залезать/залезть в
карман, К-79
класть в карман, К-80
набивать/набить карман,
К-81
положить в карман, К-80
пустой карман, К-83
толстый карман, К-82
тугой карман, К-82
тощий карман, К-83

КАРМАНАХ
ветер (свистит) в
карманах, В-70

КАРМАНЕ
без гроша в кармане, Г-415
без копейки в кармане,
Г-415
в кармане, К-84
ветер (свистит) в кармане,
В-70
дуля в кармане, К-458
кукиш в кармане, К-458
фига в кармане, К-458
шиш в кармане, Ш-67

КАРМАНОМ
тряхнуть карманом, М-272

КАРМАНУ
бить по карману, К-85
не по карману, К-86

ударить ⟨ударять⟩ по
карману, К-85

КАРМАНЫ
вывернуть
⟨выворачивать⟩ (свои)
карманы, К-77

КАРТА
карта бита ⟨убита⟩, К-87
последняя карта, К-88

КАРТЕ
стоять на карте, К-89

КАРТИНКА
как картинка, К-90

КАРТИНКЕ
как на картинке, К-90
по картинке, К-91

КАРТОЧНЫЙ
карточный домик, Д-260

КАРТОШКА
не картошка, К-92

КАРТУ
побить карту, К-95
поставить всё на одну
карту, К-93
поставить на карту, К-94
ставить всё на одну карту,
К-93
ставить на карту, К-94
убить карту, К-95

КАРТЫ
держать карты к орденам,
К-96
(и) карты в руки, К-97
мешать (все) карты, К-98
открывать/открыть (свои)
карты, К-99
попутать (все) карты, К-98
путать (все) карты, К-98
раскрывать/раскрыть
(свои) карты, К-99
смешать (все) карты, К-98
спутать (все) карты, К-98

КАРЬЕР
с места в карьер, М-96

КАРЬЕРУ
делать/сделать карьеру,
К-100

КАСАЕТСЯ
что касается (, то...), К-101

КАССЫ
не отходя от кассы, К-102

КАТАНЬЕМ
не мытьём, так катаньем,
М-318

КАТАТЬСЯ
как сыр в масле кататься,
С-736
люби ⟨любишь⟩ кататься,
люби и саночки возить,
С-12
кататься от смеха ⟨от
хохота⟩, С-406
кататься с хохоту ⟨со
смеху⟩, С-406
словно сыр в масле
кататься, С-736

КАТИСЬ
катись колбаской
⟨колбасой⟩!, К-180

КАТИТЬ
катить бочку, Б-192

КАТИТЬСЯ
катиться вниз, Г-352
катиться по наклонной
плоскости, П-197
катиться по скользкой
дорожке, П-197
катиться под горку ⟨под
гору⟩, Г-352
катиться под откос, О-150
катиться под уклон, Г-352

КАТУШКУ
на всю катушку, К-103
на полную катушку, К-103

КАФТАН
Тришкин кафтан, К-104

КАЧАТЬ
качать права, П-470

КАЧЕСТВЕ
в качестве, К-105

КАША
берёзовая каша, К-106
гречневая каша сама себя
хвалит, К-107
заваривается/заварилась
каша, К-108
каша в голове, К-109
каша во рту, К-110

КАШИ
каши маслом не
испортишь, К-116
каши не сварить ⟨не
сваришь⟩, К-111
каши просят, К-112
мало каши ел/съел, К-113

КАШТАНЫ
таскать каштаны из огня,
К-114

КАШУ
заваривать/заварить
кашу, К-115
кашу маслом не
испортишь, К-116
расхлёбывать кашу, К-117
сам кашу заварил, сам и
расхлёбывай, К-118

КВАДРАТ
возвести ⟨возводить⟩ в
квадрат, К-119

КВАДРАТЕ
в квадрате, К-120

КВАДРАТУРА
квадратура круга, К-121

КВАС
перебиваться с хлеба на
квас, Х-41

КВАСНОЙ
квасной патриотизм, П-70

КВЕРХУ
кверху дном, Д-208
кверху ногами, Н-125
кверху тормашками
⟨тормашки⟩, Т-162
лапки кверху, Л-24
поднимать/поднять лапки
кверху, Л-24

КВИНТУ
вешать/повесить нос на
квинту, Н-208

КЕМ
за кем дело стало?, Д-103
с кем поведёшься, от того
и наберёшься, П-212

КЕРОСИНОМ
дело пахнет керосином,
Д-90

КИДАТЬ
кидать в жар (и в холод),
Ж-2
кидать взгляд, В-95
кидать грязью, Г-434
кидать жребий, Ж-83
кидать камень, К-37
кидать камень в огород,
К-47
кидать камешек
⟨камешки⟩ в огород,
К-47
кидать камнем, К-37
кидать камни в огород,
К-47
кидать на ветер, В-67
кидать тень, Т-73
кидать то в жар, то в
холод, Ж-2

КИДАТЬСЯ
кидаться в глаза, Г-45
кидаться в голову, Г-280
кидаться на шею, Ш-51
кидаться наутёк, П-637

КИЕВА
язык до Киева доведёт,
Я-36

КИЕВЕ
в огороде бузина, а в
Киеве дядька, О-68

КИНЕШЬ
куда ни кинешь взгляд(ом)
⟨глазом⟩, Г-137

КИНУЛАСЬ
краска кинулась в лицо,
К-400
кровь кинулась в голову,
К-399
кровь кинулась в лицо,
К-400

КИНУТЬ
кинуть в жар (и в холод),
Ж-2
кинуть взгляд, В-95
кинуть грязью, Г-434
кинуть жребий, Ж-83
кинуть камень ⟨камнем⟩,
К-37
кинуть на ветер, В-67
кинуть палку, П-11
кинуть тень, Т-73
кинуть якорь, Я-62

КИНУТЬСЯ
кинуться в глаза, Г-45
кинуться в голову, Г-280
кинуться в ноги, Н-141
кинуться на шею, Ш-51
кинуться наутёк, П-637

КИНЬ
куда ни кинь, везде ⟨всё,
всюду⟩ клин, К-136
куда ни кинь взгляд(ом)
⟨глазом⟩, Г-137

КИПЕТЬ
в котле вариться ⟨кипеть⟩,
К-340
как* в котле вариться
⟨кипеть⟩, К-340
кипеть ключом, К-145

КИПИТ
кровь кипит, К-403

КИРПИЧА
кирпича просит, К-122

КИСЕЙНАЯ
кисейная барышня, Б-25

КИСЕЛЕ
десятая ⟨седьмая⟩ вода на
киселе, В-175

КИСЕЛЬНЫЕ
молочные реки и
кисельные берега, Р-107
молочные реки, кисельные
берега, Р-107

КИСЕЛЯ
за семь вёрст киселя есть
⟨хлебать⟩, В-43

КИСЛАЯ
кислая мина, М-165

КИСЛЫХ
профессор кислых щей,
П-592

КИСТИ
выйти ⟨выходить⟩ из-под
кисти, К-123

КИСТОЧКОЙ
наше ⟨вам⟩ с кисточкой,
К-124
сорок одно с кисточкой,
К-124

КИСТЬЮ
владеть кистью, К-125

КИТАЙСКАЯ
китайская грамота, Г-372
китайская стена, С-560

КИТАЙСКИЕ
китайские церемонии, Ц-38

КИТАХ
на трёх китах, К-126

КИШЕТЬ
кишмя кишеть, К-127

КИШКА
кишка тонка ⟨тонкая⟩,
К-128

КИШКИ
выматывать/вымотать
(все) кишки, К-129
выпустить кишки, К-130
вытягивать/вытянуть
(все) кишки, К-129
надорвать ⟨надрывать⟩
кишки, Ж-33

КИШМЯ
кишмя кишеть, К-127

КЛАДЕЗЬ
кладезь премудрости, Б-47

КЛАДИ
палец ⟨пальца⟩ в рот не
клади, П-16

КЛАДУТ
краше в гроб кладут, Г-398

КЛАНЯТЬСЯ
кланяться в ноги ⟨в
ножки⟩, Н-145

кланяться в пояс, П-467
честь имею кланяться,
Ч-140

КЛАСС
показать ⟨показывать⟩
класс, К-131

КЛАСТЬ
класть в карман, К-80
класть в кубышку, К-452
класть во главу угла, Г-21
класть душу, Д-423
класть живот (свой), Ж-55
класть жизнь, Ж-55
класть зубы на полку,
З-198
класть на лопатки, Л-135
класть на месте, М-102
класть на музыку, М-285
класть на ноты, М-285
класть на обе лопатки,
Л-135
класть на чашку ⟨чашу⟩
весов, Ч-37
класть начало, Н-38
класть оружие, О-104
класть отпечаток, О-162
класть печать, О-162
класть под сукно, С-671
класть поклоны, П-280
класть с прибором, П-513
охулки на руку не класть,
О-180
похулы на руку не класть,
О-180
разжёвывать и в рот
класть, Р-181

КЛЕВАЛ
жареный петух не клевал,
П-130

КЛЕВАТЬ
клевать носом, Н-227

КЛЕЙМО
каиново клеймо, П-139

КЛЁПКИ
клёпки (в голове) не
хватает ⟨недостаёт⟩,
В-147

КЛЁПОК
клёпок (в голове) не
хватает ⟨недостаёт⟩,
В-147

КЛЕЩАМИ
клещами вытягивать,
К-133
клещами не вытащишь
⟨не вытянешь⟩, К-132
клещами тащить, К-133

КЛИКАТЬ
кликать клич, К-139

КЛИКНУТЬ
кликнуть клич, К-139

КЛИН
вбивать/вбить клин, К-134
клин клином выбивается
⟨выбивают⟩, К-135
клин клином вышибается
⟨вышибают⟩, К-135
куда ни кинь, везде ⟨всё,
всюду⟩ клин, К-136

КЛИНОМ
земля не клином сошлась,
С-58

клин клином выбивается
⟨выбивают⟩, К-135
клин клином вышибается
⟨вышибают⟩, К-135
клином не выколотишь ⟨не
вышибешь⟩, К-137
свет клином не сошёлся,
С-58
свет не клином сошёлся,
С-58

КЛИНЬЯ
подбивать/подбить
клинья, К-138

КЛИЧ
кликать/кликнуть клич,
К-139

КЛОК
с паршивой овцы хоть
шерсти клок, О-47

КЛОЧЬЯ
в ⟨на⟩ клочья, К-140

КЛУБНИЧКИ
(попользоваться) насчёт
клубнички, К-141

КЛУБОК
клубок в горле (застрял),
К-142
клубок в горле стоит,
К-142
клубок к горлу подступил
⟨подкатил(ся)⟩, К-142

КЛЮКВА
вот так клюква!, К-143
развесистая клюква, К-144

КЛЮНУЛ
жареный петух не клюнул,
П-130

КЛЮНУТЬ
клюнуть на удочку, У-52

КЛЮЧОМ
бить ключом, К-145
забить ключом, К-145
закипеть ключом, К-145
кипеть ключом, К-145

КЛЮЮТ
куры не клюют, К-487

КЛЯТВА
аннибалова
⟨аннибаловская⟩
клятва, К-146

КНИГА
книга за семью печатями,
К-147

КНИГИ
(и) книги в руки, К-97

КНИГУ
глядеть ⟨смотреть⟩ в
книгу и видеть фигу,
К-148

КНОПКИ
нажать ⟨нажимать⟩ (на
все) кнопки, К-149

КНУТА
политика кнута и пряника,
П-298

КНЯЗИ
из грязи (да) в князи, Г-431

КОБЕЛЮ
кобелю под хвост, П-611

КОБЕЛЯ
чёрного кобеля не отмоешь добела, К-150

КОБЫЛЕ
(не) пришей кобыле хвост, К-151

КОБЫЛЫ
бред сивой кобылы, Б-205

КОВЁР
вызвать ⟨вызывать⟩ на ковёр, К-152

КОВРИЖКИ
ни за какие коврижки, К-153

КОВЫРЯТЬ
в носу ковырять, Н-234

КОГДА
были когда-то и мы рысаками, Р-393
когда б(ы), К-154
когда бы ни..., К-155
когда бы то ни было, Б-265
когда как, К-156
когда ни..., К-155
когда ни попало, П-351
когда попало, П-351
когда придётся, П-351
когда рак (на горе) свистнет, Р-71
когда угодно, У-24
смотря когда, С-422

КОГО
кто кого, К-445
на кого похож, П-441
у кого что болит, тот о том и говорит, Б-170
что у кого болит, тот о том и говорит, Б-170

КОГОТКИ
показать ⟨показывать⟩ (свои) коготки, К-158

КОГТИ
в когти, Л-21
выпускать/выпустить когти, К-158
обломать когти, К-157
показать ⟨показывать⟩ (свои) когти, К-158
рвануть ⟨рвать⟩ когти, К-159

КОГТЯХ
в когтях, Л-21

КОЕЙ
ни в коей мере, М-73

КОЕМ
ни в коем разе, С-370
ни в коем случае, С-370

КОЖА
гусиная кожа, К-160
кожа да кости, К-161
одна кожа да кости, К-161

КОЖЕ
мороз по коже дерёт, М-258
мороз по коже идёт/ пошёл, М-258
мороз по коже подирает/ подрал, М-258
мороз по коже пробегает/ пробежал, М-258

мороз по коже продирает/ продрал, М-258
мороз по коже проходит/ прошёл, М-258
мурашки бегают ⟨бегут⟩ по коже, М-291
мурашки забегали по коже, М-291
мурашки заползали по коже, М-291
мурашки побежали по коже, М-291
мурашки ползают ⟨ползут/поползли⟩ по коже, М-291
мурашки пошли по коже, М-291
мурашки пробежали по коже, М-291

КОЖИ
из кожи (вон) вылезать ⟨лезть⟩, К-162
ни кожи ни рожи, К-163
ни кожи, ни рожи, ни ведения, К-163

КОЖУ
влезать/влезть в кожу, Ш-77

КОЗЕ
на козе не объедешь, К-387
на козе не подъедешь, К-164

КОЗЁЛ
козёл отпущения, К-165

КОЗЛА
драть козла, К-166
забивать/забить «козла», К-167
как от козла молока, К-168
любовь зла — полюбишь и козла, Л-162
пускать/пустить козла в огород, К-169
что от козла молока, К-168

КОЗЛИЩ
отделить ⟨отделять⟩ овец от козлищ, О-42

КОЗНИ
строить козни, К-170

КОЗУ
как сидорову козу, К-171

КОЗЫ
отставной козы барабанщик, К-172

КОЗЫРЁК
брать/взять под козырёк, К-173
делать/сделать под козырёк, К-173

КОЗЫРЕМ
ходить козырем, К-174

КОЗЫРИ
козыри в руках ⟨в руки⟩, К-175

КОЗЫРЬ
козырь в руках ⟨в руки⟩, К-175

КОЗЫРЯХ
при своих козырях, К-176

КОЗЬЯ
козья ножка, Н-187

КОИ
в кои ⟨кои-то⟩ веки, В-26

КОЙ
кой чёрт, Ч-76
на кой бес, Ч-77
на кой дьявол, Ч-77
на кой леший, Ч-77
на кой ляд, Ч-77
на кой пёс, Ч-77
на кой прах, Ч-77
на кой хрен, Х-102
на кой чёрт, Ч-77

КОЛ
вбить ⟨забить⟩ осиновый кол (в могилу), К-177
хоть кол на голове теши, К-178

КОЛА
ни кола ни двора, К-179

КОЛБАСКОЙ
катись колбаской!, К-180

КОЛБАСОЙ
катись колбасой!, К-180

КОЛЕБЛЕТСЯ
почва колеблется под ногами, П-448

КОЛЕИ
выбивать из колеи, К-181
выбиваться из колеи, К-182
выбить из колеи, К-181
выбиться из колеи, К-182
выйти ⟨выходить⟩ из колеи, К-182
вышибать/вышибить из колеи, К-181

КОЛЕНА
до седьмого колена, К-183
преклонить ⟨преклонять⟩ колена, К-184

КОЛЕНИ
колени подгибаются, К-188
падать/пасть на колени, Н-152
поставить на колени, К-185
преклонить ⟨преклонять⟩ колени, К-184
ставить на колени, К-185
становиться/стать на колени, К-186
упасть на колени, Н-152

КОЛЕНКАХ
слаб в коленках, К-187

КОЛЕНКИ
коленки дрожат, К-188
коленки подгибаются, К-188

КОЛЕНКОЙ
давать/дать коленкой под зад, К-189
коленкой под зад, К-189

КОЛЕНКОР
другой коленкор, К-190
иной коленкор, К-190
не тот коленкор, К-190

КОЛЕНО
море по колено, М-256

КОЛЕНОМ
давать/дать коленом под зад, К-189

коленом под зад, К-189

КОЛЕНЦА
выделывать коленца, К-191
выкидывать/выкинуть коленца, К-191
откалывать/отколоть коленца, К-191

КОЛЕНЦЕ
выделывать коленце, К-191
выкидывать/выкинуть коленце, К-191
откалывать/отколоть коленце, К-191

КОЛЕНЯХ
ползать на коленях, Н-133
стоять на коленях, К-192

КОЛЁСА
вставлять палки в колёса, П-9
подмазать ⟨подмазывать⟩ колёса, К-193
совать палки в колёса, П-9
ставить палки в колёса, П-9

КОЛЁСАХ
на колёсах, К-194
турусы на колёсах, Т-240

КОЛЕСЕ
(вертеться) как* белка в колесе, Б-51
кружиться ⟨крутиться⟩ как* белка в колесе, Б-51

КОЛЕСНИЦЕ
десятая спица в колеснице, С-520
последняя спица в колеснице, С-520
пятая спица в колеснице, С-520
пятое колесо в колеснице, К-197

КОЛЕСО
как немазаное ⟨неподмазанное, несмазанное⟩ колесо, К-195
повернуть колесо истории вспять ⟨назад⟩, К-196
пятое колесо в колеснице, К-197
пятое колесо в телеге, К-197

КОЛЕТ
правда глаза колет, П-477

КОЛЕТСЯ
(и) хочется и колется, Х-93

КОЛЕЮ
войти в колею, К-198
войти в обычную ⟨привычную⟩ колею, К-198
войти в свою колею, К-198
входить в колею, К-198
входить в обычную ⟨привычную⟩ колею, К-198
входить в свою колею, К-198
попадать в колею, К-198
попадать в обычную ⟨привычную⟩ колею, К-198

попадать в свою колею,
К-198
попасть в колею, К-198
попасть в обычную
⟨привычную⟩ колею,
К-198
попасть в свою колею,
К-198

КОЛИ
коли на то пошло, П-465
коли угодно, У-21
коли уж на то пошло,
П-465
хоть глаз ⟨глаза⟩ коли,
Г-43

КОЛОДЕЦ
не плюй в колодец,
пригодится воды
напиться, К-199

КОЛОДКУ
на одну колодку, К-200

КОЛОДУ
через пень колоду ⟨пень-
колоду⟩, П-84

КОЛОКОЛА
бить во все колокола,
К-201
зазвонить ⟨звонить⟩ в ⟨во
все⟩ колокола, К-202
колокола лить, К-203
раззвонить в ⟨во все⟩
колокола, К-202
растрезвонить в ⟨во все⟩
колокола, К-202
трезвонить в ⟨во все⟩
колокола, К-202
ударить ⟨ударять⟩ в ⟨во
все⟩ колокола, К-201

КОЛОКОЛЬНИ
глядеть со своей
колокольни, К-204
смотреть со своей
колокольни, К-204

КОЛОМ
встать колом в горле,
К-206
стать колом в горле, К-206
стоять колом, К-205
стоять колом в горле,
К-206

КОЛОМЕНСКАЯ
коломенская верста, В-45

КОЛОМЕНСКУЮ
в ⟨с⟩ коломенскую версту,
В-45

КОЛОННА
пятая колонна, К-207

КОЛОСС
колосс на глиняных ногах,
К-208

КОЛОТЬ
колоть глаз ⟨глаза⟩, Г-77

КОЛПАК
под стеклянный колпак,
К-209

КОЛПАКОМ
под стеклянным колпаком,
К-209

КОЛЫБЕЛИ
в колыбели, П-77

от колыбели, П-79
с колыбели, П-79
стоять у колыбели, К-210

КОЛЬ
коль на то пошло, П-465
коль скоро, С-235
коль уж на то пошло,
П-465

КОМ
ком в горле ⟨застрял⟩,
К-142
ком в горле стоит, К-142
ком к горлу подступил
⟨подкатил(ся)⟩, К-142

КОМАНДЕ
как по команде, К-211

КОМАНДОВАТЬ
командовать парадом,
П-58

КОМАР
комар носа ⟨носу⟩ не
подточил бы ⟨не
подточит⟩, К-212

КОМБИНАТОР
великий комбинатор, К-213

КОМБИНАЦИЯ
комбинация из трёх
пальцев, К-214

КОМЕДИЮ
играть комедию, К-215
ломать комедию, К-215
разыгрывать комедию,
К-215

КОМЕДИЯ
кукольная комедия, К-216

КОММЕНТАРИИ
комментарии излишни,
К-217

КОМОК
комок в горле ⟨застрял⟩,
К-142
комок в горле стоит, К-142
комок к горлу подступил
⟨подкатил(ся)⟩, К-142

КОМОМ
первый блин (всегда)
комом, Б-80

КОМПАНИИ
для компании, К-219
при всей честной
компании, Н-30

КОМПАНИЮ
водить компанию, К-218
за компанию, К-219
поддержать компанию,
К-220
составить компанию,
К-221

КОМПАНИЯ
и компания, К-222
какая компания, К-223
не компания, К-223
тёплая компания, К-224

КОМПАШКА
тёплая компашка, К-224

КОМУ
кому какое дело, что кума
с кумом сидела, Д-109
кому не лень, Л-51

кому поп, кому попадья, а
кому попова дочка,
П-344
кому только не лень, Л-51
расскажи ⟨рассказывай⟩
это кому-нибудь
другому, Б-7

КОН
поставить ⟨ставить⟩ на
кон, К-225

КОНДАЧКА
с кондачка, К-226

КОНДИЦИИ
до кондиции, К-227

КОНДРАТИЙ
кондратий хватил, К-228

КОНДРАШКА
кондрашка пришиб
⟨стукнул, хватил⟩,
К-228

КОНЕ
на коне, К-229

КОНЕЦ
в конец, К-230
в один конец, К-231
и делу конец, Д-104
и конец, К-232
из конца в конец, К-250
как верёвочке ни виться, а
конец будет, В-38
конец венчает дело, К-233
конец — (всему) делу
венец, К-233
на какой конец?, К-234
на худой конец, К-235
найти конец, М-201
найти свой конец, М-201
один конец, К-236
под конец, К-237
положить конец, К-238
сколько верёвочке ни
виться, а конец будет,
В-38

КОНЕЧНОМ
в конечном итоге, И-93
в конечном счёте, С-718

КОНКУРЕНЦИИ
вне конкуренции, К-239

КОНКУРСА
вне конкурса, К-239

КОНТОРА
дела идут, контора пишет,
Д-55
шарашкина контора, К-240

КОНТРА
про и контра, З-1

КОНФЕТКУ
сделать конфетку, К-241

КОНЦА
без конца, К-242
без конца и (без) краю
⟨края⟩, К-243
без конца-краю, К-243
в оба конца, К-244
до конца, К-245
до конца дней, К-247
до конца ногтей, К-246
до конца своих дней, К-247
до победного конца, К-248
довести ⟨доводить⟩ до
конца, К-249

из конца в конец, К-250
конца-краю ⟨конца и
краю⟩ не видать ⟨не
видно⟩, К-251
конца-краю ⟨конца и
краю⟩ несть ⟨нет⟩,
К-251
конца не видать ⟨не
видно⟩, К-251
конца несть ⟨нет⟩, К-251
не с того конца, К-252
ни конца ни краю не
видать ⟨не видно, несть,
нет⟩, К-251

КОНЦАМИ
концы с концами не
сходятся, К-259
концы с концами сходятся,
К-259
с концами, К-253
свести ⟨сводить⟩ концы с
концами, К-263
связать ⟨связывать⟩
концы с концами, К-263

КОНЦАХ
палка о двух концах, П-7

КОНЦЕ
в конце концов, К-254

КОНЦОВ
в конце концов, К-254
концов не найти ⟨не
сыскать⟩, К-255
со всех концов, К-256

КОНЦОМ
и дело с концом, Д-104

КОНЦУ
сколько верёвку
⟨верёвочку⟩ ни вить, а
концу быть, В-38

КОНЦЫ
во все концы, К-257
(и) концы в воду, К-258
концы с концами не
сходятся, К-259
концы с концами сходятся,
К-259
отдавать/отдать концы,
К-260, К-261
прятать концы (в воду),
К-262
свести ⟨сводить⟩ концы с
концами, К-263
связать ⟨связывать⟩
концы с концами, К-263
спрятать концы (в воду),
К-262
схоронить концы (в воду),
К-262
хоронить концы (в воду),
К-262

КОНЧАЕТСЯ
всё хорошо, что хорошо
кончается, К-264

КОНЧАТЬ
кончать век, Ж-56
кончать жизнь, Ж-56
кончать свой век, Ж-56

КОНЧАТЬСЯ
кончаться ничем, К-265

КОНЧЕН
(и) кончен бал, Б-12

КОРТОЧКАХ

на корточках, К-316

КОРТОЧКИ

на корточки, К-316

КОРЧИТЬ

корчить ваньку, Д-333

корчить дурака, Д-333

корчить дурочку, Д-333

корчить из себя шута, Ш-98

корчить рожи ⟨рожу⟩, Р-146

КОРЫТА

у разбитого корыта, К-317

КОРЫТУ

к разбитому корыту, К-317

КОСА

нашла коса на камень, К-318

КОСАЯ

косая сажень в плечах, С-3

КОСО

глядеть косо, С-416

смотреть косо, С-416

КОСТЕЙ

до костей, К-319

до мозга костей, М-217

костей не соберёшь ⟨не собрать⟩, К-320

куда ворон костей не заносил, В-271

язык без костей, Я-35

КОСТИ

башня из слоновой кости, Б-32

кожа да кости, К-161

кость от кости, П-202

мыть кости, К-327

одна кожа да кости, К-161

переломать (все) кости, К-321

перемывать/перемыть кости, К-327

пересчитать кости, Р-96

плоть от плоти и кость от кости, П-202

разминать/размять кости, К-322

сложить (свои) кости, К-323

КОСТОЧКА

военная косточка, К-324

рабочая косточка, К-325

солдатская косточка, К-324

КОСТОЧКАМ

разбирать/разобрать по косточкам, К-326

КОСТОЧКИ

мыть косточки, К-327

перемывать/перемыть косточки, К-327

разминать/размять косточки, К-322

КОСТЬ

белая кость, К-328

кость от кости, П-202

плоть от плоти и кость от кости, П-202

чёрная кость, К-329

КОСТЬМИ

лечь ⟨полечь⟩ костьми, К-330

КОСТЬЮ

встать костью в глотке ⟨в горле⟩, К-206

стать костью в глотке ⟨в горле⟩, К-206

стоять костью в глотке ⟨в горле⟩, К-206

КОСТЮМЕ

в костюме Адама, К-331

в костюме Евы, К-331

КОСТЯХ

на костях, К-332

КОСУЮ

в косую сажень, С-2

КОТ

как кот на сметану, К-333

кот в мешке, К-335

кот наплакал, К-334

КОТА

купить ⟨покупать⟩ кота в мешке, К-335

тянуть кота за хвост, К-336

КОТЁЛ

как пивной котёл, К-337

общий котёл, К-338

с пивной котёл, К-337

КОТЕЛОК

котелок варит, Г-199

КОТЛЕ

в котле вариться, К-340

в котле кипеть, К-340

вариться в котле, К-339, К-340

как* в котле вариться, К-340

как* в котле кипеть, К-340

КОТЛЕТУ

сделать (отбивную) котлету, О-128

КОТОРОМ

подрубать ⟨рубить⟩ сук, на котором сидишь, С-670

КОТОРЫЙ

в который раз, Р-18

который час, Ч-12

КОТОРЫХ

до которых пор, П-358

с которых пор, П-363

КОТУ

коту под хвост, П-611

не всё коту масленица (,бывает и великий пост), К-341

КОФЕЙНОЙ

гадание на кофейной гуще, Г-450

гадать на кофейной гуще, Г-450

КОЧЕРГА

ни богу свечка ⟨свеча⟩ ни чёрту кочерга, Б-137

КОШЕЛЁК

набивать/набить кошелёк, К-81

пустой кошелёк, К-83

толстый кошелёк, К-82

тощий кошелёк, К-83

тугой кошелёк, К-82

КОШЕЛЬ

развязать ⟨развязывать⟩ кошель, М-273

КОШЕЧКА

рано пташечка запела, как бы кошечка не съела, П-612

КОШКА

драная кошка, К-342

знает кошка, чьё мясо съела, К-343

как кошка с собакой, К-344

как угорелая кошка, К-345

кошка пробежала ⟨проскочила⟩, К-346

ободранная кошка, К-342

серая кошка пробежала ⟨проскочила⟩, К-346

чёрная кошка пробежала ⟨проскочила⟩, К-346

чует кошка, чьё мясо съела, К-343

КОШКЕ

кошке под хвост, П-611

КОШКИ

в темноте все кошки серы, К-349

игра в кошки-мышки, К-347

играть в кошки-мышки, К-347

кошки скребут на душе ⟨на сердце⟩, К-348

ночью все кошки серы, К-349

КРАЕМ

краем глаза, К-350

краем уха, К-351

КРАЕУГОЛЬНЫЙ

краеугольный камень, К-44

КРАЕШКОМ

краешком глаза, К-350

краешком уха, К-351

КРАЙ

бить через край, К-352

из края в край, К-373

литься через край, К-352

на край земли, К-353

на край света, К-353

непочатый край, К-354

обетованный край, З-127

переливать через край, К-355

переливаться через край, К-352

перехватить через край, К-355

хватать/хватить через край, К-355

хлебнуть через край, К-356

через край, К-357

КРАЙНЕЙ

по крайней мере, М-74

КРАЙНЕМ

в крайнем случае, С-359

КРАЙНИЙ

на крайний случай, С-374

КРАЙНОСТИ

вдаваться в крайности, К-358

впадать в крайности, К-358

до крайности, К-359

довести ⟨доводить⟩ до крайности, К-360

по крайности, М-74

прибегать/прибегнуть к крайности, К-362

КРАЙНОСТЬ

вдаваться/вдаться в крайность, К-361

впадать/впасть в крайность, К-361

идти/пойти на крайность, К-362

КРАПИВНОЕ

крапивное семя, С-117

КРАСЕ

во всей (своей) красе, К-363

КРАСЕН

долг платежом красен, Д-234

КРАСИВ

не родись красив, а родись счастлив, Р-135

КРАСИВЫЕ

за красивые глаза, Г-35

КРАСИВЫЙ

красивый жест, Ж-23

КРАСИВЫМ

не родись красивым, а родись счастливым, Р-135

КРАСИТ

не место красит человека, а человек место, М-118

КРАСКА

краска бросилась ⟨кинулась⟩ в лицо, К-400

КРАСКАМИ

мрачными красками, К-364

розовыми красками, К-364

чёрными красками, К-364

КРАСКАХ

в мрачных красках, К-364

в розовых красках, К-364

в чёрных красках, К-364

КРАСКИ

не скупиться/не поскупиться на краски, К-368

сгустить ⟨сгущать⟩ краски, К-365

КРАСКУ

бросает/бросило в краску, К-366

ввести ⟨вводить⟩ в краску, К-367

вгонять/вогнать в краску, К-367

КРАСНА

на людях и смерть красна, М-191

на миру и смерть красна,
М-191

не красна изба углами, а
красна пирогами, И-34

КРАСНАЯ

красная девица ⟨девка,
девушка⟩, Д-49

красная цена, Ц-26

КРАСНЕЕТ

бумага не краснеет, Б-243

КРАСНОГО

для красного словца, С-339

подпускать/подпустить
красного петуха, П-132

пускать/пустить красного
петуха, П-132

ради красного словца,
С-339

КРАСНОЕ

красное словцо, С-340

КРАСНОЙ

под красной шапкой, Ш-31

проходить красной нитью,
Н-105

тянуться красной нитью,
Н-105

КРАСНУЮ

под красную шапку, Ш-31

КРАСНЫЙ

красный петух, П-131

красный угол, У-30

красный уголок, У-35

красный фонарь, Ф-15

КРАСОК

не жалеть/не пожалеть
красок, К-368

не пощадить красок, К-368

не щадить красок, К-368

КРАТ

во много крат, К-369

во сто крат, К-369

КРАШЕ

краше в гроб кладут, Г-398

КРАЮ

без конца и (без) краю,
К-243

конца-краю ⟨конца и
краю⟩ не видать ⟨не
видно⟩, К-251

конца-краю ⟨конца и
краю⟩ несть ⟨нет⟩,
К-251

моя хата с краю, Х-6

на краю гибели, К-370

на краю гроба, К-371

на краю земли, К-372

на краю могилы, К-371

на краю пропасти, К-370

на краю света, К-372

ни конца ни краю не
видать ⟨не видно⟩,
К-251

ни конца ни краю несть
⟨нет⟩, К-251

КРАЯ

без конца и (без) края,
К-243

в ваши ⟨наши⟩ края,
К-376

из голодного края, К-374

из края в край, К-373

как из голодного края,
К-374

от края (и) до края, К-375

у края гроба, К-371

у края могилы, К-371

КРАЯХ

в ваших ⟨наших⟩ краях,
К-376

КРЕДИТ

в кредит, К-377

КРЕДИТОМ

пользоваться кредитом,
К-378

КРЕНДЕЛИ

выделывать ⟨выписывать,
писать⟩ (ногами)
крендели, В-33

КРЕНДЕЛЯ

выделывать кренделя,
В-33, К-379

выделывать ⟨выписывать,
писать⟩ ногами
кренделя, В-33

выкидывать кренделя,
К-379

выписывать кренделя,
В-33, К-379

писать кренделя, В-33

КРЕПИСЬ

давши слово, держись, а не
давши, крепись, С-285

не давши слова, крепись, а
давши, держись, С-285

КРЕПКИЙ

крепкий на ухо, У-161

крепкий орех ⟨орешек⟩,
О-101

КРЕПКО

крепко стоять на ногах,
Н-134

неладно ⟨нескладно, худо⟩
скроен, да крепко сшит,
С-242

КРЕПКОЕ

крепкое слово ⟨словцо⟩,
С-316

КРЕПОК

задним умом крепок,
У-108

крепок на ухо, У-161

КРЕСТ

вот вам крест!, К-380

вот те ⟨тебе⟩ крест!,
К-380

нести крест, К-381

поставить крест, К-382

ставить крест, К-382

КРЕСТА

креста нет, К-383

КРЕСТАХ

или грудь в крестах, или
голова в кустах, Г-425

либо грудь в крестах, либо
голова в кустах, Г-425

КРЕСТИТЬ

не детей крестить, Д-188

КРЕСТНАЯ

с нами крестная сила!,
С-173

КРЕЩЕНИЕ

боевое крещение, К-384

КРИВАЯ

кривая вывезет
⟨вывозит⟩, К-385

кривая вынесет
⟨выносит⟩, К-385

куда кривая выведет
⟨вывезет, вынесет⟩,
К-386

куда кривая ни вывезет
⟨ни вынесет⟩, К-386

КРИВИТЬ

кривить душой, Д-399

рожу кривить, Р-147

КРИВОЙ

на кривой не объедешь,
К-387

КРИК

(последний) крик моды,
К-388

КРИКНУТЬ

крикнуть караул, К-72

КРИКОМ

криком кричать, К-389

КРИТИКИ

не выдерживать (никакой)
критики, К-390

ниже всякой критики,
К-390

КРИЧАТЬ

криком кричать, К-389

кричать караул, К-72

кричать на всех
перекрёстках, П-92

кричмя кричать, К-389

КРИЧИ

хоть караул кричи, К-74

КРИЧМЯ

кричмя кричать, К-389

КРОВАВОГО

до кровавого пота, П-420

КРОВИ

в крови, К-391

голубой крови, К-398

до крови, К-397

до последней капли крови,
К-58

жаждать крови, К-392

испортить крови, К-408

испортить себе крови,
К-409

кровь от крови, П-202

купаться в крови, К-393

напиться крови, К-394

насосаться крови, К-394

обагрить ⟨обагрять⟩ руки
в крови, Р-299

плоть от плоти и кровь от
крови, П-202

попортить крови, К-408

попортить себе крови,
К-409

потопить в крови, К-395

топить в крови, К-395

узы крови, У-62

утопать в крови, К-393

КРОВИНКИ

без кровинки в лице, К-396

кровинки в ⟨на⟩ лице не
осталось ⟨нет⟩, К-396

ни кровинки в ⟨на⟩ лице не
осталось ⟨нет⟩, К-396

КРОВИНОЧКИ

без кровиночки в лице,
К-396

кровиночки в ⟨на⟩ лице не
осталось ⟨нет⟩, К-396

ни кровиночки в ⟨на⟩ лице
не осталось ⟨нет⟩,
К-396

КРОВЛЕЙ

под одной кровлей, К-437

КРОВНЫЕ

кровные узы, У-62

КРОВЬ

в жилах течёт голубая
кровь, К-398

в кровь, К-397

войти в плоть и кровь,
П-199

входить в плоть и кровь,
П-199

выпить кровь, К-407

высасывать/высосать
кровь, К-407

голубая кровь, К-398

кровь бродит, К-403

кровь бросилась в голову,
К-399

кровь бросилась в лицо,
К-400

кровь говорит, К-401

кровь горит, К-403

кровь за кровь, К-402

кровь заговорила, К-401

кровь заиграла (в жилах),
К-403

кровь закипела, К-403

кровь застывает в жилах,
К-405

кровь застыла (в жилах),
К-405

кровь играет (в жилах),
К-403

кровь из носа ⟨из носу⟩,
К-412

кровь кинулась в голову,
К-399

кровь кинулась в лицо,
К-400

кровь кипит, К-403

кровь леденеет (в жилах),
К-405

кровь от крови, П-202

кровь прилила к лицу,
К-400

кровь разгорелась, К-403

кровь разыгралась, К-403

кровь с молоком, К-404

кровь стынет (в жилах),
К-405

кровь ударила в голову,
К-399

кровь холодеет (в жилах),
К-405

леденить кровь, К-406

лить кровь, К-410

лить свою кровь, К-410

облекать в плоть и кровь,
П-200

облекаться в плоть и
кровь, П-201

облечь в плоть и кровь,
П-200
облечься в плоть и кровь,
П-201
пить кровь, К-407
плоть и кровь, П-202
плоть от плоти и кровь от
крови, П-202
портить кровь, К-408
портить себе кровь, К-409
проливать/пролить (свою)
кровь, К-410
разгонять/разогнать
кровь, К-411
сосать кровь, К-407
хоть кровь из носа ⟨из
носу⟩, К-412

КРОВЬЮ
кровью умываться/
умыться, К-413
малой кровью, К-414
наливаться/налиться
кровью, К-415
написать кровью (сердца),
К-416
обагрить ⟨обагрять⟩ руки
кровью, Р-299
облекать плотью и
кровью, П-200
облекаться плотью и
кровью, П-201
облечь плотью и кровью,
П-200
облечься плотью и
кровью, П-201
писать кровью (сердца),
К-416
потом и кровью, П-434
сердце кровью
обливается/облилось,
С-138
смывать/смыть кровью,
К-417

КРОКОДИЛОВЫ
крокодиловы слёзы, С-268
КРОКОДИЛЬИ
крокодильи слёзы, С-268
КРОМЕШНАЯ
кромешная тьма, Т-249
КРОМЕШНЫЙ
ад кромешный, А-7
кромешный мрак, Т-249
КРОХИ
крохи с барского ⟨с
господского⟩ стола,
К-418
ни крохи, К-419
КРОШЕЧКИ
ни крошечки, К-419
КРОШКИ
крошки с барского ⟨с
господского⟩ стола,
К-418
ни крошки, К-419
КРУГ
давать/дать круг, К-420
делать круг, К-420
заколдованный круг, К-421
на круг, К-422
порочный круг, К-421

сделать круг, К-420
КРУГА
квадратура круга, К-121
с круга, К-425
КРУГИ
на круги своя, К-423
КРУГЛАЯ
круглая дата, Д-27
круглая копеечка, К-275
круглая сумма, С-675
КРУГЛЕНЬКАЯ
кругленькая копеечка,
С-275
кругленькая сумма, С-675
КРУГЛЫЕ
делать/сделать круглые
глаза, Г-66
КРУГЛЫЙ
круглый дурак, Д-330
круглый ноль, Н-195
круглый стол, С-586
КРУГЛЫМ
за круглым столом, С-586
круглым счётом, С-720
КРУГЛЫМИ
смотреть круглыми
глазами, Г-66
КРУГОВАЯ
круговая порука, П-391
КРУГОМ
голова идёт/пошла
кругом, Г-204
кружить кругом да около,
Х-59
петлять кругом да около,
Х-59
ходить кругом да около,
Х-59
КРУГУ
по второму ⟨третьему⟩
кругу, К-424
с кругу, К-425
КРУЖИТСЯ
кружится голова, Г-215
КРУЖИТЬ
кружить вокруг да около,
Х-59
кружить голову, Г-253
кружить кругом да около,
Х-59
КРУЖИТЬСЯ
кружиться как* белка в
колесе, Б-51
КРУЖОК
в кружок, К-426
КРУПНАЯ
крупная шишка, Ш-70
КРУПНЫХ
в крупных чинах, Ч-148
КРУПУ
как мышь на крупу, М-323
КРУТИ
как ни крути, К-427
как там ⟨тут⟩ ни крути,
К-427
КРУТИСЬ
как (там) ни крутись,
К-428
КРУТИТЬ
вола крутить, В-220

крутить голову, Г-254
крутить динамо, Д-196
крутить любовь, Р-160
крутить мозги, М-225
крутить носом, Н-228
крутить роман, Р-160
крутить хвостом, Х-24
крутить шарманку, Ш-36
КРУТИТЬСЯ
крутиться как* белка в
колесе, Б-51
крутиться ужом, У-56
КРУТО
круто приходится/
пришлось, П-552
КРУТЫЕ
укатали ⟨умыкали,
уходили⟩ бурку ⟨сивку⟩
крутые горки, С-160
КРЫЛО
под крыло, К-430
прятать/спрятать голову
под крыло, Г-272
КРЫЛОМ
под крылом, К-430
КРЫЛЫШКИ
опускать/опустить
крылышки, К-431
КРЫЛЫШКО
брать/взять под своё
крылышко, К-429
под крылышко, К-430
КРЫЛЫШКОМ
под крылышком, К-430
КРЫЛЬЯ
обрезать крылья, К-432
опускать/опустить
крылья, К-431
подрезать крылья, К-432
подсекать/подсечь
крылья, К-432
расправить ⟨расправлять⟩
крылья, К-433
связать ⟨связывать⟩
крылья, К-432
КРЫСА
бумажная крыса, К-434
как церковная крыса,
М-324
канцелярская крыса, К-434
чернильная крыса, К-434
КРЫСИНЫЙ
крысиный хвост(ик), Х-22
КРЫСЫ
крысы бегут с тонущего
корабля, К-435
крысы покидают тонущий
корабль, К-435
КРЫТЬ
крыть нечем, К-436
КРЫШЕЙ
под одной крышей, К-437
КРЮК
дать крюк, К-438
сделать крюк, К-438
КРЮКУ
дать крюку, К-438
КРЮЧКЕ
на крючке, К-439

КРЮЧОК
попадаться/попасться на
крючок, К-440
КСТАТИ
как нельзя кстати, Н-76
кстати говоря, С-206
кстати и некстати, К-441
кстати сказать, С-206
прийтись ⟨приходиться⟩
кстати, П-554
КТО
как не знаю кто, З-179
кто бы мог подумать!,
П-258
кто бы ни…, К-448
кто бы ни был, Б-260
кто бы подумал!, П-258
кто бы то ни был, Б-260
кто бы то ни было, Б-266
кто в лес, кто по дрова,
Л-55
кто во что горазд, Г-317
кто где, К-442
кто его знает, З-143
кто знает, З-143
кто как, К-443
кто как, а…, К-444
кто кого, К-445
кто-кто, а…, К-446
кто куда, К-447
кто куда, а я в сберкассу,
С-23
кто любит попа, (а) кто
попадью, (а) кто попову
дочку, П-344
кто надо, Н-10
кто ни…, К-448
кто ни попало, П-352
кто попало, П-352
кто придётся, П-352
кто рано встаёт, тому бог
(по)даёт, В-346
кто старое вспомянет
⟨помянет⟩, тому глаз
вон, С-546
кто угодно, У-25
кто что, К-449
не кто иной, как…, К-450
скажи мне, кто твой друг,
и я скажу (тебе), кто ты,
Д-310
смотря кто, С-422
спасайся, кто может,
С-505
хоть кто, К-451
КУБЫШКУ
класть в кубышку, К-452
набивать/набить
кубышку, К-452
положить в кубышку,
К-452
КУВШИННОЕ
кувшинное рыло, Р-388
КУДА
а не пошёл бы ты куда
подальше!, И-23
вон куда махнул!, Х-8
вон куда хватил!, Х-8
вот куда махнул!, Х-8
вот куда хватил!, Х-8
закон что дышло: куда
повернёшь ⟨повернул⟩,
туда и вышло, З-49

иди (ты) ⟨идите (вы)⟩ куда
    подальше!, И-23
кто куда, К-447
кто куда, а я в сберкассу,
    С-23
куда б(ы) ни..., Г-13
куда бы то ни было, Б-262
куда ветер дует, В-71
куда ворон костей не
    заносил, В-271
куда глаза глядят, Г-78
куда до, К-453
куда за, К-453
куда иголка, туда и нитка,
    И-3
куда как..., К-454
куда как нужно!, Н-259
куда кривая выведет
    ⟨вывезет, вынесет⟩,
    К-386
куда кривая ни вывезет
    ⟨ни вынесет⟩, К-386
куда Макар телят не
    гонял, М-3
куда махнул!, Х-8
куда надо, Н-10
куда ни..., Г-13
куда ни кинешь взгляд(ом)
    ⟨глазом⟩, Г-137
куда ни кинь, везде клин,
    К-136
куда ни кинь взгляд(ом),
    Г-137
куда ни кинь, всё ⟨всюду⟩
    клин, К-136
куда ни кинь глазом, Г-137
куда ни плюнь, П-205
куда ни поверни(те) ⟨ни
    повороти(те)⟩, П-214
куда ни попало, П-348
куда ни шло, Ш-81
куда ноги несут/понесут,
    Н-146
куда попало, П-348
куда придётся, П-348
куда смотрит, С-420
куда там!, К-455
куда только смотрит,
    С-420
куда тут!, К-455
куда угодно, У-20
куда уж, К-456
куда хватает ⟨хватал⟩
    глаз, Г-27
куда хватало глаз ⟨глаза,
    глазу⟩, Г-27
куда хватил!, Х-8
куда это годится!, Г-186
не знать, куда глаза
    девать/деть, Г-83
не знать, куда деваться
    ⟨деть себя, деться⟩,
    З-174
не знать, куда себя девать/
    деть, З-175
послать куда подальше,
    П-409
послать куда следует,
    П-409
пошёл бы ты куда
    подальше!, И-23

смотря куда, С-422
хоть куда, К-457
эк(а) куда хватил!, Х-8
КУДЫКИНУ
    на кудыкину гору, Г-354
КУЗОВ
    назвался груздем, полезай
    в кузов, Г-428
КУЗЬКИНУ
    показать кузькину мать,
    М-54
КУЙ
    куй железо, пока горячо,
    Ж-12
КУКАРЕКУ
    ни бе ни ме ни кукареку,
    Б-33
КУКИШ
    кукиш в кармане, К-458
    кукиш с маслом, К-459
КУКЛА
    чёртова кукла, К-460
КУКОЛЬНАЯ
    кукольная комедия, К-216
КУКУШКУ
    менять/променять
    кукушку на ястреба,
    К-461
    сменять кукушку на
    ястреба, К-461
КУЛАК
    в кулак свистать
    ⟨свистеть⟩, К-462
    зажать ⟨зажимать⟩ в
    кулак, К-463
    прыскать/прыснуть в
    кулак, К-464
    сжать ⟨сжимать⟩ в кулак,
    К-465
    смеяться в кулак, К-464
    собирать/собрать в кулак,
    К-465
    хихикать в кулак, К-464
КУЛАКАМ
    давать/дать волю
    кулакам, В-249
КУЛАКАМИ
    после драки кулаками не
    машут, Д-303
КУЛАКЕ
    в кулаке, К-466
    зажать ⟨зажимать⟩ в
    кулаке, К-463
КУЛИК
    всяк кулик своё болото
    хвалит, К-467
КУЛИСАМИ
    за кулисами, К-468
КУЛИЧКАХ
    у чёрта на куличках, Ч-105
КУЛИЧКИ
    к чёрту ⟨к чертям⟩ на
    кулички, Ч-105
КУЛУАРАХ
    в кулуарах, К-469
КУЛЬ
    куль соли съесть, П-625
КУЛЬКА
    из кулька в рогожку, К-470

КУЛЬМИНАЦИОННАЯ
    кульминационная точка,
    П-634
КУЛЬМИНАЦИОННЫЙ
    кульминационный пункт,
    П-634
КУМ
    кум королю, К-471
    ни кум ни сват, С-31
КУМА
    кому какое дело, что кума
    с кумом сидела, Д-109
КУМИР
    создать себе кумир, К-472
    сотворить себе кумир,
    К-472
    творить себе кумир, К-472
КУМИРА
    создать себе кумира,
    К-472
    сотворить себе кумира,
    К-472
    творить себе кумира,
    К-472
КУМОМ
    кому какое дело, что кума
    с кумом сидела, Д-109
КУПАТЬСЯ
    купаться в золоте, З-181
    купаться в крови, К-393
КУПИЛ
    за что купил, за то и
    продаю, К-473
КУПИЛО
    купило притупило
    ⟨притупилось⟩, К-474
КУПИТЬ
    купить кота в мешке,
    К-335
КУПОНЫ
    стричь купоны, К-475
КУР
    как кур во щи, К-476
КУРАЖЕ
    в ⟨на⟩ кураже, Г-370
КУРАЖОМ
    под куражом, Г-370
КУРАМ
    курам на смех, К-477
КУРБЕТЫ
    выделывать
    ⟨выписывать⟩ курбеты,
    К-379
КУРИЛКА
    жив курилка!, К-478
КУРИНАЯ
    куриная память, П-44
КУРИНЫЕ
    куриные мозги, М-226
КУРИТЬ
    курить фимиам, Ф-11
КУРИЦА
    как* курица лапой, К-479
    как курица с яйцом, К-480
    мокрая курица, К-481
    слепая курица, К-482
КУРИЦУ
    яйца курицу не учат, Я-60
КУРИЦЫН
    курицын сын, С-733

КУРС
    ввести ⟨вводить⟩ в курс,
    К-483
    войти ⟨входить⟩ в курс,
    К-484
    держать курс, К-485
КУРСЕ
    в курсе, К-486
КУРЫ
    куры не клюют, К-487
    строить куры, К-488
КУРЬЕРСКИХ
    (как) на курьерских, К-489
КУРЬИХ
    избушка на курьих
    ножках, И-37
КУСАТЬ
    кусать (себе) локти, Л-131
КУСКА
    куска недоедать, К-490
    перебиваться с куска на
    кусок, Х-41
КУСОК
    кусок в глотку не идёт ⟨не
    лезет, не пойдёт, не
    полезет⟩, К-491
    кусок в горло не идёт ⟨не
    лезет, не пойдёт, не
    полезет⟩, К-491
    кусок хлеба, К-492
    лакомый кусок, К-493
    перебиваться с куска на
    кусок, Х-41
    пронести ⟨проносить⟩
    кусок мимо рта, К-494
    урвать кусок, К-495
КУСОЧЕК
    лакомый кусочек, К-493
КУСТА
    пуганая ворона (и) куста
    боится, В-275
КУСТАХ
    или грудь в крестах, или
    голова в кустах, Г-425
    либо грудь в крестах, либо
    голова в кустах, Г-425
КУСТЫ
    в кусты, К-496
    глядеть в кусты, К-497
    смотреть в кусты, К-497
КУЧУ
    валить в (одну) кучу, К-498
    мешать в (одну) кучу,
    К-498
    сваливать/свалить в
    (одну) кучу, К-498
    смешать в (одну) кучу,
    К-498

Л

ЛАВКАМ
    не семеро по лавкам, Л-1
ЛАВКЕ
    слон в посудной лавке,
    С-342
ЛАВОЧКА
    одна лавочка, Ш-25

ЛАВОЧКЕ
по пьяной лавочке, Л-2

ЛАВОЧКУ
закрывать/закрыть
лавочку, Л-3
прикрывать/прикрыть
лавочку, Л-3
под пьяную лавочку, Л-2

ЛАВРАХ
покоиться на лаврах, Л-4
почивать/почить на
лаврах, Л-4

ЛАВРЫ
лавры не дают покоя
⟨спать⟩, Л-5
пожать ⟨пожинать⟩
лавры, Л-6

ЛАГЕРЯ
действовать на два лагеря,
Л-7

ЛАД
в лад, Л-8
идёт на лад, Л-9
на один лад, Л-10
на свой лад, Л-11
на тот же лад, Л-10
пошло на лад, Л-9

ЛАДАН
дышать на ладан, Л-12

ЛАДАНА
как чёрт ладана, Ч-74
как чёрт от ладана, Ч-75

ЛАДАХ
в ладах, Л-14
не в ладах, Л-15

ЛАДОНИ
как* на ладони, Л-13

ЛАДОНКЕ
как* на ладонке, Л-13

ЛАДОШКЕ
как* на ладошке, Л-13

ЛАДУ
в ладу, Л-14
не в ладу, Л-15
нет ни складу ни ладу,
С-223
ни складу ни ладу, С-223

ЛАДЫ
на все лады, Л-16
склонять на все лады, Л-17

ЛАЗАРЯ
лазаря запеть, Л-18
лазаря петь, Л-18
наобум лазаря, Л-19

ЛАЗИТ
за словом в карман не
лазит, С-332

ЛАКОМЫЙ
лакомый кусок ⟨кусочек⟩,
К-493

ЛАМПОЧКИ
до лампочки, Л-20

ЛАПАХ
в лапах, Л-21
на задних лапах, Л-22
стоять на задних лапах,
Л-22
ходить на задних лапах,
Л-22

ЛАПКАХ
на задних лапках, Л-22
стоять на задних лапках,
Л-22
ходить на задних лапках,
Л-22

ЛАПКИ
гусиные лапки, Л-23
лапки кверху, Л-24
поднимать/поднять лапки
кверху, Л-24
становиться/стать на
задние лапки, Л-25

ЛАПОЙ
как* курица лапой, К-479

ЛАПТЕМ
лаптем щи хлебать, Л-26
не лаптем щи хлебать,
Л-27

ЛАПТИ
лапти плести, Л-28

ЛАПУ
запускать/запустить лапу,
Р-343
на лапу, Л-29
накладывать/наложить
лапу, Р-352
сосать лапу, Л-30

ЛАПЧАТЫЙ
гусь лапчатый, Г-446

ЛАПШУ
вешать лапшу на уши,
Л-31
изрубить в лапшу, К-68
искрошить в лапшу, К-68
навесить ⟨навешивать⟩
лапшу на уши, Л-31
повесить лапшу на уши,
Л-31

ЛАПЫ
в лапы, Л-21

ЛАРЧИК
(а) ларчик просто
открывался, Л-32

ЛАСКАТЬ
ласкать взор ⟨глаз⟩, Г-25

ЛАСТОЧКА
одна ласточка весны не
делает, Л-33
первая ласточка, Л-34

ЛАТАТЫ
давать/дать лататы,
Д-304
задавать/задать лататы,
Д-304

ЛБОМ
лбом стенку ⟨стену,
стены⟩ не прошибёшь,
Л-35

ЛБУ
зарубить (себе) на лбу,
Н-235
на лбу написано, Л-36
семи ⟨семь⟩ пядей
⟨пяденей, пядень⟩ во
лбу, П-675
что в лоб, что по лбу,
Л-119

ЛБЫ
брить лбы, Л-115

забривать/забрить лбы,
Л-115

ЛЕБЕДИНАЯ
лебединая песня ⟨песнь⟩,
П-120

ЛЕВАЯ
левая нога захочет/хочет,
Н-119

ЛЕВОЙ
вставать левой ногой ⟨с
левой ноги⟩, Н-142
встать левой ногой ⟨с
левой ноги⟩, Н-142
левой ногой, Н-160
одной левой, Л-37

ЛЕГИОН
имя (же) им легион, И-63

ЛЁГКАЯ
лёгкая рука, Р-226

ЛЁГКИЙ
лёгкий на ногу, Н-171
лёгкий на подъём, П-262
лёгкий на помине, П-332

ЛЁГКИМ
отделаться
⟨отделываться⟩ лёгким
испугом, И-81
с лёгким паром!, П-64
с лёгким сердцем, С-145

ЛЕГКО
легко отделаться, О-139
легко сказать, С-207

ЛЁГКОГО
лёгкого поведения, П-211
легче лёгкого, Л-38

ЛЁГКОЙ
с лёгкой душой, С-145
с лёгкой руки, Р-325

ЛЁГКОМУ
по лёгкому, М-9

ЛЕГЛА
тень легла, Т-78

ЛЁГОК
лёгок на ногу, Н-171
лёгок на подъём, П-262
лёгок на помине, П-332

ЛЕГЧЕ
легче верблюду пройти в
⟨сквозь⟩ игольное ушко,
В-35
легче лёгкого, Л-38
легче на поворотах!, П-226
час от часу не легче, Ч-18

ЛЁД
биться как рыба об лёд,
Р-378
как лёд, Л-39
лёд растаял, Л-40
лёд тает, Л-40
лёд тронулся, Л-41
разбить лёд, Л-42
растопить лёд, Л-43
сломать лёд, Л-42

ЛЕДЕНЕЕТ
кровь леденеет (в жилах),
К-405

ЛЕДЕНИТЬ
леденить душу, К-406
леденить кровь, К-406

леденить сердце, К-406

ЛЕЖАТ
худые вести не лежат на
месте, В-64

ЛЕЖАТЬ
лежать в лёжку, Л-49
лежать как пласт, П-165
лежать мёртвым грузом,
Г-429
лежать на боку, Б-158
лежать на печи ⟨на печке⟩,
Б-158
лежать на плечах, П-187
лежать пластом, П-165
лежать под сукном, С-673
лежма ⟨лежнем⟩ лежать,
Л-44

ЛЕЖАЧ
под лежач камень (и) вода
не течёт, К-45

ЛЕЖАЧЕГО
лежачего не бьют, Л-45
не бей лежачего, Л-46

ЛЕЖАЧИЙ
под лежачий камень (и)
вода не течёт, К-45

ЛЕЖИТ
душа не лежит, Д-369
плохо лежит, Л-47
сердце не лежит, Д-369

ЛЁЖКУ
в лёжку, Л-48
лежать в лёжку, Л-49
повалить в лёжку, Л-50
уложить в лёжку, Л-50

ЛЕЖМЯ
лежмя лежать, Л-44

ЛЕЖНЕМ
лежнем лежать, Л-44

ЛЕЗВИЮ
ходить по лезвию ножа,
О-126

ЛЕЗЕТ
в глотку не лезет, К-491
в горло не лезет, К-491
за словом в карман не
лезет, С-332
кусок в глотку ⟨в горло⟩
не лезет, К-491
ни в какие ворота не лезет,
В-279

ЛЕЗТЬ
без мыла в душу лезть,
М-307
из кожи (вон) лезть, К-162
из шкуры (вон) лезть,
К-162
лезть в бутылку, Б-249
лезть в глаза, Г-79
лезть в голову, Г-255
лезть в гору, Г-351
лезть в душу, Д-410
лезть в петлю, П-127
лезть в пузырь, Б-249
лезть во все дырки, Д-440
лезть к чёрту в зубы, Ч-112
лезть на глаза, Г-79
лезть на рожон, Р-145
лезть на стенку ⟨на
стену⟩, С-569

[913]

ЛЕЗУТ
глаза на лоб лезут, Г-54

ЛЕЗЬ
не лезь поперёд батьки в пекло, Б-27
прежде батьки ⟨отца⟩ в петлю не лезь, Б-27
хоть в петлю лезь, П-129

ЛЕНИВАЯ
ленивая тетеря, Т-92

ЛЕНЬ
кому (только) не лень, Л-51

ЛЕПЕТ
детский лепет, Л-52
младенческий лепет, Л-52
ребячий лепет, Л-52

ЛЕПЁШКУ
разбиваться/разбиться в лепёшку, Л-53
расшибаться/расшибиться в лепёшку, Л-53

ЛЕПИТЬ
лепить ярлык ⟨ярлыки⟩, Я-67

ЛЕПТУ
внести ⟨вносить⟩ свою лепту, Л-54

ЛЕС
волков бояться – в лес не ходить, В-231
глядеть в лес, Л-57
дело не волк ⟨не медведь⟩, в лес не убежит ⟨не уйдёт⟩, Р-3
дремучий лес, Л-58
как волка ни корми, (а) он ⟨всё⟩ в лес глядит ⟨смотрит⟩, В-228
кто в лес, кто по дрова, Л-55
лес рубят – щепки летят, Л-56
работа не волк ⟨не медведь⟩, в лес не убежит ⟨не уйдёт⟩, Р-3
сколько волка ни корми, (а) он ⟨всё⟩ в лес глядит ⟨смотрит⟩, В-228
смотреть в лес, Л-57
тёмный лес, Л-58
чем дальше в лес, тем больше дров, Л-59

ЛЕСА
за деревьями леса не видеть, Д-178
из-за деревьев леса не видеть, Д-178

ЛЕСОМ
семь вёрст до небес и всё лесом, В-44

ЛЕСТНИЦЫ
спускать/спустить с лестницы, Л-60

ЛЕСУ
как в (тёмном) лесу, Л-61

ЛЕТ
в ⟨во⟩ цвете лет, Ц-14
выслуга лет, В-377
выйти ⟨выходить⟩ из лет, В-211

за давностью лет, Д-10
на склоне лет, С-224
на старости лет, С-547
по молодости лет, М-235
сколько лет, сколько зим!, Л-62
средних лет, Л-63

ЛЕТА
войти в лета, В-210
вступать/вступить в лета, В-210
входить в лета, В-210
мафусаиловы лета, В-19
многая ⟨многие⟩ лета, Л-64

ЛЕТАМ
не по летам, Г-183

ЛЕТАМИ
с летами, Г-184

ЛЕТАТЬ
высоко летать, Л-65

ЛЕТАХ
в летах, Г-185

ЛЕТЕТЬ
лететь в тартарары, Т-41
лететь вверх тормашками ⟨тормашки⟩, Т-163
лететь к чёртовой матери, Ч-113
лететь к чёрту, Ч-113
лететь к чертям ⟨собачьим⟩, Ч-113
лететь ко всем чертям, Ч-113
лететь прахом, П-498

ЛЕТО
бабье лето, Л-66

ЛЕТОПИСЬ
живая летопись, Л-67

ЛЕТУ/ЛЁТУ
кануть в Лету, Л-68
ловить на лету, Л-69
ловить с лёту, Л-69
на лету, Л-70
схватывать на лету ⟨с лёту⟩, Л-69
хватать на лету ⟨с лёту⟩, Л-69

ЛЕТЯТ
головы летят, Г-290
дрова рубят – щепки летят, Л-56
лес рубят – щепки летят, Л-56
пух да ⟨и⟩ перья летят, П-664

ЛЕЧЬ
лечь в гроб, М-206
лечь в землю, М-206
лечь в могилу, М-206
лечь костьми, К-330
лечь на бумагу, Б-245
лечь на плечи, П-190
лечь на стол, С-587
лечь под перо, Б-245
лечь свинцом на душу ⟨на сердце⟩, С-79

ЛЕШЕГО
какого лешего?, Ч-103
ни лешего, Ч-104

ЛЕШЕМУ
к лешему, Ч-110, Ч-111

ЛЕШИЙ
леший дёрнул, Ч-88
леший дёрнул за язык, Я-10
леший его знает, Ч-89
леший носит, Ч-96
леший тебя возьми ⟨дери⟩!, Ч-99
леший тебя побери ⟨подери⟩!, Ч-99
на кой леший, Ч-77

ЛЕШИМ
за каким лешим, Ч-77

ЛЕЩА
дать ⟨поддать⟩ леща, Л-71

ЛИЗАТЬ
лизать ноги, П-679
лизать пятки, П-679
лизать руки, П-679
лизать сапоги, П-679

ЛИМОН
выжатый лимон, Л-72

ЛИНИИ
идти/пойти по линии наименьшего сопротивления, Л-73
по линии, Л-74

ЛИНИЮ
вести свою линию, Л-75
гнуть свою линию, Л-75
держать линию, К-485

ЛИПКУ
обдирать/ободрать как липку, Л-76
обирать/обобрать как липку, Л-76
облупить как липку, Л-76
обчистить как липку, Л-76

ЛИРИЧЕСКОЕ
лирическое отступление, О-169

ЛИСА
Лиса Патрикеевна, Л-77

ЛИСТ
как* банный лист, Л-78
как (осиновый) лист, Л-79

ЛИСТА
с листа, Л-80

ЛИСТОК
фиговый листок, Л-81

ЛИСТОЧЕК
фиговый листочек, Л-81

ЛИТЬ
колокола лить, К-203
лить воду на мельницу, В-187
лить грязь, Г-436
лить кровь, К-410
лить помои, Г-436
лить пули ⟨пулю⟩, П-631
лить свою кровь, К-410
лить слёзы, С-269

ЛИТЬСЯ
литься через край, К-352

ЛИХА
лиха беда, Б-38
лиха беда начало ⟨начать⟩, Б-39

почём фунт лиха, Ф-33
хватить лиха, Г-363
хлебнуть лиха, Г-363

ЛИХВОЙ
с лихвой, Л-82

ЛИХОЙ
лихой глаз, Г-24

ЛИХОМ
не поминай(те) лихом, Л-83

ЛИЦА
в поте лица (своего), П-422
лица нет, Л-84
невзирая на лица, Л-85
от лица, И-57
с лица не воду пить, Л-86
смести с лица земли, Л-88
снести с лица земли, Л-88
спасть с лица, Л-87
стереть с лица земли, Л-88

ЛИЦАХ
в лицах, Л-89

ЛИЦЕ
без кровинки ⟨кровиночки⟩ в лице, К-396
в лице, Л-90
измениться в лице, Л-91
кровинки ⟨кровиночки⟩ в ⟨на⟩ лице не осталось ⟨нет⟩, К-396
меняться в лице, Л-91
на лице написано, Л-92
ни кровинки ⟨кровиночки⟩ в ⟨на⟩ лице не осталось ⟨нет⟩, К-396
перемениться в лице, Л-91

ЛИЦО
бросать/бросить в лицо, Л-93
в лицо, Л-94, Л-95
взглянуть правде в лицо, П-483
глядеть в лицо, Г-97
глядеть правде в лицо, П-483
глядеть смерти в лицо, С-394
делать страшное лицо, Г-67
краска бросилась ⟨кинулась⟩ в лицо, К-400
кровь бросилась ⟨кинулась⟩ в лицо, К-400
лицо в лицо, Г-52
лицо вытянулось, Л-96
на одно лицо, Л-97
наплевать в лицо, Г-86
плевать ⟨плюнуть⟩ в лицо, Г-86
показать своё ⟨истинное⟩ лицо, Л-98
показать своё настоящее лицо, Л-98
потерять лицо, Л-100
сделать страшное лицо, Г-67
смотреть в лицо, Г-97

смотреть правде в лицо,
П-483
смотреть смерти в лицо,
С-394
сохранить лицо, Л-99
терять лицо, Л-100
ЛИЦОМ
лицом к лицу, Л-101
не ударить лицом в грязь,
Л-102
перед лицом, Л-103
повернуться
⟨поворачиваться⟩
лицом, Л-104
показать ⟨показывать⟩
товар лицом, Т-116
ЛИЦУ
к лицу, Л-105
кровь прилила к лицу,
К-400
лицом к лицу, Л-101
ЛИЧИНОЙ
под личиной, М-32
ЛИЧИНУ
надевать/надеть личину,
М-33
носить личину, М-33
снимать/снять личину,
М-34
ЛИЧНОСТИ
перейти ⟨переходить⟩ на
личности, Л-106
ЛИШАТЬ
лишать жизни, Ж-44
лишать слова, С-283
ЛИШАТЬСЯ
лишаться жизни, Ж-45
лишаться рассудка, У-85
лишаться ума, У-85
лишаться чувств, Ч-194
ЛИШЁН
не лишён, Л-107
ЛИШЁННЫЙ
не лишённый, Л-107
ЛИШИТЬ
лишить жизни, Ж-44
лишить слова, С-283
ЛИШИТЬСЯ
лишиться жизни, Ж-45
лишиться рассудка, У-85
лишиться ума, У-85
лишиться чувств, Ч-194
ЛИШКОМ
с лишком, Л-112
ЛИШКУ
переложить лишку, Л-108
хватить лишку, Л-108
хлебнуть лишку, Л-108
ЛИШНЕ
не лишне, Л-109
ЛИШНЕГО
хватить лишнего, Л-108
шагу лишнего не сделать,
Ш-22
ЛИШНЕЕ
не лишнее, Л-109
переложить лишнее, Л-108
позволить ⟨позволять⟩
себе лишнее, Л-110

сболтнуть лишнее, Л-111
сказать лишнее, Л-111
хватить лишнее, Л-108
хлебнуть лишнее, Л-108
ЛИШНИЕ
дальние ⟨долгие⟩ проводы
– лишние слёзы, П-566
ЛИШНИЙ
лишний раз, Р-25
лишний рот, Р-177
лишний человек, Ч-48
третий лишний, Т-203
ЛИШНИМ
с лишним, Л-112
ЛИШНИХ
без лишних разговоров,
С-274
без лишних слов, С-274
ЛИШЬ
едва лишь, Е-2
лишь бы, Л-113
лишь бы как, К-20
лишь бы только, Л-113
лишь только…, К-18
разве лишь, Р-45
только лишь…, К-18
ЛОБ
брить лоб, Л-115
в лоб, Л-114
глаза на лоб лезут/
полезли, Г-54
забривать/забрить лоб,
Л-115
забрить лоб в рекруты ⟨в
солдаты⟩, Л-115
лоб в лоб, Л-116
медный лоб, Л-117
подставить ⟨подставлять⟩
(свой) лоб, Л-118
пускать/пустить (себе)
пулю в лоб, П-632
хоть пулю в лоб, П-633
что в лоб, что по лбу,
Л-119
ЛОБЗАНИЕ
иудино лобзание, П-447
ЛОВИТЬ
в мутной воде рыбу
ловить, В-177
ворон ловить, В-270
ловить блох, Б-82
ловить за хвост, Х-19
ловить каждое слово,
С-317
ловить момент, М-250
ловить на лету, Л-69
ловить на словах ⟨на
слове⟩, С-302
ловить с лёту, Л-69
ловить себя, Л-120
мух ловить, В-270
ЛОВЦА
на ловца и зверь бежит,
Л-121
ЛОДЫРЯ
лодыря гонять, Л-122
ЛОЖЕ
прокрустово ложе, Л-123
ЛОЖЕЧКОЙ
под ложечкой, Л-124

ЛОЖЕЧКУ
под ложечку, Л-125
ЛОЖИСЬ
ложись да помирай, Л-126
хоть в гроб ложись, Г-400
хоть ложись да помирай,
Л-126
ЛОЖИТСЯ
тень ложится, Т-78
ЛОЖИТЬСЯ
ложиться в землю, М-206
ложиться на бумагу, Б-245
ложиться на плечи, П-190
ложиться на стол, С-587
ложиться под перо, Б-245
ЛОЖКА
дорога ложка к обеду,
Л-127
ложка дёгтю в бочке мёда
⟨мёду⟩, Л-128
ЛОЖКЕ
в ложке воды утопить,
Л-129
в час по ⟨столовой⟩ ложке,
Ч-20
в час по чайной ложке,
Ч-20
через час по ⟨столовой⟩
ложке, Ч-20
через час по чайной ложке,
Ч-20
ЛОЖНОЕ
ложное положение, П-305
ЛОЖНОЙ
на ложной дороге, П-643
по ложной дороге, П-643
ЛОЖНОМ
на ложном пути, П-643
ЛОЖНОМУ
по ложному пути, П-643
ЛОЖНУЮ
на ложную дорогу, П-643
ЛОЖНЫЙ
ложный шаг, Ш-3
на ложный путь, П-643
ЛОКОТЬ
близко ⟨близок⟩ локоть,
да не укусишь, Л-130
ЛОКТИ
кусать (себе) локти, Л-131
ЛОКТЯ
чувство локтя, Ч-199
ЛОМАНОГО
гроша ломаного не стоит,
Г-416
ЛОМАНУЮ
ни на ломаную полушку,
Г-414
ЛОМАНЫЙ
ломаный грош цена, Г-410
ЛОМАТЬ
ломать ваньку, Д-333
ломать голову, Г-256
ломать горб, С-513
ломать дурака, Д-333
ломать дурочку, Д-333
ломать зубы, З-199
ломать комедию, К-215
ломать копья, К-288

ломать пальцы, Р-291
ломать руки, Р-291
ломать себе голову, Г-256
ломать спину, С-513
ломать хребет, Х-97
ломать шапку, Ш-30
ЛОМИТ
сила солому ломит, С-174
ЛОМИТЬ
ломить шапку, Ш-30
ЛОМИТЬСЯ
ломиться в открытую
дверь ⟨в открытые
двери⟩, Д-36
ЛОМОВАЯ
как ломовая лошадь, Л-141
ЛОМОТЬ
отрезанный ломоть, Л-132
ЛОНЕ
на лоне природы, Л-133
ЛОПАЕТСЯ
терпение лопается, Т-81
ЛОПАТКИ
во все лопатки, Л-134
класть/положить на (обе)
лопатки, Л-135
уложить на (обе) лопатки,
Л-135
ЛОПАТОЙ
грести ⟨загребать⟩
лопатой, Л-136
ЛОПАТЬСЯ
лопаться от злости, З-137
от ⟨с⟩ жиру лопаться,
Ж-79
ЛОПНИ
лопни (мои) глаза, Г-80
хоть лопни, Л-137
ЛОПНУЛ
чтоб ты лопнул!, Л-138
ЛОПНУЛО
терпение лопнуло, Т-81
ЛОПНУТЬ
лопнуть как мыльный
пузырь, П-628
лопнуть от злости, З-138
лопнуть от смеха, С-407
лопнуть со злости, З-138
лопнуть со смеху, С-407
от жиру лопнуть, Ж-79
с жиру лопнуть, Ж-79
чтоб тебе лопнуть!, Л-138
ЛОСК
в лоск, Л-139
ЛОСКУТ
в лоскут, Л-139
ЛОСКУТЫ
в лоскуты, Л-139
ЛОШАДКА
тёмная лошадка, Л-140
ЛОШАДЬ
как ломовая лошадь, Л-141
ЛУЖЁНАЯ
лужёная глотка, Г-146
ЛУЖУ
посадить в лужу, Л-143
садиться в лужу, Л-142
сажать в лужу, Л-143
сесть в лужу, Л-142

ЛУКАВО
не мудрствуя лукаво,
М-281

ЛУКАВОГО
от лукавого, Л-144

ЛУКАВЫЙ
лукавый попутал, Ч-97

ЛУКОВОЕ
горе луковое, Г-324

ЛУКУЛЛОВ
лукуллов пир, П-152

ЛУКУЛЛОВСКИЙ
лукулловский пир, П-152

ЛУНОЙ
под луной, Л-145

ЛУНЫ
с луны свалился ⟨упал⟩,
Л-146

ЛУНЬ
как лунь, Л-147

ЛУПАТЬ
лупать глазами, Г-123

ЛУПИТЬ
лупить бельма, Г-100
лупить глаза, Г-100
лупить зенки, Г-100

ЛУЧШЕ
в гостях хорошо, а дома
лучше, Г-368
лучше не надо, Л-148
лучше поздно, чем
никогда, Л-149
лучше синица в руках ⟨в
руки⟩, чем журавль в
небе, С-195
лучше сказать, С-208
лучше сквозь землю
провалиться, З-117
старый друг лучше новых
двух, Д-311
тем лучше, Л-150
ум хорошо, а два лучше,
У-80
худой мир лучше доброй
ссоры, М-185

ЛУЧШЕГО
всего лучшего!, Х-83
оставляет желать лучшего
⟨многого⟩, Л-151

ЛУЧШЕМ
в лучшем виде, В-122
в лучшем случае, С-360

ЛУЧШИЙ
отбывать/отбыть в
лучший мир, М-184
переселиться
⟨переселяться⟩ в
лучший мир, М-184
уйти ⟨уходить⟩ в лучший
мир, М-184

ЛУЧШИХ
в лучших домах
Филадельфии, Д-258

ЛЫЖИ
навострить лыжи, Л-152
направить ⟨направлять⟩
лыжи, Л-153

ЛЫКА
лыка не вяжет, Л-154

ЛЫКО
не всяко(е) лыко в строку,
Л-155
поставить всякое лыко в
строку, Л-156
ставить всякое лыко в
строку, Л-156

ЛЫКОМ
лыком не вяжет, Л-154
лыком шит(ый), Л-157
не лыком шит(ый), Л-158

ЛЫСОГО
беса лысого, Ч-106
чёрта лысого, Ч-106

ЛЬВИНАЯ
львиная доля, Д-250

ЛЮБАЯ
любая собака, С-441

ЛЮБВИ
из любви к искусству,
Л-159

ЛЮБЕЗЕН
будь любезен, Б-227

ЛЮБЕЗНОСТИ
не откажи(те) в
любезности, Л-160

ЛЮБЕЗНЫ
будьте любезны, Б-227

ЛЮБИ
люби кататься, люби и
саночки возить, С-12

ЛЮБИМОГО
оседлать своего любимого
конька, К-270
садиться/сесть на своего
любимого конька, К-270

ЛЮБИМУЮ
наступать/наступить на
любимую мозоль,
М-230

ЛЮБИТ
бог троицу любит, Б-105
денежка счёт любит, Д-171
кто любит попа, (а) кто
попадью, (а) кто попову
дочку, П-344
шутить не любит, Ш-99

ЛЮБИТЬ
просим ⟨прошу⟩ любить
да ⟨и⟩ жаловать, П-602

ЛЮБИШЬ
любишь кататься, люби и
саночки возить, С-12

ЛЮБО
любо-дорого, Л-161
любо-мило, Л-161

ЛЮБОВЬ
закрутить любовь
⟨роман⟩, Р-160
крутить любовь ⟨роман⟩,
Р-160
любовь зла — полюбишь и
козла, Л-162
покрутить любовь
⟨роман⟩, Р-160
совет да ⟨и⟩ любовь,
С-462
старая любовь не ржавеет,
Л-163

ЛЮБОЙ
в любой момент, М-248
любой ценой, Ц-29

ЛЮБОМ
в любом случае, С-361

ЛЮБОМУ
дай бог любому, Б-110

ЛЮБОПЫТНОЙ
любопытной Варваре нос
оторвали, В-7

ЛЮБЫХ
любых мастей, М-41

ЛЮБЯТ
денежки ⟨деньги⟩ счёт
любят, Д-171

ЛЮДЕЙ
как у людей, Л-164
мир не без добрых людей,
С-57
поспешишь — людей
насмешишь, Л-165
свет не без добрых людей,
С-57

ЛЮДИ
в люди, Л-172
все мы люди, все (мы)
человеки, Л-166
выбиваться/выбиться в
люди, Л-168
вывести ⟨выводить⟩ в
люди, Л-167
выйти ⟨выходить⟩ в
люди, Л-168
живут (же) люди!, Л-169
идти в люди, Л-170
люди доброй воли, Л-171
на люди, Л-172
пойти в люди, Л-170
свои люди — сочтёмся,
Л-173
уйти в люди, Л-170

ЛЮДЯХ
в людях, Л-175
жить в людях, Л-174
на людях, Л-175
на людях и смерть красна,
М-191
служить в людях, Л-174

ЛЯД
ляд тебя побери!, Ч-99
на кой ляд, Ч-77

ЛЯДУ
к ляду, Ч-110

ЛЯМКУ
потянуть ⟨тянуть⟩ лямку,
Л-176

ЛЯП
тяп да ляп, Т-257

ЛЯСЫ
поточить ⟨точить⟩ лясы,
Л-177

М

МАГ
маг и волшебник, М-1

МАГОМЕТ
если гора не идёт к

Магомету, то Магомет
идёт к горе, Г-315

МАЗАНЫ
одним миром мазаны,
М-188

МАЗИ
на мази, М-2

МАКАР
куда Макар телят не
гонял, М-3

МАКАРА
на бедного Макара все
шишки валятся, М-4

МАКАРОМ
таким макаром, М-5

МАКОВ
как ⟨что⟩ маков цвет, Ц-12

МАКОВОЙ
маковой росинки в рот не
брать/не взять, К-60
маковой росинки во рту не
было, Р-161
ни маковой росинки, Р-162
ни маковой росинки во рту
не было, Р-161

МАКОВУЮ
на маковую росинку, Р-163
ни на маковую росинку,
Р-163

МАКУШКЕ
держать ушки на макушке,
У-158
ушки на макушке, У-193

МАЛ
и стар и мал, С-542
мал золотник, да дорог,
З-182
мал мала меньше, М-6
стар и мал, С-542

МАЛА
без мала, М-16
мал мала меньше, М-6
от мала до велика, М-7

МАЛАНЬИНУ
(как) на Маланьину
свадьбу, С-28

МАЛАЯ
малая нужда, Н-254
малая толика, Т-136

МАЛЕНЬКАЯ
вагон и маленькая
тележка, В-1

МАЛЕНЬКО
есть маленько, Е-13

МАЛЕНЬКОЕ
моё дело маленькое, Д-115

МАЛЕНЬКОЙ
по маленькой, М-8

МАЛЕНЬКОМУ
по маленькому, М-9

МАЛИНА
не жизнь ⟨не житьё⟩, а
малина, Ж-57
разлюли малина, М-10

МАЛО
и горя ⟨горюшка⟩ мало,
Г-361
мало каши ел/съел, К-113
мало ли, М-11

мало ли что, М-12
мало радости, Р-10
мало того, М-13
мало того что... ещё и...,
  М-14
мало что, М-15
много званых, но мало
  избранных, З-88
ни много ни мало, М-197
нужды мало, Н-256
повесить мало, У-3
убить мало, У-3
МАЛОГО
без малого, М-16
МАЛОЕ
самое малое, М-71
МАЛОЙ
малой кровью, К-414
МАЛОМУ
по малому делу, М-9
МАЛОСТЬ
самая малость, М-17
МАЛЫЕ
малые мира сего, М-18
МАЛЫЙ
добрый малый, М-19
и старый и малый, С-542
славный малый, М-19
старый и малый, С-542
МАЛЫМ
за малым дело стало,
  Д-102
малым делом, Д-139
МАЛЬЧИК
мальчик для битья, М-20
мальчик с пальчик, М-21
МАЛЮЮТ
не так страшен чёрт, как
  его малюют, Ч-78
МАМАЕВО
мамаево нашествие, Н-44
мамаево побоище, П-210
МАМАЙ
как* Мамай прошёл,
  М-22
МАМЕНЬКИН
маменькин сынок
  ⟨сыночек⟩, С-735
МАМЕНЬКИНА
маменькина дочка, Д-301
МАНЕР
на манер, М-23
на свой манер, Л-11
МАНЕРОМ
живым манером, Р-331
МАНИЮ
как* по манию волшебного
  жезла, М-27
МАННА
манна небесная, М-24
МАННОЙ
питаться манной небесной,
  М-25
МАННЫ
как манны небесной, М-26
МАНОВЕНИЮ
как* по мановению
  волшебного жезла, М-27
как* по мановению
  волшебной палочки,
  М-27

МАРАТЬ
марать бумагу, Б-246
марать руки, Р-292
МАРАФЕТ
навести ⟨наводить⟩
  марафет, М-28
МАРКИ
высшей марки, М-29
первой марки, М-29
МАРКОЙ
под маркой, М-30
МАРКУ
выдерживать марку, М-31
держать марку, М-31
показать ⟨показывать⟩
  марку, К-131
МАРМЕЛАДОМ
антик с мармеладом, А-30
МАРТЫШКИН
мартышкин труд, Т-213
МАРУСЯ
чёрная маруся, В-272
МАРШ
шагом марш!, Ш-16
МАСКИ
снимать/снять маски,
  М-35
сорвать ⟨срывать⟩ маски,
  М-35
МАСКОЙ
под маской, М-32
МАСКУ
надевать/надеть маску,
  М-33
носить маску, М-33
сбрасывать/сбросить (с
  себя) маску, М-34
снимать/снять маску,
  М-34, М-35
сорвать ⟨срывать⟩ маску,
  М-35
МАСЛА
подливать/подлить масла
  в огонь, М-36
МАСЛЕ
ерунда на постном масле,
  Е-11
как ⟨словно⟩ сыр в масле
  кататься, С-736
чепуха на постном масле,
  Е-11
МАСЛЕНИЦА
не всё коту масленица
  (,бывает и великий
  пост), К-341
не жизнь ⟨не житьё⟩, а
  масленица, Ж-57
МАСЛО
масло масляное, М-37
МАСЛОМ
как* маслом по сердцу,
  М-38
каши ⟨кашу⟩ маслом не
  испортишь, К-116
кукиш с маслом, К-459
фига с маслом, К-459
шиш с маслом, К-459
МАСЛУ
как по маслу, М-39

МАСЛЯНОЕ
масло масляное, М-37
МАССЕ
в (общей) массе, М-40
МАСТЕЙ
всех мастей, М-41
любых мастей, М-41
разных мастей, М-41
МАСТЕР
заплечный мастер, Д-52
заплечных дел мастер,
  Д-52
мастер на все руки, М-42
МАСТЕРА
дело мастера боится, Д-85
МАСТЕРИЦА
мастерица на все руки,
  М-42
МАСТИ
к масти, М-44
одной (и той же) масти,
  М-43
той же масти, М-43
МАСТЬ
в масть, М-44
под масть, М-44
под одну масть, М-43
МАТЕРИ
впитать ⟨впитывать⟩ с
  молоком матери, М-241
всасывать/всосать с
  молоком матери, М-241
годиться в матери, Г-188
идти к чёртовой матери,
  Ч-113
к ёбаной ⟨ебене⟩ матери,
  М-50
к едрёной матери, М-45
к чёртовой матери, Ч-110,
  Ч-111
лететь к чёртовой матери,
  Ч-113
по матери, М-48
пойти к чёртовой матери,
  Ч-113
полететь к чёртовой
  матери, Ч-113
МАТЕРИИ
высокие материи, М-46
МАТЕРИНО
материно молоко на губах
  не обсохло, М-240
МАТЕРИНСКОЕ
материнское молоко на
  губах не обсохло, М-240
МАТОМ
благим матом, М-47
МАТУШКЕ
по матушке, М-48
МАТУШКИ
матушки мои!, Б-29
матушки светы!, Б-29
МАТЬ
в бога (душу) мать, М-55
в чём мать родила, М-49
вашу мать, М-55
ёб вашу ⟨твою⟩ мать,
  М-50
как мать родила, М-49

мать родная не узнает,
  М-51
мать твою за ногу!, М-52
мать твою перемать, М-55
мать честная!, М-53
повторенье — мать ученья,
  П-227
показать кузькину мать,
  М-54
так вашу ⟨твою⟩ мать,
  М-55
твою мать, М-55
МАФУСАИЛОВ
мафусаилов век, В-19
МАФУСАИЛОВЫ
мафусаиловы года ⟨лета⟩,
  В-19
МАХ
в один мах, М-56
во весь мах, Д-342
МАХА
со всего маха, М-58
МАХНУЛ
(вон) куда махнул!, Х-8
вот куда махнул!, Х-8
МАХНУТЬ
махнуть рукой, Р-333
МАХОМ
единым махом, М-56
одним махом, М-56
МАХУ
давать/дать маху, М-57
с единого маху, М-56
с маху, М-58
с одного маху, М-56
со всего маху, М-58
МАШЕРОЧКА
машерочка с машерочкой,
  Ш-47
МАШЕРОЧКОЙ
машерочка с машерочкой,
  Ш-47
шерочка с машерочкой,
  Ш-47
МАШИНА
как заведённая машина,
  М-59
МАШУТ
после драки кулаками не
  машут, Д-303
МАЯЧИТЬ
маячить перед глазами,
  Г-121
МГНОВЕНИЕ
в мгновение ока, М-60
в одно мгновение (ока),
  М-60
МЕ
ни бе ни ме (ни кукареку),
  Б-33
МЕБЕЛИ
для мебели, М-61
МЁД
вашими бы устами (да)
  мёд пить, У-145
не мёд, С-21
твоими бы устами (да)
  мёд пить, У-145
МЁДА
ложка дёгтю в бочке мёда,
  Л-128

МЕДАЛИ
   другая сторона медали,
      С-602
   оборотная ⟨обратная⟩
      сторона медали, С-602
МЕДВЕДЬ
   дело не медведь, в лес не
      убежит ⟨не уйдёт⟩, Р-3
   медведь на ухо наступил,
      М-62
   работа не медведь, в лес
      не убежит ⟨не уйдёт⟩,
      Р-3
МЕДВЕДЯ
   делить шкуру неубитого
      медведя, Ш-78
МЕДВЕЖИЙ
   медвежий угол, У-31
МЕДВЕЖЬЯ
   медвежья услуга, У-131
МЕДНАЯ
   медная глотка, Г-146
МЕДНОГО
   гроша медного не стоит,
      Г-416
МЕДНЫЕ
   на медные гроши
      ⟨деньги⟩, Д-172
   пройти (и) огни и воды
      ⟨огонь и воду⟩ и медные
      трубы, О-65
   пройти сквозь ⟨через⟩
      огни и воды ⟨огонь и
      воду⟩ и медные трубы,
      О-65
МЕДНЫЙ
   (и) в медный грош не
      ставить, Г-412
   медный грош цена, Г-410
   медный лоб, Л-117
МЕДОВИЧ
   сахар медович, С-22
МЕДОВЫЙ
   медовый месяц, М-131
МЁДОМ
   питаться акридами
      и (диким) мёдом,
      А-20
МЁДУ
   капля моего мёду, К-66
   ложка дёгтю в бочке мёду,
      Л-128
   частица моего мёду, К-66
МЕЛИ
   как рак на мели, Р-70
   мели, Емеля, твоя неделя,
      Е-10
   на мели, М-63
   сидеть на мели, М-63
МЕЛКАЯ
   мелкая сошка, С-504
МЕЛКИЙ
   истереть в мелкий
      порошок, П-386
   стереть в мелкий
      порошок, П-386
МЕЛКИМ
   рассыпаться мелким
      бесом, Б-60

МЕЛКО
   мелко плавать, П-162
МЕЛКУЮ
   разменивать на мелкую
      монету, М-65
   размениваться на мелкую
      монету, М-66
   разменять на мелкую
      монету, М-65
   разменяться на мелкую
      монету, М-66
МЕЛОЧАМ
   истратить по мелочам,
      М-65
   по мелочам, М-64
   размениваться/
      разменяться по
      мелочам, М-66
   растратить по мелочам,
      М-65
   тратить по мелочам, М-65
МЕЛОЧИ
   истратить по мелочи,
      М-65
   по мелочи, М-64
   разменивать на мелочи,
      М-65
   размениваться на мелочи,
      М-66
   разменять на мелочи,
      М-65
   разменяться на мелочи,
      М-66
   растратить по мелочи,
      М-65
   тратить по мелочи, М-65
МЕЛОЧЬ
   разменивать на (всякую)
      мелочь, М-65
   размениваться на (всякую)
      мелочь, М-66
   разменять на (всякую)
      мелочь, М-65
   разменяться на (всякую)
      мелочь, М-66
МЕЛЬ
   посадить на мель, М-68
   садиться на мель, М-67
   сажать на мель, М-68
   сесть на мель, М-67
МЕЛЬНИЦА
   ветряная мельница, М-69
МЕЛЬНИЦАМИ
   воевать с ветряными
      мельницами, М-70
   сражаться с ветряными
      мельницами, М-70
МЕЛЬНИЦУ
   лить воду на мельницу,
      В-187
МЕНЕЕ
   более или менее, Б-164
   не более (и) не менее,
      М-197
   ни более (и) ни менее,
      М-197
   тем не менее, Т-66
МЕНЬШЕ
   мал мала меньше, М-6
   не больше (и) не меньше,
      М-197

   ни больше (и) ни меньше,
      М-197
МЕНЬШЕЕ
   из двух зол меньшее, З-180
   самое меньшее, М-71
МЕНЬШЕЙ
   по меньшей мере, М-75
МЕНЯ
   без меня меня женили,
      Ж-16
   да поразит меня гром,
      Г-406
   да поразят меня силы
      небесные, Г-406
   да разразит меня бог
      ⟨господь⟩, Б-125
   да разразит меня гром,
      Г-406
   да разразят меня силы
      небесные, Г-406
   не про меня писано, П-156
   отсохни у меня рука ⟨руки
      и ноги⟩!, Р-302
   побей меня бог ⟨господь⟩,
      Б-125
   покарай меня бог
      ⟨господь⟩, Б-125
   помяни(те) меня, С-321
   попомни(те) меня, С-321
   порази меня гром (на этом
      месте), Г-406
   порази меня силы
      небесные, Г-406
   пускай поразит меня гром,
      Г-406
   пускай поразят меня силы
      небесные, Г-406
   пускай разразит меня
      гром, Г-406
   пускай разразят меня силы
      небесные, Г-406
   пускай у меня рука
      отсохнет!, Р-302
   пусть поразит меня гром,
      Г-406
   пусть поразят меня силы
      небесные, Г-406
   пусть разразит меня гром,
      Г-406
   пусть разразят меня силы
      небесные, Г-406
   пусть у меня рука
      отсохнет!, Р-302
   разрази меня бог
      ⟨господь⟩, Б-125
   разрази меня гром (на
      этом месте), Г-406
   разрази меня силы
      небесные, Г-406
   смотри(те) у меня!, С-421
   ты у меня попляшешь,
      П-355
   убей меня бог ⟨господь⟩,
      Б-125
   убей меня гром (на этом
      месте), Г-406
   чтоб у меня руки (и ноги)
      отсохли!, Р-302
МЕНЯТЬ
   менять гнев на милость,
      Г-155

   менять декорации, Д-51
   менять кукушку на
      ястреба, К-461
   менять шило на мыло,
      Ш-63
МЕНЯТЬСЯ
   меняться в лице, Л-91
МЕРА
   мера терпения
      переполнилась, Ч-36
МЕРЕ
   в полной мере, М-72
   в равной мере, О-23
   ни в какой мере, М-73
   ни в коей мере, М-73
   по крайней мере, М-74
   по меньшей мере, М-75
   по мере, М-76
   по мере возможности,
      М-77
   по мере того как..., М-78
МЕРЗОСТЬ
   мерзость запустения, М-79
МЕРИН
   как сивый мерин, М-80
МЕРИТЬ
   мерить... аршином, А-43
   мерить вёрсты, В-47
   мерить взглядом, Г-109
   мерить глазами, Г-109
   мерить... мер(к)ой, А-43
   мерить на... аршин, А-43
   мерить на... мер(к)у, А-43
   мерить на один аршин,
      А-44
   мерить на одну мер(к)у,
      А-44
   мерить на свой аршин,
      А-45
   мерить на свою мерку,
      А-45
   мерить одним аршином,
      А-44
   мерить одной мер(к)ой,
      А-44
   мерить по себе, А-45
   мерить своей меркой, А-45
   мерить своим аршином,
      А-45
МЕРКОЙ
   мерить... меркой, А-43
   мерить своей меркой, А-45
   мерять... меркой, А-43
   мерять своей меркой, А-45
МЕРКУ
   мерить на... мерку, А-43
   мерить на свою мерку,
      А-45
   мерять на... мерку, А-43
   мерять на свою мерку,
      А-45
МЕРОЙ
   мерить... мерой, А-43
   мерить одной мерой, А-44
   мерять... мерой, А-43
   мерять одной мерой, А-44
МЁРТВ
   ни жив ни мёртв, Ж-25
МЁРТВАЯ
   мёртвая хватка, Х-9

МЕРТВЕЦКИМ
мертвецким сном, С-433
МЁРТВОЙ
мёртвой буквой, Б-238
на мёртвой точке, Т-178
сдвинуть с мёртвой точки, Т-181
сдвинуться с мёртвой точки, Т-182
сойти с мёртвой точки, Т-182
МЁРТВОМУ
как мёртвому припарки, М-81
МЁРТВУЮ
запить мёртвую, Г-360
пить мёртвую, Г-360
МЁРТВЫЕ
мёртвые души, Д-390
МЁРТВЫЙ
мёртвый час, Ч-13
ни живой ни мёртвый, Ж-25
МЁРТВЫМ
лежать мёртвым грузом, Г-429
мёртвым сном, С-433
МЕРУ
в меру, М-82
знать меру, М-83
мерить на... меру, А-43
мерить на одну меру, А-44
мерять на... меру, А-43
мерять на одну меру, А-44
не в меру, М-84
через ⟨чрез⟩ меру, М-87
МЕРЫ
без меры, М-85
принимать/принять меры, М-86
сверх ⟨свыше⟩ (всякой) меры, М-87
МЕРЯТЬ
мерять... аршином, А-43
мерять вёрсты, В-47
мерять... мер(к)ой, А-43
мерять на... аршин, А-43
мерять на... мер(к)у, А-43
мерять на один аршин, А-44
мерять на одну мер(к)у, А-44
мерять на свой аршин, А-45
мерять на свою мерку, А-45
мерять одним аршином, А-44
мерять одной мер(к)ой, А-44
мерять по себе, А-45
мерять своей меркой, А-45
мерять своим аршином, А-45
МЕСИТЬ
месить грязь, Г-433
МЕСТА
взять с места, М-88
встало на свои места, М-99

живого места не осталось ⟨нет⟩, М-89
места не столь отдалённые, М-90
мокрого места не останется, М-115
не встать (мне ⟨нам⟩) с (этого) места, М-92
не мочь найти (себе) места, М-91
не находить (себе) места, М-91
не сойти мне ⟨нам⟩ с (этого) места!, М-92
не сходя с места, М-93
не у места, М-130
нет места, М-94
ни с места, М-95
поставить всё на свои места, М-98
рвануть с места, М-88
с места в карьер, М-96
сдвинуть с места, М-97
ставить всё на свои места, М-98
стало ⟨становится⟩ на свои места, М-99
у места, М-128
чтоб не встать (мне ⟨нам⟩) с (этого) места!, М-92
чтоб не сойти (мне ⟨нам⟩) с (этого) места!, М-92
МЕСТАХ
на местах, М-100
МЕСТЕ
всё на ⟨своём⟩ месте, М-101
глаза на мокром месте, Г-55
душа не на месте, Д-370
кажинный раз на этом (самом) месте, Р-22
класть на месте, М-102
мозги не на месте, М-227
на голом месте, М-105
на месте, М-102, М-103
на месте преступления, М-104
на пустом месте, М-105
на ровном месте, М-106
на своём месте, М-103
оставаться на (одном) месте, М-108
положить на месте, М-102
порази меня гром на этом месте, Г-406
провалиться (мне) на (этом) месте, М-107
разрази меня гром на этом месте, Г-406
сердце не на месте, Д-370
стоять на (одном) месте, М-108
топтаться на (одном) месте, М-108
убей меня гром на этом месте, Г-406
худые вести не лежат на месте, В-64
чтоб мне провалиться на (этом) месте, М-107

шишка на ровном месте, Ш-71
МЕСТЕЧКО
тёпленькое ⟨тёплое⟩ местечко, М-109
хлебное местечко, М-127
МЕСТО
больное место, М-110
встало на (своё) место, М-99
встать на место, М-124
злачное место, М-111
знать своё место, М-112
иметь место, М-113
место под солнцем, М-114
мокрое место останется, М-115
на место, М-116
не место, М-117
не место красит человека, а человек место, М-118
общее место, М-119
поставить всё на (своё) место, М-98
поставить на (своё) место, М-123
поставить себя на место, М-124
пустое место, М-120
свято место пусто не бывает, М-121
слабое место, М-122
ставить всё на (своё) место, М-98
ставить на (своё) место, М-123
ставить себя на место, М-124
стало ⟨становится⟩ на (своё) место, М-99
становиться/стать на место, М-124
тёпленькое ⟨тёплое⟩ место, М-109
узкое место, М-125
указать ⟨указывать⟩ его ⟨её⟩ место, М-123
уступать/уступить место, М-126
уязвимое место, М-122
хлебное место, М-127
честь и место, Ч-139
МЕСТУ
к месту, М-128
к месту и не к месту, М-129
не к месту, М-130
МЕСЯЦ
медовый месяц, М-131
МЕТАЛЛ
презренный металл, М-132
МЕТАТЬ
метать бисер перед свиньями, Б-69
метать гром и молнию ⟨громы, громы и молнии, громы-молнии⟩, Г-409
метать жребий, Ж-83
метать икру, И-54
метать петли, П-126

рвать и метать, Р-94
МЕТЁЛКУ
под метёлку, М-133
МЕТЁТ
новая метла чисто метёт, М-134
МЕТКО
редко, да метко, Р-98
МЕТЛА
новая метла чисто метёт, М-134
МЕТЛОЙ
вымести ⟨выметать⟩ железной метлой, М-135
МЕТЛУ
под метлу, М-133
МЕТНУТЬ
метнуть жребий, Ж-83
МЕХУ
на рыбьем меху, М-136
МЕЧ
вложить меч в ножны, М-137
дамоклов меч, М-138
обнажать/обнажить меч, М-139
повинную голову (и) меч не сечёт, Г-267
поднимать/поднять меч, М-139
МЕЧА
не выпускать из рук меча, Р-215
МЕЧИ
скрестить ⟨скрещивать⟩ мечи, Ш-84
МЕЧОМ
огнём и мечом, О-58
под дамокловым мечом, М-138
МЕЧТАТЬ
нечего и мечтать, Д-325
МЕЧУ
предавать/предать огню и мечу, О-60
МЕШАЕТ
не мешает, М-140
МЕШАЛО
не мешало бы, М-140
МЕШАТЬ
мешать в (одну) кучу, К-498
мешать (все) карты, К-98
МЕШАТЬСЯ
мешаться в рассудке, У-99
мешаться в уме, У-99
мешаться рассудком, У-99
мешаться умом, У-99
МЕШКЕ
покупать/купить кота в мешке, К-335
шила в мешке не утаишь, Ш-62
МЕШКИ
мешки под глазами, М-141
МЕШКОМ
из-за угла (пыльным) мешком прибит(ый) ⟨трахнутый, ударен(ный)⟩, У-13

как* из-за угла (пыльным) мешком прибит(ый) ⟨трахнутый, ударен(ный)⟩, У-13
сидеть мешком, М-142

МЕШОК
денежный мешок, М-143
золотой мешок, М-143
мешок с соломой, М-144

МЕШОЧЕК
в мешочек, М-145

МЕЩАНИН
мещанин во дворянстве, М-146

МИГ
в единый миг, М-147
в один миг, М-147
на миг, М-175

МИГНУТЬ
(и) глазом мигнуть, Г-135

МИЗИНЕЦ
на ⟨с⟩ мизинец, М-148

МИЗИНЦА
не стоить мизинца, М-149

МИКИТКИ
под микитки, М-150

МИЛ
насильно мил не будешь, Б-221
не по хорошу мил, а по милу хорош, Х-85

МИЛЕНЬКИЙ
как миленький, М-151

МИЛО
вот (это) мило!, М-152
снаружи мило, а внутри гнило, С-427

МИЛОВАЛ
бог миловал, Б-98

МИЛОГО
для милого дружка (и) семь вёрст не околица, Д-312

МИЛОЕ
милое дело, Д-112

МИЛОСТИ
милости просим ⟨прошу⟩, М-153
милости прошу к нашему шалашу, М-154
по милости, М-155

МИЛОСТЬ
вкрадываться/вкрасться в милость, М-156
войти в милость, М-157
втереться ⟨втираться⟩ в милость, М-156
входить в милость, М-157
попадать/попасть в милость, М-157
менять гнев на милость, Г-155
переменить ⟨положить, преложить⟩ гнев на милость, Г-155
сдаваться/сдаться на милость, М-158
сделай(те) божескую милость, М-161

сделай(те) милость, М-159
скажи(те) на милость, М-160
сменить ⟨сменять⟩ гнев на милость, Г-155
яви(те) божескую милость, М-161

МИЛОСТЬЮ
божьей милостью, М-162

МИЛУ
не по хорошу мил, а по милу хорош, Х-85

МИЛУЮ
за милую душу, Д-418

МИЛЫЕ
милые бранятся – только тешатся, М-163

МИЛЫМ
с милым рай и в шалаше, М-164

МИМО
пройти ⟨проходить⟩ мимо, П-597

МИНА
кислая мина, М-165

МИНИАТЮРЕ
в миниатюре, М-166

МИНОВАЛА
миновала (сия) чаша, Ч-34
миновала эта чаша, Ч-34

МИНОВАТЬ
двум смертям ⟨двух смертей⟩ не бывать, а одной не миновать, С-399
чему быть, того ⟨тому⟩ не миновать, Б-282

МИНУ
делать весёлую ⟨хорошую⟩ мину при плохой игре, М-167
подвести ⟨подводить⟩ мину, М-168
подкладывать/подложить мину, М-168
сделать весёлую ⟨хорошую⟩ мину при плохой игре, М-167

МИНУТ
без пяти минут, М-169

МИНУТА
как одна минута, М-170
минута в минуту, М-171

МИНУТКУ
на минутку, М-175
одну минутку!, М-177
сию минутку, М-178

МИНУТНОЕ
минутное дело, Д-113

МИНУТОЧКУ
на минуточку, М-175
одну минуточку!, М-177

МИНУТУ
в добрую минуту, М-172
в минуту, М-173
в одну минуту, М-174
в первую минуту, М-174
минута в минуту, М-171
на минуту, М-175

ни на минуту, М-176
одну минуту!, М-177
с минуты на минуту, М-180
сию минуту, М-178

МИНУТЫ
ни минуты, М-179
с минуты на минуту, М-180

МИНЫ
подвести ⟨подводить⟩ мины, М-168
подкладывать/подложить мины, М-168

МИР
мир не без добрых людей, С-57
мир не производил, С-59
мир праху, М-182
мир тесен, М-181
отбывать/отбыть в другой ⟨иной, лучший⟩ мир, М-184
перевернуть весь мир, М-183
переселиться ⟨переселяться⟩ в другой ⟨иной, лучший⟩ мир, М-184
пир на весь мир, П-153
уйти ⟨уходить⟩ в другой ⟨иной, лучший⟩ мир, М-184
худой мир лучше доброй ссоры, М-185

МИРА
до скончания мира, С-229
малые мира сего, М-18
не от мира сего, М-186
сильные мира сего, С-194

МИРЕ
ни за какие блага ⟨сокровища⟩ в мире, Б-73

МИРОВАЯ
мировая скорбь, С-231

МИРОВУЮ
идти/пойти на мировую, М-187

МИРОМ
одним миром мазаны, М-188
с миром, М-189

МИРУ
идти по миру, М-190
на миру и смерть красна, М-191
пойти по миру, М-190
пускать/пустить по миру, М-192
с миру по нитке, М-193
с миру по нитке – голому рубаха ⟨рубашка⟩, М-194
ходить по миру, М-190

МИТЬКОЙ
Митькой звали, П-330

МЛАД
(и) стар и млад, С-542

МЛАДЕНЦЕВ
избиение младенцев, И-36

МЛАДЕНЧЕСКИЙ
младенческий лепет, Л-52

МЛАДЕНЧЕСТВО
впадать/впасть в младенчество, Д-190

МЛАДЫХ
от ⟨с⟩ младых ногтей, Н-166

МНЕ
(а) мне-то что?, Ч-159
наказание мне, Н-21
не встать мне с (этого) места!, М-92
не сойти мне с (этого) места!, М-92
нужен ты мне!, Н-258
по мне, М-195, М-196
почём мне знать, З-176
провалиться мне в тартарары!, З-121
провалиться мне на (этом) месте, М-107
провалиться мне сквозь землю!, З-121
скажи мне, кто твой друг, и я скажу (тебе), кто ты, Д-310
тоже мне, Т-135
чтоб мне провалиться (в тартарары)!, З-121
чтоб мне провалиться на (этом) месте, М-107
чтоб мне сквозь землю провалиться!, З-121
чтоб не встать мне с (этого) места!, М-92
чтоб не сойти мне с (этого) места!, М-92

МНИТЬ
высоко мнить о себе, В-256
много мнить о себе, В-256

МНОГАЯ
многая лета, Л-64

МНОГИЕ
многие лета, Л-64

МНОГО
во много крат, К-369
много воображать о себе, В-256
много будешь знать – скоро состаришься, З-173
много бы дал, Д-11
много думать о себе, В-256
много званых, но мало избранных, З-88
много мнить о себе, В-256
много на себя брать/ взять, Б-204
много соли съесть, П-625
много чести, Ч-122
ни много ни мало, М-197
слишком много позволить ⟨позволять⟩ себе, Л-110

МНОГОГО
многого захотел ⟨хочет⟩, Х-92
оставляет желать многого, Л-151

МНОГОСТРАДАЛЬНЫЙ
Иов многострадальный,
И-71

МОГ
кто бы мог подумать!,
П-258

МОГИ
не моги, М-198

МОГИКАН
последний из могикан,
М-199
последний могикан, М-199

МОГИЛА
братская могила, М-200
горбатого могила
исправит, Г-319

МОГИЛЕ
(стоять) одной ногой в
могиле, Н-162

МОГИЛУ
вбить осиновый кол в
могилу, К-177
глядеть в могилу, М-205
забить осиновый кол в
могилу, К-177
загнать в могилу, М-204
копать могилу, М-202
копать себе могилу, М-203
лечь в могилу, М-206
найти (себе) могилу, М-201
рыть могилу, М-202
рыть себе могилу, М-203
свести (сводить) в
могилу, М-204
смотреть в могилу, М-205
сойти (сходить) в могилу,
М-206
уйти в могилу, М-206
уложить в могилу, М-204
унести (уносить) (с собой)
в могилу, М-207

МОГИЛЫ
до (самой) могилы, М-208
на краю могилы, К-371
у края могилы, К-371

МОГИЛЬНЫМ
заснуть могильным сном,
С-432
спать могильным сном,
С-436
уснуть могильным сном,
С-432

МОГУ
не могу знать, М-209
терпеть не могу, Т-85

МОДЕЛЬ
не модель, Ф-4

МОДУ
брать/взять моду, М-210

МОДЫ
(последний) крик моды,
К-388

МОЁ
моё дело, Д-114
моё дело маленькое, Д-115
моё дело сторона, Д-116
моё почтение, П-460,
П-461
помяни(те) моё слово,
С-321

попомни(те) моё слово,
С-321
с моё, М-211

МОЕГО
герой не моего романа,
Г-18
капля моего мёду, К-66
частица моего мёду, К-66

МОЕЙ
в моей власти (воле),
В-160
по моей части, Ч-24

МОЕМУ
к стыду моему, С-655

МОЕТ
рука руку моет, Р-233

МОЖАХОМ
еле можахом, М-212

МОЖАХУ
еле можаху, М-212

МОЖЕТ
быть не может!, М-214
видеть не может, В-127
всякий дурак может, Д-328
и разговора (разговору)
быть не может, Р-51
и речи быть не может,
Р-112
каждый дурак может,
Д-328
какой может быть
разговор!, Р-50
может быть, М-213
может статься, М-213
не может быть!, М-214
не может быть и речи,
Р-112
не может надышаться,
Н-14
речи быть не может, Р-112
спасайся, кто может,
С-505

МОЖЕШЬ
не откладывай на завтра
то, что можешь сделать
сегодня, О-149

МОЖНО
глаза сломать можно, Г-65
как можно!, М-216
как можно..., М-215
как это можно!, М-216
можно сказать, С-209
можно топор вешать,
Т-160
не откладывай на завтра
то, что можно сделать
сегодня, О-149
по пальцам можно
пересчитать
(перечесть), П-17
по пальцам можно
сосчитать (счесть),
П-17
разве можно!, М-216
соплёй перешибить
можно, С-490
убиться можно!, У-4
язык сломать можно, Я-46

МОЗГА
до мозга костей, М-217

мозга за мозгу заходит/
зашла, М-218

МОЗГАМ
давать/дать по мозгам,
М-219
получать/получить по
мозгам, М-220

МОЗГАМИ
ворочать мозгами, М-221
пораскинуть мозгами,
У-109
пошевелить мозгами,
М-221
раскидывать/раскинуть
мозгами, У-109
шевелить/шевельнуть
мозгами, М-221

МОЗГИ
вправить (вправлять)
мозги, М-222
давить на мозги, М-223
забивать/забить мозги,
Г-251
закрутить мозги, М-225
запудрить мозги, М-229
капать на мозги, М-224
крутить мозги, М-225
куриные мозги, М-226
мозги варят, Г-199
мозги набекрень, М-227
мозги не на месте, М-227
мозги не туда повёрнуты,
М-227
промывать/промыть
мозги, М-228
пудрить мозги, М-229
цыплячьи мозги, М-226
чугунные мозги, Г-222

МОЗГОВ
промывка мозгов, М-228

МОЗГОЙ
пошевелить (шевелить)
мозгой, М-221

МОЗГУ
гвоздём засесть (сидеть) в
мозгу, Г-12
засесть в мозгу, Г-12
мозга за мозгу заходит/
зашла, М-218
сидеть в мозгу, Г-12

МОЗОЛИТЬ
мозолить глаза, Г-81
мозолить руки, Р-293
мозолить язык, Я-32

МОЗОЛЬ
наступать на больную
мозоль, М-230
наступать на (любимую)
мозоль, М-230
наступить на больную
мозоль, М-230
наступить на (любимую)
мозоль, М-230

МОИ
батюшки мои!, Б-29
глаза бы мои не видали
(не видели), Г-51
глаза бы мои не глядели
(не смотрели), Г-51
лопни мои глаза, Г-80

матушки мои!, Б-29

МОЙ
бог (ты) мой!, Б-142
боже (ты) мой!, Б-142
ни боже мой, Б-144
через мой труп!, Т-220
язык мой — враг мой,
Я-38

МОКРАЯ
мокрая курица, К-481

МОКРОГО
мокрого места не
останется, М-115

МОКРОЕ
мокрое дело, Д-117
мокрое место останется,
М-115

МОКРОМ
глаза на мокром месте,
Г-55

МОЛ
так и так мол, Т-18

МОЛИТВАМИ
вашими (твоими)
молитвами, М-231

МОЛНИИ
метать громы и молнии
(громы-молнии), Г-409
с быстротою молнии,
Б-276

МОЛНИЮ
метать гром и молнию,
Г-409

МОЛОДЕЦ
молодец против (среди)
овец (, а против молодца
и сам овца), М-232

МОЛОДО
молодо-зелено, М-233

МОЛОДОЙ
молодой да ранний, М-237

МОЛОДОСТИ
не первой молодости,
М-234
по молодости лет, М-235

МОЛОДОСТЬ
вторая молодость, М-236

МОЛОДЦА
молодец против (среди)
овец, а против молодца
и сам овца, М-232

МОЛОДЫХ
из молодых, да ранний,
М-237
от (с) молодых ногтей,
Н-166

МОЛОКА
как от козла молока, К-168
(только) птичьего молока
недостаёт (не хватает,
нет), М-238
что от козла молока, К-168

МОЛОКЕ
обжёгся (обжёгшись) на
молоке, дуешь (будешь
дуть) и на воду, М-239

МОЛОКО
материно (материнское)
молоко на губах не
обсохло, М-240

молоко на губах не обсохло, М-240

МОЛОКОМ
впитать ⟨впитывать⟩ с
молоком матери, М-241
всасывать/всосать с
молоком матери, М-241
кровь с молоком, К-404

МОЛОТКА
с молотка, М-242

МОЛОТОМ
между молотом и
наковальней, М-243

МОЛОТЬ
молоть вздор ⟨галиматью,
ерунду, чепуху⟩, В-99
молоть языком, Я-32

МОЛОЧИШКО
детишкам ⟨ребятишкам⟩
на молочишко, Д-189

МОЛОЧНЫЕ
молочные реки и
кисельные берега, Р-107
молочные реки, кисельные
берега, Р-107

МОЛЧАЛА
чья бы корова мычала, а
твоя (бы) молчала,
К-311

МОЛЧАНИЕ
молчание – знак согласия,
М-244
слово – серебро, молчание
– золото, С-329
хранить молчание, М-245

МОЛЧАНИЕМ
обойти ⟨обходить⟩
молчанием, М-246
пройти ⟨проходить⟩
молчанием, М-246

МОЛЧАНИЯ
заговор молчания, З-30

МОЛЧАНКИ
играть в молчанки, М-247

МОЛЧАНКУ
игра в молчанку, М-247
играть в молчанку, М-247

МОЛЧАТЬ
молчать в тряпочку, Т-224

МОМЕНТ
в любой момент, М-248
в момент, М-249
в один момент, М-249
ловить момент, М-250

МОНАСТЫРЬ
в чужой монастырь со
своим уставом не ходят,
М-251
подвести ⟨подводить⟩ под
монастырь, М-252

МОНЕТА
ходячая монета, М-253

МОНЕТОЙ
отплатить ⟨отплачивать⟩
той же монетой, М-254
платить той же монетой,
М-254

МОНЕТУ
зашибать/зашибить
монету, Д-175

принимать/принять за
чистую монету, М-255
разменивать на мелкую
монету, М-65
размениваться на мелкую
монету, М-66
разменять на мелкую
монету, М-65
разменяться на мелкую
монету, М-66

МОРАЛЬ
прочитать ⟨читать⟩
мораль, Н-240

МОРГНУТЬ
глазом моргнуть, Г-135
глазом не моргнуть, Г-134
и глазом моргнуть, Г-135

МОРДОЙ
мордой не вышел, Р-390

МОРДУ
воротить/отворотить
морду, Н-210

МОРЕ
капля в море, К-64
море по колена ⟨колено⟩,
М-256
разливанное море, М-257
разливное море, М-257

МОРИТЬ
морить голодом, Г-296

МОРКОВКИНА
до морковкина заговенья,
З-29

МОРКОВКОЙ
держать хвост морковкой,
Х-10

МОРОЗ
мороз по коже ⟨по спине⟩
дерёт ⟨идёт⟩, М-258
мороз по коже ⟨по спине⟩
подирает/подрал, М-258
мороз по коже ⟨по спине⟩
пошёл, М-258
мороз по коже ⟨по спине⟩
пробегает/пробежал,
М-258
мороз по коже ⟨по спине⟩
продирает/продрал,
М-258
мороз по коже ⟨по спине⟩
проходит/прошёл,
М-258

МОРОЧИТЬ
морочить голову, Г-257

МОРСКОГО
как песку морского, П-122
со дна морского, Д-200
что песку морского, П-122

МОРСКОЙ
как песок морской, П-122
морской волк, В-226

МОРСКОМ
на дне морском, Д-200

МОРФЕЮ
в объятия к Морфею, О-37

МОРФЕЯ
в объятия Морфея, О-37
в объятиях Морфея, О-37

МОРЯ
ждать у моря погоды,
М-259

на дне моря, Д-200
нести (и) с Дона и с моря,
Д-262
сидеть у моря да ⟨и⟩
ждать погоды, М-259
со дна моря, Д-200

МОСКВА
(и) Москва не вдруг ⟨не
сразу⟩ строилась, М-260
Москва от копеечной
свечки загорелась
⟨сгорела⟩, М-261
Москва слезам не верит,
М-262

МОСКВЫ
до Москвы не
перевешаешь ⟨не
перевешать⟩, М-263

МОСТ
перебрасывать/
перебросить мост,
М-264
перекидывать/перекинуть
мост, М-264

МОСТА
хоть с моста в реку, В-191

МОСТОВУЮ
гранить мостовую, М-265

МОСТЫ
навести ⟨наводить⟩
мосты, М-266
жечь все ⟨за собой⟩
мосты, К-289
жечь (свои) мосты, К-289
сжечь ⟨сжигать⟩ все ⟨за
собой⟩) мосты, К-289
сжечь ⟨сжигать⟩ свои
мосты, К-289

МОТАТЬ
мотать дело, Д-126
мотать на ус, У-129
мотать нервы, Н-83
мотать себе на ус, У-129

МОХОМ
зарастать/зарасти мохом,
М-267
обрастать/обрасти
мохом, М-267

МОЧА
моча в голову ударила,
М-268

МОЧАЛКУ
жевать мочалку, М-269

МОЧАЛО
жевать мочало, М-269

МОЧЕНЬКИ
моченьки не стало ⟨нет⟩,
М-270

МОЧИ
изо всей мочи, М-271
мочи не стало ⟨нет⟩,
М-270
что было мочи, М-271
что есть мочи, М-271

МОЧИТЬСЯ
мочиться против ветра,
В-75

МОЧЬ
во всю мочь, М-271

не мочь найти (себе)
места, М-91
шагу не мочь сделать
⟨ступить⟩, Ш-24

МОШНА
толстая мошна, К-82
тугая мошна, К-82

МОШНОЙ
тряхнуть мошной, М-272

МОШНУ
набивать/набить мошну,
К-81
развязать ⟨развязывать⟩
мошну, М-273

МОЩИ
живые мощи, М-274
ходячие мощи, М-274

МОЮ
на мою голову, Г-261

МОЯ
будь ⟨была бы⟩ моя воля,
В-252
душа моя, Д-366
моя бы воля, В-252
моя половина, П-303
моя хата с краю, Х-6
не моя забота ⟨печаль⟩,
З-6
чья потеря, моя находка,
П-426

МРАК
кромешный мрак, Т-249

МРАКОМ
покрыт(о) мраком
неизвестности, М-275

МРАЧНЫМИ
мрачными красками,
К-364

МРАЧНЫХ
в мрачных красках, К-364

МРУТ
мухи мрут, М-302

МУДРЕНЕЕ
утро вечера мудренее,
У-152

МУДРЕНО
мудрено ли, М-276
не мудрено, М-277

МУДРЁНОГО
мудрёного нет, М-278
что мудрёного, М-278

МУДРЕЦА
на всякого ⟨каждого⟩
мудреца довольно
простоты, М-279

МУДРОСТЬ
не велика мудрость, М-280

МУДРСТВУЯ
не мудрствуя лукаво,
М-281

МУЖ
муж да ⟨и⟩ жена – одна
сатана, М-282

МУЖИК
гром не грянет, мужик не
перекрестится, Г-404

МУЗЕЙНАЯ
музейная редкость, Р-100

МУЗЫКА
другая музыка, М-283

иная музыка, М-283
не та музыка, М-283

МУЗЫКОЙ
пропадать, так с музыкой!, М-284

МУЗЫКУ
испортить музыку, О-1
класть на музыку, М-285
переложить на музыку, М-285
положить на музыку, М-285
портить музыку, О-1

МУКА
мука мученическая, М-286
перемелется — мука будет, М-287

МУКАМ
хождение по мукам, Х-75

МУКИ
муки Тантала, М-288
танталовы муки, М-288

МУЛ
как мул, О-109

МУНДИРА
защищать честь мундира, Ч-132

МУНДИРАХ
в мундирах, М-289

МУНДИРЕ
в мундире, М-289

МУР-МУР
ни мур-мур, М-290

МУРАШКИ
мурашки бегают ⟨бегут⟩ по коже ⟨по спине, по телу⟩, М-291
мурашки забегали ⟨заползали⟩ по коже ⟨по спине, по телу⟩, М-291
мурашки побежали по коже ⟨по спине, по телу⟩, М-291
мурашки ползают ⟨ползут/поползли, пошли⟩ по коже ⟨по спине, по телу⟩, М-291
мурашки пробежали по коже ⟨по спине, по телу⟩, М-291

МУРУ
разводить муру, М-292

МУТИТСЯ
в глазах мутится, Г-127
мутится в голове, Г-227

МУТИТЬ
мутить воду, В-188

МУТНОЙ
в мутной воде рыбу ловить, В-177

МУХ
до белых мух, М-293
мух ловить, В-270
мух считать, В-270

МУХА
как сонная муха, М-294
какая муха укусила, М-295
муха укусила, М-296

слышно, как муха пролетит, М-297

МУХИ
белые мухи, М-298
делать из мухи слона, М-299
едят его мухи!, М-300
как мухи, М-301
мухи дохнут, М-302
мухи мрут, М-302
мухи не обидит, М-303
сделать из мухи слона, М-299

МУХОЙ
под мухой, М-304

МУХУ
муху задавить, М-306
муху зашибить, М-306
муху проглотил, М-305
муху раздавить, М-306

МУЧЕНИЧЕСКАЯ
мука мученическая, М-286

МУШКУ
брать/взять на мушку, П-555

МЫ
были когда-то и мы рысаками, Р-393
все мы люди, все (мы) человеки, Л-166
все мы под богом ходим, Б-135
знаем мы вас!, З-142
(и) мы пахали, П-71

МЫКАТЬ
горе мыкать, Г-325
мыкать век ⟨жизнь⟩, В-20

МЫЛА
без мыла в душу влезть ⟨лезть⟩, М-307

МЫЛЕ
в мыле, М-308

МЫЛИТЬ
мылить голову, Г-258
мылить шею, Ш-54

МЫЛО
менять/сменять шило на мыло, Ш-63
на мыло!, М-309

МЫЛЬНЫЙ
лопнуть как мыльный пузырь, П-628
мыльный пузырь, П-629

МЫСЛЕЙ
без (всяких) задних мыслей, М-311

МЫСЛЕТЕ
выделывать ⟨выписывать, писать⟩ (ногами) мыслете, В-33

МЫСЛИ
без (всякой) задней мысли, М-311
гигант мысли, Г-19
прочитать ⟨читать⟩ мысли, М-310

МЫСЛИМО
мыслимо ли дело, Д-118

МЫСЛИМОЕ
мыслимое ли дело, Д-118

МЫСЛЬ
взбредать/взбрести на мысль, Г-248
войти в мысль, Г-271
вспадать/вспасть на мысль, Г-271
входить в мысль, Г-271
задняя мысль, М-311
навести ⟨наводить⟩ на мысль, М-312
прийти ⟨приходить⟩ на мысль, Г-271

МЫСЛЬЮ
растекаться мыслью по древу, М-313

МЫСЛЯМИ
собираться/собраться с мыслями, М-314

МЫСЛЯХ
в мыслях, М-315
в мыслях не иметь, М-317
держать в мыслях, М-316
и в мыслях нет, М-317
перебирать/перебрать в мыслях, У-101

МЫТЬ
мыть голову, Г-258
мыть кости ⟨косточки⟩, К-327

МЫТЬЁМ
не мытьём, так катаньем, М-318

МЫЧАЛА
чья бы корова мычала, а твоя (бы) молчала, К-311

МЫЧИТ
не мычит, не телится, М-319

МЫШИНАЯ
мышиная беготня ⟨возня⟩, В-209
мышиная суета ⟨сутолока⟩, В-209

МЫШИНЫЙ
мышиный жеребчик, Ж-19
мышиный хвост(ик), Х-22

МЫШКАМИ
под мышками, М-320

МЫШКИ
под мышки, М-320

МЫШКОЙ
под мышкой, М-320

МЫШКУ
под мышку, М-320

МЫШЬ
гора родила мышь, Г-313
как мышь, М-321, М-322
как мышь на крупу, М-323
как церковная мышь, М-324

МЯГКО
мягко выражаясь, В-371
мягко говоря, В-371
мягко стелет, да жёстко спать, С-557

МЯКИНЕ
на мякине не проведёшь, М-325

старого воробья на мякине не проведёшь, В-268

МЯКИННАЯ
мякинная башка, Г-212
мякинная голова, Г-212

МЯКИНОЙ
голова мякиной набита, Г-208

МЯСО
знает кошка, чьё мясо съела, К-343
ни рыба ни мясо, Р-381
пушечное мясо, М-326
чует кошка, чьё мясо съела, К-343

МЯСОМ
с мясом, М-327

Н

НА
на тебе, Т-50

НАБАТ
бить/забить в набат, Н-1
ударить ⟨ударять⟩ в набат, Н-1
бить набат, Н-1

НАБЕГА
с набега, Н-22

НАБЕКРЕНЬ
мозги набекрень, М-227

НАБЕРЁШЬСЯ
с кем поведёшься, от того и наберёшься, П-212

НАБИВАТЬ
набивать карман, К-81
набивать кошелёк, К-81
набивать кубышку, К-452
набивать мошну, К-81
набивать оскомину, О-111
набивать руку, Р-351
набивать себе цену, Ц-34
набивать цену, Ц-35

НАБИРАТЬ
набирать силу, С-189

НАБИРАТЬСЯ
набираться духа ⟨духу⟩, Д-358
набираться разума, У-86
набираться сил, С-168
набираться терпения, Т-83
набираться ума ⟨ума-разума⟩, У-86

НАБИТ
глаз набит, Г-23

НАБИТА
голова мякиной ⟨соломой, трухой⟩ набита, Г-208
рука набита, Р-229

НАБИТЫЙ
набитый дурак, Д-330

НАБИТЬ
битком набить, Н-2
набить карман, К-81
набить кошелёк, К-81
набить кубышку, К-452
набить мошну, К-81
набить оскомину, О-111

набить руку, Р-351
набить себе цену, Ц-34
набить цену, Ц-35
НАБИТЬСЯ
битком набиться, Н-2
НАБОР
набор слов, Н-3
НАБРАСЫВАТЬ
набрасывать тень, Т-73
НАБРАТЬ
воды в рот набрать, В-192
набрать силу ⟨силы⟩,
С-189
НАБРАТЬСЯ
набраться духа ⟨духу⟩,
Д-358
набраться разума, У-86
набраться сил, С-168
набраться терпения, Т-83
набраться ума ⟨ума-
разума⟩, У-86
НАБРОСИТЬ
набросить тень, Т-73
НАВЕРНЯКА
бить наверняка, Б-70
НАВЕСИТЬ
навесить лапшу на уши,
Л-31
НАВЕСТИ
навести глянец, Г-154
навести марафет, М-28
навести мосты, М-266
навести на мысль, М-312
навести тень, Т-73, Т-75
навести тень на плетень,
Т-75
навести тень на ясный
день, Т-75
навести тоску, Т-167
навести туман(а)
⟨туману⟩, Т-235
НАВЕШАТЬ
собак навешать, С-439
НАВЕШИВАТЬ
навешивать лапшу на уши,
Л-31
НАВОДИТЬ
наводить глянец, Г-154
наводить марафет, М-28
наводить мосты, М-266
наводить на мысль, М-312
наводить тень, Т-73, Т-75
наводить тень на плетень,
Т-75
наводить тень на ясный
день, Т-75
наводить тоску, Т-167
наводить туман(а)
⟨туману⟩, Т-235
НАВОСТРИТЬ
навострить глаза, Г-82
навострить лыжи, Л-152
навострить слух, У-185
навострить уши, У-185
НАВРЯД
навряд ли, В-323
НАВСЕГДА
раз (и) навсегда, Р-32
НАВСТРЕЧУ
делать шаг навстречу, Ш-1

идти ⟨пойти⟩ навстречу,
И-28
сделать шаг навстречу,
Ш-1
НАВЫКАТ(Е)
глаза навыкат(е), Г-56
НАВЫТЯЖКУ
стоять навытяжку, С-621
НАВЯЗАТЬСЯ
навязаться на голову ⟨на
шею⟩, Г-264
НАВЯЗНУТЬ
навязнуть в зубах, З-191
НАВЯЗЫВАТЬСЯ
навязываться на голову
⟨на шею⟩, Г-264
НАГНАТЬ
нагнать тоску, Т-167
НАГОЛОВУ
разбить ⟨разгромить⟩
наголову, Р-40
НАГОНЯТЬ
нагонять тоску, Т-167
НАГОРОДИТЬ
нагородить вздор ⟨ерунду,
околёсицу⟩, В-99
нагородить чепуху
⟨чушь⟩, В-99
НАГОТЕ
во всей ⟨своей⟩ наготе, Н-4
НАГРАДУ
в награду, Н-5
НАГРЕВАТЬ
нагревать руки, Р-284
НАГРЕТЬ
нагреть бока, Б-152
нагреть руки, Р-284
НАДАВАТЬ
надавать в шею, Ш-44
надавать по шее ⟨по
шеям⟩, Ш-44
НАДВОЕ
бабушка (ещё) надвое
гадала ⟨сказала⟩, Б-5
НАДДАВАТЬ
наддавать ходу, Х-71
НАДДАТЬ
наддать ходу, Х-71
НАДЕВАТЬ
надевать личину, М-33
надевать маску, М-33
надевать на себя хомут
⟨ярмо⟩, Х-80
надевать петлю на себя,
П-128
надевать петлю ⟨себе⟩ на
шею, П-128
надевать себе хомут на
шею, Х-80
надевать смирительную
рубаху ⟨рубашку⟩, Р-194
надевать хомут на шею,
Х-80
НАДЕЖДЕ
в надежде, Н-6
НАДЕЖДУ
питать надежду, Н-7
НАДЕЖДЫ
возлагать надежды, Н-8

питать надежды, Н-7
подавать (большие)
надежды, Н-9
НАДЁЖНЫЕ
в надёжные руки, Р-267
НАДЁЖНЫХ
в надёжных руках, Р-267
НАДЕЙСЯ
на бога надейся, а сам не
плошай, Б-129
НАДЕЛАТЬ
наделать дел ⟨делов⟩,
Д-53
наделать шума ⟨шуму⟩,
Ш-96
НАДЕТЬ
надеть личину, М-33
надеть маску, М-33
надеть на себя хомут
⟨ярмо⟩, Х-80
надеть петлю на себя,
П-128
надеть петлю ⟨себе⟩ на
шею, П-128
надеть себе хомут на шею,
Х-80
надеть смирительную
рубаху ⟨рубашку⟩, Р-194
надеть хомут на шею,
Х-80
НАДО
ведь надо же!, Н-11
ведь это же надо!, Н-11
далеко ходить не надо,
Х-58
даром не надо, В-218
за примерами ⟨примером⟩
далеко ходить не надо,
Х-58
кто надо, Н-10
куда надо, Н-10
лучше не надо, Л-148
надо быть, Б-279
надо думать, Д-323
надо же!, Н-11
надо и совесть знать,
С-456
надо и честь знать, Ч-137
надо полагать, Д-323
надо признаться, П-525
надо совесть знать, С-456
надо честь знать, Ч-137
совесть знать надо, С-454
совесть иметь надо, С-454
так и надо, Т-17
что надо, Н-12
это же надо!, Н-11
НАДОБНОСТИ
по казённой надобности,
Н-13
НАДОЛГО
всерьёз и надолго, В-341
НАДОРВАТЬ
надорвать душу, Д-424
надорвать живот
⟨животики, животы⟩,
Ж-33
надорвать кишки, Ж-33
надорвать сердце, Д-424
надорвать силы, С-192

НАДРЫВАЕТСЯ
душа надрывается, Д-367
сердце надрывается, Д-367
НАДРЫВАТЬ
надрывать глотку, Г-339
надрывать горло, Г-339
надрывать грудь, Г-426
надрывать душу, Д-424
надрывать живот
⟨животики, животы⟩,
Ж-33
надрывать кишки, Ж-33
надрывать сердце, Д-424
надрывать силы, С-192
НАДСАЖИВАТЬ
надсаживать глотку, Г-339
надсаживать горло, Г-339
надсаживать грудь, Г-426
НАДУВАТЬ
надувать в уши, У-186
надувать губки ⟨губы⟩,
Г-440
НАДУТЬ
надуть в уши, У-186
надуть губки ⟨губы⟩,
Г-440
НАДЫШАТЬСЯ
не может надышаться,
Н-14
НАДЫШИТСЯ
не надышится, Н-14
НАДЫШИШЬСЯ
перед смертью не
надышишься, С-396
НАЖАТЬ
нажать все пружины, П-75
нажать кнопки, К-149
нажать на все кнопки,
К-149
нажать на все педали,
П-75
нажать на все пружины,
П-75
НАЖИВНОЕ
дело наживное, Д-86
НАЖИМАТЬ
нажимать все пружины,
П-75
нажимать кнопки, К-149
нажимать на все кнопки,
К-149
нажимать на все педали,
П-75
нажимать на все
пружины, П-75
НАЖУЖЖАТЬ
нажужжать в уши, У-186
НАЗАД
своё слово ⟨свои слова⟩
брать своё слово
⟨свои слова⟩ назад,
С-280
брать слова ⟨слово⟩
назад, С-280
взять своё слово ⟨свои
слова⟩ назад, С-280
взять слова ⟨слово⟩ назад,
С-280
повернуть колесо истории
назад, К-196

повернуть оглобли назад,
О-50
поворачивать
⟨поворотить⟩ оглобли
назад, О-50
тому назад, Т-152
туда и назад, Т-230

НАЗВАЛСЯ
назвался груздем, полезай
в кузов, Г-428

НАЗВАНИЕ
одно название, Н-15
(одно) только название,
Н-15

НАЗВАТЬ
боюсь назвать, Б-194
назвать белое чёрным (и
чёрное белым), Ч-71
назвать вещи настоящими
именами, В-88
назвать вещи своими
⟨собственными⟩
именами, В-88
назвать чёрное белым (и
белое чёрным), Ч-71

НАЗДРАВСТВУЕШЬСЯ
на всякий чих ⟨на всякое
чиханье⟩ не
наздравствуешься, Ч-156

НАЗЛО
как назло, Н-16

НАЗОВИ
хоть горшком назови,
только в печку не ставь,
Г-356

НАЗЫВАЕМЫЙ
так называемый, Н-17

НАЗЫВАЕТСЯ
что называется, Н-18

НАЗЫВАТЬ
называть белое чёрным (и
чёрное белым), Ч-71
называть вещи
настоящими именами,
В-88
называть вещи своими
⟨собственными⟩
именами, В-88
называть чёрное белым (и
белое чёрным), Ч-71

НАИЗНАНКУ
вывернуло наизнанку,
В-358
вывернуть душу
наизнанку, Д-413
вывернуть наизнанку,
В-359
вывернуться наизнанку,
В-360
выворачивает наизнанку,
В-358
выворачивать душу
наизнанку, Д-413
выворачивать наизнанку,
В-359
выворачиваться
наизнанку, В-360
выворотило наизнанку,
В-358
выворотить наизнанку,
В-359

НАИЛУЧШЕГО
всего наилучшего, Х-83

НАИМЕНЬШЕГО
идти по линии ⟨по пути⟩
наименьшего
сопротивления, Л-73
пойти по линии ⟨по пути⟩
наименьшего
сопротивления, Л-73

НАИТИЮ
по наитию (свыше), Н-19

НАЙДЁШЬ
не знаешь, где найдёшь,
где потеряешь, З-147

НАЙТИ
концов не найти, К-255
найти дорогу к сердцу,
Д-282
найти доступ к сердцу,
Д-282
найти конец ⟨кончину⟩,
М-201
найти могилу, М-201
найти общий язык, Я-14
найти путь к сердцу, Д-282
найти самого себя, Н-20
найти свой конец, М-201
найти себе могилу, М-201
найти себя, Н-20
найти смерть, М-201
найти управу, У-122
не мочь найти (себе)
места, М-91
не найти покою ⟨покоя⟩,
П-288

НАКАЗАНИЕ
вот наказание, Н-21
наказание божеское, Н-21
наказание господне(е),
Н-21
наказание какое-то, Н-21
наказание мне, Н-21
просто наказание, Н-21
прямо наказание, Н-21
сущее наказание, Н-21
чистое наказание, Н-21
что за наказание, Н-21

НАКАЛИТЬ
накалить атмосферу, А-47

НАКАЛЯТЬ
накалять атмосферу, А-47

НАКАТИЛ
стих накатил, С-574

НАКАЧАЛИ
не было печали, (так)
черти накачали, П-137

НАКИДЫВАТЬ
накидывать петлю на
себя, П-128
накидывать петлю (себе)
на шею, П-128

НАКИНЕШЬ
на всякий роток не
накинешь платок, Р-186
на чужой роток не
накинешь платок, Р-186

НАКИНУТЬ
накинуть петлю на себя,
П-128
накинуть петлю (себе) на
шею, П-128

НАКЛАДЕ
в накладе, У-8

НАКЛАДЫВАТЬ
накладывать лапу, Р-352
накладывать на себя руки,
Р-296
накладывать отпечаток,
О-162
накладывать печать, О-162
накладывать руку, Р-352

НАКЛЕИВАТЬ
наклеивать ярлык(и), Я-67

НАКЛЕИТЬ
наклеить нос, Н-214
наклеить ярлык(и), Я-67

НАКЛОННОЙ
идти по наклонной
плоскости, П-197
катиться по наклонной
плоскости, П-197
пойти по наклонной
плоскости, П-197
покатить(ся) по наклонной
плоскости, П-197

НАКОВАЛЬНЕЙ
между молотом и
наковальней, М-243

НАКОСТЫЛЯТЬ
накостылять в шею ⟨по
шее⟩, Ш-54
накостылять шею, Ш-54

НАКРУТИТЬ
накрутить хвост(а), Х-13

НАЛЕВО
направо и налево, Н-26

НАЛЕГАЕТ
рука не налегает, Р-231

НАЛЕГЛА
рука не налегла, Р-231

НАЛЁТА
с налёта, Н-22

НАЛЁТУ
с налёту, Н-22

НАЛИВАТЬ
наливать глаза, Г-73
наливать зенки, Г-73
наливать шары, Г-73

НАЛИВАТЬСЯ
наливаться кровью, К-415

НАЛИТА
как* свинцом налита, С-78

НАЛИТЬ
налить глаза, Г-73
налить зенки, Г-73
налить шары, Г-73

НАЛИТЬСЯ
налиться кровью, К-415

НАЛОЖИТЬ
наложить лапу, Р-352
наложить на себя руки,
Р-296
наложить отпечаток,
О-162
наложить печать, О-162
наложить руку, Р-352

НАЛОМАТЬ
наломать бока, Б-152
наломать дров, Д-306
наломать шею, Ш-54

НАМ
не встать нам с (этого)
места!, М-92
не сойти нам с (этого)
места!, М-92
чтоб не встать ⟨не сойти⟩
нам с (этого) места!,
М-92

НАМАЗАТЬ
намазать пятки (салом),
П-682

НАМАЗЫВАТЬ
намазывать пятки (салом),
П-682

НАМАТЫВАТЬ
наматывать (себе) на ус,
У-129

НАМЁК
тонкий намёк на толстое
обстоятельство ⟨на
толстые
обстоятельства⟩, Н-23

НАМЁТАН
глаз намётан, Г-23

НАМЁТАННЫЙ
намётанный глаз, Г-23

НАМИ
между нами, Г-172
между нами говоря, Г-172
с нами крестная сила!,
С-173

НАМОЗОЛИТЬ
намозолить глаза, Г-81

НАМОТАТЬ
намотать дело, Д-126
намотать (себе) на ус,
У-129

НАМЫКАТЬСЯ
намыкаться горя, Г-325

НАМЫЛИТЬ
намылить голову, Г-258
намылить холку, Ш-54
намылить шею, Ш-54

НАМЯТЬ
намять бока, Б-152
намять холку, Ш-54
намять шею, Ш-54

НАНЮХАТЬСЯ
нанюхаться пороха
⟨пороху⟩, П-384

НАОБУМ
наобум лазаря, Л-19

НАПАДАЕТ
стих нападает, С-574

НАПАДАТЬ
нападать на след, С-250

НАПАЛ
едун напал, Е-4
не на дурака ⟨дуру⟩ напал,
Д-335
не на простака напал,
Д-335
не на таковского напал,
Н-24
не на такого напал, Н-24
не на того напал, Н-24
стих напал, С-574
столбняк напал, С-591
хохотун напал, Х-91

НАПАСТЬ
напасть на след, С-250

НАПЕРЁД
задом наперёд, З-33

НАПЕТЬ
напеть в уши, У-186

НАПИСАНО
на лбу написано, Л-36
на лице написано, Л-92
на роду написано, Р-138
что написано пером, того
    не вырубишь топором,
    П-103

НАПИСАТЬ
написать кровью (сердца),
    К-416

НАПИТЬСЯ
напиться крови, К-394
не плюй в колодец,
    пригодится воды
    напиться, К-199

НАПЛАКАЛ
кот наплакал, К-334

НАПЛЕВАТЬ
наплевать в глаза, Г-86
наплевать в душу, Д-430
наплевать в лицо, Г-86
наплевать в рожу, Г-86
наплевать с высокого
    дерева, Д-176

НАПОКАЗ
выставить (выставлять)
    напоказ, В-109

НАПОРОЛИСЬ
за что боролись, на то и
    напоролись, Б-181

НАПРАВИТЬ
направить лыжи, Л-153
направить на путь
    истинный (истины),
    П-658
направить путь (стопы,
    шаги), П-657

НАПРАВЛЕНИИ
в направлении, Н-25

НАПРАВЛЕНИЮ
по направлению, Н-25

НАПРАВЛЯТЬ
направлять лыжи, Л-153
направлять на путь
    истинный (истины),
    П-658
направлять путь (стопы,
    шаги), П-657

НАПРАВО
направо и налево, Н-26

НАПРАСЛИНУ
возвести (возводить)
    напраслину, Н-27

НАПРОЛОМ
идти (переть) напролом,
    И-29

НАПУДРИТЬ
напудрить голову, Г-258

НАПУСКАТЬ
напускать на себя, Н-28
напускать на себя вид,
    В-112
напускать туман(а)
    (туману) (в глаза),
    Т-235

НАПУСТИТЬ
напустить на себя, Н-28
напустить на себя вид,
    В-112
напустить туман(а)
    (туману) (в глаза),
    Т-235

НАРАСПАШКУ
душа нараспашку, Д-368

НАРОД
во (на) весь народ, Н-29

НАРОДЕ
при всём (честном) народе,
    Н-30
при народе, Н-30

НАРОЧНО
как* нарочно, Н-31

НАРУЖНОСТЬ
наружность обманчива,
    В-171

НАРУЖУ
весь наружу, В-66
всё наружу, В-66
всплывать/всплыть
    наружу, П-217
вывести (выводить)
    наружу, В-357
выплывать/выплыть
    наружу, П-217
выставить (выставлять)
    наружу, В-109

НАС
везде хорошо, где нас нет,
    Т-39
полюбите нас
    чёрненькими, а
    беленькими всякий
    полюбит, П-326
там хорошо, где нас нет,
    Т-39

НАСЕСТЕ
худые вести не сидят на
    насесте, В-64

НАСИЛУ
насилу ноги волочить
    (передвигать), Н-144
насилу ноги таскать
    (тащить, тянуть),
    Н-144

НАСИЛЬНО
насильно мил не будешь,
    Б-221

НАСКВОЗЬ
видеть насквозь, В-126

НАСКОКА
с наскока, Н-32

НАСКОКУ
с наскоку, Н-32

НАСКОЛЬКО
насколько хватает
    (хватал) глаз, Г-27
насколько хватало глаз
    (глаза, глазу), Г-27

НАСМАРКУ
идти/пойти насмарку,
    И-30

НАСМЕШИШЬ
поспешишь — людей
    насмешишь, Л-165

НАСОСАТЬСЯ
насосаться крови, К-394

НАСТАВИТЬ
наставить на путь
    истинный (истины),
    П-658
наставить на разум, У-78
наставить на ум, У-78
наставить нос, Н-214
наставить рога, Р-122
наставить фонарей, Ф-16

НАСТАВЛЕНИЕ
прочитать (читать)
    наставление, Н-240

НАСТАВЛЯТЬ
наставлять на путь
    истинный (истины),
    П-658
наставлять на разум, У-78
наставлять на ум, У-78
наставлять рога, Р-122

НАСТАИВАТЬ
настаивать на своём, С-85

НАСТАЛ
час настал, Ч-19

НАСТОРОЖИТЬ
насторожить слух (уши),
    У-185

НАСТОЯТЬ
настоять на своём, С-85

НАСТОЯЩЕГО
до настоящего дня, Д-163
до настоящего времени,
    Д-163

НАСТОЯЩЕЕ
показать своё настоящее
    лицо, Л-98

НАСТОЯЩИМИ
назвать (называть) вещи
    настоящими именами,
    В-88

НАСТРОЕНИЯ
человек настроения, Ч-51

НАСТУПАТЬ
наступать на больную
    мозоль, М-230
наступать на глотку, Г-335
наступать на горло, Г-335
наступать на (любимую)
    мозоль, М-230
наступать на ноги (на
    ногу), Н-178
наступать на пятки, П-680
наступать на хвост, Х-14

НАСТУПИЛ
медведь на ухо наступил,
    М-62
слон на ухо наступил,
    М-62

НАСТУПИТЬ
наступить на больную
    мозоль, М-230
наступить на глотку, Г-335
наступить на горло, Г-335
наступить на (любимую)
    мозоль, М-230
наступить на ноги (на
    ногу), Н-178
наступить на пятки, П-680
наступить на хвост, Х-14

НАСУЩНЫЙ
хлеб насущный, Х-39

НАСЫПАТЬ
насыпать соли на хвост,
    С-471

НАТРУБИТЬ
натрубить в уши, У-186

НАТУРА
вторая натура, Н-33
привычка — вторая
    натура, П-518
широкая натура, Н-34

НАТУРЕ
в натуре вещей, П-543

НАТЯНУТЬ
натянуть нос, Н-214

НАУТЁК
бросаться/броситься
    наутёк, П-637
кидаться/кинуться наутёк,
    П-637
пускаться/пуститься
    наутёк, П-637

НАУЧИТЬ
научить уму-разуму, У-115

НАХВАТАТЬСЯ
нахвататься верхов (вер-
    хушек, вершков), В-55

НАХОДИТ
стих находит, С-574

НАХОДИТЬ
находить дорогу к сердцу,
    Д-282
находить доступ к сердцу,
    Д-282
находить общий язык,
    Я-14
находить путь к сердцу,
    Д-282
не находить места, М-91
не находить покою
    (покоя), П-288
не находить себе места,
    М-91

НАХОДКА
чья потеря, моя находка,
    П-426

НАЧАЛ
под начал, Н-40

НАЧАЛА
для начала, Н-35

НАЧАЛО
брать (своё) начало, Н-36
вести (своё) начало, Н-37
давать/дать начало, Н-38
доброе начало полдела
    откачало, Н-39
класть начало, Н-38
лиха беда начало, Б-39
под начало, Н-40
положить начало, Н-38
хорошее начало полдела
    откачало, Н-39

НАЧАЛОМ
под началом, Н-40

НАЧАЛЬСТВУ
по начальству, Н-41

НАЧАТЬ
лиха беда начать, Б-39

начать за здравие, а
кончить ⟨свести⟩ за
упокой, З-107
начать издалека, Н-42
начать с нуля, Н-262

НАЧИНАТЬ
начинать издалека, Н-42
начинать с нуля, Н-262

НАЧИНАЯ
начиная от ⟨с⟩, Н-43

НАЧИХАЛ
не баран начихал, Б-21

НАШ
наш брат, Б-198
наш пострел везде поспел,
П-416

НАША
где наша не пропадала!,
П-573
наша берёт, Б-58
наша взяла, Б-58
наша сестра, С-155

НАШЕ
где наше не пропадало!,
П-573
наше вам ⟨с кисточкой⟩,
К-124
наше почтение, П-460
наше с кисточкой, К-124
с наше, М-211

НАШЕГО
нашего полку прибыло,
П-300
нашего поля ягода
⟨ягодки, ягоды⟩, П-327

НАШЕЙ
будет и на нашей улице
праздник, У-72

НАШЁЛ
нашёл дурака ⟨дураков⟩!,
Д-334
нашёл дурочку ⟨дуру⟩!,
Д-334
стих нашёл, С-574
столбняк нашёл, С-591

НАШЕМ
в нашем полку прибыло,
П-300

НАШЕМУ
милости прошу к нашему
шалашу, М-154

НАШЕСТВИЕ
мамаево нашествие, Н-44

НАШИ
в наши края, К-376

НАШИМ
вернёмся к нашим
баранам, Б-22
и нашим и вашим, Н-45

НАШИХ
в наших краях, К-376
знай наших!, З-149

НАШЛА
нашла коса на камень,
К-318

НАШЬЁШЬ
на чужой рот пуговицы не
нашьёшь, Р-178

НАЩУПАТЬ
нащупать почву, П-455

НАЩУПЫВАТЬ
нащупывать почву, П-455

НЕ
не до, Д-217

НЕБА
звёзд с неба не хватать,
З-89
как* гром среди ясного
неба, Г-405
как* с неба свалиться
⟨упасть⟩, Н-46
коптитель неба, Н-52
падать с неба на землю,
Н-47
подарок с неба, П-236
с неба свалиться ⟨упасть⟩,
Н-46
сойти с неба на землю,
Н-47
спускаться/спуститься ⟨с
неба⟩ на землю, Н-47
упасть с неба на землю,
Н-47
хватать звёзды с неба,
З-97

НЕБЕ
журавль в небе, Ж-85
лучше синица в руках ⟨в
руки⟩, чем журавль в
небе, С-195
на седьмом небе, Н-48
не сули журавля в небе, а
дай синицу в руки, С-195

НЕБЕС
вознести ⟨возносить⟩ до
небес, Н-49
превознести
⟨превозносить⟩ до
небес, Н-49
семь вёрст до небес (и всё
лесом), В-44

НЕБЕСНАЯ
как птица ⟨птичка⟩
небесная, П-618
манна небесная, М-24
небесная канцелярия, К-54
царица небесная, Ц-3

НЕБЕСНОГО
олух царя небесного, О-90

НЕБЕСНОЕ
царствие ⟨царство⟩
небесное, Ц-7

НЕБЕСНОЙ
как манны небесной, М-26
питаться манной небесной,
М-25

НЕБЕСНЫЕ
да поразят ⟨разразят⟩
меня силы небесные,
Г-406
отверзлись хляби
небесные, Х-46
порази меня силы
небесные, Г-406
пускай поразят ⟨разразят⟩
меня силы небесные,
Г-406
пусть поразят ⟨разразят⟩
меня силы небесные,
Г-406

разверзлись хляби
небесные, Х-46
разрази меня силы
небесные, Г-406

НЕБЕСНЫЙ
отец небесный, Ц-9
царь небесный, Ц-9

НЕБО
как небо и земля, Н-50
как небо от земли, Н-51
небо в овчинку кажется/
показалось, Н-53
небо и земля, Н-50
небо коптить, Н-52
небо с овчинку кажется/
показалось, Н-53
попадать/попасть пальцем
в небо, П-24

НЕБОЛЬШИМ
за небольшим дело стало,
Д-102
с небольшим, Н-54

НЕБОМ
витать между небом и
землёй, О-8
парить между небом и
землёй, О-8
между небом и землёй,
Н-55
под открытым небом,
Н-56

НЕБОСЬ
авось да небось, А-5
авось, небось да как-
нибудь, А-5

НЕБУ
небу жарко, Н-57

НЕВЕДЕНИИ
в блаженном неведении,
Н-58

НЕВЕЛИКА
невелика птица, П-620

НЕВЕРНЫЙ
неверный шаг, Ш-3
Фома неверный, Ф-14

НЕВЕРОЯТИЯ
до невероятия, Н-59

НЕВЕРОЯТНОСТИ
до невероятности, Н-59

НЕВЕРУЮЩИЙ
Фома неверующий, Ф-14

НЕВЕСТА
христова невеста, Н-60

НЕВЕСТКЕ
невестке в отместку, Н-61

НЕВЗВИДЕТЬ
света ⟨свету⟩ (божьего)
невзвидеть, С-67

НЕВЗИРАЯ
невзирая на, Н-62
невзирая на лица, Л-85
невзирая на то что, Н-63
невзирая ни на что, Н-64

НЕВИДАЛЬ
вот невидаль!, Н-65
какая невидаль!, Н-65
что за невидаль!, Н-65
эка(я) невидаль!, Н-65

НЕВИДАЛЬЩИНА
вот невидальщина!, Н-65

какая невидальщина!,
Н-65
что за невидальщина!,
Н-65
эка(я) невидальщина!,
Н-65

НЕВИДИМО
и видимо и невидимо,
В-128

НЕВИННОСТЬ
капитал приобрести и
невинность соблюсти,
К-55
оскорблённая невинность,
Н-66
угнетённая невинность,
Н-66

НЕВОЗМОЖНО
шагу невозможно сделать
⟨ступить⟩, Ш-24

НЕВОЗМОЖНОСТИ
до невозможности, Н-67

НЕВОЛИ
охота пуще неволи, О-176

НЕВООРУЖЁННЫМ
невооружённым глазом,
Г-138

НЕВРЕДИМ
цел и невредим, Ц-22

НЕВРЕДИМОСТИ
в целости и невредимости,
Ц-21

НЕВРЕДИМЫЙ
целый и невредимый, Ц-22

НЕВЫСОКОГО
птица невысокого полёта,
П-620

НЕГДЕ
дохнуть ⟨дыхнуть⟩ негде,
Д-299
иголки ⟨иголку⟩ негде
воткнуть, И-8
плюнуть негде, П-204
повернуться
⟨поворотиться⟩ негде,
П-215
пробу ⟨пробы⟩ ставить
негде, П-563
шагу негде ступить, Ш-23
яблоку негде упасть, Я-6

НЕГОДНЫМИ
покушение с негодными
средствами, П-292
попытка с негодными
средствами, П-292

НЕДАЛЕКО
недалеко искать, Х-58
недалеко уйти, У-64
недалеко ходить (за
примерами
⟨примером⟩), Х-58
яблоко ⟨яблочко⟩ от
яблони ⟨яблоньки⟩
недалеко падает, Я-4

НЕДЕЛЕ
семь пятниц на неделе,
П-684

НЕДЕЛЮ
без году неделя, Г-190

НЕДЕЛЯ
без году неделя, Г-190
мели, Емеля, твоя неделя,
Е-10

НЕДОБРОЙ
недоброй памяти, П-36

НЕДОБРЫЙ
в недобрый час, Ч-9

НЕДОБРЫМ
поминать/помянуть
недобрым словом, С-336

НЕДОЕДАТЬ
куска недоедать, К-490

НЕДОЛГА
вот (тебе) и вся недолга,
В-349
и вся недолга, В-349

НЕДОЛГО
недолго до беды, Г-390
недолго до греха, Г-390
недолго и до беды, Г-390
недолго и до греха, Г-390

НЕДОРОГО
недорого возьмёт, В-214

НЕДОСТАВАЛО
только этого (и)
недоставало!, Х-7
этого ещё (только)
недоставало!, Х-7

НЕДОСТАЁТ
винтика ⟨винтиков⟩ (в
голове) недостаёт, В-147
заклёпки ⟨заклёпок⟩ (в
голове) недостаёт, В-147
клёпки ⟨клёпок⟩ (в голове)
недостаёт, В-147
(только) птичьего молока
недостаёт, М-238
шариков (в голове)
недостаёт, В-147

НЕДОСТАТКА
нет недостатка, Н-68

НЕДРЕМАННОЕ
недреманное око, О-87

НЕЖДАННО
нежданно-негаданно, Н-69

НЕЖЕЛИ
прежде нежели, Ч-60

НЕЖНОСТИ
телячьи нежности, Н-70

НЕЖНЫЙ
нежный пол, П-294

НЕЗАБВЕННОЙ
незабвенной памяти, П-30

НЕЗАВИСИМО
независимо от, Н-71
независимо от того что,
Н-72

НЕЗАПАМЯТНЫХ
с незапамятных времён,
В-288

НЕИЗВЕСТНОСТИ
покрыт(о) мраком
неизвестности, М-275

НЕИМЕНИЕМ
за неимением, Н-73

НЕИМЕНИЮ
по неимению, Н-73

НЕИСПОВЕДИМЫ
неисповедимы пути
господни, П-648

НЕЙДЁТ
нейдёт в голову, Г-265
нейдёт из головы, Г-291
нейдёт из памяти, Г-291
нейдёт из ума, Г-291
нейдёт на ум, Г-265

НЕЙМЁТ
(хоть) видит око, да зуб
неймёт, О-89

НЕКОГДА
вздохнуть некогда, В-100
дохнуть ⟨дыхнуть⟩
некогда, Д-300

НЕКОМУ
бить некому, Б-71

НЕКОТОРОМ
в некотором отношении,
О-157
в некотором роде, Р-131
в некотором царстве, в
некотором государстве,
Ц-4

НЕКОТОРЫМ
некоторым образом, О-21

НЕКОТОРЫХ
в некоторых отношениях,
О-157
с некоторых пор, П-364

НЕКСТАТИ
кстати и некстати, К-441

НЕКУДА
дальше ехать некуда, Н-74
дальше идти некуда, Н-74
дальше некуда, Н-74
девать некуда, Д-47
деваться некуда, Д-48
деть некуда, Д-47
деться некуда, Д-48
иголки ⟨иголку⟩ некуда
воткнуть, И-8
плюнуть некуда, П-204
пробу ⟨пробы⟩ ставить
некуда, П-563
шагу некуда ступить, Ш-23
яблоку некуда упасть, Я-6

НЕЛАДЕН
будь ты неладен, Б-230

НЕЛАДНО
неладно скроен, да крепко
⟨плотно⟩ сшит, С-242

НЕЛЁГКАЯ
нелёгкая дёрнула, Ч-88
нелёгкая дёрнула за язык,
Я-10
нелёгкая занесла, Ч-94
нелёгкая несёт, Ч-94, Ч-95
нелёгкая носит, Ч-96
нелёгкая понесла, Ч-94,
Ч-95
нелёгкая попутала, Ч-97
нелёгкая принесла, Ч-94
нелёгкая унесла, Ч-100

НЕЛЬЗЯ
в рот нельзя взять, Р-172
дохнуть ⟨дыхнуть⟩
нельзя, Д-299
как нельзя..., Н-75
как нельзя кстати, Н-76
нельзя иголки подпустить
⟨подточить⟩, И-7

нельзя не, Н-77
нельзя отказать, О-146
нельзя отнять, О-146
нельзя подступиться,
П-257
нельзя сказать, С-210
ничего нельзя поделать,
П-241
продохнуть нельзя, П-568
слова сказать нельзя,
С-293
шагу нельзя сделать
⟨ступить⟩, Ш-24
шутить нельзя, Ш-99

НЕМАЗАНОЕ
как немазаное колесо,
К-195

НЕМАЗАНЫЙ
такой-сякой немазаный
(сухой), Т-33
такой-сякой сухой
немазаный, Т-33

НЕМИЛОСТИ
в немилости, Н-78

НЕМИЛОСТЬ
впадать/впасть в
немилость, Н-78
попадать/попасть в
немилость, Н-78

НЕМНОГИМ
за немногим дело стало,
Д-102

НЕМНОГО
есть немного, Е-13
немного погодя, П-232
немного спустя, П-232

НЕНАСЫТНАЯ
ненасытная утроба, У-153

НЕПЛОХО
неплохо подвешенный
язык, Я-47
язык неплохо подвешен
⟨привешен⟩, Я-47

НЕПОВАДНО
чтобы неповадно было,
Б-272

НЕПОДМАЗАННОЕ
неподмазанное колесо,
К-195

НЕПОКРЫТОЙ
с непокрытой головой,
Г-241

НЕПОСТИЖИМО
уму непостижимо, У-114

НЕПОЧАТЫЙ
непочатый край, К-354
непочатый угол, К-354

НЕПРАВДАМИ
правдами и неправдами,
П-480

НЕПРИКАЯННЫЙ
как неприкаянный, Н-79

НЕПРОБУДНЫМ
почить непробудным
сном, С-432
спать непробудным сном,
С-436

НЕПРОТОЛЧЁНАЯ
непротолчёная труба,
Т-206

НЕРВАХ
играть/поиграть на
нервах, Н-80

НЕРВЫ
выматывать/вымотать
нервы, Н-83
действовать на нервы,
Н-81
измотать нервы, Н-83
испортить нервы, Н-83
истрепать нервы, Н-83
мотать нервы, Н-83
подействовать на нервы,
Н-81
портить нервы, Н-83
потратить нервы, Н-82
потрепать нервы, Н-83
тратить нервы, Н-82
трепать нервы, Н-83

НЕРЕЗАНЫХ
как собак нерезаных,
С-438
что собак нерезаных,
С-438

НЕСЁТ
бог несёт, Б-102
нелёгкая несёт, Ч-94, Ч-95
нечистая сила несёт, Ч-94
чёрт несёт, Ч-94, Ч-95

НЕСИ
хоть святых (вон) неси,
С-90

НЕСКЛАДНО
нескладно скроен, да
крепко ⟨плотно⟩ сшит,
С-242

НЕСКОЛЬКИХ
в нескольких словах, С-300
в нескольких шагах, Ш-12

НЕСМАЗАННОЕ
несмазанное колесо, К-195

НЕСМОТРЯ
несмотря на, Н-84
несмотря на то что, Н-85
несмотря ни на что, Н-86

НЕСОЛОНО
несолоно хлебавши, Х-42

НЕСТИ
нести ахинею
⟨белиберду⟩, В-99
нести вздор ⟨галиматью,
дичь, ересь⟩, В-99
нести ерунду, В-99
нести и с Дона и с моря,
Д-262
нести крест, К-381
нести околёсину
⟨околёсную⟩, В-99
нести с Дона и с моря,
Д-262
нести чепуху ⟨чушь⟩, В-99

НЕСТЬ
конца несть, К-251
конца и краю ⟨конца-
краю⟩ несть, К-251
ни конца ни краю несть,
К-251
несть пророка в отечестве
своём ⟨в своём
отечестве⟩, П-581

несть числа, С-726

НЕСУТ
куда ноги несут, Н-146
ноги несут, Н-150
черти несут, Ч-94

НЕСЧАСТЬЕ
на несчастье, Н-87
не было бы счастья, да
несчастье помогло,
С-693

НЕСЧАСТЬЮ
к несчастью, Н-87
по несчастью, Н-87
товарищ по несчастью,
Т-117

НЕСЧАСТЬЯ
двадцать два несчастья,
Н-88

НЕТ
а то нет!, Н-89
в заводе нет, З-22
в ногах правды нет, Н-129
живого места нет, М-89
живой нитки нет, Н-101
житья нет, Ж-81
и в заводе нет, З-22
и в мыслях нет, М-317
и в уме нет, М-317
и ваших нет, В-9
и звания нет, З-87
и разговора ⟨разговору⟩
нет, Р-51
износа ⟨износу⟩ нет, И-53
конца и краю ⟨конца-
краю⟩ нет, К-251
конца нет, К-251
креста нет, К-383
кровинки ⟨кровиночки⟩ в
⟨на⟩ лице нет, К-396
ладу нет, С-248
лица нет, Л-84
моченьки нет, М-270
мочи нет, М-270
мудрёного нет, М-278
на вкус (и) на цвет
товарища ⟨товарищей⟩
нет, В-154
на нет и суда нет, С-658
нет бы, Т-130
нет да нет, Н-90
нет дела, Д-57
нет дураков!, Д-334
нет дыма ⟨дыму⟩ без
огня, Д-437
нет и нет, Н-90
нет и следа, С-254
нет, извини(те), И-42
нет как нет, Н-91
нет места, М-94
нет недостатка, Н-68
нет-нет да..., Н-92
нет-нет (да) и..., Н-92
нет ни складу ни ладу,
С-223
нет никакого удержу, У-45
нет ничего общего, О-33
нет перевода, П-89
нет пророка в отечестве
своём ⟨в своём
отечестве⟩, П-581
нет розы без шипов, Р-149

нет стыда в глазах, С-653
нет того чтобы, Т-130
нет, ты только подумай!,
П-259
нет удержу, У-45
нет, уж (это) извини(те),
И-42
нет хода ⟨ходу⟩, Х-70
нет худа без добра, Х-107
нет числа, С-726
нет, что вы ⟨ты⟩!, Ч-191
нет чтобы, Т-130
ни конца ни краю нет,
К-251
ни кровинки ⟨кровиночки⟩
в ⟨на⟩ лице, К-396
ни одной живой нитки нет,
Н-101
ни одной сухой нитки нет,
Н-101
ни стыда ни совести нет,
С-653
никак нет, Н-94
нужды нет, Н-257
отбою ⟨отбоя⟩ нет, О-131
погибели нет!, П-229
подступа ⟨подступу⟩ нет,
П-256
приступа ⟨приступу⟩ нет,
П-548
пропасти нет!, П-229
прохода ⟨проходу⟩ нет,
П-595
птичьего молока нет,
М-238
свести ⟨сводить⟩ на нет,
С-83
сил нет, С-169, С-170
сил нет, до чего, С-170
сил нет, как, С-170
слада ⟨сладу⟩ нет, С-248
слов(а) нет, С-277, С-278
сноса ⟨сносу⟩ нет, И-53
сойти на нет, С-685
спаса нет, С-507
спасения нет, С-507
спасу нет, С-507
спора ⟨спору⟩ нет, С-277
суда нет, С-659
сухой нитки нет, Н-101
сходить на нет, С-685
счёта ⟨счёту⟩ нет, С-726
так нет (же), Т-23
только птичьего молока
нет, М-238
управы нет, У-123
цены нет, Ц-36
чего только нет, Ч-47

НЕТОЛЧЁНАЯ
нетолчёная труба, Т-206

НЕУБИТОГО
делить шкуру неубитого
медведя, Ш-78

НЕУЗНАВАЕМОСТИ
до неузнаваемости, Н-93

НЕУЧЕНЬЕ
ученье свет, (а) неученье
тьма, У-166

НЕХОРОШО
нехорошо пахнет, П-73

НЕЧЕГО
делать нечего, Д-60

делить нечего, Д-67
нечего греха таить, Г-392
нечего и говорить, Г-166
нечего и греха таить, Г-392
нечего и думать, Д-325
нечего и мечтать, Д-325
нечего сказать, С-211
нечего терять, Т-86
от нечего делать, Д-62

НЕЧЕМ
дохнуть ⟨дыхнуть⟩ нечем,
Д-299
крыть нечем, К-436

НЕЧИСТ
на руку нечист, Р-348

НЕЧИСТАЯ
нечистая сила, С-171
нечистая сила занесла,
Ч-94
нечистая сила несёт
⟨понесла⟩, Ч-94
нечистая сила попутала,
Ч-97
нечистая сила принесла,
Ч-94

НЕЧИСТО
дело нечисто, Д-88

НЕЧИСТОМУ
к нечистому, Ч-111

НЕЧИСТЫЙ
нечистый дух, С-171
нечистый на руку, Р-348
нечистый попутал, Ч-97

НЕШУТОЧНОЕ
дело нешуточное, Д-89

НИЖАЙШЕЕ
нижайшее почтение, П-460

НИЖАЙШИМ
с нижайшим почтением,
П-463

НИЖЕ
ниже всякой критики,
К-390
ниже достоинства, Д-297
ниже пояса, П-468
ниже своего достоинства,
Д-297
тише воды, ниже травы,
В-196
тоном ниже, Т-159
удовольствие ниже
среднего, У-48

НИЗКОГО
птица низкого полёта,
П-620

НИЗКОЙ
низкой пробы, П-565

НИЗШЕЙ
низшей пробы, П-565

НИКАК
никак нет, Н-94

НИКАКИМ
никаким образом, О-22

НИКАКИМИ
никакими силами, С-176

НИКАКИХ
без никаких, Н-95
и никаких!, Н-96
(и) никаких гвоздей, Г-11

НИКАКОГО
не выдерживать никакого
сравнения, С-531
не знать никакого удержу,
У-44
нет никакого удержу, У-45

НИКАКОЙ
не выдерживать никакой
критики, К-390
не играть никакой роли,
Р-152

НИКАКОМУ
не поддаваться никакому
сравнению, С-531

НИКОГДА
беда никогда не приходит
⟨не ходит⟩ одна, Б-37
лучше поздно, чем
никогда, Л-149

НИКОИМ
никоим образом, О-22

НИКУДА
никуда не годится, Г-187
никуда не годный, Г-189
никуда не денешься ⟨не
деться⟩, Д-149

НИМ
и иже с ним, И-32

НИМИ
и иже с ними, И-32

НИТКА
как нитка с иголкой, Н-97
куда иголка, туда и нитка,
И-3

НИТКАМИ
шито белыми нитками,
Н-98

НИТКЕ
висеть на нитке, В-239
держаться на нитке, В-239
по нитке, Н-99
повиснуть на нитке, В-239
с миру по нитке, М-193
с миру по нитке — голому
рубаха ⟨рубашка⟩,
М-194

НИТКИ
до нитки, Н-100
до последней нитки, Н-100
живой нитки не осталось
⟨нет⟩, Н-101
ни одной живой нитки не
осталось ⟨нет⟩, Н-101
ни одной сухой нитки не
осталось ⟨нет⟩, Н-101
сухой нитки не осталось
⟨нет⟩, Н-101

НИТКУ
на живую нитку, Н-102

НИТОЧКЕ
висеть на ниточке, В-239
держаться на ниточке,
В-239
по ниточке, Н-99
повиснуть на ниточке,
В-239
ходить по ниточке, С-647

НИТЬ
Ариаднина нить, Н-103
нить Ариадны, Н-103

насилу ноги волочить ⟨передвигать⟩, Н-144
насилу ноги таскать ⟨тащить, тянуть⟩, Н-144
наступать/наступить на ноги, Н-178
ноги в руки, Н-140
ноги заплетаются, Н-147
ноги не будет, Н-148
ноги не держат, Н-149
ноги несут, Н-150
ноги носят, Н-150
ноги отказали, Н-151
ноги подкашиваются/ подкосились, Н-151
отсохни ⟨у меня⟩ руки и ноги!, Р-302
падать ⟨пасть⟩ в ноги, Н-152
поднимать на ноги, Н-153, Н-154
подниматься на ноги, Н-157
поднять на ноги, Н-153, Н-154
подняться на ноги, Н-157
подымать на ноги, Н-153, Н-154
поклониться в ноги, Н-145
поставить на ноги, Н-153, Н-154
протянуть ноги, Н-155
с головы на ноги, Г-294
с трудом ноги волочить ⟨передвигать⟩, Н-144
с трудом ноги таскать ⟨тащить, тянуть⟩, Н-144
сбиваться/сбиться с ноги, Н-156
ставить на ноги, Н-153, Н-154
становиться/стать на ноги, Н-157
унести ⟨уносить⟩ ноги, Н-158
упасть в ноги, Н-152
хромать на обе ноги, Н-159
чтоб ноги не было ⟨не ступало⟩, Н-148
чтоб у меня руки и ноги отсохли!, Р-302
чуть ноги волочить ⟨передвигать⟩, Н-144
чуть ноги таскать ⟨тащить, тянуть⟩, Н-144

НОГОЙ
вставать/встать левой ногой, Н-142
левой ногой, Н-160
ни в зуб ногой, З-187
ни ногой, Н-161
одной ногой в гробу, Н-162
одной ногой в могиле, Н-162
стать твёрдой ногой, Н-163
стоять одной ногой в гробу, Н-162

стоять одной ногой в могиле, Н-162
НОГОТОК
с ноготок, Н-164
НОГОТЬ
под ноготь, Н-165
НОГТЕЙ
до конца ногтей, К-246
до кончиков ногтей, К-246
от младых ⟨молодых⟩ ногтей, Н-166
с младых ⟨молодых⟩ ногтей, Н-166
НОГТЮ
к ногтю, Н-167
НОГТЯ
не стоить ногтя, М-149
НОГУ
в ногу, Н-168
взять ногу, Н-169
дать ногу, Н-169
держать ногу, Ш-2
идти в ногу, Н-170
лёгкий ⟨лёгок⟩ на ногу, Н-171
мать твою за ногу!, М-52
на барскую ногу, Н-177
на большую ногу, Н-177
на босу(ю) ногу, Н-172
на военную ногу, Н-173
на дружескую ногу, Н-135
на короткую ногу, Н-135
на новую ногу, Н-174
на ногу, Н-175
на холостую ⟨холостяцкую⟩ ногу, Н-176
на широкую ногу, Н-177
наступать/наступить на ногу, Н-178
нога в ногу, Н-168
нога за ногу, Н-120
нога на ногу, Н-121
подставить ⟨подставлять⟩ ногу, Н-188
потерять ногу, Н-156
сам чёрт ногу сломит, Ч-83
скор(ый) на ногу, Н-171
терять ногу, Н-156
тяжёл(ый) на ногу, Н-179
чёрт ногу сломит, Ч-83
шагать в ногу, Н-170
НОЕТ
сердце ноет, Д-364
НОЖ
как* нож в сердце, Н-180
нож в сердце, Н-180
нож в спину, Н-181
нож вострый, Н-182
нож острый, Н-182
под нож, Н-183, Н-192
точить нож, Н-184
НОЖА
без ножа зарезать ⟨резать⟩, Н-185
ходить по лезвию ножа, О-126
ходить по острию ножа, О-126

НОЖАХ
на ножах, Н-186
НОЖИ
точить ножи, Н-184
НОЖКА
козья ножка, Н-187
НОЖКАХ
валяться в ножках, Н-130
избушка на курьих ножках, И-37
поваляться в ножках, Н-130
НОЖКИ
кланяться в ножки, Н-145
остались рожки да ножки, Р-142
по одёжке протягивай ножки, О-71
поклониться в ножки, Н-145
НОЖКУ
подставить ⟨подставлять⟩ ножку, Н-188
НОЖНЫ
вложить меч в ножны, М-137
НОЖОМ
как ножом отрезал, Н-190
как* ножом отрезало, Н-189
как* ножом полоснуть ⟨по сердцу⟩, Н-191
как* ножом резануть ⟨резнуть⟩ ⟨по сердцу⟩, Н-191
под ножом, Н-192
с ножом к горлу, Н-193
НОЗДРЕ
не по ноздре, Н-194
НОЗДРЮ
ноздря в ноздрю, У-162
НОЗДРЯ
ноздря в ноздрю, У-162
НОЛЬ
круглый ноль, Н-195
ноль без палочки, Н-195
ноль внимания ⟨, фунт презрения⟩, Н-196
под ноль, Н-197
совершенный ноль, Н-195
НОМЕР
вот так ⟨это⟩ номер!, Ш-89
выбрасывать/выбросить номер, Н-198
выкидывать/выкинуть номер, Н-198
дохлый номер, Д-97
номер не выйдет, Н-201
номер не пройдёт, Н-201
номер не удастся, Н-201
номер один, Н-199
откалывать/отколоть номер, Н-198
пустой номер, Н-200
этот номер не выйдет ⟨не пройдёт, не удастся⟩, Н-201
НОМЕРА
выбрасывать/выбросить номера, Н-198

выкидывать/выкинуть номера, Н-198
откалывать/отколоть номера, Н-198
НОМЕРЕ
на одиннадцатом номере, Н-202
НОМЕРОМ
одиннадцатым номером, Н-202
НОРМЕ
в норме, Н-203
НОРМУ
войти ⟨входить⟩ в норму, Н-204
прийти ⟨приходить⟩ в норму, Н-204
НОРОВОМ
с норовом, Н-205
НОС
бить в нос, Н-206
бросаться/броситься в нос, Н-206
в нос, Н-207
вешать нос ⟨на квинту⟩, Н-208
водить за нос, Н-209
воротить нос, Н-210
высовывать/высунуть нос, Н-211
держать нос по ветру, Н-212
драть нос, Н-213
задирать/задрать нос, Н-213
любопытной Варваре нос оторвали, В-7
на нос, Б-201
наклеить нос, Н-214
наставить нос, Н-214
натянуть нос, Н-214
нос в нос, Н-229
нос к носу, Н-229
нос не дорос, Н-215
нос с носом, Н-229
отворотить нос, Н-210
повесить нос ⟨на квинту⟩, Н-208
под нос, Н-216
поднимать/поднять нос, Н-213
показать ⟨показывать⟩ нос, Н-217
с воробьиный нос, Н-218
с гулькин нос, Н-218
совать в нос, Н-219
совать нос, Н-220
совать под нос, Н-219
совать свой нос, Н-220
сунуть в нос, Н-219
сунуть нос, Н-220
сунуть под нос, Н-219
сунуть свой нос, Н-220
тыкать в нос, Г-101
ударило ⟨ударить⟩ в нос, Н-206
ударяет ⟨ударять⟩ в нос, Н-206
утереть нос, Н-221
уткнуть нос, Н-222

НОСА
из-под (самого) носа,
Н-223
комар носа не подточил бы
⟨не подточит⟩, К-212
короче воробьиного носа,
Н-224
кровь из носа, К-412
не видеть дальше своего
(собственного) носа,
Н-225
не видеть дальше
собственного носа,
Н-225
не казать носа, Н-226
не показать ⟨не
показывать⟩ носа, Н-226
с носа, Б-202
хоть кровь из носа, К-412

НОСИТ
бес носит, Ч-96
и как (ещё) земля носит,
З-126
и как только земля носит,
З-126
как (ещё) земля носит,
З-126
как только земля носит,
З-126
леший носит, Ч-96
нелёгкая носит, Ч-96
чёрт носит, Ч-96

НОСИТЬ
носить воду решетом,
В-189
носить камень за пазухой,
К-39
носить личину, М-33
носить маску, М-33
носить на руках, Р-274
носить оружие, О-103
носить под сердцем, С-144

НОСИТЬСЯ
носиться в воздухе, В-207

НОСОВУЮ
во всю носовую завёртку,
З-14

НОСОВЫЕ
во все носовые завёртки,
З-14

НОСОМ
и носом не ведёт/не повёл,
Б-209
клевать носом, Н-227
крутить носом, Н-228
нос с носом, Н-229
носом к носу, Н-229
носом не ведёт/не повёл,
Б-209
перед самым носом, Н-230
под (самым) носом, Н-230
поклёвывать носом, Н-227
с носом, Н-231
соваться/сунуться со
своим носом, Н-220
ткнуть носом, Н-232
тыкать носом, Н-232
уткнуться носом, Н-222
хлюпать/хлюпнуть носом,
Н-233

чуять носом, Н-267
шмыгать/шмыгнуть
носом, Н-233

НОСУ
в носу ковырять, Н-234
висеть на носу, Г-234
давать/дать по носу,
Н-238
зарубить (себе) на носу,
Н-235
комар носу не подточил бы
⟨не подточит⟩, К-212
кровь из носу, К-412
на носу, Н-236
не казать носу, Н-226
не по носу, Н-237
не показать ⟨не
показывать⟩ носу, Н-226
нос к носу, Н-229
носом к носу, Н-229
стукать/стукнуть по носу,
Н-238
ударить ⟨ударять⟩ по
носу, Н-238
хоть кровь из носу, К-412
щёлкать/щёлкнуть по
носу, Н-238

НОСЫ
показать ⟨показывать⟩
носы, Н-217

НОСЯТ
едва ноги носят, Н-143
еле ноги носят, Н-143
ноги носят, Н-150
черти носят, Ч-96

НОТАМ
как* по нотам, Н-239

НОТАЦИЮ
прочитать ⟨читать⟩
нотацию, Н-240

НОТЫ
класть на ноты, М-285
переложить на ноты,
М-285
положить на ноты, М-285

НОЧЕВАЛ
(и) не ночевал, Н-241

НОЧЕВАТЬ
дневать и ночевать, Д-203

НОЧИ
доброй ночи, Н-242
не к ночи будь помянут,
Н-243
не к ночи будь сказано,
Н-243
не к ночи сказать, Н-243
покойной ночи, Н-242
спокойной ночи, Н-242

НОЧЬ
варфоломеевская ночь,
Н-244
день и ночь, Д-155
на ночь, Н-245
на ночь глядя, Н-246

НОЧЬЮ
днём и ночью, Д-155
ночью все кошки серы,
К-349

НОША
своя ноша не тянет, Н-247

НОЩНО
денно и нощно, Д-155

НРАВУ
по нраву, Н-248

НУ
а ну-ка, Н-249
а ну тебя!, Т-51
ай да ну!, Н-252
да ну?, Д-2
да ну тебя!, Т-51
ни тпру ни ну, Т-191
ну вот ещё!, Е-28
ну да!, Н-250
ну знаете ⟨знаешь⟩ ли!,
З-148
ну и...!, Н-251
ну и гусь!, Г-448
ну и дела!, Д-58
ну и ну!, Н-252
ну и что (же)?, Ч-173
ну-ка, Н-249
ну так что ж(е), Т-11
ну тебя!, Т-51
ну тебя в болото!, Б-171
ну то-то же, Т-115
ну уж...!, Н-251
ну что, Ч-174
ну что вы!, Ч-191
ну что ж(е), Ч-180
ну что ты!, Ч-191
ну что я говорил!, Г-159
ну я вас спрашиваю!,
С-525
ну я тебя спрашиваю!,
С-525
фу-ты, ну-ты, Ф-29

НУЖДА
большая нужда, Н-253
малая нужда, Н-254
что за нужда, Н-255

НУЖДЫ
нужды мало, Н-256
нужды нет, Н-257

НУЖЕН
нужен ты мне!, Н-258

НУЖНО
далеко ходить не нужно,
Х-58
даром не нужно, В-218
за примерами
⟨примером)) далеко
ходить не нужно, Х-58
куда как нужно!, Н-259
нужно признаться, П-525
очень нужно!, Н-259
так и нужно, Т-17

НУЛЬ
нуль без палочки, Н-195
под нуль, Н-197

НУЛЮ
свести к нулю, Н-260
свестись к нулю, Н-261
сводить к нулю, Н-260
сводиться к нулю, Н-261

НУЛЯ
начать ⟨начинать⟩ с нуля,
Н-262

НУТРУ
по нутру, Н-263

НЫНЕ
да только воз и ныне там,
В-201

и ныне, и присно (, и во
веки веков), Н-264
ныне и присно, Н-264

НЫНЧЕ
не нынче-завтра, С-106

НЮНИ
распускать/распустить
нюни, Н-265

НЮХАЛ
(и) не нюхал, Н-266

НЮХАТЬ
нюхать пороха ⟨пороху⟩,
П-384

НЮХОМ
нюхом чувствовать, Н-267
нюхом чуять, Н-267

НЯНЕК
у семи нянек дитя без
глазу, Н-268

О

ОБА
в оба глаза, Г-47
в оба конца, К-244
глядеть в оба (глаза),
С-414
следить в оба, С-414
смотреть в оба (глаза),
С-414

ОБАГРИТЬ
обагрить руки в крови,
Р-299
обагрить руки кровью,
Р-299

ОБАГРЯТЬ
обагрять руки в крови,
Р-299
обагрять руки кровью,
Р-299

ОБВЕРНУТЬ
обвернуть вокруг
⟨кругом⟩ пальца, П-15

ОБВЕРТЕТЬ
обвертеть вокруг
⟨кругом⟩ пальца, П-15

ОБВЕСТИ
обвести вокруг ⟨кругом⟩
пальца, П-15

ОБВОДИТЬ
обводить вокруг ⟨кругом⟩
пальца, П-15

ОБДАВАТЬ
обдавать холодом, Х-79

ОБДАЛО
как* варом обдало, В-8

ОБДАТЬ
обдать холодом, Х-79

ОБДИРАТЬ
обдирать как липку, Л-76

ОБЕ
за обе щёки, Щ-2
класть на обе лопатки,
Л-135
на обе корки, К-296
положить на обе лопатки,
Л-135
уложить на обе лопатки,
Л-135

хромать на обе ноги,
Н-159

ОБЕДНЮ
испортить ⟨портить⟩
обедню, О-1

ОБЕДУ
дорога ложка к обеду,
Л-127

ОБЕИМИ
обеими руками
подписаться
⟨подписываться⟩, Р-255
схватиться обеими
руками, Р-264
ухватиться обеими
руками, Р-264

ОБЕРЁШЬСЯ
не оберёшься, О-2

ОБЕТОВАННАЯ
обетованная земля
⟨страна⟩, З-127

ОБЕТОВАННЫЙ
обетованный край, З-127

ОБЕЩАНИЮ
раз в год по обещанию,
Р-27

ОБЕЩАНИЯМИ
бросаться обещаниями,
С-295
кормить обещаниями, З-25

ОБЕЩАННОГО
обещанного три года
ждут, Г-182

ОБЖЁГСЯ
обжёгся на молоке, будешь
дуть и на воду, М-239
обжёгся на молоке, дуешь
и на воду, М-239

ОБЖЁГШИСЬ
обжёгшись на молоке,
будешь дуть и на воду,
М-239
обжёгшись на молоке,
дуешь и на воду, М-239

ОБЖЕЧЬ
обжечь себе пальцы
⟨руки⟩, П-25

ОБЖИГАЮТ
не боги горшки обжигают,
Б-133

ОБИВАТЬ
обивать весь порог, П-377
обивать ⟨все⟩ пороги,
П-377

ОБИДЕ
в обиде, О-3
в тесноте, да не в обиде,
Т-88

ОБИДЕЛ
бог не обидел, Б-101

ОБИДИТ
мухи не обидит, М-303

ОБИДУ
не в обиду будь сказано,
О-4
не давать в обиду, О-5
не давать себя в обиду, О-6
не даваться в обиду, О-6
не дать в обиду, О-5

не дать себя в обиду, О-6
не даться в обиду, О-6

ОБИЖЕН
богом обижен, Б-134
обижен судьбой, С-664

ОБИЖЕННЫЙ
богом обиженный, Б-134
обиженный судьбой, С-664

ОБИНЯКОВ
без обиняков, О-7

ОБИРАТЬ
обирать как липку, Л-76

ОБИТЬ
обить весь порог, П-377
обить ⟨все⟩ пороги, П-377

ОБЛАКА
уноситься в облака, О-8

ОБЛАКАМ
уноситься к облакам, О-8

ОБЛАКАХ
витать в облаках, О-8
парить в облаках, О-8

ОБЛАКОВ
свалиться с облаков, О-9
спуститься с облаков, О-9
упасть с облаков, О-9

ОБЛАМЫВАТЬ
обламывать рога, Р-123

ОБЛАСТИ
в области, О-10

ОБЛАСТЬ
отойти ⟨отходить⟩ в
область воспоминаний
⟨преданий, предания⟩,
О-11
уйти ⟨уходить⟩ в область
воспоминаний
⟨преданий, предания⟩,
О-11

ОБЛАЦЕХ
темна вода во облацех,
В-176

ОБЛЕГЧАТЬ
облегчать душу, Д-425
облегчать сердце, Д-425

ОБЛЕГЧИТЬ
облегчить душу, Д-425
облегчить сердце, Д-425

ОБЛЕКАТЬ
облекать в плоть (и
кровь), П-200
облекать плотью (и
кровью), П-200

ОБЛЕКАТЬСЯ
облекаться в плоть (и
кровь), П-201
облекаться плотью (и
кровью), П-201

ОБЛЕЧЬ
облечь в плоть (и кровь),
П-200
облечь плотью (и кровью),
П-200

ОБЛЕЧЬСЯ
облечься в плоть (и кровь),
П-201
облечься плотью (и
кровью), П-201

ОБЛИВАЕТСЯ
сердце кровью обливается,
С-138

ОБЛИВАТЬ
обливать грязью, Г-436
обливать помоями, Г-436

ОБЛИВАТЬСЯ
обливаться слезами, С-260

ОБЛИЖЕТЕ
пальчики оближете, П-28

ОБЛИЖЕШЬ
пальчики оближешь, П-28

ОБЛИЛОСЬ
сердце кровью облилось,
С-138

ОБЛИТЬ
как* холодной водой
облить, В-181
облить грязью, Г-436
облить помоями, Г-436
облить ушатом холодной
воды, В-181
облить холодной водой,
В-181

ОБЛОМАТЬ
обломать бока, Б-152
обломать зубы, З-199
обломать когти, К-157
обломать рога, Р-123

ОБЛУПИТЬ
облупить как липку, Л-76

ОБЛУПЛЕННОГО
как облупленного, О-12

ОБМАН
оптический обман, О-13

ОБМАНЧИВА
внешность обманчива,
В-171
наружность обманчива,
В-171

ОБМОЛВИТЬСЯ
не обмолвиться ни единым
словом, С-333
не обмолвиться ни
словечком ⟨ни словом⟩,
С-333
не обмолвиться словом,
С-333

ОБМОРОК
падать в обморок, О-14
упасть в обморок, О-14

ОБНАЖАТЬ
обнажать меч, М-139

ОБНАЖИТЬ
обнажить меч, М-139

ОБНИМКУ
в обнимку, О-15

ОБОБРАТЬ
обобрать как липку, Л-76

ОБОДРАННАЯ
ободранная кошка, К-342

ОБОДРАТЬ
ободрать как липку, Л-76

ОБОЙДЁННЫЙ
обойдённый судьбой,
С-664

ОБОЙТИ
обойти десятой дорогой,
Д-274
обойти за версту, В-48
обойти за три версты,
В-48

обойти молчанием, М-246
обойти сторонкой
⟨стороной⟩, С-608

ОБОЙТИСЬ
обойтись в копеечку ⟨в
копейку⟩, К-276

ОБОРВАЛОСЬ
оборвалось в груди, С-141
оборвалось в сердце, С-141
сердце оборвалось, С-141

ОБОРОНИ
боже оборони, Б-143
оборони бог, Б-143
оборони господь, Б-143

ОБОРОТ
брать в оборот, О-16
ввести ⟨вводить⟩ в
оборот, О-18
взять в оборот, О-16
принимать/принять
оборот, О-17
пускать/пустить в оборот,
О-18

ОБОРОТА
завестись ⟨заводиться⟩ с
одного оборота, П-316

ОБОРОТНАЯ
оборотная сторона
медали, С-602

ОБРАЗА
рыцарь печального образа,
Р-396

ОБРАЗОМ
главным образом, О-19
каким образом, О-20
некоторым образом, О-21
никаким образом, О-22
никоим образом, О-22
равным образом, О-23
таким образом, О-24

ОБРАЗУ
по образу и подобию, О-25
по образу пешего
хождения, О-26

ОБРАСТАТЬ
обрастать мохом, М-267

ОБРАСТИ
обрасти мохом, М-267

ОБРАТИТЬ
обратить в прах, П-495
обратить в свою веру, В-51
обратить на путь
истинный ⟨истины⟩,
П-658

ОБРАТИТЬСЯ
обратиться в прах, П-497
обратиться в слух, С-354
обратиться на путь
истинный ⟨истины⟩,
П-659

ОБРАТНАЯ
обратная сторона медали,
С-602

ОБРАТНО
брать своё слово ⟨свои
слова⟩ обратно, С-280
брать слова ⟨слово⟩
обратно, С-280
взять своё слово ⟨свои
слова⟩ обратно, С-280

взять слова ⟨слово⟩
обратно, С-280
туда и обратно, Т-230

ОБРАЩАТЬ
обращать в прах, П-495
обращать в свою веру,
В-51
обращать на путь
истинный ⟨истины⟩,
П-658

ОБРАЩАТЬСЯ
обращаться в прах, П-497
обращаться в слух, С-354

ОБРАЩЕНИЕ
обращение на ты, Т-248
пускать/пустить в
обращение, О-18

ОБРЕЗ
в обрез, О-27

ОБРЕЗАТЬ
обрезать крылья, К-432

ОБРЫВАЕТСЯ
сердце обрывается, С-141

ОБСЕВОК
не обсевок в поле, О-28

ОБСОХЛО
материно ⟨материнское⟩
молоко на губах не
обсохло, М-240
молоко на губах не
обсохло, М-240

ОБСТОЯТЕЛЬСТВА
тонкий намёк на толстые
обстоятельства, Н-23

ОБСТОЯТЕЛЬСТВО
тонкий намёк на толстое
обстоятельство, Н-23

ОБСТРЕЛ
брать/взять под обстрел,
О-29

ОБТЯЖКУ
в обтяжку, О-30

ОБУХА
плетью обуха не
перешибёшь, П-174

ОБУХОМ
бить как* обухом по
голове, О-31
как* обухом по голове,
О-31
ударить ⟨ударять⟩ как*
обухом по голове, О-31

ОБХОД
в обход, О-32

ОБХОДИТЬ
обходить десятой дорогой,
Д-274
обходить за версту, В-48
обходить за три версты,
В-48
обходить молчанием,
М-246
обходить сторонкой
⟨стороной⟩, С-608

ОБХОДНОЙ
обходной путь, П-660

ОБХОДНЫМ
обходным путём, П-660

ОБХОДНЫМИ
обходными путями, П-660

ОБЧЁЛСЯ
один-два ⟨один-другой⟩
(да) и обчёлся, Р-29
раз-два ⟨раз-другой⟩ (да)
и обчёлся, Р-29

ОБЧИСТИТЬ
обчистить как липку, Л-76

ОБЩЕГО
не иметь ничего общего,
О-33
нет ничего общего, О-33

ОБЩЕЕ
общее место, М-119

ОБЩЕЙ
в общей массе, М-40
в общей сложности, С-341

ОБЩЕМ
в общем, О-34
в общем и целом, О-35

ОБЩЕМУ
привести ⟨приводить⟩ к
общему знаменателю,
З-162

ОБЩЕСТВА
душа общества, Д-372

ОБЩИЙ
найти ⟨находить⟩ общий
язык, Я-14
общий котёл, К-338
общий язык, Я-15

ОБЩИХ
в общих чертах, Ч-108

ОБЪЕДЕШЬ
на вороных не объедешь,
К-387
на козе ⟨на кривой⟩ не
объедешь, К-387
на саврасой не объедешь,
К-387

ОБЪЕЛСЯ
белены объелся, Б-50

ОБЪЯВИТЬ
объявить бой, Б-148

ОБЪЯВЛЯТЬ
объявлять бой, Б-148

ОБЪЯТИЯ
в объятия к Морфею, О-37
в объятия Морфея, О-37

ОБЪЯТИЯМИ
с распростёртыми
объятиями, О-36

ОБЪЯТИЯХ
в объятиях Морфея, О-37
душить/задушить в
объятиях, О-38

ОБЫКНОВЕНИЮ
по обыкновению, О-39
по своему обыкновению,
О-39

ОБЫКНОВЕНИЯ
против обыкновения, О-40

ОБЫЧНАЯ
обычная история, И-86

ОБЫЧНОЕ
вернуться ⟨возвращаться⟩
в обычное русло, К-198
войти ⟨входить⟩ в
обычное русло, К-198

ОБЫЧНУЮ
войти ⟨входить⟩ в
обычную колею, К-198

попадать/попасть в
обычную колею, К-198

ОБЯЗАННОСТЬ
вменить ⟨вменять⟩ в
обязанность, О-41

ОВЕЦ
молодец против ⟨среди⟩
овец (, а против молодца
и сам овца), М-232
отделить ⟨отделять⟩ овец
от козлищ, О-42

ОВЕЧКА
заблудшая овечка ⟨овца⟩,
О-45

ОВЕЧЬЕЙ
волк в овечьей шкуре,
В-224

ОВЛАДЕВАТЬ
овладевать собой, О-43

ОВЛАДЕТЬ
овладеть собой, О-43

ОВОЩУ
всякому овощу своё время,
О-44
каждому овощу своё
время, О-44

ОВЦА
заблудшая овца, О-45
молодец против ⟨среди⟩
овец, а против молодца
и сам овца, М-232
(одна) паршивая овца всё
стадо портит, О-46

ОВЦЫ
и волки сыты, и овцы
целы, В-230
с паршивой овцы хоть
шерсти клок, О-47

ОВЧИНКА
овчинка выделки не стоит,
О-48

ОВЧИНКУ
небо в овчинку кажется/
показалось, Н-53
небо с овчинку кажется/
показалось, Н-53

ОГЛАСКУ
получать/получить
огласку, О-49

ОГЛОБЛИ
повернуть оглобли
(назад), О-50
поворачивать
⟨поворотить⟩ оглобли
(назад), О-50

ОГЛУШИТЬ
как громом оглушить,
Г-408

ОГЛЯДКИ
без оглядки, О-51

ОГЛЯДКОЙ
с оглядкой, О-52

ОГЛЯНУТЬСЯ
оглянуться не успеет ⟨не
успеешь⟩, О-53

ОГНЕЙ
меж ⟨между⟩ двух огней,
О-54

ОГНЁМ
гори огнём, О-55

гори (оно) синим ⟨ясным⟩
огнём, О-55
днём с огнём, О-56
играть с огнём, О-57
огнём и мечом, О-58
шутить с огнём, О-57

ОГНИ
пройти (и) огни и воды (и
медные трубы), О-65
пройти сквозь ⟨через⟩
огни и воды (и медные
трубы), О-65

ОГНЮ
предавать/предать огню,
О-59
предавать/предать огню и
мечу, О-60

ОГНЯ
дыма без огня не бывает,
Д-437
из огня (да) в полымя,
О-61
как огня, О-62
нет дыма без огня, Д-437
пуще огня, О-62
таскать каштаны из огня,
К-114

ОГОНЁК
на огонёк, О-63

ОГОНЬ
в огонь и в воду, О-64
идти в огонь и в воду, О-64
подливать/подлить масла
в огонь, М-36
пойти в огонь и в воду,
О-64
пройти (и) огонь и воду (и
медные трубы), О-65
пройти сквозь ⟨через⟩
огонь и воду (и медные
трубы), О-65

ОГОНЬКОМ
с огоньком, О-66

ОГОРОД
бросать камень ⟨камешек,
камешки, камни⟩ в
огород, К-47
камешек ⟨камешки⟩ в
огород, К-47
кидать камень ⟨камешек,
камешки, камни⟩ в
огород, К-47
огород городить, О-67
пускать/пустить козла в
огород, К-169

ОГОРОДЕ
в огороде бузина, а в
Киеве дядька, О-68

ОГУРЧИК
как огурчик, О-69

ОДЁЖКЕ
по одёжке встречают, по
уму провожают, О-70
по одёжке протягивай
ножки, О-71

ОДЕРЖАТЬ
одержать верх, В-53

ОДЕРЖИВАТЬ
одерживать верх, В-53

ОДИН
в один голос, Г-298

в один конец, К-231
в один мах, М-56
в один миг, М-147
в один момент, М-249
в один прекрасный день,
Д-150
в один присест, П-545
все за одного, один за всех,
О-73
грех один, Г-384
за один присест, П-545
как один, О-72
как один человек, О-72
мерить ⟨мерять⟩ на один
аршин, А-44
на один зуб, З-186
на один лад, Л-10
на один покрой, П-290
на один уровень, У-125
ни один чёрт, Ч-79, Ч-82
номер один, Н-199
один бог ведает ⟨знает⟩,
Б-138
один господь-бог ведает
⟨знает⟩, Б-138
один в один, О-75
один в одного, О-75
один в поле не воин, П-295
один-два (да) и обчёлся,
Р-29
один-другой (да) и
обчёлся, Р-29
один за всех, все за одного,
О-73
один за другим, О-74
один и тот же, Т-171
один к одному, О-75, О-76
один конец, К-236
один на один, О-77
один-одинёхонек
⟨одинёшенек⟩, О-78
один свет в окошке, С-74
один чёрт, Ч-80
один шаг, Ш-6
просто смех один, С-404
прямо смех один, С-404
садиться за один стол,
С-590
семь бед — один ответ,
Б-36
сесть за один стол, С-590
смех один, Г-384, С-404

ОДИНАКОВЫМ
с одинаковым успехом,
У-137

ОДИННАДЦАТОМ
на одиннадцатом номере,
Н-202

ОДИННАДЦАТЫМ
одиннадцатым номером,
Н-202

ОДИНОЧКУ
беда в одиночку не ходит,
Б-37
в одиночку, О-79

ОДНА
беда (никогда) не
приходит ⟨не ходит⟩
одна, Б-37
как одна, О-72
как одна копеечка
⟨копейка⟩, К-277

как одна минута, М-170
муж да ⟨и⟩ жена — одна
сатана, М-282
ни одна ⟨живая⟩ душа,
Д-376
ни одна собака, С-445
одна в одну, О-75
одна к одной, О-75
одна кожа да кости, К-161
одна лавочка, Ш-25
одна ласточка весны не
делает, Л-33
одна нога здесь, (а) другая
там, Н-123
одна-одинёхонька
⟨одинёшенька⟩, О-78
одна паршивая овца всё
стадо портит, О-46
одна радость в глазу, Р-14
одна смехота, С-404
одна тень осталась, Т-76
одна шайка ⟨шайка-
лейка⟩, Ш-25
просто одна смехота,
С-404
прямо одна смехота, С-404
только одна слава, Н-15

ОДНИ
в одни руки, Р-280

ОДНИМ
жить одним домом, Д-261
мерить ⟨мерять⟩ одним
аршином, А-44
одним глазком, Г-133
одним глазом, Г-133, Г-139
одним духом, Д-354
одним махом, М-56
одним миром мазаны,
М-188
одним росчерком пера,
Р-170
одним словом, С-334
одним ухом, К-351

ОДНИХ
в одних руках, Р-268

ОДНО
в одно мгновение (ока),
М-60
в одно прекрасное время,
Д-150
в одно слово, С-308
в одно ухо вошло, (а) в
другое вышло, У-156
в одно ухо входит, (а) в
другое выходит, У-156
всё одно, В-327
всё одно как, В-328
всё одно что, В-328
за одно спасибо, Т-3
заладила сорока Якова
одно про всякого, С-496
на одно лицо, Л-97
одно в одно, О-75
одно время, В-317
одно звание, З-86
одно к одному, О-75, О-80
одно название, Н-15
одно только звание, З-86
одно только название, Н-15
сорок одно с кисточкой,
К-124

ОДНОГО
все за одного, один за всех,
О-73
до одного, О-81
завестись ⟨заводиться⟩ с
одного оборота, П-316
из одного (и того же)
теста, Т-90
испечены из одного (и того
же) теста, Т-90
один в одного, О-75
один за всех, все за одного,
О-73
одного покроя, П-290
одного поля ягода ⟨ягодки,
ягоды⟩, П-327
птицы одного полёта,
П-622
с одного маху, М-56
сделаны из одного (и того
же) теста, Т-90
семеро одного не ждут,
Ж-10

ОДНОЙ
в одной рубашке, Р-191
двум смертям не бывать,
а одной не миновать,
С-399
двух смертей не бывать, а
одной не миновать,
С-399
до одной, О-81
мерить ⟨мерять⟩ одной
мер(к)ой, А-44
на одной ноге, Н-136
не знать ни одной
женщины, Ж-18
ни одной ⟨живой⟩ души,
Д-391
ни одной живой нитки не
осталось ⟨нет⟩, Н-101
ни одной йоты, Й-2
ни одной сухой нитки не
осталось ⟨нет⟩, Н-101
одна к одной, О-75
одной верёвкой
⟨верёвочкой⟩ связан,
В-39
одной и той же масти,
М-43
одной левой, Л-37
одной масти, М-43
одной ногой в гробу, Н-162
одной ногой в могиле,
Н-162
одной цепочкой связан,
В-39
под одной кровлей, К-437
под одной крышей, К-437
с одной стороны... с
другой (стороны), С-616
стоять на одной доске,
Д-291
стоять одной ногой в гробу
⟨в могиле⟩, Н-162

ОДНОМ
ни в одном глазе ⟨глазу⟩,
Г-141
оставаться на одном
месте, М-108
стоять в одном ряду, Р-405

стоять на одном месте,
М-108
топтаться на одном месте,
М-108
хоть бы в одном глазе
⟨глазу⟩, Г-141

ОДНОМУ
один к одному, О-75, О-76
одно к одному, О-75, О-80
одному аллаху ведомо
⟨известно⟩, Б-138
одному богу ведомо
⟨известно⟩, Б-138
одному господу ведомо
⟨известно⟩, Б-138
одному чёрту известно,
Ч-115
по одному, О-82
по одному росчерку пера,
Р-170
привести ⟨приводить⟩ к
одному знаменателю,
З-162

ОДНУ
бить в одну точку, Т-184
в одну дудку ⟨дуду⟩
дудеть, Д-320
в одну душу, Д-408
в одну минуту, М-173
валить в одну кучу,
К-498
встать на одну доску,
Д-296
как одну копеечку
⟨копейку⟩, К-283
мерить ⟨мерять⟩ на одну
мер(к)у, А-44
мешать в одну кучу, К-498
на одну колодку, К-200
ни на одну йоту, Й-1
одна в одну, О-75
одну минутку ⟨минуточку,
минуту⟩!, М-177
одну секундочку
⟨секунду⟩!, М-177
остричь под одну гребёнку,
Г-381
петь одну и ту же песню,
П-118
под одну масть, М-43
подстригать/подстричь
под одну гребёнку, Г-381
поставить всё на одну
карту, К-93
поставить на одну доску,
Д-295
сваливать/свалить в одну
кучу, К-498
смешать в одну кучу,
К-498
ставить всё на одну карту,
К-93
ставить на одну доску,
Д-295
становиться/стать на одну
доску, Д-296
стричь под одну гребёнку,
Г-381
тянуть одну и ту же
песню, П-118

ОДОЛЖЕНИЕ
сделай(те) (такое)
одолжение, М-159

ОСНОВУ
закладывать/заложить
основу, О-118
ОСНОВЫ
закладывать/заложить
основы, О-118
ОСОБАЯ
особая статья, С-554
ОСОБЕННОСТИ
в особенности, О-119
ОСОБОГО
особого рода, Р-128
ОСОБЬ
особь статья, С-554
ОСТАВАТЬСЯ
имею честь оставаться,
Ч-134
не оставаться в долгу,
Д-243
оставаться без штанов,
Ш-86
оставаться на (одном)
месте, М-108
оставаться при своих, С-87
счастливо оставаться!,
О-120
ОСТАВИТЬ
камня на камне не
оставить, К-50
оставить без внимания,
В-173
оставить в покое, П-282
оставить в стороне, С-607
оставить в тени, Т-72
оставить за собой, О-121
оставить отпечаток, О-162
оставить печать, О-162
оставить позади себя,
О-121
оставить при себе, Д-179
ОСТАВЛЯЕТ
оставляет желать лучшего
(многого), Л-151
ОСТАВЛЯТЬ
камня на камне не
оставлять, К-50
оставлять без внимания,
В-173
оставлять в покое, П-282
оставлять в стороне, С-607
оставлять в тени, Т-72
оставлять за собой, О-121
оставлять отпечаток,
О-162
оставлять печать, О-162
оставлять позади себя,
О-121
оставлять при себе, Д-179
ОСТАЁТСЯ
ничего (другого) не
остаётся, О-122
ОСТАЛАСЬ
одна тень осталась, Т-76
осталась (только) тень,
Т-76
ОСТАЛИСЬ
остались рожки да ножки,
Р-142
ОСТАЛОСЬ
живого места не осталось,
М-89

живой нитки не осталось,
Н-101
камня на камне не
осталось, К-50
кровинки в (на) лице не
осталось, К-396
кровиночки в (на) лице не
осталось, К-396
не осталось и следа, С-254
ни кровинки в (на) лице не
осталось, К-396
ни кровиночки в (на) лице
не осталось, К-396
ни одной живой нитки не
осталось, Н-101
ни одной сухой нитки не
осталось, Н-101
сухой нитки не осталось,
Н-101
ОСТАНЕТСЯ
мокрого места не
останется, М-115
мокрое место останется,
М-115
ничего (другого) не
останется, О-122
ОСТАНОВКА
остановка за, О-123
ОСТАТКА
без остатка, О-124
ОСТАТКИ
потерять (последние)
остатки совести, С-457
ОСТАТЬСЯ
не остаться в долгу, Д-243
остаться без штанов, Ш-86
остаться при своих, С-87
ОСТЁР
остёр на язык, Я-16
ОСТРАСТКУ
давать/дать острастку,
О-125
задавать/задать
острастку, О-125
ОСТРИТЬ
острить зуб(ы), З-204
ОСТРИЧЬ
остричь под одну гребёнку,
Г-381
ОСТРИЮ
ходить по острию ножа,
О-126
ОСТРОГ
острог плачет, Т-253
ОСТРЫЕ
сгладить (сглаживать)
острые углы, У-16
ОСТРЫЙ
нож острый, Н-182
острый на язык, Я-16
острый язык (язычок),
Я-17
ОСУШАТЬ
не осушать глаз, Г-29
осушать (свои) слёзы,
С-271
ОСУШАЮТСЯ
глаза не осушаются, Г-57
ОСУШИТЬ
осушить (свои) слёзы,
С-271

ОТБАВЛЯЙ
хоть отбавляй, О-127
ОТБИВАТЬ
отбивать охоту, О-179
отбивать хлеб, Х-35
ОТБИВАТЬСЯ
отбиваться от дома, Д-256
отбиваться от рук, Р-217
отбиваться руками и
ногами, Р-256
ОТБИВНУЮ
сделать отбивную
(котлету), О-128
ОТБИТЬ
отбить охоту, О-179
отбить хлеб, Х-35
ОТБИТЬСЯ
отбиться от дома, Д-256
отбиться от рук, Р-217
ОТБОЙ
бить отбой, О-129
давать/дать отбой, О-130
забить отбой, О-129
ОТБОЮ
отбою нет, О-131
ОТБОЯ
отбоя нет, О-131
ОТБРОСИТЬ
отбросить коньки, К-271
отбросить копыта, К-287
ОТБЫВАТЬ
отбывать в другой (иной,
лучший) мир, М-184
ОТБЫТЬ
отбыть в другой (иной,
лучший) мир, М-184
ОТВАЛА
до отвала, О-132
ОТВАЛУ
до отвалу, О-132
ОТВАЛИВАЮТСЯ
руки отваливаются, Р-321
ОТВАЛИЛАСЬ
челюсть отвалилась, Ч-56
ОТВАЛИЛИСЬ
руки отвалились, Р-321
ОТВАЛЯТСЯ
руки не отвалятся, Р-319
ОТВЕРЗЛИСЬ
отверзлись хляби
небесные, Х-46
ОТВЕСТИ
не отвести глаз, Г-33
нельзя отвести глаз, Г-33
отвести глаза, Г-84
отвести душу, Д-426
отвести сердце, Д-426
ОТВЕТ
в ответ, О-133
давать ответ, О-134
держать ответ, О-134
семь бед — один ответ,
Б-36
ОТВЕТА
ни ответа ни привета,
О-135
ОТВЕТЕ
в ответе, О-136
ОТВЕТИТЬ
ответить головой, Г-237

ОТВЕЧАТЬ
отвечать головой, Г-237
ОТВИСЛА
челюсть отвисла, Ч-56
ОТВОДА
для отвода глаз, О-137
ОТВОДИТЬ
не отводить глаз, Г-30
отводить глаза, Г-84
отводить душу, Д-426
отводить сердце, Д-426
ОТВОРОТИТЬ
отворотить морду, Н-210
отворотить нос, Н-210
отворотить рожу, Н-210
отворотить рыло, Н-210
ОТВОРЯЙ
пришла беда — отворяй
ворота, Б-42
ОТДАВАТЬ
дорого отдавать свою
жизнь, Ж-53
отдавать богу душу, Б-139
отдавать дань, Д-22
отдавать должное, Д-246
отдавать должную
справедливость, Д-246
отдавать жизнь, Ж-60
отдавать замуж, В-361
отдавать концы, К-260,
К-261
отдавать на откуп, О-153
отдавать полную
справедливость, Д-246
отдавать последний долг,
Д-235
отдавать руку, Р-353
отдавать руку и сердце,
Р-353
отдавать себе отчёт, О-172
отдавать сердце, С-132
отдавать честь, Ч-136
ОТДАВАТЬСЯ
отдаваться власти, В-165
отдаваться во власть,
В-165
ОТДАЛЕНИИ
держать в известном
(почтительном)
отдалении, Р-84
держаться в известном
(почтительном)
отдалении, Р-85
ОТДАЛЁННЫЕ
места не столь
отдалённые, М-90
ОТДАТЬ
дорого отдать свою
жизнь, Ж-53
отдать богу душу, Б-139
отдать дань, Д-22
отдать должное, Д-246
отдать должную
справедливость, Д-246
отдать жизнь, Ж-60
отдать замуж, В-361
отдать концы, К-260,
К-261
отдать на откуп, О-153
отдать полную
справедливость, Д-246

отдать последний долг,
Д-235
отдать последнюю рубаху
〈рубашку〉, Р-196
отдать руку, Р-353
отдать руку и сердце,
Р-353
отдать с себя последнюю
рубаху 〈рубашку〉, Р-196
отдать себе отчёт, О-172
отдать сердце, С-132
отдать честь, Ч-136
ОТДАТЬСЯ
отдаться власти, В-165
отдаться во власть, В-165
ОТДАЧИ
без отдачи, О-138
ОТДЕЛАТЬ
отделать под орех, О-98
ОТДЕЛАТЬСЯ
дёшево отделаться, О-139
легко отделаться, О-139
отделаться лёгким
испугом, И-81
счастливо отделаться,
О-139
ОТДЕЛИТЬ
отделить овец от козлищ,
О-42
отделить плевелы от
пшеницы, П-170
ОТДЕЛЫВАТЬ
отделывать под орех, О-98
ОТДЕЛЫВАТЬСЯ
отделываться лёгким
испугом, И-81
ОТДЕЛЬНОСТИ
в 〈по〉 отдельности, О-140
ОТДЕЛЯТЬ
отделять овец от козлищ,
О-42
отделять плевелы от
пшеницы, П-170
ОТДОХНУТЬ
отдохнуть душой, Д-401
отдохнуть сердцем, Д-401
ОТДУВАТЬСЯ
отдуваться своими
〈собственными〉
боками, Б-154
ОТДЫХА
не давать ни отдыха ни
срока, О-141
ОТДЫХАТЬ
отдыхать душой, Д-401
отдыхать сердцем, Д-401
ОТЕЦ
отец небесный, Ц-9
ОТЕЧЕСТВЕ
несть 〈нет〉 пророка в
отечестве своём 〈в
своём отечестве〉, П-581
ОТЖИВАТЬ
отживать своё 〈время〉,
В-21
отживать свой век, В-21
ОТЖИТЬ
отжить своё 〈время〉, В-21
отжить свой век, В-21

ОТКАЖЕШЬ
не откажешь, О-146
ОТКАЖИ
не откажи, О-142
не откажи в любезности,
Л-160
ОТКАЖИТЕ
не откажите, О-142
не откажите в
любезности, Л-160
ОТКАЖУСЬ
не откажусь, О-143
ОТКАЗА
без отказа, О-144
до отказа, О-145
ОТКАЗАЛИ
ноги отказали, Н-151
ОТКАЗАЛСЯ
не отказался бы, О-143
ОТКАЗАТЬ
не отказать в чести, Ч-124
нельзя отказать, О-146
отказать от дома, Д-257
ОТКАЗЫВАТЬ
ни в чём себе не
отказывать, О-147
отказывать от дома, Д-257
отказывать себе, О-148
ОТКАЛЫВАТЬ
откалывать коленца
〈коленце〉, К-191
откалывать номер
〈номера〉, Н-198
откалывать штуки
〈штуку〉, Ш-91
ОТКАЧАЛО
доброе начало полдела
откачало, Н-39
хорошее начало полдела
откачало, Н-39
ОТКИНУТЬ
откинуть копыта, К-287
ОТКЛАДЫВАЙ
не откладывай на завтра
то, что можешь
〈можно〉 сделать
сегодня, О-149
ОТКЛИКНЕТСЯ
как аукнется, так и
откликнется, А-49
ОТКОЛОТЬ
отколоть коленца
〈коленце〉, К-191
отколоть номер 〈номера〉,
Н-198
отколоть штуки 〈штуку〉,
Ш-91
ОТКОС
идти под откос, О-150
катиться под откос, О-150
пойти под откос, О-150
покатиться под откос,
О-150
ОТКРОВЕННО
откровенно говоря, Г-174
откровенно сказать, Г-174
ОТКРЫВАЙ
пришла беда — открывай
ворота, Б-42

ОТКРЫВАЛСЯ
(а) ларчик просто
открывался, Л-32
ОТКРЫВАТЬ
открывать Америку, А-27
открывать глаза, Г-85
открывать двери 〈дверь〉,
Д-33
открывать душу, Д-427
открывать карты, К-99
открывать новую
страницу, С-626
открывать рот 〈рты〉,
Р-180
открывать свои карты,
К-99
открывать сердце, С-133
открывать счёт, С-708
ОТКРЫВАЮТСЯ
глаза открываются, Г-60
ОТКРЫЛИСЬ
глаза открылись, Г-60
ОТКРЫТИЕ
открытие Америки, А-27
ОТКРЫТОЙ
с открытой душой, Д-404
ОТКРЫТОМ
на открытом воздухе,
В-206
ОТКРЫТУЮ
в открытую, О-151
ломиться в открытую
дверь, Д-36
ОТКРЫТЫЕ
ломиться в открытые
двери, Д-36
ОТКРЫТЫЙ
на открытый воздух,
В-206
ОТКРЫТЫМ
под открытым небом,
Н-56
с открытым забралом, З-8
с открытым сердцем,
Д-404
ОТКРЫТЫМИ
с открытыми глазами,
Г-116
ОТКРЫТЫХ
день открытых дверей,
Д-156
ОТКРЫТЬ
открыть Америку, А-27
открыть глаза, Г-85
открыть двери 〈дверь〉,
Д-33
открыть душу, Д-427
открыть карты, К-99
открыть новую страницу,
С-626
открыть рот 〈рты〉, Р-180
открыть свои карты, К-99
открыть сердце, С-133
открыть счёт, С-708
ОТКУДА
откуда ветер дует, В-71
откуда ни возьмись, В-217
откуда ни попало, П-353
откуда попало, П-353
откуда придётся, П-353

откуда прыть взялась,
П-609
откуда ты взял?, В-105
откуда что взялось!, В-106
ОТКУП
брать/взять на откуп,
О-152
отдавать/отдать на откуп,
О-153
ОТКУСИТ
дай ему палец, он и всю
руку откусит, П-3
ОТЛЕГЛО
отлегло на душе, С-126
отлегло на сердце, С-126
отлегло от души, С-126
отлегло от сердца, С-126
ОТЛЁТЕ
на отлёте, О-154
ОТЛИВАТЬ
отливать пули 〈пулю〉,
П-631
ОТЛИТЬ
отлить пули 〈пулю〉, П-631
ОТЛИЧИЕ
в отличие от, О-155
ОТМАЧИВАТЬ
отмачивать штуки
〈штуку〉, Ш-91
ОТМЕРЬ
семь раз отмерь, (а) один
(раз) отрежь, Р-37
ОТМЕСТИ
отмести с порога, П-373
ОТМЕСТКУ
в отместку, О-156
невестке в отместку, Н-61
ОТМЕТАТЬ
отметать с порога, П-373
ОТМОЕШЬ
чёрного кобеля не отмоешь
добела, К-150
ОТМОЧИТЬ
отмочить штуки 〈штуку〉,
Ш-91
ОТНЕСТИ
отнести за 〈на〉 счёт,
С-709
ОТНИМЕШЬ
не отнимешь, О-146
ОТНОСИТЬ
относить за 〈на〉 счёт,
С-709
ОТНОШЕНИИ
в некотором отношении,
О-157
в отношении, О-158
ОТНОШЕНИЮ
по отношению, О-158
ОТНОШЕНИЯ
выяснить 〈выяснять〉
отношения, О-159
ОТНОШЕНИЯХ
в некоторых отношениях,
О-157
во всех отношениях, О-**160**
ОТНЫНЕ
отныне и во веки веков,
В-27

ОТНЯЛСЯ
  язык отнялся, Я-41
ОТНЯТЬ
  нельзя отнять, О-146
ОТОГРЕВАТЬ
  отогревать змею за
    пазухой ⟨на груди⟩,
    З-139
ОТОГРЕТЬ
  отогреть змею за пазухой
    ⟨на груди⟩, З-139
ОТОЙТИ
  отойти в вечность, В-86
  отойти в область
    воспоминаний
    ⟨преданий, предания⟩,
    О-11
  отойти в прошлое, П-601
  отойти в тень, Т-77
ОТОЛЬЮТСЯ
  отольются слёзы, С-272
ОТОРВАЛИ
  любопытной Варваре нос
    оторвали, В-7
ОТОРВАЛОСЬ
  оторвалось в груди, С-141
  оторвалось в сердце, С-141
  сердце оторвалось, С-141
ОТОРВАТЬ
  не оторвать глаз, Г-33
  нельзя оторвать глаз, Г-33
  оторвать от себя, О-164
  оторвать от сердца, С-127
  с руками оторвать, Р-261
ОТОРВИ
  оторви да ⟨и⟩ брось
    ⟨выбрось⟩, О-161
ОТОШЛО
  отошло от сердца, С-126
  сердце отошло, С-140
ОТПЕЧАТОК
  класть отпечаток, О-162
  накладывать/наложить
    отпечаток, О-162
  оставить ⟨оставлять⟩
    отпечаток, О-162
  положить отпечаток,
    О-162
ОТПЛАТИТЬ
  отплатить той же
    монетой, М-254
ОТПЛАЧИВАТЬ
  отплачивать той же
    монетой, М-254
ОТПОР
  давать/дать отпор, О-163
ОТПРАВИТЬ
  отправить к праотцам,
    П-492
  отправить на тот свет,
    С-52
ОТПРАВИТЬСЯ
  отправиться к праотцам,
    П-493
  отправиться на тот свет,
    С-53
ОТПРАВЛЕНИЯ
  точка отправления, Т-177
ОТПРАВЛЯТЬ
  отправлять к праотцам,
    П-492

отправлять на тот свет,
    С-52
ОТПРАВЛЯТЬСЯ
  отправляться к праотцам,
    П-493
  отправляться на тот свет,
    С-53
ОТПРАВНАЯ
  отправная точка, Т-177
ОТПУСТИТЬ
  отпустить душу на
    покаяние, Д-428
ОТПУЩЕНИЯ
  козёл отпущения, К-165
ОТРАВЛЯТЬ
  отравлять жизнь, Ж-61
  отравлять существование,
    Ж-61
ОТРЕЖЬ
  семь раз отмерь
    ⟨примерь⟩, (а) один
    (раз) отрежь, Р-37
ОТРЕЗАЛ
  как ножом отрезал, Н-190
  как отрезал, Н-190
ОТРЕЗАЛО
  как* ножом отрезало,
    Н-189
  как отрезало, Н-189
ОТРЕЗАННЫЙ
  отрезанный ломоть, Л-132
ОТРЫВАЕТСЯ
  взгляд не отрывается,
    Г-58
  сердце отрывается, С-141
ОТРЫВАТЬ
  не отрывать глаз, Г-30
  отрывать от себя, О-164
  отрывать от сердца, С-127
ОТРЫВАЮТСЯ
  глаза не отрываются, Г-58
ОТРЫВАЯСЬ
  не отрываясь, О-165
ОТРЫВЕ
  в отрыве, О-166
ОТРЯСТИ
  отрясти прах от ⟨с⟩
    ⟨своих⟩ ног, П-494
ОТРЯХНУТЬ
  отряхнуть прах от ⟨с⟩
    ⟨своих⟩ ног, П-494
ОТСЕЧЕНИЕ
  давать голову ⟨руку⟩ на
    отсечение, Г-250
  дать голову ⟨руку⟩ на
    отсечение, Г-250
ОТСОХ
  чтоб у тебя язык отсох,
    Я-33
ОТСОХЛИ
  чтоб у меня руки (и ноги)
    отсохли!, Р-302
ОТСОХНЕТ
  пускай у меня рука
    отсохнет!, Р-302
  пусть у меня рука
    отсохнет!, Р-302
ОТСОХНИ
  отсохни руки и ноги!,
    Р-302

отсохни у меня рука!,
    Р-302
  отсохни у меня руки и
    ноги!, Р-302
  отсохни язык, Я-18
ОТСОХНУТ
  руки не отсохнут, Р-319
ОТСТАВАТЬ
  отставать от века, В-297
  отставать от времени,
    В-297
  отставать от жизни, Ж-46
ОТСТАВКУ
  давать/дать отставку,
    О-167
  получать/получить
    отставку, О-168
ОТСТАВНОЙ
  отставной козы
    барабанщик, К-172
ОТСТАТЬ
  отстать от века, В-297
  отстать от времени, В-297
  отстать от жизни, Ж-46
ОТСТУПАТЬ
  отступать в тень, Т-77
ОТСТУПИТЬ
  отступить в тень, Т-77
ОТСТУПЛЕНИЕ
  лирическое отступление,
    О-169
ОТСУТСТВИЕМ
  блистать (своим)
    отсутствием, О-170
  за отсутствием, О-171
ОТТАЩИШЬ
  за уши не оттащишь,
    У-184
ОТТОГО
  оттого что, П-435
ОТТЯНЕШЬ
  за уши не оттянешь, У-184
ОТХОДИТ
  сердце отходит, С-140
ОТХОДИТЬ
  отходить в область
    воспоминаний
    ⟨преданий, предания⟩,
    О-11
  отходить в прошлое,
    П-601
  отходить в тень, Т-77
ОТХОДЯ
  не отходя от кассы,
    К-102
ОТЦА
  прежде отца в петлю не
    лезь ⟨не суйся⟩, Б-27
ОТЦЫ
  годиться в отцы, Г-188
ОТЧАЯННАЯ
  отчаянная башка, Г-216
  отчаянная голова
    ⟨головушка⟩, Г-216
ОТЧЁТ
  давать/дать себе отчёт,
    О-172
  отдавать/отдать себе
    отчёт, О-172

ОТШИБЕ
  на отшибе, О-173
ОХАПКЕ
  в охапке, О-174
ОХАПКУ
  в охапку, О-174
ОХИ
  ахи да ⟨и⟩ охи, А-50
  охи да ⟨и⟩ ахи, А-50
  охи да ⟨и⟩ вздохи, О-175
ОХОТА
  охота пуще неволи, О-176
ОХОТКУ
  в охотку, О-177
ОХОТУ
  в охоту, О-178
  отбивать/отбить охоту,
    О-179
ОХУЛКИ
  охулки на руку не класть
    ⟨не положить⟩, О-180
ОЦЕНИВАТЬ
  оценивать по достоинству,
    Д-298
ОЦЕНИТЬ
  оценить по достоинству,
    Д-298
ОЧЕЙ
  свет очей, С-60
ОЧЕНЬ
  не очень далеко уйти, У-64
  очень нужно!, Н-259
ОЧЕРЕДИ
  в порядке живой очереди,
    П-399
  на очереди, О-181
  по очереди, О-182
  стоять на очереди, О-181
ОЧЕРЕДЬ
  в первую очередь, О-183
  в свою очередь, О-184
  вставать/встать на
    очередь, О-186
  поставить на очередь,
    О-185
  ставить на очередь, О-185
  становиться/стать на
    очередь, О-186
ОЧЕРТЯ
  очертя голову, Г-266
ОЧИ
  смежить очи, О-187
ОЧИСТКИ
  для очистки совести, О-188
ОЧКИ
  втереть ⟨втирать⟩ очки,
    О-189
  смотреть сквозь розовые
    очки, О-190
ОЧКОВ
  давать двадцать ⟨десять,
    сто⟩ очков вперёд,
    О-191
  дать двадцать ⟨десять,
    сто⟩ очков вперёд,
    О-191
ОЧУМЕЛЫЙ
  как очумелый, О-192
ОШПАРЕННЫЙ
  как ошпаренный, О-193

П

ПАВА
ни пава ни ворона, П-1
ПАВЛИНИЙ
распускать/распустить
павлиний хвост, Х-17
ПАВЛИНЬИХ
ворона в павлиньих
перьях, В-274
ПАДАЕТ
как будто* пелена падает
(с глаз), П-76
как будто* покров падает
(с глаз), П-76
завеса падает (с глаз), З-16
пелена падает (с глаз),
П-76
покров падает (с глаз),
П-76
сердце падает, С-141
тень падает, Т-78
яблоко ⟨яблочко⟩ от
яблони ⟨яблоньки⟩
недалеко падает, Я-4
ПАДАЙ
хоть стой, хоть падай,
С-584
ПАДАТЬ
падать без памяти, Ч-194
падать без сознания, Ч-194
падать без чувств, Ч-194
падать в ноги, Н-152
падать в обморок, О-14
падать духом, Д-355
падать к ногам, Н-152
падать на колени, Н-152
падать с неба на землю,
Н-47
падать с ног, Н-113
ПАДАЮТ
акции падают, А-23
ПАДЕЖАМ
просклонять ⟨склонять⟩
по всем падежам, П-2
ПАДЕЖАХ
просклонять ⟨склонять⟩
во всех падежах, П-2
ПАЗУХОЙ
держать камень за
пазухой, К-39
как у Христа за пазухой,
Х-104
носить камень за пазухой,
К-39
отогревать/отогреть змею
за пазухой, З-139
пригревать/пригреть
змею за пазухой, З-139
согревать/согреть змею за
пазухой, З-139
ПАЛА
тень пала, Т-78
ПАЛАТА
ума палата, У-94
ПАЛЁНЫМ
запахло ⟨пахнет⟩
палёным, Ж-3
ПАЛЕЦ
дай ему палец, он и всю
руку откусит, П-3

на большой палец, П-4
палец в рот не клади, П-16
палец о палец не ударить,
П-5
пальца о палец не ударить,
П-5
пальцем о палец не
ударить, П-5
ПАЛИТЬ
из пушек ⟨пушки⟩ по
воробьям палить, П-666
ПАЛКА
как палка, П-6
палка о двух концах, П-7
палка плачет, П-8
ПАЛКИ
вставлять палки в колёса,
П-9
из-под палки, П-10
совать палки в колёса, П-9
ставить палки в колёса,
П-9
ПАЛКУ
бросить палку, П-11
как собака палку, С-444
кинуть палку, П-11
перегибать/перегнуть
палку, П-12
ПАЛОЧКЕ
дерьмо на палочке, Д-185
ПАЛОЧКИ
как* по мановению
волшебной палочки,
М-27
ноль ⟨нуль⟩ без палочки,
Н-195
ПАЛЬМА
пальма первенства, П-13
ПАЛЬЦА
высасывать/высосать из
пальца, П-14
обвернуть вокруг
⟨кругом⟩ пальца, П-15
обвертеть вокруг
⟨кругом⟩ пальца, П-15
обвести вокруг ⟨кругом⟩
пальца, П-15
обводить вокруг ⟨кругом⟩
пальца, П-15
пальца в рот не клади,
П-16
пальца о палец не ударить,
П-5
ПАЛЬЦАМ
по пальцам можно
пересчитать
⟨перечесть⟩, П-17
по пальцам можно
сосчитать ⟨счесть⟩,
П-17
ПАЛЬЦАМИ
плыть меж ⟨между⟩
пальцами, П-18
показывать пальцами,
П-23
проскакивать между
пальцами, П-19
проскальзывать/
проскользнуть между
пальцами, П-19

проскочить между
пальцами, П-19
тыкать пальцами, П-23
уйти меж ⟨между⟩
пальцами, П-18
указывать пальцами, П-23
уплывать/уплыть меж
⟨между⟩ пальцами, П-18
уходить меж ⟨между⟩
пальцами, П-18
ПАЛЬЦЕВ
как свои пять пальцев,
П-20
комбинация из трёх
пальцев, К-214
плыть между пальцев,
П-18
проскакивать между
пальцев, П-19
проскальзывать/
проскользнуть между
пальцев, П-19
проскочить между
пальцев, П-19
уйти между пальцев, П-18
уплывать/уплыть между
пальцев, П-18
уходить между пальцев,
П-18
ПАЛЬЦЕМ
пальцем не двинуть, П-22
пальцем не пошевелить
⟨не пошевельнуть⟩,
П-22
пальцем не трогать/не
тронуть, П-21
пальцем не шевельнуть,
П-22
пальцем о палец не
ударить, П-5
показывать пальцем, П-23
попадать/попасть пальцем
в небо, П-24
указывать пальцем, П-23
тыкать пальцем, П-23
ПАЛЬЦЫ
глядеть сквозь пальцы,
П-27
ломать пальцы, Р-291
обжечь себе пальцы, П-25
плыть сквозь пальцы,
П-18
поглядеть сквозь пальцы,
П-27
посмотреть сквозь
пальцы, П-27
пропускать/пропустить
сквозь пальцы, П-26
проскакивать/проскочить
сквозь пальцы, П-19
смотреть сквозь пальцы,
П-27
уйти сквозь пальцы, П-18
уплывать/уплыть сквозь
пальцы, П-18
уходить сквозь пальцы,
П-18
ПАЛЬЧИК
мальчик с пальчик, М-21
ПАЛЬЧИКИ
пальчики оближете
⟨оближешь⟩, П-28

ПАМЯТИ
без памяти, П-29
блаженной памяти, П-30
в здравом уме и твёрдой
памяти, У-95
в знак памяти, З-154
в полной памяти, У-95
в твёрдой памяти, У-95
врезаться в памяти, П-42
всплывать/всплыть в
памяти, П-31
выбросить из памяти,
Г-286
выживать/выжить из
памяти, П-32
выкинуть из памяти, Г-286
вылетать/вылететь из
памяти, Г-287
выпадать/выпасть из
памяти, Г-287
выскакивать/выскочить из
памяти, Г-287
вычёркивать/вычеркнуть
из памяти, П-33
дай бог памяти, Б-112
держать в памяти, П-34
из памяти вон, Г-287
копаться в памяти, П-39
на памяти, П-35
не выходит из памяти,
Г-291
не идёт из памяти, Г-291
недоброй памяти, П-36
незабвенной памяти, П-30
нейдёт из памяти, Г-291
падать без памяти, Ч-194
перебирать/перебрать в
памяти, У-101
печальной памяти, П-36
по памяти, П-37
по старой памяти, П-38
покопаться в памяти, П-39
порыться в памяти, П-39
рыться в памяти, П-39
светлой памяти, П-30
упасть без памяти, Ч-194
ПАМЯТЬ
в память, П-40
вечная память, П-41
врезаться в память, П-42
дай бог память, Б-112
девичья память, П-44
дырявая память, П-44
если память не изменяет,
П-43
завязать ⟨завязывать⟩
узелок на память, У-60
западать/запасть в
память, Д-421
короткая память, П-44
куриная память, П-44
на память, П-45, П-46
на свежую память, П-47
привести в память, Ч-196
приводит на память, П-48
приводить в память, Ч-196
прийти в память, Ч-197
прийти на память, П-49
приходить в память, Ч-197
приходить на память,
П-49

птичья память, П-44
ПАН
  или пан, или пропал, П-50
  либо пан, либо пропал, П-50
  пан или пропал, П-50
ПАНА
  из хама не будет ⟨не сделаешь⟩ пана, Х-1
ПАНДОРЫ
  ящик Пандоры, Я-72
ПАНЕГИРИК
  петь/спеть панегирик, Д-198
ПАНЕЛЬ
  выйти ⟨выходить⟩ на панель, П-51
  идти ⟨пойти⟩ на панель, П-51
ПАНТАЛЫКУ
  сбивать с панталыку, П-52
  сбиваться с панталыку, П-53
  сбить с панталыку, П-52
  сбиться с панталыку, П-53
ПАНЫ
  паны дерутся, а у хлопцев ⟨холопов⟩ чубы болят ⟨трещат⟩, П-54
ПАРА
  два сапога пара, С-14
  не пара, П-55
  пара пустяков, П-56
ПАРАДЕ
  в полном параде, П-57
  во всём параде, П-57
  при всём параде, П-57
  при (полном) параде, П-57
ПАРАДОМ
  командовать парадом, П-58
ПАРАМИ
  под парами, П-59
ПАРАХ
  на всех парах, П-60
ПАРЕ
  в паре, П-61
  всякой твари по паре, Т-46
  каждой твари по паре, Т-46
ПАРЕНОЙ
  дешевле пареной репы, Р-110
  проще пареной репы, Р-111
ПАРЕНЬ
  первый парень на деревне ⟨на селе⟩, П-62
  свой парень в доску, Д-294
ПАРИ
  держать пари, П-63
  на пари, С-524
ПАРИТЬ
  парить в облаках ⟨в эмпиреях⟩, О-8
  парить между небом и землёй, О-8
ПАРОМ
  с лёгким паром!, П-64
ПАРТБИЛЕТ
  выложить партбилет (на стол), Б-65

положить партбилет (на стол), Б-65
ПАРУ
  задавать/задать пару, П-65
  на пару, П-66
  на пару слов, П-67
  под пару, П-68
  поддавать/поддать пару, Ж-7
  сказать пару тёплых слов, П-69
ПАРУСАХ
  на всех парусах, П-60
ПАРШИВАЯ
  (одна) паршивая овца всё стадо портит, О-46
ПАРШИВОЙ
  с паршивой овцы хоть шерсти клок, О-47
ПАСПОРТ
  волчий паспорт, Б-63
ПАСТЬ
  пасть в ноги, Н-152
  пасть духом, Д-355
  пасть жертвой, Ж-20
  пасть к ногам, Н-152
  пасть на колени, Н-152
ПАТРИКЕЕВНА
  Лиса Патрикеевна, Л-77
ПАТРИОТИЗМ
  квасной патриотизм, П-70
ПАХАЛИ
  (и) мы пахали, П-71
ПАХВЕЙ
  сбивать с пахвей, П-52
  сбиваться с пахвей, П-53
  сбить с пахвей, П-52
  сбиться с пахвей, П-53
ПАХЛО
  чтобы духом не пахло, Д-362
ПАХНЕТ
  дело пахнет керосином, Д-90
  (и) не пахнет, П-72
  нехорошо пахнет, П-73
  пахнет жареным, Ж-3
  пахнет палёным, Ж-3
  пахнет порохом, П-383
  плохо пахнет, П-73
ПАХНУТ
  деньги не пахнут, Д-170
ПАЧЕ
  паче глаза, Г-93
  паче зеницы ока, З-130
  паче ока, Г-93
  паче чаяния, Ч-40
  тем паче, Т-64
ПАЧКАТЬ
  пачкать руки, Р-292
ПАЯХ
  на паях, П-74
ПЕДАЛИ
  нажать ⟨нажимать⟩ на все педали, П-75
ПЕЙ
  пей — не хочу, Х-95
ПЕКЛО
  не лезь поперёд батьки в пекло, Б-27

хоть к чёрту в пекло, Ч-118
ПЕЛЁН
  от ⟨с⟩ пелён, П-79
ПЕЛЕНА
  как будто* пелена падает (с глаз), П-76
  как будто* пелена спадает/спала (с глаз), П-76
  как будто* пелена упала (с глаз), П-76
  пелена падает (с глаз), П-76
  пелена спадает/спала (с глаз), П-76
  пелена упала (с глаз), П-76
ПЕЛЁНКАХ
  в пелёнках, П-77
ПЕЛЁНОК
  выйти ⟨выходить⟩ из пелёнок, П-78
  от ⟨с⟩ пелёнок, П-79
ПЕНКИ
  снимать/снять пенки, П-80
ПЕНОЙ
  с пеной у рта, П-81
ПЕНЬ
  как пень, П-82
  пень берёзовый, П-83
  через пень колоду ⟨пень-колоду⟩, П-84
ПЕНЯТЬ
  пенять на себя, П-85
ПЕПЛА
  возродиться из пепла, П-86
ПЕПЛОМ
  посыпать главу ⟨голову⟩ пеплом, Г-269
  посыпать себе главу ⟨голову⟩ пеплом, Г-269
ПЕРА
  выйти ⟨выходить⟩ из-под пера, П-87
  единым росчерком пера, Р-170
  ни пуха ни пера, П-665
  одним росчерком пера, Р-170
  по единому росчерку пера, Р-170
  по одному росчерку пера, Р-170
  проба пера, П-559
  росчерком пера, Р-170
ПЕРВАЯ
  первая ласточка, Л-34
  первая скрипка, С-238
ПЕРВЕНСТВА
  пальма первенства, П-13
ПЕРВОГО
  с первого абцуга, А-3
  с первого взгляда, В-98
  с первого знакомства, З-158
  с первого слова, С-290
ПЕРВОЕ
  в первое время, В-299

на первое время, В-316
  первое время, В-299
  первое дело, Д-122
  первое слово, С-319
  по первое число, Ч-153
ПЕРВОЙ
  звезда первой величины, З-91
  не первой молодости, М-234
  не первой свежести, С-36
  первой марки, М-29
  первой руки, Р-276
ПЕРВОМ
  на первом взводе, В-93
  при первом взгляде, В-98
ПЕРВОМУ
  по первому абцугу, А-3
  по первому взгляду, В-98
ПЕРВУЮ
  в первую голову, О-183
  в первую минуту, М-174
  в первую очередь, О-183
  играть первую роль, Р-155
  играть первую скрипку, С-240
ПЕРВЫЕ
  первые шаги, Ш-13
ПЕРВЫЙ
  на первый взгляд, В-97
  на первый случай, С-375
  не ты первый, не ты последний, П-88
  первый блин (всегда) комом, Б-80
  первый встречный, В-348
  первый парень на деревне ⟨на селе⟩, П-62
  первый попавший, П-346
  первый попавшийся, П-346
  первый сорт, С-499
  первый шаг, Ш-13
  сделать первый шаг, Ш-7
ПЕРВЫМ
  первым делом, Д-141
  первым долгом, Д-141
ПЕРВЫХ
  в первых рядах, Р-401
  до первых петухов, П-135
  из первых рук, Р-210
  из первых уст, У-138
  на первых порах, П-368
  на первых ролях, Р-159
  после первых петухов, П-136
  с первых слов, С-290
  с первых шагов, Ш-14
ПЕРЕБЕГАТЬ
  перебегать дорогу ⟨дорожку⟩, Д-283
ПЕРЕБЕЖАТЬ
  перебежать дорогу ⟨дорожку⟩, Д-283
ПЕРЕБИВАТЬ
  перебивать дорогу ⟨дорожку⟩, Д-283
  перебивать хлеб, Х-35
ПЕРЕБИВАТЬСЯ
  перебиваться с гроша на копейку, Х-41

перебиваться с корочки на
    корочку, Х-41
перебиваться с куска на
    кусок, Х-41
перебиваться с хлеба на
    воду, Х-41
перебиваться с хлеба на
    квас, Х-41
перебиваться со дня на
    день, Д-211
ПЕРЕБИРАТЬ
перебирать в голове, У-101
перебирать в мыслях,
    У-101
перебирать в памяти,
    У-101
перебирать в уме, У-101
ПЕРЕБИТЬ
перебить дорогу
    ⟨дорожку⟩, Д-283
перебить хлеб, Х-35
ПЕРЕБОЛЕЛА
душа переболела, Д-364
ПЕРЕБРАСЫВАТЬ
перебрасывать мост,
    М-264
ПЕРЕБРАТЬ
перебрать в голове, У-101
перебрать в мыслях, У-101
перебрать в памяти, У-101
перебрать в уме, У-101
ПЕРЕБРОСИТЬ
перебросить мост, М-264
перебросить словечко
    ⟨слово⟩, С-335
ПЕРЕБРОСИТЬСЯ
переброситься двумя
    словами, С-335
переброситься словечком,
    С-335
переброситься словом
    ⟨словцом⟩, С-335
ПЕРЕВЕРНУЛАСЬ
душа перевернулась, Д-373
ПЕРЕВЕРНУЛОСЬ
сердце перевернулось,
    Д-373
ПЕРЕВЕРНУТЬ
перевернуть вверх
    тормашками, Т-164
перевернуть весь мир,
    М-183
перевернуть весь свет,
    М-183
перевернуть (всю) душу,
    Д-429
ПЕРЕВЕРНУТЬСЯ
перевернуться в гробу,
    Г-403
ПЕРЕВЁРТЫВАТЬ
перевёртывать вверх
    тормашками, Т-164
перевёртывать (всю) душу,
    Д-429
ПЕРЕВЁРТЫВАТЬСЯ
перевёртываться в гробу,
    Г-403
ПЕРЕВЕСТИ
перевести дух, Д-348
перевести дыхание, Д-348

перевести на рельсы, Р-108
перевести разговор на
    другое, Р-48
перевести разговор на
    другую тему, Р-48
ПЕРЕВЕШАЕШЬ
до Москвы не
    перевешаешь, М-263
ПЕРЕВЕШАТЬ
до Москвы не перевешать,
    М-263
ПЕРЕВОДА
нет перевода, П-89
ПЕРЕВОДИТЬ
переводить дух, Д-348
переводить дыхание,
    Д-348
переводить на рельсы,
    Р-108
переводить разговор на
    другое, Р-48
переводить разговор на
    другую тему, Р-48
ПЕРЕВОДЯ
не переводя духа ⟨духу⟩,
    Д-444
не переводя дыхания,
    Д-444
ПЕРЕВОРАЧИВАЕТСЯ
душа переворачивается,
    Д-373
сердце переворачивается,
    Д-373
ПЕРЕВОРАЧИВАТЬ
переворачивать вверх
    тормашками, Т-164
переворачивать (всю)
    душу, Д-429
ПЕРЕВОРАЧИВАТЬСЯ
переворачиваться в гробу,
    Г-403
ПЕРЕВОРОТИТЬ
переворотить (всю) душу,
    Д-429
ПЕРЕГИБАТЬ
перегибать палку, П-12
ПЕРЕГНУТЬ
перегнуть палку, П-12
ПЕРЕГРЫЗТЬ
перегрызть горло, Г-340
ПЕРЕДАВАТЬ
передавать эстафету, Э-2
ПЕРЕДАТЬ
передать эстафету, Э-2
ПЕРЕДВИГАТЬ
едва ⟨еле⟩ ноги
    передвигать, Н-144
насилу ноги передвигать,
    Н-144
с трудом ноги
    передвигать, Н-144
чуть ноги передвигать,
    Н-144
ПЕРЕДЕЛКАХ
бывать/побывать в
    переделках, П-95
ПЕРЕДЕЛКЕ
бывать/побывать в
    переделке, П-95

ПЕРЕДЕЛКУ
попадать/попасть в
    переделку, П-95
ПЕРЕДРЯГАХ
бывать/побывать в
    передрягах, П-95
ПЕРЕДРЯГЕ
бывать/побывать в
    передряге, П-95
ПЕРЕДРЯГУ
попадать/попасть в
    передрягу, П-95
ПЕРЕЕЗЖАЯ
переезжая сваха, С-32
ПЕРЕЖЁВЫВАТЬ
пережёвывать жвачку, Ж-8
ПЕРЕЖИВАТЬ
переживать (самого) себя,
    П-90
ПЕРЕЖИТЬ
пережить (самого) себя,
    П-90
ПЕРЕЙТИ
жизнь прожить — не поле
    перейти, Ж-54
перейти дорогу
    ⟨дорожку⟩, Д-283
перейти на личности,
    Л-106
перейти на рельсы, Р-109
перейти порог, П-372
перейти Рубикон, Р-197
перейти через порог, П-372
ПЕРЕКАТИ-ПОЛЕ
перекати-поле, П-91
ПЕРЕКАТНАЯ
голь перекатная, Г-312
ПЕРЕКИДЫВАТЬ
перекидывать мост, М-264
ПЕРЕКИНУТЬ
перекинуть мост, М-264
перекинуть словечко
    ⟨слово⟩, С-335
ПЕРЕКИНУТЬСЯ
перекинуться двумя
    словами, С-335
перекинуться словечком,
    С-335
перекинуться словом
    ⟨словцом⟩, С-335
ПЕРЕКЛАДЫВАТЬ
перекладывать на плечи,
    П-191
перекладывать с больной
    головы на здоровую,
    Г-284
ПЕРЕКРЕСТИТСЯ
гром не грянет, мужик не
    перекрестится, Г-404
ПЕРЕКРЁСТКАХ
кричать на всех
    перекрёстках, П-92
ПЕРЕЛАМЫВАТЬ
переламывать себя, П-93
ПЕРЕЛИВАТЬ
переливать из пустого в
    порожнее, П-638
переливать через край,
    К-355

ПЕРЕЛИВАТЬСЯ
переливаться через край,
    К-352
ПЕРЕЛОЖИТЬ
переложить лишку, Л-108
переложить лишнее, Л-108
переложить на музыку,
    М-285
переложить на ноты,
    М-285
переложить на плечи,
    П-191
ПЕРЕЛОМАТЬ
переломать (все) кости,
    К-321
ПЕРЕЛОМИТЬ
переломить себя, П-93
ПЕРЕМАТЬ
мать твою перемать, М-55
ПЕРЕМЕЛЕТСЯ
перемелется — мука будет,
    М-287
ПЕРЕМЕНА
перемена декораций, Д-51
ПЕРЕМЕНИТЬ
переменить гнев на
    милость, Г-155
переменить декорации,
    Д-51
переменить пластинку,
    П-164
ПЕРЕМЕНИТЬСЯ
перемениться в лице, Л-91
ПЕРЕМЁТНАЯ
сума перемётная, С-674
ПЕРЕМОЛВИТЬСЯ
перемолвиться двумя
    словами, С-335
перемолвиться словечком,
    С-335
перемолвиться словом
    ⟨словцом⟩, С-335
ПЕРЕМЫВАТЬ
перемывать кости
    ⟨косточки⟩, К-327
ПЕРЕМЫТЬ
перемыть кости
    ⟨косточки⟩, К-327
ПЕРЕПЛЁТ
брать/взять в переплёт,
    П-94
попадать/попасть в
    переплёт, П-95
ПЕРЕПЛЁТАХ
бывать/побывать в
    переплётах, П-95
ПЕРЕПЛЁТЕ
бывать/побывать в
    переплёте, П-95
ПЕРЕПОЛНИВШАЯ
капля, переполнившая
    чашу, К-67
ПЕРЕПОЛНИЛАСЬ
мера терпения
    переполнилась, Ч-36
чаша переполнилась, Ч-36
чаша терпения
    переполнилась, Ч-36
ПЕРЕПОЛНИТЬ
переполнить чашу
    терпения, Ч-38

ПЕРЕПОЛНЯТЬ
переполнять чашу
терпения, Ч-38
ПЕРЕПОЮ
с перепою, П-96
ПЕРЕПОЯ
с перепоя, П-96
ПЕРЕПРЫГНЕШЬ
не говори гоп, пока не
перепрыгнешь, Г-158
ПЕРЕПУТЬЕ
на перепутье, Р-82
ПЕРЕСЕЛИТЬСЯ
переселиться в другой
⟨иной, лучший⟩ мир,
М-184
ПЕРЕСЕЛЯТЬСЯ
переселяться в другой
⟨иной, лучший⟩ мир,
М-184
ПЕРЕСИЛИВАТЬ
пересиливать себя, П-499
ПЕРЕСИЛИТЬ
пересилить себя, П-499
ПЕРЕСКОЧИШЬ
не говори гоп, пока не
перескочишь, Г-158
ПЕРЕСТУПАТЬ
переступать ⟨через⟩ порог,
П-372
ПЕРЕСТУПИТЬ
переступить ⟨через⟩ порог,
П-372
переступить через труп,
Т-219
ПЕРЕСУДЫ
суды да ⟨и⟩ пересуды,
С-661
ПЕРЕСЧИТАТЬ
пересчитать кости, Р-96
пересчитать рёбра, Р-96
по пальцам можно
пересчитать, П-17
ПЕРЕСЫПАТЬ
пересыпать из пустого в
порожнее, П-638
ПЕРЕТРУТ
терпение и труд всё
перетрут, Т-80
ПЕРЕТЬ
переть в гору, Г-351
переть на рожон, Р-145
переть напролом, И-29
переть против рожна,
Р-144
ПЕРЕХВАТИЛО
перехватило дух, Д-345
перехватило дыхание,
Д-345
ПЕРЕХВАТИТЬ
перехватить горло, Г-341
перехватить через край,
К-355
ПЕРЕХВАТЫВАЕТ
перехватывает дух, Д-345
перехватывает дыхание,
Д-345
ПЕРЕХВАТЫВАТЬ
перехватывать горло,
Г-341

ПЕРЕХОДИТЬ
переходить дорогу
⟨дорожку⟩, Д-283
переходить на личности,
Л-106
переходить на рельсы,
Р-109
переходить ⟨через⟩ порог,
П-372
ПЕРЕЧЕСТЬ
по пальцам можно
перечесть, П-17
ПЕРЕЧНИЦА
чёртова перечница, П-97
ПЕРЕШАГИВАТЬ
перешагивать ⟨через⟩
порог, П-372
ПЕРЕШАГНУТЬ
перешагнуть ⟨через⟩ порог,
П-372
перешагнуть через труп,
Т-219
ПЕРЕШИБЁШЬ
плетью обуха не
перешибёшь, П-174
соплёй перешибёшь, С-490
ПЕРЕШИБИТЬ
соплёй перешибить
можно, С-490
ПЕРЛ
возвести ⟨возводить⟩ в
перл создания, П-98
ПЕРО
бойкое перо, П-99
браться за перо, П-100
взяться за перо, П-100
лечь под перо, Б-245
ложиться под перо, Б-245
ПЕРОМ
владеть пером, П-101
ни в сказке сказать, ни
пером описать, С-216
под пером, П-102
что написано пером, того
не вырубишь топором,
П-103
ПЕРСОНА
персона грата, П-104
персона нон грата, П-105
ПЕРСОНОЙ
собственной персоной,
П-106
ПЕРСТ
как перст, П-107
перст божий, П-108
перст провидения, П-108
перст рока, П-108
перст свыше, П-108
перст судьбы, П-108
ПЕРУ
принадлежать перу, П-109
ПЕРЦУ
задавать/задать перцу,
П-110
ПЕРЧАТКАХ
в белых перчатках, П-111
ПЕРЧАТКУ
бросать/бросить перчатку,
П-112

поднимать/поднять
перчатку, П-113
ПЁРЫШКИ
почистить ⟨чистить⟩
пёрышки, П-114
ПЕРЬЯ
пух да ⟨и⟩ перья летят/
полетят, П-664
ПЕРЬЯХ
ворона в павлиньих
перьях, В-274
ПЁС
на кой пёс, Ч-77
пёс его знает, Ч-89
пёс с тобой, Ч-98
пёс тебя возьми!, Ч-99
ПЕСЕНКА
песенка спета, П-115
ПЕСКЕ
построить ⟨строить⟩ на
песке, П-116
ПЕСКОМ
пробирать/пробрать с
песком, П-124
продирать/продрать с
песком, П-124
протереть ⟨протирать⟩ с
песком, П-124
ПЕСКУ
как песку морского, П-122
что песку морского, П-122
ПЕСНИ
из песни слова не
выкинешь, П-117
ПЕСНЬ
лебединая песнь, П-120
ПЕСНЮ
петь одну и ту же песню,
П-118
тянуть одну и ту же
песню, П-118
ПЕСНЯ
всё та же песня, П-121
длинная песня, П-119
долгая песня, П-119
лебединая песня, П-120
песня спета, П-115
прежняя песня, П-121
старая песня, П-121
ПЕСОК
как песок морской, П-122
песок сыплется, П-123
ПЕСОЧКОМ
пробирать/пробрать с
песочком, П-124
продирать/продрать с
песочком, П-124
протереть ⟨протирать⟩ с
песочком, П-124
ПЕСЦЕ
построить ⟨строить⟩ на
песце, П-116
ПЕТЛЕ
в петле, П-125
ПЕТЛИ
метать петли, П-126
ПЕТЛЮ
в петлю, П-125
лезть в петлю, П-127

надевать/надеть петлю на
себя ⟨(себе) на шею⟩,
П-128
накидывать/накинуть
петлю на себя ⟨(себе) на
шею⟩, П-128
полезть в петлю, П-127
прежде батьки в петлю не
лезь ⟨не суйся⟩, Б-27
прежде отца в петлю не
лезь ⟨не суйся⟩, Б-27
совать голову в петлю,
Г-278
соваться в петлю, Г-278
сунуть голову в петлю,
Г-278
хоть в петлю лезь, П-129
хоть в петлю полезай,
П-129
ПЕТЛЯ
петля плачет, В-36
ПЕТЛЯТЬ
петлять вокруг ⟨кругом⟩
да около, Х-59
ПЕТУХ
жареный петух не клевал/
не клюнул, П-130
красный петух, П-131
ПЕТУХА
давать/дать петуха, П-133
подпускать/подпустить
⟨красного⟩ петуха, П-132
пускать красного петуха,
П-132
пускать петуха, П-132,
П-133
пустить красного петуха,
П-132
пустить петуха, П-132,
П-133
ПЕТУХАМИ
с петухами, П-134
ПЕТУХОВ
до вторых петухов, П-135
до первых петухов, П-135
до петухов, П-135
до поздних петухов, П-135
до третьих петухов, П-135
после вторых петухов,
П-136
после первых петухов,
П-136
после третьих петухов,
П-136
ПЕТЫЙ
петый дурак, Д-330
ПЕТЬ
лазаря петь, Л-18
петь в уши, У-186
петь дифирамбы, Д-198
петь одну и ту же песню,
П-118
петь осанну, О-107
петь панегирик, Д-198
петь с твоего ⟨чужого⟩
голоса, Г-306
петь соловьём, С-472
ПЕЧАЛИ
не было печали, (так)
черти накачали, П-137

ПЕЧАЛЬ
   какая печаль, П-138
   не моя печаль, З-6
   что за печаль, П-138
ПЕЧАЛЬНОГО
   рыцарь печального образа, Р-396
ПЕЧАЛЬНОЙ
   печальной памяти, П-36
ПЕЧАТЬ
   каинова печать, П-139
   класть печать, О-162
   накладывать/наложить печать, О-162
   оставить ⟨оставлять⟩ печать, О-162
   печать Каина, П-139
   положить печать, О-162
ПЕЧАТЯМИ
   за семью печатями, П-140
   книга за семью печатями, К-147
ПЕЧЁНКАМИ
   всеми печёнками, П-141
ПЕЧЁНКАХ
   сидеть в печёнках, П-142
ПЕЧИ
   лежать на печи, Б-158
ПЕЧКЕ
   лежать на печке, Б-158
ПЕЧКИ
   от печки, П-143
   танцевать от печки, П-145
   печки-лавочки, П-144
ПЕЧЬ
   печь как блины, Б-81
ПЕШЕГО
   по образу пешего хождения, О-26
ПЕШКОМ
   под стол пешком ходит, С-589
ПИВА
   пива не сварить ⟨не сваришь⟩, К-111
ПИВНОЙ
   как ⟨с⟩ пивной котёл, К-337
ПИК
   час(ы) пик, Ч-33
ПИКОВОЕ
   пиковое положение, П-306
ПИКОВОМ
   при пиковом интересе, И-70
ПИКУ
   в пику, П-146
ПИЛЮЛИ
   поднести ⟨подносить⟩ пилюли, П-148
   преподнести ⟨преподносить⟩ пилюли, П-148
ПИЛЮЛЮ
   золотить пилюлю, П-147
   поднести ⟨подносить⟩ пилюлю, П-148
   подсластить пилюлю, П-147

позолотить пилюлю, П-147
   преподнести ⟨преподносить⟩ пилюлю, П-148
   проглотить пилюлю, П-149
   съесть пилюлю, П-149
ПИЛЮЛЯ
   горькая пилюля, П-150
   пилюля горька, П-150
ПИР
   валтасаров пир, П-151
   лукуллов(ский) пир, П-152
   пир горой, П-153
   пир на весь мир, П-153
ПИРОГАМИ
   не красна изба углами, а красна пирогами, И-34
ПИРОГИ
   вот какие пироги, П-154
ПИРРОВА
   пиррова победа, П-207
ПИРУ
   в чужом пиру похмелье, П-155
ПИРШЕСТВО
   валтасарово пиршество, П-151
ПИСАН
   дуракам ⟨дураку⟩ закон не писан, Д-337
   закон не писан, З-48
ПИСАНО
   вилами на ⟨по⟩ воде писано, В-144
   ещё вилами на ⟨по⟩ воде писано, В-144
   не про меня писано, П-156
ПИСАНОЙ
   как дурак ⟨дурень⟩ с писаной торбой, Т-161
   как с писаной торбой, Т-161
ПИСАНОМУ
   как* по писаному, П-157
ПИСАТЬ
   и пошла ⟨пошло⟩ писать, Г-439
   писать в стол ⟨в ящик⟩, С-588
   писать вавилоны, В-33
   писать вензеля, В-33
   писать крендели ⟨кренделя⟩, В-33
   писать кровью (сердца), К-416
   писать мыслете, В-33
   писать ногами вензеля ⟨крендели, кренделя, мыслете⟩, В-33
   пошла писать, Г-439
   пошла писать губерния, Г-439
   пошло писать, Г-439
ПИСТОЛЕТОМ
   держать хвост пистолетом, Х-10
ПИТАТЬ
   питать надежду ⟨надежды⟩, Н-7

ПИТАТЬСЯ
   питаться акридами (и диким мёдом), А-20
   питаться акридами и мёдом, А-20
   питаться манной небесной, М-25
   питаться святым духом, Д-356
ПИТЬ
   вашими бы устами (да) мёд пить, У-145
   давать/дать пить, Д-6
   как пить дадут ⟨даст⟩, П-158
   как пить дать, П-158
   пить брудершафт, Б-213
   пить горькую, Г-360
   пить горькую чашу (до дна), Ч-39
   пить до дна горькую ⟨полную⟩ чашу, Ч-39
   пить кровь, К-407
   пить мёртвую, Г-360
   пить на брудершафт, Б-213
   пить на ты, Б-213
   пить полную чашу, Ч-39
   пить чашу (до дна), Ч-39
   с лица не воду пить, Л-86
   твоими бы устами (да) мёд пить, У-145
ПИШЕТ
   говорит как пишет, Г-160
   дела идут, контора пишет, Д-55
ПИШИ
   пиши пропало, П-159
ПИЩА
   будет день, будет пища, Б-92
ПИЩЕ
   сидеть на пище святого Антония, П-160
ПИЩИ
   вкушать от пищи святого Антония, П-160
ПИЩУ
   бог даст день, бог даст пищу, Б-92
   бог даст день, даст и пищу, Б-92
   давать/дать пищу, П-161
ПЛАВАНИЕ
   большому кораблю большое плавание, К-290
ПЛАВАТЬ
   мелко плавать, П-162
   не учи рыбу плавать, Р-385
ПЛАКАЛИ
   плакали денежки, Д-148
ПЛАКАЛО
   чем бы дитя ни тешилось, лишь бы не плакало, Д-197
ПЛАКАТЬ
   плакать в жилетку, Ж-71
ПЛАКАТЬСЯ
   плакаться в жилетку, Ж-71

ПЛАМЕНЕМ
   гори (оно) синим ⟨ясным⟩ пламенем, О-55
ПЛАН
   на задний план, П-163
ПЛАНЕ
   на заднем плане, П-163
ПЛАСТ
   лежать как пласт, П-165
ПЛАСТИНКУ
   переменить пластинку, П-164
   сменить пластинку, П-164
ПЛАСТОМ
   лежать пластом, П-165
ПЛАТЕЖОМ
   долг платежом красен, Д-234
ПЛАТИТЬ
   платить дань, Д-22
   платить той же монетой, М-254
ПЛАТФОРМЕ
   стоять на платформе, П-166
ПЛАТЬЕ
   береги платье снову, а честь смолоду, П-167
ПЛАТЬЮ
   по платью встречают, по уму провожают, О-70
ПЛАЧЕМ
   что имеем, не храним, потерявши, плачем, И-55
ПЛАЧЕТ
   верёвка плачет, В-36
   острог плачет, Т-253
   палка плачет, П-8
   петля плачет, В-36
   тюрьма плачет, Т-253
ПЛАЧУТ
   снявши голову, по волосам не плачут, Г-276
ПЛАЧЬ
   хоть плачь, П-168
ПЛЕВАТЬ
   плевать в глаза, Г-86
   плевать в душу, Д-430
   плевать в лицо, Г-86
   плевать в потолок, П-433
   плевать в рожу, Г-86
   плевать с высокого дерева, Д-176
   плевать я хотел, П-169
ПЛЕВЕЛЫ
   отделить ⟨отделять⟩ плевелы от пшеницы, П-170
ПЛЕВКА
   плевка не стоит, П-171
ПЛЁВОЕ
   плёвое дело, Д-123
ПЛЕМЕНИ
   без роду, без племени, Р-137
   без роду и (без) племени, Р-137
   ни роду ни племени, Р-139

ПЛЕСТИ
лапти плести, Л-28
плести ахинею, В-99
плести ересь, В-99
плести околёсицу, В-99
ПЛЕТЕНИЕ
плетение словес, П-172
ПЛЕТЕНЬ
навести ⟨наводить⟩ тень
на плетень, Т-75
ПЛЕТЬЮ
плетью не вышибешь,
П-173
плетью обуха не
перешибёшь, П-174
ПЛЕЧ
гора с плеч ⟨свалилась⟩,
Г-316
как* гора с плеч
⟨свалилась⟩, Г-316
с плеч долой, П-175
сбрасывать/сбросить с
плеч, П-176
сваливать с плеч, П-176
сваливаться с плеч, П-177
свалить с плеч, П-176
свалиться с плеч, П-177
скидывать/скинуть с плеч,
П-176
спихивать/спихнуть с
плеч, П-178
стряхивать/стряхнуть с
плеч, П-176
ПЛЕЧА
с плеча, П-179, П-180
с чужого плеча, П-181
со всего плеча, П-182
ПЛЕЧАМИ
за плечами, П-183
пожать ⟨пожимать⟩
плечами, П-184
ПЛЕЧАХ
висеть на плечах, П-185
вывезти на плечах, П-186
вывезти на своих
⟨собственных⟩ плечах,
П-186
вывозить на плечах, П-186
вывозить на своих
⟨собственных⟩ плечах,
П-186
вынести на плечах, П-186
вынести на своих
⟨собственных⟩ плечах,
П-186
выносить на плечах, П-186
выносить на своих
⟨собственных⟩ плечах,
П-186
голова на плечах, Г-205
иметь голову на плечах,
Г-205
косая сажень в плечах, С-3
лежать на плечах, П-187
на плечах, П-187, П-188
своя голова на плечах,
Г-219
сидеть на плечах, П-185
ПЛЕЧЕ
язык на плече, Я-39

ПЛЕЧИ
взваливать/взвалить на
плечи, П-189
лечь на плечи, П-190
ложиться на плечи, П-190
перекладывать/
переложить на плечи,
П-191
сваливаться/свалиться на
плечи, П-190
ПЛЕЧОМ
плечо в плечо, П-192
плечо к плечу, П-192
плечо о плечо, П-192
язык на плечо, Я-39
ПЛЕЧОМ
плечом к плечу, П-192
ПЛЕЧУ
плечо к плечу, П-192
плечом к плечу, П-192
по плечу, П-193
похлопывать по плечу,
П-194
ПЛОД
запретный плод, П-195
ПЛОДЫ
вкусить ⟨вкушать⟩ плоды,
П-196
пожать ⟨пожинать⟩
плоды, П-196
ПЛОСКОСТИ
идти по наклонной
плоскости, П-197
катиться по наклонной
плоскости, П-197
пойти по наклонной
плоскости, П-197
покатиться по наклонной
плоскости, П-197
ПЛОТИ
во плоти, П-198
плоть от плоти ⟨и кость от
кости⟩, П-202
плоть от плоти и кровь от
крови, П-202
ПЛОТНО
неладно ⟨нескладно⟩
скроен, да плотно сшит,
С-242
худо скроен, да плотно
сшит, С-242
ПЛОТЬ
войти ⟨входить⟩ в плоть и
кровь, П-199
облекать в плоть ⟨и
кровь⟩, П-200
облекаться в плоть ⟨и
кровь⟩, П-201
облечь в плоть ⟨и кровь⟩,
П-200
облечься в плоть ⟨и кровь⟩,
П-201
плоть и кровь, П-202
плоть от плоти ⟨и кость от
кости⟩, П-202
плоть от плоти и кровь от
крови, П-202
ПЛОТЬЮ
облекать плотью (и
кровью), П-200

облекаться плотью ⟨и
кровью⟩, П-201
облечь плотью ⟨и кровью⟩,
П-200
облечься плотью ⟨и
кровью⟩, П-201
ПЛОХИ
шутки плохи, Ш-104
ПЛОХО
дело плохо, Д-91
не плохо ⟨бы⟩, Х-108
плохо будет, Б-219
плохо кончить, К-266
плохо лежит, Л-47
плохо пахнет, П-73
язык плохо подвешен
⟨привешен⟩, Я-42
ПЛОХОЙ
делать весёлую
⟨хорошую⟩ мину при
плохой игре, М-167
на плохой путь, П-644
на плохой дурной дороге
⟨дорожке⟩, П-644
пойти по плохой дороге
⟨дорожке⟩, Д-270
сделать весёлую
⟨хорошую⟩ мину при
плохой игре, М-167
ПЛОХОМ
на плохом пути, П-644
ПЛОХОМУ
пойти по плохому пути,
Д-270
ПЛОХУЮ
на плохую дорогу
⟨дорожку⟩, П-644
ПЛОШАЙ
на бога надейся, а сам не
плошай, Б-129
ПЛЫВЁТ
земля плывёт под ногами,
З-125
ПЛЫТЬ
плыть в руки, Р-303
плыть меж пальцами,
П-18
плыть между пальцами
⟨пальцев⟩, П-18
плыть по течению, Т-96
плыть против течения,
Т-97
плыть сквозь пальцы,
П-18
ПЛЮЙ
не плюй в колодец,
пригодится воды
напиться, К-199
ПЛЮНУТЬ
плюнуть в глаза, Г-86
плюнуть в душу, Д-430
плюнуть в лицо, Г-86
плюнуть в рожу, Г-86
плюнуть да ⟨и⟩ растереть,
П-203
плюнуть негде, П-204
плюнуть некуда, П-204
раз плюнуть, Р-35
ПЛЮНЬ
куда ни плюнь, П-205

ПЛЯСАТЬ
плясать по дудке
⟨дудочке⟩, Д-319
плясать под дудку
⟨дудочку⟩, Д-319
ПО-СВОЕМУ
всяк(ий) по-своему с ума
сходит, У-82
каждый по-своему с ума
сходит, У-82
ПОБЕГУШКАХ
на побегушках, П-206
ПОБЕДА
пиррова победа, П-207
ПОБЕДИТЕЛЕЙ
победителей не судят,
П-208
ПОБЕДНОГО
до победного конца, К-248
ПОБЕЖАЛИ
мурашки побежали по
коже, М-291
мурашки побежали по
спине ⟨по телу⟩, М-291
ПОБЕЙ
побей меня бог ⟨господь⟩,
Б-125
ПОБЕРИ
леший тебя побери!, Ч-99
лядь тебя побери!, Ч-99
прах тебя побери!, Ч-99
чёрт побери!, Ч-87
чёрт тебя побери!, Ч-99
шут тебя побери!, Ч-99
ПОБИТЬ
побить карту, К-95
ПОБИТЬСЯ
побиться об заклад, З-45
ПОБЛАЖКИ
давать/дать поблажки,
П-209
делать поблажки, П-209
сделать поблажки, П-209
ПОБЛАЖКУ
давать/дать поблажку,
П-209
делать поблажку, П-209
сделать поблажку, П-209
ПОБОИЩЕ
мамаево побоище, П-210
ПОБОЙСЯ
побойся бога, Б-130
ПОБОЯЛСЯ
бога бы побоялся, Б-130
ПОБРАЛ
чёрт бы тебя побрал!,
Ч-99
ПОБЫВАТЬ
побывать в переделках ⟨в
переделке⟩, П-95
побывать в передрягах ⟨в
передряге⟩, П-95
побывать в переплётах ⟨в
переплёте⟩, П-95
ПОВАДКУ
давать/дать повадку,
П-209
ПОВАДНО
чтобы не было повадно,
Б-272

ПОВАЛИТЬ
валом повалить, В-6
повалить в лёжку, Л-50

ПОВАЛЯТЬСЯ
поваляться в ногах ⟨в ножках⟩, Н-130

ПОВАПЛЕННЫЙ
гроб повапленный, Г-397

ПОВЕДЕНИЯ
лёгкого поведения, П-211

ПОВЕДЁШЬСЯ
с кем поведёшься, от того и наберёшься, П-212

ПОВЁЛ
бровью ⟨глазом, носом⟩ не повёл, Б-209
усом ⟨ухом⟩ не повёл, Б-209
и бровью ⟨глазом, носом⟩ не повёл, Б-209
и усом ⟨ухом⟩ не повёл, Б-209

ПОВЕРГАТЬ
повергать в прах, П-495
повергать к ногам, С-600
повергать к стопам, С-600

ПОВЕРГАТЬСЯ
повергаться в прах, П-496

ПОВЕРГНУТЬ
повергнуть в прах, П-495
повергнуть к ногам, С-600
повергнуть к стопам, С-600

ПОВЕРГНУТЬСЯ
повергнуться в прах, П-496

ПОВЕРИТЬ
поверить на слово, С-309
не поверить ⟨своим⟩ глазам, Г-102
не поверить ⟨своим⟩ ушам, У-174

ПОВЕРКУ
на поверку, П-213

ПОВЕРНЁШЬ
закон что дышло: куда повернёшь, туда и вышло, З-49

ПОВЕРНЁШЬСЯ
не повернёшься, П-215

ПОВЕРНИ(ТЕ)
как ни поверни(те), П-214
куда ни поверни(те), П-214

ПОВЕРНУЛ
закон что дышло: куда повернул, туда и вышло, З-49

ПОВЕРНУЛСЯ
язык не повернулся, Я-40

ПОВЁРНУТЫ
мозги не туда повёрнуты, М-227

ПОВЕРНУТЬ
повернуть колесо истории вспять ⟨назад⟩, К-196
повернуть оглобли ⟨назад⟩, О-50

ПОВЕРНУТЬСЯ
не повернуться, П-215

повернуться лицом, Л-104
повернуться негде, П-215

ПОВЁРТЫВАЕТСЯ
язык не повёртывается, Я-40

ПОВЕРХНОСТИ
скользить по поверхности, П-216

ПОВЕРХНОСТЬ
всплывать/всплыть на поверхность, П-217

ПОВЕСИТЬ
повесить голову, Г-247
повесить камень на шею, К-38
повесить лапшу на уши, Л-31
повесить мало, У-3
повесить нос (на квинту), Н-208
повесить себе камень на шею, К-38
повесить (себе) хомут на шею, Х-80

ПОВЕСТИ
повести себя, В-62
стоит только бровью ⟨усом⟩ повести, Б-210
только бровью ⟨усом⟩ повести, Б-210

ПОВЕСТКА
повестка дня, П-218

ПОВЕШЕННОГО
в доме повешенного не говорят о верёвке, Д-259

ПОВИННОЙ
с повинной, П-219
с повинной головой, П-219

ПОВИННУЮ
повинную голову (и) меч не сечёт, Г-267
принести ⟨приносить⟩ повинную, П-220
принести ⟨приносить⟩ повинную голову, П-220

ПОВИСАТЬ
повисать в воздухе, В-208

ПОВИСНУТЬ
повиснуть в воздухе, В-208
повиснуть на волоске, В-239
повиснуть на нитке ⟨на ниточке⟩, В-239
повиснуть на телефоне, Т-55
повиснуть на хвосте, Х-21
повиснуть на шее, Ш-43

ПОВЛЕЧЬ
повлечь за собой, В-169

ПОВОД
давать/дать повод, П-221
подавать/подать повод, П-221

ПОВОДКЕ
держать на коротком поводке, П-222

ПОВОДУ
идти на поводу, П-223
на поводу, П-223

по поводу, П-224
пойти на поводу, П-223
ходить на поводу, П-223

ПОВОРАЧИВАЕТСЯ
язык не поворачивается, Я-40

ПОВОРАЧИВАТЬ
поворачивать оглобли ⟨назад⟩, О-50

ПОВОРАЧИВАТЬСЯ
поворачиваться лицом, Л-104

ПОВОРОТ
от ворот поворот, В-277
поворот на сто восемьдесят градусов, П-225

ПОВОРОТАХ
легче ⟨полегче⟩ на поворотах!, П-226

ПОВОРОТИ(ТЕ)
как ни ни повороти(те), П-214
куда ни ни повороти(те), П-214

ПОВОРОТИЛСЯ
язык не поворотился, Я-40

ПОВОРОТИТЬ
поворотить оглобли ⟨назад⟩, О-50

ПОВОРОТИТЬСЯ
поворотиться негде, П-215

ПОВРЕДИТЬСЯ
повредиться в рассудке ⟨в уме⟩, У-99
повредиться рассудком ⟨умом⟩, У-99

ПОВТОРЕНЬЕ
повторенье — мать ученья, П-227

ПОВЫСИЛИСЬ
акции повысились, А-24

ПОВЫСИТЬ
повысить голос, Г-301
повысить тон, Г-301

ПОВЫШАТЬ
повышать голос, Г-301
повышать тон, Г-301

ПОВЫШАЮТСЯ
акции повышаются, А-24

ПОВЫШЕ
поднимай ⟨подымай⟩ повыше!, П-248

ПОГИБЕЛИ
в три погибели, П-228
гнуть в три погибели, Р-120
погибели нет!, П-229
согнуть в три погибели, Р-120

ПОГЛАДИТЬ
погладить не по шерсти ⟨не по шёрстке⟩, Ш-49
погладить по голове ⟨по головке⟩, Г-232
погладить по шерсти ⟨по шёрстке⟩, Ш-48
погладить против шерсти ⟨против шёрстки⟩, Ш-49

ПОГЛЯДЕТЬ
поглядеть другими ⟨иными⟩ глазами, Г-120
поглядеть сквозь пальцы, П-27

ПОГЛЯЖУ
как (я) погляжу, П-230

ПОГНАТЬСЯ
погнаться за двумя зайцами, З-36

ПОГОВОРКУ
войти ⟨входить⟩ в поговорку, П-411

ПОГОДУ
делать погоду, П-231

ПОГОДЫ
ждать у моря погоды, М-259
сидеть у моря да ⟨и⟩ ждать погоды, М-259

ПОГОДЯ
немного ⟨чуть⟩ погодя, П-232

ПОГОНИШЬСЯ
за двумя зайцами погонишься, ни одного не поймаешь, З-37

ПОГРЕБ
пороховой погреб, Б-190

ПОГРЕБАТЬ
погребать себя в четырёх стенах, П-233
погребать себя заживо, П-233

ПОГРЕСТИ
погрести себя в четырёх стенах, П-233
погрести себя заживо, П-233

ПОГРЕТЬ
погреть руки, Р-284

ПОДАВАТЬ
не подавать вида ⟨виду⟩, В-116
подавать большие надежды, Н-9
подавать голос, Г-302
подавать знак, З-155
подавать надежды, Н-9
подавать повод, П-221
подавать признаки жизни, П-524
подавать пример, П-532
подавать руку, Р-360
подавать руку помощи, Р-367

ПОДАВНО
и подавно, П-234

ПОДАЛЬШЕ
а не пошёл бы ты (куда) подальше!, И-23
иди (ты) (куда) подальше!, И-23
идите (вы) (куда) подальше!, И-23
от греха подальше, Г-391
послать (куда) подальше, П-409
пошёл бы ты (куда) подальше!, И-23

ПОДАРИТЬ
подарить жизнь, Ж-51

ПОДАРОК
не подарок, П-235
подарок с неба, П-236

ПОДАРОЧЕК
не подарочек, П-235

ПОДАТЬ
не подать вида ⟨виду⟩,
В-116
подать голос, Г-302
подать знак, З-155
подать повод, П-221
подать признаки жизни,
П-524
подать пример, П-532
подать руку, Р-360
подать руку помощи,
Р-367
рукой подать, Р-339

ПОДАЧИ
с подачи, П-237

ПОДБАВИТЬ
подбавить жару, Ж-7

ПОДБАВЛЯТЬ
подбавлять жару, Ж-7

ПОДБИВАТЬ
подбивать бабки, Б-3
подбивать клинья, К-138

ПОДБИТ(ЫЙ)
подбит(ый) ветерком
⟨ветром⟩, В-80

ПОДБИТЬ
подбить бабки, Б-3
подбить клинья, К-138

ПОДБОР
как* на подбор, П-238
на подбор, П-238

ПОДВЕЛО
живот ⟨животики,
животы⟩ подвело, Ж-32

ПОДВЕРНУТЬ
подвернуть хвост
⟨хвосты⟩, Х-15

ПОДВЕРНУТЬСЯ
подвернуться под руку,
Р-363

ПОДВЁРТЫВАТЬ
подвёртывать хвост
⟨хвосты⟩, Х-15

ПОДВЁРТЫВАТЬСЯ
подвёртываться под руку,
Р-363

ПОДВЕСТИ
подвести базу, Б-9
подвести итог ⟨итоги⟩,
И-92
подвести мину ⟨мины⟩,
М-168
подвести под монастырь,
М-252
подвести черту, Ч-116

ПОДВЕШЕН
язык здорово подвешен,
Я-47
язык неплохо подвешен,
Я-47
язык плохо подвешен,
Я-42

язык хорошо подвешен,
Я-47

ПОДВЕШЕННЫЙ
неплохо подвешенный
язык, Я-47
хорошо подвешенный
язык, Я-47

ПОДВИНЬСЯ
извини подвинься, И-41

ПОДВИНЬТЕСЬ
извините подвиньтесь,
И-41

ПОДВОДИТ
живот ⟨животики,
животы⟩ подводит,
Ж-32

ПОДВОДИТЬ
подводить базу, Б-9
подводить итог ⟨итоги⟩,
И-92
подводить мину ⟨мины⟩,
М-168
подводить под монастырь,
М-252
подводить черту, Ч-116

ПОДВОДНЫЕ
подводные камешки
⟨камни⟩, К-49

ПОДВОРАЧИВАТЬСЯ
подворачиваться под руку,
Р-363

ПОДГИБАЮТСЯ
колени ⟨коленки⟩
подгибаются, К-188

ПОДГОТАВЛИВАТЬ
подготавливать почву,
П-454

ПОДГОТОВИТЬ
подготовить почву, П-454

ПОДДАВАТЬ
поддавать газу, Г-2
поддавать жару, Ж-7
поддавать пару, Ж-7
поддавать ходу, Х-71

ПОДДАВАТЬСЯ
не поддаваться никакому
сравнению, С-531
не поддаваться описанию,
О-95

ПОДДАТЬ
поддать газу, Г-2
поддать жару, Ж-7
поддать леща, Л-71
поддать пару, Ж-7
поддать ходу, Х-71

ПОДДЕВАТЬ
поддевать на фуфу, Ф-35

ПОДДЕРЖАТЬ
поддержать компанию,
К-220

ПОДДЕТЬ
поддеть на удочку, У-51
поддеть на фуфу, Ф-35

ПОДЕЙСТВОВАТЬ
подействовать на нервы,
Н-81

ПОДЕЛАЕШЬ
ничего не поделаешь,
П-239

что (же) поделаешь, П-240

ПОДЕЛАТЬ
ничего не поделать, П-241
ничего нельзя поделать,
П-241
что (же) поделать, П-240

ПОДЕРИ
леший тебя подери!, Ч-99
чёрт подери!, Ч-87
чёрт тебя подери!, Ч-99
шут тебя подери!, Ч-99

ПОДЖАТЬ
поджать хвост ⟨хвосты⟩,
Х-15

ПОДЖИЛКИ
поджилки затряслись
⟨трясутся⟩, П-242

ПОДЖИМАТЬ
поджимать хвост
⟨хвосты⟩, Х-15

ПОДИ
а вот поди (ж) ты!, П-243
вот поди ж!, П-243
вот поди (ж) ты!, П-243
да вот поди (ж) ты!, П-243
поди ж!, П-243
поди (ж) ты!, П-243

ПОДИРАЕТ
мороз по коже ⟨по спине⟩
подирает, М-258

ПОДКАТИЛ
клубок к горлу подкатил,
К-142
ком(ок) к горлу подкатил,
К-142

ПОДКАТИЛСЯ
клубок к горлу
подкатился, К-142
ком(ок) к горлу
подкатился, К-142

ПОДКАТИТЬ(СЯ)
подкатить(ся) к горлу,
Г-347

ПОДКАТЫВАТЬ(СЯ)
подкатывать(ся) к горлу,
Г-347

ПОДКАШИВАЮТСЯ
ноги подкашиваются,
Н-151

ПОДКЛАДЫВАТЬ
подкладывать мину
⟨мины⟩, М-168
подкладывать свинью,
С-80

ПОДКОЛОДНАЯ
змея подколодная, З-140

ПОДКОСИЛИСЬ
ноги подкосились, Н-151

ПОДКОСИТЬ
подкосить под корень,
К-294

ПОДКОШЕННЫЙ
как подкошенный, П-244

ПОДКРУТИТЬ
подкрутить гайки, Г-8

ПОДКРУЧИВАТЬ
подкручивать гайки, Г-8

ПОДЛЕЖИТ
не подлежит сомнению,
С-479

ПОДЛИВАТЬ
подливать масла в огонь,
М-36

ПОДЛИТЬ
подлить масла в огонь,
М-36

ПОДЛОЖИТЬ
подложить мину ⟨мины⟩,
М-168
подложить свинью, С-80

ПОДМАЖЕШЬ
не подмажешь — не
поедешь, П-245

ПОДМАЗАТЬ
подмазать колёса, К-193
подмазать пятки (салом),
П-682

ПОДМАЗЫВАТЬ
подмазывать колёса, К-193
подмазывать пятки
(салом), П-682

ПОДМЕНИЛИ
как* подменили, П-246

ПОДМЁТКИ
в подмётки не годится ⟨не
станет⟩, П-247
на ходу подмётки рвёт
⟨режет⟩, Х-68
не стоить подмётки, М-149

ПОДНЕСТИ
поднести пилюли
⟨пилюлю⟩, П-148

ПОДНИМАЕТСЯ
рука не поднимается, Р-231

ПОДНИМАЙ
поднимай выше
⟨повыше⟩!, П-248

ПОДНИМАТЬ
поднимать бокал(ы),
Б-153
поднимать голову
⟨головы⟩, Г-268
поднимать голос, Г-303
поднимать знамя, З-166
поднимать лапки кверху,
Л-24
поднимать меч, М-139
поднимать на ноги, Н-153,
Н-154
поднимать на смех, С-403
поднимать на фуфу, Ф-35
поднимать на щит, Щ-6
поднимать нос, Н-213
поднимать оружие, М-139
поднимать перчатку, П-113
поднимать руку, Р-361

ПОДНИМАТЬСЯ
подниматься на ноги,
Н-157

ПОДНИМАЮТСЯ
акции поднимаются, А-24
волосы поднимаются
дыбом, В-241

ПОДНОЖКУ
давать/дать подножку,
Н-188
подставить ⟨подставлять⟩
подножку, Н-188

ПОДНОЖНЫЙ
подножный корм, К-298

ПОЖИРАТЬ
пожирать глазами, Г-107

ПОЖНЁШЬ
что посеешь, то и
пожнёшь, П-407

ПОЗВОЛЕНИЯ
с вашего позволения,
П-268
с позволения сказать,
П-269

ПОЗВОЛИТЕ
если позволите, П-270

ПОЗВОЛИТЬ
позволить роскошь, Р-164
позволить себе лишнее,
Л-110
позволить себе роскошь,
Р-164
слишком много позволить
себе, Л-110

ПОЗВОЛЯТЬ
позволять роскошь, Р-164
позволять себе лишнее,
Л-110
позволять себе роскошь,
Р-164
слишком много позволять
себе, Л-110

ПОЗДНИХ
до поздних петухов, П-135

ПОЗДНО
лучше поздно, чем
никогда, Л-149
рано или поздно, Р-77

ПОЗДОРОВИТСЯ
не поздоровится, П-271

ПОЗДОРОВУ
подобру да поздорову,
П-252

ПОЗДРАВЛЯЕМ
с чем вас и поздравляем,
П-272

ПОЗДРАВЛЯЮ
с чем вас и поздравляю,
П-272

ПОЗЕЛЕНЕЛО
в глазах позеленело, Г-127

ПОЗНАША
своя своих не познаша,
С-88

ПОЗНАЮТСЯ
друзья познаются в беде,
Д-315

ПОЗОЛОТИТЬ
позолотить пилюлю,
П-147
позолотить руку ⟨ручку⟩,
Р-376

ПОЗОНДИРОВАТЬ
позондировать почву,
П-452

ПОЗОРНОМУ
пригвождать/пригвоздить
к позорному столбу,
С-593
приковать ⟨приковывать⟩
к позорному столбу,
С-593

ПОЗУ
встать в позу, П-273

принимать/принять позу,
П-273
становиться в позу, П-273
стать в позу, П-273

ПОИГРАТЬ
поиграть на нервах, Н-80

ПОИЛЕЦ
поилец и кормилец, П-274
поилец-кормилец, П-274

ПОИЛИЦА
поилица и кормилица,
П-274
поилица-кормилица, П-274

ПОИМЕЙ(ТЕ)
поимей(те) совесть, С-454

ПОИМЕЛ
поимел бы ты совесть,
С-454

ПОИМЕТЬ
поиметь в виду, В-138

ПОИТЬ
поить и кормить, П-274
поить-кормить, П-274

ПОЙДЁТ
в глотку не пойдёт, К-491
в горло не пойдёт, К-491
кусок в глотку ⟨в горло⟩
не пойдёт, К-491
не пойдёт в голову, Г-265
не пойдёт на ум, Г-265

ПОЙМАЕШЬ
слово не воробей, вылетит
— не поймаешь, С-328

ПОЙМАН
не пойман не вор, В-265

ПОЙМАТЬ
поймать в свои сети, С-157
поймать за руку, Р-370
поймать за хвост, Х-19
поймать на словах ⟨на
слове⟩, С-302
поймать на удочку, У-51
поймать себя, Л-120

ПОЙМАТЬСЯ
пойматься на удочку, У-52

ПОЙТИ
далеко пойти, П-275
пойти в гору, Г-351
пойти в дело, Х-53
пойти в Каноссу, К-53
пойти в люди, Л-170
пойти в огонь и в воду,
О-64
пойти в ход, Х-53
пойти ва-банк, И-25
пойти вниз, Г-352
пойти впрок, И-26
пойти вразрез, И-27
пойти к венцу, В-31
пойти к чёртовой матери,
Ч-113
пойти к чёрту, Ч-113
пойти к чертям
(собачьим), Ч-113
пойти ко всем чертям,
Ч-113
пойти ко дну, Д-209
пойти на дно, Д-209
пойти на крайность, К-362
пойти на мировую, М-187

пойти на панель, П-51
пойти на поводу, П-223
пойти на попятную, П-357
пойти на попятный ⟨двор⟩,
П-357
пойти на убыль, У-7
пойти на удочку, У-52
пойти на фуфу, Ф-36
пойти навстречу, И-28
пойти насмарку, И-30
пойти по дурной дороге
⟨дорожке⟩, Д-270
пойти по линии
наименьшего
сопротивления, Л-73
пойти по миру, М-190
пойти по наклонной
плоскости, П-197
пойти по плохой дороге
⟨дорожке⟩, Д-270
пойти по плохому пути,
Д-270
пойти по пути
наименьшего
сопротивления, Л-73
пойти по рукам, Р-251,
Р-252
пойти по следам, С-599
пойти по стопам, С-599
пойти по худой дороге
⟨дорожке⟩, Д-270
пойти под венец, В-31
пойти под горку ⟨под
гору⟩, Г-352
пойти под откос, О-150
пойти под уклон, Г-352
пойти прахом, П-498
пойти против совести,
С-449
пойти против течения,
Т-97
пойти с протянутой рукой,
Р-340
пойти с сумой, М-190
пойти своей дорогой,
Д-273
пойти своим путём, Д-273

ПОКА
до тех пор пока, П-361
до тех пор пока не, П-362
пока душа держится в
теле, Д-377
пока рак (на горе)
свистнет, Р-71
пока суд да дело, С-656
пока то да сё, Т-110
пока цел, Ц-18
пока что, П-276

ПОКАЖУ
я тебе покажу!, Д-19

ПОКАЗАЛОСЬ
небо в ⟨с⟩ овчинку
показалось, Н-53

ПОКАЗАТЬ
глаза показать, Г-61
не показать вида ⟨виду⟩,
В-116
не показать глаз, Г-28
не показать носа ⟨носу⟩,
Н-226
показать, где раки
зимуют, Р-73

показать дверь, Д-38
показать зубы, З-200
показать класс, К-131
показать коготки ⟨когти⟩,
К-158
показать кузькину мать,
М-54
показать марку, К-131
показать на дверь, Д-38
показать нос ⟨носы⟩,
Н-217
показать пример, П-532
показать пферу, П-110
показать пятки, П-681
показать своё (истинное)
лицо, Л-98
показать своё настоящее
лицо, Л-98
показать свои коготки
⟨когти⟩, К-158
показать себя, П-277
показать спину, С-515
показать товар лицом,
Т-116
показать тыл, С-515
показать феферу, П-110
показать характер, Х-3
показать язык, Я-19

ПОКАЗАТЬСЯ
показаться на глаза, Г-87

ПОКАЗЫВАТЬ
не показывать вида, В-116
не показывать глаз, Г-28
не показывать носа
⟨носу⟩, Н-226
показывать дверь, Д-38
показывать зубы, З-200
показывать класс, К-131
показывать коготки
⟨когти⟩, К-158
показывать марку, К-131
показывать на дверь, Д-38
показывать нос ⟨носы⟩,
Н-217
показывать пальцами
⟨пальцем⟩, П-23
показывать пример, П-532
показывать пферу, П-110
показывать пятки, П-681
показывать свои коготки
⟨когти⟩, К-158
показывать себя, П-277
показывать спину, С-515
показывать товар лицом,
Т-116
показывать тыл, С-515
показывать феферу, П-110
показывать характер, Х-3
показывать язык, Я-19

ПОКАЗЫВАТЬСЯ
не показываться на порог,
П-370
показываться на глаза,
Г-87

ПОКАРАЙ
покарай меня бог
⟨господь⟩, Б-125

ПОКАТИ
хоть шаром покати, Ш-37

ПОКАТИТЬ
покатить бочку, Б-192

покатить по наклонной
плоскости, П-197
ПОКАТИТЬСЯ
покатиться вниз, Г-352
покатиться от смеха,
С-406
покатиться от хохота,
С-406
покатиться по наклонной
плоскости, П-197
покатиться по скользкой
дорожке, П-197
покатиться под горку ⟨под
гору⟩, Г-352
покатиться под откос,
О-150
покатиться под уклон,
Г-352
покатиться с хохоту, С-406
покатиться со смеху, С-406
ПОКАТЫВАТЬСЯ
покатываться от смеха,
С-406
покатываться от хохота,
С-406
покатываться с хохоту,
С-406
покатываться со смеху,
С-406
ПОКАЯНИЕ
отпустить душу на
покаяние, Д-428
ПОКИДАЮТ
крысы покидают тонущий
корабль, К-435
ПОКЛАДАЯ
не покладая рук, Р-216
ПОКЛЁВЫВАТЬ
поклёвывать носом, Н-227
ПОКЛЁП
возвести ⟨возводить⟩
поклёп, П-278
ПОКЛОН
на поклон, П-279
ПОКЛОНИТЬСЯ
поклониться в ноги ⟨в
ножки⟩, Н-145
поклониться в пояс, П-467
ПОКЛОНОМ
с поклоном, П-279
ПОКЛОНЫ
класть поклоны, П-280
ПОКОЕ
на покое, П-281
оставить ⟨оставлять⟩ в
покое, П-282
ПОКОЕН
будь покоен, Б-235
ПОКОИТЬСЯ
покоиться на лаврах, Л-4
ПОКОЙ
вечный покой, П-283
на покой, П-284
ПОКОЙНОЙ
покойной ночи, Н-242
ПОКОЙНЫ
будьте покойны, Б-235
ПОКОНЧИТЬ
покончить все счёты,
С-727

покончить жизнь
самоубийством, П-285
покончить с жизнью,
П-285
покончить с собой, П-285
покончить самоубийством,
П-285
покончить счёты, С-727
покончить счёты с
жизнью, П-285
ПОКОПАТЬСЯ
покопаться в памяти, П-39
ПОКОРИТЕЛЬ
покоритель сердец, П-286
ПОКОРИТЕЛЬНИЦА
покорительница сердец,
П-286
ПОКОРИТЬ
покорить сердце, С-134
ПОКОРНЕЙШЕ
покорнейше благодарю,
Б-75
покорнейше прошу, П-603
ПОКОРНЕЙШИЙ
ваш покорнейший слуга,
С-346
ПОКОРНО
покорно благодарю, Б-75
прошу покорно, П-603,
П-604
ПОКОРНЫЙ
ваш покорный слуга, С-346
слуга покорный, С-348
твой покорный слуга,
С-346
ПОКОРЯТЬ
покорять сердце, С-134
ПОКОЮ
не видеть покою, П-288
не давать покою, П-287
не знать покою, П-288
не найти ⟨не находить⟩
покою, П-288
ПОКОЯ
лавры не дают покоя, Л-5
не видеть покоя, П-288
не давать покоя, П-287
не знать покоя, П-288
не найти ⟨не находить⟩
покоя, П-288
ПОКРИВИТЬ
покривить душой, Д-399
ПОКРОВ
как будто* покров падает
⟨с глаз⟩, П-76
как будто* покров
спадает/спал ⟨с глаз⟩,
П-76
как будто* покров упал ⟨с
глаз⟩, П-76
покров падает ⟨с глаз⟩,
П-76
покров спадает/спал ⟨с
глаз⟩, П-76
покров упал ⟨с глаз⟩, П-76
снимать/снять покров,
З-18
сорвать ⟨срывать⟩
покров, З-18
ПОКРОВЫ
снимать/снять покровы,
З-18

сорвать ⟨срывать⟩
покровы, З-18
ПОКРОВОМ
под покровом, П-289
ПОКРОЙ
на один покрой, П-290
ПОКРОЯ
одного покроя, П-290
старого покроя, П-291
ПОКРУТИТЬ
покрутить любовь, Р-160
покрутить роман, Р-160
ПОКРЫТО
покрыто мраком
неизвестности, М-275
ПОКРЫШКИ
(чтоб) ни дна ни
покрышки, Д-201
ПОКУДА
покуда цел, Ц-18
ПОКУПАТЬ
покупать кота в мешке,
К-335
ПОКУШЕНИЕ
покушение с негодными
средствами, П-292
ПОЛ
нежный пол, П-294
прекрасный пол, П-294
сильный пол, П-293
слабый пол, П-294
ПОЛ-ОБОРОТА
завестись ⟨заводиться⟩ с
пол-оборота, П-316
ПОЛАГАЕТСЯ
по штату полагается,
Ш-88
ПОЛАГАТЬ
надо полагать, Д-323
ПОЛДОРОГЕ
на полдороге, П-315
ПОЛЕ
догоняй ветра в поле, В-74
жизнь прожить – не поле
перейти, Ж-54
ищи ветра в поле, В-74
ищи-свищи ветра в поле,
В-74
не обсевок в поле, О-28
поле битвы, П-296
поле боя, П-296
поле брани, П-296
один в поле не воин, П-295
поле зрения, П-297
поле сражения, П-296
поле чести, П-296
ПОЛЕГЧЕ
полегче на поворотах!,
П-226
ПОЛЕЗАЙ
назвался груздем, полезай
в кузов, Г-428
хоть в петлю полезай,
П-129
ПОЛЕЗЕТ
в глотку не полезет, К-491
в горло не полезет, К-491
за словом в карман не
полезет, С-332

кусок в глотку ⟨в горло⟩
не полезет, К-491
ПОЛЕЗЛИ
глаза на лоб полезли, Г-54
ПОЛЕЗТЬ
полезть в бутылку, Б-249
полезть в голову, Г-255
полезть в гору, Г-351
полезть в петлю, П-127
полезть в пузырь, Б-249
полезть к чёрту в зубы,
Ч-112
полезть на рожон, Р-145
полезть на стенку ⟨на
стену⟩, С-569
ПОЛЁТА
птица высокого полёта,
П-619
птица невысокого полёта,
П-620
птица низкого полёта,
П-620
птицы одного полёта,
П-622
с высоты птичьего полёта,
В-379
с птичьего полёта, В-379
ПОЛЕТЕЛИ
головы полетели, Г-290
ПОЛЕТЕТЬ
полететь в тартарары,
Т-41
полететь вверх
тормашками
⟨тормашки⟩, Т-163
полететь к чёртовой
матери, Ч-113
полететь к чёрту, Ч-113
полететь к чертям
(собачьим), Ч-113
полететь ко всем чертям,
Ч-113
полететь прахом, П-498
ПОЛЁТУ
видна птица по полёту,
П-616
видать птицу ⟨сокола⟩ по
полёту, П-616
видно птицу ⟨сокола⟩ по
полёту, П-616
ПОЛЕТЯТ
пух да ⟨и⟩ перья полетят,
П-664
ПОЛЕЧЬ
полечь костьми, К-330
ПОЛЗАТЬ
ползать в ногах, Н-133
ползать на брюхе, Б-214
ползать на коленях, Н-133
ПОЛЗАЮТ
мурашки ползают по
коже, М-291
мурашки ползают по
спине ⟨по телу⟩, М-291
ПОЛЗУТ
мурашки ползут по коже,
М-291
мурашки ползут по спине
⟨по телу⟩, М-291
ПОЛИВАТЬ
поливать грязью, Г-436

поливать помоями, Г-436

ПОЛИТИКА
политика кнута и пряника, П-298

ПОЛИТЬ
полить грязью, Г-436
полить помоями, Г-436

ПОЛИЧНЫМ
с поличным, П-299

ПОЛИШИНЕЛЯ
секрет полишинеля, С-110

ПОЛКАМ
раскладывать/разложить по полкам, П-314

ПОЛКУ
в нашем полку прибыло, П-300
зубы на полку, З-198
класть зубы на полку, З-198
нашего полку прибыло, П-300
положить зубы на полку, З-198

ПОЛНАЯ
полная чаша, Ч-35

ПОЛНИТСЯ
слухами ⟨слухом⟩ земля полнится, С-356

ПОЛНО
да и полно, П-301

ПОЛНОЙ
в полной мере, М-72
в полной памяти, У-95

ПОЛНОМ
в полном ажуре, А-12
в полном параде, П-57
в полном порядке, П-396
в полном рассудке, У-95
в полном смысле слова, С-424
в полном соку, С-469
в полном уме, У-95
на полном газу, Г-5
на полном серьёзе, С-153
на полном скаку, С-219
при полном параде, П-57

ПОЛНОСТЬЮ
целиком и полностью, Ц-20

ПОЛНОТЫ
от полноты души, П-302
от полноты сердца, П-302
от полноты чувств(а), П-302

ПОЛНУЮ
в полную силу, С-182
выпить (до дна) полную чашу, Ч-39
испить (до дна) полную чашу, Ч-39
на полную железку, Ж-11
на полную катушку, К-103
отдавать/отдать полную справедливость, Д-246
пить (до дна) полную чашу, Ч-39

ПОЛНЫЙ
в полный голос, Г-299

в полный рост, Р-167
на полный ход, Х-54
полный вперёд!, Х-55
полный ход!, Х-55

ПОЛНЫМ
полным голосом, Г-299
полным ходом, Х-62

ПОЛНЫХ
на полных рысях, Р-394

ПОЛОВИНА
дражайшая половина, П-303
моя половина, П-303

ПОЛОВИНЕ
середина на половине, С-152
серёдка на половине, С-152

ПОЛОВИНКЕ
серединка на половинке, С-152
серёдка на половинке, С-152

ПОЛОВИНКУ
серединка на половинку, С-152
серёдка на половинку, С-152

ПОЛОВИНУ
середина на половину, С-152
серёдка на половину, С-152

ПОЛОЖА
положа руку на сердце, Р-362

ПОЛОЖЕНИЕ
войти ⟨входить⟩ в положение, П-304
ложное положение, П-305
пиковое положение, П-306
положение вещей, П-307
положение хуже губернаторского, П-308
спасать/спасти положение, П-309

ПОЛОЖЕНИИ
в интересном положении, П-310
в положении, П-310

ПОЛОЖЕНИЯ
выйти из положения, П-311
выход из положения, П-311
выходить из положения, П-311
до положения риз, П-312
на высоте положения, В-378
хозяин положения, Х-77
хозяйка положения, Х-77

ПОЛОЖЕНО
по штату положено, Ш-88

ПОЛОЖИВ(ШИ)
положив(ши) руку на сердце, Р-362

ПОЛОЖИТ
как бог на душу положит, Б-113
сколько бог на душу положит, Б-123
что бог на душу положит, Б-128

ПОЛОЖИТЬ
охулки на руку не положить, О-180
положить билет (на стол), Б-65
положить в карман, К-80
положить в кубышку, К-452
положить во главу угла, Г-21
положить глаз, Г-34
положить гнев на милость, Г-155
положить голову ⟨головы⟩, Г-252
положить душу, Д-423
положить живот (свой), Ж-55
положить жизнь, Ж-55
положить за правило, П-489
положить зубы на полку, З-198
положить к ногам, Н-124
положить конец, К-238
положить на лопатки, Л-135
положить на месте, М-102
положить на музыку, М-285
положить на ноты, М-285
положить на обе лопатки, Л-135
положить на чашку ⟨чашу⟩ весов, Ч-37
положить начало, Н-38
положить оружие, О-104
положить отпечаток, О-162
положить партбилет (на стол), Б-65
положить печать, О-162
положить под сукно, С-671
положить правилом, П-489
положить с прибором, П-513
положить свои головы ⟨свою голову⟩, Г-252
положить себе за правило, П-489
положить себе правилом, П-489
похулы на руку не положить, О-180
разжевать и в рот положить, Р-181

ПОЛОЖЬ
вынь да положь, В-370

ПОЛОМАТЬ
поломать голову, Г-256
поломать копья, К-288
поломать себе голову, Г-256

ПОЛОН
полон рот, Р-179

ПОЛОСНУТЬ
как* ножом полоснуть (по сердцу), Н-191
полоснуть по сердцу, Н-191

ПОЛОТНО
как полотно, П-313

ПОЛОЧКАМ
разложить ⟨раскладывать⟩ по полочкам, П-314

ПОЛПУТИ
на полпути, П-315

ПОЛСЛОВА
на полслова, П-67
ни полслова, С-287
с полслова, П-317

ПОЛСЛОВЕ
на полслове, П-318

ПОЛТАВОЙ
как швед под Полтавой, Ш-41

ПОЛТОРА
ни два ни полтора, Д-30

ПОЛУ
из полы в полу, П-321
на полу не валяется, Д-268

ПОЛУОБОРОТА
завестись ⟨заводиться⟩ с полуоборота, П-316

ПОЛУСЛОВА
с полуслова, П-317

ПОЛУСЛОВЕ
на полуслове, П-318

ПОЛУСМЕРТИ
до полусмерти, П-319

ПОЛУСОГНУТЫХ
ходить на полусогнутых, Х-60

ПОЛУЧАТЬ
получать взбучку, Т-201
получать выволочку, Т-201
получать головомойку, Г-244
получать огласку, О-49
получать отставку, О-168
получать по мозгам, М-220
получать по рукам, Р-247
получать по шапке, Ш-29
получать сдачи, С-93
получать трёпку, Т-201

ПОЛУЧИТЬ
получить взбучку, Т-201
получить выволочку, Т-201
получить головомойку, Г-244
получить огласку, О-49
получить отставку, О-168
получить по мозгам, М-220
получить по рукам, Р-247
получить по шапке, Ш-29
получить сдачи, С-93
получить трёпку, Т-201

ПОЛУШКИ
ни полушки, Г-418

ПОЛУШКУ
ни на (ломаную) полушку, Г-414

ПОЛЫ
из-под полы, П-320
из полы в полу, П-321

ПОЛЫМЯ
из огня (да) в полымя, О-61

ПОЛЬЗОВАТЬСЯ
пользоваться кредитом, К-378

ПОЛЬЗУ
в пользу, П-322
в пользу бедных, П-323
говорить в пользу, П-324
на пользу, П-325
свидетельствовать в пользу, П-324

ПОЛЮБИТЕ
полюбите нас чёрненькими, а беленькими всякий полюбит, П-326

ПОЛЮБИШЬ
любовь зла — полюбишь и козла, Л-162

ПОЛЯ
дурная трава из поля вон, Т-194
дурную траву из ⟨с⟩ поля вон, Т-194
нашего поля ягода ⟨ягодки, ягоды⟩, П-327
одного поля ягода ⟨ягодки, ягоды⟩, П-327
своего поля ягода ⟨ягодки, ягоды⟩, П-327
сорная трава из поля вон, Т-194
сорную траву из ⟨с⟩ поля вон, Т-194
того же поля ягода ⟨ягодки, ягоды⟩, П-327
худая трава из поля вон, Т-194
худую траву из ⟨с⟩ поля вон, Т-194

ПОМАЛКИВАТЬ
помалкивать в тряпочку, Т-224

ПОМАТРОСИЛ
поматросил и бросил, П-328

ПОМЕНЯТЬСЯ
поменяться ролями, Р-157

ПОМЕРЕТЬ
помереть со смеха ⟨со смеху⟩, С-407

ПОМЕРК
свет померк в глазах, С-61

ПОМЕШАТЬСЯ
помешаться в рассудке ⟨в уме⟩, У-99
помешаться рассудком ⟨умом⟩, У-99

ПОМИЛУЙ
помилуй бог!, Б-121

ПОМИНА
и помина, П-329

ПОМИНАЙ
не поминай лихом, Л-83
поминай как звали, П-330

ПОМИНАЙТЕ
не поминайте лихом, Л-83

ПОМИНАТЬ
поминать добром, Д-222
поминать добрым словом, Д-222

поминать недобрым словом, С-336

ПОМИНЕ
(и) в помине, П-331
лёгкий ⟨лёгок⟩ на помине, П-332

ПОМИНУ
и помину, П-329

ПОМИРАЙ
(хоть) ложись да помирай, Л-126

ПОМИРАТЬ
помирать со смеха ⟨со смеху⟩, С-407

ПОМИРИТЬСЯ
помириться со своей совестью, С-459

ПОМНИТЬ
зла не помнить, З-131
не помнить себя, П-333

ПОМНЯЩИЙ
Иван, не помнящий родства, Р-136
не помнящий родства, Р-136

ПОМОГАЙ
помогай бог, Б-99

ПОМОГАЮТ
дома (и) стены помогают, С-570

ПОМОГЛО
не было бы счастья, да несчастье помогло, С-693

ПОМОЕВ
вылить ушат помоев, У-178
окатить ушатом помоев, У-178

ПОМОЖЕШЬ
слезами горю не поможешь, С-261

ПОМОЗОЛИТЬ
помозолить язык, Я-32

ПОМОИ
лить помои, Г-436

ПОМОЙКУ
выбрасывать/выбросить на помойку, П-334

ПОМОЛОТЬ
помолоть языком, Я-32

ПОМОЛЧАТЬ
помолчать в тряпочку, Т-224

ПОМОЧАХ
водить на помочах, П-335
держать на помочах, П-335
на помочах, П-336
ходить на помочах, П-336

ПОМОЧЬ
бог в помочь, Б-99
бог (на) помочь, Б-99

ПОМОЩИ
подавать/подать руку помощи, Р-367
при помощи, П-337
протягивать/протянуть руку помощи, Р-367

ПОМОЩЬ
бог в ⟨на⟩ помощь, Б-99

ПОМОЩЬЮ
с помощью, П-337

ПОМОЯМИ
обливать/облить помоями, Г-436
поливать/полить помоями, Г-436

ПОМРЁШЬ
прежде ⟨раньше⟩ смерти не помрёшь, С-393

ПОМУТИЛОСЬ
в глазах помутилось, Г-127
помутилось в голове, Г-227

ПОМЯНЕТ
кто старое помянет, тому глаз вон, С-546

ПОМЯНИ(ТЕ)
помяни(те) меня, С-321
помяни(те) моё слово, С-321

ПОМЯНУТ
не к ночи будь помянут, Н-243
не тем будь помянут, Б-234

ПОМЯНУТЬ
помянуть добром, Д-222
помянуть добрым словом, Д-222
помянуть недобрым словом, С-336

ПОМЯТЬ
помять бока, Б-152

ПОНАВЕШАТЬ
собак понавешать, С-439

ПОНЕВОЛЕ
свой своему поневоле брат ⟨друг⟩, Б-200

ПОНЕМНОЖКУ
хорошего ⟨хорошенького⟩ понемножку, Х-84

ПОНЁС
чёрт понёс, Ч-94, Ч-95

ПОНЕСЛА
нелёгкая понесла, Ч-94
нечистая сила понесла, Ч-94

ПОНЕСЛИ
черти понесли, Ч-94

ПОНЕСТИ
понести ахинею ⟨белиберду⟩, В-99
понести вздор ⟨галиматью, гиль, дичь⟩, В-99
понести ересь ⟨ерунду⟩, В-99
понести околёсину ⟨околёсицу, околёсную⟩, В-99
понести чепуху ⟨чушь⟩, В-99

ПОНЕСУТ
куда ноги понесут, Н-146

ПОНИЖАТЬ
понижать голос, Г-304
понижать тон, Т-157

ПОНИЗИТЬ
понизить голос, Г-304
понизить тон, Т-157

ПОНИМАТЬ
понимать толк, Т-138

ПОНИМАЮ
(вот) это я понимаю!, П-338

ПОНТА
для понта, П-339

ПОНЮХ
ни за понюх табаку, П-340

ПОНЮХАТЬ
понюхать пороха ⟨пороху⟩, П-384

ПОНЮШКУ
ни за понюшку табаку, П-340

ПОНЯТИЕМ
с понятием, П-341

ПОНЯТИЯ
не иметь понятия, П-342

ПОНЯТНАЯ
понятная вещь, Д-124

ПОНЯТНО
(и) ежу понятно, Е-6

ПОНЯТНОЕ
понятное дело, Д-124

ПОНЯТЬ
давать/дать понять, Д-5

ПООБИВАТЬ
пообивать (весь) порог, П-377
пообивать (все) пороги, П-377

ПООБИТЬ
пообить (весь) порог, П-377
пообить (все) пороги, П-377

ПОП
каков поп, таков и приход, П-343
кому поп, кому попадья, а кому попова дочка, П-344

ПОПА
кто любит попа, (а) кто попадью, (а) кто попову дочку, П-344
на попа, П-345

ПОПАВШИЙ
первый попавший, П-346

ПОПАВШИЙСЯ
первый попавшийся, П-346

ПОПАДАЕТ
зуб на зуб не попадает, З-184

ПОПАДАТЬ
попадать в жилку ⟨жилу⟩, Ж-73
попадать в историю, И-85
попадать в колею, К-198
попадать в милость, М-157
попадать в немилость, Н-78
попадать в обычную колею, К-198
попадать в переделку ⟨в передрягу⟩, П-95

попадать в переплёт, П-95
попадать в привычную
колею, К-198
попадать в руки, Р-305
попадать в самую жилку
⟨жилу⟩, Ж-73
попадать в самую точку,
Т-185
попадать в свою колею,
К-198
попадать в сети, С-158
попадать в тон, Т-156
попадать в точку, Т-185
попадать впросак, П-347
попадать на глаза, Г-88
попадать на заметку ⟨на
замечание⟩, З-55
попадать на зуб(ок), З-194
попадать на след, С-250
попадать на язык ⟨на
язычок⟩, Я-20
попадать пальцем в небо,
П-24
попадать под руку, Р-363

ПОПАДАТЬСЯ
попадаться в руки, Р-305
попадаться в сети, С-158
попадаться впросак, П-347
попадаться на глаза, Г-88
попадаться на зуб(ок),
З-194
попадаться на крючок,
К-440
попадаться на удочку, У-52
попадаться на язык ⟨на
язычок⟩, Я-20
попадаться под руку, Р-363

ПОПАДЁШЬ
не рой другому яму
⟨ямы⟩, сам в неё
попадёшь, Я-64

ПОПАДЬЮ
кто любит попа, (а) кто
попадью, (а) кто попову
дочку, П-344

ПОПАДЬЯ
кому поп, кому попадья, а
кому попова дочка,
П-344

ПОПАЛА
вожжа под хвост попала,
В-198
смешинка в рот попала,
С-409
шлея под хвост попала,
В-198

ПОПАЛО
где (ни) попало, П-348
как (ни) попало, П-349
какой (ни) попало, П-350
когда (ни) попало, П-351
кто (ни) попало, П-352
куда (ни) попало, П-348
откуда (ни) попало, П-353
что (ни) попало, П-354

ПОПАСТЬ
попасть в жилку ⟨жилу⟩,
Ж-73
попасть в историю, И-85
попасть в колею, К-198

попасть в милость, М-157
попасть в немилость, Н-78
попасть в обычную колею,
К-198
попасть в переделку ⟨в
передрягу⟩, П-95
попасть в переплёт, П-95
попасть в привычную
колею, К-198
попасть в руки, Р-305
попасть в самую жилку
⟨жилу⟩, Ж-73
попасть в самую точку,
Т-185
попасть в свою колею,
К-198
попасть в сети, С-158
попасть в тон, Т-156
попасть в точку, Т-185
попасть впросак, П-347
попасть на глаза, Г-88
попасть на заметку ⟨на
замечание⟩, З-55
попасть на зуб(ок), З-194
попасть на след, С-250
попасть на язык ⟨на
язычок⟩, Я-20
попасть пальцем в небо,
П-24
попасть под руку, Р-363

ПОПАСТЬСЯ
попасться в руки, Р-305
попасться в сети, С-158
попасться впросак, П-347
попасться на глаза, Г-88
попасться на зуб(ок), З-194
попасться на крючок,
К-440
попасться на удочку, У-52
попасться на язык ⟨на
язычок⟩, Я-20
попасться под руку, Р-363

ПОПЕРЁК
вдоль и поперёк, В-11

ПОПЕРЕТЬ
попереть на рожон, Р-145
попереть против рожна,
Р-144

ПОПЕРЕЧНЫЙ
встречный и поперечный
⟨встречный-
поперечный⟩, В-347
всякий встречный и
поперечный ⟨встречный-
поперечный⟩, В-347
каждый встречный и
поперечный ⟨встречный-
поперечный⟩, В-347

ПОПИШЕШЬ
ничего не попишешь,
П-239

ПОПЛАКАТЬ
поплакать в жилетку, Ж-71

ПОПЛАКАТЬСЯ
поплакаться в жилетку,
Ж-71

ПОПЛАТИТЬСЯ
поплатиться головой,
Г-236
поплатиться жизнью,
Г-236

ПОПЛЫЛА
земля поплыла под
ногами, З-125

ПОПЛЯСАТЬ
поплясать по дудке
⟨дудочке⟩, Д-319
поплясать под дудку
⟨дудочку⟩, Д-319

ПОПЛЯШЕШЬ
ты у меня попляшешь,
П-355

ПОПОЛАМ
с горем пополам, Г-393
с грехом пополам, Г-393
хоть пополам разорвись,
Р-64

ПОПОЛЗЛИ
мурашки поползли по
коже, М-291
мурашки поползли по
спине ⟨по телу⟩, М-291

ПОПОЛЬЗОВАТЬСЯ
попользоваться насчёт
клубнички, К-141

ПОПОМНИ(ТЕ)
попомни(те) меня, С-321
попомни(те) моё слово,
С-321

ПОПОРТИТЬ
попортить крови, К-408
попортить себе крови,
К-409

ПОПРИДЕРЖАТЬ
попридержать язык
⟨язычок⟩, Я-21

ПОПРОСТУ
попросту говоря, Г-175
попросту сказать, Г-175

ПОПУТАЛ
бес попутал, Ч-97
грех попутал, Ч-97
лукавый попутал, Ч-97
нечистый (дух) попутал,
Ч-97
чёрт попутал, Ч-97

ПОПУТАЛА
нелёгкая попутала, Ч-97
нечистая сила попутала,
Ч-97

ПОПУТАТЬ
попутать (все) карты, К-98

ПОПУТНОГО
попутного ветра, В-76

ПОПЫТАТЬ
попытать счастье
⟨счастья⟩, С-694

ПОПЫТКА
попытка с негодными
средствами, П-292
попытка не пытка (, а
спрос не беда), П-356

ПОПЯТНУЮ
идти на попятную, П-357
на попятную, П-357
пойти на попятную, П-357

ПОПЯТНЫЙ
идти на попятный (двор),
П-357
на попятный (двор), П-357

пойти на попятный (двор),
П-357

ПОР
до каких пор, П-358
до которых пор, П-358
до сих пор, П-359
до тех пор, П-360
до тех пор пока, П-361
до тех пор пока не, П-362
с каких пор, П-363
с которых пор, П-363
с некоторых пор, П-364
с тех пор, П-365
с тех пор как, П-366
с этих пор, П-367

ПОРА
пора (и) совесть знать,
С-456
пора (и) честь знать, Ч-137

ПОРАЗИ
порази меня гром (на этом
месте), Г-406
порази меня силы
небесные, Г-406
порази тебя гром
⟨громом⟩, Г-407

ПОРАЗИТ
да поразит меня гром,
Г-406
пускай ⟨пусть⟩ поразит
меня гром, Г-406

ПОРАЗИТЬ
как громом поразить,
Г-408

ПОРАЗЯТ
да поразят меня силы
небесные, Г-406
пускай ⟨пусть⟩ поразят
меня силы небесные,
Г-406

ПОРАСКИНУТЬ
пораскинуть мозгами,
У-109
пораскинуть умом, У-109

ПОРАХ
на первых порах, П-368

ПОРЕ
в поре, П-369
в самой поре, П-369
во всей поре, П-369

ПОРЕТ
ни шьёт ни порет, Ш-114

ПОРОГ
вот (тебе) бог, а вот порог,
Б-107
не показываться на порог,
П-370
не появляться на порог,
П-370
не пускать/не пустить на
порог, П-371
обивать/обить (весь)
порог, П-377
перейти (через) порог,
П-372
переступать/переступить
(через) порог, П-372
переходить (через) порог,
П-372
перешагивать/
перешагнуть (через)
порог, П-372

поставить в вину, В-148
поставить в известность,
　И-40
поставить в тупик, Т-238
поставить в укор, У-70
поставить в упрёк, У-70
поставить во главу угла,
　Г-21
поставить вопрос ребром,
　В-260
поставить всё на место,
　М-98
поставить всё на одну
　карту, К-93
поставить всё на своё
　место ⟨на свои места⟩,
　М-98
поставить все точки на
　⟨над⟩ и, Т-183
поставить всякое лыко в
　строку, Л-156
поставить за правило,
　П-489
поставить за честь, Ч-138
поставить знак равенства,
　З-156
поставить к стене ⟨к
　стенке⟩, С-564
поставить крест, К-382
поставить на вид, В-114
поставить на карту, К-94
поставить на колени,
　К-185
поставить на кон, К-225
поставить на место, М-123
поставить на ноги, Н-153,
　Н-154
поставить на одну доску,
　Д-295
поставить на очередь,
　О-185
поставить на рельсы,
　Р-108
поставить на своё место,
　М-123
поставить на своём, С-85
поставить на службу,
　С-351
поставить на учёт, У-167
поставить перед
　свершившимся
　⟨совершившимся⟩
　фактом, Ф-2
поставить перед фактом,
　Ф-2
поставить под вопрос,
　В-261
поставить под удар, У-39
поставить правилом,
　П-489
поставить себе за правило,
　П-489
поставить себе правилом,
　П-489
поставить себя на место,
　М-124
поставить точку, Т-186
поставить точку на ⟨над⟩
　и, Т-183
поставить фонарь, Ф-16

ПОСТЕЛЬ
слечь в постель, П-412

ПОСТНОМ
ерунда на постном масле,
　Е-11
чепуха на постном масле,
　Е-11
ПОСТОИТ
дело не постоит, Д-87
ПОСТОЛЬКУ
постольку-поскольку,
　П-414
постольку, поскольку,
　П-413
ПОСТОЯТЬ
не постоять, С-619
постоять за себя, П-415
ПОСТРЕЛ
(наш) пострел везде
　поспел, П-416
ПОСТРЕЛИВАТЬ
постреливать глазами
　⟨глазками⟩, Г-122
ПОСТРОИТЬ
построить на песке ⟨на
　песце⟩, П-116
ПОСУДНОЙ
слон в посудной лавке,
　С-342
ПОСХОДИТЬ
посходить с ума, У-92
ПОСЧИТАТЬ
посчитать за честь, Ч-138
ПОСЫЛАТЬ
(только) за смертью
　посылать, С-398
ПОСЫЛКАХ
на посылках, П-417
ПОСЫПАЛИСЬ
искры из глаз посыпались,
　И-77
ПОСЫПАТЬ
посыпать главу ⟨голову⟩
　пеплом, Г-269
посыпать себе главу
　⟨голову⟩ пеплом, Г-269
ПОТ
вгонять/вогнать в пот,
　П-418
проливать/пролить пот,
　П-419
ПОТА
до десятого пота, П-421
до кровавого пота, П-420
до седьмого пота, П-421
ПОТАЧКУ
давать/дать потачку,
　П-209
ПОТАЩИТЬ
потащить на аркане, А-39
ПОТЕ
в поте лица (своего), П-422
ПОТЕКЛИ
слюнки потекли, С-387
ПОТЁМКАХ
блуждать в потёмках,
　П-423
бродить в потёмках, П-423
в потёмках, П-424
ПОТЁМКИ
чужая душа — потёмки,
　Д-379

ПОТЁМКИНСКИЕ
потёмкинские деревни,
　Д-177
ПОТЕМНЕЛО
в глазах потемнело, Г-127
ПОТЕРИ
до потери сознания, П-425
ПОТЕРЯ
чья потеря, моя находка,
　П-426
ПОТЕРЯЕШЬ
не знаешь, где найдёшь,
　где потеряешь, З-147
ПОТЕРЯЛ
что я там ⟨тут⟩ потерял?,
　З-11
ПОТЕРЯННЫЙ
как* потерянный, П-427
ПОТЕРЯТЬ
потерять власть над
　собой, В-166
потерять всякую совесть,
　С-457
потерять голову, Г-279
потерять землю из-под
　ног, П-456
потерять землю под
　ногами ⟨под собой⟩,
　П-456
потерять из вида ⟨из
　виду⟩, В-140
потерять из глаз, В-140
потерять лицо, Л-100
потерять ногу, Н-156
потерять остатки совести,
　С-457
потерять последние
　остатки совести, С-457
потерять почву из-под ног,
　П-456
потерять почву под ногами
　⟨под собой⟩, П-456
потерять рассудок, У-85
потерять себя, Т-87
потерять совесть, С-457
потерять сознание, Ч-194
потерять счёт, С-713
потерять терпение, Т-82
потерять шаг, Н-156
ПОТЕХА
пошла потеха!, П-428
ПОТЕХЕ
делу время, (а) потехе час,
　Д-144
ПОТОВ
десять потов сгонять/
　согнать, П-429
десять потов сошло, П-430
десять потов спускать/
　спустить, П-429
пролить семь потов, П-419
семь потов сгонять/
　согнать, П-429
семь потов сошло, П-430
семь потов спускать/
　спустить, П-429
ПОТОК
поток и разграбление,
　П-431
ПОТОКУ
потоку и разграблению,
　П-431

ПОТОЛКА
с потолка, П-432
ПОТОЛОК
плевать в потолок, П-433
ПОТОМ
потом и кровью, П-434
умываться потом, П-419
ПОТОМУ
потому как, П-435
потому что, П-435
ПОТОПА
до потопа, П-436
ПОТОПИТЬ
потопить в крови, К-395
ПОТОЧИТЬ
поточить балясы, Л-177
поточить лясы, Л-177
поточить язык, Я-29
ПОТРАТИТЬ
потратить нервы, Н-82
ПОТРЕПАТЬ
потрепать нервы, Н-83
потрепать язык(ом), Я-32
ПОТРЕЩАТЬ
потрещать языком, Я-32
ПОТРОХАМИ
с потрохами, П-437
со всеми потрохами, П-437
ПОТРОХОВ
до потрохов, П-438
до самых потрохов, П-438
ПОТРЯСАТЬ
потрясать оружием, О-106
ПОТЯНУТЬ
потянуть лямку, Л-176
потянуть на аркане, А-39
ПОХЛЁБКУ
продавать за чечевичную
　похлёбку, П-439
продаваться за
　чечевичную похлёбку,
　П-439
продать за чечевичную
　похлёбку, П-439
продаться за чечевичную
　похлёбку, П-439
променять на чечевичную
　похлёбку, П-439
ПОХЛОПЫВАТЬ
похлопывать по плечу,
　П-194
ПОХМЕЛЬЕ
в чужом пиру похмелье,
　П-155
ПОХОДОМ
с походом, П-440
ПОХОЖ
на кого похож, П-441
на что похож, П-441
ПОХОЖЕ
на что это похоже?, П-442
не похоже, П-443
ни на что не похоже!,
　П-445
похоже на то, что…, П-444
похоже, что…, П-444
это ни на что не похоже!,
　П-445
ПОХОРОНИТЬ
заживо похоронить, Х-81

заживо похоронить себя,
Х-82
ПОХУЛЫ
похулы на руку не класть
⟨не положить⟩, О-180
ПОЦЕЛОВАТЬ
поцеловать замок, З-60
поцеловать пробой, З-60
ПОЦЕЛУЙ
воздушный поцелуй,
П-446
иудин поцелуй, П-447
поцелуй Иуды, П-447
ПОЧВА
почва заколебалась
⟨колеблется⟩ под
ногами, П-448
почва уплывает/уплыла
из-под ног, П-448
почва ускользает/
ускользнула из-под ног,
П-448
почва уходит/ушла из-под
ног, П-448
ПОЧВЕ
на почве, П-449
стоять на реальной почве,
П-450
стоять на твёрдой почве,
П-450
ПОЧВУ
выбивать/выбить почву
из-под ног, П-451
вышибать/вышибить
почву из-под ног, П-451
зондировать почву, П-452
иметь под собой почву,
П-453
иметь почву под ногами,
П-450
иметь твёрдую почву под
ногами, П-450
нащупать ⟨нащупывать⟩
почву, П-455
подготавливать/
подготовить почву,
П-454
позондировать почву,
П-452
потерять почву из-под ног,
П-456
потерять почву под ногами
⟨под собой⟩, П-456
прозондировать почву,
П-452
прощупать
⟨прощупывать⟩ почву,
П-455
расчистить ⟨расчищать⟩
почву, П-454
терять почву из-под ног,
П-456
терять почву под ногами
⟨под собой⟩, П-456
ПОЧЁМ
почём знать, З-172
почём зря, П-457
почём мне знать, З-176
почём фунт лиха, Ф-33
почём я знаю, З-176

ПОЧЕМУ
почему бы то ни было,
Б-268
ПОЧЕСАТЬ
почесать зубки ⟨зубы⟩,
З-205
почесать язык, Я-32
почесать языками
⟨языки⟩, Я-56
почесать языком, Я-32
почесать язычки, Я-56
ПОЧЕСТЬ
почесть за благо, Б-74
почесть за честь, Ч-138
ПОЧЁТ
почёт и уважение, П-458
ПОЧЁТЕ
в почёте, П-459
ПОЧЁТНЫЙ
почётный караул, К-73
ПОЧИВАТЬ
почивать вечным сном,
С-436
почивать на лаврах, Л-4
ПОЧИСТИТЬ
почистить пёрышки, П-114
ПОЧИТЬ
почить в бозе, Б-145
почить вечным сном,
С-432
почить на лаврах, Л-4
почить непробудным
сном, С-432
ПОЧТЕНИЕ
моё почтение, П-460,
П-461
наше почтение, П-460
нижайшее почтение, П-460
ПОЧТЕНИЕМ
с глубоким почтением,
П-463
с нижайшим почтением,
П-463
с почтением, П-462
с совершеннейшим
⟨совершенным⟩
почтением, П-463
ПОЧТЕНИИ
примите уверения в
совершеннейшем
⟨совершенном⟩
почтении, П-463
ПОЧТИ
почти что, П-464
ПОЧТИТЕЛЬНОМ
держать в почтительном
отдалении, Р-84
держать на почтительном
расстоянии, Р-84
держаться в почтительном
отдалении, Р-85
держаться на
почтительном
расстоянии, Р-85
ПОЧУВСТВОВАТЬ
давать/дать
почувствовать, Д-5
дать себя почувствовать,
Д-7
ПОШЕВЕЛИТЬ
пальцем не пошевелить,
П-22

пошевелить мозгами
⟨мозгой⟩, М-221
ПОШЕВЕЛЬНУТЬ
пальцем не пошевельнуть,
П-22
ПОШЁЛ
а не пошёл бы ты (куда)
подальше!, И-23
дым пошёл коромыслом
⟨столбом⟩, Д-436
мороз по коже ⟨по спине⟩
пошёл, М-258
пошёл бы ты (куда)
подальше!, И-23
ПОШЛА
голова пошла кругом,
Г-204
(и) пошла писать, Г-439
пошла писать губерния,
Г-439
пошла потеха!, П-428
ПОШЛИ
мурашки пошли по коже,
М-291
мурашки пошли по спине
⟨по телу⟩, М-291
ПОШЛО
дело пошло, Д-84
ежели (уж) на то пошло,
П-465
если (уж) на то пошло,
П-465
и пошло писать, Г-439
коли ⟨коль⟩ (уж) на то
пошло, П-465
пошло на лад, Л-9
пошло писать, Г-439
ПОЩАДИТЬ
не пощадить красок, К-368
ПОЯВИТЬСЯ
появиться на свет, С-54
появиться на сцену, С-686
ПОЯВЛЕНИЕ
появление на свет, С-54
ПОЯВЛЯТЬСЯ
не появляться на порог,
П-370
появляться на свет, С-54
появляться на сцену, С-686
ПОЯС
заткнуть за пояс, П-466
кланяться ⟨поклониться⟩
в пояс, П-467
ПОЯСА
ниже пояса, П-468
ПРАВА
войти в свои права,
П-469
вступать/вступить в свои
права, П-469
входить в свои права,
П-469
качать права, П-470
ПРАВАХ
на правах, П-471
на птичьих правах, П-472
на равных правах, П-473
ПРАВАЯ
правая рука, Р-228
ПРАВДА
ваша правда, П-478

великая сермяжная
правда, П-474
и то правда, П-475
не правда ли?, П-476
правда глаза колет, П-477
сермяжная правда, П-474
твоя правда, П-478
что правда, то правда,
П-479
ПРАВДАМИ
правдами и неправдами,
П-480
ПРАВДЕ
взглянуть правде в глаза
⟨в лицо⟩, П-483
глядеть правде в глаза ⟨в
лицо⟩, П-483
по правде, П-481
по правде говоря, П-482
по правде сказать, П-482
смотреть правде в глаза ⟨в
лицо⟩, П-483
ПРАВДОЙ
верой и правдой, В-41
ПРАВДУ
говорить правду-матку (в
глаза), П-484
правду говоря, П-482
правду сказать, П-482
резать правду в глаза,
П-484
резать правду-матку (в
глаза), П-484
ПРАВДЫ
в каждой шутке есть доля
правды, Ш-102
в ногах правды нет, Н-129
доля правды, Д-249
ПРАВЕДНИКА
сном праведника, С-435
ПРАВЕДНИЦЫ
сном праведницы, С-435
ПРАВЕДНЫХ
после трудов праведных,
Т-217
сном праведных, С-435
ПРАВИЛАМ
по всем правилам, П-485
по всем правилам
искусства, П-486
ПРАВИЛАХ
не в правилах, П-487
ПРАВИЛО
взять (себе) за правило,
П-489
как правило, П-488
положить (себе) за
правило, П-489
поставить (себе) за
правило, П-489
ПРАВИЛОМ
взять (себе) правилом,
П-489
положить (себе) правилом,
П-489
поставить (себе)
правилом, П-489
ПРАВИЛЬНОЙ
на правильной дороге,
П-645

по правильной дороге,
П-645
ПРАВИЛЬНОМ
на правильном пути,
П-645
ПРАВИЛЬНОМУ
по правильному пути,
П-645
ПРАВИЛЬНУЮ
на правильную дорогу,
П-645
ПРАВИЛЬНЫЙ
на правильный путь,
П-645
ПРАВЛЕНИЯ
бразды правления, Б-195
ПРАВО
право слово, С-324
ПРАВУ
по праву, П-490, П-491
ПРАЗДНИК
будет и на нашей улице
праздник, У-72
ПРАЗДНОВАТЬ
труса ⟨трусу⟩
праздновать, Т-222
ПРАОТЦАМ
отправить к праотцам,
П-492
отправиться к праотцам,
П-493
отправлять к праотцам,
П-492
отправляться к праотцам,
П-493
ПРАТЬ
прать против рожна, Р-144
ПРАХ
в прах, П-663
в пух и (в) прах, П-663
на кой прах, Ч-77
обратить в прах, П-495
обратиться в прах, П-497
обращать в прах, П-495
обращаться в прах, П-497
отрясти прах от ⟨с⟩
(своих) ног, П-494
отряхнуть прах от ⟨с⟩
(своих) ног, П-494
повергать в прах, П-495
повергаться в прах, П-496
повергнуть в прах, П-495
повергнуться в прах,
П-496
прах с тобой, Ч-98
прах тебя возьми!, Ч-99
прах тебя побери!, Ч-99
превратить в прах, П-495
превратиться в прах,
П-497
превращать в прах, П-495
превращаться в прах,
П-497
ПРАХОМ
гори всё прахом, О-55
гори (оно) прахом, О-55
идти прахом, П-498
лететь прахом, П-498
пойти прахом, П-498
полететь прахом, П-498

разлетаться/разлететься
прахом, П-498
рассыпаться прахом,
П-498
ПРАХУ
мир праху, М-181
ПРЕБЫВАТЬ
имею честь пребывать,
Ч-134
ПРЕВЗОЙТИ
превзойти (самого) себя,
П-500
ПРЕВОЗМОГАТЬ
превозмогать себя, П-499
ПРЕВОЗМОЧЬ
превозмочь себя, П-499
ПРЕВОЗНЕСТИ
превознести до небес, Н-49
ПРЕВОЗНОСИТЬ
превозносить до небес,
Н-49
ПРЕВОСХОДИТЬ
превосходить (самого)
себя, П-500
ПРЕВРАТИТЬ
превратить в прах, П-495
ПРЕВРАТИТЬСЯ
превратиться в прах,
П-497
превратиться в слух, С-354
ПРЕВРАЩАТЬ
превращать в прах, П-495
ПРЕВРАЩАТЬСЯ
превращаться в прах,
П-497
превращаться в слух,
С-354
ПРЕВЫШЕ
превыше всего, П-501
ПРЕДАВАТЬ
предавать анафеме, А-28
предавать гласности, Г-145
предавать забвению, З-2
предавать земле, З-111
предавать огню, О-59
предавать огню и мечу,
О-60
ПРЕДАВАТЬСЯ
предаваться власти, В-165
ПРЕДАНИЙ
отойти ⟨отходить⟩ в
область преданий, О-11
уйти ⟨уходить⟩ в область
преданий, О-11
ПРЕДАНИЯ
отойти ⟨отходить⟩ в
область предания, О-11
уйти ⟨уходить⟩ в область
предания, О-11
ПРЕДАТЬ
предать анафеме, А-28
предать гласности, Г-145
предать за тридцать
сребреников, С-533
предать забвению, З-2
предать земле, З-111
предать огню, О-59
предать огню и мечу, О-60
ПРЕДАТЬСЯ
предаться власти, В-165

ПРЕДЕЛА
до предела, П-502
ПРЕДЕЛЕ
на пределе, П-503
ПРЕДЛАГАТЬ
предлагать руку (и
сердце), Р-364
ПРЕДЛОГОМ
под предлогом, П-504
ПРЕДЛОЖЕНА
была бы честь
предложена, Ч-129
ПРЕДЛОЖЕНИЕ
делать/сделать
предложение, П-505
ПРЕДЛОЖИТЬ
предложить руку (и
сердце), Р-364
ПРЕДМЕТ
на какой предмет?, П-506
на предмет, П-507
на сей предмет, П-508
на тот предмет, П-508
на этот предмет, П-508
ПРЕДОСТАВИТЬ
предоставить самому себе,
П-509
предоставить слово, С-311
ПРЕДОСТАВЛЯТЬ
предоставлять самому
себе, П-509
предоставлять слово, С-311
ПРЕДПОЛАГАЕТ
человек предполагает, а
бог располагает, Ч-52
ПРЕДПОЛОЖЕНИЯХ
теряться в
предположениях, Д-229
ПРЕДЪЯВИТЬ
предъявить счёт, С-710
ПРЕДЪЯВЛЯТЬ
предъявлять счёт, С-710
ПРЕЖДЕ
прежде нежели, Ч-60
прежде чем, Ч-60
ПРЕЖНЯЯ
прежняя песня, П-121
ПРЕЗРЕНИЯ
ноль внимания, фунт
презрения, Н-196
ПРЕЗРЕННЫЙ
презренный металл, М-132
ПРЕИМУЩЕСТВУ
по преимуществу, П-510
ПРЕКЛОНИТЬ
преклонить колена
⟨колени⟩, К-184
ПРЕКЛОНЯТЬ
преклонять колена
⟨колени⟩, К-184
ПРЕКРАСНОЕ
в одно прекрасное время,
Д-150
ПРЕКРАСНЫЕ
за прекрасные глаза, Г-35
ПРЕКРАСНЫЙ
в один прекрасный день,
Д-150
прекрасный пол, П-294

ПРЕКРАСНЫХ
для прекрасных глаз, Г-35
ради прекрасных глаз,
Г-35
ПРЕЛОЖИТЬ
преложить гнев на
милость, Г-155
ПРЕМУДРОСТИ
бездна премудрости, Б-47
кладезь премудрости, Б-47
ПРЕПОДНЕСТИ
преподнести пилюли
⟨пилюлю⟩, П-148
ПРЕПОДНОСИТЬ
преподносить пилюли
⟨пилюлю⟩, П-148
ПРЕПЯТСТВИЯМИ
скачка с препятствиями,
С-222
ПРЕСТУПЛЕНИЯ
на месте преступления,
М-104
ПРЕТВОРИТЬ
претворить в жизнь, Ж-49
ПРЕТВОРЯТЬ
претворять в жизнь, Ж-49
ПРЕТЕНЗИИ
в претензии, П-511
ПРЕТКНОВЕНИЯ
камень преткновения, К-42
ПРИБАВИТЬ
прибавить газу, Г-2
прибавить ходу, Х-71
прибавить шагу, Ш-21
ПРИБАВЛЕНИЕ
прибавление семейства,
П-512
ПРИБАВЛЯТЬ
прибавлять газу, Г-2
прибавлять ходу, Х-71
прибавлять шагу, Ш-21
ПРИБЕГАТЬ
прибегать к крайности,
К-362
ПРИБЕГНУТЬ
прибегнуть к крайности,
К-362
ПРИБИРАТЬ
прибирать вожжи к рукам,
В-200
прибирать к рукам, Р-248
ПРИБИТ(ЫЙ)
из-за угла (пыльным)
мешком прибит(ый),
У-13
как* из-за угла (пыльным)
мешком прибит(ый),
У-13
ПРИБОРОМ
класть/положить с
прибором, П-513
ПРИБРАЛ
бог прибрал, Б-103
господь прибрал, Б-103
ПРИБРАТЬ
прибрать вожжи к рукам,
В-200
прибрать к рукам, Р-248
ПРИБЫЛО
в нашем полку прибыло,
П-300

нашего полку прибыло,
П-300

ПРИВЕДИ
не приведи бог, Б-119
не приведи бог сколько,
Б-120
не приведи боже, Б-119
не приведи господи, Б-119
не приведи господи
сколько, Б-120
не приведи господь, Б-119

ПРИВЁЛ
бог привёл, Б-89
случай привёл, С-378

ПРИВЕЛА
судьба привела, С-378

ПРИВЕСТИ
привести в божеский вид,
В-113
привести в память, Ч-196
привести в порядок, П-405
привести в себя, П-516
привести в сознание, Ч-196
привести в христианский
вид, В-113
привести в чувство, Ч-196
привести к единому
знаменателю, З-162
привести к общему
знаменателю, З-162
привести к одному
знаменателю, З-162
привести себя в порядок,
П-406

ПРИВЕТА
ни ответа ни привета,
О-135

ПРИВЕТОМ
с приветом, П-514, П-515

ПРИВЕШЕН
язык здорово привешен,
Я-47
язык неплохо привешен,
Я-47
язык плохо привешен,
Я-42
язык хорошо привешен,
Я-47

ПРИВОДИТ
приводит на память, П-48
приводит на ум, П-48

ПРИВОДИТЬ
приводить в божеский
вид, В-113
приводить в память, Ч-196
приводить в порядок,
П-405
приводить в себя, П-516
приводить в сознание,
Ч-196
приводить в христианский
вид, В-113
приводить в чувство,
Ч-196
приводить к единому
знаменателю, З-162
приводить к общему
знаменателю, З-162
приводить к одному
знаменателю, З-162

приводить себя в порядок,
П-406

ПРИВЫКАТЬ
не привыкать (стать),
П-517

ПРИВЫЧКА
привычка – вторая
натура, П-518

ПРИВЫЧКУ
войти ⟨входить⟩ в
привычку, П-519

ПРИВЫЧНОЕ
вернуться ⟨возвращаться⟩
в привычное русло,
К-198
войти ⟨входить⟩ в
привычное русло, К-198

ПРИВЫЧНУЮ
войти ⟨входить⟩ в
привычную колею,
К-198
попадать/попасть в
привычную колею,
К-198

ПРИВЯЗИ
держать на привязи, П-520
держать язык на привязи,
Я-9
как* с привязи сорваться,
Ц-37

ПРИГВОЖДАТЬ
пригвождать к позорному
столбу, С-593

ПРИГВОЗДИТЬ
пригвоздить к позорному
столбу, С-593

ПРИГОДИТСЯ
не плюй в колодец,
пригодится воды
напиться, К-199

ПРИГРЕВАТЬ
пригревать змею за
пазухой, З-139
пригревать змею на груди,
З-139

ПРИГРЕТЬ
пригреть змею за пазухой,
З-139
пригреть змею на груди,
З-139

ПРИДАВАТЬ
придавать божеский
⟨христианский⟩ вид,
В-113

ПРИДАТЬ
придать божеский
⟨христианский⟩ вид,
В-113

ПРИДАЧУ
в придачу, П-521

ПРИДЕРЖАТЬ
придержать язык
⟨язычок⟩, Я-21

ПРИДЕРЖИВАТЬ
придерживать язык
⟨язычок⟩, Я-21

ПРИДЁТСЯ
где придётся, П-348
как придётся, П-349

какой придётся, П-350
когда придётся, П-351
кто придётся, П-352
куда придётся, П-348
откуда придётся, П-353
что придётся, П-354

ПРИДУРЬЮ
с придурью, П-522

ПРИЖАТЬ
прижать в угол, У-32
прижать к стене ⟨к
стенке⟩, С-563
прижать хвост ⟨хвосты⟩,
Х-15, Х-16

ПРИЖИМАТЬ
прижимать в угол, У-32
прижимать к стенке ⟨к
стене⟩, С-563
прижимать хвост
⟨хвосты⟩, Х-15, Х-16

ПРИЗВАТЬ
призвать к порядку, П-404

ПРИЗМУ
сквозь призму, П-523
через призму, П-523

ПРИЗНАКИ
подавать/подать признаки
жизни, П-524

ПРИЗНАТЬСЯ
надо признаться, П-525
нужно признаться, П-525
по совести признаться,
С-452
признаться сказать, П-525

ПРИЗЫВАТЬ
призывать к порядку,
П-404

ПРИЙТИ
прийти в азарт, А-14
прийти в голову, Г-271
прийти в норму, Н-204
прийти в память, Ч-197
прийти в раж, Р-17
прийти в себя, П-553
прийти в сознание, Ч-197
прийти в ум, Г-271
прийти в чувство, Ч-197
прийти на мысль, Г-271
прийти на память, П-49
прийти на ум, Г-271

ПРИЙТИСЬ
прийтись кстати, П-554

ПРИКАЖЕШЬ
сердцу не прикажешь,
С-150

ПРИКАЗАТЬ
приказать долго жить,
П-526

ПРИКАЗНАЯ
приказная строка, С-640

ПРИКЛАДЫВАТЬСЯ
прикладываться к
бутылке, Б-248
прикладываться к ручке,
Р-373
прикладываться к рюмке
⟨к рюмочке⟩, Б-248

ПРИКЛЕИВАТЬ
приклеивать ярлык
⟨ярлыки⟩, Я-67

ПРИКЛЕИТЬ
приклеить ярлык
⟨ярлыки⟩, Я-67

ПРИКЛОНИТЬ
приклонить голову, Г-270

ПРИКЛЮЧЕНИЙ
искатель приключений,
И-73
искательница
приключений, И-73

ПРИКОВАТЬ
приковать к позорному
столбу, С-593

ПРИКОВЫВАТЬ
приковывать к позорному
столбу, С-593

ПРИКОЛЕ
на приколе, П-527

ПРИКРЫВАТЬ
прикрывать лавочку, Л-3

ПРИКРЫТЬ
прикрыть лавочку, Л-3

ПРИКУРИТЬ
давать/дать прикурить,
Д-6

ПРИКУСИТЬ
прикусить язык ⟨язычок⟩,
Я-22

ПРИКУСЫВАТЬ
прикусывать язык
⟨язычок⟩, Я-22

ПРИЛАВКА
из-под прилавка, П-528

ПРИЛЕПИТЬ
прилепить ярлык
⟨ярлыки⟩, Я-67

ПРИЛИЛА
кровь прилила к лицу,
К-400

ПРИЛИП
язык прилип к гортани,
Я-43

ПРИЛИЧИЯ
держать себя в границах
приличия, Р-75
держать себя в рамках
приличия, Р-75

ПРИЛОЖЕНА
была бы честь приложена,
Ч-129

ПРИЛОЖЕНИЕ
бесплатное приложение,
П-529

ПРИЛОЖИТЬ
приложить руки, Р-306,
Р-366
приложить руку, Р-365,
Р-366
ума приложить не мочь,
У-93

ПРИЛОЖИТЬСЯ
приложиться к ручке,
Р-373

ПРИЛОЖУ
ума не приложу, У-93

ПРИМЕР
брать/взять пример,
П-530
дурной пример
заразителен, П-535

не в пример, П-531
подавать/подать пример,
П-532
показать ⟨показывать⟩
пример, П-532

ПРИМЕРА
для примера, П-533

ПРИМЕРАМИ
за примерами далеко
ходить не надо ⟨не
нужно⟩, Х-58
за примерами далеко
ходить не приходится,
Х-58
недалеко ходить за
примерами, Х-58

ПРИМЕРОМ
за примером далеко
ходить не надо ⟨не
нужно⟩, Х-58
за примером далеко
ходить не приходится,
Х-58
недалеко ходить за
примером, Х-58

ПРИМЕРУ
к примеру, П-534
к примеру говоря, П-534
к примеру сказать, П-534

ПРИМЕРЫ
дурные примеры
заразительны, П-535

ПРИМЕРЬ
семь раз примерь, (а) один
(раз) отрежь, Р-37

ПРИМЕТЕ
держать на примете,
П-536
иметь на примете, П-536
на примете, П-537

ПРИМЕТИТЬ
слона не приметить, С-343

ПРИМЕТУ
брать/взять на примету,
П-538

ПРИМИРИТЬСЯ
примириться со своей
совестью, С-459

ПРИМИТЕ
примите уверения в
совершеннейшем
⟨совершенном⟩
почтении, П-463

ПРИНАДЛЕЖАТЬ
принадлежать перу, П-109

ПРИНАДЛЕЖНОСТИ
по принадлежности, П-539

ПРИНЁС
бог принёс, Б-102
чёрт принёс, Ч-94

ПРИНЕСЛА
нелёгкая принесла, Ч-94
нечистая сила принесла,
Ч-94
сорока на хвосте принесла,
С-498

ПРИНЕСЛИ
черти принесли, Ч-94

ПРИНЕСТИ
принести в жертву, Ж-21

принести жертву
⟨жертвы⟩, Ж-22
принести повинную
(голову), П-220

ПРИНИМАЕТ
душа не принимает, Д-371

ПРИНИМАТЬ
принимать белое за чёрное
(и чёрное за белое), Ч-71
принимать близко к
сердцу, С-149
принимать в расчёт, Р-91
принимать в соображение,
С-487
принимать во внимание,
В-172
принимать грех на душу,
Г-382
принимать за чистую
монету, М-255
принимать к сведению,
С-34
принимать к сердцу, С-149
принимать меры, М-86
принимать на веру, В-52
принимать на вооружение,
В-257
принимать на свой счёт,
С-711
принимать на себя, Б-203
принимать на себя труд,
Т-211
принимать оборот, О-17
принимать позу, П-273
принимать сторону, С-609
принимать участие, У-164
принимать чёрное за белое
(и белое за чёрное), Ч-71
принимать эстафету, Э-3

ПРИНОСИТЬ
приносить в жертву, Ж-21
приносить жертву
⟨жертвы⟩, Ж-22
приносить повинную
(голову), П-220

ПРИНЦИПА
из принципа, П-540

ПРИНЦИПЕ
в принципе, П-541

ПРИНЯТЬ
принять белое за чёрное (и
чёрное за белое), Ч-71
принять близко к сердцу,
С-149
принять в расчёт, Р-91
принять в соображение,
С-487
принять во внимание,
В-172
принять грех на душу,
Г-382
принять за чистую монету,
М-255
принять закон, З-47
принять к сведению, С-34
принять к сердцу, С-149
принять меры, М-86
принять на веру, В-52
принять на вооружение,
В-257

принять на свой счёт, С-711
принять на себя, Б-203
принять на себя труд,
Т-211
принять оборот, О-17
принять позу, П-273
принять сторону, С-609
принять участие, У-164
принять чёрное за белое (и
белое за чёрное), Ч-71
принять эстафету, Э-3

ПРИОБРЕСТИ
капитал приобрести и
невинность соблюсти,
К-55

ПРИОТКРЫВАТЬ
приоткрывать завесу, З-17

ПРИОТКРЫТЬ
приоткрыть завесу, З-17

ПРИПАДАТЬ
припадать к стопам, С-601

ПРИПАРКИ
как мёртвому припарки,
М-81

ПРИПАСТЬ
припасть к стопам, С-601

ПРИПЕВАЮЧИ
жить припеваючи, Ж-80

ПРИПЁКА
сбоку припёка, П-542

ПРИПЁКУ
сбоку-припёку ⟨сбоку
припёку⟩, П-542

ПРИПЕРЕТЬ
припереть в угол, У-32
припереть к стене ⟨к
стенке⟩, С-563

ПРИПИРАТЬ
припирать в угол, У-32
припирать к стене ⟨к
стенке⟩, С-563

ПРИПОДНИМАТЬ
приподнимать завесу, З-17

ПРИПОДНЯТЬ
приподнять завесу, З-17

ПРИРАСТАТЬ
прирастать корнями,
К-305

ПРИРАСТИ
прирасти корнями, К-305

ПРИРОДЕ
в природе вещей, П-543

ПРИРОДЫ
игра природы, И-12
на лоне природы, Л-133
от природы, П-544

ПРИСЕСТ
в один присест, П-545
за один присест, П-545

ПРИСНИТСЯ
(и) во сне не приснится,
С-428
(и) не приснится, С-428

ПРИСНО
и ныне, и присно (, и во
веки веков), Н-264
ныне и присно, Н-264

ПРИСОХ
язык присох к гортани,
Я-43

ПРИСТЕГНИ
не пришей не пристегни,
К-151

ПРИСТРАСТИЕМ
с пристрастием, П-546,
П-547

ПРИСТУПА
приступа нет, П-548

ПРИСТУПУ
приступу нет, П-548

ПРИСУТСТВИЕ
присутствие духа, П-549

ПРИТУПИЛО
купило притупило, К-474

ПРИТУПИЛОСЬ
купило притупилось,
К-474

ПРИТЧА
притча во языцех, П-550

ПРИТЯГИВАТЬ
притягивать за волосы,
В-242
притягивать за уши, В-242

ПРИТЯНУТЬ
притянуть за волосы,
В-242
притянуть за уши, В-242

ПРИХОД
каков поп, таков и приход,
П-343

ПРИХОДИТ
аппетит приходит во
время еды, А-32
беда (никогда) не
приходит одна, Б-37

ПРИХОДИТСЯ
далеко ходить не
приходится, Х-58
за примерами ⟨примером⟩
далеко ходить не
приходится, Х-58
раз на раз не приходится,
Р-33
солоно приходится, П-551
туго приходится, П-552

ПРИХОДИТЬ
приходить в азарт, А-14
приходить в голову, Г-271
приходить в норму, Н-204
приходить в память, Ч-197
приходить в раж, Р-17
приходить в себя, П-553
приходить в сознание,
Ч-197
приходить в ум, Г-271
приходить в чувство,
Ч-197
приходить на мысль, Г-271
приходить на память,
П-49
приходить на ум, Г-271

ПРИХОДИТЬСЯ
приходиться кстати, П-554

ПРИЦЕЛ
брать/взять на прицел,
П-555
далёкий прицел, П-556
дальний прицел, П-556

ПРИЧИНЕ
по причине, П-557

ПРИШЕЙ
не пришей кобыле хвост,
К-151
не пришей не пристегни,
К-151
пришей кобыле хвост,
К-151
ПРИШЁЛ
карачун пришёл, К-75
час пришёл, Ч-19
ПРИШЕСТВИЯ
до второго пришествия,
П-558
ПРИШИБ
кондрашка пришиб, К-228
ПРИШИВАТЬ
пришивать дело, Д-126
ПРИШИТЬ
пришить дело, Д-126
ПРИШЛА
пришла беда — отворяй
⟨открывай, растворяй⟩
ворота, Б-42
ПРИШЛОСЬ
солоно пришлось, П-551
туго пришлось, П-552
ПРИЩЕМИТЬ
прищемить хвост
⟨хвосты⟩, Х-16
ПРИЩЕМЛЯТЬ
прищемлять хвост
⟨хвосты⟩, Х-16
ПРИЯТНОГО
приятного аппетита!, А-34
ПРО
про и контра, З-1
ПРОБА
проба пера, П-559
ПРОБЕГАЕТ
мороз по коже ⟨по спине⟩
пробегает, М-258
ПРОБЕГАТЬ
пробегать глазами, Г-111
ПРОБЕЖАЛ
мороз по коже ⟨по спине⟩
пробежал, М-258
ПРОБЕЖАЛА
(серая) кошка пробежала,
К-346
чёрная кошка пробежала,
К-346
ПРОБЕЖАЛИ
мурашки пробежали по
коже, М-291
мурашки пробежали по
спине ⟨по телу⟩, М-291
ПРОБЕЖАТЬ
пробежать глазами, Г-111
ПРОБИВАТЬ
пробивать дорогу, Д-285
пробивать себе дорогу
⟨путь⟩, Д-284
ПРОБИЛ
час пробил, Ч-19
ПРОБИРАТЬ
пробирать с песком ⟨с
песочком⟩, П-124
ПРОБИТЬ
пробить брешь, Б-207

пробить дорогу, Д-285
пробить себе дорогу
⟨путь⟩, Д-284
ПРОБКА
как пробка, П-560
как пробка вылететь
⟨выскочить⟩, П-561
ПРОБКОЙ
пробкой вылететь
⟨выскочить⟩, П-561
ПРОБНЫЙ
пробный камень, К-46
пробный шар, Ш-33
ПРОБОЙ
поцеловать пробой, З-60
ПРОБРАТЬ
пробрать с песком ⟨с
песочком⟩, П-124
ПРОБУ
на пробу, П-562
пробу ставить негде,
П-563
пробу ставить некуда,
П-563
ПРОБУДИТЬ
пробудить зверя, З-98
ПРОБЫ
высокой ⟨высшей⟩ пробы,
П-564
низкой ⟨низшей⟩ пробы,
П-565
пробы ставить негде,
П-563
пробы ставить некуда,
П-563
чистой пробы, П-564
ПРОБЬЁШЬ
из пушки не пробьёшь,
П-668
пушкой не пробьёшь,
П-668
ПРОВАЛИВАТЬСЯ
проваливаться сквозь
землю, З-120
ПРОВАЛИЛСЯ
как* сквозь землю
провалился, З-120
ПРОВАЛИСЬ
провались (ты) к чёрту,
Ч-117
провались я, М-107
ПРОВАЛИТЬСЯ
готов сквозь землю
провалиться, З-117
лучше сквозь землю
провалиться, З-117
провалиться в тартарары,
Т-42
провалиться мне в
тартарары!, З-121
провалиться мне на (этом)
месте, М-107
провалиться мне сквозь
землю!, З-121
провалиться на (этом)
месте, М-107
провалиться с треском,
Т-202
провалиться сквозь
землю, З-120

рад сквозь землю
провалиться, З-117
хоть сквозь землю
провалиться, З-117
чтоб мне провалиться (в
тартарары)!, З-121
чтоб мне провалиться на
(этом) месте, М-107
чтоб мне сквозь землю
провалиться!, З-121
чтоб тебе провалиться (в
тартарары)!, З-122
чтоб тебе сквозь землю
провалиться!, З-122
ПРОВЕДЁШЬ
на мякине не проведёшь,
М-325
старого воробья на мякине
не проведёшь, В-268
ПРОВЕРНУТЬ
провернуть динамо, Д-196
ПРОВЕСТИ
провести в жизнь, Ж-62
провести грань, Г-379
ПРОВИДЕНИЕ
искушать провидение,
С-665
испытывать провидение,
С-665
ПРОВИДЕНИЯ
перст провидения, П-108
ПРОВОДИТЬ
проводить в жизнь, Ж-62
проводить взглядом
⟨взором⟩, Г-112
проводить глазами, Г-112
проводить грань, Г-379
ПРОВОДЫ
дальние ⟨долгие⟩ проводы
— лишние слёзы, П-566
ПРОВОЖАТЬ
провожать взглядом
⟨взором⟩, Г-112
провожать глазами, Г-112
ПРОВОЖАЮТ
по одёжке ⟨по платью⟩
встречают, по уму
провожают, О-70
ПРОГЛОТИЛ
аршин проглотил, А-42
как* аршин проглотил,
А-42
как* язык проглотил, Я-23
муху проглотил, М-305
ПРОГЛОТИТЬ
проглотить пилюлю,
П-149
проглотить язык, Я-23
ПРОГЛОТИШЬ
язык проглотишь, Я-44
ПРОГЛЯДЕТЬ
(все) глаза проглядеть,
Г-48
ПРОГНАТЬ
прогнать сквозь строй,
С-638
ПРОГОНЯТЬ
прогонять сквозь строй,
С-638

ПРОГУДЕТЬ
прогудеть (все) уши, У-188
ПРОДАВАТЬ
дорого продавать свою
жизнь, Ж-53
продавать за чечевичную
похлёбку, П-439
ПРОДАВАТЬСЯ
продаваться за
чечевичную похлёбку,
П-439
ПРОДАТЬ
дорого продать свою
жизнь, Ж-53
продать за тридцать
сребреников, С-533
продать за чечевичную
похлёбку, П-439
ПРОДАТЬСЯ
продаться за чечевичную
похлёбку, П-439
ПРОДАЮ
за что купил, за то и
продаю, К-473
ПРОДИРАЕТ
мороз по коже ⟨по спине⟩
продирает, М-258
ПРОДИРАТЬ
продирать глаза
⟨глазенапа⟩, Г-89
продирать зенки, Г-89
продирать с песком ⟨с
песочком⟩, П-124
ПРОДОЛЖЕНИЕ
в продолжение, П-567
ПРОДОХНЁШЬ
не продохнёшь, П-568
ПРОДОХНУТЬ
не продохнуть, П-568
продохнуть нельзя, П-568
ПРОДРАЛ
мороз по коже ⟨по спине⟩
продрал, М-258
ПРОДРАТЬ
продрать глаза
⟨глазенапа⟩, Г-89
продрать зенки, Г-89
продрать с песком ⟨с
песочком⟩, П-124
ПРОДУВНАЯ
продувная бестия, Б-61
продувная шельма, Б-61
ПРОЕЗЖАТЬСЯ
проезжаться на счёт
⟨насчёт⟩, С-712
проезжаться по адресу,
С-712
ПРОЕСТЬ
зубы проесть, З-197
ПРОЕХАТЬСЯ
проехаться на счёт
⟨насчёт⟩, С-712
проехаться по адресу,
С-712
ПРОЖИГАТЕЛЬ
прожигатель жизни, Ж-63
ПРОЖИГАТЕЛЬНИЦА
прожигательница жизни,
Ж-63

ПРОЖИГАТЬ
прожигать жизнь, Ж-63
ПРОЖИТЬ
жизнь прожить – не поле
перейти, Ж-54
ПРОЖУЖЖАТЬ
прожужжать (все) уши,
У-188
ПРОЗАКЛАДЫВАТЬ
голову прозакладывать,
Г-249
ПРОЗАКЛАДЫВАЮ
голову прозакладываю,
Г-249
ПРОЗОНДИРОВАТЬ
прозондировать почву,
П-452
ПРОИЗВЕСТИ
произвести на свет, С-55
ПРОИЗВОДИЛ
мир не производил, С-59
свет не производил, С-59
ПРОИЗВОДИТЬ
производить на свет, С-55
ПРОИЗВОЛ
на произвол судьбы, П-569
ПРОЙДЁТ
номер не пройдёт, Н-201
это не пройдёт, Н-201
этот номер не пройдёт,
Н-201
ПРОЙДУТ
эти штучки не пройдут,
Н-201
ПРОЙТИ
легче верблюду пройти в
⟨сквозь⟩ игольное ушко,
В-35
пройти и огни и воды
⟨огонь и воду⟩ (и
медные трубы), О-65
пройти между рук, П-18
пройти мимо, П-597
пройти молчанием, М-246
пройти огни и воды ⟨огонь
и воду⟩ (и медные
трубы), О-65
пройти сквозь огни и воды
⟨огонь и воду⟩ (и
медные трубы), О-65
пройти фуксом, Ф-30
пройти через огни и воды
⟨огонь и воду⟩ (и
медные трубы), О-65
пройти через руки, Р-308
ПРОЙТИСЬ
пройтись на счёт ⟨насчёт⟩,
С-712
пройтись по адресу, С-712
ПРОК
знать прок, Т-138
ПРОКАТИТЬ
прокатить на вороных,
В-276
ПРОКЛАДЫВАТЬ
прокладывать дорогу,
Д-285
прокладывать себе дорогу,
Д-286

ПРОКЛЯТ
будь ты (трижды)
проклят, Б-231
будь я (трижды) проклят,
Б-233
ПРОКЛЯТЫЙ
как проклятый, П-570
ПРОКРУСТОВО
прокрустово ложе, Л-123
ПРОКРУТИТЬ
прокрутить динамо, Д-196
ПРОЛАГАТЬ
пролагать дорогу, Д-285
ПРОЛЕТЕЛО
мимо рта пролетело, Р-187
ПРОЛЕТИТ
слышно, как муха
пролетит, М-297
ПРОЛИВАТЬ
проливать бальзам на
раны, Б-17
проливать кровь, К-410
проливать пот, П-419
проливать свет, С-56
проливать свою кровь,
К-410
проливать слёзы, С-269
ПРОЛИТЬ
пролить бальзам на раны,
Б-17
пролить кровь, К-410
пролить пот, П-419
пролить свет, С-56
пролить свою кровь, К-410
пролить семь потов, П-419
пролить слезу, С-265
пролить слёзы, С-269
ПРОЛОЖИТЬ
проложить дорогу, Д-285
проложить себе дорогу,
Д-286
ПРОМАХ
давать/дать промах, П-571
делать промах, П-571
не промах, П-572
сделать промах, П-571
ПРОМАШКУ
давать/дать промашку,
П-571
делать/сделать промашку,
П-571
ПРОМЕНЯТЬ
променять кукушку на
ястреба, К-461
променять на чечевичную
похлёбку, П-439
ПРОМОЧИТЬ
промочить глотку, Г-343
промочить горло, Г-343
ПРОМЫВАТЬ
промывать мозги, М-228
ПРОМЫВКА
промывка мозгов, М-228
ПРОМЫТЬ
промыть мозги, М-228
ПРОНЕСТИ
пронести кусок мимо рта,
К-494
ПРОНЗАТЬ
пронзать взглядом
⟨взором⟩, Г-113

пронзать глазами, Г-113
ПРОНЗИТЬ
пронзить взглядом
⟨взором⟩, Г-113
пронзить глазами, Г-113
ПРОНОСИТЬ
проносить кусок мимо рта,
К-494
ПРОПАДАЙ
пропадай пропадом, П-575
ПРОПАДАЛА
где наша не пропадала!,
П-573
ПРОПАДАЛО
где наше не пропадало!,
П-573
ПРОПАДАТЬ
пропадать, так с
музыкой!, М-284
ПРОПАДЁТ
не пропадёт, П-574
ПРОПАДИ
пропади пропадом, П-575
ПРОПАДИТЕ
пропадите пропадом,
П-575
ПРОПАДОМ
пропадай пропадом, П-575
пропади(те) пропадом,
П-575
ПРОПАЛ
и след пропал, С-249
или пан или пропал, П-50
либо пан либо пропал,
П-50
пан или пропал, П-50
след пропал, С-249
ПРОПАЛО
пиши пропало, П-159
что с воза ⟨возу⟩ упало,
то (и) пропало, В-213
ПРОПАСТИ
на краю пропасти, К-370
пропасти нет!, П-229
ПРОПАСТЬ
пропасть без вести, В-63
тьфу пропасть!, Ч-84
тьфу ты пропасть!, Ч-84
фу ты пропасть!, Ч-84
чёртова пропасть, П-576
что за пропасть!, Ч-101
ПРОПАЩЕЕ
пропащее дело, Д-75
ПРОПЕТЬ
пропеть дифирамбы,
Д-198
ПРОПИСАЛ
то, что доктор прописал,
Д-232
ПРОПИСАТЬ
прописать ижицу, И-33
прописать пропорцию,
П-578
ПРОПИСНАЯ
прописная истина, И-83
ПРОПЛАКАТЬ
проплакать (все) глаза,
Г-49
ПРОПОВЕДЬ
прочитать ⟨читать⟩
проповедь, Н-240

ПРОПОЙ
на пропой души, П-577
ПРОПОРЦИЮ
прописать пропорцию,
П-578
ПРОПУСКАТЬ
пропускать мимо рук,
П-26
пропускать мимо ушей,
У-182
пропускать рюмочку,
Р-398
пропускать сквозь пальцы,
П-26
пропускать стаканчик,
Р-398
пропускать стопочку, Р-398
пропускать чарочку, Р-398
ПРОПУСТИТЬ
пропустить мимо рук,
П-26
пропустить мимо ушей,
У-182
пропустить рюмочку,
Р-398
пропустить сквозь
пальцы, П-26
пропустить стаканчик,
Р-398
пропустить стопочку,
Р-398
пропустить чарочку, Р-398
ПРОРВУ
как в прорву, П-579
ПРОРВЫ
как из прорвы, П-580
ПРОРЕХИ
заткнуть ⟨затыкать⟩
прорехи, Д-441
ПРОРЕХУ
заткнуть ⟨затыкать⟩
прореху, Д-441
ПРОРОКА
несть ⟨нет⟩ пророка в
отечестве своём ⟨в
своём отечестве⟩, П-581
ПРОРОНИТЬ
не проронить ни словечка,
С-286
не проронить ни слова,
С-286
не проронить слезинки,
С-270
не проронить слезы, С-270
проронить слезу, С-265
ПРОРУБЬ
хоть в прорубь (головой),
В-191
ПРОРУХА
и на старуху бывает
проруха, С-549
ПРОСИЖИВАТЬ
просиживать штаны, Ш-87
ПРОСИМ
милости просим, М-153
просим любить да ⟨и⟩
жаловать, П-602
ПРОСИТ
есть просит, Е-14
кирпича просит, К-122

ПРОСИТСЯ
   просится на язык, Я-24
ПРОСИТЬ
   не заставить себя долго
     просить, З-76
   просить руки, Р-307
   просить честью, Ч-142
ПРОСИТЬСЯ
   проситься в руки, Р-303
ПРОСКАКИВАТЬ
   проскакивать между
     пальцами ⟨пальцев⟩,
     П-19
   проскакивать между рук
     ⟨руками⟩, П-19
   проскакивать сквозь
     пальцы, П-19
ПРОСКАЛЬЗЫВАТЬ
   проскальзывать между
     пальцами ⟨пальцев⟩,
     П-19
   проскальзывать между
     рук ⟨руками⟩, П-19
ПРОСКЛОНЯТЬ
   просклонять во всех
     падежах, П-2
   просклонять по всем
     падежам, П-2
ПРОСКОЛЬЗНУТЬ
   проскользнуть между
     пальцами ⟨пальцев⟩,
     П-19
   проскользнуть между рук
     ⟨руками⟩, П-19
ПРОСКОЧИЛА
   (серая) кошка проскочила,
     К-346
   чёрная кошка проскочила,
     К-346
ПРОСКОЧИТЬ
   проскочить между
     пальцами ⟨пальцев⟩,
     П-19
   проскочить между рук
     ⟨руками⟩, П-19
   проскочить сквозь пальцы,
     П-19
   проскочить фуксом, Ф-30
ПРОСЛУШАТЬ
   прослушать (все) уши,
     У-189
ПРОСМОТРЕТЬ
   (все) глаза просмотреть,
     Г-48
ПРОСТАКА
   не на простака напал,
     Д-335
ПРОСТИ
   прости за выражение,
     В-372
   последнее прости, П-582
   прости господи, Г-366,
     Г-367
ПРОСТИТЕ
   простите за выражение,
     В-372
ПРОСТО
   (а) ларчик просто
     открывался, Л-32
   просто наказание, Н-21

просто одна смехота,
   С-404
   просто смех (один), С-404
   просто так, П-583
ПРОСТОГО
   проще простого, П-584
ПРОСТОТА
   о святая простота!, П-585
   простота хуже воровства,
     П-586
   святая простота!, П-585
ПРОСТОТЕ
   в простоте душевной
     ⟨души⟩, П-587
   в простоте (своего) сердца,
     П-587
   по простоте душевной
     ⟨души⟩, П-587
   по простоте своего сердца,
     П-587
   по простоте сердечной,
     П-587
   по простоте сердца, П-587
ПРОСТОТЫ
   на всякого мудреца
     довольно простоты,
     М-279
   на каждого мудреца
     довольно простоты,
     М-279
ПРОСТЫЛ
   (и) след простыл, С-249
ПРОСТЫМ
   простым глазом, Г-138
ПРОСЫПА
   без просыпа, П-588
ПРОСЫПУ
   без просыпу, П-588
ПРОСЫХАТЬ
   не просыхать, П-589
ПРОСЫХАЮТ
   глаза не просыхают, Г-59
ПРОСЯТ
   каши просят, К-112
ПРОТЕРЕТЬ
   протереть глаза, Г-89,
     Г-90
   протереть глазки, Г-90
   протереть с песком ⟨с
     песочком⟩, П-124
ПРОТИВ
   за и против, З-1
   ничего не иметь против,
     И-61
ПРОТИВНОМ
   в противном случае, С-362
ПРОТИВОВЕС
   в противовес, П-590
ПРОТИРАТЬ
   протирать глаза, Г-89
   протирать с песком ⟨с
     песочком⟩, П-124
   протирать штаны, Ш-87
ПРОТОРЁННАЯ
   проторённая дорожка,
     Д-288
ПРОТРУБИТЬ
   протрубить (все) уши,
     У-188

ПРОТЯГИВАЙ
   по одёжке протягивай
     ножки, О-71
ПРОТЯГИВАТЬ
   протягивать руку
     (помощи), Р-367
ПРОТЯЖЕНИИ
   на протяжении, П-591
ПРОТЯНУТОЙ
   пойти ⟨ходить⟩ с
     протянутой рукой, Р-340
ПРОТЯНУТЬ
   протянуть ноги, Н-155
   протянуть руку, Р-367,
     Р-368
   протянуть руку помощи,
     Р-367
ПРОФЕССОР
   профессор кислых щей,
     П-592
ПРОФОРМЫ
   для проформы, Ф-22
ПРОХАЖИВАТЬСЯ
   прохаживаться на счёт
     ⟨насчёт⟩, С-712
   прохаживаться по адресу,
     С-712
ПРОХЛАДЦЕЙ
   с прохладцей, П-593
ПРОХЛАДЦЕМ
   с прохладцем, П-593
ПРОХОДА
   не давать/не дать
     прохода, П-594
   прохода нет, П-595
ПРОХОДИТ
   мороз по коже ⟨по спине⟩
     проходит, М-258
   не проходит даром, П-596
   так не проходит, П-596
ПРОХОДИТЬ
   проходить красной нитью,
     Н-105
   проходить между рук,
     П-18
   проходить мимо, П-597
   проходить молчанием,
     М-246
   проходить через руки,
     Р-308
ПРОХОДНОЙ
   проходной двор, Д-43
ПРОХОДУ
   не давать/не дать проходу,
     П-594
   проходу нет, П-595
ПРОЦЕНТОВ
   на все сто процентов,
     С-576
ПРОЧАЯ
   и прочая (и прочая), П-598
ПРОЧЕЕ
   и всё такое прочее, В-330
   и прочее (и прочее), П-598
ПРОЧИМ
   между прочим, П-599
ПРОЧИТАТЬ
   прочитать между строк
     ⟨строками⟩, С-639

   прочитать между строчек
     ⟨строчками⟩, С-639
   прочитать мораль, Н-240
   прочитать мысли, М-310
   прочитать наставление,
     Н-240
   прочитать нотацию, Н-240
   прочитать проповедь,
     Н-240
ПРОЧИХ
   при прочих равных, Р-8
ПРОЧНО
   прочно стоять на ногах,
     Н-134
ПРОЧЬ
   не прочь, П-600
   руки прочь, Р-323
   шутки прочь, Ш-103
ПРОШЁЛ
   как* Мамай прошёл, М-22
   мороз по коже ⟨по спине⟩
     прошёл, М-258
   не прошёл даром, П-596
ПРОШИБЁШЬ
   из пушки не прошибёшь,
     П-668
   лбом стенку ⟨стену,
     стены⟩ не прошибёшь,
     Л-35
   пушкой не прошибёшь,
     П-668
ПРОШЛО
   мимо рта прошло, Р-187
   так не прошло, П-596
   что было, то прошло (и
     быльём поросло), Б-275
ПРОШЛОГО
   из глубины прошлого,
     Г-151
ПРОШЛОГОДНИЙ
   как прошлогодний снег,
     С-429
ПРОШЛОЕ
   дело прошлое, Д-92
   кануть в прошлое, П-601
   отойти ⟨отходить⟩ в
     прошлое, П-601
   уйти ⟨уходить⟩ в
     прошлое, П-601
ПРОШУ
   милости прошу, М-153
   милости прошу к нашему
     шалашу, М-154
   покорнейше прошу, П-603
   прошу любить да ⟨и⟩
     жаловать, П-602
   прошу покорно, П-603,
     П-604
   прошу прощения, П-606
ПРОЩАНИЕ
   на прощание, П-605
ПРОЩЕ
   проще пареной репы, Р-111
   проще простого, П-584
   проще сказать, С-208
ПРОЩЕНИЯ
   прошу прощения, П-606
ПРОЩУПАТЬ
   прощупать почву, П-455
ПРОЩУПЫВАТЬ
   прощупывать почву, П-455

ПРОЯВИТЬ
  проявить характер, Х-3
ПРОЯВЛЯТЬ
  проявлять характер, Х-3
ПРУД
  (хоть) пруд пруди, П-607
ПРУДИ
  (хоть) пруд пруди, П-607
ПРУЖИНЫ
  нажать ⟨нажимать⟩ (на)
    все пружины, П-75
ПРЫГАЮТ
  в глазах чертенята
    ⟨чёртики⟩ прыгают,
    Г-128
ПРЫГНЕШЬ
  выше головы не
    прыгнешь, Г-289
ПРЫСКАТЬ
  прыскать в кулак, К-464
ПРЫСНУТЬ
  прыснуть в кулак, К-464
ПРЫТЬ
  во всю прыть, П-608
  откуда прыть взялась,
    П-609
ПРЯМАЯ
  прямая дорога, Д-264
ПРЯМО
  бить прямо в цель, Ц-23
  глядеть прямо в глаза,
    Г-98
  не в бровь, а прямо в глаз,
    Б-208
  прямо наказание, Н-21
  прямо одна смехота, С-404
  прямо смех (один), С-404
  смотреть прямо в глаза,
    Г-98
ПРЯМОЙ
  идти прямой дорогой,
    Д-272
  прямой путь, Д-264
ПРЯМЫМ
  идти прямым путём,
    Д-272
ПРЯНИКА
  политика кнута и пряника,
    П-298
ПРЯНИКИ
  ни за какие пряники, К-153
ПРЯТАТЬ
  прятать взгляд ⟨взор⟩,
    Г-91
  прятать глаза, Г-91
  прятать голову под крыло,
    Г-272
  прятать концы (в воду),
    К-262
ПРЯТАТЬСЯ
  прятаться в свою
    скорлупу, С-233
  прятаться за других, С-516
  прятаться за спину, С-516
  прятаться за чужую спину,
    С-516
ПРЯТКИ
  игра в прятки, П-610
  играть в прятки, П-610

ПСУ
  псу под хвост, П-611
ПТАШЕЧКА
  рано пташечка запела, как
    бы кошечка не съела,
    П-612
ПТАШКА
  вольная пташка, П-617
  ранняя пташка, П-613
ПТЕНЕЦ
  желторотый птенец, П-614
ПТИЦА
  важная птица, П-615
  видна птица по полёту,
    П-616
  вольная птица, П-617
  как птица небесная, П-618
  невелика птица, П-620
  птица высокого полёта,
    П-619
  птица невысокого полёта,
    П-620
  птица низкого полёта,
    П-620
  синяя птица, П-621
  стреляная птица, В-267
ПТИЦУ
  видать ⟨видно⟩ птицу по
    полёту, П-616
ПТИЦЫ
  птицы одного полёта,
    П-622
ПТИЧИЙ
  не верить ни в чох, ни в
    сон ни в птичий грай,
    Ч-157
ПТИЧКА
  как птичка небесная, П-618
ПТИЧЬЕГО
  птичьего молока не
    хватает ⟨недостаёт⟩,
    М-238
  птичьего молока нет,
    М-238
  с высоты птичьего полёта,
    В-379
  с птичьего полёта, В-379
  только птичьего молока не
    хватает ⟨недостаёт⟩,
    М-238
  только птичьего молока
    нет, М-238
ПТИЧЬИХ
  на птичьих правах, П-472
ПТИЧЬЯ
  птичья память, П-44
ПУБЛИКУ
  играть на публику, П-623
  работать на публику,
    П-623
ПУБЛИЧНЫЙ
  публичный дом, Д-252
ПУГАЛО
  пугало гороховое, Ш-97
ПУГАНАЯ
  пуганая ворона (и) куста
    боится, В-275
ПУГОВИЦЫ
  застёгнут(ый) на все
    пуговицы, П-624

  на чужой рот пуговицы не
    нашьёшь, Р-178
ПУД
  пуд соли съесть, П-625
  чтобы узнать человека,
    надо с ним пуд соли
    съесть, Ч-54
ПУДРИТЬ
  пудрить голову, Г-258
  пудрить мозги, М-229
ПУЗА
  от пуза, П-626
ПУЗЫРЬ
  дутый пузырь, П-627
  лезть в пузырь, Б-249
  лопнуть как мыльный
    пузырь, П-628
  мыльный пузырь, П-629
  полезть в пузырь, Б-249
ПУЛЕЙ
  пулей вылетать/вылететь,
    П-630
ПУЛИ
  лить пули, П-631
  отливать/отлить пули,
    П-631
ПУЛЮ
  лить пулю, П-631
  отливать/отлить пулю,
    П-631
  пускать/пустить (себе)
    пулю в лоб, П-632
  хоть пулю в лоб, П-633
ПУНКТ
  кульминационный пункт,
    П-634
  пункт за пунктом, П-635
ПУНКТА
  инвалид пятого пункта,
    И-67
ПУНКТАМ
  по пунктам, П-635
ПУНКТОМ
  пункт за пунктом, П-635
ПУП
  пуп земли, П-636
ПУСКАЙ
  пускай его ⟨её, их⟩, П-639
  пускай поразит меня гром,
    Г-406
  пускай поразят меня силы
    небесные, Г-406
  пускай разразит меня
    гром, Г-406
  пускай разразят меня силы
    небесные, Г-406
  пускай себе, П-639
  пускай у меня рука
    отсохнет!, Р-302
ПУСКАТЬ
  не пускать на порог, П-371
  пускать в дело, Х-56
  пускать в оборот, О-18
  пускать в обращение, О-18
  пускать в расход, Р-88
  пускать в трубу, Т-208
  пускать в ход, Х-56
  пускать камень ⟨камнем⟩,
    К-37
  пускать козла в огород,
    К-169

  пускать корни, К-303
  пускать красного петуха,
    П-132
  пускать на ветер, В-67
  пускать на глаза, Г-92
  пускать на самотёк, С-10
  пускать петуха, П-132,
    П-133
  пускать по ветру, В-82
  пускать по миру, М-192
  пускать по рукам, Р-249
  пускать пулю в лоб, П-632
  пускать пыль в глаза,
    П-672
  пускать с сумой, М-192
  пускать себе пулю в лоб,
    П-632
  пускать слезу, С-265
  пускать шпильки
    ⟨шпильку⟩, Ш-85
ПУСКАТЬСЯ
  пускаться во все тяжкие
    ⟨во вся тяжкая⟩, Т-256
  пускаться наутёк, П-637
ПУСКАЮТ
  (и) рад бы в рай, да грехи
    не пускают, Р-67
ПУСТАЯ
  пустая башка, Г-217
  пустая голова, Г-217
ПУСТИТЬ
  не пустить на порог, П-371
  пустить в дело, Х-56
  пустить в оборот, О-18
  пустить в обращение, О-18
  пустить в расход, Р-88
  пустить в трубу, Т-208
  пустить в ход, Х-56
  пустить камень ⟨камнем⟩,
    К-37
  пустить козла в огород,
    К-169
  пустить корни, К-303
  пустить красного петуха,
    П-132
  пустить на ветер, В-67
  пустить на глаза, Г-92
  пустить на самотёк, С-10
  пустить петуха, П-132,
    П-133
  пустить по ветру, В-82
  пустить по миру, М-192
  пустить по рукам, Р-249
  пустить пулю в лоб, П-632
  пустить пыль в глаза,
    П-672
  пустить с сумой, М-192
  пустить себе пулю в лоб,
    П-632
  пустить слезу, С-265
  пустить шпильки
    ⟨шпильку⟩, Ш-85
ПУСТИТЬСЯ
  пуститься во все тяжкие
    ⟨во вся тяжкая⟩, Т-256
  пуститься наутёк, П-637
ПУСТО
  разом густо, разом пусто,
    Р-62
  свято место пусто не
    бывает, М-121

чтоб пусто было, Б-273

ПУСТОГО
переливать из пустого в порожнее, П-638
пересыпать из пустого в порожнее, П-638

ПУСТОЕ
пустое дело, Д-127
пустое место, М-120

ПУСТОЙ
на пустой желудок, Ж-14
пустой звук, З-102
пустой карман, К-83
пустой кошелёк, К-83
пустой номер, Н-200

ПУСТОМ
на пустом месте, М-105

ПУСТЫМИ
с пустыми руками, Р-259

ПУСТЫНЕ
глас, вопиющий в пустыне, Г-143
глас вопиющего в пустыне, Г-143
голос, вопиющий в пустыне, Г-143

ПУСТЬ
пусть будет земля пухом, З-128
пусть его ⟨её, их⟩, П-639
пусть поразит меня гром, Г-406
пусть поразят меня силы небесные, Г-406
пусть разразит меня гром, Г-406
пусть разразит тебя бог ⟨господь⟩, Г-406
пусть разразят меня силы небесные, Г-406
пусть себе, П-639
пусть у меня рука отсохнет!, Р-302
пусть так, П-640

ПУСТЯКОВ
пара пустяков, П-56

ПУТАТЬ
путать ⟨все⟩ карты, К-98

ПУТАТЬСЯ
путаться под ногами, Н-126

ПУТЁВКА
путёвка в жизнь, П-641

ПУТЕВОДНАЯ
путеводная звезда, З-92
путеводная нить, Н-104

ПУТЁМ
идти прямым путём, Д-272
идти своим путём, Д-273
обходным путём, П-660
окольным путём, П-660
пойти своим путём, Д-273
явочным путём, П-402

ПУТИ
без пути, П-642
встать на пути, П-652
встать поперёк пути, П-652
доброго пути!, П-653

заказать ⟨заказывать⟩ (все) пути, П-656
идти по пути наименьшего сопротивления, Л-73
на дурном пути, П-644
на ложном пути, П-643
на плохом пути, П-644
на правильном пути, П-645
на пути, П-646
на хорошем пути, П-647
неисповедимы пути господни, П-648
по дурному пути, П-644
по ложному пути, П-643
по плохому пути, П-644
по правильному пути, П-645
по пути, Д-269
по хорошему пути, П-647
пойти по плохому пути, Д-270
пойти по пути наименьшего сопротивления, Л-73
пути разошлись ⟨расходятся⟩, П-649
сбивать с пути, П-650
сбиваться с пути, П-651
сбивать с пути истинного ⟨истины⟩, П-650
сбиваться с пути истинного ⟨истины⟩, П-651
сбить с пути, П-650
сбить с пути истинного ⟨истины⟩п, П-650
сбиться с пути, П-651
сбиться с пути истинного ⟨истины⟩, П-651
становиться на пути, П-652
становиться поперёк пути, П-652
стать на пути, П-652
стать поперёк пути, П-652
стоять на пути, П-652
стоять поперёк пути, П-652
счастливого пути!, П-653

ПУТЬ
в добрый путь!, П-654
вставать/встать на путь, П-662
вступать/вступить на путь, П-662
вывести ⟨выводить⟩ на путь, Д-276
держать путь, П-655
добрый путь!, П-653
заказать ⟨заказывать⟩ путь, П-656
на дурной путь, П-644
на ложный путь, П-643
на плохой путь, П-644
на правильный путь, П-645
на хороший путь, П-647
найти путь к сердцу, Д-282
направить ⟨направлять⟩ на путь истинный ⟨истины⟩, П-658

направить ⟨направлять⟩ путь, П-657
наставить ⟨наставлять⟩ на путь истинный ⟨истины⟩, П-658
находить путь к сердцу, Д-282
обратить на путь истинный ⟨истины⟩, П-658
обратиться на путь истины ⟨истинный⟩, П-659
обращать на путь истинный ⟨истины⟩, П-658
обходной путь, П-660
окольный путь, П-660
последний путь, П-661
пробивать/пробить себе путь, Д-284
прямой путь, Д-264
путь добрый!, П-653
становиться/стать на путь, П-662
счастливый путь!, П-653

ПУТЯМИ
обходными путями, П-660
окольными путями, П-660

ПУХ
в пух, П-663
в пух и (в) прах, П-663
пух да ⟨и⟩ перья летят/полетят, П-664

ПУХА
ни пуха ни пера, П-665

ПУХНЕТ
голова пухнет, Г-206

ПУХОМ
да будет земля пухом, З-128
пусть будет земля пухом, З-128

ПУХУ
рыльце в пуху, Р-392

ПУЧИТЬ
пучить бельма, Г-100
пучить глаза, Г-100
пучить зенки, Г-100

ПУШЕК
из пушек по воробьям бить ⟨палить, стрелять⟩, П-666

ПУШЕЧНОЕ
пушечное мясо, М-326

ПУШЕЧНЫЙ
на пушечный выстрел, В-383

ПУШКИ
из пушки по воробьям бить ⟨палить, стрелять⟩, П-666
из пушки не пробьёшь ⟨не прошибёшь⟩, П-668
как из пушки, П-667

ПУШКОЙ
пушкой не пробьёшь ⟨не прошибёшь⟩, П-668

ПУШКУ
брать/взять на пушку, П-669

рыльце в пушку, Р-392

ПУЩЕ
охота пуще неволи, О-176
пуще глаза, Г-93
пуще горькой редьки, Р-102
пуще зеницы ока, З-130
пуще огня, О-62

ПУЩЕЙ
для пущей важности, В-2

ПФЕФЕРУ
задавать/задать пфеферу, П-110
показать ⟨показывать⟩ пфеферу, П-110

ПШЕНИЦЫ
отделить ⟨отделять⟩ плевелы от пшеницы, П-170

ПЫЛУ
в пылу, П-670
с пылу, с жару, П-671

ПЫЛЬ
пускать/пустить пыль в глаза, П-672
пыль столбом, П-673

ПЫЛЬНАЯ
не пыльная, П-674

ПЫЛЬНЫМ
из-за угла пыльным мешком прибит(ый) ⟨трахнутый, ударен(ный)⟩, У-13
как* из-за угла пыльным мешком прибит(ый) ⟨трахнутый, ударен(ный)⟩, У-13

ПЫТКА
попытка не пытка а спрос не беда, П-356

ПЫШНЫЙ
распускать/распустить пышный хвост, Х-17

ПЫШНЫМ
пышным цветом, Ц-15

ПЬЯНКЕ
по пьянке, Л-2

ПЬЯНОГО
что у трезвого на уме, то у пьяного на языке, Т-198

ПЬЯНОЙ
по пьяной лавочке, Л-2

ПЬЯНОМУ
по пьяному делу, Л-2

ПЬЯНУЮ
под пьяную лавочку, Л-2
под пьяную руку, Р-356

ПЬЯНЫХ
с пьяных глаз, Г-40

ПЯДЕЙ
семи ⟨семь⟩ пядей во лбу, П-675

ПЯДЕНЕЙ
семи ⟨семь⟩ пяденей во лбу, П-675

ПЯДЕНЬ
семи ⟨семь⟩ пядень во лбу, П-675

ПЯДЬ
ни на пядь, Ш-5

ПЯЛИТЬ
пялить бельма, Г-100
пялить глаза, Г-100
пялить зенки, Г-100

ПЯТ
до пят, П-676
от головы до пят, Г-293
с головы до пят, Г-293

ПЯТА
ахиллесова пята, П-677

ПЯТАМ
по пятам, П-678

ПЯТАЯ
как собаке пятая нога,
С-446
пятая колонна, К-207
пятая спица в колеснице,
С-520

ПЯТИ
без пяти минут, М-169

ПЯТКА
ахиллесова пятка, П-677

ПЯТКАХ
душа в пятках, Д-374

ПЯТКИ
душа уходит/ушла в
пятки, Д-374
лизать пятки, П-679
намазать ⟨намазывать⟩
пятки (салом), П-682
наступать/наступить на
пятки, П-680
подмазать ⟨подмазывать⟩
пятки (салом), П-682
показать ⟨показывать⟩
пятки, П-681
смазать ⟨смазывать⟩
пятки (салом), П-682
только пятки засверкали,
П-683
только пятки сверкают,
П-683

ПЯТКУ
хрен в пятку, Х-100

ПЯТНИЦ
семь пятниц на неделе,
П-684

ПЯТНО
белое пятно, П-685
родимое пятно, П-686
тёмное пятно, П-687
чёрное пятно, П-687

ПЯТОГО
из пятого в десятое, П-688
инвалид пятого пункта,
И-67
с пятого на десятое, П-688

ПЯТОЕ
пятое-десятое, П-689
пятое колесо в колеснице,
К-197
пятое колесо в телеге,
К-197
пятое через десятое, П-688
через пятое на десятое,
П-688

ПЯТОЙ
инвалид пятой группы,
И-67
под пятой, П-690

ПЯТОК
от головы до пяток, Г-293
с головы до пяток, Г-293

ПЯТЬ
как свои пять пальцев,
П-20
опять двадцать пять!,
О-97

Р

РАБ
раб божий, Р-1

РАБОТА
египетская работа, Р-2
работа не волк ⟨не
медведь⟩, в лес не
убежит ⟨не уйдёт⟩, Р-3
сизифова работа, Т-214

РАБОТАЕТ
время работает, В-309

РАБОТАТЬ
работать на публику,
П-623
работать над собой, Р-4

РАБОТЕ
гореть на работе, Р-5

РАБОТУ
брать/взять в работу, О-16

РАБОЧАЯ
рабочая косточка, К-325
рабочая сила, С-172

РАБОЧЕМ
в рабочем порядке, П-400

РАБОЧИЕ
рабочие руки, Р-309

РАВЕНСТВА
поставить ⟨ставить ⟩знак
равенства, З-156

РАВНО
всё равно, В-327
всё равно как, В-328
всё равно что, В-328
равно как (и), Р-6

РАВНОЙ
в равной мере, О-23
в равной степени, О-23
на равной ноге, Н-137

РАВНЫМ
равным образом, О-23

РАВНЫХ
на равных, Р-7
на равных правах, П-473
при прочих равных, Р-8

РАД
и рад бы в рай, да грехи не
пускают, Р-67
и сам не рад, Р-9
не рад, Р-9
рад бы в рай, да грехи не
пускают, Р-67
рад или не рад, Х-94
рад не рад, Х-94
рад сквозь землю
провалиться, З-117
рад стараться, С-543
сам не рад, Р-9

РАДОВАТЬ
радовать взор, Г-36

радовать глаз, Г-36

РАДОВАТЬСЯ
извольте радоваться, И-46

РАДОСТИ
мало радости, Р-10
на радости, Р-16
с какой радости?, Р-11

РАДОСТЬ
велика радость!, Р-12
не в радость, Р-13
одна радость в глазу, Р-14
старость не радость, С-548

РАДОСТЬЮ
с радостью, Р-15

РАДОСТЯХ
на радостях, Р-16

РАДУЖНОМ
в радужном свете, С-69

РАДЫ
чем богаты, тем и рады,
Б-132

РАЖ
впадать/впасть в раж,
Р-17
войти ⟨входить⟩ в раж,
Р-17
прийти ⟨приходить⟩ в
раж, Р-17

РАЗ
в который раз, Р-18
в самый раз, Р-19
вот те (и) раз!, Р-20
вот тебе (и) раз!, Р-20
другой раз, Р-21
иной раз, Р-21
кажинный раз на этом
(самом) месте, Р-22
как раз, Р-23
как-то раз, Р-24
лишний раз, Р-25
не раз, Р-26
раз в год по обещанию,
Р-27
раз в раз, Р-28
раз-два да и обчёлся, Р-29
раз-два и готово, Р-30
раз-два и обчёлся, Р-29
раз-другой (да) и обчёлся,
Р-29
раз за разом, Р-31
раз и навсегда, Р-32
раз как-то, Р-24
раз на раз не приходится,
Р-33
раз навсегда, Р-32
раз от раза ⟨разу⟩, Р-34
раз плюнуть, Р-35
раз-раз и готово, Р-30
раз так, Т-12
раз такое дело, Д-128
самый раз, Р-36
семь раз отмерь
⟨примерь⟩, (а) один
(раз) отрежь, Р-37

РАЗА
раз от раза, Р-34

РАЗБЕГА
с разбега, Р-38

РАЗБЕГАЮТСЯ
глаза разбегаются, Г-62

РАЗБЕГУ
с разбегу, Р-38

РАЗБЕЖАЛИСЬ
глаза разбежались, Г-62

РАЗБЕРЕДИТЬ
разбередить душу, Д-406
разбередить рану ⟨раны⟩,
Р-78
разбередить сердце, Д-406

РАЗБЕРЁТ
чёрт его разберёт, Ч-89
шут его разберёт, Ч-89

РАЗБЕРИ
не разбери-бери, Р-39
не разбери-поймёшь, Р-39
не разбери-пойми, Р-39

РАЗБИВАТЬСЯ
разбиваться в лепёшку,
Л-53

РАЗБИРАЕТ
зло разбирает, З-132
злость разбирает, З-132

РАЗБИРАТЬ
разбирать по косточкам,
К-326

РАЗБИТОГО
у разбитого корыта, К-317

РАЗБИТОМУ
к разбитому корыту, К-317

РАЗБИТЬ
разбить лёд, Л-42
разбить наголову, Р-40

РАЗБИТЬСЯ
разбиться в лепёшку, Л-53

РАЗБОЙНИК
разбойник с большой
дороги, Р-41

РАЗБОРА
без разбора, Р-42

РАЗБОРОМ
с разбором, Р-43

РАЗБОРУ
без разбору, Р-42
к шапочному разбору, Р-44

РАЗБУДИТЬ
разбудить зверя, З-98

РАЗВЕ
разве вот, Р-45
разве лишь, Р-45
разве можно!, М-216
разве только, Р-45
разве что, Р-45
разве это слыхано?, С-383

РАЗВЕРЗЛИСЬ
разверзлись хляби
небесные, Х-46

РАЗВЕСИСТАЯ
развесистая клюква, К-144

РАЗВЕСИТЬ
развесить уши, У-190

РАЗВЕСТИ
развести канитель, К-52
развести руками, Р-257
развести сантименты, С-13
развести сырость, С-738

РАЗВЕШИВАТЬ
развешивать уши, У-190

РАЗВОДИТЬ
бобы разводить, Б-87

[965]

разводить антимонии, А-31
разводить бодягу, Б-140
разводить волынку, В-246
разводить канитель, К-52
разводить муру, М-292
разводить руками, Р-257
разводить сантименты, С-13
разводить сырость, С-738
разводить тары-бары ⟨тары-бары-растабары⟩, Т-43
разводить тары да бары, Т-43

РАЗВЯЗАЛСЯ
язык развязался, Я-45

РАЗВЯЗАТЬ
развязать кошель, М-273
развязать мошну, М-273
развязать руки, Р-310
развязать себе руки, Р-311
развязать язык, Я-25

РАЗВЯЗЫВАЕТСЯ
язык развязывается, Я-45

РАЗВЯЗЫВАТЬ
развязывать кошель, М-273
развязывать мошну, М-273
развязывать руки, Р-310
развязывать себе руки, Р-311
развязывать язык, Я-25

РАЗГИБАТЬ
не разгибать спины, С-517

РАЗГИБАЯ
не разгибая спины, С-518

РАЗГОВОР
вот вам и весь разговор, Р-46
вот и весь разговор, Р-46
вот тебе и весь разговор, Р-46
другой разговор, Р-47
и весь разговор, Р-46
какой ⟨может быть⟩ разговор!, Р-50
о чём разговор!, Р-50
перевести разговор на другое ⟨на другую тему⟩, Р-48
переводить разговор на другое ⟨на другую тему⟩, Р-48
разговор короткий, Р-49
что за разговор!, Р-50

РАЗГОВОРА
без всякого разговора, Р-52
и разговора быть не может, Р-51
и разговора нет, Р-51

РАЗГОВОРОВ
без всяких разговоров, Р-52
без дальних разговоров, С-274
без лишних разговоров, С-274

РАЗГОВОРУ
и разговору быть не может, Р-51

и разговору нет, Р-51

РАЗГОНА
с разгона, Р-53

РАЗГОНЕ
в разгоне, Р-54

РАЗГОНИШЬСЯ
не разгонишься, Р-55

РАЗГОНУ
с разгону, Р-53

РАЗГОНЯТЬ
разгонять кровь, К-411

РАЗГОРЕЛАСЬ
кровь разгорелась, К-403

РАЗГОРЕЛИСЬ
глаза (и зубы) разгорелись, Г-63
зубы разгорелись, Г-63

РАЗГРАБЛЕНИЕ
поток и разграбление, П-431

РАЗГРАБЛЕНИЮ
потоку и разграблению, П-431

РАЗГРОМИТЬ
разгромить наголову, Р-40

РАЗДАВИТЬ
муху раздавить, М-306
раздавить бутылку, Б-250

РАЗДЕЛАТЬ
разделать под орех, О-98

РАЗДЕЛЫВАТЬ
разделывать под орех, О-98

РАЗДОРА
яблоко раздора, Я-5

РАЗДРАЗНИТЬ
раздразнить гусей, Г-444

РАЗДУВАТЬ
раздувать кадило, К-3

РАЗДУЙ
раздуй тебя горой!, Г-349

РАЗДУТЬ
раздуть кадило, К-3

РАЗЕ
в таком разе, С-366
ни в каком разе, С-370
ни в коем разе, С-370

РАЗЕВАТЬ
разевать рот ⟨рты⟩, Р-180

РАЗЖАТЬ
разжать губы ⟨зубы⟩, Г-441

РАЗЖЕВАТЬ
разжевать и в рот положить, Р-181

РАЗЖЁВЫВАТЬ
разжёвывать и в рот класть, Р-181

РАЗЖИМАТЬ
разжимать губы ⟨зубы⟩, Г-441

РАЗЗВОНИТЬ
раззвонить в ⟨во все⟩ колокола, К-202

РАЗИНУТЬ
разинуть рот ⟨рты⟩, Р-180

РАЗЛАМЫВАЕТСЯ
башка разламывается, Г-209

голова разламывается, Г-209

РАЗЛЕТАТЬСЯ
разлетаться прахом, П-498

РАЗЛЕТЕТЬСЯ
разлететься прахом, П-498

РАЗЛИВАННОЕ
разливанное море, М-257

РАЗЛИВАТЬСЯ
разливаться соловьём, С-472

РАЗЛИВНОЕ
разливное море, М-257

РАЗЛИТЬ
водой не разлить, В-179

РАЗЛИЧНОГО
различного рода, Р-126

РАЗЛОЖИТЬ
разложить по полкам ⟨по полочкам⟩, П-314

РАЗЛЮЛИ
разлюли малина, М-10

РАЗМАХА
с размаха, Р-56
со всего размаха, Р-56

РАЗМАХОМ
с размахом, Р-57

РАЗМАХУ
с размаху, Р-56
со всего размаху, Р-56

РАЗМЕНИВАТЬ
разменивать на всякую мелочь, М-65
разменивать на мелкую монету, М-65
разменивать на мелочи ⟨мелочь⟩, М-65

РАЗМЕНИВАТЬСЯ
размениваться на всякую мелочь, М-66
размениваться на мелкую монету, М-66
размениваться на мелочи, М-66
размениваться по мелочам, М-66

РАЗМЕНЯТЬ
разменять на всякую мелочь, М-65
разменять на мелкую монету, М-65
разменять на мелочи ⟨мелочь⟩, М-65

РАЗМЕНЯТЬСЯ
разменяться на всякую мелочь, М-66
разменяться на мелкую монету, М-66
разменяться на мелочи, М-66
разменяться по мелочам, М-66

РАЗМИНАТЬ
разминать кости ⟨косточки⟩, К-322

РАЗМЯТЬ
размять кости ⟨косточки⟩, К-322

РАЗНИЦА
большая разница, Р-58

какая разница?, Р-59

РАЗНИЦЫ
две большие разницы, Р-60

РАЗНОГО
из разного теста, Т-89
испечены из разного теста, Т-89
разного рода, Р-126
сделаны из разного теста, Т-89

РАЗНОСТИ
разные разности, Р-61

РАЗНЫЕ
разные разности, Р-61

РАЗНЫХ
говорить на разных языках, Я-52
разных мастей, М-41

РАЗОБРАЛА
злость разобрала, З-132

РАЗОБРАЛО
зло разобрало, З-132

РАЗОБРАТЬ
разобрать по косточкам, К-326

РАЗОГНАТЬ
разогнать кровь, К-411

РАЗОЛЬЁШЬ
водой не разольёшь, В-179

РАЗОМ
раз за разом, Р-31
разом густо, разом пусто, Р-62

РАЗОРВАЛО
чтоб его ⟨тебя⟩ разорвало!, Р-63

РАЗОРВИСЬ
хоть (пополам) разорвись, Р-64

РАЗОШЛИСЬ
дороги разошлись, П-649
пути разошлись, П-649

РАЗРАЗИ
разрази меня бог ⟨господь⟩, Б-125
разрази меня гром (на этом месте), Г-406
разрази меня силы небесные, Г-406
разрази тебя гром ⟨громом⟩, Г-407

РАЗРАЗИТ
да разразит меня бог ⟨господь⟩, Б-125
да разразит меня гром, Г-406
да разразит тебя бог ⟨господь⟩, Г-407
пускай ⟨пусть⟩ разразит меня гром, Г-406
пусть разразит тебя бог ⟨господь⟩, Г-407

РАЗРАЗЯТ
да разразят меня силы небесные, Г-406
пускай ⟨пусть⟩ разразят меня силы небесные, Г-406

РАЗРЕЗЕ
в разрезе, Р-65
РАЗРЕШАТЬСЯ
разрешаться от бремени, Б-206
РАЗРЕШЕНИЯ
с вашего разрешения, П-268
РАЗРЕШИТЬСЯ
разрешиться от бремени, Б-206
РАЗРЫВАЕТСЯ
душа разрывается на части, С-142
сердце разрывается на части, С-142
РАЗРЫВАТЬ
разрывать на части, Ч-27
РАЗРЫВАТЬСЯ
разрываться на части, Ч-26
РАЗРЯДИТЬ
разрядить атмосферу, А-48
РАЗУ
ни разу не, Р-66
раз от разу, Р-34
РАЗУЙ
разуй бельма, Г-94
разуй глаза, Г-94
РАЗУМ
наставить ⟨наставлять⟩ на разум, У-78
ум за разум заходит/зашёл, У-79
РАЗУМА
набираться/набраться разума ⟨ума-разума⟩, У-86
РАЗУМЕЕТ
сытый голодного не разумеет, С-739
РАЗУМЕЕТСЯ
само собой разумеется, С-9
РАЗЫГРАЛАСЬ
кровь разыгралась, К-403
РАЗЫГРАТЬ
разыграть дурака ⟨дуру⟩, Д-336
разыграть роль, Р-156
РАЗЫГРЫВАТЬ
разыгрывать дурака ⟨дуру⟩, Д-336
разыгрывать комедию, К-215
разыгрывать роль, Р-156
разыгрывать шута ⟨горохового⟩, Ш-98
РАЙ
и рад бы в рай, да грехи не пускают, Р-67
на чужой спине в рай въехать, Г-323
на чужом горбу в рай въехать, Г-323
рад бы в рай, да грехи не пускают, Р-67

рай земной, Р-68
с милым рай и в шалаше, М-164
РАК
как рак, Р-69
как рак на мели, Р-70
когда рак (на горе) свистнет, Р-71
на безрыбье и рак рыба, Б-48
пока рак (на горе) свистнет, Р-71
РАКИ
знать, где раки зимуют, Р-72
показать, где раки зимуют, Р-73
узнать, где раки зимуют, Р-74
РАМКАХ
держать себя в рамках (приличия), Р-75
РАНГАХ
табель о рангах, Т-1
РАНЖИРУ
по ранжиру, Р-76
РАННИЙ
из молодых, да ранний, М-237
молодой да ранний, М-237
РАННЯЯ
ранняя пташка, П-613
РАНО
кто рано встаёт, тому бог (по)даёт, В-346
рано или поздно, Р-77
рано пташечка запела, как бы кошечка не съела, П-612
РАНУ
бередить ⟨разбередить⟩ рану, Р-78
сыпать соль на рану, С-477
РАНЫ
бередить ⟨разбередить⟩ раны, Р-78
проливать/пролить бальзам на раны, Б-17
сыпать соль на раны, С-477
РАНЬШЕ
раньше времени, В-298
раньше смерти не помрёшь ⟨не умрёшь⟩, С-393
раньше срока, В-298
раньше чем, Ч-60
РАСКАЛЫВАЕТСЯ
башка раскалывается, Г-209
голова раскалывается, Г-209
РАСКИДЫВАТЬ
раскидывать мозгами, У-109
раскидывать умом, У-109
РАСКИНУТЬ
раскинуть мозгами, У-109
раскинуть умом, У-109
РАСКЛАДЫВАТЬ
раскладывать по полкам ⟨по полочкам⟩, П-314

РАСКРЫВАТЬ
раскрывать глаза, Г-85
раскрывать душу, Д-427
раскрывать игру, И-16
раскрывать карты, К-99
раскрывать рот ⟨рты⟩, Р-180
раскрывать свои карты, К-99
РАСКРЫТЬ
раскрыть глаза, Г-85
раскрыть душу, Д-427
раскрыть игру, И-16
раскрыть карты, К-99
раскрыть рот ⟨рты⟩, Р-180
раскрыть свои карты, К-99
РАСПАХИВАТЬ
распахивать душу, Д-427
РАСПАХНУТЬ
распахнуть душу, Д-427
РАСПОЛАГАЕТ
человек предполагает, а бог располагает, Ч-52
РАСПОЛОЖЕНИЕ
расположение духа, Р-79
РАСПОРЯЖЕНИЕ
в распоряжение, Р-80
РАСПОРЯЖЕНИИ
в распоряжении, Р-80
РАСПРАВА
расправа короткая, Р-81
РАСПРАВИТЬ
расправить крылья, К-433
РАСПРАВЛЯТЬ
расправлять крылья, К-433
РАСПРОСТЁРТЫМИ
с распростёртыми объятиями, О-36
РАСПУСКАТЬ
распускать глотку, Г-344
распускать горло, Г-344
распускать нюни, Н-265
распускать павлиний хвост, Х-17
распускать пышный хвост, Х-17
распускать руки, Р-312
распускать слюни, С-385
распускать сопли, С-491
распускать хвост, Х-17
распускать язык, Я-26
РАСПУСТИТЬ
распустить глотку, Г-344
распустить горло, Г-344
распустить нюни, Н-265
распустить павлиний хвост, Х-17
распустить пышный хвост, Х-17
распустить руки, Р-312
распустить слюни, С-385
распустить сопли, С-491
распустить хвост, Х-17
распустить язык, Я-26
РАСПУТЬЕ
на распутье, Р-82
РАСПУХЛА
голова распухла, Г-206

РАССКАЖИ
расскажи это кому-нибудь другому, Б-7
расскажи это своей бабушке ⟨тёте⟩, Б-7
РАССКАЗЫВАЙ
рассказывай это кому-нибудь другому, Б-7
рассказывай это своей бабушке ⟨тёте⟩, Б-7
РАССКАЗЫВАТЬ
рассказывать сказки, С-218
РАССРОЧКУ
в рассрочку, Р-83
РАССТАВИТЬ
расставить акценты, А-22
расставить сети, С-159
РАССТАВЛЯТЬ
расставлять акценты, А-22
расставлять сети, С-159
РАССТЕГНУТЬ
расстегнуть глотку, Р-182
расстегнуть рот, Р-182
РАССТОЯНИИ
держать на известном ⟨почтительном⟩ расстоянии, Р-84
держать на расстоянии, Р-84
держаться на известном ⟨почтительном⟩ расстоянии, Р-85
держаться на расстоянии, Р-85
РАССУДИТЬ
рассудить за благо, Б-74
РАССУДКА
лишаться/лишиться рассудка, У-85
РАССУДКЕ
в здравом рассудке, У-95
в полном рассудке, У-95
в твёрдом рассудке, У-95
мешаться в рассудке, У-99
повредиться в рассудке, У-99
помешаться в рассудке, У-99
тронуться в рассудке, У-99
РАССУДКОМ
мешаться рассудком, У-99
повредиться рассудком, У-99
помешаться рассудком, У-99
тронуться рассудком, У-99
РАССУДОК
потерять ⟨терять⟩ рассудок, У-85
РАССЫПАТЬ
рассыпать бисер перед свиньями, Б-69
РАССЫПАТЬСЯ
рассыпаться мелким бесом, Б-60
рассыпаться прахом, П-498
РАСТАЯЛ
лёд растаял, Л-40

РАСТВОРЯЙ
пришла беда – растворяй ворота, Б-42

РАСТЕКАТЬСЯ
растекаться мыслью по древу, М-313

РАСТЕНИЕ
оранжерейное растение, Р-86
тепличное растение, Р-86

РАСТЕРЕТЬ
плюнуть да ⟨и⟩ растереть, П-203

РАСТИ
расти над собой, Р-87
хоть трава не расти, Т-193

РАСТОПИТЬ
растопить лёд, Л-43

РАСТРАТИТЬ
растратить по мелочам ⟨по мелочи⟩, М-65

РАСТРЕЗВОНИТЬ
растрезвонить в ⟨во все⟩ колокола, К-202

РАСТРЁПАННЫХ
в растрёпанных чувствах, Ч-195

РАСТРЯСАТЬ
растрясать жир(ок), Ж-75

РАСТРЯСТИ
растрясти жир(ок), Ж-75

РАСХЛЁБЫВАЙ
сам кашу заварил, сам и расхлёбывай, К-118

РАСХЛЁБЫВАТЬ
расхлёбывать кашу, К-117

РАСХОД
ввести ⟨вводить⟩ в расход, Р-89
вывести ⟨выводить⟩ в расход, Р-88
пускать/пустить в расход, Р-88
списать ⟨списывать⟩ в расход, Р-88

РАСХОДЫ
ввести ⟨вводить⟩ в расходы, Р-89

РАСХОДЯТСЯ
дороги расходятся, П-649
пути расходятся, П-649

РАСЧЁТ
брать в расчёт, Р-91
брать расчёт, Р-90
взять в расчёт, Р-91
взять расчёт, Р-90
принимать/принять в расчёт, Р-91
расчёт короткий, Р-81

РАСЧЁТЕ
в расчёте, Р-92, Р-93

РАСЧЁТОМ
с расчётом, Р-93

РАСЧИСТИТЬ
расчистить почву, П-454

РАСЧИЩАТЬ
расчищать почву, П-454

РАСШИБАТЬСЯ
расшибаться в лепёшку, Л-53

РАСШИБИТЬСЯ
расшибиться в лепёшку, Л-53

РВАНУТЬ
рвануть когти, К-159
рвануть с места, М-88

РВАТЬ
рвать глотку, Г-339
рвать горло, Г-339
рвать и метать, Р-94
рвать когти, К-159
рвать на себе волосы, В-243
рвать на части, Ч-27
с руками рвать, Р-262

РВАТЬСЯ
рваться в бой, Б-149
рваться на части, Ч-26

РВЁТ
на ходу подмётки рвёт, Х-68
с души рвёт, Д-393

РВЁТСЯ
где тонко, там и рвётся, Р-95
душа рвётся на части, С-142
сердце рвётся на части, С-142

РЕАЛЬНОЙ
стоять на реальной почве, П-450

РЁБРА
пересчитать рёбра, Р-96

РЕБРОМ
последний грош ребром поставить ⟨ставить⟩, К-284
последнюю копейку ребром поставить ⟨ставить⟩, К-284
поставить ⟨ставить⟩ вопрос ребром, В-260

РЕБЯТИШКАМ
ребятишкам на молочишко, Д-189

РЕБЯЧЕСКИЙ
ребяческий лепет, Л-52

РЕБЯЧЕСТВО
впадать/впасть в ребячество, Д-190

РЕВЕТЬ
реветь белугой, Б-52
ревма реветь, Р-97

РЕВМЯ
ревмя реветь, Р-97

РЕДКО
редко, да метко, Р-98

РЕДКОСТЬ
в редкость, Р-99
музейная редкость, Р-100
на редкость, Р-101

РЕДЬКА
как горькая редька, Р-102

РЕДЬКИ
пуще горькой редьки, Р-102
хрен редьки не слаще, Х-101
хуже горькой редьки, Р-102

РЕЖЕТ
на ходу подмётки режет, Х-68

РЕЗАНУТЬ
как* ножом резануть (по сердцу), Н-191

РЕЗАНЫЙ
как резаный, Р-103

РЕЗАТЬ
без ножа резать, Н-185
по живому резать, Ж-31
резать глаз ⟨глаза⟩, Г-95
резать правду в глаза, П-484
резать правду-матку (в глаза), П-484
резать слух, У-160
резать ухо ⟨уши⟩, У-160

РЕЗИНУ
тянуть резину, Р-104

РЕЗНУТЬ
как* ножом резнуть (по сердцу), Н-191

РЕЗУЛЬТАТЕ
в результате, Р-105

РЕЗЦА
выйти ⟨выходить⟩ из-под резца, Р-106

РЕКИ
молочные реки и кисельные берега, Р-107
молочные реки, кисельные берега, Р-107

РЕКРУТЫ
забрить (лоб) в рекруты, Л-115

РЕКУ
кануть в реку забвения, Л-68
хоть в реку, В-191
хоть с моста в реку, В-191

РЕЛЬСЫ
перевести ⟨переводить⟩ на рельсы, Р-108
перейти ⟨переходить⟩ на рельсы, Р-109
поставить ⟨ставить⟩ на рельсы, Р-108
становиться/стать на рельсы, Р-109

РЕПЫ
дешевле пареной репы, Р-110
проще пареной репы, Р-111

РЕЧИ
дар речи, Д-23
и речи быть не может, Р-112
не может быть и речи, Р-112
речи быть не может, Р-112

РЕЧЬ
вести речь, Р-113
о чём речь!, Р-50
речь идёт, Р-114
суконная речь, Я-28
эзоповская речь, Я-34

РЕШАТЬ
решать жизни, Ж-44

РЕШАТЬСЯ
решаться жизни, Ж-45
решаться ума, У-91

РЕШЕНИЕ
соломоново решение, Р-115

РЕШЕНО
решено и подписано, Р-116

РЕШЕТЕ
носить воду в решете, В-189
таскать воду в решете, В-189
чудеса в решете, Ч-200

РЕШЁТКОЙ
за решёткой, Р-117

РЕШЁТКУ
за решётку, Р-117

РЕШЕТОМ
носить воду решетом, В-189
таскать воду решетом, В-189
черпать воду решетом, В-189

РЕШИТЬ
решить жизни, Ж-44

РЕШИТЬСЯ
решиться жизни, Ж-45
решиться ума, У-91

РЖАВЕЕТ
старая любовь не ржавеет, Л-163

РИГУ
поехал в Ригу, Р-118

РИЗ
до положения риз, П-312

РИСК
на свой (собственный) страх и риск, С-627
риск – благородное дело, Р-119

РОБКОГО
не (из) робкого десятка, Д-186

РОВЁН
не ровён час, Ч-14

РОВНОГО
для ровного счёта, С-716

РОВНОМ
на ровном месте, М-106
шишка на ровном месте, Ш-71

РОВНЫМ
ровным счётом, С-721, С-722

РОГ
гнуть в бараний рог, Р-120
рог изобилия, Р-121
свернуть в бараний рог, Р-120
скрутить в бараний рог, Р-120
согнуть в бараний рог, Р-120

РОГА
брать/взять быка за рога, Б-256
к дьяволу на рога, Ч-105
к чёрту ⟨к чертям⟩ на рога, Ч-105

и карты в руки, К-97
и книги в руки, К-97
играть в четыре руки,
Р-290
идти в руки, Р-303
из рук в руки, Р-211
искать руки, Р-307
карты в руки, К-97
книги в руки, К-97
козыри ⟨козырь⟩ в руки,
К-175
лизать руки, П-679
ломать руки, Р-291
лучше синица в руки, чем
журавль в небе, С-195
марать руки, Р-292
мастер на все руки, М-42
мастерица на все руки,
М-42
мозолить руки, Р-293
на все руки, Р-294
на руки, Р-295
нагревать/нагреть руки,
Р-284
накладывать/наложить на
себя руки, Р-296
не брать в руки, Р-297
не с руки, Р-298
не сули журавля в небе, а
дай синицу в руки, С-195
ноги в руки, Н-140
обагрить ⟨обагрять⟩ руки
в крови ⟨кровью⟩, Р-299
обжечь себе руки, П-25
опускать/опустить руки,
Р-300
от руки, Р-301
отсохни (у меня) руки и
ноги!, Р-302
пачкать руки, Р-292
первой руки, Р-276
плыть в руки, Р-303
погреть руки, Р-284
под руки, Р-304
попадать(ся) в руки, Р-305
попасть(ся) в руки, Р-305
приложить руки, Р-306,
Р-366
пройти через руки, Р-308
просить руки, Р-307
проситься в руки, Р-303
проходить через руки,
Р-308
рабочие руки, Р-309
развязать руки, Р-310
развязать себе руки, Р-311
развязывать руки, Р-310
развязывать себе руки,
Р-311
распускать/распустить
руки, Р-312
руки в брюки, Р-313
руки вверх!, Р-314
руки загребущие (, глаза
завидущие), Р-315
руки зачесались, Р-324
руки зудят, Р-324
руки как крюки, Р-317
руки коротки, Р-316
руки-крюки, Р-317
руки не доходят/не дошли,
Р-318

руки не отвалятся, Р-319
руки не отсохнут, Р-319
руки опускаются/
опустились, Р-320
руки отваливаются/
отвалились, Р-321
руки по швам!, Р-322
руки прочь, Р-323
руки чешутся, Р-324
с лёгкой руки, Р-325
с рук на руки, Р-219
связать ⟨связывать⟩ руки,
Р-250
складывать руки, Р-326
сложа руки, Р-327
сложить руки, Р-326
средней руки, Р-328
стоять руки по швам,
Р-285
укорачивать/укоротить
руки, Р-329
умывать/умыть руки,
Р-330
чтоб у меня руки (и ноги)
отсохли!, Р-302

РУКОЙ
голой рукой, Р-254
живой рукой, Р-331
как* рукой сняло, Р-332
махнуть рукой, Р-333
под рукой, Р-334, Р-335,
Р-336, Р-337
рука с рукой, Р-232
рукой не достанешь ⟨не
достать⟩, Р-338
рукой подать, Р-339
пойти с протянутой рукой,
Р-340
ходить с протянутой
рукой, Р-340
щедрой рукой, Р-341

РУКОПИСИ
рукописи не горят, Р-342

РУКОЮ
под рукою, Р-336, Р-337

РУКУ
давать руку на отсечение,
Г-250
дай ему палец, он и всю
руку откусит, П-3
дать руку на отсечение,
Г-250
держать руку, С-611
запускать/запустить руку,
Р-343
играть на руку, Р-344
иметь руку, Р-345
на живую руку, Р-346
на руку, Р-347
на руку нечист, Р-348
на скорую руку, Р-349
на широкую руку, Р-350
набивать/набить руку,
Р-351
накладывать/наложить
руку, Р-352
нечистый на руку, Р-348
об руку, Р-232
отдавать/отдать руку (и
сердце), Р-353
охулки на руку не класть
⟨не положить⟩, О-180

под весёлую руку, Р-354
под горячую руку, Р-355
под пьяную руку, Р-356
под руку, Р-357, Р-358
под сердитую руку, Р-359
подавать руку, Р-360
подавать руку помощи,
Р-367
подать руку, Р-360
подать руку помощи,
Р-367
подвернуться
⟨подвёртываться⟩ под
руку, Р-363
подворачиваться под руку,
Р-363
поднимать/поднять руку,
Р-361
подымать руку, Р-361
позолотить руку, Р-376
поймать за руку, Р-370
положа руку на сердце,
Р-362
положив(ши) руку на
сердце, Р-362
попадать(ся) под руку,
Р-363
попасть(ся) под руку, Р-363
похулы на руку не класть
⟨не положить⟩, О-180
предлагать/предложить
руку (и сердце), Р-364
приложить руку, Р-365,
Р-366
протягивать руку
(помощи), Р-367
протянуть руку, Р-367,
Р-368
протянуть руку помощи,
Р-367
рука в руку, Р-232
рука об руку, Р-232
рука руку моет, Р-233
скор(ый) на руку, Р-369
сон на руку, С-485
схватить за руку, Р-370
сыграть на руку, Р-344
тяжёл(ый) на руку, Р-371
тянуть руку, С-614

РУЛЯ
без руля и без ветрил,
Р-372

РУСЛО
вернуться в обычное
⟨привычное⟩ русло,
К-198
вернуться в ⟨своё⟩ русло,
К-198
возвращаться в обычное
⟨привычное⟩ русло,
К-198
возвращаться в ⟨своё⟩
русло, К-198
войти в обычное
⟨привычное⟩ русло,
К-198
войти в ⟨своё⟩ русло, К-198
входить в обычное
⟨привычное⟩ русло,
К-198
входить в ⟨своё⟩ русло,
К-198

РУССКИМ
русским языком, Я-58
РУЧАТЬСЯ
ручаться головой, Г-238
РУЧКЕ
прикладываться/
приложиться к ручке,
Р-373
подойти ⟨подходить⟩ к
ручке, Р-373
РУЧКИ
до ручки, Р-374
РУЧКОЙ
делать/сделать ручкой,
Р-375
РУЧКУ
под ручку, Р-357
позолотить ручку, Р-376
РУЧЬЯ
в три ручья, Р-377
РЫБА
биться как рыба об лёд,
Р-378
как рыба, Р-379
как рыба в воде, Р-380
на безрыбье и рак рыба,
Б-48
ни рыба ни мясо, Р-381
рыба с головы воняет
⟨гниёт, тухнет⟩, Р-382
РЫБАК
рыбак рыбака видит
издалека, Р-383
РЫБАКА
рыбак рыбака видит
издалека, Р-383
РЫБЕ
как рыбе зонтик, Р-384
РЫБКЕ
как рыбке зонтик, Р-384
РЫБУ
в мутной воде рыбу
ловить, В-177
не учи рыбу плавать,
Р-385
РЫБЬЕМ
на рыбьем меху, М-136
РЫЖИЙ
я рыжий, Р-386
РЫЛА
ни уха ни рыла, У-155
с рыла, Р-387
РЫЛО
воротить рыло, Н-210
кувшинное рыло, Р-388
на рыло, Р-389
отворотить рыло, Н-210
РЫЛОМ
рылом не вышел, Р-390
РЫЛУ
не по рылу, Р-391
РЫЛЬЦЕ
рыльце в пуху ⟨в пушку⟩,
Р-392
РЫСАКАМИ
были когда-то и мы
рысаками, Р-393
РЫСЬ
во всю рысь, Р-394

этот свет, С-65
явиться ⟨являться⟩ на
    свет, С-54

СВЕТА
выходец с того света,
    В-386
на край света, К-353
на краю света, К-372
света белого ⟨божьего⟩ не
    видеть, С-66
света божьего невзвидеть,
    С-66
света не видеть, С-66
света невзвидеть, С-66
сгонять/согнать со света,
    С-68
сживать/сжить со света,
    С-68
только и света в окне ⟨в
    окошке⟩, С-74

СВЕТЕ
в радужном свете, С-69
в розовом свете, С-69
в свете, С-70 С-71
во всём белом свете, С-39
на (всём) белом свете,
    С-39
не жилец на (белом) свете,
    Ж-72
не жилец на этом свете,
    Ж-72
не знать, на каком свете,
    С-72
ни за что на свете, Ч-171

СВЕТИЛО
восходящее светило, З-90

СВЕТИТ
не светит, С-73

СВЕТЛАЯ
светлая голова, Г-218

СВЕТЛОЙ
светлой памяти, П-30

СВЕТУ
по белому ⟨белу⟩ свету,
    С-39
свету (божьего)
    невзвидеть, С-67
сгонять/согнать со свету,
    С-68
сживать/сжить со свету,
    С-68
только и свету в окне ⟨в
    окошке⟩, С-74

СВЕТЫ
батюшки светы!, Б-29
матушки светы!, Б-29

СВЕЧ
игра не стоит свеч, И-11

СВЕЧА
ни богу свеча ни чёрту
    кочерга, Б-137

СВЕЧКА
ни богу свечка ни чёрту
    кочерга, Б-137

СВЕЧКИ
Москва от копеечной
    свечки загорелась
    ⟨сгорела⟩, М-261

СВИДАНИЕМ
со свиданием, С-76

СВИДАНИЯ
до (скорого) свидания,
    С-75

СВИДАНЬИЦЕМ
со свиданьицем, С-76

СВИДЕТЕЛЬСТВОВАТЬ
свидетельствовать в
    пользу, П-324

СВИНЕЦ
свинец на душе, С-77
свинец на сердце, С-77

СВИНЦОМ
как* свинцом налита, С-78
лечь свинцом на душу,
    С-79
лечь свинцом на сердце,
    С-79

СВИНЬЕ
гусь свинье не товарищ,
    Г-447

СВИНЬЮ
подкладывать/подложить
    свинью, С-80

СВИНЬЯ
бог не выдаст, свинья не
    съест, Б-100
господь не выдаст, свинья
    не съест, Б-100
как свинья, С-81
как свинья в апельсинах,
    С-82

СВИНЬЯМ
к свиньям, Ч-110
ко всем свиньям, Ч-110

СВИНЬЯМИ
метать бисер перед
    свиньями, Б-69
рассыпать бисер перед
    свиньями, Б-69

СВИСТАТЬ
в кулак свистать, К-462

СВИСТЕТЬ
в кулак свистеть, К-462

СВИСТИТ
ветер свистит в карманах
    ⟨в кармане⟩, В-70

СВИСТНЕТ
когда рак (на горе)
    свистнет, Р-71
пока рак (на горе)
    свистнет, Р-71

СВИТЬ
свить (себе) гнездо, Г-156

СВИХНУТЬ
свихнуть с ума, У-91
свихнуть (себе) шею, Ш-58

СВИХНУТЬСЯ
свихнуться с ума, У-91

СВИЩИ
ищи да свищи, В-74

СВОБОДНО
свободно вздохнуть, В-101

СВОДИТЬ
не сводить взгляда
    ⟨взора⟩, Г-31
не сводить глаз, Г-31
сводить в гроб, Г-396
сводить в могилу, М-204
сводить к нулю, Н-260

сводить концы с концами,
    К-263
сводить на нет, С-83
сводить с ума, У-90
сводить счёты, С-728

СВОДИТЬСЯ
сводиться к нулю, Н-261

СВОЁ
брать под своё крылышко,
    К-429
брать своё, С-84
брать своё начало, Н-36
брать своё слово назад
    ⟨обратно⟩, С-280
браться не за своё дело,
    Д-69
в своё время, В-301
в своё удовольствие, У-47
вернуться в своё русло,
    К-198
вести своё начало, Н-37
взять под своё крылышко,
    К-429
взять своё, С-84
взять своё слово назад
    ⟨обратно⟩, С-280
взяться не за своё дело,
    Д-69
вмешиваться не в своё
    дело, Д-111
возвращаться в своё русло,
    К-198
войти в своё русло, К-198
всё в своё время, В-312
всему своё время, В-312
встало на своё место, М-99
всяк кулик своё болото
    хвалит, К-467
всякому овощу своё время,
    О-44
входить в своё русло,
    К-198
гнуть своё, Л-75
делать своё дело, Д-77
держать своё слово, С-313
знать своё место, М-112
каждому овощу своё
    время, О-44
каждому своё, К-4
лезть не в своё дело, Д-111
отживать/отжить своё
    (время), В-21
показать своё ⟨истинное⟩
    лицо, Л-98
показать своё настоящее
    лицо, Л-98
поставить всё на своё
    место, М-98
поставить на своё место,
    М-123
своё на уме, У-102
сделать своё дело, Д-77
сдержать своё слово, С-313
сказать своё слово, С-325
соваться не в своё дело,
    Д-111
ставить всё на своё место,
    М-98
ставить на своё место,
    М-123
стало на своё место, М-99

становится на своё место,
    М-99

СВОЕГО
в поте лица своего, П-422
в простоте своего сердца,
    П-587
господин своего слова,
    Х-78
дождаться ⟨дожидаться⟩
    своего часа, Ч-21
ждать своего часа, Ч-21
живота своего не жалеть,
    Ж-43
не видеть дальше своего
    ⟨собственного⟩ носа,
    Н-225
ниже своего достоинства,
    Д-297
ожидать своего часа, Ч-21
оседлать своего
    ⟨любимого⟩ конька,
    К-270
по простоте своего сердца,
    П-587
с высоты своего величия,
    В-380
садиться на своего
    ⟨любимого⟩ конька,
    К-270
своего поля ягода ⟨ягодки,
    ягоды⟩, П-327
своего рода, Р-129
сесть на своего
    ⟨любимого⟩ конька,
    К-270
хозяин ⟨хозяйка⟩ своего
    слова, Х-78

СВОЕЙ
в своей стихии, С-575
во всей своей красе, К-363
во всей своей наготе, Н-4
выйти ⟨выходить⟩ из
    своей скорлупы, С-234
вычёркивать/вычеркнуть
    из своей жизни, Ж-41
глядеть со своей
    колокольни, К-204
жизни своей не жалеть,
    Ж-43
играть своей жизнью,
    Ж-66
идти своей дорогой, Д-273
мерить ⟨мерять⟩ своей
    меркой, А-45
на своей собственной
    шкуре, Ш-76
на своей спине, Г-322
на своей шкуре, Ш-76
не в своей тарелке, Т-40
по своей воле, В-221
пойти своей дорогой,
    Д-273
помириться со своей
    совестью, С-459
примириться со своей
    совестью, С-459
расскажи ⟨рассказывай⟩
    это своей бабушке
    ⟨тёте⟩, Б-7
с своей стороны, С-617
своей смертью, С-397

[974]

своей чередой, Ч-69
смотреть со своей
колокольни, К-204
со своей стороны, С-617

СВОЁМ
в большинстве своём,
Б-174
в своём роде, Р-132
в своём уме, У-96
в чужом глазу сучок
видим, а в своём (и)
бревна не замечаем,
Г-140
всё на своём месте, М-101
вывезти ⟨вывозить⟩ на
своём горбу, П-186
вынести ⟨выносить⟩ на
своём горбу, П-186
единственный в своём
роде, Р-134
на своём горбу, Г-322
на своём горьком опыте,
О-96
на своём месте, М-103
настаивать/настоять на
своём, С-85
несть ⟨нет⟩ пророка в
отечестве своём ⟨в
своём отечестве⟩, П-581
поставить на своём, С-85
стоять на своём, С-86
упереться на своём, С-86

СВОЕМУ
господин своему слову,
Х-78
к стыду своему, С-655
по своему обыкновению,
О-39
свой своему поневоле брат
⟨друг⟩, Б-200
хозяин ⟨хозяйка⟩ своему
слову, Х-78

СВОИ
брать в свои руки, Р-278
брать свои слова назад
⟨обратно⟩, С-280
взвесить ⟨взвешивать⟩
свои слова, С-281
взять в свои руки, Р-278
взять свои слова назад
⟨обратно⟩, С-280
войти в свои права, П-469
встало на свои места,
М-99
вступать/вступить в свои
права, П-469
входить в свои права,
П-469
вывернуть
⟨выворачивать⟩ свои
карманы, К-77
жечь свои корабли, К-289
жечь свои мосты, К-289
как свои пять пальцев,
П-20
класть свои головы, Г-252
не в свои сани не садись,
С-11
осушать/осушить свои
слёзы, С-271
открывать/открыть свои
карты, К-99

поймать в свои сети, С-157
показать/показывать свои
коготки ⟨когти⟩, К-158
положить свои головы,
Г-252
поставить всё на свои
места, М-98
раскрывать/раскрыть
свои карты, К-99
свои люди — сочтёмся,
Л-173
свои собаки грызутся
⟨дерутся⟩, чужая не
приставай ⟨не подходи⟩,
С-447
сжечь свои корабли, К-289
сжечь свои мосты, К-289
сжигать свои корабли,
К-289
сжигать свои мосты,
К-289
сложить свои головы,
Г-252
сложить свои кости, К-323
ставить всё на свои места,
М-98
стало на свои места, М-99
становится на свои места,
М-99

СВОИМ
блистать своим
отсутствием, О-170
в Тулу со своим самоваром
не ездят, Т-231
в чужой монастырь со
своим уставом не ходят,
М-251
дойти ⟨доходить⟩ своим
(собственным) умом,
У-105
жить своим умом, У-106
идти своим путём, Д-273
мерить ⟨мерять⟩ своим
аршином, А-45
не верить своим глазам,
Г-102
не верить своим ушам,
У-174
не поверить своим глазам,
Г-102
не поверить своим ушам,
У-174
не своим голосом, Г-310
пойти своим путём, Д-273
своим горбом, Г-320
своим порядком, П-401
своим умом, У-105
своим ходом, Х-63
своим чередом, Ч-69
соваться ⟨сунуться⟩ со
своим носом, Н-220

СВОИМИ
назвать ⟨называть⟩ вещи
своими именами, В-88
отдуваться своими
боками, Б-154
своими глазами, Г-118
своими руками, Р-263
своими словами, С-299
своими собственными
глазами, Г-118

своими собственными
руками, Р-263
своими (собственными)
ушами, У-176

СВОИХ
вывезти ⟨вывозить⟩ на
своих плечах, П-186
вынести ⟨выносить⟩ на
своих плечах, П-186
до конца своих дней, К-247
на своих (на) двоих, Д-41
не видать ⟨не видеть⟩ как
своих ушей, У-181
не увидеть как своих ушей,
У-181
от своих щедрот, Щ-1
оставаться/остаться при
своих, С-87
отрясти ⟨отряхнуть⟩ прах
от ⟨с⟩ своих ног, П-494
при своих козырях, К-176
своих не узнаешь, У-61
своя своих не познаша,
С-88
стоять на своих ногах,
Н-134

СВОЙ
в свой час, Ч-10
в свой черёд, О-184
внести ⟨вносить⟩ свой
вклад, В-149
всяк сверчок знай свой
шесток, С-38
доживать свой век, В-17
есть свой хлеб, Х-31
за свой счёт, С-698
знай сверчок свой шесток,
С-38
класть живот свой, Ж-55
кончать/кончить свой век,
Ж-56
мерить ⟨мерять⟩ на свой
аршин, А-45
на свой лад, Л-11
на свой манер, Л-11
на свой салтык, Л-11
на свой собственный страх
(и риск), С-627
на свой страх (и риск),
С-627
на свой счёт, С-698
найти свой конец, М-201
отживать/отжить свой
век, В-21
подставить ⟨подставлять⟩
свой лоб, Л-118
положить живот свой,
Ж-55
принимать/принять на
свой счёт, С-711
сам не свой, С-5
свой брат, Б-199
свой в доску, Д-294
свой глаз — алмаз (, а
чужой — стекло), Г-41
свой глаз(ок) — смотрок,
Г-41
свой парень в доску, Д-294
свой своему поневоле брат
⟨друг⟩, Б-200
свой угол, У-33

совать ⟨сунуть⟩ свой нос,
Н-220

СВОРОТИТЬ
своротить гору ⟨горы⟩,
Г-358
своротить с ума, У-91

СВОЮ
в свою очередь, О-184
вести свою линию, Л-75
внести ⟨вносить⟩ свою
лепту, Л-54
войти ⟨входить⟩ в свою
колею, К-198
гнуть свою линию, Л-75
дорого отдавать/отдать
свою жизнь, Ж-53
дорого продавать/продать
свою жизнь, Ж-53
замкнуться ⟨замыкаться⟩
в свою скорлупу, С-233
класть свою голову, Г-252
лить свою кровь, К-410
мерить ⟨мерять⟩ на свою
мерку, А-45
на свою голову, Г-263
обратить ⟨обращать⟩ в
свою веру, В-51
положить свою голову,
Г-252
попадать/попасть в свою
колею, К-198
проливать/пролить свою
кровь, К-410
прятаться в свою
скорлупу, С-233
сложить свою голову,
Г-252
спрятаться в свою
скорлупу, С-233
уйти ⟨уходить⟩ в свою
скорлупу, С-233

СВОЯ
на круги своя, К-423
своя голова на плечах,
Г-219
своя ноша не тянет, Н-247
своя рубаха ⟨рубашка⟩
ближе к телу, Р-190
своя рука владыка, Р-234
своя рука есть ⟨имеется⟩,
Р-345
своя своих не познаша,
С-88
своя шкура, Ш-74

СВЫСОКА
глядеть свысока, С-418
смотреть свысока, С-418

СВЫШЕ
перст свыше, П-108
по наитию свыше, Н-19

СВЯЗАН
одной верёвкой
⟨верёвочкой⟩ связан, В-39
одной цепочкой связан,
В-39

СВЯЗАТЬ
двух слов связать не мочь,
С-275
связать концы с концами,
К-263

к себе, С-96
копать себе могилу, М-203
кусать себе локти, Л-131
ломать себе голову, Г-256
мерить ⟨мерять⟩ по себе, А-45
много воображать о себе, В-256
много думать о себе, В-256
много мнить о себе, В-256
мотать себе на ус, У-129
набивать/набить себе цену, Ц-34
надевать петлю себе на шею, П-128
надевать себе хомут на шею, Х-80
надеть петлю себе на шею, П-128
надеть себе хомут на шею, Х-80
найти себе могилу, М-201
накидывать/накинуть петлю себе на шею, П-128
наматывать/намотать себе на ус, У-129
не в себе, С-97
не мочь найти себе места, М-91
не находить себе места, М-91
не по себе, С-98
ни в чём себе не отказывать, О-147
ни хрена себе!, Х-103
ничего себе, Н-107
обжечь себе пальцы ⟨руки⟩, П-25
оставить ⟨оставлять⟩ при себе, Д-179
отдавать/отдать себе отчёт, О-172
отказывать себе, О-148
по себе, С-99
повесить себе камень на шею, К-38
повесить себе хомут на шею, Х-80
позволить себе лишнее, Л-110
позволить себе роскошь, Р-164
позволять себе лишнее, Л-110
позволять себе роскошь, Р-164
положить себе за правило, П-489
положить себе правилом, П-489
поломать себе голову, Г-256
попортить себе крови, К-409
портить себе кровь, К-409
поставить себе за правило, П-489
поставить себе правилом, П-489
посыпать себе главу ⟨голову⟩ пеплом, Г-269

предоставить ⟨предоставлять⟩ самому себе, П-509
при себе, С-100
пробивать/пробить себе дорогу ⟨путь⟩, Д-284
прокладывать/проложить себе дорогу, Д-286
пускай себе, П-639
пускать/пустить себе пулю в лоб, П-632
пусть себе, П-639
развязать ⟨развязывать⟩ себе руки, Р-311
рвать на себе волосы, В-243
рыть себе могилу, М-203
сам по себе, С-6
сам себе голова ⟨господин⟩, Х-76
сам себе хозяин, Х-76
сама себе голова ⟨госпожа⟩, Х-76
сама себе хозяйка, Х-76
свернуть себе башку, Ш-58
свернуть себе голову, Ш-58
свернуть себе шею, Ш-58
свить себе гнездо, Г-156
свихнуть себе шею, Ш-58
сделать себе имя, И-65
себе в убыток, У-9
себе дороже (стоит), Д-287
себе на голову, Г-263
себе на уме, У-103
слишком много позволить ⟨позволять⟩ себе, Л-110
сломать себе голову ⟨шею⟩, Ш-58
сломить себе голову ⟨шею⟩, Ш-58
создать себе кумир(а), К-472
составить себе имя, И-65
сотворить себе кумир(а), К-472
так себе, Т-24
творить себе кумир(а), К-472

СЕБЯ

бить себя в грудь, Г-421
брать на себя, Б-203
брать на себя смелость, С-389
брать на себя труд, Т-211
брать себя в руки, Р-279
вести себя, В-62
взять на себя, Б-203
взять на себя смелость, С-389
взять на себя труд, Т-211
взять себя в руки, Р-279
вне себя, С-101
вывести ⟨выводить⟩ из себя, В-356
выдавать/выдать себя, В-362
выйти ⟨выходить⟩ из себя, В-388
гречневая каша сама себя хвалит, К-107
давать себя знать, Д-7

давать себя чувствовать, Д-7
дать себя знать, Д-7
дать себя почувствовать, Д-7
дать себя чувствовать, Д-7
делать из себя шута, Ш-98
делать под себя, Д-61
держать себя, Д-180
держать себя в границах (приличия), Р-75
держать себя в рамках (приличия), Р-75
держать себя в руках, Р-272
держать себя в узде, У-58
забывать/забыть себя, З-9
заживо похоронить ⟨хоронить⟩ себя, Х-82
заставить ⟨заставлять⟩ себя ждать, З-77
знать про себя, З-170
из себя, С-102
изживать/изжить себя, И-48
как у себя дома, Д-254
корчить из себя шута, Ш-98
ловить себя, Л-120
много на себя брать/ взять, Б-204
надевать петлю на себя, П-128
надевать на себя хомут ⟨ярмо⟩, Х-80
надеть петлю на себя, П-128
надеть на себя хомут ⟨ярмо⟩, Х-80
найти (самого) себя, Н-20
накидывать/накинуть петлю на себя, П-128
накладывать/наложить на себя руки, Р-296
напускать на себя, Н-28
напускать на себя вид, В-112
напустить на себя, Н-28
напустить на себя вид, В-112
не давать/не дать себя в обиду, О-6
не заставить себя долго ждать, З-78
не заставить себя долго просить ⟨упрашивать⟩, З-76
не заставить себя ждать, З-78
не заставлять себя (долго) ждать, З-78
не знать, куда деть себя, З-174
не знать, куда себя девать/ деть, З-175
не помнить себя, П-333
оставить ⟨оставлять⟩ позади себя, О-121
от себя, С-103
отдать с себя последнюю рубаху ⟨рубашку⟩, Р-196

оторвать ⟨отрывать⟩ от себя, О-164
пенять на себя, П-85
переживать/пережить (самого) себя, П-90
переламывать/переломить себя, П-93
пересиливать/пересилить себя, П-499
повести себя, В-62
погребать себя в четырёх стенах, П-233
погребать себя заживо, П-233
погрести себя в четырёх стенах, П-233
погрести себя заживо, П-233
поймать себя, Л-120
показать ⟨показывать⟩ себя, П-277
поперёк себя толще, Ш-64
поперёк себя шире, Ш-64
поставить себя на место, М-124
постоять за себя, П-415
потерять себя, Т-87
превзойти (самого) себя, П-500
превзмогать/превозмочь себя, П-499
превосходить (самого) себя, П-500
привести в себя, П-516
привести себя в порядок, П-406
приводить в себя, П-516
приводить себя в порядок, П-406
прийти в себя, П-553
принимать на себя, Б-203
принимать на себя труд, Т-211
принять на себя, Б-203
принять на себя труд, Т-211
приходить в себя, П-553
про себя, С-104
разыгрывать из себя шута (горохового), Ш-98
сам за себя говорит, Г-161
сбрасывать/сбросить с себя маску, М-34
сделать под себя, Д-61
сдержать ⟨сдерживать⟩ себя, С-95
себя не забывать/не забыть, З-10
себя не слышать, П-333
снять с себя последнюю рубаху ⟨рубашку⟩, Р-196
ставить себя на место, М-124
строить из себя, С-635
строить из себя шута, Ш-98
сходить под себя, Д-61
терять себя, Т-87
у себя, С-105
углубиться ⟨углубляться⟩ в себя, У-163

уйти ⟨уходить⟩ в себя, У-163
ходить под себя, Д-61

СЕГО
до сего времени, Д-163
малые мира сего, М-18
не от мира сего, М-186
ни с того ни с сего, Т-131
сильные мира сего, С-194

СЕГОДНЯ
не откладывай на завтра то, что можешь ⟨можно⟩ сделать сегодня, О-149
не сегодня-завтра, С-106

СЕГОДНЯШНИЙ
по сегодняшний день, Д-163

СЕГОДНЯШНИМ
жить сегодняшним днём, Д-204

СЕДЛА
выбивать/выбить из седла, С-107
вышибать/вышибить из седла, С-107

СЕДЛО
как (к) корове седло, К-312
как на корове седло, К-313

СЕДЫХ
до седых волос, В-235

СЕДЬМАЯ
седьмая вода на киселе, В-175

СЕДЬМОГО
до седьмого колена, К-183
до седьмого пота, П-421

СЕДЬМОЙ
седьмой сон видеть, С-483
седьмой сон снится, С-483

СЕДЬМОМ
на седьмом взводе, В-94
на седьмом небе, Н-48

СЕЗОН
бархатный сезон, С-108

СЕЙ
до сей поры, П-359
на сей предмет, П-508
по сей день, Д-163
что сей сон значит ⟨означает⟩?, С-486

СЕКРЕТ
не секрет, С-109
секрет полишинеля, С-110

СЕКРЕТА
не делать секрета, С-111

СЕКРЕТЕ
в секрете, С-112

СЕКРЕТОМ
под секретом, С-113

СЕКРЕТУ
по секрету, С-113

СЕКУНДА
секунда в секунду, М-171

СЕКУНДОЧКУ
на секундочку, М-175
одну секундочку!, М-177

СЕКУНДУ
на секунду, М-175

одну секунду!, М-177
секунда в секунду, М-171
сию секунду, М-178

СЕКУНДЫ
ни секунды, М-179

СЕЛЕ
первый парень на селе, П-62

СЕЛУ
ни к селу ни к городу, С-114

СЕЛЬДЕЙ
как сельдей в бочке, С-115

СЕЛЬДИ
как сельди в бочке, С-115

СЁМ
о том (и) о сём, Т-112

СЕМЕЙСТВА
прибавление семейства, П-512

СЕМЕРО
не семеро по лавкам, Л-1
семеро одного не ждут, Ж-10

СЕМИ
семи пядей ⟨пяденей, пядень⟩ во лбу, П-675
у семи нянек дитя без глазу, Н-268

СЕМИМИЛЬНЫЕ
семимильные сапоги, С-16

СЕМИМИЛЬНЫМИ
семимильными шагами, Ш-11

СЕМУ
быть по сему, Б-277

СЕМЬ
для друга (и) семь вёрст не околица, Д-312
для милого дружка (и) семь вёрст не околица, Д-312
драть семь шкур, Ш-79
за семь вёрст киселя есть ⟨хлебать⟩, В-43
пролить семь потов, П-419
сдирать семь шкур, Ш-79
семь бед — один ответ, Б-36
семь вёрст до небес (и всё лесом), В-44
семь потов сгонять/согнать, П-429
семь потов сошло, П-430
семь потов спускать/спустить, П-429
семь пядей ⟨пяденей, пядень⟩ во лбу, П-675
семь пятниц на неделе, П-684
семь раз отмерь ⟨примерь⟩, (а) один (раз) отрежь, Р-37
снять семь шкур, Ш-80
содрать семь шкур, Ш-79
спускать/спустить семь шкур, Ш-80

СЕМЬЕ
в семье не без урода, С-116

СЕМЬЮ
за семью замками, З-57

за семью печатями, П-140
книга за семью печатями, К-147
под семью замками, З-57

СЕМЯ
заронить семя, И-76
крапивное семя, С-117

СЕНА
иголка в стогу сена, И-2
как* иголка в стоге ⟨в стогу⟩ сена, И-2

СЕНЕ
иголка в сене, И-2
(как) собака на сене, С-443

СЕНТЯБРЁМ
смотреть сентябрём, С-118

СЕНЬКЕ
по Сеньке (и) шапка, С-119

СЕНЬЮ
под сенью, С-120

СЕРАЯ
серая кошка пробежала ⟨проскочила⟩, К-346

СЕРДЕЦ
покоритель ⟨покорительница⟩ сердец, П-286

СЕРДЕЧНОЙ
по простоте сердечной, П-587

СЕРДИТО
(и) дёшево и сердито, Д-191

СЕРДИТУЮ
под сердитую руку, Р-359

СЕРДЦА
большого сердца, С-121
в глубине сердца, Г-149
в простоте (своего) сердца, П-587
вырвать ⟨вырывать⟩ из сердца, С-122
дама сердца, Д-20
до глубины сердца, Г-150
камень с сердца свалился, К-43
написать кровью сердца, К-416
от всего сердца, С-123
от доброго сердца, С-124
от полноты сердца, П-302
от чистого сердца, С-125
отлегло от сердца, С-126
отошло от сердца, С-126
оторвать ⟨отрывать⟩ от сердца, С-127
писать кровью сердца, К-416
по простоте (своего) сердца, П-587
с глаз долой — из сердца вон, Г-39
с замиранием сердца, З-56

СЕРДЦАХ
в сердцах, С-128

СЕРДЦЕ
бередить сердце, Д-406
большое сердце, С-129
брать/взять за сердце, Д-407

вкладывать сердце, Д-409
влагать/вложить сердце, Д-409
войти ⟨входить⟩ в сердце, Д-411
выместить ⟨вымещать⟩ сердце, С-130
держать сердце, С-131
забирать/забрать за сердце, Д-407
заглядывать/заглянуть в сердце, Д-419
закрадываться/закрасться в сердце, Д-420
иметь сердце, С-131
как* нож в сердце, Н-180
камень на сердце, К-40
кошки скребут на сердце, К-348
леденить сердце, К-406
лечь свинцом на сердце, С-79
на сердце, Д-383
надорвать ⟨надрывать⟩ сердце, Д-424
нож в сердце, Н-180
облегчать/облегчить сердце, Д-425
оборвалось в сердце, С-141
отвести ⟨отводить⟩ сердце, Д-426
отдавать руку и сердце, Р-353
отдавать сердце, С-132
отдать руку и сердце, Р-353
отдать сердце, С-132
открывать/открыть сердце, С-133
отлегло на сердце, С-126
оторвалось в сердце, С-141
покорить ⟨покорять⟩ сердце, С-134
положа руку на сердце, Р-362
положив(ши) руку на сердце, Р-362
предлагать/предложить руку и сердце, Р-364
разбередить сердце, Д-406
свинец на сердце, С-77
сердце болит, Д-364
сердце ёкает ⟨ёкнуло⟩, С-136
сердце закатилось ⟨закатывается⟩, С-135
сердце замерло ⟨замирает⟩, С-136
сердце заходится/зашлось, С-137
сердце кровью обливается/облилось, С-138
сердце надрывается, Д-367
сердце не камень, С-139
сердце не лежит, Д-369
сердце не на месте, Д-370
сердце ноет, Д-364
сердце оборвалось ⟨обрывается⟩, С-141
сердце оторвалось, С-141

от силы, С-193
подорвать ⟨подрывать⟩
    силы, С-192
порази меня силы
    небесные, Г-406
пускай поразят ⟨разразят⟩
    меня силы небесные,
    Г-406
пусть поразят ⟨разразят⟩
    меня силы небесные,
    Г-406
разрази меня силы
    небесные, Г-406
что есть ⟨было⟩ силы,
    М-271

СИЛЬНАЯ
сильная рука, Р-235

СИЛЬНЫЕ
сильные мира сего, С-194

СИЛЬНЫЙ
сильный пол, П-293

СИНИЙ
синий чулок, Ч-202

СИНИМ
гори ⟨оно⟩ синим огнём,
    О-55
гори ⟨оно⟩ синим
    пламенем, О-55

СИНИЦА
лучше синица в руках ⟨в
    руки⟩, чем журавль в
    небе, С-195
синица в руках, С-196

СИНИЦУ
не сули журавля в небе, а
    дай синицу в руки, С-195

СИНЬ
(ни) синь пороха, П-381

СИНЯ
(ни) синя пороха, П-381

СИНЯЯ
синяя птица, П-621

СИРОТА
казанская ⟨казанский⟩
    сирота, С-197

СИХ
до сих пор, П-359
от сих (и) до сих, С-198

СИЮ
сию минутку ⟨минуту⟩,
    М-178
сию секунду, М-178

СИЯ
миновала сия чаша, Ч-34

СКАЖЕШЬ
ничего не скажешь, С-199
скажешь тоже, С-200

СКАЖИ
не скажи, С-201
скажи на милость, М-160
скажи пожалуйста!, С-202
скажи мне, кто твой друг,
    и я скажу ⟨тебе⟩, кто ты,
    Д-310
слова не скажи, С-293

СКАЖИТЕ
не скажите, С-201
скажите на милость,
    М-160

скажите пожалуйста!,
    С-202

СКАЗ
и весь сказ, Р-46
вот вам ⟨тебе⟩ и весь сказ,
    Р-46

СКАЗАЛА
бабушка (ещё) надвое
    сказала, Б-5

СКАЗАНО
не в обиду будь сказано,
    О-4
не в укор будь сказано,
    У-69
не в упрёк будь сказано,
    У-69
не во гнев будь сказано,
    О-4
не к ночи будь сказано,
    Н-243
сказано – сделано, С-203

СКАЗАТЬ
боюсь сказать, Б-194
вернее сказать, С-208
(да) и то сказать, С-204
к примеру сказать, П-534
к слову сказать, С-338
как вам сказать, С-205
как сказать, С-205
как тебе сказать, С-205
кстати сказать, С-206
легко сказать, С-207
лучше сказать, С-208
можно сказать, С-209
не к ночи сказать, Н-243
нельзя сказать, С-210
нечего сказать, С-211
ни в сказке сказать, ни
    пером описать, С-216
откровенно сказать, Г-174
по правде сказать, П-482
по совести сказать, С-452
по чести сказать, Ч-126
попросту сказать, Г-175
правду сказать, П-482
признаться сказать, П-525
проще сказать, С-208
с позволения сказать,
    П-269
сказать лишнее, Л-111
сказать пару тёплых слов,
    П-69
сказать своё слово, С-325
слова сказать нельзя,
    С-293
словом сказать, С-334
так сказать, С-212
точнее сказать, С-208
чтобы не сказать..., С-213
шутка (ли) сказать, Ш-101

СКАЗКА
сказка про белого бычка,
    С-214
скоро сказка сказывается,
    а ⟨да⟩ не скоро дело
    делается, С-215

СКАЗКЕ
ни в сказке сказать, ни
    пером описать, С-216

СКАЗКИ
бабушкины сказки, С-217

бабьи сказки, С-217
рассказывать сказки, С-218

СКАЗЫВАЕТСЯ
скоро сказка сказывается,
    а ⟨да⟩ не скоро дело
    делается, С-215

СКАКУ
на всём скаку, С-219
на (полном) скаку, С-219

СКАЛИТЬ
скалить зубы, З-201

СКАМЬИ
с университетской скамьи,
    С-220
со школьной скамьи, С-220

СКАТЕРТЬ
как скатерть, П-313

СКАТЕРТЬЮ
скатертью дорога
    ⟨дорожка⟩, С-221

СКАЧКА
скачка с препятствиями,
    С-222

СКВЕРНО
скверно кончить, К-266

СКИДЫВАТЬ
скидывать с плеч, П-176
скидывать со счёта, С-719
скидывать со счетов ⟨со
    счётов⟩, С-719

СКИНУТЬ
скинуть с плеч, П-176
скинуть со счёта, С-719
скинуть со счетов ⟨со
    счётов⟩, С-719

СКИНУТЬСЯ
скинуться на троих, Т-204

СКЛАДУ
(нет) ни складу ни ладу,
    С-223

СКЛАДЫВАТЬ
складывать оружие, О-104
складывать руки, Р-326

СКЛОНЕ
на склоне дней, С-224
на склоне жизни, С-224
на склоне лет, С-224

СКЛОНИТЬ
склонить голову, Г-274

СКЛОНЯТЬ
склонять во всех падежах,
    П-2
склонять голову, Г-274
склонять имена ⟨имя⟩,
    П-2
склонять на все лады, Л-17
склонять по всем
    падежам, П-2

СКОБКАХ
в скобках, С-225

СКОБКИ
вынести ⟨выносить⟩ за
    скобки, С-226

СКОВАТЬ
сковать по рукам и (по)
    ногам, Р-250

СКОВЫВАТЬ
сковывать по рукам и (по)
    ногам, Р-250

СКОК
во весь скок, С-227

СКОЛЬЗИТЬ
скользить по верхам, В-55
скользить по поверхности,
    П-216

СКОЛЬЗКОЙ
катиться/покатиться по
    скользкой дорожке,
    П-197

СКОЛЬКО
бог знает сколько, Б-96
не ахти сколько, А-53
не бог весть сколько, Б-117
не бог знает сколько, Б-117
не приведи бог сколько,
    Б-120
не приведи господи
    сколько, Б-120
не столько... сколько...,
    С-597
сколько бог на душу
    положит, Б-123
сколько бы ни..., С-228
сколько бы то ни было,
    Б-269
сколько верёвку
    ⟨верёвочку⟩ ни вить, а
    концу быть, В-38
сколько верёвочке ни
    виться, а конец будет,
    В-38
сколько влезет, В-167
сколько волка ни корми,
    (а) он (всё) в лес глядит
    ⟨смотрит⟩, В-228
сколько голов, столько (и)
    умов, Г-192
сколько душе угодно,
    Д-385
сколько лет, сколько зим!,
    Л-62
сколько ни..., С-228
сколько ни (на) есть, Е-20
сколько угодно, У-27
сколько хватает ⟨хватал⟩
    глаз, Г-27
сколько хватало глаз
    ⟨глаза, глазу⟩, Г-27
смотря сколько, С-422
чёрт знает сколько, Ч-92
чёрт-те сколько, Ч-92

СКОНЧАНИЯ
до скончания века, С-229
до скончания мира, С-229

СКОПОМ
всем скопом, С-230

СКОР
скор на ногу, Н-171
скор на руку, Р-369

СКОРБЬ
мировая скорбь, С-231

СКОРЕЕ
скорее всего, С-232

СКОРЛУПУ
замкнуться ⟨замыкаться⟩
    в свою скорлупу, С-233
прятаться/спрятаться в
    свою скорлупу, С-233
уйти ⟨уходить⟩ в свою
    скорлупу, С-233

СКОРЛУПЫ
выйти ⟨выходить⟩ из
своей скорлупы, С-234

СКОРО
как скоро, С-235
коль скоро, С-235
много будешь знать —
скоро состаришься,
З-173
скоро сказка сказывается,
а ⟨да⟩ не скоро дело
делается, С-215

СКОРОГО
до скорого (свидания),
С-75

СКОРОМ
в скором времени, В-294

СКОРУЮ
на скорую руку, Р-349

СКОРЧИТЬ
скорчить рожу, Р-146

СКОРЫЙ
скорый на ногу, Н-171
скорый на руку, Р-369

СКРЕБЁТ
скребёт на душе, К-348
скребёт на сердце, К-348

СКРЕБУТ
кошки скребут на душе,
К-348
кошки скребут на сердце,
К-348

СКРЕЖЕТ
скрежет зубовный, С-236

СКРЕЖЕТОМ
со скрежетом зубовным,
С-236

СКРЕПЯ
скрепя сердце, С-143

СКРЕСТИТЬ
скрестить мечи, Ш-84
скрестить оружие, Ш-84
скрестить шпаги, Ш-84

СКРЕЩИВАТЬ
скрещивать мечи, Ш-84
скрещивать оружие, Ш-84
скрещивать шпаги, Ш-84

СКРИВИТЬ
рожу скривить, Р-147

СКРИПКА
вторая скрипка, С-237
первая скрипка, С-238

СКРИПКУ
играть вторую скрипку,
С-239
играть первую скрипку,
С-240

СКРИПОМ
со скрипом, С-241

СКРОЕН
неладно ⟨нескладно, худо⟩
скроен, да крепко
⟨плотно⟩ сшит, С-242

СКРОИТЬ
скроить рожу, Р-146

СКРУТИТЬ
скрутить в бараний рог,
Р-120

СКРЫВАТЬСЯ
скрываться из вида
⟨виду⟩, Г-42

скрываться из ⟨с⟩ глаз,
Г-42

СКРЫТЬСЯ
скрыться из вида ⟨виду⟩,
Г-42
скрыться из ⟨с⟩ глаз, Г-42

СКУКА
скука зелёная ⟨смертная⟩,
Т-166

СКУПИТЬСЯ
не скупиться на краски,
К-368

СКУЧНО
вместе тесно, а врозь
скучно, В-170

СЛАБ
слаб в коленках, К-187
слаб на слезу ⟨на слёзы⟩,
С-266
слаб на язык, Я-27

СЛАБА
гайка слаба, Г-7

СЛАБАЯ
слабая струна ⟨струнка⟩,
С-645

СЛАБИНУ
давать/дать слабину,
С-243

СЛАБОЕ
слабое место, М-122

СЛАБЫЙ
слабый на слезу ⟨на
слёзы⟩, С-266
слабый на язык, Я-27
слабый пол, П-294

СЛАВА
одна слава, Н-15
слава богу, С-244
слава те ⟨тебе⟩ господи,
С-244
только одна слава, Н-15

СЛАВНЫЙ
славный малый, М-19

СЛАВУ
во славу, С-245
на славу, С-246

СЛАДКО
не сладко, С-247

СЛАДА
слада нет, С-248

СЛАДУ
сладу нет, С-248

СЛАЩЕ
хрен редьки не слаще,
Х-101

СЛЕД
и след пропал, С-249
и след простыл, С-249
замести ⟨заметать⟩ след,
С-258
нападать/напасть на след,
С-250
не след, С-251
попадать/попасть на след,
С-250
след в след, С-252
след пропал, С-249
след простыл, С-249
следом в след, С-252

СЛЕДА
без следа, С-253
не осталось и следа, С-254
нет и следа, С-254

СЛЕДАМ
идти по следам, С-599
по горячим следам, С-255
по свежим следам, С-255
пойти по следам, С-599

СЛЕДИТЬ
следить в оба, С-414

СЛЕДОВАТЬ
следовать по стопам,
С-599

СЛЕДОМ
следом в след, С-252
следом за, С-256

СЛЕДУ
по горячему следу, С-255
по свежему следу, С-255

СЛЕДУЕТ
как следует, С-257
послать куда следует,
П-409

СЛЕДЫ
замести ⟨заметать⟩
следы, С-258

СЛЁЗ
до слёз, С-259

СЛЕЗАМ
Москва слезам не верит,
М-262

СЛЕЗАМИ
заливаться слезами, С-260
обливаться слезами, С-260
слезами горю не
поможешь, С-261
умываться слезами, С-260

СЛЕЗАХ
в слезах, С-262
утопать в слезах, С-263

СЛЕЗИНКИ
не проронить (ни)
слезинки, С-270

СЛЕЗОЙ
со слезой, С-264

СЛЕЗУ
пролить слезу, С-265
проронить слезу, С-265
пускать/пустить слезу,
С-265
ронять слезу, С-265
слаб(ый) на слезу, С-266

СЛЕЗЫ/СЛЁЗЫ
глотать слёзы, С-267
дальние проводы —
лишние слёзы, П-566
долгие проводы — лишние
слёзы, П-566
крокодиловы
⟨крокодильи⟩ слёзы,
С-268
лить слёзы, С-269
не проронить слезы, С-270
осушать (свои) слёзы,
С-271
осушить (свои) слёзы,
С-271
отольются слёзы, С-272

проливать/пролить слёзы,
С-269
ронять слёзы, С-269
слаб(ый) на слёзы, С-266

СЛЕПАЯ
слепая курица, К-482

СЛЕТАТЬ
слетать с губ, Я-51
слетать с уст, Я-51
слетать с языка, Я-51

СЛЕТЕТЬ
слететь с губ, Я-51
слететь с уст, Я-51
слететь с языка, Я-51

СЛЕЧЬ
слечь в постель, П-412

СЛИВКИ
снимать/снять сливки,
С-273

СЛИЗАЛА
как* корова языком
слизала, К-310

СЛИЗНУЛА
как* корова языком
слизнула, К-310

СЛИЗНУЛО
как языком слизнуло,
К-310

СЛИПАЮТСЯ
глаза слипаются, Г-64

СЛИШКОМ
зайти ⟨заходить⟩ слишком
далеко, З-85
слишком далеко хватить,
З-85
слишком жирно (будет),
Б-217
слишком много
позволять/позволить
себе, Л-110
это уж(е) слишком, Э-8

СЛОВ
без дальних слов, С-274
без лишних слов, С-274
двух слов связать не мочь,
С-275
игра слов, И-13
на пару слов, П-67
набор слов, Н-3
с первых слов, С-290
с слов, С-279
с чужих слов, С-276
сказать пару тёплых слов,
П-69
слов нет, С-277, С-278
со слов, С-279

СЛОВА
боек ⟨бойкий⟩ на слова,
Я-7
брать (свои) слова назад
⟨обратно⟩, С-280
в полном смысле слова,
С-424
взвесить ⟨взвешивать⟩
свои слова, С-281
взять (свои) слова назад
⟨обратно⟩, С-280
владеть даром слова,
С-331
выбирать слова, В-375

[981]

перемолвиться словом,
С-335
поминать/помянуть
добрым словом, Д-222
поминать/помянуть
недобрым словом, С-336
словом сказать, С-334

СЛОВУ
господин своему слову,
Х-78
к слову, С-337, С-338
к слову говоря, С-338
к слову сказать, С-338
от слова к слову, С-289
хозяин ⟨хозяйка⟩ своему
слову, Х-78

СЛОВЦА
для красного словца, С-339
ради красного словца,
С-339

СЛОВЦО
закидывать/закинуть
словцо, С-315
замолвить словцо, С-305
красное словцо, С-340
крепкое словцо, С-316

СЛОВЦОМ
переброситься словцом,
С-335
перекинуться словцом,
С-335
перемолвиться словцом,
С-335

СЛОЖА
сложа руки, Р-327

СЛОЖИТЬ
сложить голову ⟨головы⟩,
Г-252
сложить кости, К-323
сложить оружие, О-104
сложить руки, Р-326
сложить свои головы
⟨свою голову⟩, Г-252
сложить свои кости, К-323

СЛОЖНОСТИ
в общей сложности, С-341

СЛОМАЕШЬ
глаза сломаешь, Г-65
язык сломаешь, Я-46

СЛОМАТЬ
глаза сломать можно, Г-65
сломать голову, Ш-58
сломать зубы, З-199
сломать лёд, Л-42
сломать рога, Р-123
сломать себе голову, Ш-58
сломать (себе) шею, Ш-58
язык сломать можно, Я-46

СЛОМИТ
сам чёрт голову ⟨ногу⟩
сломит, Ч-83
чёрт голову ⟨ногу⟩
сломит, Ч-83

СЛОМИТЬ
сломить голову, Ш-57,
Ш-58
сломить рога, Р-123
сломить себе голову, Ш-58
сломить себе шею, Ш-58
сломить шею, Ш-57, Ш-58

СЛОМЯ
сломя голову, Г-275

СЛОН
слон в посудной лавке,
С-342
слон на ухо наступил,
М-62

СЛОНА
делать/сделать из мухи
слона, М-299
слона не приметить, С-343

СЛОНОВ
слонов слонять, С-345

СЛОНОВОЙ
башня из слоновой кости,
Б-32

СЛОНУ
как слону дробина
⟨дробинка⟩, С-344
что слону дробина
⟨дробинка⟩, С-344

СЛОНЫ
слоны слонять, С-345

СЛОНЯТЬ
слонов ⟨слоны⟩ слонять,
С-345

СЛУГА
ваш покорнейший слуга,
С-346
ваш покорный слуга, С-346
слуга двух господ, С-347
слуга покорный, С-348
твой покорный слуга,
С-346

СЛУЖБА
дружба дружбой, а служба
службой, Д-314

СЛУЖБУ
не в службу, а в дружбу,
С-349
поставить на службу,
С-351
сослужить службу, С-350
ставить на службу, С-351

СЛУЖИТЬ
служить в людях, Л-174

СЛУХ
абсолютный слух, С-352
на слух, С-353
навострить слух, У-185
насторожить слух, У-185
обратиться ⟨обращаться⟩
в слух, С-354
превратиться
⟨превращаться⟩ в слух,
С-354
резать слух, У-160

СЛУХАМ
по слухам, С-355

СЛУХАМИ
слухами земля полнится,
С-356

СЛУХОМ
слухом земля полнится,
С-356

СЛУХУ
ни слуху ни духу, С-357
по слуху, С-353

СЛУЧАЕ
в данном случае, С-358

в крайнем случае, С-359
в лучшем случае, С-360
в любом случае, С-361
в противном случае, С-362
в случае, С-363, С-364
в случае ежели ⟨если⟩,
С-367
в случае чего, С-365
в таком случае, С-366
в том случае ежели
⟨если⟩, С-367
в худшем случае, С-368
в этом случае, С-366
во всяком случае, С-369
ни в каком случае, С-370
ни в коем случае, С-370
при случае, С-371

СЛУЧАЙ
в случай, С-363
на всякий пожарный
случай, С-372
на всякий случай, С-373
на крайний случай, С-374
на первый случай, С-375
на случай, С-376
на случай если, С-377
на тот случай если, С-377
случай привёл, С-378

СЛУЧАЮ
от случая к случаю, С-382
по случаю, С-379
по такому случаю, С-380
по этому случаю, С-380

СЛУЧАЯ
дело случая, Д-94
игра случая, И-14
не упускать/не упустить
случая, С-381
от случая к случаю, С-382

СЛЫХАННОЕ
слыханное ли дело, Д-129

СЛЫХАНО
где это слыхано?, С-383
разве это слыхано?, С-383
слыхано ли дело, Д-129

СЛЫХАТЬ
слыхом не слыхать, С-384

СЛЫХИВАТЬ
слыхом не слыхивать,
С-384

СЛЫХОМ
слыхом не слыхать ⟨не
слыхивать⟩, С-384

СЛЫШАЛ
слышал звон, да не знает
⟨не знаешь⟩, где он, З-99

СЛЫШАТЬ
земли под собой не
слышать, З-113
не слышать ног под собой,
Н-114
себя не слышать, П-333

СЛЫШНО
слышно, как муха
пролетит, М-297

СЛЮБИТСЯ
стерпится, слюбится,
С-573

СЛЮНИ
распускать/распустить
слюни, С-385

СЛЮНКИ
глотать слюнки, С-386
слюнки потекли ⟨текут⟩,
С-387

СМАЗАТЬ
смазать пятки (салом),
П-682

СМАЗЫВАТЬ
смазывать пятки (салом),
П-682

СМАТЫВАТЬ
сматывать удочки, У-49

СМЕЖИТЬ
смежить глаза, О-187
смежить очи, О-187

СМЕЙ(ТЕ)
не смей(те), С-388

СМЕЛО
глядеть смело в глаза,
Г-98
кончил дело — гуляй
смело, Д-110
смотреть смело в глаза,
Г-98

СМЕЛОСТЬ
брать/взять на себя
смелость, С-389
смелость города берёт,
С-390

СМЕНИТЬ
сменить гнев на милость,
Г-155
сменить декорации, Д-51
сменить пластинку, П-164

СМЕНЯТЬ
сменять гнев на милость,
Г-155
сменять кукушку на
ястреба, К-461
сменять шило на мыло,
Ш-63

СМЕРИТЬ
смерить взглядом, Г-109
смерить глазами, Г-109

СМЕРТЕЙ
двух смертей не бывать, а
одной не миновать,
С-399

СМЕРТИ
вопрос жизни и ⟨или⟩
смерти, В-259
глядеть смерти в глаза ⟨в
лицо⟩, С-394
до смерти, С-391
на одре смерти, О-83
при смерти, С-392
прежде смерти не
помрёшь ⟨не умрёшь⟩,
С-393
раньше смерти не
помрёшь ⟨не умрёшь⟩,
С-393
смотреть смерти в глаза
⟨в лицо⟩, С-394

СМЕРТНАЯ
скука смертная, Т-166

СМЕРТНОМ
на смертном одре, О-83

СМЕРТНЫЙ
как смертный грех, Г-387

смертный грех, Г-389
смертный час, Ч-15
СМЕРТНЫМ
смертным боем, Б-141
СМЕРТЬ
как смерть, С-395
на людях и смерть красна,
М-191
на миру и смерть красна,
М-191
найти смерть, М-201
не на живот, а на смерть,
Ж-58
не на жизнь, а на смерть,
Ж-58
СМЕРТЬЮ
за смертью посылать,
С-398
играть жизнью и
смертью, Ж-66
играть со смертью, Ж-66
между жизнью и смертью,
Ж-67
перед смертью не
надышишься, С-396
своей смертью, С-397
только за смертью
посылать, С-398
СМЕРТЯМ
двум смертям не бывать,
а одной не миновать,
С-399
СМЕСТИ
смести с лица земли, Л-88
СМЕТАНУ
как кот на сметану, К-333
СМЕТЬ
не сметь дохнуть
〈дыхнуть〉, С-400
шагу не сметь сделать
〈ступить〉, Ш-24
СМЕХ
и смех и горе, С-401
и смех и грех, С-401
как* на смех, С-402
курам на смех, К-477
на смех, С-405
поднимать/поднять на
смех, С-403
подымать на смех, С-403
просто смех (один), С-404
прямо смех (один), С-404
смех да и только, С-404
смех и горе, С-401
смех и грех, С-401
смех один, Г-384, С-404
СМЕХА
валяться от смеха, С-406
для смеха, С-405
кататься от смеха, С-406
лопнуть от смеха, С-407
подохнуть 〈подыхать〉 от
смеха, С-407
покатиться
〈покатываться〉 от
смеха, С-406
смеха ради, С-405
треснуть от смеха, С-407
СМЕХОТА
одна смехота, С-404

просто одна смехота,
С-404
прямо одна смехота, С-404
смехота да и только, С-404
СМЕХУ
валяться со смеху, С-406
для смеху, С-405
кататься со смеху, С-406
лопнуть со смеху, С-407
не до смеху, Ш-112
подохнуть 〈подыхать〉 со
смеху, С-407
покатиться
〈покатываться〉 со
смеху, С-406
помереть 〈помирать〉 со
смеху, С-407
треснуть со смеху, С-407
умереть 〈умирать〉 со
смеху, С-407
уморить со смеху, С-408
СМЕШАТЬ
смешать в 〈одну〉 кучу,
К-498
смешать все карты, К-98
смешать карты, К-98
смешать с грязью, Г-437
смешать с дерьмом, Г-437
СМЕШИВАТЬ
смешивать с грязью, Г-437
смешивать с дерьмом,
Г-437
СМЕШИНКА
смешинка в рот попала,
С-409
СМЕШНОГО
до смешного, С-410
СМЕЯТЬСЯ
смеяться в кулак, К-464
СМИГНУВ(ШИ)
не смигнув(ши), С-411
СМИРИТЕЛЬНУЮ
надевать/надеть
смирительную рубаху
〈рубашку〉, Р-194
СМИРНО
по стойке смирно, С-585
стойка смирно, С-585
СМОЖЕТ
всякий дурак сможет,
Д-328
каждый дурак сможет,
Д-328
СМОКОВНИЦА
бесплодная смоковница,
С-412
СМОЛОДУ
береги платье снову, а
честь смолоду, П-167
береги честь смолоду,
П-167
СМОЛЬ
как смоль, С-413
СМОТАТЬ
смотать удочки, У-49
СМОТРЕЛ
как* в воду смотрел, В-184
на свет (божий) не
смотрел бы, С-48

СМОТРЕЛИ
глаза бы (мои) не
смотрели, Г-51
СМОТРЕТЬ
как сыч смотреть, С-740
смотреть бирюком, Б-67
смотреть большими
глазами, Г-66
смотреть букой, Б-240
смотреть в глаза, Г-96,
Г-97
смотреть в гроб, М-205
смотреть в книгу и видеть
фигу, К-148
смотреть в корень, К-295
смотреть в кусты, К-497
смотреть в лес, Л-57
смотреть в лицо, Г-97
смотреть в могилу, М-205
смотреть в оба, С-414
смотреть в оба глаза,
С-414
смотреть в рот, Р-184
смотреть волком, В-233
смотреть вон, С-415
смотреть глазами, Г-119
смотреть другими
глазами, Г-120
смотреть женихом, Ж-17
смотреть из рук, Р-221
смотреть именинником
〈именинницей〉, И-59
смотреть иными глазами,
Г-120
смотреть косо, С-416
смотреть круглыми
глазами, Г-66
смотреть на вещи, В-89
смотреть на сторону, С-613
смотреть не на что, С-417
смотреть по сторонам,
С-604
смотреть правде в глаза 〈в
лицо〉, П-483
смотреть прямо в глаза,
Г-98
смотреть сверху вниз,
С-418
смотреть свысока, С-418
смотреть сентябрём, С-118
смотреть сквозь пальцы,
П-27
смотреть сквозь розовые
очки, О-190
смотреть смело в глаза,
Г-98
смотреть смерти в глаза
〈в лицо〉, С-394
смотреть снизу вверх,
С-419
смотреть со своей
колокольни, К-204
смотреть фертом, Ф-8
сычом смотреть, С-740
СМОТРИ
смотри у меня!, С-421
того и смотри, Г-153
СМОТРИТ
как волка ни корми, (а) он
(всё) в лес смотрит,
В-228

куда (только) смотрит,
С-420
сколько волка ни корми,
(а) он (всё) в лес
смотрит, В-228
чего смотрит, С-420
что смотрит, С-420
СМОТРИТЕ
смотрите у меня!, С-421
СМОТРОК
свой глаз(ок) — смотрок,
Г-41
СМОТРЯ
смотря где, С-422
смотря как 〈какой〉, С-422
смотря когда, С-422
смотря кто, С-422
смотря куда, С-422
смотря по, С-423
смотря сколько, С-422
смотря что, С-422
СМОТРЯТ
дарёному 〈даровому〉
коню в зубы не смотрят,
К-272
СМЫВАТЬ
смывать кровью, К-417
СМЫКАТЬ
не смыкать глаз, Г-32
СМЫЛО
как* водой смыло, В-180
СМЫСЛЕ
в полном смысле слова,
С-424
в смысле, С-425
СМЫТЬ
смыть кровью, К-417
СНА
со сна, С-426
СНАРУЖИ
снаружи мило, а внутри
гнило, С-427
СНЕ
во сне не приснится 〈не
снилось〉, С-428
и во сне не приснится 〈не
снилось〉, С-428
спит и во сне видит, С-519
СНЕГ
как прошлогодний снег,
С-429
как* снег на голову, С-430
СНЕГА
зимой снега не
выпросишь, С-431
СНЕГУ
зимой снегу не
выпросишь, С-431
СНЕСТИ
не снести головы, Г-292
снести с лица земли, Л-88
СНИЖАТЬ
снижать тон, Т-157
СНИЗИТЬ
снизить тон, Т-157
СНИЗУ
глядеть снизу вверх, С-419
смотреть снизу вверх,
С-419

СНИЛОСЬ
во сне не снилось, С-428
и во сне не снилось, С-428
(и) не снилось, С-428

СНИМАТЬ
снимать завесу, З-18
снимать личину, М-34
снимать маски, М-35
снимать маску, М-34, М-35
снимать пенки, П-80
снимать покров(ы), З-18
снимать (последнюю)
рубашку, Р-195
снимать с учёта, У-170
снимать сливки, С-273
снимать со счёта ⟨со
счетов, со счётов⟩, С-719
снимать стружку, С-644
снимать шляпу, Ш-82

СНИМАТЬСЯ
сниматься с учёта, У-171

СНИТСЯ
десятый сон снится, С-483
седьмой сон снится, С-483

СНОВУ
береги платье снову, а
честь смолоду, П-167

СНОМ
заснуть вечным
⟨могильным⟩ сном,
С-432
заснуть последним сном,
С-432
мертвецким сном, С-433
мёртвым сном, С-433
ни сном ни духом, С-434
почивать вечным сном,
С-436
почить вечным сном,
С-432
почить непробудным
сном, С-432
сном праведника
⟨праведницы,
праведных⟩, С-435
спать вечным
⟨могильным⟩ сном,
С-436
спать непробудным сном,
С-436
спать последним сном,
С-436
уснуть вечным
⟨могильным⟩ сном,
С-432
уснуть последним сном,
С-432

СНОСА
сноса нет, И-53

СНОСЕ
на сносе, С-437

СНОСИТЬ
не сносить головы, Г-292

СНОСУ
сносу нет, И-53
сносу не знать, И-53

СНОСЯХ
на сносях, С-437

СНЯВШИ
снявши голову, по волосам
не плачут, Г-276

СНЯЛО
как* рукой сняло, Р-332

СНЯТЬ
снять голову, Г-277
снять завесу, З-18
снять личину, М-34
снять маски, М-35
снять маску, М-34, М-35
снять пенки, П-80
снять покров(ы), З-18
снять последнюю рубаху,
Р-196
снять последнюю
рубашку, Р-195, Р-196
снять рубашку, Р-195
снять с себя последнюю
рубаху ⟨рубашку⟩, Р-196
снять с учёта, У-170
снять семь шкур, Ш-80
снять сливки, С-273
снять со счёта ⟨со счетов,
со счётов⟩, С-719
снять стружку, С-644
снять три шкуры, Ш-80
снять шкуру, Ш-80
снять шляпу, Ш-82

СНЯТЬСЯ
сняться с учёта, У-171

СОБАК
как собак нерезаных,
С-438
что собак нерезаных,
С-438
собак вешать/навешать,
С-439
собак понавешать, С-439

СОБАКА
вот в чём собака зарыта,
С-440
вот в этом и зарыта
собака, С-440
вот где собака зарыта,
С-440
вот здесь и зарыта собака,
С-440
вот тут ⟨тут-то⟩ и зарыта
собака, С-440
всякая собака, С-441
каждая собака, С-441
как собака, С-442
как собака на сене, С-443
как собака палку, С-444
любая собака, С-441
ни одна собака, С-445
собака на сене, С-443

СОБАКЕ
как собаке пятая нога,
С-446
собаке под хвост, П-611

СОБАКИ
свои собаки грызутся
⟨дерутся⟩, чужая не
подходи ⟨не приставай⟩,
С-447

СОБАКОЙ
как кошка с собакой, К-344

СОБАКУ
собаку съесть, С-448

СОБАЧИЙ
собачий сын, С-734

СОБАЧЬЕ
не твоё собачье дело,
Д-120

СОБАЧЬИМ
к чертям собачьим, Ч-110
идти к чертям собачьим,
Ч-113
лететь к чертям собачьим,
Ч-113
пойти к чертям собачьим,
Ч-113
полететь к чертям
собачьим, Ч-113

СОБАЧЬЯ
собачья дочь, Д-302
собачья жизнь, Ж-64

СОБЕРЁШЬ
костей не соберёшь, К-320

СОБИРАТЬ
собирать в кулак, К-465

СОБИРАТЬСЯ
собираться с духом, Д-358
собираться с мыслями,
М-314
собираться с силами,
С-177

СОБИРАЮТСЯ
тучи собираются над
головой, Т-245

СОБЛЮСТИ
капитал приобрести и
невинность соблюсти,
К-55

СОБОЙ
бороться с (самим) собой,
Б-182
владеть собой, В-159
влечь за собой, В-169
жечь за собой мосты,
К-289
земли под собой не
слышать ⟨не чуять⟩,
З-113
иметь под собой почву,
П-453
не слышать ног под собой,
Н-114
не чувствовать ног под
собой, Н-114
не чуять ног под собой,
Н-114
овладевать/овладеть
собой, О-43
оставить ⟨оставлять⟩ за
собой, О-121
повлечь за собой, В-169
покончить с собой, П-285
потерять власть над
собой, В-166
потерять землю под
собой, П-456
потерять почву под собой,
П-456
работать над собой, Р-4
расти над собой, Р-87
с собой, С-100
сам собой, С-7
самим собой, С-8
само собой, С-9
само собой разумеется,
С-9

сжечь ⟨сжигать⟩ за собой
мосты, К-289
справиться ⟨справляться⟩
с собой, О-43
терять власть над собой,
В-166
терять землю под собой,
П-456
терять почву под собой,
П-456
унести ⟨уносить⟩ с собой в
могилу, М-207

СОБОЮ
сам собою, С-7
само собою, С-9
само собою разумеется,
С-9

СОБРАЛИСЬ
тучи собрались (над
головой), Т-245

СОБРАТЬ
костей не собрать, К-320
собрать в кулак, К-465

СОБРАТЬСЯ
собраться с духом, Д-358
собраться с мыслями,
М-314
собраться с силами, С-177

СОБСТВЕННО
собственно говоря, Г-176

СОБСТВЕННОГО
не видеть дальше (своего)
собственного носа,
Н-225

СОБСТВЕННОЙ
на своей собственной
шкуре, Ш-76
на собственной спине,
Г-322
на собственной шкуре,
Ш-76
собственной персоной,
П-106

СОБСТВЕННОМ
вариться в собственном
соку, С-470
вывезти ⟨вывозить⟩ на
собственном горбу,
П-186
вынести ⟨выносить⟩ на
собственном горбу,
П-186
на собственном горбу,
Г-322

СОБСТВЕННЫЕ
в собственные руки, Р-281

СОБСТВЕННЫЙ
за собственный счёт, С-698
на свой собственный страх
(и риск), С-627
на собственный счёт,
С-698
собственный угол, У-33

СОБСТВЕННЫМ
бить его собственным
оружием, О-105
бороться его собственным
оружием, О-105
дойти ⟨доходить⟩ (своим)
собственным умом,
У-105

[985]

запеть ⟨петь⟩ соловьём,
С-472

разливаться соловьём,
С-472

СОЛОВЬЯ
соловья баснями не
кормят, С-473

СОЛОМЕННАЯ
соломенная вдова, В-10

СОЛОМЕННЫЙ
соломенный вдовец, В-10

СОЛОМИНКУ
схватиться за соломинку,
С-474

утопающий хватается (и)
за соломинку, У-149

хвататься за соломинку,
С-474

СОЛОМОЙ
голова соломой набита,
Г-208

мешок с соломой, М-144

СОЛОМОНОВО
соломоново решение, Р-115

СОЛОМУ
сила солому ломит, С-174

СОЛОНО
солоно досталось, П-551

солоно приходится/
пришлось, П-551

СОЛЬ
аттическая соль, С-475

соль земли, С-476

сыпать соль на рану
⟨раны⟩, С-477

хлеб да ⟨и⟩ соль!, Х-38

СОМКНУТЬ
не сомкнуть глаз, Г-32

сомкнуть ряды, Р-404

СОМНЕНИЕ
брать/взять под сомнение,
С-478

СОМНЕНИЮ
не подлежит сомнению,
С-479

СОМНЕНИЯ
без (всякого) сомнения,
С-480

вне (всякого) сомнения,
С-480

СОН
десятый сон видеть, С-483

как* сквозь сон, С-481

на сон грядущий, С-482

не верить ни в чох, ни в
сон ни в птичий грай,
Ч-157

седьмой сон видеть, С-483

седьмой сон снится, С-483

сквозь сон, С-484

сон в руку, С-485

что сей сон значит
⟨означает⟩?, С-486

СОННАЯ
как сонная муха, М-294

сонная тетеря, Т-93

СОННОЕ
сонное царство, Ц-5

СООБРАЖАТЬ
соображать на троих,
Т-204

СООБРАЖЕНИЕ
брать/взять в
соображение, С-487

принимать/принять в
соображение, С-487

СООБРАЖЕНИЕМ
с соображением, У-110

СООБРАЗЕН
ни с чем не сообразен,
С-488

СООБРАЗИТЬ
сообразить на троих,
Т-204

СООБРАЗНЫЙ
ни с чем не сообразный,
С-488

СООТВЕТСТВИИ
в соответствии с, С-489

СОПЛЁЙ
соплёй перешибёшь, С-490

соплёй перешибить
можно, С-490

СОПЛИ
распускать/распустить
сопли, С-491

СОПЛЯХ
на соплях, С-492

СОПРОВОЖДЕНИИ
в сопровождении, С-493

СОПРОТИВЛЕНИЯ
идти по линии ⟨по пути⟩
наименьшего
сопротивления, Л-73

пойти по линии ⟨по пути⟩
наименьшего
сопротивления, Л-73

СОР
вынести ⟨выносить⟩ сор
из избы, С-494

СОРВАЛСЯ
голос сорвался
⟨срывается⟩, Г-300

СОРВАТЬ
сорвать голову, Г-277

сорвать голос, Г-305

сорвать завесу, З-18

сорвать зло, З-133

сорвать маски ⟨маску⟩,
М-35

сорвать покров(ы), З-18

сорвать сердце, З-133

СОРВАТЬСЯ
как* с привязи сорваться,
Ц-37

как* с цепи сорваться,
Ц-37

сорваться с губ, Я-51

сорваться с уст, Я-51

сорваться с языка, Я-51

СОРИТЬ
сорить деньгами, Д-165

СОРНАЯ
сорная трава из поля вон,
Т-194

СОРНУЮ
сорную траву из ⟨с⟩ поля
вон, Т-194

СОРОК
сорок бочек арестантов,
Б-186

сорок одно с кисточкой,
К-124

сорок сороков, С-495

СОРОКА
заладила сорока Якова
(одно про всякого),
С-496

как сорока, С-497

сорока на хвосте принесла,
С-498

СОРОКОВ
сорок сороков, С-495

СОРОЧКЕ
родиться в сорочке, Р-192

СОРТ
первый сорт, С-499

СОСАТЬ
сосать кровь, К-407

сосать лапу, Л-30

сосать сок ⟨соки⟩, С-467

СОСЕНКЕ
с бору по сосенке, Б-185

СОСЕНКИ
и с бору и с сосенки, Б-185

с бору да с сосенки, Б-185

СОСЛУЖИТЬ
сослужить службу, С-350

СОСНАХ
заблудиться в трёх соснах,
С-500

СОСТАВИТЬ
составить компанию,
К-221

составить себе имя, И-65

СОСТАРИШЬСЯ
много будешь знать —
скоро состаришься,
З-173

СОСТОЯНИЕ
состояние духа, Р-79

СОСТОЯНИИ
в состоянии, С-501

СОСТОЯТЬ
состоять на учёте, У-172

СОСТРОИТЬ
состроить рожу, Р-146

СОСЧИТАТЬ
не сосчитать, С-695

по пальцам можно
сосчитать, П-17

СОТВОРИТЬ
сотворить себе кумир(а),
К-472

СОУСОМ
ни под каким соусом,
С-502

под соусом, С-503

СОХРАНИ
боже сохрани, Б-143

сохрани бог ⟨господь⟩,
Б-143

СОХРАНИТЬ
сохранить лицо, Л-99

СОХРАННОСТИ
в целости и сохранности,
Ц-21

СОЧТЁМСЯ
свои люди — сочтёмся,
Л-173

СОЧТЕНЫ
дни сочтены, Д-205

СОЧТЁШЬ
не сочтёшь, С-695

СОШЁЛСЯ
свет клином не сошёлся,
С-58

свет не клином сошёлся,
С-58

СОШКА
мелкая сошка, С-504

СОШЛАСЬ
земля не клином сошлась,
С-58

СОШЛО
десять потов сошло, П-430

семь потов сошло, П-430

СОШЬЁШЬ
шубы не сошьёшь, Ш-94

СПАДАЕТ
завеса спадает (с глаз),
З-16

как будто* пелена спадает
(с глаз), П-76

как будто* покров спадает
(с глаз), П-76

пелена спадает (с глаз),
П-76

покров спадает (с глаз),
П-76

СПАДАТЬ
спадать с тела, Т-52

СПАЛ
(как будто*) покров спал (с
глаз), П-76

СПАЛА
завеса спала (с глаз), З-16

(как будто*) пелена спала
(с глаз), П-76

СПАСА
спаса нет, С-507

СПАСАЙСЯ
спасайся, кто может,
С-505

СПАСАТЬ
спасать положение, П-309

СПАСЕНИЯ
спасения нет, С-507

якорь спасения, Я-63

СПАСИБО
за (одно) спасибо, Т-3

и на том спасибо, С-506

спасибо и на этом, С-506

спасибо на добром слове,
С-304

СПАСТИ
спасти положение, П-309

СПАСТЬ
спасть с лица, Л-87

спасть с тела, Т-52

СПАСУ
спасу не стало, С-507

спасу нет, С-507

СПАТЬ
лавры не дают спать, Л-5

мягко стелет, да жёстко
спать, С-557

спать вечным
⟨могильным⟩ сном,
С-436

спать непробудным сном,
С-436
спать последним сном,
С-436
СПЁРЛО
дух спёрло, Д-345
дыхание спёрло, Д-345
СПЕСЬ
сбивать/сбить спесь,
С-508
сшибать/сшибить спесь,
С-508
СПЕТА
песенка ⟨песня⟩ спета,
П-115
СПЕТЬ
спеть панегирик, Д-198
СПЕХУ
не к спеху, С-509
СПЕША
не спеша, С-510
СПИНЕ
мороз по спине дерёт
⟨идёт⟩, М-258
мороз по спине подирает/
подрал, М-258
мороз по спине пошёл,
М-258
мороз по спине пробегает/
пробежал, М-258
мороз по спине
продирает/продрал,
М-258
мороз по спине проходит/
прошёл, М-258
мурашки бегают ⟨бегут⟩
по спине, М-291
мурашки забегали
⟨заползали⟩ по спине,
М-291
мурашки побежали по
спине, М-291
мурашки ползают
⟨ползут/поползли⟩ по
спине, М-291
мурашки пошли по спине,
М-291
мурашки пробежали по
спине, М-291
на своей спине, Г-322
на собственной спине,
Г-322
на чужой спине в рай
въехать, Г-323
СПИНОЙ
за спиной, С-511
стоять за спиной, С-512
СПИНУ
гнуть спину, С-513, С-514
ломать спину, С-513
нож в спину, Н-181
показать ⟨показывать⟩
спину, С-515
прятаться/спрятаться за
(чужую) спину, С-516
СПИНЫ
не разгибать спины, С-517
не разгибая спины, С-518
СПИСАТЬ
списать в расход, Р-88

списать в тираж, Т-100
СПИСЫВАТЬ
списывать в расход, Р-88
списывать в тираж, Т-100
СПИТ
спит и (во сне) видит,
С-519
СПИХИВАТЬ
спихивать с плеч, П-178
спихивать с шеи, П-178
СПИХНУТЬ
спихнуть с плеч, П-178
спихнуть с шеи, П-178
СПИЦА
десятая спица в колеснице,
С-520
последняя спица в
колеснице, С-520
пятая спица в колеснице,
С-520
СПИЧКА
как спичка, С-521
СПЛЕЧА
рубить сплеча, Р-198
СПЛОШЬ
сплошь да ⟨и⟩ рядом,
С-522
СПЛЫЛ
был да сплыл, Б-257
СПОКОЙНОЙ
со спокойной совестью,
С-461
спокойной ночи, Н-242
СПОКОЙСТВИЕ
олимпийское спокойствие,
С-523
СПОКОН
спокон века ⟨веков⟩, В-22
СПОР
на спор, С-524
СПОРА
спора нет, С-277
СПОРТИВНОГО
из спортивного интереса,
И-68
СПОРУ
спору нет, С-277
СПОРЯТ
о вкусах не спорят, В-155
СПОТЫКАЕТСЯ
конь (и) о четырёх ногах,
да (и то ⟨и тот⟩)
спотыкается, К-268
СПРАВЕДЛИВОСТЬ
отдавать должную
справедливость, Д-246
отдавать (полную)
справедливость, Д-246
отдать должную
справедливость, Д-246
отдать (полную)
справедливость, Д-246
СПРАВИТЬСЯ
справиться с собой, О-43
СПРАВЛЯТЬСЯ
справляться с собой, О-43
СПРАВОЧНИК
живой справочник, Э-1
СПРАШИВАЮ
ну я вас ⟨тебя⟩
спрашиваю!, С-525

я вас ⟨тебя⟩ спрашиваю!,
С-525
СПРОС
попытка не пытка а спрос
не беда, П-356
СПРОСА
без спроса, С-526
СПРОСУ
без спросу, С-526
СПРОСЯСЬ
не спросясь броду, не суйся
в воду, Б-211
СПРЯТАТЬ
спрятать голову под
крыло, Г-272
спрятать концы (в воду),
К-262
СПРЯТАТЬСЯ
спрятаться в свою
скорлупу, С-233
спрятаться за других,
С-516
спрятаться за (чужую)
спину, С-516
СПУД
под спуд, С-528
СПУДА
из-под спуда, С-527
СПУДОМ
под спудом, С-528
СПУСКА
не давать/не дать спуска,
С-529
СПУСКАТЬ
десять потов спускать,
П-429
не спускать взгляда
⟨взора⟩, Г-31
не спускать глаз, Г-31
семь потов спускать, П-429
спускать жир(ок), Ж-75
спускать на тормозах,
Т-165
спускать с лестницы, Л-60
спускать с рук, Р-220
спускать семь шкур, Ш-80
спускать три шкуры, Ш-80
спускать шкуру, Ш-80
СПУСКАТЬСЯ
спускаться (с неба) на
землю, Н-47
СПУСКУ
не давать/не дать спуску,
С-529
СПУСТИТЬ
десять потов спустить,
П-429
семь потов спустить,
П-429
спустить жир(ок), Ж-75
спустить на тормозах,
Т-165
спустить с лестницы, Л-60
спустить с рук, Р-220
спустить семь шкур, Ш-80
спустить три шкуры, Ш-80
спустить шкуру, Ш-80
СПУСТИТЬСЯ
спуститься на землю, Н-47

спуститься с неба на
землю, Н-47
спуститься с облаков, О-9
СПУСТЯ
немного спустя, П-232
спустя рукава, Р-240
СПУТАТЬ
спутать (все) карты, К-98
спутать по рукам и (по)
ногам, Р-250
СПУТНИК
спутник жизни, С-530
СПУТНИЦА
спутница жизни, С-530
СПУТЫВАТЬ
спутывать по рукам и (по)
ногам, Р-250
СПЯТИТЬ
спятить с ума, У-91
СРАВНЕНИЕ
не идти в сравнение, С-531
не идти ни в какое
сравнение, С-531
СРАВНЕНИИ
в сравнении, С-532
СРАВНЕНИЮ
не поддаваться никакому
сравнению, С-531
по сравнению, С-532
СРАВНЕНИЯ
не выдерживать (никакого)
сравнения, С-531
СРАЖАТЬСЯ
сражаться с ветряными
мельницами, М-70
СРАЖЕНИЯ
поле сражения, П-296
СРАЗУ
(и) Москва не сразу
строилась, М-260
СРЕБРЕНИКОВ
предать ⟨продать⟩ за
тридцать сребреников,
С-533
тридцать сребреников,
С-534
СРЕДНЕГО
удовольствие ниже
среднего, У-48
СРЕДНЕЙ
средней руки, Р-328
СРЕДНЕМ
в среднем, С-535
СРЕДНИХ
средних лет, Л-63
СРЕДСТВА
цель оправдывает
средства, Ц-24
СРЕДСТВАМ
не по средствам, С-536
СРЕДСТВАМИ
покушение с негодными
средствами, П-292
попытка с негодными
средствами, П-292
СРОВНЯТЬ
сровнять с землёй, З-112
СРОК
дай(те) срок, С-537

[988]

СРОКА
не давать ни отдыха ни срока, О-141
раньше срока, В-298

СРЫВАЕТСЯ
голос срывается, Г-300

СРЫВАТЬ
срывать голос, Г-305
срывать завесу, З-18
срывать зло, З-133
срывать маски ⟨маску⟩, М-35
срывать покров(ы), З-18
срывать сердце, З-133
срывать цветы удовольствия, Ц-17

СРЫВАТЬСЯ
срываться с губ, Я-51
срываться с уст, Я-51
срываться с языка, Я-51

ССОРЫ
худой мир лучше доброй ссоры, М-185

СТАВИТЬ
(и) в грош не ставить, Г-412
(и) в медный грош не ставить, Г-412
ни в грош не ставить, Г-412
ни во что не ставить, Г-412
последний грош ребром ставить, К-284
последнюю копейку ребром ставить, К-284
пробу ⟨пробы⟩ ставить негде ⟨некуда⟩, П-563
ставить в вину, В-148
ставить в известность, И-40
ставить в тупик, Т-238
ставить в укор, У-70
ставить в упрёк, У-70
ставить во главу угла, Г-21
ставить вопрос ребром, В-260
ставить всё на место, М-98
ставить всё на одну карту, К-93
ставить всё на своё место ⟨на свои места⟩, М-98
ставить все точки на ⟨над⟩ и, Т-183
ставить всякое лыко в строку, Л-156
ставить за честь, Ч-138
ставить знак равенства, З-156
ставить к стене ⟨к стенке⟩, С-564
ставить крест, К-382
ставить на вид, В-114
ставить на карту, К-94
ставить на колени, К-185
ставить на кон, К-225
ставить на место, М-123
ставить на ноги, Н-153, Н-154
ставить на одну доску, Д-295
ставить на очередь, О-185

ставить на рельсы, Р-108
ставить на своё место, М-123
ставить на службу, С-351
ставить на учёт, У-167
ставить палки в колёса, П-9
ставить перед свершившимся ⟨совершившимся⟩ фактом, Ф-2
ставить перед фактом, Ф-2
ставить под вопрос, В-261
ставить под удар, У-39
ставить рога, Р-122
ставить рогатки, Р-125
ставить себя на место, М-124
ставить точки на ⟨над⟩ и, Т-183
ставить точку, Т-186
ставить точку на ⟨над⟩ и, Т-183
ставить фонарь, Ф-16

СТАВКУ
делать/сделать ставку, С-538

СТАДНОЕ
стадное чувство, Ч-198

СТАДО
как стадо баранов, С-539
(одна) паршивая овца всё стадо портит, О-46

СТАКАНЕ
буря в стакане воды, Б-247

СТАКАНЧИК
пропускать/пропустить стаканчик, Р-398

СТАЛИ
волосы стали дыбом, В-241

СТАЛКИВАТЬСЯ
сталкиваться на узкой дороге ⟨дорожке⟩, Д-289

СТАЛО
во что бы то ни стало, С-540
житья не стало, Ж-81
за кем дело стало?, Д-103
за малым дело стало, Д-102
за небольшим дело стало, Д-102
за немногим дело стало, Д-102
за тем дело стало, Д-103
за чем дело стало?, Д-103
моченьки ⟨мочи⟩ не стало, М-270
спасу не стало, С-507
стало быть, С-541
стало на место, М-99
стало на своё место ⟨на свои места⟩, М-99

СТАНЕТ
в подмётки не станет, П-247
дело не станет, Д-87

СТАНОВАЯ
становая жила, Х-98

СТАНОВИТСЯ
становится на место, М-99
становится на своё место ⟨на свои места⟩, М-99

СТАНОВИТЬСЯ
становиться в позу, П-273
становиться в тупик, Т-239
становиться на дороге, П-652
становиться на дыбы, Д-434
становиться на задние лапки, Л-25
становиться на колени, К-186
становиться на место, М-124
становиться на ноги, Н-157
становиться на одну доску, Д-296
становиться на очередь, О-186
становиться на пути, П-652
становиться на путь, П-662
становиться на рельсы, Р-109
становиться на сторону, С-609
становиться на учёт, У-168
становиться под знамёна ⟨под знамя⟩, З-167
становиться поперёк горла, Г-332
становиться поперёк дороги, П-652
становиться поперёк пути, П-652
становиться стеной, С-566

СТАНОВОЙ
становой хребет, Х-98

СТАНОВЯТСЯ
волосы становятся дыбом, В-241

СТАР
и стар и мал ⟨млад⟩, С-542
стар и мал ⟨млад⟩, С-542

СТАРАТЬСЯ
рад стараться, С-543

СТАРАЯ
старая дева, Д-46
старая карга, К-76
старая любовь не ржавеет, Л-163
старая песня, П-121

СТАРИНЕ
по старине, С-544

СТАРИНКЕ
по старинке, С-544

СТАРИНОЙ
тряхнуть стариной, С-545

СТАРОГО
старого воробья на мякине не проведёшь, В-268
старого закала, З-43
старого покроя, П-291

СТАРОЕ
кто старое вспомянет

⟨помянет⟩, тому глаз вон, С-546

СТАРОЙ
по старой памяти, П-38
старой закваски, З-43

СТАРОСТИ
на старости лет, С-547

СТАРОСТЬ
старость не радость, С-548

СТАРУХУ
и на старуху бывает проруха, С-549

СТАРЫЙ
и старый и малый, С-542
старый волк, В-227
старый воробей, В-267
старый друг лучше новых двух, Д-311
старый и малый, С-542
старый хрен, Х-99

СТАТИ
с какой стати?, С-550

СТАТОЧНОЕ
статочное ли дело, Д-130

СТАТЬ
не занимать стать, З-63
не привыкать стать, П-517
ни стать ни сесть, С-551
ни стать ни сесть не уметь, С-552
под стать, С-553
стать в копеечку ⟨в копейку⟩, К-276
стать в позу, П-273
стать в тупик, Т-239
стать выше, С-620
стать горой, Г-350
стать грудью, Г-427
стать колом в горле, К-206
стать костью в глотке ⟨в горле⟩, К-206
стать на дороге, П-652
стать на дыбы, Д-434
стать на задние лапки, Л-25
стать на колени, К-186
стать на место, М-124
стать на ноги, Н-157
стать на одну доску, Д-296
стать на очередь, О-186
стать на пути, П-652
стать на путь, П-662
стать на рельсы, Р-109
стать на сторону, С-609
стать на учёт, У-168
стать под знамёна ⟨под знамя⟩, З-167
стать поперёк горла, Г-332
стать поперёк дороги, П-652
стать поперёк пути, П-652
стать стеной, С-566
стать твёрдой ногой, Н-163

СТАТЬСЯ
может статься, М-213

СТАТЬЯ
особая статья, С-554
особь статья, С-554

СТАТЬЯМ
по всем статьям, С-555

СТЁКЛЫШКО
как стёклышко, С-556

СТЕКЛЯННЫЙ
под стеклянный колпак, К-209

СТЕКЛЯННЫМ
под стеклянным колпаком, К-209

СТЕЛЕТ
мягко стелет, да жёстко спать, С-557

СТЕЛЬКА
как стелька, С-558

СТЕЛЬКУ
в стельку, С-558

СТЕН
и у стен бывают ⟨есть⟩ уши, С-559

СТЕНА
китайская стена, С-560
стена в ⟨об⟩ стену, С-561

СТЕНАХ
в четырёх стенах, С-562
погребать себя в четырёх стенах, П-233
погребать себя заживо, П-233
погрести себя в четырёх стенах, П-233
погрести себя заживо, П-233

СТЕНЕ
поставить к стене, С-564
прижать ⟨прижимать⟩ к стене, С-563
припереть ⟨припирать⟩ к стене, С-563
ставить к стене, С-564
что стене горох, С-565

СТЕНКА
стенка в ⟨об⟩ стенку, С-561

СТЕНКЕ
поставить к стенке, С-564
прижать ⟨прижимать⟩ к стенке, С-563
припереть ⟨припирать⟩ к стенке, С-563
ставить к стенке, С-564
что стенке горох, С-565

СТЕНКИ
как от стенки горох, С-565

СТЕНКУ
как в стенку горох ⟨горохом⟩, С-565
как об стенку горох ⟨горохом⟩, С-565
лбом стенку не прошибёшь, Л-35
лезть/полезть на стенку, С-569
стенка в стенку, С-561
стенка об стенку, С-561
хоть головой об стенку бейся, Г-242

СТЕНОЙ
вставать/встать стеной, С-566
как за каменной стеной, С-567
становиться/стать стеной, С-566

стоять стеной, С-568

СТЕНУ
как в стену горох ⟨горохом⟩, С-565
как на каменную стену, Г-353
как об стену горох ⟨горохом⟩, С-565
лбом стену не прошибёшь, Л-35
лезть/полезть на стену, С-569
стена в стену, С-561
стена об стену, С-561
хоть головой об стену бейся, Г-242

СТЕНЫ
дома (и) стены помогают, С-570
и стены имеют уши, С-559
как от стены горох, С-565
лбом стены не прошибёшь, Л-35
стены имеют уши, С-559

СТЕПЕНИ
в высшей степени, С-571
в равной степени, О-23

СТЕПЬ
не в ту степь, С-572

СТЕРЕТЬ
стереть в (мелкий) порошок, П-386
стереть грани ⟨грань⟩, Г-376
стереть с лица земли, Л-88

СТЁРЛИСЬ
стёрлись грани, Г-377

СТЕРПИТ
бумага всё стерпит, Б-243

СТЕРПИТСЯ
стерпится, слюбится, С-573

СТИРАТЬ
стирать грани ⟨грань⟩, Г-376

СТИРАЮТСЯ
стираются грани, Г-377

СТИСНУТЬ
стиснуть зубы, З-203

СТИХ
стих накатил, С-574
стих нападает/напал, С-574
стих находит/нашёл, С-574

СТИХИИ
в своей стихии, С-575

СТО
во сто крат, К-369
давать/дать сто очков вперёд, О-191
на все сто, С-576
на все сто процентов, С-576
не имей сто рублей, (а) имей сто друзей, Р-199
поворот на сто восемьдесят градусов, П-225

СТОГЕ
как* иголка в стоге сена, И-2

СТОГУ
иголка в стогу сена, И-2
как* иголка в стогу сена, И-2

СТОЕРОСОВАЯ
дубина стоеросовая, Д-317

СТОЕРОСОВЫЙ
болван стоеросовый, Д-317
дурак стоеросовый, Д-317

СТОИМ
на том стоим, С-577
на том стояли, стоим и стоять будем, С-577

СТОИТ
гроша ломаного не стоит, Г-416
гроша медного не стоит, Г-416
дым стоит коромыслом ⟨столбом⟩, Д-436
и гроша не стоит, Г-416
игра не стоит свеч, И-11
клубок в горле стоит, К-142
ком(ок) в горле стоит, К-142
на чём свет стоит, С-49
не стоит, С-578
не стоит труда, Т-216
ни гроша не стоит, Г-416
ничего не стоит, С-579
овчинка выделки не стоит, О-48
плевка не стоит, П-171
себе дороже стоит, Д-287
стоит того, С-580
стоит только бровью повести ⟨шевельнуть⟩, Б-210
стоит только усом повести ⟨шевельнуть⟩, Б-210
чего стоит, С-582, С-583
чего-нибудь да стоит, С-581
что стоит, С-583

СТОИТЬ
выеденного яйца не стоить, Я-59
не стоить мизинца, М-149
не стоить ногтя, М-149
не стоить подмётки, М-149

СТОЙ
хоть стой, хоть падай, С-584

СТОЙКА
стойка смирно, С-585

СТОЙКЕ
по стойке смирно, С-585

СТОЛ
выложить (парт)билет на стол, Б-65
круглый стол, С-586
лечь ⟨ложиться⟩ на стол, С-587
писать в стол, С-588
под стол пешком ходит, С-589
положить (парт)билет на стол, Б-65
садиться/сесть за один стол, С-590

СТОЛА
крохи с барского ⟨с господского⟩ стола, К-418
крошки с барского ⟨с господского⟩ стола, К-418

СТОЛБ
стоять как столб, С-592

СТОЛБНЯК
столбняк напал ⟨нашёл⟩, С-591

СТОЛБОВАЯ
столбовая дорога, Д-265

СТОЛБОМ
дым идёт/пошёл столбом, Д-436
дым (стоит) столбом, Д-436
пыль столбом, П-673
стоять столбом, С-592

СТОЛБУ
пригвождать/пригвоздить к позорному столбу, С-593
приковать ⟨приковывать⟩ к позорному столбу, С-593

СТОЛБЫ
геркулесовские ⟨геркулесовы⟩ столбы, С-594

СТОЛЕ
на столе, С-595

СТОЛЕЧКО
и (вот) на столечко, С-598
ни (вот) на столечко, С-598

СТОЛКНУТЬСЯ
столкнуться на узкой дороге ⟨дорожке⟩, Д-289

СТОЛОВОЙ
в час по столовой ложке, Ч-20
через час по столовой ложке, Ч-20

СТОЛОМ
за круглым столом, С-586

СТОЛПОТВОРЕНИЕ
вавилонское столпотворение, С-596

СТОЛПЫ
геркулесовские ⟨геркулесовы⟩ столпы, С-594

СТОЛЬ
места не столь отдалённые, М-90

СТОЛЬКО
и вот (на) столько, С-598
и на столько, С-598
не столько... сколько..., С-597
ни (вот) на столько, С-598
сколько голов, столько (и) умов, Г-192

СТОПАМ
идти по стопам, С-599
повергать/повергнуть к стопам, С-600

пойти по стопам, С-599
припадать/припасть к
    стопам, С-601
следовать по стопам,
    С-599

СТОПОЧКУ
пропускать/пропустить
    стопочку, Р-398

СТОПЫ
направить ⟨направлять⟩
    стопы, П-657

СТОРОНА
другая сторона медали,
    С-602
моё дело сторона, Д-116
оборотная ⟨обратная⟩
    сторона медали, С-602

СТОРОНАМ
глядеть по сторонам,
    С-604
зевать по сторонам, С-603
озираться по сторонам,
    С-604
смотреть по сторонам,
    С-604

СТОРОНЕ
в стороне, С-605
на стороне, С-606
оставить ⟨оставлять⟩ в
    стороне, С-607

СТОРОНКЕ
в сторонке, С-605

СТОРОНКОЙ
обойти ⟨обходить⟩
    сторонкой, С-608

СТОРОНОЙ
обойти ⟨обходить⟩
    стороной, С-608

СТОРОНУ
брать сторону, С-609
в сторону, С-610
взять сторону, С-609
вставать/встать на
    сторону, С-609
держать сторону, С-611
и шатко и валко и на
    сторону, Ш-38
на сторону, С-612
ни шатко ни валко ни на
    сторону, Ш-39
принимать/принять
    сторону, С-609
смотреть на сторону, С-613
становиться/стать на
    сторону, С-609
тянуть сторону, С-614
шутки в сторону, Ш-103

СТОРОНЫ
на все четыре стороны,
    С-615
с какой стороны подойти
    ⟨подступиться⟩, Б-163
с одной стороны... с
    другой (стороны), С-616
с ⟨со⟩ своей стороны,
    С-617
со стороны, С-618

СТОЯЛИ
на том стояли, стоим и
    стоять будем, С-577

СТОЯТЬ
едва ⟨еле⟩ стоять на
    ногах, Н-131
крепко стоять на ногах,
    Н-134
на ногах не стоять, Н-131
на том стояли, стоим и
    стоять будем, С-577
не стоять, С-619
прочно стоять на ногах,
    Н-134
с трудом стоять на ногах,
    Н-131
стоять в глазах, Г-121
стоять выше, С-620
стоять горой, Г-350
стоять грудью, Г-427
стоять за спиной, С-512
стоять как столб, С-592
стоять колом, К-205
стоять колом в горле,
    К-206
стоять костью в глотке ⟨в
    горле⟩, К-206
стоять на дороге, П-652
стоять на задних лапах
    ⟨лапках⟩, Л-22
стоять на карте, К-89
стоять на коленях, К-192
стоять на ногах, Н-134
стоять на месте, М-108
стоять на одной доске,
    Д-291
стоять на одном месте,
    М-108
стоять на очереди, О-181
стоять на платформе,
    П-166
стоять на пути, П-652
стоять на реальной почве,
    П-450
стоять на своём, С-86
стоять на своих
    ⟨собственных⟩ ногах,
    Н-134
стоять на твёрдой почве,
    П-450
стоять на учёте, У-172
стоять навытяжку, С-621
стоять над душой, Д-405
стоять одной ногой в гробу
    ⟨в могиле⟩, Н-162
стоять перед глазами,
    Г-121
стоять поперёк горла,
    Г-333
стоять поперёк дороги,
    П-652
стоять поперёк пути,
    П-652
стоять руки по швам,
    Р-285
стоять стеной, С-568
стоять столбом, С-592
стоять у колыбели, К-210
стоять фертом, Ф-8
твёрдо стоять на ногах,
    Н-134
чуть стоять на ногах,
    Н-131

СТРАЖЕ
на страже, С-622

СТРАЖЕЙ
под стражей, С-623

СТРАЖУ
брать/взять под стражу,
    С-624
на стражу, С-622

СТРАНА
обетованная страна, З-127

СТРАНИЦУ
вписать новую страницу,
    С-625
открывать/открыть
    новую страницу, С-626

СТРАННАЯ
странная вещь, Д-131

СТРАННОЕ
странное дело, Д-131

СТРАХ
на свой собственный
    страх, С-627
на свой собственный страх
    и риск, С-627
на свой страх, С-627
на свой страх и риск, С-627
не за страх, а за совесть,
    С-628

СТРАХА
рыцарь без страха и
    упрёка, Р-395
страха ради иудейска,
    С-629
у страха глаза велики,
    С-630

СТРАХЕ
в страхе (божием), С-631
в страхе божьем, С-631

СТРАХОМ
под страхом, С-632

СТРАШЕН
не так страшен чёрт, как
    его малюют, Ч-78

СТРАШНО
страшно подступиться,
    П-257

СТРАШНОЕ
делать/сделать страшное
    лицо, Г-67

СТРАШНОЙ
со страшной силой, С-181

СТРАШНЫЕ
делать/сделать страшные
    глаза, Г-67

СТРЕКАЧА
давать/дать стрекача,
    С-633
задавать/задать стрекача,
    С-633

СТРЕЛОЙ
стрелой вылетать/
    вылететь, П-630

СТРЕЛОЧНИК
всегда виноват
    стрелочник, С-634
стрелочник виноват, С-634

СТРЕЛЬНУТЬ
стрельнуть глазами
    ⟨глазками⟩, Г-122

СТРЕЛЯНАЯ
стреляная птица, В-267

СТРЕЛЯНЫЙ
стреляный волк, В-227
стреляный воробей, В-267

СТРЕЛЯТЬ
из пушек ⟨пушки⟩ по
    воробьям стрелять,
    П-666
стрелять глазами
    ⟨глазками⟩, Г-122

СТРЕЧКА
давать/дать стречка,
    С-633
задавать/задать стречка,
    С-633

СТРИЧЬ
стричь купоны, К-475
стричь под одну гребёнку,
    Г-381

СТРОИЛАСЬ
(и) Москва не вдруг ⟨не
    сразу⟩ строилась, М-260

СТРОИТЬ
строить глазки, Г-132
строить дурочку, Д-333
строить из себя, С-635
строить из себя шута,
    Ш-98
строить козни, К-170
строить куры, К-488
строить на песке ⟨на
    песце⟩, П-116
строить рожи ⟨рожу⟩,
    Р-146

СТРОЙ
ввести ⟨вводить⟩ в строй,
    С-636
войти в строй, С-637
вступать/вступить в
    строй, С-637
входить в строй, С-637
прогнать ⟨прогонять⟩
    сквозь строй, С-638

СТРОК
прочитать ⟨читать⟩
    между строк, С-639

СТРОКА
приказная строка, С-640

СТРОКАМИ
прочитать ⟨читать⟩
    между строками, С-639

СТРОКУ
не в строку, С-641
не всяко(е) лыко в строку,
    Л-155
поставить ⟨ставить⟩
    всякое лыко в строку,
    Л-156

СТРОЧЕК
прочитать ⟨читать⟩
    между строчек, С-639

СТРОЧКАМИ
прочитать ⟨читать⟩
    между строчками, С-639

СТРОЯ
выбывать/выбыть из
    строя, С-643
вывести ⟨выводить⟩ из
    строя, С-642
выйти ⟨выходить⟩ из
    строя, С-643

СТРУЖКУ
снимать/снять стружку,
С-644

СТРУНА
слабая струна, С-645

СТРУНЕ
в струне, С-646

СТРУНКА
слабая струнка, С-645

СТРУНКЕ
ходить по струнке, С-647

СТРУНКУ
в струнку, С-648
ходить в струнку, С-647

СТРУНУ
в струну, С-648
задевать/задеть (за)
больную
⟨чувствительную⟩
струну, С-649
затронуть (за) больную
⟨чувствительную⟩
струну, С-649
тронуть (за) больную
⟨чувствительную⟩
струну, С-649

СТРУЮ
вливать/влить живую
⟨свежую⟩ струю, С-650
внести ⟨вносить⟩ живую
⟨свежую⟩ струю, С-650

СТРЯХИВАТЬ
стряхивать с плеч, П-176

СТРЯХНУТЬ
стряхнуть с плеч, П-176

СТУКАТЬ
стукать по носу, Н-238

СТУКНУЛ
кондрашка стукнул, К-228

СТУКНУТЬ
стукнуть по носу, Н-238

СТУЛЬЕВ
сидеть между двух
стульев, С-651

СТУЛЬЯМИ
сидеть между двумя
стульями, С-651

СТУПАЛА
нога не ступала, Н-122
чтоб нога не ступала,
Н-148

СТУПАЛО
чтоб ноги не ступало,
Н-148

СТУПЕ
толочь воду в ступе, В-190
чёрт в ступе, Ч-86

СТУПИТЬ
не давать/не дать шагу
ступить, Ш-19
шагу не мочь ⟨не сметь⟩
ступить, Ш-24
шагу невозможно ступить,
Ш-24
шагу негде ступить, Ш-23
шагу некуда ступить, Ш-23
шагу нельзя ступить, Ш-24

СТУЧАТЬСЯ
стучаться в двери ⟨в
дверь⟩, Д-37

СТЫД
стыд не дым, глаза не
выест, С-652

СТЫДА
нет стыда в глазах, С-653
ни стыда ни совести нет,
С-653
сгорать/сгореть от ⟨со⟩
стыда, С-654

СТЫДУ
к стыду моему ⟨своему⟩,
С-655

СТЫНЕТ
кровь стынет (в жилах),
К-405

СУД
пока суд да дело, С-656
шемякин суд, С-657

СУДА
на нет и суда нет, С-658
суда нет, С-659

СУДЕБ
вершитель судеб, В-58
волею судеб, В-223
по воле судеб, В-223

СУДИТЬ
судить да ⟨и⟩ рядить,
С-660
судить-рядить, С-660

СУДЫ
суды да ⟨и⟩ пересуды,
С-661

СУДЬБА
не судьба, С-662
судьба привела, С-378

СУДЬБАМИ
какими судьбами?, С-663

СУДЬБОЙ
обижен(ный) судьбой,
С-664
обойдённый судьбой,
С-664

СУДЬБУ
искушать судьбу, С-665
испытывать судьбу, С-665

СУДЬБЫ
баловень судьбы, Б-16
волею судьбы, В-223
игра судьбы, И-14
ирония судьбы, И-72
на произвол судьбы, П-569
от судьбы не уйдёшь,
С-666
перст судьбы, П-108
по воле судьбы, В-223
по иронии судьбы, И-72

СУДЯ
судя по, С-667
судя по тому что, С-668

СУДЯТ
победителей не судят,
П-208

СУЕТ
суета сует (и всяческая
суета), С-669

СУЕТА
мышиная суета, В-209
суета сует (и всяческая
суета), С-669

СУЙСЯ
не зная ⟨не спросясь⟩
броду, не суйся в воду,
Б-211
прежде батьки ⟨отца⟩ в
петлю не суйся, Б-27

СУК
подрубать сук, на котором
сидишь, С-670
рубить сук, на котором
сидишь, С-670

СУКИН
сукин сын, С-734

СУКНО
класть/положить под
сукно, С-671

СУКНОМ
держать под сукном, С-672
лежать под сукном, С-673

СУКОННАЯ
суконная речь, Я-28

СУКОННЫЙ
суконный язык, Я-28

СУЛИ
не сули журавля в небе, а
дай синицу в руки, С-195

СУМА
сума перемётная, С-674

СУМАСШЕДШИЙ
сумасшедший дом, Д-253

СУММА
кругленькая ⟨круглая⟩
сумма, С-675

СУММЕ
в сумме, С-676

СУМНЯСЯ
ничтоже сумняся, С-677

СУМНЯШЕСЯ
ничтоже сумняшеся, С-677

СУМОЙ
идти/пойти с сумой, М-190
пускать/пустить с сумой,
М-192
ходить с сумой, М-190

СУМЫ
довести ⟨доводить⟩ до
сумы, М-192
дойти ⟨доходить⟩ до
сумы, М-190

СУНУТЬ
сунуть в нос, Н-219
сунуть голову в петлю,
Г-278
сунуть нос, Н-220
сунуть под нос, Н-219
сунуть свой нос, Н-220

СУНУТЬСЯ
сунуться в глаза, Г-99
сунуться на глаза, Г-99
сунуться со своим носом,
Н-220

СУРДИНКОЙ
под сурдинкой, С-678

СУРДИНКУ
под сурдинку, С-678

СУРОК
как сурок, С-679

СУТИ
по сути (дела), С-680

СУТОЛОКА
мышиная сутолока, В-209

СУТЬ
суть дела, С-681

СУХИМ
выйти ⟨выходить⟩ сухим
из воды, В-195
держать порох сухим,
П-378

СУХОЙ
ни одной сухой нитки не
осталось ⟨нет⟩, Н-101
сухой нитки не осталось
⟨нет⟩, Н-101
такой-сякой немазаный
сухой, Т-33
такой-сякой сухой
немазаный, Т-33

СУЧКА
без сучка без задоринки,
С-682
без сучка и задоринки,
С-682
ни сучка ни задоринки,
С-683

СУЧОК
в чужом глазу сучок
видим, а в своём (и)
бревна не замечаем,
Г-140

СУЧЬЯ
сучья дочь, Д-302

СУЩЕЕ
сущее наказание, Н-21

СУЩЕСТВОВАНИЕ
отравлять существование,
Ж-61

СУЩЕСТВУ
по существу, С-684
по существу говоря, С-684

СУЩНОСТИ
в сущности (говоря), С-684

СХВАТИТЬ
схватить быка за рога,
Б-256
схватить за глотку, Г-335
схватить за горло, Г-335
схватить за грудки, Г-420
схватить за руку, Р-370
схватить за хвост, Х-19

СХВАТИТЬСЯ
схватиться обеими
руками, Р-264
схватиться за голову, Г-281
схватиться за соломинку,
С-474

СХВАТЫВАТЬ
схватывать на лету, Л-69
схватывать с лёту, Л-69

СХОДИТ
всяк(ий) по-своему с ума
сходит, У-82
каждый по-своему с ума
сходит, У-82

СХОДИТСЯ
гора с горой не сходится, а
человек с человеком
(всегда) сойдётся, Г-314

СХОДИТЬ
не сходить с уст, Я-50

не сходить с языка, Я-50
сходить в гроб, М-206
сходить в могилу, М-206
сходить на нет, С-685
сходить под себя, Д-61
сходить с рук, Р-222
сходить с ума, У-92
сходить со сцены, С-688

СХОДЯ
не сходя с места, М-93

СХОДЯТСЯ
концы с концами (не) сходятся, К-259

СХОРОНИТЬ
схоронить концы (в воду), К-262

СЦЕНУ
выступать/выступить на сцену, С-686
появиться ⟨появляться⟩ на сцену, С-686
сделать сцену, С-687
устраивать ⟨устроить⟩ сцену, С-687
явиться ⟨являться⟩ на сцену, С-686

СЦЕНЫ
делать сцены, С-687
сойти ⟨сходить⟩ со сцены, С-688
устраивать сцены, С-687

СЦИЛЛОЙ
между Сциллой и Харибдой, С-689

СЧАСТЛИВ
не родись красив, а родись счастлив, Р-135
счастлив твой бог, Б-124

СЧАСТЛИВО
счастливо оставаться!, О-120
счастливо отделаться, О-139

СЧАСТЛИВОГО
счастливого пути!, П-653

СЧАСТЛИВОЙ
родиться под счастливой звездой, З-93

СЧАСТЛИВУЮ
верить в счастливую звезду, З-94

СЧАСТЛИВЫЙ
счастливый путь!, П-653

СЧАСТЛИВЫМ
не родись красивым, а родись счастливым, Р-135

СЧАСТЬЕ
на счастье, С-690
не в деньгах счастье, Д-166
попытать счастье, С-694
счастье твоё, С-691

СЧАСТЬЮ
к счастью, С-692
по счастью, С-692

СЧАСТЬЯ
баловень счастья, Б-16
не было бы счастья, да несчастье помогло, С-693

попытать счастья, С-694

СЧЕСТЬ
не счесть, С-695
по пальцам можно счесть, П-17
счесть за благо, Б-74
счесть за честь, Ч-138

СЧЁТ
в счёт, С-696
гамбургский счёт, С-697
денежка счёт любит, Д-171
денежки ⟨деньги⟩ счёт любят, Д-171
за свой счёт, С-698
за собственный счёт, С-698
за счёт, С-699, С-700
за чужой счёт, С-705
закрывать/закрыть счёт, С-701
знать счёт деньгам, С-702
на свой счёт, С-698
на собственный счёт, С-698
на счёт, С-703, С-704
на чужой счёт, С-705
на этот счёт, С-706
не в счёт, С-707
не идти в счёт, С-707
открывать/открыть счёт, С-708
отнести за ⟨на⟩ счёт, С-709
относить за ⟨на⟩ счёт, С-709
потерять счёт, С-713
предъявить ⟨предъявлять⟩ счёт, С-710
принимать/принять на свой счёт, С-711
проезжаться/проехаться на счёт, С-712
пройтись на счёт, С-712
прохаживаться на счёт, С-712
терять счёт, С-713

СЧЁТА
без счёта, С-714
в два счёта, С-715
для ровного счёта, С-716
не знать счёта деньгам, С-717
сбрасывать/сбросить со счёта, С-719
скидывать/скинуть со счёта, С-719
снимать/снять со счёта, С-719
счёта нет, С-726

СЧЁТЕ
в конечном счёте, С-718
в последнем счёте, С-718

СЧЕТОВ/СЧЁТОВ
сбрасывать/сбросить со счетов ⟨со счётов⟩, С-719
скидывать/скинуть со счетов ⟨со счётов⟩, С-719
снимать/снять со счетов ⟨со счётов⟩, С-719

СЧЁТОМ
круглым счётом, С-720

ровным счётом, С-721, С-722

СЧЕТУ/СЧЁТУ
без счёту, С-714
на счету, С-723, С-724
по большому счёту, С-725
счёту нет, С-726

СЧЁТЫ
кончить (все) счёты, С-727
покончить (все) счёты, С-727
покончить счёты с жизнью, П-285
свести ⟨сводить⟩ счёты, С-728
что за счёты!, С-729

СЧИТАННЫЕ
считанные дни, Д-206

СЧИТАТЬ
ворон считать, В-270
галок считать, В-270
мух считать, В-270
не считать денег, Д-147
не считать за человека, Ч-53
ни во что не считать, Г-412
ни за что считать, Г-412
считать за честь, Ч-138
считать звёзды, З-96
считать каждую копейку, К-285
считать копейки ⟨копейку⟩, К-285

СЧИТАЮТ
цыплят по осени считают, Ц-40

СШИБАТЬ
сшибать гонор, С-508
сшибать с ног, Н-112
сшибать спесь, С-508
сшибать форс, С-508

СШИБИТЬ
сшибить гонор, С-508
сшибить с ног, Н-112
сшибить спесь, С-508
сшибить форс, С-508

СШИТ
неладно ⟨нескладно, худо⟩ скроен, да крепко ⟨плотно⟩ сшит, С-242

СЪЕДЕНИЕ
на съедение, С-730

СЪЕЛ
мало каши съел, К-113

СЪЕЛА
знает кошка, чьё мясо съела, К-343
рано пташечка запела, как бы кошечка не съела, П-612
чует кошка, чьё мясо съела, К-343

СЪЕСТ
бог не выдаст, свинья не съест, Б-100
господь не выдаст, свинья не съест, Б-100

СЪЕСТЬ
зубы съесть, З-197
куль соли съесть, П-625

много соли съесть, П-625
поедом съесть, Е-19
пуд соли съесть, П-625
собаку съесть, С-448
съесть гриб, Г-394
съесть живьём, С-731
съесть пилюлю, П-149
чтобы узнать человека, надо с ним пуд соли съесть, Ч-54

СЫГРАТЬ
сыграть в ящик, Я-71
сыграть ва-банк, И-25
сыграть на руку, Р-344
сыграть роль, Р-156
сыграть труса, Т-222
сыграть штуку, Ш-109
сыграть шутку, Ш-109

СЫН
блудный сын, С-732
вражий сын, С-734
курицын сын, С-733
собачий сын, С-734
сукин сын, С-734
чёртов сын, С-734

СЫНОВЬЯ
годиться в сыновья, Г-188

СЫНОК
маменькин сынок, С-735

СЫНОЧЕК
маменькин сыночек, С-735

СЫПАТЬ
сыпать деньгами, Д-165
сыпать соль на рану ⟨раны⟩, С-477

СЫПЛЕТСЯ
песок сыплется, П-123

СЫР
как ⟨словно⟩ сыр в масле кататься, С-736

СЫР-БОР
весь сыр-бор (загорелся), С-737
сыр-бор горит, С-737
сыр-бор загорелся, С-737

СЫРОСТЬ
развести ⟨разводить⟩ сырость, С-738

СЫСКАТЬ
концов не сыскать, К-255

СЫТ
сыт по горло, Г-345

СЫТОЕ
на сытое брюхо, Ж-15

СЫТЫ
и волки сыты, и овцы целы, В-230

СЫТЫЙ
на сытый желудок, Ж-15
сытый голодного не разумеет, С-739

СЫЧ
как сыч глядеть, С-740
как сыч жить, С-741
как сыч сидеть, С-740
как сыч смотреть, С-740

СЫЧОМ
сычом глядеть, С-740
сычом жить, С-741

сычом сидеть, С-740
сычом смотреть, С-740

СЮ
по сю пору, П-359

СЮДА
и туда и сюда, Т-226
ни туда (и) ни сюда, Т-227
то туда, то сюда, Т-228
туда да сюда, Т-226
туда и сюда, Т-226
туда, сюда, Т-226

СЮДЫ
ни туды (и) ни сюды,
   Т-227

СЯК
и так и сяк, Т-6
так и сяк, Т-6
так или сяк, Т-21
так ли, сяк ли, Т-21
то так, то сяк, Т-30
хоть так, хоть сяк, Т-21

СЯКОЙ
такой и сякой, Т-33

СЯМ
там и сям, Т-38
то там, то сям, Т-241

Т

ТА
всё та же песня, П-121
не та музыка, М-283

ТАБАК
дела ⟨дело⟩ табак, Д-95
другой табак, К-190
иной табак, К-190
не тот табак, К-190

ТАБАКУ
ни за понюх ⟨понюшку⟩
   табаку, П-340

ТАБЕЛЬ
табель о рангах, Т-1

ТАЕТ
лёд тает, Л-40
тает во рту, Р-188

ТАИТЬ
нечего (и) греха таить,
   Г-392
чего (и) греха таить,
   Г-392
что (и) греха таить, Г-392

ТАЙНЫ
не делать тайны, С-111

ТАК
вот так...!, Т-2
вот так клюква!, К-143
вот так номер!, Ш-89
вот так так!, Р-20
вот так фунт!, Ф-31
вот так штука!, Ш-89
вот это номер!, Ш-89
давно бы так!, Д-9
за так, Т-3
и так, Т-4
и так далее, Т-5
и так и сяк, Т-6
и так и так, Т-7
и так и эдак ⟨этак⟩, Т-7
как аукнется, так и
   откликнется, А-49

как бы не так!, К-14
как не так!, К-14
надо же так!, Н-11
не мытьём, так катаньем,
   М-318
не так ли?, Т-8
не так страшен чёрт, как
   его малюют, Ч-78
не так уж далеко уйти,
   У-64
не так чтоб(ы), Т-9
ни за так, Т-10
ну так что ж(е), Т-11
пропадать, так с
   музыкой!, М-284
просто так, П-583
пусть так, П-640
раз так, Т-12
так вашу мать, М-55
так вот, Т-13
так держать!, Д-181
так его!, Т-14
так же как (и), Т-15
так и, Т-16
так и быть, Б-280
так и есть, Е-21
так и знай(те), З-151
так и надо, Т-17
так и нужно, Т-17
так и сяк, Т-6
так и так, Т-7, Т-18
так и так дескать, Т-18
так и так мол, Т-18
так и эдак ⟨этак⟩, Т-7
так или иначе, Т-19
так или сяк, Т-21
так как, Т-20
так ли, сяк ли, Т-21
так ли, этак ли, Т-21
так на так, Т-22
так называемый, Н-17
так не проходит/не
   прошло, Т-596
так нет (же), Т-23
так оно и есть, Е-21
так разе, С-366
так себе, Т-24
так сказать, С-212
так-сяк, Т-6
так твою мать, М-55
так-то и так-то, Т-18
так-то (оно) так, а ⟨да,
   но⟩, Т-25
так только, Т-26
так тому и быть, Б-281
так точно, Т-27
так что, Т-28
так что ж(е), Т-11
так чтоб(ы), Т-29
то так, то сяк, Т-30
то так, то так, Т-30
то так, то этак, Т-30
хоть бы и так, Т-31
хоть так, хоть сяк, Т-21
хоть так, хоть этак, Т-21
хотя бы и так, Т-31
что до... так..., Ч-178
что так?, Ч-187
что-то не так, Ч-190
чтоб я так жил!, Ж-69

ТАКИМ
с таким же успехом, У-137

таким макаром, М-5
таким образом, О-24

ТАКОВ
и был таков, Б-258
каков поп, таков и приход,
   П-343

ТАКОВОЙ
как таковой, Т-32

ТАКОВСКОГО
не на таковского напал,
   Н-24

ТАКОГО
не на такого напал, Н-24
такого рода, Р-130
что ж(е) такого?, Ч-181
что ж(е) тут такого?, Ч-181
что (тут) такого?, Ч-181

ТАКОЕ
есть такое дело, Д-99
и всё такое (прочее), В-330
раз такое дело, Д-128
сделай(те) такое
   одолжение, М-159
что ж(е) такое?, Ч-181
чёрт знает что такое!,
   Ч-93
что такое, Ч-188
это чёрт знает что такое!,
   Ч-93

ТАКОЙ
есть такой грех, Г-385
какой такой..., К-25
такой и сякой, Т-33
такой-сякой, Т-33
такой-сякой немазаный
   сухой, Т-33
такой-сякой сухой
   немазаный, Т-33
такой-то (и такой-то), Т-34

ТАКОМ
в таком духе, Д-350
в таком же духе, Д-350
в таком разе, С-366
в таком роде, Р-133
в таком случае, С-366
с таком, Т-35

ТАКОМУ
по такому случаю, С-380

ТАКТ
в такт, Т-36

ТАЛАНТ
зарывать/зарыть талант
   (в землю), Т-37

ТАМ
да только воз и ныне там,
   В-201
да что там говорить, Г-167
все там будем, Б-215
где там!, К-455
где тонко, там и рвётся,
   Р-95
где уж там!, К-455
где хотенье, там и уменье,
   Х-86
здесь и там, Т-38
как бы там ни было, Б-263
как там ни верти, К-427
как там ни вертись, К-428
как там ни крути, К-427
как там ни крутись, К-428

какое там!, К-21
какой там...!, К-26
куда там!, К-455
одна нога здесь, (а) другая
   там, Н-123
там и здесь, Т-38
там и сям, Т-38
там и тут, Т-38
там хорошо, где нас нет,
   Т-39
то там, то сям, Т-241
то там, то тут, Т-241
то тут, то там, Т-241
тут и там, Т-38
чего там, Ч-189
чего я там не видал ⟨не
   видел⟩?, В-118
что там, Ч-189
что там говорить, Г-167
что я там забыл?, З-11
что я там потерял?, З-11

ТАНТАЛА
муки Тантала, М-288

ТАНТАЛОВЫ
танталовы муки, М-288

ТАНЦЕВАТЬ
танцевать от печки, П-145

ТАРАБАРСКАЯ
тарабарская грамота,
   Г-372

ТАРАЩИТЬ
таращить глаза, Г-100

ТАРЕЛКЕ
не в своей тарелке, Т-40

ТАРТАРАРЫ
лететь/полететь в
   тартарары, Т-41
провалиться в тартарары,
   Т-42
провалиться мне в
   тартарары!, З-121
чтоб мне провалиться в
   тартарары!, З-121
чтоб тебе провалиться в
   тартарары!, З-122

ТАРЫ
разводить тары да бары,
   Т-43
тары да бары, Т-44

**ТАРЫ-БАРЫ(-
   РАСТАБАРЫ)**
разводить тары-бары
   ⟨тары-бары-
   растабары⟩, Т-43
тары-бары, Т-44
тары-бары-растабары,
   Т-44

ТАСКАЕТ
чёрт таскает, Ч-96

ТАСКАТЬ
едва ⟨еле⟩ ноги таскать,
   Н-144
насилу ноги таскать, Н-144
с трудом ноги таскать,
   Н-144
таскать воду в решете,
   В-189
таскать воду решетом,
   В-189
таскать каштаны из огня,
   К-114

ТАСКАЮТ
чуть ноги таскать, Н-144
ТАСКАЮТ
черти таскают, Ч-96
ТАСКУ
давать/дать таску, Т-45
задавать/задать таску,
Т-45
ТАЩИТЬ
едва ⟨еле⟩ ноги тащить,
Н-144
клещами тащить, К-133
насилу ноги тащить, Н-144
с трудом ноги тащить,
Н-144
тащить за уши, У-191
тащить на аркане, А-39
чуть ноги тащить, Н-144
ТВАРИ
всякой твари по паре, Т-46
каждой твари по паре,
Т-46
ТВЁРДАЯ
твёрдая рука, Р-236
ТВЁРДО
твёрдо стоять на ногах,
Н-134
ТВЁРДОЙ
в здравом уме и твёрдой
памяти, У-95
в твёрдой памяти, У-95
стать твёрдой ногой, Н-163
стоять на твёрдой почве,
П-450
ТВЁРДОМ
в твёрдом рассудке, У-95
ТВЁРДУЮ
иметь твёрдую почву под
ногами, П-450
ТВЁРДЫЙ
твёрдый орех ⟨орешек⟩,
О-101
ТВОЁ
за твоё здоровье!, З-105
не твоё собачье дело,
Д-120
с твоё, М-211
счастье твоё, С-691
твоё здоровье!, З-105
ТВОЕГО
говорить с твоего голоса,
Г-306
петь с твоего голоса, Г-306
ТВОЕМУ
к твоему сведению, С-33
ТВОИМ
к твоим услугам, У-134
ТВОИМИ
твоими бы устами (да)
мёд пить, У-145
твоими молитвами, М-231
ТВОЙ
счастлив твой бог, Б-124
твой покорный слуга,
С-346
что твой..., Т-47
ТВОРИТЬ
творить себе кумир(а),
К-472
ТВОЮ
ёб твою мать, М-50

мать твою за ногу!, М-52
мать твою перемать, М-55
так твою мать, М-55
твою мать, М-55
ТВОЯ
воля твоя, В-254
мели, Емеля, твоя неделя,
Е-10
твоя берёт, Б-58
твоя взяла, Б-58
твоя правда, П-478
ТЕ
вот те (и) здравствуй(те)!,
З-109
вот те и на!, Р-20
вот те и раз!, Р-20
вот те крест!, К-380
вот те на!, Р-20
вот те раз!, Р-20
вот те фунт!, Ф-31
слава те господи, С-244
ТЕБЕ
вот тебе!, Т-48
вот тебе, бабушка, и
Юрьев день!, Б-6
вот тебе бог, а вот порог,
Б-107
вот тебе и..., Т-49
вот тебе и весь разговор,
Р-46
вот тебе и весь сказ, Р-46
вот тебе и вся недолга,
В-349
вот тебе и здравствуй(те)!,
З-109
вот тебе и на!, Р-20
вот тебе и раз!, Р-20
вот тебе крест!, К-380
вот тебе на!, Р-20
вот тебе раз!, Р-20
говорю ⟨говорят⟩ тебе,
Г-177
доложу (я) тебе, Д-247
как тебе сказать, С-205
на тебе!, Т-50
по тебе, М-196
слава тебе господи, С-244
чтоб тебе лопнуть!, Л-138
чтоб тебе сквозь землю
провалиться!, З-122
чтоб тебе треснуть!,
Л-138
я тебе дам!, Д-19
я тебе задам!, Д-19
я тебе покажу!, Д-19
ТЕБЯ
а ну тебя!, Т-51
вот я тебя, Я-1
да ну тебя!, Т-51
да разразит тебя бог
⟨господь⟩, Г-407
дуй тебя горой!, Г-349
леший тебя возьми
⟨дери⟩!, Ч-99
леший тебя побери
⟨подери⟩!, Ч-99
ляд тебя побери!, Ч-99
ну тебя!, Т-51
ну тебя в болото!, Б-171
ну я тебя спрашиваю!,
С-525

пёс тебя возьми!, Ч-99
порази тебя гром
⟨громом⟩, Г-407
прах тебя возьми
⟨побери⟩!, Ч-99
пусть разразит тебя бог
⟨господь⟩, Г-407
раздуй тебя горой!, Г-349
разрази тебя гром
⟨громом⟩, Г-407
чёрт тебя возьми ⟨дери⟩!,
Ч-99
чёрт тебя побери
⟨подери⟩!, Ч-99
чёрт бы тебя брал ⟨взял,
драл⟩!, Ч-99
чёрт бы тебя побрал
⟨подрал⟩!, Ч-99
чтоб тебя!, Р-63
чтоб тебя разорвало!,
Р-63
чтоб у тебя язык отсох,
Я-33
шут тебя возьми ⟨дери⟩!,
Ч-99
шут тебя побери
⟨подери⟩!, Ч-99
я тебя, Я-1
я тебя спрашиваю!, С-525
ТЁКУ
давать/дать тёку, Д-304
задавать/задать тёку,
Д-304
ТЕКУТ
слюнки текут, С-387
ТЕЛА
спадать/спасть с тела,
Т-52
ТЕЛЕ
в теле, Т-53
держать в чёрном теле,
Т-54
еле-еле душа в теле, Д-363
пока душа держится в
теле, Д-377
ТЕЛЕГЕ
пятое колесо в телеге,
К-197
ТЕЛЕЖКА
вагон и маленькая
тележка, В-1
ТЕЛЕФОНЕ
висеть на телефоне, Т-55
повиснуть на телефоне,
Т-55
ТЕЛЕЦ
златой ⟨золотой⟩ телец,
Т-56
ТЕЛИТСЯ
не мычит, не телится,
М-319
ТЕЛО
войти ⟨входить⟩ в тело,
Т-57
ТЕЛОМ
душой и телом, Д-397
ни душой ни телом, Д-400
ТЕЛУ
мурашки бегают ⟨бегут⟩
по телу, М-291

мурашки забегали
⟨заползали⟩ по телу,
М-291
мурашки побежали по
телу, М-291
мурашки ползают
⟨ползут, поползли⟩ по
телу, М-291
мурашки пошли по телу,
М-291
мурашки пробежали по
телу, М-291
своя рубаха ⟨рубашка⟩
ближе к телу, Р-190
ТЕЛЯТ
куда Макар телят не
гонял, М-3
ТЕЛЯЧИЙ
телячий восторг, В-281
ТЕЛЯЧЬИ
телячьи нежности, Н-70
ТЕМ
а между тем, Т-58
вместе с тем, Т-59
вслед за тем, В-345
за всем тем, В-338
за тем дело стало, Д-103
меж тем, Т-60
меж тем как, Т-61
между тем, Т-60
между тем как, Т-61
не тем будь помянут,
Б-234
перед тем как, Т-62
по тем временам, В-291
с тем же успехом, У-137
с тем чтобы, Т-63
со всем тем, В-338
тем более, Т-64
тем более что, Т-65
тем временем, В-293
тем лучше, Л-150
тем не менее, Т-66
тем паче, Т-64
тем самым, Т-67
чем богаты, тем и рады,
Б-132
чем... тем..., Ч-63
ТЕМНА
от темна до темна, Т-68
с темна до темна, Т-68
темна вода во облацех,
В-176
ТЁМНАЯ
тёмная лошадка, Л-140
ТЕМНЕЕТ
в глазах темнеет, Г-127
ТЁМНОЕ
тёмное пятно, П-687
ТЁМНОМ
как в тёмном лесу, Л-61
ТЕМНОТЕ
в темноте все кошки серы,
К-349
ТЁМНУЮ
делать/сделать тёмную,
Т-69
устраивать/устроить
тёмную, Т-69
ТЁМНЫЙ
тёмный лес, Л-58

[995]

какой бы то ни было,
Б-264

кидать то в жар, то в
холод, Ж-2

когда бы то ни было,
Б-265

коли ⟨коль⟩ (уж) на то
пошло, П-465

кто бы то ни был, Б-260

кто бы то ни было, Б-266

куда бы то ни было, Б-262

на то, Т-107

на то и, Т-107

не всё то золото, что
блестит, З-183

не то, Т-103

не то... не то, Т-114

не то что, Т-108

не то что... а, Т-108

не то что... но, Т-108

не то чтоб(ы)..., Т-108

не то чтоб(ы)... а, Т-108

не то чтоб(ы)... но, Т-108

невзирая на то что, Н-63

несмотря на то что, Н-85

ни то ни сё, Т-109

но и то, Т-106

ну то-то же, Т-115

пока то да сё, Т-110

похоже на то, что..., П-444

почему бы то ни было,
Б-268

сколько бы то ни было,
Б-269

то бишь, Т-111

то да сё, Т-112

то есть, Т-113

то и дело, Д-132

то и знай, З-152

то и сё, Т-112

то ли будет, Б-218

то ли дело, Д-133

то ли ещё будет, Б-218

то ли... то ли..., Т-114

то-сё, Т-112

то так, то сяк, Т-30

то так, то так, Т-30

то так, то этак, Т-30

то там, то сям, Т-241

то там, то тут, Т-241

то-то же, Т-115

то-то и есть, Т-105

то-то и оно ⟨оно-то⟩,
Т-105

то-то оно и есть, Т-105

то туда, то сюда, Т-228

то тут, то там, Т-241

то, что доктор прописал,
Д-232

чей бы то ни было, Б-270

что будет, то будет, Б-220

что бы то ни было, Б-271

что было, то прошло (и
быльём поросло), Б-275

что до... то..., Ч-178

что касается, то..., К-101

что посеешь, то и
пожнёшь, П-407

что правда, то правда,
П-479

что-то не то, Ч-190

ТОБОЙ
бог с тобой, Б-104

господь с тобой, Б-104

пёс с тобой, Ч-98

прах с тобой, Ч-98

хрен с тобой, Ч-98

Христос с тобой, Б-104

чёрт с тобой, Ч-98

шут с тобой, Ч-98

ТОВАР
показать ⟨показывать⟩
товар лицом, Т-116

ТОВАРИЩ
гусь свинье не товарищ,
Г-447

товарищ по несчастью,
Т-117

ТОВАРИЩА
на вкус (и) на цвет
товарища нет, В-154

ТОВАРИЩЕЙ
на вкус (и) на цвет
товарищей нет, В-154

ТОГДА
тогда как, Т-118

ТОГО
без того, Т-125

более того, Б-165

больше того, Б-165

в силу того что, С-185

ввиду того что, Т-119

вместо того чтобы, Т-120

выходец с того света,
В-386

для того чтобы, Т-121

до того, Т-122

до того как, Т-123

до того, что..., Т-124

и без того, Т-125

и того, Т-126

из (одного и) того же
теста, Т-90

испечён не из того теста,
Т-89

испечены из (одного и)
того же теста, Т-90

кроме того, Т-127

мало того, М-13

мало того что... ещё и...,
М-14

не без того, Т-128

не более того, Б-168

не больше того, Б-168

не из того теста, Т-89

не на того напал, Н-24

не с того конца, К-252

не того, Т-129

независимо от того что,
Н-72

нет того чтобы, Т-130

ни с того ни с сего, Т-131

по мере того как, М-78

после того как, Т-132

ради того чтобы, Т-121

с кем поведёшься, от того
и наберёшься, П-212

сверх того, Т-133

сделан не из того теста,
Т-89

сделаны из (одного и) того
же теста, Т-90

стоит того, С-580

того гляди, Г-153

того же поля ягода
⟨ягодки, ягоды⟩, П-327

того и гляди, Г-153

того и жди, Г-153

того и смотри, Г-153

чему быть, того не
миновать, Б-282

ТОГУ
рядиться в тогу, Т-134

ТОЖЕ
скажешь тоже, С-200

тоже мне, Т-135

ТОЙ
вставать/встать не с той
ноги, Н-142

не из той оперы, О-94

одной и той же масти,
М-43

отплатить ⟨отплачивать⟩
той же монетой, М-254

платить той же монетой,
М-254

с той поры, П-365

той же масти, М-43

ТОЛИКА
малая толика, Т-136

ТОЛК
взять в толк, Т-137

знать толк, Т-138

понимать толк, Т-138

ТОЛКНУТЬ
ни в зуб толкнуть, З-187

ТОЛКОМ
с толком, Т-139

ТОЛКУ
без толку, Т-140

добиться толку (нельзя),
Т-141

не добиться толку, Т-141

сбивать с толку, Т-142

сбиваться с толку, Т-143

сбить с толку, Т-142

сбиться с толку, Т-143

ТОЛОЧЬ
толочь воду (в ступе),
В-190

ТОЛСТАЯ
толстая мошна, К-82

ТОЛСТОЕ
тонкий намёк на толстое
обстоятельство, Н-23

ТОЛСТЫЕ
тонкий намёк на толстые
обстоятельства, Н-23

ТОЛСТЫЙ
толстый карман, К-82

толстый кошелёк, К-82

ТОЛЩЕ
поперёк себя толще, Ш-64

ТОЛЬКО
в чём только душа
держится, Д-363

вы только подумайте!,
П-259

да и только, Т-144

да только воз и ныне там,
В-201

едва только, Е-2

едва только... Е-2

и как только земля держит
⟨носит, терпит⟩, З-126

и только, Т-146

как только..., К-18

как только земля держит
⟨носит, терпит⟩, З-126

кому только не лень, Л-51

куда только смотрит,
С-420

лишь бы только, Л-113

лишь только..., К-18

милые бранятся — только
тешатся, М-163

нет, вы только
подумайте!, П-259

нет, ты только подумай!,
П-259

одно только звание, З-86

одно только название, Н-15

осталась только тень, Т-76

подумать только!, П-259

разве только, Р-45

смех да и только, С-404

смехота да и только, С-404

стоит только бровью
повести ⟨шевельнуть⟩,
Б-210

стоит только усом повести
⟨шевельнуть⟩, Б-210

так только, Т-26

только слава, Н-15

только бровью повести
⟨шевельнуть⟩, Б-210

только бы..., Л-113

только держись!, Д-182

только за смертью
посылать, С-398

только и..., Т-145

только и видел, В-125

только и видели, В-125

только и всего, Т-146

только и делает, З-144

только и знает, З-144

только и света ⟨свету⟩ в
окне ⟨в окошке⟩, С-74

только... как..., Т-147

только лишь..., К-18

только название, Н-15

только одна слава, Н-15

только птичьего молока не
хватает ⟨недостаёт⟩,
М-238

только птичьего молока
нет, М-238

только пятки сверкают/
засверкали, П-683

только слава, Н-15

только-только... как...,
Т-147

только усом повести
⟨шевельнуть⟩, Б-210

только что, Т-148

только что... как..., Т-147

только что не, Т-149

только этого (и) не хватало
⟨недоставало⟩!, Х-7

ты только подумай!,
П-259

хоть горшком назови,
только в печку не ставь,
Г-356

чего ⟨чего-чего⟩ только
    нет, Ч-47
чуть только..., К-18
это только цветики
    ⟨цветки, цветочки⟩, а
    ягодки (будут) впереди,
    Ц-16
этого ещё только не
    хватало ⟨недоставало⟩!,
    Х-7

ТОМ
в том духе, Д-350
в том же духе, Д-350
в том случае ежели
    ⟨если⟩, С-367
в том-то и дело, Д-70
в том-то и штука, Д-70
в том числе (и), Ч-152
дело в том..., Д-78
и на том спасибо, С-506
на том стоим, С-577
на том стояли, стоим и
    стоять будем, С-577
о том (и) о сём, Т-112
при всём (при) том, В-338

ТОМУ
благодаря тому что, Т-150
и тому подобное, П-251
к тому же, Т-151
подобно тому как, П-249
судя по тому что, С-668
так тому и быть, Б-281
тому назад, Т-152
чему быть, тому не
    миновать, Б-282

ТОН
в тон, Т-153
давать/дать тон, Т-154
задавать/задать тон, Т-154
не в тон, Т-155
повысить ⟨повышать⟩
    тон, Г-301
под тон, Т-153
попадать/попасть в тон,
    Т-156
понижать/понизить тон,
    Т-157
сбавить ⟨сбавлять⟩ тон,
    Т-157
снижать/снизить тон,
    Т-157

ТОНКА
кишка тонка, К-128

ТОНКАЯ
кишка тонкая, К-128

ТОНКИЙ
тонкий намёк на толстое
    обстоятельство ⟨на
    толстые
    обстоятельства⟩, Н-23

ТОНКО
где тонко, там и рвётся,
    Р-95

ТОНОМ
тоном выше, Т-158
тоном ниже, Т-159

ТОПИТЬ
топить в крови, К-395

ТОПОР
можно топор вешать,
    Т-160

(хоть) топор вешай, Т-160

ТОПОРОМ
что написано пером, того
    не вырубишь топором,
    П-103

ТОПТАТЬСЯ
топтаться на (одном)
    месте, М-108

ТОРБОЙ
как дурак с (писаной)
    торбой, Т-161
как дурень с (писаной)
    торбой, Т-161
как с писаной торбой, Т-161

ТОРМАШКАМИ
вверх тормашками, Т-162
кверху тормашками, Т-162
лететь вверх тормашками,
    Т-163
перевернуть
    ⟨перевёртывать⟩ вверх
    тормашками, Т-164
переворачивать вверх
    тормашками, Т-164
полететь вверх
    тормашками, Т-163

ТОРМАШКИ
вверх тормашки, Т-162
кверху тормашки, Т-162
лететь/полететь вверх
    тормашки, Т-163

ТОРМОЗАХ
спускать/спустить на
    тормозах, Т-165

ТОРНАЯ
торная дорога, Д-266

ТОРЧАТЬ
торчать над душой, Д-405

ТОСКА
тоска зелёная, Т-166

ТОСКУ
заливать/залить тоску,
    Г-327
навести ⟨наводить⟩ тоску,
    Т-167
нагнать ⟨нагонять⟩ тоску,
    Т-167

ТОТ
есть тот грех, Г-385
и тот и другой, Т-168
на тот же лад, Л-10
на тот предмет, П-508
на тот случай если, С-377
не тот, Т-169
не тот коленкор, К-190
не тот табак, К-190
ни тот ни другой, Т-170
один и тот же, Т-171
отправить на тот свет,
    С-52
отправиться на тот свет,
    С-53
отправлять на тот свет,
    С-52
отправляться на тот свет,
    С-53
тот же, Т-172
тот и другой, Т-168
тот или другой, Т-173
тот или иной, Т-173

тот свет, С-62
Федот, да не тот, Ф-5

ТОЧИТЬ
точить балясы, Л-177
точить зуб(ы), З-204
точить лясы, Л-177
точить нож(и), Н-184
точить язык, Я-29

ТОЧКА
и точка, Т-174
кульминационная точка,
    П-634
отправная точка, Т-177
точка в точку, Т-175
точка зрения, Т-176
точка отправления, Т-177

ТОЧКЕ
на мёртвой точке, Т-178
на точке замерзания, Т-178

ТОЧКИ
до точки, Т-179, Т-180
поставить (все) точки на
    ⟨над⟩ и, Т-183
сдвинуть с мёртвой точки,
    Т-181
сдвинуться с мёртвой
    точки, Т-182
сойти с мёртвой точки,
    Т-182
ставить (все) точки на
    ⟨над⟩ и, Т-183

ТОЧКУ
бить в одну точку, Т-184
попадать/попасть в
    (самую) точку, Т-185
поставить точку, Т-186
поставить точку на ⟨над⟩
    и, Т-183
ставить точку, Т-186
ставить точку на ⟨над⟩ и,
    Т-183
точка в точку, Т-175

ТОЧНЕЕ
точнее сказать, С-208

ТОЧНО
бить точно обухом по
    голове, О-31
вертеться точно белка в
    колесе, Б-51
кружиться точно белка в
    колесе, Б-51
крутиться точно белка в
    колесе, Б-51
так точно, Т-27
точно аршин проглотил,
    А-42
точно банный лист, Л-78
точно белка в колесе, Б-51
точно бельмо в ⟨на⟩ глазу,
    Б-55
точно в воду глядел, В-184
точно в воду канул, В-185
точно в воду опущенный,
    В-186
точно в воду смотрел,
    В-184
точно в котле вариться,
    К-340
точно в котле кипеть,
    К-340

точно варом обдало, В-8
точно ветром сдувало,
    В-78
точно ветром сдуло
    ⟨сдунуло⟩, В-78
точно вкопанный, В-150
точно водой смыло, В-180
точно гора с плеч
    (свалилась), Г-316
точно гром среди ясного
    неба, Г-405
точно иголка в стоге ⟨в
    стогу⟩ сена, И-2
точно из-за угла
    (пыльным) мешком
    прибит(ый)
    ⟨трахнутый,
    ударен(ный)⟩, У-13
точно из земли, З-115
точно из-под земли, З-115
точно корова языком
    слизала ⟨слизнула⟩,
    К-310
точно курица лапой, К-479
точно Мамай прошёл,
    М-22
точно на иголках, И-5
точно на ладони ⟨на
    ладонке, на ладошке⟩,
    Л-13
точно на подбор, П-238
точно на пожар, П-265
точно на смех, С-402
точно нарочно, Н-31
точно нож в сердце, Н-180
точно ножом отрезало,
    Н-189
точно ножом полоснуть
    (по сердцу), Н-191
точно ножом резануть
    ⟨резнуть⟩ (по сердцу),
    Н-191
точно обухом по голове,
    О-31
точно пелена падает (с
    глаз), П-76
точно пелена спадает/
    спала (с глаз), П-76
точно пелена упала (с
    глаз), П-76
точно по волшебству,
    В-245
точно по манию
    волшебного жезла, М-27
точно по мановению
    волшебного жезла, М-27
точно по мановению
    волшебной палочки,
    М-27
точно по писаному, П-157
точно подменили, П-246
точно покров падает (с
    глаз), П-76
точно покров спадает/спал
    (с глаз), П-76
точно покров упал (с глаз),
    П-76
точно потерянный, П-427
точно рукой сняло, Р-332
точно с неба свалиться,
    Н-46

точно с неба упасть, Н-46
точно с привязи сорваться,
Ц-37
точно с цепи сорваться,
Ц-37
точно свинцом налита,
С-78
точно сквозь землю
провалился, З-120
точно сквозь сон, С-481
точно снег на голову, С-430
точно ужаленный, У-54
точно холодной водой
облить ⟨окатить⟩, В-181
точно язык проглотил,
Я-23
ударить ⟨ударять⟩ точно
обухом по голове, О-31

ТОЧНОСТИ
в точности, Т-187
до точности, Т-188

ТОЧЬ-В-ТОЧЬ
точь-в-точь, Т-175
точь-в-точь как, Т-189

ТОШНОТЫ
до тошноты, Т-190

ТОЩИЙ
на тощий желудок, Ж-14
тощий карман, К-83
тощий кошелёк, К-83

ТПРУ
ни тпру ни ну, Т-191

ТРАВА
дурная трава из поля вон,
Т-194
как трава, Т-192
сорная трава из поля вон,
Т-194
трава травой, Т-192
хоть трава не расти, Т-193
худая трава из поля вон,
Т-194

ТРАВИТЬ
травить баланду, Б-14
травить душу, Д-432
травить сердце, Д-432

ТРАВЛЕНЫЙ
травленый волк, В-227
травленый зверь, В-227

ТРАВОЙ
трава травой, Т-192
травой поросло, Б-274

ТРАВУ
дурную траву из ⟨с⟩ поля
вон, Т-194
сорную траву из ⟨с⟩ поля
вон, Т-194
худую траву из ⟨с⟩ поля
вон, Т-194

ТРАВЫ
тише воды, ниже травы,
В-196

ТРАГЕДИЮ
делать/сделать трагедию,
Т-195
устраивать/устроить
трагедию, Т-195

ТРАТИТЬ
тратить нервы, Н-82
тратить по мелочам ⟨по
мелочи⟩, М-65

тратить порох, П-380

ТРАХНУТЫЙ
из-за угла (пыльным)
мешком трахнутый,
У-13
как* из-за угла (пыльным)
мешком трахнутый,
У-13

ТРЕБОВАЛОСЬ
что и требовалось
доказать, Т-196

ТРЕВОГУ
бить/забить тревогу, Т-197

ТРЕЗВОГО
что у трезвого на уме, то у
пьяного на языке, Т-198

ТРЕЗВОН
задавать/задать трезвон,
Т-199

ТРЕЗВОНИТЬ
трезвонить в колокола,
К-202
трезвонить во все
колокола, К-202

ТРЕЗВОНУ
задавать/задать трезвону,
Т-199

ТРЕПАТЬ
трепать нервы, Н-83
трепать язык(ом), Я-32

ТРЁПКУ
давать/дать трёпку, Т-200
задавать/задать трёпку,
Т-200
получать/получить трёпку,
Т-201

ТРЕСКОМ
провалиться с треском,
Т-202

ТРЕСНИ
хоть тресни, Л-137

ТРЕСНУЛ
чтоб ты треснул!, Л-138

ТРЕСНУТЬ
треснуть от смеха ⟨со
смеху⟩, С-407
чтоб тебе треснуть!, Л-138

ТРЕТИЙ
третий лишний, Т-203

ТРЕТЬЕГО
третьего дня, Д-214

ТРЕТЬЕМ
на третьем взводе, В-94

ТРЕТЬЕМУ
по третьему кругу, К-424

ТРЕТЬИ
в третьи руки, Р-282

ТРЕТЬИХ
до третьих петухов, П-135
из третьих рук, Р-209
из третьих уст, У-139
после третьих петухов,
П-136

ТРЁХ
в трёх шагах, Ш-12
заблудиться в трёх соснах,
С-500
комбинация из трёх
пальцев, К-214

на трёх китах, К-126

ТРЕЩАТЬ
трещать по (всем) швам,
Ш-40
трещать языком, Я-32

ТРЕЩИТ
башка трещит, Г-209
голова трещит, Г-209
за ушами трещит, У-175

ТРИ
в три дуги, П-228
в три погибели, П-228
в три ручья, Р-377
в три шеи, Ш-52
в три этажа, Э-4
видеть на три аршина в
землю ⟨под землёй, под
землю⟩, А-46
гнуть в три дуги, Р-120
гнуть в три погибели,
Р-120
драть (по) три шкуры,
Ш-79
обещанного три года
ждут, Г-182
обойти ⟨обходить⟩ за три
версты, В-48
от горшка три вершка,
Г-355
с три короба, К-308
сдирать (по) три шкуры,
Ш-79
снять три шкуры, Ш-80
согнуть в три дуги, Р-120
согнуть в три погибели,
Р-120
содрать (по) три шкуры,
Ш-79
спускать/спустить три
шкуры, Ш-80

ТРИДЕВЯТОЕ
тридевятое государство,
Ц-6
тридевятое царство, Ц-6

ТРИДЕВЯТЬ
за тридевять земель, З-110

ТРИДЕСЯТОЕ
тридесятое государство,
Ц-6
тридесятое царство, Ц-6

ТРИДЦАТЬ
предать ⟨продать⟩ за
тридцать сребреников,
С-533
тридцать сребреников,
С-534

ТРИЖДЫ
будь ты трижды проклят,
Б-231
будь я трижды проклят,
Б-233

ТРИШКИН
Тришкин кафтан, К-104

ТРОГАТЬ
пальцем не трогать, П-21

ТРОИТСЯ
троится в глазах, Г-129

ТРОИХ
скинуться на троих, Т-204
соображать/сообразить
на троих, Т-204

ТРОИЦУ
бог троицу любит, Б-105

ТРОНУЛСЯ
лёд тронулся, Л-41

ТРОНУТЬ
не тронуть волоска, В-238
пальцем не тронуть, П-21
тронуть (за) больную
струну, С-649
тронуть (за)
чувствительную струну,
С-649

ТРОНУТЬСЯ
тронуться в рассудке ⟨в
уме⟩, У-99
тронуться рассудком
⟨умом⟩, У-99

ТРОЯНСКИЙ
троянский конь, К-269

ТРУБА
дела ⟨дело⟩ труба, Д-95
иерихонская труба, Т-205
непротолчёная
⟨нетолчёная⟩ труба,
Т-206

ТРУБИ
хоть в трубу ⟨в трубы⟩
труби, Т-209

ТРУБИТЬ
в трубу ⟨в трубы⟩
трубить, Т-210
во все трубы трубить,
Т-210

ТРУБОЙ
держать хвост трубой,
Х-10

ТРУБУ
в трубу трубить, Т-210
вылетать/вылететь в
трубу, Т-207
выпустить в трубу, Т-208
пускать/пустить в трубу,
Т-208
хоть в трубу труби, Т-209

ТРУБЫ
в трубы трубить, Т-210
во все трубы трубить,
Т-210
пройти (и) огни и воды
⟨огонь и воду⟩ и медные
трубы, О-65
пройти сквозь ⟨через⟩
огни и воды ⟨огонь и
воду⟩ и медные трубы,
О-65
хоть в трубы труби, Т-209

ТРУД
брать/взять на себя труд,
Т-211
давать/дать себе труд,
Т-212
египетский труд, Р-2
мартышкин труд, Т-213
принимать/принять на
себя труд, Т-211
сизифов труд, Т-214
терпение и труд всё
перетрут, Т-80

ТРУДА
без труда, Т-215

ТЯЖКАЯ
    пускаться/пуститься во вся тяжкая, Т-256

ТЯЖКИЕ
    пускаться/пуститься во все тяжкие, Т-256

ТЯНЕТ
    с души тянет, Д-393
    своя ноша не тянет, Н-247

ТЯНУТЬ
    едва ⟨еле⟩ ноги тянуть, Н-144
    насилу ноги тянуть, Н-144
    с трудом ноги тянуть, Н-144
    тянуть волынку, В-246
    тянуть время, В-319
    тянуть душу, Д-433
    тянуть жилы, Ж-74
    тянуть за душу, Д-433
    тянуть за уши, У-191
    тянуть за язык, Я-30
    тянуть канитель, К-52
    тянуть кота за хвост, К-336
    тянуть лямку, Л-176
    тянуть на аркане, А-39
    тянуть одну и ту же песню, П-118
    тянуть резину, Р-104
    тянуть руку, С-614
    тянуть сок(и), С-467
    тянуть сторону, С-614
    чуть ноги тянуть, Н-144

ТЯНУТЬСЯ
    тянуться красной нитью, Н-105

ТЯП
    тяп да ляп, Т-257
    тяп-ляп, Т-257

У

УБЕЙ
    убей бог, Б-125
    убей меня бог, Б-125
    убей меня господь, Б-125
    убей меня гром (на этом месте), Г-406
    хоть убей, У-1

УБЕЙТЕ
    хоть убейте, У-1

УБИВАТЬ
    убивать время, В-320
    убивать двух зайцев, З-38

УБИТА
    карта убита, К-87

УБИТЫЙ
    как убитый, У-2

УБИТЫМ
    с убитым видом, В-136

УБИТЬ
    убить бобра, Б-86
    убить время, В-320
    убить двух зайцев, З-38
    убить карту, К-95
    убить мало, У-3

УБИТЬСЯ
    убиться можно!, У-4

УБОЙ
    как на убой, У-5
    на убой, У-5

УБУДЕТ
    не убудет, У-6

УБЫЛЬ
    идти/пойти на убыль, У-7

УБЫТКЕ
    в убытке, У-8

УБЫТОК
    в убыток, У-9
    ввести ⟨вводить⟩ в убыток, Р-89
    вгонять/вогнать в убыток, Р-89
    себе в убыток, У-9

УВАЖЕНИЕ
    почёт и уважение, П-458

УВЕРЕНИЯ
    примите уверения в совершенном ⟨совершеннейшем⟩ почтении, П-463

УВИДЕТЬ
    увидеть свет, С-63

УВИДИМ
    поживём — увидим, П-267

УВЫ
    увы и ах!, У-10

УГЛА
    из-за угла, У-12
    из-за угла (пыльным) мешком прибит(ый) ⟨трахнутый, ударен(ный)⟩, У-13
    из угла в угол, У-11
    как* из-за угла (пыльным) мешком прибит(ый) ⟨трахнутый, ударен(ный)⟩, У-13
    класть/положить во главу угла, Г-21
    поставить ⟨ставить⟩ во главу угла, Г-21

УГЛАМ
    по углам, У-14

УГЛАМИ
    не красна изба углами, а красна пирогами, И-34

УГЛОМ
    под углом (зрения), У-15

УГЛУБИТЬСЯ
    углубиться в себя, У-163

УГЛУБЛЯТЬСЯ
    углубляться в себя, У-163

УГЛЫ
    сгладить ⟨сглаживать⟩ (острые) углы, У-16

УГЛЯХ
    как на (горячих) углях, У-36

УГНЕТЁННАЯ
    угнетённая невинность, Н-66

УГОВОР
    уговор дороже денег, У-17

УГОДИШЬ
    на всех не угодишь, У-18

УГОДНИК
    дамский угодник, У-19

    женский угодник, У-19

УГОДНО
    где угодно, У-20
    если угодно, У-21
    как душе угодно, Д-382
    как угодно, У-22
    какой угодно, У-23
    когда угодно, У-24
    коли угодно, У-21
    кто угодно, У-25
    куда угодно, У-20
    не угодно ли, У-26
    сколько душе угодно, Д-385
    сколько угодно, У-27
    что душе угодно, Д-387
    что угодно, У-28

УГОДУ
    в угоду, У-29

УГОЛ
    глухой угол, У-31
    загнать ⟨загонять⟩ в угол, У-32
    из угла в угол, У-11
    красный угол, У-30
    медвежий угол, У-31
    непочатый угол, К-354
    прижать ⟨прижимать⟩ в угол, У-32
    припереть ⟨припирать⟩ в угол, У-32
    свой угол, У-33
    собственный угол, У-33
    угол зрения, У-34

УГОЛОК
    красный уголок, У-35

УГОЛЬЯХ
    как на (горячих) угольях, У-36

УГОРЕЛАЯ
    как угорелая кошка, К-345

УГОРЕЛЫЙ
    как угорелый, У-37

УГРЫЗЕНИЕ
    угрызение совести, У-38

УДАВИТСЯ
    за грош удавится, К-282
    за копейку удавится, К-282

УДАР
    поставить ⟨ставить⟩ под удар, У-39
    удар хватил, У-40

УДАРЕ
    в ударе, У-41

УДАРЕН(НЫЙ)
    из-за угла (пыльным) мешком ударен(ный), У-13
    как* из-за угла (пыльным) мешком ударен(ный), У-13

УДАРИЛ
    ударил час, Ч-19

УДАРИЛА
    кровь ударила в голову, К-399
    моча в голову ударила, М-268

УДАРИЛО
    ударило в нос, Н-206

УДАРИТЬ
    не ударить лицом в грязь, Л-102
    палец о палец не ударить, П-5
    пальца ⟨пальцем⟩ о палец не ударить, П-5
    ударить в голову, Г-280
    ударить в колокола, К-201
    ударить в набат, Н-1
    ударить в нос, Н-206
    ударить во все колокола, К-201
    ударить как* обухом по голове, О-31
    ударить по карману, К-85
    ударить по носу, Н-238
    ударить по рукам, Р-243
    ударить челом, Ч-55

УДАРИТЬСЯ
    удариться в амбицию, А-26
    удариться в сантименты, С-13
    удариться об заклад, З-45

УДАРОМ
    под ударом, У-42

УДАРЯЕТ
    ударяет в нос, Н-206

УДАРЯТЬ
    ударять в голову, Г-280
    ударять в колокола, К-201
    ударять в набат, Н-1
    ударять в нос, Н-206
    ударять во все колокола, К-201
    ударять как* обухом по голове, О-31
    ударять по карману, К-85
    ударять по носу, Н-238
    ударять по рукам, Р-243
    ударять челом, Ч-55

УДАРЯТЬСЯ
    ударяться в амбицию, А-26
    ударяться в сантименты, С-13

УДАСТСЯ
    (этот) номер не удастся, Н-201

УДЕЛЬНЫЙ
    удельный вес, В-61

УДЕРЖУ
    без (всякого) удержу, У-43
    не знать (никакого) удержу, У-44
    нет (никакого) удержу, У-45

УДИВИТЕЛЬНОЕ
    удивительное дело, Д-134

УДИВЛЕНИЕ
    на удивление, Д-192

УДИЛА
    закусить ⟨закусывать⟩ удила, У-46

УДОВОЛЬСТВИЕ
    в своё удовольствие, У-47
    удовольствие ниже среднего, У-48

УДОВОЛЬСТВИЯ
    срывать цветы удовольствия, Ц-17

что у трезвого на уме, то у
пьяного на языке, Т-198
УМЕНЬЕ
где хотенье, там и уменье,
Х-86
УМЕРЕТЬ
умереть со смеху, С-407
УМЕТЬ
ни стать ни сесть не
уметь, С-552
УМЕЩАЕТСЯ
не умещается в голове,
Г-228
не умещается в сознании,
Г-228
УМИРАЙ
хоть умирай, У-112
УМИРАТЬ
умирать со смеху, С-407
УМНАЯ
умная голова
〈головушка〉, Г-221
УМОВ
сколько голов, столько 〈и〉
умов, Г-192
УМОЛКУ
без умолку, У-104
УМОМ
дойти своим умом, У-105
дойти 〈своим〉
собственным умом,
У-105
доходить своим умом,
У-105
доходить 〈своим〉
собственным умом,
У-105
жить своим умом, У-106
жить собственным умом,
У-106
жить чужим умом, У-107
задним умом крепок,
У-108
мешаться умом, У-99
повредиться умом, У-99
помешаться умом, У-99
пораскинуть умом, У-109
раскидывать/раскинуть
умом, У-109
с умом, У-110
своим умом, У-105
тронуться умом, У-99
УМОПОМРАЧЕНИЯ
до умопомрачения, У-111
УМОРИТЬ
уморить со смеху, С-408
УМРЁШЬ
прежде смерти не умрёшь,
С-393
раньше смерти не умрёшь,
С-393
УМРИ
хоть умри, У-112
УМУ
научить уму-разуму, У-115
ни уму ни сердцу, У-113
по одёжке встречают, по
уму провожают, О-70
по платью встречают, по
уму провожают, О-70

уму непостижимо, У-114
учить уму-разуму, У-115
УМЫВАТЬ
умывать руки, Р-330
УМЫВАТЬСЯ
кровью умываться, К-413
умываться потом, П-419
умываться слезами, С-260
УМЫКАЛИ
умыкали бурку 〈сивку〉
крутые горки, С-160
УМЫТЬ
умыть руки, Р-330
УМЫТЬСЯ
кровью умыться, К-413
УНЁС
чёрт унёс, Ч-100
УНЕСЛА
нелёгкая унесла, Ч-100
УНЕСТИ
унести в могилу, М-207
унести ноги, Н-158
унести с собой в могилу,
М-207
УНИВЕРСИТЕТ
ходячий университет, Э-1
УНИВЕРСИТЕТСКОЙ
с университетской скамьи,
С-220
УНИСОН
в унисон, У-116
УНОСИ
хоть святых 〈вон〉 уноси,
С-90
УНОСИТЬ
уносить в могилу, М-207
уносить ноги, Н-158
уносить с собой в могилу,
М-207
УНОСИТЬСЯ
уноситься в облака 〈к
облакам〉, О-8
УПАВШИМ
с упавшим сердцем, С-147
УПАДА
до упада, У-117
УПАДУ
до упаду, У-117
УПАЛ
как будто* покров упал 〈с
глаз〉, П-76
покров упал 〈с глаз〉, П-76
с луны упал, Л-146
УПАЛА
завеса упала 〈с глаз〉, З-16
как будто* пелена упала 〈с
глаз〉, П-76
пелена упала 〈с глаз〉,
П-76
тень упала, Т-78
УПАЛИ
акции упали, А-23
УПАЛО
сердце упало, С-141
что с воза 〈возу〉 упало,
то 〈и〉 пропало, В-213
УПАСИ
боже упаси, Б-143
упаси бог, Б-143

упаси господь, Б-143
УПАСТЬ
как* с неба упасть, Н-46
с неба упасть, Н-46
упасть без памяти, Ч-194
упасть без сознания, Ч-194
упасть без чувств, Ч-194
упасть в ноги, Н-152
упасть в обморок, О-14
упасть духом, Д-355
упасть к ногам, Н-152
упасть на колени, Н-152
упасть с неба на землю,
Н-47
упасть с облаков, О-9
яблоку негде 〈некуда〉
упасть, Я-6
УПЕРЕТЬСЯ
упереться на своём, С-86
упереться руками и
ногами, Р-256
УПИРАТЬСЯ
упираться руками и
ногами, Р-256
УПЛЫВАЕТ
земля уплывает из-под
ног, П-448
почва уплывает из-под
ног, П-448
УПЛЫВАТЬ
уплывать меж〈ду〉
пальцами, П-18
уплывать между пальцев,
П-18
уплывать сквозь пальцы,
П-18
УПЛЫЛА
земля уплыла из-под ног,
П-448
почва уплыла из-под ног,
П-448
УПЛЫТЬ
уплыть меж〈ду〉 пальцами,
П-18
уплыть между пальцев,
П-18
уплыть сквозь пальцы,
П-18
УПОКОЙ
начать за здравие, а
кончить 〈свести〉 за
упокой, З-107
УПОР
в упор, У-118
в упор не видеть, У-119
делать упор, У-120
сделать упор, У-120
УПОРА
до упора, У-121
УПОТРЕБИТЬ
употребить во зло, З-134
УПРАВУ
найти управу, У-122
УПРАВЫ
управы нет, У-123
УПРАШИВАТЬ
не заставить себя долго
упрашивать, З-76
УПРЁК
не в упрёк будь сказано,
У-69

поставить в упрёк, У-70
ставить в упрёк, У-70
УПРЁКА
рыцарь без страха и
упрёка, Р-395
УПУСКАТЬ
не упускать случая, С-381
упускать из вида 〈виду〉,
В-141
упускать из 〈с〉 глаз, В-141
УПУСТИТЬ
не упустить случая, С-381
упустить из вида 〈виду〉,
В-141
упустить из 〈с〉 глаз, В-141
УРА
на ура, У-124
УРВАТЬ
урвать кусок, К-495
УРОВЕНЬ
в уровень, У-125
на 〈один〉 уровень, У-125
УРОВНЕ
на уровне, У-126
УРОДА
в семье не без урода, С-116
УРОК
дать урок, У-127
УС
〈и〉 в ус 〈себе〉 не дуть,
У-128
мотать 〈себе〉 на ус, У-129
наматывать/намотать
〈себе〉 на ус, У-129
УСАМ
сам с усам, У-130
УСАМИ
сами с усами, У-130
УСКОЛЬЗАЕТ
земля ускользает из-под
ног, П-448
почва ускользает из-под
ног, П-448
УСКОЛЬЗАТЬ
ускользать из рук, Р-223
УСКОЛЬЗНУЛА
земля ускользнула из-под
ног, П-448
почва ускользнула из-под
ног, П-448
УСКОЛЬЗНУТЬ
ускользнуть из рук, Р-223
УСЛУГА
медвежья услуга, У-131
услуга за услугу, У-132
УСЛУГАМ
готовый к услугам, У-133
к вашим услугам, У-134
к твоим услугам, У-134
к услугам, У-135
УСЛУГУ
услуга за услугу, У-132
УСНУТЬ
уснуть вечным сном, С-432
уснуть могильным сном,
С-432
уснуть последним сном,
С-432
УСОМ
и 〈даже〉 усом не ведёт/не
повёл, Б-209

по уши, У-187
повесить лапшу на уши,
Л-31
притягивать/притянуть за
уши, В-242
прогудеть (все) уши, У-188
прожужжать (все) уши,
У-188
прослушать (все) уши,
У-189
протрубить (все) уши,
У-188
развесить ⟨развешивать⟩
уши, У-190
резать уши, У-160
стены имеют уши, С-559
тащить за уши, У-191
тянуть за уши, У-191
уши вянут, У-192
УШКИ
держать ушки на макушке,
У-158
ушки на макушке, У-193
УШКО
за ушко да на солнышко,
У-194
легче верблюду пройти в
⟨сквозь⟩ игольное ушко,
В-35
УШЛА
душа ушла в пятки, Д-374
земля ушла из-под ног,
П-448
почва ушла из-под ног,
П-448
УЩЕРБ
в ущерб, У-195
УЩЕРБЕ
на ущербе, У-196
УЯЗВИМОЕ
уязвимое место, М-122

Ф

ФАВОР
в фавор, Ф-1
ФАВОРЕ
в фаворе, Ф-1
ФАКТОМ
поставить перед
(свершившимся
⟨совершившимся⟩)
фактом, Ф-2
ставить перед
(свершившимся
⟨совершившимся⟩)
фактом, Ф-2
ФАСОН
давить фасон, Ф-3
держать фасон, Ф-3
не фасон, Ф-4
ФЕДОТ
Федот, да не тот, Ф-5
ФЕНЕ
к едрене ⟨едрёной⟩ фене,
Ф-6
к ядрёной фене, Ф-6
ФЕНИ
до фени, Ф-7

ФЕРТОМ
глядеть фертом, Ф-8
смотреть фертом, Ф-8
стоять фертом, Ф-8
ходить фертом, Ф-8
ФЕФЕРУ
задавать/задать феферу,
П-110
показать ⟨показывать⟩
феферу, П-110
ФИБРАМИ
всеми фибрами души, Ф-9
ФИГ
на фиг, Ф-10
ФИГА
до фига, Ч-102
фига с маслом, К-459
ни фига, Ч-104
фига в кармане, К-458
ФИГОВЫЙ
фиговый листок
⟨листочек⟩, Л-81
ФИГУ
глядеть в книгу и видеть
фигу, К-148
смотреть в книгу и видеть
фигу, К-148
ФИЗИОНОМИЯ
физиономия вытянулась,
Л-96
ФИКС
идея фикс, И-21
ФИЛАДЕЛЬФИИ
в лучших домах
Филадельфии, Д-258
ФИЛЬКИНА
филькина грамота, Г-373
ФИМИАМ
воскурять фимиам, Ф-11
жечь фимиам, Ф-11
курить фимиам, Ф-11
ФЛАГОМ
под флагом, Ф-12
ФОКУС
выкидывать/выкинуть
фокус, Ф-13
ФОКУСЫ
выкидывать/выкинуть
фокусы, Ф-13
ФОМА
Фома неверный
⟨неверующий⟩, Ф-14
ФОНАРЕЙ
наставить фонарей, Ф-16
ФОНАРЬ
красный фонарь, Ф-15
поставить фонарь, Ф-16
ставить фонарь, Ф-16
ФОНАРЯ
до фонаря, Ф-7
ФОНД
золотой фонд, Ф-17
ФОНТАН
заткнуть фонтан, Ф-18
не фонтан, Ф-19
ФОРМЕ
в форме, Ф-20
во всей форме, Ф-21
по (всей) форме, Ф-21

ФОРМУ
в форму, Ф-20
ФОРМЫ
для формы, Ф-22
ФОРС
держать форс, Ф-23
сбивать/сбить форс, С-508
сшибать/сшибить форс,
С-508
ФОРСА
для форса, Ф-24
ФОРСУ
для форсу, Ф-24
ФОРТЕЛИ
выкидывать/выкинуть
фортели, Ф-13
ФОРТЕЛЬ
выкидывать/выкинуть
фортель, Ф-13
ФОРТУНЫ
баловень фортуны, Б-16
ФОРУ
давать/дать фору, Ф-25
ФРОНТ
во фронт, Ф-26
ФРОНТА
на два фронта, Ф-27
ФРОНТОМ
единым фронтом, Ф-28
ФРУНТ
во фрунт, Ф-26
ФУ
фу-ты, Ф-29
фу-ты, ну-ты, Ф-29
фу ты пропасть!, Ч-84
фу ты чёрт!, Ч-84
ФУКСОМ
выйти фуксом, Ф-30
пройти фуксом, Ф-30
проскочить фуксом, Ф-30
ФУНДАМЕНТ
закладывать/заложить
фундамент, О-118
ФУНТ
вот так фунт!, Ф-31
вот те фунт!, Ф-31
не фунт изюма ⟨изюму⟩,
Ф-32
ноль внимания, фунт
презрения, Н-196
почём фунт лиха, Ф-33
ФУТЛЯРЕ
человек в футляре, Ч-50
ФУФУ
на фуфу, Ф-34
поддевать/поддеть на
фуфу, Ф-35
поднимать/поднять на
фуфу, Ф-35
подымать на фуфу, Ф-35
пойти на фуфу, Ф-36
сойти на фуфу, Ф-36

Х

ХАЛИФ
халиф на час, К-36
ХАМА
из хама не будет ⟨не
сделаешь⟩ пана, Х-1

ХАРАКТЕР
выдержать
⟨выдерживать⟩
характер, Х-2
показать ⟨показывать⟩
характер, Х-3
проявить ⟨проявлять⟩
характер, Х-3
ХАРАКТЕРАМИ
не сойтись характерами,
Х-4
ХАРАКТЕРЕ
в характере, Х-5
ХАРАКТЕРОМ
не сойтись характером,
Х-4
ХАРИБДОЙ
между Сциллой и
Харибдой, С-689
ХАТА
моя хата с краю, Х-6
ХАХАНЬКИ
всё хаханьки да хиханьки,
Х-28
всё хиханьки да хаханьки,
Х-28
хаханьки да хиханьки,
Х-28
хиханьки да хаханьки,
Х-28
ХВАЛИТ
всяк кулик своё болото
хвалит, К-467
гречневая каша сама себя
хвалит, К-107
ХВАТАЕТ
винтика ⟨винтиков⟩ (в
голове) не хватает, В-147
заклёпки ⟨заклёпок⟩ (в
голове) не хватает, В-147
клёпки ⟨клёпок⟩ (в голове)
не хватает, В-147
куда хватает глаз, Г-27
насколько хватает глаз,
Г-27
пороха ⟨пороху⟩ не
хватает, П-385
птичьего молока не
хватает, М-238
сколько хватает глаз, Г-27
совести хватает, С-453
только птичьего молока не
хватает, М-238
хватает духу, Д-360
шариков (в голове) не
хватает, В-147
ХВАТАЕТСЯ
утопающий хватается (и)
за соломинку, У-149
ХВАТАЛ
куда хватал глаз, Г-27
насколько хватал глаз,
Г-27
сколько хватал глаз, Г-27
ХВАТАЛО
ещё чего не хватало!, Х-7
куда хватало глаз ⟨глаза,
глазу⟩, Г-27
насколько хватало глаз
⟨глаза, глазу⟩, Г-27

сколько хватало глаз
⟨глаза, глазу⟩, Г-27
только этого (и) не
хватало!, Х-7
этого ещё (только) не
хватало!, Х-7

ХВАТАТЬ
звёзд с неба не хватать,
З-89
хватать быка за рога,
Б-256
хватать верхи ⟨верхушки,
вершки⟩, В-55
хватать за глотку, Г-335
хватать за горло, Г-335
хватать за грудки, Г-420
хватать за душу, Д-407
хватать за сердце, Д-407
хватать за хвост, Х-19
хватать звёзды с неба,
З-97
хватать на лету, Л-69
хватать с лёту, Л-69
хватать через край, К-355

ХВАТАТЬСЯ
хвататься за бока, Ж-35
хвататься за голову, Г-281
хвататься за живот ⟨за
животики, за животы⟩,
Ж-35
хвататься за соломинку,
С-474

ХВАТИЛ
вон ⟨вот⟩ куда хватил!,
Х-8
кондратий хватил, К-228
кондрашка хватил, К-228
куда хватил!, Х-8
удар хватил, У-40
эк(а) ⟨куда⟩ хватил!, Х-8

ХВАТИЛО
пороха ⟨пороху⟩ не
хватило, П-385
совести хватило, С-453
хватило духу, Д-360

ХВАТИТЬ
далеко хватить, З-85
слишком далеко хватить,
З-85
хватить горюшка ⟨горя⟩,
Г-363
хватить греха на душу,
Г-382
хватить лиха, Г-363
хватить лишку, Л-108
хватить лишнего
⟨лишнее⟩, Л-108
хватить через край, К-355

ХВАТКА
мёртвая хватка, Х-9

ХВОСТ
в хвост и в гриву, Х-12
вожжа под хвост попала,
В-198
держать хвост морковкой,
Х-10
держать хвост
пистолетом, Х-10
держать хвост трубой,
Х-10

задирать/задрать хвост,
Х-11
и в хвост и в гриву, Х-12
кобелю под хвост, П-611
коту ⟨кошке⟩ под хвост,
П-611
крысиный хвост, Х-22
ловить за хвост, Х-19
мышиный хвост, Х-22
накрутить хвост, Х-13
наступать/наступить на
хвост, Х-14
насыпать соли на хвост,
С-471
не пришей кобыле хвост,
К-151
опускать/опустить хвост,
Х-15
подвернуть
⟨подвёртывать⟩ хвост,
Х-15
поджать ⟨поджимать⟩
хвост, Х-15
поймать за хвост, Х-19
прижать ⟨прижимать⟩
хвост, Х-15, Х-16
пришей кобыле хвост,
К-151
прищемить ⟨прищемлять⟩
хвост, Х-16
псу под хвост, П-611
распускать павлиний
хвост, Х-17
распускать ⟨пышный⟩
хвост, Х-17
распустить павлиний
хвост, Х-17
распустить ⟨пышный⟩
хвост, Х-17
собаке под хвост, П-611
схватить за хвост, Х-19
тянуть кота за хвост,
К-336
укоротить хвост, Х-18
ухватить за хвост, Х-19
хватать за хвост, Х-19
шлея под хвост попала,
В-198

ХВОСТА
накрутить хвоста, Х-13

ХВОСТЕ
в хвосте, Х-20
висеть на хвосте, Х-21
на хвосте, Х-21
повиснуть на хвосте, Х-21
сорока на хвосте принесла,
С-498

ХВОСТИК
крысиный хвостик, Х-22
мышиный хвостик, Х-22

ХВОСТИКОМ
с хвостиком, Х-23

ХВОСТОМ
вертеть хвостом, Х-24
вильнуть хвостом, Х-25
вилять хвостом, Х-26
завертеть хвостом, Х-24
завилять хвостом, Х-26
закрутить ⟨крутить⟩
хвостом, Х-24
с хвостом, Х-23

ХВОСТЫ
опускать/опустить
хвосты, Х-15
подвернуть
⟨подвёртывать⟩
хвосты, Х-15
поджать ⟨поджимать⟩
хвосты, Х-15
прижать ⟨прижимать⟩
хвосты, Х-15, Х-16
прищемить ⟨прищемлять⟩
хвосты, Х-16

ХИТРА
голь на выдумки хитра,
Г-311

ХИТРОСТЬ
не большая хитрость, Х-27
не велика хитрость, Х-27

ХИХАНЬКИ
всё хаханьки да хиханьки,
Х-28
всё хиханьки да хаханьки,
Х-28
хаханьки да хиханьки,
Х-28
хиханьки да хаханьки,
Х-28

ХИХИКАТЬ
хихикать в кулак, К-464

ХЛЕБ
водить хлеб-соль, Х-29
даром хлеб есть, Х-30
есть свой хлеб, Х-31
есть хлеб, Х-32
есть чужой хлеб, Х-32
забывать/забыть хлеб-
соль, Х-33
зря хлеб есть, Х-30
и то хлеб, Х-34
отбивать/отбить хлеб,
Х-35
перебивать/перебить хлеб,
Х-35
посадить на хлеб и (на)
воду, Х-37
садиться на хлеб и (на)
воду, Х-36
сажать на хлеб и (на) воду,
Х-37
сесть на хлеб и (на) воду,
Х-36
хлеб да ⟨и⟩ соль!, Х-38
хлеб насущный, Х-39
хлеб-соль!, Х-38, Х-40

ХЛЕБА
кусок хлеба, К-492
на хлеба, Х-43
перебиваться с хлеба на
воду, Х-41
перебиваться с хлеба на
квас, Х-41

ХЛЕБАВШИ
несолоно хлебавши, Х-42

ХЛЕБАТЬ
за семь вёрст киселя
хлебать, В-43
лаптем щи хлебать, Л-26
не лаптем щи хлебать,
Л-27

ХЛЕБАХ
на хлебах, Х-43

ХЛЕБЕ
сидеть на хлебе и (на)
воде, Х-44

ХЛЕБНОЕ
хлебное местечко ⟨место⟩,
М-127

ХЛЕБНУТЬ
хлебнуть горюшка ⟨горя⟩,
Г-363
хлебнуть лиха, Г-363
хлебнуть лишку, Л-108
хлебнуть лишнее, Л-108
хлебнуть через край, К-356

ХЛЕБОМ
хлебом не корми, Х-45

ХЛОПАТЬ
хлопать глазами, Г-123
хлопать ушами, У-177

ХЛОПНУТЬ
хлопнуть дверью, Д-39

ХЛОПОТ
не было у бабы хлопот,
(так) купила (баба)
порося, Б-2

ХЛОПЦЕВ
паны дерутся, а у хлопцев
чубы болят ⟨трещат⟩,
П-54

ХЛЮПАТЬ
хлюпать носом, Н-233

ХЛЮПНУТЬ
хлюпнуть носом, Н-233

ХЛЯБИ
отверзлись хляби
небесные, Х-46
разверзлись хляби
небесные, Х-46

ХМЕЛЕМ
под хмелем, Х-48

ХМЕЛЬ
хмель вылетел ⟨выскочил,
вышел⟩ из головы, Х-47

ХМЕЛЬКОМ
под хмельком, Х-48

ХМЕЛЮ
во хмелю, Х-49

ХНЫ
хоть бы хны, Х-50

ХОД
давать задний ход, Х-51
давать ход, Х-52
дать задний ход, Х-51
дать ход, Х-52
идти в ход, Х-53
на полный ход, Х-54
пойти в ход, Х-53
полный ход!, Х-55
пускать/пустить в ход,
Х-56

ХОДА
не давать/не дать хода,
Х-69
нет хода, Х-70

ХОДЕ
в ходе, Х-57

ХОДЕНЁМ
заходить ⟨ходить⟩
ходенём, Х-73

ХОДИМ
все (мы) под богом ходим,
Б-135

ХОДИТ
беда в одиночку не ходит, Б-37
беда (никогда) не ходит одна, Б-37
за словом в карман не ходит, С-332
под стол пешком ходит, С-589
сапожник (всегда) ходит без сапог, С-19

ХОДИТЬ
волков бояться — в лес не ходить, В-231
далеко ходить не надо ⟨не нужно, не приходится⟩, Х-58
за примерами ⟨примером⟩ далеко ходить не надо ⟨не нужно⟩, Х-58
за примерами ⟨примером⟩ далеко ходить не приходится, Х-58
недалеко ходить (за примерами ⟨примером⟩), Х-58
ходить в струнку, С-647
ходить вокруг ⟨кругом⟩ да около, Х-59
ходить гоголем, Г-178
ходить козырем, К-174
ходить на головах ⟨на голове⟩, Г-230
ходить на задних лапах ⟨лапках⟩, Л-22
ходить на поводу, П-223
ходить на полусогнутых, Х-60
ходить на помочах, П-336
ходить на цыпочках, Ц-42
ходить по лезвию ножа, О-126
ходить по миру, М-190
ходить по ниточке, С-647
ходить по острию ножа, О-126
ходить по рукам, Р-251, Р-252
ходить по струнке, С-647
ходить по трупам, Т-221
ходить под себя, Д-61
ходить с протянутой рукой, Р-340
ходить с сумой, М-190
ходить фертом, Ф-8
ходить ходенём ⟨ходнем, ходором⟩, Х-73
ходить ходуном, Х-73

ХОДНЕМ
заходить ⟨ходить⟩ ходнем, Х-73

ХОДОК
не ходок, Х-61

ХОДОМ
полным ходом, Х-62
своим ходом, Х-63
черепашьим ходом, Х-64

ХОДОРОМ
заходить ⟨ходить⟩ ходором, Х-73

ХОДУ
в большом ходу, Х-65

в ходу, Х-65
дать ходу, Х-66
на ходу, Х-67
на ходу подмётки рвёт ⟨режет⟩, Х-68
наддавать/наддать ходу, Х-71
не давать/не дать ходу, Х-69
нет ходу, Х-70
поддавать/поддать ходу, Х-71
прибавить ⟨прибавлять⟩ ходу, Х-71
с ходу, Х-72

ХОДУНОМ
заходить ⟨ходить⟩ ходуном, Х-73

ХОДЫ
знать все ходы-выходы ⟨ходы и выходы⟩, Х-74

ХОДЯТ
в чужой монастырь со своим уставом не ходят, М-251

ХОДЯЧАЯ
ходячая монета, М-253
ходячая энциклопедия, Э-1

ХОДЯЧИЕ
ходячие мощи, М-274

ХОДЯЧИЙ
ходячий университет, Э-1

ХОЖДЕНИЕ
хождение по мукам, Х-75

ХОЖДЕНИЯ
по образу пешего хождения, О-26

ХОЗЯИН
сам себе хозяин, Х-76
хозяин положения, Х-77
хозяин своего слова ⟨своему слову⟩, Х-78

ХОЗЯЙКА
сама себе хозяйка, Х-76
хозяйка положения, Х-77

ХОЗЯЙСКОЕ
дело хозяйское, Д-96

ХОЛКУ
намылить холку, Ш-54
намять холку, Ш-54

ХОЛОД
бросать в жар и (в) холод, Ж-2
бросать то в жар, то в холод, Ж-2
бросить в жар и (в) холод, Ж-2
кидать в жар и (в) холод, Ж-2
кидать то в жар, то в холод, Ж-2
кинуть в жар и (в) холод, Ж-2

ХОЛОДЕЕТ
кровь холодеет (в жилах), К-405

ХОЛОДНО
ни жарко ни холодно, Ж-4
ни тепло ни холодно, Ж-4

ни холодно ни жарко, Ж-4

ХОЛОДНОЙ
вылить ушат холодной воды, В-181
как* холодной водой облить ⟨окатить⟩, В-181
облить ушатом холодной воды, В-181
облить холодной водой, В-181
окатить ушатом холодной воды, В-181
окатить холодной водой, В-181

ХОЛОДОМ
обдавать/обдать холодом, Х-79

ХОЛОПОВ
паны дерутся, а у холопов чубы болят ⟨трещат⟩, П-54

ХОЛОСТОЙ
холостой выстрел, В-384

ХОЛОСТУЮ
на холостую ногу, Н-176

ХОЛОСТЯЦКУЮ
на холостяцкую ногу, Н-176

ХОМУТ
вешать (себе) хомут на шею, Х-80
надевать на себя хомут, Х-80
надевать (себе) хомут на шею, Х-80
надеть на себя хомут, Х-80
надеть (себе) хомут на шею, Х-80
повесить (себе) хомут на шею, Х-80

ХОРОНИТЬ
заживо хоронить, Х-81
заживо хоронить себя, Х-82
хоронить концы (в воду), К-262

ХОРОШ
не по хорошу мил, а по милу хорош, Х-85
хорош гусь!, Г-448

ХОРОШЕГО
всего хорошего!, Х-83
хорошего понемножку, Х-84

ХОРОШЕЕ
хорошее дело!, Д-135
хорошее начало полдела откачало, Н-39

ХОРОШЕЙ
на хорошей дороге, П-647
по хорошей дороге, П-647

ХОРОШЕМ
на хорошем пути, П-647

ХОРОШЕМУ
по хорошему пути, П-647

ХОРОШЕНЬКОГО
хорошенького понемножку, Х-84

ХОРОШЕНЬКОЕ
хорошенькое дело!, Д-135

ХОРОШИЕ
в хорошие руки, Р-267

ХОРОШИЙ
на хороший путь, П-647

ХОРОШИХ
в хороших руках, Р-267

ХОРОШО
в гостях хорошо, а дома лучше, Г-368
везде хорошо, где нас нет, Т-39
всё хорошо, что хорошо кончается, Х-85
там хорошо, где нас нет, Т-39
ум хорошо, а два лучше, У-80
хорошо подвешенный язык, Я-47
язык хорошо подвешен ⟨привешен⟩, Я-47

ХОРОШУ
не по хорошу мил, а по милу хорош, Х-85

ХОРОШУЮ
делать хорошую мину при плохой игре, М-167
на хорошую дорогу, П-647
сделать хорошую мину при плохой игре, М-167

ХОТЕЛ
плевать я хотел, П-169

ХОТЕНЬЕ
где хотенье, там и уменье, Х-86
на всякое хотенье есть терпенье, Х-87

ХОТИТЕ
если хотите, Х-88
как хотите, Х-89
какой хотите, К-27

ХОТЬ
хоть брось, Б-212
хоть бы..., Х-90
хоть бы в одном глазе ⟨глазу⟩, Г-141
хоть бы и так, Т-31
хоть бы хны, Х-50
хоть бы что, Ч-175
хоть в воду, В-191
хоть в гроб ложись, Г-400
хоть в омут (головой), В-191
хоть в петлю лезь ⟨полезай⟩, П-129
хоть в прорубь (головой), В-191
хоть в реку, В-191
хоть в трубу ⟨в трубы⟩ труби, Т-209
хоть видит око, да зуб неймёт, О-89
хоть волком вой, В-234
хоть выжми, В-365
хоть глаз(а) выколи ⟨коли⟩, Г-43
хоть головой об стенку ⟨стену⟩ бейся, Г-242
хоть горшком назови, только в печку не ставь, Г-356

хоть завались, З-13
хоть зарежь(те), З-71
хоть к чёрту (в зубы), Ч-118
хоть к чёрту в пекло, Ч-118
хоть к чёрту на рога, Ч-118
хоть к чертям, Ч-118
хоть какой, К-27
хоть караул кричи, К-74
хоть ко всем чертям, Ч-118
хоть кол на голове теши, К-178
хоть кровь из носа ⟨из носу⟩, К-412
хоть кто, К-451
хоть куда, К-457
хоть ложись да помирай, Л-126
хоть лопни, Л-137
хоть на выставку, В-381
хоть отбавляй, О-127
хоть плачь, П-168
хоть пополам разорвись, Р-64
хоть пруд пруди, П-607
хоть пулю в лоб, П-633
хоть разорвись, Р-64
хоть с моста в реку, В-191
хоть святых (вон) выноси ⟨неси, уноси⟩, С-90
хоть сквозь землю провалиться, З-117
хоть стой, хоть падай, С-584
хоть так, хоть сяк, Т-21
хоть так, хоть этак, Т-21
хоть топор вешай, Т-160
хоть трава не расти, Т-193
хоть тресни, Л-137
хоть ты что, Ч-176
хоть убей(те), У-1
хоть умирай, У-112
хоть умри, У-112
хоть шаром покати, Ш-37
ХОТЯ
хотя бы..., Х-90
хотя бы и так, Т-31
ХОХМЫ
для хохмы, С-405
ХОХОТА
валяться от хохота, С-406
кататься от хохота, С-406
покатиться ⟨покатываться⟩ от хохота, С-406
ХОХОТУ
валяться с хохоту, С-406
кататься с хохоту, С-406
покатиться ⟨покатываться⟩ с хохоту, С-406
ХОХОТУН
хохотун напал, Х-91
ХОЧЕТ
ишь чего хочет, Х-92
левая нога хочет, Н-119
многого хочет, Х-92
ХОЧЕТСЯ
(и) хочется и колется, Х-93
ХОЧЕШЬ
если хочешь, Х-88

как хочешь, Х-89
какой хочешь, К-27
хочешь не хочешь, Х-94
ХОЧУ
бери — не хочу, Х-95
ешь — не хочу, Х-95
знать не хочу, З-169
пей — не хочу, Х-95
ХОШЬ
хошь не хошь, Х-94
ХРАБРОГО
не (из) храброго десятка, Д-187
ХРАНИМ
что имеем, не храним, потерявши, плачем, И-55
ХРАНИТЬ
хранить молчание, М-245
ХРАПАКА
задавать/задать храпака, Х-96
ХРАПОВИЦКОГО
задавать/задать храповицкого, Х-96
ХРЕБЕТ
гнуть хребет, С-513, С-514
ломать хребет, Х-97
становой хребет, Х-98
ХРЕН
на кой хрен, Х-102
на хрен, Х-102
старый хрен, Х-99
хрен в голову, Х-100
хрен в пятку, Х-100
хрен его знает, Ч-89
хрен редьки не слаще, Х-101
хрен с тобой, Ч-98
ХРЕНА
на хрена, Х-102
ни хрена, Ч-104
ни хрена себе!, Х-103
ХРИСТА
как у Христа за пазухой, Х-104
Христа ради, Х-105
ХРИСТИАНСКИЙ
привести ⟨приводить⟩ в христианский вид, В-113
придавать/придать христианский вид, В-113
ХРИСТОВА
христова невеста, Н-60
ХРИСТОМ
Христом-богом, Х-106
ХРИСТОС
Христос с тобой, Б-104
ХРОМАТЬ
хромать на обе ноги, Н-159
ХРОНОЛОГИЧЕСКАЯ
хронологическая канва, К-51
ХУДА
нет худа без добра, Х-107
ХУДАЯ
худая трава из поля вон, Т-194

ХУДО
не худо (бы), Х-108
худо-бедно, Х-109
худо будет, Б-219
худо скроен, да крепко ⟨плотно⟩ сшит, С-242
художник от слова худо, Х-110
ХУДОГО
не говоря худого слова, С-284
ХУДОЖНИК
художник от слова худо, Х-110
ХУДОЙ
на худой конец, К-235
пойти по худой дороге ⟨дорожке⟩, Д-270
худой глаз, Г-24
худой мир лучше доброй ссоры, М-185
ХУДУЮ
худую траву из ⟨с⟩ поля вон, Т-194
ХУДШЕМ
в худшем случае, С-368
ХУДЫЕ
худые вести не лежат на месте, В-64
худые вести не сидят на насесте, В-64
ХУЖЕ
положение хуже губернаторского, П-308
простота хуже воровства, П-586
хуже горькой редьки, Р-102

Ц

ЦАРЕ
при царе Горохе, Ц-1
ЦАРЁМ
с царём в голове, Ц-2
ЦАРИЦА
царица небесная, Ц-3
ЦАРСТВЕ
в некотором царстве, в некотором государстве, Ц-4
ЦАРСТВИЕ
царствие небесное, Ц-7
ЦАРСТВО
сонное царство, Ц-5
тридевятое ⟨тридесятое⟩ царство, Ц-6
царство небесное, Ц-7
ЦАРЬ
царь и бог, Ц-8
царь небесный, Ц-9
ЦАРЯ
без царя в голове, Ц-10
олух царя небесного, О-90
царя Гороха, Ц-11
ЦВЕТ
как маков цвет, Ц-12
на вкус (и) на цвет товарища ⟨товарищей⟩ нет, В-154

что маков цвет, Ц-12
ЦВЕТЕ
в розовом цвете, С-69
в цвете лет ⟨сил⟩, Ц-14
во цвете лет ⟨сил⟩, Ц-14
в чёрном цвете, Ц-13
ЦВЕТИКИ
это ещё ⟨только⟩ цветики, а ягодки (будут) впереди, Ц-16
ЦВЕТКИ
это ещё ⟨только⟩ цветки, а ягодки (будут) впереди, Ц-16
ЦВЕТОК
тепличный цветок, Р-86
ЦВЕТОМ
пышным цветом, Ц-15
ЦВЕТОЧКИ
это ещё ⟨только⟩ цветочки, а ягодки (будут) впереди, Ц-16
ЦВЕТЫ
срывать цветы удовольствия, Ц-17
ЦЕЛ
пока цел, Ц-18
покуда цел, Ц-18
цел и невредим, Ц-22
ЦЕЛИ
бить мимо цели, Ц-19
ЦЕЛИКОМ
целиком и полностью, Ц-20
ЦЕЛОМ
в общем и целом, О-35
ЦЕЛОСТИ
в целости и невредимости, Ц-21
в целости и сохранности, Ц-21
в целости-сохранности, Ц-21
ЦЕЛЫ
и волки сыты, и овцы целы, В-230
ЦЕЛЫЙ
целый и невредимый, Ц-22
целый короб, К-307
ЦЕЛЬ
бить в цель, Ц-23
цель оправдывает средства, Ц-24
бить прямо в цель, Ц-23
ЦЕЛЬЮ
с целью, Ц-25
ЦЕЛЯХ
в целях, Ц-25
ЦЕНА
грош цена (в базарный день), Г-410
красная цена, Ц-26
ломаный грош цена, Г-410
медный грош цена, Г-410
ЦЕНЕ
в цене, Ц-27
ЦЕНОЙ
дорогой ценой, Ц-28
любой ценой, Ц-29

ЦЕНТР
центр тяжести, Ц-30
ЦЕНУ
знать себе цену, Ц-31
знать цену, Ц-32
знать цену деньгам
⟨копейке⟩, Ц-33
набивать себе цену, Ц-34
набивать цену, Ц-35
набить себе цену, Ц-34
набить цену, Ц-35
узнавать/узнать цену,
Ц-32
ЦЕНЫ
цены нет, Ц-36
ЦЕПИ
как* с цепи сорваться,
Ц-37
ЦЕПОЧКОЙ
одной цепочкой связан,
В-39
ЦЕРЕМОНИИ
китайские церемонии, Ц-38
ЦЕРКОВНАЯ
как церковная крыса,
М-324
как церковная мышь,
М-324
ЦУГУНДЕР
на цугундер, Ц-39
ЦЫПЛЯТ
цыплят по осени считают,
Ц-40
ЦЫПЛЯЧЬИ
цыплячьи мозги, М-226
ЦЫПОЧКАХ
на цыпочках, Ц-41
ходить на цыпочках, Ц-42
ЦЫПОЧКИ
на цыпочки, Ц-41

Ч

ЧАДУ
в чаду, Ч-1
как ⟨будто⟩ в чаду, Ч-1
ЧАЁК
на чаёк, Ч-3
ЧАИ
гонять чаи, Ч-2
ЧАЙ
на чай, Ч-3, Ч-4
чай да ⟨и⟩ сахар!, Ч-5
чай с сахаром!, Ч-5
ЧАЙНОЙ
в ⟨через⟩ час по чайной
ложке, Ч-20
ЧАРОЧКУ
пропускать/пропустить
чарочку, Р-398
ЧАС
адмиральский час, Ч-6
битый час, Ч-7
в добрый час!, Ч-8
в недобрый час, Ч-9
в свой час, Ч-10
в час по (столовой) ложке,
Ч-20

в час по чайной ложке,
Ч-20
делу время, (а) потехе час,
Д-144
звёздный час, Ч-11
калиф на час, К-36
который час, Ч-12
мёртвый час, Ч-13
не в добрый час, Ч-9
не ровён час, Ч-14
последний час, Ч-15
с часу на час, Ч-31
смертный час, Ч-15
тихий час, Ч-13
ударил час, Ч-19
халиф на час, К-36
час в час, Ч-16
час добрый!, Ч-8
час настал, Ч-19
час от часу, Ч-17
час от часу не легче, Ч-18
час пришёл, Ч-19
час пробил, Ч-19
час пик, Ч-33
через час по (столовой)
ложке, Ч-20
через час по чайной ложке,
Ч-20
ЧАСА
дождаться ⟨дожидаться⟩
своего часа, Ч-21
ждать своего часа, Ч-21
ожидать своего часа, Ч-21
ЧАСАМ
не по дням, а по часам,
Д-215
по часам, Ч-22
ЧАСАХ
на часах, Ч-23
ЧАСТИ
в части, Ч-25
душа разрывается на
части, С-142
по большей части, Ч-30
по моей части, Ч-24
по части, Ч-25
разрывать на части, Ч-27
разрываться на части,
Ч-26
рвать на части, Ч-27
рваться на части, Ч-26
сердце разрывается на
части, С-142
ЧАСТИЦА
частица моего мёду, К-66
ЧАСТНОСТИ
в частности, Ч-28
ЧАСТЬ
избирать/избрать благую
часть, Ч-29
ЧАСТЬЮ
большей частью, Ч-30
ЧАСУ
с часу на час, Ч-31
час от часу, Ч-17
час от часу не легче, Ч-18
ЧАСЫ
как часы, Ч-32
часы пик, Ч-33
ЧАША
миновала (сия) чаша, Ч-34

миновала эта чаша, Ч-34
полная чаша, Ч-35
чаша переполнилась, Ч-36
чаша терпения
переполнилась, Ч-36
ЧАШКУ
бросать/бросить на чашку
весов, Ч-37
класть на чашку весов,
Ч-37
на чашку чаю ⟨чая⟩, Ч-4
положить на чашку весов,
Ч-37
ЧАШУ
бросать/бросить на чашу
весов, Ч-37
выпить (горькую) чашу (до
дна), Ч-39
допить (горькую) чашу (до
дна), Ч-39
испить (горькую) чашу (до
дна), Ч-39
капля, переполнившая
чашу, К-67
класть на чашу весов, Ч-37
переполнять/переполнить
чашу (терпения), Ч-38
пить (горькую) чашу (до
дна), Ч-39
положить на чашу весов,
Ч-37
ЧАЮ
на чашку чаю, Ч-4
ЧАЯ
на чашку чая, Ч-4
ЧАЯНИЯ
паче чаяния, Ч-40
против всякого чаяния,
Ч-40
сверх всякого чаяния, Ч-40
ЧАЯТЬ
души не чаять, Д-389
ЧЕГО
в случае чего, С-365
до чего..., Ч-41
ещё чего!, Ч-42
ещё чего не хватало!, Х-7
ишь чего захотел ⟨хочет⟩,
Х-92
как бы чего не вышло,
В-392
не для чего, Ч-43
не с чего, Ч-44
с чего, Ч-45
с чего ты взял?, В-105
сил нет, до чего, С-170
чего бы не дал, Д-11
чего греха таить, Г-392
чего доброго, Д-221
чего ж(е), Ч-180
чего и греха таить, Г-392
чего изволите, И-44
чего-нибудь да стоит,
С-581
чего ради, Ч-46
чего смотрит, С-420
чего стоит, С-582, С-583
чего там, Ч-189
чего только нет, Ч-47
чего тут, Ч-189

чего уж там ⟨тут⟩, Ч-189
чего-чего (только) нет,
Ч-47
чего я здесь не видал ⟨не
видел⟩?, В-118
чего я там не видал ⟨не
видел⟩?, В-118
чего я тут не видал ⟨не
видел⟩?, В-118
ЧЕЙ
чей бы то ни было, Б-270
ЧЕЛОВЕК
гора с горой не сходится, а
человек с человеком
(всегда) сойдётся, Г-314
как один человек, О-72
лишний человек, Ч-48
не место красит человека,
а человек место, М-118
последний человек, Ч-49
человек в футляре, Ч-50
человек настроения, Ч-51
человек предполагает, а
бог располагает, Ч-52
ЧЕЛОВЕКА
не место красит человека,
а человек место, М-118
не считать за человека,
Ч-53
чтобы узнать человека,
надо с ним пуд соли
съесть, Ч-54
ЧЕЛОВЕКИ
все мы люди, все (мы)
человеки, Л-166
ЧЕЛОМ
бить челом, Ч-55
ударить ⟨ударять⟩ челом,
Ч-55
ЧЕЛЮСТЬ
челюсть отвалилась, Ч-56
челюсть отвисла, Ч-56
ЧЕМ/ЧЁМ
более чем..., Б-166
больше чем..., Б-166
в чём был, Б-259
в чём дело?, Д-71
в чём душа держится,
Д-363
в чём мать родила, М-49
в чём только душа
держится, Д-363
вот в чём собака зарыта,
С-440
ещё ни о чём не говорить,
Г-165
как ни в чём не бывало,
Б-253
за что дело стало?, Д-103
лучше поздно, чем
никогда, Л-149
лучше синица в руках ⟨в
руки⟩, чем журавль в
небе, С-195
на чём свет стоит, С-49
не далее чем, Д-13
не дальше чем, Д-13
ни в чём себе не
отказывать, О-147
ни о чём не говорить,
Г-165

не то что... а, Т-108
не то что... но..., Т-108
не что иное, как..., Ч-170
невзирая на то что, Н-63
невзирая ни на что, Н-64
независимо от того что,
   Н-72
несмотря на то что, Н-85
несмотря ни на что, Н-86
нет, что вы ⟨ты⟩!, Ч-191
ни во что не ставить ⟨не
   считать⟩, Г-412
ни за что, Ч-171, Ч-172
ни за что на свете, Ч-171
ни за что ни про что, Ч-172
ни за что считать, Г-412
ни во что не похоже!,
   П-445
ну и что (же)?, Ч-173
ну так что ж(е), Т-11
ну что, Ч-174
ну что ж(е), Ч-180
ну что вы!, Ч-191
ну что ты!, Ч-191
ну что я говорил!, Г-159
откуда что взялось!, В-106
оттого что, П-435
пока что, П-276
потому что, П-435
похоже на то, что..., П-444
похоже, что..., П-444
почти что, П-464
разве что, Р-45
смотреть не на что, С-417
смотря что, С-422
судя по тому что, С-668
так что, Т-28
так что ж(е), Т-11
тем более что, Т-65
то, что доктор прописал,
   Д-232
только что, Т-148
только что... как..., Т-147
только что не, Т-149
у кого что болит, тот о
   том и говорит, Б-170
уж на что, Ч-167
хоть бы что, Ч-175
хоть ты что, Ч-176
чёрт знает что, Ч-93
чёрт знает что такое!,
   Ч-93
чёрт-те что, Ч-93
что б..., Ч-177
что бог даст, Б-127
что бог на душу положит,
   Б-128
что бог послал, Б-126
что будет, то будет, Б-220
что бы..., Ч-177
что бы ни..., Ч-186
что бы то ни было, Б-271
что было духу, Д-361
что было мочи, М-271
что было сил(ы), М-271
что было, то прошло (и
   быльём поросло), Б-275
что в лоб, что по лбу,
   Л-119
что взять, В-216
что возьмёшь, В-216

что вы!, Ч-191
что вы говорите!, Г-168
что говорить, Г-167
что греха таить, Г-392
что делается!, Д-59
что делать, П-240
что до... (то ⟨так⟩...),
   Ч-178
что душе угодно, Д-387
что, ежели ⟨ежели б(ы)⟩,
   Ч-179
что, если ⟨если б(ы)⟩,
   Ч-179
что есть духу, Д-361
что есть мочи, М-271
что есть сил(ы), М-271
что ж, Ч-180
что ж такого ⟨такое⟩?,
   Ч-181
что ж тут такого?, Ч-181
что же, Ч-180
что же делать, П-240
что же поделаешь
   ⟨поделать⟩, П-240
что же такого ⟨такое⟩?,
   Ч-181
что же тут такого?, Ч-181
что же это, Ч-180
что за..., Ч-182
что за беда, Б-43
что за важность!, В-3
что за вопрос!, В-262
что за гусь!, Г-448
что за дело, Д-108
что за дьявол!, Ч-101
что за наказание, Н-21
что за невидаль
   ⟨невидальщина⟩!, Н-65
что за новости ⟨новость⟩!,
   Н-110
что за нужда, Н-255
что за печаль, П-138
что за пропасть!, Ч-101
что за разговор!, Р-50
что за счёты, С-729
что за чёрт!, Ч-101
что значит, З-177
что и говорить, Г-167
что и греха таить, Г-392
что и требовалось
   доказать, Т-196
что имеем, не храним,
   потерявши, плачем,
   И-55
что к чему, Ч-183
что касается (, то...), К-101
что ли, Ч-184
что маков цвет, Ц-12
что мудрёного, М-278
что надо, Н-12
что называется, Н-18
что написано пером, того
   не вырубишь топором,
   П-103
что ни..., Ч-185, Ч-186
что ни говори(те), Г-163
что ни (на) есть, Е-22, Е-23
что ни попало, П-354
что ни... то..., Ч-185
что ни шаг, Ш-8
что от козла молока, К-168

что песку морского, П-122
что поделаешь
   ⟨поделать⟩, П-240
что попало, П-354
что посеешь, то и
   пожнёшь, П-407
что правда, то правда,
   П-479
что придётся, П-354
что с воза ⟨возу⟩ упало,
   то (и) пропало, В-213
что сей сон значит
   ⟨означает⟩?, С-486
что слону дробина
   ⟨дробинка⟩, С-344
что смотрит, С-420
что собак нерезаных,
   С-438
что стоит, С-583
что стене ⟨стенке⟩ горох,
   С-565
что так?, Ч-187
что такого, Ч-181
что такое, Ч-188
что там, Ч-189
что там говорить, Г-167
что твой..., Т-47
что-то не так ⟨не то⟩,
   Ч-190
что тут, Ч-189
что тут говорить, Г-167
что тут такого?, Ч-181
что ты!, Ч-191
что ты говоришь!, Г-168
что у кого болит, тот о
   том и говорит, Б-170
что у трезвого на уме, то у
   пьяного на языке, Т-198
что угодно, У-28
что уж там, Ч-189
что уж тут, Ч-189
что-что, а..., Ч-192
что это, Ч-180
что я говорил!, Г-159
что я там забыл
   ⟨потерял⟩?, З-11
что я тут забыл
   ⟨потерял⟩?, З-11
чуть что, Ч-193
чуть что не..., Ч-206
это ещё что за новости
   ⟨новость⟩!, Н-110
это ни на что не похоже!,
   П-445
это чёрт знает что такое!,
   Ч-93

ЧТОБ
не так чтоб, Т-9
не то чтоб... а ⟨но⟩, Т-108
так чтоб, Т-29
чтоб его (разорвало)!, Р-63
чтоб мне провалиться (в
   тартарары)!, З-121
чтоб мне провалиться на
   (этом) месте, М-107
чтоб мне сквозь землю
   провалиться!, З-121
чтоб не встать (мне
   ⟨нам⟩) с (этого) места!,
   М-92
чтоб не сойти (мне ⟨нам⟩)
   с (этого) места!, М-92

чтоб ни дна ни покрышки,
   Д-201
чтоб нога не была ⟨не
   ступала⟩, Н-148
чтоб ноги не было ⟨не
   ступало⟩, Н-148
чтоб пусто было, Б-273
чтоб тебе лопнуть!, Л-138
чтоб тебе провалиться (в
   тартарары)!, З-122
чтоб тебе сквозь землю
   провалиться!, З-122
чтоб тебе треснуть!, Л-138
чтоб тебя (разорвало)!,
   Р-63
чтоб ты лопнул
   ⟨треснул⟩!, Л-138
чтоб у меня руки (и ноги)
   отсохли!, Р-302
чтоб у тебя язык отсох,
   Я-33
чтоб я так жил!, Ж-69

ЧТОБЫ
а не то чтобы, Т-108
вместо того чтобы, Т-120
для того чтобы, Т-121
не так чтобы, Т-9
нет бы, Т-130
нет того чтобы, Т-130
нет чтобы, Т-130
ради того чтобы, Т-121
с тем чтобы, Т-63
так чтобы, Т-29
чтобы духом не пахло,
   Д-362
чтобы духу не было, Д-362
чтобы не было повадно,
   Б-272
чтобы не сказать..., С-213
чтобы неповадно было,
   Б-272
чтобы узнать человека,
   надо с ним пуд соли
   съесть, Ч-54

ЧУБЫ
паны дерутся, а у хлопцев
   ⟨холопов⟩ чубы болят
   ⟨трещат⟩, П-54

ЧУВСТВ
лишаться/лишиться
   чувств, Ч-194
от полноты чувств, П-302
падать без чувств, Ч-194
упасть без чувств, Ч-194

ЧУВСТВА
от полноты чувства, П-302

ЧУВСТВАХ
в растрёпанных чувствах,
   Ч-195

ЧУВСТВИТЕЛЬНУЮ
задевать/задеть (за)
   чувствительную струну,
   С-649
затронуть (за)
   чувствительную струну,
   С-649
тронуть (за)
   чувствительную струну,
   С-649

ЧУВСТВО
привести ⟨приводить⟩ в
   чувство, Ч-196

прийти ⟨приходить⟩ в чувство, Ч-197
стадное чувство, Ч-198
чувство локтя, Ч-199

ЧУВСТВОВАТЬ
давать себя чувствовать, Д-7
давать чувствовать, Д-5
дать себя чувствовать, Д-5
не чувствовать ног под собой, Н-114
нюхом чувствовать, Н-267

ЧУГУННАЯ
чугунная голова, Г-222

ЧУГУННЫЕ
чугунные мозги, Г-222

ЧУДЕСА
чудеса в решете, Ч-200

ЧУДНОЕ
чудное дело, Д-131

ЧУДО
чудо как..., Ч-201

ЧУЕТ
чует кошка, чьё мясо съела, К-343

ЧУЖАЧКА
на чужачка, Д-24

ЧУЖАЯ
свои собаки грызутся ⟨дерутся⟩, чужая не подходи ⟨не приставай⟩, С-447
чужая душа — потёмки, Д-379

ЧУЖИЕ
в чужие руки, Р-283

ЧУЖИМ
жить чужим умом, У-107
чужим горбом, Г-321

ЧУЖИМИ
чужими руками, Р-265
чужими руками жар загребать, Р-266

ЧУЖИХ
с чужих слов, С-276

ЧУЖОГО
говорить с чужого голоса, Г-306
петь с чужого голоса, Г-306
с чужого плеча, П-181

ЧУЖОЙ
в чужой монастырь со своим уставом не ходят, М-251
есть чужой хлеб, Х-32
за чужой счёт, С-705
за чужой щекой зуб не болит, Щ-3
заедать/заесть чужой век, В-18
на чужой счёт, С-705
на чужой роток не накинешь платок, Р-186
на чужой рот пуговицы не нашьёшь, Р-178
на чужой спине в рай въехать, Г-323

ЧУЖОМ
в чужом глазу сучок

видим, а в своём ⟨и⟩ бревна не замечаем, Г-140
в чужом пиру похмелье, П-155
копаться в чужом грязном белье, Б-53
на чужом горбу в рай въехать, Г-323
рыться в чужом грязном белье, Б-53

ЧУЖУЮ
заедать/заесть чужую жизнь, В-18
прятаться/спрятаться за чужую спину, С-516

ЧУЛОК
синий чулок, Ч-202

ЧУМЫ
как чумы, Ч-203

ЧУТОЧКИ
ни чуточки, Ч-204

ЧУТЬ
чуть было не..., Ч-205
чуть держаться на ногах, Н-131
чуть дышать, Д-445
чуть ли не..., Ч-206
чуть не, Ч-207
чуть ноги волочить ⟨передвигать⟩, Н-144
чуть ноги таскать ⟨тащить, тянуть⟩, Н-144
чуть погодя, П-232
чуть свет, С-64
чуть стоять на ногах, Н-131
чуть только..., К-18
чуть что, Ч-193
чуть что не..., Ч-206
чуть-чуть было не..., Ч-205
чуть-чуть не, Ч-207

ЧУЧЕЛО
чучело гороховое, Ш-97

ЧУШЬ
городить/нагородить чушь, В-99
нести/понести чушь, В-99
пороть чушь, В-99

ЧУЯТЬ
земли под собой не чуять, З-113
не чуять ног под собой, Н-114
нюхом чуять, Н-267
чуять носом, Н-267

ЧЬЯ
чья бы корова мычала, а твоя (бы) молчала, К-311
чья возьмёт, В-215
чья потеря, моя находка, П-426

Ш

ШАГ
делать шаг навстречу, Ш-1

держать шаг, Ш-2
идти шаг в шаг, Н-170
ложный шаг, Ш-3
на шаг, Ш-4
неверный шаг, Ш-3
ни на шаг, Ш-5
один шаг, Ш-6
первый шаг, Ш-13
потерять шаг, Н-156
сделать первый шаг, Ш-7
сделать шаг навстречу, Ш-1
терять шаг, Н-156
что ни шаг, Ш-8
шаг в шаг, Н-168
шаг вперёд, Ш-9
шаг за шаг, Ш-10
шаг за шагом, Ш-10

ШАГА
сбиваться/сбиться с шага, Н-156

ШАГАМИ
гигантскими шагами, Ш-11
семимильными шагами, Ш-11

ШАГАТЬ
шагать в ногу, Н-170
шагать по трупам, Т-221

ШАГАХ
в двух шагах, Ш-12
в нескольких шагах, Ш-12
в трёх шагах, Ш-12

ШАГИ
направить ⟨направлять⟩ шаги, П-657
первые шаги, Ш-13

ШАГОВ
с первых шагов, Ш-14

ШАГОМ
черепашьим шагом, Ш-15
шаг за шагом, Ш-10
шагом марш!, Ш-16

ШАГУ
в шагу, Ш-17
на каждом шагу, Ш-18
не давать/не дать шагу сделать ⟨ступить⟩, Ш-19
ни шагу, Ш-20
ни шагу не сделать, Ш-22
прибавить ⟨прибавлять⟩ шагу, Ш-21
шагу лишнего не сделать, Ш-22
шагу не мочь сделать ⟨ступить⟩, Ш-24
шагу не сделать, Ш-22
шагу невозможно сделать ⟨ступить⟩, Ш-24
шагу негде ступить, Ш-23
шагу некуда ступить, Ш-23
шагу нельзя сделать ⟨ступить⟩, Ш-24

ШАЙКА
одна шайка ⟨шайка-лейка⟩, Ш-25

ШАЛАШЕ
с милым рай и в шалаше, М-164

ШАЛАШУ
милости прошу к нашему шалашу, М-154

ШАЛЬНАЯ
шальная голова, Г-223

ШАЛЬНЫЕ
шальные деньги, Д-174

ШАПКА
на воре шапка горит, В-266
по Сеньке ⟨и⟩ шапка, С-119

ШАПКАМИ
шапками закидать, Ш-26

ШАПКЕ
давать/дать по шапке, Ш-27
по шапке, Ш-28
получать/получить по шапке, Ш-29

ШАПКОЙ
под красной шапкой, Ш-31

ШАПКУ
ломать ⟨ломить⟩ шапку, Ш-30
под красную шапку, Ш-31

ШАПОЧНОЕ
шапочное знакомство, З-159

ШАПОЧНОМУ
к шапочному разбору, Р-44

ШАПОЧНЫЙ
шапочный знакомый, З-161

ШАР
белый шар, Ш-32
пробный шар, Ш-33
чёрный шар, Ш-34

ШАРАП
на шарап, Ш-35

ШАРАШКИНА
шарашкина контора, К-240

ШАРИКОВ
шариков (в голове) не хватает ⟨недостаёт⟩, В-147

ШАРИТЬ
шарить взглядом, Г-124
шарить глазами, Г-124

ШАРМАНКУ
вертеть шарманку, Ш-36
крутить шарманку, Ш-36
завести ⟨заводить⟩ шарманку, Ш-36

ШАРОМ
хоть шаром покати, Ш-37

ШАРЫ
заливать/залить шары, Г-73
наливать/налить шары, Г-73

ШАТАЕТ
ветром шатает, В-77

ШАТКО
и шатко и валко (и на сторону), Ш-38
ни шатко ни валко (ни на сторону), Ш-39

ШВАМ
вытягивать/вытянуть руки по швам, Р-285
держать руки по швам, Р-285
руки по швам!, Р-322
стоять руки по швам, Р-285

трещать по (всем) швам,
Ш-40
ШВАХ
дело швах, Д-91
ШВЕД
как швед (под Полтавой),
Ш-41
ШВЕЦ
и швец, и жнец, и в дуду
⟨и на дуде⟩ игрец, Ш-42
ШВЫРНУТЬ
швырнуть на ветер, В-67
ШВЫРЯТЬ
швырять на ветер, В-67
швырять деньгами, Д-165
ШВЫРЯТЬСЯ
швыряться деньгами,
Д-165
ШЕВЕЛИТЬ
шевелить мозгами
⟨мозгой⟩, М-221
ШЕВЕЛЬНУЛ
(и) бровью не шевельнул,
Б-209
ШЕВЕЛЬНУТЬ
пальцем не шевельнуть,
П-22
стоит только бровью
⟨усом⟩ шевельнуть,
Б-210
только бровью ⟨усом⟩
шевельнуть, Б-210
шевельнуть мозгами,
М-221
ШЕЕ
висеть на шее, Ш-43
виснуть на шее, Ш-53
давать/дать по шее, Ш-44
жить на шее, Ш-45
камень на шее, К-41
надавать по шее, Ш-44
накостылять по шее, Ш-54
повиснуть на шее, Ш-43
сидеть на шее, Ш-45
ШЕИ
в три шеи, Ш-52
спихивать/спихнуть с шеи,
П-178
ШЁЛКОВЫЙ
как шёлковый, Ш-46
ШЕЛКУ
в долгу как в шелку, Д-242
ШЕЛЬМА
продувная шельма, Б-61
ШЕМЯКИН
шемякин суд, С-657
ШЕРОЧКА
шерочка с машерочкой,
Ш-47
ШЕРСТИ
гладить не по шерсти,
Ш-49
гладить по шерсти, Ш-48
гладить против шерсти,
Ш-49
не по шерсти, Ш-50
погладить не по шерсти,
Ш-49
погладить по шерсти,
Ш-48

погладить против шерсти,
Ш-49
против шерсти, Ш-50
с паршивой овцы хоть
шерсти клок, О-47
ШЁРСТКЕ
гладить не по шёрстке,
Ш-49
гладить по шёрстке, Ш-48
не по шёрстке, Ш-50
погладить не по шёрстке,
Ш-49
погладить по шёрстке,
Ш-48
ШЁРСТКИ
гладить/погладить против
шёрстки, Ш-49
против шёрстки, Ш-50
ШЕСТОК
всяк сверчок знай свой
шесток, С-38
знай сверчок свой шесток,
С-38
ШЕЮ
бросаться/броситься на
шею, Ш-51
в шею, Ш-52
вешать (себе) камень на
шею, К-38
вешать (себе) хомут на
шею, Х-80
вешаться на шею, Ш-53
гнуть шею, С-514
давать/дать в шею, Ш-44
кидаться/кинуться на
шею, Ш-51
мылить шею, Ш-54
навязаться
⟨навязываться⟩ на шею,
Г-264
надавать в шею, Ш-44
надевать петлю (себе) на
шею, П-128
надевать (себе) хомут на
шею, Х-80
надеть петлю (себе) на
шею, П-128
надеть (себе) хомут на
шею, Х-80
накидывать/накинуть
петлю (себе) на шею,
П-128
накостылять (в) шею,
Ш-54
наломать шею, Ш-54
намылить шею, Ш-54
намять шею, Ш-54
повесить (себе) камень на
шею, К-38
повесить (себе) хомут на
шею, Х-80
посадить на шею, Ш-56
садиться на шею, Ш-55
сажать на шею, Ш-56
свернуть себе шею, Ш-58
свернуть шею, Ш-57, Ш-58
свихнуть (себе) шею, Ш-58
сесть на шею, Ш-55
сломать (себе) шею, Ш-58
сломить себе шею, Ш-58
сломить шею, Ш-57, Ш-58

ШЕЯМ
давать/дать по шеям,
Ш-44
надавать по шеям, Ш-44
ШИВОРОТ
за шиворот, Ш-59
шиворот-навыворот, Ш-60
ШИК
задавать/задать шик,
Ш-61
ШИКУ
задавать/задать шику,
Ш-61
ШИЛА
шила в мешке не утаишь,
Ш-62
ШИЛО
менять/сменять шило на
мыло, Ш-63
ШИПОВ
нет розы без шипов, Р-149
ШИРЕ
держи карман шире, К-78
поперёк себя шире, Ш-64
ШИРОКАЯ
широкая душа, Н-34
широкая натура, Н-34
ШИРОКИЙ
широкий жест, Ж-23
ШИРОКУЮ
выбиваться/выбиться на
широкую дорогу, Д-277
выйти ⟨выходить⟩ на
широкую дорогу, Д-277
на широкую ногу, Н-177
на широкую руку, Р-350
ШИРЬ
во всю ширь, Ш-65
ШИТ
лыком шит, Л-157
не лыком шит, Л-158
ШИТО
шито белыми нитками,
Н-98
шито да ⟨и⟩ крыто, Ш-66
шито-крыто, Ш-66
ШИТЫЙ
лыком шитый, Л-157
не лыком шитый, Л-158
ШИТЬ
не шубу шить, Ш-94
шить дело, Д-126
ШИШ
шиш в кармане, Ш-67
шиш с маслом, К-459
ШИША
ни шиша, Ш-68
ШИШИ
на какие шиши, Ш-69
ШИШКА
большая шишка, Ш-70
важная шишка, Ш-70
крупная шишка, Ш-70
шишка на ровном месте,
Ш-71
ШИШКИ
все шишки валятся на
голову, Ш-72
на бедного Макара все
шишки валятся, М-4

ШКИРКУ
брать/взять за шкирку,
Ш-73
ШКОЛЬНОЙ
со школьной скамьи, С-220
ШКУР
драть семь шкур, Ш-79
сдирать семь шкур, Ш-79
снять семь шкур, Ш-80
содрать семь шкур, Ш-79
спускать/спустить семь
шкур, Ш-80
ШКУРА
своя шкура, Ш-74
ШКУРЕ
в шкуре, Ш-75
волк в овечьей шкуре,
В-224
на своей собственной
шкуре, Ш-76
на своей шкуре, Ш-76
на собственной шкуре,
Ш-76
ШКУРУ
влезать/влезть в шкуру,
Ш-77
делить шкуру неубитого
медведя, Ш-78
драть шкуру, Ш-79
снять шкуру, Ш-80
содрать шкуру, Ш-79
спускать/спустить шкуру,
Ш-80
ШКУРЫ
драть (по) две ⟨три⟩
шкуры, Ш-79
из шкуры (вон) вылезать,
К-162
из шкуры (вон) лезть,
К-162
сдирать (по) две ⟨три⟩
шкуры, Ш-79
снять три шкуры, Ш-80
содрать (по) две ⟨три⟩
шкуры, Ш-79
спускать/спустить три
шкуры, Ш-80
ШЛЕЯ
шлея под хвост попала,
В-198
ШЛО
куда ни шло, Ш-81
ШЛЯПЕ
дело в шляпе, Д-79
ШЛЯПОЧНОЕ
шляпочное знакомство,
З-159
ШЛЯПУ
снимать/снять шляпу,
Ш-82
ШМЫГАТЬ
шмыгать носом, Н-233
ШМЫГНУТЬ
шмыгнуть носом, Н-233
ШНЫРЯТЬ
шнырять глазами, Г-125
ШОРАХ
держать в шорах, Ш-83
ШОРЫ
брать/взять в шоры, Ш-83

ШПАГИ
скрестить ⟨скрещивать⟩ шпаги, Ш-84

ШПИЛЬКИ
подпускать/подпустить шпильки, Ш-85
пускать/пустить шпильки, Ш-85

ШПИЛЬКУ
подпускать/подпустить шпильку, Ш-85
пускать/пустить шпильку, Ш-85

ШТАНОВ
оставаться/остаться без штанов, Ш-86

ШТАНЫ
просиживать штаны, Ш-87
протирать штаны, Ш-87

ШТАТСКОМ
искусствовед в штатском, И-78

ШТАТУ
по штату полагается ⟨положено⟩, Ш-88

ШТУКА
в том-то и штука, Д-70
вот так штука!, Ш-89
не велика штука, Ш-90
не штука, Ш-90

ШТУКИ
выкидывать/выкинуть штуки, Ш-91
откалывать/отколоть штуки, Ш-91
отмачивать/отмочить штуки, Ш-91
удрать штуки, Ш-91

ШТУКУ
выкидывать/выкинуть штуку, Ш-91
откалывать/отколоть штуку, Ш-91
отмачивать/отмочить штуку, Ш-91
сыграть штуку, Ш-109
удрать штуку, Ш-91

ШТУЧКИ
эти штучки не пройдут, Н-201

ШТЫК
как штык, Ш-92

ШТЫКИ
в штыки, Ш-93

ШУБУ
не шубу шить, Ш-94

ШУБЫ
шубы не сошьёшь, Ш-94

ШУМА
наделать шума, Ш-96

ШУМИТ
шумит в голове, Г-231

ШУМОК
под шумок, Ш-95

ШУМУ
наделать шуму, Ш-96

ШУТ
шут гороховый, Ш-97
шут его знает, Ч-89

шут его разберёт, Ч-89
шут с тобой, Ч-98
шут тебя возьми ⟨дери⟩!, Ч-99
шут тебя побери ⟨подери⟩!, Ч-99

ШУТА
делать из себя шута, Ш-98
какого шута?, Ч-103
корчить из себя шута, Ш-98
на какого шута, Ч-77
на шута, Ч-77
ни шута, Ч-104
разыгрывать (из себя) шута (горохового), Ш-98
строить из себя шута, Ш-98

ШУТИТ
не шутит, Ш-99
чем чёрт не шутит, Ч-85

ШУТИТЬ
шутить с огнём, О-57
шутить не любит, Ш-99
шутить нельзя, Ш-99
шутки ⟨шутку⟩ шутить, Ш-105

ШУТКА
не шутка, Ш-100
шутка ли, Ш-101
шутка (ли) сказать, Ш-101
шутка шуткой, Ш-106

ШУТКАМИ
шутки шутками, Ш-106

ШУТКЕ
в каждой шутке есть доля правды, Ш-102

ШУТКИ
для шутки, Ш-107
ради шутки, Ш-107
шутки в сторону, Ш-103
шутки коротки ⟨короткие⟩, Р-49
шутки плохи, Ш-104
шутки прочь, Ш-103
шутки шутить, Ш-105
шутки шутками, Ш-106

ШУТКОЙ
шутка шуткой, Ш-106

ШУТКУ
в шутку, Ш-107
не на шутку, Ш-108
сыграть шутку, Ш-109
шутку шутить, Ш-105

ШУТОК
без шуток, Ш-110
кроме шуток, Ш-111
не до шуток, Ш-112

ШУТОЧНОЕ
шуточное (ли) дело, Д-89

ШУТУ
к шуту, Ч-111

ШУТЯ
не шутя, Ш-113

ШЬЁТ
ни шьёт ни порет, Ш-114

Щ

ЩАДИТЬ
не щадить красок, К-368

ЩЕДРОЙ
щедрой рукой, Р-341

ЩЕДРОТ
от своих щедрот, Щ-1
от щедрот, Щ-1

ЩЕЙ
профессор кислых щей, П-592

ЩЕКИ/ЩЁКИ
за обе щеки ⟨щёки⟩, Щ-2

ЩЕКОЙ
за чужой щекой зуб не болит, Щ-3

ЩЁЛКАТЬ
щёлкать зубами, З-190
щёлкать как орехи ⟨орешки⟩, О-100
щёлкать по носу, Н-238

ЩЁЛКНУТЬ
щёлкнуть по носу, Н-238

ЩЕМИТ
сердце щемит, Д-364

ЩЕНКАМИ
борзыми щенками, Щ-4

ЩЕПКА
как щепка, Щ-5

ЩЕПКИ
дрова рубят — щепки летят, Л-56
лес рубят — щепки летят, Л-56

ЩИ
как кур во щи, К-476
лаптем щи хлебать, Л-26
не лаптем щи хлебать, Л-27

ЩИТ
поднимать/поднять на щит, Щ-6
подымать на щит, Щ-6

ЩИТЕ
на щите, Щ-7

ЩИТОМ
со щитом, Щ-8

ЩУЧЬЕМУ
(как) по щучьему веленью, В-29
словно по щучьему веленью, В-29

Э

ЭДАК
(и) так и эдак, Т-7

ЭЗОПОВ
эзопов язык, Я-34

ЭЗОПОВСКАЯ
эзоповская речь, Я-34

ЭЗОПОВСКИЙ
эзоповский язык, Я-34

ЭК
эк (куда) хватил!, Х-8

ЭКА
эка важность!, В-3
эка куда хватил, Х-8
эка невидаль ⟨невидальщина⟩!, Н-65
эка хватил, Х-8

ЭКАЯ
экая невидаль ⟨невидальщина⟩!, Н-65

ЭМПИРЕЯХ
витать в эмпиреях, О-8
парить в эмпиреях, О-8

ЭНЦИКЛОПЕДИЯ
живая энциклопедия, Э-1
ходячая энциклопедия, Э-1

ЭСТАФЕТУ
передавать/передать эстафету, Э-2
принимать/принять эстафету, Э-3

ЭТА
миновала эта чаша, Ч-34

ЭТАЖА
в три этажа, Э-4

ЭТАК
и так и этак, Т-7
так и этак, Т-7
так ли, этак ли, Т-21
то так, то этак, Т-30
хоть так, хоть этак, Т-21

ЭТАПНЫМ
этапным порядком, Э-5

ЭТАПУ
по этапу, Э-5

ЭТИ
эти штучки не пройдут, Н-201

ЭТИХ
с этих пор, П-367

ЭТО
ведь это же надо!, Н-11
виданное ли (это) дело, Д-72
вот это да!, Э-6
вот это мило!, М-152
вот это номер!, Ш-89
вот это я понимаю!, П-338
где ж(е) это видано?, В-119
где это видано?, В-119
где это слыхано?, С-383
как это можно!, М-216
куда это годится!, Г-186
на что это похоже?, П-442
нет, уж это извини(те), И-42
разве это слыхано?, С-383
расскажи это кому-нибудь другому, Б-7
расскажи это своей бабушке ⟨тёте⟩, Б-7
рассказывай это кому-нибудь другому, Б-7
рассказывай это своей бабушке ⟨тёте⟩, Б-7
что (же) это, Ч-180
это ещё цветики ⟨цветки, цветочки⟩, а ягодки (будут) впереди, Ц-16
это ещё что за новости ⟨новость⟩!, Н-110
это же надо!, Н-11
это не пройдёт, Н-201
это ни на что не похоже!, П-445
это самое, Э-7
это слишком, Э-8

это только цветики 〈цветки, цветочки〉, а ягодки (будут) впереди, Ц-16
это уж(е) слишком, Э-8
это чёрт знает что такое!, Ч-93
это я понимаю!, П-338

ЭТОГО
до этого времени, Д-163
не встать мне 〈нам〉 с этого места!, М-92
не сойти мне 〈нам〉 с этого места!, М-92
только этого (и) не хватало 〈недоставало〉!, Х-7
чтоб не встать 〈не сойти〉 мне 〈нам〉 с этого места!, М-92
этого ещё (только) не хватало 〈недоставало〉!, Х-7

ЭТОЙ
с этой поры, П-367

ЭТОМ
в этом 〈же〉 духе, Д-350
в этом роде, Р-133
в этом случае, С-366
вот в этом и зарыта собака, С-440
кажинный раз на этом (самом) месте, Р-22
не жилец на этом свете, Ж-72
порази меня гром на этом месте, Г-406
при этом, Э-9
провалиться (мне) на этом месте, М-107
разрази меня гром на этом месте, Г-406
спасибо и на этом, С-506
убей меня гром на этом месте, Г-406
чтоб мне провалиться на этом месте, М-107

ЭТОМУ
по этому случаю, С-380

ЭТОТ
этот номер не выйдет, Н-201
этот номер не пройдёт 〈не удастся〉, Н-201
на этот предмет, П-508
на этот счёт, С-706
этот свет, С-65

ЭТУ
об эту пору, П-390

Ю

ЮБКЕ
в юбке, Ю-1
ЮБКУ
держаться за бабью юбку, Ю-2
держаться за юбку, Ю-2
ЮМОР
юмор висельника, Ю-3

ЮРЬЕВ
вот тебе, бабушка, и Юрьев день!, Б-6

Я

Я
а что я говорил!, Г-159
будь я (трижды) проклят, Б-233
вот это я понимаю!, П-338
вот я тебя!, Я-1
доложу я вам 〈тебе〉, Д-247
как я погляжу, П-230
кто куда, а я в сберкассу, С-23
не я буду, Б-223
ну что я говорил!, Г-159
ну я вас спрашиваю!, С-525
ну я тебя спрашиваю!, С-525
от а до я, А-1
плевать я хотел, П-169
почём я знаю, З-176
провались я, М-107
скажи мне, кто твой друг, и я скажу 〈тебе〉, кто ты, Д-310
чего я здесь не видал 〈не видел〉?, В-118
чего я там 〈тут〉 не видал 〈не видел〉?, В-118
что я говорил!, Г-159
что я там 〈тут〉 забыл 〈потерял〉?, З-11
чтоб я так жил!, Ж-69
это я понимаю!, П-338
я вас спрашиваю!, С-525
я думаю!, Д-326
я не я, Я-2
я не я буду, Б-223
я рыжий, Р-386
я тебе!, Д-19
я тебе дам 〈задам〉!, Д-19
я тебе покажу!, Д-19
я тебя!, Я-1
я тебя спрашиваю!, С-525
я уж(е) не говорю, Г-173

ЯБЛОКАХ
в яблоках, Я-3
ЯБЛОКО
яблоко от яблони 〈яблоньки〉 недалеко падает, Я-4
яблоко раздора, Я-5
ЯБЛОКУ
яблоку негде упасть, Я-6
яблоку некуда упасть, Я-6
ЯБЛОНИ
яблоко 〈яблочко〉 от яблони недалеко падает, Я-4
ЯБЛОНЬКИ
яблоко 〈яблочко〉 от яблоньки недалеко падает, Я-4
ЯБЛОЧКО
яблочко от яблони

〈яблоньки〉 недалеко падает, Я-4
ЯВИ(ТЕ)
яви(те) божескую милость, М-161
ЯВИТЬСЯ
явиться на свет, С-54
явиться на сцену, С-686
ЯВЛЯТЬСЯ
являться на свет, С-54
являться на сцену, С-686
ЯВОЧНЫМ
явочным порядком 〈путём〉, П-402
ЯГОДА
нашего поля ягода, П-327
одного 〈своего〉 поля ягода, П-327
того же поля ягода, П-327
ЯГОДКИ
нашего поля ягодки, П-327
одного 〈своего〉 поля ягодки, П-327
того же поля ягодки, П-327
это ещё 〈только〉 цветики 〈цветки, цветочки〉, а ягодки (будут) впереди, Ц-16
ЯГОДЫ
нашего поля ягоды, П-327
одного 〈своего〉 поля ягоды, П-327
того же поля ягоды, П-327
ЯДРЁНА
ядрёна вошь!, В-284
ЯДРЁНОЙ
к ядрёной фене, Ф-6
ЯЗЫК
бес дёрнул за язык, Я-10
боек 〈бойкий〉 на язык, Я-7
высунув(ши) 〈высуня〉 язык, Я-8
держать язык за зубами, Я-9
держать язык на привязи, Я-9
дёрнуло за язык, Я-10
длинный язык, Я-11
закусить язык, Я-22
злой на язык, Я-12
злой язык, Я-13
как будто* язык проглотил, Я-23
леший дёрнул за язык, Я-10
мозолить язык, Я-32
найти 〈находить〉 общий язык, Я-14
нелёгкая дёрнула за язык, Я-10
неплохо подвешенный язык, Я-47
общий язык, Я-15
остёр 〈острый〉 на язык, Я-16
острый язык, Я-17
отсохни язык, Я-18
показать 〈показывать〉 язык, Я-19

помозолить язык, Я-32
попадать(ся) на язык, Я-20
попасть(ся) на язык, Я-20
попридержать язык, Я-21
поточить язык, Я-29
потрепать язык, Я-32
почесать язык, Я-32
придержать 〈придерживать〉 язык, Я-21
прикусить 〈прикусывать〉 язык, Я-22
проглотить язык, Я-23
просится на язык, Я-24
развязать 〈развязывать〉 язык, Я-25
распускать/распустить язык, Я-26
слаб(ый) на язык, Я-27
суконный язык, Я-28
типун на язык, Т-98
точить язык, Я-29
трепать язык, Я-32
тянуть за язык, Я-30
укоротить язык, Я-31
хорошо подвешенный язык, Я-47
чёрт дёрнул за язык, Я-10
чесать язык, Я-32
чтоб у тебя язык отсох, Я-33
эзопов(ский) язык, Я-34
язык без костей, Я-35
язык до Киева доведёт, Я-36
язык заплетается, Я-37
язык зачесался, Я-48
язык здорово подвешен 〈привешен〉, Я-47
язык мой — враг мой, Я-38
язык на плече 〈на плечо〉, Я-39
язык не ворочается, Я-40
язык не повернулся 〈не повёртывается〉, Я-40
язык не поворачивается/не поворотился, Я-40
язык неплохо подвешен 〈привешен〉, Я-47
язык отнялся, Я-41
язык плохо подвешен 〈привешен〉, Я-42
язык прилип к гортани, Я-43
язык присох к гортани, Я-43
язык проглотишь, Я-44
язык развязался 〈развязывается〉, Я-45
язык сломаешь, Я-46
язык сломать можно, Я-46
язык хорошо подвешен 〈привешен〉, Я-47
язык чешется, Я-48

ЯЗЫКА
без языка, Я-49
не сходить с языка, Я-50
слетать/слететь с языка, Я-51
слова не идут с языка, С-292

сорваться ⟨срываться⟩ с
языка, Я-51

ЯЗЫКАМИ
почесать ⟨чесать⟩
языками, Я-56

ЯЗЫКАХ
говорить на разных
языках, Я-52

ЯЗЫКЕ
вертеться на языке, Я-53
на языке, Я-54
что у трезвого на уме, то у
пьяного на языке, Т-198

ЯЗЫКИ
высунув(ши) ⟨высуня⟩
языки, Я-8
злые языки, Я-55
почесать ⟨чесать⟩ языки,
Я-56

ЯЗЫКОМ
болтать языком, Я-57
как* корова языком
слизала ⟨слизнула⟩,
К-310
как языком слизнуло,
К-310
молоть/помолоть языком,
Я-32
потрепать языком, Я-32
потрещать языком, Я-32
почесать языком, Я-32
русским языком, Я-58

трепать языком, Я-32
трещать языком, Я-32
чесать языком, Я-32

ЯЗЫКУ
давать/дать волю языку,
В-251

ЯЗЫЦЕХ
притча во языцех, П-550

ЯЗЫЧКИ
почесать ⟨чесать⟩ язычки,
Я-56

ЯЗЫЧОК
закусить язычок, Я-22
острый язычок, Я-17
попадать(ся) на язычок,
Я-20
попасть(ся) на язычок,
Я-20
попридержать язычок,
Я-21
придержать
⟨придерживать⟩
язычок, Я-21
прикусывать/прикусить
язычок, Я-22

ЯЙЦА
выеденного яйца не
стоить, Я-59
яйца курицу не учат, Я-60

ЯЙЦО
выеденное яйцо, Я-61

ЯЙЦОМ
как курица с яйцом, К-480

ЯКОВА
заладила сорока Якова
(одно про всякого),
С-496

ЯКОРЬ
бросить якорь, Я-62
кинуть якорь, Я-62
якорь спасения, Я-63

ЯМУ
выкопать ⟨вырыть⟩ яму,
Я-65
копать яму, Я-65
не рой другому яму, сам в
неё попадёшь, Я-64
рыть яму, Я-65

ЯНУС
двуликий Янус, Я-66

ЯРЛЫК
лепить ярлык, Я-67
наклеивать/наклеить
ярлык, Я-67
приклеивать/приклеить
ярлык, Я-67
прилепить ярлык, Я-67

ЯРЛЫКИ
лепить ярлыки, Я-67
наклеивать/наклеить
ярлыки, Я-67
приклеивать/приклеить
ярлыки, Я-67

прилепить ярлыки, Я-67

ЯРМО
надевать/надеть на себя
ярмо, Х-80

ЯСНОГО
как* гром среди ясного
неба, Г-405

ЯСНОЕ
ясное дело, Д-137

ЯСНОСТИ
замнём для ясности, Я-68

ЯСНЫЙ
навести ⟨наводить⟩ тень
на ясный день, Т-75

ЯСНЫМ
гори (оно) ясным огнём
⟨пламенем⟩, О-55

ЯСТРЕБА
менять/променять
кукушку на ястреба,
К-461
сменять кукушку на
ястреба, К-461

ЯТЬ
на ять, Я-69

ЯЩИК
в долгий ящик, Я-70
писать в ящик, С-588
сыграть в ящик, Я-71
ящик Пандоры, Я-72

ABOUT THE AUTHOR

Sophia Lubensky is Associate Professor of Slavic Languages at the State University of New York at Albany. She has M.A.'s in Classics and English, and obtained her Ph.D. in linguistics from the University of Leningrad, now St. Petersburg. She emigrated to the United States in 1976. Professor Lubensky lives in Albany, New York.